SECOND COLLEGE EDITION

WEBSTER'S
NEW WORLD
DICTIONARY

of the

American Language

SECOND COLLEGE EDITION

WEBSTER'S NEW WORLD DICTIONARY

of the

American Language

David B. Guralnik, *Editor in Chief*

THE WORLD PUBLISHING COMPANY

New York and Cleveland

CONTENTS

Editorial Staff .... *vi*

Foreword .... *vii*

Guide to the Use of the Dictionary .... *ix*

    I. The Main Entry Word
    II. Pronunciation
    III. Part-of-Speech Labels
    IV. Inflected Forms
    V. The Etymology
    VI. The Definitions
    VII. Usage Labels & Notes
    VIII. Field Labels
    IX. Scientific Names of Plants & Animals
    X. Idiomatic Phrases
    XI. Run-in Derived Entries
    XII. The Synonymy

Language and the Dictionary *by Charlton Laird* .... *xv*

Etymology *by William E. Umbach* .... *xxxi*

Americanisms *by Mitford M. Mathews* .... *xxxiii*

Abbreviations and Symbols Used in This Dictionary .... *xxxv*

A DICTIONARY OF THE AMERICAN LANGUAGE 1–1656

Colleges and Universities of the United States 1657

Junior Colleges of the United States 1670

Colleges and Universities of Canada 1677

Other Institutions of Higher Education in Canada 1678

Guide to Punctuation and Mechanics 1680

    Marks of Punctuation
    Numbers
    Capitalization
    Abbreviations

Manuscript Form 1684
    Footnotes
    Terms and Abbreviations Used in Scholarly Writing
    Bibliography
    Proofreading and Proofreaders' Marks

Tables of Weights and Measures 1688

Special Signs and Symbols 1690

EDITORIAL STAFF

Editor in Chief – DAVID B. GURALNIK

Managing Editor – SAMUEL SOLOMON

Special Consulting Editor & Editor, Americanisms – MITFORD M. MATHEWS

Etymological Editor – WILLIAM E. UMBACH

Associate Editors – CLARK C. LIVENSPARGER (*Supervising*), THOMAS LAYMAN,
ANDREW N. SPARKS, CHRISTOPHER T. HOOLIHAN, PAUL B. MURRY,
RUTH KIMBALL KENT, WILLIAM S. CHISHOLM (*Pronunciation*)

Assistant Editors – ELEANOR RICKEY STEVENS, JONATHAN L. GOLDMAN,
ROSLYN BLOCK, JUDITH CLARK, LOIS AARON

Research & Office Assistants – VIRGINIA C. BECKER, DOROTHY H. BENEDICT,
CYNTHIA SADONICK, ANGIE WEST, DOROTHY FITZGIBBONS, AGNES BRDAR,
GOLDIE F. SOLOMON, GERTRUDE TULLAR, IRENE KAUFFMAN,
DOROTHY TROUTMAN, CHRISTINE PHILLIPS

Chief Proofreader – SHIRLEY M. MILLER   *Illustrator* – ANITA S. ROGOFF

Cartographer – NORMAN CLARK ADAMS

SPECIAL CONTRIBUTING EDITORS

NORMAN A. ALLDRIDGE, Associate Chairman, Department of Biology, Case Western Reserve University HOLT ASHLEY, Professor, Department of Aeronautics and Astronautics, Stanford University W. E. BARNES, Canadian journalist NORMAN A. CLEMENS, Assistant Professor of Psychiatry, School of Medicine, Case Western Reserve University CHARLES C. DAVIS, Professor, Department of Biology, Memorial University of Newfoundland and Case Western Reserve University LOYD D. EASTON, Professor of Philosophy, Department Chairman, Ohio Wesleyan University U. WOLFGANG FETSCH, Chairman, Department of Applied Music, Conservatory of Music, University of the Pacific PAUL R. FIELDS, Senior Chemist, Argonne National Laboratory MORRIS FINDER, Associate Professor of English Education, State University of New York at Albany LEONARD J. GOSS, Director, Cleveland Zoological Park JACOB O. KAMM, Economist & financial consultant HAROLD E. LEIDNER, Attorney at Law RICHARD P. LEVY, Associate Professor of Medicine, School of Medicine, Case Western Reserve University ARTHUR LOESSER (deceased), Chairman of Piano Department, Cleveland Institute of Music ASHLEY MONTAGU, Anthropologist, Princeton, New Jersey HERBERT PENZL, Professor of Germanic Philology, University of California at Berkeley PETER PESCH, Associate Professor of Astronomy, Case Western Reserve University RICHARD W. POHL, Professor of Botany & Curator of the Herbarium, Iowa State University MAURICE W. SASIENI, Professor of Mathematics, Case Western Reserve University LORENZO D. TURNER, Professor of English, Roosevelt University, & specialist in African languages JOHN R. VAN ATTA, Biophysicist, Carnation Research Laboratories C. F. VOEGELIN, Professor of Anthropology and Linguistics, Indiana University, & specialist in Amerindian languages JAMES E. WALTER, Professor of Finance, University of Pennsylvania J. MARVIN WELLER, Professor Emeritus of Geology, University of Chicago, & Research Associate, Field Museum of Natural History EVERARD M. WILLIAMS, Professor & Head of Department of Electrical Engineering, Carnegie-Mellon University ARTHUR YASPAN, Associate Professor, Department of Mathematics, Polytechnic Institute of Brooklyn

FOREWORD

The appearance of *Webster's New World Dictionary of the American Language*, College Edition, on the lexicographical scene in 1953 elicited, in the first major review of that work (*Library Journal*, May, 1953), the encomium "a great advance in American lexicography." In the years immediately following, others made their own assessment of that work, scholars, teachers, students, writers, and workers in every field of endeavor. Unanimity in assessing so complex an undertaking, and one so dependent upon subjective evaluation, is hardly to be expected, but the consensus, as evidenced by rapidly growing acceptance of the dictionary on college campuses and its regular appearance on the bookshelves and desks of researchers, professional persons, and the like, suggested substantial agreement with that first assessment.

Efforts were continually made to maintain the currency of the dictionary through annual, later biennial, updating. These efforts were for a time successful, at least in incorporating the more visible of the newest accretions to the language into the written record of that language. Eventually, however, it became apparent that the flood of new terms inundating the staff's citation file, the subtle changes in pronunciation reflected in the aural citations, and the changes in group attitudes toward numerous locutions had made a total revision of the dictionary mandatory. The first decades of the second half of the 20th century have witnessed not only a population explosion, but an information explosion of unprecedented proportions. Rapid advances in the physical sciences and in technology are bringing with them countless new terms and new applications of established terms. Vast sociological and political upheavals have had lexical consequences, and the young of our land, both alienated and unalienated, have made full, vigorous contribution to the slang sector of the language. Free borrowing from other languages, always a salient feature of English, continues unabated (see Dr. Umbach's article *Etymology*, on p. xxxi).

The science of lexicography makes it possible for the dictionary staff of our times to keep up with these shifts and turns in language and to accumulate large stores of data with which to work. It is still, however, the art of the lexicographer that must be employed in sifting the masses of data, selecting those items and details that fall properly within the scope of the dictionary under construction, and assembling these into an instructive, useful, and graceful whole. Most often, a period of incubation is required for new words to prove their vitality and establish their right to entry in the dictionary. Sometimes, however, the swift current of events brings startling changes, and the items of vocabulary resulting from such events are firmly fixed in our speech from the day of their coinage. Not long before this work went to press, we witnessed a milestone in the human saga, man's first, halting steps on the moon's surface, an event that demanded the insertion of such an entry as *mascon* and a biographical listing of Neil Armstrong, whose feat—and feet—made history.

Those who are familiar with the first College Edition of *Webster's New World Dictionary* will find here the same reassuringly large and clear type and the same single alphabetical listing that makes it unnecessary to leaf through numerous supplementary lists of biographical and geographical entries, proper names, and abbreviations. They will also find in this Second College Edition the same devotion to careful, detailed definitions as in the previous edition and the same generous use of illustrative examples to help clarify both meaning and usage. As they continue to use this new work, they will, however, discover many thousands of new entries and new meanings not to be found in the earlier edition, many of them, indeed, not to be found in any other dictionary. They will discover, too, small but significant changes in the diacritical key that lend phonemic precision to the pronunciations, and they will discover the changes that the record shows have taken place in the prevalence of certain pronunciations since the first edition. Such change is a phenomenon that has always characterized living languages, and it is a special characteristic of the language of America.

The users of this dictionary will find, again, that each entry block has been ordered to show logical semantic extension from the etymology through the earlier uses of the word to the current, often specialized or informal applications. The result is a single coherent paragraph that clearly shows the history and development of the word and the relationship among the meanings, rather than an assemblage of fragmented bits of disconnected information. The etymologies, always a strong feature of the *New World Dictionary*, have been carefully reviewed by Dr. Umbach, who has incorporated the latest etymological findings and has still further extended the practice of showing cognate relationships between words in English and between English words and those in other Indo-European languages. For the first time in any general dictionary of the language, the origins of American place names have been included, prepared by Dr. Mathews, where these could be ascertained. Also for the first time in any general dictionary, every Americanism has been clearly identified as such (see the "Guide to the Use of the Dictionary," paragraph I.,E. on p. ix and Dr. Mathews' article *Americanisms* on p. xxxiii).

Foreword

The art of the lexicographer is further displayed in the help that is given the user of the dictionary who must decide the aptness of any term or phrase to the use he wishes to make of it. The editors of this work believe that one who consults a college dictionary is entitled to the informed collective determination by the staff as to whether a particular term is appropriate to a standard or formal context or is suitable only in an informal context or as an item of slang, whether a given word is current or obsolete or archaic or now rare, whether it is current only as a regional, or dialectal, term, and whether it is, in spite of widespread usage, held in low repute by those who take a stricter, or purist, view of these matters. The issue is not one of "permissiveness" versus "authoritarianism." No lexicographer, at least in this country, has been given a mandate either to permit or to disallow any usage. He has, however, assumed the responsibility of informing the public of the state of the language as of the time during which his dictionary was being compiled. The status of any usage, as determined by the trained lexicographer after a careful study of current writings and speech and disregarding the crotchets and prejudices of individuals, is a part of the record and should be incorporated among the data made available to the writer and student.

The absence from this dictionary of a handful of old, well-known vulgate terms for sexual and excretory organs and functions is not due to a lack of citations for these words from current literature. On the contrary, the profusion of such citations in recent years would suggest that the terms in question are so well known as to require no explanation. The decision to eliminate them as part of the extensive culling process that is the inevitable task of the lexicographer was made on the practical grounds that there is still objection in many quarters to the appearance of these terms in print and that to risk keeping this dictionary out of the hands of some students by introducing several terms that require little if any elucidation would be unwise. In a similar vein, it was decided in the selection process that this dictionary could easily dispense with those true obscenities, the terms of racial or ethnic opprobrium, that are, in any case, encountered with diminishing frequency these days.

The vocabulary entered was chosen to meet the needs of students and others in this particular period of history, and so it will be seen that there is here a heavier proportion of terms from the sciences than was true for the previous edition. In response to numerous requests, it was decided to include the taxonomic designation, or scientific name, for every animal and plant entered. The taxa shown herein reflect the process of continuous adjustment and reclassification that is taking place in this discipline. In general, the technical definitions were written by, or prepared in direct consultation with, leading specialists in every field.

Population figures for geographical entries and other similar statistical data have been checked with authoritative sources. Unofficial estimates have been avoided; only the latest official counts or estimates were considered reliable.

On the editorial staff page preceding this foreword are listed the names of those who labored to produce the dictionary. Titular designations, however descriptive in intention, often fail to describe adequately the roles and responsibilities carried out. For example, Dr. Mitford M. Mathews, dean of American lexicographers and editor of the *Dictionary of Americanisms*, has over the past decade had a lively impact on nearly every aspect of this work to a degree improperly conveyed by the designation "Special Consulting Editor."

A major advantage in the preparation of the second edition of a dictionary is the inevitable exposure to the collective wisdom of those who have put the first edition to the test of repeated usage. Over the years we have benefited immeasurably from the suggestions, queries, emendations, and citations offered by scholars, experts, and lay people throughout the United States and, indeed, throughout the world. However desirable, it would be impractical to attempt to acknowledge individually those many who have given us, and in many instances continue to give us, aid and advice. They will know who they are and, we trust, will accept our generalized thanks.

Special acknowledgment must be made of those scholars who participated in the staff's planning sessions and whose good counsel has served us so well in the execution of those plans: Professor Charlton Laird (whose article *Language and the Dictionary* on p. xv you are urged to read), Professor Donald Lloyd, and the late Professor George Grauel. Our thanks are also herewith extended to the many individuals at institutions and agencies, private and governmental, who so graciously served as sources of information and verification, and to those persons who served as regular informants on matters of pronunciation and usage. Special thanks are due the editors and custodians of the unpublished records of the Linguistic Atlas of the North-Central States for making those materials available to us, to Miss Dorothy Fey, of the United States Trademark Association, for her invaluable help in determining whether terms suspected of being trademarks do currently in fact have such status, and to Professor Frederick McLeod for his expert assistance in the preparation of the supplementary "Guide to Punctuation, Mechanics, and Manuscript Form." For their helpful cooperation in solving a number of problems in typography, thanks are due to Mr. Donald M. Snyder and Mr. Willis Larson of the American Typesetting Company.

The editors of *Webster's New World Dictionary of the American Language*, Second College Edition, firmly believe that the years of work expended on its production will be well justified by the many services it will perform for those who turn to it. To ensure that the greatest possible benefit is obtained from this reference work, the user is urged to read the "Guide to the Use of the Dictionary" on the following pages.

David B. Guralnik
Editor in Chief

GUIDE TO THE USE OF THE DICTIONARY

I. THE MAIN ENTRY WORD

A. *Arrangement of Entries*

All main entries, including single words, hyphenated and unhyphenated compounds, proper names, prefixes, suffixes, and abbreviations, are listed in strict alphabetical order and are set in large, boldface type.

black (blak) *adj.* . . .
Black (blak), **Hugo (La Fayette)** . . .
black alder . . .
black-and-blue (-ən blo͞o′) *adj.* . . .
black·ber·ry (-ber′ē) *n.* . . .
bldg. . . .
-ble (b'l) . . .

Note that in the biographical entry only the last, or family, name (that part preceding the comma) has been considered in alphabetization. When two or more persons with the same family name are entered, they are dealt with in a single entry block, arranged in alphabetical order by first names. Biographical and geographical names that are identical in form are kept in separate blocks.

Jack·son (jak′s'n) [after Andrew JACKSON] **1.** capital of Miss., in the SW part, on the Pearl River: pop. 144,000 **2.** city in S Mich.: pop. 51,000 **3.** city in W Tenn.: pop. 34,000
Jack·son (jak′s'n) **1. Andrew,** (nickname *Old Hickory*) 1767–1845; U.S. general; 7th president of the U.S. (1829–37) **2. Robert H(oughwout),** 1892–1954; U.S. jurist; associate justice, Supreme Court (1941–54) **3. Thomas Jonathan,** (nickname *Stonewall Jackson*) 1824–63; Confederate general in the Civil War

The name prefixes "Mac" and "Mc" are listed in strict alphabetical order.

MacDowell, Edward Alexander
mace
MacLeish, Archibald
make
maser
McCormack, John
McKinley, William

Strict alphabetical order is also followed for "Saint" and "St." when they appear as a part of proper names other than the names of canonized persons.

Saint Bernard (dog)
Saint-Gaudens, Augustus
squint
St. Clair (river)
steel
St. Helena (island)

Canonized persons are alphabetized by their given names, which appear in boldface. The designation "Saint" follows in lightface type, either directly after a comma or, within a proper-name block, at the beginning of a numbered sense. Thus **Augustine,** the saint, will be found in the A's, but **St. Augustine,** the city in Florida, will be found in the S's.

B. *Variant Spellings & Forms*

When variant spellings of a word are some distance apart alphabetically, the definition for the word appears at the spelling known or judged to be the one most frequently used. Other spellings of the word are cross-referred to that spelling in small capitals, and unless such a cross-reference indicates that the variant is British, dialectal, slang, obsolete, or the like, each form given is as acceptable in standard American usage as the one carrying the definition, though usually not as commonly used.

aes·the·si·a . . . *n. same as* ESTHESIA
kerb . . . *n. Brit. sp. of* CURB (*n.* 5)

If two variant spellings are alphabetically close to each other, they appear together as a joint boldface entry. In some such cases, usage is about evenly divided between them. In still others, the evidence of collected citations indicates a greater frequency of occurrence for the one given

first. In no case is the first spelling considered "more correct" or the one necessarily to be preferred.

the·a·ter, the·a·tre . . . *n.* . . .

If one variant spelling, or several, are alphabetically close to the main-entry spelling and pronounced exactly like it but are somewhat or considerably less frequent in usage, such spellings are given at the end of the entry block in small boldface.

Par·chee·si . . . : also sp. **par·che′si, par·chi′si**

In some cases, the variants may involve diacritics, hyphens, or the like.

co·op·er·ate, co-op·er·ate . . . *vi.* . . . Also **co·öp′er·ate′**

When words having exactly the same meaning would fall alphabetically next to or close to each other, the less frequently used word is given in small boldface at the end of the definition for the predominant word.

laud·a·to·ry . . . *adj.* . . . : also **laud′a·tive**
-lep·sy . . . : also **-lep′si·a**

C. *Cross-references*

In all main entries that consist simply of a cross-reference to another entry of the same meaning, the entry cross-referred to is in small capitals.

gay·e·ty . . . *n.* . . . *same as* GAIETY
aer·o·plane . . . *n.* . . . *Brit. var. of* AIRPLANE
slap-bang . . . *—adj. colloq. var. of* SLAPDASH
me·grim . . . *n.* . . . *obs. var. of* MIGRAINE
yellow daisy ☆*popular name for* BLACK-EYED SUSAN
☆**ma·jor·ette** . . . *n. short for* DRUM MAJORETTE
log·o . . . *n. clipped form of* LOGOTYPE

D. *Homographs*

Main entries that are spelled alike but are different in meaning and origin, as **bat** (a club), **bat** (the animal), and **bat** (to wink), in addition to being entered in separate blocks are marked by superscript numbers immediately following the boldface spellings.

bat[1] . . . *n.* . . .
bat[2] . . . *n.* . . .
bat[3] . . . *vt.* . . .

When these need to be referred to in etymologies, definitions, etc., the cross-reference is made to the numbered homograph.

Main entries that differ from others with the same spelling by having such markings as accents, hyphens, etc. or by being capitalized are not considered homographs and are not marked with superscripts.

E. *Americanisms*

Words and phrases having their origin in the United States, as well as those senses of previously existing words or phrases that first came into use in this country, are marked as Americanisms by an open star (☆). (See article *Americanisms* by Mitford M. Mathews, p. xxxiii.)

If the star precedes the entry word, all senses in the block and run-in derivatives, if given, are Americanisms.

☆**las·so** . . . *n.* . . . a long rope or leather thong with a sliding noose at one end, used to catch cattle or wild horses *—vt.* to catch with a lasso *—***las′so·er** *n.*

If the star precedes a particular part of speech, all senses of that part of speech are Americanisms.

squid . . . *n.* . . . *—*☆*vi.* **squid′ded, squid′ding 1.** to take on an elongated squidlike shape due to strong air pressure: said of a parachute **2.** to fish for squid or with squid as bait

If the star precedes a single definition or part of a definition, only that definition or part is an Americanism.

liv·er·y . . . *n.* . . . **4.** *a)* . . . *b)* . . . ☆*c) same as* LIVERY STABLE
load . . . *n.* . . . ☆**6.** the amount of work carried by or assigned to a person, group, etc. [the class *load* of a teacher, the *caseload* of a social worker]
stuff . . . *n.* . . . **6.** something to be drunk, swallowed etc.; specif., a medicine or ☆[Slang] a drug, as heroin. . .

F. Foreign Terms

Foreign words and phrases encountered with some frequency in English speech and writing but not completely naturalized are marked with a double dagger (‡) preceding the boldface entry. The user of the dictionary is thus signaled that such terms are generally printed in italics or underlined in writing.

‡au na·tu·rel . . . [Fr.] . . .

Commonly used abbreviations for non-English terms are not marked with the sign (‡). Their etymologies show the language of origin and the full, unabbreviated form of the term.

i.e. [L. *id est*] that is (to say)
R.S.V.P., r.s.v.p. [Fr. *répondez s'il vous plaît*] please reply

G. Prefixes, Suffixes, & Combining Forms

Prefixes and initial combining forms are indicated by a hyphen following the entry form.

hem·i- . . . *a prefix meaning* half [*hemisphere*]

Suffixes and terminal combining forms are indicated by a hyphen preceding the entry form.

-la·try . . . *a combining form meaning* worship of or excessive devotion to [*idolatry*]

The very full coverage given these forms, which are also pronounced when pronunciation in isolation is feasible, makes it possible for the reader to understand and pronounce countless complex terms not entered in the dictionary but formed with affixes and words that are entered.

H. Syllabification

Center dots in the entry words indicate where the words can be divided if they need to be broken at the end of a written or printed line. In actual copy, a hyphen is used in place of the center dot. For example, **her·biv·o·rous** can be broken at the end of a line variously (**her-** or **herbiv-** or **herbivo-**), depending on how much space is available before the right-hand margin is reached.

The syllabifications used in this dictionary are in the main those in general use by printers since the 18th century. While they are not scientifically based on a consistent system, either morphological or phonological, they have developed as the most practical solution to a complicated problem. The only useful purpose of syllable markings is to signal the reader at the end of a line of written or printed matter and help him to anticipate what is to follow on the next line. More often than not, a syllabification based on a phonological division of the word best serves this purpose. Sometimes, especially when affixes or other fixed clusters are involved, a division based on the morphemes of a word is preferable. The syllabifications shown in this dictionary conform in most instances with those in use by the Government Printing Office.

Complicating any system is the fact that our language is in a continual flux and that changes in pronunciation and spelling gradually occur over a period of time. Thus, the syllabification shown at the entry word may be in conflict with one or more of the alternative pronunciations (e.g., **recondite**). Similarly, if a shift of stress occurs for a new part of speech (e.g., **progress**), the syllabification shown will properly apply only to the use of the word as the first part of speech given. In such a case a writer may wish to alter the syllabification (as from **prog·ress** for the noun to **pro·gress** for the verb) to accommodate the only real purpose of the syllable markings, that is, their signaling function. The variant pronunciation shown will usually, but not always, serve as a guide to such change.

All the syllables of a word are marked for the sake of consistency (e.g., **might·y, a·ban·don**). It is not, however, customary in writing or printing to break a word after the first syllable or before the last if that syllable consists of only a single letter, or, in the case of a long word, of only two.

II. PRONUNCIATION

A. Introduction

The pronunciations recorded in this dictionary are those used by cultivated speakers in normal, relaxed conversation. For technical words of a kind that occur in conversation, a relaxed pronunciation is recorded, but for more recondite ones that are found mostly in writing and are not often spoken, a formal pronunciation based essentially on analogy is given.

The pronunciations are symbolized in as broad a manner as is consistent with accuracy so that speakers of every variety of American English can easily read their own pronunciations into the symbols used here. For some words, variant pronunciations that are dialectal, British, Canadian, slang, etc. are given along with the standard American pronunciations. Contextual differences in pronunciation also have been indicated wherever practicable, as by showing variants in unstressed or shifted stress form. See Charlton Laird's article, *Language and the Dictionary*, p. xv, for further discussion of American pronunciation.

B. Key to Pronunciation

An abbreviated form of this key appears at the bottom of every alternate page of the vocabulary.

Symbol	Key Words	Symbol	Key Words
a	asp, fat, parrot	b	bed, fable, dub
ā	ape, date, play	d	dip, beadle, had
ä	ah, car, father	f	fall, after, off
		g	get, haggle, dog
e	elf, ten, berry	h	he, ahead, hotel
ē	even, meet, money	j	joy, agile, badge
		k	kill, tackle, bake
i	is, hit, mirror	l	let, yellow, ball
ī	ice, bite, high	m	met, camel, trim
		n	not, flannel, ton
ō	open, tone, go	p	put, apple, tap
ô	all, horn, law	r	red, port, dear
o͞o	ooze, tool, crew	s	sell, castle, pass
oo	look, pull, moor	t	top, cattle, hat
yo͞o	use, cute, few	v	vat, hovel, have
yoo	united, cure, globule	w	will, always, swear
oi	oil, point, toy	y	yet, onion, yard
ou	out, crowd, plow	z	zebra, dazzle, haze
u	up, cut, color	ch	chin, catcher, arch
ur	urn, fur, deter	sh	she, cushion, dash
		th	thin, nothing, truth
ə	a in ago	th	then, father, lathe
	e in agent	zh	azure, leisure
	i in sanity	ŋ	ring, anger, drink
	o in comply	'	[see explanatory note
	u in focus		below and also *For-*
ər	perhaps, murder		*eign sounds* below]

The qualities of most of the symbols above can be readily understood from the key words in which they are shown, and a speaker of any dialect of American English will automatically read his own pronunciation into any symbol shown here. A few explanatory notes on some of the more complex of these symbols follow.

ä This symbol represents essentially the low back vowel of *car*, but may also represent the low central vowel sometimes heard in New England for *bath*. Certain words shown with ä, such as *alms* (ämz), *hot* (hät), *rod* (räd), etc., are heard in the speech of some persons with vowel variation, ranging all the way to ô (ômz), (hôt), (rôd), etc. Such variation, though not generally recorded in this dictionary, may be assumed.

e This symbol represents the mid front vowel of *ten*, and is also used, followed by *r*, to represent the vowel sound of *care* (ker). For this sound, vowels ranging from ā (kār *or* kā'ər) to a (kar) are sometimes heard and, though not here recorded, may be assumed as variants.

ē This symbol represents the high front vowel of *meet* and is also used for the vowel in the unstressed final syllable of such words as *lucky* (luk'ē), *pretty* (prit'ē), etc. In such contexts, reduction to i (luk'i), (prit'i), etc. is often heard. Such variants, though not here recorded, may be assumed.

i This symbol represents the high front unrounded vowel of *hit* and is also used for the vowel in the unstressed syllables of such words as *garbage* (gär'bij), *goodness* (good'nis), *preface* (pref'is), *deny* (di nī'), *curate* (kyoor'it), etc. In such contexts, reduction to ə is commonly heard: (gär'bəj), (good'nəs), (pref'əs), (də nī'), (kyoor'ət), etc. Such variants, though not here recorded, may be assumed. This symbol is also used, followed and hence colored by *r*, to represent the vowel sound of *dear* (dir). For this sound, vowels ranging to ē (dēr *or* dē'ər) are sometimes heard and, though not here recorded, may be assumed as variants.

ô This symbol represents the mid to low back vowel of *all*. When followed by *r*, as in *more* (môr), vowels ranging to ō (mōr *or* mō'ər) are often heard and, though not here recorded, may be assumed as variants. Certain words shown with ô, such as *cough* (kôf), *lawn* (lôn), etc., are heard in the speech of some persons with vowel variation ranging all the way to ä (käf), (län), etc. Such variation, though not generally recorded in this dictionary, may be assumed.

ur and **ər** These two clusters of symbols represent respectively the stressed and unstressed r-colored vowels heard successively in the two syllables of *murder* (mur'dər). Where these symbols are shown, some speakers, especially in the South and along the Eastern seaboard, will, as a matter of course, pronounce them without the r-coloration, that is, by "dropping their r's." Such pronunciations, though not here recorded, may be inferred as variants.

ə This symbol, called the schwa, represents the mid central relaxed vowel of neutral coloration heard in the unstressed syllables of *ago, agent, focus*, etc. The degree and quality of the dulling of such vowels vary from word to word and from speaker to speaker. In many contexts, as for *-itis* (īt'əs), the vowel is often raised to i (īt'is). Such variants when not shown may be inferred.

t This symbol represents the voiceless alveolar stop of *top* or *hat*. When it appears between vowels, especially before an unstressed vowel, as in *later* (lāt'ər), or before a syllabic *l*, as in *cattle* (kat*'*l), it is often heard as a voiced sound that approaches the sound of *d* in *ladle*. Although such variants are not shown in this dictionary, the symbol (t) is generally placed in the same syllable with the preceding vowel to help the reader infer the voiced alternative.

ʊ This symbol represents the voiced velar nasal sound indicated in spelling by the *ng* of *sing* and occurring also for *n* before the back consonants *k* and *g*, as in *drink* (driŋk) and *finger* (fiŋ'gər).

' The apostrophe occurring before an *l*, *m*, or *n* indicates that the following consonant is a syllabic consonant; that is, that it forms the nucleus of a syllable with no appreciable vowel sound accompanying it, as in *apple* (ap*'*l) or *happen* (hap*'*n). In the speech of some persons, certain syllabic consonants are replaced with syllables containing reduced vowels, as in (hap'ən). Such variants, though not entered here, may be inferred. See *Foreign sounds*, below.

Foreign sounds

Most of the symbols in the key above have been used to transcribe pronunciations in foreign languages, although it should be understood that these sounds will vary somewhat from language to language. The additional symbols below will suffice to cover those situations that cannot be adequately dealt with using the general key. Several of these symbols are, again, intended to convey varying sounds in different languages, where the similarities are sufficient to permit the use of a single symbol.

à This symbol, representing the *a* in French *bal* (bàl) can best be described as intermediate between (a) and (ä).

ë This symbol represents the sound of the vowel cluster in French *coeur* (kër) and can be approximated by rounding the lips as for (ō) and pronouncing (c).

ö This symbol variously represents the sound of *eu* in French *feu* (fö) or of *ö* (or *oe*) in German *Göthe* (or *Goethe*) (gö'tə) and can be approximated by rounding the lips as for (ō) and pronouncing (ā).

ô This symbol represents a range of sounds varying from (ō) to (ô) and heard with such varying quality in French *coq* (kôk), German *doch* (dôkh), Italian *poco* (pô'kô), Spanish *torero* (tô re'rô), etc.

ü This symbol variously represents the sound of *u* in French *duc* (dük) and in German *grün* (grün) and can be approximated by rounding the lips as for (ōō) and pronouncing (ē).

kh This symbol represents the voiceless velar or uvular fricative as in German *doch* (dôkh). It can be approximated by arranging the speech organs as for (k) but allowing the breath to escape in a stream, as in pronouncing (h).

H This symbol represents a sound similar to the preceding but formed by friction against the forward part of the palate, as in German *ich* (iH). It is sometimes misheard, and hence pronounced, by English speakers as (sh).

n This symbol indicates that the vowel sound immediately preceding it is nasalized; that is, the nasal passage is left open so that the breath passes through both the mouth and nose in voicing the vowel, as in French *mon* (mōn).

r This symbol represents any of various sounds used in languages other than English for the consonant *r*. It may represent the tongue-point trill or uvular trill of the *r* in French *reste* (rest) or *sur* (sür), German *Reuter* (roi'tər), Italian *ricotta* (rē kôt'tä), Russian *gorod* (gô'rôd), etc.

' The apostrophe is used after final *l* and *r*, in certain French pronunciations, to indicate that they are voiceless after an unvoiced consonant, as in *lettre* (let*'*r'). In Russian words the "soft sign" in the Cyrillic spelling is indicated by (y'). The sound can be approximated by pronouncing an unvoiced (y) directly after the consonant involved, as in *Sevastopol* (se'väs tô'pəl y').

C. General Styling of Pronunciation

Pronunciations are given inside parentheses, immediately following the boldface entry. A single space is used between syllables. A primary, or strong, stress is indicated by a heavy stroke (') immediately following the syllable so stressed. A secondary, or weak, stress is indicated by a lighter stroke (') following the syllable so stressed All notes, labels, or other matter inside the parentheses other than the actual pronunciation symbols are in italics.

D. Truncation

Variant pronunciations are truncated wherever possible, with only that syllable or those syllables in which change occurs shown. A hyphen after the truncated variant marks it as initial; one before the variant, as terminal; and hyphens before and after the variant, as internal.

ab·duct (ab dukt', əb-) . . .
fu·tu·ri·ty (fyoo toor'ə tē, -tyoor'-, -choor'-) . . .
rec·ti·tude (rek'tə tōōd', -tyōōd') . . .

Truncations of variant pronunciations involving different parts of speech in the same entry block appear as follows:

pre·cip·i·tate (pri sip'ə tāt'; *also, for adj. & n.,* -tit) . . .

Truncated pronunciations are also given for a series of words with the same base after the pronunciation of the base has been established.

ju·di·ca·ble (jōō'di kə b'l) . . .
ju·di·ca·tive (-kāt'iv, -kə tiv) . . .
ju·di·ca·to·ry (-kə tôr'ē) . . .

Similarly, with a series containing compounds and derived forms:

time·keep·er (tīm'kē'pər) . . .
time-lapse (-laps') . . .
time·less (-lis) . . .
time loan . . .
time·ly (-lē) . . .

Full pronunciations are given with words in a series of the following kind when there is a shift in stress affecting the base.

bi·o·ce·no·sis (bī'ō si nō'sis) . . .
bi·o·chem·is·try (-kem'is trē) . . .
bi·o·cide (bī'ə sīd') . . .
bi·o·cli·ma·tol·o·gy (bī'ō klī'mə täl'ə jē) . . .
bi·o·de·grad·a·ble (-di grā'də b'l) . . .

E. *Variants*

Where two or more pronunciations for a single word are given, the order in which they are entered does not necessarily mean that the first is preferred to or more correct than the one or ones that follow. In most cases, the order indicates that on the basis of available information, the form given first is the one most frequent in general cultivated use. Where usage is about evenly divided, since one form must be given first, the editors' preference generally prevails. Unless a variant is qualified, as by *now rarely* or *occasionally* or some such note, it is understood that any pronunciation here entered represents a standard use.

Compounds or phrases of two or more separate, unhyphenated words (e.g., **bill of attainder** or **launch pad**), each of which has been entered and pronounced separately in the dictionary, are not repronounced.

III. PART-OF-SPEECH LABELS

Part-of-speech labels are given for lower-case main entries that are solid or hyphenated forms, except prefixes, suffixes, and abbreviations. The following labels for the parts of speech into which words are classified in traditional English grammar are used in this dictionary. They appear in boldface italic type following the pronunciations.

n.	noun	*prep.*	preposition
vt.	transitive verb	*conj.*	conjunction
vi.	intransitive verb	*pron.*	pronoun
adj.	adjective	*interj.*	interjection
adv.	adverb		

In addition, the following labels are sometimes used:

n.pl. plural noun
v.aux. auxiliary verb
v.impersonal impersonal verb
n.fem. feminine noun
n.masc. masculine noun

When an entry word is used as more than one part of speech, long dashes introduce each different part of speech in the entry block and each part-of-speech label appears in boldface italic type.

round¹ . . . *adj.* . . . *—n.* . . . *—vt.* . . . *—vi.* . . . *—adv.* . . . *—prep.* . . .

Two or more part-of-speech labels are given jointly for an entry when the definition or definitions, or the cross-reference, will suffice for both or all.

lip-read . . . *vt., vi.* . . . to recognize (a speaker's words) by lip reading . . .
hal·lo, hal·loa . . . *interj., n., vi., vt.* same as HALLOO

Part-of-speech labels are not used for names of persons and places, or for given names, figures in religion, mythology, literature, etc. However, usages have sometimes developed from these that can be classified as parts of speech and these are indicated.

A·don·is . . . *Gr. Myth.* a handsome young man loved by Aphrodite: he was killed by a wild boar *—n.* any very handsome young man . . .

It is theoretically possible to use almost any word as whatever part of speech is required, although most such uses would be only for the nonce. Thus any transitive verb can be used absolutely as an intransitive verb, with the object understood (e.g., he *defined* the word; you must *define* discriminatively). Such absolute uses are entered only when they are relatively common. In the same way nouns used as adjectives (e.g., a *cloth* cover; a *family* affair) are indicated only for the most frequent uses.

IV. INFLECTED FORMS

Inflected forms regarded as irregular or offering difficulty in spelling are entered in small boldface immediately following the part-of-speech labels. They are truncated where possible, and syllabified and pronounced where necessary.

A. *Plurals of Nouns*

Plurals formed regularly by adding -*s* to the singular (or -*es* after *s, x, z, ch,* and *sh*), as *bats, boxes,* are not normally indicated.

Plurals are shown when formed irregularly, as for nouns with a -*y* ending that changes to -*ies,* and for those with an -*o* ending, those inflected by internal change, those having variant forms, those having different forms for different meanings, compound nouns, etc.

cit·y . . . *n., pl.* **cit′ies** . . .
bo·le·ro . . . *n., pl.* -**ros** . . .
tooth . . . *n., pl.* **teeth** (tēth) . . .
a·moe·ba . . . *n., pl.* -**bas, -bae** (-bē) . . .
die² . . . *n., pl.* for 1 & 2, **dice** (dīs); for 3 & 4 **dies** (dīz)
son-in-law . . . *n., pl.* **sons′-in-law′** . . .

If an irregular plural is so altered in spelling that it would appear at some distance from the singular form, it is entered additionally in its proper alphabetical place.

lice . . . *n. pl. of* LOUSE

B. *Principal Parts of Verbs*

Verb forms regarded as regular and not normally indicated include:
a) present tenses formed by adding -*s* to the infinitive (or -*es* after *s, x, z, ch,* and *sh*), as *waits, searches;*
b) past tenses and past participles formed by simply adding -*ed* to the infinitive with no other changes in the verb form, as *waited, searched;*
c) present participles formed by simply adding -*ing* to the infinitive with no other change in the verb form, as *waiting, searching.*

Principal parts are given for irregular verbs, including those in which the final *e* is dropped in forming the present participle, those which always or optionally repeat the final consonant in all principal parts, those in which -*y* changes to -*ie* in the past tense and past participle, and those inflected by internal change.

Where two inflected forms are given for a verb, the first is the form for the past tense and the past participle, and the second is the form for the present participle.

make . . . *vt.* **made, mak′ing** . . .
sip . . . *vt., vi.* **sipped, sip′ping** . . .

Where three forms are given, separated from one another by commas, the first represents the past tense, the second the past participle, and the third the present participle.

swim . . . *vi.* **swam, swum, swim′ming** . . .

Where there are alternative forms for any of the principal parts, these are indicated as follows:

trav·el . . . *vi.* -**eled** or -**elled, -el·ing** or -**el·ling** . . .
drink . . . *vt.* **drank** or archaic **drunk** (druŋk), **drunk** or now colloq. **drank** or archaic **drunk′en, drink′ing** . . .

If a principal part of a verb is so altered in spelling that it would appear at some distance from the infinitive form, it is entered additionally in its proper alphabetical place.

said . . . *pt. & pp. of* SAY

C. *Comparatives & Superlatives of Adjectives & Adverbs*

Comparatives and superlatives formed by simply adding -*er* or -*est* to the base, as *taller, tallest,* are not indicated. Those formed irregularly, as by adding -*r* and -*st* (*rare, rarer, rarest*), by changing final -*y* to -*i-* (*happy, happier, happiest*), or by some radical change in form (*good, better, best* or *well, better, best*), are indicated with the positive form.

The positive form is also noted at the comparative and superlative forms when these are entered and defined at some distance from it.

best . . . *adj. superl. of* GOOD . . . —*adv. superl. of* WELL²

Conjugations are given for those irregular verbs that are used as auxiliaries (**be, have,** etc.) and declensions are given for the personal pronouns. The various conjugated and declined forms for these important elements, both current and archaic, are also entered separately.

V. THE ETYMOLOGY

Etymology has been made a strong feature of this dictionary because it is believed that insights into the current usage of a word can be gained from a full knowledge of the word's history and that a better understanding of language generally can be achieved from knowing how words are related to other words in English and to words in other Indo-European languages. Particular attention is paid to showing these relationships as fully as possible and to carrying the

etymologies back where possible (either directly or through cross-reference) to the Indo-European base.

Etymologies appear in entry blocks inside heavy boldface brackets that make them clearly distinguishable in their position before the definitions proper. The symbols, as < for "derived from," and the abbreviations of language labels, etc. used in the etymologies are dealt with in full in the Abbreviations and Symbols list immediately preceding page 1 of the vocabulary.

The form and content of a typical etymology is demonstrated in the following entry for **life.**

life (līf) *n., pl.* **lives** [ME. < OE. *lif,* akin to ON. *lif,* life, G. *leib,* body < IE. base **leibh,* to live, whence L. (*cae*)*lebs,* unmarried, orig., living alone (cf. CELIBATE)] **1.** that property of plants and animals which makes it possible . . .

The first portion of this etymology, dealing with the history of the word within English itself, indicates that in Middle English the word is found in the same form and with the same meaning as in Modern English, and that this form derives from the Old English word *lif.* Cognate forms from other Germanic languages are next introduced by the words *akin to,* the first cognate, Old Norse *lif,* with the same meaning, "life," and the other, German *leib,* with an interestingly related meaning, "body." The word is then taken back to the reconstructed Indo-European base (its hypothetical character is indicated by an *) and its meaning, "to live." Following is a Latin word derived from this base, *caelebs* (note the similarity in the last syllable), whose meaning, "unmarried," although seemingly unrelated to the meaning of the base, is shown to be directly related through the original meaning, "living alone." Finally there is a cross-reference (in small capitals) to an English word in the dictionary, *celibate,* which derives from the Latin word *caelebs* and which the user can consult further if he is interested. Thus we have traveled back in the history of an entry word across language barriers to the very root of the word and forward again to a modern English word related to it.

Some words are etymologized by means of cross-references (in small capitals) to their component elements, which are dealt with separately in the dictionary.

pro·to·ste·le . . . *n.* [PROTO- + STELE] . . .
si·lox·ane . . . *n.* [SIL(ICON) + OX(YGEN) + -ANE] . . .
splurge . . . *n.* [echoic blend of SPL(ASH) + (S)URGE] . . .

Note that in two of the etymologies above, the parentheses are used to set off parts dropped in telescoping the words that were used to form the entry word. It is always the whole word, however, that will be found in the dictionary.

No etymology is shown where one would be superfluous, as because the elements making up the word are immediately apparent to the user (e.g., **preconscious**) or because the definition that follows clearly explains the derivation (e.g., **bluebottle**).

Where no etymology can be ascertained and no reasonable conjecture can be made, that fact is indicated by the following: [< ?]

A special effort has been made to include as many etymologies as possible for place names in the United States.

VI. THE DEFINITIONS

A. *Order of Senses*

The senses of an entry have, wherever possible, been arranged in semantic order from the etymology to the most recent sense so that there is a logical, progressive flow showing the development of the word and the relationship of its senses to one another (see, for example, the entries **stock** and **common**). In longer entries, where the treatment would not greatly disturb the semantic flow, technical senses have been entered, with special field labels in alphabetical order, usually following the general senses, to facilitate their being found quickly. For the same reason, senses that are colloquial, slang, archaic, obsolete, dialectal, or the like are generally entered, with suitable usage labels, just before the technical senses. Sometimes labeled senses will appear earlier in the block, if it is desirable to tie them in semantically with general or standard senses. Obsolete senses that bridge the gap between the etymology and the definitions proper often occur first. Such senses are generally preceded by "originally" or "formerly" rather than by a formal usage label.

B. *Numbering & Grouping of Senses*

Senses are numbered consecutively within any given part of speech in boldface numerals. Numeration is begun anew for each part of speech and for each idiomatic phrase.

aim . . . *vi., vt.* . . . **1.** . . . **2.** . . . **3.** . . . **4.** . . . —*n.* **1.** . . . **2.** . . . **3.** . . . **4.** . . . —**take aim 1.** . . . **2.** . . .

Where a primary sense of a word can easily be subdivided into several closely related meanings, this has been done; such meanings are indicated by italicized letters after the pertinent numbered or labeled sense. The words "especially" or "specifically" (abbreviated "esp." and "specif.") are

often used after an introductory definition to introduce such a grouping of related senses.

hack[2] . . . *n*. . . . . **1.** *a)* a horse for hire *b)* a horse for all sorts of work *c)* a saddle horse *d)* an old, worn-out horse **2.** a person hired to do routine, often dull, writing; literary drudge . . .

low[1] . . . *n*. something low; specif., ☆*a)* that gear of a motor vehicle, etc. producing the lowest speed and the greatest power; also, an arrangement similar to this in an automatic transmission *b)* a low level, point, degree, etc. /the stock market *low* for the day/ ☆*c) Meteorol.* an area of low barometric pressure . . .

Where a basic word has very many senses that can conveniently be arranged under a few major headings, such a division has been made (e.g., **go, time**). The sections, indicated by boldface Roman numerals, are then further subdivided into numbered (and, where necessary, lettered) senses.

C. *Capitalization*

If a main-entry word is capitalized in all its senses, the entry word itself is printed with a capital letter (e.g., **European**).

If a capitalized main-entry word has a sense or senses that are uncapitalized, these are marked with the corresponding small-boldface, lower-case letter followed by a short dash and enclosed in brackets.

Pur·i·tan . . . *n*. . . . **1.** . . . **2.** [p-] . . . —*adj.* **1.** . . . **2.** [p-] . . .

Conversely, capitalized letters are shown where pertinent with lower-case entries. In some instances these designations are qualified by the self-explanatory "usually," "often," "also," or "occas." in italics.

north . . . *n*. . . **1.** . . . **2.** . . . **3.** . . . **4.** [*often* N-] . . . —*adj.* **1.** . . . **2.** . . . **3.** [N-] . . .

D. *Plural Forms*

In a singular noun entry, the designation "[*pl.*]" (or "[*often pl.*]," "[*usually pl.*]," etc.) before a definition indicates that it is (or *often, usually*, etc. is) the plural form of the entry word that has the meaning given in the definition.

lim·it . . . *n*. . . . **1.** . . . **2.** [*pl.*] bounds; boundary lines . . .
look . . . *vi.* . . —*n.* **1.** . . . **2.** . . . **3.** [Colloq.] *a)* [*usually pl.*] appearance; the way something seems to be . . . *b)* [*pl.*] personal appearance, esp. of a pleasing nature . . .

If such a plural sense is construed as singular, the designation "*with sing. v.*" is added inside the brackets.

bone . . . *n.* . . . **7.** *a)* [*pl.*] flat sticks used as clappers in minstrel shows ☆*b)* [*pl., with sing. v.*] the end man in a minstrel show . . .

The note "*usually used in pl.*" at the end of a singular noun definition means that although the definition applies to the given singular form of the entry word, the word is usually used in the plural.

lead[2] (led) *n.* . . . **1.** . . . **2.** anything made of this metal; specif., *a)* . . . *b)* any of the strips of lead used to hold the individual panes in ornamental windows: *usually used in pl.* . . .

If a plural noun entry is construed as singular, the designation "[*with sing. v.*]" is placed after the *n.pl.* label or, in some cases, with the numbered sense to which it applies.

☆**ger·i·at·rics** . . . *n.pl.* [*with sing. v.*] . . . the branch of medicine that deals with the diseases and hygiene of old age . . .
a·cous·tics . . . *n.pl.* **1.** . . . **2.** [*with sing. v.*] . . .

E. *Prepositions Accompanying Verbs*

Where certain verbs are, in usage, invariably or usually followed by a specific preposition or prepositions, this has been indicated in the following ways: the preposition has been worked into the definition, italicized and enclosed in parentheses, or a note has been added in parentheses indicating that the preposition is so used.

strike . . . *vi.* . . . **10.** to come suddenly or unexpectedly; fall, light, etc. (*on* or *upon*) /to *strike* on the right combination/
strike . . . *vi.* . . . ☆**17.** *U.S. Navy* to try hard to qualify (*for* a rating) . . .
fig[2] . . . *vt.* . . . . to dress showily (with *out* or *up*) . . .
hit . . . *vi.* . . . **3.** to knock, bump, or strike (usually with *against*) . . .

Such uses of verbs with specific prepositions should not be confused with verb sets consisting of a verb form with an adverb, which are entered as idiomatic phrases under the key verb (e.g., **make out, make over,** and **make up** at the entry **make**).

F. *Objects of Transitive Verbs*

In definitions of transitive verbs the specific or generalized objects of the verb, where given, are enclosed in parentheses since such objects are not part of the definition.

ob·serve . . . *vt.* . . . **1.** to adhere to, follow, keep, or abide by (a law, custom, duty, rule, etc.) **2.** to celebrate or keep (a holiday, etc.) according to custom **3.** *a)* to notice or perceive (something) *b)* to pay special attention to . . .

In 3*b* above, it will be noted no object is shown; the definition is formulated so that it is apparent that the verb takes an object. In some such cases the transitive verb can be defined jointly with the intransitive verb.

chis·el . . . —*vi., vt.* . . . **1.** to cut or shape with a chisel . . .

G. *Additional Information & Notes*

Additional information or any note or comment on the definition proper is preceded by a colon.

mag·ne·to·sphere . . . *n.* . . . that region surrounding a planet in which the planetary magnetic field is stronger than the interplanetary field: the earth's magnetosphere extends about 3.5 million miles in the direction away from the sun . . .
ma·ture . . . *adj.* . . . **4.** due; payable: said of a note, bond, etc. . . .
mil·li·gram . . . *n.* . . . : also, chiefly Brit. sp., **mil′li·gramme′**: abbrev. **mg.** (*sing. & pl.*)

If the note or comment applies to all the senses or parts of speech preceding it, it begins with a capital letter and no colon introduces it.

old hat [Slang] **1.** old-fashioned; out-of-date **2.** well-known or familiar to the point of being trite or commonplace Used predicatively

Where the explanatory material consists of a series of items, as in geographical and chemical definitions, the colon precedes the first item and the others are separated by semicolons (e.g., **hydrogen, Ohio**).

H. *Illustrative Examples of Entry Words in Context*

Examples of usage have been liberally supplied, enclosed in lightface slant brackets, with the word that is being illustrated set in italics. These brief illustrative examples are helpful in clarifying meaning, discriminating a large stock of senses for a basic word, showing level of usage or special connotation, and supplying added information.

com·mon . . . *adj.* . . . **1.** belonging equally to, or shared by, every one or all /the *common* interests of a group/ **2.** belonging or relating to the community at large; public /*common* carriers/ **3.** widely existing; general; prevalent /*common* knowledge/ **4.** widely but unfavorably known /a *common* criminal/ **5.** met with or occurring frequently; familiar; usual /a *common* sight/ **6.** not of the upper classes; of the masses /the *common* man/

I. *Internal Entry Words*

Entry words occasionally occur within definitions, parenthesized and in small boldface type. In such cases, the meaning of the inserted entry word is made clear in the definition.

☆**time clock** a clock with a mechanism for recording on a card (**timecard**) the time an employee begins and ends a work period

J. *Cross-references*

Entry words (or tables, illustrations, etc.) to which the reader is being cross-referred are given in small capitals.

ca·tab·o·lism . . . *n.* . . . : opposed to ANABOLISM
con·sub·stan·ti·a·tion . . . *n.* . . . : cf. TRANSUBSTANTIATION
fa . . . *n.* . . . : see SOLFEGGIO
Gem·i·ni . . . : see ZODIAC, illus.
natural law 1. . . . **2.** . . . : see LAW (sense 8 *a*) . . .
natural selection . . . : see also DARWINIAN THEORY
sol[1] . . . *n.* . . . : see MONETARY UNITS, table

VII. USAGE LABELS & NOTES

It is generally understood that usage varies among groups of people according to locality, level of education, social environment, occupation, etc. More specifically, it must be remembered, usage varies for an individual in any given day depending upon the particular situation in which he is involved and the purpose his language must serve. The language that a scientist uses in preparing a report on his work may be quite different from the language he uses in writing a letter to a friend. What is good usage in a literary essay may not be the best usage in the lyrics to a popular song or in casual conversation. None of the modes of using language in the cases cited is in an absolute sense more correct than any of the others. Each is right for its occasion and any attempt to interchange styles can result in inappropriate language. Certain occasions call for language

that is more or less formal, and others, language that is more or less informal.

Dictionaries can reasonably be expected to assign usage labels to those terms that the record shows are regularly used in informal or highly informal contexts. The editors of this dictionary decided that the familiarity of the conventional usage designations makes their use advisable if the meaning of these labels is clearly understood in advance. The labels, and what they are intended to indicate, are given below. If the label, which is placed in brackets (and in some cases abbreviated), occurs directly after a part-of-speech label or after a boldface entry term, it applies to all the senses given with that part of speech or that term; if it occurs after a numeral or letter, it applies only to the sense so numbered or lettered.

Colloquial: The term or sense is generally characteristic of conversation and informal writing. It is not to be regarded as substandard or illiterate.

Slang: The term or sense is not generally regarded as conventional or standard usage but is used, even by the best speakers, in highly informal contexts. Slang consists of both coined terms and of new or extended meanings attached to established terms. Slang terms either pass into disuse in time or come to have a more formal status.

Obsolete: The term or sense is no longer used but occurs in earlier writings.

Archaic: The term or sense is rarely used today except in certain restricted contexts, as in church ritual, but occurs in earlier writings.

Poetic: The term or sense is used chiefly in poetry, especially in earlier poetry, or in prose where a poetic quality is desired.

Dialect: The term or sense is used regularly only in some geographical areas or in a certain designated area (*South, Southwest, West,* etc.) of the United States.

British (or *Canadian, Scottish,* etc.): The term or sense is characteristic of British (or Canadian, etc.) English rather than of that spoken in the United States. When preceded by *chiefly,* the label indicates an additional, though less frequent, American usage. *British dialect* indicates that the term or sense is used regularly only in certain geographical areas of Great Britain, usually in northern England.

In addition to the above usage labels, supplementary information is often given after the definition, indicating whether the term or sense is generally regarded as vulgar, substandard, or derogatory, used with ironic, familiar, or hyperbolic connotations, etc. Where there are some objections to common usages, that fact is also indicated (e.g., **who, whom**).

VIII. FIELD LABELS

Labels for specialized fields of knowledge and activity appear in italics (in abbreviated form where practical) immediately before the sense involved. In long entry blocks having many general and specialized senses, these labels, arranged in alphabetical order, help the user to quickly find the special sense or senses he is seeking.

form . . . *n.* . . . 17. *Gram.* . . . 18. *Linguis.* . . . 19. *Philos.* . . . 20. *Printing* . . .
hit . . . *vt.* . . . ☆12. *Baseball* . . . ☆13. *Card Games* . . .

IX. SCIENTIFIC NAMES OF PLANTS & ANIMALS

When the name of an animal or plant is entered in this dictionary, its scientific name is included parenthetically in the definition.

All animals and plants have been given Modern Latin or Latinized names by biologists in accordance with rules prescribed by international codes of zoological and botanical nomenclature and have been systematically classified into certain categories, or taxa, that discriminate the similarities and differences among organisms.

Taxonomists are continuously studying and comparing basic materials in order to classify organisms more precisely or to modify, when necessary, current classifications. The taxonomic designations used in this dictionary reflect the most recent and most reliable information available from such constant scrutiny, including current revisions in classification.

The basic taxa are phylum or division, class, order, family, genus, and species. When these or any additional taxonomic names appear in this dictionary, they are enclosed in parentheses and, in conformity with the international codes, have an initial capital with the regular exception of the names of species and taxa ranking below species.

The scientific name of every species of animal or plant is an italicized binomial that consists of the capitalized name of the genus followed by the uncapitalized specific name or

epithet. In those taxa where a trinomial is used, as for a variety, the third term is uncapitalized and italicized.

car·rot . . . *n.* . . . 1. a biennial plant (*Daucus carota*) of the parsley family . . .
mus·tard . . . *n.* . . . 1. any of several annual plants (genus *Brassica*) . . . —*adj.* designating or of a family (Cruciferae) of plants . . .
cab·bage[1] . . . *n.* . . . 1. a common vegetable (*Brassica oleracea capitata*) of the mustard family . . .
chor·date . . . *n.* . . . any of a phylum (Chordata) of animals . . .
mam·mal . . . *n.* . . . any of a large class (Mammalia) of . . . vertebrates . . .
car·ni·vore . . . *n.* . . . any of an order (Carnivora) of fanged, flesh-eating mammals . . .
wolf . . . *n.* . . . 1. *a*) any of a large group of wild, flesh-eating, doglike mammals (genus *Canis*) . . .
☆**gray wolf** a large, gray wolf (*Canis lupus*) . . .

X. IDIOMATIC PHRASES

Idiomatic phrases are run in on an entry block alphabetically after the definition or definitions of the main-entry word, each phrasal entry set in small boldface with a dash preceding it. Such phrases have been entered wherever possible under the key word.

busi·ness . . . *n.* . . . . —**business is business** . . . —**do business with** . . . —☆**give** (or **get**) **the business** . . . —**mean business** . . .

Alternative forms are indicated inside parentheses, as above in **give** (or **get**) **the business**. In the phrase (**at**) **full tilt** under the entry **tilt**, both the longer phrase, **at full tilt**, and the shorter, **full tilt**, are being recorded.

XI. RUN-IN DERIVED ENTRIES

It is possible in English to form an almost infinite number of derived forms simply by adding certain prefixes or suffixes to the base word. It has been the purpose of the editors to include as run-in entries in small boldface type only those words one might reasonably expect to encounter in literature or ordinary usage, and then only when the meaning of such derived words can be immediately understood from the meanings of the base word and the affix. Thus, **greatness, liveliness,** and **newness** are run in at the end of the entries for **great, lively,** and **new,** the meanings of the derived forms being clearly understood from the base word and the suffix -**ness,** which is found as a separate entry in this dictionary and means "state, quality, or instance of being." Many words formed with common suffixes such as -**able,** -**er,** -**less,** -**like,** -**ly,** -**tion,** etc. are similarly treated as run-in entries with the base word from which they are derived. All such entries are syllabled and either accented to show stress in pronunciation or, where necessary, pronounced in full or in part. Each run-in derived form is preceded by a dash.

If two synonymous run-in derived forms share a part-of-speech label, the more frequently used form appears first and the part-of-speech label is given after the second form. Note the plural form following the first run-in:

prac·ti·cal . . . *adj.* . . . . —**prac′ti·cal′i·ty** (-kal′ə tē), *pl.* -**ties, prac′ti·cal·ness** *n.*

When a derived word has a meaning or meanings different from those which can be deduced from the sum of its parts, it has been entered in a block of its own, pronounced, and fully defined (e.g., **producer**).

XII. THE SYNONYMY

The dictionary contains many short paragraphs in which synonyms are listed and discriminated. Each such synonymy is entered after that word in the group which may generally be considered the most basic or comprehensive. Although synonyms have similar or closely related meanings, they are not always interchangeable with one another. The subtle differences that distinguish them are of great importance to precision in language. These distinctions are briefly stated and typical examples of usage given where these will be helpful.

The abbreviation *SYN.* in boldface italic capitals at the left indented margin of an entry block introduces a synonymy for the main-entry word. Each of the words discriminated in the paragraph carries, at its own place of entry in the vocabulary, a cross-reference to that synonymy. Thus, following the entry for **guffaw,** there is a note "—*SYN.* see LAUGH."

In many cases antonyms are given at the end of the synonymy and these, in turn, may receive discriminative treatment themselves, following their own entries in the dictionary.

LANGUAGE AND THE DICTIONARY

by Charlton Laird

I. *The Making of Dictionaries*

Language can be thought of as articulate mind, as the means of becoming human, as the record of wit at play, as the right hand of thought, or as the great reservoir of symbol, but as a working tool it results from the use man has made of it. The general record of that use is the dictionary, a useful tool in the twin senses that it has many uses and that use has formed its contents.

Although this introduction is intended to promote the first of these understandings, that a dictionary has manifold uses, this end may be served by observing the second, that man has shaped language by his use of it, and that dictionary makers work from this fact. All good recent dictionaries have been based directly or indirectly on this principle, that any language at any time will be what it is because of the way the previous and current users of the language have employed it. Literally, no one can discover how a language is being employed, since language is always changing, and the shifts and innovations may become apparent only later. Practically, however, we have devices for discovering what a language has been, what it is now, and even what it is becoming. Modern lexicographers profit from these techniques and can, through the dictionaries they edit, tell us how the language is being used, and how we can use it well.

Not always has man enjoyed such tools. Men have always sought to order information, using language to do so, but early lists of words have, in the main, not survived. The modern dictionary has a more recent origin, seeming to stem from linguistic confusion during the Middle Ages in Europe, when Latin was the universal learned language but was known to relatively few people, with most communication relying upon a welter of vernacular tongues and dialects, many of them highly regional. Fluent readers of Latin did not know all the local languages with which they came in contact, and most speakers of local dialects knew Latin only imperfectly. Accordingly, we find medieval manuscripts in which a Latin word like *puer* will have a vernacular equivalent like *boy* written above it. Similarly, *hyde and gaine* was an early English phrase for as much land as a man could till and the profit he might expect from it, but a priest involved in canon law, born in Rome, educated in Paris, and now serving in London, could not be assumed to know this. Accordingly, such an English phrase might be adorned with a gloss, for example, a synonym in Latin, or perhaps the Anglo-Norman used in the courts.

Such a gloss when combined with the glossed word becomes, in effect, a simple dictionary entry. It provides the word itself, an accepted spelling of it, and by implication, since the spelling was roughly phonetic, a suggested pronunciation. It implies something about the grammar, since presumably the word or phrase could be used in the same way in either language, and it offers an acceptable usage. It even provides a definition of sorts, since the gloss includes a synonym in another language. Thus the user of such manuscripts had ready-made materials for a simple dictionary if he wished so to use them; he had only to assemble them in some kind of order, preferably alphabetical.

Such books were compiled. The earliest we know in English was called *Promptorium Parvulorum* (the title might be translated *A Treasure House for the Children*), apparently intended for youngsters learning Latin, though it probably served some of their elders as well. Such collections became the ancestors of bilingual dictionaries; Shakespeare, for example, could have used quite a good Italian-English dictionary published by one John Florio just before 1600, and at about this time dictionaries of English began to appear, although from our point of view they are poor things. They were small, and like *A Treasure House for the Children* and the bilingual dictionaries, they were calculated to help people ignorant of a language or of a dialect of it, in this case a social dialect, learn the speech of the supposedly best people. A typical introduction to one of these dictionaries of English is likely to explain that the book is intended for foreigners, artisans, farmers, and the like—presumably gentlemen and professional people would know the fashionable dialect already. The entries themselves are devoted to what were called "hard words" or to meanings assumed to be rare. Even as late as 1676, Elisha Coles in compiling *An English Dictionary Explaining Difficult Terms*, the best English dictionary of its day, defines a horse only as "a rope fasten'd to the foremast shrouds, to keep the sprit-sail sheats clear of the anchor-flukes."

Apparently he saw no reason to waste good printed paper on the more common uses of the word, and even in the next century, Nathaniel Bailey, often called "the father of English lexicography," dismisses the Englishman's favorite equine quadruped with the epithet, "a Beast well known," adding only that the word could be used for both the male and the female.

Thus the essential problems involved in dictionary making appeared early, presenting such questions as these: For whom is a dictionary made? To what purposes should it be put? What words should be included, and what uses recognized? And most difficult of all, what should be said about the words included, particularly, how should they be defined? The early answers were limited and practical; dictionaries were conceived to be helpful little books, useful to persons ignorant of language in one way or another, including children, foreigners, and underprivileged adults.

Meanwhile, more sophisticated philosophies and better editorial practices were being developed on the European continent. Two ideas predominated: (1) that all important words, and all of the most important material about these words, should be included in the dictionary, even though much of the resulting matter would be familiar to many people, and (2) information about the word should be based upon recorded evidence, upon samples of the language as it is known to have been used. Thus the job of the lexicographer was now being seen as the studying, the ordering, the evaluating, and the interpreting of linguistic evidence, and not merely the digesting of what the editor happens to know or prefers to believe. In effect, this means that the lexicographer must first collect vast numbers of citations, selected for their revealing qualities, from all sorts of writers; he must then study these citations for their significance, consulting experts if necessary, and order the result into a book. A dictionary so prepared can be described as edited on historical principles.

As a matter of course, these two basic ideas did not spring full-blown from any single brain, nor were they immediately grasped in their entirety. Consider one of the best-known definitions from the best-known English lexicographer, Samuel Johnson, who wrote as follows: "OATS. *n.* A grain which in England is generally given to horses, but in Scotland supports the people." Johnson was here quite possibly twitting his friend and biographer, the Scotsman James Boswell, and the witticism would have been appropriate in Johnson's satirical writings or in his table talk, but it is palpably a poor definition, at least partly because it comes from Johnson's wit, his playfulness, his prejudices, or something of the sort, and not from the recorded use of the word. If a contemporary Chinese, presented with an oat, had relied only on Johnson's dictionary, he would not have known how to recognize the object or even what to do with it, being neither a horse nor a Scotsman. Similarly, early lexicographers, inheriting little tradition as to what constitutes use, tended to consult the writings of famous literary figures, and thus to miss technical words, and if they had little objective evidence concerning a term, they took the easiest way to a ready answer by resorting to their own memories. Such an editor, being well-informed, would usually have been right, but a modern lexicographer refuses such shortcuts, feeling that in the end his product will be more objective and more reliable if he restricts "use" to documented use. On the other hand, he has learned to supplement written use with oral use, which earlier recorders of the language mainly ignored.

If modern lexicography arrived a little late on the island of Britain, it thrived in the good soil of the English-speaking peoples. Bailey, mentioned above, was conversant with the best Continental lexicography of his day, and he embodied its principles in *An Universal Etymological Dictionary* (first edition, 1721), which Johnson used as the basis of his great *Dictionary of the English Language* (1755). As a result, Johnson has been popularly credited with developing much that he only inherited from Bailey, who had imported it from abroad. Yet if, confirmed conservative that he was, Johnson has been given too much credit as an innovator, he can scarcely be given too much as an editor. He brought to his work a sharpened command of his native language, a mind stored with the Latin and Greek classics, indefatigable energy, and a disciplined judgment. The result was that, probably without a close second, he did more to bring order and good sense into our concept of English meaning than any other man before or since. All subsequent

Language and the Dictionary

English and American dictionaries have stemmed from him and the lexicographical tradition he inspired.

For whatever reasons—and they are not entirely clear—dictionaries have become a sort of specialty of the English-speaking world. A possible explanation may be sought in the size of the vocabulary, since English seems to have more words and more uses for words—many more than two million named uses—than any other known language. Speakers of English have uncommon need for dictionaries, and Americans, who constitute the largest single body of English speakers and who have been uncommonly well provided with the means of buying reference works, have augmented this need through what would seem to be a mania for linguistic correctness, a zeal for rectitude which they have built into their elaborate school system. Thus, for whatever reason, the speakers of no other known language have ever brought to fruition such a work as the *Oxford English Dictionary* (also called *A New English Dictionary on Historical Principles*), whose editors endeavored to trace every use of every word that has ever gained wide currency in the native tongue. The creation of the modern American desk dictionary is scarcely less remarkable.

American lexicography has its own glories and its own character. The founder of the American school was Noah Webster, whose *An American Dictionary of the English Language* (1828 and frequently revised and enlarged) was a truly remarkable work, especially for its day and place, a New World still very much a colony, socially and intellectually, of the Old. Webster was as untiring and self-assertive as Samuel Johnson himself, and if he was less well read and probably less intellectually endowed, he suffered from no false modesty and he possessed a genius for definition. His work was rivaled in many ways by that of his one-time employee, Joseph E. Worcester, and the "War of the Dictionaries" waged between the successors to Webster's volume and Worcester's *A Dictionary of the English Language* (1860) lent to lexicography the zest of a sporting event. Dictionaries were news in the New World, and a great century of dictionary making was crowned by the labors of William Dwight Whitney and his colleagues in editing *The Century Dictionary: an Encyclopedic Lexicon of the English Language* (1889 and following), a work variously printed in as many as fourteen volumes, probably the best dictionary in English of its day published on either side of the Atlantic Ocean—the *Oxford* was then being edited but was thirty-five years from complete publication.

Modern desk dictionaries grow in part from the great descriptive dictionaries like the *Oxford*, but they are also distinct from these works, not merely smaller imitations of them. They resemble the more comprehensive, purely descriptive dictionaries in that they are based upon use, use revealed in objectively collected evidence, and when necessary evaluated by experts, although in the interests of economy—economy of space, and thus eventually of economy in cost—and for convenience in handling, desk dictionaries are made to rely upon this evidence more or less indirectly. All editors of desk dictionaries depend in part upon the citations assembled for descriptive dictionaries; for example, all editors of English dictionaries must rely in part upon the *Oxford*, and upon the more specialized dictionaries like the *Middle English Dictionary* and *A Dictionary of Americanisms* that were inspired by it. No commercial publisher of a desk dictionary could afford to pay for the reading that has gone into assembling the citations used in such works, and endeavoring to do so would be both foolish and wasteful. In addition, all good desk dictionaries rely upon reading done by their own staffs (*Webster's New World Dictionary* also maintains a corps of full-time readers constantly collecting citations), although, on the whole, this material is digested by the lexicographers and only the results are printed in the ensuing volume.

Like the descriptive dictionaries, the desk dictionaries have their own history and tradition, from which their modern philosophy stems. Many of the practices embodied in desk dictionaries go back to the dictionaries of "hard words," whose editors tended to put into their books anything they thought the users would want. Johnson and Webster prided themselves on what they called the purity—that is, the elegance—of the language they included in their volumes, but the makers of the smaller, highly practical works did not. Elisha Coles (d. 1680), who wrote into his dictionary what he called "canting terms," the language of the underworld, defended them by insisting, "'Tis no disparagement" to understand such terms, since "it may chance to save your throat from being cut." For other practical purposes he included proper names from the Bible, along with "all the Market-towns (and other considerable places) in England, with all the places of note in other Countries." Studying rival dictionaries he noticed that for most purposes "Some are too little, some are too big," and accordingly he endeavored to make a book of just the right size and with just the right content to combat "Confusion and Barbarity."

Practical wordbooks proliferated, and editors learned to assemble more useful collections. Less than a century after Coles, the lexicographer Benjamin Martin, although he was still dismissing a horse as "a beast well known," devoted a paragraph to the town of Horsham, pointing out that it has "two bailiffs and burgage-holders"; he gives us dates of the fairs held there and records that the place is "distant from London 28 computed, and 35 measured miles." Martin's younger contemporary, John Ash, provided brief statements about historical and mythological figures. This tradition, of including biographical and encyclopedic entries within an alphabetical list of words to be defined, matured in the great *Century Dictionary* mentioned above; as its full title suggests, it is a concise encyclopedia as well as a great descriptive dictionary, with articles by specialists, an atlas, and a dictionary of proper names. Its editors endeavored to include, copiously, any material they assumed the user of the book might want when he looked up a word. Thus one can distinguish the modern desk dictionary by observing that it is based upon the principles of the *Century Dictionary*, that like their predecessors of the *Century* the new generation of lexicographers has profited from the most recent linguistic discoveries, but that the sorts of material which were spread through the *Century's* fourteen volumes have here been comprised in one.

II. *Linguistics and Lexicography*

Recent linguistic developments warrant our examination, since they have entered extensively into lexicography, and editors of desk dictionaries, especially, have been alert to utilize them. Most changes in language are slow; language must have required millenia to form into anything like an ordered system. Even writing, a secondary development, took thousands of years to evolve into an adequate complex of skills. Devices and understandings which promote the study and use of language, however, may be rapid and sweeping, and recent decades have witnessed a linguistic revolution, a revolution that embodies new thinking and new tools with which to implement new thought.

Since they are fundamental, we might take the ideas first; until scholars had learned to think straight about language and had sufficient reliable evidence from which to think, new tools could not be expected, or at a minimum could not be refined. Some of the most important of these new understandings might be phrased as follows: (1) languages rest upon use; (2) they have been shaped and directed by man's nature; (3) they change and grow; (4) they tend to proliferate; and (5) in their development they are at once centrifugal and centripetal, working through dialects. These principles are neither exclusive nor definitive, but they should warrant more detailed consideration.

1. *Language rests upon use; anything used long enough by enough people will become standard.* As we have seen in our sketch of the growth of lexicography, the importance of use has been recognized for some centuries. Dictionaries became possible in any real sense only when this principle concerning language use could be applied, but even lexicographers appreciated its implications only gradually as they worked with it, and as they became convinced that users of reference books would tolerate the changes that such a principle dictates. They understood, at least vaguely, that if use determines language it must also determine usage, what is fashionable in language. However, they did not at once apply this principle to dictionaries in an orderly manner, partly because they knew that people want to be told what is right and what is wrong, and partly because they misunderstood the nature and the power of the dictionary.

A dictionary, like any other delicate tool, can be misused, and if it is misused it will not work well. The readiest way to misuse it will follow from a misunderstanding of its nature and purpose. The Academie Française, for example, embarked upon its great dictionary to save the French language from decay; the academy assumed that French was so nearly perfect that it could only decline if it was permitted to change, and the members thought to arrest change by putting the language into a vast book. They did succeed in making one of the first good dictionaries, but they did not stop the French language from changing, and it has gone on doing so quite rapidly, as have most European tongues, and seems not to be the worse for that. So far as we know, no language has ever decayed from within in the sense that it has become progressively less useful; no speech has ever languished from not having been put into a dictionary, and no moribund tongue has ever been saved as a functioning tool by being enshrined in a book. Dictionaries have great powers, but rescuing doomed languages is not one of them. Many tongues have been destroyed as an incidence to military, social, or economic conquest, but although individual locutions can and do waste away, change in language seems mainly to be a sign of growth, not of decay. A good dictionary can promote order in inevitable growth. It will also promote stability in the language by preserving evidence of the past, but it should not be treated mainly as a means to ensure linguistic atrophy.

Similarly, lexicographers were a long time learning that they need not—or at least they could not—purify a language. Of course there is no such thing as a "pure" language. All languages are corrupt, if we conceive that change is to be equated with corruption, and all languages are mixtures, since all have borrowed from other languages. In moderate quantities, both change from within and borrowing from without seem to help languages thrive—perhaps we should call such phenomena fertilization, not corruption—but many of the earlier lexicographers did not understand this. Samuel Johnson, mentioned above, collected subscriptions

to his great dictionary on the theory that he would refine and purify the language. The American, Noah Webster, asserted with great confidence that single-handedly he would be able to standardize American speech.

Both failed in their efforts to police language, however much they may have triumphed otherwise, and lived to learn that language can be described, that within limits it can be influenced, but that it cannot be controlled. Johnson tells us that he "found our speech copious without order, and energetic without rules; wherever I turned my view, there was perplexity to be disentangled, and confusion to be regulated." He found that in spelling, "caprice has long wantoned without control." Accordingly, he had "endeavoured to proceed with a scholar's reverence for antiquity, and a grammarian's regard to the genius of our tongue." He cautioned that we must not allow "our written language to comply with the corruption of oral utterance." He could scarcely have had much foresight regarding the manner in which the written language was to follow the oral during the subsequent two centuries, but he had grown to understand the language enough so that he appears distinctly nostalgic when he concludes, "I am not yet so lost in lexicography as to forget that *words are the daughters of earth, and that things are the sons of heaven.* Language is only the instrument of science, and words are but the signs of ideas; I wish, however, that the instrument might be less apt to decay, and that signs might be permanent, like the things which they denote." Similarly, Webster, although he had earlier been concerned with "correcting a vicious pronunciation, which prevailed extensively among the common people of this country," had gained perspective by the time he had spent half a lifetime compiling a dictionary. With the years, he became more concerned to "complete a system for instruction of the citizens of this country in the language," and to do so he had discovered that he must study "the origin and progress of our language." He was learning that to deal with language he had to rely upon language more, upon the knowledge of even oral speech, and upon prejudice less. Neither Johnson nor Webster ever grasped what use means in understanding and employing language, but they knew the principle, and as they worked with language they approached the practice.

With the years, lexicographers grew to understand more clearly the role of use in language, and to apply linguistic findings to dictionary making. Philology, which studied the history and growth of language, provided an insight into modern use and usage by tracing the phantasmagoric play of language change. Meanwhile, once lexicographers had learned to select citations to determine and illuminate meaning, they observed, also, that citations could be chosen for other purposes, notably to refine statements about usage. Now, quite recently, scholars have developed a new technique, known as *dialect* or *linguistic geography*, essentially a controlled device for language sampling. We shall need to consider it more particularly when we raise problems concerning dialects, but for the moment we may notice that it is already bringing more order into our statements about usage, and that it promises eventually to provide answers to all sorts of linguistic questions, perhaps especially to problems of usage, with something approaching scientific accuracy.

2. *However language started, it has been shaped and directed by man's mind, his society, and his vocal equipment.* How early man's shaping power was exerted on language we know not, because we know not how, when, or where language originated, but we can infer some things about its beginning. Language seems to be universal among men but not to exist outside the human tradition. All men of whom we know anything speak a native language, and whereas other creatures—bees, ants, monkeys and apes, porpoises, and many more—can communicate within limits, none of these creatures, so far as we know, have developed communications systems sufficiently elaborate so that we can properly use the word *language* to describe them. Human linguistic systems may well have developed from more primitive communicative devices, as the human body presumably developed from the simpler vertebrates; quite probably they did, but the differences between language and the nonhuman signaling devices are so great that we must assume that the growth of language is uniquely associated with human beings, and that once language became possible it developed with a rapidity beyond that of either biological or geophysical evolution, and in accordance with its own laws and principles.

Theoretically, language could have had a single origin, multiple origins, or no origin at all—if by *origin* we mean a single action or a relatively brief series of actions closely limited in time and space. Unique inventions are possible; in fact, for many devices they seem to be the rule. Anthropologists believe, for example, that the wheel was invented only once, or at the most very few times, and that all uses of the wheel spread from few centers. So language might have spread, but logic would encourage one to doubt it. The wheel, however it has proliferated, utilizes a simple principle; language, on the other hand, is anything but simple. It employs sound, which must be used in various patterns, and it relies upon extensive and dexterous handling of the tongue, a bundle of muscles which requires long and purposive training. It grows from brains, brains functioning

in many ways, including the development of a sense of meaning, the amassing of great bodies of linguistic phenomena, and the generating of a sense for grammar. That anything so complex, anything so rooted in physical and mental skills not easily acquired, could have been brought to a functioning state by any one person at any one time, or even by relatively few people cooperating for a brief time, seems highly improbable. Such skepticism gains confirmation, apparently, from the fact that people learn language over a relatively long period, and that the child learns various linguistic activities which must coalesce before he can command anything that can properly be called language.

All this variety in linguistic evidence seems to accord with the fact that we have not been able to find a single plausible explanation for the origin of language. Various theorists have suggested that language sprang from cries of fear, from expressions of love and sympathy, from exclamations associated with the dance, from work songs, from patterns of chattering—the thesis most pursued at this writing—from the imitation of sounds, especially the sounds of babies and of wild creatures. This last guess must have some validity; certainly such words as *whippoorwill* rely upon echoic practices, upon what is formally called *onomatopoeia.* An Algonquian word for an owl, *uhu*, must have a similar origin, along with words like *murmur* and *choo-choo*, and terms like *mama*, *daddy*, and *baby*, the latter clearer in the pronunciation of French *bébé*. All these theses seem rather too limited to account for much, however, and especially because language as we know it is more the product of the human mind than it is the product of the human vocal apparatus.

A somewhat more plausible thesis associates language with symbol and the human power to generate and control symbols. According to this theory, man, surrounded by a bewildering world, ordered what was otherwise inexplicable by reducing it to symbols. Indisputably, the mind does work through symbols, which have the great advantage of being at once concrete, and thus readily apprehensible, and capable of almost indefinite expansion. Indisputably, also, although art supplies striking symbols and many of them, language provides incomparably the greatest body of symbols, and on the whole those that are the most readily defined. At a minimum, all words are symbols, and many locutions involve very complex symbols—the word *cross* is a symbol for the object, a cross, but it also comprises much of the symbolism involved in the cross itself.

This thesis, if a little vague, dovetails with other plausible guesses, notably that language is intimately associated with the nature of man and that it must have grown slowly. It permits us to assume that man as an organism, art and civilization as social phenomena, and language as a means of thought and growth are so interreliant that no one of them could have developed without each of the others, that they grew by being continually interactive. When man was sufficiently human so that he became capable of language, language as organized symbol provided him with the means of cultivating his own humanity, including his mental and artistic powers, and these made society possible, which in turn permitted the greater development of man and of man's prime tool, language.

Thus language need never have had a beginning, except as man can be defined as a beginning, man with his creative desire and his aptitude for symbol, his love of rhythm and ritual, his innate playfulness, his physical dexterity, and his remarkable aural and oral abilities. Man as we know him would not have been possible without language, without the use of language over long periods. Similarly, language was not possible without man, without man improving his own invention, in many ways and over many millennia. Society as we know it, of course, was not possible without both man and language. By this thesis, then, language grew as part of a sort of multiple hen-and-egg sequence, with better hens producing better eggs to hatch into better hens. If so, language resulted not from a single action but from interaction, and prolonged interaction at that.

Certainly, this is what has happened in historic time. We cannot imagine that any complex society was possible without language; we know of no very complex society that has existed without written language; and we cannot conceive modern society without mass media. There were no Einsteins or Freuds among unsophisticated men; a potential Einstein among the Cro-Magnons would have had no body of thought organized by language. Similarly, how could modern medical terminology be supported without modern medicine? In our day, mankind, language, and society have grown as an interreliant trilogy, and we have no reason to suppose that such interreliance has been restricted to modern, or even historic, times. This understanding of the nature of language and of its growth provides the basis for our convictions as to what a dictionary should be and our awareness of what it can do. Such a book consists of a listing of symbols, symbols in the simple sense that words are symbols, and the etymologies of these words and the considerations of their use and meanings shadow forth the symbolic power of words. Furthermore, this thesis, that the nature of man shapes the nature of his language, can be observed even in the minutiae of human communication, as we shall see when we consider the third principle.

3. *Language grows and changes, and although unbridled*

change may be harmful, language possesses its own inner restraints, and most change in language is apparently healthful —or, at the least, not readily amenable to conscious, human interdiction. This principle is a corollary of the second; if always in flux, we must assume that any given language will be changing at any given time, whether individual users of the language are aware of these developments, or dislike the changes if they become aware. Even if a language were to die, that would be change, and as we have observed, languages do die, but not of themselves. Most languages that have flourished during the millennia of linguistic time must have died; some have vanished when their speakers were killed, as have most Amerindian tongues. Some have been overrun by other languages; the Norse and French spoken in England were smothered by English. Others have survived only in such changed form that we call them by new names; Latin has reappeared in modern languages like French and Spanish. But all languages seem to have served their users well, and so far as we know none has ever died because of its inadequacy or from internal linguistic change. Languages do not commit suicide or suffer from senility. Accordingly, we must assume that language change is at least as much growth as it is decay, that new forms, new devices, new principles compensate, and usually more than compensate, for any losses. And if we know relatively little about how language got started, we know a great deal about how it has grown.

Here our knowledge is both specific and philosophic. For example, the plural of the word *lip* is formed by adding the hissing sound associated with the letter *s*. On the other hand, the plural of the word *bug*, although it is spelled with an *s*, is made by adding a buzzing sound associated with the letter *z*, in phonemics /z/. At this point anyone familiar with sounds would notice that the consonants /p/ and /s/ are voiceless, that is, they are made without vibration of the vocal cords, whereas /g/ and /z/ are voiced, made with vibration of the vocal cords. He would be likely to guess that formerly these signs of the plural had all been the same, whether voiced or unvoiced, and that they had changed so that the voiced or voiceless sounds present a continuing sequence. But what about words like *hues* or *toes*, in which the plural uses the voiced sound /z/ although it is not preceded by a voiced consonant? Again, the answer is easy, since all vowels in English are voiced. Thus we can start generating principles like the following: In English all recently formed plurals will be made of the voiceless fricative /s/ if the signal of the plural is preceded by a voiceless consonant, and will be formed with the corresponding voiced fricative /z/ if it is preceded by a voiced sound, whether vowel or consonant. We could now state a broader postulate, making it tentative until we have supporting evidence, somewhat as follows: In language, sounds may be influenced by adjacent sounds.

Thus, in language, we can observe that sounds significant for speech may be influenced by the nature of the human vocal apparatus. Nor is this intimate relationship between man and speech restricted to sound. Similar phenomena can be observed in vocabulary, even perhaps in grammar. For example, the vaulting of man into space has inspired a flood of new words and new uses of old words. *Sputnik*, a Russian word for a satellite, has become an English word for a Russian satellite, and a Russian voyager into space has become a *cosmonaut*, a word related to dozens of terms in Western languages deriving from Greek *kosmos*. Words already with us have taken on new uses; a word like *orbit* has been long in the language, but not as a verb meaning to project an object into space so that it will go into orbit. Similarly, the great urbanization of modern American society, and the resulting need to deal with urban problems, have led to terms like *city planning*, *urban renewal*, and *zoning* in the sense that buildings constructed within a given area must be restricted to certain uses.

Usage, what might be called the etiquette of language, can also change, and sometimes quite rapidly. For example, *like* has now extensively replaced *as* in *as it should* and in similar locutions, and this change has engendered its proportion of fury, probably because it has been blazoned in full-page advertisements. That is, this use of *like* has become a problem in usage. Actually, this is only one of many shifts among *like* and *as*, most of which have not become problems in usage, because so few people noticed them that they went unchallenged. For example, Richard Mulcaster, a school-teacher contemporary of Shakespeare, discussing the forms of Latin words, could write, "when theie be used English like." This can scarcely be called bad grammar or bad usage either; if anybody in the sixteenth century knew what was correct and proper in English it would have been Mulcaster —courtier, writer on language, and university professor. If he had been writing two centuries later, he might well have used a construction like, "When they are used as they are in English," and now, after another two centuries, many speakers would say, "like they are in English." In the end, the language will probably work as well one way as the other, but while the change is taking place, purists will feel that the new locution is "wrong," or "bad grammar," and even careful but tolerant speakers may be irked by the innovation if they happen to notice it. Usually they do not. For some time *any more* has been moving into the semantic area formerly served by *now*, and becoming *anymore*. This drift

might well infuriate purists, but to date it is not doing so. *Any more* has not become a problem in modern usage because few users of the language have noticed the change, and those have mainly been professional linguists, on the whole not the sort of people who readily lose their tempers—at least not about usage.

Meanwhile, grammar, in the broader sense of the way in which language works, has changed very slowly. Nonetheless, we must assume that grammar, like all other aspects of language, changes constantly although in the main imperceptibly. Some thousands of years ago the ancestor of English, called Indo-European, was what we may describe as a highly synthetic language. That is, the language worked chiefly by altering the form of linguistic units or by putting linguistic units together. During the subsequent millennia the grammar changed so much that variations in form, like those apparent in *go–goes* and *boy–boys*, are rare, and the grammar works by word order and through other devices in which words have grammatical use, whether or not they have much meaning. Hundreds of millions of speakers must have been involved in this change, but so far as we know nobody ever noticed it until recent centuries, when scholars were able to compare the current form of the language with earlier recorded and reconstructed forms. Apparently grammar changes so slowly that most people assume that it does not alter fundamentally, and hence they never examine it to see whether it may not be changing. And anyhow, the change is so gradual that only an expert is likely to detect it, and even he may miss most of the contemporary drift in grammar.

Thus we must assume that some change is inevitable in language, and if we cannot confidently say that it is healthful, certainly it helps the language adapt to new responsibilities, and most language change does no harm. Theoretically, it could do harm. If English changed so rapidly that constitutions had no meaning, contracts written last year could no longer be understood, and last year's novels were now gibberish, we should be worse off. But only under the most extreme circumstances does language ever change so fast that it ceases to be useful as a means of communication, so fast that common locutions rapidly lose their currency. This has happened, and could happen again. In Jamaica, for example, languages have been so blended that no one of them has survived in readily recognizable form; this is what is called *creolizing*, and it may account for the difference between modern French and the other Romance languages, but even creolizing does not last long. Soon another language grows from the wreckage of the earlier tongues and finds means to serve its users well. Any such change for English is not predictable in the near future. Barring some major disaster, we may expect English to change continually and in an orderly manner, and however much individual users of the language may deprecate particular changes, the language itself is not likely to suffer.

4. *Languages tend to proliferate.* Awareness of this phenomenon, that filial relationships in language are much like those among human beings, that the concept of family seems to be as pertinent in linguistics as it is in society, helps the lexicographer understand the language with which he is dealing.

Ignoring the present for the moment, we can observe that languages have proliferated in the past. Consider the word for *horse* in Romance languages; in Italian it is now spelled *cavallo* and in Spanish *caballo*. This is surely not coincidence, especially because the differences are mainly in spelling, not in sound. The French is *cheval*, but we know that French has changed enough so that it uses *ch* to spell the sound /š/ or (sh), while other Romance languages have a spelling *c* and a sound /k/. Thus, even if we did not know Latin, we would guess that it included a word for *horse* that would have been spelled something like *caballus*. We do know Latin, of course, and the word *caballus* appears frequently in it. Furthermore, what is true of *caballus* is true, also, of other Latin words, that they occur with minor differences in the various Romance languages, with the differences falling into regular patterns. Thus we could infer that languages like Italian, Spanish, and French stand in relation to Latin roughly as children do to their parents. But we need not guess; we have the record in thousands of manuscripts of this proliferation and of growth from Latin into the daughter languages.

But what about Latin? Was it part of a family of languages, very much as one's grandfather was part of a family? This would be the obvious guess, but it was not confirmed until the past century, when almost simultaneous observations by an Englishman, Sir William Jones, working in India, and a Dane, Rasmus Rask, led to the conclusion that most European languages descend from one common ancestor, the reconstructed language called Indo-European. Nor was this the end; once scholars had the key to the relationships of European languages, that they had a common ancestor and had proliferated from that common source, the next question was obvious: Were not all languages, whether surviving or extinct, related by descent to other languages? The flood of confirmation was overwhelming, so that scholars have now been able to relate practically all languages to other languages, living or dead. A few, like Basque, along the mountainous border of Spain and France, for which no relatives have been discovered, are presumably

the sole survivors of once-numerous language families that formerly spread over wide areas. Similarly, in the Americas, some native tongues are still labeled *language isolates*, although presumably many of these languages are not without relatives, and their seeming isolation reflects mainly our ignorance and our inability to work with considerable time depths in Amerindian studies.

This understanding of the relationships of languages provided the basis for the growth of philology in the past century and led to revolutions in our concepts of language. It is the foundation for our practice of etymology. Its implications, however, are not restricted to etymology, and it influences, directly or indirectly, almost everything that goes into the making of a modern dictionary, as will appear when we consider a fifth and final principle.

5. *Languages are at once centrifugal and centripetal.* Languages tend to break into dialects and at the same time to pull together. In a broad way we have noticed both these forces; we have just observed languages breaking up into families of languages, and earlier we noted that the parts of a language tend to coalesce into some kind of ordered system. Both these tendencies, however, will warrant more particular examination, especially for the role played by dialects in linguistic change, since dialects appear to be natural and inevitable in language, and hence essential to its study.

Let us take the first, that some forces in language tend to be centrifugal. Every person speaks in his own way, and his individual way of using the language is called his *idiolect*. Of course it is not a permanent thing; no person of sixty-five speaks as he did when he was fifteen, nor, for that matter, does any person speak at any time in precisely the way he would have spoken a year earlier—or theoretically a day earlier—but for practical purposes we can speak of an individual's idiolect, which we can define as the total of all his speech habits at the moment. This idiolect will participate in speech habits having a wider currency, a spread of linguistic practice which we may call a *dialect*, something between an idiolect and a language. This definition will require that we distinguish the concept *language*.

Presumably, languages are so diverse that the speakers of one are not intelligible to speakers of the other without special preparation. A Frenchman cannot understand a German without learning his tongue; French and German are different languages. Not all cases are so clear; French and Spanish and Italian are presumably separate languages, but it is said that a traveler may go from southern Spain to southern Italy, following the Mediterranean coast, and never pass through a community whose inhabitants cannot understand the inhabitants of the neighboring communities. The dialects of southeast Spain blend into Catalan, which blends into the dialects that have survived from Old French and Provençal, and into the dialects of northwest Italy. In most parts of the world, however, the lines between languages are relatively distinct, while dialects work within languages. A dialect can be defined roughly as a way of using a language which involves a considerable number of speakers and is sufficiently distinctive to contrast with other dialects, but not so distinctive that its speakers are mutually unintelligible to other speakers of the language. Confusion among languages, if it troubles the lexicographer at all, troubles the American lexicographer but little; dialects, on the other hand, present problems, many of them, and to dialects we must turn.

Within limits, languages work by dialect and change by dialect. To understand these phenomena, we should recall that language is always changing, and that every person has his own idiolect. Take the familiar case of dwellers in the Appalachian valleys. White settlers settled there during the eighteenth century, and many of their descendants have remained there. These settlers brought their own idiolects, reflecting various dialects. Their ancestors had come mostly from the vicinity of London and its environs, and from southeast England generally; naturally, they spoke with the peculiarities of those areas. They were mainly lower middle-class or upper lower-class folk, with some admixtures from British jails, and they included indentured servants, long since freed, who also spoke the language associated during the seventeenth and early eighteenth centuries with servants, semiskilled workmen, farmers, and the like. They brought lower middle-class and upper lower-class dialects, superimposed upon their regional speech. In addition, most of the Appalachian settlers had spent some time in Maryland, Virginia, or North Carolina, and they brought with them habits of speech acquired in the New World. Once they had settled into a mountain valley, their idiolects coalesced into speech which would be somewhat different from English spoken anywhere else, since it would be a combination of a number of idiolects, each of them unique. Furthermore, their language could change, as all languages do, but since the speakers were isolated it would change differently than did any other body of language, English or anything else.

Thus, after a time, the mountain valley would have its own way of speaking, a set of speech manners in which all persons who grew up in the valley would participate, a set of speech habits that would not be common to any other body of speakers, although it would still be recognizable as English, and even in its peculiarities, it would no doubt have much in common with similar dialects in nearby valleys.

Theoretically, if the mountain valley remained isolated long enough, the speech would change so much that it would not be understood outside the valley and could be classified as a separate language, not English but a descendant of English. That, of course, does not usually happen. It presumably did happen when dialects of Latin became so diverse that we now think of them as Italian, French, and Spanish; but most dialects do not remain sufficiently isolated and for periods long enough to become mutually unintelligible. It has happened frequently in the past, but the mere fact that there are many more dialects than languages suggests that it does not usually happen, and with the great growth of modern communications it may cease entirely some time in the future.

The sort of dialects discussed in the paragraph above may be called regional or geographical dialects. They are dialects cultivated by relative isolation in space. But space is not the only circumstance that keeps people apart. They may be separated, also, by social and economic forces, by anything approaching a caste system, by the means of making a living, even by religion. A worker on an assembly line may be as much insulated from the chairman of the board of directors as though the two of them lived in separate countries. Two surgeons, one working in Houston and the other in Brooklyn, will have no difficulty discussing the procedures in an operation, but neither could discuss surgical techniques with the janitor in his own hospital. Thus, along with regional dialects we find social, occupational, and other dialects, and every user of language participates more or less in more than one. Everybody lives somewhere, and hence he participates in a regional dialect, perhaps in several—among educated younger Americans, usually in several. Everybody has some social status, and hence is subject to the influence of at least one social dialect. Everybody has some kind of occupation, or he associates with people who do have something in common occupationally. Everybody, always and inevitably, speaks in dialects; his use of the language resembles that of some users, and does not so closely resemble the speech of some other users.

From this principle we can derive several corollaries useful in understanding how dictionaries are made and how they should be used. First we might note that all languages are composed of dialects and that except for very limited idiolectal characteristics, no language exists outside dialects. An Amerindian language recently discovered in Alaska is of such restricted currency that it is known only to a few hundred speakers, yet it has been preserved in dialects and subdialects. To use language, one must use dialects, and inevitably dialects must be taken into account when dictionaries are prepared. Similarly, if dictionaries are used well they must be consulted in light of the fact that all language works through dialects.

Next we might observe that all dialects are natural, useful, and linguistically equal. They have all grown naturally, in response to the needs of the users of the dialect. Needs vary; most lawyers need more words as well as different words from those required by most migrant agricultural workers, but presumably the dialect of each serves the needs of each, and has its own reasons for existence. One dialect may be more fashionable than another; it may have wider use, geographically and culturally. A Boston psychiatrist who speaks a Back Bay dialect may attract wealthier patients than one who speaks a dialect of the neighboring ghetto, but we are misunderstanding language and the nature of language if we assume that the Back Bay speaker is "correct" and the ghetto speaker "incorrect." The Back Bay speaker, having had the advantage of careful schooling, may use the language more precisely, more tastefully, and more vigorously than does the ghetto speaker—although, again, he may not. There is more or less effective use of language, more or less fashionable use of language, but to introduce the concept of correctness is usually only to confuse one's thinking. In mathematics, the correct answer for two-times-two is four, and answers like three and five are incorrect—incorrect for everybody, not just for mathematicians or for Back Bay dwellers—but in language, the difference between *I saw* and *I seen* is not well described by saying that one is correct and the other incorrect. The difference is that *I saw* is characteristic of most of the fashionable dialects, and *I seen* is not; the locutions have different impacts. Anyone who wishes to be accepted in the United States as a cultured person had better say *I saw* and avoid *I seen*, but such choices are too subtle and varied to be well described by the rigid distinction involved in correctness. Linguistic preferences tend to grow from dialects and to reflect their complexities; in the main, they are best understood on that basis.

Thus, centrifugal forces are omnipresent and inevitable in language. All languages tend all the time to break up. Individuals speak idiolects; groups speak dialects; dialects have always the potential of diverging into languages. During the thousands of years which we can study objectively, and the other thousands for which we can infer causes only by extrapolating from results, these forces promoting diversity have worked so powerfully and persistently that man has developed thousands of languages and vast numbers of dialects. On the other hand, man seems to have an innate need of order and innate powers of promoting it. Without this sense of order, without the

tendency to regularize, to standardize, to organize by analogy, language in any real sense would have been impossible. Language is extremely complex, much more complex than most users can imagine, so complex that nobody could learn to use a language well if it were not standardized into relatively few patterns. The earliest languages we have discovered—to say nothing of the more recent languages serving highly sophisticated peoples—have all been organized into systems, and we have evidence that all men, unconsciously and sometimes consciously, are ordering language.

III. Words and Dictionaries

Once the nature and working of language have been surveyed, the answers to many of the problems become obvious, problems involved in both the making and the using of dictionaries. About some of these problems the dictionary user can do little. The lexicographer may lose sleep over his word list, wondering how he can assure himself that he has discovered all the new words that have infiltrated the language, and—somewhat more difficult—how he can discover all the new uses developed from old words. The user of the dictionary, however, need not be much concerned over such questions, at least not after he has opened the book. He may decide not to buy or use a specific dictionary because he believes the word list to be inadequate, but once he is committed to using a book, he can do nothing about the entries. They are there, or they are not. He can, however, do much to make the best use of the entries that do appear. Meanwhile, he should understand that any dictionary will have inherent limitations, for even a good tool is not good for everything.

A dictionary is a reference work; it is not a course in composition. Many writers find that a desk dictionary is their most valuable writing aid, but the purchase of a dictionary will not assure the owner that he will thereby become a fluent speaker or a lucid writer. A dictionary can help its user to understand his linguistic tools; it can provide him quickly and conveniently with information pertinent to the problems of writing, speaking, reading, and listening, but the best dictionary can be no more than a ready aid. The skillful use of a language, oral or written, is far too complex and difficult to be subsumed in a volume, and in any event, a dictionary is intended to provide information for the use of language, not to give rhetorical advice.

It should have the further virtue that it tells no lies. It may leave many questions unanswered. If it is an honest book, inevitably it will, for in a world in which much is uncertain, a good lexicographer endeavors to assert only what he has reason to believe is true. Even so laudable and limited an ambition as this, however, presents its impasses, and one of these the lexicographer faces as soon as he starts to prepare his manuscript. Finding words to put into a word list may be exacting and onerous, because words are multitudinous and in their own ways furtive. But the lexicographer faces a more fundamental uncertainty because, although he assumes he must organize his book on the basis of words, he does not know what a word is, and nobody at this date can tell him. This dilemma will require a bit of detail.

All known languages comprise two sorts of ingredients, linguistic units and means of manipulating these units. The second we call grammar and the first vocabulary, which is our immediate concern. Units of vocabulary become involved with calling up meaning, although we shall need to take notice hereafter that meaning itself is not very measurable or definable stuff. In most communications systems, meaning is associated with sound, and in a written language this complex of sound and meaning is represented by some graphic symbol, sometimes known as a *grapheme*. That is, a word, whether spoken, written, or only thought, is commonly supposed to be what has been defined as "the smallest unit of speech that has meaning when taken by itself."

But what determines one of these units? Presumably *mother* is a unit in the sense of maternal ancestor. Is it the same word or different words—since it seems to have different meanings—in "the mother of Parliaments," and in "the mother of months," by which Swinburne may have meant something like *year* or *season*? Is it also the same word that appears in "mother of vinegar" because that *mother* may be related to a folk term in Dutch, supposedly derived from the ancestor of English *mother*? If so, would it be a different word if an etymologist were to discover that this guess is wrong, and that the word was borrowed from Egyptian? Do we have two more or no more words for *mother* in "A mother hen will mother a gosling" because the words work differently in a sentence? Are *mother* and *mothers* two words because they have different meanings, and are *mothers* and *mother's* two words because they have different uses, and were they one word in the Middle Ages when they were spelled the same way? Are *cheque* and *check* two words because they are spelled in two ways although they have the same sound and some of the same meanings? Is *gutter* one word because it has only one spelling although some uses of the word probably come from Old Norse and some from Old French, and some may be influenced by both? How many words is *campfire girls' camp ground*? Is it one because it is the name of a place, or three or four or five words for various other reasons?

Confronted with these confusions, along with some others, scientific students of language tend to avoid the term *word* because they cannot define it in any way that sharply accords with its use. Many modern students of language prefer in their linguistic analysis to start with sound and structure and to recognize working units of sound which they call *phonemes* (for a more detailed discussion see VII, "Pronunciation and the Dictionary"). These sounds, which roughly resemble sounds associated with letters, modern students build up into working units of language, which they call *morphemes*. Morphemes, in turn, somewhat resemble words, but differ, notably in that they are more accurately definable. For example, take the graphemes *girl* and *girls*. The first, *girl*, would be a word by the traditional identification, and it would be a morpheme to the structuralist. Here, as frequently, the two approaches provide the same result, but not for the second grapheme, *girls*. In the older description, this, also, is a word, and most dictionaries would treat it as the same word as *girl*, although here appearing in the plural form. In some modern analysis, however, often called *structural analysis* or *structural linguistics*, *girls* is a phrase, made up of two morphemes, the first morpheme *girl* and the second, *s* in spelling or /z/ in sound. This second element, of course, is not a word, since it cannot be used alone, but to the structuralist it is a morpheme because it is a working unit of language; it can be employed in *boys*, *politicians*, or *antiperfectabilitarians* and it always has a known and describable use. The structuralists thus would call *girl* a free morpheme, because it can be used by itself, and *s* or /z/ a bound morpheme because it is a working unit of language but can work only with at least one other morpheme.

Thus the modern student, insofar as he relies upon an analysis like this one, has a tolerably straightforward and consistent statement because he relies on sound and structure, and he brooks no interference from spelling, which is arbitrary, or from meaning, which is hard to measure. This sort of scientific order, however, has not much helped the lexicographer, who is still faced with the necessity of some kind of alphabetical listing that must rely upon spelling, and he is centrally concerned with meaning, which the structuralist has generally rejected as not scientific or too difficult to be dealt with in the present state of our knowledge. Accordingly, the lexicographer finds that he must continue to work with words, unscientific though they may be. Nobody has as yet succeeded in making a general dictionary based upon morphemes, if anybody has seriously tried to, and indeed such a reference work would present problems as yet scarcely broached. But even if a manual of morphemic vocabulary—one hesitates to call such a work a dictionary—could be prepared, the general public, not as yet familiar with concepts like the phoneme and the morpheme, would be unable to use it.

Accordingly, the maker of a general dictionary finds that he must continue to base his book on words, and that he must act as though he knows what a word is. Practically, the concept of the word is indispensable, although scientifically words may be nonexistent. The lexicographer must make the most of them and do with them what he can. In this he has some help, if not much from modern approaches, since lexicography has such a long tradition that certain locutions are assumed to be words. They are recorded in dictionaries, are taught in the schools, are written into publishers' style sheets, and are familiar to all literate users of the language. Also, he has working principles. On the whole, he assumes that words from different origins are different words. Thus he calls *bushy* and *bosky* different words, because they come from different languages, respectively from Old English and Old Norse. They differ less in meaning than does the word *horse* in various uses, which can refer to a beast, a sawing frame, a mass of earth inside a vein of coal, and the like. They differ less in sound than does *idea* as spoken in Boston and Dallas. In spelling they are less disparate than *shivaree* and *charivari*, along with recognized alternate spellings of hundreds of other words. Thus lexicographers generally assume that two graphemes, even if they are identical in form and even though they have closely similar meanings, along with overlapping pronunciations, are not the same word and never will be if they come from different sources.

Of course there are other esoterica that the lexicographer must bear in mind when he tries to determine which are words and which are variants of the same words. How does one know that *trap* and *tramp* are two words although they came from the same original? How does one decide how many *tramp*-words and *trap*-words there are? Fortunately, the user of the dictionary need not know the principles on which the decisions are made, but some understanding of the basic uncertainties and the working complexities may encourage in him tolerance of lexicographical inconsistencies. In practice, dictionaries can be made with more or less understanding, with more or less persistent care, but the fact is that there is no one right list of the words in English nor is there ever likely to be one. That two dictionaries have somewhat differing word lists does not mean that either is thereby wrong, or that either is carelessly made. The word lists of all good dictionaries will reflect somewhat similar principles, but these are so numerous and so uncertainly weighted that no two bodies of scholars could possibly produce identical lists, unless one copied from another. Any

Language and the Dictionary

comparison of two dictionaries will produce variations; the admirable *Century Dictionary*, for example, used *light* as seven entry words, whereas many other dictionaries, equally well edited, reduce *light* to two or three. Neither is necessarily right nor necessarily better than the other; a word list is not a list of the English words. It is a selection from the available graphemes, or word-shapes, and if they have been intelligently selected on principles that reflect the nature of the language in question, they will serve as an orderly basis for presenting linguistic facts in a usable sequence.

IV. *The Shapes of Words*

Once a lexicographer has decided which forms he will recognize as words, he has to ask himself what shape they will take, how they will be represented on a page. Some problems are relatively simple, spelling for example. Spelling may be troublesome to the speller, but it presents few difficult problems to either the maker or the user of a dictionary. Formerly, English spelling was so chaotic that there was no right way to spell a word, and few people bothered to try. Now all this is changed. The modern practice is to be very rigid about spelling, so rigid that in this area, as perhaps in no other in language, one may properly use the word *correct*. The form *jail* is certainly a correct spelling of a word for a building to implement incarceration. This word was formerly spelled *gaol*, and it is still so spelled by many Britons, and hence we should say, and many dictionaries do say, that both are correct. One might even recognize that for dialectal purposes *jale* or *jell* would be possible "correct" spellings, but nobody would recognize *lija* or *loag* as the word *jail*, and, hence, if these are considered spellings at all, they must be incorrect spellings. Of all the possible combinations of letters in English, only a very few, usually for most purposes only one, can be considered a correct spelling.

The most fruitful source of variant spellings, of course, are words borrowed from other languages; words like *theater* borrowed as French *theatre* may or may not be Anglicized, and *smörgåsbord* may or may not retain its native diacritical marks. The most unstable are words taken from languages using a script not based on the Latin alphabet, from Russian, Arabic, or Chinese, for example, since such words may be variously transliterated, as in *jin, djin, djinn, djinni, jinni, ginnee, ginii, jinee, genie, djineeya, ginii,* and many more, when misunderstanding of distinctions of sex and number are added to the confusion of alphabetic variety.

Confusion, when there is any, arises mainly from failure to recall a fact taken note of above, that a dictionary is descriptive, not prescriptive. That is, if a dictionary offers the spelling *jinn* as a collective term for Mohammedan spirits of a rank below that of angels, the dictionary does not mean to say that all other spellings are incorrect. It is saying that this is a generally acceptable spelling, one that the user can employ with confidence. The recommending of a form may imply something more; as a matter of fact, the editors of the dictionary may have argued long and heatedly as to which spelling or spellings to use as entries, and when they finally selected one or a few they were doubtless reflecting the fact that one spelling is more common, is closer to an accepted system of transliteration, or something. They are offering an accepted spelling, usually the most acceptable spelling, but they are not prescribing one and proscribing all others.

Some aspects of written form in words are not readily normalized because they reflect essential instabilities in usage. Consider the problem of compounding, where we might notice the relatively simple case of *grizzly*. Members of the Lewis and Clark party, and doubtless many other pioneers and frontiersmen, saw a large animal, obviously a bear by its form and manner, but previously unknown to them. It differed from other bears they knew or had heard of, which were brown, black, or white, in that its generally brownish cast was tempered with yellowish, grayish, or silvery hairs. The creature could be aptly described as a bear having a grizzly color, and a *grizzly bear* he became. It is also possible that he became first a *grisly bear*, because of his ferocity, but however the bear acquired his qualifying adjective, the principle is the same, that two known words were put together to provide a name for a new object. When the word was applied to a desert plant, however, the term became a *grizzly-bear cactus*, and when the term *grizzly* was applied to a certain sort of mining employee he became a *grizzlyman*. Now we should ask why we have two words, *grizzly bear*, along with a hyphenated word *grizzly-bear*, and a new compound written solid, *grizzlyman*. The answer is relatively simple. *Grizzly bear* is two words because we are reticent to combine an adjective with a following noun unless the referent having a compound name becomes so familiar that it is thought of for itself rather than mainly within a generic classification, as have *redbird, yellowbelly,* and *greenback. Grizzly-bear* as a modifier is hyphenated because we tend to hyphenate independent words if they become modifiers, and *grizzlyman* is written solid because the first part of the compound is a noun, not an adjective. A *grizzlyman* is not a man with grizzly hair; in the days before the job and the word became mainly obsolete, a *grizzlyman* was a mining employee who worked with the *grizzly*, a screen of parallel iron bars.

Thus, human minds working as they do, and human experiences being what they are, growing languages tend to acquire compounds. In fact, compounding has been unusually characteristic of American English, probably because Americans encountered so many new phenomena suggestive of familiar phenomena but still to be distinguished from the old, and more recently because Americans have been much involved in inventions, devising new objects and new methods described in such compounds as *air surveillance, radar installation, radiometeorograph,* and *low-cost housing.* But as objects become familiar, their names tend to be written solid; if grizzly bears had been as common on city streets as streetcars used to be, they would no doubt have become *grizzlybears.* Thus words and phrases that develop from compounding tend always to be unstable until they are written solid, and there is always a new crop of compounds not yet written as single, nonhyphenated terms. Lexicographers and editors must constantly reexamine compounds and frequently they must change their decisions, inserting hyphens here, taking them out there.

Hence, dictionaries that differ in age will differ in practice, and even contemporary books may differ, especially if use is so divided that the editor is uncertain which form to prefer—users of dictionaries generally want answers, not explanations of editorial dilemmas. Outer space, of course, is a lively area of uncertainty at this writing; presumably *spacecraft* is no longer *space craft,* and *space diseases* will probably not be *spacediseases* for a long time, if ever, but how about *space platform, space age, space suit,* and *space port?* The lexicographer can endeavor to be hospitable to the new and not too inconsistent with the old, but he has no guaranteed answer. The user of a dictionary can appropriately understand the principles of compounding, as an aid to his thinking and his memory, but he must also recognize that in a complex and fluid pattern of usage some decisions must be arbitrary, and he will do well to select a recent, carefully edited dictionary, and follow it. At worst, he can then explain that he is accepting the usage of a certain book, and if he has chosen well he will be as consistent as one can hope to be in a shifty world.

Capitalization, although more nearly subject to standards than is compounding, is also inherently unstable. Words that are names, and hence are capitalized in the English writing system, become the terms for classes of objects, or for part of a compound, and eventually develop into common nouns and are written with an initial lower-case letter. Thus *China ware,* which came from China, has become *chinaware; French dressing* is now *french dressing,* and the House of Bourbon, which gave its name to Bourbon County, Kentucky, finds it has given its name also to a lower-case whiskey, *bourbon.* All this is now well past and thoroughly enshrined in dictionaries, but what about a *New York cut* of steak, a *Mexican jumping bean,* and *New Zealand spinach?* A lexicographer, every time he reedits a dictionary, must ask himself which of such words can now appropriately be considered common nouns and written without capital letters, and sometimes, in spite of his understanding of the principles of capitalization, while utilizing the best sampling of usage his budget will accommodate, he must be arbitrary. In that event he does not mean to imply that the other alternative answer cannot possibly be right. Here, as elsewhere, he is being descriptive and selective.

The complications just discussed, matters like spelling, hyphenation, and capitalization, are often called mechanics. They involve the writing system, and they are not extensively involved in dialects; *idea* is spelled in mainly one way, however it is pronounced in Boston, Houston, and Chicago. Other linguistic decisions, however, do involve dialects, and consequently the choices are much more numerous, much more subtle and complex than the choices between the use of an upper-case or a lower-case letter.

V. *Dictionaries, Dialects, and Dialect Geography*

Dialects, as we have seen, permeate all aspects of language, but some of them do not much plague either makers or users of dictionaries. A physicist may speak a professional dialect among his colleagues that is incomprehensible to the layman because it is seeded with technical terminology. The lexicographer must record this vocabulary, but doing so is not complicated; since physicists publish extensively, the lexicographer has plentiful evidence to delineate the technical vocabulary they use, and since physicists are generally scrupulous about detail and orderly in their habits, they are likely to standardize their own linguistic practices. Furthermore, they will be the authorities; the lexicographer can accept their use as standard practice, and if he cannot understand the physicist's terms he can always find a physicist to explain them.

No such simplicity, however, characterizes the impact of dialects upon either pronunciation or grammatical usage. For the former, regional or geographical dialects are the most important; for the latter, social dialects prevail, and each of these is extremely complex, so complex that no entirely satisfactory statement has ever been made about them, or is likely to be made in the near future. The problem is, and long has been, to find out how various sorts of people use the language. For example, although *ain't* was common in the best circles in New England a century and a half ago, all literate people know that it is now commonly deprecated

in most cultured speech. On the other hand, all listeners to radio or television will know that it can be heard somewhat more commonly among literate speakers in parts of the deep South than in most other areas. But who uses this locution, for what purposes, and in what circumstances? Until recently, even the best informed students could make little more than educated guesses.

Now, however, the lexicographer has one of those new tools referred to above, called *linguistic* or *dialect geography*. It acquired its name through the fact that when it was developed in Europe, it was used mainly to determine the geographical spread of regional dialects and to trace the movements of languages. It can be used, however, to answer almost any question about the current and recent use of language, and even to predict future language developments. The technique is slow, costly in time and money, and since it has been pursued extensively for English only since the early 1930's, the practice is still in its infancy and available materials are inadequate. In spite of these limitations, we are now able to discuss American English with a confidence, and with a fund of detail, that would have been inconceivable a few decades ago. Furthermore, alert lexicographers are learning to make use of this evidence.

Linguistic studies of this nature resemble the well-known opinion poll in that they rely upon carefully drawn questions and a relatively small number of selected informants. The success of the technique depends upon the skill with which a questionnaire is drafted, the patience and care with which it is used, and the intelligence with which the results are interpreted. In the classic use of the device a skilled dialectologist assembles a series of questions and subjects calculated to elicit the desired information. For instance, in this country early linguistic geographers observed that the terms for sledding head first down a snow-covered hill—a score of variants from *belly-bump* to *belly-womp*—and terms for calling farm animals varied widely and fell into patterns. One can see why; coasting has long been popular sport in rural America, but early immigrants came extensively from the mild climates of England and Ireland. They would have brought few coasting terms with them, and the native terms would have had various origins and distinct local growth. Similarly, farm animals are not much called in well-hedged England, where they cannot stray widely, but when such animals were turned loose in the pastures of the New World, calling became a useful farm practice having relatively distinct regional distributions. Chickens are called in Pennsylvania by shouting *Bee!*, but not in Virginia, where *Coo-chee!* and *Coo-chikie!* are common, nor in New England, where *Biddie* and *Widdie* predominate, with *Coop* in highly restricted areas in parts of Rhode Island and eastern Long Island.

Once a suitable questionnaire has been drawn and checked for significance, the onerous job begins, that of locating suitable informants and conducting extensive interviews with them, interviews that last many hours and may extend over a fortnight or so for each informant. The results of these interviews are assembled and tabulated, and in the final operation of the project are studied by specialists to determine dialect areas and describe the speech involved. The older dialectologists worked by transcribing data onto maps, consolidating these data, and printing the results cartographically, with isoglosses to reveal the spread of dialect terms and their possible consolidation into the borderlines of dialect areas. More recently, dialect geographers have been experimenting with printed questionnaires, distributed by mail, and have analyzed the results with the aid of computers. At this writing, such procedures seem to show great promise; dialect geography may become much cheaper and faster in the near future than it is now, and accordingly dialect studies may be more detailed and more numerous.

VI. *American English Dialects*

Employing such studies, scholars have now drafted a generally plausible description of regional dialects in the United States. Hans Kurath, the pioneer of linguistic geography in this country, demonstrated that to explain what has happened in American regional speech, we must understand the dialects that built up along the Atlantic seaboard, especially in the eighteenth century. Kurath identified three of these: Northern in New England and much of New York, extending as far south as a secondary dialect area centered on New York City; Midland speech, dominant in much of New Jersey, Pennsylvania, and northern Delaware; and Southern, which is heard along the east coast from Chesapeake Bay south.

These three dialects moved west, but in devious ways, as migration responded to geography, politics, and the like. For a time the Appalachian Mountains, Indian hostility, and British and French control of the Mississippi-Ohio-Missouri River system deterred westward migration. When the central basin was opened to settlement after the War of 1812, speakers from New York and New England moved along the Erie Canal and the Great Lakes, Midland speakers from Pennsylvania were drawn down the Ohio River, and upland Southern speakers from what Kurath called the Virginia Piedmont worked through the mountain gaps into Kentucky and Tennessee. Two groups moved less than might have been expected; in New England, the growth

of manufacturing and shipping absorbed many of the potential emigrants, and to the south, the great prosperity of the plantation areas and the military competence of the Cherokee delayed the movement that eventually swept along the Gulf of Mexico.

The further western movement was even more diverse. The Northern dialect skirted the Great Lakes, but by the time it had reached the Upper Mississippi it was much blunted and splintered; for example, New England *stoneboat* and *stone drag* found their way as far as Idaho, Washington, and Oregon, but are less common than terms from Midland, *sled* and *sledge*. To the south, the Highland speakers fanned out rapidly in all three directions, north into the old Northwest Territory—Lincoln, as was characteristic of his time, was born in Kentucky but nurtured in Illinois—west into Arkansas and Missouri, south into the tier of States along the Gulf, where they encountered the delayed movement from the Southern tidewater along the Gulf of Mexico. This southern movement declined so sharply during and after the Civil War that Southern terms are found only scatteringly through the Far West.

Thus the Midland dialect, which looks relatively insignificant as it appears on the dialect map of the Atlantic coast, took over vast western areas almost by default, and thus became the basic dialect for much of the western plains and beyond. For this rapid but heterogeneous spread there are at least three reasons. First, it was the only blend dialect; it could blend with Northern or with Southern, which could not well blend much with each other. Thus the important string of Great Lakes cities—Chicago, Detroit, Cleveland, and others, even Milwaukee to the north—although historically within the Northern dialect area, tended to draw Midland speakers to them and merge into the Midland speech area. Second, since the westward movement of both Northern and Southern speakers moderated after the Civil War—albeit for very different reasons—the Midland speakers fanned out from their channel along the Ohio River, as earlier the Highland Southerners had fanned out from their gaps through the mountains, and this penetration was encouraged by the ease with which immigrants could move up tributary rivers into Northern territory. Third, when the great non-English immigration swelled the population during the late nineteenth and early twentieth centuries, the flood moved mainly into the West, which had already been pioneered by Midland speakers. Inasmuch as these immigrants included Welsh and Scotsmen, they brought with them dialects closer to American Midland than to either of the other basic American bodies of speech.

Thus the Midland dialect has a curious configuration. With a narrow eastern base in New Jersey, Delaware, and Pennsylvania, it occupies a relatively constricted trough along the Ohio River, and then, with various crosscurrents and backwashes, it broadens to include much of the western portion of the Middle West, of the Southwest, the Great Basin, and the Pacific coastal States, including the most populous State, California, and the Northwest. Midland speech in the West is anything but pure; Northern forms are common, along with some Southernisms—many Confederate prisoners were shipped west and turned loose— and a considerable number of pockets appear. One area of San Francisco shows strong links with Boston, probably because of 49ers who sailed around Cape Horn, and another reflects speech patterns that must have worked north from Old Mexico. The Church of Christ of Latter-Day Saints has provided the center for a subdialect, which includes Northernisms from upper New York, where the religion started, Southernisms from Missouri where the Saints sojourned, and Midland speech from Iowa and Illinois, from whence the church moved west.

Of course these dialect areas are not sharp, not nearly so sharp as are such areas in most of Europe, or, so far as we know, in most of Asia or Africa. Dialect areas blend into one another, and many Americans speak some blending of regional as well as social dialects. Notable, for example, is the blending of speech south of Lakes Erie and Michigan. Here three lines of western movement were fairly close together, that along the lakes, that to the south along the Ohio River, and that from still farther south pouring through mountain valleys like the Shenandoah. These three movements brought Northern, Midland, and Southern users respectively. Doubtless these bodies of dialect speakers were tolerably distinct at one time, but secondary northward and southward crosscurrents affected them, perhaps especially those population drifts set up by the magnetic attraction of cities like Chicago and Detroit, which pulled Midland and Southern speakers toward the lakes. Similarly, a community like Louisville, Kentucky, is enough the daughter of the Midland movement down the Ohio River, and is sufficiently within the territory of Southern speakers in Kentucky and southern Indiana, that some dialect lines run north and some south of the city. West of the Mississippi River, major dialect divisions become even more blended. Far Western settlement came from so many sources by such intermingled channels, and the whole was so confused by backwashes and crosscurrents—Californians followed mining to Nevada and Idaho, Texans followed cattle to Wyoming and Montana—that vast stretches of Western speech now reflect various minglings and combinations not as yet very well understood.

Language and the Dictionary

VII. *Pronunciation and the Dictionary*

With some sketch of American dialects to think from, we are ready to consider, insofar as the welter of evidence admits of consideration, the vexed problem of pronunciation, and what to do about it in dictionaries. No one has solved this problem; no one has succeeded in reflecting pronunciation in a dictionary, and so complex must be the solution that one suspects nobody ever will, perhaps especially for modern American English. If the problem is essentially unsolvable from the editor's point of view—although the lexicographer may do better or worse with it—it is further confused by users of dictionaries, who on the whole tend to misuse their books more on questions of pronunciation than in most other areas. Here, at least, something can be said.

As a matter of fact, the problem of pronunciation is not so crucial as is sometimes supposed. A speaker having little formal education may expose the state of his culture more quickly by his pronunciation than in any other way, but his pronunciation may damage him less than he believes, and he can do less about it deliberately than he is likely to imagine. Recent American presidents have come from New England, New York, the Middle West, the South, and the Far West; they spoke various dialects, but studies of their success in attracting voters suggest that their accents had little to do with their popularity, except that some listeners, intrigued by pronunciations strange to them, may therefore have listened more closely. Furthermore, most people cannot or will not learn much pronunciation deliberately; they learn pronunciation young and they learn it unconsciously. They cannot hear themselves, and for the most part they do not know how they speak. If they try consciously to "correct" speech they conceive to be "wrong," they are likely to change only relatively few pronunciations, and those only part of the time. But many users of the language want to speak well and some of them try hard to do so; they expect a dictionary to help them, and a modern lexicographer labors to provide help, even though with reservations.

Dictionary makers have not always done so. Early editors acted as though they thought pronunciation was none of their business; such conduct simplified life, if it did not improve the product. Bailey, and Johnson after him, contented himself by marking stressed syllables, and Webster did little more. He was aware that Thomas Sheridan, and especially John Walker, had made serious efforts to describe British pronunciation, but he professed to have discovered more than 12,000 errors in the stressed syllables alone in Walker's *Critical Pronouncing Dictionary*, which would have been an average of something like one mistake per word. In his own dictionary he seems to have been more concerned with identifying the use of letters than with describing sounds. He recognized "a mass of errors and contradictions" in the speech of his contemporaries, which he apparently attributed to "the spirit of innovation," which should be "reprobated and resisted." In this he trusted the good sense of the users of English, at least the "respectable" users, but not his fellow editors; "I am persuaded," he writes, "that there are *ten* differences among these orthoepists [phonologists] where there is *one* in the actual pronunciation of respectable people in England and the United States." He was determined, he wrote, to "present to my fellow citizens the English language, in its genuine purity, as we have received the inheritance from our ancestors," but he never explained to these fellow citizens what the genuine pure sounds were nor how they were to be used.

Webster's younger contemporary, Joseph Worcester, did better. In his work published in 1860, he marked the quality of all vowels, and many consonants, using a system of diacritical marks, some of which were reproduced at the bottoms of pages. Even so, one cannot from his volume discover how words are pronounced, or who pronounced them in accordance with his system. For *bear* he gives a phonetic equivalent *bar*, but one of his tables indicates that his symbol *a* is what he calls an "obscure" vowel, whereas a second table calls it "long before r," and he tells us how to pronounce this sound only by indicating that it is the sound heard also in *bare* and *fair*. Apparently any sound was all right, so long as the speaker was consistent. Not all of Webster's "respectable people" would have employed the same sound. Worcester's fellow townsman in what might have been called Greater Boston, Ralph Waldo Emerson, apparently pronounced *bear* with a diphthong, with a sound that certainly was not obscure and probably was not followed by an r, perhaps something like (be′ə)—for the symbols used here and below, see Key to Pronunciation. At any rate, he rhymed *bear* and *woodpecker*, a similarity which nothing in Worcester or Webster suggests is to be associated with respectable people, although the Reverend Mr. Emerson was respectable on almost any count.

Some difficulties arose because lexicographers did not understand the problem and had inadequate tools with which to work. Webster knew about dialects, but he had no real understanding of them, and as a practical matter he seems to have assumed that whatever was spoken in New Haven was the pure language we had been bequeathed by our ancestors. As a practical matter, also, users of his dictionary assumed that whatever pronunciation appeared there was "preferred."

So far as dialects are concerned, Worcester did little better, for he was concerned with being correct, with following a model; in fact, the question was not whether each speaker should try to imitate one best speech, but whether for an American that speech had to be the practices of London. Worcester declared that "it is advisable for American writers and speakers to conform substantially to the best models, wherever they may be found," but since no American city "holds a corresponding rank as a center of intelligence and fashion," he was glad to observe that London was already the American standard. He asserted "there is, undoubtedly, a more general conformity to London usage in pronunciation, throughout the United States, than there is throughout Great Britain." Whatever he meant by this statement, one can observe that Worcester's pronunciations often paralleled those in British dictionaries, that American dialects mainly stem from those of southeastern England, including London, and that Worcester, who traveled but little in this or any other country, must have known mainly the dialects of southern New England. One must notice, also, that travelers from London were generally horrified at the language they heard in the New World; they called it "vulgar," "uncouth," and "barbarous," not the English language in any real sense, apparently a jargon degenerating into gibberish. For Worcester the problem of pronunciation resolved itself into the existence of "irregularities" and the disagreements among the experts. "The language, as it respects pronunciation," he wrote, "has many irregularities, which cannot be subjected to any general rules."

By the early decades of the twentieth century, phonetic studies were improved, but dictionaries were still being used much as they had been in Webster's day. Scholars were providing more accurate descriptions of human sounds; the International Phonetic Alphabet was being devised and promoted, and more linguistic evidence had been collected, some of it on dialectal bases. Dictionaries were greatly improved, but even the best of them remained patchy, especially in their treatments of pronunciation. Speakers continued to use wordbooks pretty much as had their ancestors, and many publishers encouraged them in their reliance upon dictionaries as prescriptions for correct speech. Users assumed, as they generally still assume, that there is one correct, uncorrupted pronunciation, or at least one that is better than all others, provided one can distinguish it from what Worcester had called "irregularities," and that this pronunciation will be prescribed in "the dictionary." One has only to look up the word in the entry list and sound out the pronunciation there; that will be the correct pronunciation and the only correct pronunciation unless a second one is provided, in which case the first will be the best, or, to phrase the matter a little more delicately, it will be "preferred."

So much for the past. What can now be done to confront the same old problem, the need for simplicity in the Babel of human sound? The modern lexicographer gets some help, if not much, in fuller understanding and better tools. Basically, he can rely upon a principle we have noticed elsewhere, that a dictionary is intended to be descriptive and helpful, not mainly prescriptive or monitory. If a dictionary offers a pronunciation for *government* having three syllables and none having two syllables—as all dictionaries I have checked do—they are not thereby implying that former President Franklin D. Roosevelt was guilty of a gross blunder when he pronounced the word something like (guv′m'nt) as, in accordance with his regional and class dialects, he consistently did. They are saying that a pronunciation with three syllables is widely or universally accepted, and they may also be implying that such a pronunciation characterizes more literate speakers than does any other, that it is a more widely disseminated pronunciation than any other, that it has the strongest tradition and hence may be assumed to be the most stable, that it reflects the ideal of cultivated speakers if not their consistent practice, or something of the sort. They may also be reflecting the fact that in many dictionaries the listed pronunciations are restricted arbitrarily to two, and there are probably at least two pronunciations of *government* with three syllables that are, on some counts, more "acceptable" than more syncopated pronunciations.

The lexicographer can rely, also, on a widely understood concept of dialects, that there are both social and geographical dialects, and if he wishes to prefer one of these to another he can frankly say so. He will prefer the pronunciations of literate speakers as against illiterate speakers, not because he wishes to insult the illiterate, but because, if anyone wishes to correct, or refine, or improve his speech he is likely to wish to seem more literate rather than less so. Regional dialects are more difficult. Presumably, all regional speakers are equally "correct," and one dialect is as good as another; on the other hand, they cannot all be adequately reflected in a desk dictionary. Some can readily be eliminated; a desk dictionary will not include the Gullah pronunciations, however picturesque and charming the talk may be along Goose Creek, North Carolina, because few people know Gullah or wish to imitate it. But what about a choice between a widely current pronunciation and a

supposedly prestigious pronunciation? Earlier American editors, as we have seen, tended to listen to their neighbors if they were as independent as was Webster—which meant mainly New England neighbors—or to copy earlier lexicographers, who would have been mainly British lexicographers, or to look to fashionable London, especially, of course, to the English court. The practice continued; for the word *ask* the pronunciation with the so-called broad *a* [äsk] was often "preferred," presumably because it was common in New England, but it was not the most widely used by literate speakers in the United States. The modern lexicographer, studying the results of linguistic geography surveyed in the previous section, may consciously base his pronunciations on a dual standard, the social dialect of literate speakers and the regional dialect of the Midlands, the upper Middle West, and much of the Far West. At the very least he will give extensive notice in his variant pronunciations to this largest single body of English speech.

The lexicographer gets help, also, from the concept of the phoneme, which can be defined roughly as the spread of sound which the users of a language at any given time and place recognize as a minimal working unit. Sound is precise, but not as human beings use sound, and still less as they conceive it. A given sound can be recorded and reduced to a wave which will differ from the waves derivable from other sounds. Human vocal apparatus, however, is not precise enough to repeat such sounds exactly, and human concepts are still less capable of apprehending them, or bothering with distinctions that seem to have no value. Accordingly, users of the language associate various sounds with purposive speech, or with a letter to represent such speech. For example, any modern American who pronounces the words *tip, mutter*, and *fought* will produce three distinct sounds which he is likely to associate with the letter *t*. For the first he is likely to put the tip of his tongue just back of his front teeth, and flip it a bit as he draws it down. For the t-sound in *mutter* he is likely to touch the roof of his mouth somewhat farther back with the tongue rather flattened, striking almost a glancing blow not quite with the tip of the tongue. For the final sound in *fought* he returns the tongue toward the teeth, but presses it more firmly against the roof of the mouth. These are three quite distinct sounds, but users of the language, either speakers or hearers, do not consciously distinguish them; the sounds are conceived by the users of the language as one, and consequently they are accepted by a phonologist as one of many possible linguo-alveolar voiceless stops which he calls allophones of one phoneme, written /t/. Similarly, any analysis of the consonant sounds in *dead* and *eddy* will reveal several allophones of /d/, but /d/ and /t/ will be different phonemes, because they are involved in significant distinctions, in the differences between *bit* and *bid* or between *mat* and *mad*.

This concept of the phoneme has its lexicographical uses. The modern dictionary editor is likely still to use symbols somewhat as his predecessor did, as indications of phonetically describable sounds, partly because he knows that most users of dictionaries do not understand the concept of the phoneme, but he is likely to be thinking of these symbols as though they represent phonemes. Or, to put this in another way, the older editors were aware of the spread of sound, but they inclined to treat this variety as something exceptional, even something reprehensible, whereas the modern editor knows that sounds as they are used always appear in greater or lesser spread, and he has an orderly system well worked out to deal with this natural fluidity of language. Thus, when a modern lexicographer records the pronunciation of *ask* as [ask], he is more likely to be giving the user a phonemic indication of the sound than a phonetic prescription for it.

Now that the phoneme has been described, I am in a position to indicate how I am using symbols for sound in this essay. There is today no universally accepted set of symbols; accordingly, since the reader will have the list handy, I shall use the symbols in the Key to Pronunciation (see the front endpaper) insofar as that list will serve, and shall make some other provision when I must enlarge upon it. In accordance with what is now common practice, I shall enclose these symbols within square brackets if I am using them as phonetic indications of a supposed sound; I shall place them between slant lines if I am using them as indications of phonemes. Perhaps I should add that many linguists, particularly those concerned with determining the phonemes of a language, rely upon one of several relatively objective definitions, for example, that employed by various members of the Prague school, that a phoneme is a bundle of sounds, some of which are contrastive. I have preferred the definition above since it seems to me more practicable, especially for laymen, once the phonemes of a language are determined.

The modern lexicographer has better means of describing sound than had any of his predecessors, but actually he may be less confident than they, partly because he is better informed and thus more aware than they of the multiplicity of his problems, and partly because we do not as yet have a generally accepted, guaranteed unalterable description of the sounds in American English. Until recently, all American phonetic descriptions grew from the work of the philologists; then, in the 1920's, the concept of the phoneme was im-

ported, notably by Leonard Bloomfield in his monumental *Language*. Bloomfield's statement, applied to American speech especially by Bernard Bloch, George L. Trager, and Henry Lee Smith, became, with the wide acceptance of structural linguistics, the basis of the standard description.

Meanwhile, linguistic geography was developing; it has led to a still different description, growing from a somewhat different analysis and resting on the extensive dialectal evidence assembled by the linguistic geographers (see especially, Hans Kurath, *A Phonology and Prosody of Modern English*, Ann Arbor: University of Michigan Press, 1964, although involved also is the work of Raven I. McDavid and others). This system relies upon a basic analysis into free and checked vowels. These terms, *checked* and *free*, have been widely used to suggest the differences between a vowel in a syllable which is not closed or checked by a consonant, like *spa* /spä/, as against one which is checked, like *spot* /spät/. Phonologists have long recognized that sounds which have been described as the "same" in quality will differ in quality, length, and various other characteristics in the open as against the checked position. The Kurath-McDavid description, however, provides also for free and checked vowels, which will differ of themselves, and can differ even further by position. For example, the vowels in *foot* and *boot* are both in the checked position, but Kurath makes his major distinction between these two vowels by calling that in *foot* [ʊ] checked and that in *boot* [u] free—respectively [oo] and [o͞o] in the system I am using. Kurath's description provides, also, for much more extensive appearance of glides after American vowels, and he notes that they differ, depending upon the position of the tongue when the vowel is sounded and upon the influence of checking, whether in the position of the vowel or the vowel itself.

Thus the modern lexicographer, facing the essentially unsolvable problem of reflecting pronunciation in a transcription or two, is both better and worse off than his predecessor. He is likely to be more aware than were earlier editors that no two speakers ever pronounce a given word alike, and that the same speaker will not repeat a pronunciation, particularly not in different surroundings. For *the* he may say something like /thē/ or /thēə/ in "She is my daughter, but not *the* daughter I meant," something like /thə/ in *the daughter* as ordinarily spoken, and something like /th/ in *the answer*. The modern lexicographer has excellent phonological statements at his disposal, but the modern experts agree neither as to the best phonological approach nor the resulting descriptions. The modern lexicographer has better understanding of the spread of sound than did his predecessor, and he has, in the phoneme, a better tool with which to deal with phonetic spread, but the new tool, as we shall see later, works better for grammar than for phonology. He has vastly improved collections of dialectal variants, and greatly refined descriptions of American dialects, but in some ways this new wealth only compounds and confounds his problem.

Here we should remind ourselves of the blending that is characteristic of American dialects. In the British Isles, the dialectal forms are extremely numerous, but they tend to fall into definable patterns, so that a lexicographer can, if he wishes, restrict his pronunciations to those of a certain dialect and be tolerably consistent. Nothing of the sort is possible, apparently, for American speech; dialects can be described so that they are recognizable, and some words will follow dialect lines rather closely, but others will not. The modern lexicographer, and especially the modern American lexicographer, finds himself plagued, as was Worcester, by irregularities. Although he probably means something rather different by *irregularities* than did Worcester, the earlier editor's description still has pertinence, that the variants "cannot be subjected to any general rules."

Take, for example, what Kurath calls the checked vowel /ɪ/. In *milk* one can expect variants which in the system of transcription I am using would start a little farther back and higher than [ä], through [a], [e], to [i], including a sound not represented in the system I am using, often transcribed as an *i* with a line through it. On the other hand, transcriptions for *hill*, which presumably contains the same high front checked vowel, would not have the lower transcriptions that appear for *milk*, but would have some farther back, perhaps as far back as [u]. The sounds represented by *i* in *within* would have still different spreads, and the sounds in learned words like *ichthyosaurus* would have variants higher and farther forward, even, with some speakers, free as against checked. Not less confused are the vowels in words like *park* and *car*, or the diphthongs in words like *cow* and *out;* here the diphthong tends to start higher in the North than in the South and is less likely to become a triphthong, but the variations are many, both North and South, and the occurrences inconsistent. Thus the recognized patterns of American dialects help, but they help less than lexicographers could wish.

Earlier we noticed that no one had ever reduced American English pronunciation to a simple, adequate, alphabetical list. The editors of the present dictionary tried hard to render that statement obsolete, but they would be the first to say they have not been able to do so. They have, however, made use of the latest evidence and the most modern techniques, and they have produced a set of transcriptions that

will serve most purposes for most persons, at least for those who will learn how to use it in relation to what can be expected of it. They have made such use as they could of dialect, relying for a social level upon the literate use of the largest body of American speakers having a relatively uniform speech, and for regional dialects those that have stemmed from Midland with some admixture of Northern. They have tried to reflect this speech phonemically rather than phonetically; that is, when they provide *car* with the transcribed equivalent /kär/ they are saying only that the word can be pronounced with any of a variety of pure vowels or diphthongs, with a low mid vowel central among them, as these vowels may or may not be altered in quality by a following /r/ or a retroflex. They are also saying that a speaker who wishes to recognize these symbols as phonetics can feel safe in doing so, that a pronunciation like [kär] is universally acceptable, although not universally used. They are not, however, condemning the speaker who has no postvocalic /r/ in his dialect—as many of the best speakers do not, notably in New England and the South. The editors can only trust that such speakers will recognize that the pronunciation /kär/, like all pronunciations, reflects a dialect, and that speakers of other dialects will make the appropriate adjustments.

This procedure would work fairly well if American dialects were consistent. Within limits they are; most speakers either have a postvocalic /r/ or they do not have one; *dear* and *here* rhyme in most dialects, and thus the editor, if he uses one or the other and warns his readers which he is using, can hope that readers can construct a whole series of equivalents, and if the choices are not many the problem is not difficult. But for some sounds the allophonic spread is extensive and complex, and individual words do not follow clear patterns. Take *tauter*, *daughter*, and *water*, words which would rhyme in many idiolects. The first, *tauter* has few variants, and they follow common dialectal patterns; the latter two, *daughter* and *water*, have many variants but not the same ones. Using the diacritical system of the current dictionary, a pronunciation of *water* as (ōō ôt'ə) is common in the New York City area, but for *daughter* (dōō ôt'ə) is not common anywhere; in some areas *daughter* can be heard as (dôr'tər), but *water* can probably not be much heard as (wôr'tər). As the editor of the dictionary put it in a letter to me, "We consulted a number of informants, geographically dispersed . . . about their practices in connection with a representative list of words with [ä] or [ô], including *squabble*, *water*, *caught*, *wad*, *broad*, *fog*, *loss*, etc. About all we could determine from their returns (and also from material on this very point in the atlas project for the North Central States) was that chaos prevails, that there is no fixed pattern that we could determine, and that we would have to be pretty darn arbitrary about entering words in such a category." Of course an editor does not like to be arbitrary, and the difficulty is that we users of the dictionary have no real way of finding out how unhappy the editors were when they had to be more or less arbitrary with individual entries.

The user of the dictionary should remind himself, also, that the editors are employing, with their own refinements, standardizing devices which have been developed during the years, of which one of the most useful is called "full-form" pronunciation. The editors know that no two speakers will pronounce a given word in the same way, and that even a single speaker will not pronounce the same word identically in two uses, since his speech will be altered by various circumstances, especially by the context in which the word appears. Thus, possible pronunciations of any word are infinite, but the lexicographer must reduce this infinity, particularly in a desk dictionary, to what the user needs most to know, and for this purpose he employs full-form for most words. That is, the editors record what they conceive a careful speaker would be likely to say if he were asked how to pronounce a word. Thus the current dictionary gives (bī' 'n bī') for *by-and-by*, although the editors know that the same speaker would give more attention to the *and* if he were singing the phrase in the old song, "in the sweet by-and-by." In actual speech, this same careful speaker might say (bīm'bī'), since a succeeding /b/ is likely to influence a preceding nasal and promote the development of /m/ as against /n/, and a terminal vowel in an open syllable tends to develop a glide in modern American speech. The editors know all this, but they have little chance to explain it, and their full-form equivalent probably gives as clear an understanding of the word as is possible in brief compass. For extreme cases they have made exceptions, notably for connecting words, auxiliaries, prefixes, and the like. The following entries are instructive:

and (ənd, ən, 'n, 'm; *stressed,* and)
have (hav, həv, əv; *before* "to," haf)
de- (di, də; *with some slight stress,* dē)

Such extensive treatment helps for a few words; applied generally, it would waste space and confuse users of the dictionary.

For the remainder, the editors have been liberal in the use of alternative pronunciations and have conserved space by truncation wherever practicable. They have endeavored to restrict pronunciations to no more than two or three; a rough check suggests that they have provided alternatives for nearly half the entries, which is very high, higher, I suspect, than for any other desk dictionary. However that

may be, the user of the book may be surprised—I was—to observe for how many words most of the literate pronunciations could be suggested through two well-selected transcriptions. For a relatively few entries the editors have recognized as many as four variants, but usually with enough truncation so that the section devoted to pronunciation remains brief; that is, they repeat in alternate transcriptions only the portions of the word that show variety. Thus the entry for *futurity* offers the following: (fyōō toor'ə tē, -tyoor'-, -choor'-), and that for *nausea* provides the following: (nô'shə, -sē ə, -zē ə, -zhə). The editors could easily have carried this variety further. For example, the voiceless /p/ in *newspaper* influences the preceding voiced /z/ sufficiently so that many speakers will voice the terminal sound in *news* more than they do the same sound in the compound. The unprinted editing materials used in preparing the dictionary show that the editors considered reflecting this tendency but decided against doing so, probably because the resulting variants are not very sharply distinguished. The editors recognized (nōōz'pā'pər, nyōōz'-), but they also considered as possibilities (nōōs'pā'pər) and (nyōōs' pā'pər).

VIII. *Usage and Linguistic Levels*

As we have seen, dialects of all sorts affect all aspects of language, but concepts of usage, particularly usage in what is felt to be grammatical correctness or propriety, are notably linked to social dialects. Presumably all dialects are equal in at least one sense, that each has a use for a body of speakers. A platoon sergeant who can speak the dialects of his men may survive better than one who can speak only the language of literary criticism, but not all dialects are equally fashionable, nor for learned, commercial, professional, and polite purposes, equally useful. This fact has led to the concept of language levels, that is, that different sorts of language are appropriate for different purposes, on different occasions, and among different kinds of persons. No agreement has been reached as to how these are to be distinguished and described, but a widely recognized classification identifies four levels of speech as follows: *formal speech*, suitable for governmental and legal documents, for solemn pronouncements, for scholarly and scientific writing addressed to specialists, and the like; *standard speech*, the oral or written use characteristic of literate, cultured persons when they are using the language with considerable care, but do not find themselves in a situation requiring formal usage; *informal* or *familiar speech*, the use of the same body of speakers using the language in a somewhat more relaxed manner, and *vulgate*, speech not generally accepted by the literate community. These levels, if they can be said to have any real existence, are neither sharp nor permanent. *Hadn't ought* as against *ought not* will be considered vulgate in some groups but not in others. *Providing* was formerly considered vulgate for *provided* in a sentence like, "I will join, provided I do not have to attend meetings," but is now commonly used in the United States, except at the formal level. Some other labels, perhaps especially *colloquial* and *slang*, do not fit very neatly into these categories; neither would be characteristic of formal speech and not much of standard, but they appear commonly and appropriately at the other levels. *Colloquial* is often defined as "characteristic of conversation and informal writing." *Slang* refers to a great variety of locutions, but most of them are thought of as transient, or at least of such recent origin that they may be expected to become so.

This concept of linguistic levels, although more practical and nearer the truth than the older approach in which specific locutions were labeled right and others wrong, some good and others bad, does not simplify the problem of usage for the user of the language. The older approach had the virtues of simplicity and ease, if not of truth and good sense. One can readily say "That is a bad word; never use it," but all words have use, or they could not exist. Many a word, frowned on in the classroom and the glossary of usage, does more than its share of the work of the world. But deciding what work a word can appropriately do is not easy. Good usage requires wide knowledge and tasteful discrimination; it cannot be learned easily, but at the worst, one who thinks of language on the basis of levels of usage is approaching his speech problem in a sensible, realistic way, and he need not feel that his reference books are loftily giving him fibs for answers. And for the simpler problems, the answers are essentially the same anyhow. The modern linguist would not say that *ain't* is a bad word, but he would say, "Unless you have very good reasons, don't use it."

Of course language levels are vague and shifty, and trying to provide labels for them causes gray hair and ulcers in editorial offices. To date, nobody has been able to devise language labels that will be at once objective and permanent, although the methodology of linguistic geography is beginning to provide the means of being objective about the present and of predicting the future. Consider, for example, the word *guts*. Webster seems not to have known the word in the sense of the intestinal regions, or as personal fortitude, but he labeled the singular, when applied to the stomach, as "low." His rival, Worcester, on the other hand observed that the word was "commonly used in the plural," and let it go at that. Later, the *Century* still considered the use meaning "the whole digestive system" low, even though

the editors cited John Dryden translating a classical author, and if Dryden on the classics was low, one wonders who was not. Soon after, the *New International*, second edition, recognized both uses, but labeled the use meaning "courage" as "slang" and that meaning "the intestines" as "now coarse." The first edition of the present dictionary continued the label for *guts* as "courage," calling it "slang," but somewhat tempered the use meaning "intestines," with the words "now generally regarded as an indelicate usage." The current edition labels one use "slang" and one "colloquial." Thus, we are probably safe in saying that at no time in the last 150 years could the persons best qualified to speak agree as to how low, coarse, slangy, indelicate, or colloquial *guts* might be, or how to describe this degree of indelicacy with a label. Meanwhile *gut* as an attributive has long been used among medical practitioners, in compounds like *catgut*, and it has developed as a synonym for *basic* in expressions like *gut issues*. The verb, as in *to gut a building*, is standard. And so it goes; usage is not very sharply measurable and is much too subtle to be measured satisfactorily with a few usage labels.

As a result, books treating usage are likely to follow one of three attitudes. Usage manuals tend to treat relatively few debated locutions and to discuss them at length. Such books can be very useful in resolving difficult problems, but their word list is inevitably limited. The great reference dictionaries can provide sufficient quotations so that if their editors select quotations to reveal usage as well as meaning, they can put before the user enough information so that he can make up his own mind. The editors of such a dictionary can, in effect, say to the user, "Here is a quotation from a prizefighter; if you want to talk like a prizefighter, this is the way to do it, but if you do not want to, here are other citations that will suggest how you may talk differently." Obviously, neither of these approaches will serve for a desk dictionary, which must be handy to use, must treat all words in good standing that present problems in usage, and must provide quick answers if not always detailed ones.

Here we might recall the tradition of the desk dictionary, that it has always been intended to give the user what he wants and needs, or the nearest approach to it that can be compressed into brief compass. Users of dictionaries want usage labels and with good reason. The public mostly trusts such labels too much, but however unscientific usage labels may be, they provide the only succinct means yet devised, handy for both the maker and the user of a dictionary, with which a speaker or writer can be quickly warned of the limited usage of a word, and can be given some indication of the limits. If the user of a dictionary is troubled about the propriety of *guts*, he is at least alerted if he knows that a well-informed lexicographer thought the word questionable enough to attach a restrictive label to it. Of course the lexicographer is not saying that the word is equally indelicate at all times, in all places, and forever, but if the user of a dictionary will recall that the book is intended to be helpful, and within limits descriptive but not prescriptive, usage labels can have their place.

Some matters of usage are random, not to say whimsical. Many a newspaper editor who has shown no great sensitivity to tautology will scrupulously edit out all occurrences of "consensus of opinion" because style sheets traditionally point out that any consensus must involve opinion. Some dicta as to usage grow from various sorts of pedantry: the double negative was frowned upon because it was thought to be illogical; a verbal or adverbial particle at the end of a sentence was discouraged because it had mistakenly been called a preposition; and speakers who quite logically said, "He is older than me," have been rebuked on the dubious thesis that the sentence really is "He is older than I [am old]." Some questions of usage, however, are deeply rooted in the history of the language, mainly that of the verb.

Verb forms in Indo-European, from which English descends, were distinguished in part by what is called radical change, that is, change in the radix, or root. A few such changes have survived, and are familiar in some of our commonest verbs, as in *sing, sang, sung; ride, rode, ridden; and eat, ate, eaten*. Verbs were not the most numerous sort of words in Indo-European, but several hundred of them continued into Old English. Some time before our earliest written English documents, however, our ancestors had ceased to use these radical-changing patterns when they made new verbs, and had developed instead a pattern employing added endings, notably /t/ and its voiced variant /d/, along with unstressed vowels if they were needed for ease in pronunciation. These forms were involved in past tenses, and in past participles.

This new means of verb-forming coincided roughly with a great period of verb-making in English. For whatever reasons, and they were probably many, English found use for more verbs; our ancestors had participated in several migrations, had adapted to the sea, were changing from hunters and fishers to farmers and town dwellers, and were encountering new cultures, especially the Roman civilization and its derivatives to the north. All of these circumstances would have encouraged new vocabulary, particularly the contacts with Mediterranean cultures, which promoted the borrowing of great numbers of words from Latin and later from French and Greek. This new vocabulary included verbs, and all of them developed in accordance with the new

verbal pattern, with no radical changes but with added endings. Such verbs spawned by the hundreds; soon they were much the more numerous and from their inception they had been the simpler; often they would have been the more fashionable. If a great person had a French wig, a *cheveler*, he would inevitably have been called *chevelered*. To invent a past participle to describe him by using the older verbal pattern would have been awkward linguistically and shocking to polite society. Many of the old verbs, like *dwinan*, faded away and were replaced by new words borrowed from abroad having the new endings—in this instance, with words like *vanish* and *disappear*—or with one of the new phrases like *go away*. Most of the old verbs that survived changed to the new form; *dwinan* had a related word which has given us *dwindle*, but with the new past and past participle, *dwindled*.

As we have seen, whenever changes occur in language, dialects will be involved. The shift from the old type of verb to the new was never completed, and it took place differently and at different rates in various dialects, both regional and social dialects. For example, *helped* and *holp* as past forms of *help* were for a time about equally common, the new form *helped* fashionable among some groups, *holp* surviving in others, perhaps notably among the conservative landed gentry. On the other hand, although *seed* developed as a past of *see*, it succumbed to the older *saw*. When the older forms were not lost entirely, they were usually reduced to two or three, but which two or three was not uniform, as confusions among *have drank* and *have drunk*, *ate* and *eat* (pronounced /ēt/ or /et/) amply testify. The result was confusion; most of the old forms disappeared, but in accordance with no consistent pattern, so that historically one can justify *I seen* and *I seed* as well as *I saw*, *have corven* as well as *have carved*, *drinked* as well as *drank* or *drunk*. Some words became fashionable and others unfashionable, not so much on the basis of the correctness of the words on any linguistic or historical basis as upon the wealth, social standing, and residence of the speakers.

By now, of course, most surviving forms are firmly labeled standard or vulgate, but the process of creating new verb forms continues, scatteringly, but for the whole phenomenon, revealingly. The verb *slay* has the old preterite *slew* and the past participle *slain*, but in slang uses, a preterite of the newer type *slayed* has developed (*They beat us on their field, but in the return game we slayed 'em*). Meanwhile, since *slew* is nearly obsolete in most dialects, *slayed* may become standard, if *slay* survives at all. As for *slain*, although it was once extremely common, being formal speech in a passive expression meaning *died* (*He was* [or *became*] *slain* occurs regularly in the *Anglo-Saxon Chronicle* for "he died," even from disease or senility), its almost complete disappearance from modern use would encourage the growth of *slayed* as a new past participle. Similarly, *fly* has the old preterite *flew*, which seems not to be declining, but the newer preterite has developed in some specialized uses; we can say that the batter *flied out*, but to say he *flew out* would mean something quite different. Thus, variant verb forms have long presented usage problems, and are still creating them, partly because the outcasts stem from a heritage generally as honorable as that of the forms arbitrarily made legitimate.

IX. *Dictionaries and Meaning*

Now we come to meaning, the core of any dictionary more adequate than the pocket abridgments intended for ready spelling reference. Most users, when they consult a dictionary seriously, want to confirm old but hazy notions of meaning, or to introduce themselves to unfamiliar meanings. Similarly, the lexicographer concerns himself most seriously with meaning, for here he has no adequate methods and few objective answers. Etymology may require highly informed, elaborate research, but good research will produce a high percentage of demonstrably accurate answers. Spelling is relatively easy, and even pronunciation, usage, and the like are more or less amenable to careful, informed research. But nobody knows what meaning is or how to define it; extensive research will help, but in the last analysis definitions are only as good as the trained brains that draft them. In semantics, more than anywhere else, lexicography approaches both philosophy and art.

Part of the difficulty arises from the fact that, in any strict sense, words do not have intrinsic meaning. The meanings and the senses of words are in the users of the language, in the speakers and writers, in the hearers and readers. The words are stimuli that call forth senses of meaning, one sense in the speaker or writer, a somewhat different sense in the hearer or reader, and in reality a different sense in each hearer or reader, since no word can ever have quite the same impact on any two people, nor, if one wishes to push the investigation far enough, does a word have precisely the same meaning any two times it is used. Thus, the lexicographer, when he tries to define a term, is not trying to put into words an ideal, objectively existing meaning which could be completely and exactly revealed if his defining practices were without flaw.

He is trying to describe what he trusts is a consensus, even though a mainly unconscious consensus, of the ways in which users believe they are employing the word, for interestingly enough, the fact that words have no objective meaning does not prevent users from believing they have. In fact,

users believe this so strongly that they will fight about the meanings of words, and these fights are national and international as well as personal. Constitutions are drafted, laws are made, cases at law are decided, and books and articles and newspapers are written on the tacit assumption that words do have meanings. On this assumption the maker of dictionaries must work. He knows that although philosophically he cannot describe meaning, he can attempt to describe the common convictions about a word, aware that language can function and can serve mankind on this working assumption, that for practical purposes words can be defined.

Within limits, meanings can be pinned down. Most words have what are called referents, something to which they refer. The name *Rabbi Abraham ben Meir Ibn Ezra* probably refers to only one poet-grammarian, since it is unlikely that there was another Spanish Jewish divine by the same name. Similarly, as usually used, *Jesus* has only one referent, although the word is used as a given name in some countries. That is, proper names presumably have referents, one referent to a name, since theoretically the proper name attaches to only one object, even though the same linguistic shape may be the proper name for another object or kind of object. Molly Mog, the heroine of *The Fair Maid of the Inn*, is quite different from a Molly Maguire Riot and different also from the sheep in one of Chaucer's tales "that was called Molly." Similarly, almost any concrete term is likely to have an identifiable referent. Words like *goat* and *automobile* refer only to one referent at a time, whether it be a single object or class of objects. But the concept of referents has its limits; no two people would be likely to agree as to what *truth* refers to, except that they would agree that it does not refer to something false. The concept becomes even less useful with grammatical terms like *but*, *a*, and *of*. In the consideration of many other words, for instance, terms like *full*, *somewhat*, and *beautiful*, the concept of referents seems to do little more than confuse the issue.

Furthermore, even for those words that have identifiable referents, a word obviously does more than identify an object. Almost always and inevitably it has more meaning than that. The mere fact that a word is heard or read assures us that it will do more. A word like *Hiroshima*, although it has as its referent a certain Japanese city, today means more than just a specific community. A word like *Mary*, whatever its referent, is likely to mean more to all Christians than to most Buddhists, more to Roman Catholics than to Unitarians, more to nuns than to most cowboys. Here an old distinction is useful, if not very precise— the difference between a word's denotation and its connotation. The denotation has been defined as the total of all the word's referents. Its connotation concerns the personal and especially the emotional impact that the word can arouse. Obviously, neither of these identifications will bear examination, but every word has some sort of recognized use, some denotation that can be generally described and will be roughly the same for all people, and most words will call up associations that will be unique in each person. These connotations will vary greatly, in degree as well as character; presumably words like *God* and *mother* will have strong connotations for all English-speaking persons, even though different connotations for each person, whereas *ichthyology* and *symbiosis* will move few readers deeply.

Thus at best a lexicographer cannot hope to survey the power and the working of a word, but practically he can do much to order meaning and to distill it into a refined statement. After all, definition is an ancient study, and the semanticist has well-tried techniques at his disposal. Troglodytes must have argued in caves about what one another meant, and the earliest orderly thinkers of whom we have any record were aware that they could not think or speak with any precision unless they could first agree upon the terms they were using. Often they could rely upon what is called *stipulative defining*, defining by mutual or tacit agreement for limited purposes. A speaker may say, "When I use the term *subsistence level*, I am accepting the current estimate of the Department of Labor." Obviously, some families could subsist in low-cost communities on incomes that would not suffice for families in certain other communities, but if a speaker has stipulated what he means by *subsistence level*, he can govern his statements accordingly, and his hearers can make appropriate adjustments.

The lexicographer can use this device only to a limited degree, but he has other techniques at his disposal. Perhaps the readiest definitions are provided by synonyms, words that theoretically have the same meaning. One can say that *Hund* in German means *dog* in English, because the words have the same referent, but an American who has not encountered the term *bushbaby* might call to mind a faulty referent until he is told it is a British and African designation for a galago, a small monkey. Definition by synonym, however, has its limits. Strictly speaking, there are no synonyms; no word means just what another word means. *Digit* is a synonym of *finger*, roughly speaking, but each means both more and less than the other; a German would not use *Hund* in all the ways in which a speaker of English uses *dog*. And for many words there are, in effect, no synonyms at all; for example, *phenylalanine* probably has no synonym, unless one wishes to accept $C_9H_{11}O_2N$ as a word, and even a common term like *eye* has, in effect, no synonym,

because the implications of *optic* are quite different, although the words have the same referent.

Perhaps the most generally accurate mode of defining, sometimes called *analytic definition*, works by placing an object within a known class and identifying it within that class. For example, the present dictionary defines a cow as "the mature female of domestic cattle (genus *Bos*)." That is, the cow is placed within a category, the genus *Bos*, and the modifying details are so chosen that they exclude all creatures not cows and presumably include all creatures that can be called cows in this use of the word. Anyone who does not know what the genus *Bos* is can find out, since Latin genus names are extensively described in scientific works, and good dictionaries, like the present one, may include related English terms derived from the genus name, in this instance, for example, *bovid*. If one wishes to pursue the search further, he is likely to find that the Bovidae are ruminants distinguished by a polycotyledonary placenta; by nondeciduous, hollow, unbranched horns, and usually by the presence of a gall bladder.

As a means of identification this system works so well that, properly handled, it can be used to describe animals, plants, insects, and the like so accurately that a specimen need seldom be confused with any other specimen. Scientists use this system of taxonomic classification extensively. For less learned purposes, however, the method may be less useful, partly because scientific generic terms are esoterica with which few laymen are concerned. The average city dweller, passing a field of various large quadrupeds, might not know which horns would eventually prove to be deciduous, or which creatures possessed gall bladders and polycotyledonary placentas. Consequently, for most purposes, most lexicographers, even when they employ this relatively exact type of definition, find that they can profitably combine it with another, known as *descriptive definition*, indicating how the object appeals to the senses. Thus the present dictionary, although it identifies the so-called American buffalo as *Bison bison*, a bovine mammal, adds that it has "a shaggy mane, short curved horns, and a humped back," and that it stands from five and a half to six feet high. These details are not, of course, discrete; they will not differentiate a bison from all other creatures, but they will be more useful to most users of a desk dictionary than will arcane but discrete details about the placenta.

The possible processes of definition are too numerous to be developed here in any complexity, but a brief survey may be useful. Definition by example may provide helpful insights; the present dictionary defines one use of *covert* as "a hiding place for game, as underbrush, a thicket, etc." Definition by purpose, use, or origin can be revealing; the definition just quoted suggests something about the use of *covert*, implying a game's-eye view of the use of underbrush. One can hardly see how *covert* in this sense could be defined more accurately, revealingly, and succinctly, than by this deft combination of category ("a hiding place for game"), plus examples ("underbrush, a thicket, etc."), plus the distinction between brush used as a hiding place and brush not so used. Similarly, any good definition of a typewriter or a typesetting machine would certainly require some indication of the purpose of the device. Brief, although not usually very precise, definition can be achieved through contrast, through the use of antonyms—*up* is the opposite of *down*—or through negation, as an *agnostic* is "a person who believes one cannot know whether there is a God."

Etymology may be useful in definition. The word *definition* comes from Latin *de finibus*, meaning "concerning boundaries," and in one sense *definition* is setting limits to things, including words. Even figures of speech may be useful in defining, but on the whole they are not very useful in semantics as the lexicographer must practice it; "my love is like a red, red rose" may be good poetry, but it is not precise or universal enough to be very good lexicography.

Thus the handling of meaning, as an editor of a dictionary must conceive it, is not mainly based upon an understanding of the nature of meaning itself. It requires, of course, clear, penetrating thought; anyone who doubts this should select some common word, look it up in two dictionaries having independent developments, and then ask himself seriously how one set of definitions differs from the other, in scope, in analysis of overlapping and intermingling uses, in conceptions as embodied in word choice. Anyone who attempts this seriously is not likely to forget the experience. Having made such an analysis, the lexicographer must then ask himself what combination of all the possible devices for definition will serve him best for this particular word. When that decision has been reached, he has still to write the definition, an activity which requires unusual precision, clarity, and simplicity in the use of language.

X. *Grammar and the Dictionary*

One more aspect of language must concern us, grammar as it pertains to the dictionary. Some earlier editors of dictionaries provided surveys of grammar; both Johnson and Webster felt moved or obligated to do so, although neither understood the complexity of grammar, and these grammatical statements are among the least enduring of their works. Such practices have gone out of fashion; grammar is now a serious and lively study, if not now often undertaken in introductions to dictionaries, and no such

survey as Webster's will be attempted here. Lexicographers, however, must deal with grammar. The grammatical functioning of a word is part of its being, and users of desk dictionaries turn to such volumes seeking grammatical aid. This introduction will consider grammar as it influences dictionaries and as it is reflected in them, although grammar as an area of study will be left to works more specifically devoted to that subject.

Grammatical labels present the lexicographer—and these days perhaps particularly the American lexicographer—with difficult problems. The whole theory of parts of speech does not fit English very well, and the traditional definitions of these parts are not sharply applicable to modern American grammar. The concept and the terms stem from Latin, where they were much more appropriate. For example, the Latin word *audiremini*, an imperfect, passive subjunctive form meaning something like "you would be heard," can be recognized at once as a verb, and it could scarcely be anything else. With a few exceptions, this is true of most classical Latin words. Usually anyone conversant with Latin knows at once the part of speech of any word he encounters, and he knows it by the shape, especially by the inflectional ending.

The converse is true of English, where parts of speech can seldom be recognized by formal appearance. There are exceptions; words ending in *-ly* are typically adverbs, unless they happen to be like *homely*, which is usually an adjective, *rely*, which is usually a verb, *holly*, which is usually a noun, and the like. Words ending in *-ness* tend to be nouns and those ending in *-ize* to be verbs, but few words have such endings. Consider a shape like *out*. It is a preposition in *out the window*, a noun in *the catcher made an out*, a verb in *truth will out*, an adjective in *the batter is out*, probably an adverb in *carried out to sea*, and, like almost all words, it can be used as an interjection. That is, *out* as form can be almost anything; one can determine its part of speech only on the basis of use, and even this device has limits. In "Father put him out" the *out* can be thought of as part of the verb *put out* or as a modifier; if it is a modifier and if the *him* is a baseball player, the *out* is perhaps an adjective, but if the *him* is a cat *out* is more likely an adverb. Consider "They went walking"; is there such a thing as the verb *go walking*, or is *went* an auxiliary? No dictionary I have consulted accepts either possibility. Or is *walking* a noun, some sort of complement? If we now add a phrase so that the sentence becomes "They went walking down the highway," the word that formerly looked verbal or nominal seems to be some sort of modifier, although whether adjectival or adverbial might pose a good question. In the sentence "The man looked up the street," the particle *up* would seem to be a preposition if the man was standing in the street, but part of a verb if he was consulting a map or a reference work. Subtleties of this sort, which seem to be characteristic of an analytic grammar like that of modern English, can scarcely be well revealed by a few labels.

At this writing, and for the near future, that is essentially what the lexicographer has, a limited set of labels, not very precise and not sharply applicable to English. He has elaborate devices to elucidate meaning and extensive means to record phonology, but only a meager system to reveal grammar. Since he cannot, especially in a popular work, use arcane terms in his apparatus, an editor cannot take much advantage of terminology being developed in recent grammatical approaches; he is in effect restricted to inherited labels, mostly for the traditionally recognized parts of speech. These he can redefine if he wishes, but if he does, he is likely to have little assurance that he and users of his book will employ these terms in the same way.

Consider a few grammatical labels. Most users of dictionaries, if they find *n.* after a word, assume that the word is a substantive, "the name of a person, place, or thing." But most such names can be used also as modifiers (an *Amazon* warrior, a *city* problem, *lion* cubs) and if nominal forms cannot be distinguished from adjectives by the conventional definition, neither can they be distinguished from pronouns by saying that "a pronoun is a word that can be used in place of a noun." Most nouns can replace other nouns (The *parent* spanked his *child*; The *father* spanked his *son*), and pronouns are not exclusively substitutes for anything. They are relationships or signal words having nominal force, doing both more and less than nouns, but they seldom characterize or describe as nouns do, and they reveal relationships as nouns cannot. We have already seen that adjectives do more than modify nouns; and although the conventional definition of adverbs was so broad as to include modification of "a verb, an adjective, or another adverb," it was not broad enough, since what seem to be adverbs can modify whole clauses or various parts of them. Verbs are supposed to be definable, but in many sentences one has trouble distinguishing verbs from verbals or even from complements, as in *He set about trying to get his accounts put in order*.

Meanwhile, in spite of the inherent limitations of grammatical labels, we should notice that the linguistic facts which the older grammarians endeavored to approach through the parts of speech are very real. Words do work differently; most nouns and verbs cannot function as prepositions or adverbs, for example. Thus a modern lexicographer, when he puts an *n.* after *out*, is not likely to mean that the form *out* is a noun and that it cannot be anything else unless he says so. Of course, if an editor has space enough, he can sharpen the definition of a noun as the name of something. He can notice that it is the sort of word that can be a subject and can fit into unique patterns. It can be preceded by a determiner (*the*), by an adjective (*infirm*), which can in turn be preceded by an intensifier (*very*), and these words can be built into patterns like *the very infirm old man*, but they cannot enter into a string like *man infirm old the very*. With some exceptions a noun can be made into a plural by adding /s/ or /z/, and the exceptions can be treated in various subsidiary rules. With enough such rules, a noun can be described with some certainty, but the process becomes cumbersome, so cumbersome that even inadequate grammars run to several volumes. It is a further fact that the grammar of modern English cannot be well described only by identifying parts of speech, however these classes of words are defined.

Meanwhile, parts of speech labels do have their uses, and lexicographers have become extremely skillful in making the most of grammatical designations. Labels, even though they are imprecise and limited, have practical applications. Man has always needed names for things, and words have grown to fill these needs. Man has needed to refine concepts represented in such names, and he has been able to do so by developing words to sharpen or otherwise alter the impacts of names. If we now call one sort of word a noun and the other an adjective, to say that an adjective can modify a noun helps us understand the working of language, even though our definitions of noun and adjective are not the whole truth and nothing but the truth. Grammatical labels have many side applications; they can be utilized, for example, in limiting meaning. As was apparent in the discussion of words like *out*, meaning and grammatical use are intimately related, and just as we have to rely on meaning in determining grammar we can use grammar to distinguish meanings. *Out* as a noun has very limited meanings; it has quite different meanings as adjective and adverb. And lexicographers work hard to make labels for parts of speech descriptive of the use of the language. Even the briefest look at the present edition, when compared with the earlier version—which was in turn strong in just this—will reveal that the editors have been alert to the recently developed attributive uses of nouns, to the current growth of verbal devices, and the like.

How does a lexicographer view his grammatical labels? All lexicographers scrupulously attempt to define the grammatical terms they employ, but we have seen that they are not very sure what these labels mean, and they are still less sure that their whole system is adequate. Their uncertainty, however, arises not from their own doing. Lexicographers are not, except incidentally, grammatical theoreticians, and they find themselves trying to provide grammatical identifications with no well worked-out understanding based upon a generally accepted grammatical philosophy. They know that the older statement, if it was ever adequate for Latin, is certainly not adequate for modern English, and yet it has been replaced by no other universally accepted approach. Never, since men have tried to think seriously about English, have grammatical statements concerning it stemmed from such a variety of assumptions. This variety, not to say confusion, may be intriguing for the grammarian, who finds himself involved in revolutions that stimulate new proposals and provide fresh insights, but faced with the practical problem of producing a reliable book, the lexicographer lacks the simple, authoritative assurances that would simplify his editing.

The lexicographer's dilemma will perhaps be best revealed through an examination of recent grammatical thought as it applies to English. Here one scarcely knows where to begin, since the cleavages are so great and the lines of thought so numerous that no one can today be sure which distinctions are primary and which secondary, but one that is surely important grows out of the kind of linguistic evidence the grammarian depends upon. The older approach relied upon language already in existence. That is, the grammarian made up a sentence, or he took a sentence he found written or could record as having been spoken. He derived his concept of the working of the language from such samples, and the result was called *grammar*, and is now often referred to as *sentence-interpreting grammar*. But a sense for grammar must have existed in the user of the language before these bits of language came into existence; otherwise the speaker could not have uttered them for purposive reasons and unless this same sense of the language was present also in hearers and readers, the sentences could not have been understood. That is, the grammar of a language must exist in the user of the language as well as in the language as it has already been used, and this conviction can be embodied in what might be called a *sentence-producing grammar*, or more frequently, a *generative grammar*. The two resulting kinds of statements would inevitably be different, but theoretically they should both be valid, and they should both be interesting and probably useful. As we have seen, all of the older grammatical statements tended to be sentence-interpreting, so much so that grammar was assumed to be the process of interpreting sentences through their internal working, but recent grammatical attempts have tended to favor generative approaches.

Language and the Dictionary

At this writing, the grammatical statement that is exciting the most learned interest is one called *stratificational grammar*. It has been worked out by Prof. Sydney M. Lamb of Yale University and others interested in machine translation, developing ideas formulated by the Dane, Louis Hjelmslev, under the title *glossematics*, which utilizes both generative and interpretative devices. This grammar does not start with such minutiae as words or phonemes, but with great forces which are conceived to work through language at all levels; thus, although the stratificational approach can be used to tell what sort of thing a word is, it presumably explains sounds, words, sentences, and larger areas of language, combining in one vast system what has formerly been thought of as both grammar and rhetoric, along with quite a bit of psychology and philosophy. The working of these forces is rather more suggestive of electronics than what was formerly called grammar, and in fact it deals with what Lamb calls *impulses*.

These impulses are supposed to appear in English, and perhaps in all languages, in three contrastive pairs, *and/or*, *upward/downward*, and *ordered/unordered*. Indisputably, such phenomena do appear in English. One can make choices as he generates a sentence, and *and/or* is such a choice, since a speaker can combine clauses, with or without other changes in the clauses themselves. Similarly, within sentences, some portions are directed toward other portions or from them, but in stratificational grammar *upward* is defined as "toward meaning" and *downward* as "toward expression." Thus, to use Lamb's statement, "Impulses move downward during the production process and upward during the decoding process." Similarly, some components of language appear in ordered systems, and some seem not to. These six impulses can be combined into eight nodes, as follows: Unordered Downward And, Unordered Downward Or, Unordered Upward And, Unordered Upward Or, Ordered Downward And, Ordered Downward Or, Ordered Upward And, and Ordered Upward Or. They work on lexemic, morphemic, and phonemic levels and in what are called tactic, knot, and sign patterns. The whole statement rapidly becomes complicated and rests upon concepts and terms for these concepts that are not well understood, and at best the results are described as "highly tentative."

Obviously, however intriguing stratificational grammar may be, it will not today help a dictionary editor much if he is faced with the problem of producing a useful book. Certainly it has some validity, but it may not be valid and true in the sense that it will provide an adequate working approach to a description of the language. Even if it does provide the best philosophical approach to grammatical process—and Lamb and others have demonstrated that it can be used to make sharp distinctions in the complex area of modern English verbal expressions—no such extensive description has as yet been attempted. And if the lexicographer had such a system, he could not use it; how many users of a reference work would feel enlightened to know that a given locution involved portmanteau realization or Unordered Upward And? Thus, for the present, stratificational grammar can do little more for the lexicographer than to remind him that perhaps his grammatical designations, also, should be thought of as "tentative."

Almost contemporary with stratificational grammar is *tagmemics*, associated especially with the name of Prof. Kenneth L. Pike and some of his former students at the University of Michigan. As stratification is suggestive of electronics, tagmemics suggests physics, and its major terminology is adopted from that discipline, relying upon *particle*, *wave*, and *field*. The term *tagmemics* itself is a coined word from Greek *tagmeme*, a chunk of something, but the grammatical forces which this approach utilizes would seem to be much more subtle and fluid than anything associated with a definable physical body. Tagmemics is like stratification in that it takes all language as its province, and that it relies somewhat upon describing the generative process. It utilizes what tagmemics call "the principle of trimodalism," that is, that all language must be looked upon from the three points of view mentioned above, that of particles, dividing language into discrete, contrastive units; that of wave, viewing "unsegmental physical continua"; and that of field, "orderly systems of relationships." Tagmemic theory postulates that language can be described adequately only after it has been examined in all three ways, but if so, these approaches are so fluid and as yet so scatteringly applied that the lexicographer cannot hope to employ tagmemics in grammatical designations in the near future.

One recent approach, *transformational grammar*, although it is not much older than tagmemics, has developed so rapidly and been adapted so skillfully into textbooks that it is becoming widely usable. Stemming from the work of Prof. Zellig Harris of the University of Pennsylvania and more particularly from Noam Chomsky and his colleagues at Massachusetts Institute of Technology, transformational grammar uses the method of mathematics and is notably generative. For simplicity, the system makes use of what are called *transforms*, but we shall not need to go into them to understand what a transformationalist means when he uses a grammatical label, where the essential concept is embodied in what are called *slots*, in an approach known as *string grammar* because it works by describing strings of linguistic units.

A transformationalist accepts the fact we have noticed earlier, that a native user of the language has developed a sense for its grammar. He senses the rules within him, and the grammarian needs only to formalize these intuited rules into an organized grammatical statement. A user of English knows that English sentences have subjects and that these subjects function with verbs; therefore a sentence can be defined as S——>NP + VP. This rule can be expanded as "A sentence can be written as a noun phrase plus a verb phrase." Other rules will make clear that a noun phrase can be anything like *man* and all that goes along with it to serve as a subject, and that a verb phrase is something like *lives* and whatever goes along with that to make what is called a predicate in the older terminology. Each of these, NP and VP can be called a slot, and each can include subsidiary slots; *the very old man* is a series of four phonemes (or words, since the generative grammarians have less trouble with words than do some linguists) filling four slots.

Thus for a transformationalist, a noun is a word or anything else that can fill a noun slot. Of course, describing a slot can become complicated; theoretically, one could describe all the possible kinds of grammatical units that could fit into a noun slot, but for most purposes the transformationalist does not have to do this. He relies upon the grammatical sense in the users of the language; even a very small child will know that, in a sequence of nonsense syllables like *The gupo was dubbying the midyup*, the *gupo* was doing something called *dubbying* and hence *gupo* fits into one kind of slot and may not fit into the slot occupied by *dubbying*. In theory, also, the transformationalist could provide language labels that the lexicographer could use, but practically he has not done so. He can distinguish anything that belongs to what he calls a noun form class, and thus could fit into a noun slot, but this sort of statement occurs rather far into his analysis, and his analysis rapidly becomes complex. The systems now current would be complicated for a lexicographer to use, and difficult for the users of his book to interpret.

The oldest of the new grammars, if one may use such a seeming contradiction in terms, is called variously *structural analysis*, *structural grammar*, or *structural linguistics*. Although structuralists work, as did the traditional grammarians, with bodies of language already extant, they are to be contrasted with their predecessors in that of all modern grammarians they are the most concerned with being scientific. Structuralists have labored to produce objectively accurate grammatical observations, limiting themselves to conclusions for which they believe they have demonstrable evidence. They have worked from the minutiae of language toward what they have called *deep grammar*, *metalinguistics*, *megalinguistics*, and the like. To them we mainly owe the concepts of the phoneme and the morpheme, discussed earlier. The structuralist, seeking the basis for objective grammar, distrusted such approaches as those through function and meaning, used by traditional grammarians, and observed that two parts of language, sound and sequence, are measurable. Of these, sequence was relatively easy; language appears when spoken in some order, and the written order stems from the spoken order. However, for a time sound presented problems, since it is so complex that it was not readily usable for grammatical purposes. This lack was supplied by the phoneme. Science requires units of measurement, and although the phoneme is not an accurate unit, since it will vary from time to time and from language to language, even from grammarian to grammarian, it provides a working unit. With it the structuralist can say that phonemes have describable privilege of occurrence, that is, they can occur in some ways but not in others. The phonemes /r/, /s/, and /t/, for example, can occur in the cluster /rst/ as in the word *first*, as /str/ as in the word *distress*, and as /rts/ as in the word *smarts*, but not as /trs/; the phoneme /n/ can appear terminally and medially as in *bringing* /briŋ'in/, but in Modern English not initially, except in non-native words like *ngaio*/ŋi'ɔ/. Such statements, although they were interesting phonologically, were of little help to grammarians, but once the concept of the morpheme was added to that of the phoneme, the grammarian had a set of tools with which he could describe any body of language whatever.

As we have seen above, a phoneme is a working unit of sound, but a morpheme is whatever combination of phonemes may constitute a working unit of language. As a matter of fact, the morphemes we considered above are what are called *segmental morphemes*, since they can be segmented; the combination, sometimes called a *phrase*, *boys* /boiz/, can be broken by an immediate constituent cut into the morpheme /boi/ plus the morpheme /z/.

All languages include also patterns of sound which cannot be broken up in this way, and which are accordingly called *suprasegmental morphemes*. For example, an utterance that can be written *You are going tomorrow* can be distinguished from one that would be written *You are going tomorrow?* by different sequences of stress, tone (called *pitch*), and pause (which structuralists prefer to designate more accurately as *juncture*). Such nonsequential patterns of sound can be used, also, to distinguish words not firmly identifiable by segmental patterns alone; in a typical example of *light*, *house*, and *keeper* put together in a sequence,

the various standard stress, pitch, and juncture patterns can be used to distinguish the keeper of a lighthouse from a housekeeper that is not hefty, or from someone engaged in light housekeeping.

The system works by what are called *IC* (immediate constituent) cuts. Starting with any body of language, the materials are cut into immediate constituents until the whole has been reduced to a sequence of Chinese boxes of which the smallest will contain phonemes. The first cut will produce independent clauses, if the sentence contains more than one, and the second cut will separate verbs from complements. Thus far, a structural approach provides little more than a graphic way of doing what the older approach by function had done, but it works simply and positively. Now consider a sentence like *Any sufficiently alert pitcher had better go about trying to put the runner out by catching him off base.* Obviously the first cut will occur between *pitcher* and *had*. To the left of this cut, the second will be either after *any* or before *pitcher*—structuralists have not always agreed on this point—but whichever cut is second, this half of the sentence will give us a string of *any* (a determiner), *sufficiently* (an intensifier), alert (an adjective), and *pitcher* (a noun). Here the method is simple, relatively objective, and it produces an analysis of a very common English structure that has been understood the better because of structural approaches. Now let us look to the right of this first cut; here the next cut should separate the verb from the complement, and subsequent cuts should reduce the verb and the complement to their parts, but where should these cuts fall? The complement would seem to be *runner*, or *runner* plus *him*, but how can we, with a single cut, separate these words from what comes before, after, and between them? The cut can surely not come after *had*, since all that follows is not something the pitcher had, but even if we cut there arbitrarily, where will subsequent cuts fall? The main verbal idea seems to be involved in *put out* or *catching off base*, although *had, go, about, trying*, and probably *better* seem also to be involved in the verb, and some of those words may be involved also in the complement. Of course a problem like this can be resolved; cuts can be devised, but their rectitude is not always obvious. They must involve arbitrary decisions, and the results tend to be complex and not very revealing. At best, they are not very helpful in editing dictionaries or instructing the young.

Thus structural linguistics, while it did much to loosen up American thinking about grammar and to provide insights through which subsequent grammatical approaches have profited, has not of itself provided an adequate description of modern English grammar. It was obviously more objective than the traditional grammar; applied to simple structures it was easy to handle and sometimes revealing, but like a good many other grammatical statements, it readily became complex, and in recent years it has been giving way to transformational grammar, which, as we have seen, may soon give way to something else.

Meanwhile, it has bequeathed to the lexicographer at least one concept he finds useful, that of privilege of occurrence. To say that a noun has privilege of occurrence after adjectives, or after determiners, but not immediately after intensifiers, that it has privilege of occurrence with verbs in conjunction with certain pitch, stress, and juncture patterns may be too cumbersome for dictionary designations, but the general concept of privilege of occurrence is not complicated, and since it can be combined with the grammatical sense of the native user of the language, it can be readily applied.

The modern lexicographer, when he prints *n.* after a word, is more likely to be thinking—if he needs to think at all beyond using his own grammatical sense—that this word is of the class that can be used as a subject, and not so likely to be thinking of it as "the name of a person, place, or thing." In this way, if he is not telling an absolute, objective truth, if he is not placing the word in a guaranteed, definable category, he is at least describing for his user one way in which the word can be used. He can say to himself here, as he has elsewhere, that he is being descriptive of what the language can be used for, not prescriptive of how it should be used.

XI. *Conclusion*

English dictionaries, as they approach their four hundredth anniversary, reflect sweeping changes. A casual inspection of Robert Cawdrey's *A Table Alphabeticall* (1604), supposedly the first English dictionary, would suggest neither the *Oxford* nor the present volume. As the language has grown, and especially as our knowledge of both the nature of language and the functioning of the English language has grown, dictionaries have changed so much in character that they have almost changed in kind. Cawdrey, referring to his entries, mentions their propriety for "simple children," and makes his bow to "Men of Judgement (for whom they [the entries] were not writ)." But it is precisely for men of judgment, and for those who aspire to become men and women of judgment and creativity, that modern dictionaries are writ. They are no longer restricted to providing admonitions for foreigners, children, and benighted adults. They pillage a vast world of reliable information; they have refined the methods of linguistic description, and they have become man's best single aid to clear thinking, adequate expression, and lucid communication.

Since dictionaries have changed much, we need not be surprised if they change more. The great *Oxford*, the work of dozens of scholars during three quarters of a century, was planned to last for all time. It was only nicely started before its word list was seen to be incomplete; some of its etymologies are now hopelessly outdated; its grammatical observations are inadequate and are becoming rapidly less adequate; even the citations cry for supplementation. Obsolescence will start plaguing the present dictionary upon publication, as it is already damaging other desk dictionaries recently printed.

Meanwhile, one can observe that we have here a dictionary well calculated to defy time, as well as time can be defied in a transient world, one which for a reasonable period will serve its users well if they can become expert in its use. The editors of the present dictionary have been uncommonly alert to take advantage of the fresher thought and the newer techniques in language study; this is a matter of fact. They seem, also, to have been uncommonly sensitive in their application of this new material in their lexicographical thinking and writing; that is a matter of my personal judgment, based upon my reading of their entries. Whether or not I am right about that, this is obviously an excellent book, which will be of more or less help to its users, depending upon their employment of it. Insofar as my observation is valid, most users of dictionaries today get much less from their volumes than they might, because they do not know how dictionaries are made or why they are made that way. The preceding introduction is intended to promote dictionary use by furthering lexicographical understanding; its ends might be summarized as follows:

1. A modern dictionary is descriptive rather than prescriptive; it tries to inform about language, aware that only the writer or speaker, the reader or listener, can apply linguistic knowledge to linguistic use.

2. A desk dictionary is intended to be helpful; language is unbelievably multifarious, and a dictionary, especially a book intended for ready reference, must excel by the intelligence and skill with which its contents are selected, not only by the extent of its contents.

3. A dictionary designed for convenience must be arbitrary. Users want firm answers, but truth is shifty; a skillful editor may be able to suggest some alternatives, to hint at gradations, but in the end only an understanding of the need for and the limits of pat replies can permit a dictionary to become the subtle tool it should be.

A dictionary, at its best, is a mine of incomplete answers, but in a world where profound answers are vague and most answers are partly wrong, a collection of well-founded answers about man's most useful tool, language, can be a boon.

ETYMOLOGY

by William E. Umbach

The study of the origin and development of words, their forms and meanings, may strike the layman as an esoteric pursuit, perhaps of dubious value. It was not always so. In seeking the *etymon*, the "true sense" of a word, the Greeks were engaging in no idle quest; they, like much earlier primitive man, sensed a mysterious relationship between the word and that for which it stands. To know how to pronounce the word correctly could give the user power over the thing or being, a principle of great importance in the exercise of witchcraft. But conversely it could also be dangerous to pronounce the names of certain beings, for to do so might arouse the anger of the immanent spirit. Thus some taboo names eventually disappeared through silence. The English name *bear*, for example, is derived from an ancient term meaning "the brown one," used to avoid calling the beast by its true name. Other peoples used similar evasions: the ancient Hindus and Slavs called the same animal "the honey-eater" (Sanskrit *madhvad-*, Old Slavic *medvedi*), and the Celts knew him as "the honey pig" (Welsh *melfochyn*). Still other names were perhaps felt to be too sacred to pronounce; thus the name of the God of the Hebrews was replaced by *Adonai*, literally "my Lord," and since it was conventional in ancient Hebrew manuscripts to write only the consonants and skip the vowels, the modern names are at best only scholarly conjectures.

The ancient notion that there is a single, true meaning for a word has been replaced by the concept that words are essentially nothing more than conventional symbols whose use and pronunciation may vary even from person to person, let alone generation to generation. Over the course of the centuries such variations may so alter the form and meaning that only patient study can trace the course by which the modern word has come to its present sense and form.

In this process of unraveling the fabric of modern languages, the etymologist comes upon evidence of the effect which the associations of ancient and modern peoples have had upon the range of concepts and objects represented by the vocabulary, as well as upon the form and content of the word symbols for them. Much worn and altered, many prehistoric artifacts of language are still in active use, and may be identified in numerous languages. Thus the names of family members—father, mother, brother—appear in relatively similar form in numerous languages; *mother*, for example, is represented by German *mutter*, Old Irish *mathir*, Old Slavic *mati* (genitive form *matere*), Latin *mater*, Greek *meter*, and Sanskrit *matar*. The familiar *mouse* is represented by German *maus*, Old Saxon and Old Norse *mus*, Latin *mus*, and Sanskrit *muṣ*. Such similarities are certainly not pure coincidence, and the etymologist is concerned with the nature of their relationships.

It is well known that a number of modern languages, among them French, Spanish, Portuguese, and Italian, have come into being as a result of gradual changes of Latin. Examination of older manuscripts clearly reveals the stages in the development of each of the modern languages, and makes it possible to identify certain regular patterns of change by which each of the modern representatives of Latin came to have its unique form and character.

In the same way, historical retracing of other languages reveals a similar gradual development of some modern languages from a common parent tongue which may not, however, be as well documented as is Latin. Thus it is clear that English is closely related to Dutch and German, that this group is in turn related to the Scandinavian languages and to the language of the medieval Goths, and that all of these, known as the Germanic languages, are ultimately derived from an unrecorded ancient language known to scholars as proto-Germanic or Primitive Germanic.

Similar studies of the various Celtic languages, of the Slavic languages, and of some other groups, indicate that each group has had its common parent. But this process of historical reconstruction has gone farther, to reveal that the groups of languages already mentioned, together with many others, all have been derived from a still more ancient, unrecorded language which scholars call Indo-European. From this hypothetical language have derived a number of related languages, whose principal branches are Indo-Iranian, Armenian, Tocharian, Greek, Albanian, Italic, Celtic, Germanic, and Balto-Slavic.

Indo-European, it is important to note, includes only a small fraction of all of the world's languages, although at least one half of all of the world's population has a language of this family as its mother tongue. Similar families have been identified, but there is only fragmentary evidence of a still older relationship between Indo-European and the others. Yet regardless of genetic relationship, there is abundant evidence in the vocabulary of many languages that words have been borrowed by those who encountered names for new ideas or objects in the languages of other peoples with whom they came into contact. Such borrowings might be between languages belonging to one family, or between languages totally unrelated. Thus Greek includes words originally of Sanskrit, or even of Semitic or Egyptian origin, and some of these loanwords have in time come to be a part of our modern English vocabulary (see *costmary, gum, sack, canna, hyssop*). Numerous among the Greek loanwords from Semitic languages are those related to the Judeo-Christian religion, which were introduced through the Septuagint and the New Testament, and which continue in many modern languages, English among them (see *Beelzebub, Sabbath, Messiah*). Latin, like Greek, contains many loanwords which are now a part of our own vocabulary (see *car, biretta, gantry, lantern*).

It was inevitable, in the many encounters of different peoples during the migrations of the Middle Ages, that a residue of borrowed words would remain in various languages even after some of the groups had moved on to new homes, or had lost their separate identity and with it their own language. English has derived from French many words which had been borrowed from Germanic tribes, Franks, Goths, Norsemen, as well as from Celts; from Italian, loanwords from the Goths and Lombards, and from the Arabs; and from Spanish, words borrowed from Gothic as well as from the Arabs and Celts.

The process is still going on in the modern languages, and the vocabulary of English, more than that of any other language, has been enriched by its appropriation of foreign words. In some modern nations, notably France and Germany, there have been repeated efforts to avoid the intrusion of foreign words and to substitute native coinages to take their place. English, throughout its history, has had all of the delicate sensitivity of a powerful vacuum cleaner. Thus the warp of genetic derivation is interwoven with the woof of great numbers of words borrowed from related and unrelated languages; the resulting fabric has a richness and variety unequalled by any other language past or present.

Genetically, English is a descendant of the Germanic dialects spoken by the Angles, Saxons, and Jutes who invaded the British islands, beginning about the middle of the fifth century. They were members of a group of tribes whose homes had been near the North Sea, and who spoke a language similar to those of two other groups of tribes, one living along the Weser and Rhine rivers, and the other near the Elbe. The usual designation for the language of these three groups, taken together, is West Germanic, in contrast to that of the Germanic tribes of the Scandinavian area (North Germanic), and that of the tribes of the Oder-Vistula area (East Germanic).

In the years following the migrations of the Angles and Saxons, each of the three West Germanic language groups underwent changes which have resulted in the present differences between the descendant languages. The Elbe river group, beginning about 500 A.D., migrated to the south, occupying the central and southern highland areas, especially Bavaria, Austria, and Swabia, and spilling over the Alps into Northern Italy. Their language experienced in varying degree those phonetic changes known as the Second German Sound Shift, which differentiates the various dialects of High German from the Low German group (of which English is a part). Thus High German *wasser* corresponds to English *water*, *pfund* to *pound*, *helfen* to *help*, *sitzen* to *sit*, *zu* to *to*. The Weser-Rhine dialects developed into the

languages of the mainland Saxons (Old Saxon, modern Plattdeutsch) and Franks (Dutch, Flemish). Those Franks who, during the late fifth and early sixth centuries, occupied portions of the old Roman province of Gallia eventually gave their name (*Francia*, modern *France*) to the area, but lost their language in the competition with dialects of the Vulgar Latin of the decaying Roman Empire.

The Anglo-Saxon tribes, on invading the British islands, encountered inhabitants speaking various Celtic languages, and found areas in which the earlier Roman occupation had left some Latin influence on vocabulary. To this day, the place name *Chester*, either independently or as a prefixed or suffixed element, is a reminder of the Latin *castra*, "camp," from which Old English borrowed it in the form *ceaster* (thus *Winchester, Chesterfield, Rochester*). A second form of Latin invasion, the coming of Christian missionaries, from 597 on, supplemented the earlier Latin remains, as has the influence of the church until our own day. Other invaders, chiefly Danes and Norsemen, added to the complex. As various groups established settlements, they added to the dialect differences already present between the tribes of the Anglo-Saxon invasion. But in the main the Scandinavian settlers, whose North Germanic language had many similarities to that of the North Sea subgroup of West Germanic, gradually adopted the language (Old English) of the Anglo-Saxon group, while adding to it many of their own words, some of which appear in modern English as *husband, sky, skin, scathe, club, gape,* and the suffix *-by.*

Old English, under these conditions, was composed of numerous dialects, some of whose differences went back to those between the dialects of the Angles, Saxons, and Jutes. But interwoven with these hereditary variations were the many strands, often local or regional, of Celtic, Latin, and Scandinavian influence. To this already complex pattern the Norman invasion and conquest (1066–69) eventually brought lasting new motifs. The Normans, descendants of Scandinavian invaders who had settled on the south coast of the English Channel some centuries earlier, spoke a form of French. This became the official language of the court after the Conquest. It came, in time, also to be the language of the merchants and the learned. The common people continued to speak their various dialects of English, but French influence gradually added significant elements to the vocabulary, especially in the areas of law and government. By 1200 the language had altered to such an extent that it is designated as Middle English. It is significant that about half of the vocabulary of modern English is of Romance origin.

Since the Norman invasion, the influences which have altered the texture of the English vocabulary have not come from actual intrusions of a foreign people, although immigrants from various places have made their contributions (*pal*, a comrade, and *rye*, a gentleman, for example, are from the language of the Gypsies). As the English-speaking peoples have themselves invaded other areas, or have established trade relations, in America, Africa, Asia, and the islands of the South Pacific, there have come the influences of exotic objects and foreign cultures: *tobacco, cannibal, banana, taro, quinine, mango, jujitsu, pajama, jodhpur, manioc, pagoda, tapioca;* the long list grows year by year.

Study of classical and ancient civilizations has added, through direct appropriation, vast numbers of words from Latin and Greek; science and invention have mined the rich metal of the same languages to coin names of new creations or concepts: *halogen, pentstemon, triskaidekaphobia, metronome, acrophobia, helium, aerodynamic, neurotomy, euphenics.* Even the stripteaser calls upon Greek (*ecdysiast*).

Worldwide exploration, followed by jet travel and instantaneous communication, has made the remote and isolated familiar and even commonplace, and foreign names have become part of the common tongue. Indeed, to read the menu of even a simple meal is to recapitulate a portion of the experience of English-speaking people with remote places: potatoes or yams, hamburger with ketchup, tomatoes or succotash, a lettuce salad with Roquefort dressing or mayonnaise, and perhaps chocolate cake—none would have appeared in Old English, and only the lettuce salad and cake (but not chocolate) in Middle English.

In America a flood of new words has resulted from confrontation with the native Indian population, with the French in Canada and in the lower Mississippi basin, with the Spanish in the Southwest, and with African natives who came against their will, as well as with immigrants from all parts of the world who came for freedom, fortune, or the excitement and danger of the frontier. From the Indians, the settlers learned the names of *squash, hominy, pemmican, raccoon, skunk, chipmunk, caribou, tamarack, toboggan, tomahawk, moccasin, persimmon,* and *wampum;* from the French: *lagniappe, prairie, craps, praline, picayune, brioche, butte, crevasse, chowder;* from the Spanish: *corral, chaps, lariat, poncho, bonanza, placer, savvy, canyon, ranch, hackamore, hoosegow, loco.* The Chinese brought us *chop suey, chow mein,* and *tong* wars. From the Japanese, we learned of the *kudzu* vine, *nisei,* and *hara-kiri.* The Swedish immigrants acquainted us with the *smorgasbord,* the Czechs with the *sokol.* Germans added to the vocabulary not only many items of the diet (*pretzel, pumpernickel, zwieback, smearcase, wieners*), but *steins, delicatessens, kindergartens, turners, loafers, hoodlums,* the adjective *dumb* (in the sense "stupid"), the verb *canoodle,* and—recently, in connection with rocketry and space travel—the term *glitch.* The Yiddish-speaking portion of our population brought, from homes in Germany and in other parts of Europe, *gefillte fish, bagels, blintzes, borscht, kibitzers, shtick, schmaltz,* and the expressive *phooey.* From Italian immigrants, we have gained *spaghetti, macaroni, ravioli, pizza, minestrone, arugula,* and the *mafia.* The Dutch have given us *coleslaw, cookies, bedspreads, dope, crullers, boss, snoop,* and *spook.* And from Africa, black people brought *jazz, goobers, juke* boxes, *jumbo, voodoo, gumbo, okra,* the *marimba, yams,* and the verb *tote.* Chiefly through Spanish, we have gained from Nahuatl, the language of the Aztecs, *tomato, avocado, chocolate, chili, tamale, mesquite, peyote,* and *coyote.*

Together with the many words which English has inherited or borrowed (even if somewhat altered in form and meaning), the vocabulary possesses others which have been the product of conscious invention (*rayon, nylon, Emmy, Corfam*), of contracting or clipping longer words (*bus, hi-fi, prof*) or combining initial letters (*radar, laser*), of imitation of sounds (*blimp, whiz*), of scribal or typographical errors (*celt, collimate, cycad*) of use of personal or place names for objects or processes (*frisbee, watt, pasteurize, tuxedo*), and of the intentional merging of words (*brunch, smog*). Some are effusions of an exuberant whimsy (*hornswoggle*) or of a capricious transposition of sounds (*sockdolager*). Occasionally a borrowed word is translated (*masterpiece*), or altered by the process of folk etymology to conform to an assumed proper form (*carryall, shamefaced, country dance, singletree, sparrowgrass*). Some words have been created (by "back-formation") on the assumption that they were the root forms from which others had been created (*diagnose* from *diagnosis; evaluate* from *evaluation; edit* from *editor; shay* from *chaise*). And the language of very fastidious people contains, without their being aware of the fact, words from the argot of thieves, convicts, gamblers, and harlots.

Words, like poetry, can be treated as arbitrary mathematical symbols or formulas. Sometimes this is necessary and expedient. But to do so can be like treating a diamond simply as a material for the cutting of refractory substances. Seen as the product of perhaps three thousand years of human experience, a word may not only have many facets, but may somehow reflect with brilliant intensity the concentrated experience or insights of the generations. It is still true that words can have a mysterious power to conjure up images, or evoke visions, or stir up emotions deep-seated in the shared experience of mankind.

Thus the etymologist is engaged in no esoteric pursuit, but one which can help bring to the use of the magnificent complex which is the English language an understanding of meanings, distinctions, and implications which are not merely conventional but rooted in the long history through which we have received it.

AMERICANISMS

by Mitford M. Mathews

Early in the seventeenth century English settlers brought the English language within the borders of the present United States. In using the language in this new environment they began immediately and necessarily to modify it. As time passed more colonists came and the settled areas along the Atlantic coast became larger. Modifications in the English brought from the homeland multiplied. For a long time neither the users of this changed form of English nor those who remained in England paid particular attention to what was happening to the language here.

Those in England who first noticed the changes viewed the matter with easy tolerance. But in time, because of circumstances unnecessary to detail here, this attitude changed to one of alarm and criticism. Those in this country of sufficient education and culture to know or care about this linguistic matter were divided in their thinking. Some were disposed to agree with their overseas critics and to counsel stricter adherence to orthodox use of the language; others were of a decidedly contrary view.

The results of the Revolutionary War increased the satisfaction some patriots felt for their own kind of English. In 1783 Congress, discussing a commercial treaty with Holland, found that the English translation of the treaty was not clear in some parts. James Madison suggested that Congress instruct John Adams, Minister to the Netherlands, to substitute, with the consent of the Netherlanders, a more correct version of it "in the American language." In 1812, John Adams in a letter to a friend expressed the view that Americans "ought to have an American Dictionary: after which I should be willing to lay a tax of an eagle a volume upon all English Dictionaries that should ever be imported."

Noah Webster was the most intelligent and vocal of the early champions of the American language. In the preface of his first dictionary, a small one of 1806, he wrote: "In each of the countries peopled by Englishmen, a distinct dialect of the language will gradually be formed; the principal of which will be that of the United States. In fifty years from this time, the *American English* will be spoken by more people, than all the other dialects of the language, and in one hundred and thirty years, by more people than any other language on the globe, not excepting Chinese."

The additions to and modifications of the English language shown in American English have ceased to arouse protestations of alarm. The language of the United States has spread remarkably, though not quite to the extent predicted by Webster. Writing in 1944 Frederick Bodmer said: "The daily speech of nearly half of the world's population belongs to the Indo-European family, within which its Anglo-American representative takes first rank. Anglo-American is now the *mother* language of over 200 millions, not to mention those who habitually use it as a means of cultural collaboration or rely on it for world communication."[1]

Among the great lexicographers who have regarded contributions to the language made in this country as entirely worthy of inclusion in dictionaries were Sir James Murray and his fellow editors of what is known as the *Oxford English Dictionary*. In his president's report of 1880 to the Philological Society, Dr. Murray made grateful acknowledgment of the help the Society's undertaking had received from American readers. He said: "In connection with the Reading, I cannot sufficiently express my appreciation of the kindness of our friends in the United States, where the interest taken in our scheme, springing from a genuine love of our common language, its history, and a warm desire to make the Dictionary worthy of that language, has impressed me very deeply. I do not hesitate to say that I find in Americans an ideal love for the English language as a glorious heritage, and a pride in being intimate with its grand memories, such as one does find sometimes in a classical scholar in regard to Greek, but which is rare indeed in Englishmen towards their own tongue; and from this I draw the most certain inferences as to the lead which Americans must at no distant date take in English scholarship."

Dr. Murray mentioned especially the help given the Dictionary "by men of Academic standing in the States. The number of Professors in American Universities and Colleges included among our readers is very large; and in several instances a professor has put himself down for a dozen works, which he has undertaken to read personally, and with the help of his students. We have had no such help from any college or university in Great Britain; only one or two Professors of English in this country have thought the matter of sufficient importance to talk to their students about it, and advise them to help us."

In concluding his expression of appreciation for his American helpers and well-wishers, Dr. Murray said: "By far the greater part of the material supplied by these American readers, it may be noted, was of the same type as that furnished by the British contributors, that is, it was mainly drawn from literary or scientific works written in standard English, or without noticeable American features in vocabulary or idiom. It was thus very serviceable in supplementing the English evidence, but failed to a very large extent to bring out the special developments of the language in the American colonies and the United States. Much of the material for these was specially supplied during the progress of the Dictionary by one or two workers, notably by Mr. Albert Matthews of Boston."

Although Dr. Murray did not have all the material he would gladly have accepted to enable him fully "to bring out the special developments of the language in the American colonies and the United States," he did extremely well with what Mr. Matthews and another helper or two supplied him. For example, he included *Belittle*, v., and wrote: "The word appears to have originated in U.S.; whence in recent English use in sense 3." At the time (1781–82) Thomas Jefferson coined this word, it was immediately set upon by critics in England, who shuddered at what awaited the language here in the way of further degradation at the hands of those who could for a moment tolerate such a monster. John Pickering, one of the foremost American scholars of his time, mentioned the word somewhat apologetically as "sometimes heard here in conversation; but in writing, it is, I believe, peculiar to that gentleman [i.e. Jefferson]."

Dr. Henry Bradley, who edited L in the *OED*, gave *Lengthy*, a., his usual treatment, though this word had earlier been among those vigorously mauled by professional inspectors and censors of American linguistic atrocities. Bradley said of it: "Before the 19th c. found only in American writers; in many of the early British instances it is referred to as an Americanism." And he added a note: "We have 10 examples from Jefferson between 1782 and 1786; Washington and A. Hamilton also use the word very frequently. T. Paine (quot. 1796), though of English birth, resided much in America." These examples referred to were no doubt supplied by Mr. Matthews of Boston, who continued his investigation of *Lengthy*, and much later supplied Sir William Craigie for his use in the *Dictionary of American English* an example of 1689.

In the *OED* the amount of United States material is far greater than the editors of that work were aware. Many terms and senses that originated in this country escaped identification. Confronted as the editors were with material from thousands of authors it was not possible for them in every instance to distinguish between the work of United States writers and that of British authors.

When Dr. Bradley was editing *Saccharine*, all the material he printed was of British origin. The earliest example he had of the word in the sense of an artificial sweetener contained a faint hint that additional research should be

---

[1]Frederick Bodmer, *The Loom of Language*, (W. W. Norton & Co., 1944), pp. 409–10.

done on this meaning of the term. This quotation began: "The inventors [*sc.* Fahlberg and List] name the new substance 'saccharine' . . ." The further investigating suggested here brings out the fact that Fahlberg did his work at Johns Hopkins under the direction of the celebrated American scientist, Ira Remsen, and that List was young Fahlberg's uncle who supplied the money for him to set up a small laboratory in New York where he perfected for commercial use the product that he and Professor Remsen had unexpectedly obtained in an experiment involving benzoic acid.

Similarly, when Dr. C. T. Onions was editing *Zein* he must have noticed that the earliest example he had of the use of the term clearly suggested that an earlier might be secured. His quotation was: "1822 *Q, Jrnl. Sci.* XIII. 402 The zëine of John Gorham, is obtained from Indian corn, by infusing it in water." The hint which Dr. Onions did not take has now been acted upon.

John Gorham turns out to have been the celebrated Dr. John Gorham, Professor of Chemistry at Harvard University. In 1820 he made an analysis of some corn of two types grown in the Boston neighborhood. One type had small yellow grains, and the other was the so-called Virginia corn, with large, flat, white grains. Later that year Dr. Gorham published an article, *"Chemical Analysis of Indian Corn."* In this he explained precisely how he had proceeded, and described carefully the substance he had obtained: "This substance I shall call *zeine,* not from any wish to multiply vegetable principles, nor because I think it is of any importance, but merely that it may be definitely described and designated without circumlocution."

It is especially in the *OED Supplement* (1933) that the labeling of United States terms and meanings becomes particularly noticeable. The reason for this was that the major part of Sir William Craigie's work on the *Supplement* was done while he was in this country and could draw on the increasingly large amount of American evidence he and his students were collecting at Chicago. The practice so well carried out in the *OED* of identifying United States terms and meanings was likewise followed by the *Century Dictionary* and continued as well in the large single volume dictionaries. The contributions made by these larger general dictionaries, added to what has been made available in smaller works of a more restricted scope, have increased greatly the evidence now available for distinguishing between English and what has been called from early times American English.

The plan followed in these larger works of calling attention to terms and meanings that originated in the United States has been adopted in smaller dictionaries. For some reason, the labeling of such terms in these dictionaries has lagged considerably behind what is known in the pertinent area. In the present edition of *Webster's New World,* on the other hand, a painstaking effort has been made to identify all the terms and meanings which, from the evidence at present available, appear to have become a part of the English language in the United States. This identification has usually been by means of a small star placed before the terms and meanings involved. The star has been withheld from abbreviations and, usually, from proper names. The mark, when appropriate, on the terms for which the abbreviations are given has been considered sufficient.

The number of proper names included in this edition of the dictionary is especially large. Among these are many terms used in this country as names of Indian tribes, streams, States and cities. In its treatment of these, the dictionary follows a policy not found in others of a comparable scope. Proper names of the kind referred to are etymologized, when this is possible, and in other cases the reason for the application of the name is usually given. In either case the status of the word, either as an original or as an adaptation, is clearly indicated, thus obviating the need for the star in connection with them.

On this feature of the dictionary full use has been made of the work of scholars especially interested in the study of American place names. Their work is full of interest and value. It is especially appropriate for a dictionary with the scope of the present one to give its users what has been found out about such names as Abilene, Anchorage, Denver, Estes Park, Governors Island, Imperial Valley, Juneau, Laramie, Seattle, and others too numerous to mention.

From the outset, in the work on the Americanisms in this dictionary, care was exercised not to appropriate Canadianisms as though they too originated south of our common border. Distinguishing between these two forms of English often presents insuperable difficulties, but accuracy in the effort has been increased by the recent appearance of a well edited *Dictionary of Canadianisms on Historical Principles* (Toronto, 1967). The value and interest of this work has been pointed out elsewhere.[2]

Notwithstanding the exclusions just enumerated, the star has been used on thousands of words and meanings. Despite the diligence and care exercised on the half million or so words, meanings, and phrases dealt with, perfection cannot be claimed for the effort to distinguish between what is native and what is not. Still, enough has been done here to cause one to ponder well what the Durants have recently written about American civilization's being "still in the stage of racial mixture." There is food for thought in their statement that: "When, out of this mixture, a new homogenous type is formed, America may have its own language (as different from English as Spanish is from Italian)."[3]

[2]Mitford M. Mathews, "A Dictionary of Canadianisms," *Journal of English Linguistics,* March, 1969.
[3]Will and Ariel Durant, *The Lessons of History,* (Simon and Schuster, 1968), p. 31.

ABBREVIATIONS AND SYMBOLS USED IN THIS DICTIONARY

abl. ablative
acc. accusative
adj. adjective
adv. adverb
Aeron. Aeronautics
Afr. African
Afrik. Afrikaans
Agric. Agriculture
Alb. Albanian
alt. alternative
Am. American
AmInd. American Indian
AmSp. American Spanish
Anat. Anatomy
Anglo-Fr. Anglo-French
Anglo-Ind. Anglo-Indian
Anglo-Ir. Anglo-Irish
Anglo-L. Anglo-Latin
Anglo-N. Anglo-Norse
Anglo-Norm. Anglo-Norman
Ar. Arabic
Aram. Aramaic
Archaeol. Archaeology
Archit. Architecture
Arith. Arithmetic
Arm. Armenian
Armor. Armoric
art. article
assoc. association
Assyr. Assyrian
Astrol. Astrology
Astron. Astronomy
at. no. atomic number
at. wt. atomic weight
aug. augmentative
Av. Avestan
Bab. Babylonian
Beng. Bengali
Biochem. Biochemistry
Biol. Biology
Bohem. Bohemian
boil. pt. boiling point
Bot. Botany
Braz. Brazilian
Bret. Breton
Brit. British
Bulg. Bulgarian
C Celsius; Central
c. century (in etym.); circa
Canad. Canadian
CanadFr. Canadian French
cap. capital
Catal. Catalonian
caus. causative
Celt. Celtic
cent. century
cf. compare
Ch. Chaldean
Chem. Chemistry
Chin. Chinese
Chr. Chronicles
Class. Classical
Col. Colossians
comb. combination
comp. compound
compar. comparative
conj. conjunction
contr. contracted; contraction
Cop. Coptic
Cor. Corinthians
Corn. Cornish
cu. cubic
Cym. Cymric
Dan. Daniel; Danish
dat. dative
deriv. derivative
Deut. Deuteronomy
Dial., dial. dialectal
dim. diminutive
Du. Dutch
DuFl. Dutch Flemish
E East; eastern
E. East; English (in etym. & pronun.)
EC east central
Ec. Ecclesiastic
Eccl. Ecclesiastes
Eccles. Ecclesiastical
Ecol. Ecology
Econ. Economics
Educ. Education

e.g. for example
Egypt. Egyptian
Elec. Electricity
Eng. English
Eph. Ephesians
equiv. equivalent
Esk. Eskimo
esp. especially
est. estimated
Esth. Esther
Eth. Ethiopic
etym. etymology
Ex. example; Exodus
exc. except
Ezek. Ezekiel
F Fahrenheit
fem. feminine
ff. following (entry, sense, etc.)
fig. figurative; figuratively
Finn. Finnish
Fl. Flemish
fl. flourished
Fr. French
Frank. Frankish
freq. frequentative
Fris. Frisian
ft. feet
fut. future
G. German (in etym. & pronun.)
Gael. Gaelic
Gal. Galatians
gal. gallon
Gaul. Gaulish
Gen. Genesis
gen. genitive
Geog. Geography
Geol. Geology
Geom. Geometry
Ger. German
ger. gerund
Gmc. Germanic
Goth. Gothic
Gr. Greek
Gram. Grammar
Gym. Gymnastics
Hab. Habakkuk
Hag. Haggai
Haw. Hawaiian
Heb. Hebrew; Hebrews
Hind. Hindi
Hort. Horticulture
Hos. Hosea
Hung. Hungarian
hyp. hypothetical
Ice. Icelandic
IE. Indo-European
i.e. that is
imper. imperative
imperf. imperfect
in. inch; inches
incl. including
Ind. Indian
indic. indicative
inf. infinitive
infl. influenced
intens. intensive
interj. interjection
Ir. Irish
Iran. Iranian
irreg. irregular
Isa. Isaiah
It. Italian
Jap. Japanese
Jas. James
Jav. Javanese
Jer. Jeremiah
Josh. Joshua
Judg. Judges
KJV King James Version
Kor. Korean
L Late
L. Latin
Lam. Lamentations
L.(Ec.) Ecclesiastic Latin
Lett. Lettish
Lev. Leviticus
LGr. Late Greek
LGr.(Ec.) Ecclesiastic Late Greek
Linguis. Linguistics
lit. literally

Abbreviations and Symbols

Lith. Lithuanian
LL. Late Latin
LL.(Ec.) Ecclesiastic Late Latin
lb. pound
LME. Late Middle English
LWS. Late West Saxon
LXX Septuagint
M Middle; Medieval
Mac., Macc. Maccabees
Mal. Malachi
Math. Mathematics
Matt. Matthew
MDu. Middle Dutch
ME. Middle English
Mech. Mechanics
Med. Medicine
melt. pt. melting point
met. metropolitan
Meteorol. Meteorology
Mex. Mexican
MFr. Middle French
MGr. Medieval Greek
MHG. Middle High German
mi. mile; miles
Mic. Micah
Mil. Military
ML. Medieval Latin
ML.(Ec.) Ecclesiastic Middle Latin
MLowG. Middle Low German
Mod, Mod. Modern
ModE. Modern English
ModGr. Modern Greek
ModHeb. Modern Hebrew
ModL. Modern Latin
Mongol. Mongolic
Myth. Mythology
N North; northern
N. North
n. noun
Nah. Nahum
Naut., naut. nautical usage
NC north central
NE northeastern
Neh. Nehemiah
neut. neuter
n.fem. feminine form of noun
n.masc. masculine form of noun
nom. nominative
Norm, Norm. Norman
Norw. Norwegian
n.pl. plural form of noun
n.sing. singular form of noun
N.T. New Testament
Num. Numbers
NW northwestern
O Old
Ob. Obadiah
Obs., obs. obsolete
occas. occasionally
OE. Old English
OFr. Old French
OHG. Old High German
OIr. Old Irish
OIt. Old Italian
OL. Old Latin
ON. Old Norse
ONormFr. Old Norman French
orig. origin; originally
OS. Old Saxon
O.T. Old Testament
oz. ounce
P Primitive
part. participle
pass. passive
Per. Persian
perf. perfect
pers. person
Peruv. Peruvian
Pet. Peter
PGmc. Primitive Germanic
Phil. Philippians
Philem. Philemon
Philos. Philosophy
Phoen. Phoenician
Phonet. Phonetics
Photog. Photography
phr. phrase
Phys. Ed. Physical Education
Physiol. Physiology
PidE. Pidgin English
pl. plural
Poet. Poetic
Pol. Polish
pop. popular; population
Port. Portuguese
poss. possessive
pp. past participle

Pr. Provençal
prec. preceding
prep. preposition
pres. present
pret. preterit
prin. pts. principle parts
priv. privative
prob. probably
pron. pronoun
pronun. pronunciation
Prov. Proverbs; Provincial
prp. present participle
Ps. Psalms
pseud. pseudonym
Psychol. Psychology
pt. past tense
qt. quart; quarts
R.C.Ch. Roman Catholic Church
redupl. reduplication
refl. reflexive
resp. respelling
Rev. Revelation
Rom. Roman; Romans
R.S.F.S.R. Russian Soviet Federated Socialist Republic
RSV Revised Standard Version
Russ. Russian
S South; southern
S. South
Sam. Samuel
Sans. Sanskrit
SC south central
Scand. Scandinavian
Scot, Scot. Scottish
SE southeastern
Sem. Semitic
Serb. Serbian
sing. singular
Sinh. Sinhalese
Slav. Slavic
S. of Sol. Song of Solomon
Sp. Spanish
sp. spelled; spelling
specif. specifically
sp. gr. specific gravity
sq. square
S.S.R. Soviet Socialist Republic
subj. subjunctive
superl. superlative
SW southwestern
Sw. Swedish (in etym. & pronun.)
Swed. Swedish
Syr. Syriac
Tag. Tagalog
Tat. Tatar
Theol. Theology
Thess. Thessalonians
Tibet. Tibetan
Tim. Timothy
Tit. Titus
transl. translation
Turk. Turkish
TV television
ult. ultimately
UN United Nations
unc. uncertain
U.S. United States
U.S.S.R. Union of Soviet Socialist Republics
v. verb
var. variant; variety
v.aux. auxiliary verb
Vet. Veterinary Medicine
vi. intransitive verb
VL. Vulgar Latin
voc. vocative
vt. transitive verb
Vulg. Vulgate
W West; western
W. Welsh; West
WAfr. West African
Wal. Walloon
WC west central
WGmc. West Germanic
WInd. West Indian
WS. West Saxon
yd. yard
Yid. Yiddish
Zech. Zechariah
Zeph. Zephaniah
Zool. Zoology

‡ foreign word or phrase
☆ Americanism
* hypothetical
+ plus
< derived from
? uncertain; possibly; perhaps
& and

A

A, a (ā) *n., pl.* **A's, a's** 1. the first letter of the English alphabet: from the Greek *alpha*, a borrowing from the Phoenician 2. a sound of *A* or *a:* in English, the low front vowel (a) of *hat*, the low central or low back vowel (ä) of *father*, the mid front vowel (ā) of *bake*, or the low back vowel (ô) of *call* 3. a type or impression for *A* or *a* 4. *a* symbol *for* the first in a sequence or group —*adj.* 1. of *A* or *a* 2. first in a sequence or group

A (ā) *n.* 1. an object shaped like *A* 2. *Chem. the former symbol for* argon ☆3. *Educ.* a grade indicating excellence [an *A* in history] 4. *Music a)* the sixth tone or note in the ascending scale of C major *b)* a key, string, etc. producing this tone *c)* the scale having this tone as the keynote —*adj.* 1. shaped like *A* ☆2. first-class; A 1: see A ONE

a¹ (ə; *stressed,* ā) *adj.,* **indefinite article** [form of *an* before consonants: see AN, *adj.*] 1. one; one sort of [we planted a tree] 2. each; any one [a gun is dangerous] *A* connotes a thing not previously noted or recognized, in contrast with *the,* which connotes a thing previously noted or recognized 3. [orig. a prep. < OE. *an, on,* in, on, at] to each; in each; for each; per [once a day] Before words beginning with a consonant sound or a sounded *h, a* is used [a child, a home, a uniform, a eunuch]; before words beginning with a vowel sound or a silent *h, an* is used [an ultimatum, an honor]

a² (ə) *prep.* [OE. *of,* from, of] [Obs.] of [Inns a Court]

a³ (ə) *pron.* [Dial.] 1. he 2. she 3. it 4. they 5. I

a, a' (ô, ä) *adj.* [Scot.] all

a⁻¹ (ə) [weakened form of OE. *an, on,* in, on, at: cf. ON] *a prefix meaning:* 1. in, into, on, at, to [aboard, ashore, abed] 2. in the act or state of [asleep, a-crying, a-wishing]

a⁻² (ə) *a prefix of various origins and meanings:* 1. [OE. *a-,* out of, up] up, out: now generally used as an intensive [awake, arise] 2. [OE. *of-, af-*] off, of [akin] 3. (ā, a, ə) [Gr. *a-, an-,* not] not, without [amentia, agnostic]: before vowels *an-* is used [anesthetic] 4. *same as* AB-: used before *m, p, v* [aversion] 5. *same as* AD-: used before *sc, sp, st* [ascription]

A. 1. Absolute 2. America(n) 3. angstrom unit

a. 1. about 2. acre(s) 3. adjective 4. alto 5. ampere 6. anode 7. anonymous 8. answer 9. are (unit of area)

☆**a·a** (ä′ä) *n.* [Haw. *a'ā*] solidified lava with a rough, splintery surface: cf. PAHOEHOE

AA, A.A. 1. Alcoholics Anonymous 2. antiaircraft

A.A. Associate in (or of) Arts

AAA, A.A.A. 1. Amateur Athletic Association 2. American Automobile Association

A.A.A.L. American Academy of Arts and Letters

A.A.A.S. American Association for the Advancement of Science

Aa·chen (ä′kən; *G.* ä′khən) city in North Rhine-Westphalia, W West Germany, on the Belgian border: pop. 176,000: Fr. name, AIX-LA-CHAPELLE

Aal·borg (ôl′bôr) seaport in N Jutland, Denmark, on Lim Fjord: pop. 86,000

Aalst (älst) *Fl. name of* ALOST

A & R Artist(s) and Repertoire: with reference to those officials of commercial recording companies who select the performers and supervise the production of recordings

Aar (är) river in Switzerland, flowing into the Rhine: c. 180 mi.

aard·vark (ärd′värk′) *n.* [obs. Afrik., earth pig < D. *aarde,* EARTH + *vark,* pig, FARROW¹] a burrowing African mammal (*Orycteropus afer*) active chiefly at night, that feeds on ants and termites: it is squat and heavy with a long, sticky tongue and a long head, ending in a round, piglike snout

aard·wolf (-woolf′) *n., pl.* **-wolves** (-woolvz′) [Afrik., earth wolf] a South African mammal (*Proteles cristatus*) resembling a hyena in appearance and behavior but feeding chiefly on termites and insect larvae

Aar·e (ä′rə) *same as* AAR

Aar·gau (är′gou) canton in N Switzerland: 542 sq. mi.; pop. 384,000: Fr. name, ARGOVIE

Aar·hus (ôr′hoos) seaport in E Jutland, Denmark, on the Kattegat: pop. 120,000

Aar·on (er′ən, ar′-) [LL. < Gr. *Aarōn* < Heb. *aharōn,* lit., the exalted one] 1. a masculine name 2. *Bible* the older brother of Moses and first high priest of the Hebrews: Ex. 4

Aa·ron·ic (er än′ik, ar-) *adj.* 1. of or characteristic of Aaron 2. Levitical ☆3. designating or of the second, and lesser, order of priests in the Mormon Church

A.A.U. Amateur Athletic Union

A.A.U.P. American Association of University Professors

A.A.U.W. American Association of University Women

Ab¹ *Chem.* alabamine

Ab² (äb; *Heb.* äv) *n.* [Heb.] the eleventh month of the Jewish year: see JEWISH CALENDAR

ab- (ab, əb) [L.] *a prefix meaning* away, from, from off, down [abdicate]: shortened to *a-* before *m, p, v;* often *abs-* before *c* or *t* [abstract]

A.B. [ModL. *Artium Baccalaureus*] Bachelor of Arts

A.B., a.b. able-bodied (seaman)

a.b. *Baseball* (times) at bat

a·ba (ä′bə) *n.* [Ar.] 1. a coarse fabric of wool or hair fiber with a felted finish 2. a loose, sleeveless robe worn by Arabs

a·ba·cá (ab′ə kə, äb′-) *n.* [Tag.] 1. *same as* MANILA HEMP 2. a Philippine plant (*Musa textilis*) of the banana family, whose fibers yield Manila hemp

a·back (ə bak′) *adv.* [OE. *on bæc,* at or on the back] 1. [Archaic] backward; back 2. *Naut. a)* backward against the mast, as the sails of a square-rigged vessel in a wind from straight ahead *b)* in an unmanageable condition because of a sudden shift of wind to the opposite side of the sails —**taken aback** startled and confused; surprised

ab·a·cus (ab′ə kəs, ə bak′əs) *n., pl.* **ab′a·cus·es** (-iz), **ab′a·ci′** (-sī′) [L. < Gr. *abax,* counting board] 1. a frame with beads or balls sliding back and forth on wires or in slots, for doing or teaching arithmetic 2. *Archit.* a slab forming the uppermost part of the capital of a column

A·ba·dán (ä′bä dän′) 1. island in the Shatt al Arab, SW Iran 2. city on this island: an oil refining center: pop. 302,000

A·bad·don (ə bad′ən) [Heb., destruction, abyss] *Bible* 1. the place of the dead; nether world: Job 26:6 2. the angel of hell, Apollyon: Rev. 9:11

ABACUS

a·baft (ə baft′, -bäft′) *adv.* [ME. *o baft* < OE. *on,* on + *bæftan < be,* by + *æftan,* AFT] at or toward the stern or rear of a ship; aft —*prep. Naut.* behind; back of

☆**ab·a·lo·ne** (ab′ə lō′nē) *n.* [AmSp. < Calif. Ind. *aulun*] a marine mollusk (genus *Haliotis*) with an oval, somewhat spiral shell perforated near the edge and lined with mother-of-pearl

a·ban·don (ə ban′dən) *vt.* [ME. *abandonen* < OFr. *abandoner < metire a bandon,* to put under (someone else's) ban,

relinquish: see BAN¹] **1.** to give up (something) completely or forever [to *abandon* all hope] **2.** to leave, as in danger or out of necessity; forsake; desert **3.** to yield (oneself) completely, as to a feeling, desire, etc. —*n.* unrestrained freedom of actions or emotions; surrender to one's impulses [to shout in wild *abandon*] —**a·ban'don·ment** *n.*
SYN.—**abandon** implies leaving a person or thing, either as a final, necessary measure [to *abandon* a drought area] or as a complete rejection of one's responsibilities, claims, etc. [she *abandoned* her child]; **desert** emphasizes leaving in willful violation of one's obligation, oath, etc. [the soldier *deserted* his post]; **forsake** stresses renouncing a person or thing formerly dear to one [to *forsake* one's friends, ideals, etc.]; **quit**, basically implying to leave or give up, is now commonly used to mean stop [she *quit* her job] See also RELINQUISH —*ANT.* **reclaim**

a·ban·doned (ə ban'dənd) *adj.* **1.** given up; forsaken; deserted **2.** shamefully wicked; immoral and shameless **3.** unrestrained

‡**à bas** (à'bä') [Fr.] down with: an expression of disapproval: opposed to VIVE

a·base (ə bās') *vt.* **a·based', a·bas'ing** [ME. *abessen* < OFr. *abaissier* < ML. *abassare*, to lower, bring down < L. *ad* (see A-²) + LL. *bassus*, low] **1.** to humble or humiliate [he *abased* himself before the king] **2.** [Archaic] to lower; cast down —*SYN.* see DEGRADE —**a·base'ment** *n.*

a·bash (ə bash') *vt.* [ME. *abaishen* < OFr. *esbahir*, to astonish < L. *ex* + *ba*, interj. of surprise] to make ashamed and ill at ease; make self-conscious; disconcert —*SYN.* see EMBARRASS —**a·bash'ed·ly** (-id lē) *adv.* —**a·bash'ment** *n.*

a·bate (ə bāt') *vt.* **a·bat'ed, a·bat'ing** [ME. *abaten* < OFr. *abattre*, to beat down: see A-² & BATTER¹] **1.** to make less in amount, degree, force, etc. **2.** to deduct **3.** *Law* to put a stop to (a suit or action), end (a nuisance), etc.; terminate —*vi.* to become less in amount, degree, force, etc.; diminish; subside —*SYN.* see WANE —**a·bat'a·ble** *adj.* —**a·bat'er,** *Law* **a·ba'tor** (-ər, -ôr) *n.*

a·bate·ment (-mənt) *n.* [ME. < OFr.; see prec.] **1.** a lessening or reduction **2.** an amount deducted; extent of a reduction **3.** *Law* the termination of a suit, quashing of a nuisance, etc.

ab·a·tis, ab·at·tis (ab'ə tis) *n., pl.* **ab'a·tis, ab'at·tis** [Fr. < *abattre*, to beat down: see ABATE] **1.** a barricade of felled trees with branches facing the enemy **2.** a barbed-wire entanglement for defense

A battery an electric battery of low voltage used to heat the filament of certain electron tubes, etc.

ab·at·toir (ab'ə twär', ab'ə twär') *n.* [Fr. < *abattre*, to beat down, fell: see ABATE] a slaughterhouse

ab·ax·i·al (ab'ak'sē 'l) *adj.* away from the axis [an *abaxial* ray of light]

ab·ba (ab'ə) *n.* [LGr. < Aram.] father: title of a bishop in the Syriac, Coptic, and Ethiopian Christian churches — [A-] *Bible* God: Mark 14:36

ab·ba·cy (ab'ə sē) *n., pl.* **-cies** [LL. *abbatia* < L. *abbas:* see ABBOT] an abbot's position, jurisdiction, or term of office

Ab·bas·id (ə bas'id, ab'ə sid) *n.* any caliph of the dynasty that ruled at Bagdad (750–1258 A.D.) and claimed descent from Mohammed's uncle, Abbas —*adj.* of this dynasty

ab·ba·tial (ə bā'shəl) *adj.* [Fr. < ML. *abbatialis* < LL. *abbatia:* see ABBACY] of an abbot, abbess, or abbey

ab·bé (a'bā; *Fr.* à bā') *n.* [Fr. < LL. *abbas:* see ABBOT] a French title of respect given to a priest, minister, etc.

ab·bess (ab'es) *n.* [ME. *abbes* < OFr. *abesse* < LL. *abbatissa*, fem. of *abbas:* see ABBOT] a woman who is head of an abbey of nuns

Ab·be·vil·li·an (ab'ə vil'ē ən, ab vil'-) *adj.* [< *Abbeville*, town in N France] designating or of a lower paleolithic culture characterized by the use of stone hand axes for chopping

ab·bey (ab'ē) *n.* [ME. *abbeie* < OFr. *abaie* < LL. *abbatia*, ABBACY] **1.** a monastery headed by an abbot or a convent of nuns headed by an abbess **2.** the monks or nuns in such a place, collectively **3.** a church or building belonging to an abbey —*SYN.* see CLOISTER

ab·bot (ab'ət) *n.* [OE. *abbod* < LL. *abbas* < Gr. < Aram. *abbā*, father] a man who is head of an abbey of monks

Ab·bot (ab'ət), **Charles Greeley** 1872– ; U.S. astrophysicist

Ab·bots·ford (ab'əts fərd) estate (1812–32) of Sir Walter Scott, on the Tweed River in Scotland

Ab·bott (ab'ət) **1.** Jacob, 1803–79; U.S. clergyman & author of children's books **2.** Lyman, 1835–1922; U.S. clergyman, editor, & author: son of *prec.*

abbr., abbrev. 1. abbreviated **2.** abbreviation

ab·bre·vi·ate (ə brē'vē āt') *vt.* **-at'ed, -at'ing** [< LL. *abbreviatus*, pp. of *abbreviare* < L. *ad-* + *breviare* < *brevis*, short] **1.** to make shorter **2.** to shorten (a word or phrase) by leaving out or substituting letters —*SYN.* see SHORTEN —**ab·bre'vi·a'tor** (-ər) *n.*

ab·bre·vi·a·tion (ə brē'vē ā'shən) *n.* [MFr. *abréviation* < LL. *abbreviatio:* see ABBREVIATE] **1.** a making shorter **2.** the fact or state of being made shorter **3.** a shortened form of a word or phrase, as *N.Y.* for *New York, Mr.* for *Mister, lb.* for *pound, ctn* for *cotangent*

ABC American Broadcasting Company

A B C (ā'bē'sē') *n., pl.* **A B C's 1.** [*usually pl.*] the alphabet **2.** the basic or simplest elements (of a subject); rudiments

ABC soil a vertical section of soil made up of three distinct layers: the top layer (*A-horizon*) is mostly humus, the

middle layer (*B-horizon*) is of clay and other oxidized material, and the bottom layer (*C-horizon*) consists of loose rock and other mineral materials

Abd-el-Ka·dir (əb dool'kä'dir; *E.* ab'del-) 1807?–83; leader of the Arabs during their war against French conquest of Algeria: also **Abd-al-Kadir**

Abd-el-Krim (əb dool krēm'; *E.* ab'del krim') 1881?–1963; Moroccan leader of the Berbers against the Spanish, and later the French, in the Rif region of Morocco (1920–26): sometimes written **Abdel Krim**

Abd-er-Rah·man Khan (äb'dər rə män' khän') *same as* ABDUR RAHMAN KHAN

Ab·di·as (ab dī'əs) *Douay Bible* name for OBADIAH

ab·di·cate (ab'də kāt') *vt., vi.* **-cat'ed, -cat'ing** [< L. *abdicatus*, pp. of *abdicare*, to deny, renounce < *ab-*, off + *dicare*, to proclaim, akin to *dicere*, to say: cf. DICTION] **1.** to give up formally (a high office, throne, authority, etc.) **2.** to surrender or repudiate (a right, responsibility, etc.) —**ab'di·ca'tion** *n.* —**ab'di·ca'tor** *n.*
SYN.—**abdicate** most commonly refers to the formal giving up by a sovereign of his throne, but sometimes describes a surrender of any prerogative; **renounce**, often interchangeable with **abdicate**, is the more frequent usage when the voluntary surrender of any right, claim, title, practice, etc. is meant, and often suggests sacrifice [she *renounced* the pleasures of society]; **resign** is applied to the deliberate giving up of a position, unexpired term, etc. by formal notice —*ANT.* **assume**

ab·do·men (ab'də mən; also ab dō'mən, əb-) *n.* [L.] **1.** in higher vertebrates *a)* the part of the body between the diaphragm and the pelvis, containing the stomach, intestines, etc.; belly *b)* the area of the trunk covering this part **2.** in insects and crustaceans, the posterior or hind part of the body, beyond the thorax

ab·dom·i·nal (ab dä'mə n'l, əb-) *adj.* [ModL. *abdominalis* < L. *abdomen*] of, in, on, or for the abdomen

ab·du·cent (ab dōōs''nt, əb-; -dyōōs'-) *adj.* [< L. *abducens*, prp. of *abducere:* see ABDUCT] *Physiol.* that abducts

ab·duct (ab dukt', əb-) *vt.* [< L. *abductus*, pp. of *abducere*, to lead away < *ab-*, away + *ducere*, to lead: see DUCT] **1.** to take (a person) away unlawfully and by force or fraud; kidnap **2.** *Physiol.* to move or pull (a part of the body) away from the median axis or from another part [a muscle that *abducts* the thumb]: opposed to ADDUCT —**ab·duc'tor** (-ər) *n.*

ab·duc·tion (ab duk'shən, əb-) *n.* **1.** an abducting or being abducted **2.** *Law* the carrying off of a person by force or fraud; esp., the kidnapping of a woman for marriage, prostitution, etc. **3.** *Physiol. a)* an abducting of a part of the body *b)* the changed position resulting from this

Abd-ul-A·ziz (äb'dool ä zēz') 1830–76; sultan of Turkey (1861–76)

Abd-ul-Ha·mid II (-hä mēd') 1842–1918; sultan of Turkey (1876–1909)

Abd-ul-Me·djid, Abd-ul-Me·jid (-me jēd') 1823–61; sultan of Turkey (1839–61)

Ab·dur Rah·man Khan (äb'dər rə män' khän') 1844?–1901; amir of Afghanistan (1880–1901)

a·beam (ə bēm') *adv.* [A-¹, on + BEAM] **1.** at right angles to a ship's length or keel **2.** abreast (*of*) the middle of a ship's side

a·be·ce·dar·i·an (ā'bē sē der'ē ən) *n.* [ML. *abecedarius* < *A, B, C, D*] **1.** a person learning the alphabet; beginning student **2.** any beginner or novice —*adj.* **1.** of the alphabet **2.** elementary

a·bed (ə bed') *adv., adj.* [ME. *abedde* < OE. *on bedde:* see A-¹ & BED] in bed; on a bed

A·bed·ne·go (ə bed'ni gō') [Heb., prob. < *abed nebo*, servant of Nebo] *Bible* one of the three captives who came out of the blazing furnace miraculously unharmed: Dan. 3

A·bel (ā'b'l) [L. < Gr. *Abel* < Heb. *hebel*, lit., breath] **1.** a masculine name **2.** *Bible* the second son of Adam and Eve, killed by his brother Cain: Gen. 4

Ab·é·lard (à bā làr'), **Pierre** 1079–1142; Fr. philosopher, teacher, & theologian: Eng. name Peter **Ab·e·lard** (ab'ə-lärd'): see also HÉLOÏSE

a·bele (ə bēl') *n.* [Du. *abeel* < OFr. *abel, aubel* < ML. *albellus*, dim. of L. *albus*, white] *same as* WHITE POPLAR

A·be·lian group (ə bēl'yən) [after Niels H. *Abel* (1802–29), Norw. mathematician] *Math.* a commutative group

Ab·er·deen (ab'ər dēn') **1.** county of E Scotland, on the North Sea: 1,971 sq. mi.; pop. 321,000: also **Ab'er·deen'shire** (-shir) **2.** its county seat, a seaport: pop. 184,000 **3.** (ab'ər dēn') town in NW Md.: pop. 12,000: site of Aberdeen Proving Ground of the U.S. Army —**Ab'er·do'ni·an** (-dō'nē ən) *adj., n.*

Aberdeen An·gus (aŋ'gəs) [after ABERDEEN, Scotland + ANGUS] ☆any of a breed of black, hornless cattle, originally from Scotland, raised for beef

ab·er·rant (a ber'ənt, ə-) *adj.* [< L. *aberrans*, prp. of *aberrare*, to go astray < *ab-*, from + *errare*, to wander: see ERR] **1.** turning away from what is right, true, etc. **2.** deviating from what is normal or typical —*n.* an aberrant person or thing —**ab·er'rance** (-əns), **ab·er'ran·cy** (-ən sē) *n.*

ab·er·ra·tion (ab'ər ā'shən) *n.* [L. *aberratio* < *aberrare:* see ABERRANT] **1.** a departure from what is right, true, correct, etc. **2.** a deviation from the normal or the typical **3.** mental derangement or lapse **4.** *Astron.* a small apparent change in position of a heavenly body, caused by the orbital motion of the earth and the motion of light rays from the

body 5. *Optics a)* the failure of light rays from one point to converge to a single focus *b)* an error in a lens or mirror causing such failure: see CHROMATIC ABERRATION, SPHERICAL ABERRATION —**ab'er·ra'tion·al** *adj.*

a·bet (ə bet') *vt.* **a·bet'ted, a·bet'ting** [ME. *abetten* < OFr. *abeter*, to incite < *a-*, to + *beter*, to bait < ON. *beita*: see BAIT] to incite, sanction, or help, esp. in wrongdoing —**a·bet'ment** *n.* —**a·bet'tor** (-ər), **a·bet'ter** *n.*

a·bey·ance (ə bā'əns) *n.* [Anglo-Fr. *abeiance* < OFr. *abeance*, expectation < *a-*, to, at + *bayer*, to gape, wait expectantly < Gaul. **batare*] 1. temporary suspension, as of an activity or function 2. *Law* a state of not having been determined or settled, as of lands the present ownership of which has not been established

ab·hor (əb hôr', ab-) *vt.* **-horred', -hor'ring** [L. *abhorrere* < *ab-*, away, from + *horrere*, to shudder] to shrink from in fear, disgust, or hatred; detest —*SYN.* see HATE —**ab·hor'rer** *n.*

ab·hor·rence (əb hôr'əns, ab-; -här'-) *n.* 1. an abhorring; loathing; detestation 2. something abhorred; something repugnant —*SYN.* see AVERSION

ab·hor·rent (-ənt) *adj.* [< L. *abhorrens*, prp. of *abhorrere*, ABHOR] 1. causing fear, disgust, etc.; detestable [an *abhorrent* crime] 2. feeling abhorrence 3. opposed or contrary (*to*) [*abhorrent* to his principles] —*SYN.* see HATEFUL —**ab·hor'rent·ly** *adv.*

a·bide (ə bīd') *vi.* **a·bode'** or **a·bid'ed, a·bid'ing** [OE. *abidan* < *a-*, intens. + *bidan*, to remain: see BIDE] 1. to stand fast; remain; go on being 2. [Archaic or Poet.] to stay; reside (*in* or *at*) —*vt.* 1. to await 2. to submit to; put up with —**abide by** 1. to live up to (a promise, agreement, etc.) 2. to submit to and carry out (a rule, decision, etc.) —*SYN.* see CONTINUE, STAY —**a·bid'ance** *n.* —**a·bid'er** *n.*

a·bid·ing (ə bīd'iŋ) *adj.* continuing without change; enduring; lasting

Ab·i·djan (äb'i jän') seaport and capital of the Ivory Coast: pop. 258,000

Ab·i·gail (ab'ə gāl') [Heb. *abīgayil*, lit., father is rejoicing] a feminine name: dim. *Abby, Gail* —*n.* [a-] [< *Abigail*, name of a maid in *The Scornful Lady* by Beaumont and Fletcher (1616)] a lady's maid

Ab·i·lene (ab'ə lēn') [ult. < Luke 3:1 < ?] city in C Tex.: pop. 90,000

a·bil·i·ty (ə bil'ə tē) *n., pl.* **-ties** [ME. *abilite* < OFr. *habilité* < L. *habilitas* < *habilis*: see ABLE] 1. a being able; power to do (something physical or mental) 2. skill, expertness, or talent

-a·bil·i·ty (ə bil'ə tē) *pl.* **-ties** [L. *-ubilitas*: see -ABLE & -ITY] a *n.*-forming suffix corresponding to -ABLE [*durability, washability*]

‡**ab in·i·ti·o** (ab' in ish'ē ō') [L.] from the beginning

ab in·tra (ab in'trə) [L.] from within

ab·i·o·gen·e·sis (ab'ē ō jen'ə sis, ā'bī ō-) *n.* [ModL. < Gr. *a-*, without + BIOGENESIS] *same as* SPONTANEOUS GENERATION —**ab'i·o·ge·net'ic** (-ō net'ik) *adj.* —**ab'i·o·ge·net'i·cal·ly** *adv.*

ab·i·o·ge·nist (ab'ē äj'ə nist, ā'bī äj'-) *n.* a person who believes in abiogenesis

ab·ject (ab'jekt, ab jekt') *adj.* [ME. < L. *abjectus*, pp. of *abjicere*, to throw away < *ab-*, from + *jacere*, to throw: see JET] 1. of the lowest degree; miserable; wretched [*abject* poverty] 2. lacking self-respect; degraded [an *abject* coward] —*SYN.* see BASE² —**ab'ject·ly** *adv.* —**ab'ject·ness, ab·jec'tion** (-jek'shən) *n.*

ab·jure (əb joor', ab-) *vt.* **-jured', -jur'ing** [ME. *abjuren* < L. *abjurare* < *ab-*, from, away + *jurare*, to swear: see JURY¹] 1. to give up (rights, allegiance, etc.) on oath; renounce 2. to give up (opinions) publicly; recant —**ab·ju·ra·tion** (ab'jə rā'shən) *n.* —**ab·jur·a·to·ry** (əb-joor'ə tôr'ē) *adj.* —**ab·jur'er** *n.*

ab·lac·ta·tion (ab'lak tā'shən) *n.* [LL. *ablactatio* < L. *ablactare*, to wean < *ab-*, from + *lac*, milk] the act or process of weaning

ab·late (ab lāt') *vt.* **-lat'ed, -lat'ing** [back-formation < *ablation*] 1. to remove, as by surgery 2. *Astrophysics* to wear away, melt, or vaporize (surface material) by entering into or passing through the atmosphere at supersonic speed 3. *Geol.* to wear away, as by erosion —*vi.* to undergo ablation —**ab·la'tion** *n.*

ab·la·tive (ab'lə tiv; *for adj.* 2, ab lā'tiv) *n.* [L. *ablativus* < *ablatus*, pp. of *auferre* < *ab-*, away + *ferre*, to carry] 1. the grammatical case in Latin, Sanskrit, and certain other languages expressing removal, deprivation, direction from, or source, cause, agency, etc. 2. a word or phrase in this case —*adj.* 1. of or in the ablative 2. *Astrophysics* that ablates, as the protective coating material on the nose cone of a space missile

ablative absolute *Latin Gram.* a grammatically independent phrase in the ablative case, used to express time, cause, or circumstance: sometimes applied to English constructions thought to resemble the Latin

ab·laut (äb'lout, ab'-; *G.* äp'lout) *n.* [G. < *ab-*, off, from + *laut*, sound] patterned change of base vowels in related words to show changes in tense, meaning, etc., as in the Indo-European languages (Ex.: drink, drank, drunk) —*adj.* of or characterized by ablaut

a·blaze (ə blāz') *adj.* [A-¹, on + BLAZE¹] 1. flaming; gleaming 2. greatly excited; eager

a·ble (ā'b'l) *adj.* **a'bler** (-blər), **a'blest** (-blist) [ME. < OFr. *hable, habile* < L. *habilis*, easily handled, apt < *habere*, to have, hold: see HABIT] 1. having enough power, skill, etc. (*to do* something) 2. having much power of mind; skilled; talented [an *able* teacher] 3. *Law* legally qualified, authorized, or competent to do a specified act —*SYN.*—**able** implies power or ability to do something [*able* to make payments] but sometimes suggests superior power or skill [an *able* orator]; **capable** usually implies the mere meeting of ordinary requirements [a *capable* machinist]; **competent** and **qualified** both imply the possession of the requisite qualifications for the specified work, situation, etc., but **qualified** stresses compliance with specified requirements [a *competent* critic of modern art, a *qualified* voter] —*ANT.* inept

-a·ble (ə b'l) [ME. < OFr. < L. *-abilis*] an *adj.*-forming suffix meaning: 1. able to [*durable*] 2. capable of being [*drinkable*] 3. worthy of being [*lovable*] 4. having qualities of [*comfortable*] 5. tending or inclined to [*peaceable*] Also **-ible, -ble**

a·ble-bod·ied (ā'b'l bäd'ēd) *adj.* healthy and strong

able-bodied seaman a trained seaman, more highly skilled than an ordinary seaman: also **able seaman**

a·bloom (ə bloom') *adj.* [A-¹ + BLOOM¹] in bloom; in flower

ab·lu·ent (ab'loo wənt) *adj.* [L. *abluens*, prp. of *abluere*: see ABLUTION] that makes clean —*n.* any substance used for cleaning

ab·lu·tion (ab loo'shən, əb-) *n.* [ME. *ablucioun* < L. *ablutio* < *abluere* < *ab-*, off + *luere*, to LAVE¹] 1. a washing of the body, esp. as a religious ceremony 2. the liquid used for such washing —**ab·lu'tion·ar·y** (-er'ē) *adj.*

a·bly (ā'blē) *adv.* in an able manner; skillfully

-a·bly (ə blē, -bli) an *adv.*-forming suffix corresponding to -ABLE [*peaceably*]

ABM anti-ballistic missile

☆**Ab·na·ki** (ab nä'kē) *n.pl.* [Algonquian, lit., those of the east] Indians of an Algonquian confederacy formerly centering in Maine

ab·ne·gate (ab'nə gāt') *vt.* **-gat'ed, -gat'ing** [< L. *abnegatus*, pp. of *abnegare* < *ab-*, away, from + *negare*, to deny] to deny and refuse; give up (rights, claims, etc.); renounce —**ab'ne·ga'tor** *n.*

ab·ne·ga·tion (ab'nə gā'shən) *n.* [L. *abnegatio*: see ABNEGATE] a giving up of rights, etc.; self-denial; renunciation

Ab·ner (ab'nər) [L. < Heb. *'abnēr*, lit., the father is a light] a masculine name

ab·nor·mal (ab nôr'm'l, əb-) *adj.* [earlier *anormal* < Fr. *anormal, anomal* < LL. *anomalus* < Gr. *anōmalos* (see ANOMALOUS) infl. by L. *abnormis* < *ab-*, from + *norma*, NORM] not normal; not average; not typical; not usual; irregular, esp. to a considerable degree —*SYN.* see IRREGULAR —**ab·nor'mal·ly** *adv.*

ab·nor·mal·i·ty (ab'nôr mal'ə tē) *n.* 1. the quality or condition of being abnormal 2. *pl.* **-ties** an abnormal thing; malformation

abnormal psychology the study of the behavior of abnormal people, esp. that of the neurotic, psychotic, or feeble-minded

ab·nor·mi·ty (ab nôr'mə tē) *n., pl.* **-ties** [< L. *abnormis* (see ABNORMAL) + -ITY] [Rare] abnormality or monstrosity

a·board (ə bôrd') *adv.* [ME. *abord* < OFr. *a bord*] 1. on board; on, in, or into a ship, airplane, etc. 2. alongside —*prep.* on board of; on; in —☆**all aboard!** 1. get on] get in]: a warning to passengers that the train, car, airplane, etc. will start soon 2. everyone (is) aboard!: a signal to the driver or pilot that he may start

a·bode¹ (ə bōd') *n.* [ME. *abad, abood* < pp. of *abiden*, ABIDE] 1. a staying in a place; sojourn 2. a place where one lives or stays; home; residence

a·bode² (ə bōd') *alt. pt.* and *pp.* of ABIDE

a·bol·ish (ə bäl'ish) *vt.* [ME. *abolisshen* < OFr. *aboliss-*, extended stem of *abolir* < L. *abolescere*, to decay little by little, inceptive of *abolere*, to retard, destroy: formed, with *ab-*, from, to contrast with *adolere*, to increase, grow] to do away with completely; put an end to; esp., to make (a law, etc.) null and void —**a·bol'ish·er** *n.* —**a·bol'ish·ment** *n.* *SYN.*—**abolish** denotes a complete doing away with something, as an institution, custom, practice, condition, etc. [to *abolish* slavery, ignorance, etc.]; **annul** and **abrogate** stress a canceling by authority or formal action [the marriage was *annulled*, the law *abrogated* certain privileges]; **rescind, revoke,** and **repeal** all agree in describing the setting aside of laws, orders, permits, etc. [to *rescind* an order, *revoke* a charter, *repeal* an Amendment] —*ANT.* establish

ab·o·li·tion (ab'ə lish'ən) *n.* [Fr. < L. *abolitio*: see ABOLISH] 1. an abolishing or being abolished; annulment 2. [*occas.* A-] the abolishing of slavery in the U.S. —**ab'o·li'-tion·ar'y** (-er'ē) *adj.*

ab·o·li·tion·ist (-ist) *n.* a person in favor of abolishing some law, custom, etc.; specif., [*occas.* A-] one who favored the abolition of slavery in the U.S. —**ab'o·li'tion·ism** *n.*

fat, āpe, cär; ten, ēven; is, bīte; gō, hôrn, tōōl, look; oil, out; up, fur; get; joy; yet; chin; she; thin, then; zh, leisure; ŋ, ring; ə for *a* in *ago*, *e* in *agent*, *i* in *sanity*, *o* in *comply*, *u* in *focus*; ' as in *able* (ā'b'l); Fr. bâl; ë, Fr. coeur; ö, Fr. feu; Fr. mon; ö, Fr. coq; ü, Fr. duc; r, Fr. cri; H, G. ich; kh, G. doch. See inside front cover. ☆ Americanism; ‡foreign; *hypothetical; < derived from

ab·o·ma·sum (ab'ə mā'səm) *n., pl.* **-ma'sa** (-sə) [ModL. < L. *ab-*, from + *omasum*, bullock's tripe] the fourth, or digesting, chamber of the stomach of a cud-chewing animal, as the cow: see RUMINANT, illus.

☆**A-bomb** (ā'bäm) *n. same as* ATOMIC BOMB —*vt.* to attack or destroy with an atomic bomb

a·bom·i·na·ble (ə bäm'ə nə b'l) *adj.* [ME. *abhominable* (sp. infl. by folk etymological derivation < L. *ab homine*, away from man, inhuman) < OFr. *abominable* < L. *abominabilis* < *abominari*: see ABOMINATE] 1. nasty and disgusting; vile; loathsome 2. highly unpleasant; disagreeable; very bad [*abominable* taste] —*SYN.* see HATEFUL —**a·bom'i·na·bly** *adv.*

Abominable Snowman a large, hairy, manlike animal reputed to live in the Himalayas

a·bom·i·nate (ə bäm'ə nāt') *vt.* **-nat'ed, -nat'ing** [< L. *abominatus*, pp. of *abominari*, to regard as an ill omen: see AB- & OMEN] 1. to have feelings of hatred and disgust for; loathe; abhor 2. to dislike very much —**a·bom'i·na'tor** *n.*

a·bom·i·na·tion (ə bäm'ə nā'shən) *n.* 1. an abominating; great hatred and disgust; loathing 2. anything hateful and disgusting

‡**à bon mar·ché** (à bôn mår shā') [Fr.] at a good bargain; cheap

ab·o·rig·i·nal (ab'ə rij'ə n'l) *adj.* [ABORIGIN(ES) + -AL] 1. existing (in a place) from the beginning or from earliest days; first; indigenous 2. of or characteristic of aborigines —*n.* an aboriginal animal or plant —*SYN.* see NATIVE —**ab'o·rig'i·nal·ly** *adv.*

ab·o·rig·i·ne (ab'ə rij'ə nē') *n., pl.* **-nes'** [L., first inhabitant < *ab-*, from + *origine*, the beginning: see ORIGIN] 1. any of the first or earliest known inhabitants of a region; native 2. [*pl.*] the native animals or plants of a region

a·born·ing (ə bôr'niŋ) *adv.* while being born or created [the plan died *aborning*]

a·bort (ə bôrt') *vi.* [L. *abortire* < *abortus*, pp. of *aboriri*, to miscarry, pass away, orig., to set (as the sun) < *ab-*, from + *oriri*, to arise] 1. to give birth before the fetus is viable; have a miscarriage 2. to fail to be completed 3. *Biol.* to fail to develop; stay rudimentary —*vt.* 1. to cause to have an abortion 2. to check (a disease) before fully developed ☆3. to cut short (an action or operation of an aircraft, guided missile, etc.), as because of some failure in the equipment

a·bor·ti·cide (ə bôr'tə sīd') *n.* [ABORTI(ON) + -CIDE] 1. destruction of the fetus in the womb 2. an abortifacient

a·bor·ti·fa·cient (ə bôr'tə fā'shənt) *adj.* [ABORTI(ON) + -FACIENT] causing abortion —*n.* a drug or device that causes abortion

a·bor·tion (ə bôr'shən) *n.* [L. *abortio*: see ABORT] 1. expulsion of a fetus from the womb before it is sufficiently developed to survive; miscarriage: called **criminal abortion** when unlawfully induced 2. an aborted fetus 3. anything immature and incomplete, as a deformed creature, a badly developed plan, etc. 4. *Biol. a)* arrest of development *b)* an organ whose development has been arrested

☆**a·bor·tion·ist** (-ist) *n.* a person who effects an abortion or abortions, esp. unlawfully

a·bor·tive (ə bôr'tiv) *adj.* [ME. *abortif* < L. *abortivus*: see ABORT] 1. coming to nothing; unsuccessful; fruitless 2. *Biol.* arrested in development; rudimentary 3. *Med. a)* causing abortion *b)* halting a disease process 4. [Obs.] born prematurely —*SYN.* see FUTILE

ABO system the system of antigens found on human red blood cells, together with the corresponding antibodies of these antigens: the antigens inherited determine the major blood types

A·bou·kir (ä'bōō kir') *same as* ABUKIR

a·bou·li·a (ə bōō'lē ə) *n. same as* ABULIA

a·bound (ə bound') *vi.* [ME. *abounden* < OFr. *abonder* < L. *abundare*, to overflow < *ab-*, away + *undare*, to rise in waves < *unda*, a wave] 1. to be plentiful; exist in large numbers or amounts [tropical plants *abound* in the jungle] 2. to have plenty; be filled; be wealthy (*in*) or teem (*with*) [a land that *abounds* in grain, woods that *abound* with game]

a·bout (ə bout') *adv.* [ME. *aboute* < OE. *onbutan*, around < *on*, on + *be*, by + *utan*, outside < *ut*, out: all senses develop from the sense of "around"] 1. on every side; all around [look *about*] 2. here and there; in all directions [travel *about*] 3. in circumference; around the outside [ten miles *about*] 4. near [standing somewhere *about*] 5. in the opposite direction; to a reversed position [turn it *about*] 6. in succession or rotation [play fair—turn and turn *about*] 7. nearly; approximately [*about* four years old] 8. [Colloq.] all but; almost [just about ready] —*adj.* [used only in the predicate] 1. astir; on the move [he is up and *about* again] 2. in the vicinity; prevalent [typhoid is *about*] —*prep.* 1. around; on all sides of 2. here and there in; everywhere in 3. near to 4. with; on (one's person) [have your wits about you] 5. concerned with; attending to [go *about* your business] 6. intending; on the point of (followed by an infinitive) [I am *about* to say something] 7. having to do with; concerning [a book *about* ships] 8. in connection with —**how** (or **what**) **about** [Colloq.] 1. what is your wish, opinion, or information concerning? [how *about* going to a movie?] 2. isn't (that) interesting? [how *about* that!]

a·bout-face (ə bout'fās', -fās'; for v. ə bout'fās') *n.* 1. a sharp turn to the opposite direction, esp. in response to a military command 2. a sharp change in attitude or opinion —*vi.* **-faced', -fac'ing** to turn or face in the opposite direction

a·bout-ship (ə bout'ship') *vi.* to tack a ship

a·bove (ə buv') *adv.* [ME. *above* (n) < OE. *abufan, onbufan,* overhead, above < *on-*, intens. + *bufan < be*, by + *ufan,* over, on high] 1. in, at, or to a higher place; overhead; up 2. in or to heaven 3. at a previous place (in a piece of writing): often used in hyphenated compounds [*above*-mentioned] 4. higher in power, status, etc. —*prep.* 1. higher than; over; on top of 2. beyond; past [the road *above* the village] 3. at a point uppermost of 4. superior to; better than [*above* the average] 5. too honorable to engage in [not *above* cheating] 6. in excess of; more than [*above* fifty dollars] —*adj.* placed, found, mentioned, etc. above or earlier [as stated in the *above* rules] —*n.* something that is above —**above all** most of all; mainly

a·bove·board (-bôrd') *adv., adj.* [ABOVE + BOARD (table): orig. a cardplayer's term for cards in plain view] without dishonesty or concealment [be open and *aboveboard* with me]

‡**ab o·vo** (ab ō'vō) [L., from the egg] from the beginning, or origin

ab·ra·ca·dab·ra (ab'rə kə dab'rə) *n.* [LL., prob. of Balkan origin, but assumed to be < LGr. *Abraxas,* the almighty God] 1. a word supposed to have magic powers, and hence used in incantations, on amulets, etc. 2. a magic spell or formula 3. foolish or meaningless talk; gibberish

a·brad·ant (ə brād'nt) *adj.* abrading —*n.* an abrasive

ab·rade (ə brād') *vt., vi.* **ab·rad'ed, ab·rad'ing** [L. *abradere* < *ab-*, away + *radere*, to scrape] to scrape or rub off; wear away by scraping or rubbing —**ab·rad'er** *n.*

A·bra·ham (ā'brə ham') [Heb., lit., father of many: the original form, *A bram,* means "father is exalted": see Gen. 17:5] 1. a masculine name: dim. *Abe* 2. *Bible* the first patriarch and ancestor of the Hebrews: Gen. 12-25 —**in Abraham's bosom** 1. at rest with one's dead ancestors 2. in a state of heavenly bliss, peace, etc.

Abraham, Plains of plateau in the city of Quebec, on the St. Lawrence: site of a battle (1759) in which the British under Wolfe defeated the French under Montcalm, giving Britain control of Canada

A·bram (ā'brəm) *same as* ABRAHAM

a·bran·chi·ate (ā braŋ'kē it, -āt') *adj.* [< Gr. *a-*, not + *branchia,* gills + -ATE¹] without gills —*n.* an animal without gills Also **a·bran'chi·al** (-əl)

ab·ra·sion (ə brā'zhən) *n.* [LL. *abrasio* < L. *abradere*: see ABRADE] 1. a scraping or rubbing off, as of skin 2. a wearing away by rubbing or scraping, as of rock by wind, water, etc. 3. an abraded spot or area

ab·ra·sive (ə brā'siv) *adj.* [< L. *abrasus,* pp. of *abradere,* to ABRADE + -IVE] causing abrasion —*n.* a substance used for grinding, polishing, etc., as sandpaper or emery

‡**a·bra·zo** (ä brä'thō) *n., pl.* **-zos** (-thōs) [Sp.] an embrace or hug, esp. in greeting a person

ab·re·act (ab'rē akt') *vt.* back-formation < ABREACTION] *Psychoanalysis* to relieve (a repressed emotion), as by talking about it

ab·re·ac·tion (-ak'shən) *n.* [AB- + REACTION, after G. *abreagierung*] *Psychoanalysis* the process of abreacting (a repressed emotion)

a·breast (ə brest') *adv., adj.* [A-¹ + BREAST] 1. side by side, as in going or facing forward (often with *of* or *with*) 2. informed (*of*) or conversant (*with*) recent developments

a·bridge (ə brij') *vt.* **a·bridged', a·bridg'ing** [ME. *abregen* < OFr. *abregier* < LL. *abbreviare:* see ABBREVIATE] 1. to reduce in scope, extent, etc.; shorten 2. to shorten by using fewer words but keeping the main contents; condense 3. to lessen or curtail (rights, authority, etc.) 4. [Rare] to deprive (*of* rights, privileges, etc.) —*SYN.* see SHORTEN —**a·bridg'a·ble, a·bridge'a·ble** *adj.* —**a·bridg'er** *n.*

a·bridg·ment, a·bridge·ment (ə brij'mənt) *n.* [ME. *abregement* < OFr. < *abregier:* see ABRIDGE] 1. an abridging or being abridged; reduction 2. a curtailment, as of rights 3. an abridged or condensed form of a book, etc.

SYN.—**abridgment** describes a work condensed from a larger work by omitting the less important parts, but keeping the main contents more or less unaltered; an **abstract** is a short statement of the essential contents of a book, court record, etc. often used as an index to the original material; **brief** and **summary** both imply a statement of the main points of the matter under consideration [the *brief* of a legal argument], **summary**, especially, connoting a recapitulating statement; a **synopsis** is a condensed, orderly treatment, as of the plot of a novel, that permits a quick general view of the whole; a **digest** is a concise, systematic treatment, generally more comprehensive in scope than a synopsis, and, in the case of technical material, often arranged under titles for quick reference; an **epitome** is a statement of the essence of a subject in the shortest possible form —*ANT.* expansion

a·broach (ə brōch') *adv., adj.* [ME. *abroche < a-,* on + *broche,* skewer, spit: see BROACH] 1. opened so that the liquid contents can come out; broached 2. in motion; astir

a·broad (ə brôd') *adv.* [ME. *abrode < on brod:* see ON & BROAD] 1. broadly; far and wide 2. in circulation; current [a report is *abroad* that he has won] 3. outside one's house; outdoors [to stroll *abroad*] 4. outside one's own country; to or in foreign countries 5. wide of the mark; in error —**from abroad** from a foreign land or lands

ab·ro·gate (ab'rə gāt') *vt.* **-gat'ed, -gat'ing** [< L. *abrogatus,*

pp. of *abrogare*, to repeal < *ab-*, away + *rogare*, to ask, propose] to cancel or repeal by authority; annul —*SYN.* see ABOLISH —**ab′ro·ga·ble** (-gə b′l) *adj.* —**ab′ro·ga′tion** (-gā′shən) *n.* —**ab′ro·ga′tive** *adj.* —**ab′ro·ga′tor** *n.*

a·brupt (ə brupt′) *adj.* [L. *abruptus*, pp. of *abrumpere*, to break off < *ab-*, off + *rumpere*, to break] 1. coming, happening, or ending suddenly; sudden; unexpected 2. curt or gruff in behavior or speech; brusque 3. very steep, as a precipice 4. jumping from topic to topic without proper transitions; jerky and disconnected 5. *Geol.* suddenly cropping out [*abrupt* strata] —*SYN.* see STEEP[1], SUDDEN —**a·brupt′ly** *adv.* —**a·brupt′ness** *n.*

a·brup·tion (ə brup′shən) *n.* [L. *abruptio:* see ABRUPT] a sudden breaking away (of parts of a mass)

A·bruz·zi (ä brōōt′tsē), Duke of the (Prince *Luigi Amedeo of Savoy-Aosta*) 1873–1933; It. naval officer, mountain climber, & explorer

A·bruz·zi e Mo·li·se (e mō′lē ze) region of C Italy, on the Adriatic: 5,883 sq. mi.; pop. 1,585,000

abs- (abs, əbs) *same as* AB-: used before *t* or *c*

Ab·sa·lom (ab′sə ləm) [L. < Heb. *'abshālōm*, lit., the father is peace] *Bible* David's favorite son, killed after rebelling against his father: II Sam. 18

ab·scess (ab′ses) *n.* [L. *abscessus < abscidere*, to go from < *ab(s)-*, from + *cedere*, to go: the notion was formerly held that humors go from the body into the swelling] a swollen, inflamed area in body tissues, in which pus gathers —*vi.* to form an abscess —**ab′scessed** *adj.*

ab·scise (ab sīz′) *vi., vt.* [< L. *abscisus*, pp. of *abscidere*, to cut off < *abs-*, var. of *ab-*, AB- + *caedere*, to cut (see -CIDE)] to separate by abscission

ab·scis·sa (ab sis′ə, əb-) *n., pl.* -**sas**, -**sae** (-ē) [L. *abscissa* (*linea*), (a line) cut off, fem. of *abscissus*, pp. of *abscindere*, to cut off < *ab-*, from, off + *scindere*, to cut] in a coordinate system, the distance of a point from the vertical axis as measured along a line parallel to the horizontal axis: cf. ORDINATE

ABSCISSA
(PP′′, abscissa of P;
PP′, ordinate of P)

ab·scis·sion (ab sizh′ən) *n.* [L. *abscissio:* see ABSCISSA] 1. a cutting off, as by surgery 2. the normal separation of fruit, leaves, etc. from plants by the development of a thin layer of pithy cells at the base of their stems

ab·scond (ab skänd′, əb-) *vi.* [L. *abscondere < ab(s)-*, from, away + *condere*, to hide: see RECONDITE] to go away hastily and secretly; run away and hide, esp. in order to escape the law —**ab·scond′er** *n.*

ab·sence (ab′s′ns) *n.* [ME. < OFr. < L. *absentia:* see ABSENT, *adj.*] 1. the condition of being absent, or away 2. the time of being away 3. the fact of being without; lack [in the *absence* of evidence]

ab·sent (ab′s′nt; *for v.* ab sent′) *adj.* [ME. < OFr. < L. *absens*, prp. of *abesse < ab-*, away + *esse*, to be] 1. not present; away 2. not existing; lacking 3. not attentive; absorbed in thought —*vt.* to keep (oneself) away [to *absent* oneself from classes]

ab·sen·tee (ab′s′n tē′) *n.* a person who is absent, as from work, school, etc. —*adj.* designating or of a landlord who lives some distance away from the land or buildings that he owns

☆**absentee ballot** a ballot to be marked and delivered to a board of elections by a person (**absentee voter**) before an election during which he will be absent from his voting district

ab·sen·tee·ism (-iz′m) *n.* absence from work, school, etc., esp. when deliberate or habitual

‡**ab·sen·te re·o** (ab sen′tē rē′ō) [L.] in the absence of the defendant

ab·sent·ly (ab′s′nt lē) *adv.* in an absent or preoccupied manner; inattentively

ab·sent-mind·ed (-mīn′did) *adj.* 1. so dreamy or lost in thought as to not pay attention to what one is doing or what is going on around one 2. habitually forgetful —**ab′sent-mind′ed·ly** *adv.* —**ab′sent-mind′ed·ness** *n.*
SYN.—**absent-minded** suggests an aimless wandering of the mind away from the immediate situation, often implying a habitual tendency of this kind [the *absent-minded* professor]; **abstracted** suggests a withdrawal of the mind from the immediate present and a serious concern with some other subject; **preoccupied** implies that the attention cannot be readily turned to something new because of its concern with a present matter; **distrait** suggests inability to concentrate, often emphasizing such a condition as a mood; **distraught** implies a similar inability to concentrate, specifically because of worry, grief, etc.; **inattentive** implies a failure to pay attention, emphasizing such behavior as a lack of discipline

absent without leave *Mil.* absent from duty without official permission but with no intention of deserting: abbrev. **AWOL, A.W.O.L., awol, a.w.o.l.**

ab·sinthe, ab·sinth (ab′sinth) *n.* [ME. < OFr. < L. *absinthium* < Gr. *apsinthion* < OPer.] 1. wormwood (*Artemisia absinthium*) or its essence 2. a green, bitter liqueur with the flavor of wormwood and anise

ab·sinth·ism (ab′sin thiz′m) *n.* a diseased condition caused by habitually drinking too much absinthe

‡**ab·sit o·men** (ab′sit ō′mən) [L.] may there be no (ill) omen (in it)!

ab·so·lute (ab′sə lōōt′, ab′sə lōōt′) *adj.* [ME. *absolut* < L. *absolutus*, pp. of *absolvere*, to loosen from: see ABSOLVE] 1. perfect; complete; whole [*absolute* silence] 2. not mixed; pure [*absolute* alcohol] 3. not limited by a constitution, parliament, etc.; unrestricted [an *absolute* ruler] 4. positive; definite [an *absolute* certainty] 5. not doubted; actual; real [an *absolute* truth] 6. not dependent on, or without reference to, anything else; not relative 7. *Gram. a)* forming part of a sentence, but not in the usual relations of syntax: in the sentence "The weather being good, they went," *the weather being good* is an *absolute* construction *b)* used without an explicit object: said of a verb usually transitive, such as *steal* in the sentence "Thieves steal." *c)* used alone, with the noun understood: said of a pronoun or an adjective, such as *ours* and *brave* in the sentence "Ours are the brave." 8. *Law* without condition or encumbrance [*absolute* ownership] 9. *Physics* of the absolute-temperature scale —*n.* something that is absolute —**the Absolute** *Philos.* that which is thought of as existing in and by itself, without relation to anything else —**ab′so·lute′ly** *adv.* —**ab′so·lute′ness** *n.*

absolute altitude the altitude of an aircraft over the surface of the land or water below

absolute ceiling the maximum altitude above sea level at which a given aircraft can keep normal horizontal flight

absolute magnitude the apparent magnitude a star would have at a distance of ten parsecs from the earth

absolute music music that does not seek to suggest a story, scene, etc. but is concerned purely with tone, structure, etc.: distinguished from PROGRAM MUSIC

absolute pitch 1. the pitch of a tone as determined by its rate of vibration 2. the ability to identify the pitch of any tone heard, or to sing a given tone without having any identified pitch sounded beforehand

absolute temperature temperature measured from absolute zero on the Kelvin scale or on the Rankine scale

absolute value 1. the value of a number, regardless of a prefixed plus or minus sign; the positive square root of the square of a number [the *absolute value* of −4 is 4] 2. the modulus of a complex number

absolute zero a point of temperature, theoretically equal to −273.15° C or −459.67° F: the hypothetical point at which a substance would have no molecular motion and no heat

ab·so·lu·tion (ab′sə lōō′shən) *n.* [ME. *absoluciun* < OFr. *absolution* < L. *absolutio < absolvere*, to loosen from: see ABSOLVE] 1. a formal freeing (from guilt or obligation); forgiveness 2. *a)* remission (*of* sin or penalty for it); specif., in some churches, such remission formally given by a priest in the sacrament of penance *b)* the formula by which such remission is stated

ab·so·lut·ism (ab′sə lōō′tiz′m) *n.* 1. the doctrine or system of government under which the ruler has unlimited powers; despotism 2. the quality of being absolute; positivism 3. *Philos.* any doctrine involving the existence of an absolute 4. *Theol.* predestination —**ab′so·lut′ist** *n., adj.*

ab·sol·u·to·ry (ab säl′yōō tôr′ē) *adj.* [L. *absolutorius < absolvere:* see ABSOLVE] absolving; that absolves

ab·solve (əb zälv′, ab-; -sälv′) *vt.* -**solved′**, -**solv′ing** [ME. *absolven* < L. *absolvere < ab-*, from + *solvere:* see SOLVE] 1. to pronounce free from guilt or blame; acquit 2. *a)* to give religious absolution to *b)* to remit (a sin) 3. to free (from a duty, promise, etc.) —**ab·solv′ent** *adj., n.* —**ab·solv′er** *n.*
SYN.—**absolve** implies a setting free from responsibilities or obligation [*absolved* from her promise] or from the penalties for their violation; **acquit** means to release from a specific charge by a judicial decision, usually for lack of evidence; to **exonerate** is to relieve of the blame for a wrongdoing; to **pardon** is to release from punishment for an offense [the prisoner was *pardoned* by the governor]; **forgive** implies giving up all claim to punishment as well as any resentment or vengeful feelings; to **vindicate** is to clear (a person or thing under attack) through evidence of the unfairness of the charge, criticism, etc. —*ANT.* **blame**

ab·sorb (əb zôrb′, ab-; -sôrb′) *vt.* [L. *absorbere < ab-*, from + *sorbere*, to drink in, suck] 1. to suck up; drink in [blotting paper *absorbs* ink] 2. to take up fully the attention, energy, or time of; engross 3. to take in and incorporate; assimilate 4. to assume the burden of (costs, expenses, etc.) 5. to take in (a shock, jolt, etc.) with little or no recoil or reaction 6. to take in and not reflect [light rays are *absorbed* by black surfaces, cork ceilings *absorb* sound] —**ab·sorb′a·bil′i·ty** *n.* —**ab·sorb′a·ble** *adj.* —**ab·sorb′er** *n.*

ab·sorbed (əb zôrbd′, ab-; -sôrbd′) *adj.* 1. taken in, sucked up, assimilated, etc. 2. greatly interested; wholly occupied [*absorbed* in reading]

ab·sorb·ent (əb zôr′b′nt, ab-; -sôr′-) *adj.* [L. *absorbens*, prp. of *absorbere:* see ABSORB] capable of absorbing moisture, light rays, etc. —*n.* a thing or substance that absorbs —**ab·sorb′en·cy** *n.*

☆**absorbent cotton** raw cotton made absorbent by the removal of its wax: used for surgical dressings, etc.

fat, āpe, cär; ten, ēven; is, bīte; gō, hôrn, tōōl, look; oil, out; up, fur; get; joy; yet; chin; she; thin, *then*; zh, leisure; ŋ, ring; ə for *a* in *ago*, *e* in *agent*, *i* in *sanity*, *o* in *comply*, *u* in *focus*; ′ as in *able* (ā′b′l); Fr. bâl; ë, Fr. coeur; ö, Fr. feu; ô, Fr. mon; ô, Fr. coq; ü, Fr. duc; r, Fr. cri; H, G. ich; kh, G. doch. See inside front cover. ☆ Americanism; ‡foreign; *hypothetical; < derived from

ab·sorb·ing (əb zôr'biŋ, ab-; -sôr'-) *adj.* very interesting; engrossing *[an absorbing tale]*

ab·sorp·tion (əb zôrp'shən, ab-; -sôrp'-) *n.* [L. *absorptio < absorbere:* see ABSORB] 1. an absorbing or being absorbed 2. the fact or state of being much interested or engrossed 3. *Biol.* the passing of nutrient material into the blood stream or lymph 4. *Physics a)* a taking in and not reflecting *b)* partial loss in power of light or radio waves passing through a medium —**ab·sorp'tive** (-tiv) *adj.* —**ab'sorp·tiv'i·ty** *n.*

ab·stain (əb stān', ab-) *vi.* [ME. *absteinen < OFr. abstenir < L. abstinere,* to hold back *< ab(s)-,* from + *tenere,* to hold: see TENANT] to hold oneself back; voluntarily do without; refrain *(from)* *[to abstain from smoking]* —SYN. see REFRAIN —**ab·stain'er** *n.*

ab·ste·mi·ous (əb stē'mē əs, ab-) *adj.* [L. *abstemius,* abstaining from alcoholic liquor *< ab(s)-,* from + root of *temetum,* strong drink] 1. moderate, esp. in eating and drinking; not self-indulgent; temperate 2. characterized by abstinence

ab·sten·tion (əb sten'shən, ab-) *n.* [L. *abstentio < abstinere:* see ABSTAIN] the act or an instance of abstaining —**absten'tious** *adj.*

ab·sterge (ab sturj') *vt.* **-sterged', -sterg'ing** [L. *abstergere < ab(s)-,* away + *tergere,* to wipe] 1. to wipe away; clean 2. to purge —**ab·ster'gent** *adj., n.*

ab·ster·sion (ab stur'shən) *n.* [< L. *abstersus,* pp. of *abstergere:* see ABSTERGE] 1. a cleansing 2. a purging —**ab·ster'sive** *adj.*

ab·sti·nence (ab'stə nəns) *n.* [ME. < OFr. < L. *abstinentia < prp.* of *abstinere:* see ABSTAIN] 1. the act of voluntarily doing without some or all food, drink, or other pleasures 2. the practice of abstaining from alcoholic liquors —**ab'sti·nent** *adj.* —**ab'sti·nent·ly** *adv.*

ab·stract (ab strakt', ab'strakt) *adj.* [< L. *abstractus,* pp. of *abstrahere,* to draw from, separate *< ab(s)-,* from + *trahere,* to DRAW] 1. thought of apart from any particular instances or material objects; not concrete 2. expressing a quality thought of apart from any particular or material object *[beauty is an abstract word]* 3. not easy to understand; abstruse 4. theoretical; not practical or applied 5. designating or of art abstracted from reality, in which designs or forms may be definite and geometric or fluid and amorphous: a generic term that encompasses various nonrealistic contemporary schools —*n.* (ab'strakt) 1. a brief statement of the essential thoughts of a book, article, speech, court record, etc.; summary 2. *(also* ab strakt') an abstract thing, condition, idea, etc. —*vt.* (ab strakt') 1. to take away; remove 2. to take dishonestly; steal 3. to think of (a quality) apart from any particular instance or material object that has it; also, to form (a general idea) from particular instances 4. (ab'strakt) to summarize; make an abstract of —SYN. see ABRIDGMENT —**in the abstract** in theory as apart from practice —**ab·stract'er** *n.* —**ab·stract'ly** *adv.* —**ab·stract'ness** *n.*

ab·stract·ed (ab strak'tid) *adj.* 1. removed or separated *(from* something) 2. withdrawn in mind; preoccupied; absent-minded —SYN. see ABSENT-MINDED —**ab·stract'ed·ly** *adv.* —**ab·stract'ed·ness** *n.*

☆**abstract expressionism** a post-World War II movement in painting characterized by emphasis on the artist's spontaneous and self-expressive application of paint in creating a nonrepresentational composition

ab·strac·tion (ab strak'shən) *n.* [ME. *abstraccioun < LL. abstractio:* see ABSTRACT] 1. an abstracting or being abstracted; removal 2. formation of an idea, as of the qualities or properties of a thing, by mental separation from particular instances or material objects 3. an idea so formed, or a word or term for it *["honesty" and "whiteness" are abstractions]* 4. an unrealistic or impractical notion 5. mental withdrawal; preoccupation; absent-mindedness 6. an abstract quality; abstract character 7. a picture, statue, etc. that is wholly or partly abstract

ab·strac·tion·ism (-iz'm) *n.* the theory and practice of the abstract, esp. in art —**ab·strac'tion·ist** *adj., n.*

ab·strac·tive (ab strak'tiv) *adj.* 1. that abstracts or can abstract 2. of or having to do with abstraction —**ab·strac'tive·ly** *adv.*

abstract of title a brief history of the ownership of a piece of real estate, from the original grant through the present holder, including a statement of liens to which it may be subject

ab·strict (ab strikt') *vt., vi.* to undergo, or produce by, abstriction

ab·stric·tion (ab strik'shən) *n.* [< L. *ab-,* from + *strictio,* a binding *< strictus,* pp. of *stringere:* see STRINGENT] *Bot.* the cutting off of spores from a spore-bearing branch by the formation of dividing tissues (septa), as in certain fungi

ab·struse (ab strōōs', əb-) *adj.* [L. *abstrusus,* pp. of *abstrudere,* to thrust away *< ab(s)-,* away + *trudere,* to THRUST] hard to understand; deep; recondite —**ab·struse'ly** *adv.* —**ab·struse'ness** *n.*

ab·surd (əb surd', ab-; -zurd') *adj.* [Fr. *absurde < L. absurdus,* not to be heard of *< ab-,* intens. + *surdus,* dull, deaf, insensible] so clearly untrue or unreasonable as to be laughable or ridiculous —**ab·surd'ly** *adv.* —**ab·surd'ness** *n.* SYN.—**absurd** means laughably inconsistent with what is judged as true or reasonable *[an absurd hypothesis]*; **ludicrous** is applied to what is laughable from incongruity or exaggeration *[a ludicrous*

facial expression]; **preposterous** is used to describe anything flagrantly absurd or ludicrous; **foolish** describes that which shows lack of good judgment or of common sense *[don't take foolish chances]*; **silly** and **ridiculous** apply to whatever excites amusement or contempt by reason of its extreme foolishness, **silly** often indicating an utterly nonsensical quality —ANT. **sensible, logical**

ab·surd·i·ty (əb sur'də tē, ab-; -zur'-) *n.* 1. the quality or state of being absurd; foolishness; nonsense 2. *pl.* **-ties** an absurd idea or thing

A·bu-Bakr (ä boo'bak'ər) 573-634 A.D.; successor of Mohammed & 1st caliph of Islam (632-634 A.D.); father of AISHA: also A·bu'-Bekr' (-bek'ər)

A·bu Dha·bi (ä'boo dä'bē) largest sheikdom of the Trucial States, on the Persian Gulf: c. 4,000 sq. mi.

A·bu·kir (ä'boo kir') bay near Alexandria, Egypt: site of the victory (1798) of the British under Nelson over the French

a·bu·li·a (ə byoo'lē ə, -boo'-) *n.* [ModL. < Gr. *aboulia,* indecision *< a-,* without + *boulē,* will, determination] *Psychol.* loss of the ability to exercise will power and make decisions —**a·bu'lic** (-lik) *adj.*

A·bul Ka·sim (ä bool' kä sēm') (L. name *Albucasis*) ?-1013?; Arab surgeon & medical encyclopedist, in Spain

a·bun·dance (ə bun'dəns) *n.* [ME. *aboundaunce < OFr. abondaunce < L. abundantia < abundans:* see ABOUND] 1. a great supply; more than sufficient quantity 2. great plenty; wealth

a·bun·dant (-dənt) *adj.* [ME. *aboundaunt < OFr. abondaunt < L. abundans:* see ABOUND] 1. very plentiful; more than sufficient; ample 2. well-supplied; rich *(in* something) *[woods abundant in game]* —SYN. see PLENTIFUL —**a·bun'dant·ly** *adv.*

a·buse (ə byoōz'; *for n.* ə byoōs') *vt.* **a·bused', a·bus'ing** [ME. *abusen < OFr. abuser < L. abusus,* pp. of *abuti,* to misuse *< ab-,* away, from + *uti,* to use] 1. to use wrongly; misuse *[to abuse a privilege]* 2. to hurt by treating badly; mistreat 3. to use insulting, coarse, or bad language about or to; scold harshly; revile 4. [Obs.] to deceive —*n.* 1. wrong, bad, or excessive use 2. mistreatment; injury 3. a bad, unjust, or corrupt custom or practice 4. insulting or coarse language 5. [Obs.] deception —SYN. see WRONG —**a·bus'er** (ə byoo'zər) *n.*

A·bu Sim·bel (ä'boo sim'bel) village in S Egypt, on the Nile: site of two temples built (13th cent. B.C.) in the face of a cliff for Ramses II

a·bu·sive (ə byoos'iv) *adj.* [Fr. *abusif < L. abusivus < abusus:* see ABUSE] 1. involving or characterized by abuse or misuse; abusing; mistreating 2. coarse and insulting in language; scurrilous; harshly scolding —**a·bu'sive·ly** *adv.* —**a·bu'sive·ness** *n.*

a·but (ə but') *vi.* **a·but'ted, a·but'ting** [ME. *aboutien < OFr. abouter,* to join end to end *< a-,* to + *bout,* end] to end *(on)* or lean *(upon)* at one end; border *(on)*; terminate *(against)* —*vt.* to end at; border upon

a·bu·ti·lon (ə byoot'l än') *n.* [ModL. < Ar. *aubūtīlūn]* any of a number of related plants or shrubs (genus *Abutilon)* of the mallow family, with showy flowers of white, yellow, or red

a·but·ment (ə but'mənt) *n.* 1. the act or an instance of abutting 2. something that abuts or borders upon something else 3. the point of contact between a support and the thing supported 4. *a)* that part of a support which carries the weight of an arch and resists its pressure *b)* the supporting structure at either end of a bridge

ABUTMENT

a·but·tals (ə but'lz) *n.pl.* abutting parts of land; boundaries

☆**a·but·ter** (-ər) *n.* the owner of an abutting, or adjacent, piece of land

a·buzz (ə buz') *adj.* 1. filled with buzzing 2. full of activity, talk, etc.

a·by, a·bye (ə bī') *vt.* **a·bought'** (-bôt') *pt. & pp.* [ME. *abien < OE. abycgan < a-,* for + *bycgan,* BUY] [Archaic] to pay the penalty for

A·by·dos (ə bī'däs) 1. ancient city in Asia Minor, on the Hellespont 2. ancient city in C Egypt, near the Nile

Ab·y·la (ab'ə lə) ancient name of a peninsula, now in Ceuta, N Africa: see PILLARS OF HERCULES

a·bysm (ə biz'm) *n.* [OFr. *abisme < ML. abysmus,* altered after suffix *-ismus* (see -ISM) < L. *abyssus:* see ABYSS] [Poet.] an abyss

a·bys·mal (ə biz'm'l) *adj.* 1. of or like an abyss; bottomless; unfathomable 2. wretched to the point of despair; immeasurably bad *[abysmal poverty]* —**a·bys'mal·ly** *adv.*

a·byss (ə bis') *n.* [L. *abyssus < Gr. abyssos < a-,* without + *byssos,* bottom] 1. a deep fissure in the earth; bottomless gulf; chasm 2. anything too deep for measurement; profound depth *[abyss of shame, of time, etc.]* 3. the ocean depths 4. *Theol.* the primeval void or chaos before the Creation —**a·bys'sal** (ə bis'l) *adj.*

abyssal rock plutonic rock

Ab·ys·sin·i·a (ab'ə sin'ē ə, -sin'yə) same as ETHIOPIA —**Ab'ys·sin'i·an** *adj., n.*

ac- (ak, ək, ik) *same as* AD-: used before *c* or *q*

-ac (ak, ək) [Fr. *-aque < L. -acus < Gr. -akos* (or directly < any of these)] *an adj.-forming suffix meaning:* 1. characteristic of *[elegiac, demoniac]* 2. of; relating to *[cardiac,*

coeliac] **3.** affected by or having *[maniac]* The resulting adjectives are sometimes used as nouns

Ac *Chem.* actinium

AC, A.C., a.c. alternating current

A/C, a/c *Bookkeeping* **1.** account **2.** account current

A.C. 1. [L. *Ante Christum*] before Christ **2.** Athletic Club

a·ca·cia (ə kā′shə) *n.* [ME. < OFr. *acacie* < L. *acacia* < Gr. *akakia*, shittah tree, thorny tree; prob. < *akē*, a point, thorn < IE. base **ak-:* see ACID] **1.** any of several trees, shrubs, or other plants (genus *Acacia*) of the legume family, with clusters of yellow or white flowers: many are cultivated as ornamentals, and some yield gum arabic or dyes **2.** the flower **3.** *same as* GUM ARABIC ☆**4.** the locust tree (see LOCUST, sense 3): also called **false acacia 5.** [Chiefly South] the albizzia tree

acad. 1. academic **2.** academy

Ac·a·deme (ak′ə dēm′, ak′ə dēm′) [< Gr. *akadēmeia*, the grove of *Akadēmos*, figure in ancient Greek legend] the grove near ancient Athens where Plato taught —*n.* [a-] [Poet.] *a)* a school; esp., a college or university *b)* the academic world

ac·a·de·mi·a (ak′ə dē′mē ə) *n.* [L.: see ACADEMY] the academic world; academe

ac·a·dem·ic (ak′ə dem′ik) *adj.* [L. *academicus* < *academia:* see ACADEMY] **1.** of colleges, universities, etc.; scholastic; scholarly **2.** having to do with general or liberal rather than technical or vocational education **3.** of or belonging to an academy of scholars, artists, etc. **4.** following fixed rules or conventions; pedantic or formalistic *[an academic style of painting]* **5.** merely theoretical; having no direct practical application *[an academic question]* Also **ac′a·dem′i·cal** —*n.* an academic person; esp., a teacher or student at a college or university

ac·a·dem·i·cal·ly (-ik lē, -ik ′l ē) *adv.* **1.** in relation to an academy **2.** in an academic manner; pedantically **3.** from an academic point of view

ac·a·dem·i·cals (-ik ′lz) *n.pl.* traditional academic clothing; cap and gown

☆**academic freedom** freedom of a teacher or student to hold and express views without fear of arbitrary interference by officials

a·cad·e·mi·cian (ə kad′ə mish′ən, ak′ə də-) *n.* [Fr. *académicien*] **1.** a member of an academy (sense 4) **2.** an artist, writer, etc. who follows certain academic rules or conventions

ac·a·dem·i·cism (ak′ə dem′ə siz′m) *n.* the quality of being academic; esp., formal or pedantic quality, spirit, etc.: also **a·cad·e·mism** (ə kad′ə miz′m)

a·cad·e·my (ə kad′ə mē) *n.*, *pl.* -**mies** [Fr. *académie* < L. *academia* < Gr. *akadēmeia:* see ACADEME] **1.** [A-] Academe; hence, Plato's followers or his philosophy **2.** a private secondary or high school **3.** a school offering instruction or training in a special field *[a music academy]* **4.** an association of scholars, writers, artists, etc., for advancing literature, art, or science

☆**Academy Award** any of the annual achievement awards given by the Academy of Motion Picture Arts and Sciences: see OSCAR

A·ca·di·a (ə kā′dē ə) [Fr. *Acadie*, prob. < native name of Nova Scotia] **1.** French colony (1604–1713) on the NE coast of N. America: it included what are now the Canadian provinces of Nova Scotia and New Brunswick **2.** parish of SC Louisiana settled by Acadian exiles —**A·ca′di·an** *adj.*, *n.*

Acadia National Park national park mostly on Mount Desert Island, Me.: 48.8 sq. mi.

☆**Acadian chickadee** a chickadee (*Parus hudsonicus littoralis*) found near the Atlantic coast from Labrador to N New York: it has a brown cap and black throat

☆**Acadian flycatcher** a yellowish or greenish flycatcher (*Empidonax virescens*) found in E N. America

☆**Acadian owl** *same as* SAW-WHET OWL

ac·a·jou (ak′ə zhōō′) *n.* [Fr., CASHEW] **1.** mahogany, esp. as used in French cabinetmaking **2.** the cashew

ac·a·leph (ak′ə lef′) *n.* [< Gr. *akalēphē*, a nettle] any of several invertebrate animals, as jellyfishes, that swim or float about in the open sea; coelenterate or ctenophore (former class Acalephes, phylum Zoophyta): also **ac′a·lephe′** (-lēf′)

a·can·thine (ə kan′thin) *adj.* of or resembling an acanthus or its leaves

a·can·tho- (ə kan′thə), **a·canth-** (ə kanth′) [< Gr. *akantha*, thorn < *akē*, point] *a combining form meaning* thorn, like a thorn *[acanthocephalan]*

a·can·tho·ceph·a·lan (ə kan′thə sef′ə lən) *n.* [ACANTHO- + CEPHAL- + -AN] any of a phylum (Acanthocephala) of intestinal worms having a proboscis bearing rows of thornlike hooks and lacking a digestive tract

a·can·thoid (ə kan′thoid) *adj.* spiny; spine-shaped: also **a·can′thous** (-thəs)

ac·an·thop·ter·yg·i·an (ak′′n thäp′tə rij′ē ən) *n.* [< ACANTHO- + Gr. *pterygion*, a fin: see PTERO-] any of a superorder or order (Acanthopterygii) of spiny-finned fishes, as the basses, perches, etc.

a·can·thus (ə kan′thəs) *n.*, *pl.* -**thus·es, -thi** (-thī) [L. <

Gr. *akanthos:* see ACANTHO-] **1.** any of a genus (*Acanthus*) of thistlelike plants of the acanthus family with lobed, often spiny leaves and long spikes of white or colored flowers, found in the Mediterranean region **2.** *Archit.* a motif or conventional representation of the leaf of this plant, used esp. on the capitals of Corinthian columns — *adj.* designating a family (Acanthaceae) of plants including bear's-breech or acanthus

a cap·pel·la (ä′ kə pel′ə; *It.* ä′ kä pel′lä) [It., in chapel style < L. *ad*, to, according to + LL. *capella*, CHAPEL] without instrumental accompaniment: said of choral singing

‡**a ca·pric·cio** (ä′ kä prēt′chō) [It. < *a*, at + *capriccio:* see CAPRICE] *Music* at pleasure; at whatever tempo and with whatever expression the performer likes

A·ca·pul·co (ak′ə pool′kō, äk′-) seaport in SW Mexico: a winter resort: pop. 29,000

ac·a·ri·a·sis (ak′ə rī′ə sis) *n.* [ModL.: see ACARID & -ASIS] an infestation with acarids or mites, or the resulting skin disease

ac·a·rid (ak′ə rid) *n.* [< Gr. *akari*, mite < *akarēs*, tiny, lit., too short to cut < *a-*, not + *keirein*, to cut, akin to SHEAR] any of a large order (Acarina) of small arachnids, including the ticks and mites

Ac·ar·na·ni·a (ak′är nā′nē ə) region on the W coast of ancient Greece: with Aetolia, a province (**Aetolia and Acarnania**) of modern Greece

ac·a·roid (ak′ə roid′) *adj.* of or like an acarid

acaroid resin (or **gum**) an alcohol-soluble resin taken from various grass trees, used in varnishes, as a paper coating, etc.

ac·a·rol·o·gy (ak′ə räl′ə jē) *n.* [see ACARID & -LOGY] the scientific study of mites and ticks —**ac′a·rol′o·gist** *n.*

a·car·pel·ous, a·car·pel·lous (ā kär′p′l əs) *adj.* [A-² + CARPEL + -OUS] *Bot.* without carpels

a·car·pous (ā kär′pəs) *adj.* [Gr. *akarpos* < *a-*, without + *karpos*, fruit] *Bot.* bearing no fruit; sterile

a·cat·a·lec·tic (ā kat′ə lek′tik) *adj.* [LL. *acatalecticus* < Gr. *akatalēktos*, incessant < *a-*, without + *katalēgein:* see CATALECTIC] *Prosody* having the full number of syllables, esp. in the final foot, or of metrical feet —*n.* an acatalectic line or verse

a·cau·dal (ā kô′d′l) *adj.* [A-² + CAUDAL] having no tail: also **a·cau·date** (ā kô′dāt)

a·cau·les·cent (ā′kô les′′nt, ak′ô-) *adj.* [A-² + CAULESCENT] *Bot.* having no stem or only a very short stem: also **a·cau·lous** (ā kô′ləs) —**a′cau·les′cence** *n.*

acc. 1. accepted **2.** accompanied **3.** account **4.** accusative

Ac·cad (ak′ad, äk′äd) *same as* AKKAD —**Ac·ca·di·an** (ə kā′dē ən) *adj.*, *n.*

ac·cede (ak sēd′) *vi.* -**ced′ed, -ced′ing** [L. *accedere* < *ad-*, to + *cedere*, to go, yield] **1.** to enter upon the duties (of an office); attain (*to*) **2.** to give assent; give in; agree (*to*) **3.** to become a party (*to* a treaty) between nations —*SYN.* see CONSENT —**ac·ced′ence** *n.* —**ac·ced′er** *n.*

ac·cel·er·an·do (ak sel′ə ran′dō, -rän′-; *It.* ät che′le rän′dō) *adv.*, *adj.* [It., prp. of *accelerare* < L.: see ACCELERATE] *Music*, with gradually quickening tempo

ac·cel·er·ant (ak sel′ər ənt, ak-) *adj.* [L. *accelerans*, prp. of *accelerare:* see ACCELERATE] accelerating —*n.* **1.** something that increases the speed of a process **2.** *Chem. same as* CATALYST

ac·cel·er·ate (ak sel′ə rāt′, ak-) *vt.* -**at′ed, -at′ing** [< L. *acceleratus*, pp. of *accelerare* < *ad-*, to + *celerare*, to hasten < *celer*, swift < IE. base **kel-*, to drive, whence OE. *haldan*, HOLD¹] **1.** to increase the speed of **2.** to cause to develop or progress more quickly **3.** *Physics* to cause a change in the rate of velocity of (a moving body) **4.** to cause to happen sooner —*vi.* to go, progress, or develop faster

ac·cel·er·a·tion (ak sel′ə rā′shən, ak-) *n.* **1.** an accelerating or being accelerated **2.** change in the velocity of a moving body or the rate of such change

acceleration of gravity the acceleration of a freely falling object, caused by the force of gravity: it is expressed in terms of the rate of increase of velocity per second (980.665 cm., or 32.17 ft., per second per second)

ac·cel·er·a·tive (ak sel′ə rāt′iv, ak-) *adj.* of, causing, or increasing acceleration

ac·cel·er·a·tor (-rāt′ər) *n.* **1.** a person or thing that accelerates or increases the speed of something; specif., *a)* a device, such as the foot throttle of an automobile, for increasing the speed of a machine *b)* a nerve or muscle that speeds up a motion **2.** *Chem.* a substance that speeds up a reaction **3.** *Nuclear Physics* a betatron, cyclotron, or similar device that accelerates charged particles to high energies **4.** *Photog.* a chemical that speeds up developing

☆**ac·cel·er·om·e·ter** (ak sel′ə räm′ə tər, ak-) *n.* [ACCELER(ATE) + -o- + -METER] an instrument for measuring acceleration, as of an aircraft, or for detecting vibrations, as in machinery

ac·cent (ak′sent, -s′nt; *for v. also* ak sent′) *n.* [Fr. < L. *accentus* < *ad-*, to + *cantus*, pp. of *canere*, to sing: a L. rendering of Gr. *prosōdia* (see PROSODY), orig. referring to the pitch scheme of Gr. verse] **1.** the emphasis (by stress,

pitch, or both) given to a particular syllable or word in speaking it **2.** a mark used in writing or printing to show the placing and kind of this emphasis, as in the primary (ˊ) and secondary (ˋ) accenting of English (ac·cel′er·a′tor, ac′a·dem′i·cal·ly, etc.) **3.** a mark used to distinguish between various sounds of the same letter [in French there are acute (ˊ), grave (ˋ), and circumflex (ˆ) accents] **4.** the pitch contour of a phrase **5.** tone of the voice; hence **6.** a distinguishing regional or national manner of pronouncing [Irish accent, Southern accent] **7.** [pl.] [Poet.] speech; words; utterance [to speak in accents mild] **8.** a distinguishing style of expression [the accent of Beethoven] **9.** a striking or prominent feature of any artistic composition [the classical accent of a pillar] **10.** an object or detail that lends emphasis, as by contrast with that which surrounds it **11.** special emphasis or attention [to put the accent on highway construction] **12.** a mark used with a number or letter, as in mathematics to indicate a variable (aˊ), or in measurement of length (10′5″, ten feet five inches) or of time (3′16″, three minutes sixteen seconds) **13.** Music a) emphasis or stress on a note or chord b) a mark showing this **14.** Music & Prosody rhythmic stress or beat —vt. **1.** to pronounce (a syllable, word, or phrase) with special stress **2.** to mark with an accent in writing or printing **3.** to stress or emphasize; accentuate

ac·cen·tu·al (ak sen′choo wəl, ək-) adj. [< L. accentus (see ACCENT) + -AL] **1.** of or having to do with accent **2.** having rhythm based on stress rather than on the length of sounds [German poetry is basically accentual] —**ac·cen′tu·al·ly** adv.

ac·cen·tu·ate (ak sen′choo wāt′, ək-) vt. -at′ed, -at′ing [< ML. accentuatus, pp. of accentuare < L. accentus, ACCENT] **1.** to pronounce or mark with an accent or stress **2.** to emphasize; heighten the effect of —**ac·cen′tu·a′tion** n.

ac·cept (ək sept′, ak-) vt. [ME. accepten < OFr. accepter < L. acceptare < accipere < ad-, to + capere, to take] **1.** to take (what is offered or given); receive, esp. willingly **2.** to receive favorably; approve [to accept a theory] **3.** to agree or consent to; acquiesce in [he will not accept defeat] **4.** to believe in **5.** to understand as having a certain meaning **6.** to respond to in the affirmative [to accept an invitation] **7.** to receive (a committee report) as satisfactory according to parliamentary procedure **8.** Business to agree, as by a signed promise, to pay (a bill or draft) **9.** Law to receive with intent to retain and adopt —vi. to accept something offered —**SYN.** see RECEIVE —**ac·cept′er** n.

ac·cept·a·ble (ək sep′tə b'l, ak-) adj. worth accepting; satisfactory or, sometimes, merely adequate —**ac·cept′a·bil′i·ty, ac·cept′a·ble·ness** n. —**ac·cept′a·bly** adv.

ac·cept·ance (ək sep′təns, ak-) n. **1.** an accepting or being accepted **2.** approving reception; approval; acceptability **3.** belief in; assent **4.** an unconditional written order to pay a certain sum of money at a set future time: it is signed by the party to whom the money is to be paid and becomes effective when signed by the party who is to pay: cf. BANK ACCEPTANCE, TRADE ACCEPTANCE **5.** Law an express or implied act by which one accepts an obligation, offer, contract, etc. together with all its legal consequences

ac·cept·ant (-tənt) adj. readily accepting; receptive

ac·cep·ta·tion (ak′sep tā′shən) n. [LL. acceptatio: see ACCEPT] **1.** the generally accepted meaning (of a word or expression) **2.** [Archaic] acceptance

ac·cept·ed (ək sep′tid, ak-) adj. generally regarded as true, valid, proper, etc.; conventional; approved

ac·cep·tor (ək sep′tər, ak-) n. [L.] **1.** one who accepts; specif., a person who signs a promise to pay a draft or bill of exchange **2.** Electronics an impurity, as gallium, boron, etc., whose atoms in a semiconductor ostensibly produce positive, mobile charges while remaining bound in the crystal structure with unit negative charge

ac·cess (ak′ses) n. [ME. & OFr. acces < L. accessus, pp. of accedere: see ACCEDE] **1.** the act of coming toward or near to; approach **2.** a way or means of approaching, getting, using, etc. **3.** the right to enter, approach, or use; admittance **4.** increase or growth **5.** an outburst; paroxysm [an access of anger] **6.** the onset (of a disease); attack

ac·ces·sa·ry (ək ses′ə rē, ak-) adj., n., pl. -ries same as ACCESSORY

ac·ces·si·ble (ək ses′ə b'l, ak-) adj. [< LL. accessibilis < L. accessus, ACCESS] **1.** that can be approached or entered **2.** easy to approach or enter **3.** that can be got; obtainable **4.** open to the influence of (with to) [he is not accessible to pity] —**ac·ces′si·bil′i·ty, ac·ces′si·ble·ness** n. —**ac·ces′si·bly** adv.

ac·ces·sion (ak sesh′ən, ək-) n. [Fr. < L. accessio < accessus, ACCESS] **1.** the act of coming to or attaining (a throne, power, etc.) [the accession of a new king] **2.** assent; agreement **3.** a) increase by addition b) an item added, as to a library or museum **4.** an outburst; paroxysm; access **5.** Law a) addition to property by improvements or natural growth b) the owner's right to the increase in value due to such additions —☆vt. to record (a book, etc.) as a new accession —**ac·ces′sion·al** adj.

ac·ces·so·ri·al (ak′sə sôr′ē əl) adj. [< ML. accessorius (see ACCESSORY) + -AL] of or like an accessory; supplementary

ac·ces·so·ry (ək ses′ə rē, ak-) adj. [ML. accessorius < L. accessus, pp. of accedere, ACCEDE] **1.** extra; additional; helping in a secondary or subordinate way **2.** Geol.

occurring infrequently or in negligible amounts in a specified rock; accidental or nonessential [accessory minerals are disregarded in classifying rocks] **3.** Law acting as an accessory; helping in an unlawful act —n., pl. -ries [ME. accessorie < ML.: see the adj.] **1.** something extra; thing added to help in a secondary way; specif., a) an article worn or carried to complete one's costume, as purse, gloves, etc. b) a piece of optional equipment for convenience, comfort, appearance, etc. [the accessories of an automobile] **2.** Law a person who, though absent, helps another to break or escape the law; accomplice —**accessory before** (or **after**) **the fact** a person who, though absent at the commission of a felony, aids or abets the accused before (or after) its commission

accessory fruit a fruit (often classified botanically as a false fruit) having enlarged accessory structures in addition to those formed from the ovary, as the strawberry, in which the fleshy tissue is the enlarged receptacle and the true fruits are the small, dry achenes borne on its surface

☆**access time** in computers, a) the interval of time between the moment when data is requested from a storage unit and the moment when it is delivered b) the interval of time between the moment when data is presented for storage and the moment when storage is completed

‡**ac·ciac·ca·tu·ra** (ät chäk′kä tōō′rä; E. ə chäk′ə tur′ə) n. [It. < acciaccare, to crush < accia, ax < L. ascia: see AX] Music a short grace note sounded together with the principal note or chord, but quickly released: it is shown as a small eighth note with a diagonal line through the stem

ac·ci·dence (ak′sə dəns) n. [ME. accidens, inflection < L. accidentia, that which happens < accidens: see ACCIDENT: cf. CASE¹] **1.** the part of grammar that deals with the inflection of words **2.** the elementary or first parts of a subject; rudiments

ac·ci·dent (ak′sə dənt) n. [ME. < OFr. < L. accidens, prp. of accidere, to fall upon, happen < ad-, to + cadere, to fall] **1.** a happening that is not expected, foreseen, or intended **2.** an unpleasant and unintended happening, sometimes resulting from negligence, that results in injury, loss, damage, etc. **3.** fortune; chance [to meet by accident] **4.** an attribute or quality that is not essential **5.** Geog. & Geol. an irregular formation **6.** Law an unforeseen event that occurs without anyone's fault or negligence

ac·ci·den·tal (ak′sə den′t'l) adj. [ME. < LL. accidentalis: see ACCIDENT] **1.** happening by chance; fortuitous **2.** belonging but not essential; attributive; incidental **3.** Music of an accidental —n. **1.** a nonessential quality or attribute **2.** Music a) a sign, as a sharp, flat, or natural, placed before a note to show a change of pitch from that indicated by the key signature b) the tone indicated by such a sign —**ac′ci·den′tal·ly** adv.

SYN.—**accidental** describes that which occurs by chance [an accidental encounter] or outside the normal course of events [an accidental attribute]; **fortuitous**, which frequently suggests a complete absence of cause, now usually refers to chance events of a fortunate nature; **casual** describes the unpremeditated, random, informal, or irregular quality of something [a casual visit, remark, dress, etc.]; **incidental** emphasizes the nonessential or secondary nature of something [an incidental consideration]; **adventitious** refers to that which is added extrinsically and connotes a lack of essential connection

accident insurance insurance against injury due to accident

ac·ci·dent-prone (ak′sə dənt prōn′) adj. having an apparent tendency or inclination to become involved in accidents —**ac′ci·dent-prone′ness** n.

ac·ci·die (ak′sə dē), **ac·cid·i·a** (ak sid′ē ə) n. same as ACEDIA

ac·cip·i·ter (ak sip′ə tər) n. [L. < *acupeter, swift-winged < IE. base *acu-, swift + *peter, wing: cf. PTERO-] **1.** any of a genus (Accipiter) of small hawks with short wings and long tails, as Cooper's hawk **2.** any hawk, falcon, eagle, or other bird of prey except the owl —**ac·cip′i·trine** (-ə trin) adj., n.

ac·claim (ə klām′) vt. [L. acclamare < ad-, to + clamare, to cry out] **1.** to greet with loud approval; applaud **2.** to announce or acknowledge with applause; hail [they acclaimed him president] —vi. to shout approval —n. loud applause, approval, or welcome —**SYN.** see PRAISE —**ac·claim′er** n.

ac·cla·ma·tion (ak′lə mā′shən) n. [L. acclamatio, a shouting: see ACCLAIM] **1.** an acclaiming or being acclaimed **2.** loud applause, approval, or welcome **3.** a vote by voice; esp., an enthusiastic approving vote without an actual count [elected by acclamation] —**ac·clam·a·to·ry** (ə klam′ə tôr′ē) adj.

ac·cli·mate (ak′lə māt′, ə klī′mət) vt., vi. -mat′ed, -mat′ing [Fr. acclimater: see AD- & CLIMATE] to accustom or become accustomed to a different climate, environment, or circumstances, as by physiological or psychological changes —**ac′cli·ma′tion** n.

ac·cli·ma·tize (ə klī′mə tīz′) vt., vi. -tized′, -tiz′ing same as ACCLIMATE —**ac·cli′ma·ti·za′tion** n.

ac·cliv·i·ty (ə kliv′ə tē) n., pl. -ties [L. acclinitas < acclivis, uphill < ad-, up + clivus, hill < IE. root *klei-, to incline: see DECLINE] an upward slope of ground: opposed to DECLIVITY

ac·cli·vous (ə klī′vəs) adj. [L. acclivus, var. of acclivis: see ACCLIVITY] sloping upward

ac·co·lade (ak′ə lād′, ak′ə lād′) *n.* [Fr. < Pr. *acolada* < It. *accollata*, fem. pp. of *accollare*, to embrace < L. *ad*, to + *collum*, neck] 1. an embrace formerly used in conferring knighthood 2. a touch on the shoulder with the flat side of a sword, now used in conferring knighthood 3. anything done or given as a sign of great respect, approval, appreciation, etc. 4. *Music* a vertical line joining two or more staffs

ac·com·mo·date (ə käm′ə dāt′) *vt.* **-dat′ed, -dat′ing** [< L. *accommodatus*, pp. of *accommodare* < *ad-*, to + *commodare*, to fit < *commodus*: see COMMODE] 1. to make fit; adjust; adapt [to *accommodate* oneself to changes] 2. to reconcile (differences) 3. to help by supplying (*with* something) 4. to do a service or favor for 5. to have space for [a table to *accommodate* six diners] 6. to provide lodging for —*vi.* to become adjusted, as the lens of the eye in focusing on objects at various distances —*SYN.* see ADAPT, CONTAIN —ac·com′mo·dat′ive *adj.* —ac·com′mo·da′tor *n.*

ac·com·mo·dat·ing (-dāt′iŋ) *adj.* willing to please; ready to help; obliging —ac·com′mo·dat′ing·ly *adv.*

ac·com·mo·da·tion (ə käm′ə dā′shən) *n.* 1. an accommodating or being accommodated; adaptation (*to* a purpose); adjustment 2. reconciliation of differences 3. willingness to do favors or services 4. a help or convenience 5. [*pl.*] lodgings; room and board 6. [*pl.*] traveling space, as in a railroad train or airplane; seat, berth, etc. 7. the self-adjustment of the lens of the eye for focusing on objects at various distances 8. the act of making or endorsing an accommodation paper

accommodation ladder a ladder or stairway hung over a ship's side, usually at the gangway

accommodation paper (or **bill** or **note**) a bill of exchange cosigned by one party as maker, acceptor, or endorser without requiring collateral or a fee, in order to lend his credit reputation to the second party

☆**accommodation train** a railroad train that stops at all or nearly all stations

ac·com·pa·ni·ment (ə kump′ni mənt, ə kum′pə nē mənt) *n.* 1. anything that accompanies something else; thing added, usually for order or symmetry 2. *Music* a part, usually instrumental, performed together with the main part for richer effect [the piano *accompaniment* to a song]

ac·com·pa·nist (ə kum′pə nist) *n.* a person who plays or sings an accompaniment: also **ac·com′pa·ny·ist** (-nē ist)

ac·com·pa·ny (ə kum′pə nē, ə kump′nē) *vt.* **-nied, -ny·ing** [MFr. *acompaignier* < *ac-*, to + OFr. *compagnon*: see COMPANION[1]] 1. to go or be together with; attend 2. to send (*with*); add to; supplement [to *accompany* words with acts] 3. to play or sing a musical accompaniment for or to —*vi.* to perform a musical accompaniment

SYN.—**accompany** means to go or be together with as a companion, associate, attribute, etc., and usually connotes equality of relationship [he *accompanied* her to the theater]; **attend** implies presence either in a subordinate position or to render services, etc. [Dr. Jones *attended* the patient]; **escort** and **convoy** are both applied to the accompanying, as by an armed guard, of persons or things needing protection (**convoy**, esp. in the case of sea travel and **escort**, in the case of land travel); **escort** also implies an accompanying as a mark of honor or an act of courtesy; **chaperon** implies accompaniment, for reasons of propriety, of young unmarried people by an older or married person

ac·com·plice (ə käm′plis) *n.* [< ME. *a complice* (the article *a* is merged, after *accomplish*) < OFr. *complice* < LL. *complex*, accomplice: see COMPLEX] a person who knowingly participates with another in an unlawful act; partner in crime —*SYN.* see ASSOCIATE

ac·com·plish (ə käm′plish, -kum′-) *vt.* [ME. *accomplisshen* < OFr. *accompliss-*, extended stem of *acomplir* < VL. *adcomplere* < L. *ad-*, intens. + *complere*: see COMPLETE] 1. to do; succeed in doing; complete (a task, time, or distance) 2. to make complete; perfect —*SYN.* see PERFORM, REACH —ac·com′plish·a·ble *adj.*

ac·com·plished (-plisht) *adj.* 1. done; done successfully; completed 2. skilled; proficient [an *accomplished* pianist] 3. trained in the social arts and manners; polished

ac·com·plish·ment (-plish mənt) *n.* 1. an accomplishing or being accomplished; completion 2. something accomplished or done successfully; work completed; achievement 3. a social art or skill: *usually used in pl.*

ac·cord (ə kôrd′) *vt.* [ME. *acorden* < OFr. *acorder* < VL. *adcordare* < L. *ad-*, to + *cor* (gen. *cordis*), HEART] 1. to make agree or harmonize; reconcile 2. to grant or concede; bestow —*vi.* to be in agreement or harmony (*with*) —*n.* 1. mutual agreement; harmony 2. an informal agreement, as between countries 3. harmony of sound, color, etc. 4. [Obs.] consent; permission —*SYN.* see AGREE —of one's own accord willingly, without being asked —with one accord all agreeing; with no one dissenting

ac·cord·ance (-'ns) *n.* [ME. < OFr. *accordance* < *acordant*: see ACCORDANT] 1. agreement; harmony; conformity [in *accordance* with the plans] 2. the act of granting

ac·cord·ant (-'nt) *adj.* [ME. < OFr. *acordant*, prp. of *acorder*: see ACCORD] in agreement or harmony (*with* or *to*) —ac·cord′ant·ly *adv.*

ac·cord·ing (-iŋ) *adj.* agreeing; in harmony —*adv.* accordingly —**according as** 1. to the degree that; in proportion

as 2. depending on whether; if —**according to** 1. in agreement with 2. in the order of [arranged *according to* size] 3. as stated in or reported by

ac·cord·ing·ly (-iŋ lē) *adv.* 1. in a way that is fitting and proper; correspondingly 2. therefore

ac·cor·di·on (ə kôr′dē ən) *n.* [G. *akkordion* (prob. < It. *accordare*, to be in tune: see ACCORD + *-ion* as in CLARION): coined (1829)] a musical instrument with keys, metal reeds, and a bellows: it is played by alternately pulling out and pressing together the bellows to force air through the reeds, which are opened by fingering the keys —*adj.* having folds, or folding, like the bellows of an accordion [*accordion* pleats] **ac·cor′di·on·ist** *n.*

ACCORDION

ac·cost (ə kôst′, -käst′) *vt.* [Fr. *accoster* < It. *accostare*, to bring side by side < VL. *adcostare* < L. *ad-*, to + *costa*, rib, side] 1. to approach and speak to; greet first, before being greeted, esp. in an intrusive way 2. to solicit for sexual purposes: said of a prostitute, etc.

ac·couche·ment (ə kōōsh′mənt; Fr. ä kōōsh män′) *n.* [Fr. < *accoucher*, put to bed, give birth < OFr. *acoucher*, lie down < L. *ad-*, to + *collocare*: see COUCH] confinement for giving birth to a child; childbirth

ac·cou·cheur (a′kōō shur′; Fr. ä kōō shër′) *n.* [Fr.: see ACCOUCHEMENT] a doctor who attends childbirth cases; male midwife or obstetrician

ac·cou·cheuse (-shooz′; Fr. -shöz′) *n.* [Fr., fem. of ACCOUCHEUR] a midwife

ac·count (ə kount′) *vt.* [ME. *acounten* < OFr. *aconter* < *a-*, to + *conter*, to tell < L. *computare*: see COMPUTE] to consider or judge to be; deem; value —*vi.* 1. to furnish a reckoning (*to* someone) of money received and paid out. 2. to make satisfactory amends (*for*) [he will *account* for his crime] 3. to give satisfactory reasons or an explanation (*for*) [can he *account* for his actions?] 4. to be the cause, agent, or source of (with *for*) 5. to do away with as by killing (with *for*) [he *accounted* for five of the enemy] —*n.* 1. a counting; calculation 2. [*often pl.*] a record of the financial data pertaining to a specific asset, liability, income item, expense item, or net-worth item 3. *same as* BANK ACCOUNT 4. *a*) a record of the financial transactions relating to a specific person, property, business, etc. *b*) *same as* CHARGE ACCOUNT *c*) a business or firm that is a customer or client, esp. on a regular, credit basis [one of our best *accounts*] 5. worth; importance [a thing of small *account*] 6. an explanation 7. a report; description; story —**call to account** 1. to demand an explanation of 2. to reprimand —**give a good account of oneself** to acquit oneself creditably —**on account** 1. on a charge account; on the installment plan 2. as partial payment —**on (someone's) account** for (someone's) sake —**on account of** 1. because of 2. for (someone's) sake —**on no account** not under any circumstances —**take account of** 1. to take into consideration; allow for 2. to take notice; note —**take into account** to take into consideration —**turn to account** to get use or profit from

ac·count·a·ble (ə koun′tə b'l) *adj.* 1. obliged to account for one's acts; responsible 2. capable of being accounted for; explainable —*SYN.* see RESPONSIBLE —ac·count′a·bil′i·ty (-bil′ə tē), ac·count′a·ble·ness *n.* —ac·count′a·bly *adv.*

ac·count·an·cy (ə koun′t'n sē) *n.* the keeping or inspecting of commercial accounts; work of an accountant

ac·count·ant (ə kount′'nt) *n.* a person whose work is to inspect, keep, or adjust accounts: see CERTIFIED PUBLIC ACCOUNTANT

account book a book in which business accounts are set down

account current a record of business transactions that shows the total amount of money owed as of the date of the summarizing statement

account executive an executive in an advertising agency or similar organization who supervises the organization's accounts, maintaining direct contact with established clients and acquiring new ones

ac·count·ing (ə koun′tiŋ) *n.* 1. the principles or practice of systematically recording, presenting, and interpreting financial accounts 2. a statement of debits and credits 3. a settling or balancing of accounts

ac·cou·ple·ment (ə kup′'l mənt) *n.* [Fr. < *accoupler*, to couple up < OFr. *acoupler* < ML. *accopulare* < L. *ad-*, to + *copulare*, to COUPLE] 1. Archit. the placing of columns in pairs close together 2. Carpentry a brace or tie of timber

ac·cou·ter (ə kōōt′ər) *vt.* [Fr. *accoutrer*, earlier *accoustrer*; prob. < *à-*, to + OFr. *costure* < VL. *consutura*, seam, sewing < L. *consuere*, to sew < *con-*, together + *suere*: see SEW] to outfit; equip, esp. for military service

ac·cou·ter·ment, ac·cou·tre·ment (ə kōōt′ər mənt, -kōō′trə-) *n.* 1. an accoutering or being accoutered 2. [*pl.*]

a) personal outfit; clothes; dress *b)* a soldier's equipment except clothes and weapons

ac·cou·tre (ə kōōt′ər) *vt.* **-tred** (-ərd), **-tring** (ə kōōt′ər iŋ, -kōō′triŋ) *same as* ACCOUTER

Ac·cra (ə krä′) capital of Ghana, on the Gulf of Guinea: pop. 491,000

ac·cred·it (ə kred′it) *vt.* [Fr. *accréditer*, to give credit or authority < *à*, to + *crédit*: see CREDIT] **1.** to bring into credit or favor **2.** to authorize; give credentials to [an *accredited* representative] **3.** to believe in; take as true **4.** to certify as meeting certain set standards [colleges may be *accredited* by regional associations] **5.** to attribute; credit [an action *accredited* to him] —*SYN.* see AUTHORIZE —**ac·cred′it·a′tion** (-ə tā′shən) *n.*

ac·crete (ə krēt′) *vi.* **-cret′ed, -cret′ing** [< L. *accretus,* pp. of *accrescere:* see ACCRETION] **1.** to grow by being added to **2.** to grow together; adhere —*vt.* to cause to adhere or unite (*to*) —*adj. Bot.* grown together

ac·cre·tion (ə krē′shən) *n.* [L. *accretio* < *accrescere,* to increase < *ad-,* to + *crescere,* to grow: see CRESCENT] **1.** growth in size, esp. by addition or accumulation **2.** a growing together of parts normally separate **3.** accumulated matter [the *accretion* of earth on the shore] **4.** a part added separately; addition **5.** a whole resulting from such growth or accumulation **6.** *Law* the addition of soil to land by gradual, natural deposits —**ac·cre′tive** (-tiv) *adj.*

ac·cru·al (ə krōō′əl) *n.* **1.** the act or process of accruing **2.** the amount that accrues: also **ac·crue′ment**

ac·crue (ə krōō′) *vi.* **-crued′, -cru′ing** [ME. *acreuen* < OFr. *acreu,* pp. of *acroistre,* increase < L. *accrescere:* see ACCRETION] **1.** to come as a natural growth, advantage, or right (*to*) **2.** to be added periodically as an increase: said esp. of interest on money

acct. account

☆**ac·cul·tu·rate** (ə kul′chə rāt′) *vi., vt.* **-rat′ed, -rat′ing** [back-formation < *acculturation*] to undergo, or alter by, acculturation

☆**ac·cul·tu·ra·tion** (ə kul′chə rā′shən) *n.* [AC- + CULTUR(E) + -ATION] *Sociology* **1.** the process of conditioning a child to the patterns or customs of a culture **2.** the process of becoming adapted to a new or different culture with more or less advanced patterns **3.** the mutual influence of different cultures in close contact —**ac·cul′tu·ra·tive** *adj.*

ac·cum·bent (ə kum′bənt) *adj.* [L. *accumbens,* prp. of *accumbere* < *ad-,* to + *cubare,* to recline] **1.** lying down **2.** *Bot.* lying against some other part —**ac·cum′ben·cy** *n.*

ac·cu·mu·late (ə kyōōm′yə lāt′) *vt., vi.* **-lat′ed, -lat′ing** [< L. *accumulatus,* pp. of *accumulare* < *ad-,* to + *cumulare,* to heap: see CUMULUS] to pile up, collect, or gather together, esp. over a period of time —**ac·cu′mu·la·ble** (-lə b'l) *adj.*

ac·cu·mu·la·tion (ə kyōōm′yə lā′shən) *n.* **1.** an accumulating or being accumulated; collection **2.** accumulated or collected material; heap **3.** the addition to capital of interest or profits

ac·cu·mu·la·tive (ə kyōōm′yə lāt′iv, -lət-) *adj.* **1.** resulting from accumulation; cumulative **2.** tending to accumulate **3.** acquisitive —**ac·cu′mu·la·tive·ly** *adv.* —**ac·cu′mu·la′tive·ness** *n.*

ac·cu·mu·la·tor (-lāt′ər) *n.* [L.] **1.** a person or thing that accumulates **2.** an apparatus that collects and stores energy; specif., [Brit.] a storage battery **3.** a type of shock absorber **4.** a device or circuit unit combining one or more of the functions of storage, arithmetic, and control, as in a computer, cash register, etc.

ac·cu·ra·cy (ak′yər ə sē) *n.* the quality or state of being accurate or exact; precision; exactness

ac·cu·rate (ak′yər it) *adj.* [L. *accuratus,* pp. of *accurare* < *ad-,* to + *curare,* to take care < *cura,* care] **1.** careful and exact **2.** free from mistakes or errors; precise **3.** adhering closely to a standard [an *accurate* thermometer] —*SYN.* see CORRECT —**ac′cu·rate·ly** *adv.* —**ac′cu·rate·ness** *n.*

ac·curs·ed (ə kur′sid, -kurst′) *adj.* [ME. *acursed,* pp. of *acursen,* pronounce a curse upon, excommunicate < *a-* + *cursien:* see CURSE] **1.** under a curse; ill-fated **2.** deserving to be cursed; damnable; abominable —**ac·curs′ed·ly** *adv.* —**ac·curs′ed·ness** *n.*

ac·curst (ə kurst′) *adj. same as* ACCURSED

ac·cus·al (ə kyōō′z'l) *n. same as* ACCUSATION

ac·cu·sa·tion (ak′yə zā′shən) *n.* **1.** an accusing or being accused **2.** the crime or wrong of which a person is accused

ac·cu·sa·ti·val (ə kyōō′zə tī′v'l) *adj.* of the accusative case

ac·cu·sa·tive (ə kyōō′zə tiv) *adj.* [ME. *acusatif* < L. *accusativus* < *accusare:* see ACCUSE: L. mistranslation of Gr. grammatical term correctly rendered *causativus,* causative, by Priscian: the goal or terminating point of an action was orig. considered to be its cause] **1.** *Linguis.* designating, of, or in the case expressing the goal of an action or motion, as, in Latin grammar, the case occurring in the direct object of a verb and after certain prepositions: also sometimes used of the objective case in English **2.** accusatory —*n.* **1.** the accusative case **2.** a word in this case —**ac·cu′sa·tive·ly** *adv.*

ac·cu·sa·to·ri·al (ə kyōō′zə tôr′ē əl) *adj.* [L. *accusatorius:* see ACCUSE] of, or in the manner of, an accuser

ac·cu·sa·to·ry (ə kyōō′zə tôr′ē) *adj.* making or containing an accusation; accusing

ac·cuse (ə kyōōz′) *vt.* **ac·cused′, ac·cus′ing** [ME. *acusen* < OFr. *acuser* < L. *accusare,* to call to account < *ad-,* to +

causa, a cause, case, or lawsuit] **1.** to find at fault; blame **2.** to bring formal charges against (*of* doing wrong, breaking the law, etc.) —**the accused** *Law* the person who is formally charged with commission of a crime —**ac·cus′er** *n.* —**ac·cus′ing·ly** *adv.*

SYN.—**accuse** is used with reference to finding fault for offenses of varying gravity [to *accuse* one of murder, to *accuse* one of carelessness]; **charge** usually implies an accusation of a legal or formal nature; **indict** describes the action of a grand jury, etc. in finding a case against a person and ordering him brought to trial; **arraign** refers to the actual process of calling the person before the court and informing him of the charges against him; **impeach** is applied to charging a public official with misconduct of office, but in nonlegal usage denotes a challenging of a person's motives, etc.

ac·cus·tom (ə kus′təm) *vt.* [ME. *accustomen* < OFr. *acostumer* < *a-,* to + *costume:* see CUSTOM] to make familiar by custom, habit, or use; habituate (*to*)

ac·cus·tomed (ə kus′təmd) *adj.* **1.** customary; usual; characteristic [he spoke with *accustomed* ease] **2.** wont or used (*to*); in the habit of [*accustomed* to obeying orders] —*SYN.* see USUAL

ace (ās) *n.* [ME. *as, aas* < L. *as,* unit, unity] **1.** a unit "one" in dice, playing cards, or dominoes **2.** a playing card, domino, etc. marked with one spot **3.** *a)* a score made by a serve, as in tennis, that one's opponent is unable to return *b)* such a serve **4.** the act of getting a golf ball into a hole on the drive from the tee; hole in one **5.** a combat pilot who has destroyed a number of enemy planes **6.** an expert in any activity —*adj.* [Colloq.] first-rate; expert [an *ace* salesman] —*vt.* **aced** (āst), **ac′ing 1.** to score an ace against, as in tennis **2.** to score an ace on (a particular hole) in golf —**within an ace of** on the verge of; very close to

-a·ce·a (ā′shə, ā′shē ə) [L., neut. pl. of *-aceus*] a plural suffix used in forming the zoological names of classes or orders: see -ACEOUS

-a·ce·ae (ā′ri ē′) [L., fem. pl. of *-aceus*] a plural suffix used in forming botanical names of families: see -ACEOUS

a·ce·di·a (ə sē′dē ə) *n.* [LL. < Gr. *akēdia* < *a-,* not + *kēdos,* care: see HATE] spiritual sloth and indifference

☆**ace-high** (ās′hī′) *adj.* [orig. a poker term for a hand containing an ace, esp. as completing a straight] [Colloq.] held in high esteem; respected

☆**ace in the hole 1.** *Stud Poker* an ace dealt and kept face down until the deal is over **2.** [Slang] any advantage held in reserve until needed

A·cel·da·ma (ə sel′də mə) [L. < Gr. *Akeldama* < Aram. *haḳol demā′,* field of blood] *Bible* the field near Jerusalem bought with the money given Judas for betraying Jesus: Acts 1:19; Matt. 27:8 —*n.* a place of bloodshed

a·cen·tric (ā sen′trik) *adj.* having no center; off-center

-a·ceous (ā′shəs) [L. *-aceus*] *an adj.-forming suffix meaning* of the nature of, like, belonging to, producing, or characterized by [*herbaceous*]: often used to form adjectives corresponding to zoological and botanical nouns ending in -ACEA, -ACEAE

a·ceph·a·lous (ā sef′ə ləs) *adj.* [LL. *acephalus* < Gr. *akephalos* < *a-,* without + *kephalē,* head] **1.** headless; specif., *Zool.* having no part of the body differentiated as the head **2.** having no leader

☆**a·ce·qui·a** (ə säk′yə, -sä′kē ə) *n.* [Sp. < Ar.] in the Southwest, an irrigation canal

ac·er·ate (as′ə rāt′, -ər it) *adj.* [L. *aceratus,* needlelike < *acus* (gen. *aceris*), a pin, needle] *Bot.* needle-shaped

a·cerb (ə surb′) *adj.* [Fr. *acerbe* < L *acerbus,* bitter] **1.** sour in taste **2.** sharp, bitter, or harsh in temper, language, etc.

ac·er·bate (as′ər bāt′) *vt.* **-bat′ed, -bat′ing** [< L. *acerbatus,* pp. of *acerbare,* to make harsh or bitter] **1.** to make sour or bitter **2.** to irritate; vex

a·cer·bi·ty (ə sur′bə tē) *n., pl.* **-ties** [Fr. *acerbité* < L. *acerbitas* < *acerbus,* bitter < IE. base **ak-:* see ACID] **1.** a sour, astringent quality **2.** sharpness, bitterness, or harshness of temper, words, etc.

ac·er·ose[1] (as′ə rōs′) *adj.* [< L. *acus* (gen. *aceris*), a needle < IE. base **ak-* (see ACID); form infl. by next entry] *Bot.* shaped like a needle; having a sharp, stiff point: see LEAF FORMS, illus.

ac·er·ose[2] (as′ə rōs′) *adj.* [L. *acerosus,* full of chaff < *acus* (gen. *aceris*): see EAR[2]] **1.** like chaff **2.** mixed with chaff

a·cer·vate (ə sur′vat, as′ər vāt′) *adj.* [L. *acervatus,* pp. of *acervate,* to heap up < *acervus,* heap] *Bot.* growing in tight clusters or heaps —**a·cer′vate·ly** *adv.*

a·ces·cent (ə ses′′nt) *adj.* [Fr. < L. *acescens,* prp. of *acescere,* to turn sour < *acere:* see ACETO-] becoming sour; likely to sour —**a·ces′cence** *n.*

a·cet- (ə sēt′, -set′; as′it) *same as* ACETO-

ac·e·tab·u·lum (as′ə tab′yoo ləm) *n., pl.* **-la** (-lə), **-lums** [L., orig. vinegar cup < *acetum:* see ACETO-] **1.** *Anat.* the cup-shaped socket of the hipbone, into which the thighbone fits **2.** *Zool. a)* a sucker of a leech, octopus, etc. *b)* the socket into which an insect's leg fits —**ac′e·tab′u·lar** (-lər) *adj.*

ac·e·tal (as′ə tal′) *n.* [ACET- + -AL] a colorless, slightly soluble, volatile liquid, $CH_3CH(OC_2H_5)_2$, formed by the imperfect oxidation of alcohol and used in medicine as a hypnotic

ac·et·al·de·hyde (as′ə tal′də hīd′) *n.* [ACET- + ALDEHYDE] a colorless, soluble, volatile liquid, CH_3CHO, used as a solvent and in making various organic compounds: it has a sharp odor and is extremely flammable

ac·et·am·ide (as'ə tam'īd, -id; ə set'ə mīd') *n.* [ACET- + AMIDE] a white, crystalline organic substance, CH_3CONH_2, the amide of acetic acid: it is used in the preparation of lacquers and explosives and in many organic syntheses

ac·et·an·i·lide (as'ə tan'ə lid', -'l id) *n.* [ACET- + ANIL-(INE) + -IDE] a white, crystalline organic substance, $CH_3CONHC_6H_5$, produced by the action of acetic acid on aniline: used as a drug to lessen pain and fever

ac·e·tate (as'ə tāt') *n.* [ACET- + -ATE²] 1. a salt or ester of acetic acid 2. *same as* CELLULOSE ACETATE 3. an article or material made with an acetate or with cellulose acetate

ac·e·tat·ed (-id) *adj.* treated with acetic acid

a·ce·tic (ə sēt'ik, -set'-) *adj.* [< L. *acetum*: see ACETO-] of, like, containing, or producing acetic acid or vinegar

acetic acid a sour, colorless, liquid compound, CH_3COOH, having a sharp odor: it is found in vinegar and is used with alcohols to produce esters used as paint solvents

acetic anhydride a colorless liquid, $C_4H_6O_3$, decomposable by water to acetic acid, used as a reagent in organic synthesis

a·cet·i·fy (ə set'ə fī', -sēt'-) *vt., vi.* -fied', -fy'ing to change into vinegar or acetic acid —a·cet·i·fi·ca'tion *n.*

ac·e·tim·e·ter (as'ə tim'ə tər) *n. same as* ACETOMETER

ac·e·tin (as'ə t'n) *n.* [ACET- + -IN¹] a thick, colorless liquid, $C_3H_5(OH)_2COCCH_3$, soluble in water; glyceryl monoacetate: it is used in making dynamite and as a solvent

ac·e·to- (ə sēt'ō, as'ə tō') [< L. *acetum*, vinegar < pp. of *acere*, to be sour < IE. base *ak-: see ACID] a combining form meaning of, or from, acetic acid

ac·e·tom·e·ter (as'ə täm'ə tər) *n.* an instrument used to find the amount of acetic acid in a definite quantity of vinegar or other liquid

ac·e·tone (as'ə tōn') *n.* [ACET- + -ONE] a colorless, flammable, volatile liquid, CH_3COCH_3, used as a paint remover and as a solvent for certain oils and other organic compounds: it also occurs in the urine, esp. in diabetes —ac'e·ton'ic (-tän'ik) *adj.*

acetone body a ketone body

ac·e·to·phe·net·i·din (ə set'ō fə net'ə din) *n.* [ACETO- + PHENETIDIN(E)] a white, crystalline powder, $CH_3CONHC_6H_4OC_2H_5$, used to reduce fever and to relieve headaches and muscular pains; phenacetin: also **a·ce'to·phen'e·tide'** (-fen'ə tīd')

ac·e·tous (as'ə təs, ə sēt'əs) *adj.* [ACET- + -OUS] of, producing, or like vinegar; sour: also **ac'e·tose'** (-tōs')

a·ce·tum (ə sēt'əm) *n.* [L.: see ACETO-] *Pharmacy* vinegar or a solution of a drug in dilute acetic acid

ac·e·tyl (ə sēt'l, as'ə t'l) *n.* the radical CH_3CO, derived from acetic acid: found only in compounds —ac·e·tyl·ic (as'ə til'ik) *adj.*

ac·et·y·late (ə set''l āt', -sēt'-) *vt.* -lat'ed, -lat'ing to combine an acetyl radical with (an organic compound) —a·cet'y·la'tion *n.*

ac·e·tyl·cho·line (as'ə t'l kō'lēn) *n.* [ACETYL + CHOLINE] an alkaloid, $C_7H_{17}O_3N$, extracted from ergot and used in medicine to lower blood pressure and increase peristalsis: it is formed naturally in body tissues and is important in the transmission of nerve impulses

a·cet·y·lene (ə set''l ēn') *n.* [ACETYL + -ENE] a colorless, poisonous, highly flammable gaseous hydrocarbon, $CH:CH$, produced by the reaction of water and calcium carbide: it is used as the starting material in the synthesis of many organic compounds, for lighting, and as a fuel with oxygen to produce a hot flame, as in a blowtorch

acetyl promazine an orange-colored oil, $C_{19}H_{22}N_2OS$, used as a tranquilizer and to relieve nausea

ac·e·tyl·sal·i·cyl·ic acid (ə set''l sal'ə sil'ik, as'ə t'l-) aspirin

ace·y-deuc·y (ās'ē dōōs'ē) *n.* [< ACE + DEUCE¹] a variation of the game of backgammon

A·chae·a (ə kē'ə) ancient province in the N Peloponnesus

A·chae·an (ə kē'ən) *adj.* 1. of Achaea, its people, or its culture 2. loosely, Greek —*n.* 1. a native or inhabitant of Achaea 2. loosely, a Greek

A·chai·a (ə kā'ə, -kī'-) 1. *same as* ACHAEA 2. smaller province of modern Greece —A·chai'an *adj., n.*

A·cha·tes (ə kāt'ēz) in Virgil's *Aeneid*, a loyal companion of Aeneas —*n.* a loyal friend

ache (āk) *vi.* ached, ach'ing [orig. *ake* < ME. *aken* < OE. *acan*, akin to LowG. *äken*, to smart & MDu. *akel*, sorrow, shame < IE. base *agos-*, fault, guilt, sin: sp. *ache* through confusion with the *n.*] 1. to have or give dull, steady pain 2. to feel sympathy, pity, etc. (*for*) 3. [Colloq.] to yearn or long: with *for* or an infinitive —*n.* (āk; *before 1700*, āch) [ME. < OE. *ece*, *æce* < the *v.*] a dull, continuous pain

a·chene (ā kēn', ə-) *n.* [ModL. *achenium* < Gr. *a-*, not + *chainein*, to gape] any small, dry fruit with one seed, whose thin outer covering (pericarp) does not burst when ripe —a·che'ni·al' (-kē'nē əl) *adj.*

A·cher·nar (ā'kər när') [Ar. *Akher-nahr*, lit., the latter part] the brightest star in the S constellation Eridanus

Ach·er·on (ak'ə rän') [L. < Gr., associated with *achos*, pain, hence "river of woe"] 1. *Gr. & Rom. Myth.* the river in Hades across which Charon ferried the dead 2. Hades; infernal regions

A·cheu·le·an, A·cheu·li·an (ə shōō'lē ən) *adj.* [Fr. *Acheulien* < *St. Acheul*, France, where remains were found] designating or of a lower and middle paleolithic culture characterized by skillfully made bifacial tools of stone

‡**à·che·val** (à shə vál') [Fr.] 1. on horseback; astraddle 2. straddling (an issue)

a·chieve (ə chēv') *vt.* a·chieved', a·chiev'ing [ME. *acheven* < OFr. *achever*, to finish < *a-*, to + *chief*: see CHIEF] 1. to do; succeed in doing; accomplish 2. to get or reach by exertion; attain; gain [to *achieve* one's goals] —*vi.* to bring about a desired result —SYN. see PERFORM, REACH —a·chiev'a·ble *adj.*

a·chieve·ment (-mənt) *n.* 1. the act of achieving 2. a thing achieved, esp. by skill, work, courage, etc.; feat; exploit

achievement quotient *Psychol.* the ratio of a person's achieved educational age (as shown by testing what has been learned) to his mental age

A·chil·les (ə kil'ēz) [L. < Gr. *Achilleus*] *Gr. Myth.* Greek warrior and leader in the Trojan War, who killed Hector and was killed by Paris with an arrow that struck his only vulnerable spot, his heel: he is the hero of Homer's *Iliad*

Achilles' heel (one's) vulnerable or susceptible spot

Achilles' tendon the tendon connecting the back of the heel to the muscles of the calf of the leg

A·chit·o·phel (ə kit'ə fel') *same as* AHITHOPHEL

ach·la·myd·e·ous (ak'lə mid'ē əs) *adj.* [< A.² + Gr. *chlamys* (gen. *chlamydos*), a cloak, coat + -EOUS] *Bot.* having neither sepals nor petals; without a perianth

a·chlor·hy·dri·a (ā'klôr hī'drē ə) *n.* [ModL. < A.² + CHLOR- + HYDR- + -IA] a stomach disorder in which the stomach fails to secrete hydrochloric acid —a'chlor·hy'dric (-hī'drik) *adj.*

a·chon·drite (ā kän'drīt) *n.* [A.² + CHONDRITE] a stony meteorite that contains no chondrules —a'chon·drit'ic (-drit'ik) *adj.*

a·chon·dro·pla·sia (ā'kän drə plā'zhə, -zhē ə) *n.* [ModL.: see A.² & CHONDRO- & -PLASIA] a congenital disorder of bone formation that results in deformities and dwarfing of the skeleton —a·chon'dro·plas'tic (-plas'tik) *adj.*

ach·ro·mat·ic (ak'rə mat'ik, ā'krə-) *adj.* [Gr. *achrōmatos* < *a-*, without + *chrōma*, color + -IC] 1. colorless 2. refracting white light without breaking it up into its component colors 3. forming visual images whose outline is free from prismatic colors [an *achromatic* lens] 4. *Biol.* a) staining poorly with the usual stains b) made of achromatin 5. *Music* without accidentals; diatonic [an *achromatic* scale] —ach'ro·mat'i·cal·ly *adv.*

a·chro·ma·tin (ā krō'mə tin) *n.* [A.² + CHROMATIN] *Biol.* that material of the cell nucleus not easily colored by the usual stains

a·chro·ma·tism (-tiz'm) *n.* the condition or quality of being achromatic; lack of color: also **a·chro'ma·tic'i·ty** (-tis'ə tē)

a·chro·ma·tize (ā krō'mə tīz') *vt.* -tized', -tiz'ing to make achromatic; rid of color

a·chro·ma·tous (ā krō'mə təs) *adj.* [Gr. *achrōmatos*: see ACHROMATIC] without color, or without enough color

a·chro·mic (ā krō'mik) *adj.* [< Gr. *achrōmos* < *a-*, not + *chrōma*, color + -IC] without color: also **a·chro'mous** (-məs)

☆**A·chro·my·cin** (ā'krə mī'sin) [*achro-* (< Gr. *achrōmos*, see prec.) + MYC- + -IN¹] *a trademark for* TETRACYCLINE

ach·y (āk'ē) *adj.* ach'i·er, ach'i·est having an ache, or dull, steady pain

a·cic·u·la (ə sik'yoo lə) *n., pl.* -lae' (-lē') [LL., dim. of L. *acus*: see ACEROSE¹] *Biol., Geol.* a needlelike spine, prickle, or crystal —a·cic'u·lar (-lər) *adj.*

a·cic·u·late (-lit, -lāt') *adj.* 1. having aciculae 2. having marks like scratches made by a needle: also **a·cic'u·lat'ed** (-lāt'id)

a·cic·u·lum (-ləm) *n., pl.* -lums, -la (-lə) [ModL. < *acicula*] 1. an acicula 2. *Zool.* a bristlelike part; seta

ac·id (as'id) *adj.* [L. *acidus*, sour < IE. base *ak-*, sharp, pointed: cf. EAR²] 1. sharp and biting to the taste; sour; tart 2. sharp or sarcastic in temperament or speech 3. that is, or has the properties of, an acid 4. having too heavy a concentration of acid —*n.* 1. a sour substance 2. [Slang] *same as* LSD 3. *Chem.* any compound that can react with a base to form a salt, the hydrogen of the acid being replaced by a positive ion; in modern theory, a substance that produces the positive ion of the solvent in which the acid is dissolved: in water solution an acid tastes sour, turns blue litmus paper red, and, in the dissociation theory, produces free hydrogen ions —SYN. see SOUR —ac'id·ly *adv.* —ac'id·ness *n.*

ac·i·dan·the·ra (as'ə dan'thər ə) *n.* [ModL. < Gr. *akis* (gen. *akidis*), a pointed object, dart (for IE. base see ACID) + ModL. *anthera*, ANTHER] any of several bulbous, African plants (genus *Acidanthera*) of the iris family, with cream-colored, long-tubed blossoms: they are often grown as potted ornamental plants

ac·id-fast (as'id fast', -fäst') *adj.* that does not readily lose its color when exposed to acids after being stained [the *acid-fast* tubercle bacillus]

ac·id-form·ing (-fôrm′iŋ) *adj.* **1.** forming an acid in chemical reaction; acidic **2.** yielding a large acid residue in metabolism: said of foods

a·cid·ic (ə sid′ik) *adj.* **1.** *same as* ACID-FORMING **2.** acid **3.** containing an excess of an acid-forming substance: rocks with much silica (an acidic oxide) are called *acidic* rocks

a·cid·i·fi·er (ə sid′ə fī′ər) *n.* anything that acidifies; any substance producing an acid effect

a·cid·i·fy (ə sid′ə fī′) *vt., vi.* -**fied′**, -**fy′ing** **1.** to make or become sour or acid **2.** to change into an acid —**a·cid′i·fi′a·ble** *adj.* —**a·cid′i·fi·ca′tion** (-fi kā′shən) *n.*

ac·i·dim·e·ter (as′ə dim′ə tər) *n.* a device used to find the amount or strength of acid present in a solution —**a·cid·i·met·ric** (ə sid′ə met′rik) *adj.* —**ac′i·dim′e·try** (-ə trē) *n.*

a·cid·i·ty (ə sid′ə tē) *n., pl.* -**ties** [Fr. *acidité* < L. *aciditas* < *acidus*: see ACID] **1.** acid quality or condition; sourness **2.** the degree of this **3.** hyperacidity

acid number a number indicating the amount of free acid present in a substance, equal to the number of milligrams of potassium hydroxide needed to neutralize the free fatty acids present in one gram of fat or oil: also called **acid value**

a·cid·o·phil (ə sid′ə fil) *n.* [ACID + -o- + -PHIL] **1.** a cell, substance, or element easily stained by acid dyes, as one of a group of cells in the anterior pituitary **2.** an organism that has an affinity for and grows well in an acid environment —**a·cid·o·phil·ic** (as′ə dō fil′ik) *adj.*

ac·i·doph·i·lus milk (as′ə däf′ə ləs) milk with acidophilic bacteria added: used, esp. formerly, as a health food

ac·i·do·sis (as′ə dō′sis) *n. Med.* a condition in which the body's alkali reserve is below normal, as because of faulty metabolism —**ac′i·dot′ic** (-dät′ik) *adj.*

acid test [orig., a *test* of gold by *acid*] a crucial, final test that proves the value or quality of something

a·cid·u·late (ə sij′oo lāt′) *vt.* -**lat′ed**, -**lat′ing** [< L. *acidulus* (see ff.) + -ATE¹] to make somewhat acid or sour —**a·cid′u·la′tion** *n.*

a·cid·u·lous (-ləs) *adj.* [L. *acidulus*, dim. of *acidus*: see ACID] **1.** somewhat acid or sour **2.** somewhat sarcastic Also **a·cid′u·lent** (-lənt) —*SYN.* see SOUR

ac·i·er·ate (as′ē ə rāt′) *vt.* -**at′ed**, -**at′ing** [Fr. *acier*, steel < LL. *aciarium* < L. *acies*, sharpness < *acer*, sharp < base *ac*- (see ACID) + -ATE¹] to change into steel

ac·i·form (as′ə fôrm′) *adj.* [< L. *acus*, needle + -FORM] needle-shaped; sharp

ac·i·nac·i·form (as′ə nas′ə fôrm′) *adj.* [< L. *acinaces*, short sword < Gr. *akinakēs*, of Per. origin + -FORM] *Bot.* shaped like a scimitar

a·cin·i·form (ə sin′ə fôrm′) *adj.* [< L. *acinus*, grape, grape-stone + -FORM] formed like a cluster of grapes

ac·i·nus (as′i nəs) *n., pl.* -**ni′** (-nī′) [ModL.: see prec.] *Anat.* one of the small sacs of a compound or racemose gland —**ac′i·nar** (-nər), **ac′i·nous** (-nəs), **ac′i·nose′** (-nōs′) *adj.*

-a·cious (ā′shəs, -shis) [< L. -*ax* (gen-. -*acis*) + -OUS] an *adj.*-forming suffix meaning characterized by, inclined to, full of [*tenacious, fallacious*]

-ac·i·ty (as′ə tē) [Fr. -*acité* < L. -*acitas*] a *n.*-forming suffix corresponding to -ACIOUS [*tenacity*]

ack-ack (ak′ak′) *n.* [echoic; prob. telephonic expansion of abbrev. A.A., antiaircraft artillery] [Slang] an antiaircraft gun or its fire

ac·knowl·edge (ək näl′ij, ak-) *vt.* -**edged**, -**edg·ing** [earlier *aknowledge* < ME. *knowlechen* < *knowleche* (see KNOWL-EDGE): influenced by ME. *aknowen* < OE. *oncnawan*, to understand, know, with Latinized prefix] **1.** to admit to be true or as stated; confess **2.** to recognize the authority or claims of **3.** to recognize and answer (a greeting or greeter, an introduction, etc.) **4.** to express thanks for **5.** to state that one has received (a letter, gift, favor, payment, etc.) **6.** *Law* to admit or affirm as genuine; certify in legal form [*to acknowledge* a deed] —**ac·knowl′edge·a·ble** *adj.*

SYN.—**acknowledge** implies the reluctant disclosure of something one might have kept secret [he *acknowledged* the child as his]; **admit** describes assent that has been elicited by persuasion and implies a conceding of a fact, etc. [I'll *admit* you're right]; **own** denotes an informal acknowledgment of something in connection with oneself [to *own* to a liking for turnips]; **avow** implies an open, emphatic declaration, often as an act of affirmation; **confess** is applied to a formal acknowledgment of a sin, crime, etc., but in a weakened sense is used interchangeably with **admit** in making simple declarations [I'll *confess* I don't like him] —*ANT.* deny

ac·knowl·edged (-ijd) *adj.* commonly recognized or accepted [the *acknowledged* leader of the group]

ac·knowl·edg·ment, ac·knowl·edge·ment (-ij mənt) *n.* **1.** an acknowledging or being acknowledged; admission; avowal **2.** something done or given in acknowledging, as an expression of thanks **3.** recognition of the authority or claims of **4.** a legal avowal or certificate

a·clin·ic line (ā klin′ik) [Gr. *aklinēs* < *a*-, not + *klinein* (see INCLINE) + -IC] an imaginary line around the earth near the equator, where the lines of force of the earth's magnetic field are parallel with the surface of the earth and where a magnetic needle will consequently not dip: also called MAGNETIC EQUATOR

ACLS American Council of Learned Societies

ACLU, A.C.L.U. American Civil Liberties Union

ac·me (ak′mē) *n.* [Gr. *akmē*, a point, top, age of maturity < IE. base *ak*-: see ACID] the highest point; point of culmination; peak —*SYN.* see SUMMIT

ac·ne (ak′nē) *n.* [ModL., ? orig. error for Gr. *akmē*: see ACME] a common skin disease, esp. among adolescents and young adults, characterized by chronic inflammation of the sebaceous glands, usually causing pimples on the face, back, and chest

ac·node (ak′nōd) *n.* [< L. *acus* (see ACEROSE¹) + NODE] *same as* ISOLATED POINT

a·cock (ə käk′) *adv., adj.* in a cocked or tilted fashion [with hat *acock*]

ac·o·lyte (ak′ə lit′) *n.* [ME. *acolit* < ML. *acolytus* < Gr. *akolouthos*, follower < *a*-, copulative + *keleuthos*, a way] **1.** *R.C.Ch.* a member of the highest of the four minor orders, whose duty it is to serve at Mass **2.** *same as* ALTAR BOY **3.** an attendant; follower; helper

A.Com. Associate in (or of) Commerce

A·con·ca·gua (ä′kôn kä′gwä) mountain of the Andes in W Argentina: 22,835 ft.: highest peak in the Western Hemisphere

ac·o·nite (ak′ə nīt′) *n.* [L. *aconitum* < Gr. *akoniton*] **1.** any of a genus (*Aconitum*) of plants of the buttercup family, with blue, purple, or yellow hoodlike flowers: most of these plants are poisonous: see MONKSHOOD, WOLFSBANE **2.** a drug made from dried roots of monkshood, formerly used as a cardiac and respiratory sedative Also **ac′o·ni′tum** (-nīt′əm)

a·corn (ā′kôrn) *n.* [ME. *akorn* < OE. *æcern*, nut, mast of trees; akin to Goth. *akran*, ON. *akarn* < IE. base *2g*-, to grow, fruit: form infl. by association with OE. *ac*, oak + *corn*, grain] the fruit of the oak tree; oak nut

☆**acorn duck** *same as* WOOD DUCK

☆**acorn squash** a kind of winter squash, acorn-shaped with ridged, dark-green skin and sweet, yellow flesh

☆**acorn tube** *Radio* a small vacuum tube with an envelope shaped like an acorn: it has been replaced by the lighthouse tube

a·cous·tic (ə koos′tik) *adj.* [Fr. *acoustique* < Gr. *akoustikos*, of or for hearing < *akouein*, to hear < IE. base akin to HEAR] **1.** having to do with hearing or with sound as it is heard **2.** of acoustics

a·cous·ti·cal (-ti k'l) *adj.* acoustic; specif., having to do with the control of sound [*acoustical* tile absorbs sounds]

a·cous·ti·cal·ly (-tik lē, -tik 'l ē) *adv.* with reference to acoustics; from the standpoint of acoustics

ac·ous·ti·cian (a′koos ti′shən) *n.* an expert in acoustics

a·cous·tics (ə koos′tiks) *n.pl.* **1.** the qualities of a room, theater, etc. that have to do with how clearly sounds can be heard or transmitted in it **2.** [*with sing. v.*] the branch of physics dealing with sound, esp. with its transmission

‡**a cou·vert** (à koo ver′) [Fr.] under cover; secure

ac·quaint (ə kwānt′) *vt.* [ME. *aqueinten* < OFr. *acointier* < ML. *adcognitare* < L. *ad*, to + *cognitus*, pp. of *cognoscere*, to know thoroughly < *con*-, with + *gnoscere*: see KNOW] **1.** to let know; give knowledge of; make aware; inform [to *acquaint* oneself with the facts] **2.** to cause to know personally; make familiar with [are you *acquainted* with my brother?] —*SYN.* see NOTIFY

ac·quaint·ance (ə kwānt′'ns) *n.* **1.** knowledge (of something) got from personal experience or study of it [an intimate *acquaintance* with the plays of Jonson] **2.** the state or relation of being acquainted (*with* someone) **3.** a person or persons whom one knows, but not intimately —**make someone's acquaintance** become an acquaintance of someone —**ac·quaint′ance·ship′** *n.*

ac·qui·esce (ak′wē es′) *vi.* -**esced′**, -**esc′ing** [Fr. *acquiescer*, to yield to < L. *acquiescere* < *ad*-, to + *quiescere*: see QUIET] to agree or consent quietly without protest, but without enthusiasm (often with *in*) [to *acquiesce* in a decision] —*SYN.* see CONSENT

ac·qui·es·cence (-es′'ns) *n.* the act of acquiescing; agreement or consent without protest

ac·qui·es·cent (-es′'nt) *adj.* acquiescing; agreeing or consenting without protest —**ac′qui·es′cent·ly** *adv.*

ac·quire (ə kwīr′) *vt.* -**quired′**, -**quir′ing** [L. *acquirere* < *ad*-, to + *quaerere*, to seek] **1.** to get or gain by one's own efforts or actions [to *acquire* an education] **2.** to get or come to have as one's own [to *acquire* certain traits] —*SYN.* see GET —**ac·quir′a·ble** *adj.*

acquired character *Biol.* a modification of structure or function caused by environmental factors: now generally regarded as not inheritable: also **acquired characteristic**

ac·quire·ment (ə kwir′mənt) *n.* **1.** an acquiring or being acquired **2.** something acquired, as a skill or ability gained by learning

ac·qui·si·tion (ak′wə zish′ən) *n.* [L. *acquisitio* < pp. of *acquirere*: see ACQUIRE] **1.** an acquiring or being acquired **2.** something or someone acquired or added

ac·quis·i·tive (ə kwiz′ə tiv) *adj.* [LL. *acquisitivus* < pp. of L. *acquirere*: see ACQUIRE] eager to acquire; good at getting and holding wealth, etc.; grasping —*SYN.* see GREEDY —**ac·quis′i·tive·ly** *adv.* —**ac·quis′i·tive·ness** *n.*

ac·quit (ə kwit′) *vt.* -**quit′ted**, -**quit′ting** [ME. *aquiten* < OFr. *aquiter*, to free < ML. *acquitare*, to settle a claim < L. *ad*, to + *quietare*: see QUIET] **1.** to release from a duty, obligation, etc. **2.** to clear (a person) of a charge, as by declaring him not guilty; exonerate **3.** to bear or conduct (oneself); behave **4.** [Archaic] to pay (a debt or claim) —*SYN.* see ABSOLVE, BEHAVE —**ac·quit′ter** *n.*

ac·quit·tal (ə kwit′'l) *n.* [ME. *aquital* < Anglo-Fr. *aqui-taille*: see ACQUIT] **1.** an acquitting; discharge (of duty,

obligation, etc.) **2.** *Law* a setting free or being set free by judgment of the court

ac·quit·tance (-'ns) *n.* [ME. *aquitaunce* < OFr. *aquitance:* see ACQUIT + -ANCE] **1.** a settlement of, or release from, debt or liability **2.** a record of this; receipt

A·cre (ā′kər, ä′-; *for 2* ä′krə) **1.** seaport in NW Israel, on the Mediterranean: pop. 28,000: Heb. name, AKKO **2.** federal territory of westernmost Brazil: 59,139 sq. mi.; pop. 160,000

a·cre (āk′ər) *n.* [ME. < OE. *æcer*, field (akin to Goth. *akrs*, OHG. *ackar*, G. *acker*) < IE. base *agros*, field, lit., place to which cattle are driven < *agō-* (L. *agere*), to drive, do; akin to Sans. *ájrah*, plain, country, Gr. *agros*, country, L. *ager*, field] **1.** a measure of land, 43,560 sq. ft. **2.** [*pl.*] specific holdings in land; lands **3.** [*pl.*] [Colloq.] a large quantity **4.** [Obs.] field: see GOD'S ACRE

a·cre·age (āk′ər ij, ā′krij) *n.* [ACRE + -AGE] the number of acres in a piece of land; acres collectively

☆**a·cre-foot** (āk′ər foot′) *n.* the quantity of water (43,560 cu. ft.) that would cover one acre to a depth of one foot

☆**a·cre-inch** (-inch′) *n.* one twelfth of an acre-foot, or 3,630 cubic feet

ac·rid (ak′rid) *adj.* [< L. *acris*, sharp < IE. base *ak-* (see ACID); form infl. by ACID] **1.** sharp, bitter, stinging, or irritating to the taste or smell **2.** bitter or sarcastic in speech, etc. —**a·crid·i·ty** (a krid′ə tē, ə-), **ac′rid·ness** *n.* —**ac′rid·ly** *adv.*

ac·ri·dine (ak′rə dēn′, -din) *n.* [ACRID + -INE[4]] a colorless, crystalline compound, $C_{13}H_9N$, found in coal tar: certain dyes and drugs are made from it

ac·ri·fla·vine (ak′rə flā′vēn, -vin) *n.* [ACRI(DINE) + FLA- VINE] a brownish, odorless powder, $C_{14}H_{14}N_3Cl$, prepared from acridine and used as an antiseptic

ac·ri·mo·ni·ous (ak′rə mō′nē əs) *adj.* [ML. *acrimoniosus:* see ACRIMONY] bitter and caustic in temper, manner, or speech —**ac′ri·mo′ni·ous·ly** *adv.* —**ac′ri·mo′ni·ous·ness** *n.*

ac·ri·mo·ny (ak′rə mō′nē) *n., pl.* -nies [L. *acrimonia*, sharpness < *acer*, sharp < IE. base *ak-*: see ACID] bitter- ness or harshness of temper, manner, or speech; asperity

a·crit·i·cal (ā krit′i k′l) *adj.* **1.** not critical; having no tendency to criticism or critical judgment **2.** *Med.* showing no signs of a crisis

ac·ro- (ak′rō, ak′rə) [< Gr. *akros*, at the point, end, or top < IE. base *ak-*: see ACID] *a combining form meaning:* **1.** pointed [*acrocephaly*] **2.** highest, topmost, at the extremities [*acrospire*]

ac·ro·bat (ak′rə bat′) *n.* [Fr. *acrobate* < Gr. *akrobatos*, walking on tiptoe < *akros* (see ACRO-) + *bainein*, to walk, go] an expert performer of tricks in tumbling or on the trapeze, tightrope, etc.; skilled gymnast —**ac′ro·bat′ic** *adj.* —**ac′ro·bat′i·cal·ly** *adv.*

ac·ro·bat·ics (ak′rə bat′iks) *n.pl.* [*also with sing. v.*] **1.** the art, skill, or tricks of an acrobat **2.** any difficult or intri- cate tricks requiring great skill or agility [*mental acrobatics*]

ac·ro·car·pous (ak′rə kär′pəs) *adj.* [ACRO- + -CARPOUS] bearing fruit at the end of the stalk, as some mosses

ac·ro·ceph·a·ly (ak′rō sef′ə lē) *n.* [< ACRO- + Gr. *kephalē*, head: see CEPHALIC] *same as* OXYCEPHALY —**ac′ro·ce·phal′- ic** (-sə fal′ik), **ac′ro·ceph′a·lous** (-sef′ə ləs) *adj.*

ac·ro·gen (ak′rə jən) *n.* [ACRO- + -GEN] a plant, such as a fern or moss, having a perennial stem with the growing point at the tip —**a·crog·e·nous** (ə kräj′ə nəs), **ac′ro·gen′ic** (-jen′ik) *adj.* —**a·crog′e·nous·ly** *adv.*

a·cro·le·in (ə krō′lē in) *n.* [ACR(ID) + L. *olere*, to smell + -IN[1]] a yellowish or colorless, pungent liquid, $CH_2:CHCHO$, a decomposition product of glycerol and glycerides, used as a tear gas

ac·ro·lith (ak′rə lith′) *n.* [L. *acrolithus* < Gr. *akrolithos* < *akros* (see ACRO-) + *lithos*, stone] in early Greek sculpture, a statue with stone head, hands, and feet, and a wooden trunk

ac·ro·meg·a·ly (ak′rō meg′ə lē) *n.* [Fr. *acromégalie:* see ACRO- & MEGALO-] a disease in which there is enlargement of the bones of the head, hands, and feet, resulting from a tumor of the pituitary gland that causes overproduction of growth hormone —**ac′ro·me·gal′ic** (-mə gal′ik) *adj.*

a·cro·mi·on (ə krō′mē ən) *n.* [Gr. *akrōmion* < *akrōmia*, point of the shoulder < *akros* (see ACRO-) + *ōmos*, the shoul- der] the outer extremity of the shoulder blade, or scapula

a·cron·i·cal, a·cron·y·cal (ə krän′ə k′l) *adj.* [Gr. *akrony- chos*, at sunset < *akros* (see ACRO-) + *nyx*, NIGHT] *Astron.* happening at sunset, as the rising of a star

☆**ac·ro·nym** (ak′rə nim) *n.* [ACRO- + Gr. *onyma*, NAME] a word formed from the first (or first few) letters of a series of words, as *radar*, from radio detecting and ranging —**ac′- ro·nym′ic** *adj.*

a·crop·e·tal (ə kräp′ə t′l) *adj.* [ACRO- + -PETAL] *Bot.* developing upward from the base toward the apex: said of certain types of inflorescence —**a·crop′e·tal·ly** *adv.*

ac·ro·pho·bi·a (ak′rə fō′bē ə) *n.* [ACRO- + PHOBIA] an abnormal fear of being in high places

a·crop·o·lis (ə kräp′′l is) *n.* [Gr. *akropolis* < *akros* (see ACRO-) + *polis*, city] the fortified upper part of an ancient Greek city, esp. [A-] that of Athens, on which the Parthe- non was built

ac·ro·spire (ak′rō spīr′) *n.* [ACRO- + Gr. *speira*, a spiral] *Bot.* the spiral primary bud of germinating grain

a·cross (ə krôs′) *adv.* [ME. *acros* < *a-*, on, in + *cros*, cross, after Anglo-Fr. *an croix*] **1.** crossed; crosswise **2.** from one side to the other **3.** on or to the other side —*prep.* **1.** from one side to the other of, or so as to cross **2.** on or to the other side of; over; through **3.** into contact with by chance [he came *across* an old friend]

across-the-board (-thə bôrd′) *adj.* **1.** *Horse Racing* com- bining win, place, and show, as a bet **2.** including or affect- ing all classes or groups

a·cros·tic (ə krôs′tik) *n.* [Gr. *akrostichos* < *akros* (see ACRO-) + *stichos*, line of verse] a verse or arrangement of words in which certain letters in each line, such as the first or last, when taken in order spell out a word, motto, the alphabet, etc. —*adj.* of or like an acrostic —**a·cros′ti·cal·ly** *adv.*

ac·ry·late (ak′rə lāt′) *n.* [ACRYL(IC) + -ATE[2]] **1.** a salt of acrylic acid containing the radical $C_3H_3O_2$ **2.** *same as* ACRYLIC RESIN

a·cryl·ic (ə kril′ik) *adj.* [ACR(OLEIN) + -YL + -IC] **1.** desig- nating or of a colorless, pungent acid, $CH_2:CHCOOH$, obtained by the oxidation of acrolein **2.** designating or of a series of olefin acids with the general formula $C_nH_{2n-2}O_2$

acrylic fiber any of a group of synthetic fibers derived from a compound of hydrogen cyanide and acetylene, and made into fabrics

acrylic resin any of a group of transparent thermoplastic resins, as Lucite, formed by polymerizing esters of acrylic acid or methacrylic acid

ac·ry·lo·ni·trile (ak′rə lō nī′tril) *n.* [< ACRYL(IC) + NITRILE] a colorless liquid, $CH_2:CH \cdot C:N$, boiling at 78°C: it is used in synthetic polymerization and in making acrylic fibers, synthetic rubber, and soil conditioners

A.C.S. American Chemical Society

act (akt) *n.* [ME. < OFr. *acte* < L. *actus*, a doing or moving, *actum*, thing done, pp. of *agere*, to do < IE. base *ag-*, to drive, seen also in Gr. *agein*, to lead] **1.** a thing done; deed **2.** an action; doing [caught in the *act* of stealing] **3.** a decision (of a court, legislature, etc.); law; decree **4.** a document formally stating what has been done, made into law, etc. **5.** one of the main divisions of a drama or opera **6.** any of the separate performances on a variety program **7.** a show of feeling or behavior that is not sincere and is put on just for effect —*vt.* [ME. *acten* < L. *actus:* see the *n.*] **1.** to play the part of **2.** to perform in (a play) **3.** to behave in a way that befits [don't *act* the child] —*vi.* **1.** to perform on the stage; play a role **2.** to behave as though playing a role **3.** to be suited to performance: said of a play or a role **4.** to behave; comport oneself [act like a lady] **5.** to do something [we must *act* now to forestall disaster] **6.** to serve or function [the fence *acts* as a barrier] **7.** to serve as spokesman or substitute (*for*) [he's *acting* for the committee] **8.** to have an effect [acids *act* on metal] **9.** to appear to be [he *acted* very angry] —**act out** *Psy- chiatry* to behave in a way that unconsciously expresses (feelings that were repressed in an earlier situation) —☆**act up** [Colloq.] **1.** to be playful **2.** to misbehave **3.** to become inflamed, painful, etc.

act. active

act·a·ble (ak′tə b'l) *adj.* that can be acted: said of a play, a role, etc. —**act′a·bil′i·ty** (-bil′ə tē) *n.*

Ac·tae·on (ak tē′ən) [L. < Gr. *Aktaiōn*] *Gr. Myth.* a hunter who made Artemis angry by watching her bathe: she changed him into a stag, and he was torn to pieces by his own dogs

‡**Ac·ta Sanc·to·rum** (äk′tä säŋk tō′rəm, ak′tə saŋk tôr′- əm) [L., Acts of the Saints] *R.C.Ch.* a collection of lives of the saints and martyrs

actg. acting

☆**ACTH** [< adrenocorticotrophic hormone] a polypeptide hormone of the anterior part of the pituitary gland that stimulates the growth and hormone production of the adrenal cortex

ac·tin (ak′tin) *n.* [< L. *actus* (see ACT) + -IN[1]] a protein in muscles: see ACTOMYOSIN

ac·tin- (ak′tin) *same as* ACTINO-

ac·ti·nal (ak′ti n'l, ak tī′n'l) *adj.* [ACTIN- + -AL] of the oral region of a radiate animal, the region from which the rays or tentacles grow

act·ing (ak′tiŋ) *adj.* **1.** adapted for performance on a stage [an *acting* version of a play] **2.** that acts; functioning **3.** temporarily taking over the duties (of a specified position) [the *acting* chairman] —*n.* the act, art, or occupation of performing in plays —*SYN.* see TEMPORARY

ac·tin·i·a (ak tin′ē ə) *n., pl.* -i·ae (-i ē), -i·as [ModL. < Gr. *aktis* (gen. *aktinos*), a ray] any of a genus (*Actinia*) of sea anemones —**ac·tin′i·an** *adj., n.*

ac·tin·ic (ak tin′ik) *adj.* having to do with actinism —**ac·tin′i·cal·ly** *adv.*

actinic rays light rays of short wavelength, occurring in the violet and ultraviolet parts of the spectrum, that produce chemical changes, as in photography

ac·ti·nide series (ak′tə nid′) [< ACTINIUM] a group of radioactive chemical elements from element 89 (actinium)

through element 103 (lawrencium): it resembles the lanthanide series in electronic structure: see Group III of PERIODIC TABLE (chart)

ac·tin·i·form (ak tin′ə fôrm′) *adj.* [< ACTIN- + -FORM] *Zool.* having radial form; rayed

ac·tin·ism (ak′tən iz′m) *n.* [ACTIN- + -ISM] that property of ultraviolet light, X rays, or other radiations, by which chemical changes are produced

ac·tin·i·um (ak tin′ē əm) *n.* [ModL. < Gr. *aktis* (gen. *aktinos*), ray] a radioactive chemical element found with uranium and radium in pitchblende and other minerals and formed in reactors by the neutron irradiation of radium: symbol, Ac; at. wt., 227 (?); at. no., 89; sp. gr., 10 ±; melt. pt., 1050°C

ac·ti·no- (ak′tə nō, ak tin′ə) [< Gr. *aktis* (gen. *aktinos*), ray] *a combining form meaning:* **1.** of actinism or actinic rays [*actinometer*] **2.** *Biol.* of radiated structure [*actinomycosis*]

ac·tin·o·graph (ak tin′ə graf′) *n. Photog.* an actinometer

ac·ti·noid (ak′tə noid′) *adj.* having a radial form, as an actinozoan

ac·tin·o·lite (ak tin′ə līt′) *n.* a greenish type of amphibole: asbestos is the fibrous variety

ac·ti·nol·o·gy (ak′tə näl′ə jē) *n.* the science of light rays and their chemical effects

ac·ti·nom·e·ter (ak′tə näm′ə tər) *n.* **1.** *Physics* an instrument for measuring the intensity of the sun's rays, or the actinic effect of light rays **2.** *Photog.* same as EXPOSURE METER —**ac′ti·no·met′ric** (-nə met′rik) *adj.* —**ac′ti·nom′·e·try** (-näm′ə trē) *n.*

ac·ti·no·mor·phic (ak′ti nə môr′fik) *adj. Biol.* having radial symmetry, as a flower or a starfish: also **ac′ti·no·mor′phous**

ac·ti·no·my·cete (ak′tə nō mī sēt′, -mī′sēt) *n.* a tiny organism (order Actinomycetales, including esp. the genus *Actinomyces*), intermediate between a bacterium and an imperfect fungus, that occurs in soil, water, or decomposing organic matter: many are parasitic and cause various diseases in man, other mammals, and plants; some (the streptomyces) are an important source of antibiotics —**ac′ti·no·my·ce′tous** (-sēt′əs) *adj.*

ac·ti·no·my·cin (-mī′s′n) *n.* [< ModL. *actinomyces*, a genus of bacteria: see ACTINO-, -MYCETE, & -IN¹] any of various antibiotic polypeptides derived from a genus (*Streptomyces*) of soil bacteria: active against certain bacteria and fungi

ac·ti·no·my·co·sis (-mī kō′sis) *n.* an infection caused by certain actinomycetes, that results in bony degeneration of the jaws, and abscesses in the lungs, intestines, etc. of man and other mammals

ac·ti·non (ak′tə nän′) *n.* [ModL. < ACTINIUM + -ON] an isotope of radon, formed by the radioactive decay of actinium: at. wt., 217

ac·ti·no·u·ra·ni·um (ak′tə nō′yoo rā′nē əm) *n.* [< ACTINIUM + URANIUM] the uranium isotope of mass number 235

ac·ti·no·zo·an (ak′ti nō zō′ən) *n.* [ACTINO- + Gr. *zōion*, an animal] same as ANTHOZOAN

ac·tion (ak′shən) *n.* [ME. *accion* < OFr. *action* < L. *actio* < pp. of *agere*: see ACT] **1.** the doing of something; state of being in motion or of working **2.** an act or thing done **3.** [*pl.*] behavior; habitual conduct **4.** habitual activity characterized by energy and boldness [a man of *action*] **5.** the effect produced by something [the *action* of a drug] **6.** the way of moving, working, etc., as of a machine, an organ of the body, etc. **7.** the moving parts or mechanism, as of a gun, piano, etc. **8.** *a*) the sequence of happenings in a story or play; plot *b*) any of such happenings **9.** a legal proceeding by which one seeks to have a wrong put right; lawsuit **10.** *a*) a military encounter *b*) military combat in general **11.** the appearance of animation in a painting, sculpture, etc. **12.** [Slang] activity or excitement; specif., gambling activity —*SYN.* see BATTLE¹ —**bring action** to start a lawsuit —**see action** to participate in military combat —**take action 1.** to become active **2.** to start a lawsuit

ac·tion·a·ble (-ə b′l) *adj. Law* that gives cause for an action, or lawsuit

☆**action painting** a form of abstract expressionism in which such methods as the spattering or dripping of paint are used to create bold, fluid, apparently random compositions

Ac·ti·um (ak′tē əm, -shē əm) cape on the NW coast of Acarnania (in ancient Greece): the forces of Mark Antony and Cleopatra were defeated by those of Octavian in a naval battle near Actium (31 B.C.)

ac·ti·vate (ak′tə vāt′) *vt.* **-vat′ed, -vat′ing 1.** to make active; cause to engage in activity **2.** to put (an inactive military unit) on an active status by assigning personnel, equipment, etc. to it **3.** to make radioactive **4.** to make capable of reacting or of accelerating a chemical reaction **5.** to treat (sewage) with air so that aerobes will become active in it, thus purifying it —**ac′ti·va′tion** *n.*

activated carbon a form of highly porous carbon that can easily adsorb gases, vapors, and colloidal particles: it is made by destructive distillation of wood, peat, etc., followed by heating the resultant product to high temperatures with steam or carbon dioxide: also called **activated charcoal, active carbon**

ac·ti·va·tor (ak′tə vāt′ər) *n.* **1.** a thing or person that activates **2.** *Chem.* a catalyst

ac·tive (ak′tiv) *adj.* [ME. & OFr. *actif* < L. *activus* < base *act-* as in *actus*, pp. of *agere*: see ACT] **1.** that is acting, functioning, working, moving, etc. **2.** capable of acting, functioning, etc. **3.** causing action, motion, or change **4.** characterized by much action or motion; lively, busy, agile, quick, etc. [an *active* mind, an *active* boy] **5.** actual, not just nominal; participating [an *active* interest, to play an *active* role] **6.** necessitating action or work **7.** *a*) currently in operation, in effect, in progress, etc. [an *active* law, an *active* disease] *b*) in eruption [an *active* volcano] **8.** *Business* producing profit or interest [*active* funds] **9.** *Gram. a*) denoting the voice or form of a verb whose subject is shown as performing the action of the verb: opposed to PASSIVE *b*) in or of the active voice *c*) showing action rather than state of being: said of verbs like *throw* and *walk* —*n.* **1.** an active member of an organization **2.** *Gram.* the active voice —**ac′tive·ly** *adv.* —**ac′tive·ness** *n.* *SYN.*—**active** implies a state of motion, operation, etc. ranging from cases of normal functioning to instances of quickened activity [he's still *active* at eighty; an *active* market]; **energetic** suggests a concentrated exertion of energy or effort [an *energetic* workout]; **vigorous** implies forcefulness, robustness, and strength as an inherent quality [a *vigorous* plant]; **strenuous** is applied to things that make trying demands on one's strength, energy, etc. [a *strenuous* trip]; **brisk** implies liveliness and vigor of motion [a *brisk* walk] See also AGILE

☆**active duty** (or **service**) full-time service, esp. in the armed forces

active immunity immunity (to a disease) due to the production of antibodies by the body

ac·tiv·ism (ak′tə viz′m) *n.* the doctrine or policy of taking positive, direct action to achieve an end, esp. a political or social one —**ac′tiv·ist** *adj., n.*

ac·tiv·i·ty (ak tiv′ə tē) *n., pl.* **-ties 1.** the quality or state of being active; action **2.** energetic action; liveliness; alertness **3.** a normal function of the body or mind **4.** an active force **5.** any specific action or pursuit [recreational *activities*]

ac·tiv·ize (ak′tə vīz′) *vt.* **-ized′, -iz′ing** to activate

act of God *Law* an occurrence, esp. a disaster, that is due entirely to the forces of nature and that could not reasonably have been prevented

ac·to·my·o·sin (ak′tə mī′ə sin) *n.* a complex of two proteins (actin and myosin) in muscle tissue, interacting with ATP to bring about muscular contraction

Ac·ton (ak′t′n) city in SE England: suburb of London: pop. 65,000

Ac·ton (ak′t′n), Lord (*John Emerick Edward Dalberg-Acton;* 1st Baron Acton) 1834-1902; Eng. historian

ac·tor (ak′tər) *n.* [ME. *actour*, a doer, steward, plaintiff < L. *actor*, a doer, advocate < base *act-*: see ACT] **1.** a person who does something or participates in something **2.** a person, esp. a man, who acts in plays, movies, etc.

ac·tress (ak′tris) *n.* [see -ESS] a woman or girl who acts in plays, movies, etc.

Acts (akts) [*with sing. v.*] a book of the New Testament, ascribed to Luke: full title, **The Acts of the Apostles**

ac·tu·al (ak′choo wəl, -shoo-) *adj.* [ME. < LL. *actualis*, active, practical < L. *actus*: see ACT] **1.** existing in reality or in fact; not merely possible, but real; as it really is [the *actual* cost of the dam] **2.** existing at present or at the time —*SYN.* see TRUE

ac·tu·al·i·ty (ak′choo wal′ə tē, -shoo-) *n.* **1.** the state of being actual; reality **2.** *pl.* **-ties** an actual thing or condition; fact

ac·tu·al·ize (ak′choo wə līz′, -shoo-) *vt.* **-ized′, -iz′ing 1.** to make actual or real; realize in action **2.** to make realistic —**ac′tu·al·i·za′tion** (-li zā′shən) *n.*

ac·tu·al·ly (ak′choo wəl ē, -shoo-; -chə lē, -shə lē) *adv.* as a matter of actual fact; really

actual sin *Theol.* any sin committed by a person of his free will: distinguished from ORIGINAL SIN

ac·tu·ar·i·al (ak′choo wer′ē əl) *adj.* **1.** of actuaries or their work **2.** calculated by actuaries

ac·tu·ar·y (ak′choo wer′ē) *n., pl.* **-ies** [L. *actuarius*, clerk < *actus*: see ACT] a person whose work is to calculate statistically risks, premiums, etc. for insurance

ac·tu·ate (ak′choo wāt′) *vt.* **-at′ed, -at′ing** [< ML. *actuatus*, pp. of *actuare* < L. *actus*: see ACT] **1.** to put into action or motion **2.** to cause to take action [what motives *actuated* him?] —**ac′tu·a′tion** *n.* — **ac′tu·a′tor** *n.*

ac·u·ate (ak′yoo wət, -wāt′) *adj.* [< L. *acus*, needle (see ACEROSE¹) + -ATE¹] having a sharp point

a·cu·i·ty (ə kyōō′ə tē) *n.* [Fr. *acuité* < ML. *acuitas* < L. *acus*, needle: see ACEROSE¹] acuteness; keenness, as of thought or vision

a·cu·le·ate (ə kyōō′lē it, -āt′) *adj.* [L. *aculeatus*] having an aculeus or aculei

a·cu·le·us (ə kyōō′lē əs) *n., pl.* **-le·i′** (-ī′) [L., dim. of *acus*, needle: see ACEROSE¹] **1.** *Bot.* a prickle **2.** *Zool.* a sting

a·cu·men (ə kyōō′mən; *now also* ak′yoo mən) *n.* [L., a point, sting, mental acuteness < *acuere*, to sharpen < IE. base *ak-*: see ACID] keenness and quickness in understanding and dealing with a situation; shrewdness

a·cu·mi·nate (ə kyōō′mə nit; *for v.* -nāt′) *adj.* [L. *acuminatus*, pp. of *acuminare*, to sharpen < *acumen*: see prec.] pointed; tapering to a point [an *acuminate* leaf]: see LEAF,

illus. —vt. **-nat'ed, -nat'ing** to make sharp or pointed —**a·cu'mi·na'tion** n.

ac·u·punc·ture (ak'yoo puŋk'chər) n. [< L. acus, needle (see ACEROSE[1]) + PUNCTURE] the ancient practice, esp. as carried on by the Chinese, of piercing parts of the body with needles in seeking to treat disease or relieve pain

a·cute (ə kyōot') adj. [L. acutus, pp. of acuere, sharpen: see ACUMEN] **1.** having a sharp point **2.** keen or quick of mind; shrewd **3.** sensitive to impressions [acute hearing] **4.** severe and sharp, as pain, jealousy, etc. **5.** severe but of short duration; not chronic: said of some diseases **6.** very serious; critical; crucial [an acute shortage of workers] **7.** shrill; high in pitch **8.** of less than 90 degrees [an acute angle] —**a·cute'ly** adv. —**a·cute'ness** n.
SYN.—acute suggests severe intensification of an event, condition, etc. that is sharply approaching a climax [an acute shortage]; **critical** is applied to a turning point which will decisively determine an outcome [the critical battle of a war]; **crucial** comes into contrast with **critical** where a final determining a line of action rather than a decisive turning point is involved [a crucial debate on foreign policy] See also SHARP

acute accent a mark (´) used to show: **1.** the quality or length of a vowel, as in French idée **2.** primary stress, as in typewriter **3.** any stress on a spoken sound or syllable, as in scanning poetry

-a·cy (ə sē, ə si) [variously < Fr. -atie < L. -acia, -atia < Gr. -ateia] a n.-forming suffix meaning quality, condition, position, etc. [celibacy, curacy]

a·cy·clic (ā sī'klik, -sik'lik) adj. **1.** not cyclic; not in cycles **2.** Chem. having the structure of an open chain rather than a closed ring

ac·yl (as'əl) n. [AC(ID) + -YL] a radical, RCO-, derived from an organic acid by the removal of the OH group

a·cyl·o·in (ə sil'ō in) n. [ACYL + (BENZ)OIN] any of a group of ketones with the general formula $RCH(OH)COR$, including esp. benzoin

☆**ad**[1] (ad) n. [Colloq.] an advertisement

ad[2] (ad) n. Tennis advantage (sense 4): said of the first point scored after deuce —**ad in** server's advantage —**ad out** receiver's advantage

ad- (ad, əd, id) [L. ad-, to, at, toward; akin to AT] a prefix meaning variously motion toward, addition to, nearness to [admit; adjoin; adrenal]: assimilated in words of Latin origin to ac- before c or q, af- before f, ag- before g, al- before l, an- before n, ap- before p, ar- before r, as- before s, at- before t, and a- before sc, sp, and st: many apparent English occurrences of this prefix are Latinizations, often erroneous, of French or even of English words: see ADVANCE, ADMIRAL, ACCURSED, ACKNOWLEDGE

-ad[1] (ad, əd, id) [Gr. -as, -ad-] a suffix meaning of or relating to, used in forming: **1.** the names of collective numerals [monad] **2.** the names of some poems [Iliad] **3.** the names of some plants [cycad]

-ad[2] (ad) [L. ad, toward] a suffix meaning toward, in the direction of [caudad]

AD Mil. active duty

A.D. [L. Anno Domini, in the year of the Lord] of the Christian era: used with dates

A·da, A·dah (ā'də) [Heb. 'ādhā, beauty] a feminine name

A.D.A. 1. American Dental Association **2.** Americans for Democratic Action: also **ADA**

a·dac·ty·lous (ā dak't'l əs) adj. [A-[2] + DACTYL + -OUS] lacking fingers or toes from birth

ad·age (ad'ij) n. [Fr. < L. adagium, adagio < ad-, to + aio, I say] an old saying that has been popularly accepted as a truth —**SYN.** see SAYING

a·da·gio (ə dä'jō, -zhō; -jē ō', -zhē ō') adv. [It. ad agio, lit., at ease] Music slowly and leisurely —adj. slow —n., pl. **-gios 1.** a slow movement or passage in music **2.** a slow ballet dance, esp. for a mixed couple, requiring skillful balancing

Ad·a·line (ad'l in') a feminine name: see ADELINE

Ad·am (ad'əm) [Heb. < ādām, a human being] **1.** Bible the first man: Gen. 1-5 **2.** a masculine name —**not know (a person) from Adam** not know (a person) at all —**the old Adam** the supposed human tendency to sin

Ad·am (ad'əm) adj. [after Robert and James Adam, 18th-c. Brit. architects, its originators] relating to a style of English furniture and architecture with straight lines and ornamentation of garlands, etc.

Ad·am-and-Eve (ad'əm 'n ēv') n. same as PUTTYROOT

ad·a·mant (ad'ə mənt, -mant') n. [ME. & OFr. < L. adamas (gen. adamantis), the hardest metal < Gr. adamas (gen. adamantos) < a-, not + daman, to subdue: cf. TAME] **1.** in ancient times, a hard stone or substance that was supposedly unbreakable **2.** [Poet.] unbreakable hardness —adj. **1.** too hard to be broken **2.** not giving in or relenting; unyielding —**SYN.** see INFLEXIBLE —**ad'a·mant·ly** adv.

ad·a·man·tine (ad'ə man'tēn, -tin, -tin) adj. [ME. < L. adamantinus, hard as steel < Gr. adamantinos] **1.** of or like adamant; very hard; unbreakable **2.** unyielding; firm

Ad·am·ite (ad'ə mīt') n. **1.** a human being; person thought of as descended from Adam **2.** a person who goes naked in imitation of Adam, as did members of some early religious sects —**Ad'am·it'ic** (-mit'ik) adj.

Ad·ams (ad'əmz) **1. Charles Francis,** 1807–86; U.S. statesman: son of John Quincy **2. Henry (Brooks),** 1838–1918; U.S. historian & writer: son of prec. **3. James Trus·low** (trus'lō), 1878–1949; U.S. historian **4. John,** 1735–1826; 2d president of U.S. (1797–1801) **5. John Quin·cy** (kwin'sē), 1767–1848; 6th president of U.S. (1825–29): son of prec. **6. Maude,** (born Maude Kishadden) 1872–1953; U.S. actress **7. Samuel,** 1722–1803; Am. statesman & Revolutionary leader

Adams, Mount [after John (and John Quincy) ADAMS] **1.** mountain of the Cascade range, S Wash.: 12,307 ft. **2.** peak of the White Mountains, N.H.: 5,798 ft.

Adam's apple the projection formed in the front of the throat by the thyroid cartilage, seen chiefly in men

☆**ad·ams·ite** (ad'əm zīt') n. [after Roger Adams (1889–), U.S. chemist] a yellow, odorless crystalline compound, $NH(C_6H_4)_2AsCl$, developed for use, in a vaporous form, in chemical warfare

☆**Ad·am's-nee·dle** (ad'əmz nē'd'l) n. any of several species of the yucca plant, esp. BEAR GRASS (sense 1)

A·da·na (ä'dä nä') city in S Turkey: pop. 232,000

a·dapt (ə dapt') vt. [Fr. adapter < L. adaptare < ad-, to + aptare, to fit: see APT] **1.** to make fit or suitable by changing or adjusting **2.** to adjust (oneself) to new or changed circumstances —vi. to adjust oneself
SYN.—adapt implies a modifying so as to suit new conditions and suggests flexibility [to adapt oneself to a new environment]; **adjust** describes the bringing of things into proper relation through the use of skill or judgment [to adjust brakes; to adjust differences]; **accommodate** implies a subordinating of one thing to the needs of another and suggests concession or compromise [he accommodated his walk to the halting steps of his friend]; **conform** means to bring or act in harmony with some standard pattern, principle, etc. [to conform to specifications]

a·dapt·a·ble (ə dap'tə b'l) adj. **1.** that can be adapted or made suitable **2.** able to adjust oneself to new or changed circumstances —**a·dapt'a·bil'i·ty** (-bil'ə tē) n.

ad·ap·ta·tion (ad'əp tā'shən) n. [Fr. < ML. adaptatio: see ADAPT] **1.** an adapting or being adapted **2.** a thing resulting from adapting [this play is an adaptation of a novel] **3.** a change in structure, function, or form that produces better adjustment of an animal or plant to its environment **4.** the adjustment of a sense organ to variations in the degree of stimulation **5.** Sociology a gradual change in behavior to conform to the prevailing cultural patterns —**ad'ap·ta'tion·al** adj.

a·dapt·er, a·dap·tor (ə dap'tər) n. **1.** a person or thing that adapts **2.** a contrivance for adapting apparatus to new uses **3.** a connecting device for parts that would not otherwise fit together

a·dap·tion (ə dap'shən) n. same as ADAPTATION

a·dap·tive (-tiv) adj. **1.** showing adaptation **2.** able to adapt —**a·dap'tive·ly** adv.

A·dar (ä där') n. [Heb.] the sixth month of the Jewish year: see JEWISH CALENDAR

Adar She·ni (shä'nē) [Heb., lit., second Adar] see JEWISH CALENDAR

‡**ad as·tra per as·pe·ra** (ad' as'trə pər as'pər ə) [L.] to the stars through difficulties

ad·ax·i·al (ad ak'sē əl) adj. Bot. designating or on the side toward the axis or stem

A.D.C., ADC aide-de-camp

‡**ad cap·tan·dum vul·gus** (ad' kap tan'dəm vul'gəs) [L.] for catching, or pleasing, the crowd

add (ad) vt. [ME. adden < L. addere, to add < ad-, to + dare, to give] **1.** to join or unite (to) so as to increase the quantity, number, size, etc. **2.** to state further **3.** to combine (numbers) into a sum; calculate the total of —vi. **1.** to cause an increase; be an addition (to) [this adds to my pleasure] **2.** to find a sum by doing arithmetic —**add up 1.** to calculate the total of **2.** to equal the expected sum [these figures don't add up] **3.** to seem reasonable [his excuse just doesn't add up] —**add up to 1.** to reach a total of **2.** to mean; signify —**add'a·ble, add'i·ble** adj.

Ad·dams (ad'əmz) **Jane** 1860–1935; U.S. social worker & writer; founder of Hull House in Chicago

ad·dax (ad'aks) n., pl. **-dax·es, -dax:** see PLURAL, II, D, 1 [L. < native Afr. word] a large antelope (Addax nasomaculatus) of northern Africa and Arabia, with long, twisted horns

added line same as LEGER LINE

ad·dend (ad'end, ə dend') n. [< ADDENDUM] Math. a number or quantity to be added to another

ad·den·dum (ə den'dəm) n., pl. **-den'da** (-də) [L., gerundive of addere: see ADD] **1.** a thing added or to be added **2.** an appendix or supplement to a book, etc. **3.** the part of a gear tooth that projects beyond the pitch circle, or the distance that it projects

add·er[1] (ad'ər) n. **1.** one who adds ☆**2.** an adding machine

ADDAX
(40-44 in. high at shoulder)

ad·der² (ad'ər) n. [ME. < nadder (by faulty separation of a nadder) < OE. nædre < IE. base *nɔtr, *nētr (whence L. natrix, watersnake)] 1. a small, poisonous snake of Europe; common viper (Vipera berus) 2. any of various other snakes, as the poisonous puff adder of Africa, the harmless milk snake of North America, etc.

☆**ad·der's-mouth** (ad'ərz mouth') n. any of a number of related orchids (genus Malaxis) with greenish flowers

ad·der's-tongue (-tuŋ') n. ☆1. same as DOGTOOTH VIOLET 2. a fern (genus Ophioglossum) with a narrow spike somewhat resembling a snake's tongue

ad·dict (ə dikt'; for n. ad'ikt) vt. [< L. addictus, pp. of addicere, to give assent < ad-, to + dicere, to say: see DICTION] 1. to give (oneself) up (to some strong habit): usually in the passive voice 2. to cause (someone) to become addicted to some habit —n. a person addicted to some habit, esp. to the use of a narcotic drug

ad·dic·tion (ə dik'shən) n. the condition of being addicted (to a habit); specif., the habitual use of narcotic drugs

ad·dic·tive (-tiv) adj. relating to or causing addiction

☆**adding machine** a machine that automatically performs addition (and often subtraction, division, etc.) when certain keys are pressed

Ad·dis A·ba·ba (ä'dis ä'bə bə, ə bä'bə) capital of Ethiopia, in the C part: pop. 443,000

Ad·di·son (ad'ə s'n), **Joseph** 1672–1719; Eng. essayist & poet —**Ad'di·so'ni·an** (-sō'nē ən) adj.

Ad·di·son's disease (ad'ə s'nz) [after Thomas Addison (1793–1860), Eng. physician who identified it] a disease caused by failure of the adrenal glands: it is characterized by weakness, low blood pressure, and brownish discoloration of the skin

ad·dit·a·ment (ə dit'ə mənt) n. [L. additamentum] a thing added; addition

ad·di·tion (ə dish'ən) n. [ME. addicion < OFr. addition < L. additio < addere: see ADD] 1. an adding of two or more numbers to get a number called the sum 2. a joining of a thing to another thing 3. a thing or part added; increase; specif., a room or rooms added to a building 4. Law an identifying title or mark of status after a person's name (Ex.: John Smith, Esq.) —in addition (to) besides; as well (as)

ad·di·tion·al (-əl) adj. added; more; extra —**ad·di'tion·al·ly** adv.

ad·di·tive (ad'ə tiv) adj. [LL. additivus: see ADD] 1. showing or relating to addition 2. to be added —n. a substance added to another in small quantities to produce a desired effect, as a preservative added to food, an antiknock added to gasoline, etc.

ad·dle (ad'l) adj. [ME. adel in adel-eye, addle-egg, a transl. of L. ovum urinae, egg of urine, confused form of ovum urinum (a rendering of Gr. ourion ōon, wind-egg) < OE. adela; akin to MLowG. adele, mud] 1. rotten: said of an egg 2. muddled; confused: now usually in compounds [addlebrained] —vt., vi. -dled, -dling 1. to make or become rotten 2. to make or become muddled or confused

ad·dle-brained (-brānd') adj. having an addle brain; muddled; stupid: also **ad'dle-head'ed**, **ad'dle-pat'ed**

ad·dress (ə dres'; for n., esp. 2, 3, & 4, also ad'res) vt. [ME. adressen, to guide, direct < OFr. adresser < a-, to + dresser < VL. *directiare, to direct < dirigere: see DIRECT] 1. to direct (spoken or written words to) 2. to speak to or write to [to address an audience]: sometimes used reflexively [he addressed himself to both of us] 3. to write the destination on (a letter or parcel) 4. to use a proper form in speaking to [address the judge as Your Honor] 5. to apply (oneself) or direct (one's energies) 6. a) to take a stance and aim the club at (a golf ball) b) to take a stance in facing (a target in archery, one's partner in a square dance, etc.) 7. [Obs.] to make ready; prepare —n. 1. a written or spoken speech, esp. a formal one 2. the place to which mail, etc. can be sent to one; place where one lives or works 3. the writing on an envelope, parcel, etc. showing its destination 4. the location in a computer's storage compartment of an item of information, identified by a number or other code 5. skill and tact in handling situations 6. conversational manner 7. [pl.] attentions paid in courting or wooing —SYN. see SPEECH —**ad·dress'er**, **ad·dres'sor** n.

☆**ad·dress·ee** (ad'res ē', ə dres'ē') n. the person to whom mail, etc. is addressed

☆**ad·dress·o·graph** (ə dres'ə graf') a trademark for a machine that automatically prints addresses on letters, etc. from prepared stencils —n. such a machine

ad·duce (ə dōōs', -dyōōs') vt. -duced', -duc'ing [L. adducere, to lead or bring to < ad-, to + ducere: see DUCT] to give as a reason or proof; cite as an example —**ad·duc'er** n. —**ad·duc'i·ble**, **ad·duce'a·ble** adj.

ad·du·cent (ə dōōs'nt, ə-; -dyōōs'-) adj. [L. adducens, prp. of adducere: see ADDUCE] Physiol. that adducts

ad·duct (ə dukt', a-) vt. [< L. adductus, pp. of adducere: see ADDUCE] Physiol. to pull (a part of the body) toward the median axis: said of a muscle: opposed to ABDUCT —**ad·duc'tive** (-duk'tiv) adj. —**ad·duc'tor** n.

ad·duc·tion (a duk'shən, ə-) n. [ME. adduccioun < ML. adductio < L. adductus, pp. of adducere: see ADDUCE] 1. an adducing or citing 2. Physiol. a) an adducting of a part of the body b) the changed position resulting from this

Ade (ād), **George** 1866–1944; U.S. humorist

-ade (ād; occas. äd, ad) [Fr. -ade; Pr., Port., or Sp. -ada; It. -ata; all ult. < L. -ata, fem. ending of pp. of verbs of the first conjugation] a suffix meaning: 1. the act of [blockade] 2. the result or product of [pomade] 3. participant(s) in an action [brigade] 4. [after LEMONADE] drink made from [limeade]

A·de·la (ad'l ə, ad'ə lə, ə del'ə) a feminine name: dim. Della; var. Adelia; Fr. Adèle: see ADELAIDE

Ad·e·laide (ad'l ād') [Fr. Adélaïde < Ger. Adelheid < OHG. Adalheidis, Adalheit, lit., nobility < adal, nobility + -heit, noun suffix akin to E. -hood] 1. a feminine name: dim. Addie; var. Adeline, Adela 2. capital of South Australia, on the SE coast: pop. (incl. suburbs) 615,000

Ad·el·bert (ə del'bərt, ad'l-) a masculine name: see ALBERT

A·dele (ə del') a feminine name: see ADELA

A·de·li·a (ə dēl'ē ə, -dēl'yə) a feminine name: see ADELA

A·dé·lie Coast (ad'l ē; Fr. à dā lē') region in Antarctica, south of Australia, claimed by France: 150,000 sq. mi.: also **Adélie Land**

Ad·e·li·na (ad'l ī'nə, -ē'nə) a feminine name: see ADELINE

Ad·e·line (ad'l in', -ēn') a feminine name: var. Adelina, Aline: see ADELAIDE

a·demp·tion (ə demp'shən) n. [< L. ademptio, a taking away < adimere, to take away < ad-, to + emere, to take, buy: cf. REDEEM] Law the extinction of a legacy by an act of the testator before his death, as by his disposal of the bequeathed property

A·den (äd'n, ād'n) 1. former Brit. colony & protectorate in SW Arabia, on the Gulf of Aden: since 1967, part of SOUTHERN YEMEN 2. seaport in this region: pop. 99,000 3. **Gulf of,** gulf of the Arabian Sea, between the S coast of Arabia and E Africa

ad·en- (ad'n) same as ADENO-

A·de·nau·er (ad'n our; G. ä'dən ou'ər), **Kon·rad** (kän'rad; G. kōn'rät) 1876–1967; Ger. statesman; chancellor of the Federal Republic of Germany (1949–63)

ad·e·nine (ad'n ēn') n. [ADEN- + -INE⁴] a white, crystalline purine base, C₅H₅N₅, derived from nucleic acid formed in the pancreas, spleen, etc.

ad·e·ni·tis (ad'n ī'tis) n. [ADEN- + -ITIS] glandular inflammation

ad·e·no- (ad'n ō) [< Gr. adēn, gland] a combining form meaning of a gland or glands [adenovirus]

ad·e·no·car·ci·no·ma (-kär'sə nō'mə) n. [ADENO- + CARCINOMA] a malignant tumor of glandular origin or with a glandlike cell arrangement

ad·e·noid (ad'n oid') adj. [ADEN- + -OID] 1. glandlike or glandular 2. of or like lymphoid tissue

ad·e·noi·dal (ad'n oid'l) adj. 1. adenoid 2. having adenoids 3. having the characteristic difficult breathing or nasal tone due to enlarged adenoids

ad·e·noids (ad'n oidz') n.pl. growths of lymphoid tissue in the upper part of the throat, behind the nose: they can swell up and obstruct breathing and speech

ADENOIDS

ad·e·no·ma (ad'n ō'mə) n. [ADEN- + -OMA] a benign tumor of glandular origin or with a glandlike cell arrangement —**ad'e·nom'a·tous** (-äm'ə təs) adj.

a·den·o·sine (ə den'ə s'n, -sēn') n. [arbitrary blend < ADENINE + RIBOSE] a white, odorless, crystalline powder, C₁₀H₁₃N₅O₄, obtained from the hydrolysis of yeast nucleic acid, and consisting of a glucoside of adenine and ribose: see also ADP, ATP

ad·e·no·vi·rus (ad'n ō vi'rəs) n. [ADENO- + VIRUS] any of a group of viruses that cause a variety of respiratory diseases in man

ad·ept (ə dept'; for n. ad'ept) adj. [L. adeptus, pp. of adipisci, to arrive at < ad-, to + apisci, to pursue, attain: used in ML. of alchemists claiming to have arrived at the philosopher's stone] highly skilled; expert —n. an expert —**ad·ept'ly** adv. —**ad·ept'ness** n.

ad·e·qua·cy (ad'ə kwə sē) n. the quality or state of being adequate

ad·e·quate (ad'ə kwət) adj. [L. adaequatus, pp. of adaequare < ad-, to + aequare, to make equal < aequus, level, equal] 1. enough or good enough for what is required or needed; sufficient; suitable. 2. barely satisfactory; acceptable but not remarkable —SYN. see SUFFICIENT —**ad'e·quate·ly** adv. —**ad'e·quate·ness** n.

‡**a deux** (á dö') [Fr.] 1. of or for two 2. intimate

‡**ad ex·tre·mum** (ad' iks trē'məm) [L., at the extreme] at last; finally

ad fin. [L. ad finem] to the end; at the end

ad·here (ad hir', ad-) vi. -hered', -her'ing [L. adhaerere < ad-, to + haerere, to stick] 1. to stick fast; stay attached 2. to stay firm in supporting or approving [to adhere to a leader, to adhere to a plan] —SYN. see STICK —**ad·her'er** n.

ad·her·ence (əd hir'əns, ad-) n. the act of adhering; specif., attachment (to a person, cause, etc.); devotion and support

ad·her·ent (-hir'ənt) adj. [Fr. < L. adhaerens, prp. of adhaerere: see ADHERE] 1. sticking fast; attached 2. Bot. grown together; adnate —n. a supporter or follower (of a person, cause, etc.) —SYN. see FOLLOWER

ad·he·sion (əd hē'zhən, ad-) n. [Fr. < L. adhaesio < pp.

of *adhaerer*: see ADHERE] **1.** the act of sticking (*to* something) or the state of being stuck together **2.** devoted attachment; adherence **3.** a thing that adheres **4.** *Med. a)* the joining together, by fibrous tissue, of bodily parts or tissues that are normally separate: it typically results from inflammation *b)* the bands of fibrous tissue abnormally joining these bodily parts, etc. **5.** *Physics* the force that holds together the molecules of unlike substances whose surfaces are in contact: distinguished from COHESION

ad·he·sive (əd hēs′iv, -hē′ziv; ad-) *adj.* [Fr. *adhésif* < L. *adhaesus*, pp. of *adhaerere*: see ADHERE] **1.** sticking and not coming loose; clinging **2.** gummed; sticky —*n.* an adhesive substance, as glue —**ad·he′sive·ly** *adv.* —**ad·he′sive·ness** *n.*

adhesive tape tape with a sticky substance on one side, variously used, as for holding bandages in place

ad·hib·it (ad hib′it) *vt.* [< L. *adhibitus*, pp. of *adhibere*, to summon < *ad-*, to + *habere*, to have] **1.** to let in; admit **2.** to affix **3.** to administer, as a remedy —**ad·hi·bi·tion** (ad′hə bish′ən) *n.*

ad hoc (ad′ häk′) [L., to this] for this specific purpose; for a special case only, without general application [an *ad hoc* committee]

ad hom·i·nem (ad′ hä′mə nem′) [L., lit., to the man] appealing to one's prejudices rather than to reason, as by attacking one's opponent rather than debating the issue

ad·i·a·bat·ic (ad′ē ə bat′ik) *adj.* [< Gr. *adiabatos*, not to be passed < *a-*, not + *dia*, through + *bainein*, to go] *Physics* involving expansion or compression without loss or gain of heat —**ad′i·a·bat′i·cal·ly** *adv.*

ad·i·aph·o·rous (ad′ē af′ər əs) *adj.* [Gr. *adiaphoros* < *a-*, not + *diaphoros*, different < *diapherein*, to differ < *dia-*, through + *pherein*, to BEAR¹] **1.** morally neutral or indifferent **2.** *Med.* neither harmful nor helpful

a·dieu (ə dyōō′, -dōō′; *Fr.* à dyö′) *interj., n., pl.* **a·dieus′;** *Fr.* **a·dieux′** (-dyö′) [ME. < OFr. *a dieu*, to God (I commend you) < L. *ad*, to + *Deum*, acc. of *Deus*, God; current use chiefly from ModFr. (< OFr.)] goodbye; farewell

A·di·ge (ä′dē jā) river in N Italy, flowing into the Gulf of Venice: c. 250 mi.

ad in·fi·ni·tum (ad in′fə nīt′əm, äd-) [L., to infinity] endlessly; forever; without limit: abbrev. **ad inf.**

‡**ad i·ni·ti·um** (ad′ i nish′ē əm) [L.] at or to the beginning: abbrev. **ad init.**

ad in·te·rim (ad in′tər im) [L.] **1.** in the meantime **2.** temporary Abbrev. **ad int.** —SYN. see TEMPORARY

☆**a·di·os** (a′dē ōs′, ä′-; *Sp.* ä dyōs′) *interj.* [< Sp. *adiós* < L. *ad* + *Deum*: see ADIEU] goodbye; farewell

ad·i·po·cere (ad′ə pə sir′) *n.* [Fr. *adipocire* < L. *adeps* (gen. *adipis*), fat + *cera*, wax] a fatty or waxy substance produced in decomposing dead bodies exposed to moisture

ad·i·pose (ad′ə pōs′) *adj.* [ModL. *adiposus* < L. *adeps* (gen. *adipis*), fat] of, like, or containing animal fat; fatty —*n.* fat in the connective tissue of an animal's body

ad·i·pos·i·ty (ad′ə päs′ə tē) *n.* **1.** the state of being fat; obesity **2.** a tendency to become obese

Ad·i·ron·dack Mountains (ad′ə rän′dak) mountain range in the Appalachians, in NE New York: highest peak, Mt. MARCY: also **Adirondacks**

ad·it (ad′it) *n.* [L. *aditus*, pp. of *adire*, to approach < *ad-*, to + *ire*, to go] an approach or entrance; specif., an almost horizontal passageway into a mine

adj. 1. adjective **2.** adjourned **3.** adjutant

ad·ja·cen·cy (ə jā′sən sē) *n.* **1.** the quality or state of being adjacent; nearness **2.** *pl.* **-cies** an adjacent thing

ad·ja·cent (ə jā′sənt) *adj.* [L. *adjacens*, prp. of *adjacere*, to lie near < *ad-*, to + *jacere*, to lie, lit., cast oneself down] near or close (*to* something); adjoining —**ad·ja′cent·ly** *adv.* SYN.—**adjacent** things may or may not be in actual contact with each other but they are not separated by things of the same kind [*adjacent* angles, *adjacent* farmhouses]; that which is **adjoining** something else touches it at some point or along a line [*adjoining* rooms]; things are **contiguous** when they touch along the whole or most of one side [*contiguous* farms]; **tangent** implies contact at a single, nonintersecting point with a curved line or surface [a line *tangent* to a circle]; **neighboring** things lie near to each other [*neighboring* villages]

adjacent angles two angles having the same vertex and a side in common

ad·jec·ti·val (aj′ik tī′v'l) *adj.* **1.** of an adjective **2.** having the nature or function of an adjective **3.** adjective-forming [an *adjectival* suffix] —**ad′jec·ti′val·ly** *adv.*

ad·jec·tive (aj′ik tiv) *n.* [ME. & OFr. *adjectif* < L. *adjectivus*, that is added < *adjectus*, pp. of *adjicere*, to add to < *ad-*, to + *jacere*, to throw]

ADJACENT ANGLES

1. any of a class of words used to limit or qualify a noun or other substantive [*good, every,* and *Aegean* are *adjectives*] **2.** any phrase or clause similarly used —*adj.* **1.** of an adjective **2.** having the nature or function of an adjective **3.** dependent or subordinate **4.** *Law* of or relating to practice and procedure; procedural —**ad′jec·tive·ly** *adv.*

ad·join (ə join′) *vt.* [ME. *ajoinen* < OFr. *ajoindre* < L.

adjungere < *ad-*, to + *jungere*: see JOIN] **1.** to be next to; be contiguous to **2.** to unite or annex (*to* a person or thing) —*vi.* to be next to each other; be in contact

ad·join·ing (-iŋ) *adj.* touching at some point or along a line; contiguous —SYN. see ADJACENT

ad·journ (ə jurn′) *vt.* [ME. *ajournen* < OFr. *ajourner* < *a jorn*, at the (specified) day < *a*, at + *jorn*, day < L. *diurnum*, daily < *dies*, day] to put off or suspend until a future time [to *adjourn* a meeting] —*vi.* **1.** to close a session or meeting for the day or for a time [Congress *adjourned* for the summer] **2.** [Colloq.] to move from a place of meeting (*to* another place) [let's *adjourn* to the patio] SYN.—**adjourn** is applied to the action of a deliberative body, etc. in bringing a session to a close, with the intention of resuming at a later date; **prorogue** applies to the formal dismissal of a parliament by the crown, subject to reassembly; to **dissolve** an assembly is to terminate it as constituted, so that an election must be held to reconstitute it; **postpone** implies the intentional delaying of an action until a later time; **suspend** denotes the breaking off of proceedings, privileges, etc. for a time, sometimes for such an indefinite time as to suggest cancellation [to *suspend* a sentence]

ad·journ·ment (-mənt) *n.* **1.** an adjourning or being adjourned **2.** the time of being adjourned

ad·judge (ə juj′) *vt.* **-judged′, -judg′ing** [ME. *ajugen* < OFr. *ajugier* < L. *adjudicare* < *ad-*, to + *judicare*, to judge, decide < *judex*, JUDGE] **1.** to judge or decide by law **2.** to declare or order by law **3.** to sentence judicially; condemn [to *adjudge* a man to prison] **4.** to give or award (costs, etc.) by law **5.** [Rare] to regard; deem

ad·ju·di·cate (ə jōō′də kāt′) *vt.* **-cat′ed, -cat′ing** [< L. *adjudicatus*, pp. of *adjudicare*, ADJUDGE] *Law* to hear and decide (a case) —*vi.* to serve as a judge (*in* or *on* a dispute or problem) —**ad·ju′di·ca′tor** *n.* —**ad·ju′di·ca·to′ry** (-kə tôr′ē) *adj.*

ad·ju·di·ca·tion (ə jōō′də kā′shən) *n.* **1.** the act of adjudicating **2.** *Law a)* a judge's decision *b)* a decree in bankruptcy determining the status of the bankrupt —**ad·ju′di·ca′tive** (-kāt′iv, -kə tiv) *adj.*

ad·junct (aj′uŋkt) *n.* [< L. *adjunctus*, pp. of *adjungere*, ADJOIN] **1.** a thing added to something else, but secondary or not essential to it **2.** a person connected with another as a helper or subordinate associate **3.** *Gram.* a word or phrase that qualifies or modifies another word or other words **4.** *Logic* a nonessential attribute —*adj.* added or connected in a secondary or subordinate way —**ad′junct·ly** *adv.*

ad·junc·tive (ə juŋk′tiv) *adj.* [LL. *adjunctivus*] that constitutes an adjunct —**ad·junc′tive·ly** *adv.*

ad·ju·ra·tion (aj′oo rā′shən) *n.* [L. *adjuratio*, a swearing to < pp. of *adjurare*, ADJURE] **1.** a solemn charge or command **2.** an earnest entreaty

ad·jure (ə joor′) *vt.* **-jured′, -jur′ing** [ME. *adjuren* < L. *adjurare* < *ad-*, to + *jurare*: see JURY¹] **1.** to command or charge solemnly, often under oath or penalty **2.** to entreat solemnly; appeal to earnestly —**ad·jur′er, ad·ju′ror** *n.* —**ad·jur′a·to′ry** (-ə tôr′ē) *adj.*

ad·just (ə just′) *vt.* [ME. *ajusten* < OFr. *ajoster*, to join < *a-*, to + *joster* (see JOUST); infl. by OFr. *juste* < L. *justus*, JUST¹] **1.** to change so as to fit, conform, make suitable, etc. [to *adjust* oneself to new conditions] **2.** to make accurate by regulating [to *adjust* a watch] **3.** to settle or arrange rightly [to *adjust* accounts] **4.** to resolve or bring into accord [to *adjust* differences] **5.** to decide how much is to be paid in settling (an insurance claim) **6.** *Mil.* to correct (the gun sight, one's aim, etc.) in firing —*vi.* to come into conformity, as with one's surroundings —SYN. see ADAPT —**ad·just′a·ble** *adj.* —**ad·jus′tor** *n.*

ad·just·ment (-mənt) *n.* **1.** an adjusting or being adjusted **2.** a means or device by which parts are adjusted to one another [the *adjustment* on a micrometer] **3.** the settlement of how much is to be paid in cases of loss or claim, as by an insurance company **4.** a lowering of price, as of damaged or soiled goods

ad·ju·tan·cy (aj′ə tən sē) *n., pl.* **-cies** the rank or office of a military adjutant

ad·ju·tant (aj′ə tənt) *n.* [< L. *adjutans*, prp. of *adjutare*, to aid < *adjuvare*, to help, assist < *ad-*, to + *juvare*, to help] **1.** an assistant **2.** *Mil.* a staff officer who serves as an administrative assistant to the commanding officer **3.** *a)* a very large stork (*Leptoptilos dubius*) about 5 ft. tall, of India and Africa, with a bare head and neck and a large, thick bill: it flies gracefully but walks in an amusingly pompous way *b)* a similar but smaller stork (*Leptoptilos javanicus*) found in the same countries: also called **lesser adjutant**

adjutant general *pl.* **adjutants general 1.** an officer in the army who is the chief administrative assistant of the commanding general of a corps or higher echelon **2.** [A-G-] *U.S. Army* the general in charge of the department that handles all records, circulars, correspondence, personnel management, etc.

ADJUTANT
STORK
(to 60 in. high)

ad·ju·vant (aj'ə vənt) *adj.* [L. *adjuvans*, prp. of *adjuvare*: see ADJUTANT] that helps or aids; auxiliary —*n.* 1. a person or thing that helps 2. a substance added to a drug to aid its action

Ad·ler (äd'lər) 1. Alfred, 1870–1937; Austrian psychiatrist & psychologist 2. (ad'lər) Felix, 1851–1933; U.S. educator & social reformer: founder of the Ethical Cultural Movement

ad·lib (ad'lib') *vt.*, *vi.* **-libbed'**, **-lib'bing** [<AD LIBITUM] [Colloq.] to improvise (words, gestures, etc. not in the script); extemporize —*n.* [Colloq.] the act of ad-libbing or an ad-libbed remark: also **ad lib** —*adj.* [Colloq.] spoken or done extemporaneously —*adv.* [Colloq.] extemporizing freely: also **ad lib**

ad lib., ad libit. ad libitum

ad lib·i·tum (ad' lib'i təm) [ML. < L. *ad*, at + *libitum* < *libet*, it pleases: see LOVE] at pleasure; as one pleases: used esp. as a musical direction that the marked section may be altered or omitted to suit the performer

‡**ad lit·ter·am** (ad lit'ər əm) [L.] to the letter; exactly

ad loc. [L. *ad locum*] at or to the place

Adm. 1. Admiral 2. Admiralty

adm. 1. administration 2. administrative 3. admitted

☆**ad·man** (ad'man') *n.*, *pl.* **-men'** a man whose work or business is advertising: also **ad man**

ad·meas·ure (ad mezh'ər) *vt.* **-ured, -ur·ing** [ME. *amesuren* < OFr. *admesurer* < ML. *admensurare*: see AD- & MEASURE] to measure out shares of; apportion

ad·meas·ure·ment (-mənt) *n.* 1. the act of admeasuring 2. size or dimensions 3. an apportioning

Ad·me·tus (ad mēt'əs) [L. < Gr. *Admētos*, lit., wild, unbroken] *Gr. Myth.* a king of Thessaly, husband of ALCESTIS

ad·min·i·cle (ad min'ə k'l) *n.* [L. *adminiculum*, support, orig., a support for the hand, dim. < *ad-*, to + *manus*, hand] a thing that helps or supplements; auxiliary —**ad·min·ic·u·lar** (ad'mə nik'yə lər) *adj.*

ad·min·is·ter (əd min'ə stər, ad-) *vt.* [ME. *aministren* < OFr. *aministrer* < L. *administrare* < *ad-*, to + *ministrare*, to serve] 1. to manage or direct (the affairs of a government, institution, etc.) 2. to give out or dispense, as punishment or justice 3. to give or apply (medicine, etc.) 4. to direct the taking of (an oath, pledge, etc.) 5. *Law* to act as executor or administrator of (an estate) —*vi.* 1. to act as manager or administrator 2. to furnish help or be of service [*adminis*er to an invalid's needs/ —*SYN.* see GOVERN —**ad·min'is·tra·ble** (-ə strə b'l) *adj.* —**ad·min'is·trant** (-ə strənt) *n.*, *adj.*

ad·min·is·trate (ad min'ə strāt', ad-) *vt.* **-trat'ed, -trat'ing** to administer

ad·min·is·tra·tion (ad min'ə strā'shən, ad-) *n.* [ME. *administracioun* < OFr. *administration* < L. *administratio* < pp. of *administrare*, ADMINISTER] 1. the act of administering; management; specif., the management of governmental or institutional affairs 2. administrators collectively; specif., [*often* A-] the officials who make up the executive branch of a government and their policies and principles 3. their term of office 4. the administering (of punishment, medicine, a sacrament, an oath, etc.) 5. *Law* the management and settling (of an estate) by an administrator or executor

ad·min·is·tra·tive (əd min'ə strāt'iv, ad-; -strə tiv) *adj.* of or connected with administration; executive —**ad·min'is·tra'tive·ly** *adv.*

ad·min·is·tra·tor (əd min'ə strāt'ər, ad-) *n.* 1. a person who administers 2. a person who has considerable executive ability 3. *Law* a person appointed by a court to settle an estate: cf. EXECUTOR —**ad·min'is·tra'trix** (-strā'triks) *n. fem.*, *pl.* **-tri·ces** (-tri sēz), **-trix·es**

ad·mi·ra·ble (ad'mər ə b'l) *adj.* [ME. < L. *admirabilis* < *admirari*: see ADMIRE] inspiring or deserving admiration or praise; excellent; splendid —**ad'mi·ra·bil'i·ty** (-bil'ə tē) *n.* —**ad'mi·ra·bly** *adv.*

ad·mi·ral (ad'mər əl, -mrəl) *n.* [ME. *admirail*, *amirail* < OFr. *amiral*, *amiral* < Ar. *amīr a' ālī*, high leader; sp. infl. by ADMIRABLE] 1. the commanding officer of a navy or fleet 2. a naval officer of high rank; specif., *U.S. Navy* a four-star admiral, ranking below a fleet admiral and above a vice admiral: see also FLEET ADMIRAL, VICE ADMIRAL, REAR ADMIRAL 3. [Archaic] a vessel carrying the admiral; flagship 4. [orig. ADMIRABLE] *Zool.* any one of certain colorful butterflies (genera *Basilarchia* and *Pyrameis*) with unusually small forelegs —**ad'mi·ral·ship'** *n.*

ad·mi·ral·ty (-tē) *n.*, *pl.* **-ties** [ME. *admiralte* < OFr. *admiralté*] 1. the rank, position, or authority of an admiral 2. a) [*often* A-] the governmental department or officials in charge of naval affairs, as in England b) maritime law or court

Admiralty Islands group of small islands in the Bismarck Archipelago: pop. 19,000: also **Admiralties**

Admiralty Range mountain range in Victoria Land, Antarctica, northwest of the Ross Sea

ad·mi·ra·tion (ad'mə rā'shən) *n.* [ME. *admiracion* < L. *admiratio* < *admirari*: see ADMIRE] 1. the act of admiring 2. the sense of wonder, delight, and pleased approval inspired by anything fine, skillful, beautiful, etc. 3. a thing or person inspiring such feelings 4. [Archaic] the act of wondering

ad·mire (əd mīr', ad-) *vt.* **-mired', -mir'ing** [OFr. *admirer* < L. *admirari* < *ad-*, at + *mirari*, to wonder] 1. to regard with wonder, delight, and pleased approval 2. to have high regard for 3. [Dial.] to like or wish (*to* do something) 4. [Archaic] to marvel at —*SYN.* see REGARD —**ad·mir'er** *n.* —**ad·mir'ing·ly** *adv.*

ad·mis·si·ble (əd mis'ə b'l, ad-) *adj.* [Fr. < ML. *admissibilis* < L. *admissus*, pp. of *admittere*, ADMIT] 1. that can be properly accepted or allowed [*admissible* evidence] 2. that ought to be admitted —**ad·mis'si·bil'i·ty** (-bil'ə tē) *n.* —**ad·mis'si·bly** *adv.*

ad·mis·sion (əd mish'ən, ad-) *n.* [ME. < L. *admissio* < *admissus*, pp. of *admittere*, ADMIT] 1. an admitting or being admitted; entrance 2. the right to enter; access 3. a fee paid for the right to enter; entrance fee 4. a conceding, or granting of the truth of something 5. an acknowledging, or confessing to some crime, fault, etc. 6. a thing conceded, acknowledged, or confessed —**ad·mis'sive** (-mis'iv) *adj.*

Admission Day any of several legal holidays celebrated individually by certain States commemorating their admission into the Union

ad·mit (əd mit', ad-)' *vt.* **-mit'ted, -mit'ting** [ME. *amitten* < L. *admittere* < *ad-*, to + *mittere*, to send] 1. to permit to enter or use; let in 2. to entitle to enter [this ticket *admits* two] 3. to allow; leave room for 4. to have room for; hold [the hall *admits* 2,500 people] 5. to concede or grant 6. to acknowledge or confess 7. to permit to practice certain functions [he was *admitted* to the bar] —*vi.* 1. to give entrance (*to* a place) 2. to allow or warrant (with *of*) —*SYN.* see ACKNOWLEDGE, RECEIVE

ad·mit·tance (-'ns) *n.* 1. an admitting or being admitted 2. permission or right to enter 3. *Elec.* the ratio of effective current to effective voltage in a circuit carrying an alternating current; the reciprocal of impedance

ad·mit·ted·ly (əd mit'əd lē) *adv.* by admission or general agreement; confessedly [I am *admittedly* afraid/

ad·mix (ad miks') *vt.*, *vi.* [back-formation, after MIX < *admixt*, mixed with < L. *admixtus*: see ADMIXTURE] to mix (a thing) in; mix with something

ad·mix·ture (-chər) *n.* [< L. *admixtus*, pp. of *admiscere* < *ad-*, to + *miscere*, to mix + -URE] 1. a mixture 2. a thing or ingredient added in mixing

ad·mon·ish (əd män'ish, ad-) *vt.* [ME. *amonesten* <OFr. *amonester* < ML. *admonestare*, ult. < L. *admonere* < *ad-*, to + *monere*, to warn] 1. to caution against specific faults; warn 2. to reprove mildly 3. to urge or exhort 4. to inform or remind, by way of a warning —*SYN.* see ADVISE —**ad·mon'ish·ing·ly** *adv.* —**ad·mon'ish·ment** *n.*

ad·mo·ni·tion (ad'mə nish'ən) *n.* [ME. *amonicioun* < OFr. *amonition*, *admonition* < L. *admonitio* < *admonere*] 1. an admonishing, or warning to correct some fault 2. a mild rebuke; reprimand

ad·mon·i·tor (əd män'ə tər, ad-) *n.* [L. < *admonere*: cf. ADMONISH] a person who admonishes

ad·mon·i·to·ry (-ə tôr'ē) *adj.* admonishing; warning

ad·nate (ad'nāt) *adj.* [< L. *adnatus*, pp. of *adnasci*, to be born < *ad-*, to + *nasci*: see NATAL] *Biol.* congenitally joined together: said of unlike parts —**ad·na'tion** *n.*

ad nau·se·am (ad' nô'zē əm, äd'-; -shē-, -sē-, -zhē-) [L., to nausea] to the point of disgust; to a sickening extreme

ad·nex·a (ad nek'sə) *n.pl.* [ModL. < L., neut. pl. of *adnexus* < *adnectere*: see ANNEX] *Anat.* accessory parts or appendages of an organ [the ovaries are *adnexa* of the uterus] —**ad·nex'al** *adj.*

a·do (ə doō') *n.* [ME. *ado* < northern dial. inf. *at do*, to do] fuss; trouble; excitement

☆**a·do·be** (ə dō'bē) *n.* [Sp. < Ar. *aṭ-ṭōba*, the brick < *al*, the + Cop. *tōbe*, brick] 1. unburnt, sun-dried brick 2. the clay of which such brick is made 3. a building made of adobe, esp. in the Southwest

ad·o·les·cence (ad'l es'ns) *n.* [ME. & OFr. < L. *adolescentia* < *adolescens*] 1. the state or quality of being adolescent 2. the time of life between puberty and maturity; youth

ad·o·les·cent (-'nt) *adj.* [Fr. < L. *adolescens*, prp. of *adolescere*, to come to maturity, be kindled, burn < *adalescere* < *ad-*, to + *alescere*, to increase, grow up < *alere*, to feed, sustain; akin to OE. *ald* (see OLD), Goth. *alan*, to grow] 1. developing from childhood to maturity; growing up 2. of or characteristic of adolescence; youthful, exuberant, immature, unsettled, etc. —*n.* a boy or a girl from puberty to adulthood; person in his teens —*SYN.* see YOUNG

Ad·olph (ad'älf, ā'dôlf) [L. *Adolphus* < OHG. *Adolf*, *Adulf*, lit., noble wolf < *adal*, nobility + *wolf*, wolf] a masculine name: equiv. L. *Adolphus*, Fr. *Adolphe*, Ger. *Adolf*

‡**Ad·o·nai** (ä'dō nī', -noi'; *E.* a'də nā'ī) [Heb., my Lord; ? < Phoen. *adōn*, lord] God; Lord: used in Hebrew reading as a substitute for the "ineffable name" JHVH (see JEHOVAH)

A·don·is (ə dän'is, -dō'nis) [L. < Gr. *Adōnis*] *Gr. Myth.* a handsome young man loved by Aphrodite: he was killed by a wild boar —*n.* any very handsome young man —**A·don'ic** (-ik) *adj.*

a·dopt (ə däpt') *vt.* [L. *adoptare* < *ad-*, to + *optare*, to choose] 1. to choose and bring into a certain relationship; specif., to take into one's own family by legal process and raise as one's own child 2. to take up and use (an idea, a practice, etc.) as one's own 3. to choose and follow (a

course) **4.** to vote to accept (a committee report, motion, etc.) **5.** to select as a required textbook —**a·dopt'a·ble** *adj.* —**a·dopt'er** *n.* —**a·dop'tion** *n.*

a·dop·tive (ə däp'tiv) *adj.* [L. *adoptivus*] **1.** having to do with adoption **2.** that has become so by the act of adoption [*adoptive* parents] —**a·dop'tive·ly** *adv.*

a·dor·a·ble (ə dôr'ə b'l) *adj.* [Fr. < L. *adorabilis*] **1.** [Now Rare] worthy of adoration or love **2.** [Colloq.] delightful; charming —**a·dor'a·bil'l·ty, a·dor'a·ble·ness** *n.* —**a·dor'a·bly** *adv.*

ad·o·ra·tion (ad'ə rā'shən) *n.* [Fr. < L. *adoratio*] **1.** a worshiping or paying homage, as to a divinity **2.** great love, devotion, and respect

a·dore (ə dôr') *vt.* **a·dored', a·dor'ing** [ME. *adouren* < OFr. *adourer* < L. *adorare,* to worship < *ad-,* to + *orare,* to speak < *os* (gen. *oris*), a mouth] **1.** to worship as divine **2.** to love greatly or honor highly; idolize **3.** [Colloq.] to like very much —*SYN.* see REVERE —**a·dor'er** *n.* —**a·dor'ing·ly** *adv.*

a·dorn (ə dôrn') *vt.* [ME. *adornen* (altered after L.) < OFr. *aourner* < L. *adornare* < *ad-,* to + *ornare,* to deck out] **1.** to be an ornament to; add beauty, splendor, or distinction to **2.** to put decorations on; ornament
SYN. —**adorn** is used of that which adds to the beauty of something by gracing it with its own beauty [*roses adorned* her hair]; **decorate** implies the addition of something to render attractive what would otherwise be plain or bare [to *decorate* a wall with pictures]; **ornament** is used with reference to accessories which enhance the appearance [a crown *ornamented* with jewels]; **embellish** suggests the addition of something highly ornamental or ostentatious for effect; to **beautify** is to lend beauty to, or heighten the beauty of; **bedeck** emphasizes the addition of showy things [*bedecked* with jewelry]

a·dorn·ment (-mənt) *n.* **1.** an adorning or being adorned **2.** a decoration or ornament

A·do·wa (ä'də wä') *same as* ADUWA

a·down (ə doun') *adv., prep.* [ME. *adoun* < OE. *adun:* see DOWN] [Poet.] down

ADP [A(DENOSINE) D(i)P(hosphate)] a substance, $C_{10}H_{15}N_5$-$O_{10}P_2$, found in all living cells and vital to the energy processes of life: during the oxidation of carbohydrates ADP is converted to ATP, and the resulting energy is stored in the ATP molecule, which is converted back to ADP in the process of releasing the energy, as in muscular contraction

‡ad quem (ad' kwem') [L.] to or at which

A·dras·tus (ə dras'təs) *Gr. Myth.* a king of Argos who led the SEVEN AGAINST THEBES

‡ad rem (ad' rem') [L., to (the) thing] to the point at issue; to the matter in hand

ad·re·nal (ə drē'n'l) *adj.* [AD- + RENAL] **1.** near the kidneys **2.** of or from the adrenal glands —*n.* an adrenal gland

adrenal gland either of a pair of endocrine organs lying immediately above the kidney, consisting of an inner medulla which produces epinephrine and norepinephrine, and an outer cortex which produces a variety of steroid hormones

☆Ad·ren·al·in (ə dren'l in) [ADRENAL + -IN¹: so named (1901) by Dr. J. Takamine, U.S. chemist who first isolated it] *a trademark for* EPINEPHRINE —*n.* [a-] epinephrine: also **ad·ren'al·ine** (-in)

ad·ren·er·gic (ad'rə nur'jik) *adj.* [< ADREN(AL) + Gr. *erg*(on), WORK + -IC] **1.** releasing epinephrine or a similar substance [the *adrenergic* nerves of the sympathetic nervous system] **2.** like epinephrine in chemical activity [an *adrenergic* drug]

ad·re·no- (ə drē'nō) *a combining form meaning:* **1.** adrenal glands [*adrenocortical*] **2.** epinephrine [*adrenergic*] Also, before a vowel, **adren-**

ad·re·no·cor·ti·cal (ə drē' nō kôr'ti k'l) *adj.* of, or produced in, the cortex of the adrenal glands

ad·re·no·cor·ti·co·tro·phic (-kôr'ti kō träf'ik) *adj.* [< ADRENO- + CORTIC(AL) + TROPHIC] that can stimulate the cortex of the adrenal glands: also **ad·re'no·cor'ti·co·trop'ic**

adrenocorticotrophic hormone *same as* ACTH

A·dri·an (ā'drē ən) [L. *Adrianus, Hadrianus* < *Adria, Hadria,* name of two Italian cities] **1.** masculine name **2. Adrian IV** (*Nicholas Breakspear*) 1100?–59; Pope (1154–59): the only Eng. Pope **3. E(dgar) D(ouglas),** 1st Baron, 1889–   ; Eng. neurophysiologist

A·dri·an·o·ple (ā'drē ə nō'p'l) *former name of* EDIRNE

A·dri·an·o·po·lis (-năp'ə lis) *ancient Rom. name of* EDIRNE

A·dri·at·ic (Sea) (ā'drē at'ik) sea between Italy and Yugoslavia: it is an arm of the Mediterranean —**A'dri·at'ic** *adj.*

a·drift (ə drift') *adv., adj.* **1.** floating freely without being steered; not anchored; drifting **2.** without any particular aim or purpose

a·droit (ə droit') *adj.* [Fr. *à,* to + *droit,* right < L. *directus,* pp. of *dirigere,* DIRECT] skillful in a physical or mental way; clever; expert [his *adroit* handling of an awkward situation] —*SYN.* see DEXTEROUS —**a·droit'ly** *adv.* —**a·droit'ness** *n.*

ad·sci·ti·tious (ad'sə tish'əs) *adj.* [< L. *adscitus,* pp. of *adsciscere,* to receive with knowledge, approve < *ad-,* to + *sciscere,* to seek to know < *scire,* to know] added from an external source; supplemental

ad·script (ad'skript) *adj.* [L. *adscriptus,* pp. of *adscribere* < *ad-,* to + *scribere,* to write] written after

ad·scrip·tion (ad skrip'shən) *n. same as* ASCRIPTION

ad·sorb (ad sôrb', -zôrb') *vt.* [< AD- + L. *sorbere* (cf. ABSORB)] to collect (a gas, liquid, or dissolved substance) in condensed form on a surface —**ad·sorb'a·ble** *adj.*

ad·sor·bate (ad sôr'bāt, -zôr'-) *n.* a gas, liquid, etc. taken up by adsorption

ad·sor·bent (-bənt) *adj.* that is capable of adsorbing —*n.* a thing or substance that adsorbs

ad·sorp·tion (ad sôrp'shən, -zôrp'-) *n.* [< ADSORB, after ABSORPTION] an adsorbing or being adsorbed; adhesion of the molecules of a gas, liquid, or dissolved substance to a surface —**ad·sorp'tive** *adj.*

ad·su·ki bean (ad sōōk'ē, -zōōk'-) *same as* ADZUKI BEAN

ad·u·lar·i·a (aj'ə ler'ē ə) *n.* [It. < Fr. *adulaire* < *Adula,* a group of mountains in Switzerland + *-aire, -ARY*] a translucent kind of orthoclase, as the moonstone

ad·u·late (aj'ə lāt') *vt.* **-lat'ed, -lat'ing** [< L. *adulatus,* pp. of *adulari,* to fawn upon] to praise too highly or flatter servilely —**ad'u·la'tion** *n.* —**ad'u·la'tor** *n.* —**ad'u·la·to'ry** (-lə tôr'ē) *adj.*

a·dult (ə dult', ad'ult) *adj.* [L. *adultus,* pp. of *adolescere:* see ADOLESCENT] **1.** grown up; mature in age, size, strength, etc. **2.** of or for adult persons [an *adult* novel] —*n.* **1.** a man or woman who is fully grown up; mature person **2.** an animal or plant that is fully developed **3.** a person who has reached an age set by law that qualifies him for full legal rights, in common law generally 21 years —*SYN.* see RIPE —**a·dult'hood** *n.* —**a·dult'ness** *n.*

a·dul·ter·ant (ə dul'tər ənt) *n.* a substance that adulterates —*adj.* adulterating; making inferior or impure

a·dul·ter·ate (ə dul'tə rāt'; *for adj.* -tər it) *vt.* **-at'ed, -at'ing** [< L. *adulteratus,* pp. of *adulterare,* to falsify < *adulter,* an adulterer, counterfeiter < *ad-,* to + *alter,* other, another] to make inferior, impure, not genuine, etc. by adding a harmful, less valuable, or prohibited substance —*adj.* **1.** guilty of adultery; adulterous **2.** adulterated; not genuine —**a·dul'ter·at'or** *n.*

a·dul·ter·at·ed (-rāt'id) *adj.* **1.** made inferior, impure, etc. by adulterating **2.** that does not conform to legal standards of purity, processing, labeling, etc.

a·dul·ter·a·tion (ə dul'tə rā'shən) *n.* **1.** an adulterating or being adulterated **2.** an adulterated substance, commodity, etc.

a·dul·ter·er (ə dul'tər ər) *n.* [altered, after L. *adulterare,* from ME. *avowterer, avouter* < OFr. *avoutre* < *avoutrer,* to commit adultery < L. *adulterare:* see ADULTERATE] a person (esp. a man) guilty of adultery —**a·dul'ter·ess** (-tər is, -tris) *n.fem.*

a·dul·ter·ine (ə dul'tər in, -tə rīn') *adj.* [L. *adulterinus* < *adulter:* see ADULTERATE] **1.** of adultery **2.** due to adulteration

a·dul·ter·ous (-tər əs) *adj.* relating to, characterized by, or guilty of, adultery —**a·dul'ter·ous·ly** *adv.*

a·dul·ter·y (ə dul'tər ē) *n., pl.* **-ter·ies** [L. *adulterium* < *adulter:* see ADULTERATE] voluntary sexual intercourse between a married man and a woman not his wife, or between a married woman and a man not her husband

ad·um·bral (ad um'brəl) *adj.* [see ff.] in shadow; shady

ad·um·brate (ad um'brāt, ad'əm brāt') *vt.* **-brat·ed, -brat·ing** [< L. *adumbratus,* pp. of *adumbrari,* to shade < *ad-,* to + *umbra,* shade] **1.** to outline in a shadowy way; sketch **2.** to suggest beforehand; foreshadow in a vague way **3.** to obscure; overshadow —**ad'um·bra'tion** (-brā'shən) *n.* —**ad·um'bra·tive** (-tiv) *adj.*

a·dunc (ə dunk') *adj.* [L. *aduncus* < *ad-,* to + *uncus,* hooked, a hook < IE. base **ang-, ank-:* see ANGLE¹] curving inward, as a parrot's beak: also **a·dun·cous** (ə dun'kəs)

a·dust (ə dust') *adj.* [L. *adustus,* pp. of *adurere,* to burn up < *ad-,* to + *urere,* to burn: see EMBER¹] **1.** scorched; burned **2.** parched **3.** sunburned **4.** sallow and melancholy

A·du·wa (ä'doo wä') town in N Ethiopia: pop. c. 10,000

adv. 1. ad valorem **2.** adverb **3.** adverbial **4.** advertisement **5.** advisory **6.** advocate **7.** [L. *adversus*] against

ad val. ad valorem

ad va·lo·rem (ad' və lôr'əm) [L.] in proportion to the value: a phrase applied to certain duties levied on imports according to their invoiced value

ad·vance (ad vans', -väns') *vt.* **-vanced', -vanc'ing** [ME. *avance* < OFr. *avancer,* to forward < VL. **abantiare* < L. *ab-,* from + *ante,* before: spelling *ad-* by association with L. *ad,* to, forward] **1.** to bring forward; move forward [to *advance* a chessman] **2.** to raise in rank, importance, etc.; promote **3.** to help or hasten the success or completion of; further [to *advance* a project] **4.** to put forward; propose **5.** to bring closer to the present; specif., *a)* to cause (a future event) to happen earlier *b)* to assign a later date to (a past event) **6.** to raise the rate of; increase [to *advance* prices] **7.** to pay (money) before due **8.** to lend —*vi.* **1.** to go forward; move ahead **2.** to make progress; im-

prove; develop **3.** to rise in rank, importance, etc. **4.** to rise in price or cost; increase —*n.* **1.** a moving forward **2.** an improvement; progress *[new advances in science]* **3.** a rise in value or cost **4.** *[pl.]* approaches to curry favor, become acquainted, etc.; overtures *(to someone)* **5.** a payment made before due, as of wages **6.** a loan —*adj.* **1.** in front *[advance guard]* **2.** beforehand; ahead of time *[advance information]* —**in advance 1.** in front **2.** before due; ahead of time —**ad·vanc′er** *n.*
SYN.—**advance** is used to describe assistance in hastening the course of anything or in moving toward an objective; to **promote** is to help in the establishment, development, or success of something *[to promote good will]*; **forward** emphasizes the idea of action as an impetus *[concessions were made to forward the pact]*; **further** emphasizes assistance in bringing a desired goal closer *[to further a cause]*—*ANT.* **retard, check**
ad·vanced (-vanst′, -vänst′) *adj.* **1.** in advance; moved forward; in front **2.** far on in life; old **3.** ahead or beyond in progress, complexity, etc. *[advanced studies]* **4.** higher than usual *[a movie at advanced prices]* —*SYN.* see LIBERAL
☆**advanced credit** (or **standing**) credit toward a degree allowed to a student by a college for courses taken elsewhere
advance guard a detachment of troops sent ahead to reconnoiter and protect the line of march
ad·vance·ment (əd vans′mənt, -väns′-) *n.* **1.** an advancing or being advanced **2.** promotion, as to a higher rank **3.** progress or improvement; furtherance **4.** *Law* money or property given as an advance share in the estate of a person who later dies without making a will: it is deducted from the total share of the recipient in the intestate's estate
ad·van·tage (əd van′tij, -vän′-) *n.* [ME. *avantage, avauntage* < OFr. *avantage* < *avant,* before < L. *ab ante,* from before] **1.** a more favorable position; superiority (often with *of* or *over*) **2.** a favorable or beneficial circumstance, event, etc. **3.** gain or benefit **4.** *Tennis* the first point scored after deuce: often shortened to *ad* or *vantage* —*vt.* **-taged, -tag·ing** to give an advantage to; be a benefit or aid to —**have the advantage of** to have an advantage over —**take advantage of 1.** to make use of for one's own benefit **2.** to impose upon in a selfish way —**to advantage** so as to result in a good effect
ad·van·ta·geous (ad′vən tā′jəs) *adj.* resulting in advantage; favorable; profitable —**ad′van·ta′geous·ly** *adv.*
ad·vec·tion (ad vek′shən) *n.* [AD- + (CON)VECTION] the transference of heat by horizontal currents of air —**ad·vec′tive** (-tiv) *adj.*
Ad·vent (ad′vent) *n.* [ME. & OFr. *avent* < ML. *adventus* < pp. of L. *advenire,* to come < *ad-,* to + *venire,* COME] **1.** the period including the four Sundays just before Christmas **2.** *Theol. a)* the birth of Christ *b) same as* SECOND COMING **3.** [a-] a coming or arrival
☆**Ad·vent·ism** (ad′vən tiz′m) *n.* the belief that Christ's second coming to earth and the Last Judgment will soon occur
☆**Ad·vent·ist** (ad′vən tist, əd ven′tist) *n.* a member of a Christian sect based on Adventism —*adj.* of Adventism or Adventists
ad·ven·ti·tia (ad′ven tish′ə, -tish′ē ə) *n.* [ModL. < L., for *adventicia,* neut. pl. of *adventicius,* ADVENTITIOUS] the outer covering of an organ, as of an artery: it is made up chiefly of connective tissue
ad·ven·ti·tious (ad′vən tish′əs) *adj.* [L. *adventicius,* coming from abroad: see ADVENT] **1.** added from outside; not inherent; accidental **2.** occurring in unusual or abnormal places *[adventitious* leaves on a plant*]* —*SYN.* see ACCIDENTAL —**ad′ven·ti′tious·ly** *adv.* —**ad′ven·ti′tious·ness** *n.*
ad·ven·tive (ad ven′tiv) *adj.* [L. *adventus:* see ADVENT) + -IVE] not native to the environment —*n.* a plant or animal that is not native to the environment
Advent Sunday the first Sunday in Advent
ad·ven·ture (əd ven′chər) *n.* [ME. & OFr. *aventure* < VL. *adventura,* lit., a happening < L. *advenire:* see ADVENT] **1.** the encountering of danger **2.** an exciting and dangerous undertaking **3.** an unusual, stirring experience, often of a romantic nature **4.** a venture or speculation in business or finance **5.** a liking for danger, excitement, etc. *[a man full of adventure]* —*vt.* **-tured, -tur·ing 1.** to put in danger; risk; venture **2.** to be bold about; dare —*vi.* **1.** to engage in daring undertakings **2.** to take a risk
ad·ven·tur·er (-ər) *n.* **1.** a person who has or likes to have adventures **2.** *same as* SOLDIER OF FORTUNE **3.** a financial speculator **4.** a person who seeks to become rich, powerful, etc. by dubious schemes
ad·ven·ture·some (-səm) *adj.* willing to take risks; adventurous
ad·ven·tur·ess (-is) *n.* a woman adventurer, specif. one who seeks to become rich and socially accepted by exploiting her charms, by scheming, etc.
ad·ven·tur·ism (-iz′m) *n.* actions or tactics, esp. in politics or international relations, that are regarded as recklessly daring and involving the risk of serious consequences —**ad·ven′tur·ist** *n., adj.*
ad·ven·tur·ous (-əs) *adj.* [ME. *aventurous* < OFr. *aventuros* < *aventure,* ADVENTURE] **1.** fond of adventure; willing to take chances; daring **2.** full of danger; risky —**ad·ven′tur·ous·ly** *adv.* —**ad·ven′tur·ous·ness** *n.*
ad·verb (ad′vurb) *n.* [ME. *adverbe* < L. *adverbium* < *ad-,* to + *verbum,* a word] **1.** any of a class of words used generally to modify a verb, an adjective, another adverb, a phrase, or a clause, by expressing time, place, manner, degree, cause, etc.: English adverbs often end in *-ly* **2.** any phrase or clause similarly used; adverbial
ad·ver·bi·al (ad vur′bē əl, əd-) *adj.* **1.** of an adverb **2.** having the nature or function of an adverb **3.** used to form an adverb *[an adverbial* suffix*]* —*n.* one or more words that occur in positions that adverbs regularly occupy *[the man built houses mornings, with help, when he had money, etc.]* —**ad·ver′bi·al·ly** *adv.*
‡**ad ver·bum** (ad′ vur′bəm) [L., to a word] word for word; verbatim
ad·ver·sar·y (ad′vər ser′ē) *n., pl.* **-sar′ies** [ME. & OFr. *adversarie* < L. *adversarius* < *adversus,* ADVERSE] a person who opposes or fights against another; opponent; enemy —*SYN.* see OPPONENT —**the Adversary** Satan
ad·ver·sa·tive (ad vur′sə tiv, əd-) *adj.* [LL. *adversativus* < *adversatus,* pp. of *adversari,* to be opposed to < *adversus,* ADVERSE] expressing opposition or antithesis —*n.* an adversative word (Ex.: *but, yet, however)*
ad·verse (ad vurs′, əd-; ad′vərs) *adj.* [ME. < OFr. *avers, advers* < L. *adversus,* turned opposite to, pp. of *advertere,* ADVERT] **1.** moving or working in an opposite or contrary direction; opposed *[adverse* river currents*]* **2.** unfavorable; harmful *[the adverse* effects of a drought*]* **3.** opposite in position **4.** *Bot.* turned toward the stem —**ad·verse′ly** *adv.*
ad·ver·si·ty (ad vur′sə tē, əd-) *n.* [ME. & OFr. *aversite* < L. *adversitas* < *adversus,* ADVERSE] **1.** a state of wretchedness or misfortune; poverty and trouble **2.** *pl.* **-ties** an instance of misfortune; calamity
ad·vert (ad vurt′, əd-) *vi.* [ME. *adverten* < OFr. *avertir* < L. *advertere* < *ad-,* to + *vertere,* to turn: see VERSE] to call attention or turn one's attention *(to);* refer or allude
ad·vert·ent (-′nt) *adj.* [L. *advertens,* prp. of *advertere,* ADVERT] paying attention; attentive; heedful —**ad·vert′ence, ad·vert′en·cy** *n.* —**ad·vert′ent·ly** *adv.*
ad·ver·tise (ad′vər tīz′) *vt.* **-tised′, -tis′ing** [ME. *advertisen* < OFr. *a(d)vertiss-,* extended stem of *advertir,* to warn, call attention to < L. *advertere,* ADVERT] **1.** to tell about or praise (a product, service, etc.) publicly, as through newspapers, handbills, radio, etc., so as to make people want to buy it **2.** to make known; give notice of —*vi.* **1.** to call the public's attention to things for sale or rent, help wanted, etc., as by printed notices; sponsor advertisements **2.** to ask *(for)* publicly by printed notice, etc. *[advertise* for a servant*]* —**ad′ver·tis′er** *n.*
ad·ver·tise·ment (ad′vər tīz′mənt; əd vur′tiz mənt, -tis-) *n.* **1.** the act of advertising **2.** a public notice or announcement, usually paid for, as of things for sale, needs, etc.
ad·ver·tis·ing (ad′vər tī′ziŋ) *n.* **1.** printed or spoken matter that advertises; advertisements collectively **2.** the business or occupation of preparing and issuing advertisements
ad·ver·tize (ad′vər tīz′) *vt., vi.* **-tized′, -tiz′ing** *same as* ADVERTISE —**ad′ver·tize′ment** *n.*
ad·vice (əd vīs′) *n.* [ME. & OFr. *avis* < ML. *advisum* < *advisus,* pp. of *advidere* < L. *ad-,* at + *videre,* to look] **1.** opinion given as to what to do or how to handle a situation; counsel **2.** *[usually pl.]* information or report *[diplomatic advices]*
ad·vis·a·ble (əd vīz′ə b'l) *adj.* proper to be advised or recommended; being good advice —**ad·vis′a·bil′i·ty, ad·vis′a·ble·ness** *n.* —**ad·vis′a·bly** *adv.*
ad·vise (əd vīz′) *vt.* **-vised′, -vis′ing** [ME. *avisen,* orig., to consider < OFr. *aviser* < ML. *advisare* < *advisum:* see ADVICE] **1.** to give advice or an opinion to; counsel **2.** to offer as advice; recommend **3.** to notify; inform *[he was advised* of the facts*]* —*vi.* **1.** to discuss something and get advice; consult *(with* a person*)* **2.** to give advice —**ad·vis′er, ad·vi′sor** *n.*
SYN.—**advise** implies the making of recommendations as to a course of action by someone with actual or supposed knowledge, experience, etc.; **counsel** implies the giving of advice after careful deliberation and suggests that weighty matters are involved; **admonish** suggests earnest, gently reproving advice concerning a fault, error, etc., given by someone fitted to do so by age or position; to **caution** is to give advice that puts one on guard against possible danger, failure, etc.; **warn,** often interchangeable with **caution,** is used when a serious danger or penalty is involved
ad·vised (əd vīzd′) *adj.* showing or resulting from thought or advice; considered: now chiefly in WELL-ADVISED, ILL-ADVISED
ad·vis·ed·ly (əd vī′zid lē) *adv.* with due consideration; deliberately
ad·vise·ment (əd vīz′mənt) *n.* [ME. & OFr. *avisement* < *aviser,* ADVISE] careful consideration —**take under advisement** to consider carefully
ad·vi·so·ry (əd vī′zər ē) *adj.* **1.** advising or given the power to advise **2.** relating to, or containing, advice —*n., pl.* **-ries** a report or warning, esp. one issued by the Weather Bureau about weather conditions
ad·vo·ca·cy (ad′və kə sē) *n.* [ME. & OFr. *advocacie* < ML. *advocatia* < L. *advocatus:* see ADVOCATE] the act of advocating, or speaking or writing in support *(of* something*)*
ad·vo·cate (ad′və kit, -kāt′; *for v.* -kāt′) *n.* [ME. & OFr. *avocat* < L. *advocatus,* a counselor < *advocare,* to summon (for aid) < *ad-,* to + *vocare,* to call] **1.** a person who pleads another's cause; specif., a lawyer **2.** a person who speaks

or writes in support of something [an *advocate* of lower taxes] —*vt.* **-cat'ed, -cat'ing** [< the *n.*] to speak or write in support of; be in favor of —*SYN.* see SUPPORT —**ad'vo·ca'tor** *n.*

ad·vo·ca·tion (ad'və kā'shən) *n.* 1. [Obs.] advocacy 2. *Scot. & Papal Law* the transfer by a superior court to itself of an action pending in an inferior court

ad·voc·a·to·ry (ad väk'ə tôr'ē, ad'və kə-) *adj.* 1. of an advocate 2. of advocacy; advocating

‡**ad·vo·ca·tus di·a·bo·li** (ad'və kāt'əs dī ab'ə lī', äd'vō·kä'təs dē äb'ə lē') [L.] *same as* DEVIL'S ADVOCATE

ad·vow·son (ad vou'z'n) *n.* [ME. & OFr. *avoueson* < L. *advocatio*, a summoning, calling to: see ADVOCATE] *Eng. Law* the right to name the holder of a church benefice

advt. *pl.* **advts.** advertisement

ad·y·na·mi·a (ad'i nā'mē ə, ā'dī-) *n.* [ModL. < Gr. < *a-*, without + *dynamis*, power] *Med.* lack of vital force as a result of illness; debility —**ad'y·nam'ic** (-nam'ik) *adj.*

ad·y·tum (ad'i təm) *n., pl.* **ad'y·ta** (-tə) [L. < Gr. *adyton*, neut. of *adytos*, not to be entered < *a-*, not + *dyein*, to enter] 1. the innermost room or shrine in certain old temples, to be entered only by priests 2. a sanctum

adz, adze (adz) *n.* [ME. *adis, adse* < OE. *adesa*, adz, ax] an axlike tool for trimming and smoothing wood, etc., with a curved blade at right angles to the handle

ad·zu·ki bean (ad zōok'ē) [Jap. *azuki*] 1. a bushy bean plant (*Phaseolus angularis*) of China and Japan, with black or white pods 2. its small, brownish bean

Æ, A.E. see George William RUSSELL ADZ

ae (ā) *adj.* < OE. *an*, whence E. *one*] [Scot.] one

æ 1. a diphthong in some Latin words, equivalent to *ai* in Greek, usually written *ae* or replaced by *e* in modern spelling of derived English words, as in *demon* (*daemon*), *ether* (*aether*), etc., and pronounced (ē, i, *or* e) 2. an Old English ligature symbolizing a low front unrounded vowel like that in Modern English *hat* 3. a character in the International Phonetic Alphabet symbolizing this vowel

nc. [L. *uetatts*] aged (a specified number of years); at the age of

Ae·a·cus (ē'ə kəs) [L. < Gr. *Aiakos*] *Gr. Myth.* a king of Aegina who after he died became one of the three judges of the dead in the lower world, with Minos and Rhadamanthus

A.E. and P. Ambassador Extraordinary and Plenipotentiary

A.E.C., AEC Atomic Energy Commission

ae·cid·i·um (ē sid'ē əm) *n., pl.* **-cid'i·a** (-sid'ē ə) [ModL., dim. < Gr. *aikia*, harm, injury] an aecium —**ae·cid'i·al** *adj.*

ae·ci·o·stage (ēs'ē ə stāj') *n.* [<AECIUM + STAGE] the period in their life cycle during which certain rust fungi produce aecia

ae·ci·um (ēs'ē əm, ēsh'-) *n., pl.* **-ci·a** (-ē ə) [ModL. < Gr. *aikia*, injury] a cuplike spore fruit produced by certain rust fungi, in which chains of spores are developed —**ae'ci·al** *adj.*

a·ë·des (ā ē'dēz) *n., pl.* **a·ë'des** [ModL. < Gr. *aēdēs*, unpleasant < *a-*, not + *hēdys*, SWEET] any of a large genus (*Aëdes*) of mosquitoes, esp. a mosquito (*Aëdes aegypti*) that carries the virus of yellow fever and dengue

ae·dile (ē'dīl) *n.* [L. *aedilis* < *aedes*, building: see EDIFY] in ancient Rome, an official in charge of buildings, roads, sanitation, public games, etc.

A.E.F., AEF American Expeditionary Force (or Forces)

Ae·ge·an (ē jē'ən) *adj.* 1. in or of the Aegean Sea 2. designating or of the culture of the Bronze Age people who lived in the Aegean Islands and nearby regions

Aegean Islands the islands in the Aegean Sea; specif., an administrative division of Greece, including Lesbos, Samos, Chios, the Cyclades, and the Dodecanese

Aegean (Sea) sea between Greece and Turkey: it is an arm of the Mediterranean

Ae·geus (ē'joos, ē'jē əs) [L. < Gr. *Aigeus*] *Gr. Myth.* a king of Athens who drowned himself when he thought his son Theseus was dead

Ae·gi·na (ē jī'nə) island off the SE coast of Greece: 32 sq. mi.: Mod. Gr. names, AIGINA, AIYINA

Ae·gir (ē'gər, ē'-) [ON.] *Norse Myth.* the god of the sea

ae·gis (ē'jis) *n.* [L. < Gr. *aigis*, shield of Zeus, goatskin < ? *aix* (gen. *aigos*), goat, hence ? orig. the short goatskin cloak of Zeus] 1. *Gr. Myth.* a shield borne by Zeus and, later, by his daughter Athena and occasionally by Apollo 2. a protection 3. sponsorship; auspices

Ae·gis·thus (ē jis'thəs) [L. < Gr. *Aigisthos*] *Gr. Myth.* the son of Thyestes and lover of Clytemnestra: he helped her to kill her husband, Agamemnon

Ae·gos·pot·a·mi (ē'gos pät'ə mī') small river in ancient Thrace, flowing into the Hellespont: at its mouth, the Spartan fleet under Lysander defeated the Athenian fleet (405 B.C.) ending the Peloponnesian War

Ae·gyp·tus (ē jip'təs) *Gr. Myth.* a king of Egypt whose fifty sons married the fifty daughters of his brother Danaus: cf. DANAIDES

Ael·fric (al'frik) 955?–1020?; Eng. abbot & writer: called *the Grammarian*

-ae·mi·a (ē'mē ə, ēm'yə) *same as* -EMIA

Ae·ne·as (i nē'əs) [L. < Gr. *Aineias*] *Gr. & Rom. Myth.* a Trojan, son of Anchises and Venus, and hero of Virgil's *Aeneid*: escaping from ruined Troy, Aeneas wandered for years before coming to Latium

Ae·ne·id (i nē'id) a Latin epic poem by Virgil, about Aeneas and his adventures

a·ë·ne·ous (ā ē'nē əs) *adj.* [L. *aeneus* < *aes*, copper, bronze: cf. ORE] having the color and luster of brass

Ae·o·li·a (ē ō'lē ə) *same as* AEOLIS

Ae·o·li·an (ē ō'lē ən) *adj.* 1. of Aeolis, its people, language, etc. 2. of Aeolus; hence 3. [*often* a-] of the wind: see EOLIAN —*n.* 1. an inhabitant of Aeolis; member of the Greek tribes that settled in ancient Thessaly, Boeotia, Lesbos, and Asia Minor 2. *same as* AEOLIC

aeolian harp a box with an opening in it across which gut strings of varying thickness are stretched, tuned in unison: when air blows over them, the strings produce a sequence of rising and falling harmonies

Ae·o·lic (ē äl'ik) *n.* a dialect of ancient Greek associated with the reputed descendants of the Aeolians —*adj. same as* AEOLIAN (sense 1)

Ae·o·lis (ē'ə lis) ancient region on the NW coast of Asia Minor, settled by the Aeolians

ae·o·lo·trop·ic (ē'ə lə träp'ik) *adj.* [< Gr. *aiolos*, varying + -TROPIC] *same as* ANISOTROPIC —**ae'o·lot'ro·py** (-lä'trə pē) *n.*

Ae·o·lus (ē'ə ləs) [L. < Gr. *Aiolos*] 1. *Gr. Myth.* the god of the winds 2. a king of Thessaly, the legendary forefather of the Aeolians

ae·on (ē'ən, ē'än) *n. same as* EON

ae·o·ni·an (ē ō'nē ən) *adj.* [Gr. *aiōnios*: see EON] lasting forever; eternal

ae·py·or·nis (ē'pē ôr'nis) *n.* [ModL. < Gr. *aipys*, high, steep + *ornis*, bird: see ORNITHO-] any of a genus (*Aepyornis*) of very large, extinct, flightless birds of Madagascar

aer- (er, ar, ā'ər) *same as* AERO-: words beginning with *aer-* are still sometimes written **aër**

aer·ate (er'āt', ā'ər-) *vt.* **-at'ed, -at'ing** [AER- + -ATE[1]] 1. to expose to air, or cause air to circulate through 2. to supply oxygen to (the blood) by the process of respiration 3. to charge (liquid) with gas, as in making soda water —**aer·a'tion** *n.*

aer·a·tor (-ər) *n.* a person or thing that aerates; specif., a device for aerating a liquid, or a fumigating device

aer·i- (er'ē, ā'ər i, ar'ē) *same as* AERO-

aer·i·al (er'ē əl, ā ir'ē əl) *adj.* [< L. *aerius* < *aer* (see AIR) + -AL] 1. of, in, or by the air 2. like air; light as air 3. not substantial; unreal; imaginary 4. high up; lofty 5. of, for, from, or by means of aircraft or flying [an *aerial* photograph] 6. *Bot.* growing in the air instead of in soil or water —*n.* an antenna (sense 2) —**aer'i·al·ly** *adv.*

aer·i·al·ist (er'ē əl ist) *n.* an acrobat who performs on a trapeze, high wire, etc.

aerial ladder a ladder that can be extended for reaching high places, esp. one mounted on a fire engine

☆**aerial railway** an arrangement of overhead cables or rails with cars suspended from them, used to carry people or things across a canyon, river, etc.

aer·ie (er'ē, ir'ē) *n.* [ME. *eire, aire* < OFr. *aire* < ML. *aeria*, area, prob. ult. < L. *ager*, field (see ACRE), but sp. & meaning infl. by L. *aer*, air & ME. *ei*, egg] 1. the nest of an eagle or other bird of prey that builds in a high place 2. a house or stronghold on a high place 3. the young of an eagle, hawk, etc., in the nest

aer·if·er·ous (er if'ər əs) *adj.* transmitting air

aer·i·form (er'ə fôrm') *adj.* like air; esp., insubstantial

aer·i·fy (er'ə fī') *vt.* **-fied', -fy'ing** 1. to change into air or gas 2. to put air into; aerate —**aer'i·fi·ca'tion** (-fi kā'shən) *n.*

aer·o (er'ō, ā'ə rō') *adj.* of or for aeronautics or aircraft

aer·o- (er'ō, ar'-; -ə; ā'ə rō') [< Gr. *aēr*, air] *a combining form meaning:* 1. air; of the air [*aerolite*] 2. of aircraft or flying [*aerobatics*] 3. gas; of gases [*aerodynamics*]

aer·o·bac·ter (er'ō bak'tər) *n.* [ModL.: see AERO- & BACTERIA] any of a genus (*Aerobacter*) of bacteria normally found in the intestine

aer·o·bal·lis·tics (er'ō bə lis'tiks) *n.pl.* [*with sing. v.*] the ballistics of projectiles dropped or launched from aircraft

aer·o·bat·ics (er'ə bat'iks) *n.pl.* [AERO- + (ACRO)BATICS] 1. spectacular feats done with an airplane, as loops, rolls, etc. 2. [*with sing. v.*] the art of performing such feats; stunt flying —**aer'o·bat'ic** *adj.*

aer·obe (er'ōb) *n.* [< AERO- + Gr. *bios*, life] a microorganism that can live and grow only where free oxygen is present

aer·o·bic (er ō'bik) *adj.* 1. able to live, grow, or take place only where free oxygen is present 2. of or produced by aerobes

aer·o·bi·um (er ō'bē əm) *n., pl.* **-bi·a** (-bē ə) [ModL.: see AEROBE] an aerobe

aer·o·do·net·ics (er'ō də net'iks) *n.pl.* [with sing. v.] [Gr. *aerodonetos*, soaring, air-tossed < *aēr*, air + *donein*, to shake + -ICS] the science of soaring in a glider

aer·o·drome (er'ə drōm') *n. Brit. var. of* AIRDROME

aer·o·dy·nam·ics (er'ō dī nam'iks) *n.pl.* [with sing. v.] the branch of aeromechanics that deals with the forces (resistance, pressure, etc.) exerted by air or other gases in motion —aer'o·dy·nam'ic *adj.* —aer'o·dy·nam'i·cal·ly *adv.* —aer'o·dy·nam'i·cist (-ə sist) *n.*

aer·o·dyne (er'ə dīn') *n.* any aircraft that is heavier than air and derives its lift chiefly from aerodynamic forces

aer·o·em·bo·lism (er'ō em'bə liz'm) *n.* [AERO- + EMBOLISM] **1.** same as DECOMPRESSION SICKNESS **2.** nitrogen bubbles formed in the blood or tissues during decompression sickness

aer·o·gel (er'ə jel') *n.* [AERO- + GEL] a colloidal substance formed by replacing the liquid in a gel with gas

aer·og·ra·phy (er ä'grə fē) *n.* same as METEOROLOGY: term used esp. in the U.S. Navy —aer'og'ra·pher *n.* —aer·o·graph·ic (er'ə graf'ik) *adj.*

aer·o·lite (er'ə līt') *n.* [AERO- + -LITE] a stony meteorite —aer'o·lit'ic (-lit'ik) *adj.*

aer·ol·o·gy (er äl'ə jē) *n.* the branch of meteorology concerned with the study of air, esp. in the upper atmosphere —aer·o·log·ic (er'ə läj'ik) *adj.* —aer·ol'o·gist (-ə jist) *n.*

aer·o·me·chan·ics (er'ō mə kan'iks) *n.pl.* [with sing. v.] the branch of mechanics that deals with air or other gases in motion or equilibrium: it includes aerodynamics and aerostatics —aer'o·me·chan'ic *adj.*

aer·o·med·i·cine (er'ō med'ə s'n) *n.* a branch of medicine concerned with the diseases and disorders that are incident to flight in the earth's atmosphere; cf. SPACE MEDICINE —aer'o·med'i·cal *adj.*

aer·o·me·te·or·o·graph (-mē'tē ôr'ə graf') *n.* a meteorograph of a type used in an aircraft or balloon to record meteorologic data aloft

aer·om·e·ter (er äm'ə tər) *n.* an instrument for measuring the weight and density of air or other gases —aer'o·met'ric (-ə met'rik) *adj.* —aer·om'e·try (-ə trē) *n.*

aer·o·naut (er'ə nôt', -nät') *n.* [Fr. *aéronaute* < Gr. *aēr*, air + *nautēs*, sailor] the pilot of a balloon or dirigible: now chiefly a historical term

aer·o·nau·ti·cal (er'ə nôt'ik 'l, -nät'-) *adj.* of or concerning aeronautics: also **aer'o·nau'tic** —aer'o·nau'ti·cal·ly *adv.*

aeronautical chart a topographic map of an area of the earth's surface, esp. designed as an aid to aircraft navigation

aer·o·nau·tics (-iks) *n.pl.* [with sing. v.] the science, art, or work of designing, making, and operating aircraft

aer·o·neu·ro·sis (er'ō nyoo rōs'is, -noo-) *n.* a nervous disorder of airplane pilots caused by the tension of excessive flying, characterized by abdominal pains, digestive disturbances, etc.

aer·on·o·my (er än'ə mē) *n.* [AERO- + -NOMY] the science dealing with the physics and chemistry of the upper atmosphere

aer·o·pause (er'ō pôz') *n.* [AERO- + PAUSE] a region at the upper level of the earth's atmosphere, regarded as the boundary between the atmosphere and outer space

aer·o·pha·gi·a (er'ə fā'jē ə) *n.* an abnormal, spasmodic swallowing of air: often a symptom of hysteria

aer·o·pho·bi·a (-fō'bē ə) *n.* an abnormal fear of air, esp. of drafts

aer·o·phore (er'ə fôr') *n.* [AERO- + -PHORE] a device for supplying air to the lungs of an infant born not breathing or to workers in mines, under water, etc.

aer·o·plane (er'ə plān') *n.* [Fr. *aéroplane* < *aéro-*, AERO- + base of *planer*, to soar: see PLANE[4]] *Brit. var. of* AIRPLANE

aer·o·pulse (-puls') *n.* same as PULSEJET (ENGINE)

aer·o·scope (-skōp') *n.* an apparatus for gathering bacteria, dust, etc. from the air, for microscopic examination —aer'o·scop'ic (-skäp'ik) *adj.*

aer·o·sol (-sôl', -säl', -sōl') *n.* [AERO- + SOL[3]] a suspension of colloidal particles in a gas —*adj.* **1.** designating or of a small container in which gas under pressure is used to aerate and dispense liquid through a valve in the form of a spray or foam **2.** dispensed by such a container [an *aerosol* insecticide, *aerosol* shaving cream]

☆**aer·o·space** (er'ō spās') *n.* [altered < *air/space* < AIR + SPACE] the earth's atmosphere and the space outside it, considered as one continuous field—*adj.* of aerospace, or of spacecraft or missiles designed for flight in aerospace

aer·o·sphere (-sfir') *n.* the atmosphere surrounding the earth

aer·o·stat (-stat') *n.* [Fr. *aérostat:* see AERO- & -STAT] a dirigible, balloon, or other aircraft that is lifted and sustained by virtue of one or more containers filled with a gas lighter than air

aer·o·stat·ics (er'ō stat'iks) *n.pl.* [with sing. v.] [AERO- + STATICS] the branch of aeromechanics that deals with the equilibrium of air or other gases, and with the equilibrium of solid bodies, such as aerostats, floating in air or other gases —aer'o·stat'ic *adj.*

aer·o·sta·tion (-stā'shən) *n.* [Fr. *aérostation* < *aérostat*, AEROSTAT] the art or science of operating aerostats

aer·o·ther·a·peu·tics (-ther'ə pyoot'iks) *n.pl.* [with sing. v.] the treatment of disease by the use of air, esp. by exposing the patient to changes of atmospheric pressure: also **aer'o·ther'a·py** (-ther'ə pē)

aer·o·ther·mo·dy·nam·ics (-thur'mō dī nam'iks) *n.pl.* [with sing. v.] the study of the relationship of heat and mechanical energy in gases, esp. air

ae·ru·gi·nous (i roo'ji nəs) *adj.* [L. *aeruginosus* < *aerugo* < *aes*, copper: see ORE] bluish-green, like copper rust

aer·y[1] (er'ē, ā'ər ē) *adj.* [L. *aerius* < *aer*, AIR] [Poet.] airy; of or like air

aer·y[2] (er'ē, ir'ē) *n.* same as AERIE

Aes·chi·nes (es'ki nēz') 389–314 B.C.; Athenian orator; rival of Demosthenes

Aes·chy·lus (es'kə ləs) 525?–456 B.C.; Gr. writer of tragedies —Aes·chy·le·an (es'kə lē'ən) *adj.*

Aes·cu·la·pi·an (es'kyoo lāp'ē ən) *adj.* **1.** of Aesculapius **2.** medical —*n.* [*a:*] a physician

Aes·cu·la·pi·us (es'kyoo lāp'ē əs) [L. < Gr. *Asklēpios*] *Rom. Myth.* the god of medicine and of healing, son of Apollo: identified with the Gr. ASCLEPIUS

Ae·sir (ā'sir, ē'-) *n.pl.* [ON., pl. of *ass*, a god, akin to OE. *os* (see OSCAR)] the principal gods of Norse mythology, including Odin, Thor, Balder, Loki, Freya, and Tyr

Ae·sop (ē'säp, ēs'əp) real or legendary Gr. author of fables: supposed to have lived 6th cent. B.C.

Ae·so·pi·an (ē sōp'ē ən) *adj.* **1.** of Aesop or characteristic of his fables **2.** concealing real purposes or intentions; dissembling [*Aesopian* language]

aes·the·si·a (es thē'zhə, -zhē ə, -zē ə) *n.* same as ESTHESIA

aes·thete (es'thēt') *n.* [Gr. *aisthētēs*, a person who perceives: see AESTHETIC] **1.** a person highly sensitive to art and beauty **2.** a person who artificially cultivates artistic sensitivity or makes a cult of art and beauty

SYN.—aesthete, although applied to one highly sensitive to art and beauty, is often used derogatorily to connote effeteness, decadence, etc.; dilettante refers to one who appreciates art as distinguished from one who creates it, but is used disparagingly of one who dabbles superficially in the arts; a connoisseur is one who has expert knowledge or a keen discrimination in matters of art and, by extension, in any matters of taste [a *connoisseur* of fine foods]; virtuoso, in this comparison, denotes a collector or connoisseur of art objects, and is sometimes used derogatorily to suggest faddishness

aes·thet·ic (es thet'ik) *adj.* [Gr. *aisthētikos*, sensitive < *aisthanesthai*, to perceive < IE. base *awis-*, hence akin to L. *audire*, to hear] **1.** of or in relation to aesthetics **2.** of beauty **3.** sensitive to art and beauty; showing good taste; artistic Also **aes·thet'i·cal** —*n.* the aesthetic principle

aes·thet·i·cal·ly (-ik lē, -ik 'l ē) *adv.* **1.** in an aesthetic manner **2.** from the point of view of aesthetics

aes·the·ti·cian (es'thə tish'ən) *n.* a student of, or expert in, aesthetics

aes·thet·i·cism (es thet'ə siz'm) *n.* **1.** the doctrine that aesthetic principles underlie all human values **2.** *a)* sensitivity to art and beauty *b)* the artificial cultivation of artistic sensitivity

aes·thet·ics (es thet'iks) *n.pl.* [with sing. v.] [< AESTHETIC] the study or theory of beauty and of the psychological responses to it; specif., the branch of philosophy dealing with art, its creative sources, its forms, and its effects

aes·ti·val (es'tə v'l, es tī'v'l) *adj.* same as ESTIVAL

aes·ti·vate (es'tə vāt') *vi.* same as ESTIVATE

aes·ti·va·tion (es'tə vā'shən) *n.* same as ESTIVATION

aet., aetat. [L. *aetatis*] aged (a specified number of years); at the age of

Aeth·el·stan (eth'l stan') same as ATHELSTAN

ae·ther (ēth'ər) *n.* same as ETHER

ae·the·re·al (i thir'ē əl) *adj.* same as ETHEREAL

ae·ti·ol·o·gy (ē'tē äl'ə jē) *n.* same as ETIOLOGY

Aet·na (et' nə) same as ETNA

Ae·to·li·a (ē tō' lē ə) ancient region on the Gulf of Corinth: see ACARNANIA —Ae·to'li·an *adj.*, *n.*

af- (af, əf, if) same as AD-: used before *f*

AF, A.F., A.-F. Anglo-French

a.f., A.F. audio frequency

AF & AM, A.F.A.M. Ancient Free and Accepted Masons

a·far (ə fär') *adv.* [ME. *a ferr* < *a*, on + *feor*, far] [Poet. or Archaic] at or to a distance —**from afar** from a distance

AFB Air Force Base

A.F.C., AFC automatic frequency control

a·feard, a·feared, (ə fird') *adj.* [orig. pp. of ME. *aferen*, to frighten < OE. *afaeran* < *a-* + *faeran*, to frighten < *faer*, FEAR] [Dial. or Archaic] frightened; afraid

a·fe·brile (ā fē'brəl, -feb'rəl) *adj.* having no fever

af·fa·ble (af'ə b'l) *adj.* [ME. *affabyl* < L. *affabilis* < *ad-*, to + *fari*, to speak: see FAME] **1.** pleasant and easy to approach or talk to; friendly **2.** gentle and kindly [an *affable* smile] —*SYN.* see AMIABLE —**af'fa·bil'i·ty** (-bil'ə tē) *n.* —**af'fa·bly** *adv.*

af·fair (ə fer') *n.* [ME. *afere* < OFr. *afaire* < *a faire*, to do < L. *ad-*, to + *facere*, to do[1]] **1.** a thing to be done; business **2.** [*pl.*] matters of business or concern **3.** any matter, occurrence, or thing **4.** a social function or gathering **5.** an event that becomes a matter of public controversy **6.** [<*love affair*] an amorous relationship between two people not married to each other; an amour

af·faire (ə fer') *n.* [Fr.] same as AFFAIR (senses 5 & 6)

†**af·faire d'a·mour** (à fer' dà moor') [Fr.] a love affair

‡**af·faire de coeur** (-də kër') [Fr., lit., affair of the heart] a love affair

‡**af·faire d'hon·neur** (-dô nër') [Fr., lit., an affair of honor] a duel

af·fect¹ (ə fekt′) vt. [ME. affecten < L. affectare, to strive after < affectus, pp. of afficere, to influence, attack < ad-, to + facere, to DO¹] 1. to have an effect on; influence; produce a change in [bright light affects the eyes] 2. to move or stir the emotions of [his death affected us deeply] —n. 1. [Obs.] a disposition or tendency 2. (af′ekt) [G. affekt < L. affectus, state of mind or body: see the v.] Psychol. a) an emotion or feeling attached to an idea, object, etc. b) a stimulus or motive arousing an emotion, feeling, or mood c) in general, emotion or emotional response
SYN.—affect implies the producing of an effect strong enough to evoke a reaction; to influence is to affect in such a way as to produce a change in action, thought, nature, or behavior [to influence legislation]; impress is used of that which produces a deep or lasting effect on the mind; touch and the stronger move, as considered here, are both applied to the arousing of emotion, sympathy, etc., but move also denotes an influencing so as to effect a change; sway emphasizes the influencing of a person so as to turn him from a given course [threats will not sway us]
af·fect² (ə fekt′) vt. [ME. affecten < OFr. affecter < L. affectare, AFFECT¹] 1. to like to have, use, wear, be in, etc. [she affects plaid coats] 2. to make a pretense of being, having, feeling, liking, etc.; feign [to affect indifference] 3. [Archaic] to aim at; seek —SYN. see ASSUME
af·fec·ta·tion (af′ek tā′shən) n. [L. affectatio < pp. of affectare, AFFECT²] 1. an affecting or pretending to like, have, etc.; show or pretense 2. artificial behavior meant to impress others; mannerism for effect —SYN. see POSE¹
af·fect·ed¹ (ə fek′tid) adj. [pp. of AFFECT¹] 1. attacked by disease; afflicted 2. influenced; acted upon 3. emotionally moved or touched
af·fect·ed² (ə fek′tid) adj. [pp. of AFFECT²] 1. assumed for effect; artificial 2. behaving in an artificial way to impress people; full of affectation —af·fect′ed·ly adv.
af·fect·ing (ə fek′tiŋ) adj. emotionally touching; evoking pity, sympathy, etc. —SYN. see MOVING
af·fec·tion (ə fek′shən) n. [ME. affecciun < OFr. affection < L. affectio, a state of feeling < pp. of afficere: see AFFECT¹] 1. a mental or emotional state or tendency; disposition or feeling 2. fond or tender feeling; warm liking 3. a disease; ailment 4. an attribute or property of a thing 5. an affecting or being affected —SYN. see DISEASE, LOVE —af·fec′tion·al adj.
af·fec·tion·ate (-it) adj. [altered after -ATE¹ < Fr. affectionné] 1. full of affection; tender and loving 2. [Obs.] mentally disposed; inclined
af·fec·tive (ə fek′tiv) adj. [Fr. affectif < ML. affectivus < L. affectus] of, or arising from, affects, or feelings; emotional —af·fec′tive·ly adv. —af·fec·tiv·i·ty (af′ek tiv′i·tē) n.
af·fen·pin·scher (äf′ən pin′shər, af-; -chər) n. [G., lit., monkey terrier < affe (see APE) + pinscher: see DOBERMAN PINSCHER] any of a breed of small dogs, with a stiff, wiry coat of black, red, or gray and a monkeylike expression
af·fer·ent (af′ər ənt, -er-) adj. [< L. afferens, prp. of afferre < ad-, to + ferre, to BEAR¹] Physiol. bringing inward to a central part; specif., designating nerves that transmit impulses to the central nervous system, as to the brain: opposed to EFFERENT
af·fi·ance (ə fī′əns) n. [ME. affaunce < OFr. afiance < afier, to trust in < ML. affidare < ad-, to + fidare, to trust < L. fidere: see FIDELITY] 1. [Archaic] trust or faith 2. a plighting of faith; promise of marriage; betrothal —vt. -anced, -anc·ing to pledge, esp. in marriage; betroth —af·fi′anced adj.
☆**af·fi·ant** (ə fī′ənt) n. [< prp. of OFr. afier: see AFFIANCE] Law a person who makes an affidavit; deponent
af·fi·da·vit (af′ə dā′vit) n. [ML., he has made oath; perf. tense of affidare: see AFFIANCE] Law a written statement made on oath before a notary public or other person authorized to administer oaths
af·fil·i·ate (ə fil′ē āt′; for n. -it) vt. -at′ed, -at′ing [< ML. affiliatus, pp. of affiliare, to adopt as a son < L. ad-, to + filius, son] 1. to take in as a member or branch 2. to connect or associate (oneself with) 3. to trace the origins or source of; specif., to determine legally the paternity of —vi. to associate oneself; join —n. an affiliated individual or organization; member
af·fil·i·a·tion (ə fil′ē ā′shən) n. an affiliating or being affiliated; connection, as with an organization, club, etc.
af·fine (ə fīn′) adj. [< L. affinis: see AFFINITY] Math. of or having to do with a transformation in which finite quantities remain finite and infinite quantities remain infinite
af·fined (ə fīnd′) adj. [< Fr. affiné, related: see AFFINITY] 1. joined or connected in some way; related 2. [Obs.] under obligation; bound
af·fin·i·ty (ə fin′ə tē) n., pl. -ties [ME. affinite < OFr. afinite < L. affinitas < affinis, adjacent, related by marriage < ad-, to + finis, end] 1. relationship by marriage: distinguished from CONSANGUINITY 2. close relationship; connection 3. similarity of structure, as of species or languages, implying common origin; family resemblance 4. a natural liking or sympathy; esp., a mutual attraction between a man and a woman 5. a person of the opposite sex who especially attracts one 6. the force that causes

the atoms of certain elements to combine and stay combined —af·fin′i·tive adj.
af·firm (ə furm′) vt. [ME. affermen < OFr. affermer < L. affirmare, to present as fixed < ad-, to + firmare, to make firm < firmus: see FIRM¹] 1. to say positively; declare firmly; assert to be true: opposed to DENY 2. to make valid; confirm; uphold; ratify (a law, decision, or judgment) —vi. Law to declare solemnly, but not under oath; make affirmation —SYN. see ASSERT —af·firm′a·ble adj. —af·firm′er, Law af·firm′ant (-′nt) n.
af·firm·ance (-′ns) n. [ME. affermance < OFr. affermance < L. affirmans, prp. of affirmare, AFFIRM] 1. an affirming or declaring 2. a confirming 3. Law an upholding by a higher court of a lower court's judgment or order
af·fir·ma·tion (af′ər mā′shən) n. 1. the act of affirming 2. something affirmed; positive declaration; assertion 3. Law a solemn declaration, but not under oath: permitted to one who has conscientious objections to taking oaths
af·firm·a·tive (ə fur′mə tiv) adj. [ME. affirmatif < L. affirmativus < affirmare, AFFIRM] 1. saying that something stated is true; answering "yes" [an affirmative reply] 2. a) bold or confident in asserting [affirmative people] b) optimistic or hopeful; not negative or cynical 3. Logic affirming something about a subject ["all men are mortal" is an affirmative proposition] —n. 1. a word or expression indicating assent or agreement 2. an affirmative statement or proposition —in the affirmative 1. in assent or agreement 2. with an affirmative answer; saying "yes" —the affirmative the side upholding the proposition being debated —af·firm′a·tive·ly adv.
af·fix (ə fiks′; for n. af′iks) vt. [< L. affixus, pp. of affigere, to fasten to < ad-, to + figere, FIX] 1. to fasten; attach [to affix a label to a bottle] 2. to add at the end; append —n. [Fr. affixe < L. affixus: see the v.] 1. a thing affixed 2. Linguis. a prefix, suffix, or infix —af′fix·al adj.
af·fix·a·tion (af′ik sā′shən) n. 1. affixture 2. Linguis. the adding of affixes to roots or bases in order to vary function, modify meaning, etc.: distinguished from COMPOSITION
af·fix·ture (ə fiks′chər) n. an affixing or being affixed
af·fla·tus (ə flāt′əs) n. [L. < pp. of afflare, to blow on < ad-, to + flare, to blow < IE. base *bhel-: see BLADDER] inspiration or powerful impulse, as of an artist or poet
af·flict (ə flikt′) vt. [< L. afflictare, to injure, vex < afflictus, pp. of affligere, to strike down < ad-, to + fligere, to strike, hit] 1. to cause pain or suffering to; distress very much 2. [Obs.] to overthrow
af·flic·tion (ə flik′shən) n. [ME. afflicciun < OFr. affliction < L. afflictio] 1. an afflicted condition; pain; suffering 2. anything causing pain or distress; calamity
SYN.—affliction implies pain, suffering, or distress imposed by illness, loss, misfortune, etc.; trial suggests suffering that tries one's endurance, but in a weaker sense refers to annoyance that tries one's patience; tribulation describes severe affliction continuing over a long and trying period; misfortune is applied to a circumstance or event involving adverse fortune and to the suffering or distress occasioned by it
af·flic·tive (-tiv) adj. [< L. afflictivus: see AFFLICT] causing pain or misery —af·flic′tive·ly adv.
af·flu·ence (af′loo wəns; now sometimes af loo′-) n. [< L. affluentia < affluere, to flow to < ad-, to + fluere, to flow] 1. a flowing toward; influx 2. great plenty; abundance 3. an abundance of riches; wealth; opulence
af·flu·ent (-wənt) adj. [ME. < L. affluens, prp. of affluere: see AFFLUENCE] 1. flowing freely 2. plentiful; abundant 3. wealthy; prosperous; rich [the affluent society] —n. a stream flowing into a river; tributary —af′flu·ent·ly adv. —SYN. see RICH
af·flux (af′luks) n. [L. affluxus < pp. of affluere: see AFFLUENCE] a flow toward a point, as of blood to an organ
af·ford (ə fôrd′) vt. [ME. aforthen < OE. geforthian, to advance < forthian, to further] 1. to have enough or the means for; bear the cost of without serious inconvenience: generally used with can or be able [we can afford a car; can you afford the time?] 2. to be able (to do something) without risking serious consequences: generally used with can [I can afford to speak frankly] 3. to give; yield; supply; furnish [music affords her pleasure]
af·for·est (ə fôr′əst, -fär′-) vt. [ML. afforestare: see AD- & FOREST] to turn (land) into forest; plant many trees on —af·for′est·a′tion (-əs tā′shən) n.
af·fran·chise (ə fran′chīz′) vt. -chised′, -chis′ing [< extended stem of Fr. affranchir < OFr. afranchir < a, to + franchir: see FRANCHISE] to make free; enfranchise
af·fray (ə frā′) n. [ME. affrai, an attack, alarm < OFr. esfrai < esfraer, to frighten < ML. *exfridare < L. ex, out of + Gmc. base frith-, peace] a noisy brawl or quarrel; public fight or riot; breach of the peace —vt. [ME. affraien < OFr. esfraer] [Archaic] to frighten
af·fri·cate (af′rə kit) n. [L. affricatus, pp. of affricare, to rub against < ad-, to + fricare, to rub] Phonet. any of the complex sounds produced when slowly released stop consonants are followed immediately by fricatives at the same point of articulation: the English affricates are those heard in batch (IPA t∫) and badge (IPA dʒ), voiceless and voiced respectively —af·fric·a·tive (ə frik′ə tiv) adj., n.

af·fri·ca·tion (af'rə kā'shən) n. Phonet. the slow release of a stop consonant that results in an affricate

af·fright (ə frīt') vt. [ME. afrighten < OE. afyrhtan: see FRIGHT] [Archaic] to frighten; terrify —n. [Archaic] great fright, or terror, or a cause of terror

af·front (ə frunt') vt. [ME. afronten < OFr. afronter, to encounter face to face < ML. *affrontare < ad-, to + frons, forehead] 1. to insult openly or purposely; offend; slight 2. to confront defiantly 3. [Archaic] to come before; meet; face —n. an open or intentional insult; slight to one's dignity —SYN. see OFFEND

af·fron·tive (ə frun'tiv) adj. [Archaic] affronting; openly insulting

af·fu·sion (a fyōō'zhən) n. [ML. affusio < L. affusus, pp. of affundere < ad-, to + fundere, to pour: see FOUND³] a pouring on, as of water in baptism

Afg., Afgh. Afghanistan

Af·ghan (af'gan, -gən) n. 1. a native or inhabitant of Afghanistan 2. former name of PASHTO (language of Afghanistan) 3. any of a breed of swift hunting hound, originally from the Near East, with silky hair and a long, narrow head 4. [a-] a soft blanket or shawl, crocheted or knitted, esp. in a geometrical design —adj. of Afghanistan, its people, language, etc.

af·ghan·i (af gan'ē) n., pl. -is [Pashto, lit., Afghan] the monetary unit and a coin of Afghanistan: see MONETARY UNITS, table

Af·ghan·i·stan (af gan'ə stan') country in SW Asia, between Iran and West Pakistan: c. 250,000 sq. mi.; pop. 16,516,000; cap. Kabul

a·fi·cio·na·do (ə fish'ə nä'dō, -fesh'-; -fis'ē ə-, -yə-; Sp. ä fē'syō nä' thō) n., pl. -dos (-dōz; Sp. -thōs) [Sp., pp. of aficionar < ML. *affectionare, to like, be devoted to < L. affectio: see AFFECTION] a devoted follower of some sport, art, etc.; devotee

a·field (ə fēld') adv. 1. in, on, or to the field 2. away (from home) 3. off the right path; astray

a·fire (ə fīr') adv., adj. 1. on fire; burning 2. greatly excited

a·flame (ə flām') adv., adj. 1. in flames; burning 2. glowing [aflame with color] 3. greatly excited

af·la·tox·in (af'lə täk'sin) n. [< A(spergillus) fla(vus), (the fungus) + TOXIN] any of several carcinogenic substances produced by a fungus found esp. on peanuts

AFL-CIO American Federation of Labor and Congress of Industrial Organizations: a labor organization formed by merger in 1955

a·float (ə flōt') adv. 1. floating freely; not grounded; esp., floating on the surface; not sinking 2. on board ship; at sea 3. flooded [the lower deck is afloat] 4. drifting about 5. in circulation; current [rumors are afloat] 6. free of trouble, debt, etc. [he kept the business afloat]

a·flut·ter (ə flut'ər) adv., adj. in a flutter

a·foot (ə foot') adv. 1. on foot; walking 2. in motion or operation; in progress; astir

a·fore (ə fôr') adv., prep., conj. [ME. afore, aforn < OE. onforan, before: see A-¹ & FORE] [Archaic & Dial. except in compounds and nautical use] before

a·fore·men·tioned (ə fôr'men'shənd, -chənd) adj. mentioned before or previously

a·fore·said (-sed') adj. spoken of before; mentioned previously

a·fore·thought (-thôt') adj. thought out beforehand; premeditated

a·fore·time (-tīm') adv. [Archaic] in times now past; formerly

a for·ti·o·ri (ā fôr'tē ôr'ē, -shē ôr'ē; -ī) [L., for a stronger (reason)] all the more: said of a conclusion that follows with even greater logical necessity than another already accepted in the argument

☆**a·foul** (ə foul') adv., adj. in a collision or a tangle —run (or fall) afoul of to become entangled with; get into conflict or trouble with

Afr- same as AFRO-

Afr. 1. Africa 2. African

a·fraid (ə frād') adj. [ME. affraied, pp. of affraien, AFFRAY] feeling fear; frightened; apprehensive (followed by of, that, or an infinitive): often used colloquially to indicate regretful realization, etc. [I'm afraid I can't go]

SYN.—afraid is applied to a general feeling of fear or disquiet and is the broadest in application of all the words considered here [to be afraid of the dark, to be afraid to die]; frightened implies a sudden, usually temporary seizure of fear [the child was frightened by the dog]; timid implies a lack of courage or self-confidence and suggests overcautiousness, shyness, etc. [he is timid about investing money]; timorous and fearful suggest a feeling of disquiet and a tendency to worry rather than an alarming fear [fearful of making an error]; terrified suggests a feeling of intense, overwhelming fear [he stood terrified as the tiger charged] —ANT. brave, bold, self-controlled

☆**A-frame** (ā'frām') adj. designating or of a structural framework, as of a house, with steeply angled sides meeting at the top like the sides of the letter A —n. a structure with such a framework

a·freet (af'rēt, ə frēt') n. [Ar. 'ifrīt] Arabic Myth. a strong, evil demon or jinni

a·fresh (ə fresh') adv. again; anew

Af·ri·ca (af'ri kə) second largest continent, situated in the Eastern Hemisphere, south of Europe: c. 11,500,000 sq. mi.; pop. c. 345,000,000

Af·ri·can (af'ri kən) adj. of Africa, its peoples (esp. Negro peoples), their cultures, etc. —n. 1. a member of an indigenous ethnic group of Africa, esp. a Negro 2. any native or inhabitant of Africa

Af·ri·can·ist (-ist) n. 1. a student of or expert in African cultures, languages, etc. 2. an advocate of national independence for new African states or of pan-Africanism

☆**Af·ri·can·ize** (-īz') vt. -ized', -iz'ing 1. to staff with native Negro Africans [to Africanize the Nigerian civil service] 2. to give an African outlook, character, etc. to —Af'ri·can·i·za'tion n.

African lily an African plant (Agapanthus africanus) of the lily family, with blue or white funnel-shaped flowers

African sleeping sickness same as SLEEPING SICKNESS (sense 1)

African violet any of several tropical African plants (genus Saintpaulia) with violet, white, or pinkish flowers and hairy, dark-green leaves, often grown as house plants

Af·ri·kaans (af'ri känz', -käns', -kanz') n. [Afrik. < Afrika, Africa] an official language of South Africa, a development from 17th-cent. Dutch

Af·ri·kan·der (af'ri kan'dər) n. [Afrik. < Du. Afrikaner, with d after Hollander] 1. earlier form of AFRIKANER 2. a breed of cattle with a hump, developed in South Africa from a hairy indigenous breed 3. a hardy breed of sheep developed in South Africa from an indigenous breed

Af·ri·ka·ner (af'ri kän'ər) n. [Du.] a South African of European, esp. Dutch, ancestry; Boer

af·rit (af'rēt, ə frēt') n. same as AFREET

☆**Af·ro** (af'rō) adj. [see ff.] 1. designating or of a full, bouffant hair style, as worn by some Negroes 2. [Colloq.] Afro-American —n. an Afro hair style

Af·ro- (af'rō) [< L. Afer, an African] a combining form meaning: 1. Africa 2. African

☆**Af·ro-A·mer·i·can** (af'rō ə mer'ə kən) adj. of Negro Americans, their culture, etc. —n. a Negro American

Af·ro-A·sian (af'rō ā'zhən) adj. of Africa and Asia jointly [an Afro-Asian conference]

Af·ro-A·si·at·ic (af'rō ā'zhē at'ik) adj. designating or of a family of African and Asiatic languages including Berber, Cushitic, Semitic, Chad, and ancient Egyptian

aft (aft, äft) adv. [ME. afte < OE. æftan (akin to Goth. aftana, from behind < afta, behind, farthest back) < IE. base *af-, off, away; aft is now felt to be the positive of which AFTER is the comparative] at, near, or toward the stern of a ship or the rear of an aircraft

aft. afternoon

af·ter (af'tər, äf'-) adv. [ME. < OE. æfter (akin to OHG. aftar & MHG. after) < of-, off + -ter, old compar. suffix] 1. behind in place 2. behind in time; later; next —prep. 1. behind in place; in back of 2. behind in time; later than 3. in search of 4. as a result of; on account of [after what has happened, he won't go] 5. in spite of [after all we had done, he was still ungrateful] 6. following next to in rank or importance 7. in the manner of; patterned on the model of [a novel after Dickens' style] 8. for; in honor of [a child named after Lincoln] 9. concerning [she asked after you] —conj. following the time when; later than —adj. 1. next; later 2. nearer the rear (esp. of a ship or aircraft)

af·ter·birth (-burth') n. the placenta and fetal membranes expelled from the womb after childbirth

af·ter·brain (-brān') n. same as METENCEPHALON (sense 1)

af·ter·burn·er (-bur'nər) n. 1. a device attached to the tail pipe of some jet engines, utilizing hot exhaust gases to burn extra fuel for additional thrust 2. an auxiliary device, as on internal-combustion engines and incinerators, for burning undesirable exhaust gases produced during the original combustion

af·ter·care (-ker') n. care or treatment of a patient recovering from an illness, operation, etc.

af·ter·clap (-klap') n. an unexpected aftereffect

af·ter·damp (-damp') n. an asphyxiating gas left in a mine after an explosion of firedamp

af·ter·deck (-dek') n. the part of a ship's deck toward the stern

af·ter·ef·fect (-ə fekt') n. an effect coming later, or as a secondary result

af·ter·glow (-glō') n. 1. the glow remaining after a light has gone, as after sunset 2. the pleasant feeling one has after an enjoyable experience

af·ter·im·age (-im'ij) n. Psychol. an image or sensation that remains or returns after the external stimulus has been withdrawn

af·ter·life (-līf') n. 1. a life after death 2. the part of one's life after a previous part; one's later years

af·ter·math (-math') n. [AFTER + dial. math < OE. mæth, cutting of grass < mawan, to mow, with -th suffix] 1. a second crop, as of grass that grows after the earlier mowing 2. a result or consequence, esp. an unpleasant one

af·ter·most (-mōst') adj. [altered, after MOST < ME. aftemeste < OE. æftemest, superl. of æfter, AFTER] 1. hindmost; last 2. nearest to the stern

af·ter·noon (af'tər nōōn', af'tər nōōn'; äf'-) n. 1. the time of day from noon to evening 2. a later period —adj. of, in, or for the afternoon

af·ter·noons (-nōōnz') adv. during every afternoon or most afternoons

af·ter·pains (af'tər pānz', äf'-) n.pl. pains from contractions of the uterus following childbirth

af·ter·piece (-pēs′) *n.* a short sketch presented after a longer dramatic production

af·ter·sen·sa·tion (-sen sā′shən) *n. Psychol.* an afterimage of peripheral origin

af·ter·shaft (-shaft′, -shäft′) *n.* a feather growing from the inner surface of the stem of another feather

af·ter·shock (-shäk′) *n.* a minor earthquake following a greater one and originating at or near the same place

af·ter·taste (-tāst′) *n.* 1. a taste lingering on in the mouth after eating, drinking, or smoking 2. the feeling remaining after an experience

af·ter·thought (-thôt′) *n.* 1. an idea, explanation, part, etc. coming or added later 2. a thought coming too late, after the occasion for which it was apt

af·ter·time (-tīm′) *n.* the time to come; future

af·ter·ward (-wərd) *adv.* [OE. *æfterweard:* see AFTER & -WARD] at a later time; subsequently: also **af·ter·wards**

ag- (ag, əg) *same as* AD-: used before *g*

Ag [L. *argentum*] *Chem.* silver

Ag. August

AG Adjutant General

A.G. Attorney General

a·ga (ä′gə) *n.* [Turk.] in Turkey and other Moslem countries, a title of respect for important officials

a·gain (ə gen′; *Canad. also & Brit. always* -gān′) *adv.* [ME. *agen, agein* < OE. *ongean, ongean* < *on-*, up to, toward + *gegn,* direct: orig. separable prefix meaning "directly up to," hence, "facing, opposite"] 1. [Rare] back in response; in return [answer *again*] 2. back into a former position or condition [he is well *again*] 3. once more; a second time; anew [try *again*] 4. besides; further [*again,* we should note] 5. on the other hand; from the contrary standpoint [he may, and then *again* he may not] 6. [Obs.] in the opposite direction; back —**again and again** often; repeatedly —**as much again** twice as much

a·gainst (ə genst′; *also, esp. Canad. & Brit.* -gänst′) *prep.* [ME. *ayeynst,* opposite to, facing < OE. *ongegn, ongean* (see AGAIN), with adv. gen. *-es* + unhistoric *-t*] 1. in opposition to; contrary to [fight *against* evil, *against* one's will] 2. toward so as to press on or strike [push *against* the door, throw the ball *against* the wall] 3. opposite to the course or direction of [drive *against* the traffic] 4. in contrast with [green *against* the gold] 5. next to; adjoining [the house *against* the church] 6. in preparation for; for the possibility of [we provided *against* a poor crop] 7. as a debit or charge on [many bills were entered *against* his account] —*conj.* [Archaic] by the time that; before —**over against** 1. opposite to 2. as compared with

Aga Khan III (ä′gə kän′) (*Aga Sultan Sir Mohammed Shah*) 1877–1957; spiritual leader of the Ismailian sect of Moslems (1885–1957): succeeded by his grandson **Aga Khan IV** (*Shah Karim al-Husainy*), born 1938

ag·a·ma (ag′ə mə) *n.* [ModL. < Sp.; ? of WInd. origin] 1. any of a genus (*Agama*) of Old World lizards, some of which can change color like the chameleon 2. any of a group of Old World lizards related to these

Ag·a·mem·non (ag′ə mem′nän, -nən) [Gr.] *Gr. Myth.* king of Mycenae and commander in chief of the Greek army in the Trojan War, killed by his wife Clytemnestra

a·ga·mete (ā′gə mēt′, ā gam′ēt) *n.* [ModL. *agameta:* see A-² & GAMETE] a sporelike, asexual reproductive cell in certain protozoa

a·gam·ic (ə gam′ik) *adj.* [Gr. *agamos,* not married < *a-,* not + *gamos,* marriage] *Biol.* 1. asexual; having no sexual union 2. able to develop without fertilization by the male —**a·gam′i·cal·ly** *adv.*

ag·a·mo·gen·e·sis (ag′ə mō jen′ə sis, ə gam′ə-) *n.* [ModL. < Gr. *agamos* (see AGAMIC) + -GENESIS] *Biol.* 1. asexual reproduction by fission (as in the amoeba), budding, etc. 2. development of a germ cell into a new individual without fertilization; parthenogenesis

ag·a·mous (ag′ə məs) *adj.* [Gr. *agamos,* AGAMIC] *Biol.* 1. asexual 2. having no gametes

A·ga·ña (ä gän′yə) capital of Guam: pop. 2,000

ag·a·pan·thus (ag′ə pan′thəs) *n.* [ModL. < Gr. *agapē,* love + *anthos,* a flower] *same as* AFRICAN LILY

a·gape¹ (ə gāp′) *adv., adj.* [A-¹ + GAPE] 1. with or as with the mouth wide open, in surprise, wonder, etc.; gaping 2. wide open

ag·a·pe² (ä′gä pā′, ag′ə pē) *n.* [LL.(Ec.) < Gr. *agapē,* love] 1. a meal that early Christians ate together: see LOVE FEAST 2. *Christian Theol. a)* God's love for man; divine love *b)* spontaneous, altruistic love

a·gar-a·gar (ä′gär ä′gär, ag′ər äg′ər) *n.* [Malay] 1. a gelatinous product made from seaweed and used as a base for bacterial cultures, as a laxative, in jellied and preserved foods, etc. 2. a base containing agar-agar Also **a′gar**

ag·ar·ic (ə ger′ik, ag′ər ik) *n.* [L. *agaricum,* larch fungus < Gr. *agaricon,* tree fungus < *Agaria,* a Sarmatian town] any gill fungus, as the common edible mushroom, a corky fungus parasitic on trees, etc.

Ag·as·siz (ag′ə sē) 1. **Alexander,** 1835–1910; U.S. zoologist, geologist, & oceanographer, born in Switzerland: son of *ff.* 2. (**Jean**) **Louis** (**Rodolphe**), 1807–73; U.S. zoologist & geologist, born in Switzerland

ag·ate (ag′ət) *n.* [ME. *agaten* < OFr. *agate* < ML. *agate* < L. *achates* < Gr. *achatēs* < ?] 1. a hard, semiprecious stone, a variety of chalcedony, with striped or clouded coloring 2. any of various tools having agate parts, as a burnishing instrument with a tip of agate 3. a little ball made of this stone or of glass, used in playing marbles ☆4. a small size of type, 5½ point

☆**agate line** a measure of advertising space, one column wide and 1/14 inch deep, used as a unit for rate purposes in newspapers, etc.

ag·ate·ware (-wer′) *n.* 1. pots and pans of iron or steel enameled to look like agate 2. pottery made to look like agate

Ag·a·tha (ag′ə thə) [L. < Gr. *Agathē,* lit., good, fem. of *agathos,* good] a feminine name

a·ga·ve (ə gä′vē) *n.* [ModL. < Gr. *Agauē,* a proper name, lit., illustrious, fem. of *agauos,* famous] any of several related plants (genus *Agave*) of the agave family, as the century plant, having tall flower stalks that rise from thick, fleshy leaves: some agaves yield a fiber used for rope —*adj.* designating a family (Agavaceae) of desert plants

a·gaze (ə gāz′) *adv., adj.* gazing

agcy. agency

age (āj) *n.* [ME. < OFr. *aage* < ML. **aetaticum* < L. *aetas,* contr. < *aevitas,* akin to *aevum,* age, eternity < IE. base **aiw-,* whence AYE¹] 1. the time that a person or a thing has existed since birth or beginning 2. the lifetime 3. a stage of life [she is at the awkward *age*] 4. the condition of being old; old age [wearied with *age*] 5. a generation 6. *a)* any interval of geological time; specif., an interval corresponding to a stage in rock strata *b)* any prehistoric cultural period in human development [the Stone *Age*] *c)* a period characterized by some person or by some outstanding feature or influence [the Elizabethan *age,* the Space *Age*] 7. [*often pl.*] [Colloq.] a long time —*vi.* **aged, ag′ing** 1. to grow old or show signs of growing old 2. to ripen or become mature —*vt.* 1. to make, or make seem, old or mature 2. to cause to ripen or become mature over a period of time under fixed conditions [to *age* cheese] —SYN. see PERIOD —**of age** having reached the age when one is qualified for full legal rights [a man comes *of* age at twenty-one]

-age (ij, əj) [OFr. < LL. *-alicum,* belonging to, related to] a *noun-forming suffix meaning:* 1. act, condition, or result of [*marriage, cleavage, usage*] 2. amount or number of [*acreage*] 3. cost of [*postage*] 4. place of [*steerage*] 5. collection of [*peerage, rootage*] 6. home of [*hermitage*] The suffix appears in many words borrowed directly from French into Middle English [*savage, voyage*]

a·ged (ā′jid *for 1 & 2*; ājd *for 3 & 4*) *adj.* 1. old; grown old 2. characteristic of old age 3. brought to a desired state of aging 4. of the age of [a boy, *aged* ten years] —**the aged** (ā′jid) old people

age·less (āj′lis) *adj.* 1. seemingly not growing older 2. eternal —**age′less·ly** *adv.*

age·long (-lôŋ′) *adj.* lasting a very long time

a·gen·cy (ā′jən sē) *n., pl.* **-cies** [ML. *agentia* < prp. of L. *agere:* see AGENT] 1. active force; action; power 2. that by which something is done; means; instrumentality 3. the business of any person, firm, etc. empowered to act for another 4. the business office or district of such a person, firm, etc. 5. an administrative division of government with specific functions

☆**agency shop** 1. a contract arrangement between an employer and the union representing the majority of employees, that requires those who do not wish to be members to pay the union a fee instead of union dues 2. a factory, business establishment, etc. in which this arrangement is in effect

a·gen·da (ə jen′də) *n., pl.* **-das** [L., neut. pl. of *agendum,* gerundive of *agere,* to do, ACT] program of things to be done; specif., a list of things to be dealt with at a meeting, etc.

a·gen·dum (-dəm) *n., pl.* **-da** (-də) *same as* AGENDA

a·gen·e·sis (ā jen′ə sis) *n.* [A-² + GENESIS] congenital absence (of an organ or other part of the body)

a·gent (ā′jənt) *n.* [L. *agens* (gen. *agentis*), prp. of *agere,* ACT] 1. a person or thing that performs an action or brings about a certain result, or that is able to do so 2. an active force or substance producing an effect [a chemical *agent*] 3. a person, firm, etc. empowered to act for another ☆4. a representative of a government agency [revenue *agent*] ☆5. [Colloq.] a traveling salesman

SYN.—an **agent** is, generally, a person or thing that acts or is capable of acting, or, in this comparison, one who or that which acts, or is empowered to act, for another [the company's *agent*]; **factor** now usually denotes an agent for the sale of goods; a **deputy** is a public official to whom certain authority has been delegated by his superior; **proxy** implies the delegation of power to substitute for another in some formal or ceremonial detail [some stockholders vote by *proxy*]

a·gen·tial (ā jen′shəl) *adj.* 1. of an agent 2. of an agency 3. acting as an agent

a·gen·tive (ā′jən tiv) *adj.* [AGENT + -IVE, after (GENIT)IVE] of or producing a grammatical form that denotes the doer

of some action —*n.* an agentive affix or form, as the suffix -*ant* of *defendant* —a'gen·ti'val (-ti'v'l) *adj.*

‡a·gent pro·vo·ca·teur (à zhäɴ' prô vô kä tër') *pl.* a·gents pro·vo·ca·teurs (à zhäɴ' prô vô kä tër') [Fr.] a person hired to join a labor union, political party, etc. in order to incite its members to actions that will make them or their organization liable to penalty

age of consent *Law* the age of a girl before which sexual intercourse with her, regardless of whether she has consented, is statutory rape

age-old (āj'ōld') *adj.* ages old; centuries old; ancient

ag·er·a·tum (aj'ə rāt'əm) *n.* [ModL. < Gr. *agēraton*, a kind of plant < *agēratos*, not growing old < *a*-, not + *gēras*, old age] any of several plants (genus *Ageratum*) of the composite family that produce small, thick heads of usually bluish flowers: they are widely used as border plants in gardens

A·ges·i·la·us (II) (ə jes'ə lā'əs) 442?-360? B.C.; king of Sparta during the decline of its supremacy in ancient Greece

Ag·ge·us (a jē'əs) *Douay Bible name for* HAGGAI

☆ag·gie (ag'ē) *n.* an agate (sense 3)

‡ag·gior·na·men·to (äd jôr'nä men'tô) *n.* [It.] the act of bringing up to date the principles, methods, ideas, etc., as of an institution

ag·glom·er·ate (ə gläm'ə rāt'; *for adj. &* -ə rit) *vt., vi.* -at'ed, -at'ing [< L. *agglomeratus*, pp. of *agglomerare* < *ad*-, to + *glomerare*, to form into a ball < IE. base *glem-, var. of *gel-, form a ball, sphere, hence akin to CLIMB, CLENCH] to gather into a cluster, mass, or ball —*adj.* gathered into a mass or ball; clustered —*n.* 1. a jumbled heap, mass, etc. 2. *Geol.* a mass of fragments of volcanic rock fused by heat —ag·glom'er·a'tive (-āt'iv, -ə tiv) *adj.*

ag·glom·er·a·tion (ə gläm'ə rā'shən) *n.* 1. an agglomerating or being agglomerated 2. a jumbled heap, mass, etc.

ag·glu·ti·nant (ə glōōt'n ənt) *adj.* [L. *agglutinans*, prp. of *agglutinare*: see ff.] sticking together; adhesive —*n.* a sticky or adhesive substance

ag·glu·ti·nate (ə glōōt'n it; *for v.* -āt') *adj.* [L. *agglutinatus*, pp. of *agglutinare*, to cement to < *ad*-, to + *glutinare* < *gluten*, glue < IE. base *glei-: see CLAY] 1. stuck together, as with glue 2. *Linguis.* forming words by agglutination —*vt., vi.* -nat'ed, -nat'ing 1. to stick together, as with glue; join by adhesion 2. *Linguis.* to form (words) by agglutination 3. *Med. & Bacteriology* to clump, as microorganisms, blood cells, etc.

ag·glu·ti·na·tion (ə glōōt'n ā'shən) *n.* 1. an agglutinating or being agglutinated 2. a mass of agglutinated parts 3. *Linguis.* in some languages, the systematic combining of independent words into compounds without marked change of form or loss of meaning 4. *Med. & Bacteriology* the clumping together of microorganisms, blood cells, etc. suspended in fluid

ag·glu·ti·na·tive (ə glōōt'n āt'iv) *adj.* 1. tending to agglutinate; sticking together 2. *Linguis.* characterized by agglutination

ag·glu·ti·nin (ə glōōt'n in) *n.* a substance causing agglutination of bacteria, blood cells, etc.

ag·glu·tin·o·gen (ag'lōō tin'ə jən) *n.* any antigen which stimulates the production of agglutinins —ag'glu·tin'o·gen'ic (-jen'ik) *adj.*

ag·grade (ə grād') *vt.* -grad'ed, -grad'ing [AG- + GRADE] to build up the level or slope of (a river bed, valley, etc.) by the deposit of sediment —ag·gra·da·tion (ag'rə dā'shən) *n.*

ag·gran·dize (ə gran'dīz', ag'rən-) *vt.* -dized', -diz'ing [< extended stem of Fr. *agrandir*, to augment < *a*-, to + *grandir*, to increase < L. *grandire* < *grandis*, great] 1. to make greater, more powerful, richer, etc.: often used reflexively 2. to make seem greater or more exalted —ag·gran'dize·ment (-diz mənt) *n.* —ag·gran'diz'er *n.*

ag·gra·vate (ag'rə vāt') *vt.* -vat'ed, -vat'ing [< L. *aggravatus*, pp. of *aggravare*, to make heavier < *ad*-, to + *gravis*, heavy] 1. to make worse; make more burdensome, troublesome, etc. 2. [Colloq.] to exasperate; annoy; vex —*SYN.* see INTENSIFY

ag·gra·va·tion (ag'rə vā'shən) *n.* 1. the act of aggravating, or making worse, or the condition of being aggravated 2. a thing or circumstance that aggravates 3. [Colloq.] exasperation; annoyance

ag·gre·gate (ag'rə gət; *for v.* -gāt') *adj.* [L. *aggregatus*, pp. of *aggregare*, to lead to a flock, add to < *ad*-, to + *gregare* to herd < *grex* (gen. *gregis*), a herd] 1. gathered into, or considered as, a whole; total [the *aggregate* number of unemployed] 2. *Bot. a)* massed into a dense head or cluster, as a flower *b)* formed of closely clustered carpels, as the raspberry 3. *Geol.* made up of a mixture of mineral fragments, crystals, or similar materials [an *aggregate* rock] —*n.* 1. a group or mass of distinct things gathered into, or considered as, a total or whole 2. the sand or pebbles added to cement in making concrete or mortar 3. an aggregate rock —*vt.* -gat'ed, -gat'ing 1. to gather into a whole or mass 2. to amount to; total —*SYN.* see SUM —in the aggregate taken all together; on the whole —ag'gre·gate·ly *adv.*

ag·gre·ga·tion (ag'rə gā'shən) *n.* 1. an aggregating or being aggregated 2. a group or mass of distinct things or individuals

ag·gre·ga·tive (ag'rə gāt'iv) *adj.* 1. aggregating or tending to aggregate 2. taken collectively or as a whole

ag·gress (ə gres') *vi.* [< L. *aggressus*, pp. of *aggredi*, to attack, go to < *ad*-, to + *gradi*, to step] to start a quarrel or be the first to attack

ag·gres·sion (ə gresh'ən) *n.* [Fr. < L. *aggressio*: see AGGRESS] 1. an unprovoked attack or warlike act; specif., the use of armed force by a state in violation of its international obligations 2. the practice or habit of being aggressive, or quarrelsome 3. *Psychiatry* forceful, attacking behavior, either constructively self-assertive and self-protective or destructively hostile to others or to oneself

ag·gres·sive (ə gres'iv) *adj.* 1. aggressing or inclined to aggress; starting fights or quarrels 2. ready or willing to take issue or engage in direct action; militant 3. full of enterprise and initiative; bold and active; pushing 4. *Psychiatry* of or involving aggression —ag·gres'sive·ly *adv.* —ag·gres'sive·ness *n.*

SYN.—aggressive implies a bold and energetic pursuit of one's ends, connoting, in derogatory usage, a ruthless desire to dominate and, in a favorable sense, enterprise, initiative, etc.; militant implies a vigorous, unrelenting espousal of a cause, movement, etc. and rarely suggests the furthering of one's own ends; assertive emphasizes self-confidence and a persistent determination to express oneself or one's opinions; pushing is applied derogatorily to a forwardness of personality that manifests itself in officiousness, rudeness, etc.

ag·gres·sor (-ər) *n.* [LL.] a person, nation, etc. that is guilty of aggression, or makes an unprovoked attack

ag·grieve (ə grēv') *vt.* -grieved', -griev'ing [ME. *agreven* < OFr. *agrever*, to aggravate < L. *aggravare*, AGGRAVATE] 1. to cause grief or injury to; offend 2. to injure in one's legal rights —*SYN.* see WRONG

ag·grieved (ə grēvd') *adj.* 1. having a grievance; offended; wronged 2. injured in one's legal rights

a·gha (ä'gə, ag'ə) *n. same as* AGA

a·ghast (ə gast', -gäst') *adj.* [ME. *agast*, pp. of *agasten*, to terrify < *a*- + *gasten* < OE. *gæstan*, to terrify < *gast*, GHOST] feeling great horror or dismay; terrified; horrified

ag·ile (aj'l; *chiefly Brit.* -īl) *adj.* [Fr. < L. *agilis* < *agere*, ACT] 1. quick and easy of movement; deft and active 2. keen and lively [an *agile* wit] —ag'ile·ly *adv.* —a·gil·i·ty (ə jil'ə tē) *n.*

SYN.—agile and nimble both imply rapidity and lightness of movement, agile emphasizing dexterity in the use of the limbs and nimble, deftness in the performance of some act; quick implies rapidity and promptness, seldom indicating, out of context, the degree of skillfulness; spry suggests nimbleness or alacrity, esp. as displayed by vigorous elderly people; sprightly implies animation or vivacity and suggests gaiety, lightness, etc. —*ANT.* torpid, sluggish, lethargic

Ag·in·court (aj'in kôrt'; *Fr.* à zhaɴ kōōr') town in N France, near Calais: site of a battle (1415) won by England in the Hundred Years' War with France

ag·i·o (aj'ē ō') *n., pl.* -os' [Fr. < It. *aggio* < OFr. *agiet*, premium < LL. *adjectum*, something added < L. *adjectus*: see ADJECTIVE] a fee paid to exchange one kind of money for another or to exchange depreciated money for money of full value

ag·i·o·tage (-ə tij) *n.* [Fr. < *agioter*, to job in stocks < *agio*, AGIO] *same as* MONEY-CHANGING

ag·i·tate (aj'ə tāt') *vt.* -tat'ed, -tat'ing [< L. *agitatus*, pp. of *agitare*, to put in motion < *agere*, ACT] 1. to move violently; stir up or shake up 2. to excite or disturb the feelings of 3. to keep discussing so as to stir up interest in and support for —*vi.* to stir up interest and support through speeches and writing so as to produce changes [to *agitate* for better working conditions] —*SYN.* see DISTURB

ag·i·tat·ed (-id) *adj.* shaken; perturbed; excited —ag'i·tat'ed·ly *adv.*

ag·i·ta·tion (aj'ə tā'shən) *n.* 1. an agitating or being agitated; violent motion or stirring 2. emotional disturbance or excitement 3. discussion meant to stir up people and produce changes

‡a·gi·ta·to (ä'jē tä'tô) *adj., adv.* [It. < L. *agitatus*: see AGITATE] *Music* fast and with excitement: a direction to the performer

ag·i·ta·tor (aj'ə tāt'ər) *n.* 1. a person who tries to stir up people in support of a social or political cause: often used in an unfavorable sense 2. an apparatus for shaking or stirring, as in a washing machine

ag·it·prop (ag'it präp') *adj.* [Russ. < *agitatsiya*, agitation (< Fr.: see AGITATION) + *propaganda* (< G.: see PROPAGANDA)] of or for agitating and propagandizing: a term originally used in the Communist movement, esp. of certain plays, leaflets, etc.

A·gla·ia (ə glā'ə, -glī'-) [L. < Gr. *Aglaia*, lit., brightness] *Gr. Myth.* one of the three Graces

a·gleam (ə glēm') *adv., adj.* gleaming

ag·let (ag'lit) *n.* [ME. < OFr. *aguillette*, dim. of *aiguille* < L. *acula*, dim. of *acus*, a needle: see ACEROSE[1]] the metal tip at the end of a cord or lace

a·gley (ə glē', -glī', -glā') *adv.* [A-[1] + Scot. *gley* squint] [Scot.] awry; off to one side

a·glit·ter (ə glit'ər) *adv., adj.* glittering

a·glow (ə glō') *adv., adj.* in a glow (of color or emotion)

ag·nail (ag'nāl') *n.* [ME. *angnail* < OE. *angnægl*, a corn (on the toe or foot) < *ange*, pain (akin to ANGER) + *nægl*, nail (metal): orig. in reference to the nail-head appearance of the excrescence] 1. a sore or swelling around a fingernail or toenail 2. a hangnail

...riginally used for airplane wings 2. a similar ...oth used for shirts, etc.

...t an epiphyte

...et an atmospheric condition that causes an aircraft ...e sudden, short drops while in flight

... (-pôrt′) *n.* a place where aircraft can land and ...f, usually equipped with hangars, facilities for refuel... ...d repair, accommodations for passengers, etc.

...wer 1. the power of a nation, esp. military power, ...d upon its aeronautical development; total capacity of ...tion for air war 2. that part of the military establish... ...t responsible for the employment of this power

...pressure the pressure of atmospheric or compressed air

...proof (-pro͞of′) *adj.* not penetrable by air —*vt.* to make ...rproof

... **pump** a machine for removing or compressing air or for ...orcing it through something

...**ir raid** an attack by aircraft, esp. bombers, against a surface target, as a city

☆**air rifle** a rifle operated by compressed air, that shoots BB's, etc.

air sac any of the air-filled cavities in a bird's body, having connections to the lungs

air·scape (-skāp′) *n.* [AIR + (LAND)SCAPE] a view of the earth from a high position, as from an aircraft

air scoop a device on an aircraft for taking in air during flight, as to supply a carburetor, for ventilation, etc.

air·screw (-skro͞o′) *n.* [Brit.] an airplane propeller

air shaft 1. a passage through which fresh air can enter a tunnel, mine, etc. 2. *same as* AIR WELL

air·ship (-ship′) *n.* any self-propelled aircraft that is lighter than air and can be steered; dirigible

air·sick (-sik′) *adj.* sick or nauseated from traveling in an aircraft —**air′sick′ness** *n.*

air·space (-spās′) *n.* 1. space for maneuvering an aircraft flying in formation 2. the space extending upward above an area of the earth's surface; specif., the space above a nation over which it can maintain jurisdiction 3. the space above private land reasonably needed for its quiet enjoyment

air·speed (-spēd′) *n.* the speed of an aircraft relative to the air through which it moves rather than to the ground

air-sprayed (er′sprād′) *adj.* sprayed by means of compressed air

air spring *same as* AIR CUSHION (sense 2)

air·stream (-strēm′) *n.* a stream of air; esp., the relative stream of air set up around an aircraft in flight

air·strip (-strip′) *n.* a hard-surfaced area, as at an airhead, adapted with minimal improvements for use as a temporary airplane runway

airt (ert) *n.* [< Gael. *aird*, height, direction < IE. base **ardi-*, whence Gr. *ardis*, point of an arrow] [Scot.] any of the cardinal points of the compass; direction —*vt.* [Scot.] to guide or direct

air·tight (er′tīt′) *adj.* 1. too tight for air or gas to enter or escape 2. giving no opening for attack; invulnerable [an *airtight* alibi]

air-to-air (er′tə er′) *adj.* launched from an aircraft and directed at a target in the air [*air-to-air* missile]

air-to-ground (-ground′) *adj.* launched from an aircraft and directed at a land target [*air-to-ground* missile]

air valve a valve by which the entrance or escape of air can be regulated

air vesicle *Bot.* a space filled with air, found in many floating water plants

air·waves (er′wāvz′) *n.pl.* the medium through which radio signals are transmitted

air·way (-wā′) *n.* 1. *same as* AIR SHAFT (sense 1) 2. a specific route for air traffic, provided with navigational aids 3. [*pl.*] airwaves 4. *Med.* *a*) a respiratory passageway *b*) a device used to bring air to the lungs during anesthesia

☆**air well** an open shaft passing through the floors of a building for ventilation

air·wor·thy (-wur′thē) *adj.* fit and safe for flying: said of aircraft —**air′wor′thi·ness** *n.*

air·y (er′ē) *adj.* **air′i·er, air′i·est** 1. in the air; high up 2. of air 3. open to the air; breezy 4. unsubstantial as air; visionary 5. light as air; delicate; graceful 6. light-hearted; vivacious; gay 7. characterized by levity; flippant 8. [Colloq.] putting on airs, affected

A·i·sha (ä′ē shä′) 611?–678? A.D.; Mohammed's favorite wife; daughter of ABU-BAKR

aisle (īl) *n.* [ME. *ile* < OFr. *aile*, wing, section of a building (see AILERON); E. *-s-* through confusion with ISLE] 1. a part of a church alongside the nave, choir, or transept, set off by a row of columns or piers 2. a passageway between rows of seats 3. a narrow passageway, as between rows of trees —**aisled** (īld) *adj.*

Aisne (ān) river in N France, flowing into the Oise: 175 mi.

aitch (āch) *n.* [ME. & OFr. *ache* < LL. **accha, aha;* combination of primary vowel (ä) with consonantal symbols intended to exemplify the former quality of the sound] the letter H, h —*adj.* shaped like an H

aitch·bone (āch′bōn′) *n.* [by faulty separation of ME. *a nache bone* < OFr. *nache*, buttock < VL. **natica*, dim. < L. *natis*, buttock] 1. the rump bone 2. a cut of beef around the rump bone

Aix-en-Pro·vence (eks än prô väns′) city in S France, near Marseilles: pop. 68,000 Also called **Aix**

Aix-la-Cha·pelle (eks lå shå pel′) *Fr. name for* AACHEN

Ai·yi·na (ā yē′nə) *Mod. Gr. name of* AEGINA

A·jac·cio (ä yät′chô) capital of Corsica: birthplace of Napoleon: pop. 41,000

a·jar[1] (ə jär′) *adv., adj.* [ME. *on char, a-char* < OE. *cier*, a turn: see CHORE] slightly open [the door stood *ajar*]

a·jar[2] (ə jär′) *adv., adj.* [A-[1] + JAR, *v.*] not in harmony

A·jax (ā′jaks) [L. < Gr. *Aias*] *Gr. Myth.* 1. a strong, brave Greek warrior who killed himself when Achilles' armor was given to Odysseus: called **Ajax Tel·a·mon** (tel′ə män) 2. one of the swiftest runners among the Greek warriors: called **Ajax the Less**

Aj·mer (uj mir′) 1. city in NW India, in Rajasthan state: pop. 231,000 2. former state (1950–1956) of NW India, transferred to Rajasthan state

Aj·mer-Mer·wa·ra (uj mir′mer wä′rä) former province of NW India: in 1950, it became the state of AJMER

a k a, a.k.a. also known as: used before an alias, as in police records [George Desmond *a k a* George Destry]

A·kan (ä′kän) *n.* 1. a language spoken in a large part of Ghana and in parts of the Ivory Coast 2. a member of an Akan-speaking people

Ak·bar (ak′bär) 1542–1605; Mogul emperor of Hindustan (1556–1605): called **Akbar the Great**

AKC American Kennel Club

A·kha·ia (ə kā′ə) *see* ACHAIA

A·khe·na·ten, A·khe·na·ton (ä′ke nä′t'n) *same as* IKHNATON

a·kim·bo (ə kim′bō) *adv., adj.* [ME. *in kenebowe*, lit., in keen bow, i.e., in a sharp curve; a folk etym. from ON. *kengboginn*, bow-bent < *keng*, bent + *bogi*, a bow] with hands on hips and elbows bent outward [with arms *akimbo*]

ARMS AKIMBO

a·kin (ə kin′) *adj.* 1. of one kin; related through a common ancestor 2. having similar qualities; similar

Ak·kad (ak′ad, äk′äd) 1. ancient region in N Babylonia: it flourished c. 2800 B.C.–1100 B.C. 2. its chief city, for a time the capital of Babylonia —*n.* 1. a native or inhabitant of ancient Akkad 2. *same as* AKKADIAN

Ak·ka·di·an (ə kā′dē ən, -kä′-) *adj.* of ancient Akkad, its people, their language, etc. —*n.* an extinct Semitic language of the Mesopotamian region

Ak·ko (ä kō′) *Heb. name of* ACRE, city in Israel

Ak·ron (ak′rən) [< Gr. *akron*, highest point] city in N Ohio; center of rubber manufacturing: pop. 275,000 (met. area 679,000)

Ak·sum (äk′soom) capital of an ancient kingdom in NE Africa, part of which became Ethiopia —**Ak′sum·ite′** (-īt′) *adj., n.*

ak·va·vit (äk′və vēt′, ak′-) *n.* [Dan. < L. *aqua vitae:* see AQUA VITAE] *same as* AQUAVIT

al-[1] (al) [< Ar. *al*] *a prefix meaning* the: used to make a noun definite [*algebra, alchemy*]

al-[2] (al, əl) *same as* AD-: used before *l*

-al (əl, ′l) [Fr., *-al, -el* < L. *-alis*] 1. *an adj.-forming suffix meaning* of, like, or suitable for [*comical, hysterical, theatrical*] 2. a suffix of nouns which were originally adjectives [*perennial, annual*]: also used for nouns formed by analogy with these 3. [ME. *-aile* < OFr. *-aille* < L. *-alia*, neut. pl. of *-alis*] *a n.-forming suffix meaning* the act or process of [*avowal*] 4. [< AL(DEHYDE)] *Chem. a n.-forming suffix denoting:* *a*) an aldehyde [*furfural*] *b*) a barbiturate [*phenobarbital*]

Al *Chem.* aluminum

A.L. 1. American League 2. American Legion

a·la (ā′lə) *n., pl.* **a′lae** (-lē) [L., a wing: see AILERON] 1. *Zool.* a wing 2. a winglike structure, as a lobe of the ear or a side petal of a butterfly-shaped corolla

à la, a la (ä′lə, -lä; al′ə; *Fr.* à là) [Fr.] 1. to, in, or at the 2. in the manner or style of 3. according to

ALA, A.L.A. American Library Association

Al·a·bam·a (al′ə bam′ə) [< Fr. < native (? Choctaw) place and tribal name] 1. Southern State of SE U.S., on the Gulf of Mexico: admitted, 1819; 51,609 sq. mi.; pop. 3,444,000; cap. Montgomery: abbrev. **Ala., AL** 2. river flowing through C and SW Ala. into the Mobile River: c. 315 mi. —**Al′a·bam′i·an** (-ē ən) *adj., n.*

al·a·bam·ine (al′ə bam′ēn) *n.* [ALABAM(A) + -INE[4]] a name proposed in 1931 for what was erroneously thought to be chemical element 85, found in monazite sands in Alabama: cf. ASTATINE

al·a·bas·ter (al′ə bas′tər) *n.* [ME. & OFr. *alabastre* < L. *alabaster* < Gr. *alabastros*, earlier *alabastos*, vase for perfumes (often made of alabaster), prob. < Egypt. **'a-la-baste*, vessel of (the goddess) Bast] 1. a translucent, whitish, fine-grained variety of gypsum, used for statues, vases, etc. 2. a semitranslucent variety of calcite found esp. in stalactites and stalagmites: it is sometimes streaked or mottled like marble —**al′a·bas′trine** (-trin) *adj.*

‡**à la bonne heure** (à là bô nër′) [Fr., lit., at the good hour] well and good; well done!

a la carte (ä′lə kärt′, al′ə-) [Fr. *à la carte*, lit., by the bill of fare] with a separate price for each item on the menu: opposed to TABLE D'HÔTE

ag·nate (ag′nāt) *n.* [L. *agnatus* < pp. of *agnasci*, to be born in addition to < *ad-*, to + *nasci*, to be born] a relative through male descent or on the father's side —*adj.* 1. related through male descent or on the father's side 2. akin —**ag·nat·ic** (ag nat′ik) *adj.* —**ag·na′tion** (-nā′shən) *n.*

Ag·nes (ag′nis) [Fr. *Agnès* < L. *Agnes, Hagnes* < Gr. *hagnē*, fem. of *hagnos*, chaste] 1. a feminine name: dim. *Aggie* 2. Saint, 3d-cent. virgin martyr: see also SAINT AGNES'S EVE

Ag·new (ag′no͞o), **Spi·ro Theodore** (spir′ō) 1918– ; vice president of the U.S. (1969–)

ag·no·men (ag nō′mən) *n., pl.* **ag·nom′i·na** (-näm′ə nə) [L. < *ad-*, to + *gnomen:* see COGNOMEN] 1. in ancient Rome, a name added to the cognomen, esp. as an epithet honoring some achievement 2. a nickname

ag·nos·tic (ag näs′tik, -nôs′-) *n.* [coined by Thos. Huxley in 1870 < Gr. *agnōstos*, unknown, unknowable < *a-*, not + base of *gignōskein*, to know: see KNOW] a person who believes that the human mind cannot know whether there is a God or an ultimate cause, or anything beyond material phenomena —*adj.* of or characteristic of an agnostic or agnosticism —*SYN.* see ATHEIST —**ag·nos′ti·cal·ly** *adv.*

ag·nos·ti·cism (ag näs′tə siz'm, -nôs′-) *n.* the doctrine of agnostics: distinguished from ATHEISM

Ag·nus De·i (äg′noos dā′ē; ag′nəs dē′ī) [L., Lamb of God] 1. a representation of Christ as a lamb, often holding a cross or flag 2. *R.C.Ch.* *a*) a little wax disk with a lamb pictured on it, blessed by the Pope *b*) a prayer in the Mass, beginning *Agnus Dei* *c*) music for this 3. an Anglican anthem, beginning "O Lamb of God"

a·go (ə gō′) *adj.* [ME. *agon*, pp. of *agon*, to depart < OE. *agan*, to pass away < *a-*, away + *gan:* see GO[1]] gone by; past; before now: used following the noun [years *ago*] —*adv.* in the past [long *ago*]

a·gog (ə gäg′, -gôg′) *adv., adj.* [ME. *agogge* < OFr. *a gogue*, < *a-* + *gogue*, joke, joyfulness] in a state of eager anticipation, excitement, or interest

à go-go, a go-go (ə gō′gō′) *same as* GO-GO

-a·gogue, -a·gog (ə gäg′, -gôg′) [< Gr. *agōgos*, leading < *agein*, to lead: see ACT] *a combining form meaning* leading, directing, inciting [*demagogue*]

a·gon (ä′gōn, -gän) *n., pl.* **a′gons, a·go·nes** (ə gō′nēz) [Gr. *agōn*, assembly, contest < *agein*, to lead: see ACT] 1. any of various competitions (athletic, literary, etc.) for prizes at ancient Greek games 2. the conflict of characters, as in classical Greek drama

ag·o·nal (ag′ə n'l) *adj.* of or connected with the agony of dying

a·gone (ə gôn′, -gän′) *adj., adv.* [ME. *agon*, AGO] [Archaic] ago; past

a·gon·ic (ə gän′ik, ā-) *adj.* [< Gr. *agōnos* < *a-*, without + *gōnia*, an angle] forming no angle

agonic line an imaginary line on the earth's surface along which true north and magnetic north are identical, and a compass needle makes no angle with the meridian

ag·o·nist (ag′ə nist) *n.* [back-formation < ANTAGONIST] a muscle whose contraction is counteracted by the opposite movement of another muscle, the antagonist

ag·o·nis·tic (ag′ə nis′tik) *adj.* [Gr. *agōnistikos*, fit for contest < *agōn*, AGON] 1. of ancient Greek athletic contests 2. contesting; combative 3. strained for effect Also **ag′o·nis′ti·cal** —**ag′o·nis′ti·cal·ly** *adv.*

ag·o·nize (ag′ə nīz′) *vi.* **-nized′, -niz′ing** [LL. *agonizare* < Gr. *agōnizesthai*, to contend for a prize < *agōn*, a contest < *agein:* see ACT] 1. to make convulsive efforts; struggle 2. to be in agony; be in great pain —*vt.* to cause great pain to; torture —**ag′o·niz′ing** *adj.* —**ag′o·niz′ing·ly** *adv.*

ag·o·ny (ag′ə nē) *n., pl.* **-nies** [ME. *agonie* < L. *agonia* < Gr. *agōnia*, a contest for victory < *agōn*, AGON] 1. very great mental or physical pain 2. death pangs 3. a convulsive struggle 4. a sudden, strong outburst (*of* emotion) [an *agony* of joy] —*SYN.* see DISTRESS

ag·o·ra[1] (ag′ə rə) *n., pl.* **-rae′** (-rē′), **-ras** (-rəz) [Gr. < *ageirein*, to assemble < IE. base **ger-:* see GREGARIOUS] in ancient Greece, an assembly or a place of assembly, esp. a market place

a·go·ra[2] (ä′gō rä′) *n., pl.* **-rot′** (-rōt′) [ModHeb. *'āgōrāh*] an Israeli monetary unit and coin equal to 1/100 of the pound

ag·o·ra·pho·bi·a (ag′ər ə fō′bē ə) *n.* [AGORA[1] + -PHOBIA] an abnormal fear of being in open or public places

a·gou·ti, a·gou·ty (ə go͞o′tē) *n., pl.* **-tis, -ties:** see PLURAL II, D, 1 [Fr. < Sp. *agutí* < Guarani] a rodent (family Dasyproctidae) related to the guinea pig, found in the West Indies and Central and South America: it is about as big as a rabbit and has grizzled fur

AGOUTI
(17-25 in. long)

agr. 1. agricultural 2. agriculture 3. agriculturist

A·gra (ä′grə) 1. city in Uttar Pradesh, N India: site of the Taj Mahal: pop. 509,000 2. region of India that with *Oudh* formed United Provinces: cf. UTTAR PRADESH

a·graffe, a·grafe (ə graf′) *n.* [Fr. *agrafe* < *agrafer*, to hook < OFr. *agraper*, to fasten < *grapon*, hook < Frank. *krappo* (see GRAPE); form infl. by OFr. *grafe*, pointed tool < L. *graphium*, stylus < Gr. *grapheion*, a chisel] 1. a hook and a loop, used as a clasp for armor or clothing 2. a metal bracket for holding stones together

A·gram (ä′gräm) *Ger. name of* ZAGREB

a·gran·u·lo·cy·to·sis (ā gran′yə lō′sī tō′sis) *n.* [< *agranulocyte* (< A-[2] + GRANULE + -CYTE) + -OSIS] a disorder characterized by the absence of granulocytes from the circulating blood and resulting in high fever, great weakness, and ulceration of the mucous membranes

ag·ra·pha (ag′rə fə) *n.pl.* [Gr., neut. pl. of *agraphos*, unwritten: see A-[2] + GRAPHIC] sayings ascribed to Jesus but not found in the Gospels

a·graph·i·a (ā graf′ē ə) *n.* [ModL. < Gr. *a-*, without + *graphein*, to write] a brain disorder resulting in a partial or total loss of the ability to write —**a·graph′ic** *adj.*

a·grar·i·an (ə grer′ē ən) *adj.* [< L. *agrarius* < *ager*, a field, country] 1. relating to land or to the ownership or division of land 2. of agriculture or farmers generally —*n.* a person who advocates agrarian reform, or a more equitable division of land

a·grar·i·an·ism (-iz'm) *n.* the principles of, or a political movement for, agrarian reform

a·gree (ə grē′) *vi.* **-greed′, -gree′ing** [ME. *agreen* < OFr. *agreer*, to receive kindly < OFr. *a gre*, favorably < *a* (L. *ad*), to + *gre*, good will < L. *gratus*, pleasing] 1. to consent or accede (*to*); say "yes" 2. to be in harmony or accord [their versions *agree*] 3. to be of the same opinion; concur (*with*) 4. to arrive at a satisfactory understanding (*about* prices, terms, etc.) 5. to be suitable, healthful, etc. (followed by *with*) [this climate does not *agree* with him] 6. *Gram.* to be inflected so as to correspond in number, person, case, or gender —*vt.* to grant or acknowledge: followed by a noun clause [we *agreed* that it was true]

SYN.—**agree** implies a being or going together without conflict and is the general term used in expressing an absence of inconsistencies, inequalities, unfavorable effects, etc.; **conform** emphasizes agreement in form or essential character; **accord** emphasizes fitness for each other of the things that are being considered together; **harmonize** implies a combination or association of different things in a proportionate, orderly, or pleasing arrangement [*harmonizing* colors]; **correspond** is applied to that which matches, complements, or is analogous to something else [their Foreign Office *corresponds* to our State Department]; **coincide** stresses the identical character of the things considered [their interests *coincide*]; **tally** is applied to a thing that corresponds to another thing as a counterpart or duplicate: see also CONSENT —*ANT.* **differ**

a·gree·a·ble (-ə b'l) *adj.* [ME. & OFr. *agreable* < *agreer*, AGREE] 1. pleasing or pleasant [an *agreeable* odor] 2. willing or ready to consent 3. conformable or in accord —*SYN.* see PLEASANT —**a·gree′a·bil′i·ty** (-bil′ə tē), **a·gree′a·ble·ness** *n.* —**a·gree′a·bly** *adv.*

a·greed (ə grēd′) *adj.* settled or determined by mutual consent [pay the *agreed* price]

a·gree·ment (ə grē′mənt) *n.* 1. the act or fact of agreeing, or of being in harmony or accord 2. an understanding or arrangement between two or more people, countries, etc. 3. a contract 4. *Gram.* correspondence, as between subject and verb, in number, person, etc.

a·gres·tic (ə gres′tik) *adj.* [< L. *agrestis*, rural < *ager*, field (see ACRE) + -IC] 1. rural; rustic 2. crude; uncouth

☆**ag·ri·busi·ness** (ag′rə biz′nis) *n.* [AGRI(CULTURE) + BUSINESS] farming and the businesses associated with farming, as the processing of farm products, the manufacturing of farm equipment and fertilizers, etc.

A·gric·o·la (ə grik′ə lə) 1. (**Gnaeus Julius**), 37–93 A.D.; Rom. general; governor of Britain 2. **Geor·gi·us** (jôr′jē əs), (L. name of *Georg Bauer*) 1490–1555; Ger. scholar who made the first scientific classification of minerals: called the *Father of Mineralogy*

ag·ri·cul·ture (ag′ri kul′chər) *n.* [Fr. < L. *agricultura* < *ager*, a field (see ACRE) + *cultura*, cultivation] the science and art of farming; work of cultivating the soil, producing crops, and raising livestock —**ag′ri·cul′tur·al** *adj.* —**ag′ri·cul′tur·al·ly** *adv.*

ag·ri·cul·tur·ist (ag′ri kul′chər ist) *n.* 1. an agricultural expert 2. a farmer Also **ag′ri·cul′tur·al·ist**

Ag·ri·gen·to (ä′grē jen′tô) city in S Sicily: site of ancient Greek and Roman ruins: pop. 47,000

Ag·ri·gen·tum (ag′rə jen′təm) *ancient L. name of* AGRIGENTO

ag·ri·mo·ny (ag′rə mō′nē) *n., pl.* **-nies** [ME. < OE. *agrimonia* & OFr. *aigremoine*, both < L. *agrimonia*, altered after *ager*, field < *argemonia* < Gr. *argemōnē*] 1. any plant of a genus (*Agrimonia*) in the rose family, typically having little yellow flowers on spiky stalks and bearing fruits that look like burs 2. *same as* HEMP AGRIMONY 3. *same as* BUR MARIGOLD

ag·ri·ol·o·gy (ag′rē äl′ə jē) *n.* [< Gr. *agrios*, wild + -LOGY] the study of the customs of nonliterate peoples whose culture is marked by a simple technology

A·grip·pa (ə grip′ə) 1. (**Marcus Vipsanius**), 63–12 B.C.;

Rom. military leader & statesman; commander of Octavian's fleet at ACTIUM 2. see HEROD AGRIPPA I & II

Ag·rip·pi·na (II) (ag'ri pī'nə, -pē'-), **(Julia)** 15?–59 A.D.; mother of Nero & sister of Caligula: called *Agrippina the Younger*

ag·ro- (ag'rō) [Gr. < *agros*, a field] *a combining form meaning* field, earth, soil

ag·ro·bi·ol·o·gy (ag'rō bī äl'ə jē) *n.* the science of plant growth and nutrition as applied to improvement of crops and control of soil —**ag'ro·bi'o·log'ic** (-bī'ə läj'ik), **ag'ro·bi'o·log'i·cal** *adj.* —**ag'ro·bi'o·log'i·cal·ly** *adv.*

ag·ro·chem·i·cal (ag'rō kem'i k'l) *n.* 1. a chemical used to improve the quality and quantity of farm products 2. a chemical derived from agricultural products, as furfural

a·grol·o·gy (ə gräl'ə jē) *n.* the science of agricultural production —**a·grol'o·gist** *n.*

ag·ro·nom·ics (ag'rə näm'iks) *n.pl.* [*with sing. v.*] *same as* AGRONOMY

a·gron·o·my (ə grän'ə mē) *n.* [Fr. *agronomie* < OFr. *agronome*, agriculturist < Gr. *agronomos*, overseer of the public lands < *agros* (see ACRE) + *-nomos* < *nemein*, to deal out, manage] the science and economics of crop production; management of farm land —**ag·ro·nom·ic** (ag'rə näm'ik), **ag'ro·nom'i·cal** *adj.* —**a·gron'o·mist** *n.*

ag·ros·tol·o·gy (ag'rəs täl'ə jē) *n.* [< L. *agrostis* < Gr. *agrōstis*, kind of grass < *agros*, a field + -LOGY] the branch of botany dealing with grasses

a·ground (ə ground') *adv., adj.* on or onto the shore, the bottom, a reef, etc. [*the ship ran aground*]

agt. agent

☆**a·guar·dien·te** (ä'gwär dyen'tā) *n.* [Sp., lit., fiery water <*agua* (< L. *aqua*, water) + *ardiente*, burning (< L. *ardens*: see ARDENT)] any of various common alcoholic liquors of Spain, Latin America, etc.

A·guas·ca·lien·tes (ä'gwäs kä lyen'tās) 1. small, inland state of C Mexico: 2,499 sq. mi.; pop. 263,000 2. its capital: pop. 148,000

a·gue (ā'gyōō) *n.* [ME. < OFr. *ague* < ML. (*febris*) *acuta*, violent (fever): see ACUTE] 1. a fever, usually malarial, marked by regularly recurring chills 2. a chill; fit of shivering —**a'gu·ish** *adj.*

☆**a·gue·weed** (ā'gyōō wēd') *n.* 1. a variety (*Gentiana quinquefolia*) of gentian 2. *same as* BONESET

A·gui·nal·do (ä'gē näl'dô), **E·mi·lio** (e mē'lyô) 1869–1964; Filipino leader in the Philippine movement for independence

A·gul·has (ə gul'əs; *Port.* ä gōō'lyäsh), **Cape** southernmost point of Africa

ah (ä, ô, ôn, an, än) *interj.* [natural exclamation similar to Fr. & L. *ah*, Gr. *a*, ON. *æ*, OHG. *ā*, Sans. *ā*] an exclamation expressing pain, delight, regret, disgust, surprise, etc., according to the manner of expression

A.H. [L. *Anno Hegirae*] in the year of the Hegira

a.h., a-h ampere-hour

a·ha (ä hä') *interj.* an exclamation expressing satisfaction, pleasure, triumph, etc., often mixed with irony or mockery

A·hab (ā'hab) [Heb., lit., father's brother] *Bible* a wicked king of Israel, husband of Jezebel: I Kings 16:29–22:40

A·has·u·e·rus (ə haz'yoo wer'əs; -hazh'oo-; -wir'-)[of Per. origin] *Bible* either of two kings of the Medes and Persians, esp. the one (often identified as Xerxes I) who took Esther as his wife: Esth. 1, Ezra 4:6

‡**à haute voix** (ä ōt' vwä') [Fr., in high voice] aloud

a·head (ə hed') *adv., adj.* 1. in or to the front 2. forward; onward 3. toward the future; in advance 4. winning or leading 5. having something as a profit or advantage —**ahead of** in advance of; before —**get ahead** to advance socially, financially, etc. —**get ahead of** to outdo or excel

a·hem (ə hem': *conventionalized pronun.*) *interj.* a cough or similar noise in the throat, made to get someone's attention, give a warning, fill a pause, etc.

a·him·sa (ə him'sä) *n.* [Sans. *ahimsā*, non-injury < *a-*, not + *himsā*, injury < IE. base **gheis-*, to wound < **ghei-*, to hurl, projectile, whence GOAD] *Buddhism, Jainism, etc.* the doctrine that all life is one and sacred, resulting in the principle of nonviolence toward all living creatures

a·his·tor·ic (ā'his tôr'ik) *adj.* not related to or concerned with documented history: also **a'his·tor'i·cal** —**a'his·tor'i·cal·ly** *adv.*

A·hith·o·phel, A·hit·o·phal (ə hit'ə fel') [Heb. *'achīthōphel*, lit., brother is foolishness] *Bible* a counselor of David and associate of Absalom in rebellion against David: II Sam. 15–17

Ah·med·a·bad, Ah·mad·a·bad (ä'məd ə bäd') city in W India, capital of Gujarat state: pop. 1,206,000

Ah·med·na·gar, Ah·mad·na·gar (ä'məd nug'ər) city in Maharashtra state, W India: pop. 119,000

A-ho·ri·zon (ā'hə rī'z'n) *n.* the uppermost soil zone, containing humus: see ABC SOIL

a·hoy (ə hoi') *interj.* [interj. *a* + *hoy*, var. of HEY] *Naut.* a call used in hailing [*ship ahoy!*]

AHQ Army Headquarters

Ah·ri·man (ä'ri mən) [Per. *Ahrīman*, prob. < Avestan *aṅra mainyu*, the evil (lit., hostile) spirit] *Zoroastrianism* the spirit of evil: see ORMAZD

A·hu·ra Maz·da (ä'hoo rə maz'də) *same as* ORMAZD

Ah·vaz, Ah·waz (ä väz', -väz') city in SW Iran, the capital of Khuzistan province: pop. 155,000

Ah·ve·nan·maa Islands (ä've nän mä') group of Finnish islands at the entrance to the Gulf of Bothnia: 572 sq. mi.; pop. 21,000: *Swed. name*, ALAND ISLANDS

ai[1] (ī) *interj.* an exclamation of pain, sorrow, pity, etc.

a·i[2] (ä'ē) *n., pl.* **a'is** (-ēz) [Tupi *ai*, *hai* < the animal's cry] a S. American sloth (*Bradypus tridactylus*) with three toes

A.I.A. American Institute of Architects

A.I.C. American Institute of Chemists

AID Agency for International Development

aid (ād) *vt., vi.* [ME. *aiden* < OFr. *aider* < L. *adjutare*, freq. of *adjuvare*: see ADJUTANT] to give help or relief (to); assist —*n.* [ME. & OFr. *aide* < the *v.*] 1. help; assistance 2. a helper; assistant 3. a helpful device 4. an officer in the army, navy, etc. who is assistant to a superior; aide 5. *Eng. History* *a*) a payment in money made by a vassal to his lord *b*) a special tax or subsidy paid to the king *c*) an exchequer loan —*SYN.* see HELP

A·i·da (ä ē'də) the title character of an Italian opera by Giuseppe Verdi (1871); an Ethiopian princess enslaved in Egypt

aide (ād) *n.* [Fr.: see AID] 1. an assistant 2. an aide-de-camp

aide-de-camp, aid-de-camp (ād'də kamp') *n., pl.* **aides-de-camp, aids-de-camp** [Fr., lit., camp assistant] an officer in the army, navy, etc. serving as assistant and confidential secretary to a superior

‡**aide-mé·moire** (ed mā mwär') *n.* [Fr.] a memorandum of a discussion, proposed agreement, etc.

aid·man (ād'man') *n., pl.* **-men** (-men') *Mil.* an enlisted man in a medical corps attached to a combat unit

☆**aid station** *Mil.* a medical station in a forward area where the sick and wounded are given emergency treatment

A.I.E.E. American Institute of Electrical Engineers

Ai·gi·na (e'yē nä) *Mod. Gr. name of* AEGINA

ai·glet (ā'glit) *n. same as* AGLET

ai·grette, ai·gret (ā'gret, ā gret') *n.* [see EGRET] 1. the long, white, showy plumes of the egret, once worn for ornament by women 2. any ornament, as of jewels, like this

ai·guille (ā gwēl', ā'gwēl) *n.* [Fr.: see AGLET] 1. a peak of rock shaped like a needle 2. an instrument for drilling holes in rock or masonry

ai·guil·lette (ā'gwi let') *n.* [Fr.: see AGLET] a gilt cord hung in loops from the shoulder of certain military uniforms

Ai·ken (āk'n), **Conrad (Potter)** 1889– ; U.S. poet and fiction writer

ail (āl) *vt.* [ME. *eilen* < OE. *eglian*, to afflict with dread, trouble < *egle*, harmful, akin to Goth. *agls*, infamous, ON. *agi*, whence AWE] to be the cause of pain or distress to; trouble —*vi.* to be in poor health, esp. over a period of time

ai·lan·thus (ā lan'thəs) *n., pl.* **-thus·es** [ModL., altered after Gr. *anthos*, flower < *ailanto*, the native name in Malacca] any tree or shrub of a genus (*Ailanthus*) of the quassia family, having pointed leaflets, fine-grained wood, and clusters of small, greenish flowers with an unpleasant odor: see TREE OF HEAVEN —**ai·lan'thic** *adj.*

ailanthus moth a large moth (*Philosamia cynthia*) native to eastern Asia and cultivated in the eastern U.S., whose larvae (**ailanthus silkworms**) feed on ailanthus leaves and produce an inferior silk

Ai·leen (ī lēn', ā-) *var. of* EILEEN

ai·le·ron (ā'lə rän') *n.* [Fr. < OFr. *aleron*, wingtip < *aile*, wing < L. *ala*, wing, armpit < **agsla* < IE. base **aks-*: see AXLETREE] a movable hinged section in or near the trailing edge of an airplane wing for controlling the rolling movements of the airplane

ail·ing (āl'iŋ) *adj.* in poor health; sickly —*SYN.* see SICK[1]

ail·ment (āl'mənt) *n.* any bodily or mental disorder; illness, esp. a mild, chronic one —*SYN.* see DISEASE

ai·lu·ro·pho·bi·a (ī lur'ə fō'bē ə) *n.* [ModL. < Gr. *ailouros*, cat + -PHOBIA] an abnormal fear of cats —**ai·lu'ro·phobe'** (-fōb') *n.*

aim (ām) *vi., vt.* [ME. *aimen* < OFr. *esmer* (< L. *aestimare*: see ESTIMATE) & *aesmer* < ML. *adaestimare* < L. *ad-* + *aestimare*] 1. to point (a weapon) or direct (a blow, remark, etc.) so as to hit 2. to direct (one's efforts) [*we aimed at full victory*] 3. to try or intend (*to* do or be something) 4. [Obs.] to guess or conjecture —*n.* 1. the act of aiming 2. the direction of a missile, blow, remark, etc. 3. the object to be attained; intention or purpose 4. [Obs.] a guess or conjecture —*SYN.* see INTENTION —**take aim** 1. to point a weapon, as by viewing along a sight at a target 2. to direct a missile, blow, etc.

aim·less (-ləs) *adj.* having no aim or purpose —**aim'less·ly** *adv.* —**aim'less·ness** *n.*

ain (ān) *adj.* [Scot. & Brit. Dial.] own

ain't (ānt) [early assimilation, with lengthened and raised vowel, of *amn't*, contr. of *am not*; later confused with *a'nt* (*are not*), *i'nt* (*is not*), *ha'nt* (*has not, have not*)] [Colloq.] am not: also a dialectal or substandard contraction for *is not, are not, has not,* and *have not*: *ain't* was formerly standard for *am not* and is still defended by some authorities as a proper colloquial contraction for *am not* in interrogative constructions [*I'm going too, ain't I?*]

Ain·tab (īn täb') *former name of* GAZIANTEP

Ai·nu (ī'nōō) *n.* [Ainu, lit., man] 1. a member of an indigenous, light-skinned ethnic group of Japan, now living mostly on Hokkaido and Sakhalin 2. the language of this people, unrelated to any other known language —*adj.* of the Ainus, their language, etc.

A·ïr (ä'ir) mountainous region of the S Sahara, in N Niger: c. 30,000 sq. mi.: former name, ASBEN

air (er) *n.* [ME. < OFr. *aer* < L. *aer*, < Gr. *aēr*, air, mist] 1. the elastic, invisible mixture of gases (chiefly nitrogen and oxygen, as well as hydrogen, carbon dioxide, argon, neon, helium, etc.) that surrounds the earth; atmosphere 2. space above the earth; sky 3. a movement of air; breeze; wind 4. *same as* COMPRESSED AIR 5. an outward appearance; general impression or feeling given by something [*an air of luxury fills the room*] 6. a person's bearing, manner, or appearance 7. [*pl.*] affected, superior manners and graces 8. public expression or publicity [*give air to your opinions*] 9. transportation by aircraft 10. the medium through which radio signals are transmitted: a figurative use 11. *Music* *a*) a song or tune *b*) the main melody in a harmonized composition, usually the soprano or treble part —*adj.* of aircraft, air forces, etc. [*air power*] —*vt.* 1. to let air into or through; put where air can dry, cool, freshen, etc. 2. to make known publicly; publicize —*vi.* to become aired, dried, cooled, etc. —*SYN.* see MELODY —☆**give (or get) the air** [Slang] to reject (or be rejected), as a lover —**in the air** 1. current or prevalent 2. not decided; not settled; still imaginary —**on (or off) the air** *Radio & TV* that is (or is not) broadcasting or being broadcast —**take the air** to go outdoors, as for fresh air —**up in the air** 1. not settled; not decided 2. [Colloq.] angry; highly excited, agitated, etc. —**walk on air** to feel very happy, lively, or exalted

air alert 1. a state of readiness by air force units, in which aircraft are put into the air for immediate response to orders 2. the signal for getting into such an alert 3. popularly, an alerting, as of civilians, against an air attack

air base an air force establishment for the operation, maintenance, and supply of aircraft and air organizations

air bladder a sac with air or gas in it, found in most fishes and in other animals and some plants: also called **air cell**: see also SWIM BLADDER

air·boat (er'bōt') *n.* ☆a light, flat-bottomed boat driven by a propeller revolving in the air

air·borne (-bôrn') *adj.* 1. carried by or through the air [*airborne bacteria, airborne troops*] 2. supported only by aerodynamic forces; aloft or flying

☆**air brake** 1. a brake operated by the action of compressed air on a piston 2. popularly, *same as* SPEED BRAKE

☆**air·bra·sive** (er'brā'siv) *n.* a method of preparing teeth for filling by wearing down the surface with an abrasive substance blown into the cavity by a jet of air

☆**air·brush** (brush') *n.* a kind of atomizer operated by compressed air and used for spraying on paint or other liquid: also **air brush** —**air'brush'** *vt.*

air·burst (-burst') *n.* an explosion of a bomb, artillery shell, etc. in the air

☆**air·bus** (er'bus') *n.* [AIR(PLANE) + BUS] an airplane designed for mass transportation of passengers; esp., an extremely large, short-range airplane of this kind

air chamber a cavity or compartment full of air, esp. one used in hydraulics to equalize the flow of a fluid

air coach a commercial airplane with lower passenger rates and less luxurious accommodations than first class

air cock a small tap or valve for controlling the entrance or escape of air from a pipe, chamber, etc.

☆**air command** *U.S. Air Force* the largest organizational unit, made up of two or more air forces

☆**air-con·di·tion** (er'kən dish'ən) *vt.* to provide with air conditioning —**air'-con·di'tioned** *adj.*

☆**air conditioner** a device for air conditioning

☆**air conditioning** a method of filtering air and regulating its humidity and temperature in buildings, cars, etc.

air-cooled (er'kōōld') *adj.* 1. cooled by having air passed over, into, or through it [*an air-cooled engine*] 2. air-conditioned —**air'-cool'** *vt.*

Air Corps the former aviation branch of the U.S. Army

air corridor a passage in the air for aircraft, esp. one established by international agreement

air cover 1. protection given by aircraft to land, sea, or air forces 2. the aircraft giving such protection

air·craft (er'kraft', -kräft') *n., pl.* **-craft'** any machine designed to travel through the air, whether heavier or lighter than air; airplane, dirigible, balloon, helicopter, etc.; sometimes, in a restricted sense, an airplane

aircraft carrier a warship that carries airplanes, serves as their base and servicing station, and has a large, flat deck for taking off and landing

air crew the crew of an aircraft in flight

air curtain (or door) a downward draft of air at an open entrance for maintaining even temperatures within

air cushion 1. a cushion inflated with air 2. *Mech.* a device for lessening shock by means of the elasticity of compressed air

air cylinder an air-filled cylinder, esp. one fitted with a piston for absorbing the recoil of a gun

☆**air division** *U.S. Air Force* an organizational unit lower than an air force, usually made up of two or more wings

☆**air·drome** (er'drōm') *n.* [AIR + -DROME] the physical facilities of an air base, excluding personnel

air·drop (-dräp') *n.* the act of ... by parachuting them from ... *vt.* **-dropped', -drop'pi**...

air-dry (er'drī') *vt.* ... the air —*adj.* so dry ... upon exposure to the a...

Aire·dale (er'dāl') *n.* [a... *Aire* in Yorkshire, Englan... breed of large terrier havi... wiry, tan coat with black m...

☆**air express** a method or sys... transporting parcels rapidly ... lines

air·field (er'fēld') *n.* a field where ... craft can take off and land; spec... the landing field of an airport

air·flow (-flō') *n.* a flow of air; specif., the flow of air around a moving automobile, aircraft, etc. —*adj.* 1. allowing free flow of air 2. streamlined

air·foil (-foil') *n.* a part with a flat or curved surface, as a wing, rudder, etc., designed to keep an aircraft up or con... ments by reacting in certain specific way... through which it moves

air force 1. the aviation branch of the armed ... country 2. *U.S. Air Force* an organizational u... than an air command, usually made up of sev... divisions

air·frame (-frām') *n.* the structural framework and c... ing of an airplane, rocket, etc., not including the en... and its related parts

air gas dry air charged with vapor from petroleum or som... other hydrocarbon, used for lighting or heating

air·glow (-glō') *n.* the faint glow in the night sky, only partially visible, thought to be caused by photochemical reactions in the upper atmosphere

air gun 1. a gun operated by means of compressed air 2. a gunlike device used for spraying paint, insecticide, etc. by means of compressed air

air·head (-hed') *n.* [AIR + (BEACH)HEAD] an area seized in warfare, esp. by an airborne assault, and held to ensure the continuous bringing in of troops and materiel by air

air hole 1. a hole that permits passage of air 2. an unfrozen or open place in ice covering a body of water 3. *same as* AIR POCKET

air·i·ly (er'ə lē) *adv.* in an airy or gay, light manner; jauntily; breezily

air·i·ness (-ē nis) *n.* 1. the quality or state of being airy, or full of fresh air 2. gay lightness; jauntiness

air·ing (-iŋ) *n.* 1. exposure to the air for drying, freshening, etc. 2. exposure to public knowledge [*to give a scandal an airing*] 3. a walk or ride outdoors

air jacket a compartment filled with air, surrounding some part of a machine, esp. for checking heat transmission

air lane a route for travel by air; airway

air·less (-lis) *adj.* 1. without air or without fresh air 2. without wind or breeze

air·lift (-lift') *n.* a system of transporting troops, supplies, etc. by aircraft, as when ground routes are blocked —*vt.* to transport by airlift

☆**air·line** (-līn') *n.* 1. the shortest distance between two points on the earth's surface; great-circle route between two places; beeline: also **air line** 2. a system or company for moving freight and passengers by aircraft 3. a route for travel by air —*adj.* of or on an airline [*airline personnel*]

air·lin·er (-lī'nər) *n.* a large airline-operated aircraft for carrying passengers

air lock 1. an airtight compartment, with adjustable air pressure, between places that do not have the same air pressure, as between the working compartment of a caisson and the outside 2. a blockage, as in a water pipe, caused by trapped air

☆**air·mail** (-māl') *n.* 1. the system of transporting mail by aircraft 2. mail transported by aircraft —*vt.* to send by airmail

air·man (-mən) *n., pl.* **-men** (-mən) 1. an aviator 2. an enlisted man or woman in the U.S. Air Force, specif. one in any of the four lowest grades

air mass *Meteorol.* a large body of air maintaining virtually uniform conditions of temperature and moisture in a horizontal cross section as it moves

Air Medal a U.S. military decoration awarded for meritorious achievement while participating in aerial flight

air-mind·ed (er'mīn'dəd) *adj.* interested in or promoting aviation, aircraft, air power, etc.

☆**air·mo·bile** (er'mō'b'l) *adj.* *Mil.* designating ground troops that are moved about by aircraft for engaging in ground combat

air·plane (er'plān') *n.* [altered, after AIR, from earlier AEROPLANE] an aircraft, heavier than air, that is kept aloft by the aerodynamic forces of air upon its wings and is driven forward by a screw propeller or by other means, as jet propulsion

airplane cloth 1. a strong, plain-weave cloth of linen or

air p... cotton, ... cotton cl... ☆air pla... ☆air pock... to make... take o... ing a... air po... base... a na... me... air... air...

a·lack (ə lak′) *interj.* [A(H) + LACK] [Archaic] an exclamation of regret, surprise, dismay, etc.

a·lack·a·day (ə lak′ə dā′) *interj.* [for earlier *alack the day*, woe to the day] [Archaic] alack

a·lac·ri·ty (ə lak′rə tē) *n.* [ME. & OFr. *alacrite* < L. *alacritas*, liveliness < *alacer*, lively] eager willingness or readiness, often manifested by quick, lively action [she sprang to the door with *alacrity*] —a·lac′ri·tous *adj.*

A·la Dag, A·la Dagh (ä′lä däkh′) mountain chain of the Taurus range, S Turkey: highest peak, c. 12,000 ft.

A·lad·din (ə lad′'n) [Ar. *A′l-ad-dīn*, lit., height of faith < *a′lā*, height + *al*, the + *dīn*, faith] a boy in *The Arabian Nights* who found a magic lamp and a magic ring, with which he could call up a jinni to do his bidding

‡à la fran·çaise (à là frän sez′) [Fr.] in the French manner

A·la·gez (ä′lä gyôs′) *same as* ARAGATS

A·la·go·as (ä′lä gō′əs) state of NE Brazil, on the Atlantic: 11,016 sq. mi.; pop. 1,271,000

A·lai Mountains (ä lī′) mountain range in the S Kirghiz S.S.R.: highest peaks, c. 16,500 ft.

☆à la king (ä′lə kiŋ′) [lit., in kingly style] diced and served in a cream sauce containing mushrooms, pimentos, and green peppers [chicken *à la king*]

Al·a·man·ni (al′ə man′ī) *n.pl. same as* ALEMANNI —Al′a·man′nic (-ik) *adj.*

Al·a·me·da (al′ə mē′də, -mä′-) [Sp., see ff.] city on an island in San Francisco Bay, Calif.: pop. 71,000

al·a·me·da (al′ə mē′də, -mä′-) *n.* [Sp. < *álamo*, poplar tree] in the Southwest, a walk that is shaded, esp. by alamos

Al·a·mine (al′ə mēn′) [AL(uminum) + AMINE] *a trademark for* a straight-chain or branched-chain fatty amine of high molecular weight, or a mixture of such amines: these amines are used as corrosion inhibitors, emulsifiers, etc.

Al·a·mo (al′ə mō′) Franciscan mission at San Antonio, Tex.: scene of a siege and massacre of Texans by Mexican troops (1836)

☆al·a·mo (al′ə mō′, ä′lə-) *n., pl.* **-mos′** [Sp. *álamo*, poplar tree] [Southwest] a poplar tree, esp. a cottonwood

a·la·mode (al′ə mōd′) *n.* a thin, shiny silk

a la mode (al′ə mōd′, äl′ə-) [Fr. *à la mode*] **1.** in the fashion; stylish **2.** made or served in a certain style, as (pie or cake) with ice cream, or (beef) braised and prepared with vegetables in sauce Also **à la mode, alamode**

Al·a·mo·gor·do (al′ə mə gôr′dō) city in S N.Mex.: pop. 23,000

‡à la mort (à là môr′; *E.* al′ə môrt′) [Fr., lit., to the death] **1.** very ill, almost to the point of death **2.** dejected; melancholy **3.** mortally

Al·an (al′ən) [ML. *Alanus*, of Breton origin] a masculine name: var. *Allan, Allen*

Al·an·a·dale (al′ən ə dāl′) *n. same as* ALLAN-A-DALE

A·land Islands (ō′lənd, ä′-) *Swed. name of* AHVENANMAA ISLANDS

‡à l'an·glaise (à län glez′) [Fr.] in the English manner

al·a·nine (al′ə nēn′) *n.* [G. *alanin* < *aldehyd*, ALDEHYDE + *-in*, -INE⁴] a naturally occurring nonessential amino acid, $CH_3CH(NH_2)COOH$: it is a colorless crystal, soluble in water, and is used in biochemical research and in studies of amino-acid metabolism

a·lar (ā′lər) *adj.* [L. *alaris* < *ala*, a wing: see AILERON] **1.** of or like a wing **2.** having wings

A·lar·cón (ä′lär kōn′), **Pe·dro An·to·nio de** (pe′ᵭrō än-tō′nyō de) 1833–91; Sp. writer

A·lar·cón y Men·do·za (ē men dō′thä), **Juan Ru·iz de** (hwän′ rōō′ēth de) 1581?–1639; Sp. dramatist, born in Mexico

Al·a·ric (al′ə rik) **1.** 370–410 A.D.; king of the Visigoths (395?–410); captured Rome (410) **2. Alaric II** ?–507 A.D.; king of the Visigoths (484?–507); issued a code of laws

a·larm (ə lärm′) *n.* [ME. & OFr. *alarme* < It. *all′arme*, to arms] **1.** [Archaic] a sudden call to arms **2.** a signal, sound, cry, etc. that is a warning of danger **3.** a mechanism designed to warn of danger or trespassing [a burglar *alarm*] **4.** the bell, buzzer, etc. of an alarm clock **5.** fear caused by the sudden realization of danger **6.** *Fencing* a quick stamp on the ground with the advancing foot —*vt.* **1.** to warn of approaching danger **2.** to make suddenly afraid or anxious; frighten —*SYN.* see FEAR, FRIGHTEN

alarm clock a clock that can be set to ring, buzz, or flash a light at any particular time, as to awaken a person from sleep: see also CLOCK RADIO

a·larm·ing (-iŋ) *adj.* that alarms, or makes suddenly afraid or anxious; frightening —a·larm′ing·ly *adv.*

a·larm·ist (-ist) *n.* **1.** a person who habitually spreads alarming rumors, exaggerated reports of danger, etc. **2.** a person easily frightened and likely to anticipate the worst —*adj.* of or like an alarmist —a·larm′ism *n.*

a·lar·um (ə ler′əm, -lär′-) *n.* [Archaic or Poet.] alarm (esp. sense 1)

a·la·ry (ā′lər ē, al′ər ē) *adj.* [L. *alarius* < *ala*, a wing: see AILERON] of or shaped like a wing; alar

a·las (ə las′, -läs′) *interj.* [ME. < OFr. *a las, helas* < *a-*, *he* ah + *las*, wretched < L. *lassus*, weary] an exclamation of sorrow, pity, regret, or worry

A·las·ka (ə las′kə) [Esk. *Alákshak*, native name for the mainland portion of NW North America] **1.** State of the U.S. in NW N. America, separated from Asia by the Bering Strait: it was bought from Russia in 1867; admitted, 1959; 586,400 sq. mi.; pop. 302,000; cap. Juneau: abbrev. **Alas.**, **AK 2. Gulf of**, inlet of the Pacific in the S coast of Alaska between the Alaska Peninsula and the Alexander Archipelago —A·las′kan *adj.*, *n.*

Alaska Highway highway between Dawson Creek, Brit. Columbia and Fairbanks, Alas.: 1,523 mi.: built by the U.S. in 1942, the Canadian section was turned over to Canada in 1946: popular name, ALCAN HIGHWAY

☆Alaskan malamute any of a breed of large, strong dog with a thick coat of gray or black-and-white and a bushy tail: it was developed as a sled dog by the Alaskan Eskimo

Alaska Peninsula peninsula extending SW from the mainland of Alaska

Alaska Range mountain range in SC Alaska: highest peak, Mount MCKINLEY

☆Alaska Standard Time a standard time used in a zone which includes central Alaska, corresponding to the mean local time of the 150th meridian west of Greenwich, England: it is ten hours behind Greenwich time: equivalent to *Hawaiian Standard Time:* see TIME, chart

a·late (ā′lāt) *adj.* [L. *alatus* < *ala*, a wing: see AILERON] having wings or winglike attachments: also **a′lat·ed**

alb (alb) *n.* [ME. *albe* (< OE. *albe* < ML. *alba*), *aube* < OFr. *aube* < ML. *alba* (*vestis*), white (cloak), fem. of L. *albus*, white] a long, white linen robe with sleeves tapering to the wrist, worn by a priest at Mass

Alb. 1. Albania **2.** Albanian

Al·ba (äl′bä) **Duke of**, *same as* Duke of ALVA

al·ba (äl′bə, al′-) *n.* [Pr., dawn < ML. < L. *albus*, white] the conventionalized morning song of Provençal troubadour literature, a form of aubade

al·ba·core (al′bə kôr′) *n., pl.* **-cores′, -core′**: see PLURAL, II, D, 1 [Port. < Ar. *al*, the + *bakūrah*, albacore] **1.** a warm-water tuna (*Thunnus alalunga*) with unusually long pectoral fins, important as a game and food fish **2.** *same as* TUNA¹ **3.** any of several related saltwater fishes, as the bonito

ALB

Al·ba Lon·ga (al′bə lôŋ′gə) city in ancient Latium, near where Rome is today: legendary birthplace of Romulus and Remus

Al·ban (ôl′bən, ôl′-) [L. *Albanus* < *Alba*, name of several Italian cities] **1.** a masculine name **2.** Saint, 3d or 4th cent.; Brit. martyr: his day is June 22

Al·ba·ni·a (al bā′nē ə, -bān′yə) country in the W Balkan Peninsula, on the Adriatic: 11,099 sq. mi.; pop. 2,019,000; cap. Tirana

Al·ba·ni·an (-bā′nē ən, -bān′yən) *adj.* of Albania, its people, language, etc. —*n.* **1.** a native or inhabitant of Albania **2.** the language of the Albanians, constituting a subfamily of the Indo-European family of languages

Al·ba·ny (ôl′bə nē) [after the Duke of York and *Albany*, later JAMES II] **1.** capital of N.Y., on the Hudson: pop. 115,000: see SCHENECTADY **2.** city in SW Ga.: pop. 73,000

al·ba·tross (al′bə trôs′, -träs′) *n., pl.* **-tross′es, -tross′**: see PLURAL, II, D, 1 [altered, prob. after L. *albus*, white < Sp. *alcatraz*, lit., pelican < Port. *alcatruz*, orig. bucket < Ar. *al qāḍūs*, water container < Gr. *kados*, cask, jar; prob. < Heb. *kad*, water jug] any of several large, web-footed birds (family Diomedea) related to the petrel and found chiefly in the South Seas: they have long, narrow wings and a large, hooked beak in which, like the pelican, they were formerly reputed to carry water

al·be·do (al bē′dō) *n.* [LL.(Ec.), whiteness < L. *albus*, white: see ALBUM] **1.** *Astron.* the reflecting power of a planet or satellite, expressed as a ratio of reflected light to the total amount falling on the surface **2.** *Physics* the degree to which a surface reflects cosmic rays or neutron currents that strike it

Al·bee (ôl′bē), **Edward** 1928– ; U.S. playwright

al·be·it (ôl bē′it, al-) *conj.* [ME. *al be it*, al(though) it be] although; even though

Al·be·marle Sound (al′bə märl′) [after George Monk (1608–70), Duke of *Albemarle*] arm of the Atlantic extending into NE N.C.: c. 60 mi.

Al·bé·niz (äl bā′nith, -nis), **Isaac (Manuel Francisco)** 1860–1909; Sp. composer & pianist

Al·ber·ich (äl′ber iH) [G. < MHG. *alb*, elf + *rich* (OHG. *rihhi*), ruler, king, realm] *Ger. Legend* the king of the dwarfs and leader of the Nibelungs

Al·bert (al′bərt) [Fr. < OHG. *Adalbrecht*, lit., bright through nobility < *adal*, nobility + *beraht*, bright] **1.** a masculine name: dim. *Al, Bert;* var. *Adelbert, Elbert;* fem.

ALBATROSS (wingspread to 7 ft.)

Alberta, Albertine **2. Albert I**, 1875–1934; king of Belgium (1909–34) **3.** Prince, (*Albert of Saxe-Coburg Gotha*) 1819–61; husband (Prince Consort) of Queen Victoria of England

Albert, Lake lake in W Uganda, bordering on the Congo (sense 2): 2,064 sq. mi.

Al·ber·ta (al bur′tə) [fem. of ALBERT] **1.** a feminine name: var. *Albertina, Albertine* **2.** [after Princess Louise *Alberta*, 4th daughter of Queen Victoria] province of SW Canada: 255,285 sq. mi.; pop. 1,463,000; cap. Edmonton: abbrev. **Alta.**

Albert Canal ship canal in Belgium, from Liège to Antwerp: 81 mi.

Al·ber·ti (äl ber′tē), **Le·on Bat·tis·ta** (le ōn′ bät tēs′tä) 1404–72; It. architect and painter

Al·ber·ti·na (al′bər tē′nə) a feminine name: see ALBERTA

Al·ber·tine (al′bər tēn′) a feminine name: see ALBERTA

al·bert·ite (al′bər tīt′) n. [after *Albert* county, New Brunswick, where found] a bituminous, shiny, asphaltlike mineral: broken pieces have convex and concave surfaces

Albert Memorial monument to Prince Albert of England in Kensington Gardens, London: 175 ft. high

Albert Ny·an·za (nī an′zə, nē-) *same as* Lake ALBERT

Al·ber·tus Mag·nus (al bur′təs mag′nəs), Saint (*Count von Bollstädt*) 1193?–1280; Ger. scholastic philosopher; teacher of Thomas Aquinas

al·bes·cent (al bes′'nt) *adj.* [L. *albescens*, prp. of *albescere*, to become white < *albus*, white] turning white —**al·bes′·cence** (-'ns) *n.*

Al·bi·gen·ses (al′bə jen′sēz) *n.pl.* [ML. after *Albi*, town in S France] a religious sect that flourished in the south of France c. 1020–1250 A.D. and was finally suppressed for heresy —**Al′bi·gen′si·an** (-sē ən) *adj., n.*

al·bi·nism (al′bə niz′m) *n.* the condition of being an albino —**al·bin·ic** (al bin′ik) *adj.*

al·bi·no (al bī′nō; *chiefly Brit.* -bē′-) *n., pl.* **-nos** [Port., lit., whitish < *albo* < L. *albus*, white] **1.** a person whose skin, hair, and eyes lack normal coloration because of genetic factors: albinos have a white skin, whitish hair, and pink eyes **2.** any animal or plant abnormally lacking in color

Al·bi·on (al′bē ən) [L. < Celt., of non-IE. origin, but understood as if < L. *albus*, white: the cliffs of southern England are white] [Poet.] England

al·bite (al′bīt) *n.* [< L. *albus*, white + -ITE[1]] a whitish, glassy mineral, NaAlSi₃O₈, of the feldspar family, breaking into pieces that have oblique surfaces

al·biz·zi·a (al biz′ē ə) *n.* [ModL., after Filippo degli *Albizzi*, 18th-c. It. naturalist] a tall, ornamental tree (genus *Albizzia*) of the legume family, native to warm or tropical climates

Al·bo·in (al′boin, -bō in) ?–573? A.D.; king of the Lombards (569?–573?); conqueror of N Italy

Al·bu·ca·sis (al′byoo kās′is) *L. name of* ABUL KASIM

al·bu·gin·e·ous (al′byoo jin′ē əs) *adj.* [ML. *albugineus* < L. *albugo*, white spot < *albus*, white] of or resembling the white of the eye

al·bum (al′bəm) *n.* [L., neut. of *albus*, white] **1.** a bound or loose-leaf book with blank pages for mounting pictures, stamps, etc., or for collecting autographs **2.** a booklike holder for phonograph records **3.** a set of records in such a holder **4.** a single long-playing record or tape recording, as of a set of related musical works or readings **5.** a book that is an anthology, a collection of pictures, or the like

al·bu·men (al byoo′mən; *occas.* al′byə mən) *n.* [L. < *albus*, white] **1.** the white of an egg **2.** the nutritive protein substance in germinating plant and animal cells **3.** *same as* ALBUMIN

al·bu·men·ize (-īz′) *vt.* **-ized′, -iz′ing** to cover or treat with albumen or an albuminous solution

al·bu·min (al byoo′mən) *n.* [ALBUM(EN) + -IN[1]] any of a class of complex proteins found in milk, egg, muscle, blood, and in many vegetable tissues and fluids: albumins are soluble in water, coagulated by heat, and are hydrolyzed to a number of amino acids

al·bu·mi·nate (al byoo′mə nāt′) *n.* a compound of an albumin with an acid or base

al·bu·mi·noid (-noid′) *adj.* resembling albumin —*n.* **1.** a protein **2.** a scleroprotein

al·bu·mi·nous (-nəs) *adj.* of, like, or containing albumin or albumen

al·bu·mi·nu·ri·a (al byoo′mə nyoor′ē ə, -noor′-) *n.* the abnormal presence of albumin in the urine

al·bu·mose (al′byoo mōs′) *n.* any of a class of chemical compounds derived from albumins by the action of certain enzymes

Al·bu·quer·que (al′bə kur′kē, -byə-) [after the Duke of *Albuquerque*, Viceroy of Mexico (1702–11)] city in C N.Mex.; pop. 244,000

Al·bu·quer·que (äl′boo ker′kə), **Af·fon·so de** (ə fōn′soo də) 1453–1515; Port. navigator; established Port. colonies in the East

al·bur·num (al bur′nəm) *n.* [L., neut. of *alburnus*, whitish < *albus*, white] *same as* SAPWOOD

Al·cae·us (al sē′əs) fl. 600 B.C.; Gr. lyric poet

Al·ca·ic (al kā′ik) *adj.* of Alcaeus or in the form of his verse —*n.* [*usually pl.*] verse by Alcaeus or in his metrical patterns; four-stanza odes, with four lines to a stanza and four feet to a line

al·cai·de, al·cay·de (al kī′dē; *Sp.* äl kä′ē the) *n.* [Sp. < Ar. *al qā′īd*, the leader < *qāda*, to lead] **1.** a commander or

governor of a Spanish fortress **2.** a jailer or warden of a Spanish prison

☆**al·cal·de** (al kal′dē; *Sp.* äl käl′de) *n.* [Sp. < Ar. *al-qādi*, the judge < *qada*, to judge] the mayor of a Spanish or Spanish-American town, with certain judicial powers

Al·can Highway (al′kan) [AL(ASKA) + CAN(ADA)] *same as* ALASKA HIGHWAY

Al·ca·traz (al′kə traz′) [< Sp. *Isla de Alcatraces*, Island of Pelicans] small island in San Francisco Bay: site of a Federal prison (1934–63)

al·ca·zar (al′kə zär′, al kaz′ər; *Sp.* äl kä′thär) *n.* [Sp. *alcázar* < Ar. *al-qasr*, the castle] a palace or fortress of the Moors in Spain; specif., [A-] such a palace in Seville, later used by the Spanish kings

Al·ces·tis (al ses′tis) [L. < Gr. *Alkēstis*] *Gr. Myth.* the wife of Admetus, king of Thessaly: she offered her life to save that of her husband, but was rescued from Hades by Hercules

al·che·mist (al′kə mist) *n.* a practitioner of alchemy —**al′che·mis′tic** (-mis′tik), **al′che·mis′ti·cal** *adj.*

al·che·mize (-mīz′) *vt.* **-mized′, -miz′ing** to transmute by or as by alchemy

al·che·my (al′kə mē) *n.* [ME. *alchymie* < OFr. *alchimie* < ML. *alchemia* < Ar. *al-kimiyā* < ? Gr. *chymeia* < *cheein*, to pour: see FOUND[3]] **1.** an early form of chemistry, with philosophical and magical associations, studied in the Middle Ages: its chief aims were to change baser metals into gold and to discover the elixir of perpetual youth **2.** a method or power of transmutation; esp., the seemingly miraculous change of a thing into something better —**al·chem·ic** (al kem′ik), **al·chem′i·cal** *adj.* —**al·chem′i·cal·ly** *adv.*

Al·ci·bi·a·des (al′sə bī′ə dēz′) 450–404 B.C.; Athenian politician & general in the Peloponnesian War

Al·ci·des (al sī′dēz) [L. < Gr. *Alkeidēs*] *a name for* HERCULES

al·ci·dine (al′sə din′) *adj.* [ModL. *alcidinus*: see AUK] belonging to a family (Alcidae) of diving birds that have a stocky body, short tail and wings, and webbed feet, as the puffins and murres

Al·cin·o·üs (al sin′ə wəs) *Gr. Myth.* father of NAUSICAÄ

Alc·me·ne (alk mē′nē) [L. < Gr. *Alkmēnē*] *Gr. Myth.* the mother of Hercules: see AMPHITRYON

al·co·hol (al′kə hôl′, -häl′) *n.* [ML. < Ar. *al kuhl*, powder of antimony: the change of meaning occurred in European usage] **1.** a colorless, volatile, pungent liquid, C₂H₅OH: it can be burned as fuel, is used in industry and medicine, and is the intoxicating element of whiskey, wine, beer, and other fermented or distilled liquors: also called *ethyl alcohol* **2.** any intoxicating liquor with this liquid in it **3.** the drinking of such liquors [*alcohol* was his downfall] **4.** any of a series of organic compounds the simplest of which are like common alcohol in construction, as wood alcohol, a very poisonous liquid: all alcohols contain a hydroxyl group and form esters in reactions with organic acids

al·co·hol·ic (al′kə hôl′ik, -häl′-) *adj.* **1.** of or containing alcohol **2.** caused by alcohol or liquor containing it **3.** suffering from alcoholism —*n.* a person who has chronic alcoholism or who habitually drinks alcoholic liquor to excess —**al′co·hol′i·cal·ly** *adv.*

☆**Alcoholics Anonymous** an organization of alcoholics and former alcoholics who seek, through mutual counseling, to avoid lapses into drinking

al·co·hol·ism (al′kə hôl′iz′m, -häl′-) *n.* the habitual drinking of alcoholic liquor to excess, or a diseased condition caused by this

al·co·hol·ize (-īz′) *vt.* **-ized′, -iz′ing** **1.** to saturate or treat with alcohol **2.** to convert into alcohol

al·co·hol·om·e·ter (-äm′ə tər) *n.* an instrument for determining the percentage of alcohol in a liquid

Al·co·ran (al′kō ran′, -rän′) *n.* [ME. & OFr. *alcoran* < Ar. *al qor′ān*: see KORAN] [Archaic] the Koran

Al·cott (ôl′kət) **1.** (**Amos**) **Bron·son** (brän′s'n), 1799–1888; U.S. philosopher and educational reformer **2. Louisa May**, 1832–88; U.S. novelist: daughter of *prec.*

al·cove (al′kōv) *n.* [Fr. < Sp. *alcoba* < Ar. *al-qubba* < *al*, the + *qubba*, an arch, vault] **1.** a recessed section of a room, as a breakfast nook **2.** a secluded bower in a garden; summerhouse

Al·cuin (al′kwin) 735?–804 A.D.; Eng. theologian & writer; adviser in the court of Charlemagne

Al·cy·o·ne (al sī′ə nē′) [L. < Gr. *Alkyonē*, daughter of Aeolus] the brightest star in the Pleiades

Ald., Aldm. Alderman

Al·da (äl′də), **Frances** (born *Frances Davis*) 1883–1952; U.S. operatic soprano, born in New Zealand

Al·dan (äl dän′) river in the EC R.S.F.S.R., flowing north and east into the Lena River: c. 1,700 mi.

Al·deb·a·ran (al deb′ər ən) [Ar. *al-dabarān* < *al*, the + *dabarān*, following < *dabar*, to follow] a brilliant red star of the first magnitude in the constellation Taurus

al·de·hyde (al′də hīd′) *n.* [< AL(COHOL) + ModL. *dehyd-(rogenatum)* < L. *de*, without + HYDROGEN] **1.** a colorless, volatile fluid, CH₃CHO, with a strong, unpleasant odor, obtained from alcohol by oxidation **2.** any of a class of organic compounds containing the CHO group, as formaldehyde —**al′de·hy′dic** (-hī′dik) *adj.*

Al·den (ôl′d'n), **John** 1599?–1687; Pilgrim settler in Plymouth Colony; character in Longfellow's poem "The Courtship of Miles Standish"

‡al·den·te (äl den'tā; E. al den'tē) [It., lit., to the tooth] firm to the bite; chewy

al·der (ôl'dər) n. [ME. alder, aller < OE. alor, aler < IE. base *el-: see ELM] any of a small group of trees and shrubs (genus Alnus) of the birch family, having toothed leaves and woody cones, and growing in cool, moist soil in temperate climates: the bark is used in dyeing and tanning and the wood for bridges and piles because it resists underwater rot

al·der·man (ôl'dər mən) n., pl. -men (-mən) [ME. < OE. ealdorman, chief, prince < eald, old + man] 1. in some U.S. cities, a member of the municipal council, usually representing a certain district or ward 2. in England and Ireland, a senior member of a county or borough council 3. Anglo-Saxon History the chief officer in a shire —al'der·man·cy (-sē) n. —al'der·man'ic (-man'ik) adj.

Al·der·ney (ôl'dər nē) one of the Channel Islands of Great Britain: 3 sq. mi.; pop. 1,500 —n., pl. -neys any of a breed of small dairy cattle originally from this island

Al·der·shot (ôl'dər shät') borough in Hampshire, England: pop. 33,000: site of a military training camp

Al·dine (ôl'dīn, -dēn) adj. [Ald(us) + -INE] from the press of Aldus MANUTIUS and his family, who published fine editions of the classics (c. 1494–1597) at Venice and Rome —n. an Aldine book, edition, or type

al·dol (al'dôl) n. [Fr. < ald(éhyde), aldehyde (see ALDE-HYDE) + -ol, -OL²] a clear, colorless, syrupy liquid, CH₃CHOHCH₂CHO, obtained by condensation of acetaldehyde: used as a solvent, in organic synthesis, and as a hypnotic and sedative

al·dose (al'dōs) n. [ALD(EHYDE) + -OSE¹] Chem. any sugar containing the aldehyde group, -CHO

al·do·ste·rone (al däs'ta rōn', al'dōs-) n. [< ALD(EHYDE) + STER(OL) + -ONE] a steroid hormone C₂₁H₂₈O₅, produced synthetically and by the adrenal cortex glands: believed to be the chief regulator of sodium, potassium, and chloride metabolism

al·do·ste·ron·ism (-iz'm) n. the condition arising from too great a secretion of aldosterone, resulting in hypertension and excessive excretion of potassium

Al·drich (ôl'drich), Thomas Bailey 1836–1907; U.S. poet & novelist

☆al·drin (al'drin) n. [G., after Kurt Alder, 20th-c. G. chemist] an insecticide containing a naphthalene derivative, C₁₂H₈Cl₆, especially effective against insects resistant to DDT

ale (āl) n. [ME. ale < OE. ealu < IE. base *alu(d)-, bitter, beer, alum] a fermented drink made from malt and hops, like beer, but produced by rapid fermentation at a relatively high temperature

a·le·a·to·ric (ā/lē a tôr'ik) adj. 1. same as ALEATORY ☆2. designating music resulting from purely random successions of tones and noises

a·le·a·to·ry (ā'lē a tôr'ē) adj. [L. aleatorius, of gambling < aleator, gambler < alea, chance, a dice game] of or depending on chance, luck, or contingency

A·lec·to (a lek'tō) [L. < Gr. Alēktō] Gr. Myth. one of the three Furies

a·lee (a lē') adv., adj. Naut. on or toward the lee; leeward

al·e·gar (al'a gar, ā'la-) n. [ME. alegre < ale (see ALE) + egre, sour < OFr. aigre: see VINEGAR] a vinegar resulting from the fermentation of ale; sour ale

ale·house (āl'hous') n. a place where ale is sold and served; saloon; tavern

Aleichem, Sholom see SHOLOM ALEICHEM

A·le·mán (ä'le män') 1. Ma·te·o (mä tā'ō), 1547?–1614?; Sp. novelist 2. Mi·guel (mē gel'), 1902– ; Mex. statesman; president of Mexico (1946–52)

Al·e·man·ni (al'a man'ī) n.pl. [ML., pl. of Alemannus < OHG. aleman, a German] the Germanic tribes which invaded and settled in Alsace and part of Switzerland in the early 5th cent. A.D.: they were conquered by Clovis in 496 A.D. —Al'e·man'nic (-ik) adj.

Al·e·man·nic (-ik) n. any of several German dialects spoken in southwestern Germany, Alsace, and Switzerland

Alembert, Jean le Rond d' see D'ALEMBERT

a·lem·bic (a lem'bik) n. [ME. & OFr. alambic < ML. alambicus < Ar. al-anbīq < al, the + anbīq, a still < Gr. ambix, a cup] 1. an apparatus of glass or metal, formerly used for distilling 2. anything that refines or purifies

A·len·con (a len'sən; Fr. à län sōn') n. [after Alençon, town in NW France, where it was originally made] a needlepoint lace with a solid design on a net background

a·leph (ä'lif) n. [Heb., lit., ox, leader] the first letter of the Hebrew alphabet (א)

a·leph·null (ä'lif nul') n. Math. in the theory of sets, the least infinite cardinal number; the cardinal number of the unending set of whole numbers {1,2,3,4, . . . }: also, the symbol (א₀) for this

ALEMBIC

A·lep·po (a lep'ō) city in NW Syria: pop. 496,000: Arabic name, HALEB

a·lert (a lurt') adj. [Fr. alerte, earlier à l'erte < It. all' erta, on the watch < alla, at the + erta, a lookout < VL. *ergere, for L. erigere, to ERECT] 1. watchful and ready, as in facing danger 2. quick in thought or action; active; nimble —n. 1. a warning signal as of an expected air raid; alarm 2. the period during which such a warning is in effect —vt. to warn to be ready or watchful [the troops were alerted] —SYN. see INTELLIGENT, WATCHFUL —on the alert watchful; vigilant —a·lert'ly adv. —a·lert'ness n.

-a·les (ā'lēz) [L. pl. of -alis] a suffix used in forming the scientific Latin names of orders of plants

A·les·san·dri·a (ä'les sän'drē ä) city in NW Italy, in Piedmont region: pop. 92,000

a·leu·rone (al'ya rōn') n. [Gr. aleuron, wheat meal, flour + -ONE] finely granulated protein present in seeds generally and forming the outer layer of cereal seeds —al'eu·ron'ic (-rän'ik) adj.

A·leut (a loot', al'oot) n. [< Russ. < ? Chukchi aliuit, islanders] 1. pl. A·leuts', A·leut' any of a native people of the Aleutian Islands and of certain parts of mainland Alaska 2. either of the two languages of these people

A·leu·tian (a loo'shan) adj. 1. of the Aleutian Islands 2. of the Aleuts, their culture, etc. —n. an Aleut

Aleutian Islands chain of islands extending c. 1,200 miles SW from the tip of the Alaska Peninsula: with the W half of the Alaska Peninsula they constitute a district of Alaska: 15,501 sq. mi.; pop. 8,000

ale·wife (āl'wīf') n., pl. -wives' (-wīvz') 1. a woman who keeps an alehouse ☆2. [<?] a N. American fish (Alosa pseudoharengus) resembling the herring, found in the ocean and in some fresh water: used for food and in fertilizers

Al·ex·an·der (al'ig zan'dər) n. [L. < Gr. Alexandros, lit., defender of men < alexein, to defend + anēr (gen. andros), man] 1. a masculine name: dim. Aleck, Alex, Sandy; equiv. Fr. Alexandre, It. Alessandro, Sp. Alejandro; fem. Alexandra, Alexandrina 2. Alexander I a) 1777–1825; czar of Russia (1801–25): grandson of CATHERINE THE GREAT b) 1876–1903; king of Serbia (1889–1903): assassinated c) 1888–1934; king of Yugoslavia (1921–34): assassinated 3. Alexander II 1818–81; czar of Russia (1855–81): emancipated the serfs: assassinated: son of NICHOLAS I 4. Alexander III a) (Orlando Bandinelli) ?–1181; Pope (1159–81) b) 1845–94; czar of Russia (1881–94): son of Alexander II 5. Alexander VI (Rodrigo Lanzol y Borgia) 1431–1503; Pope (1492–1503): father of Cesare & Lucrezia BORGIA —n. [also a-] ☆a cocktail made of gin, brandy, or rum, with creme de cacao and sweet cream

Alexander, Sir Harold R(upert) L(eofric) G(eorge), 1st Viscount Alexander of Tunis, 1891–1969; Brit. general & statesman; governor-general of Canada (1946–52)

Alexander Archipelago group of c. 1,100 islands off the coast of SE Alaska

Alexander I Island island of Antarctica, just west of the base of the Antarctic Peninsula: c. 235 mi. long

Alexander Nev·ski (nef'skē) 1220?–63; Russ. military hero, statesman, & saint

Alexander Se·ver·us (si vir'as) 208?–235 A.D.; Rom. emperor (222–235 A.D.)

Alexander the Great 356–323 B.C.; king of Macedonia (336–323); military conqueror who helped spread Greek culture from Asia Minor & Egypt to India: also Alexander III

Al·ex·an·dra (al'ig zan'dra) [fem. of ALEXANDER] a feminine name: dim. Sandra; var. Alexandrina

Al·ex·an·dret·ta (al'ig zan dret'a) former name of ISKENDERUN

Al·ex·an·dri·a (al'ig zan'drē a) 1. seaport in Egypt, on the Mediterranean at the W end of the Nile delta: pop. 1,513,000: founded by Alexander the Great and, later, a center of Hellenistic culture 2. [< prec., but with allusion to the Alexander family, owners of the town site] city in NE Va., near Washington, D.C.: pop. 111,000 3. city in C La.: pop. 42,000

Al·ex·an·dri·an (-an) adj. 1. of Alexander the Great or his rule 2. of Alexandria, Egypt, or the late Hellenic culture that flourished there 3. Prosody alexandrine

Al·ex·an·dri·na (al'ig zan drē'na) a feminine name: see ALEXANDRA

al·ex·an·drine (al'ig zan'drin, -drēn) n. [Fr. alexandrin: so called from being used in OFr. poems on Alexander the Great] [occas. A-] Prosody an iambic line having normally six feet; iambic hexameter —adj. of an alexandrine

al·ex·an·drite (al'ig zan'drīt) n. [after the Russian czar Alexander II] a variety of chrysoberyl that appears dark green in daylight and deep red under artificial light: it is used in jewelry

A·lex·an·drou·po·lis (ä'lek sän droo'pô lēs) seaport in NE Greece, on the Aegean: pop. 19,000

a·lex·i·a (a lek'sē a) n. [ModL. < Gr. a-, without + lexis, speech < legein, to speak] a loss of the ability to read, caused by lesions of the brain; word blindness

a·lex·i·phar·mic (a lek'sa fär'mik) adj. [Gr. alexipharmakos < alexein, to avert + pharmakon, a drug, poison] acting

fat, āpe, cär; ten, ēven; is, bīte; gō, hôrn, tōōl, look; oil, out; up, fur; get; joy; yet; chin; she; thin, then; zh, leisure; ŋ, ring; ə for a in ago, e in agent, i in sanity, o in comply, u in focus; ' as in able (ā'b'l); Fr. bāl; ë, Fr. coeur; ö, Fr. feu; Fr. mon; ô, Fr. coq; ü, Fr. duc; r, Fr. cri; H, G. ich; kh, G. doch. See inside front cover. ☆ Americanism; ‡foreign; *hypothetical; <derived from

as an antidote; counteracting poison —*n.* an antidote

A·lex·is (ə lek′sis) [Gr., lit., help < *alexein*, to defend] 1. a masculine name 2. **Alexis (I)** 1629–76; czar of Russia (1645–76): father of *Peter the Great*

A·lex·i·us I (ə lek′sē əs) (*Alexius Comnenus*) 1048–1118; emperor of the Byzantine Empire (1081–1118)

al·fal·fa (al fal′fə) *n.* [Sp. < Ar. *al-faṣfaṣah*, the best fodder] a deep-rooted plant (*Medicago sativa*) of the legume family, with small divided leaves, purple cloverlike flowers, and spiral pods, used extensively in the U.S. for fodder, pasture, and as a cover crop

Al·fie·ri (äl fye′ rē), Count **Vit·to·ri·o** (vēt tō′ryō) 1749–1803; It. dramatist & poet

☆**al·fil·a·ri·a, al·fil·e·ri·a** (al fil′ə rē′ə) *n.* [AmSp. *alfilerillo* < Sp. *alfiler*, a pin < Ar. *al-khilāl*, thorn] a European plant (*Erodium cicutarium*) of the geranium family, grown in the western U.S. for fodder

‡**al fi·ne** (äl fē′ne) [It.] *Music* to the end: a direction to continue to the end of a repeated section

Al·fon·so XIII (al fän′zō, -sō; *Sp.* äl fōn′sō) 1886–1941; king of Spain (1902–31): deposed

☆**al·for·ja** (al fôr′hä) *n.* [Sp. < Ar. *al-khorj*] a leather or canvas saddlebag used in the western U.S.

Al·fred (al′frid) [OE. *Ælfred*, lit., elf-counsel, hence, wise counselor < *ælf*, elf + *ræd*, counsel] a masculine name: dim. *Al, Alf, Fred;* fem. *Alfreda*

Al·fre·da (al frē′də) a feminine name: see ALFRED

Alfred the Great 849–900? A.D.; king of Wessex (871–900?); put an end to Danish conquests in England; promoted English culture

al·fres·co (al fres′kō) *adv.* [It. < *al* (for *a il*), in the + *fresco*, cool: see FRESCO] in the open air; outdoors —*adj.* outdoor Also **al fresco**

alg. algebra

al·gae (al′jē) *n.pl., sing.* **al′ga** (-gə) [pl. of L. *alga*, seaweed < IE. base *el-, ol-*, to be moldy, putrid, whence Sw. *ul*, rancid, Du. *uilig*, rotten] a group of plants (subkingdom Thallophyta), variously one-celled, colonial, or filamentous, containing chlorophyll and other pigments (esp. red and brown), and having no true root, stem, or leaf: algae are found in water or damp places, and include seaweeds, pond scum, etc. —**al′gal** (-gəl) *adj.*

☆**al·gae·cide** (al′jə sid′) *n.* [ALGAE + -CIDE] a substance used to prevent or get rid of algae, esp. of green scum from a swimming pool

al·gar·ro·ba, al·ga·ro·ba (al′gə rō′bə) *n.* [Sp. < Ar. *al-kharrūbah* < *al*, the + *kharrūbah*, carob] 1. the carob tree or its pods ☆2. the mesquite tree or its pods

al·ge·bra (al′jə brə) *n.* [ME. & ML. < Ar. *al-jabr*, the reunion of broken parts < *al*, the + *jabara*, to reunite] 1. a mathematical system used to generalize certain arithmetical operations by permitting letters or other symbols to stand for numbers: it is used esp. in the solution of polynomial equations 2. a special application of this system in which the fundamental arithmetical operations of addition and multiplication are replaced by general binary operations, with properties to be defined: see also BOOLEAN ALGEBRA 3. a textbook or treatise dealing with algebra —**al′ge·bra′ist** (-brā′ist) *n.*

al·ge·bra·ic (al′jə brā′ik) *adj.* 1. of, used in, or characteristic of algebra 2. finite in the number of arithmetic operations involved Also **al′ge·bra′i·cal** —**al′ge·bra′i·cal·ly** *adv.*

algebraic number a root of a polynomial equation with coefficients that are whole numbers

Al·ge·cir·as (al′ji sir′əs, -sī′rəs; *Sp.* äl′he thē′räs) seaport in S Spain, on the Strait of Gibraltar: pop. 65,000

Al·ger (al′jər), **Horatio** 1832–99; U.S. writer of boys' stories

Al·ge·ri·a (al jir′ē ə) country in N Africa, on the Mediterranean: under French control from 1847 to 1962: c. 919,000 sq. mi.; pop. 13,547,000; cap. Algiers —**Al·ge′ri·an** *adj., n.*

Al·ge·rine (al′jə rēn′) *adj.* Algerian —*n.* 1. a native of Algeria, esp. one of Berber, Arab, or Moorish descent 2. [a-] a soft woolen cloth with bright-colored stripes

Al·ger·non (al′jər nən) [apparently < OFr. *al grenon*, with a mustache] a masculine name: dim. *Algie, Algy*

-al·gi·a (al′ji·ə, -jē ə) [< Gr. *algos*, pain < *algein*, to feel pain] *a n.-forming suffix meaning pain [neuralgia]*

al·gid (al′jid) *adj.* [Fr. *algide* < L. *algidus*, cold < *algere*, to be cold < IE. *algh-*, frost, cold] cold; chilly —**al·gid·i·ty** (al jid′ə tē) *n.*

Al·giers (al jirz′) capital of Algeria; seaport on the Mediterranean: pop. 884,000: a base of Barbary pirates until its capture by the French in 1830

al·gin (al′jən) *n.* [< ALG(AE) + -IN¹] 1. *same as* ALGINIC ACID 2. a colloidal polysaccharide derived from alginic acid and used as a stabilizer and emulsifier

al·gin·ic acid (al jin′ik) [ALGIN + -IC] a gelatinous material, (C₆H₈O₆)ₙ, extracted from brown seaweed or kelp: used in jellies, plastics, medicine, etc.

al·go- (al′gō, -gə) [< Gr. *algos*, pain] *a combining form meaning pain [algophobia]*

al·goid (al′goid) *adj.* [ALG(AE) + -OID] like algae

Al·gol (al′gäl) [Ar. *al ghūl*, lit., the ghoul] a bright variable star in the constellation Perseus: it is a binary and loses most of its brightness when eclipsed by its dark companion

al·go·lag·ni·a (al′gə lag′nē ə) *n.* [ModL. < ALGO- + Gr. *lagneia*, lust] abnormal sexual pleasure derived from inflicting or suffering pain; masochism or sadism

al·gol·o·gy (al gäl′ə jē) *n.* [< ALG(AE) + -LOGY] the branch of botany that deals with algae —**al·go·log·i·cal** (al′gə läj′i k'l) *adj.* —**al·gol′o·gist** *n.*

al·gom·e·ter (al gäm′ə tər) *n.* [< Gr. *algos*, pain + -METER] a device for measuring the intensity of pain caused by pressure —**al·go·met·ric** (al′gə met′rik), **al′go·met′ri·cal** *adj.* —**al·gom′e·try** *n.*

Al·gon·ki·an (al gän′kē ən) *adj., n.* 1. *same as* ALGONQUIAN 2. *Geol. same as* Late PRECAMBRIAN

Al·gon·kin (al gän′kin) *n. same as* ALGONQUIN

Al·gon·qui·an (al gän′kē ən, -kwē-) *adj.* [< ALGONQUIN] designating or of a widespread and important family of over twenty languages used by a number of N. American Indian tribes, including the Arapaho, Cheyenne, Blackfoot, Chippewa, Fox, Shawnee, Ottawa, and others —*n.* 1. this family of languages 2. a member of any tribe using one of these languages

Al·gon·quin (al gän′kwin, -kin) *n.* [< an AmInd. word of uncertain form and meaning] 1. a member of a tribe of Algonquian Indians who live in the area of the Ottawa River, Canada 2. the Algonquian dialect of this tribe

Algonquin Park Provincial park in SE Ontario, Canada: 2,740 sq. mi.

al·go·pho·bi·a (al′gə fō′bē ə) *n.* [ALGO- + -PHOBIA] a fear of pain to an abnormal degree

al·go·rism (al′gə riz′m) *n.* [ME. & OFr. *algorisme* < ML. *algorismus* < Ar. *al-Khowārazmi*, lit., native of Khwarazm (Khiva), mathematician of the 9th c. A.D.] 1. the Arabic system of numerals; decimal system of counting 2. the act or skill of computing with any kind of numerals

al·go·rithm (-*ith*′m) *n.* [altered (after ARITHMETIC) < ALGORISM] *Math.* any special method of solving a certain kind of problem; specif., the repetitive calculations used in finding the greatest common divisor of two numbers (called in full **Euclid's algorithm**)

al·gum (al′gum) *n.* [Heb. *algūm*] a tree mentioned in the Bible: II Chr. 2:8: see ALMUG

Al·ham·bra (al ham′brə) [Sp. < Ar. *al ḥamrā'*, lit., the red (house)] 1. palace of the Moorish kings near Granada, Spain, built during the 13th and 14th cent. 2. city in SW Calif.: suburb of Los Angeles: pop. 62,000

Al·ham·bresque (al′ham bresk′) *adj.* like the Alhambra, especially in richness of ornamentation

A·li (ä′lē, ä lē′) 1. 600?–661 A.D.; 4th caliph of Islam (656–661), considered the 1st caliph by the SHIITES: son-in-law of MOHAMMED 2. **Mehemet,** *see* MEHEMET ALI

a·li·as (ā′lē əs, āl′yəs) *n., pl.* **a′li·as·es** [L., at another time < *alius*, other: see ELSE] an assumed name; another name —*adv.* otherwise named; called by the assumed name of [Bell *alias* Jones] —*SYN.* see PSEUDONYM

A·li Ba·ba (ä′lē bä′bə, al′ē bab′ə) in *The Arabian Nights*, a poor woodcutter who finds the treasure of the forty thieves in a cave: he makes the door of the cave open by saying "Open sesame!"

al·i·bi (al′ə bī′) *n., pl.* **-bis′** [L., contr. < *alius ibi*, elsewhere] 1. *Law* the defensive plea or fact that an accused person was elsewhere than at the scene of the crime with which he is charged ☆2. [Colloq.] an excuse —☆*vi.* **-bied′, -bi′ing** [Colloq.] to offer an excuse

al·i·ble (al′ə b'l) *adj.* [L. *alibilis* < *alere*, to feed, nourish] [Rare] nourishing

A·li·can·te (ä′lē kän′te; *E.* al′ə kan′tē) seaport in SW Spain, on the Mediterranean: pop. 133,000

Al·ice (al′is) [ME. *Alys, Aeleis* < OFr. *Aliz, Aaliz* < *Adaliz* < OHG. *Adalheidis:* see ADELAIDE] a feminine name: dim. *Elsie;* var. *Alicia*

A·li·ci·a (ə lish′ə, -ē ə) a feminine name: see ALICE

al·i·cy·clic (al′ə sī′klik) *adj.* [ALI(PHATIC) + CYCLIC: used to transl. G. *alizyklisch*, of similar formation] *Chem.* of or relating to cyclic organic compounds derived from corresponding aliphatic compounds by ring formation

al·i·dade (al′ə dād′) *n.* [Fr. < Sp. *alidada* < Ar. *al 'iḍādah*, a rule] 1. a part of an optical or surveying instrument, consisting of the vernier, indicator, etc. 2. a surveying instrument consisting of a telescope mounted on a rule marked off in degrees, used in topographic mapping Also **al′i·dad′** (-dad′)

al·ien (āl′yən, -ē ən) *adj.* [ME. & OFr. < L. *alienus* < *alius*, other: see ELSE] 1. belonging to another country or people; foreign 2. strange; not natural [cruel words *alien* to his lips] 3. opposed or repugnant [beliefs *alien* to one's religion] 4. of aliens —*n.* 1. a foreigner 2. a foreign-born resident in a country who has not become a naturalized citizen 3. an outsider —*vt.* to transfer (land, etc.)

SYN.—**alien** is applied to a resident who bears political allegiance to another country; **foreigner,** to a visitor or resident from another country, esp. one with a different language, cultural pattern, etc.; **stranger,** to a person from another region who is unacquainted with local people, customs, etc.; **immigrant,** to a person who comes to another country to settle; **émigré,** to one who has left his country to take political refuge elsewhere See also EXTRINSIC—*ANT.* citizen, subject, national

al·ien·a·ble (-ə b'l) *adj.* capable of being alienated or transferred to a new owner —**al′ien·a·bil′i·ty** (-ə bil′ə tē) *n.*

al·ien·age (-ij) *n.* the legal status of an alien

al·ien·ate (-āt′) *vt.* **-at′ed, -at′ing** [< L. *alienatus*, pp. of *alienare* < *alius*, other: see ELSE] 1. to transfer the ownership of (property) to another 2. to make unfriendly; estrange [his behavior *alienated* his friends] 3. to cause to

be withdrawn or detached, as from one's society **4.** to cause a transference of (affection) —**al'ien·a'tor** n.

al·ien·a·tion (āl'yə nā'shən, -ē ə-) n. [ME. & OFr. < L. alienatio, separation, aversion, aberration (of the mind): see ALIENATE] **1.** an alienating or being alienated **2.** mental derangement; insanity

al·ien·ee (āl yə nē', -ē ə-) n. [ALIEN, v. + -EE¹] a person to whom property is transferred or conveyed

al·ien·ism (āl'yən iz'm, -ē ən iz'm) n. **1.** alienage **2.** psychiatry: an earlier term

al·ien·ist (-ist) n. [Fr. aliéniste < L. alienatio: see ALIENATION] a psychiatrist: term now used esp. of a psychiatrist who testifies in a court of law

al·ien·or (-ôr', -ər) n. [Anglo-Fr. < OFr. aliener: see ALIEN & -OR] a person from whom property is transferred or conveyed

a·lif (ä'lif) n. [Ar., akin to Heb. āleph: see ALEPH] the first letter of the Arabic alphabet (ʾ)

al·i·form (al'ə fôrm', ā'lə-) adj. [< L. ala (see AILERON) + -FORM] shaped like a wing; alar

A·li·garh (al'i gär', ä'li gur') city in N India, in Uttar Pradesh: pop. 185,000

a·light¹ (ə līt') vi. **a·light'ed** or **a·lit'**, **a·light'ing** [ME. alighten < alihtan < a-, out, off + lihtan, to dismount, render light < liht: see LIGHT²(to dismount)] **1.** to get down or off; dismount **2.** to come down after flight; descend and settle **3.** [Rare] to come (on or upon) accidentally

a·light² (ə līt') adj. [ME. aliht, pp. of alihten < OE. alihtan, to light up] **1.** lighted; burning **2.** lighted up

a·lign (ə līn') vt.[Fr. aligner < a, to + ligner < ligne, LINE¹] **1.** to bring into a straight line; adjust by line **2.** to bring (parts or components, as the wheels of a car) into proper coordination **3.** to bring into agreement, close cooperation, etc. [he aligned himself with the liberals] —vi. to come or fall into line; line up

a·lign·ment (-mənt) n. **1.** an aligning or being aligned; esp., a) arrangement in a straight line b) a condition of close cooperation [a new alignment of European nations] **2.** a line or lines formed by aligning **3.** Engineering a ground plan, as of a fieldwork, railroad, etc.

THESE LETTERS ARE IN ALIGNMENT
THESE LETTERS ARE OUT OF ALIGNMENT

a·like (ə līk') adj. [ME. olike < OE. gelic, onlike & ON. (g)likr, alikr < PGmc. *galik- < *ga- (< IE. ge-, perfective prefix) + *lik-: see LIKE¹] like one another; showing resemblance; similar: usually used in the predicate—adv. **1.** in the same manner; similarly **2.** to the same degree; equally —**a·like'ness** n.

al·i·ment (al'ə mənt; for v. al'ə ment') n. [L. alimentum < alere, to nourish] **1.** anything that nourishes; food **2.** means of support —vt. to supply with aliment; nourish —**al'i·men'tal** (-men't'l) adj.

al·i·men·ta·ry (al'ə men'tər ē) adj. [L. alimentarius: see ALIMENT] **1.** connected with food or nutrition **2.** nourishing **3.** furnishing support or sustenance

alimentary canal (or **tract**) the passage in the body through which food passes and in which it is digested, extending from the mouth through the esophagus, stomach, and intestines to the anus

al·i·men·ta·tion (al'ə men tā'shən) n. [Fr. < ML. alimentatio < L. alimentum: see ALIMENT] **1.** a nourishing or being nourished **2.** nourishment; nutrition **3.** support; sustenance —**al'i·men'ta·tive** (-men'tə tiv) adj.

al·i·mo·ny (al'ə mō'nē) n. [L. alimonia, food, support < alere, to nourish] **1.** orig., supply of the means of living; maintenance **2.** an allowance that a court orders paid to a woman (or rarely, a man) by her (or his) spouse or former spouse after a legal separation or divorce or while legal action on this is pending

A·line (ə lēn') a feminine name: see ADELINE

a·line (ə līn') vt., vi. **a·lined'**, **a·lin'ing** same as ALIGN —**a·line'ment** n.

Al·i·oth (al'ē äth) [Ar.] the brightest star in the handle of the Big Dipper

A·li Pa·sha (ä'lē pä shä') 1741–1822; Turk. governor of Albania & part of Greece, including Janina: deposed & assassinated: called the Lion of Janina

al·i·ped (al'ə ped') adj. [L. alipes < ala, wing (see AILERON) + pes (gen. pedis), FOOT] having a winglike membrane connecting the toes of the feet, as the bat —n. an aliped creature

al·i·phat·ic (al'ə fat'ik) adj. [< Gr. aleiphar (gen. aleiphatos), fat, oil + -IC] Chem. of or obtained from fat; fatty; specif., of or belonging to a class of carbon compounds, esp. the saturated or unsaturated compounds, in which the carbon atoms are joined in open chains

al·i·quant (al'ə kwənt) adj. [L. aliquantus, some, moderate < alius, other + quantus, how large, how much] Math. designating a part of a number that does not divide the number evenly but leaves a remainder [8 is an aliquant part of 25]: cf. ALIQUOT

al·i·quot (al'ə kwət) adj. [L., some, several < alius, other + quot, how many] Math. designating a part of a number that divides the number evenly and leaves no remainder [8 is an aliquot part of 24]: cf. ALIQUANT

Al·i·son (al'ə s'n) [ME. Alisoun < OFr. Alyz (see ALICE) + -on, suffix of obscure meaning] a feminine name

a·lit (ə lit') alt. pt. & pp. of ALIGHT¹

a·li·un·de (ā'lē un'dē, äl'ē-) adv., adj. [L., lit., from another place] Law from some other source [evidence clarifying a document but not deriving from the document itself is evidence aliunde]

a·live (ə līv') adj. [ME. alyfe, on live < OE. on life; on, in + life, dat. case of lif, LIFE] [usually used in the predicate] **1.** having life; living **2.** in existence, operation, etc.; unextinguished [to keep old memories alive] **3.** lively; alert Alive is also used interjectionally in such phrases as man alive! sakes alive! etc. —SYN. see LIVING —**alive to** fully aware of; perceiving [alive to the risks involved] —**alive with** teeming with; full of (living or moving things) [a garden alive with bees]

a·liz·a·rin (ə liz'ər in) n. [G. < Fr. & Sp. alizari, dried madder root < Ar. al aṣārah, the juice < aṣara, to press] a reddish-yellow crystalline compound, $C_{14}H_8O_4$, produced by oxidizing anthracene and used in dyeing wool, cotton, and silk and in the manufacture of dyestuffs: it was originally made from madder: also **a·liz'a·rine** (-in, -ēn)

al·ka·hest (al'kə hest') n. [Fr. < ML. alchahest: apparently coined by Paracelsus] the hypothetical universal solvent sought by the alchemists

al·ka·les·cence (al'kə les''ns) n. the quality of being alkaline or somewhat alkaline: also **al'ka·les'cen·cy** (-'n sē) —**al'ka·les'cent** adj.

al·ka·li (al'kə lī') n., pl. **-lies'**, **-lis'** [ME. alkaly < Ar. al-qali, for al-qili, the ashes (of saltwort) < qalai, to roast in a pan] **1.** any base or hydroxide, as soda, potash, etc., that is soluble in water and gives a high concentration of hydroxyl ions in solution; specif., any of the hydroxides and carbonates of the alkali metals **2.** any soluble mineral salt or mixture of salts found in soils, as in some deserts, and capable of neutralizing acids

al·kal·ic (al kal'ik) adj. Geol. **1.** designating rocks in which a) the ratio of alkali to silica is greater than some arbitrary amount b) the ratio of alkali to lime is less than some arbitrary amount **2.** designating rocks that contain an unusually large amount of sodium and potassium minerals

☆**alkali flat** the nearly level site of an undrained and completely evaporated pond or lake in an arid region, covered with a hard, dry mixture of alkaline salts and sediment

alkali metal Chem. any of the elements of group I of the periodic table; specif., lithium, sodium, potassium, rubidium, cesium, and francium

al·ka·lim·e·ter (al'kə lim'ə tər) n. an instrument for measuring the amount of alkali in a substance or solution

al·ka·line (al'kə lin, -līn') adj. **1.** of, like, or having the properties of an alkali **2.** containing an alkali —**al'ka·lin'·i·ty** (-lin'ə tē) n.

alkaline-earth metals (al'kə lin ʉrth', -līn'-) Chem. elements in group II of the periodic table, including calcium, strontium, barium, and sometimes beryllium, magnesium, and radium: the oxides of these metals are called the **alkaline earths**

al·ka·lin·ize (al'kə lin īz') vt. **-ized'**, **-iz'ing** same as ALKALIZE —**al'ka·lin·i·za'tion** n.

al·ka·lize (al'kə līz') vt. **-lized'**, **-liz'ing** [ALKAL(INE) + -IZE] to make alkaline —**al'ka·li·za'tion** n.

al·ka·loid (-loid') n. [ALKAL(I) + -OID] any of a number of colorless, crystalline, bitter organic substances, such as caffeine, morphine, quinine, and strychnine, having alkaline properties and containing nitrogen: they are found in plants and, sometimes, animals and can have a strong toxic effect on the human or animal system —**al'ka·loid'al** adj.

al·ka·lo·sis (al'kə lō'sis) n. [ALKAL(I) + -OSIS] a condition of abnormally high alkalinity of the body tissues and fluids: cf. ACIDOSIS

al·kane (al'kān) n. [ALK(YL) + (METH)ANE] any hydrocarbon of the methane series

al·ka·net (al'kə net') n. [ME. alknet < Sp. alcaneta, dim. of alcana < Ar. al-ḥinnā, the henna] **1.** a) a perennial plant (Alkanna tinctoria) of the borage family, whose roots yield a red dye, found in SE Europe and Asia Minor b) the root of this plant c) the dark-red coloring matter, $C_{16}H_{16}O_5$, present in this root **2.** any of several other plants (genus Anchusa) of the borage family, grown for their red dyes or as garden plants **3.** same as PUCCOON (sense 1)

al·kan·na (al kan'ə) n. same as ALKANET (senses 1 & 2)

al·kan·nin (-in) n. same as ALKANET (sense 1 c)

al·kene (al'kēn) n. [ALK(YL) + -ENE] any of a series of unsaturated open-chain hydrocarbons containing a double bond and having the general formula C_nH_{2n}

Alk·maar (älk'mär) city in NW Netherlands: pop. 48,000

Al·ko·ran (al'kō rän', -rän') n. the Koran

al·kyd (al'kid) n. [ALKY(L) + (ACI)D] any of several synthetic resins made by heating together a polybasic acid, such as phthalic or maleic acid, and a polyhydric alcohol, such as glycerin or a glycol: these resins are used in paints, varnishes, and lacquers: also **alkyd resin**

al·kyl (al'kil) n. [ALK(ALI) + -YL] a noncyclic saturated hydrocarbon radical with the general formula C_nH_{2n+1}-: also **alkyl radical** —**al·kyl'ic** adj.

fat, āpe, cär; ten, ēven; is, bīte; gō, hôrn, tōōl, look; oil, out; up, fʉr; get; joy; yet; chin; she; thin, then; zh, leisure; ŋ, ring; ə for a in ago, e in agent, i in sanity, o in comply, u in focus; ' as in able (ā'b'l); Fr. bâl; ë, Fr. coeur; ö, Fr. feu; Fr. mon; δ, Fr. coq; ü, Fr. duc; r, Fr. cri; H, G. ich; kh, G. doch. See inside front cover. ☆ Americanism; ‡foreign; *hypothetical; <derived from

al·ky·la·tion (al′kə lā′shən) *n.* the introduction of the alkyl group into hydrocarbons, esp. in petroleum-refining processes for producing high-octane hydrocarbons —**al′ky·late′** (-lāt′) *n., vt.* -**lat′ed, -lat′ing**

al·kyne, al·kine (al′kīn) *n.* [ALKY(L) + -(I)NE[4]] any of a series of unsaturated open-chain hydrocarbons containing a triple bond and having the general formula C_nH_{2n-2}

all (ôl) *adj.* [ME. *al, all* < OE. *eall* < IE. base *al-no-s*, beyond, exceeding, whence L. *ultra*] **1.** the whole extent or quantity of [*all* New England, *all* the gold] **2.** the entire number of [*all* the men went] **3.** every one of [*all* men must eat] **4.** the greatest possible; as much as possible [said in *all* sincerity] **5.** any; any whatever [true beyond *all* question] **6.** every: now used only in such phrases as *all manner of men* **7.** alone; only [life is not *all* pleasure] **8.** seeming to be nothing but [he was *all* arms and legs] ☆**9.** [Dial.] completely used up, consumed, over with, etc. [the bread is *all*] —*pron.* **1.** [*with pl. v.*] everyone [*all* must die] **2.** [*with pl. v.*] every one [*all* of us are here, *all* of the pencils are sharpened] **3.** everything; the whole affair [*all* is over between them] **4.** every part or bit [*all* of it is gone] —*n.* **1.** everything one has [give your *all*] **2.** a totality; whole —*adv.* **1.** wholly; entirely; altogether; quite [*all* worn out, riding *all* through the night] **2.** apiece [a score of thirty *all*] —**after all** nevertheless; in spite of everything —**all but 1.** all except **2.** nearly; almost —☆**all in** [Colloq.] very tired; fatigued —**all in all 1.** considering everything **2.** as a whole **3.** everything —**all over 1.** ended **2.** everywhere; in or on every part of; throughout **3.** [Colloq.] as one characteristically is [that's Mary *all over*] —**all the** as much of (something) as [that's *all the* help you'll get] —**all the** (**better, worse,** etc.) so much the (better, worse, etc.) —**all the** (**farther, closer,** etc.) [Colloq. or Dial.] as (far, close, etc.) as —**all the same 1.** nevertheless **2.** of no importance —☆**as** (or **like**) **all get-out** [Colloq.] to a considerable degree; greatly [angry *as all get-out*] —**at all 1.** in the least; to the slightest degree **2.** in any way **3.** under any considerations —**for all** in spite of; despite —**in all** altogether; all being counted

all- (ôl) *a combining form meaning:* **1.** wholly, entirely, or exclusively [*all*-American] **2.** for every [*all*-purpose] **3.** of everything; of every part [*all*-inclusive]

‡**al·la bre·ve** (äl′lä bre′ve) [It., lit., according to the breve] *Music* the time signature C, representing 2/2 time, in which the half note receives the beat

Al·lah (al′ə, ä′lə, ä lä′) [Ar. *Allāh* < *al*, the + *ilāh*, god, akin to Heb. *elōah*, God] *the Moslem name for God*

Al·la·ha·bad (al′ə hä bäd′) city in N India, at the juncture of the Jumna and Ganges rivers: pop. 431,000

☆**all-A·mer·i·can** (ôl′ə mer′ə kən) *adj.* **1.** made up entirely of Americans or American parts **2.** representative of the U.S. as a whole, or chosen as the best in the U.S. **3.** of all the Americas —*n.* **1.** a hypothetical football or other team made up of college players voted the best of the year in the U.S. **2.** a player chosen for such team

Al·lan (al′ən) a masculine name: see ALAN

Al·lan-a-dale (al′ən ə dāl′) *Eng. Legend* a member of Robin Hood's band

al·lan·to·ic (al′ən tō′ik) *adj.* **1.** of or in the allantois **2.** having an allantois

al·lan·toid (ə lan′toid) *adj.* [Gr. *allantoeidēs*: see ALLANTOIS] of or like the allantois; sausage-shaped

al·lan·to·is (ə lan′tə wis) *n., pl.* **al·lan·to·i·des** (al′ən tō′ə dēz′) [ModL. < Gr. *allantoeidēs*, sausage-shaped < *allas*, sausage + *eidos*, form] a membranous pouch in the embryos of most vertebrates: it is an organ of respiration and excretion in the fetuses of birds and reptiles: in mammals it contributes to the formation of the placenta

‡**al·lar·gan·do** (äl′lär gän′dō) *adj., adv.* [It.] *Music* gradually slower and with more power: a direction to the performer

☆**all-a·round** (ôl′ə round′) *adj.* having many abilities, talents, or uses; not specialized; versatile

al·lay (ə lā′) *vt.* -**layed′, -lay′ing** [ME. *alaien, alleggen*, with confusion of form and meaning of OE. *alecgan* (< *a-*, down + *lecgan*, to lay) & OFr. *alegier* (<LL. *alleviare*: see ALLEVIATE)] **1.** to put (fears, etc.) to rest; quiet; calm **2.** to lessen, relieve, or alleviate (pain, grief, etc.) —*SYN.* see RELIEVE —**al·lay′er** *n.*

all-clear (ôl′klir′) *n.* a siren or other signal that an air raid or practice alert is over

‡**al·lée** (à lā′) *n.* [Fr. < OFr. *alee:* see ALLEY[1]] a walk or passage, esp. between two rows of evenly planted trees

al·le·ga·tion (al′ə gā′shən) *n.* [ME. *allegacioun* < OFr. *allegation* < L. *allegatio* < *allegare:* see ALLEGE] **1.** the act of alleging **2.** something alleged; assertion **3.** an assertion made without proof **4.** *Law* an assertion, made in a pleading, which its maker proposes to support with evidence

al·lege (ə lej′) *vt.* -**leged′, -leg′ing** [ME. *aleggen*, to produce as evidence; form < OFr. *esligier* < VL. *exlitigare* < *ex-*, out of + *litigare* (see LITIGATE); meaning infl. by OFr. *alleguer*, declare on oath < L. *allegare*, to send, mention, adduce < *ad-*, to + *legare*, to send] **1.** to assert positively, or declare; affirm; esp., to assert without proof **2.** to offer as a plea, excuse, etc. [in his defense he *alleged* temporary insanity] **3.** [Archaic] to cite as an authority (*for* or *against*) —**al·lege′a·ble** *adj.*

al·leged (ə lejd′, ə lej′id) *adj.* **1.** so declared, but without proof [the *alleged* assassin] **2.** called by this term, but perhaps improperly so; so-called [his *alleged* friends] —**al·leg′ed·ly** (-id lē) *adv.*

Al·le·ghe·ny (al′ə gā′nē) [< AmInd. (? Delaware), of unc. meaning] river in W Pennsylvania, joining the Monongahela at Pittsburgh to form the Ohio: 325 mi.

Allegheny Mountains mountain range of the Appalachian system, in C Pa., Md., W.Va., and Va.: highest peaks, over 4,800 ft. Also **Al′le·ghe′nies**

al·le·giance (ə lē′jəns) *n.* [ME. *alligeaunce*, altered (after *allegeaunce*, a formal declaration < *aleggen*, ALLEGE) of OFr. *ligeance* < *lige, liege* (see LIEGE); sense affected by association with L. *ligare*, to bind] **1.** the duty that was owed by a vassal to his feudal lord **2.** the obligation of support and loyalty to one's ruler, government, or country **3.** loyalty or devotion, as to a cause, person, etc. —**al·le′giant** (-jənt) *adj., n.*

SYN.—**allegiance** refers to the duty of a citizen to his government or a similarly felt obligation to support a cause, leader, etc.; **fidelity** implies strict adherence to an obligation, trust, etc.; **loyalty** suggests a steadfast devotion of an unquestioning kind that one may feel for one's family, friends, or country; **fealty**, now chiefly a literary word, suggests faithfulness that one has sworn to uphold; **homage** implies respect, reverence, or honor rendered to a person because of his rank, achievement, etc. —*ANT.* **faithlessness, disaffection**

al·le·gor·i·cal (al′ə gôr′i k'l, -gär′-) *adj.* **1.** of or characteristic of allegory **2.** that is or contains an allegory Also **al′le·gor′ic** —**al′le·gor′i·cal·ly** *adv.*

al·le·go·rist (al′ə gôr′ist, -gər ist) *n.* a person who writes allegories —**al′le·go·ris′tic** (-gə ris′tik) *adj.*

al·le·go·rize (al′ə gə rīz′, -gô rīz′) *vt.* -**rized′, -riz′ing** [OFr. *allegoriser* < LL. *allegorizare:* see ff. & -IZE] **1.** to make into or treat as an allegory **2.** to interpret in an allegorical sense —*vi.* to make or use allegories —**al′le·go·ri·za′tion** *n.*

al·le·go·ry (al′ə gôr′ē) *n., pl.* -**ries** [ME. *allegorie* < L. *allegoria* < Gr. *allēgoria*, description of one thing under the image of another < *allos*, other (see ELSE) + *agoreuein*, to speak in assembly < *agora*, AGORA[1]] **1.** a story in which people, things, and happenings have a hidden or symbolic meaning: allegories are used for teaching or explaining ideas, moral principles, etc. **2.** the presenting of ideas by means of such stories; symbolical narration or description **3.** any symbol or emblem

al·le·gret·to (al′ə gret′ō) *adj., adv.* [It., dim. of *allegro:* see ALLEGRO] *Music* moderately fast; faster than *andante* but slower than *allegro:* a direction to the performer —*n., pl.* -**tos** an allegretto movement or passage

al·le·gro (ə leg′rō, -lä′grō) *adj., adv.* [It. < L. *alacer*, brisk, sprightly, cheerful] *Music* fast; faster than *allegretto* but not so fast as *presto:* a direction to the performer —*n., pl.* -**gros** a fast movement or passage

al·lele (ə lēl′) *n.* [G. *allel* < Gr. *allēlōn*, of one another] either of a pair of genes located at the same position on both members of a pair of chromosomes and conveying characters that are inherited alternatively in accordance with Mendelian law (see ELSE) —**al·le′lic** (-lē′lik, -lel′ik) *adj.* —**al·lel′ism** (-lēl′iz′m, -lel′-) *n.*

al·le·lo·morph (ə lel′ə môrf′, ə lē′lə-) *n.* [< ALLELE + -MORPH] *same as* ALLELE —**al·le′lo·mor′phic** *adj.*

al·le·lu·ia (al′ə lōō′yə) *interj., n.* [L. < Gr. *allēlouia* < Heb. *hallelū-yāh*, HALLELUJAH] *same as* HALLELUJAH

al·le·mande (al′ə mand′) *n.* [Fr. < *allemand*, German < OFr. *aleman* < ML. *alamannus:* see ALEMANNI] **1.** any of various stately German dances of the 16th, 17th, and 18th cent., in 2/2 time. **2.** music for such a dance, or a piece like this in rhythm, formerly used as the movement preceding the prelude in a suite **3.** a figure in a square dance in which two dancers join right or left hands and make a turn

Al·len (al′ən) **1.** a masculine name: see ALAN **2. Ethan,** 1738–89; Am. Revolutionary soldier who led the Green Mountain Boys in the capture of Fort Ticonderoga

Al·len·by (al′ən bē), **Edmund Henry Hyn·man** (hin′mən), 1st Viscount, 1861–1936; Brit. army officer; commander of Brit. expeditionary forces in Egypt (1918); high commissioner of Egypt (1919–25)

Allen Park [after Lewis *Allen*, early settler] city in SE Mich.: suburb of Detroit: pop. 41,000

Al·len·town (al′ən toun′) [after Wm. *Allen*, the founder] city in E Pa., on the Lehigh River: pop. 110,000 (met. area, incl. Bethlehem, 544,000)

Al·lep·pey, Al·lep·ey (ə lep′ē) seaport on the Malabar Coast, in Kerala state, India: pop. 139,000

☆**al·ler·gen** (al′ər jən) *n.* [G. < *allergie*, ALLERGY + -*gen*, -GEN] a substance inducing an allergic state or reaction —**al′ler·gen′ic** (-jen′ik) *adj.*

☆**al·ler·gic** (ə lur′jik) *adj.* **1.** of or caused by allergy **2.** having an allergy **3.** averse or disinclined (*to*): a humorous usage [*allergic* to study]

☆**al·ler·gist** (al′ər jist) *n.* a doctor who specializes in treating allergies

☆**al·ler·gy** (al′ər jē) *n., pl.* -**gies** [G. *allergie* < Gr. *allos*, other (see ELSE) + -*ergeia*, as in *energeia* (see ENERGY)] **1.** a hypersensitivity to a specific substance (such as a food, pollen, dust, etc.) or condition (as heat or cold) which in similar amounts is harmless to most people: it is manifested in a physiological disorder **2.** a strong aversion

☆**al·le·thrin** (al′ə thrin) *n.* [< *all(ene)* < *allylene* < ALLYL

+ -ENE) + (PYR)ETHR(UM) + -IN[1] a thick, pale yellow, synthetic liquid insecticide, C₁₉H₂₆O₃, similar in structure to pyrethrin

al·le·vi·ate (ə lē'vē āt') vt. -at'ed, -at'ing [ME. alleviaten < LL. alleviatus, pp. of alleviare, for L. allevare < ad-, to + levis, light] 1. to make less hard to bear; lighten or relieve (pain, suffering, etc.) 2. to reduce or decrease [to alleviate poverty] —SYN. see RELIEVE —al·le'vi·a'tor n. —al·le'vi·a·to'ry (-ə tôr'ē) adj.

al·le·vi·a·tion (ə lē'vē ā'shən) n. 1. an alleviating or being alleviated 2. a thing that alleviates

al·le·vi·a·tive (ə lē'vē āt'iv, -ə tiv) adj. alleviating or tending to alleviate —n. a thing that alleviates

al·ley[1] (al'ē) n., pl. -leys [ME. aly < OFr. alee < aler (Fr. aller), to go < ML. alare, contr. < L. ambulare, to walk] 1. a lane in a garden or park, bordered by trees or shrubs 2. a narrow street or walk; specif., a lane behind a row of buildings or between two rows of buildings that face on adjacent streets 3. Bowling a) the long, narrow lane along which the balls are rolled: now usually LANE b) [occas. pl.] a bowling establishment 4. Tennis either of the narrow lanes on opposite sides of the court, that extend the singles area for playing doubles —☆up (or down) one's alley [Slang] suited to one's tastes or abilities

al·ley[2] (al'ē) n., pl. -leys [< ALABASTER, formerly used for marbles] a fine marble used as the shooter in playing marbles

☆alley cat a homeless, mongrel cat

al·ley-oop (al'ē ōōp') interj. [< Fr. allez (imper. of aller, to go), used as interjection of encouragement, surprise, exhortation + oop < ?] an exclamation accompanying the act of lifting, rising, etc.

☆al·ley·way (al'ē wā') n. 1. an alley between buildings 2. any narrow passageway

all-fired (ôl'fird') adj. [altered < hell-fired] [Slang] complete; total —adv. [Slang] completely; extremely

All Fools' Day same as APRIL FOOLS' DAY

all fours 1. all four limbs of an animal or human being [the cat landed on all fours] 2. any of several card games that are based on scoring four particular points

all hail [Archaic] all health: a greeting

All·hal·lows (ôl'hal'ōz) n. [ME. alhalwes < OE. ealle halgan: ooo ALL & HALLOW] [Archaic] same as ALL SAINTS' DAY: also called All'hal'low·mas (-hal'ō məs)

All·hal·low·tide (-hal'ō tid') n. [ME. alle halwen tid: see ALLHALLOWS & TIDE[1]] [Archaic] the time or season of Allhallows

all·heal (ôl'hēl') n. 1. same as SELFHEAL 2. Brit. name for VALERIAN

al·li·a·ceous (al'ē ā'shəs) adj. [< L. allium, garlic + -ACEOUS] 1. of a group of strong-smelling bulb plants of the lily family, including the onion, garlic, etc. 2. having the smell or taste of onions or garlic

al·li·ance (ə li'əns) n. [ME. aliaunce < OFr. aleiance < alier: see ALLY] 1. an allying or being allied; specif., a union or joining, as of families by marriage 2. a close association for a common objective, as of nations, political parties, etc. 3. the agreement made for such an association 4. the countries, groups, etc. forming such a connection 5. similarity or relationship in characteristics, structure, etc.; affinity

SYN.—alliance refers to any association entered into for mutual benefit; league, often interchangeable with alliance, stresses formality of organization and definiteness of purpose; coalition implies a temporary alliance of opposing parties, etc., as in times of emergency; confederacy and confederation in political usage refer to a combination of independent states for the joint exercise of certain governmental functions, as defense or customs; union implies a close, permanent alliance and suggests complete unity of purpose and interest

al·li·cin (al'ə sin) n. [< alliin, an amino acid found in garlic oil (< L. allium, garlic + -IN[1]) + -(I)C + -IN[1]] a somewhat unstable, colorless, oily liquid, C₆H₁₀OS₂, extracted from garlic and used as an antibacterial substance

al·lied (ə lid'; also, esp. for 3, al'id) adj. 1. united by kinship, treaty, agreement, etc. 2. closely related [Danish and Swedish are allied languages] 3. [A-] of the Allies —SYN. see RELATED

Al·lier (à lyā') river in C France, flowing northward into the Loire: c. 250 mi.

Al·lies (al'iz'; rarely, ə liz') n.pl. [see ALLY] 1. in World War I, the nations allied by treaty against Germany and the other Central Powers; orig., Great Britain, France, and Russia, later joined by the U.S., Italy, Japan, etc. 2. in World War II, the nations associated against the Axis, esp. Great Britain, the Soviet Union, and the U.S.: see UNITED NATIONS

al·li·ga·tor (al'ə gāt'ər) n., pl. -tors, -tor: see PLURAL, II, D, 1 [Sp. el lagarto < el, the & L. lacerta, lacertus: see LIZARD] 1. a large reptile (genus Alligator) of the crocodile group, found in tropical rivers and marshes of the U.S. and China: its snout is shorter and blunter than the crocodile's 2. a scaly leather made from an alligator's hide ☆3. a machine, tool, etc. with a strong, movable, often toothed jaw

alligator pear [altered (? by folk etym. because of the appearance of the skin) < avogato: see AVOCADO] same as AVOCADO

☆alligator snapper a large fresh-water turtle (Macrochelys temminckii) of the SE U.S. and the Mississippi Valley, found chiefly in rivers and bayous: it may weigh up to 200 pounds

all-im·por·tant (ôl'im pôr't'nt) adj. highly important; necessary; essential

all-in·clu·sive (-in klōōs'iv) adj. including everything; comprehensive

al·lit·er·ate (ə lit'ə rāt') vi. -at'ed, -at'ing [< ALLITERATION] 1. to constitute or show alliteration 2. to use alliteration —vt. to cause to show alliteration

al·lit·er·a·tion (ə lit'ə rā'shən) n. [ML. alliteratio < L. ad-, to + littera, LETTER[1]] repetition of an initial sound, usually of a consonant or cluster, in two or more words of a phrase, line of poetry, etc. (Ex.: "What a tale of terror now their turbulency tells!")

al·lit·er·a·tive (ə lit'ə rā'tiv, -ər ə tiv) adj. of, showing, or using alliteration —al·lit'er·a·tive·ly adv.

al·li·um (al'ē əm) n. [L., garlic] any strong-smelling bulb plant of a genus (Allium) of the lily family, as the onion, garlic, leek, etc.

al·lo- (al'ə, -ō) [< Gr. allos, other: see ELSE] a combining form signifying variation, departure from the normal, reversal [allonym, allomorph]

al·lo·cate (al'ə kāt') vt. -cat'ed, -cat'ing [< ML. allocatus, pp. of allocare < L. ad, to + locare, to place < locus: see LOCUS] 1. to set apart for a specific purpose [to allocate funds for housing] 2. to distribute in shares or according to a plan; allot 3. to fix the location of; locate —SYN. see ALLOT —al'lo·ca·ble (-kə b'l) adj.

al·lo·ca·tion (al'ə kā'shən) n. 1. an allocating or being allocated 2. a thing or amount allocated

al·loch·tho·nous (ə läk'thə nəs) adj. [ALLO- + (AUTO)-CHTHON + -OUS] originating elsewhere; not native to a place

al·lo·cu·tion (al'ə kyōō'shən) n. [L. allocutio < alloqui, to speak to < ad-, to + loqui, to speak] a formal address, esp. one warning or advising with authority

al·lod (al'äd) n. same as ALLODIUM

al·lo·di·al (ə lō'dē əl) adj. of an allodium; freehold

al·lo·di·um (-əm) n. [ML., < Frank. alōd, full and free possession < all, all + *od, akin to OE. ead, wealth] Law land owned independently, free of any superior claim, and without any rent, payment in service, etc.; a freehold estate: opposed to FEUD[2]

al·log·a·my (ə läg'ə mē) n. [ALLO- + -GAMY] the process of cross-fertilizing; cross-fertilization —al·log'a·mous (-məs) adj.

al·lo·graph (al'ə graf') n. [ALLO- + -GRAPH] 1. any of the ways a unit of a writing system, as the letter of an alphabet, is formed or shaped 2. any of the units or combination of units that can represent a single phoneme, morpheme, syllable, etc.

al·lom·er·ism (ə läm'ər iz'm) n. [ALLO- + Gr. meros, part + -ISM] variation in chemical make-up without change in crystalline form —al·lom'er·ous (-əs) adj.

al·lom·e·try (ə läm'ə trē) n. [ALLO- + -METRY] the study and measurement of the relative growth of a part of an organism in comparison with the whole

al·lo·morph (al'ə môrf') n. [ALLO- + -MORPH] 1. Mineralogy a) any of the crystalline forms of a substance existing in more than one such form b) same as PARAMORPH 2. Linguis. any of the variant forms of a morpheme as conditioned by position or adjoining sounds —al'lo·mor'phic adj. —al'lo·mor'phism n.

al·lo·nym (al'ə nim') n. [ALL(O)- + Gr. onyma, NAME] another name, usually historical, adopted by an author [the journalist's allonym was Cincinnatus]

al·lo·path (al'ə path') n. a person who practices or advocates allopathy: also al·lo·pa·thist (ə läp'ə thist)

al·lop·a·thy (ə läp'ə thē) n. [G. allopathie (see ALLO- & -PATHY), after Gr. allopatheia, subjection to external influences] treatment of disease by remedies that produce effects different from or opposite to those produced by the disease: loosely applied to the general practice of medicine today, but in strict usage opposed to HOMEOPATHY —al·lo·path·ic (al'ə path'ik) adj. —al'lo·path'i·cal·ly adv.

al·lo·pat·ric (al'ə pat'rik) adj. [<ALLO- + Gr. patra, native village (< patēr, FATHER) + -IC] Biol. of or pertaining to species of organisms occurring in different, but often adjacent areas —al'lo·pat'ri·cal·ly adv. —al·lop·a·try (ə läp'ə trē) n.

al·lo·phane (al'ə fān') n. [ALLO- + -PHANE, after Gr. allophanēs, appearing otherwise: so named because it changes appearance under the blowpipe] a translucent, hydrated silicate of aluminum of varying composition and color, typically occurring in the form of stalactites or as incrustations on chalk and sandstone

al·lo·phone (-fōn') n. [ALLO- + PHONE[1]] Linguis. any of the variant forms of a phoneme as conditioned by position or adjoining sounds [the relatively short (a) of mat and the relatively long (a) of mad are allophones]

al·lo·plasm (al'ə plaz'm) n. [ALLO- + -PLASM] Biol. 1. the special form of protoplasm from which cilia, flagella, etc.

fat, āpe, cär; ten, ēven; is, bīte; gō, hôrn, tōōl, look; oil, out; up, fur; get; joy; yet; chin; she; thin, then; zh, leisure; ŋ, ring; ə for a in ago, e in agent, i in sanity, o in comply, u in focus; ' as in able (ā'b'l); Fr. bâl; ë, Fr. coeur; ö, Fr. feu; Fr. mon; ô, Fr. coq; ü, Fr. duc; r, Fr. cri; H, G. ich; kh, G. doch. See inside front cover. ☆ Americanism; ‡foreign; *hypothetical; <derived from

develop **2.** *same as* METAPLASM—**al'lo·plas'mic** (-plaz'-mik), **al'lo·plas·mat'ic** (-plaz mat'ik) *adj.*

al·lo·pol·y·ploi·dy (al'ə päl'ə ploi'dē) *n.* [ALLO- + POLY-PLOID + -Y³] the state of having two or more sets of chromosomes derived from parents of different species or widely differing strains—**al'lo·pol'y·ploid'** *n., adj.*

☆**al·lo·sau·rus** (al'ə sôr'əs) *n.* [ModL.: see ALLO- & -SAURUS] any of a genus (*Allosaurus*) of large carnivorous, Jurassic dinosaurs: also **al'lo·saur'**

al·lot (ə lät') *vt.* **-lot'ted, -lot'ting** [OFr. *aloter* < *a-*, to + *loter* < *lot*, LOT] **1.** to distribute by lot or in arbitrary shares; apportion **2.** to give or assign as one's share [each speaker is *allotted* five minutes]
SYN.—**allot** and **assign** both imply the giving of a share or portion with no indication of uniform distribution, **assign** having the extra connotation of authoritativeness [I was *assigned* the task of *allotting* the seats]; **apportion** connotes the just, proportionate, often uniform distribution of a fixed number of portions; **allocate** usually implies the allowance of a fixed amount for a specific purpose [to *allocate* $50 for books]

al·lot·ment (-mənt) *n.* **1.** an allotting or being allotted **2.** a thing allotted; portion; share **3.** *Mil.* a portion of one's pay regularly deducted, as for one's dependents, insurance premiums, etc.

al·lo·trope (al'ə trōp') *n.* an allotropic form

al·lo·trop·ic (al'ə träp'ik) *adj.* of or characterized by allotropy: also **al'lo·trop'i·cal**—**al'lo·trop'i·cal·ly** *adv.*

al·lot·ro·py (ə lät'rə pē) *n.* [< Gr. *allotropos*, of or in another manner < *allos*, other + *tropos*, way, manner] the property that certain chemical elements have of existing in two or more different forms, as carbon in the form of charcoal, diamond, lampblack, etc.: also **al·lot'ro·pism**

‡**all' ot·ta·va** (äl' lōt tä'vä) [It., lit., according to the octave] *Music* to be played an octave higher or an octave lower, as indicated

al·lot·tee (ə lät'ē') *n.* a person to whom something is allotted

all-out (ôl'out') *adj.* complete or wholehearted [an *all-out* effort]

all·o·ver (ôl'ō'vər) *adj.* **1.** over the whole surface **2.** with the pattern repeated over the whole surface [*allover* embroidery]—*n.* cloth, etc. with such a pattern

al·low (ə lou') *vt.* [ME. *alowen* < OFr. *alouer* < ML. *allocare* < L. *ad-*, to + *locus*, a place; associated with OFr. *alouer* < L. *allaudare*, to extol < *ad-*, to + *laudare*, to praise] **1.** to let do, happen, etc.; permit; let [we weren't *allowed* to go] **2.** to let have [she *allowed* herself no sweets] **3.** to let enter or stay [dogs are not *allowed*] **4.** to admit (a claim or the like); acknowledge as true or valid **5.** to provide or allot (a certain amount, period of time, etc.) for a purpose [*allow* an inch for shrinkage] **6.** [Dial.] *a)* to think; give as one's opinion *b)* to intend—*SYN.* see LET!—**allow for** to make allowance, provision, etc. for; keep in mind [*allow for* the difference in their ages]—**allow of** to be subject to; admit of

al·low·a·ble (-ə b'l) *adj.* that can be allowed; permissible—**al·low'a·bly** *adv.*

al·low·ance (-əns) *n.* **1.** the act of allowing, permitting, admitting, etc. [the *allowance* of a claim] **2.** something allowed as a share; specif., an amount of money, food, etc. given regularly to a child, dependent, etc. or to military personnel for a specific purpose [travel *allowance*] **3.** a reduction in the price of something in consideration of a large order or of turning in a used article, etc. **4.** the amount by which something is allowed to be more or less than stated, as to compensate for the weight of the container, inaccuracy of machining, etc.—*vt.* **-anced, -anc·ing 1.** to put on an allowance or a ration **2.** to apportion economically—**make allowance** (or **allowances**) to take circumstances, limitations, etc. into consideration—**make allowance** (or **allowances**) **for 1.** to forgive or excuse because of mitigating factors **2.** to leave room, time, etc. for; allow for

Al·lo·way (al'ə wā') village in Scotland, in Ayr county: birthplace of Robert Burns

al·low·ed·ly (ə lou' id lē) *adv.* by allowance or admission; admittedly

al·loy (al'oi; *also, and for v. usually,* ə loi') *n.* [ME. *alai* < Anglo-Fr. *alei* (OFr. *aloi*) < *aleier*: see the *v.*] **1.** the relative purity of gold or silver; fineness **2.** a substance that is a mixture, as by fusion, of two or more metals, or of a metal and something else **3.** *a)* formerly, a less valuable metal mixed with a more valuable one, often to give hardness *b)* something that lowers the value or quality of another thing when mixed with it—*vt.* [Fr. *aloyer* < OFr. *aloier, aleier* < L. *alligare* < *ad-*, to + *ligare*, to bind: cf. ALLY] **1.** to make (a metal) less pure by mixing with a less valuable metal **2.** to mix (metals) to form an alloy **3.** to debase by mixing with something inferior

All·port (ôl'pôrt), **Gordon W(illard)** 1897–　　; U.S. psychologist

all-pur·pose (ôl'pur'pəs) *adj.* for every pertinent purpose; useful in many ways

all-right (-rit') *adj.* [Slang] honest, honorable, good, excellent, etc.: used before the noun it modifies

all right 1. satisfactory; adequate **2.** unhurt; safe **3.** correct **4.** yes; very well: used in reply to a question or merely to preface or resume one's remarks **5.** [Colloq.] certainly [he's the one who did it, *all right*]

all-round (ôl'round') *adj. same as* ALL-AROUND

All Saints' Day an annual church festival (November 1) in honor of all the saints

all·seed (-sēd') *n.* any of various plants producing many seeds, as knotgrass or goosefoot

All Souls' Day in certain Christian churches, a day (usually November 2) of services and prayer for the dead

all·spice (-spis') *n.* **1.** *a)* the berry of a West Indian tree (*Pimenta officinalis*) of the myrtle family *b)* the spice made from this berry: so called because its flavor seems to combine the tastes of several spices **2.** the tree itself

☆**all-star** (-stär') *adj.* made up entirely of outstanding or star performers

all-time (-tim') *adj.* unsurpassed up to the present time [an *all-time* record]

al·lude (ə lōōd') *vi.* **-lud'ed, -lud'ing** [L. *alludere*, to joke, jest < *ad-*, to + *ludere*, to play] to refer in a casual or indirect way (*to*)—*SYN.* see REFER

al·lure (ə loor') *vt., vi.* **-lured', -lur'ing** [ME. *aluren* < OFr. *alurer* < *a-*, to + *lurer*, to lure; associated with Fr. *allure*, gait, way of walking, love affair < *aller* (see ALLEY¹)] to tempt with something desirable; attract; entice; fascinate—*n.* the power to entice or attract; fascination—*SYN.* see ATTRACT

al·lure·ment (-mənt) *n.* **1.** the act of alluring **2.** alluring quality; fascination; charm **3.** something that allures

al·lur·ing (-in) *adj.* tempting strongly; highly attractive; charming—**al·lur'ing·ly** *adv.*

al·lu·sion (ə lōō'zhən, a-) *n.* [LL. *allusio*, a playing with < *allusus*, pp. of *alludere*: see ALLUDE] **1.** the act of alluding **2.** an indirect reference; casual mention

al·lu·sive (ə lōōs'iv, a-) *adj.* **1.** containing an allusion **2.** using allusion; full of allusions—**al·lu'sive·ly** *adv.*—**al·lu'sive·ness** *n.*

al·lu·vi·al (ə lōō'vē əl) *adj.* [< L. *alluvius* (see ALLUVION) + -AL] of, found in, or made up of, alluvium—*n. same as* ALLUVIUM

☆**alluvial cone** a steeply sloping, cone-shaped mass of alluvium formed where a swift stream suddenly slows down, as where an upland stream emerges abruptly into a level plain

alluvial fan a gradually sloping mass of alluvium that widens out like a fan from the place where a stream slows down little by little as it enters a plain, etc.

al·lu·vi·on (ə lōō'vē ən) *n.* [Fr. < L. *alluvio*, an overflowing < *alluere* < *ad-*, to + *luere*, to wash, akin to *lavere:* see LATHER] **1.** the washing of water against a shore or bank **2.** an overflowing; flood **3.** *same as* ALLUVIUM **4.** *Law* a gradual addition to land along a river, lake, etc., as through the deposit of sedimentary material

al·lu·vi·um (ə lōō'vē əm) *n., pl.* **-vi·ums, -vi·a** (-vē ə) [L., neut. of *alluvius:* see ALLUVION] sand, clay, etc. gradually deposited by moving water, as along a river bed or the shore of a lake—*SYN.* see WASH

al·ly (ə li'; *also, and for n. usually,* al'i) *vt.* **-lied', -ly'ing** [ME. *alien* < OFr. *alier* < L. *alligare* < *ad-*, to + *ligare*, to bind] **1.** to unite or associate for a specific purpose, as families by marriage, nations by treaty, or companies by agreement: generally used reflexively or in the passive **2.** to relate by similarity of structure, certain qualities, etc.: usually in the passive [the onion is *allied* to the lily]—*vi.* to become allied—*n., pl.* **-lies 1.** a country, person, or group joined with another or others for a common purpose: see also ALLIES **2.** a plant, animal, or thing closely related in structure, etc. to another **3.** an associate; helper; auxiliary—*SYN.* see ASSOCIATE

al·lyl (al'il) *n.* [ALL (IUM) + -YL] *Chem.* the univalent radical $CH_2:CHCH_2$, found in oil of garlic, etc.—**al·lyl·ic** (ə lil'ik) *adj.*

allyl alcohol a poisonous, pungent, colorless liquid, $CH_2:CHCH_2OH$, used in resins, plasticizers, herbicides, etc.

allyl resin any of several thermosetting vinyl resins derived from esters of allyl alcohol and dibasic acids: they are highly resistant to chemicals, moisture, abrasion, and heat, and are used as laminating adhesives in varnishes, etc.

allyl thiourea *same as* THIOSINAMINE

Al·ma (al'mə) [L., fem of *almus*, nourishing, bountiful] a feminine name

al·ma, al·mah (al'mə) *n.* [Ar. 'ālimah, learned (in music and dancing)] an Egyptian dancing girl: also **al'me, al'meh** (-me)

Al·ma-A·ta (äl'mə ä'tə) capital of the Kazakh S.S.R., in the SE part: pop. 623,000

Al·ma·gest (al'mə jest') *n.* [ME. < OFr. *almageste* < Ar. *al majistī* < *al*, the + Gr. *megistē* (*syntaxis*), greatest (work)] **1.** a vast work on astronomy and mathematics compiled by Ptolemy c. 150 A.D. **2.** [a-] any of several medieval works like this, on astrology, alchemy, etc.

al·ma ma·ter (al'mə mät'ər; mät'ər) [L., fostering mother] **1.** the college or school that one attended **2.** its official anthem, or hymn

al·ma·nac (ôl'mə nak', al'-) *n.* [ME. *almenak* < ML. *almanachus* < LGr. *almenichiaka*, calendar, ? of Coptic origin] **1.** a yearly calendar of days, weeks, and months, with astronomical data, weather forecasts, etc. **2.** a book published annually, containing information, usually statistical, on many subjects

al·man·dine (al'mən dēn', -din) *n.* [altered < *alabandine* < L. *alabandina*, precious gem < *Alabanda*, city in the

interior of Caria] a purplish-red garnet containing ferrous iron and aluminum: also **al′man·dite′** (-dīt′)

al·Man·sur (al′man soor′) *see* MANSUR

Al·ma-Tad·e·ma (al′mə tad′i mə) Sir **Lawrence** 1836-1912; Eng. painter, born in the Netherlands

Al·me·lo (äl′mə lō′) city in E Netherlands: pop. 56,000

Al·me·rí·a (äl′me rē′ä) seaport in SE Spain, on the Mediterranean: pop. 89,000

al·might·y (ôl mīt′ē) adj. [ME. almihtig < OE. ealmihtig < eal, all + mihtig, mighty] 1. having unlimited power; all-powerful 2. [Slang] great; extreme [an almighty nuisance] —adv. [Slang] extremely —**the Almighty God** —☆**the almighty dollar** [Colloq.] money regarded figuratively as a god, or source of great power —**al·might′i·ly** adv. —**al·might′i·ness** n.

al·mond (ä′mənd, am′ənd; al′mənd, äl′-) n. [ME. almande < OFr. amande < ML. amandola < L. amygdala < Gr. amygdalē] 1. a) the edible, nutlike kernel of the small, dry, peachlike fruit of a tree (Prunus amygdalus) growing in warm regions b) the tree itself 2. anything shaped like an almond, oval and pointed at one or both ends 3. the light-tan color of the almond shell —adj. 1. made of almonds 2. having an almond flavor 3. almond-shaped 4. almond-colored

al·mon·er (al′mən ər, ä′mən-) n. [ME. almoiner < OFr. almosnier < almosne, act of mercy < LL. *alemosyna < eleemosyna: see ALMS] a distributor of alms, as for a church, wealthy family, etc.

al·most (ôl′mōst, ôl′mōst′) adv. [OE. eallmæst: see ALL & MOST] very nearly but not completely; all but

alms (ämz) n., pl. **alms** [ME. almesse < OE. ælmesse < LL. eleemosyna < Gr. eleēmosynē, alms < eleos, pity] 1. money, food, clothes, etc. given to poor people 2. [Obs.] a deed of mercy —**alms′giv′er** n. —**alms′giv′ing** n.

alms·house (-hous′) n. 1. formerly, a home for people too poor to support themselves; poorhouse 2. [Brit.] a privately endowed home for the disabled or aged poor

alms·man (-mən) n., pl. **-men** (-mən) [Now Rare] a person, esp. a man, supported by alms —**alms′wom′an** (-woom′ən) n.fem., pl. **-wom′en** (-wim′in)

al·muce (al′myōōs) n. [ML. almutia, cowl or hood < Ar. al, the + mustaka, fur cloak with long sleeves] a fur-lined hood or hooded cape, formerly worn by the clergy

al·mug (al′mug) n. [Heb., orig. error for algūm] Bible a tree, probably sandalwood, from whose wood Solomon made the pillars of the Temple: I Kings 10:12

al·ni·co (al′ni kō′) n. [AL(UMINUM) + NI(CKEL) + CO-(BALT)] any of various alloys of iron containing cobalt, nickel, aluminum, and occasionally copper, titanium, or niobium: used in making strong permanent magnets

al·od (al′əd) n. same as ALLODIUM

a·lo·di·um (ə lō′dē əm) n. same as ALLODIUM —**a·lo′di·al** adj.

al·oe (al′ō) n., pl. **-oes** [ME. < L. < Gr. aloē < ? Heb. ′ahālīm, aloe wood < Sans. agaru] 1. any of a large genus (Aloe) of plants of the lily family, native to South Africa, with fleshy leaves that are spiny along the edge and with drooping clusters of tubular, red or yellow flowers 2. [pl., with sing. v.] a bitter, laxative drug made from the juice of certain aloe leaves 3. [pl., with sing. v.] the aromatic heartwood of several trees of a genus (Aquilaria) of the mezereum family, native to the East Indies and southeast Asia —**al′o·et′ic** (-et′ik) adj.

a·loft (ə lôft′) adv. [ME. < o, on, on + loft < ON. lopt: see LOFT] 1. high up; far above the ground 2. in the air; flying 3. high above the deck of a ship; esp., at the masthead

☆**a·lo·ha** (ə lō′ə, ä lō′hä) n., interj. [Haw., lit., love] a word used as a greeting or farewell

al·o·in (al′ō in) n. a bitter, crystalline cathartic prepared from the aloe

a·lone (ə lōn′) adj., adv. [ME. < al, ALL + one, ONE] 1. apart from anything or anyone else [the hut stood alone on the prairie] 2. without involving any other person [to walk alone] 3. without anything further; with nothing more; only [the carton alone weighs two pounds] 4. without equal or peer [to stand alone as an example of courage] As an adjective, alone generally follows the word it modifies —**let alone** 1. to refrain from bothering or interfering with 2. not to speak of [we hadn't a dime, let alone a dollar] —**let well enough alone** to be content with things as they are and not try to improve them

SYN.—alone, unqualified, denotes the simple fact of being by oneself or itself; solitary conveys the same sense but suggests more strongly the lack of companionship or association [a solitary tree in the meadow]; lonely, and the more poetic lone, convey a heightened sense of solitude and gloom [the lonely sentinel walks his post]; lonesome suggests a longing or yearning for companionship, often for a particular person [the child is lonesome for his mother] —ANT. accompanied

a·long[1] (ə lôn′) prep. [ME. < OE. andlang, along, orig. turned toward < and-, over against + -lang > PGmc. *langha- < IE. base lenk-, to bend: cf. LING[2]] 1. on or beside the length of; over or throughout the length of [along the wall there is a hedge] 2. in conformity with [to

think along certain lines] —adv. 1. in a line; lengthwise 2. progressively forward or onward [he walked along by himself] 3. as a companion [come along with us] 4. with one [she took her camera along] ☆5. on its way; advanced [the program was well along when he arrived] ☆6. [Colloq.] approaching [along toward evening] —**all along** all the time; from the very beginning —**along with** 1. together with 2. in addition to —☆**be along** [Colloq.] to come or arrive [I'll be along later] —**get along** 1. to go forward 2. to contrive 3. to succeed 4. to agree 5. [Colloq.] to go away

a·long[2] (ə lôn′) adv. [ME. < OE. gelang, depending] [Brit. Dial.] owing to (with of or on)

a·long·shore (ə lôn′shôr′) adv. along the shore; near or beside the shore

a·long·side (-sīd′) adv. at or by the side; side by side —prep. at the side of; side by side with —**alongside of** at the side of; beside; adjoining

a·loof (ə lōōf′) adv. [a-, on + loof < Du. loef, LUFF, to windward] at a distance but in view; apart —adj. 1. at a distance; removed 2. distant in sympathy, interest, etc.; reserved and cool [her manner was aloof] —**a·loof′ly** adv. —**a·loof′ness** n.

a·lo·pe·ci·a (al′ə pēsh′ē·ə, -pēsh′ə) n. [L., baldness, fox mange < Gr. alōpekia < alōpēx, a fox] loss of hair on the head; baldness

‡**a·lors** (á lôr′) interj. [Fr.] well then! and so: a generalized exclamation

A·lost (á lōst′) city in WC Belgium: pop. 45,000: Fl. name, AALST

a·loud (ə loud′) adv. 1. loudly [to cry aloud] 2. with the normal voice [read the letter aloud]

a·low (ə lō′) adv. [ME. aloue < on, on + loue: see LOW[1]] Naut. below

Al·o·ys·i·us (al′ə wish′əs) [ML. Aloisius; prob. < OFr. Loeis: see LOUIS] a masculine name

alp (alp) n. [< L. Alpes, the Alps, high mountains; prob. < a non-IE. root appearing also in ALBION] a high mountain, esp. in Switzerland: see ALPS

al·pac·a (al pak′ə) n., pl. **-pac′as, -pac′a**: see PLURAL, II, D, 1 [Sp. < Aymara allpaca] 1. a domesticated S.American mammal (Lama pacos) related to the llama and guanaco, with fleecy brown or black wool 2. its wool 3. a thin cloth woven from this wool, often mixed with other fibers 4. a glossy, generally black cloth of cotton and wool, used for linings, suits, etc.

ALPACA (3 ft. high at shoulder)

al·pen·glow (al′pən glō′) n. [partial transl. of G. alpenglühen < alpen, of the Alps + glühen, glow] a reddish glow seen on mountain tops before sunrise or after sunset

al·pen·horn (-hôrn′) n. [G., Alpine horn] a curved, wooden, powerful-sounding horn, from five to twelve or more feet long, used by Swiss Alpine herdsmen for signaling

al·pen·stock (-stäk′) n. [G., Alpine staff] a strong iron-pointed staff used by mountain climbers

al·pes·trine (al pes′trin) adj. [ML. alpestris < Alpes: see ALP] 1. of the Alps or any mountainous region 2. Bot. growing in subalpine regions

al·pha (al′fə) n. [Gr. < Phoen. name whence Heb. āleph: see ALEPH] 1. the first letter of the Greek alphabet (A,α) 2. the beginning of anything 3. Astron. the brightest star in a constellation 4. Chem. designating the first of two or more positions in which the substituting atom or radical appears relative to some particular carbon atom in an organic compound: usually written α-: the other positions, in order, are beta (β-), gamma (γ-), delta (δ-), etc.

alpha and omega 1. the first and last letters of the Greek alphabet 2. the beginning and the end: cf. Rev. 1:8

al·pha·bet (al′fə betum′) n. [LL. alphabetum < LGr. alphabētos < Gr. alpha + bēta, the first two letters of the Greek alphabet] 1. the letters of a language, arranged in a traditional order 2. a system of characters, signs, or symbols used to indicate letters or speech sounds 3. the first elements or principles, as of a branch of knowledge —vt. **-bet′ed -bet′ing** to alphabetize

al·pha·bet·i·cal (al′fə bet′i k′l) adj. 1. of or using an alphabet 2. arranged in the regular order of the alphabet Also **al′pha·bet′ic** —**al′pha·bet′i·cal·ly** adv.

al·pha·bet·ize (al′fə bə tīz′) vt. **-ized′, -iz′ing** 1. to arrange in alphabetical order 2. to express by or provide with an alphabet —**al′pha·bet′i·za′tion** (-i zā′shən) n.

alpha iron an allotropic form of iron stable below 760°C: it is soft and magnetic, and has a crystal structure

al·pha·nu·mer·ic (al′fə nōō mer′ik, -nyōō-) adj. [ALPHA-(BET) + NUMERIC(AL)] having or using both alphabetical and numerical symbols

alpha particle a positively charged particle given off by

certain radioactive substances: it consists of two protons and two neutrons, and is converted into an atom of helium by the acquisition of two electrons

alpha ray 1. *same as* ALPHA PARTICLE **2.** a stream of alpha particles, less penetrating than a beta ray

Al·phe·us (al fē′əs) [L. < Gr. *Alpeios*] *Gr. Myth.* a river god who pursued Arethusa until she was changed into a fountain by Artemis

Al·phon·so (al fän′zō, -sō) [Sp. *Alfonso* < Gmc. **Athalfuns* < **athal*, akin to OHG. < *adal*, nobility + *funs*, ready] a masculine name

alp·horn (alp′hôrn′) *n. same as* ALPENHORN

al·pho·sis (al fōs′is) *n.* [ModL. < Gr. *alphos*, dull-white leprosy] abnormal absence of skin pigment, as in albinism

Al·pine (al′pīn) *adj.* [L. *alpinus* < *Alpes*, the Alps] **1.** of the Alps or their inhabitants **2.** [a-] *a)* of or like high mountains *b)* growing in high altitudes above the timberline **3.** designating or of a physical type of the Caucasoid peoples exemplified by the broad-headed, brown-haired, medium-statured people of the Alps: see also MEDITERRANEAN, NORDIC

al·pin·ist (al′pə nist) *n.* [*also* A-] a mountain climber

Alps (alps) mountain system in SC Europe extending from S France through Switzerland, Italy, Germany, and Austria into Yugoslavia and Albania: highest peak, Mont BLANC

al·read·y (ôl red′ē) *adv.* **1.** by or before the given or implied time **2.** even now or even then *[he was already two days late]* Also used colloquially at the end of a phrase to express impatience *[that's enough already!]*

al·right (ôl rīt′) *adv. a disputed var. sp. of* ALL RIGHT

Al·sace (al säs′, -sas′; al′sas; *Fr.* ål zås′) former province of NE France (1648–1790)

Al·sace-Lor·raine (-lô rān′, -lə-; *Fr.* -lô ren′) region in NE France consisting of the former provinces of Alsace and Lorraine: under German control, 1871–1919 and 1940–1944: since 1945, divided into three departments of France

Al·sa·tian (al sā′shən) *adj.* [after *Alsatia*, older name for Alsace < ML. *Alisatia*] **1.** of Alsace, its people, etc. **2.** of Whitefriars, a district in London —*n.* **1.** a native or inhabitant of Alsace **2.** the Alemannic dialect spoken by the Alsatians **3.** a German shepherd dog

al·sike (al′sīk, ôl′-) *n.* [after *Alsike*, town in Sweden] a European clover (*Trifolium hybridum*) with white or pinkish flowers, grown for fodder: also **alsike clover**

Al Si·rat (al′ si rät′; *Ar.* as si rät′) [Ar., the road] *Islam* **1.** the true faith of the Koran **2.** the narrow bridge over hellfire to Paradise

al·so (ôl′sō) *adv.* [ME. *al so, al swo* < OE. *eallswa* < *eal*, ALL + *swa*, SO[1]] in addition; likewise; too; besides; sometimes used with conjunctive force as an equivalent of *and*

☆**al·so-ran** (-ran′) *n.* **1.** a horse that fails to finish first, second, or third in a race **2.** [Colloq.] any loser in a race, competition, election, etc.

alt (alt) *adj.* [It. *alto* < L. *altus*, high: see ALTITUDE] *Music* high in pitch —*n.* **1.** the first octave above the treble staff **2.** a tone in this octave

alt. 1. alternate **2.** alternating **3.** altitude **4.** alto

Alta. Alberta (Canada)

Al·ta·de·na (al′tə dē′nə) [< L. *alta*, fem. of *altus*, high + (PASA)DENA, which is at a lower elevation] suburb of Los Angeles, adjacent to Pasadena: pop. 42,000

Al·ta·ic (al tā′ik) *adj.* **1.** of the Altai Mountains or the people living there **2.** designating or of a family of languages including Turkic, Mongolic, and Tungusic —*n.* this family of languages

Al·tai Mountains (al′tī) mountain system in SC R.S.F.S.R., NW China, and W Mongolian People's Republic: highest peak, c. 15,000 ft.

Al·ta·ir (al tä′ir) [Ar. *al tā′ir*, the bird] the brightest star in the constellation Aquila

Al·ta·mi·ra (äl′tä mē′rä) cave in N Spain, near Santander, containing paleolithic drawings

al·tar (ôl′tər) *n.* [ME. *alter* < OE. & OFr. *alter*; both < L. *altare*, high altar < *altus*, high: see ALTITUDE] **1.** a place, esp. a raised platform, where sacrifices or offerings are made to a god, an ancestor, etc. **2.** a table, stand, etc. used for sacred purposes in a place of worship, as the Communion table in Christian churches —**lead to the altar** to marry

altar boy a boy or man who helps a priest, vicar, etc. at religious services, esp. at Mass

al·tar·piece (-pēs′) *n.* an ornamental carving, painting, etc. above and behind an altar

alt·az·i·muth (alt′az′ə məth) *n.* [ALT(ITUDE) + AZIMUTH] an instrument for simultaneously measuring the altitude and azimuth of a star, planet, etc.

Alt·dorf (ält′dôrf) town in Switzerland near Lake Lucerne: pop. 7,000: scene of the William Tell legend

al·ter (ôl′tər) *vt.* [ME. *alteren* < ML. *alterare* < L. *alter*, other] **1.** to make different in details but not in substance; modify **2.** to resew parts of (a garment) for a better fit **3.** to castrate or spay —*vi.* to become different; change; vary —*SYN.* see CHANGE —**al′ter·a·ble** *adj.*

al·ter·ant (-ənt) *adj.* [ML. *alterans*, prp. of *alterare*, ALTER] causing alteration —*n.* **1.** a thing that causes alteration **2.** *Dyeing* a substance used to change a color

al·ter·a·tion (ôl′tə rā′shən) *n.* **1.** an altering or being altered **2.** the result of this; change

al·ter·a·tive (ôl′tə rāt′iv, -tər ə tiv) *adj.* [ME. & OFr. *alteratif* < ML. *alterativus*: see ALTER] **1.** causing or tending to cause alteration **2.** *Med.* gradually restoring to health —*n.* an alterative medicine or treatment

al·ter·cate (ôl′tər kāt′, al′-) *vi.* **-cat′ed**, **-cat′ing** [< L. *altercatus*, pp. of *altercari*, to dispute < *alter*, other] to argue angrily; quarrel

al·ter·ca·tion (ôl′tər kā′shən, al′-) *n.* an angry or heated argument —*SYN.* see QUARREL[2]

al·tered chord (ôl′tərd) *Music* a chord in which one or more tones have been chromatically altered by sharps, flats, or naturals foreign to the key

al·ter e·go (ôl′tər ē′gō, al′-; eg′ō) [L., lit., other I] **1.** another aspect of oneself **2.** a very close friend or constant companion

†**al·ter i·dem** (al′tər ī′dem, ôl′-; id′em) [L.] another of the same kind; second self

al·ter·nant (ôl′tər nənt) *adj.* alternating —*n. Linguis.* any of the variant forms of an alternation

al·ter·nate (ôl′tər nit, al′-; *for v.* -nāt′) *adj.* [L. *alternatus*, pp. of *alternare*, to do by turns < *alternus*, one after the other < *alter*, other] **1.** occurring by turns; succeeding each other; one and then the other *[alternate stripes of blue and white]* **2.** every other; every second *[to report on alternate Tuesdays]* **3.** being one of two or more choices; alternative **4.** *Bot. a)* growing along the stem singly at different intervals, first on one side then the other, etc. *b)* placed at intervals between other parts —*n.* a person standing by to take the place of another if necessary; substitute —*vt.* **-nat′ed**, **-nat′ing 1.** to do or use by turns **2.** to make happen or arrange by turns —*vi.* **1.** to act, happen, etc. by turns; follow successively *[good times alternate with bad]* **2.** to take turns **3.** to exchange places, etc. regularly **4.** *Elec.* to reverse direction periodically: said of a current —*SYN.* see INTERMITTENT —**al′ter·nate·ly** *adv.*

ALTERNATE LEAVES

alternate angles two angles at opposite ends and on opposite sides of a line crossing two others

alternating current an electric current that reverses its direction periodically

al·ter·na·tion (ôl′tər nā′shən, al′-) *n.* **1.** the act of alternating; occurrence, position, etc. of things by turns **2.** *Linguis.* the occurrence of a variant of a morpheme or phoneme

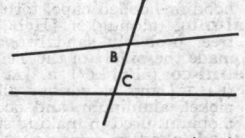

ALTERNATE ANGLES (B, C)

alternation of generations the occurrence of generations in alternate order, esp. of one that reproduces sexually with one that reproduces asexually

al·ter·na·tive (ôl tur′nə tiv, al-) *adj.* [ML. *alternativus*: see ALTERNATE] providing or being a choice between two (or, less strictly, among more than two) things *[alternative routes]* —*n.* **1.** a choice between two or among more than two things **2.** either or any one of the things to be chosen **3.** something remaining to be chosen *[is there an alternative to going?]* —*SYN.* see CHOICE —**al·ter′na·tive·ly** *adv.*

alternative conjunction a conjunction joining elements which are to be understood as alternatives (Ex.: or; neither . . . nor)

al·ter·na·tor (ôl′tər nāt′ər, al′-) *n.* an electric generator or dynamo producing alternating current

Alt·geld (ôlt′geld), **John Peter** 1847–1902; U.S. statesman; governor of Ill. (1892–96); instituted social reforms

Al·the·a (al thē′ə) [L. *Althaea* < Gr. *Althaia*, lit., healer < *althainein*, to heal] a feminine name

al·the·a, al·thae·a (al thē′ə) *n.* [L. *althaea* < Gr. *althaia*, wild mallows] **1.** any plant of a genus (*Althea*) in the mallow family, as the hollyhock, typically with tall spikes of showy flowers **2.** *same as* ROSE OF SHARON (sense 1)

alt·horn (alt′hôrn′) *n.* a brass-wind instrument, the alto saxhorn: also **alto horn**

al·though (ôl thō′) *conj.* [ME. < *all, al*, emphatic, even + *though*] in spite of the fact that; granting that; though: now sometimes spelled **altho**

al·ti- (al′tə) *same as* ALTO-

al·ti·graph (al′tə graf′) *n.* [ALTI- + -GRAPH] an altimeter that records altitude automatically on a chart

al·tim·e·ter (al tim′ə tər; *also, chiefly Brit.*, al′tə mēt′ər) *n.* [ALTI- + -METER] an instrument for measuring the altitude or height above a given reference level, as the sea or ground: in aircraft it is usually an aneroid barometer with a dial marked in feet or meters

al·tim·e·try (-trē) *n.* [< ALTIMETER] the science or practice of measuring altitudes, as with an altimeter

†**al·ti·pla·no** (äl′tē plä′nō) *n.* [AmSp. < Sp. *alti-* (< L. *altus*, high) + *plano*, a plain < VL. < L. *planus*, PLANE[3]] a high plateau, as in Bolivia

al·ti·tude (al′tə tōōd′, -tyōōd′) *n.* [L. *altitudo* < *altus*, high, orig. pp. of *alere*, to nourish, cause to grow: cf. OLD] **1.** height; esp., the height of a thing above the earth's surface or above sea level **2.** a high place or region: *usually used in pl.* **3.** a high level, rank, etc. **4.** *Astron.* the angular height of a planet, star, etc. above the horizon **5.** *Geom.*

the perpendicular distance from the base of a figure to its highest point or to the side parallel to the base —*SYN.* see HEIGHT —**al'ti·tu'di·nal** (-'n əl) *adj.*

al·to (al'tō) *n., pl.* **-tos** [It. < L. *altus,* high] **1.** the range of the lowest female voice (contralto) or, esp. formerly, the highest male voice (countertenor) **2.** *a)* a voice or singer with such range *b)* an instrument with the second highest range within a family of instruments, as the alto saxophone *c)* a part for such a voice or instrument —*adj.* **1.** singing or playing within this range **2.** for this range

al·to- (al'tō) [< L. *altus,* high] *a prefix meaning* high

alto clef the C clef on the third line; viola clef

al·to·cu·mu·lus (al'tō kyōō'myə ləs) *n.* [ALTO- + CUMULUS] a formation of white or gray clouds in many shapes, most commonly rounded, found at intermediate heights

al·to·geth·er (ôl'tə geth'ər, ôl'tə geth'ər) *adv.* [ME. *altogedere:* see ALL & TOGETHER] **1.** wholly; completely [not *altogether* wrong] **2.** in all; all being counted [he wrote six books *altogether*] **3.** everything being considered; on the whole [*altogether* a great success] Distinguished from **all together** —**in the altogether** [Colloq.] nude

Al·ton (ôl't'n) [after *Alton* Easton, son of its founder] city in SW Ill., on the Mississippi: pop. 40,000

Al·to·na (äl'tō nä) former seaport of N Germany: since 1937, part of the city of Hamburg

Al·too·na (al tōō'nə) [< ALTONA] city in C Pa.: pop. 63,000

al·to·re·lie·vo (al'tō ri lē'vō) *n., pl.* **-vos** [< It. *alto,* high + *relievo,* relief; sp. infl. by RELIEF] *same as* HIGH RELIEF

‡al·to·ri·lie·vo (äl'tō rē lye'vō) *n., pl.* **al'ti·ri·lie'vi** (äl'tē-rē lye'vē) [It.] *same as* ALTO-RELIEVO

al·to·stra·tus (al'tō strāt'əs, -strat'-) *n.* [ALTO- + STRATUS] a formation of gray to bluish clouds found at intermediate heights in continuous dense layers or thick patches

al·tri·cial (al trish'əl) *adj.* [ModL. *altricialis* < L. *altrix,* a nurse, fem. of *altor,* one who nourishes < *alere,* to feed: cf. OLD] designating or of birds whose newly hatched young are helpless and hence confined to the nest for some time: opposed to PRECOCIAL

al·tru·ism (al'trōō iz'm) *n.* [Fr. *altruisme* < It. *altrui* or Fr. *autrui,* of or to others < L. *alter,* another] **1.** unselfish concern for the welfare of others; selflessness **2.** *Ethics* the doctrine that the general welfare of society is the proper goal of an individual's actions: opposed to EGOISM —**al'tru·ist** *n.*

al·tru·is·tic (al'trōō is'tik) *adj.* of or motivated by altruism —*SYN.* see PHILANTHROPIC —**al'tru·is'ti·cal·ly** *adv.*

al·u·del (al'yoo del') *n.* [OFr. < Sp. < Ar. *al uthāl*] *Chem.* a pear-shaped vessel open at both ends so that several such vessels may be fitted into one another to form a series: used in the sublimation of iodine, in condensing mercury vapor, etc.

al·u·la (al'yoo lə) *n., pl.* **-lae** (-lē) [ModL. dim. of *ala,* wing: see AILERON] the terminal part of a bird's wing corresponding to the thumb, consisting of three or more quills; bastard wing

al·um¹ (al'əm) *n.* [ME. & OFr. < L. *alumen,* alum; for IE. base see ALE] **1.** a double sulfate of ammonium or a univalent metal (as sodium or potassium) and of a trivalent metal (as aluminum, iron, or chromium): it is used as an astringent, as an emetic, and in the manufacture of baking powders, dyes, and paper; the commonest form is potash alum (potassium aluminum sulfate), KAl(SO₄)₂·12H₂O **2.** aluminum sulfate: erroneous use

☆a·lum² (ə lum') *n.* [Colloq.] an alumnus or alumna

a·lu·mi·na (ə lōō'mə nə) *n.* [ModL. < L. *alumen. aluminis*), ALUM¹] an oxide of aluminum, Al₂O₃, present in bauxite and clay and found as different forms of corundum, including emery, sapphires, rubies, etc.

a·lu·mi·nate (-nāt') *n.* a salt of aluminum hydroxide reacting as an acid in an alkaline solution

a·lu·mi·nif·er·ous (ə lōō'mə nif'ər əs) *adj.* yielding or containing aluminum, alumina, or alum

al·u·min·ium (al'yoo min'yəm, -ē əm) *n. Brit. var. of* ALUMINUM

a·lu·mi·nize (ə lōō'mə nīz') *vt.* **-nized', -niz'ing** to cover, or treat, with aluminum

a·lu·mi·no·ther·my (ə lōō'mə nō thur'mē) *n.* a metallurgical process in which aluminum reduces another metal from its oxide, simultaneously releasing great heat

a·lu·mi·nous (ə lōō'mə nəs) *adj.* [L. *aluminosus*] of or containing alum, alumina, or aluminum

a·lu·mi·num (ə lōō'mə nəm) *n.* [ModL. < L. *alumen* (gen. *aluminis*), alum] one of the chemical elements, a silvery, lightweight, easily worked metal that resists corrosion and is found abundantly, but only in combination: symbol, Al; at. wt., 26.9815; at. no., 13; sp. gr., 2.699; melt. pt., 660.1°C; boil. pt., 2327°C —*adj.* of, containing, or made of aluminum

aluminum hydroxide a white powder, Al(OH)₃, prepared from aluminum salts: used in dyeing, waterproofing fabrics, etc.

aluminum oxide *same as* ALUMINA

aluminum sulfate a white crystalline salt, Al₂(SO₄)₃, made by treating bauxite or clay with sulfuric acid: it is used in sizing paper, purifying water, fixing dyes, tanning, etc.

☆a·lum·na (ə lum'nə) *n., pl.* **-nae** (-nē) [L., fem. of ALUMNUS] a girl or woman alumnus

a·lum·nus (-nəs) *n., pl.* **-ni** (-nī) [L., a pupil, foster son < *alere,* to nourish: cf. OLD] ☆a person, esp. a boy or man, who has attended or is a graduate of a particular school, college, or university

☆al·um·root (al'əm rōōt') *n.* any of several N. American plants of a genus (*Heuchera*) in the saxifrage family, with tiny, bell-shaped flowers and an astringent root

A·lun·dum (ə lun'dəm) [AL(UMINA) + (COR)UNDUM] *a trademark for* a synthetic aluminum oxide abrasive similar to natural corundum or emery

al·u·nite (al'yə nīt') *n.* [Fr. < *alun* < L. *alumen,* alum] a mineral consisting of hydrated potassium aluminum sulfate, KAl₃(OH)₆(SO₄)₃: also called **alumstone**

Al·va (al'və; *Sp.* äl'vä), **Duke of,** (*Fernando Álvarez de Toledo*) 1508–82; Sp. general who suppressed a revolt in the Low Countries

Al·vah, Al·va (al'və) [Heb. *'alvāh, 'alvān;* often associated with L. *albus,* white] a masculine name: var. **Al'van** (-vən)

Al·va·ra·do (äl'və rä' thō), **Pe·dro de** (pe' thrō de) 1495– _1541; Sp. general with Cortés in the conquest of Mexico

Ál·va·rez Quin·te·ro (äl'vä reth kēn te'rō), **Joa·quín** (hwä kēn') 1873–1944, and his brother **Se·ra·fín** (se'rä fēn') 1871–1938; Sp. playwrights who collaborated

al·ve·o·lar (al vē'ə lar) *adj.* **1.** of or like an alveolus or the alveoli; socketlike **2.** *Anat. a)* relating to the part of the jaws containing the sockets of the teeth *b)* designating the ridge of the gums behind the upper front teeth *c)* relating to the air pockets in the lungs **3.** *Phonet.* formed, as English *t, d, s,* by touching or approaching the alveolar ridge with the tip of the tongue —*n. Phonet.* an alveolar sound

al·ve·o·late (-lit) *adj.* [L. *alveolatus,* hollowed out < *alveolus,* ALVEOLUS] honeycombed; full of small cavities: also **al·ve·o·lat'ed** (-lāt'id) —**al·ve'o·la'tion** *n.*

al·ve·o·lus (-ləs) *n., pl.* **-li'** (-lī') [L., dim. of *alveus,* a hollow, cavity < *alvus,* the belly, womb < IE. base *au-lo-s,* whence Gr. *aulos,* flute, Lith. *aulỹs,* beehive] **1.** *Anat., Zool.* a small cavity or hollow, as a cell of a honeycomb, air cell of a lung, tooth socket, etc. **2.** [*usually pl.*] the alveolar ridge; teethridge

Al·vin (al'v'n) [G. *Alwin,* lit., noble friend < OHG. *adal,* nobility + *wini,* friend] a masculine name

al·vine (al'vin, -vin) *adj.* [< L. *alvus,* belly: see ALVEOLUS] of the abdomen or intestines

al·way (ôl'wā) *adv.* [Archaic or Poet.] always

al·ways (ôl'wiz, -wāz) *adv.* [ME., adv. gen. of *alwei, alway* < OE. *ealne weg:* see ALL + WAY] **1.** at all times; on all occasions; invariably [*always* be courteous] **2.** all the time; continually; forever [*always* present in the atmosphere] **3.** at any time; whenever one wishes [you can *always* leave if the show gets boring] **4.** in every instance; with no exception [Labor Day is *always* the first Monday of September]

al·yce clover (al'is) [prob. < ModL. *Alysicarpus,* name of the genus (< Gr. *halysis,* chain + *-carpus,* -CARPOUS] a tropical annual legume (*Alysicarpus vaginalis*) sometimes used as a cover crop and for fodder

a·lys·sum (ə lis'əm) *n.* [ModL. < Gr. *alysson,* madwort < *alyssos,* curing madness < *a-,* without + *lyssa,* madness, rage] **1.** any plant of a genus (*Alyssum*) in the mustard family, with white or yellow flowers and grayish leaves **2.** *same as* SWEET ALYSSUM

am (am, em; *unstressed* əm) [OE. *eom, am,* akin to Sans. *asmi* < *as-,* is + *-mi,* first person pron.: see BE] *1st pers. sing., pres. indic., of* BE

Am *Chem.* americium

AM amplitude modulation

Am. 1. America **2.** American

A.M., AM [L. *Artium Magister*] master of arts

A.M., a.m., AM [L. *ante meridiem*] before noon: used to designate the time from midnight to noon

AMA, A.M.A. American Medical Association

am·a·da·vat (am'ə də vat') *n.* [Ind., after AHMADABAD, whence it was exported] a small bird (*Estrilda amandava*) of India, kept as a caged pet for its singing ability

Am·a·dis of Gaul (am'ə dis) [Sp. *Amadis,* lit., love of God] the title character of a medieval prose romance in Spanish

am·a·dou (am'ə dōō') *n.* [Fr. < ModPr. *amadú,* tinder, kindling < L. *amator,* lover] a spongy material made from certain fungi, as the agaric, and used as punk for lighting fires or, in medicine, to halt bleeding

A·ma·ga·sa·ki (ä'mä gä sä'kē) city on the S coast of Honshu, Japan, near Osaka: pop. 478,000

a·mah (ä'mə) *n.* [Anglo-Ind. < Port. *ama*] in the Orient, a woman servant, esp. one who serves as a baby's nurse

a·main (ə mān') *adv.* [A-¹, on + MAIN³] [Archaic or Poet.] **1.** forcefully; vigorously **2.** at or with great speed **3.** hastily; suddenly **4.** greatly

Am·a·lek (am'ə lek) *Bible* **1.** a grandson of Esau: Gen. 36:9-12 **2.** the descendants of Amalek, collectively: Ex. 17:8-16 —**Am'a·lek·ite'** (-lə kīt') *n.*

a·mal·gam (ə mal'gəm) *n.* [ME. < ML. *amalgama,* prob.

< Ar. *al malgham* < Gr. *malagma*, an emollient < *malassein*, to soften < IE. base **mel-*, to crush: see MILL] **1.** any alloy of mercury with another metal or other metals [silver *amalgam* is used as a dental filling] **2.** a combination or mixture; blend

a·mal·gam·a·ble (-gəm ə b'l) *adj.* that can be amalgamated

a·mal·ga·mate (-gə māt') *vt., vi.* -**mat'ed,** -**mat'ing 1.** to combine in an amalgam **2.** to join together into one; unite; combine [five companies were *amalgamated* into a corporation] —**a·mal'ga·mat'ive** *adj.*

a·mal·ga·ma·tion (ə mal'gə mā'shən) *n.* **1.** an amalgamating or being amalgamated **2.** the result of amalgamating; mixture, blend, merger, etc. **3.** *Metallurgy* the extraction of a precious metal from its ore by alloying it with mercury

a·mal·ga·mat·or (ə mal'gə māt'ər) *n.* **1.** a person or thing that amalgamates **2.** a machine for the amalgamation of silver, etc. from its ore

Am·al·thae·a, Am·al·the·a (am''l thē'ə) [L. < Gr. *Amaltheia*] *Gr. & Rom. Myth.* the goat that nursed Zeus (Jupiter): one of its horns was called the CORNUCOPIA

A·man·da (ə man'də) [L., lit., worthy to be loved < the gerund stem of *amare,* to love] a feminine name: dim. *Mandy*

am·a·ni·ta (am'ə nīt'ə) *n.* [< Gr. *amanitai,* pl., a kind of fungus] any of several very poisonous fungi (genus *Amanita*) with white spores: see FLY AGARIC

a·man·u·en·sis (ə man'yoo wen'sis) *n., pl.* -**ses** (-sēz) [L. < *a-* (*ab*), from + *manu,* abl. of *manus,* a hand + *-ensis,* relating to] an assistant who takes dictation or copies something already written; secretary: now a somewhat jocular usage

A·ma·pá (ä'mə pä') federal territory of N Brazil, on the Atlantic: c. 53,000 sq. mi.; pop. 69,000

am·a·ranth (am'ə ranth') *n.* [L. *amarantus* < Gr. *amarantos,* unfading < *a-,* not + *marainein,* to die away] **1.** any of a genus (*Amaranthus*) of plants of the amaranth family, usually with colorful leaves and, in some species, showy, tassellike heads of flowers, as the love-lies-bleeding, pigweed, tumbleweed, etc. **2.** [Poet.] an imaginary flower that never fades or dies **3.** a dark purplish red —*adj.* designating a family (Amaranthaceae) of plants including the amaranths and cockscombs

am·a·ran·thine (am'ə ran'thin) *adj.* **1.** of or like the amaranth **2.** unfading or undying **3.** dark purplish-red

am·a·relle (am'ə rel') *n.* [G. < ML. *amarellum,* dim. < L. *amarus,* sour, bitter < IE. **umros* < base **om-,* bitter, whence Sans. *amlá-,* sour, Du. *amper,* sharp, raw] a horticultural variety of the sour cherry, having a colorless juice

Am·a·ril·lo (am'ə ril'ō) [Sp., yellow; reason for the name unknown] city in NW Tex.: pop. 127,000

am·a·ryl·lis (am'ə ril'əs) *n.* [< L. & Gr. *Amaryllis,* a shepherdess' name in poems by Virgil and Theocritus] **1.** *a)* any of several plants (genus *Amaryllis*) of a family (Amaryllidaceae), bearing several white, purple, pink, or red lilylike flowers on a single stem, as the belladonna lily *b)* any of several plants of genera formerly grouped with or closely related to the amaryllis **2.** [A-] a shepherdess: a conventional name used in pastoral poetry

a·mass (ə mas') *vt.* [Fr. *amasser* < ML. *amassare* < *a-,* to + L. *massare,* to form a lump < L. *massa,* a lump or MASS] **1.** to pile up; collect together **2.** to accumulate (esp. wealth) —**a·mass'er** *n.* —**a·mass'ment** *n.*

am·a·teur (am'ə chər, -tər, -toor, -tyoor) *n.* [Fr. < L. *amator,* lover < *amare,* to love] **1.** a person who engages in some art, science, sport, etc. for the pleasure of it rather than for money; a nonprofessional; specif., an athlete who is variously forbidden by rule to profit from his athletic activity **2.** a person who does something without professional skill —*adj.* **1.** of or done by an amateur or amateurs **2.** being an amateur or made up of amateurs **3.** amateurish

SYN.—**amateur** refers to one who does something for the pleasure of it rather than for pay and often implies a relative lack of skill; a **dilettante** is an amateur in the arts, but the word is also applied disparagingly to a superficial dabbler in the arts; **novice** and **neophyte** refer to one who is a beginner, hence inexperienced, in some activity, **neophyte** carrying additional connotations of youthful enthusiasm; **tyro** refers to an inexperienced but selfassertive beginner and generally connotes incompetence —*ANT.* professional, expert

am·a·teur·ish (am'ə choor'ish, -toor'-, -tyoor'-) *adj.* like an amateur; inexpert; unskillful —**am'a·teur'ish·ly** *adv.* —**am'a·teur'ish·ness** *n.*

am·a·teur·ism (am'ə chər iz'm, -tər-, -toor-, -tyoor-) *n.* **1.** an amateurish method or quality **2.** the nonprofessional status of an amateur

A·ma·ti (ä mät'ē; *E.* ə mät'ē) **1.** It. family of violin-makers of Cremona, Italy (fl. 16th-17th cent.) **2.** Ni·co·lò (nē'kō-lō'), 1596-1684; violin-maker of this family; teacher of GUARNERI & STRADIVARI —*n.* a violin made by any member of the Amati family

am·a·tive (am'ə tiv) *adj.* [< ML. *amativus,* lovable < pp. of L. *amare,* to love] of or inclined to love, esp. sexual love —**am'a·tive·ly** *adv.* —**am'a·tive·ness** *n.*

am·a·tol (am'ə tôl', -täl') *n.* [< AM(MONIUM) + TOL-(UENE)] a powerful explosive made up of ammonium nitrate and trinitrotoluene (TNT)

am·a·to·ry (am'ə tôr'ē) *adj.* [L. *amatorius* < *amator,* lover < pp. of *amare,* to love] of, causing, or showing love, esp. sexual love

am·au·ro·sis (am'ô rō'sis) *n.* [ModL. < Gr. *amaurōsis* < *amauros,* dark < *a-,* intens. + *mauros,* dark] partial or total blindness —**am'au·rot'ic** (-rät'ik) *adj.*

a·maze (ə māz') *vt.* **a·mazed', a·maz'ing** [ME. (only in pp. *amased*) < OE. *amasian:* see MAZE] **1.** to fill with great surprise or sudden wonder; astonish **2.** [Obs.] to bewilder —*n.* [Poet.] amazement —*SYN.* see SURPRISE —**a·maz'-ed·ly** (-id lē) *adv.* —**a·maz'ing** *adj.* —**a·maz'ing·ly** *adv.*

a·maze·ment (-mənt) *n.* **1.** an amazed condition; great wonder; astonishment **2.** [Obs.] bewilderment

Am·a·zon (am'ə zän', -zən) [so named by Spaniards, who believed its shores inhabited by female warriors: see *n.* below] river in S. America, flowing from the Andes in Peru across N Brazil into the Atlantic: c. 3,300 mi. —*n.* [L. < Gr. *Amazōn,* of unknown origin, but derived by folk etym. < *a-,* without + *mazos,* breast, hence the story that the Amazons cut off one breast to facilitate archery] **1.** *Gr. Myth.* any of a race of female warriors supposed to have lived in Scythia, near the Black Sea **2.** [a-] a large, strong, masculine woman **3.** a small, greenish parrot (genus *Amazona*) of Central and South America, often kept as a pet **4.** a species of ant (genus *Polyergus*) that makes slaves of other ants: also **Amazon ant**

A·ma·zo·nas (ä'mə zō'näs) state of NW Brazil: c. 615,000 sq. mi.; pop. 722,000; cap. Manaus

Am·a·zo·ni·an (am'ə zō'nē ən) *adj.* **1.** of, like, or characteristic of an Amazon **2.** [*often* a-] warlike and masculine: said of a woman **3.** of the Amazon River or the country around it

am·a·zon·ite (am'ə zə nīt') *n.* [after the AMAZON River] a green kind of microcline, often cut and polished for use as a gem: also called **Amazon stone**

Amb. Ambassador

am·bage (am'bij) *n., pl.* -**bag·es** (-bij iz; am bā'jēz) [ME. & OFr. *ambages* < L. < *amb-,* around + *agere,* to go] [Archaic] **1.** a winding pathway: *usually used in pl.* **2.** [*pl.*] a roundabout, indirect way of talking or doing things —**am·ba'gious** (-bā'jəs) *adj.*

Am·ba·la (əm bä'lä) city in N India, in Punjab state: pop. 106,000

am·ba·ry, am·ba·ri (am bä'rē) *n.* [Hind. *ambārī*] same as KENAF

am·bas·sa·dor (am bas'ə dər, ə m-) *n.* [ME. *ambassatour* < MFr. *ambassateur* < OIt. *ambasciatore* < Pr. *ambais-sador* < **ambaissa,* mission, task < Goth. *andbahti,* office, service < Celt. **amb(i)actos,* a messenger, servant (whence L. *ambactus,* a vassal) < IE. **ambhi-,* about (cf. AMBI-) + base **ag̑-,* to move (cf. ACT)] **1.** the highest-ranking diplomatic representative appointed by one country or government to represent it in another **2.** a special representative: an ☆**ambassador-at-large** is one accredited to no particular country; an **ambassador extraordinary** is one on a special diplomatic mission; an **ambassador plenipotentiary** is one having the power to make treaties **3.** an official messenger or agent with a special mission —**am·bas·sa·do'ri·al** (-dôr'ē əl) *adj.* —**am·bas'sa·dor·ship'** *n.*

am·bas·sa·dress (-ə dris) *n.* [Now Rare] **1.** a woman ambassador **2.** the wife of an ambassador

am·ber (am'bər) *n.* [ME. *aumbre,* amber, ambergris < OFr. *ambre* < Ar. *'anbar,* ambergris] **1.** a yellow or brownish-yellow translucent fossil resin found along some seacoasts and used in jewelry, pipestems, etc.: it is hard, easily polished, and quickly electrified by friction **2.** the color of amber —*adj.* **1.** made of or like amber **2.** having the color of amber

am·ber·gris (-grēs', -gris') *n.* [ME. *ambregris* < OFr. *ambre gris* < *ambre* (see AMBER) + *gris* < Frank. **grīs,* akin to MHG., OS., Du. *gris,* gray] a grayish, waxy substance from the intestinal canal of sperm whales, often found floating in tropical seas: it is used in some perfumes

☆**am·ber·jack** (am'bər jak') *n.* [AMBER + JACK[1] (fish): from its color] any of several large food and game fishes (genus *Seriola*) found in the Mediterranean and in warm waters of the Atlantic

Am·ber·lite (am'bər līt') [AMBER + -LITE] *a trademark for* various insoluble cross-linked polymers used in commercial processes and in pharmacy

am·ber·oid (-oid') *n.* a material made to resemble amber, formed of small pieces of amber or some other resin pressed together under high temperature

am·bi- (am'bə, -bi) [L., akin to Gr. *amphi* < IE. base **ambhi-,* around, var. *ambho(u)-,* whence BOTH: cf. EMBASSY] *a combining form meaning* both [ambidextrous]

am·bi·ance (am'bē əns; *Fr.* än byäns') *n.* [Fr.: see AMBIENT] an environment or its distinct atmosphere; milieu: also **am'bi·ence** (-əns)

am·bi·dex·ter (am'bə dek'stər) *adj.* [ML. < L. *ambi-* (see AMBI-) + *dexter,* right hand] [Archaic] same as AMBIDEX-TROUS —*n.* [Archaic] an ambidextrous person

am·bi·dex·trous (-dek'strəs) *adj.* [< AMBIDEXTER + -OUS] **1.** able to use both hands with equal ease **2.** very skillful or versatile **3.** deceitful; double-dealing —**am'bi·dex·ter'i·ty** (-dek ster'ə tē) *n.* —**am'bi·dex'trous·ly** *adv.*

am·bi·ent (am'bē ənt) *adj.* [L. *ambiens,* prp. of *ambire,* to go around < *ambi-,* around + *ire,* to go] surrounding; on all sides

am·bi·gu·i·ty (am'bə gyoo'ə tē) *n.* [ME. *ambiguite* < L.

ambiguitas] **1.** the quality or state of being ambiguous **2.** *pl.* **-ties** an ambiguous word, statement, etc.
am·big·u·ous (am big′yoo wəs) *adj.* [L. *ambiguus* < *ambigere*, to wander < *ambi-*, about, around + *agere*, to do, ACT] **1.** having two or more possible meanings **2.** not clear; indefinite; uncertain; vague —*SYN.* see OBSCURE —**am·big′u·ous·ly** *adv.* —**am·big′u·ous·ness** *n.*
am·bit (am′bit) *n.* [L. *ambitus*, a going about, revolution < pp. of *ambire*: see AMBIENT] **1.** a circuit or circumference **2.** the limits or scope; bounds
am·bi·tend·en·cy (am′bə tend′ən sē) *n.* *Psychol.* the existence of conflicting tendencies in an individual
am·bi·tion (am bi′shən) *n.* [ME. < OFr. < L. *ambitio*, a going around (to solicit votes) < pp. of *ambire*: see AMBIENT] **1.** a strong desire to gain a particular objective; specif., the drive to succeed, or to gain fame, power, wealth, etc. **2.** the objective strongly desired —*vt.* [Rare] to be ambitious for
am·bi·tious (-shəs) *adj.* [ME. *ambicious* < L. *ambitiosus*, seeking favor < *ambitio*: see prec.] **1.** full of or showing ambition **2.** greatly desirous (*of* something); eager for **3.** demanding great effort, skill, enterprise, etc. [an *ambitious* undertaking] —**am·bi′tious·ly** *adv.*
SYN.—**ambitious** implies a striving for advancement, wealth, fame, etc., and is used with both favorable and unfavorable connotations; **aspiring** suggests a striving to reach some lofty end regarded as somewhat beyond one's normal expectations [an *aspiring* young poet]; **enterprising** implies an energetic readiness to take risks or undertake new projects in order to succeed; **emulous** suggests ambition characterized by a competitive desire to equal or surpass another
am·biv·a·lence (am biv′ə ləns) *n.* [AMBI- + VALENCE] simultaneous conflicting feelings toward a person or thing, as love and hate —**am·biv′a·lent** *adj.* —**am·biv′a·lent·ly** *adv.*
am·bi·ver·sion (am′bi vur′zhən) *n.* [AMBI- + (INTRO)VERSION] *Psychol.* a condition or character trait that includes elements of both introversion and extroversion —**am′bi·vert** *n.*
am·ble (am′b'l) *vi.* **-bled, -bling** [ME. *amblen* < OFr. *ambler* < L. *ambulare*, to walk] **1.** to move at a smooth, easy gait by raising first both legs on one side, then both on the other: said of a horse, etc. **2.** to go easily and unhurriedly; walk in a leisurely manner —*n.* **1.** a horse's ambling gait **2.** a leisurely walking pace —**am′bler** (-blər) *n.*
am·blyg·o·nite (am blig′ə nīt′) *n.* [G. *amblygonit* < Gr. *amblygōnios*, obtuse-angled < *amblys*, dull + *gōnia*, an angle + *-it*, -ITE[1]] a pale-green or white crystalline mineral, Li(AlF)PO4: it is an ore of lithium and occurs in pegmatitic rocks
am·bly·o·pi·a (am′blē ōp′ē ə) *n.* [ModL. < Gr. *amblys*, dull + *ōps*, EYE] a loss in sharpness of vision, esp. when not traceable to any intrinsic eye disease —**am′bly·o′pic** (-ō′pik, -äp′ik) *adj.*
am·bo (am′bō) *n., pl.* **am′bos, am·bo·nes** (am bō′nēz) [ML. < Gr. *ambōn*] a pulpit or raised reading stand in early Christian churches
am·bo·cep·tor (am′bō sep′tər, -bō-) *n.* [L. *ambo*, both + (RE)CEPTOR] *Bacteriology* an antibody able to damage or destroy a microorganism or other cell by connecting complement to it
Am·boi·na (am boi′nə) **1.** one of the Molucca Islands, southwest of Ceram, in Indonesia: 314 sq. mi. **2.** its capital, a naval base: pop. 55,000
Amboina (wood) the mottled, curled wood of an Asiatic tree (*Pterocarpus indicus*), used in making furniture: also sp. **Am·boy′na (wood)**
Am·boise (än bwäz′) town in WC France, near Tours: pop. 6,000: site of the royal residence, 1483-1560
am·broid (am′broid) *n.* same as AMBEROID
Am·brose (am′brōz) [L. *Ambrosius* < Gr. *ambrosios*: see AMBROSIA] **1.** a masculine name **2.** Saint, 340?-397 A.D.; Bishop of Milan: his day is Dec. 7 —**Am·bro·si·an** (am brō′zhē ən) *adj.*
am·bro·sia (am brō′zhə, -zhē ə) *n.* [L. < Gr. < *ambrotos*, immortal < *a-*, not + *brotos*, mortal < **mrotos* < IE. base **mer-*, to die, **mr-to*, dead: cf. MORTAL] **1.** *Gr. & Rom. Myth.* the food of the gods and immortals **2.** anything that tastes or smells delicious **3.** any of a genus (*Ambrosia*) of plants of the ragweed family
am·bro·sial (am brō′zhəl, -zhē əl) *adj.* **1.** of or fit for the gods; divine **2.** like ambrosia; delicious; fragrant Also **am·bro′sian** (-zhən)
Ambrosian chant a type of liturgical chant introduced by Saint Ambrose, characterized by a greater ornamentation of melody than in the Gregorian chant, which superseded it
☆**am·bro·type** (am′brə tip′, -brō-) *n.* [< Gr. *ambrotos*, immortal (see AMBROSIA) + -TYPE] an early kind of photograph, consisting of a glass negative backed by a dark surface so as to appear positive
am·bry (am′brē) *n., pl.* **-bries** [ME. *almerie* < OFr. *armarie* < L. *armarium*, chest for tools or arms < *arma*, weapons] [Archaic] a cupboard, locker, or pantry
ambs·ace (āmz′ās′, amz′-) *n.* [ME. *ambesas* < OFr. *ambes as* < L. *ambas as* < *ambas*, both + *as*: see AMBI- + ACE]

[Now Rare] **1.** double aces, the lowest throw at dice **2.** bad luck **3.** the most worthless or least thing possible
am·bu·la·crum (am′byoo lā′krəm) *n., pl.* **-cra** (-krə) [ModL. < L., tree-lined walk < *ambulare*, to walk] in echinoderms (starfishes, sea urchins, etc.), that part of a radiating limb containing a double row of perforated plates through which the tube feet extend —**am′bu·la′cral** *adj.*
am·bu·lance (am′byə ləns) *n.* [Fr. < (*hôpital*) *ambulant* < prp. of L. *ambulare*, to walk] **1.** orig., a mobile field hospital **2.** a specially equipped automobile or other vehicle for carrying the sick or wounded
☆**am·bu·lance-chas·er** (-chās′ər) *n.* [Slang] a lawyer who encourages victims of accidents to sue for damages as his clients
am·bu·lant (am′byə lənt) *adj.* [< L. *ambulans*, prp. of *ambulare*, to walk] moving about; walking
am·bu·late (-lāt′) *vi.* **-lat′ed, -lat′ing** [< L. *ambulatus*, pp. of *ambulare*, to walk] to move about; walk —**am′bu·la′tion** *n.*
am·bu·la·to·ry (-lə tôr′ē) *adj.* [L. *ambulatorius* < *ambulare*, to walk] **1.** of or for walking **2.** able to walk and not confined to bed [an *ambulatory* patient] **3.** moving from one place to another; movable **4.** *Law* that can be changed or revoked [an *ambulatory* will] —*n., pl.* **-ries** any covered or sheltered place for walking, as in a cloister —*SYN.* see ITINERANT
am·bus·cade (am′bəs kād′; *also, for n.,* am′bəs kād′) *n., vi.* **-cad′ed, -cad′ing** [Fr. *embuscade* < *embusquer*, to ambush, altered (after It. *imboscare*) < OFr. *embuschier*: see AMBUSH] *same as* AMBUSH —**am′bus·cad′er** *n.*
am·bush (am′boosh) *n.* [OFr. *embusche* < *embuschier*: see the *v.*] **1.** an arrangement of persons in hiding to make a surprise attack **2.** *a)* the persons in hiding *b)* their place of hiding **3.** the act of so lying in wait to attack —*vt., vi.* [ME. *embusshen* < OFr. *embuschier*, to lay an ambush < ML. *imboscare*, to set an ambush < *in-* + *boscus*, woods < Frank. *busk*, akin to BUSH[1]] **1.** to hide in ambush **2.** to attack from ambush —**am′bush·ment** *n.*
A.M.D.G. [L. *ad majorem Dei gloriam*] to the greater glory of God: Jesuit motto
A.M.E. African Methodist Episcopal (church)
a·me·ba (ə mē′bə) *n., pl.* **-bas, -bae** (-bē) *same as* AMOEBA —**a·me′bic, a·me′ban** *adj.* —**a·me′boid** *adj.*
am·e·bi·a·sis (am′i bī′ə sis) *n.* [ModL. *amoebiasis*: see AMOEBA & -IASIS] infestation with amoebas, esp. with a protozoan (*Endamoeba histolytica*) parasitic in the intestines
amebic dysentery a form of dysentery caused by an amoeba (*Endamoeba histolytica*)
a·me·bo·cyte (ə mē′bə sīt′) *n.* same as AMOEBOCYTE
a·meer (ə mir′) *n.* same as AMIR
A·me·lia (ə mēl′yə, -ē ə) [of Gmc. origin; lit., prob. diligent < base of *amal*, work] a feminine name
a·mel·io·rant (ə mēl′yər ənt) *n.* a thing that ameliorates
a·mel·io·rate (ə mēl′yə rāt′) *vt., vi.* **-rat′ed, -rat′ing** [< Fr. *améliorer* < OFr. *ameillorer* < *a-*, to + *meillor* < L. *melior*, better] to make or become better; improve —*SYN.* see IMPROVE —**a·mel′io·ra·ble** (-yər ə b'l) *adj.* —**a·mel′io·ra′tion** (-yə rā′shən) *n.* —**a·mel′io·ra·tive** (-yə rāt′iv, -yər ə tiv) *adj.* —**a·mel′io·rat′or** (-yə rāt′ər) *n.*
A·men (ä′mən) *same as* AMON
a·men (ā′men′, ä′-) *interj.* [ME. & OE. < L. < Gr. < Heb. *āmēn*, truly, certainly] may it be so! so it is!: used after a prayer or to express approval —*adv.* [Archaic] verily —*n.* a speaking or writing of "amen"
a·me·na·ble (ə mē′nə b'l, -men′ə-) *adj.* [Anglo-Fr. < OFr. *amener*, to bring about, lead in < *a-*, to + *mener*, to lead < L. *minare*, to drive (animals) < *minari*, to threaten: see MENACE] **1.** responsible or answerable **2.** able to be controlled or influenced; responsive; submissive [a person *amenable* to suggestion; an illness *amenable* to treatment] **3.** that can be tested by (with *to*) [*amenable* to the laws of physics] —*SYN.* see OBEDIENT —**a·me′na·bil′i·ty** (-bil′ə tē) *n.* —**a·me′na·bly** *adv.*
amen corner ☆in some rural Protestant churches, the seats to the minister's right, once occupied by those leading the responsive amens
a·mend (ə mend′) *vt.* [ME. *amenden* < OFr. *amender* < L. *emendare*, to correct: see EMEND] **1.** to make better; improve **2.** to remove the faults of; correct; emend **3.** to change or revise (a legislative bill, law, constitution, etc.) —*vi.* to improve one's conduct —**a·mend′a·ble** *adj.* —**a·mend′er** *n.*
☆**a·mend·a·to·ry** (ə men′də tôr′ē) *adj.* tending or serving to amend; corrective
a·mend·ment (ə mend′mənt) *n.* [ME. < OFr. *amendement* < *amender*, AMEND] **1.** a change for the better; improvement **2.** a correction of errors, faults, etc. **3.** *a)* a revision or addition proposed or made in a bill, law, constitution, etc. *b)* the process of making such changes
a·mends (ə mendz′) *n.pl.* [ME. < OFr., pl. of *amende*, a fine: see AMEND] [*sometimes with sing. v.*] something given or done to make up for injury, loss, etc. that one has caused [to make *amends* for rudeness]
A·men·ho·tep (ä′mən hō′tep) any of four pharaohs of

Egypt who ruled during the 16th, 15th, & 14th cent. B.C.,
esp. *a*) **Amenhotep III** (reigned 1411?–1375? B.C.) *b*)
Amenhotep IV *same as* IKHNATON Also **A·men·o·phis**
(am'ə nō'fis)

a·men·i·ty (ə men'ə tē, -mē'nə-) *n.*, *pl.* **-ties** [ME. & OFr.
amenite < L. *amoenitas* < *amoenus*, pleasant] **1.** pleasant
quality; attractiveness **2.** *a*) an attractive or desirable
feature, as of a place, climate, etc. *b*) anything that adds
to one's comfort; convenience **3.** [*pl.*] the courteous acts
and pleasant manners of polite social behavior

a·men·or·rhe·a, a·men·or·rhoe·a (ā men'ə rē'ə) *n.*
[ModL. < Gr. *a-*, not + *mēn*, month + *rheein*, to flow]
abnormal absence or suppression of menstruation

A·men-Ra (ä'mən rä') *same as* AMON-RE

am·ent[1] (am'ənt, ā'mənt) *n.* [< L. *amentum*, thong, strap]
a tasselike spike of small, closely clustered, unisexual
flowers lacking petals and sepals, as on a willow, birch,
or poplar

a·ment[2] (ā'ment, -mənt) *n.* [back-formation < AMENTIA] a
person with a severe congenital mental deficiency; feeble-
minded person

am·en·ta·ceous (am'ən tā'shəs) *adj.* [AMENT[1] + -ACEOUS]
Bot. **1.** of or like an ament or aments **2.** amentiferous

a·men·tia (ā men'shə, ə) *n.* [L., madness < *amens*, senseless < *a-* (*ab*), away, from + *mens*, mind] a severe congenital mental deficiency; feeble-mindedness: cf. DEMENTIA

am·en·tif·er·ous (am'ən tif'ər əs) *adj.* [< AMENT[1] +
-FEROUS] *Bot.* bearing aments

a·merce (ə murs') *vt.* **a·merced', a·merc'ing** [ME. *amercen*
< Anglo-Fr. *amercier* < OFr. *a merci*, at the mercy of]
1. to punish by imposing an arbitrarily determined fine
2. to punish generally —**a·merce'ment** *n.*

A·mer·i·ca (ə mer'ə kə) [ModL., name associated in 1507 by
Martin Waldseemüller (1470?–1522?), Ger. cosmographer,
with *Americus* Vespuccius, Latinized form of *Amerigo*
VESPUCCI, but < ? Sp. *Amerrique*, name of a mountain
range in Nicaragua, used by early explorers for the newly
discovered lands < AmInd. (? Carib) *Americ*] **1.** North
America and South America considered together **2.**
North America **3.** South America ☆**4.** the United States of
America —**the Americas** America (*entry*)

A·mer·i·can (ə mer'ə kən) *adj.* **1.** of or in America ☆**2.** of,
in, or characteristic of the U.S., its people, etc. [the
American language] —*n.* **1.** a native or inhabitant of
America; specif., *a*) an American Indian ☆*b*) a citizen of
the U.S. ☆**2.** the English language as spoken in the U.S.

☆**A·mer·i·ca·na** (ə mer'ə kan'ə, -kä'nə) *n.pl.* [AMERIC(A)
+ -ANA] books, papers, objects, facts, etc. having to do
with America, its people, and its history

☆**American aloe** *same as* CENTURY PLANT

☆**American Beauty** a variety of hybrid, perennial red rose

☆**American chameleon** a common arboreal lizard of the
SE U.S., Cuba, and Mexico: see CHAMELEON (sense 2)

☆**American cheese** a kind of fairly hard, mild Cheddar
cheese, popular in the U.S.

American dialects regional varieties of spoken American
English identified by differences in syntax, vocabulary,
and pronunciation: principal dialect areas are now generally distinguished as Northern, Midland, and Southern

American eagle the bald eagle of N.America, shown on
the coat of arms of the U.S.

American English the English language as spoken and
written in the U.S.; American

American Expeditionary Forces the U.S. troops in
Europe during World War I

American Federation of Labor a federation of labor
unions of the U.S. and Canada, founded in 1881: merged
with the Congress of Industrial Organizations in 1955

American Indian *same as* INDIAN (*n.* 2)

☆**A·mer·i·can·ism** (ə mer'ə kən iz'm) *n.* **1.** a custom,
characteristic, or belief of or originating in the U.S. **2.** a
word, phrase, or usage originating in or peculiar to American English **3.** devotion or loyalty to the U.S., or to its
traditions, customs, institutions, etc.

A·mer·i·can·ist (-ist) *n.* **1.** a student of America, its
history, geology, etc. **2.** an anthropologist specializing in
the study of American Indians and their cultures

☆**American ivy** *same as* VIRGINIA CREEPER

☆**A·mer·i·can·ize** (ə mer'ə kə nīz') *vt.*, *vi.* **-ized', -iz'ing** to
make or become American in character, manners, methods,
ideals, etc.; assimilate to U.S. customs, speech, etc.
—**A·mer'i·can·i·za'tion** (ə mer'ə kə nī zā'shən) *n.*

American Legion an organization of veterans of the
armed forces of the U.S., founded in 1919

☆**American plan** a system of hotel operation in which the
price charged to guests covers room, service, and meals:
distinguished from EUROPEAN PLAN

American Revolution 1. a sequence of actions by American colonists from 1763 to 1783 protesting British domination and culminating in the Revolutionary War **2.** the
Revolutionary War (1775–83), fought by the American
colonies to gain independence from England

American Samoa possession of the U.S. since 1899, consisting of seven islands in the S Pacific, north of Tonga:
76 sq. mi.; pop. 28,000; cap. Pago Pago on Tutuila Island

American screw gauge a standard gauge for checking the
diameter of wood screws and machine screws

American Standard Version a revision of the King James
Version of the Bible, published in 1901: issued by members

of the American committee who had helped produce the
Revised Version (1881, 1885) in England

☆**American widgeon** *same as* BALDPATE

☆**am·er·ic·i·um** (am'ə rish'ē əm, -ris'-) *n.* [ModL. <
AMERIC(A) + -IUM] a chemical element, one of the transuranic elements produced by the beta decay of an isotope of plutonium: symbol, Am; at. wt., 243.13; at. no.,
95; sp. gr., 13.67; melt. pt., 995°C; boil. pt., 2607°C (est.)

☆**Am·er·ind** (am'ə rind') *n.* [AMER(ICAN) + IND(IAN)] an
American Indian or Eskimo —**Am'er·in'di·an** *adj.*, *n.*
—**Am'er·in'dic** *adj.*

A·mers·foort (ä'mərs fōrt') city in C Netherlands: pop.
74,000

Ames (āmz) [after Oakes *Ames*, railroad official] city in C
Iowa, north of Des Moines: pop. 40,000

ames·ace (āmz'ās') *n. same as* AMBSACE

am·e·thyst (am'ə thist) *n.* [ME. *ametist* < OFr. *ametiste* <
L. *amethystus* < Gr. *amethystos*, not drunken (the Greeks
believed that the amethyst prevented intoxication) < *a-*,
not + *methystos*, drunken < *methyein*, to be drunken <
methy, strong drink < IE. **medhu-*, honey, MEAD[1]] **1.** a
purple or violet variety of quartz, used in jewelry **2.**
popularly, a purple variety of corundum, used in jewelry
3. purple or violet —**am'e·thys'tine** (-this'tin, -tēn) *adj.*

am·e·tro·pi·a (am'ə trōp'ē ə) *n.* [ModL. < Gr. *ametros*,
disproportionate + -OPIA] any condition of imperfect
refraction of the eye, as nearsightedness, farsightedness, or
astigmatism —**am'e·tro'pic** (-trōp'ik, -träp'ik) *adj.*

☆**Am·ex** (am'eks) *n.* the American Stock Exchange

Am·for·tas (äm fôr'təs) [MHG. *Anfortas*] *Medieval Legend*
the leader of the knights of the Holy Grail: cf. PARSIFAL

AMG Allied Military Government

Am·ha·ra (äm hä'rä) province of NW Ethiopia, formerly
a kingdom

Am·har·ic (am har'ik, äm här'-) *n.* the Semitic language
used officially in Ethiopia, a subfamily of the Afro-Asiatic
family of languages

Am·herst (am'ərst), Baron **Jeffrey** 1717–97; Eng. general;
led Brit. forces that won control of Canada

†**a·mi** (à mē') *n.*, *pl.* **a·mis'** (-mē') [Fr.] a (man or boy)
friend

a·mi·a·ble (ā'mē ə b'l, ām'yə-) *adj.* [ME. < OFr. < LL.
amicabilis, friendly < L. *amicus*, friend: confused with OFr.
amable < L. *amabilis*, worthy of love; both from L.
amare, to love] **1.** having a pleasant and friendly disposition; good-natured **2.** [Obs.] lovely or lovable —**a'mi·a·
bil'i·ty** (-bil'ə tē) *n.* —**a'mi·a·bly** *adv.*
SYN.—**amiable** and **affable** suggest qualities of friendliness, easy
temper, etc. that make one likable, **affable** also implying a readiness to be approached, to converse, etc.; a **good-natured** person
is one who is disposed to like as well as be liked and is sometimes
easily imposed on; **obliging** implies a ready, often cheerful, desire
to be helpful [the *obliging* clerk took my order]; **genial** suggests
good cheer and sociability [our *genial* host]; **cordial** suggests
graciousness and warmth [a *cordial* greeting] —*ANT.* surly,
ill-natured

am·i·an·thus (am'ē an'thəs) *n.* [altered, after ANTHO- <
L. *amiantus*, asbestos < Gr. *amiantos* (*lithos*), lit., unspotted
(stone) < *a-*, not + *miainein*, to stain or spot] a kind of
asbestos with long, silky fibers

am·i·ca·ble (am'i kə b'l) *adj.* [LL. *amicabilis*: see AMIABLE]
friendly in feeling; showing good will; peaceable [an
amicable discussion] —**am'i·ca·bil'i·ty** (-bil'ə tē) *n.* —
am'i·ca·bly *adv.*

am·ice (am'is) *n.* [ME. < OFr. *amit* < L. *amictus*, a cloak;
confused with OFr. *aumuce* < ML. *almutia*: see ALMUCE]
1. an oblong white linen cloth worn about the neck and
shoulders by a priest at Mass **2.** an almuce

a·mi·cus cu·ri·ae (ə mī'kəs kyoor'i ē', ə mē'kəs kyoor'ē ī')
[L., friend of the court] *Law* a person who offers, or is called
in, to advise a court on some legal matter

a·mid (ə mid') *prep.* [ME. *amidde* < *on middan* < *on*, at +
middan, middle] in the middle of; among

am·ide (am'id, -id) *n.* [AM(MONIA) + -IDE] **1.** any of a
group of organic compounds containing the CO·NH₂
radical (e.g., acetamide) or an acid radical in place of one
hydrogen atom of an ammonia molecule (e.g., sulfanilamide) **2.** any of the ammono bases in which one hydrogen
atom of the ammonia molecule is replaced by a metal (e.g.,
sodamide) —**a·mid·ic** (ə mid'ik) *adj.*

am·i·din (am'ə din) *n.* [Fr. *amid(on)* < L. *amylum*, starch
+ -IN] *Chem.* a transparent, water-soluble substance made
by heating starch in water

am·i·dine (am'ə dēn') *n.* [AMID(E) + -INE⁴] any nitrogen
base having the general formula $RC(:NH)NH_2$; these bases
are crystalline solids soluble in alcohol and ether

a·mi·do (ə mē'dō, am'ə dō') *adj.* of an amide or amides

a·mi·do- (ə mē'dō, am'ə dō') [< AMIDE] *a combining form
meaning* having one hydrogen atom in the ammonia
molecule replaced by an acid radical

a·mi·do·gen (ə mē'də jən, ə mid'ə jən) *n.* [AMIDO- + -GEN]
the hypothetical monovalent radical NH₂

am·i·dol (am'ə dōl', -dôl') *n.* [AMID(O)- + (PHEN)OL] a
colorless crystalline compound, $C_6H_8ON_2 \cdot HCl$, used as a
developer in photography

☆**am·i·done** (am'ə dōn') *n.* [G. *amidon* < (dimethyl)ami-
(no)- + d(iphenyl) + (heptan)one] *same as* METHADONE

a·mid·ships (ə mid'ships') *adv.* in or toward the middle of
a ship; midway between bow and stern: also **a·mid'ship'**

a·midst (ə midst′) *prep.* [ME. *amidde*, with adv. gen. *-s* + unhistoric *-t*] *same as* AMID

‡a·mie (à mē′) *n., pl.* **a·mies′** (-mē′) [Fr., fem. of *ami*] a (woman or girl) friend

A·miel (à myel′), **Hen·ri Fré·dé·ric** (än rē′ frā dā rēk′) 1821–81; Swiss writer & philosopher

Am·i·ens (à myan*t*; *E.* am′ē ənz) city in N France, on the Somme River: pop. 105,000

☆**a·mi·go** (ə mē′gō; *Sp.* ä mē′gð) *n., pl.* **-gos** (-gōz; *Sp.* -gôs) [Sp. < L. *amicus:* see AMIABLE] a friend

a·mine (ə mēn′; am′ēn, -in) *n.* [AM(MONIA) + -INE⁴] *Chem.* a derivative of ammonia in which hydrogen atoms have been replaced by radicals containing hydrogen and carbon atoms (e.g., methylamine, CH_3NH_2) —**a·mi′nic** (-mē′nik, -min′ik) *adj.*

a·mi·no (ə mē′nō, am′ə nō′) *adj.* of or containing the NH_2 radical in combination with certain organic radicals

a·mi·no- (ə mē′nō, am′ə nō′) [< AMINE] *a combining form meaning* having one hydrogen atom in the ammonia molecule replaced by an alkyl or other nonacid radical

amino acids 1. a group of nitrogenous organic compounds that serve as units of structure of the proteins and are essential to human metabolism **2.** chemical compounds in which a hydrogen atom in the alkyl group attached to the COOH (carboxyl) group of an organic acid is replaced by an NH_2 group

a·mi·no·ben·zo·ic acid (ə mē′nō ben zō′ik, am′ə nō′-) any of several crystalline substances with the same formula, NH_2C_6COOH, used in the manufacture of dyes, drugs, etc.: see also PARA-AMINOBENZOIC ACID

a·mi·no·phe·nol (-fē′nōl) *n.* any of several white or light-red crystalline compounds, $NH_2C_6H_4OH$, esp. such a compound (*p-* **aminophenol**) used in making dyes and as a photographic developer

a·mi·no·py·rine (ə mē′nō pī′rēn, am′ə nō-) *n.* [< (*dimethyl*)-*amine* + (ANTI)PYRINE] a colorless, crystalline powder, $C_{13}H_{17}N_3O$, sometimes used to reduce fever or pain

amino resin a thermosetting resinous product made by condensation of a compound containing an amine (e.g., melamine or urea) with an aldehyde (e.g., formaldehyde): also called **amino plastic**

a·mi·no·tri·a·zole (-trī′ə zōl′) *n.* [AMINO- + TRIAZOLE] a white, crystalline, soluble powder, $C_2H_5N_4$, used for killing weeds or other undesired vegetation

a·mir (ə mir′) *n.* [Ar. *amîr*] in certain Moslem countries, a ruler, prince, or commander: see also EMIR

☆**Am·ish** (ä′mish, am′ish) *n.pl.* [after Jacob *Ammann* (or *Amen*), the founder] Mennonites of a strict sect founded in the 17th cent. —*adj.* designating or of this sect

a·miss (ə mis′) *adv.* [ME. *amis, on-mis:* scc A-¹ + MISS¹] in a wrong way; astray, wrongly, faultily, improperly, etc. —*adj.* wrong, faulty, improper: used only in the predicate

a·mi·to·sis (ā′mi tō′sis, am′ə-) *n.* [A-², not + MITOSIS] *Biol.* cell division in which the nucleus and cytoplasm divide by simple constriction and without halving of chromosomes; direct cell division: opposed to MITOSIS —**am′i·tot′ic** (-tät′ik) *adj.* —**am′i·tot′i·cal·ly** *adv.*

am·i·trol (am′ə trōl′) *n.* [AMI(NO)- + TR(IAZ)OL(E)] *same as* AMINOTRIAZOLE: also **am′i·trole′** (-trōl′)

a·mi·ty (am′ə tē) *n., pl.* **-ties** [ME. *amite* < OFr. *amistie* < VL. **amicitas* < L. *amicus*, friend < *amare*, to love] friendly, peaceful relations, as between nations or groups; friendship

Am·man (äm′än) capital of Jordan, in the NW part: pop. 296,000: site of the Biblical city *Rabbah*

am·me·ter (am′mēt′ər) *n.* [AM(PERE) + -METER] an instrument for measuring the strength of an electric current in terms of amperes

am·mine (am′ēn, -in) *n.* [AMM(ONIA) + -INE⁴] *Chem.* **1.** a molecule of ammonia (NH_3) as found in certain complex compounds **2.** any of the complex compounds containing this molecule

am·mi·no- (ə mē′nō, am′ə nō′) *a combining form meaning* containing one or more ammines

am·mo (am′ō) *n.* [Slang] ammunition

Am·mon¹ (am′ən) [L. < Fr. *Ammōn* < Egypt. *Åmen*] Amon, the ancient Egyptian god: identified by the Greeks (and Romans) with Zeus (and Jupiter)

Am·mon² (am′ən) [Heb. *'ammōn*, lit., prob. populous] *Bible* **1.** a son of Lot: Gen. 19:38 **2.** an ancient kingdom east and north of the Dead Sea —**Am′mo·nite′** (-ə nīt′) *n., adj.*

am·mo·nia (ə mōn′yə) *n.* [< (SAL) AMMONIAC] **1.** a colorless, pungent gas, NH_3, composed of nitrogen and hydrogen: its compounds are used as fertilizers, in medicine, etc. **2.** a water solution of this gas: in full, **ammonia water**

am·mo·ni·ac (ə mō′nē ak′) *n.* [ME. *ammoniak* < ML. *armoniac* < L. *ammoniacum* < Gr. *ammōniakon*, gum resin from a plant said to grow near the temple of Jupiter AMMON¹ in Libya] a pungent gum resin obtained from the stems of a plant (*Dorema ammoniacum*) of the parsley family, found in Iran, S Siberia, and N India: used in perfumes, porcelain cements, and formerly in medicine

am·mo·ni·a·cal (am′ə nī′ə k′l) *adj.* of, like, or containing ammonia

am·mo·ni·ate (ə mō′nē āt′; *for n.* -it) *vt.* **-at′ed, -at′-ing** to mix or combine with ammonia —*n.* any of several compounds containing ammonia —**am·mo′ni·a′tion** *n.*

am·mo·nic (ə mō′nik, -män′ik) *adj.* of or from ammonia or ammonium

am·mo·ni·fi·ca·tion (ə mō′nə fi kā′shən, -män′ə-) *n.* **1.** infusion with ammonia or ammonium compounds **2.** the production of ammonia by bacterial action in the decay of nitrogenous organic matter

am·mo·ni·fy (ə mō′nə fī′, -män′ə-) *vt.* **-fied′, -fy′ing** to cause to undergo ammonification —*vi.* to undergo ammonification

am·mo·nite¹ (am′ə nīt′) *n.* [ModL. *Ammonites*, name of the genus < L. (*cornu*) *Ammonis*, (horn) of Ammon < *Jupiter* AM-MON¹, whose statues were represented with ram's horns] any of the flat, usually coiled fossil shells of an extinct order (Ammonoidea) of cephalopod mollusks dominant in the Mesozoic era —**am′mo·nit′ic** (-nit′ik) *adj.*

AMMONITE
(5 in.–6 ft.)

am·mo·nite² (am′ə nīt′) *n.* [AM-MON(IA) + -ITE¹] a fertilizer produced from animal waste

am·mo·ni·um (ə mō′nē əm) *n.* [ModL., coined by Berzelius < AMMONIA] the radical NH_4, present in salts produced by the reaction of ammonia with an acid: its compounds are like those of the alkali metals

ammonium chloride a white crystalline compound, NH_4Cl, produced by the reaction of ammonia with hydrochloric acid: it is used in medicine, and also in dry cells, fertilizers, dyes, etc., and as a flux in soldering: also called **sal ammoniac**

ammonium hydroxide an alkali, NH_4OH, formed by dissolving ammonia in water

ammonium nitrate a colorless, crystalline salt, NH_4NO_3, used in some explosives and as a fertilizer

ammonium sulfate an ammonium salt, $(NH_4)_2SO_4$, made chiefly from synthetic ammonia and used in making fertilizers, in treating water, etc.

am·mo·no (am′ə nō′) *adj.* **1.** of or containing ammonia **2.** derived from ammonia: used to describe compounds bearing the same relation to ammonia as certain other compounds bear to water [sodium amide, $NaNH_2$, is an *ammono* base corresponding to sodium hydroxide, NaOH]

am·mo·no- (am′ə nō′) [< AMMONIA] *a combining form meaning* of ammonia, containing ammonia

am·mo·no·tel·ic (am′ə nō tel′ik) *adj.* [AMMONO- + TELIC] excreting ammonia as the main nitrogenous waste: characteristic chiefly of freshwater fishes, frogs, etc. —**am·mo·not·el·ism** (am′ə nät′ 'l iz′m) *n.*

am·mu·ni·tion (am′yə nish′ən) *n.* [Fr. *amunition*, by faulty separation of *la munition:* see MUNITIONS] **1.** anything hurled by a weapon or exploded as a weapon, as bullets, gunpowder, shot, shells, bombs, grenades, rockets, etc. **2.** any means of attack or defense [the facts provided him with *ammunition* for his argument] **3.** [Archaic] any military supplies

am·ne·sia (am nē′zhə, -zhē ə) *n.* [ModL. < Gr. *amnēsia*, forgetfulness < *a-*, not + *mnasthai*, to remember < IE. base *men-, *mnā-*, to think, be alert, whence L. *mens*, mind, E. MAN] partial or total loss of memory caused by brain injury, or by shock, repression, etc. —**am·ne′si·ac′** (-zē ak′), **am·ne′sic** (-sik, -zik) *adj., n.*

am·nes·tic (am nes′tik) *adj.* < Gr. *amnēstos*, forgotten (see AMNESTY) + -IC] causing amnesia

am·nes·ty (am′nəs tē) *n., pl.* **-ties** [Fr. *amnestie* < L. *amnestia* < Gr. *amnēstia*, a forgetting: see AMNESIA] **1.** a general pardon, esp. for political offenses against a government **2.** [Archaic] a deliberate overlooking, as of an offense —*vt.* **-tied, -ty·ing** to grant amnesty to; pardon

am·ni·on (am′nē ən, -än′) *n., pl.* **-ni·ons, -ni·a** (-ə) [Gr., dim. of *amnos*, lamb] **1.** the innermost membrane of the sac enclosing the embryo of a mammal, reptile, or bird: it is filled with a watery fluid (**amniotic fluid**) **2.** a similar membrane of certain invertebrates, esp. insects —**am′ni·ot′ic** (-ät′ik), **am′ni·on′ic** (-än′ik) *adj.*

am·o·bar·bi·tal (am′ō bär′bə tôl′) *n.* [AM(YL)O- + BARBITAL] a colorless crystalline compound, $C_{11}H_{18}O_3N_2$, used as a sedative and hypnotic

am·o·di·a·quin (-dī′ə kwin′) *n.* [AM(IN)O- + DI(HYDRO-CHLORIDE) + *-a-* + QUIN(OLINE)] a compound, $C_{20}H_{22}ClN_3O$, whose hydrochloride form is used in treating malaria: also **am′o·di′a·quine′** (-kwēn′)

a·moe·ba (ə mē′bə) *n., pl.* **-bas, -bae** (-bē) [ModL. < Gr. *amoibē*, change < *ameibein*, to change] **1.** a microscopic, one-celled animal (genus *Amoeba*) found in soil and water: it moves by making continually changing protrusions of its body, feeds by engulfing bits of food, and multiplies by fission **2.** any of several similar, microscopic animals (genus *Endamoeba*) parasitic in higher animals and man

am·oe·bae·an, am·oe·be·an (am′ə bē′ən) *adj.* [< L. *amoebaeum* (*carmen*) < Gr. (*asma*) *amoibaion*, responsive (song)

< *amoibē*: see AMOEBA] answering or responding to each other, as successive strophes of a verse dialogue

am·oe·bi·a·sis (am'i bī'ə sis) *n. same as* AMEBIASIS

a·moe·bic (ə mē'bik) *adj.* **1.** of or like an amoeba or amoebas **2.** caused by amoebas Also **a·moe'ban** (-bən)

amoebic dysentery *same as* AMEBIC DYSENTERY

a·moe·bo·cyte (ə mē'bə sīt') *n.* [< AMOEBA + -CYTE] any cell capable of moving like an amoeba, esp. one that floats freely in the blood or other body fluids, as a white blood corpuscle

a·moe·boid (ə mē'boid) *adj.* like or characteristic of an amoeba, as in constantly changing shape

a·mok (ə muk') *adj., adv.* [Malay *amoq*, engaging furiously in battle] in a frenzy to kill; in a violent rage —*n.* among Malays, the condition of being amok —**run** (or **go**) **amok 1.** to rush about in a frenzy to kill **2.** to lose control of oneself and do or attempt violence

☆**a·mo·le** (ə mō'lā) *n.* [MexSp. < Nahuatl] **1.** the root of any of various plants of the southwestern U.S. and Mexico, used as a substitute for soap **2.** any of these plants

A·mon (ä'mən) [Egypt., lit., hidden one] orig., a local deity of Egyptian Thebes associated with life and reproduction: later, one of the chief deities of Egypt, identified with Re: see ÅMON-RE

a·mong (ə mun') *prep.* [ME. < OE. *on gemang*, in the company (of) < *on*, in + *gemang*, a mingling, crowd < *gemengan*, MINGLE] **1.** in the company of; surrounded by; included with [you are *among* friends] **2.** from place to place in [he passed *among* the crowd] **3.** in the number or class of [fairest *among* women] **4.** by or with many of [popular *among* businessmen] **5.** as compared with [one *among* thousands] **6.** with a portion for each of [the estate was divided *among* the relatives] **7.** with one another [don't quarrel *among* yourselves] **8.** *a*) by the concerted action of *b*) in the joint possession of

a·mongst (ə munst') *prep.* [AMONG + adv. gen. -*s* + unhistoric -*t*] *same as* AMONG

A·mon-Re (ä'mən rā') [Egypt. *Åmen-Rē'*; *Åmen*, lit., hidden one + *Rē'*, sun] the ancient Egyptian sun god: also **A'mon-Ra'** (-rä')

a·mon·til·la·do (ə män'tə lä'dō; *Sp.* ä môn'tē lyä'tħô) *n.* [< Sp. < *Montilla*, a town in Spain + -*ado*, -ATE²] a pale, relatively dry sherry

a·mor·al (ā môr'əl, -mär'-) *adj.* **1.** not to be judged by criteria of morality; neither moral nor immoral **2.** without moral sense or principles; incapable of distinguishing between right and wrong —**a·mor·al·i·ty** (ā'mə ral'ə tē) *n.* —**a·mor'al·ly** *adv.*

am·o·ret·to (am'ə ret'ō) *n., pl.* -**ret'ti** (-ret'ē) [It., dim. of *amore* < L. *amor*, love] an infant cupid, as in Italian art of the 16th cent.

am·o·rist (am'ər ist) *n.* [L. *amor*, love + -IST] a person much occupied with love and lovemaking

Am·o·rite (am'ə rīt') *n.* [Heb. *'emōrī*] any of an ancient Semitic people of c. 2000 B.C.: in the Bible, regarded as descended from Canaan, son of Ham: Gen. 10:16

am·o·rous (am'ər əs) *adj.* [ME. < OFr. *amoureus* < LL. *amorosus*, loving < L. *amor*, love < *amare*, to love] **1.** full of love or fond of making love **2.** in love; enamored or fond (*of*) **3.** full of or showing love or sexual desire [*amorous* words] **4.** of sexual love or lovemaking —**am'o·rous·ly** *adv.* —**am'o·rous·ness** *n.*

‡**a·mor pa·tri·ae** (ä'môr pä'tri ē) [L.] love of one's country; patriotism

a·mor·phous (ə môr'fəs) *adj.* [ModL. *amorphus* < Gr. *amorphos* < *a-*, without + *morphē*, form] **1.** without definite form; shapeless **2.** of no definite type; anomalous **3.** unorganized; vague **4.** *Biol.* without definite or specialized structure, as some lower forms of life **5.** *Chem. & Mineralogy* lacking a definite crystalline form; not crystalline —**a·mor'phism** (-fiz'm) *n.* —**a·mor'phous·ly** *adv.* —**a·mor'phous·ness** *n.*

a·mort (ə môrt') *adj.* [altered by faulty separation, as if *all amort* (after AMORTIZE) < Fr. *à la mort* < *à*, to + *la*, the + *mort* < L. *mors* (gen. *mortis*), death] [Archaic] dead or dying; spiritless

am·or·tise (am'ər tīz', ə môr'-) *vt.* -**tised'**, -**tis'ing** [Chiefly Brit.] *same as* AMORTIZE

am·or·ti·za·tion (am'ər ti zā'shən, ə môr'tə-) *n.* **1.** an amortizing or being amortized **2.** money put aside for amortizing a debt, etc. Also **a·mor·tize·ment** (ə môr'tiz·mənt)

am·or·tize (am'ər tīz', ə môr'-) *vt.* -**tized'**, -**tiz'ing** [ME. *amortisen* < extended stem of OFr. *amortir*, to extinguish, sell in mortmain (< ML. *amortire*); or < ML. *amortizare*; both ML. forms < L. *ad*, to + *mors*, death] **1.** to put money aside at intervals, as in a sinking fund, for gradual payment of (a debt, etc.) either at or before maturity **2.** *Accounting* to write off (expenditures) by prorating over a fixed period **3.** *Law* to reduce, transfer, or sell (property) in mortmain —**am'or·tiz'a·ble** *adj.*

A·mos (ä'məs) [Heb. *'āmōs*, lit., borne (by God?)] **1.** a masculine name **2.** *Bible a*) a Hebrew prophet of the 8th cent. B.C. *b*) the book containing prophecies attributed to him

a·mount (ə mount') *vi.* [ME. *amounten*, to ascend < OFr. *amonter* < *amont*, upward < *a-* (L. *ad*), to + *mont* < L. *montem*, acc. sing. of *mons*, MOUNTAIN] **1.** to add up; equal in total [the bill *amounts* to $4.50] **2.** to be equal in mean-

ing, value, or effect [her failure to reply *amounts* to a refusal] —*n.* **1.** the sum of two or more quantities; total **2.** a principal sum plus its interest **3.** the whole meaning, value, or effect **4.** a quantity [a fair *amount* of resistance] —*SYN.* see SUM

a·mour (ə moor') *n.* [Fr. < Pr. *amor* < L. *amor*, love] a love affair, esp. of an illicit or secret nature

‡**a·mour-pro·pre** (à moor prô'pr') *n.* [Fr.] self-esteem

A·moy (ä moi') **1.** seaport on an island in Taiwan Strait, SE China: pop. 600,000 **2.** the island

amp. 1. amperage **2.** ampere; amperes

am·pe·lop·sis (am'pə läp'sis) *n.* [ModL. < Gr. *ampelos*, vine + *opsis*, appearance] a climbing vine or shrub of a genus (*Ampelopsis*) in the grape family, widely grown as ornamentals

am·per·age (am'pər ij, am pir'-) *n.* the strength of an electric current, measured in amperes

am·pere (am'pir) *n.* [after ff.] the standard unit for measuring the strength of an electric current; rate of flow of charge in a conductor or conducting medium of one coulomb per second

Am·père (än per'), **An·dré Ma·rie** (än drā' má rē') 1775-1836; Fr. physicist & mathematician

am·pere-hour (am'pir our') *n.* a standard unit for measuring the quantity of electricity, equal to the flow of a current of one ampere for one hour, or to an elapsed current drain of 3,600 coulombs

ampere turn the amount of magnetomotive force produced by an electric current of one ampere flowing around one turn of a wire coil

am·per·sand (am'pər sand') *n.* [< *and per se and*, lit., (the sign) & by itself (is) *and*] a sign (& or &·), meaning *and:* it represents the Latin word *et* (and)

☆**am·phet·a·mine** (am fet'ə mēn', -min) *n.* [alpha-methyl-beta-phenyl-ethyl-amine] a colorless, volatile liquid, $C_9H_{13}N$, used in its sulfate or phosphate forms as a drug to overcome mental depression, fatigue, etc., and to lessen the appetite in dieting

am·phi- (am'fi, -fē, -fə; *often assimilated to* an'fi) [< Gr. *amphi*, AMBI-] *a prefix meaning:* **1.** on both sides or on both ends [*amphistylar*] **2.** around or about **3.** of both kinds [*amphibiotic*]

am·phi·ar·thro·sis (am'fē är thrōs'is) *n.* [AMPHI- + Gr. *arthrōsis*, a jointing < *arthron*, a joint: see ARTHRO-] *Anat.* a form of jointing in which an elastic cartilage connects the bones and motion is limited

am·phi·as·ter (am'fē as'tər) *n.* [AMPHI- + -ASTER¹] in mitosis, the long spindle with asters at either end that forms during the prophase, or first stage

am·phib·i·an (am fib'ē ən) *n.* [< ModL. *Amphibia*, name of the class < Gr. *amphibia*, neut. pl.: see AMPHIBIOUS] **1.** any of a class (Amphibia) of vertebrates, including frogs, toads, newts, and salamanders, that usually begin life in the water as tadpoles with gills, and later develop lungs:

AMPHIBIAN (sense 4)

they are cold-blooded and scaleless **2.** any amphibious animal or plant **3.** any aircraft that can take off from and come down on either land or water **4.** a tank or other vehicle that can travel on either land or water —*adj.* **1.** of amphibians **2.** *same as* AMPHIBIOUS

am·phi·bi·ot·ic (am'fi bī ät'ik) *adj.* [< Gr. *amphibios* (see AMPHIBIOUS) + -IC] *Zool.* that lives in water in one stage of development, and on land in another

am·phib·i·ous (am fib'ē əs) *adj.* [Gr. *amphibios*, living a double life < *amphi-*, AMPHI- + *bios*, life] **1.** that can live both on land and in water **2.** that can operate or travel on both land and water **3.** designating, of, or for a military operation involving the landing of assault troops on a shore from seaborne transports **4.** having two natures or qualities; of a mixed nature —**am·phib'i·ous·ly** *adv.*

am·phi·blas·tu·la (am'fi blas'choo lə) *n., pl.* -**lae** (-lē) -**las** [AMPHI- + BLASTULA] a hollow, half-flagellated ball of cells that constitutes the free-swimming developmental stage of many marine sponges

am·phi·bole (am'fə bōl') *n.* [Fr. < LL. *amphibolus*, ambiguous < Gr. *amphibolos* < *amphiballein*, to throw around, doubt < *amphi-*, AMPHI- + *ballein*, to throw] any of a group of rock-forming minerals, as hornblende or asbestos, composed largely of silica, calcium, iron, and magnesium: they are common constituents of igneous and metamorphic rocks —**am'phi·bol'ic** (-bäl'ik) *adj.*

am·phib·o·lite (am fib'ə līt') *n.* [AMPHIBOL(E) + -ITE²] a rock consisting largely of amphibole and plagioclase with little or no quartz

am·phi·bol·o·gy (am'fi bäl'ə jē) *n., pl.* -**gies** [ME. *amphibologie* < LL. *amphibologia* (altered after words ending in *-logia*, -LOGY) < L. *amphibolia* < Gr. *amphibolia*, ambiguity < *amphiballein*: see AMPHIBOLE] **1.** double or doubtful meaning; ambiguity, esp. from uncertain grammatical construction **2.** an ambiguous phrase, proposition, etc. Also **am·phib'o·ly** (am fib'ə lē), *pl.* -**lies** —**am'phi·bol'ic** (-bäl'ik), **am'phi·bo'lous** (-ə ləs) *adj.*

am·phi·brach (am'fi brak') *n.* [L. *amphibrachys* < Gr. *amphibrachys*, lit., short before and after < *amphi-* + *brachys*, short] a metrical foot in Greek and Latin verse consisting of one long syllable between two short ones, or,

in English, of one accented syllable between two unaccented ones (Ex.: ǀĕxplôsĭon ǀ)

am·phi·chro·ic (am'fĭ krō'ĭk) *adj.* [AMPHI- + Gr. *chroa*, color + -IC] *Chem.* exhibiting either of two colors under varying conditions, as litmus

am·phi·coe·lous (-sē'ləs) *adj.* [Gr. *amphikoilos* < *amphi-*, AMPHI- + *koilos*, hollow] concave on both sides, as the vertebrae of fishes

am·phic·ty·on (am fĭk'tē ən) *n.* [L. (pl.) *Amphictyones* < Gr. *Amphiktyones* < *amphiktiones*, those that dwelt around, next neighbors] a delegate to the council or assembly of an amphictyony

am·phic·ty·o·ny (am fĭk'tē ə nē) *n.*, *pl.* -nies [Gr. *amphiktyonia*: see AMPHICTYON] in ancient Greece, a confederation of states established around a religious center, as at Delphi —**am·phic'ty·on'ic** (-än'ĭk) *adj.*

am·phi·go·ry (am'fĭ gôr'ē) *n.*, *pl.* -ries [Fr. *amphigouri*] a piece of nonsense writing, as in burlesque

am·phim·a·cer (am fĭm'ə sər) *n.* [< L. *amphimacrus* < Gr. *amphimakros*, lit., long at both ends < *amphi-*, AMPHI- + *makros*, long] a metrical foot in Greek and Latin verse consisting of one short syllable between two long ones, or, in English, of one unaccented syllable between two accented ones (Ex.: ǀhōsĭtātĕ ǀ)

am·phi·mix·is (am'fĭ mĭk'sĭs) *n.* [ModL. < AMPHI- ǀ Gr. *mixis*, a mixing] *Biol.* 1. the uniting of male and female germ cells from two individuals in reproduction 2. crossbreeding

Am·phi·on (am fī'ən) [L. < Gr. *Amphiōn*] *Gr. Myth.* the son of Zeus and Antiope: he built a wall around Thebes by charming the stones into place with a lyre

am·phi·ox·us (am'fē äk'səs) *n.* [< AMPHI- + Gr. *oxys*, sharp] the lancelet, a small chordate sea animal (genus *Branchiostoma*)

am·phi·pod (am'fĭ päd') *n.* [AMPHI- + -POD] any of several crustaceans with one set of feet for jumping or walking and another set for swimming, as the sand flea

am·phi·pro·style (am'fĭ prō'stīl, am fĭp'rə stīl') *adj.* [L. *amphiprostylos* < Gr. *amphiprostylos*: see AMPHI- & PROSTYLE] *Archit.* having rows of columns at the front and back, but none along the sides —*n.* an amphiprostyle building

am·phis·bae·na (am'fĭs bē'nə) *n.* [ME. *amphibena* < L. *amphisbuena* < Gr. *amphisbaina* < *amphis-*, AMPHI- + *bainein*, to go] a mythical serpent with a head at each end of its body

am·phis·bae·ni·an (-nē ən) *n.* [see prec.] a wormlike tropical lizard (genus *Amphisbaena*) with a head and tail that look very much alike

am·phi·sty·lar (am'fĭ stī'lər) *adj.* [AMPHI- + Gr. *stylos*, pillar + -AR] *Archit.* having columns at both front and back or on both sides

am·phi·the·a·ter, am·phi·the·a·tre (am'fĭ thē'ə tər) *n.* [L. *amphitheatrum* < Gr. *amphitheatron*: see AMPHI- + THEATER] 1. a round or oval building with an open space (arena) surrounded by rising rows of seats 2. a scene of contest; arena 3. a sloping gallery in a theater 4. a lecture hall with a sloping gallery, for observing surgical procedures in a medical school or hospital 5. a level place surrounded by rising ground —**am'phi·the·at'ric** (-thēat'rik), **am'phi·the·at'ri·cal** *adj.* —**am'phi·the·at'ri·cal·ly** *adv.*

am·phi·the·ci·um (am'fĭ thē'shē əm, -sē-) *n.*, *pl.* -ci·a (-shē ə, -sē'ə) [ModL. < AMPHI- + Gr. *thēkion*, dim. of *thēkē*, a case, container] *Bot.* the outer layer of cells in the spore case of a moss

Am·phi·tri·te (am'fĭ trīt'ē) [L. < Gr. *Amphitritē*] *Gr. Myth.* one of the Nereids, goddess of the sea and wife of Poseidon

am·phi·tro·pous (am fĭt'rə pəs) *adj.* [AMPHI- + -TROPOUS] *Bot.* having a half-inverted ovule, so that the micropyle and chalaza are at equal distances from the placenta

Am·phi·try·on (am fĭt'rē ən) [L. < Gr. *Amphitryōn*] *Gr. Myth.* a king of Thebes: his wife, Alcmene, became the mother of Hercules by Zeus, who seduced her by appearing in the likeness of Amphitryon

am·pho·ra (am'fər ə) *n.*, *pl.* -rae (-ē), -ras [L. < Gr. *amphoreus*, a jar with two handles, contr. < *amphiphoreus* < *amphi-* (see AMPHI-) + *phoreus*, bearer < *pherein*, BEAR] a tall jar with a narrow neck and base, and two handles, used by the ancient Greeks and Romans

am·pho·ter·ic (am'fə ter'ĭk) *adj.* [< Gr. *amphoteros*, compar. form of *amphō*, both. var. of AMPHI-] *Chem.* having both acid and basic properties

am·pho·ter·i·cin B (-ter'ə sin) [AMPHOTERIC + -IN¹] an antibiotic compound, C₄₆H₇₃NO₂₀, used in treating certain diseases caused by parasitic fungi

am·ple (am'p'l) *adj.* [ME. & OFr. < L. *amplus*, prob. < **amlos* < IE. base **am-*, to contain] 1. large in size, extent, scope, etc.; spacious 2. more than enough; abundant 3. enough to fulfill the needs or purpose; adequate—*SYN.* see PLENTIFUL —**am'ple·ness** *n.*

AMPHORA

am·plex·i·caul (am plek'sə kôl') *adj.* [< L. *amplexus*, pp. of *amplectari*, to twine around + *caulis*, stem (cf. HOLE)] *Bot.* growing directly from the main stem and clasping or encircling the stem: said of some leaves, as those of corn

am·pli·a·tion (am'plē ā'shən) *n.* [L. *ampliatio* < *ampliare*, to widen < *amplus*: see AMPLE] [Archaic] an enlarging or something added to enlarge

am·pli·dyne (am'plə dīn') *n.* [AMPLI(FIER) + DYNE] a direct-current amplifier producing a large output current from a small current in the field windings by means of a short circuit across one pair of brushes to provide a second magnetic field

am·pli·fi·ca·tion (am'plə fĭ kā'shən) *n.* 1. an amplifying or being amplified 2. matter, details, etc. added to amplify a statement, report, etc. 3. a statement, etc. with something added

am·pli·fi·er (am'plə fī'ər) *n.* 1. a person or thing that amplifies 2. *Electronics* a device, esp. one with electron tubes or semiconductors, used to increase the strength of an electrical signal

am·pli·fy (am'plə fī') *vt.* -fied', -fy'ing [ME. *amplifien* < OFr. *amplifier* < L. *amplificare* < *amplus* (see AMPLE) + *facere*, to make] 1. to make larger or stronger; increase or extend (power, authority, etc.) 2. to develop more fully, as with details, examples, statistics, etc. [to *amplify* a point in a debate] 3. [Rare] to give a magnified account of; exaggerate 4. *Electronics* to increase the strength of (an electrical signal) by means of an amplifier —*vi.* to speak or write at length; expatiate

am·pli·tude (am'plə tōōd', -tyōōd') *n.* [L. *amplitudo* < *amplus*: see AMPLE] 1. the quality of being ample or the amount or degree to which a thing extends; largeness 2. an amount that is more than enough; abundance; fullness 3. scope or breadth, as of mind 4. the angular distance of a star from the true east or west point of the horizon, at the moment of its rising or setting 5. the extreme range of a fluctuating quantity, as an alternating current, swing of a pendulum, etc., generally measured from the average or mean to the extreme

amplitude modulation 1. the changing of the amplitude of the transmitting radio wave in accordance with the signal being broadcast 2. a broadcasting system that uses this Distinguished from FREQUENCY MODULATION

am·ply (am'plē) *adv.* to an ample degree; liberally; fully

am·pul (am'pool, -pul) *n.* [Fr. < L. *ampulla*, AMPULLA] a small, sealed glass container for one dose of a sterile medicine to be injected hypodermically: also **am'pule** (-pyool), **am'poule** (-pōōl)

am·pul·la (am pul'ə, -pool'-) *n.*, *pl.* -pul'lae (-ē) [ME. *ampulle* < OE. *ampulla* or OFr. *ampoule*, both < L. *ampulla*, dim. of *ampora*, for *amphora*, AMPHORA] 1. a nearly round bottle with two handles, used by the ancient Greeks and Romans 2. a container used in churches for holy oil, consecrated wine, etc. 3. *Anat.* a sac or dilated part of a tube or canal, as of a milk duct in a mammary gland —**am·pul'lar** (-ər) *adj.*

am·pul·la·ceous (am'pə lā'shəs) *adj.* [L. *ampullaceus*] shaped like an ampulla or a bladder

am·pu·tate (am'pyə tāt') *vt.* -tat'ed, -tat'ing [< L. *amputatus*, pp. of *amputare* < *am-*, for *ambi-*, AMBI- + *putare*, to trim, prune < IE. **putos*, participial form of base **peu-*, to strike, chop: cf. PAVE] to cut off (an arm, leg, etc.), esp. by surgery —**am'pu·ta'tion** *n.* —**am'pu·ta'tor** *n.*

am·pu·tee (am'pyə tē') *n.* [AMPUT(ATE) + -EE¹] a person who has had a limb or limbs amputated

Am·rao·ti (əm rou'tē) city in Maharashtra state, C India: pop. 138,000: also **Am·ra·va·ti** (um'rə vä'tē)

am·ri·ta (əm rēt'ə) *n.* [< Sans. *amṛta*, deathless, hence drink that makes immortal < IE. base **mer-*: see AMBROSIA] *Hindu Myth.* 1. the ambrosial drink granting immortality 2. the immortality granted by this

Am·rit·sar (əm rit'sər) city in N India, in Punjab state: pop. 376,000

Am·ster·dam (am'stər dam') constitutional capital of the Netherlands, on the IJsselmeer: pop. 866,000: see also The HAGUE

amt. amount

☆**am·trac** (am'trak') *n.* [AM(PHIBIOUS) + TRAC(TOR)] a small amphibious vehicle with tractor treads, used in sea-to-shore operations in World War II

amu, AMU atomic mass unit

a·muck (ə muk') *adj.*, *adv.* same as AMOK

A·mu Dar·ya (ä'moo' där'yä) river in C Asia rising in the Hindu Kush and flowing into the Aral Sea: c. 1,500 mi.: ancient name, OXUS

am·u·let (am'yə lit) *n.* [Fr. *amulette* < L. *amuletum*] something worn on the body because of its supposed magic power to protect against injury or evil; a charm

A·mund·sen (ä'moon sən), **Ro·ald** (rō'äl) 1872–1928; Norw. explorer; 1st to reach the South Pole (1911)

Amundsen Sea part of the Pacific Ocean bordering on Antarctica, east of the Ross Sea

A·mur (ä moor') river in NE Asia, flowing along the

U.S.S.R.–China border across Khabarovsk Territory into Tatar Strait: c. 2,700 mi.

a·muse (ə myŏŏz′) vt. **a·mused′, a·mus′ing** [Fr. amuser < à, at + OFr. muser, to stare fixedly < ML. musus, mouth, muzzle] 1. to keep pleasantly or enjoyably occupied or interested; entertain [we amused ourselves with games] 2. to make laugh, smile, etc. by being comical or humorous 3. [Obs.] to engage or distract the attention of —**a·mus′a·ble** adj. —**a·mus′er** n.

SYN.—**amuse** suggests the agreeable occupation of the mind, esp. by something that appeals to the sense of humor [the monkey's antics amused him]; to **divert** is to take the attention from serious thought or worry to something gay or light; **entertain** implies planned amusement or diversion, often with some intellectual appeal [another guest entertained us with folk songs]; **beguile** suggests the occupation of time with an agreeable activity, largely to dispel boredom or tedium —ANT. bore

a·muse·ment (-mənt) n. 1. the condition of being amused 2. something that amuses or entertains; entertainment

☆**amusement park** an outdoor place with various devices for entertainment, as a merry-go-round, roller coaster, etc., refreshment booths, and the like

amusement tax a tax on various forms of entertainment, paid on admissions to theaters, etc.

a·mu·si·a (ā′myŏŏ′zē·ə) n. [ModL. < Gr. amousos, unmusical < a-, without + mousa, MUSIC] Psychol. a disorder characterized by inability to recognize or reproduce musical sounds

a·mus·ing (ə myŏŏ′ziŋ) adj. 1. entertaining; diverting 2. causing laughter or mirth —SYN. see FUNNY —**a·mus′ing·ly** adv.

a·mu·sive (-ziv) adj. amusing or tending to amuse

A·my (ā′mē) [ME. Amye < OFr. Amee, lit., beloved < fem. pp. of aimer, to love < L. amare] a feminine name

a·myg·da·la (ə mig′də lə) n., pl. -lae (-lē) [ME. amigdale < L. amygdala < Gr. amygdalē, an almond] Anat. an almond-shaped structure, as a tonsil

a·myg·da·la·ceous (ə mig′də lā′shəs) adj. [L. amygdalaceus: see AMYGDALA] of or relating to a group of shrubs and trees (chiefly of the genus Prunus) with fleshy fruit that contains a single hard seed or stone, as the peach, almond, cherry, etc.

a·myg·dale (ə mig′dāl) n. [< L. amygdala, almond (see AMYGDALA): from the typical shape] any of the small mineral masses (usually calcite, chalcedony, quartz, or a zeolite) deposited in cavities in a solidified igneous rock, produced during its molten stage by expanding gas: also **a·myg′dule** (-dŏŏl, -dyŏŏl)

a·myg·da·lin (ə mig′də lən) n. [AMYGDAL(A) + -IN¹] a crystalline glucoside, C₂₀H₂₇NO₁₁, present in bitter almonds: it is used as a flavoring agent

a·myg·da·loid (-loid′) n. [AMYGDAL(A) + -OID] igneous rock containing amygdales —adj. 1. almond-shaped 2. of or like amygdaloid; containing amygdales

a·myg·da·loid·al (ə mig′də loid′'l) adj. same as AMYGDALOID

am·yl (am′il) n. [AM(YLUM) + -YL] any of various isomeric forms of the monovalent radical C₅H₁₁ —**a·myl·ic** (ə mil′ik) adj.

am·yl- (am′il) same as AMYLO-

am·y·la·ceous (am′ə lā′shəs) adj. of or like starch

amyl alcohol a colorless, sharp-smelling alcohol, C₅H₁₁OH, obtained by the fermentation of starchy substances and also present in fusel oil

am·yl·ase (am′ə lās′) n. an enzyme that helps change starch into sugar: it is found in saliva, pancreatic juice, etc.: see also DIASTASE

am·yl·ene (-lēn′) n. any of several isomeric hydrocarbons having the formula C₅H₁₀

amyl nitrite a volatile liquid, C₅H₁₁NO₂, that is inhaled to relieve arterial spasms, esp. in angina pectoris

am·y·lo- (am′ə lō) [< AMYLUM] a combining form meaning: 1. of starch [amylogen] 2. of amyl

a·myl·o·gen (ə mil′ə jən) n. the water-soluble part of the starch granule

am·y·loid (am′ə loid′) n. 1. a starchy food or substance 2. a nearly transparent, waxy deposit resulting from degeneration of bodily tissues

am·y·lol·y·sis (am′ə läl′ə sis) n. the changing of starch into soluble substances by the action of enzymes or by hydrolysis with dilute acids —**am′y·lo·lyt′ic** (-lō lit′ik) adj.

am·y·lo·pec·tin (am′ə lō pek′tən) n. a nearly insoluble substance derived from the outer part of starch granules: it is a polymer of glucose

am·y·lop·sin (am′ə läp′sin) n. [AMYLO- + (TRY)PSIN] the enzyme (amylase) of pancreatic juice: it splits starch into glucose

am·y·lose (am′ə lōs′) n. 1. the inner, water-soluble content of starch 2. any of a group of complex carbohydrates of the general formula (C₆H₁₀O₅)ₙ, as cellulose or starch, which are converted by hydrolysis into two or more simple sugars

am·y·lum (am′ə ləm) n. [L. < Gr. amylon, starch, short for amylon (aleuron), (meal) not ground at the mill < a-, not + mylē, MILL¹] Chem. a technical name for STARCH

a·my·o·to·ni·a (ā mī′ə tō′nē ə) n. [A-² (not) + ModL. myotonia < MYO- + -tonia < Gr. tonos: see TONE] a condition in which the muscle tissues lack normal vigor and tension; lack of muscle tone

☆**Am·y·tal** (am′ə tôl′, -tal′) a trademark for AMOBARBITAL

an¹ (ən, 'n; stressed, an) adj., indefinite article [weakened variant of ONE < OE. an, the numeral one; the older and fuller form of A¹] 1. one; one sort of [to bake an apple pie] 2. each; any one [pick an apple from the tree] 3. to each; in each; for each; per [two an hour] The chief grammatical function of an (or a) is to connote a thing not previously noted or recognized, the connoting a thing previously noted or recognized; an now replaces a before all words beginning with a vowel sound or mute h [an orange, an honor]; older usage also favored an before h in an unstressed initial syllable [an hotel], and British usage favors an before the sound (yŏŏ, yoo) [an union, an eulogy] See also A¹, adj.

an², **an′** (an) conj. [ME. < and, AND] 1. [Dial.] and 2. [Archaic] if

an-¹ (an) same as A-² (not, without): used before vowels

an-² (an, ən) same as AD-: used before n

-an (ən, in, 'n) [Fr. -ain, -en < L. -anus, of, belonging to; also directly < L.] an adj.-forming and n.-forming suffix meaning: 1. (one) belonging to or having some relation to [diocesan] 2. (one) born in or living in [American] 3. (one) believing in or following [Mohammedan]

AN, A.N., A.-N. Anglo-Norman

an. 1. [L. anno] in the year 2. anonymous

an·a¹ (an′ə) adv. [Gr. ana, apiece, of each] of each (ingredient referred to): used in doctors' prescriptions

a·na² (ā′nə, ä′-; an′ə) n. [< -ANA] a collection of anecdotes, reminiscences, etc., esp. by or about a particular person

an·a- (an′ə) [L. < Gr. ana, up, on, again, apiece] a prefix meaning: 1. up, upward [anadromous] 2. back, backward [anagram] 3. again [Anabaptist] 4. throughout [analysis] 5. according to, similar to [analogy]

-a·na (an′ə, ä′nə, ā′nə) [neut. pl. of L. -anus] a n.-forming suffix meaning sayings, writings, anecdotes, or facts of [Americana]

an·a·bae·na (an′ə bē′nə) n. [ModL. < Gr. anabainein: see ANABASIS] 1. a freshwater alga (genus Anabaena), often growing in reservoirs, that may make the water taste or smell fishy 2. a mass of such algae

An·a·bap·tist (an′ə bap′tist) n. [ModL. anabaptista < LL. anabaptismus < Gr.(Ec.) anabaptismos, second baptism < anabaptizein < ana-, again + baptizein, to BAPTIZE] a member of a 16th.cent. sect of the Reformation, originating in Switzerland, that denied the validity of infant baptism, practiced baptism of adults, and advocated religious and social reforms —adj. of this sect —**An′a·bap′tism** n.

an·a·bas (an′ə bas′) n. [ModL. < Gr. anabas < anabainein (see ANABASIS): so named from its habit of climbing] any of a number of related freshwater fishes (suborder Anabantoidei) of Africa and SE Asia: they can live for a long time out of water: cf. CLIMBING PERCH

A·nab·a·sis (ə nab′ə sis) [Gr. < anabainein, to go up < ana-, up + bainein, to go < IE. base *gwem-: see COME] 1. the unsuccessful military expedition (401–400 B.C.) of Cyrus the Younger to overthrow Artaxerxes II 2. a book about this by Xenophon —n. [a-] pl. -ses′ (-sēz′) any large military expedition

an·a·bat·ic (an′ə bat′ik) adj. [Gr. anabatikos: see ANABASIS] moving upward: said of air currents or winds

an·a·bi·o·sis (an′ə bī ō′sis) n. [ModL. < Gr. < anabioein, to come to life again < ana-, again + bioein, to live < bios: see BIO-] a state of suspended animation, as in certain minute arthropods when desiccated —**an′a·bi·ot′ic** (-ät′ik) adj.

a·nab·o·lism (ə nab′ə liz′m) n. [< Gr. anabolē, a rising up < ana-, up + bolē, a stroke < ballein, to throw + -ISM] the process in a plant or animal by which food is changed into living tissue; constructive metabolism: opposed to CATABOLISM —**an·a·bol·ic** (an′ə bäl′ik) adj.

an·a·branch (an′ə branch′) n. [< ana(stomosing) branch] 1. a river branch that reenters the main stream 2. a river branch that becomes absorbed by sandy ground

a·nach·ro·nism (ə nak′rə niz′m) n. [MGr. anachronismos < anachronizein, to refer to a wrong time < ana-, against + chronos, time] 1. the representation of something as existing or occurring at other than its proper time, esp. earlier 2. anything that is or seems to be out of its proper time in history —**a·nach′ro·nis′tic, a·nach′ro·nous** (-nəs) adj. —**a·nach′ro·nis′ti·cal·ly** adv.

an·a·clas·tic (an′ə klas′tik) adj. [Gr. anaklastos, reflected < anaklan < ana-, back + klan, to bend + -IC] Optics of, caused by, or causing refraction

an·a·cli·nal (an′ə klī′n'l) adj. [see ANACLITIC] Geol. progressing in a direction opposite to that in which the rock strata dip, as a valley

an·a·clit·ic (-klit′ik) adj. [< Gr. anaklitos, for reclining < anaklinein, to lean upon < ana-, on + klinein, to LEAN¹] Psychoanalysis having the libido dependent upon another instinct

an·a·co·lu·thon (an′ə kə lŏŏ′thän) n., pl. -tha (-thə), -thons [Gr., neut. of anakoulouthos, inconsequent < an-, not + akolouthos, following: see ACOLYTE] 1. a change from one grammatical construction to another within the same sentence, sometimes as a rhetorical device 2. a sentence in which this occurs (Ex.: Romeo and Juliet, I, iii "A man, young lady! lady, such a man as all the world— why, he's a man of wax!") —**an′a·co·lu′thic** adj.

An·a·con·da (an′ə kän′də) city in SW Mont., known for its copper refinery: pop. 10,000

an·a·con·da (an′ə kän′də) n. [orig. used in Eng. for a Ceylonese snake < ? Sinhalese *henakandayā*, whip snake] 1. a very long, heavy, South American snake (*Eunectes murinus*) of the boa family 2. any similar large snake that crushes its victim in its coils

A·nac·re·on (ə nak′rē ən, -rē än′) 6th cent. B.C.; Gr. lyric poet

A·nac·re·on·tic (ə nak′rē än′tik) adj. of or like the poetry of Anacreon, as in praising love and conviviality —n. an Anacreontic poem or verse: *often used in pl.*

an·a·cru·sis (an′ə krōōs′is) n. [ModL. < Gr. *anakrousis* < *anakrouein*, to push back < *ana-*, back + *krouein*, to strike] 1. one or more unaccented syllables at the beginning of a line of verse which properly begins with an accented syllable 2. *Music* same as UPBEAT

ANACONDA (to 30 ft. long)

an·a·dem (an′ə dem′) n. [L. *anadema* < *anadein*, to bind up, wreathe < *ana-*, up + *dein*, to bind: see DIADEM] [Poet.] a wreath or garland for the head

an·a·di·plo·sis (an′ə di plōs′is) n. [L. < Gr. *anadiplōsis* < *anadiploun*, to double < *ana-*, up, again + *diploos*, double: cf. DOUBLE] the repetition of a key word, esp. the last one, at the beginning of the next sentence or clause (Ex.: "He gave his life; life was all he could give.")

a·nad·ro·mous (ə nad′rə məs) adj. [Gr. *anadromos* < *ana-*, upward + *dromos*, a running < *dramein*, to run] going up rivers to spawn: said of salmon, shad, etc.

A·na·dyr, A·na·dir (ä nä dir′) river in NE Siberia, flowing into the Bering Sea: c. 700 mi.

Anadyr (or **Anadir**) **Range** mountain range in NE Siberia: highest peaks, c. 7,500 ft.

a·nae·mi·a (ə nē′mē ə, -myə) n. same as ANEMIA

an·aer·obe (an er′ōb, an′ə rōb′) n. [< ModL. *anaerobium*: see ANAEROBIUM] a microorganism that can live and grow where there is no free oxygen: anaerobes get oxygen by the decomposition of compounds containing it

an·aer·o·bic (an′er ō′bik, -ə rō′-) adj. 1. of or produced by anaerobes 2. able to live and grow where there is no air or free oxygen, as certain bacteria

an·aer·o·bi·um (bē əm) n., pl. -bi·a (-bē ə) [ModL. < Gr. *an-* (see A-²) + *aero-*, AERO- + *bios*, life] same as ANAEROBE

an·aes·the·sia (an′əs thē′zhə) n. same as ANESTHESIA —an′aes·thet′ic (-thet′ik) adj., n. —an·aes·the·tist (ə nes′thə tist) n. —an·aes·the·tize′ vt. -tized′, -tiz′ing

an·a·glyph (an′ə glif′) n. [Gr. *anaglyphē* < *ana-*, up + *glyphein*, to carve out: see CLEAVE¹] 1. an ornament, as a cameo, carved in low relief 2. a photograph made up of two slightly different views, in contrasting colors, of the same subject: when looked at through a pair of corresponding color filters, the picture seems three-dimensional

an·a·go·ge, an·a·go·gy (an′ə gō′jē) n. [ME. *anagogie* < ML. *anagogia* < Gr. *anagōgē*, a leading up < *ana-*, up + *agein*, to lead: cf. ACT] mystical interpretation, as of the Scriptures, intended to reveal a hidden, spiritual meaning —an′a·gog′ic (-gäj′ik), an′a·gog′i·cal adj. —an′a·gog′i·cal·ly adv.

an·a·gram (an′ə gram′) n. [ModL. *anagramma* < Gr. *anagrammatizein*, to transpose letters < *ana-*, back + *gramma*, letter < *graphein*, to write] 1. a word or phrase made from another by rearranging its letters (Ex.: *now* —*won, dread* — *adder*) 2. [pl., with sing. v.] a game whose object is to make words by arranging letters from a common pool or by forming anagrams from other words —an′a·gram·mat′ic (-grə mat′ik), an′a·gram·mat′i·cal adj. —an′a·gram·mat′i·cal·ly adv.

A·na·heim (an′ə him′) [< Santa *Ana* (St. ANNE) + G. *heim*, home] city in SW Calif.: pop. 167,000 (met. area, with Garden Grove & Santa Ana, 1,420,000)

a·nal (ā′n'l) adj. [ModL. *analis* < L. *anus*, anus] 1. of or near the anus 2. *Psychoanalysis* a) designating or of the second stage of psychosexual development in which interest centers in excretory functions b) designating or of such traits in the adult as orderliness, stinginess, obstinacy, etc., regarded as unconscious psychic residues of that stage: cf. ORAL —a′nal·ly adv.

anal. 1. analogous 2. analogy 3. analysis 4. analytic

an·al·cite (ə nal′sit) n. [< Gr. *analkēs*, weak + -ITE¹: so named by J. D. DANA because of its weak electric power] a zeolite occurring in traprock: also **an·al′cime** (-sim, -sēm)

an·a·lects (an′ə lekts′) n.pl. [L. *analecta* < Gr. *analegein*, to collect < *ana-*, up + *legein*, to gather] collected literary excerpts or passages: also **an·a·lec·ta** (an′ə lek′tə) —the **Analects** a collection of Confucius' teachings

an·a·lem·ma (an′ə lem′ə) n. [L., a sundial showing latitude and meridian < Gr. *analēmma*, a support, substructure < *analambanein*: see ANALEPTIC] a scale of the sun's daily declination shown on a globe of the earth, usually in the form of an elongated 8 crossing the equator

an·a·lep·tic (an′ə lep′tik) adj. [Gr. *analēptikos*, restorative < *analambanein*, to recover < *ana-*, up + *lambanein*, to take] *Med.* restorative; esp., counteracting drowsiness or the effects of sedatives —n. an analeptic drug

an·al·ge·si·a (an′′l jē′zē ə, -sē ə, -zhē ə) n. [ModL. < Gr. *analgēsia* < *an-*, without + *algēsia*, pain < *algos*, pain] a state of not feeling pain although fully conscious

an·al·ge·sic (-zik, -sik) adj. of or causing analgesia —n. a drug that produces analgesia

an·a·log computer (an′ə lôg′, -läg′) a computer that manipulates numerical representations of physical-quantity data (as lengths), the way a slide rule does: electronic analog computers work on voltages instead of numbers: cf. DIGITAL COMPUTER

an·a·log·i·cal (an′ə läj′ə k'l) adj. [L. *analogicus*] of, expressing, or based upon analogy: also **an′a·log′ic** —an′a·log′i·cal·ly adv.

a·nal·o·gist (ə nal′ə jist) n. a person who looks for analogies or uses them in reasoning

a·nal·o·gize (-jiz′) vi. -gized′, -giz′ing to use, or reason by, analogy —vt. to explain or liken by analogy

a·nal·o·gous (-gəs) adj. [L. *analogus* < Gr. *analogos*: see ANALOGY] 1. similar or comparable in certain respects 2. *Biol.* similar in function but not in origin and structure —a·nal′o·gous·ly adv.

an·a·logue, an·a·log (an′ə lôg′, -läg′) n. [Fr. *analogue* < L. *analogus*: see ANALOGY] a thing or part that is analogous —adj. of or by means of an analog computer: in this sense usually **analog**

a·nal·o·gy (ə nal′ə jē) n., pl. -gies [ME. & OFr. *analogie* < L. *analogia* < Gr. *analogia*, proportion < *analogos*, in due ratio < *ana-*, according to + *logos*, ratio: see LOGIC] 1. similarity in some respects between things otherwise unlike; partial resemblance 2. an explaining of something by comparing it point by point with something similar 3. *Biol.* similarity in function between parts dissimilar in origin and structure: cf. HOMOLOGY 4. *Linguis.* the process by which new or less familiar words, constructions, or pronunciations conform to the pattern of older or more familiar (and often unrelated) ones [*energize* is formed from *energy* by analogy with *apologize* from *apology*] 5. *Logic* the inference that certain admitted resemblances imply probable further similarities —SYN. see LIKENESS

an·al·pha·bet·ic (an al′fə bet′ik) adj., n. illiterate

a·nal·y·sand (ə nal′ə sand′) n. [< ANALYS(IS) + -and < L. -andus, gerundive suffix] a person who is undergoing psychoanalysis

an·a·lyse (an′ə liz′) vt. -lysed′, -lys′ing *Chiefly Brit. sp. of* ANALYZE

a·nal·y·sis (ə nal′ə sis) n., pl. -ses′ (-sēz′) [ML. < Gr., a dissolving < *ana-*, up, throughout + *lysis*, a loosing < *lyein*, to LOOSE] 1. a separating or breaking up of any whole into its parts, esp. with an examination of these parts to find out their nature, proportion, function, interrelationship, etc. 2. a statement of the results of this process 3. same as PSYCHOANALYSIS 4. *Chem.* a) the separation of compounds and mixtures into their constituent substances for the purpose of determining the nature (*qualitative analysis*) or the proportion (*quantitative analysis*) of the constituents b) the determination of the nature or proportion of one or more constituents of a substance, whether separated out or not 5. *Linguis.* the use of word order and uninflected function words rather than inflection to express syntactic relationships 6. *Math.* a branch of mathematics, including algebra and calculus, that deals with properties of related variables, esp. properties associated with limits —**in the last** (or **final**) **analysis** after all factors have been considered

an·a·lyst (an′ə list) n. [Fr. *analyste*] 1. a person who analyzes [a news *analyst*] 2. a psychoanalyst

an·a·lyt·ic (an′ə lit′ik) adj. [ML. *analyticus* < Gr. *analytikos* < *analytos*, soluble: see ANALYSIS] 1. *Linguis.* expressing syntactic relationships by the use of uninflected function words instead of inflections, as in English, *more often* instead of *oftener* 2. same as ANALYTICAL 3. *Logic* necessarily true, with its denial resulting in self-contradiction; tautologous [*an analytic proposition*]

an·a·lyt·i·cal (-i k'l) adj. 1. of analysis or analytics 2. skilled in or using analysis 3. that separates into constituent parts 4. same as ANALYTIC (sense 1) —an′a·lyt′i·cal·ly adv.

analytic geometry the branch of geometry in which position is indicated by algebraic symbols and solutions are obtained by algebraic analysis

analytic psychology the system of psychology developed by C. G. Jung as a variant of psychoanalysis

an·a·lyt·ics (an′ə lit′iks) n.pl. [with sing. v.] the part of logic having to do with analyzing

an·a·lyze (an′ə liz′) vt. -lyzed′, -lyz′ing [Fr. *analyser* < *analyse*, ANALYSIS] 1. to separate (a thing, idea, etc.) into its parts so as to find out their nature, proportion, function, interrelationship, etc. 2. to examine in detail so as to determine the nature or tendencies of 3. to psychoanalyze 4. *Chem.* to separate (compounds or mixtures) into their constituent substances in order to determine the nature or the proportion of the constituents 5. *Gram.* to resolve (a

fat, āpe, cär; ten, ēven; is, bīte; gō, hôrn, tōōl, look; oil, out; up, fur; get; joy; yet; chin; she; thin, then; zh, leisure; ŋ, ring; ə for a in ago, e in agent, i in sanity, o in comply, u in focus; ' as in able (ā′b'l); Fr. bâl; ë, Fr. coeur; ö, Fr. feu; Fr. mon; ô, Fr. coq; ü, Fr. duc; r, Fr. cri; H, G. ich; kh, G. doch. See inside front cover. ✿Americanism; ‡foreign; *hypothetical; <derived from

sentence) into its grammatical elements —**an'a·lyz'a·ble** *adj.* —**an'a·lyz'er** *n.*

an·am·ne·sis (an'am nē'sis) *n.* [Gr. *anamnēsis* < *anamimnēskein* < *ana-*, again + *mimnēskein*, to call to mind, akin to *mnasthai*: see AMNESIA] 1. a recollecting of past events 2. *Med.* the case history of a patient —**an'am·nes'tic** (-nes'tik) *adj.*

an·a·mor·phism (an'ə môr'fiz'm) *n.* [ANA- + -MORPH + -ISM] *Geol.* ☆deformation and change in rocks from great pressure and heat deep below the earth's surface

an·a·mor·pho·scope (an'ə môr'fə skōp') *n.* [ANAMORPHO- (SIS) + -SCOPE] a special lens or mirror for making images normal again after distortion by anamorphosis

an·a·mor·pho·sis (an'ə fə sis, -môr fō'sis) *n.*, *pl.* -**ses** (-sēz) [Gr. *anamorphōsis*, a forming anew < *ana-*, again + *morphoun*, to form] 1. a distorted image which looks normal when viewed with a special device 2. *Biol.* a gradual change of form by evolution

An·a·ni·as (an'ə nī'əs) [Gr.] *Bible* a man who fell dead when Peter rebuked him for withholding from the apostles a part of the proceeds from a sale of his land: Acts 5:1–10

an·a·pest, an·a·paest (an'ə pest') *n.* [L. *anapaestus* < Gr. *anapaistos* < *ana-*, back + *paiein*, to strike] 1. a metrical foot in Greek and Latin verse consisting of two short syllables followed by a long one, or, in English, of two unaccented syllables followed by an accented one 2. a line of verse made up of such feet (Ex.: "Ănd thĕ shéen |ŏf thĕir spéars | wăs líke stárs |ŏn thĕ séa") —**an'a·pes'tic**, **an'a·paes'tic**, *adj.*, *n.*

an·a·phase (an'ə fāz') *n.* [ANA- + PHASE] *Biol.* the stage in mitosis, after the metaphase and before the telophase, in which the divided chromosomes move apart toward the poles of the spindle

a·naph·o·ra (ə naf'ər ə) *n.* [L. < Gr. < *ana-*, up, back + *pherein*, to BEAR¹] 1. the rhetorical device of repeating a word or phrase at the beginning of successive clauses or sentences 2. *Linguis.* the device of syntactical cross reference through pronouns, auxiliary verbs, etc.

an·aph·ro·dis·i·ac (an af'rə diz'ē ak) *adj.* that lessens sexual desire —*n.* a drug, etc. that lessens sexual desire

an·a·phy·lax·is (an'ə fə lak'sis) *n.* [ModL. < Gr. *ana-*, intens. + *phylaxis*, a guarding < *phylassein*, to guard] a condition of hypersensitivity to proteins or other substances, caused by previous exposure to the substance and resulting in shock or other physical reactions —**an'a·phy·lac'tic** (-lak'tik) *adj.*

an·a·plas·tic (an'ə plas'tik) *adj. Med.* characterized by a reversion to a more primitive, imperfectly developed form: said of cells

an·ap·tyx·is (an'ap tik'sis) *n.* [ModL. < Gr. *anaptyxis*, an opening, gaping < fut. stem of *anaptyssein*, to unfold, open < *ana-*, up + *ptyssein*, to fold] *Linguis.* the insertion of an extra vowel into a consonant group, usually one containing a liquid or nasal, as in a three-syllable pronunciation of *athlete* (ath'ə lēt') —**an'ap·tyc'tic** (-tik'tik) *adj.*

An·a·pur·na (än'ə poor'nə, an'-) *same as* ANNAPURNA

an·arch (an'ärk) *n.* [< Gr. *anarchos*, without a leader < *an-*, without + *archos*, leader: see -ARCH] an anarchist

an·ar·chic (an är'kik) *adj.* 1. of, like, or involving anarchy 2. advocating anarchy 3. tending to bring about anarchy; lawless Also **an·ar'chi·cal** —**an·ar'chi·cal·ly** *adv.*

an·ar·chism (an'ər kiz'm) *n.* [ANARCH(Y) + -ISM] 1. the theory that all forms of government interfere unjustly with individual liberty and should be replaced by the voluntary association of cooperative groups 2. resistance, sometimes by terrorism, to organized government

an·ar·chist (-kist) *n.* 1. a person who believes in or advocates anarchism 2. a person who promotes anarchy, as by flouting or ignoring rules, duties, orderly behavior, etc. —**an'ar·chis'tic** *adj.*

an·ar·chy (-kē) *n.*, *pl.* -**chies** [Gr. *anarchia*: see ANARCH] 1. the complete absence of government 2. political disorder and violence; lawlessness 3. disorder in any sphere of activity

an·ar·thri·a (an är'thrē ə) *n.* [ModL. < Gr. < *anarthros*, inarticulate (< *an-*, without + *arthron*, articulation, joint: see ARTHRO-)] complete inability to produce articulate speech

an·a·sar·ca (an'ə sär'kə) *n.* [ME. < ML. < Gr. *ana*, throughout + *sarx*, flesh] generalized edema, or dropsy —**an'a·sar'cous** *adj.*

An·a·sta·sia (an'ə stā'shə, -zhə) [LL., fem. of *Anastasius* < Gr. *Anastasios*, lit., of the resurrection] a feminine name

an·as·tig·mat (an as'tig mat') *n.* an anastigmatic lens

an·as·tig·mat·ic (an as'tig mat'ik, an'ə stig-) *adj.* free from, or corrected for, astigmatism; specif., designating a compound lens made up of one converging and one diverging lens so that the astigmatism of one is neutralized by the equal and opposite astigmatism of the other

a·nas·to·mose (ə nas'tə mōz') *vt.*, *vi.* -**mosed'**, -**mos'ing** [Fr. *anastomoser*] to join by anastomosis

a·nas·to·mo·sis (ə nas'tə mō'sis) *n.*, *pl.* -**ses** (-sēz) [ModL. < Gr. *anastomōsis*, opening < *ana-*, again + *stomoein*, to provide with a mouth < *stoma*, mouth] 1. interconnection between blood vessels, veins in a leaf, channels of a river, etc. 2. a surgical joining of one hollow or tubular organ to another, as of the severed ends of the intestine after resection —**a·nas'to·mot'ic** (-mät'ik) *adj.*

a·nas·tro·phe (ə nas'trə fē) *n.* [Gr. *anastrophē* < *anas-*

trephein < *ana-*, back + *strephein*, to turn] reversal of the usual order of the parts of a sentence; inversion (Ex.: "Came the dawn")

anat. 1. anatomical 2. anatomist 3. anatomy

an·a·tase (an'ə tāz') *n.* [Fr. < Gr. *anatasis*, prolongation: so named because of its long crystals] *same as* OCTAHEDRITE

a·nath·e·ma (ə nath'ə mə) *n.*, *pl.* -**mas** [LL.(Ec.) < Gr., thing devoted to evil; previously, anything devoted < *anatithenai*, to set up, dedicate < *ana-*, up + *tithenai*, to set: see FACT] 1. a thing or person accursed or damned 2. a thing or person greatly detested 3. a formal curse or condemnation excommunicating a person from a church or damning something 4. any strong curse

a·nath·e·ma·tize (ə nath'ə mə tīz') *vt.*, *vi.* -**tized'**, -**tiz'-ing** to utter an anathema (against); curse —*SYN.* see CURSE —**a·nath'e·ma·ti·za'tion** *n.*

An·a·to·li·a (an'ə tō'lē ə) 1. formerly, Asia Minor 2. the part of modern Turkey that is in Asia

An·a·to·li·an (-ən) *adj.* 1. of Anatolia or its people 2. designating or of a group of extinct Indo-European languages of ancient Anatolia, including Hittite —*n.* a native or inhabitant of Anatolia

an·a·tom·i·cal (an'ə täm'i k'l) *adj.* [< Gr. *anatomikos*, skilled in anatomy (see ANATOMY) + -ICAL] 1. of or connected with anatomy 2. structural Also **an'a·tom'ic** —**an'a·tom'i·cal·ly** *adv.*

a·nat·o·mist (ə nat'ə mist) *n.* [Fr. *anatomiste*] 1. a person skilled in anatomy 2. a person who analyzes in great detail

a·nat·o·mize (-mīz') *vt.*, *vi.* -**mized'**, -**miz'ing** [ME. *anatomisen* < ML. *anatomizare*: see ANATOMY] 1. to dissect (an animal or plant) in order to examine the structure 2. to analyze in great detail —**a·nat'o·mi·za'tion** *n.*

a·nat·o·my (ə nat'ə mē) *n.*, *pl.* -**mies** [ME. & OFr. *anatomie* < LL. *anatomia* < Gr. *anatomia*, *anatomē*, a cutting up < *analemnein* < *ana-*, up + *temnein*, to cut: cf. ESTEEM] 1. the dissecting of an animal or plant in order to determine the position, structure, etc. of its parts 2. the science of the morphology or structure of animals or plants 3. the structure of an organism or body, or a model of it as dissected 4. a detailed analysis 5. [Archaic] a skeleton

a·nat·ro·pous (ə nat'rə pəs) *adj.* [ModL. *anatropus*: see ANA- & -TROPOUS] *Bot.* completely inverted so that its micropyle is bent down to the attaching stalk: said of an ovule

a·nat·to (ä nät'ō) *n. same as* ANNATTO

An·ax·ag·o·ras (an'ik sag'ər əs) 500?–428? B.C.; Gr. philosopher from Ionia who taught in Athens

A·nax·i·man·der (ə nak'si man'dər) 611?–547? B.C.; Gr. philosopher, astronomer, & mathematician

anc. 1. ancient 2. anciently

-ance (əns, 'ns; *also often* ənts, 'nts) [Fr. *-ance* < L. *-antia*, *-entia*, or directly < L.] a *n.-forming suffix meaning:* 1. the act of *[utterance]* 2. the quality or state of being *[vigilance]* 3. a thing that *[conveyance]* 4. a thing that is *[dissonance, inheritance]* A word ending in -*ance* may combine two or more of the above meanings

an·ces·tor (an'ses'tər, -səs-) *n.* [ME. & OFr. *ancestre* < L. *antecessor*, one who goes before < pp. of *antecedere* < *ante-*, before + *cedere*, to go] 1. any person from whom one is descended, esp. one earlier in a family line than a grandparent; forefather; forebear 2. an early type of animal from which later kinds have evolved 3. anything regarded as a precursor or forerunner of a later thing 4. *Law* the deceased person from whom an estate has been inherited —**an'ces'-tress** (-trəs) *n.fem.*

an·ces·tral (an ses'trəl) *adj.* of or inherited from an ancestor or ancestors —**an·ces'tral·ly** *adv.*

an·ces·try (an'ses'trē, -səs-) *n.*, *pl.* -**tries** [ME. *ancestrie* < OFr. *ancesserie* < *ancestre*, ANCESTOR] 1. family descent or lineage 2. ancestors collectively 3. noble or distinguished descent

An·chi·ses (an kī'sēz) [L. < Gr. *Anchisēs*] *Rom. Myth.* the father of Aeneas

an·chor (aŋ'kər) *n.* [ME. *anker* < OE. *ancor* < L. *anc(h)ora* < Gr. *ankyra*, an anchor, hook < IE. base *ank-*, to bend: cf. ANKLE] 1. a heavy object, usually a shaped iron weight with flukes, lowered by cable or chain to the bottom of water to keep a ship from drifting 2. any device that holds something else secure 3. anything that gives or seems to give stability or security —*vt.* to keep from drifting, giving way, etc., by or as by an anchor —*vi.* 1. to lower the anchor 2. to become fixed —**at anchor** anchored —**drop** (or **cast**) **anchor** 1. to throw or lower the anchor overboard 2. to stay or settle (*in* a place) —**drag anchor** 1. to drift because of the failure of the anchor to hold 2. to lose ground; slip or fail —**ride at anchor** to be anchored: said of ships —**weigh anchor** 1. to raise the anchor 2. to leave; go away

ANCHOR

An·chor·age (aŋ'kər ij, aŋ'krij) [from the anchoring there of early supply ships] seaport in S Alas., on Cook Inlet: pop. 48,000

an·chor·age (aŋ'kər ij, -krij) *n.* 1. money charged for the right to anchor, as in a port 2. an anchoring or being anchored 3. a place to anchor 4. something that can be firmly held on to or relied on

☆**anchor ice** ice that sometimes forms at the bottom of an otherwise unfrozen stream or lake, often covering stones, etc.

an·cho·rite (aŋ′kə rīt′) n. [ME. < OFr. anachorete < LL. anachoreta < Gr. anachōrētēs, one retired < anachōrein < ana-, back + chōrein, to retire < IE. base *ĝhē-, ĝhēi, to be missing, leave, GO¹] a person who lives alone and apart from society for religious meditation; hermit; recluse: also **an′cho·ret** (-rit) —**an′cho·ress** (-ris) n.fem. —**an′cho·rit′ic** (-rit′ik), **an′cho·ret′ic** (-ret′ik) adj.

anchor man 1. the end man in a tug of war 2. the final contestant, as on a relay team or bowling team 3. Radio & TV that member of a team of newscasters who coordinates the reports broadcast from various sources

an·cho·vy (an′chō′vē, -chə-; an′chō′vē) n., pl. **-vies, -vy:** see PLURAL, II, D, 1 [Port. anchova, prob. < VL. *apiuva < L. aphya < Gr. aphyē, small fry] any of a family (Engraulidae) of very small, herringlike fishes found mostly in warm seas: anchovies, esp. the European species (Engraulis encrasicholus), are used as a relish, either canned in oil or made into a salty paste

anchovy pear 1. a West Indian fruit that tastes like a mango 2. the tree (Grias cauliflora) that it grows on

an·chu·sa (aŋ kyŏŏ′sə, an chŏŏ′sə; -zə) n. [L. anchusa < Gr. anchousa] same as ALKANET (senses 1 a & 2)

an·chu·sin (-s′n, -z′n) n. same as ALKANET (sense 1 c)

an·chy·lose (aŋ′kə lōs′) vt., vi. **-losed′, -los′ing** same as ANKYLOSE —**an′chy·lo′sis** (-lō′sis) n.

‡**an·cien ré·gime** (än syan′ rā zhēm′) [Fr., old order] the former social and governmental system, esp. that in France before the Revolution of 1789

an·cient¹ (ān′shənt) adj. [ME. auncient < OFr. ancien < VL. *anteanus < L. ante, before] 1. of times long past; belonging to the early history of the world, esp. before the end of the Western Roman Empire 2. having existed a long time; very old 3. old-fashioned; antiquated 4. [Archaic] having the wisdom, dignity, etc. of age; venerable —n. 1. a person who lived in ancient times 2. an aged person —SYN. see OLD —**the ancients** 1. the people who lived in ancient times 2. the ancient or classical writers and artists, esp. of Greco-Roman times —**an′cient·ness** n.

an·cient² (ān′shənt) n. [confusion of ENSIGN with earlier ancien, ancient] [Archaic] 1. an ensign, or flag 2. a person carrying an ensign

ancient history 1. history from the beginning of recorded events to the end of the Roman Empire in the West in 476 A.D. 2. [Colloq.] something of the recent past that is well known or no longer important

an·cient·ly (-lē) adv. in ancient times

Ancient of Days God or a heavenly judge: cf. Dan. 7:13

an·cient·ry (-rē) n. [Archaic] 1. the quality or state of being ancient 2. ancient times; antiquity

an·cil·lar·y (an′sə ler′ē) adj. [< L. ancillaris < ancilla, maidservant, dim. of fem. of anculus, servant] 1. subordinate (often with to) 2. that serves as an aid; helping; auxiliary

an·ci·pi·tal (an sip′ə t′l) adj. [< L. anceps (gen. ancipitis), two-headed, two-sided < an- for ambi-, on both sides (see AMBI-) + caput, HEAD] Bot. two-edged, as the flat stems of certain grasses: also **an·cip′i·tous** (-təs)

an·con (aŋ′kän) n., pl. **an·co·nes** (aŋ kō′nēz) [L. < Gr. ankon, elbow < ankos, a bend: for base see ANKLE] Archit. a bracketlike projection supporting a cornice; console

An·co·na (äŋ kō′nä) seaport in C Italy, on the Adriatic; pop. 105,000

-an·cy (ən sē, 'n sē; also often, ənt sē, 'nt sē) same as -ANCE

an·cy·los·to·mi·a·sis (aŋ′kə läs′tə mī′ə sis, -sə läs′-; -lōs′-) n. [ModL. < ancylostoma, hookworm genus < Gr. ankylos, crooked (cf. ANKLE) + stoma, the mouth + -IASIS] technical name for HOOKWORM DISEASE

and (and, ən, an, 'n, 'm; stressed, and) conj. [ME. and, an < OE. and, ond; akin to G. und, OHG. unti, OS. endi, ON. enn; the original meaning was "thereupon, then, next"] 1. also; in addition; moreover; as well as: used to join elements of equal grammatical value [apples and pears, a red and white dress, he begged and borrowed] 2. plus; added to [6 and 2 equals 8] 3. as a consequence or result [he told her and she wept] 4. in contrast; but [vegetable oil is digestible and mineral oil is not] 5. [Colloq.] to; in order to [try and come today] 6. [Archaic] then [and it came to pass] 7. [Obs.] if And is sometimes used colloquially as a superfluous element connecting clauses in conversation

An·da·lu·sia (an′də lōō′zhə, -shə) region, formerly a province, of S Spain

An·da·lu·sian (-zhən, -shən) adj. of Andalusia, its people, etc. —n. 1. a native or inhabitant of Andalusia 2. the Spanish dialect of Andalusia

an·da·lu·site (-sīt) n. [< ANDALUSIA, where it was discovered] a silicate of aluminum, Al₂SiO₅, found in rhombic crystals of different colors

An·da·man Islands (an′də mən) group of islands in the Bay of Bengal, southwest of Burma: with the Nicobar Islands, constituting a territory of India (**Andaman and Nicobar Islands**), 3,215 sq. mi.; pop. 64,000

Andaman Sea part of the Indian Ocean, west of the Malay Peninsula and east of the Andaman and Nicobar Islands

an·dan·te (än dän′tā, an dan′tē) adj., adv. [It., prp. of andare, to walk] Music moderate in tempo; slower than allegretto but faster than adagio —n. an andante movement or passage

an·dan·ti·no (än′dän tē′nō, an′dan-) adj., adv. [It., dim. of andante] Music slightly varied from andante; esp. now, slightly faster than andante —n., pl. **-nos** an andantino movement or passage

An·de·an (an dē′ən, an′dē ən) adj. of the Andes Mountains or their inhabitants

An·der·sen (an′dər s'n), **Hans Christian** 1805–75; Dan. novelist, poet, & writer of fairy tales

Andersen Nexø, Martin see Martin Andersen NEXØ

An·der·son (an′dər s'n) [after a Delaware Indian, Chief Anderson] city in EC Ind.: pop. 71,000

Anderson 1. **Carl David,** 1905– ; U.S. physicist; discovered the positron (1932) 2. **Judith,** 1898– ; U.S. actress, born in Australia 3. **Marian,** 190?– ; U.S. contralto 4. **Max·well** (maks′wel, -wəl), 1888–1959; U.S. playwright 5. **Sher·wood** (shur′wood), 1876–1941; U.S. novelist & short-story writer

An·der·son·ville (an′dər s'n vil′) [for Major Robt. Anderson (1805–71), U.S. Army] town in C Ga.: site of a Confederate prison in the Civil War

an·des·ite (an′də zīt′) n. [< ANDES + -ITE¹] a fine-grained rock resembling granite, consisting of plagioclase feldspar with dark ferromagnesian minerals and little or no quartz

An·des (Mountains) (an′dēz) mountain system extending the length of W S. America: highest peak, ACONCAGUA

An·dhra Pra·desh (än′drä prə desh′) state of S India: 106,052 sq. mi.; pop. 35,983,000; cap. Hyderabad

and·i·ron (and′ī′ərn) n. [ME. aundiren (with ending altered by association with IRON) < OFr. andier < Gaul. *andera, andiron, heifer (so named from use of bull's head as ornamentation on andirons) < IE. base *andh-, to sprout, bloom, whence Gr. anthos (cf. ANTHO-)] either of a pair of metal supports with ornamented front uprights, used to hold the wood in a fireplace

☆**and/or** either and or or, according to what is meant [personal and/or real property]

An·dor·ra (an dôr′ə, -där′-) 1. republic in the E Pyrenees, between Spain and France: c. 180 sq. mi.; pop. 19,000 2. its capital: pop. c. 1,000: also called **Andorra la Vel·la** (lä väl′yə) —**An·dor′ran** adj., n.

ANDIRONS

an·dra·dite (an′drə dīt′) n. [after J.B. de Andrada (1763?–1838), Braz. geologist] a variety of iron garnet containing calcium, Ca₃Fe₂Si₃O₁₂, varying from light green to black in color

An·drás·sy (än′dräsh ē) 1. **Count Gyu·la** (dyoo′lä), 1823–90; Hung. statesman; 1st prime minister of Hungary (1867–71) 2. **Count Gyula,** 1860–1929; Hung. statesman; son of prec.

An·dre (än′drā, an′drē), **Major John** 1751–80; Brit. officer hanged as a spy in the Am. Revolution

Andrea del Sarto see Andrea del SARTO

An·dre·ev same as ANDREYEV

An·drew (an′drōō) [OFr. Andrieu < L. Andreas < Gr. Andreas < andreios, manly < anēr (gen. andros), man] 1. a masculine name: dim. Andy; equiv. L. Andreas, Fr. André, It. Andrea, Sp. Andrés 2. Bible one of the twelve apostles; brother of Simon Peter: also called Saint Andrew: his day is Nov. 30

An·drewes (an′drōōz), **Lancelot** 1555–1626; Eng. bishop & theologian; one of the divines who prepared the Authorized Version of the Bible

An·drews (an′drōōz), **Roy Chapman** 1884–1960; U.S. naturalist, explorer, & writer

An·dre·yev (än drā′yef), **Le·o·nid Ni·ko·la·ye·vich** (le′ô nēd′ nē kô lä yā′vich) 1871–1919; Russ. playwright, novelist, & short-story writer

an·dro- (an′drə, -drō) [< Gr. anēr (gen. andros), man, male < IE. base *aner, *ner-, vital force, man, whence Sans. nár-, man, human being, Cym. ner, hero, L. Nero, lit., strong] a combining form meaning: 1. man, male, masculine [androgynous] 2. anther, stamen

An·dro·cles (an′drə klēz′) [L. < Gr. Androklēs] Rom. Legend a slave who escaped death when thrown into the arena with a lion because the lion recognized him as the man who had once extracted a thorn from its foot: also **An′dro·clus** (-kləs)

an·droe·ci·um (an drē′shē əm, -sē əm) n., pl. **-ci·a** (-shē ə, -sē ə) [ModL. < ANDRO- + Gr. oikos, house] Bot. the stamens and the parts belonging to them, collectively; all the microsporophylls of a flower

an·dro·gen (an′drə jən) n. a male sex hormone or synthetic substance that can give rise to masculine characteristics —**an′dro·gen′ic** (-jen′ik) adj.

an·drog·e·nous (an dräj′ə nəs) adj. Biol. producing male offspring

an·dro·gyne (an′drə jin) *n.* an androgynous plant
an·drog·y·nous (an drãj′ə nəs) *adj.* [L. *androgynus* < Gr. *androgynos* < *anēr* (gen. *andros*), man + *gynē*, woman] **1.** both male and female in one; hermaphroditic **2.** *Bot.* bearing both staminate and pistillate flowers in the same inflorescence or cluster —**an·drog′y·ny** (-ə nē) *n.*
an·droid (an′droid) *n.* [ANDR(O)- + -OID] in science fiction, an automaton made to resemble a human being
An·drom·a·che (an drãm′ə kē) [L. < Gr. *Andromachē*] *Gr. Myth.* the faithful wife of Hector
An·drom·e·da (an drãm′ə də) [L. < Gr. *Andromedē*] **1.** *Gr. Myth.* an Ethiopian princess whom Perseus rescued from a sea monster and then married **2.** *Astron.* a N constellation containing the brightest and the nearest of the spiral nebulas, just south of Cassiopeia
An·dros (an′drəs), Sir **Edmund** 1637–1714; Eng. governor of colonies in America
an·dro·sphinx (an′drə sfiŋks′) *n.* a sphinx with the head of a man and the body of a lion
an·dros·ter·one (an drãs′tə rōn′) *n.* [ANDRO- + STER(OL) + -ONE] a steroid, $C_{19}H_{30}O_2$, produced by the metabolism of certain hormones and having weak activity as a male sex hormone
-an·drous (an′drəs) [< Gr. *anēr* (gen. *andros*): see ANDRO-)] *an adj.-forming suffix meaning* having stamens: used in forming botanical adjectives [*monandrous*]
An·dvar·i (än′dwä′rē, änd′vä′rē) *Norse Myth.* a dwarf from whom Loki stole gold and a magic ring
ane (ān) *adj., pron.* [OE. *an*, one] [Scot.] one
-ane (ān) [arbitrary formation] *a suffix denoting* a hydrocarbon of the paraffin series [*methane, ethane*]
a·near (ə nir′) *adv., prep.* [Dial. or Poet.] near
an·ec·dot·age (an′ik dōt′ij) *n.* [ANECDOT(E) + (DOT)AGE] **1.** a collection of anecdotes **2.** senility, as characterized by the telling of rambling anecdotes: a humorous usage
an·ec·dot·al (-dōt′'l) *adj.* **1.** of or like an anecdote **2.** full of anecdotes
an·ec·dote (an′ik dōt′) *n.* [Fr. < ML. *anecdota* < Gr. *anekdota*, neut. pl. of *anekdotos*, unpublished < *an-*, not + *ekdotos* < *ekdidonai* < *ek-*, out + *didonai*, to give] **1.** [*pl.*] originally, little-known, entertaining facts of history or biography **2.** a short, entertaining account of some happening, usually personal or biographical —*SYN.* see STORY[1]
an·ec·dot·ic (an′ik dãt′ik) *adj.* **1.** anecdotal **2.** fond of telling anecdotes Also **an′ec·dot′i·cal**
an·ec·dot·ist (an′ik dōt′ist) *n.* a person who tells or collects anecdotes
an·e·cho·ic (an′e kō′ik) *adj.* [AN-[1] + ECHOIC] free from echoes; completely absorbing sound waves or radar signals [*an anechoic chamber*]
a·nele (ə nēl′) *vt.* -**neled′**, -**nel′ing** [ME. *anelien* < *an-*, on + *elien* < *ele*, oil < OE. *ele* < L. *oleum*] [Archaic] to anoint, esp. in the Anointing of the Sick
a·ne·mi·a (ə nē′mē ə, -myə) *n.* [ModL. < Gr. *anaimia* < *a-, an-*, without + *haima*, blood] **1.** *Med.* a condition in which there is a reduction of the number of red blood corpuscles or of the total amount of hemoglobin in the blood stream or of both, resulting in a paleness, generalized weakness, etc. **2.** lack of vigor or vitality; lifelessness — **a·ne′mic** (-mik) *adj.* —**a·ne′mi·cal·ly** *adv.*
a·ne·mo- (an′ə mə, ə nem′ə) [< Gr. *anemos*, the wind] *a combining form meaning* wind [*anemometer*]
a·nem·o·graph (ə nem′ə graf′) *n.* an instrument for recording the velocity and direction of the wind —**a·nem′o·graph′ic** *adj.*
an·e·mol·o·gy (an′ə mäl′ə jē) *n.* the study of winds
an·e·mom·e·ter (-mäm′ə tər) *n.* a gauge for determining the force or speed of the wind, and sometimes its direction; wind gauge
an·e·mom·e·try (-mäm′ə trē) *n.* the process of determining the speed and direction of the wind with an anemometer —**an·e·mo·met·ric** (an′ə mō met′rik) *adj.*
a·nem·o·ne (ə nem′ə nē′) *n.* [L. < Gr. *anemōnē*, altered, after *anemos*, wind < ? Sem. name] **1.** *Bot.* any of a number of related plants of a genus (*Anemone*) of the buttercup family, with cup-shaped flowers that are usually white, pink, red, or purple **2.** *Zool.* same as SEA ANEMONE
a·nem·o·phi·lous (an′ə mäf′'l əs) *adj.* fertilized by the wind, as plants to which pollen is blown —**an′e·moph′i·ly** (-'l ē) *n.*
a·nem·o·scope (ə nem′ə skōp′) *n.* an instrument for showing or recording the direction of the wind
an·e·mo·sis (an′ə mō′sis) *n.* [ModL. < Gr. *anemos*, the wind + -OSIS] *same as* WIND SHAKE
a·nent (ə nent′) *prep.* [ME. *anent* (with unhistoric -*t*) < OE. *onemn, on efen*, lit., on even (with), level (with)] [Now Rare] concerning; as regards; about
an·er·gy (an′ər jē) *n.* [ModL. *anergia* < Gr. *an-*, without + *ergon*, WORK] *Med.* a condition in which the body fails to respond to the injection of an antigen —**an·er·gic** (an ur′jik) *adj.*
an·er·oid (an′ər oid) *adj.* [< Gr. *a-*, without + *nēros*, liquid + -OID] not using liquid —*n.* same as ANEROID BAROMETER
aneroid barometer a barometer with a needle connected to the top of a metal box in which a partial vacuum is maintained: a change in atmospheric pressure causes the top of the box to bend in or out, thus moving the needle
an·es·the·sia (an′əs thē′zhə, -zhē ə, -zē ə) *n.* [Gr. *anaisthēsia* < *an-*, without + *aisthēsis*, feeling < *aisthanesthai*: see

AESTHETIC] **1.** a partial or total loss of the sense of pain, temperature, touch, etc., produced by disease ☆**2.** a loss of sensation induced by an anesthetic and limited to a specific area (**local anesthesia**) or involving a loss of consciousness (**general anesthesia**)
☆**an·es·the·si·ol·o·gist** (an′əs thē′zē äl′ə jist) *n.* a doctor who specializes in anesthesiology
☆**an·es·the·si·ol·o·gy** (-jē) *n.* the science of anesthesia and anesthetics
☆**an·es·thet·ic** (an′əs thet′ik) *adj.* [< Gr. *anaisthētos* + -IC] **1.** relating to, with, or characterized by anesthesia **2.** producing anesthesia —*n.* a drug, gas, etc. used to produce anesthesia, as before surgery —**anesthetic to** incapable of feeling or responding to —**an′es·thet′i·cal·ly** *adv.*
an·es·the·tist (ə nes′thə tist) *n.* a nurse or other person trained to administer anesthetics
an·es·the·tize (-tīz′) *vt.* -**tized′**, -**tiz′ing** to cause anesthesia in; give an anesthetic to —**an·es′the·ti·za′tion** *n.*
an·es·trus (an es′trəs) *n.* [AN-[1] + ESTRUS] in the breeding cycle of many mammals, the period of sexual inactivity during two periods of estrus —**an·es′trous** (-trəs) *adj.*
A·ne·to (ä ne′tō), **Pi·co de** (pē′kō *the*) highest mountain in the Pyrenees, in Spain: 11,168 ft.: Fr. name, Pic de NÉTHOU
an·eu·rin (an′yər in) *n.* [A-[2] + NEUR- + -IN[1]] *same as* THIAMINE
an·eu·rysm, an·eu·rism (an′yər iz′m) *n.* [ModL. *aneurisma* < Gr. *aneurysma* < *ana-*, up + *eurys*, broad] a sac formed by local enlargement of the weakened wall of an artery, caused by disease or injury —**an′eu·rys′mal, an′eu·ris′mal** (-yə riz′m′l) *adj.*
a·new (ə nōō′, -nyōō′) *adv.* [ME. *aneue* < *of neue*: see A-[1] + NEW] **1.** once more; again **2.** in a new manner or form
an·frac·tu·os·i·ty (an frak′chōō wäs′ə tē) *n.* **1.** the quality or state of being anfractuous **2.** *pl.* -**ties** a winding channel, passage, etc.
an·frac·tu·ous (an frak′chōō wəs) *adj.* [L. *anfractuosus* < *anfractus*, pp. of *anfringere* < *an-* (for *ambi-*), around + *frangere*, to BREAK[1]] full of twists, turns, and windings; roundabout; tortuous
An·ga·ra (än′gä rä′) river in SC Siberia, flowing from Lake Baikal to the Yenisei River: c. 1,100 mi.
an·ga·ry (aŋ′gə rē) *n.* [L. *angaria*, enforced service < Gr. *angaria*, impressment for the public service < *angaros*, a mounted courier, prob. < OPer. term akin to Assyr. *agarru*, hired laborer] *International Law* the right of a belligerent to use or destroy a neutral's property if necessary, with the obligation of full indemnification
an·ge·kok, an·ga·kok (aŋ′gə käk) *n.* [Esk.] an Eskimo medicine man
an·gel (ān′j′l) *n.* [ME. *aungel* < OFr. *angel* or OE. *engel*, or directly < L. *angelus* (whence OFr. & OE. forms) < Gr. *angelos*, messenger < Iran.: cf. ANGARY] **1.** *Theol. a)* a messenger of God *b)* a supernatural being, either good or bad, to whom are attributed greater than human power, intelligence, etc. **2.** a guiding spirit or influence [*one's good angel*] **3.** a conventionalized image of a white-robed figure in human form with wings and a halo **4.** a person regarded as beautiful, good, innocent, etc. **5.** an English gold coin, last issued in 1634, stamped with the archangel Michael and the dragon ☆**6.** [Colloq.] a supporter who provides money, as for producing a play —☆*vt.* [Slang] to support with money —*SYN.* see SPONSOR
An·ge·la (an′jə lə) [contr. of *Angelica* < ML. *angelica*, angelic < L. *angelicus*: see ANGELIC] a feminine name: var. *Angelina, Angelina, Angeline*
☆**An·gel·e·no** (an′jə lē′nō) *n., pl.* -**nos** [AmSp. < (Los) ANGEL(ES) + Sp. -*eño*, suffix denoting inhabitant of given location] a native or inhabitant of Los Angeles
Angel Falls or **Fall** waterfall in SE Venezuela: over 3,200 ft.
an·gel·fish (ān′j′l fish′) *n., pl.* -**fish′**, -**fish′es**: see FISH **1.** a shark (genus *Squatina*) with winglike pectoral fins **2.** any of a number of bright-colored tropical fishes (genus *Holacanthus*) with spiny fins
☆**angel food cake** a light, spongy, white cake made with egg whites and no shortening: also **angel cake**
an·gel·ic (an jel′ik) *adj.* [L. *angelicus* < Gr. *angelikos* < *angelos*: see ANGEL] **1.** of an angel or the angels; spiritual; heavenly **2.** like an angel in beauty, goodness, innocence, etc. Also **an·gel′i·cal** (-i k′l) —**an·gel′i·cal·ly** *adv.*
An·gel·i·ca (an jel′i kə) a feminine name: see ANGELA
an·gel·i·ca (-i kə) *n.* [ML. (*herba*) *angelica*, lit., the angelic (herb) < *angelicus* (see ANGELIC): so named from its medical uses] any of a number of related plants (genus *Angelica*) of the parsley family, with tall stalks, large divided leaves, clusters of white or greenish flowers, and roots and fruit used in flavoring, perfumes, medicine, etc.
☆**angelica tree** *same as* HERCULES'-CLUB
An·gel·i·co (an jel′ə kō′), **Fra** (frä) (*Giovanni da Fiesole*) 1387–1455; It. painter
An·ge·li·na (an′jə lē′nə, -lī′-) a feminine name: see ANGELA
An·ge·line (an′jə lin′) a feminine name: see ANGELA
An·gell (ān′j′l) **1. James Row·land** (rō′lənd), 1869–1949; U.S. educator & psychologist **2. Sir Norman** (*Ralph Norman Angell Lanc*), 1874–1967; Brit. economist, writer, & pacifist
an·gel·ol·o·gy (ān′j′l äl′ə jē) *n.* the branch of theology dealing with angels

An·ge·lus, an·ge·lus (an'jə ləs) *n.* [L. (see ANGEL): so named from the opening words, "Angelus Domini"] *R.C.Ch.* **1.** a prayer said at morning, noon, and evening in commemoration of the Incarnation **2.** the bell rung to announce the time for this prayer

an·ger (aŋ'gər) *n.* [ME. *anger* < ON. *angr*, distress, sorrow < IE. base *angh-*, constricted, seen in L. *angustus*, narrow, tight, *angustia*, tightness, distress (cf. ANGUISH), Gr. *anchonē* (see ANGINA), G. *eng*, narrow, *angst*, fear] **1.** a feeling of displeasure resulting from injury, mistreatment, opposition, etc., and usually showing itself in a desire to fight back at the supposed cause of this feeling **2.** [Dial.] an inflammation of a sore or wound **3.** [Obs.] pain or trouble —*vt.* [ME. *angren* < ON. *angra*, to distress] **1.** to make angry; enrage **2.** [Dial.] to make painfully inflamed —*vi.* to become angry
SYN.—**anger** is broadly applicable to feelings of resentful or revengeful displeasure; **indignation** implies righteous anger aroused by what seems unjust, mean, or insulting; **rage** suggests a violent outburst of anger in which self-control is lost; **fury** implies a frenzied rage that borders on madness; **ire**, chiefly a literary word, suggests a show of great anger in acts, words, looks, etc.; **wrath** implies deep indignation expressing itself in a desire to punish or get revenge —**ANT. pleasure, forbearance**

An·gers (än zhā'; *E.* an'jərz) city in NW France: pop. 115,000

An·ge·vin, An·ge·vine (an'jə vən) *adj.* [Fr.] **1.** of or from Anjou **2.** of or belonging to the Plantagenet line of English kings (1154–1399) —*n.* **1.** a native or inhabitant of Anjou **2.** a person of the Plantagenet royal line

an·gi·na (an jī'nə, an'jə nə) *n.* [L., quinsy < Gr. *anchonē*, a strangling < *anchein*, to squeeze: see ANGER] **1.** any inflammatory disease of the throat, esp. one characterized by spasmodic suffocation **2.** a localized spasm of pain or any condition marked by such spasms; specif., *same as* ANGINA PECTORIS —**an·gi'nal, an·gi·nose** (an'jə nōs'), **an·gi·nous** (-nəs) *adj.*

angina pec·to·ris (pek'tər is) [L., angina of the breast] a condition marked by recurrent pain in the chest and left arm, caused by a sudden decrease of the blood supply to the heart muscle

an·gi·o- (an'jē ō, -ə) [< Gr. *angeion*, case, capsule < *angos*, vessel] *a combining form meaning:* **1.** seedcase [*angiosperm*] **2.** blood vessel or lymph vessel [*angioma*]

an·gi·og·ra·phy (an'jē äg'rə fē) *n.* [ANGIO- + -GRAPHY] the process of making X-ray pictures of blood vessels, by first injecting a radiopaque substance

an·gi·ol·o·gy (an'jē äl'ə jē) *n.* the study of blood vessels and lymph vessels

an·gi·o·ma (an'jē ō'mə) *n., pl.* **-ma·ta** (-mə tə), **-mas** [ANGI(O)- + -OMA] a tumor made up mainly of blood vessels and lymph vessels —**an'gi·om'a·tous** (-äm'ə təs, -ō'mə təs) *adj.*

an·gi·o·sperm (an'jē ə spurm') *n.* any of a class (Angiospermae) of plants, including all the flowering plants, characterized by having the seeds enclosed in an ovary: opposed to GYMNOSPERM —**an'gi·o·sper'mous** *adj.*

Ang·kor (aŋ'kôr) an accumulation of Khmer ruins in NW Cambodia, consisting mainly of **Angkor Thom** (tōm), the capital of the Khmer civilization

Angkor Vat (vät) or **Wat** (wät) ancient Khmer temple in Angkor

Angl. 1. Anglican **2.** Anglicized

an·gle¹ (aŋ'g'l) *n.* [ME. & OFr. < L. *angulus*, a corner, angle < Gr. *ankylos*, bent, crooked: for IE. base, see ANKLE] **1.** the shape made by two straight lines meeting in a point, or by two plane surfaces meeting along a line **2.** the space between such lines or surfaces **3.** the amount of difference in direction between them, measured in degrees **4.** a sharp or projecting corner **5.** an aspect, as of something viewed or considered; point of view [to examine a problem from all *angles*] **6.** [Colloq.] *a)* a disingenuous personal motive *b)* a tricky method for achieving a purpose —*vt., vi.* **-gled**, **-gling 1.** to move or bend at an angle or by means of angles **2.** [Colloq.] to give a specific aspect, bias, or point of view to (a story, report, etc.) —**SYN.** see PHASE

an·gle² (aŋ'g'l) *vi.* **-gled, -gling** [< ME. *angel* < OE. *angul*, fishhook, hook: for IE. base see ANKLE] **1.** to fish with a hook and line **2.** to scheme or use tricks to get something [he *angled* for her attention]

an·gled (aŋ'g'ld) *adj.* **1.** set at an angle **2.** having an angle or angles

angle iron a piece of structural iron or steel in the form of an angle; esp., such a piece in a right angle, used for joining or reinforcing two beams, girders, etc.

angle of attack *Aeron.* the acute angle between the chord of an airfoil and the line of relative air flow

angle of incidence 1. the angle that a light ray or electromagnetic wave striking a surface makes with a line perpendicular to the reflecting surface **2.** [Chiefly Brit.] *same as* ANGLE OF ATTACK

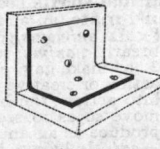

ANGLE IRON

angle of repose the maximum angle of slope at which sand, loose rock, etc., will remain in place without sliding, as on a hillside

angle of view *Optics* the angle subtended by two lines drawn from the corners of the objective to the center of a lens

☆**an·gle·pod** (-päd') *n.* any of a genus (*Gonolobus*) of the milkweed family, esp. a vine (*Gonolobus laevis*) of the SE U.S., bearing angular pods

an·gler (aŋ'glər) *n.* [< ANGLE²] **1.** a fisherman who uses hook and line **2.** a person who schemes and uses tricks to get something **3.** a saltwater fish (*Lophius piscatorius*) that feeds on other fish, luring them into its large mouth by means of a filament that grows from its head; also, any of several similar fishes

ANGLER FISH
(to 4 ft. long)

An·gles (aŋ'g'lz) *n.pl.* [L. *Angli* < PGmc. source of OE. *Angle*, *Ængle*, the Angles < *Angel*, *Angul*, district in Holstein, lit., hook (cf. ANGLE²): so named from its shape] a Germanic people of the northern lowlands that settled in eastern England in the 5th cent. A.D.: the name *England* is from *Englaland* (land of the Angles), and *English* is from *Englisc* (of the Angles)

An·gle·sey, An·gle·sea (aŋ'g'l sē') **1.** county of NW Wales, consisting of a large island and several small adjacent islands: 276 sq. mi.; pop. 52,000 **2.** the large island of this county

an·gle·site (aŋ'glə sīt') *n.* [after ANGLESEY, where it was discovered] a native lead sulfate, PbSO₄, occurring, usually with galena, in colorless or variously colored orthorhombic crystals

☆**an·gle·worm** (aŋ'g'l wurm') *n.* an earthworm: so called because used as fishing bait

An·gli·a (aŋ'glē ə) [see ANGLES] *L. name of* ENGLAND

An·gli·an (-ən) *adj.* **1.** of Anglia; English **2.** of the Angles, their culture, dialect, etc. —*n.* **1.** a member of the Angles **2.** the Old English dialects spoken by the Angles in Mercia and Northumbria

An·glic (aŋ'glik) *n.* a simplified form of English for international communication: developed by R.E. Zachrisson (1880–1937), Swed. linguist —*adj.* Anglian

An·gli·can (aŋ'gli kən) *adj.* [ML. *Anglicanus* < *Anglicus*, of England, of the ANGLES] **1.** of England, its people, or their culture **2.** of the Church of England or of any other church in the Anglican Communion —*n.* a member of the Church of England or of another church in the Anglican Communion —**An'gli·can·ism** *n.*

Anglican Communion the informal organization of the Church of England and derived churches with closely related faith and forms, including the Anglican Church of Canada, the Protestant Episcopal Church in the U.S., the Episcopal Church of Scotland, etc.

‡**An·gli·ce** (aŋ'glə sē) *adv.* [ML. < *Anglicus*] in English; as the English term it [*Livorno*, *Anglice* Leghorn]

An·gli·cism (aŋ'glə siz'm) *n.* [ML. *Anglicus* (see ANGLICAN) + -ISM] **1.** a word or idiom peculiar to English, esp. British English; Briticism **2.** a typically English trait, custom, etc. **3.** the quality of being English

An·gli·cist (-sist) *n.* a student of or authority on the English language and literature

An·gli·cize (aŋ'glə sīz') *vt., vi.* **-cized', -ciz'ing** [ML. *Anglicus* (see ANGLICAN) + -IZE] to change to English idiom, pronunciation, customs, manner, etc. —**An'gli·ci·za'tion** (-si zā'shən) *n.*

☆**An·gli·fy** (-fī') *vt.* **-fied', -fy'ing** to Anglicize

an·gling (aŋ'gliŋ) *n.* [< ANGLE²] the act or skill of fishing with hook and line

An·glo (aŋ'glō) *n., pl.* **-glos** [short for ANGLO-AMERICAN] [Southwest] a white person of non-Mexican descent

An·glo- (aŋ'glō) [< L. *Anglus*, sing. of *Angli*, ANGLES] *a combining form meaning:* **1.** English [*Anglo*-American, *Anglophile*] **2.** Anglican [*Anglo*-Catholic]

☆**An·glo-A·mer·i·can** (-ə mer'ə kən) *adj.* **1.** English and American; of or between England and the U.S. **2.** of Anglo-Americans —*n.* an American of English birth or ancestry

An·glo-Cath·o·lic (-kath'ə lik, -kath'lik) *n.* a member of the Church of England who stresses its continuous tradition with the Catholic Church before and after the Reformation —*adj.* of Anglo-Catholics or their beliefs and practice

An·glo-E·gyp·tian Sudan (-i jip'shən) *former name of* SUDAN (the country)

An·glo-French (-french') *adj.* **1.** English and French; of or between England and France **2.** of Anglo-French —*n.* the French spoken in England from the Norman Conquest through the Middle Ages: see NORMAN FRENCH

An·glo-Fri·sian (-frizh'ən) *adj.* designating or of the subgroup of West Germanic from which Old English and

Old Frisian developed —n. the reconstructed common ancestral language of Old English and Old Frisian

An·glo-In·di·an (-in′dē ən) adj. 1. English and Indian; of or between England and India 2. of Anglo-Indians or their English speech —n. 1. an English citizen living in India 2. a person of both English and Indian ancestry 3. words borrowed into English from the languages of India

☆**An·glo·ma·ni·a** (-mā′nē ə) n. an exaggerated liking for and imitation of English customs, manners, institutions, etc. —**An′glo·ma′ni·ac′** (-ak′) n.

An·glo-Nor·man (-nôr′mən) adj. 1. English and Norman 2. of the Anglo-Normans or their language —n. 1. a Norman settler in England after the Norman Conquest 2. the Anglo-French dialect spoken by such settlers

An·glo·phile (aŋ′glə fīl′) n. [often a-] a person who strongly admires or is devoted to England, its people, customs, influence, etc.

An·glo·phil·i·a (aŋ′glə fil′ē ə) n. [often a-] extreme admiration for England, its people, customs, etc.

An·glo·phobe (aŋ′glə fōb′) n. [often a-] a person who hates or fears England, its people, customs, influence, etc.

☆**An·glo·pho·bi·a** (aŋ′glə fō′bē ə) n. [often a-] hatred or fear of England, its people, customs, etc. —**An′glo·pho′bic** (-fō′bik, -fäb′ik) adj.

An·glo-Sax·on (-sak′s'n) n. [< ML. Anglo-Saxones: see ANGLES & SAXON] 1. a member of the Germanic peoples (Angles, Saxons, and Jutes) who invaded England (5th-6th cent. A.D.) and were there at the time of the Norman Conquest 2. their language, OLD ENGLISH 3. modern English, esp. plain, blunt language of Old English origin 4. a person of English nationality or descent —adj. 1. of the Anglo-Saxons, their language, or culture 2. of their descendants; English

An·go·la (aŋ gō′lə, an-) Port. overseas territory on the SW coast of Africa: 481,351 sq. mi.; pop. 5,258,000; cap. Luanda

An·go·ra (aŋ gôr′ə, an-) n. [after Angora, former name of ANKARA] 1. a kind of cat with long, silky fur: in full, **Angora cat** 2. a) a kind of goat raised for its long, silky hair: in full, **Angora goat** b) this hair (**Angora wool**) or the cloth made from this hair; mohair 3. a) a long-eared rabbit, raised for its long, silky hair: in full, **Angora rabbit** b) this hair c) a soft yarn made from this hair and woven into sweaters, etc. Also **angora**, for senses 2 b, 3 b, 3 c

an·gos·tu·ra (**bark**) (aŋ′gəs toor′ə, -tyoor′-) n. [after Angostura (former name of CIUDAD BOLÍVAR, lit., (in Sp.) narrowness, so named because located on the narrows of the Orinoco] the bitter aromatic bark of either of two S. American trees (Galipea officinalis or Cusparia trifoliata) of the rue family, used as a medicinal tonic and as a flavoring in bitters

an·gry (aŋ′grē) adj. **-gri·er, -gri·est** [ME. angri, troubled < ANGER] 1. feeling, showing, or resulting from anger [an angry reply] 2. wild and stormy, as if angry [an angry sea] 3. inflamed and sore [an angry wound] —**an′gri·ly** (-grə lē) adv. —**an′gri·ness** (-grē nis) n.

angry young men [often A- Y- M-] a group of young writers in Great Britain after World War II, bitterly critical of upper-class and middle-class values, practices, etc.

‡**Angst** (äŋst) n. [G.] [often a-] a gloomy, often neurotic feeling of generalized anxiety and depression

ang·strom (aŋ′strəm) n. [after ff.] one hundred-millionth of a centimeter, a unit used in measuring the length of light waves: also **angstrom unit**

Ång·ström (ôŋ′strəm; E. aŋ′strəm), **An·ders Jöns** (än′ders yöns′) 1814–74; Swed. physicist

An·guil·la (aŋ gwil′ə) island of the Leeward group, constituting, with St. Christopher and Nevis islands, a Brit. self-governing territory in the West Indies: 35 sq. mi.; pop. 6,000

an·guish (aŋ′gwish) n. [ME. angwisshe < OFr. anguisse < L. angustia, tightness, distress: see ANGER] great suffering, as from worry, grief, or pain; agony —vt. to cause to feel anguish —vi. to feel anguish —SYN. see DISTRESS

an·guished (-gwisht) adj. 1. feeling anguish 2. showing or resulting from anguish

an·gu·lar (aŋ′gyə lər) adj. [L. angularis < angulus: see ANGLE¹] 1. having or forming an angle or angles; having sharp corners 2. measured by an angle [angular distance] 3. with bones that jut out; gaunt 4. without ease or grace; stiff [an angular stride] —**an′gu·lar·ly** adv. —**an′gu·lar·ness** n.

an·gu·lar·i·ty (aŋ′gyə ler′ə tē) n., pl. **-ties** 1. the quality or condition of being angular 2. [pl.] angular forms; sharp corners; angles

an·gu·late (aŋ′gyə lit; also, and for v. always, -lāt′) adj. [L. angulatus, pp. of angulare, to make angular < angulus, ANGLE¹] having angles or corners —vt., vi. **-lat′ed, -lat′ing** to make or become angular —**an′gu·late·ly** adv.

an·gu·la·tion (aŋ′gyə lā′shən) n. 1. the act of angulating 2. an angular form, part, or position

An·gus (aŋ′gəs) [Gael. Aonghas & Ir. Aonghus < aon, one] 1. a masculine name 2. Celtic Myth. the god of love 3. county of E Scotland, on the North Sea: 873 sq. mi.; pop. 280,000; county seat, Forfar: former name, FORFAR or FORFARSHIRE

ang·wan·ti·bo (aŋ gwän′tə bō′) n., pl. **-bos′** [Efik] a small lemur (Arctocebus calabarensis) of W African forests, with a long, sharp nose and a small tail

An·halt (än′hält) former state of C Germany: since 1945 a part of East Germany

☆**an·hin·ga** (an hiŋ′gə) n. [Port. < Tupi name] same as DARTER (sense 2)

An·hwei (än′hwā′) province of E China: c. 54,000 sq. mi.; pop. 33,560,000; cap. Hofei: also sp. **An′hui′**

an·hy·dride (an hī′drīd) n. [< Gr. anhydros (see ANHYDROUS) + -IDE] 1. an oxide that reacts with water to form an acid or a base 2. any compound formed by the removal of the elements of water, usually from an acid

an·hy·drite (-drīt) n. [< Gr. anhydros (see ANHYDROUS) + -ITE¹] anhydrous calcium sulfate, CaSO₄, a granular, white or light-colored mineral resembling marble, often found together with rock salt

an·hy·drous (-drəs) adj. [Gr. anhydros < an-, without + hydōr, water: see HYDRO-] 1. without water 2. Chem. having no water of crystallization; not hydrated

a·ni (ä′nē) n., pl. a′nis (-nēz) [Port. < native name in Brazil] an American bird (genus Crotophaga), generally black, belonging to the cuckoo family

an·il (an′il) n. [Fr. < Port. < Ar. an-nil < al, the + nil, blue < Sans. nīla, dark blue] 1. a West Indian shrub (Indigofera suffruticosa) of the legume family, from which indigo is made 2. same as INDIGO

an·ile (an′īl, ā′nil) adj. [L. anilis < anus, old woman < IE. base *an-, designation of male or female ancestor (whence G. ahn, grandfather), orig. < baby talk] of or like an old woman; infirm; weak —**a·nil·i·ty** (ə nil′ə tē) n.

an·i·line (an′'l in, -ēn′, -īn′) n. [ANIL + -INE⁴] a colorless, poisonous, oily liquid, C₆H₅NH₂, a derivative of benzene used in making dyes, resins, varnishes, and rocket fuel, and in organic synthesis

aniline dye 1. any dye made from aniline 2. any dye that is chemically like aniline; commonly, any dye produced synthetically from coal-tar products

an·i·ma (an′ə mə) n. [L.] life principle; soul

an·i·mad·ver·sion (an′ə mad vur′zhən, -məd-; -shən) n. [L. animadversio < pp. of animadvertere: see ANIMADVERT] 1. a critical, esp. unfavorable, comment (on or upon something) 2. the act of criticizing adversely

an·i·mad·vert (-vurt′) vi. [L. animadvertere, to observe, censure < animum (acc. of animus, mind) + advertere, to turn: see ANIMUS & ADVERT] to comment (on or upon), esp. with disapproval; criticize adversely

an·i·mal (an′ə m'l) n. [L., living being < anima, animus, breath, air, life principle, soul < IE. base *an(e)-, to breathe, exhale, whence Sans. anilas, wind, breath, OE. antha, excitement, anger] 1. any living organism except a plant or bacterium: most animals can move about voluntarily and have specialized sense organs that enable them to react more quickly than plants to stimuli: animals are unable to make their own food, the way plants do, from inorganic matter by photosynthesis 2. any such organism other than a human being, esp. a mammal or, sometimes, any four-footed creature 3. a brutish, debased, or inhuman person —adj. 1. of, like, or derived from animals 2. physical rather than mental or spiritual; specif., sensual, gross, bestial, etc. —SYN. see CARNAL —**the animal** animal nature; animality [it's the animal in him] —**an′i·mal·ly** adv.

☆**animal cracker** a small, sweet cracker shaped like any of various animals

an·i·mal·cule (an′ə mal′kyool) n. [ModL. animalculum, dim.: see ANIMAL] a very small animal, esp. one that cannot be seen without a microscope —**an′i·mal′cu·lar** (-kyə lər) adj.

an·i·mal·cu·lum (-kyoo ləm) n., pl. **-la** (-lə) [see ANIMALCULE] same as ANIMALCULE

animal husbandry the care and raising of domesticated animals, as cattle, horses, sheep, etc.

an·i·mal·ism (an′ə m'l iz'm) n. 1. the activity, appetites, nature, etc. of animals 2. the doctrine that man is a mere animal with no soul or spiritual quality —**an′i·mal·ist** n. —**an′i·mal·is′tic** adj.

an·i·mal·i·ty (an′ə mal′ə tē) n. [Fr. animalité < LL. animalitas: see ANIMAL] 1. animal characteristics or nature 2. the animal kingdom; animal life 3. the animal instincts or nature in man

an·i·mal·ize (an′ə mə līz′) vt. **-ized′, -iz′ing** 1. to change into animal matter 2. to make (a person) resemble a beast; brutalize; dehumanize —**an′i·mal·i·za′tion** (-li zā′-shən) n.

animal magnetism 1. former var. of HYPNOTISM 2. the power to attract others in a physical or sensual way

animal spirits healthy, lively vigor

an·i·mate (an′ə māt′; for adj. -mit) vt. **-mat′ed, -mat′ing** [< L. animatus, pp. of animare, to make alive, fill with breath < anima: see ANIMAL] 1. to give life to; bring to life 2. to make gay, energetic, or spirited 3. to stimulate to action or creative effort; inspire 4. to give motion to; put into action [the breeze animated the leaves] 5. to make move so as to seem lifelike [to animate puppets] 6. to produce as an animated cartoon [to animate a fairy tale] —adj. 1. living; having life, esp. animal life 2. lively; vigorous; spirited

SYN.—**animate** implies a making alive or lively [an animated conversation] or an imparting of motion or activity [an animated doll]; to **quicken** is to rouse to action that which is lifeless or inert [the rebuff quickened his resolution]; **exhilarate** implies an enlivening or elevation of the spirits; **stimulate** implies a rousing from

inertia, inactivity, or lethargy, as if by goading; **invigorate** means to fill with vigor or energy in a physical sense [an *invigorating* tonic]; **vitalize** implies the imparting of vigor or animation in a non-physical sense [to *vitalize* a dull story] —*ANT.* **deaden, depress, enervate** See also LIVING

an·i·mat·ed (-māt'id) *adj.* **1.** alive or seeming alive; living or lifelike **2.** showing animation; lively; gay —*SYN.* see LIVELY, LIVING —**an'i·mat'ed·ly** *adv.*

☆**animated cartoon** a motion picture made by photographing a series of drawings, each showing a stage of movement slightly changed from the one before, so that the figures in them seem to move when the drawings are projected in rapid succession

an·i·mat·er (-māt'ər) *n. same as* ANIMATOR

an·i·ma·tion (an'ə mā'shən) *n.* **1.** an animating or being animated **2.** an animate condition; life **3.** vivacity; brisk, lively quality **4.** the preparation of animated cartoons **5.** *same as* ANIMATED CARTOON

an·i·ma·tism (an'ə mə tiz'm) *n.* the belief that inanimate things have consciousness or personality

‡**a·ni·ma·to** (ä'nē mä'tô) *adj., adv.* [It.] *Music* with animation: a direction to the performer

an·i·ma·tor (an'ə māt'ər) *n.* [L.] **1.** a person or thing that animates **2.** an artist who draws animated cartoons; specif., one who draws the progressive changes in movement

an·i·mé (an'ə mā', -mē') *n.* [Fr. < Port. or Sp. *anime*, prob. < native (Tupi) name] any of various resins obtained from certain tropical trees and used in making varnish; esp., a variety of copal

an·i·mism (an'ə miz'm) *n.* [Fr. *animisme* & G. *animismus*, both < L. *anima*, soul: see ANIMAL & -ISM] **1.** the doctrine that all life is produced by a spiritual force separate from matter **2.** the belief that all natural phenomena have souls independent of their physical being **3.** a belief in the existence of spirits, demons, etc. —**an'i·mist** *n.* —**an'i·mis'tic** *adj.*

an·i·mos·i·ty (an'ə mäs'ə tē) *n., pl.* **-ties** [ME. *animosite* < L. *animositas*, boldness, spirit < *animosus*, spirited < *animus*: see ANIMUS] a feeling of strong dislike or hatred; ill will; hostility —*SYN.* see ENMITY

an·i·mus (an'ə məs) *n.* [L., soul, mind, disposition, passion, akin to *anima*: see ANIMAL] **1.** an animating force or underlying purpose; intention **2.** a feeling of strong ill will or hatred; animosity

an·i·on (an'ī'ən) *n.* [a special application. orig. by Faraday, of Gr. *anion*, thing going up, neut. prp. of *anienai*, to go up < *ana-*, up + *ienai*, to go] the negatively charged atom or radical in an ionic compound: in electrolysis, anions move toward the anode: opposed to CATION —**an·i·on·ic** (an'ī än'ik) *adj.*

an·ise (an'is) *n.* [ME. & OFr. *anis* < L. *anisum* < Gr. *aneson*, orig. *anēthon* < foreign native name] **1.** a plant (*Pimpinella anisum*) of the parsley family, with small, white or yellow flowers **2.** its fragrant seed, used for flavoring and as a medicine for expelling intestinal gas

an·i·seed (an'ə sēd') *n. same as* ANISE (sense 2)

an·i·sei·ko·ni·a (an i'sī kō'nē ə) *n.* [ModL. < *aniso-* (see ANISO-) + Gr. *eikon* (see ICON), an image + ModL. *-ia*, -IA] a condition in which the image seen by one eye is larger than that seen by the other eye —**an·i'sei·kon'ic** (-kän'ik) *adj.*

an·i·sette (an'ə set', -zet') *n.* [Fr., dim. < *anis*: see ANISE] a sweet, anise flavored liqueur

an·i·so- (an i'sə) [< Gr. *anisos*, unequal < *an-*, not + *isos*, equal] *a combining form meaning* not equal, not alike [*anisomerous*]: also, before a vowel, **anis-**

an·i·so·gam·ete (an i'sə gam'ēt, -gə mēt') *n. same as* HETEROGAMETE —**an·i·sog·a·mous** (an'i säg'ə məs) *adj.* —**an'i·sog'a·my** (-mē) *n.*

an·i·sole (an'ə sōl') *n.* [Fr. *anisol* < *anis* (see ANISE) + *-ol*, -OLE] a colorless, fragrant liquid, C₆H₅OCH₃, made by heating phenol with methyl alcohol: it is used in making perfumes

an·i·som·er·ous (an'i säm'ər əs) *adj.* [ANISO- + -MEROUS] *Bot.* having an unequal number of parts in the floral whorls

an·i·so·met·ric (an'i sō met'rik) *adj.* [AN-¹ + ISOMETRIC] not isometric; with asymmetrical parts

an·i·so·me·tro·pi·a (an'ə mə trō'pē ə) *n.* [ANISO- + METR(O)-¹ + -OPIA] a condition of the eyes in which they have unequal refractive power —**an·i'so·me·trop'ic** (-träp'ik) *adj.*

an·i·so·trop·ic (-träp'ik) *adj.* [AN-¹ + ISOTROPIC] **1.** *Bot.* having unequal responses to external stimuli **2.** *Physics* having properties, as conductivity, speed of transmission of light, etc., that vary according to the direction in which they are measured —**an·i·sot'ro·py** (an'i sät'rə pē), **an'i·sot'ro·pism** (-piz'm) *n.* —**an·i'so·trop'i·cal·ly** *adv.*

A·ni·ta (ə nēt'ə) [Sp. dim.: see ANNA] a feminine name: dim. *Nita*

An·jou (an'jōō; Fr. äṇ zhōō') former province of W France: Anjou gave rise to the Plantagenet house of England through Henry II, son of Geoffrey (IV) Plantagenet, Count of Anjou

An·ka·ra (aṇ'kər ə, äṇ'-) capital of Turkey, in the central part: pop. 650,000

an·ker·ite (aṇ'kə rīt') *n.* [G. *ankerit*, after the 19th-cent.

Austrian mineralogist *Anker*] a mineral much like dolomite but with iron replacing an important part of the magnesium

ankh (aṇk) *n.* [Egypt., life, soul] a cross with a loop at the top, an ancient Egyptian symbol of life

An·king (än'kiṇ') city in Anhwei province, China, on the Yangtze River: pop. 121,000

an·kle (aṇ'k'l) *n.* [ME. *ancle, ancleou* < OE. *ancleow* (& ? ON. *ǫkkla*) < IE. base *ang-*, limb, var. of *ank-*, to bend: cf. ANGLE¹] **1.** the joint that connects the foot and the leg **2.** the part of the leg between the foot and calf

ANKH

an·kle·bone (-bōn') *n.* the bone of the ankle; talus

an·klet (aṇ'klit) *n.* **1.** anything worn around the ankle as a fetter, ornament, or support **2.** a short sock worn by children or women, esp. by girls

an·kus (aṇ'kəs) *n.* [Hind. *aṅkus* < Sans. *aṅkuçá-ḥ*, hook, fishhook, elephant goad < IE. base *ank-*, to bend, whence ANGLE², ANKLE] a pointed spike with a hook, used, esp. in India, for goading or leading an elephant

an·ky·lo·saur (aṇ'kə lō sôr') *n.* [< ModL. *ankylosauria*, name of the suborder < Gr. *ankylos*, crooked (for IE. base see ANGLE¹) + *saurus*, lizard (see -SAURUS)] any of a number of heavily armored, herbivorous dinosaurs of the Cretaceous

an·ky·lose (aṇ'kə lōs') *vt., vi.* **-losed', -los'ing** [< ANKY-LOSIS] to stiffen or join by ankylosis

an·ky·lo·sis (aṇ'kə lō'sis) *n.* [Gr. *ankylōsis* < *ankyloun*, to crook, stiffen < *ankylos*, crooked, bent: for IE. base see ANKLE] **1.** *Med.* a stiffening of a joint, caused by the pathological joining of bones or fibrous parts **2.** *Zool.* a joining of bones or fibrous parts into a single part —**an'ky·lot'ic** (-lät'ik) *adj.*

an·ky·los·to·mi·a·sis (aṇ'kə läs'tə mī'ə sis, -lōs'-) *n. same as* ANCYLOSTOMIASIS

an·lace (an'ləs) *n.* [ME. *anelas*, altered by metathesis < OFr. *alenas, alesnaz* < *alesne*, awl < Gmc. *alisna* (whence G. *else*, sail-maker's awl) + *-az* (< L. *-aceus*)] a broad, tapering medieval dagger

☆**an·la·ge** (än'lä'gə) *n., pl.* **-gen** (-gən), **-ges** (-gəz) [G., foundation < *anlegen*, lay out] [*also* A-] **1.** the basis of a later development; foundation **2.** *same as* PRIMORDIUM

Ann (an) a feminine name: see ANNA

ann. 1. annual **2.** annuity

An·na (an'ə) [Fr. *Anne* < L. *Anna* < Gr. *Anna* < Heb. *ḥannāh*, lit., grace] a feminine name: dim. *Annie, Nan, Nancy*; var. *Ann, Anne, Hannah*; equiv. Fr. *Anne, Annette, Nannette*, Sp. *Ana*

an·na (an'ə, ä'nə) *n.* [Hindi *ānā*] a former monetary unit and coin of India, Pakistan, and Burma, equal to 1/16 of one rupee

An·na·bel, An·na·belle (an'ə bel') [? altered < *Amabel* < L. *amabilis*, lovable < *amare*, to love: now associated with ANNA & BELLE] a feminine name

an·na·berg·ite (an'ə bur'gīt) *n.* [< *Annaberg*, town in Germany + -ITE¹] a green monoclinic mineral, Ni₃(AsO₄)₂·8H₂O, found in association with other nickel ores and produced by the hydration of their arsenides

an·nal·ist (an'l ist) *n.* a person who writes annals —**an'nal·is'tic** *adj.*

an·nals (an'l'z) *n.pl.* [L. *annalis*, pl. *annales* < *annus*, year] **1.** a written account of events year by year in chronological order **2.** historical records or chronicles; history **3.** any journal containing reports of discoveries in some field, meetings of a society, etc.

An·nam (an am', an'am) region & former Fr. protectorate in EC Indochina: since 1954, divided between North Vietnam and South Vietnam

An·na·mese (an'ə mēz', -mēs') *n., pl.* **-mese' 1.** one of a Mongolian people in the region of Annam and Cochin China **2.** the language of these people; Vietnamese —*adj.* of the Annamese, their language, etc. Also **An'na·mite'** (-mīt')

An·nap·o·lis (ə nap'ə lis) [< *Anna* (cf. ANNE) + Gr. *polis*, city] capital of Md., on Chesapeake Bay: pop. 30,000: site of U.S. Naval Academy

An·na·pur·na (än'ə poor'nə, an'ə pur'nə) mountain mass of the Himalayas, in C Nepal: highest peak, c. 26,500 ft.: also sp. **An'a·pur'na**

Ann Ar·bor (an är'bər) [prob. after *Ann* Allen, early settler, and the woody site] city in SE Mich.: pop. 100,000

an·nat·to (ə nät'ō) *n.* [of WInd. origin] a dye of reddish yellow made from pulp around the seeds of a tropical tree (*Bixa orellana*): it is used for coloring butter, cheese, varnishes, etc.

Anne (an) **1.** a feminine name: see ANNA **2.** 1665–1714; queen of Great Britain and Ireland (1702–14); last of the Stuart monarchs **3.** Saint, according to New Testament Apocrypha, the mother of the Virgin Mary: her day is July 26

an·neal¹ (ə nēl') *vt.* [ME. *anelen* < OE. *anǣlan*, to burn < *an-, on-*, on + *ǣlan*, to burn < *al, ǣl*, fire] **1.** to heat (glass, metals, etc.) and then cool slowly to prevent brittleness **2.** to strengthen and temper (the mind, will, etc.) **3.**

[Archaic] to fire or glaze, as in a kiln —**an·neal'er** *n.*

an·neal² (ə nēl') *vt.* [Archaic] *same as* ANELE

Anne Boleyn *see* BOLEYN

an·ne·lid (an'ʼl id) *n.* [Fr. *annélide* < *annelés*, ringed < L. *annellus*, dim. of *anulus*, a ring: see ANNULAR] any of a phylum (Annelida) of worms with a body made of joined segments or rings, as the earthworm, leech, etc. —*adj.* of this phylum —**an·nel·i·dan** (ə nel'ə dən) *adj.*

Anne of Austria 1601–66; wife of Louis XIII of France; regent (1643–61) during minority of Louis XIV

Anne of Cleves (klēvz) 1515–57; 4th wife of Henry VIII of England

An·nette (an et', ə net') a feminine name: see ANNA

an·nex (ə neks'; *for n.* an'eks) *vt.* [ME. *annexen* < OFr. *annexer* < L. *annexus*, pp. of *annectere* < *ad-*, to + *nectere*, to tie, bind] **1.** to add on or attach, as a smaller thing to a larger; append **2.** to add to as a condition, consequence, etc. **3.** to incorporate into a country, state, etc. the territory of (another country, state, etc.) **4.** to take or appropriate, esp. without asking **5.** [Archaic] to join; connect —*n.* something added on; specif., *a*) a wing added to a building *b*) a nearby building used as an addition to the main building *c*) a section added to a document, record, etc.; addendum —**an·nex·a·tion** (an'ek sā'shən) *n.* —**an'nex·a'tion·ist** *n.*

an·nexe (an'eks) *n.* [Fr.] *Brit. var. of* ANNEX (senses *a* & *b*)

an·nex·ment (ə neks'mənt) *n.* [Rare] something annexed

☆**An·nie Oak·ley** (an'ē ōk'lē) [after woman rifle expert (1860–1926) ? because her small targets resembled punched tickets] [Slang] a free ticket; pass

an·ni·hi·la·ble (ə nī'ə lə b'l) *adj.* that can be annihilated

an·ni·hi·late (ə nī'ə lāt') *vt.* **-lat·ed, -lat·ing** [< LL. *annihilatus*, pp. of *annihilare*, to bring to nothing < L. *ad*, to + *nihil*, nothing] **1.** to destroy completely; put out of existence; demolish [an atomic bomb can *annihilate* a city] **2.** to consider or cause to be of no importance or without effect; nullify [to *annihilate* another's ambition] **3.** to kill **4.** to conquer decisively; crush —**an·ni'hi·la'tion** *n.* —**an·ni'hi·la'tive** *adj.* —**an·ni'hi·la'tor** *n.*

an·ni·ver·sa·ry (an'ə vur'sər ē) *n., pl.* **-ries** [ME. *anniversarie* < ML. *anniversaria* (*dies*), anniversary (day) < L. *anniversarius* < *annus*, year + *versum*, pp. of *vertere*, to turn] **1.** the date on which some event occurred in an earlier year **2.** the celebration of such an event on that date in following years —*adj.* **1.** that is an anniversary **2.** of or connected with an anniversary

‡**an·no Do·mi·ni** (än'ō dō̍'mə nē, an'-; -däm'ə-; -nī) [L., lit., in the year of the Lord] in the (given) year since the beginning of the Christian Era

‡**an·no mun·di** (mun'dē, moon'dē) [L., lit., in the year of the world] in the (given) year since the supposed creation of the world

an·no·tate (an'ə tāt', -ō-) *vt., vi.* **-tat·ed, -tat·ing** [< L. *annotatus*, pp. of *annotare* < *ad-*, + *notare*, to note, mark < *nota*: see NOTE] to provide critical or explanatory notes for (a literary work, etc.) —**an'no·ta'tive** *adj.* —**an'no·ta'tor** *n.*

an·no·ta·tion (an'ə tā'shən, -ō-) *n.* **1.** an annotating or being annotated **2.** a critical or explanatory note or notes

an·nounce (ə nouns') *vt.* **-nounced', -nounc'ing** [OFr. *anoncier* < L. *annuntiare*, to make known < *ad-*, to + *nuntiare*, to report < *nuntius*, messenger: cf. NUNCIO] **1.** to declare publicly; give notice of formally; proclaim **2.** to say or tell **3.** to make known the arrival of **4.** to make known through the senses [footsteps *announced* his return] **5.** *Radio & TV* to be an announcer for —*vi.* **1.** to serve as a radio or television announcer ☆**2.** to make known publicly one's candidacy or one's political endorsement of another (with *for*) —*SYN.* see DECLARE

an·nounce·ment (-mənt) *n.* **1.** an announcing or being announced **2.** something announced **3.** a written or printed notice [an engraved wedding *announcement*]

an·nounc·er (-ər) *n.* a person who announces; specif., one who introduces radio or television programs, identifies the station, reads the news, etc.

‡**an·no ur·bis con·di·tae** (än'ō ʉr'bis kän'də tē, an'ō) [L.] in the (given) year of the founded city: the ancient Roman way of reckoning dates from Rome's founding, c. 753 B.C.

an·noy (ə noi') *vt.* [ME. *anoien* < OFr. *anoier* < VL. *inodiare* < *in odio habere* (or *esse*), to have (or be) in hate: see ODIUM] **1.** to irritate, bother, or make somewhat angry, as by a repeated action, noise, etc. **2.** to harm by repeated attacks; harry; molest —*vi.* to be annoying —**an·noy'er** *n.* **SYN.**—**annoy** implies temporary disturbance of mind caused by something that displeases one or tries one's patience; **vex** implies a more serious source of irritation and greater disturbance, often intense worry; **irk** stresses a wearing down of one's patience by persistent annoyance; **bother** implies minor disturbance of one's peace of mind and may suggest mild perplexity or anxiety; to **tease** is to annoy by persistent, irritating actions, remarks, etc.; **plague** suggests mental torment comparable to the physical suffering caused by an affliction —**ANT.** comfort, soothe

an·noy·ance (-əns) *n.* **1.** an annoying or being annoyed **2.** a thing or person that annoys

an·noy·ing (-iŋ) *adj.* irritating; vexing; bothersome —**an·noy'ing·ly** *adv.*

an·nu·al (an'yoo wəl, -yool) *adj.* [ME. & OFr. *annuel* < L. *annualis*, yearly < *annus*, year < IE. **atnos* < *at-*, to go,

year, whence Goth. *athnam* (dat. pl.), years, Sans. *átati*, he goes] **1.** of or measured by a year **2.** that comes or happens once a year; yearly **3.** for a year's time, work, etc. [an *annual wage*] **4.** living or lasting for only one year or season [an *annual plant*] —*n.* **1.** a book or magazine published once a year; yearbook, as one brought out by the senior class in a school or college, with pictures and reports of the preceding school year **2.** a plant that lives only one year or season —**an'nu·al·ly** *adv.*

annual ring any of the concentric rings seen in cross sections of the stems of most trees and shrubs: each ring is a layer of wood that is a year's growth

an·nu·i·tant (ə noō'ə tənt, -nyoō'-) *n.* a person receiving an annuity

an·nu·i·ty (ə noō'ə tē, -nyoō'-) *n., pl.* **-ties** [ME. & OFr. *annuite* < ML. *annuitas* < L. *annuus*, annual < *annus*: see ANNUAL] **1.** a payment of a fixed sum of money at regular intervals of time, esp. yearly **2.** an investment yielding fixed payments during the holder's lifetime, for a stated number of years, or in perpetuity

an·nul (ə nul') *vt.* **-nulled', -nul'ling** [ME. *annullen* < OFr. *anuller* < LL. *annullare*, to bring to nothing < L. *ad-*, to + *nullum*, nothing, neut. of *nullus*: see NULL] **1.** to do away with; put an end to **2.** to make no longer binding under the law; invalidate; cancel —*SYN.* see ABOLISH

an·nu·lar (an'yoo lər) *adj.* [L. *anularis* < *anulus*, a ring < *anus*, a ring] of, like, or forming a ring —*SYN.* see ROUND¹ —**an'nu·lar'i·ty** (-ler'ə tē) *n.* —**an'nu·lar·ly** *adv.*

annular eclipse an eclipse in which a ring of sunlight can be seen around the disk of the moon

annular ligament *Anat.* the ligament surrounding the ankle joint or wrist joint

an·nu·late (an'yoo lit, -lāt') *adj.* [L. *anulatus* < *anulus*: see ANNULAR] **1.** provided or marked with rings; ringed **2.** made up of rings Also **an'nu·lat'ed**

an·nu·la·tion (an'yoo lā'shən) *n.* **1.** formation of rings **2.** a ring or ringlike structure

an·nu·let (an'yoo lət) *n.* [< L. *anulus*, a ring + -ET] **1.** a small ring **2.** *Archit.* a ringlike molding where the shaft of a column joins the capital

an·nul·ment (ə nul'mənt) *n.* **1.** an annulling or being annulled **2.** an invalidation, as of a marriage, by the decree of a court

an·nu·lus (an'yoo ləs) *n., pl.* **-li'** (-lī') **-lus·es** [< L. *anulus* (incorrectly *annulus*)] any ring or ringlike part, mark, etc.

an·nun·ci·ate (ə nun'sē āt', -shē-) *vt.* **-at'ed, -at'ing** [< L. *annuntiatus*, pp. of *annuntiare*, ANNOUNCE] to announce

an·nun·ci·a·tion (ə nun'sē ā'shən, -shē-) *n.* [LL. *annuntiatio*: see ANNOUNCE] **1.** an announcing or being announced **2.** an announcement **3.** [A-] *Eccles. a*) the angel Gabriel's announcement to Mary that she was to give birth to Jesus: Luke 1:26–38 *b*) the church festival on March 25 commemorating this

an·nun·ci·a·tor (ə nun'sē āt'ər, -shē-) *n.* [LL. *annuntiator*] **1.** a person or thing that announces ☆**2.** an electric indicator, as a light or buzzer, used in hotels, offices, etc. to show the source of calls

Annunzio, Gabriele D' *see* D'ANNUNZIO

an·ode (an'ōd) *n.* [special application, by Faraday, of Gr. *anodos*, a way up < *ana-*, up + *hodos*, way] **1.** in an electrolytic cell, the positively charged electrode, toward which current flows **2.** in an electron tube, the principal electrode for collecting electrons, operated at a positive potential with respect to the cathode **3.** in a battery that is a source of electric current, the negative electrode —**an·o·dal** (an ō'd'l), **an·od·ic** (an äd'ik) *adj.*

an·o·dize (an'ə dīz') *vt.* **-dized', -diz'ing** to put a protective, often colored, oxide film on (a light metal) by an electrolytic process in which the metal serves as the anode

an·o·dyne (an'ə din') *adj.* [L. *anodynus* < Gr. *anōdynos* < *an-*, without + *odynē*, pain] relieving or lessening pain; soothing —*n.* anything that relieves pain or soothes —**an'o·dyn'ic** (-din'ik) *adj.*

a·noint (ə noint') *vt.* [ME. *anointen* < OFr. *enoindre* < L. *inungere* < *in-*, on + *ungere*, to smear] **1.** to rub oil or ointment on **2.** to put oil on in a ceremony of making sacred or consecrating to high office —**a·noint'er** *n.* —**a·noint'ment** *n.*

Anointing of the Sick *R.C.Ch.* the sacrament in which a priest prays for and anoints with oil a person dying or in danger of death from sickness or injuries incurred

a·nom·a·lism (ə näm'ʼl iz'm) *n.* [Rare] **1.** the state of being anomalous **2.** an anomaly

a·nom·a·lis·tic (ə näm'ə lis'tik) *adj.* **1.** tending to be anomalous **2.** of an anomaly

a·nom·a·lous (ə näm'ə ləs) *adj.* [L. *anomalus* < Gr. *anōmalos* < *an-*, not + *homalos* < *homos*, the same: see SAME] **1.** deviating from the regular arrangement, general rule, or usual method; abnormal **2.** being, or seeming to be inconsistent, contradictory, or improper —*SYN.* see IRREGULAR —**a·nom'a·lous·ly** *adv.* —**a·nom'a·lous·ness** *n.*

anomalous water *same as* POLYWATER

a·nom·a·ly (-lē) *n., pl.* **-lies** [L. *anomalia* < Gr. *anōmalia*, inequality: see ANOMALOUS] **1.** departure from the regular arrangement, general rule, or usual method; abnormality **2.** anything anomalous **3.** *Astron.* a planet's angular distance from its perihelion, measured as if viewed from the sun

an·o·mie, an·o·my (an'ə mē) *n.* [Fr. < Gr. *anomia*, law-

lessness < *a*-, without + *nomos*, law: see -NOMY] lack of purpose, identity, or ethical values in a person or in a society; disorganization, rootlessness, etc. —**a·nom·ic** (ə nämʹik) *adj.*

a·non (ə nänʹ) *adv.* [ME. < OE. *on an*, acc., in one, together, straightway] **1.** [Archaic] immediately; at once **2.** *a*) soon; shortly *b*) at another time Now nearly archaic or a self-conscious usage —**ever and anon** now and then; once in a while

anon. anonymous

an·o·nym (anʹə nim) *n.* [Fr. *anonyme* < Gr. *anōnymos*, ANONYMOUS] **1.** a person whose name is not known; anonymous person **2.** an assumed name; pseudonym

an·o·nym·i·ty (anʹə nimʹə tē) *n.* the condition or fact of being anonymous

a·non·y·mous (ə nänʹə məs) *adj.* [Gr. *anōnymos* < *an*-, without + *onyma* < *onoma*, name: see NAME] **1.** with no name known or acknowledged **2.** given, written, etc. by a person whose name is withheld **3.** not easily distinguished from others or from one another because of a lack of individual features or character —**a·nonʹy·mous·ly** *adv.*

a·noph·e·les (ə näfʹə lēzʹ) *n.* [ModL. < Gr. *anōphelēs*, harmful < *an*-, without + *ophelēs*, use, help] any mosquito of a genus (*Anopheles*) that can carry the malaria parasite and transmit the disease —**a·nophʹe·line** (-linʹ, -lin) *adj.*

a·no·rak (äʹnə räkʹse ə) *n.* [Esk. (Greenland) *ánorâq*] a heavy jacket with a hood, worn in the cold north

an·o·rex·i·a (anʹə rekʹsē ə) *n.* [ModL. < Gr. *anorexia* < *an*-, without + *orexis*, a desire for < *oregein*, to reach after: for IE. base see RIGHT] chronic lack of appetite for food —**anʹo·retʹic** (-retʹik) *adj.*

an·or·thite (an ôrʹthit) *n.* [< Gr. *an*-, not + *orthos*, straight + -ITE¹] a plagioclase feldspar, CaAl₂(SiO₄)₂, found in basic igneous rocks —**anʹor·thitʹic** (-thitʹik) *adj.*

an·or·tho·site (an ôrʹthə sitʹ) *n.* [< Fr. *anorthose* < Gr. *an*-, not + *orthos*, straight + -ITE¹] an igneous rock, made up almost entirely of plagioclase feldspar —**an·orʹtho·sitʹic** (-sitʹik) *adj.*

an·os·mi·a (an äzʹmē ə, -äsʹ-) *n.* [ModL. < Gr. *an*-, without + *osmē*, smell] total or partial loss of the sense of smell —**an·osʹmic** (-mik) *adj.*

an·oth·er (ə nuthʹər) *adj.* [ME. *an other*; OE. uses *ōther* in same sense] **1.** one more; an additional [have *another* cup of tea] **2.** a different; not the same [in *another* city, at *another* time] **3.** one of the same sort as; some other [*another* Caesar] —*pron.* **1.** one additional **2.** a different one **3.** one of the same kind

An·ouilh (ä nüʹyʹ; E. än wēʹ), Jean (zhän) 1910– ; Fr. playwright

an·ox·e·mi·a (anʹäk sēʹmē ə) *n.* [AN-¹, not + OX(YGEN) + -EMIA] a reduction in the normal amount of oxygen in the blood, as at high altitudes —**anʹox·eʹmic** (-mik) *adj.*

an·ox·i·a (an äkʹsē ə) *n.* [AN-, not + OX(YGEN) + -IA] *Med.* **1.** total deprivation of oxygen **2.** *same as* HYPOXIA —**an·oxʹic** (-sik) *adj.*

ans. answer

an·sate (anʹsāt) *adj.* [L. *ansatus* < *ansa*, a handle] having a handle or handlelike part

ansate cross *same as* ANKH

An·sel (anʹsʹl) [L. *Anselmus* < Lombard *Anselhelm* < *ansi*, a god + *helma*, HELM²] a masculine name

An·selm (anʹselm), Saint 1033–1109; archbishop of Canterbury (1093–1109), born in Italy: his day is April 21

an·ser·ine (anʹsər inʹ, -in) *adj.* [L. *anserinus* < *anser*, GOOSE] **1.** of or like a goose **2.** stupid; foolish

An·shan (änʹshänʹ) city in NE China, in Liaoning province: pop. 2,500,000

an·swer (anʹsər, änʹ-) *n.* [ME. *andsware* < OE. *andswaru* < *and*-, against + *swerian*, to SWEAR] **1.** something said or written in return to a question, argument, letter, etc. **2.** any act in response or retaliation [his answer was a well-aimed blow] **3.** a solution to a problem **4.** *Law* a written pleading by which the defendant replies to the plaintiff's charges; defense **5.** *Music* the repetition by one instrument or voice of a theme first stated by another; specif., the transposition of the subject in the exposition of a fugue — *vi.* **1.** to reply in words, by an action, etc. **2.** to react to a stimulus; respond (*to*) [the horse *answered* to its rider's touch] **3.** to serve the purpose; be sufficient **4.** to be responsible or liable (*to* a person *for* an action, accusation, etc.) **5.** to be in conformity; correspond (*to*) [he *answers* to the description] —*vt.* **1.** *a*) to reply to in words, by an action, etc. *b*) to say or write in reply **2.** to respond to the signal of (a telephone, doorbell, etc.) **3.** to fulfill satisfactorily; comply with; be sufficient for; serve [the makeshift tent *answered* their *purpose*] **4.** to defend oneself against (an accusation, criticism, etc.); refute **5.** to agree with; conform to; suit [the *answers* the description] **6.** [Obs.] to atone for —**answer back** [Colloq.] to reply forcefully, rudely, or impertinently; talk back

SYN.—**answer** implies a saying, writing, or acting in return, as required by the situation or by courtesy [to *answer* a letter, the phone, etc.]; **respond** implies an appropriate reaction made voluntarily or spontaneously to that which serves as a stimulus [to *respond* to an appeal]; **reply** in its strictest application refers to an answer that satisfies in detail the question asked; **retort** suggests a reply, esp. one that is sharp or witty, provoked by a charge, criticism, etc.; **rejoin** implies an answer, originally to a reply, now often to an objection —*ANT.* question, ask, inquire

an·swer·a·ble (-ə bʹl) *adj.* **1.** subject to being called to account; responsible **2.** that can be answered or shown to be wrong [an *answerable* argument] **3.** [Archaic] in proportion; corresponding —*SYN.* see RESPONSIBLE

ant (ant) *n.* [ME. *amete* < OE. *æmete*; akin to OHG. *âmeiza* < *â*-, off + *meizan*, Goth. *maitan*, OE. **mætan*, to cut; hence, lit., "the cutter off"] any of a family (Formicidae) of black, brown, or red insects, generally wingless, that live in colonies with a complex division of labor by groups

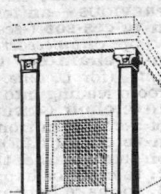

WORKER ANT

an't (ant, änt, änt) [Chiefly Dial. or Brit. Colloq.] are not: also variously heard at different levels of usage as an assimilated form for *am not*, and as a contracted form for *is not*, *have not*, and *has not*: see also AIN'T

ant- (ant) *same as* ANTI-: used before a vowel

-ant (ənt, 'nt) [Fr. -*ant* < L. -*antem* or -*entem*, acc. prp. ending] **1.** *an adj.-forming suffix meaning* that has, shows, or does [*defiant*, *radiant*] **2.** *a n.-forming suffix meaning* a person or thing that [*occupant*, *accountant*]

ant. **1.** antenna **2.** antonym

an·ta (anʹtə) *n.*, *pl.* **-tae** (-tē), **-tas** [L.] *Archit.* a pier or square column formed by enlarging the end of a wall on either side of a door or in a corner

ANTA American National Theatre and Academy

ant·ac·id (antʹasʹid) *adj.* that neutralizes acids; counteracting acidity —*n.* an antacid substance, such as sodium bicarbonate

An·tae·us (an tēʹəs) [L. < Gr. *Antaios*] *Gr. Myth.* a giant wrestler who was invincible as long as he was touching his mother, the earth —**An·taeʹan** *adj.*

ANTAE

an·tag·o·nism (an tagʹə nizʹm) *n.* [Gr. *antagōnisma* < *antagōnizesthai*: see ANTAGONIZE] **1.** the state of being opposed or hostile to another or to each other; opposition or hostility **2.** an opposing force, principle, etc.; specif., a mutually opposing action that can take place between organisms, muscles, drugs, etc. —*SYN.* see ENMITY

an·tag·o·nist (-nist) *n.* [LL. *antagonista* < Gr. *antagōnistēs* < *antagōnizesthai*: see ANTAGONIZE] **1.** a person who opposes or competes with another; adversary; opponent **2.** a muscle, drug, etc. that acts in opposition to or counteracts another —*SYN.* see OPPONENT

an·tag·o·nis·tic (an tagʹə nisʹtik) *adj.* showing antagonism; acting in opposition; opposing or mutually opposed —**an·tagʹo·nisʹti·cal·ly** *adv.*

an·tag·o·nize (an tagʹə nizʹ) *vt.* **-nized**ʹ, **-niz**ʹing [Gr. *antagōnizesthai*, to struggle against < *anti*-, against + *agōnizesthai*: see AGONIZE] **1.** to act in opposition to; oppose or counteract **2.** to incur the dislike of; make an enemy of

An·ta·kya (änʹtä kyäʹ) *Turk.* name of ANTIOCH (sense 1)

ant·al·ka·li (ant alʹkə līʹ) *n.*, *pl.* **-lies**, **-lis** a substance that neutralizes an alkali or counteracts alkalinity

ant·al·ka·line (-lʹn, -linʹ) *adj.* neutralizing an alkali or counteracting alkalinity —*n.* an antalkali

ant·arc·tic (ant ärkʹtik; -ärʹ-) *adj.* [ME. *antartik* < OFr. *antartique* < L. *antarcticus* < Gr. *antarktikos*, southern < *anti*-, opposite + *arktikos*, ARCTIC] of or near the South Pole or the region around it —**the Antarctic** *same as* ANTARCTICA

Ant·arc·ti·ca (-ti ka) land area about the South Pole, completely covered by an ice shelf: c. 5,000,000 sq. mi.: it is almost entirely within the Antarctic Circle: sometimes called a continent

Antarctic Circle [also a- c-] an imaginary circle parallel to the equator, 66°33ʹ south of it

Antarctic Ocean popularly, the parts of the Atlantic, Pacific, and Indian oceans surrounding Antarctica

Antarctic Peninsula peninsula in Antarctica, extending toward S. America: c. 800 mi. long

An·tar·es (an terʹēz) [Gr. *Antarēs* < *anti*-, like + *Arēs*, Mars: so named because of its color] a giant red star of the first magnitude, the brightest in the constellation Scorpio

ant bear a large anteater (*Myrmecophaga jubata*) of tropical S. America, with a long, shaggy tail

ant cow any aphid from which ants get honeydew

☆**an·te** (anʹtē) *n.* [L., before] **1.** *Poker* the stake that each player must put into the pot before receiving cards or drawing new ones to his hand **2.** [Colloq.] the amount one must pay as his share —*vt.*, *vi.* **-ted** or **-teed**, **-te·ing** **1.** *Poker* to put in (one's stake) **2.** [Colloq.] to pay (one's share) —**ante up** to ante up

an·te- (anʹti, -tə, -tē) [< L. *ante*, before] *a prefix meaning:* **1.** before, prior (to) [*antecedent*, ante-Victorian] **2.** before, in front (of) [*anteroom*, antepenult]

ant·eat·er (ant′ēt′ər) *n.* any of several mammals that feed mainly on ants, as the pangolin, aardvark, echidna, ant bear, etc.: anteaters have a long, sticky tongue and a long snout

☆**an·te·bel·lum** (an′ti bel′əm) *adj.* [L. *ante bellum*] before the war; specif., before the American Civil War

an·te·cede (an′tə sēd′) *vt., vi.* -**ced′ed**, -**ced′ing** [L. *antecedere* < *ante-*, before + *cedere*, to go] to go before in rank, place, or time; precede

an·te·ced·ence (-sēd′′ns) *n.* [L. *antecedentia*] **1.** the act of going before or the fact of being prior; precedence **2.** *Astron.* retrograde motion

an·te·ced·en·cy (-sēd′′n sē) *n.* the fact or condition of being antecedent

an·te·ced·ent (-sēd′′nt) *adj.* [ME. & OFr. < L. *antecedens*, prp. of *antecedere*: see ANTECEDE] going or coming before in time, order, or logic; prior; previous; preceding —*n.* **1.** any happening or thing prior to another **2.** anything logically preceding **3.** [*pl.*] one's ancestry, past life, training, etc. **4.** *Gram.* the word, phrase, or clause to which a pronoun refers [*"man"* is the *antecedent* of *"who"* in *"the man who spoke"]* **5.** *Logic* the conditional part of a hypothetical proposition **6.** *Math.* the first term of a ratio —SYN. see CAUSE, PREVIOUS —**an′te·ced′ent·ly** *adv.*

an·te·ces·sor (-ses′ər) *n.* [ME. *antecessour* < L. *antecessor* < pp. of *antecedere*: see ANTECEDE] [Rare] a predecessor

an·te·cham·ber (an′ti chām′bər) *n.* [Fr. *antichambre* < *anti-* (for L. *ante*, before) + *chambre*, CHAMBER] a smaller room leading into a larger or main room

an·te·choir (-kwir′) *n.* a partially or wholly enclosed part of a chapel in front of the choir

an·te·date (-dāt′) *vt.* -**dat′ed**, -**dat′ing 1.** to put a date on that is earlier than the actual date [*to antedate a check]* **2.** to come or happen at an earlier date than; come before **3.** to make happen earlier; accelerate **4.** to set an earlier date for **5.** [Archaic] to anticipate —*n.* a date fixed for a historical event, writing, etc. that is earlier than the actual one

an·te·di·lu·vi·an (an′ti də lōō′vē ən) *adj.* [< ANTE- + L. *diluvium*, a flood + -AN] **1.** of the time before the Biblical Flood **2.** very old, old-fashioned, or primitive —*n.* an antediluvian person or thing

an·te·fix (an′ti fiks′) *n., pl.* -**fix′es** [L. *antefixus*: see ANTE- & FIX] a small decorative fixture put at the eaves of a roof of a classic building to hide the ends of the tiles —**an′te·fix′al** *adj.*

an·te·lope (an′tə lōp′) *n., pl.* -**lopes′**, -**lope′**: see PLURAL, II, D, 1 [ME. & OFr. *antelop* < ML. *antalopus* < Gr. *antholops*, deer] **1.** *a)* any of a group of swift, cud-chewing, hollow-horned, deerlike animals (family Bovidae) related to oxen, sheep, and goats ☆*b)* a pronghorn **2.** leather made from the hide of an antelope

an·te·me·rid·i·an (an′ti mə rid′ē ən) *adj.* [L. *antemeridianus* < *ante-*, before + *meridianus*, of midday] before noon [*an antemeridian repast]*

an·te me·ri·di·em (an′tē mə rid′ē əm) [L.] before noon: abbrev. A.M., a.m., AM

an·te·mor·tem (an′ti môr′təm) *adj.* [L. *ante mortem*, before death] made or done just before one's death

an·te·na·tal (-nāt′′l) *adj.* before birth; prenatal

an·ten·na (an ten′ə) *n.* [L., earlier *antemna*, sail yard] **1.** *pl.* -**nae** (-ē), -**nas** either of a pair of movable, jointed sense organs on the head of an insect, crab, lobster, etc.; feeler **2.** *pl.* -**nas** *Radio & TV* an arrangement of wires, metal rods, etc. used in sending and receiving the electromagnetic waves; aerial

an·ten·nule (an ten′yool) *n.* [ANTENN(A) + -ULE] *Zool.* a small antenna

an·te·pen·di·um (an′ti pen′dē əm) *n., pl.* -**di·a** (-ə), -**di·ums** [ML. < L. *ante*, before + *pendere*, to hang] a screen or veil hanging from the front of an altar, pulpit, etc.

an·te·pe·nult (-pē′nəlt) *n.* [contr. < L. *(syllaba) antepaenultima* < *ante-*, before + *paenultima*, the last but one < *paene*, almost + fem. of *ultimus*, last] the third last syllable in a word, as *-lu-* in *an·te·di·lu·vi·an*

an·te·pe·nul·ti·mate (-pi nul′tə mət) *adj.* [< ANTEPENULT (after ULTIMATE] third last; third from the end —*n.* **1.** anything third from the end **2.** an antepenult

an·te·ri·or (an tir′ē ər) *adj.* [L., compar. of *ante*, before] **1.** at or toward the front; forward: opposed to POSTERIOR **2.** coming before in time, order, or logic; previous; earlier —**an·te′ri·or·ly** *adv.*

an·te·room (an′ti rōōm′, -room′) *n.* a room leading to a larger or more important room; waiting room

an·te·type (an′ti tīp′) *n.* an earlier form; prototype

an·te·ver·sion (an′ti vur′shən, -zhən) *n.* [LL. *anteversio* <

GIANT ANTEATER
(about 5-7 ft. long,
including tail)

ANTELOPE
(to 70 in. high
at shoulder)

L. *anteversus*, pp. of *antevertere*, ANTEVERT] a displacing of a bodily organ, esp. the uterus, in which its axis is inclined farther forward than is normal

an·te·vert (an′ti vurt′) *vt.* [L. *antevertere* < *ante-*, before + *vertere*, to turn] to cause anteversion of

ant·he·li·on (ant′hēl′yən, -ē ən; an thēl′-) *n., pl.* -**li·a** (-yə, -ē ə), -**li·ons** [ModL. < Gr. *anthēlion* < *anti-*, against + *hēlios*, sun] a halo around an object's shadow cast by the sun on a cloud or bank of mist at high altitudes or in polar regions

ant·hel·min·tic (ant′hel min′tik, an′thel-) *adj.* [ANT- + Gr. *helmins*, worm + -IC] killing or ejecting intestinal worms —*n.* an anthelmintic medicine

an·them (an′thəm) *n.* [ME. *antefne* < OE. *antefn* < ML. *antifona*, *antiphona* < Gr. *antiphōna* < *anti-*, over against + *phōnē*, voice] **1.** formerly, a religious song sung antiphonally **2.** a religious choral song usually based on words from the Bible **3.** a song of praise or devotion, as to a nation, college, etc.

an·the·mi·on (an thē′mē ən) *n., pl.* -**mi·a** (-ə) [Gr. *anthemion*, a flower < *anthos*: see ANTHO-] a flat decoration of floral or leaf forms, used in painting and relief sculpture

an·ther (an′thər) *n.* [Fr. *anthère* < ModL. *anthera* (in L., medicine composed of flowers) < Gr. *antheros*, blooming < *anthein*, to bloom < *anthos*: see ANTHO-] the part of a stamen that contains the pollen

an·the·rid·i·um (an′thə rid′ē əm) *n., pl.* -**id′i·a** (-ə) [ModL. < *anthera* (see ANTHER) + Gr. dim. suffix *-idion*] in flowerless and seedless plants (cryptogams), the organ in which the male sex cells are developed —**an·ther·id′i·al** *adj.*

an·ther·o·zo·id (an′thər ə zō′id, an′thər ə zoid′) *n.* [< ModL. *anthera*, ANTHER + ZOOID] a spermatozoid developing in the antheridium

an·the·sis (an thē′sis) *n.* [Gr. *anthēsis* < *anthein*: see ANTHO-] the state of full bloom in a flower

ant·hill (ant′hil′) *n.* the soil carried away by ants in digging their underground nest, heaped in a mound around its entrance

an·tho- (an′thə, -thō) [< Gr. *anthos*, a flower < IE. *andhos*, flower, vegetation < base *andh-*, to project, bloom] a prefix meaning flower [*anthocarpous]*

an·tho·car·pous (an′thə kär′pəs) *adj.* designating or of a multiple fruit, as the pineapple or strawberry, formed from the ovaries of several blossoms

an·tho·cy·a·nin (-sī′ə nin) *n.* [ANTHO- + Gr. *kyan(os)*, blue + -IN] a soluble, reddish-blue pigment in flowers and plants: also **an′tho·cy′an** (-sī′ən)

an·tho·di·um (an thō′dē əm) *n., pl.* -**di·a** (-ə) [ModL. < Gr. *anthōdēs*, flowerlike < *anthos*: see ANTHO-] the flower head of a composite plant, or the involucre of such a head, as in daisies or asters

an·thol·o·gize (an thäl′ə jīz′) *vi.* -**gized′**, -**giz′ing** to make anthologies —*vt.* to make an anthology of or include in an anthology —**an·thol′o·gist** (-jist) *n.*

an·thol·o·gy (-jē) *n., pl.* -**gies** [Gr. *anthologia*, a garland, collection of short poems < *anthologos*, gathering flowers < *anthos*, flower + *legein*, to gather] a collection of poems, stories, excerpts, etc., chosen by the compiler —**an·tho·log·i·cal** (an′thə läj′i k'l) *adj.*

An·tho·ny (an′thə nē; *also, for 1, 2, 3,* -tə-) [with unhistoric *-h-* < L. *Antonius*, name of a Roman gens] **1.** a masculine name: dim. *Tony*; var. *Antony*; equiv. L. *Antonius*, It. & Sp. *Antonio*, Fr. *Antoine*, G. *Anton*; fem. *Antonia* **2.** Saint *a)* (*Anthony the Great*) 251?-356? A.D.; Egypt. hermit; founder of Christian monasticism: his day is Jan. 17 *b)* (*Anthony of Padua*) 1195-1231; Franciscan friar in France & Italy, born in Portugal: his day is June 13 **3. Mark**, *see* ANTONY **4. Susan B**(rownell), 1820-1906; U.S. leader in the movement for women's suffrage

an·tho·phore (an′thə fôr′) *n.* [< Gr. *anthophoros*, flower-bearing < *anthos*, a flower + *pherein*, to BEAR[1]] an elongation of the internode between the calyx and corolla in some plants, forming a stalklike part on which the pistils and corolla are carried

-an·thous (an′thəs) [< Gr. *anthos*: see ANTHO-] *an adj.-forming suffix meaning* having flowers (of a specified kind or number) [*monanthous]*

an·tho·zo·an (an′thə zō′ən) *n.* [< ModL. *Anthozoa*, name of the class < ANTHO- + Gr. *zōia*, pl. of *zōion*, animal + -AN] any of a class (Anthozoa) of saltwater coelenterates, comprising corals, sea anemones, sea fans, etc. —*adj.* of the anthozoans

an·thra·cene (an′thrə sēn′) *n.* [< Gr. *anthrax*, coal + -ENE] a crystalline hydrocarbon, $C_6H_4(CH)_2C_6H_4$, a product of coal-tar distillation used in making alizarin dyes and as a detector of radiation

an·thra·cite (-sīt′) *n.* [Gr. *anthrakitis*, kind of coal < *anthrax*, coal] hard coal, which gives much heat but little flame and smoke —**an′thra·cit′ic** (-sit′ik) *adj.*

an·thrac·nose (an thrak′nōs′) *n.* [< Gr. *anthrax*, coal, carbuncle + *nosos*, disease] any of various fungus diseases of plants, in which roundish dead spots appear chiefly on leaves or fruit

an·thra·coid (an′thrə koid′) *adj.* resembling anthrax

an·thra·nil·ic acid (an′thrə nil′ik) [ANTHR(ACENE) + ANIL(INE) + -IC] a yellow crystalline compound, $NH_2C_6H_4-COOH$, used in the manufacture of dyes, drugs, etc.

an·thra·qui·none (-kwi nōn′) *n.* [ANTHRA(CENE) + QUINONE] a yellow crystalline ketone, $C_6H_4(CO)_2C_6H_4$,

produced from anthracene by oxidation: it is used in the manufacture of certain dyes and dye intermediates

an·thrax (an′thraks) *n.* [ME. *antrax* < L. *anthrax*, virulent ulcer < Gr. *anthrax*, (burning) coal, hence ulcer, carbuncle] **1.** an infectious disease of wild and domesticated animals, esp. cattle and sheep, which is caused by a bacillus (*Bacillus anthracis*) and can be transmitted to man: it is characterized by black pustules **2.** any such pustule

an·thro·po- (an′thrə pə, -pō) [< Gr. *anthrōpos*, man] *a combining form meaning* man, human [*anthropology*]: also, before a vowel, **anthrop-**

an·thro·po·cen·tric (an′thrə pə sen′trik) *adj.* [ANTHROPO- + -CENTRIC] **1.** that considers man as the central fact, or final aim, of the universe **2.** conceiving of everything in the universe in terms of human values

an·thro·po·gen·e·sis (-jen′ə sis) *n.* the study of man's origin and development: also **an·thro·pog·e·ny** (an′thrə-pȧj′ə nē) —**an′thro·po′ge·net′ic** (-pō′jə net′ik) *adj.*

an·thro·pog·ra·phy (an′thrə pȧg′rə fē) *n.* the branch of anthropology that deals with the distribution of man according to his physical characteristics, languages, etc.

an·thro·poid (an′thrə poid′) *adj.* **1.** resembling man; manlike; esp., designating or of any of the most highly developed apes, including the chimpanzee, gorilla, orangutan, and gibbon **2.** apelike [a brutish man with *anthropoid* features] —*n.* any anthropoid ape —**an′thro·poi′dal** *adj.*

an·thro·pol·o·gist (an′thrə pȧl′ə jist) *n.* a student of or specialist in anthropology

an·thro·pol·o·gy (-jē) *n.* the study of man, esp. of the variety, physical and cultural characteristics, distribution, customs, social relationships, etc. of mankind: often restricted to the study of the institutions, myths, etc. of nonliterate peoples —**an′thro·po·log′i·cal** (-pə lȧj′i k′l), **an′thro·po·log′ic** *adj.* —**an′thro·po·log′i·cal·ly** *adv.*

an·thro·pom·e·try (-pȧm′ə trē) *n.* the science dealing with measurement of the human body to determine differences in individuals, groups, etc. —**an′thro·po·met′ric** (-pə me′trik), **an′thro·po·met′ri·cal** *adj.* —**an′thro·po·met′ri·cal·ly** *adv.*

an·thro·po·mor·phic (an′thrə pə môr′fik) *adj.* of, characterized by, or resulting from anthropomorphism —**an′-thro·po·mor′phi·cal·ly** *adv.*

an·thro·po·mor·phism (an′thrə pə môr′fiz′m) *n.* [AN-THROPOMORPH(OUS) + -ISM] the attributing of human shape or characteristics to a god, animal, or inanimate thing —**an′thro·po·mor′phist** (-fist) *n.*

an·thro·po·mor·phize (-môr′fīz) *vt., vi.* **-phized, -phiz·ing** to attribute human shape or characteristics to (a god, animal, etc.)

an·thro·po·mor·pho·sis (-môr′fə sis) *n.* [ANTHROPO- + (META)MORPHOSIS] a changing into human form

an·thro·po·mor·phous (-môr′fəs) *adj.* [Gr. *anthrōpomorphos* < *anthrōpos*, a man + *morphē*, form, shape] having human shape and appearance

an·thro·pop·a·thy (-pȧp′ə thē) *n.* [ML. *anthropopathia* < Gr. *anthrōpopatheia*, humanity < *anthrōpos*, man + *pathos*, suffering] the attributing of human feelings and passions to a god, animal, etc.: also **an′thro·pop′a·thism** (-thiz′m)

an·thro·poph·a·gi (-pȧf′ə jī′) *n.pl., sing.* **-a·gus** (-ə gəs) [L. < Gr. *anthrōpophagos*, a man-eater < *anthrōpos*, man + *phagos* < *phagein*, to eat] cannibals

an·thro·poph·a·gite (-jīt′) *n.* [see prec.] a cannibal

an·thro·poph·a·gy (-jē) *n.* [see ANTHROPOPHAGI] cannibalism —**an′thro·poph′a·gous** (-gəs), **an′thro·po·phag′ic** (-pə faj′ik) *adj.*

an·thu·ri·um (an thoor′ē əm) *n.* [ModL. < Gr. *anthos*, flower + *oura*, tail] any of a genus (*Anthurium*) of tropical American plants of the arum family, having a long-stalked spike, surrounded at the base by a flaring, heart-shaped, white or colored spathe

an·ti (an′tī, -tē) *n., pl.* **-tis** [< ANTI-, in various compounds] [Colloq.] a person opposed to some policy, proposal, action, etc. *adj.* [Colloq.] opposed; against

an·ti- (an′tī; *also variously* -tē, -tĭ, -tə) [Gr. *anti-, ant-* < *anti*, against < IE. *anti*, facing, opposite, near, whence L. *ante*, opposite, before < base *ant-s*, front, forehead] *a prefix meaning:* **1.** against, hostile to [*antilabor*, *anti-Semitism*] **2.** that counteracts, that operates against [*antiaircraft*] **3.** that prevents, cures, or neutralizes [*antitoxin*] **4.** opposite, reverse [*antiperistalsis*] **5.** rivaling [*antipope*]

an·ti·air·craft (an′tē er′kraft, -kräft) *adj.* used for defense against hostile aircraft [an *antiaircraft* gun]

an·ti·ar (an′tē är′) *n.* [Jav. *antjar*] **1.** the upas tree of Java **2.** a poison made from its gum resin: also called **an′ti·ar·in** (-ə rin)

an·ti·bac·te·ri·al (an′tī bak tir′ē əl; *see* ANTI-) *adj.* that checks the growth or effect of bacteria

an·ti·bal·lis·tic missile (-bə lis′tik) a ballistic missile intended to intercept and destroy another ballistic missile in flight

an·ti·bar·y·on (-bar′ē än′, -ber′-) *n.* an antiparticle of the baryon, as an antineutron, antiproton, or antihyperon

an·ti·bi·o·sis (-bī ō′sis) *n.* [ModL. < ANTI- + Gr. *biōsis*,

way of life < *bios*, life] *Biol.* an association between organisms which is harmful to one of them or between bacteria, etc. and an antagonistic antibiotic

☆**an·ti·bi·ot·ic** (-bī ät′ik, -bē-) *adj.* **1.** of antibiosis **2.** destroying, or inhibiting the growth of bacteria and other microorganisms. **3.** of antibiotics —*n.* any of certain chemical substances produced by various microorganisms, specif. bacteria, fungi, and actinomycetes, and having the capacity, in dilute solutions, to inhibit the growth of or to destroy bacteria and other microorganisms: the antibiotics, including penicillin, streptomycin, tetracycline, etc., are used in the treatment of various infectious diseases

☆**an·ti·bod·y** (an′ti bäd′ē) *n., pl.* **-bod′ies** a protein produced in the body in response to contact of the body with an antigen, and having the specific capacity of neutralizing, hence creating immunity to, the antigen

an·tic (an′tik) *adj.* [It. *antico* < L. *antiquus*: see ANTIQUE] **1.** [Archaic] fantastic and queer; grotesque: also **an′tick 2.** odd and funny; ludicrous —*n.* **1.** a playful, silly, or ludicrous act, trick, etc.; prank; caper **2.** [Archaic] a clown or buffoon —*vi.* **-ticked, -tick·ing** to perform antics; caper

an·ti·cat·a·lyst (an′ti kat′′l ist; *see* ANTI-) *n.* a substance that slows down a chemical reaction

an·ti·cath·ode (-kath′ōd) *n.* in an X-ray tube, the piece opposite the cathode, serving as the target for the cathode's discharge

an·ti·chlor (an′ti klôr′; *see* ANTI-) *n.* [ANTI- + CHLOR(INE)] any substance for removing excess chlorine from textiles or other substances that have been bleached

an·ti·cho·lin·er·gic (an′ti kō′lə nur′jik, -käl′ə-; *see* ANTI-) *adj.* [ANTI- + CHOLINERGIC] having the ability to retard the activity of organs that receive their nerve impulses through the parasympathetic nervous system —*n.* an anticholinergic drug, as an alkaloid of belladonna

an·ti·cho·lin·es·ter·ase (-nes′tə rās′) *n.* a substance that inhibits the action of a cholinesterase, as the drug aserine or the insecticide parathion

an·ti·christ (an′ti krist′; *see* ANTI-) *n.* [ME. *anticrist* < OFr. *antecrist* < LL. *antichristus* < Gr. *antichristos* < *anti-*, against + *Christos*, Christ] **1.** an opponent of or disbeliever in Christ **2.** [A-] *Bible* the great antagonist of Christ, expected to spread universal evil before the end of the world but finally to be conquered at Christ's second coming: I John 2:18 **3.** a false Christ

an·tic·i·pant (an tis′ə pənt) *adj.* [L. *anticipans*, prp. of *anticipare*: see ff.] expecting; anticipating (with *of*) —*n.* a person who anticipates

an·tic·i·pate (an tis′ə pāt′) *vt.* **-pat′ed, -pat′ing** [< L. *anticipatus*, pp. of *anticipare* < *ante-*, before + *capere* < *capere*, to take] **1.** to look forward to; expect [to *anticipate* a pleasant vacation] **2.** to make happen earlier; precipitate **3.** to prevent by action in advance; forestall [to *anticipate* an opponent's blows] **4.** to foresee (a command, wish, etc.) and perform in advance [to *anticipate* a request] **5.** to use or enjoy in advance [to *anticipate* a legacy] **6.** to be ahead of in doing or achieving [did the Vikings *anticipate* Columbus in discovering America?] **7.** to pay (a debt) before due —*vi.* to speak of or consider a matter prematurely —*SYN.* see EXPECT —**an·tic′i·pa′tor** *n.*

an·tic·i·pa·tion (an tis′ə pā′shən) *n.* **1.** an anticipating or being anticipated **2.** something anticipated or expected **3.** foreknowledge; presentiment **4.** *Law* the assignment or taking of income from a trust fund before it is due **5.** *Music* the sounding of a tone in advance of the chord to which the tone belongs

an·tic·i·pa·tive (an tis′ə pāt′iv) *adj.* inclined to anticipate; of or full of anticipation —**an·tic′i·pa′tive·ly** *adv.*

an·tic·i·pa·to·ry (-pə tôr′ē) *adj.* anticipating; of or expressing anticipation —**an·tic′i·pa·to′ri·ly** *adv.*

an·ti·cler·i·cal (an′ti kler′ə k′l; *see* ANTI-) *adj.* opposed to the clergy or church hierarchy, esp. to its influence in public affairs —**an′ti·cler′i·cal·ism** *n.*

an·ti·mac·tic (-kli mak′tik) *adj.* of, having, or like an anticlimax —**an′ti·cli·mac′ti·cal·ly** *adv.*

an·ti·cli·max (-klī′maks) *n.* **1.** a sudden drop from the dignified or important in thought or expression to the commonplace or trivial, sometimes for humorous effect **2.** a descent, as in a series of events, which is in ludicrous or disappointing contrast to a preceding rise

an·ti·cli·nal (-klī′n′l) *adj.* [< ANTI- + Gr. *klinein*, to LEAN¹ + -AL] **1.** inclined in opposite directions **2.** of or like an anticline

an·ti·cline (an′ti klīn′; *see* ANTI-) *n.* [< prec., after IN-CLINE, DECLINE] *Geol.* a sharply arched fold of stratified rock from whose central axis the strata slope downward in opposite directions: opposed to SYNCLINE

an·ti·cli·no·ri·um (an′ti klī nôr′ē-əm; *see* ANTI-) *n., pl.* **-ri·a** (-ə) [ModL. < ANTICLINE + Gr. *oros*, mountain] *Geol.* a large, generally anticlinal structure consisting of a succession of anticlines and synclines: opposed to SYNCLINORIUM

ANTICLINE

an·ti·co·ag·u·lant (-kō ag′yə lənt) *n.* a drug or substance that delays or prevents the clotting of blood

An·ti·cos·ti (an′tə käs′tē) [< ? AmInd. *natiscotec,* lit., where bears are hunted] island at the mouth of the St. Lawrence River, in the province of Quebec, Canada: c. 3,000 sq. mi.; pop. 500

an·ti·cy·clone (an′ti sī′klōn; see ANTI-) *n. Meteorol.* an atmospheric condition of high barometric pressure extending over a wide area and moving slowly, generally eastward in the temperate zones, with the winds at the edge blowing outward —**an·ti·cy·clon·ic** (-sī klän′ik) *adj.*

an·ti·de·pres·sant (-də pres′ənt) *adj. Psychiatry* designating or of any drug used primarily to treat emotional depression —*n.* an antidepressant drug

an·ti·dote (an′tə dōt′) *n.* [ME. & OFr. *antidote* < L. *antidotum* < Gr. *antidoton* < *anti-,* against + *dotos,* given < *didonai,* to give] 1. a remedy to counteract a poison 2. anything that works against an evil or unwanted condition —**an′ti·dot′al** *adj.*

an·ti·drom·ic (an′ti dräm′ik; see ANTI-) *adj.* [< ANTI- + Gr. *dromos,* a running (see -DROME) + -IC] *Physiol.* conveying nerve impulses in a direction opposite to the normal

an·ti·e·lec·tron (-ə lek′trän) *n. same as* POSITRON

an·ti·en·er·gis·tic (-en′ər jis′tik) *adj.* resisting applied energy

An·tie·tam (an tēt′əm) [AmInd. < ?] creek in W Md.: its juncture with the Potomac is the site of a Civil War battle (1862)

an·ti·fe·brile (an′ti fē′brəl, -feb′rəl; see ANTI-) *adj.* [ANTI- + FEBRILE] reducing or relieving fever —*n.* an antifebrile drug

☆**an·ti·fed·er·al·ist** (-fed′ər ə list, -fed′rə-) *n.* 1. a person opposed to federalism 2. [A-] a person who opposed the adoption of the U.S. Constitution —*adj.* [A-] designating or of a former political party, later allied with the Jeffersonian Republican party, which opposed the Federalists

☆**an·ti·freeze** (an′ti frēz′; see ANTI-) *n.* a substance of low freezing point added to a liquid, esp. to the water in the radiator of an automobile engine, or to gasoline in the tank, to prevent freezing

an·ti·fric·tion (an′ti frik′shən; see ANTI-) *adj.* reducing friction —*n.* a device, lubricant, etc. for reducing friction

☆**an·ti·gen** (an′tə jən) *n.* [ANTI- + -GEN] an enzyme, toxin, or other substance, usually of high molecular weight, to which the body reacts by producing antibodies —**an′ti·gen′ic** (-jcn′ik) *adj.*

An·tig·o·ne (an tig′ə nē′) [L. < Gr. *Antigonē*] *Gr. Myth.* the daughter of Oedipus and Jocasta: she defied her uncle, Creon, by performing funeral rites for her brother, Polynices

An·tig·o·nus (I) (an tig′ə nəs) 382?–301 B.C.; Macedonian general under Alexander the Great; king of Macedonia (306–301): called *Cyclops*

An·ti·gua (an tē′gə, -gwə) self-governing island of the Leeward group in the West Indies: it is under Brit. protection: 108 sq. mi.; pop. 57,000; chief town, St. John's

an·ti·he·lix (an′ti hē′liks; see ANTI-) *n., pl.* **-hel′i·ces′** (-hel′ə sēz′), **-he′lix·es** (-hē′lik siz) the rounded piece of cartilage inside the outer rim (helix) of the ear

an·ti·he·ro (an′ti hir′ō; see ANTI-) *n.* the protagonist of a novel, play, etc. who lacks the stature or virtues of a traditional hero

an·ti·his·ta·mine (-his′tə mēn′, -mən) *n.* any of several drugs used to minimize the action of histamine in such allergic conditions as hay fever and hives —**an′ti·his′ta·min′ic** (-his′tə min′ik) *adj.*

an·ti·hy·per·on (-hī′pə rän′) *n.* the antiparticle of the hyperon

☆**an·ti·knock** (-näk′) *n.* a substance added to the fuel of internal-combustion engines to do away with or reduce noise resulting from too rapid combustion

an·ti·la·bor (an′ti lā′bər; see ANTI-) *adj.* opposed to labor unions or to the interests of workers

An·ti-Leb·a·non (an′ti leb′ə nən) mountain range in W Syria, east of and parallel to the Lebanon Mountains: highest peak, Mount HERMON

an·ti·lep·ton (an′ti lep′tən; see ANTI-) *n.* an antiparticle (positron, positive mu meson, or antineutrino) of the lepton

an·ti·lith·ic (-lith′ik) *adj.* [ANTI- + LITHIC] *Med.* preventing the formation or development of calculi, as of the urinary tract —*n.* an antilithic substance

An·til·les (an til′ēz) main island group of the West Indies, including all but the Bahamas: see GREATER ANTILLES, LESSER ANTILLES —**An·til·le·an** (-ē ən; an′tə-lē′ən) *adj.*

an·ti·log·a·rithm (an′ti lôg′ə rith′m, -läg′-; see ANTI-) *n.* the number corresponding to a logarithm [the *antilogarithm* of 1 is 10]

an·til·o·gy (an til′ə jē) *n., pl.* **-gies** [Gr. *antilogia* < *antilogos* < *anti-,* against + *logos* < *legein,* to speak] a contradiction in ideas, statements, or terms

an·ti·ma·cas·sar (an′ti mə kas′ər; see ANTI-) *n.* [ANTI- + *macassar* (oil), an oil, orig. imported from Macassar, used as a hair dressing] a small cover on the back or arms of a chair, sofa, etc. to prevent soiling

an·ti·mag·net·ic (an′ti mag net′ik; see ANTI-) *adj.* constructed of metals that resist magnetism [an *antimagnetic* watch]

an·ti·ma·lar·i·al (-mə ler′ē əl) *adj.* preventing or relieving malaria —*n.* an antimalarial drug

an·ti·masque, an·ti·mask (an′ti mask′, -mäsk′; see ANTI-) *n.* a comic sketch, often a burlesque, between the acts of a masque

an·ti·mat·ter (-mat′ər) *n.* a form of matter in which the electrical charge or other property of each constituent particle is the reverse of that in the usual matter of our universe: an atom of antimatter has a nucleus of antiprotons and antineutrons surrounded by positrons

an·ti·mere (-mir′) *n. Zool.* either of the corresponding parts opposite each other on both sides of an organism's axis —**an′ti·mer′ic** (-mer′ik) *adj.*

an·ti·mis·sile (-mis′′l) *adj.* designed as a defense against ballistic missiles

an·ti·mo·ni·al (an′tə mō′nē əl) *adj.* of or containing antimony —*n.* a medicine, etc. containing antimony

an·ti·mon·ic (-män′ik, -mō′nik) *adj.* 1. of or containing antimony 2. *Chem.* designating or of compounds of pentavalent antimony

an·ti·mo·nous (an′tə mō′nəs) *adj.* 1. of or like antimony 2. *Chem.* designating or of compounds of trivalent antimony Also **an′ti·mo′ni·ous** (-mō′nē əs)

an·ti·mon·soon (an′ti män sōōn′; see ANTI-) *n.* the air current above a monsoon, moving in the opposite direction

an·ti·mo·ny (an′tə mō′nē) *n.* [ME. *antimonie* < OFr. *antimoine* < ML. *antimonium*] a silvery-white, brittle, metallic chemical element of crystalline structure, found only in combination: used in alloys with other metals to harden them and increase their resistance to chemical action; compounds of antimony are used in medicines, pigments, matches, and fireproofing: symbol, Sb; at. wt., 121.75; at. no., 51; sp. gr., 6.684 (at 25°C); melt. pt., 630.5°C; boil. pt., 1640°C

antimony glance *same as* STIBNITE

an·ti·mo·nyl (an′tə mə nil′, an′tə mō′n′l) *n.* [ANTIMON(Y) + -YL] *Chem.* the univalent radical SbO, found in certain salts, notably antimonyl potassium tartrate

antimonyl potassium tartrate a poisonous, colorless or white crystalline powder, an antimonous tartrate, KSbOC₄H₄O₆, used as an emetic and as a mordant in dyeing

antimony trisulfide a black or orange-red crystalline compound, Sb₂S₃, used as a pigment, in pyrotechnics and matches, for fireproofing fabrics and paper, etc.

an·ti·neu·tri·no (an′ti nōō trē′nō, -nyōō-; see ANTI-) *n.* the antiparticle of the neutrino, with no charge and a rest mass close to zero: it is emitted during radioactive decay

☆**an·ti·neu·tron** (-nōō′trän, -nyōō-) *n.* the antiparticle of the neutron, with the same mass and spin as the neutron but with a magnetic moment that is opposite in sign

an·ti·node (an′ti nōd′; see ANTI-) *n. Physics* the point of maximum vibration located halfway between two adjacent nodes in a vibrating body

an·ti·no·mi·an (an′ti nō′mē ən; see ANTI-) *n.* [< ANTINOMY + -AN] [*also* A-] *Christian Theol.* a believer in the doctrine that faith alone, not obedience to the moral law, is necessary for salvation —*adj.* of this doctrine —**an′ti·no′mi·an·ism** *n.*

an·tin·o·my (an tin′ə mē) *n., pl.* **-mies** [L. *antinomia* < Gr. *antinomia* < *anti-,* against + *nomia* < *nomos,* law] 1. the opposition of one law, regulation, etc. to another 2. a contradiction or inconsistency between two apparently reasonable principles or laws

an·ti·nov·el (an′ti näv′′l; see ANTI-) *n.* [transl. of Fr. *antiroman,* term coined by Sartre] a work of prose fiction in which the author's intention is to violate such traditional aspects of the novel as plot, character development, concept of a hero, etc.

an·ti·nu·cle·on (an′ti nōō′klē än, -nyōō′-; see ANTI-) *n.* the antiparticle of a nucleon; an antiproton or antineutron

An·ti·och (an′tē äk′) 1. capital of ancient Syria (until 64 B.C.): now, a city in S Turkey: pop. 46,000: Turk. name, ANTAKYA 2. city in ancient Pisidia, Asia Minor

An·ti·o·chus (an tī′ə kəs) any of thirteen kings of the Selucid dynasty of Syria; esp., *a)* **Antiochus III** 242–187 B.C.; king (223–187): called **Antiochus the Great** *b)* **Antiochus IV** -163? B.C.; king (175?–163?): his suppression of the Jews led to the Maccabean revolt: called **Antiochus E·piph·a·nes** (i pif′ə nēz′)

an·ti·ox·i·dant (an′tē äk′sə dənt; see ANTI-) *n.* a substance that slows down the oxidation of oils, fats, etc. and thus helps to check deterioration: antioxidants are often added commercially to foods, soaps, etc. —*adj.* serving to check oxidation

an·ti·par·al·lel (an′ti par′ə lel′) *adj.* designating lines or planes that make equal but opposite angles with two other lines or planes

an·ti·par·ti·cle (an′ti pär′tə k′l; see ANTI-) *n.* any of the constituent particles of antimatter: see ANTIMATTER

an·ti·pas·to (an′ti pas′tō; *It.* än′tē päs′tō) *n.* [It. < *anti-* (L. *ante*), before + *pasto* < L. *pastus,* food < *pascere,* to feed] a dish of salted fish, meat, olives, etc., served as an appetizer

An·tip·a·ter (an tip′ə tər) 398?–319 B.C.; Macedonian general under Alexander the Great

an·ti·pa·thet·ic (an′ti pə thet′ik; see ANTI-) *adj.* [< ANTIPATHY after PATHETIC] 1. having antipathy 2. opposed or antagonistic in character, tendency, etc. —**an′ti·pa·thet′i·cal** *adj.* —**an′ti·pa·thet′i·cal·ly** *adv.*

an·tip·a·thy (an tip′ə thē) *n., pl.* **-thies** [L. *antipathia* < Gr. *antipatheia* < *anti-,* against + *patheia* < *pathein,* to

suffer: see PATHOS] **1.** a strong or deep-rooted dislike; aversion **2.** the object of such dislike **3.** [Obs.] an opposition in character, nature, tendency, etc. —*SYN.* see AVERSION

an·ti·pe·ri·od·ic (an'ti pir'ē äd'ik; *see* ANTI-) *adj.* preventing the periodic return of attacks of disease, as of certain fevers —*n.* an antiperiodic medicine

an·ti·per·i·stal·sis (-per'ə stal'sis, -stôl'-) *n. Physiol.* reverse peristaltic action in which the contents of the intestines, etc. are moved backward

an·ti·per·son·nel (-pur'sə nel') *adj.* directed against, or intended to destroy, people rather than material objects [*antipersonnel* mines]

an·ti·per·spir·ant (-pur'spər ənt) *n.* an astringent substance applied to the skin to reduce perspiration

an·ti·phlo·gis·tic (-flə jis'tik) *adj.* counteracting inflammation —*n.* an antiphlogistic substance

an·ti·phon (an'tə fän') *n.* [ML. *antiphona* < Gr. *antiphona:* see ANTHEM] **1.** a hymn, psalm, etc. chanted or sung in responsive, alternating parts **2.** anything composed for responsive chanting or singing **3.** verses chanted or a piece of plainsong sung before or after a psalm, canticle, etc.

an·tiph·o·nal (an tif'ə n'l) *adj.* of or like an antiphon; sung or chanted in alternation: also **an·ti·phon·ic** (an'tə fän'ik) —*n.* an antiphonary

an·tiph·o·nar·y (an tif'ə ner'ē) *n., pl.* **-nar'ies** [ME. *antiphonere* < OFr. *antifonier* < ML. *antiphonarium:* see ANTIPHON] a collection of antiphons, esp. a book of responsive prayers

an·tiph·o·ny (an tif'ə nē) *n., pl.* **-nies** [< Gr. *antiphōnos* (see ANTHEM), after SYMPHONY] **1.** the opposition of sounds **2.** harmony produced by this **3.** an antiphon **4.** antiphonal chanting or singing **5.** any response or echo

an·tiph·ra·sis (an tif'rə sis) *n.* [L. < Gr. < *anti-*, against + *phrazein*, to speak] the use of words or phrases in a sense opposite to the usual one, as for ironical effect

an·ti·pode (an'tə pōd') *n., sing. of* ANTIPODES anything diametrically opposite; exact opposite

an·tip·o·des (an tip'ə dēz') *n.pl.* [ML. < L. < Gr., pl. of *antipous*, with the feet opposite < *anti-*, opposite + *pous*, FOOT] **1.** any two places directly opposite each other on the earth **2.** [*with pl. or sing. v.*] a place on the opposite side of the earth; in British usage, New Zealand and Australia **3.** two opposite or contrary things **an·tip'o·dal** *adj.* — **an·tip'o·de·an** (-dē'ən) *adj.*, *n.*

an·ti·pope (an'ti pōp'; *see* ANTI-) *n.* a pope set up against the one chosen by church laws, as in a schism

an·ti·pro·ton (an'ti prō'tän; *see* ANTI-) *n.* the antiparticle of the proton, with the same mass as the proton but a negative charge

an·ti·py·ret·ic (-pī ret'ik) *adj.* reducing fever —*n.* anything that reduces fever

an·ti·py·rine (-pī'rēn, -rin) *n.* [ANTIPYR(ETIC) + -INE⁴] a white, crystalline powder, $C_{11}H_{12}N_2O$, used to relieve pain and to reduce fever

antiq. 1. antiquarian **2.** antiquity; antiquities

an·ti·quar·i·an (an'tə kwer'ē ən) *adj.* **1.** of antiques or antiquities **2.** of antiquaries **3.** of, or dealing in, rare old books —*n.* an antiquary —**an'ti·quar'i·an·ism** *n.*

an·ti·quar·y (an'tə kwer'ē) *n., pl.* **-quar'ies** [L. *antiquarius* < *antiquus:* see ANTIQUE] a person who collects or studies relics and ancient works of art

an·ti·quate (an'tə kwāt') *vt.* **-quat'ed, -quat'ing** [< L. *antiquatus*, pp. of *antiquare* < *antiquus:* see ANTIQUE] **1.** to make old or obsolete; cause to become old-fashioned **2.** to give an antique look to —**an'ti·qua'tion** *n.*

an·ti·quat·ed (-id) *adj.* **1.** no longer used or useful; obsolete, old-fashioned, out-of-date, etc. **2.** aged —*SYN.* see OLD

an·tique (an tēk') *adj.* [Fr. < L. *antiquus*, ancient, old < *ante*, before] **1.** of ancient times; ancient; old **2.** out-of-date; old-fashioned **3.** in the style of classical antiquity **4.** of, or in the style of, a former period **5.** dealing in antiques —*n.* **1.** anything from ancient times; relic **2.** the ancient style, esp. of Greek or Roman sculpture, architecture, etc. **3.** a piece of furniture, silverware, etc. made in a former period, generally more than 100 years ago **4.** *Printing* a variety of boldface type —*vt.* **-tiqued', -tiqu'ing** to make look antique —*SYN.* see OLD —**an·tique'ly** *adv.* —**an·tique'ness** *n.*

an·tiq·ui·ty (an tik'wə tē) *n., pl.* **-ties** [ME. & OFr. *antiquite* < L. *antiquitas* < *antiquus:* see prec.] **1.** the early period of history, esp. before the Middle Ages **2.** the quality of being ancient or old; great age [a statue of great *antiquity*] **3.** the people of ancient times **4.** [*pl.*] *a)* relics, monuments, etc. of the distant past *b)* ancient manners, customs, etc.

an·ti·ra·chit·ic (an'ti rə kit'ik; *see* ANTI-) *adj.* that cures or prevents rickets —*n.* a remedy or preventive for rickets

an·ti·re·mon·strant (-ri män'strənt) *n.* a person opposed to remonstrance or remonstrants; specif., [A-] any of a group of Dutch Calvinists who opposed the Arminian Remonstrants

an·tir·rhi·num (-rī'nəm) *n.* [L. < Gr. *antirrhinon*, snapdragon < *anti-*, like + *rhis* (gen. *rhinos*), nose] any of a genus (*Antirrhinum*) of plants of the figwort family, with showy white, yellow, red, or purplish flowers, including the common snapdragon

An·ti·sa·na (än'tē sä'nä) volcanic mountain of the Andes, in NC Ecuador: c. 18,800 ft.

an·ti·scor·bu·tic (an'ti skôr byōō'tik; *see* ANTI-) *adj.* that cures or prevents scurvy —*n.* a remedy or preventive for scurvy

antiscorbutic acid *same as* VITAMIN C

an·ti·Sem·ite (-sem'īt) *n.* an anti-Semitic person

an·ti·Se·mit·ic (-sə mit'ik) *adj.* **1.** having or showing prejudice against Jews **2.** discriminating against or persecuting Jews **3.** of or caused by such prejudice or hostility —**an'ti·Se·mit'i·cal·ly** *adv.* —**an'ti·Sem'i·tism** (-sem'ə-tiz'm) *n.*

an·ti·sep·sis (-sep'sis) *n.* [ANTI- + SEPSIS] **1.** the technique of preventing infection, the growth of microorganisms, etc. **2.** the condition of being antiseptic **3.** the use of antiseptics

an·ti·sep·tic (-tik) *adj.* **1.** preventing infection, decay, etc. by inhibiting the action of microorganisms **2.** using antiseptics **3.** free from infection or infectious agents; sterile **4.** untouched by life, its problems, emotions, etc. [an *antiseptic* mind] —*n.* any substance that inhibits the action of microorganisms —**an'ti·sep'ti·cal·ly** *adv.*

an·ti·sep·ti·cize (-sep'tə siz') *vt.* **-cized', -ciz'ing** to make antiseptic; apply antiseptics to

an·ti·se·rum (an'ti sir'əm; *see* ANTI-) *n.* a serum with antibodies in it

☆**an·ti·slav·er·y** (an'ti slā'vər ē; -vrē; *see* ANTI-) *adj.* against slavery

an·ti·so·cial (-sō'shəl) *adj.* **1.** avoiding association with others; unsociable **2.** against the basic principles of society; harmful to the welfare of the people generally —*SYN.* see UNSOCIAL

an·ti·spas·mod·ic (-spaz mäd'ik) *adj.* relieving or preventing spasms —*n.* an antispasmodic drug

an·ti·stat·ic (-stat'ik) *adj.* reducing static electric charges, as on textiles, waxes, polishes, etc., by retaining enough moisture to provide electrical conduction

An·tis·the·nes (an tis'thə nēz') 444?-365? B.C.; Gr. philosopher; founder of Cynicism

an·tis·tro·phe (an tis'trə fē) *n.* [L. < Gr. *antistrophē* < *antistrephein*, to turn about < *anti-*, against, opposite + *strephein*, to turn] **1.** the return movement, left to right, made by the chorus of an ancient Greek play in answering the previous strophe **2.** that part of a choric song performed while making this movement **3.** in a Pindaric ode, the stanza, usually in the same or similar form, which follows the strophe **4.** in poems with contrasting or parallel stanza systems, a stanza of the second system —**an·ti·stroph·ic** (an'tə sträf'ik) *adj.*

an·ti·tank (an'ti taŋk'; *see* ANTI-) *adj.* for use against tanks in war

an·tith·e·sis (an tith'ə sis) *n., pl.* **-ses'** (-sēz') [L. < Gr. < *antithenai* < *anti-*, against + *tithenai*, to place: see DO¹] **1.** a contrast or opposition of thoughts, usually in two phrases, clauses, or sentences (Ex.: you are going; I am staying) **2.** the second part of such an expression **3.** a contrast or opposition: see also DIALECTIC (sense 3) **4.** the exact opposite [joy is the *antithesis* of sorrow]

an·ti·thet·i·cal (an'tə thet'i k'l) *adj.* [Gr. *antithetikos*] **1.** of or containing antithesis **2.** exactly opposite Also **an'ti·thet'ic** —*SYN.* see OPPOSITE —**an'ti·thet'i·cal·ly** *adv.*

an·ti·tox·ic (an'ti täk'sik; *see* ANTI-) *adj.* of, containing, or acting as an antitoxin

an·ti·tox·in (-täk'sin) *n.* **1.** a circulating antibody formed by the body to act against a specific toxin **2.** a serum containing an antitoxin: taken from the blood of an immunized animal, such a serum is injected into a person to prevent a specific disease, as botulism, tetanus, diphtheria, etc.

an·ti·trades (an'ti trādz'; *see* ANTI-) *n.pl.* **1.** winds that blow steadily above and opposite to the trade winds **2.** the prevailing westerly winds of the Temperate Zone

an·ti·tra·gus (an tit'rə gəs) *n., pl.* **-gi'** (-jī') the fleshy, cartilaginous protrusion at the rear of the external ear, opposite the tragus

☆**an·ti·trust** (an'ti trust'; *see* ANTI-) *adj.* opposed to or regulating trusts, or business monopolies, cartels, etc.

an·ti·tus·sive (-tus'iv) *adj.* [ANTI- + TUSSIVE] reducing the severity of coughing —*n.* an antitussive preparation

an·ti·type (an'ti tīp'; *see* ANTI-) *n.* [LL. *antitypus* < Gr. *antitypos* < *anti-*, against, corresponding to + *typos*, form, figure] **1.** the person or thing represented or foreshadowed by an earlier type or symbol **2.** an opposite type —**an'ti·typ'i·cal** (-tīp'ə k'l), **an'ti·typ'ic** *adj.* —**an'ti·typ'i·cal·ly** *adv.*

an·ti·un·i·verse (-yōō'nə vərs) *n.* a universe made up of antimatter, postulated to exist far out in space

an·ti·ven·in (an'ti ven'ən; *see* ANTI-) *n.* [ANTI- + VEN(OM) + -IN¹] **1.** an antitoxin for venom, as of snakes, produced by gradually increased injections of the specific venom **2.** a serum containing this antitoxin

an·ti·viv·i·sec·tion (-viv'ə sek'shən) *n.* opposition to medical research on living animals —**an'ti·viv'i·sec'tion·ist** *n., adj.*

---

fat, āpe, cär; ten, ēven; is, bīte; gō, hôrn, tōol, look; oil, out; up, fur; get; joy; yet; chin; she; thin, then; zh, leisure; ŋ, ring; ə for a in ago, e in agent, i in sanity, o in comply, u in focus; ' as in able (ā'b'l); Fr. bal; ë, Fr. coeur; ö, Fr. feu; Fr. mon; ô, Fr. coq; ü, Fr. duc; r, Fr. cri; H, G. ich; kh, G. doch. See inside front cover. ☆Americanism; ‡foreign; *hypothetical; <derived from

ant·ler (ant'lər) *n.* [ME. *aunteler* < OFr. *antoillier* < ML. **anteoculare* < *ante-*, before + *ocularis*, of the eyes] **1.** the branched, deciduous horn of any animal of the deer family **2.** any branch of such a horn —**ant'lered** (-lərd) *adj.*

Ant·li·a (ant'lē ə) [ModL. *Antlia* (*Pneumatica*), lit., (air) pump < L. *antlia*, a water pump < Gr. *antlia*, bilgewater < *antlos*, hold (of a ship): name introduced by N. L. de Lacaille (1713–1762), Fr. astronomer] a S constellation northwest of Centaurus, between Argo and Hydra

ant lion 1. the large-jawed larva of several species of insects (family Myrmeleontidae) that lies hidden in a cone-shaped pit which it has dug and feeds on ants, etc. that fall in **2.** the winged adult insect: in full, **ant lion fly**

An·to·fa·gas·ta (än'tō fä gäs'tä) seaport in N Chile: pop. 89,000

An·toi·nette (an'twa net', -tə-) a feminine name: dim. *Nettie, Netty:* see ANTONIA

Antoinette, Marie *see* MARIE ANTOINETTE

An·to·ni·a (an tō'nē ə, -nyə) [L., fem. of *Antonius:* see ANTHONY] a feminine name: var. *Antoinette*

An·to·ni·nus (an'tə nī'nəs), **Marcus Aurelius** *see* AURELIUS

Antoninus Pius 86–161 A.D.; Rom. emperor (138–161)

an·to·no·ma·sia (an'tə nō mā'zhə) *n.* [L. < Gr. < *antonomazein*, to call by another name < *anti-*, instead of + *onomazein*, to name < *onoma*, NAME] **1.** the use of an epithet or title in place of a name, as in calling a judge *his honor* **2.** the use of a proper name instead of a common noun, as in calling a philanderer a *Don Juan*

An·to·ny (an'tə nē) **1.** a masculine name **2.** Mark or Marc, (L. name *Marcus Antonius*) 83?–30 B.C.; Rom. general & member of the second triumvirate

an·to·nym (an'tə nim') *n.* [with altered sense (as if < ANTI-) < Gr. *antōnymia*, a pronoun < *anti-*, equal to, instead of, opposite (cf. ANTI-) + *ōnyma*, NAME] a word that is opposite in meaning to another word [*sad* is an *antonym* of *happy*]

an·ton·y·mous (an tän'ə məs) *adj.* of, or having the nature of, an antonym —*SYN.* see OPPOSITE

an·tre (an'tər) *n.* [Fr. < L. *antrum* < Gr. *antron*, cave: cf. ANTRUM] [Archaic or Poet.] a cave; cavern

An·trim (an'trim) county of NE Northern Ireland: 1,204 sq. mi.; pop. 700,000; county seat, Belfast

an·trorse (an trôrs') *adj.* [ModL. *antrorsus:* see ANTERIOR & VERSUS] *Biol.* upward or forward —**an·trorse'ly** *adv.*

an·trum (an'trəm) *n., pl.* **-tra** (-trə), **-trums** [L. < Gr. *antron*, cave < IE. **antrom*, ? akin to **ant-*, breath: cf. ANIMAL] *Anat.* a cavity; esp., either of a pair of sinuses in the upper jaw

☆**AN·TU** (an'tōō) [αlpha-naphthyl-*t*hiourea] a *trademark* for an odorless gray powder, C₁₀H₇NHCSNH₂, used to kill rats —*n.* [a-] this powder

An·tung (än'doon'; *E.* an toon') seaport in Liaoning province, NE China, at the mouth of the Yalu River: pop. 370,000

Ant·werp (an'twərp) **1.** province of N Belgium: 1,104 sq. mi.; pop. 1,482,000 **2.** its capital, on the Scheldt River: pop. 247,000 Fl. name **Ant·wer·pen** (änt'ver/pən)

A·nu·bis (ə nyōō'bis, -nōō'-) [L. < Gr. *Anoubis* < Egypt. *Anpu*] an Egyptian god, depicted with the head of a jackal, who led the dead to judgment: identified with the Greek Hermes

a·nu·cle·ar (ā'nōō'klē ər, -nyōō'-) *adj. Biol.* without a nucleus or nuclei

an·u·ran (ə nyoor'ən) *adj., n.* [< Gr. *an-*, not + *oura*, tail + -AN] *same as* SALIENTIAN

an·u·re·sis (an'yoo rē'sis) *n.* [ModL. < AN-¹ + Gr. *ourēsis*, urination < *ourein:* see URINE] **1.** partial or total inability to void urine secreted by the kidneys **2.** *same as* ANURIA —**an'u·ret'ic** (-ret'ik) *adj.*

an·u·ri·a (an yoor'ē ə) *n.* [ModL.: see AN-¹ & -URIA] failure of the kidneys to secrete urine —**an·u'ric** *adj.*

an·u·rous (-yoor'əs) *adj.* [see ANURAN & -OUS] having no tail, as a frog or toad

a·nus (ā'nəs) *n., pl.* **a'nus·es, a'ni** (-nī) [L., ring, anus] the opening at the lower end of the alimentary canal

an·vil (an'vil) *n.* [ME. *anvelt* < OE. *anfilt* < *an-*, on + **fiitan*, to hit, beat < IE. base **pel(d)-*, to beat into motion, whence (IM)PEL: cf. FELT¹] **1.** an iron or steel block on which metal objects are hammered into shape **2.** the incus, one of the three bones of the middle ear: see EAR¹, illus.

anx·i·e·ty (an zī'ə tē) *n., pl.* **-ties** [L. *anxietas* < *anxius:* see ff.] **1.** a state of being uneasy, apprehensive, or worried about what may happen; concern about a possible future event **2.** *Psychiatry* an intense state of this kind, characterized by varying degrees of emotional disturb-

ance and psychic tension **3.** an eager but often uneasy desire [*anxiety* to do well] —*SYN.* see CARE

anx·ious (aŋk'shəs, aŋ'-) *adj.* [L. *anxius* < *angere*, to choke, give pain < IE. base **angh-:* see ANGER] **1.** having or showing anxiety; uneasy in mind; apprehensive; worried **2.** causing or full of anxiety [an *anxious* hour] **3.** eagerly wishing [*anxious* to do well] —*SYN.* see EAGER¹ —**anx'ious·ly** *adv.* —**anx'ious·ness** *n.*

☆**anxious seat** a bench near the preacher at revival meetings, for those with a troubled conscience who seek salvation: also **anxious bench**

an·y (en'ē) *adj.* [ME. *ani* < OE. *ænig* < *an*, ONE, akin to G. *einig*, ON. *einigr*] **1.** one, no matter which, of more than two [*any* pupil may answer] **2.** some, no matter how much or how little, how many, or what kind [he can't tolerate *any* criticism] **3.** without limit [entitled to *any* number of admissions] **4.** even one; the least amount or number of [I haven't *any* dimes] **5.** every [*any* child can do it] **6.** of considerable size or extent [we won't be able to travel *any* distance before nightfall] —*pron. sing. & pl.* any one or ones; any amount or number —*adv.* to any degree or extent; at all [is he *any* better this morning?]

an·y·bod·y (-bud'ē, -bäd'ē) *pron.* **1.** any person; anyone **2.** a person of fame, importance, etc.

an·y·how (-hou') *adv.* **1.** no matter in what way **2.** no matter what else may be true; in any case **3.** in a careless way; haphazardly

an·y·more (-môr') *adv.* now; nowadays: used in negative constructions [he doesn't live here *anymore*]: ☆dialectal in affirmative constructions [that's hard to get *anymore*]: also **any more**

an·y·one (-wun') *pron.* any person; anybody

any one 1. any single **2.** any single person or thing

☆**an·y·place** (-plās') *adv.* [Colloq.] in, at, or to any place; anywhere —**get anyplace** [Colloq.] to have any success

an·y·thing (-thiŋ') *pron.* any object, event, fact, etc. —*n.* a thing, no matter of what kind —*adv.* in any way; at all [is he *anything* like his father?] —**anything but** by no means; not at all

an·y·way (-wā') *adv.* **1.** in any manner or way **2.** at least; nevertheless; anyhow **3.** haphazardly; carelessly: also [Colloq. or Dial.] **an'y·ways'**

an·y·where (-hwer', -wer') *adv.* **1.** in, at, or to any place **2.** [Colloq.] at all; to any extent —☆**anywhere from** [Colloq.] any amount, rate, time, etc. between (stated limits) [*anywhere from* five to ten dollars] —**get anywhere** [Colloq.] to have any success

an·y·wheres (-hwerz', -werz') *adv.* [Colloq.] *same as* ANYWHERE

an·y·wise (-wīz') *adv.* [ME. *ani wise* < OE. (on) *ænige wisan:* see ANY & WISE²] in any manner or way; at all

An·zac (an'zak') *n.* [an acronym formed from the title] a soldier in the Australian and New Zealand Army Corps —*adj.* of the Anzacs

An·zi·o (an'zē ō; *It.* än'tsyð) port on the W coast of Italy, south of Rome: pop. 10,000: site of Allied beachhead (Jan., 1944) in the invasion of Italy, World War II

A/o, a/o account of

☆**A-OK** (ā'ō kā') *adj.* [A(LL) OK] [Colloq.] excellent, fine, in working order, etc.: a generalized term of commendation: also **A'-O·kay'**

A one (ā' wun') [orig. a designation of first-class ships, as in Lloyd's Register, *A* indicating the excellent condition of the hull, *1* that of the equipment] [Colloq.] first-class; first-rate; superior: also **A 1, A number 1**

A·o·ran·gi (ä'ō räŋ'gē) *same as* Mount COOK

a·o·rist (ā'ə rist) *n.* [Gr. *aoristos*, indefinite < *a-*, without + *horizein*, to define < *horos*, a limit: cf. HORIZON] a past tense of Greek verbs, denoting an action without indicating whether completed, continued, or repeated —*adj.* designating or in this tense

a·o·ris·tic (ā'ə ris'tik) *adj.* **1.** of or in the aorist **2.** indefinite

a·or·ta (ā ôr'tə) *n., pl.* **-tas, -tae** (-tē) [ModL. < Gr. *aortē* < *aeirein*, to raise, heave] the main artery of the body carrying blood from the left ventricle of the heart to arteries in all organs and parts: see HEART, illus. —**a·or'tic, a·or'tal** *adj.*

Aosta, Valle d' *see* VALLE D'AOSTA

a·ou·dad (ä'oo dad', ou'dad') *n.* [Fr. < Moorish *audad*] a wild North African sheep (*Ammotragus lervia*) with large curved horns and a heavy growth of hair from the throat to the knees

‡**à ou·trance** (à' ōō träns') [Fr.] to the utmost; to the bitter end; to the death

ap- (ap, əp) **1.** *same as* AD-: used before *p*- **2.** *same as* APO-: used before a vowel

a·pace (ə pās') *adv.* [ME. *apas:* see A-¹ & PACE¹] at a fast pace; with speed; swiftly

A·pach·e (ə pach'ē) *n., pl.* **A·pach'e, A·pach'es** [AmSp., prob. < Zuni *ápachu*, enemy] **1.** a member of a tribe of nomadic Indians of N Mexico and the SW U.S. **2.** any of their five Athapascan languages

a·pache (ə pash', -päsh'; *Fr.* à pàsh') *n., pl.* **a·pach'es** (-iz; *Fr.* à pàsh') [Fr., lit., Apache: first used of Parisian thieves in 1902 by Victor Moris, French journalist] a gangster or thug of Paris —*adj.* designating a dance, performed as an exhibition in cabarets, etc., which represents an apache handling his girl in a brutal, masterful way

ANTLERS
(49–77 in. long)

ANVIL

Ap·a·lach·ee Bay (ap/ə lach/ē) [< AmInd. (? Choctaw) tribal name] inlet of the Gulf of Mexico, on the NW coast of Florida

Ap·a·lach·i·co·la (ap/ə lach/ə kō/lə) [< AmInd. (? a tribal name] river in NW Fla., flowing into the Gulf of Mexico: with the Chattahoochee River, 500 mi.

a·pa·nage (ap/ə nij) n. *same as* APPANAGE

☆**a·pa·re·jo** (ap/ə rā/hō) n., pl. **-jos** [Sp.] [Chiefly Southwest] a kind of packsaddle made of a stuffed leather pad

a·part (ə pärt/) adv. [ME. < OFr. *a part* < L. *ad*, to, at + *partem*, acc. of *pars*, a part, side] 1. to one side; at a distance; aside 2. separately or away in place or time / born two years *apart*/ 3. reserved for a particular purpose 4. separately or independently in function, use, etc. / viewed *apart*/ 5. in or to pieces / to take a motor *apart*/ 6. aside; notwithstanding / all joking *apart*/ —adj. [used only in the *predicate*] separated; not together —**apart from** other than; besides —**take apart** to reduce (a whole) to its parts —**tell apart** to distinguish one from another

a·part·heid (ə pärt/hāt, -hīt; -āt, -īt) n. [Afrik., apartness] the policy of strict racial segregation and discrimination against the native Negroes and other colored peoples as practiced in South Africa

a·part·ment (ə pärt/mənt) n. [Fr. *appartement* < It. *appartamento* < *appartare*, to separate < *parte*, PART] 1. a room or suite of rooms to live in; esp., one suite in an apartment house ☆2. an apartment house —adj. of, in, or for an apartment or apartments

☆**apartment house** a building in which the rooms are arranged in suites as apartments: also **apartment building**

ap·a·tet·ic (ap/ə tet/ik) adj. [Gr. *apatētikos*, deceiving < *apatē*, deceit] Zool. serving to disguise or conceal by camouflaging; imitative / the *apatetic* coloration or form of some animals/

ap·a·thet·ic (ap/ə thet/ik) adj. [< APATHY, after PATHETIC] 1. feeling little or no emotion; unmoved 2. not interested; indifferent; listless —SYN. see IMPASSIVE —**ap/a·thet/i·cal·ly** adv.

ap·a·thy (ap/ə thē) n., pl. **-thies** [Fr. *apathie* < L. *apathia* < Gr. *apatheia* < *a-*, without + *pathos*, emotion < *pathein*, to feel] 1. lack of emotion or of interest; listless condition; unconcern; indifference

ap·a·tite (ap/ə tīt/) n. [< Gr. *apatē*, deceit + -ITE¹: so named from being mistaken for other minerals] any of a group of minerals consisting essentially of calcium phosphate and usually containing fluorine, chlorine, or hydroxyl or carbonate ions: apatites commonly occur in sedimentary or igneous rocks and as the inorganic component of bones and teeth as small, hexagonal crystals of green, blue, or yellow

APC [*a*cetylsalicylic acid, *p*henacetin, and *c*affeine] aspirin, phenacetin, and caffeine, usually in a white tablet (**APC tablet**) used for reducing fevers, relieving headaches, etc.

ape (āp) n. [ME. < OE. *apa*; akin to G. *affe* < Gmc. **apan*, prob. < OSlav. *opica*] 1. any of a family (Pongidae) of large, tailless monkeys that can stand and walk in an almost erect position; specif., a chimpanzee, gorilla, orangutan, or gibbon 2. any monkey 3. a person who imitates; mimic 4. a person who is uncouth, gross, clumsy, etc. —vt. **aped, ap/ing** to imitate or mimic —SYN. see IMITATE —**go ape** [Slang] to become mad; also, to become wildly enthusiastic —**ape/like/** adj. —**ap/er** n.

a·peak (ə pēk/) adv. Naut. in a vertical or nearly vertical position

A·pel·doorn (ä/pəl dōrn/) city in EC Netherlands: pop. 112,000

A·pel·les (ə pel/ēz) fl. 4th cent. B.C.; Gr. painter

ape-man (āp/man/) n. any of several extinct primates, as Pithecanthropus, with structural characteristics intermediate between ape and man

Ap·en·nines (ap/ə ninz/) mountain range along the length of C Italy: highest peak, 9,560 ft.

‡**a·per·cu** (å per sü/; E. ap/ər sōō/) n., pl. **-cus** (-sü/; E -sōōz/) [Fr.] 1. a quick impression or insight 2. a brief digest or survey

a·pe·ri·ent (ə pir/ē ənt) adj., n. [L. *aperiens*, prp. of *aperire*: see APERTURE] laxative —SYN. see PHYSIC

a·pe·ri·od·ic (ā/pir ē äd/ik) adj. 1. not periodic; occurring irregularly 2. Physics without periodic vibrations

a·pe·ri·tif (ä/pā rə tēf/) n. [Fr. *apéritif* < L. *apertus*: see APERTURE] an alcoholic drink, esp. a wine, taken before meals to stimulate the appetite

ap·er·ture (ap/ər chər; by dissimilation, -ə char) n. [L. *apertura* < *apertus*, pp. of *aperire*, to open < IE. **ap-wer-*, to uncover < **ap(o)-*, away + **uer-*, to close, cover: cf. OPERCULUM] 1. an opening; hole; gap 2. the opening, or the diameter of the opening, in a camera, telescope, etc. through which light passes into the lens

ap·er·y (āp/ər ē) n., pl. **-er·ies** 1. an aping; mimicking 2. a silly or mischievous act

a·pet·a·lous (ā pet/'l əs) adj. Bot. without petals

a·pex (ā/peks) n., pl. **a/pex·es, ap·i·ces** (ap/ə sēz/, ā/pə-) [L., a point < ? *apere*, to fasten: see APT] 1. the highest point; peak; vertex 2. the pointed end; tip 3. the highest point of interest, excitement, etc.; climax ☆4. Mining the

edge or outcrop of a vein nearest the surface —SYN. see SUMMIT

aph- (af) *same as* APO-

aph·a·nite (af/ə nīt/) n. [< Gr. *aphanēs*, invisible + -ITE¹] rock so closely grained that its individual crystals cannot be seen by the unaided eye —**aph/a·nit/ic** (-nit/ik) adj.

a·pha·si·a (ə fā/zhə, -zhē ə) n. [ModL. < Gr. *aphasia* < *aphatos*, unuttered < *a-*, not + *phatos* < *phanai*, to speak < IE. base **bhā-*, to speak, whence L. *fari*, *fama*, OE. *bann*: see BAN¹] a total or partial loss of the power to use or understand words, usually caused by brain disease or injury —**a·pha/sic** (-zik), **a·pha/si·ac/** (-zē ak/) adj., n.

a·phe·li·on (ə fē/lē ən) n., pl. **-li·ons, -li·a** (-ə) [ModL., altered (after Gr. *apo*, from + *hēlios*, sun) < *aphelium*, coined from same Gr. elements by Kepler after L. *apogaeum*: see APOGEE] the point farthest from the sun in the orbit of a planet or comet, or of a man-made satellite in orbit around the sun: opposed to PERIHELION

APHELION
(planet at aphelion A and at perihelion P)

a·phe·li·o·tro·pism (ə fē/lē al/trə piz/m) n. [AP- + HELIOTROPISM] a tendency of certain plants to turn away from the sun; negative heliotropism —**a·phe/li·o·trop/ic** (-ə tιäp/ik) adj.

a·pher·e·sis, a·phaer·e·sis (ə fer/ə sis) n. [L. *aphaeresis* < Gr. *aphairesis* < *aphairein*, to take away < *apo-*, away + *hairein*, to take] the dropping of a letter, syllable, or phoneme at the beginning of a word (Ex.: '*cause* for *because*) —**aph·e·ret·ic** (af/ə ret/ik) adj.

aph·e·sis (af/ə sis) n. [Gr., a letting go < *apo*, from + *hienai*, to send] loss of a short unaccented vowel at the beginning of a word, a form of apheresis (Ex.: *squire* for *esquire*) —**a·phet·ic** (ə fet/ik) adj. —**a·phet/i·cal·ly** adv.

A·pi·a (ä pē/ə) seaport and the capital of Western Samoa, on Upolu island: pop. 22,000

a·phid (ā/fid, af/id) n. [ModL. *aphis* (pl. *aphides*), coined by Linnaeus < Gr. *apheidēs*, unsparing, lavish, prob. in reference to their rapid multiplication] any of a group of small homopterous insects (family Aphididae) that suck the juice from plants; plant louse —**a·phid·i·an** (ə fid/ē ən) adj.

a·phis (ā/fis, af/is) n., pl. **aph·i·des** (af/ə dēz/) n. [ModL.] an aphid; specif., one of a widespread genus (*Aphis*)

aphis lion any of the larvae of lacewing flies: so called because they feed upon aphids

APHID
(1/25 to 1/4 of an inch)

a·pho·ni·a (ā fō/nē ə, ə-) n. [ModL. < Gr. *aphōnia* < *aphōnos*, voiceless < *a-*, without + *phōnē*, sound, voice < *phanai*: see APHASIA] loss of voice due to an organic or functional disorder

a·phon·ic (ā/fän/ik) adj. [< Gr. *aphōnos* (see prec.) + -IC] 1. of or having aphonia 2. Phonet. a) not pronounced b) voiceless

aph·o·rism (af/ə riz/m) n. [Fr. *aphorisme* < Gr. *aphorismos*, definition, aphorism < *aphorizein*, to divide, mark off < *apo-*, from + *horizein*, to bound: see HORIZON] 1. a short, concise statement of a principle 2. a short, pointed sentence expressing a wise or clever observation or a general truth; maxim; adage —SYN. see SAYING

aph·o·ris·tic (af/ə ris/tik) adj. 1. of or like an aphorism 2. full of or using aphorisms —**aph/o·ris/ti·cal·ly** adv.

aph·o·rize (af/ə rīz/) vi. **-rized/, -riz/ing** to write or speak in aphorisms —**aph/o·rist** n.

a·pho·tic (ā/fōt/ik) adj. [< Gr. *aphōs, aphōtos* < *a-*, without + *phōs, phōtos*, light + -IC] without light; specif., pertaining to that part (**aphotic zone, aphotic region**) of the ocean below a depth of about 300 ft. to which sunlight sufficient for photosynthesis does not penetrate

aph·ro·dis·i·ac (af/rə diz/ē ak/) adj. [Gr. *aphrodisiakos* < *Aphroditē*] arousing or increasing sexual desire —n. any aphrodisiac drug or other agent

Aph·ro·di·te (af/rə dīt/ē) [Gr. *Aphroditē*, associated by the Greeks with *aphros*, foam, but of Oriental origin] Gr. Myth. the goddess of love and beauty: see also VENUS —n. [a-] a spotted, brown butterfly (*Argynnis aphrodite*) of N. America

aph·tha (af/thə, ap/-) n., pl. **-thae** (-thē) [ModL. < L. *aphthae* (pl.) < Gr. *aphthai*, pl. of *aphtha*, an eruption, thrush < *haptein*, to inflame] a small, white spot or pustule that is caused by a fungus and appears in the mouth, on the lips, or in the gastrointestinal tract in certain diseases, as thrush —**aph/thous** (-thəs) adj.

a·phyl·lous (ā/fil/əs) adj. [Gr. *aphyllos* < *a-*, without + *phyllon*, a leaf] lacking leaves, as most cactuses

a·pi·a·ceous (ā/pē ā/shəs) adj. [< ModL. *apiaceae*, carrot family < L. *apium*, parsley, celery + -OUS] *same as* UMBELLIFEROUS

a·pi·an (ā/pē ən) adj. [L. *apianus* < *apis*, bee] of a bee or bees

a·pi·ar·i·an (ā′pē er′ē ən) *adj.* having to do with bees or the care of bees

a·pi·a·rist (ā′pē ə rist, -er′ist) *n.* a person who keeps bees

a·pi·ar·y (ā′pē er′ē) *n., pl.* **-ar′ies** [L. *apiarium,* beehive < *apis,* bee] a place where bees are kept for their honey, generally consisting of a number of hives

ap·i·cal (ap′ə k'l, ā′pə-) *adj.* [< L. *apex* (gen. *apicis*), APEX] **1.** of, at, or constituting the apex **2.** *Phonet.* articulated with the apex of the tongue —*n.* a sound so articulated, as the *l, t,* or *d* of *lighted*

ap·i·ces (ap′ə sēz′, āp′ə-) *n. alt. pl.* of APEX

a·pic·u·late (ə pik′yoo lit, -lāt′) *adj.* [ModL. *apiculatus* < *apiculus,* dim. of L. *apex,* APEX] ending abruptly in a small point, as some leaves

a·pi·cul·ture (ā′pə kul′chər) *n.* [< L. *apis,* bee + CULTURE] the raising and care of bees; beekeeping —**a′pi·cul′tur·al** *adj.* —**a′pi·cul′tur·ist** *n.*

a·piece (ə pēs′) *adv.* [ME. *a pece:* see A¹ & PIECE] for each one; each

à pied (à pyä′) [Fr.] on foot; afoot

A·pis (ā′pis) [L. < Gr. < Egypt. *Hapi,* lit., hidden] the sacred bull worshiped by the ancient Egyptians as the embodiment of a god

ap·ish (āp′ish) *adj.* **1.** like an ape **2.** imitative in an unreasoning way **3.** silly, affected, mischievous, etc. —**ap′ish·ly** *adv.* —**ap′ish·ness** *n.*

a·piv·o·rous (ā piv′ər əs) *adj.* [< L. *apis,* bee + -VOROUS] feeding on bees, as some birds

a·pla·cen·tal (ā′plə sen′t'l) *adj.* having no placenta, as the kangaroo

ap·la·nat·ic (ap′lə nat′ik) *adj.* [A-² + Gr. *planatikos,* wandering < *planan,* to stray < IE. base *plā-no-:* see FLOOR] *Optics* corrected for distortion, lack of sharpness, etc.: said of a lens

a·plen·ty (ə plen′tē) *adj., adv.* [A-¹ + PLENTY] [Colloq.] in abundance

ap·lite (ap′līt) *n.* [< Gr. *haploos,* simple (see HAPLO-) + -ITE¹] a light-colored, fine-grained granitic rock consisting chiefly of quartz and orthoclase feldspar —**ap·lit·ic** (ap lit′ik) *adj.*

a·plomb (ə pläm′, -plum′, -plôm′) *n.* [Fr., lit., perpendicularity, equilibrium < *a,* to + *plomb,* the metal lead: see PLUMB] self-possession; assurance; poise —*SYN.* see CONFIDENCE

ap·ne·a, ap·noe·a (ap nē′ə, ap′nē ə) *n.* [ModL. < Gr. *apnoia* < *a-,* without + *pnoie,* wind: cf. PNEUMATIC & SNEEZE] **1.** temporary stopping of breathing **2.** asphyxia —**ap·ne′ic, ap·noe′ic** *adj.*

ap·o- (ap′ə) [< Gr. *apo,* off, from off] *a prefix meaning:* **1.** off, from, or away from [*apogamy*] **2.** detached [*apocarp*]

APO Army Post Office

Apoc. **1.** Apocalypse **2.** Apocrypha **3.** Apocryphal

a·poc·a·lypse (ə päk′ə lips′) *n.* [L. *apocalypsis* < Gr. *apokalypsis* < *apokalyptein,* to disclose < *apo-,* from + *kalyptein,* to cover < IE. base *kel-:* see HALL] **1.** any of various Jewish and Christian pseudonymous writings (c.200 B.C.—c.300 A.D.) depicting symbolically the ultimate destruction of evil and triumph of good; specif., [A-] the last book of the New Testament; book of Revelation **2.** a disclosure regarded as prophetic; revelation —**a·poc′a·lyp′tic** (-lip′tik), **a·poc′a·lyp′ti·cal** *adj.* —**a·poc′a·lyp′ti·cal·ly** *adv.*

a·po·car·pous (ap′ə kär′pəs) *adj. Bot.* having separate or partially joined carpels, as the strawberry

ap·o·chro·mat·ic (ap′ə krō mat′ik) *adj. Optics* corrected to prevent distortion of the image and the occurrence of refracted colors along its edges: said of a lens

a·poc·o·pate (ə päk′ə pāt′) *vt.* **-pat′ed, -pat′ing** [ML. *apocopatus* < Gr. *apokopē:* see APOCOPE] to shorten by apocope —**a·poc·o·pa′tion** *n.*

a·poc·o·pe (ə pē′) *n.* [Gr. *apokopē,* a cutting off < *apokoptein,* to cut off < *apo-,* from + *koptein,* to cut off] the cutting off or dropping of the last sound or sounds of a word (Ex.: *mos′* for *most*)

ap·o·crine (ap′ə krin′, -krin) *adj.* [< APO- + Gr. *krinein,* to separate: see CRISIS] designating a type of glandular secretion in which part of the secreting cell is thrown off along with the secretion

a·poc·ry·pha (ə päk′rə fə) *n.pl.* [ME. *apocrifa* < LL. *apocrypha,* pl. of *apocryphus* < Gr. *apokryphos,* hidden, obscure < *apokryptein* < *apo-,* away + *kryptein,* to hide: see CRYPT] **1.** any writings, anecdotes, etc. of doubtful authenticity or authorship **2.** [A-] fourteen books of the Septuagint that are rejected in Judaism and regarded by Protestants as not canonical: eleven of them are fully accepted in the Roman Catholic canon **3.** [A-] various writings falsely attributed to Biblical characters or kept out of the New Testament because not accepted as resulting from revelation

a·poc·ry·phal (-f'l) *adj.* **1.** of doubtful authorship or authenticity **2.** not genuine; spurious; counterfeit **3.** [A-] of or like the Apocrypha —*SYN.* see FICTITIOUS

a·poc·y·na·ceous (ə päs′ə nā′shəs) *adj.* [< ModL. *Apocynaceae,* the dogbane family < Gr. *apokynon,* dogbane < *apo-,* from + *kyōn,* dog < IE. *kwon-:* see CANINE, HOUND¹] of the dogbane family of plants, which are mainly tropical, with simple leaves and a milky, often poisonous juice

ap·od (ap′əd) *adj.* same as APODAL —*n.* an apodal animal, such as a snake or a legless lizard

ap·o·dal (ap′ə d'l) *adj.* [< Gr. *apous, apodos,* footless < *a-,* without + *pous,* FOOT + -AL] *Zool.* **1.** lacking feet or legs, as snakes **2.** lacking pelvic fins Also **ap′o·dous** (-dəs)

ap·o·dic·tic (ap′ə dik′tik) *adj.* [L. *apodicticus* < Gr. *apodeiktikos,* proving clearly < *apodeiknynai,* to show by argument < *apo-,* from + *deiknynai,* to show] that can clearly be shown or proved; absolutely certain or necessarily true: also **ap′o·deic′tic** (-dīk′tik) —**ap′o·dic′ti·cal·ly** *adv.*

a·pod·o·sis (ə päd′ə sis) *n., pl.* **-ses′** (-sēz′) [Gr., a giving back < *apo-,* back + *didonai,* to give] the clause expressing the conclusion or result in a conditional sentence: opposed to PROTASIS

ap·o·en·zyme (ap′ō en′zīm) *n.* the part of an enzyme that consists wholly of protein and that, together with a coenzyme, forms a complete enzyme

a·pog·a·my (ə päg′ə mē) *n.* [APO- + -GAMY] the development of a plant without the union of gametes; development of a sporophyte from a gametophyte without fertilization —**ap·o·gam·ic** (ap′ə gam′ik), **a·pog′a·mous** (-məs) *adj.*

ap·o·gee (ap′ə jē′) *n.* [Fr. *apogée* < ML. *apogaeum* < Gr. *apogaion* < *apo-,* from + *gaia, gē,* earth] **1.** the point farthest from the earth in the orbit of the moon or of a man-made satellite: opposed to PERIGEE **2.** the highest or farthest point —**ap′o·ge′an** (-jē′ən), **ap′o·ge′al** *adj.*

ap·o·ge·ot·ro·pism (ap′ə jē ä′trə piz′m) *n.* [APO- + GEOTROPISM] *Bot.* a tendency to grow or move away from the earth or from the pull of gravity; negative geotropism

EARTH

P ———————— A

APOGEE
(moon at apogee A
and at perigee P)

a·po·lit·i·cal (ā′pə lit′ə k'l) *adj.* not concerned or connected with political matters —**a′po·lit′i·cal·ly** *adv.*

A·pol·li·naire (à pô lē ner′), **Guil·laume** (gē yōm′) (born *Wilhelm Kostrowitzki*) 1880–1918; Fr. poet & essayist, born in Italy

A·pol·lo (ə päl′ō) [L. < Gr. *Apollōn*] *Gr. & Rom. Myth.* the god of music, poetry, prophecy, and medicine, represented as exemplifying manly youth and beauty: later identified with HELIOS —*n.* any handsome young man —**Ap·ol·lo·ni·an** (ap′ə lō′nē ən) *adj.*

A·pol·lyon (ə päl′yən) [Gr. *apollyōn,* destroying, ruining < *apollynai, apolluein,* to destroy < *apo-,* from + *lyein,* to LOOSE] **1.** *Bible* the angel of the bottomless pit; Satan: Rev. 9:11 **2.** an evil spirit subdued by the hero, Christian, of Bunyan's *Pilgrim's Progress*

a·pol·o·get·ic (ə päl′ə jet′ik) *adj.* [Fr. *apologétique* < LL. *apologeticus* < Gr. *apologētikos,* suitable for defense < *apologeisthai:* see APOLOGY] **1.** defending in writing or speech; vindicating **2.** showing realization of and regret for a fault, wrong, etc.; making apology Also **a·pol′o·get′i·cal** —*n.* a formal defense, often written, of a belief, cause, etc. —**a·pol′o·get′i·cal·ly** *adv.*

a·pol·o·get·ics (-iks) *n.pl.* [with sing. v.] [see APOLOGETIC] the branch of theology having to do with the defense and proofs of Christianity

ap·o·lo·gi·a (ap′ə lō′jē ə) *n.* [LL.(Ec.)] an apology, esp. a formal defense of an idea, religion, etc.

a·pol·o·gist (ə päl′ə jist) *n.* [Fr. *apologiste:* see APOLOGY] a person who writes or speaks in defense or justification of a doctrine, faith, action, etc.

a·pol·o·gize (-jīz′) *vi.* **-gized′, -giz′ing** **1.** to make an apology; acknowledge, and express regret for, a fault, wrong, etc. **2.** to make a formal defense in speech or writing —**a·pol′o·giz′er** *n.*

ap·o·logue (ap′ə lôg′, -läg′) *n.* [Fr. < L. *apologus* < Gr. *apologos*] a short allegorical story with a lesson or moral; fable

a·pol·o·gy (ə päl′ə jē) *n., pl.* **-gies** [LL.(Ec.) *apologia* < Gr. *apologia,* a speaking in defense < *apologeisthai,* to speak in defense < *apo-,* from + *logos,* speech: see LOGIC] **1.** a formal spoken or written defense of some idea, religion, philosophy, etc. **2.** an acknowledgment of some fault, injury, insult, etc., with an expression of regret and a plea for pardon **3.** an inferior substitute; makeshift [he is a poor *apology* for an actor]

ap·o·mict (ap′ə mikt) *n.* [< *apomictic,* of apomixis < ff., with suffix as if < Gr. *miktos,* mixed + -IC] a plant that reproduces by apomixis or that has been produced by apomixis —**ap′o·mic′tic** *adj.*

ap·o·mix·is (ap′ə mik′sis) *n.* [ModL. < Gr. *apo,* from + *mixis,* a mingling] nonsexual reproduction; esp., apogamy

ap·o·mor·phine (ap′ə môr′fēn) *n.* a crystalline alkaloid, C₁₇H₁₇NO₂, produced by synthesis from morphine: used as an emetic and expectorant

ap·o·neu·ro·sis (ap′ə noo rō′sis, -nyoo-) *n., pl.* **-ses** (-sēz) [ModL. < Gr. *aponeurōsis* < *apo-,* from + *neuron,* a nerve, end of the muscle] a fibrous membrane that covers certain muscles and connects them with tendons —**ap′o·neu·rot′ic** (-rät′ik) *adj.*

ap·o·pemp·tic (ap′ə pemp′tik) *adj.* [< Gr. *apopemptikos* < *apopempein,* to send off < *apo-,* away + *pempein,* to send: cf. POMP] [Archaic] of farewell or leavetaking; valedictory [an *apopemptic* song]

a·poph·a·sis (ə päf′ə sis) *n.* [LL. < Gr. *apophasis,* denial

< *apophanai*, to deny < *apo-*, away + *phanai*, say, assert]
Rhetoric the artful mention of something by denying that it
will be mentioned (Ex.: we will not remind you of his
many crimes)

ap·o·phthegm (ap′ə them′) *n. same as* APOTHEGM

a·poph·y·ge (ə päf′ə jē′) *n.* [Gr. *apophygē* < *apopheugein*,
to flee away < *apo-*, from + *pheugein*, to flee < IE. base
**bheug-*: cf. FUGITIVE] *Archit.* the concave curve where the
end of a column spreads into its base or capital

a·poph·yl·lite (-ə lit′) *n.* [< APO- + Gr. *phyllon*, a leaf +
-ITE: so named from its flaking off under the blowpipe] a
tetragonal mineral, KCa(Si₂O₅)₄F·8H₂O, occurring in
square, transparent prisms or grayish-white, layerlike
masses

a·poph·y·sis (-ə sis) *n., pl.* **-ses** (-sēz′) [Gr. *apophysis*, an
offshoot < *apo-*, from + *phyein*, to grow] 1. *Anat.* a natural
outgrowth or process on a vertebra or other bone 2. *Bot.* a
swelling at the base of the capsule in some mosses —**a·poph′y·
se′al** (-sē′əl) *adj.*

ap·o·plec·tic (ap′ə plek′tik) *adj.* [LL. *apoplecticus* < Gr.
apoplēktikos < *apoplēktos*, stricken: see APOPLEXY] 1. of,
like, or causing apoplexy 2. having apoplexy 3. on the
apparent verge of apoplexy *[apoplectic* with rage*]* Also
ap′o·plec′ti·cal —a person having or likely to have
apoplexy —**ap′o·plec′ti·cal·ly** *adv.*

ap·o·plex·y (ap′ə plek′sē) *n.* [ME. & OFr. *apoplexie* < L.
apoplexia < Gr. *apoplēxia* < *apoplēssein*, to strike down,
disable by a stroke < *apo-*, from + *plēssein*, to strike < IE.
base **plāk-*: see PLAGUE] sudden paralysis with total or
partial loss of consciousness and sensation, caused by the
breaking or obstruction of a blood vessel in the brain; stroke

a·port (ə pôrt′) *adv. Naut.* on or to the left, or port, side

ap·o·se·mat·ic (ap′ə si mat′ik) *adj.* [APO- + SEMATIC] *Zool.*
serving to warn off potential attackers, as the coloration of
some poisonous animals —**ap′o·se·mat′i·cal·ly** *adv.*

ap·o·si·o·pe·sis (ap′ə sī′ə pē′sis) *n.* [L. < Gr. *aposiōpēsis*
< *aposiōpan*, to be silent < *apo-*, from + *siōpan*, to be
silent] a sudden breaking off of a thought in the middle of
a sentence as if one were unable or unwilling to continue
(Ex.: the horrors I saw there—but I dare not tell them)
—**ap′o·si′o·pet′ic** (-pet′ik) *adj.*

a·po·spor·y (ap′ə spôr′ē) *n.* the formation of a gametophyte from a sporophyte cell which has not undergone
reduction division: a form of apomixis in which spore formation does not occur

a·pos·ta·sy (ə päs′tə sē) *n., pl.* **-sies** [ME. *apostasie* <
LL.(Ec.) *apostasia* < Gr. *apostasia* < *apo-*, away + *stasis*,
a standing] an abandoning of what one has believed in,
as a faith, cause, principles, etc.

a·pos·tate (-tāt′, -tit) *n.* [ME. & OFr. < ML. *apostata* <
Gr. *apostatēs*: see prec.] a person guilty of apostasy;
renegade —*adj.* guilty of apostasy

a·pos·ta·tize (-tə tīz′) *vi.* **-tized′, -tiz′ing** [ML. *aposta-
tizare*] to become an apostate

a pos·te·ri·o·ri (ā′ päs tir′ē ôr′ī, -ôr′ē) [ML., lit., from
what comes later < *a* (L. *ab*), from + L. *posteriori*, abl. of
posterius, compar. of *posterius*, subsequent] 1. from effect
to cause, or from particular instances to a generalization;
inductive 2. based on observation or experience; empirical
Opposed to A PRIORI

a·pos·til, a·pos·tille (ə päs′til) *n.* [Fr. *apostille* < *à*, to +
postille, marginal note < ML. *postilla* < L. *post illa*, lit.,
after this] a note, esp. one in the margin

a·pos·tle (ə päs′'l) *n.* [ME. < OFr. *apostle* & OE. *apostol*,
< LL.(Ec.) *apostolus* < Gr. *apostolos*, a person sent forth <
apostellein < *apo-*, from + *stellein*, to send] 1. a person sent
out on a special mission; specif., [*usually* A-] any of the
twelve disciples sent out by Christ to teach the gospel:
originally, Andrew, Bartholomew, James (the younger, son
of Alphaeus), James (the elder) and John (sons of Zebedee),
Jude (or Lebbaeus or Thaddaeus), Judas Iscariot, Matthew
(or Levi), Philip, Simon the Canaanite, Simon (called
Peter), and Thomas (or Didymus); Paul, the "Apostle to
the Gentiles," was not among the original twelve; Judas
was replaced by Matthias 2. the first Christian missionary
in a place 3. any of a group of early Christian missionaries
4. an early advocate or leader of a new principle or movement, esp. one aimed at reform 5. any of the twelve
administrative officials of the Mormon Church

Apostles' Creed an ancient statement of belief in the basic
Christian doctrines, formerly ascribed to the Apostles: it
begins, "I believe in God the Father Almighty. . . ."

a·pos·to·late (ə päs′t′l it, -ə lāt′) *n.* [ME. *apostolat* <
LL.(Ec.) *apostolatus* < *apostolus*: see APOSTLE] the office,
duties, or period of activity of an apostle

ap·os·tol·ic (ap′əs täl′ik) *adj.* [ME. *apostolik* < LL.(Ec.)
apostolicus < Gr. *apostolikos*] 1. of an apostle 2. of the
Apostles, their teachings, work, or times 3. held to derive
from the Apostles in a direct line of succession 4. [*often* A-]
of the Pope; papal Also **ap′os·tol′i·cal** —**a·pos·to·lic·i·ty**
(ə päs′tə lis′ə tē) *n.*

apostolic delegate a church official empowered to represent the Pope in a country that does not have diplomatic
relations with the Vatican

Apostolic Fathers 1. a group of early Christian religious
writers, followers or disciples of the apostles 2. a collection
of writings attributed to them

apostolic see 1. a see, or bishopric, founded by an apostle
2. [A- S-] *R.C.Ch.* the Pope's see, believed to have been
founded at Rome by Peter

apostolic succession the doctrine that the religious authority and mission conferred by Jesus on Saint Peter and
the other Apostles have come down through an unbroken
succession of bishops (in the *R.C.Ch.*, bishops of Rome, or
Popes)

a·pos·tro·phe¹ (ə päs′trə fē) *n.* [L. < Gr. *apostrophē*, a
turning away from the audience to address one person <
apostrephein < *apo-*, from + *strephein*, to turn] words
addressed to a person or thing, whether absent or present,
generally in an exclamatory tone and as a digression in a
speech or literary writing —**ap·os·troph·ic** (ap′ə sträf′ik)
adj.

a·pos·tro·phe² (ə päs′trə fē) *n.* [Fr. < LL. *apostrophus* <
Gr. *apostrophos* (*prosōdia*), averted (accent) < same base
as prec.] the mark (′) used: 1. to show the omission of a
letter or letters from a word (Ex.: *it's* for *it is*, *o*′ for *of*) 2.
to indicate the possessive case of English nouns and some
pronouns (Ex.: *Mary's* dress, the *girls*′ club, *one's* duty)
3. in forming some plurals, as of figures and letters (Ex.:
five *6's*, dot the *i's*) —**ap·os·troph·ic** (ap′ə sträf′ik) *adj.*

a·pos·tro·phize (-fiz′) *vt., vi.* **-phized′, -phiz′ing** to speak
or write an apostrophe (to)

apothecaries' measure a system of liquid measure used in
pharmacy: see TABLES OF WEIGHTS AND MEASURES in
Supplements

apothecaries' weight a system of weights used in pharmacy: see TABLES OF WEIGHTS AND MEASURES in Supplements

a·poth·e·car·y (ə päth′ə ker′ē) *n., pl.* **-car′ies** [ME.
apotecarie < OFr. *apotecaire* < ML. *apothecarius*, shopkeeper, apothecary (in LL., warehouseman) < L. *apotheca*,
storehouse < Gr. *apothēkē* < *apo-*, away + *tithenai*, to put]
a pharmacist, or druggist: apothecaries formerly also
prescribed drugs

ap·o·the·ci·um (ap′ə thē′sē əm, -shē əm) *n., pl.* **-ci·a** (-ə)
[ModL. < Gr. *apothēkion, dim. of *apothēkē*: see APOTHE-
CARY] *Bot.* an open cuplike structure containing sacs in
which sexual spores are developed, as in lichens and certain
fungi —**ap′o·the′ci·al** (-shəl, -shē əl) *adj.*

ap·o·thegm (ap′ə them′) *n.* [< Gr. *apophthegma*, a terse,
pointed saying < *apophthengesthai* < *apo-*, from +
phthengesthai, to cry out, utter] a short, pithy saying
(Ex.: "Brevity is the soul of wit") —**ap·o·theg·mat·ic**
(ap′ə theg mat′ik), **ap′o·theg·mat′i·cal** *adj.*

ap·o·them (ap′ə them′) *n.* [ModL. < APO- + Gr. *thema*,
that which is placed: see THEME] *Math.* the perpendicular
from the center of a regular polygon to any one of its sides

a·poth·e·o·sis (ə päth′ē ō′sis, ap′ə thē′ə sis) *n., pl.* **-ses′**
(-sēz′) [L. < Gr. *apotheōsis* < *apotheoun*, to deify < *apo-*,
from + *theos*, a god] 1. the act of raising a person to the
status of a god; deification 2. the glorification of a person
or thing 3. a glorified ideal

a·poth·e·o·size (ə päth′ē ə sīz′, ap′ə thē′ə sīz′) *vt.* **-sized′,
-siz′ing** [APOTHEO(SIS) + -IZE] 1. to raise to the status of a
god; deify 2. to glorify; idealize

app. 1. apparatus 2. appendix 3. appointed 4. approved
5. approximate

ap·pal (ə pôl′) *vt.* **-palled′, -pal′ling** *same as* APPALL

Ap·pa·la·chi·a (ap′ə lā′chə, -chē ə; -lach′ə) the highland
region of the E U.S. including the C and S Appalachian
Mountains and the Piedmont Plateau from N Pa. through
N Ala.: it is characterized generally by economic depression and poverty

Ap·pa·la·chi·an Mountains (-lā′chən, -chē ən; -lach′ən)
[< ? *Apalachee* Indians < ?] mountain system in E N.
America, extending from S Quebec to N Ala.: c. 1,500 mi.;
highest peak, Mount MITCHELL: also **Appalachians** —
Ap′pa·la′chi·an *adj.*

☆**Appalachian tea** any of various plants, as withe rod,
whose leaves were used locally for tea in pioneer times

ap·pall (ə pôl′) *vt.* [ME. *apallen* < OFr. *apalir* < *a-*, to +
palir, to grow pale < L. *palescere* < *pallere*, to be pale <
L. *pallidus*, PALLID] to fill with horror or dismay; shock
—*SYN.* see DISMAY

ap·pal·ling (-iŋ) *adj.* causing horror, shock, or dismay —
ap·pal′ling·ly *adv.*

☆**ap·pa·loo·sa** (ap′ə lōō′sə) *n.* [altered < *a palouse*: so
named after the *Palouse* Indians or the *Palouse* River (in
NW Idaho and SE Washington), near which the horses
were raised; ult. < a Nez Percé word] any of a sturdy breed
of Western saddle horses distinguished by black and white
spotted markings on the rump and loins

ap·pa·nage (ap′ə nij) *n.* [Fr. *apanage* < ML. *appanagium*
< *appanare*, to equip, lit., provide with bread < L. *ad*, to +
panis, bread] 1. money, land, etc. granted by a monarch
for the support of his younger children 2. a person's
rightful extra gain; perquisite 3. an accompanying endowment; adjunct

ap·pa·ra·tus (ap′ə rat′əs, -rāt′-) *n., pl.* **-ra′tus, -ra′tus·es**
[L., a making ready, preparation < *apparare* < *ad-*, to +

fat, āpe, cär; ten, ēven; is, bīte; gō, hôrn, tōōl, look; oil, out; up, fur; get; joy; yet; chin; she; thin, *then*; zh, leisure; ŋ, ring;
ə for *a* in ago, *e* in agent, *i* in sanity, *o* in comply, *u* in focus; ′ as in able (ā′b'l); Fr. bâl; ë, Fr. coeur; ö, Fr. feu; Fr. mon; δ, Fr. coq;
ü, Fr. duc; r, Fr. cri; H, G. ich; kh, G. doch. See inside front cover. ☆Americanism; ‡foreign; *hypothetical; <derived from

parare, to prepare] **1.** the instruments, materials, tools, etc. needed for a specific use, experiment, or the like **2.** any complex device or machine for a specific use **3.** *Physiol.* a set of organs having a specific function /the digestive *apparatus)* **4.** the means or system by which something is kept in action or a desired result is obtained; organization /the *apparatus* of government/ **5.** the notes, indexes, glossaries, etc. of a scholarly edition of a text: in full **apparatus crit·i·cus** (krit′i kəs)

ap·par·el (ə per′əl, -par′-) *n.* [ME. *appareil* < OFr. *apareil* < VL. **appariculum*, equipment < L. *apparare:* see AP-PARATUS] **1.** clothing; garments; attire **2.** anything that clothes or adorns /the white *apparel* of winter/ **3.** [Archaic] a ship's outfit or furnishings, as rigging, anchor, guns, etc. —*vt.* **-eled** or **-elled, -el·ing** or **-el·ling 1.** to clothe; dress **2.** to adorn; bedeck

ap·par·ent (ə per′ənt, -par′-) *adj.* [ME. *aparaunt* < OFr. *aparant* < L. *apparens,* prp. of *apparere,* APPEAR] **1.** readily seen; visible **2.** readily understood or perceived; evident; obvious **3.** appearing (but not necessarily) real or true; seeming See also HEIR APPARENT —*SYN.* see EVIDENT —**ap·par′ent·ly** *adv.* —**ap·par′ent·ness** *n.*

ap·pa·ri·tion (ap′ə rish′ən) *n.* [ME. *apparicioun* < OFr. *apparition* < ML. *apparitio,* epiphany, appearance (in L., attendance, service) < *apparere,* APPEAR] **1.** anything that appears unexpectedly or in an extraordinary way; esp., a strange figure appearing suddenly and thought to be a ghost **2.** the act of appearing or becoming visible —**ap′pa·ri′tion·al** *adj.*

ap·pa·ri·tor (ə per′ə tər, -par′-) *n.* [L. < *apparere,* APPEAR] formerly, an officer who carried out the orders of a civil or ecclesiastical court

ap·pas·si·o·na·ta (ə päs′ē ə nät′ə) *adj.* [It.] *Music* impassioned

ap·peal (ə pēl′) *vt.* [ME. *apelen* < OFr. *apeler* < L. *appellare,* to accost, apply to, appeal; iterative < *appellere,* to prepare < *ad-,* to + *pellere:* see COMPEL] **1.** to make a request to a higher court for the rehearing or review of (a case) **2.** [Obs.] to accuse or of a crime —*vi.* **1.** to appeal a law case to a higher court **2.** to make an urgent request (*to* a person *for* help, sympathy, etc.) **3.** to resort or turn (*to*) for decision, justification, etc. /to *appeal* to logic/ **4.** to be attractive, interesting, etc.; arouse a favorable response /her argument *appealed* to me/ —*n.* **1.** a call upon some authority or person for a decision, opinion, etc. **2.** an urgent request for help, sympathy, etc. **3.** a quality in a person or thing that arouses interest, sympathy, desire, etc.; attraction **4.** [Obs.] an accusation **5.** *Law* a) the transference of a case to a higher court for rehearing or review b) a request for this c) the right to this d) a case thus transferred —**ap·peal′a·ble** *adj.* —**ap·peal′ing** *adj.* —**ap·peal′ing·ly** *adv.*

SYN.—**appeal** implies an earnest, sometimes urgent request and in legal usage connotes resort to a higher court or authority; **plead,** applied to formal statements in court answering to allegations or charges, carries into general usage the implication of entreaty by argument /he *pleaded* for tolerance/; **sue** implies respectful or formal solicitation for relief, a favor, etc.; **petition** implies a formal request, usually in writing and in accordance with established rights; **pray** and **supplicate** suggest humility in entreaty and imply that the request is addressed to God or to a superior authority, **supplicate** in addition suggesting a kneeling or other abjectly prayerful attitude

ap·pear (ə pir′) *vi.* [ME. *aperen* < OFr. *aparoir* < L. *apparere* < *ad-,* to + *parere,* to come forth, be visible, akin to Gr. *peparein,* to display] **1.** to come into sight **2.** to come into being /freckles *appear* on his face every summer/ **3.** to become understood or apparent /it *appears* he's right/ **4.** to seem; look /to *appear* to be in good health/ **5.** to present oneself formally, as in court **6.** to come before the public /he will *appear* in Hamlet/ **7.** to be published /the magazine *appears* monthly/

ap·pear·ance (-əns) *n.* [ME. & OFr. *apparence* < LL. *apparentia* < prp. of *apparere,* APPEAR] **1.** the act or an instance of appearing **2.** the look or outward aspect of a person or thing **3.** anything that appears; thing seen **4.** [Archaic] an apparition **5.** an outward show; pretense /to give the *appearance* of being busy/ **6.** [*pl.*] the way things seem to be /from all *appearances* he's innocent/ —**keep up appearances** to maintain an outward show of being proper, decorous, well-off, etc. —**make an appearance 1.** to put in an appearance **2.** to appear publicly —**put in an appearance** to be present for a short time, as at a party, meeting, etc.

SYN.—**appearance** and **look** refer generally to the outward impression of a thing, but the former often implies mere show or pretense /an *appearance* of honesty/ and the latter (often in the plural) refers specifically to physical details /the *look* of an abandoned house, good *looks*/; **aspect** also refers to physical details, esp. to facial features or expression /a man of handsome *aspect*/ or to the distinguishing features at a given time or place /in spring the yard had a refreshing *aspect*/; **semblance,** which also refers to the outward impression as contrasted with the inner reality, usually does not imply deception /a *semblance* of order/; **guise** is usually used of a deliberately misleading appearance /under the *guise* of patriotism/

ap·pease (ə pēz′) *vt.* **-peased′, -peas′ing** [ME. *apaisen* < OFr. *apaisier* < *a-,* to + *pais,* peace < L. *pax,* PEACE] **1.** to pacify or quiet, esp. by giving in to the demands of

2. to satisfy or relieve /water *appeases* thirst/ —*SYN.* see PACIFY —**ap·peas′a·ble** *adj.* —**ap·peas′er** *n.*

ap·pease·ment (-mənt) *n.* **1.** an appeasing or being appeased **2.** the policy of giving in to the demands of a hostile or aggressive power in an attempt to keep the peace

‡ap·pel (à pel′) *n.* [Fr., lit., an appeal, call < *appeler,* APPEAL] *Fencing* a sharp stamp with the foot, usually accompanying a stroke on the opponent's blade, to help gain an opening

ap·pel·lant (ə pel′ənt) *adj.* [Fr. < prp. of *appeler,* APPEAL] *Law* relating to appeals; appealing —*n.* a person who appeals, esp. to a higher court

ap·pel·late (-it) *adj.* [L. *appellatus,* pp. of *appellare,* APPEAL] *Law* relating to or having jurisdiction to review appeals /an *appellate* court/

ap·pel·la·tion (ap′ə lā′shən) *n.* [L. *appellatio* < pp. of *appellare,* APPEAL] **1.** the act of calling by a name **2.** a name or title that describes or identifies a person or thing; designation

ap·pel·la·tive (ə pel′ə tiv) *adj.* [L. *appellativus* < pp. of *appellare,* APPEAL] **1.** having to do with the giving of names; naming **2.** relating to a common noun: an earlier usage —*n.* **1.** a name or title **2.** a common noun: an earlier usage

ap·pel·lee (ap′ə lē′, ə pel′ē′) *n.* [Fr. *appelé,* pp. of *appeler,* APPEAL] *Law* the defendant in an appeal; person appealed against

ap·pend (ə pend′) *vt.* [ME. *appenden* < OFr. *apendre* < L. *appendere* < *ad-,* to + *pendere,* to suspend] to attach or affix; add as a supplement or appendix

ap·pend·age (ə pen′dij) *n.* **1.** anything appended; adjunct **2.** *Biol.* any subordinate or external organ or part, as a branch of a tree or the tail of a dog

ap·pend·ant, ap·pend·ent (-dənt) *adj.* [Fr., prp. of *appendre,* APPEND] **1.** attached or added as an appendage **2.** associated with as a consequence **3.** *Law* belonging to as a subsidiary right —*n.* **1.** an appendage **2.** *Law* a subsidiary right attached to and passing with a major one

☆ap·pen·dec·to·my (ap′ən dek′tə mē) *n., pl.* **-mies** [AP-PEND(IX) + -ECTOMY] the surgical removal of the vermiform appendix

☆ap·pen·di·ci·tis (ə pen′də sīt′əs) *n.* [< APPENDIX + -ITIS] inflammation of the vermiform appendix

ap·pen·di·cle (ə pen′də k'l) *n.* [L. *appendicula,* dim. of *appendix*] a small appendage or appendix

ap·pen·dic·u·lar (ap′ən dik′yə lər) *adj.* of an appendix or appendicle; specif., of a limb or the extremities of a vertebrate

ap·pen·dix (ə pen′diks) *n., pl.* **-dix·es, -di·ces′** (-də sēz′) [L., appendage < *appendere,* APPEND] **1.** additional or supplementary material at the end of a book or other writing **2.** *Anat.* an outgrowth of an organ; esp., a small saclike appendage (**vermiform appendix**) extending from the caecum of the large intestine: it has no known function

Ap·pen·zell (ap′ən zel′; *G.* ä′pən tsel′) canton of NE Switzerland: 161 sq. mi.; pop. 63,000

ap·per·ceive (ap′ər sēv′) *vt.* **-ceived′, -ceiv′ing** [ME. *aperceiven* < OFr. *aperceivre* < L. *ad,* to + *percipere,* PERCEIVE] **1.** *Psychol.* to assimilate and interpret (new ideas, impressions, etc.) by the help of past experience **2.** [Obs.] to perceive

ap·per·cep·tion (-sep′shən) *n.* [Fr. *aperception* < *apercevoir,* APPERCEIVE] **1.** the act or process of apperceiving **2.** the state or fact of the mind in being conscious of its own consciousness —**ap′per·cep′tive** *adj.*

ap·per·tain (ap′ər tān′) *vi.* [ME. *apertenen* < OFr. *apertenir* < L. *appertinere* < *ad-,* to + *pertinere:* see PER-TAIN] to belong properly as a function, part, etc.; have to do with; relate; pertain

ap·pe·ten·cy (ap′ə tən sē) *n., pl.* **-cies** [L. *appetentia,* a longing after < prp. of *appetere:* see ff.] **1.** a strong desire; craving; appetite **2.** an instinctive tendency; propensity **3.** a natural attraction, as between some chemical elements; affinity Also **ap′pe·tence** (-təns)

ap·pe·tite (ap′ə tīt′) *n.* [ME. & OFr. *appetit* < L. *appetitus,* eager desire for < *appetere,* to strive after < *ad-,* to + *petere,* to seek] **1.** a desire to satisfy some craving of the body; specif., a desire for food or, sometimes, a desire for some specific food **2.** any strong desire or craving /an *appetite* for knowledge/ —**ap′pe·ti′tive** (-tīt′iv) *adj.*

ap·pe·tiz·er (-tī′zər) *n.* [APPETIZ(ING) + -ER] **1.** a small portion of a tasty food or a drink to stimulate the appetite at the beginning of a meal **2.** a bit of something that excites a desire for more

ap·pe·tiz·ing (-tī′zin) *adj.* [transl. of Fr. *appétissant,* formed as if prp. of (unrecorded) **appetissier* < base of *appétit,* APPETITE] **1.** stimulating the appetite **2.** savory; delicious —**ap′pe·tiz′ing·ly** *adv.*

Ap·pi·an Way (ap′ē ən) [after the Roman censor *Appius Claudius Caecus,* by whom it was begun c. 312 B.C.] ancient Roman paved highway from Rome to Capua to Brundisium (Brindisi): c. 350 mi.

ap·plaud (ə plôd′) *vt., vi.* [L. *applaudere* < *ad-,* to + *plaudere,* to clap hands, strike] **1.** to show approval or enjoyment (of) by clapping the hands or by cheering, stamping the feet, etc. **2.** to praise; approve; commend —**ap·plaud′er** *n.* —**ap·plaud′ing·ly** *adv.*

ap·plause (ə plôz′) *n.* [L. *applausus,* pp. of *applaudere,* APPLAUD] approval or praise, esp. as shown by clapping hands, cheering, etc.

ap·ple (ap'l) n. [ME. appel < OE. æppel, fruit, apple (also, eyeball, anything round), akin to OIr. aball (W. afall), apple tree & L. Abella, name of a Campanian town] **1.** a round, firm, fleshy, edible fruit with a green, yellow, or red skin and small seeds **2.** any of the trees (genus Malus) it grows on, widely distributed in temperate regions **3.** any of various plants bearing applelike fruits, or growths, as the May apple, love apple, etc.

☆**apple butter** a kind of jam made from apples stewed with spices

apple cart a huckster's handcart for selling apples in the street, etc. —**upset the** (or **one's**) **apple cart** to disrupt a procedure, spoil one's plans, etc.

apple green a clear yellowish green

ap·ple·jack (-jak') n. [APPLE + JACK (nickname)] ☆apple brandy, an alcoholic drink made from apple cider

☆**apple maggot** the larva of a fruit fly (Rhagoletis pomonella) that infests apples and other fruits

apple of discord 1. Gr. Myth. a golden apple marked "For the most beautiful," claimed by Athena, Hera, and Aphrodite, and awarded by Paris to Aphrodite: in return, she helped him kidnap the beautiful Helen, thus starting the Trojan War **2.** anything causing trouble, discord, or jealousy

apple of one's eye 1. the pupil of one's eye **2.** any person or thing that one cherishes

ap·ple-pie order (ap''l pī') [Colloq.] neat, orderly condition

☆**apple polisher** [Slang] a person who curries favor by gifts, flattery, etc., as a child bringing his teacher an apple

ap·ple·sauce (-sôs') n. **1.** a dessert or relish made of apples cooked to a pulp in water or, sometimes, puréed in a blender ☆**2.** [Slang] nonsense; hokum

Ap·ple·seed (ap''l sēd'), **Johnny** (nickname of John Chapman) 1775–1845; U.S. frontiersman who planted apple trees throughout the Midwest

Ap·ple·ton (ap''l tən) [after S. Appleton (?–1853), Boston philanthropist] city in E Wis.: pop. 57,000

Appleton layer [after Sir Edward V. Appleton (1892–), Eng. scientist] the F₂ layer of the ionosphere: see F LAYER

ap·pli·ance (ə pli'əns) n. **1.** [Rare] the act of applying; application **2.** a device or machine for performing a specific task, esp. one that is worked mechanically or by electricity [stoves, irons, etc. are household appliances] —SYN. see IMPLEMENT

ap·pli·ca·ble (ap'li kə b'l) adj. [ML. applicabilis < L. applicare, APPLY + -abilis, -ABLE] that can be applied; appropriate —SYN. see RELEVANT —**ap'pli·ca·bil'i·ty** (-bil'ə tē) n.

ap·pli·cant (ap'li kənt) n. [< L. applicans, prp. of applicare, APPLY] a person who applies, as for employment, help, etc.

ap·pli·ca·tion (ap'lə kā'shən) n. [ME. applicacioun < L. applicatio, a binding on, joining to < pp. of applicare, APPLY] **1.** the act of applying; specif., a) the act of putting something on [the application of cosmetics] b) the act of putting something to use [a job calling for the application of many skills] **2.** anything applied, esp. a remedy **3.** a way of applying or method of being used [a scientific principle having many applications in industry] **4.** an asking for something; request [an application for employment] **5.** a form to be filled out with pertinent data in applying for something, as for employment **6.** continued mental or physical effort; close attention; diligence **7.** relevance or practicality [this idea has no application to the case]

ap·pli·ca·tive (ap'lə kāt'iv, -kə tiv) adj. applying or capable of being applied, as to some practical use; applicatory

ap·pli·ca·tor (-kāt'ər) n. [< L. applicatus (pp. of applicare, APPLY) + -OR] **1.** any device for applying medicine or paint, polish, etc. **2.** a person who applies a substance, as roofing, siding, etc.

ap·pli·ca·to·ry (-kə tôr'ē) adj. that can be applied or used; practical

ap·plied (ə plīd') adj. used in actual practice or to work out practical problems [applied science]

ap·pli·qué (ap'lə kā') n. [Fr., pp. of appliquer < L. applicare: see ff.] a decoration or trimming made of one material attached by sewing, gluing, etc. to another —adj. applied as such a decoration —vt. -quéd', -qué'ing **1.** to decorate with appliqué **2.** to put on as appliqué

ap·ply (ə plī') vt. -plied', -ply'ing [ME. applien < OFr. aplier < L. applicare, to attach to < ad-, to + plicare, to fold] **1.** to put on or spread on; place so as to be touching [to apply a salve to the skin] **2.** to put to some practical or specific use [to apply one's knowledge to a problem] **3.** to refer to a person or thing with (an epithet or suitable term) **4.** to concentrate (one's faculties) on; employ (oneself) diligently [to apply oneself to one's work] —vi. **1.** to make a formal request (to someone for something) **2.** to be appropriate, suitable, or relevant [this principle always applies] —**ap·pli'er** n.

ap·pog·gia·tu·ra (ə päj'ə toor'ə) n. [It. < appoggiare, to rest, lean < VL. appodiare, to support < L. ad-, to + *podiare, to support < L. podium, PODIUM] Music an auxiliary melodic note, often making a dissonance with its accompanying harmony, modifying, preceding, and usually rhythmically more prominent than the principal note toward which it progresses in a single scale step as a rule

ap·point (ə point') vt. [ME. apointen < OFr. apointer, to arrange, make ready < VL. *appunctare < L. ad, to + punctum, POINT] **1.** to set (a date, place, etc.); decide upon officially; decree [to appoint a time for a meeting] **2.** to name or select officially for an office, position, etc. [to appoint a chairman] **3.** to furnish and arrange: now usually in well-appointed, etc. **4.** Law to decide the disposition of (property) by special authority —vi. to make appointments to an office, position, etc. —SYN. see FURNISH

ap·point·ee (ə poin'tē', ap'oin tē') n. a person appointed to some position

ap·point·ive (ə poin'tiv) adj. of or filled by appointment [an appointive position]

ap·point·ment (ə point'mənt) n. **1.** an appointing or being appointed; specif., a naming or selecting for an office, position, etc. **2.** a person so selected **3.** a position held in this way **4.** an arrangement to meet someone or be somewhere at a set time; engagement **5.** [pl.] furniture; equipment **6.** Law the designation of beneficiaries and the assignment of property to them by an appointor

ap·poin·tor (ə poin'tər, -tôr') n. Law a person given special authority (power of appointment) by a will or deed to dispose of property

Ap·po·mat·tox (**Court House**) (ap'ə mat'əks) [< Algonquian tribal name] former village in C Va., near Lynchburg, where Lee surrendered to Grant (April 9, 1865), ending the Civil War: now a national monument

ap·por·tion (ə pôr'shən) vt. [OFr. apportionner: see AD- & PORTION] to divide and distribute in shares according to a plan —SYN. see ALLOT

ap·por·tion·ment (-mənt) n. **1.** an apportioning or being apportioned **2.** a proportional distribution or assignment, as of U.S. Representatives among the States, or of State legislators among counties, etc.

ap·pos·a·ble (ə pōz'ə b'l) adj. that can be apposed; specif., that can move so as to touch each of the four fingers [the human thumb is apposable]

ap·pose (ə pōz') vt. -posed', -pos'ing [Fr. apposer < L. appositus, pp. of apponere, to put near to < ad-, to + ponere, to put] **1.** to put side by side; place opposite or near **2.** [Archaic] to put or apply (something) to another thing

ap·po·site (ap'ə zit) adj. [L. appositus: see APPOSE] suited to the purpose; appropriate; apt —SYN. see RELEVANT —**ap'po·site·ly** adv. **ap'po·site·ness** n.

ap·po·si·tion (ap'ə zish'ən) n. [L. appositio, a setting before < appositus: see APPOSE] **1.** an apposing or being apposed; putting side by side **2.** the position resulting from this **3.** Gram. a) the placing of a word or expression beside another so that the second explains and has the same grammatical construction as the first b) the relationship between such terms (Ex.: my cousin is in apposition with Mary in "Mary, my cousin, is here") —**ap'po·si'tion·al** adj. —**ap'po·si'tion·al·ly** adv.

ap·pos·i·tive (ə päz'ə tiv) adj. of or in apposition —n. a word, phrase, or clause in apposition —**ap·pos'i·tive·ly** adv.

ap·prais·al (ə prā'z'l) n. **1.** an appraising or being appraised **2.** an appraised value or price; esp., an expert valuation for taxation, tariff duty, sale, etc.; estimate Also **ap·praise'ment**

ap·praise (ə prāz') vt. -praised', -prais'ing [ME. apreisen < OFr. apreiser < LL. appretiare < L. ad, to + pretium, PRICE; E. sp. infl. by PRAISE] **1.** to set a price for; decide the value of, esp. officially **2.** to estimate the quantity of **3.** to judge the quality or worth of —SYN. see ESTIMATE —**ap·prais'a·ble** adj. —**ap·prais'ing·ly** adv.

ap·pre·ci·a·ble (ə prē'shə b'l, -shē ə-) adj. [ME. & OFr. < ML. appretiabilis < LL. appretiare, APPRAISE] enough to be perceived or estimated; noticeable; measurable [an appreciable difference] —SYN. see PERCEPTIBLE —**ap·pre'ci·a·bly** adv.

ap·pre·ci·ate (ə prē'shē āt') vt. -at'ed, -at'ing [< LL. appretiatus, pp. of appretiare, APPRAISE] **1.** to think well of; understand and enjoy; esteem **2.** to recognize and be grateful for **3.** to estimate the quality or worth of, esp. favorably **4.** to be fully or sensitively aware of; notice with discrimination ☆**5.** to raise the price or value of: opposed to DEPRECIATE —☆vi. to rise in value —**ap·pre'ci·a'tor** n. —**ap·pre'ci·a·to·ry** (-shə tôr'ē, -shē ə-) adj.

SYN.—**appreciate**, in this comparison, implies sufficient critical judgment to see the value or to enjoy [he appreciates good music]; to **value** is to rate highly because of worth [I value your friendship]; to **prize** is to value highly or take great satisfaction in [he prizes his Picasso collection]; to **treasure** is to regard as precious and implies special care to protect from loss; to **esteem** is to hold in high regard and implies warm attachment or respect [an esteemed statesman]; to **cherish** is to prize or treasure, but connotes greater affection for or attachment to the thing cherished [she cherished her friends] See also UNDERSTAND —ANT. despise, disdain

ap·pre·ci·a·tion (ə prē'shē ā'shən) n. **1.** the act or fact of appreciating; specif., a) proper estimation or enjoyment b) grateful recognition, as of a favor c) sensitive awareness

or enjoyment, as of art **2.** a judgment or evaluation ☆**3.** a rise in value or price: opposed to DEPRECIATION

ap·pre·ci·a·tive (ə prē′shə tiv, -shē ə-; -shē āt′iv) *adj.* feeling or showing appreciation —**ap·pre′ci·a·tive·ly** *adv.* — **ap·pre′ci·a·tive·ness** *n.*

ap·pre·hend (ap′rə hend′) *vt.* [ME. *apprehenden* < L. *apprehendere*, to take hold of < *ad-*, to + *prehendere*: see PREHENSILE] **1.** to take into custody; capture or arrest **2.** to take hold of mentally; perceive; understand **3.** to anticipate with anxiety; dread **4.** [Obs.] to seize —*vi.* to understand

ap·pre·hen·si·ble (-hen′sə b'l) *adj.* [L. *apprehensibilis* < pp. of *apprehendere*, APPREHEND] that can be apprehended —**ap′pre·hen′si·bil′i·ty** (-bil′ə tē) *n.*

ap·pre·hen·sion (-hen′shən) *n.* [ME. *apprehencioun* < L. *apprehensio* < pp. of *apprehendere*, APPREHEND] **1.** capture or arrest **2.** mental grasp; perception or understanding **3.** a judgment or opinion **4.** an anxious feeling of foreboding; dread

ap·pre·hen·sive (-hen′siv) *adj.* [ME. < ML. *apprehensivus* < pp. of L. *apprehendere*, APPREHEND] **1.** able or quick to apprehend, or understand **2.** having to do with perceiving or understanding **3.** anxious or fearful about the future; uneasy —**ap′pre·hen′sive·ly** *adv.* —**ap′pre·hen′sive·ness** *n.*

ap·pren·tice (ə pren′tis) *n.* [ME. *aprentis* < OFr. *aprentiz* < *aprendre*, to teach < L. *apprehendere*, APPREHEND] **1.** a person under legal agreement to work a specified length of time for a master craftsman in a craft or trade in return for instruction and, formerly, support **2.** a person who is acquiring a trade, craft, or skill under specified conditions, usually as a member of a labor union **3.** any learner or beginner; novice —*vt.* -ticed, -tic·ing to place or accept as an apprentice —**ap·pren′tice·ship′** *n.*

ap·pressed (ə prest′, a-) *adj.* [< L. *appressus*, pp. of *apprimere* < *ad-*, to + *primere*, to press] pressed close to or flat against a surface

ap·prise, ap·prize (ə prīz′) *vt.* **-prised′** or **-prized′**, **-pris′ing** or **-priz′ing** [< Fr. *appris*, pp. of *apprendre*, to teach, inform < L. *apprehendere*, APPREHEND] to inform or notify —*SYN.* see NOTIFY

ap·prize, ap·prise (ə prīz′) *vt.* **-prized′** or **-prised′**, **-priz′ing** or **-pris′ing** [ME. *apprisen* < OFr. *apreiser*, APPRAISE] *same as* APPRAISE

ap·proach (ə prōch′) *vi.* [ME. *aprochen* < OFr. *aprochier* < LL.(Ec.) *appropiare* < L. *ad*, to + *propius*, compar. of *prope*, near] to come closer or draw nearer —*vt.* **1.** to come near or nearer to **2.** to be like or similar to; approximate **3.** to bring near (*to* something) **4.** to make advances, a proposal, or a request to **5.** to begin dealing with [to *approach* a task] —*n.* **1.** a coming closer or drawing nearer **2.** an approximation or similarity **3.** an advance or overture (*to* someone): *usually used in pl.* **4.** a path, road, or other means of reaching a person or place; access **5.** *Aeron.* the act of bringing an aircraft into position for landing, bombing a target, etc. **6.** *Golf* a stroke from the fairway, meant to knock the ball onto the putting green

ap·proach·a·ble (-ə b'l) *adj.* **1.** that can be approached; accessible **2.** easily approached; friendly; receptive — **ap·proach′a·bil′i·ty** (-bil′ə tē) *n.*

ap·pro·bate (ap′rə bāt′) *vt.* **-bat′ed**, **-bat′ing** [ME. *approbaten* < L. *approbatus*, pp. of *approbare*, APPROVE] [Now Rare] to approve or sanction

ap·pro·ba·tion (ap′rə bā′shən) *n.* **1.** official approval, sanction, or commendation **2.** [Obs.] proof

ap·pro·ba·tive (ap′rə bāt′iv) *adj.* [Fr. *approbatif* < LL. *approbativus*] showing approbation or approval: also **ap·pro·ba·to·ry** (ə prō′bə tôr′ē)

ap·pro·pri·a·ble (ə prō′prē ə b'l) *adj.* that can be appropriated

ap·pro·pri·ate (ə prō′prē āt′; *for adj.* -it) *vt.* **-at′ed**, **-at′ing** [ME. *appropriaten* < LL. *appropriatus*, pp. of *appropriare*, to make one's own < L. *ad-*, to + *proprius*, one's own] **1.** to take for one's own or exclusive use **2.** to take improperly, as without permission **3.** to set aside for a specific use or certain person [to *appropriate* funds for the schools] —*adj.* right for the purpose; suitable; fit; proper —*SYN.* see FIT¹ —**ap·pro′pri·ate·ly** (-it lē) *adv.* —**ap·pro′pri·ate·ness** *n.* — **ap·pro′pri·a′tive** (-āt′iv) *adj.* —**ap·pro′pri·a′tor** *n.*

ap·pro·pri·a·tion (ə prō′prē ā′shən) *n.* **1.** an appropriating or being appropriated **2.** a thing appropriated; esp., money set aside for a specific use

ap·prov·al (ə prōō′v'l) *n.* **1.** the act of approving **2.** favorable attitude or opinion **3.** formal consent or sanction — **on approval** for the customer to examine and decide whether to buy or return

ap·prove (ə prōōv′) *vt.* **-proved′**, **-prov′ing** [ME. *aproven* < OFr. *aprover* < L. *approbare* < *ad-*, to + *probare*, to try, test < *probus*, good] **1.** to give one's consent to; sanction; confirm **2.** to be favorable toward; think or declare to be good, satisfactory, etc. **3.** [Archaic] to prove or show (often used reflexively) **4.** [Obs.] to prove by testing —*vi.* to give approval; have a favorable opinion (*of*) —**ap·prov′a·ble** *adj.* —**ap·prov′er** *n.* —**ap·prov′ing·ly** *adv.*

SYN.—**approve**, the most general of the following terms, means simply to regard as good or satisfactory; **endorse** adds the further implication of active support or advocacy [to *endorse* a candidate for office]; **sanction** implies authoritative approval [a practice *sanctioned* by the charter]; **certify** implies official approval because of compliance with the requirements or standards [a *certified* public

accountant]; **ratify** implies official approval of that which has been done by one's representative [to *ratify* a peace treaty] —*ANT.* disapprove, reject

approx. 1. approximate **2.** approximately

ap·prox·i·mal (ə präk′sə məl) *adj.* [L. *approximare* (see ff.) + -AL] *Anat.* side by side; adjoining

ap·prox·i·mate (ə präk′sə mit; *for v.* -māt′) *adj.* [ME. < LL. *approximatus*, pp. of *approximare*, to come near < L. *ad*, to + *proximus*, superl. of *prope*, near] **1.** near in position; close together **2.** much like; resembling **3.** more or less correct or exact —*vt.* **-mat′ed**, **-mat′ing 1.** to come near to; approach or be almost the same as [this painting *approximates* reality] **2.** to bring near; make approach (*to* something) —*vi.* to come near; be almost the same — **ap·prox′i·mate·ly** *adv.*

ap·prox·i·ma·tion (ə präk′sə mā′shən) *n.* **1.** the act or state of approximating, or coming close **2.** an estimate, guess, or mathematical result that is approximately correct or close enough to exactness for a particular purpose

ap·pur·te·nance (ə pur′t'n əns) *n.* [ME. < Anglo-Fr. *apurtenance* < OFr. *apertenance* < prp. of L. *appertinere*, APPERTAIN] **1.** anything that appertains; thing added to a more important thing; adjunct **2.** [*pl.*] apparatus or equipment; accessories **3.** *Law* an additional, subordinate right or privilege

ap·pur·te·nant (-ənt) *adj.* appertaining or pertinent; accessory —*n.* an appurtenance

Apr. April

a·prax·i·a (ə prak′sē ə) *n.* [ModL. < Gr. *apraxia*, nonaction: see A-² & PRAXIS] complete or partial loss of memory of how to perform complex muscular movements, resulting from damage to certain areas of the brain — **a·prax′ic** (-prak′sik), **a·prac′tic** (-prak′tik) *adj.*

a·près (a′prā′; Fr. à pre′) *prep.* [Fr.] after: often used in hyphenated compounds [an *après*-ski party]

‡**a·près moi le dé·luge** (a′pre mwä′ lə dā lüzh′) [Fr.] after me the deluge: a saying attributed to Louis XV of France

a·pri·cot (ap′rə kät′, ā′prə-) *n.* [Fr. *abricot* < Port. *albricoque* < Ar. *al-birqūq* < MGr. *praikokion* < L. *praecoquus*, early matured (fruit) < *prae-*, beforehand + *coquere*, to COOK, ripen] **1.** a small, yellowish-orange fruit, somewhat resembling the peach and plum, to which it is related **2.** the tree (*Prunus armeniaca*) that it grows on **3.** a yellowish-orange color

A·pril (ā′prəl) *n.* [altered, after the L., from ME. *Avril* < OFr. *avrill* < L. *aprilis* < *apero-*, latter, second (in the ancient Rom. calendar, the year began with March), akin to Sans. *aparah*, latter, Goth. *afar*, after] the fourth month of the year, having 30 days: abbrev. **Apr., Apl., Ap.**

April fool a victim of jokes played on April Fools' Day

April Fools' Day April 1; All Fools' Day, when practical jokes are played on the unsuspecting

a pri·o·ri (ä′ prē ôr′ē, ā′ prī ôr′ī) [L. < *a*, *ab*, from + *prior*, compar. of *prius*, first] **1.** from cause to effect or from a generalization to particular instances; deductively **2.** of such reasoning; deductive **3.** based on theory instead of experience or experiment **4.** before examination or analysis Opposed to A POSTERIORI

a·pri·or·i·ty (ā′prī ôr′ə tē, -prē-) *n.* **1.** the quality or fact of being a priori **2.** the use of a priori reasoning

a·pron (ā′prən, -pərn) *n.* [by faulty separation of *a napron* < ME. *napron* < OFr. *naperon* < *nape*, a cloth < L. *mappa*, a cloth, napkin] **1.** a garment of cloth, leather, etc. worn over the front part of the body, usually to protect one's clothes **2.** anything like an apron in appearance or use; specif., *a*) a covering or extending part for protecting or shielding a structure, machine, etc. *b*) a waterproof protecting shield in an open vehicle *c*) the hard-surfaced area, often paved, in front of an airplane hangar *d*) a broadened part of an automobile driveway, as where it joins the roadway *e*) the part of a proscenium stage in front of the arch *f*) an endless belt for carrying things *g*) a protective work of planking or other material along a river bank, below a dam, etc. *h*) *Geol.* a sheet of sand or gravel deposited by streams in front of a glacial moraine —*vt.* to put an apron on or provide an apron for —**a′pron·like′** *adj.*

apron string a string for tying an apron on —**tied to one's mother's** (or **wife's**, etc.) **apron strings** dominated by one's mother (or wife, etc.)

ap·ro·pos (ap′rə pō′) *adv.* [Fr. *à propos*, to the purpose < L. *ad*, to + *propositus*, pp. of *proponere*, PROPOUND] **1.** at the right time; opportunely **2.** by the way: used to introduce a remark —*adj.* fitting the occasion; relevant; apt — *SYN.* see RELEVANT —**apropos of** in connection with; with regard to

A.P.S. American Physical Society

apse (aps) *n.* [L. *apsis*, APSIS] **1.** a semicircular or polygonal projection of a building, esp. one at the east end of a church, with a domed or vaulted roof **2.** *same as* APSIS (sense 1)

ap·si·dal (ap′sid 'l) *adj.* of an apse or apsis

ap·sis (ap′sis) *n., pl.* **-si·des′** (-sə dēz′) [L. *apsis*, an arch < Gr. *hapsis*, a fastening < *haptein*: see APT] **1.** that point in the orbit of the moon, a planet, etc. nearest to (**lower apsis**), or that farthest from (**higher apsis**), the center of attraction **2.** *same as* APSE (sense 1) —**line of apsides** a line joining the lower and higher apsides, forming the major axis of the orbit

apt (apt) *adj.* [ME. & OFr. *apte* < L. *aptus*, pp. of *apere* < IE. base **ap-*, to grasp, reach, whence Gr. *haptein*, to

fasten] **1.** suited to its purpose; appropriate; fitting [an *apt* remark] **2.** tending or inclined; likely [*apt* to rain] **3.** quick to learn or understand [an *apt* student] **4.** [Archaic] ready; prepared —*SYN.* see FIT[1], LIKELY, QUICK —**apt′ly** *adv.* —**apt′ness** *n.*

apt. *pl.* **apts.** apartment

ap·ter·al (ap′tər əl) *adj.* [Gr. *apteros* (see APTEROUS) + -AL] **1.** *Archit.* having columns at one or both ends, but not along the sides **2.** *Zool. same as* APTEROUS

ap·ter·ous (-əs) *adj.* [Gr. *apteros* < *a-*, without + *pteron*, a wing] *Biol.* having no wings or winglike parts

ap·ter·yg·i·al (ap′tə rij′ē əl) *adj.* [< Gr. *apterygos* < *a-*, without + *pteryx*, a wing + -AL] *Zool.* lacking paired fins or limbs

ap·ter·yx (ap′tər iks) *n.* [Gr. *a-*, without + *pteryx*, wing] *same as* KIWI

ap·ti·tude (ap′tə tōōd′, -tyōōd′) *n.* [ME. < ML. *aptitudo* < L. *aptus*: see APT] **1.** the quality of being apt or appropriate; fitness **2.** a natural tendency or inclination **3.** a natural ability or talent **4.** quickness to learn or understand —*SYN.* see TALENT

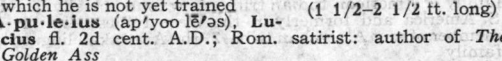

☆**aptitude test** a test for determining the probability of a person's success in some activity in which he is not yet trained

APTERYX
(1 1/2–2 1/2 ft. long)

A·pu·le·ius (ap′yōo lē′əs), Lu·cius fl. 2d cent. A.D.; Rom. satirist: author of *The Golden Ass*

A·pu·li·a (ə pyōōl′yə, -ē ə) region on the SE coast of Italy: 7,469 sq. mi.; pop. 3,410,000

A·pu·re (ä pōō′re) river in WC Venezuela, flowing into the Orinoco: c. 350 mi.

A·pus (ā′pəs) [ModL., bird of paradise, lit., footless (see APODAL)] a S constellation near the south celestial pole

a·py·ret·ic (ā′pī ret′ik) *adj.* [Gr. *apyretos*: see A-[2] & PYRETIC] *Med.* without fever

A·qa·ba (ä′kə bä′), Gulf of arm of the Red Sea between the Sinai Peninsula and NW Saudi Arabia

aq·ua (ak′wə, äk′-, äk′-) *n.*, *pl.* **aq′uas, aq′uae** (-wē) [L. < IE. *akwa-*: cf. ISLAND] water; csp., *Pharm.* a solution of a substance in water —*adj.* [< *aquamarine*] bluish-green

aqua am·mo·ni·ae (ə mō′ni ē′) [ModL., lit., water of ammonia] a water solution of ammonia; ammonia water; ammonium hydroxide: also **aqua ammonia**

☆**aq·ua·cade** (ak′wə kād′, äk′-) *n.* [AQUA + *-cade*, as in (CAVAL)CADE] an aquatic exhibition or entertainment consisting of swimming, diving, etc., often to music

aq·ua·cul·ture (-kul′chər) *n.* [AQUA + CULTURE] the regulation and cultivation of ocean plants and animals for human use or consumption; saltwater farming —**aq′ua·cul′tur·al** *adj.*

aqua for·tis (fôr′təs) [L., strong water] *same as* NITRIC ACID

Aq·ua-lung (äk′wə luŋ′, ak′-) [AQUA + LUNG] *a trademark for* a kind of self-contained underwater breathing apparatus: see SCUBA —*n.* such an apparatus: usually **aq′ua·lung′**

aq·ua·ma·rine (ak′wə mə rēn′, äk′-) *n.* [L. *aqua marina*, sea water] **1.** a transparent, pale bluish-green variety of beryl, used in jewelry **2.** its color —*adj.* bluish-green

☆**aq·ua·naut** (ak′wə nôt′) *n.* [AQUA + (ASTRO)NAUT] **1.** a person trained to live and work in a watertight underwater chamber in and from which he can conduct oceanographic experiments **2.** *same as* SKINDIVER

AQUALUNG

☆**aq·ua·plane** (ak′wə plān′, äk′-) *n.* [AQUA + PLANE[4]] a board that is towed by a motorboat while a person stands on it for a ride over the water —*vi.* **-planed′, -plan′ing** to ride on such a board as a sport

aqua pu·ra (pyoor′ə) [L.] pure water; esp., distilled water

aqua re·gi·a (rē′jē ə) [L., lit., kingly water: it dissolves the "noble metals," gold and platinum] a mixture of nitric and hydrochloric acids

aq·ua·relle (ak′wə rel′, äk′-) *n.* [Fr. < It. *acquerella*, water color < *acqua* < L. *aqua*, water] a kind of painting in transparent water colors —**aq′ua·rel′list** *n.*

a·quar·ist (ə kwer′ist) *n.* **1.** a person who keeps an aquarium as a hobby **2.** the curator or director of an aquarium (sense 2)

a·quar·i·um (ə kwer′ē əm) *n.*, *pl.* **-i·ums, -i·a** (-ə) [L., neut. of *aquarius*, of water < *aqua*, water] **1.** a tank, usually with glass sides, or a pool, bowl, etc., for keeping live water animals and water plants **2.** a building where such collections are exhibited

A·quar·i·us (ə kwer′ē əs) [L., the water carrier < *aqua*, water] **1.** a large S constellation, near the celestial equator **2.** the eleventh sign of the zodiac (♒), entered by the sun about January 21: see ZODIAC, illus.

a·quat·ic (ə kwät′ik, -kwat′-) *adj.* [L. *aquaticus* < *aqua*, water] **1.** growing or living in or upon water [*aquatic* plants] **2.** done in or upon the water [*aquatic* sports] —*n.* **1.** an aquatic plant or animal **2.** [*pl.*, *often with sing. v.*] aquatic sports or performances —**a·quat′i·cal·ly** *adv.*

aq·ua·tint (ak′wə tint′, äk′-) *n.* [Fr. *aquatinte* < It. *acqua tinta*, dyed in water < L. *aqua*, water + *tintus*, pp. of *tingere*, to dye, tinge] **1.** a process by which spaces rather than lines are etched with acid, producing tones that give the effect of a wash drawing or water color **2.** an etching made in this way —*vt.* to etch in this way

aq·ua·vit (ak′wə vēt′, äk′-) *n.* [G. < L. *aqua vitae*: see AQUA VITAE] a Scandinavian alcoholic liquor distilled from grain or potatoes, flavored with caraway seeds, and usually drunk as an apéritif

aqua vi·tae (vīt′ē) [L., water of life] **1.** *Alchemy* alcohol **2.** brandy or other strong liquor

aq·ue·duct (ak′wə dukt′) *n.* [L. *aquaeductus* < *aquae*, gen. of *aqua*, water + *ductus*, pp. of *ducere*, to lead] **1.** a large pipe or conduit made for bringing water from a distant source **2.** a bridgelike structure for carrying a water conduit or canal across a river or valley **3.** *Anat.* a passage or canal

a·que·ous (ā′kwē əs, ak′wē-) *adj.* [ML. *aqueus*: see AQUA & -OUS] **1.** of, like, or containing water; watery **2.** formed by the action of water, as certain rocks made of sediment **3.** of the aqueous humor

aqueous humor a watery fluid in the space between the cornea and the lens of the eye: see EYE, illus.

aq·ui·cul·ture (ak′wi kul′chər, äk′-) *n. same as* AQUA-CULTURE —**aq′ui·cul′tur·al** *adj.*

☆**aq·ui·fer** (ak′wə fər, äk′-) *n.* [ModL.: see AQUA & -FER] an underground layer of porous rock, sand, etc. containing water, into which wells can be sunk —**a·quif·er·ous** (ə-kwif′ər əs) *adj.*

Aq·ui·la (ak′wi lə; *occas.* ə kwil′ə) [L., eagle] a N constellation in the Milky Way, nearly centered on the celestial equator

aq·ui·le·gi·a (ak′wə lē′jē ə) *n.* [ModL. < ML. *aquileia* < L. *aquila*, eagle: so named because of the spurred flower] *same as* COLUMBINE

A·qui·le·ia (ā′kwē le′yä) town in NE Italy, near the Adriatic: in ancient times, a Roman city of military and commercial importance

aq·ui·line (ak′wə lin′, -lən) *adj.* [L. *aquilinus* < *aquila*, eagle] **1.** of or like an eagle **2.** curved or hooked like an eagle's beak [an *aquiline* nose]

A·qui·nas (ə kwī′nəs), Saint Thomas 1225?–74; It. theologian & philosopher: called *the Angelic Doctor*: cf. THOMISM

Aq·ui·taine (ak′wə tān′) lowland region of SW France: orig., a division of Gaul, later, a duchy under the French crown, still later a French province renamed *Guyenne*: L. name Aq′ui·ta′ni·a (-tā′nē ə)

‡**a quo** (ä kwō′, ā′) [L.] from which

ar- *same as* AD-: used before *r*

-ar (ər) [< ME. *-er* < OFr. *-er, -ier, -air* < L. *-aris*; or directly < L. *-aris*; also < L. *-arius*, a suffix of nouns of agency] **1.** *an adj.-forming suffix meaning* of, relating to, like, of the nature of [*singular, polar*] **2.** *a n.-forming suffix* denoting agency [*bursar, vicar*] In some nouns formed after *scholar*, etc., *-ar* is equivalent to *-er*

Ar *Chem.* argon

AR 1. Airman Recruit **2.** Army Regulation

Ar. 1. Arabic **2.** Aramaic

ar. 1. arrival **2.** arrives

A.R. Autonomous Republic

a.r. [L. *anno regni*] in the year of the reign

A·ra (ā′rə) [L., an altar] a S constellation

Ar·ab (ar′əb, er′-; *also, esp. for* 4, *or dial. or facetiously,* ā′rab) *n.* **1.** a native or inhabitant of Arabia **2.** any of a Semitic people native to Arabia but now widely scattered throughout surrounding lands; commonly, a Bedouin **3.** any of a breed of swift, graceful horses native to Arabia **4.** a waif left to roam the streets; street Arab —*adj. same as* ARABIAN

Arab. 1. Arabian **2.** Arabic

Ar·a·bel·la (ar′ə bel′ə, er′-) [? by dissimilation < ANNA-BEL] a feminine name: dim. *Bella*

ar·a·besque (ar′ə besk′, er′-) *n.* [Fr. < It. *arabesco* < *Arabo*, Arab < Ar. *'arab*: with reference to the designs in Moorish architecture] **1.** a complex and elaborate design of intertwined flowers, foliage, geometrical patterns, etc. painted or carved in low relief **2.** *Ballet* a position in which one leg is extended straight backward and the arms are extended, one forward and one backward **3.** *Music* a light, whimsical composition with many delicately ornamental passages; also, any ornamental passage typical of such a composition —*adj.* of, done in, or like arabesque; fantastic and elaborate

ARABESQUE

A·ra·bi·a (ə rā′bē ə) peninsula in SW Asia, between the

Red Sea and the Persian Gulf, largely a desert region: c. 1,000,000 sq. mi.

A·ra·bi·an (-ən) *adj.* of Arabia or the Arabs —*n. same as* ARAB (senses 1 & 3)

Arabian coffee a tall, widely cultivated shrub (*Coffea arabica*) yielding coffee beans that are the chief source of commercially produced coffee

Arabian Desert 1. desert in E Egypt, between the Nile valley and the Red Sea **2.** popularly, the desert area of Arabia

Arabian Nights, The a collection of ancient tales from Arabia, India, Persia, etc.: also called **The Arabian Nights' Entertainment, The Thousand and One Nights**

Arabian Peninsula *same as* ARABIA

Arabian Sea part of the Indian Ocean, between India and Arabia

Ar·a·bic (ar'ə bik, er'-) *adj.* **1.** of Arabia **2.** of the Arabs, their language, culture, etc. **3.** [a-] designating an acid, $C_5H_{10}O_5$, found in gum arabic —*n.* the Semitic language of the Arabs, spoken in Arabia, Syria, Jordan, Iraq, northern Africa, etc. in various dialects

Arabic numerals the figures 1, 2, 3, 4, 5, 6, 7, 8, 9, and the 0 (zero), orig. used in India: also called *Hindu-Arabic numerals*

a·rab·i·nose (ə rab'ə nōs', ar'ə bə-) *n.* [ARAB(IC) + -IN[1] + -OSE[1]] a pentose sugar, $HOCH_2(CHOH)_3CHO$, obtained esp. from certain vegetable gums

Ar·ab·ist (ar'ə bist, er'-) *n.* an expert in Arabic; student of Arabic linguistics or literature

ar·a·ble (ar'ə b'l, er'-) *adj.* [Fr. < L. *arabilis* < *arare*, to plow] suitable for plowing and, hence, for producing crops —*n.* arable land —**ar'a·bil'i·ty** (-bil'ə tē) *n.*

Arab League confederation of the countries of Algeria, Iraq, Jordan, Kuwait, Lebanon, Libya, Morocco, Saudi Arabia, Sudan, Syria, Tunisia, United Arab Republic, and Yemen

Ar·a·by (ar'ə bē, er'-) [Archaic or Poet.] *same as* ARABIA

A·rach·ne (ə rak'nē) [L. < Gr. *Arachnē* < *arachnē*, spider] *Gr. Myth.* a girl turned into a spider by Athena for challenging the goddess to a weaving contest

a·rach·nid (ə rak'nid) *n.* [ModL. *Arachnida*, the arachnids < Gr. *arachnē*, spider] any of a large class (Arachnida) of arthropods that have four pairs of legs and that breathe by means of lunglike sacs or breathing tubes: some arachnids, such as mites and ticks, have bodies without exterior segmentation, others, such as spiders, have bodies divided into two segments, and still others, such as scorpions, have bodies of several segments—**a·rach'ni·dan** (-ni dən) *adj., n.*

a·rach·noid (-noid) *adj.* [< Gr. *arachnē*, spider + -OID] **1.** *Anat.* designating the middle of three membranes (between the dura mater and the pia mater) covering the brain and the spinal cord **2.** *Bot.* covered with or consisting of soft, fine hairs or fibers **3.** *Zool.* of or like an arachnid —*n.* **1.** *Anat.* the arachnoid membrane **2.** *Zool.* an arachnid

A·rad (ä räd') city in W Romania, on the Mureş River: pop. 115,000

A·ra·fu·ra Sea (ä'rə fōō'rə) part of the South Pacific Ocean, between Australia and New Guinea

A·ra·gats (ä'rä gäts') extinct volcano in NW Armenian S.S.R.: 13,435 ft.: also ALAGEZ

Ar·a·gon (ar'ə gän', -gən) region in NE Spain: from the 11th to the 15th cent., a kingdom which at various times included the Balearic Islands, Sardinia, Sicily, etc.

Ar·a·gon (a rà gōn') **Louis** (lwē) 1897– ; Fr. poet, novelist, & journalist

Ar·a·go·nese (ar'ə gə nēz', er'-) *adj.* of Aragon, its people, language, etc. —*n.* **1.** *pl.* **-nese'** a native or inhabitant of Aragon **2.** the Spanish dialect spoken in Aragon

a·rag·o·nite (ə rag'ə nīt', ar'ə gə-) *n.* [after ARAGON, in Spain] an orthorhombic mineral made up of calcium carbonate, $CaCO_3$: it resembles calcite, but it is heavier and harder, has less distinct cleavage, and occurs less frequently

A·ra·gua·ia (ä'rə gwä'yə) river in C Brazil, flowing north into the Tocantins: c. 1,500 mi.

ar·ak (ar'ək) *n. same as* ARRACK

A·ra·kan Yo·ma (ar'ə kan' yō'mə) mountain range in W Burma: highest peak, c. 10,000 ft.

A·raks (ä räks') *Russ. name of* ARAS river

Ar·al Sea (ar'əl) inland body of salt water in the SW Asiatic U.S.S.R., east of the Caspian Sea: c. 24,600 sq. mi.: also **Lake Aral**

Ar·am (er'əm) [Heb.] *Biblical name for* ancient Syria

Aram. Aramaic

Ar·a·mae·an, Ar·a·me·an (ar'ə mē'ən, er'-) *n.* **1.** any member of a people who lived in ancient Syria (Aram) and Mesopotamia **2.** their Aramaic language —*adj.* **1.** of these people **2.** of their language

Ar·a·ma·ic (-mā'ik) *n.* a group of northwest Semitic languages spoken in Biblical times, including specifically the language used in Palestine after the captivity and spoken by Jesus and his disciples

a·ra·ne·id (ə rā'nē id) *n.* [< L. *aranea*, spider (akin to Gr. *arachnē*, spider) + -ID] *Zool.* a spider —**ar·a·ne·id·an** (ar'ə nē'i dən) *adj.*

☆**A·rap·a·ho** (ə rap'ə hō') *n., pl.* **-ho** [< ? Crow, lit., enemy < *a-*, with + *raxpé*, skin + *-ahu*, lots, many] **1.** a member of a tribe of Indians who formerly lived in the area between the North Platte and Arkansas rivers and now live in Wyoming and Oklahoma **2.** their Algonquian language

ar·a·pai·ma (ar'ə pī'mə) *n.* [Port. < a Tupian word] an edible, large-scaled river fish (*Arapaima gigas*) of S. America, sometimes reaching a weight of 500 lb.

Ar·a·rat (ar'ə rat', er'-) mountain in E Turkey, near the Armenian and Iranian borders: supposed landing place of Noah's Ark (Gen. 8:4): higher of its two peaks, c. 17,000 ft.

ar·a·ro·ba (ar'ə rō'bə, är'-) *n.* [Port. < Braz. (Tupi) name] **1.** a bitter, yellow powder used in medicine and obtained from cavities in the trunk of a Brazilian tree (*Andira araroba*) **2.** this tree

A·ras (ä räs') river flowing from E Turkey along the southwest border of the U.S.S.R., into the Kura River and the Caspian Sea: c. 650 mi.: Russ. name, ARAKS

Ar·au·ca·ni·an (ar'ô kä'nē ən, ə rô'-) *n.* [< Sp. *Araucano* < *Arauco*, region (now a province) in Chile < Araucanian *rau*, clay + *ko*, water] **1.** a member of a group of tribes of S. American Indians of Chile and the Argentine pampas **2.** their language —*adj.* of the Araucanians Also **A·rau·can** (ə rô'kən)

ar·au·car·i·a (ar'ô ker'ē ə, er'-) *n.* [ModL. < Sp. *Araucano*, Araucanian tribe] any of a genus (*Araucaria*) of cone-bearing trees with flat, scalelike needles, native to the Southern Hemisphere and grown as ornamentals in other areas —**ar'au·car'i·an** *adj., n.*

A·ra·wak (ä'rä wäk', ar'ə wak') *n.* a member of any tribe of the Arawakan Indians

A·ra·wa·kan (ä'rä wä'kən) *adj.* of the largest linguistic family of American Indian tribes, now found chiefly in NE S. America and formerly in the West Indies —*n.* **1.** a member of any Arawakan tribe **2.** the Arawakan linguistic family

A·rax·es (ə rak'sēz) *ancient name of* ARAS river

ar·ba·lest, ar·ba·list (är'bə list) *n.* [ME. *arbelaste* < OFr. *arbaleste* < L. *arcuballista* < *arcus*, a bow + *ballista*, BALLISTA] a medieval crossbow consisting of a steel bow set crosswise in a wooden shaft with a mechanism to bend the bow: it propelled arrows, balls, or stones —**ar'ba·lest'·er** (-les'tər) *n.*

Ar·be·la (är bē'lə) ancient Persian city near which Alexander the Great defeated Darius III of Persia (331 B.C.): modern name, ERBIL or ARBIL

Ar·bil (är'bil) *same as* ERBIL, city in Iraq

ar·bi·ter (är'bə tər) *n.* [L., orig., one who goes to a place, a witness, judge < *ad-*, to + *baetere*, to come, go] **1.** a person selected to judge a dispute; umpire; arbitrator **2.** a person fully authorized or qualified to judge or decide —*SYN.* see JUDGE

ar·bi·tra·ble (är'bə trə b'l) *adj.* that can be arbitrated; subject to arbitration

ar·bi·trage (är'bə trij; *also, for 2,* är'bə träzh') *n.* [Fr. < *arbitrer*, to judge < L. *arbitrari*: see ARBITRATE] **1.** [Archaic] arbitration **2.** a buying of bills of exchange, stocks, etc. in one market and selling them at a profit in another market

ar·bi·tral (är'bə trəl) *adj.* [Fr. < L. *arbitralis*: see ARBITER] of arbiters or arbitration

ar·bit·ra·ment (är bit'rə mənt) *n.* [ME. & OFr. *arbitrement* < L. *arbitrari*: see ARBITRATE] **1.** arbitration **2.** an arbitrator's verdict or award **3.** the power to judge or right to decide

ar·bi·trar·y (är'bə trer'ē) *adj.* [L. *arbitrarius* < *arbiter*, ARBITER] **1.** not fixed by rules but left to one's judgment or choice; discretionary [*arbitrary* decision, *arbitrary* judgment*]* **2.** based on one's preference, notion, whim, etc.; capricious **3.** absolute; despotic —*SYN.* see DICTATORIAL —**ar'bi·trar'i·ly** *adv.* —**ar'bi·trar'i·ness** *n.*

ar·bi·trate (är'bə trāt') *vt.* **-trat'ed, -trat'ing** [< L. *arbitratus*, pp. of *arbitrari*, to give a decision < *arbiter*, ARBITER] **1.** to give to an arbitrator to decide; settle by arbitration **2.** to decide (a dispute) as an arbitrator —*vi.* **1.** to act as an arbitrator (*in* a dispute, *between* persons) **2.** to submit a dispute to arbitration —**ar'bi·tra'tive** *adj.*

ar·bi·tra·tion (är'bə trā'shən) *n.* the act of arbitrating; specif., the settlement of a dispute by a person or persons chosen to hear both sides and come to a decision —**ar'bi·tra'tion·al** *adj.*

ar·bi·tra·tor (är'bə trāt'ər) *n.* **1.** a person selected to judge a dispute; arbiter, esp. one, as in collective bargaining negotiations, named with the consent of both sides **2.** a person authorized to judge or decide

ar·bi·tress (är'bə tris) *n.* a woman arbiter

ar·bor[1] (är'bər) *n.* [ME. *erber* < OFr. *erbier, herbier* < LL. *herbarium,* HERBARIUM] **1.** a place shaded by trees or shrubs or, esp., by vines on a latticework; bower **2.** [Obs.] a garden or lawn; also, an orchard

ar·bor[2] (är'bər) *n., pl.* **ar'bo·res'** (-bə rēz') [L., a tree, beam] *Bot.* a tree

ar·bor[3] (är'bər) *n.* [Fr. *arbre,* tree, axis < L. *arbor,* tree, beam] *Mech.* **1.** a shaft; beam **2.** a spindle; axle **3.** a bar that holds cutting tools

ar·bo·ra·ceous (är'bə rā'shəs) *adj.* [ARBOR[2] + -ACEOUS] **1.** of or like a tree; treelike **2.** wooded

Arbor Day a tree-planting day observed individually by the States of the U.S., usually in spring

ar·bo·re·al (är bôr'ē əl) *adj.* [L. *arboreus,* of a tree < *arbor,* tree + -AL] **1.** of or like a tree **2.** living in trees or adapted for living in trees

ar·bored (är'bərd) *adj.* **1.** having an arbor, or bower **2.** having trees on both sides or all around

ar·bo·re·ous (är bôr′ē əs) *adj.* **1.** *same as* ARBOREAL **2.** full of trees **3.** *same as* ARBORESCENT

ar·bo·res·cent (är′bə res′'nt) *adj.* [L. *arborescens*, prp. of *arborescere*, to become a tree < *arbor*, tree] treelike in shape or growth; branching —**ar′bo·res′cence** *n.*

ar·bo·re·tum (-rēt′əm) *n., pl.* **-re′tums, -re′ta** (-rēt′ə) [L. < *arbor*, tree] a place where many kinds of trees and shrubs are grown for exhibition or study

ar·bo·ri·cul·ture (är′bər ə kul′chər, är bôr′-) *n.* [< L. *arbor*, tree + *cultura*, culture] the scientific cultivation of trees and shrubs —**ar′bo·ri·cul′tur·ist** *n.*

ar·bor·ist (-ist) *n.* a specialist in the planting and maintenance of trees

ar·bor·i·za·tion (är′bər i zā′shən) *n.* [ARBOR² + -IZ(E) + -ATION] **1.** a treelike formation or arrangement **2.** the forming of such an arrangement

ar·bor·ous (är′bər əs) *adj.* of or made up of trees

ar·bor·vi·tae (-vīt′ē) *n.* [L., tree of life] **1.** *Bot.* any of several trees or shrubs (genus *Thuja*) of the cypress family, with flattened sprays of scalelike leaves **2.** *Anat.* the treelike structure of the white substance in a longitudinal section of the cerebellum Also, esp. for sense 2, **arbor vitae**

ar·bour (är′bər) *n. Brit. sp.* of ARBOR¹

Ar·buth·not (är buth′nət, är′beth nät′), **John** 1667–1735; Scot. writer & physician

ar·bu·tus (är byōot′əs) *n.* [L., wild strawberry tree] **1.** any of a genus (*Arbutus*) of trees or shrubs of the heath family, with dark-green leaves, clusters of white or pinkish flowers, and strawberrylike berries **2.** a related trailing plant (*Epigaea repens*) with clusters of white or pink flowers

arc (ärk) *n.* [ME. *ark* < OFr. *arc* < L. *arcus*, a bow, arch < IE. base *arqu-*, bowed, curved, whence ARROW] **1.** orig., the part of a circle that is the apparent path of a heavenly body above and below the horizon **2.** a bowlike curved line or object **3.** *Elec.* the band of sparks or incandescent light formed when an electric discharge is conducted from one electrode or conducting surface to another, characterized by relatively high current and low potential difference between electrodes: in full, **electric arc 4.** *Geom.* **a)** any part of a curve, esp. of a circle **b)** the angular measurement of this —*adj.* *Trigonometry* designating an inverse function [*arc sine x* is an angle whose sine is *x*] —*vi.* **arced** or **arcked, arc′ing** or **arck′ing 1.** to move in a curved course **2.** *Elec.* to form an arc

Arc, Jeanne d' (zhän därk′) *see* JOAN OF ARC

ARC, A.R.C. American Red Cross

ar·cade (är kād′) *n.* [Fr. < Prov. *arcada* < ML. *arcata* < L. *arcus*, arch: see ARC] **1.** a passage having an arched roof **2.** any covered passageway, esp. one with shops along the sides **3.** *Archit.* **a)** a line of arches and their supporting columns **b)** an arched building —*vt.* **-cad′ed, -cad′ing** to make into or provide with an arcade

Ar·ca·di·a (är kā′dē ə) **1.** *a)* an ancient pastoral district of the C Peloponnesus *b)* prefecture of the C Peloponnesus of modern Greece, on the Aegean **2.** city in SW Calif.: suburb of Los Angeles: pop. 43,000 —*n.* any place of rural peace and simplicity

Ar·ca·di·an (-ən) *adj.* **1.** of Arcadia **2.** rustic, peaceful, and simple; pastoral —*n.* **1.** a native or inhabitant of Arcadia **2.** a person of simple habits and tastes

Ar·ca·dy (är′kə dē) *poetic name for* ARCADIA

ar·cane (är kān′) *adj.* [< L. *arcanus*: see ff.] **1.** hidden or secret **2.** understood by only a few; esoteric

ar·ca·num (-kā′nəm) *n., pl.* **-na** (-nə), **-nums** [L., neut. of *arcanus*, shut in, hidden < *arcere*, to shut up: for IE. base see EXERCISE] **1.** secret or hidden knowledge **2.** a secret; mystery **3.** a secret remedy; elixir

ar·ca·ture (är′kə chər) *n.* [< ML. *arcata:* see ARCADE] *Archit.* **1.** a small arcade **2.** a closed or false arcade, as for ornament

‡**arc-bou·tant** (ár′bōō tän′) *n., pl.* **arcs-bou·tants** (ár′ bōō tän′) [Fr.] *Archit.* a flying buttress

arc furnace an electric furnace in which the heat comes from an arc between an electrode and the material being heated

arch¹ (ärch) *n.* [ME. < OFr. *arche* < ML. *arca* < L. *arcus*, arch: see ARC] **1.** a curved structure, as of masonry, that supports the weight of material over an open space, as in a bridge, doorway, etc. **2.** any similar structure, as a monument **3.** the form of an arch **4.** anything shaped like an arch; specif., an archlike anatomical part [the dental *arch*, *arch* of the foot, etc.] —*vt.* **1.** to provide with an arch or arches **2.** to cause to take the form of an arch; curve or bend —*vi.* **1.** to form an arch **2.** to span as an arch

ARCHES
(A, semicircular; B, horseshoe; C, pointed)

arch² (ärch) *adj.* [< ARCH-, with changed meaning because of use in *archknave, archrogue*] **1.** main; chief; principal [the *arch* villain] **2.** clever; crafty **3.** gaily mischievous; pert [an *arch* look]

arch- (ärch; *in* "*archangel*" & *its derivatives*, ärk) [ME. *arche-* < OE. *arce-* < L. *archi-, arch-* < Gr. *archos*, ruler] *a prefix meaning* main, chief, principal: used in forming titles of rank [*archduke, archbishop*]

-arch (ärk; *occas.* ərk) [< Gr. *archos*, ruler < *archein*, to rule, orig., to be first, begin] *a n.-forming suffix meaning* ruler [*matriarch, monarch*]

arch. 1. archaic **2.** archaism **3.** archipelago **4.** architect **5.** architectural **6.** architecture

Ar·chae·an (är kē′ən) *adj. same as* ARCHEAN

ar·chae·o- (är′kē ō, -ə) [< Gr. *archaios*, ancient < *archē*, the beginning] *a combining form meaning* ancient, original [*archaeology*]

ar·chae·ol·o·gy (är′kē äl′ə jē) *n.* [ARCHAEO- + -LOGY] the scientific study of the life and culture of ancient peoples, as by excavation of ancient cities, relics, artifacts, etc. —**ar′chae·o·log′i·cal** (-ə läj′i k'l) *adj.* —**ar′chae·o·log′i·cal·ly** *adv.* —**ar′chae·ol′o·gist** *n.*

ar·chae·op·ter·yx (-äp′tər iks) *n.* [ModL. < ARCHAEO- + Gr. *pteryx*, wing] an extinct reptilelike bird (genus *Archaeopteryx*) of the Jurassic Period, which had teeth, a lizardlike tail, and well-developed wings

ar·chae·or·nis (-ôr′nəs) *n.* [ModL. < ARCHAE(O)- + Gr. *ornis*, bird] an extinct bird (genus *Archaeornis*) of the Jurassic Period, that resembled the archaeopteryx

Ar·chae·o·zo·ic (-ə zō′ik) *adj. same as* ARCHEOZOIC

ar·cha·ic (är kā′ik) *adj.* [Gr. *archaikos* < *archaios*, old, ancient] **1.** belonging to an earlier period; ancient **2.** antiquated; old-fashioned **3.** that has ceased to be used except for special purposes, as in poetry, church ritual, etc. [*thou* is an archaic form of *you*] —*SYN.* see OLD —**ar·cha′i·cal·ly** *adv.*

ar·cha·ism (är′kē iz'm, -kā-) *n.* [Fr. *archaisme* < Gr. *archaismos* < *archaios*, old] **1.** the use or imitation of archaic words, technique, etc. **2.** an archaic word, usage, style, practice, etc. —**ar′cha·ist** *n.* —**ar′cha·is′tic** (-is′tik) *adj.* —**ar′cha·is′ti·cal·ly** *adv.*

ar·cha·ize (-īz′) *vt.* **-ized′, -iz′ing** to make archaic or make seem archaic —*vi.* to use archaisms

arch·an·gel (ärk′ān′j'l) *n.* [ME. < OFr. *archangel* or LL. *archangelus* < Gr. *archangelos* < *archos*, chief, first + *angelos*, ANGEL] **1.** a chief angel; angel of high rank **2.** an angelica plant (*Angelica archangelica*)

Arch·an·gel (ärk′ān′j'l) **1.** seaport in NW R.S.F.S.R., on the White Sea: pop. 303,000: Russ. name, ARKHANGELSK **2.** Gulf of, *a former name of* DVINA BAY

ar·chan·thro·pine (ärk an′thrə pīn′) *n.* [< ModL. *archanthropinae*, name of the subdivision: see ARCHI- & ANTHROPO- & -INAE] an extinct primate with structural characteristics intermediate between ape and man; an ape-man

arch·bish·op (ärch′bish′əp) *n.* [ME. *archebishop* < OE. *arcebisceop* < LL.(Ec.) *archiepiscopus* < LGr. *archiepis-kopos* < Gr. *archos*, chief + *episkopos*, overseer: see BISHOP] a bishop of the highest rank; a chief bishop, who presides over an archbishopric or archdiocese

arch·bish·op·ric (-ə prik) *n.* [ME. *archebischoprriche* < OE. *arcebiscoprice* < *arcebisceop* (see ARCHBISHOP) + *rice*, jurisdiction < PGmc. *rikja* (whence G. *reich*, realm): for IE. base see REGAL] **1.** the office, rank, duties, or term of an archbishop **2.** the church district over which an archbishop has jurisdiction

arch·dea·con (-dēk′'n) *n.* [ME. *archedeken* < OE. *arcediacon* < LL.(Ec.) *archidiaconus* < LGr. *archidiakonos* < Gr. *archos*, chief + *diakonos*, servant, minister] a church official ranking just below a bishop or an archpriest: in the Anglican Church he has supervisory duties under the bishop

arch·dea·con·ry (-dēk′'n rē) *n., pl.* **-ries 1.** the office, rank, duties, or jurisdiction of an archdeacon **2.** an archdeacon's residence

arch·di·o·cese (-dī′ə sis, -sēs′) *n.* the diocese of an archbishop —**arch′di·oc′e·san** (-dī äs′ə sən) *adj.*

arch·du·cal (-dōōk′'l, -dyōōk′'l) *adj.* of an archduke or archduchy

arch·duch·ess (-duch′is) *n.* **1.** the wife or widow of an archduke **2.** a princess of the former Austrian royal family

arch·duch·y (-duch′ē) *n., pl.* **-ies** [Fr. *archiduché:* see ARCHI- & DUCHY] the territory ruled by an archduke or archduchess

arch·duke (-dōōk′, -dyōōk′) *n.* a chief duke, esp. a prince of the former Austrian royal family

Ar·che·an (är kē′ən) *adj.* [< Gr. *archaios*, ancient < *archē*, beginning] *Geol.* designating or occurring in the earlier part of the Precambrian Era; esp., designating the highly crystalline, partly igneous and partly sedimentary rocks formed during that time —**the Archean** the Archean Era or its rocks: see GEOLOGY, chart

arched (ärcht) *adj.* **1.** furnished or covered with an arch or arches **2.** having the form of an arch; curved

ar·che·go·ni·ate (är′kə gō′nē it) *adj.* having archegonia —*n.* a plant having archegonia

ar·che·go·ni·um (-nē əm) *n., pl.* **-ni·a** (-nē ə) [ModL., dim. < Gr. *archegonos*, the first of a race < *archos*, first + *gonos*, offspring] the flask-shaped female reproductive

organ in mosses, ferns, etc.: also **ar′che·gone′** (-gōn′) —**ar′che·go′ni·al** *adj.*

arch·en·e·my (ärch′en′ə mē) *n., pl.* **-mies** a chief enemy —**the archenemy** Satan

ar·chen·ter·on (är ken′tə rän′) *n.* [ARCH(I)- + Gr. *enteron*, intestine] the cavity at the center of an embryo in the gastrula stage of development, forming a primitive digestive tract —**ar·chen·ter·ic** (är′kən ter′ik) *adj.*

ar·che·o- (är′kē ō, -ə) *same as* ARCHAEO-

ar·che·ol·o·gy (är′kē äl′ə jē) *n. same as* ARCHAEOLOGY

Ar·che·o·zo·ic (är′kē ə zō′ik) *adj.* [ARCHEO- + ZO- + -IC] *same as* Early PRECAMBRIAN

arch·er (är′chər) *n.* [ME. & OFr. < VL. *arcarius*, bowman < L. *arcus*, a bow] a person who shoots with bow and arrow; bowman —[A-] the constellation Sagittarius

Arch·er (är′chər), **William** 1856–1924; Scottish dramatic critic, playwright, & translator

arch·er·fish (är′chər fish′) *n., pl.* **-fish′, -fish′es:** see FISH² a small freshwater fish (*Toxotes jaculator*) of the East Indies and Thailand: it captures insects, etc. by knocking them into the water with a tiny jet of water shot from its mouth

arch·er·y (är′chər ē) *n.* [ME. & OFr. *archerie:* see ARCHER] 1. the practice, art, or sport of shooting with bow and arrow 2. an archer's bows, arrows, and other equipment 3. archers collectively

ar·che·spore (är′kə spôr′) *n.* [ModL. *archesporium:* see ARCHI- & SPORE] a cell or group of cells from which the spore mother cells develop: also **ar′che·spo′ri·um** (-spôr′ē əm) —**ar′che·spo′ri·al** *adj.*

ar·che·type (är′kə tīp′) *n.* [L. *archetypus* < Gr. *archetypon* < *archos*, first + *typos:* see TYPE, *n.*] 1. the original pattern, or model, from which all other things of the same kind are made; prototype 2. a perfect example of a type or group —*SYN.* see MODEL —**ar′che·typ′al** (-tīp′əl), **ar′che·typ′i·cal** (-tip′i k′l) *adj.* —**ar′che·typ′al·ly** (-tīp′ə lē), **ar′che·typ′i·cal·ly** *adv.*

arch·fiend (ärch′fēnd′) *n.* a chief fiend —**the archfiend** Satan

ar·chi- (är′kə, -kē, -ki) [see ARCH-] *a prefix meaning:* 1. chief, first [*archidiaconal*] 2. *Biol.* primitive, original [*archiplasm*]

Ar·chi·bald (är′chə bôld′) [of Gmc. origin (akin to OHG. *Erchanbald*), prob. nobly bold] a masculine name: dim. *Archie, Archy*

ar·chi·blast (är′kə blast′) *n.* [ARCHI- + -BLAST] *Biol.* 1. egg protoplasm 2. the outer of the two layers of an embryo in an early stage of development

ar·chi·carp (-kärp′) *n.* [ARCHI- + -CARP] *Bot.* the female reproductive organ in an ascomycetous fungus, giving rise to spore sacs (*asci*) after fertilization

ar·chi·di·ac·o·nal (är′kə dī ak′ə n′l) *adj.* [ME. < ML. *archidiaconalis*] of an archdeacon or archdeaconry —**ar′chi·di·ac′o·nate** (-ak′ə nit) *n.*

ar·chi·e·pis·co·pal (är′kē ə pis′kə p′l) *adj.* [see ARCHI- & EPISCOPACY] of an archbishop or archbishopric —**ar′chi·e·pis′co·pate** (-pət, -pāt′) *n.*

ar·chil (är′kil, -chil) *n.* [ME. *orchell* < OFr. *orchel* < It. *orcello*] 1. any of a number of lichens (genera *Roccella, Dendrographa, Lecanora*) yielding purple dyes 2. any of these dyes

ar·chi·mage (är′kə māj′) *n.* [< Gr. *archimagos*, chief of the magi: see ARCHI- & MAGI] a great magician or wizard

ar·chi·man·drite (är′kə man′drīt′) *n.* [LL.(Ec.) *archimandrita* < LGr. *archimandritēs* < *archi-*, ARCHI- + *mandra*, enclosure, monastery] *Orthodox Eastern Ch.* the head of a monastery or of a number of monasteries

Archimedean (or **Archimedes′**) **screw** an ancient water-raising device attributed to Archimedes, made up of a spiral tube coiled about a shaft or of a large screw in a cylinder, revolved by hand

Ar·chi·me·des (är′kə mē′dēz) 287?–212 B.C.; Gr. mathematician & inventor, born in Syracuse (Sicily) —**Ar·chi·me·de·an** (är′kə mē′dē ən, är′kə mi dē′ən) *adj.*

ar·chine, ar·chine (är shēn′) *n. same as* ARSHIN

arch·ing (är′chiŋ) *adj.* forming an arch —*n.* 1. an arched part 2. a series of arches

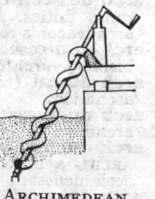

ARCHIMEDEAN SCREW

ar·chi·pel·a·go (är′kə pel′ə gō′) *n., pl.* **-goes′, -gos′** [It. *arcipelago* < MGr. *archipelagos*, orig., the Aegean Sea < Gr. *archi-*, chief + *pelagos*, sea] 1. a sea with many islands 2. a group or chain of many islands —**ar′chi·pe·lag′ic** (-pə laj′ik) *adj.*

Ar·chi·pen·ko (är′ki pen′kō), **Alexander** 1887–1964; U.S. sculptor, born in Russia

ar·chi·plasm (är′kə plaz′m) *n. same as* ARCHOPLASM

ar·chi·tect (är′kə tekt′) *n.* [L. *architectus* < Gr. *architektōn* < *archos*, chief + *tektōn*, carpenter < IE. *tekth-*, to build, weave (cf. TECHNIC)] 1. a person whose profession is designing and drawing up plans for buildings, bridges, etc. and generally supervising the construction 2. any similar designer in a specialized field [a naval *architect*] 3. any planner, builder, or creator [the *architects* of our Constitution]

ar·chi·tec·ton·ic (är′kə tek tän′ik) *adj.* [L. *architectonicus*

< Gr. *architektonikos* < *architektōn*, ARCHITECT] 1. of or relating to architecture or architectural methods, principles, etc. 2. having structure or design of a kind thought of as architectural 3. *Philos.* having to do with the systematizing of knowledge —*n. same as* ARCHITECTONICS —**ar′chi·tec·ton′i·cal·ly** *adv.*

ar·chi·tec·ton·ics (-tän′iks) *n.pl.* [*with sing. v.*] 1. the science of architecture 2. structural design [the *architectonics* of a symphony] 3. *Philos.* the science of systematizing knowledge

ar·chi·tec·tur·al (-tek′chər əl) *adj.* 1. of or connected with architecture 2. having the qualities of architecture — **ar′chi·tec′tur·al·ly** *adv.*

ar·chi·tec·ture (är′kə tek′chər) *n.* [Fr. < L. *architectura:* see ARCHITECT] 1. the science, art, or profession of designing and constructing buildings, bridges, etc. 2. a building, or buildings collectively 3. a style of construction [Elizabethan *architecture*] 4. design and construction [the *architecture* of a beehive] 5. any framework, system, etc.

ar·chi·trave (är′kə trāv′) *n.* [Fr. < It. < L. *archi-* + *trabs*, a beam] *Archit.* 1. the lowest part of an entablature, a beam resting directly on the tops, or capitals, of the columns; epistyle 2. the molding around a doorway, window, etc.

ar·chi·val (är′kī′v'l, är kī′v'l) *adj.* of, in, or containing archives

ar·chives (är′kīvz) *n.pl.* [Fr., pl. of *archif* < L. *archivum* < Gr. *archeion*, town hall < *archē*, the beginning, government] 1. a place where public records, documents, etc. are kept 2. the public records, documents, etc. kept in such a place

ar·chi·vist (är′kə vist, är′kī′vist) *n.* [ML. *archivista*] a person having charge of archives

ar·chi·volt (är′kə vōlt′) *n.* [It. *archivolto* < ML. *archivoltum:* see ARCH¹ & VAULT¹] *Archit.* 1. the inner curve of an arch or the structural parts of this 2. an ornamental molding on the wall side of an arch

arch·ly (ärch′lē) *adv.* in an arch manner; pertly and mischievously

arch·ness (-nis) *n.* the quality of being arch, or saucily mischievous

ar·chon (är′kän′, -kən) *n.* [Gr. *archōn* < *archein*, to be first, rule] 1. one of the nine chief magistrates of ancient Athens 2. a ruler

ar·cho·plasm (är′kə plaz′m) *n.* [ModL. *archoplasma* < ARCH- (with -o-, as if < Gr. *archōn*, ARCHON) + -PLASM] a supposedly specialized portion of the cytoplasm formerly thought to be involved in the formation of the aster and spindle during mitosis

arch·priest (ärch′prēst′) *n.* 1. formerly, a priest who acted as a bishop's chief assistant; dean 2. a chief priest

arch·way (ärch′wā′) *n.* 1. a passageway under an arch 2. an arch framing a passage

-ar·chy (är kē; *occas. also* ər kē) [Gr. *-archia* < *archein*, to rule] *a noun-forming suffix meaning* ruling, that which is ruled [*matriarchy, monarchy*]

☆**arc lamp** a lamp in which the light is produced by an arc between electrodes: also **arc light**

arc·tic (ärk′tik, är′-) *adj.* [ME. *artik* < OFr. *artique* < L. *arcticus* < Gr. *arktikos*, lit., of the (constellation of the) Bear (Gr. *arktos*), northern, arctic] 1. of, characteristic of, or near the North Pole or the region around it 2. very cold; frigid —**the Arctic** the region around the North Pole

arctic char a kind of trout (*Salvelinus alpinus*) of N Canada and Alaska

Arctic Circle [*also* a- c-] an imaginary circle parallel to the equator, 66°33′ north of it

arctic fox any of a widespread species (*Alopex lagopus*) of foxes of the Arctic region, having fur almost pure white in winter and smoky-gray in summer

Arctic Ocean ocean surrounding the North Pole, north of the Arctic Circle: c. 5,500,000 sq. mi.

☆**arc·tics** (är′tiks, ärk′-) *n.pl.* [< ARCTIC] high, warm, waterproof overshoes, usually with buckles

Arc·tu·rus (ärk toor′əs, -tyoor′-) [L. < Gr. *Arktouros* < *arktos*, a bear + *ouros*, a guard] a giant red star of the first magnitude, the brightest in the constellation Boötes

ar·cu·ate (är′kyoo wit, -wāt′) *adj.* [L. *arcuatus*, pp. of *arcuare*, to arch, bend like a bow < *arcus*, a bow: see ARC] curved like a bow; arched —**ar′cu·ate·ly** *adv.*

ar·cu·a·tion (är′kyoo wā′shən) *n.* [L. *arcuatio:* see ARCUATE] 1. a curving or being curved like a bow 2. the use of arches in building 3. a row of arches

arc welding a method of fusing metal parts together under the extreme heat produced by an electric arc

-ard (ərd) [OFr. < MHG. *-hart* < *hart*, bold, hardy] *a noun-forming suffix denoting* one who carries an action, or has some quality, to excess [*sluggard, drunkard*]

ARD acute respiratory disease

ar·deb (är′deb) *n.* [colloq. Ar. *ardabb*, for Ar. *al irdabb*; prob. ult. < Gr. *artabē*, a Persian measure] a unit of dry measure used in Egypt, equal to 5.6189 bushels

Ar·den (är′d'n) wooded area in Warwickshire, Eng.: site of a former forest, the setting of Shakespeare's *As You Like It*

Ar·den-Ar·cade (-är kād′) suburb of Sacramento, in C Calif.: pop. 82,000

Ar·dennes (är den′) wooded plateau in NE France, S Belgium, and Luxembourg

ar·dent (är′d′nt) *adj.* [L. *ardens*, prp. of *ardere*, to burn] 1. warm or intense in feeling; passionate *[ardent love]* 2. intensely enthusiastic or devoted; zealous *[an ardent disciple]* 3. glowing; radiant 4. burning; aflame —*SYN.* see PASSIONATE —**ar′den·cy** (-d′n sē) *n.* —**ar′dent·ly** *adv.*

ardent spirits strong alcoholic liquor; whiskey, gin, etc.

ar·dor (är′dər) *n.* [ME. & OFr. *ardour* < L. *ardor*, a flame, fire < *ardere*, to burn] 1. emotional warmth; passion 2. eagerness; enthusiasm; zeal 3. intense heat; fire —*SYN.* see PASSION

ar·dour (är′dər) *n. Brit. sp.* of ARDOR

ar·du·ous (är′joo wəs) *adj.* [L. *arduus*, steep] 1. difficult to do; laborious; onerous 2. using much energy; strenuous 3. steep; hard to climb —*SYN.* see HARD —**ar′du·ous·ly** *adv.* —**ar′du·ous·ness** *n.*

are[1] (är; *unstressed* ər) [OE. (Northumbrian) *aron* < base found also in AM & ART[2]] *pl. & 2d pers. sing., pres. indic.,* of BE

are[2] (er, är) *n.* [Fr. < L. *area:* see AREA] a unit of surface measure in the metric system, equal to 100 square meters (119.6 sq. yd.)

ar·e·a (er′ē ə) *n.* [L., vacant place, courtyard, prob. (in sense: "arid, bare place") < *arere*, to be dry] 1. orig., a level surface or piece of ground 2. a part of the earth's surface; region; tract 3. the measure of a bounded region on a plane or of the surface of a solid 4. a yard of a building 5. a part of a house, lot, district, city, etc. having a specific use or character *[dining area, play area, slum area,* commercial *area]* 6. a part of any surface, as of an organism, or a particular zone, as of the cerebral cortex 7. scope or extent, as of an operation —**ar′e·al** *adj.*

☆**area code** any of the groups of three numerals assigned as a telephone code to each of the more than 120 areas into which the U.S. and Canada are divided

☆**area rug** a rug intended to cover only part of a floor

☆**ar·e·a·way** (-wā′) *n.* 1. a sunken yard or court leading into a cellar, for entrance or light and air 2. a passageway between buildings or parts of a building

ar·e·ca (ar′ə kə, er′-; ə rēk′ə) *n.* [Port., prob. < Malayalam *adekka*] any of a genus (*Areca*) of palm trees, native to Asia and Australia, with a smooth, slender trunk and feathery compound leaves; the betel palm

A·re·ci·bo (ä′re sē′bō) seaport in N Puerto Rico: pop. 35,000

a·re·na (ə rē′nə) *n.* [L. *arena, harena,* sand, sandy place, arena] 1. the central part of an ancient Roman amphitheater, where gladiatorial contests and shows took place 2. any place or building like this *[an arena for boxing matches]* 3. any sphere of struggle or conflict *[the arena of politics]* 4. the central stage in an arena theater

ar·e·na·ceous (ar′ə nā′shəs, er′-) *adj.* [L. *arenaceus:* see ARENA] 1. sandy 2. growing in sand

☆**arena theater** 1. a theater having a central stage without a proscenium, surrounded by seats 2. the techniques, methods, etc. used in such a theater

ar·e·nic·o·lous (ar′ə nik′ə ləs, er′-) *adj.* [< L. *arena*, sand + -COLOUS] living or growing in sand

ar·e·nite (ar′ə nit′, er′-) *n.* [L. *arena, harena,* sand, ARENA + -ITE[1]] sandstone or other fragmental rock made up chiefly of sand grains

aren't (ärnt) are not: also occasionally used as a substitute for a contraction of *am not* in interrogative constructions: see also AIN'T

a·re·o·la (ə rē′ə lə) *n., pl.* **-lae** (-lē′), **-las** [L., dim. of *area:* see AREA] 1. a small space, as between the veins of a leaf or the ribs of an insect's wing 2. *Anat.* a small area around something, as the dark ring around a nipple 3. *Biol.* a small hollow in a surface —**a·re′o·lar** (-lər) *adj.* —**a·re′o·late** (-lit) *adj.* —**ar·e·o·la·tion** (ar′ē ə lā′shən, ə rē′ə-) *n.*

ar·e·ole (ar′ē ōl′, er′-) *n.* [Fr.] *same as* AREOLA

Ar·e·o·pa·gite (ar′ē äp′ə jit′, er′-; -gīt′) *n.* [L. *Areopagites* < Gr. *Areiopagitēs*] any member of the Areopagus in ancient Athens

Ar·e·op·a·git·i·ca (-äp′ə jit′ə kə) a pamphlet (1644) by John Milton opposing censorship of printed matter and praising freedom of thought

Ar·e·op·a·gus (-äp′ə gəs) [L. < Gr. *Areiopagos* < *Areios*, of Ares + *pagos*, hill] rocky hill northwest of the Acropolis, Athens —*n.* 1. the high court of justice that met there 2. any supreme court

A·re·qui·pa (ä′re kē′pä) city in S Peru: pop. 157,000

Ar·es (er′ēz) [L. < Gr. *Arēs*] *Gr. Myth.* the god of war, son of Zeus and Hera: identified with the Roman god Mars

a·rête (ə rāt′) *n.* [Fr., lit., fish skeleton, awn of wheat, ridge < OFr. *areste* < VL. *aresta* < L. *arista*, awn of grain] a sharp, narrow ridge or crest of a mountain

Ar·e·thu·sa (ar′ə thōō′zə, er′-; -thyōō′-; -sə) [L. < Gr. *Arethousa*] *Gr. Myth.* a woodland nymph, changed into a stream by Artemis so that she might escape her pursuer, Alpheus —*n.* [a-] a N. American orchid (*Arethusa bulbosa*) with one long, narrow leaf and rose-purple flower

A·re·ti·no (ä′re tē′nō), **Pie·tro** (pye′trō) 1492–1556; It. satirical writer

A·rez·zo (ä ret′tsō) commune in C Italy: pop. 74,000

Arg. 1. Argentina 2. Argyll

ar·gal (är′g′l) *n. same as* ARGOL

---

ar·ga·la (är′gə lə) *n.* [Hind. *hargīla*] 1. a stork of India, the adjutant 2. an African stork, the marabou

ar·ga·li (är′gə lē) *n., pl.* **-lis, -li:** *see* PLURAL, II, D, 1 [Mongol.] a wild sheep (*Ovis ammon*) of Asia, with large, curved horns

ARGALI (3–4 ft. high at shoulder)

Ar·gand burner (är′gənd) [after its inventor, Aimé *Argand* (1755–1803), Swiss chemist] a gas or oil burner with a cylindrical wick, designed to let air flow inside and outside the flame

ar·gent (är′jənt) *n.* [Fr. < L. *argentum* < IE. base **ar(e)g-*, gleaming, whitish (whence Gr. *argyros,* silver)] 1. [Archaic or Poet.] silver 2. [Obs.] silver coin; money —*adj.* [Poet.] silvery: also **ar·gen·tal** (är jen′t′l)

Ar·gen·teuil (à r zhän tö′i) city in N France, on the Seine near Paris: pop. 82,000

ar·gen·tic (är jen′tik) *adj.* [< L. *argentum* (see ARGENT) + -IC] of or containing silver, esp. divalent silver

ar·gen·tif·er·ous (är′jən tif′ər əs) *adj.* [< L. *argentum* (see ARGENT) + -FEROUS] containing silver, as ore

Ar·gen·ti·na (är′jən tē′nə) country in S S. America: 1,084,120 sq. mi.; pop. 23,983,000; cap. Buenos Aires

Ar·gen·tine (är′jən tēn′, -tin′) *adj.* of Argentina, its people, or culture —*n.* a native or inhabitant of Argentina Also **Ar′gen·tin′e·an** (-tin′ē ən) —**the Argentine** Argentina

ar·gen·tine (är′jən tin, -tin′, -tēn′) *adj.* [Fr. & OFr. *argentin* < *argent,* ARGENT] of or like silver; silvery —*n.* silver or any silvery substance

ar·gen·tite (-tīt′) *n.* [< L. *argentum* (see ARGENT) + -ITE[1]] native silver sulfide, Ag₂S, a monoclinic, dark-gray mineral that is an important ore of silver

ar·gen·tous (är jen′təs) *adj.* [< L. *argentum* (see ARGENT) + -OUS] of or containing monovalent silver

ar·gil·la·ceous (är′jə lā′shəs) *adj.* [L. *argillaceus* < *argilla*, clay < Gr. *argilla* < *argos,* white] like or containing clay

ar·gil·lite (är′jə līt′) *n.* [L. *argilla* (see prec.) + -ITE[1]] a hardened mudstone showing no slatelike cleavage

ar·gi·nase (är′jə nās′) *n.* [< ff. + -ASE] an animal enzyme, found esp. in the liver of mammals, important in the hydrolysis of arginine to form urea

ar·gi·nine (-nēn′, nin′) *n.* [G. *arginin* < ? Gr. *arginoeis,* white, gleaming (its first discovered salts were silvery) + -in, -INE[4]] a colorless amino acid, C₆H₁₄O₂N₄, necessary in nutrition, obtained from plant and animal proteins by hydrolysis or by the action of bacteria in digestion

Ar·give (är′gīv, -jīv) *adj.* 1. of ancient Argos or Argolis 2. Greek —*n.* 1. a native of Argos or Argolis 2. any Greek: Homeric name

Ar·go (är′gō) [L. < Gr. *Argō*] 1. *Gr. Myth.* the ship on which Jason sailed to find the Golden Fleece 2. formerly, a large S constellation between Canis Major and the Southern Cross: now subdivided into four constellations

ar·gol (är′g′l) *n.* [ME. *argoile* < Anglo-Fr. *argoil*] tartar in its crude form as deposited in wine casks

Ar·go·lis (är′gə lis) province on the NE coast of the Peloponnesus, Greece: 873 sq. mi.; pop. 89,000: in ancient times, a region dominated by the city of Argos

ar·gon (är′gän) *n.* [< Gr. *argon,* neut. of *argos,* inert, idle < *a-,* without + *ergon,* WORK] one of the chemical elements, an inert, colorless, odorless gas constituting nearly one percent of the atmosphere: it is used in incandescent light bulbs, radio tubes, welding, etc.: symbol, Ar; at. wt., 39.948; at. no., 18; density, 1.784 g/l (0°C); melt. pt., −189.2°C; boil. pt., −185.7°C

Ar·go·naut (är′gə nôt′, -nät′) *n.* 1. *Gr. Myth.* [*Argonauta* < Gr. *Argonautēs* < *Argō,* Jason's ship + *nautēs,* sailor < *naus,* ship] *Gr. Myth.* any of the men who sailed with Jason to search for the Golden Fleece ☆2. [also a-] a person who took part in the California gold rush of 1848–49 3. [a-] *Zool. same as* PAPER NAUTILUS

Ar·gonne (är′gän; *Fr.* àr gôn′) wooded region in NE France, near the Belgian border

Ar·gos (är′gäs, -gəs) city in the NE Peloponnesus, Greece: pop. 17,000: ancient Argos dominated the Peloponnesus until the rise of Sparta

ar·go·sy (är′gə sē) *n., pl.* **-sies** [earlier *ragusy* < It. (*nave*) *Ragusea,* (vessel of) RAGUSA (see sense 2); sp. influenced by the ARGO) [Poet.] 1. a large ship, esp. a merchant ship 2. a fleet of such ships

ar·got (är′gō, -gət) *n.* [Fr., orig. (in thieves' jargon), the company of beggars (*argoter,* to beg, prob. < *ergot,* claw, spur, hence orig. "get one's claws into")] the specialized vocabulary and idioms of those in the same work, way of life, etc., as the secret jargon of criminals: see SLANG[1] —*SYN.* see DIALECT

Ar·go·vie (àr gō vē′) *Fr. name of* AARGAU

ar·gu·a·ble (är′gyoo wə b′l) *adj.* 1. that can be argued about 2. that can be supported by argument

ar·gu·a·bly (-blē) *adv.* as can be supported by argument

ar·gue (är′gyoo) *vi.* **-gued, -gu·ing** [ME. *arguen* < OFr. *arguer* < L. *argutare,* to prattle, freq. of *arguere,* to make

clear, prove < IE. base *ar(e)g-, gleaming; OFr. meaning and form influenced by *arguere*] **1.** to give reasons (*for* or *against* a proposal, proposition, etc.) **2.** to have a disagreement; quarrel; dispute —*vt.* **1.** to give reasons for and against; discuss; debate **2.** to try to prove by giving reasons; maintain; contend **3.** to give evidence of; seem to prove; indicate (his manners *argue* a good upbringing] **4.** to persuade (*into* or *out of* an opinion, etc.) by giving reasons —*SYN.* see DISCUSS —**ar′gu·er** n.

ar·gu·fy (är′gyə fī′) *vt., vi.* **-fied′, -fy′ing** [(ARGU(E) + -FY] [Colloq. or Dial.] to argue, esp. about something petty or merely for the sake of arguing; wrangle

ar·gu·ment (är′gyə mənt) *n.* [Fr. < L. *argumentum*, evidence, proof < *arguere:* see ARGUE] **1.** a reason or reasons offered for or against something **2.** the offering of such reasons; reasoning **3.** discussion in which there is disagreement; dispute; debate **4.** a short statement of subject matter, or a brief synopsis of a plot; summary **5.** [Archaic] proof or evidence **6.** [Obs.] a topic; theme **7.** *Math.* an independent variable whose value determines that of a function (the number is the *argument* of which the logarithm is the function]

SYN.—**argument** refers to a discussion in which there is disagreement and suggests the use of logic and the bringing forth of facts to support or refute a point; **dispute** basically refers to a contradiction of an assertion and implies vehemence or anger in debate; **controversy** connotes a disagreement of lengthy duration over a matter of some weight or importance (the Darwinian *controversy*]

ar·gu·men·ta·tion (är′gyə men tā′shən, -mən-) *n.* [Fr. < L. *argumentatio* < *argumentare:* see ARGUE] **1.** the process of arriving at reasons and conclusions; arguing or reasoning **2.** discussion in which there is disagreement; debate

ar·gu·men·ta·tive (-men′tə tiv) *adj.* [Fr. *argumentatif*] **1.** of or containing argument; controversial **2.** apt to argue; contentious Also **ar′gu·men′tive** —**ar′gu·men·ta·tive·ly** *adv.*

‡ar·gu·men·tum (-men′təm) *n.* [L.] an argument: used with Latin phrases, AD HOMINEM, AD REM, etc.

Ar·gus (är′gəs) [L. < Gr. *Argos* < *argos*, bright] *Gr. Myth.* a giant with a hundred eyes, ordered by Hera to watch Io: after he was killed by Hermes, his eyes were put in the tail of the peacock —*n.* **1.** any alert watchman **2.** [a-] an East Indian pheasant (genus *Argusianus*) resembling the peacock

Ar·gus-eyed (-īd′) *adj.* keenly observant; vigilant

ar·gy-bar·gy (är′gē bär′gē) *n.* [earlier dial. *argle-bargle*, reduplicative alteration (? after HAGGLE) < ARGUE + BARGAIN] [Dial. or Colloq.] argument; haggle

ar·gyle (är′gīl) *adj.* [< ARGYLL: the pattern is adapted from a clan tartan of Argyll] knitted or woven in a pattern of diamond-shaped figures of different colors —*n.* [*pl.*] argyle socks

Ar·gyll (är′gīl) county on the W coast of Scotland: 3,110 sq. mi.; pop. 60,000: also **Ar′gyll·shire′** (-shir′)

ar·gy·ro·dite (är jir′ə dīt′) *n.* [< Gr. *argyrōdēs*, rich in silver < *argyros*, silver + -ITE¹] a lustrous, gray mineral, Ag₈GeS₆, made up of silver, germanium, and sulfur

a·ri·a (är′ē ə, er′-) *n.* [It. < L. *aer*, AIR] an air or melody in an opera, cantata, or oratorio, esp. for solo voice with instrumental accompaniment

-a·ri·a (er′ē ə, ä′rē ə) [ModL. < L. *-arius*] *Bot. & Zool.* a plural *n.-forming suffix used for* taxonomic groups

Ar·i·ad·ne (ar′ē ad′nē, er′-) [L. < Gr. *Ariadnē*] *Gr. Myth.* king Minos' daughter, who gave Theseus the thread by which he found his way out of the labyrinth

Ar·i·an¹ (er′ē ən, ar′-) *n., adj. same as* ARYAN

Ar·i·an² (er′ē ən, ar′-) *adj.* [L. *Arianus* < *Arius*] of Arius or Arianism —*n.* a believer in Arianism

-ar·i·an (er′ē ən, ar′-) [L. *-arius*, -ary + *-anus*, -an] *an adj.-& n.-forming suffix denoting:* **1.** age (octogenarian] **2.** sect [Unitarian] **3.** social belief (utilitarian] **4.** occupation (antiquarian]

Ar·i·an·ism (er′ē ə niz′m, ar′-) *n.* the doctrines of Arius, who taught that Jesus was not of the same substance as God, but a created being exalted above all other creatures

a·ri·bo·fla·vin·o·sis (ā rī′bə flā′və nōs′is) *n.* [A-² + RIBOFLAVIN + -OSIS] a disorder resulting from a lack of riboflavin, characterized by cracking of the corners of the mouth and disturbances of vision

A·ri·ca (ä rē′kä) seaport in N Chile, just south of the Peru border: pop. 47,000: see also TACNA

ar·id (ar′id, er′-) *adj.* [L. *aridus* < *arere*, to be dry] **1.** lacking enough water for things to grow; dry and barren **2.** not interesting; lifeless; dull —*SYN.* see DRY —**a·rid·i·ty** (ə rid′ə tē), **ar′id·ness** n. —**ar′id·ly** *adv.*

Ar·i·el (er′ē əl, ar′-) [< Gr. *ariēl* < Heb. *arī′ēl*, lion of God: a name applied to Jerusalem in the Old Testament] **1.** in Shakespeare's *The Tempest*, an airy spirit who was the servant of Prospero **2.** a satellite of the planet Uranus

ar·i·el (er′ē əl, ar′-) *n.* [Ar. *aryal*] a gazelle (*Gazella arabica*) of Asia and Africa

Ar·i·es (er′ēz, ar′-; -ĭ ēz′) [L., the Ram] **1.** a northern constellation between Pisces and Taurus, supposedly outlining a ram **2.** the first sign of the zodiac (♈), which the sun enters about March 21: see ZODIAC, illus.

ar·i·et·ta (ar′ē et′ə, er′-, är′-) *n.* [It., dim. of *aria*, ARIA] a short aria: also **ar′i·ette′** (-ē et′)

a·right (ə rīt′) *adv.* in a right way; correctly; rightly

☆**A·ri·ka·ra** (ə rē′kə rə) *n.* [< Pawnee, lit., horns, from their hair style with hornlike bones inserted] **1.** a member of a village tribe of Plains Indians who live on the Missouri River in North Dakota **2.** their Caddoan language

ar·il (ar′il, er′-) *n.* [ModL. *arillus* < ML., dried grape < L. *aridus*, dry] an additional covering that forms on certain seeds after fertilization, developing from the stalk of the ovule

ar·il·late (-ə lāt′) *adj.* covered with an aril

ar·il·lode (-ə lōd′) *n.* [< ModL. *arillus* (see ARIL) + -ODE²] a false aril, developing from an opening in the covering of the ovule instead of from its stalk

Ar·i·ma·the·a, Ar·i·ma·thae·a (ar′ə mə thē′ə) town in Judea, ancient Palestine

A·rim·i·num (ə rim′ə nəm) *ancient name of* RIMINI

ar·i·ose (ar′ē ōs′, er′ē ōs′) *adj.* [< ARIOSO] songlike; melodic: distinguished from RECITATIVE

a·ri·o·so (är′ē ōs′ō; *It.* ä ryô′sô) *adj.* [It. < *aria*, ARIA] like an aria; melodious —*adv.* in the style of an aria —*n.* an arioso composition

A·ri·os·to (ä′rē ôs′tô), **Lo·do·vi·co** (lô′dô vē′kô) 1474–1533; It. poet: author of *Orlando Furioso*

-ar·i·ous (er′ē əs, ar′-) [< L. *-arius* + -OUS] *an adj.-forming suffix meaning* relating to, connected with (hilarious, vicarious]

a·rise (ə rīz′) *vi.* **a·rose′** (-rōz′), **a·ris′en** (-riz′'n), **a·ris′ing** [ME. *arisen* < OE. *arisan* < *a-*, out + *risan*, to RISE] **1.** to get up, as from sleeping or sitting; rise **2.** to move upward; ascend **3.** to come into being; originate **4.** to result or spring (*from* something) —*SYN.* see RISE

a·ris·ta (ə ris′tə) *n., pl.* **-tae** (-tē) [L.] **1.** the beardlike part of grain or grasses; awn **2.** a bristlelike process, as on the antennae of certain insects —**a·ris′tate** (-tāt) *adj.*

Ar·is·tar·chus of Samos (ar′is tär′kəs) fl. 3d cent. B.C.; Gr. astronomer

Ar·is·ti·des (ar′əs tī′dēz) 530?–468? B.C.; Athenian general & statesman: called *the Just*

Ar·is·tip·pus (ar′əs tip′əs) 435?–356? B.C.; Gr. philosopher; founder of the Cyrenaic school

ar·is·toc·ra·cy (ar′ə stä′krə sē, er′-) *n., pl.* **-cies** [L. *aristocratia* < Gr. *aristokratia* < *aristos*, best + *-kratia*, rule < *kratein*, to rule] **1.** orig., government by the best citizens **2.** government by a privileged minority or upper class, usually of inherited wealth and social position **3.** a country with this form of government; oligarchy **4.** a privileged ruling class; nobility **5.** those considered the best in some way (an *aristocracy* of scientists] **6.** aristocratic quality or spirit

a·ris·to·crat (ə ris′tə krat′, ar′is-) *n.* **1.** a member of the aristocracy; nobleman **2.** a person with the tastes, manners, beliefs, etc. of the upper class **3.** a person who believes in aristocracy as a form of government

a·ris·to·crat·ic (ə ris′tə krat′ik, ar′is-) *adj.* **1.** of, characteristic of, or favoring aristocracy as a form of government **2.** of an aristocracy or upper class **3.** like or characteristic of an aristocrat: used in either a favorable sense (proud, distinguished, etc.) or an unfavorable (snobbish, haughty, etc.) —**a·ris′to·crat′i·cal·ly** *adv.*

Ar·is·toph·a·nes (ar′ə stä′fə nēz′) 448?–380? B.C.; Athenian writer of satirical comic dramas

Ar·is·to·te·li·an (ar′is tə tēl′yən, -tē′lē ən) *adj.* of or characteristic of Aristotle or his philosophy —*n.* **1.** a follower of Aristotle or his philosophy **2.** a person who tends to be empirical or practical in his thinking, rather than metaphysical or idealistic —**Ar′is·to·te′li·an·ism** n.

Aristotelian logic 1. Aristotle's method of deductive logic, characterized by the syllogism **2.** the formal logic developed from Aristotle's

Ar·is·tot·le (ar′is tät′'l, er′-) 384–322 B.C.; Gr. philosopher, pupil of Plato: noted for his works on logic, metaphysics, ethics, politics, etc.

a·rith·me·tic (ə rith′mə tik; *for adj.* ar′ith met′ik, er′-) *n.* [ME. *arsmetrike* < OFr. *arismetrique* (influenced in form by L. *ars metrica*, the art of measurement) < L. *arithmetica* < Gr. (*hē*) *arithmētikē* (*technē*), (the) counting (art) < *arithmētikos*, arithmetical < *arithmein*, to count < *arithmos*, number] **1.** the science or art of computing by positive, real numbers, specif. by adding, subtracting, multiplying, and dividing **2.** knowledge of or skill in this science (her *arithmetic* is poor] —*adj.* of, based on, or using arithmetic: also **ar′ith·met′i·cal** —**ar′ith·met′i·cal·ly** *adv.*

a·rith·me·ti·cian (ar′ith mə tish′ən, ə rith′mə-) *n.* a person skilled in arithmetic

arithmetic mean the average obtained by dividing a sum by the number of its addends

arithmetic progression a sequence of terms each of which, after the first, is derived by adding to the preceding one a constant quantity (the *common difference*, or *constant*) [5, 9, 13, 17, etc. are in *arithmetic progression*]

A·ri·us (ə rī′əs, ar′ē əs) 256?–336 A.D.; Alexandrian theologian, born in N. Africa: see ARIANISM

‡a ri·ve·der·ci (ä rē′ve der′chē) [It.] *older form of* ARRIVE-DERCI

Ar·i·zo·na (ar′ə zō′nə, er′-) [AmSp. < Papago *Arizonac*, "little springs"] State of the SW U.S., on the Mexican border: admitted, 1912; 113,909 sq. mi.; pop. 1,772,000; cap. Phoenix: abbrev. **Ariz., AZ** —**Ar′i·zo′nan** (-nən), **Ar′i·zo′ni·an** (-nē ən) *adj., n.*

Ar·ju·na (är jōō′nə) the hero of the Hindu epic, the *Mahabharata*

ark (ärk) *n.* [OE. *earc* < L. *arca* < *arcere*, to shut up, enclose] **1.** *Bible* the huge boat in which Noah, his family, and two of every kind of creature survived the Flood: Gen. 6 ☆**2.** formerly, a large, flat-bottomed river boat **3.** a place or thing furnishing protection; refuge **4.** *a) same as* ARK OF THE COVENANT *b)* an enclosure in a synagogue or temple for the scrolls of the Torah **5.** [Obs. or Dial.] a chest or coffer

Ar·kan·sas (är′k'n sô′) [< Fr. < Siouan tribal name; ? "downstream people"] **1.** State of the SC U.S.: admitted, 1836; 53,104 sq. mi.; pop. 1,923,000; cap. Little Rock: abbrev. Ark., AR **2.** (*also* är kan′zəs) river flowing from Colorado southeast into the Mississippi: 1,450 mi. — **Ar·kan·san** (är kan′z'n) *adj., n.*

Ar·khan·gelsk (är khän′gelsk) *Russ. name of* ARCHANGEL

ark of the covenant the chest containing the two stone tablets inscribed with the Ten Commandments, kept in the holiest part of the ancient Jewish Tabernacle: Ex. 25:10

ar·kose (är′kōs) *n.* [Fr.] a sandstone containing unweathered feldspar, usually formed from granite

Ark·wright (ärk′rīt′), Sir **Richard** 1732–92; Eng. inventor of a cotton-spinning machine

Arl·berg (ärl′berkh′; *E.* ärl′bərg) **1.** mountain pass in W Austria **2.** railroad tunnel beneath this pass: c. 6 1/2 mi. long

Arles (ärlz; *Fr.* ârl) city in SE France, on the Rhone River: pop. 42,000

arles (ärlz) *n.pl.* [*with sing. v.*] [ME.; prob. via OFr. < L. *arrhula*, dim. of *arra*, earnest money, contr. < *arrabo* < Gr. *arrabōn*, prob. < Heb. *'ērābōn*, pledge] [Scot. or Eng. Dial.] money paid in advance to confirm a pledge; earnest

Ar·ling·ton (är′liŋ tən) [orig. after an Eng. place name] **1.** urban county in NE Va., across the Potomac from Washington, D.C.: pop. 174,000: site of a national cemetery (**Arlington National Cemetery**) **2.** suburb of Boston, in E Mass.: pop. 54,000 **3.** city in NE Tex.: suburb of Fort Worth: pop. 91,000

Arlington Heights [see prec.] village in NE Ill.: suburb of Chicago: pop. 65,000

arm¹ (ärm) *n.* [ME. < OE. *earm*; akin to Goth. *arms*, OHG. *arm*: for IE. base see ART¹] **1.** an upper limb of the human body; part between shoulder and hand **2.** anything resembling this in structure or function; esp., *a)* the forelimb of a vertebrate animal *b)* any limb of an invertebrate animal *c)* a branch of a tree **3.** anything commonly in contact with the human arm; esp., *a)* a sleeve of a garment *b)* a support for the arm on a chair, sofa, etc. **4.** anything thought of as armlike, esp. in being attached or connected to something larger [*an arm* of the sea, a yard*arm*, the *arm* of a balance, the *arm* of a phonograph, an *arm* of the government, etc.] **5.** power to seize, control, etc. [the long *arm* of the law] ☆**6.** *Sports* ability to pitch or throw a ball —**arm in arm** with arms interlocked, as two persons walking together —**at arm's length** at a distance; not friendly or intimate; aloof —**put the arm on** [Slang] **1.** to arrest or restrain, as with force **2.** to seek to borrow money from —**with open arms** in a warm and friendly way —**arm′less** (-lis) *adj.* —**arm′like′** *adj.*

arm² (ärm) *n.* [ME. & OFr. *armes*, pl. < L. *arma*, implements, weapons, akin to *armus*, shoulder, upper arm < IE. base **ar-*, to join, fit, whence ARM¹, ART¹; for semantic development cf. ARM¹, sense 3] **1.** any instrument used in fighting; weapon: *usually used in pl.*: see *also* SMALL ARMS **2.** [*pl.*] warfare; fighting **3.** [*pl.*] *a)* heraldic insignia: see COAT OF ARMS *b)* insignia of countries, corporations, etc. **4.** [a merging with ARM¹ (see sense 4)] any combatant branch of the military forces —*vt.* [ME. *armen* < OFr. *armer* < L. *armare*, to arm < *arma*: see the n.] **1.** to provide with weapons, tools, etc. **2.** to provide with something that protects or fortifies **3.** to prepare to attack or to meet attack [reporters *armed* with questions] **4.** to make ready or equip with parts needed for operation [to *arm* a missile with a warhead] —*vi.* **1.** to equip oneself with weapons, as in preparing for war **2.** to prepare for any struggle —*SYN.* see FURNISH —**bear arms 1.** to carry or be equipped with weapons **2.** to serve as a combatant in the armed forces —**take up arms 1.** to go to war or rise in rebellion **2.** to enter a dispute —**to arms!** get ready to fight! —**under arms** equipped with weapons; ready for war —**up in arms 1.** prepared to fight **2.** indignant

ar·ma·da (är mä′də, -mä′-) *n.* [Sp., an armed force < L. *armata*, fem. of *armatus*, pp. of *armare*: see ARM², v.] **1.** a fleet of warships **2.** [A-] such a fleet sent against England by Spain in 1588 but destroyed: also **Spanish Armada 3.** a fleet of military aircraft

ar·ma·dil·lo (är′mə dil′ō) *n., pl.* **-los** [Sp., dim. of *armado* < L. *armatus*: see ARMADA] any of a family (Dasypodidae) of burrowing mammals of Texas and Central and South America, having an armorlike covering of bony plates and either no teeth at all or very simple, undifferentiated, rootless teeth: armadillos move about mostly at night, and some species roll up into a ball when attacked

Ar·ma·ged·don (är′mə ged′'n) *n.* [LL. *Armagedon* < Gr. *Harmagedōn* < ? Heb. *har*, mountain + *meghiddo*, the plain of Megiddo, proverbial scene of decisive battles] **1.** *Bible* the place where the last, decisive battle between the forces of good and evil is to be fought before the Day of Judgment: Rev. 16:16 **2.** any great, decisive battle

Ar·magh (är mä′) **1.** county of SE Northern Ireland: 512 sq. mi.; pop. 121,000 **2.** its county seat: pop. 10,000

Ar·ma·gnac (är′mən yak′; *Fr.* âr må nyåk′) *n.* [*sometimes* a-] brandy distilled from wine in the district of Armagnac in Gascony, France

ar·ma·ment (är′mə mənt) *n.* [L. *armamentum*, pl. *armamenta*, implements, ship's tackle < *armare*: see ARM²] **1.** [*often pl.*] all the military forces and equipment of a nation **2.** a large force for offense or defense **3.** all the guns and other military equipment of a warship, warplane, tank, fortification, etc. **4.** an arming or being armed for war **5.** anything serving to protect or defend

☆**ar·ma·men·tar·i·um** (är′mə mən ter′ē əm) *n., pl.* **-i·a** (-ə) [L., an arsenal < *armamenta*: see ARMAMENT] an aggregate of resources, apparatus, etc., specif. for work in the field of medicine

ar·ma·ture (är′mə chər) *n.* [L. *armatura*, arms, equipment < *armatus*, pp. of *armare*; all senses from that of "armored, protected": see ARM²] **1.** any protective covering: see ARMOR (senses 1 & 2) **2.** any part or structure of an organism useful for defense or offense, as claws, teeth, burs, etc. **3.** a soft iron bar placed across the poles of a magnet to keep it from losing magnetic power **4.** *a)* the laminated iron core with wire wound around it in which electromotive force is produced by magnetic induction in a generator or motor: usually a revolving part, but in an alternating-current machine often stationary *b)* the vibrating part in an electric relay or bell **5.** *Sculpture* a framework for supporting the plastic material in modeling

arm·chair (ärm′cher′) *n.* a chair with supports at the sides for one's arms or elbows —*adj.* offering opinions or advice although not actually participating [an *armchair* general]

armed (ärmd) *adj.* **1.** provided with arms (weapons), armor, etc. **2.** having arms (limbs) of a specified kind [long-*armed*]

armed forces all the military, naval, and air forces of a country or group of countries

Ar·me·ni·a (är men′ē ə, -mēn′yə) **1.** former kingdom of SW Asia, south of the Caucasus Mts.: now divided between the U.S.S.R., Turkey, and Iran **2.** *same as* ARMENIAN SOVIET SOCIALIST REPUBLIC

Ar·me·ni·an (-ən, -yən) *adj.* of Armenia, its people, language, etc. —*n.* **1.** a native or inhabitant of Armenia **2.** the language of the Armenians, constituting a subfamily of the Indo-European family of languages

Armenian Soviet Socialist Republic a republic of the U.S.S.R., in Transcaucasia: 11,500 sq. mi.; pop. 2,100,000; cap. Yerevan: also called ARMENIA

Ar·men·tières (âr män tyer′) town in N France, near the Belgian border: pop. 25,000

ar·met (är′met) *n.* [Fr. < Sp. *almete* < OFr. *helmet* < *helme*, helmet < Frank. *helm*, HELM¹] a type of round medieval helmet with a movable visor

arm·ful (ärm′fool) *n., pl.* **-fuls**: *see* -FUL as much as the arms or one arm can hold

arm·hole (-hōl′) *n.* an opening for the arm in a garment

ar·mi·ger (är′mə jər) *n.* [L. < *arma*, arms + *gerere*, to carry] **1.** orig., an armorbearer for a knight; squire **2.** a person entitled to display armorial bearings

ar·mil·lar·y (är′mə ler′ē) *adj.* [< L. *armilla*, armlet, bracelet < *armus*, upper arm: see ARM²] **1.** of, like, or made up of circles or rings **2.** *Astron.* designating a model of the celestial sphere (**armillary sphere**) used since ancient times, formed of rings fixed in the position of the great circles such as the tropics, the ecliptic, the meridian, etc.

Ar·min (är′min) [L. *Arminius;* of Gmc. origin < ? bases *aran*, eagle + *wini*, friend] a masculine name: equiv. Fr. *Armand:* see HERMAN

arm·ing (är′min) *n.* **1.** the act of one who arms **2.** a part put on something to make it complete or ready for use **3.** [Obs.] heraldic arms

Ar·min·i·an·ism (är min′ē ən iz′m) *n.* the doctrines of Jacobus Arminius, which stressed man's free will as against Calvinistic predestination —**Ar·min′i·an** *adj., n.*

Ar·min·i·us (är min′ē əs) **1.** (G. name *Hermann*) 17? B.C.–21 A.D.; Germanic tribal leader **2. Ja·co·bus** (jə kō′bəs), (born *Jacob Harmensen*) 1560-1609; Du. theologian: see ARMINIANISM

ar·mip·o·tent (är mip′ə tənt) *adj.* [L. *armipotens < arma*, arms + *potens*, POTENT] [Rare] mighty in battle

ar·mi·stice (är′mə stis) *n.* [Fr. < L. *arma*, arms + *-stitium* (as in *solstitium*, SOLSTICE) < *sistere*, to cause to stand, redupl. < *stare*, to STAND still] a temporary stopping of warfare by mutual agreement, as a truce preliminary to the signing of a peace treaty

Armistice Day November 11, the anniversary of the armistice of World War I in 1918: see VETERANS DAY

arm·let (ärm′lit) *n.* [ARM¹ + -LET] **1.** a band worn for ornament around the arm, esp. the upper arm **2.** a small arm or inlet of the sea

arm·lock (-läk′) *n. Wrestling* a hold in which one con-

testant's arm is locked by an arm and a hand of the other
ar·moire (är mwär′) *n.* [Fr. < OFr. *armarie*, AMBRY] a
large, usually ornate cupboard or clothespress
ar·mor (är′mər) *n.* [ME. *armure* < OFr. *armure* < L.
armatura < *armare:* see ARM²] **1.**
covering worn to protect the body
against weapons **2.** any defensive
or protective covering, as on animals
or plants, or the metal plating on
warships, warplanes, etc. **3.** the
armored forces and vehicles of an
army; tanks, reconnaissance cars,
etc. **4.** a quality or condition serving
as a defense difficult to penetrate
—*vt., vi.* to put armor or armor plate on
ar·mor·bear·er (-ber′ər) *n.* a person
who carried the armor or weapons
of a warrior
ar·mor-clad (-klad′) *adj.* covered
with armor
ar·mored (är′mərd) *adj.* **1.** covered
with armor or armor plate **2.**
equipped with, or making use of,
armored vehicles [an *armored* divi-
sion]

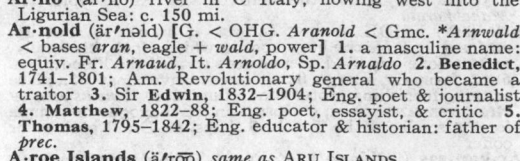

Labels on figure: HELMET, BEAVER, GORGET, PAULDRON, BREASTPLATE, TASSE, GAUNTLET, CUISSE, KNEEPIECE, GREAVE, SOLLERET

ARMOR

armored cable an electric cable covered with metal tape
or wire for mechanical protection
☆**armored car** any of various vehicles covered with armor
plate, as a truck for carrying money to or from a bank;
specif., *Mil.* a wheeled motor vehicle with armor plate,
usually carrying a mounted machine gun and used esp.
for reconnaissance
☆**armored scale** a scale insect (family Diaspididae)
characterized by a hard, waxy secretion that covers the
body: many armored scales, such as the San Jose scale,
are serious pests of trees and shrubs
ar·mor·er (är′mər ər) *n.* **1.** formerly, a person who made
or repaired armor and arms **2.** a maker of firearms **3.**
Mil. an enlisted man in charge of the maintenance and
repair of the small arms of his unit, warship, etc.
ar·mo·ri·al (är môr′ē əl) *adj.* [< ARMORY + -AL] of coats of
arms; heraldic
Ar·mor·ic (är môr′ik, -mär′-) *adj.* of Armorica, its people,
language, etc. —*n.* a native or inhabitant of Armorica
2. the language of Armorica; Breton Also **Ar·mor′i·can**
Ar·mor·i·ca (är môr′i kə, -mär′-) ancient region of Gaul,
between the mouths of the Loire and Seine rivers, nearly
equivalent to Brittany
armor plate a protective covering of specially hardened
steel plates, as on a tank —**ar′mor-plat′ed** *adj.*
ar·mor·y (är′mər ē) *n., pl.* **-mor·ies** [altered, by association
with ARMOR, from OFr. *armoierie*, science of heraldry <
armoier, to blazon coats of arms < *arme*, ARM²] **1.** a storehouse for weapons; arsenal **2.** an aggregate of resources,
etc. ☆**3.** a building housing the drill hall and offices of a
unit of the National Guard ☆**4.** a place where firearms are
made **5.** heraldry **6.** [Archaic] *a)* armor *b)* armorial
bearings
ar·mour (är′mər) *n., vi., vt. Brit. sp.* of ARMOR
arm·pit (ärm′pit′) *n.* the hollow under the arm at the
shoulder; axilla
arm·rest (-rest′) *n.* a support on which to rest one's arm,
as on the inside of an automobile door
Arm·strong (ärm′strôn′) **1. Louis,** 1900–71; U.S. jazz
musician **2. Neil,** 1930– ; U.S. astronaut: first man to
step on the moon
ar·mure (är′myoor) *n.* [Fr., ARMOR] **1.** a woven fabric with
a small pebbled pattern **2.** [Obs.] armor
ar·my (är′mē) *n., pl.* **-mies** [ME. & OFr. *armee* < *armer*, to
ARM²] **1.** a large, organized body of soldiers for waging war,
esp. on land **2.** a military unit, usually two or more army
corps, together with auxiliary troops; field army **3.** [often
A-] a large organization of persons for a specific cause [the
Salvation *Army*] **4.** any large number of persons, animals,
etc. considered as a whole [the *army* of the unemployed]
Army Air Forces the former aviation branch of the U.S.
Army (1941–47), replaced by the U.S. Air Force
army ant any of a number of ants that travel in large
groups and devour insects and animals in their path; esp.,
such an ant (genus *Eciton*) of the American tropics
army of occupation an army that goes into a defeated
country to enforce peace terms, keep order, etc.
Army of the United States during World War II, the
overall army forces of the U.S., including the Regular
Army, the Organized Reserves, the National Guard, and
Selective Service personnel: cf. UNITED STATES ARMY
☆**army worm** any of the larvae of certain moths, esp. any of
the black-striped green and yellow larvae of a species
(*Leucania unipuncta*) that travel in large groups, ruining
crops and grass
Arne (ärn), **Thomas Augustine** 1710–78; Eng. composer
Arn·hem (ärn′hem) city on the Rhine, in E Netherlands:
pop. 130,000
ar·ni·ca (är′ni kə) *n.* [ModL.] **1.** any of a number of plants
(genus *Arnica*) bearing bright yellow flowers on long stalks
with clusters of leaves at the base **2.** a preparation made
from certain of these plants (esp. *Arnica montana* or *Arnica
cordifolia*), formerly much used for treating sprains,
bruises, etc.

Ar·no (är′nō) river in C Italy, flowing west into the
Ligurian Sea: c. 150 mi.
Ar·nold (är′nəld) [G. < OHG. *Aranold* < Gmc. *Arnwald*
< bases *aran*, eagle + *wald*, power] **1.** a masculine name:
equiv. Fr. *Arnaud*, It. *Arnoldo*, Sp. *Arnaldo* **2. Benedict,**
1741–1801; Am. Revolutionary general who became a
traitor **3. Sir Edwin,** 1832–1904; Eng. poet & journalist
4. Matthew, 1822–88; Eng. poet, essayist, & critic **5.
Thomas,** 1795–1842; Eng. educator & historian: father of
prec.
A·roe Islands (ä′rōō) *same as* ARU ISLANDS
ar·oid (ar′oid′, er′-) *n.* any plant of the arum family
a·roint (ə roint′) *vt.* [< ?; first occurs in Shakespeare
(*Macbeth* I, iii, 6)] [Obs.] begone; avaunt (usually followed
by *thee*): used in the imperative
a·ro·ma (ə rō′mə) *n.* [LL. *aroma* < Gr. *arōma*, sweet spice]
1. a pleasant, often spicy odor; fragrance, as of a plant, a
wine, cooking, etc. **2.** any smell or odor **3.** a characteristic
quality or atmosphere [a city with the *aroma* of Paris]
—*SYN.* see SMELL
ar·o·mat·ic (ar′ə mat′ik, er′-) *adj.* [ME. *aromatik* < OFr.
aromatique < L. *aromaticus* < Gr. *aromatikos* < *arōma*,
sweet spice] **1.** of or having an aroma; smelling sweet or
spicy; fragrant or pungent **2.** *Chem.* of or designating a
derivative of benzene or a compound whose molecule contains one or more benzene rings: many of these derivatives
and compounds have a recognizable odor —*n.* an aromatic
plant, chemical, etc. —**ar′o·mat′i·cal·ly** *adv.*
a·ro·ma·tize (ə rō′mə tīz′) *vt.* **-tized′, -tiz′ing 1.** to make
aromatic **2.** *Chem.* to change into an aromatic compound
—**a·ro′ma·ti·za′tion** (-ti zā′shən) *n.*
A·roos·took (ə rōōs′tək) [AmInd. < ?] river in N Me.,
flowing into the St. John River in New Brunswick, Canada:
c. 140 mi.
a·rose (ə rōz′) *pt.* of ARISE
a·round (ə round′) *adv.* [ME. < *a-*, on + *round;* all senses
derive from those of "circling, within a circle"] **1.** round;
esp., *a)* in a circle; along a circular course or circumference
b) in or through a course or circuit, as from one place to
another *c)* on all sides; in every direction *d)* in circumference *e)* in or to the opposite direction, belief, etc. *f)* in
various places; here and there *g)* in succession or sequence
[his turn came *around*] *h)* in every part of; throughout [the
year *around*] **2.** [Colloq.] within a close periphery; nearby
[stay *around*] ☆**3.** [Colloq.] to a (specified or understood)
place [come *around* to see us] —*prep.* **1.** round; esp., *a)* so
as to encircle, surround, or envelop; about *b)* on the circumference, border, or outer part of *c)* on all sides of; in
every direction from *d)* in various places in or on *e)* so as
to rotate or revolve about (a center or axis) ☆**2.** somewhat
close to; about [*around* five pounds, *around* 1890] —*adj.*
[used only in the predicate] **1.** on the move; about [he's up
and *around* now] **2.** existing; living [when dinosaurs were
around] Cf. ROUND¹ —☆**have been around** [Colloq.] to have
had wide experience; be sophisticated See also phrases
under BRING, COME, GET, etc.
a·rouse (ə rouz′) *vt.* **a·roused′, a·rous′ing** [A-², intens. +
ROUSE¹] **1.** to awaken, as from sleep **2.** to stir, as to action
or strong feeling **3.** to evoke (some action or feeling); excite
[to *arouse* pity] —*vi.* to become aroused —*SYN.* see
INCITE, STIR¹ —**a·rous′al** *n.*
Arp (ärp), **Jean** (zhän) (or **Hans**) 1887–1966; Fr. painter &
sculptor, born in Alsace
Ar·pad (är′päd) ?–907 A.D.; Magyar leader; national hero
of Hungary
ar·peg·gio (är pej′ō, -pej′ē ō, -pä′jō) *n., pl.* **-gios** (-ōz)
[It. < *arpeggiare*, to play on a harp < *arpa*, a harp < LL.
harpa, of Gmc. origin: see HARP] **1.** the playing of the notes
of a chord in quick succession instead of simultaneously
2. a chord so played
ar·pent (är′pənt; *Fr.* är pän′) *n.* [Fr., ult. < Gaul. *arepen-
nis*] an old French unit of land measurement, still used in
parts of Quebec and Louisiana, equal to about 5/6 acre
ar·que·bus (är′kwə bəs) *n. same as* HARQUEBUS
arr. 1. arranged **2.** arrangements **3.** arrival
ar·rack (ar′ək) *n.* [Fr. *arak* < Ar. *'araq*, sweat, palm sap,
liquor] in the Orient, strong alcoholic drink, esp. that made
from rice, molasses, or coconut milk
ar·raign (ə rān′) *vt.* [ME. *arreinen* < OFr. *araisnier* < ML.
adrationare < L. *ad*, to + *ratio*, reason] **1.** to bring before a
law court to hear and answer charges **2.** to call to account
or in question; accuse —*SYN.* see ACCUSE —**ar·raign′ment** *n.*
Ar·ran (ar′ən) island in the Firth of Clyde, Bute county
in SW Scotland: 165 sq. mi.
ar·range (ə rānj′) *vt.* **-ranged′, -rang′ing** [ME. *arengen* <
OFr. *arengier* < *renc*, rank: see RANGE] **1.** to put in the
correct, proper, or suitable order **2.** to sort systematically;
classify **3.** to make ready; prepare or plan [to *arrange* a
program of entertainment] **4.** to arrive at an agreement
about; settle **5.** *Music* to adapt (a composition) to other
instruments or voices than those for which it was written,
or to the style of a certain band or orchestra —*vi.* **1.** to
come to an agreement (*with* a person, *about* a thing) **2.** to
make plans; provide or prepare [*arrange* to be here later]
3. *Music* to write arrangements, esp. as a profession —
ar·rang′er *n.*
ar·range·ment (-mənt) *n.* **1.** an arranging or being arranged **2.** the way in which something is
arranged **3.** something made by arranging parts in a par-

ticular way **4.** [*usually pl.*] a preparation; plan [*arrangements* have been made for the party] **5.** a settlement or adjustment, as of a dispute, difference, etc. **6.** *Music a)* adaptation of a composition to other instruments or voices than those for which it was originally written, or to the style of a certain band or orchestra *b)* the composition as thus adapted

ar·rant (ar′ənt, er′-) *adj.* [var. of ERRANT] **1.** that is plainly bad; out-and-out; notorious [an *arrant* fool] **2.** *obs. sp. of* ERRANT (sense 1) —**ar′rant·ly** *adv.*

ar·ras (ar′əs, er′-) *n.* [ME., after *Arras*, city in France, where it was made] **1.** an elaborate kind of tapestry **2.** a wall hanging, esp. of tapestry

ar·ray (ə rā′) *vt.* [ME. *arraien* < OFr. *areer* < ML. *arredare*, to put in order < *ad-*, to + Gmc. base *raid-* (< IE. *reidh-*, ride, move), whence RIDE, ROAD, READY] **1.** to place in order; marshal (troops for battle, etc.) **2.** to dress in fine or showy attire; deck out —*n.* **1.** an orderly grouping or arrangement, esp. of troops **2.** troops in order; military force **3.** an impressive display of assembled persons or things **4.** fine clothes; finery **5.** *Math. & Statistics* a systematic arrangement of numbers or symbols in tabulated form

ar·ray·al (-əl) *n.* **1.** the act or process of arraying **2.** something arrayed

ar·rear·age (ə rir′ij) *n.* [ME. *arerage* < OFr. *arierage* < *ariere*: see ARREARS] **1.** the state of being in arrears **2.** arrears **3.** a thing kept in reserve

ar·rears (ə rirz′) *n.pl.* [ME. *arrers* < *arrere*, backward < OFr. *ariere* < VL. *aretro* < L. *ad*, to + *retro*, behind] **1.** unpaid and overdue debts **2.** any obligation not met on time; unfinished business, work, etc. —**in arrears** (or **arrear**) behind in paying a debt, doing one's work, etc.

ar·rest (ə rest′) *vt.* [ME. *aresten* < OFr. *arester* < VL. *arrestare* < L. *ad-*, to + *restare*, to stop, stay back] **1.** to stop or check the motion, course, or spread of **2.** to seize or take into custody by authority of the law **3.** to catch and keep (one's attention, sight, etc.) —*n.* [ME. & OFr. *arest* < the *v.*] **1.** an arresting or being arrested; esp., a taking or being taken into custody by authority of the law **2.** a thing for checking motion —**under arrest** in legal custody, as of the police —**ar·rest′er, ar·res′tor** (-ər) *n.*

ar·rest·ing (-iŋ) *adj.* attracting attention; interesting; striking —**ar·rest′ing·ly** *adv.*

Ar·rhe·ni·us (ä rā′nē oos; *E.* ə rā′nē əs), **Svan·te Au·gust** (svän′te ou′goost) 1859–1927; Swed. physical chemist; first to present the theory of ionization

ar·rhyth·mi·a (ə rith′mē ə, -rith′-) *n.* [ModL. < Gr. *arrhythmia*, lack of rhythm < *a-*, without + *rhythmos*, measure] any irregularity in the rhythm of the heart's beating —**ar·rhyth′mic, ar·rhyth′mi·cal** (-rith′mik ′l, -rith′-) *adj.* —**ar·rhyth′mi·cal·ly** *adv.*

ar·ride (ə rīd′) *vt.* -**rid′ed, -rid′ing** [L. *arridere* < *ad-* + *ridere*, to laugh] [Archaic] to please

ar·rière-ban (ar′ē er′ban′; *Fr.* à ryer bän′) *n.* [Fr., altered by folk-etym., after *arrière* (see ARREARS) < OFr. *harbon* < OHG. *hariban*, conscription < *hari*, army + *ban*, command under penalty] **1.** in medieval France, a king's calling of his vassals to do their military duty **2.** the vassals so assembled

‡**ar·rière-pen·sée** (-pän sā′) *n.* [Fr., lit., a backthought] a mental reservation; ulterior motive

ar·ris (ar′əs, er′-) *n.* [OFr. *areste*: see ARÊTE] *Archit.* the edge made by two straight or curved surfaces coming together at an angle, as in a molding

ar·riv·al (ə rīv′l) *n.* [ME. & OFr. *arivaille* < *ariver*: see ARRIVE] **1.** the act of arriving **2.** a person or thing that arrives or has arrived

ar·rive (ə rīv′) *vi.* -**rived′, -riv′ing** [ME. *ariven* < OFr. *ar(r)iver* < VL. *arripare*, come to shore, land < L. *ad-*, to + *ripa*, shore] **1.** to reach one's destination; come to a place **2.** to come [the time has *arrived* for action] **3.** to attain success, fame, etc. [he has *arrived* professionally] —**arrive at 1.** to reach by traveling **2.** to reach by work, thinking, development, etc.

‡**ar·ri·ve·der·ci** (ä rē′ve der′chē) *interj.* [It.] until we meet again; goodbye: implies temporary parting

‡**ar·ri·viste** (á rē vēst′) *n.* [Fr. < *arriver* (see ARRIVE) + *-iste*, -IST] a person who has recently gained power, wealth, success, etc. and is regarded as an upstart; parvenu

ar·ro·ba (ə rō′bə; *Sp.* ä rō′bä) *n.* [Sp. < Ar. *al rub′*, the quarter (of the unit of weight *al qintar*)] **1.** a Spanish unit of weight used in some Spanish-American countries, equal to 25.36 pounds **2.** a Portuguese unit of weight used in Brazil, equal to 32.38 pounds **3.** a unit of liquid measure used in some Spanish-speaking countries, varying from 13 to 17 quarts

ar·ro·gance (ar′ə gəns, er′-) *n.* [ME. & OFr. < L. *arrogantia*] the quality or state of being arrogant; overbearing pride or self-importance Also **ar′ro·gan·cy**

ar·ro·gant (-gənt) *adj.* [ME. & OFr. < L. *arrogans*, prp. of *arrogare*, ARROGATE] full of or due to unwarranted pride and self-importance; overbearing; haughty —*SYN.* see PROUD —**ar′ro·gant·ly** *adv.*

ar·ro·gate (-gāt′) *vt.* -**gat′ed, -gat′ing** [< L. *arrogatus*, pp.

of *arrogare*, to claim < *ad-*, to, for + *rogare*, to ask] **1.** to claim or seize without right; appropriate (to oneself) arrogantly **2.** to ascribe or attribute without reason — **ar′ro·ga′tion** *n.*

‡**ar·ron·disse·ment** (à rôn dēs män′) *n., pl.* **-ments** (-män′) [Fr. < *arrondir*, to make round] **1.** in France, the largest administrative subdivision of a department **2.** a municipal subdivision, as of Paris

ar·row (ar′ō, er′-) *n.* [OE. *earh, arwe*; akin to Goth. *arhwa-* (for IE. base see ARC); original sense of *arrow* was "belonging to the bow"] **1.** a slender shaft, usually pointed at one end and feathered at the other, for shooting from a bow **2.** anything like an arrow in form, speed, purpose, etc. **3.** a sign (←) used to indicate direction or position

ar·row·head (-hed′) *n.* **1.** the separable, pointed head or tip of an arrow, made formerly of flint or stone, now usually of metal **2.** anything shaped like an arrowhead; specif., an indicating mark, part of a cuneiform character, etc.: the sign (<) as used throughout this dictionary marks the derivation of a word or word form from another **3.** a marsh plant (genus *Sagittaria*) with arrow-shaped leaves and small, white, cuplike flowers

ar·row·root (-rōōt′, -root′) *n.* [so named from use as antidote for poisoned arrows] **1.** any of a number of tropical plants with starchy roots; esp., a West Indian plant (*Maranta arundinacea*, family Marantaceae) with large leaves, white flowers, and roots yielding an easily digestible starch **2.** starch derived from an arrowroot, esp. the West Indian one

☆**ar·row·wood** (-wood′) *n.* any of various trees or shrubs, as certain viburnums, with long straight stems used by N. American Indians to make arrows

ar·row·worm (-wurm′) *n.* any of certain saltwater worms (phylum Chaetognatha) with a long, arrow-shaped, almost completely transparent body: they feed on plankton

ar·row·y (-ē) *adj.* **1.** having the shape or speed of an arrow **2.** of or full of arrows

☆**ar·roy·o** (ə roi′ō, -ə) *n., pl.* **-os** [Sp. < L. *arrugia*, shaft or pit in a gold mine)] [Southwest] **1.** a dry gully **2.** a rivulet or stream

Ar·ru Islands (ä′rōō) *same as* ARU ISLANDS

ar·sa·nil·ic acid (är′sə nil′ik) [ARS(ENIC)[1] + ANIL(INE) + -IC] a poisonous, white crystalline powder, $C_6H_4NH_2AsO·(OH)_2$, used in the manufacture of arsenical medicinal compounds and some azo dyes

arse (ärs) *n.* [ME. *ars* < OE. *ears, ærs* < IE. base *orsos*] the buttocks: now a vulgar term

ar·se·nal (är′s'n əl, -snəl) *n.* [It. *arsenale*, a dock < Ar. *dār* (*ēṣ*) *ṣinā′a*, wharf, workshop < *dār*, house + *ṣinā′a*, craft, skill] **1.** a place for making or storing weapons and other munitions **2.** a store or collection [an *arsenal* of facts used in a debate]

ar·se·nate (är′sə nāt′, -s′n it) *n.* [ARSEN(IC)[1] + -ATE[2]] a salt or ester of arsenic acid

ar·se·nic[1] (är′s'n ik′, -snik) *n.* [ME. *arsenik* < OFr. *arsenic* < L. *arsenicum* < Gr. *arsenikon*, yellow orpiment; ult. (? via Syr. *zarnīka*) < Per. *zar*, gold; associated in Gr. with *arsenikos*, strong, masculine] **1.** a silvery-white, brittle, very poisonous chemical element, compounds of which are used in making insecticides, glass, medicines, etc.: symbol, As; at. wt., 74.9216; at. no., 33; sp. gr., 5.727: sublimes at 615°C **2.** loosely, arsenic trioxide, As_2O_3 or As_4O_6, a poisonous compound of arsenic used to exterminate insects and rodents: it is a white powder and has no taste

ar·sen·ic[2] (är sen′ik) *adj.* of or containing arsenic, esp. arsenic with a valence of five

arsenic acid a white, poisonous, crystalline compound, H_3AsO_4, used to make insecticides, etc.

ar·sen·i·cal (är sen′ə k'l) *adj.* [ML. *arsenicalis*] of or containing arsenic —*n.* a drug, fungicide, insecticide, etc. whose effect depends on its arsenic content

ar·se·nide (är′sə nid′) *n.* a compound of arsenic and an element or a radical, in which arsenic has a negative valence of three

ar·se·ni·ous (är sē′nē əs) *adj.* of or containing arsenic, esp. arsenic with a valence of three

ar·se·nite (är′sə nit′) *n.* a salt or ester of arsenious acid

ar·se·niu·ret·ed, ar·se·niu·ret·ted (är sen′yoo ret′id, -sen′-) *adj.* [< *arseniuret*, old name for arsenide < L. *arsenicum*, arsenic + ModL. *-uret*, formerly equiv. to -IDE] combined with arsenic

ar·se·no- (är′sə nō′, är sen′ə) *a combining form meaning* having arsenic as a constituent

ar·se·no·py·rite (är′s'n ō pi′rit) *n.* a hard, brittle, monoclinic, silvery-white mineral, FeAsS, an important ore of arsenic

ar·se·nous (är′s'n əs) *adj. same as* ARSENIOUS

‡**ars gra·ti·a ar·tis** (ärz′ grä′shē ə är′tis; grä′tē ə) [L.] art for art's sake

ar·shin, ar·shine (är shēn′) *n.* [Russ.] a Russian unit of linear measure equal to 28 inches

ar·sine (är sēn′, är′sēn) *n.* [ARS(ENIC)[1] + -INE[4]] **1.** arseniureted hydrogen, AsH₃, a very poisonous, inflammable gas that smells like garlic **2.** any of its derivatives

ar·sis (är′sis) *n., pl.* **-ses** (-sēz) [L. < Gr. *arsis*, a lifting up,

omission < *airein*, to lift, raise up] **1.** in classical poetry, the unaccented part of a foot of verse **2.** the accented part of a foot of verse: usage due to a misunderstanding of the original Greek **3.** *Music* the unaccented part of a measure; upbeat

‡**ars lon·ga, vi·ta bre·vis** (ärz′ lôŋ′gə vīt′ə brev′is; vēt′ə) [L.] art (is) long, life (is) short

ar·son (är′s'n) *n.* [OFr. < LL. *arsio*, fire < L. *arsus*, pp. of *ardere*, to burn] the crime of purposely setting fire to another's building or property, or to one's own, as to collect insurance —**ar′son·ist** *n.*

ars·phen·a·mine (ärs fen′ə mēn′, -min) *n.* [ARS(ENIC)[1] + PHEN(YL) + AMINE] a yellowish arsenical powder, C₁₂H₁₄As₂Cl₂N₂O₂·2H₂O, formerly used in treating syphilis and other infections

‡**ars po·e·ti·ca** (ärz′ pō et′i kə) [L.] the art of poetry

art[1] (ärt) *n.* [ME. < OFr. *arte* < L. *artis*, gen. of *ars*, art < IE. base *ar-*, to join, fit together, whence ARM², ARTICULATE, RATIO] **1.** human ability to make things; creativity of man as distinguished from the world of nature **2.** skill; craftsmanship **3.** any specific skill or its application [the *art* of making friends] **4.** any craft, trade, or profession, or its principles [the cobbler's *art*, the physician's *art*] **5.** creative work or its principles; making or doing of things that display form, beauty, and unusual perception: art includes painting, sculpture, architecture, music, literature, drama, the dance, etc.: see also FINE ART **6.** any branch of creative work, esp. painting, drawing, or work in any other graphic or plastic medium **7.** products of creative work; paintings, statues, etc. **8.** pictorial and decorative material accompanying the text in a newspaper, magazine, or advertising layout **9.** *a)* [Archaic] learning *b)* a branch of learning; specif., [*pl.*] the liberal arts (literature, music, philosophy, etc.) as distinguished from the sciences **10.** artful behavior; cunning **11.** sly or cunning trick; wile: *usually used in pl.* —*adj.* **1.** of or for works of art or artists [*art* gallery, *art* colony] **2.** produced with an especially artistic technique, or exhibiting such productions [*art* movie, *art* theater]

SYN—**art**, the word of widest application in this group, denotes in its broadest sense merely the ability to make something or to execute a plan; **skill** implies expertness or great proficiency in doing something; **artifice** implies skill used as a means of trickery or deception; **craft** implies ingenuity in execution, sometimes even suggesting trickery or deception; in another sense, **craft** is distinguished from **art** in its application to a lesser skill involving little or no creative thought

art² (ärt) *archaic 2d pers. sing., pres. indic., of* BE: *used with* thou

-art (ərt) *same as* -ARD

art. **1.** article **2.** artificial

ar·tal (är′täl) *n., pl. of* ROTL

Ar·ta·xer·xes (är′tə zurk′sēz) any of several kings of ancient Persia, esp. *a)* **Artaxerxes I** king (465?–424? B.C.): son of XERXES I *b)* **Artaxerxes II** king (404?–358? B.C.): see CUNAXA

ar·te·fact (är′tə fakt′) *n. same as* ARTIFACT

ar·tel (är tel′) *n.* [Russ. *artel'* < It. *artieri*, *pl.*, workmen, artisans] a group of people working collectively and sharing the income and liability; kind of cooperative found esp. in the Soviet Union

Ar·te·mis (är′tə mis) [L. < Gr. *Artemis*] Gr. Myth. the goddess of the moon, wild animals, and hunting, Apollo's twin sister: identified with the Roman goddess Diana

ar·te·mis·i·a (är′tə miz′ē ə, -mēz′-; -yə) *n.* [L., mugwort < Gr. *artemisia* < *Artemis*; reason for name unknown] any of a genus (*Artemisia*) of aromatic herbs or shrubs of the composite family, with small greenish heads, including wormwood, absinthe, and sagebrush

ar·te·ri·al (är tir′ē əl) *adj.* [Fr. *artérial* (now *artériel*) < ML. *arterialis*: see ARTERY] **1.** of or like an artery or arteries **2.** designating or of the blood in the arteries, which has undergone oxygenation in the lungs or gills and is brighter red than the blood in the veins **3.** designating or of a main road or channel with many branches —**ar·te′ri·al·ly** *adv.*

ar·te·ri·al·ize (-īz′) *vt.* **-ized′, -iz′ing** to change (venous blood) into arterial blood by oxygenation —**ar·te′ri·al·i·za′tion** (-i zā′shən) *n.*

ar·te·ri·o- (är tir′ē ō, -ə) [< Gr. *artēria*, artery] a combining form meaning artery, of the arteries

ar·te·ri·og·ra·phy (är tir′ē ä′grə fē) *n.* [ARTERIO- + -GRAPHY] X-ray examination of arteries after injection of radiopaque dyes

ar·te·ri·ole (är tir′ē ōl′) *n.* [ModL. *arteriola*, dim. of L. *arteria*, ARTERY] any of the smaller blood vessels, intermediate in size and position between arteries and capillaries —**ar·te′ri·o′lar** (-ō′lər) *adj.*

ar·te·ri·o·scle·ro·sis (är tir′ē ō sklə rō′sis) *n.* [ARTERIO- + SCLEROSIS] a thickening, and loss of elasticity, of the walls of the arteries, as in old age —**ar·te′ri·o·scle·rot′ic** (-rät′ik) *adj.*

ar·te·ri·o·ve·nous (-vē′nəs) *adj.* designating or of arteries and veins

ar·te·ri·tis (är′tə rīt′əs) *n.* [ModL.: see ARTERY & -ITIS] any inflammatory disorder of the arteries

ar·ter·y (är′tər ē) *n., pl.* **-ies** [L. *arteria*, windpipe, artery < Gr. *artēria*, prob. < *aeirein*, to raise, attach] **1.** any one of the system of large, thick-walled tubes that carry

blood directly from the heart to the principal parts of the body: cf. VEIN, CAPILLARY **2.** a main road or channel [a traffic *artery*]

ar·te·sian well (är tē′zhən) [Fr. *artésien*, lit., of ARTOIS (OFr. *Arteis*), where such a well existed] a well drilled deep enough to reach water that is draining down from higher surrounding ground above the well so that the pressure will force a flow of water upward

ARTESIAN WELL

Ar·te·vel·de (är′tə vel′də) **1.** Jacob van, 1290?–1345; Fl. statesman **2.** Philip van, 1340?–81; Fl. leader: son of *Jacob* Also **Ar′te·veld′** (-veld′)

art·ful (ärt′f'l) *adj.* **1.** skillful or clever, esp. in achieving a purpose **2.** sly or cunning; crafty [an *artful* swindle] **3.** done with, using, or showing considerable art or skill **4.** artificial; imitative —**art′ful·ly** *adv.* —**art′ful·ness** *n.*

arthr- *same as* ARTHRO-

ar·thral·gia (är thral′jə) *n.* neuralgic pain in a joint or joints

ar·thri·tis (är thrīt′is) *n.* [Gr. < *arthron* (see ff.) + -ITIS] inflammation of a joint or joints —**ar·thrit·ic** (är thrit′ik) *adj.*

ar·thro- (är′thrə, -thrō) [< Gr. *arthron*, a joint < var. of IE. base *ar-*, to join, fit: see ART¹] *a combining form meaning* joint, of the joints

ar·thro·mere (är′thrə mir′) *n.* [ARTHRO- + -MERE] any of the body segments of an arthropod —**ar′thro·mer′ic** (-mer′ik) *adj.*

ar·thro·pod (-päd′) *n.* [ARTHRO- + -POD] any member of a large phylum (Arthropoda) of invertebrate animals with jointed legs and a segmented body, such as insects, crustaceans, arachnids, myriapods, and trilobites —**ar·throp·o·dal** (är thräp′ə d'l), **ar·throp·o·dan** (-dən), **ar·throp′o·dous** (-dəs) *adj.*

ar·thro·spore (-spôr′) *n.* [ARTHRO- + SPORE] a spore produced by the breaking up of a fungus hypha into individual cells

Ar·thur (är′thər) [ML. *Arthurus*] **1.** a masculine name: dim. *Art*; equiv. It. *Arturo* **2.** a legendary king of Britain who led the knights of the Round Table: such a king is supposed to have lived in the 6th cent. **3.** Chester Alan, 1830–86; 21st president of the U.S. (1881–85) —**Ar·thu·ri·an** (är thoor′ē ən) *adj.*

ar·ti·choke (är′tə chōk′) *n.* [It. *articiocco* < Sp. *alcarchofa* < Ar. *al-ḥaršūf*] **1.** a thistlelike plant (*Cynara scolymus*) of the composite family **2.** its flower head, cooked as a vegetable **3.** *short for* JERUSALEM ARTICHOKE

ar·ti·cle (är′ti k'l) *n.* [ME. & OFr. < L. *articulus*, dim. of *artus*, a joint: see ART¹] **1.** one of the sections or items of a written document, as of a constitution, treaty, contract, etc. **2.** [*pl.*] the parts of a formal declaration, or of a body of rules, beliefs, etc., considered as a whole **3.** a complete piece of writing, as a report or essay, that is part of a newspaper, magazine, or book **4.** a thing of a certain kind; separate item [an *article* of luggage] **5.** a thing for sale; commodity **6.** *Gram.* any one of the words *a*, *an*, or *the* (and their equivalents in other languages), used as adjectives: *a* and *an* are the *indefinite articles* and *the* is the *definite article* —*vt.* **-cled, -cling 1.** [Archaic] to set forth (charges) in an indictment **2.** to bind by the articles of an agreement or contract [an *articled* apprentice] —*vi.* [Archaic] to bring charges (*against*)

Articles of Confederation the first constitution of the thirteen original States: it was adopted in 1781 and replaced by the present Constitution, which went into effect in 1789

Articles of War formerly, the code of laws governing members of the U.S. Army: see UNIFORM CODE OF MILITARY JUSTICE

ar·tic·u·lar (är tik′yə lər) *adj.* [L. *articularis* < *articulus*, a joint: see ARTICLE] of a joint or joints [an *articular* inflammation]

ar·tic·u·late (är tik′yə lit; *for v.* -lāt′) *adj.* [L. *articulatus*, pp. of *articulare*, to separate into joints, utter distinctly < *articulus*, a joint: see ARTICLE] **1.** having parts connected by joints; jointed: usually **ar·tic′u·lat′ed 2.** made up of distinct syllables or words that have meaning, as human speech **3.** able to speak **4.** expressing oneself easily and clearly **5.** well formulated; clearly presented [an *articulate* argument] —*vt.* **-lat′ed, -lat′ing 1.** to put together by joints; joint **2.** to arrange in connected sequence; fit together; correlate [to *articulate* a science program for all grades] **3.** to utter distinctly; pronounce carefully; enunciate **4.** to express clearly **5.** *Phonet.* to produce (a speech sound) by moving an articulator;

ARTICHOKE

phonate —*vi.* 1. to speak distinctly; pronounce clearly 2. to be jointed or connected 3. *Phonet.* to produce a speech sound —ar·tic′u·late·ly *adv.* —ar·tic′u·late·ness, ar·tic′u·la·cy (-lə sē) *n.* —ar·tic′u·la′tive (-lāt′iv) *adj.*

ar·tic·u·la·tion (är tik′yə lā′shən) *n.* [ME. *articulacioun* < L. *articulatio:* see ARTICULATE] 1. a jointing or being jointed 2. the way in which parts are joined together 3. utterance or enunciation; way of talking or pronouncing 4. a spoken sound, esp. a consonant 5. a joint between bones or similar parts 6. *Bot. a)* a joint in a stem or between two separable parts, as a branch and leaf *b)* a node or space between two nodes

ar·tic·u·lat·or (är tik′yə lāt′ər) *n.* 1. a person or thing that articulates 2. *Phonet.* any organ in the mouth or throat which, when moved, helps to give speech sounds their characteristic acoustic properties —ar·tic′u·la·to′ry *adj.*

ar·ti·fact (är′tə fakt′) *n.* [L. *artis,* gen. of *ars,* ART¹ + *factum,* thing made (see FACT)] 1. any object made by human work; esp., a simple or primitive tool, weapon, vessel, etc. 2. *Histology* any structure or changed appearance produced artificially or by death

ar·ti·fice (är′tə fis) *n.* [Fr. < L. *artificium,* craft < *artifex,* artist, master of a trade < *ars,* ART¹ + *facere,* to make] 1. skill or ingenuity 2. a clever expedient 3. trickery or craft 4. a sly or artful trick —*SYN.* see ART¹, TRICK

ar·tif·i·cer (är tif′ə sər) *n.* [ME. < OFr. *artificier* < ML. *artificiarius:* see prec. & -ER] 1. a skillful maker of things; skilled craftsman 2. a person who devises; inventor 3. a military or naval mechanic

ar·ti·fi·cial (är′tə fish′əl) *adj.* [ME. < OFr. < L. *artificialis < artificium,* ARTIFICE] 1. made by human work or art, not by nature; not natural 2. made in imitation of or as a substitute for something natural; simulated [*artificial* teeth] 3. unnatural in an affected way [an *artificial* smile] 4. pretended; feigned 5. *Bot.* cultivated; not native, as a garden plant —ar·ti·fi′ci·al′i·ty (-fish′ē al′ə tē) *n., pl.* -ties —ar′ti·fi′cial·ly *adv.*

SYN.—**artificial** is applied to anything made by human work, esp. if in imitation of something natural [*artificial* hair]; **synthetic** is applied to a substance that is produced by chemical synthesis and is used as a substitute for a natural substance which it resembles [*synthetic* dyes]; **ersatz,** which refers to an artificial substitute, always implies an inferior substance [*ersatz* coffee made of acorns]; **counterfeit** and **spurious** are applied to a careful imitation deliberately intended to deceive [*counterfeit* money, a *spurious* signature] —*ANT.* natural

artificial horizon 1. a gyroscopic instrument on an aircraft for indicating the true horizon and the position of the craft with reference to it; flight indicator 2. a level mirror, as the surface of mercury in a shallow basin, used in measuring the altitude of a celestial body

artificial insemination the impregnation of a female by artificial introduction of semen taken from a male

artificial respiration the maintenance of breathing by artificial means, as by forcing breath into the mouth or by creating and relaxing pressure externally on the chest cavity at regular intervals

ar·til·ler·ist (är til′ər ist) *n.* 1. a student of gunnery 2. an artilleryman; gunner

ar·til·ler·y (är til′ər ē) *n.* [ME. < OFr. *artillerie* < Pr. *artilla,* fortifications < ML. *articula;* ult. < L. *ars,* handicraft, skill, ART¹] 1. formerly, apparatus for hurling heavy missiles, as catapults, arbalests, etc. 2. guns of large caliber, too heavy to carry; mounted guns (excluding machine guns), as cannon or missile launchers: artillery may be mobile, stationary, or mounted on ships, airplanes, etc. 3. the science of guns; gunnery ☆4. [Slang] small arms: a facetious or hyperbolic usage —**the artillery** the branch of an army specializing in the use of heavy mounted guns

ar·til·ler·y·man (-mən) *n., pl.* -men (-mən) a soldier in the artillery

ar·ti·o·dac·tyl (är′tē ō dak′t′l) *n.* [Gr. *artios,* even + *daktylos,* finger or toe] any of an order (Artiodactyla) of hoofed mammals having an even number of toes, such as the camel or deer —ar′ti·o·dac′ty·lous (-t′l əs) *adj.*

ar·ti·san (är′tə z′n, -s′n) *n.* [Fr. < It. *artigiano;* ult. < L. *ars,* ART¹] a skilled workman or craftsman

art·ist (är′tist) *n.* [ML. *artista,* craftsman, artisan < L. *ars,* craft, ART¹] 1. a person who works in or is skilled in any of the fine arts, esp. in painting, drawing, sculpture, etc. 2. a person who does anything very well, with imagination and a feeling for form, effect, etc. 3. *same as* ARTISTE

ar·tiste (är tēst′) *n.* [Fr., ARTIST] 1. a professional person in any of the performing arts 2. a person very skilled in his work: often humorous or facetious

ar·tis·tic (är tis′tik) *adj.* [Fr. *artistique*] 1. of art or artists 2. done skillfully and tastefully; aesthetically satisfying 3. keenly sensitive to aesthetic values —ar·tis′ti·cal·ly *adv.*

art·ist·ry (är′tis trē) *n.* artistic quality, ability, work, or workmanship

art·less (ärt′lis) *adj.* 1. lacking skill or art 2. uncultured; ignorant 3. not artistic; clumsy; crude 4. without arti-

ficiality; simple; natural 5. without guile or deceit; ingenuous; innocent —*SYN.* see NAIVE —art′less·ly *adv.* —art′less·ness *n.*

☆**art·mo·bile** (ärt′mō bēl′) *n.* [ART¹ + (AUTO)MOBILE] a traveling art collection transported and exhibited in a trailer truck

‡**art nou·veau** (är nōō vō′) [from the name of an art gallery (c. 1895) carrying examples of the work] a movement in arts and crafts of the late 19th and early 20th cent., characterized by curvilinear designs styled from nature

Ar·tois (är twä′) region and former province of N France

art·sy-craft·sy (ärt′sē kraft′sē, -kräft′-) *adj.* [Colloq.] having to do with arts and crafts: usually used in a disparaging sense to connote faddishness, dilettantism, superficiality, etc.: also **art′y-craft′y**

art·y (ärt′ē) *adj.* art′i·er, art′i·est [Colloq.] having or showing artistic pretensions —art′i·ness *n.*

arty. artillery

A·ru·ba (ä rōō′bä) island of the Netherlands Antilles, north of the coast of Venezuela: 73 sq. mi.; pop. 59,000

a·ru·gu·la (ə rōōg′ə lə) *n.* [It. dial., dim. < Pr. *auruga,* rocket, ult. < L. *eruca,* kind of colewort: cf. ROCKET²] *same as* ROCKET² (sense 2)

A·ru Islands (ä′rōō) group of islands of Indonesia, in the Arafura Sea southwest of New Guinea: c. 3,300 sq. mi.

ar·um (er′əm, ar′-) *n.* [L. < Gr. *aron,* the wake robin] any of a family (Araceae) of plants bearing small flowers on a thick, fleshy spike, enveloped within a large, hoodlike leaf, as the jack-in-the-pulpit

a·run·di·na·ceous (ə run′di nā′shəs) *adj.* [L. *arundinaceus < arundo,* reed, cane] of or like a reed

a·rus·pex (ə rus′peks) *n., pl.* -pi·ces (-pə sēz′) *same as* HARUSPEX

A.R.V. American (Standard) Revised Version (of the Bible), printed in 1901

Ar·vad·a (är vad′ə) [after Hiram *Arvada* Haskins, a member of the founding family] city in NC Colo.: suburb of Denver: pop. 47,000

-ar·y (er′ē; *chiefly Brit.* ər i) [L. *-arius, -aria, -arium*] 1. *an adj.-forming suffix meaning* relating to, connected with [*auxiliary, elementary*] 2. *a noun-forming suffix meaning: a)* a person or thing connected with [*missionary, dictionary*] *b)* a place for [*granary, aviary*] 3. [L. *aris*] *a noun- and adj.-forming suffix meaning* like, of the same kind [*military*]

Ar·y·an (ar′ē ən, er′-; -yən) *adj.* [< Sans. *ārya,* noble, lord (used as tribal name to distinguish from indigenous races), whence Avestan *airya-nam,* IRAN; akin to Gr. *aristos,* best] 1. formerly, designating or of the Indo-European language family 2. *same as* INDO-IRANIAN 3. of the Aryans —*n.* 1. formerly, the hypothetical parent language of the Indo-European family 2. a person belonging to, or supposed to be a descendant of, the prehistoric peoples who spoke this language *Aryan* has no validity as an ethnological term, although it has been so used, notoriously and variously by the Nazis to mean "a Caucasian of non-Jewish descent," "a Nordic," etc.

ar·yl (ar′əl, er′-) *n.* [G. < *aromatisch,* aromatic + -yl, -YL] an organic radical derived from an aromatic hydrocarbon by the removal of one hydrogen atom

ar·y·te·noid (ar′ə tē′noid, ə rit′n oid′) *adj.* [Gr. *arytainoeidēs,* ladle-shaped < *arytaina,* a ladle cup + *eidos,* form] 1. designating or of either of two small cartilages at the back of the larynx, connected with the vocal cords 2. relating to any of certain muscles in the larynx —*n.* an arytenoid cartilage or muscle

as¹ (az; *unstressed* əz) *adv.* [weakened form of ALSO; ME. *as, ase* < OE. *alswa, ealswa < al, eall,* all + *swa,* so; lit., wholly so, just as] 1. to the same amount or degree; equally [he's just *as* happy at home] 2. for instance; thus [a card game, *as* bridge] 3. when set off or related in a specified way [romanticism *as* contrasted with classicism] —*conj.* 1. to the same amount or degree that [it flew straight *as* an arrow] 2. in the same manner that; according to the way that [do *as* you are told] 3. at the same time that; while [she wept *as* she spoke] 4. because [*as* you object, we won't go] 5. that the consequence is [the question is so obvious *as* to need no reply] 6. though [tall *as* he was he couldn't reach the apples] 7. [Colloq.] that [I don't know *as* I should] —*pron.* 1. a fact that [he is tired, *as* anyone can see] 2. that (preceded by *such* or *the same*) [the same color *as* yours] —*prep.* 1. in the role, function, capacity, or sense of [he poses *as* a friend] 2. like [the risk is *as* nothing compared to the gain] —**as ... as** a correlative construction used to indicate the equality or sameness of two things [*as* large *as, as* heavy *as, as* many *as,* etc.]: see also GOOD, WELL², MUCH, FAR, etc. for certain idiomatic phrases with *as* —**as for** with reference to; concerning —**as it is** (or one) would if 2. that [it seems *as if* she's never happy] —☆**as is** [Colloq.] just as it is; without any changes: said of damaged goods being sold —**as it were** as if it were so; so to speak —**as of** up to, on, or from (a specified time) —**as though** same as AS IF —**as to** 1. with reference to; concerning 2. as if to

as² (as) *n., pl.* **as′ses** (-əz, -ēz) [L.] 1. an ancient Roman unit of weight, equal to about twelve ounces; libra, or

Roman pound **2.** an ancient Roman coin of copper alloy

as- (as, əs) *same as* AD-: used before *s*

As *Chem.* arsenic

AS., A.S., A.-S. Anglo-Saxon

As. **1.** Asian **2.** Asiatic

A.S. Associate in (or of) Science

A·sa (ās′ə) [Heb. *āsā*, lit., healer] **1.** a masculine name **2.** *Bible* a king of Judah, who opposed idolatry: I Kings 15:8–24

ASA American Standards Association

as·a·fet·i·da, as·a·foet·i·da (as′ə fet′ə də) *n.* [ML. *asa* < Per. *āzā*, gum + L. *fetida, foetida,* FETID] a bad-smelling gum resin obtained from various Asiatic plants (genus *Ferula*) of the parsley family: it was formerly used to treat some illnesses or, in folk medicine, to repel disease

as·a·rum (as′ə rəm) *n.* [L., hazelwort, wild spikenard < Gr. *asaron*] the dried rhizomes and roots of a plant (*Asarum canadense*) from which an aromatic oil used in perfumery is extracted

As·ben (äs ben′) *former name of* AÏR

as·bes·tos, as·bes·tus (as bes′təs, az-) *n.* [ME. *asbestus* < L. *asbestos* < Gr. *asbestos,* inextinguishable < *a-,* not + *sbestos* < *sbennynai,* to extinguish: first applied in Gr. & L. to unslaked lime or a mineral other than asbestos (Gr. *amiantos*)] any of several grayish amphiboles or similar minerals that separate into long, threadlike fibers: because certain varieties do not burn, do not conduct heat or electricity, and are often resistant to chemicals, they are used for making fireproof materials, electrical insulation, roofing, filters, etc. —*adj.* woven of or containing asbestos —**as·bes′tine** (-tin) *adj.*

as·bes·to·sis (as′bes tō′sis) *n.* [ModL.: see ASBESTOS & -OSIS] a form of pneumoconiosis caused by inhaling asbestos fibers

As·bur·y (az′ber′ē, -bər-), **Francis** 1745–1816; 1st Methodist bishop in U.S.

Asbury Park [after Bishop ASBURY] city in EC N.J., on the Atlantic: an ocean resort: pop. 17,000

As·ca·lon (as′kə län′) *same as* ASHKELON

As·ca·ni·us (as kā′nē əs) [L.] *Rom. Myth.* son of Aeneas

ASCAP (as′kap′) American Society of Composers, Authors, and Publishers

as·ca·ri·a·sis (as′kə rī′ə sis) *n.* [ModL.: see ASCARID & -IASIS] infestation with ascarids or a disease caused by this; esp., infestation of the intestines by roundworm (*Ascaris lumbricoides*)

as·ca·rid (as′kə rid) *n.* [Gr. *askarides,* pl. of *uskaris,* intestinal worm] any of a genus (*Ascaris*) of parasitic roundworms

as·cend (ə send′) *vi.* [ME. *ascenden* < OFr. *ascendre* < L. *ascendere* < *ad-,* to + *scandere,* to climb] **1.** to go up; move upward; rise **2.** to proceed from a lower to a higher level or degree, as in rank, pitch, etc. **3.** to slope or lead upward **4.** to go back in time or line of ancestry —*vt.* **1.** to move upward along; mount; climb [*to ascend* stairs] **2.** to move toward the source of [*to ascend* a river] **3.** to succeed to (a throne) —**as·cend′a·ble, as·cend′i·ble** *adj.*

as·cend·an·cy, as·cend·en·cy (-ən sē) *n.* a position in which one has control or power; supremacy; domination: also **as·cend′ance, as·cend′ence**

as·cend·ant, as·cend·ent (-ənt) *adj.* [L. *ascendens,* prp. of *ascendere*] **1.** rising; ascending **2.** in control; dominant; superior **3.** *Bot. same as* ASCENDING —*n.* **1.** a dominating position; ascendancy **2.** an ancestor: opposed to DESCENDANT **3.** *Astrol.* the sign of the zodiac just above the eastern horizon at any given moment —**in the ascendant** at or heading toward the height of power, influence, fame, etc.

as·cend·er (-ər) *n.* **1.** a person or thing that ascends **2.** *Typography* the extension or upward stroke of any of the tall lower-case letters, as *b, d, k,* etc. **3.** any of these letters

as·cend·ing (-in) *adj.* **1.** that ascends **2.** *Bot.* rising or curving upward from a trailing position, as the stems of certain vines and shrubs

As·cen·sion (ə sen′shən) small island in the S Atlantic: part of the Brit. colony of St. Helena: 34 sq. mi.; pop. 500

as·cen·sion (ə sen′shən) *n.* [ME. *ascensioun* < OFr. *ascension* < L. *ascensio,* a rising < pp. of *ascendere,* ASCEND] **1.** the act of ascending; ascent **2.** [A-] Ascension Day —**the Ascension** *Bible* the bodily ascent of Jesus into heaven on the fortieth day after the resurrection: Acts 1:9 —**as·cen′sion·al** *adj.*

Ascension Day the fortieth day after Easter, celebrating the Ascension

as·cen·sive (ə sen′siv) *adj.* [< L. *ascensus,* pp. of *ascendere* + -IVE] ascending; rising

as·cent (ə sent′) *n.* [< ASCEND, after DESCENT] **1.** the act of ascending, rising, or climbing **2.** an advancement, as in rank, fame, etc. **3.** *a)* a way leading up; upward slope; acclivity *b)* the amount of such slope [*an ascent* of three degrees] **4.** a going back in time or in line of ancestry

as·cer·tain (as′ər tān′) *vt.* [ME. *acertainen* < OFr. *acertainer* < *a-,* to + *certain,* CERTAIN] **1.** to find out with certainty **2.** [Archaic] to make certain or definite —*SYN.* see LEARN —**as′cer·tain′a·ble** *adj.* —**as′cer·tain′ment** *n.*

as·cet·ic (ə set′ik) *adj.* [Gr. *askētikos,* exercised, austere < *askein,* to work, train the body] of or characteristic of ascetics or asceticism; self-denying; austere: also **as·cet′i·cal** —*n.* **1.** a person who leads a life of contemplation and rigorous self-denial for religious purposes **2.** anyone who

lives with strict self-discipline and abstinence —*SYN.* see SEVERE —**as·cet′i·cal·ly** *adv.*

as·cet·i·cism (-ə siz′m) *n.* **1.** the practices or way of life of an ascetic **2.** the religious doctrine that one can reach a higher spiritual state by rigorous self-discipline and self-denial

Asch (ash), **Sho·lem** (shō′ləm) 1880–1957; U.S. novelist & playwright in Yiddish, born in Poland

As·cham (as′kəm), **Roger** 1515–68; Eng. writer & classical scholar; tutor of Queen Elizabeth I

as·ci (as′ī) *n., pl. of* ASCUS

as·cid·i·an (ə sid′ē ən) *n.* [Gr. *askidion:* see ff.] any of a class (Ascidiacea) of water animals of the subphylum Tunicata, usually sac-shaped with a tough, cellulose outer covering: sea squirts are ascidians

as·cid·i·um (-əm) *n., pl.* **-i·a** (-ə) [ModL. < Gr. *askidion,* dim. of *askos,* wineskin, bladder] *Bot.* a pitcherlike leaf or structure, as of the pitcher plant or bladderwort

as·ci·tes (ə sīt′ēz) *n.* [L. < Gr. *askitēs,* kind of dropsy < *askos:* see prec.] an accumulation of fluid in the peritoneal cavity of the abdomen

as·cle·pi·a·da·ceous (as klēp′ē ə dā′shəs) *adj.* [< L. *asclepias,* the common swallowwort (< Gr. *asklēpias* < *Asklēpios,* Asclepius) + -ACEOUS] belonging to the milkweed family of plants —**as·cle′pi·ad′** (-ad′) *n.*

As·cle·pi·a·de·an (as klēp′ē ə dē′ən) *adj.* [< Gr. *Asklēpiadēs,* Gr. poet, inventor of the verse] designating or of a form of classical verse consisting typically of a spondee, two (or three) choriambs, and an iamb —*n.* an Asclepiadean verse

As·cle·pi·us (as klēp′ē əs) [L. < Gr. *Asklēpios*] *Gr. Myth.* the god of healing and medicine, corresponding to the Roman Aesculapius

as·co·carp (as′kə kärp′) *n.* [< Gr. *askos,* bladder + -CARP] *Bot.* a structure shaped like a globe, cup, or disk, containing spore sacs; sac fruit of an ascomycetous fungus —**as′co·car′pous** (-kär′pəs) *adj.*

as·co·go·ni·um (as′kə gō′nē əm) *n., pl.* **-ni·a** (-ə) [ModL. < Gr. *askos,* bladder + *gonos,* offspring < *gignesthai,* to be born] *Bot.* the female gametangium, or archicarp, in an ascomycetous fungus

as·co·my·cete (as′kə mī sēt′) *n.* [< ModL. *Ascomycetes,* a class of fungi < Gr. *askos,* bladder + *mykēs* (gen. *mykētos*), fungus] any of a class (Ascomycetes) of fungi, including the mildews, yeasts, gill fungi, etc., which reproduce through spores developed in saclike structures (called *asci*) —**as′co·my·ce′tous** *adj.*

a·scor·bate (ə skôr′bāt) *n.* a salt of ascorbic acid

a·scor·bic acid (ə skôr′bik) [A-³ + SCORB(UTIC) + -IC] *same as* VITAMIN C

as·co·spore (as′kə spôr′) *n.* [< Gr. *askos,* bladder + SPORE] any of the spores in an ascus

as·cot (as′kət, -kät′) *n.* [A-] a famous horse-racing meet held annually at Ascot Heath, Berkshire, England **2.** a kind of necktie or scarf with very broad ends hanging from the knot, one upon the other: supposedly developed for wear at the Ascot

ASCOT

as·cribe (ə skrīb′) *vt.* **-cribed′, -crib′ing** [ME. *ascriben* (also *ascriven* < OFr. *ascriv-,* stem of *ascrire*) < L. *ascribere* < *ad-,* to + *scribere,* to write] **1.** to assign (*to* a supposed cause); impute; attribute **2.** to regard as belonging (*to*) or coming from someone [poems *ascribed* to Homer] —**as·crib′a·ble** *adj.*

SYN.—**ascribe,** in this comparison, implies assignment to someone of something that may reasonably be deduced [*to ascribe* a motive to someone]; **attribute** implies assignment of a quality, factor, or responsibility that may reasonably be regarded as applying [*to attribute* an error to carelessness]; **impute** usually implies the assignment of something unfavorable or accusatory [*to impute* evil to someone]; **assign** implies the placement of something in a particular category because of some quality, etc. attributed to it [*to assign* a poem to the 17th century]; **credit** implies belief in the possession by someone of some quality, etc. [*to credit* one with intelligence]; **attach** implies the connection of something with something else as being appropriate to it [different people *attach* different meanings to words]

as·crip·tion (ə skrip′shən) *n.* [L. *ascriptio* < pp. of *ascribere,* ASCRIBE] **1.** the act of ascribing or being ascribed **2.** a statement that ascribes; specif., a prayer or text ascribing glory to God

as·cus (as′kəs) *n., pl.* **as·ci** (as′ī) [ModL. < Gr. *askos,* bladder] in ascomycetous fungi, a sac in which spores are produced and meiosis occurs

as·dic, AS·DIC (az′dik) *n.* [**a**(llied) **s**(ubmarine) **d**(evices) **i**(nvestigation) **c**(ommittee)] a British submarine-detection apparatus similar to sonar

-ase (ās, āz) [abstracted < (DIAST)ASE] a *n.-forming suffix* denoting an enzyme, esp. one of vegetable origin [*amylase*]

a·sep·sis (ā sep′sis, ə-) *n.* **1.** the condition of being aseptic **2.** aseptic treatment or technique

a·sep·tic (-tik) *adj.* not septic; free from or keeping away disease-producing or putrefying microorganisms —**a·sep′ti·cal·ly** *adv.*

a·sex·u·al (ā sek′shoo wəl) *adj.* **1.** having no sex or sexual

organs; sexless **2.** designating or of reproduction without the union of male and female germ cells: budding, fission, etc. are types of asexual reproduction **—a·sex'u·al'i·ty** (-shoō wal'ə tē) *n.* **—a·sex'u·al·ly** *adv.*

As·gard (as'gärd, az'-) [ON. *Asgarthr < āss*, god + *garthr*, YARD²] *Norse Myth.* the home of the gods and slain heroes: also **As·garth** (äs'gär*th*)

ash¹ (ash) *n.* [ME. *asshe* (usually in pl.) < OE. *æsce* < IE. base **as-*, to burn, whence ARID, Goth. *azgo*, ON. *aske*] **1.** the white or grayish powder remaining after something has been thoroughly burned **2.** fine, volcanic lava **3.** the silvery-gray color of wood ash; pallor See also ASHES

ash² (ash) *n.* [ME. *asshe* < OE. *æsc* < IE. base *os-ko *ōsen, whence G. *esche*, L. *ornus* (mountain ash), ON. *askr*] **1.** any of a genus (*Fraxinus*) of timber and shade trees belonging to the olive family, having pinnate leaves, winged fruit, and tough, elastic wood with a straight, close grain **2.** the wood

a·shamed (ə shāmd') *adj.* [pp. of obs. *ashame*, to shame < ME. *aschamien*, to make ashamed < OE. *ascamian:* see SHAME] **1.** feeling shame because something bad, wrong, or foolish was done **2.** feeling humiliated or embarrassed, as from a sense of inadequacy or inferiority **3.** reluctant because fearing shame beforehand **—a·sham·ed·ly** (ə shā'mid lē) *adv.*

SYN.—ashamed implies embarrassment, and sometimes guilt, felt because of one's own or another's wrong or foolish behavior [*ashamed* of his tears]; **humiliated** implies a sense of being humbled or disgraced [*humiliated* by my failure]; **mortified** suggests humiliation so great as to seem almost fatal to one's pride or self-esteem [she was *mortified* by his obscenities]; **chagrined** suggests embarrassment coupled with irritation or regret over what might have been prevented [*chagrined* at his error] **—ANT.** proud

A·shan·ti (ə shän'tē, -shan'-) region in C Ghana: orig.: a native kingdom, it was a protectorate in the Gold Coast from 1901 to 1957: 9,700 sq. mi.; pop. 1,109,000; cap. Kumasi **—n. 1.** *pl.* **A·shan'ti, -tis** any member of the W African people of Ashanti **2.** the Akan dialect spoken by these people

ash blond 1. silvery blond or light brownish gray **2.** a person with hair of this color **—ash'-blond'** *adj.*

☆**ash·can** (ash'kan') *n.* **1.** a large can for ashes and trash **2.** naval slang for DEPTH CHARGE Also **ash can**

☆**Ashcan School** [orig.: hostile critical term] a group (formed c. 1908) of U.S. painters who promoted realistic painting based on the direct observation of everyday, esp. urban events

ash·en¹ (ash'ən) *adj.* **1.** of ashes **2.** like ashes, esp. in color; pale; pallid **—SYN.** see PALE¹

ash·en² (ash'ən) *adj.* [Archaic] **1.** of the ash tree **2.** made of its wood

Ash·er (ash'ər) *Bible* **1.** the eighth son of Jacob **2.** the tribe of Israel descended from him

ash·es (ash'iz) *n.pl.* [see ASH¹] **1.** the unburned particles and white or grayish powder remaining after a thing has been burned **2.** the part of the body left after cremation **3.** a dead person; human remains **4.** ruins or remains, as of a destroyed civilization

Ashe·ville (ash'vil) [after Samuel *Ashe* (1725–1813), governor of N.C.] city in W North Carolina: pop. 58,000

Ash·ke·lon (ash'kə län') ancient city in Palestine, on the Mediterranean

Ash·ke·naz·im (ash'kə naz'im; äsh'kə näz'im) *n.pl.*, *sing.* **-naz', -naz'i** (-ē) [Heb., pl. of *Ashkenāzi*, a German Jew, earlier, a German < *Ashkenaz*, name of an ancient kingdom (cf. Jer. 51:27), after *Ashkenaz*, second son of Gomer (cf. Gen. 10:3), prob. akin to Akkadian *Ishkuzai* (whence Gr. *Skythoi*, the Scythians)] the Jews who settled in middle and northern Europe after the Diaspora, or their descendants: distinguished from SEPHARDIM **—Ash'ke·naz'ic** *adj.*

Ash·kha·bad (äsh'khä bäd') capital of the Turkmen S.S.R. in the SC part, near the Iranian border: pop. 226,000

ash·lar, ash·ler (ash'lər) *n.* [ME. *assheler* < OFr. *aisseler* < *aissele*, shingle, dim. < *ais*, board < L. *assis*, board, akin to *asser*, beam, plank] **1.** a square, hewn stone used in building **2.** a thin, dressed, square stone used for facing masonry walls **3.** masonry made of either kind of ashlar

ash·man (ash'man') *n.*, *pl.* **-men'** (-men') ☆a man who hauls away ashes and trash

a·shore (ə shôr') *adv.*, *adj.* **1.** to or on the shore [rowing the boat *ashore*] **2.** to or on land [an old sailor in sad retirement *ashore*]

ash·ram (ash'rəm) *n.* [Sans. *āśrama < ā*, towards + *śrama*, fatigue, exhaustion, religious penance < IE. base **klem-*, tired, weak, whence W. *claf*, sick] a secluded place for a community of Hindus leading a life of simplicity and religious meditation

Ash·ton-un·der-Lyne (ash'tən un'dər līn') city in NW England, near Manchester: pop. 50,000

Ash·to·reth (ash'tə reth') [Heb.; ? akin to APHRODITE] the ancient Phoenician and Syrian goddess of love and fertility: identified with ASTARTE

ash·tray (ash'trā') *n.* a container for smokers' tobacco ashes: also **ash tray**

A·shur (ä'shoor) [Assyr.] **1.** *Assyr. Myth.* the chief deity, god of war and empire **2.** ancient city on the upper Tigris River: the original capital of Assyria **3.** Assyria: the original name

A·shur·ba·ni·pal (ä'shoor bän'i päl') ?–626? B.C.; king of Assyria (668?–626?)

Ash Wednesday the first day of Lent and seventh Wednesday before Easter: so called from the practice of putting ashes on the forehead as a sign of penitence

ash·y (ash'ē) *adj.* **ash'i·er, ash'i·est 1.** of, like, or covered with ashes **2.** of ash color; pale; pallid

A·sia (ā'zhə; *chiefly Brit.* -sha) largest continent: situated in the Eastern Hemisphere, bounded by the Arctic, Pacific, and Indian oceans, and separated from N Europe by the Ural Mountains: c. 16,900,000 sq. mi.; pop. c. 2,035,351,000

Asia Minor large peninsula in W Asia, between the Black Sea and the Mediterranean, including most of Asiatic Turkey: cf. ANATOLIA

A·sian (ā'zhən; *chiefly Brit.* -shən) *adj.* of or characteristic of Asia or its people **—n.** a native or inhabitant of Asia

Asian influenza pandemic influenza caused by a strain of the influenza virus first isolated in Singapore in 1957: also **Asian flu**

A·si·at·ic (ā'zhē at'ik) *adj.*, *n. same as* ASIAN, which is now generally the preferred term

Asiatic beetle a beetle (*Anomala orientalis*) of Asian origin, harmful to grasses

Asiatic cholera an acute, severe, infectious disease characterized by profuse diarrhea, intestinal pain, and dehydration

a·side (ə sīd') *adv.* [ME. < *on side*] **1.** on or to one side [pull the curtains *aside*] **2.** away; in reserve [put the book *aside* for me] **3.** out of the way; out of one's mind [lay the proposal *aside* temporarily] ☆**4.** apart; notwithstanding [joking *aside*, I mean it] **—n. 1.** words spoken by an actor in such a way that they are heard by the audience but supposedly not by the other actors **2.** a written digression [a novelist's *aside* to the reader] **—☆aside from 1.** with the exception of **2.** apart from; besides

as·i·nine (as'ə nīn) *adj.* [L. *asininus < asinus*, ass] of or like an ass; esp., having qualities regarded as characteristic of asses; stupid, silly, obstinate, etc. **—SYN.** see SILLY **—as'i·nine'ly** *adv.*

as·i·nin·i·ty (as'ə nin'ə tē) *n.* **1.** the quality or state of being asinine; stupidity **2.** *pl.* **-ties** an asinine act or remark

A·sir (ä sir') province of SW Saudi Arabia, on the Red Sea

-a·sis (ə sis, -səs) [L. < Gr.] a *n.-forming suffix* meaning a condition resembling or a condition characterized by [*elephantiasis, psoriasis*]

ask (ask, äsk) *vt.* [ME. *askien* < OE. *ascian* < IE. base **ais-*, to wish, desire, whence Sans. *ēṣati*, seeks, OHG. *eiscōn*, to inquire, demand] **1.** to use words in seeking the answer to (a question); try to find out about by inquiring **2.** to put a question to (a person); inquire of **3.** to request; solicit; beg **4.** to demand or expect as a price [they *ask* ten dollars for it] **5.** to be in need of or call for (a thing) **6.** to invite **7.** [Archaic] to publish (banns); also, to publish the banns of **—vi. 1.** to make a request (*for*) **2.** to inquire (*about, after,* or *for*) **3.** to behave in such a way as to appear to be looking (*for* trouble, punishment, etc.) **—ask'er** *n.* **—ask'ing** *n.*

SYN.—ask and the more formal **inquire** and **query** usually denote no more than the seeking of an answer or information, but **query** also often implies doubt as to the correctness of something [the printer *queried* the spelling of several words]; **question** and **interrogate** imply the asking of a series of questions [to *question* a witness, **interrogate** adding the further implication of systematic examination [to *interrogate* a prisoner of war]; **catechize** is equivalent to **interrogate** but implies the expectation of certain fixed answers, esp. with reference to religious doctrine; **quiz**, used esp. in schools, implies a short, selective questioning to test factual knowledge of some subject **—ANT. answer, tell**

a·skance (ə skans') *adv.* [ME. *ascaunce*; form < *ase quances < as(e)*, as + OFr. *quanses*, how if < VL. *quam si* < L. *quam*, how + *si*, if; meaning < ME. *askoin* < *a-*, on + *skwyn* < Du. *schuin*, sidewise] **1.** with a sidewise glance; obliquely **2.** with suspicion, disapproval, etc.

a·skant (ə skant') *adv.* [Archaic or Poet.] askance

as·kar·i (äs'kä rē, ə skär'ē) *n.* [Ar. '*askari*] a native African soldier or policeman, esp. one in the service of a colonial power

As·ke·lon, As·ka·lon (äs'kə län') *same as* ASHKELON

a·skew (ə skyoō') *adv.* [A-¹ + SKEW] to one side; awry; crookedly **—adj.** to one side; awry

☆**asking price** the price asked by a seller, esp. when he is willing to accept less after bargaining

a·slant (ə slant') *adv.* on a slant; slantingly; obliquely **—prep.** on a slant across **—adj.** slanting

a·sleep (ə slēp') *adj.* **1.** in a condition of sleep; sleeping **2.** inactive; dull; sluggish **3.** numb except for a prickly feeling [my arm is *asleep*] **4.** dead **—adv.** into a sleeping or inactive condition

a·slope (ə slōp') *adv.* slopingly; at a slant **—adj.** sloping

---

fat, āpe, cär; ten, ēven; is, bīte; gō, hôrn, toōl, look; oil, out; up, fur; get; joy; yet; chin; she; thin, then; zh, leisure; ŋ, ring; ə for *a* in *ago*, *e* in *agent*, *i* in *sanity*, *o* in *comply*, *u* in *focus*; ' as in *able* (ā'b'l); Fr. bal; ë, Fr. coeur; ö, Fr. feu; Fr. mon; ô, Fr. coq; ü, Fr. duc; r, Fr. cri; H, G. ich; kh, G. doch. See inside front cover. ☆ Americanism; ‡foreign; *hypothetical; <derived from

As·ma·ra (äs mä′rä) capital of Eritrea, in N Ethiopia: pop. 120,000

As·mo·de·us (az′mə dē′əs, as′-) [L. *Asmodaeus* < Gr. *Asmodaios* < Heb. *ashmadai*] an evil spirit or chief demon in Jewish legends

As·nières (ä nyer′) city in France: NW suburb of Paris: pop. 82,000

a·so·cial (ā sō′shəl) *adj.* 1. not social; not gregarious; characterized by withdrawal from others 2. showing little concern for the welfare of others; selfish —*SYN.* see UN-SOCIAL

A·so·ka (ə sōk′ə) ?-232 B.C.; king of India (273?-232); 1st Indian ruler to embrace Buddhism

A·so·san, A·so·san (ä′sō sän′) a large volcanic crater in C Kyushu, Japan, with five cones: highest cone, 5,223 ft.; crater, c. 15 mi. wide

asp¹ (asp) *n.* [ME. < OFr. *aspe* < L. *aspis* < Gr. *aspis*] any of several small, poisonous snakes of Africa, Arabia, and Europe, as the horned viper, common European viper, Egyptian cobra, etc.

asp² (asp) *n.* [Archaic] an aspen

as·par·a·gine (ə spar′ə jēn′, -sper′-) *n.* [Fr. < L. *asparagus* (see ASPARAGUS) + Fr. *-ine*, *-INE⁴*] a nonessential amino acid, $NH_2COCH_2CH(NH_2)COOH$, found in the sprouts of many seeds: it is a constituent of many proteins

as·par·a·gus (-gəs) *n.* [L. < Gr. *asparagos* < IE. base *sp(h)er(e)g-*, to spring up, sprout, whence Av. *sparegha-*, sprout, SPRING, SPARK¹] 1. any of a genus (*Asparagus*) of plants of the lily family, with small, scalelike leaves, many flat or needlelike branches, and whitish flowers 2. the tender shoots of one of these plants (*Asparagus officinalis*), used as a vegetable

as·par·tic acid (as pär′tik) [coined after prec.] a nonessential amino acid, $COOHCH_2CH(NH_2)COOH$ occurring in proteins in white prisms or colorless leaflets, used in organic synthesis

As·pa·si·a (as pā′zhē ə, -zhə) fl. 5th cent. B.C.; clever, influential woman of Athens; mistress of Pericles

A.S.P.C.A. American Society for the Prevention of Cruelty to Animals

as·pect (as′pekt) *n.* [ME. < L. *aspectus*, pp. of *aspicere*, to look at < *ad-*, to, at + *spicere*, *specere*, to look] 1. the way one appears; looks; mien 2. the appearance of a thing as seen from a specific point; view 3. the appearance or interpretation of an idea, problem, situation, etc. as considered from a specific viewpoint 4. a facing in a given direction 5. a side facing in a given direction; exposure [the eastern *aspect* of the house] 6. [Archaic] a glance; gaze 7. *Astrol.* the position of stars in relation to each other or to the observer, as it supposedly influences human affairs 8. *Gram.* the form that a verb takes to indicate duration or completion of action: e.g., he *was eating* (imperfect aspect); he *ate* (perfect aspect) 9. *Physics* the position of a plane (flat surface) in relation to a liquid or gaseous substance through which it is moving or which is moving past it —*SYN.* see APPEARANCE, PHASE

as·pen (as′pən) *n.* [ME. *aspe* (aspen, in compounds) < OE. *æspe* < IE. base *apsa*, whence Lith. *apušė*, OPrus. *abse*] any of several kinds of poplar tree (genus *Populus*) with flattened leafstalks that cause the leaves to flutter in the least breeze —*adj.* of or like an aspen; esp., [Poet.] fluttering, trembling

as·per (as′pər) *n.* [< Fr. *aspre* < MedGr. *aspron* < L. *asper* (*nummus*), rough (coin)] a former silver coin of Turkey and Egypt, later a money of account equal to 1/120 of a piaster

As·per·ges (ə sper′jez, ə spur′jēz) *n.* [2d pers. sing., fut. indic., of L. *aspergere*: see ASPERSE] *R.C.Ch.* 1. [*also a-*] the sprinkling of altar, clergy, and people with holy water before High Mass 2. a hymn sung during this ceremony, beginning *Asperges me*

as·per·gil·lo·sis (as′pər ji lō′sis) *n.* an infection caused by a fungus (genus *Aspergillus*), characterized by small, inflamed lesions of the skin, respiratory tract, bones, etc.

as·per·gil·lum (as′pər jil′əm) *n.*, *pl.* -**gil′la** (-ə), -**gil′lums** [ML. < L. *aspergere* (see ASPERSE) + neut. dim. *-illum*] *R.C.Ch.* a brush or perforated container for sprinkling holy water: also **as′per·gill** (-jil)

as·per·gil·lus (-jil′əs) *n.*, *pl.* -**gil′li** (-ī) [ModL.: see ASPERGILLUM: so named from appearing similar to the aspergillum] any of a genus (*Aspergillus*) of fungi bearing chains of spores attached to stalks on the swollen end of a threadlike branch

as·per·i·ty (as per′ə tē, ə sper′-) *n.*, *pl.* -**ties** [ME. & OFr. *asprete* < L. *asperitas*, roughness < *asper*, rough < IE. *apo-spero-*, repellent < *apo-*, away + *sper-*, to flick away, push] 1. roughness or harshness, as of surface, sound, weather, etc. 2. harshness or sharpness of temper

as·perse (ə spurs′) *vt.* -**persed′**, -**pers′ing** [< L. *aspersus*, pp. of *aspergere*, to sprinkle on < *ad-*, to + *spargere*, to sprinkle, strew] 1. [Rare] to sprinkle water on, as in baptizing 2. to spread false or damaging charges against; besmirch the reputation of; slander

as·per·sion (ə spur′zhən, -shən) *n.* [L. *aspersio*: see ASPERSE] 1. a sprinkling with water, as in baptizing 2. the act of defaming 3. a damaging or disparaging remark; slander; innuendo

as·per·so·ri·um (as′pər sôr′ē əm) *n.*, *pl.* -**ri·a** (-ə), -**ri·ums** (-əmz) [ML. < L. *aspersus*: see ASPERSE] *R.C.Ch.* 1. a basin, font, etc. for holy water 2. *same as* ASPERGILLUM

as·phalt (as′fôlt) *n.* [ML. *asphaltus* < Gr. *asphaltos*, prob. < *a-*, not + *sphallein*, to cause to fall, injure: ? so named because of use as protective substance for walls] 1. a brown or black tarlike substance, a variety of bitumen, found in a natural state or obtained by evaporating petroleum 2. a mixture of this with sand or gravel, for cementing, paving, roofing, etc. —*vt.* to pave, roof, etc. with asphalt —**as·phal′tic** *adj.*

as·phal·tite (as′fôl tīt′) *n.* a solid, complex hydrocarbon with a relatively high melting point, found in natural deposits: a purer form of asphalt

☆**asphalt jungle** the crowded city, esp. regarded as a place of predatory behavior in a struggle for survival

as·phal·tum (-fôl′təm) *n. same as* ASPHALT

as·pho·del (as′fə del′) *n.* [L. *asphodelus* < Gr. *asphodelos*] 1. any of a genus (*Asphodeline*) of plants of the lily family, having fleshy roots, narrow leaves, and white or yellow flowers like lilies 2. any of a genus (*Asphodelus*) of plants like these, but with leafless flower stems

as·phyx·i·a (as fik′sē ə) *n.* [ModL. < Gr., a stopping of the pulse < *a-*, not + *sphyzein*, to throb] loss of consciousness as a result of too little oxygen and too much carbon dioxide in the blood: suffocation causes asphyxia

as·phyx·i·ant (-ənt) *adj.* causing or tending to cause asphyxia —*n.* an asphyxiant substance or condition

as·phyx·i·ate (-āt′) *vt.* -**at′ed**, -**at′ing** 1. to cause asphyxia in 2. to suffocate —*vi.* to undergo asphyxia —**as·phyx′i·a′tion** *n.* —**as·phyx′i·a′tor** *n.*

as·pic (as′pik) *n.* [Fr. < OFr. *aspe*, ASP¹; *-ic* by association with Pr. *espic*, a plant used in treating snake bite] 1. [Archaic] an asp 2. [Fr., apparently so named from its asplike colorfulness] a jelly of meat juice, tomato juice, etc., molded, often with meat, seafood, etc., and eaten as a relish

as·pi·dis·tra (as′pə dis′trə) *n.* [ModL. < Gr. *aspis*, a shield + *astron*, a star] any of a genus (*Aspidistra*) of plants of the lily family, with dark, inconspicuous flowers and stiff, glossy, evergreen leaves: cultivated as a house plant

as·pir·ant (as′pər ənt, ə spīr′ənt) *adj.* [L. *aspirans*, prp. of *aspirare*: see ASPIRE] aspiring —*n.* a person who aspires, as after honors, high position, etc.

as·pi·rate (as′pə rāt′; *for n. & adj.* -pər it) *vt.* -**rat′ed**, -**rat′ing** [< L. *aspiratus*, pp. of *aspirare*: see ASPIRE] 1. to begin (a word) or precede (a sonorous speech sound) by the gradual glottal closure represented by English *h* 2. to follow (a consonant, esp. a stop consonant, as *p*, *t*, and *k*) with a puff of suddenly released breath 3. to suck in or draw in, as by inhaling [*aspirating* dust into the lungs] 4. *Med.* to remove (fluid or gas), as from a body cavity, by suction —*n.* 1. the speech sound represented by English *h* or Greek ʻ (see ROUGH BREATHING) 2. an expiratory breath puff such as follows initial *p*, *t*, *k* in English —*adj.* preceded or followed by an aspirate: also **as′pi·rat′ed**

as·pi·ra·tion (as′pə rā′shən) *n.* [L. *aspiratio*, a blowing or breathing < pp. of *aspirare*, ASPIRE] 1. *a)* strong desire or ambition, as for advancement, honor, etc. *b)* the thing so desired 2. a breathing in, as of dust into the lungs 3. *Med.* removal of fluid or gas by suction, as from a body cavity 4. *Phonet.* *a)* the act of pronouncing with an aspirate *b)* an aspirate

as·pi·ra·tor (as′pə rāt′ər) *n.* [see ASPIRATE] any apparatus for moving air, fluids, etc. by suction; specif., an apparatus using suction to remove a fluid or gas from a body cavity

as·pi·ra·to·ry (ə spīr′ə tôr′ē) *adj.* [ASPIRAT(E) + -ORY] of or suited for breathing or suction

as·pire (ə spīr′) *vi.* -**pired′**, -**pir′ing** [ME. *aspiren* < L. *aspirare*, to breathe upon, aspire to < *ad-*, to + *spirare*, to breathe] 1. to be ambitious (*to* get or do something, esp. something lofty or grand); yearn or seek (*after*) 2. [Archaic] to rise high; tower —**as·pir′er** *n.*

as·pi·rin (as′pər in, as′prin) *n.* [G. < a(*cetyl*) + *spir*(*säure*), salicylic acid (< ModL. *Spiraea*, SPIRAEA + G. *säure*, acid: so named because found in spiraea blossoms) + -IN¹] 1. a white, crystalline powder, acetylsalicylic acid, $C_9H_8O_4$, used for reducing fever, relieving headaches, etc. 2. a tablet of this

as·pir·ing (ə spīr′iŋ) *adj.* striving for or desirous of reaching some (usually lofty) goal —*SYN.* see AMBITIOUS —**as·pir′ing·ly** *adv.*

a·squint (ə skwint′) *adv.*, *adj.* [ME. *of skwyn* (see ASKANCE): infl. by SQUINT] with a squint; out of the corner of the eye

As·quith (as′kwith), **Herbert Henry,** 1st Earl of Oxford and Asquith, 1852-1928; Brit. statesman; prime minister (1908-16)

ass¹ (as) *n.* [ME. *asse* < OE. *assa*, *assen* < L. *asinus*] 1. any of a genus (*Equus*) of animals resembling horses but having longer ears and a shorter mane, as the common wild ass (*Equus asinus*) of Africa: donkeys and burros are domesticated asses: in fables the ass is represented as obstinate and stupid 2. a stupid or silly person; fool

ass² (as) *n.* [var. of ARSE] [Slang] the buttocks: a vulgar term

as·sa·fet·i·da, as·sa·foet·i·da (as′ə fet′ə də) *n. same as* ASAFETIDA

as·sa·gai (as′ə gī′) *n.* [Port. *azagaia* < Ar. *az-zaghāyah* < *az*, for *al*, the + *zaghāyah*, spear, of Berber origin] 1. a slender spear or javelin with an iron tip, used in southern Africa 2. a tree (*Curtisea faginea*) of the dogwood family, whose hard wood is used to make such spears —*vt.* to pierce with an assagai

as·sai¹ (ə sī′) *n.* [Braz. Port. *assahy* < Tupi name] any of a genus (*Euterpe*, esp. *Euterpe oleracea*) of Brazilian palms bearing a small, dark-purple, fleshy, edible fruit

‡**as·sa·i²** (äs sä′ē) *adv.* [It.] *Music* very: used in indicating tempo [*adagio assai*]

as·sail (ə sāl′) *vt.* [ME. *assailen* < OFr. *asaillir* < VL. *assalire*, for L. *assilire*, to leap on < *ad*, to + *salire*, to leap] 1. to attack physically and violently; assault 2. to attack with arguments, questions, doubts, etc. 3. to begin working on (a task, problem, etc.) with vigor and determination 4. to have a forceful effect on [a loud noise *assailed* his ears] —*SYN.* see ATTACK —**as·sail′a·ble** *adj.* —**as·sail′er** *n.* —**as·sail′ment** *n.*

as·sail·ant (-ənt) *n.* [Fr. *assaillant*, prp. of *assaillir*, ASSAIL] a person who assails or attacks; attacker

As·sam (ə sam′, as′am) state of NE India, on the borders of Bhutan and East Pakistan: 47,091 sq. mi.; pop. 11,873,000; cap. Shillong

As·sa·mese (as′ə mēz′, -mēs′) *adj.* of Assam, its people, language, etc. —*n.* 1. *pl.* **-mese′** a native or inhabitant of Assam 2. the Indic language of the Assamese

as·sas·sin (ə sas′′n) *n.* [Fr. < Ar. *hashshāshīn*, hashish users < *hashish*, hemp] 1. [A-] a member of a secret sect of Moslems who killed Christian leaders during the Crusades, supposedly while under the influence of hashish 2. a murderer who strikes suddenly and by surprise: now generally used of the killer of a politically important person

as·sas·si·nate (-āt′) *vt.* **-nat′ed, -nat′ing** [< ML. *assassinatus*, pp. of *assassinare*, to kill < *assassinus*, ASSASSIN] 1. to murder (esp. a politically important person) by surprise attack 2. to harm or ruin (one's reputation, etc.), as by slander, vilification, etc. —*SYN.* see KILL¹ —**as·sas′si·na′tion** *n.*

assassin bug any of a number of large, often brightly colored bugs (family Reduviidae) that kill and devour other insects

as·sault (ə sôlt′) *n.* [ME. *assaut* < OFr. *assaut, assalt* < VL. *assaltus* < L. *ad*, to + *saltare*, to leap] 1. a violent attack, either physical or verbal 2. rape: a euphemism 3. *Law* an unlawful threat or unsuccessful attempt to do physical harm to another, causing a present fear of immediate harm 4. *Mil.* a) a sudden attack upon a fortified place b) the close-combat phase of an attack —*vt., vi.* 1. to make an assault (upon) 2. to rape —*SYN.* see ATTACK —**as·sault′ive** *adj.*

assault and battery *Law* the carrying out of threatened physical harm or violence; an intentional and unlawful beating

as·say (as′ā, a sā′; *for v.* a sā′, ə-) *n.* [ME. & Anglo-Fr. *assai* < OFr. *essai*, trial, test < L. *exagium*, a weighing < *ex-*, out + *agere*, to transact, ACT] 1. an examination or testing 2. the analysis of an ore, alloy, drug, etc. to determine the nature, proportion, or purity of the ingredients 3. a substance to be thus tested or analyzed 4. the result or report of such an analysis 5. [Archaic] an attempt —*vt.* 1. to make an assay of; test; analyze 2. to try; attempt —☆*vi.* to be shown by analysis to contain a specified proportion of some component [this ore *assays* high in gold] —**as·say′er** *n.*

as·se·gai (as′ə gī′) *n., vt. same as* ASSAGAI

as·sem·blage (ə sem′blij) *n.* [Fr. < *assembler*, ASSEMBLE] 1. an assembling or being assembled 2. a group of persons or things gathered together; assembly 3. a form of art involving the assembly and arrangement of unrelated objects, parts, and materials in a kind of sculptural collage

as·sem·ble (-b′l) *vt., vi.* **-bled, -bling** [ME. *assemblen* < OFr. *assembler* < VL. *adsimulare* < L. *ad-*, to + *simul*, together] 1. to gather into a group; collect ☆2. to fit or put together the parts of (a machine, etc.) —*SYN.* see GATHER —**as·sem′bler** *n.*

as·sem·bly (-blē) *n., pl.* **-blies** [ME. *assemble* < OFr. *assemblee* < *assembler*, ASSEMBLE] 1. an assembling or being assembled 2. a group of persons gathered together, as for worship, instruction, entertainment, etc. 3. a legislative body; specif., [A-] in some States of the U.S., the lower house of the legislature 4. a fitting together of parts to make a whole, as in manufacturing automobiles, etc. 5. the parts to be thus fitted together 6. a call, as by bugle or drum, for soldiers to assemble in ranks

☆**assembly line** in many factories, an arrangement whereby each worker performs a specialized operation in assembling the work as it is passed along, often on a slowly moving belt or track

as·sem·bly·man (-mən) *n., pl.* **-men** (-mən, -men′) a member of a legislative assembly; specif., [A-] in some States of the U.S., a member of the lower house of the legislature

as·sent (ə sent′) *vi.* [ME. *assenten* < OFr. *assenter* < L. *assentari* < *assentire* < *ad-*, to + *sentire*, to feel] to express acceptance of an opinion, proposal, etc.; agree (*to*); concur —*n.* consent or agreement; concurrence —*SYN.* see CONSENT —**as·sent′er** *n.*

as·sen·ta·tion (as′en tā′shən) *n.* [L. *assentatio* < pp. of *assentari*, ASSENT] immediate and usually flattering or hypocritical assent

as·sert (ə surt′) *vt.* [< L. *assertus*, pp. of *asserere*, to join to,

claim < *ad-*, to + *serere*, to join, bind] 1. to state positively; declare; affirm 2. to maintain or defend (rights, claims, etc.) —**assert oneself** to insist on one's rights, or on being recognized —**as·sert′er, as·ser′tor** *n.*

SYN.—to **assert** is to state positively with great confidence but with no objective proof [he *asserted* that man's nature would never change]; to **declare** is to assert openly or formally, often in the face of opposition [they *declared* their independence]; **affirm** implies deep conviction in one's statement and the unlikelihood of denial by another [I cannot *affirm* that he was there]; **aver** connotes implicit confidence in the truth of one's statement from one's own knowledge of the matter; **avouch** implies firsthand knowledge or authority on the part of the speaker; **warrant**, in this comparison, is colloquial, and implies positiveness by the speaker [I *warrant* he'll be late again] —*ANT.* deny, controvert

as·ser·tion (ə sur′shən) *n.* [L. *assertio*, formal declaration: see ASSERT] 1. the act of asserting 2. something asserted; positive statement; declaration

as·ser·tive (-tiv) *adj.* [ML. *assertivus*] characterized by assertion; positive or confident in a persistent way —*SYN.* see AGGRESSIVE —**as·ser′tive·ly** *adv.* —**as·ser′tive·ness** *n.*

asses' bridge *same as* PONS ASINORUM

as·sess (ə ses′) *vt.* [ME. *assessen* < OFr. *assesser* < ML. *assessare*, to impose a tax, set a rate < L. *assessus*, pp. of *assidere*, to sit beside, assist (in office), in ML., to assess < *ad-*, to + *sedere*, to SIT¹] 1. to set an estimated value on (property, etc.) for taxation 2. to set the amount of (a tax, a fine, damages, etc.) 3. to impose a fine, tax, or special payment on (a person or property) 4. to impose (an amount) as a fine, tax, etc. 5. to estimate or determine the significance, importance, or value of; evaluate

as·sess·ment (-mənt) *n.* 1. the act of assessing 2. an amount assessed See also SPECIAL ASSESSMENT

as·ses·sor (-ər) *n.* [ME. & OFr. *assessour* < L. *assessor* < *assessus:* see ASSESS] 1. a person who sets valuations, as on property, for taxation 2. an assistant; esp., an advisory assistant, as an expert in some field serving as a consultant to a judge —**as·ses·so·ri·al** (as′ə ses′ē əl) *adj.*

as·set (as′et) *n.* [earlier *assets* < Anglo Fr. *assetz* (in legal phrase *aver assetz*, to have enough) < OFr. *assez*, enough < VL. *ad satis*, sufficient < L. *ad*, to + *satis*, enough] 1. anything owned that has exchange value 2. a valuable or desirable thing to have [charm is her chief *asset*] 3. [*pl.*] *Accounting* all the entries on a balance sheet showing the entire resources of a person or business, tangible and intangible, as accounts and notes receivable, cash, inventory, equipment, real estate, good will, etc. 4. [*pl.*] *Law* a) property, as of a business, bankrupt, etc. b) the property of a deceased person available to his estate for the payment of debts and legacies

as·sev·er·ate (ə sev′ə rāt′) *vt.* **-at′ed, -at′ing** [< L. *asseveratus*, pp. of *asseverare*, to assert strongly < *ad-*, to + *severus*, earnest, severe] to state seriously or positively; assert —**as·sev′er·a′tion** *n.*

As·shur (ä′shoor) *same as* ASHUR

as·sib·i·late (ə sib′ə lāt′) *vt.* **-lat′ed, -lat′ing** [AS- + SIBILATE] to substitute a sibilant sound for in pronouncing [to *assibilate* the *t* of *bastion* (bas′chən)]

as·si·du·i·ty (as′ə dyōō′ə tē, -dōō′-) *n., pl.* **-ties** [L. *assiduitas*, constant presence < *assidere*, to assist: see ASSESS] 1. the quality or condition of being assiduous; diligence 2. [*pl.*] constant personal attention

as·sid·u·ous (ə sij′oo wəs) *adj.* [L. *assiduus:* see prec.] 1. done with constant and careful attention 2. diligent; persevering —*SYN.* see BUSY —**as·sid′u·ous·ly** *adv.* —**as·sid′u·ous·ness** *n.*

as·sign (ə sīn′) *vt.* [ME. *assignen* < OFr. *assigner* < L. *assignare*, to mark out, allot < *ad-*, to + *signare*, SIGN] 1. to set apart or mark for a specific purpose; designate [assign a day for the meeting] 2. to place at some task or duty; appoint [I was *assigned* to watch the road] 3. to give out as a task; allot [the teacher *assigned* a new lesson] 4. to ascribe; attribute [jealousy was *assigned* as the motive for the crime] 5. *Law* to transfer (a claim, right, property, etc.) to another —*vi.* to transfer property, etc. to another —*n.* [usually *pl.*] an assignee —*SYN.* see ALLOT, ASCRIBE —**as·sign′a·bil′i·ty** (ə bil′ə ti) *n.* —**as·sign′a·ble** *adj.* —**as·sign′er,** *Law* **as·sign′or** (, ôr′) *n.*

as·sig·nat (as′ig nat′; *Fr.* à sē nyà′) *n.* [Fr. < L. *assignatus*, pp. of *assignare*, ASSIGN] a piece of paper currency issued during the French Revolution with confiscated lands as the security

as·sig·na·tion (as′ig nā′shən) *n.* [ME. & OFr. *assignacion* < L. *assignatio* < pp. of *assignare*, ASSIGN] 1. an assigning or being assigned 2. anything assigned 3. an appointment to meet, esp. one made secretly by lovers; tryst; rendezvous

as·sign·ee (ə sī′nē′) *n.* [Fr. *assigné:* see ASSIGN] *Law* 1. a person to whom a claim, right, property, etc. is transferred 2. a person appointed to act for another

as·sign·ment (ə sīn′mənt) *n.* 1. an assigning or being assigned; appointment; allotment 2. anything assigned or allotted, as a lesson, task, etc. 3. *Law* a) a transfer of a claim, right, property, etc. b) a paper, as a deed, authorizing this —*SYN.* see TASK

as·sim·i·late (ə sim′ə lāt′) *vt.* **-lat′ed, -lat′ing** [< L.

assimilatus, pp. of *assimilare* < *ad-,* to + *similare,* to make similar to < *similis,* like] **1.** to change (food) into a form that can be taken up by, and made part of, the body tissues; absorb into the body **2.** to absorb and incorporate into one's thinking **3.** to absorb (groups of different cultures) into the main cultural body **4.** to make like or alike; cause to resemble (with *to*) **5.** [Now Rare] to compare or liken **6.** *Linguis.* to cause to undergo assimilation —*vi.* **1.** to become like or alike **2.** to be absorbed and incorporated —**as·sim'i·la·ble** (-ə lə b'l) *adj.*

as·sim·i·la·tion (ə sim'ə lā'shən) *n.* [L. *assimilatio*] an assimilating or being assimilated; specif., *a)* the cultural absorption of a minority group into the main cultural body *b) Phonet.* the process whereby a sound, influenced by a contiguous or neighboring sound, tends to become like it in position and type of articulation [the *p* in *cupboard* has been lost by *assimilation* to *b*] *c) Physiol.* the change of digested food into the protoplasm of an animal; also, the absorption and incorporation of nutritive elements by plants, as in the process of photosynthesis

as·sim·i·la·tion·ism (-iz'm) *n.* the policy of completely absorbing minority cultural groups into the main cultural body, esp. by intermarriage —**as·sim'i·la'tion·ist** *n.*

as·sim·i·la·tive (ə sim'ə lāt'iv) *adj.* of or causing assimilation; assimilating: also **as·sim·i·la·to·ry** (ə sim'/'lə tôr'ē)

As·sin·i·boine (ə sin'ə boin') [< Fr. < Ojibwa, name of a Dakota tribe, lit., "one who cooks with heated stones"] river in SC Canada flowing from E Saskatchewan through S Manitoba into the Red River at Winnipeg: c. 600 mi.

As·si·si (ə sēs'ē; *It.* äs sē'zē) town in C Italy: birthplace of St. Francis: pop. 25,000

as·sist (ə sist') *vt.* [ME. *assisten* < OFr. *assister* < L. *assistere* < *ad-,* to + *sistere,* to make stand < *stare,* to STAND] **1.** to give help to; aid **2.** to work with as a helper or assistant —*vi.* to give help; aid —*n.* **1.** an instance or act of helping **2.** *Baseball* the act of a player who throws or deflects a batted ball in such a way that a teammate can make a putout **3.** *Ice Hockey* the act of a player who passes the puck in such a way that a teammate can score a goal —*SYN.* see HELP —**assist at** to be present at; attend

as·sis·tance (ə sis'təns) *n.* [ME. & OFr. < ML. *assistentia:* see ASSIST] the act of assisting or the help given; aid

as·sis·tant (-tənt) *adj.* [ME. *assistent* < prp. of L. *assistere*] assisting; helping; that serves as a helper —*n.* **1.** a person who assists or serves in a subordinate position; helper **2.** a thing that aids

☆**assistant professor** a college teacher ranking above an instructor and below an associate professor

As·siut (ä syōōt') *same as* ASYUT

as·size (ə sīz') *n.* [ME. & OFr. *assise,* court session < *asseoir* < L. *assidere:* see ASSESS] **1.** orig., a legislative assembly or any of its decrees **2.** [*pl.*] court sessions held periodically in each county of England to try civil and criminal cases **3.** [*pl.*] the time or place of such sessions **4.** an inquest, the writ instituting it, or the verdict **5.** [Archaic] *a)* a law regulating standards of price, measure, weight, ingredients, etc. for goods to be sold *b)* these standards as formerly prescribed

assn. association

assoc. **1.** associate **2.** associated **3.** association

as·so·ci·a·ble (ə sō'shē ə b'l, -shə b'l) *adj.* [Fr.] that can be associated or connected in the mind

as·so·ci·ate (ə sō'shē āt', -sē-; *for n. & adj., usually* -it) *vt.* **-at'ed, -at'ing** [< L. *associatus,* pp. of *associare,* to join to, unite with < *ad-,* to + *sociare,* to join, unite with < *socius,* companion] **1.** to join together; connect; combine **2.** to bring (a person) into relationship with oneself or another as companion, partner, friend, etc. **3.** to connect in the mind [to *associate* rain with grief] —*vi.* **1.** to join (with another or others) as a companion, partner, friend, etc. **2.** to join together; unite —*n.* **1.** a person with whom one is associated; friend, partner, fellow worker, etc. **2.** a member of less than full status, as of a society, institute, etc. **3.** anything joined with another thing or things ☆**4.** a degree or certificate granted by a junior college to those who have completed the regular two-year course [an *Associate* in (or of) Arts] —*adj.* **1.** joined with others in some venture, work, etc. [an *associate* justice] **2.** having less than full status [an *associate* membership] **3.** accompanying; connected

SYN.—**associate** refers to a person who is frequently in one's company, usually because of some work or project shared in common [business *associates*]; **colleague** denotes a fellow worker, esp. in one of the professions, and may or may not imply a close, personal relationship [his *colleagues* at the university]; **companion** always refers to a person who actually accompanies one and usually implies a close, personal relationship [a dinner *companion,* the *companions* of one's youth]; **comrade** refers to a close associate and implies a sharing in activities and fortunes [comrades in arms]; **ally** now usually refers to a government joined with another or others in a common pursuit, esp. war; a **confederate** is one who joins with another or others for some common purpose, specif. in some unlawful act; an **accomplice** is one who unites with others, either as a principal or a subordinate, with criminal intent to commit an offense See also JOIN

☆**associate professor** a college teacher ranking above an assistant professor and below a full professor

as·so·ci·a·tion (ə sō'sē ā'shən, -shē-) *n.* [ML. *associatio,* a joining with: see ASSOCIATE] **1.** the act of associating **2.**

the state of being associated; companionship; fellowship; partnership **3.** an organization of persons having common interests, purposes, etc.; society; league **4.** a connection in the mind between ideas, sensations, memories, etc. **5.** the use of such connections as a literary device or psycho-analytic technique **6.** a group of plants, often of several species or genera, living together in the same environment and exhibiting a basic uniformity **7.** *Chem.* the joining of two or more molecules of the same or different substances into a larger aggregate, as in polymerization —**as·so'ci·a'tion·al** *adj.*

association football soccer: so called from the British controlling body, the National Football Association

as·so·ci·a·tive (ə sō'shē āt'iv, -sē-; -shə tiv) *adj.* [ML. *associativus*] **1.** of, characterized by, or causing association, as of ideas **2.** *Math.* of or pertaining to an operation in which the result is the same regardless of the way the elements are grouped, as, in addition, $2 + (3 + 4) = (2 + 3) + 4$ and, in multiplication, $2(3 \times 4) = (2 \times 3)4$

as·soil (ə soil') *vt.* [ME. *assoilen* < OFr. *assoil,* pres. indic. form of *assoldre* < L. *absolvere,* ABSOLVE] [Archaic] **1.** to absolve or acquit **2.** to atone for

as·so·nance (as'ə nəns) *n.* [Fr. < L. *assonans,* prp. of *assonare,* to sound to < *ad-,* to + *sonare,* to sound] **1.** likeness of sound, as in a series of words or syllables **2.** a partial rhyme in which the stressed vowel sounds are alike but the consonant sounds are unlike, as in *late* and *make* —**as'so·nant** (-nənt) *adj., n.*

as·sort (ə sôrt') *vt.* [OFr. *assorter* < *a-* (L. *ad*), to + *sorte,* SORT] **1.** to separate into classes according to sorts or kinds; classify **2.** to supply with an assortment of goods —*vi.* **1.** to be of the same sort; match or harmonize (*with*) **2.** to associate or consort (*with*) —**as·sort'a·tive** (-ə tiv) *adj.* —**as·sort'er** *n.*

as·sort·ed (-id) *adj.* **1.** of different sorts; of various kinds; miscellaneous **2.** sorted into groups according to kind **3.** matched [a poorly *assorted* pair]

as·sort·ment (-mənt) *n.* **1.** an assorting or being assorted; classification **2.** an assorted, or miscellaneous, group or collection; variety

As·souan (ä swän') *same as* ASWAN

ASSR, A.S.S.R. Autonomous Soviet Socialist Republic

asst. assistant

as·suage (ə swāj') *vt.* **-suaged', -suag'ing** [ME. *aswagen* < OFr. *assuagier* < L. *ad,* to + *suavis,* SWEET] **1.** to lessen (pain, distress, etc.); allay **2.** to calm (passion, anger, etc.); pacify **3.** to satisfy or slake (thirst, appetite, etc.) —*SYN.* see RELIEVE —**as·suage'ment** *n.*

As·suan (ä swän') *same as* ASWAN

as·sua·sive (ə swā'siv) *adj.* [< ASSUAGE, after PERSUASIVE] soothing; allaying

as·sume (ə sōōm', -syōōm') *vt.* **-sumed', -sum'ing** [ME. *assumen* < L. *assumere,* to take up, claim < *ad-,* to + *sumere,* to take] **1.** to take on or put on (the appearance, form, role, etc. of) **2.** to seize; usurp [to *assume* control] **3.** to take upon oneself; undertake [to *assume* an obligation] **4.** to take for granted; suppose (something) to be a fact **5.** to pretend to have; feign [to *assume* an air of innocence] **6.** [Archaic] *a)* to take in or receive *b)* to take into association —**as·sum'a·ble** *adj.* —**as·sum'er** *n.*

SYN.—**assume** implies the putting on of a false appearance but suggests a harmless or excusable motive [an *assumed* air of bravado]; **pretend** and **feign** both imply a profession or display of what is false, the more literary **feign** sometimes suggesting an elaborately contrived situation [to *pretend* not to hear, to *feign* deafness]; to **affect** is to make a show of being, having, using, wearing, etc., usually for effect [to *affect* a British accent]; **simulate** emphasizes the imitation of typical signs involved in assuming an appearance or characteristic not one's own [to *simulate* interest] See also PRESUME

as·sumed (ə sōōmd', -syōōmd') *adj.* **1.** pretended; put on; fictitious **2.** taken for granted

as·sum·ing (ə sōō'miŋ, -syōō'-) *adj.* taking too much for granted; presumptuous

as·sump·sit (ə sump'sit) *n.* [L., he has undertaken; 3d pers. sing., perf. indic., of *assumere,* ASSUME] *Law* **1.** an agreement or promise, written, spoken, or implied, and not under seal **2.** an action to recover damages for the non-fulfillment of such an agreement

as·sump·tion (ə sump'shən) *n.* [ME. *assumpcioun* < L. *assumptio* < pp. of *assumere,* ASSUME] **1.** a supposed bodily ascent into heaven **2.** [A-] *R.C.Ch. a)* the dogma of the taking up of the body and soul of the Virgin Mary into heaven after her death *b)* a church festival on August 15 celebrating this **3.** the act of assuming; a taking upon oneself, taking over, or taking for granted **4.** anything taken for granted; supposition **5.** presumption —**as·sump'tive** *adj.*

As·sur (ä'soor) *same as* ASHUR

as·sur·ance (ə shoor'əns) *n.* [ME. *assuraunce* < OFr. *asseurance* < ML. *assecurantia*] **1.** the act of assuring **2.** the state of being assured; sureness; confidence; certainty **3.** something said or done to inspire confidence, as a promise, positive statement, etc.; guarantee **4.** belief in one's own abilities; self-confidence **5.** impudent forwardness; presumption **6.** [Chiefly Brit.] insurance —*SYN.* see CERTAINTY, CONFIDENCE

As·sur·ba·ni·pal (ä'soor bän'i päl') *same as* ASHUR-BANIPAL

as·sure (ə shoor′) *vt.* **-sured′, -sur′ing** [ME. *assuren* < OFr. *asseurer* < ML. *assecurare* < L. *ad*, to + *securus*, SECURE] **1.** to make (a person) sure of something; convince **2.** to give confidence to; reassure [the news *assured* us] **3.** to declare to or promise confidently [I *assure* you I'll be there] **4.** to make (a doubtful thing) certain; guarantee **5.** to make safe or secure **6.** [Brit.] to insure against loss

as·sured (ə shoord′) *adj.* **1.** made sure; certain **2.** confident; sure of oneself **3.** insured —*n.* **1.** the person to whom an insurance policy is payable **2.** the person whose life or property is insured —**as·sur·ed·ly** (ə shoor′id lē) *adv.* —**as·sur′ed·ness** *n.*

as·sur·er (ə shoor′ər) *n.* a person or thing that gives assurance; specif., [Brit.] an insurance underwriter

as·sur·gent (ə sur′jənt) *adj.* [L. *assurgens*, prp. of *assurgere*, to rise up, swell < *ad*-, to + *surgere*, to rise] **1.** rising **2.** *Bot. same as* ASCENDING

Assyr. Assyrian

As·syr·i·a (ə sir′ē ə) ancient empire in SW Asia in the region of the upper Tigris River: at its height (7th cent. B.C.), it extended from the head of the Persian Gulf to Egypt and Asia Minor: original cap. Ashur; later cap. Nineveh

As·syr·i·an (-ən) *adj.* of Assyria, its people, language, or culture —*n.* **1.** a native or inhabitant of Assyria **2.** the Akkadian Semitic language of the Assyrians

As·syr·i·ol·o·gy (ə sir′ē äl′ə jē) *n.* the study of the civilization of ancient Assyria —**As·syr′i·ol′o·gist** *n.*

As·tar·te (as tär′tē) [L. < Gr. *Astartē*; of Sem. origin, akin to Phoen. *Ashtareth*] a Semitic goddess of fertility and sexual love, worshiped by the Phoenicians and others: see also ASHTORETH, ISHTAR

a·stat·ic (ā stat′ik) *adj.* [Gr. *astatos*, unstable < a-, not + *statos*, standing] **1.** unstable; unsteady **2.** *Physics* not taking a definite position or direction [an *astatic* needle is not affected by the earth's magnetism] —**a·stat′i·cal·ly** *adv.* —**a·stat′i·cism** (-ə siz′m) *n.*

☆**as·ta·tine** (as′tə tēn′) *n.* [< Gr. *astatos*, unstable + -INE⁴] a radioactive chemical element formed from bismuth when it is bombarded by alpha particles: symbol, At; at. wt., 210 (?); at. no., 85

as·ter (as′tər) *n.* [L. < Gr. *astēr*, star: see ASTRAL] **1.** any of a large genus (*Aster*) of plants of the composite family, with purplish, blue, pink, or white daisylike flowers **2.** *same as* CHINA ASTER **3.** *Zool.* a structure shaped like a star, formed around the centrosome in the cytoplasm of an animal cell during mitosis

as·ter- (as′tər) [< Gr. *astēr*, star] a *combining form denoting* relationship to a star [*asterism, asteroid*]

-as·ter¹ (as′tər) [see prec.] a *n.-forming suffix meaning* star or starlike structure [*diaster*]

-as·ter² (as′tər) [L. dim. suffix] a *n.-forming suffix denoting* inferiority or worthlessness [*poetaster*]

as·te·ri·a·ted (as tir′ē āt′id) *adj.* [< Gr. *asterios*, starred (< *astēr*, STAR) + -AT(E)¹ + -ED] **1.** having radiate form; star-shaped **2.** *Mineralogy* having asterism

NEW ENGLAND ASTER

as·ter·isk (as′tər isk) *n.* [LL. *asteriscus* < Gr. *asteriskos*, dim. of *astēr*, a STAR] a starlike sign (*) used in printing to indicate footnote references, omissions, etc.: it is used throughout this dictionary to indicate hypothetical forms of words —*vt.* to mark with this sign

as·ter·ism (-iz′m) *n.* [Gr. *asterismos*, a marking with stars < *asterizein*, to mark with stars < *astēr*, a STAR] **1.** *Astron.* a group or cluster of stars **2.** *Mineralogy* a starlike figure produced in some crystals by reflected or transmitted light **3.** *Printing* three asterisks placed in triangular form (*⁎* or ⁎*⁎) to call special attention to a passage

a·stern (ə sturn′) *adv.* [A-¹ + STERN²] **1.** behind a ship or aircraft **2.** at or toward the back of a ship or aircraft **3.** backward, in a reverse direction

a·ster·nal (ā stur′n'l) *adj.* [A-² + STERNAL] **1.** not joined to the sternum **2.** without a sternum

as·ter·oid (as′tə roid′) *adj.* [Gr. *asteroeidēs* < *astēr*, STAR + *eidēs*, -OID] starlike; shaped like a star or starfish —*n.* **1.** *Astron.* any of the numerous very small planets (the largest c. 490 miles in diameter), with orbits between those of Mars and Jupiter; planetoid **2.** *Zool. same as* STARFISH

as·the·ni·a (as thē′nē ə) *n.* [ML. < Gr. *astheneia*, weakness < a-, without + *sthenos*, strength] a lack or loss of bodily strength; bodily weakness

as·then·ic (as then′ik) *adj.* [Gr. *asthenikos*] **1.** of or having asthenia **2.** designating or of a constitutional body type of slender physique

as·the·no·pi·a (as′thə nō′pē ə) *n.* [ModL. < Gr. *asthenēs*, weak (see ASTHENIA) + -OPIA] a strained condition of the eyes, often with headache, dizziness, etc. —**as′the·nop′ic** (-näp′ik) *adj.*

as·then·o·sphere (as then′ə sfir′) *n.* [< Gr. *asthenēs*, weak (see ASTHENIA) + -SPHERE] a zone within the earth some distance below the surface, which consists of weak material, subject to plastic deformation, underlying the stronger lithosphere

asth·ma (az′mə; *chiefly Brit.* as′-) *n.* [Gr., a panting, asthma] a chronic disorder characterized by wheezing, coughing, difficulty in breathing, and a suffocating feeling, usually caused by an allergy to ingested substances

asth·mat·ic (az mat′ik; *chiefly Brit.* as-) *adj.* [L. *asthmaticus* < Gr. *asthmatikos*] of or having asthma: also **asth·mat′i·cal** —*n.* a person who has asthma —**asth·mat′i·cal·ly** *adv.*

As·ti (äs′tē) commune in Piedmont, NW Italy: center of a winegrowing region: pop. 60,000

as·tig·mat·ic (as′tig mat′ik) *adj.* **1.** of or having astigmatism **2.** correcting astigmatism **3.** having or resulting from a distorted view or judgment —**as′tig·mat′i·cal·ly** *adv.*

a·stig·ma·tism (ə stig′mə tiz′m) *n.* [< Gr. a-, without + *stigma, stigmatos*, a mark, puncture + -ISM] **1.** an irregularity in the curvature of a lens, including the lens of the eye, so that light rays from an object do not meet in a single focal point, resulting in an indistinct or distorted image **2.** a distorted view or judgment, as because of bias

a·stir (ə stur′) *adv., adj.* [A-¹ + STIR¹] **1.** in motion; in excited activity **2.** out of bed

ASTM American Society for Testing Materials

As·to·lat (as′tə lät′) an English town in Arthurian legend

a·stom·a·tous (ā stäm′ə təs, -stō′mə-) *adj.* [A-² + STOMATOUS] *Biol.* without a stoma or stomata

As·ton (as′t'n), **Francis William** 1877–1945; Eng. chemist & physicist: noted for his work on isotopes

as·ton·ied (ə stän′ēd) *adj.* [pp. of ME. *astonien*, ASTONISH] [Archaic] bewildered, dazed, astounded, etc.

as·ton·ish (ə stän′ish) *vt.* [altered < ME. *astonien* < OFr. *estoner* < VL. **extonare* (for L. *attonare*) < *ex*-, intens. + *tonare*, to THUNDER] to fill with sudden wonder or great surprise; amaze —*SYN.* see SURPRISE —**as·ton′ish·ing** *adj.* —**as·ton′ish·ing·ly** *adv.*

as·ton·ish·ment (-mənt) *n.* **1.** the state of being astonished; great amazement **2.** anything that astonishes

As·tor (as′tər) **1. John Jacob,** 1763–1848; U.S. fur merchant & financier, born in Germany **2. Viscountess, (born** *Nancy Witcher Langhorne*) 1879–1964; 1st woman member of the Brit. House of Commons (1919–45); born in the U.S.

As·tor·i·a (as tôr′ē ə) seaport in NW Oreg., on the Columbia River: site of first American settlement in the Northwest, 1811: pop. 10,000

as·tound (ə stound′) *vt.* [< ME. *astouned, astoned*, pp. of *astonien*, ASTONISH] to bewilder with sudden surprise; astonish greatly; amaze —*adj.* [Archaic] amazed; astonished —*SYN.* see SURPRISE —**as·tound′ing** *adj.* —**as·tound′ing·ly** *adv.*

astr. **1.** astronomer **2.** astronomy **3.** astronomical

as·tra·chan (as′trə kən) *n. same as* ASTRAKHAN

a·strad·dle (ə strad′'l) *adv.* in a straddling position

As·trae·a (as trē′ə) [L. < Gr. *Astraia* < *astraios*, starry < *astron*, STAR] *Gr. Myth.* a goddess, variously identified with justice or innocence, the last deity to leave the earth after the fabled Golden Age

as·tra·gal (as′trə g'l) *n.* [L. *astragalus* < Gr. *astragalos*, anklebone, vertebra, architectural molding] **1.** *Anat. same as* ASTRAGALUS **2.** *Archit.* a small, convex molding, sometimes cut like beading

as·trag·a·lus (ə strag′ə ləs) *n., pl.* **-li′** (-lī′) [L., ASTRAGAL] **1.** *Anat.* older term for the talus, or anklebone, in man **2.** *Archit. same as* ASTRAGAL

As·tra·khan (as′trə kan′; *Russ.* äs′trə khän′y′) city in SW U.S.S.R., on the Volga River delta near the Caspian Sea: pop. 342,000

as·tra·khan (as′trə kən) *n.* **1.** a loosely curled fur, a kind of karakul, made from the pelt of very young lambs originally bred near Astrakhan **2.** a wool fabric with a pile cut and curled to look like this

as·tral (as′trəl) *adj.* [L. *astralis* < *astrum*, star < Gr. *astron* < *astēr* < IE. base **ster*-, whence E. STAR, L. *stella*, Bret. *sterenn*] **1.** of, from, or like the stars **2.** *Zool.* of an aster in mitosis **3.** *Theosophy* designating or of a universal substance supposedly existing at a level just beyond normal human perception

astral lamp an oil lamp having a tubular wick and designed so that the ring-shaped reservoir does not cast its shadow downward

a·stray (ə strā′) *adv.* [ME. < pp. of OFr. *estraier*, STRAY] **1.** off the right path **2.** so as to be in error

as·trict (ə strikt′) *vt.* [< L. *astrictus*, pp. of *astringere*: see ASTRINGE] [Rare] **1.** to bind; constrict; limit **2.** to restrict legally or morally —**as·tric′tion** *n.*

a·stride (ə strīd′) *adv.* [A-¹ + STRIDE] **1.** with a leg on either side; astraddle **2.** with legs far apart —*prep.* **1.** with a leg on either side of (a horse, etc.) **2.** extending over or across on either side of (a horse, etc.)

as·tringe (ə strinj′) *vt.* **-tringed′, -tring′ing** [L. *astringere*, to contract < *ad*-, to + *stringere*, draw: see STRICT] [Rare] to constrict; compress

as·trin·gent (ə strin′jənt) *adj.* [L. *astringens*, prp. of *astringere*: see ASTRINGE] **1.** that contracts body tissue and checks secretions, capillary bleeding, etc.; styptic **2.** having a harsh, biting quality [an *astringent* style of writing] —*n.*

---

an astringent substance, drug, etc. —**as·trin′gen·cy** *n.* —**as·trin′gent·ly** *adv.*

as·tro- (as′trō, -trə) [< Gr. *astron*, a star: see ASTRAL] *a combining form meaning:* **1.** of a star, or stars [*astrophysics*] **2.** *Zool.* of an aster in mitosis [*astrosphere*]

as·tro·bi·ol·o·gy (as′trō bī äl′ə jē) *n.* the branch of biology that investigates the existence of living organisms on planets other than earth

as·tro·com·pass (as′trə kum′pəs) *n.* an instrument for determining the direction of an aircraft by sighting upon a heavenly body

as·tro·cyte (-sīt′) *n.* [ASTRO- + -CYTE] a star-shaped cell of the brain and spinal cord— **as′tro·cyt′ic** (-sit′ik) *adj.*

as·tro·dome (-dōm′) *n.* a domelike transparent structure for housing astronomical or navigational instruments; specif., such a structure mounted on top of an aircraft fuselage for the navigator

as·tro·dy·nam·ics (as′trō dī nam′iks) *n.pl.* [*with sing. v.*] the branch of dynamics dealing with the motion and gravitation of natural and artificial objects in space

astrol. **1.** astrologer **2.** astrological **3.** astrology

as·tro·labe (as′trə lāb′) *n.* [ME. *astrelabie* < OFr. *astrelabe* < ML. *astrolabium* < Gr. *astrolabon* < *astron*, a star (see ASTRAL) + *lambanein*, to take] an instrument formerly used to find the altitude of a star, etc.: it was replaced by the sextant

as·trol·o·gy (ə sträl′ə jē) *n.* [ME. *astrologie* < L. & Gr. *astrologia*, astronomy, astrology < *astron*, star (see ASTRAL) + -*logia*, -LOGY] **1.** orig., primitive astronomy **2.** a pseudo-science claiming to foretell the future by studying the supposed influence of the relative positions of the moon, sun, and stars on human affairs —**as·trol′o·ger** *n.* —**as·tro·log·i·cal** (as′trə läj′i k'l) *adj.* —**as′tro·log′i·cal·ly** *adv.*

as·trom·e·try (ə sträm′ə trē) *n.* [ASTRO- + -METRY] that branch of astronomy dealing with the measurement of the positions and changes of positions of planets, stars, etc. —**as·tro·met·ric** (as′trə met′rik) *adj.*

astron. **1.** astronomer **2.** astronomical **3.** astronomy

as·tro·naut (as′trə nôt′) *n.* [< Fr. *astronaute:* see ff.] a person trained to make rocket flights in outer space

as·tro·nau·tics (as′trə nôt′iks) *n.pl.* [*with sing. v.*] [< Fr. *astronautique* (coined 1927): see ASTRO- & AERONAUTICS] the science that deals with spacecraft and with travel in outer space, esp. to the moon and to other planets — **as′tro·nau′ti·cal** *adj.* —**as′tro·nau′ti·cal·ly** *adv.*

as·tro·nav·i·ga·tion (as′trō nav′ə gā′shən) *n.* same as CELESTIAL NAVIGATION —**as′tro·nav′i·ga′tor** *n.*

as·tron·o·mer (ə strän′ə mər) *n.* an expert in astronomy

as·tro·nom·i·cal (as′trə näm′i k'l) *adj.* **1.** of or having to do with astronomy **2.** extremely large, as the numbers or quantities used in astronomy Also **as′tro·nom′ic** —**as′-tro·nom′i·cal·ly** *adv.*

astronomical latitude the angle between the direction of gravity at the observer's position and the plane of the celestial equator

astronomical unit a unit of length equal to the mean radius of the earth's orbit (c. 93 million mi.) used in measuring distances in astronomy

as·tron·o·my (ə strän′ə mē) *n.* [ME. & OFr. *astronomie* < L. *astronomia* < Gr. *astronomia* < *astron*, star (see ASTRAL) + *nomos*, law, system of laws < *nemein*, to arrange] **1.** the science of the stars, planets, and all other heavenly bodies, dealing with their composition, motion, relative position, size, etc. **2.** *pl.* **-mies** a book or treatise on this

as·tro·pho·tog·ra·phy (as′trō fə tä′grə fē) *n.* photography as used in investigating astronomical phenomena

as·tro·phys·ics (-fiz′iks) *n.pl.* [*with sing. v.*] the science of the physical properties and phenomena of the stars, planets, and all other heavenly bodies —**as′tro·phys′i·cal** *adj.* —**as′tro·phys′i·cist** (-ə sist) *n.*

as·tro·sphere (as′trə sfir′) *n.* [ASTRO- + SPHERE] *Biol.* **1.** same as CENTROSPHERE **2.** all of an aster except the centrosome

as·tu·cious (as tōō′shəs, -tyōō′-) *adj.* [Fr. *astucieux*] same as ASTUTE

As·tu·ri·as (as toor′ē əs; *Sp.* äs tōōr′yäs) former kingdom and province of NW Spain, on the Bay of Biscay —**As·tu′ri·an** *adj., n.*

as·tute (ə stōōt′, -styōōt′) *adj.* [L. *astutus* < *astus*, craft, cunning] having or showing a clever or shrewd mind; cunning; crafty; wily —*SYN.* see SHREWD —**as·tute′ly** *adv.* —**as·tute′ness** *n.*

As·ty·a·nax (as tī′ə naks′) *Gr. Myth.* the young son of Hector and Andromache: he was killed at Troy by the Greek conquerors

a·sty·lar (ā stī′lər) *adj.* [< A-² + Gr. *stylos*, pillar + -AR] *Archit.* having no columns or pilasters

A·sun·ción (ä sōōn syōn′) capital of Paraguay, a seaport on the Paraguay River: pop. 305,000

a·sun·der (ə sun′dər) *adv.* [ME. < OE. *on sundran* < *on,* on + *sundor:* see SUNDER] **1.** into parts or pieces **2.** apart or separate in direction or position

A·sur (ä′soor) same as ASHUR

As·wan (äs wän′, as-; as′wän′) city in S Egypt, just below the first cataract of the Nile: pop. 48,000: site of a dam providing irrigation for the surrounding region: a larger dam (**Aswan High Dam**) has been constructed five miles farther south: also spelled ASSUAN, ASSOUAN: ancient name, SYENE

a·swarm (ə swôrm′) *adj.* filled or crowded (*with*); swarming [*the park aswarm with people*]

a·syl·lab·ic (ā′sə lab′ik) *adj.* not syllabic

a·sy·lum (ə sī′ləm) *n.* [L. < Gr. *asylon* < *a-*, without + *sylē*, right of seizure] **1.** formerly, a sanctuary, as a temple, where criminals, debtors, etc. were safe from arrest **2.** a place where one is safe and secure; refuge **3.** the protection given by a sanctuary or refuge or by one country to refugees from another country **4.** an institution for the care of the mentally ill, or of the aged, the poor, etc.: in this sense, largely replaced by such terms as *mental* (or *psychiatric*) *hospital, nursing home,* etc. —*SYN.* see SHELTER

a·sym·me·try (ā sim′ə trē) *n.* [Gr. *asymmetria* < *a-*, without + *symmetria*] lack of symmetry —**a·sym·met·ri·cal** (ā′sə met′ri k'l), **a′sym·met′ric** *adj.* —**a′sym·met′ri·cal·ly** *adv.*

as·ymp·tote (as′im tōt′) *n.* [ModL. *asymptotus* < Gr. *asymptōtos* < *a-*, not + *symptōtos*, self-intersecting < *syn-*, together + *piptein*, to fall] *Math.* a straight line always approaching but never meeting a curve; tangent to a curve at infinity — **as′ymp·tot′ic** (-tät′ik), **as′ymp·tot′i·cal** *adj.* —**as′ymp·tot′i·cal·ly** *adv.*

ASYMPTOTE
(A, asymptote of curve C)

a·syn·chro·nism (ā siŋ′krə niz′m, -sin′-) *n.* lack of synchronism; failure to occur at the same time —**a·syn′-chro·nous** *adj.* —**a·syn′chro·nous·ly** *adv.*

a·syn·de·ton (ə sin′də tän′) *n.* [LL. < Gr. *asyndeton* < *a-*, not + *syndetos*, united with < *syndein*, to bind together < *syn-*, together + *dein*, to bind] *Rhetoric* the practice of leaving out the usual conjunctions between coordinate sentence elements (Ex.: smile, shake hands, part) —**as·yn·det·ic** (as′'n det′ik) *adj.* —**as′yn·det′i·cal·ly** *adv.*

As·yut (ä syōōt′) city in C Egypt, on the Nile: pop. 122,000: also sp. ASSIUT

at¹ (at; *unstressed* ət) *prep.* [ME. < OE. *æt* akin to Goth., OS., ON. *at* & L. *ad*, at, in, to] **1.** on; in; near; by [*at* the office, *at* the edge of town] **2.** to or toward as the goal or object [look *at* her, swing *at* the ball, don't shout *at* me] **3.** through [come in *at* the front door] **4.** from [get the facts *at* their source] **5.** attending [*at* the party] **6.** occupied in; busy with [*at* work] **7.** in a condition or state of [*at* war] **8.** in the manner of [*at* a trot] **9.** because of; in response to [terrified *at* the sight, to smile *at* a remark] **10.** according to [*at* his discretion] **11.** with reference to [good *at* tennis] **12.** in the amount, degree, number, price, etc. of [*at* twenty miles per hour, *at* five cents each] **13.** from an interval of [visible *at* half a mile] **14.** on or close to the time or age of [*at* five o'clock, *at* once, *at* sixty-five] **15.** during the period of [to happen *at* night] Basically, *at* is the preposition of general (usually static) location; it is replaced by *in, on, over, under, by* when more precise indications of locality are needed

at² (ät, at) *n., pl.* **at** a unit of money in Laos, equal to 1/100 kip

at- (ət) *same as* AD-: used before *t*

At *Chem.* astatine

AT antitank

at. **1.** airtight **2.** atmosphere **3.** atomic

at·a·bal (at′ə bal′) *n.* [Sp. < Ar. colloq. *aṭ-ṭabl* < *al,* the + *ṭabl,* drum] a kind of kettledrum or tabor used by the Moors

☆**At·a·brine** (at′ə brin, -brēn′) [G. *atebrin* < ? *a(n)t(if)-ebrin:* see ANTI-, FEBRILE, -INE⁴] *a trademark for* quinacrine hydrochloride, C₂₃H₃₀ClN₃O·2HCl·2H₂O, a synthetic drug used in treating malaria and other diseases —*n.* [a-] this drug

A·ta·ca·ma Desert (ä′tä kä′mä) desert area in N Chile, containing valuable nitrate deposits: c. 30,000 sq. mi.

at·a·ghan (at′ə gan′) *n.* a Moslem sword: see YATAGHAN

A·ta·hual·pa (ä′tə wäl′pə) 1502?–33; last Inca king of Peru (1525–33)

At·a·lan·ta (at′'l an′tə) [L. < Gr. *Atalantē*] *Gr. Myth.* a beautiful, swift-footed maiden who offered to marry any man able to defeat her in a race: Hippomenes won by dropping three golden apples, which she stopped to pick up, along the way

at·a·man (at′ə man′) *n., pl.* **-mans′** [Russ. *atamanu*] a Cossack chief; hetman

☆**at·a·mas·co lily** (at′ə mas′kō) [AmInd. (Virginian) *attamusco,* lit., stained with red] any of a genus (*Zephyranthes*) of bulbous plants of the amaryllis family, with hollow stems, grassy leaves, and funnel-shaped flowers of purple-tinged white or pink or yellow

a·tap (a′tap) *n.* [Malay, roof, thatch] **1.** thatch for native huts in Malaya, made of leaves of the nipa palm **2.** same as NIPA

at·a·rac·tic (at′ə rak′tik) *n.* [< Gr. *ataraktos,* calm, undisturbed < *ataraxia:* see ATARAXIA] a tranquilizing drug —*adj.* of or having to do with tranquilizing drugs or their effects Also at′a·rax′ic (-rak′sik)

at·a·rax·i·a (at′ə rak′sē ə) *n.* [Gr. < *a-*, not + *tarassein,* to disturb] calmness of the mind and emotions; tranquillity: also at′a·rax′y (-rak′sē)

Ataturk *see* KEMAL ATATURK

at·a·vism (at′ə viz′m) *n.* [Fr. *atavisme* < L. *atavus,* father

of a great-grandfather, ancestor < *at-*, beyond + *avus*, grandfather < IE. **ati*, beyond + **avos*, maternal grandfather] **1.** appearance in an individual of some characteristic found in a remote ancestor but not in nearer ancestors **2.** *a)* such a characteristic *b)* an individual with such a characteristic: also **at'a·vist** —**at'a·vis'tic, a·tav·ic** (ə tav'ik) *adj.* —**at'a·vis'ti·cal·ly** *adv.*

a·tax·i·a (ə taks'sē ə) *n.* [Gr., disorder < *ataktos*, disorderly < *a-*, not + *taktos* < *tassein*, to arrange] total or partial inability to coordinate voluntary bodily movements, esp. muscular movements —**a·tax'ic** *adj., n.*

At·ba·ra (ät'bä rä) river flowing from N Ethiopia through NE Sudan into the Nile: c. 500 mi.

A·te (ā'tē) [Gr. *atē*] *Gr. Myth.* the goddess personifying criminal folly or reckless ambition in man, bringing on him punishment by Nemesis

ate (āt; *Brit.,* or *U.S. dial.,* et) *pt. of* EAT

-ate¹ (āt *for 1;* it, āt *for 2 & 3*) [< L. *-atus*, pp. ending of verbs of 1st conjugation] **1.** *a v.*-forming *suffix meaning: a)* to become [*evaporate, maturate*] *b)* to cause to become [*invalidate, sublimate*] *c)* to form or produce [*ulcerate, salivate*] *d)* to provide or treat with [*vaccinate, refrigerate*] *e)* to put in the form of, or form by means of [*delineate, triangulate*] *f)* to arrange for [*orchestrate*] *g)* to combine, infuse, or treat with [*chlorinate, oxygenate*] **2.** *an adj.*-forming *suffix meaning: a)* of or characteristic of [*collegiate, roseate*] *b)* having or filled with [*proportionate, passionate*] *c) Biol.* having or characterized by [*spatulate, caudate*] **3.** *an adj.*-forming *suffix roughly equivalent to the past participial ending* -ed [*animate* (*animated*), *determinate* (*determined*)]

-ate² (āt, it) [L. *-atus*, a noun ending] *a n.*-forming *suffix denoting:* **1.** an office, function, agent, official, or group of officials [*episcopate, potentate, directorate*] **2.** a person or thing that is the object of (an action) [*legate, mandate*] **3.** [L. *-atum*, neut. of *-atus*] *Chem.* a salt made from (an acid with a name ending in *-ic*) [*acetate, nitrate*]

at·e·brin (at'ə brin) *n.* [G.] *same as* ATABRINE

at·e·lec·ta·sis (at'ə lek'tə sis) *n.* [ModL. < Gr. *atelēs*, incomplete (< *a*, without + *telos*, an end, completion) + *ektasis*, a stretching out] the collapse of all or part of a lung

at·el·ier (at'l yā'; *Fr.* à ta lyā') *n.* [Fr. < OFr. *astelier* < *astele*, a shaving, splinter < VL. *astella* < L. *assula*, dim. of *assis*, board] a studio or workshop, esp. one used by an artist or couturier

a tem·po (ä tem'pō) [It.] *Music* in time: a direction to the performer to return to the preceding tempo

A·te·ri·an (ə tir'ē ən) *adj.* [Fr. *atérien* < Bir-el-*Ater*, Algeria] designating or of an upper paleolithic culture of northern Africa, characterized by arrowheads with barbs and tangs, etc.

Ath·a·bas·ca, Ath·a·bas·ka (ath'ə bas'kə) **1.** river rising in the Rocky Mountains of SW Alberta, Canada, and flowing northeast into Lake Athabasca: 765 mi. **2.** lake extending across the N Alberta-Saskatchewan border: 3,058 sq. mi. usually **Lake Athabasca**

Ath·a·bas·can, Ath·a·bas·kan (ath'ə bas'kən) *adj., n. same as* ATHAPASCAN

ath·a·na·si·a (ath'ə nā'zhə, -zhē ə) *n.* [Gr. < *a-*, not + *thanatos*, death] endless existence; immortality: also **a·than·a·sy** (ə than'ə sē)

Ath·a·na·sian Creed (-zhən, -zhē ən) a statement of Christian faith of unknown authorship, formerly attributed to Athanasius: it maintains belief in the Trinity as opposed to Arianism

Ath·a·na·sius (ath'ə nā'shəs), Saint 296?–373 A.D.; Alexandrian bishop; patriarch of Alexandria (328–373) & opponent of Arianism: his day is May 2: called *the Great* —**Ath·a·na·sian** (-zhən) *adj., n.*

Ath·a·pas·can, Ath·a·pas·kan (ath'ə pas'kən, -kan) *adj.* [< Cree *athap-askaw*, lit., grass here and there < *athap*, in succession + *-askaw*, grass, reeds] designating or of the most widely scattered linguistic family of N. American Indians, ranging from Alaska to northern Mexico and including the Navajo and Apache tribes —*n.* **1.** an Indian of this family **2.** a language of this family

a·the·ism (ā'thē iz'm) *n.* [< Fr. *athéisme* < Gr. *atheos*, godless < *a-*, without + *theos*, god] **1.** the belief that there is no God, or denial that God or gods exist **2.** godlessness —**a'the·is'tic, a'the·is'ti·cal** *adj.* —**a'the·is'ti·cal·ly** *adv.*

a·the·ist (-ist) *n.* [Fr. *athéiste:* see ATHEISM] a person who believes that there is no God

SYN.—an **atheist** rejects all religious belief and denies the existence of God; an **agnostic** questions the existence of God, heaven, etc. in the absence of material proof and in unwillingness to accept supernatural revelation; **deist,** a historical term, was applied to 18th-cent. rationalists who believed in God as a creative, moving force but who otherwise rejected formal religion and its doctrines of revelation, divine authority, etc.; **freethinker,** the current parallel term, similarly implies rejection of the tenets and traditions of formal religion as incompatible with reason; **unbeliever** is a more negative term, simply designating, without further qualification, one who does not accept any religious belief; **infidel** is applied to a person not believing in a certain religion or the prevailing religion —ANT. theist

ath·el·ing (ath'l iŋ) *n.* [OE. *ætheling* < *æthele*, noble] a nobleman or prince of the Anglo-Saxons

Ath·el·stan (ath'l stan') 895–940 A.D.; king of the Mercians & West Saxons (925–940); assumed the title of king of England: grandson of *Alfred the Great*

A·the·na (ə thē'nə) [Gr. *Athēnē*] *Gr. Myth.* the goddess of wisdom, skills, and warfare: identified by the Romans with Minerva: also **A·the'ne** (-nē)

Ath·e·nae·um, Ath·e·ne·um (ath'ə nē'əm) [L. *Athenaeum* < Gr. *Athēnaion*] **1.** the temple of Athena at Athens, where writers and scholars met **2.** a Roman school of law, literature, etc. founded by Hadrian —*n.* [a-] ☆**1.** a literary or scientific club **2.** any building or hall used as a library or reading room

A·the·na (ä thē'ne) *Gr. name of* ATHENS

A·the·ni·an (ə thē'nē ən) *adj.* of Athens, esp. ancient Athens, its people, or culture —*n.* **1.** a native or inhabitant of Athens **2.** a citizen of ancient Athens

Ath·ens (ath'nz) **1.** capital of Greece, in the SE part: pop. 1,853,000: Athens became established as the center of Greek culture in the 5th cent. B.C., when it was the capital of ancient Attica: Gr. names, ATHENAI, ATHINAI **2.** city in NE Ga.: pop. 44,000

a·ther·man·cy (ā thur'mən sē) *n.* [< Gr. *a-*, not + *thermansis*, heating < *thermainein*, to heat < *thermē*, heat + *-cy*] the property of not transmitting infrared or heat rays —**a·ther'ma·nous** (-mə nəs) *adj.*

ath·er·o·ma (ath'ə rō'mə) *n., pl.* **-mas, -ma·ta** (-mə tə) [ModL. < Gr. *athērōma*, tumor filled with grainy matter] a condition marked by the depositing of small fatty nodules on the inner walls of the arteries, and by degeneration of the affected areas; also, such a nodule —**ath'er·o'ma·tous** (-mə təs) *adj.*

ath·er·o·scle·ro·sis (ath'ər ō sklə rō'sis) *n.* [ModL. < ATHEROMA + SCLEROSIS] a thickening of, and loss of elasticity in, the inner walls of arteries, accompanied by the formation of atheromas —**ath'er·o·scle·rot'ic** (-rät'ik) *adj.*

A·thi·nai (ä thē'ne) *Gr. name of* ATHENS

a·thirst (ə thurst') *adj.* [ME. *ofthurst* < AS. *ofthyrsted*, pp. of *ofthyrstan* < *of-*, intens. + *thyrstan*, to THIRST] **1.** [Archaic or Poet.] thirsty **2.** eager; longing (*for* a thing)

ath·lete (ath'lēt') *n.* [L. *athleta* < Gr. *athlētēs*, contestant in the games < *athlein*, to contest for a prize < *athlos*, a contest, *athlon*, a prize] a person trained in exercises, games, or contests requiring physical strength, skill, stamina, speed, etc.

athlete's foot a common fungous infection of the skin of the feet; ringworm of the feet

athlete's heart enlargement of the heart, caused by continued, heavy physical exertion

ath·let·ic (ath let'ik) *adj.* [L. *athleticus* < Gr. *athlētikos*] **1.** of, like, or proper to athletes or athletics **2.** physically strong, skillful, active, etc. **3.** designating or of a constitutional type of robust, muscular physique —**ath·let'i·cal·ly** *adv.*

ath·let·i·cism (ath let'ə siz'm) *n.* **1.** addiction to athletics **2.** an athletic quality

ath·let·ics (-iks) *n.pl.* [*sometimes with sing. v.*] sports, games, exercises, etc. requiring physical strength, skill, stamina, speed, etc.

ath·o·dyd (ath'ə did) *n.* [a(ero)- th(erm)o- dy(namic) d(uct)] *same as* RAMJET

at-home (ət hōm') *n.* an informal reception at one's home, usually in the afternoon

Ath·os (ath'äs, ā'thäs), **Mount 1.** autonomous monastic district occupying the easternmost prong of the Chalcidice peninsula, NE Greece: 131 sq. mi.; pop. 2,700 **2.** mountain on this peninsula: 6,670 ft.

a·thwart (ə thwôrt') *prep.* [A-¹ + THWART] **1.** across; from one side to the other of **2.** against; in opposition to **3.** *Naut.* across the course or length of —*adv.* **1.** crosswise; across at a slant **2.** so as to block or thwart

-at·ic (at'ik) [< Fr. or L.; Fr. *-atique* < L. *-aticus* < Gr. *-atikos* < base ending *-at* + suffix *-ikos, -*IC] *an adj.*-forming *suffix meaning* of, of the kind of: used in adjectives of Greek and Latin origin [*lymphatic, chromatic*]

a·tilt (ə tilt') *adj., adv.* **1.** in a tilted, or inclined, position **2.** tilting, as with a lance

a·tin·gle (ə tiŋ'g'l) *adj.* tingling, as with excitement

-a·tion (ā'shən) [< Fr. or L.; Fr. *-ation* < L. *-ation(em)*, suffix formed from *-at-* of pp. of *-are* verbs (1st conjugation)] *a n.*-forming *suffix meaning:* **1.** the act of [*alteration*] **2.** the condition of being [*gratification*] **3.** the result of [*compilation*]

-a·tive (ə tiv, āt'iv) [< Fr. or L.; Fr. *-atif*, fem. *-ative* < L. *-ativus*] *an adj.*-forming *suffix meaning* of or relating to, serving to, tending to [*demonstrative, informative, talkative*]

☆**At·ka mackerel** (at'kə) [< *Atka* Island, in the Aleutians] a commercially important ocean fish (*Pleurogrammus monopterygius*) of the northern Pacific, esp. the area off the Aleutian Islands: also called **Atka fish**

At·kin·son (at'kin s'n), (**Justin**) **Brooks** 1894– ; U.S. journalist & drama critic

Atl. Atlantic

---

fat, āpe, cär; ten, ēven; is, bīte; gō, hôrn, tōōl, look; oil, out; up, fur; get; joy; yet; chin; she; thin, *then*; zh, leisure; ŋ, ring; ə for *a* in *ago, e* in *agent, i* in *sanity, o* in *comply, u* in *focus;* ' as in *able* (ā'b'l); Fr. bal; ë, Fr. coeur; ö, Fr. feu; Fr. mon; ô, Fr. coq; ü, Fr. duc; r, Fr. cri; H, G. ich; kh, G. doch. See inside front cover. ☆ Americanism; ‡foreign; *hypothetical; < derived from

At·lan·ta (ət lan′tə, at-) [< Western & *Atlantic* Railroad] capital of Ga., in the NC part; pop. 497,000 (met. area 1,390,000)

At·lan·te·an (at′lan tē′ən; ət lan′tē ən, at-) *adj.* [L. *Atlanteus*, of Atlas, of the Atlantic < *Atlas*, ATLAS] 1. of or like Atlas; strong 2. of Atlantis

at·lan·tes (ət lan′tēz, at-) *n.pl. sing.* **at·las** (at′ləs) [L. < Gr. *Atlantes*, pl. of *Atlas*] *Archit.* supporting columns for an entablature, carved in the form of standing or kneeling figures of men

At·lan·tic (ət lan′tik, at-) [L. *Atlanticum* (*mare*), Atlantic (ocean) < *Atlanticus*, of the Atlas Mountains < *Atlas*, ATLAS] ocean touching the American continents to the west and Europe and Africa to the east: c. 31,830,000 sq. mi.; greatest known depth, 30,246 ft. —*adj.* designating, of, in, on, or near this ocean

Atlantic City city in SE N.J., on the Atlantic: an ocean resort: pop. 48,000

Atlantic Standard Time a standard time used in a zone which includes Bermuda, Nova Scotia, New Brunswick, and E Quebec, corresponding to the mean local time of the 60th meridian west of Greenwich, England: it is four hours behind Greenwich time: see TIME, chart

At·lan·tis (ət lan′tis, at-) [L. < Gr.] legendary island or continent supposed to have existed in the Atlantic west of Gibraltar and to have sunk into the sea

At·las (at′ləs) [L. < Gr. < prothetic *a-* + *tlan*, bearing < IE. base *tel-*, *tla-*, to lift, bear, whence TOLERATE, THOLE[2]] *Gr. Myth.* a Titan compelled to support the heavens on his shoulders —*n.* 1. any person who carries a great burden 2. [a-] *a*) a book of maps: Atlas supporting the earth was often pictured on the front page of such books *b*) a book of tables, charts, illustrations, etc. on a specific subject or subjects [an anatomical *atlas*] ☆3. an intercontinental ballistic missile of the U.S. Air Force 4. [a-] *Anat.* the topmost vertebra of the neck 5. [a-] *Archit. sing. of* ATLANTES

Atlas Mountains mountain system in NW Africa, extending across Morocco, Algeria, and Tunisia: c. 1,500 mi.; highest peak (in Morocco), c. 13,600 ft.

At·li (ät′lē) [ON. < Goth. *Attila*, ATTILA] *Norse Myth.* a king of the Huns, killed by his wife, Gudrun, because he had killed her brothers for Sigurd's treasure

atm. 1. atmosphere 2. atmospheric

at·man (ät′mən) *n.* [Sans., breath, soul, Supreme Spirit < IE. *ēt-men*, breath, whence OE. *æthm*, G. *atem*] *Hinduism* 1. the individual soul or ego 2. [A-] the universal soul; source of all individual souls

at·mom·e·ter (at măm′ə tər) *n.* [ATMO(SPHERE) + -METER] an instrument for measuring the rate of evaporation of water into the atmosphere, under varying conditions

at·mos·phere (at′məs fir′) *n.* [ModL. *atmosphaera* < Gr. *atmos*, vapor + *sphaira*, sphere] 1. the gaseous envelope (air) surrounding the earth: it consists of oxygen, nitrogen, and other gases, extends to a height of about 22,000 miles, and rotates with the earth 2. the gaseous mass surrounding any star, planet, etc. 3. the air in any given place 4. a pervading or surrounding influence or spirit; general mood or social environment 5. the general tone of a work of art [a play with a fateful *atmosphere*] 6. [Colloq.] an interesting, often exotic, effect produced by decoration, furnishings, etc. [a restaurant with *atmosphere*] 7. *Physics* a unit of pressure equal to 14.69 lb. per sq. in.

at·mos·pher·ic (at′məs fer′ik, -fir′-) *adj.* 1. of or in the atmosphere [*atmospheric* lightning] 2. caused or produced by the atmosphere [*atmospheric* pressure] 3. having or giving atmosphere or an atmosphere [*atmospheric* music] Also **at′mos·pher′i·cal** —**at′mos·pher′i·cal·ly** *adv.*

atmospheric pressure the pressure due to the weight of the earth's atmosphere, equal at sea level to about 14.69 lb. per sq. in.

at·mos·pher·ics (-iks) *n.pl.* 1. *Radio a*) disturbances in reception, produced by natural electric discharges, as in a storm; static *b*) the phenomena producing these disturbances 2. prevailing mood or influence

at. no. atomic number

at·oll (a′tôl, ă′-; -täl; -tōl) *n.* [< Maldive Is. term < ? Malayalam *aḍal*, uniting] a ring-shaped coral island nearly or completely surrounding a lagoon

at·om (at′əm) *n.* [ME. *attome* < OFr. *atome* < L. *atomus* < Gr. *atomos*, uncut, indivisible, atom < *a-*, not + *tomos* < *temnein*, to cut] 1. orig., any of the indivisible particles postulated by philosophers as the basic component of all matter 2. a tiny particle of anything; jot 3. *Chem. & Physics* any of the smallest particles of an element that combine with similar particles of other elements to produce compounds: atoms combine to form molecules, and consist of a complex arrangement of electrons revolving about a positively charged nucleus containing (except for hydrogen) protons and neutrons and other particles —**the atom** atomic (i.e., nuclear) energy

atom bomb same as ATOMIC BOMB —**at′om-bomb′** *vt.*

a·tom·ic (ə täm′ik) *adj.* 1. of an atom or atoms 2. of, using, or powered by atomic energy [an *atomic* submarine]

ATOLL

3. involving the use of atomic bombs [*atomic* warfare] 4. having its atoms in an uncombined form [*atomic* oxygen] 5. very small; minute —**a·tom′i·cal·ly** *adv.*

☆**Atomic Age** the period characterized by the use of atomic energy, regarded as beginning with the creation of the first self-sustaining nuclear chain reaction on December 2, 1942

☆**atomic bomb** an extremely destructive type of bomb, the power of which results from the immense quantity of energy suddenly released when a very rapid chain reaction of nuclear fission is set off by neutron bombardment in the atoms of a charge of plutonium or of the uranium isotope with an atomic mass of 235 (U 235): first used in warfare (1945) by the United States against the Japanese cities of Hiroshima and Nagasaki

atomic clock an extremely accurate clock whose precision depends upon the very constant frequency at which atoms (or molecules) of certain substances, as of cesium, rubidium, or ammonia, absorb or emit electromagnetic radiation

☆**atomic cocktail** a dose of medicine to be swallowed, containing a radioactive element, used in medical treatment and diagnosis, as of cancer

atomic disintegration a process resulting in the change of a radioactive nucleus, either by emission of an alpha, beta, or gamma ray or by fission, and producing a change in the original mass, atomic number, or energy

atomic energy the energy released from an atom in nuclear reactions or by radioactive decay; esp., the energy released in nuclear fission or nuclear fusion

a·tom·ic·i·ty (at′ə mis′ə tē) *n.* 1. the condition of being made up of atoms 2. *Chem. a*) the number of atoms in a molecule *b*) the number of replaceable atoms or groups of atoms in the molecule of a compound *c*) same as VALENCE

atomic mass the mass of a given atom, usually expressed in atomic mass units: it is the atomic weight multiplied by the atomic mass unit

atomic mass unit a unit of mass, exactly one twelfth the mass of a neutral atom of the most abundant isotope of carbon, C^{12}: one atomic mass unit equals 1.6605×10^{-24} gram and is equivalent to 931.48 mev in energy

atomic number *Chem.* a number representing the relative position of an element in the periodic table, in which the elements are arranged in the order of their nuclear charges; number representing the positive charge or the number of protons in the nucleus of the atom of an element: isotopes have the same atomic numbers but different atomic weights

☆**atomic pile** *an early name for* NUCLEAR REACTOR

a·tom·ics (ə täm′iks) *n.pl.* [*with sing. v.*] the science dealing with atomic structure and, esp., atomic energy

atomic structure *Physics* a conventionalized, hypothetical concept of an atom, regarded as consisting of a central, positively charged nucleus and a number of negatively charged electrons revolving about it in various orbits: the number and arrangement of the electrons vary in the different elements

atomic theory the theory that all material objects and substances are composed of atoms, and that various phenomena are explained by the properties and interactions of these atoms

atomic volume *Chem.* the quotient obtained by dividing the atomic weight of an element by its specific gravity

atomic weight *Chem.* a number representing the weight of one atom of an element as compared with an arbitrarily selected number representing the weight of one atom of another element taken as the standard (now usually carbon at 12)

at·om·ism (at′ə miz′m) *n.* [ATOM + -ISM] *Philos.* the theory that the universe is made up of tiny, simple, indivisible particles that cannot be destroyed —**at′om·ist** *n., adj.*

at·om·is·tic (at′ə mis′tik) *adj.* 1. of atoms or atomism 2. made up of a number of unrelated elements —**at′om·is′ti·cal·ly** *adv.*

at·om·ize (at′ə mīz′) *vt.* **-ized′, -iz′ing** 1. to separate into atoms 2. to reduce (a liquid) to a fine spray 3. to destroy by atomic weapons 4. to separate into many parts or fragments; disintegrate —**at′om·i·za′tion** *n.*

☆**at·om·iz·er** (at′ə mī′zər) *n.* a device used to shoot out a fine spray, as of medicine or perfume

☆**atom smasher** same as ACCELERATOR (sense 3)

at·o·my[1] (at′ə mē) *n., pl.* **-mies** [by division of *anatomy* as an *atomy*, by association with ATOM] [Archaic] a skeleton

at·o·my[2] (at′ə mē) *n., pl.* **-mies** [< L. *atomi*, pl. of *atomus*, ATOM] [Archaic] 1. an atom; tiny thing 2. a tiny being; pygmy

a·ton·al (ā tōn′'l) *adj.* having atonality; lacking tone —**a·ton′al·ism** *n.* —**a·ton′al·ist** *n.* —**a·ton′al·is′tic** *adj.* —**a·ton′al·ly** *adv.*

a·to·nal·i·ty (ā′tō nal′ə tē) *n. Music* lack of tonality through intentional disregard of key; also, use of the tones of the chromatic scale as separate entities, unrelated to any central keynote

a·tone (ə tōn′) *vi.* **a·toned′, a·ton′ing** [ME. *at onen*, to become reconciled < *at one*, in accord: see AT & ONE] 1. to make amends or reparation (*for* wrongdoing, a wrongdoer, etc.) 2. [Obs.] to be in agreement —*vt.* [Obs.] 1. to make amends for; expiate 2. to bring into agreement; reconcile

a·tone·ment (-mənt) *n.* 1. the act of atoning 2. satisfaction given for wrongdoing, injury, etc.; amends; expiation

ATOMIZER

3. [A-] *Theol.* a) the effect of Jesus' sufferings and death in redeeming mankind and bringing about the reconciliation of God to man b) this reconciliation **4.** [Obs.] agreement or reconciliation

a·ton·ic (ā tän'ik, ə-) *adj.* [ML. *atonicus* < Gr. *átonos:* see ATONY] **1.** caused or characterized by atony **2.** unaccented: said of a word or syllable —*n.* an unaccented syllable or word —**a·to·nic·i·ty** (ā'tō nis'ə tē) *n.*

at·o·ny (at'n ē) *n.* [Fr. *atonie* < LL. *atonia* < Gr. *atonia,* languor < a-, not + tonos, tone < teinein, to stretch] lack of bodily tone or muscle tone

a·top (ə täp') *adv.* on the top; at the top —*prep.* on the top of

-a·tor (āt'ər) [ME. -*atour* < OFr. < L. -ator: see -ATE¹ & -OR] a n.-forming suffix meaning one who or that which acts or does [improvisator]

-a·to·ry (ə tôr'ē, ə tō'rē) [L. -atorius < -ator, n. ending + -ius, adj. suffix] an adj.-forming suffix meaning of, characterized by, produced by [accusatory, exclamatory]

ATP [A(DENOSINE) t(ri)p(hosphate)] a substance, C₁₀H₁₆P₃O₁₃N₅, found in muscle tissue, important in the metabolism of all organisms, and the immediate source of energy as for muscular contractions: see also ADP

at·ra·bil·ious (a'trə bil'yəs) *adj.* [< L. *atra bilis,* black bile; sp. after BILIOUS: cf. MELANCHOLY] melancholy, morose, cross, etc.: also **at'ra·bil'iar** (-yər)

a·trem·ble (ə trem'b'l) *adv.* [Poet.] trembling

A·treus (ā'trōōs, ā'trē əs) [L. < Gr.] *Gr. Myth.* a king of Mycenae and father of Agamemnon and Menelaus: to avenge the treachery of his brother, Thyestes, he killed Thyestes' sons and served their flesh to him at a banquet

a·trip (ə trip') *adj.* [A-¹ + TRIP] *Naut.* raised just off the bottom: said of an anchor

a·tri·um (ā'trē əm) *n.,* pl. **a'tri·a** (-ə), **a'tri·ums** [L.] **1.** the central court or main room of an ancient Roman house **2.** a hall or entrance court **3.** *Anat.* a chamber or cavity, esp. either of the upper chambers of the heart; auricle —**a'tri·al** (-əl) *adj.*

a·tro·cious (ə trō'shəs) *adj.* [< L. *atrocis,* gen. of *atrox,* fierce, cruel < ater, black + -OUS] **1.** very cruel, evil, brutal, etc. **2.** appalling or dismaying **3.** [Colloq.] very bad, unpleasant, offensive, inferior, etc. [an atrocious joke] —*SYN.* see OUTRAGEOUS —**a·tro'cious·ly** *adv.* —**a·tro'cious·ness** *n.*

a·troc·i·ty (ə träs'ə tē) *n.,* pl. **-ties** [L. *atrocitas* < *atrox:* see ATROCIOUS] **1.** atrocious behavior or condition; brutality, cruelty, etc. **2.** an atrocious act **3.** [Colloq.] a very displeasing or tasteless thing

at·ro·phy (a'trə fē) *n.* [Fr. *atrophie* < L. *atrophia* < Gr. *atrophia,* a wasting away < a-, not + trephein, to nourish] a wasting away, esp. of body tissue, an organ, etc., or the failure of an organ or part to grow or develop, as because of insufficient nutrition —*vi.* **-phied, -phy·ing** to waste away or fail to develop —*vt.* to cause atrophy in —**a·troph·ic** (ə träf'ik) *adj.*

at·ro·pine (at'rə pēn', -pin) *n.* [< ModL. *Atropa,* deadly nightshade < Gr. *Atropos* (see ATROPOS) + -INE⁴] a poisonous, crystalline alkaloid, C₁₇H₂₃O₃N, obtained from belladonna and similar plants: used to relieve spasms and dilate the pupil of the eye: also **at'ro·pin** (-pin)

At·ro·pos (a'trə päs') [L. < Gr. *Atropos,* lit., not to be turned < a-, not + trepein, to turn] *Gr. Myth.* that one of the three Fates who is represented as cutting the thread of life

att. 1. attention **2.** attorney

at·ta·bal (at'ə bal') *n.* same as ATABAL

at·tach (ə tach') *vt.* [ME. *attachen* < OFr. *atacher,* altered by substitution of prefix < estachier, to attach < estache, a post, stake < Frank. *stakka (for base see STAKE)] **1.** to fasten by sticking, tying, etc. **2.** to make (a person or thing) part of; join (often used reflexively) [he attached himself to us] **3.** to connect by ties of affection, attraction, etc. **4.** to add or affix (a signature, codicil, etc.) **5.** to ascribe [I attach great significance to the news] **6.** to appoint by authority or order **7.** *Law* to take (property or a person) into custody of a court by writ **8.** *Mil.* to join (troops, a unit, etc.) temporarily to some other unit —*vi.* to be fastened or joined; adhere; belong [a moral obligation attaches to high rank] —*SYN.* see ASCRIBE, TIE —**at·tach'a·ble** *adj.*

at·ta·ché (at'ə shā'; chiefly Brit. ə tash'ā; Fr. ȧ tȧ shā') *n.* [Fr., pp. of *attacher,* ATTACH] a person with special duties on the diplomatic staff of an ambassador or minister to another country [press attaché, military attaché]

attaché case a flat, rectangular case for carrying documents, papers, etc.

at·tach·ment (ə tach'mənt) *n.* **1.** the act of attaching something **2.** anything used for attaching; fastening **3.** affectionate regard or devotion **4.** anything added or attached **5.** an accessory for an electrical appliance, machine, etc. **6.** *Law* a) a taking of a person, property, etc. into custody b) a writ authorizing this —*SYN.* see LOVE

at·tack (ə tak') *vt.* [Fr. *attaquer* < It. *attaccare* < OFr. *atachier,* ATTACH] **1.** to use force against in order to harm; start a fight with; strike out at with physical or military force; assault **2.** to speak or write against, esp. with vigor;

criticize, denounce, censure, etc. **3.** to begin working on energetically; undertake (a problem, task, etc.) vigorously **4.** to begin acting upon harmfully or destructively [the disease attacked him suddenly] —*vi.* to make an assault —*n.* **1.** the act of attacking **2.** any hostile offensive action, esp. with armed forces; onslaught **3.** the onset of a disease, or the recurrence of a chronic disease **4.** a beginning of any task, undertaking, etc. **5.** act or manner of such beginning **6.** *Music* promptness and precision in beginning a passage or phrase —**at·tack'er** *n.*

SYN.—**attack** implies vigorous, aggressive action, whether in actual combat or in an undertaking [to attack a city, a problem, etc.]; **assail** means to attack by repeated blows, thrusts, etc. [assailed by reproaches]; **assault** implies a sudden, violent attack or onslaught and suggests direct contact and the use of force; **beset** implies an attack or onset from all sides [beset with fears]; **storm** suggests a rushing, powerful assault that is stormlike in its action and effect; **bombard** means to attack with artillery or bombs, and in figurative use suggests persistent, repetitious action [to bombard a speaker with questions] —*ANT.* **defend, resist**

at·tain (ə tān') *vt.* [ME. *attainen* < OFr. *ataindre* < L. *attingere* < ad-, to + tangere, to touch] **1.** to gain through effort; accomplish; achieve **2.** to reach or come to; arrive at [he attained the age of ninety] —*vi.* to succeed in reaching or coming (to a goal) —*SYN.* see REACH —**at·tain'a·bil'i·ty** *n.* —**at·tain'a·ble** *adj.*

at·tain·der (ə tān'dər) *n.* [ME. *atteindre* < OFr. *ataindre:* see ATTAIN] **1.** forfeiture of property and loss of civil rights of a person sentenced to death or outlawed: see BILL OF ATTAINDER **2.** [Obs.] dishonor

at·tain·ment (ə tān'mənt) *n.* **1.** an attaining or being attained **2.** anything attained, as an acquired skill; accomplishment

at·taint (ə tānt') *vt.* **-taint'ed, -taint'ing,** archaic pp. **-taint'** [ME. *atteinten,* to convict < OFr. *ateint,* pp. of *ataindre:* see ATTAIN] **1.** to punish by attainder **2.** [Archaic] to disgrace or dishonor **3.** [Archaic] to infect **4.** [Archaic] to accuse **5.** [Obs.] to prove guilty —*n.* **1.** an attainder **2.** [Archaic] a taint; disgrace **3.** [Obs.] a touch or hit in tilting

at·tain·ture (ə tān'chər) *n.* [Obs.] **1.** attainder **2.** dishonor

at·tar (at'ər) *n.* [Per. *atar,* fragrance < Ar. *'itr,* perfume] an essential oil or perfume made from the petals of flowers, esp. of damask roses (**attar of roses**)

at·tem·per (ə tem'pər) *vt.* [ME. *attempren* < OFr. *atemprer* < L. *attemperare,* to fit, adjust < ad-, to + temperare, to control, TEMPER] **1.** to modify or reduce by mixture **2.** to control the temperature of **3.** to moderate (anger, etc.) **4.** to adapt (to)

at·tempt (ə tempt') *vt.* [ME. *attempten* < OFr. *attempter* < L. *attemptare,* to try, solicit < ad-, to + temptare, to try, attack] **1.** to make an effort to do, get, have, etc.; try; endeavor **2.** [Archaic] to tempt —*n.* **1.** a try; an endeavor **2.** an attack, as on a person's life —*SYN.* see TRY —**attempt the life of** to try to kill —**at·tempt'a·ble** *adj.*

at·tend (ə tend') *vt.* [ME. *attenden* < OFr. *atendre,* to wait, expect < L. *attendere,* to stretch toward, give heed to < ad-, to + tendere, stretch: see TEND²] **1.** [Now Rare] to take care or charge of; look after **2.** a) to wait on; minister to; serve b) to serve as doctor to during an illness **3.** to accompany; go with **4.** to accompany as a circumstance or result [success attended his efforts] **5.** to be present at [to attend a concert] **6.** [Archaic] to await **7.** [Archaic] to pay attention to —*vi.* **1.** to pay attention, give heed **2.** to be in readiness; wait (with on or upon) **3.** to devote or apply oneself (to) **4.** to give the required care or attention; see (to) **5.** [Obs.] to wait or delay —*SYN.* see ACCOMPANY

at·tend·ance (ə ten'dəns) *n.* [ME. < OFr. *atendance* < atendre: see ATTEND] **1.** the act of attending **2.** the persons or number of persons attending **3.** the degree of regularity in attending

at·tend·ant (-dənt) *adj.* [ME. < OFr., prp.] **1.** attending or serving [an attendant nurse] **2.** being present **3.** accompanying as a circumstance or result [attendant difficulties] —*n.* **1.** a person who attends or serves [an attendant at the zoo, a queen's attendants] **2.** a person present **3.** an accompanying thing; concomitant

at·tent (ə tent') *adj.* [L. *attentus,* pp. of *attendere:* see ATTEND] [Archaic] attentive

‡at·ten·tat (ȧ tän tȧ') *n.* [Fr.] an attempt, esp. an unsuccessful one, at an act of political violence

at·ten·tion (ə ten'shən) *n.* [L. *attentio* < pp. of *attendere:* see ATTEND] **1.** a) the act of keeping one's mind closely on something or the ability to do this; mental concentration b) mental readiness for such concentration **2.** notice or observation [her smile caught my attention] **3.** care or consideration [the matter will receive his immediate attention] **4.** a) thoughtful consideration for others b) an act of consideration, courtesy, or devotion: usually used in pl. [a suitor's attentions to a woman] **5.** *Mil.* a) the erect, motionless posture of soldiers in readiness for another command b) a command to assume this posture

at·ten·tive (ə ten'tiv) *adj.* [ME. & OFr. *attentif* < ML. *attentivus:* see ATTEND] **1.** paying attention; observant **2.** considerate, courteous, devoted, etc. [an attentive husband]

—*SYN*. see THOUGHTFUL —**at·ten′tive·ly** *adv.* —**at·ten′-tive·ness** *n.*

at·ten·u·ate (ə ten′yoo wāt′; *for adj.* -wit) *vt.* -**at′ed, -at′-ing** [< L. *attenuatus*, pp. of *attenuare*, to make thin < *ad-*, to + *tenuare* < *tenuis*, THIN] 1. to make slender or thin 2. to dilute; rarefy 3. to lessen in severity, value, amount, intensity, etc.; weaken 4. *Bacteriology* to make (a virus, etc.) less deadly 5. *Electronics* to reduce the strength of (an electrical impulse) —*vi.* to become thin, weak, etc. — *adj.* 1. attenuated 2. *Bot.* tapering gradually to a point —**at·ten′u·a·ble** (-wə b'l) *adj.* —**at·ten′u·a′tion** *n.* — **at·ten′u·a′tor** *n.*

at·test (ə test′) *vt.* [Fr. *attester* < L. *attestari* < *ad-*, to + *testari*, to bear witness < *testis*, a witness] 1. to declare to be true or genuine 2. to certify by oath or signature 3. to serve as proof of; demonstrate; make clear 4. to place (a person) on oath —*vi.* to bear witness; certify or testify (*to*) —*n.* [Archaic] attestation —**at·test′er, at·tes′tor** *n.*

at·tes·ta·tion (a′tes tā′shən) *n.* 1. the act of attesting 2. testimony

At·tic (at′ik) *adj.* [L. *Atticus* < Gr. *Attikos*] 1. of Attica 2. of or characteristic of Athens, its people, culture, etc.; Athenian 3. classical; simple, restrained, etc.: said of a style —*n.* 1. the Greek dialect of Attica, the literary language of ancient Greece 2. an Athenian

at·tic (at′ik) *n.* [Fr. *attique*, an attic < *Attique*, ATTIC, used as an architectural term] 1. a low wall or story above the cornice of a classical façade 2. the room or space just below the roof of a house; garret

At·ti·ca (at′i ka) [Gr. *Attikē*] province occupying a peninsula of SE Greece: 1,400 sq. mi.; pop. 2,058,000: in ancient times, a region dominated by Athens, its chief city: see GREECE, map

Attic faith unshakable faith

At·ti·cism (at′ə siz'm) *n.* [Gr. *Attikismos* < *Attikos*, ATTIC] [*also* a-] 1. an Attic idiom, style, custom, etc. 2. a graceful, restrained phrase —**At′ti·cize′** (-sīz′) *vt.*, *vi.* -**cized′, -ciz′ing**

Attic salt, Attic wit graceful, piercing wit

At·ti·la (at′'l ə, ə til′ə) [Goth., lit., little father] 406?–453 A.D.; king of the Huns (433?–453): called the *Scourge of God*

at·tire (ə tīr′) *vt.* -**tired′, -tir′ing** [ME. *atiren* < OFr. *atirier*, to put in order, arrange < *a tire*, in a row, in order; *a* (L. *ad*), to + *tire*, order, row, dress < ? Gmc. base whence G. *zier*, ornament, OE. *tir*, glory] to dress, esp. in fine garments; clothe; array —*n.* 1. clothes, esp. fine or rich apparel; finery 2. *Heraldry* a stag's antlers

at·ti·tude (at′ə tood′, -tyood′) *n.* [Fr. < It. *attitudine*, attitude, aptness < LL. *aptitudinis*, gen. of *aptitudo* < L. *aptus*, APT] 1. the position or posture assumed by the body in connection with an action, feeling, mood, etc. [to kneel in an *attitude* of prayer] 2. a manner of acting, feeling, or thinking that shows one's disposition, opinion, etc. [a friendly *attitude*] 3. one's disposition, opinion, mental set, etc. 4. *Aeron.* the position of an aircraft or spacecraft in relation to a given line or plane, as the horizon —*SYN*. see POSTURE —**strike an attitude** to assume a posture or pose, often an affected or theatrical one —**at′ti·tu′di·nal** *adj.*

at·ti·tu·di·nize (at′ə tood′'n iz′, -tyood′-) *vi.* -**nized′, -niz′ing** [It. *attitudine* (see ATTITUDE) + -IZE] to strike an attitude; pose

Att·lee (at′lē), **Clement Richard, 1st Earl Attlee,** 1883–1967; Brit. statesman; prime minister (1945–51)

at·to- (at′ō) [< Dan. *atten*, eighteen < ODan. *attan* < *atta*, eight + -*tjan*, -teen] *a combining form meaning* one quintillionth; the factor 10⁻¹⁸ [*attosecond*]

at·torn (ə turn′) *vi.* [ME. *attournen* < OFr. *atourner* < *a-* (L. *ad*), to + *torner*, TURN] 1. orig., to transfer homage and service from one feudal lord to another 2. to agree to continue as tenant under a new landlord —**at·torn′ment** *n.*

at·tor·ney (ə tur′nē) *n., pl.* -**neys** [ME. *attourne* < OFr. *atourne*, (one) appointed, pp. of *atourner*: see prec.] any person legally empowered to act as agent for, or in behalf of, another; esp., a lawyer —*SYN*. see LAWYER

attorney at law a lawyer

attorney general *pl.* **attorneys general, attorney generals** 1. the chief law officer and representative in legal matters of a national or State government, and legal adviser to the chief executive 2. [A- G-] the head of the United States Department of Justice and member of the President's Cabinet

at·tract (ə trakt′) *vt.* [ME. *attracten* < L. *attractus*, pp. of *attrahere*, to draw to < *ad-*, to + *trahere*, to DRAW] 1. to draw to itself or oneself; make approach or adhere [a magnet *attracts* iron and steel] 2. to get the admiration, attention, etc. of; allure [her beauty *attracted* people] —*vi.* to be attractive —**at·tract′a·ble** *adj.* —**at·tract′er, at·trac′tor** *n.*

SYN.—**attract** implies the exertion of a force such as magnetism to draw a person or thing and connotes susceptibility in the thing drawn; **allure** implies attraction by that which seductively offers pleasure, delight, reward, etc.; **charm** suggests the literal or figurative casting of a spell and implies very pleasing qualities in the agent; **fascinate** and **enchant** both also suggest a magical power, **fascinate** stressing irresistibility and **enchant** the evoking of great admiration; **captivate** implies a capturing of the attention or affection, but suggests a light, passing influence —*ANT.* repel

at·trac·tion (ə trak′shən) *n.* [ME. *attraccioun* < OFr.

attraction < L. *attractio*] 1. the act of attracting 2. power of attracting; esp., charm or fascination 3. anything that attracts or is meant to attract [movies are sometimes called *attractions*] 4. *Physics* the mutual action by which bodies or particles of matter tend to draw together or cohere: opposed to REPULSION

attraction sphere *Biol.* the central area of an aster, including the centrosome

at·trac·tive (-tiv) *adj.* [ME. < LL. *attractivus*] that attracts or has the power to attract; esp., pleasing, charming, pretty, etc. —**at·trac′tive·ly** *adv.* —**at·trac′tive·ness** *n.*

attrib. 1. attribute 2. attributive

at·tri·bute (ə trib′yoot; *for n.* a′trə byōot′) *vt.* -**but·ed, -but·ing** [< L. *attributus*, pp. of *attribuere*, to assign < *ad-*, to + *tribuere*, to assign < *tribus*: see TRIBE] 1. to set down or think of as belonging to, produced by, resulting from, or originating in; assign or ascribe [the play is *attributed* to Shakespeare] 2. to ascribe as a quality or characteristic peculiar to one —*n.* 1. a characteristic or quality of a person or thing 2. an object used in literature or art as a symbol for a person, office, etc. [winged feet are the *attribute* of Mercury] 3. *Gram.* a word or phrase used as an adjective —*SYN*. see ASCRIBE, QUALITY —**at·trib′ut·a·ble** (-yoo tə b'l) *adj.* —**at·tri·bu·tion** (a′trə byōo′shən) *n.*

at·trib·u·tive (ə trib′yoo tiv) *adj.* [Fr. *attributif*] 1. attributing 2. of or like an attribute 3. *Gram.* joined directly to (in English, generally preceding) the substantive that it modifies: said of an adjective —*n.* an attributive adjective [black in *black cat* is an *attributive*] —**at·trib′u·tive·ly** *adv.*

at·trit·ed (ə trīt′id) *adj.* [< L. *attritus*: see ATTRITION] worn down by friction or attrition

at·tri·tion (ə trish′ən) *n.* [ME. *attricioun* < L. *attritio* < *attritus*, pp. of *atterere*, to wear, rub away < *ad-*, to + *terere*, to rub: for IE. base see THROW] 1. the act or process of wearing away or grinding down by friction 2. any gradual wearing or weakening, esp. to the point of exhaustion [a siege is a battle of *attrition*] 3. the loss in the personnel of an organization due to natural causes such as death, retirement, etc. 4. *Theol.* an imperfect degree of repentance, caused by shame or fear of punishment: distinguished from CONTRITION

At·tu (at′ōō) westernmost island of the Aleutians

at·tune (ə tōōn′, -tyōōn′) *vt.* -**tuned′, -tun′ing** [AD- + TUNE] 1. to tune 2. to bring into harmony or agreement [old methods not *attuned* to the times]

atty. attorney

Atty. Gen. Attorney General

at. vol. atomic volume

a·twain (ə twān′) *adv.* [ME.: see A-¹ & TWAIN] [Archaic or Poet.] in two [cut *atwain*]

a·tween (ə twēn′) *prep., adv.* [Archaic or Dial.] between

a·twit·ter (ə twit′ər) *adv., adj.* twittering

at. wt. atomic weight

a·typ·i·cal (ā tip′i k'l) *adj.* not typical; not characteristic; abnormal: also **a·typ′ic** —**a·typ′i·cal·ly** *adv.*

‡**au** (ō) [Fr., contr. of *à le* < *à*, to + *le*, masc. form of def. article, the] *equivalent of* À LA: used with masc. nouns

Au [L. *aurum*] *Chem.* gold

A.U., AU angstrom unit

‡**au·bade** (ō bàd′) *n.* [Fr. < Sp. *albada* < *alba*, dawn: see ALBA] a piece of music, as a love song, suitable for performance at sunrise, or in the morning: the counterpart of SERENADE

Au·ber (ō ber′), **Da·niel (Francois Esprit)** (dà nyel′) 1782–1871; Fr. composer of operas

‡**au·berge** (ō berzh′) *n.* [Fr.] an inn

au·ber·gine (ō′bər zhēn′) *n.* [Fr. < Catal. *albergina* < Ar. *al-bādhinjān* < Per. *badindjan*] 1. eggplant 2. the color of eggplant, a dark purple

Au·ber·vil·liers (ō ber vē lyā′) city in France: NE suburb of Paris: pop. 71,000

Au·brey (ô′brē) [Fr. *Aubri* < G. *Alberich* < OHG. *alb*, elf + *rihhi*, ruler, control] a masculine name

au·brie·tia (ô brē′shə) *n.* [ModL. < *Claude Aubriet*, 18th-c. Fr. painter of floral and animal subjects] any of a genus (*Aubrietia*) of plants of the mustard family native to the Middle East, with showy, purplish flowers: often grown in rock gardens: also **au·bre′tia**

Au·burn (ô′bərn) [ult. after the family in Goldsmith's "The Deserted Village"] city in WC N.Y.: pop. 35,000

au·burn (ô′bərn) *adj., n.* [ME. *auburne* < OFr. *auborne* < L. *alburnus* < *albus*, white; meaning infl. by ME. *brun*, BROWN] reddish brown

‡**Au·bus·son** (ō bü sōn′) *adj.* [< *Aubusson*, town in C France] designating or of tapestries or tapestrylike rugs of a kind made in the Aubusson region of France

A.U.C. 1. [L. *ab urbe condita*] from the founding of the city (of Rome, 753? B.C.) 2. [L. *anno urbis conditae*] in a (specified) year from the founding of the city

Auck·land (ôk′lənd) seaport of N North Island, New Zealand: pop. 149,000 (met. area 515,000)

‡**au con·traire** (ō kôn trer′) [Fr.] on the contrary

‡**au cou·rant** (ō kōō rän′) [Fr., lit., with the current] fully informed on current matters; up-to-date

auc·tion (ôk′shən) *n.* [L. *auctio*, an increasing, sale by increase of bids < *auctus*, pp. of *augere*, to increase: see AUGMENT] 1. a public sale at which items are sold one by one, each going to the last and highest of a series of competing bidders 2. auction bridge 3. the bidding in bridge

—*vt.* to sell at auction —*SYN.* see SELL —**auction off** to sell at auction —☆**put up at auction** to offer for sale at an auction

auction bridge a variety of the game of bridge in which the players bid for the right to declare the trump or no-trump: the extra tricks the declarer wins beyond his bid count toward a game: see also CONTRACT BRIDGE

auc·tion·eer (ôk′shə nir′) *n.* a person whose work is selling things at auction —*vt.* to sell at auction

auc·to·ri·al (ôk tôr′ē əl) *adj.* [< L. *auctor*, author + -AL] of or by an author

au·cu·ba (ô′kyoo bə) *n.* [ModL. < Jap. *aokuba* < *aoku*, green] any of a genus (*Aucuba*) of evergreen shrubs, grown for their variegated foliage and red berries

aud. 1. audit 2. auditor

au·da·cious (ô dā′shəs) *adj.* [< L. *audacia*, audacity < *audax*, bold < *audere*, to be bold, to dare] 1. bold or daring; fearless 2. not restrained by a sense of shame, propriety, or decorum; rudely bold; brazen —*SYN.* see BRAVE — **au·da′cious·ly** *adv.* —**au·da′cious·ness** *n.*

au·dac·i·ty (ô das′ə tē) *n.* [ME. *audacite* < L. *audacia:* see prec.] 1. bold courage; daring 2. shameless or brazen boldness; insolence; impudence 3. *pl.* -**ties** an audacious act or remark —*SYN.* see TEMERITY

Au·den (ôd′'n), **W**(ystan) **H**(ugh) 1907–   ; U.S. poet, born in England

au·di·ble (ô′di b'l) *adj.* [ML. *audibilis* < L. *audire*, to hear] that can be heard; loud enough to be heard —*n.* ☆*Football* a play decided upon and called by the quarterback at the line of scrimmage —**au′di·bil′i·ty** (-bil′ə tē) *n.* —**au′di·bly** *adv.*

au·di·ence (ô′dē əns, ôd′yəns) *n.* [ME. & OFr. < L. *audientia*, a hearing, listening < *audiens*, prp. of *audire*, to hear < IE. *awiz-dh-io* < base *awis-*, to perceive physically, grasp, whence AESTHETE] 1. a group of persons assembled to hear and see a speaker, a play, a concert, etc. 2. all those persons who are tuned in to a particular radio or TV program ☆3. all those persons who pay attention to what one writes or says; one's public 4. the act or state of hearing 5. an opportunity to have one's ideas heard; a hearing 6. a formal interview with a person in high position

au·di·ent (-ənt) *adj.* [L. *audiens:* see AUDIENCE] listening; giving attention

au·dile (ô′dil) *adj.* [< L. *audire*, to hear + -ILE] auditory —*n. Psychol.* a person who relies mainly on his sense of hearing or whose imagery is chiefly in terms of sound

au·di·o (ô′dē ō) *adj.* [< L. *audire*, to hear] 1. of frequencies corresponding to sound waves that can normally be heard by the human ear ☆2. of or relating to the reproduction of sound, esp. to the sound phase of a telecast, as distinguished from the *video* (or picture) portion

au·di·o- (ô′dē ō) [see prec.] *a combining form meaning* of hearing or sound *[audiometer]*

au·di·o-fre·quen·cy (ô′dē ō frē′kwən sē) *adj.* of the band of audible sound frequencies or corresponding electric current frequencies, about 20 to 20,000 hertz

au·di·o·gram (ô′dē ə gram′) *n.* a graph showing the percentage of hearing loss in a particular ear, as indicated by an audiometer

au·di·ol·o·gy (ô′dē äl′ə jē) *n.* the science of hearing; esp., the evaluation of hearing defects and the rehabilitation of those who have such defects —**au′di·o·log′i·cal** (-ə läj′i k'l) *adj.* —**au′di·ol′o·gist** *n.*

au·di·om·e·ter (ô′dē äm′ə tər) *n.* an instrument for measuring the sharpness and range of hearing through the use of controlled amounts of sound —**au′di·om′e·try** (-trē) *n.* —**au′di·o·met′ric** (-ō met′rik) *adj.* —**au′di·om′e·trist** *n.*

au·di·o·phile (ô′dē ə fil′) *n.* a devotee of high-fidelity sound reproduction on record players, tape recorders, etc.

au·di·o-vis·u·al (ô′dē ō vizh′oo wəl) *adj.* 1. involving both hearing and sight 2. designating or of such materials or aids in teaching besides books as motion pictures, film-strips, recordings, radio, etc.

☆**au·di·phone** (ô′də fōn′) *n.* [AUDIO- + -PHONE] a device for the hard of hearing that transmits sound to the auditory nerves through the bones of the head

au·dit (ô′dit) *n.* [ME. < L. *auditus*, a hearing, pp. of *audire*, to hear] 1. a formal, often periodic examination and checking of accounts or financial records to verify their correctness 2. a settlement or adjustment of accounts 3. an account thus examined and adjusted 4. a final statement of account by auditors 5. any thorough examination and evaluation of a problem 6. [Archaic] a hearing, esp. by a court —*vt., vi.* 1. to examine and check (accounts, claims, etc.) ☆2. to attend (a college class) as a listener receiving no credits

au·di·tion (ô dish′ən) *n.* [L. *auditio* < pp. of *audire*, to hear] 1. the act or sense of hearing 2. a hearing to test the fitness of an actor, musician, etc., as for a particular job — ☆*vt.* to give an audition to —*vi.* to perform in an audition

au·di·tive (ô′də tiv) *adj.* [Rare] auditory

au·di·tor (ô′də tər) *n.* [ME. < L. < *audire*, to hear] 1. a hearer or listener 2. a person who is authorized to audit accounts ☆3. a person who audits classes

au·di·to·ri·um (ô′də tôr′ē əm) *n.* [L., neut. of *auditorius:*

see prec.] 1. a room for the gathering of an audience, as in a school, library, etc. 2. a building or hall for speeches, concerts, etc.

au·di·to·ry (ô′də tôr′ē) *adj.* [L. *auditorius* < *auditor*, AUDITOR] of hearing or the sense of hearing —*n., pl.* -**ries** [L. *auditorium*] [Archaic] 1. an assembly of hearers; audience 2. an auditorium —**au′di·tor′i·ly** *adv.*

Au·drey (ô′drē) [ult. < OE. *æthelthryth*, lit., noble might < *æthel*, noble + *thryth*, might, strength, etc.] a feminine name

Au·du·bon (ôd′ə bän′), **John James** 1785–1851; U.S. ornithologist, naturalist, & painter, born in Haiti; famed for his paintings of N.American birds

☆**Audubon Society** any of a number of affiliated groups organized for the conservation of wildlife and other natural resources

Au·er (ou′ər), **Leopold** 1845–1930; Hung. violinist & teacher, mainly in Russia

au fait (ō fā′) [Fr., lit., to the fact, in fact] 1. acquainted with the facts; well-informed 2. proficient; expert

‡**Auf·klä·rung** (ouf′kler′oon) *n.* [G. < *aufklären*, to enlighten < *auf-*, up + *klären*, to clear < *klar*, clear] *same as* the ENLIGHTENMENT

‡**au fond** (ō fôn′) [Fr.] at bottom; basically

‡**auf Wie·der·se·hen** (ouf vē′dər zā′ən) [G.] till we see each other again; goodbye: implies temporary parting

Aug. August

aug. augmentative

Au·ge·an (ô jē′ən) *adj.* [< L. *Augeas* < Gr. *Augeias*] 1. *Gr. Legend* of King Augeas or his stable, which held 3,000 oxen and remained uncleaned for 30 years until Hercules cleaned it in one day by diverting a river (or two rivers) through it 2. very filthy or corrupt

au·ger (ô′gər) *n.* [by faulty separation of ME. *a nauger* < OE. *nafogar*, nave drill < *nafu*, nave (of a wheel) + *gar*, a spear] 1. a tool with a spiral cutting edge for boring holes in wood, etc.: it is larger than a gimlet 2. a similar but larger tool, as for boring holes in the earth

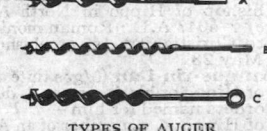

TYPES OF AUGER
(A, screw auger; B, ship auger; C, lip-ring auger)

Au·ger effect (ō zhā′) [after Pierre V. *Auger*, 1899–, Fr. physicist] the excitation of electrons within an atom initiated by the absorption of energy, as from cosmic rays, and accompanied by the emission of an electron

Auger shower a shower of electrons, photons, etc. resulting from the collision of primary cosmic rays with atomic nuclei in the atmosphere

aught (ôt) *n.* [ME. < OE. *awiht* < *a*, an one + *wiht*, a creature, WIGHT¹] 1. anything whatever *[for aught I know]* 2. [< *a naught* (see NAUGHT), wrongly divided *an aught*] a zero —*adv.* [Archaic] to any degree; at all

Au·gier (ō zhyā′), (**Guillaume Victor**) **Émile** (ā mēl′) 1820–89; Fr. playwright

au·gite (ô′jit) *n.* [L. *augites* < Gr. *augitēs*, a precious stone < *augē*, bright, shining] a black complex silicate mineral of vitreous luster occurring in igneous rocks; kind of pyroxene

aug·ment (ôg ment′; *for n.* ôg′ment) *vt.* [ME. *augmenten* < OFr. *augmenter* < L. *augmentare* < *augmentum*, an increase < *augere*, to increase < IE. base *aug-*, to multiply, increase, whence Gr. *auxein*, EKE¹, WAX²] 1. to make greater, as in size, quantity, strength, etc.; enlarge 2. *Gram.* to add an augment to —*vi.* to become greater; increase —*n.* 1. [Obs.] an increase 2. *Gram.* a prefixed vowel or a lengthening or diphthongization of the initial vowel to show past time in Greek and Sanskrit verbs —*SYN.* see INCREASE —**aug·ment′a·ble** *adj.* —**aug·ment′er** *n.*

aug·men·ta·tion (ôg′mən tā′shən) *n.* [ME. *augmentacioun* < ML. *augmentatio* < pp. of L. *augmentare:* see AUGMENT] 1. an augmenting or being augmented 2. a thing that augments; addition; increase 3. *Music* variation of a theme by lengthening, usually doubling, the time value of the notes

aug·ment·a·tive (ôg men′tə tiv) *adj.* [Fr. *augmentatif*] 1. augmenting or capable of augmenting 2. *Gram.* increasing the force of an idea expressed by a word or denoting increased size, intensity, etc. —*n.* an augmentative prefix, suffix, word, etc.; intensifier (Ex.: *perdurable*, eat *up*)

aug·ment·ed interval (ôg men′tid) *Music* an interval that is a half step greater than the corresponding major or perfect interval

Augmented Roman see INITIAL TEACHING ALPHABET

au gra·tin (ō grät′'n, ō-; grat′-) [Fr., lit., with scrapings] made with a lightly browned crust of bread crumbs and grated cheese

Augs·burg (ôgz′bərg; *G.* ouks′boork) city in Bavaria, S West Germany: pop. 210,000

au·gur (ô′gər) *n.* [L., orig., a priest at rituals of fertility and increase; prob. < OL. *augos*, *augeris*, increase, growth < *augere* (see AUGMENT); meaning infl. by *auspex*, AUSPEX] 1. in ancient Rome, any of a body of officials who interpreted omens as being favorable or unfavorable in connec-

tion with an undertaking 2. a fortuneteller; prophet; soothsayer —*vt.*, *vi.* [L. *augurari* < the *n.*] 1. to foretell or prophesy from omens 2. to be an omen (of) —**augur ill** (or **well**) to be a bad (or good) omen

au·gu·ry (ô′gyər ē) *n.*, *pl.* **-ries** [ME. *augurie* < L. *augurium*, divination < *augur*, AUGUR] 1. the practice of divination from omens 2. a formal ceremony conducted by an augur 3. an omen; sign; portent; indication

Au·gust (ô′gəst) [ME. < L. *Augustus* < *Augustus* Caesar: see ff.] a masculine name: see AUGUSTUS —*n.* the eighth month of the year, having 31 days: abbrev. Aug., Ag.

au·gust (ô gust′) *adj.* [L. *augustus*, orig., prob. "consecrated by the augurs"] 1. inspiring awe and reverence; imposing and magnificent 2. worthy of respect because of age and dignity, high position, etc.; venerable —*SYN.* see GRAND —**au·gust′ly** *adv.* —**au·gust′ness** *n.*

Au·gus·ta (ô gus′tə, ə-) [L., fem. of *Augustus*] 1. a feminine name 2. city in E Ga., on the Savannah River: pop. 60,000 3. capital of Me., on the Kennebec River: pop. 22,000

Au·gus·tan (ô gus′tən) *adj.* 1. of or characteristic of Augustus Caesar, his reign (27 B.C.–14 A.D.), or his times 2. of or characteristic of any age having standards or tastes like those of Augustus' age, as the period of Pope and Addison in England 3. classical; elegant —*n.* a writer living in an Augustan age

Augustan age 1. the period of Latin literature during the reign of Augustus Caesar, when elegance and form were highly valued 2. the similar period of English literature, c. 1690–1745: limited by some to the reign of Queen Anne (1702–1714)

Au·gus·tine (ô′gəs tēn′; ô gus′t'n, ə-) [L. *Augustinus*, dim. of *Augustus*] 1. a masculine name: var. *Austin, Augustin*; equiv. Fr. & G. *Augustin*, It. *Agostino* 2. Saint *a*) 354–430 A.D.; early Christian church father, born in Numidia; bishop of Hippo in North Africa: his day is August 28 *b*) ?–604? A.D.; Roman monk sent to convert the English to Christianity; 1st archbishop of Canterbury: his day is May 28

Au·gus·tin·i·an (ô′gəs tin′ē ən) *adj.* 1. of Saint Augustine of Hippo or his doctrines 2. designating or of any of several orders named for him —*n.* 1. a follower of Saint Augustine of Hippo 2. a member of an Augustinian religious order —**Au′gus·tin′i·an·ism, Au·gus′tin·ism** (ô gus′tə niz′m, ə-) *n.*

Au·gus·tus (ô gus′təs, ə-) [L. < *augustus*, AUGUST] 1. a masculine name: dim. *Gus, Gustus;* fem. *Augusta;* equiv. Fr. *Auguste,* G. *August,* It. *Augusto* 2. *(Gaius Julius Caesar Octavianus)* 63 B.C.–14 A.D.; 1st Roman emperor (27 B.C.–14 A.D.): grandnephew of Julius Caesar: also called *Octavian*

au jus (ō zhōō′, ō jōōs′; *Fr.* ō zhü′) [Fr., with the juice] served in its natural juice or gravy: said of meat

auk (ôk) *n.* [dial. *alk* < ON. *alka*] any of a number of related diving birds (family Alcidae) of northern seas, with a heavy body, webbed feet, a short tail, and short wings used as paddles

auk·let (ôk′lit) *n.* [AUK + -LET] any of several small kinds of auk

†au lait (ō le′) [Fr.] with milk

auld (ôld, äld) *adj.* [Dial. & Scot.] old

auld lang syne (ôld′ laŋ′ zin′; äld′; sin′) [Scot., lit., old long since] old times; the good old days (of one's youth, etc.)

au·lic (ô′lik) *adj.* [Fr. *aulique* < L. *aulicus* < Gr. *aulikos*, princely < *aulē*, a court] of a court; courtly

†au na·tu·rel (ō nà tü rel′) [Fr.] 1. in the natural state 2. naked 3. cooked or served simply

aunt (ant, änt) *n.* [ME. & OFr. *aunte* < L. *amita*, paternal aunt] 1. a sister of one's mother or father 2. the wife of one's uncle

aunt·ie, aunt·y (an′tē, än′-) *n.* aunt: a familiar or affectionate form

†au pair (ō per′) [Fr., lit., as an equal] designating, of, or in an arrangement in which services are exchanged on an even basis [an *au pair* girl who helped with the housework in return for room and board]

au·ra (ôr′ə) *n.*, *pl.* **-ras, -rae** (-ē) [ME. < L. < Gr., akin to *aēr*, air] 1. an invisible emanation or vapor, as the aroma of flowers 2. a particular atmosphere or quality that seems to arise from and surround a person or thing [enveloped in an *aura* of grandeur] 3. *Med.* a warning sensation that precedes a seizure or other neurological disorder

au·ral[1] (ôr′əl) *adj.* of an aura

au·ral[2] (ôr′əl) *adj.* [< L. *auris*, ear + -AL] of or received through the ear or the sense of hearing —**au′ral·ly** *adv.*

Au·rang·zeb (ôr′əŋ zeb′, ou′rəŋ-) 1618–1707; last influential Mogul emperor of Hindustan (1658–1707): also **Au′rang·zib′** (-zib′), **Au′rang·zebe′** (-zēb′)

au·rar (ou′rär) *n.*, *pl.* of EYRIR

au·re·ate (ôr′ē it) *adj.* [ME. *aureat* < LL. *aureatus* < L. *aureus* < *aurum*, gold] 1. golden; gilded 2. splendid or brilliant, often affectedly so

Au·re·li·a (ô rē′lē ə, -rēl′yə) [L., lit., golden < *aurum*, gold] a feminine name

Au·re·li·an (ô rē′lē ən, -rēl′yən) *(Lucius Domitius Aurelianus)* 212?–275 A.D.; Roman emperor (270–275)

Au·re·li·us (ô rē′lē əs, -rēl′yəs), **Marcus** *(Marcus Aurelius*

Antoninus) 121–180 A.D.; Roman emperor (161–180) & Stoic philosopher

au·re·ole (ôr′ē ōl′) *n.* [ME. < L. *aureola (corona)*, golden (crown) < L. *aureolus*, dim. of *aureus:* see AUREATE] 1. a radiance encircling the head or body, as in religious paintings, etc.; halo; glory 2. a band or fringe of light around the sun, etc., as when seen in a mist or during an eclipse; sun's corona Also **au·re·o·la** (ô rē′ə lə)

☆**Au·re·o·my·cin** (ôr′ē ō mīs′′n) [< L. *aureus*, golden (from its color) + Gr. *mykēs*, fungus + -IN[1]] *a trademark for* CHLORTETRACYCLINE

au·re·voir (ō′rə vwär′, ôr′ə-) [Fr. < *au*, to the + *revoir*, seeing again < L. *revidere*, to see again < *re-*, again + *videre*, to see] until we meet again; goodbye: implies temporary parting

au·ric (ôr′ik) *adj.* [< L. *aurum*, gold] 1. of or containing gold 2. *Chem.* designating or of compounds in which gold has a valence of three

au·ri·cle (ôr′ə k'l) *n.* [ME. < L. *auricula*, dim. of *auris*, EAR[1]] 1. *Anat. a)* the external part of the ear; pinna *b*) an atrium of the heart 2. *Biol.* an earlike part or organ

au·ric·u·la (ô rik′yoo lə) *n.*, *pl.* **-las, -lae′** (-lē′) [see prec.] 1. a species of primrose *(Primula auricula)* with leaves shaped like a bear's ear 2. *same as* AURICLE

au·ric·u·lar (-lər) *adj.* [ME. *auriculer* < ML. *auricularis* < L. *auricula:* see AURICLE] 1. of or near the ear, or having to do with the sense of hearing 2. received by or spoken directly into the ear; private [an *auricular* confession] 3. shaped like an ear 4. of an auricle —*n.* any of the feathers covering the opening of a bird's ear: *usually used in pl.* —**au·ric′u·lar·ly** *adv.*

au·ric·u·late (-lit, -lāt′) *adj.* [< L. *auricula* (see AURICLE) + -ATE[1]] having ears or earlike parts

au·rif·er·ous (ô rif′ər əs) *adj.* [L. *aurifer* < *aurum*, gold + *ferre*, to BEAR[1] + -OUS] bearing or yielding gold

au·ri·form (ôr′ə fôrm′) *adj.* [< L. *auris*, ear + -FORM] ear-shaped

Au·ri·ga (ô rī′gə) [ME. < L., lit., charioteer < *aurea*, bridle + *agere*, to drive] a N constellation between Perseus and Gemini

Au·rig·na·cian (ô′ri nyā′shən, -rig nā′-) *adj.* [Fr. *Aurignacien* < *Aurignac*, village in southern France, in whose caves artifacts were discovered] designating or of an upper paleolithic culture, characterized by artifacts of bone, flint scrapers, and two-edged blades, and the employment of primitive artistic designs

au·rochs (ôr′äks) *n.*, *pl.* **au′rochs** [G. *auerochs* < OHG. *urohso* < *uro*, aurochs (< IE. base *wer-*, damp, whence URINE & names of male animals, as L. *verres*, boar, Sans. *vṛsabha*, bull) + *ohso*, OX] 1. a nearly extinct European bison *(Bos bonasus)* 2. *same as* URUS

AUROCHS (72 in. high at shoulder)

Au·ro·ra (ô rôr′ə, ə-) [L., lit., dawn: for IE. base see EAST] 1. *Rom. Myth.* the goddess of dawn: identified with the Greek Eos 2. [immediately or ult. < prec.] *a)* city in NE Ill., near Chicago: pop. 74,000 *b*) city in NC Colo., near Denver: pop. 75,000 —*n.* [a-] *pl.* **-ras, -rae** (-ē) 1. the dawn 2. *same as* AURORA AUSTRALIS or AURORA BOREALIS —**au·ro′ral, au·ro′re·an** (-ē ən) *adj.*

aurora aus·tra·lis (ô strā′lis) [L., lit., southern aurora: see AURORA & AUSTRAL] luminous bands or streamers of light in the Southern Hemisphere, that are the counterpart of the aurora borealis; southern lights

aurora bo·re·a·lis (bôr′ē al′is) [L., lit., northern aurora: see AURORA & BOREAS] luminous bands or streamers of light sometimes appearing in the night sky of the Northern Hemisphere, believed to be electrical discharges in the ionized air; northern lights

au·rous (ôr′əs) *adj.* [< L. *aurum*, gold + -OUS] 1. of or containing gold 2. *Chem.* designating or of compounds in which gold has a valence of one

au·rum (ôr′əm) *n.* [L.] gold: symbol, Au

Au·rung·zeb (ôr′əŋ zeb′) *same as* AURANGZEB

AUS Army of the United States

Au·schwitz (ou′shvits) city in SW Poland: pop. 34,000: site of a Nazi concentration camp notorious as an extermination center: Pol. name, OŚWIĘCIM

aus·cul·tate (ôs′kəl tāt′) *vt.*, *vi.* **-tat′ed, -tat′ing** [< pp. of L. *auscultare*] to examine by auscultation —**aus′cul·ta′tor** *n.* —**aus·cul·ta·to·ry** (ôs kul′tə tôr′ē) *adj.*

aus·cul·ta·tion (ôs′kəl tā′shən) *n.* [L. *auscultatio*, a listening < *auscultare*, to listen < *aus-*, base of *auris*, EAR[1] + *cultare*, by metathesis < **clutare* < IE. base **kel-*, to incline] 1. a listening 2. a listening, often with the aid of a stethoscope, to sounds in the chest, abdomen, etc. so as to determine the condition of the heart, lungs, etc.

aus·pex (ôs′peks) *n.*, *pl.* **aus′pi·ces′** (-pə sēz′) [L., contr. of *avispex* < *avis*, bird + *spicere*, to see] in ancient Rome, an augur, or diviner, esp. one who watched for omens in the flight of birds

aus·pi·cate (ôs′pə kāt′) *vt.* **-cat′ed, -cat′ing** [< pp. of *auspicari*, to take the auspices < *auspex*, AUSPEX] [Now Rare] to begin formally or auspiciously, as with a ceremony invoking good fortune

aus·pice (ôs′pis) *n.*, *pl.* **aus′pi·ces′** (-pə sēz′) [Fr. < L.

auspicium, omen < *auspex*, AUSPEX] **1.** a watching for omens in the flight of birds; divination **2.** an omen; esp., a favorable omen or sign **3.** [*pl.*] approval and support; guiding sponsorship; patronage [a plan under government *auspices*]

aus·pi·cial (ôs pish'l) *adj.* **1.** of augury **2.** auspicious

aus·pi·cious (-əs) *adj.* [< L. *auspicium*, AUSPICE + -OUS] **1.** of good omen; boding well for the future; favorable; propitious **2.** favored by fortune; successful; prosperous —*SYN.* see FAVORABLE —**aus·pi'cious·ly** *adv.* —**aus·pi'cious·ness** *n.*

Aust. **1.** Australia **2.** Austria

Aus·ten (ôs'tən), **Jane** 1775–1817; Eng. novelist

aus·ten·ite (ôs'tə nīt') *n.* [Fr., after Sir Wm. C. Roberts-*Austen* (1843–1902), Eng. metallurgist] a nonmagnetic solid solution of carbon or iron carbide in some iron, obtained in high carbon steels by rapid quenching and deforming at high temperatures

Aus·ter (ôs'tər) [L.] [Poet.] the south wind: a personification

aus·tere (ô stir') *adj.* [ME. < OFr. < L. *austerus*, harsh < Gr. *austēros*, dry, harsh < *auein*, to dry < *auos*, dry < IE. base *saus, dry, whence SEAR[1] **1.** having a severe or stern look, manner, etc.; forbidding **2.** showing strict self-discipline and self-denial; ascetic **3.** very plain; lacking ornament or luxury [*austere* surroundings] **4.** [Rare] grave; sober —*SYN.* see SEVERE —**aus·tere'ly** *adv.*

aus·ter·i·ty (ô ster'ə tē) *n., pl.* -ties [ME. & OFr. *austerite* < L. *austeritas*] **1.** the quality or condition of being austere **2.** an austere act, habit, practice, or manner **3.** tightened economy, as because of shortages of consumers' goods

Aus·ter·litz (ôs'tər lits; *G.* ou'stər lits) town in C Czechoslovakia, near Brno: scene of Napoleon's victory (1805) over the combined Russian and Austrian armies: pop. 4,500: Czech. name, SLAVKOV

Aus·tin[1] (ôs'tən) **1.** a masculine name: see AUGUSTINE **2.** [after S.F. AUSTIN[2]] capital of Tex., in the C part, on the Colorado River: pop. 252,000 —*adj., n.* [Chiefly Brit.] Augustinian

Austin[2] **1.** Alfred, 1835–1913; Eng. poet; poet laureate (1896–1913) **2.** John, 1790–1859; Eng. jurist **3.** Stephen (Fuller), 1793–1836; Am. pioneer; founded 1st Am. colony in Texas in early 1820's

Austl. **1.** Australasia **2.** Australia

aus·tral (ôs'trəl) *adj.* [L. *australis*, southern < *auster*, south wind, the south: for IE. base see EAST; shift in meaning from "east" prob. due to false assumption concerning direction of axis of Italy] **1.** southern; southerly **2.** [A-] Australian

Aus·tral·a·sia (ôs'trə lā'zhə; *chiefly Brit.* -shə) generally, the islands of the SW Pacific; sometimes, specif., *a)* Australia and New Zealand and adjacent islands *b)* Australia, New Zealand, New Guinea, the Malay Archipelago and all islands south of the equator and between E longitudes 100 and 180 *c)* Oceania —**Aus'tral·a'sian** *adj., n.*

Aus·tral·ia (ô strāl'yə) [ModL. < L. (*terra*) *australis*, southern (land): see AUSTRAL] **1.** island continent in the Southern Hemisphere between the S Pacific and Indian oceans **2.** country comprising this continent and Tasmania: a member of the Brit. Commonwealth: 2,971,081 sq. mi.; pop. 12,446,000; cap. Canberra: official name, **the Commonwealth of Australia** —**Aus·tral'ian** *adj., n.*

Australian Alps mountain range in SE Australia, in the states of Victoria and New South Wales: highest peak, Mount KOSCIUSKO

Australian Antarctic Territory region in Antarctica, south of Tasmania, claimed by Australia: c. 2,472,000 sq. mi.

☆**Australian ballot** an official ballot listing candidates for election to public office and distributed inside the polling place to be marked by the voter in secret: it originated in Australia and is widely used in the U.S.

Australian Capital Territory federal territory within New South Wales, consisting of an area in the SE part and a port at Jervis Bay: site of Canberra, Australian capital: 939 sq. mi.; pop. 89,000

Australian crawl *Swimming* an earlier form of the crawl stroke, in which each arm stroke is accompanied by a flutter kick of the opposite leg, resulting in a two-beat stroke

Australian terrier a small, sturdy terrier with a wire-haired, blue-black or silver-black coat with tan markings: it was originally bred in Australia

Aus·tra·loid (ôs'trə loid') *adj.* [AUSTRAL(IA) + -OID] designating or of an ethnic group that includes the Australian aborigines, the Veddas of Ceylon, the Ainu, etc. —*n.* any member of this group

AUSTRALIAN TERRIER
(10 in. high at shoulder)

aus·tral·o·pith·e·cine (ô strā'lō pith'ə sēn', -stral'ō-; ôs'trə-) *adj.* [ModL. *australopithecinus* < *Australopithecus*, lit., South African ape < L. *australis*, southern (see AUSTRAL) + ModL. -*pithecus* (see

PITHECANTHROPUS ERECTUS)] of or relating to a genus (*Australopithecus*) of extinct apelike men from southern Africa that made tools and walked erect

Aus·tra·sia (ôs trā'zhə; *chiefly Brit.* -shə) [ML. < OHG. *ostar:* see ff.] easternmost part of the kingdom of the Merovingian Franks from the 6th to the 8th cent., composed of what is now NE France, Belgium, and W Germany

Aus·tri·a (ôs'trē ə) [ML. < OHG. *ostarrih* < *ostar* < *ostan*, EAST + *rihhi*, realm] country in C Europe: part of Austria-Hungary (1867–1918) until proclaimed a republic after the Versailles Treaty: 32,375 sq. mi.; pop. 7,371,000; cap. Vienna: Ger. name, ÖSTERREICH —**Aus'tri·an** *adj., n.*

Aus·tri·a-Hun·ga·ry (-huŋ'gər ē) former monarchy in C Europe (1867–1918) consisting of territory that became Austria, Hungary, and Czechoslovakia, as well as parts of Poland, Romania, Yugoslavia, and Italy: it was dissolved by the Versailles Treaty: in 1910, c. 260,000 sq. mi.; pop. c. 50,000,000 —**Aus'tro-Hun·gar'i·an** *adj.*

Aus·tro-[1] (ôs'trō) *a combining form meaning* Austria [*Austro*-Hungarian]

Aus·tro-[2] (ôs'trō) [< L. *auster:* see AUSTRAL] *a combining form meaning:* **1.** South; Southern **2.** Australian

Aus·tro-As·i·at·ic (ôs'trō ā'zhē at'ik) *adj.* [AUSTRO-[2] + ASIATIC] designating or of a family of languages widely scattered throughout southeastern Asia, including Mon, Khmer, Vietnamese, etc.

Aus·tro·ne·sia (ôs'trō nē'zhə; *chiefly Brit.* -shə) [AUSTRO-[2] + Gr. *nēsos*, island + -IA] **1.** islands of the C and S Pacific **2.** island area extending from Madagascar east to Hawaii and Easter Island

Aus·tro·ne·sian (-zhən; *chiefly Brit.* -shən) *adj.* **1.** of Austronesia, its peoples, etc. **2.** *same as* MALAYO-POLYNESIAN

aut- (ôt) *same as* AUTO-, used before vowels

au·ta·coid (ôt'ə koid') *n.* [AUT- + Gr. *akos*, cure, remedy + -OID] an organic substance, such as a hormone, carried by the bloodstream or other body fluids from the part of the body where it is formed to another part on which it has activating effects

au·tar·chy (ô'tär kē) *n., pl.* -chies [Gr. *autarchia* < *autarchos*, autocrat, absolute ruler < *autos*, self + *archos*, first, ruler] **1.** absolute rule or sovereignty; autocracy **2.** a country under such rule **3.** *same as* AUTARKY —**au·tar'chic, au·tar'chi·cal** *adj.*

au·tar·ky (ô'tär kē) *n.* [Gr. *autarkeia*, self-sufficiency < *autos*, self + *arkein*, to achieve, suffice] economic self-sufficiency, esp. on a national basis; national policy of getting along without imports —**au·tar'kic, au·tar'ki·cal** *adj.*

au·te·cious (ô tē'shəs) *adj. same as* AUTOECIOUS

aut·e·col·o·gy (ôt'i käl'ə jē) *n.* [AUT- + ECOLOGY] the ecological study of a single organism, or of a single species of organism: cf. SYNECOLOGY

‡**au·teur** (ō tër') *n., pl.* **au·teurs'** (-tër') [Fr., author] a film-maker, esp. a director, notable for his creativity and personal style

auth. **1.** author **2.** authority **3.** authorized

au·then·tic (ô then'tik, ə-) *adj.* [ME. *autentike* < OFr. *autentique* < LL. *authenticus* < Gr. *authentikos*, genuine < *authentēs*, one who does things himself < *autos*, self + -*hentēs* < IE. base *sen-, to prepare, achieve] **1.** that can be believed or accepted; trustworthy; reliable [an *authentic* news report] **2.** that is in fact as represented; genuine; real [an *authentic* antique] **3.** legally attested or executed, as a deed, affidavit, etc. **4.** [Obs.] authoritative —**au·then'ti·cal·ly** *adv.*

SYN.—**authentic** implies reliability and trustworthiness, stressing that the thing considered is in agreement with fact or actuality [an *authentic* report]; **genuine** is applied to that which really is what it is represented to be, emphasizing freedom from admixture, adulteration, sham, etc. [*genuine* silk; *genuine* grief]; **bona fide** is properly used when a question of good faith is involved; **veritable** implies correspondence with the truth and connotes absolute affirmation [a *veritable* fool] —*ANT.* spurious, counterfeit, sham

au·then·ti·cate (ô then'tə kāt', ə-) *vt.* -cat'ed, -cat'ing [< ML. *authenticatus*, pp. of *authenticare* < LL. *authenticus*] **1.** to make authentic or valid **2.** to establish the truth of; verify **3.** to prove to be genuine or as represented —*SYN.* see CONFIRM —**au·then'ti·ca'tion** *n.* —**au·then'ti·ca'tor** (-kāt'ər) *n.*

au·then·tic·i·ty (ô'thən tis'ə tē) *n.* the quality or state of being authentic; reliability; genuineness

au·thor (ô'thər) *n.* [ME. *autour* < OFr. *auteur* < L. *auctor*, enlarger, author < *augere*, to increase: see AUGMENT] **1.** one who makes or originates something; creator; originator ["*author* of liberty"] **2.** the writer (*of* a book, article, etc.) **3.** an author's writings [to translate French *authors* into English] —*vt.* to be the author of —**au·tho·ri·al** (ô thôr'ē əl) *adj.*

au·thor·ess (ô'thər is) *n.* [Now Rare] a woman writer

au·thor·i·tar·i·an (ə thôr'ə ter'ē ən, -thär'-) *adj.* [AU-THORIT(Y) + -ARIAN] believing in, relating to, or characterized by unquestioning obedience to authority, as that of a dictator, rather than individual freedom of judgment and action —*n.* a person who advocates, practices, or enforces such obedience —**au·thor'i·tar'i·an·ism** *n.*

au·thor·i·ta·tive (ə thôr′ə tāt′iv, -thär′-) *adj.* [ML. *auctoritativus*] **1.** having or showing authority; official **2.** based on competent authority; reliable because coming from one who is an expert or properly qualified [an *authoritative* biography] **3.** asserting authority; fond of giving orders; dictatorial —**au·thor′i·ta′tive·ly** *adv.* —**au·thor′i·ta′tive·ness** *n.*

au·thor·i·ty (ə thôr′ə tē, -thär′-) *n., pl.* -**ties** [ME. & OFr. *autorite* < L. *auctoritas* < *auctor*, AUTHOR] **1.** *a)* the power or right to give commands, enforce obedience, take action, or make final decisions; jurisdiction *b)* the position of one having such power [a person in *authority*] **2.** such power as delegated to another; authorization; warrant [he has my *authority* to do it] **3.** power or influence resulting from knowledge, prestige, etc. **4.** *a)* the citation of a writing, decision, etc. in support of an opinion, action, etc. *b)* the writing, etc. cited **5.** reliability of a source or witness **6.** *a)* [pl.] persons, esp. in government, having the power or right to enforce orders, laws, etc. *b)* a government agency that administers a project **7.** a person with much knowledge or experience in some field, whose information or opinion is hence reliable; expert **8.** self-assurance and expertness that comes with experience [the pianist's performance lacked *authority*] —*SYN.* see INFLUENCE, POWER

au·thor·i·za·tion (ô′thər i zā′shən) *n.* **1.** an authorizing or being authorized **2.** legal power or right; sanction

au·thor·ize (ô′thə rīz′) *vt.* -**ized**, -**iz′ing** [ME. *autorisen* < OFr. *autoriser* < ML. *auctorizare* < L. *auctor*, AUTHOR] **1.** to give official approval to or permission for [the city *authorized* a housing project] **2.** to give power or authority to; empower; commission **3.** to give justification for; warrant —**au′thor·iz′er** *n.*

SYN.—**authorize** implies the giving of power or right to act, ranging in application from a specific legal power to discretionary powers in dealings of any kind; to **commission** a person is to authorize as well as instruct him to perform a certain duty, as the execution of an artistic work, or to appoint him to a certain rank or office; **accredit** implies the sending of a person, duly authorized and with the proper credentials, as an ambassador, delegate, etc.; **license** implies the giving of formal legal permission to do some specified thing and often emphasizes regulation [to *license* hunters]

au·thor·ized (-rīzd′) *adj.* **1.** established or justified by authority **2.** given authority [my *authorized* agent]

Authorized Version the revised English translation of the Bible published in England in 1611 with the authorization of King James I: also called *King James Version*

au·thor·less (ô′thər lis) *adj.* with the author or authors unknown; anonymous

au·thor·ship (-ship′) *n.* **1.** the profession or occupation of a writer. **2.** the origin (of a book, etc.) with reference to its author [a story of unknown *authorship*] **3.** the source (of an idea, deed, etc.) with reference to its originator

Auth. Ver. Authorized Version

☆**au·tism** (ô′tiz′m) *n.* [AUT- + -ISM] *Psychol.* a state of mind characterized by daydreaming, hallucinations, and disregard of external reality —**au·tis′tic** *adj.*

☆**au·to** (ôt′ō) *n., pl.* -**tos** an automobile —*vi.* -**toed**, -**to·ing** to go by automobile: an earlier usage

au·to- (ôt′ō, -ə; ät′-) [Gr. *autos*, self] *a combining form meaning:* **1.** of or for oneself; self [autobiography] **2.** by oneself or itself [automobile]

au·to·an·ti·bod·y (ôt′ō an′tə bäd′ē) *n.* an antibody that acts against a component substance of the body in which it is produced

‡**Au·to·bahn** (ou′tō bän′; *E.* ôt′ə bän′) *n., pl.* -**bahn′en** (-bä′nən) [G. < *auto(mobil)*, AUTOMOBILE + *bahn*, a course, highway] in Germany, an automobile expressway

au·to·bi·og·ra·pher (ôt′ə bī ä′grə fər, -bē-) *n.* a person who writes the story of his own life

au·to·bi·og·ra·phy (-bī ä′grə fē, -bē-) *n., pl.* -**phies 1.** the art or practice of writing one's own biography **2.** the story of one's own life written or dictated by oneself —**au′to·bi′o·graph′i·cal** (-bī′ə graf′i k′l), **au′to·bi′o·graph′ic** *adj.* —**au′to·bi′o·graph′i·cal·ly** *adv.*

☆**au·to·bus** (ôt′ō bus) *n. same as* BUS

au·to·ca·tal·y·sis (ôt′ō kə tal′ə sis) *n.* the catalysis of a reaction by one of the products produced in the reaction

au·to·ceph·a·lous (-sef′ə ləs) *adj.* [see AUTO- & -CEPHA-LOUS] self-governing; independent: said of certain churches within the communion of the Orthodox Eastern Church

au·toch·thon (ô täk′thən) *n., pl.* -**thons**, -**tho·nes′** (-thə nēz′) [Gr. *autochthōn*, sprung from the land itself < *autos*, self + *chthōn*, earth, ground] **1.** any of the earliest known inhabitants of a place; aborigine **2.** any indigenous animal or plant —**au·toch′tho·nous** (-thə nəs), **au·toch′-tho·nal** *adj.* —**au·toch′tho·nous·ly** *adv.*

au·to·clave (ôt′ə klāv′) *n.* [Fr. < *auto-*, AUTO- + L. *clavis*, key] a container for sterilizing, cooking, etc. by super-heated steam under pressure —*vt.* -**claved′**, -**clav′ing** to sterilize or cook by means of such a device

au·to·coid (-koid′) *n. same as* AUTACOID

au·toc·ra·cy (ô täk′krə sē) *n., pl.* -**cies** [Gr. *autokrateia*, absolute power < *autokratēs*: see AUTOCRAT] **1.** government in which one person has absolute power; dictatorship; despotism **2.** a country with this kind of government **3.** unlimited power or authority of one person over others

au·to·crat (ôt′ə krat′) *n.* [Fr. *autocrate* < Gr. *autokratēs*, absolute ruler < *autos*, self + *kratos*, power, rule: see -CRAT]

1. a ruler with absolute power; dictator; despot **2.** anyone having unlimited power over others **3.** any domineering, self-willed person —**au′to·crat′ic**, **au′to·crat′i·cal** *adj.* —**au′to·crat′i·cal·ly** *adv.*

au·to-da-fé (ôt′ō də fā′, out′-) *n., pl.* **au′tos-da-fé** [Port., lit., act of the faith < *auto* (< L. *actus*, ACT) + *da*, of the + *fé* (< L. *fides*, faith)] **1.** the public ceremony in which the Inquisition pronounced judgment and passed sentence on those tried as heretics **2.** the execution by the secular power of the sentence thus passed; esp., the public burning of a heretic

‡**au·to de fe** (ou′tō de fe′) *pl.* **au′tos de fe′** (ou′tōs) [Sp.] *same as* AUTO-DA-FÉ

au·to·di·dact (ôt′ō dī′dakt) *n.* [< Gr. *autodidaktos*, self-taught: see AUTO- & DIDACTIC] a person who is self-taught —**au′to·di·dac′tic** (-dī dak′tik) *adj.*

au·to·dyne (ôt′ə dīn′) *adj.* [AUTO- + DYNE] designating or of a system of heterodyne radio reception in which a single tube serves both as oscillator and first detector —*n.* **1.** an autodyne system **2.** an autodyne receiver

au·toe·cious (ô tē′shəs) *adj.* [AUTO- + Gr. *oikos*, house + -OUS] *Biol.* passing the entire life cycle on one host, as certain parasites do, esp. rust fungi —**au·toe′cious·ly** *adv.* —**au·toe′cism** (-siz′m) *n.*

au·to·er·o·tism (ôt′ō er′ə tiz′m) *n.* [AUTO- + EROTISM: term coined by Havelock Ellis] **1.** pleasurable sensations or tensions arising in the erogenous body zones without external stimulation **2.** self-initiated activity aimed at reducing sexual excitations, as in masturbation Also **au′to·e·rot′i·cism** (-i rät′ə siz′m) —**au′to·e·rot′ic** (-i rät′ik) *adj.* —**au′to·e·rot′i·cal·ly** *adv.*

au·tog·a·my (ô täg′ə mē) *n.* [AUTO- + -GAMY] **1.** self-fertilization, as in a flower receiving pollen from its own stamens **2.** internal self-fertilization in algae, fungi, protozoa, etc. by the fusion of gametes or nuclei within the same individual —**au·tog′a·mous** (-məs) *adj.*

au·to·gen·e·sis (ôt′ō jen′ə sis) *n.* [AUTO- + GENESIS] *same as* SPONTANEOUS GENERATION —**au′to·ge·net′ic** (-jə net′ik) *adj.* —**au′to·ge·net′i·cal·ly** *adv.*

au·tog·e·nous (ô täj′ə nəs) *adj.* [Gr. *autogenēs* (< *autos*, self + *genesis*, birth) + -OUS] **1.** self-generated or self-generating **2.** produced in or obtained from one's own body [an *autogenous* vaccine] Also **au·to·gen·ic** (ôt′ə jen′ik) —**au·tog′e·nous·ly** *adv.*

au·to·gi·ro, au·to·gy·ro (ôt′ə jī′rō) *n., pl.* -**ros** [orig. a trademark, *Autogiro* < AUTO- + Gr. *gyros*, a circle] an aircraft that moves forward by means of a propeller and is supported in the air mainly by means of a large rotor mounted horizontally above the fuselage and turned by air pressure rather than motor power: largely superseded by the HELICOPTER

au·to·graph (ôt′ə graf′) *n.* [L. *autographum*, neut. of *autographus* < Gr. *autographos*, written with one's own hand < *autos*, self + *graphein*, to write] **1.** a person's own signature or handwriting **2.** a thing written in one's own handwriting; original manuscript; holograph —*vt.* **1.** to write (something) with one's own hand **2.** to write one's signature on or in

au·to·graph·ic (ôt′ə graf′ik) *adj.* **1.** of, for, or like an autograph or autographs **2.** written in one's own hand-writing **3.** that makes a record automatically, as some instruments —**au′to·graph′i·cal·ly** *adv.*

au·tog·ra·phy (ô täg′rə fē) *n.* [< AUTOGRAPH] **1.** the writing of something with one's own hand **2.** a person's own handwriting **3.** autographs in general

au·to·harp (ôt′ō härp′) *n.* [AUTO- + HARP] a type of zither for playing chordal accompaniments by means of a series of dampers worked by keys

au·to·hyp·no·sis (ôt′ō hip nōs′is) *n.* the act of hypnotizing oneself or the state of being so hypnotized —**au′to·hyp·not′ic** (-nät′ik) *adj.*

au·to·im·mune (-i myoōn′) *adj.* initiating or resulting from the production of autoantibodies, sometimes with damage to normal components of the body —**au′to·im·mu′ni·ty** *n.*

au·to·in·fec·tion (-in fek′shən) *n.* infection from a source within the organism itself, as from harmful bacteria previously present but heretofore away from vulnerable areas

au·to·in·oc·u·la·tion (-in äk′yə lā′shən) *n.* **1.** inoculation of a patient with a vaccine prepared from microorganisms from his own body **2.** a spreading of infection from one part to other parts in the body

au·to·in·tox·i·ca·tion (-in täk′sə kā′shən) *n.* poisoning by toxic substances generated within the body

☆**au·to·ist** (ôt′ō ist) *n. same as* MOTORIST

au·to·ki·net·ic (ôt′ō ki net′ik) *adj.* [AUTO- + KINETIC] that moves automatically; self-moving

☆**au·to·load·ing** (ôt′ō lō′din) *adj. same as* SEMIAUTOMATIC (sense 2)

au·tol·o·gous (ô täl′ə gəs) *adj.* [AUTO- + (HOMO)LOGOUS] derived from the same organism or from one of its parts [an *autologous* graft]

au·tol·y·sate (ôt′ə li′sāt, ô täl′ə sāt′) *n.* [AUTOLYS(IS) + -ATE²] a product of autolysis

au·to·ly·sin (ôt′ə li′sin, ô täl′ə sin) *n.* [AUTOLYS(IS) + -IN¹] a substance that produces autolysis

au·tol·y·sis (ô täl′ə sis) *n.* [AUTO- + -LYSIS] the destruction of cells or tissues by enzymes within them, as after death or in some diseases —**au·to·lyt·ic** (ôt′ə lit′ik) *adj.*

au·to·lyze (ôt′ə līz′) *vt., vi.* **-lyzed′, -lyz′ing** to affect with or undergo autolysis

au·to·mat (ôt′ə mat′) *n.* [G. < Gr. *automatos:* see AUTOMATIC] a restaurant in which patrons get food from small compartments with doors opened by putting coins into slots

au·tom·a·ta (ô täm′ə tə) *n. alt. pl. of* AUTOMATON

☆**au·to·mate** (ôt′ə māt′) *vt.* **-mat′ed, -mat′ing** [back-formation < *automation*] **1.** to convert (a factory, process, etc.) to automation **2.** to use the techniques of automation in [*automated* teaching]

au·to·mat·ic (ôt′ə mat′ik) *adj.* [Gr. *automatos*, self-moving, self-thinking (< *autos*, self + component < IE. *mntos, thinking < base **men-*, to think, whence MIND, MEMORY) + -IC] **1.** done without conscious thought or volition, as if mechanically, or from force of habit **2.** involuntary or reflex, as some muscle or gland action **3.** *a)* moving, operating, etc. by itself; regulating itself [*automatic* machinery] *b)* done with automatic equipment [an *automatic* landing] **4.** *Firearms a)* using the force of the explosion of a shell to eject the empty cartridge case, place the next cartridge into the breech, and fire it, so that shots continue in rapid succession until the trigger is released *b)* popularly, *same as* SEMIAUTOMATIC —*n.* **1.** an automatic (or, popularly, semiautomatic) pistol, rifle, etc. **2.** any automatic machine —*SYN.* see SPONTANEOUS —**au′to·mat′i·cal·ly** *adv.*

automatic direction finder a type of radio compass that indicates automatically the direction of the station to which it is tuned, used esp. on aircraft

au·to·ma·tic·i·ty (ôt′ə mə tis′ə tē) *n.* the condition of being automatic or the degree of this

automatic pilot a gyroscopic instrument that automatically keeps an aircraft, missile, etc. to a predetermined course and attitude; gyropilot

☆**au·to·ma·tion** (ôt′ə mā′shən) *n.* [AUTOMA(TIC) + -TION] **1.** in manufacturing, a system or method in which many or all of the processes of production, movement, and inspection of parts and materials are automatically performed or controlled by self-operating machinery, electronic devices, etc. **2.** any system or method resembling this in using self-operating equipment, electronic devices, etc. to replace human beings in doing routine or repetitive work [*automation* in teaching] **3.** the condition of being automated

au·tom·a·tism (ô täm′ə tiz′m) *n.* [AUTOMAT(IC) + -ISM] **1.** the quality or condition of being automatic **2.** automatic action **3.** *Philos.* the theory that the human or animal body is a machine governed by physical laws and that consciousness does not control but only accompanies its actions **4.** *Physiol. a)* action independent of outside stimulus *b)* action not controlled by the will *c)* the power of such action **5.** *Psychol.* an automatic or unconscious action, as a tic **6.** free expression of the unconscious mind by releasing it from the control of the conscious: a surrealist concept —**au·tom′a·tist** *n.*

au·tom·a·tize (-tīz′) *vt.* **-tized′, -tiz′ing 1.** to make automatic **2.** *same as* AUTOMATE —**au·tom′a·ti·za′tion** *n.*

au·tom·a·ton (ô täm′ə tän′, -tən) *n., pl.* **-tons′, -ta** (-tə) [Gr., neut. of *automatos:* see AUTOMATIC] **1.** anything that can move or act of itself **2.** an apparatus that automatically performs certain actions by responding to preset controls or encoded instructions **3.** an electronic machine, control device, etc. equipped with a computer and designed to operate automatically in response to instructions previously fed into the computer **4.** a person or animal acting in an automatic or mechanical way

☆**au·to·mo·bile** (ôt′ə mə bēl′, -mō-; ôt′ə mə bēl′; ôt′ə mō′bēl) *n.* [Fr.: see AUTO- & MOBILE] a passenger car, usually four-wheeled, propelled by an engine or motor, esp. an internal-combustion engine, that is part of it, meant for traveling on streets or roads; motorcar —*vi.* **-biled′, -bil′ing** [Now Rare] to drive or ride in an automobile —**au′to·mo·bil′ist** *n.*

au·to·mo·tive (ôt′ə mōt′iv) *adj.* [AUTO- + -MOTIVE] **1.** moving by means of its own power; self-moving **2.** of or having to do with automobiles or motor vehicles

au·to·nom·ic (-näm′ik) *adj.* **1.** occurring involuntarily; automatic **2.** of or controlled by the autonomic nervous system **3.** *Biol.* resulting from internal causes, as through a mutation —**au′to·nom′i·cal·ly** *adv.*

autonomic nervous system the sympathetic and parasympathetic divisions of the nervous system, that control the motor functions of the heart, lungs, intestines, glands, and other internal organs, and of the smooth muscles, blood vessels, and lymph vessels

au·ton·o·mist (ô tän′ə mist) *n.* a person desiring or advocating autonomy

au·ton·o·mous (-məs) *adj.* [Gr. *autonomos*, independent < *autos*, self + *nomos*, law] **1.** of or having to do with autonomy **2.** *a)* having self-government *b)* functioning independently without control by others **3.** *Biol. a)* existing, functioning, or developing independently of other parts or forms *b)* making its own food; autotrophic: said of a green plant or of any of certain bacteria and other lower organisms in which photosynthesis or chemosynthesis

takes place *c)* resulting from internal causes; autonomic

au·ton·o·my (-mē) *n.* [Gr. *autonomia*] **1.** the fact or condition of being autonomous; self-government; independence **2.** *pl.* **-mies** any state that governs itself

au·to·phyte (ôt′ə fīt′) *n.* [AUTO- + -PHYTE] *Bot.* any plant that makes its own food from inorganic matter —**au′to·phyt′ic** (-fit′ik) *adj.* —**au′to·phyt′i·cal·ly** *adv.*

au·to·pi·lot (-pī′lət) *n. same as* AUTOMATIC PILOT

au·to·plas·ty (-plas′tē) *n.* [AUTO- + -PLASTY] the repairing of injuries by grafting in tissue from another part of the patient's body —**au′to·plas′tic** *adj.*

au·top·sy (ôt′äp·sē, ôt′əp sē) *n., pl.* **-sies** [ML. & Gr. *autopsia*, a seeing with one's own eyes < *autos*, self + *opsis*, a sight, appearance] **1.** an examination and dissection of a dead body, esp. by a coroner, to discover the cause of death, damage done by disease, etc.; post-mortem **2.** a detailed critical analysis of a book, play, etc., or of some event

au·to·ra·di·o·graph (ôt′ō rā′dē ə graf′) *n.* [AUTO- + RADIOGRAPH] an X-ray photograph made by bringing an object containing radioactive material into close contact with the emulsion on a film or plate: it shows the pattern of radioactivity in the object: also **au′to·ra′di·o·gram** —**au′to·ra′di·o·graph′ic** *adj.* —**au′to·ra′di·og′ra·phy** (-ä′grə fē) *n.*

au·to·some (ôt′ə sōm′) *n.* [AUTO- + (CHROMO)SOME] any chromosome that is not a sex chromosome; specif., either of a pair of like chromosomes in a diploid cell —**au′to·so′mal** (-sō′məl) *adj.*

au·to·sta·bil·i·ty (ôt′ō stə bil′ə tē) *n. Mech.* stability of a thing due either to inherent qualities or to some automatic stabilizing device

‡**au·to·stra·da** (ou′tō strä′dä) *n., pl.* **-stra′de** (-strä′de) [It. < *auto*, contr. < *automobile* (< Fr.: see AUTOMOBILE) + *strada*, road < LL. *strata:* see STREET] in Italy, an automobile expressway

au·to·sug·ges·tion (ôt′ō səg jes′chən, -sə jes′-; -jesh′-) *n.* suggestion to oneself arising within one's own mind and having effects on one's thinking and bodily functions

au·to·tel·ic (-tel′ik) *adj.* [< Gr. *autotelēs*, complete in itself (see AUTO- & TELEOLOGY) + -IC] having an end in itself; engaged in for its own sake, as some creative art —**au′to·tel′ism** *n.*

au·tot·o·mize (ô tät′ə mīz′) *vi., vt.* **-mized′, -miz′ing** to undergo or cause to undergo autotomy

au·tot·o·my (-mē) *n.* [AUTO- + -TOMY] the reflex action by which a leg, claw, tail, etc., as of a lobster, starfish, or lizard, is dropped off from the body when the part is damaged or the animal is under attack —**au·to·tom·ic** (ôt′ə täm′ik) *adj.*

au·to·tox·e·mi·a, au·to·tox·ae·mi·a (ôt′ō täk sē′mē ə) *n.* [AUTO- + TOXEMIA] *same as* AUTOINTOXICATION

au·to·tox·in (ôt′ə täk′sin) *n.* any toxin or poison produced within the body —**au′to·tox′ic** *adj.*

au·to·trans·form·er (ôt′ō trans′fôr′mər) *n. Elec.* a transformer with at least part of the windings common to both the primary and the secondary circuits

au·to·troph·ic (ôt′ə träf′ik) *adj.* [AUTO- + TROPHIC] making its own food by photosynthesis, as a green plant, or by chemosynthesis, as any of certain bacteria —**au′to·troph′** (-träf′) *n.* —**au′to·troph′i·cal·ly** *adv.*

☆**au·to·truck** (ôt′ō truk′) *n.* [AUTO(MOBILE) + TRUCK¹] *same as* MOTOR TRUCK

au·to·type (ôt′ə tīp′) *n.* [AUTO- + -TYPE] **1.** any facsimile **2.** *Photog. a)* an early process of reproducing in monochrome by a carbon pigment *b)* a picture thus reproduced —**au′to·typ′ic** (-tip′ik) *adj.* —**au′to·typ′y** (-tīp′ē) *n.*

au·tox·i·da·tion (ô täk′sə dā′shən) *n.* [AUT- + OXIDATION] *Chem.* the oxidation of a substance by its exposure to air —**au·tox′i·da′tive** (-tiv) *adj.*

au·tumn (ôt′əm) *n.* [ME. *autumpne* < OFr. *autompne* < L. *autumnus, auctumnus;* prob. of Etruscan origin] **1.** the season that comes between summer and winter; fall **2.** any period of maturity or of beginning decline —*adj.* of, in, characteristic of, or like autumn —**au·tum·nal** (ô tum′n'l) *adj.* —**au·tum′nal·ly** *adv.*

autumn crocus any of the colchicum plants, that bloom in autumn and resemble the crocus

au·tun·ite (ôt′ə nīt′) *n.* [*Autun*, town in France + -ITE¹] a light-yellow, hydrated, uranium calcium phosphate: it is radioactive and occurs in the form of tetragonal crystals or scales

Au·vergne (ō vurn′; *Fr.* ō ver′ny′) **1.** region and former province of SC France **2.** mountain range in SC France: highest peak, 6,188 ft.: in full **Auvergne Mountains**

‡**aux** (ō; *before vowel sounds* ōz) [Fr., contr. of *à les* < *à*, to + *les*, pl. def. art., the] *equivalent of* AU and À LA: used with pl. nouns

aux. auxiliary

Aux Cayes (ō kā′) *same as* LES CAYES

aux·e·sis (ôg zē′sis) *n.* [ModL. < Gr. *auxēsis*, growth < *auxein*, to grow, increase: see AUXIN] *Biol.* a process in which cells grow larger but in which no cell division takes place —**aux·et′ic** (-zet′ik) *adj.*

aux·il·ia·ry (ôg zil′yər ē, -zil′ər-) *adj.* [L. *auxiliaris*, helpful

< *auxilium*, aid < pp. of *augere*, AUGMENT] **1.** giving help or aid; assisting or supporting **2.** acting in a subsidiary, or subordinate, capacity **3.** additional; supplementary; reserve **4.** having an engine that can be used for supplementary power, as a sailing vessel **5.** designating or of any of the noncombat ships, as tankers, tenders, etc., that form the service fleet of a navy —*n.*, *pl.* **-ries 1.** an auxiliary person or thing **2.** [*pl.*] foreign or allied armed forces aiding those of a country at war **3.** an assisting or supplementary group or organization [*this club has a women's auxiliary*] **4.** an auxiliary vessel or ship **5.** *same as* AUXILIARY VERB

auxiliary verb a verb that helps form tenses, aspects, moods, or voices of other verbs, as *have, be, may, can, must, do, shall, will*

aux·in (ôk′sin) *n.* [< Gr. *auxein*, to increase (see AUGMENT) + -IN[1]] an organic compound, a kind of plant hormone, produced in the fruits, seeds, etc. of plants or made synthetically, that promotes longitudinal growth of plant shoots and that also controls bud growth, root formation, etc. —**aux·in·ic** (ôk sin′ik) *adj.*

aux·o·chrome (ôk′sə krōm′) *n.* [< Gr. *auxanein*, to increase (< *auxein:* see prec.) + CHROME] an atom group, as $-NH_2$ or -OH, that develops a color from a chromogen or that intensifies the color of a chromophore and that keeps organic dyes bonded to the fibers of a fabric

Av., av. avenue

av. 1. average **2.** avoirdupois

A.V. Authorized Version (of the Bible)

a.v., a/v, A/V ad valorem

av·a·da·vat (av′ə də vat′) *n. same as* AMADAVAT

a·vail (ə vāl′) *vi., vt.* [ME. *availen* < OFr. *a* (L. *ad*), to + *valoir*, to be worth < L. *valere*, to be strong: see VALUE] to be of use, help, worth, or advantage (to), as in accomplishing an end [*will force alone avail us?*] —*n.* **1.** effective use or help; advantage [*he tried, but to no avail*] **2.** [*pl.*] net proceeds; profits: chiefly in legal writings —**avail oneself of** to take advantage of (an opportunity, etc.); utilize

a·vail·a·bil·i·ty (ə vā′lə bil′ə tē) *n.* **1.** the quality or condition of being available **2.** *pl.* **-ties** an available person or thing

a·vail·a·ble (ə vā′lə b'l) *adj.* **1.** that one can avail himself of; that can be used; usable **2.** that can be got, had, or reached; handy; accessible **3.** [Obs.] that can avail ☆**4.** *Politics a)* having qualifications that would make one a strong candidate for an elective office *b)* willing and able to run for office —**a·vail′a·bly** *adv.*

av·a·lanche (av′ə lanch′, -länch′) *n.* [Fr. (altered after *avaler*, to descend) < *lavanche* < LL. *labina*, slippery place < L. *labes*, a falling down < *labi*, to slip, glide down] **1.** a mass of loosened snow, earth, rocks, etc. suddenly and swiftly sliding down a mountain, often growing as it descends **2.** anything that comes suddenly in overwhelming number [*an avalanche of mail, of blows, etc.*] —*vi., vt.* **-lanched′, -lanch′ing** to come down (on) like an avalanche

☆**avalanche lily** a wildflower (*Erythronium montanum*) of the lily family, native to the mountain meadows of Washington and Oregon and blooming among the snowbanks

Av·a·lon, Av·al·lon (av′ə län′) [Fr. < ML. *Avallonis* (*insula*) < W. (*ynys yr*) *Afallon*, (island of) apples] *Celtic Legend* the isle of the dead, an island paradise in the west where King Arthur and other heroes were taken after death

Avalon Peninsula peninsula forming the SE corner of Newfoundland, Canada

a·vant-garde (ä vänt′gärd′; *Fr.* å vän gård′) *n.* [Fr., lit., advance guard] the leaders in new or unconventional movements, esp. in the arts; vanguard —*adj.* of such movements, ideas, etc. —**avant′-gard′ism** *n.* —**avant′-gard′ist** *n.*

av·a·rice (av′ər is) *n.* [ME. & OFr. < L. *avaritia* < *avarus*, greedy < *avere*, to desire] too great a desire to have wealth; greed for riches; cupidity

av·a·ri·cious (av′ə rish′əs) *adj.* full of avarice; greedy for riches —*SYN.* see GREEDY —**av′a·ri′cious·ly** *adv.* —**av′a·ri′cious·ness** *n.*

a·vast (ə vast′, -väst′) *interj.* [< Du. *hou'vast, houd vast*, hold fast] *Naut.* stop! cease! halt!

av·a·tar (av′ə tär′) *n.* [Sans. *avatāra* < *ava-*, down + base of *tarati*, he goes, passes beyond] **1.** *Hinduism* a god's coming down in bodily form to the earth; incarnation of a god **2.** any incarnation or embodiment, as of a quality or concept in a person

a·vaunt (ə vônt′, -vänt′) *interj.* [ME. < OFr. *avant*, forward < LL. *abante* < L. *ab*, from + *ante*, before] [Archaic] begone! go away!

avdp. avoirdupois

a·ve (ä′vā, ā′vē) *interj.* [L., imperative of *avere*, to be well] **1.** hail! **2.** farewell! —*n.* **1.** the salutation *ave* **2.** [A-] the prayer AVE MARIA

Ave., ave. avenue

A·vel·la·ne·da (ä ve′yä ne′thä; *locally, also* ä ve′zhä-) city in E Argentina, on the Río de la Plata: suburb of Buenos Aires: pop. 330,000

A·ve Ma·ri·a (ä′vā mə rē′ə, -vē) [ME. < L. (Luke 1:28)] **1.** "Hail, Mary," the first words of the Latin version of a prayer to the Virgin Mary used in the Roman Catholic Church **2.** this prayer **3.** a musical setting of this

a·venge (ə venj′) *vt., vi.* **a·venged′, a·veng′ing** [ME. *avengen* < OFr. *avengier* < *a-* (L. *ad*), to + *vengier* < L. *vindicare*, to claim: see VINDICATE] **1.** to get revenge for (an injury, wrong, etc.) **2.** to take vengeance on behalf of, as for a wrong —**a·veng′er** *n.*

SYN.—**avenge** implies the infliction of deserved or just punishment for wrongs or oppressions; **revenge** implies the infliction of punishment as an act of retaliation, usually for an injury against oneself, and connotes personal malice, bitter resentment, etc. as the moving force

av·ens (av′inz) *n.* [ME. & OFr. *avence* < ML. *avencia*] any of a genus (*Geum*) of small plants of the rose family, with compound leaves and variously colored, usually yellow, flowers

Av·en·tine (av′'n tīn′, -tēn′) *see* SEVEN HILLS OF ROME

a·ven·tu·rine (ə ven′chər in) *n.* [Fr. < It. (*vetro*) *avventurino*, aventurine (glass): so named from resembling the mineral *avventurina* (< *avventura*, chance), so named from its rarity: see ADVENTURE] **1.** a kind of glass flecked with spangles, as from copper filings or bits of chromic oxide **2.** a translucent quartz shot through with sparkling bits of mica, etc.

av·e·nue (av′ə nōō′, -nyōō′) *n.* [Fr. < *avenir*, to happen, come < L. *advenire:* see ADVENT] **1.** a roadway, pathway, or drive, often bordered with trees; specif., [Brit.] one leading from the main road to the house on an estate **2.** a way of approach to something [*books are avenues to knowledge*] ☆**3.** a street, esp. a wide, principal one; often, one running at right angles to others called "streets"

a·ver (ə vur′) *vt.* **a·verred′, a·ver′ring** [ME. *averren* < OFr. *averrer*, to confirm < L. *ad*, to + *verus*, true] **1.** to declare to be true; state positively; affirm **2.** *Law* to state or declare formally; assert; allege —*SYN.* see ASSERT —**a·ver′ment** *n.*

av·er·age (av′rij, -ər ij) *n.* [altered (after ME. *average*, feudal service < *aver*, drafthorse) < Fr. *avarie*, damage to ship or goods, mooring charges < It. *avaria* < Ar. *'awār*, damaged goods; order of main sense development (in *n.*), 6 *a*, 6 *c*, 1, 2, etc.] **1.** the numerical result obtained by dividing the sum of two or more quantities by the number of quantities; an arithmetical mean **2.** an approximation to this [*an average of C in school work*] **3.** usual or normal kind, amount, quality, rate, etc. [*an intelligence above the average*] **4.** a number or value that typifies a set of values of which it is a function, as a median or mode ☆**5.** *see* BATTING AVERAGE **6.** *Marine Law a)* a loss incurred by damage to a ship at sea or to its cargo *b)* an incurring of such loss *c)* the equitable division of such loss among the interested parties *d)* a charge arising from such loss *e)* any of various small charges paid by the master of a ship, as for pilotage or towage —*adj.* **1.** constituting a numerical average [*his average speed is high*] **2.** intermediate in value, rate, etc.; hence, normal; ordinary [*an average student*] **3.** *Marine Law* assessed in accordance with the laws of average —*vi.* **-aged, -ag·ing 1.** to be or amount to on an average [*the children average six years of age*] **2.** to buy or sell more shares, goods, etc. so as to get a better average price —*vt.* **1.** to calculate the average or mean of **2.** to do, take, etc. on an average [*to average six hours of sleep a night*] **3.** to divide proportionately among more than two [*they averaged the loss among themselves*] —**average out** to arrive at an average eventually —**on the average** as an average quantity, rate, etc.

SYN.—**average** refers to the result obtained by dividing a sum by the number of quantities added [*the average of 7, 9, 17 is 33 ÷ 3, or 11*] and in extended use is applied to the usual or ordinary kind, instance, etc.; **mean** commonly designates a figure intermediate between two extremes [*the mean temperature for a day with a high of 56° and a low of 34° is 45°*] and figuratively implies moderation [*the golden mean*]; the **median** is the middle number or point in a series arranged in order of size [*the median grade in the group 50, 55, 85, 88, 92 is 85; the average is 74*]; **norm** implies a standard of average performance for a given group [*a child below the norm for his age in reading comprehension*] See also NORMAL

A·ver·nus (ə vur′nəs) [L.] **1.** a small lake in an extinct volcano near Naples, Italy, at the edge of which the entrance to Hades was anciently said to be: It. name **A·ver·no** (ä ver′nô) **2.** *Rom. Myth.* Hades; hell

A·ver·ro·ës, A·ver·rho·ës (ə ver′ ō ēz′) (Ar. *ibn-Rushd*) 1126–98; Arab philosopher & physician in Spain & Morocco

Av·er·ro·ism (av′ə rō′iz'm) *n.* the teachings of Averroës, applying Aristotelian philosophy to religion

a·verse (ə vurs′) *adj.* [L. *aversus*, pp. of *avertere*, AVERT] **1.** not willing or inclined; reluctant; opposed (*to*) **2.** *Bot.* turned away from the main stem or axis —*SYN.* see RELUCTANT —**a·verse′ly** *adv.* —**a·verse′ness** *n.*

a·ver·sion (ə vur′zhən, -shən) *n.* [L. *aversio* < *aversus:* see prec.] **1.** an intense or definite dislike; antipathy; repugnance **2.** the object arousing such dislike **3.** [Obs.] the act of turning away

SYN.—**aversion** and **antipathy** both imply an ingrained feeling against that which is disagreeable or offensive, **aversion** stressing avoidance or rejection, and **antipathy**, active hostility; **repugnance** emphasizes the emotional resistance or opposition one offers to that which is incompatible with one's ideas, tastes, etc.; **loathing** suggests a feeling of extreme disgust or intolerance; **revulsion** suggests a drawing back or away from in disgust, horror, etc.; **abhorrence** implies a feeling of extreme aversion or repugnance —*ANT.* **attraction, affinity**

a·vert (ə vurt′) *vt.* [L. *avertere*, to turn away < *a-* (*ab-*), from + *vertere*, to turn] **1.** to turn away [*to avert one's glance from an ugly sight*] **2.** to keep from happening;

ward off; prevent [he apologized to *avert* trouble] —*SYN.* see PREVENT

A·ves·ta (ə ves′tə) *n.* [< Per.] the sacred writings of the ancient Zoroastrian religion and of its present-day form among the Parsees

A·ves·tan (-tən) *adj.* 1. of the Avesta 2. of the Indo-European, Iranian language in which the Avesta was written —*n.* this language, closely related to Old Persian

avg. average

☆**av·gas** (av′gas′) *n.* [AV(IATION) GAS(OLINE)] gasoline for aircraft

a·vi·an (ā′vē ən) *adj.* [< L. *avis*, bird + -AN] of or having to do with birds —*n.* a bird

a·vi·ar·y (ā′vē er′ē) *n.*, *pl.* -**ar′ies** [L. *aviarium* < *avis*, bird] a large cage or building for keeping many birds

a·vi·ate (ā′vē āt′; *occas.* av′ē-) *vi.* -**at′ed**, -**at′ing** [back-formation < AVIATION] to fly in, esp. to operate, an aircraft

a·vi·a·tion (ā′vē ā′shən; *occas.* av′ē-) *n.* [Fr. < L. *avis*, bird] 1. the art or science of flying airplanes 2. the development and operation of heavier-than-air craft, including airplanes and piloted or guided rocket ships 3. aircraft, esp. military aircraft, collectively

aviation medicine a branch of medicine that embraces aeromedicine and space medicine

a·vi·at·or (ā′vē āt′ər; *occas.* av′ē-) *n.* [Fr. *aviateur*] an airplane pilot; flier

a·vi·a·trix (ā′vē ā′triks; *occas.* av′ē-) *n.* a woman aviator: also [Rare] **a′vi·a·tress** (-tris)

Av·i·cen·na (av′i sen′ə) (Ar. *ibn-Sina*) 980–1037; Arab physician & philosopher in Persia

a·vi·cul·ture (ā′və kul′chər, av′ə-) *n.* [< L. *avis*, bird + *cultura*, culture] the raising and care of birds —**a′vi·cul′-tur·ist** *n.*

av·id (av′id) *adj.* [L. *avidus* < *avere*, to desire] 1. having an intense desire or craving; greedy [*avid* for power] 2. eager and enthusiastic [an *avid* reader of books] —*SYN.* see EAGER[1] —**a·vid·i·ty** (ə vid′ə tē) *n.* —**av′id·ly** *adv.*

av·i·din (av′ə din) *n.* [AVID + -IN[1]: so named because of its peculiar biotin-binding capacity] a protein substance found in raw egg white: in some experimental animals it suppresses biotin

a·vi·fau·na (ā′və fô′nə) *n.* [< L. *avis*, bird + FAUNA] the birds of a specified region or time —**a′vi·fau′nal** *adj.*

A·vi·gnon (à vē nyôn′) city in SE France, on the Rhone River: seat of the papacy (1309–77): pop. 73,000

a·vi·on·ics (ā′vē än′iks; *occas.* av′ē-) *n.pl.* [AVI(ATION) + (ELECTR)ONICS] [*with sing. v.*] the branch of electronics dealing with the development, manufacture, and use of electronic devices and equipment in aviation and astronautics —**a′vi·on′ic** *adj.*

a·vir·u·lent (ā′vir′yə lənt, -ə lənt) *adj.* not virulent or no longer virulent, as certain bacteria

a·vi·ta·min·o·sis (ā′vīt′ə mi nō′sis) *n.* [A-[2] + VITAMIN + -OSIS] any disease caused by a deficiency of vitamins

☆**a·vo·ca·do** (av′ə kä′dō, äv′-) *n.*, *pl.* -**dos** [Sp., altered (by folk-etym., after *avocado*, now *abogado*, advocate) < MexSp. *agua-cate* < Nahuatl *ahuacatl*] 1. a thick-skinned, pear-shaped tropical fruit, yellowish green to purplish black, with a single large seed and yellow, buttery flesh, used in salads; alligator pear 2. the tree (*Persea americana*, of the laurel family) that it grows on

AVOCADO

av·o·ca·tion (av′ə kā′shən) *n.* [L. *avocatio*, a calling away < pp. of *avocare* < *a-* (*ab-*), away + *vocare*, to call] 1. something one does in addition to his vocation or regular work, and usually for pleasure; hobby 2. [Now Rare] one's regular work; vocation 3. [Obs.] the fact of being called away or distracted from something —**av′o·ca′tion·al** *adj.*

a·voc·a·to·ry (ə väk′ə tôr′ē) *adj.* [< ML. *avocatorius*: see AVOCATION] that summons back, or recalls

av·o·cet (av′ə set′) *n.* [Fr. *avocette* < It. *avocetta*] any of a genus (*Recurvirostra*) of long-legged wading birds with webbed feet and a slender bill that curves upward

A·vo·ga·dro (ä′vō gä′drō; *E.* äv′ə gä′drō), **A·me·de·o** (ä′me de′ô) (*Conte di Quaregna*) 1776–1856; It. chemist & physicist

Avogadro constant (or **number**) the number of molecules contained in one mole (molecular weight in grams) of a substance: the symbol used for this number is N, and N is equal to 6.02252 x 10²³ particles per mole

Avogadro's law the theory, formulated by Avogadro, that equal volumes of all gases under identical conditions of temperature and pressure contain equal numbers of molecules

a·void (ə void′) *vt.* [ME. *avoiden* < Anglo-Fr. *avoider* < OFr. *esvuidier*, to empty < *es-* (< L. *ex*), out + *vuidier*: see VOID] 1. to make void; annul, invalidate, or quash (a plea, etc. in law) 2. to keep away from; evade; shun [*to avoid* crowds] 3. to keep from happening [*to avoid* breakage] 4. [Obs.] to void; empty 5. [Obs.] to go away

from; leave —*SYN.* see ESCAPE —**a·void′a·ble** *adj.* —**a·void′a·bly** *adv.*

a·void·ance (-′ns) *n.* 1. the act of avoiding, or shunning something 2. the act of making void; annulment

av·oir·du·pois (av′ər də poiz′, av′ər də poiz′) *n.* [ME. *aver de poiz* < OFr. *aveir de peis* < *aveir*, goods (< L. *habere*, to have) + *de* (< L. *de*), from + *peis* (< L. *pensum*), weight] 1. *same as* AVOIRDUPOIS WEIGHT ☆2. [Colloq.] heaviness or weight, esp. of a person

avoirdupois weight an English and American system of weights based on a pound of 16 ounces: see TABLES OF WEIGHTS AND MEASURES in Supplements

A·von (ā′vən, -vän; av′ən) any of three rivers in England; esp., the one in the SW part, on which lies Stratford, Shakespeare's birthplace

‡**à vo·tre san·té** (à vô′tr′ sän tā′) [Fr.] to your health: a toast in drinking

a·vouch (ə vouch′) *vt.* [ME. *avouchen* < OFr. *avochier*, to affirm positively < L. *advocare*: see ADVOCATE] 1. to vouch for; guarantee 2. to declare the truth of; assert; affirm 3. to acknowledge openly; avow —*SYN.* see ASSERT —**a·vouch′ment** *n.*

a·vow (ə vou′) *vt.* [ME. *avowen* < OFr. *avouer* < L. *advocare*: see ADVOCATE] 1. to declare openly or admit frankly 2. to acknowledge or claim (oneself) to be [he *avowed* himself a patriot] —*SYN.* see ACKNOWLEDGE —**a·vow′er** *n.*

a·vow·al (ə vou′əl) *n.* open acknowledgment or declaration; frank admission

a·vowed (ə voud′) openly declared or frankly acknowledged [his *avowed* purpose] —**a·vow′ed·ly** (ə vou′id lē) *adv.*

a·vul·sion (ə vul′shən) *n.* [L. *avulsio* < *a-*, from + pp. of *vellere*, to pull] 1. a separation by force; specif., *Med.* the tearing away of a structure or part by surgical traction or by accident 2. a structure, part, etc. separated by force 3. the sudden transference of a piece of land from one person's property to another's without change of ownership, as by a change in the course of a stream

a·vun·cu·lar (ə vuŋ′kyə lər) *adj.* [< L. *avunculus*, maternal uncle, dim. of *avus*, ancestor (see ATAVISM) + -AR] of, like, or in the relationship of, an uncle

aw (ô, ä) *interj.* an exclamation of protest, dislike, disgust, sympathy, etc.

AW Articles of War

a·wa (ə wä′, -wô′) *adv.* [Scot.] away

a·wait (ə wāt′) *vt.* [ME. *awaiten* < ONormFr. *awaitier* < *a-* (L. *ad*), to + *waitier*, WAIT] 1. to wait for; expect 2. to be in store for; be ready for 3. [Obs.] to watch for so as to confront —*vi.* 1. to wait 2. [Obs.] to attend —*SYN.* see EXPECT

a·wake (ə wāk′) *vt.* **a·woke′** or **a·waked′**, **a·waked′**, **a·wak′-ing;** *occas.* Brit. pp. **a·woke′** or **a·wok′en** [a merging of two words: ME. *awaken* < OE. *awacan* (*on-* + *wacan*, to arise, awake) & ME. *awakien* < OE. *awacian* (*on-* + *wacian*, to be awake, watch)] 1. to rouse from sleep; wake 2. to rouse from inactivity; activate; stir up 3. to call forth (memories, fear, etc.) 4. to make aware (with *to*) —*vi.* 1. to come out of sleep; wake 2. to become active 3. to become aware (with *to*) —*adj.* [< obs. pp. *awaken*] 1. not asleep 2. active or alert

a·wak·en (ə wāk′'n) *vt.*, *vi.* [ME. *awakenen* < OE. *awæchnian*, to awaken < *on-* + *wæcnian*, to awake, come into being] to awake; wake up; rouse —*SYN.* see STIR[1] —**a·wak′en·er** *n.*

a·wak·en·ing (-iŋ) *n.*, *adj.* 1. (a) waking up 2. (an) arousing or reviving, as of impulses, religion, etc.

a·ward (ə wôrd′) *vt.* [ME. *awarden* < Anglo-Fr. *awarder* < ONormFr. *eswarder* < *es-* (< L. *ex*) + Gmc. *wardon: see GUARD] 1. to give by the decision of a law court or arbitrator [the plaintiff was *awarded* damages] 2. to give as the result of judging the relative merits of those in competition; grant [to *award* a prize for the best essay] —*n.* 1. a decision, as by a judge or arbitrator 2. something awarded; prize —*SYN.* see REWARD —**a·ward′a·ble** *adj.*

a·ware (ə wer′) *adj.* [ME. < OE. *gewær* < *wær*, cautious] 1. orig., on one's guard; vigilant 2. knowing or realizing; conscious; informed —**a·ware′ness** *n.*

SYN.—**aware** implies having knowledge of something through alertness in observing or in interpreting what one sees, hears, feels, etc. [to be *aware* of a fact]; **conscious** implies awareness of a sensation, feeling, fact, condition, etc. and may suggest mere recognition or a focusing of attention [*conscious* of a draft in the room, *conscious* humor]; one is **cognizant** of something when one has certain or special knowledge of it through observation or information [*cognizant* of the terms of the will]; **sensible** implies awareness of something that is not expressed directly or explicitly [*sensible* of their solemn grief]

a·wash (ə wôsh′, -wäsh′) *adv., adj.* 1. just above the surface of the water so that breakers, tide, etc. flow over 2. floating on the water 3. flooded with water

a·way (ə wā′) *adv.* [ME. < OE. *aweg* < phr. *on weg* < *on*, on + *weg*, way, in the sense "from this (that) place"] 1. from any given place; off [*to run away*] 2. in another place, esp. the proper place [*to put one's tools away*] 3. in another direction [*look away*, turn *away*] 4. by a considerable time or distance; far [*away* behind] 5. so as to be removed; aside [*to clear snow away*, to get *away* from the

subject/ **6.** from one's possession [to give *away* a secret/ **7.** out of existence [the sound faded *away*/ **8.** at once [fire *away*/ **9.** without stopping; continuously [he worked *away* all night/ **10.** into action or movement [*away* we go!/ —*adj.* **1.** not present; absent; gone [he is *away*/ **2.** at a distance [a mile *away*/ ☆**3.** not played on the home team's field [an *away* game/ **4.** (having one's golf ball) in a position to be played first because it lies farthest from the cup ☆**5.** *Baseball* out [one *away* in the last half of the 4th/ —*interj.* **1.** begone! **2.** let's go! —**away with 1.** take away **2.** go or come away Used generally as an imperative expression without a verb—**do away with 1.** to get rid of; put an end to **2.** to kill —**where away?** in what direction?: said of something being sighted from a ship

awe (ô) *n.* [ME. *age, aghe, awe* < ON. *agi* < IE. base **agh-*, to be depressed, afraid, whence OE. *ege,* Goth. *agis,* Gr. *achos*] **1.** a mixed feeling of reverence, fear, and wonder, caused by something majestic, sublime, sacred, etc. **2.** [Archaic] the power of inspiring intense fear or fearful reverence **3.** [Obs.] terror; dread —*vt.* **awed, aw'ing** to inspire awe in; fill with awe —**stand** (or **be**) **in awe of** to respect and fear

SYN.—**awe** refers to a feeling of fearful or profound respect or wonder inspired by the greatness, superiority, grandeur, etc. of a person or thing and suggests an immobilizing effect; **reverence** is applied to a feeling of deep respect mingled with love for something one holds sacred or inviolable and suggests a display of homage, deference, etc.; **veneration** implies worshipful reverence for a person or thing regarded as hallowed or sacred and specifically suggests acts of religious devotion; **dread,** as it comes into comparison here, suggests extreme fear mixed with awe or reverence [a *dread* of divine retribution/

a·wear·y (ə wir′ē) *adj.* [Poet.] weary; tired (*of*)

a·weath·er (ə weth′ər) *adv., adj.* [A-[1] + WEATHER] *Naut.* in the direction from which the wind is blowing; at or to windward

a·weigh (ə wā′) *adj.* [A-[1] + WEIGH[2]] *Naut.* clearing the bottom; being weighed: said of an anchor

awe·less, aw·less (ô′lis) *adj.* feeling no awe

awe·some (ô′səm) *adj.* [AWE + -SOME[1]] **1.** inspiring awe **2.** showing awe —**awe'some·ly** *adv.* —**awe'some·ness** *n.*

awe-struck (ô′struk′) *adj.* filled with awe: also **awe'-strick'en** (-strik′ən)

aw·ful (ô′fəl) *adj.* [ME. *awful, agheful:* see AWE & -FUL] **1.** inspiring awe; highly impressive **2.** causing fear; dreadful; terrifying; appalling **3.** full of awe; reverential **4.** [Colloq.] *a*) very bad, ugly, unpleasant, etc. [an *awful* joke/ *b*) great [an *awful* bore] —☆*adv.* [Colloq.] very; extremely —**aw'ful·ness** *n.*

aw·ful·ly (ô′fə lē, ô′flē) *adv.* **1.** in a way to inspire awe ☆**2.** [Colloq.] in a bad or offensive way [to behave *awfully*] **3.** [Colloq.] very; very much; extremely

a·while (ə wīl′, -hwīl′) *adv.* [ME. < OE. *ane hwile,* a while] for a while; for a short time

awk·ward (ôk′wərd) *adj.* [ME. *aukward* < ON. *ǫfugr,* turned backward + OE. *-weard, -WARD*] **1.** not having grace or skill; clumsy, as in form or movement; bungling [an *awkward* dancer, an *awkward* style] **2.** inconvenient to use; hard to handle; unwieldy [an *awkward* tool] **3.** inconvenient; uncomfortable; cramped [an *awkward* position] **4.** showing or resulting from lack of social poise; embarrassed or embarrassing [an *awkward* remark] **5.** not easy to deal with; delicate [an *awkward* situation] **6.** [Obs.] perverse or untoward —**awk'ward·ly** *adv.* —**awk'ward·ness** *n.*

SYN.—**awkward** implies unfitness for smooth, easy functioning and has the broadest application of the terms here, suggesting ungracefulness, unmanageableness, inconvenience, tactlessness, embarrassment, etc. [an *awkward* implement, step, position, remark, etc.]; **clumsy,** emphasizing stiffness or bulkiness, suggests a lack of flexibility or dexterity, unwieldiness, etc. [a *clumsy* build, *clumsy* galoshes]; **maladroit** and **inept** both imply tactlessness in social relations; **maladroit** often emphasizing this as a tendency and **inept** stressing inappropriateness of a particular act or remark —ANT. deft, handy, graceful

awl (ôl) *n.* [ME. *alle, awel* < OE. *æl, awel* < IE. base **ēlā,* whence Sans. *ārā,* OHG. *āla,* ON. *alr*] a small, pointed tool for making holes in wood, leather, etc.

awl·wort (ôl′wurt′) *n.* a small water plant (*Subularia aquatica*) of the mustard family, bearing clusters of awl-shaped leaves around the root

awn (ôn) *n.* [ME. *aune* < ON. *ǫgn* (pl. *agnir*) < IE. **aken* (< base **ak,* sharp), whence OE. *egenu,* Goth. *ahana,* L. *agua*] any of the bristly fibers on a head of barley, oats, etc., or, usually, such fibers collectively; beard —**awned** *adj.* —**awn'less** *adj.*

awn·ing (ôn′niŋ) *n.* [< ? MFr. *auvans,* pl. of *auvent,* cloth shade for store window + -ING] a structure of canvas, metal, etc. extended before a window or door or over a patio, deck, etc. as a protection from the sun or rain

a·woke (ə wōk′) *alt. pt. and occas. Brit. pp. of* AWAKE

a·wok·en (ə wōk′'n) *occas. Brit. pp. of* AWAKE

A·WOL, a·wol (ā′wôl′) *adj.* [A(BSENT) W(ITH)O(UT) L(EAVE)] *same as* ABSENT WITHOUT LEAVE —*n.* one who is AWOL

a·wry (ə rī′) *adv., adj.* [ME. *a wrie:* see A-[1] &

AWN

WRY] **1.** with a twist to a side; not straight; askew **2.** wrong; amiss [our plans went *awry*]

ax, axe (aks) *n., pl.* **ax'es** [ME. < OE. *eax, æx* < IE. base **agw(e)si,* whence Goth. *aqizi,* Gr. *axinē,* L. *ascia*] **1.** a tool for chopping trees and splitting wood: it has a long wooden handle and a metal head with a blade usually on only one side **2.** any similar tool or weapon, as a battle-ax, headsman's ax, etc. —*vt.* **axed, ax'ing 1.** to trim, split, etc. with an ax **2.** to cut off, remove, get rid of, etc. —☆**get the ax** [Colloq.] **1.** to be executed by beheading **2.** to be discharged from one's job —☆**have an ax to grind** [Colloq.] to have an object of one's own to gain or promote

ax. 1. axiom **2.** axis

Ax·el (ak′s'l) [Sw.] a masculine name

a·xe·nic (ā zē′nik, -zen′ik) *adj.* [< A-[2] + XEN(O)- + -IC] devoid of all living organisms except those of a single species [an *axenic* culture medium/

ax·es[1] (ak′siz) *n. pl. of* AX

ax·es[2] (ak′sēz) *n. pl. of* AXIS[1]

ax·i·al (ak′sē əl) *adj.* **1.** of or like an axis **2.** forming an axis **3.** around, on, or along an axis

axial flow the flow of air parallel to the longitudinal axis of the engine of a jet aircraft

ax·i·al·ly (ak′sē ə lē) *adv.* in the direction or line of the axis

axial skeleton in vertebrates, the skull, vertebral column, sternum, and ribs without the arms and legs

ax·il (ak′sil) *n.* [< L. *axilla,* AXILLA] the upper angle formed by a leaf, twig, etc. and the stem from which it grows

ax·ile (ak′sil, -sil) *adj.* [AX(IS)[1] + -ILE] *Bot.* in or of the axis

axile placentation *Bot.* placentation in an ovary consisting of several carpels whose edges are folded in to form a round structure of tissue at the middle on which the ovules are borne

ax·il·la (ak sil′ə) *n., pl.* **-il'lae** (-ē), **-il'las** [L., armpit: see AXIS[1]] **1.** the armpit **2.** *Bot.* an axil

ax·il·lar (ak′sə lər) *adj. same as* AXILLARY —*n.* one of the stiff feathers on the underside of a bird's wing where it joins the body

ax·il·la·ry (ak′sə ler′ē) *adj.* [Fr. *axillaire*] **1.** *Anat.* of or near the axilla **2.** *Bot.* of, in, or growing from an axil —*n. same as* AXILLAR

ax·i·ol·o·gy (ak′sē äl′ə jē) *n.* [< Gr. *axios,* worthy (see ff.) + -LOGY] the branch of philosophy dealing with the nature of value and the types of value, as in morals, aesthetics, religion, and metaphysics —**ax'i·o·log'i·cal** (-ə läj′i k'l) *adj.* —**ax'i·o·log'i·cal·ly** *adv.*

ax·i·om (ak′sē əm) *n.* [Fr. *axiome* < L. *axioma* < Gr. *axiōma,* authority, authoritative sentence < *axioun,* to think worthy < *axios,* worthy < base of *agein,* to weigh] **1.** a statement universally accepted as true; maxim **2.** an established principle or law of a science, art, etc. **3.** *Logic, Math.* a statement that needs no proof because its truth is obvious; self-evident proposition [Euclid's *axiom* that things equal to the same thing are equal to each other/

ax·i·o·mat·ic (ak′sē ə mat′ik) *adj.* [Gr. *axiōmatikos*] of or like an axiom; self-evident or aphoristic —**ax'i·o·mat'i·cal·ly** *adv.*

ax·is[1] (ak′sis) *n., pl.* **ax'es** (-sēz) [L., axle, axis < IE. base **aks-* (< **ag-,* to drive), whence OE. *eax,* ON. *ǫxull,* Gr. *axōn,* L. *axilla*] **1.** a real or imaginary straight line on which an object rotates or is regarded as rotating [the *axis* of a planet/ **2.** a real or imaginary straight line around which the parts of a thing, system, etc. are symmetrically or evenly arranged or composed [the *axis* of a picture] **3.** a main line of motion, development, etc. **4.** an alignment between countries, groups, etc. for promoting their purposes **5.** *Aeron.* any of three straight lines, the first running lengthwise through the center of the body of a flight vehicle, the second at right angles to this in the plane of symmetry, and the third perpendicular to the first two at their point of intersection **6.** *Anat. a*) the second cervical vertebra *b*) any of various axial or central parts **7.** *Bot. a*) the main stem of a plant *b*) the central system of a cluster **8.** *Geom. a*) a straight line through the center of a plane figure or solid, esp. one around which the parts are symmetrically arranged *b*) a straight line for measurement or reference, as in a graph: see also ABSCISSA, ORDINATE **9.** *Optics a*) a straight line through the centers of both surfaces of a lens *b*) a straight line from the object of vision to the fovea of the eye —**the Axis** the countries aligned against the United Nations in World War II: originally applied to Nazi Germany and Fascist Italy (**Rome-Berlin Axis**), later extended to include Japan, etc. (**Rome-Berlin-Tokyo Axis**)

ax·is[2] (ak′sis) *n.* [L.] any of a subgenus (*Axis*) of small, white-spotted deer of India and southern Asia, with slender, sparsely branched antlers

ax·le (ak′s'l) *n.* [ME. *axel* (only in comp. *axeltre*): see ff.] **1.** a rod on which a wheel turns, or one connected to a wheel so that they turn together **2.** *a*) a bar connecting two opposite wheels, as of an automobile *b*) the spindle at either end of such a bar

ax·le·tree (-trē′) *n.* [ME. *axeltre* < ON. *ǫxultre* < *ǫxull,* axle (see AXIS[1]) + *tre,* beam, TREE] a bar connecting two opposite wheels of a carriage, wagon, etc.

Ax·min·ster (aks′min stər) *n.* [after *Axminster,* town in SW England, where it was first made by hand] a type of carpet with a cut pile, woven in various colors and patterns

ax·o·lotl (ak'sə lät''l) *n.* [Sp. < Nahuatl, lit., water toy] any of various members of a genus (*Ambystoma*) of dark salamanders of Mexico and the western U.S., that mature sexually and breed while remaining in the larval stage

ax·on (ak'sän) *n.* [ModL. < Gr. *axōn*, AXIS[1]] that part of a nerve cell through which impulses travel away from the cell body

ax·seed (aks'sēd') *n.* [AX + SEED: so named from the shape of the pods] *same as* CROWN VETCH

Ax·um (äk'soom) *same as* AKSUM

ay (ā) *interj.* a sound used in northern England to express sorrow, distress, etc.: also used in the phrase *ay me!*

A·ya·cu·cho (ä'yä kōō'chō) city in SC Peru: site of a battle (1824) which marked the end of Spanish rule in S.America: pop. 24,000

ay·ah (ä'yə) *n.* [Anglo-Ind. < Hindu *āya* < Port. *aia*, governess] a native nursemaid or lady's maid in India

aye[1] (ā) *adv.* [ME. *ai, ay* < ON. *ei* < IE. base *aiw-*, vital force: cf. AGE] [Poet.] always; ever: also sp. **ay**

aye[2] (ī) *adv.* [< ? prec.] yes; yea —*n.* an affirmative vote or a person voting affirmatively Also sp. **ay** —**aye, aye** [*Naut.*] I understand and will obey: used in response to a command

aye-aye (ī'ī') *n.* [Fr. < Malagasy; echoic of its cry] a lemur (*Daubentonia madagascarensis*) of Madagascar, with shaggy, generally yellowish-white fur, large ears, pointed claws, and a long, bushy tail

Ay·er (ā'ər), **Alfred Jules** 1910– ; Brit. philosopher

A·ye·sha, A·ye·shah (ä'ē shä') *same as* AISHA

a·yin (ä'yin) *n.* [Heb. 'ayin] the sixteenth letter of the Hebrew alphabet (ּ y)

Ay·ma·ra (ī'mə rä') *n.* **1.** *pl.* **-ras', -ra'** a member of a S. American Indian tribe living largely in Bolivia and Peru and believed to have been the builders of a great ancient culture, later supplanted by the Incan **2.** their language —**Ay'ma·ran'** *adj., n.*

Ayr (er, ar) **1.** county of SW Scotland, on the Firth of Clyde: 1,131 sq. mi.; pop. 348,000 **2.** its county seat, a seaport: pop. 46,000

Ayr·shire (-shir) *same as* AYR (sense 1) —*n.* any of a breed of dairy cattle which are brownish-red and white in varying proportions, originally from the country of Ayr

A·yub Khan (ä'yoob kän'), **Mohammad** 1907– ; Pakistani military leader; president of Pakistan (1958–69)

☆ **a·yun·ta·mien·to** (ə yoon'tə myen'tō) *n., pl.* **-tos** [Sp.] formerly, the administrative council or town hall of a Spanish or Spanish-American city or town

A·yut·tha·ya (ä yoo'tä yä) city in C Thailand, on the Chao Phraya River: former capital (1350–1767): pop. 33,000 Also sp. **Ayuthia, Ayudhya**

az- (az) *same as* AZO-

az. azimuth

a·zal·ea (ə zāl'yə) *n.* [ModL. < Gr., fem. of *azaleos*, dry: so called because it thrives in dry soil] **1.** any of various flowering shrubs (genus *Rhododendron*) of the heath family: the flowers are of various colors, and the leaves are usually shed each season **2.** the flower of any of these plants

‡ **a·zan** (ä zän') *n.* [< Ar. *ādhan*] the Moslem summons to prayer: it is called five times a day by the muezzin, from a minaret on the mosque

A·za·ña (ä thä'nyä), **Ma·nuel** (mä nwel') 1880–1940; Sp. statesman; president of the Spanish Republic (1936–39) until its overthrow by Franco

A·za·zel (ə zā'z'l, az'ə zel') [Heb. 'asā'sēl, lit., removal] in Milton's *Paradise Lost*, one of the angels who rebelled with Satan: see also Lev. 16:7–10, 21–26

a·zed·a·rach (ə zed'ə rak') *n.* [< Fr. *azédarac* < Sp. *acedaraque* < Ar. *azādirah* < Per. *azād dirāḥt*, lit., free tree] **1.** the chinaberry tree **2.** the bark of this tree, formerly used in medicine as a cathartic, emetic, etc.

a·ze·o·trope (ā zē'ə trōp') *n.* [< A-[2] + Gr. *zein*, to boil (see YEAST) + -TROPE] a liquid mixture that maintains a constant boiling point and that produces a vapor of the same composition as the mixture —**a·ze·o·trop·ic** (ā'zē ə träp'ik) *adj.*

Az·er·bai·jan (äz'ər bī jän', az'-) **1.** region of NW Iran: former province, in 1928 it was divided into two provinces

AXOLOTL (to 10 in. long)

AYE-AYE (34–41 in. long, including tail)

(**Eastern** and **Western Azerbaijan**); chief city, Tabriz **2.** the Azerbaijan Soviet Socialist Republic

Azerbaijan Soviet Socialist Republic republic of the U.S.S.R., on the Caspian Sea, in Transcaucasia: 33,436 sq. mi.; pop. 4,500,000; cap. Baku Also sp. **Azerbaidzhan** (or **Azerbaydzhan**) **Soviet Socialist Republic**

A·zer·bai·ja·ni (-jä'nē) *n., pl.* **-nis, -ni 1.** a native or inhabitant of Azerbaijan **2.** one of a Turkic people of Azerbaijan **3.** the Turkic dialect spoken there

az·ide (az'īd, ā'zīd) *n.* [AZ- + -IDE] a compound containing the monovalent group -N3

A·zil·ian (ə zil'yən) *adj.* [< Mas d'*Azil*, cavern in the French Pyrenees, where traces were found] denoting or of a stage of prehistoric culture after the Magdalenian and before the Neolithic, characterized by painted stone pebbles and by harpoon heads made from antlers

az·i·muth (az'ə məth) *n.* [ME. & OFr. *azimut* < Ar. *as-sumūt* < *as* < *al*, the + *sumūt*, pl. of *samt*, way, path] *Astron., Surveying, etc.* distance in angular degrees in a clockwise direction from the north point or, in the Southern Hemisphere, south point; arc of the horizon measured clockwise from such a point to a vertical circle passing from the zenith through the center of a star —**az'i·muth'al** *adj.*

az·ine (az'ēn, -in) *n.* [AZ- + -INE[4]] any of a group of organic chemical compounds with a 6-membered ring containing one or more nitrogen atoms: the group consists of the diazines, triazines, etc.

az·lon (az'län) *n.* [AZ- + (NY)LON] any of a group of textile fibers manufactured from a regenerated protein such as casein

az·o (az'ō, ā'zō) *adj.* [< AZOTE] pertaining to or containing the divalent radical -N:N- [*azo dyes*]

az·o- (az'ō, ā'zō) [< AZOTE] *a prefix meaning:* **1.** containing nitrogen [*azole*] **2.** containing the divalent radical -N:N- [*azobenzene*]

az·o·ben·zene (-ben'zēn, -ben zēn') *n.* an orange-red crystalline compound, $C_{12}H_{10}N_2$, derived from nitrobenzene in an alkaline solution and used in organic synthesis

a·zo·ic (ə zō'ik) *adj.* [Gr. *azōos* (< *a-*, without + *zōē*, life) + -IC] [Now Rare] without life; specif., designating or of the Older Precambrian (Archean) era, before life appeared on the earth

az·ole (az'ōl) *n.* [AZ- + -OLE] any of a group of chemical compounds with a 5-membered ring containing one or more nitrogen atoms: the group consists of the diazoles, triazoles, etc.

a·zon·al (ā zōn'l) *adj.* designating or of zones, or layers, of soil that cannot be sharply distinguished from one another because, for example, they are of recent formation

A·zores (ā'zōrz, ə zōrz') group of Portuguese islands in the N Atlantic, west of Portugal: 890 sq. mi.; pop. 596,000; chief city, Ponta Delgada

az·ote (az'ōt, ə zōt') *n.* [Fr. (coined by G. de Morveau) < Gr. *a-*, not + *zōē*, life: the gas does not support life] *a former name for* NITROGEN

az·o·te·mi·a (az'ə tē'mē ə) *n.* [ModL.: see AZOTE & -EMIA] the accumulation of nitrogenous substances in the blood, resulting from failure of the kidneys to remove them —**az'o·te'mic** (-tē'mik) *adj.*

az·oth (az'äth) *n.* [< Ar. *az zā'uq* < *al*, the + *zā'uq*, mercury < *zístan*, to live] *Alchemy* **1.** the metal mercury; quicksilver **2.** Paracelsus' universal remedy

az·o·tize (az'ə tīz') *vt.* **-tized', -tiz'ing** [AZOT(E) + -IZE] **1.** to nitrogenize **2.** to change to an azo compound

a·zo·to·bac·ter (ə zōt'ə bak'tər) *n.* [ModL.: see AZOTE & BACTERIA] any of a genus (*Azotobacter*) of large, rod-shaped, nitrogen-fixing bacteria found in certain soils

A·zov (ā'zôf; *Russ.* ä'zôf), **Sea of** northern arm of the Black Sea, in S European U.S.S.R.: c. 14,000 sq. mi.

Az·ra·el (az'rē əl) [Heb. 'azra'ēl, lit., help of God] the angel who, according to ancient Jewish and Moslem belief, parts the soul from the body at death

Az·tec (az'tek) *n.* [< Nahuatl *Aztatlán*, name of their legendary place of origin] **1.** a member of a people who lived in Mexico and had an advanced civilization before the conquest of Mexico by Cortés in 1519 **2.** their Uto-Aztecan language, usually called Nahuatl **3.** the branch of the Uto-Aztecan family to which Nahuatl belongs —*adj.* of the Aztecs, their language, culture, etc.: also **Az'tec·an**

az·ure (azh'ər) *adj.* [ME. *asur* < OFr. *azur* (with omission of initial *l-*, as if *l'azur*) < Ar. *lāsaward* < Per. *lāzhuward*, lapis lazuli] of or like the color of a clear sky; sky-blue —*n.* **1.** sky blue or any similar blue color **2.** [Poet.] the blue sky

az·u·rite (azh'ə rīt') *n.* [AZUR(E) + -ITE[1]] **1.** a brilliantly blue, monoclinic mineral, $2CuCO_3·Cu(OH)_2$: it is an ore of copper **2.** a semiprecious gem made from this mineral

az·y·gous (az'i gəs) *adj.* [Gr. *azygos*, unmatched < *a-*, not + *zygon*, YOKE] not one of a pair; having no mate; odd [*an azygous muscle*]

B

B, b (bē) *n.*, *pl.* **B's, b's** **1.** the second letter of the English alphabet: from the Greek *beta*, a borrowing from the Phoenician **2.** the sound of *B* or *b*, normally a voiced bilabial stop **3.** a type or impression for *B* or *b* **4.** *a symbol for* the second in a sequence or group —*adj.* **1.** of *B* or *b* **2.** second in a sequence or group

B¹ (bē) *n.* **1.** an object shaped like *B* **2.** *Chem.* boron ☆**3.** *Educ.* a grade indicating above average but not outstanding work [a *B* in French] **4.** *Music a)* the seventh tone or note in the ascending scale of C major *b)* a key, string, etc. producing this tone *c)* the scale having this tone as the keynote —*adj.* **1.** shaped like *B* ☆**2.** second-class; inferior to the best [a class *B* motion picture]

B² *Chess* bishop

B- bomber

B. 1. Baumé **2.** Bible **3.** British **4.** Brotherhood

B., b. 1. bachelor **2.** bacillus **3.** *Baseball a)* base *b)* baseman *c)* bat **4.** *Music* bass or basso **5.** battery **6.** bay **7.** bi-cuspid **8.** bolivar **9.** boliviano **10.** book **11.** born **12.** brother

B/- **1.** bag **2.** bale

ba (bä) *n. Egypt. Myth.* the soul, symbolized by a bird with a human head

Ba *Chem.* barium

B.A. 1. [L. *Baccalaureus Artium*] Bachelor of Arts **2.** British Academy

baa (bä) *n.* [echoic] the cry of a sheep or goat —*vi.* to make this cry; bleat

Ba·al (bā'əl, bāl) *n.*, *pl.* **Ba'al·im** (-im), **Ba'als** [LL. < Heb. *ba'al*] **1.** among some ancient Semitic peoples, orig., any of a number of local fertility gods; later, a chief god **2.** a false god; idol —**Ba'al·ish** *adj.* —**Ba'al·ism** *n.* —**Ba'al·ist, Ba'al·ite'** (-īt') *n.*

Baal·bek (bäl'bek) town in NE Lebanon: pop. 9,600: site of ruins of ancient Heliopolis

Baal Shem Tov, Baal Shem Tob (bäl' shem' tōv') (born *Israel ben Eliezer*) 1700?–60; Jewish religious leader in Poland; founder of Hasidism

baas (bäs) *n.* [Afrik. < Du., master, foreman, BOSS¹] master; sir: term of address used in South Africa by a native Negro speaking to a white man

baas·kaap (bäs'käp') *n.* [Afrik. < *baas* (see prec.) + MDu. *-scap*, -SHIP] the policy of absolute domination of the native peoples by white settlers in South Africa

Bab (bäb) *n.* [a shortening of *Bāb-ud-Dīn*, lit., Gate of the Faith] a Persian title taken by the founder of Babism

Bab. Babylonian

‡**ba·ba au rhum** (bá bá' ō rôm) [Fr.] a batter cake raised with yeast and saturated in rum before serving

Ba·bar (bä'bər) *same as* BABER

ba·bas·su (bä'bä sōō') *n.* [Port. *babaçú*] a Brazilian palm (*Orbignya speciosa*) whose edible nuts furnish an oil used in making soap, margarine, etc.

☆**bab·bitt** (bab'it) *n.* [after George *Babbitt*] Babbitt metal —*vt.* to line or cover with Babbitt metal

☆**bab·bitt, Bab·bitt** (bab'it) *n.* [after George *Babbitt*, title character of a satirical novel (1922) by Sinclair Lewis] a smugly conventional person interested chiefly in business and social success and indifferent to cultural values; Philistine —**bab'bitt·ry, Bab'bitt·ry** *n.*

Babbitt, Irving 1865–1933; U.S. educator & critic

☆**Babbitt metal** [after Isaac *Babbitt* (1799–1862), U.S. inventor] a soft alloy of tin, copper, and antimony in various proportions, used to reduce friction in bearings, etc.

bab·ble (bab''l) *vi.* **-bled, -bling** [ME. *bablen*; like similar forms (Norw. *bable*, Sw. *babbla*, G. *babbeln*, to prattle, L. *balbutire*, to stammer, Sans. *balbuthah*, stammerer), of echoic origin] **1.** to make incoherent sounds, as a baby does; prattle **2.** to talk foolishly or too much; blab **3.** to make a low, bubbling sound, as a brook does when flowing over stones —*vt.* **1.** to say indistinctly or incoherently **2.** to say foolishly or inadvisedly; blab —*n.* **1.** confused, incoherent talk or vocal sounds **2.** foolish or meaningless talk **3.** a low, bubbling sound —**bab'bler** *n.*

babe (bāb) *n.* [ME.; like similar forms (W. *baban*, Alb. *bebe*, L., Gr., & G. *papa*, MHG. *babe*, old woman, Lith. *boba*, mother) formed in imitation of baby cries] **1.** a baby; infant **2.** a naive, gullible, or helpless person: also **babe in the woods** ☆**3.** [Slang] a girl or young woman

Ba·bel (bā'b'l, bab'l) [Heb. *bābel* < Assyr.-Bab. *Bāb-ilu*, Babylon, lit., gate of God (? transl. of Turanian *Ca-*

dimirra, Gate of God)] *Bible* a city in Shinar in which Noah's descendants tried to build a very high tower and were prevented from doing so by a confusion of tongues: Gen. 11:1–9 —*n.* **1.** an impracticable scheme **2.** [*also* b-] *a)* a confusion of voices, languages, or sounds; tumult *b)* a place of such confusion

Ba·bel (bä'b'l), **I·saak** (**Emmanuilovich**) (ē säk') 1894–1941; Russ. writer

Bab el Man·deb (bab' el man'deb) strait joining the Red Sea and the Gulf of Aden: 20 mi. wide

Ba·ber (bä'bər) (born *Zahir ud-Din Muhammed*) 1483–1530; founder & first emperor (1526–30) of the Mogul dynasty of India

Ba·bi (bä'bē) *n. same as* BABISM, BABIST

☆**ba·biche** (bä bēsh') *n.* [< CanadFr. < Algonquian] [Chiefly Canad.] thongs or lacings made of rawhide, eel skins, sinew, etc., used for tying or weaving, esp. in snowshoes

babies' breath (bā'bēz) *same as* BABY'S BREATH

bab·i·ru·sa, bab·i·rous·sa, bab·i·rus·sa (bab'ə rōōs'ə, bä'bə-) *n.* [Malay *bābī*, hog + *rūsa*, deer] a wild hog (*Babirusa alfurus*) of southeast Asia and eastern India that has a pair of hornlike tusks curving up backward from each jaw

Bab·ism (bäb'iz'm) *n.* a Persian religion founded c. 1844 by the Bab (Mirza Ali Muhammed): it forbids begging, drinking alcoholic liquors, buying and selling slaves, having more than one wife, etc.: cf. BAHAISM —**Bab'ist, Bab'ite** *n.*, *adj.*

bab·ka (bäb'kə) *n.* [< Pol. dim. of *baba*, lit., old woman] a light, sweet, usually cylindrical, yeast cake containing raisins, often glazed and flavored with rum

ba·boon (ba bōōn', bə-) *n.* [ME. *babewyne* < OFr. *babuin*, ape, fool < *baboue*, lip (of animals) < *bab*, echoic (see BABBLE)] any of various large and fierce short-tailed monkeys (mainly genus *Papio*) of Africa and Arabia, having a doglike snout and teeth, a large head with cheek pouches, and bare calluses on the rump —**ba·boon'er·y** *n.* —**ba·boon'ish** *adj.*

BABOON
(35-58 in. long,
including tail)

ba·bu, ba·boo (bäb'ōō) *n.* [Hind. *bābu*] **1.** a Hindu title equivalent to Mr., Sir, or Esq. **2.** a native clerk in India who can write English

ba·bul (bə bōōl') *n.* [Per. *babūl*] a spiny acacia tree (*Acacia arabica*) of the legume family, found in northern Africa and parts of Asia, that furnishes gum arabic, tannin, and wood for carving

Ba·bur (bä'bər) *same as* BABER

☆**ba·bush·ka** (bə boosh'kə) *n.* [Russ., grandmother] a kerchief or scarf worn on the head by a woman or girl and tied under the chin

ba·by (bā'bē) *n.*, *pl.* **-bies** [ME. *babi*, dim.: see BABE] **1.** a very young child; infant **2.** a person who behaves like an infant; helpless or timid person **3.** a very young animal **4.** the youngest or smallest in a group ☆**5.** [Slang] *a)* a girl or young woman *b)* any person or thing —*adj.* **1.** of or for an infant [*baby* food] **2.** extremely young **3.** small of its kind **4.** infantile or childish —*vt.* **-bied, -by·ing 1.** to treat like a baby; pamper; coddle **2.** [Colloq.] to handle with great care [to *baby* a new car] —*SYN.* see INDULGE —**ba'by·hood'** *n.* —**ba'by·ish** *adj.* —**ba'by·ish·ly** *adv.*

BABUSHKA

☆**baby beef** meat from a prime heifer or steer fattened for butchering when one to two years old

☆**baby blue-eyes** (blōō'īz') an American plant (*Nemophila menziesii*) with bell-shaped flowers

☆**baby carriage** a light carriage for wheeling a baby about; perambulator: also **baby buggy**

baby grand a small grand piano, about five feet long

Bab·y·lon (bab'ə lən, -län') [L. < Gr. *Babylōn* < Heb. *bābel*: see BABEL] ancient city on the lower Euphrates River, the capital of Babylonia, famous for wealth, luxury, and wickedness —*n.* any city or place of great wealth, luxury, and vice

Bab·y·lo·ni·a (bab′ə lō′nē ə) [L. < Gr. *Babylōnia* < *Babylōn*: see BABY-LON] ancient empire in SW Asia, in the lower valley of the Tigris & Euphrates rivers: it flourished c. 2100–689 B.C. and again, as Chaldea or "New Babylonia," c. 625–538 B.C.

Bab·y·lo·ni·an (bab′-ə lō′nē ən) *adj.* **1.** of Babylon, its people, etc. **2.** of Babylonia **3.** luxurious, unrestrained, wicked, etc. —*n.* **1.** a native or inhabitant of Babylon or Babylonia **2.** the Akkadian language of the ancient Babylonians

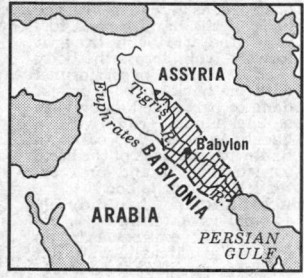

BABYLONIA (c. 2100 B.C.)

Babylonian Captivity 1. the exile of the Jews, deported by Nebuchadnezzar into Babylonia in 597 B.C. and permitted to return by Cyrus in 538 B.C. **2.** the period of forced residence of the Popes at Avignon, France (1309–77): so called after the exile of the Jews

ba·by's breath (bā′bēz breth′) **1.** any of several species (genus *Gypsophila*) of the pink family, having small, delicate, white or pink flowers **2.** any of several species of bedstraw (genus *Galium*) of the madder family

☆**ba·by-sit** (bā′bē sit′) *vi.* **-sat′, -sit′ting** [back-formation < ff.] to act as a baby sitter

☆**baby sitter** a person hired to take care of a child or children, as when the parents are away for the evening

‡**bac·ca·lau·ré·at** (bá kä lō rä ä′) *n.* [Fr.] in France, the diploma awarded to students who have completed secondary school (*lycée*) and have passed the two-part examination that makes them eligible to enter a university

bac·ca·lau·re·ate (bak′ə lôr′ē it) *n.* [ML. *baccalaureatus*; as if < L. *bacca laureus*, laurel berry, but actually < ML. *baccalaris*, vassal farmer, young nobleman seeking to become a knight < ? Gaul. *bakalākos*, a staff-bearer, shepherd < L. *baculum*, staff] **1.** the degree of bachelor of arts, bachelor of science, etc. ☆**2.** an address or sermon delivered to a graduating class at commencement: also **baccalaureate address** (or **sermon**)

bac·ca·rat, bac·ca·ra (bak′ə rä′, bäk′-, bak′ə rä′) *n.* [Fr. *baccara* < ?] a gambling game played with cards, somewhat like the game of twenty-one

bac·cate (bak′āt) *adj.* [L. *baccatus* < *bacca*, berry] **1.** like a berry, as in form **2.** bearing berries

Bac·chae (bak′ē) *n.pl.* [L. < Gr. *Bakchai* < *Bakchos*, Bacchus] **1.** *Gr. Myth.* women companions of Bacchus **2.** priestesses of Bacchus **3.** the women who took part in the Bacchanalia

bac·cha·nal (bak′ə nəl, -nal′; bak′ə nal′) *n.* [L., place devoted to Bacchus] **1.** a worshiper of Bacchus; bacchant or bacchante **2.** a drunken carouser **3.** [*pl.*] the Bacchanalia **4.** a dance or song in honor of Bacchus **5.** a drunken party; orgy —*adj.* **1.** of Bacchus or his worship; bacchanalian **2.** carousing

Bac·cha·na·li·a (bak′ə nāl′yə, -nā′lē ə) *n.pl.* **1.** an ancient Roman festival in honor of Bacchus **2.** [b-] a drunken party; orgy —**bac′cha·na′li·an** (-nā′lē ən) *adj., n.*

bac·chant (bak′ənt; bə kant′, -känt′) *n., pl.* **bac′chants, bac·chan·tes** (bə kan′tēz, -kän′-) [< L. *bacchans*, prp. of *bacchari*, to celebrate the feast of Bacchus] **1.** a priest or worshiper of Bacchus **2.** a drunken carouser —*adj.* **1.** worshiping Bacchus **2.** given to carousing—**bac·chan′tic** *adj.*

bac·chan·te (bə kan′tē, -kän′-; -kant′) *n.* [Fr.: see prec.] **1.** a priestess or woman votary of Bacchus **2.** a woman who carouses

Bac·chus (bak′əs) [L. < Gr. *Bakchos*] an ancient Greek and Roman god of wine and revelry: earlier called Dionysus by the Greeks —**Bac′chic, bac′chic** *adj.*

bac·ci- (bak′sə, -sē) [< L. *bacca, baca*, berry] a combining form meaning berry [*baccivorous*]

bac·cif·er·ous (bak sif′ər əs) *adj.* [L. *baccifer* < *bacca*, berry + *ferre*, to BEAR[1] + -OUS] producing berries

bac·ci·form (bak′sə fôrm′) *adj.* shaped like a berry

bac·civ·or·ous (bak siv′ər əs) *adj.* feeding on berries

☆**bach** (bach) *vi.* [< BACHELOR] [Slang] to live alone or keep house for oneself, as a bachelor: usually in the phrase **to bach it** —*n.* [Slang] a bachelor

Bach (bäkh; *E. occas.* bäk) **1. Jo·hann Christian** (yō′hän), 1735–82; Ger. organist & composer: son of *ff.* **2. Johann Sebastian,** 1685–1750; Ger. organist & composer **3. Karl Philipp Emanuel,** 1714–88; Ger. composer: son of **2**

bach·e·lor (bach′l ər, bach′lər) *n.* [ME. *bacheler* < OFr. *bachelier* < ML. *baccalaris*: see BACCALAUREATE] **1.** orig., in the feudal system, a young knight and landholder who served under another's banner: also **bach′e·lor-at-arms′ 2.** an unmarried man **3.** a person who is a BACHELOR OF ARTS (or SCIENCE, etc.) **4.** a young male animal, specif. a fur seal, that has not yet mated —*adj.* of or for a bachelor —**bach′e·lor·hood′, bach′e·lor·ship′** *n.*

☆**bachelor girl** [Colloq.] an unmarried young woman who works and leads an independent life

Bachelor of Arts (or ☆**Science,** etc.) **1.** a degree given by a college or university to a person who has completed a four-year course or its equivalent in the humanities or related studies (or in science, etc.) **2.** a person who has this degree

bachelor's button any of a genus (*Centaurea*) of plants of the composite family, that have scaly, vase-shaped involucres and long-stalked heads with showy white, pink, or blue marginal flowers, including the cornflower and knapweed

bac·il·lar·y (bas′ə ler′ē, bə sil′ər ē) *adj.* [ModL. *bacillarius*: see BACILLUS] **1.** rod-shaped; bacilliform **2.** consisting of rodlike structures **3.** of, like, characterized by, or caused by bacilli Also **ba·cil·lar** (bə sil′ər)

ba·cil·li (bə sil′ī) *n. pl. of* BACILLUS

ba·cil·li·form (bə sil′ə fôrm′) *adj.* rod-shaped; shaped like a bacillus

ba·cil·lus (bə sil′əs) *n., pl.* **-cil′li** (-ī) [ModL. < LL., little rod < L. *bacillum*, dim. of *baculus*, a stick < IE. base *bak-*, staff, whence PEG, Gr. *baktron*] **1.** any of a genus (*Bacillus*) of rod-shaped bacteria which occur in chains, produce spores, and are active only in the presence of oxygen **2.** any rod-shaped bacterium: distinguished from COCCUS, SPIRILLUM **3.** [*usually pl.*] loosely, any of the bacteria, esp. those causing disease

☆**bac·i·tra·cin** (bas′ə trās′'n) *n.* [arbitrary blend < BACI-(LLUS) + (Margaret) *Trac*(*y*), name of Am. girl (1936—) from whose wounds the strain was isolated + -IN[1]] an antibiotic obtained from a strain of bacteria (*Bacillus subtilis*) and used in the treatment of certain bacterial infections, esp. of the body surface

back[1] (bak) *n.* [ME. *bak* < OE. *bæc*; akin to ON. *bak*, OHG. *bahho*] **1.** the part of the body opposite to the front; in man and many other animals, the part to the rear or top reaching from the nape of the neck to the end of the spine **2.** the backbone or spine **3.** the part of a chair that supports one's back **4.** the part of a garment or harness that fits on the back of a person or animal **5.** physical strength [put some *back* into the work] **6.** the rear or hinder part of anything; part behind or opposite the front [the *back* of the room, the *back* of his leg] **7.** the part or side of anything that is less often used, seen, etc. [the *back* of the hand; the *back* of a carpet, textile, etc.; the *back* of a knife] **8.** *a*) the part of a book where the sections are sewed or glued together; part covered by the spine *b*) the spine of a book **9.** *Mining* the roof or overhead part of an underground passage **10.** *Sports a*) a player in a position more or less behind the front line, as a quarterback or fullback in football *b*) the position of such a player —*adj.* **1.** at the rear or back; behind **2.** distant or remote [*back* country] **3.** of or for a time in the past [a *back* copy of a newspaper, *back* pay] **4.** in a backward direction; returning; reversed [a *back* step] **5.** *Phonet.* articulated with the tongue toward the back of the mouth, as (ōō) in *cool* —*adv.* [ME. *bac* < *abac* < OE. *on bæc*, backward] **1.** at, to, or toward the rear; backward **2.** to or toward a former position or location **3.** into or toward a previous condition **4.** to or toward an earlier time **5.** so as to keep in reserve or concealment [to hold *back* information] **6.** in return or requital [to pay one *back*] —*vt.* **1.** to cause to move backward, or to the rear (often with *up*) **2.** to be at the back of; stand behind **3.** to support or help, as with money, endorsement, etc. **4.** to make a wager in support of; bet on **5.** to get on the back of; mount **6.** to provide with a back or backing **7.** to form the back of **8.** to sign on the back; endorse —*vi.* **1.** *a*) to move or go backward [to *back* into a room] *b*) to move (*into* a desired position) through the faulty performance of an opponent [to *back* into a championship] **2.** to shift counterclockwise (in the Northern Hemisphere): said of the wind: opposed to VEER[1] **3.** to have the back in a certain place or direction [the house *backs* on a lake] —*SYN.* see SUPPORT —**back and fill 1.** to handle sails so that they alternately spill wind and fill with wind **2.** to zigzag ☆**3.** to vacillate, as in a decision —**back and forth** to and fro; from side to side —☆**back down** to withdraw from a position or a claim —**back off** to move back a short distance —**back out (of) 1.** to withdraw from an enterprise **2.** to refuse to keep a promise or engagement —**back up 1.** to support or help **2.** to move or go backward: also **back away, back out,** etc. **3.** to accumulate as the result of a stoppage [traffic *backed up* for a mile] —**back water 1.** to use oars, a propeller, etc. to move backward or prevent drifting ☆**2.** to withdraw from a position or a claim —**behind one's back** without one's knowledge or consent —**be (flat) on one's back** to be ill, bedridden, or helpless —☆**get off one's back** [Slang] to stop nagging or harassing one —**get (or put) one's back up 1.** to make or become angry, as a cat arching its back **2.** to be obstinate —☆**go back on** [Colloq.] **1.** to be faithless or disloyal to; betray **2.** to fail to keep

(a promise, one's word, etc.) —☆(**in**) **back of** at or to the rear of; behind —**turn one's back on** 1. to show anger, contempt, etc. toward by turning away from 2. to ignore the plight of; desert; fail —**with one's back to the wall** in a desperate position, as a fighter cornered and unable to retreat

back² (bak) n. [Du. *bak* < LL. *bacca*, water bowl] a vat or tub used in certain industrial processes

back·ache (bak'āk') n. an ache or pain in the back

Back Bay a wealthy residential district in Boston

back·bench·er (-ben'chər) n. a member of a legislature, esp. of the British House of Commons, who is not a leader in his party

back·bend (-bend') n. an acrobatic stunt in which the body is bent backward from a standing position until the hands touch the ground

back·bite (-bīt') vt., vi. -**bit'**, -**bit'ten** or -**bit'**, -**bit'ing** [ME. *bakbiten*: see BACK¹ & BITE] to speak maliciously about (an absent person); slander —**back'bit'er** (-bīt'ər) n.

back·board (-bôrd') n. 1. a board that forms or supports the back of something ☆2. *Basketball* a board or flat surface just behind the basket

back·bone (-bōn') n. [ME. *bakbon*: see BACK¹ & BONE] 1. the column of bones along the center of the back of man and many animals, made up of separate bones (vertebrae) connected by muscles and tendons; spine 2. main support; firmest part 3. a main ridge or range of mountains 4. will power, courage, determination, etc. 5. *same as* BACK¹ (n. 8) —SYN. see FORTITUDE —**back'boned'** adj.

back·break·ing (-brāk'iŋ) adj. requiring great physical exertion; very tiring

back court 1. *Basketball* the half of the court which contains the basket a team is defending 2. *Tennis* the area on either side of the court extending from the service line to the base line at the back of the court

back·cross (-krôs') vt., vi. to cross, or breed (a hybrid) with one of its parents or with another organism genetically equivalent to such a parent —n. an instance or result of such a breeding

back·date (bak'dāt') vt. -**dat'ed**, -**dat'ing** to date before the actual date; predate

back·door (bak'dôr') adj. 1. of a rear entrance 2. secret; underhand; surreptitious

back·down (-doun') n. [Colloq.] a backing down; withdrawal from a position, claim, etc.

back·drop (-dräp') n. 1. a curtain hung at the back of a stage, often painted to represent some scene 2. background or setting, as of an event

backed (bakt) adj. having a back or backing: *often used in hyphenated compounds meaning* having a (specified kind of) back [*canvas-backed*]

back·er (bak'ər) n. 1. a person who supports or gives help, as to a protégé or undertaking; patron; sponsor 2. a person who bets on a contestant —SYN. see SPONSOR

☆**back·field** (-fēld') n. *Football* the players whose usual position is behind the line of scrimmage; esp., the offensive unit that carries the ball

back·fill (-fil') vt. to refill (an excavation) as with the earth, etc. previously removed —n. material used in refilling an excavation

back·fire (-fīr') n. ☆1. a fire started to stop an advancing prairie fire or forest fire by creating a burned area in its path 2. a premature explosion in a cylinder of an internal-combustion engine, preventing the completion of the compression stroke and reversing the direction of the piston 3. an explosive force toward the breech, rather than through the muzzle, of a firearm —vi. -**fired'**, -**fir'ing** ☆1. to use or set a backfire 2. to explode as a backfire 3. to have an unexpected and unwelcome result; go awry; boomerang [his plan *backfired*]

back·for·ma·tion (-fôr mā'shən) n. 1. a word actually formed from, but looking as if it were the base of, another word (Ex.: *burgle* from *burglar*) 2. the process of forming such a word

back·gam·mon (-gam'ən) n. [BACK¹ + GAMMON²] a game played on a special board by two people: each has fifteen pieces, which he moves according to the throw of dice

back·ground (-ground') n. 1. the part of a scene or picture that is or seems to be toward the back 2. surroundings, esp. those behind something and providing harmony or contrast; surface against which something is seen 3. a less important or unobtrusive place or position [to stay in the *background*]

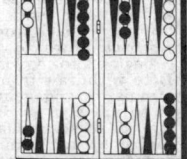

BACKGAMMON BOARD

4. the whole of one's study, training, and experience [the right *background* for the job] 5. a) the circumstances or conditions surrounding something b) the events leading up to something c) information which will help to explain something 6. music (in full, **background music**) or sound effects used as a subordinated accompaniment to dialogue or action, as in movies, radio, or television 7. any of various unwanted, interfering effects produced or registered by apparatus of various kinds, as static in radio or radiation due to cosmic rays

back·hand (-hand') n. 1. handwriting that slants backward, up to the left 2. a kind of stroke, as in tennis, with the back of the hand turned forward, the arm being brought forward from across the body —adj. 1. done or performed with the back of the hand 2. done or performed as or with a backhand —adv. with a backhand —vt. ☆to catch (a ball) with the back of the hand turned inward and arm extended across the body

back·hand·ed (-han'did) adj. 1. *same as* BACKHAND 2. expressing or expressed in an indirect or sarcastic way; not sincere; equivocal [a *backhanded* compliment] 3. *Sports* performed with the back of the hand turned inward and the arm extended across the body [a *backhanded* catch] —adv. with a backhand

Backhandwriting

BACKHAND STROKE

back·house (-hous') n. a small building behind the main one; esp., a privy

back·ing (-iŋ) n. 1. something placed in back or forming a back for support or strength 2. support or aid given to a person or cause; endorsement 3. those giving such support or aid 4. [Slang] a musical accompaniment

back·lash (-lash') n. 1. a) a quick, sharp recoil b) any sudden or violent reaction; specif., strong political or social reaction resulting from fear or resentment of a movement, candidate, etc. 2. a snarl in a reeled fishing line, resulting from an imperfect cast 3. the jarring reaction of loose or worn parts; also, the play in these parts

back·list (-list') n. all the books of a publisher that are kept in print over a relatively long period of time —vt. to include in a backlist

☆**back·log** (-lôg', -läg') n. 1. a large log at the back of a fire, as in a fireplace 2. a reserve of something stored, saved, etc. 3. an accumulation of unfilled orders, unfinished work, etc. —vi., vt. -**logged'**, -**log'ging** to accumulate as a backlog

☆**back number** 1. an old issue of a periodical 2. [Colloq.] an old-fashioned person or thing

back order an order not yet filled

back·ped·al (-ped''l) vi. -**ped'aled** or -**ped'alled**, -**ped'al·ing** or -**ped'al·ling** 1. to press backward on the pedals of a bicycle in braking ☆2. to move backward quickly in boxing to avoid a blow ☆3. to retreat from a previously held opinion

back·rest (-rest') n. a support for or at the back

Back River river in Northwest Territories, Canada, flowing northeast into the Arctic Ocean: 605 mi.

☆**back road** a road that is away from the main road; country road, esp. an unpaved one

back·scat·ter·ing (-skat'ər iŋ) n. the scattering of rays or particles at angles to the original direction of motion of greater than 90°: also **back'scat'ter**

back seat a secondary or inconspicuous position

☆**back-seat driver** (-sēt') a passenger in an automobile who offers unwanted advice about driving

back·set (-set') n. 1. a setback; relapse; reverse 2. a backward current; eddy

back·sheesh, back·shish (bak'shēsh', bäk'-) n. *same as* BAKSHEESH

▶**back·side** (bak'sīd') n. [ME. *bak side*] 1. the back or hind part 2. the rump; buttocks

☆**back·sight** (-sīt') n. *Surveying* 1. a sight taken backwards, in an opposite direction 2. a flag or marker for a location that has been made

☆**back·slap·per** (-slap'ər) n. [Colloq.] a person who is friendly in a way that is effusive or too hearty —**back'slap'** vt. -**slapped'**, -**slap'ping**

back·slide (-slīd') vi. -**slid'**, -**slid'** or -**slid'den**, -**slid'ing** to slide backward in morals or religious enthusiasm; become less virtuous, less pious, etc. —**back'slid'er** n.

back·space (-spās') vi. -**spaced'**, -**spac'ing** to move a typewriter carriage back along the same line one space at a time by depressing a special key (**backspacer**)

back·spin (-spin') n. a backward spin given to a propelled ball, wheel, etc. that causes it, upon hitting the ground, to bound backward

back·stage (-stāj') adv. in or to that part of the stage or theater behind the proscenium, esp. the wings, the dressing rooms, etc. —adj. 1. situated backstage 2. of or relating to the life of people in show business 3. of or relating to secret or private activities or dealings

back·stairs (-sterz') adj. involving intrigue or scandal; secret: also **back'stair'**

back·stay (-stā') n. 1. a stay or rope extending aft from a masthead to the side or stern of the ship 2. a support for the back

back·stitch (-stich') n. a stitch made by doubling the thread back on part of the stitch before —vt., vi. to sew with backstitches

back·stop (-stäp') n. ☆1. a) a fence, screen, etc. serving to stop balls from going too far: in baseball the backstop is behind the catcher b) [Slang] the catcher in baseball

2. anything that supports or bolsters —*vt.* **-stopped′, -stop′-ping** to act as a backstop for

☆**back·stretch** (-strech′) *n.* the part of a race track farthest from the grandstand and opposite and parallel to the homestretch

back·stroke (-strōk′) *n.* **1.** a stroke backward, or a back-handed stroke **2.** a stroke made by a swimmer lying face upward; esp., a racing stroke in which the arms are stretched alternately over the head and the legs are moved in a flutter kick —*vi.* **-stroked′, -strok′ing** to perform a backstroke —*vt.* to hit with a backstroke

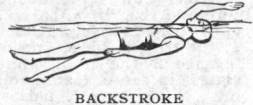

BACKSTROKE

back·swept (-swept′) *adj.* sloping away from the front

back swimmer a hemipterous water bug (family Notonectidae) that swims rapidly on its back by use of its long, oarlike legs

back·sword (-sôrd′) *n.* **1.** a sword sharpened on only one edge; broadsword **2.** a hilted, saberlike stick used in fencing practice or as a singlestick

back talk [Colloq.] saucy or insolent retorts

back-to-back (bak′tə bak′) *adj.* [< use in stud poker to describe a pair dealt consecutively, one face down and the next face up] ☆[Colloq.] one right after another; consecutive

☆**back·track** (-trak′) *vi.* **1.** to return by the same path **2.** to withdraw from a position, attitude, etc.

back·up, back-up (-up′) *adj.* **1.** standing by as an alternate or auxiliary [a *backup* pilot] **2.** supporting [a *backup* effort] —*n.* the act or result of backing up; specif., *a)* an accumulation because of a stoppage *b)* a support or help

back·ward (-wərd) *adv.* [ME. *bakward*, for *abakward* < *abak* (< OE. *on bæc*, back) + *-ward* (< OE. *-weard*, toward)] **1.** toward the back or rear; behind **2.** with the back or rear foremost **3.** in reverse [to spell a word *backward*] **4.** in a way contrary to the normal or usual way **5.** toward earlier times; into the past **6.** from a better to a worse state —*adj.* **1.** turned or directed toward the rear or in the opposite way **2.** hesitant, bashful, or shy, as in meeting people **3.** late in developing or growing; retarded; slow —**bend over backward 1.** to try to an unusual degree (to please, pacity, etc.) **2.** to counterbalance a tendency, prejudice, etc. by an extreme effort in the opposite direction: also **lean over backward** —**back′ward·ly** *adv.* —**back′ward·ness** *n.*

back·wards (-wərdz) *adv.* [ME. *bakwardes* ‖ prec. ‖ adv. gen. -(e)s] same as BACKWARD

back·wash (-wôsh′, -wäsh′) *n.* **1.** water moved backward, as by a ship, an oar, etc. **2.** a backward current or flow, as of air from an airplane propeller **3.** a reaction or commotion caused by some event

back·wa·ter (-wôt′ər, -wät′-) *n.* **1.** water moved backward or held back by a dam, tide, etc. **2.** stagnant water in a small stream or inlet **3.** a place or condition regarded as stagnant, backward, etc. [a cultural *backwater*] —*adj.* like a backwater; backward

☆**back·woods** (-woodz′, -woodz′) *n.pl.* [occas. *with sing. v.*] **1.** heavily wooded areas far from centers of population **2.** any remote, thinly populated place —*adj.* in, from, or characteristic of the backwoods: also **back′wood′** —**back′-woods′man** *n.*, *pl.* **-men**

Ba·co·lod (bä kô′lôd) seaport on Negros island, the Philippines: pop. 138,000

ba·con (bāk′'n) *n.* [ME. & OFr. < OS. *baco*, side of bacon, akin to OHG. *bahho*, BACK] salted and smoked meat from the back or sides of a hog: see PORK, illus. —**bring home the bacon** [Colloq.] **1.** to earn a living **2.** to succeed; win

Ba·con (bāk′'n) **1. Francis,** Baron Verulam, Viscount St. Albans, 1561–1626; Eng. philosopher, essayist, & statesman **2. Nathaniel,** 1647?–76; Am. colonist born in England: leader of a rebellion (1676) which sought social reform **3. Roger,** 1214?–94; Eng. philosopher & scientist

Ba·co·ni·an (bā kō′nē ən) *adj.* **1.** of Francis Bacon, his philosophy, or his style of writing **2.** designating or of the theory alleging that Francis Bacon wrote Shakespeare's works —*n.* **1.** one who believes in the philosophy of Francis Bacon **2.** an adherent of the Baconian theory

bact. 1. bacteriology **2.** bacterium

bac·te·re·mi·a (bak′tə rē′mē ə) *n.* [BACTER(IA) + -EMIA] the presence of bacteria in the bloodstream

bac·te·ri- (bak′tər ə) same as BACTERIO-

bac·te·ri·a (bak tir′ē ə) *n.pl.*, *sing.* **-ri·um** (-əm) [ModL., pl. of *bacterium* < Gr. *baktērion*, dim. of *baktron*, a staff: see BACILLUS] typically one-celled microorganisms which have no chlorophyll, multiply by simple division, and can be seen only with a microscope: they occur in three main forms, spherical (cocci), rod-shaped (bacilli), and spiral (spirilla); some bacteria cause diseases such as pneumonia, tuberculosis, and anthrax, and others are necessary for fermentation, nitrogen fixation, etc. —**bac·te′ri·al** *adj.* —**bac·te′ri·al·ly** *adv.*

bac·te·ri·cide (bak tir′ə sīd′) *n.* [BACTERI- + -CIDE] an agent or substance that destroys bacteria —**bac·te′ri·cid′al** *adj.*

bac·te·ri·o- (bak tir′ē ə) [< BACTERIUM] *a combining form meaning* of bacteria [bacteriostasis]

bac·te·ri·ol·o·gy (bak tir′ē äl′ə jē) *n.* the study of bacteria, either as a branch of medicine or as a science important in food processing, agriculture, industry, etc. —**bac·te′ri·o·log′ic** (-ē ə läj′ik), **bac·te′ri·o·log′i·cal** *adj.* —**bac·te′ri·o·log′i·cal·ly** *adv.* —**bac·te·ri·ol′o·gist** *n.*

bac·te·ri·ol·y·sis (bak tir′ē äl′ə sis) *n.* [BACTERIO- + -LYSIS] the dissolution or destruction of bacteria —**bac·te′ri·o·lyt′ic** (-ə lit′ik) *adj.*

bac·te·ri·o·phage (bak tir′ē ə fāj′) *n.* [BACTERIO- + -PHAGE] any virus that is parasitic upon certain bacteria, disintegrating them —**bac·te′ri·oph′a·gy** (-äf′ə jē) *n.*

bac·te·ri·os·co·py (bak tir′ē äs′kə pē) *n.* [BACTERIO- + -SCOPY] the microscopic study of bacteria

bac·te·ri·o·sta·sis (bak tir′ē ə stā′sis) *n.* [ModL.: see BACTERIO- & STASIS] an arresting of the growth or multiplication of bacteria —**bac·te′ri·o·stat′** (-ə stat′) *n.* —**bac·te′ri·o·stat′ic** *adj.*

bac·te·ri·um (bak tir′ē əm) *n. sing. of* BACTERIA

bac·te·rize (bak′tə rīz′) *vt.* **-rized′, -riz′ing** to affect by bacterial action —**bac′te·ri·za′tion** *n.*

bac·te·roid (-roid′) *adj.* resembling bacteria: also **bac′te·roid′al** —*n.* a structurally modified form of bacterium

Bac·tri·a (bak′trē ə) ancient country between the Hindu Kush & the upper Amu Darya, in what is now NE Afghanistan —**Bac′tri·an** *adj.*, *n.*

Bactrian camel a camel (*Camelus bactrianus*) with two humps, native to central Asia: it is shorter and hairier than the Arabian camel

ba·cu·li·form (ba kyōō′lə fôrm′, bak′yoo-) *adj.* [< L. *baculus*, a stick + -FORM] shaped like a rod

bac·u·line (bak′yə lin, -līn′) *adj.* [< L. *baculum*, a stick + -INE¹] of a rod, or punishment administered with a rod

bac·u·lum (bak′yə ləm) *n.*, *pl.* **-la** (-lə), **-lums** [L., a stick] a slim bone that supports rigidity of the penis in certain mammals, as the whale

bad¹ (bad) *adj.* **worse, worst** [ME. *bad*, *badde* < ? OE. *bæddel*, hermaphrodite] **1.** *a)* not good; not as it should be [a *bad* attitude, a *bad* deal] *b)* defective in quality; below standard; inadequate [*bad* plumbing] **2.** unfit; unskilled [a *bad* writer] **3.** not pleasant; unfavorable; disagreeable [*bad* news] **4.** rotten; spoiled [a *bad* apple] **5.** incorrect; faulty; erroneous [*bad* spelling] **6.** *a)* wicked; immoral *b)* not behaving properly; mischievous **7.** causing injury; harmful [*bad* for one's health] **8.** severe [a *bad* storm] **9.** ill; in poor health **10.** sorry; distressed [he feels *bad* about it]: cf. BADLY **11.** offensive; disgusting [a *bad* smell] **12.** *Law* defective; not valid; void [a *bad* title] —*adv.* [Colloq.] badly —*n.* **1.** anything that is bad; bad quality or state **2.** wickedness —**go to the bad** [Colloq.] to become wicked, shiftless, etc.; degenerate —☆**in bad** [Colloq.] **1.** in trouble **2.** in disfavor —**not bad** [Colloq.] good; fairly good; not unsatisfactory: also **not half bad, not so bad** —**the bad** those who are wicked —**bad′ness** *n.*

SYN.—**bad**, in this comparison, is the broadest term, ranging in implication from merely unsatisfactory to utterly depraved; **evil** and **wicked** connote willful violation of a moral code, but **evil** often has ominous or malevolent implications [an *evil* hour] and **wicked** is sometimes weakened in a playful way to mean merely mischievous [*wicked* wit]; **ill,** which is slightly weaker than **evil** in its implications of immorality, is now used chiefly in certain idiomatic phrases [*ill*-gotten gains]; **naughty** today implies mere mischievousness or disobedience [a *naughty* child] —ANT. **good, moral**

bad² (bad) **1.** archaic *pt.* of BID¹ **2.** obs. *pt.* of BIDE

Ba·da·joz (bä′thä hôth′) city in SW Spain, on the border of Portugal: pop. 102,000

Ba·da·lo·na (bä′thä lô′nä) seaport in NE Spain: suburb of Barcelona: pop. 120,000

Ba·dar·i·an (bä där′ē ən) *adj.* [*Badari* (village in Egypt where artifacts were found) + -AN] designating or of a neolithic culture of upper Egypt, characterized by cattle-breeding, fine pottery, and a large range of ornaments

bad blood a feeling of (mutual) enmity

bad·der·locks (bad′ər läks′) *n.* [< ?] a dark-brown seaweed (*Alaria esculenta*) used as a food in northern Europe

bade (bad; *occas.* bād) *alt. pt.* of BID¹

☆**bad egg** [Slang] a mean or dishonest person: also **bad actor, bad apple, bad hat, bad lot,** etc.

Ba·den (bäd′'n) **1.** region of SW Germany: formerly a duchy **2.** former state of West Germany, made up of the S part of this region: see BADEN-WÜRTTEMBERG **3.** same as BADEN-BADEN

Ba·den-Ba·den (bäd′'n bäd′'n) city in SW West Germany: well-known as a health resort: pop. 40,000

Ba·den-Pow·ell (bäd′'n pō′əl), Sir **Robert Stephenson Smyth,** 1st Baron, 1857–1941; Brit. general: founder of Boy Scouts & Girl Guides

Ba·den-Würt·tem·berg (bäd′'n vür′təm berk′; *E.*-wurt′'m burg′) state of SW West Germany: formed (1951) by a merger of Baden (sense 2), Württemberg, & Hohenzollern: 13,800 sq. mi.; pop. 8,257,000; cap. Stuttgart

badge (baj) *n.* [ME. *bage*, *bagge*] **1.** a distinctive token, emblem, or sign worn to show rank, membership, achievement, etc. **2.** any distinguishing mark, sign, or symbol

—*vt.* **badged, badg′ing** to mark or provide with a badge

badg·er (baj′ər) *n., pl.* **-ers, -er:** see PLURAL II, D, 1 [16th-c. term for earlier *brock* < ? obs. n. & personal name *badger*, grain dealer] **1.** any of several carnivorous, burrowing mammals (genera *Taxidea* and *Meles*) of North America, Europe, and Asia, with a broad back, thick short legs, and long claws on the forefeet **2.** the fur of a badger **3.** in Australia, *same as a)* WOMBAT *b)* BANDICOOT **4.** [B-] *a*

BADGER
(body 16-28 in. long)

nickname for an inhabitant of Wisconsin, called the **Badger State** —*vt.* to torment as if baiting a badger; nag at —*SYN.* see BAIT

☆**badger game** [Slang] the blackmailing of a man by maneuvering him into a compromising situation with a woman

bad·i·nage (bad′ə näzh′, bad′'n ij) *n.* [Fr. < *badiner*, to jest, make merry < *badin*, fool < Pr. *badar*, to gape < ML. *badare*, to gape, trifle] playful, teasing talk; banter —*vt.* **-naged′, -nag′ing** to tease with playful talk

☆**bad·lands** (bad′landz′) *n.pl.* **1.** any section of barren land where rapid erosion has cut the loose, dry soil or soft rocks into strange shapes **2.** [B-] any of several such sections in the W U.S., esp. in SW S.Dak.: also **Bad Lands** —*SYN.* see WASTE

bad·ly (bad′lē) *adv.* **1.** in a bad manner; harmfully, unpleasantly, incorrectly, wickedly, etc. **2.** [Colloq.] very much; greatly [to want something *badly*] *Badly* is often used with adjectival force to mean "sorry" or "distressed" [to feel *badly* about a loss]

☆**bad·man** (bad′man′) *n., pl.* **-men′** (-men′) a cattle thief, desperado, or hired gunman of the old West

bad·min·ton (bad′min t′n) *n.* [after *Badminton*, estate of the Duke of Beaufort] a game in which a feathered cork (*shuttlecock*) is batted back and forth with light rackets across a net by opposing players or pairs of players

bad-tem·pered (bad′tem′pərd) *adj.* having a bad temper or cranky disposition; irritable

Bae·de·ker (bā′də kər) *n.* **1.** any of a series of guidebooks to foreign countries first published in Germany by Karl Baedeker (1801–59) **2.** loosely, any guidebook

Baf·fin (baf′in), **William** 1584–1622; Eng. navigator & explorer

Baffin Bay [after prec., its discoverer] arm of the N Atlantic, between Greenland & Baffin Island

Baffin Island large island off the NE coast of Canada, in Franklin District of Northwest Territories: c. 200,000 sq. mi.; pop. 2,000

baf·fle (baf′'l) *vt.* **-fled, -fling** [16th-c. Scot.; prob. respelling (as *duff* for *dough*, *Affleck* for *Auchinleck*) of obs. Scot. *bauchle*] **1.** to confuse so as to keep from understanding or solving; puzzle; confound **2.** to interfere with; hinder; impede **3.** to check the interference of (low-frequency sound waves) in a radio, phonograph, etc. by the use of a baffle —*vi.* to struggle without result —*n.* **1.** a baffling or being baffled **2.** an obstructing device, as a wall or screen to hold back or turn aside the flow of liquids, gases, etc.: also **baf′fle-plate′ 3.** a mounting or partition used to check the transmission of sound waves between the front and rear of the loudspeaker of a radio, phonograph, etc. —*SYN.* see FRUSTRATE —**baf′fle·ment** *n.* —**baf′fler** *n.* —**baf′fling** *adj.*

bag (bag) *n.* [ME. *bagge* < ON. *baggi*] **1.** a nonrigid container made of fabric, paper, leather, etc., with an opening at the top that can be closed; sack or pouch **2.** a piece of hand luggage; suitcase **3.** a woman's handbag or purse **4.** *a)* a container for game *b)* the amount of game caught or killed **5.** a bagful **6.** anything shaped like a bag. **7.** any thing or part shaped or bulging like a bag [*bags* under the eyes, *bags* at trouser knees] **8.** an udder or similar pouchlike membrane or sac **9.** [*pl.*] [Brit. Colloq.] trousers ☆**10.** [Slang] one's special sphere of interest, milieu, talent, obsession, etc. **11.** [< BAGGAGE, sense 3*a*] [Slang] an unattractive woman **12.** *Baseball* a base —*vt.* **bagged, bag′ging 1.** to make bulge **2.** to enclose within a bag **3.** to seize; capture **4.** to kill in or as in hunting **5.** [Slang] to obtain or collect —*vi.* **1.** to swell like a full bag **2.** to hang loosely —**bag and baggage** [Colloq.] **1.** with all one's possessions **2.** completely; entirely —☆**be in the bag** [Slang] having its success assured; certain —**be left holding the bag** [Colloq.] to be left to suffer the bad consequences or the blame

ba·gasse (bə gas′) *n.* [Fr. < Pr. *bagasso*, refuse from processing of grapes or olives < Gallo-Roman **bacacea* < L. *baca*, berry] the part of sugar cane left after the juice has been extracted, or the residue of certain other processed plants: it is used for fuel and in making fiberboard

bag·a·telle (bag′ə tel′) *n.* [Fr. < It. *bagatella*, dim. < L. *baca*, berry] **1.** something of little importance or value; trifle **2.** a game somewhat like billiards, played with nine balls on a table having nine holes spaced in a diamond shape at one end **3.** a short musical composition, esp. for the piano

Bag·dad (bag′dad, bäg däd′) *same as* BAGHDAD

Bage·hot (baj′ət), **Walter** 1826–77; Eng. economist, journalist, & critic

ba·gel (bā′g'l) *n.* [Yid. *beygel* < G. dial. *beugel*, a ring-shaped pastry (akin to G. *bügel*, stirrup, orig. ring), dim. < G. *beugen*, to bend: for IE. base see BOW[1]] a hard bread roll made of yeast dough twisted into a small doughnutlike shape, cooked in simmering water, then baked

bag·ful (bag′fool′) *n., pl.* **-fuls′ 1.** the amount that a bag will hold **2.** a large amount

bag·gage (bag′ij) *n.* [ME. & OFr. *bagage* < *bagues*, baggage < ML. *baga*, chest, bag, prob. < ON. *baggi*, bag] **1.** the trunks, bags, and other equipment of a traveler; luggage **2.** the supplies and gear of an army **3.** *a)* [associated, in sense "camp follower" with "army baggage," but < Fr. *bagasse*, harlot < OFr. *baiasse*, ult. < Ar. *bagīja*, adulteress, prostitute] formerly, a prostitute or wanton *b)* a saucy, impudent, or lively girl **4.** burdensome, superfluous, or outdated ideas, practices, etc.

bagged (bagd) *adj.* [Slang] drunk; intoxicated

bag·ging (bag′in) *n.* cloth for making bags; sacking

bag·gy (bag′ē) *adj.* **-gi·er, -gi·est 1.** puffed or swelling in a baglike way **2.** hanging loosely; unpressed [*baggy* trousers] —**bag′gi·ly** *adv.* —**bag′gi·ness** *n.*

Bagh·dad (bag′dad, bäg däd′) capital of Iraq, on the Tigris River: pop. c. 1,000,000: formerly a caliphate

bag·man (-mən) *n., pl.* **-men** (-mən) **1.** [Brit.] a traveling salesman ☆**2.** [Slang] a go-between in offering bribes, collecting money as for the numbers racket, etc.

bagn·io (ban′yō, bän′-) *n., pl.* **-ios** [It. *bagno* < L. *balneum*, bathing place < Gr. *balaneion*, bath] **1.** [Obs.] a Turkish or Italian bathhouse **2.** [Obs.] in the Orient, a prison **3.** a house of prostitution; brothel

bag·pipe (bag′pīp′) *n.* [*often pl.*] a shrill-toned musical instrument with one double-reed pipe operated by finger stops and one or more drone pipes, all of them sounded by air forced with the arm from a leather bag, which is kept filled by the breath: now chiefly a Scottish instrument —**bag′pip′er** *n.*

BAGPIPE

ba·guette, ba·guet (ba get′) *n.* [Fr. *baguette*, a rod < It. *bacchetta*, dim. of *bacchio*, a pole, cudgel < L. *baculum*, a staff] **1.** a gem, etc. cut in the shape of a narrow oblong, often tapered at one end **2.** this shape **3.** *Archit.* a small, convex molding

Ba·gui·o (bä′gē ō′; Sp. bä′gyō) city in NW Luzon: summer capital of the Philippines: pop. 58,000

bag·wig (bag′wig′) *n.* a wig with the back hair held in a cloth bag or snood: worn in the 18th cent.

☆**bag·worm** (-wurm′) *n.* the larva of any of various moths (family Psychidae) that builds a cocoon like a bag and feeds on the leaves of various trees

bah (bä, ba) *interj.* an exclamation expressing contempt, scorn, or disgust

‡**ba·ha·dur** (bə hô′door, -hä′-) *n.* [Hind. *bāhadur*, hero, brave] a Hindu title of respect

Ba·hai (bə hī′, ba hä′ē) *n., pl.* **Ba·hais′ 1.** a believer in Bahaism **2.** *same as* BAHAISM —*adj.* of Bahaism or a Bahai Also written **Baha'i**

Ba·ha·ism (bə hä′iz'm, -hī′-) *n.* [Ar. *ba-hā*, splendor + -ISM] a modern religion, developed orig. in Iran from Babism, that stresses principles of universal brotherhood, social equality, etc. —**Ba·ha′ist** *n., adj.*

Ba·ha·mas (bə hä′məz, -hä′-) group of islands in the West Indies, southeast of Fla. and north of Cuba: self-governing Brit. colony: 4,404 sq. mi.; pop. 131,000; cap. Nassau: also **Bahama Islands** —**Ba·ha′mi·an** *adj., n.*

Ba·ha·sa Indonesia (bä′hä′sä) *see* INDONESIAN

Ba·ha Ul·lah, Ba·ha·ul·lah (bä hä′ōō lä′) (born *Husayn Ali*) 1817–92; Persian founder of Bahaism

Ba·hi·a (bä ē′ä; E. bä hē′ə) **1.** state on the EC coast of Brazil: c. 216,000 sq. mi.; pop. 5,991,000; cap. Salvador **2.** *former name of* SALVADOR

Ba·hi·a Blan·ca (bä ē′ə blän′kä) seaport on the E coast of C Argentina: pop. 150,000

Bah·rain, Bah·rein (bä rān′) group of islands in the Persian Gulf, off the Arabian coast, constituting an independent Arab sheikdom: a member of the Brit. Commonwealth: 231 sq. mi.; pop. 185,000

baht (bät) *n., pl.* **bahts, baht** [Thai *bāt*] **1.** the monetary unit of Thailand: see MONETARY UNITS, table **2.** a coin of this value

Ba·hu·tu (bä hoo′too) *n., pl.* **-tus, -tu 1.** any member of an agricultural people of Burundi and Rwanda **2.** their Bantu language

Bai·kal (bī käl′), **Lake** large lake in SE Siberia, near the Mongolian border: deepest lake in the world, c. 5,700 ft.: c. 12,000 sq. mi.

bail[1] (bāl) *n.* [ME. & OFr., power, control, custody < *baillir*, to keep in custody, deliver < L. *bajulare*, to bear a burden < *bajulus*, porter, carrier] **1.** money or credit deposited with the court to get an arrested person temporarily released on the assurance that he will appear for trial, etc. at the proper time **2.** the release thus brought about **3.** the person or persons giving bail —*vt.* **1.** to

deliver (goods) in trust for a special purpose **2.** to set (an arrested person) free on bail or have (an arrested person) set free by giving bail (often with *out*) **3.** to help out of financial or other difficulty (often with *out*) —**go bail for** to furnish bail for

bail² (bāl) *n.* [ME. & OFr. *baille*, bucket < VL. *bajula*, vessel < *bajulare*: see prec.] a bucket or scoop for dipping up water and removing it from a boat —*vi.*, *vt.* **1.** to remove water from (a boat) as with a bail **2.** to dip out (water, etc.) as with a bail Usually with *out* —**bail out** to make a parachute jump from an aircraft —**bail′er** *n.*

bail³ (bāl) *n.* [ME. *beil* < ON. *beygla* < *beygja*, to bend, arch; ult. < IE. base *bheugh-*, whence BOW¹] **1.** a hoop-shaped support for holding up the cloth of a canopy, etc. **2.** a hoop-shaped handle for a bucket, kettle, etc. **3.** a movable bar on a typewriter to hold the paper against the platen

bail⁴ (bāl) *n.* [ME. < OFr. *baile*, ult. < L. *bajulus*, porter] **1.** [*pl.*] formerly, an outer fortification made of stakes; palisades **2.** a bar or pole to keep animals separate in a barn **3.** *Cricket* either of two sticks laid across the three stumps to form a wicket

bail·a·ble (-ə b'l) *adj.* **1.** that may be released on bail **2.** allowing payment of bail

bail bond a surety bond (money or property) offered or deposited by one charged in a court or by other persons to insure the defendant's appearance at trial

Bai·le Átha Cliath (bä′lä klē′ə) *Gael. name of* DUBLIN

bail·ee (bā lē′) *n.* [BAIL⁴ + -EE¹] the party to whom property is delivered under contract of bailment

bai·ley (bā′lē) *n.*, *pl.* **-leys** [ME. *baili*, var. of *baile*, BAIL⁴] the outer wall or court of a medieval castle: term still kept in some proper names, as in OLD BAILEY

Bai·ley (bā′lē), **Nathan(iel)** ?–1742; Eng. lexicographer

Bai·ley bridge (bā′lē) [after Sir D. C. *Bailey* (1901–), Eng. inventor] *Mil. Engineering* a portable bridge consisting of a series of prefabricated steel sections in the form of lattices

bai·lie (bā′lē) *n.* [Scot. < ME. *baili* < OFr. *baili* < *bailif*: see BAILIFF] **1.** in Scotland, a municipal official corresponding to an alderman in England **2.** [Obs. or Dial.] *same as* BAILIFF

bai·liff (bā′lif) *n.* [ME. *bailif* < OFr. *bailif* < *baillir*, to govern, keep in custody: see BAIL¹] **1.** a deputy sheriff who serves processes, etc. **2.** a court officer who guards the jurors, maintains order in the courtroom, etc. **3.** in England, an administrative official of a district, with power to collect taxes, serve as a magistrate, etc. **4.** [Chiefly Brit.] an overseer or steward of an estate

bai·li·wick (bā′lə wik) *n.* [ME. < *bailif*, BAILIFF + *wik* < OE. *wic*, village] **1.** the district within which a bailiff has jurisdiction **2.** one's particular area of activity, authority, interest, etc.

bail·ment (bāl′mənt) *n.* **1.** the providing of bail for an arrested person **2.** the delivering of goods by one party to another to be held in trust for a specific purpose and returned when that purpose is ended

bail·or (bā′lôr′, bā′lər) *n. Law* the party who delivers property to another under contract of bailment

bails·man (bālz′mən) *n.*, *pl.* **-men** a person who acts as surety or gives bail for another

‡bain-ma·rie (ban mä rē′) *n.*, *pl.* **bains-ma·rie′** (ban-) [Fr. < ML. *balneum Mariae*, lit., bath of Maria; faulty transl. of Gr. *kaminos Marias*, furnace of Mary (altered after the Virgin *Mary*), for *Miriam*, sister of Moses, reputed in legend to have been an alchemist] a kind of double boiler or steam table

Bai·ram (bī räm′) *n.* [Turk. *bairam*] either of two Moslem festivals following the fast of Ramadan

bairn (bern) *n.* [ME. *bearn* < OE. *bearn* < *beran*, to BEAR¹] [Scot.] a son or daughter; child

bait (bāt) *vt.* [ME. *baiten* < ON. *beita*, to make bite, caus. < *bita*, to BITE] **1.** *a)* to set attacking dogs against [people formerly *baited* chained bears for sport] *b)* to attack as such dogs do **2.** to torment or harass with unprovoked, vicious, repeated attacks **3.** to tease or goad, so as to provoke a reaction **4.** to put food, etc. on (a hook or trap) to lure animals or fish **5.** to lure; tempt; entice **6.** [Archaic] to feed (animals) during a break in a journey —*vi.* [Archaic] to stop for food during a journey —*n.* **1.** food, etc. put on a hook or trap to lure fish or animals **2.** anything used as a lure; enticement **3.** [Archaic] a stop for rest or food during a journey —**bait′er** *n.*

SYN.—to **bait** is to torment or goad and implies malicious delight in the persecution [Jew-*baiting*]; to **badger** is to pester so persistently as to bring to a state of frantic confusion; to **hound** is to pursue or attack relentlessly until the victim succumbs [he was *hounded* out of office]; **heckle** denotes the persistent questioning and taunting of a public speaker so as to annoy or confuse him; **hector** implies a continual bullying or nagging in order to intimidate or break down resistance; **torment**, in this comparison, suggests continued harassment so as to cause acute suffering [*tormented* by her memories]; **ride** is colloquial and implies harassing or teasing by ridiculing, criticizing, etc. [they were *riding* the rookie unmercifully from the dugout]

baize (bāz) *n.* [OFr. *baie*, pl. *baies*, baize < L. *badius*, chestnut-brown] a thick woolen cloth made to resemble felt and often dyed green, used to cover billiard tables, etc.

Ba·ja Ca·li·for·nia (bä′hä kä′lē fôr′nyä) peninsula in Mexico, between the Pacific & the Gulf of California: the northern section (**Baja California**) is a state: 27,655 sq. mi.; pop. 670,000; cap. Mexicali; the southern section (**Baja California Sur**) is a federal territory: 27,979 sq. mi.; pop. 89,000; cap. La Paz

bake (bāk) *vt.* **baked, bak′ing** [ME. *baken* < OE. *bacan* < IE. *bhog-* < base *bhe-*, to warm, bake, whence Gr. *phōgein*, to roast & BATH¹] **1.** to cook (food) by dry heat, esp. in an oven **2.** to make dry and hard by heat; fire (esp. glazed stoneware) **3.** to expose (oneself) to the rays of the sun, a lamp, etc. **4.** [Obs.] to harden or cake —*vi.* **1.** to bake bread, pastry, etc. **2.** to become baked **3.** to become dry and hard in the sun: said of soil —*n.* **1.** the act of baking **2.** a product of baking ☆**3.** a social affair at which a certain kind of food, often baked, is served **4.** [Scot.] a cracker

☆**baked Alaska** a dessert consisting of a cake layer covered with ice cream, topped with sweetened, stiffly beaten egg whites, and browned quickly in an oven

bake·house (-hous′) *n.* a bakery

☆**Ba·ke·lite** (bā′kə līt′) [after L. H. *Baekeland*, U.S. (Belgian-born) chemist (1863–1944)] *a trademark for* a synthetic resin and plastic made from formaldehyde and phenol —*n.* [**b-**] this resin

bak·er (bāk′ər) *n.* [ME. *bakere* < OE. *bæcere* < *bacan*, BAKE] **1.** a person whose work or business is baking bread, pastry, etc. ☆**2.** a small, portable oven

Bak·er (bāk′ər) **1. George Pierce,** 1866–1935; U.S. author & professor of drama **2. Newton D(iehl),** 1871–1937; U.S. statesman; secretary of war (1916–21) **3. Ray Stan·nard** (stan′ərd), (pseud. *David Grayson*) 1870–1946; U.S. author

Baker Island small uninhabited island in the C Pacific, near the equator, a possession of the U.S.

baker's dozen thirteen: supposedly from bakers' former practice of adding an extra roll to each dozen sold to avoid any risk of penalty for short measure

Bak·ers·field (bāk′ərz fēld′) [after Col. T. *Baker*, early landowner] city in SC Calif.: pop. 70,000

☆**bak·er·y** (bāk′ər ē, bāk′rē) *n.* **1.** *pl.* **-er·ies** a place where bread, pastries, etc. are baked or sold **2.** baked goods; bread, pastries, etc.

bake·shop (bāk′shäp′) *n.* a bakery

☆**baking powder** a leavening agent that raises dough by the gas (carbon dioxide) produced when baking soda and acid react in the presence of water: it usually contains baking soda mixed with either starch or flour and cream of tartar or other acid-forming substance, as anhydrous sodium aluminum sulfate

☆**baking soda** sodium bicarbonate, NaHCO₃, used as a leavening agent and as an antacid

‡bak·la·va (bäk′lə vä′) *n.* [Turk. *baklawa*] a rich Turkish or Greek dessert made of thin, flaky layers of pastry with chopped nuts, honey, etc. between

bak·sheesh, bak·shish (bak′shēsh) *n.* [via Turk. or Ar. < Per. *bakhshish* < *bakhshidan*, to give: for IE. base see -PHAGOUS] in Turkey, Egypt, India, etc., a tip, gratuity, or alms

Bakst (bäkst), **Lé·on Ni·ko·la·e·vich** (lā′ôn ni′kô lä′yə vich) 1866–1924; Russ. painter and stage designer

Ba·ku (bä kōō′) capital of the Azerbaijan S.S.R., port on the Caspian Sea: pop. 1,147,000

Ba·ku·nin (bä koo′nyin; *E.* bə kyōō′nin), **Mi·kha·il A·lek·san·dro·vich** (mē khä ēl′ ä′lyik sän′drô vich) 1814–76; Russ. anarchist

bal. **1.** balance **2.** balancing

Ba·laam (bā′ləm) *Bible* a prophet hired to curse the Israelites: when he beat his donkey, the animal rebuked him: Num. 22–24

Ba·la·ki·rev (bä lä′kē ryef), **Mi·li A·lek·sey·e·vich** (mē′lē ä′lyik sā′yə vich) 1837–1910; Russ. composer

Bal·a·kla·va (bäl′ə klä′və) seaport in the Crimea, U.S.S.R.: site of the incident in the Crimean War celebrated in Tennyson's "Charge of the Light Brigade"

bal·a·lai·ka (bäl′ə līk′ə) *n.* [Russ.] a Russian stringed instrument somewhat like a guitar but with a triangular body and usually three strings

bal·ance (bal′əns) *n.* [ME. & OFr. < ML. *balancia* < LL. *bilanx*, having two scales < L. *bis*, twice + *lanx*, a dish, scale] **1.** an instrument for weighing, esp. one that opposes equal weights, as in two matched shallow pans hanging from either end of a lever supported exactly in the middle; scales **2.** the imaginary scales of fortune or fate, as an emblem of justice or the power to decide **3.** the power or ability to decide **4.** a state of equilibrium or equipoise; equality in amount, weight, value, or importance, as between two things or the

BALALAIKA

parts of a thing **5.** bodily equilibrium or stability [he kept his *balance* on the tightrope] **6.** mental or emotional stability **7.** *a)* the pleasing harmony of various elements in a design, painting, musical composition, etc.; harmonious proportion *b)* a setting of clauses, phrases, ideas, etc. in parallel constructions for rhetorical effect **8.** a weight, force, effect, etc. that counteracts another or causes equilibrium; counterpoise **9.** the point along an object's length at which there is equilibrium: in full, **balance point 10.** *a)* equality of debits and credits in an account *b)* the excess of credits over debits or of debits over credits **11.** the amount still owed after a partial settlement **12.** whatever is left over; remainder **13.** the act of balancing **14.** *same as* BALANCE WHEEL —*vt.* **-anced, -anc·ing 1.** to weigh in or as in a balance **2.** to compare as to relative importance, value, etc. **3.** to counterpoise or counteract; make up for; offset **4.** to bring into or keep in a state of equilibrium or equipoise; keep steady; poise [to *balance* oneself on stilts] **5.** to bring into proportion, harmony, etc. **6.** to make or be proportionate to; make or be equal to in weight, force, effect, etc. **7.** *a)* to find any difference which may exist between the debit and credit sides of (an account); also, to equalize the debit and credit sides of (an account) *b)* to settle (an account) by paying debts **8.** *Dancing* to move toward and then back from (a partner) —*vi.* **1.** to be in equilibrium **2.** to be equal in value, weight, etc. **3.** to have the credit and debit sides equal to each other **4.** to waver slightly; tilt and return to equilibrium **5.** *Dancing* to balance partners —*SYN.* see REMAINDER, SYMMETRY —**in the balance** in a critical, undecided state —**on balance** considering everything; all in all —**bal′ance·a·ble** *adj.*

balance of (international) payments a balance estimated for a given time period showing an excess or deficit in payments between one country and another country or other countries for all public and private business transactions, including exports and imports, grants, debt payments, etc.

balance of power 1. a distribution of military and economic power among nations that is sufficiently even to keep any one of them from being too strong or dangerous **2.** the power of a minority to give control to a larger group by allying with it

balance of trade the difference in value between all the merchandise imports and exports of a country

bal·anc·er (bal′ən sər) *n.* **1.** a person or thing that balances **2.** an acrobat **3.** either of the balancing organs of a fly, mosquito, etc.; halter

balance sheet a financial statement summarizing the assets, liabilities, and net worth of an individual or a business at a given date: so called because the sum of the assets equals the total of the liabilities plus the net worth

balance wheel a wheel that swings back and forth to regulate the movement of a timepiece, music box, etc.

Bal·an·chine (bal′ən shēn′), **George** (born *Georgi Melitonovitch Balanchivadze*) 1904–   ; U.S. choreographer born in Russia

bal·as (bal′əs) *n.* [ME. *baleis* < OFr. *balais* < ML. *balascius* < Ar. *balakhsh* < Per. *Badakhshān*, name of province in Afghanistan where the gem occurs] a pink or orange type of ruby spinel, a semiprecious stone

bal·a·ta (bal′ə tə) *n.* [Sp. < Tupi or Galibi *balata*] **1.** any of a genus (*Mimusops*) of tropical American trees of the sapodilla family **2.** the dried milky sap of these trees, a rubberlike gum that is used in making transmission belts, golf ball covers, etc.

Ba·la·ton (bä′lä tôn), **Lake** lake in W Hungary: largest lake in C Europe: c. 260 sq. mi.

Bal·bo·a (bal bō′ə) seaport in the Canal Zone, near the Pacific entrance to the canal: pop. 2,500

bal·bo·a (bal bō′ə) *n.* [Sp., after If.] a silver coin, the monetary unit of Panama: see MONETARY UNITS, table

Bal·bo·a (bal bō′ə; *Sp.* bäl bō′ä), **Vas·co Nú·ñez de** (väs′kō nōō′nyeth *the*) 1475?–1517?; Sp. explorer: first European to discover the Pacific Ocean (1513)

bal·brig·gan (bal brig′ən) *n.* [after *Balbriggan*, town in Ireland] **1.** a knitted cotton material used for hosiery, underwear, etc. **2.** [*pl.*] garments made of balbriggan —*adj.* made of balbriggan

bal·co·ny (bal′kə nē) *n., pl.* **-nies** [It. *balcone* < Langobardic **balko-*, akin to OHG. *balcho*, beam] **1.** a platform projecting from the wall of a building and enclosed by a railing or balustrade **2.** an upper floor of rows of seats in a theater or auditorium, often jutting out over the main floor; gallery —**bal′co·nied** *adj.*

bald (bôld) *adj.* [ME. *balled*, associated with *bal*, BALL[1], but prob. ult. < IE. base **bhel-*, gleaming, white, whence Gr. *phalos*, white, *phalakros*, bald, OPrus. *ballo*, forehead] **1.** having white fur or feathers on the head, as some animals and birds **2.** having no hair on all or part of the scalp **3.** not covered by natural growth [*bald* hills] **4.** bare; plain; unadorned [the *bald* facts] **5.** frank and blunt [a *bald* statement] —*SYN.* see BARE[1] — **bald′ly** *adv.* —**bald′ness** *n.*

BALCONY

bal·da·chin, bal·da·quin (bal′də kin, bôl′-) *n.* [< It. or Fr., Fr. *baldaquin* < It. *baldacchino* < *Baldacco*, Baghdad, where the cloth was manufactured] **1.** a rich brocade, formerly made of silk and gold **2.** a canopy of this or other material, carried in church processions or placed over an altar or throne **3.** a marble or stone structure like a canopy, built over an altar

☆**bald·cy·press** (bôld′sī′pris) *n.* any of a genus (*Taxodium*) of cone-bearing trees of the baldcypress family, esp. a species (*Taxodium distichum*) that grows in the swamps of the SE U.S. and sheds its small, pointed needles in the fall: also **bald cypress** —*adj.* designating a family (*Taxodiaceae*) of trees including the redwoods, big trees, etc.

☆**bald eagle** a large, strong eagle (*Haliæetus leucocephalus*) of North America: the adult has a white-feathered head and neck: see AMERICAN EAGLE

Bal·der (bôl′dər) [ON. *Baldr*, lit., bold, dangerous] *Norse Myth.* the god of light, peace, virtue, and wisdom, son of Odin and Frigg: he was killed by the trickery of Loki: also spelled **Baldr**

bal·der·dash (bôl′dər dash′) *n.* [orig. (17th c.), a senseless mixture of liquids, as of milk and ale] senseless talk or writing; nonsense

bald·faced (bôld′fāst′) *adj.* ☆brazen; shameless [a *bald-faced* lie]

bald·head (-hed′) *n.* **1.** a person who has a bald head **2.** any of various birds with a patch of white on the head, as the baldpate —**bald′head′ed** *adj.*

bald·ing (bôl′diŋ) *adj.* becoming bald

bald·pate (bôld′pāt′) *n.* **1.** a baldheaded person **2.** a common North American duck (*Mareca americana*) the male of which has a glossy, white crown and a wine-colored breast; American widgeon

bal·dric (bôl′drik) *n.* [ME. *bauderik* < OFr. *baudrei* < Frank. **balti*, belt < L. *balteus*, whence BELT] a belt worn over one shoulder and across the chest to support a sword, bugle, etc.

Bald·win (bôld′win) [ME. < OFr. *Baldewin, Baudoin* < MHG. *Baldewin*, lit., bold friend < OHG. *bald* (akin to OE. *beald*, bold) + *wini*, friend] **1.** a masculine name **2. James Mark**, 1861–1934; U.S. psychologist & philosopher **3. Stanley**, 1st Earl Baldwin of Bewdley, 1867–1947; Brit. statesman; prime minister (1923–24; 1924–29; 1935–37) —☆*n.* [after Col. Loammi *Baldwin* (1740–1807), Mass. apple grower] a moderately tangy, red winter apple

Bald·win (bôld′win) [after the *Baldwin* family, prominent in the town's history] suburb of New York City, on Long Island: pop. 35,000

Baldwin I 1058–1118; crusader & king of Jerusalem (1100–18)

Bald·win Park [after E. J. *Baldwin*, local rancher] city in SW Calif.: suburb of Los Angeles: pop. 47,000

Bâle (bäl) *Fr. name for* BASEL

bale[1] (bāl) *n.* [ME. < OFr. *bale, balle* < OHG. *balla*, a ball] a large bundle, esp. a standardized quantity of goods, as ginned cotton, hay, straw, etc., compressed, bound, and sometimes wrapped —*vt.* **baled, bal′ing** to make into a bale or bales —*SYN.* see BUNDLE —**bal′er** *n.*

bale[2] (bāl) *n.* [ME. *bale, baelu* < OE. *bealu*] [Poet.] **1.** evil; disaster; harm **2.** sorrow; woe

bale[3] (bāl) *n.* [Archaic] *same as* BALEFIRE

Ba·le·ar·es (bä′le ä′res) Sp. province comprising the Balearic Islands: 1,935 sq. mi.; pop. 443,000; cap. Palma

Bal·e·ar·ic Islands (bal′ē er′ik) group of islands in the Mediterranean, off the E coast of Spain, constituting a province of Spain

ba·leen (bə lēn′) *n.* [ME. & OFr. *baleine* < L. *ballaena* < Gr. *phallaina*, whale < *phallos* (see PHALLUS): so named from the shape of the whale] *same as* WHALEBONE

bale·fire (bāl′fir′) *n.* [ME. *balefir* < OE. *bælfyr*, fire of the funeral pyre < *bæl*, great fire (akin to ON. *bal*) + *fyr*, fire] **1.** an outdoor fire; bonfire **2.** a beacon fire **3.** [Obs.] a funeral pyre

bale·ful (bāl′fəl) *adj.* [ME. < OE. *bealoful < bealu*, calamity + *-ful*, full] **1.** harmful or threatening harm or evil; ominous; deadly **2.** [Archaic] sorrowful; wretched —*SYN.* see SINISTER —**bale′ful·ly** *adv.* —**bale′ful·ness** *n.*

Balfe (balf), **Michael William** 1808–70; Brit. operatic composer & singer, born in Ireland

Balfour (bal′foor), **Arthur James**, 1st Earl of Balfour, 1848–1930; Brit. statesman & philosopher; prime minister (1902–05)

Balfour Declaration a declaration by the British government (November, 1917) favoring the establishment in Palestine of a Jewish "National Home"

Ba·li (bä′lē, bal′ē) island of Indonesia, east of Java: c. 2,100 sq. mi.; pop. (with nearby islets) 1,783,000

bal·i·bun·tal, bal·i·bun·tl (bal′ē bunt′'l) *n.* [< *Bali-(nog)*, village on Luzon, Philippines + Tag. *buntál*, a kind of palm fiber] a fine, lightweight, shiny straw from the Philippines, used for hats: often shortened to **bal′i**

Ba·li·nese (bä′lə nēz′, bal′ə-) *adj.* of Bali, its people, language, or culture —*n.* **1.** *pl.* **-nese′** a native or inhabitant of Bali **2.** the Indonesian language of the Balinese

balk (bôk) *n.* [ME. *balke* < OE. *balca*, a bank, ridge < IE. base **bhel-ĝ-*, a beam, whence OE. *balken*, beam, Gr. *phalanx*, L. *fulcrum*] **1.** a ridge of unplowed land between furrows **2.** a roughly hewn piece of timber **3.** the tie beam of a house **4.** something that obstructs or thwarts; check;

hindrance, disappointment, etc. **5.** a blunder; error **6.** *Baseball* an illegal motion by the pitcher, such as an un-completed motion to throw to a base, while one foot is on the rubber: it entitles each base runner to advance one base **7.** *Billiards* any of the outer spaces between the cushions and the balklines in balkline billiards —*vt.* **1.** to miss or let slip by **2.** to obstruct or thwart; foil **3.** [Obs.] to make balks in (land) —*vi.* **1.** to stop and obstinately refuse to move or act **2.** to hesitate or recoil (*at*) **3.** to make a balk, as in baseball —*SYN.* see FRUSTRATE —**balk′er** *n.*

Bal·kan (bôl′kən) *adj.* **1.** of the Balkans, their people, etc. **2.** of the Balkan Mountains

Bal·kan·ize (bôl′kə nīz′) *vt., vi.* **-ized′, -iz′ing** [*sometimes* **b-**] to break up into small, mutually hostile political units, as the Balkans after World War I —**Bal′kan·i·za′tion** *n.*

Balkan Mountains mountain range extending across C Bulgaria, from the Yugoslav border to the Black Sea: highest peak, c. 7,800 ft.

Balkan Peninsula peninsula in SE Europe, between the Adriatic & the Black seas

Bal·kans (bôl′kənz) countries of the Balkan Peninsula (Yugo-slavia, Bulgaria, Albania, Greece, & the European part of Turkey) & Romania: also **Balkan States**

Balkh (bälkh) town in N Afghanistan: in ancient times it was the capital of Bactria

Bal·khash (bäl khash′), **Lake** large salt lake in the SE Kazak S.S.R.: c. 6,700 sq. mi.

BALKAN PENINSULA

balk·line (bôk′lin′) *n. Billiards* **1.** a line at one end of a table, from behind which a player must cue off or resume playing when his ball has left the table **2.** any of four lines drawn on a table, parallel to the sides and ends so as to form eight outer spaces: in **balkline billiards**, a player may not make more than one or two caroms in any space on the cushion side of a balkline without driving a ball out of that space

balk·y (bôk′ē) *adj.* **balk′i·er, balk′i·est** in the habit of balking; stubbornly resisting —*SYN.* see CONTRARY

ball¹ (bôl) *n.* [ME. *bal* < OE. *beallu* < IE. base *bhel-*, to swell, whence BOWL¹, BLADDER, ON. *bollr*, OHG. *balla*, Gr. *phallos*, L. *follis* & *flare*] **1.** any round, or spherical, object; sphere; globe **2.** a planet or star, esp. the earth **3.** *a)* a round or egg-shaped object used in various games *b)* any of several such games, esp. baseball **4.** a throw or pitch of a ball; esp., the style of delivery of a baseball or other ball [a fast *ball*] **5.** *a)* a solid missile or projectile for a cannon or firearm *b)* such projectiles for firearms, collectively **6.** *a)* a rounded part of the body [the *ball* of the foot] *b)* [*pl.*] [Slang] the testicles: a vulgar usage ☆**7.** *Baseball* a pitch that is wide of the plate or goes above the shoulder or below the knee of the batter and is not struck at by him **8.** *Horticulture* the roots of a plant, bound and packed for shipping —*vi., vt.* to form into a ball —**ball up** [see BOLLIX] ☆[Slang] to muddle or confuse —☆**be on the ball** [Slang] to be alert; be efficient —☆**carry the ball** [Colloq.] to assume responsibility; take command —☆**get** (or **keep**) **the ball rolling** [Colloq.] to start (or maintain) some action —**have something on the ball** [Slang] to have ability —**play ball** ☆**1.** to begin or resume playing a ball game ☆**2.** to begin or resume any activity ☆**3.** [Colloq.] to cooperate

ball² (bôl) *n.* [Fr. *bal* < OFr. *baller*, to dance < LL. *ballare* < Gr. *ballein*, to throw (with sense of *ballizein*, to dance, jump about)] **1.** a formal social dance **2.** [Slang] an enjoyable time or experience

Ball (bôl), **John** ?–1381; Eng. priest: executed as an insti-gator of the peasants' revolt led by Wat Tyler

bal·lad (bal′əd) *n.* [ME. *balad* < OFr. *ballade*, dancing song < OProv. *ballada*, (poem for a) dance < *balar*, to dance < LL. *ballare*: see BALL²] **1.** a romantic or sentimental song with the same melody for each stanza **2.** a song or poem that tells a story in short stanzas and simple words, with repetition, refrain, etc.: most old ballads are of unknown authorship and have been handed down orally in more than one version **3.** a slow, sentimental popular song, esp. a love song

bal·lade (bə läd′, ba-) *n.* [Fr.: see prec.] **1.** a verse form that has three stanzas of eight or ten lines each and an envoy of four or five lines: the last line of each stanza and of the envoy is the same **2.** a musical composition of a romantic or narrative nature, esp. for piano

bal·lad·eer (bal′ə dir′) *n.* a ballad singer

bal·lad·mon·ger (bal′əd muŋ′gər, -mäŋ′-) *n.* **1.** a seller of popular ballads, esp. one who hawked them in the streets **2.** an inferior poet; poetaster

bal·lad·ry (bal′ə drē) *n.* **1.** ballads in general **2.** the art of composing ballads

ballad stanza the four-line stanza commonly used in ballads, generally rhymed *abcb*

☆**ball and chain 1.** a heavy metal ball fastened by a chain to a prisoner's body to keep him from escaping **2.** [Slang] one's wife

ball-and-sock·et joint (bôl′ən säk′it) a joint, as that of the hip or shoulder, formed by a ball in a socket, allowing lim-ited movement in any direction

Bal·la·rat (bal′ə rat′) city in SC Victoria, Australia: pop., with suburbs, 58,000

bal·last (bal′əst) *n.* [LowG. < ODan. *barlast* < *bar*, bare, waste + *last*, a load] **1.** any-thing heavy carried in a ship, aircraft, or vehicle to give sta-bility or in a balloon or airship to help control altitude **2.** anything giving stability and firmness to character, human relations, etc. **3.** crushed rock or gravel, as that placed between and below the ties of a railroad —*vt.* **1.** to furnish with ballast; stabilize **2.** to fill in (a railroad bed, etc.) with ballast

BALL-AND-SOCKET JOINTS

ball bearing 1. a bearing in which the moving parts revolve or slide on freely rolling metal balls so that friction is reduced **2.** any of such metal balls

ball cock a device consisting of a valve connected by a lever with a floating ball which shuts the valve when raised and opens it when lowered, as in flush toilets

bal·le·ri·na (bal′ə rē′nə) *n.* [It. < *ballare*: see BALL²] a woman ballet dancer

bal·let (bal′ā, ba lā′) *n.* [Fr. *ballette* < It. *balletto*, dim. < *ballo*, a dance: see BALL²] **1.** *a)* an intricate group dance using pantomime and conventionalized movements to tell a story, usually with costumes and scenery *b)* the music for such a dance **2.** dancing of this kind **3.** a company of dancers of ballet —**bal·let·ic** (ba let′ik) *adj.*

bal·let·o·mane (bə let′ə mān′) *n.* [Fr. < It. *balletto* (see prec.) + Fr. *manie*, mania] a person enthusiastic about the ballet —**bal′let·o·ma′ni·a** (-mā′nē ə) *n.*

ball-flow·er (bôl′flou′ər) *n. Archit.* a decoration in a mold-ing that looks like a ball held in the petals of a flower

bal·lis·ta (bə lis′tə) *n., pl.* **-tae** (-tē) [L. < Gr. *ballein*, to throw] a device, resembling a large mounted crossbow, used in ancient warfare to hurl heavy stones and similar missiles

bal·lis·tic (bə lis′tik) *adj.* **1.** of or connected with ballistics **2.** of the motion and force of projectiles

ballistic missile a long-range missile that is guided by preset mechanisms in the first part of its flight, but is a free-falling object as it approaches its target

bal·lis·tics (bə lis′tiks) *n.pl.* [*with sing. v.*] **1.** the science dealing with the motion and impact of projectiles, such as bullets, rockets, bombs, etc. **2.** the study of the effects of firing on a firearm or bullet, cartridge, etc. —**bal·lis·ti·cian** (bal′əs tish′ən) *n.*

☆**ball lightning** lightning in the form of a short-lived, reddish, glowing ball, up to about a foot in diameter, infrequently reported floating in the air or moving rapidly along the ground before disintegrating

bal·lo·net (bal′ə net′) *n.* [Fr. *ballonnet*, dim. of *ballon*, BALLOON] any of several auxiliary gas containers within a balloon or airship, which can be inflated or deflated during flight to control altitude

bal·loon (bə lōōn′) *n.* [Fr. *ballon*, altered (after *balle*, ball) < It. *pallone*, large ball < *palla*, ball < Lombard **palla* (OHG. *balla*), BALL¹] **1.** a large, airtight bag that rises and floats above the earth when filled with hot air or a gas lighter than air, such as hydrogen or helium **2.** a bag of this sort with an attached car or gondola for carrying passengers or instruments **3.** a small, inflatable rubber bag, used as a toy **4.** the outline enclosing the words said by a character in a cartoon, as in comic strips —*vt.* to cause to swell like a balloon; inflate —*vi.* **1.** to ascend or ride in a balloon **2.** to swell; expand —*adj.* like a balloon; large, round, and soft —**bal·loon′ist** *n.*

balloon sail a large, light sail used on yachts together with or instead of the customary working sails

balloon tire a wide, deep-walled pneumatic tire holding a large volume of air at low pressure to lessen the shock of bumps

☆**balloon vine** a tropical American vine (*Cardiospermum halicacabum*) bearing inflated triangular pods with large, black seeds

bal·lot (bal′ət) *n.* [It. *ballotta, pallotta*, dim. of *palla*: see BALLOON] **1.** orig., a ball, now a ticket, paper, etc., by which a vote is registered **2.** act or method of voting, esp. secret voting by the use of ballots or voting machines **3.** the right to vote **4.** the total number of votes cast in an election **5.** a list of people running for office; ticket —*vi.* [It. *ballottare*] to decide by means of the ballot; vote —**bal′lot·er** *n.*

bal·lotte·ment (bə lät′mənt) *n.* [Fr. < *ballotter*, to toss <

ballotte: see BALLOT] *Med.* **1.** palpation sometimes used to determine pregnancy by pushing up against the uterus with the finger so as to feel any downward pressure exerted by an embryo as it sinks back into place in the amniotic fluid **2.** palpation of the abdominal wall to test for floating kidney

☆**ball·park** (bôl′pärk′) *n.* a stadium for playing baseball

ball·play·er (bôl′plā′ər) *n.* a baseball player

☆**ball point pen** a pen having instead of a point a small ball bearing that picks up its ink by rolling against an ink reservoir: also **ball′-point′, ball′point′** *n.*

ball·room (-rōōm′) *n.* a large hall for dancing

ballroom dancing a kind of dancing in which two people dance as partners to a waltz, fox trot, etc.

☆**bal·lute** (ba lōōt′) *n.* [BALL(OON) + (PARACH)UTE] a balloonlike device made of heat-resistant materials and inflated by stored gas, designed for deceleration, as of spacecraft reentering the atmosphere

ball valve a valve that works by the action of a ball resting on the inlet hole: the pressure of rising fluid raises the ball and opens the hole; when the pressure is removed, the ball drops and closes the hole

☆**bal·ly·hoo** (bal′ē hōō′; *also, for v.* bal′ē hōō′) *n.* [erroneously associated with *Ballyhooly,* village in Ireland: origin obscure] **1.** loud talk; noisy uproar **2.** loud, exaggerated, or sensational advertising or propaganda —*vt., vi.* -hooed′, -hoo′ing [Colloq.] to advertise or promote by sensational methods —**bal′ly·hoo′er** *n.*

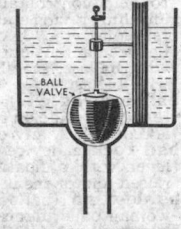

BALL VALVE

balm (bäm; *occas.* bälm) *n.* [ME. *baume* < OFr. *basme* < L. *balsamum,* balsam < Gr. *balsamon* < Sem. (Heb. *bāsām,* Ar. *basām*)] **1.** an aromatic gum resin obtained from certain trees and plants (esp. of the genus *Commiphora*) and used as medicine; balsam **2.** any fragrant ointment or aromatic oil for healing or anointing **3.** anything healing or soothing, esp. to the mind or temper [sleep was a *balm* to his troubles] **4.** any of various aromatic plants of the mint family, as the lemon balm **5.** pleasant odor; fragrance

bal·ma·caan (bal′mə kan′) *n.* [after *Balmacaan,* Inverness, Scotland] a loose overcoat with raglan sleeves

balm of Gilead [in allusion to Jer. 8:22] **1.** *a)* a small evergreen tree (*Commiphora opobalsamum*) native to Asia and Africa *b)* the resinous juice of this tree, used in ancient times in an aromatic ointment **2.** anything healing or soothing; balm ☆**3.** *same as* BALSAM FIR ☆**4.** a hybrid poplar (*Populus gileadensis*) of the northern U.S. and eastern Canada, with sticky, aromatic buds

Bal·mor·al (bal môr′əl, -mär′-) *n.* [< *Balmoral* Castle, Scotland] **1.** a striped or figured woolen petticoat formerly worn beneath a skirt that was looped up in front **2.** [*also* **b-**] *a)* a kind of laced walking shoe *b)* a round, brimless Scottish cap, flat on top

balm·y (bäm′ē; *occas.* bäl′mē) *adj.* **balm′i·er, balm′i·est** **1.** having the qualities of balm; soothing, mild, pleasant, etc. [a *balmy* day] **2.** [var. of BARMY] [Brit. Slang] crazy or foolish —**balm′i·ly** *adv.* —**balm′i·ness** *n.*

bal·ne·al (bal′nē əl) *adj.* [< L. *balneum,* bath + -AL] of a bath or bathing

bal·ne·ol·o·gy (bal′nē äl′ə jē) *n.* [< L. *balneum,* bath + -LOGY] the study of the therapeutic use of various sorts of bathing, as in mineral springs, etc.

☆**ba·lo·ney** (bə lō′nē) *n.* [altered < ? *bologna,* sausage] **1.** bologna **2.** [Slang] foolish or exaggerated talk or behavior; nonsense —*interj.* [Slang] nonsense!: an exclamation of skepticism

☆**bal·sa** (bôl′sə) *n.* [Sp.] **1.** a tropical American tree (*Ochroma lagopus*) that yields an extremely light and buoyant wood used for airplane models, rafts, etc. **2.** the wood **3.** a raft, esp. one made up of a frame resting on cylindrical floats

bal·sam (bôl′səm) *n.* [OE. < L. *balsamum:* see BALM] **1.** any of various oily or gummy aromatic resins obtained from certain of a family (Balsaminaceae) of trees **2.** any of various aromatic, resinous oils or fluids **3.** any aromatic preparation made with balsam, as certain medical dressings **4.** anything healing or soothing; balm **5.** any of various plants or trees that yield balsam, as the balsam fir **6.** any of various species of the impatiens, esp. a fleshy annual garden flower (*Impatiens balsamina*) —**bal·sam·ic** (bôl sam′ik) *adj.*

☆**balsam fir** an evergreen tree (*Abies balsamea*) of the pine family, native to Canada and the northern U.S., that has flat needles, yields Canada balsam and a soft wood used chiefly for pulpwood and is often used as a Christmas tree

balsam of Peru a viscous liquid resin obtained from a Central American tree (*Myroxylon pereirae*) of the legume family: it is used in some medical preparations

balsam of To·lu (tō lōō′) [see TOLU (BALSAM)] a fragrant oleoresin obtained from the bark of a S. American tree (*Myroxylon toluiferum*) of the legume family: it is used in cough mixtures, etc.

☆**balsam poplar** a poplar (*Populus balsamifera*) native to the northeastern U.S. and Canada: its buds are coated with a fragrant resin

Bal·sas (bäl′säs) river in SC Mexico, flowing into the Pacific: c. 450 mi.: in full, **Río de las Balsas**

Bal·tic (bôl′tik) *adj.* **1.** of the Baltic Sea **2.** of the Baltic States **3.** of a branch of the Indo-European language family that includes Lithuanian, Latvian, and Old Prussian —*n.* **1.** the Baltic Sea **2.** the Baltic branch of Indo-European

Baltic Sea sea in N Europe, south & east of the Scandinavian Peninsula and west of the U.S.S.R., joining the North Sea: c. 160,000 sq. mi.

Baltic States former independent countries of Latvia, Lithuania, & Estonia

Bal·ti·more (bôl′tə môr′; *locally* -mər) [see ff.] seaport in N Md., on Chesapeake Bay: pop. 906,000 (met. area 2,071,000)

Baltimore, Lord, 1st Baron Baltimore (*George Calvert*) 1580?-1632; Eng. statesman: founder of Maryland

BALTIC SEA & STATES

Baltimore oriole [so named from having the colors of the coat of arms of Lord *Baltimore* (son of prec.), colonial proprietor of Maryland] a N. American oriole (*Icterus galbula*) that has an orange body with black on the head, wings, and tail

Bal·to-Sla·vic (bôl′tō släv′ik, -slav′-) *n.* a subfamily of Indo-European languages, including the Baltic and Slavic branches —*adj.* of this subfamily

Ba·lu·chi (bə lōō′chē) *n.* **1.** the Iranian language spoken in Baluchistan **2.** *pl.* **-chis, -chi** a native or inhabitant of Baluchistan

Ba·lu·chi·stan (bə lōō′chə stan′, -stän′) region in West Pakistan and SE Iran, formerly comprising *a)* a province of Pakistan, including a union of native states (**Baluchistan States**) and *b)* a province of Iran

bal·us·ter (bal′əs tər) *n.* [Fr. *balustre* < It. *balaustro,* pillar < *balausto,* flower of the wild pomegranate < L. *balaustium* < Gr. *balaustion:* from some resemblance in shape] any of the small posts that support the upper rail of a railing, as on a staircase

bal·us·trade (bal′ə strād′) *n.* [Fr. *balustrade* < It. *balaustrata* < *balaustro:* see prec.] a railing held up by balusters, as on a staircase

Bal·zac (bál zák′; E. bôl′zak), **Ho·no·ré de** (ô nô rā′ də) 1799-1850; Fr. novelist

Ba·ma·ko (bä mä kō′) capital of Mali, a port on the upper Niger River: pop. 120,000

Bam·berg (bam′bərg; *G.* bäm′berk) city in N Bavaria, West Germany: pop. 75,000

bam·bi·no (bam bē′nō, bäm-) *n., pl.* **-nos, -ni** (-nē) [It., dim. of *bambo,* childish] **1.** a child; baby **2.** any image of the infant Jesus

bam·boo (bam bōō′) *n.* [Malay *bambu*] any of a number of semitropical or tropical grasses (subfamily Bambusoideae) often resembling trees, with perennial, jointed stems that are woody, hard, springy, and often hollow and sometimes grow to heights of 120 feet: the stems are used in light construction and for furniture, canes, etc., and the young shoots of some species are eaten —*adj.* **1.** of bamboo **2.** made of bamboo stems

bamboo curtain [*often* B- C-] the barrier of political and ideological differences that separate China from the West

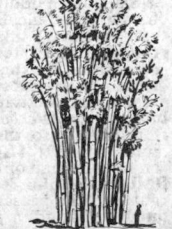

BAMBOO

bam·boo·zle (bam bōō′z'l) *vt.* -zled, -zling [c. 1700; cant form; origin obscure] **1.** to deceive or cheat by trickery; dupe **2.** to confuse or puzzle —**bam·boo′zle·ment** *n.* —**bam·boo′zler** *n.*

ban¹ (ban) *vt.* **banned, ban′ning** [ME. *bannen* < OE. *bannan,* to summon, proclaim < IE. base **bha-,* to speak, whence L. *fari,* to speak, Gr. *phanai,* to say, ON. & OHG. *bann,* command, prohibition] **1.** to prohibit, as by official order, from doing, using, appearing, happening, etc.; forbid; censor [to *ban* fraternities, to *ban* a movie] **2.** [Archaic] to curse; condemn —*n.* [ME. < the *v.;* also < OFr. *ban,* decree < OHG. *bann*] **1.** in medieval times, a proclamation, esp. an official calling of vassals to arms **2.** an excommunication or condemnation by church authorities **3.** a curse **4.** an official order forbidding something; prohibition **5.** strong public disapproval or condemnation intended to prevent something **6.** a sentence or decree of outlawry —SYN. see FORBID

ban² (bän) *n., pl.* **ba·ni** (bä′nē) a Romanian coin equal to 1/100 leu

ba·nal (bā′n'l; bə nal′, -näl′) *adj.* [Fr. < OFr., designating objects (such as ovens or mills) belonging to feudal serfs

(hence common, ordinary) < *ban*, decree, legal control: see BAN¹] dull or stale as because of overuse; trite; hackneyed; commonplace —*SYN.* see INSIPID —**ba·nal·i·ty** (bə nal′ə tē) *n., pl.* **-ties** —**ba′nal·ly** *adv.*

ba·nan·a (bə nan′ə) *n.* [Sp. & Port. < native name in W. Africa, as in Mandingo *banāna*] **1.** any of a genus (*Musa*) of treelike tropical plants, with long, broad leaves and large clusters of edible fruit; esp., a species (*Musa sapientum*) widely cultivated in the Western Hemisphere **2.** the fruit: it is narrow and somewhat curved, and has a sweet, creamy flesh covered by a yellowish or reddish skin

banana oil 1. amyl acetate, CH₃CO₂C₅H₁₁, a colorless liquid with an odor somewhat like that of bananas: it is used in flavorings, in making lacquers, etc. **2.** [Old Slang] insincere or foolish talk

banana republic any small Latin American country that has a one-crop economy controlled by foreign capital

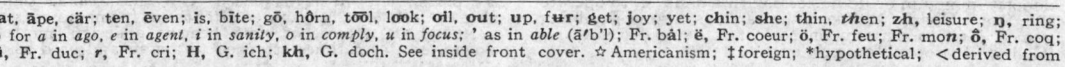
BANANA

banana spider a large, yellowish, tropical crab spider (*Heteropoda venatoria*) occasionally found in bunches of bananas shipped to the temperate zone

Ba·na·ras (bə när′əz) *former name of* VARANASI

Ba·nat (bä nät′) agricultural region in the Danube River basin in NE Yugoslavia & W Romania: formerly, a part of Hungary (1779–1919)

Ban·bur·y tarts (ban′ber′ē, bam′-; *esp.* Brit. -bər i) [after *Banbury*, Oxfordshire, England, noted for its cakes] small baked pastries filled with mincemeat

Ban·croft (ban′krôft, baṇ′-; -kräft), George 1800–91; U.S. historian & statesman

band¹ (band) *n.* [ME. < ON. *band* (akin to OE. *bend*); also (in meaning "thin strip") < Fr. *bande*, flat strip < OFr. *bende* < ML. *benda* < Goth. *binda* < *bindan*, BIND] **1.** something that binds, ties together, restrains, etc. **2.** *a)* a strip or ring of wood, metal, rubber, etc. fastened around something to bind or tie it together *b)* a finger ring [a wedding *band*] **3.** a contrasting strip or stripe running across or along the edge of a material, or separating different sorts of material **4.** a narrow strip of cloth used to bind, line, decorate, etc.; binding; banding [*hatband*, *neckband*] **5.** [*usually pl.*] two strips hanging in front from the neck, as part of certain academic, legal, or clerical dress **6.** a belt to drive wheels or pulleys in machinery **7.** any of the separate divisions on a long-playing phonograph record containing individual selections **8.** *a)* a specific range of wavelengths or frequencies, as in radio broadcasting or sound or light transmission *b)* any of the stripes of color in a spectrum **9.** *Archit.* a thin layer or molding **10.** *Mining* a thin layer of ore or metal —*vt.* [OFr. *bander* < the *n.*] **1.** to put a band on or around; tie with a band **2.** to mark with a band for identification [to *band* migratory birds]

band² (band) *n.* [Fr. *bande*, a troupe, division (orig., prob., those following the same sign) < It. *banda* < Goth. *bandwa*, a sign < *bindan*, BIND] **1.** a group of people joined together for a common purpose **2.** a group of musicians playing together, esp. upon wind and percussion instruments [brass *band*, a dance *band*] —*vi., vt.* to gather or unite for a common purpose (usually with *together*) —*SYN.* see TROOP

band·age (ban′dij) *n.* [Fr. < *bande*, BAND¹] a strip of cloth, esp. gauze, or other dressing used to bind or cover an injured part of the body —*vt.* **-aged, -ag·ing** to put a bandage on (an injured part or person)

☆**Band-Aid** (ban′dād′) [BAND(AGE) + AID] *a trademark for* a small prepared bandage of gauze and adhesive tape for minor wounds —*n.* [b-] a bandage of this type: also **band′aid′**

ban·dan·na, ban·dan·a (ban dan′ə) *n.* [Hind. *bāndhnū*, a method of dyeing < Sans. *bandhana*, tying (so named because the cloth is tied to prevent certain parts from receiving the dye) < IE. *bhendh-*, BIND] a large, colored handkerchief, usually with a figure or pattern

Ban·da Sea (bän′də) part of the S Pacific Ocean, west of New Guinea & south of the Moluccas

band·box (band′bäks′) *n.* [orig. made to hold *neckbands*, or collars] a light box of wood or pasteboard to hold hats, collars, etc.

ban·deau (ban dō′, ban′dō) *n., pl.* **-deaux** (-dōz′, -dōz) [Fr. < OFr. *bendel* < *bende*, BAND¹] **1.** a narrow ribbon, esp. one worn around the head to hold the hair in place **2.** a narrow brassiere

☆**band·ed rattlesnake** (ban′did) *same as* TIMBER RATTLESNAKE

‡**ban·de·ril·la** (bän′de rēl′yä) *n.* [Sp., small banner < *bandera* < Fr. *banniere*, BANNER] any of several barbed darts with little streamers attached to them, which the banderillero in a bullfight tries to stick into the neck and shoulders of the bull

‡**ban·de·ril·le·ro** (-rē lye′rō) *n.* [Sp. < prec.] a man whose task in a bullfight is to stick banderillas into the neck and shoulders of the bull

ban·de·role, ban·de·rol (ban′də rōl′) *n.* [Fr. *banderole* < It. *banderuola*, dim. of *bandiera* < Fr. *banniere*, BANNER] **1.** a narrow flag or pennant, esp. one attached to a lance or carried at the masthead of a ship **2.** a ribbonlike scroll, or a sculptured representation of one, carrying an inscription or symbol

ban·di·coot (ban′di kōōt′) *n.* [< Telugu *pandikokku*, pig rat] **1.** a very large rat (genus *Bandicota*) found esp. in India and Ceylon, which destroys rice fields and gardens **2.** any of several ratlike animals (family Peramelidae) of Australia and nearby islands, which carry their young in pouches and feed on insects and plants

ban·dit (ban′dit) *n., pl.* **-dits, ban·dit·ti** (ban dit′ē) [It. *bandito* < *bandire*, to outlaw < Gmc. **bann* (see BAN¹), with sp. infl. by It. *banda*, BAND²] **1.** a robber, esp. one who robs travelers on the road; brigand; highwayman **2.** anyone who steals, cheats, exploits, etc. —**ban′dit·ry** *n.*

Ban·djer·ma·sin, Ban·djar·ma·sin (bän′jər mä′sin) *same as* BANJERMASIN

band·mas·ter (band′mas′tər, -mäs′-) *n.* the leader or conductor of a military or brass band

ban·dog (ban′dôg′) *n.* [ME. *bande dogge*: see BAND¹ + DOG] **1.** orig., a dog kept tied up as a watchdog or because it is ferocious **2.** any mastiff or bloodhound

ban·do·leer, ban·do·lier (ban′də lir′) *n.* [Fr. *bandoulière* < Sp. *bandolera* < *banda*, a scarf, sash, ult. < Goth. *bandwa*: see BAND²] a broad belt worn over one shoulder and across the chest, with pockets for carrying ammunition, etc.

ban·dore (ban dôr′, ban′dôr) *n.* [Sp. *bandurria* < LL. *pandura* < Gr. *pandoura*, musical instrument] an ancient musical instrument somewhat like a guitar

band-pass filter (band′pas′) *Electronics* a combination of filters which will pass frequencies within a desired range but will virtually cut out other frequencies

☆**band saw** a power saw consisting of an endless toothed steel belt that runs over pulleys

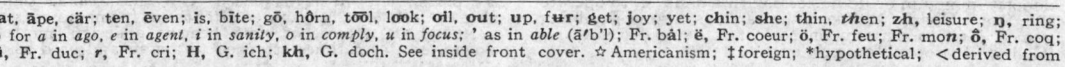
BANDOLEER

band shell an outdoor platform for concerts, having a concave, nearly hemispherical back serving as a sounding board

bands·man (bandz′mən, banz′-) *n., pl.* **-men** (-mən) a member of a band of musicians

band·stand (band′stand′, ban′-) *n.* **1.** an outdoor platform for a band or orchestra, usually with a roof **2.** any platform for a musical band, as in a ballroom

Ban·dung (bän′dooṇ, ban dooṇ′) city in W Java, Indonesia: pop. 973,000: site of a conference (1955) of 30 African and Asian nations

☆**band·wag·on** (band′wag′ən, ban′-) *n.* a high, gaily decorated wagon for a band of musicians to ride in, as in a parade—**on the bandwagon** [Colloq.] on the popular or apparently winning side, as in an election

band·width (band′width′) *n.* the range of frequencies within a radiation band required to transmit a particular signal

ban·dy¹ (ban′dē) *vt.* **-died, -dy·ing** [Fr. *bander*, to bandy at tennis, bend, unite, connect by binding: see BAND¹, *v.*] **1.** to toss or hit back and forth, as a ball **2.** to pass (gossip, rumor, etc.) about freely and carelessly **3.** to give and take; specif., to exchange (words) in an angry or argumentative manner

ban·dy² (ban′dē) *n., pl.* **-dies** [Fr. *bandé*, pp. of *bander*, to tie, bend (as a bow): see BAND¹, *v.*] **1.** an old game, much like field hockey **2.** a club bent at one end, used to strike the ball in this game —*adj.* bent or curved outward: bowed

ban·dy·leg·ged (-leg′id, -legd′) *adj.* having bandy legs; bowlegged

bane (bān) *n.* [ME. < OE. *bana* < IE. base **bhen-*, to strike, wound, whence Avestan *banta-*, ill, infirm, Goth. *banja*, wound, stroke] **1.** [Poet.] deadly harm; ruin; death **2.** the cause of distress, death, or ruin **3.** deadly poison: now obsolete except in *ratsbane*, etc.

bane·ber·ry (bān′ber′ē) *n., pl.* **-ries 1.** any of a genus (*Actaea*) of plants of the buttercup family, with clusters of fleshy, white or red, often poisonous berries **2.** the berry of any of these plants

bane·ful (bān′fəl) *adj.* causing distress, death, or ruin; deadly —*SYN.* see PERNICIOUS —**bane′ful·ly** *adv.*

Banff (bamf) **1.** county in NE Scotland, on the North Sea: 630 sq. mi.; pop. 46,000: also **Banff′shire** (-shir) **2.** its county seat: pop. 3,300 **3.** town in Banff National Park: summer & winter resort: pop. 4,000

Banff National Park Canadian national park on the E slopes of the Rockies, SW Alberta: 2,585 sq. mi.

bang¹ (baṇ) *vt.* [ON. *banga*, to pound, hammer; akin to G. *bengel*, cudgel] **1.** to hit with a resounding blow; strike hard and noisily **2.** to shut (a door, etc.) noisily **3.** to handle violently —*vi.* **1.** to make a loud noise, as through

concussion or explosion **2.** to move noisily or strike sharply (*against* something) —*n.* **1.** a hard, noisy blow or impact **2.** a loud, sudden noise, as of hitting or exploding ☆**3.** *a*) [Colloq.] a display of enthusiasm or vigor /to start with a *bang*/ *b*) [Slang] a thrill; excitement *c*) [Colloq.] sudden force or effectiveness /the idea hit him with a *bang*/ —*adv.* **1.** hard, noisily, and suddenly /to run *bang* against a wall/ **2.** suddenly or exactly /be stopped *bang* in the middle/ —*interj.* a sound in imitation of a shot or explosion —**bang up** to do physical damage to

☆**bang²** (baŋ) *vt.* [< ?] to cut (hair) short and straight across —*n.* [*usually pl.*] banged hair worn across the forehead

bang³ (baŋ) *n. same as* BHANG

Ban·ga·lore (baŋ′gə lôr′) city in S India, the capital of Mysore state: pop. 1,207,000

ban·ga·lore torpedo (baŋ′gə lôr′) [< ? prec.] *Mil.* a piece of metal tubing filled with high explosive, used esp. to blast a path through a barbed-wire entanglement or to detonate buried mines

☆**bang·board** (baŋ′bôrd′) *n.* [BANG¹ + BOARD] a large board mounted along one side of a wagon, against which cornhuskers toss the ears of corn, causing them to rebound into the wagon

Bang·ka (bäŋ′kä) island of Indonesia, off the SE coast of Sumatra: tin-mining center: 4,610 sq. mi.; pop. 252,000

Bang·kok (baŋ′käk) capital of Thailand, a seaport on the Chao-Phraya River, near the Gulf of Siam: pop. 1,669,000 (met. area 2,300,000): official name, KRUNG THEP

ban·gle (baŋ′g'l) *n.* [Hindi *bangri*, glass bracelet] **1.** a decorative bracelet, armlet, or anklet **2.** a disk-shaped ornament, esp. one hanging from a bracelet

Ban·gor (baŋ′gôr) [? after an old hymn tune] city in S Maine, on the Penobscot River: pop. 33,000

Bang's disease (baŋz) [after B.L.F. *Bang* (1848–1932), Dan. veterinarian] an infectious disease of cattle, caused by a bacterium (*Brucella abortus*) and often resulting in abortion

bang·tail (baŋ′tāl′) *n.* ☆[Slang] a racehorse

Ban·gui (bäŋ gē′) capital of the Central African Republic, on the Ubangi River: pop. 83,000

bang-up (baŋ′up′) *adj.* [Colloq.] very good; excellent

Bang·we·u·lu (baŋ′wē ōō′lōō) shallow lake in N Zambia: c. 1,900 sq. mi.

ba·ni (hä′nē) *n. pl. of* BAN²

ban·ian¹ (ban′yən) *n. same as* BANYAN

ban·ian² (ban′yən) *n.* [Port. < Ar. *banyān* < Gujarati *vaniyo* < Sans. *vanij*, merchant] a Hindu merchant

ban·ish (ban′ish) *vt.* [ME. *banischen* < extended stem of OFr. *banir* < ML. **bannire* < Frank. **bannjan*, to order or prohibit under penalty < *ban*, akin to BAN¹] **1.** to put out of the country as a punishment; exile **2.** to send or put away; get rid of; dismiss /to *banish* cares, to *banish* wrinkles/ —**ban′ish·ment** *n.*

SYN.—**banish** implies removal from a country (not necessarily one's own) as a formal punishment; **exile** implies compulsion to leave one's own country, either because of a formal decree or through force of circumstance; **expatriate** suggests more strongly voluntary exile and often implies the acquiring of citizenship in another country; to **deport** is to send (an alien) out of the country, either because of unlawful entry or because his presence is regarded as undesirable; to **transport** is to banish (a convict) to a penal colony; **ostracize** today implies forced exclusion from society, or a certain group, as because of disgrace /he was *ostracized* for his part in the scandal/

ban·is·ter (ban′əs tər) *n.* [altered < BALUSTER] **1.** [Now Rare] a baluster **2.** [*often pl.*] a railing held up by balusters, as along a staircase **3.** the railing itself

Ban·jer·ma·sin, Ban·jar·ma·sin (bän′jər mä′sin) seaport in S Borneo, near the Java Sea: pop. 214,000

☆**ban·jo** (ban′jō) *n., pl.* -jos, -joes [of Afr. origin, prob. akin to Kimbundu (a Bantu language) *mbanza*, an instrument resembling the banjo] a stringed musical instrument having a long neck and a circular body covered on top with tightly stretched skin: the strings, usually four or five, are plucked with the fingers or a plectrum —**ban′jo·ist** *n.*

bank¹ (baŋk) *n.* [Fr. *banque* < It. *banca*, orig. table, moneylenders' exchange table < OHG. *bank*, bench: see ff.] **1.** an establishment for receiving, keeping, lending, or, sometimes, issuing money and making easier the exchange of funds by checks, notes, etc. **2.** the office or building of such an establishment **3.** *same as* PIGGY BANK **4.** *a*) the fund or pool held by the banker or dealer in some gambling games; also, the dealer *b*) the entire monetary pool of a gambling establishment *c*) a common fund of pieces used in playing a game **5.** *Med. a*) any place for gathering and distributing blood for transfusions or parts of the body for transplantation *b*) any reserve thus gathered /an eye (i.e., corneal) *bank*/ —*vi.* **1.** to deposit money in or do business with a bank **2.** to operate or manage a bank **3.** to keep the bank, as in some gambling games —*vt.* to deposit (money) in a bank —☆**bank on** [Colloq.] to depend on; rely on

BANJO

bank² (baŋk) *n.* [ME. *banke* < (prob. via Anglo-N. **banki*) ON. *bakki*, akin to OHG. & Du. *bank* & OE. *benc*, BENCH] **1.** a long mound or heap, as of ground, clouds, or snow; ridge **2.** a steep rise or slope, as of a hill **3.** a stretch of rising land at the edge of a body of water, esp. a stream **4.** a shoal or shallow place, as in a sea or lake; esp., a raised part of a continental shelf **5.** the sloping of an airplane laterally to avoid slipping sideways on a turn **6.** the sloping of a road, racing track, etc. laterally along a curve **7.** the cushioned inner rim of a billiard table **8.** *Mining* the face or top end of the body of ore —*vt.* **1.** to heap dirt around for protection from cold, light, etc.; embank **2.** to arrange (a fire) by covering with ashes, adding fuel, etc. so that it will burn low and keep longer **3.** to heap or pile up so as to form a bank **4.** to construct (a curve in a road, etc.) so that it slopes up from the inside edge **5.** to slope (an airplane) laterally on a turn, with the inside wing low and the outside wing high so as to prevent slipping sideways **6.** *Billiards a*) to stroke (a ball) so that it recoils from a cushion *b*) to make (a shot) in this way —*vi.* **1.** to take the form of a bank or banks **2.** to fly an airplane with lateral slope on a turn —*SYN.* see SHOAL², SHORE¹

bank³ (baŋk) *n.* [ME. *banke* < OFr. *banc*, bench < Frank. or OHG. *bank*: see prec.] **1.** *a*) a bench for rowers in a galley *b*) the rowers **2.** a row or tier of oars **3.** a row or tier of objects /a *bank* of lights/ **4.** a row of keys in a keyboard or console **5.** any of the subheads under a newspaper headline —*vt.* to arrange in a bank

Ban·ka (bäŋ′kä) *same as* BANGKA

☆**bank·a·ble** (baŋ′kə b'l) *adj.* acceptable to a bank

bank acceptance a draft or bill of exchange drawn on a bank and accepted by it

☆**bank account** money deposited in a bank and subject to withdrawal by the depositor

bank annuities British government bonds; consols

bank bill 1. a bank note **2.** a bill of exchange issued or accepted by a bank

bank·book (baŋk′book′) *n.* the book in which the account of a depositor in a bank is recorded; passbook

bank discount interest deducted in a lump sum by a bank from a loan when the loan is made: it is computed from the date of the loan to the date of the final payment on the basis of the original amount of the loan

bank draft a draft or bill of exchange drawn by a bank on another bank

bank·er¹ (-ər) *n.* [< BANK¹, by analogy with Fr. *banquier*] **1.** a person who owns or manages a bank **2.** the keeper of the bank in some gambling games

bank·er² (baŋ′kər) *n.* [< BANK²] a person or boat engaged in cod fishing on the Newfoundland banks

bank·er³ (baŋ′kər) *n.* [BANK³, in obs. sense "bench" + -ER] workbench of a bricklayer, mason, or sculptor

bank holiday 1. any weekday on which banks are closed, as for a legal holiday **2.** any period during which banks are closed by government order, as during a financial crisis **3.** [Brit.] any of several legal holidays, usually on a Monday, when banks, schools, etc. are closed

bank·ing (-kiŋ) *n.* the work of a banker; business of operating a bank

banking house a company in the business of banking

bank note a promissory note issued by a bank, payable on demand: it is a form of paper money

bank paper 1. bank notes collectively **2.** any bankable notes, bills, etc.

bank rate a standard rate of discount set by a central bank or banks

bank·roll (baŋk′rōl′) *n.* a supply of money; available funds —*vt.* [Colloq.] to supply with money; finance

bank·rupt (baŋk′rupt′, -rəpt) *n.* [Fr. *banqueroute* < It. *banca rotta* < *banca*, bench (see BANK¹) + *rotta*, broken < L. *rupta*, fem. pp. of *rumpere*, to break] **1.** a person legally declared unable to pay his debts: the property of a bankrupt is administered for the benefit of his creditors and divided among them **2.** anyone unable to pay his debts **3.** a person who lacks a certain quality or has failed completely in some way /a political *bankrupt*/ —*adj.* **1.** that is a bankrupt; insolvent **2.** lacking in some quality; destitute /morally *bankrupt*/ **3.** that has failed completely; ruined /a *bankrupt* foreign policy/ —*vt.* to cause to become bankrupt

bank·rupt·cy (-rupt′sē, -rəp sē) *n., pl.* -cies **1.** the state or an instance of being bankrupt **2.** complete failure; ruin; destitution

Banks (baŋks), Sir **Joseph** 1743–1820; Eng. botanist

bank·si·a (baŋk′sē ə) *n.* [after prec.] an Australian evergreen (genus *Banksia*) with clusters of showy yellow flowers and long, narrow leaves

Bank·side (baŋk′sīd′) district on the S. bank of the Thames, London: former site of many theaters, including the Shakespearean Globe Theater

Banks Island (baŋks) westernmost island of the Canadian Arctic islands: c. 26,000 sq. mi.

‡**ban·lieue** (bän lyö′) *n., pl.* -**lieues′** (-lyö′) [Fr.] a residential suburb of a city

ban·ner (ban′ər) *n.* [ME. *banere* < OFr. *baniere* < **bandiere*, place where the flag is placed (< WGmc. **banda*, sign, akin to Goth. *bandwa*), altered after *banir*, to announce (see BANISH)] **1.** a piece of cloth bearing a design, motto, slogan, etc., sometimes attached to a staff and used as a

battle standard **2.** a flag [the Star-Spangled *Banner*] **3.** a headline extending across a newspaper page **4.** a long strip of cloth with an advertisement, greeting, etc. lettered on it —*adj.* foremost; leading; excelling [a *banner* year in sales]

ban·ner·et[1] (ban/ər it, -ə ret/) *n.* a small banner: also **ban'ner·ette'**

ban·ner·et[2] (ban/ər it, -ə ret/) *n.* [ME. & OFr. *baneret* < *baniere*, BANNER] formerly, a knight allowed to lead his men into battle under his own banner and ranking just above a knight bachelor

ban·ne·rol (ban/ə rōl/) *n. same as* BANDEROLE

ban·nis·ter (ban/əs tər) *n. same as* BANISTER

ban·nock (ban/ək) *n.* [ME. *bannok* < Gael. *bannach*, a cake] [Scot.] a thick, flat cake made of oatmeal or barley meal baked on a griddle

Ban·nock·burn (ban/ək burn/) town in C Scotland: site of a battle (1314) in which the Scots under Robert Bruce secured their independence from England

banns (banz) *n.pl.* [see BAN[1]] the proclamation, generally made in church on three successive Sundays, of an intended marriage

ban·quet (baŋ/kwit, baŋ/-) *n.* [Fr. < It. *banchetto*, dim. of *banca*: see BANK[1]] **1.** an elaborate meal; feast **2.** a formal dinner for many people, usually with toasts and speeches —*vt.* to honor with or entertain at a banquet —*vi.* to dine at a banquet —**ban'quet·er** *n.*

ban·quette (baŋ ket/) *n.* [Fr., dim. of Norm. *banque*, earthwork < Du. *bank*, BANK[2]] **1.** a gunners' platform extending along the inside of a trench or parapet ✿**2.** [South] a raised way; sidewalk **3.** an upholstered bench, esp. one along a wall in a restaurant

Ban·quo (baŋ/kwō, baŋ/-) a character in Shakespeare's *Macbeth*: the ghost of Banquo appears to Macbeth, who had ordered his murder

ban·shee, ban·shie (ban/shē) *n.* [Ir. *bean sidhe* < *bean*, woman + *sith*, fairy] *Irish & Scot. Folklore* a female spirit believed to wail outside a house as a warning that a death will occur soon in the family

ban·tam (ban/təm) *n.* [after *Bantam*, former Du. residency in Java] **1.** [often B-] any of various small, domestic fowls, many of which are dwarf varieties of standard breeds **2.** a small but aggressive person **3.** a bantamweight —*adj.* like a bantam; small and aggressive

ban·tam·weight (-wāt/) *n.* a boxer or wrestler between a flyweight and a lightweight (in boxing, 113–118 pounds)

ban·ter (ban/tər) *vt.* [17th-c. slang < ? BANDY[1]] to tease or make fun of in a playful, good-natured way —*vi.* to exchange banter (*with* someone) —*n.* good-natured teasing, ridicule, or joking —**ban'ter·er** *n.* **ban'ter·ing·ly** *adv.*

Ban·ting (ban/tiŋ), Sir **Frederick Grant** 1891–1941; Canad. physiologist: co-discoverer of insulin (1922)

bant·ling (bant/liŋ) *n.* [altered < G. *bänkling*, bastard < *bank*, a bench] [Archaic] a young child; brat: a term of contempt

Ban·tu (ban/tōō) *n., pl.* **-tus, -tu** [Bantu *ba-ntu*, mankind, men < *ba*, var. of *aba*, pl. personal prefix + *-ntu*, a person] **1.** any member of a large group of Negroid tribes of equatorial and southern Africa **2.** any of a group of languages belonging to the Niger-Congo subfamily of the Congo-Kordofanian family of languages —*adj.* of the Bantus or their languages

ban·yan (ban/yən) *n.* [so called in allusion to such a tree on the S Iranian coast at the E end of the Persian Gulf, under which the *banians* (see BANIAN[2]) had built a pagoda] an East Indian fig tree (*Ficus benghalensis*) from whose branches grow shoots that take root and form new trunks over a relatively wide area

ban·zai (bän/zī/) *interj.* [Jap.] a Japanese greeting, battle cry, and cheer, meaning "May you live ten thousand years!"

BANYAN

ba·o·bab (bā/ō bab/, bä/-) *n.* [prob. EAfr. native name] a tall tree (*Adansonia digitata*) of the bombax family, having a thick trunk, and found in Africa and India: fiber from its bark is used for making rope, paper, etc. and the gourdlike fruit has an edible pulp

bap., bapt. baptized

bap·ti·si·a (bap tiz/ē ə, -tizh/ə) *n.* [ModL., name of the genus < Gr. *baptisis*, a dipping: see BAPTIZE] any plant of a genus (*Baptisia*) of the pea family, including a common wildflower of the southern U.S.

bap·tism (bap/tiz'm) *n.* [ME. & OFr. *baptesme* < L. *baptisma*, a dipping under, LL.(Ec.), Christian baptism, < Gr. *baptisma*, immersion < *baptizein*: see BAPTIZE] **1.** a baptizing or being baptized; specif., the ceremony or sacrament of admitting a person into Christianity or a specific Christian church by dipping him in water or sprinkling water on him, as a symbol of washing away sin and of spiritual purification **2.** any experience or ordeal

that initiates, tests, or purifies —**bap·tis'mal** (-tiz/m'l), *adj.* —**bap·tis'mal·ly** *adv.*

baptism of fire [transl. of Gr. *baptisma pyros* (see Matt. 3:11)] **1.** the first time that new troops are under fire or in combat **2.** any experience that tests one's courage, strength, etc. for the first time

bap·tist (bap/tist) *n.* [ME. & OFr. *baptiste* < LL.(Ec.) *baptista*, a baptizer (esp. John the Baptist) < Gr. *baptistēs*: see BAPTIZE] **1.** a person who baptizes, specif. [B-] John the Baptist **2.** [B-] a member of a Protestant denomination holding that baptism should be given only to believers after confession of faith and by immersion rather than sprinkling

bap·tis·ter·y (bap/tis trē, -tis tər ē) *n., pl.* **-ter·ies** [L. *baptisterium*, place for bathing, LL.(Ec.), baptismal font, < Gr. *baptistērion* < *baptizein*, BAPTIZE] **1.** a place, esp. a part of a church, used for baptizing **2.** a baptismal font or tank Also **bap'tis·try** (-trē), *pl.* **-tries**

bap·tize (bap/tīz, bap tīz/) *vt.* **-tized, -tiz·ing** [ME. *baptisen* < OFr. *baptiser* < LL. *baptizare* < Gr. *baptizein*, to immerse, baptize, substituted for earlier *baptein*, to dip, used in post-classical Gr. chiefly in sense "to dip in dye"] **1.** to dip (a person) into, or sprinkle with, water as a symbol of admission into Christianity or a specific Christian church **2.** to subject to an initiation or an ordeal that purifies or cleanses **3.** to give a first name to as part of the baptismal ceremony; christen —*vt.* to administer baptism —**bap'tiz·er** *n.*

bar[1] (bär) *n.* [ME. & OFr. *barre* < ML. *barra*, bar, barrier, prob. < Gaul. **barros*, the bushy end, akin to Ir. *bar*, branch] **1.** any piece of wood, metal, etc. longer than it is wide or thick, often used as a barrier, fastening, lever, etc. **2.** *a*) an oblong piece or mass of something solid [bar of soap, chocolate bar] *b*) any of various small metal strips worn to show military or other rank **3.** a thing that blocks the way or prevents entrance, departure, or further movement: cf. SAND BAR **4.** anything that hinders or prevents [illiteracy is a *bar* to success] **5.** a strip, stripe, band, or broad line, as of light or color **6.** *a*) the railing enclosing the part of a law court where the judges or lawyers sit, or where prisoners are brought to trial *b*) this part of the law court **7.** *a*) a law court or system of courts *b*) any place of judgment [the *bar* of public opinion] **8.** *a*) lawyers collectively *b*) the legal profession **9.** *a*) a counter at which alcoholic drinks and sometimes food are served *b*) an establishment or room with such a counter *c*) an article of furniture, often on wheels, from which drinks, etc. are served **10.** a handrail held onto while doing ballet exercises **11.** the mouthpiece of a horse's bit, or the part of a horse's mouth into which it is fitted **12.** in lace making and other needlework, a loop or tie that connects parts of a pattern **13.** *Heraldry* a horizontal stripe on a shield or bearing **14.** *Law a*) the defeat or nullifying of a claim or action *b*) anything that brings this about **15.** *Music a*) a vertical line across a staff, dividing it into measures *b*) a measure *c*) same as DOUBLE BAR **16.** *Zool.* either of the ends of the wall of a horse's hoof, curving inward toward the center of the sole —*vt.* **barred, bar'ring 1.** to fasten with or as with a bar **2.** to obstruct by means of a bar or bars; shut off; close **3.** to oppose, prevent, or forbid, as by legal action **4.** to keep out; exclude [he was *barred* from the contest] **5.** to set aside; dismiss [barring certain possibilities] **6.** to mark with stripes —*prep.* excluding; excepting [the best hotel in town, *bar* none] —*SYN.* see HINDER[1], SHOAL[2] —**cross the bar** to die

bar[2] (bär) *n.* [G. < Gr. *baros*, weight, akin to *barys*, heavy: see GRAVE[1]] **1.** a metric unit of pressure equal to one million dynes per square centimeter **2.** formerly, a unit of acoustical pressure equal to one dyne per square centimeter: cf. MICROBAR

BAR Browning automatic rifle

Bar. Baruch

bar. **1.** barometer **2.** barrel **3.** barrister

Ba·rab·bas (bə rab/əs) [Heb., son of Abba] *Bible* the prisoner whom the people wanted freed rather than Jesus: Matt. 27:16–21

Bar·a·nof Island (ber/ə nôf/) island in Alexander Archipelago, Alas.: c. 1,600 sq. mi.; largest city, Sitka

bar·a·the·a (ber/ə thē/ə) *n.* [19th c.; ? coined] a soft fabric made of silk and wool or rayon and cotton

barb[1] (bärb) *n.* [ME. & OFr. *barbe* < L. *barba*, BEARD] **1.** a thin, somewhat beardlike growth near the mouth of certain animals **2.** a piece of white linen for covering the throat and sometimes the chin, worn by certain nuns **3.** a sharp point curving or projecting in an opposite direction from the main point of a fishhook, harpoon, arrow, etc. **4.** sharpness; sting [the *barb* of his wit made us wince] **5.** a cutting remark **6.** one of the hairlike branches growing from the shaft of a feather: see FEATHER, illus. **7.** *Bot. a*) a hooked hair or bristle *b*) an awn —*vt.* to provide with a barb or barbs

barb[2] *n.* [Fr. *barbe*, Barbary horse < It. *barbero* < Ar. *Barbar*, BERBER] **1.** a horse of a breed native to Barbary, noted for speed, strength, and gentle behavior **2.** a breed of pigeon similar to the carrier pigeon

Bar·ba·dos (bär bā/dōz, -dōs/; *occas.* bär/bə dōz/) country

on the easternmost island of the West Indies: formerly a Brit. dependency, since 1966 a member of the Brit. Commonwealth: 166 sq. mi.; pop. 245,000; cap. Bridgetown
—**Bar·ba′di·an** (-dē ən) *adj.*, *n.*

Bar·ba·ra (bär′bər ə, -brə) [L., fem. of *barbarus* (see BARBAROUS) lit., foreign, strange] a feminine name: dim. *Babs*, *Barb*

bar·bar·i·an (bär ber′ē ən) *n.* [< L. *barbarus*, BARBAROUS] 1. orig., an alien or foreigner: in the ancient world applied esp. to non-Greeks, non-Romans, or non-Christians 2. a member of a people or group with a civilization regarded as primitive, savage, etc. 3. *a*) a person who lacks culture *b*) a coarse or unmannerly person; boor 4. a savage, cruel person; brute —*adj.* of or like a barbarian; esp., *a*) uncivilized; crude *b*) savage; cruel; barbarous —**bar·bar′i·an·ism** *n.*
SYN.—**barbarian** basically refers to a civilization regarded as primitive, usually without further connotation [the Anglo-Saxons were a *barbarian* people]; **barbaric** suggests the crudeness and lack of restraint regarded as characteristic of primitive peoples [*barbaric* splendor]; **barbarous** connotes the cruelty and brutality regarded as characteristic of primitive peoples [*barbarous* warfare]; **savage** implies a more primitive civilization than **barbarian** and connotes even greater fierceness and cruelty [a *savage* inquisition] —*ANT.* **civilized**

bar·bar·ic (bär ber′ik) *adj.* [ME. *barbarik* < L. *barbaricus* < Gr. *barbarikos*: see BARBAROUS] 1. of, like, or characteristic of barbarians; uncivilized; primitive 2. wild, crude, and unrestrained —*SYN.* see BARBARIAN —**bar·bar′i·cal·ly** *adv.*

bar·ba·rism (bär′bər iz'm) *n.* [L. *barbarismus* < Gr. *barbarismos*: see BARBAROUS] 1. *a*) the use of words and expressions not standard in a language *b*) a word or expression of this sort (Ex.: "youse" for "you"): see also IMPROPRIETY, SOLECISM 2. the state of being primitive or lacking civilization 3. a barbarous action, custom, etc. 4. brutal behavior; barbarity

bar·bar·i·ty (bär ber′ə tē) *n.*, *pl.* **-ties** 1. cruel or brutal behavior; inhumanity 2. a cruel or brutal act 3. a crude or coarse taste, manner, form, etc.

bar·ba·rize (bär′bə rīz′) *vt.* **-rized′**, **-riz′ing** [ML. *barbarizare* < Gr. *barbarizein*, to behave like a barbarian] to make barbarous; coarsen, brutalize, etc. —*vi.* to become barbarous —**bar′ba·ri·za′tion** *n.*

Bar·ba·ros·sa (bär′bə räs′ə, rōs′-, -rôs′-), **Frederick** [It. < *barba*, beard + *rossa*, red: so named from his beard] *see* FREDERICK I (of the Holy Roman Empire)

bar·ba·rous (bär′bər əs) *adj.* [L. *barbarus* < Gr. *barbaros*, foreign, strange, ignorant < **barbar*, of echoic origin, used for unintelligible speech of foreigners (Sans. *barbara-*, stammering, non-Aryan; Sumerian *barbar*, foreigner)] 1. orig., foreign or alien; in the ancient world, non-Greek, non-Roman, or non-Christian 2. characterized by substandard usages in speaking or writing; also, not classical 3. characteristic of barbarians; primitive or lacking in civilization 4. uncultured, crude, coarse, rough, etc. 5. cruel; brutal 6. harsh in sound; raucous —*SYN.* see BARBARIAN —**bar′ba·rous·ly** *adv.* —**bar′ba·rous·ness** *n.*

Bar·ba·ry (bär′bər ē) [< L. *Barbaria*, lit., a foreign country: see BERBER] region in N Africa, between Egypt & the Atlantic, inhabited chiefly by Berbers

Barbary ape a tailless, apelike monkey (*Macaca sylvana*) of North Africa and Gibraltar, easily tamed

Barbary Coast 1. the coastal regions of Barbary, once centers of piracy 2. the waterfront district in San Francisco before the earthquake of 1906, known for its saloons, gambling places, & brothels

Barbary States North African states of Tripolitania, Tunisia, Algeria, & Morocco when they were semi-independent under Turkish rule (16th–19th cent.)

bar·bas·co (bär bas′kō) *n.*, *pl.* **-cos**, **-coes** [AmSp., altered < *verbasco*, mullein < L. *verbascum*] a Mexican plant (*Dioscorea floribunda*) having a large, inedible root that yields extracts used in making synthetic steroidal hormones

bar·bate (bär′bāt) *adj.* [L. *barbatus*, bearded < *barba*, BEARD] 1. bearded 2. *Bot.* having hairlike tufts, or awns, as oats, barley, etc.

bar·be·cue (bär′bə kyōō′) *n.* [Sp. *barbacoa* < Taino, lit., framework of sticks] 1. orig., a raised framework for smoking, drying, or broiling meat 2. a hog, steer, etc. broiled or roasted whole over an open fire, sometimes in an open pit 3. any meat broiled on a spit over an open fire ☆4. a party or picnic at which such meat is served 5. a restaurant that specializes in barbecuing 6. a portable outdoor grill —*vt.* **-cued′**, **-cu′ing** 1. to prepare (meat) outdoors by roasting on a spit or broiling on a grill, usually over a charcoal fire 2. to broil or cook (meat) with a highly seasoned sauce (**barbecue sauce**) containing vinegar, tomatoes, spices, etc.

barbed (bärbd) *adj.* 1. having a barb or barbs 2. stinging; cutting [*barbed* words]

☆**barbed wire** strands of wire twisted together, with barbs at regular, close intervals, used for fencing or military barriers

bar·bel (bär′b'l) *n.* [ME. & OFr. < ML. *barbellus* < L. *barbula*, dim. of *barbus* < *barba*, BEARD] 1. a threadlike growth from the lips or jaws of certain fishes: it is an organ of touch 2. any of several large European freshwater fishes (genus *Barbus*) with such growths

bar·bell (bär′bel′) *n.* [BAR[1] + (DUMB)BELL] a metal bar or rod to which disks of varying weights are attached at each end, used for weightlifting exercises: also **bar bell, bar-bell**

BARBELL

bar·bel·late (bär′bə lāt′, bär bel′it) *adj.* [ModL. *barbellatus* < *barbella*, dim. < L. *barbula*: see BARBEL] *Bot.* covered with short, hooked bristles or hairs

bar·ber (bär′bər) *n.* [ME. & OFr. *barbour*, ult. < L. *barba*, BEARD] a person whose work or trade is cutting and dressing hair, shaving and trimming beards, etc. —*vt.* to cut the hair of, shave, trim the beard of, etc. —*vi.* to work as a barber

Bar·ber (bär′bər), **Samuel** 1910– ; U.S. composer

☆**barber college** a school for teaching the trade of barbering

barber pole a pole with spiral stripes of red and white, used as a symbol of the barber's trade

bar·ber·ry (bär′ber′ē; *esp. Brit.* -bər i) *n.*, *pl.* **-ries** [ME. *berberie* (infl. by *berie*, BERRY) < ML. *barberis* < Ar. *barbāris* < *ambar bāris* < *amīr bāris*] 1. any of a genus (*Berberis*) of spiny shrubs, with sour, red berries and yellow flowers: it is often used for hedges 2. the berry —*adj.* designating a family (Berberidaceae) of mostly spiny plants including the May apple, mahonia, and umbrella leaf

☆**bar·ber·shop** (bär′bər shäp′) *n.* a barber's place of business —*adj.* [Colloq.] designating, or characterized by, the close harmony of male voices, esp. in sentimental songs [a *barbershop* quartet]

barber's itch an inflammation of the hair follicles of the face and neck, caused by various fungi (genera *Trichophyton* and *Microsporum*): so called because it can be contracted in unsanitary barbershops

bar·bet (bär′bit) *n.* [Fr., dim. of *barbe*, BEARD] any of many kinds of brightly colored tropical birds (family Capitonidae) that have a large, strong bill with bristles growing at its base

bar·bette (bär bet′) *n.* [Fr.; ? fig. use of orig. sense, "veil with which nuns cover the breast" < *barbe*, BEARD] 1. a platform for guns in a fort, high enough to permit firing over the walls 2. the armored structure around a gun platform on a warship

bar·bi·can (bär′bi kən) *n.* [ME. < OFr. *barbicane* < ML. *barbacana*, prob. < Per. *barbar-khānah*, house on a wall] a defensive tower or similar fortification at a gate or bridge leading into a town or castle

bar·bi·cel (bär′bə sel′) *n.* [ModL. *barbicella*, dim. of L. *barba*, BEARD] any of the tiny, hairlike extensions growing from the barbules of a feather: barbicels have many little hooks (*hamuli*) that hold barbules together

bar·bi·tal (bär′bi tôl′) *n.* [BARBIT(URIC ACID) + -AL] diethylbarbituric acid, $C_8H_{12}O_3N_2$, a drug in the form of a white powder, used to induce sleep

bar·bi·tu·rate (bär bich′ər it, -āt′; bär′bə tyoor′it, -toor′-) *n.* [BARBITUR(IC ACID) + -ATE[2]] any salt or ester of barbituric acid, used as a sedative or to induce sleep

bar·bi·tu·ric acid (bär′bə tyoor′ik, -toor′-) [< G. *barbitursäure* (< ? ModL. *Usnea barbata*, lit., bearded moss + *ursäure*, a ureide of acid character < *urea*, urea + *säure*, acid) + -IC] a white, odorless, crystalline acid, $C_4H_4O_3N_2$, used in the manufacture of sedatives and hypnotics, in making dyes, and as a polymerization catalyst

Bar·bi·zon School (bär′bə zän′; *Fr.* bár bē zōn′) a group of French romantic landscape painters (including Millet, Corot, Théodore Rousseau, and Daubigny) who settled in Barbizon, a village in N France in the mid-19th cent.

Bar·bu·da (bär bōō′də) island dependency of Antigua, in the Leeward Islands of the West Indies: 62 sq. mi.; pop. 1,000

bar·bule (bär′byōōl) *n.* [L. *barbula*, dim. of *barba*, BEARD] 1. a very small barb; barbel 2. any of the threadlike parts fringing each side of the barb of a feather: cf. BARBICEL

Bar·busse (bàrb′ker′), **Hen·ri** (än rē′) 1873–1935; Fr. novelist & journalist

barb·wire (bärb′wir′) *n.* *same as* BARBED WIRE

Bar·ca (bär′kə) ancient Greek colony in Cyrenaica, N Africa

bar·ca·role, bar·ca·rolle (bär′kə rōl′) *n.* [Fr. < It. (Venetian) *barcarola* < *barcarolo*, gondolier < *barca*, BARK[3]] 1. a song sung by Venetian gondoliers 2. any piece of music imitating this

Bar·ce·lo·na (bär′sə lō′nə; *Sp.* bär′the lō′nä) seaport in NE Spain, on the Mediterranean: pop. 1,696,000

B.Arch. Bachelor of Architecture

bar·chan (bär′kän; bär′kən) *n.* [Russ. *barkhan*] a crescent-shaped sand dune formed in certain inland desert regions, with the convex side to windward

bar chart *same as* BAR GRAPH

Bar Coch·ba (bär kōkh′və) *same as* BAR KOKBA

bard[1] (bärd) *n.* [Gael. & Ir.] 1. an ancient Celtic poet and singer of epic poems, who accompanied himself on the harp

2. any of various other national minstrels or epic poets **3.** a poet —**bard′ic** adj.

bard² (bärd) n. [Fr. barde < Sp. or It. barda, leather armor for horses < Ar. barda′a, saddle pad] a piece of armor for a horse —vt. to put bards on (a horse) Also sp. **barde**

Bard of Avon William Shakespeare: so called from his birthplace, Stratford-on-Avon

bare¹ (ber) adj. [ME. bar < OE. bær < IE. base *bhoso-s < ? *bhes, to rub off] **1.** a) without the natural or customary covering [bare wooden floors] b) without clothing; naked [bare legs] **2.** without equipment, supplies, or furnishings; empty [a bare room, a bare larder] **3.** without embellishment; unadorned; simple; plain [the bare facts] **4.** without tools or weapons [to use one's bare hands] **5.** threadbare **6.** no more than; mere [a bare subsistence wage] —vt. **bared, bar′ing** to make bare; uncover; strip; expose —**lay bare** to open to view; uncover; expose —**bare′ness** n.

SYN.—**bare**, in this comparison, implies the absence of the conventional or appropriate covering [bare legs, bareheaded]; **naked** implies the absence of clothing, either entirely or from some part, and connotes a revealing of the body [a naked bosom]; **nude**, which is somewhat euphemistic for **naked**, is commonly applied to the undraped human figure in art; **bald** suggests a lack of natural covering, esp. of hair on the head; **barren** implies a lack of natural covering, esp. vegetation, and connotes destitution and fruitlessness [barren lands]. See also STRIP. —ANT. covered, clothed

bare² archaic pt. of BEAR¹

bare·back (ber′bak′) adv., adj. on a horse with no saddle

bare·faced (-fāst′) adj. **1.** with the face uncovered, unmasked, or beardless **2.** unconcealed; open **3.** shameless; brazen; audacious —**bare′fac′ed·ly** (-fās′id lē) adv. —**bare′fac′ed·ness** n.

bare·foot (-foot′) adj., adv. with bare feet; without shoes and stockings —**bare′foot′ed** adj.

ba·rège, ba·rege (bə rezh′) n. [Fr. < Barèges, town in France] a gauzy cloth of silk and wool, or cotton and wool, used for veils, dresses, etc.

bare·hand·ed (ber′han′did) adj., adv. **1.** with hands uncovered or unprotected **2.** without weapons, appropriate means, etc.

bare·head·ed (-hed′id) adj., adv. wearing no hat or other covering on the head

Ba·reil·ly, Ba·re·li (bə rā′lē) city in Uttar Pradesh, N India: pop. 273,000

bare·leg·ged (ber′leg′id, -legd′) adj., adv. with the legs bare; without stockings on

bare·ly (ber′lē) adv. **1.** without covering or disguise; plainly [stating the unpleasant facts barely] **2.** only just; no more than; scarcely [barely enough to eat] **3.** meagerly; scantily [a barely furnished room]

Bar·ents Sea (ber′ənts, bär′-) part of the Arctic Ocean, north of Europe & south of Spitsbergen & Franz Josef Land

bare·sark (ber′särk′) n. [alt. (after BARE¹ + SARK) < BERSERK] a frenzied fighter; berserker —adv. without armor on

☆**barf** (bärf) vi., vt. [echoic] [Slang] to vomit

☆**bar·fly** (bär′flī′) n., pl. -flies′ [Slang] a person who spends much time drinking in barrooms

bar·gain (bär′g'n) n. [ME. & OFr. bargaine < bargaignier, to haggle < Frank. *borganjan, to lend, akin to BORROW] **1.** a mutual agreement or contract in which the parties settle on what should be given or done by each **2.** the terms of such an agreement **3.** such an agreement considered in terms of its worth to one of the parties [to make a bad bargain] **4.** something offered, bought, or sold at a price favorable to the buyer —vi. **1.** to discuss the details of a transaction, contract, treaty, etc., trying to get the best possible terms **2.** to make a bargain, or agreement —vt. to sell or trade to another by bargaining; barter —**bargain for** **1.** to try to get cheaply **2.** to expect; anticipate; count on: also **bargain on** —**into the bargain** beyond what has been agreed on; in addition —**bar′gain·er** n.

☆**bargain counter** a store counter on which goods are displayed for sale at reduced prices

barge (bärj) n. [ME. < OFr. < ML. barga] **1.** a large boat, usually flat-bottomed, for carrying heavy freight on rivers, canals, etc. **2.** a large pleasure boat, esp. one used for state ceremonies, pageants, etc. **3.** a flagship's boat reserved for use by flag officers **4.** [Slang] any clumsy boat —vt. **barged, barg′ing** to carry by barge —vi. **1.** to move slowly and clumsily **2.** to come or go (in or into) in a rude, abrupt, or clumsy way **3.** to collide heavily or clumsily; run (into)

barge·board (-bôrd′) n. [see BARGE COUPLE] a board, often ornate, attached along the barge couples of a gabled roof, as in Tudor and Gothic architecture

barge couple [ME. berge, a sloping roof (< ? OFr. berge, a slope) + COUPLE] either of the pair of outside rafters forming the projection of a gabled roof

barge course the overhang of a projecting gable roof

bar·gee (bär jē′) n. [BARG(E) + -EE] [Brit.] a bargeman

barge·man (bärj′mən) n., pl.

BARGEBOARD

-men (-mən) a man who operates, or works aboard, a barge

bar·ghest (bär′gest) n. [? akin to G. berg geist, mountain spirit] Eng. Folklore a doglike goblin whose appearance supposedly foreshadows death or bad luck

bar graph a graph in which parallel bars represent in proportional lengths the figures given in a set of data

Bar Harbor [after a local sand bar] resort town on Mount Desert Island, Me.: pop. 3,800

Ba·ri (bä′rē) seaport in SE Italy, on the Adriatic: pop. 330,000

bar·ic (ber′ik) adj. [< Gr. barys, weighty + -IC] Physics of weight or pressure, esp. that of the atmosphere; barometric

ba·ril·la (bə ril′ə) n. [Sp. barrilla < Galician baril, very good < Ar. bari, excellent] crude soda ash obtained by burning various saltworts and related plants (genera Salsola and Halogeton) of the Mediterranean area

bar·ite (ber′īt) n. [< Gr. barys, weighty + -ITE¹] a white, unusually heavy, orthorhombic mineral composed mainly of barium sulfate: it is the chief source of barium and its compounds and is used in making paint

bar·i·tone (bar′ə tōn′, ber′-) n. [It. baritono < Gr. barytonos, deep-toned < barys, heavy, deep + tonos, TONE] **1.** the range of a male voice between bass and tenor, from the second A below middle C to the first F above **2.** a male voice of this range, or a man with such a voice **3.** any wind instrument with a similar range; specif., a three-valved brass-wind instrument of the saxhorn family **4.** a musical part for such a voice or instrument —adj. of, for, or having the range of a baritone

bar·i·um (ber′ē əm) n. [ModL. < Gr. barys, heavy] a silver-white, slightly malleable, metallic chemical element, found as a carbonate or sulfate and used in alloys: symbol Ba; at. wt., 137.34; at. no., 56; sp. gr., 3.5; melt. pt., 729°C; boil. pt., 1637°C

barium chloride a poisonous compound, $BaCl_2$, consisting of flat white crystals that are soluble in water: it is used in making rat poison, in tanning leather, etc.

barium peroxide a gray-white powder, BaO_2, used as a bleach and in the preparation of hydrogen peroxide: also **barium dioxide**

barium sulfate an odorless, tasteless, white powder, $BaSO_4$, insoluble in water: it is used as a paint pigment, as a filler for paper, textiles, etc., and as an opaque substance swallowed to help in the examination of X-rays of the stomach and intestines

bark¹ (bärk) n. [ME. < ON. borkr, akin to G. borke] **1.** the outside covering of the stems and roots of trees and woody plants **2.** some kinds of this matter used in tanning, dyeing, etc. **3.** cinchona, a medicinal bark —vt. **1.** to treat with a bark infusion, as in leather tanning **2.** to take the bark off; specif., to peel a ring of bark from (a tree) **3.** [Colloq.] to scrape some skin off [to bark one's shin] —SYN. see SKIN

bark² (bärk) vi. [ME. berken < OE. beorcan, akin to ON. berkja, of echoic origin] **1.** to make the characteristic sharp, abrupt cry of a dog **2.** to make a sound like this [the engine barked] **3.** to speak or shout sharply; snap **4.** [Colloq.] to cough ☆**5.** [Slang] to advertise a show, sale, etc. by shouting about it in public —vt. to say or advertise with a bark or shout —n. **1.** the sharp, abrupt sound made by a dog **2.** any sharp, abrupt sound or utterance like this —☆**bark up the wrong tree** to misdirect one's attack, energies, etc.

bark³ (bärk) n. [Fr. barque < It. & L. barca, small boat < Gr. baris, Egyptian boat < Coptic bari, small boat] **1.** [Poet.] any boat, esp. a small sailing boat **2.** a sailing vessel with its two forward masts square-rigged and its rear mast rigged fore-and-aft

☆**bark beetle** any of a family (Scolytidae) of small beetles, the larvae and adults of which burrow under the bark of trees, esp. conifers, and feed on the inner bark, sometimes causing extensive damage

BARK (sense 2)

bar·keep·er (bär′kēp′ər) n. **1.** an owner or manager of a bar where alcoholic drinks are sold **2.** a bartender Also ☆**bar′keep′**

☆**bark·en·tine** (bär′kən tēn′) n. [< BARK³ after BRIGANTINE] a sailing vessel with its foremast square-rigged and its two other masts rigged fore-and-aft

bark·er¹ (bär′kər) n. a person or machine that takes bark off a tree, log, etc.

bark·er² (bär′kər) n. **1.** an animal, person, or thing that makes a barking sound **2.** a person in front of a side show, theater, store, etc. who tries to attract customers by loud, animated talking

Bar·king (bär′kiŋ) city in SE England: suburb of London: pop. 72,000

Bar Kok·ba, Bar Kokh·ba (bär kôkh′vä) (born Simon of Kozeba) ?–135 A.D.; Jewish leader of a revolt against the Romans (131–135)

bar·ley (bär′lē) *n.* see PLURAL, II, D, 3 [ME. *barli* < OE. *bærlic, adj.,* of barley < *bere,* barley + -*lic* (-LY¹) < IE. base **bhares,* whence FARINA, ON. *barr,* grain] **1.** a cereal grass (*Hordeum vulgare* and related species) with dense, bearded spikes of flowers, each made up of three single-seeded spikelets **2.** its grain, used in making malts, in soups, and as a feed for animals

bar·ley·corn (-kôrn′) *n.* [ME. *barli-corn*] **1.** barley or a grain of barley **2.** formerly, a unit of length equal to 1/3 inch

Barleycorn, John see JOHN BARLEYCORN

barley sugar a clear, hard candy made by melting sugar, formerly with a barley extract added

barley water [Chiefly Brit.] a drink made by boiling barley in water

Bar·low (bär′lō), **Joel** 1754–1812; U.S. poet & diplomat

barm (bärm) *n.* [ME. *berme* < OE. *beorma,* yeast < IE. base **bher-,* to surge up, whence FERMENT, BREATH] the foamy yeast that appears on the surface of malt liquors as they ferment

bar·maid (bär′mād′) *n.* a waitress who serves alcoholic drinks in a bar

bar·man (-mən) *n., pl.* -**men** (-mən) a bartender

Bar·me·cide feast (bär′mə sīd′) [< the name of a prince in *The Arabian Nights* who served such a feast] **1.** a pretended feast with no food **2.** any pretended or illusory generosity or hospitality —**Bar′me·ci′dal** (-sīd′'l) *adj.*

bar mitz·vah, bar miz·vah (bär mits′və; *Heb.* bär′mits vä′) [Heb. *bar mitswāh,* son of the commandment] [*also* B- M-] **1.** a Jewish boy who has arrived at the age of religious responsibility, thirteen years *☆*2. the ceremony celebrating this event

barm·y (bär′mē) *adj.* **barm′i·er, barm′i·est 1.** full of barm; yeasty or foamy **2.** [Brit. Slang] silly; idiotic

barn (bärn) *n.* [ME. < OE. *bern, berern* < *bere,* BARLEY + *ærn,* a building, house] **1.** a farm building for sheltering harvested crops, livestock, machines, etc. *☆*2. a large building for streetcars, trucks, etc. **3.** [arbitrary use, from phr. *as big as a barn*] *Nuclear Physics* a unit of measure of the degree of probability that a nuclear reaction will occur: 1 barn = a magnitude of 10⁻²⁴ sq. cm. per nucleus: see CROSS SECTION

Bar·na·bas (bär′nə bəs) [ME. < LL. (Vulgate: Acts 4:36) < Gr. < Aram. *barnebhū′āh,* son of exhortation] **1.** a masculine name: dim. *Barney;* var. *Barnaby* **2.** *Bible* a Levite of Cyprus, a Christian apostle & missionary companion of Paul

Bar·na·by (bär′nə bē) a masculine name: see BARNABAS

bar·na·cle (bär′nə k'l) *n.* [ME. *bernacle,* earlier *bernak* < Fr. *bernicle* & Breton *bernik,* kind of shellfish (ult. ? via Gaul. **berna,* Ir. *berna,* split < IE. base **bher-,* to slit)] **1.** *same as* BARNACLE GOOSE **2.** any of a number of salt-water shellfish (subclass Cirripedia) that attach themselves to rocks, wharves, ship bottoms, etc. and to whales **3.** a person or thing hard to get rid of —**bar′na·cled** *adj.*

barnacle goose [from the popular notion that it grew from the BARNACLE] a European wild goose (*Branta leucopsis*)

bar·na·cles (-k'lz) *n.pl.* [ME. & OFr. *bernac,* kind of bit] **1.** nose pincers for controlling an unruly horse **2.** an instrument of torture like such pincers

Bar·nard (bär′nərd) **1.** a masculine name: see BERNARD **2. George Gray,** 1863–1938; U.S. sculptor

Bar·na·ul (bär′nä ōōl′) city in the SC R.S.F.S.R., on the Ob River: pop. 382,000

*☆***barn dance** a party, orig. held in a barn, at which people dance square dances

Barnes (bärnz), **Harry Elmer** 1889– ; U.S. historian & sociologist

Bar·ne·veldt (bär′nə velt′), **Jan van Ol·den** (yän′ vän ōl′dən) 1547–1619; Du. statesman & patriot

barn owl any of a family (Tytonidae) of owls, esp. a widely distributed species (*Tyto alba*), usually brown and gray with a spotted white breast, found chiefly in hollow trees and barns

Barns·ley (bärnz′lē) city in NC England: pop. 75,000

barn·storm (bärn′stôrm′) *vi., vt.* [BARN + STORM, *vi.* 3: from occas. use of barns as auditoriums] **1.** to go about (the country) performing plays, giving lectures or campaign speeches, playing exhibition games, etc., esp. in small towns and rural districts **2.** [from the use of barns as hangars] in the early days of aviation, to tour (the country) giving short airplane rides, exhibitions of stunt flying, etc. —**barn′storm′er** n.

barn swallow a common swallow (*Hirundo rustica*) with a long, deeply forked tail: it usually nests on rafters in barns

Bar·num (bär′nəm), **P(hineas) T(aylor)** 1810–91; U.S. showman and circus operator

barn·yard (bärn′yärd′) *n.* the yard or ground near a barn, often enclosed —*adj.* **1.** of a barnyard **2.** like or fit for a barnyard; earthy, smutty, etc.

*☆***barnyard golf** [Colloq.] the game of horseshoes

bar·o- (bar′ə, ber′ə-; -ō) [< Gr. *baros,* weight < *barys,* heavy] *a prefix meaning* of pressure, esp. atmospheric pressure [*barograph*]

Ba·ro·da (bə rō′də) **1.** city in Gujarat state, W India: pop. 295,000 **2.** former state of W India: merged with Bombay state, 1948

bar·o·gram (bar′ə gram′) *n.* a linear record of variations in atmospheric pressure, traced by a barograph

bar·o·graph (-graf′) *n.* a barometer that records variations in atmospheric pressure automatically on a revolving cylinder —**bar′o·graph′ic** *adj.*

Ba·ro·ja (bä rō′hä), **Pí·o** (pē′ō) 1872–1956; Sp. novelist

ba·rom·e·ter (bə räm′ə tər) *n.* [BARO- + -METER] **1.** an instrument for measuring atmospheric pressure, as by an evacuated and graduated glass tube (**mercury barometer**) in which a column of mercury rises or falls as the pressure of the atmosphere increases or decreases (see also ANEROID BAROMETER): barometers are used in forecasting changes in the weather or finding height above sea level **2.** anything that reflects or indicates change [the stock market is a *barometer* of business] —**bar·o·met·ric** (bar′ə met′rik), **bar′o·met′ri·cal** *adj.* —**bar′o·met′ri·cal·ly** *adv.*

barometric gradient the rate of decrease in barometric pressure in a given region at a particular time

barometric pressure the pressure of the atmosphere as indicated by a barometer: in a mercury barometer it averages 29.92 inches of mercury at sea level

bar·on (bar′ən, ber′-) *n.* [ME. & OFr. *baron* < Frank. **baro,* freeman, man < IE. base **bher-,* to carry, whence BAIRN, BEAR¹] **1.** in the Middle Ages, a feudal tenant of the king or of any higher-ranking lord; nobleman **2.** a member of the lowest rank of the British hereditary peerage **3.** this rank or its title **4.** a European or Japanese nobleman of like rank *☆*5. a man having great or absolute power in some field of business or industry; magnate [an oil *baron*] **6.** *a)* a double sirloin of beef *b)* a saddle of mutton or lamb

bar·on·age (bar′ə nij, ber′-) *n.* [ME. & OFr. *barnage* < prec.] **1.** the barons as a class **2.** the peerage **3.** the rank, title, status, or domain of a baron

bar·on·ess (-nis) *n.* [ME. & OFr. *baronesse*] **1.** a baron's wife, widow, or (in some European countries) daughter **2.** a lady with a barony in her own right

bar·on·et (-nit, -net′) *n.* [ME., dim. of *baron*] **1.** a man holding the lowest hereditary British title, below a baron but above a knight: a baronet is addressed as "Sir," and may add *Bart.* to his name, as Sir John Doe, Bart. **2.** this title

bar·on·et·age (-ij) *n.* **1.** baronets as a class **2.** *same as* BARONETCY

bar·on·et·cy (-sē) *n., pl.* -**cies** the title, rank, or status of a baronet

ba·rong (bə rôn′, -räŋ′) *n.* [native name; prob. akin to PARANG] a heavy sheath knife used by the Moros of the Philippines

ba·ro·ni·al (bə rō′nē əl) *adj.* **1.** of a baron or barons **2.** fit for a baron; grand, showy, etc. [a *baronial* mansion]

bar·on·y (bar′ə nē, ber′-) *n., pl.* -**nies** [ME. & OFr. *baronie*] **1.** a baron's domain **2.** the rank, title, or status of a baron

‡**ba·ronne** (bà rôn′) *n.* [Fr.] baroness

ba·roque (bə rōk′) *adj.* [Fr., orig., irregular < Port. *barroco,* imperfect pearl] **1.** *a)* of, characteristic of, or like a style of art and architecture characterized by much ornamentation and curved rather than straight lines *b)* of, characteristic of, or like a style of music characterized by highly embellished melodies and fugal or contrapuntal forms **2.** designating or of the period in which these styles flourished (c. 1550–1750) **3.** of the late or decadent baroque period style; rococo **4.** fantastically overdecorated; gaudily ornate **5.** irregular in shape: said of pearls —*n.* baroque style, baroque art, etc.

bar·o·scope (bar′ə skōp′) *n.* [BARO- + -SCOPE] an instrument for indicating changes in atmospheric pressure —**bar′o·scop′ic** (-skäp′ik) *adj.*

Ba·rot·se·land (bə rät′sē land′) former Brit. protectorate in W Northern Rhodesia: it now constitutes a province (**Barotse**) of Zambia: 44,920 sq. mi.

ba·rouche (bə rōōsh′) *n.* [G. *barutsche* < It. *baroccio* altered < *biroccio* < ML. **birotium,* two-wheeled cart < LL. *birotus,* two-wheeled < *bi-,* BI-¹ + *rota,* wheel] a four-wheeled carriage with a collapsible hood, two double seats opposite each other, and a box seat in front for the driver

barque (bärk) *n. same as* BARK³

*☆***bar·quen·tine** (bär′kən tēn′) *n. same as* BARKENTINE

Bar·qui·si·me·to (bär kē′sē mä′tō) city in NW Venezuela: pop. 200,000

bar·rack (bar′ik, ber′-) *n.* [Fr. *baraque* < Sp. *barraca,* cabin, mud hut < *barro,* clay, mud < VL. **barrum,* clay] **1.** [Rare] an improvised hut **2.** [*pl.,* often with sing. v.] *a)* a building or group of buildings for housing soldiers *b)* a large, plain, often temporary building for housing workmen, etc. —*vt., vi.* to house in barracks

barracks bag a large cloth bag to hold a soldier's equipment and personal possessions

bar·ra·coon (bar′ə kōōn′) *n.* [< Sp. *barracón,* aug. of *barraca,* a hut, cabin: see BARRACK] at the time of the slave trade, an enclosure or barracks for temporarily confining slaves awaiting transportation

bar·ra·cu·da (bar′ə kōō′də, ber′-) *n., pl.* -**da, -das:** see PLURAL, II, D, 2 [Sp., prob. < native WInd. name] any of a family (Sphyraenidae) of fierce, pikelike fishes of tropical seas: some species are edible

bar·rage¹ (bə räzh′, -räj′) *n.* [Fr., in *tir de barrage,* firing barrier: see ff.] **1.** a curtain of artillery fire laid down to keep enemy forces from moving, or to cover or prepare the way for one's own forces, esp. in attack **2.** a heavy, prolonged attack of words, blows, etc. —*vi., vt.* -**raged′, -rag′-**

ing to lay down a barrage (against); subject to a barrage
bar·rage[2] (bär′ij) *n.* [Fr. < *barrer*, to stop < *barre*, BAR[1]] a man-made barrier in a stream, river, etc. to deepen the water or channel it for irrigation; dam
bar·rage balloon (bə räzh′, -räj′) any of a number of anchored balloons with cables or nets attached for entangling low-flying attacking airplanes
bar·ra·mun·da (bar′ə mun′də, ber′-) *n., pl.* **-da, -das:** see PLURAL, II, D, 2 [< native name] an edible Australian fish (*Neoceratodus forsteri*) with both gills and lungs
bar·ra·mun·di (-dē) *n., pl.* **-di, -dis, -dies:** see PLURAL, II, D, 2 *same as* BARRAMUNDA
☆**bar·ran·ca** (bə raŋ′kə) *n.* [Sp.] a deep ravine or hole, or a steep cliff, esp. in the southwestern U.S.: also **bar·ran′co** (-kō), *pl.* **-cos**
Bar·ran·quil·la (bä′rän kē′yä) seaport in NW Colombia, on the Magdalena River: pop. 498,000
bar·ra·tor, bar·ra·ter (bar′ə tər, ber′-) *n.* [ME. *baratour* < OFr. *barateor*, swindler < *barater*, to cheat < *barate*, fraud, strife < ON. *baratta*, quarrel] a person guilty of barratry
bar·ra·try (-trē) *n.* [Fr. *baraterie*, orig., misuse of office < *barater*: see BARRATOR] 1. orig., the buying or selling of ecclesiastical or civil positions 2. the criminal offense of habitually bringing about quarrels or lawsuits 3. *Maritime Law* fraud, or gross negligence showing fraud, on the part of a ship's officers or crew that results in loss to the owners —**bar′ra·trous** (-trəs) *adj.*
Barr body (bär) [after Dr. M. L. *Barr* (1908–), Canad. anatomist] a structure found on the inside of the nuclear membrane of female cells that takes a dark stain and indicates by its presence the sex of the individual: also called *sex chromatin body*
‡**barre** (bär) *n.* [Fr.] the practice bar in a ballet studio
barred (bärd) *adj.* 1. having bars or stripes 2. closed off with bars 3. forbidden or excluded
barred owl a variety of large, N. American owl (*Strix varia*) with bars of brown feathers across the breast
bar·rel (bar′əl, ber′-) *n.* [ME. *barel* < OFr. *baril* < ML. *barillus;* origin obscure] 1. a large, wooden, cylindrical container with flat, circular ends and sides that bulge outward, made usually of staves bound together with hoops 2. the capacity or contents of a standard barrel, esp. as a unit of measure (in the U.S., usually 31 1/2 gal.; in Gr. Brit., 36 imperial gal.; in dry measure, various amounts, as 196 lb. of flour, 200 lb. of pork or fish, etc.) 3. a revolving cylinder, wound with a chain or rope [the *barrel* of a windlass] 4. any hollow or solid cylinder [the *barrel* of a fountain pen] 5. the tube of a gun, through which the projectile is fired 6. the cylindrical case containing the mainspring of a clock or watch 7. the piston chamber of a pump 8. the quill of a feather 9. [Colloq.] a great amount [a *barrel* of fun] —*vt.* **-reled** or **-relled**, **-rel·ing** or **-rel·ling** to put or pack in a barrel or barrels —☆*vi.* [Slang] to go at high speed —☆**have (someone) over a barrel** [Slang] to have (someone) completely at one's mercy, esp. financially
☆**barrel chair** a kind of upholstered chair with an upright, rounded back
bar·rel-chest·ed (-ches′tid) *adj.* having an especially broad, deep chest for one's height
☆**bar·rel·house** (-hous′) *n.* 1. formerly, a small, cheap saloon with a row of racked barrels along the wall 2. an early form of jazz characterized by an unrestrained style with a strong beat and a driving rhythm
barrel organ a mechanical musical instrument having a cylinder studded with pins which open pipe valves or strike metal tongues when the cylinder is revolved, producing a tune; hand organ
barrel roll a complete revolution made by an airplane around its longitudinal axis while in flight
barrel vault *Archit.* a vault shaped like half a cylinder
bar·ren (bar′ən, ber′-) *adj.* [ME. *barain* < OFr. *baraigne, brehaigne,* orig. used of land] 1. that cannot produce offspring; sterile [a *barren* woman] 2. not bearing or pregnant at the regular time: said of animals or plants 3. not producing crops or fruit; having little or no vegetation [*barren* soil] 4. not bringing useful results; unproductive; unprofitable [a *barren* plan] 5. lacking appeal, interest, or meaning; dull; boring 6. empty; devoid [*barren* of creative spirit] —*n.* 1. an area of unproductive land 2. [*usually pl.*] land with shrubs, brush, etc. and sandy soil —*SYN.* see BARE[1], STERILE —**bar′ren·ly** *adv.* —**bar′ren·ness** *n.*
Barren Grounds (or **Lands**) vast tundra region of N Canada, west of Hudson Bay
‡**bar·re·ra** (bä rā′rä) *n.* [Sp.] 1. the protecting wall enclosing the bull ring at bullfights 2. [*pl.*] the first row of seats in a bullfight arena
Bar·rès (bà res′), (**Auguste**) **Mau·rice** (mô rēs′) 1862–1923; Fr. novelist, essayist, & politician
bar·re·try (bar′ə trē, ber′-) *n. same as* BARRATRY
Bar·rett (-it), **Elizabeth** *see* Elizabeth Barrett BROWNING
bar·rette (bə ret′, bä-) *n.* [Fr., dim. of *barre*, BAR[1]] a small bar or clasp for holding a girl's or woman's hair in place
bar·ri·cade (bar′ə kād′, ber′-; *also, esp. for v.* bar′ə kād′) *n.* [Fr. < It. *barricata*, pp. of *barricare*, to fortify (< ? Fr. or Sp. *barrica*, barrel, prob. akin to BARREL: from use of casks

as barriers)] 1. a barrier thrown up hastily for defense, as in street fighting 2. any barrier or obstruction —*vt.* **-cad′ed**, **-cad′ing** 1. to shut in or keep out with a barricade 2. to put up barricades in; obstruct
Bar·rie (bar′ē, ber′-), Sir **James M(atthew)** 1860–1937; Brit. novelist & playwright, born in Scotland
bar·ri·er (bar′ē ər, ber′-) *n.* [ME. *barrere* < OFr. *barriere* < *barre*, BAR[1]] 1. orig., a fortress, stockade, etc. for defending an entrance or gate 2. a thing that prevents passage or approach; obstruction, as a fence, wall, etc. 3. anything that holds apart, separates, or hinders [racial *barriers, barriers* to progress] 4. a customs gate on a country's border 5. [*sometimes* B-] the part of the antarctic ice sheet that extends into the sea 6. [*pl.*] a high fence of stakes enclosing the area in which a tournament of knights was held 7. *Horse Racing* the movable gate used to keep the horses in line at the starting point —*SYN.* see OBSTACLE
barrier bar (or **beach**) a ridge of sand and gravel thrown up parallel to a coast line by the waves
barrier reef a long ridge of coral near and parallel to the coast line, separated from it by a lagoon: see GREAT BARRIER REEF
bar·ring (bär′iŋ) *prep.* unless there should be; excepting [*barring* rain, we leave tonight]
bar·ri·o (bär′ē ō) *n., pl.* **-os** [Sp. < Ar. *barri*, rural < *barr*, land, open country] in Spanish-speaking countries, a district or suburb of a city
bar·ris·ter (bar′is tər, ber′-) *n.* [< BAR[1] (*n.* 8) + *-ister*, as in MINISTER, CHORISTER] in England, a qualified member of the legal profession who presents and pleads cases in court; counselor-at-law: distinguished from SOLICITOR —*SYN.* see LAWYER
☆**bar·room** (bär′rōōm′) *n.* a room with a bar or counter at which alcoholic drinks are sold
bar·row[1] (bar′ō, ber′-) *n.* [ME. *barwe* < OE. *bearwe*, basket, barrow < *beran*, BEAR[1]] 1. *same as* HANDBARROW 2. *same as* WHEELBARROW 3. a small cart with two wheels, pushed by hand; pushcart
bar·row[2] (bar′ō, ber′-) *n.* [ME. *berwe* < OE. *beorg*, hill < IE. base **bhere̱gh-*, high, raised up, whence G. *berg, burg,* L. *fortis*] 1. a heap of earth or rocks marking a grave, esp. an ancient one; tumulus 2. a mountain; hill: now used only in English place names
bar·row[3] (bar′ō, ber′-) *n.* [ME. *barow* < OE. *bearg* < IE. base **bher-*, to cut, whence L. *ferire*, to strike, stab] a castrated pig
Bar·row (bar′ō, ber′-), **Point** [after Sir John *Barrow* (1764–1848), Eng. geographer] northernmost point of Alas.; cape on the Arctic Ocean
Bar·row-in-Fur·ness (-in fur′nəs) seaport in N Lancashire, England, on the Irish Sea: pop. 65,000: also called **Barrow**
barrow pit [Chiefly Western] a ditch dug along a road
Bar·ry·more (bar′ē môr′, ber′-) family of U.S. actors including 1. **Ethel,** 1879–1959 2. **John,** 1882–1942 3. **Lionel,** 1878–1954 4. **Maurice,** (born *Herbert Blythe*) 1847–1905: father of *Ethel, John,* & *Lionel*
bar sinister *popular term in literature for* BEND SINISTER
Bart. Baronet
☆**bar·tend·er** (bär′ten′dər) *n.* a man who mixes and serves alcoholic drinks at a bar
bar·ter (bär′tər) *vi.* [ME. *bartren* < OFr. *barater*, to barter, trick: see BARRATOR] to trade by exchanging goods or services without using money —*vt.* to give (goods or services) in return for other goods or services; trade —*n.* 1. the act or practice of bartering 2. anything bartered —*SYN.* see SELL —**barter away** to give or trade for too small a return —**bar′ter·er** *n.*
Barth (bärt), **Karl** 1886–1968; Swiss theologian —**Barth′i·an** *adj.*
Bar·thol·di (bár tôl dē′), **Fré·dé·ric Au·guste** (frā dā rēk′ ô güst′) 1834–1904; Fr. sculptor of the Statue of Liberty
Bar·thol·o·mew (bär thäl′ə myōō′) [ME. *Bartelmeus* < LL. (Vulgate) *Bartholomaeus* < Gr. *Bartholomaios* < Aram., lit., son of Talmai] 1. a masculine name: dim. *Bart;* equiv. Fr. *Barthélomé,* It. *Bartolomeo,* G. *Bartholomäus,* Sp. *Bartolomé* 2. *Bible* one of the twelve apostles: identified by some authorities with NATHANAEL: also called *Saint Bartholomew:* his day is Aug. 24
bar·ti·zan (bär′ti zən, bär′tə zan′) *n.* [revived by Sir Walter Scott from a Scot. form altered < ME. *bretasce*, BRATTICE] a small, overhanging turret on a tower or battlement, originally for defense or as a lookout
Bart·lett (bärt′lət), **John** 1820–1905; U.S. editor & publisher: compiler of a book of quotations
☆**Bartlett pear** [after Enoch *Bartlett* of Roxbury, Mass., the distributor] a large, juicy variety of pear
Bar·tók (bär′tôk), **Bé·la** (bā′lä) 1881–1945; Hung. composer & compiler of Hung. folk songs

BARTIZAN

fat, āpe, cär; ten, ēven; is, bīte; gō, hôrn, tōōl, look; oil, out; up, fur; get; joy; yet; chin; she; thin, then; zh, leisure; ŋ, ring; ə for *a* in *ago, e* in *agent, i* in *sanity, o* in *comply, u* in *focus;* ' as in *able* (ā′b'l); Fr. bàl; ë, Fr. coeur; ö, Fr. feu; Fr. mon; ô, Fr. coq; ü, Fr. duc; r, Fr. cri; H, G. ich; kh, G. doch. See inside front cover. ☆ Americanism; ‡foreign; *hypothetical; < derived from

Bar·to·lom·me·o (bär′tō lôm mā′ō), Fra (born *Bartolommeo di Pagholo del Fattorino*) 1475?–1517; Florentine painter

Bar·ton (bär′t'n), **Clara** (born *Clarissa Harlowe Barton*) 1821–1912; U.S. philanthropist; founder of the American Red Cross (1881)

Ba·ruch (bə rōōk′), **Bernard Man·nes** (man′əs) 1870–1965; U.S. financier & statesman

Bar·uch (ber′ək) [Heb., lit., blessed] *Bible* **1.** Jeremiah's scribe: Jer. 36:4–6 **2.** a book of the Old Testament Apocrypha attributed to him

bar·y·on (bar′ē än′, ber′-) *n.* [< Gr. *barys*, heavy (see GRAVE[1]) + (ELECTR)ON] one of a class of heavy atomic particles, including the proton, neutron, and the hyperons

ba·ry·ta (bə rīt′ə) *n.* [ModL. < ff.] **1.** barium oxide **2.** barium hydroxide —**ba·ryt′ic** (-rit′ik) *adj.*

ba·ry·tes (-ēz) *n.* [ModL. < Gr. *barytēs*, weight < *barys*, heavy] *same as* BARITE

bar·y·tone (bar′ə tōn′, ber′-) *adj., n. same as* BARITONE

bas·al (bā′s'l) *adj.* **1.** of, at, or forming the base **2.** being the base or basis; basic; fundamental **3.** *Bot.* growing from the base of a stem —**bas′al·ly** *adv.*

basal anesthesia *Med.* anesthesia induced as a preliminary to further and deeper anesthesia

basal metabolism the quantity of energy used by any organism at rest; amount of heat produced by the human · organism fourteen to eighteen hours after eating and when at complete rest in a warm environment for thirty to sixty minutes but not asleep: it is measured by the rate (**basal metabolic rate**) at which heat is given off, and is expressed in calories per hour per square meter of skin surface

ba·salt (bə sôlt′; bās′ôlt, bas′-) *n.* [earlier *basaltes* < L., a dark Ethiopian marble, term used by Pliny for *basanites* < Gr. *basanitēs*, species of slate used to test gold] **1.** a dark, tough, fine-grained to dense, extrusive volcanic rock commonly occurring in sheetlike lava flows **2.** a kind of unglazed, black pottery designed by Josiah Wedgwood: also **ba·salt′ware′** —**ba·sal·tic** (bə sôl′tik) *adj.*

‡**bas bleu** (bä blö′) [Fr.] *same as* BLUESTOCKING

bas·cule (bas′kyōōl) *n.* [Fr., a seesaw] a device that works like a seesaw, being balanced so that when one end is lowered the other end is raised

bascule bridge a kind of drawbridge counterweighted so that it can be raised and lowered easily

base[1] (bās) *n., pl.* **bas′es** (-əz) [ME. < OFr. *bas* < L. *basis*, BASIS] **1.** the thing or part on which something rests; lowest part or bottom; foundation **2.** the fundamental or main part, as of a plan, organization, system, theory, etc. **3.** the principal or essential ingredient, or the one serving as a vehicle [paint with an oil *base*] **4.** anything from which a start is made; basis **5.** a goal, starting place, or safety point in certain games; specif., *Baseball* any of the four goals which must be reached safely one after the other to score a run **6.** the point of attachment of a part of the body [the *base* of the thumb] **7.** a center of operations or source of supply; headquarters, as of a military operation or exploring expedition **8.** *a)* the bottommost layer or coat, as of paint *b)* a makeup cream to give a desired color to the skin, esp. in the theater **9.** *Archit.* the lower part of a column, pier, wall, etc. **10.** *Chem.* a substance which forms a salt when it reacts with an acid; in terms of the theory of the dissociation of electrolytes, a compound, such as sodium hydroxide, which liberates hydroxyl ions in aqueous solutions; in terms of the modern theory of acids and bases, a substance that removes hydrogen ions (protons) from an acid and combines with them in a chemical reaction **11.** *Dyeing* a substance used for fixing colors **12.** *Geom.* the line or plane upon which a figure is thought of as resting [the *base* of a triangle] **13.** *Heraldry* the lower portion of a shield **14.** *Linguis.* any morpheme to which prefixes, suffixes, etc. are or can be added; stem or root **15.** *Math. a)* a whole number made the fundamental number, and raised to various powers to produce the major counting units, of a number system; radix *b)* the number that when raised to the logarithm of a given number produces the given number *c)* in business, etc., a figure or sum upon which certain calculations are made —*adj.* forming a base —*vt.* **based, bas′ing 1.** to make or form a base or foundation for **2.** to put or rest (*on*) as a base or basis [to base a guess on past experience] **3.** to place or station (*in* or *at* a base) —☆**off base 1.** *Baseball* not touching the base **2.** [Slang] taking a position, attitude, etc. that is unsound or in error

SYN.—**base**, as compared here, refers to a part or thing at the bottom acting as a support or underlying structure [the *base* of a lamp]; **basis**, conveying the same idea, is the term preferred for nonphysical things [the *basis* of a theory]; **foundation** stresses solidity in the underlying or supporting thing and often suggests permanence and stability in that which is built on it [the *foundation* of a house]; **groundwork**, closely synonymous with **foundation**, is principally applied to nonphysical things [the *groundwork* of a good education]

base[2] (bās) *adj.* [ME. & OFr. *bas* < VL. *bassus*, thick,

BASCULE BRIDGE

stumpy, low] **1.** having or showing little or no honor, courage, or decency; mean; ignoble; contemptible [a *base* coward, *base* ingratitude] **2.** of a menial or degrading kind [*base* servitude] **3.** inferior in quality **4.** [Now Rare] not classical or cultivated [*base* Latin] **5.** of comparatively low worth [iron is a *base* metal, gold a precious one] **6.** debased or counterfeit [*base* coin] **7.** *a)* having the low feudal status of villein *b)* held by one having this status [*base* tenure] **8.** [Archaic] low in height; short **9.** [Archaic] of servile, humble, or illegitimate birth **10.** [Obs.] low or inferior in place or position **11.** [Obs.] *same as* BASS[1] —*n.* [Obs.] *same as* BASS[1] —**base′ly** *adv.* —**base′ness** *n.*

SYN.—**base** implies a putting of one's own interests ahead of one's obligations, as because of greed or cowardice [*base* motives]; **mean** suggests a contemptible pettiness of character or conduct [his *mean* attempts to slander her]; **ignoble** suggests a lack of high moral or intellectual qualities [to work for an *ignoble* end]; **abject** implies debasement and a contemptible lack of self-respect [an *abject* servant]; **sordid** connotes the depressing drabness of that which is mean or base [the *sordid* details of their affair]; **vile** suggests disgusting foulness or depravity [*vile* epithets]; **low** suggests rather generally coarseness, vulgarity, depravity, etc., specif. in reference to taking grossly unfair advantage [so *low* as to kick a cripple's crutch]; **degrading** suggests a lowering or corruption of moral standards [the *degrading* aspects of army life] —ANT. **noble, moral, virtuous**

base·ball (bās′bôl′) *n.* ☆**1.** a game played with a hard, rawhide-covered ball and wooden bat by two opposing teams of nine players each: it is played on a field with four bases forming a diamond-shaped circuit which a runner must complete to score a run ☆**2.** the ball used

☆**base·board** (-bôrd′) *n.* **1.** a board or molding covering the edge of a wall next to the floor **2.** any board at or forming a base

base·born (-bôrn′) *adj.* **1.** of humble birth or origin **2.** of illegitimate birth **3.** mean or ignoble in character or spirit

☆**base·burn·er, base-burn·er** (-bur′nər) *n.* any stove or furnace in which more coal is fed automatically from above when that at the base is consumed

☆**base hit** *Baseball* a play in which the batter hits the ball and gets on base without benefit of an opponent's error and without forcing out a runner already on base

Ba·sel (bä′z'l) **1.** city in NW Switzerland, on the Rhine: pop. 213,000 **2.** canton of NW Switzerland: 179 sq. mi.; pop. 397,000

base·less (bās′lis) *adj.* having no basis in fact; unfounded —**base′less·ness** *n.*

base level *Geol.* **1.** the level below which a particular stream cannot erode its bed **2.** the theoretical limit below which dry lands cannot be eroded; sea level

base line 1. a line serving as a base; specif., *Surveying* a horizontal line measured with special accuracy to provide a base for survey by triangulation ☆**2.** *Baseball* the lane, six feet wide, between any two consecutive bases **3.** *Tennis* the line at the back at either end of the court

☆**base·man** (-mən) *n., pl.* **-men** (-mən) *Baseball* an infielder stationed at first, second, or third base

base map an outline map on which data may be plotted

base·ment (bās′mənt) *n.* [BASE[1] + -MENT] **1.** the foundation or lower part of a wall or structure **2.** the lowest story of a building, below the main floor and wholly or partly below the surface of the ground

basement complex a mass of rocks, often metamorphic and igneous, underlying stratified sedimentary rocks

ba·sen·ji (bə sen′jē) *n.* [Bantu < *ba-*, plural prefix + *senji*, altered < Fr. *singe*, a monkey: so named because of the monkeylike tail and face] any of an African breed of small dog that has a silky, reddish-brown coat and does not make a true barking sound

☆**base on balls** *Baseball same as* WALK

base pay the basic rate of pay for a particular job exclusive of overtime pay, bonuses, etc.

☆**base runner** *Baseball* any member of the team at bat who is on base or is trying to reach a base

bas·es[1] (bās′əz) *n. pl. of* BASE[1]

ba·ses[2] (bā′sēz) *n. pl. of* BASIS

bash (bash) *vt.* [echoic; akin to (? <) ON. *basca*, to strike] [Colloq.] to strike with a violent blow; smash (*in*) —*n.* **1.** [Colloq.] a violent blow **2.** [Slang] a gala event or party —**have a bash at** [Slang] to make an attempt at

Ba·shan (bā′shan) *Bible* fertile region east & northeast of the Sea of Galilee, in ancient Palestine

ba·shaw (bə shô′) *n.* [see PASHA] **1.** *same as* PASHA **2.** an important or self-important person

bash·ful (bash′fəl) *adj.* [(A)BASH + -FUL] **1.** timid, shy, and easily embarrassed **2.** showing an embarrassed timidity —*SYN.* see SHY[1] —**bash′ful·ly** *adv.* —**bash′ful·ness** *n.*

bash·i·ba·zouk (bash′ē bə zōōk′) *n.* [Turk. *bashi-bozuq* < *bashi*, headdress + *bozuq*, disorderly, unkempt] a member of the Turkish irregulars, troops notorious in the 19th cent. for their brutality

Bash·kir (bash kir′) *n., pl.* **-kirs′, -kir′ 1.** any member of a Turkic Moslem people of SW R.S.F.S.R. **2.** their language

bas·ic (bā′sik) *adj.* **1.** of, at, or forming a base; fundamental; essential **2.** constituting a basis or introduction; elementary [*basic* military training] **3.** *a) Chem.* of, having the nature of, or containing a base; alkaline *b)* designating, of, or resulting from a process of manufacturing steel in which the refractory lining of the furnace is a basic sub-

stance, as magnesite, and the basic slag in the charge serves as the refining agent **4.** *Geol.* designating or of igneous rocks with less than about 52 percent silica —*n.* **1.** a basic principle, factor, etc.: *usually used in pl.* **2.** basic military training —**bas′i·cal·ly** *adv.*

Basic English [British, American, Scientific, International, Commercial] a simplified form of the English language for international communication and for first steps into full English, devised by C. K. Ogden: it consists of a selected vocabulary of 850 essential words and is copyrighted

ba·sic·i·ty (bə sis′ə tē) *n. Chem.* **1.** the quality or condition of being a base **2.** the capacity of an acid to react with a base, measured by the number of chemical equivalents of a base with which one gram molecular weight of the acid reacts

basic oxygen process a procedure used in certain processes for refining steel in which oxygen is introduced into the melt to produce higher temperatures, conserve fuel, increase production, etc.

basic slag a slag of steel manufacture having low silica (and high alkaline) content: also used as a fertilizer

ba·sid·i·o·my·cete (bə sid′ē ō mī′sēt, -mi sēt′) *n.* [< BASIDIUM + -MYCETE] *Bot.* any of a class (Basidiomycetes) of fungi, including the mushrooms, rusts, smuts, and puffballs, that produce spores on basidia —**ba·sid′i·o·my·ce′tous** (-mi sēt′əs) *adj.*

ba·sid·i·o·spore (bə sid′ē ō spôr′) *n.* [< BASIDIUM + SPORE] a spore produced on a basidium —**ba·sid′i·o·spo′rous** (-spôr′əs) *adj.*

ba·sid·i·um (bə sid′ē əm) *n., pl.* **-i·a** (-ə) [ModL. < Gr. *basis*, base + ModL. thin suffix *-idium*] *Bot.* any of a number of club-shaped cells in basidiomycetous fungi, bearing a definite number of external spores (usually four) on short, slender stalks —**ba·sid′i·al** *adj.*

bas·i·fixed (bās′ə fikst′) *adj. Bot.* attached at the base

bas·i·fy (bās′ə fī′) *vt.* to change into a base; alkalize

Bas·il (baz′′l, bā′z′l) [L. *Basilius* < Gr. *Busileios*, lit., kingly < *basileus*, king] **1.** a masculine name **2.** Saint (called *Basil the Great*, 330?–379? A.D.; Gr. prelate, born in Cappadocia; bishop of Caesarea: his day is June 14 —**Ba·sil·i·an** (bə zil′ē ən, -sil′-) *adj.*

bas·il (baz′′l, bā′z′l) *n.* [ME. & OFr. *basile* < ML. *basilicum* < Gr. *basilikon* (*phyton*), basil, lit., royal (plant) < *basileus*, king] any of a group of fragrant plants of the mint family, esp. a white-flowered garden herb (*Ocimum basilicum*) whose leaves are used for flavoring in cooking

Ba·si·lan (bä sē′län) **1.** city comprising a group of islands in the Philippines, southwest of Mindanao: pop. 181,000 **2.** largest island of this group

bas·i·lar (bas′ə lər) *adj.* [ModL. *basilaris* < L. *basis*, BASIS] of or at the base, esp. of the skull: also **bas′i·lar′y** (-ler′ē)

ba·sil·ic (bə sil′ik) *adj.* [Fr. *basilique* < L. *basilicus* < Gr. *basilikos*: see BASIL] **1.** designating or of a large vein of the upper arm, on the inner side of the biceps muscle **2.** of a basilica; basilican **3.** [Obs.] kingly: also **ba·sil′i·cal**

ba·sil·i·ca (bə sil′i kə) *n., pl.* **-cas** [L. < Gr. *basilikē* (*stoa*), royal (portico) < *basilikos*: see BASIL] **1.** orig., a royal palace **2.** in ancient Rome, a rectangular building with a broad nave ending in an apse, and flanked by colonnaded aisles, used as a courtroom, public hall, etc. **3.** a Christian church built in this style **4.** *R.C.Ch.* any of a number of churches granted certain ceremonial rights —**ba·sil′i·can** (-kən) *adj.*

Ba·sil·i·ca·ta (bä sē′lē kä′tä) region in S Italy, on the Gulf of Taranto: 3,856 sq. mi.; pop. 648,000

bas·i·lisk (bas′ə lisk′) *n.* [ME. < L. *basiliscus* < Gr. *basiliskos*, dim. of *basileus*, king] **1.** a mythical lizardlike monster with supposedly fatal breath and glance, fabled to have been hatched by a serpent from a cock's egg: see also COCKATRICE **2.** any of several tropical American lizards (genus *Basiliscus*) with an erectile crest on the back and tail and an inflatable pouch on the head **3.** an obsolete kind of cannon

ba·sin (bās′′n) *n.* [ME. & OFr. *bacin* < VL. *baccinum* < *bacca*, water vessel] **1.** a round, wide, shallow container, as for holding water to wash in **2.** its contents or capacity **3.** a washbowl or sink **4.** any shallow, rounded hollow or depression, often containing water, as a pond **5.** a bay or harbor [yacht *basin*] **6.** all the land drained by a river and its branches **7.** a great hollow in the earth's surface filled by an ocean **8.** *Geol.* a wide, depressed area in which the rock layers all incline toward a center

bas·i·net (bas′ə nit) *n.* [ME. & OFr. *bacinet*, dim. of *bacin*, BASIN] a light, steel, medieval helmet

ba·si·on (bās′ē ən) *n.* [ModL. < Gr. *basis*: see BASIS] the midpoint of the front border of the foramen magnum

ba·sip·e·tal (bə sip′i t′l) *adj.* [< BASIC + -PETAL] *Bot.* developing or moving from the apex toward the base of the stem: used to describe the development of tissues or movement of hormones in plants

ba·sis (bā′sis) *n., pl.* **ba′ses** (-sēz) [L. < Gr., a base, pedestal < *bainein*, to go < IE. base *gwem-*, to go, come, whence COME, L. *venire*] **1.** the base, foundation, or chief supporting factor of anything **2.** the principal constituent of any-

thing **3.** the fundamental principle or theory, as of a system of knowledge —*SYN.* see BASE[1]

bask (bask, bäsk) *vi.* [ME. *basken*, to wallow (in blood); found only in Gower & Lydgate; < ?; modern use apparently due to Shakespeare's misunderstanding of Lydgate] **1.** to warm oneself pleasantly, as in the sunlight **2.** to enjoy a warm or pleasant feeling from being in a certain environment or situation [to *bask* in someone's favor] —*vt.* [Archaic] to expose to warmth

Bas·ker·ville (bas′kər vil), **John** 1706–75; Eng. printer & type designer

bas·ket (bas′kit, bäs′-) *n.* [ME.; origin obscure] **1.** a container made of interwoven cane, rushes, strips of wood, etc. and often having a handle or handles **2.** the amount that a basket will hold **3.** anything like a basket in shape or use **4.** the structure hung from a balloon to carry personnel and equipment ☆**5.** *Basketball* *a)* the goal, a round, open net hanging from a metal ring attached to a raised backboard *b)* a toss of the ball through this net, counted as a score when properly made

☆**bas·ket·ball** (-bôl′) *n.* **1.** a game played by two opposing teams of five players each, usually in a zoned floor area: points are scored by tossing a ball through a raised goal (basket) at the opponent's end of the playing court: the game was invented in 1891 by James A. Naismith of Springfield, Mass. **2.** the large, round, inflated ball used in this game

basket hilt a hilt with a basketlike guard for the hand, as on some swords —**bas′ket-hilt′ed** *adj.*

Basket Maker **1.** any of several early American Indian cultures of the southwestern U.S. (c. 100–700 A.D.) characterized by great skill in basket making and by the later development of basket molds for the construction and drying of mud pottery **2.** a member of the people who produced this culture

bas·ket-of-gold (-əv gōld′) *n.* a yellow-flowered perennial plant (*Alyssum saxatile*) of the mustard family, often used in borders

bas·ket·ry (bas′kə trē, bäs′-) *n.* **1.** the craft of making baskets **2.** baskets collectively; basketwork

basket star any of a genus (*Gorgonocephalus*) of small sea animals related to the starfish with narrow, branching, interlaced arms or rays: also called **basket fish**

basket weave a weave of fabrics resembling the weave used in basket making

bas·ket·work (bas′kit wurk′) *n.* work that is interlaced or woven like a basket; wickerwork

basking shark a large shark (*Cetorhinus maximus*) with small, weak teeth that feeds on plankton: often found basking on the surface in northern seas

Basle (bäl) *older name for* BASEL

bas mitz·vah, bas miz·vah (häs mits′və) *same as* BAT MITZVAH

bas·net (bas′nit) *n. same as* BASINET

ba·so·phile (bās′ə fil′, -fil′) *n.* [< BASIC + -PHILE] *Biol.* a cell or tissue that is readily stained with basic dyes: also **ba′so·phil′** (-fil′) —**ba′so·phil′ic** (-fil′ik) *adj.*

Basque (bask, bäsk) *n.* [Fr. < Sp. *Vasco*, ult. < L. *Vascones*, the Basques] **1.** any member of a certain people living in the western Pyrenees **2.** their language, which is unrelated to any other known language —*adj.* of the Basques, their language, etc.

basque (bask) *n.* [Fr. < Pr. *basto* < ?; altered by association with Fr. *basquine*, kind of petticoat < Sp. *basquina* < *basco*, *vasco*, BASQUE] a woman's tightfitting bodice or tunic

Basque Provinces region comprising three provinces in N Spain, inhabited by Basques: Sp. name, VASCONGADAS

Bas·ra (bus′rə, buz′-) port in SE Iraq, on the Shatt al Arab: pop. 328,000

bas-re·lief (bä′rə lēf′, bas′-) *n.* [Fr. < It. *basso-rilievo*: see BAS SO & RELIEF] sculpture in which figures are carved in a flat surface so that they project only a little from the background

bass[1] (bās) *n.* [ME. *bas*, BASE[2]; sp. influenced by It. *basso*] **1.** the range of the lowest male voice, below baritone **2.** a male voice of this range, or a man with such a voice **3.** a low, deep sound or tone, as of such a voice **4.** an instrument of the lowest range; specif., a double bass **5.** a musical part for such a voice or instrument —*adj.* of, for, or having the range of a bass

bass[2] (bas) *n., pl.* **bass, bass′es**: see PLURAL, II, D, 2 [ME. *bas*, earlier *bars* < OE. *baers* < IE. *bhor(s)-*, point, bristle (in reference to the dorsal fins), whence ON. *barr*, needle, G. *Barsch*, perch] any of various families of spiny-finned food and game fishes of fresh or salt water: cf.

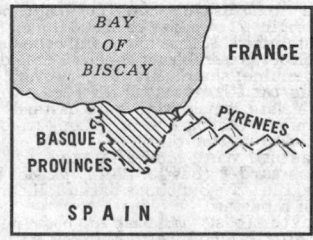

BASQUE PROVINCES

BLACK BASS, STRIPED BASS, ROCK BASS, CALICO BASS, WHITE BASS

bass³ (bas) *n.* **1.** *same as* BAST **2.** *same as* BASSWOOD

bass clef (bās) *Music* **1.** a sign on a staff, indicating the position of F below middle C on the fourth line: see CLEF, illus. **2.** the range of notes on a staff so marked

bass drum (bās) the largest and lowest-toned of the double-headed drums

bas·set¹ (bas'it) *n.* [OFr., short-legged dog, orig., short, dim. of *basse*, fem. of *bas*, BASE²] a kind of hound with a long body, short, crooked forelegs, and long, drooping ears, used in hunting: also **basset hound**

bas·set² (bas'it) *n.* [< ? Fr. *basset*, dim. of *basse*: see prec.] *Geol., Mining same as* OUTCROP —*vi.* to appear at or emerge above the surface

Basse·terre (bäs ter') seaport on St. Christopher island in the Leeward Islands, West Indies: capital of the Brit. self-governing territory of St. Christopher, Nevis, & Anguilla: pop. 16,000

Basse-Terre (bäs ter') **1.** W island of the two major islands of Guadeloupe, West Indies **2.** seaport on this island; capital of Guadeloupe: pop. 14,000 Also **Basse Terre**

basset horn a kind of clarinet pitched in F, between the B-flat clarinet and the bass clarinet in size

bass horn 1. orig., a brass-wind instrument related to the serpent **2.** a tuba

bas·si·net (bas'ə net') *n.* [altered (after Fr. *bassin*, BASIN) < Fr. *bercelonnette*, dim. of *berceau*, cradle] a basketlike bed for an infant: it is often hooded and set on a stand having casters

bass·ist (bās'ist) *n.* a person who plays the double bass

bas·so (bäs'ō, bäs'-; *It.* bäs'sō) *n., pl.* **bas'sos**; *It.* **bas'si** (-sē) [It., low < VL. *bassus*] a bass voice or singer

bas·soon (bə sōōn', ba-) *n.* [Fr. *basson* < It. *bassone* < prec.] a double-reed bass wood-wind instrument having a long, curved stem attached to the mouthpiece —**bas·soon'ist** *n.*

basso pro·fun·do (prə fun'dō, prō foon'-) [< It. *basso*, low + *profondo*, deep < L. *profundus*, PROFOUND] **1.** a very deep bass voice **2.** a man with such a voice

bas·so-re·lie·vo (-rə lē'vō) *n., pl.* **-vos** [It. *basso-rilievo*] *same as* BAS-RELIEF

‡bas·so-ri·lie·vo (bäs'sō rē lye' vō) *n., pl.* **bas'si-ri·lie'vi** (bäs'sē rē lye'vē) [It.] *same as* BAS-RELIEF

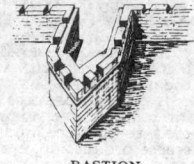

BASSOON

Bass Strait (bas) strait between Australia & Tasmania: 80–150 mi. wide

bass viol (bās) **1.** *same as* VIOLA DA GAMBA **2.** *same as* DOUBLE BASS

☆**bass·wood** (bas'wood') *n.* **1.** any of a genus (*Tilia*) of trees of the linden family, with light, soft, durable wood; linden **2.** its wood **3.** the tulip tree or its wood

bast (bast) *n.* [ME. < OE. *bæst*, inner bark of trees] **1.** phloem, a kind of plant tissue: see PHLOEM **2.** fiber obtained from phloem, used in making ropes, mats, etc.

‡bas·ta (bäs'tä) *interj.* [It.] (it is) enough!

bas·tard (bas'tərd) *n.* [ME. < OFr.; origin uncertain: *bast-* (also in *fils de bast*) < ? Goth. *bansts*, barn] **1.** a person born of parents not married to each other; illegitimate child **2.** anything spurious, inferior, or varying from standard **3.** a person regarded with contempt, hatred, pity, resentment, etc. or, sometimes, with playful affection: a vulgar usage —*adj.* **1.** of illegitimate birth or of uncertain origin **2.** of a size or shape that differs from the normal or standard **3.** that is not truly the designated thing but that closely resembles it [*gneiss* is called *bastard* granite] **4.** not genuine; sham; inferior —**bas'tard·ly** *adj.*

bas·tard·ize (bas'tər dīz') *vt.* **-ized', -iz'ing 1.** to make, declare, or show to be a bastard **2.** to make corrupt or inferior; debase —*vi.* [Rare] to become inferior —**bas'·tard·i·za'tion** *n.*

bastard wing *same as* ALULA

bas·tard·y (bas'tər dē) *n., pl.* **-ies** [ME. & OFr. *bastardie*] **1.** the state of being a bastard; illegitimacy **2.** the begetting of a bastard

baste¹ (bāst) *vt.* **bast'ed, bast'ing** [ME. *basten* < OFr. *bastir* < OHG. *bastian*, to sew with bast] to sew with long, loose stitches so as to keep the parts together until properly sewed; tack

baste² (bāst) *vt.* **bast'ed, bast'ing** [< OFr. *basser*, to moisten < *bassiner*, to moisten < *bassin*, BASIN] to moisten (meat) with melted butter, drippings, etc. while roasting — **bast'er** *n.*

baste³ (bāst) *vt.* **bast'ed, bast'ing** [ON. *beysta*] **1.** to beat soundly; thrash **2.** to attack with words; abuse

Bas·ti·a (bäs'tē ə) seaport on the NE coast of Corsica: pop. 50,000

bas·tille, bas·tile (bas tēl') *n.* [ME. *bastile* (Fr. *bastille*) < OFr. *bastir*, to build: see BASTION] **1.** in ancient warfare, a tower for defense or attack; small fortress **2.** a prison —**the Bastille** a state prison in Paris, stormed and destroyed (1789) in the French Revolution: its destruction is commemorated on Bastille Day, July 14

bas·ti·na·do (bas'tə nād'ō, -nā'dō) *n., pl.* **-does** [Sp.

bastonada < *bastón*, a stick] **1.** a beating or blow with a stick, usually on the soles of the feet, esp. as a method of punishment **2.** a rod, stick, or cudgel Also **bas'ti·nade'** (-nād') —*vt.* **-doed, -do·ing** to inflict the bastinado on

bast·ing (bās'tin) *n.* [< BASTE¹] **1.** the act of sewing with loose, temporary stitches **2.** loose, temporary stitches or the thread used for them

bas·tion (bas'chən; *occas.* -tē ən) *n.* [Fr. < It. *bastione* < *bastia* < *bastire*, to build < Gmc. *bastjan*, to make with bast, thatch, build < *bast*, bast] **1.** a projection from a fortification, arranged to give a wider firing range **2.** any fortified place; strong defense or bulwark: often used figuratively —**bas'tioned** *adj.*

Bas·togne (bas tōn'; *Fr.* bä stōn'y') town in SE Belgium: besieged by the German Army (1944) during a fierce counteroffensive in World War II

BASTION

Ba·su·to (bə sōōt'ō) *n.* any of a Bantu people living in the region of Lesotho (Basutoland)

Ba·su·to·land (bə sōōt'ō land') *former name of* LESOTHO

bat¹ (bat) *n.* [ME. < OE. *batt*, cudgel (prob. < W. *bat* < IE. base *bhat-*, to strike) & < OFr. *batte*, pestle < *battre*, BATTER¹] **1.** any stout club, stick, or cudgel **2.** a club used to strike the ball in baseball and cricket **3.** a ping-pong paddle, squash racket, etc. ☆**4.** a turn at batting, as in baseball [to be at *bat*] **5.** [Brit.] a batsman at cricket **6.** [*usually pl.*] cotton batting, esp. of an inferior quality; batt **7.** a jockey's riding crop **8.** [Colloq.] a blow or hit ☆**9.** [Slang] a drinking bout; spree **10.** [Brit. Colloq.] fast pace; speed **11.** *Ceramics* a plaster disk on which the clay is based in modeling —*vt.* **bat'ted, bat'ting 1.** to strike with or as with a bat **2.** to have a batting average of: see BATTING AVERAGE —*vi.* **1.** to use a bat, as in games **2.** to take a turn at batting —☆**bat around** [Slang] **1.** to travel or roam about **2.** to consider or discuss (an idea, plan, etc.) freely and informally —☆**bat out** [Slang] to create or compose quickly or hastily —☆**go to bat for** [Colloq.] to intervene on behalf of; defend —☆**(right) off the bat** [Colloq.] immediately

bat² (bat) *n.* [altered < ME. *bakke* < Scand.: OSw. *backa*] any of an order (Chiroptera) of mouselike flying mammals with a furry body and membranous wings: the insectivores are usually seen flying at night when they capture their prey by echolocation —**blind as a bat** quite blind —☆**have bats in the** (or **one's**) **belfry** [Slang] to be insane; have crazy notions

bat³ (bat) *vt.* **bat'ted, bat'ting** [ME. *baten*, to flap (wings) < OFr. *battre*, BATTER¹] **1.** to wink; blink; flutter —**not bat an eye** (or **eyelash**) [Colloq.] not show surprise

Ba·taan (bə tan', -tän') peninsula on SW Luzon, the Philippines: in World War II, scene of a Japanese victory over American-Filipino forces after bitter fighting

Ba·ta·vi·a (bə tā'vē ə) *former* (*Du.*) *name of* JAKARTA

batch¹ (bach) *n.* [ME. *bache* < OE. *bacan*, BAKE] **1.** the amount (of bread, etc.) produced at one baking **2.** the amount of material, as dough, needed for one operation **3.** the quantity of anything made in one operation or lot **4.** a number of things or persons taken as a group; lot; set

☆**batch**² (bach) *same as* BACH

bate¹ (bāt) *vt.* **bat'ed, bat'ing** [ME. < *abaten*, ABATE] **1.** to abate, lessen, lower, etc. **2.** [Archaic] to deprive (of) — **with bated breath** with the breath held in because of fear, excitement, etc.

bate² (bāt) *vt., vi.* **bat'ed, bat'ing** [prob. var. of BAIT; akin to G. *beissen*, to soak in lye] *Tanning* to soften by soaking in an alkaline solution —*n.* an alkaline solution for this purpose

☆**ba·teau** (ba tō') *n., pl.* **-teaux'** (-tōz') [Fr. < OFr. *batel* < OE. *bat*, boat] a lightweight, flat-bottomed river boat with tapering ends, used chiefly in Canada and Louisiana —*adj.* designating a wide, shallow neckline, as on a woman's dress, extending to the shoulders

bat·fish (bat'fish') *n., pl.* **-fish'**, **-fish'es**: see FISH² [BAT² + FISH²] any of various strangely shaped marine fishes; esp., *a)* any of a family (Ogcocephalidae) of angler fishes *b)* a stingray (*Aetobatus californicus*) of California *c)* *same as* FLYING GURNARD

bat·fowl (bat'foul') *vi.* [BAT¹ + FOWL] to catch birds at night by blinding them with a light, and netting or hitting them when they fly toward it —**bat'fowl'er** *n.*

Bath (bath, bäth) city in SW England: pop. 83,000: health resort known for its hot springs

bath¹ (bath, bäth) *n., pl.* **baths** (ba*th*z, bä*th*z; baths, bäths) [ME. < OE. *bæth* < IE. base *bhe-*, to warm, whence BAKE] **1.** a washing or dipping of a thing, esp. the body, in water or other liquid, steam, etc. **2.** water or other liquid for bathing, or for dipping, cleaning, soaking, regulating

BAT
(3 1/2 in. long)

temperature, etc.   3. a container for such liquid   4. a bathtub   5. a bathroom   6. *a)* a building or set of rooms for bathing   *b)* [*pl.*] in ancient Greece and Rome, a building used for public bathing, relaxation, etc. and as a social center   7. [*often pl.*] a resort where bathing is part of the medical treatment; spa   8. the condition of being covered with a liquid   9. *Chem. a)* a material that acts as a medium for regulating the temperature of things put in or on it   *b)* the container for this   10. *Metallurgy* molten metal in a furnace   11. *Photog.* the solution used in developing and fixing —*vt., vi.* [Brit.] *same as* BATHE

bath² (bäth) *n.* [Heb.] an ancient Hebrew liquid measure, variously estimated as equaling from 6 to 10 gal.

Bath brick [after BATH, England, where first made] a brick-shaped piece of earth containing carbonate of lime or of calcium, used for cleaning polished metal

Bath chair a hooded wheelchair of a kind used at Bath, England

bathe (bā*th*) *vt.* **bathed, bath′ing** [ME. *bathen* < OE. *bathian* < *bæth*, BATH¹] 1. to put into a liquid; immerse 2. to give a bath to; wash 3. to wet or moisten [sweat *bathed* his brow] 4. to cover or envelop as if with liquid [the trees are *bathed* in moonlight] —*vi.* 1. to take a bath; bathe oneself 2. to go into or be in a body of water so as to swim, cool oneself, etc. 3. to soak oneself in some substance or influence —*n.* [Brit.] a bathing in the sea, a pool, etc.; a swim —**bath·er** (bā*th*′ər) *n.*

ba·thet·ic (bə thet′ik) *adj.* [< BATHOS by analogy with PATHETIC] characterized by bathos —**ba·thet′i·cal·ly** *adv.*

bath·house (bäth′hous′, bäth′-) *n.* 1. a public building where people can take baths ☆2. a building used by bathers for changing clothes

☆**Bath·i·nette** (bath′ə net′, bäth′-) [< BATH¹, after BASSINET] *a trademark for* a portable folding bathtub for babies, made of rubberized cloth, etc. —*n.* [b-] a bathtub of this kind

bathing cap a tightfitting cap of rubber, plastic, etc. worn to keep the hair from getting wet in swimming

☆**bathing suit** a garment worn for swimming; swimsuit

bath·mat (bath′mat′, bäth′-) *n.* a mat used in or next to a bathtub, as to prevent slipping

batho- (bath′ə, -ō) [< Gr. *bathos*, depth] *a combining form meaning* depth [*bathometer*]

bath·o·lith (bath′ə lith′) *n.* [BATHO- + -LITH] a large, deep-seated rock intrusion, usually granite, often forming the base of a mountain range, and uncovered only by erosion: also **bath′o·lite′** (-līt′)

ba·thom·e·ter (bə thäm′ə tər) *n.* [BATHO- + -METER] an instrument for measuring water depths

ba·thos (bā′thäs, -thôs) *n.* [Gr. *bathos*, depth] 1. an abrupt change from the lofty to the ordinary or trivial in writing or speech; anticlimax 2. false pathos; sentimentality 3. hackneyed quality; triteness —*SYN.* see PATHOS

☆**bath·robe** (bath′rōb′, bäth′-) *n.* a long, loose coat for wear to and from the bath, in lounging, etc.

bath·room (-rōōm′) *n.* a room with a bathtub, toilet, washstand, etc.

Bath·she·ba (bath shē′bə, bath′shi bə) [Heb. *Bathsheba*, lit., daughter of Sheba, daughter of the oath] *Bible* the mother of Solomon by King David, whom she married after he had sent her first husband, Uriah, to death in battle: II Sam. 11

☆**bath·tub** (bath′tub′, bäth′-) *n.* a tub, now usually a bathroom fixture, in which to take a bath

Bath·urst (bath′ərst, bäth′-) capital of Gambia; a seaport on the Atlantic: pop. 28,000

bath·y- (bath′ə) [< Gr. *bathys*, deep] *a combining form meaning* deep, of the sea depths [*bathysphere*]

bath·y·al (bath′ē əl) *adj.* [BATHY- + -AL] designating or of the ocean depths

ba·thym·e·try (bə thim′ə trē) *n.* [BATHY- + -METRY] 1. the science of measuring the depths of oceans, seas, etc. 2. the study of the depth range and distribution of marine life —**bath·y·met·ric** (bath′ə met′rik), **bath′y·met′ri·cal** *adj.* —**bath′y·met′ri·cal·ly** *adv.*

bath·y·scaph (bath′ə skaf′) *n.* [Fr., coined by A. PICCARD < Gr. *bathys*, deep + *skaphē*, boat] a deep-sea diving apparatus for reaching great depths without a cable: it consists of a navigable, ballasted, submarine-shaped float filled with a fluid lighter than water, and a steel observation cabin: also **bath′y·scaphe′** (-skaf′, -skäf′)

☆**bath·y·sphere** (-sfir′) *n.* [BATHY- + -SPHERE; coined c. 1930 by C. W. BEEBE] a round, watertight observation chamber lowered by cables into sea depths

BATHYSCAPH

bath·y·ther·mo·graph (bath′ə thur′mə graf) *n.* [BATHY- + THERMOGRAPH] a device for measuring the temperature of the oceans to depths of 900 ft.

ba·tik (bə tēk′, bat′ik) *n.* [Malay] 1. a method of dyeing designs on cloth by coating with removable wax the parts not to be dyed 2. cloth so decorated or a design made in this way —*adj.* of or like batik

bat·ing (bāt′iŋ) *prep.* [prp. of BATE¹] [Archaic] except for; excluding

ba·tiste (ba tēst′, bə-) *n.* [Fr. < OFr. *baptiste*: so called from the supposed original maker, *Baptiste* of Cambrai] a fine, thin cloth of cotton, linen, rayon, wool, etc.

bat·man (bat′mən) *n., pl.* **-men** (mən) [bat, packsaddle (only in comb.) < Fr. *bat* < OFr. *bast* < ML. *bastum* + MAN] the orderly of an officer in the British army

☆**bat mitz·vah, bat miz·vah** (bät mitz′və; Heb. bät′mits vä′) [Heb. *bat mitswäh*, daughter of the commandment] [*also* B- M-] 1. a Jewish girl who, in Conservative and Reform congregations, undergoes a ceremony analogous to that of a bar mitzvah 2. the ceremony itself

ba·ton (bə tän′, ba-) *n.* [Fr. *baton* < OFr. *baston* < VL. *basto*, a stick] 1. a staff serving as a symbol of office 2. a short, narrow, diagonal bend on a coat of arms: in England, such a bend placed sinisterly and cut short at both ends indicated bastardy: cf. BEND SINISTER 3. a slender stick used by a conductor in directing an orchestra, choir, etc. ☆4. a hollow metal rod, with a knob at one end, twirled in a showy way by a drum major or drum majorette 5. the short, light rod passed from one runner to the next in a relay race 6. [Brit.] a policeman's billy; truncheon

Bat·on Rouge (bat′n rōōzh′) [Fr. transl. of Choctaw *itu-úma*, red pole, a boundary mark] capital of La., on the Mississippi: pop. 166,000

ba·tra·chi·an (bə trā′kē ən) *adj.* [< ModL. *Batrachia* < Gr. *batracheios*, relating to frogs < *batrachos*, frog] of, like, or concerning amphibians without tails, as frogs and toads —*n.* an amphibian without a tail; frog or toad

bats (bats) *adj.* [Slang] insane; crazy

bats·man (bats′mən) *n., pl.* **-men** (-mən) the batter in cricket

batt (bat) *n. same as* BAT¹ (*n.* 6)

bat·tal·ion (bə tal′yən) *n.* [Fr. *bataillon* < It. *battaglione* < *battaglia* < VL. *battalia*, BATTLE¹] 1. a large group of soldiers arrayed for battle 2. any large group joined together in some activity 3. *U.S. Army* a tactical unit made up of three or more companies, batteries, or analogous units: it is normally commanded by a lieutenant colonel and is the basic building unit of a division

bat·ten¹ (bat′n) *n.* [var. of BATON] 1. a sawed strip of wood, flooring, etc. 2. a strip of wood put over a seam between boards as a fastening or covering 3. a short, flexible strip of wood inserted in a sail to keep it flat 4. a strip used to fasten canvas over a ship's hatchways —*vt.* 1. to fasten with battens 2. to supply or strengthen with battens —**batten down the hatches** to fasten canvas over the hatches, esp. in preparing for a storm

bat·ten² (bat′n) *vi.* [ON. *batna*, to improve < IE. base *bhad-*, good, whence BETTER¹] 1. to grow fat; thrive 2. to be well fed or wealthy at another's expense —*vt.* to fatten up; overfeed

bat·ten³ (bat′n) *n.* [Fr. *battant*, orig. prp. of *battre* < OFr. *batre*: see ff.] in a loom, the movable frame that presses into place the threads of a woof

bat·ter¹ (bat′ər) *vt.* [ME. *bateren* < OFr. *batre* < VL. *battere* < L. *battuere*, to beat; also, in part, freq. of BAT¹, *v.*] 1. to beat or strike with blow after blow; pound 2. to break to bits by pounding 3. to injure by pounding, hard wear, or use —*vi.* to pound noisily and repeatedly —*n. Printing* 1. a broken place on the face of type or of a plate 2. the imperfect impression resulting from this

bat·ter² (bat′ər) *n.* the baseball or cricket player whose turn it is to bat

bat·ter³ (bat′ər) *n.* [ME. & OFr. *bature*, prob. < *batre*: see BATTER¹] a flowing mixture of flour, milk, eggs, etc. for making cakes, pancakes, etc.

bat·ter⁴ (bat′ər) *vt., vi.* [origin obscure] to slope gradually upward and backward —*n.* a gradual upward and backward slope, as of the outer face of a wall

bat·ter·ing ram (bat′ər iŋ ram′) 1. an ancient military machine having a heavy wooden beam, sometimes with an iron ram's head at its end, for battering down gates, walls, etc. 2. any bar, log, etc. used like this to force entrance

BATTERING RAM

Bat·ter·sea (bat′ər sē) metropolitan borough of London, on the south bank of the Thames: pop. 103,000

bat·ter·y (bat′ər ē, bat′rē) *n., pl.* **-ter·ies** [Fr. *batterie* < *battre*: see BATTER¹] 1. the act of battering, beating, or pounding 2. machinery used in battering 3. a group of similar things arranged, connected, or used together; set or series; array [a *battery* of microphones, a

battery of school achievement tests*]* ☆4. *Baseball* the pitcher and the catcher 5. *Elec.* a connected group of cells (or popularly, a single cell) storing an electrical charge and capable of furnishing a current 6. *Law* any illegal beating or touching of another person either directly or with an object: see ASSAULT AND BATTERY 7. *Mil.* *a)* an emplacement for heavy guns or a fortification equipped with such guns *b)* a set of heavy guns, rockets, etc. *c)* the men who operate such guns: usually the basic unit of artillery, equivalent to an infantry company 8. *Music* the percussion instruments of an orchestra 9. *Navy* the guns, or a specific set of the guns, of a warship —**in battery** in firing position after recovery from the recoil of a previous discharge: said of a heavy gun —**the Battery** a park in New York City, at the S tip of Manhattan: 21 acres: also called **Battery Park**

bat·tik (bat′ik) *n., adj., vt. same as* BATIK

bat·ting (bat′iŋ; *for 2, often* bat′'n) *n.* 1. the action of a person who bats, as in baseball ☆2. [see BATT] cotton, wool, or synthetic fiber wadded into sheets and used in bandages, quilts, etc.

☆**batting average** 1. a number expressing the average effectiveness of a baseball player's batting, figured by dividing the number of safe hits by the number of times at bat 2. [Colloq.] the average level of competence or success reached by a person in any activity

bat·tle[1] (bat′'l) *n.* [ME. & OFr. *bataille* < VL. *battalia* < L. *battualia*, exercises of gladiators and soldiers in fighting and fencing < *battuere:* see BATTER[1]] 1. a fight, esp. a large-scale engagement, between armed forces on land, at sea, or in the air 2. armed fighting; combat or war 3. any fight or struggle; conflict 4. [Archaic] a battalion —*vt.* **-tled, -tling** to oppose as in a battle; fight —*vi.* 1. to take part in a battle; fight 2. to struggle; contend —**give** (or **do**) **battle** to engage in battle; fight —**bat′tler** *n.*

SYN.—**battle** denotes a conflict between armed forces in a war and implies a large-scale, prolonged contest over a particular area; **engagement**, the more formal term, stresses the actual meeting of opposing forces, with no restrictive connotation as to duration; a **campaign** is a series of military operations with a particular objective and may involve a number of battles; **encounter** usually suggests a chance meeting of hostile forces; **skirmish** refers to a brief, light encounter between small detachments; **action** stresses the detailed operations of active fighting *[*killed in *action]*; **combat**, the most general of these terms, simply implies armed fighting, without further qualification

bat·tle[2] (bat′'l) *vt.* [Archaic] to build battlements on (a fort, etc.)

bat·tle-ax, bat·tle-axe (-aks′) *n.* 1. a heavy ax with a wide blade, formerly used as a weapon of war ☆2. [Slang] a woman who is harsh, domineering, etc.

Battle Creek [after an encounter (1824) between surveyors and Indians] city in SW Mich.: pop. 39,000

battle cruiser a large warship with longer range and greater speed and maneuverability than a battleship, but less heavily armored

battle cry a cry or slogan used to encourage those in a battle, struggle, contest, etc.

bat·tle·dore (bat′'l dôr′) *n.* [ME. *batildore* < ? Pr. *batedor*, beater] 1. a flat paddle or racket used to hit a shuttlecock back and forth in a game (called **battledore and shuttlecock**) similar to badminton 2. this game

battle fatigue *same as* COMBAT FATIGUE

bat·tle·field (bat′'l fēld′) *n.* 1. the site of a battle 2. any area of conflict Also **bat′tle·ground′**

battle group in a pentomic military organization, a major unit of an infantry or airborne division, made up of five companies

bat·tle·ment (-mənt) *n.* [ME. *batelment* < OFr. *batailler*, to fortify with battlements < *bataille*, fortification on a wall or tower < ? VL. **battacula*, place of battle < *battere*, BATTER[1]] 1. a low wall with open spaces for shooting, built on top of a castle wall, tower, or fort 2. an architectural decoration like this —**bat′tle·ment′ed** (-men′tid) *adj.*

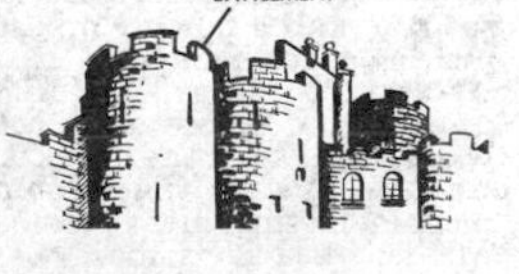
BATTLEMENT

battle royal *pl.* **battles royal** 1. a fight or bout involving several or many contestants; free-for-all 2. a long, bitterly fought battle 3. a heated dispute

bat·tle-scarred (-skärd′) *adj.* having scars from wounds received in combat or in fights

☆**bat·tle·ship** (-ship′) *n.* any of a class of large warships with the biggest guns and very heavy armor

battle stations the places to which soldiers, sailors, warships, etc. are assigned for a battle or an emergency

☆**bat·tle·wag·on** (-wag′ən) *n.* [Slang] a battleship

bat·tue (ba to͞o′, -tyo͞o′) *n.* [Fr., fem. pp. of *battre*, to beat: cf. BATTER[1]] 1. a beating of underbrush and woods to drive game out toward hunters 2. a hunt of this kind 3. any mass killing

bat·ty (bat′ē) *adj.* **-ti·er, -ti·est** [< BAT[2] + -Y[2]] 1. of or like a bat 2. [Slang] *a)* mentally deranged; insane; crazy *b)* odd; eccentric

Ba·tu·mi (bä to͞o′mē) seaport in the Georgian S.S.R., on the Black Sea: pop. 82,000: also called **Ba·tum′** (-to͞om′)

bat·wing (bat′wiŋ′) *adj.* shaped like a bat's wing

bau·ble (bô′b'l) *n.* [ME. *babel* < OFr. *baubel, belbel*, prob. redupl. of *bel* < L. *bellus*, pretty] 1. a showy but worthless or useless thing; trinket, trifle, etc. 2. [Archaic] a jester's baton with an ornament at the end

Bau·cis (bô′sis) *Gr. Myth.* a poor, old woman who, with her husband, Philemon, showed such hospitality to the disguised Zeus and Hermes that the grateful gods turned their humble cottage into a temple

baud (bôd) *n.* [after J. M. E. *Baudot*, 19th-c. Fr. inventor] 1. a unit of signaling speed in telegraphic code 2. the number of bits per second that can be transmitted in a given computer system

bau·de·kin (bô′də kən) *n.* [ME. < OFr. *baudequin*] [Archaic] *same as* BALDACHIN

Baude·laire (bōd ler′), (**Pierre**) **Charles** (shȧrl) 1821–67; Fr. poet & essayist

Bau·douin I (bō dwan′) 1930– ; king of Belgium (1951–): son of LEOPOLD III

bau·drons (bô′drənz) *n.* [Scot.] a cat: an epithet used without an article

Bau·er (bou′ər), **Harold** 1873–1951; U.S. pianist, born in England

Bau·haus (bou′hous′) [G. < *bauen*, to build + *haus*, a house] the architectural school of Walter Gropius, founded in Germany, 1919: it promoted a synthesis of painting, sculpture, and architecture and the adaptation of science and technology to architecture

baulk (bôk) *n., vt., vi. same as* BALK

Baum (bôm, bäm), **Lyman Frank** 1856–1919; U.S. writer of children's books, including the *Oz* books

Bau·mé (bō mā′) *adj.* [after Antoine *Baumé* (1728–1804), Fr. chemist] designating or of either of two hydrometer scales used to indicate specific gravity

baum marten (boum) [< G. *baummarder* < *baum*, tree + *marder*, marten] the brown fur of the European marten

baux·ite (bôk′sīt, bō′zīt) *n.* [Fr. < (*Les*) *Baux*, town near Arles] the claylike ore, mainly hydrated aluminum oxide, from which aluminum is obtained

Ba·var·i·a (bə ver′ē ə) state of S West Germany: formerly a duchy, a kingdom, & a republic: 27,239 sq. mi.; pop. 9,976,000; cap. Munich: Ger. name, BAYERN

Ba·var·i·an (-ən) *adj.* of Bavaria, its people, dialect, etc. —*n.* 1. a native or inhabitant of Bavaria 2. the High German dialect of the Bavarians and Austrians

Bavarian cream a dessert made with gelatin, whipped cream, eggs, and fruit flavoring

baw·bee (bô′bē) *n.* [prob. < *siller* (Scot. for SILVER) *bawby*, jocular for name of the laird of *Sillebawby*, a mint master] [Scot.] a halfpenny or any small coin

baw·cock (bô′käk′) *n.* [< Fr. *beau*, fine + *coq*, COCK[1]] [Archaic] a good fellow

bawd (bôd) *n.* [ME. *baude*, lewd person < ? OFr. *baud*, gay, licentious (< Frank. *bald*, bold), whence Fr. *baudet*, donkey, also (in Picardy) loose woman] 1. [Now Literary] a person, now esp. a woman, who keeps a brothel; madam 2. [Rare] a prostitute

bawd·ry (bô′drē) *n.* [ME. & OFr. *bauderie*, gaiety: see BAWD] 1. obscene language; bawdiness 2. [Archaic] the occupation of a bawd

bawd·y (bô′dē) *adj.* **bawd′i·er, bawd′i·est** characteristic of a bawd; indecent, obscene, salacious, etc. —**bawd′i·ly** *adv.* —**bawd′i·ness** *n.*

bawd·y·house (-hous′) *n.* a house of prostitution

bawl (bôl) *vi., vt.* [ME. *baulen* (found only in gerund) < ML. *baulare*, to bark & ? ON. *baula*, to low like a cow; both of echoic origin] 1. to shout or call out noisily; bellow; yell 2. to weep and wail loudly —*n.* 1. an outcry; bellow 2. a noisy weeping —**bawl out** 1. to shout or call out ☆2. [Slang] to scold angrily —**bawl′er** *n.*

Bax·ter (bak′stər), **Richard** 1615–91; Eng. Puritan minister

bay[1] (bā) *n.* [ME. *bai* < OFr. *baie* < ML. *baia*, prob. a misunderstanding (by Isidore of Seville) of L. *Baiae*, a favorite Roman coastal resort, hence any bathing resort] 1. a part of a sea or lake, indenting the shore line; wide inlet not so large as a gulf ☆2. any level land area making an indentation, as into a woods, range of hills, etc.

bay[2] (bā) *n.* [ME. *bai* < OFr. *baée* < *baer, bayer*, to gape, yawn < VL. *batare*, to gape] 1. *a)* an opening or alcove marked off by pillars, columns, etc. *b)* a recess in a wall, as for a window *c) same as* BAY WINDOW 2. a part of a building projecting from the main part; wing 3. a compartment or space; specif., *a)* a bin in a barn, for storing hay or grain *b)* a compartment in an aircraft *[*bomb *bay*, cargo *bay]* 4. *same as* SICK BAY

bay[3] (bā) *vi.* [ME. *baien, abaien* < OFr. *baier, abaier* < VL. **adbatare* < *ad*, at + *batare*, to gape] to bark or howl in long, deep tones —*vt.* 1. to bark at; howl at 2. to chase with yelps and barks 3. to bring to or hold at bay 4. to utter in long, deep tones —*n.* 1. the sound of baying 2. the situation of or as of a hunted animal forced to turn and fight —**at bay** 1. with escape cut off; cornered 2. unable to advance; held off *[*the bear kept the hunters *at bay]* —**bring to bay** to force into a situation that makes escape impossible; corner

bay[4] (bā) *n.* [ME. *bai* < OFr. *baie* < L. *baca*, berry] 1. *same as* LAUREL (*n.* 1) 2. [*pl.*] *a)* a wreath of bay leaves, a classical token of honor given to poets and conquerors *b)* honor; fame 3. any of various trees or shrubs resembling the laurel, as rosebay

bay⁵ (bā) *adj.* [ME. *bai* < OFr. *baie* < L. *badius*] reddish-brown: said esp. of horses —*n.* **1.** a horse (or other animal) of this color **2.** reddish brown

ba·ya·dere, ba·ya·deer (bā′ya dir′) *n.* [Fr. *bayadère;* Port. *bailadeira,* dancer < *bailar,* dance < LL. *ballare:* see BALL²] a fabric or design with horizontal stripes, usually brightly colored —*adj.* striped horizontally

Ba·ya·món (bä′yä môn′) city in NE Puerto Rico, near San Juan: pop. 146,000

bay antler *same as* BEZ ANTLER

bay·ard (bā′ərd) *n.* [ME. & OFr. *baiard* < *baie,* BAY⁵ + *-ard,* -ARD] [Archaic] a bay horse —[B-] a magic horse in medieval romances

Ba·yard (bā yàr′; E. bā′ərd), Chevalier de (born *Pierre Terrail*) 1473?–1524; Fr. military hero: known as *chevalier sans peur et sans reproche* (the fearless & irreproachable knight)

bay·ber·ry (bā′ber′ē, -bər ē) *n., pl.* **-ries** ☆**1.** *a)* any of a genus (*Myrica*) of shrubs, as the wax myrtle, having a small, berrylike fruit covered with a wax used in making candles *b)* the fruit **2.** a tropical American tree (*Pimenta racemosa*) of the myrtle family, that yields an aromatic oil used in the preparation of bay rum

Bay City city in E Mich., a river port: pop. 49,000

Bay·ern (bī′ərn) *Ger. name of* BAVARIA

Ba·yeux Tapestry (bä yöö′; *Fr.* bà yö′) an embroidered length of linen, 231 feet long and 19 1/2 inches wide, probably of the 11th cent., in the museum of Bayeux, in NW France, picturing incidents of the Norman conquest and events leading up to it

Bay·kal (bī käl′), Lake *same as* Lake BAIKAL

Bayle (bel), **Pierre** 1647–1706; Fr. critic & philosopher

bay leaf the aromatic leaf of the laurel, dried and used as a spice in cooking

☆**bay lynx** a common wildcat (*Lynx rufus*) of N. America

bay·o·net (bā′ə nit, -net′; bā′ə net′) *n.* [Fr. *bayonnette* < *Bayonne,* France, where first made] **1.** a detachable, daggerlike blade put on the muzzle end of a rifle, for hand-to-hand fighting **2.** a part like a bayonet in shape, manner of attachment, etc.

BAYONET

—*vt., vi.* **-net′ed** or **-net′ted, -net′ing** or **-net′ting** to stab, prod, or kill with a bayonet

Ba·yonne (bā yōn′; *for 2 Fr.* bà yōn′) **1.** city in NE N.J.: pop. 73,000 **2.** city in SW France: pop. 37,000

☆**bay·ou** (bī′ōō, -ō) *n.* [AmFr. < Choctaw *bayuk,* small stream] in some parts of the southern U.S., a sluggish, marshy inlet or outlet of a lake, river, etc.

Bay·reuth (bī roit′, bī′roit) city in NE Bavaria: pop. 61,000: known for its annual Wagnerian music festivals

bay rum an aromatic liquid formerly obtained from leaves of a bayberry tree, now made of certain oils, water, and alcohol: it is used in medicines and cosmetics

Bay State *nickname of* MASSACHUSETTS —**Bay Stater**

Bay·town (bā′toun′) city in SE Tex., on Galveston Bay, near Houston: pop. 44,000

bay window 1. a window or set of windows jutting out from the wall of a building and forming an alcove within, esp. one rising from ground level ☆**2.** [Slang] a large, protruding belly

bay·wood (bā′wood′) *n.* a soft, light kind of mahogany (*Swietenia macrophylla*) from the bay region of SE Mexico

ba·zaar (bə zär′) *n.* [Per. *bāzār,* a market] **1.** in Oriental countries, a market or street of shops and stalls **2.** a shop for selling various kinds of goods **3.** a sale of various articles, usually to raise money for a club, church, etc.

ba·zoo (bə zōō′) *n.* [prob. < Du. *bazuin,* trumpet] [Slang] **1.** the mouth **2.** the nose **3.** loud or boastful talk

☆**ba·zoo·ka** (bə zōō′kə) *n.* [extension of BAZOO: name applied by Bob Burns (189?–1956), U.S. comedian, to a comic horn consisting of two gas pipes and a whiskey funnel] a weapon of metal tubing, for aiming and launching electrically fired, armor-piercing rockets

b.b., bb base on balls

B.B.A. Bachelor of Business Administration

B battery an electric battery used in the plate circuit and the screen-grid circuit of certain vacuum tubes: it is usually made up of a number of dry cells in series

BBC British Broadcasting Corporation

bbl. *pl.* **bbls.** barrel

☆**BB (shot)** [a designation of the size] a size of shot measuring .18 of an inch in diameter, fired from an air rifle (**BB gun**) or shotgun

B.C. 1. before Christ **2.** British Columbia

B.C.E. 1. Bachelor of Civil Engineering **2.** before the Common Era

BCG (vaccine) [*bacillus Calmette-Guérin,* after A.L.C. *Calmette* (1863–1933) & A.F.M. *Guérin* (1816–95), Fr. physicians who developed it] a vaccine prepared from an attenuated strain of the tubercle bacillus and used for immunization against tuberculosis

bch. *pl.* **bchs.** bunch

B.Ch.E. Bachelor of Chemical Engineering

B.C.L. 1. Bachelor of Canon Law **2.** Bachelor of Civil Law

B complex *same as* VITAMIN B (COMPLEX)

BC soil a soil that contains the B and C horizons only: see ABC SOIL

bd. *pl.* **bds. 1.** board **2.** bond **3.** bound

B/D bank draft

b/d barrels per day

B.D. 1. Bachelor of Divinity **2.** bills discounted

bdel·li·um (del′ē əm) *n.* [ME. < L. < Gr. *bdellion;* of Oriental origin (as in Assyr. *budulḫu,* Heb. *b'dōlakh*)] **1.** a myrrhlike gum resin **2.** any of a genus (*Commiphora*) of trees yielding this **3.** *Bible* a jewel variously interpreted as being a carbuncle (Gen. 2:12), a crystal (Num. 11:7), or a pearl (rabbinical interpretation)

bd. ft. board foot (or feet)

bdl. *pl.* **bdls.** bundle

bds. (bound in) boards

be (bē; *unstressed* bi) *vi.* **was** or **were, been, being** [ME. *been, beon* < OE. *beon:* be is a defective verb with parts from three unrelated stems: 1) the IE. substantive verb, base **es-,* as in Sans. *ásmi, asti,* Goth. *im, ist,* E. *am, is;* 2) IE. base **wes-,* stay, remain, as in Sans. *vasati,* lingers, stays, Goth. *wisan, was, wēsun,* remain, be, E. *was, were;* 3) IE. base **bheu-,* grow, become, as in Sans. *bhávati,* occurs, is there, L. *fieri (fis, fit, fimus),* be, become, occur: see BOND²] **I.** as a substantive verb, *be* means: **1.** to exist; live [*Caesar is no more*] **2.** to happen or occur [*when will the wedding be?*] **3.** to remain or continue [*will he be here long?*] **4.** to come to; belong [*peace be with you*] **5.** to have a place or position [*the door is on your left*] **II.** as a copula, *be* links its subject to a predicate nominative, adjective, or pronoun so as to express attribution or identity, and by extension, value, cause, signification, etc.; it is sometimes equivalent to the mathematical sign (=) (Ex.: Mrs. Siddons *was* an actress, he *is* handsome, that coat *is* fifty dollars, let x *be* y) **III.** as an auxiliary, *be* is used: **1.** with the past participle of a transitive verb to form the passive voice [*he will be whipped*] **2.** with the past participle of certain intransitive verbs to form an archaic perfect tense [*Christ is risen*] **3.** with the present participle of another verb to express continuation [*the player is running with the ball*] **4.** with the present participle or infinitive of another verb to express futurity, possibility, obligation, intention, etc. [*he is going next week, she is to wash the dishes*] *Be* is conjugated in the present indicative: (I) *am,* (he, she, it) *is,* (we, you, they) *are;* in the past indicative: (I, he, she, it) *was,* (we, you, they) *were;* archaic forms are (thou) *art, wert, wast;* the present subjunctive is *be,* the past subjunctive were —**be off** go away

be- (bi, bə; *with some slight stress* bē) [OE. *be-, bi-* (G. *be-,* Goth. *bi-),* at, near < *be, bi,* BY] *a prefix of various uses and meanings:* **I.** *prefixed to verbs:* **1.** *with the general meaning of* around [*besprinkle, beset*] **2.** *as an intensifier, with the general meanings of* completely, thoroughly, excessively [*bedeck, besmear*] **3.** *as a privative, with the general meaning of* away [*bereave, betake*] **4.** *as a transitive prefix, with the general meaning of* about [*bethink, bemoan*] **II.** *prefixed to nouns (sometimes adjectives) to form transitive verbs:* **1.** *with the general sense of* make [*besot, bepretty, bedirty*] **2.** *with the general senses of* furnish with, cover with, affect by, treat as [*befriend, bedizen, becloud*] **III.** *prefixed to past participles in* -ed *used as adjectives, with the general senses of* covered with, furnished with, furnished with to excess [*bemedaled, bewhiskered*]

Be *Chem.* beryllium

Bé. Baumé

B/E, b.e. bill of exchange

B.E. 1. Bachelor of Education **2.** Bachelor of Engineering

beach (bēch) *n.* [E. dial., orig., pebbles, shingles; origin obscure] **1.** a nearly level stretch of pebbles and sand beside a sea, lake, etc., often washed by high water; sandy shore; strand **2.** an area of shore as a place for swimming, sunbathing, etc. —*vt., vi.* to ground (a boat) on a beach —*SYN.* see SHORE¹ —☆**on the beach** *Naut.* not aboard a ship; ashore; hence, unemployed

☆**beach ball** a large, inflated ball for playing with on beaches, in swimming pools, etc.

beach·comb·er (-kō′mər) *n.* **1.** a long wave rolling ashore; comber **2.** a man who loafs on beaches or wharves, esp. on a South Sea island, living on what he can beg or find

☆**beach flea** any of various small crustaceans (order Amphipoda) found on sea beaches, that jump like fleas

beach grass any of a genus (*Ammophila*) of deeply rooted, tough, perennial grasses that grow on sandy beaches and are often planted to combat beach erosion

beach·head (-hed′) *n.* **1.** a position established by invading troops on an enemy shore **2.** a position gained as a secure starting point for any action; foothold

beach-la-mar (bēch′lə mär′) *n. same as* BÊCHE-DE-MER (sense 2)

beach ridge a ridge just inland from a beach, consisting of sand and gravel built up by storm waves

☆**beach umbrella** a large umbrella used as a sunshade on beaches, in gardens, etc.

☆**beach wagon** *earlier name for* STATION WAGON

bea·con (bēk'n) *n*. [ME. *beken* < OE. *beacen, becn*, a sign, signal < IE. **bhau-* < base **bha-*, gleam, shine, whence PHENOMENON] **1.** a signal fire, esp. one on a hill, pole, etc. **2.** any light for warning or guiding **3.** a lighthouse **4.** a radio transmitter that sends out signals for the guidance of aircraft, as at night or in fog **5.** a person or thing that warns, offers encouragement or guidance, etc. —*vt*. **1.** to light up (darkness, etc.) **2.** to provide or mark with beacons —*vi*. to shine or serve as a beacon

Bea·cons·field (bēk'nz fēld'), Earl of, *see* DISRAELI

bead (bēd) *n*. [ME. *bede*, prayer, prayer bead < OE. *bed* < *biddan*, to pray, ask (see BID¹)] **1.** a small, usually round piece of glass, wood, metal, etc., pierced for stringing **2.** [*pl*.] a rosary (sense 2*a*) **3.** [*pl*.] a string of beads; necklace **4.** any small, round object, as the sight at the muzzle end of a gun barrel **5.** a drop or bubble [*beads of sweat*] **6.** *a*) a bubble in an effervescing liquid *b*) foam or a head, as on beer **7.** a globule of metal, as gold or silver, obtained by refining in a cupel **8.** the inner edge of the outer wall of a rubber tire, fitting on the rim **9.** *Archit. a*) a narrow, half-round molding *b*) a molding composed of small rounded ornaments, like a string of beads **10.** *Chem.* a beadlike mass usually formed inside the loop of a platinum wire by the action of a flux, such as borax, upon the oxide or salt of certain metals: used in identifying metals in their compounds, since the metal determines the color of the bead —*vt*. **1.** to decorate or string with beads or beading **2.** to string like beads —*vi*. to form a bead or beads —☆**draw a bead on** to take careful aim at —**say** (or **tell** or **count**) **one's beads** to say prayers with a rosary

bead·house (-hous') *n*. an almshouse where the inmates were required to pray for its benefactors

bead·ing (-iŋ) *n*. **1.** beads or decorative work in beads on dresses, purses, etc. **2.** a molding, edge, or pattern resembling a row of beads **3.** a narrow, half-round molding **4.** *a*) a narrow trimming of lacelike loops, as on a garment *b*) an openwork trimming through which a ribbon can be run

bea·dle (bē'd'l) *n*. [ME. *bidel* (< OE. *bydel*, akin to *beodan*, to BID¹, order), *bedel* < OFr. *bedel* < Frank. **bidal*, akin to OE. form] **1.** formerly, a minor parish officer in the Church of England, who kept order in church **2.** *same as* SEXTON (sense 2) **3.** [Obs.] a messenger of a law court

bea·dle·dom (-dəm) *n*. [prec. + -DOM] fussiness and stupidity of minor officials; petty bureaucracy

bead·roll (bēd'rōl') *n*. **1.** a list of names **2.** [Archaic] *R.C.Ch.* a list of the dead for whose souls prayers are to be said

☆**bead·ru·by** (-roo'bē) *n*., *pl*. **-bies** a small wildflower (*Maianthemum canadense*) of the lily family, with white flowers and red berries shaped like beads, found in the N U.S. and in Canada

beads·man (bēdz'mən) *n*., *pl*. **-men** (-mən) [ME. *bedeman* < *bede*, prayer (see BEAD) + *man*, MAN] **1.** a person who prays for another's soul, esp. one hired to do so **2.** a person in a poorhouse **3.** [Scot.] a beggar —**beads'wom·an** *n.fem.*, *pl*. **-wom'en**

bead·work (bēd'wurk') *n*. **1.** decorative work in beads **2.** beaded molding; beading

bead·y (bē'dē) *adj.* **bead'i·er, bead'i·est 1.** small, round, and glittering like a bead [*the beady eyes of a snake*] **2.** decorated with beads

bea·gle (bē'g'l) *n*. [ME. *begle* < ? Fr. *bégueule*, widethroat (with reference to its bark)] a small hound with a smooth coat, short legs, and drooping ears, used in hunting small game

beak (bēk) *n*. [ME. *bek* < OFr. *bec* < L. *beccus* < Gaul.] **1.** a bird's bill, esp. the large, sharp, horny bill of a bird of prey **2.** a beaklike part or thing, as the protruding mouthpart of various insects, fishes, etc., or the spout of a pitcher **3.** the metal-covered ram projecting from the prow of an ancient warship **4.** [Slang] the nose, esp. if large and hooked **5.** *Archit.* the outward-sloping upper surface of the drip of a cornice, by which water is directed away from the wall beneath —**beaked** (bēkt; *occas.* bēk'id) *adj.* —**beak'less** *adj.* —**beak'like** *adj.*

BEAGLE
(13-15 in. high
at shoulder)

beak·er (bēk'ər) *n*. [ME. *biker* < ON. *bikarr*, a cup < VL. *bicarium, becarium* < LL. *bacarium* < L. *bacar*, wine glass] **1.** a large or ornate cup; goblet **2.** a jarlike container of glass or metal with a lip for pouring, used by chemists, druggists, etc. **3.** the contents or capacity of a beaker

be-all and end-all (bē'ôl'ənd end'ôl') **1.** a thing or person regarded as incapable of improvement; acme; ultimate **2.** chief or all-important element

beam (bēm) *n*. [ME. < OE., a tree, piece of wood, column, akin to G. *baum*, Du. *boom*, tree] **I. 1.** orig., the squared-off trunk of a tree

BEAKER

2. *a*) a long, thick piece of wood, metal, or stone, used in building *b*) such a piece used as a horizontal support for a roof, ceiling, etc. **3.** one of the two large rollers of a loom **4.** the barlike, horizontal part of a plow, to which the handles, share, etc. are attached **5.** the crossbar of a balance; also, occasionally, the balance itself **6.** the main shaft of a deer's antlers **7.** any of the heavy, horizontal crosspieces of a ship **8.** a ship's breadth at its widest point **9.** the side of a ship or the direction extending outward on either side at right angles to the fore-and-aft line of a ship, aircraft, etc. **10.** [Slang] the width of the hips **11.** *Mech.* a lever that is moved back and forth by a piston rod and transmits its motion to the crank, etc. **II.** [orig. transl. of L. *columna lucis*, column of light] **1.** a slender shaft or stream of light or other radiation, as of X-rays, nuclear particles, etc.: also used figuratively **2.** a radiant look, smile, etc. **3.** a stream of radio or radar signals sent continuously in one direction from a landing field, harbor, etc. as a guide for incoming aircraft or ships —*vt*. **1.** to give out (shafts of light); radiate in a beam or beams **2.** to direct or aim (a radio signal, program, etc.) —*vi*. **1.** to shine brightly; be radiant **2.** to smile warmly —**beam in one's own eye** [after Matt. 7:3, Luke 6:41] a major moral flaw in oneself which one ignores while criticizing minor faults in others —**off the beam 1.** not following the direction of a guiding beam, as an airplane ☆**2.** [Colloq.] *a*) going in the wrong direction *b*) wrong; incorrect —**on the beam 1.** in a direction at right angles to the keel of a ship; abeam **2.** following the direction of a guiding beam, as an airplane ☆**3.** [Colloq.] *a*) going in the right direction *b*) working or functioning well; alert, keen, quick, etc.

beam-ends (bēm'endz') *n.pl.* the ends of a ship's beams (*n*. 7) —**on the beam-ends 1.** tipping so far to the side as to be in danger of overturning **2.** at the end of one's resources, money, etc.

beam·ing (-iŋ) *adj.* **1.** sending out beams; shining **2.** radiant as with joy; bright; cheerful —**beam'ing·ly** *adv*.

beam·ish (-ish) *adj.* [BEAM + -ISH; used (? in sense of *happy*) by Lewis Carroll in *Through the Looking Glass*] beaming; radiant; cheerful

beam·y (-ē) *adj.* **beam'i·er, beam'i·est 1.** sending out beams of light; radiant; bright **2.** beamlike; broad; massive **3.** *Naut.* having a broad beam (*n*. 8)

bean (bēn) *n*. [ME. *ben* < OE. *bean*, akin to ON. *baun*, G. *bohne* < ? IE. base **bhabhā*, whence L. *faba*, bean] **1.** any of various plants of the legume family; esp., any of several species of a genus (*Phaseolus*) including the kidney bean, string bean, lima bean, etc. **2.** the edible, smooth, kidney-shaped seed of any of these plants **3.** a pod with such seeds, eaten as a vegetable when still unripe **4.** the bean-shaped seed of some other plants [*coffee bean*] **5.** any of these plants ☆**6.** [Slang] the head, brain, or mind ☆**7.** [*pl*.] [Slang] even a little amount: used in negative constructions [*not to know beans about something*] —☆*vt*. [Slang] to hit on the head; specif., *Baseball* to hit on the head with a pitched ball —**full of beans** [Slang] **1.** full of energy and vitality; lively; ebullient ☆**2.** mistaken; in error —☆**spill the beans** [Colloq.] to divulge secret information —**bean'like'** *adj.*

☆**bean·bag** (-bag') *n*. **1.** a small cloth bag filled with beans, for throwing in certain games **2.** such a game

☆**bean ball** [Slang] *Baseball* a pitch aimed at the batter's head, in violation of the rules

☆**bean beetle** any of a number of beetles and weevils attacking legumes, esp. the MEXICAN BEAN BEETLE

bean caper any of a genus (*Zygophyllum*) of plants having buds used as capers

☆**bean·er·y** (bē'nər ē) *n*., *pl*. **-er·ies** [BEAN + -ERY: so named from serving baked beans as a chief dish] [Colloq.] a cheap restaurant

bean·ie (bē'nē) *n*. [BEAN (*n*. 6) + -IE] [Colloq.] any of various kinds of skullcap worn as by children or by freshmen at some colleges

☆**bean·pole** (bēn'pōl') *n*. **1.** a long stick put upright in the ground for bean plants to climb on **2.** [Colloq.] a tall, lean person

bean·shoot·er (-shoot'ər) *n*. *same as* PEASHOOTER

bean·stalk (-stôk') *n*. the main stem of a bean plant

☆**bean tree** any of various trees bearing podlike fruit, as the catalpa, carob, etc.

☆**bean weevil** any of a family (Lariidae) of small, hardy beetles whose larvae develop in growing bean plants and also in dried beans and peas

bear¹ (ber) *vt*. **bore** or *archaic* **bare, borne** or **born** (see vt. 3), **bear'ing** [ME. *beren* < OE. *beran* < IE. base **bher-*, to carry, bring, whence L. *ferre*, Gr. *pherein*, Sans. *bharati* (he bears)] **1.** *a*) to hold and take along; carry; transport *b*) to hold in the mind [*to bear a secret*] **2.** to possess as a part, characteristic, attribute, etc.; have or show [*the letter bore his signature*] **3.** to give birth to: the passive past participle in this sense is **born** when *by* does not follow **4.** to bring forth; produce or yield [*fruit-bearing trees, coal-bearing strata*] **5.** to support or hold up; sustain **6.** to sustain the burden of; take on; take care of [*to bear the cost*] **7.** *a*) to undergo successfully; withstand; endure [*her work won't bear scrutiny*] *b*) to put up with; tolerate [*she can't bear him*] **8.** to call for; require [*his actions bear watching*] **9.** to carry or conduct (oneself) **10.** to carry over or hold (a sentiment) [*to bear a grudge*] **11.** to bring

and tell (a message, tales, etc.) **12.** to move or push as if carrying [the crowd *bore* us along] **13.** to give, offer, or supply [to *bear* witness] —*vi.* **1.** to be productive [the tree *bears* well] **2.** *a)* to lie in a given direction [the lighthouse *bears* due east] *b)* to point or be aimed toward (with *on* or *upon*) [artillery deployed to *bear* on the fort] *c)* to move in a given direction [*bear* right at the corner] **3.** to have bearing (*on*); have a relation [his story *bears* on the crime] **4.** to tolerate; put up patiently (*with*) **5.** to be oppressive; weigh [grief *bears* heavily on her] —**bear a hand 1.** to give help **2.** *Naut.* get to work!: a command —**bear away** to keep or change a ship's course away from the wind —**bear down 1.** to press or push down; exert pressure **2.** to make a strong effort —**bear down on 1.** to press down on; exert pressure on **2.** to make a strong effort toward accomplishing **3.** to come or go toward; approach —**bear out** to show to be true; support or confirm —**bear up** to endure, as under a strain; keep up one's spirits —**bring to bear on** (or **upon**) to cause to have an effect on [he brought his influence to *bear* on the lawmakers] *SYN.*—**bear** implies a putting up with something that distresses, annoys, pains, etc., without suggesting the way in which one sustains the imposition; **suffer** suggests passive acceptance of or resignation to that which is painful or unpleasant; **endure** implies a holding up against prolonged pain, distress, etc. and stresses stamina or patience; **tolerate** and the more informal **stand** both imply self-imposed restraint of one's opposition to what is offensive or repugnant; **brook**, a literary word, is usually used in the negative, suggesting determined refusal to put up with what is distasteful See also CARRY

bear² (ber) *n., pl.* **bears, bear**: see PLURAL, II, D, 1 [ME. *bere* < OE. *bera* < IE. base *bhero-s*, brown, brown animal, whence L. *fiber*, Avestan *bawra-*, BEAVER¹] **1.** any of a number of large, heavy mammals (family Ursidae) that eat any sort of food, walk flat on the soles of their feet, and have shaggy fur and a very short tail: bears are native to temperate and arctic zones **2.** [B-] either of two constellations in the Northern Hemisphere, the Great Bear (also called *Ursa Major*, etc.) and the Little Bear (also called *Ursa Minor*, etc.): see also BIG DIPPER, LITTLE DIPPER **3.** a person who is clumsy, rude, gruff, churlish, etc. **4.** a person who believes prices on the stock or commodity markets are going to decline, esp. one who sells shares, etc. in the expectation of buying them later at a lower price: opposed to BULL¹ —*adj.* falling in price [a *bear* market] —**be a bear for punishment** to be able to withstand much rough treatment; be rugged, tough, determined, etc. —**bear'like'** *adj.*

bear·a·ble (-ə b'l) *adj.* that can be borne or endured; tolerable —**bear'a·bly** *adv.*

bear·bait·ing (-bāt'iŋ) *n.* an old form of diversion in which dogs were made to torment a chained bear

bear·ber·ry (-ber'ē) *n., pl.* **-ries 1.** any of a genus (*Arctostaphylos*) of trailing plants of the heath family, having small, leathery leaves, white or pinkish flowers, and red berries ☆**2.** a local name for any of various other unrelated plants, as the cowberry, cascara, etc.

bear·cat (-kat') *n.* **1.** same as BINTURONG **2.** same as PANDA ☆**3.** [Colloq.] a person or thing having exceptional power, strength, energy, etc.

beard (bird) *n.* [ME. & OE. < IE. base *bhardhā*, whence L. *barba*, Russ. *borodá*, G. *bart*] **1.** the hair growing on the lower part of a man's face; whiskers **2.** this hair, esp. on the chin and cheek, when worn long or trimmed in various shapes **3.** any beardlike part, as of certain animals **4.** a hairy outgrowth on the head of certain grains, grasses, etc.; awn **5.** anything that projects like a beard; barb or hook **6.** the part of a printing type that lies between the face and the shoulder —*vt.* **1.** to face or oppose courageously or brazenly, as if grasping by the beard; defy **2.** to provide with a beard —**beard'ed** *adj.*

Beard (bird) **1. Charles Austin,** 1874–1948; U.S. historian, often in collaboration with his wife, **Mary,** 1876–1958 **2. Daniel Carter,** 1850–1941; U.S. author & illustrator: a founder of the Boy Scouts of America

beard·less (bird'lis) *adj.* **1.** having no beard **2.** too young to have a beard **3.** young, callow, etc.

Beards·ley (birdz'lē), **Aubrey Vincent** 1872–98; Eng. artist & illustrator

☆**beard·tongue** (bird'tuŋ') *n.* [so named from the bearded, tonguelike stamen] *same as* PENSTEMON

bear·er (ber'ər) *n.* **1.** a person or thing that bears, carries, or supports **2.** a plant or tree that produces fruit or blooms **3.** [Rare] a pallbearer **4.** a person presenting for payment a check, note, money order, etc. —*adj.* made out to the bearer [bearer bonds]

bear garden 1. a place for bearbaiting or similar pastimes **2.** any rough, noisy, rowdy place

☆**bear grass 1.** any of several plants (genus *Yucca*) of the agave family, with a thick tuft of swordlike leaves at the base of a flowering stalk **2.** a western American plant (*Xerophyllum tenax*) of the lily family, with stiff, grasslike leaves and spikes of small, white flowers

bear·ing (ber'iŋ) *n.* **1.** way of carrying and conducting oneself; carriage; manner; mien **2.** a support or supporting part **3.** *a)* the act, power, or period of producing young, fruit, etc. *b)* ability to produce *c)* anything borne or produced, as a crop, fruit, etc. **4.** an enduring; endurance **5.** *a)* direction relative to one's own position or to the compass *b)* [*pl.*] position, as of a ship, established by determining the bearing from it of several known points *c)* [*pl.*] awareness or recognition of one's position or situation [to lose one's *bearings*] **6.** relevant meaning; application; relation [the evidence had no *bearing* on the case] **7.** *Archit.* the part of a lintel or beam that rests on supports **8.** *Heraldry* any figure on the field; charge **9.** *Mech.* any part of a machine in or on which another part revolves, slides, etc. —*adj.* that bears, or supports weight [a *bearing* wall]
SYN.—**bearing,** in this comparison denoting manner of carrying or conducting oneself, refers to characteristic physical and mental posture; **carriage,** also applied to posture, specif. stresses the physical aspects of a person's bearing [an erect *carriage*]; **demeanor** refers to behavior as expressing one's attitude or a specified personality trait [a demure *demeanor*]; **mien,** a literary word, refers to one's bearing and manner [a man of melancholy *mien*]; **deportment** refers to one's behavior with reference to standards of conduct or social conventions; **manner** is applied to customary or distinctive attitude, actions, speech, etc. and, in the plural, refers to behavior conforming with polite conventions

bearing rein *same as* CHECKREIN (sense 1)

bear·ish (ber'ish) *adj.* **1.** bearlike; rude, rough, surly, etc. **2.** directed toward or causing a lowering of prices in the stock exchange —**bear'ish·ly** *adv.*

Bé·arn (bā är', -ärn') region & former province in SW France, in the Pyrenees

Bear River river flowing through Utah, Wyo., & Ida. into Great Salt Lake: c. 350 mi.

bear's-breech (berz'brēch') *n. same as* ACANTHUS (sense 1)

bear's-ear (-ir') *n. same as* AURICULA (sense 1)

bear·skin (ber'skin') *n.* **1.** the pelt, fur, or hide of a bear **2.** anything made from this, as a rug or coat **3.** a tall fur cap worn as part of some uniforms

☆**bear·wood** (-wood') *n. same as* CASCARA (sense 1)

beast (bēst) *n.* [ME. & OFr. *beste* < L. *bestia*] **1.** orig., any animal except man **2.** any large, four-footed animal; sometimes, specif., a domesticated animal **3.** qualities or impulses like an animal's [the *beast* in him] **4.** a person who is brutal, gross, vile, etc.

beast·ie (bēs'tē) *n.* [Chiefly Scot.] a little animal

beast·ly (bēst'lē) *adj.* **-li·er, -li·est 1.** of, like, or characteristic of a beast; bestial, brutal, etc. **2.** [Colloq.] disagreeable; unpleasant —*adv.* [Brit. Colloq.] very [*beastly* bad news] —**beast'li·ness** *n.*

beast of burden any animal used for carrying things

beast of prey any animal that hunts and kills other animals for food

beat (bēt) *vt.* **beat, beat'en, beat'ing** [ME. *beten* < OE. *beatan* < IE. base *bhau-*, *bhu-*, to strike, beat, whence L. *fustis*, club, BEETLE², BUTT¹&²] **1.** to hit or strike repeatedly; pound **2.** to punish by striking repeatedly and hard; whip, flog, spank, etc. **3.** to dash repeatedly against [waves *beat* the shore] **4.** *a)* to form by repeated treading or riding [to *beat* a path through grass] *b)* to keep walking on [to *beat* the pavements] **5.** to shape or flatten by hammering; forge **6.** to mix by stirring or striking repeatedly with a utensil; whip (an egg, cream, etc.) **7.** to move (esp. wings) up and down; flap; flail **8.** to hunt through; search [the posse *beat* the countryside for the fugitive] **9.** to make, force, or drive by or as by hitting, flailing, or pounding [to *beat* one's way through a crowd, to *beat* chalk dust from erasers] **10.** *a)* to defeat in a race, contest, or struggle; overcome *b)* to outdo or surpass *c)* to act, arrive, or finish before **11.** to mark (time or rhythm) by tapping, etc. **12.** to sound or signal, as by a drumbeat **13.** [Colloq.] to baffle or puzzle ☆**14.** [Colloq.] to cheat or trick ☆**15.** [Slang] to avoid the penalties associated with (a charge, indictment, etc.); escape (a rap) —*vi.* **1.** to strike, hit, or dash repeatedly and, usually, hard **2.** to move or sound rhythmically; throb, pulsate, vibrate, tick, etc. **3.** to strike about in or hunt through underbrush, woods, etc. for game **4.** to take beating or stirring [this cream doesn't *beat* well] **5.** *a)* to make a sound by being struck, as a drum *b)* to beat a drum, as to sound a signal **6.** [Colloq.] to win **7.** *Naut.* to progress by tacking into the wind **8.** *Radio* to combine two waves of different frequencies, thus producing an additional frequency equal to the difference between these —*n.* **1.** a beating, as of the heart **2.** any of a series of blows or strokes **3.** any of a series of movements or sounds; throb **4.** a habitual path or round of duty [a policeman's *beat*] **5.** *a)* the unit of musical rhythm [four *beats* to a measure] *b)* the accent or stress in the rhythm of verse or music *c)* the gesture of the hand, baton, etc. used to mark this ☆**6.** [Colloq.] a person or thing that surpasses [you never saw the *beat* of it] ☆**7.** *same as* BEATNIK; also, [often B-] any of a group of U.S. writers whose work grows out of and expresses beat attitudes **8.** *Acoustics* the regularly recurring amplification of sound produced by two simultaneous tones of nearly equal frequency ☆**9.** *Journalism* a publishing of news before rival newspapers;

scoop **10.** *Naut.* a tack into the wind **11.** *Radio* one cycle of a frequency formed by beating —*adj.* **1.** [Slang] tired out; exhausted, physically or emotionally ☆**2.** of or belonging to a group of young persons, esp. of the 1950's, rebelling against conventional attitudes, dress, speech, etc., largely as an expression of social disillusionment —**beat about 1.** to hunt or look through or around **2.** *Naut.* to tack into the wind —**beat back** to force to retreat; drive back —**beat down 1.** to shine steadily with dazzling light and intense heat, as the sun **2.** to put down; suppress **3.** [Colloq.] to force to a lower price —☆**beat it!** [Slang] go away! —**beat off** to drive back; repel —☆**beat out** *Baseball* to get (a base hit) by reaching first base safely on a hit that does not leave the infield —☆**beat up (on)** [Slang] to give a beating to; thrash —**on the beat** in tempo —**to beat the band** (or **hell, the devil,** etc.) [Slang] with great energy and vigor; fast and furiously

SYN.—**beat,** the most general word in this comparison, conveys the basic idea of hitting or striking repeatedly, whether with the hands, feet, an implement, etc.; **pound** suggests heavier, more effective blows than **beat** [to *pound* with a hammer]; **pummel** implies the beating of a person with the fists and suggests a continuous, indiscriminate rain of damaging blows; **thrash,** originally referring to the beating of grain with flail, suggests similar broad, swinging strokes, as in striking a person repeatedly with a stick, etc.; **flog** implies a punishing by the infliction of repeated blows with a stick, strap, whip, etc.; **whip,** often used as an equivalent of **flog,** specifically suggests lashing strokes or motions; **maul** implies the infliction of repeated heavy blows such as to bruise or lacerate Most of these terms are used loosely, esp. by journalists, in describing a decisive victory in a contest

beat·en (bēt''n) *adj.* [alternative pp. of BEAT] **1.** struck with repeated blows; whipped **2.** shaped or made thin by hammering **3.** flattened by treading; much traveled [a *beaten* path] **4.** a) defeated b) crushed by defeat **5.** tired out **6.** searched through for game —**off the beaten track** (or **path**) **1.** away or apart from others of its kind **2.** unusual, unfamiliar, original, etc.

beat·er (bēt'ər) *n.* **1.** a person or thing that beats **2.** an implement or utensil for beating **3.** a person who drives game from cover in a hunt

be·a·tif·ic (bē'ə tif'ik) *adj.* [L. *beatificus*: see BEATIFY] **1.** making blissful or blessed **2.** showing happiness or delight; blissful [a *beatific* smile] —**be'a·tif'i·cal·ly** *adv.*

be·at·i·fi·ca·tion (bē at'ə fi kā'shən) *n.* [Fr.] **1.** a beatifying or being beatified **2.** *R.C.Ch.* the process of determining the sanctity of a person who has died and declaring him to be among the blessed in heaven: he is then entitled to public veneration and is usually, but not necessarily, canonized

be·at·i·fy (bē at'ə fī') *vt.* -**fied'**, -**fy'ing** [Fr. *béatifier* < LL. *beatificare* < *beatus*, happy + *facere*, to make] **1.** to make blissfully happy; bless **2.** *R.C.Ch.* to pronounce the beatification of by papal decree

beat·ing (bēt'iŋ) *n.* **1.** the act of a person or thing that beats **2.** a whipping or thrashing **3.** a throbbing; pulsation **4.** a defeat

be·at·i·tude (bē at'ə tōōd', -tyōōd') *n.* [Fr. *béatitude* < L. *beatitudo* < *beatus*, happy, blessed] perfect blessedness or happiness —**the Beatitudes** the pronouncements in the Sermon on the Mount, which begin "Blessed are the poor in spirit": Matt. 5:3–12

☆**beat·nik** (bēt'nik) *n.* [BEAT, *adj.* **2** + Russ. (via Yid.) -nik, equiv. to -ER] a member of the beat group

Be·a·trice (bē'ə tris) [It. < L. *beatrix*, she who makes happy < *beatus*: see BEATITUDE] **1.** a feminine name: dim. *Bea*; var. *Beatrix* **2.** (also It. be'ä trē'che) a Florentine woman (*Beatrice Portinari*, 1266–1290) loved by Dante and immortalized in his *Divine Comedy*

Beat·ty (bēt'ē), **David, 1st Earl Beatty,** 1871–1936; Brit. admiral

☆**beat-up** (bēt'up') *adj.* [Slang] in a worn-out condition; dilapidated, battered, shabby, etc.

beau (bō) *n., pl.* **beaus, beaux** (bōz) [Fr., a dandy < *beau, bel,* pretty < L. *bellus,* pretty] **1.** [Now Rare] a dandy **2.** the sweetheart or courter of a woman or girl

Beau Brum·mell (brum'əl) **1.** (born *George Bryan Brummell*), 1778–1840; Eng. gentleman famous for his fashionable dress and manners **2.** any dandy or fop

‡**beau·coup** (bō kōō') *adj.* [Fr.] very much; very many

Beau·fort scale (bō'fərt) [after Sir Francis Beaufort (1774–1857), Brit. naval officer who devised the original scale c. 1805] a scale of wind force, used officially by the members of the World Meteorological Organization

Beaufort number	Miles per hour	International description
0	up to 1	Calm
1	1 – 3	Light air
2	4 – 7	Light breeze
3	8 – 12	Gentle breeze
4	13 – 18	Moderate breeze
5	19 – 24	Fresh breeze
6	25 – 31	Strong breeze
7	32 – 38	Moderate gale
8	39 – 46	Fresh gale
9	47 – 54	Strong gale
10	55 – 63	Whole gale
11	64 – 72	Storm
12 – 17	73 – 136	Hurricane

Beaufort Sea part of the Arctic Ocean, north of Alaska & northwest of Canada

‡**beau geste** (bō zhest') *pl.* **beaux gestes** (bō zhest') [Fr.] **1.** a fine or beautiful gesture **2.** an act or offer that seems fine, noble, etc., but is empty

Beau·har·nais (bō ár ne'), **Josephine de** *see* JOSEPHINE & HORTENSE

beau i·de·al (ī dē'əl) [Fr. *beau idéal*] **1.** ideal beauty **2.** the perfect type or conception [the *beau ideal* of fashion]: a sense due to mistranslation

Beau·jo·lais (bō'zhə lā') *n.* a rich red wine from the region of Beaujolais near Burgundy, France

Beau·mar·chais (bō mär she'), **Pierre Augustin Caron de** (pyer ō güs tan' kà rōn' də) 1732–99; Fr. dramatist

beau monde (bō' mänd'; *Fr.* bō' mōnd') [Fr., lit., elegant world] fashionable society

Beau·mont (bō'mänt) [< ? surname: ult. < Fr., lit., beautiful hill] city in SE Tex.: pop. 116,000

Beau·mont (bō'mänt), **Francis** 1584–1616; Eng. dramatist who collaborated with John FLETCHER

Beau·re·gard (bō'rə gärd', bôr'ə-), **P(ierre) G(ustave) T(outant) de** 1818–93; Confederate general in the Civil War

☆**beaut** (byōōt) *n.* [Slang] one that is beautiful or superlative in some way: often used ironically [his alibi was a *beaut*]

beau·te·ous (byōōt'ē əs) *adj.* beautiful —*SYN.* see BEAUTIFUL —**beau'te·ous·ly** *adv.*

☆**beau·ti·cian** (byōō tish'ən) *n.* a person who does hair styling, manicuring, etc. in a beauty shop; cosmetologist

beau·ti·ful (byōōt'ə fəl) *adj.* having beauty; very pleasing to the eye, ear, mind, etc. —**the beautiful 1.** that which has beauty; the quality of beauty **2.** those who are beautiful —**beau'ti·ful·ly** (-ə flē, -ə fəl ē) *adv.*

SYN.—**beautiful** is applied to that which gives the highest degree of pleasure to the senses or to the mind and suggests that the object of delight approximates one's conception of an ideal; **lovely** refers to that which delights by inspiring affection or warm admiration; **handsome** implies attractiveness by reason of pleasing proportions, symmetry, elegance, etc. and carries connotations of masculinity, dignity, or impressiveness; **pretty** implies a dainty, delicate, or graceful quality in that which pleases and carries connotations of femininity or diminutiveness; **comely** applies to persons only and suggests a wholesome attractiveness of form and features rather than a high degree of beauty; **fair** suggests beauty that is fresh, bright, or flawless and, when applied to persons, is used esp. of complexion and features; **good-looking** is closely equivalent to **handsome** or **pretty,** suggesting a pleasing appearance but not expressing the fine distinctions of either word; **beauteous,** equivalent to **beautiful** in poetry and lofty prose, is now often used in humorously disparaging references to beauty —*ANT.* **ugly**

beau·ti·fy (byōōt'ə fī') *vt.* -**fied'**, -**fy'ing** to make beautiful or more beautiful —*vi.* to become beautiful —*SYN.* see ADORN —**beau'ti·fi·ca'tion** (-fi kā'shən) *n.* —**beau'ti·fi'er** *n.*

beau·ty (byōōt'ē) *n., pl.* -**ties** [ME. *beaute* < OFr. *bealte* < VL. *bellitas* < L. *bellus,* pretty, lovely] **1.** the quality attributed to whatever pleases or satisfies the senses or mind, as by line, color, form, texture, proportion, rhythmic motion, tone, etc., or by behavior, attitude, etc. **2.** a thing having this quality **3.** good looks **4.** a very good-looking woman **5.** any very attractive feature —*adj.* [Slang] best, nicest, most satisfying, etc. [a *beauty* play]

beauty bush a hardy shrub (*Kolkwitzia amabilis*) of the honeysuckle family, having tubular pink flowers and white bristly hairs on the stalks

☆**beauty culture** the skill or occupation of a beautician; cosmetology

☆**beauty shop** (or **salon** or **parlor**) a place where women go for hair styling and tinting, manicuring, etc.

beauty sleep [Colloq.] **1.** sleep before midnight, popularly thought to be most restful **2.** any extra sleep

beauty spot 1. a tiny black patch applied to the face or back to emphasize the beauty or whiteness of the skin: a former fashion among women **2.** a natural mark or mole on the skin **3.** any place noted for its beauty

Beau·voir (bō vwär'), **Si·mone de** (sē mōn' də) 1908– ; Fr. existentialist writer

beaux (bōz; *Fr.* bō) *n. alt. pl.* of BEAU

‡**beaux-arts** (bō zàr'; *E.* bōz ärt') *n.pl.* [Fr.] the fine arts

‡**beaux-es·prits** (bō zes prē') *n. pl.* of BEL-ESPRIT

bea·ver¹ (bē'vər) *n.* [ME. *bever* < OE. *beofor*; for IE. base see BEAR²] **1.** *pl.* -**vers, -ver:** see PLURAL, II, D, 1 a) any of a genus (*Castor*) of large rodents with soft, brown fur, chisellike teeth, webbed hind feet, and a flat, broad tail, that are equally at home on land or in the water, where they build dams of mud and twigs b) its fur **2.** a man's high silk hat, originally made of this fur **3.** a heavy cloth of felted wool, used for overcoats, etc. ☆**4.** [Colloq.] a hard-working, conscientious person

BEAVER
(32–47 in. long, including tail)

bea·ver² (bē'vər) *n.* [ME. *bavier* < OFr. *baviere,* beaver of a helmet, orig., bib < *bave,* saliva, foam] **1.** a movable piece of armor on the lower part of a medieval helmet, for protecting the mouth and chin **2.** later, the visor of a helmet

☆**Bea·ver·board** (-bôrd′) *a trademark for* artificial board made of compressed wood fiber, used for walls, partitions, etc. —*n.* [b-] fiberboard of this kind

Bea·ver·brook (bē′vər brook′), 1st Baron (*William Max·well Aitkin*) 1879–1964; Brit. newspaper publisher & statesman, born in Canada

be·bee·rine (bi bē′rēn, -rin) *n.* [< ff. + -INE⁴] an alkaloid drug, C₃₆H₃₈N₂O₆, similar to quinine, obtained from the bark of the bebeeru tree

be·bee·ru (bi bē′rōo) *n.* [< native name in Guiana] a tropical S. American evergreen tree (*Nectandra rodiaei*) of the laurel family

Be·bel (bā′bəl), (**Ferdinand**) **Au·gust** (ou goost′) 1840–1913; Ger. socialist leader & writer

☆**be·bop** (bē′bäp′) *n.* [? from sound made on a trumpet] *orig. name for* BOP²

be·calm (bi käm′) *vt.* 1. to make quiet or still; calm 2. to make (a sailing vessel) motionless from lack of wind: usually in passive voice

be·came (bi kām′) *pt. of* BECOME

be·cause (bi kôz′, -kuz′) *conj.* [ME. *bi cause* < *bi*, by + *cause*] 1. for the reason or cause that; on account of the fact that; since 2. the reason that; that: used to introduce a noun clause —**because of** by reason of; on account of

bec·ca·fi·co (bek′ə fē′kō) *n.*, *pl.* **-cos** [It. < *beccare*, to peck + *fico*, a fig] any of several small European songbirds, eaten as a delicacy esp. in Italy

bé·cha·mel (bāsh′ə mel′) *n.* [Fr. < Louis de *Béchamel*, steward to Louis XIV] a white sauce made of cream, butter, flour, etc.

be·chance (bi chans′, -chäns′) *vt.*, *vi.* **-chanced′, -chanc′-ing** [Now Rare] to happen (to); befall

‡**bêche-de-mer** (besh də mer′) *n.* [Fr., worm of the sea; altered < Port. *bicho do mar*, sea slug] 1. *pl.* **bêches-de-mer′** (besh-) *same as* TREPANG 2. a mixed trade language, largely a pidgin variety of English, spoken by both natives and whites in island areas of the SW Pacific

Bech·u·a·na (bech′oo wän′ə) *n.* 1. *pl.* **-nas, -na** a member of a Bantu-speaking people living in Botswana 2. their language

Bech·u·a·na·land (bech′oo wän′ə land′) *former name of* BOTSWANA

beck¹ (bek) *n.* [< BECKON] 1. a gesture of the hand, head, etc., meant to summon 2. [Scot.] a bow or curtsy —*vt., vi.* [Archaic] to summon by a beck; beckon —**at the beck and call** of at the service of; obedient to the wishes of

beck² (bek) *n.* [ME. *bek* < ON. *bekkr*, akin to G. *bach*, brook & E. dial. *bache*] [Chiefly Brit. Dial.] a little stream, esp. one with a rocky bottom

Beck·en·ham (bek′′n əm) residential suburb just south of London: pop. 77,000

beck·et (bek′ət) *n.* [origin obscure] a contrivance, as a looped rope, large hook and eye, or grommet, used for fastening loose ropes, oars, spars, etc.

Beck·et (bek′ət), Saint **Thomas à** 1118?–1170; Eng. prelate; archbishop of Canterbury: murdered after opposing Henry II: his day is Dec. 29

becket bend *same as* SHEET BEND

Beck·ett (bek′ət), **Samuel** 1906– ; Ir. poet, novelist, & playwright in France, writing mostly in French

beck·on (bek′′n) *vi., vt.* [ME. *beknen* < OE. *beacnian*, to make signs < *beacen*, BEACON] 1. to call or summon by a silent gesture 2. to seem enticing (to); attract; lure [the woods *beckon*] —*n.* a summoning gesture

be·cloud (bi kloud′) *vt.* 1. to cloud over; darken 2. to confuse; muddle

be·come (bi kum′) *vi.* **-came′, -come′, -com′ing** [ME. *bicumen* < OE. *becuman*: see BE- & COME] 1. to come to be [to become ill] 2. to grow to be; change or develop into by growth [the tadpole *becomes* a frog] —*vt.* 1. to befit; suit [modesty *becomes* her] 2. to be right for or suitable to in appearance [that hat *becomes* you] —**become of** to happen to; be the fate of

be·com·ing (bi kum′iŋ) *adj.* 1. that is suitable or appropriate; fit 2. suitable to the wearer [a *becoming* gown] —*n.* the fact of coming into existence —**be·com′ing·ly** *adv.*

Bec·que·rel (be krel′; E. bek′ə rel′) 1. **Alex·an·dre Ed·mond** (à lek sän′dr′ ed mōn′), 1820–91; Fr. physicist: father of *Antoine Henri* 2. **An·toine Cé·sar** (än twän′ sā zàr′), 1788–1878; Fr. physicist: pioneer in electrochemistry: father of *prec.* 3. **Antoine Hen·ri** (än rē′), 1852–1908; Fr. physicist: discoverer of radioactivity in uranium

Becquerel rays [after A.H. BECQUEREL] rays given off by radioactive substances: now called GAMMA RAYS

bed (bed) *n.* [ME. & OE. < IE. base *bhedh-, to dig, whence G. *bett*, L. *fossa*, ditch, W. *bedd*, Bret. *béz*, a grave; orig. sense "a sleeping hollow in the ground"] 1. a thing for sleeping or resting on; specif., a piece of furniture consisting usually of a bedstead, spring, mattress, and bedding 2. *same as* BEDSTEAD 3. *same as* BEDTIME 4. any place used for sleeping or reclining 5. such a place regarded as the scene of sexual intercourse or procreation 6. *a*) a plot of soil where plants are raised *b*) the flowers or vegetables growing in this 7. *a*) the bottom of a river, lake, etc. *b*) a

place on the ocean floor where something grows in abundance [oyster *bed*] 8. an enclosing substance, as rock in which shells, minerals, etc. are lodged 9. any flat surface used as a foundation or support, as the earth, gravel, etc. under the rails and ties of a railroad 10. *a*) a layer of cement or mortar in which stone or brick is laid *b*) the underside of a brick, slate, or tile 11. a pile or heap resembling a bed, esp. in softness or shape [a *bed* of leaves] 12. a geological layer; stratum [a *bed* of coal] —*vt.* **bed′ded, bed′ding** 1. to provide with a sleeping place 2. to put to bed 3. [Archaic] to have sexual intercourse with 4. to fix or place firmly; embed 5. to plant in a bed of earth 6. to make (earth) into a bed for plants 7. to lay out flat like a bed; arrange in layers —*vi.* 1. to go to bed; rest; sleep 2. to form in layers; stratify —**be brought to bed (of)** [Archaic] to give birth (to) —**bed and board** 1. sleeping accommodations and meals 2. home; the married state —☆**bed down** to prepare and use a sleeping place —**get up on the wrong side of the bed** to be cross or grouchy —**put to bed** 1. to get (a child, invalid, etc.) ready for sleep 2. to lock (type, plates, etc.) into a form and place on a printing press 3. [Slang] to get an edition of (a newspaper, etc.) ready for the press —**take to one's bed** to go to bed because of illness, etc.

B.Ed. Bachelor of Education

be·daub (bi dôb′) *vt.* 1. to make daubs on; smudge or smear over 2. to ornament showily; overdecorate

be·daz·zle (bi daz′′l) *vt.* **-daz′zled, -daz′zling** to dazzle thoroughly; bewilder; confuse

bed·bug (bed′bug′) *n.* a small, wingless, bloodsucking insect (*Cimex lectularius*) with a broad, flat, reddish-brown body and an unpleasant odor: it infests beds, furniture, walls, etc. and is active mainly at night

bed·cham·ber (-chām′bər) *n.* a bedroom

bed·clothes (-klōz′, -klōthz′) *n.pl.* sheets, blankets, comforters, etc. used on a bed

bed·cov·er (-kuv′ər) *n.* a cover for a bed; coverlet; bedspread

bed·der (-ər) *n.* a plant suitable for a garden bed

BEDBUG
(3/16 in. long)

bed·ding (-iŋ) *n.* 1. mattresses and bedclothes 2. straw, hay, etc., used to bed animals 3. a bottom layer; base 4. *Geol.* stratification —*adj.* suitable for planting in a garden bed

bedding plane *Geol.* the surface separating two successive layers of stratified rock

Bed·does (bed′ōz), **Thomas Lov·ell** (luv′′l) 1803–49; Eng. poet & playwright

bed·dy-bye (bed′ē bī′) *n.* bed or bedtime: orig. a nursery word, now facetious

Bede (bēd), Saint 673–735 A.D.; Eng. historian & theologian: his day is May 27: called the **Venerable Bede**

be·deck (bi dek′) *vt.* to cover with decorations; adorn — *SYN.* see ADORN

bede·house (bēd′hous′) *n. same as* BEADHOUSE

bedes·man (bēdz′mən) *n.*, *pl.* **-men** (-mən) *same as* BEADSMAN —**bedes′wom·an** *n.fem.*, *pl.* **-wom·en**

be·dev·il (bi dev′′l) *vt.* **-iled** or **-illed, -il·ing** or **-il·ling** 1. to plague diabolically; torment; harass 2. to possess as with a devil; bewitch 3. to confuse completely; muddle 4. to corrupt; spoil —**be·dev′il·ment** *n.*

be·dew (bi dōo′, -dyōo′) *vt.* to make wet with or as if with drops of dew

bed·fast (bed′fast′, -fäst′) *adj. same as* BEDRIDDEN

bed·fel·low (-fel′ō) *n.* 1. a person who shares one's bed 2. associate, ally, confederate, etc.

Bed·ford (bed′fərd) 1. county seat of Bedfordshire: pop. 65,000 2. *same as* BEDFORDSHIRE

Bedford cord [? after *Bedford*, England; ? after New *Bedford*, Mass.] a heavy cloth with vertical ribs like corduroy

Bed·ford·shire (-shir, -shər) county in SC England: 473 sq. mi.; pop. 404,000

be·dight (bi dit′) *adj.* [pp. of obs. *bedight* < ME. *bidighten*, to equip, deck out < *bi-*, BE- + *dighten*, to prepare, set in order < OE. *dihtan*, to arrange, compose, write < L. *dictare*: see DICTATE] [Archaic or Poet.] bedecked; arrayed

be·dim (bi dim′) *vt.* **-dimmed′, -dim′ming** to make (the eyes or the vision) dim; darken or obscure

Bed·i·vere (bed′ə vir′), Sir *Arthurian Legend* the loyal knight who was with the dying King Arthur and saw him off to Avalon

be·diz·en (bi dī′z′n, -diz′′n) *vt.* [BE- + DIZEN] [Now Rare] to dress or decorate in a cheap, showy way —**be·diz′en·ment** *n.*

bed jacket a woman's short, loose upper garment sometimes worn in bed over a nightgown

bed·lam (bed′ləm) *n.* [ME. *Bedlem, Bethlem*, var. of Bethlehem] [B-] an old insane asylum in full, *St. Mary of Bethlehem*), later a hospital for the mentally ill in London —*n.* 1. [Archaic] any insane asylum 2. any place or condition of noise and confusion

bed·lam·ite (-īt') *n.* [prec. + -ITE²] [Archaic] an insane person; madman

bed linen bed sheets, pillowcases, etc., whether of linen or not

Bed·ling·ton terrier (bed'liŋ t'n) [after *Bedlington*, a town in N England] a blue or liver-colored, woolly-coated terrier resembling a small lamb

Bed·loe's Island (bed'lōz) [after Isaac *Bedloe*, first owner] *former name of* LIBERTY ISLAND

bed molding *Archit.* a molding below a projecting part, esp. between the corona and frieze

bed of roses [Colloq.] a situation or position of ease and luxury

Bed·ou·in (bed'oo win) *n., pl.* -**ins**, -**in** [Fr. *bédouin* < Ar. *baddāwīn*, pl. of *badawī*, desert dweller < *badw*, desert] [*also* b-] **1.** an Arab of any of the nomadic desert tribes of Arabia, Syria, or North Africa **2.** any wanderer or nomad —*adj.* of or like the Bedouins

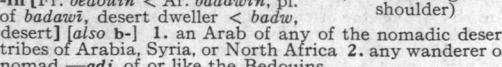

BEDLINGTON TERRIER
(15–16 in. high at shoulder)

bed·pan (bed'pan') *n.* **1.** *same as* WARMING PAN ☆**2.** a shallow pan for use as a toilet by a person confined to bed

bed·plate (-plāt') *n.* a plate forming the base, as of a machine

bed·post (-pōst') *n.* any of the vertical supporting posts at the corners of some beds

be·drag·gle (bi drag''l) *vt.* -**gled, -gling** to make wet, limp, and dirty, as by dragging through mire —**be·drag'gled** *adj.*

bed·rail (bed'rāl') *n.* a rail along the side of a bed

bed rest 1. a period of resting in bed **2.** a device used to prop a patient up in bed

bed·rid·den (-rid''n) *adj.* [ME. *bedrede(n)* < OE. *bedreda* < *bed* (BED) + *rida*, rider < *ridan*, to ride] having to stay in bed, usually for a long period, because of illness, infirmity, etc.: also **bed'rid'**

☆**bed·rock** (-räk') *n.* **1.** solid rock beneath the soil and superficial rock **2.** a secure foundation **3.** the very bottom **4.** basic principles or facts

☆**bed·roll** (-rōl') *n.* a portable roll of bedding, generally for sleeping outdoors

bed·room (-rōōm') *n.* a room with a bed, for sleeping in —*adj.* **1.** having to do with sex or sexual affairs [a *bedroom* farce] **2.** housing those who spend their days at work in a nearby metropolis [*bedroom* suburbs]

bed·side (-sīd') *n.* the side of a bed; space beside a bed [a nurse at his *bedside*] —*adj.* **1.** near a bed [a *bedside* table] **2.** as regards patients [a doctor's *bedside* manner]

bed-sit·ting room (bed'sit'iŋ) [Brit.] a combined bedroom and sitting room serving as a one-room apartment: also **bed'-sit'ter** *n.*

bed·sore (-sôr') *n.* a sore on the body of a bedridden person, caused by chafing or pressure

☆**bed·spread** (-spred') *n.* a cover spread over the blanket on a bed, mainly for ornament

☆**bed·spring** (-spriŋ') *n.* **1.** a framework of springs placed in a bedstead to support the mattress **2.** any of these springs

bed·stead (-sted') *n.* a framework for supporting the spring and mattress of a bed

bed·straw (-strô') *n.* [from its former use as straw for beds] any of a genus (*Galium*) of small plants of the madder family, with square stems, stalkless whorled leaves, and small, white or colored flowers

bed·time (-tīm') *n.* one's usual time for going to bed

bedtime story 1. a story told to children at bedtime **2.** a pleasant but unconvincing account or explanation

bed·ward (-wərd) *adv.* on the way to bed: also **bed'wards**

bed-wet·ting (-wet'iŋ) *n.* urinating in bed

bee¹ (bē) *n.* [ME. < OE. *beo* < IE. base *bhei*, whence G. *biene*, OPrus. *bitte*, OIr. *bech*] any of a large number of broad-bodied, four-winged, hairy insects (superfamily Apoidea) that gather pollen and nectar, have biting as well as sucking mouth parts, and often live in organized colonies; esp., the honeybee —**have a bee in one's bonnet 1.** to be preoccupied or obsessed with one idea **2.** to be not quite sane

bee² (bē) *n.* [altered (prob. after prec.) < dial. *bean*, a social gathering to assist < ME. *bene*, extra feudal service, a favor, boon < OE. *ben*, compulsory service, request, akin to ON. *bon*: see BOON¹] ☆ a meeting of people for working at something together for competition or amusement [a sewing *bee*, spelling *bee*]

bee³ (bē) *n.* [ME. *bei*, bracelet < OE. *beah* < *bugen*, to bend: see BOW¹] *Naut.* a piece of wood on each side of the bowsprit of a ship, used for fastening stays from the mast or foremast: in full, **bee block**

bee⁴ (bē) *n.* the letter B

☆**bee balm 1.** *same as* OSWEGO TEA **2.** *same as* LEMON BALM

Bee·be (bē'bē), (Charles) **William** 1877–1962; U.S. naturalist, explorer, & writer

☆**bee bird** *same as* BEE MARTIN

bee·bread (-bred') *n.* a yellowish-brown mixture of pollen and honey, made and eaten by some bees

beech (bēch) *adj.* [ME. *beche* < OE. *boece, bece*: see BOOK] designating a family (Fagaceae) of trees including the beeches, oaks, and chestnuts —*n.* **1.** any of a genus (*Fagus*) of trees of the beech family, with smooth, gray bark, hard wood, dark-green leaves, and edible three-

cornered nuts **2.** the wood of any of these trees —**beech'en** *adj.*

Bee·cham (bē'chəm), Sir **Thomas** 1879–1961; Eng. orchestral conductor

☆**beech·drops** (bēch'dräps') *n.pl.* [*with sing. v.*] a wiry N. American plant (*Epifagus virginiana*) of the broomrape family with brown stems and small clusters of whitish-purple flowers, parasitic on beech roots

Bee·cher (bē'chər) **1. Henry Ward**, 1813–87; U.S. clergyman & lecturer: brother of Harriet Beecher STOWE **2. Lyman**, 1775–1863; U.S. clergyman & theologian: father of *prec.* & of Harriet Beecher STOWE

beech·mast (bēch'mast', -mäst') *n.* beechnuts, esp. as they lie on the ground

beech·nut (-nut') *n.* the small, three-cornered, edible nut of the beech tree

beech·wood (-wood') *n.* the wood of the beech tree

bee eater any of a family (Meropidae) of small, brightly colored, tropical, Old World birds that feed on bees and other insects

beef (bēf) *n., pl.* **beeves**; also, and for 5 always, **beefs** (bēfs) [ME. < OFr. *boef* < L. *bovis*, gen. of *bos*, ox (apparently an Oscan-Umbrian cognate form, replacing L. *vos*) < IE. *gwous*, whence Sans. *gauh*, Gr. *bous*, OIr. *bo*, E. COW¹] **1.** a full-grown ox, cow, bull, or steer, esp. one bred and fattened for meat **2.** meat from such an animal; specif., a whole dressed carcass **3.** such animals collectively ☆**4.** [Colloq.] *a)* human flesh or muscle *b)* strength; brawn ☆**5.** [Slang] a complaint —☆*vi.* [Slang] to complain or protest —**beef up** to strengthen by addition, reinforcement, etc.

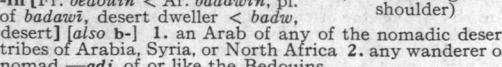

BEEF CUTS

☆**beef cattle** cattle bred and fattened for meat

beef·eat·er (-ēt'ər) *n.* **1.** a person who eats beef, typified as a large, well-fed, red-faced person **2.** *same as* YEOMAN OF THE GUARD **3.** a guard at the Tower of London **4.** [Slang] an Englishman

☆**bee fly** any of a family (Bombyliidae) of flies that look like bees and feed on nectar and pollen

beef·steak (bēf'stāk') *n.* a slice of beef, esp. from the loin, cut thick for broiling or frying

beef tea a drink made from beef extract or by boiling lean strips of beef

beef·wood (-wood') *n.* a hard, heavy, dark red or brown wood from a tropical tree (*Manilkara bidentata*), used for flooring, furniture, etc.

beef·y (bēf'ē) *adj.* **beef'i·er, beef'i·est** fleshy and solid; muscular and heavy; brawny —**beef'i·ness** *n.*

☆**bee gum** [Chiefly South] **1.** a hollow gum tree or log used as a hive by bees **2.** a beehive, esp. one made from such a tree

bee·hive (bē'hīv') *n.* **1.** a box or other shelter for a colony of domestic bees, in which they make and store honey **2.** a place of great activity

bee·keep·er (-kēp'ər) *n.* a person who keeps bees for producing honey; apiarist —**bee'keep'ing** *n.*

bee killer any of various insects that kill bees and other insects with their piercing beaks, as the robber flies (family Asilidae)

☆**bee·line** (-līn') *n.* a straight line or direct route: from the belief that a bee usually flies straight back to its hive after getting nectar —**make a beeline for** [Colloq.] to go straight toward

Be·el·ze·bub (bē el'zə bub') [LL.(Ec.) < Gr.(Ec.) *Beelzeboub* < Heb. *Ba'al zebūb*, lit., god of flies < *ba'al* (see BAAL) + *zebub*, a fly: prob. deliberate pejorative alteration < Ugaritic *Ba'al zebul*, lit., lord of the lofty dwelling (< *zbl*, exalted one, eminence)] **1.** *Bible* the chief devil; Satan: also **Be·el'ze·bul'** (-bool') **2.** any devil **3.** in Milton's *Paradise Lost*, Satan's chief lieutenant among the fallen angels

☆**bee martin** *see* KINGBIRD

☆**bee moth** a moth (*Galleria mellonella*) whose larvae, hatched in beehives, eat the wax of the honeycomb

been (bin, ben; *Canad. also and Brit. usually* bēn) [ME. *ben* < OE. *beon*: see BE] *pp.* of BE

beep (bēp) *n.* [echoic] **1.** the brief, high-pitched sound of a horn, as on an automobile or bicycle **2.** a brief, high-pitched electronic signal, used in warning, direction-finding etc. —*vi.* to make such a sound —*vt.* to cause to make such a sound

☆**bee plant** any plant that particularly attracts bees; esp., a pungent plant (*Cleome serrulata*) of the caper family or the California figwort (*Scrophularia californica*)

beer (bir) *n.* [ME. & OE. *beor*, akin to G. *bier*; only in WGmc.; a monastic (6th c.) borrowing < VL. *biber*, beverage (< L. *bibere*, IMBIBE); orig. used to distinguish the drink made with hops (*beer*) from the older drink (*ale*) then made without] **1.** an alcoholic, fermented beverage made from grain, esp. malted barley, and flavored with hops; specif., such a beverage produced by slow fermentation at a relatively low temperature: cf. ALE **2.** any of several soft drinks made from extracts of roots and plants [ginger *beer*]

Beer·bohm (bir′bōm), Sir (**Henry**) **Max**(**imilian**) 1872–1956; Eng. satirist, caricaturist, & critic

Beer·she·ba (bir shē′ba) ancient city in S Israel, the principal city of the Negev: pop. 62,000

beer·y (bir′ē) *adj.* **beer′i·er, beer′i·est** **1.** of or like beer **2.** showing the effects of drinking beer; drunken, tipsy, maudlin, etc. —**beer′i·ness** *n.*

beest·ings (bēs′tiŋz) *n.pl.* [*often with sing. v.*] [ME. *bestinge* < OE. *bysting* < *beost*, beestings] the first milk of a cow after having a calf; cow's colostrum

bees·wax (bēz′waks′) *n.* a tallowlike substance that honeybees secrete and use for building their honeycomb: it is used in candles, polishes, etc.

bees·wing (-wiŋ′) *n.* a gauzy film that forms in some old wines, esp. port

beet (bēt) *n.* [ME. & OE. *bete* < L. *beta*] **1.** any of a genus (*Beta*) of plants of the goosefoot family, with edible leaves and a thick, fleshy, white or red root **2.** the root of any of these plants: some varieties are eaten as a vegetable, some serve as a source of sugar, and some are used for fodder

Bee·tho·ven (bā′tō vən), **Lud·wig van** (lŏŏt′viH vän) 1770–1827; Ger. composer

bee·tle[1] (bēt′'l) *n.* [ME. *bitil* < OE. *bitela* < *bitan*, BITE] **1.** any of an order (Coleoptera) of insects, with biting mouth parts and hard front wings that cover the membranous hind wings when these are folded **2.** any insect resembling a beetle

bee·tle[2] (bēt′'l) *n.* [ME. & OE. (Anglian) *betel*, mallet, hammer, ult. connected with BEAT] **1.** a heavy mallet, usually wooden, for driving wedges, tamping earth, etc. **2.** a household mallet or pestle for mashing or beating **3.** a club used in finishing handmade linen **4.** a machine for finishing cloth by beating it over or between rollers —*vt.*

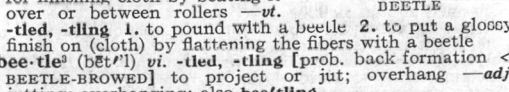

CATERPILLAR HUNTER BEETLE

-tled, -tling 1. to pound with a beetle **2.** to put a glossy finish on (cloth) by flattening the fibers with a beetle

bee·tle[3] (bēt′'l) *vi.* **-tled, -tling** [prob. back formation < BEETLE-BROWED] to project or jut; overhang —*adj.* jutting; overhanging; also **bee′tling**

☆**beet leaf·hop·per** (lēf′häp′ər) a small insect (*Eutettix tenellus*) that carries and transmits a very destructive plant virus

bee·tle-browed (bēt′'l broud′) *adj.* [ME. *bitelbrouwed* < ? *bitel*, sharp, cruel + *brouwe*, BROW] **1.** having bushy or overhanging eyebrows **2.** frowning; scowling

☆**bee tree 1.** a hollow tree used as a hive by bees **2.** *same as* BASSWOOD (sense 1)

beet sugar sugar extracted from sugar beets

beeves (bēvz) *n. alt. pl.* of BEEF

bef. before

B.E.F. British Expeditionary Force (or Forces)

be·fall (bi fôl′) *vi.* **-fell′, -fall′en, -fall′ing** [ME. *bifallen* < OE. *befeallan*, to fall, fall to as a share or right < *be-* + *feallan*, FALL] **1.** to come to pass; happen; occur **2.** [Archaic] to be fitting; pertain —*vt.* to happen to [what *befell* them?]

be·fit (bi fit′) *vt.* **-fit′ted, -fit′ting** to be suitable or proper for; be suited or becoming to

be·fit·ting (-iŋ) *adj.* proper or right; suitable —**be·fit′·ting·ly** *adv.*

be·fog (bi fôg′, -fäg′) *vt.* **-fogged′, -fog′ging 1.** to cover with or envelop in fog; make foggy **2.** to make obscure or muddled; confuse; bewilder [to *befog* an issue, to *befog* one's mind]

be·fool (bi fōōl′) *vt.* **1.** to play a trick on; fool or deceive **2.** to treat as a fool

be·fore (bi fôr′) *adv.* [ME. *biforen* < OE. *beforan* < *be-*, by + *foran*, before] **1.** in advance; in front; ahead **2.** in the past; previously [I've heard this song *before*] **3.** at an earlier time; sooner [come at ten, not *before*] —*prep.* **1.** ahead of in time, space, order, rank, or importance **2.** just in front of [he paused *before* the door] **3.** into the sight, notice, presence, etc. of [a thought flashed *before* her mind, he stood *before* his accuser] **4.** being considered, judged, or decided by [the matter *before* the committee] **5.** earlier than; prior to [the left *before* noon] **6.** still to be reached, accomplished, etc. by [the hardest task was *before* them] **7.** in preference to; rather than [to choose death *before* dishonor] —*conj.* **1.** earlier than the time that [drop in *before* you go] **2.** sooner than; rather than [I'd die *before* I'd tell]

be·fore·hand (-hand′) *adv., adj.* **1.** ahead of time; in advance **2.** in anticipation; exercising forethought

be·fore·time (-tīm′) *adv.* [Archaic] formerly

be·foul (bi foul′) *vt.* [ME. *befoulen* < OE. *befylan*: see BE- & FOUL] **1.** to make filthy; dirty; soil **2.** to cast aspersions on; slander

be·friend (bi frend′) *vt.* to act as a friend to; help

be·fud·dle (bi fud′'l) *vt.* **-fud′dled, -fud′dling 1.** to fuddle or confuse (the mind, a person, etc.) **2.** to stupefy with alcoholic liquor —**be·fud′dle·ment** *n.*

beg (beg) *vt.* **begged, beg′ging** [ME. *beggen* < Anglo-Fr. *begger* < OFr. *begard*, beggar < MDu. *beggaert*] **1.** to ask for as charity or as a gift [he *begged* a dime] **2.** to ask for earnestly as a kindness or favor —*vi.* **1.** to ask for alms; be a beggar **2.** to ask humbly; entreat —**beg off** to ask to be released from —**beg the question 1.** to use an argument that assumes as proved the very thing one is trying to prove **2.** loosely, to evade the issue —**go begging** to fail to find a taker; be unwanted

SYN.—**beg** implies humbleness or earnestness in asking for something and is now often used in polite formulas [I *beg* to differ, I *beg* to report]; **solicit** stresses courtesy and formality in requesting something [we *solicit* your aid, he *solicits* our trade]; **entreat** implies the use of all the persuasive power at one's command; **beseech** suggests fervor or passion in the asking and connotes anxiety over the outcome; **implore** is stronger still, suggesting desperation or great distress; **importune** suggests persistence in entreating, often to the point of becoming offensive

be·gan (bi gan′) *pt.* of BEGIN

be·get (bi get′) *vt.* **be·got′,** or archaic **be·gat′** (-gat′), **be·got′ten** or **be·got′, be·get′ting** [ME. *begeten*, to obtain, beget < OE. *begitan*, to acquire: see BE- & GET] **1.** to be the father or sire of; procreate **2.** to bring into being; produce [tyranny *begets* rebellion] —**be·get′ter** *n.*

beg·gar (beg′ər) *n.* [ME. *beggere* < OFr. *begard:* see BEG] **1.** a person who begs, or asks for charity, esp. one who lives by begging; mendicant **2.** a person who is very poor; pauper **3.** a person; fellow: often used jokingly or affectionately —*vt.* **1.** to make a beggar of; make poor **2.** to make seem inadequate or useless [her beauty *beggars* description] —**beg′gar·dom** (-dəm) *n.*

beg·gar·ly (-lē) *adj.* like or fit for a beggar; very poor, worthless, inadequate, etc. —**beg′gar·li·ness** *n.*

☆**beg·gar's-lice** (beg′ərz līs′) *n., pl.* **beg′gar's-lice′ 1.** any of various genera of plants (as *Cynoglossum, Hackelia,* and *Lappula*) of the borage family, with dry, prickly fruits that adhere to fur or clothing **2.** the fruit of any of these plants Also **beg′gar-lice′**

☆**beg·gar's-ticks** (-tiks′) *n., pl.* **beg′gar's-ticks′ 1.** any of a genus (*Desmodium*) of plants of the legume family, having prickly seed pods **2.** a segment of such a seed pod **3.** *a*) *same as* BUR MARIGOLD *b*) the prickly seed of a bur marigold **4.** *same as* BEGGAR'S-LICE Also **beg′gar-ticks′**

☆**beg·gar·weed** (beg′ər wēd′) *n.* any of several tick trefoils; esp., a West Indian plant (*Desmodium tortuosum*) of the legume family, grown in the southeastern U.S. for soil improvement

beg·gar·y (beg′ər ē) *n., pl.* **-ies** [ME. *beggerie* < *beggere,* BEGGAR] **1.** extreme poverty **2.** the act of begging or state of being a beggar **3.** beggars as a group

Beg·hard (beg′ərd, bə gärd′) *n.* [ML. *beghardus, begardus* < OFr. *begard:* see BEG] a member of any of several lay brotherhoods in Belgium, Holland, Germany, etc. in the 13th century

be·gin (bi gin′) *vi.* **be·gan′, be·gun′, be·gin′ning** [ME. *biginnen* < OE. *beginnan,* akin to G. *beginnen,* Goth. *duginnan*] **1.** to start doing, acting, going, etc.; get under way **2.** to come into being; arise **3.** to have a first part or element [the Bible *begins* with Genesis] **4.** to be or do in the slightest degree (with an infinitive) [they don't *begin* to compare] —*vt.* **1.** to cause to start; set about; commence **2.** to cause to come into being; originate **3.** to be the first part or element of

SYN.—**begin,** the most general of these terms, indicates merely a setting into motion of some action, process, or course [to *begin* eating]; **commence,** the more formal term, is used with reference to a ceremony or an elaborate course of action [to *commence* a court action]; **start** carries the particular implication of leaving a point of departure in any kind of progression [to *start* a journey, the boulder *started* a landslide]; **initiate,** in this connection, refers to the carrying out of the first steps in some course or process, with no indication of what is to follow [to *initiate* peace talks]; **inaugurate** suggests a formal or ceremonial beginning or opening [to *inaugurate* a new library] —**ANT.** end, finish, conclude

be·gin·ner (-ər) *n.* **1.** a person who begins anything **2.** a person just beginning to do or learn something; inexperienced, unskilled person; novice

be·gin·ning (-iŋ) *n.* **1.** a starting or commencing **2.** the time or place of starting; birth; origin; source [English democracy had its *beginning* in the Magna Charta] **3.** the first part [the *beginning* of a book] **4.** [*usually pl.*] an early stage or example [the *beginnings* of scientific agriculture] —**SYN.** see ORIGIN

be·gird (bi gurd′) *vt.* **-girt′** or **-gird′ed, -girt′, -gird′ing** [ME. *bigirden* < OE. *begyrdan* < *be-* + *gyrdan:* see BE- & GIRD[1]] **1.** to bind around; gird **2.** to encircle; surround; encompass

be·gone (bi gôn′, -gän′) *interj., vi.* (to) be gone; go away; get out: usually in the imperative

be·gon·ia (bi gōn′yə) *adj.* [after Michel *Bégon* (1638–1710), Fr. governor of Santo Domingo, a patron of science] designating a family (Begoniaceae) of tropical plants —*n.* any of a genus (*Begonia*) of plants of this family, grown for

their handsome, ornamental leaves or their clustered, showy flowers

be·got (bi gät′) *pt. & alt. pp.* of BEGET

be·got·ten (-'n) *alt. pp.* of BEGET

be·grime (bi grim′) *vt.* **-grimed′, -grim′ing** to cover with grime; make dirty; soil

be·grudge (bi gruj′) *vt.* **-grudged′, -grudg′ing** 1. to feel ill will or resentment at the possession or enjoyment of (something) by another [to *begrudge* another's fortune] 2. to give with ill will or reluctance [he *begrudges* her every cent] 3. to regard with displeasure or disapproval —*SYN.* see ENVY —**be·grudg′ing·ly** *adv.*

be·guile (bi gīl′) *vt.* **-guiled′, -guil′ing** 1. to mislead by cheating or tricking; deceive 2. to deprive (*of* or *out of*) by deceit; cheat [he was *beguiled* of his money] 3. to pass (time) pleasantly; while away [he *beguiled* his days with reading] 4. to charm or delight —*SYN.* see AMUSE, DECEIVE, LURE —**be·guile′ment** *n.* —**be·guil′er** *n.*

Beg·uin (beg′in; *Fr.* bā gan′) *n.* [OFr. < *begard:* see BEG] same as BEGHARD

Beg·uine (beg′ēn; *Fr.* bā gēn′) *n.* [OFr. < *begard:* see BEG] a member of any of several lay sisterhoods, not bound by permanent vows, that began in the Low Countries in the 12th century

be·guine (bi gēn′) *n.* [AmFr. béguine < Fr. *béguin,* infatuation, fancy (< *phr. avoir un béguin pour,* to have a fancy for), earlier, a child's cap with strings, orig., a nun's cap < MFr. *Béguine:* see prec.] a rhythmic native dance of Martinique, whose music has been popularized in the U.S.

be·gum (bē′gəm) *n.* [Anglo-Ind. < Hind. *begam,* lady < Turk., princess, fem. of *beg,* bey] in India, a Moslem princess or lady of high rank

be·gun (bi gun′) *pp.* of BEGIN

be·half (bi haf′, -häf′) *n.* [ME., in phrase *on (mi) behalfe, on (my) side* < OE. *be,* by + *healf,* half, side] support, interest, side, etc. [I speak in his *behalf*] —**in** (or **on**) **behalf of** in the interest of; for —**on behalf of** speaking for; representing

be·have (bi hāv′) *vt., vi.* **-haved′, -hav′ing** [see BE- & HAVE] 1. to conduct (oneself or itself) in a specified way; act or react 2. to conduct (oneself) in a correct or proper way; do the right things

SYN.—**behave,** used reflexively (as also the other words in this comparison), implies action in conformity with the required standards of decorum [did the children *behave* themselves?]; **conduct** implies the direction or guidance of one's actions in a specified way [he *conducted* himself well at the trial]; **demean** suggests behavior or appearance that is indicative of the specified character trait [he *demeaned* himself like a gracious host]; **deport** and **comport** suggest behavior in accordance with the fixed rules of society [they always *deport* themselves like gentlemen]; **acquit** suggests behavior in accordance with the duties of one's position or with one's obligations [the rookie *acquitted* himself like a major leaguer]

be·hav·ior (bi hāv′yər) *n.* [< BEHAVE by analogy with ME. *havior,* property < OFr. *aveir* < *avoir,* to have] 1. the way a person behaves or acts; conduct; manners 2. an organism's muscular or glandular responses to stimulation, esp. those that can be observed 3. the way a machine, element, etc. acts or functions —**be·hav′ior·al** *adj.* —**be·hav′ior·al·ly** *adv.*

behavioral science any of several studies, as sociology, anthropology, etc., that examine human activities in an attempt to discover recurrent patterns and to formulate rules about man's social behavior

☆**be·hav·ior·ism** (-iz′m) *n.* [BEHAVIOR + -ISM: coined (1913) by John B. Watson, U.S. psychologist] the doctrine that observed behavior provides the only valid data of psychology: it rejects the concept of mind and consciousness —**be·hav′ior·ist** *n., adj.* —**be·hav′ior·is′tic** *adj.*

be·hav·iour (bi hāv′yər) *n. Brit. sp.* of BEHAVIOR

be·head (bi hed′) *vt.* [ME. *bihevden* < OE. *beheafdian* < *be- + heafod,* the head] to cut off the head of; decapitate

be·held (bi held′) *pt. & pp.* of BEHOLD

be·he·moth (bi hē′məth, bē′ə-) *n.* [Heb. *behēmōth,* intens. pl. of *behēmāh,* beast < ? Egypt. *p-ehe-mau,* water ox] 1. *Bible* a huge animal, assumed to be the hippopotamus: Job 40:15–24 2. any animal or thing that is huge or very powerful

be·hest (bi hest′) *n.* [ME. *bihest* (with unhistoric *-t*) < OE. *behæs,* a vow: see BE- & HEST] an order, command, or earnest request; bidding

be·hind (bi hīnd′) *adv.* [ME. *bihinden* < OE. *behindan:* see BE- & HIND[1]] 1. in or to the rear or back [to walk *behind*], to look *behind*] 2. at an earlier time; in the past [my joy lies *behind*] 3. in a former place, condition, etc. [the girl he left *behind*] 4. in or into a retarded state [to drop *behind* in one's studies] 5. in or into arrears [to fall *behind* in one's dues] 6. slow in time; late [the train was running *behind*] 7. [Archaic] in reserve; yet to come —*prep.* 1. remaining after [the dead leave their wealth *behind* them] 2. in the rear of; back of [he sat *behind* me] 3. inferior to in position, achievement, etc. 4. later than [to be *behind* schedule] 5. on the other or farther side [of; beyond [*behind* the hill] 6. gone by or ended for [his apprenticeship was *behind* him] 7. supporting or advocating [Congress is *behind* the plan] 8. *a)* hidden by; not yet revealed about [there's something *behind* this news] *b)* in the circumstances surrounding or antecedent to —*adj.* that follows, as in a line [the person *behind*] —*n.* [Colloq.] the buttocks

be·hind·hand (-hand′) *adv., adj.* 1. behind in paying

debts, rent, etc.; in arrears 2. behind time; slow; late 3. behind or slow in progress, advancement, etc.

be·hold (bi hōld′) *vt.* **-held′, -held′** or archaic **-hold′en, -hold′ing** [ME. *biholden* < OE. *bihealdan,* to hold, keep hold of: see BE- & HOLD[1]] to hold in view or attention; look at; see; regard —*interj.* look! see! —*SYN.* see SEE[1] —**be·hold′er** *n.*

be·hold·en (-ən) *adj.* [ME., pp. of prec.] obliged to feel grateful; owing thanks; indebted [I am *beholden* to you for your advice]

be·hoof (bi hoof′) *n.* [ME. *bihove,* profit, benefit < OE. *behofe* (dat. of **bihof*) < WGmc. **behaffjan* < *be- + *hafjan:* see HEAVE] behalf, benefit, interest, advantage, sake, etc.

be·hoove (-hoov′) *vt.* **-hooved′, -hoov′ing** [ME. *bihofian* < OE. *behofian,* to have need of < prec.] to be necessary for or incumbent upon [it behooves you to think for yourself] —*vi.* [Now Rare] to be morally necessary or proper [he spoke courteously, as it *behooved*]

be·hove (-hōv′) *vt., vi.* **-hoved′, -hov′ing** [Chiefly Brit.] same as BEHOOVE

Beh·ring (bā′riŋ), **Emil Adolf von** (ā′mēl ä′dôlf fôn) 1854–1917; Ger. bacteriologist: developed tetanus & diphtheria antitoxins

Bei·der·becke (bī′dər bek′), **Bix** (biks) (born *Leon Bismarck Beiderbecke*) 1903–31; U.S. jazz musician

beige (bāzh) *n.* [Fr., orig., natural color of wool < ? It. *bambagia,* cotton < ML. *bambax:* see BOMBAST] 1. a soft wool fabric, formerly undyed and unbleached 2. its characteristic sandy color; grayish tan —*adj.* grayish-tan

be·ing (bē′iŋ) *n.* [see BE] 1. the state or fact of existing or living; existence or life 2. fundamental or essential nature 3. one who lives or exists, or is assumed to do so [a human *being,* a divine *being*] 4. all the physical and mental qualities that make up a person; personality 5. *Philos. a)* fulfillment of possibilities; essential completeness *b)* that which exists, can exist, or can be logically conceived —**being as** (or **that**) [Dial. or Colloq.] since; because —**for the time being** for the present; for now

Bei·ra (bā′rä) seaport in Mozambique, on the Mozambique Channel: pop. c. 50,000

Bei·rut (bā root′; bā′root) capital of Lebanon: seaport on the Mediterranean: pop. c. 500,000

be·jab·bers (bi jab′ərz) *interj.* [euphemism for *by Jesus*] an exclamation used variously to express surprise, pleasure, anger, annoyance, etc.: also used as a slang noun of indefinite meaning in such phrases as **beat** (or **scare**) **the bejabbers out of:** also **be·ja′bers** (-jā′bərz), **be·je′sus** (-jē′zəs)

be·jew·el (bi joo′əl) *vt.* **-eled** or **-elled, -el·ing** or **-el·ling** to cover or decorate with or as with jewels

Bel (bāl) [Akkadian form of BAAL] *Babylonian Myth.* the god of heaven and earth

☆**bel** (bel) *n.* [after A. G. BELL] *Physics* a unit for expressing in logarithms the ratios of power, equal to 10 decibels: cf. DECIBEL

be·la·bor (bi lā′bər) *vt.* 1. to beat severely; hit or whip 2. to attack with words; scold or criticize 3. *popularly,* same as LABOR, *vt.*

Be·las·co (bə las′kō), **David** 1859?–1931; U.S. theatrical producer, playwright, & actor

be·lat·ed (bi lāt′id) *adj.* [BE- + LAT(E) + -ED] 1. late or too late; tardy 2. [Archaic] overtaken by night —**be·lat′ed·ly** *adv.* —**be·lat′ed·ness** *n.*

be·lay (bi lā′) *vt., vi.* **-layed′, -lay′ing** [ME. *bileggen* < OE. *belecgan,* to make fast < *be- + lecgan,* to lay] 1. to make (a rope) secure by winding around a belaying pin, cleat, piton, etc.; hold fast 2. [Naut. Colloq.] to hold; stop [*belay* there!] 3. to secure (a person, as a mountain climber, or thing) by a rope —*n.* action, method, or place of securing a hold for a rope in mountain climbing

belaying pin a removable wooden or metal pin in the rail of a ship, around which ropes can be fastened

bel can·to (bel′ kän′tō) [It., lit., beautiful song] a style of singing characterized by brilliant vocal display and purity of tone

belch (belch) *vi., vt.* [ME. *belchen* < OE. *bealcian,* to bring up, emit, splutter out] 1. to expel (gas) through the mouth from the stomach; eructate 2. to utter (curses, orders, etc.) violently 3. to vomit 4. to throw forth (its contents) violently, often in spasms [the volcano *belched* flame] —*n.* 1. the act of belching; eructation 2. a thing belched

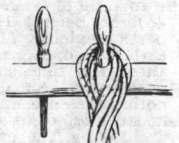

BELAYING PIN

bel·dam, bel·dame (bel′dəm) *n.* [*bel-* < Fr. *belle* (see BELLE) + DAME] 1. an old woman; esp., a hideous old woman; hag 2. [Obs.] a grandmother

be·lea·guer (bi lē′gər) *vt.* [Du. *belegeren,* to besiege < *be-,* by + *legeren,* to camp < *leger* (akin to LAIR, a camp] 1. to besiege by encircling, as with an army 2. to beset, as with difficulties; harass

Be·lém (be len′) seaport in NE Brazil, on the Pará River in the Amazon delta: capital of Pará state: pop. 402,000: also called PARÁ

bel·em·nite (bel′əm nīt′) *n.* [< Gr. *belemnon,* a dart, arrow, prob. akin to *ballein,* to throw + -ITE[1]] the cigar-

shaped fossil shell of an extinct genus (*Belemnites*) of cuttlefish of the Mesozoic Era

‡**bel·es·prit** (bel'es prē') *n., pl.* **beaux·es·prits** (bō zes prē') [Fr., lit., beautiful spirit] a clever, cultured person

Bel·fast (bel'fast, -fäst) seaport & capital of Northern Ireland, on the North Channel: pop. 410,000

Bel·fort (bel fôr') city in E France: pop. 48,000

bel·fry (bel'frē) *n., pl.* **-fries** [ME. *belfrei*, altered after *belle* (BELL¹) < *berfrai* < OFr. *berfroi* < OHG. *bergfrid*, lit., protector of peace < *bergen*, to protect + *frid*, peace] 1. a movable tower used in ancient warfare for attacking walled positions 2. a bell tower, esp. one that is part of a building, placed at the top 3. the part of a tower or steeple that holds the bell or bells

Belg. 1. Belgian 2. Belgium

bel·ga (bel'gə) *n.* [L., a Belgian] a former Belgian money of account, established in 1926 and abolished after World War II

Bel·gae (-jē) *n.pl.* [L. < Gaul., lit., the angry ones] an ancient Gallic people of northern France and Belgium

Bel Geddes *see* Norman Bel GEDDES

Bel·gian (bel'jən) *adj.* of Belgium, its people, etc. —*n.* a native or inhabitant of Belgium

Belgian Congo former Belgian colony in C Africa: see CONGO (sense 2)

Belgian hare a large, reddish-brown domestic rabbit

Bel·gic (bel'jik) *adj.* [L. *Belgicus* < *Belgae*] 1. of Belgium 2. of the Netherlands 3. of the Belgae

Bel·gium (bel'jəm) kingdom in W Europe, on the North Sea: 11,779 sq. mi.; pop. 9,499,000; cap. Brussels: Fr. name **Bel·gique** (bel zhēk'); Fl. name **Bel·gi·ë** (bel'gē ə)

Bel·grade (bel'grād, -gräd; bel grād', -gräd') capital of Yugoslavia: port on the Danube: pop. 598,000

Bel·gra·vi·a (bel grā'vē ə) a residential area surrounding Belgrave Square in London: in Victorian times, inhabited by the fashionable —**Bel·gra'vi·an** *adj., n.*

Be·li·al (bē'lē əl, bēl'yəl) *n.* [ME. < LL. (Vulgate: Deut. 13:13) < Heb. *beliya'al*, worthlessness] in the *Old Testament*, wickedness or worthlessness as an evil force —1. in the *New Testament*, Satan 2. in Milton's *Paradise Lost*, one of the fallen rebel angels

be·lie (bi lī') *vt.* **-lied', -ly'ing** [ME. *bilien* < OE. *beleogan*, to deceive by lying < *be-* + *leogan*, LIE²] 1. [Archaic] to tell lies about 2. to give a false idea of; disguise or misrepresent [his smile *belies* his anger] 3. to leave unfulfilled; disappoint [war *belied* hopes for peace] 4. to show to be untrue; prove false [her cruelty *belied* her kind words] —**be·li'er** *n.*

be·lief (bə lēf') *n.* [ME. *bileve* < *bi-*, BE- + *-leve*, contr. < *ileve* < OE. *geleafa*: see BELIEVE] 1. the state of believing; conviction or acceptance that certain things are true or real 2. faith, esp. religious faith 3. trust or confidence [I have *belief* in his ability] 4. anything believed or accepted as true; esp., a creed, doctrine, or tenet 5. an opinion; expectation; judgment [my *belief* is that he'll come]
SYN.—**belief**, the term of broadest application in this comparison, implies mental acceptance of something as true, even though absolute certainty may be absent; **faith** implies complete, unquestioning acceptance of something even in the absence of proof and, esp., of something not supported by reason; **trust** implies assurance, often apparently intuitive, in the reliability of someone or something; **confidence** also suggests such assurance, esp. when based on reason or evidence; **credence** suggests mere mental acceptance of something that may have no solid basis in fact See also OPINION —*ANT.* **doubt, incredulity**

be·lieve (bə lēv') *vt.* **-lieved', -liev'ing** [ME. *bileven* < *bi-*, BE- + *-leven*, contr. < *ileven* < OE. *geliefan* < IE. base *leubh-*, to like, desire, whence L. *libido*, LOVE, LIEF] 1. to take as true, real, etc. 2. to have confidence in a statement or promise of (another person) 3. to suppose or think —*vi.* 1. to have trust or confidence (*in*) as being true, real, good, etc. 2. to have religious faith 3. to suppose or think —**be·liev'a·bil'i·ty** *n.* —**be·liev'a·ble** *adj.* —**be·liev'a·bly** *adv.* —**be·liev'er** *n.*

be·like (bi līk') *adv.* [Archaic] quite likely; probably

Be·lin·da (bə lin'də) [< Gmc. *Betlindis:* Bet- (< ?) + *-lindis,* prob. akin to OHG. *lind,* ON. *linnr,* snake < IE. base *lento-,* flexible, whence L. *lentus*] a feminine name: dim. *Linda*

Bel·i·sa·ri·us (bel'ə ser'ē əs) 505?-565 A.D.; Byzantine general under Justinian I

Be·li·tong, Be·li·tung (be lē'tən) *same as* BILLITON

☆**be·lit·tle** (bi lit'l) *vt.* **-tled, -tling** [coined c. 1780 by Jefferson] to make seem little, less important, etc.; speak slightingly of; depreciate —*SYN.* see DISPARAGE —**be·lit'-tle·ment** *n.* —**be·lit'tler** *n.*

Be·lize (bə lēz') seaport on the Caribbean coast of British Honduras: the former capital: pop. 38,000

bell¹ (bel) *n.* [ME. & OE. *belle* < IE. base *bhel-*, to sound, roar (orig. ? echoic), whence ON. *belja*, to roar, BELLOW] 1. a hollow object, usually cuplike, made of metal or other hard material which rings when struck, as by a clapper inside 2. such an object rung to mark the hours or the beginning and end of a period of time 3. the sound made by a bell 4. anything shaped like a bell, as a flower, the flare of a horn, etc. 5. [*pl.*] a musical instrument made up

of a series of tuned metal bars or hollow tubes that are sounded by striking 6. *Naut. a)* a bell rung every half hour to mark the periods of the watch: the series of rings begins at *one bell* (12:30, 4:30, and 8:30 o'clock) and ends at *eight bells* (4:00, 8:00, and 12:00 o'clock) *b)* any of these half-hour periods —*vt.* 1. to attach a bell or bells to 2. to shape like a bell —*vi.* to flare out like a bell

bell² (bel) *n.* [ME. *bellen* < OE. *bellan:* see prec.] a bellow; roar —*vi.* to utter long, deep sounds, as a hound in pursuit of game; bay; bellow

Bell (bel) 1. Alexander Graham, 1847–1922; U.S. inventor of the telephone, born in Scotland 2. pseudonym of the BRONTË sisters

Bel·la (bel'ə) a feminine name: see ARABELLA, ISABELLA

bel·la·don·na (bel'ə dän'ə) *n.* [ModL. < It. *bella donna,* lit., beautiful lady, a folk etym. (infl. by cosmetic use for dilating the eye) for ML. *bladona,* nightshade, prob. < Gaul.] 1. a poisonous European plant (*Atropa belladonna*) of the nightshade family, with purplish or reddish bell-shaped flowers and shiny black berries; deadly nightshade: it is the source of atropine 2. *same as* ATROPINE

belladonna lily a tropical American bulbous plant (*Amaryllis belladonna*) of the agave family, grown for its large pink, white, or red flowers

‡**bel·la fi·gu·ra** (bel'lä fē gōō'rä) [It.] a good impression; fine appearance

Bel·la·my (bel'ə mē), **Edward** 1850–98; U.S. writer & political theorist; author of *Looking Backward*

bell·bird (bel'burd') *n.* any of various birds that make bell-like sounds, as the wood thrush

bell-bot·tom (-bät'əm) *adj.* designating trousers that flare at the ankles: also **bell'-bot'tomed**

☆**bell·boy** (-boi') *n. same as* BELLMAN (sense 2)

bell buoy a buoy with a warning bell rung by the motion of the waves

☆**bell captain** a person in charge of a group of bellmen

Belle (bel) [Fr.: see ff.] a feminine name

belle (bel) *n.* [Fr., fem. of *beau:* see BEAU] a pretty woman or girl; often, one who is the prettiest or most popular [the *belle* of the ball]

Bel·leau Wood (be lō') small forest in France, east of Paris: site of a battle (1918) in World War I

Bel·leek (ware) (bə lēk') [after *Belleek,* town in Northern Ireland, where it is made] a fine, glossy, often iridescent pottery resembling porcelain

‡**belle é·poque** (be lā pôk') [*occas.* B- E-] the era of elegance and gaiety that characterized fashionable Parisian life in the period preceding World War I

Belle Isle, Strait of strait between Labrador & Newfoundland: 10–15 mi. wide

Bel·ler·o·phon (bə ler'ə fän') [L. < Gr. *Bellerephōn*] *Gr. Myth.* the hero who killed the monster Chimera, aided by the winged horse Pegasus

belles-let·tres (bel let'rə) *n.pl.* [Fr., lit., beautiful letters, fine literature] literature as one of the fine arts; fiction, poetry, drama, etc. as distinguished from technical and scientific writings

bel·let·rist (bel let'rist) *n.* a writer of belles-lettres — **bel'le·tris'tic** *adj.*

Belle·ville (bel'vil) [Fr., lit., beautiful town] city in SW Ill.: pop. 42,000

Belle·vue (bel'vyōō') [Fr., lit., beautiful view] city in NW Wash.: suburb of Seattle: pop. 61,000

Bell·flow·er (bel'flou'ər) city in SW Calif.: suburb of Los Angeles: pop. 51,000

bell·flow·er (bel'flou'ər) *adj.* designating a large family (Campanulaceae) of flowering plants —*n.* any of a genus (*Campanula*) of plants of this family, with showy, bell-shaped flowers of white, pink, or blue, widely distributed in the temperate zones

☆**bell·hop** (-häp') *n. same as* BELLMAN (sense 2)

bel·li·cose (bel'ə kōs') *adj.* [ME. < L. *bellicosus* < *bellicus,* of war < *bellum,* war < OL. *dvellum:* for IE. base see DUEL] of a quarrelsome or hostile nature; eager to fight or quarrel; warlike —*SYN.* see BELLIGERENT —**bel'li·cose'ly** *adv.* — **bel·li·cos·i·ty** (bel'ə käs'ə tē) *n.*

bel·lied (bel'ēd) *adj.* having a belly, esp. of a specified kind [the yellow-*bellied* sapsucker]

bel·lig·er·ence (bə lij'ər əns) *n.* belligerent or aggressively hostile attitude, nature, or quality

bel·lig·er·en·cy (-ən sē) *n.* 1. the state of being at war or of being recognized as a belligerent 2. *same as* BELLIGERENCE

bel·lig·er·ent (bə lij'ər ənt) *adj.* [L. *belligerans,* prp. of *belligerare,* to wage war < *bellum,* war (see BELLICOSE) + *gerere,* to carry on] 1. at war; designating or of a state recognized under international law as being engaged in a war 2. of fighting 3. seeking war; warlike 4. showing a readiness to fight or quarrel [a *belligerent* gesture or tone] —*n.* a belligerent person, group, or nation — **bel·lig'er·ent·ly** *adv.*
SYN.—**belligerent** implies a taking part in war or fighting or in actions that are likely to provoke fighting [*belligerent* nations;] **bellicose** implies a warlike or hostile nature, suggesting a readiness to fight [a *bellicose* mood]; **pugnacious** and **quarrelsome** both

connote aggressiveness and a willingness to initiate a fight, but **quarrelsome** more often suggests pettiness and eagerness to fight for little or no reason; **contentious** suggests an inclination to argue or quarrel, usually with annoying persistence —*ANT.* **peaceful, friendly**

Bel·ling·ham (bel′iŋ ham′) seaport in NW Wash., at the N end of Puget Sound: pop. 39,000

Bel·lings·hau·sen Sea (bel′iŋz hou′z'n) part of the S Pacific Ocean, west of the Antarctic Peninsula

Bel·li·ni (bel lē′nē) **1. Gen·ti·le** (jen tē′le), 1429?–1507; Venetian painter: son of *Jacopo* **2. Gio·van·ni** (jō vän′nē), 1430?–1516; Venetian painter: teacher of Titian & Giorgione: son of *ff.* **3. Ja·co·po** (yä′kô pô), 1400?–70; Venetian painter **4. Vin·cen·zo** (vēn chen′tsô), 1801–35; It. operatic composer

bell jar a bell-shaped container or cover made of glass, used to keep gases, air, moisture, etc. in or out: also **bell glass**

bell·man (bel′mən) *n., pl.* **-men** (-mən) **1.** *same as* TOWN CRIER ☆**2.** a man or boy employed by a hotel, club, etc. to carry luggage and do errands

bell metal an alloy of copper and tin used in bells

bell-mouthed (-mouthd′, -mout͟ht′) *adj.* having a flaring mouth or opening like that of a bell

Bel·loc (bel′äk), **(Joseph) Hi·laire (Pierre)** (hi ler′) 1870–1953; Eng. writer, born in France

Bello Horizonte *former spelling of* BELO HORIZONTE

Bel·lo·na (bə lō′nə) [L. < *bellum*: see BELLICOSE] *Rom. Myth.* the goddess of war, wife or sister of Mars

bel·low (bel′ō) *vi.* [ME. *belwen* < OE. *bylgan*: for IE. base see BELL[1]] **1.** to roar with a powerful, reverberating sound, as a bull, elephant, etc. **2.** to cry out loudly, as in anger or pain —*vt.* to utter loudly or powerfully —*n.* the sound of bellowing; roar

bel·lows (bel′ōz; *occas.* -əz) *n. sing. & pl.* [ME. *belwes*, orig. pl. of *beli*: see BELLY] **1.** a device that produces a stream of air through a narrow tube when its sides are pressed together: used for blowing fires, in pipe organs, etc. **2.** anything like a bellows, as the folding part of some cameras, the lungs, etc.

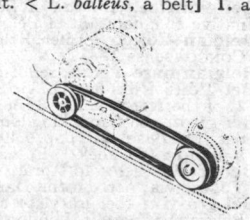

NOZZLE

ENTRANCE FOR AIR

VALVE

BELLOWS

Bel·lows (bel′ōz), **George (Wesley)** 1882–1925; U.S. painter

bell·weth·er (bel′wet͟h′ər) *n.* **1.** a male sheep, usually wearing a bell, that leads the flock **2.** a leader, esp. of a sheeplike crowd

bell·wort (-wurt′) *n.* **1.** any of a genus (*Uvularia*) of perennial woodland plants of the lily family, native to N. America, with conspicuous, drooping yellow flowers **2.** [Chiefly Brit.] any of various bellflowers

bel·ly (bel′ē) *n., pl.* **-lies** [ME. *beli* < OE. *belg*, leather bag, purse, bellows < IE. base *bhelgh-*, to swell, bag (< *bhel-*, to inflate), whence Ir. *bolg*, sack, belly, ON. *bylgja*, billow, Goth. *balgs*, leather bottle] **1.** the lower front part of the human body between the chest and thighs; abdomen **2.** the underside of an animal's body **3.** the abdominal cavity **4.** the stomach **5.** an appetite for food **6.** the deep interior [the *belly* of a ship] **7.** any part, surface, or section that curves outward or bulges, as the swelling part of a sail in the wind, the fleshy middle part of a muscle, or the upper surface of a violin **8.** the front part or underside of anything: opposed to BACK[1] **9.** [Archaic] the womb —*vt., vi.* **-lied, -ly·ing** to swell out; curve out; bulge

bel·ly·ache (-āk′) *n.* pain in the abdomen or bowels —☆*vi.* **-ached′, -ach′ing** [Slang] to complain or grumble

bel·ly·band (-band′) *n.* **1.** a girth or cinch around an animal's belly, as for keeping a saddle or harness in place **2.** a cloth band formerly put around a baby's abdomen to prevent protrusion of the navel

bel·ly·but·ton (-but′'n) *n.* [Colloq.] the navel: also **belly button**

belly dance a dance of eastern Mediterranean origin characterized by a twisting of the abdomen, sinuous hip movements, etc. —**belly′dance′** *vi.* —**belly dancer**

☆**bel·ly-flop** (-fläp′) *vi.* **-flopped′, -flop′ping** [Colloq.] **1.** to dive awkwardly so that the belly strikes flat against the water **2.** to throw oneself on a sled, with the belly downward, and coast, as down a hill Also **bel′ly-bump′, bel′ly-whop′, bel′ly-slam′,** etc.

bel·ly·ful (-fool′) *n.* **1.** enough or more than enough to eat **2.** [Slang] enough or more than enough of anything; all that one can bear

☆**belly laugh** [Colloq.] **1.** a hearty laugh **2.** anything that provokes such a laugh, as a line in a play

Bel·mon·te (bel môn′te), **Juan** 1892–1962; Sp. matador

Be·lo Ho·ri·zon·te (be′lô rē zôn′te) city in SE Brazil: capital of Minas Gerais state: pop. 693,000

Be·loit (bə loit′) [< Fr. *bel*, beautiful + (DETR)OIT] city in S Wis.: pop. 36,000

be·long (bi lôŋ′) *vi.* [ME. *bilangen* < *be-*, intens. + OE. *langian*, belong] **1.** to have a proper or suitable place [the chair *belongs* in the corner, she *belongs* in the movies] **2.** to be part of; be related or connected (*to*) **3.** to be associated; be a member (with *to*) **4.** to be owned (with *to*) **5.** [Slang] to be the owner (with *to*) [who *belongs* to this toothbrush?]

be·long·ing (-iŋ) *n.* **1.** a thing that belongs to one **2.** [*pl.*] possessions; property **3.** close relationship; affinity; rapport [a feeling of *belonging*]

Be·lo·rus·sia (byel′ō rush′ə) *same as* BYELORUSSIA

Be·lo·stok (byel′ō stôk′) *Russ. name of* BIALYSTOK

be·lov·ed (bi luv′id, -luvd′) *adj.* [ME., pp. of *biluven*: see BE- & LOVE] dearly loved —*n.* a beloved person

be·low (bi lō′) *adv., adj.* [see BE- & LOW[1]] **1.** in or to a lower place; beneath **2.** in a lower place on the page or on a later page (of a book, etc.) **3.** in or to hell **4.** on earth **5.** on or to a lower floor or deck **6.** in or to a lesser rank, amount, function, etc. **7.** *Music* in a lower pitch —*prep.* **1.** lower than, as in position, rank, worth, etc. **2.** unworthy of; beneath [it is *below* her to say that]

Bel·sen (bel′z'n) village in West Germany, near Hanover: with the nearby village of Bergen, the site of a Nazi concentration camp and extermination center

Bel·shaz·zar (bel shaz′ər) [Heb. *bēlshatstsar* < Bab. *belsharra-uṣur*, lit., may Bel protect the king] *Bible* the last king of Babylon, who was warned of defeat by the handwriting on the wall: Dan. 5

belt (belt) *n.* [ME. & OE., ult. < L. *balteus*, a belt] **1.** a strip or band of leather or other material worn around the waist to hold clothing up, support tools, etc., or as an ornament or sign of rank: see also SAFETY BELT **2.** any encircling thing like this **3.** a series of armored plates around a ship at the water line **4.** a wide, endless strap or band for transferring motion from one wheel or pulley to another or others, or for carrying things **5.** an area or zone distinguished from others in some way [the corn *belt*] ☆**6.** an encircling or beltlike road, highway, or route **7.** [Slang] a hard blow; cuff ☆**8.** [Slang] *a*) a drink or big gulp, esp. of liquor *b*) pleasurable excitement; thrill —*vt.* **1.** to surround or encircle with or as with a belt; girdle **2.** to fasten or attach with or as with a belt **3.** to strike with a belt ☆**4.** [Colloq.] to sing loudly and lustily with a driving rhythm (usually with *out*) **5.** [Slang] to strike with force ☆**6.** [Slang] *a*) to take one or more drinks of (liquor): often with *down b*) to drink heavily —*vi.* [Colloq.] to move at high speed —**below the belt** unfair(ly); foul: orig. said of a blow to the groin in boxing —**tighten one's belt** **1.** to endure hunger, privation, etc. as best one can **2.** to live more thriftily —**under one's belt** [Colloq.] as part of one's experience or training; to one's credit [ten years of civil service *under his belt*]

TRANSMISSION BELT

Bel·tane (bel′tān) *n.* [Scot. < Gael. *Bealtainn*] **1.** May 1 (Old Style) **2.** the ancient Celtic May Day

belt·ed (bel′tid) *adj.* **1.** wearing a belt, esp. as a mark of distinction [a *belted* knight] **2.** having or marked by a band or stripe

belt·ing (-tiŋ) *n.* **1.** material for making belts **2.** belts collectively **3.** [Slang] a beating

☆**belt line** a railroad, trolley line, etc. that makes a circuit, as around a large urban area

be·lu·ga (bə lōō′gə) *n., pl.* **-ga, -gas**: see PLURAL, II, D, 2 [< Russ. < *byeli*, white] **1.** a large, white sturgeon (*Huso huso*) of the Black Sea and the Caspian Sea **2.** a large white dolphin (*Delphinapterus leucas*) of northern seas; white whale

bel·ve·dere (bel′və dir′, bel′və dir′) *n.* [It., beautiful view < *bel* (L. *bellus*), beautiful + *vedere* (L. *videre*), to see] a summerhouse on a height, or an open, roofed gallery in an upper story, built for giving a view of the scenery —**[B-]** a court in the Vatican, housing a collection of classical art

be·ma (bē′mə) *n., pl.* **be′ma·ta** (-mə tə), **be′mas** [Gr. *bēma*, platform, lit., a step < base of *bainein*, to go] **1.** in ancient Greece, a speaker's platform **2.** *Judaism* a platform in a synagogue, from which the Scripture is read **3.** *Orthodox Eastern Church* the enclosed area surrounding the altar

be·mean (bi mēn′) *vt. same as* DEMEAN[2]

be·mire (bi mir′) *vt.* **-mired′, -mir′ing 1.** to make dirty with or as with mire, mud, etc. **2.** to cause to bog down in mud

be·moan (bi mōn′) *vt., vi.* [ME. *bimaenen* < OE. *bemaenan*: see BE- & MOAN] to moan about or deplore (a loss, grief, etc.); lament [to *bemoan* one's fate]

be·mock (bi mäk′) *vt.* to mock or mock at

be·muse (bi myōōz′) *vt.* **-mused′, -mus′ing** [BE- + MUSE] **1.** to muddle or stupefy, as with liquor **2.** to plunge in thought; preoccupy: usually in the passive voice —**be·muse′ment** *n.*

ben[1] (ben) *n.* [Heb. *bēn*] son (of) [Rabbi *Ben* Ezra]

ben[2] (ben) *n.* [Scot. < Gael. *beann*, a peak] [Scot. & Ir.] a mountain peak [*Ben* Nevis]

ben[3] (ben) *adv., prep.* [Scot. < ME. *binne* < OE. *be-* + *innan*, in] [Scot.] within; inside —*adj.* [Scot.] inner —*n.* [Scot.] the inner room or living room of a cottage

ben·act·y·zine (bə nak′tə zēn′) *n.* [arbitrary coinage] a crystalline drug used as a tranquilizer in treating anxiety and psychoneurosis

☆**Ben·a·dryl** (ben′ə dril) *a trademark for* an antihistamine

used to treat a variety of allergic disorders —*n.* [b-] this drug

be·name (bi nām′) *vt.* -named′, -named′ or -nempt′ or -nempt′ed, -nam′ing [Archaic] to name; call

Be·na·res (bə nä′rēz) *former name of* VARANASI

Be·na·ven·te (y Mar·ti·nez) (be′nä ven′te ē mär te′neth), Ja·cin·to (hä then′tô) 1866–1954; Sp. playwright

bench (bench) *n.* [ME. < OE. *benc* (cf. BANK²)] 1. a long, hard seat for several persons, with or without a back 2. a seat between the two sides of a boat 3. the place where judges sit in a court 4. [*sometimes* B-] *a*) the status or office of a judge *b*) judges collectively *c*) a law court 5. *a*) an official's seat or his office, status, etc. *b*) the officials in this office ☆6. *a*) a seat on which the players on a sports team sit when not on the field *b*) auxiliary players collectively 7. *a*) a stand upon which dogs are exhibited and judged at a dog show *b*) a dog show 8. a strong table on which work with tools is done, often one that is part of a machine; worktable 9. a terrace along the bank of a body of water, often marking a former shore line 10. a shelf in rock or in mine workings —*vt.* 1. to provide with benches 2. to place on a bench, esp. an official one 3. to exhibit at a dog show ☆4. *Sports* to take or keep (a player) out of a game —**on the bench** 1. presiding in a law court; serving as a judge ☆2. *Sports* not taking part in the game, as an auxiliary player

bench·er (ben′chər) *n.* a person who sits on a bench, as a judge or member of a British Parliament

☆**bench jockey** [Slang] *Sports* a player on the bench who taunts opposing players, the umpire, etc.

Bench·ley (bench′lē), **Robert (Charles)** 1889–1945; U.S. humorist

bench man one who works at a bench, esp. one who does radio and television repair work

bench mark 1. a surveyor's mark made on a permanent landmark of known position and altitude: it is used as a reference point in determining other altitudes 2. a standard or point of reference in measuring or judging quality, value, etc. Also **bench′mark′** *n.*

☆**bench show** an exhibition of small animals, esp. dogs, competing for awards on the basis of how closely they conform to ideal standards for the breed

bench warrant an order issued by a judge or law court for the arrest of a person charged with contempt of court or a criminal offense

bend¹ (bend) *vt.* **bent** or archaic **bend′ed, bend′ing** [ME. *benden* < OE. *bendan*, to confine with a string < OE. *bend*: see BAND¹]; hence, to fetter, bend (a bow) 1. orig., to cause tension in (a bow, etc.), as by drawing with a string 2. to force (an object) into a curved or crooked form, or (*back*) to its original form, by turning, pulling, pressing, etc. 3. to turn from a straight line [*he bent* his steps from the path] 4. to make submit or give in [*to bend* another's will to one's wishes] 5. to turn or direct (one's eyes, attention, energy, etc. *to*) 6. to cause to have a fixed purpose; determine: used in the passive voice [*he was bent* on success] 7. to incline or tend (*to* or *toward*) 8. *Naut.* to fasten (sails or ropes) into position —*vi.* 1. to turn or be turned from a straight line or from some direction or position 2. to yield by curving or crooking, as from pressure 3. to crook or curve the body from a standing position; stoop (*over* or *down*) 4. to give in; yield [*he bent* to her wishes] 5. [Archaic] to direct one's attention, energy, etc. (*to* something) —*n.* 1. a bending or being bent 2. a bent or curving part, as of a river 3. *Shipbuilding* a wale —**SYN.** see CURVE —**round the bend** [Brit. Colloq.] crazy, mad, insane, etc. —**bend′a·ble** *adj.*

bend² (bend) *n.* [ME. < prec.] 1. any of various knots used to tie one rope to another or to something else 2. *Tanning* one half of a trimmed hide, or butt —☆**the bends** [Colloq.] *same as* DECOMPRESSION SICKNESS

bend³ (bend) *n.* [OFr. *bende*: see BAND¹] *Heraldry* a stripe or band on a coat of arms, from the upper left to the lower right corner (as seen by the viewer)

☆**Ben Day process** [after *Benjamin Day* (1838–1916), N.Y. printer] *Photoengraving* a process for adding tone or shading in reproducing line drawings, etc. by the use of patterns of dots, stipples, or the like: also **Ben′day′** (or **ben′day′**) **process**

bend·er (ben′dər) *n.* 1. a person or thing that bends ☆2. [Slang] a drinking bout; spree

Ben·di·go (ben′di gō′) city in C Victoria, Australia: pop., with suburbs, 43,000

bend sinister *Heraldry* a band or stripe on a coat of arms, from the upper right to the lower left corner (as seen by the viewer): it signifies bastardy in the family line

be·neath (bi nēth′) *adv., adj.* [ME. *binethe* < OE. *beneothan* < *be-* + *neothan*, down: see NETHER] 1. in a lower place; below 2. just below something; underneath —*prep.* 1. below; lower than 2. directly under; underneath 3. covered by [*beneath* blankets] 4. under the influence or control of 5. inferior to or lower than in rank, quality, worth, etc. 6. unworthy of [*it is beneath* him to cheat]

ben·e·dic·i·te (ben′ə dis′ə tē′; *for n. 2 usually* bā′nā dē′chē tā′) *interj.* [L. < *benedicere*: see BENEDICTION] bless

you! —*n.* 1. the invocation of a blessing, as in asking grace at meals 2. [B-] the canticle that begins *Benedicite, omnia opera Domini, Domino* (Bless the Lord, all ye works of the Lord)

Ben·e·dick (ben′ə dik) in Shakespeare's *Much Ado About Nothing,* a bachelor who falls in love with and marries the clever Beatrice —*n.* [b-] *same as* BENEDICT

Ben·e·dict (ben′ə dikt′) [L. *Benedictus,* lit., blessed: see BENEDICTION] 1. a masculine name: var. *Bennet, Bennett* 2. Saint, 480?–543? A.D.; It. monk: founder of the Benedictine order: his day is March 21: also called **St. Benedict of Nur·si·i** (nur′sē ə) 3. **Benedict XIV** (*Prospero Lambertini*) 1675–1758; Pope (1740–58) 4. **Benedict XV** (*Giacomo della Chiesa*) 1854–1922; Pope (1914–22)

ben·e·dict (-dikt′) *n.* [< BENEDICK] a recently married man, esp. one who seemed to be a confirmed bachelor

Ben·e·dict (-dikt′), **Ruth Fulton** 1887–1948; U.S. anthropologist

Ben·e·dic·tine (ben′ə dik′tin; *also, and for n. 2 usually,* -tēn) *adj.* [Fr. *bénédictin*] 1. of Saint Benedict 2. designating or of the monastic order based on his teachings, founded c. 529 A.D. —*n.* 1. a Benedictine monk or nun 2. [b-] a liqueur, containing aromatic herbs and spices, orig. made by Benedictine monks in France

ben·e·dic·tion (ben′ə dik′shən) *n.* [ME. *benediccioun* < L. *benedictio* < *benedicere,* to speak well of, in ML (Ec.), to hallow, bless, < *bene,* well + *dicere,* to speak] 1. a blessing 2. an invocation of divine blessing, esp. at the end of a religious service 3. blessedness 4. [B-] *R.C.Ch.* a devotional service during which a consecrated Host is exposed in a monstrance and a solemn blessing is given with the Host —**ben′e·dic′to·ry** (-tər ē) *adj.*

Ben·e·dic·tus (-tәs) *n.* [L., blessed, pp. of *benedicere:* see BENEDICTION] 1. Zacharias' hymn (see Luke 1:68) beginning "Benedictus," sung daily at Lauds 2. a short hymn of praise, also beginning "Benedictus," used in the Mass: Matt. 21:9 3. music for either of these hymns

ben·e·fac·tion (ben′ə fak′shən, ben′ə fak′shən) *n.* [LL. *benefactio* < L. *benefacere,* to do (something) well, do a good deed < *bene,* well + *facere,* to do] 1. the act of doing good or helping others, esp. by giving money for charitable purposes 2. the money or help given

ben·e·fac·tor (ben′ə fak′tər) *n.* [ME. < LL.: see prec.] a person who has given help, esp. financial help; patron —**ben′e·fac′tress** (-tris) *n.fem.*

be·nef·ic (bə nef′ik) *adj.* [L. *beneficus* < *benefacere:* see BENEFACTION] beneficent

ben·e·fice (ben′ə fis) *n.* [ME. < OFr. < L. *beneficium,* a kindness, service, promotion < prec.] 1. land held by a feudal tenant for services rendered the owner 2. an endowed church office providing a living for a vicar, rector, etc. 3. its income —*vt.* **-ficed, -fic·ing** to provide with a benefice

be·nef·i·cence (bə nef′ə s'ns) *n.* [ME. < L. *beneficentia* < *benefacere:* see BENEFACTION] 1. the fact or quality of being kind or doing good; charity 2. a charitable act or generous gift

be·nef·i·cent (-s'nt) *adj.* 1. showing beneficence; doing good 2. resulting in benefit —**be·nef′i·cent·ly** *adv.*

ben·e·fi·cial (ben′ə fish′əl) *adj.* [ME. < OFr. < LL. *beneficialis* < L. *benefacere:* see BENEFACTION] 1. producing benefits; advantageous; favorable 2. receiving benefit 3. *Law* for one's own benefit [*beneficial* interest] —**ben′e·fi′cial·ly** *adv.*

ben·e·fi·ci·ar·y (ben′ə fish′ē er′ē, -fish′ər ē) *adj.* [L. *beneficiarius*] of or holding a benefice —*n., pl.* **-ar·ies** 1. a holder of a benefice 2. anyone receiving benefit 3. a person named to receive the income or inheritance from a will, insurance policy, trust, etc. 4. *Law* a person for whose benefit a trust has been created

ben·e·fit (ben′ə fit) *n.* [ME. *benefet* < OFr. *bienfait,* a kindness < L. *benefactum,* meritorious act < *benefacere:* see BENEFACTION] 1. [Archaic] a kindly, charitable act; benefaction 2. anything contributing to an improvement in condition; advantage; help 3. [*often pl.*] payments made by an insurance company, public agency, welfare society, etc. as during sickness, retirement, unemployment, etc. or for death 4. any public performance, bazaar, dance, etc. the proceeds of which are to help a certain person, group, or cause —*vt.* **-fit·ed, -fit·ing** to do good to or for; aid —*vi.* to receive advantage; profit

benefit of clergy 1. the exemption which the medieval clergy had from trial or punishment except in a church court 2. an administering or sanctioning by the church [*marriage without benefit of clergy*]

benefit society (or **association**) an organization which, by means of dues, secures for its members certain benefits, such as life insurance, hospitalization, etc.

Be·ne·lux (ben′ə luks′) [< BE(LGIUM), NE(THERLANDS), LUX(EMBURG)] economic union of Belgium, Netherlands, & Luxemburg established by treaty in 1958: in full, **Benelux Economic Union**

be·nempt (bi nempt′) [Archaic] *alt. pp.* of BENAME: also **be·nempt′ed**

Be·neš (ben′esh), **E·du·ard** (e′dŏŏ ärt′) 1884–1948; Czech

statesman: president of Czechoslovakia (1935–38; 1946–48); president of government in exile (1939–45)

Be·nét (bə nā′) **1. Stephen Vincent,** 1898–1943; U.S. poet & writer **2. William Rose,** 1886–1950; U.S. poet, novelist, & editor: brother of *prec.*

be·nev·o·lence (bə nev′ə ləns) *n.* [ME. & OFr. < L. *benevolentia:* see BENEVOLENT] **1.** an inclination to do good; kindliness **2.** a kindly, charitable act or gift; beneficence **3.** a forced loan formerly levied by some English kings on their subjects

be·nev·o·lent (-lənt) *adj.* [ME. & OFr. < L. *benevolens* < *bene,* well + *volens,* prp. of *velle,* to wish] **1.** doing or inclined to do good; kindly; charitable **2.** characterized by or resulting from benevolence —**be·nev′o·lent·ly** *adv.*

Beng. Bengali

Ben·gal (ben gôl′, beŋ-; beŋ′gəl) **1.** region in the NE part of the Indian peninsula, divided (1947) between India & Pakistan: see EAST BENGAL, WEST BENGAL **2. Bay of,** part of the Indian Ocean, east of India & west of Burma & the Malay Peninsula

Ben·ga·lese (ben′gə lēz′, beŋ′-) *adj.* of Bengal or its people —*n., pl.* **-lese′** a native of Bengal

Ben·gal·i (ben gôl′ē, beŋ-) *n.* **1.** a native of Bengal **2.** the Indo-European, Indic language of Bengal —*adj.* of Bengal, its people, or their language

ben·ga·line (beŋ′gə lēn′, beŋ′gə lēn′) *n.* [Fr. < *Bengal,* whence the cloth was imported] a heavy, corded cloth of silk, rayon, or the like and either wool or cotton

Bengal light a firework or flare with a steady blue light, used, esp. formerly, as a signal, etc.

Ben·gha·zi, Ben·ga·si (ben gä′zē, beŋ-) seaport on the coast of Libya, one of its two capitals: pop. 80,000

Ben-Gu·ri·on (ben goor′ē ən), **David** 1886– ; Israeli statesman, born in Poland: prime minister of Israel (1948–53; 1955–63)

Be·ni (bā′nē) river in NW Bolivia, joining the Mamoré to form the Madeira: c. 1,000 mi.

be·night·ed (bi nīt′id) *adj.* [ME., pp. of *binighten:* see BE- & NIGHT] **1.** caught or surrounded by darkness or night **2.** intellectually or morally backward; ignorant; unenlightened

be·nign (bi nīn′) *adj.* [ME. & OFr. *benigne* < L. *benignus,* good, lit., well-born < *bene,* well (cf. sense development of GENTLE) + *genus,* birth: see GENUS] **1.** good-natured; kindly **2.** favorable; beneficial **3.** *Med.* doing little or no harm; not malignant —*SYN.* see KIND —**be·nign′ly** *adv.*

be·nig·nant (bi nig′nənt) *adj.* [< BENIGN, by analogy with MALIGNANT] **1.** kindly or gracious, sometimes in a patronizing way **2.** favorable; beneficial —**be·nig′nan·cy** *n., pl.* **-cies**

be·nig·ni·ty (-nə tē) *n., pl.* **-ties** [ME. & OFr. *benignite* < L. *benignitas:* see BENIGN] **1.** benignancy; kindliness **2.** a kind act; favor

Be·nin (be nēn′) **1.** former native kingdom in W Africa, now a province of Nigeria: it was the center of what came to be known as the Slave Coast **2. Bight of,** N part of the Gulf of Guinea, just west of the Niger delta

ben·i·son (ben′ə z′n, -s′n) *n.* [ME. *benisoun* < OFr. *beneisson* < L. *benedictio*] a blessing; benediction

Ben·ja·min (ben′jə mən) [Heb. *binyāmin,* lit., son of the right hand; hence, favorite son] **1.** a masculine name: dim. *Ben, Benny* **2.** *Bible a)* Jacob's youngest son *b)* the tribe of Israel descended from him **3. Judah Philip,** 1811–84; U.S. lawyer; Confederate secretary of state (1862–65)

ben·ja·min (ben′jə mən) *n.* [alt. < *benjoin:* see BENZOIN] *same as* BENZOIN (sense 1)

☆**ben·ne, ben·e** (ben′ē) *n.* [< Mende (Sierra Leone) *bene*] *same as* SESAME (sense 1)

Ben·nett (ben′it) **1.** a masculine name: see BENEDICT: also **Bennet 2. (Enoch) Arnold,** 1867–1931; Eng. novelist **3. James Gordon,** 1795–1872; U.S. journalist, born in Scotland: founder of the New York *Herald* **4. Richard Bedford,** 1st Viscount, 1870–1947; Canad. statesman: prime minister of Canada (1930–35)

Ben Ne·vis (ben nē′vis; nev′is) mountain in WC Scotland: highest peak in the British Isles: 4,406 ft.

Ben·ning·ton (ben′iŋ tən) [after *Benning* Wentworth (1696–1770), 1st gov. of New Hampshire] town in SW Vt.: a Revolutionary War battle was fought near here (1777): pop. 8,000

☆**ben·ny** (ben′ē) *n., pl.* **-nies** [Slang] an amphetamine pill, esp. Benzedrine, used as a stimulant

Be·no·ni (bə nō′nē) city in the Transvaal, South Africa: gold-mining center: pop. 141,000

bent¹ (bent) *pt. and pp. of* BEND¹ —*adj.* **1.** made curved or crooked; not straight **2.** strongly inclined or determined (with *on*) [she is *bent* on going] **3.** set in a course; bound [travelers westward *bent*] —*n.* **1.** an inclining; tendency **2.** a mental leaning; propensity [a *bent* for music, a criminal *bent*] **3.** a framework transverse to the length of a structure, for supporting lateral as well as vertical loads —*SYN.* see INCLINATION —**to** (or **at**) **the top of one's bent** (or at) the limit of one's capacity or ability

bent² (bent) *n.* [ME. < OE. *beonot,* bent, a rush < WGmc. *binut,* as in G. *binse*] **1.** any of a genus (*Agrostis*) of wiry, low-growing grasses that spread by putting out runners and are often used for lawns and golf greens: also called **bent′grass 2.** the stiff flower stalk of certain grasses **3.** [Archaic] a heath; moor

Ben·tham (ben′thəm), **Jeremy** 1748–1832; Eng. philosopher, economist, & jurist

Ben·tham·ism (-thə miz′m) *n.* the utilitarian philosophy of Jeremy Bentham, which holds that the greatest happiness of the greatest number should be the ultimate goal of society and of the individual —**Ben′tham·ite′** (-mīt′) *n.*

ben·thos (ben′thäs) *n.* [ModL. < Gr. *benthos,* depth of the sea] all the plants and animals living on or closely associated with the bottom of a body of water, esp. the ocean —**ben′thic** (-thik), **ben·thon′ic** (-thän′ik) *adj.*

Bent·ley (bent′lē) **1. Eric (Russell),** 1916– ; U.S. drama critic & stage director, born in England **2. Richard,** 1662–1742; Eng. classical scholar & critic

Ben·ton (ben′tən) **1. Thomas Hart,** 1782–1858; U.S. senator (1821–51) **2. Thomas Hart,** 1889– ; U.S. painter: grandnephew of *prec.*

☆**ben·ton·ite** (ben′tə nīt′) *n.* [from Fort *Benton* (after Senator BENTON) in Montana, where it is found] a porous clay, produced by the decomposition of volcanic ash, that is able to absorb much water and swell greatly as a result

bent·wood (bent′wood′) *adj.* designating furniture made of wood permanently bent into various forms by heat, moisture, and pressure

Be·nue (bā′nwā) river in W Africa, a tributary of the Niger, flowing through Cameroun and Nigeria: 870 mi.

be·numb (bi num′) *vt.* [< ME. *bi-numen,* pp. of *binimen,* to take away < OE. *beniman* < *be-* + *niman,* to take; *-b* by analogy with DUMB] **1.** to make numb physically **2.** to deaden the mind, will, or feelings of [*be-numbed* by grief]

benz- (benz) *same as* BENZO-

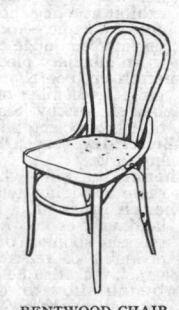

BENTWOOD CHAIR

ben·zal·de·hyde (ben zal′də hīd′) *n.* [BENZ- + ALDEHYDE] a clear, pleasant-smelling liquid, C_6H_5CHO, found in the oil of the bitter almond and used in making dyes, perfumes, flavorings, etc.

☆**Ben·ze·drine** (ben′zə drēn′) [BENZ- + (EPH)EDRINE] *a trademark for* AMPHETAMINE —*n.* [b-] this drug

ben·zene (ben′zēn, ben zēn′) *n.* [BENZ(OIC) + -ENE] a clear, flammable, poisonous, aromatic liquid, C_6H_6, obtained by scrubbing coal gas with oil and by the fractional distillation of coal tar: it is used as a solvent for fats and in making lacquers, varnishes, many dyes, and other organic compounds

benzene hex·a·chlo·ride (hek′sə klôr′īd) a compound, $C_6H_6Cl_6$, used as an insecticide

benzene ring a structural unit believed to exist in the molecules of aromatic organic compounds, consisting of a ring of six atoms of carbon with alternate double bonds between the carbon atoms: in the molecule of benzene six atoms of hydrogen are believed to be attached to the ring, one to each atom of carbon, but in derivatives of benzene one or more atoms of hydrogen are replaced by atoms of other elements or by groups of atoms: also called **benzene nucleus**

ben·zi·dine (ben′zə dēn′) *n.* [< BENZENE] a white, crystalline organic base, $NH_2C_6H_4C_6H_4NH_2$, used in the manufacture of certain dyes

BENZENE RING

ben·zine (ben′zēn, ben zēn′) *n.* [BENZ(OIC) + -INE⁴, orig. applied to BENZENE] a mixture of hydrocarbons, a colorless, flammable liquid, obtained in the fractional distillation of petroleum and used as a motor fuel and as a solvent for fats and oils in dry cleaning, etc.: in chemistry, called *ligroin*

ben·zo- (ben′zō, -zə) [see BENZENE] *a combining form meaning:* **1.** relating to benzene **2.** the bivalent radical C_6H_4—

ben·zo·ate (ben′zō āt′) *n.* [BENZO- + -ATE²] a salt or ester of benzoic acid

benzoate of soda *same as* SODIUM BENZOATE

ben·zo·caine (ben′zə kān′, -zō-) *n.* [BENZO- + (CO)CAINE] a white, crystalline, odorless powder, $C_6H_4NH_2COOC_2H_5$, used in ointments as a local anesthetic and to protect against sunburn

ben·zo·ic (ben zō′ik) *adj.* [BENZO(IN) + -IC] of or derived from benzoin

benzoic acid a white, crystalline organic acid, C_6H_5COOH, produced commercially from toluene and used as an antiseptic and preservative and in aniline dyes

ben·zo·in (ben′zō in, -zoin) *n.* [Fr. *benjoin* < It. *benzoino* < Ar. *lubān jāwi,* incense of Java; *lu-* dropped because falsely assumed to be the article] **1.** a balsamic resin obtained from certain tropical Asiatic trees (genus *Styrax*) and used in medicine and perfumery and as incense **2.** any of a genus (*Lindera*) of aromatic plants of the laurel family; esp., the spicebush of eastern N. America **3.** *Chem.* a white, crystal-

line substance, $C_{14}H_{12}O_2$, used in making antiseptic ointments

ben·zol (ben′zōl, -zôl) *n.* [BENZ- + -OL[1]] *same as* BENZENE: as used in the chemical industry, the term sometimes denotes a mixture distilling below 100° C, 70 percent of which is benzene

ben·zo·phe·none (ben′zō fi nōn′, -fē′nōn) *n.* [BENZO- + PHEN(OL) + -ONE] a white, crystalline organic compound, $C_6H_5COC_6H_5$, classified as a ketone: it is produced by the distillation of calcium benzoate and is used as an intermediate compound in the formation of certain other organic compounds

ben·zo·py·rene (ben′zō pī′rēn) *n.* [BENZO- + *pyrene*, a crystalline hydrocarbon, $C_{16}H_{10}$ < PYR- + -ENE] an aromatic hydrocarbon, $C_{20}H_{12}$, found in coal tar, cigarette smoke, etc. and known to be a cause of cancer in animals: also **benz·py·rene** (benz′pī′rēn)

ben·zo·yl (ben′zō il) *n.* [BENZO- + -YL] a univalent radical, C_6H_5CO, found in benzoic acid and in certain derivatives of the acid

ben·zyl (ben′zil) *n.* [BENZ- + -YL] a univalent radical, $C_6H_5CH_2$, found in organic compounds derived from toluene

Be·o·grad (be ô′grät) *Serbo-Croatian name of* BELGRADE

Be·o·wulf (bā′ə woolf′) [< ?; prob. understood in OE. as *beo*, bee + *wulf*, wolf, hence as a kenning for "bear"] hero of the Old English folk epic of that name, an Anglian poem probably composed c. 700 A.D.: Beowulf slays Grendel and Grendel's mother, reigns as king, and dies after a fight with a dragon

be·queath (bi kwēth′, -kwēth′) *vt.* -queathed′, -queath′ing [ME. *bequethen* < OE. *becwethan*, to declare, give by will < *be-* + *cwethan*, to say: see QUOTH] **1.** to leave (property) to another by last will and testament **2.** to hand down; pass on [he *bequeathed* his talent to his son] —**be·queath′al** (-əl) *n.*

be·quest (-kwest′) *n.* [ME. *biquest* < *be-* + OE. *cwis*, a saying < *cwethan*, to speak (see QUOTH): -*t* is unhistoric] **1.** the act of bequeathing **2.** anything bequeathed

Bé·ran·ger (bā rän zhā′), **Pierre Jean de** (pyer zhän′ də) 1780–1857; Fr. lyric poet

Be·rar (bā rär′) administrative division of the former Indian state of Central Provinces and Berar

be·rate (bi rāt′) *vt.* -rat′ed, -rat′ing [BE- + RATE[2], *vt.*] to scold or rebuke severely —SYN. see SCOLD

Ber·ber (bur′bər) *n.* [Ar., earlier *Barbar* < L. *Barbari*, lit., foreigners, barbarians: see BARBAROUS] **1.** any of a Moslem people living in northern Africa **2.** their language, a subfamily of the Afro-Asiatic family of languages —*adj.* of the Berbers, their culture, or their language

Ber·ber·a (bur′bər ə) seaport in Somalia, on the Gulf of Aden: pop. 20,000

ber·ber·ine (bur′bə rēn′, -bər in) *n.* [ModL. *berberina* < *Berberis*, name of the genus < ML. *barberis*, barberry] a bitter, yellow alkaloid, $C_{20}H_{17}NO_4 \cdot 6H_2O$ or $C_{20}H_{19}NO_5 \cdot 6H_2O$, obtained from barberry and other plants: it is used in dyeing and as a drug

ber·ceuse (ber sooz′; *Fr.* ber söz′) *n., pl.* -ceus′es (-sooz′iz; *Fr.* -söz′) [Fr. < *bercer*, to rock, lull to sleep] **1.** a lullaby **2.** a piece of instrumental music that has a rocking or lulling effect

Berch·tes·ga·den (berk′tis gäd′'n; *G.* berH′təs gä′dən) resort town in SE Germany, in the Bavarian Alps

Ber·dya·ev (bir dyä′yif), **Ni·ko·lai** (**Alexsandrovich**) (nē kô lī′) 1874–1948; Russ. religious philosopher, in France after 1922

be·reave (bi rēv′) *vt.* -reaved′ or -reft′ (-reft′), -reav′ing [ME. *bireven* < OE. *bereafian*, to deprive, rob < *be-* + *reafian*; akin to G. *berauben*, to rob: see REAVE[1]] **1.** to deprive or rob; dispossess: now usually in the pp. (bereft) [*bereft* of hope or happiness] **2.** to leave in a sad or lonely state, as by loss or death **3.** [Obs.] to take away by force —**the bereaved** the survivors of a recently deceased person —**be·reave′ment** *n.*

Ber·e·ni·ce (ber nēs′, bur′nis, ber′ə nī′sē) a feminine name: see BERNICE

Ber·e·ni·ce's Hair (ber′ə nī′sēz) *same as* COMA BERENICES

Ber·en·son (ber′ən sən), **Bernard** 1865–1959; U.S. art critic, born in Russia

be·ret (bə rā′) *n.* [Fr. *béret* < Pr. *berret* < LL. *birrettum*: see BIRETTA] a flat, round cap of felt, wool, etc.

be·ret·ta (bə ret′ə) *n. same as* BIRETTA

Ber·e·zi·na (ber′ə zē′nə; *Russ.* be rez′i nä′) river in Byelorussia, flowing into the Dnepr: c. 365 mi.: site of a fierce battle (1812) during Napoleon's retreat from Moscow

berg (burg) *n. same as* ICEBERG

Berg (berkh; *E.* berg), **Al·ban** (äl′bän) 1885–1935; Austrian composer

BERET

Ber·ga·ma (ber′gə mä′) town in W Turkey, on the site of ancient Pergamum: pop. 22,000

Ber·ga·mo (ber′gä mō′) commune in Lombardy, N Italy: pop. 120,000

ber·ga·mot (bur′gə mät′) *n.* [Fr. *bergamote* < It. *bergamotta* < Turk. *beg-armûdī*, prince's pear; form influenced by BERGAMO] **1.** a pear-shaped citrus fruit (*Citrus bergamia*) grown in S Europe for its oil, used in perfumery **2.** this oil ☆**3.** any of several aromatic N. American herbs (genus *Monarda*) of the mint family, as horsemint, Oswego tea, etc.

Ber·gen (ber′gən; *E.* bur′-) **1.** seaport in SW Norway: pop. 117,000 **2.** village in NW Germany: see BELSEN

Ber·ge·rac (bur′zhə rak′; *Fr.* ber zhə răk′), **Cy·ra·no de** (sir′ə nō′ də; *Fr.* sē rä nō′ də) 1619–55; Fr. writer & soldier, famous for his large nose: title character of a poetic drama by Edmond Rostand (1897)

ber·gère, ber·gere (ber zher′) *n.* [Fr., lit., shepherdess, fem. of *berger*, a shepherd < OFr. *bergier* < VL. *berbecarius*, altered < **vervecarius* < L. *vervex*, a wether] an upholstered armchair, or one with caned seat, back, and sides and loose cushions, esp. in an 18th-cent. French style

Berg·son (berg sôn′; *E.* berg′sən), **Hen·ri** (än rē′) 1859–1941; Fr. philosopher —**Berg·so·ni·an** (berg sō′nē ən) *adj., n.*

Berg·son·ism (berg′sən iz'm) *n.* the philosophy of Bergson, which maintains that there is an original life force (*élan vital*) carried through all successive generations, that time or duration is being, and that reality is apprehended by intuition

ber·i·ber·i (ber′ē ber′ē) *n.* [Sinh. *beri*, weakness] a deficiency disease caused by lack of vitamin B_1, thiamine, in the diet: it is characterized by nerve disorders, swelling of the body, etc.

Be·ring (bā′rin; *E.* ber′in, bir′-), **Vi·tus** (vē′toos) 1680–1741; Dan. navigator & explorer, in the service of Russia

Bering Sea (ber′in, bir′-) [after prec.] part of the N Pacific Ocean, between NE Siberia & Alas.: c. 878,000 sq. mi.

Bering Standard Time a standard time used in a zone which includes W Alaska and the Aleutian Islands, corresponding to the mean local time of the 165th meridian west of Greenwich, England: it is eleven hours behind Greenwich time: see TIME, chart

BERING SEA

Bering Strait strait between Siberia & Alas., joining the Pacific & Arctic oceans: average width, c. 50 mi.

Berke·le·ian (bär′klē ən, bur′-; bər klē′ən) *adj.* of George Berkeley or his philosophy —*n.* a person who believes in Berkeley's philosophy

Berke·le·ian·ism (-iz'm) *n.* the philosophy of George Berkeley, which holds that physical objects exist only in being perceived by a mind

Berke·ley (bur′klē) [after G. BERKELEY] city in Calif., on San Francisco Bay, just north of Oakland: pop. 117,000

Berke·ley (bär′klē, bur′klē) **1. George,** 1685–1753; Ir. philosopher & bishop **2. Sir William,** 1606–77; Brit. colonial governor of Virginia (1641–52; 1660–76)

☆**berke·li·um** (bur′klē əm) *n.* [< University of California at BERKELEY, where first isolated] a radioactive chemical element initially produced by bombarding americium with high-energy alpha particles in a cyclotron, later prepared by intense neutron irradiation of plutonium: symbol, Bk; at. wt., 248(?); at. no., 97

Berk·shire (burk′shir, -shər; *Brit.* bärk′-) county in SC England: 725 sq. mi.; pop. 539,000; county seat, Reading: also called **Berks** —*n.* any of a breed of medium-sized hogs, black with white spots

Berkshire Hills region of wooded hills and mountains in W Mass.: resort area: also called **Berkshires**

Ber·lin (bər lin′; *G.* ber lēn′) city in E Germany, 110 miles east of the West German border: capital of Germany (1871–1945): after World War II, it was divided into four sectors of occupation (U.S., British, French, and Soviet); the eastern sector (**East Berlin**) is the capital of East Germany: pop. 1,071,000; the three western sectors (**West Berlin**) are associated with West Germany: pop. 2,200,000 —**Ber·lin′er** *n.*

ber·lin (bər lin′, bur′lin) *n.* [after BERLIN, where it was first used] **1.** a four-wheeled closed carriage with a footman's platform behind, separate from the body **2.** [*sometimes* B-] a fine, soft wool yarn: also called **Berlin wool**

Ber·lin (bər lin′), **Ir·ving** (born *Israel Baline*) 1888– ; U.S. composer of popular songs, born in Russia

Ber·li·oz (ber′lē ōz′; *Fr.* ber lyôz′), (**Louis**) **Hector** 1803–69; Fr. composer

berm, berme (bʉrm) *n.* [Fr. *berme* & Du. *berm* < MDu. *baerm* < IE. base **bherem-*, to project, form an edge, whence BRIM] 1. a ledge or space between the ditch and parapet in a fortification ☆2. a ledge or shoulder, as along the edge of a paved road

Ber·me·jo (ber me′hō) river in N Argentina, flowing into the Paraguay River; c. 1,000 mi.

Ber·mond·sey (bʉr′mən zē) metropolitan borough of London, on the south bank of the Thames: pop. 51,000

Ber·mu·da (bər myōō′də) [after Juan de *Bermúdez*, Sp. explorer who discovered it (c. 1515)] group of islands in the W Atlantic, c. 580 miles southeast of N.C.: a self-governing Brit. colony: 20 1/2 sq. mi.; pop. 48,000; cap. Hamilton —**Ber·mu′dan, Ber·mu′di·an** *adj., n.*

Bermuda collar a narrow, pointed collar on a woman's dress or blouse

☆**Bermuda grass** a creeping perennial grass (*Cynodon dactylon*) widely grown in warm climates as a lawn or pasture grass, esp. in the southern U.S.

☆**Bermuda onion** a large onion with a mild flavor, grown in Texas, California, etc.

☆**Bermuda shorts** short trousers extending to just above the knee: often worn with knee-length stockings

Bern, Berne (bʉrn; *Fr.* bern) 1. capital of Switzerland & of Bern canton: pop. 167,000 2. canton of WC Switzerland: 2,658 sq. mi.; pop. 921,000 —**Ber·nese** (bər nēz′, -nēs′) *adj., n.*

Ber·na·dotte (bʉr′nə dät′; *Fr.* ber nà dôt′), **Jean Baptiste Jules** 1763–1844; Fr. marshal under Napoleon I: as Charles XIV (John) he was king of Sweden & Norway (1818–44)

Ber·nard (bər närd′, bʉr′nərd; *for 2* ber när′) [Fr. < OHG. *Berinhard*, lit., bold as a bear < *bero*, BEAR[2] + *hart*, bold, HARD] 1. a masculine name: dim. *Bernie*; var. *Barnard*; equiv. Ger. *Bernhard* 2. **Claude** (klōd), 1813–78; Fr. physiologist

Ber·nar·din de Saint-Pierre (ber när dan′ də san pyer′), **Jacques Hen·ri** (zhäk än rē′) 1737–1814; Fr. writer

Ber·nard·ine (bʉr′nər din, -dēn′) *adj.* 1. of Saint Bernard of Clairvaux 2. of the order of Cistercian monks founded by him in 1115 —*n.* a monk belonging to this order

Bernard of Clair·vaux (kler vō′), Saint 1090?–1153; Fr. monk & theological writer: founder of Cistercian order: his day is Aug. 20

Bernard of Men·thon (män tōn′), Saint 11th cent.; Fr. monk who founded hospices in the Swiss Alps: his day is May 28

Ber·nese Alps (bər nēz′, -nēs′) range of the Alps, in SW Switzerland: highest peak, Finsteraarhorn

Bern·hardt (bʉrn′härt′; *Fr.* ber när′), **Sarah** (born *Rosine Bernard*) 1844–1923; Fr. actress

Ber·nice (bər nēs′, bʉr′nis) [L. *Berenice* < Gr. *Berenikē*, lit., victory-bringing] a feminine name: var. *Berenice*

ber·ni·cle goose (bʉr′nə k'l, bär′-) *same as* BARNACLE GOOSE

Ber·ni·ni (ber nē′nē), **Gio·van·ni Lo·ren·zo** (jō vän′nē lō ren′tsō) 1598–1680; It. baroque sculptor, architect, & painter

Ber·noul·li, Ber·nouil·li (ber nōō′lē; *Fr.* ber nōō yē′) family of Swiss mathematicians & scientists, esp. *a*) **Daniel**, 1700–82; known for his work on hydrodynamics: son of *Jean b*) **Jacques**, 1654–1705; known for his work on calculus: brother of *ff. c*) **Jean**, 1667–1748; known for his work on calculus

Bernoulli's principle [after D. BERNOULLI] the statement that an increase in the speed of a fluid produces a decrease in pressure and a decrease in the speed produces an increase in pressure

Bern·stein (bʉrn′stīn′), **Leonard** 1918– ; U.S. conductor & composer

ber·ret·ta (bə ret′ə) *n. same as* BIRETTA

ber·ried (ber′ēd) *adj.* 1. bearing berries 2. like a berry, as in shape 3. bearing eggs: said of lobsters, crayfish, etc.

ber·ry (ber′ē) *n., pl.* **-ries** [ME. & OE. *berie*, a berry, grape, akin to ON. *ber*, Goth. *weina-basi*, lit., wineberry] 1. any small, juicy, fleshy fruit, as a strawberry, raspberry, etc. 2. the dry seed or kernel of various plants, as a coffee bean, wheat grain, etc. 3. an egg of a lobster, crayfish, etc. 4. *Bot.* a fleshy fruit with a soft wall and thin skin, as the tomato, grape, or cranberry —*vi.* **-ried, -ry·ing** 1. to bear berries 2. to look for and pick berries —**ber′ry·like′** *adj.*

Ber·ry, Ber·ri (be rē′) region & former province in C France: chief city, Bourges

ber·seem (bər sēm′) *n.* [Ar. *barsim* < Copt. *bersīm*, clover] an Egyptian clover (*Trifolium alexandrinum*) of the legume family, grown as a forage crop

ber·serk (bər sʉrk′, -zʉrk′; bʉr′sərk) *n.* [see ff.] a berserker —*adj., adv.* in or into a state of violent or destructive rage or frenzy

ber·serk·er (bər sʉr′kər, -zʉr-; bʉr′sər kər) *n.* [ON. *berserkr*, warrior clothed in bearskin < *ber*, a bear + *serkr*, coat] 1. *Norse Legend* a warrior who worked himself into a frenzy before a battle 2. a person who acts like a berserker

berth (bʉrth) *n.* [< base of BEAR[1]] 1. enough space at sea to keep clear of another ship, the shore, etc. 2. space for anchoring or tying up 3. a ship's place of anchorage 4. a position, place, office, job, etc. [*a berth* as chief engineer on the ship] 5. *a*) a built-in bed or bunk, as in a ship's cabin or a Pullman car *b*) any sleeping place —*vt.* 1. to

put into a berth 2. to furnish with a berth —*vi.* to come into or occupy a berth —**give a wide berth to** to stay at a prudent distance from; keep well clear of

Ber·tha (bʉr′thə) [G. < OHG. *Berahta*, lit., bright one < *beraht*, bright, shining; akin to OE. *beorht, bryht*, bright] a feminine name —*n.* [b-] [Fr. *berthe* < Fr. form of the name] a woman's wide collar, often of lace, and usually extending over the shoulders

Ber·til·lon system (bʉr′tə län′; *Fr.* ber tē yōn′) [after Alphonse *Bertillon* (1855–1914), Fr. anthropologist who developed it] a system of identifying people through records of body measurements, markings or deformities, coloring, etc.: fingerprinting was later incorporated into the system

Ber·tram (bʉr′trəm) [G. < OHG. *Berahtram, Berahtraban* < *beraht*, bright + *hraban*, RAVEN[1]] a masculine name: dim. *Bertie*; var. *Bertrand*

Ber·trand (-trənd) a masculine name: see BERTRAM

Ber·wick (ber′ik) county in SE Scotland, on the North Sea: 457 sq. mi.; pop. 22,000: also called **Ber′wick·shire** (-shir)

Ber·wyn (bʉr′win) [after *Berwyn* Mts., Wales] city in NE Ill.: suburb of Chicago: pop. 53,000

ber·yl (ber′əl) *n.* [ME. & OFr. *beril* < L. *beryllus* < Gr. *bēryllos*, sea-green gem < Prakrit *veruliya* < *veluriya*, of Dravidian origin, prob. < *Vēḷūr* (now *Bēlūr*), city in S India] beryllium aluminum silicate, $Be_3Al_2Si_6O_{18}$, a very hard, lustrous mineral that is a source of beryllium and that occurs in hexagonal crystals, usually blue, green, pink, or yellow in color: emerald and aquamarine are two gem varieties of beryl

be·ryl·li·um (bə ril′ē əm) *n.* [ModL. < prec.] a hard, silver-white, rare, metallic chemical element, found only in combination with others: it forms strong, hard alloys with several metals, including copper and nickel, and is used widely as a moderator in atomic reactors: symbol, Be; at. wt., 9.0122; at. no., 4; sp. gr., 1.85; melt. pt., 1284°C; boil. pt., 2970°C

Ber·ze·li·us (ber sā′lē oos; *E.* bər zē′lē əs), **Baron Jons Ja·kob** (yöns′ yä′kôp) 1779–1848; Swed. chemist

Bes (bes) [Egypt. *besa*] *Egypt. Myth.* a god of pleasure and guardian of the home

Be·san·çon (bə zän sōn′) city in E France, on the Doubs River: pop. 96,000

Bes·ant (bez′'nt), **Annie** (born *Annie Wood*) 1847–1933; Brit. theosophist; leader in India's movement for independence

be·seech (bi sēch′) *vt.* **-sought′** or **-seeched′, -seech′ing** [ME. *bisechen* < OE. *besecan*: see BE- & SEEK] 1. to ask (someone) earnestly; entreat; implore 2. to ask for earnestly; solicit eagerly; beg for —*SYN.* see BEG —**be·seech′ing·ly** *adv.*

be·seem (bi sēm′) *vi.* [ME. *bisemen*: see BE- & SEEM] to be suitable or appropriate (to): what appears to be the direct object of the verb (e.g., *him* in "it ill beseems him") is really the indirect object

be·set (bi set′) *vt.* **-set′, -set′ting** [ME. *bisetten* < OE. *besettan*: see BE- & SET] 1. to cover or set thickly with; stud 2. to attack from all sides; harass or besiege 3. to surround or hem in —*SYN.* see ATTACK —**be·set′ment** *n.*

be·set·ting (-iŋ) *adj.* constantly harassing or attacking [*a besetting* temptation]

☆**be·show** (bi shō′) *n.* [AmInd. *bishowk*] *same as* SABLEFISH

be·shrew (bi shrōō′) *vt.* [ME. *bishrewen*: see BE- & SHREW] [Archaic] to curse: mainly in mild imprecations [*beshrew* thee]

be·side (bi sīd′) *prep.* [ME. < OE. *bi sidan*: see BY & SIDE] 1. by or at the side of; alongside; near 2. in comparison with [*beside* yours my share seems small] 3. in addition to; besides 4. other than; aside from [who, *beside* him, is qualified?] 5. not pertinent to [that's *beside* the point] —*adv.* [Archaic] in addition —**beside oneself** wild or upset, as with fear, rage, etc.

be·sides (-sīdz′) *adv.* [ME. < prec. + adv. gen. -(e)s] 1. in addition; as well 2. except for that mentioned; else 3. moreover; furthermore —*prep.* 1. in addition to; as well 2. other than; except

be·siege (bi sēj′) *vt.* **-sieged′, -sieg′ing** [ME. *bisegen* < be- + *segen*, to lay siege to < *sege*, seat, SIEGE] 1. to hem in with armed forces, esp. for a sustained attack; lay siege to 2. to close in on; crowd around 3. to overwhelm, harass, or beset [*besieged* with queries] —**be·sieg′er** *n.*

be·smear (bi smir′) *vt.* [ME. *bismeren* < OE. *bismerian*: see BE- & SMEAR] to smear over; bedaub; soil

be·smirch (bi smʉrch′) *vt.* [BE- + SMIRCH] 1. to make dirty; soil 2. to bring dishonor to; sully

be·som (bē′zəm) *n.* [ME. *besme* < OE. *besma*, broom, rod < WGmc. **besman*, whence G. *besen*] 1. a broom, esp. one made of twigs tied to a handle 2. *same as* BROOM (*n.* 1)

be·sot (bi sät′) *vt.* **-sot′ted, -sot′ting** 1. to make a sot of; stupefy or confuse, as with alcoholic drink 2. to make silly or foolish —**be·sot′ted** *adj.*

be·sought (bi sôt′) *alt. pt.* and *pp.* of BESEECH

be·span·gle (bi span′g'l) *vt.* **-span′gled, -span′gling** to cover with or as with spangles

be·spat·ter (bi spat′ər) *vt.* to spatter, as with mud or slander; soil or sully by spattering

be·speak (bi spēk′) *vt.* **-spoke′** or archaic **-spake** (-spāk′), **-spo′ken** or **-spoke′, -speak′ing** [ME. *bispeken* < OE.

besprecan: see BE- & SPEAK] **1.** to speak for in advance; engage beforehand; reserve *[to bespeak* a box at the opera*]* **2.** to be indicative of; show *[his charity bespeaks* a generous nature*]* **3.** to foreshadow; point to *[today's events bespeak* a bright future*]* **4.** [Archaic or Poet.] to speak to; address

be·spec·ta·cled (bi spek′t'ə k'ld) *adj.* wearing spectacles

be·spoke (bi spōk′) *pt.* and *alt. pp.* of BESPEAK —*adj.* [Brit.] custom or custom-made; making or made to order Also **be·spo′ken**

be·spread (bi spred′) *vt.* **-spread′, -spread′ing** to spread over or cover

be·sprent (bi sprent′) *adj.* [ME. *bespreynt,* pp. of *besprengen* < OE. *besprengan* < *be-* + *sprengan,* caus. < *springan,* SPRING] [Poet.] sprinkled; strewed

be·sprin·kle (bi spriŋ′k'l) *vt.* **-kled, -kling** to sprinkle over (*with* something)

Bess (bes) a feminine name: see ELIZABETH[1]

Bes·sa·ra·bi·a (bes′ə rā′bē ə) region in SW European Russia, mostly in the Moldavian S.S.R., ceded by Romania in 1940 —**Bes′sa·ra′bi·an** *adj., n.*

Bes·se·mer process (bes′ə mər) [after Sir Henry *Bessemer* (1813–98), Eng. engineer who developed it] a method of making steel by blasting air through molten pig iron in a large container (**Bessemer converter**) to burn away the carbon and other impurities

best (best) *adj. superl.* of GOOD [ME. *best, besst* < OE. *betst* < IE. base **bhad-,* good, whence Goth. *batists,* best, Sans. *bhadra-ḥ,* fortunate, good] **1.** of the most excellent sort; surpassing all others **2.** most suitable, most desirable, most favorable, most profitable, etc. **3.** being almost the whole; largest *[it took the best* part of an hour*]* —*adv. superl.* of WELL[2] **1.** in the most excellent manner; in the most suitable way **2.** in the highest degree; to the greatest extent; most —*n.* **1.** people of the highest worth, ability, or reputation *[among the best* in his profession*]* **2.** the thing, condition, circumstance, action, etc. that is most excellent, most suitable, etc. **3.** the most one can do; utmost *[to do one's best]* **4.** advantage *[to get the best* of an opponent*]* **5.** one's finest clothes —*vt.* to win out over; defeat or outdo —**all for the best** turning out to be good or fortunate after all —**as best one can** as well as one can —**at best 1.** under the most favorable conditions or interpretation **2.** at most —**at one's best** in one's best mood, form, health, etc. —**get (or have) the best of 1.** to outdo, overcome, or defeat **2.** to outwit —**had best** ought to; would be prudent or wise to —**make the best of** to do as well as one can with —**with the best** as ably as the most able

be·stead (bi sted′) *adj.* [ME. *bistad* < bi, be- + *stad,* placed < ON. *staddr,* prp. of *stethja,* to fix, place] [Archaic] situated; placed —*vt.* **-stead′ed, -stead′, -stead′ing** [Archaic] to help; avail

bes·tial (bes′chəl, -tyəl; bēs′-) *adj.* [ME. & OFr. < LL. *bestialis*] **1.** of beasts or lower animals **2.** like a beast in qualities or behavior; brutish or savage; brutal, coarse, vile, etc.

bes·ti·al·i·ty (bes′chē al′ə tē, -tē-; bēs′-) *n., pl.* **-ties 1.** bestial quality, character, or behavior **2.** a bestial act or practice **3.** sexual relations between a person and an animal

bes·tial·ize (bes′chə līz′, -tyə-; bēs′-) *vt.* **-ized, -iz′ing** to make bestial; brutalize

bes·ti·ar·y (bes′chē er′ē, -tē-; bēs′-) *n., pl.* **-ar′ies** [ML. *bestiarium* < L. *bestiarius,* relating to beasts < *bestia,* BEAST] a type of medieval natural history book with moralistic or religious fables about actual and mythical animals

be·stir (bi stur′) *vt.* **-stirred′, -stir′ring** [ME. *bistiren* < OE. *bestyrian:* see BE- & STIR[1]] to stir to action; exert or busy (oneself)

☆**best man** the principal attendant of the bridegroom at a wedding

be·stow (bi stō′) *vt.* [ME. *bistowen:* see BE- & STOW] **1.** to give or present as a gift (often with *on* or *upon*) **2.** to apply; devote *[to bestow* much time on a project*]* **3.** [Archaic] to put or place, as in storage **4.** [Archaic] to provide lodgings for; house **5.** [Obs.] to give in marriage —*SYN.* see GIVE —**be·stow′al** *n.*

be·strew (bi strōō′) *vt.* **-strewed′, -strewed′** or **-strewn′, -strew′ing** [ME. *bistrewen* < OE. *bestreowian:* see BE- & STREW] **1.** to cover over (a surface); strew **2.** to scatter over or about **3.** to lie scattered over or about *[papers bestrewed* the streets*]*

be·stride (bi strīd′) *vt.* **-strode′, -strid′den, -strid′ing** [ME. *bistriden* < OE. *bestridan:* see BE- & STRIDE] **1.** to sit on, mount, or stand over with a leg on each side; straddle **2.** [Archaic] to stride over or across

☆**best seller** a book, phonograph record, etc. currently outselling most others

bet[1] (bet) *n.* [prob. aphetic < ABET; but ? akin to G. *wette,* bet] **1.** an agreement between two persons that the one proved wrong about the outcome of something will do or give a stipulated thing or pay a stipulated sum of money to the other; wager **2.** *a)* the proposition or terms of such an agreement *b)* the thing or sum thus staked *c)* the thing or person that something is or may be thus staked on *[this* team is a poor *bet]* **3.** a person, thing, or action likely to bring about a desired result *[he's the best bet* for the job*]* —*vt.* **bet** or **bet′ted, bet′ting 1.** to declare in or as in a bet *[I bet* he'll be late*]* **2.** to stake (money, etc.) in a bet **3.** to wager with (someone) —*vi.* to make a bet or bets (*on, against, with*); wager —☆**you bet** (you)! [Colloq.] certainly!

bet[2] (bät, bet) *n. same as* BETH

bet. between

be·ta (bāt′ə; *chiefly Brit.* bēt′ə) *n.* [L. < Gr. *bēta* < Heb. *bēth,* lit., house; of Phoen. origin] **1.** the second letter of the Greek alphabet (B, β) **2.** the second of a group or series **3.** *Astron.* the second brightest star in a constellation —*adj. Chem. see* ALPHA

beta decay radioactive disintegration of a nucleus with the accompanying emission of a beta particle: the residual nucleus has one more unit of positive charge after electron emission and one less after positron emission

beta emitter a radioactive element, either natural or artificial, which transforms into another element by emitting a beta particle

Be·ta fiber (bāt′ə) [after *Beta,* a trademark] a nonflammable glass fiber made into fabrics, insulation, etc.

be·ta·ine (bēt′ə ēn′, -in) *n.* [L. *beta,* beet + -INE[4]] a crystalline basic organic compound, $(CH_3)_3NCH_2COO$, found in the residues from the preparation of beet sugar or prepared synthetically

be·take (bi tāk′) *vt.* **-took′, -tak′en, -tak′ing** [ME. *bitaken:* see BE- & TAKE] **1.** to go (used reflexively) *[he betook* himself to his own kingdom*]* **2.** to direct or devote (oneself) *[betake* yourself to your studies*]*

be·ta·naph·thol (bāt′ə naf′thōl, -nap′-; -thȯl) *n.* a colorless, crystalline isomer of naphthol, $C_{10}H_8O$, used in medicine as an antiseptic and parasiticide

beta particle an electron or positron ejected at high velocity from the nucleus of an atom undergoing beta decay

beta ray 1. *same as* BETA PARTICLE **2.** a stream of beta particles

☆**be·ta·tron** (bāt′ə trän′) *n.* [BETA (RAY) + (ELEC)TRON] an electron accelerator which uses a rapidly changing magnetic field to accelerate the particles and maintain them in a focused circular path

be·tel (bēt′'l) *n.* [Port. < Malay *veṭṭilui*] a tropical Asiatic climbing plant (*Piper betle*) of the pepper family, whose leaf is chewed along with lime and betel nut by some Asian peoples

Be·tel·geuse, Be·tel·geux (bet′'l jooz′, bāt′-, bēt′-; jōōz′; *occas.* -gōōz′) [Fr. *Bételgeuse* < Ar. *bayt al jauza,* lit., house of the twins] a variable, very large, red, first-magnitude star, second brightest in the constellation Orion: its average diameter (c. 700,000,000 mi.) is several times greater than that of the earth's orbit

betel nut the fruit of the betel palm, chewed together with lime and leaves of the betel (plant) by some Asian peoples

betel palm a palm (*Areca cathecu*) grown in SE Asia

bête noire (bāt′ nwär′; *Fr.* bet nwȧr′) *pl.* **bêtes noires** (bāt′ nwärz′; *Fr.* bet nwȧr′) [Fr., lit., black beast] a person or thing feared, disliked, and avoided

beth (bāth, beth; *Heb.* bāt, bās) *n.* [Heb. *bēth:* see BETA] the second letter of the Hebrew alphabet (ב)

Beth·a·ny (beth′ə nē) [LL. (Vulgate) *Bethania* < Gr. *Bēthania* < Heb., lit., house of dates (or figs)] ancient town in Palestine, near Jerusalem, at the foot of the Mount of Olives: John 11:1, Acts 1:9

Be·the (bā′tē), **Hans Al·brecht** (häns äl′breHt) 1906– ; U.S. theoretical physicist, born in Germany

Beth·el (beth′əl) ancient town in Palestine, just north of Jerusalem

beth·el (beth′əl) *n.* [LL. (Vulgate) < Heb. *bēth 'ēl,* house of God] **1.** a spot where God is worshiped, marked by a pillar: Gen. 28:17–19 **2.** a holy place ☆**3.** a church or other place of worship for seamen **4.** [Brit.] a place of worship for non-Anglican Protestants

Be·thes·da (bə thez′də) [after the Biblical *Bethesda* (in RSV, *Bethzatha*) John 5:2] suburb of Washington, D.C., in C Md.: pop. 72,000

be·think (bi thiŋk′) *vt.* **-thought′, -think′ing** [ME. *bithenchen* < OE. *bethencan:* see BE- & THINK[1]] to bring (oneself) to think of, consider, or recollect; remind (oneself) —*vi.* [Archaic] to ponder

Beth·le·hem (beth′lə hem′, -lē əm) [LL. (Vulgate) < Gr. *Bēthleem* < Heb. *bēth lehem,* lit., house of bread] **1.** ancient town in Judea, Palestine: birthplace of Jesus (Matt. 2:1): now, a town in W Jordan: pop. 24,000 **2.** city in E Pa.: steel-producing center: pop. 73,000: see ALLENTOWN

Beth·mann-Holl·weg (bāt′män hȯl′vāk), **The·o·bald von** (tā′ō bält′ fȯn) 1856–1921; chancellor of Germany (1909–17)

Beth·nal Green (beth′nəl) metropolitan borough of London, north of the Thames: pop. 46,000

be·tide (bi tīd′) *vt.* **-tid′ed, -tid′ing** [ME. *bitiden* < be- + OE. *tidan,* to happen < *tid,* time: see TIDE[1]] to happen (to); befall

be·times (bi tīmz′) *adv.* [ME. *bitimes* < *bi-,* by + *time,* TIME + adv. gen. *-(e)s*] **1.** early or early enough *[he awoke betimes]* **2.** [Archaic] promptly; quickly

‡bê·tise (be tēz′) *n.*, *pl.* -tises′ (-tēz′) [Fr. < *bête*, beast < OFr. *beste*: see BEAST] 1. a foolish act, remark, suggestion, etc. 2. stupidity or foolishness

be·to·ken (bi tō′k'n) *vt.* [ME. *betocnen* < *be-* + *toknen* < OE. *tacnian*, to mark < *tacen*, TOKEN] 1. to be a token or sign of; indicate; show 2. to show beforehand; presage

bet·o·ny (bet′'n ē) *n.*, *pl.* -nies [ME. *betonike* < OE. *betonice* < LL. *betonica*, altered < L. *vettonica*, after the *Vettones*, an ancient tribe in Gaul] any of a genus (*Stachys*) of plants of the mint family, having spikes of white, yellow, or lavender flowers and formerly used in medicine

be·tray (bi trā′) *vt.* [ME. *bitraien* < *be-* + *traien*, betray < OFr. *trair* < L. *tradere*, to hand over: see TREASON] 1. *a*) to help the enemy of (one's country, cause, etc.); be a traitor to *b*) to deliver or expose to an enemy traitorously 2. to break faith with; fail to meet the hopes of [he betrayed my trust in him] 3. to lead astray; deceive; specif., to seduce and then desert 4. to reveal unknowingly or against one's wishes [his face *betrays* his fear] 5. to reveal or show signs of; indicate [the house *betrays* its age] 6. to disclose (secret information, confidential plans, etc.) —*SYN.* see DECEIVE, REVEAL —be·tray′al *n.* —be·tray′er *n.*

be·troth (bi trō*th*′, -trô*th*′) *vt.* [ME. *bitrouthen* < *be-* + *treuthe* < OE. *treowth*, truth] 1. to promise in marriage [to *betroth* a daughter] 2. [Archaic] to promise to marry

be·troth·al (-əl) *n.* a betrothing or being betrothed; mutual pledge to marry; engagement

be·trothed (-trō*th*d′, -trô*th*t′) *adj.* engaged to be married —*n.* the person to whom one is betrothed

bet·ta (bet′ə) *n.* [ModL.] any of a genus (*Betta*) of brightly colored, tropical, freshwater fishes of SE Asia, esp. an aquarium species (*Betta splendens*)

bet·ted (bet′id) *alt. pt.* and *pp.* of BET[1]

bet·ter[1] (bet′ər) *adj. compar.* of GOOD [ME. *bettere, betere* < OE. *betera*: see BEST] 1. of a more excellent sort; surpassing another or others 2. more suitable, more desirable, more favorable, more profitable, etc. 3. being more than half; larger [it cost the *better* part of his pay] 4. improved in health or disposition —*adv. compar.* of WELL[2] 1. in a more excellent manner; in a more suitable way 2. in a higher degree; to a greater extent 3. more [it took *better* than an hour] —*n.* 1. a person superior in authority, position, etc. [obey your *betters*] 2. the thing, condition, circumstance, action, etc. that is more excellent, more suitable, etc. 3. advantage [to get the *better* of a rival] —*vt.* 1. to outdo; surpass 2. to make better; improve —*vi.* to become better —*SYN.* see IMPROVE —**better off** 1. in a better situation or condition 2. having more income, wealth, etc. —**for the better** to a better or improved condition —**get** (or **have**) **the better of** 1. to outdo 2. to outwit

bet·ter[2] (bet′ər) *n. same as* BETTOR

better half [Slang] one's wife or, less often, one's husband

bet·ter·ment (-mənt) *n.* 1. a making or being made better; improvement ☆2. *Law* an improvement that increases the value of property and is more extensive than mere repairs

Bet·ter·ton (bet′ər tən), Thomas 1635?–1710; Eng. actor

bet·tor (-ər) *n.* a person who bets

Bet·ty (bet′ē) a feminine name: see ELIZABETH[1]

be·tween (bi twēn′) *prep.* [ME. *bitwene* < OE. *betweonum* < *be*, by + *tweonum*, dat. of **tweon*, akin to Goth. *tweihnai*, by twos, in pairs: for IE. base see TWO] 1. in or through the space that separates (two things) 2. in or of the time, amount, or degree that separates (two things); intermediate to [*between* blue and green] 3. that connects or relates to [a bond *between* friends] 4. along a course that connects [the road runs *between* here and there] 5. by the joint action of [*between* them they landed the fish] 6. in the combined possession of [they had fifty dollars *between* them] 7. to the exclusion of all but both of [they divided it *between* them] 8. from one or the other of [choose *between* love and duty] 9. because of the combined effect of [*between* work and studies she has no time left] *Between* is sometimes used where more than two are involved, if the relationship is thought of as of each individually with each of the others [a treaty *between* four powers] —*adv.* 1. in an intermediate space, position, or function 2. in an intermediate time; in the interval —**between ourselves** in confidence; as a secret: also **between you and me** —**in between** 1. in an intermediate position 2. in the midst of; surrounded by

be·tween·brain (-brān′) *n. same as* DIENCEPHALON

be·tween·times (-tīmz′) *adv.* at intervals: also be·tween′-whiles′

be·twixt (bi twikst′) *prep., adv.* [ME. *bitwix* < OE. *betwix* < *be-* + a form related to *twegen*, TWAIN; *-t* is unhistoric] between: now archaic except in the phrase **betwixt and between**, in an intermediate position; neither altogether one nor altogether the other

Beu·lah (byōō′lə) [Heb. *be 'ūlāh*, married] 1. the land of Israel: Isa. 62:4 2. in Bunyan's *Pilgrim's Progress*, a country of peace and rest near the end of life's journey: short for **Land of Beulah** 3. a feminine name

bev, Bev (bev) *n.*, *pl.* bev, Bev [B(ILLION) E(LECTRON-) V(OLTS)] a unit of energy equal to one billion (10⁹) electron-volts

☆bev·a·tron (bev′ə trän′) *n.* [< BEV + -*tron*, as in CYCLO-TRON] a synchrotron for accelerating protons and other atomic particles to an energy level of six or more billion electron-volts

bev·el (bev′l) *n.* [prob. < OFr. **baivel*, dim. < *baif*, gaping: see BAY[2]] 1. a tool consisting of a rule with a movable arm, used in measuring or marking angles and in fixing surfaces at an angle: also **bevel square** 2. an angle other than a right angle 3. sloping part or surface, as the angled edge of plate glass —*adj.* sloped; beveled —*vt.* -eled or -elled, -el·ing or -el·ling to cut to an angle other than a right angle —*vi.* to slope at an angle; slant

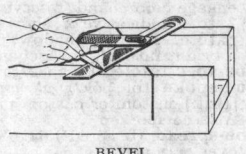

BEVEL

bevel gear a gearwheel meshed with another so that their shafts are at an angle of less than 180°

bev·er·age (bev′rij, -ər ij) *n.* [ME. < OFr. *bevrage* < *bevre* < L. *bibere*, IM-BIBE] any liquid for drinking, esp. other than water

BEVEL GEAR

Bev·er·idge (bev′ər ij) 1. Albert Jeremiah, 1862–1927; U.S. statesman & historian 2. Sir William Henry, 1st Baron, 1879–1963; Eng. economist, born in India

Bev·er·ley, Bev·er·ly (bev′ər lē) [lit., beaver lea < ME. *bever*, BEAVER[1] + *ley*, LEA[1]] a feminine name

Bev·er·ly (bev′ər lē) city in NE Mass.: pop. 38,000

Beverly Hills [after *Beverly* Farms, in Mass.] city in Calif., surrounded by Los Angeles: pop. 34,000

bev·y (bev′ē) *n.*, *pl.* bev′ies [ME. *bevey* < Anglo-Fr. *bevée* < OFr., a drinking bout < *bevre*: see BEVERAGE] 1. a group, esp. of girls or women 2. a flock: now chiefly of quail 3. any group or collection —*SYN.* see GROUP

be·wail (bi wāl′) *vt.* [ME. *biwailen*: see BE- & WAIL] to wail over or complain about; lament; mourn

be·ware (bi wer′) *vi., vt.* -wared′, -war′ing [associated with BE- & WARE[2], but prob. < OE. *bewarian*, to keep watch < *be-* + *warian*, to watch, be wary] to be wary or careful (of); be on one's guard (against)

be·wil·der (bi wil′dər) *vt.* [BE- + WILDER] 1. to confuse hopelessly, as by something complicated or involved; befuddle; puzzle 2. [Archaic] to cause to be lost, as in a wilderness *SYN.* see PUZZLE **be·wil′dered** (-dərd) *adj.* —**be·wil′der·ing·ly** *adv.*

be·wil·der·ment (-mənt) *n.* 1. the fact or condition of being bewildered 2. a confusion; jumble

be·witch (bi wich′) *vt.* [ME. *biwicchen* < *be-* + *wicchen* < OE. *wiccian* < *wicca*: see WITCH] 1. to use witchcraft or magic on; cast a spell over 2. to attract and delight irresistibly; enchant; fascinate; charm —**be·witch′ing** *adj.* —**be·witch′ing·ly** *adv.*

be·witch·ment (-mənt) *n.* 1. power to bewitch 2. a bewitching or being bewitched 3. a spell that bewitches Also **be·witch′er·y** (-ər ē), *pl.* -er·ies

be·wray (bi rā′) *vt.* [ME. *biwreien* < *be-* + OE. *wregan*, to inform] [Archaic] to divulge; reveal; betray

Bex·ley (beks′lē) city in SE England, near London: pop. 90,000

bey (bā) *n.* [Turk. *bey, beg*] 1. in the Ottoman Empire, the governor of a minor Turkish district or province 2. a Turkish title of respect and former title of rank 3. the former native ruler of Tunis

Beyle (bāl), Ma·rie Hen·ri (mả rē′ än rē′) see STENDHAL

be·yond (bi yänd′) *prep.* [ME. *biyonde* < OE. *begeondan* < *be-* + *geond*, yonder, across] 1. on or to the far side of; farther on than; past [*beyond* the river] 2. farther on in time than; later than [*beyond* the visiting hours] 3. outside the reach, possibility, or understanding of [*beyond* help, *beyond* belief] 4. more or better than; exceeding; surpassing [a success *beyond* one's expectations] 5. in addition to [he had no experience *beyond* school training] —*adv.* 1. farther out; farther away 2. in addition; besides —**the beyond** 1. whatever is beyond or far away 2. whatever follows death; afterlife: often **the great beyond**

Bey·routh (bā rōōt′, bā′rōōt) *same as* BEIRUT

bez·ant (bez′nt, bə zant′) *n.* [ME. *besant* < OFr. *besant* < L. *byzantius* (*nummus*), Byzantine (coin) < *Byzantium*] 1. the solidus, a gold coin issued in Byzantium: see SOLIDUS (sense 1) 2. *Archit., Heraldry* an ornamental flat disk or circular figure representing such a coin

bez antler (bez, bâz) [< OFr. *bes-* < L. *bis*, twice + ANTLER] the second branch from the base of a deer's horn: also called **bez tine, bay antler**

☆be·zazz (bə zaz′) *n. same as* PIZAZZ

bez·el (bez′l) *n.* [OFr. **bisel* (Fr. *biseau*), sloping edge < *biais*, bias] 1. a sloping surface, as the cutting edge of a chisel 2. the slanting faces of a cut jewel, esp. those of the upper half 3. the groove and flange holding a gem or a watch crystal in place

Bé·ziers (bā zyā′) city in S France: pop. 74,000

be·zique (bi zēk′) *n.* [Fr. *bésigue*; ? akin to It. *bazzica*, card game < *bazza*, trick (at cards) < Ar. *bazza*, to capture] a card game resembling pinochle, but using a double deck of 64 cards, two of each card above the six

be·zoar (bē′zôr) *n.* [Fr. *bézoard* < Sp. *bezoar* < Ar. *bāzahr* < Per. *pādzahr* < *pād*, expelling + *zahr*, poison] a concretion found in the stomach or intestines of some animals, esp.

ruminants, and formerly thought to be an antidote for poisons

bf, b.f. boldface

B/F brought forward

B.F.A. Bachelor of Fine Arts

bg. pl. **bgs.** bag

☆**B-girl** (bē′gurl′) n. [< b(ar) girl] a woman employed by a bar to entice men into buying drinks freely

Bha·ga·vad-Gi·ta (bug′ə vad gē′tə) n. [Sans. Bhagavad-gitā, Song of the Blessed One] a philosophical dialogue that is a sacred Hindu text, found in the Mahabharata, one of the ancient Sanskrit epics

bhak·ti (buk′tē) n. [Sans., lit., a share < IE. base *bhag-, to allot, whence Gr. phagein, to eat, OBulg. bogat', rich: see BAKSHEESH] Hinduism devotion to one god with all the tasks and activities of life selflessly directed to his service

bhang (baŋ) n. [Hind. < Sans. bhangā, hemp] 1. the hemp plant, or its tough fiber 2. its dried leaves and flowers, which have narcotic and intoxicating properties 3. a preparation, such as hashish, made from these leaves and flowers Also sp. **bang**

Bha·rat (bu′rut) Hindu name for INDIA (sense 2)

Bhav·na·gar, Bhau·na·gar (bou nug′ər) seaport in W India, on the Arabian Sea: pop. 176,000

bhees·ty, bhees·tie (bēs′tē) n., pl. **-ties** [Hind. bhisti < Per. bihishti, lit. (prob. ironically) one from paradise] in India, a water carrier, as for troops

Bhn Brinell hardness number

Bho·pal (bō päl′) 1. city in C India: capital of Madhya Pradesh state: pop. 223,000 2. former state of C India: since 1956, part of Madhya Pradesh

B-horizon n. the second soil zone, in which material leached from the overlying zone is concentrated: see ABC SOIL

bhp brake horsepower

Bhu·ba·nes·war (boo′və nāsh′vər) city in E India, noted for its Hindu shrines: capital of Orissa: pop. 17,000

Bhu·tan (boo tän′) independent monarchy in the Hima-layas, north of the Indian state of Assam: its external affairs are directed by India: c. 18,000 sq. mi.: pop. 750,000 —**Bhu·tan·ese** (boot′n ēz′) adj., n., pl. **-ese′**

bi-[1] (bī) [L. bi- < OL. dui- < IE. base *dwi- < *dwo-, TWO] a prefix meaning: 1. having two [biangular, bicapsular] 2. doubly, on both sides, in two ways or directions [biconvex, bilingual] 3. coming, happening, or issued every two [biennial, biweekly] 4. coming, happening, or issued twice during every [bimonthly, biyearly]; often replaced by semi- or half-, to avoid confusion with preceding sense 5. using two or both [bilabial, bimanual] 6. joining two, combining or involving two [bilateral, bipartisan] 7. Bot., Zool. twice, doubly, in pairs [bifurcate, bipinnate] 8. Chem. a) having twice as many atoms or chemical equivalents for a definite weight of the other constituent of the compound [sodium bicarbonate] b) in organic compounds, having a combina-tion of two radicals of the same composition [biphenyl]: usually replaced by di- except in the names of acid salts [sodium bisulfate] Also, before a vowel, **bin-**; before c or s, **bis-**

bi-[2] (bī) same as BIO-

Bi Chem. bismuth

Bi·a·fra (bē äf′rə) 1. region (Eastern Region) of Nigeria: fought an unsuccessful war for independence (1967–70): 29,484 sq. mi. 2. **Bight of,** eastern part of the Gulf of Guinea, on the W coast of Africa

bia·ly (byä′lē) n., pl. **-lys** [Yid. < ff., where orig. made] a flat bread roll made with gluten flour and topped with chopped onions, etc.: also sp. **biali**

Bia·ly·stok (byä′lis tôk′) city in NE Poland: pop. 134,000

bi·an·gu·lar (bī aŋ′gyoo lər) adj. having two angles

bi·an·nu·al (-an′yoo wəl, -yool) adj. coming twice a year; semiannual: see also BIENNIAL —**bi·an′nu·al·ly** adv.

bi·an·nu·late (-an′yoo lit, -lāt′) adj. Zool. having two rings or bands of color, etc.

Bi·ar·ritz (bē′ə rits′; Fr. byà rēts′) resort town in SW France, on the Bay of Biscay: pop. 25,000

bi·as (bī′əs) n., pl. **bi′as·es** [Fr. biais, a slope, slant] 1. a slanting or diagonal line, cut or sewn across the weave of cloth, as in making seams, binding tape, etc. 2. a mental leaning or inclination; partiality; prejudice; bent 3. Bowls a) the bulge or weight in the side of the ball that causes it to roll in a curve b) this curve or tendency to curve c) the force causing this 4. Radio the fixed voltage applied to an electrode circuit to control the mode of operation, usually measured with the cathode voltage as reference 5. Math. the difference between the estimated value and the true value of a statistic obtained by random sampling —adj. slanting; diagonal —adv. 1. diagonally 2. [Obs.] awry —vt. **-ased** or **-assed, -as·ing** or **-as·sing** 1. to cause to have a bias; influence; prejudice 2. Radio to apply a bias to (an electrode) —SYN. see PREJUDICE —**on the bias** diagonally; obliquely; specif., cut or sewed diagonally across the weave

bi·ath·lon (bī ath′lən, -län) n. [BI-[1] + Gr. athlon, a contest] in the winter Olympic games, an event combining a ski run and marksmanship

bi·aur·al (bī ôr′əl) adj. same as BINAURAL

bi·au·ric·u·late (bī′ô rik′yoo lit) adj. [BI-[1] + AURICULATE] Anat. having two auricles: also **bi′au·ric′u·lar** (-lər)

bi·ax·i·al (bī ak′sē əl) adj. having two axes, as some crystals —**bi·ax′i·al·ly** adv.

bib (bib) vt., vi. **bibbed, bib′bing** [ME. bibben < L. bibere, to drink] [Archaic] to drink; imbibe; tipple —n. 1. an apron-like cloth or plastic napkin tied under a child's chin at meals 2. the front upper part of an apron or overalls

Bib. 1. Bible 2. Biblical

bib and tucker [Colloq.] an outfit of clothes; esp., **best bib and tucker** best, or most formal, clothes

bi·bas·ic (bī bās′ik) adj. [Rare] Chem. same as DIBASIC

bibb (bib) n. [< BIB, n.: so named because in position it resembles a child's bib] 1. a bibcock 2. a wooden bracket supporting the trestletrees of a ship's mast

bib·ber (bib′ər) n. a person who bibs; drinker; toper

☆**bibb lettuce** (bib) [so named after Jack Bibb (1789–1884), Kentucky horticulturist who developed it] a kind of lettuce formed in loose heads of very crisp, dark-green leaves

bib·cock (bib′käk′) n. [BIB + COCK[1]: from the position of the nozzle] a faucet whose nozzle is bent downward

BIBCOCK

‡**bi·be·lot** (bē blō′; E. bib′lō, -ə lō′) n. [Fr. < OFr. beubelot < belbel, BAUBLE] 1. a small object whose value lies in its beauty or rarity; trinket 2. a book of unusually small size

bi·bi·va·lent (bī′bī vā′lənt) adj. Chem. separating into two bivalent ions: said of electrolytes

Bibl., bibl. 1. Biblical 2. bibliographical

Bi·ble (bī′b'l) n. [ME. & OFr. < ML. biblia < Gr. biblia, collection of writings, in LGr.(Ec.), the Scriptures, pl. of biblion, book < biblos, papyrus < Byblos (now Dschebel), Phoen. city from which papyrus was imported] 1. the sacred book of Christianity; Old Testament and New Testament: the Roman Catholic (Douay) Bible also in-cludes all of the Apocrypha except the two additional books of Esdras and the Prayer of Manasses 2. the Holy Scriptures of Judaism, identical with the Old Testament of Christianity 3. a copy or particular edition of the Scriptures 4. any collection or book of writings sacred to a religion [the Koran is the Moslem Bible] 5. [b-] any book regarded as authoritative or official See also AUTHORIZED VERSION, REVISED STANDARD VERSION, DOUAY BIBLE, VULGATE, SEPTUAGINT, APOCRYPHA

BOOKS OF THE BIBLE

(Names used in the Douay Bible, when different, are in parentheses)

Old Testament

Genesis	Proverbs
Exodus	Ecclesiastes
Leviticus	Song of Solomon (Canticle
Numbers	of Canticles)
Deuteronomy	Isaiah (Isaias)
Joshua (Josue)	Jeremiah (Jeremias)
Judges	Lamentations
Ruth	Ezekiel (Ezechiel)
I Samuel (I Kings)	Daniel
II Samuel (II Kings)	Hosea (Osee)
I Kings (III Kings)	Joel
II Kings (IV Kings)	Amos
I Chronicles (I	Obadiah (Abdias)
Paralipomenon)	Jonah (Jonas)
II Chronicles (II	Micah (Micheas)
Paralipomenon)	Nahum
Ezra (I Esdras)	Habakkuk (Habacuc)
Nehemiah (II Esdras)	Zephaniah (Sophonias)
Esther	Haggai (Aggeus)
Job	Zechariah (Zacharias)
Psalms	Malachi (Malachias)

Old Testament Apocrypha

I Esdras (III Esdras)	Additions to Daniel, including
II Esdras (IV Esdras)	the Song of the Three Holy
Tobit (Tobias)	Children, the Story of Susan-
Judith	na, and the Idol Bel and the
Additions to Esther	Dragon
Wisdom of Solomon	Prayer of Manasses
Ecclesiasticus	I Maccabees (I Machabees)
Baruch	II Maccabees (II Machabees)

New Testament

Matthew	Ephesians	Hebrews
Mark	Philippians	James
Luke	Colossians	I Peter
John	I Thessalonians	II Peter
The Acts	II Thessalonians	I John
Romans	I Timothy	II John
I Corinthians	II Timothy	III John
II Corinthians	Titus	Jude
Galatians	Philemon	Revelation
		(Apocalypse)

Bible belt [coined c. 1925 by H. L. MENCKEN] those regions of the U.S., particularly areas in the South, where fundamentalist beliefs prevail and Christian clergymen are especially influential

Bible paper a thin, strong, opaque paper used for printing many Bibles, dictionaries, etc.

Bib·li·cal (bib′li k'l) *adj.* [*also* b-] **1.** of or in the Bible **2.** in keeping with or according to the Bible; like that in the Bible —**Bib′li·cal·ly** *adv.*

Bib·li·cist (-sist) *n.* **1.** a person who takes the words of the Bible literally **2.** an expert on the Bible; specialist in Biblical literature —**Bib′li·cism** *n.*

bib·li·o- (bib′lē ō, -ə) [< Gr. *biblion*: see BIBLE] *a combining form meaning:* **1.** book, of books [*bibliophile*] **2.** of the Bible [*bibliolatry*]

bib·li·o·film (bib′lē ə film′) *n.* a kind of microfilm used esp. for reproducing pages of books

bibliog. 1. bibliographer **2.** bibliography

bib·li·o·graph (bib′lē ə graf′) *vt.* [back-formation < ff.] **1.** to supply (a book, article, etc.) with a bibliography **2.** to prepare a bibliography of

bib·li·og·ra·pher (bib′lē äg′rə fər) *n.* [< Gr. *bibliographos*, writer of books < *biblion*, a book + *graphos* < *graphein*, to write + -ER] **1.** an expert in bibliography **2.** a person who compiles a bibliography

bib·li·og·ra·phy (bib′lē äg′rə fē) *n.*, *pl.* -**phies** [Gr. *bibliographia*: see BIBLE & -GRAPHY] **1.** the study of the editions, dates, authorship, etc. of books and other writings **2.** a book containing such information **3.** a list of sources of information on a given subject, period, etc., or of the literary works of a given author, publisher, etc. **4.** a list of the books, articles, etc. used or referred to by an author —**bib′li·o·graph′ic** (-ə graf′ik), **bib′li·o·graph′i·cal** *adj.* —**bib′li·o·graph′i·cal·ly** *adv.*

bib·li·ol·a·try (bib′lē äl′ə trē) *n.* [BIBLIO- + -LATRY] **1.** excessive adherence to a literal interpretation of the Bible **2.** excessive veneration of books —**bib′li·ol′a·ter** *n.* —**bib′li·ol′a·trous** *adj.*

bib·li·o·man·cy (bib′lē ə man′sē) *n.* [BIBLIO- + -MANCY] prediction based on a Bible verse or literary passage chosen at random

bib·li·o·ma·ni·a (bib′lē ə mā′nē ə, -nyə) *n.* [BIBLIO- + -MANIA] a craze for collecting books, esp. rare ones —**bib′li·o·mane′** (-mān′) *n.* —**bib′li·o·ma′ni·ac** *n.*, *adj.* —**bib′li·o·ma·ni′a·cal** (-mə nī′ə k'l) *adj.*

bib·li·op·e·gy (bib′lē äp′ə jē) *n.* [BIBLIO- + Gr. *pēgia* < *pēgnynai*, to fasten, bind] the art of bookbinding

bib·li·o·phile (bib′lē ə fīl′) *n.* [BIBLIO- + -PHILE] **1.** a person who loves or admires books, esp. for their style of binding, printing, etc. **2.** a collector of books Also **bib′li·o·phil′** (-fil′), **bib′li·oph·i·list** (bib′lē äf′ə list) —**bib′li·o·phil′ic** (-ə fil′ik) *adj.* —**bib′li·oph′i·lism** (-äf′ə liz′m), **bib′li·oph′i·ly** (-äf′ə lē) *n.* —**bib′li·oph′i·lis′tic** (-äf′ə lis′tik) *adj.*

bib·li·o·pole (bib′lē ə pōl′) *n.* [L. *bibliopola* < Gr. *bibliopōlēs* < *biblion*, a book + *pōlein*, to sell] a bookseller, esp. one dealing in rare works: also **bib·li·op·o·list** (bib′lē äp′ə list) —**bib′li·o·pol′ic** (-ə päl′ik) *adj.* —**bib′li·op·o·ly** (bib′lē äp′ə lē) *n.* —**bib′li·op′o·lism** *n.*

bib·li·o·the·ca (bib′lē ə thē′kə) *n.* [L. < Gr. *bibliothēkē*, library, bookcase < *biblion*, a book + *thēkē* < *tithenai*, to place] **1.** a book collection; library **2.** a bookseller's catalogue —**bib′li·o·the′cal** *adj.*

Bib·list (bib′blist) *n. same as* BIBLICIST

bib·u·lous (bib′yoo ləs) *adj.* [L. *bibulus* < *bibere*, to drink: see IMBIBE] **1.** highly absorbent **2.** addicted to or fond of alcoholic liquor —**bib′u·lous·ly** *adv.* —**bib′u·lous·ness** *n.*

bi·cam·er·al (bī kam′ər əl, -kam′rəl) *adj.* [BI-¹ + CAMERAL] made up of or having two legislative chambers [Congress is a *bicameral* legislature] —**bi·cam′er·al·ism** *n.*

bi·cap·su·lar (bī kap′sə lər, -syoo lər) *adj. Bot.* having two capsules or a capsule with two cells

bi·car·bon·ate (bī kär′bə nit, -nāt′) *n.* [BI-¹ + CARBONATE] an acid salt of carbonic acid containing the radical HCO_3

bicarbonate of soda *same as* SODIUM BICARBONATE

bice (bīs) *n.* [ME. & OFr. *bis*, dusky, dark] **1.** a grayish blue, duller than azure **2.** a grayish-blue or green pigment made from smalt or azurite

bi·cen·te·nar·y (bī′sen ten′ər ē, bī sen′tə ner′ē) *adj.*, *n.*, *pl.* -**ies** *same as* BICENTENNIAL

bi·cen·ten·ni·al (bī′sen ten′ē əl) *adj.* **1.** happening once in a period of 200 years **2.** lasting for 200 years —☆*n.* a 200th anniversary or its celebration

bi·ceph·a·lous (bī sef′'l əs) *adj.* [BI-¹ + CEPHALOUS] two-headed: also **bi·ce·phal·ic** (bī′sə fal′ik)

bi·ceps (bī′seps) *n.*, *pl.* -**ceps** *or* -**ceps·es** [L. < *bis*, two + *caput*, head] **1.** a muscle having two heads, or points of origin; esp., the large muscle in the front of the upper arm or the corresponding muscle at the back of the thigh **2.** loosely, strength or muscular development, esp. of the arm

bi·chlo·ride (bī klôr′īd) *n.* **1.** a binary compound containing two atoms of chlorine for each atom of another element; dichloride **2.** bichloride of mercury

bichloride of mercury *same as* MERCURIC CHLORIDE

bi·chro·mate (bī krō′māt) *n. same as* DICHROMATE

bi·cip·i·tal (bī sip′ə t'l) *adj.* [< L. *bicipitis*, gen. of *biceps*, BICEPS] *Anat.* **1.** with two heads or points of origin, as a biceps muscle **2.** of a biceps

bick·er (bik′ər) *vi.* [ME. *bikeren*, ? akin to Fris. *bikkern*, hack, gnaw] **1.** to have a petty quarrel; squabble **2.** to move with quick, rippling or pattering noises [a *bickering* brook] **3.** to flicker, twinkle, etc. —*n.* **1.** a bickering; petty quarrel **2.** a rippling or pattering sound —**bick′er·er** *n.*

Bi·col (bi kōl′) *n. same as* BIKOL

bi·col·or (bī′kul′ər) *adj.* [L. < *bis*, two + *color*, COLOR] of two colors: also **bi′col′ored**

bi·con·cave (bī′kän kāv′, bī kän′kāv) *adj.* concave on both surfaces [a *biconcave* lens]

bi·con·vex (bī′kän veks′, bī kän′veks) *adj.* convex on both surfaces [a *biconvex* lens]

bi·corn (bī′kôrn) *adj.* [L. *bicornis* < *bis*, twice + *cornu*, HORN] **1.** having two horns or hornlike parts **2.** crescent-shaped Also **bi·cor·nu·ate** (bī kôr′nyoo wit)

bi·cor·po·ral (bī kôr′pər əl, -prəl) *adj.* having two bodies or main parts: also **bi·cor·po·re·al** (bī′kôr pôr′ē əl)

bi·cron (bī′krän) *n.* [BI(LLION) + (MI)CRON] one billionth (.000000001) of a meter: symbol μμ

bi·cus·pid (bī kus′pid) *adj.* [< BI-¹ + L. *cuspidis*, gen. of *cuspis*, pointed end] having two points [a *bicuspid* tooth]: also **bi·cus′pi·date′** (-pi dāt′) —*n.* any of eight adult teeth with two-pointed crowns; premolar tooth

BICUSPID

bicuspid valve *same as* MITRAL VALVE

bi·cy·cle (bī′si k'l) *n.* [Fr.: see BI-¹ & CYCLE] a vehicle consisting of a tubular metal frame mounted on two large, wire-spoked wheels, one behind the other, and equipped with handle bars and a saddlelike seat: it is propelled by foot pedals or, sometimes, by a small gasoline motor —*vi.*, *vt.* -**cled**, -**cling** to ride or travel on a bicycle —**bi′cy·clist**, **bi′cy·cler** *n.*

bi·cy·clic (bī sī′klik, -sik′lik) *adj.* **1.** of or forming two cycles, circles, etc. **2.** *Chem.* containing two fused rings in the molecule Also **bi·cy′cli·cal**

bid¹ (bid) *vt.* **bade** *or* **bid** *or archaic* **bad**, **bid′den** *or* **bid**, **bid′ding**; for vt. 3, 6, 8 & for vi., the pt. & pp. are always **bid** [ME. *bidden*, to ask, plead, pray < OE. *biddan* < IE. base *bheidh-*, to urge, compel; meaning and form merged with ME. *beden*, to offer, present < OE. *beodan*, to command, decree < IE. base *bheudh-*, to be alert, announce] **1.** orig., to beseech or implore **2.** to command, ask, or tell [do as you are *bidden*] **3.** to offer (a certain amount) as the price or fee that one will pay or accept **4.** to declare openly [to bid defiance] **5.** to express in greeting or taking leave [bid farewell to your friends] ☆**6.** [Colloq.] to offer membership to [the fraternity may bid five new men] **7.** [Archaic or Dial.] to invite **8.** *Card Games* to state (the number of tricks or points one expects to take) and declare (a suit or no-trump) —*vi.* to make a bid —*n.* **1.** a bidding of an amount **2.** the amount bid **3.** a chance to bid **4.** an attempt or try [a bid for fame] ☆**5.** [Colloq.] an invitation, esp. to become a member **6.** *Card Games* a) the act of bidding   b) the number of tricks or points stated   c) a player's turn to bid —**bid fair** to seem likely (to be or do something) —☆**bid in** at an auction, to bid more than the best offer in an attempt to raise the final purchasing price —**bid up**, to raise the amount bid

bid² (bid) *obs. pp. of* BIDE

bi·dar·ka (bi där′kə) *n.* [< Russ. *baidarka*, dim. of *baidara*, canoe, coracle] a sealskin-covered canoe used by Eskimos of Alaska: also **bi·dar′kee** (-kē)

bid·da·ble (bid′ə b'l) *adj.* **1.** ready to do as bidden; obedient; docile **2.** worth bidding on [a *biddable* bridge hand]

bid·den¹ (bid′'n) *alt. pp. of* BID¹

bid·den² (bid′'n) *obs. pp. of* BIDE

bid·der (bid′ər) *n.* a person who bids, as at an auction

bid·ding (-iŋ) *n.* **1.** a command or request **2.** an invitation or summons **3.** the bids or the making of bids in a card game or auction —**do the bidding of** to be obedient to; carry out the orders of

Bid·dle (bid′'l) **1. John**, 1615–62; Eng. theologian; founder of Eng. Unitarianism **2. Nicholas**, 1786–1844; U.S. financier

bid·dy (bid′ē) *n.*, *pl.* -**dies** [< ?] **1.** a chicken or chick; esp., a hen ☆**2.** [Slang] a woman, esp. an elderly woman regarded contemptuously as eccentric, gossipy, etc.

bide (bid) *vi.* **bode** *or* **bid′ed**, **bid′ed**, **bid′ing** [ME. *biden* < OE. *bidan*, to stay, wait < IE. base *bheidh-* (cf. BID¹), prob. in sense "compel oneself," hence, delay] [Archaic or Dial.] **1.** to stay; continue **2.** to dwell; reside **3.** to wait —*vt.* [Archaic or Dial.] to endure or tolerate —**bide one's time** *pt.* **bid′ed** to wait patiently for an opportunity

bi·den·tate (bī den′tāt) *adj.* [BI-¹ + DENTATE] having two teeth or toothlike parts

bi·det (bi dā′) *n.* [Fr., lit., small pony, nag (prob. < Gaul. *bid*, small): fig. use from straddling stance assumed by the user] a low, bowl-shaped, porcelain bathroom fixture equipped with running water, used for bathing the crotch

bi·don·ville (bē dôn vēl′) *n.* [Fr. slang < *bidonner*, to guzzle, swig < *bidon*, wine jug, orig. soldier's water bottle] in N Africa, a shantytown on the outskirts of a city, characterized by squalor and extreme poverty

Bie·der·mei·er (bē′dər mī′ər) *adj.* [G. < (*Gottlieb*) *Biedermeier*, fictitious author of stodgy poems published (1855–57, and later) by Adolf Kussmaul and Ludwig Eichrodt to

satirize German bourgeois tastes] designating or of a style of mid-19th-cent. German furniture design, essentially a heavy, stolid variation of French Empire

Biel (bēl) city in NW Switzerland: pop. 67,000

bield (bēld) *n., vt.* [Scot.] shelter

Bie·le·feld (bē′lə felt′) city in NW West Germany, in North Rhine-Westphalia: pop. 175,000

‡**bien en·ten·du** (byan nän tän dü′) [Fr., lit., well understood] certainly; to be sure

Bienne (byen) *Fr.* name of BIEL

bi·en·ni·al (bī en′ē əl) *adj.* [< L. *biennium*, period of two years < *bis*, twice + *annus*, year + -AL] 1. happening every two years 2. lasting or living for two years —*n.* 1. a biennial event or occurrence 2. *Bot.* a plant that lasts two years, usually producing flowers and seed the second year —**bi·en′ni·al·ly** *adv.*

‡**bien·ve·nue** (byan və nü′) *n.* [Fr., lit., well come] a welcome

Bien·ville (byan vēl′), sieur de (born *Jean Baptiste Le Moyne*) 1680–1768; Fr. colonizer & governor of Louisiana; founder of New Orleans

bier (bir) *n.* [ME. *bere* < OE. *bǣr*: for IE. base see BEAR[1]] 1. a platform or portable framework on which a coffin or corpse is placed 2. a coffin and its supporting platform

Bierce (birs), **Ambrose (Gwinett)** 1842–1914?; U.S. satirical writer

biest·ings (bēs′tiŋz) *n.pl. same as* BEESTINGS

bi·fa·cial (bī fā′shəl) *adj.* 1. having two faces or main surfaces 2. *Bot.* having two unlike opposite surfaces

bi·far·i·ous (bī fer′ē əs) *adj.* [L. *bifarius*, twofold < *bis*, twice + *fari*, to speak] *Bot.* arranged in two rows

☆**biff** (bif) *n.* [prob. echoic] [Slang] a blow; strike; hit —*vt.* [Slang] to strike; hit

bi·fid (bī′fid) *adj.* [L. *bifidus*, forked < *bis*, twice + *findere*, to cleave, divide] divided into two equal parts by a cleft, as the end of a snake's tongue; forked —**bi·fid′i·ty** (-fid′ə tē) *n.* —**bi′fid·ly** *adv.*

bi·fi·lar (bī fī′lər) *adj.* [BI-[1] + FILAR] having or involving the use of two threads, as certain sensitive measuring instruments —**bi·fi′lar·ly** *adv.*

bi·flag·el·late (bī flaj′ə līt, -lāt′) *adj.* [BI-[1] + FLAGELLATE] *Biol.* having two whiplike parts, as certain protozoa

bi·flex (bī′fleks) *adj.* [see BI-[1] & FLEX[2]] having two bends or curves

☆**bi·fo·cal** (bī fō′k'l; *also, esp. for the n.,* bī′fō′k'l) *adj.* adjusted to two different focal lengths —*n.* a lens with one part ground to adjust the eyes for close focus, as for reading, and the other ground for distant focus

☆**bi·fo·cals** (bī′fō′k'lz) *n.pl.* a pair of glasses with bifocal lenses

bi·fo·li·ate (bī fō′lē it, -āt′) *adj.* [BI-[1] + FOLIATE] *Bot.* having two leaves

bi·fo·li·o·late (bī fō′lē ə lit, -lāt′) *adj.* [BI-[1] + FOLIOLATE] *Bot.* having two leaflets

bi·forked (bī′fôrkt′) *adj. same as* BIFURCATE

bi·form (bī′fôrm′) *adj.* [L. *biformis:* see BI-[1] & FORM] having, or incorporating the features of, two forms

Bif·rost (bēf′räst) [ON. *bifrost*, lit., the tremulous way: *bif-* < *bifask*, to tremble + *rost*, a distance] *Norse Myth.* the rainbow bridge of the gods from Asgard, their home, to Midgard, the earth

bi·fur·cate (bī′fər kāt′, bī fur′kāt; *for adj. also* -kit) *adj.* [ML. *bifurcatus* < L. *bifurcus* < *bi-* + *furca*, FORK] having two branches or peaks; forked —*vt., vi.* -cat′ed, -cat′ing to divide into two parts or branches —**bi′fur·cate′ly** *adv.*

bi·fur·ca·tion (bī′fər kā′shən) *n.* 1. the act or fact of bifurcating 2. the place where this occurs

big (big) *adj.* **big′ger, big′gest** [ME. < Gmc. base *bugja*, swollen up, thick (whence BUG[1] & Norw. dial. *bugge*, big man) < IE. base *bhu-, *bu-*, to blow out, whence L. *bucca*, puffed cheek] 1. *a)* of great size, extent, or capacity; large *b)* great in force or intensity [*a big* wind] 2. *a)* full-grown *b)* elder [*his big* sister] 3. *a)* far advanced in pregnancy (*with*) *b)* filled or swelling (*with*) 4. loud 5. important or outstanding [*to do big* things] 6. boastful; pompous; extravagant [*big* talk] 7. generous; noble [*a big* heart] *Big* is much used in combination to form adjectives [*big*-bodied, *big*-headed, *big*-souled, etc.] —*adv.* [Colloq.] 1. pompously; boastfully; extravagantly [*to talk big*] 2. impressively 3. in a broad way; showing imagination [*think big!*] —*SYN.* see LARGE —**big′ness** *n.*

big·a·mist (big′ə mist) *n.* a person who commits bigamy

big·a·mous (-məs) *adj.* [LL. *bigamus*] 1. constituting or involving bigamy 2. guilty of bigamy —**big′a·mous·ly** *adv.*

big·a·my (-mē) *n., pl.* **-mies** [ME. & OFr. *bigamie* < LL. *bigamus* < *bis*, twice + Gr. *gamos*, marriage] the act of marrying a second time while a previous marriage is still legally in effect: when done knowingly, it is a criminal offense

big·ar·reau (big′ə rō′, big′ə rō′) *n.* [Fr. < Prov. *bigarreu* < *bigarra*, fleck] [*also* B-] any of several varieties of sweet cherry, heart-shaped and firm-fleshed: also **big′a·roon′** (-rōōn′)

big-bang theory a theory of cosmology holding that the expansion of the universe began with a gigantic explosion

Big Ben 1. the great bell in the Parliament clock tower in London 2. the clock itself

Big Bend National Park national park in SW Tex., in the bend formed by the Rio Grande: 1,094 sq. mi.

☆**Big Board** 1. the listing of the securities that are bought and sold on the New York Stock Exchange 2. the New York Stock Exchange

big brother 1. one's older brother ☆2. [*often* B- B-] a man who undertakes the role of friend and mentor to a disadvantaged boy, as through a social agency 3. [< concept in G. ORWELL's novel *1984*] [*usually* B- B-] the state or some other organization regarded as ruthlessly invading the privacy of the individual in seeking to exercise control over him

☆**Big Dipper** a dipper-shaped group of stars in the constellation Ursa Major (Great Bear)

bi·gem·i·ny (bī jem′ə nē) *n.* [*bigemin(ate)*, in two pairs (< BI-[1] + GEMINATE) + -Y[3]] the state of occurring in pairs, as a rhythm of the heartbeat consisting of pairs of beats —**bi·gem′i·nal** *adj.*

bi·ge·ner·ic (bī′jə ner′ik) *adj.* designating or of hybrids derived from two different genera

big·eye (big′ī′) *n.* any of a family (Priacanthidae) of small, red, tropical fishes with large eyes, rough scales, and a short body

hig game 1. large wild animals hunted for sport, as lions, tigers, moose, etc. 2. the object of any important or dangerous undertaking

big·gie (big′ē) *n.* [Colloq.] *same as* BIGWIG

big·gin (big′in) *n.* [Fr. *béguin*, a cap worn by the BEGUINES] [Brit. Dial.] 1. a cap or hood, esp. for a child 2. a nightcap

big·ging, big·gin (big′in) *n.* [ME. < *biggen*, to build, dwell < ON. *byggja*, to build, dwell, akin to OE. *bogian*, to dwell: for IE. base see BONDAGE] [Brit. Dial.] a building

big·gish (big′ish) *adj.* somewhat big

☆**big·head** (-hed′) *n.* 1. [Colloq.] conceit; egotism: also **big head** 2. any of certain diseases of animals, esp. sheep, characterized by the swelling of tissues about the head —**big′head′ed** *adj.*

big·heart·ed (-här′tid) *adj.* quick to give or forgive; generous or magnanimous —**big′heart′ed·ly** *adv.*

Big·horn (big′hôrn′) river flowing from NW Wyo. into the Yellowstone River in S Mont.: c. 450 mi.: also **Big Horn**

☆**big·horn** (hôrn′) *n., pl.* **-horns**, **-horn**: see PLURAL, II, D, 1 any of a number of animals with large horns, esp. a large, wild, shaggy-haired sheep (*Ovis canadensis*) of the Rocky Mountains

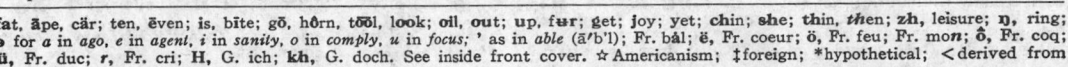

Bighorn Mountains range of the Rocky Mountains in N Wyo. and S Mont.: highest peak, 13,165 ft.: also **Big Horn Mountains**

☆**big house, the** [Slang] a penitentiary

bight (bīt) *n.* [ME. *byht* < base of *bugan* (see BOW[1]); akin to Du. & G. *bucht*] 1. orig., a bend, angle, or hollow, specif. of a body structure 2. a loop or slack part in a rope 3. a curve in a river, coastline, etc. 4. a bay formed by such a curve —*vt.* to fasten with a bight

☆**big-league** (big′lēg′) *adj.* [after the *big* (i.e., major) *leagues* in professional baseball] [Colloq.] of or at the highest level in one's profession or field of activity

big lie, the 1. a gross falsification or misrepresentation of the facts, with constant repetition and embellishment to lend credibility 2. the propaganda technique, as in politics, of using this device

big mouth ☆[Slang] a person who talks too much, esp. in an opinionated or gossipy way —**big′-mouthed′** *adj.*

big·no·ni·a (big nō′nē ə) *n.* [after the Abbé *Bignon*, 18th-c. Fr. librarian to the king] any of a genus (*Bignonia*) of tropical American vines, that bear tendrils, compound leaves, and trumpet-shaped, yellow or reddish flowers

big·ot (big′ət) *n.* [Fr. < OFr., a term of insult used of Normans, apparently a Norman oath < ? ME. *bi god*, by God] 1. a person who holds blindly and intolerantly to a particular creed, opinion, etc. 2. a narrow-minded, prejudiced person —*SYN.* see ZEALOT —**big′ot·ed** *adj.* —**big′ot·ed·ly** *adv.*

big·ot·ry (big′ə trē) *n., pl.* **-ries** [Fr. *bigoterie*] the behavior, attitude, or beliefs of a bigot; intolerance; prejudice

☆**big shot** [Slang] a person regarded as important or influential: also **big noise, big wheel,** etc.

☆**big stick** [from Theodore ROOSEVELT's phrase "speak softly and carry a big stick"] [*also* B- S-] a policy of acting or negotiating from a position backed by a show of strength

☆**big-tick·et** (big′tik′it) *adj.* having a high price tag

☆**big time** [Slang] 1. formerly, vaudeville performed in the top-ranking, big-city theatrical circuits, at high pay 2. the level regarded as highest in any profession, occupation, etc. 3. a very enjoyable time

BIGHORN
(3–4 ft. high
at shoulder)

☆**big top** [Colloq.] 1. the main tent of a circus 2. the life or work of circus performers

big tree a giant California evergreen (*Sequoiadendron giganteum*) of the baldcypress family, found in the high Sierra and often exceeding 300 ft. in height; giant sequoia

big·wig (-wig′) n. [Colloq.] an important and influential person

Bi·har (bi här′) state of NE India: 67,198 sq. mi.; pop. 46,456,000; cap. Patna

Bi·ha·ri (bi här′ē) n. 1. pl. **-ris, -ri** a native or inhabitant of Bihar 2. the Indic dialects spoken by the people of Bihar

bi·jou (bē′zhōō, bi zhōō′) n., pl. **-joux** (-zhōōz, -zhōōz′) [Fr. < Bret. *bizou*, a ring < *biz*, finger] 1. a jewel 2. something small and exquisite; trinket

bi·jou·te·rie (bi zhōōt′ər ē) n. [Fr. < prec.] jewelry or trinkets generally or collectively

bi·ju·gate (bī′joo gāt′, bi jōō′git) adj. [BI-¹ + JUGATE] having two pairs of leaflets, as some pinnate leaves: also **bi′ju·gous** (-gəs)

Bi·kan·er (bē′kə nir′) city in NW India, in the Thar Desert, Rajasthan state: pop. 151,000

☆**bike** (bīk) n., vt., vi. **biked, bik′ing** [< BICYCLE] [Colloq.] 1. bicycle 2. motorcycle

bi·ki·ni (bi kē′nē) n. [< *Bikini*, atoll in the Marshall Islands, site of atomic bomb tests in 1946] an extremely brief two-piece bathing suit for women

Bi·kol (bi kōl′) n. 1. a member of a Christianized Malayan people of Luzon and neighboring islands 2. their Indonesian language

bi·la·bi·al (bī lā′bē əl) adj. 1. having two lips; bilabiate 2. *Phonet.* made by stopping or constricting the air stream at the closed or nearly closed lips, as the English stops *p* and *b*, the Spanish fricative *b*, etc. —n. a bilabial sound

bi·la·bi·ate (-bē it, -āt′) adj. [BI-¹ + LABIATE] *Bot.* having two lips, as the corolla of flowers of the mint family

bil·an·der (bil′ən dər, bī′lən-) n. [< Du. *bijlander*, lit., coaster < *bij*, by + *land*, land] a small, two-masted ship used on the canals and along the coast of the Netherlands, etc.

bi·lat·er·al (bī lat′ər əl) adj. [BI-¹ + LATERAL] 1. of, having, or involving two sides, halves, factions, etc. 2. affecting both sides equally; reciprocal *[a bilateral* trade agreement*]* 3. arranged symmetrically on opposite sides of an axis —**bi·lat′er·al·ism** n. —**bi·lat′er·al·ly** adv.

Bil·ba·o (bil bä′ō) seaport in N Spain, near the Bay of Biscay: pop. 351,000

bil·ber·ry (bil′ber′ē; chiefly Brit. -bər ē) n., pl. **-ries** [< Scand.; cf. Dan. *bøllebær*, lit., ball berry < ON. *bollr*, BALL¹ + *ber*, BERRY] 1. any of several N. American species of blueberries (genus *Vaccinium*) 2. its dark-blue fruit

bil·bo (bil′bō) n., pl. **-boes** [after BILBAO, once famous for its ironworks] 1. [pl.] a long iron bar with shackles that slide back and forth on it, for fettering a prisoner's feet 2. [Archaic] a sword or rapier

‡**Bil·dungs·ro·man** (bil′doonks rô män′) n., pl. **-ma′ne** (-mä′nə) [G.] a novel that details the psychological development of the principal character

bile (bīl) n. [Fr. < L. *bilis*] 1. the bitter, yellow-brown or greenish fluid secreted by the liver and found in the gallbladder: it is discharged into the duodenum and helps in digestion, esp. of fats 2. a) either of two bodily humors (**black bile**, or melancholy, and **yellow bile**, or choler) in ancient physiology b) bitterness of spirit; choler; anger

bi·lec·tion (bi lek′shən) n. same as BOLECTION

bile·stone (bīl′stōn′) n. same as GALLSTONE

bilge (bilj) n. [var. of BULGE] 1. the bulge of a barrel or cask 2. the rounded, lower part of a ship's hull or hold 3. stagnant, dirty water that gathers there: also **bilge water** 4. [Slang] worthless or silly talk or writing; nonsense —vt., vi. **bilged, bilg′ing** to break open in the bottom or bilge area: said of a vessel

bilge keel a beam fastened lengthwise on either side of a ship's bottom to prevent heavy rolling, damage to the bilges, etc.: also **bilge piece**

bilg·y (bil′jē) adj. looking or smelling like bilge water

bil·har·zi·a (bil här′zē ə) n. [ModL., after Theodor *Bilharz* (1825–1862), Ger. helminthologist] 1. same as SCHISTOSOME 2. same as SCHISTOSOMIASIS

bil·har·zi·a·sis (bil′här zī′ə sis) n. [see prec. & -IASIS] same as SCHISTOSOMIASIS

bil·i·ar·y (bil′ē er′ē, bil′yər ē) adj. [Fr. *biliaire*] 1. of or involving the bile 2. bile-carrying 3. bilious

bi·lin·e·ar (bī lin′ē ər) adj. of or involving two lines

bi·lin·gual (bī liŋ′gwəl) adj. [< L. *bilinguis* (< *bis*, two + *lingua*, tongue) + -AL] 1. of or in two languages 2. using or capable of using two languages, esp. with equal or nearly equal facility —**bi·lin′gual·ism** n. —**bi·lin′gual·ly** adv.

bil·ious (bil′yəs) adj. [Fr. *bilieux* < L. *biliosus* < *bilis*, bile] 1. of the bile 2. having or resulting from some ailment of the bile or the liver 3. having the appearance of one who has such an ailment 4. bad-tempered; cross —**bil′ious·ly** adv. —**bil′ious·ness** n.

bil·i·ru·bin (bil′ə roō′bin) n. [< L. *bilis*, bile + *ruber*, RED + -IN] a yellowish-red substance, $C_{33}H_{36}N_4O_6$, occurring in bile and, in jaundice, found in the urine and blood

bi·lit·er·al (bī lit′ər əl) adj. [BI-¹ + L. *litera*, letter + -AL] made up of two letters —n. any two-letter linguistic element

bil·i·ver·din (bil′ə vʉr′d'n) n. [< L. *bilis*, bile + obs. Fr.

verd, green (see VERDURE) + -IN¹] a dark-green substance, $C_{33}H_{34}N_4O_6$, related to bilirubin, occurring in bile

bilk (bilk) vt. [? altered < BALK] 1. to balk or thwart 2. to cheat or swindle; defraud 3. to get away without paying (a debt, etc.) 4. to manage to get away from; elude *[to bilk* the police*]* —n. 1. a bilking or being bilked; hoax 2. a person who cheats; swindler —**bilk′er** n.

Bill (bil) [< *Will:* see WILLIAM] a masculine nickname: dim. *Billy*

bill¹ (bil) n. [ME. *bille* < Anglo-L. *billa*, altered < ML. *bulla*, sealed document < L. *bulla*, knob, bubble] 1. a statement, usually itemized, of charges for goods or services; invoice 2. a statement or list, as a menu, theater program, ship's roster, etc. 3. a poster or handbill, esp. one announcing a circus, show, etc. 4. the entertainment offered in a theater 5. a draft of a law proposed to a lawmaking body 6. a bill of exchange 7. any promissory note ☆8. a) a bank note or piece of paper money b) [Slang] a hundred dollars or a hundred-dollar bill 9. [Obs.] a written document, esp. one with a seal 10. *Law* a written declaration of charges or complaints filed in a legal action —vt. 1. to make out a bill of (items); list 2. to present a statement of charges to 3. a) to advertise or announce by bills or posters b) to book or engage (a performer or performance) 4. to post bills or placards throughout (a town, etc.) 5. to enter on a bill of consignment; book for shipping —☆**fill the bill** [Colloq.] to be satisfactory; meet the requirements —**bill′a·ble** adj.

bill² (bil) n. [ME. & OE. *bile* < IE. base *bhei*, to strike] 1. the horny jaws of a bird, usually projecting to a point; beak 2. a beaklike mouth part, as of a turtle 3. the point of an anchor fluke ☆4. [Colloq.] the peak, or visor, of a cap —vi. 1. to touch bills together 2. to caress lovingly: now only in the phrase **bill and coo**, to kiss, talk softly, etc. in a loving way

bill³ (bil) n. [ME. *bil* < OE. *bill:* for IE. base see prec.] 1. an ancient weapon having a hook-shaped blade with a spike at the back, mounted on a long staff 2. same as BILLHOOK

bill⁴ (bil) n. [prob. < BELL²] [Rare] the cry of the bittern

bill·a·bong (bil′ə bäŋ′) n. [Australian native term < *billa*, water + ?] in Australia, 1. a backwater channel that forms a lagoon or pool 2. a river branch that reenters the main stream

☆**bill·board¹** (bil′bôrd′) n. [BILL¹ + BOARD] a signboard, usually outdoors, for advertising posters

bill·board² (-bôrd′) n. [BILL² + BOARD] a ledge behind the cathead of a ship, on which the fluke of a secured anchor rests

☆**bill·bug** (-bug′) n. [BILL² + BUG¹] any of a number of weevils (esp. genus *Calendra*) whose larvae feed upon numerous plants, esp. cereal grasses, corn, etc.

bill·er (-ər) n. 1. a person whose work is making out bills 2. a machine used in making out bills

bil·let¹ (bil′it) n. [ME. < Anglo-Fr., dim. of *bille*, BILL¹] 1. a written order to provide quarters or lodging for military personnel, as in private buildings 2. a) the quarters thus assigned or occupied b) the sleeping place assigned to a sailor on ship 3. a position, job, or situation 4. [Archaic] a brief document or letter; note —vt. 1. to assign to lodging by billet 2. to assign to a post 3. to serve a billet on —vi. to be billeted or quartered

bil·let² (bil′it) n. [ME. < OFr. *billette*, dim. of *bille* < Gaul. *bilia*, tree trunk, akin to Ir. *bile*, tree] 1. a) a short, thick piece of firewood b) [Obs.] a wooden club 2. a) a small, unfinished bar of iron or steel, usually less than 25 sq. in. in cross section b) a similar, generally smaller, bar made from a nonferrous metal 3. *Archit.* a log-shaped insert in a Norman molding 4. [? < another source] *Saddlery* a) that part of a belt or strap which fits into a buckle b) a loop for securing the loose end of a buckled strap

bil·let-doux (bil′ē dōō′; Fr. bē ye dōō′) n., pl. **bil·lets-doux** (bil′ē dōōz′; Fr. bē ye dōō′) [Fr., lit., sweet letter] a love letter

☆**bill·fish** (bil′fish′) n., pl. **-fish′, -fish′es**: see FISH² any of various fishes with long, narrow jaws that resemble a beak, as many gars, the needlefish, etc.

☆**bill·fold** (-fōld′) n. a flat, folding case, usually of leather, for carrying paper money, cards, etc. in the pocket; wallet

bill·head (-hed′) n. a letterhead used for statements of charges

bill·hook (-hook′) n. a tool with a curved or hooked blade at one end, for pruning and cutting

bil·liard (bil′yərd) adj. of or for billiards —n. a point scored in billiards by a carom

bil·liards (-yərdz) n. [Fr. *billard*, the game; orig., a stick, cue < *bille:* see BILLET²] 1. a game played with three hard balls on an oblong table covered with cloth, esp. baize, and having raised, cushioned edges: a long tapering stick (called a *cue*) is used to hit and move the balls 2. any of a number of similar games: pool is sometimes called **pocket billiards**

Bil·lie (bil′ē) [fem. dim. of WILLIAM] a feminine name

bill·ing (bil′iŋ) n. 1. the listing of the actors' names on a playbill, theater marquee, etc. 2. the order in which the names are listed

Bil·lings (bil′iŋz) [after F. *Billings* (1823–90), railroad president] city in S Mont., on the Yellowstone River: pop. 62,000

Bil·lings (bil′iŋz), **Josh** (jäsh) (pseud. of *Henry Wheeler Shaw*) 1818–85; U.S. humorist

bil·lings·gate (bil'iŋz gāt') *n.* [after a fish market in London, notorious for the foul language used there] foul, vulgar, abusive talk

bil·lion (bil'yən) *n.* [Fr. contr. < *bi-*, BI-¹ + *million*] **1.** in the U.S. and France, a thousand millions (1,000,000,000) **2.** in Great Britain and Germany, a million millions (1,000,000,000,000) **3.** an indefinite but very large number: a hyperbolic use —*adj.* amounting to one billion in number

bil·lion·aire (bil'yə ner') *n.* [prec. + (MILLION)AIRE] a person whose wealth comes to at least a billion dollars, pounds, francs, etc.

bil·lionth (bil'yənth) *adj.* **1.** coming last in a series of a billion **2.** designating any of the billion equal parts of something —*n.* **1.** the last in a series of a billion **2.** any of the billion equal parts of something

Bil·li·ton (bi lē'tän) island of Indonesia, southwest of Borneo: 1,866 sq. mi.; pop. 102,000

bill of attainder a legislative enactment against a person, pronouncing him guilty, without trial, of an alleged crime (esp. treason) and inflicting the punishment of death and attainder upon him: prohibited in the U.S. by the Constitution

bill of exchange a written order to pay a certain sum of money to the person named or to his account; draft

bill of fare a list of the foods served; menu

bill of goods a shipment of goods sent to an agent for sale —**sell (someone) a bill of goods** ☆[Colloq.] to persuade (someone) by deception or misrepresentation to accept, believe, or do something

bill of health a certificate stating whether there is infectious disease aboard a ship or in the port which the ship is leaving: it is given to the captain for him to show at the next port —**clean bill of health 1.** a bill of health certifying the absence of infectious disease **2.** [Colloq.] a good record; favorable report, as after an investigation

bill of lading a contract issued to a shipper by a transportation agency, listing the goods shipped, acknowledging their receipt, and promising delivery to the person named

bill of rights 1. a list of the rights and freedoms assumed to be essential to a group of people **2.** [B- R-] an act of the British Parliament passed in 1689, to confirm certain rights of the people and of Parliament ☆**3.** [B- R-] the first ten amendments to the Constitution of the U.S., which guarantee certain rights to the people, as freedom of speech, assembly, and worship

bill of sale a written statement certifying that the ownership of something has been transferred by sale

bil·lon (bil'ən) *n.* [Fr. < *bille*, small log: see BILLET²] an alloy of gold or silver with a heavy proportion of another metal, as copper: used in some coins

bil·low (bil'ō) *n.* [ON. *bylgja*: see BELLY] **1.** a large wave; great swell of water **2.** any large swelling mass or surge, as of smoke, sound, etc. —*vi.* to surge, swell, or rise like or in a billow —*vt.* to make billow or surge —*SYN.* see WAVE

bil·low·y (bil'ə wē) *adj.* -**low·i·er**, -**low·i·est** swelling in or as in a billow or billows —**bil'low·i·ness** *n.*

bill·post·er (bil'pōs'tər) *n.* a person hired to fasten advertisements or notices on walls, billboards, etc.: also **bill'stick'er** —**bill'post'ing** *n.*

bil·ly¹ (bil'ē) *n., pl.* -**lies** [< BILLET²] a club or heavy stick; truncheon, esp. one carried by a policeman

bil·ly² (bil'ē) *n., pl.* -**lies** [< Australian *billycan* < ? native term *billa*, water (as in BILLABONG) + CAN²] [Austral.] a can or kettle used in outdoor cooking

bil·ly·cock (bil'i käk') *n.* [< 18th-c. *bully-cocked*, worn in the style of a bully] [Brit. Colloq.] a type of felt hat with a low, round crown, as a derby

billy goat [< the nickname *Billy*, dim. of BILL] a male goat

bi·lo·bate (bi lō'bāt) *adj.* having or divided into two lobes: also **bi·lo'bat·ed, bi·lobed'**

bi·loc·u·lar (bi läk'yoo lər) *adj.* [BI-¹ + LOCULAR] *Biol.* having or divided into two cells or chambers: also **bi·loc'u·late** (-lit, -lāt')

Bi·lox·i (bə läk'sē) *n.* **1.** any member of a tribe of Siouan Indians who lived in the lower Mississippi Valley **2.** their Siouan language, now extinct **3.** city in S Miss., on the Gulf of Mexico: pop. 48,000

☆**bil·sted** (bil'sted) *n.* [origin obscure] *same as* SWEET GUM

bil·tong (bil'tôŋ, -täŋ) *n.* [Afrik. < *bil*, rump (from which it is cut) + *tong*, tongue (from the shape)] in South Africa, sun-dried strips of meat

bi·ma·nous (bi mā'nəs, bim'ə-) *adj.* [ModL. *bimanus* < L. *bi-*, BI-² + *manus*, hand] having two hands

bi·man·u·al (bi man'yoo wəl) *adj.* [BI-¹ + MANUAL] using or requiring both hands —**bi·man'u·al·ly** *adv.*

☆**bim·bo** (bim'bō) *n.* [earlier, a guy, fellow, youth < It., a child, baby, akin to *bambino*] [Slang] a woman, esp. a sexually promiscuous one

bi·mes·tri·al (bi mes'trē əl) *adj.* [L. *bimestris* < *bi-* + *mensis*, month + -AL] **1.** lasting two months **2.** occurring every two months; bimonthly

bi·met·al (bi'met''l) *adj. same as* BIMETALLIC —*n.* a bimetallic substance

bi·me·tal·lic (bi'mə tal'ik) *adj.* [Fr. *bimétallique* < *bi-* + *métallique*, metallic] **1.** of, containing, or using two metals, often two metals bonded together **2.** of or based on bimetallism

bi·met·al·lism (bi met''l iz'm) *n.* **1.** the use of two metals, usually gold and silver, as the monetary standard, with fixed values in relation to each other **2.** the doctrine, actions, or policies supporting this —**bi·met'al·list** *n.*

bi·mod·al (bi mōd''l) *adj. Statistics* having two modes —**bi·mo·dal·i·ty** (bi'mō dal'ə tē) *n.*

bi·mo·lec·u·lar (bi'mə lek'yə lər) *n.* consisting of or relating to two molecules

bi·month·ly (bi munth'lē) *adj., adv.* **1.** once every two months **2.** twice a month: in this sense, *semimonthly* is the preferred term —*n., pl.* -**lies** a publication appearing once every two months

bi·morph (bi'môrf) *n. Electronics* an assembly of two crystals cemented together and used to increase the voltage from a given stress, as in a pickup, microphone, etc.

bi·mor·phe·mic (bi'môr fē'mik) *adj.* involving or consisting of two morphemes

bi·mo·tored (bi mōt'ərd) *adj. same as* TWIN-ENGINED

bin (bin) *n.* [ME. < OE., manger, crib < ? Celt.] a box or other receptacle, or an enclosed space, esp. for storing foods or other articles for a time —*vt.* **binned, bin'ning** to put or store in a bin

bin- (bin) *same as* BI-¹: used before a vowel

bi·nal (bi'n'l) *adj.* [ModL. *binalis* < L. *bini*, two by two] twofold

bi·na·ry (bi'nər ē) *adj.* [ME. *binarie* < L. *binarius* < *bini*, two by two < *bis*, double] **1.** made up of two parts or things; twofold; double **2.** designating or of a number system in which the base used is two, each number being expressed in powers of two by using only two digits, specif. 0 and 1 **3.** designating or of a musical form consisting of two main sections **4.** *Chem.* composed of two elements or radicals, or of one element and one radical [*binary* compounds] —*n., pl.* -**ries 1.** something made up of two parts or things **2.** *same as* BINARY STAR

binary fission asexual reproduction in animals, esp. protists, by a simple splitting of the body into two approximately equal parts

binary star two stars revolving around a common center of gravity; double star

bi·nate (bi'nāt) *adj.* [ModL. *binatus* < L. *bini*: see BINARY] *Bot.* occurring in pairs [*binate* leaves] —**bi'nate·ly** *adv.*

bin·au·ral (bi nôr'əl, bin nôr'əl) *adj.* [BIN- + AURAL²] **1.** having two ears **2.** of or involving the use of both ears **3.** designating or of sound reproduction or transmission in which at least two sources of sound are used to give a stereophonic effect —**bin·au'ral·ly** *adv.*

bind (bind) *vt.* **bound, bind'ing** [ME. *binden* < OE. *bindan* < IE. base *bhendh-*, whence Sans. *badhnāti*, he binds, Goth. *bindan*, ON. *binda*, BAND¹, BEND¹] **1.** to tie together; make fast or tight, as with a rope or band **2.** to hold or restrain as if bound or tied down [*bound* by convention] **3.** to gird or encircle with a belt, girdle, etc.; wrap or fasten around **4.** to bandage (often with *up*) **5.** to make stick together; make cohere **6.** to tighten the bowels of; constipate **7.** to strengthen, secure, or ornament the edges of by a band, as of tape **8.** to fasten together the printed pages of (a book) and enclose them within a protective cover **9.** to secure or make firm (a bargain, contract, etc.) **10.** to obligate by duty, love, etc. **11.** to compel, as by oath, legal restraint, or contract **12.** to make an apprentice of; indenture: often with *out* or *over* **13.** to unite or hold, as by a feeling of loyalty or love —*vi.* **1.** to do the act of binding **2.** to be or become tight, hard, or stiff **3.** to be constricting or restricting **4.** to stick together **5.** to be obligatory or binding in force —*n.* **1.** anything that binds ☆**2.** [Colloq.] a difficult or restrictive situation; jam [to be in a *bind*] **3.** *Music* a curved line connecting two successive notes; tie or slur —*SYN.* see TIE —**bind over** to put under legal bond to appear at a specified time and place, as before a law court

bind·er (bin'dər) *n.* **1.** a person who binds; specif., a bookbinder **2.** a thing that binds or holds together; specif., *a*) a band, cord, etc. *b*) a material that binds things together [tar is a *binder* for gravel in paving] *c*) a detachable cover with clasps or the like for holding sheets of paper together ☆**3.** *Agric. a*) a device attached to a reaper, for tying grain in bundles *b*) a machine that both reaps and binds grain **4.** *Law* a temporary memorandum of a contract, in effect pending execution of the final contract

☆**bind·er·y** (bin'dər ē, -drē) *n., pl.* -**er·ies** a place where books are bound

bind·ing (-diŋ) *n.* **1.** the action of a person or thing that binds **2.** a thing that binds, as *a*) the fastenings on a ski for the boot *b*) a band or bandage *c*) tape used in sewing for strengthening seams, edges, etc. *d*) the covers and backing of a book **3.** a cohesive substance for holding a mixture together —*adj.* **1.** that binds; restrictive **2.** that holds one to an agreement, promise, etc.; obligatory —**bind'ing·ly** *adv.*

binding energy 1. the energy needed to separate an atom into its constituent neutrons and protons **2.** the energy required to remove a particle from a nucleus

fat, āpe, cär; ten, ēven; is, bīte; gō, hôrn, tōol, look; oil, out; up, fur; get; joy; yet; chin; she; thin, then; zh, leisure; ŋ, ring; ə for a in ago, e in agent, i in sanity, o in comply, u in focus; ' as in able (ā'b'l); Fr. bȧl; ë, Fr. coeur; ö, Fr. feu; Fr. mon; ô, Fr. coq; ü, Fr. duc; r, Fr. cri; H, G. ich; kh, G. doch. See inside front cover. ☆ Americanism; ‡foreign; *hypothetical; <derived from

☆**bin·dle** (bin′d'l) *n.* [prob. < G. *bündel*, bundle] [Slang] a bundle of bedding carried by a hobo

☆**bin·dle·stiff** (-stif′) *n.* [Slang] a migratory worker; hobo

bind·weed (bīnd′wēd′) *n.* any of a number of vines (esp. genus *Convolvulus*) of the morning-glory family, which twine around their support

bine (bīn) *n.* [dial. form of BIND] **1.** any climbing, twining stem, as of the hop, woodbine, etc. **2.** a plant having such stems

Bi·net-Si·mon test (bi nā′si′mən) [after Fr. psychologists who devised it, Alfred *Binet* (1857–1911), Théodore *Simon* (1873–1961)] an intelligence test that consists of questions, problems, and things to do, graded in terms of mental age: often **Binet test:** see also INTELLIGENCE QUOTIENT (IQ)

binge (binj) *n.* [? < dial. *binge*, to soak] [Colloq.] **1.** a drunken celebration or spree **2.** a completely unrestrained action [a shopping *binge*]

Bing·en (biŋ′ən) city in W West Germany, on the Rhine: pop. 19,000

Bing·ham·ton (biŋ′əm tən) [after Wm. *Bingham* (1752–1804), land donor] city in SC N.Y.: pop. 64,000

☆**bin·go** (biŋ′gō) *n.* [< ?] a gambling game, like lotto, usually with many players

Bi·ni (bē′nē) *n.* **1.** *pl.* **-nis, -ni** any member of an agricultural people of S Nigeria **2.** their Kwa language

bin·na·cle (bin′ə k'l) *n.* [formerly *bittacle* < Port. *bitacola*, binnacle < L. *habitaculum*, dwelling place < *habitare*, to inhabit] the case enclosing a ship's compass, usually located near the helm

bin·oc·u·lar (bī näk′yə lər; *also, esp. for n.,* bi-) *adj.* [< L. *bini*, double + *ocularis*, of the eyes < *oculus*, EYE] using, or for the use of, both eyes at the same time —*n.* [*usually pl.*] a binocular instrument, as field glasses or opera glasses —**bin·oc′u·lar′i·ty** (-lar′ə tē) *n.* —**bin·oc′u·lar·ly** *adv.*

bi·no·mi·al (bī nō′mē əl) *n.* [< LL. *binomius* < *bi-* + Gr. *nomos*, law + -AL] **1.** a mathematical equation or expression consisting of two terms connected by a plus or minus sign **2.** a two-word scientific name of a plant or animal: see BINOMIAL NOMENCLATURE —*adj.* **1.** having two names **2.** composed of two terms **3.** of binomials —**bi·no′mi·al·ly** *adv.*

BINOCULARS

binomial coefficient *Math.* the coefficient of any component derived from the expansion of $(x + a)^n$

binomial distribution *Statistics* the distribution of the probability of a specified number of successes in a given number of independent trials, in each of which the probability of success is the same

binomial nomenclature (or **system**) the scientific system of giving a double name to each plant and animal, consisting of the name of the genus followed by that of the species (Ex.: *Prunus armeniaca*, apricot)

binomial theorem a general formula for writing any power of a binomial without multiplying out: discovered by Omar Khayyám and generalized by Sir Isaac Newton (Ex.: $(a + b)^2 = a^2 + 2ab + b^2$)

bin·tu·rong (bin′too rông′) *n.* [Malay] a variety of civet (*Arctictis binturong*) of SE Asia, with tufted ears and a long, hairy, prehensile tail

bi·nu·cle·ate (bī nōō′klē it, -āt′; -nyo͞o′l'-) *adj.* of or having two nuclei or centers: also **bi·nu′cle·at′ed, bi·nu′cle·ar**

Bin·yon (bin′yən), (Robert) Laurence 1869–1943; Eng. poet & art critic

bi·o- (bī′ō, -ə) [Gr. < *bios*, life < IE. base *gwei-*, to live, whence Sans. *jīvātu-ḥ*, life, OIr. *biu*, living, L. *vivere*, to live, E. QUICK] *a combining form meaning* life, of living things, biological [*biography, biochemistry*]

bi·o·as·say (bī′ō as′ā, -a sā′) *n.* [BIO- + ASSAY] a technique for determining the power of a drug or other substance by measuring its effects on a test specimen against those of a standard substance

bi·o·as·tro·nau·tics (bī′ō as′trə nô′tiks) *n.pl.* [*with sing. v.*] the science that deals with the physical responses of living things to the environment of space and space travel

Bí·o-Bí·o (bē′ō bē′ō) river in C Chile, flowing into the Pacific at Concepción: c. 240 mi.

bi·o·cat·a·lyst (bī′ō kat′'l ist) *n.* a substance, as an enzyme or hormone, that activates or speeds up a biochemical reaction —**bi′o·cat′a·lyt′ic** (-kat′ə lit′ik) *adj.*

bi·o·cel·late (bī äs′ə lāt′) *adj.* [BI-¹ + OCELLATE] *Zool.* having two simple eyes or eyelike markings

bi·o·ce·nol·o·gy (bī′ō si näl′ə jē) *n.* [BIO- + CENO- + -LOGY] the branch of biology that deals with communities of organisms and their reactions to their environment and to each other

bi·o·ce·no·sis (bī′ō si nō′sis) *n.* [ModL. < BIO- + Gr. *koinōsis*, a mingling < *koinoun*, to share, make common < *koinos*, common: see COENO-] a community of biologically integrated and interdependent plants and animals: also **bi′o·coe·no′sis** (-sē nō′sis), **bi′o·ce′nose** (-sē′nōs)

bi·o·chem·i·cal (-kem′i k'l) *adj.* of biochemistry; having to do with chemical processes in living organisms —*n.* a biochemical substance —**bi′o·chem′i·cal·ly** *adv.*

bi·o·chem·is·try (-kem′is trē) *n.* the branch of chemistry that deals with plants and animals and their life processes; biological chemistry —**bi′o·chem′ist** *n.*

bi·o·cide (bī′ə sīd′) *n.* [BIO- + -CIDE] a poisonous chemical substance that can kill living organisms

bi·o·cli·ma·tol·o·gy (bī′ō klī′mə täl′ə jē) *n.* the science that deals with the effects of climate on living matter —**bi′o·cli·mat′ic** (-klī mat′ik) *adj.*

bi·o·de·grad·a·ble (-di grā′də b'l) *adj.* [BIO- + DEGRAD(E) + -ABLE] capable of being readily decomposed by biological means, esp. by bacterial action: said of some detergents with reference to disposal in sewage

bi·o·e·col·o·gy (-ē käl′ə jē) *n.* [BIO- + ECOLOGY] the science that deals with the interrelations of communities of animals and plants with their environment

bi·o·en·gi·neer·ing (-en′jə nir′iŋ) *n.* a science dealing with the application of engineering science and technology to problems of biology and medicine: also called **biomedical engineering**

bi·o·fla·vo·noid (-flā′və noid′, -flav′ə-) *n.* a derivative of a flavone compound that helps maintain the capillary walls, reducing the likelihood of hemorrhaging

biog. **1.** biographer **2.** biographical **3.** biography

bi·o·gen·e·sis (bī′ō jen′ə sis) *n.* [BIO- + GENESIS] **1.** the principle that living organisms originate only from other living organisms closely similar to themselves **2.** the generation of organisms in this way —**bi′o·ge·net′ic** (-jə net′ik), **bi′o·ge·net′i·cal** *adj.* —**bi′o·ge·net′i·cal·ly** *adv.*

bi·og·e·ny (bī äj′ə nē) *n.* same as BIOGENESIS

bi·o·ge·o·chem·i·cal cycle (bī′ō jē′ō kem′i k'l) the cycle in which nitrogen, carbon, and other inorganic elements of the soil, atmosphere, etc. of a region are converted into the organic substances of animals or plants of the region and released back into the environment

bi·o·ge·og·ra·phy (bī′ō jē äg′rə fē) *n.* the branch of biology that deals with the geographical distribution of plants and animals —**bi′o·ge′o·graph′ic** (-jē′ə graf′ik), **bi′o·ge′o·graph′i·cal** *adj.*

bi·og·ra·pher (bī äg′rə fər, bē-) *n.* a writer of a biography or biographies

bi·o·graph·i·cal (bī′ə graf′i k'l) *adj.* **1.** of, having to do with, or characteristic of biography or biographies **2.** giving the story of, or based on, a person's life Also **bi′o·graph′ic** —**bi′o·graph′i·cal·ly** *adv.*

bi·og·ra·phy (bī äg′rə fē, bē-) *n.* [Gr. *biographia*: see BIO- & -GRAPHY] **1.** the histories of individual lives, considered as a branch of literature **2.** *pl.* **-phies** an account of a person's life, described by another; life story

bi·o·herm (bī′ō hurm′) *n.* [< BIO- + Gr. *herma*, a reef] **1.** a reeflike mass or mound of limestone built by organisms, as corals, and surrounded by rock of a different kind: cf. BIOSTROME **2.** *same as* CORAL REEF

biol. **1.** biological **2.** biologist **3.** biology

bi·o·log·ic (bī′ə läj′ik) *adj., n.* same as BIOLOGICAL

bi·o·log·i·cal (-i k'l) *adj.* **1.** of or connected with biology; of plants and animals **2.** of the nature of living matter **3.** used in or produced by practical biology —*n.* a biological product —**bi′o·log′i·cal·ly** *adv.*

biological clock any of various rhythm patterns in organisms, associated with recurrent natural cycles, as of tides, days and nights, seasons, etc.

biological warfare the deliberate use of disease-spreading microorganisms, toxins, etc. in warfare

biologic species a group of organisms of similar genetic endowment that interbreed regularly and successfully

bi·ol·o·gy (bī äl′ə jē) *n.* [BIO- + -LOGY] **1.** the science that deals with the origin, history, physical characteristics, life processes, habits, etc. of plants and animals: it includes botany, zoology, and their subdivisions **2.** animal and plant life, as of a given area **3.** biological history, principles, etc. —**bi·ol′o·gist** *n.*

bi·o·lu·mi·nes·cence (bī′ō lōō′mə nes′'ns) *n.* **1.** the production of light by living organisms, as by fireflies **2.** such light —**bi′o·lu′mi·nes′cent** *adj.*

bi·ol·y·sis (bī äl′ə sis) *n.* [BIO- + -LYSIS] the destruction of life, as by microorganisms —**bi′o·lyt′ic** (bī′ə lit′ik) *adj.*

bi·o·mass (bī′ō mas′) *n.* [BIO- + MASS²] the total mass or amount of living organisms in a particular area or volume

bi·o·math·e·mat·ics (bī′ō math′ə mat′iks) *n.pl.* [*with sing. v.*] the science that deals with the application of mathematical methods to the structure and functions of living organisms

bi·ome (bī′ōm) *n.* [< BIO- + -ome, group, mass < ModL. -oma < Gr. -ōma] an extensive community of plants and animals whose makeup is determined by soil and climatic conditions

bi·o·me·chan·ics (bī′ō mə kan′iks) *n.pl.* [with sing. v.] the application of the principles and techniques of mechanics to the structure, functions, and capabilities of living organisms —**bi′o·me·chan′i·cal** *adj.*

bi·o·med·i·cine (bī′ō med′ə s'n) *n.* a branch of medicine that is combined with research in biology —**bi′o·med′i·cal** *adj.*

bi·o·met·rics (-met′riks) *n.pl.* [with sing. v.] that branch of biology which deals with its data statistically and by quantitative analysis —**bi′o·met′ric, bi′o·met′ri·cal** *adj.* —**bi′o·met′ri·cal·ly** *adv.*

bi·om·e·try (bī äm′ə trē) *n.* **1.** calculation of the probable human life span **2.** *same as* BIOMETRICS

Bi·on (bī′än, -ən) fl. 2d cent. B.C.; Gr. pastoral poet

☆**bi·on·ics** (bī än′iks) *n.pl.* [*with sing. v.*] [< Gr. *bion*, living, prp. of *bioun*, to live (see BIO-) + -ICS] the science of designing instruments or systems modeled after living organisms

bi·o·nom·ics (bī′ō näm′iks) *n.pl.* [*with sing. v.*] [< BIO- + Gr. *nomos*, law] *same as* ECOLOGY (sense 1)

bi·o·phys·ics (-fiz′iks) *n.pl.* [*with sing. v.*] the study of biological phenomena using the principles and techniques of physics —**bi′o·phys′i·cal** *adj.* —**bi′o·phys′i·cist** *n.*

bi·o·plasm (bī′ō plaz′m) *n.* living matter; protoplasm

bi·op·sy (bī′äp′sē) *n., pl.* -**sies** [see BIO- & -OPSIS] *Med.* the removal of bits of living tissue, fluids, etc. from the body for diagnostic examination

bi·o·sat·el·lite (bī′ō sat′′l it′) *n.* a recoverable spacecraft designed for the study of the physiological effects of cosmic radiation, weightlessness, etc. on terrestrial forms of life in space

bi·o·sci·ence (bī′ō sī′əns) *n.* any science whose systematized knowledge is applied to the functions or problems of living organisms

bi·o·scope (bī′ə skōp′) *n.* [BIO- + -SCOPE] an early kind of motion-picture projector

bi·os·co·py (bī äs′kə pē) *n.* [BIO- + -SCOPY] *Med.* an examination to find out whether life is present

-**bi·o·sis** (bī ō′sis, bē-) [< Gr. *biōsis*, way of life < *bios*: see BIO-] *a combining form meaning* a (specified) way of living [*symbiosis*]

bi·o·sphere (bī′ə sfir′) *n.* [BIO- + SPHERE] **1.** the zone of the earth, extending from its crust out into the surrounding atmosphere, which contains living organisms **2.** all the living organisms of the earth

bi·o·sta·tis·tics (bī′ō stə tis′tiks) *n.pl.* [*with sing. v.*] the science that applies the methods of statistics to biological data —**bi′o·sta·tis′ti·cal** *adj.* —**bi′o·stat′is·ti′cian** (-stat′əs tish′ən) *n.*

bi·o·strome (bī′ō strōm′) *n.* [< BIO- + Gr. *strōma*, a mattress, bed, rug < IE. base **ster-*, to spread out, whence STRAW, STREW] a thin limestone layer consisting predominantly of marine fossils, as corals: cf. BIOHERM

bi·o·syn·the·sis (bī′ō sin′thə sis) *n.* the formation of chemical compounds by the cells of living organisms, as in photosynthesis —**bi′o·syn·thet′ic** (-sin thet′ik) *adj.* —**bi′o·syn·thet′i·cal·ly** *adv.*

bi·o·sys·te·mat·ics (-sis′tə mat′iks) *n.pl.* [*with sing. v.*] the study of morphological and other problems basic to taxonomic systems —**bi′o·sys′te·mat′ic** *adj.*

bi·o·ta (bī ōt′ə) *n.* [ModL.: see BIOTIC] the plant and animal life of a region

bi·o·tech·nol·o·gy (bī′ō tek näl′ə jē) *n.* the use of the data and techniques of engineering and technology for the study and solution of problems concerning living organisms

bi·o·te·lem·e·try (-tə lem′ə trē) *n.* the use of telemeters to monitor the physical condition or responses of animals, men, etc. at great distances, as in spacecraft

bi·o·ther·a·py (bī′ō ther′ə pē) *n.* the treatment of disease by means of substances, as serums, vaccines, penicillin, etc., secreted by or derived from living organisms

bi·ot·ic (bī ät′ik) *adj.* [Gr. *biōtikos* < *bios*: see BIO-] of life, or caused by living organisms: also **bi·ot′i·cal**

-**bi·ot·ic** (bī ät′ik, bē-) *a combining form meaning* of or having a (specified) way of living [*symbiotic*]

bi·o·tin (bī′ə tin) *n.* [BIOT(IC) + -IN¹] a bacterial growth factor, $C_{10}H_{16}O_3N_2S$, one of the vitamin B group, found in liver, egg yolk, and yeast

bi·o·tite (bī′ə tīt′) *n.* [after J. B. Biot (1774–1862), Fr. naturalist] a dark-brown or black mineral of the mica family, found in igneous and metamorphic rocks

bi·o·tope (bī′ə tōp′) *n.* [< BIO- + Gr. *topos*, a place: see TOPIC] a small area with a uniform environment occupied by a unified community of organisms

bi·o·type (-tīp′) *n.* a group of plants or animals having the same fundamental constitution in terms of genetic or hereditary factors —**bi′o·typ′ic** (-tip′ik) *adj.*

bi·pack (bī′pak′) *n. Photog.* two adjacent films with different color sensitivities, intended to be exposed one through the other

bi·pa·ri·e·tal (bī′pə rī′ə t′l) *adj.* of or connected with the prominent rounded part of the two parietal bones

bip·a·rous (bip′ər əs) *adj.* [BI-¹ + -PAROUS] **1.** bearing two offspring at a birth **2.** *Bot.* dividing into two branches

bi·par·ti·san (bī pär′tə z′n, -s′n) *adj.* of, representing, or supported by two parties —**bi·par′ti·san·ship′** *n.*

bi·par·tite (bī pär′tīt) *adj.* [L. *bipartitus*, pp. of *bipartire* < *bi-*, two + *partire*, to divide] **1.** having two parts **2.** having two corresponding parts, one each for the two parties to a contract **3.** with two involved or participating [a *bipartite* alliance] **4.** *Bot.* divided in two nearly to the base, as some leaves —**bi·par′tite·ly** *adv.*

bi·par·ti·tion (bī′pär tish′ən) *n.* partition, or division, into two parts

bi·ped (bī′ped) *n.* [L. *bipes* < *bi-* + *pedis*, gen. of *pes*, FOOT] any two-footed animal —*adj.* two-footed: also **bi·ped′al**

bi·pet·al·ous (bī pet′′l əs) *adj.* having two petals

bi·phen·yl (bī fen′′l, -fē′n′l) *same as* DIPHENYL (sense 1)

bi·pin·nate (bī pin′āt, -it) *adj.* having pinnate leaflets on stems that grow opposite each other on a main stem —**bi·pin′nate·ly** *adv.*

bi·plane (bī′plān′) *n.* an airplane with two sets of wings, one above the other

bi·pod (bī′päd′) *n.* [BI-¹ + -POD] a two-legged stand, as for an automatic rifle

bi·po·lar (bī pō′lər) *adj.* **1.** of or having two poles **2.** of or involving both of the earth's polar regions **3.** characterized by two directly opposite opinions, natures, etc. —**bi·po·lar·i·ty** (bī′pō lar′ə tē) *n.*

BIPINNATE LEAF
(of acacia)

bi·pro·pel·lant (bī′prə pel′ənt) *n.* a propellant system for rockets consisting of a fuel and an oxidizer kept in separate tanks and brought together only in the combustion chamber

bi·quad·rate (bī kwäd′rit, -rāt) *n. Math.* the square of the square; fourth power

bi·quad·rat·ic (bī′kwäd rat′ik) *adj. Math.* of or involving the biquadrate, or fourth power, of a quantity —*n.* **1.** a biquadrate **2.** an algebraic equation of the fourth power

bi·quar·ter·ly (bī kwôr′tər lē) *adj.* happening or appearing twice in every three-month period

bi·ra·cial (bī rā′shal) *adj.* consisting of or involving two races, esp. Negroes and whites

bi·ra·di·al (bī rā′dē əl) *adj. Biol.* having both bilateral and radial symmetry

bi·ra·mous (bī rā′məs) *adj.* [BI-¹ + RAMOUS] having two branches, as the two end branches found on the appendages of crustaceans

birch (burch) *n.* [ME. *birche* < OE. *beorc* < IE. base **bhereg̑-*, to shine, white, whence BRIGHT] **1.** any of a genus (*Betula*) of trees and shrubs of northern climates, having smooth bark easily peeled off in thin sheets, and hard, close-grained wood **2.** the wood of any of these trees **3.** a birch rod or bunch of twigs used for whipping —*vt.* to beat with a birch —*adj.* of birch: also **birch′en**

☆**Birch·er** (bur′chər) *n.* a member or supporter of the John Birch Society, an extreme rightist political organization: also **Birch′ite** (-chīt)

birch partridge [Canad.] *same as* RUFFED GROUSE

bird (burd) *n.* [ME. *brid* < OE. *bridd*, bird, orig. a young bird] **1.** any of a class (Aves) of warm-blooded, two-legged, egg-laying vertebrates with feathers and wings **2.** a small game bird: distinguished from WATERFOWL **3.** a clay pigeon in trapshooting **4.** a shuttlecock ☆**5.** [Slang] a person, esp. a mildly eccentric one **6.** [Slang] a sound of disapproval made by the lips fluttering **7.** [Slang] a rocket or guided missile —*vi.* **1.** to shoot or catch birds **2.** to engage in bird watching —**bird in the hand** something sure or definite because already in one's possession: opposed to **bird in the bush**, something unsure, tentative, etc. —**birds of a feather** people with the same characteristics or tastes —**eat like a bird** to eat very little food —☆**for the birds** [Slang] ridiculous, foolish, worthless, useless, etc. —**the birds and the bees** [Colloq.] the rudimentary facts concerning sexual matters, as they might be explained to a child —**bird′er** *n.*

☆**bird-bath** (-bath′, -bäth′) *n.* a basinlike garden ornament for birds to bathe in

☆**bird-brain** (-brān′) *n.* [Colloq.] a stupid or silly person; nitwit

bird-call (-kôl′) *n.* **1.** the sound or song of a bird **2.** an imitation of this **3.** a device for imitating bird sounds Also **bird call**

☆**bird dog 1.** a dog trained for hunting birds, as a pointer **2.** [Colloq.] a person whose work is searching, as for new talent, missing persons, etc.

☆**bird-dog** (-dôg′) *vt.* -**dogged′**, -**dog′ging** [Colloq.] to search out diligently or pursue doggedly

bird-foot (-foot′) *n. same as* BIRD'S-FOOT

☆**bird grass** a local name for **1.** ROUGH BLUEGRASS **2.** KNOTGRASS

☆**bird-house** (-hous′) *n.* **1.** a small box, often resembling a house, for birds to live in **2.** a building for exhibiting birds

bird·ie (bur′dē) *n.* **1.** any small bird: a child's word ☆**2.** *Golf* a score of one stroke under par for a hole

bird-lime (burd′līm′) *n.* **1.** a sticky substance spread on

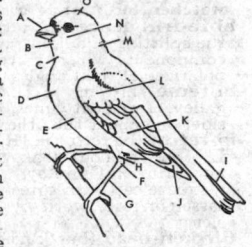

BIRD
(A, bill; B, chin; C, throat; D, breast; E, abdomen; F, heel; G, tarsus; H, tibia; I, tail feathers; J, primaries; K, secondaries; L, wing coverts; M, nape; N, auriculars or ear coverts; O, crown)

twigs to catch birds **2.** anything that snares —*vt.* **-limed′, -lim′ing** to spread or catch with birdlime

bird louse any of an order (Mallophaga) of small, wingless insects with biting mouthparts, that live as external parasites on birds

bird·man (-man′, -mən) *n., pl.* **-men** (-men′, -mən) **1.** a person whose work deals with birds, as an ornithologist or taxidermist **2.** [Colloq.] an aviator

bird of ill omen 1. a bearer of bad news **2.** an unlucky person

bird of paradise 1. any of a family (Paradiseaidae) of brightly colored birds found in and near New Guinea **2.** any of several tropical African plants (genus *Strelitzia*) of the banana family, having several brilliant orange and blue flowers protruding from a green spathe in a form that resembles a bird in flight

bird of passage 1. any migratory bird **2.** anyone who travels or roams about constantly

bird of peace the dove

bird of prey any of a number of birds, as the eagle, hawk, owl, etc., that feed upon mammals and other birds, which they capture and kill

bird pepper the tropical American, wild red pepper (*Capsicum frutescens*) of the nightshade family, with small, very pungent fruits

bird·seed (-sēd′) *n.* seed for feeding caged birds

Birds·eye (burdz′ī′), **Clarence** 1886–1956; U.S. inventor of methods of quick-freezing foods

bird's-eye (burdz′ī′) *n.* **1.** any of several plants (esp. of the genera *Primula* and *Veronica*) having flowers with centers and petals of contrasting colors **2.** a pattern of small, diamond-shaped figures, each with a dot in the center, woven into cottons and linens **3.** a cotton or linen cloth with such a pattern: used for diapers, napkins, etc. —*adj.* **1.** seen from above or at a distance, as by a bird in flight; hence, general; overall, but cursory [a *bird's-eye* view] **2.** having markings that resemble birds' eyes [*bird's-eye* maple]

bird's-foot (-foot′) *n., pl.* **-foots′** any of various plants whose leaves or flowers resemble a bird's foot, as the bird's-foot trefoil

bird's-foot trefoil a perennial plant (*Lotus corniculatus*) of the legume family, with clusters of brilliant yellow flowers, used for forage and hay

☆**bird's-foot violet** a N. American violet (*Viola pedata*) having divided leaves and large blue or purple flowers

bird·shot (burd′shät′) *n.* small shot, for shooting birds

bird watching the observation of wild birds in their habitat, esp. as a hobby: also **bird′watch′ing** *n.* —**bird watcher, bird′watch′er** *n.*

bi·re·frin·gence (bī′ri frin′jəns) *n.* [BI-¹ + REFRINGENCE] the splitting of a light ray, generally by a crystal, into two components which travel at different velocities and are polarized at right angles to each other —**bi′re·frin′gent** *adj.*

bi·reme (bī′rēm) *n.* [L. *biremis* < *bi-* + *remus*, oar] a galley of ancient times, having two rows of oars on each side, one under the other

bi·ret·ta (bə ret′ə) *n.* [It. *berretta* < LL. *birrettum*, dim. of L. *birrus*, a hood, cloak, prob. < Celt. base appearing in Cym. *byrr*, MIr. *berr*, short] a square cap with three projections and a tassel on top, worn by Roman Catholic clergy

Bir·ken·head (bur′k'n hed′) *n.* seaport in W England, at the mouth of the Mersey River: pop. 144,000

birl (burl) *vt., vi.* [earlier *pirl*, to spin, ? echoic, after WHIRL, PURL] **1.** to spin with a whirring sound ☆**2.** to revolve (a floating log) by treading

BIRETTA

birle, birl (burl) *vt.* [ME. *birlen*, to serve a drink < OE. *byrelian*, akin to *byrele*, cup-bearer, butler, prob. < base of *beran*, to BEAR¹] [Obs. except Scot.] to pour (a drink) or ply with drink —*vi.* [Obs. except Scot.] to carouse

birl·ing (burl′iŋ) *n.* ☆a competitive game among lumberjacks in which each tries to keep his balance while revolving a floating log with his feet —**birl′er** *n.*

Bir·ming·ham (bur′miŋ əm *for 1;* -ham′ *for 2*) **1.** industrial city in C England: pop. 1,116,000 **2.** [after prec.] city in NC Ala.: iron and steel center: pop. 301,000 (met. area 739,000)

Bi·ro (bir′ō) [Brit.] *a trademark for* a kind of ball point pen —*n.* [b-] *pl.* **-os** such a pen

Bir·o·bi·dzhan, Bir·o·bi·jan (bir′ō bi jän′) region in E Siberia, set aside for Jewish agricultural colonization in 1934: officially an autonomous region of the R.S.F.S.R., called *Jewish Autonomous Region:* 13,895 sq. mi.

birr (bur) *n.* [ME. *bir* < ON. *byrr*, impetus, strong wind] **1.** onrush or driving force; impetus **2.** a vibrant whirring sound —*vi.* to make or move with a birr

birth (burth) *n.* [ME. *birthe, burde* < OE. *byrde, gebyrde* < *beran*, to BEAR¹] **1.** the act of bringing forth offspring **2.** the act of being born; nativity **3.** origin or natal background [a Spaniard by *birth*] **4.** good or noble lineage [a man of *birth*] **5.** the beginning of anything [the birth of a nation] **6.** an inherited or natural inclination or talent [an actor by *birth*] **7.** [Archaic] a person or thing born or produced —*vi., vt.* [Dial.] to give birth (to) —**give birth to 1.** to bring forth

(offspring) **2.** to be the cause or origin of; originate; create

☆**birth control** control of how many children a woman will have and when she will have them, specif. through the control of conception

birth·day (-dā′) *n.* **1.** the day of a person's birth or a thing's beginning **2.** the anniversary of this day

birth·mark (-märk′) *n.* a skin blemish present at birth

birth·place (-plās′) *n.* **1.** the place of one's birth **2.** the place where something originated

birth·rate (-rāt′) *n.* the number of births per year per thousand of population in a given community, area, or group: sometimes other units of time or population are used in giving the birth rate: also **birth rate**

birth·right (-rīt′) *n.* **1.** a right or the rights that a person has because he was born in a certain family, nation, etc. **2.** the rights of the first-born son —*SYN.* see HERITAGE

☆**birth·root** (-rōōt′, -root′) *n.* any of various trilliums whose short, thick rootstocks were supposed by the American Indians to be of help in childbirth

birth·stone (-stōn′) *n.* a precious or semiprecious gem symbolizing the month of one's birth: the usual list, beginning with that of January, is as follows: garnet, amethyst, bloodstone, diamond, emerald, pearl, ruby, sardonyx, sapphire, opal, topaz, and turquoise

birth·wort (-wurt′) *n.* any of a genus (*Aristolochia*) of plants with unusual coloring and S-shaped flowers: formerly supposed to be of help in childbirth

‡**bis** (bēs) *interj.* [L., twice < OL. *duis* < base of *duo*, TWO] again; once more: used by audiences in France, etc. instead of *encore!*: in written music, it is a direction to repeat the passage indicated

bis- (bis) *same as* BI-¹: used before *c* or *s*

Bi·sa·yan (bi sä′yən) *n., adj. same as* VISAYAN

Bis·cay, Bay of (bis′kā, -kē) part of the Atlantic, north of Spain & west of France

bis·cuit (bis′kit) *n., pl.* **-cuits, -cuit** [ME. *bisquit* < OFr. *bescuit* (alt. after cognate It. *biscotto*) < ML. *bis coctum,* (bread) baked twice < L. *bis* (see BI-¹) + pp. of *coquere,* COOK] **1.** [Chiefly Brit.] a crisp, unleavened wafer; cracker or cookie ☆**2.** *a)* a quick bread, made light by baking powder, soda, or yeast, and baked in small pieces *b)* any of these pieces **3.** light brown; tan **4.** pottery or porcelain after the first firing and before glazing

‡**bise** (bēz) *n.* [Fr. < Frank. *bisa*] a cold north or northeast wind blowing down from the Swiss Alps

bi·sect (bī sekt′, bī′sekt) *vt.* [< ML. *bisectus,* pp. of *bisecare* < L. *bi-* + *secare,* to cut] **1.** to cut in two **2.** *Geom.* to divide into two equal parts —*vi.* to divide; fork — **bi·sec′tion** *n.* —**bi·sec′tion·al** *adj.*

bi·sec·tor (-ər) *n.* a thing that bisects; specif., a straight line that bisects an angle or line

bi·sec·trix (bī sek′triks) *n., pl.* **bi·sec·tri·ces** (bī′sek trī′sēz) *Crystallography* either of the two lines bisecting the acute and obtuse angles formed by the optic axes in a biaxial crystal

bi·ser·rate (bī ser′āt, -it) *adj.* **1.** *Bot.* having serrations along the serrations, as some leaves; doubly serrate **2.** *Zool.* notched on both sides, as some antennae

bi·sex·u·al (bī sek′shōō wəl) *adj.* **1.** of both sexes **2.** having both male and female organs, as certain animals and plants; hermaphroditic **3.** sexually attracted by both sexes —*n.* one that is bisexual —**bi·sex′u·al′i·ty** (-shōō wal′ə tē), **bi·sex′u·al·ism** *n.* —**bi·sex′u·al·ly** *adv.*

bish·op (bish′əp) *n.* [ME. < OE. *bisceop* < LL. *episcopus,* an overseer (in Eccles. use, bishop) < Gr. *episkopos,* overseer (in NT., bishop) < *epi-,* upon + *skopos* < *skopein,* to look] **1.** a high-ranking Christian clergyman having authority, variously, over other clergy and usually supervising a diocese or church district **2.** a chessman that can move in a diagonal direction across any number of empty squares of the same color **3.** a hot, sweet drink of port wine flavored with an orange stuck with cloves

bish·op·ric (bish′ə prik) *n.* [ME. *bischopriche* < OE. *bisceoprice* < prec. + *rice,* jurisdiction, kingdom] **1.** the church district controlled by a bishop; diocese **2.** the office, authority, or rank of a bishop

BISHOP

bish·op's-cap (bish′əps kap′) *n.* ☆any of a genus (*Mitella*) of small woodland plants of the saxifrage family, with two-lobed seedcases shaped like a bishop's hat

Bis·marck (biz′märk) [after Otto von BISMARCK] capital of N.Dak., on the Missouri River: pop. 35,000

Bis·marck (biz′märk), **Prince Otto (Eduard Leopold) von** 1815–98; Prussian chancellor of the German Empire (1871–90), which he unified: called the *Iron Chancellor*

Bismarck Archipelago group of islands northeast of New Guinea: part of the Australian-administered trust territory of New Guinea: 19,800 sq. mi.; pop. 183,000

bis·muth (biz′məth) *n.* [G. *wismut* < LowG. *wesemod* < ?] a hard, brittle, metallic element that is grayish-white with a tinge of red, used chiefly in making alloys of low melting point: symbol, Bi; at. wt., 208.980; at. no., 83; sp. gr., 9.78; melt. pt., 271.3°C; boil. pt., 1560°C —**bis′muth·al** *adj.*

bis·mu·thic (biz′məth ik; biz myōō′thik, -muth′ik) *adj.* containing bismuth, esp. with a valence of five

bis·muth·ous (biz′məth əs) *adj.* containing bismuth, esp. with a valence of three

bi·son (bīs′'n, bī′z'n) *n.*, *pl.* **bi′son** [Fr. < L., wild ox < Gmc. *wisunt* < IE. *wis-onto-* < base *weis*: see FITCHEW] any of a number of related four-legged bovine mammals with a shaggy mane, short, curved horns, and a humped back, as the American buffalo (*Bison bison*) or the wisent

bisque¹ (bisk) *n.* [Fr.] 1. a rich, thick, creamy soup made from shellfish or from rabbit, fowl, etc. 2. a thick, strained, creamy vegetable soup 3. an ice cream containing ground macaroons or nuts

BISON
(5 1/2–6 ft. high at shoulder)

bisque² (bisk) *n.* [< BISCUIT] 1. biscuit ceramic ware, specif. such ware left unglazed in the finished state 2. a red-yellow color

bisque³ (bisk) *n.* [Fr.] a handicap of one point per set in tennis, one turn per game in croquet, or one or more strokes per game at match play in golf

Bis·sau (bi sou′) seaport & capital of Portuguese Guinea, on the W coast of Africa: pop. 20,000

bis·sex·tile (bi seks′t'l, bī-; -tīl) *adj.* [L. *bisextilis*, containing an intercalary day < *bisextus* < *bis*, twice + *sextus*, sixth: Feb. 24 (sixth day before the calends of March) was reckoned twice every fourth year] 1. denoting the extra day (February 29) in a leap year 2. designating or of a leap year —*n.* a leap year

bis·ter, bis·tre (bis′tər) *n.* [Fr. *bistre*] 1. a yellowish-brown to dark-brown pigment made from the soot of burned wood 2. any of various colors in this range

bis·tort (bis′tôrt) *n.* [Fr. *bistorte* < ModL. *bistorta*, lit., twice twisted < L. *bis*, twice + *tortus*, pp. of *torquere*, to twist] any of several perennial northern and alpine plants (genus *Polygonum*) of the buckwheat family, whose twisted roots furnish an astringent

bis·tou·ry (bis′too rē) *n.*, *pl.* **-ries** [Fr. *bistouri* < *bistourner*, to deform, castrate < OFr. *bestorner*, distort] a small, slender surgical knife with a straight or curved blade and a very sharp point

bis·tro (bis′trō; *Fr.* bē strō′) *n.* [Fr. (Parisian) slang, wine shop, wine seller, orig. (dial. of Anjou & Poitou), a shepherd] 1. a small wine shop or restaurant where wine is served 2. a small nightclub or bar

bi·sul·cate (bī sul′kāt) *adj.* [BI-¹ + SULCATE] 1. having two grooves 2. *Zool.* *a*) cloven *b*) cloven-hoofed

bi·sul·fate (bī sul′fāt) *n.* an acid sulfate; compound containing the monovalent HSO₄⁻ radical

bi·sul·fide (bī sul′fīd) *n.* 1. hydrosulfide 2. erroneously, a disulfide

bi·sul·fite (-fīt) *n.* compound containing the monovalent HSO₃⁻ radical

bit¹ (bit) *n.* [ME. < OE. *bite*, a bite < *bitan*, BITE] 1. the metal mouthpiece on a bridle, used for controlling the horse 2. anything that curbs or controls 3. the part of a pipestem held in the mouth 4. the part of a key that actually turns the lock 5. the cutting part of any tool, as the blade of a plane 6. a drilling or boring tool for use in a bitstock, drill press, etc.: see BRACE AND BIT, illus. —*vt.* **bit′ted, bit′ting** 1. *a*) to put a bit into the mouth of (a horse) *b*) to train to the bit 2. to check or curb 3. to make the bit on (a key) —**take** (or **get**) **the bit in one's teeth** 1. to clench the bit between the teeth, so that it fails to restrain: said of horses 2. to be beyond control

bit² (bit) *n.* [ME. *bite* < OE. *bita*, a piece, morsel, bit < *bitan*, to BITE] 1. *a*) a small piece or quantity *b*) a small extent or limited degree: often used with *a* and having adverbial force [a *bit* bored] *c*) a short time; moment [wait a *bit*] ☆2. [orig. used of a small silver coin worth 1/8 of the Spanish peso (hence, normally 12 1/2 cents)] [Colloq.] an amount equal to 12 1/2 cents: now usually in *two bits*, *four bits*, etc. ☆3. *a*) a small part or short performance in a play or entertainment *b*) [Colloq.] any stereotyped or repeated action, expression, etc. [resorting to the aggrieved *bit*] —*adj.* very small [a *bit* role] —**bit by bit** little by little; gradually —**do one's bit** to do one's share —**every bit** altogether; entirely

bit³ (bit) *pt.* and alt. *pp.* of BITE

bit⁴ (bit) *n.* [b(*inary*) (dig*it*)] a single digit in a binary number system; specif., a unit of information equal to the amount of information obtained by learning which of two equally likely events occurred

bi·tar·trate (bī tär′trāt) *n.* an acid tartrate; compound containing the monovalent C₄H₅O₆⁻ radical

bitch (bich) *n.* [ME. *bicche* < OE. *bicce*; akin to ON. *bikkja*] 1. the female of the dog, wolf, fox, etc. 2. a woman, esp. a bad-tempered, malicious, or promiscuous woman: a coarse term of contempt or hostility 3. [Slang] anything especially unpleasant or difficult —*vi.* [Slang] to complain —**bitch up** [< BOTCH¹] [Slang] to botch; spoil by bungling —**bitch′i·ness** *n.* —**bitch′y, -i·er, -i·est** *adj.*

bite (bīt) *vt.* **bit, bit′ten** or **bit, bit′ing** [ME. *biten* < OE.

bitan < IE. base *bheid-*, to split, crack, whence FISSURE, BITTER] 1. to seize, pierce, or cut with the teeth or with parts like jaws 2. to cut into, as with a sharp weapon 3. to sting, as an insect 4. to hurt in a sharp, stinging way 5. to eat into; corrode 6. to seize or possess [often by a lust for power] 7. to cheat or trick: usually in the passive —*vi.* 1. *a*) to press or snap the teeth (*into*, *at*, etc.) *b*) to have a tendency to do this 2. to cause a biting sensation or have a biting effect 3. to get or keep a tight hold; grip [the car wheels *bit* into the snow] 4. to seize a bait 5. to be caught, as by a trick —*n.* 1. the act of biting 2. biting quality; sting [a *bite* to his words] 3. a wound, bruise, or sting from biting 4. *a*) amount of food bitten off; mouthful or morsel *b*) food *c*) a meal, esp. a light meal or snack 5. a tight hold or grip 6. an edge or surface that grips ☆7. [Colloq.] an amount cut off or sum deducted [the tax takes quite a *bite* from his paycheck] ☆8. [Slang] money or price asked; cost; expense (with *the*): usually used in the phrase **put the bite on**, to press for a loan, gift, or bribe of money 9. *Dentistry* the way the upper and lower teeth meet 10. *Etching* the corrosion of the metal plate by the acid —☆**bite off more than one can chew** [Colloq.] to attempt more than one is capable of

bite·wing (-wiŋ′) *n. Dentistry* an X-ray film with a projecting edge that is clamped by the teeth to hold the film in place for an exposure

Bi·thyn·i·a (bə thin′ē ə) ancient kingdom in NW Asia Minor, in what is now Turkey

bit·ing (bīt′iŋ) *adj.* 1. cutting; sharp 2. sarcastic; caustic —*SYN.* see INCISIVE —**bit′ing·ly** *adv.*

biting midge any of a family (Ceratopogonidae) of tiny flies with piercing and sucking mouthparts

Bi·to·la (bē′tô lə) city in Macedonia, S Yugoslavia: pop. 49,000: also **Bi·tolj** (bē′tôl′y′)

bit·stock (bit′stäk′) *n.* a handle for holding and turning bits; brace

bitt (bit) *n.* [< ?] *Naut.* any of the deck posts, often in pairs, around which ropes or cables are wound and held fast —*vt.* to wind around a bitt

bit·ten (bit′'n) *alt. pp.* of BITE

bit·ter (bit′ər) *adj.* [ME. < OE. *biter* < base of *bitan*, BITE] 1. designating or having a sharp, often unpleasant taste; acrid, as quinine or peach stones 2. causing or showing sorrow, discomfort, or pain; grievous 3. sharp and disagreeable; harsh; severe; piercing [a *bitter* wind] 4. characterized by strong feelings of hatred, resentment, cynicism, etc. —*adv.* in a way that is bitter; bitterly —*n.* 1. a bitter quality or thing [take the *bitter* with the sweet] 2. [Brit.] bitter, strongly hopped ale: cf. BITTERS —*vt.*, *vi.* to make or become bitter —**bit′ter·ly** *adv.* —**bit′ter·ness** *n.*

bitter almond a variety of almond whose bitter seeds yield hydrocyanic acid upon hydrolysis

bitter apple *same as* COLOCYNTH

bitter cassava a species of cassava (*Manihot esculenta*) whose poisonous roots when processed yield tapioca starch

bitter end [archaic *bitter*, turn of cable about a bitt; with cable out to the bitter end, no freedom of action remains; meaning infl. by BITTER (*adj.* 2)] *Naut.* 1. that end of a rope or cable that is wound around a bitt 2. the inboard end of a rope or cable —**to the bitter end** 1. until the end, however difficult or distressing 2. until death

☆**bit·ter-end·er** (-en′dər) *n.* [Colloq.] a person who persists in a hopeless cause; one who will not give in

bit·tern¹ (bit′ərn) *n.*, *pl.* **-terns**, **-tern**: see PLURAL, II, D, 1 [ME. *bitor* < OFr. *butor*, prob. < L. *butio* < echoic base *bu-*] any of various wading birds (esp. genus *Botaurus*) of the heron family, noted for the resounding, thumping call of the male

bit·tern² (bit′ərn) *n.* [prob. < dial. *bittering* < BITTER + -ING] the bitter liquid left after the crystallization of salt from brine

☆**bit·ter·nut** (bit′ər nut′) *n.* a hickory tree (*Carya cordiformis*) of the eastern U.S., with yellow buds and thin-shelled bitter nuts

bitter principle any of various bitter substances found in plants, as lupulin, aloin, etc.

bit·ter·root (-root′, -root′) *n.* a western N. American flowering plant (*Lewisia rediviva*) of the purslane family, having fleshy, edible roots and pink or white flowers

Bitterroot Range range of the Rocky Mountains, along the Ida.-Mont. border: highest peak, 10,961 ft.

bit·ters (bit′ərs) *n.pl.* a liquor containing bitter herbs, roots, etc. and usually alcohol, used as a medicine or tonic and as an ingredient in some cocktails

bit·ter·sweet (bit′ər swēt′) *n.* ☆1. a N. American twining woody vine (*Celastrus scandens*), bearing clusters of small orange fruits which open to expose the brightly-red seeds 2. a poisonous climbing European vine (*Solanum dulcamara*) of the nightshade family, with purple flowers and red berries, now widely found as a weed in N. America 3. *a*)

BITTERN
(to 31 in. including bill)

bitterness and sweetness combined *b*) pleasure mixed with overtones of sadness —*adj.* **1.** both bitter and sweet, as dark chocolate made with little sugar **2.** pleasant with overtones of sadness

☆**bit·ter·weed** (-wēd′) *n.* any of various plants which have a bitter taste, as ragweed, sneezeweed, etc.

bit·ty (bit′ē) *adj.* **-ti·er, -ti·est** [< BIT² + -Y³] tiny: a playful term or child's term: cf. ITTY-BITTY

bi·tu·men (bi tōō′mən, bī-; -tyōō′-) *n.* [L. < Celt. (or ? Oscan-Umbrian) name < IE. base *gwet*, resin, whence Sans. *jatu*, gum, E. CUD, Bret. *bezuen* & L. *betulla*, birch] **1.** orig., asphalt found in a natural state; mineral pitch **2.** any of several hard or semisolid materials obtained as asphaltic residue in the distillation of coal tar, wood tar, petroleum, etc., or occurring as natural asphalt —**bi·tu′mi·noid′** (-mə noid′) *adj.*

bi·tu·mi·nize (-mə nīz′) *vt.* **-nized′, -niz′ing** to impregnate with, or convert into, bitumen —**bi·tu′mi·ni·za′tion** (-mə ni zā′shən) *n.*

bi·tu·mi·nous (-mə nəs) *adj.* [Fr. *bitumineux* < L. *bitumineus*] **1.** of the nature of bitumen **2.** containing or made with bitumen

bituminous coal coal that yields pitch or tar when it burns and produces much smoke and ashes; soft coal

bi·va·lence (bī vā′ləns, biv′ə-) *n.* the quality or state of being bivalent: also **bi·va′len·cy** (-lən sē)

bi·va·lent (-lənt) *adj.* **1.** *Chem.* *a*) having two valences *b*) having a valence of two **2.** *Biol.* double: said of a chromosome formed by two similar chromosomes that lie close together or appear to join completely during meiosis —*n.* such a double chromosome; dyad

bi·valve (bī′valv′) *n.* any of a class (Pelecypoda) of mollusks having two valves or shells hinged together, as a mussel, clam, etc. —*adj.* having two valves, or two shells hinged together: also **bi′valved′**

biv·ou·ac (biv′wak, -ōō wak′) *n.* [Fr. < OHG. *biwacht*, outpost < *bi-*, by + *wacht*, a guard] **1.** orig., a night guard to avoid surprise attack **2.** a temporary encampment (esp. of soldiers) in the open, with only tents or improvised shelter —*vi.* **-acked, -ack·ing** to encamp in the open

bi·week·ly (bī wēk′lē) *adj., adv.* **1.** once every two weeks **2.** twice a week: in this sense, *semiweekly* is the preferred term —*n., pl.* **-lies** a publication that appears once every two weeks

bi·year·ly (bī yir′lē) *adj., adv.* **1.** once every two years; biennial(ly) **2.** twice a year: in this sense, *semiyearly, semiannual(ly),* or *biannual(ly)* is preferred

☆**biz** (biz) *n.* [Slang] business [show *biz*]

bi·zarre (bi zär′) *adj.* [Fr. < It. *bizarro*, angry, fierce, strange < Sp. *bizarro*, bold, knightly < Basque *bizar*, a beard] **1.** odd in manner, appearance, etc.; grotesque; queer; eccentric **2.** marked by extreme contrasts and incongruities of color, design, or style **3.** unexpected and unbelievable; fantastic [a *bizarre* sequence of events] —*SYN.* see FANTASTIC —**bi·zarre′ly** *adv.* —**bi·zarre′ness** *n.*

Bi·zer·te (bi zur′tə, -tē; Fr. bē zert′) seaport in northernmost Tunisia, near Tunis: pop. 47,000: also sp. **Bi·zer′ta** (-zur′tə)

Bi·zet (bē zā′), **Georges** (zhôrzh) (born *Alexandre César Léopold Bizet*) 1838–75; Fr. composer

B.J. Bachelor of Journalism

Björn·son (byôrn′sôn), **Björn·stjer·ne** (byörn′styer′nə) 1832–1910; Norw. novelist, dramatist, & poet

Bk *Chem.* berkelium

bk. *pl.* **bks.** **1.** bank **2.** block **3.** book

bkcy. bankruptcy

bkg. banking

bkpt. bankrupt

bks., Bks. barracks

bkt. **1.** basket(s) **2.** bracket

bl. **1.** bale(s) **2.** barrel(s) **3.** black

B/L *pl.* **BS/L** bill of lading

B.L. Bachelor of Laws

blab (blab) *vt., vi.* **blabbed, blab′bing** [ME. *blabben*: see ff.] **1.** to give away (a secret) in idle chatter **2.** to chatter; prattle —*n.* **1.** loose chatter; gossip **2.** a person who blabs

blab·ber (blab′ər) *vt., vi.* [ME. *blabberen*, freq. of *blabben*, like ON. *blabbra*, MDu. *blabberen*, of echoic origin] [Dial. or Colloq.] to blab or babble —*n.* [< BLAB + -ER] a person who blabs

blab·ber·mouth (-mouth′) *n.* [Colloq.] a person who blabs or babbles

black (blak) *adj.* [ME. *blak* < OE. *blæc* < IE. base *bhleg-*, burn, gleam, whence L. *flagrare*, flame, burn; orig. sense, "sooted, smoke-black from flame"] **1.** opposite to white; of the color of coal or pitch: see COLOR **2.** having dark-colored skin and hair; esp., Negro **3.** *a*) totally without light; in complete darkness *b*) very dark **4.** without cream, milk, etc.: said of coffee **5.** soiled; dirty **6.** wearing black clothing **7.** evil; wicked; harmful **8.** disgraceful **9.** full of sorrow or suffering; sad; dismal; gloomy **10.** disastrous **11.** sullen or angry [*black* looks] **12.** without hope [a *black* future] **13.** inveterate; confirmed; deep-dyed [a *black* villain] **14.** humorous or satirical in a morbid or cynical way [*black* comedy] —*n.* **1.** *a*) black color *b*) a black pigment, paint, or dye **2.** any substance or thing that is black **3.** a fleck, spot, or area that is black **4.** black clothes, esp. when worn in mourning **5.** a person with a dark-colored skin; esp., a Negro: *black* is now the term preferred by some **6.** com-

plete darkness or absence of light —*vt., vi.* **1.** to make black; blacken **2.** to polish with blacking —**black out** **1.** to cover (writing, printing, etc.) with black pencil marks or paint **2.** to cause a blackout in **3.** to lose consciousness; faint **4.** to lose all memory of an event or fact —☆**in the black** [from the practice of entering a credit item in account books with black ink] operating at a profit —☆**into the black** into a profitable condition financially —**black′ish** *adj.* —**black′ness** *n.*

Black (blak), **Hugo (La Fayette)** 1886– ; U.S. jurist; associate justice, Supreme Court (1937–)

☆**black alder** an eastern N. American deciduous shrub (*Ilex verticillata*) of the holly family, with bright-red berries and glossy leaves that turn black in the fall

black-a-moor (-ə moor′) *n.* [< BLACK + MOOR] [Archaic] a dark-skinned person; specif., an African Negro

black-and-blue (-ən blōō′) *adj.* discolored from congestion of blood under the skin, as a bruise

Black and Tan a member of the British troops sent to Ireland to help put down disturbances during the Sinn Fein rebellion (1919–1921)

☆**black-and-tan terrier** (-ən tan′) *same as* MANCHESTER TERRIER

black and white **1.** writing or print [to put an agreement down in *black and white*] **2.** a drawing or picture done in black and white

Black Angus *same as* ABERDEEN ANGUS

black art *same as* BLACK MAGIC

black·ball (-bôl′) *n.* **1.** orig., a small, black ball used as a vote against a person or thing **2.** a secret ballot or vote against a person or thing —*vt.* **1.** to vote against; esp., to vote against letting (a person) join one's organization **2.** to exclude from social life, etc.; ostracize

black bass (bas) any of a genus (*Micropterus*) of freshwater fishes of N. America, highly prized as a game fish

black bear **1.** the common N. American bear (*Euarctos americanus*) that lives in forests and feeds mainly on roots and berries **2.** any of several large, dark-colored bears of Asia

Black·beard (-bird′) (born *Edward Teach* or *Thatch*) ?–1718; Eng. pirate

black·bee·tle (-bēt′'l) *n. same as* ORIENTAL ROACH

black belt a black-colored belt or sash awarded to an expert in judo or karate: a beginner wears a *white belt*, and increasing degrees of skill are symbolized by belts of other colors, culminating in the black belt

black·ber·ry (-ber′ē; *chiefly Brit.* -bər i) *n., pl.* **-ries** **1.** the fleshy, purple or black, edible fruit of various brambles (genus *Rubus*) of the rose family **2.** a bush or vine bearing this fruit

☆**blackberry lily** an ornamental plant (*Belamcanda chinensis*) of the iris family, bearing orange flowers with red spots and a cluster of black seeds that resembles a blackberry

black bindweed a European twining plant (*Polygonum convolvulus*) of the buckwheat family, with heart-shaped leaves and triangular black seed pods: now found in America as a weed

black·bird (-burd′) *n.* any of various birds the male of which is almost entirely black, as the purple grackle, cowbird, red-winged blackbird, common English thrush, etc.

black·board (-bôrd′) *n.* a large, smooth, usually dark surface of slate or other material on which to write or draw with chalk; chalkboard

black·bod·y (-bäd′ē) *n.* an ideal surface or body that can absorb completely all the radiation striking it

black book a book containing names of those blacklisted —**be in one's black book** to be regarded unfavorably by one —**little black book** [Colloq.] an address book with the names of available women companions

black box [Slang] an intricate, compact assemblage of electronic equipment

black bread a dark, coarse bread, esp. of rye flour

black buck a long-horned Indian antelope (*Antilope cervicapra*), brownish-black above and white below

Black·burn (blak′bərn) **1.** city in NW England, in Lancashire: textile center: pop. 105,000 **2.** Mount, mountain in the Wrangell Mountains, SE Alas.: 16,523 ft.

black·cap (-kap′) *n.* **1.** any of various birds with a black, caplike crown, as the chickadee, a European warbler (*Sylvia atricapilla*), etc. ☆**2.** *same as* BLACK RASPBERRY

black·cock (-käk′) *n., pl.* **-cocks, -cock:** see PLURAL, II, D, 1 the male of the black grouse

☆**black crappie** *see* CRAPPIE

black·damp (-damp′) *n.* a suffocating gas, chiefly carbon monoxide, found in mines; chokedamp

Black Death a deadly disease, probably bubonic plague, which devastated Europe and Asia in the 14th cent.

black diamond **1.** [*pl.*] coal **2.** carbonado (n. 2)

black·en (blak′'n) *vi.* [ME. *blaknen* < *blak*, black] to become black or dark —*vt.* **1.** to make black; darken **2.** to slander; defame; vilify —**black′en·er** *n.*

Black·ett (blak′it), **P(atrick) M(aynard) S(tuart)** 1897– ; Eng. nuclear physicist

black eye **1.** an eye with a very dark iris **2.** a discoloration of the skin or flesh surrounding an eye, resulting from a sharp blow or contusion ☆**3.** [Colloq.] shame or dishonor, or a cause or source of this

☆**black-eyed pea** (blak′īd′) *same as* COWPEA (sense 2)

black-eyed Su·san (sōō'z'n) ☆any of several common N. American wildflowers (genus *Rudbeckia*) of the composite family, with heads of yellow ray flowers around a dark, cone-shaped center

black·face (blak'fās') *adj.* **1.** having a black or blackened face **2.** *Printing* bold-faced —*n.* ☆**1.** black makeup used by performers, as in minstrel shows, in gross caricature of Negroes **2.** *Printing* boldface

black·fel·low (-fel'ō) *n.* a member of any dark-skinned native tribe of Australia: patronizing term

black·fin (-fin') *n.* **1.** a snapper (*Lutianus buccanella*) of the West Indies ☆**2.** a whitefish (*Coregonus nigripinnis*) of northeastern N. America

black·fish (-fish') *n., pl.* **-fish', -fish'es:** see FISH² ☆**1.** any of a genus (*Globicephala*) of small, black, toothed whales **2.** any of a number of dark fishes, as the sea bass, tautog, etc. **3.** an edible, minnowlike, freshwater fish (*Dallia pectoralis*) of Siberia and Alaska: reputed to revive after being frozen

black flag the flag of piracy, usually with a white skull and crossbones on a black background; Jolly Roger

☆**black fly** any of various small, dark, biting flies (family Simuliidae) of N. American forests and mountains, whose larvae live attached to rocks in swift water

Black·foot (-foot') *n., pl.,* esp. for those in Canada, **-feet'; -foot'** [transl. of Blackfoot *siksika;* ? in reference to moccasins] **1.** any member of an Algonquian Indian tribe consisting of three subtribes (the Blackfoot proper, the Blood, and Piegan) of Montana, Saskatchewan, and Alberta **2.** their language **3.** any member of the Blackfoot subtribe

Black Forest wooded, mountain region in SW Germany

Black Friar a Dominican friar

black frost a severe frost that blackens growing plants

black gram *same as* URD

black grouse a large grouse (*Lyrurus tetrix*) of Europe and Asia: the male is almost entirely black

black·guard (blag'ərd; *chiefly Brit. & Canad.* -ärd) *n.* [BLACK + GUARD] **1.** orig., the lowest servants of a large household, in charge of pots and pans **2.** *a)* a person who uses abusive language *b)* scoundrel; villain —*adj.* **1.** vulgar, low, etc. **2.** abusive —*vt.* to abuse with words; rail at; revile —**black'guard·ly** *adj., adv.*

black guillemot *see* GUILLEMOT

☆**black gum** any of a genus (*Nyssa*) of tall N. American gum trees found in moist forests and having simple alternate leaves and sour, purple fruits

Black Hand [< symbol used by group in letters of extortion] **1.** a group of Sicilian immigrant blackmailers and terrorists who operated in New York in the early 20th cent. **2.** any similar secret society

☆**black haw 1.** any of several eastern U.S. shrubs (genus *Viburnum*) of the honeysuckle family, having blue-black fruits **2.** *same as* SHEEPBERRY

Black Hawk 1767–1838; Am. Indian chief of the Sauk: leader in the Black Hawk War against the U.S. (1832)

black·head (blak'hed') *n.* **1.** any of certain birds black about the head and neck, esp. the scaup duck **2.** a black-tipped plug of dried fatty matter in a pore of the skin; comedo ☆**3.** an infectious disease of turkeys, chickens, etc. caused by a protozoan (*Histomonas meleagridis*) **4.** a larva of a freshwater mussel encysted in the gills, etc. of a fish

black·heart (-härt') *n.* **1.** a dark, heart-shaped, sweet cherry with purplish flesh **2.** a plant disease, esp. of potatoes, that turns the internal tissues black

black·heart·ed (-här'tid) *adj.* wicked; evil

Black Hills mountainous region in SW S.Dak. & NE Wyo.: highest peak, 7,242 ft.

Black Hole 1. a small dungeon at Calcutta: on the night of June 20, 1756, 123 of the 146 Europeans reputedly confined there were said to have died from heat and lack of air **2.** [b- h-] any dungeon

black horehound a foul-smelling weed (*Ballota nigra*) of the mint family, native to Europe

black·ing (-in) *n.* a black polish, as for shoes

black·jack (-jak') *n.* [see JACK-] **1.** a large beer mug, formerly made of leather coated with tar **2.** *same as* BLACK FLAG ☆**3.** a small, leather-covered bludgeon with a flexible handle ☆**4.** an eastern U.S. scrub oak (*Quercus marilandica*) of the beech family, with fan-shaped leaves ☆**5.** *a)* the card game TWENTY-ONE *b)* a combination of an ace and a face card or ten, equaling 21 points in this game **6.** a dark variety of sphalerite, a native zinc sulfide —☆*vt.* **1.** to hit with a blackjack **2.** to force (a person) to do something by threatening, as if with a blackjack

☆**black knot** a disease of cherry and plum trees caused by a fungus (*Plowrightia morbosa*), in which hard, black swellings appear on twigs and branches

black lead graphite, as used in lead pencils, etc.

black·leg (-leg') *n.* **1.** an acute, usually fatal, infectious disease of young cattle and sheep caused by a bacterium (*Clostridium chauvoei*) **2.** a disease of cabbage and related plants caused by a fungus (*Phoma lingam*) **3.** a disease of potatoes caused by a bacterium (*Erwinia atroseptica*) **4.** [Colloq.] a gambler who cheats **5.** [Brit.] a strikebreaker

black letter a kind of heavy-faced type: also called *Gothic* or *Old English*

black light ultraviolet or infrared radiation used for fluorescent effects, photography, etc. in the dark

black·list (-list') *n.* a list of persons who have been censured and who are being discriminated against, refused employment, etc. —*vt.* to put on a blacklist

black lung (disease) a pneumoconiosis caused by the inhalation of coal dust

black·ly (-lē) *adv.* **1.** drearily; gloomily **2.** angrily; menacingly **3.** in a sinister manner

black magic magic with an evil purpose; sorcery

black·mail (-māl') *n.* [lit., black rent < ME. *male*, rent, tribute < OE. *mal*, lawsuit, terms < ON. *mal*, lawsuit, discussion; infl. in ME. by OFr. *maille*, a coin] **1.** formerly, a tribute paid to freebooters and bandits along the Scottish border to assure safety from looting **2.** *a)* payment extorted to prevent disclosure of information that would bring disgrace or ruin if made public *b)* the extortion of such payment —*vt.* **1.** to get or try to get blackmail from **2.** to coerce (*into* doing something) as by threats —**black'mail'er** *n.*

☆**Black Ma·ri·a** (mə rī'ə) [Old Slang] a patrol wagon

black mark a mark indicating something unfavorable in one's record

black market a place or system for selling goods illegally, esp. in violation of rationing —**black'-mar'ket** *vt., vi.* —**black marketeer** (or **marketer**)

Black Mass, black mass 1. a Requiem Mass, at which the clergy is dressed in black **2.** a blasphemous parody of the Mass by worshipers of Satan

black measles a severe form of measles with a hemorrhagic rash

black medic a weedy annual plant (*Medicago lupulina*) of the legume family, with small yellow flowers and pods with a single seed, sometimes grown for forage

black mold bread mold

Black Mountains highest range of the Appalachians, in W N.C.: highest peak, Mount MITCHELL

Black·mun (blak'mən), **Harry Andrew** 1908– ; associate justice, U.S. Supreme Court (1970–)

☆**Black Muslim** a member of a militant Islamic sect of American Negroes that advocates asceticism, racial separation, and the establishment of Negro States: members of the sect call themselves simply "Muslims"

☆**black nationalism** a movement advocating the establishment of a separate Negro nation within the U.S.

black nightshade a poisonous plant (*Solanum nigrum*) of the nightshade family, with white, star-shaped flowers and dark berries, widespread as a weed in N. America

☆**black oak** *a local name for* any of various N. American oaks with dark bark or foliage

black·out (-out') *n.* **1.** *a)* the extinguishing of all stage lights to end a play or scene *b)* a comic stage skit ending with a quick blackout **2.** an elimination or concealing of all lights that might be visible to enemy air raiders, etc. at night **3.** a temporary loss of consciousness or vision **4.** a loss of memory of an event or fact **5.** suppression or concealment, as of news by censorship

black pepper see PEPPER (*n.* 1 *a*)

☆**black·poll** (-pōl') *n.* a N. American warbler (*Dendroica striata*), the male of which has a black crown

Black·pool (blak'pōōl') city in NW England, on the Irish Sea: resort: pop. 151,000

☆**black power** political and economic power as sought by black Americans in the struggle for civil rights

Black Prince *name for* EDWARD (Prince of Wales)

☆**black raspberry** a shrub (*Rubus occidentalis*) of the rose family, with long prickly canes that root at the tips and bear juicy, purple-black fruits

Black Rod 1. in England, the chief usher (in full, **Gentleman Usher of the Black Rod**) to the Order of the Garter and the House of Lords: so called from his symbol of office, an ebony rod **2.** a similar official in other British Commonwealth parliaments

☆**black rot** any of various bacterial or fungous diseases of plants that cause discoloration and decay

☆**black rust** any of several diseases of grasses, cereals, etc. caused by a fungus (genus *Puccinia*) that attacks the leaves and stem

Black Sea sea surrounded by European U.S.S.R., Asia Minor, & the Balkan Peninsula: c. 160,000 sq. mi.

black sheep a person regarded as not so respectable or successful as the rest of his family or group

Black Shirt a member of any fascist organization (specif., of the Italian Fascist party) having a black-shirted uniform: also **Black'shirt'** *n.*

black·smith (blak'smith') *n.* [< *black metal*, former name for iron] a smith who works in iron, including the making and fitting of horseshoes

☆**black·snake** (-snāk') *n.* **1.** any of various black or dark-colored snakes, esp. a slender, harmless snake (*Coluber constrictor*) found in the U.S. **2.** a long, heavy whip of braided leather or rawhide Also **black snake**

☆**black spruce 1.** a small coniferous tree (*Picea mariana*) of the pine family found in the cold bogs of NE N. America **2.** its soft, light wood

---

fat, āpe, cär; ten, ēven; is, bīte; gō, hôrn, tōōl, look; oil, out; up, fur; get; joy; yet; chin; she; thin, *then*; zh, leisure; ŋ, ring; ə for *a* in *ago, e* in *agent, i* in *sanity, o* in *comply, u* in *focus;* ' as in *able* (ā'b'l); Fr. bâl; ë, Fr. coeur; ö, Fr. feu; Fr. mon; ð, Fr. coq; ü, Fr. duc; r, Fr. cri; H, G. ich; kh, G. doch. See inside front cover. ☆Americanism; ‡foreign; *hypothetical; <derived from

Black·stone (blak′stōn; *Brit.* -stən), Sir **William** 1723–80; Eng. jurist & writer on law
black·strap molasses (blak′strap′) ☆crude, dark, thick molasses
☆**black·tailed deer** (-tāld′) **1.** a large deer (*Odocoileus columbianus*) of the coastal mountains from N California to British Columbia **2.** *same as* MULE DEER Also **black′tail′** *n.*
black tea tea withered and fermented before being dried by heating
black·thorn (-thôrn′) *n.* **1.** a thorny, white-flowered shrub (*Prunus spinosa*) of the rose family with purple or black, plumlike fruit; sloe **2.** a cane or stick made of the stem of this shrub ☆**3.** a variety of hawthorn of the eastern U.S.
black tie 1. a black bow tie, properly worn with a tuxedo **2.** a tuxedo and the proper accessories
black·top (blak′täp′) *n.* a bituminous mixture, usually asphalt, used as a surface for roads, etc. —*vt.* **-topped′**, **-top′ping** to cover with blacktop
Black Volta *see* VOLTA
black vomit 1. vomit characteristic of yellow fever, dark because of the blood in it **2.** yellow fever
Black·wall hitch (-wôl′) a kind of knot: see KNOT², illus.
☆**black walnut 1.** a tall walnut tree (*Juglans nigra*) native to eastern N. America **2.** its hard, heavy, dark-brown wood, used in making furniture, gunstocks, etc. **3.** its edible, oily nut
black·wa·ter fever (blak′wôt′ər, -wät′-) a severe, often fatal, form of malaria characterized by the passing of dark urine
Black·well (blak′wəl), **Elizabeth** 1821–1910; first woman physician in the U.S., born in England
Black·wells Island (blak′welz) [< name of early owner] *former name of* WELFARE ISLAND
☆**black widow** an American spider (*Latrodectus mactans*) the female of which has a glossy black body with reddish markings underneath, and a very poisonous bite: so called because the female sometimes eats its mate
blad·der (blad′ər) *n.* [ME. *bladre* < OE. *blæddre* < IE. base *bhle-*, var. of *bhel*: see BALL¹] **1.** a bag of membranous tissue in the bodies of many animals, capable of inflation to receive and contain liquids or gases: the *urinary bladder* in the pelvic cavity holds urine flowing from the kidneys **2.** a thing resembling such a bag [a football *bladder*] **3.** a vesicle or blister **4.** *a)* an inflated covering of certain fruits *b)* an air sac, as in some water plants
bladder campion a perennial plant (*Silene cucubalus*) of the pink family, with an inflated calyx
bladder kelp any of various giant seaweeds, with air bladders that buoy up the leafy portions
bladder ket·mie (ket′mē) [Fr. *ketmie*, mallow < ML. *ketmia* < Ar.] *same as* FLOWER-OF-AN-HOUR
blad·der·nose (-nōz′) *n. same as* HOODED SEAL
blad·der·nut (-nut′) *n.* **1.** any of a family of shrubs or small trees (esp. genus *Staphylea*) with bladderlike, inflated pods **2.** one of these pods
blad·der·worm (-wurm′) *n. same as* CYSTICERCUS
blad·der·wort (-wurt′) *n.* any of a large genus (*Utricularia*) of chiefly aquatic plants, having finely divided leaves with bladders on them that trap small insects and crustaceans
bladder wrack any of various seaweeds (genera *Ascophyllum* and *Fucus*), having flattened plant bodies and conspicuous air bladders
blad·der·y (blad′ər ē) *adj.* **1.** like a bladder **2.** having a bladder or bladders
blade (blād) *n.* [ME. *blad* < OE. *blæd*, a leaf < IE. base *bhlē-*, *bhel*, to swell, sprout, whence L. *flos*, flower, E. BLOOM¹] **1.** *a)* the leaf of a plant, esp. of grass *b)* the flat, expanded part of a leaf; lamina **2.** *a)* a broad, flat section or surface, as of an oar, propeller, arm, rotary vane, etc. *b)* the propeller arm or rotary vane itself **3.** a flat bone [the shoulder *blade*] **4.** the cutting part of a tool, instrument, or weapon **5.** the metal runner of an ice skate **6.** a sword **7.** a swordsman **8.** a gay, dashing young man **9.** *Phonet.* the flat part of the tongue, behind the tip —*adj.* designating or of chops, roasts, etc., as of beef or veal, that are cut across the shoulder blade section —**blad′ed** *adj.*
‡**blague** (bläg) *n.* [Fr.] a practical joke, playful deception, raillery, etc.
☆**blah** (blä) *n., interj.* [Slang] nonsense —*adj.* [Slang] **1.** unappetizing **2.** uninteresting, dull, lifeless, etc.
blain (blān) *n.* [ME. *bleine* < OE. *blegen*, a blister: for IE. base see BALL¹] an inflamed sore or swollen place; pustule or blister
Blaine (blān), **James G(illespie)** 1830–93; U.S. statesman; secretary of state (1881, 1889–92)
Blake (blāk) **1.** **Robert**, 1599–1657; Eng. admiral **2.** **William**, 1757–1827; Eng. poet & artist
blam·a·ble, blame·a·ble (blām′ə b'l) *adj.* [ME.] that deserves blame; culpable —**blam′a·bly** *adv.*
blame (blām) *vt.* **blamed, blam′ing** [ME. *blamen* < OFr. *blasmer*, to speak evil of < LL. *blasphemare*, BLASPHEME]

1. to accuse of being at fault; condemn (*for* something); censure **2.** to find fault with (*for* something) **3.** to put the responsibility of, as an error, fault, etc. (*on* someone or something) —*n.* **1.** the act of blaming; accusation; condemnation; censure **2.** responsibility for a fault or wrong **3.** [Archaic] blameworthiness; fault —*SYN.* see CRITICIZE —**be to blame** to be blamable; be at fault
blamed (blāmd) *adj., adv.* [Colloq.] damned: a mild expletive
blame·ful (blām′f'l) *adj.* **1.** finding or imputing blame; blaming **2.** deserving to be blamed; blameworthy —**blame′ful·ly** *adv.* —**blame′ful·ness** *n.*
blame·less (-lis) *adj.* free from blame —**blame′less·ly** *adv.* —**blame′less·ness** *n.*
blame·wor·thy (-wur′thē) *adj.* deserving to be blamed —**blame′wor′thi·ness** *n.*
Blanc (blän), **(Jean Joseph Charles) Louis** (lwē) 1811–82; Fr. socialist & historian, born in Spain
Blanc, Mont (mōn blän′) mountain in E France, near the Italian border: highest peak in the Alps: 15,781 ft.
Blan·ca Peak (blaŋ′kə) [Sp. *blanca*, white (with snow)] highest peak of the Sangre de Cristo range, S Colo.: 14,317 ft.
blanc fixe (blaŋk fiks; Fr. blän fēks′) [Fr., permanent white] *same as* BARIUM SULFATE
blanch (blanch, blänch) *vt.* [ME. *blanchen* < OFr. *blanchir* < *blanc*, white: see BLANK] **1.** to make white; take color from **2.** to make pale **3.** to bleach (endive, celery, etc.) by earthing up or covering so as to keep away light and improve the appearance, flavor, or tenderness **4.** *a)* to scald (as vegetables being prepared for freezing) *b)* to scald (almonds) so as to remove the skins **5.** *Metallurgy* to brighten with acid or by coating with tin —*vi.* to whiten; turn pale —**blanch′er** *n.*
Blanche, Blanch (blanch) [Fr., lit., white, fem. of *blanc*: see BLANK] a feminine name: equiv. Ger. & Sp. *Blanca*, It. *Bianca*
blanc·mange (blə mänzh′, -mänj′) *n.* [Fr. < *blanc*, white + *manger*, to eat] a sweet, molded jellylike dessert made with starch or gelatin, milk, flavoring, etc.
bland (bland) *adj.* [L. *blandus*, mild, prob. < IE. base *mldu-*, soft, var. of *mel*: see MILL¹] **1.** pleasantly smooth; agreeable; suave [a *bland*, ingratiating manner] **2.** *a)* mild and soothing; not sharp, harsh, etc. [*bland* medicine] *b)* tasteless, insipid, dull, etc. —*SYN.* see SOFT, SUAVE —**bland′ly** *adv.* —**bland′ness** *n.*
blan·dish (blan′dish) *vt., vi.* [ME. *blandishen* < OFr. *blandiss-*, extended stem of *blandir*, to flatter < L. *blandiri*, to flatter < *prec.*] to flatter or coax in persuading; cajole —**blan′dish·er** *n.* —**blan′dish·ing·ly** *adv.*
blan·dish·ment (-mənt) *n.* **1.** the act of blandishing; cajolery **2.** a flattering or ingratiating act or remark, etc. meant to persuade: *usually used in pl.*
blank (blaŋk) *adj.* [ME. < OFr. *blanc* < Frank. *blank*, white, gleaming, akin to OE. *blanca*, white steed < IE. base *bhleg-*, to shine: see BLACK] **1.** orig., colorless or white **2.** *a)* not written on; not marked; empty [a *blank* sheet of paper] *b)* having empty spaces to be filled in **3.** having an empty, vacant, or monotonous look or character **4.** *a)* without interest or expression [*blank* looks] *b)* showing incomprehension or confusion **5.** empty of thought; lacking ideas [a *blank* mind] **6.** unproductive; barren [*blank* years] **7.** utter; complete [a *blank* denial] **8.** lacking certain elements or characteristics, as a wall without an opening **9.** damn: a euphemistic usage —*n.* **1.** an empty space, esp. one to be filled out in a printed form **2.** a printed form or document with such empty spaces **3.** an emptiness; vacant place or time; void **4.** *a)* the center spot of a target *b)* anything aimed at or pointed at **5.** a manufactured article yet to be cut to a pattern or marked with a design [a key *blank*] **6.** a lottery ticket that fails to win **7.** a powder-filled cartridge without a bullet: in full, **blank cartridge 8.** a mark, usually a dash (—), indicating an omitted word, esp. an oath or curse —*vt.* ☆**1.** to hold (an opponent) scoreless in a game **2.** to stamp out with a die from flat stock —**blank out** to cancel or obscure by covering over; void —**draw a blank 1.** to draw a lottery ticket that fails to win **2.** [Colloq.] *a)* to be unsuccessful in any attempt *b)* to be unable to remember a particular thing —**blank′ly** *adv.* —**blank′ness** *n.*
blank check 1. a check form that has not been filled in **2.** a check carrying a signature only and allowing the bearer to fill in any amount **3.** permission to use an unlimited amount of money, authority, etc.
blank endorsement an endorsement naming no payee, making the endorsed amount payable to the bearer
blan·ket (blaŋ′kit) *n.* [ME. < OFr., dim. of *blanc*, white: see BLANK] **1.** a large piece of cloth, often of soft wool, used for warmth as a bed cover or a covering for animals **2.** anything used as or resembling a blanket; covering [a *blanket* of leaves] —*adj.* covering a group of conditions or requirements; including many or all items [a *blanket* insurance policy] —*vt.* **1.** to cover with or as with a blanket; overspread; overlie **2.** to apply uniformly to: said of regulations or rates **3.** to cut off the wind of (a sailboat, etc.) by passing close to windward, as in yacht racing **4.** to suppress; hinder; obscure [a powerful radio station *blankets* a weaker one] **5.** to toss in a blanket, as in hazing
☆**blan·ket·flow·er** (-flou′ər) *n. same as* GAILLARDIA

BLADDERWORT

blanket stitch a kind of buttonhole stitch with the stitches spaced relatively far apart, used to reinforce the edge of thick material, as that used for blankets

☆**blan·ke·ty-blank** (blaŋ′kə tē blaŋk′) *adj., adv.* [see BLANK, *n.* 8] [Slang] damned: a humorous euphemism

blank verse unrhymed verse; esp., unrhymed verse having five iambic feet per line, as in Elizabethan drama: cf. FREE VERSE

blare (bler) *vt., vi.* blared, blar′ing [ME. *bleren, bloren,* to wail, bellow: for IE. base see BLEAR] **1.** to sound out with loud, harsh, trumpetlike tones **2.** to announce or exclaim loudly —*n.* **1.** a loud, brassy sound **2.** harsh brilliance or glare, as of color

blar·ney (blär′nē) *n.* [see BLARNEY STONE] smooth talk used in flattering or coaxing —*vt., vi.* -neyed, -ney·ing to engage in blarney (with)

Blarney stone a stone in Blarney Castle in the county of Cork, Ireland, said to impart skill in blarney to those who kiss it

Blas·co I·bá·ñez (bläs′kō ē bä′nyeth), **Vi·cen·te** (vē then′te) 1867–1928; Sp. novelist

bla·sé (blä zā′, blä′zā) *adj.* [Fr., pp. of *blaser,* to satiate] having indulged in pleasure so much as to be unexcited by it; satiated and bored

blas·pheme (blas fēm′, blas′fēm) *vt.* -phemed′, -phem′ing [ME. *blasfemen* < OFr. *blasfemer* < LL. (Vulgate) *blasphemare* < Gr. *blasphēmein,* to speak evil of, in LGr.(Ec.), blaspheme] **1.** to speak irreverently or profanely of or to (God or sacred things) **2.** to curse or revile —*vi.* to utter blasphemy —**blas·phem′er** *n.*

blas·phe·mous (blas′fə məs) *adj.* [ME. *blasfemous* < L. *blasphemus* < Gr. *blasphēmos*] characterized by blasphemy; irreverent or profane —**blas′phe·mous·ly** *adv.*

blas·phe·my (-mē) *n., pl.* -mies [ME. *blasfemie* < OFr. *blasphemie* < L. *blasphemia* < Gr. *blasphēmia:* see BLASPHEME] **1.** profane or contemptuous speech, writing, or action concerning God or anything held as divine **2.** any remark or action held to be irreverent or disrespectful
SYN.—blasphemy, the strongest of the following terms, is used esp. of any remark deliberately mocking or contemptuous of God; **profanity** extends the concept to irreverent remarks referring to any person or thing regarded as sacred; **swearing** and **cursing,** in this connection, both refer to the utterance of profane oaths and imprecations, the latter, esp., to the calling down of evil upon someone or something

blast (blast, bläst) *n.* [ME. < OE. *blæst,* puff of wind < IE. base *bhel-,* to inflate, blow up: see BALL[1]] **1.** a gust of wind; strong rush of air **2.** the sound of a sudden rush of air or gas, as through a trumpet **3.** a strong, artificially created jet of air, steam, exhaust gases, etc. **4.** the steady current of air forced into a blast furnace **5.** an abrupt and damaging influence; specif., any disease of plants that causes them to wither; blight **6.** *a)* an explosion, as of dynamite *b)* a charge of explosive causing this *c)* a wave of air of increased pressure followed by one of lower pressure radiating from an explosion ☆**7.** a strong, sudden outburst, as of criticism ☆**8.** *Sports* a strong, driving hit, as of a baseball ☆**9.** [Slang] a gay, hilarious time; esp., a gay or wild party —*vi.* **1.** to make a loud, harsh sound **2.** to set off explosives, gunfire, etc. **3.** to suffer or wither from a blight —*vt.* **1.** to damage or destroy by or as if by a blight; wither; ruin **2.** to blow up or move with or as with an explosive; explode ☆**3.** to attack or criticize sharply ☆**4.** *Sports* to drive (a ball) far with a sharp blow of the bat or club —*SYN.* see WIND[2] —☆**blast off** to take off with explosive force and begin its flight: said of a rocket or ballistic missile —(at) **full blast** at full speed or capacity —**blast′er** *n.*

-blast (blast) [< Gr. *blastos,* a sprout: see BLASTEMA] *a combining form meaning* formative, embryonic [*mesoblast*]

blast·ed (blas′tid, bläs′-) *adj.* **1.** blighted; withered; destroyed **2.** damned; confounded: a mild expletive

blas·te·ma (blas tē′mə) *n., pl.* -mas, -ma·ta (-mə ta) [Gr. *blastēma,* a bud < *blastanein,* to bud or sprout] the undifferentiated embryonic tissue from which cells, tissues, and organs are developed —**blas·te′mic, blas′te·mat′ic** (-tə-mat′ik) *adj.*

blast furnace a towerlike furnace for separating metal, esp. iron, from the impurities in the ore: a blast of air is forced into the furnace from below to produce the intense heat needed

blas·tie (blas′tē, bläs′-) *n.* [BLAST, *vi.* 3 + -IE] [Scot.] a dwarf

blas·to- (blas′tō, -tə) [see -BLAST] *a combining form meaning* of an embryo; having to do with germination [*blastoderm, blastogenesis*]: also, before a vowel, **blast-**

blas·to·coele, blas·to·cele (blas′tə sēl′) *n.* [BLASTO- + -COELE] the segmentation cavity of a developing ovum or of the blastula: see BLASTULA, illus.

blas·to·cyst (-sist′) *n.* [BLASTO- + -CYST] *same as* BLASTULA

blas·to·derm (-dɜrm′) *n.* [BLASTO- + -DERM] the part of a fertilized ovum that gives rise to the germinal disk from which the embryo develops —**blas′to·der′mic** *adj.*

blas·to·disc, blas·to·disk (-disk′) *n.* *same as* GERMINAL DISC

☆**blast·off, blast-off** (blast′ôf′) *n.* the launching of a rocket, ballistic missile, space vehicle, etc.

blas·to·gen·e·sis (blas′tə jen′ə sis) *n.* [BLASTO- + -GENE-SIS] **1.** reproduction by asexual means, as by budding in corals **2.** the theory that the germ plasm transmits hereditary characters: opposed to PANGENESIS

blas·to·mere (blas′tə mir′) *n.* [BLASTO- + -MERE] any of the cells resulting from the first few divisions of the ovum after fertilization —**blas′to·mer′ic** (-mer′ik) *adj.*

blas·to·my·cete (blas′tō mī sēt′, -mī′sēt) *n.* [BLASTO- + -MYCETE] any of a group (Blastomycetes) of yeastlike fungi that cause diseases in man and animals

blas·to·my·co·sis (-mī kō′sis) *n.* [BLASTO- + MYCOSIS] any disease caused by a blastomycete

blas·to·pore (blas′tə pôr′) *n.* [BLASTO- + PORE[2]] the opening into the gastrula cavity

blas·to·sphere (-sfir′) *n.* [BLASTO- + -SPHERE] *same as* BLASTULA

blas·tu·la (blas′choo lə) *n., pl.* -las, -lae (-lē) [ML., dim. < Gr. *blastos,* a germ, sprout] an embryo at the stage of development in which it consists of one or several layers of cells around a central cavity, forming a hollow sphere —**blas′tu·lar** (-lər) *adj.* —**blas′tu·la′tion** (-lā′shən) *n.*

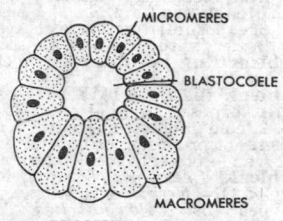
MICROMERES
BLASTOCOELE
MACROMERES
BLASTULA

blat (blat) *vi.* **blat′ted, blat′ting** [var. of BLEAT] to make a sound like that of a sheep or calf; bleat —*vt.* to blurt out; blab —*n.* a blatting sound

bla·tan·cy (blāt′n sē) *n., pl.* -cies a blatant quality or thing

bla·tant (blāt′nt) *adj.* [coined by E. SPENSER, prob. < L. *blaterare,* to babble, or E. dial. *blate,* to bellow] **1.** disagreeably loud or boisterous; offensively noisy; clamorous **2.** glaringly conspicuous or obtrusive [*blatant* ignorance] —*SYN.* see VOCIFEROUS —**bla′tant·ly** *adv.*

blath·er (blath′ər) *n.* [ON. *blathr*] foolish talk; loquacious nonsense —*vi., vt.* to talk on and on foolishly —**blath′er·er** *n.*

blath·er·skite (-skīt′) *n.* [< prec. + Scot. *skate,* a term of contempt] a talkative, foolish person

blau·bok (blou′bäk′) *n., pl.* -boks, -boks: see PLURAL, II, D, 2 [obs. Afrik. *blauwbok;* lit., blue buck] a large, bluish-gray antelope (*Hippotragus leucophaeus*) of Cape Province, South Africa, now extinct

Bla·vat·sky (blə vät′skē, -vat′-), **Helena Pe·trov·na** (pə trôv′nə) (born *Helena Hahn*) 1831–91; Russ. theosophist in U.S. and elsewhere: called **Madame Blavatsky**

blaw (blô) *vt., vi.* [Brit. Dial. or Scot.] to blow

blaze[1] (blāz) *n.* [ME. *blase* < OE. *blæse, blase,* a torch, flame < IE. base *bhles-,* shine < *bhel-:* see BLACK] **1.** a brilliant mass or burst of flame; strongly burning fire **2.** any very bright, often hot, light or glare [the *blaze* of searchlights] **3.** a sudden, spectacular occurrence; showy outburst [a *blaze* of oratory] **4.** a brightness; vivid display; flash **5.** [pl.] hell: a euphemism, esp. in the phrase **go to blazes!** —*vi.* **blazed, blaz′ing** **1.** to burn rapidly or brightly; flame **2.** to give off a strong, vivid light; shine very brightly; glare **3.** to be deeply stirred or excited, as with anger —*vt.* [Rare] to cause to blaze —**blaze away 1.** to fire a gun rapidly a number of times **2.** to speak heatedly
*SYN.—***blaze** suggests a hot, intensely bright, relatively large and steady fire [the *blaze* of a burning house]; **flame** generally refers to a single, shimmering, tonguelike emanation of burning gas [the *flame* of a candle]; **flicker** suggests an unsteady, fluttering flame, esp. one that is dying out [the last *flicker* of his oil lamp]; **flare** implies a sudden, bright, unsteady light shooting up into darkness [the *flare* of a torch]; **glow** suggests a steady, warm, subdued light without flame or blaze [the *glow* of burning embers]; **glare** implies a steady, unpleasantly bright light [the *glare* of a bare light bulb]

blaze[2] (blāz) *n.* [< ON. *blesi:* for IE. base see prec.] **1.** a light-colored spot on an animal's face ☆**2.** a mark made on a tree, as to mark a trail, by cutting off a piece of bark —☆*vt.* **blazed, blaz′ing** to mark (a tree or trail) with blazes —☆**blaze a way** (or **path,** etc.) **in** to pioneer in (a sphere of activity)

blaze[3] (blāz) *vt.* **blazed, blaz′ing** [ME. *blasen,* to blow < OE. or ON. form akin to G. *blasen* < IE. base *bhlē-,* to blow up: see BALL[1]; infl. by BLAZON] to make known publicly; spread the news of; proclaim

blaz·er (blā′zər) *n.* [< BLAZE[1] + -ER] a lightweight, singlebreasted sports jacket in a solid, often bright color or with stripes

blazing star ☆**1.** *a)* any of a genus (*Liatris*) of American wildflowers of the composite family, with showy, usually lavender flowers *b)* a white-flowered plant (*Chamaelirium luteum*) of the lily family, native to the E U.S. **2.** [Obs.] a comet

bla·zon (blā′z'n) *n.* [ME. *blasoun* < OFr. *blason,* a shield,

blazon] **1.** a coat of arms; heraldic shield, emblem, or banner **2.** a technical description or illustration of a coat of arms in accordance with the rules of heraldry **3.** showy display —*vt.* [< the *n.*; mistakenly associated with BLAZE³] **1.** to make known far and wide; proclaim (often with *forth, out,* or *abroad*)⫽ **2.** to describe technically or portray (coats of arms) **3.** *a)* to portray in colors *b)* to adorn colorfully or showily —**bla′zon·er** *n.* —**bla′zon·ment** *n.*

bla·zon·ry (-rē) *n., pl.* **-ries** [see BLAZON] **1.** the description or illustration of coats of arms **2.** a coat of arms; heraldic emblem **3.** any brilliant display

bldg. building

-ble (b'l) *same as* -ABLE

bleach (blēch) *vt.* [ME. *blechen* < OE. *blǣcan* < *blac* < IE. base *bhlēig-*, to gleam, whence BLEAK¹,²] **1.** to decolorize by means of chemicals or by exposure to the sun's rays **2.** to whiten; blanch —*vi.* to become white, colorless, or pale —*n.* **1.** a bleaching or whitening **2.** any substance used for bleaching **3.** the degree of whiteness resulting from bleaching —**bleach′er** *n.*

☆**bleach·ers** (-ərz) *n.pl.* [< prec., in reference to the effects of exposure] a section of cheaper seats, usually bare benches in tiers without a roof, for spectators at sporting events

bleaching powder chloride of lime or any other powder used in bleaching

bleak¹ (blēk) *adj.* [ME. *bleik* < ON. *bleikr*, pale: see BLEACH] **1.** exposed to wind and cold; unsheltered; treeless; bare **2.** cold and cutting; harsh **3.** not cheerful; gloomy; dreary **4.** not promising or hopeful [a *bleak* future] **5.** [Obs.] pale; wan —**bleak′ly** *adv.* —**bleak′ness** *n.*

bleak² (blēk) *n., pl.* **bleak, bleaks** [< ON. *bleikja* < *bleikr:* see prec.] a small, slender European fish (*Alburnus lucidus*) of the carp family, with silvery scales, an extract of which is used in making artificial pearls

blear (blir) *adj.* [ME. *blere*, watery, rheumy < the *v.*] **1.** made dim by tears, mucus, etc.: said of eyes **2.** blurred; dim; indistinct; misty —*vt.* [ME. *bleren*, to have watery eyes, akin to G. *plärren*, to bawl, cry < IE. base *bhlē-*, to howl, weep (of echoic origin), whence BLARE, BLEAT, L. *flere*, to weep] **1.** to dim (the eyes) with tears, mucus, etc. **2.** to blur (a surface or an outline)

blear·y (-ē) *adj.* **blear′i·er, blear′i·est 1.** dim or blurred as the eyes are from lack of rest or when one first awakens **2.** having blurred vision —**blear′i·ly** *adv.* —**blear′i·ness** *n.*

blear·y-cyed (-ˌīd′) *adj.* having bleary eyes: also **blear′eyed′**

bleat (blēt) *vi.* [ME. *bleten* < OE. *blǣtan:* see BLEAR] **1.** to make its characteristic cry: said of a sheep, goat, or calf **2.** to make a sound like this cry **3.** to speak foolishly, whiningly, or querulously —*vt.* to say or express in a bleating voice —*n.* **1.** the cry of a sheep, goat, or calf **2.** any sound or utterance like this —**bleat′er** *n.*

bleb (bleb) *n.* [< sound produced in forming a bubble with the lips] **1.** a small swelling on the skin or on plants; blister; vesicle **2.** an air bubble, as in water or glass —**bleb′by** *adj.*

bleed (blēd) *vi.* **bled** (bled), **bleed′ing** [ME. *bleden* < OE. *bledan* < *blod*, blood < ? IE. base *bhlō-* (var. of *bhel-*, to swell), to spurt forth, sprout: cf. BALL¹, BLOOM¹] **1.** to emit or lose blood **2.** to suffer wounds or die in a battle or cause **3.** to feel pain, grief, or sympathy; suffer **4.** to ooze; esp., to ooze sap, juice, etc., as bruised plants **5.** to run together, as dyes in wet cloth **6.** to come through a covering coat of paint, as certain stains **7.** to be printed to the edge of a page, wrapper, etc. so that a part is later trimmed off: said of pictures, designs, etc. —*vt.* **1.** to draw blood from; leech **2.** to ooze (sap, juice, etc.) ☆**3.** to take sap or juice from **4.** *a)* to empty slowly of liquid, air, or gas *b)* to draw off (liquid, air, or gas) slowly **5.** *a)* to print (a picture, design, etc.) so that a small part at the edge is cut off when the paper is trimmed *b)* to trim (a page) so as to bleed some of the printed matter **6.** [Colloq.] to get money from, esp. by extortion —*n.* the part of a printed picture, design, etc. that overruns the margin to be trimmed —*adj.* having such an overrunning part [a *bleed* page]

bleed·er (-ər) *n.* **1.** a person who draws blood from another **2.** a person who bleeds profusely; hemophiliac **3.** *Electronics* an auxiliary resistor used chiefly for discharging a high-voltage capacitor

bleeding heart 1. any of a genus (*Dicentra*) of plants with fernlike leaves and drooping clusters of pink or reddish, heart-shaped flowers **2.** a person regarded as too sentimental or too liberal in his approach to social problems

bleep (blēp) *n., vi.* [echoic] *same as* BEEP —*vt.* to censor (something said), as in a telecast by substituting a beep

blem·ish (blem′ish) *vt.* [ME. *blemishen* < OFr. *blemiss-*, extended root of *blemir*, to injure, prob. via Frank. *blesmjan*, to cause to turn pale < *blesmi*, akin to BLAZE²] to mar, as by some flaw or fault; spoil the perfection of —*n.* **1.** a mark that mars the appearance, as a stain, spot, scar, etc. **2.** any flaw, defect, or shortcoming —*SYN.* see DEFECT

blench¹ (blench) *vt., vi.* [var. of BLANCH] to make or become pale; whiten; bleach

blench² (blench) *vi.* [ME. *blenchen*, move suddenly, avoid < OE. *blencan*, to deceive, akin to G. *blinken*, ult. < IE. base of BLANK] to shrink back, as in fear; flinch; quail

blend (blend) *vt.* **blend′ed** or **blent, blend′ing** [ME. *blenden* < OE. *blendan* & ON. *blanda*, to mix < IE. base *bhlendh-*,

to glimmer indistinctly, whence BLIND, BLUNDER] **1.** to mix or mingle (varieties of tea, tobacco, etc.), esp. so as to produce a desired flavor, color, grade, etc. **2.** to mix or fuse thoroughly, so that the parts merge and are no longer distinct [green results from *blending* blue and yellow] —*vi.* **1.** to mix, merge, or unite **2.** to pass gradually or imperceptibly into each other, as colors **3.** to go well together; harmonize —*n.* **1.** the act of blending; thorough mixture **2.** the result of blending; a mixture of varieties [a *blend* of coffee] **3.** *Linguis.* a word formed by combining parts of other words (Ex.: *galumph, smog*) —*SYN.* see MIX

blende (blend) *n.* [G. *blende* < *blenden*, to blind, deceive: so named because it resembles galena, but contains no lead] **1.** sphalerite, an ore of zinc or zinc sulfide **2.** any of certain other sulfides, esp. metallic sulfides, having a fairly bright luster

☆**blended whiskey** whiskey that is a blend of straight whiskey and neutral spirits or of two or more straight whiskeys

blend·er (blen′dər) *n.* **1.** a person or thing that blends ☆**2.** an electrical appliance that can chop, cream, whip, mix, or liquefy foods

blending inheritance the blending of characteristics of the parents in the offspring, as in a pink flower that results from the mating of a red flower with a white one

Blen·heim (blen′əm) village in W Bavaria, Germany: site of a battle (1704) in the War of the Spanish Succession in which the English-Austrian army under Marlborough defeated the Franco-Bavarian forces: Ger. name, BLINDHEIM

Blenheim spaniel [after *Blenheim* Palace, seat of the Duke of Marlborough, where the dogs were bred] a variety of toy spaniel that is white with reddish-brown spots

blen·ny (blen′ē) *n., pl.* **-nies, -ny:** see PLURAL, II, D, 1 [L. *blennius* < Gr. *blennos* < *blenna*, slime, mucus] any of a large family (Blenniidae) of small fishes with long, many-rayed dorsal fins and a tapering body covered with a slimy substance —**blen′ni·oid′** (-ē oid′) *adj.*

blent (blent) *alt. pt. & pp.* of BLEND

bleph·a·ri·tis (blef′ə rīt′əs) *n.* [BLEPHAR(O)- + -ITIS] inflammation of the eyelids

bleph·a·ro- (blef′ər ə) [< Gr. *blepharon*, eyelid] *a combining form meaning* eyelid, eyelids: also, before a vowel, **blephar-**

Blér·i·ot (bler′ē ō′; *Fr.* blā ryō′), **Louis** 1872-1936; Fr. aeronautical engineer & aviation pioneer

bles·bok (bles′bäk′) *n., pl.* **-bok′, -boks′:** see PLURAL, II, D, 2 [Afrik. < *bles*, BLAZE² + *bok*, BUCK¹] a South African antelope (*Damaliscus albifrons*) that has a large, white mark on its face: also **bles′buck′** (-buk′)

bless (bles) *vt.* **blessed** or **blest, bless′ing** [ME. *blessen, bletsien* < OE. *bletsian, bledsian* < *blod*, blood: rite of consecration by sprinkling the altar with blood] **1.** to make or declare holy by a spoken formula or a sign; hallow; consecrate **2.** to ask divine favor for [the minister *blessed* the congregation] **3.** to favor or endow (*with*) [to be *blessed* with eloquence] **4.** to make happy or prosperous; gladden [he *blessed* us with his leadership] **5.** to think (oneself) happy; congratulate (oneself) **6.** to praise or glorify [to *bless* the Lord] **7.** to make the sign of the cross over or upon **8.** [Obs., except in prayers, exclamations, etc.] to keep or protect from harm, evil, etc. —**bless me** (or **you, him,** etc.)! an exclamation of surprise, pleasure, dismay, etc.

BLESBOK
(35-47 in. high
at shoulder)

bless·ed (bles′id; *occas.* blest) *adj.* **1.** holy; sacred; consecrated **2.** enjoying great happiness; blissful **3.** of or in eternal bliss: a title applied to a person who has been beatified **4.** bringing comfort or joy **5.** confounded; cursed: an ironical oath —**the blessed** people who are blessed; specif., *Theol.* those dead whose souls are in heaven —**bless′ed·ly** *adv.* —**bless′ed·ness** *n.*

blessed event the birth of a child; also, a newborn child: a jocular usage

Blessed Sacrament *R.C.Ch.* the Eucharist

Blessed Virgin the Virgin Mary

bless·ing (-iŋ) *n.* **1.** the act or prayer of one who blesses; invocation or benediction **2.** a grace said before or after eating **3.** the gift of divine favor **4.** good wishes or approval **5.** anything that gives happiness or prevents misfortune; special benefit or favor

blest (blest) *alt. pt. & pp.* of BLESS —*adj.* blessed

blet (blet) *n.* [Fr. *blet, blette*, overripe, soft] decay in over-ripe fruit

bleth·er (bleth′ər) *n., vi., vt. same as* BLATHER

bleu cheese (bloo; *Fr.* blö) [Fr. *bleu*, blue] *same as* BLUE CHEESE

blew (bloo) *pt.* of BLOW¹ & BLOW³

Bli·da (blē′dä) city in NC Algeria: pop. 93,000

Bligh (blī), **William** 1754-1817; Eng. naval officer: commander of the *Bounty*, whose crew mutinied

blight (blīt) *n.* [? akin to ME. *blichening*, blight, rust (on grain) < *bliknen*, to lose color < ON. *blikja*, turn pale]

1. any atmospheric or soil condition, parasite, or insect that kills, withers, or checks the growth of plants **2.** any of several plant diseases, as rust, mildew, or smut **3.** anything that destroys, prevents growth, etc. [slums are a *blight* on a city] **4.** a person or thing that withers one's hopes or ambitions **5.** the condition or result of being blighted —*vt.* **1.** to cause a blight in or on; wither **2.** to destroy **3.** to disappoint or frustrate —*vi.* to suffer blight

blight·er (-ər) *n.* **1.** a person or thing that blights **2.** [Brit. Slang] a mean or contemptible fellow

bli·mey (blī′mē) *interj.* [contr. < (*God*) *blind me*] a British exclamation of surprise, wonder, etc.

blimp (blimp) *n.* [echoic of sound caused by thumping the airship bag with a finger: prob. coined (1915) by A. D. Cunningham, Brit. Naval Air officer] [Colloq.] **1.** a small, nonrigid or semirigid airship **2.** [< Col. *Blimp*, creation of Brit. cartoonist David Low (1891–1933)] a pompous, smug, highly conservative person —**blimp′ish** *adj.*

blind (blīnd) *adj.* [ME. & OE.: see BLEND] **1.** without the power of sight; unable to see; sightless **2.** of or for sightless persons **3.** not able or willing to notice, understand, or judge [a *blind* search] **5.** disregarding evidence, sound logic, etc. [*blind* love, *blind* faith] **6.** reckless; unreasonable **7.** out of sight; hard to see; hidden [a *blind* driveway] **8.** dense; impenetrable [a *blind* hedge] **9.** closed at one end [a *blind* duct] **10.** not controlled by intelligence [*blind* destiny] **11.** *a*) insensible *b*) [Slang] drunk **12.** illegible; indistinct [a *blind* letter] **13.** not bearing flowers or fruit, as imperfect plants **14.** *Aeron.* by the use of instruments only [*blind* flying] **15.** *Archit. a*) having no opening [a *blind* wall] *b*) walled up [a *blind* window] **16.** *Bookbinding* without gilding or coloring [*blind* tooling] —*vt.* **1.** to make sightless **2.** to make temporarily unable to see; dazzle **3.** to deprive of the power of insight or judgment **4.** to make dim; obscure **5.** to outshine or eclipse **6.** to hide or conceal —*n.* **1.** anything that obscures or prevents sight **2.** *a*) anything that keeps out light, as a window shade or shutter *b*) *same as* VENETIAN BLIND **3.** a place of concealment, as for a hunter; ambush **4.** *a*) a person or thing used to deceive or mislead; decoy *b*) a person who in his dealings is really acting for another —*adv.* **1.** blindly; specif., so as to be blind, insensible, etc. **2.** recklessly **3.** *Aeron.* by the use of instruments alone [to fly *blind*] **4.** sight unseen [to buy a thing *blind*] —**the blind** people who are blind —**blind′ly** *adv.* —**blind′ness** *n.*

blind alley 1. an alley or passage shut off at one end **2.** any undertaking, idea, etc. that leads to nothing

☆**blind date** [Colloq.] **1.** a social engagement arranged for a man and a woman who are strangers to each other **2.** either person involved

blind·er (blīn′dər) *n.* either of two leather flaps on a bridle that keep the horse from seeing to the sides

☆**blind·fish** (blīnd′fish′) *n., pl.* -**fish′**, -**fish′es**: see FISH² any of a number of small fishes with functionless eyes, found in underground streams, waters of caves, etc.

blind·fold (-fōld′) *vt.* [altered (after FOLD¹) < ME. *blindfeld*, struck blind, pp. of *blindfellen* < OE. *(ge)blindfellian*: see BLIND + FELL²] **1.** to cover the eyes of with a cloth or bandage **2.** to hinder the sight or understanding of —*n.* **1.** a cloth used to cover the eyes **2.** anything that hinders the sight or understanding —*adj.* **1.** with the eyes covered **2.** reckless; heedless —*adv.* **1.** blindly **2.** recklessly; heedlessly

blind gut 1. *same as* CECUM **2.** a section of the intestinal tract with one end closed off either by surgery or as a result of disease

Blind·heim (blint′hīm) *Ger.* name for BLENHEIM

blind·man's buff (blīnd′manz buf′) [*buff* contr. < BUFFET¹] a game in which a blindfolded player has to catch and identify another: also **blind′man's bluff′** (bluf′)

☆**blind pig** [Old Slang] *same as* SPEAK-EASY

blind spot 1. the small area, insensitive to light, in the retina of the eye where the optic nerve enters **2.** an area where vision is hindered or obscured **3.** a lack of sensitivity to a particular thing; prejudice, or area of ignorance, that one has but is often unaware of **4.** an area where radio reception is poor

☆**blind staggers** the staggers: see STAGGER (*n.* 3)

blind·sto·ry (blīnd′stôr′ē) *n., pl.* -**ries** *Archit.* **1.** a windowless story **2.** in Gothic churches, a gallery (triforium) without windows, above the main arches

☆**blind tiger** [Old Slang] *same as* SPEAK-EASY

blind·worm (-wurm′) *n.* a legless lizard (*Anguis fragilis*) of the Old World: it has a dark, snakelike body with greenish or yellow spots or stripes, a small head, very small eyes, and a brittle tail

blin·i (blin′ē) *n.pl., sing.* **blin** [Russ.] small, thin pancakes, commonly served with caviar and sour cream: also **blin′is** (-ēz): cf. BLINTZ

blink (bliŋk) *vi.* [ME. *blenken, blenchen* (see BLENCH²)] **1.** to close the eyelids and open them quickly one or more times, either as a reflex or a conscious act **2.** to flash on and off; twinkle or glimmer **3.** to look with eyes half-shut, winking, as in a glare **4.** *a*) to look (*at*) as if not seeing; disregard;

ignore; condone [to *blink* at a mistake] *b*) to look (*at*) with wonder or shock [he *blinked* at the weight of the players] **5.** [Obs.] to look with a glance —*vt.* **1.** to wink (the eyes) rapidly **2.** to cause (eyes, light, etc.) to wink or blink **3.** to get rid of (tears, eye drops, etc.) by blinking (with *away* or *from*) **4.** to close the eyes to (a fact or situation); evade or avoid **5.** to signal (a message) by flashing a light, etc. —*n.* **1.** a blinking of the eyes **2.** a brief flash of light; twinkle or glimmer **3.** [Chiefly Scot.] a quick look; glimpse **4.** *a*) a shining reflection on the horizon caused by ice masses at sea *b*) a dull, leaden appearance of the sky on the horizon caused by the absence of reflecting ice —*SYN.* see WINK —☆**on the blink** [Slang] not working right; out of order

blink·ard (-ərd) *n.* [Now Rare] **1.** a person who habitually blinks his eyes **2.** a person who fails to perceive or understand; stupid person

blink·er (-ər) *n.* ☆**1.** *a*) a flashing warning light at crossings *b*) a light for signaling messages in flashes **2.** [*pl.*] *a*) blinders, esp. as worn by a race horse that tends to shy *b*) a kind of goggles —*vt.* to put blinkers, or blinders, on

☆**blintz** (blints) *n.* [Yid. *blintze* < Russ. *blinyets*, dim. of *blin*, pancake] a thin pancake rolled with a filling of cottage cheese, fruit, etc.

blip (blip) *n.* [echoic of a brief sound] **1.** a luminous image on an oscilloscope, as in a radar set **2.** a quick, sharp sound —*vi.* **blipped, blip′ping** to make a blip or series of blips

bliss (blis) *n.* [ME. *blisse* < OE. *bliss, bliths,* joy < *blithe,* BLITHE] **1.** great joy or happiness **2.** spiritual joy; heavenly rapture **3.** any cause of bliss —*SYN.* see ECSTASY —**bliss′ful** *adj.* —**bliss′ful·ly** *adv.* —**bliss′ful·ness** *n.*

blis·ter (blis′tər) *n.* [ME. < Du. *bluister* or OFr. *blestre* < ON. *blastr:* for IE. base see BALL¹] **1.** a raised patch of skin, specif. of epidermis, filled with watery matter and caused by a burn or by rubbing **2.** something used or applied to cause a blister **3.** anything resembling a blister, as on a plant, a coat of paint, etc. **4.** a bulging, bubblelike projection, usually transparent, used for observation, protection, etc. on an aircraft, train, car, etc. **5.** a similar, transparent, rigid shell, used to package, protect, and display an article of merchandise —*vt.* **1.** to cause blisters to form on **2.** to beat severely **3.** to lash with words —*vi.* to have or form a blister or blisters —**blis′ter·y** *adj.*

blister beetle any of several small green, gray, black, or striped beetles (family Meloidae), as the Spanish fly, some of which are harmful to plants: the dried and ground bodies of the Spanish fly and certain other species were used medically as a blistering agent

blister copper copper that is 96 to 99 percent pure, produced by smelting: it has a blistery surface caused by sulfur dioxide bubbles

☆**blister rust** a destructive disease of white pines, caused by a fungus (*Cronartium ribicola*) that produces orange-colored blisters on the bark and branch tips

blithe (blīth, blith) *adj.* [ME. < OE., ult < IE. base *bhlei-,* to shine, gleam] showing a gay, cheerful disposition; carefree —**blithe′ly** *adv.* —**blithe′ness** *n.*

blith·er·ing (blith′ər in) *adj.* [*blither,* var. of BLETHER + -ING] talking without sense; jabbering

blithe·some (blīth′sam, blith′-) *adj.* blithe; lighthearted —**blithe′some·ly** *adv.* —**blithe′some·ness** *n.*

B.Litt., B.Lit. [L. *Baccalaureus Lit(t)erarum*] Bachelor of Letters (or Literature)

blitz (blits) *n.* [< ff.] **1.** a sudden, destructive attack, as by aircraft or tanks **2.** any sudden, overwhelming attack —*vt.* **1.** to subject to a blitz; overwhelm and destroy ☆**2.** to hold (an opponent) scoreless in gin rummy ☆**3.** *Football* to charge (the opposing passer) through gaps in the line; red-dog

blitz·krieg (-krēg′) *n.* [G. < *blitz,* lightning + *krieg,* war] **1.** sudden, swift, large-scale offensive warfare intended to win a quick victory **2.** any swift, sudden, overwhelming attack

☆**bliz·zard** (bliz′ərd) *n.* [dial. *bliz,* violent blow (? akin to G. *blitz,* lightning) + -ARD] **1.** orig., *a*) a sharp or violent blow *b*) a shot or burst of shots **2.** a violent storm with powdery, driving snow and extremely cold winds

blk. **1.** black **2.** block **3.** bulk

bloat¹ (blōt) *adj.* [ME. *blout,* soft < ON. *blautr,* ult. < IE. base *bhel-,* to swell: see BALL¹] bloated; puffed up —*vt., vi.* **1.** to swell, as with water or air **2.** to puff up, as with pride —*n.* ☆**1.** a bloated person or thing ☆**2.** [Slang] a drunkard ☆**3.** *Vet.* a gassy swelling of the abdomen caused by watery forage or eating too fast

bloat² (blōt) *vt.* < ME. *blote,* soft with moisture < ON. *blautr,* soaked: see prec.] to cure or preserve (herring, mackerel, etc.) by soaking in salt water, smoking, and half-drying

bloat·er¹ (-ər) *n.* [< BLOAT²] a fat herring or mackerel that has been bloated, or cured

bloat·er² (-ər) *n.* [< BLOAT¹] a small freshwater fish (*Coregonus hoyi*) found in the Great Lakes and in the lakes of eastern Canada

blob (bläb) *n.* [see BLEB] **1.** a drop or small lump of a thick, viscous substance [a *blob* of jelly] **2.** a small spot or splash of color **3.** something of vague or indefinite form

[a hazy *blob* on the horizon] —*vt.* **blobbed, blob′bing** to splash or mark, as with blobs

bloc (bläk) *n.* [Fr. & OFr. < LowG. *block*, log, plant] 1. an alliance, often temporary, of political parties in a legislature ☆2. a group of legislators who, without regard to party affiliation, act together to advance some common interest of their constituents [the farm *bloc*] 3. a group of nations joined or acting together in support of one another [the African-Asian *bloc*]

Bloch (bläk; *G.* blōkh), **Ernest** 1880–1959; U.S. composer, born in Switzerland

block (bläk) *n.* [ME. *blokke* < MDu. or OFr. *bloc* < LowG.: see BLOC] 1. any large, solid piece of wood, stone, or metal, often with flat surfaces 2. a blocklike stand or platform on which hammering, chopping, etc. is done [a butcher's *block*, headsman's *block*] ☆3. an auctioneer's platform 4. *a)* a mold upon which things are shaped, as hats *b)* the shape of a hat 5. anything that stops movement or progress; obstruction, obstacle, or hindrance 6. a pulley or system of pulleys in a frame, with a hook, loop, etc. for attachment 7. any solid piece of material used to strengthen or support 8. a large, hollow building brick [a cement *block*] 9. a child's wooden or plastic toy brick ☆10. a large building with many units in it, or a group of buildings regarded as a unit ☆11. *a)* a city square *b)* one side of a city square 12. any number of persons or things regarded as a unit; bloc [a *block* of tickets, a trade *block*] 13. the metal casting that houses the cylinders of an internal-combustion engine 14. [Slang] a person's head 15. *Med. a)* an interruption of normal function in a part of the body [heart *block*, kidney *block*] *b)* an interruption of the passage of impulses through a nerve by means of pressure or anesthetics 16. *Printing* a piece of engraved wood, linoleum, etc. with a design or picture 17. *Psychiatry* a sudden interruption in speech or thought processes, resulting from deep emotional conflict, repression, etc. 18. *Railroading* a length of track governed by signals: see BLOCK SYSTEM ☆19. *Sports* an interruption, restraining, or thwarting of an opponent's play or movement 20. *Stamp Collecting* a set of four or more undetached stamps forming a rectangle —*vt.* [Fr. *bloquer* < the *n.*] 1. to impede the passage or progress of; obstruct 2. to blockade 3. to create difficulties for; stand in the way of; hinder 4. *a)* to shape or mold on or as on a block *b)* to stamp with a block 5. to form into blocks 6. to strengthen or support with blocks 7. to restrict or prohibit the use, conversion, or flow of (currency, assets, etc.) 8. to sketch or outline with little or no detail (often with *out*) 9. *Games, Sports* to hinder (an opponent or his play), whether legally or as a foul 10. *Med.* to prevent the transmission of impulses in (a nerve), esp. by anesthetizing 11. *Railroading* to run (trains) by the block system: see BLOCK SYSTEM —*vi.* 1. to have a mental block (*on*) 2. *Sports* to block an opponent —*adj.* 1. made or formed in a block or blocks [block coal] 2. set out like or involving a city block 3. *Stenography* having no indentation in address, heading, or paragraphs —*SYN.* see HINDER[1] —**block up** 1. to fill in (a passage, space, etc.) so as to obstruct 2. to elevate on blocks —**go to the block** 1. to be beheaded 2. to be up for sale in an auction —**knock someone's block off** [Slang] give a beating to; thrash —☆**on the block** up for sale or auction —**block′er** *n.*

block·ade (blä kād′) *n.* [BLOCK + -ADE] 1. a shutting off of a port or region of a belligerent state by the troops or ships of the enemy in order to prevent passage in or out in time of war 2. any blocking action designed to isolate another nation and cut off communication and commerce with it 3. the force that maintains a blockade 4. any strategic barrier —*vt.* **-ad′ed, -ad′ing** to subject to a blockade —☆**run the blockade** to go past or through a blockade —**block·ad′er** *n.*

☆**blockade runner** a ship or person that tries to go through or past a blockade

block·age (bläk′ij) *n.* a blocking or being blocked

block and tackle an arrangement of one or more pulley blocks, with rope or cables, for pulling or hoisting large, heavy objects

block·bust·er (-bus′tər) *n.* [Colloq.] 1. a large, aerial bomb that can demolish a large area ☆2. a particularly powerful, forceful, or effective person or thing; specif., an expensive or pretentious movie, novel, etc. intended to have wide popular appeal ☆3. a real-estate dealer who engages in blockbusting

☆**block·bust·ing** (-bus′tin) *n.* [Colloq.] the practice of inducing homeowners in a particular neighborhood to sell their homes quickly, often at a loss, by creating the fear that actual or prospective purchases by members of a minority group will bring a loss of value

☆**block diagram** *Geol.* a three-dimensional perspective representation of geologic or topographic features showing a surface area and usually two vertical cross sections

block·head (-hed′) *n.* a stupid person

BLOCKS (sense 6)

block·house (-hous′) *n.* 1. formerly, a strong wooden fort with a projecting second story and openings in the walls for the defenders to shoot from ☆2. any building of squared timber or logs ☆3. *a) Mil.* a small defensive structure of concrete *b)* a dome-shaped, heavily reinforced structure, with periscopes and detecting instruments, to protect observers of missile launchings, nuclear explosions, etc.

BLOCKHOUSE

blocking capacitor *Elec.* a capacitor for preventing the passage of direct current

block·ish (-ish) *adj.* like a block; stupid; dull

Block Island [after Adriaen *Block*, 17th-c. Du. explorer] island off the coast of R.I.: summer resort: pop. 500

block lava lava formed in sharp, angular, rough-surfaced blocks

block letter a printed or hand-printed letter that is simple in form, as sans-serif

block line a rope or cable used in a block and tackle

☆**block mountain** a mountain produced by faulting and the uplifting of large blocks of rock

block plane a carpenter's small plane for cutting across the grain on board ends

block printing printing of designs, drawings, etc. with engraved blocks coated with ink or dyes

block system a system of dividing a railroad track into several sections (*blocks*) and regulating the trains by automatic signals (**block signals**) so that there is usually no more than one train in one section

block·y (-ē) *adj.* **block′i·er, block′i·est** 1. having contrasting blocks or patches 2. of or like a block; stocky; chunky —**block′i·ness** *n.*

Bloem·fon·tein (blōom′fän tān′) city in C South Africa: capital of Orange Free State province & the national judicial capital: pop. 145,000

Blois (blwä) town in C France, on the Loire River: pop. 34,000

Blok (blôk; *E.* bläk; **Al·ex·an·dr Al·ex·an·dro·vich** (ä lyik sän′dr′ ä′lyik sän′drô vyich) 1880–1921; Russ. poet

bloke (blōk) *n.* [word found in Shelta, Irish tinkers' argot] [Chiefly Brit. Slang] a man; fellow; chap

blond (bländ) *adj.* [Fr. < ? Gmc.] 1. having yellow or yellowish-brown hair, often along with fair skin and blue or gray eyes 2. *a)* yellow or yellowish-brown: said of hair *b)* pink-and-white: said of skin 3. light-colored [blond furniture] —*n.* 1. a blond person 2. blonde (lace) —**blond′-ness** *n.*

blonde (bländ) *adj. same as* BLOND —*n.* 1. a blond woman or girl 2. a type of silk bobbin lace: so called because originally flaxen in color

Blood (blud) *n., pl.* **Blood** any member of a subtribe of the Blackfoot Indians

blood (blud) *n.* [ME. *blod, blode* < OE. *blod:* see BLEED] 1. the fluid, usually red, circulating in the heart, arteries, and veins of vertebrates: it carries oxygen and cell-building material to, and carbon dioxide and waste matter away from, the body tissues 2. a similar fluid in invertebrate animals 3. the spilling of blood; murder 4. the essence of life; life; lifeblood 5. the life fluid, sap, or juice of a plant 6. passion, temperament, or disposition 7. parental heritage; family line; lineage 8. racial heritage; race: a loose unscientific usage, for there are no ethnic differences in blood 9. relationship by descent in the same family line; kinship 10. descent from nobility or royalty 11. descent from purebred stock 12. a dandy or fop 13. people, esp. youthful people [new *blood* in an organization] —*vt.* 1. to let (a hunting dog) taste, smell, or see the blood of its prey 2. to initiate (a hunter) by staining his face with blood of the prey 3. to initiate (a person) in any new experience —**bad blood** anger; hatred —**blood is thicker than water** family ties are stronger than others —**have (someone's) blood on one's head** to be responsible for (someone's) death or misfortune —**in cold blood** 1. with cruelty; unfeelingly 2. dispassionately; deliberately —**make one's blood boil** to make one angry or resentful —**make one's blood run cold** to frighten or terrify one

☆**blood bank** 1. a place where whole blood or blood plasma is typed, processed, and stored for future use 2. any reserve of blood for use in transfusion

blood bath a killing of many people; massacre

blood brother 1. a brother by birth 2. a person bound to one by the ceremony of mingling his blood with one's own —**blood brotherhood**

blood count a count of the number of red corpuscles and white corpuscles in a given volume of blood

blood·cur·dling (-kurd′lin) *adj.* very frightening; causing terror or horror

blood·ed (blud′id) *adj.* 1. having (a specific kind of) blood [hot-blooded] ☆2. of fine stock or breed; pedigreed; thoroughbred; purebred

blood·fin (-fin′) *n.* a small silvery S. American fish (*Aphyocharax rubripinnis*) with red fins, often kept in aquariums

blood group any of several groups into which any person's blood is classified with reference to the type of agglutinogen of its corpuscles

blood·guilt (-gilt′) *n.* the state or fact of being responsible for, or guilty of, murder or bloodshed: also **blood′guilt′i·ness** —**blood′guilt′y** *adj.*

blood heat the normal temperature of human blood, approximately 98.6°F

blood·hound (-hound′) *n.* [ME. *blodhond:* see BLOOD (*n.* 11) & HOUND[1]] 1. any of a breed of large dogs with a smooth coat, wrinkled face, drooping ears, and a keen sense of smell: bloodhounds are used in tracking escaped prisoners, fugitives, etc. 2. a person who pursues keenly or relentlessly; sleuth

blood·i·ly (-′l ē) *adv.* 1. in a bloody manner 2. cruelly; savagely

blood·i·ness (-ē nəs) *n.* the state of being bloody

blood·less (-ləs) *adj.* 1. without blood 2. without bloodshed 3. not having enough blood; anemic or pale 4. having little energy or vitality 5. unfeeling; cruel —**blood′less·ly** *adv.* —**blood′less·ness** *n.*

BLOODHOUND
(to 27 in. high
at shoulder)

blood·let·ting (-let′iŋ) *n.* [ME. *blodleting:* see BLOOD & LET[1]] 1. the opening of a vein to remove blood; bleeding; phlebotomy 2. bloodshed

blood·line (-līn′) *n.* a direct line of descent, esp. of a domestic animal; pedigree, strain

☆**blood·mo·bile** (-mō bēl′, -mə-) *n.* [BLOOD + (AUTO)-MOBILE] a traveling unit equipped for collecting blood from donors for blood banks

blood money 1. money paid to a hired killer 2. money paid as compensation to the next of kin of a murdered person; wergeld 3. money gotten ruthlessly at the expense of others' lives or suffering

blood plasma the fluid part of blood, as distinguished from the corpuscles

blood platelet any of the minute, disklike elements of the blood that are essential for normal clotting

blood poisoning any of various diseases in which the blood contains microorganisms, their toxins, or other poisonous matter; septicemia: a nontechnical term

blood pressure the pressure exerted by the blood against the inner walls of the blood vessels, esp. the arteries: it varies with health, age, emotional tension, etc.

blood pudding a large sausage made of blood, esp. pig's blood, and suet, enclosed in a casing

blood-red (-red′) *adj.* 1. stained red with blood 2. having the deep-red color of blood

blood relation (or **relative**) a person related by birth

blood·root (-rōōt′, -root′) *n.* ☆a spring-blooming, N. American wildflower (*Sanguinaria canadensis*) of the poppy family, with a single white flower and lobed leaf arising from a rootstock that yields a red juice

blood·shed (-shed′) *n.* the shedding of blood; killing

blood·shot (-shät′) *adj.* [ME. *blodshoten* < *blod,* BLOOD + pp. of *schoten,* SHOOT] red because the small blood vessels are swollen or broken: said of the eyes

blood sport any pastime, as fox-hunting or cockfighting, in which killing is involved

blood·stain (-stān′) *n.* a dark discoloration caused by a blot or smear of blood

blood·stained (-stānd′) *adj.* 1. soiled or discolored with blood 2. guilty of murder

blood·stone (-stōn′) *n.* a semiprecious, dark-green variety of quartz spotted with red jasper, used as a gem: the usual birthstone for March

blood·stream (-strēm′) *n.* the blood flowing through the circulatory system of a body

blood·suck·er (-suk′ər) *n.* 1. an animal that sucks blood, esp. a leech 2. a person who extorts or takes from others all that he can —**blood′suck′ing** *adj.,* *n.*

blood test an examination of a small amount of a person's blood for diagnosis, classification, etc.

blood·thirst·y (-thur′stē) *adj.* eager to hurt or kill; murderous; very cruel —**blood′thirst′i·ly** *adv.* —**blood′-thirst′i·ness** *n.*

blood type *same as* BLOOD GROUP

blood typing the classification of human blood to determine compatible blood groups for transfusion

blood vessel any of the many tubes through which the blood circulates; artery, vein, or capillary

blood·worm (-wurm′) *n.* 1. any of various small, red annelid worms 2. the wormlike red larva of various midges, esp. of the dipteran family, found in fresh water

blood·wort (-wurt′) *n.* 1. any of a family (Haemodoraceae) of perennial plants, with red roots and juice 2. an old-world plant (*Sanguisorba officinalis*) of the rose family ☆3. any of several American plants with red roots, stems, etc., as the bloodroot

blood·y (blud′ē) *adj.* **blood′i·er, blood′i·est** [ME. *blodi* < OE. *blodig*] 1. of, like, or containing blood 2. covered or stained with blood; bleeding 3. involving bloodshed; with much killing or wounding 4. bloodthirsty; cruel 5. having the red color of blood 6. [Brit. Slang] cursed; damned: a

vulgar usage —*adv.* [Brit. Slang] very; a vulgar usage —*vt.* **blood′ied, blood′y·ing** to cover or stain with blood

Bloody Mary 1. *epithet* of MARY I ☆2. a drink made of vodka and tomato juice

☆**bloo·ey, bloo·ie** (blōō′ē) *adj.* [Slang] not in working condition: chiefly in **go blooey,** to go out of order

bloom[1] (blōōm) *n.* [ME. *blom* < ON. *blomi,* flowers and foliage on trees < IE. base *bhlō-,* to spring up, as in L. *flos* (gen. *floris*), Gr. *phyllon,* leaf, whence FLOWER: cf. BLEED] 1. a flower; blossom 2. flowers collectively, as of a plant 3. the state or time of flowering 4. a state or time of most health, beauty, vigor, or freshness; prime 5. a youthful, healthy glow (of cheeks, skin, etc.) 6. the grayish, powdery coating on various fruits, as the plum, grape, etc., and on some leaves 7. any similar coating, as on new coins 8. a mass of planktonic algae in lakes, ponds, or the sea, as in the development of red tides 9. the bouquet, as of wine —*vi.* 1. to bear a flower or flowers; blossom 2. to reach a prime condition, as in health, vigor, beauty, perfection, etc.; flourish 3. to glow with color, health, etc. —*vt.* [Archaic] to cause to bloom, flower, or flourish

bloom[2] (blōōm) *n.* [OE. *bloma,* lump of metal] 1. a spongy mass of wrought iron ready for further working 2. a thick bar of iron or steel obtained by rolling or hammering an ingot

bloom·er[1] (blōō′mər) *n.* 1. a plant with reference to its blooming [an early *bloomer*] 2. a person in his bloom or prime 3. [short for *blooming error*] [Slang] a foolish or stupid mistake

☆**bloom·er[2]** (blōō′mər) *n.* [after A. J. BLOOMER, who advocated it] 1. formerly, a costume for women or girls, consisting of a short skirt and loose trousers gathered at the ankles 2. [*pl.*] *a*) baggy trousers gathered at the knee, formerly worn by girls and women for athletics *b*) an undergarment somewhat like this

Bloom·er (blōō′mər), **Amelia Jenks** (jeŋks) 1818–94; U.S. social reformer & feminist

Bloom·field (blōōm′fēld′) [after Jos. *Bloomfield* (1753–1823), early governor of N.J.] suburb of Newark, in NE N.J.: pop. 52,000

Bloom·field (-fēld′), **Leonard** 1887–1949; U.S. linguist

bloom·ing (blōō′miŋ) *adj.* 1. flowering; blossoming 2. thriving; flourishing 3. [Colloq.] utter; complete [a *blooming* idiot]

Bloom·ing·ton (blōō′miŋ tən) *n.* [prob. from the abundance of flowers settlers found there] city in SC Ind.: pop. 43,000 2. [? after prec.] city in C Ill.: pop. 40,000 3. [? after *Bloomington,* Ind.] city in E Minn., near Minneapolis: pop. 82,000

bloom·y (blōō′mē) *adj.* 1. full of blooms or blossoms 2. having a bloom (powdery coating)

☆**bloop** (blōōp) *vt.* [Slang] Baseball 1. to hit (a pitched ball) as a blooper 2. to get (a hit) in this way

☆**bloop·er** (-ər) *n.* [*bloop,* echoic of a vulgar noise + -ER] [Slang] 1. a foolish or stupid mistake; blunder 2. *Baseball a*) a ball batted up in a low arc so that it falls between the infield and outfield, usually for a hit *b*) a ball that is pitched to the batter in a high lob

blos·som (bläs′əm) *n.* [ME. *blosme* < OE. *blostma, blostm:* for IE. base see BLOOM[1]] 1. a flower or bloom, esp. of a fruit-bearing plant 2. a state or time of flowering —*vi.* 1. to have or open into blossoms; bloom 2. to begin to thrive or flourish; develop —**blos′som·y** *adj.*

blot[1] (blät) *n.* [ME. < ?] 1. a spot or stain, esp. of ink 2. anything that spoils or mars, esp. by providing an unpleasant contrast [that shack is a *blot* on the landscape] 3. a moral stain; disgrace —*vt.* **blot′ted, blot′ting** 1. to make blots on; spot; stain; blur 2. to stain (a reputation); disgrace 3. to erase or get rid of [memories *blotted* from one's mind] 4. to dry by soaking up the wet liquid, as with blotting paper —*vi.* 1. to make blots 2. to become blotted 3. to be absorbent —**blot out** 1. to darken or hide entirely; obscure 2. to kill or destroy

blot[2] (blät) *n.* [prob. < MDu. *bloot* or Dan. *blot,* naked, uncovered] 1. *Backgammon* an exposed piece, liable to capture 2. [Archaic] a weak point; fault; failing

blotch (bläch) *n.* [? extension of BLOT[1]] 1. a discolored patch or blemish on the skin 2. any large blot or stain —*vt.* to cover or mark with blotches

blotch·y (-ē) *adj.* **blotch′i·er, blotch′i·est** 1. like a blotch 2. covered with blotches —**blotch′i·ness** *n.*

blot·ter (blät′ər) *n.* 1. a piece of blotting paper ☆2. a book for recording events as they occur [a police *blotter* is a record of arrests and charges]

blotting paper a thick, soft, absorbent paper used to dry a surface that has just been written on in ink

blot·to (-ō) *adj.* [< ? BLOT[1]] [Slang] very drunk; unconscious because of drinking too much

blouse (blous, blouz) *n.* [Fr., (18th c.) workman's smock; < ? Pr. (*lano*) *blouso,* short (wool), prob. < Langobardic *bloz,* bare] 1. a loose, smocklike outer garment of varying length, worn by certain European peasants and workmen 2. a loose, shirtlike garment extending to the waistline or just below, worn by women and children 3. the coat or jacket of a service uniform or dress uniform of

the armed forces **4.** a sailor's jumper —*vi.*, *vt.* **bloused** (bloust, blouzd), **blous'ing** to gather in and drape at the waistline

blous·on (bloo͞s'än; Fr. bloo zōn') *adj.* [Fr., extended < *blouse*] styled with a long, full, bloused top, as a dress —*n.* a blouson dress, dress top, etc.

blow[1] (blō) *vi.* **blew, blown, blow'ing** [ME. *blowen* < OE. *blawan* < IE. base *bhle-, *bhlo-: see BLAST, BALL[1]] **1.** to move with some force: said of the wind or a current of air **2.** to send forth air with or as with the mouth **3.** to pant; be breathless **4.** to make or give sound by blowing or being blown **5.** to spout water and air from the lungs, as whales do **6.** to be carried by the wind or a current of air [the paper *blew* away] **7.** to be stormy **8.** to burst suddenly, as a tire, or melt, as a fuse (often with *out*) **9.** to lay eggs: said of flies **10.** [Colloq.] to brag; boast ☆**11.** [Slang] to go away; leave —*vt.* **1.** to cause air to come from (a bellows, blower, etc.) **2.** to send out (breath, tobacco smoke, etc.) from the mouth **3.** to force air onto, into, or through **4.** to drive by blowing **5.** to give out or spread (news) **6.** *a)* to sound (a wind instrument) by blowing *b)* to make (a sound or signal) by blowing **7.** to cool, warm, dry, or soothe by blowing on or toward **8.** to shape or form (glass, soap bubbles, etc.) by blown air or gas **9.** to clean or clear by blowing through [to *blow* one's nose] **10.** to cause to burst or break by an explosion **11.** to cause (a horse) to pant **12.** to lay or deposit eggs in **13.** to melt (a fuse, etc.) **14.** [Colloq.] to spend (money) freely or wastefully; squander **15.** [Colloq.] to treat (*to* something) ☆**16.** [Colloq.] to forget or fluff (one's lines) in a show ☆**17.** [Slang] to go away from; leave [he *blew* town] ☆**18.** [Slang] to bungle and fail in [we had our chance and *blew* it] **19.** [Slang] *pp.* **blowed** to damn: used in euphemistic oaths —*n.* **1.** the act of blowing **2.** *a)* a blast of air *b)* the time of, or amount of metal refined in, each blast of air in a Bessemer converter **3.** a strong wind; gale **4.** a boast **5.** [Slang] a braggart —**blow hot and cold** [orig. with reference to the scent in hunting] to be favorable toward something and then opposed to it; vacillate —☆**blow in** [Slang] **1.** to arrive **2.** to spend all (one's money) —**blow off 1.** to let steam or hot water out from (a boiler) **2.** [Colloq.] to give vent to one's feelings, as by loud or long talking —☆**blow one's stack** (or **top** or **lid**) [Slang] to lose one's temper; fly into a rage —**blow out 1.** *a)* to put out (a fire or flame) by blowing *b)* to be put out by wind or air **2.** to blow (*vi.* 8) **3.** to dispel (itself) after a time: said of a storm —**blow over 1.** to move away, as rain clouds **2.** to pass over or by; be forgotten —**blow up 1.** to fill with or as with air or gas **2.** to burst or explode **3.** to arise and become more intense, as a storm **4.** to enlarge (a photograph) **5.** to exaggerate (an incident, rumor, etc.) **6.** [Colloq.] to lose one's temper or poise

blow[2] (blō) *n.* [ME. *blowe*, akin to G. *bleuen*, Goth. *bliggwan*, to strike] **1.** a hard hit or stroke with the fist, a weapon, etc. **2.** a sudden attack or forcible effort **3.** any sudden calamity or misfortune; shock —**at a** (or **one**) **blow** by one action; with a single effort —**come to blows** to begin fighting one another

blow[3] (blō) *vi.* **blew, blown, blow'ing** [ME. *blowen* < OE. *blowan*; akin to G. *blühen*: for IE. base see BLOOM[1]] [Poet.] to bloom; blossom —*n.* **1.** a mass of blossoms **2.** the state of flowering **3.** any splendid display

☆**blow·by** (-bī') *adj.* designating or of a device attached to the crankcase vent of an automobile engine to burn off exhaust fumes and thus reduce air pollution

blow-by-blow (-bī'blō') *adj.* told in great detail [a *blow-by-blow* account of a debate]

blow·er (-ər) *n.* **1.** a person who blows **2.** any device for producing a current of air or blowing air into a room, from a furnace, etc. **3.** [Brit. Slang] the telephone

☆**blow·fish** (-fish') *n.*, *pl.* **-fish', -fish'es:** see FISH[2] same as PUFFER

blow·fly (-flī') *n.*, *pl.* **-flies'** [BLOW[1] (*vi.* 9) + FLY[2]] any of a family (Calliphoridae) of two-winged flies that deposit eggs or living larvae in carrion and meat and sometimes in open wounds, etc.

☆**blow·gun** (-gun') *n.* a long, tubelike weapon through which darts or pellets are blown

☆**blow·hard** (-härd') *n.* [Slang] a loudly boastful person

blow·hole (-hōl') *n.* **1.** a nostril in the top of the head of whales and certain other cetaceans, through which they breathe **2.** a hole through which gas or air can escape **3.** a hole in the ice to which seals, whales, etc. come to get air **4.** a crack in rock along a shore through which waves force water up in a spout **5.** a flaw in cast metal caused by an air or gas bubble

blown[1] (blōn) *pp.* of BLOW[1] —*adj.* **1.** swollen or bloated **2.** out of breath, as from exertion **3.** flyblown **4.** made by blowing or by using a blowpipe, etc.

blown[2] (blōn) *pp.* of BLOW[3] —*adj.* having bloomed; in full bloom: often **full'-blown'**

blow·off (-ôf', -äf') *n.* **1.** a blowing off of steam, water, etc. **2.** a valve for effecting this **3.** [Slang] a boaster

blow·out (-out') *n.* **1.** the act or result of blowing out; specif., *a)* the bursting of a tire *b)* the melting of an electric fuse from too much current **2.** [Slang] a party, banquet, or celebration

blow·pipe (-pīp') *n.* **1.** a tube for forcing air or gas into a flame to intensify and concentrate its heat **2.** a metal tube used in blowing glass **3.** same as BLOWGUN

☆**blow·torch** (-tôrch') *n.* a small gasoline torch that shoots out a hot flame intensified by a blast of air: it is used to melt metal, remove old paint, etc.

BLOWTORCH

blow·tube (-too͞b', -tyoo͞b') *n.* **1.** same as BLOWPIPE (sense 2) **2.** same as BLOWGUN

blow·up (-up') *n.* **1.** an explosion **2.** an enlarged photograph **3.** [Colloq.] an angry or hysterical outburst

blow·y (-ē) *adj.* **blow'i·er, blow'i·est** windy

blowz·y (blou'zē) *adj.* **blowz'i·er, blowz'i·est** [< obs. *blouze*, wench] **1.** fat, ruddy, and coarse-looking **2.** slovenly; frowzy Also **blows'y**

BLS Bureau of Labor Statistics

bls. 1. bales **2.** barrels

B.L.S. Bachelor of Library Science

blub·ber[1] (blub'ər) *n.* [ME. *blober*, a bubble; prob. of echoic origin: see BLEB] **1.** the fat of the whale and other sea mammals, from which an oil is obtained **2.** unsightly fat on the human body

blub·ber[2] (-ər) *vi.* [ME. *bloberen*, to bubble (see prec.)] to weep loudly, like a child —*vt.* **1.** to say while blubbering **2.** to wet, disfigure, or swell with weeping —*n.* loud weeping; a blubbering —*adj.* thick or swollen —SYN. see CRY —**blub'ber·er.** *n.*

blub·ber·y (-ər ē) *adj.* **1.** of or full of blubber **2.** like blubber in appearance, texture, etc.; fat **3.** swollen or disfigured, as by blubbering

blu·cher (bloo͞'chər, -kər) *n.* [after ff.] **1.** a heavy half boot **2.** a kind of shoe in which the upper laps over the vamp, which is of one piece with the tongue

Blü·cher (blü'Har; E. bloo͞'chər, -kər), **Geb·hard Le·be·recht von** (gep'härt lā'bə reHt' fôn) 1742–1819; Prussian field marshal: helped defeat Napoleon at Waterloo

BLUCHER

bludg·eon (bluj'n) *n.* [? altered < MFr. *bougeon*, dim. of *bouge*, a club] a short club with a thick, heavy, or loaded end —*vt.*, *vi.* **1.** to strike with or as with a bludgeon **2.** to bully or coerce

blue (bloo͞) *adj.* [ME. & OFr. *bleu* < Frank. *blao* < IE. base *bhlē-wos, light-colored, blue, blond, yellow, whence L. *flavus*, yellow, Cym. *blawr*, gray, OE. *blǣwen*, blue, G. *blau*] **1.** having the color of the clear sky or the deep sea **2.** [infl. by ME. *blo* < ON. *blā*, livid] livid: said of the skin **3.** sad and gloomy; depressed or depressing **4.** balefully murky [the air was *blue* with oaths] **5.** puritanical; rigorous **6.** wearing blue garments [*Blue* Nuns] **7.** [Colloq.] indecent; risqué; suggestive —*n.* **1.** the color of the clear sky or the deep sea; any color between green and violet in the spectrum **2.** any blue pigment or dye **3.** bluing **4.** anything colored blue, as the second ring of an archer's target **5.** *a)* blue clothing *b)* [often B-] a person or group wearing a blue uniform; ☆specif., a Union soldier *c)* [*pl.*] a sailor's blue uniform **6.** same as BLUESTOCKING ☆**7.** [*pl.*] [short for BLUE DEVILS] [Colloq.] a depressed, unhappy feeling (with *the*) ☆**8.** [*pl.*] [also, *and always for sense c, with sing. v.*] *a)* Negro folk music characterized by minor harmonies, typically slow tempo, and melancholy words (often with *the*) *b)* the form of jazz that evolved from this (often with *the*) *c)* a song or composition in this style —*vt.* **blued, blu'ing** to make blue **1.** to make blue **2.** to use bluing on or in —*vi.* to become blue —**once in a blue moon** very seldom; almost never —**out of the blue** as if from the sky; without being expected or foreseen —**the blue 1.** the sky **2.** the sea

☆**blue baby** a baby born with cyanosis as a result of a congenital heart lesion or incomplete lung expansion

Blue·beard (-bird') *n.* a character in an old folk tale who married and then murdered one wife after another

blue·bell (-bel') *n.* any of various plants (esp. of the genera *Campanula* and *Mertensia*) with blue, bell-shaped flowers, as the harebell or some other bellflower

blue·ber·ry (-ber'ē, -bər ē) *n.*, *pl.* **-ries** [ME. *bloberi* < blo, blue + *berie*, berry] ☆**1.** any of a genus (*Vaccinium*) of shrubs of the heath family, bearing small, edible, blue-black berries with tiny seeds and a whitish, waxy bloom: cf. HUCKLEBERRY ☆**2.** any of the berries

☆**blue·bill** (-bil') *n.* any of various American ducks with bluish bills; esp., the scaup

blue·bird (-burd') *n.* ☆any of a genus (*Sialia*) of small N. American songbirds: the male usually has a blue or bluish back and an orange or reddish breast

blue blood 1. descent from nobility or royalty **2.** a person of such descent; aristocrat; nobleman: also **blue'blood'** *n.* —**blue'-blood'ed** *adj.*

blue·bon·net (-bän'it) *n.* **1.** a broad, flat cap of blue woolen, formerly worn in Scotland **2.** a Scotsman ☆**3.** ☆*a)* any of a genus (*Lupinus*) of wildflowers with blue blossoms, common in the southwestern U.S.; esp., a Texan flower (*Lupinus subcarnosus*) *b)* [Chiefly Scot.] a cornflower with blue blossoms Also **blue bonnet**

blue book 1. [*also* B- B-] an official government report or registry, often having a blue cover ☆**2.** a book listing people who are socially prominent ☆**3.** a blank booklet with a blue paper cover, in which college students can write examination answers: also **blue'book'** *n.*

blue·bot·tle (-bät''l) *n.* **1.** any of several plants with blue, bottle-shaped flowers, as the cornflower, grape hyacinth, or closed gentian **2.** any of several blue-colored blowflies; esp., a large species (*Cynomyia cadaverina*) with a steel-blue abdomen and a hairy body

blue cheese a cheese similar to Roquefort, but usually made of cow's milk

☆**blue-chip** (-chip') *adj.* [after the high-value *blue chips* of poker] **1.** designating any high-priced stock with a good record of earnings and price stability **2.** [Colloq.] excellent, valuable, etc.

blue·coat (-kōt') *n.* a person wearing a blue coat or uniform; specif., ☆*a*) a U.S. soldier of the 19th cent. ☆*b*) a policeman

☆**blue-col·lar** (-käl'ər) *adj.* [from the color of many work shirts] designating or of industrial workers, esp. the semiskilled and unskilled

☆**blue crab** a blue, edible swimming crab (*Callinectes sapidus*) of the Atlantic coast of the U.S.

☆**Blue Cross** (any of) a system of nonprofit health-insurance organizations offering hospitalization and, variously, medical benefits to subscribers, esp. to groups of employees and their families

☆**blue-curls** (-kurlz') *n.* any of a genus (*Trichostema*) of plants of the mint family, with downy, narrow leaves and blue flowers: also **blue curls**

blue devils 1. delirium tremens or its hallucinations **2.** a depressed feeling; the blues

☆**blue-eyed grass** (-īd') any of a genus (*Sisyrinchium*) of small, grasslike plants of the iris family, with flat blue or white flowers

☆**blue·fish** (-fish') *n.*, *pl.* **-fish', -fish'es:** see FISH[2] **1.** an important commercial food fish (*Pomatomus saltatrix*) of a bluish color, common along the Atlantic coast of N. America **2.** any of various other bluish fishes

blue flag ☆any of several species of iris with blue flowers, growing as wildflowers in marshy places

blue fox 1. a mutant of the arctic fox in which the fur has a bluish or smoky-gray cast at all seasons **2.** this fur

☆**blue·gill** (-gil') *n.* a freshwater sunfish (*Lepomis macrochirus*) of a bluish color

☆**blue·grass** (-gras', -gräs') *n.* **1.** any of a large genus (*Poa*) of temperate and arctic forage grasses, as Kentucky **bluegrass 2.** [< ff.] [*often* B-] Southern string-band folk music

Bluegrass Country (or **Region**) region in C Ky. where there is much bluegrass: also called **the Bluegrass**

blue-green algae (-grēn') any of a division (Cyanophyta) of microscopic algae that contain a blue pigment which obscures the chlorophyll

blue gum a large Australian tree (*Eucalyptus globulus*) of the myrtle family, having smooth, deciduous bark and aromatic leaves: grown extensively in California

☆**blue-hearts** (-härts') *n.*, *pl.* **-hearts'** a hairy perennial plant (*Buchnera americana*) of the southern U.S., with deep-purple flowers

blue·ing (-iŋ) *n.* same as BLUING

blue·ish (-ish) *adj.* same as BLUISH

blue·jack (-jak') *n.* **1.** *same as* COPPER SULFATE ☆**2.** a small oak (*Quercus incana*) of the S U.S.

blue·jack·et (-jak'it) *n.* an enlisted man in the U.S. or British navy

☆**blue jay** any of a number of noisy, often crested, American birds (genera *Cyanocitta* and *Aphelocoma*), with a bluish upper part: also **blue'jay'** *n.*

☆**blue law 1.** any of the strict puritanical laws prevalent in colonial New England **2.** a law prohibiting dancing, shows, sports, business, etc. on Sunday

blue·line (-līn') *n.* either of the two blue lines that divide an ice hockey rink into three equal zones

blue mold any of various species of a fungus (genus *Penicillium*) that produce bluish masses of spores: some species yield penicillin and some are used to ripen certain cheeses

Blue Mountains heavily forested mountain range of NE Oreg. & SE Wash.: highest peak, c. 9,000 ft.

Blue Nile *see* NILE

blue·nose (-nōz') *n.* [Colloq.] ☆**1.** a puritanical person, esp. one who tries to impose his moral views on others **2.** [B-] a Nova Scotian: so called from the cold climate

blue note *Jazz* a slightly flatted note, esp. the third or seventh note of the scale

blue-pen·cil (-pen's'l) *vt.* **-ciled** or **-cilled, -cil·ing** or **-cil·ling** to edit, cross out, or correct with or as with a blue pencil

BLUE JAY (12 in. long)

blue peter [prob. < *blue repeater*, signal flag used in Brit. Navy] a blue signal flag with a white square in the center, used to announce a ship's sailing, etc.

☆**blue-plate special** (-plāt') an inexpensive restaurant meal served at a fixed price on a large plate, orig. blue, with compartments

☆**blue-point** (-point') *n.* [< *Blue Point*, Long Island, near which beds of such oysters are located] a small oyster, usually eaten raw

blue·print (-print') *n.* **1.** a photographic reproduction in white on a blue background, as of architectural or engineering plans **2.** any exact or detailed plan or outline —*vt.* to make a blueprint of

☆**blue racer** a long, blue-green N. American variety of blacksnake, that can move very rapidly

blue ribbon 1. orig., the blue silk ribbon of the British Order of the Garter **2.** first prize in a competition

blue-rib·bon (-rib'ən) *adj.* [Colloq.] **1.** pre-eminent or outstanding of its kind ☆**2.** designating or of a jury especially selected as for educational background or experience

Blue Ridge Mountains easternmost range of the Appalachians, extending from S Pa. to N Ga.

☆**blue-sky** (-skī') *adj.* [see ff.] of no value; worthless

☆**blue-sky law** [Colloq.] [said to be so named from the comment made by a proponent of the first such law that certain business groups were trying to "capitalize the blue skies"] a law regulating the sale of stocks, bonds, etc., for the protection of the public from fraud

☆**blue-stem** (-stem') *n.* any of various tufted grasses (genus *Andropogon*) grown in the U.S. for hay and forage

blue-stock·ing (-stäk'iŋ) *n.* [from the unconventional blue worsted stockings worn by the leading figure at literary meetings in 18th-c. London] a learned, bookish, or pedantic woman

blue·stone (-stōn') *n.* **1.** a blue-gray sandstone **2.** *same as* COPPER SULFATE

☆**blue streak** [Colloq.] anything regarded as like a streak of lightning in speed, vividness, etc. —**talk a blue streak** to talk much and rapidly

blu·et (blōō'it) *n.* [Fr. *bleuet*, dim. of *bleu*, BLUE] ☆a small plant (*Houstonia caerulea*) of the madder family, having little, pale blue, four-lobed flowers

blue vitriol *same as* COPPER SULFATE

blue·weed (-wēd') *n.* a bristly weed (*Echium vulgare*) with blue flowers and pink buds

blue whale a whalebone whale (*Balaenoptera musculus*) with a gray or blue-gray back and yellowish or grayish belly: the largest animal that ever lived, reaching a length of over 100 ft.

☆**blue-winged teal** (-wiŋd') a small N. American duck (*Anas discors*) found on ponds and rivers

☆**bluff**[1] (bluf) *vt.*, *vi.* [17th c.: prob. < Du. *bluffen* or *verbluffen*, to baffle, mislead] **1.** to mislead or seek to mislead (a person) by a false, bold front **2.** to frighten (a person) by threats that cannot be made good **3.** to manage to get (one's way) by bluffing **4.** *Poker* to try to mislead (other players) by betting or raising the bet while holding poor cards —*n.* **1.** the act or practice of bluffing **2.** a person who bluffs —SYN. see BLUNT —**bluff'er** *n.*

bluff[2] (bluf) *adj.* [orig. a nautical term < Du. *blaf*, flat, broad] **1.** having, or ascending steeply with, a broad, flat front **2.** having a rough and frank but affable manner —*n.* a high, steep, broad-faced bank or cliff —**bluff'ly** *adv.* —**bluff'ness** *n.*

☆**blu·ing** (blōō'iŋ) *n.* a blue liquid, powder, etc. used in rinsing white fabrics to prevent yellowing

blu·ish (-ish) *adj.* somewhat blue

Blum (blōōm), **Le·on** (lā'än) 1872-1950; Fr. socialist statesman

blun·der (blun'dər) *vi.* [ME. *blunderen*, freq. < ON. *blunda*, to shut the eyes, akin to Sw. dial. *blundra*, to do blindly < IE. base *bhlendh-*: see BLEND] **1.** to move clumsily or carelessly; flounder; stumble **2.** to make a foolish or stupid mistake —*vt.* **1.** to say stupidly, clumsily, or confusedly; blurt (*out*) **2.** to do clumsily or poorly; bungle —*n.* a foolish or stupid mistake —SYN. see ERROR —**blun'der·er** *n.* —**blun'der·ing·ly** *adv.*

blun·der·buss (-bus') *n.* [Du. *donderbus*, thunder box; altered after prec.] **1.** an obsolete short gun with a large bore and a broad, flaring muzzle, accurate only at close range **2.** a person who blunders

blunge (blunj) *vt.* blunged, blung'ing [< ? PLUNGE] *Ceramics* to mix (clay) with water —**blung'er** *n.*

blunt (blunt) *adj.* [ME. < ?] **1.** slow to perceive, feel, or understand; dull **2.** having a dull edge or point; not sharp **3.** plain-spoken and abrupt —*vt.* **1.** to make (an edge or point) dull **2.** to make dull or insensitive **3.** to make less effective —*vi.* to develop a dull edge or point —**blunt'ly** *adv.* —**blunt'ness** *n.*

SYN.—**blunt** implies a candor and tactlessness that show little

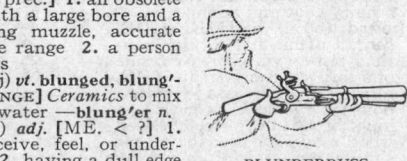

BLUNDERBUSS

regard for another's feelings ["You're a fool," was his *blunt* reply]; **bluff** suggests a coarse heartiness of manner and a good nature that causes the candor to seem inoffensive [a *bluff* old gardener]; **brusque** implies apparent rudeness, as evidenced by abruptness of speech or behavior [a *brusque* rejection]; **curt** suggests a terseness of expression that implies a lack of tact or courtesy [a *curt* dismissal]; **gruff** suggests bad temper and roughness of speech and manner, connoting, in addition, a harshness or throatiness in utterance [a *gruff* sergeant] See also DULL —ANT. suave, tactful

blur (blur) *vt., vi.* **blurred, blur'ring** [16th c.; ? akin to BLEAR] 1. to smear or stain without obliterating; blot; smudge 2. to make or become hazy or indistinct in outline or shape 3. to make or become dim or dull —*n.* 1. the state of being blurred 2. an obscuring stain or blot 3. anything indistinct or hazy to the sight or the mind 4. [Archaic] a moral stain —**blur'ry** *adj.* —**blur'ri·ness** *n.*

☆**blurb** (blurb) *n.* [arbitrary coinage (c. 1907) by Gelett Burgess, "to sound like a publisher"] [Colloq.] an advertisement or announcement, as on a book jacket, esp. one that is highly laudatory —*vi.* to state in a blurb

blurt (blurt) *vt.* [16th–17th c.; prob. of echoic origin] to say suddenly, without stopping to think (with *out*)

blush (blush) *vi.* [ME. *blushen*, to shine brightly, blush, glance < OE. *blyscan*, akin to *blyse*, torch < IE. base *bhles-*, to shine, gleam, whence BLAZE[1]] 1. to become red in the face from shame, embarrassment, or confusion 2. to be ashamed or embarrassed (usually with *at* or *for*) 3. to be or become rosy —*vt.* 1. to reveal by blushing 2. to redden —*n.* 1. a reddening of the face, as from shame 2. a rosy color [the *blush* of youth] —*adj.* rosy [*blush*-pink] —**at first blush** [orig. ME. sense] at first sight; without further consideration —**blush'er** *n.* —**blush'ful** *adj.*

blus·ter (blus'tər) *vi.* [ME. *blustren*, to blow violently < or akin to LowG. *blüstern, blistern;* for IE. base see FLUCTU-ATE] 1. to blow stormily: said of wind 2. to speak or conduct oneself in a noisy, swaggering, or bullying manner —*vt.* 1. to force by blustering; bully 2. to say noisily and aggressively —*n.* 1. stormy blowing or noisy commotion 2. noisy swaggering or bullying talk —**blus'ter·er** *n.* — **blus'ter·ing·ly** *adv.* —**blus'ter·y, blus'ter·ous** *adj.*

blvd. boulevard

BM 1. bench mark 2. [Colloq.] bowel movement

b.m. board measure

B.M.E. Bachelor of Mining Engineering

B.Mech.E. Bachelor of Mechanical Engineering

B.M.E.W.S. Ballistic Missile Early Warning System

BMOC, B.M.O.C. big man on (the) campus

BMR basal metabolic rate

B.Mus. Bachelor of Music

Bn., bn. battalion

B.N., b.n. bank note

☆**bo, 'bo** (bō) *n., pl.* **bos** or **boes, 'bos** or **'boes** [Slang] a hobo

BO, B.O. 1. body odor 2. box office

B/O, B/o *Bookkeeping* brought over

b.o. 1. back order 2. bad order 3. branch office 4. broker's order 5. buyer's option

bo·a (bō'ə) *n.* [L., a large water serpent] 1. any of a number of tropical and subtropical snakes (family Boidae) that crush their prey in their coils, as the anaconda, boa constrictor, etc. 2. a woman's long scarf, as of fur or feathers, worn around the neck or shoulders

Bo·ab·dil (bō'əb dēl') [born *Abu-Abdullah;* ruled as *Mohammed XI*) ?–1538?; last Moorish king of Granada

boa constrictor a species of boa (*Constrictor constrictor*), pale brown with dark crossbars, which reaches a length of 10–15 feet

Bo·ad·i·ce·a (bō'ad ə sē'ə) ?–62 A.D.; queen of the Iceni in ancient Britain, who led a vain revolt against the Romans (61 A.D.)

Bo·a·ner·ges (bō'ə nur'jēz) [LL. (Vulgate) < Gr. (NT.) *boanerges;* prob. ult. < Heb. *b'nāi regesh,* sons of wrath] the Apostles John and James: an epithet used by Jesus: Mark 3:17

boar (bôr) *n., pl.* **boars, boar:** see PLURAL, II, D, 1 [ME. *bor* < OE. *bar;* akin to G. (dial.) *bär,* Du. *beer;* only in WGmc.] 1. an uncastrated male hog or pig 2. a wild hog (*Sus scrofa*) of Europe, Africa, and Asia, with a hairy coat and a long snout

board (bôrd) *n.* [ME. & OE. *bord,* a plank, flat surface (nautical senses via OFr. *bord,* side of a ship < Gmc. cognate of OE. form) < IE. base *bhrdho-,* board < *bheredh-,* to cut] 1. a long, broad, flat piece of sawed wood ready for use; thin plank 2. a flat piece of wood or similar material, often rectangular, for some special use [a *checkerboard,* bulletin *board,* ironing *board,* diving *board*] 3. *a)* any of various construction materials manufactured in thin, flat, rectangular sheets [*fiberboard*] *b)* pasteboard or stiff paper, often used for book covers 4. *a)* a table for meals, esp. when spread with food *b)* food served at a table; esp., meals provided regularly for pay 5. a council table 6. a group of persons who manage or control a business, school system, etc.; council [a *board* of trade, *board* of education] ☆7. *a)* a posted or printed list of the stocks sold, and their prices, on a particular stock exchange

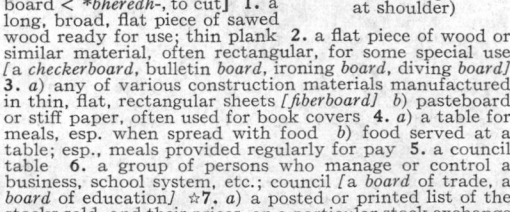

BOAR
(36 in. high
at shoulder)

b) the stock exchange listing these stocks 8. the side of a ship: usually in compounds [*overboard*] 9. a rim, border, or coast: now only in *seaboard* 10. *Naut. a)* a course sailed against the wind; tack *b)* the distance made in a single tack ☆11. *Basketball* a backboard 12. [*pl.*] *Hockey* the sideboards —*vt.* 1. to cover or close (*up*) with boards 2. to provide with meals, or room and meals, regularly for pay 3. to put (a person) where board is supplied 4. to come alongside (a ship) esp. with hostile purpose 5. to come over the rail and onto the deck of (a ship) ☆6. to get on (a train, bus, etc.) 7. [Obs.] to accost —*vi.* to receive meals, or room and meals, regularly for pay —☆**across the board** 1. *Horse Racing* to win, place, and show: said of betting 2. including or affecting all classes or groups —**go by the board** 1. to fall or be swept overboard 2. to be got rid of, lost, ruined, etc. —**on board** 1. on or in a ship ☆2. on or in an aircraft, bus, etc. —**the boards** the stage (of a theater)

board·er (bôr'dər) *n.* 1. a person who regularly gets his meals, or room and meals, at another's home for pay 2. a person who boards a ship, aircraft, etc., esp. one of the crew detailed to board a hostile ship

☆**board foot** *pl.* **board feet** a unit of measure of lumber, equal to a board one foot square and one inch thick

board·ing (bôr'diŋ) *n.* 1. a structure or covering of boards 2. boards collectively; light timber

board·ing·house (-hous') *n.* a house where meals, or room and meals, can be had for pay: also **boarding house**

boarding school a school providing lodging and meals for the pupils: cf. DAY SCHOOL

☆**board measure** measurement of lumber in board feet

board of health a local government agency that supervises public health

board of trade ☆1. *same as* CHAMBER OF COMMERCE 2. [B- T-] a British governmental department supervising commerce and industry 3. a commodities exchange dealing in grain, etc.

☆**board room** a room in which a board of administrators or directors regularly holds meetings

☆**board rule** a measuring device with a graduated scale for finding out quickly how many board feet there are in a quantity of lumber

☆**board·walk** (bôrd'wôk') *n.* 1. a walk made of thick boards 2. a walk, often made of wood and elevated, placed along a beach or sea front

boar·fish (bôr'fish') *n., pl.* **-fish', -fish'es:** see FISH[2] any of various fishes with a projecting snout like a boar's

boar·hound (-hound') *n.* a great Dane or other large dog used in hunting wild boar

boar·ish (-ish) *adj.* like a boar; swinish, fierce, etc.

Bo·as (bō'az, -as), **Franz** (fränts) 1858–1942; U.S. anthropologist, born in Germany

boast[1] (bōst) *vi.* [ME. *bosten < bost, n. <* Anglo-Fr.] 1. to talk about deeds, abilities, etc., either one's own or those of someone close to one, in a manner showing too much pride and satisfaction; brag 2. to be vainly proud; exult —*vt.* 1. to brag about 2. to glory in having or doing (something); be proud of [the town *boasts* a fine new library] —*n.* 1. the act of one who boasts 2. anything boasted of —**boast'er** *n.* —**boast'ing·ly** *adv.*

SYN.—**boast,** the basic term in this list, merely suggests pride or satisfaction, as in one's deeds or abilities [you may well *boast* of your efficiency]; **brag** suggests greater ostentation and overstatement [he *bragged* of what he would do in the race]; **vaunt,** a formal, literary term, implies greater suavity but more vainglory than either of the preceding [*vaunt* not in your triumph]; **swagger** suggests a proclaiming of one's superiority in an insolent or overbearing way; **crow** suggests loud boasting in exultation or triumph [stop *crowing* over your victory]

boast[2] (bōst) *vt.* [< ?] to do preliminary shaping on (sculpture, stonework, etc.) with a broad chisel

boast·ful (-fəl) *adj.* inclined to brag; boasting —**boast'ful·ly** *adv.* —**boast'ful·ness** *n.*

boat (bōt) *n.* [ME. *bot <* OE. *bat <* IE. base *bheid-,* to split (in the sense "hollowed-out tree trunk"): cf. FISSURE] 1. a small, open vessel or watercraft propelled by oars, sails, or engine 2. a large vessel; ship: landsman's term 3. a boat-shaped dish [a gravy *boat*] —*vt.* to lay or carry in the boat [*boat* the oars] —*vi.* to go in a boat; row, sail, or cruise —**in the same boat** in the same unfavorable situation —**miss the boat** [Colloq.] to fail to make the most of an opportunity —☆**rock the boat** [Colloq.] to disturb or challenge the status quo

boat-billed heron (bōt'bild') a nocturnal, tropical American wading bird (*Cochlearius cochlearius*) found near fresh water and related to the night herons: it has a large, broad bill

boat·er (-ər) *n.* [BOAT + -ER: orig. worn when boating] a stiff hat of braided straw, with a flat crown and brim and a wide hatband

boat·hook (-hook') *n.* a long pole with a metal hook on one end, for maneuvering boats, logs, or rafts

boat·house (-hous') *n.* a building for storing a boat or boats, sometimes equipped with recreational facilities

boat·ing (-iŋ) *n.* the act or recreation of rowing, sailing, or cruising

boat·load (-lōd') *n.* 1. all the freight or passengers that a boat can carry or contain 2. the load carried by a boat

boat·man (-mən) *n., pl.* **-men** (-mən) a man who operates, works on, rents, or sells boats —**boat'man·ship'** *n.*

☆**boat neck** a bateau neckline —**boat′necked′** *adj.*

boat·swain (bō′s'n) *n.* a ship's warrant officer or petty officer in charge of the deck crew, the rigging, anchors, boats, etc.

boat train a train scheduled to be at a port in time for prompt transfer of passengers to or from a ship

Bo·az (bō′az) [Heb. *bō′az,* lit., swiftness] *Bible* Ruth's second husband: Ruth 4:13

bob[1] (bäb) *n.* [ME. *bobbe,* hanging cluster; senses 6–9, 11 < the *v.,* 10 < *bobsled,* etc.] **1.** [Brit. Dial.] a hanging cluster **2.** any knoblike hanging weight or pendant [a plumb *bob]* **3.** a short curl or knob of hair **4.** a docked tail, as of a horse **5.** a woman's or girl's short haircut **6.** a quick, jerky motion, like that of a cork on water **7.** *a)* a float on a fishing line *b)* clustered bait used on a fishing line **8.** a type of Scottish dance **9.** a quick curtsy ☆**10.** a bobsled or bob skate **11.** [Archaic] a tap or light blow **12.** [Archaic] a short refrain in a song —*vt.* **bobbed, bob′bing** [ME. *bobben,* to knock against; also < *bobbe,* hanging cluster] **1.** to knock against lightly; rap **2.** to make move up and down with short, jerky motions **3.** to cut (hair, a tail, etc.) short; dock —*vi.* **1.** to move or act in a bobbing manner; move suddenly or jerkily **2.** to curtsy quickly **3.** to fish with a bob **4.** to try to catch suspended or floating fruit with the teeth (with *for)* —**bob up** to come up unexpectedly; appear suddenly

bob[2] (bäb) *n., pl.* **bob** [< ? *Bob,* nickname for ROBERT] [Brit. Slang] a shilling

bob·ber (bäb′ər) *n.* **1.** a person or thing that bobs **2.** a float for a fishing line

bob·ber·y (bäb′ər ē) *n., pl.* **-ber·ies** [Anglo-Ind. < Hind. *bāp-rē,* O father!, exclamation of sorrow or surprise] a hubbub or commotion

bob·bin (bäb′in) *n.* [Fr. *bobine < bobiner,* to wind] **1.** a reel or spool for thread or yarn, used in spinning, weaving, machine sewing, etc. **2.** a small notched pin of wood, bone, or ivory, used in making bobbin lace

bob·bi·net (bäb′ə net′, bäb′ə net′) *n.* [< BOBBIN + NET[1]] a machine-made netted fabric of hexagonal mesh

bobbin lace a lace whose design is laid out on a pillowlike pad with pins around which thread is drawn and interlaced by means of bobbins

bob·ble (bäb′'l) *n.* [freq. of BOB[1], *v.*] **1.** a bobbing, up-and-down movement **2.** any of the tufted balls forming a decorative fringe, as on a tablecloth ☆**3.** [Colloq.] an awkward mistake; error; specif., *Sports* an awkward juggling of the ball in trying to catch or hold on to it —*vi.* **-bled, -bling 1.** to move jerkily; bob ☆**2.** [Colloq.] to make an error —*vt.* [Colloq.] to deal with awkwardly or unskillfully; specif., to make a bobble with (a ball); muff; bungle

bob·by (bäb′ē) *n., pl.* **-bies** [after Sir Robert (*Bobby*) Peel (1788–1850), who reorganized the London police force] [Brit. Colloq.] a policeman

☆**bobby pin** [from use with *bobbed* hair] a small metal hairpin with the sides pressing close together

☆**bobby socks** (or **sox**) [< BOB[1] (*vt.* 3)] [Colloq.] girls' socks that reach just above the ankle

☆**bob·by·sox·er, bob·by·sox·er** (-säk′sər) *n.* [< the prec.] [Colloq.] a girl in her early teens, esp. one who conforms to current adolescent fads

☆**bob·cat** (bäb′kat′) *n., pl.* **-cats′, -cat′:** see PLURAL, II, D, 1 [so called from its short tail] *same as* BAY LYNX

‡**bo·bèche** (bō besh′) *n.* [Fr.] a disk of glass, metal, etc. with a center hole, placed across the top of a candlestick to catch the candle drippings

☆**bob·o·link** (bäb′ə liŋk′) *n.* [earlier *boblincoln:* echoic, after its call] a migratory songbird (*Dolichonyx oryzivorus*) of N. American fields and meadows

☆**bob skate** a skate with two parallel runners

☆**bob·sled** (bäb′sled′) *n.* **1.** formerly, a long sled made of two short sleds joined together, or either of the short sleds **2.** a long sled that has two sets of runners one behind the other and is equipped with steering apparatus and brakes, ridden down a prepared run by a team of four or two men in a race against time —*vi.* **-sled′ded, -sled′ding** to ride or race on a bobsled

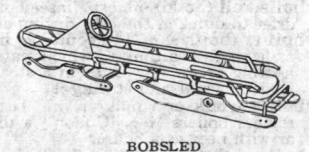

BOBSLED

bob·stay (-stā′) *n.* a rope or chain for tying down a bowsprit to keep the ship from bobbing

bob·tail (-tāl′) *n.* **1.** a tail cut short; docked tail **2.** a horse or dog with a bobtail —*adj.* **1.** having a bobtail **2.** cut short; abbreviated —*vt.* **1.** to dock the tail of **2.** to cut short; curtail

☆**bob·white** (bäb′hwīt′, -wīt′) *n., pl.* **-whites′, -white′:** see PLURAL, II, D, 1 [echoic, after its call] a small N. American quail (*Colinus virginianus*) having markings of brown and white on a gray body; partridge

☆**boc·cac·cio** (bə kä′chō) *n.* [It. *boccaccio < boccaccia,* large mouth, disparaging dim. of *bocca,* mouth < L. *bucca]* a

large-mouthed marine rockfish (*Sebastodes paucispinis*) found along the California coast

Boc·cac·cio (bō kä′chē ō′; *It.* bô kät′chō), **Gio·van·ni** (jō vän′nē) 1313–75; It. author of the *Decameron*

Boc·che·ri·ni (bō′ke rē′nē; *E.* bōk′ə rē′nē), **Lu·i·gi** (loō ē′jē) 1743–1805; It. composer

boc·cie, boc·ce, boc·ci (bäch′ē) *n.* [It. *bocce,* (wooden) balls, pl. of *boccia,* akin to Fr. *bosse:* see BOSS[2]] an Italian game similar to bowls, usually played on a long clay court, or alley

Boc·cio·ni (bôt chō′nē), **Um·ber·to** (oom ber′tō) 1882–1916; It. futurist painter & sculptor

Boche (bôsh, bäsh; *Fr.* bôsh) *n., pl.* **Boch′es** (-iz; *Fr.* bôsh) [Fr. slang, contr. < *tête de caboche,* hard head, head of cabbage (see CABBAGE[1]) [*also* b-] a German, esp. a German soldier in World War I: hostile term

Bo·chum (bō′khoom) city in North Rhine-Westphalia, W West Germany, in the Ruhr valley: pop. 358,000

☆**bock** (bäk) *n.* [G. < *bockbier,* contr. < *oanbock-, ambock-,* Bavarian dial. pronun. of *Einbecker bier < Einbeck,* Hanover, where first brewed] a dark beer traditionally drunk in the early spring: also **bock beer**

bode[1] (bōd) *vt.* **bod′ed, bod′ing** [ME. *bodien < OE. bodian < boda,* messenger, prob. < IE. base of BID[1]] **1.** to be an omen of; presage **2.** [Archaic] to announce in advance; predict —**bode ill** (or **well**) to be a bad (or good) omen

bode[2] *archaic pt. of* BIDE

bo·de·ga (bō dā′gə, -dē′-) *n.* [Sp., a grocery shop, wine cellar < L. *apotheca:* see APOTHECARY] **1.** a small grocery store **2.** a wine shop

Bo·den·heim (bōd′'n hīm′), **Maxwell** 1893–1954; U.S. poet & novelist

Bo·den·see, Boden See (bō′dən zā′) *Ger. names of* Lake CONSTANCE

bo·dhi·satt·va (bō′də sut′və) *n.* [Sans., lit., one enlightened in essence < *bodhi,* enlightenment (< IE. base *bheudh-,* to be alert, recognize, whence OE. *beodan,* to command: see BID[1]) + *saliva,* being, existence (< IE. *sent-,* participial stem of base *es-,* to be, whence IS)] *Buddhism* a person who has achieved great moral and spiritual wisdom and is a potential Buddha, esp. such a person who rejects nirvana in order to assist suffering mankind

bod·ice (bäd′is) *n.* [altered < *bodies,* pl. of BODY, in obs. sense of "part of dress above the waist"] **1.** the upper part of a woman's dress **2.** a kind of vest worn over a blouse or dress by women or girls, usually laced in front **3.** [Archaic] a corset; stays

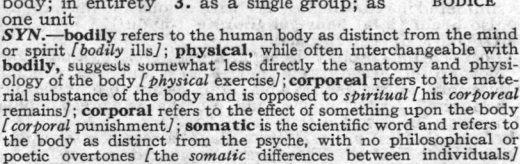

BODICE

bod·ied (-ēd) *adj.* having a body or substance, esp. of a specified kind [able-*bodied,* full-*bodied* flavor]

bod·i·less (-ē lis) *adj.* without a body; having no material substance; incorporeal

bod·i·ly (-'l ē) *adj.* [ME. *bodilich < bodi,* BODY] **1.** physical: opposed to MENTAL[1] **2.** of, in, by, or to the body —*adv.* **1.** in person; in the flesh [to be *bodily* present] **2.** as a single body; in entirety **3.** as a single group; as one unit

SYN.—**bodily** refers to the human body as distinct from the mind or spirit [bodily ills]; **physical,** while often interchangeable with **bodily,** suggests somewhat less directly the anatomy and physiology of the body [*physical* exercise]; **corporeal** refers to the material substance of the body and is opposed to *spiritual* [his *corporeal* remains]; **corporal** refers to the effect of something upon the body [*corporal* punishment]; **somatic** is the scientific word and refers to the body as distinct from the psyche, with no philosophical or poetic overtones [the *somatic* differences between individuals] —ANT. **mental, psychic, spiritual**

bod·ing (bō′diŋ) *n.* [ME. *bodynge, bodunge < OE. bodung < bodian,* BODE[1]] an omen; foreboding —*adj.* ominous; foreboding —**bod′ing·ly** *adv.*

bod·kin (bäd′k'n) *n.* [ME. *boidekyn, bodekin < ?*] **1.** a pointed instrument for making holes in cloth **2.** a long, ornamental hairpin **3.** a thick, blunt needle for drawing ribbon or tape through openwork **4.** [Obs.] a dagger or stiletto **5.** *Printing* a kind of awl for picking out letters from set type

Bod·lei·an (bäd′lē ən, bäd lē′ən) *adj.* [after Sir Thomas *Bodley* (1545–1613), Eng. statesman & scholar who restored it] designating or of the Oxford University library

Bo·do·ni (bə dō′nē) *n.* a style of type designed by the Italian printer, Giambattista Bodoni (1740–1813)

bod·y (bäd′ē) *n., pl.* **bod′ies** [ME. *bodi, bodig < OE. bodig,* trunk, chest, orig. sense "cask," akin to MLowG. *boddike,* tub for brewing, OHG. *botah,* prob. < It. *bottega,* shop < L. *apotheca,* storehouse, esp. storeroom for wine: see APOTHECARY] **1.** the whole physical structure and substance of a man, animal, or plant **2.** *a)* the trunk or torso of a man or animal *b)* the part of a garment that covers the trunk **3.** a dead person; corpse **4.** the flesh or material substance, as opposed to the spirit **5.** [Colloq.] a human being; person **6.** a group of people or things regarded or functioning as a unit [a *body* of soldiers, an advisory *body*] **7.** the majority

of a number of people or things **8.** the main or central part of anything; specif., *a)* the part of an automobile, truck, etc. that holds the load or passengers; part of a vehicle that is not the chassis *b)* the hull of a ship *c)* the fuselage of an aircraft *d)* the main part of a piece of writing as distinguished from headings and introductory or supplementary matter *e)* the sound box of a stringed instrument **9.** anything having real or material substance or form; any physical or perceptible object **10.** any of the natural objects seen in the visible heavens [the sun, moon, planets, stars, etc. are heavenly *bodies*] **11.** a separate portion or mass of matter [a *body* of land or water] **12.** substance, density, or consistency, as of a liquid, fabric, etc. **13.** richness of tone or flavor **14.** *Law* a person or something legally regarded as a person **15.** *Printing* the shank of a type —*vt.* **bod′ied, bod′y·ing 1.** to give a body or substance to; make substantial **2.** to make part of; embody —**body forth 1.** to give shape or form to **2.** to symbolize or represent —**keep body and soul together** to stay alive (in adverse circumstances)
SYN.—**body** refers to the whole physical substance of a person or animal, whether dead or alive; **corpse** and the euphemistic **remains** refer to a dead human body; **carcass** is used of the dead body of an animal or, contemptuously, of a human being; **cadaver** refers primarily to a dead human body used for dissection in medical studies
body check *Hockey* the act, variously legal or illegal, of checking the progress of the puck-carrier by bumping him with the body —**bod′y-check′** *vt., vi.*
body corporate *Law* a corporation
☆**body English** [cf. ENGLISH, sense 6] a follow-through motion of the body, as after bowling a ball, in a semi-involuntary or joking effort to control the ball's movement
bod·y·guard (-gärd′) *n.* a person or group of persons, usually armed, assigned to guard someone
body politic the people who collectively constitute a political unit under a government
body snatcher a person who steals corpses from graves, as formerly to sell them for anatomical dissection
body stocking a tightfitting garment, usually of one piece, that covers the torso and, sometimes, the legs
boehm·ite (bām′īt) *n.* [G. *böhmit*, after J. *Böhm*, 20th-c. mineralogist] a crystalline mineral, hydrous aluminum oxide, AlO(OH), commonly present in bauxite
Boe·o·ti·a (bē ō′shə, -shē ə) province of EC Greece, northwest of Attica: c. 1,100 sq. mi.; pop. 114,000: in ancient times, a region dominated by the city of Thebes
Boe·o·tian (-shən) *adj.* of or like Boeotia or its people, who were reputed to be dull and stupid —*n.* **1.** a native or inhabitant of Boeotia **2.** a dull, stupid person
Boer (bôr, boor, bō′ər) *n.* [Du. *boer*, peasant: see BOOR] a South African whose ancestors were Dutch colonists —*adj.* of the Boers
Boer War a war (1899–1902) in which Great Britain defeated the Boers of South Africa
Bo·e·thi·us (bō ē′thē əs), (**Anicus Manlius Severinus**) 480?–524? A.D.; Roman philosopher
‡**boeuf bour·gui·gnon** (bĕf boor gē nyôn′) [Fr., beef of Burgundy] a dish consisting of seasoned cubes of beef simmered in red wine together with onions and mushrooms: also **boeuf (à la) bour·gui·gnonne′** (-nyôn′)
BOF basic oxygen furnace
☆**boff** (bäf) *n.* [prob. < It. *buffa*, a jest, or *buffo*, a puff, gust of wind: cf. BUFFOON] [Slang] **1.** *a)* a loud, hearty laugh *b)* a joke, an incident in a play, etc. meant to produce such a laugh **2.** a play, movie, song, etc. that is a great popular success; hit Also **bof·fo·la** (bə fō′lə)
bof·fin (bäf′in) *n.* [< ?] [Brit. Slang] a research scientist
☆**bof·fo** (bäf′ō) *adj.* [Slang] very popular or successful —*n.* [Slang] a boff
bog (bäg, bôg) *n.* [< Gael. & Ir. *bog*, soft, moist (Ir. *bogach*, a bog)] wet, spongy ground; a small marsh or swamp —*vt., vi.* **bogged, bog′ging** to sink or become stuck in or as in a bog (often with *down*); mire
bog asphodel any of several plants (genus *Narthecium*) of the lily family, esp. a yellow-blossomed, grasslike wildflower (*Narthecium americanum*) found in bogs
bog·bean (bäg′bēn′, bôg′-) *n. same as* BUCKBEAN
bo·gey (bō′gē) *n., pl.* **-geys 1.** *same as* BOGY¹ ☆**2.** [after Col. *Bogey*, imaginary partner assumed to play a first-rate game] *Golf a)* par, esp. for an average player *b)* now usually, one stroke more than par on a hole —☆*vt.* **-geyed, -gey·ing** *Golf* to score one over par on (a hole)
bog·gle (bäg′'l) *vi.* **-gled, -gling** [< Scot. *bogle*, specter; prob. < ME. *bugge*, specter (as in BUGBEAR); now associated with BUNGLE] **1.** to be startled or frightened (*at*) **2.** to hesitate (*at*); have scruples **3.** to equivocate; quibble (with *at*) **4.** to bungle or botch —*n.* **1.** an act or instance of boggling **2.** *same as* BOGLE
bog·gy (bäg′ē, bôg′-) *adj.* **-gi·er, -gi·est 1.** like a bog; marshy **2.** full of bogs —**bog′gi·ness** *n.*
bo·gie¹ (bō′gē) *n., pl.* **-gies 1.** *same as* BOGY¹ ☆**2.** *same as* BOGEY (sense 2)
bo·gie² (bō′gē) *n., pl.* **-gies** [< North Brit. Dial.] **1.** a low, swiveled undercarriage at either end of a railroad car **2.** any wheel of the several pairs supporting the tread of an armored tank or tractor **3.** [North Brit. Dial.] a low, heavy cart or truck
bo·gle (bō′g'l) *n.* [see BOGGLE] a bogy, or goblin

bog oak the wood of oak found preserved in peat bogs
Bo·gor (bō′gôr) city in W Java, Indonesia: pop. 147,000
Bo·go·tá (bō′gə tä′) capital of Colombia, in the central part of the country, on an Andean plateau: pop. 1,697,000
bog·trot·ter (bäg′trät′ər, bôg′-) *n.* a person who lives in or wanders among bogs
☆**bo·gus** (bō′gəs) *adj.* [orig. (slang), counterfeiter's apparatus: < ?] not genuine; spurious —*SYN.* see FALSE
bog·wood (bäg′wood, bôg′-) *n.* a black, heavy wood from certain trees preserved in peat bogs
bo·gy¹ (bō′gē, boog′ē) *n., pl.* **-gies** [see BOGGLE & BUG²] **1.** an imaginary evil being or spirit; goblin **2.** anything one especially, and often needlessly, fears; bugbear
bo·gy² (bō′gē) *n., pl.* **-gies** *same as* BOGIE²
bo·gy·man, bo·gey·man (bō′gē man′, boog′ē-) *n., pl.* **-men′** (-men′) an imaginary frightful being, esp. one used as a threat to children in disciplining them
Bo·he·mi·a (bō hē′mē ə) region, formerly a province, of W Czechoslovakia: earlier, a kingdom, then a province of Austria-Hungary —*n.* [often b-] **1.** Bohemians (sense 4) collectively **2.** community of such people
Bo·he·mi·an (-ən) *n.* **1.** a native or inhabitant of Bohemia **2.** *same as* CZECH (*n.* 2) **3.** [Fr. *Bohémien:* from the fact that the gypsies passed through Bohemia to reach W Europe] a gypsy **4.** [often b-] a person, esp. an artist, poet, etc., who lives in an unconventional, nonconforming way —*adj.* **1.** of Bohemia, its people, or their language; Czech **2.** [often b-] like or characteristic of a Bohemian (*n.* 4) —**Bo·he′mi·an·ism** *n.*
Bohemian Forest wooded mountain region along the border between Bohemia & Bavaria
Böh·me (bö′mə), **Ja·kob** (yä′kôp) 1575–1624; Ger. theosophist & mystic: also **Böhm** (böm)
Böh·mer·wald, Böh·mer Wald (bö′mər vält′) *Ger. name of* BOHEMIAN FOREST
Bo·hol (bə hôl′) island in the SC Philippines, between Cebu & Leyte: 1,492 sq. mi.
Bohr (bôr), **Niels (Henrik David)** (nēlz) 1885–1962; Dan. nuclear & theoretical physicist
Bohr theory a theory, proposed by Niels Bohr in 1913, stating that electrons revolve in definite orbits around a nucleus, and that radiation is absorbed or emitted only when an electron is transferred from one orbit to another
Bo·iar·do (bō yär′dō), **Mat·te·o Ma·ri·a** (mät tā′ō mä rē′ä) 1434?–94; It. poet
boil¹ (boil) *vi.* [ME. *boilen* < OFr. *boillir* < L. *bullire* < *bulla*, a bubble, knob, prob. < IE. base *bu-l-, to blow up, cause to swell] **1.** to bubble up and vaporize by being heated **2.** to reach the vaporizing stage **3.** to seethe or churn when boiling liquids **4.** to be agitated, as with rage **5.** to cook in boiling water or other liquid —*vt.* **1.** to heat to the boiling point **2.** to cook, process, or separate in boiling water or other liquid —*n.* the act or state of boiling —**boil away** to evaporate as a result of boiling —**boil down 1.** to lessen in quantity by boiling **2.** to make more terse; condense; summarize —**boil over 1.** to come to a boil and spill over the rim **2.** to lose one's temper; get excited
SYN.—**boil,** the basic word, refers to the vaporization of a liquid over direct heat or, metaphorically, to great agitation, as with rage [it made my blood *boil]*; **seethe** suggests violent boiling with much bubbling and foaming or, in an extended sense, violent excitement [the country *seethed* with rebellion]; **simmer** implies a gentle, continuous cooking at or just below the boiling point or, metaphorically, imminence of eruption, as in anger or revolt; **stew** refers to slow, prolonged boiling or, in an extended colloquial sense, unrest caused by worry or anxiety
boil² (boil) *n.* [orig., & still dial., *bile* < ME. *byle* < OE. *byle, byl* (akin to G. *beule*) < IE. base of prec.] an inflamed, painful, pus-filled swelling on the skin, caused by infection
Boi·leau-Des·pré·aux (bwä lō′dā prā ō′), **Ni·co·las** (nē kô lä′) 1636–1711; Fr. critic & poet: also **Boileau**
boiled oil (boild) oil, esp. linseed oil, heated, with an added drier to quicken the oil's drying action in paints
boil·er (boi′lər) *n.* **1.** a container in which things are boiled or heated **2.** a tank in which water is turned to steam for heating or for power, as in a steam engine **3.** a tank for heating water and storing it
boil·er·mak·er (-māk′ər) *n.* **1.** a worker who makes or repairs boilers ☆**2.** [Colloq.] a drink of whiskey in beer or with beer as a chaser
boil·er·plate (-plāt′) *n.* **1.** steel rolled in large flat plates, used in making steam boilers ☆**2.** [Colloq.] the stereotyped news, feature, and editorial items that are syndicated to small publications: also **boiler plate**
boiler suit [Brit.] overalls or coveralls
boiling point the temperature at which a specified liquid boils; temperature at which the vapor pressure of a specified liquid equals the atmospheric pressure: water at sea level boils at 212°F or 100°C, but a change in external pressure raises or lowers its boiling point
Bois de Bou·logne (bwäd boo lôn′y′; E. bwä′ də boo lōn′) park on the W outskirts of Paris
Boi·se (boi′sē, -zē) [< Fr. *boisé*, wooded] capital of Ida., in the SW part: pop. 75,000: also **Boise City**
bois·ter·ous (bois′tər əs) *adj.* [ME. *boistreous*, crude, coarse, altered < *boistous*, unmannerly, violent < ? OFr. *boisteus*, limping, rough] **1.** rough and stormy; turbulent **2.** *a)* noisy and unruly; rowdy *b)* noisy and lively; loud and exuberant **3.** [Obs.] rough, coarse, or bulky —*SYN.*

see VOCIFEROUS—**bois′ter·ous·ly** adv.—**bois′ter·ous·ness** n.

‡**boîte** (bwȧt) n. [Fr., lit., box] a small nightclub or cabaret

Boj·er (boi′ər), **Jo·han** (yō hän′) 1872–1959; Norw. novelist & playwright

Bok (bäk), **Edward William** 1863–1930; U.S. editor & writer, born in the Netherlands

Bo·kha·ra (bō khä′rä; E. bō kär′ə) same as BUKHARA

Bol. 1. Bolivia 2. Bolivian

bo·la (bō′lə) n. [Sp., a ball < L. bulla, a bubble: see BOIL¹] a weapon made of a long cord or thong with heavy balls at the ends, used for throwing at and entangling cattle, etc.: also **bo′las** (-ləs)

bold (bōld) adj. [ME. < OE. beald, bold, brave, akin to G. bald: orig. sense, "swollen up" < IE. base *bhel-: see BALL¹] 1. showing a readiness to take risks or face danger; daring; fearless 2. too free in behavior or manner; taking liberties; impudent; shameless 3. steep or abrupt, as a cliff 4. prominent and clear; striking and sharp [to write a bold hand] 5. printed in boldface 6. forceful in expression 7. [Obs.] confident —SYN. see BRAVE —**make bold** to be so bold as (to); dare —**bold′ly** adv. —**bold′ness** n.

BOLA

bold·face (bōld′fās′) n. a type with a heavy, dark face: the words listed in this dictionary are in boldface

bold·faced (-fāst′) adj. 1. impudent or forward in manner 2. printed in boldface

bole¹ (bōl) n. [ME. bol < ON. bolr < IE. base *bhl-, var. of *bhel-, to swell up: see BALL¹] a tree trunk

bole² (bōl) n. [ME. & OFr. bol < ML. bolus, clay < Gr. bōlos, lump of earth] a variety of easily pulverized, reddish clay —**bo·lar** (bō′lər) adj.

bo·lec·tion (bō lek′shən) n. [< ?] Archit. a molding that projects beyond the surface of a panel

bo·le·ro (bə ler′ō, bō-) n., pl. -ros [Sp. < bola, a ball < OFr. boule < L. bulla, bubble: see BOIL¹] 1. a Spanish dance done to castanets and lively music in 3/4 time 2. the music for this dance 3. a sleeveless or sleeved jacket that ends at the waist and is open at the front

bo·le·tus (bə lēt′əs) n. [L. < ?] any of a genus (Boletus) of fleshy fungi, with thick stems and caps, often brightly colored

Bol·eyn (bool′in, bə lin′), **Anne** 1507?–36; 2d wife of Henry VIII of England: mother of ELIZABETH I

bo·lide (bō′līd, -lid) n. [Fr. < L. bolidis, gen. of bolis, fiery meteor < Gr. bolis, missile, arrow] a brilliant shooting meteor, esp. one that explodes

Bol·ing·broke (bäl′iŋ brook′, bōl′iŋ brŏk′), first Viscount, (born Henry St. John) 1678–1751; Eng. statesman & political writer

bo·li·var (bä lē′vər; Sp. bō lē′vär), n., pl. **bo·li·var·es** (bō′li·vä′res), **bo·li′vars** [after ff.] the monetary unit of Venezuela: see MONETARY UNITS, table

Bol·í·var (bäl′ə vər; Sp. bō lē′vär), **Si·món** (sī′mən; Sp. sē mōn′) 1783–1830; S. American general & revolutionary leader, born in Caracas: hero of S. American fight for independence from Spain

Bo·liv·i·a (bə liv′ē ə) inland country in WC S. America: 424,000 sq. mi.; pop. 3,748,000; capitals, La Paz & Sucre —**Bo·liv′i·an** adj., n.

bo·liv·i·a (bə liv′ē ə) n. [< prec.] a soft woolen cloth resembling plush

bo·liv·i·a·no (bə liv′ē ä′nō; Sp. bō lē′vyä′nō) n., pl. -nos [AmSp. < BOLIVIA] the former monetary unit of Bolivia: replaced (1963) by the PESO BOLIVIANO

boll (bōl) n. [ME. bolle, boll, BOWL¹] the roundish seed pod of a plant, esp. of cotton or flax

bol·lard (bäl′ərd) n. [< ?] a strong post on a ship or dock, for holding a hawser fast

bol·lix (bäl′iks) vt. [euphemistic respelling of nautical slang < ME. ballokes < OE. beallucas, testicles (akin to BALL¹), used as an extension of BALL¹) ☆[Slang] to make a muddle of; bungle; botch (usually with up)

☆**boll weevil** a small, grayish weevil (Anthonomus grandis) with a long beak, whose larvae, when hatched in the immature bolls of cotton plants, destroy the bolls

☆**boll·worm** (bōl′wurm′) n. 1. a kind of moth larva (Platyedra gossypiella) that feeds on cotton bolls, ears of corn, tomatoes, etc. 2. same as CORN EARWORM

bo·lo (bō′lō) n., pl. -los [Sp. < native name] a large, single-edged knife used in the Philippines as a weapon or cutting tool; kind of machete

Bo·lo·gna (bə lō′nyä; E. bə lō′nə) commune in NC Italy, at the foot of the Apennines: pop. 482,000 —n. [usually b-] (bə lō′nē; occas. -nyə, -nə) a large, smoked sausage of beef, pork, or veal, or of a mixture of these: also **bologna sausage**

Bo·lo·gnese (bō′lə nēz′, -nyēz′) n., pl. -gnese′ a native or inhabitant of Bologna —adj. of Bologna, its people, or their dialect

☆**bo·lo·graph** (bō′lə graf′, -gräf′) n. [bolo- (as in ff.) + -GRAPH] a record of variations registered by a bolometer —**bo′lo·graph′ic** adj.

☆**bo·lom·e·ter** (bō läm′ə tər) n. [< Gr. bolē, ray, lit., something thrown < ballein, to throw + -METER] Physics a very sensitive instrument for measuring and recording the intensity of small amounts of radiant energy —**bo·lo·met·ric** (bō′lə met′rik) adj. —**bo′lo·met′ri·cal·ly** adv.

☆**bo·lo·ney** (bə lō′nē) n. same as BALONEY

☆**bolo tie** [altered < bola tie: from its resemblance to the BOLA] a man's string tie held together with an ornamented slide device

Bol·she·vik (bōl′shə vik′, bäl′-) n., pl. -viks, -vi′ki (-vē′kē) [Russ. (1903) < bolshe, the larger, majority] [also b-] 1. orig., a member of a majority faction (Bolsheviki) of the Social Democratic Party of Russia, which formed the Communist Party after seizing power in the 1917 Revolution 2. a Communist, esp. of the Soviet Union 3. loosely, any radical: hostile usage —adj. of, characteristic of, or like the Bolsheviks or Bolshevism —**Bol′she·vism** n. —**Bol′she·vist** n., adj. —**Bol′she·vize′** (-vīz′) vt. -vized′, -viz′ing

☆**bol·son** (bōl′sən; Sp. bōl sōn′) n. [Sp., lit., big purse] in the SW U.S., a flat desert valley surrounded by mountains and draining into a shallow lake in the center

bol·ster (bōl′stər) n. [ME. & OE., akin to ON. bolstr, G. polster, ult. < IE. base *bhel-, to swell: see BALL¹] 1. a long, narrow cushion or pillow 2. a soft pad for easing pressure on any part of the body 3. any bolsterlike object or support; specif., a) a capping piece over a post to extend the bearing area under a beam b) the connecting part between the volutes of an Ionic capital —vt. to prop up as with a bolster; support, strengthen, or reinforce (often with up)

bolt¹ (bōlt) n. [ME. & OE., akin to G. bolzen < IE. base *bhcld-, to knock, strike] 1. a short, heavy arrow with a thick, blunt head, shot from a crossbow 2. a flash of lightning; thunderbolt 3. a sudden dash or movement 4. a sliding bar for locking a door, gate, etc. 5. a similar bar in a lock, moved by a key 6. a metal rod or pin, usually threaded, having a head, and used with a nut to hold parts together 7. a roll (of cloth, paper, etc.) of a given length 8. a jet or column (of some liquid) ☆9. a bolting or withdrawal from one's party or group 10. Firearms a sliding bar that pushes the cartridge into place, closes the breech, and extracts the empty cartridge case after firing —vt. 1. [Archaic] to shoot (an arrow, etc.) 2. to say suddenly or unexpectedly; blurt (out) 3. to swallow (food) hurriedly; gulp down 4. to hold together or fasten with or as with a bolt 5. to roll (cloth, etc.) into bolts ☆6. to withdraw support from or abandon (a party, group, etc.) —vi. 1. to dash out suddenly; spring; dart 2. to start suddenly and run away, as a horse 3. to swallow food hurriedly ☆4. to withdraw support from or abandon a party, group, etc. 5. Horticulture to produce seed prematurely —adv. 1. [Archaic] directly or suddenly 2. straight as an arrow; erectly [to sit bolt upright] —**bolt from the blue** 1. a thunderbolt from a clear sky 2. a sudden, unforeseen occurrence, often an unfortunate one —**shoot one's bolt** to do one's utmost; exhaust one's capabilities

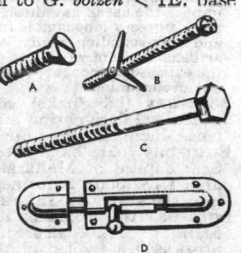

BOLTS
(A, stove; B, toggle; C, machine; D, door)

bolt² (bōlt) vt. [ME. bulten < OFr. buleter < dissimilated < *bureter < bure (< VL. *bura), coarse cloth; akin to It. burattare < buratto, sieve] 1. to sift (flour, grain, etc.) so as to separate and grade 2. to inspect and separate, as good from bad; examine closely

bolt·er¹ (bōlt′ər) n. 1. a horse that bolts, or runs away ☆2. a person who withdraws from his political party, group, etc.

bolt·er² (-tər) n. a device for bolting, or sifting, flour, etc.

Bol·ton (bōlt′'n) city in NW England: pop. 160,000

☆**bol·to·ni·a** (bōl tōn′ē ə, -yə) n. [ModL., after James Bolton, 18th-c. Eng. naturalist] any of a genus (Boltonia) of perennial American plants of the composite family with white or purplish asterlike heads

bolt·rope (bōlt′rōp′) n. [BOLT¹ + ROPE] a rope sewn into the edge seam of a sail to prevent tearing

bo·lus (bō′ləs) n., pl. **bo′lus·es** [L. < Gr. bōlos, a lump] 1. a small, round lump or mass, as of chewed food 2. Vet. a large pill

bomb (bäm) n. [Fr. bombe < It. bomba < It. bombus < Gr. bombos, deep and hollow sound: of echoic origin] 1. an explosive, incendiary, or chemical-filled container, for dropping or hurling, or for detonating by a timing mechanism 2. a sudden, surprising occurrence, esp. an unpleasant

one **3.** a small container with compressed gas in it [an aerosol *bomb*] **4.** a heavily shielded apparatus with radioactive material in it, used in radiotherapy [a cobalt *bomb*] ☆**5.** [Slang] a complete failure: said esp. of a theatrical performance **6.** *Geol.* a mass of lava, usually globular, ejected from a volcano by explosion —*vt.* to attack, damage, or destroy with a bomb or bombs —*vi.* [Slang] to have a failure

bom·bard (bäm bärd′, bəm-; *for n.* bäm′bärd) *vt.* [Fr. *bombarder* < *bombarde*, mortar < *bombe*, BOMB] **1.** to attack with or as with artillery or bombs **2.** to keep attacking or pressing with questions, suggestions, etc. **3.** to direct a stream of particles, as neutrons, against the atomic nuclei of (an element) to produce nuclear transformations —*n.* the earliest type of cannon, originally hurling round stones —*SYN.* see ATTACK —**bom·bard′ment** *n.*

bom·bar·dier (bäm′bə dir′, -bər-) *n.* [Fr. < *bombarde*: see BOMBARD] **1.** a member of the air crew of a bomber who operates the bombsight and releases the bombs **2.** a noncommissioned artillery officer in the British and Canadian armies **3.** [Archaic] an artilleryman

bom·bar·don (bäm′bər dən, bäm bär′-) *n.* [It. *bombardone* < *bombarda*, mortar < Fr. *bombarde*: see BOMBARD] **1.** an early type of bassoon **2.** a bass or contrabass tuba, used in military bands **3.** an organ stop with a bass reed

bom·bast (bäm′bast) *n.* [OFr. *bombace* < ML. *bombax*, cotton < *bambax*, cotton (with form infl. by L. *bombyx*, silk, silkworm < Gr. *bombyx*) < LGr. *bambax* < Gr. *pambax* < Per. *pambak*, cotton] **1.** orig., a soft material used for padding **2.** talk or writing that sounds grand or important but has little meaning; pompous language

bom·bas·tic (bäm bas′tik) *adj.* using or characterized by high-sounding but unimportant or meaningless language; pompous; grandiloquent —**bom·bas′ti·cal·ly** *adv.*

SYN.—**bombastic** refers to speech or writing that is pompous and inflated and suggests extravagant verbal padding and little substance; **grandiloquent** suggests an overreaching eloquence and implies the use of grandiose, high-flown language and an oratorical tone; **flowery** language is full of figurative and ornate expressions and high-sounding words; **euphuistic** is applied to an extremely artificial style of writing in which there is a straining for effect at the expense of thought; **turgid** implies such inflation of style as to obscure meaning

bom·bax (bäm′baks) *adj.* [ModL. < ML., cotton: see BOMBAST] designating a family (Bombacaceae) of tropical trees, including the kapok tree, the baobab, and the balsa

Bom·bay (bäm′bā′) **1.** seaport in W India, on the Arabian Sea: capital of Maharashtra state: pop. 2,772,000 (met. area 4,152,000) **2.** former state of W India: divided (1960) into the states of Gujarat & Maharashtra

bom·ba·zine (bäm′bə zēn′, bäm′bə zēn′) *n.* [Fr. *bombasin* < ML. *bombacinium*, silk texture < *bombax*: see BOMBAST] a twilled cloth of silk or rayon with worsted, often dyed black

bomb bay a compartment in the fuselage of a bomber that can be opened to release bombs

‡**bom·bé** (bôn bā′) *adj.* [Fr. < *bombe*, BOMB (because of the shape)] having a rounded, outward curve on the front or sides [a *bombé* china cabinet]

‡**bombe** (bônb) *n.* [Fr.: see BOMB] a frozen dessert consisting of a round mold of ice or ice cream filled with a light, frothy center made of eggs, sugar, etc.

bomb·er (bäm′ər) *n.* **1.** an airplane designed for dropping bombs **2.** a person who bombs

bom·bi·nate (bäm′bə nāt′) *vi.* -**nat′ed**, -**nat′ing** [< ModL. *bombinatus*, pp. of *bombinare*, altered < L. *bombitare*, to buzz < *bombus*, a buzzing: see BOMB] to buzz, as a fly —**bom′bi·na′tion** *n.*

bomb·proof (bäm′prōōf′) *adj.* capable of withstanding the force of ordinary bombs

bomb·shell (-shel′) *n.* **1.** a bomb **2.** any sudden, shocking surprise

bomb·sight (-sīt′) *n.* an instrument on a bomber for aiming the bombs

bom·by·cid (bäm′bə sid) *n.* [< L. *bombyx* (see BOMBAST) + -ID] any of a family (Bombycidae) of moths found chiefly in tropical regions, as the silkworm moth

Bo·mu (bō′mōō) river in C Africa, that forms the border between the Central African Republic and the Congo (sense 2): c. 500 mi.

☆**bo·na·ci** (bō′nə sē′) *n.* [AmSp. *bonasi*] any of various groupers (genus *Mycteroperca*) found near Florida, the West Indies, etc.: important as food fishes

bo·na fi·de (bō′nə fīd′, bän′ə; bō′nə fī′dē) [L.] in good faith; without dishonesty, fraud, or deceit —*SYN.* see AUTHENTIC

☆**bo·nan·za** (bə nan′zə, bō-) *n.* [Sp., fair weather, prosperity < VL. *bonacia*, altered (after L. *bonus*, good) < L. *malacia*, calm at sea < Gr. *malakia* < *malakos*, soft] **1.** a very rich vein or pocket of ore **2.** any source of wealth or profits

Bo·na·parte (bō′nə pärt′; Fr. bô nå pårt′) a Corsican family including NAPOLEON I and his four brothers: **1. Jerome,** 1784–1860; king of Westphalia (1807–13) **2. Joseph,** 1768–1844; king of Naples (1806–08) & of Spain (1808–13) **3. Louis,** 1778–1846; king of Holland (1806–10); father of LOUIS NAPOLEON **4. Lucien,** (*Prince of Canico*) 1775–1840; Fr. government official See also NAPOLEON II, LOUIS NAPOLEON

Bo·na·part·ism (bō′nə pär′tiz'm) *n.* **1.** belief in and support of Napoleon Bonaparte and his actions, methods, and doctrines **2.** the methods, doctrines, etc. of any military-political dictator like Napoleon Bonaparte — **Bo′na·part′ist** *n.*

Bon·a·ven·tu·ra (bän′ə ven tyoor′ə), **Saint** (born *Giovanni Fidanza*) 1221–74; It. theologian & scholastic philosopher: his day is July 14: also **Bon·a·ven·ture** (bän′ə ven/chər)

bon·bon (bän′bän′; Fr. bôn bôn′) *n.* [Fr. *bon*, good, emphasized by repetition] a small piece of candy, as a chocolate-covered cream

bond¹ (bänd) *n.* [ME. *bond, band*: see BAND¹] **1.** anything that binds, fastens, or restrains **2.** [*pl.*] *a*) shackles *b*) [Archaic] imprisonment; captivity **3.** a uniting force; tie; link [the *bonds* of friendship] **4.** a binding agreement; covenant **5.** a duty or obligation imposed by a contract, promise, etc. **6.** a substance or device, as glue, solder, or a chain, which holds things together or unites them **7.** *same as* BOND PAPER **8.** *Chem. a*) a unit of combining capacity equivalent to one atom of hydrogen: represented in structural formulas by a dash or dot *b*) the means or mechanism by which atoms or groups of atoms are combined in molecules **9.** *Commerce a*) an agreement by an agency holding taxable goods that taxes on them will be paid before they are sold *b*) the condition of goods kept in a warehouse until taxes are paid *c*) an insurance contract by which a bonding agency guarantees payment of a specified sum to an employer, etc., in the event of a financial loss caused him by the act of a specified employee or by some contingency over which the payee has no control **10.** *Finance* an interest-bearing certificate issued by a government or business, promising to pay the holder a specified sum on a specified date: it is a common means of raising capital funds **11.** *Law a*) a written obligation to pay specified sums, or to do or not do specified things *b*) an amount paid as surety or bail *c*) [Archaic] a bondsman, or surety **12.** *Masonry* the way in which bricks, stones, etc. are lapped upon one another in building —*vt.* **1.** to connect or fasten with or as with a bond; bind **2.** to furnish a bond, or bail, and thus become a surety for (someone) **3.** to place or hold (goods) in or under bond **4.** to issue interest-bearing certificates on; mortgage **5.** to put under bonded debt **6.** to arrange (timbers, bricks, etc.) in a pattern that gives strength —*vi.* to connect, hold together, or solidify by or as by a bond —**bottled in bond** bottled and stored in bonded warehouses for the length of time stated on the label, as some whiskey —**bond′a·ble** *adj.* —**bond′er** *n.*

bond² (bänd) *n.* [ME. *bonde* < OE. *bonda*: see ff.] [Obs.] a serf or slave —*adj.* in serfdom or slavery

bond·age (bän′dij) *n.* [ME. < Anglo-L. *bondagium* < OE. *bonda* < ON. *bonde*, orig. prp. of *bua*, to prepare, inhabit, akin to G. *bauen*, to build < IE. base *bheu-*, to grow, develop, whence Sans. *bhū-*, earth, Gr. *phyein*, to grow, E. BE] **1.** serfdom or slavery **2.** subjection to some force, compulsion, or influence **3.** *same as* VILLEINAGE —*SYN.* see SERVITUDE

bond·ed (-did) *adj.* **1.** subject to or secured by a bond or bonds **2.** placed in a bonded warehouse (see ff.)

bonded warehouse a warehouse, certified by the government and guaranteed by a bonding agency, where goods may be stored until duties or taxes are paid

bond·hold·er (bänd′hōl′dər) *n.* an owner of bonds issued by a company, government, or person

bond·maid (-mād′) *n.* a girl or woman bondservant or slave

bond·man (-mən) *n., pl.* -**men** (-mən) **1.** a feudal serf **2.** a man or boy bondservant —**bond′wom′an** *n.fem., pl.* -**wom′en**

☆**bond paper 1.** rag paper used for bonds and other documents **2.** a strong, superior stock of paper with a hard surface, used for letterheads, etc.

bond·ser·vant (-sur′vənt) *n.* **1.** a person bound to service without pay **2.** a slave

bonds·man (bändz′mən, bänz′-) *n., pl.* -**men** (-mən) **1.** *same as* BONDMAN **2.** a person who takes responsibility for another by furnishing a bond; surety

bon·duc (bän′duk′) *n.* [Fr. < Ar. *bunduq*, hazelnut < Gr. *pontikon* (*karyon*), lit., PONTIC (nut) ☆*same as* KENTUCKY COFFEE TREE

Bône (bōn) seaport in NE Algeria, on the Mediterranean: pop. 164,000

bone (bōn) *n.* [ME. *bon* < OE. *ban*, bone, esp. of a limb, akin to G. *bein*, a leg; only Gmc.] **1.** any of the separate parts of the hard tissue forming the skeleton of most full-grown vertebrate animals **2.** this hard tissue **3.** [*pl.*] the skeleton **4.** [*pl.*] the body, living or dead **5.** a bonelike substance or part, as whalebone **6.** a thing made of bone or of bonelike material; specif., *a*) a corset stay *b*) [*pl.*] [Colloq.] dice **7.** *a*) [*pl.*] flat sticks used as clappers in minstrel shows ☆*b*) [*pl., with sing. v.*] an end man in a minstrel show **8.** *same as* BONE WHITE —*vt.* **boned**, **bon′ing 1.** to remove the bones from **2.** to put whalebone or other stiffening into **3.** to fertilize with bone meal —*vi.* ☆[Slang] to study hard and hurriedly, as in preparation for an examination; cram (usually with *up*) —☆**feel in one's bones** to think or be certain without any real reason; have a presentiment —**have a bone to pick** to have something to quarrel or complain about —**make no bones**

about [Colloq.] **1.** to make no attempt to hide; admit freely **2.** to have no objection to or qualms about
bone ash a white porous ash prepared by burning bones in the open air and consisting chiefly of calcium phosphate: used in making bone china: also **bone earth**
bone-black (-blak/) *n.* a fine charcoal made by burning animal bones in closed containers: used as a pigment, in refining sugar, etc.: also **bone black**
bone china translucent china made with white clay to which bone ash or calcium phosphate has been added
boned (bōnd) *adj.* **1.** having (a specific kind of) bone [brittle-*boned*] **2.** having the bones taken out **3.** having stays of whalebone, etc.
bone-dry (bōn/drī/) *adj.* **1.** dry as a bone that has lain exposed to the air; very dry **2.** absolutely abstaining from, or prohibiting the use of, alcoholic drinks
☆**bone-fish** (-fish/) *n.*, *pl.* **-fish', -fish'es:** see FISH² any of various silvery marine fishes (family Albulidae) that feed on the bottom in shallow waters; esp., a game and food fish (*Albula vilpes*) of tropical seas
☆**bone-head** (-hed/) *n.* [Slang] a stupid person; fool
bone-less (-lis) *adj.* without bones; specif., with the bones removed [*boneless* sardines]
☆**bone meal** crushed or finely ground bones, used as feed for stock or as fertilizer
bone of contention a matter for argument; subject about which there is disagreement
bone oil a thick, black oil obtained by the dry distillation of bones
☆**bon-er** (bōn/ər) *n.* [Slang] a stupid or silly blunder —*SYN.* see ERROR
☆**bone-set** (-set/) *n.* any of several plants of the composite family; esp., a plant (*Eupatorium perfoliatum*) with flat clusters of white flowers used in folk medicine
bone white an off shade of white varying from grayish white to beige-white
bon-fire (bän/fīr/) *n.* [ME. *banefyre*, lit., bone fire; later, funeral pyre] a large fire built out-of-doors
bong (bôŋ, bäŋ) *n.* [echoic] a deep ringing sound, as of a large bell or gong —*vi.* to make this sound
bon-go¹ (bäŋ/gō) *n.*, *pl.* **-gos** [native African name] any of various large African antelopes (genus *Boöcercus*), having a reddish-brown coat with white stripes
bon-go² (bäŋ/gō) *n.*, *pl.* **-gos** [AmSp. < ?] either of a pair of small joined drums, each of different pitch, struck with the fingers: in full **bongo drum**
Bon-heur (bô nër/), **Ro-sa** (rō zà/) born *Marie Rosalie Bonheur*) 1822–99; Fr. painter of animals
bon-ho-mie, bon-hom-mie (bän/ə mē/, bän/ə mē; *Fr.* bô nô mē/) *n.* [Fr. < *bonhomme* < *bon*, good + *homme*, man] good nature; pleasant, affable manner; amiability —**bon'ho-mous** (bän/ə məs) *adj.* —**bon'ho-mous-ly** *adv.*

BONGO DRUMS

bon-i-face (bän/ə fās/) *n.* [after Boniface, landlord in Farquhar's comedy, *The Beaux' Stratagem*] a tavernkeeper, innkeeper, restaurateur, etc.
Bon-i-face (bän/ə fās/, -fäs/) **1.** Saint, (born *Winfrid* or *Wynfrith*) 680?–754? A.D.; Eng. monk & missionary in Germany; his day is June 5 **2. Boniface VIII** (born *Benedetto Gaetani*) 1235?–1303; Pope (1294–1303)
bon-i-ness (bō/nē nis) *n.* the quality or condition of being bony
Bo-nin Islands (bō/nin) group of small Japanese islands in the W Pacific, south of Honshu: 40 sq. mi.; pop. 220
bo-ni-to (bə nēt/ō) *n.*, *pl.* **-tos, -toes:** see PLURAL, II, D, 1 [Sp.] any of several saltwater fishes of the mackerel family, related to the tuna; esp., a large game and food fish (*Sarda sarda*) of the Atlantic and Mediterranean
‡**bon jour** (bôn zhoor/) [Fr.] good day; good morning
bon mot (bôn' mō/; *Fr.* bôn mō/) *pl.* **bons mots** (bôn' môz/; *Fr.* bôn mō/) [Fr., lit., good word] an apt, clever, or witty remark
Bonn (bän) city in W West Germany, on the Rhine: capital of the Federal Republic of Germany (West Germany): pop. 142,000
Bon-nard (bô når/), **Pierre** (pyer) 1867–1947; Fr. impressionist painter
‡**bonne** (bôn) *n.* [Fr., fem. of *bon*, good] **1.** a maidservant **2.** a nursemaid
‡**bonne nuit** (nwē/) [Fr.] good night
bon-net (bän/it) *n.* [ME. & OFr. *bonet* < ML. *bonitum* aphetic < *abonnis*, kind of cap] **1.** a flat, brimless cap, worn by men and boys in Scotland **2.** *a*) a hat with a chin ribbon, worn by children and women *b*) [Colloq.] any hat worn by women or girls ☆**3.** *short for* WAR BONNET **4.** *a*) a metal covering, hood, or cowl, as over a fireplace, stove, or chimney for draft or ventilation *b*) [Brit.] an automobile hood **5.** *Naut.* a strip of canvas fastened by lacing to the bottom of a sail to increase sail area —*vt.* to put a bonnet on
bon-ny, bon-nie (bän/ē) *adj.* **-ni-er, -ni-est** [< Fr. *bon*, good < L. *bonus*] [Now Chiefly Scot. or Eng. Dial.] **1.**

handsome or pretty, with a healthy, cheerful glow **2.** fine; pleasant —**bon'ni-ly** *adv.* —**bon'ni-ness** *n.*
bon-ny-clab-ber (bän/ē klab/ər) *n.* [Ir. *bainne*, milk + *clabar*, clabber < *claba*, thick] thickly curdled milk
bon-sai (bän sī/) *n.* [Jap., lit., tray arrangement] **1.** the art of dwarfing and shaping trees and shrubs in shallow pots by pruning, controlled fertilization, etc. **2.** *pl.* **bon-sai'** such a tree or shrub
‡**bon soir** (bôn swår/) [Fr.] good evening
bon-spiel (bän/spēl, -spəl) *n.* [prob. < Du. *bondspel*] [Scot.] a curling match between two clubs, towns, etc.

BONSAI

bon-te-bok (bän/tə bäk/) *n.*, *pl.* **-bok', -boks':** see PLURAL, II, D, 2 [Afrik. < Du. *bont*, variegated + *bok*, BUCK¹] a large, dark-brown antelope (*Damaliscus pygargus*) of South Africa, white on the face and rump
‡**bon ton** (bôn tôn/) [Fr., lit., good tone] **1.** stylishness **2.** fine manners **3.** fashionable society
bo-nus (bō/nəs) *n.*, *pl.* **bo'nus-es** [L., good < OL. *dvonus*] anything given in addition to the customary or required amount; specif., *a*) extra payment over and above salary given to an employee as an incentive or reward *b*) a payment made by a government to veterans of military service *c*) [Brit.] a dividend to insurance policyholders; also, an extra dividend to stockholders
SYN.—**bonus** refers to anything given over and above the regular wages, salary, remuneration, etc. [a Christmas *bonus*, a soldier's *bonus*]; a **bounty** is a reward given by a government for a specific undertaking considered in the public interest, as the production of certain crops, the destruction of vermin, etc.; **premium**, as compared here, implies a reward or prize offered as an inducement to buy, sell, compete, etc. [a toy given as a *premium* with each package]; **dividend** refers to a prorated share in an amount distributed among stockholders, policyholders, etc. from profits or surplus
bonus stock shares of stock, usually common, given by a corporation as a bonus with the purchase of another class of stock or bonds
bon vi-vant (bän' vi vänt'; *Fr.* bôn vē vän') *pl.* **bons vi-vants** (bän' vi vänts'; *Fr.* bôn vē vän') [Fr.] a person who enjoys good food and drink and other luxuries
bon voy-age (bän' voi äzh'; *Fr.* bôn vwå yåzh') [Fr.] pleasant journey: a farewell to a traveler
bon-y (bō/nē) *adj.* **bon'i-er, bon'i-est 1.** of or like bone **2.** having many bones **3.** having large or protruding bones **4.** thin; emaciated
bonze (bänz) *n.* [Fr. < Port. *bonzo* < Jap. *bonsō*, prob. < Chin. *fan seng*, religious person] a Buddhist monk
boo (boo) *interj.*, *n.*, *pl.* **boos** [echoic] a prolonged sound made to express disapproval, scorn, etc., or, more abruptly, to startle —*vi.* **booed, boo'ing** to make this prolonged sound —*vt.* to shout "boo" at
☆**boob** (boob) *n.* [< BOOBY] [Slang] a stupid or foolish person —*vi.* [Brit. Slang] to make a stupid mistake
☆**boo-boo, boo-boo** (boo/boo) *n.*, *pl.* **-boos'** [Fr.] [Slang] a stupid or foolish mistake; blunder **2.** a minor injury or bruise: chiefly a child's usage
boo-by (boo/bē) *n.*, *pl.* **-bies** [prob. < Sp. *bobo*, stupid < L. *balbus*, stammering] **1.** a stupid or foolish person; nitwit **2.** any of a number of gannetlike marine diving birds (genus *Sula*) that feed on fish of warm seas **3.** the player who gets the poorest score in a game, or does worst in a contest
booby hatch 1. a hood over a hatchway on a ship ☆**2.** [Slang] an institution for the mentally ill
☆**booby prize** a prize, usually a ridiculous one, given in fun to whoever has done worst in a game, race, etc.
booby trap 1. any scheme or device for tricking a person unawares **2.** a bomb or mine set to be exploded by some action of the intended victim, as when some seemingly harmless object is lifted —**boo'by-trap'** *vt.*
☆**boo-dle** (boo/d'l) *n.* [< Du. *boedel*, property, estate] [Slang] **1.** the entire lot or group; caboodle **2.** counterfeit money **3.** something given as a bribe; graft **4.** the loot taken in a robbery
☆**boo-gie-woo-gie** (boog/ē woog/ē, boo/gē woo/gē) *n.* [echoic; ? suggested by the characteristic "walking" bass; ? redupl. of *boogie*, var. of *bogy* (hobgoblin)] **1.** a style of jazz piano playing in which repeated bass figures in 8/8 rhythm accompany melodic variations in the treble **2.** any jazz music in this style
boo-hoo (boo/hoo/) *vi.* **-hooed', -hoo'ing** [echoic] to weep noisily —*n.*, *pl.* **-hoos'** noisy weeping
book (book) *n.* [ME. *bok* < OE. *boc*, pl. *bec* < PGmc. *bokiz*, beech, beechwood tablets carved with runes < IE. base *bhago-s*, beech, whence Gr. *phagos*, L. *fagus*, E. BEECH] **1.** *a*) a number of sheets of paper, parchment, etc. with writing or printing on them, fastened together along one edge, usually between protective covers *b*) a literary or scientific work, anthology, etc. so prepared; distinguished

by length and form from a magazine, tract, etc. **2.** any of the main divisions of a long written or printed work, as of the Bible **3.** *a)* a book of blank or ruled sheets or printed forms for the entry of accounts, records, notes, etc. [an account *book*] *b)* the record or account kept in such a book **4.** something regarded as a subject for study [the *book* of life] **5.** the body of facts, traits, or circumstances connected with a person or subject, esp. as being understandable, evident, etc. [an open *book*] or obscure, done with, etc. [a closed *book*] **6.** [*pl.*] studies; lessons **7.** the words of an opera or musical play; libretto: distinguished from SCORE **8.** a booklike package, as of matches or tickets **9.** a list or record of bets made and the odds given, as by bookmakers on horse races **10.** *Bridge*, etc. a specified number of cards or tricks making a set —*vt.* **1.** to record in a book; list **2.** to engage ahead of time, as rooms, transportation, performers or performances, etc. **3.** to record charges against on a police record —*adj.* in, from, or according to books or accounts —**bring to book 1.** to force to explain; demand an accounting from **2.** to reprimand —**by the book** according to the rules; in the prescribed or usual way —**close the books** *Bookkeeping* to make no further entries, balance the books, and draw up statements from them —**in one's book** in one's opinion —**in one's good** (or **bad**) **books** in (or out of) one's favor, or good graces —☆**in the book** in all that is known and practiced in connection with a particular activity [to know every trick *in the book*] —**keep books** to keep a record of business transactions —**know like a book** to know well or fully —**make book** [Slang] to make or accept a bet or bets —☆**one for the books** [Colloq.] something notably surprising, shocking, or unexpected —**on the books 1.** recorded **2.** listed; enrolled —**the Book** the Bible —**the book** [Colloq.] any set of rules, pronouncements, etc. regarded as authoritative —☆**throw the book at** [Slang] **1.** to place every possible pertinent charge against (an accused person) **2.** to deal out the maximum in punishment, penalty, etc. to —**without book 1.** without reading the lines; from memory **2.** without authority —**book′er** *n.*

book·bind·ing (-bīn′diŋ) *n.* the art, trade, or business of binding books —**book′bind′er** *n.* —**book′bind′er·y** *n., pl.* **-ies**

book·case (-kās′) *n.* a set of shelves or a cabinet for holding books

book club ☆an organization that sells books, usually at reduced prices, to members who undertake to buy a minimum number of them annually

book·end (-end′) *n.* an ornamental weight or bracket put at the end of a row of books to keep them upright

book·ie (-ē) *n.* [Slang] *Horse Racing* a bookmaker

book·ing (-iŋ) *n.* an engagement, as for a lecture, performance, etc.

book·ish (-ish) *adj.* **1.** of or connected with books **2.** inclined to read and study; literary; scholarly **3.** having mere book learning **4.** pedantic; stodgy —**book′ish·ly** *adv.* —**book′ish·ness** *n.*

book jacket *same as* DUST JACKET

book·keep·ing (-kēp′iŋ) *n.* the work of keeping a systematic record of business transactions —**book′keep′er** *n.*

book learning knowledge gained from reading or formal education, as distinguished from practical experience: also **book′lore′** (-lôr′) *n.* —**book′-learn′ed** (-lur′nid) *adj.*

book·let (-lit) *n.* a small book, often with paper covers

book louse any of a group of small, usually wingless, insects (order Corrodentia), esp. one of a family (Atropidae) that often infest and destroy old books

book·mak·er (-māk′ər) *n.* **1.** a maker of books; compiler, publisher, or manufacturer **2.** a person in the business of taking bets, as on horse races —**book′mak′ing** *n.*

book·man (-mən) *n., pl.* **-men** (-mən) **1.** a literary or scholarly man **2.** a man whose work is making, publishing, or selling books

book·mark (-märk′) *n.* anything slipped between the pages of a book to mark a place

☆**book matches** safety matches made of paper and fastened into a small cardboard folder

☆**book·mo·bile** (-mō bēl′, -mə-) *n.* [BOOK + (AUTO)- MOBILE] a traveling lending library transported in a truck, trailer, etc. to small towns or rural areas lacking permanent libraries

book of account 1. a book to keep accounts in; ledger **2.** any of the records needed for auditing the accounts of a business; journal

Book of Common Prayer the official book of services and prayers for the Church of England or, with some minor modifications, for other Anglican churches

☆**Book of Mormon** the sacred book of the Mormon Church: see MORMON

Book of the Dead in ancient Egypt, a book of prayers and charms meant to help the soul in the afterworld

book·plate (-plāt′) *n.* a label, often specially designed, pasted in a book to identify its owner

book·rack (-rak′) *n.* **1.** a rack or shelf for books **2.** *same as* BOOKSTAND

book·rest (-rest′) *n. same as* BOOKSTAND

book review an article or talk in which a book, esp. a new book, is discussed and critically analyzed

book scorpion any of various small arachnids (order Pseudoscorpionida) resembling a scorpion without a tail,

found beneath stones, in old papers and books, etc.

book·sell·er (-sel′ər) *n.* the owner or manager of a bookstore

book·shelf (-shelf′) *n., pl.* **-shelves′** a shelf on which books are kept

☆**book·stack** (-stak′) *n.* a series of bookshelves, one over the other, as in a library

book·stall (-stôl′) *n.* **1.** a stand, booth, or counter, often one outdoors, where books are sold **2.** [Brit.] a newsstand

book·stand (-stand′) *n.* **1.** a stand for holding a book open before a reader **2.** *same as* BOOKSTALL

☆**book·store** (-stôr′) *n.* a store where books are sold: also **book′shop′**

book value 1. the value of any of the assets of a business as shown on its account books **2.** *a)* the net worth of a business, or the value of its capital stock, as shown by the excess of assets over liabilities *b)* the value, on this basis, of a single share of stock

book·worm (-wurm′) *n.* **1.** any of a number of insects or insect larvae that harm books by feeding on the binding, paste, etc. **2.** a person who spends much time reading or studying

Bool·e·an algebra (boo′lē ən) [after George *Boole* (1815– 64), Eng. mathematician] a mathematical system, orig. devised for the analysis of symbolic logic, in which all variables have the value of either zero or one: widely used in digital computers

boom¹ (boom) *vi.* [ME. *bummen*, to hum; like Du. *bommen*, G. *bummen*, of echoic orig.] to make a deep, hollow, resonant sound —*vt.* to speak or indicate with such a sound [the clock *boomed* the hour] —*n.* **1.** a booming sound, as of thunder, heavy guns, etc. **2.** the resonant cry of certain animals, as the bullfrog

boom² (boom) *n.* [Du., a tree, beam, pole; same word ult. as E. BEAM] **1.** a spar extending from a mast to hold the bottom of a sail outstretched **2.** [< use of ship's boom for this purpose] a long beam extending as from an upright to lift or carry something and guide it as needed [the *boom* of a derrick, a microphone *boom*] **3.** a barrier of chains or poles to obstruct navigation ☆**4.** *Lumbering a)* a barrier across a river or around an area of water to prevent floating logs from dispersing *b)* the area in which logs are thus confined **5.** *Aeron.* a retractable metal tube for transferring fuel from one plane to another in flight —*vt.* **1.** to stretch out (sails) as with a boom so as to take maximum advantage of a wind abaft the beam and hence make speed ☆**2.** *Lumbering* to place a boom in (a river, lake, etc.) —*vi.* **1.** to sail with maximum speed (usually with *along*) ☆**2.** to go rapidly along; move with speed or vigor —☆**lower the boom** [Colloq.] to act suddenly and forcefully in dealing out punishment or criticism, in defeating, etc.

☆**boom³** (boom) *vi.* [< ? prec. *vi.;* later associated with BOOM¹] to increase suddenly in size, importance, activity, etc.; undergo swift, vigorous growth; flourish [business *boomed*] —*vt.* **1.** to cause to increase suddenly or grow swiftly; make flourish [the war *boomed* the aircraft industry] **2.** to promote vigorously; popularize [they proposed him for mayor] —*n.* **1.** swift, vigorous growth or development **2.** a period of business prosperity, industrial expansion, etc. **3.** a sudden favorable turn in business or political prospects —*adj.* of, characteristic of, or resulting from a boom in business, etc. [a boom town]

boom·er·ang (boom′ə raŋ′) *n.* [< Australian native name] **1.** a flat, curved stick that can be thrown so that it will return to a point near the thrower: it is used as a weapon by Australian aborigines **2.** something that goes contrary to the expectation of the person doing or saying it and results in his disadvantage or harm —*vi.* to act as a boomerang; result in harm to the originator

Boom·er State (boom′ər) *nickname for* OKLAHOMA

☆**boom·let** (boom′lit) *n.* a small boom, as in business

boon¹ (boon) *n.* [ME. *bone* < ON. *bon*, a petition, prayer < IE. base **bha-*, to speak, whence BAN¹, L. *fari*, to speak: E. meaning prob. infl. by ff.] **1.** welcome benefit; blessing **2.** [Archaic] a request or the favor requested

boon² (boon) *adj.* [ME. & OFr. *bon* < L. *bonus*, good] **1.** [Archaic or Poet.] kind, generous, pleasant, etc. **2.** merry; convivial: now only in **boon companion**, a close friend who often joins one in seeking fun

boon·docks, the (boon′däks′) *n.pl.* [orig. World War II military slang < Tag. *bundok*, mountain] [Colloq.] **1.** a jungle or a wild, heavily wooded area; wilderness ☆**2.** any remote rural or provincial region; hinterland —**boon′dock′** *adj.*

☆**boon·dog·gle** (boon′dôg′'l, -däg′-) *vi.* **-gled, -gling** [orig. dial. n., ornamental leather strap; modern sense c. 1935] [Colloq.] to do trifling, pointless work —*n.* trifling, pointless work —**boon′dog′gler** *n.*

Boone (boon), **Daniel** 1734–1820; Am. frontiersman

boor (boor) *n.* [Du. *boer* < MDu. *gheboer*, fellow dweller < *ghe-*, with, co- + *bouwen*, to build, cultivate; akin to G. *bauer:* for IE. base see BONDAGE] **1.** orig., a peasant or farm worker **2.** a rude, awkward, or ill-mannered person **3.** [B-] *same as* BOER

boor·ish (-ish) *adj.* like or characteristic of a boor; rude; awkward; ill-mannered —*SYN.* see RUDE —**boor′ish·ly** *adv.* —**boor′ish·ness** *n.*

☆**boost** (boost) *vt.* [< ?] **1.** to raise by or as by a push from

behind or below; push up **2.** to urge others to support; promote [to *boost* a program] **3.** to make higher or greater; increase in amount, power, etc. [to *boost* taxes, *boost* electric current] —**n. 1.** a push to help propel a person or thing upward or forward **2.** an act that helps or promotes **3.** an increase in amount, power, etc.
☆**boost·er** (boos′tər) *n.* **1.** a person who boosts; enthusiastic supporter **2.** *Elec.* a device for controlling or varying the voltage in a circuit **3.** *Radio & TV* an amplifier between the antenna and the receiver **4.** any device that provides added power, thrust, or pressure **5.** any of the early stages of a multistage rocket; also, a rocket system that launches a spacecraft or other payload: also **booster rocket 6.** *same as* BOOSTER SHOT
☆**boost·er·ism** (-iz′m) *n.* the practice of boosting or promoting a city, resort, etc.
☆**booster shot** (or **injection**) an injection of a vaccine or other antigen some time after the initial series of injections, for maintaining immunity
boot[1] (boot) *n.* [ME. & OFr. *bote*] **1.** *a)* a protective covering of leather, rubber, cloth, etc., for the foot and part or all of the leg [riding *boot*] *b)* an overshoe *c)* a man's shoe reaching at least to the ankle **2.** a boot-shaped instrument of torture for crushing the foot and leg **3.** [Brit.] the trunk, or baggage compartment, of an automobile **4.** a patch for the inner surface of an automobile tire to protect a break or weak spot in the casing **5.** *a)* a box that holds the reed in a reed pipe of an organ **6.** *a)* a kick *b)* [Colloq.] pleasurable excitement; thrill ☆**7.** [Slang] a navy or marine recruit, esp. one in a training camp —*vt.* **1.** to put boots on **2.** to torture with the boot **3.** to kick **4.** [Slang] to put (a person) out of a place or job; dismiss ☆**5.** *Baseball* to make an error in fielding (a grounder) —**bet your boots** to be certain; rely on it —**die with one's boots on** to die in action —☆**lick the boots of** to be servile toward; fawn on —**the boot** [Slang] discharge, as from work; dismissal
boot[2] (boot) *n., vt., vi.* [ME. *bote* < OE. *bot*, advantage, remedy; akin to BETTER[1], BEST] [Archaic or Poet.] remedy; profit; benefit —**to boot** besides; in addition
boot·black (-blak′) *n.* a person whose work is shining shoes and boots
☆**boot camp** [Colloq.] a station where navy or marine recruits receive basic training
☆**boot·ee** (boo tē′; *for 2* boot′ē) *n.* [BOOT[1] + -EE[1]] **1.** a short boot or light overshoe worn by women and children **2.** a baby's soft, knitted or cloth shoe
Bo·ö·tes (bō ō′tēz) [L. < Gr. *boötēs*, lit., plowman < *bous*, ox] a N constellation including the bright star Arcturus
booth (booth; *chiefly Canad. & Brit.* booth) *n., pl.* **booths** (boothz) [ME. *both* < ON. *buth*, temporary dwelling < *bua*, to prepare, dwell, akin to BONDAGE] **1.** a temporary shed or shelter **2.** a stall for the sale of goods, as at markets and fairs **3.** a small temporary structure or enclosure for voting at elections **4.** a small permanent structure or enclosure to house a sentry, public telephone, etc. **5.** a small, partially enclosed compartment with a table and seats, as in some restaurants
Booth (booth) **1. Bal·ling·ton** (bal′in tən), 1859–1940; founder of Volunteers of America (1896): son of *William* **2. Edwin** (**Thomas**), 1833–93; U.S. actor: son of *Junius Brutus* **3. Evangeline Cor·y** (kôr′ē), 1865–1950; U.S. general of Salvation Army, born in England: daughter of *William* **4. John Wilkes** (wilks), 1838–65; U.S. actor; assassin of Abraham Lincoln: son of *Junius Brutus* **5. Junius Brutus**, 1796–1852; U.S. actor, born in England **6. William**, 1829–1912; Eng. revivalist; founder of the Salvation Army (1865)
Boo·thi·a (boo′thē ə), **Gulf of** inlet of the Arctic Ocean between Boothia Peninsula & Baffin Island
Boothia Peninsula peninsula in Franklin District, Northwest Territories, Canada
bootie *var. sp. of* BOOTEE
boot·jack (boot′jak′) *n.* [BOOT + JACK[1]] a device to grip a boot heel, for helping a person to pull off boots
Boo·tle (boot′'l) seaport in NW England, adjoining Liverpool: pop. 83,000
☆**boot·leg** (boot′leg′) *vt., vi.* **-legged′, -leg′ging** [in allusion to concealing objects in the leg of a high boot] to make, carry, or sell (esp. liquor) illegally —*adj.* **1.** bootlegged; illegal **2.** *Football* designating a play in which the ball carrier fakes

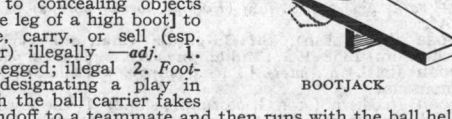

BOOTJACK

a handoff to a teammate and then runs with the ball held hidden behind a hip —*n.* **1.** the part of a boot that covers the leg **2.** something bootlegged; esp., bootlegged liquor —**boot′leg′ger** *n.*
boot·less (-lis) *adj.* [BOOT[2] + -LESS] without benefit; useless —**boot′less·ly** *adv.* —**boot′less·ness** *n.*
☆**boot·lick** (-lik′) *vt., vi.* [Colloq.] to try to gain favor with (someone) by fawning, servility, etc. —**boot′lick′er** *n.*

boots (boots) *n., pl.* **boots** [Brit.] a servant who shines shoes, as in a hotel
boots and saddles [? confusion of Fr. *boute-selle!*, lit., put saddle!] a cavalry bugle call used as the first signal for mounted drill or other mounted formation
boot·strap (boot′strap′) *n.* a strap on a boot for pulling it on —*adj.* undertaken or effected without the help of others [a *bootstrap* operation] —**lift** (or **raise**) **oneself by the** (or **one's own**) **bootstraps** to achieve success by one's own unaided efforts
boot tree *same as* SHOE TREE
boo·ty (boot′ē) *n., pl.* **-ties** [MLowG. *bute*, akin to G. *beute*; infl. by BOOT[2]] **1.** loot taken from the enemy; spoils of war **2.** anything seized by force or robbery; plunder **3.** any valuable gain, prize, or gift: a humorous usage —*SYN.* see SPOIL
booze (booz) *vi.* **boozed, booz′ing** [Du. *buizen*: see BOUSE[1]] [Colloq.] to drink too much alcoholic liquor —*n.* [Colloq.] **1.** an alcoholic drink; liquor **2.** a drinking spree —**booz′er** *n.*
booz·y (-ē) *adj.* **booz′i·er, booz′i·est** [Colloq.] drunk, esp. habitually so —**booz′i·ly** *adv.*
☆**bop**[1] (bäp) *vt.* **bopped, bop′ping** [echoic] [Slang] to hit; punch —*vi.* [Slang] to fight —*n.* [Slang] a blow
☆**bop**[2] (bäp) *n.* [clipped form of BE-BOP] a style of jazz, characterized by complex rhythms, experimental harmonic structures, and instrumental virtuosity
Bopp (bôp), **Franz** (fränts) 1791–1867; Ger. philologist
bor. borough
bo·ra (bôr′ə) *n.* [It. dial. for *borea* < L. *boreas*, BOREAS] a fierce, cold northeasterly wind of the Adriatic Sea
bo·rac·ic (bə ras′ik) *adj.* [< BORAX + -IC] *same as* BORIC
bo·ra·cite (bôr′ə sīt′) *n.* [< BORAX + -ITE[1]] a mineral, $Mg_6Cl_2B_{14}O_{26}$, found either in hard, crystalline form or as a soft, white mass, and having pyroelectric properties
bor·age (bôr′ij, bur′-) *n.* [ME. < OFr. *bourage* < ML. *borrago, burrago* < ? *burra*, coarse hair] any of a family (Boraginaceae) of plants; esp., an annual plant (*Borago officinalis*) with brilliant blue flowers and hairy leaves sometimes used in salads
bo·ral (bôr′əl) *n.* [BOR(ON) + AL(UMINUM)] a mixture of boron carbide, B_4C, and aluminum, used in reactor control and as a shielding material
bo·rane (bôr′ān) *n.* [BOR(ON) + -ANE] any of various compounds of boron and hydrogen, used as a fuel in rockets, as a reducing agent, etc.
bo·rate (-āt) *n.* a salt or ester of boric acid —*vt.*, **-rat·ed, -rat·ing** to treat or mix with borax or boric acid —**bo′rat·ed** *adj.*
bo·rax (bôr′aks) *n.* [ME. < OFr. *boras* < ML. *borax* < Ar. *bauraq* < Per. *būrah*] **1.** a white, crystalline salt, $Na_2B_4O_7$, with an alkaline taste, used as a flux in soldering metals and in the manufacture of glass, enamel, artificial gems, soaps, antiseptics, etc. ☆**2.** [from the furniture formerly given as premiums by manufacturers of borax soap] cheap, poorly made merchandise, esp. furniture
☆**bo·ra·zon** (bôr′ə zän′) *n.* [BOR(ON) + AZ- + -ON] a crystalline modification of boron nitride, somewhat harder than diamond and far more resistant to heat
Bor·deaux (bôr dō′) seaport in SW France, on the Garonne River: pop. 250,000 —*n.* red or white wine from the region around Bordeaux
Bordeaux mixture a mixture of lime, water, and copper sulfate, used as a spray on trees and plants to kill insects and fungi
bor·del (bôr′d'l) *n.* [ME. < OFr., dim. of *borde*, hut < Frank. (& OHG.) *bord*, BOARD] [Archaic] a bordello
bor·del·lo (bôr del′ō) *n.* [It. < OFr.] a house of prostitution; brothel
bor·der (bôr′dər) *n.* [ME. & OFr. *bordure* < *border*, to border < OHG. *bord*, margin: see BOARD] **1.** an edge or a part near an edge; margin; side **2.** a dividing line between two countries, states, etc. or the land along it; frontier **3.** a narrow strip, often ornamental, along an edge; fringe; edging **4.** an ornamental strip of flowers or shrubs along the edge of a garden, walk, etc. —*vt.* **1.** to provide with a border **2.** to extend along the edge of; bound —*adj.* of, forming, or near a border —**border on** (or **upon**) **1.** to be next to or adjoining **2.** to be like; almost be [his grief *borders on* madness] —**the Border** the district on and near the boundary between Scotland and England —**bor′dered** *adj.*
SYN.—**border** refers to the boundary of a surface and may imply the limiting line itself or the part of the surface immediately adjacent to it; **margin** implies a bordering strip more or less clearly defined by some distinguishing feature [the *margin* of a printed page]; **edge** refers to the limiting line itself or the terminating line at the sharp convergence of two surfaces [the *edge* of a box]; **rim** is applied to the edge of a circular or curved surface; **brim** refers to the inner rim at the top of a vessel, etc.; **brink** refers to the edge at the top of a steep slope All of these terms have figurative application [the *border* of good taste, a *margin* of error, an *edge* on one's appetite, the *rim* of consciousness, a mind filled to the *brim*, the *brink* of disaster]
‡**bor·de·reau** (bôr′də rō′) *n., pl.* **-reaux′** (-rō′) [Fr.] a memorandum, esp. one that gives a list of documents

bor·der·er (bôr′dər ər) *n.* a person living near a border

bor·der·land (-land′) *n.* 1. *a*) land constituting or near a border *b*) hinterland (sense 2) 2. a vague or uncertain condition that is not quite one thing or the other

bor·der·line (-līn′) *n.* a boundary; dividing line —*adj.* on a boundary; specif., on the boundary of what is acceptable, valid, or normal and hence having a questionable or indefinite status

Border States Slave States bordering on the Free States before the Civil War; Missouri, Kentucky, Virginia, Maryland, and Delaware

bor·dure (bôr′jər) *n.* [Fr.: see BORDER] *Heraldry* a border around the field of a coat of arms

bore¹ (bôr) *vt.* **bored, bor′ing** [ME. *boren* < OE. *borian*, to bore < *bor*, auger < IE. base **bher-*, to cut with a sharp point] 1. to make a hole in or through with a drill or other rotating tool 2. to make (a hole, tunnel, well, etc.) by or as by drilling 3. to force (one's way), as through a crowd 4. to weary by being dull, uninteresting, or monotonous —*vi.* 1. to bore a hole or passage 2. to be drilled by a tool [soft materials *bore* easily] 3. to move forward slowly but steadily, as if by boring —*n.* [ME. < the *v.*; also < ON. *bora*, a hole] 1. a hole made by or as by boring 2. *a*) the hollow part inside a tube, pipe, or cylinder, as of a gun barrel *b*) the inside diameter of such a hollow part; gauge; caliber 3. a person or thing that wearies by being dull, uninteresting, etc.

bore² (bôr) *n.* [ME. *bare*, a wave < ON. *bara*, a billow, prob. < IE. base **bher-*, to well up, boil] a high, abrupt tidal wave in a narrow channel, having great force

bore³ (bôr) *pt. of* BEAR¹

bo·re·al (bôr′ē əl) *adj.* [LL. *borealis* < ff.] 1. northern 2. of the north wind 3. of or pertaining to the northern zone of plant and animal life lying just below the tundra and usually characterized by coniferous forests

Bo·re·as (-əs) [L. < Gr. *Boreas*, north wind; ? orig., wind from the mountains < IE. base meaning "mountain," as in OSlav. *gora*, mountain] 1. *Gr. Myth.* the god of the north wind 2. the north wind personified

bore·dom (bôr′dəm) *n.* the condition of being bored or uninterested; ennui

bor·er (bôr′ər) *n.* 1. a tool for boring or drilling 2. a person whose work is to bore holes 3. an insect or worm that bores holes in trees, fruit, etc. 4. a shipworm

bore·some (-səm) *adj.* boring; tiresome

Bor·ges (bôr′hes), **Jor·ge Luis** (hôr′hā lwēs) 1900– ; Argentinian poet, short-story writer, & critic

Bor·ghe·se (bôr gā′ze) family of It. nobility, orig. of Siena, later of Rome: its members achieved prominence from the 16th to the 19th cent.

Bor·gia (bôr′jä) 1. **Ce·sa·re** (che′zä re), 1476?–1507; It. military leader & cardinal: son of Pope ALEXANDER VI 2. **Lu·cre·zia** (lōō kre′tsyä), 1480–1519; duchess of Ferrara; patroness of the arts: sister of *prec.*

Bor·glum (bôr′gləm), **(John) Gut·zon** (gut′s'n) 1867–1941; U.S. sculptor and painter

Borgne (bôrn), **Lake** inlet of the Gulf of Mexico, in SE La., east of New Orleans

Bo·ri (bôr′ē), **Lu·cre·zia** (lōō krät′syə) (born *Lucrecia Borja González de Riabeno*) 1888–1960; U.S. operatic soprano, born in Spain

bo·ric (bôr′ik) *adj.* of or containing boron

boric acid a white, crystalline compound, H₃BO₃, with the properties of a weak acid, used as a mild antiseptic and in the manufacture of cements, enamels, etc.

bo·ride (-īd) *n.* [BOR(ON) + -IDE] a compound consisting of boron and one other element or radical

bor·ing (bôr′iŋ) *adj.* 1. for making holes 2. wearying by being dull, uninteresting, etc. —*n.* 1. the action of one that bores 2. a hole made by boring 3. [*pl.*] chips, flakes, etc. made by boring

Bor·is (bôr′is) [Russ., lit., fight] 1. a masculine name 2. **Boris III** 1894–1943; king of Bulgaria (1918–43)

born (bôrn) *alt. pp. of* BEAR¹ (which see) —*adj.* 1. brought into life or being 2. by birth: used in hyphenated compounds [French-*born*] 3. having certain qualities or abilities innately, as if from birth; natural [a *born* athlete] 4. being as specified from birth [nobly *born*] 5. [Dial. or Colloq.] since birth [in all my *born* days]

Born (bôrn), **Max** 1882–1970; Ger. nuclear physicist, in England (1933–53)

borne (bôrn) *alt. pp. of* BEAR¹ (which see)

Bor·ne·o (bôr′nē ō) large island in the Malay Archipelago, southwest of the Philippines: the S portion (KALIMANTAN) is a part of Indonesia; the N portion is composed of the Malaysian states of Sabah & Sarawak, and of BRUNEI: total area, 288,000 sq. mi.

bor·ne·ol (bôr′nē ōl′, -ôl′) *n.* [< prec. + -OL¹] a white, crystalline terpene alcohol, C₁₀H₁₈O, resembling camphor, found in the trunk of a tree native to Borneo and Sumatra and used in perfumery, as an antiseptic, etc.

Born·holm (bôrn′hōlm) Danish island in the Baltic Sea, south of Sweden: 227 sq. mi.; pop. 49,000

born·ite (bôr′nīt) *n.* [after Ignatius von *Born* (1742–91), Austrian metallurgist] an isometric mineral, an ore of copper, Cu₅FeS₄, that is brownish red but quickly tarnishes to an iridescent purple when it is fractured

Bor·nu (bôr nōō′) former sultanate in WC Africa, around Lake Chad: now mostly in N Nigeria

Bo·ro·din (bô′rə din; *Russ.* bō′rō dyēn′), **A·lek·san·dr Por·fir·e·vich** (ä′lyik sän′dr′ pôr fir′yi vich) 1833–87; Russ. composer

Bor·o·di·no (bôr′ə dē′nō) Russian village just west of Moscow: site of a battle (1812) in which the Russian army retreated before Napoleon's army

bo·ron (bôr′än) *n.* [< BOR(AX) + -*on* as in (CARB)ON] a nonmetallic chemical element occurring only in combination, as with sodium and oxygen in borax, and produced in the form either of a brown amorphous powder or very hard, brilliant crystals: its compounds are used in the preparation of boric acid, water softeners, soaps, enamels, glass, pottery, etc.: symbol, B; at. wt., 10.811; at. no., 5; sp. gr., 2.34; melt. pt., 2300°C; boil. pt., 2550°C

boron carbide a compound of boron and carbon, B₄C, almost as hard as diamond: used as an abrasive and in control rods for nuclear reactors

bo·ro·sil·i·cate (bôr′ō sil′ə kit, -kāt′) *n.* any of several salts derived from both boric acid and silicic acid and found in certain minerals, such as tourmaline

bor·ough (bur′ō, bur′-) *n.* [ME. *burgh* < OE. *burg, burh*, town, fortified place, akin to G. *burg* < IE. **bhrgh*, fortified elevation < base **bheregh-*, high, whence BARROW², BURGUNDY] 1. in certain States of the U.S., a self-governing, incorporated town 2. any of the five administrative units of New York City 3. in England *a*) a town with a municipal corporation and rights to self-government granted by royal charter *b*) a town that sends one or more representatives to Parliament *c*) [Obs.] any fortified town larger than a village

borough English a former custom in some parts of England by which the youngest son succeeded to land holdings

bor·row (bär′ō, bôr′-) *vt., vi.* [ME. *borwen* < OE. *borgian*, to borrow, lend, be surety for, akin to *beorgan*, to protect & BOROUGH] 1. to take or receive (something) with the understanding that one will return it or an equivalent 2. to adopt or take over as one's own [to *borrow* a theory] 3. to adopt and naturalize from another language [the word *depot* was *borrowed* from French] 4. *Arith.* in subtraction, to take (a unit of ten) from the next higher denomination in the minuend and add it to the next lower: done when the number to be subtracted is the greater 5. [Dial.] to lend —☆**borrow trouble** to worry about anything needlessly or before one has to —**bor′row·er** *n.*

Bor·row (bär′ō), **George Henry** 1803–81; Eng. linguist & writer, esp. on gypsy life

Bors (bôrs, bôrz), Sir a knight of King Arthur's Round Table, nephew of Sir Lancelot

borsch (bôrsh; *Russ.* bôrshch) *n.* [Russ. *borshch*] a Russian beet soup, served either hot or cold, usually with sour cream: also **borsht** (bôrsht)

☆**borsch** (or **borsht**) **circuit** [jocular, from the characteristic Jewish cuisine] [Slang] summer resort hotels in the Catskills and White Mountains, where entertainment is provided for the guests

Bor·stal (bôr′stəl) *n.* [< *Borstal*, town in England] [sometimes b-] any of a number of British correctional institutions to which convicted young offenders (17 to 21 years old) are sent for reeducation and training

bort (bôrt) *n.* [< ? OFr. *bourt, bourde*, bastard] a dark-colored, poorly crystallized variety of diamond used for industrial purposes as an abrasive: also **bortz** (bôrts)

bor·zoi (bôr′zoi) *n.* [Russ., swift] any of a breed of large dog with a narrow head, long legs, and silky coat; Russian wolfhound

BORZOI
(28-31 in. high at shoulder)

bos·cage (bäs′kij) *n.* [ME. *boskage* < OE. *boscage* < Frank. (& OHG.) *busk*, forest, thicket: see BUSH¹] a natural growth of trees or shrubs; wooded place

Bosch (bäs, bôs), **Hier·on·y·mus** (hi rän′ə məs) (born *Jerome van Aken*) 1450?–1516; Du. painter

bosch·bok, bosh·bok (bäsh′bäk′) *n., pl.* -**bok′**, -**boks′**: see PLURAL, II, D, 2 [obs. Afrik. < Du. *bosch*, BUSH¹ + *bok*, BUCK¹] same as BUSHBUCK

bosch·vark (-värk′) *n.* [obs. Afrik. < Du. *bosch*, BUSH¹ + *vark*, pig] a wild hog (*Potamochoerus porcus*) of South Africa

Bose (bōs, bôsh), Sir **Ja·ga·dis Chan·dra** (jə gə dēs′ chun′drə) 1858–1937; Indian physicist & plant physiologist

bosh¹ (bäsh) *n., interj.* [Turk., empty, worthless] [Colloq.] nonsense

bosh² (bäsh) *n.* [< ? G. *böschung*, slope] 1. the lower part of the shaft of a blast furnace, where the walls begin to slope 2. a trough for cooling hot metal

bosk (bäsk) *n.* [ME. *bosk, boske*, BUSH¹] a small wooded place; grove; thicket: also **bos·kage** (bäs′kij)

bos·ket (bäs′kit) *n.* [Fr. *bosquet* < It. *boschetto*, dim. of *bosco* < ML. *boscus*: see BUSH¹] a small grove; thicket

Bos·kop man (bäs′käp) [fossil remains found (1914) near *Boskop*, in Transvaal] a Middle Stone Age man of S Africa, thought to be the direct ancestor of the modern Bushman and Hottentot

bosk·y (bäs′kē) *adj.* [BOSK + -Y²] covered with trees or shrubs; wooded; sylvan

bo's'n (bōs'n) *n. contracted form of* BOATSWAIN
Bos·ni·a (bäz'nē ə) **and Hercegovina** federal republic of Yugoslavia, in the central part: 19,745 sq. mi.; pop. 3,278,000; cap. Sarajevo: Bosnia, formerly an independent kingdom, annexed Hercegovina from Serbia in the late 14th cent. —**Bos'ni·an** *adj., n.*

bos·om (booz'əm, bŏŏ'zəm) *n.* [ME. < OE. *bosm,* prob. < IE. base **bhou-, *bhū-,* to grow, swell] **1.** the human breast; specif., a woman's breasts **2.** a thing thought of as like this [the bosom of the sea] **3.** the breast regarded as the source of feelings or the seat of inmost thoughts **4.** the enclosing space formed by the breast and arms in embracing **5.** the inside; central part; midst [in the bosom of one's family] **6.** *a)* the part of a dress, shirt, etc. that covers the breast *b)* the space inside this part of a garment —*vt.* **1.** to embrace; cherish **2.** to conceal in the bosom; hide —*adj.* cherished; intimate [a bosom companion] —**SYN.** see BREAST
bos·omed (-əmd) *adj.* having a (specified kind of) bosom [small-bosomed]
bos·om·y (-əm ē) *adj.* having large breasts
bos·on (bō'sän) *n.* [after Sir J. C. BOSE + -ON] a subatomic particle, as a photon or any of certain mesons, that does not obey the Pauli exclusion principle
Bos·po·rus (bäs'pər əs) strait between the Black Sea and the Sea of Marmara: c. 20 mi. long: also **Bos'pho·rus** (-fər əs) See DARDANELLES, map
☆**bos·que** (bäs'kā) *n.* [Sp.] [Chiefly Southwest] a clump or grove of trees
bos·quet (bäs'kit) *n. same as* BOSKET
☆**boss**[1] (bôs, bäs) *n.* [Du. *baas,* a master, orig., uncle] **1.** a person in authority over employees, as an employer, a manager, or a foreman **2.** a person who controls a political machine or organization, as in a county: often **political boss** —*vt.* **1.** to act as boss of **2.** [Colloq.] to order (a person) about; act bossy with —*adj.* **1.** [Colloq.] chief **2.** [Slang] excellent; fine
boss[2] (bôs, bäs) *n.* [ME. & OFr. *boce* (Fr. *bosse*), a hump, swelling, akin to It. *boccia,* ball, bud] **1.** a raised part or protruding ornament on a flat surface; a decorative knob, stud, etc. **2.** *Archit.* an ornamental projecting piece, as at the intersection of the ribs of an arched roof **3.** *Geol.* a protuberant body of igneous rock laid bare by erosion **4.** *Mech.* the enlarged part of a shaft —*vt.* to decorate with raised ornaments, metal studs, etc.
boss[3] (bôs) *n.* [< ?] [Colloq.] *a pet name for* a cow
bos·sa no·va (bäs'ə nō'və) [Port., lit., new bump, new tendency < *bossa,* a bump (akin to Fr. *bosse,* BOSS[2]) + *nova* (< L. *nova,* fem. of *novus,* NEW)] **1.** jazz samba music originating in Brazil, with a light, flowing line **2.** a dance for couples performed to this music
Bos·sier City (bō'zhər) [after Pierre E. J. B. *Bossier,* 19th-c. legislator] city in NW La., on the Red River opposite Shreveport: pop. 42,000
☆**boss·ism** (bôs'iz'm, bäs'-) *n.* domination or control by bosses, esp. of a political machine or party
Bos·suet (bô swe') Jacques Bé·nigne (zhäk bā nēn'y') 1627–1704; Fr. bishop & orator
☆**boss·y**[1] (bôs'ē, bäs'-) *adj.* **boss'i·er, boss'i·est** [BOSS[1] + -Y[2]] [Colloq.] domineering or dictatorial —**boss'i·ness** *n.*
boss·y[2] (-ē) *adj.* [BOSS[2] + -Y[2]] decorated with bosses; studded
boss·y[3] (-ē) *n.* [BOSS[3] + -Y[1]] *a pet name for* a cow
Bos·ton (bôs't'n, bäs'-) [after *Boston,* port in NE England] capital of Mass., on an arm (**Boston Bay**) of Massachusetts Bay: pop. 641,000 (met. area 2,754,000) —**Bos·to·ni·an** (bôs tō'nē ən, bäs-) *adj., n.*
bos·ton (bôs't'n, bäs'-) *n.* [Fr.] **1.** a card game for four players, using two decks of cards: terms used in the game refer to the siege of Boston (1775–76) ☆**2.** a kind of waltz
☆**Boston brown bread** a dark, sweetened, steamed bread made of cornmeal, rye or wheat flour, etc. and molasses
☆**Boston bull** *same as* BOSTON TERRIER
☆**Boston cream pie** a cake of two layers with icing and a creamy filling
☆**Boston fern** a cultivated fern (*Nephrolepis exaltata bostoniensis*) with compound leaves, used as a house plant.
☆**Boston ivy** a climbing vine (*Parthenocissus tricuspidata*) of the grape family, having shield-shaped leaves and purple berries: often grown to cover walls
Boston Massacre an outbreak (1770) in Boston against British troops, in which several citizens were killed
☆**Boston rocker** a type of 19th-cent. American rocking chair, having a curved wooden seat and a high back formed of spindles held in place by a broad headpiece
Boston Tea Party a protest (1773) against the British duty on tea imported by the American colonies: colonists disguised as Indians boarded British ships in Boston harbor and dumped the tea overboard

BOSTON ROCKER

☆**Boston terrier** any of a breed of small dog having a smooth coat of brindle or black with white markings: it originated as a cross between a bulldog and a bull terrier

bo·sun (bōs'n) *n. alt. sp. of* BOATSWAIN
Bos·well (bäz'wel, -wəl), **James** 1740–95; Scot. lawyer & writer: biographer of Samuel Johnson
Bos·worth Field (bäz'wərth) field in Leicestershire, England: scene of a battle (1485) in which Richard III was killed; the crown passed to the victor, the Earl of Richmond (Henry VII)
bot (bät) *n.* [ME. < ? Gael. *botus,* belly worm < *boiteag,* maggot] the larva of the botfly
bot. 1. botanical **2.** botanist **3.** botany **4.** bottle
bo·tan·i·cal (bə tan'i k'l) *adj.* [ML. *botanicus* < Gr. *botanikos* < *botanē,* a plant, herb < *boskein,* to feed, graze + -AL] **1.** of plants and plant life **2.** of or connected with the science of botany **3.** of or belonging to a botanical species Also **bo·tan'ic** —*n.* a vegetable drug prepared from bark, roots, herbs, etc. —**bo·tan'i·cal·ly** *adv.*
botanical garden a place where collections of plants and trees are kept for scientific study and exhibition
bot·a·nist (bät'n ist) *n.* [Fr. *botaniste*] a student of or specialist in botany
bot·a·nize (-īz') *vi.* **-nized', -niz'ing 1.** to gather plants for botanical study **2.** to study plants, esp. in their natural environment —*vt.* to investigate the plant life of (a region) —**bot'a·niz'er** *n.*
bot·a·ny (bät'n ē) *n.* [BOTAN(ICAL) + -Y[3]] **1.** the science, a branch of biology, that deals with plants, their life, structure, growth, classification, etc. **2.** the plant life of an area **3.** the characteristics or properties of a plant or plant group
Bot·a·ny Bay (bät'n ē) bay on the SE coast of Australia, near Sydney: site of a former Brit. penal colony
Botany wool [< prec., orig. source of export] merino wool of high quality
botch[1] (bäch) *vt.* [ME. *bocchen,* to repair < ? Du. *botsen,* to patch] **1.** to repair or patch clumsily **2.** to spoil by poor work or poor performance; bungle —*n.* **1.** a badly patched place or part **2.** a bungling or unskillful piece of work —**botch'er** *n.* —**botch'y** *adj.*
botch[2] (bäch) *n.* [ME. *bocche* < ONormFr. *boche* (OFr. *boce*): see BOSS[2]] [Obs. or Brit. Dial.] a boil, sore, or ulcer
bot·fly (bät'flī') *n., pl.* **-flies'** [see BOT] any of a number of related flies (families Gasterophilidae and Oestridae) resembling small bumblebees: the larvae are parasitic in horses, sheep, etc.
both (bōth) *adj., pron.* [ME. *bothe* < OE. *ba tha,* both these < *ba,* fem. nom. & acc. of *begen,* both + *tha,* nom. & acc. pl. of *se,* that, the: akin to ON. *bathir,* OS. *bethia,* MDu. *bede,* G. *beide:* cf. AMBI-] the two; the one and the other [both birds sang loudly, both were small] —*conj., adv.* together; equally; as well: used correlatively with *and* [both tired *and* hungry]
Bo·tha (bō'tə), **Louis** 1862–1919; South African statesman; 1st prime minister (1910–19)
both·er (bäth'ər) *vt., vi.* [earlier *bodder* (in Swift); prob. Anglo-Ir. for POTHER] **1.** to cause worry, trouble, or annoyance (to); harass, pester, etc. **2.** to bewilder or fluster **3.** to take the time or trouble; concern (oneself) [don't *bother* to reply] —*n.* **1.** a cause or condition of worry or irritation; trouble; fuss **2.** a person who gives trouble —*interj.* a mild expression of annoyance, etc. —**SYN.** see ANNOY
both·er·a·tion (bäth'ə rā'shən) *n., interj.* [Colloq.] bother
both·er·some (bäth'ər səm) *adj.* causing bother; annoying; troublesome; irksome
Both·ni·a (bäth'nē ə), **Gulf of** arm of the Baltic Sea, between Finland & Sweden
bo tree (bō) [Singh. *bo* < Pali *bodhi* < *bodhi-taru* < *bodhi,* wisdom, enlightenment + *taru,* tree] the sacred fig tree (PIPAL) of Buddhism: Gautama is believed to have got heavenly inspiration under such a tree
bot·ry·oid·al (bä'trē oid'l) *adj.* [Gr. *botryoeidēs* < *botrys,* bunch of grapes + *-eidēs, -OID + -AL*] resembling a bunch of grapes: also **bot'ry·oid**
bot·ry·o·my·co·sis (-ō mī kō'sis) *n.* [< Gr. *botrys,* bunch of grapes + MYCOSIS] a disease of horses caused by a micrococcus (*Staphylococcus aureus*) producing a tumorous growth esp. in the shoulder, or at the cut end of the spermatic cord after castration
bots (bäts) *n.pl.* [with sing. v.] a condition of horses, cattle, etc. caused by the presence in the stomach or intestines of the parasitic larvae of botflies
Bot·swa·na (bät swä'nə) country in S Africa, north of South Africa: formerly the Brit. protectorate of Bechuanaland, it is now a member of the Brit. Commonwealth: 222,000 sq. mi.; pop. 629,000; cap. Gaberones
bott (bät) *n. same as* BOT
Bot·ti·cel·li (bät'ə chel'ē; It. bôt'tē chel'ē), **San·dro** (sän'drô) (born *Alessandro di Mariano dei Filipepi*) 1445?–1510; It. Renaissance painter
bot·tle[1] (bät'l) *n.* [ME. *botel* < OFr. *bouteille* < ML. *butticula,* a bottle < LL. *buttis,* a cask] **1.** a container, esp. for liquids, usually made of glass, earthenware, or plastic and having a relatively narrow neck **2.** the amount that a bottle holds **3.** milk from an infant's nursing bottle **4.** alcoholic liquor —*vt.* **-tled, -tling 1.** to put into a bottle or

bottles 2. to store under pressure in a tank or cylinder [*bottled* gas] —**bottle up** 1. to shut in, as enemy troops 2. to hold in or suppress, as emotions —☆**hit the bottle** [Slang] to drink much alcoholic liquor —**bot′tle·ful′** n., pl. -**fuls′** —**bot′tler** n.

bot·tle² (bät′'l) n. [ME. & OFr. *botel*, dim. of *botte* < MDu. *bote*, a bundle] [Brit. Dial.] a bundle, as of hay

☆**bottle club** a so-called club in which patrons, nominally members, are served liquor from bottles purportedly belonging to them, without regard to liquor control laws

bot·tle·neck (-nek′) n. 1. the neck of a bottle 2. any place, as a narrow road, where traffic is slowed up or halted 3. any point at which movement or progress is slowed up because much must be funneled through it [a *bottleneck* in production] —vt. to act as a bottleneck in

bot·tle·nose (-nōz′) n. any of several dolphins (genus *Tursiops*) gray or greenish above and lighter below, with a bottle-shaped snout

bottle tree any of a genus (*Brachychiton*) of Australian trees, some of which have a swollen, bottle-shaped trunk

bot·tom (bät′əm) n. [ME. *botme* < OE. *botm*, *bodan*, ground, soil < IE. base *bhudh-men*, whence L. *fundus*, ground, Gr. *pythmen*, bottom, G. *boden*] 1. the lowest part 2. a) the lowest or last place or position [the *bottom* of the class] b) Baseball the second half (*of* an inning) 3. the part on which something rests; base 4. the underside or which-ever end is underneath [the *bottom* of a crate] 5. the seat of a chair 6. the part farthest in; inner end, as of a bay or lane 7. the bed or ground beneath a body of water ☆8. [*often pl.*] *same as* BOTTOM LAND 9. a) the part of a ship's hull nor-mally below water; keel b) a ship; esp., a cargo ship 10. [*usually pl.*] the lower unit of a two-piece garment, as pajama trousers 11. fundamental or basic meaning or cause; source 12. endurance; stamina 13. [Colloq.] the buttocks —adj. of, at, or on the bottom; lowest, last, undermost, basic, etc. —vt. 1. to provide with a bottom, as a chair 2. to find the basic meaning or cause of; fathom 3. to place (*on* or *upon* a foundation); base —vi. 1. to reach or rest upon the bottom 2. to be based or established —**at bottom** fundamentally; actually —**be at the bottom of** to be the underlying cause of; be the real reason for —☆**bet one's bottom dollar** [Slang] to bet one's last dollar; bet everything one has —☆**bottom out** to level off at a low point, as prices —**bottoms up!** [Colloq.] drink deep!: a toast

☆**bottom land** low land through which a river flows, rich in alluvial deposits; flood plain

bot·tom·less (-lis) adj. 1. having no bottom 2. seeming to have no bottom; very deep, endless, etc. —**the bottomless pit** the underworld; hell

bot·tom·most (-mōst′) adj. at the very bottom; lowest, last, most basic, etc.

bot·tom·ry (bät′əm rē) n. [< BOTTOM n. 9, after Du. *bodemerij*, bottomry] a contract by which a shipowner borrows money for equipment, repairs, or a voyage, pledging the ship as security

bot·u·lin (bäch′ə lin) n. the toxin causing botulism

bot·u·li·nus (bäch′ə lī′nəs) n. a bacterium (*Clostridium botulinum*) that produces the toxin causing botulism

bot·u·lism (bäch′ə liz'm) n. [G. *botulismus* < L. *botulus*, sausage + -*ismus*, -ISM: so named from German cases involving sausages] poisoning resulting from the toxin produced by a certain bacillus sometimes found in foods improperly canned or preserved: it is characterized by profound muscular paralysis including disturbances of vision and breathing

Bot·vin·nik (bôt′vē nyik), **Mik·ha·il** (mē khä ēl′) 1911– ; Russ. chess master

Bou·cher (bōō shā′), **Fran·çois** (frän swä′) 1703–70; Fr. painter in the rococo style

Bou·ci·cault (bōō′sē kō′), **Di·on** (dē′än) (born *Dionysius Lardner Boursiquot*) 1820?–90; Brit. playwright & actor, born in Ireland

bou·clé, bou·cle (bōō klā′) n. [Fr., pp. of *boucler*, to buckle, curl, bulge: see BUCKLE²] 1. a curly wool, silk, or cotton yarn that gives the knitted or woven fabric made from it a tufted or knotted texture 2. the fabric made from this yarn

Bou·dic·ca (bōō dik′ə) *same as* BOADICEA

bou·doir (bōōd′wär, bood′-; bōō dwär′, boo-) n. [Fr., lit., pouting room < *bouder*, to pout, sulk + -*oir*, as in *parloir*] a woman's bedroom, dressing room, or private sitting room

bouf·fant (bōō fänt′) adj. [Fr., prp. of *bouffer*, to puff out] puffed out; full, as some skirts, hair styles, etc.

‡**bouffe** (boof) n. *same as* OPÉRA BOUFFE

Bou·gain·ville (bōō′gən vil′) largest of the Solomon Islands, in the Australian trust territory of New Guinea: 3,880 sq. mi.; pop. (with nearby Buka island) 64,000

Bou·gain·ville (bōō gan vēl′), **Louis An·toine de** (lwē än twän′ də) 1729–1811; Fr. navigator & explorer

bou·gain·vil·le·a, bou·gain·vil·lae·a (bōō′gən vil′ē ə) n. [ModL., after prec.] any of a genus (*Bougainvillea*) of woody tropical vines of the four-o'clock family, having inconspicuous flowers surrounded by large, showy, purple or red bracts

bough (bou) n. [ME. < OE. *bog*, shoulder or arm, hence twig or branch < IE. *bhāgus*, elbow and forearm, whence G. *bug*, upper arm or leg, BOW³] branch of a tree, esp. a main branch

bought (bôt) pt. & pp. of BUY —adj. [Dial.] *same as* BOUGHTEN

bought·en (-'n) adj. [Dial.] bought at a store and not homemade

bou·gie (bōō zhē′; bōō′zhē, -jē) n. [Fr., wax candle < *Bougie*, Algerian seaport (< ML. *Bugia* < Ar. *Buġaya*) whence wax candles were imported] 1. a wax candle 2. Med. a slender instrument introduced into a body canal, esp. the urethra or rectum, as for dilating it

bouil·la·baisse (bōō'lyə bäs′, boo′lə-; Fr. bōō yà bes′) n. [Fr. < Pr. *boulh-abaisso*, lit., boils and settles < *bouli* (Fr. *bouillir*), to boil + *abaissa* (Fr. *abaisser*): see ABASE] a chowder made with several kinds of fish and shellfish, vegetables, seasoning, etc.

bouil·lon (bool′yän, -yən; Fr. bōō yōn′) n. [Fr. < *bouillir*, BOIL¹] a clear broth, usually of beef

bouillon cube a small cube of concentrated stock for making bouillon

Bou·lan·ger (bōō län zhā′), **Na·dia** (**Juliette**) (nà dyà′) 1887– ; Fr. music teacher & conductor

Boul·der (bōl′dər) [from the abundance of large rocks there] city in NC Colo.: pop. 67,000

boul·der (bōl′dər) n. [ME. *bulder*, short for *bulderstan* < Scand., as in Sw. *bullersten*, lit., noisy stone < *bullra*, to roar (akin to BELLOW) + *sten*, STONE] any large rock worn smooth and round by weather and water

boulder clay unstratified material left by a glacier, con-sisting of boulders and rocks in a clay matrix

Boulder Dam former name of HOOVER DAM

bou·le¹ (bōō′lē) n. [Gr. *boulē*] in ancient Greece, orig., an advisory council of elders; later, a representative assembly with legislative and administrative functions

boule² (bōōl) n. [Fr., ball] 1. [*usually pl.*] a French game similar to bowls, or boccie 2. a gambling game somewhat like roulette 3. a small rounded mass, as of synthetic sapphire or ruby, produced by the fusion of alumina, suitably tinted, in a furnace

boule³, boulle n. *same as* BUHL

boul·e·vard (bool′ə värd′) n. [Fr., orig., top surface of a military rampart < MDu. *bolwerc*, BULWARK] ☆a broad, well-made street, often one lined with trees, grass plots, etc.

‡**boule·var·dier** (bōōl vär dyā′) n. [Fr.] a man who fre-quents the cafés on the boulevards of Paris; hence, any man about town

‡**boule·ver·se·ment** (bōōl vers män′) n. [Fr.] a confused reversal of things; overthrow; upset; turmoil

Bou·logne (bōō lōn′; Fr. bōō lôn′y′) port in N France, on the English Channel: pop. 49,000; also **Bou·logne′-sur-Mer′** (-sür mer′)

Bou·logne-Bil·lan·court (-bē yän kōōr′) city in France, on the Seine: SW suburb of Paris: pop. 107,000

bounce (bouns) vt. **bounced, bounc′ing** [ME. *bounsen*, to thump; akin to Du. *bonzen* & LowG. *bunsen*, to thump, strike] 1. orig., to bump or thump 2. to cause to hit against a surface so as to spring back [to *bounce* a ball] ☆3. [Slang] to put (an undesirable person) out by force ☆4. [Slang] to discharge from employment —vi. 1. to spring back from a surface after striking it; rebound 2. to move suddenly; spring; jump [to *bounce* out of bed] ☆3. [Slang] to be re-turned to the payee by a bank as a worthless check, be-cause of insufficient funds in the drawer's account —n. 1. a) a bouncing; rebound b) a leap or jump 2. capacity for bouncing [the ball has lost its *bounce*] 3. [Brit.] impu-dence; bluster ☆4. [Colloq.] a) energy, zest, dash, etc. b) the ability to regain one's spirit or optimism —☆**bounce back** [Colloq.] to recover strength, spirits, good humor, etc. quickly —☆**the bounce** [Slang] dismissal or forcible ejection [to give (or get) *the bounce*] —**bounc′y** adj.

bounc·er (boun′sər) n. a person or thing that bounces; specif., ☆[Slang] a man hired to remove very disorderly people from a nightclub, restaurant, etc.

bounc·ing (-sin) adj. big, healthy, strong, etc.

bouncing Bet (bet) a perennial plant (*Saponaria offici-nalis*) of the pink family, with clusters of pinkish flowers; soapwort: its sap forms a lather with water

bound¹ (bound) vi. [Fr. *bondir*, to leap, make a noise, orig., to echo back < LL. *bombitare*, to buzz, hum < L. *bombus*, a humming (see BOMB)] 1. to move with a leap or series of leaps 2. to spring back from a surface after striking it, as a ball; bounce; rebound —vt. to cause to bound or bounce —n. 1. a jump; leap 2. a springing back from a surface after striking it; bounce —SYN. see SKIP

bound² (bound) pt. & pp. of BIND —adj. 1. confined by or as by binding; tied 2. closely connected or related 3. cer-tain; sure; destined [*bound* to lose] 4. under compulsion; obliged [legally *bound* to accept] 5. constipated 6. pro-vided with a binding or attached cover, as a book 7. [Colloq.] having one's mind made up; resolved [a team *bound* on winning] 8. Linguis. designating a form, or morpheme, that never occurs by itself (Ex.: -*ing* in *singing*, *dis-* in *discredit*) —**bound up in** (or **with**) 1. deeply de-voted to 2. implicated or involved in

bound³ (bound) adj. [ME., pp. of *bounen*, to prepare < *boun*, ready < ON. *buinn*, pp. of *bua*, to prepare: see BONDAGE] 1. ready to go or going; headed (often with *for*) [*bound* for home? 2. [Archaic] ready; prepared

bound⁴ (bound) n. [ME. *bounde* < OFr. *bunne*, *bodne* < ML. *bodina*, *butina*, boundary, boundary marker] 1. a bound-ary; limit 2. [pl.] an area near, alongside, or enclosed by

a boundary —*vt.* **1.** to provide with bounds; limit; confine **2.** to be a limit or boundary to ☆**3.** to name the boundaries of (a state, etc.) —*vi.* to have a boundary (*on* another country, etc.) —*SYN.* see LIMIT —**out of bounds 1.** beyond the boundaries or limits, as of a playing field **2.** not to be entered or specified; forbidden

-bound (bound) *a combining form meaning* going or headed in (a specified direction) [*southbound*]

bound·a·ry (boun'drē, -dər ē) *n., pl.* **-ries** [altered after BOUND⁴ < ML. *bunnarium* (ult. of same orig.)] any line or thing marking a limit; bound; border

boundary layer a very thin layer of fluid immediately next to a solid body, that flows more slowly than the rest of the fluid

bound·en (boun'dən) *adj.* [old pp. of BIND] **1.** held under obligation; indebted **2.** that one is bound by; obligatory [*one's bounden duty*]

bound·er (-dər) *n.* [BOUND¹ + -ER] [Chiefly Brit. Colloq.] a man whose behavior is ungentlemanly; cad

bound·less (-lis) *adj.* having no bounds; unlimited; vast —**bound'less·ly** *adv.* —**bound'less·ness** *n.*

boun·te·ous (boun'tē əs) *adj.* [ME. *bountevous* < OFr. *bontive:* see BOUNTY] mod. spelling as if < BOUNTY] **1.** giving freely and generously, without restraint **2.** provided in abundance; plentiful —**boun'te·ous·ly** *adv.* —**boun'te·ous·ness** *n.*

boun·ti·ful (-tə f'l) *adj.* **1.** giving freely and graciously; generous **2.** provided in abundance; plentiful —**boun'ti·ful·ly** *adv.* —**boun'ti·ful·ness** *n.*

boun·ty (-tē) *n., pl.* **-ties** [ME. *bounte* < OFr. *bonte* < L. *bonitas,* goodness < *bonus,* good] **1.** generosity in giving **2.** something given freely; generous gift **3.** a reward, premium, or allowance, esp. one given by a government for killing certain harmful animals, raising certain crops, etc. —*SYN.* see BONUS

bounty jumper in the U.S. Civil War, a man who accepted the cash bounty offered for enlisting and then deserted

bou·quet (bō kā'; *also, and for 2 usually,* boō-) *n.* [Fr., a plume, nosegay, older *bosquet* < OFr. *boschet:* see BOSKET] **1.** a bunch of cut flowers **2.** a fragrant smell or aroma; esp., the characteristic aroma of a wine or brandy —*SYN.* see SCENT

Bour·bon (boor'bən) the ruling family of France (1589 1793; 1814–48, from 1830–48 as the ORLÉANS branch); of Spain (1700–1808; 1813–1931); of Naples & Sicily (1734–1806; 1815 60), united as the kingdom of Two Sicilies, 1815; and of various duchies & principalities in Italy at various times within the periods 1748–1807 & 1815–60, including Parma, Piacenza, Lucca, & Etruria —*n.* [*also* **b-**] a political and social reactionary

bour·bon (bur'bən, boor'-) *n.* [< *Bourbon* County, Kentucky, where it has been produced] [*sometimes* **B-**] ☆a whiskey distilled from a fermented mash of not less than 51% corn grain and stored in charred, new oak containers for not less than two years —*adj.* designating, of, or made with such whiskey

☆**Bour·bon·ism** (boor'bən iz'm) *n.* [*also* **b-**] advocacy or support of conservative government, like that of the Bourbons; extreme political and social reaction

bour·don (boor'dən) *n.* [Fr. < ML. *burdo,* drone (bee), wind instrument: see BURDEN²] **1.** a bass stop on the organ, usually of the sixteen-foot pipes **2.** the drone of a bagpipe

bourg (boorg) *n.* [Fr. < OHG. *burg,* town: see BOROUGH] **1.** a medieval town or village, esp. one near a castle **2.** a market town in France

bour·geois (boor zhwä', boor'zhwä) *n., pl.* **bour·geois'** [Fr. < OFr. *burgeis* < ML. *burgeis* < LL. *burgus,* castle, fortress < Gmc. **burgs:* see BOROUGH] **1.** orig., a freeman of a medieval town **2.** a self-employed person such as a shopkeeper or businessman **3.** a member of the bourgeoisie, or middle class **4.** a person whose beliefs, attitudes, and practices are conventionally middle class —*adj.* of or characteristic of a bourgeois or the bourgeoisie; middle-class: also used variously to mean commonplace, conventional, respectable, smug, materialistic, etc. —**bour·geoise'** (-zhwäz') *n.fem.*

bour·geoi·sie (boor'zhwä'zē') *n.* [*with sing. or pl. v.*] [Fr. < *bourgeois:* see prec.] **1.** the social class between the aristocracy or very wealthy and the working class, or proletariat; middle class **2.** in Marxist doctrine, capitalists as a social class antithetical to the proletariat

bour·geon (bur'jən) *n., vt., vi.* same as BURGEON

Bourges (boorzh) city in C France: pop. 61,000

Bour·get (boor zhā'), **Paul (Charles Joseph)** 1852–1935; Fr. novelist & essayist

Bour·gogne (boor gôn'y') Fr. name of BURGUNDY

Bour·gui·ba (boor gē'bə), **Ha·bib ben A·li** (hä bēb' ben ä'lē) 1904– ; president of Tunisia (1957–)

Bourke-White (burk'hwīt', -wīt'), **Margaret** 1906– ; U.S. photographer

bourn¹, bourne¹ (bôrn, boorn) *n.* [ME. *burne* < OE. *burna,* metathetic for *brunna:* see BURN²] a brook or stream

bourn², bourne² (bôrn, boorn) *n.* [Fr. *borne* < OFr. *bunne:* see BOUND⁴] [Archaic] **1.** a limit; boundary **2.** a goal; objective **3.** a domain

Bourne·mouth (bôrn'məth, boorn'-) resort city in S England, on the English Channel: pop. 151,000

bour·rée (boo rā') *n.* [Fr. < *bourrir,* to beat wings, whir] **1.** a lively, 17th-cent. French dance in duple time **2.** music for this dance, or a composition or movement of similar rhythm

bourse (boors) *n.* [Fr., a purse, exchange < OFr. *borse* < ML. *bursa,* a purse, bag < Gr. *byrsa,* a hide] an exchange where securities or commodities are regularly bought and sold; specif., [**B-**] the stock exchange of Paris or of any of certain other European cities

bouse¹ (boōz, bouz) *n., vi.* **boused, bous'ing** [ME. *bous(en)* < MDu. *buse(n),* drink] *earlier form of* BOOZE —**bous'y** *adj.*

bouse² (bous, bouz) *vt., vi.* **boused, bous'ing** [< ?] *Naut.* to pull up by means of a tackle; hoist

bou·stro·phe·don (boō'strə fēd'n) *adj.* [Gr. *boustrophēdon,* lit., turning like oxen in plowing < *bous,* ox + *strephein,* to turn] designating or of an ancient form of writing in which the lines run alternately from right to left and left to right

bout (bout) *n.* [for earlier *bought* < ME. *bught,* akin to MLowG. *bucht,* BIGHT; form & meaning prob. infl. by *'bout* < *about*] **1.** [Dial.] a going and coming back again, as across a field in plowing; turn **2.** a struggle; contest or match [a boxing *bout*] **3.** a period of time taken up by some activity, illness, etc.; spell [a *bout* of the flu, a *bout* of floor scrubbing]

bou·tique (boō tēk') *n.* [Fr. < Gr. *apothēkē:* see APOTHECARY] a small shop, or a small department in a store, where fashionable, usually expensive, clothes and other articles are sold

bou·ton·niere, bou·ton·nière (boōt''n ir', -er', -yer') *n.* [Fr. *boutonnière,* a buttonhole] a flower or flowers worn in a buttonhole, as of a lapel

bou·var·di·a (boō vär'dē ə) *n.* [ModL., after C. *Bouvard,* 17th-c. Fr. physician] any of a genus (*Bouvardia*) of plants of the coffee family, cultivated for the showy flowers, often used in brides' bouquets

bou·zou·ki (boō zoō'kē) *n.* [ModGr. *mpouzouki,* prob. < Turk.] a stringed musical instrument of Greece, somewhat like a mandolin, used to accompany folk dances and singers

bo·vid (bō'vid) *adj.* [< ModL. *Bovidae,* name of the family < L. *bovis,* gen. of *bos:* see ff.] of the ox family of ruminants, having characteristically a pair of hollow, unbranched horns, and including cattle, sheep, goats, antelopes, etc.

bo·vine (-vīn, -vin, -vēn) *adj.* [LL. *bovinus* < L. *bovis,* gen. of *bos,* ox: for IE. base see COW¹] **1.** of an ox or cow **2.** having oxlike qualities; thought of as oxlike or cowlike; slow, dull, stupid, stolid, etc. —*n.* an ox, cow, or related animal

bow¹ (bou) *vi.* [ME. *bouen* < OE. *bugan,* to bend < IE. base **bheugh-,* to bend, whence G. *biegen;* the n. is 17th c.] **1.** [Dial.] to bend or stoop **2.** to bend the head or body in respect, agreement, worship, recognition, etc. **3.** to yield or submit, as to authority **4.** to express assent, greeting, etc. by bowing —*vt.* **1.** [Dial.] to bend **2.** to bend (the head) in respect, prayer, shame, etc. **3.** to indicate (agreement, thanks, etc.) by bowing **4.** to weigh (*down*); overwhelm; crush [the load *bowed* him down] —*n.* a bending of the head or body, as in respect, greeting, etc. —**bow and scrape** to be too polite and ingratiating —**bow out 1.** to leave or retire formally or ceremoniously **2.** (or **in**) to usher out (or in) with a bow —**take a bow** to acknowledge an introduction, applause, etc. as by bowing

bow² (bō) *n.* [ME. *boue* < OE. *boga* < base of prec.] **1.** anything curved or bent [a *rainbow,* *oxbow*] **2.** a curve; bend **3.** a device for shooting arrows, made of a flexible, curved strip of wood, metal, etc. with a tightly drawn cord connecting the two ends **4.** a bowman or archer **5.** *a)* a slender stick strung along its length with horsehairs and drawn across the strings of a violin, cello, etc. to play it *b)* a stroke with such a bow **6.** a bowknot or a decorative knot, as of ribbon, with two or more loops **7.** either of the side-pieces of a pair of glasses extending over the ears; temple —*adj.* bow-shaped; curved; bent —*vt., vi.* **1.** to bend or curve in the shape of a bow **2.** *Music* to play (a violin, etc.) with a bow

bow³ (bou) *n.* [ME. *boue* < LowG. or Scand.: LowG. *būg,* Du. *boeg.* Sw. *bog,* shoulder, shoulders of a ship, bows; akin to BOUGH] **1.** the front part of a ship, boat, or airship; prow **2.** the oarsman nearest the bow **3.** *Naut.* a direction at a 45° angle left or right from dead ahead —*adj.* of or near the bow; forward: opposed to STERN²

bow compass (bō) a pair of drawing compasses whose legs are joined by a flexible steel band instead of a hinge, the angle between being adjusted by a screw

Bow·ditch (bou'dich), **Nathaniel** 1773–1838; U.S. mathematician, astronomer, & navigator

bowd·ler·ize (boud'lə rīz', bōd'-) *vt.* **-ized, -iz'ing** [after Thomas *Bowdler* (1754–1825), Eng. editor who in 1818 published an expurgated Shakespeare] to remove passages considered offensive from (a book, etc.); expurgate —**bowd'ler·ism** *n.* —**bowd'ler·i·za'tion** *n.*

---

fat, āpe, cär; ten, ēven; is, bīte; gō, hôrn, tōōl, look; oil, out; up, fur; get; joy; yet; chin; she; thin, *then;* zh, leisure; ŋ, ring; ə for *a* in *ago, e* in *agent, i* in *sanity, o* in *comply, u* in *focus;* ' as in *able* (ā'b'l); Fr. bäl; ë, Fr. coeur; ö, Fr. feu; ô, Fr. mon; ô̤, Fr. coq; ü, Fr. duc; r, Fr. cri; H, G. ich; kh, G. doch. See inside front cover. ☆ Americanism; ‡foreign; *hypothetical; <derived from

bow·el (bou′əl, boul) *n.* [ME. *bouel* < *boele* < OFr. *buele* < ML. *botellum*, intestine < L. *botellus*, dim. of *botulus*, sausage] **1.** an intestine, esp. of a human being; gut; entrail: *usually used in pl.* **2.** [*pl.*] the interior or inner part [the *bowels* of the mountain] **3.** [*pl.*] [Archaic] the inside of the body, regarded as the source of pity, tenderness, etc.; hence, tender emotions —*vt.* **-eled** or **-elled**, **-el·ing** or **-el·ling** to disembowel —**move one's bowels** to pass waste matter from the large intestine; defecate

bowel movement 1. the passing of waste matter from the large intestine **2.** waste matter thus passed; feces

bow·er[1] (bou′ər) *n.* [ME. *bour* < OE. *bur*, room, hut, dwelling, akin to G. *bauer*, bird cage: for IE. base see BONDAGE] **1.** a place enclosed by overhanging boughs of trees or by vines on a trellis; arbor **2.** [Poet.] a rustic cottage or retreat **3.** [Archaic] a lady's boudoir —*vt.* to form into a bower; enclose with boughs, etc. —**bow′er·y** *adj.*

☆**bow·er**[2] (bou′ər) *n.* [G. *bauer*, peasant (akin to prec.): so called from the figure sometimes used as the jack] either of the two highest cards in certain games: the jack of trumps (**right bower**) or the jack of the other suit of the same color (**left bower**): if a joker is used, it is called the **best bower**

bow·er[3] (bou′ər) *n.* [< BOW[3]] the heaviest anchor of a ship, normally carried at the bow

bow·er·bird (-burd′) *n.* any of certain birds (family Ptilonorhynchidae) of Australia and New Guinea: the male builds a mating bower, variously decorated, to attract the female

☆**bow·er·y** (bou′ər ē, bou′rē) *n.*, *pl.* **-er·ies** [Du. *bouwerij*, farm < *bouer*, *boer*, farmer: see BOOR] a farm or plantation of an early Dutch settler of New York —**the Bowery** a street in New York City, or the district around this street, characterized by flophouses, saloons, etc.

☆**bow·fin** (bō′fin′) *n.* a primitive freshwater fish (*Amia calva*) of E N. America, with a rounded tail fin and a long, narrow fin on its back

bow-front (-frunt′) *adj.* having a front with a convex curve [a *bow-front* chest]

bow hand (bō) the hand that holds the bow in archery or in playing a violin, cello, etc.

bow·head (-hed′) *n.* a whale (*Balaena mysticetus*) with a very large head and an arched upper jaw that yields whalebone

☆**bow·ie knife** (bōō′ē, bō′-) [after Col. James *Bowie* (1799?–1836) or ? his brother, Rezin, Am. frontiersmen] a steel knife about fifteen inches long, with a single edge, usually carried in a sheath, originally by American frontiersmen as a weapon

bow·ing (bō′iŋ) *n.* the manner or technique of using the bow in playing a violin, cello, etc.

bow·knot (bō′nät′) *n.* a decorative knot in a string, ribbon, etc., usually with two loops and two ends: it is untied by pulling the ends

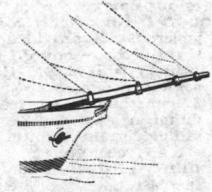

BOWIE KNIFE

bowl[1] (bōl) *n.* [ME. *bolle* < OE. *bolla*, cup, bowl < IE. base **bhel-*, to swell, inflate (cf. BALL[1]); infl. in OE. by cognate L. *bulla*, bubble, ball] **1.** a deep, rounded container or dish, open at the top **2.** a large drinking cup **3.** *a)* any intoxicating drink *b)* convivial drinking **4.** a thing or part shaped like a bowl; specif., *a)* the hollowed-out part of a spoon or smoking pipe *b)* the basin of a toilet sink or a water closet *c)* a hollow land formation ☆**5.** an amphitheater, or stadium **6.** the capacity or contents of a bowl —**bowl′like** *adj.*

bowl[2] (bōl) *n.* [ME. & OFr. *boule* < L. *bulla*, bubble, knob: see BOIL[1]] **1.** a heavy ball rolled on a level surface in bowling, esp. a weighted one used on a bowling green: see BOWLS **2.** a roll of the ball in bowling or bowls **3.** a roller, drum, or wheel, as in some machines —*vi.* **1.** to participate or take a turn in bowling or in the game of bowls **2.** to throw a bowl, usually underhand, so as to make it roll **3.** to move swiftly and smoothly [the car *bowled* steadily along] **4.** *Cricket* to throw a ball to the batsman —*vt.* **1.** to throw so as to make roll; roll **2.** to make a score of in bowling [to *bowl* 180] **3.** to cause to move along swiftly and smoothly, as on wheels **4.** *Cricket* to put (a batsman *out*) by bowling the balls off the wicket —**bowl over 1.** to knock over with or as with something rolled **2.** [Colloq.] to astonish and confuse; stagger

bowl·der (bōl′dər) *n. same as* BOULDER

bow·leg (bō′leg′) *n.* **1.** a leg with outward curvature **2.** the condition or degree of such curvature

bow·leg·ged (-leg′id, -legd′) *adj.* having bowlegs

bowl·er[1] (bōl′ər) *n.* a person who bowls

bowl·er[2] (-ər) *n.* [< *Bowler*, name of a 19th-c. London hat manufacturer] [Brit.] a derby hat

bow·line (bō′lin, -līn′) *n.* [ME. *boueline*, prob. < Scand., as in Dan. *bovline*: for bases see BOW[3] & LINE[1]] **1.** a rope running forward from the middle of a square sail's weather edge to the bow, used to keep the sail taut when the ship is sailing into the wind **2.** *same as* BOWLINE KNOT —**on a bowline** with sails set so as to head close to the wind; closehauled

bowline knot a knot used to tie off a loop so that it will not slip

bowl·ing (bōl′iŋ) *n.* **1.** a game in which a heavy ball is

bowled along a wooden lane in an attempt to knock over large, wooden pins, now usually ten, set upright at the far end **2.** *same as* BOWLS **3.** the playing of either of these games **4.** *Cricket* the act of pitching the ball to the batsman

bowling alley 1. the long, narrow wooden lane used in bowling **2.** [*often pl.*] a building or hall with a number of such lanes

Bowling Green [after the local popularity of the game of bowls] city in S Ky.: pop. 36,000

bowling green a smooth, level lawn for playing the game of bowls

bowls (bōlz) *n.* **1.** a game played on a smooth lawn with weighted wooden balls which are rolled in an attempt to make them stop near a target ball (the *jack*); lawn bowling **2.** the game of ninepins, tenpins, or skittles

bow·man[1] (bō′mən) *n.*, *pl.* **-men** (-mən) a man armed with bow and arrows; archer

bow·man[2] (bou′mən) *n.*, *pl.* **-men** (-mən) the oarsman nearest the bow of a boat

bowse (booz, bouz) *n.*, *vi.* **bowsed**, **bows′ing** [Archaic] *same as* BOOZE

bow·shot (bō′shät′) *n.* the distance that an arrow can travel when shot from a bow

bow·sprit (bou′sprit, bō′-) *n.* [ME. *bouspret*, prob. < Du. *boegspriet* < *boeg*, BOW[3] + *spriet*, SPRIT] a large, tapered spar extending forward from the bow of a sailing vessel

bow·string (bō′striŋ′) *n.* **1.** a cord stretched from one end of an archer's bow to the other **2.** any strong, light cord —*vt.* **-stringed′** or **-strung′**, **-string′ing** to strangle with a bowstring; garrote

bowstring hemp 1. *a popular name for* SANSEVIERIA **2.** hemplike fiber from the leaves of certain sansevierias

BOWSPRIT

bow tie (bō) a small necktie tied in a bowknot

bow window (bō) a bay window built in a curve

bow-wow (bou′wou′) *n.* [echoic] **1.** the bark of a dog, or a sound in imitation of it **2.** a dog: a child's word —*vi.* to bark as or like a dog

bow·yer (bō′yər) *n.* [BOW[2] + -YER] a person who makes or deals in bows for shooting arrows

box[1] (bäks) *n.* [ME. & OE., a container, box < ML. *buxis* < L. *buxus*, boxwood < Gr. *pyxos*] **1.** any of various kinds of containers, usually rectangular and lidded, made of cardboard, wood, or other stiff material; case; carton **2.** the contents or capacity of a box **3.** [Chiefly Brit.] a gift, esp. a Christmas present, in a box **4.** [< the tool box under the seat] the driver's seat on a coach **5.** a boxlike thing, opening, or compartment **6.** a small, enclosed group of seats, as in a theater, stadium, etc. **7.** a small booth or shelter for men on outdoor duty **8.** a small country house used by sportsmen [a grouse *box*] **9.** *same as* BOX STALL **10.** a space or section for a certain person or group [a press *box*, jury *box*] **11.** a short newspaper article or advertisement enclosed in borders ☆**12.** *Baseball* any of certain designated areas for the batter, pitcher, first-base and third-base coaches, and catcher **13.** *Mech.* a protective casing for a part [a journal *box*] —*vt.* **1.** to provide with a box **2.** to put into a box, etc., as for storage or shipment **3.** to boxhaul —*adj.* **1.** shaped or made like a box **2.** packaged in a box —**box in 1.** *same as* BOX UP (sense 1) **2.** to block (another racer) so as to prevent him from getting ahead —**box the compass 1.** to name the thirty-two points of the compass in order: compasses were kept in boxes **2.** to make a complete circuit, returning to the starting point —**box up 1.** to keep in; surround or confine ☆**2.** to encase with sheathing boards, or laths —**in a box** [Colloq.] in difficulty or a dilemma —**box′like** *adj.*

box[2] (bäks) *n.* [ME. < ?] a blow struck with the hand or fist, esp. on the ear or the side of the head —*vt.* **1.** to strike with such a blow **2.** to engage in a boxing match with —*vi.* to fight with the fists; engage in boxing

box[3] (bäks) *n.* [ME. & OE. < L. *buxus* < Gr. *pyxos*] **1.** any of a genus (*Buxus*) of evergreen shrubs or small trees of the box family with small, leathery leaves: some species are used as hedge plants or shaped as garden ornaments **2.** *same as* BOXWOOD —*adj.* designating a family (Buxaceae) of evergreen shrubs and trees including pachysandra

☆**box·ber·ry** (bäks′ber′ē) *n.*, *pl.* **-ries 1.** *same as* WINTERGREEN (sense 1) **2.** *same as* PARTRIDGEBERRY

☆**box·board** (bäks′bôrd′) *n.* stiff paperboard used for making boxes

☆**box calf** tanned calf leather characterized by square markings

box camera a simple camera shaped like a box and having a fixed focus and, usually, a single shutter speed

☆**box·car** (-kär′) *n.* **1.** a fully enclosed railroad freight car **2.** [*pl.*] [Slang] a throw of two sixes (twelve) at dice

box coat 1. a type of heavy overcoat, formerly worn by coachmen **2.** an overcoat that fits loosely, hanging straight from the shoulders

☆**box elder** a medium-sized, fast-growing N. American maple (*Acer negundo*), with compound leaves

Box·er (bäk′sər) *n.* [< BOX[2]; E. transl. of Chin. phrase

I-He-Chuan, "righteous-uniting-band," misunderstood as "righteous-uniting-fists"] a member of a Chinese society that led an unsuccessful uprising (the **Boxer Rebellion,** 1900) against foreign powers and foreigners in China, as a result of which China was forced to make economic and territorial concessions

box·er (bäk′sər) *n.* **1.** a man who boxes; pugilist; prize fighter **2.** [G. < *boxen,* to BOX²: from its aggressive appearance] any of a breed of medium-sized dog with a sturdy body and a smooth fawn or brindle coat: it is related to the bulldog

☆**boxer shorts** men's undershorts with an elastic waistband and the loose, full cut of prizefighters' trunks

box·haul (bäks′hôl′) *vt.* to change the course of a sailing ship) by veering around sharply instead of tacking normally

box·ing¹ (bäk′siŋ) *n.* the skill or sport of fighting with the fists, esp. in padded leather mittens (**boxing gloves**)

box·ing² (-siŋ) *n.* **1.** the act or process of packing a box or boxes **2.** a boxlike covering or casing **3.** material used for boxes

Boxing Day in England, Canada, etc. the first weekday after Christmas, a legal holiday marked (in England) by the giving of Christmas boxes to employees, postmen, etc.

box kite a kite with an oblong, box-shaped framework, open at the ends and along the middle

☆**box lunch** an individual boxed lunch of sandwiches, fruit, etc., esp. as prepared by a caterer

box office **1.** a place where admission tickets are sold, as in a theater ☆**2.** [Colloq.] *a)* the power of a show or performer to attract a paying audience *b)* a show, etc. considered with regard to this power

box pleat (or **plait**) a double pleat with the under edges folded toward each other

☆**box score** a summary in boxlike form of a baseball game, showing the number of hits, runs, errors, etc.

box seat a seat in a box at a theater, stadium, etc.

☆**box spring** a bedspring consisting of a boxlike, cloth-enclosed frame containing rows of coil springs

BOX PLEAT

☆**box stall** a large, enclosed stall, for a single horse, cow, etc.

☆**box supper** a social gathering, as at a church, at which box lunches donated by women are auctioned off to raise funds

box·thorn (-thôrn′) *n. same as* MATRIMONY VINE

☆**box turtle** (or **tortoise**) any of several N. American land turtles (genus *Terrapene*) with a hinged shell that can be completely closed

box·wood (-wood′) *n.* **1.** the hard, close-grained wood of the box shrub or tree **2.** the box shrub or tree

box·y (bäk′sē) *adj.* like a box, as in shape, plainness, confining quality, etc.

boy (boi) *n.* [ME. *boie,* servant, commoner, knave, boy < ? EFris. *boi,* akin to G. *bube*] **1.** a male child from birth to the age of physical maturity; lad; youth **2.** a man regarded as immature or callow **3.** any man; fellow: familiar term **4.** a male domestic worker or servant: a patronizing term applied esp. by Caucasians to nonwhites **5.** a bellboy, messenger boy, etc. **6.** [Colloq.] a son [Mrs. Dill's oldest *boy*] —☆*interj.* [Slang] an exclamation of pleasure, surprise, etc.: often **oh, boy!**

bo·yar (bō yär′, boi′ər) *n.* [Russ. *boyarin,* pl. *boyare,* grandee] **1.** a member of the privileged aristocracy in Czarist Russia, ranking just below the ruling princes: the rank was abolished by Peter I **2.** formerly, a member of the privileged aristocracy in Romania Also **bo·yard** (-yärd′, -ərd)

boy·cott (boi′kät) *vt.* [after Captain C. C. *Boycott,* land agent ostracized by his neighbors during the Land League agitation in Ireland in 1880] **1.** to join together in refusing to deal with, so as to punish, coerce, etc. **2.** to refuse to buy, sell, or use [to *boycott* a newspaper] —*n.* an act or instance of boycotting

Boyd (boid) [Celt.] a masculine name

☆**boy·friend** (boi′frend′) *n.* [Colloq.] **1.** a sweetheart, beau, or escort of a girl or woman **2.** a boy who is one's friend

boy·hood (-hood′) *n.* [see -HOOD] **1.** the time or state of being a boy **2.** boys collectively

boy·ish (-ish) *adj.* of, like, or fit for a boy or boys — **boy′ish·ly** *adv.* —**boy′ish·ness** *n.*

Boyle (boil), **Robert** 1627–91; Brit. chemist & physicist, born in Ireland

Boyle's law the statement that for a body of ideal gas at constant temperature the volume is inversely proportional to the pressure

Boyne (boin) river in E Ireland: site of a battle (1690) in which William III of England defeated James II, who had been deposed

boy scout **1.** a member of the **Boy Scouts,** a world-wide boys' organization, founded in England (1908), that stresses outdoor life and service to others ☆**2.** [Slang] a man regarded as being very naive or idealistic: disparaging term

☆**boy·sen·ber·ry** (boi′z'n ber′ē, bois′'n-) *n., pl.* **-ries** [after

Rudolph *Boysen,* U.S. horticulturist who developed it c. 1935] a large berry, dark red or almost black when ripe, probably a cross of varieties of raspberry, loganberry, and blackberry

Boz (bäz; *orig.* bōz) *see* Charles DICKENS

Boz·caa·da (bōz′jä dä′) *Turk. name of* TENEDOS

☆**bo·zo** (bō′zō) *n., pl.* **-zos** [< ?] [Slang] a fellow; man, esp. one who is rough, burly, uncouth, etc.

bp. **1.** birthplace **2.** bishop

B/P, BP, b.p. bills payable

b/p blueprint

b.p. **1.** below proof **2.** bill of parcels **3.** boiling point

BPD, bpd barrels per day

B.P.E. Bachelor of Physical Education

B.Ph., B.Phil. Bachelor of Philosophy

B.Pharm. Bachelor of Pharmacy

bpl. birthplace

B.P.O.E. Benevolent and Protective Order of Elks

Br *Chem.* bromine

Br. **1.** Breton **2.** Britain **3.** British

br. **1.** branch **2.** brand **3.** bronze **4.** brother **5.** brown

B/R, b.r. bills receivable

☆**bra** (brä) *n.* [< BRASSIERE] a brassiere

Bra·bant (brə bant′, -bänt′) **1.** former independent duchy of W Europe: since 1830, divided between the Netherlands (*North Brabant* province) & Belgium (provinces *Antwerp* & *Brabant*) **2.** province of C Belgium: 1,300 sq. mi.; pop. 2,085,000; *cap.* Brussels

brab·ble (brab′'l) *vi.* **-bled, -bling** [< Du. *brabbelen,* to stammer] [Archaic] to quarrel noisily over trifles; squabble —*n.* quarrelsome chatter

brace¹ (brās) *vt.* **braced, brac′ing** [ME. *bracen* < OFr. *bracer,* to brace, embrace < L. *brachia,* pl. of *brachium,* an arm < Gr. *brachiōn,* arm, upper arm < *brachys,* short (in reference to the longer lower arm)] **1.** to tie or bind on firmly **2.** to tighten, esp. by stretching **3.** to strengthen or make firm by supporting the weight of, resisting the pressure of, etc.; prop up **4.** to equip or support with braces **5.** to make ready for an impact, shock, etc.: often used reflexively **6.** to give vigor or energy to; stimulate; invigorate **7.** to get a firm hold with (the hands or feet) ☆**8.** [Slang] to ask a loan or handout from — *n.* [ME. < OFr., armful, fathom < L. *brachia*] **1.** two of a kind; a couple; pair **2.** a device that clasps or connects to keep something firmly in place; fastener **3.** [*pl.*] [Brit.] suspenders **4.** a device for setting up or maintaining tension, as a guy wire **5.** either of the signs [], used to connect or enclose words, lines, or staves of music **6.** a device, as a beam, used as a support, to resist strain or pressure, etc.; prop **7.** *a)* any of various devices for supporting a weak or deformed part of the body *b)* [*often pl.*] a device worn on irregularly aligned teeth to force them to grow into proper occlusion **8.** a tool for holding and rotating a drilling bit ☆**9.** [Colloq.] a rigid position of exaggerated attention, as that assumed by underclassmen at military academies —*SYN.* see PAIR —☆**brace up** [Colloq.] to call forth one's courage, resolution, etc., as after defeat or disappointment

brace² (brās) *n.* [Fr. *bras* (de vergue), brace (of a yard) < L. *brachium:* see prec.] *Naut.* a rope passed through a block at the end of a yard, by which the yard is swung from the deck —*vt. Naut.* to turn (a yard) by means of a brace

brace and bit a tool for boring, consisting of a removable drill (*bit*) in a rotating handle (*brace*)

brace·let (brās′lit) *n.* [ME. < OFr., dim. of *bracel, brachel* < L. *brachiale,* armlet < *brachium,* an arm: see BRACE¹] **1.** an ornamental band or chain worn about the wrist or arm **2.** [Colloq.] a handcuff: *usually used in pl.* —**brace′-let·ed** *adj.*

brac·er¹ (brā′sər) *n.* [ME. < OFr. *brasseure* < *brasse,* arms < L. *brachia,* pl.: see BRACE¹] a leather guard worn on the arm holding the bow in archery, for protection against the bowstring

brac·er² (-sər) *n.* **1.** a person or thing that braces ☆**2.** [Slang] a drink of alcoholic liquor

☆**bra·ce·ro** (brə ser′ō; *Sp.* brä sä′rŏ) *n., pl.* **-ros** [Sp. < *brazo,* an arm < L. *brachium* (see BRACE¹)] a Mexican farm laborer brought into the U.S. temporarily for migrant work in harvesting crops

brach (brach) *n.* [ME. & OFr. *brache,* back-formation < *brachez,* pl. of *brachet,* hunting dog, ult. < Frank. **brak,* akin to OHG. *brakko*) [Archaic] a female hound; bitch: also **brach′et** (-it)

bra·chi·al (brāk′ē əl, brak′-) *adj.* [L. *brachialis* < *brachium,* an arm: see BRACE¹] **1.** of or like an arm **2.** of an armlike part, as a wing or fin

bra·chi·ate (brāk′ē āt′, brak′-; *also, for adj.,* -it) *adj.* [BRACHI(O)- + -ATE¹] having widely spreading branches, alternately arranged —*vi.* **-at′ed, -at′ing** to swing arm over arm from one hold to the next, as certain apes and monkeys do —**bra′chi·a′tion** *n.*

bra·chi·o- (brāk′ē ə, brak′-) [< L. *brachium:* see BRACE¹]

a combining form meaning of an arm or the arms [*brachiopod*]: also **bra′chi-**

bra·chi·o·pod (-päd′) *n.* [prec. + -POD] a member of a phylum (Brachiopoda) of marine animals with hinged upper and lower shells enclosing two armlike parts with tentacles, that are used for guiding minute food particles to the mouth

bra·chi·um (brāk′ē əm, brak′-) *n., pl.* **-chi·a** (-ə) [L.: see BRACE[1]] **1.** the part of the arm that extends from shoulder to elbow **2.** *Biol.* any armlike part or process **3.** *Zool.* a limb corresponding to the human arm

brach·y- (brak′i, -ə) [< Gr. *brachys*, short < IE. base *mр̆ghu-*, short, whence L. *brevis*, E. MERRY] *a combining form meaning* short [*brachycephalic*]

brach·y·ce·phal·ic (brak′i sə fal′ik) *adj.* [BRACHY- + -CEPHALIC] having a relatively short or broad head; having a head whose width is 81 percent or more of its length: also **brach′y·ceph′a·lous** (-sef′ə ləs): see also CEPHALIC INDEX —**brach′y·ceph′a·ly** (-sef′ə lē) *n.*

brach·y·cra·ni·al (-krā′nē əl) *adj.* [BRACHY- + CRANIAL] broad-skulled with a cranial index of 81 or more: also **brach′y·cra′nic** (-krā′nik) —**brach′y·cra′ny** (-krā′nē) *n.*

brach·y·dac·tyl·ic (-dak til′ik) *adj.* [BRACHY- + DACTYL + -IC] having abnormally short fingers or toes: also **brach′y·dac′ty·lous** (-dak′t'l əs) —**brach′y·dac′ty·ly** (-dak′t'l ē) *n.*

bra·chyl·o·gy (bra kil′ə jē) *n.* [ML. *brachylogia*: see BRACHY- & -LOGY] **1.** conciseness of speech; brevity **2.** *pl.* **-gies** an abridged expression

bra·chyp·ter·ous (bra kip′tər əs) *adj.* [BRACHY- + -PTEROUS] having incompletely developed or very short wings, as certain insects

brach·y·u·ran (brak′ē yoor′ən) *adj.* [BRACHY- + Gr. *oura*, a tail + -AN] designating or of any of a suborder (Brachyura) of crustaceans having five pairs of legs, stalked eyes, and a short abdomen folded beneath the main body, and comprising the common crabs: also **brach′y·u′rous** (-yoor′əs) —*n.* such a crustacean; crab

brac·ing (brās′iŋ) *adj.* invigorating; stimulating; refreshing —*n.* **1.** a device that braces; support **2.** a system of braces

brack·en (brak′'n) *n.* [ME. *braken* < ON. *brakni*, whence Sw. *brakan*] **1.** any of a genus (*Pteridium*) of large, coarse, weedy ferns, as the brake, occurring in meadows, woods, and esp. wastelands **2.** a growth of such ferns

brack·et (brak′it) *n.* [earlier *bragget* < Fr. *braguette*, codpiece, dim. of *brague*, knee pants, ult. < Gaulish *braca*, pants] **1.** an architectural support projecting from a wall, as a corbel **2.** any angle-shaped support, esp. one in the form of a right triangle **3.** a wall shelf or shelves held up by brackets **4.** a wall fixture, as for a small electric lamp **5.** either of the pair of signs [ ], used to enclose a word or words inserted as

BRACKETS

for explanation, the quantities in a single mathematical term, etc.: braces and parentheses are sometimes also called *brackets* **6.** the part of a classified, graded grouping that falls within specified limits [the $5,000 to $10,000 income *bracket*] **7.** *a)* the interval between the ranges of two rounds of artillery fire, one over and the other short of the target, used to find the correct range *b)* such a pair of rounds —*vt.* **1.** to provide or support with brackets **2.** to enclose within brackets **3.** to group, classify, or associate together [Grant and Lee are *bracketed* in history] **4.** to fire a bracket of artillery rounds at (a target)

bracket fungus any of various fleshy or woody basidiomycetous fungi having fruiting bodies growing like shelves from the trunk or branches of trees

brack·ish (brak′ish) *adj.* [earlier Scot. *brack* < MDu. *brak*, salty + -ISH] **1.** somewhat salty, as the water of some marshes near the sea **2.** having an unpleasant taste; nauseating —**brack′ish·ness** *n.*

bract (brakt) *n.* [L. *bractea*, thin metal plate] a modified leaf, usually small and scalelike, sometimes large and brightly colored, growing at the base of a flower or on its stalk —**brac·te·al** (brak′tē əl) *adj.*

brac·te·ate (brak′tē it) *adj.* having bracts

brac·te·o·late (brak′tē ə lāt′) *adj.* having bractlets

bract·let (brakt′lit) *n.* a small or secondary bract at the base of a flower: also **brac·te·ole** (brak′tē ōl′)

brad (brad) *n.* [ME. *brod* < ON. *broddr*, a spike] a thin wire nail of uniform thickness with a small head, sometimes off-center —*vt.* **brad′ded**, **brad′ding** to fasten with brads

brad·awl (-ôl′) *n.* a straight awl with a chisel edge, used to make holes, as for brads

Brad·dock (brad′ək), **Edward** 1695–1755; Brit. general, born in Scotland: commander of the Brit. forces in the French & Indian War

Brad·ford (brad′fərd) city in N England, in Yorkshire: pop. 297,000

Brad·ford (brad′fərd) **1. Gamaliel,** 1863–1932; U.S. biographer **2. William,** 1590–1657; 2d governor of Plymouth Colony

Brad·ley (brad′lē) **1. A**(ndrew) **C**(ecil), 1851–1935; Eng. educator & literary critic **2. Henry,** 1845–1925; Eng. lexicographer **3. Omar Nelson,** 1893– ; U.S. general

Brad·street (brad′strēt′), **Anne** (born *Anne Dudley*) 1612?–72; Am. poet, born in England

brad·y- (brad′ē) [< Gr. *bradys*, slow] *a combining form meaning* slow, delayed, tardy [*bradycardia*]

Bra·dy (brā′dē), **Mathew B.** 1823?–96; U.S. photographer, esp. of Lincoln & the Civil War

brad·y·car·di·a (brad′i kär′dē ə) *n.* [< BRADY- + Gr. *kardia*, heart] abnormally slow heartbeat

brad·y·kin·in (brad′ə kin′in, -kī′nin; brā′dē-) *n.* [< BRADY- + Gr. *kinein*, to move] a polypeptide substance released from blood plasma by snake venoms and certain other enzymes, which slows intestinal contractions, lowers blood pressure, etc.

brae (brā) *n.* [ME. *bra*, *bro* < ON. *bra*, eyelid, brow, river bank: see BRAID] [Scot.] a sloping bank; hillside

brag (brag) *vt., vi.* **bragged**, **brag′ging** [ME. *braggen*, prob. < OFr. *braguer*, to flaunt, brag; ? akin to BRAY[1]] to boast —*n.* **1.** boastful talk or manner **2.** [Colloq.] anything boasted of; boast **3.** a braggart **4.** an old card game, much like poker —*adj.* **brag′ger, brag′gest 1.** [Archaic] *a)* spirited *b)* boastful ☆**2.** first-rate; excellent —*SYN.* see BOAST[1] —**brag′ger** *n.*

Bra·ge (brä′gə) *same as* BRAGI

Bragg (brag) **1. Brax·ton** (brak′stən), 1817–76; Confederate general **2. Sir William Henry,** 1862–1942; Eng. physicist **3. Sir** (**William**) **Lawrence,** 1890–1971; Eng. physicist, born in Australia: son of *prec.*

brag·ga·do·ci·o (brag′ə dō′shē ō, -dō′shō) *n., pl.* **-os** [coined by Spenser < BRAG + It. ending] **1.** a braggart **2.** vain, noisy boasting or bragging

brag·gart (brag′ərt) *n.* [OFr. *bragard* < *braguer*: see BRAG] an offensively boastful person —*adj.* bragging; boastful

Bra·gi (brä′gē) *Norse Myth.* the god of poetry and eloquence, son of Odin and Frigg

Bra·he (brä′ə), **Ty·cho** (tü′kō) 1546–1601; Dan. astronomer

Brah·ma[1] (brä′mə; *for n.* brā′-) [Hindi < Sans. *brahman*, worship, prayer] *Hinduism* **1.** the supreme and eternal essence or spirit of the universe **2.** the chief member of the trinity (Brahma, Vishnu, and Siva) and creator of the universe —☆*n. same as* BRAHMAN (sense 2)

Brah·ma[2] (brä′mə, brä′-) *n.* [< BRAHMAPUTRA] [*also* b-] any of an Asiatic breed of large domestic fowl with feathered legs and small tail and wings

Brah·man (brä′mən; *for* 2 brä′-) *n., pl.* **-mans** [Hindi < Sans. *brāhmana* < *brahman*, worship, prayer] **1.** a member of the priestly Hindu caste, which is the highest ☆**2.** a breed of domestic cattle developed from the zebu of India and having a large hump over the shoulders: it is well adapted to hot climates, as of the South and Southwest, and is used in crossbreeding for beef cattle —**Brah·man·ic** (brä man′ik), **Brah·man′i·cal** *adj.*

Brah·ma·ni, Brah·ma·nee (brä′mə nē′) *n.* a woman of the Brahman caste

Brah·man·ism (brä′mən iz′m) *n.* the religious doctrines and system of the Brahmans

Brah·ma·pu·tra (brä′mə pōō′trə) river flowing through Tibet, Assam (India), & East Pakistan to join the Ganges at the Bay of Bengal: c. 1,800 mi.

Brah·min (brä′mən) *n.* **1.** a Brahman (sense 1) **2.** a cultured person from a long-established upper-class family, esp. of New England, regarded as haughty or conservative —**Brah·min·ic** (brä min′ik), **Brah·min′i·cal** *adj.*

Brah·min·ism (-iz′m) *n.* **1.** *same as* BRAHMANISM **2.** the characteristic spirit, attitude, etc. of Brahmins

Brahms (brämz; *G.* bräms), **Jo·han·nes** (yō hän′əs) 1833–97; Ger. composer

braid (brād) *vt.* [ME. *breiden*, to dart, twist, pull < OE. *bregdan*, to move quickly < IE. base *bherek-*, to gleam, flash, whence ON. *bra*, E. BREAM[1]] **1.** to interweave three or more strands of (hair, straw, etc.) **2.** to make by such interweaving [to *braid* a rug] **3.** *a)* to arrange (the hair) in a braid or braids *b)* [Chiefly Poet.] to tie up (the hair) in a ribbon or band **4.** to trim or bind with braid —*n.* **1.** a band or strip formed by braiding **2.** a length of braided hair **3.** a woven band of cloth, tape, ribbon, etc., used to bind or decorate clothing —**braid′er** *n.*

braid·ing (-iŋ) *n.* **1.** braids collectively **2.** trimming with or of braid

brail (brāl) *n.* [ME. < OFr. *braiel*, a cincture, belt for trousers < *braie* < L. *braca*, pl. *bracae*, breeches < Gaulish *braca*] any of the small ropes attached to the leech of a sail for hauling it in before furling —*vt.* to haul (*in*) with brails

Brä·i·la (brə ē′lä) city in E. Romania, on the Danube: pop. 122,000

Braille (brāl) *n.* [after Louis *Braille* (1809–52), blind Fr. teacher who devised it] [*also* b-] **1.** a system of printing and writing for the blind, in which characters are formed by patterns of raised dots which are felt with the fingers **2.** the characters used in this system —*vt.* **Brailled, Brail′ling** to print or write in such characters

	1	2	3	4	5	6	7
	a	b	c	d	e	f	g
	8	9	0				
	h	i	j				
	k	l	m	n	o	p	q
	r	s	t	u	v	w	x
	y	z					

BRAILLE ALPHABET
AND NUMERALS

brain (brān) *n.* [ME. < OE. *brægen* < IE. base *mregh-m(n)o-*, skull, brain, whence Gr. *bregma*, forehead] **1.** the mass of nerve tissue in the cranium of vertebrate animals, an enlarged extension of the spinal cord: it is the main part of the nervous system, the center of thought, and the organ that receives sensory impulses and transmits motor impulses: it is made up of gray matter (the outer cortex of nerve cells) and white matter (the inner mass of nerve fibers) **2.** a comparable organ in invertebrate animals **3.** *a)* [*often pl.*] intelligence; mental ability *b)* [Colloq.] a person of great intelligence *c)* [Colloq.] the main organizer or planner of a group activity; chief controller or director —*vt.* **1.** to dash out the brains of **2.** [Slang] to hit hard on the head —**beat** (or **rack, cudgel,** etc.) **one's brains** to try hard to remember, understand, or solve something —**have on the brain** to be obsessed by —**pick (someone's) brains** [Slang] to extract information, ideas, etc. from (someone) and use them to one's own advantage

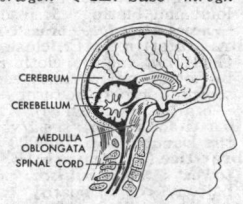
CEREBRUM
CEREBELLUM
MEDULLA OBLONGATA
SPINAL CORD
BRAIN OF MAN

brain·case (-kās') *n.* same as BRAINPAN
☆**brain·child** (-chīld') *n.* [Colloq.] an idea, plan, etc. regarded as produced by one's mental labor
brain drain [Colloq.] depletion of the intellectual or professional resources of a country, region, etc., esp. through emigration
brain fever meningitis of the brain
brain·less (-lis) *adj.* foolish or stupid —**brain'less·ly** *adv.* —**brain'less·ness** *n.*
brain·pan (-pan') *n.* the part of the cranium containing the brain
brain·pow·er (-pou'ər) *n.* mental ability; intellectual power
brain·sick (-sik') *adj.* having or caused by a mental disorder —**brain'sick·ly** *adv.* —**brain'sick·ness** *n.*
☆**brain·storm** (-stôrm') *n.* **1.** a series of sudden, violent cerebral disturbances **2.** [Colloq.] a sudden inspiration, idea, or plan —*vi.* to engage in brainstorming
☆**brain·storm·ing** (-stôr'miŋ) *n.* the unrestrained offering of ideas or suggestions by all members of a conference to seek solutions to problems
Brain·tree (brān'trē') [after *Braintree*, town in Essex, England] suburb of Boston, in E Mass.: pop. 35,000
☆**brain trust** a group of experts acting as administrative advisers, specif. during the Roosevelt New Deal —**brain truster**
brain·wash (brān'wôsh', -wäsh') *vt.* [Colloq.] to indoctrinate so intensively and thoroughly as to effect a radical transformation of beliefs and mental attitudes
brain wave 1. rhythmic electric impulses given off by nerve centers in the brain during rest, resulting in oscillations on an electroencephalogram **2.** [Colloq.] a sudden inspiration; brainstorm
brain·y (-ē) *adj.* **brain'i·er, brain'i·est** [Colloq.] having a good mind; intelligent —**brain'i·ness** *n.*
braise (brāz) *vt.* **braised, brais'ing** [Fr. *braiser* < *braise*, live coals < Gmc. *brasa*, glowing coals] to cook (meat) by browning in fat and then simmering in a covered pan with a little liquid
brake[1] (brāk) *n.* [ME.; prob. taken as sing. of BRACKEN] a large, coarse fern, a variety of bracken
brake[2] (brāk) *n.* [ME. < MLowG. *brake* or ODu. *braeke*, flax brake < *breken*, to break; senses 2-6 variously infl. by OFr. *brac* (form of *bras*, an arm) & BREAK[1]] **1.** a device for beating or crushing flax or hemp so that the fiber can be separated **2.** a heavy harrow for breaking up clods of earth **3.** a handle or lever on a machine [a pump *brake*] **4.** a machine for turning or bending the edges of sheet metal **5.** *a)* any device for slowing or stopping the motion of a vehicle or machine, as by causing a block or band to press against a moving part *b)* anything that slows down or stops motion or progress **6.** [Obs.] the rack, former instrument of torture —*vt.* **braked, brak'ing 1.** to break up (flax, clods of earth, etc.) into smaller pieces **2.** to slow down or stop with or as with a brake —*vi.* **1.** to operate a brake or brakes **2.** to be slowed down or stopped by a brake —**brake'less** *adj.*
brake[3] (brāk) *n.* [< or akin to MLowG. *brake*, stumps, broken branches, akin to OE. *brecan*, to break] a clump or area of brushwood, briers, etc.; thicket
brake[4] (brāk) *n.* same as BREAK[2]
brake[5] (brāk) *archaic pt.* of BREAK[1]
brake·age (-ij) *n.* **1.** the action or application of a brake **2.** braking capacity
brake band a flexible, lined band that serves as a braking force by creating friction when tightened about the drum of a brake, as in an automobile
brake drum the metal cylinder, as on the hub of a wheel, to which the brake band is applied in braking

brake horsepower the actual horsepower of an engine, measured by a brake attached to the drive shaft and recorded on a dynamometer
brake lining a material of asbestos, minerals, fine wire, etc. riveted or bonded to a brake band to create the friction necessary for braking
☆**brake·man** (-mən) *n., pl.* **-men** (-mən) a railroad worker who operated the brakes on a train, but is now chiefly assistant to the conductor
☆**brake shoe** a block curved to fit the shape of a wheel and forced against it to act as a brake
brakes·man (brāks'mən) *n., pl.* **-men** (-mən) *Brit. var.* of BRAKEMAN
Bra·man·te (brä män'te), **Do·na·to d'A·gno·lo** (dō nä'tô dä nyô'lô) 1444-1514; It. architect
bram·ble (bram'b'l) *n.* [ME. *brembel* < OE. *bræmel* < *brom*, BROOM (akin to G. *brombeere*, blackberry) < IE. base **bh(e)rem-*, form a point, edge] **1.** any of a genus (*Rubus*) of generally prickly shrubs of the rose family, as the raspberry, blackberry, dewberry, etc. **2.** any prickly shrub or vine —**bram'bly** *adj.*
bram·bling (-bliŋ) *n.* [earlier *bramline*, prob. < prec.] a bright-colored finch (*Fringilla montifringilla*) of Europe and Asia
Bran (bran) [< ? Ir. *bran*, raven] *Celtic Myth.* a giant king of Britain
bran (bran) *n.* [ME. *bran, bren* < OFr. *bren*] the skin or husk of grains of wheat, rye, oats, etc. separated from the flour, as by sifting
branch (branch) *n.* [ME. *branche* < OFr. *brance* < LL. *branca*, a claw, paw] **1.** any woody extension growing from the trunk or main stem, or from a main limb, of a tree **2.** anything physically resembling a branch, as a tine of a deer's antler ☆**3.** *a)* one of the streams into which a river or large creek may divide, usually near the mouth *b)* a large tributary flowing into a river ☆**4.** [Chiefly Southern] a small stream, as a brook, rivulet, or run, flowing usually into a creek ☆**5.** same as BRANCH WATER **6.** any part or extension of a main body or system; specif., *a)* a division or part of a body of learning [optics is a *branch* of physics] *b)* a division of a family descending from a common ancestor *c)* a subdivision of a family of languages *d)* a division or a separately located unit of an organization [a suburban *branch* of a library] —*vi.* **1.** to put forth branches; spread in or divide into branches; ramify **2.** to come out (*from* the trunk or stem) as a branch —*vt.* **1.** to separate into branches **2.** to embroider with a pattern of flowers, foliage, etc. —**branch off 1.** to separate into branches; fork **2.** to go off in another direction; diverge —**branch out 1.** to put forth branches **2.** to extend the scope of interests, activities, etc. —**branched** (brancht) *adj.* —**branch'like'** *adj.*
branched chain *Chem.* a nonlinear chain of atoms in which one or more series of atoms branches off another chain of atoms
bran·chi·ae (braŋ'kē ē) *n.pl., sing.* **-chi·a** (-ə) [L., pl. of *branchia* < Gr. *branchia*, pl. of *branchion*, a fin] the gills of a fish —**bran'chi·al** *adj.* —**bran'chi·ate** (-kē it) *adj.*
bran·chi·o- (braŋ'kē ō) [< Gr. *branchia*, gills] a combining form meaning gills [*branchiopod*]
bran·chi·o·pod (braŋ'kē ə päd') *n.* [prec. + -POD] any of a subclass (Branchiopoda) of crustaceans with many pairs of flattened, leaflike limbs, as the brine shrimp, fairy shrimp, water flea, etc.
☆**branch water 1.** water from a small stream or brook **2.** water, esp. ordinary tap water, as used for mixing with whiskey, etc.
Bran·cuşi (brän'kōōsh), **Con·stan·tin** (kôn'stən tēn') 1876-1957; Romanian sculptor, in Paris after 1904
brand (brand) *n.* [ME. < OE. *brand, brond*, a flame, torch, sword < base of *biernan, brinnan, vi.*, to burn: see BURN[1]] **1.** a stick that is burning or partially burned **2.** a mark burned on the skin with a hot iron, formerly used to punish and identify criminals, now used on cattle to show ownership **3.** the iron thus used **4.** a mark of disgrace; stigma **5.** *a)* an identifying mark or label on the products of a particular company; trademark *b)* the kind or make of a commodity [a new *brand* of cigarettes] *c)* a special kind or variety [a *brand* of nonsense] **6.** [Archaic or Poet.] a sword —*vt.* **1.** to mark with or as with a brand [a scene *branded* in his memory] **2.** to put a mark of disgrace on; stigmatize —**brand'er** *n.*
Bran·deis (bran'dīs, -dīz), **Louis Dem·bitz** (dem'bits) 1856-1941; U.S. jurist; associate justice, Supreme Court (1916-39)
Bran·den·burg (bran'dən burg'; *G.* brän'dən boork') **1.** former state of East Germany, earlier a province of Prussia **2.** city in C East Germany, west of Berlin: pop. 87,000
Bran·des (brän'dəs, bran'-), **Georg Morris** (born *Georg Morris Cohen*) 1842-1927; Dan. literary critic
bran·died (bran'dēd) *adj.* flavored or blended with brandy
bran·dish (bran'dish) *vt.* [ME. *brandischen* < extended stem of OFr. *brandir* < Gmc. *brand*: see BRAND] to wave, shake, or exhibit in a menacing, challenging, or exultant way; flourish —*n.* the act of brandishing something

brand·ling (brand'liŋ) n. [BRAND, n. + -LING¹: so named from the color] 1. a small, red or yellowish worm used for fish bait 2. a young salmon

☆**brand name** the name by which a certain brand or make of commodity is known; esp., the widely advertised name of a widely distributed product —**brand'-name'** adj.

brand-new (bran'nōō', -nyōō'; brand'-) adj. [orig., fresh from the fire: see BRAND] 1. entirely new; recently made and not used before 2. recently acquired

bran·dy (bran'dē) n., pl. -dies [earlier brandywine < Du. brandewijn, lit., burnt wine: so called from being distilled] 1. an alcoholic liquor distilled from wine 2. a similar liquor distilled from the fermented juice of a specified fruit [cherry brandy] —vt. -died, -dy·ing to flavor, mix, or preserve with brandy

Bran·dy·wine (bran'dē wīn') [< ?] creek in SE Pa. & N Del.: site of a battle (1777) in which the British under Howe defeated the Americans under Washington

branks (braŋks) n.pl. [NormFr. branques < Gael. brancas, instrument of punishment, prob. ult. akin to G. pranger, pillory] a device formerly used to punish noisy, quarrelsome women, consisting of an iron curb for the tongue, held in place by a frame around the head

☆**bran·ni·gan** (bran'ə gən) n. [prob. < surname Brannigan] [Slang] a noisy quarrel or fight; brawl

bran·ny (bran'ē) adj. of, like, or containing bran

brant (brant) n., pl. brants, brant: see PLURAL, II, D, 1 [< ?] any of a genus (Branta) of small, dark wild geese of Europe and N. America; esp., a variety (Branta bernicla) found chiefly in the E U.S. and N Canada

Brant (brant), **Joseph** (born Thayendanegea) 1742–1807; Mohawk Indian chief: fought for the British in the French & Indian War & the Revolutionary War

bran·tail (bran'tāl') n. [< brandtail] a local Brit. name for REDSTART (sense 1)

Brant·ford (brant'fərd) city in SE Ontario, Canada: pop. 60,000

Braque (bräk), **Georges** (zhôrzh) 1882–1963; Fr. painter

brash¹ (brash) adj. [orig., dial. & Scot.; < ?] 1. brittle or fragile, as some wood 2. hasty and reckless; rash; impetuous 3. offensively bold; pushing, presumptuous, impudent, etc. —n. 1. same as PYROSIS 2. [Scot.] a sudden shower —**brash'ly** adv. —**brash'ness** n.

brash² (brash) n. [Fr. brèche < OHG. brecha, fragment < brehhan, to BREAK¹] broken pieces or fragments, as of rock or floating ice

bra·sier (brā'zhər) n. same as BRAZIER

Bra·sil (brä zēl') Port. name of BRAZIL

bra·sil·e·in (brə zil'ē in) n. same as BRAZILEIN

Bra·sí·lia (brä zē'lyä) capital of Brazil, constituting a federal district in the EC part: pop. 141,000

bras·il·in (braz'l in, brə zil'-) n. same as BRAZILIN

Bra·şov (brä shôv') city in C Romania: pop. 137,000

brass (bras, bräs) n., pl. brass'es: see PLURAL, II, D, 3 [ME. bras < OE. bræs, brass, bronze] 1. a yellowish metal that is essentially an alloy of copper and zinc 2. things made of brass, as fittings, ornaments, implements, etc. 3. [often pl.] brass-wind musical instruments 4. a brass memorial tablet, as in the floor or wall of a medieval English church, often bearing an effigy of the deceased 5. [Colloq.] bold impudence; effrontery 6. [Obs. Slang] money 7. [often with pl. v.] [Slang] a) military officers of high rank: see BRASS HAT b) any high officials, executives, etc. 8. Machinery the lining or bushing of a bearing —adj. made of or containing brass —vt. to coat with brass

bras·sage (-ij) n. [Fr. < brasser, to stir, orig., to brew < VL. *braciare < L. brace, grain used to prepare malt < Gaul. bracis, orig., steeped, softened grain < IE. *merk-, to soften, decay (< base *mer-, to pulverize: cf. MORTAR)] a charge made by a government to cover the expense of coining

bras·sard (brə särd', bras'ärd) n. [Fr., ult. < bras, an arm] 1. armor for the arm from elbow to shoulder: also **brassart** (bras'ärt) 2. an arm band with a distinctive design that identifies the wearer in some way

brass band a band of mainly brass-wind instruments

‡**bras·se·rie** (bràs rē'; E. bras'ə rē') n. [Fr. < MFr. < brasser, to brew: see BRASSAGE] a bar where food and drink are served

brass hat [Slang] 1. a military officer of high rank: so called from the gold braid often on the cap 2. any high official, executive, etc.

brass·ie (bras'ē) n. [< BRASS: orig. made with a brass plate on the bottom of the head] a golf club with a wooden head and medium loft, used for long fairway shots: now usually called number 2 wood

bras·siere, bras·sière (brə zir') n. [Fr., orig. (14th c.) arm guard < bras, an arm] an undergarment worn by women to support the breasts or give a desired contour to the bust

☆**brass knuckles** linked metal rings or a metal bar with holes for the fingers, worn for rough fighting

brass tacks ☆[Colloq.] basic facts; practical details; really important matters: usually used in the phrase get (or come) down to brass tacks

brass·ware (bras'wer', bräs'-) n. articles made of brass

brass winds (windz) musical instruments made of coiled metal tubes and having a cup-shaped mouthpiece — **brass'-wind'** adj.

brass·y (-ē) adj. brass'i·er, brass'i·est 1. of or decorated

with brass 2. like brass, as in color 3. cheap and showy 4. loud and blaring 5. insolently bold; impudent; brazen —**brass'i·ly** adv. —**brass'i·ness** n.

brat (brat) n. [ME., cloak of coarse cloth < OE. bratt < Gael. bratt, mantle, cloth, rag: present sense ? from child's bib or apron] a child, esp. an impudent, unruly child: scornful or playful term —**brat'ti·ness, brat'tish·ness** n. —**brat'ty, brat'tish** adj.

Bra·ti·sla·va (brä'ti slä'və) city in S Czechoslovakia, on the Danube: pop. 266,000

brat·tice (brat'əs) n. [ME. bretice < OFr. bretesche, wooden tower < ML. brittisca, prob. < OHG. brittissa, lattice, balcony < bret, board] 1. formerly, a temporary breastwork or parapet put up during a siege 2. Mining a partition of wood, creosote-impregnated cloth, etc., used to form ventilation passages —vt. -ticed, -tic·ing to furnish with a brattice

brat·tle (brat''l) n., vi. -tled, -tling [echoic] [Scot.] rattle or clatter

brat·wurst (brat'wərst; G. brät'voorsht) n. [G. < OHG. < brato, lean meat (akin to OE. bræd, meat) + wurst, sausage] highly seasoned, fresh sausage of veal and pork, for grilling, frying, etc.

Braun·schweig (broun'shvīk') Ger. name of BRUNSWICK

braun·schwei·ger (broun'shwī'gər; G. broun'shvī'gər) n. [G. Braunschweiger (wurst), lit., Brunswick (sausage) < Braunschweig, Brunswick] smoked liver sausage

bra·va·do (brə vä'dō) n. [altered < Sp. bravada < bravo, BRAVE] pretended courage or defiant confidence where there is really little or none

brave (brāv) adj. [Fr. < It. bravo, brave, bold, orig., wild, savage < L. barbarus, BARBAROUS] 1. willing to face danger, pain, or trouble; not afraid; having courage 2. showing to good effect; having a fine appearance 3. fine, grand, or splendid [a brave new world] —n. 1. any brave man ☆2. [< 17th-c. NAmFr.] a North American Indian warrior 3. [Archaic] a bully —vt. braved, brav'ing 1. to face with courage 2. to defy; dare 3. [Obs.] to make splendid, as in dress —vi. [Obs.] to boast —**brave'ly** adv. — **brave'ness** n.

SYN.—**brave** implies fearlessness in meeting danger or difficulty and has the broadest application of the words considered here; **courageous** suggests constant readiness to deal with things fearlessly by reason of a stout-hearted temperament or a resolute spirit; **bold** stresses a daring temperament, whether displayed courageously, presumptuously, or defiantly; **audacious** suggests an imprudent or reckless boldness; **valiant** emphasizes a heroic quality in the courage or fortitude shown; **intrepid** implies absolute fearlessness and esp. suggests dauntlessness in facing the new or unknown; **plucky** emphasizes gameness in fighting against something when one is at a decided disadvantage —ANT. **craven, cowardly**

brav·er·y (brā'vər ē) n. [Fr. braverie, gallantry, splendor < prec.] 1. the quality of being brave; courage; valor 2. fine appearance, show, or dress; showiness

‡**bra·vis·si·mo** (brä vis'sē mō') interj. [It., superl. of BRAVO¹] very well done! splendid!

bra·vo¹ (brä'vō) interj. [It.: see BRAVE, adj.] well done! very good! excellent! —n., pl. -vos a shout of "bravo!" —**bra'va** (-vä) interj., n.fem.

bra·vo² (brä'vō) n., pl. -voes, -vos; It. -vi (-vē) [It.: < BRAVE] a hired killer; assassin; desperado

bra·vu·ra (brə vyoor'ə; It. brä vōō'rä) n. [It., bravery, spirit < bravo, BRAVE] 1. a bold attempt or display of daring; dash 2. Music a) a brilliant passage or piece that displays the performer's skill and technique b) brilliant technique —adj. characterized by bravura

braw (brô, brä) adj. [< BRAVE] [Scot.] 1. finely dressed 2. fine; excellent

brawl¹ (brôl) vi. [ME. braulen, to cry out, quarrel < ? Du. brallen, to boast] 1. to quarrel or fight noisily 2. to flow noisily over rapids, falls, etc.: said of water —n. 1. a rough, noisy quarrel or fight; row 2. [Slang] a noisy party, with much drinking of liquor —**brawl'er** n.

brawl² (brôl) n. [Fr. branle < branler, to sway, toss about, swing, ult. < Gmc. brand, sword: see BRAND] 1. an old French country dance 2. the music for this

brawn (brôn) n. [ME. braun < OFr. braon, fleshy or muscular part, buttock < Frank. brado, meat, calf (of leg), akin to OHG. brato, OE. bræde] 1. strong, well-developed muscles 2. muscular strength 3. [Brit.] cooked boar's flesh 4. same as HEADCHEESE

brawn·y (-ē) adj. brawn'i·er, brawn'i·est [< BRAWN] strong and muscular —**brawn'i·ness** n.

brax·y (brak'sē) n. [? akin to OE. broc, disease] any of various intestinal disorders of sheep, esp. one resembling anthrax —adj. having braxy

bray¹ (brā) vi. [ME. braien < OFr. braire < VL. bragire, to cry out] to make the loud, harsh cry of a donkey, or a sound, esp. a laugh, like this —vt. to utter loudly and harshly —n. the loud, harsh cry of a donkey, or a sound like this

bray² (brā) vt. [ME. braien < OFr. breier, to pound, pulverize, prob. < Frank. *brekan, to break] 1. to crush or pound into a powder, as in a mortar 2. to spread thin, as ink

bray·er (-ər) n. [see prec.] Printing a roller used for spreading ink by hand

braze¹ (brāz) vt. brazed, braz'ing [Fr. braser, to solder, var. of braiser, BRAISE] to solder with a metal having a high

melting point, esp. with an alloy of zinc and copper —**braz′er** *n.*

braze² (brāz) *vt.* **brazed, braz′ing** [ME. *brasen* < OE. *bræsian* < *bræs,* BRASS] **1.** to make of, or coat with, brass or a brasslike substance **2.** to make hard like brass —**braz′er** *n.*

bra·zen (brā′z′n) *adj.* [ME. *brasen* < OE. *bræsen* < *bræs,* BRASS] **1.** of brass **2.** like brass in color or other qualities **3.** showing no shame; bold; impudent **4.** having the ringing sound of brass; harsh and piercing —**brazen it out** to act in a bold way as if one need not be ashamed —**bra′zen·ly** *adv.* —**bra′zen·ness** *n.*

bra·zen-faced (-fāst′) *adj.* having, or uttered with, a brazen expression; impudent; shameless

bra·zier¹ (brā′zhər) *n.* [Fr. *brasier:* see BRAISE] a metal pan, bowl, etc. to hold burning coals or charcoal, as for warming a room or grilling food

bra·zier² (brā′zhər) *n.* [ME. *brasiere* < *bras:* see BRASS] a person who works in brass

Bra·zil (brə zil′) [< Port. *Brazil,* short for *terra de brasil,* land of brazilwood] country in C & NE South America, on the Atlantic: c. 3,287,000 sq. mi.; pop. 84,829,000; cap. Brasília: Port. name, BRASIL: official name, **United States of Brazil** —**Bra·zil′ian** (-yən) *adj., n.*

bra·zil (brə zil′) *n.* [ME. *brasile* < Sp. & Port. *brasil;* prob. ult. (because of color) < Gmc. *brasa:* see BRAISE] **1.** *same as* BRAZILWOOD **2.** a red dye from this wood

bra·zil·e·in (-ē′ən) *n.* [< BRAZIL + -IN¹] a bright-red dye, $C_{16}H_{12}O_5$, obtained by oxidizing brazilin

braz·i·lin (braz′′l in, brə zil′-) *n.* [BRAZIL + -IN¹] a bright-yellow compound, $C_{16}H_{14}O_5$, obtained from brazilwood as a crystalline powder and used as a dye and indicator

Brazil nut 1. any of the hard-shelled, three-sided, oily, edible seeds of a tree, that grow in clusters, like segments of an orange, in large, round hard-shelled fruits **2.** the gigantic (100–150 ft.) tree (*Bertholletia excelsa*) of S. America, on which these seeds grow

bra·zil·wood (brə zil′wood′) *n.* [see BRAZIL] a reddish wood obtained from several tropical American trees (genus *Caesalpinia*) of the legume family: it yields a red dye and is also used in making cabinets and violin bows

Bra·zos (brä′zəs, braz′əs) [Sp., arms, branches (of a river)] river in C & SE Tex., flowing into the Gulf of Mexico: 870 mi.

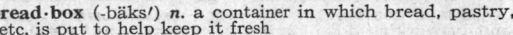

BRAZIL NUTS

Braz·za·ville (brä′zə vil′; *Fr.* brà zà vēl′) capital of the Congo (sense 3), on the Congo River: pop. 136,000

breach (brēch) *n.* [ME. *breche* < OE. *bryce* < *brecan,* to break < IE. base *bhreg-,* to break, crash; infl. by OFr. *breche* < OHG. *brecha,* of same orig.] **1.** orig., a breaking or being broken **2.** a failure to observe the terms, as of a law or promise, the customary forms, etc.; violation; infraction **3.** an opening made by a breakthrough, as in a wall, line of defense, etc. **4.** a broken or torn place or part **5.** a breaking of waves over or upon a ship, sea wall, etc. **6.** a whale's leap clear of the water **7.** a break in friendly relations —*vt.* to make a breach in; break open or through —*vi.* to leap clear of the water: said of a whale

breach of promise a breaking of a promise, esp. a promise to marry

breach of the peace *Law* any unnecessary disturbance of the public peace

breach of trust *Law* a violation of duty by a person holding property in trust

bread (bred) *n.* [ME. *bred* < OE. *bread,* crumb, morsel < IE. base *bhreu-,* var. of *bhereu-,* to well up, ferment, whence BREW, BURN¹; L. *fervere,* to boil] **1.** a food baked from a leavened, kneaded dough made with flour or meal, water, yeast, etc. **2.** any baked food like bread but made with a batter [*quick breads, cornbread*] **3.** food generally **4.** the means of living; livelihood [to earn one's *bread*] **5.** [*Slang*] money —*vt.* to cover with bread crumbs before cooking —**bread and butter** one's means of subsistence; livelihood —**break bread** to partake of food; eat —**cast one's bread upon the waters** to be generous or do good deeds without expecting something in return —**know which side one's bread is buttered on** to know what is to one's economic interest; know where the good that one has comes from

bread-and-but·ter (-'n but′ər) *adj.* **1.** relating to subsistence or to the product, work, etc. basically relied on for earnings **2.** basic, commonplace, everyday, etc. ☆**3.** expressing thanks, as a letter sent to one's host after a visit

bread·bas·ket (-bas′kit, -bäs′-) *n.* **1.** a region that supplies much grain **2.** [Slang] the stomach or abdomen

☆**bread·board** (-bôrd′) *n.* **1.** a board on which dough is kneaded **2.** a board on which bread is sliced **3.** a usually portable board on which experimental electronic circuits or diagrams can be laid out

bread·box (-bäks′) *n.* a container in which bread, pastry, etc. is put to help keep it fresh

bread·fruit (-frōōt′) *n.* **1.** a large, round, usually seedless fruit with a starchy pulp: when baked, it looks and tastes like bread **2.** the tropical tree (*Artocarpus altilis*) of the mulberry family, on which it grows

☆**bread line** a line of people waiting to be given food as government relief or private charity

bread mold a fungus (*Rhizopus nigricans*) often found on decaying vegetable matter or bread

☆**bread·root** (-rōōt′, -root′) *n.* **1.** a low-growing plant (*Psoralea esculenta*) of the legume family, common on the prairies of western N. America **2.** its edible starchy root

☆**bread·stuff** (-stuf′) *n.* **1.** ground grain or flour for making bread **2.** bread

breadth (bredth, bretth) *n.* [ME. *bræde* < OE. *brædu* < *brad,* broad; *-th* by analogy with LENGTH] **1.** the distance from side to side of a thing; width **2.** a piece of a given and regular width [a *breadth* of linoleum] **3.** lack of narrowness or of restriction [true *breadth* of understanding] **4.** *Art* an effect of unity and inclusiveness achieved as by subordinating details

breadth·ways (-wāz′) *adj.* in the direction of the breadth: also **breadth′wise′** (-wīz′)

bread·win·ner (bred′win′ər) *n.* a person who supports those dependent upon him by his earnings

break¹ (brāk) *vt.* **broke, bro′ken, break′ing** [ME. *breken* < OE. *brecan* < IE. base *bhreg-,* whence L. *frangere* & BREACH, BREECH, FRAGILE] **1.** to cause to come apart by force; split or crack sharply into pieces; smash; burst **2.** to cut open the surface of (soil, the skin, etc.) **3.** to cause the failure of by force or extralegal measures [to *break* a strike] **4.** to make unusable or inoperative by cracking, disrupting, etc. **5.** to tame or make obedient with or as with force **6.** *a)* to cause to get rid (of a habit) *b)* to get rid of (a habit) **7.** to lower in rank or grade; demote **8.** *a)* to reduce to poverty or bankruptcy *b)* to ruin the chance for success of *c)* to wreck the health, spirit, etc. of **9.** to surpass (a record) **10.** to fail to follow the terms of (a law, promise, agreement, etc.); violate **11.** *a)* to open or enter by force [to *break* a safe] *b)* to escape from by force [to *break* prison] **12.** to disrupt the order or completeness of; make irregular [the troops *broke* formation and ran] **13.** to interrupt (a journey, electric circuit, etc.) **14.** to reduce the force of by interrupting (a fall, the wind, etc.) **15.** to bring to a sudden end [to *break* a tie] **16.** to cut through or penetrate (silence, darkness, etc.) **17.** to make known; tell; disclose **18.** *a)* to decipher [to *break* a code] *b)* to succeed in solving [to *break* a criminal case] **19.** to make (a will) invalid by legal process **20.** to prove (an alibi) to be false **21.** to begin; open; start **22.** to exchange (a bill or coin) for smaller units —*vi.* **1.** to split into pieces; come apart; burst **2.** to scatter; disperse [to *break* and run] **3.** to force one's way (*through* obstacles or resistance) **4.** to quarrel; stop associating (*with*) **5.** to become unusable or inoperative; go out of order **6.** to suffer a sudden fall in prices, financial condition, etc. **7.** to change suddenly, as by a sharp rise, fall, turn, shift, etc. [his voice *broke,* the hot spell *broke*] **8.** *a)* to move away suddenly; burst forth *b)* to move apart after a clinch in boxing ☆**9.** to move into a gait other than the directed one, as in harness racing **10.** to begin suddenly to utter, perform, etc. (with *into, forth in,* or *out in*) [to *break into* song] **11.** to come suddenly into being, evidence, or general knowledge [day was *breaking,* the story *broke*] **12.** to appear suddenly above water, as a periscope, fish, etc. ☆**13.** to stop activity temporarily [we *broke* for lunch] **14.** *a)* to fall apart slowly; disintegrate *b)* to dash apart, as a wave on the shore **15.** to suffer a collapse of health, vitality, spirit, etc. **16.** to change into a diphthong: said of vowels ☆**17.** to curve near the plate: said of a pitched baseball ☆**18.** to begin a game of pool by dispersing the racked balls **19.** [Colloq.] to happen in a certain way [things were *breaking* badly] —*n.* **1.** a breaking open or apart; breach; fracture **2.** *a)* a breaking in, out, or forth ☆*b)* a sudden move away or toward; rush; dash **3.** the result of a breaking; broken place; separation; crack **4.** a beginning or appearance [the *break* of day] **5.** an interruption of a regular or continuous arrangement, action, etc. **6.** the result of this; a gap, interval, pause, omission, rest, etc. **7.** a breach in friendly relations **8.** [*pl.*] a series of dots used as punctuation; suspension points (Ex.: Came the dawn . . .) **9.** a sudden change, as in weather ☆**10.** an escape, as from prison ☆**11.** a sudden lowering or drop, as of prices **12.** an imperfection; flaw **13.** an unbroken series or sequence, as of points in billiards ☆**14.** the shot that scatters the racked balls in a game of pool ☆**15.** a failure in bowling to knock down all the pins with two balls ☆**16.** [Colloq.] an improper or untimely action or remark ☆**17.** [Slang] a chance piece of luck, often specif. of good luck **18.** *Music a)* the point where one register changes to another *b)* the abrupt change in quality of a voice or instrument at this point *c)* a transitional or ornamental phrase between regular divisions of a jazz composition —**break away 1.** to leave suddenly; get away; escape

2. to start too soon, as in a race —**break down 1.** to go out of working order **2.** to give way to tears or emotion **3.** to have a physical or nervous collapse **4.** to crush or overcome (opposition, etc.) **5.** to separate into parts; analyze —**break in 1.** to enter forcibly or unexpectedly **2.** to interrupt **3.** to train (a beginner) ☆**4.** to work the stiffness out of (new equipment) by use or wear —**break in on** (or **upon**) **1.** to intrude on **2.** to interrupt —**break off 1.** to stop abruptly, as in talking **2.** to stop being friendly or intimate —**break out 1.** to begin suddenly **2.** to escape suddenly **3.** to become covered with pimples or a rash **4.** *a*) *Naut.* to bring out of stowage for use [*break out* the foul weather gear] *b*) [Colloq.] to bring out (anything) for use —**break up 1.** to separate; disperse: also, esp. as a command, **break it up 2.** to take apart; dismantle and scrap **3.** to put a stop to **4.** [Colloq.] to end a relationship ☆**5.** [Colloq.] to distress or upset greatly ☆**6.** [Colloq.] to laugh or make laugh uncontrollably *SYN.*—**break,** the most general of these terms, expresses their basic idea of separating into pieces as a result of impact, stress, etc.; **smash** and **crash** add connotations of suddenness, violence, and noise; **crush** suggests a crumpling or pulverizing pressure; **shatter,** sudden fragmentation and a scattering of pieces; **crack,** incomplete separation of parts or a sharp, snapping noise in breaking; **split,** separation lengthwise, as along the direction of grain or layers; **fracture,** the breaking of a hard or rigid substance, as bone or rock; **splinter,** the splitting of wood, etc. into long thin, sharp pieces All of these terms are used figuratively to imply great force or damage [to *break* one's heart, *smash* one's hopes, *crush* the opposition, *shatter* one's nerves, etc.]

break² (brāk) *n.* [< ?] a former large, four-wheeled carriage for six or more passengers

break·a·ble (-ə b'l) *adj.* that can be, or is liable to be, broken —*n.* a thing easily broken; fragile article

break·age (-ij) *n.* **1.** an act or instance of breaking **2.** things or quantity broken **3.** loss or damage due to breaking **4.** the sum allowed for such loss or damage

break·a·way (-ə wā′) *adj.* **1.** breaking away from a given position, procedure, group, etc. ☆**2.** designed to break or shatter harmlessly upon slight impact, as a theatrical prop used in staging a fight —*n.* a breakaway movement, stage prop, etc.

☆**break·bone fever** (-bōn′) same as DENGUE

break·down (-doun′) *n.* **1.** an act, instance, or result of breaking down; specif., *a*) a failure to work or function properly [*breakdown* of a machine, of authority, etc.] *b*) a failure of health; physical, mental, or emotional collapse *c*) decomposition *d*) a separation into parts or categories; analysis **2.** a lively, shuffling, American country dance

break·er¹ (-ər) *n.* **1.** a person or thing that breaks; specif., *a*) a device or structure in which rock, coal, etc. are broken up *b*) a wave that breaks into foam against a shore or reef —*SYN.* see WAVE

break·er² (brāk′ər) *n.* [Sp. *barrica,* akin to BARREL] a small water keg, often carried in lifeboats

break·fast (brek′fəst) *n.* [BREAK¹ + FAST²] the first meal of the day —*vi.* to eat breakfast —*vt.* to give breakfast to —**break′fast·er** *n.*

☆**breakfast food** any prepared cereal for eating at breakfast

break·front (brāk′frunt′) *adj.* having a front with the continuity of the main surface broken, as by a projecting section —*n.* a breakfront cabinet

breaking and entering the deliberate and unpermitted putting aside of any obstacle to an entrance, which if left untouched would prevent entrance, followed by entry into a house or other structure owned by another: also called **breaking and entry**

breaking point 1. the point at which material breaks under strain **2.** the point at which one's endurance, self-control, etc. collapses under trial

break·neck (-nek′) *adj.* likely to cause an accident; highly dangerous [*breakneck* speed]

break·out (-out′) *n.* **1.** a sudden, forceful escape, as from prison or enemy troop encirclement **2.** a skin eruption

break·through (-thrōō′) *n.* **1.** the act, result, or place of breaking through against resistance, as in warfare **2.** a strikingly important advance or discovery in any field of knowledge or activity

break·up (-up′) *n.* the act or an instance of breaking up; specif., *a*) a dispersion *b*) a disintegration or decay *c*) a collapse *d*) a stopping or ending

break·wa·ter (-wôt′ər, -wät′-) *n.* a barrier to break the impact of waves, as before a harbor

bream¹ (brēm; *also, esp. for 2,* brim) *n., pl.* **bream, breams:** see PLURAL, II, D, 2 [ME. *breme* < OFr. *bresme* < Frank. *brahsima:* for IE. base see BRAID] **1.** a European freshwater fish (*Abramis brama*) related to the minnows **2.** any of various saltwater fishes (family Sparidae) ☆**3.** any of a number of freshwater sunfishes, as the bluegill

bream² (brēm) *vt.* [< ? Du. *brem,* furze (see BRAMBLE): burning furze was orig. used in process] to clean (a ship's bottom) by applying heat and then scraping

breast (brest) *n.* [ME. *brest* < OE. *breost* < IE. base *bhreus-,* to swell, sprout] **1.** either of two milk-secreting glands protruding from the upper, front part of a woman's body **2.** a corresponding gland in a female primate **3.** a corresponding undeveloped gland in the male **4.** figura-

tively, a source of nourishment **5.** the upper, front part of the body, between the shoulders, neck, and abdomen **6.** the part of a garment, etc. that is over the breast **7.** the breast regarded as the center of emotions **8.** anything likened to the breast [the *breast* of the sea] **9.** *Mining* the face that is being worked at the end of an excavation or tunnel —*vt.* **1.** to oppose the breast to; face **2.** to face or meet firmly; move forward against —**beat one's breast** to make an exaggerated display of one's feelings of guilt, remorse, etc. —**make a clean breast of** to confess (guilt, etc.) fully

SYN.—**breast** refers to the front part of the human torso from the shoulders to the abdomen, or it designates either of the female mammary glands; **bosom** refers to the entire human breast but, except in euphemistic applications [a big-*bosomed* matron], is now more common in figurative usage where it implies the human breast as a source of feeling, a protective, loving enclosure, etc. [the *bosom* of his family]; **bust,** as considered here, almost always implies the female breasts and is the conventional term in referring to silhouette, form, etc., as in garment fitting, beauty contests, etc.

breast·bone (-bōn′) *n. same as* STERNUM

Breas·ted (bres′tid), **James Henry** 1865–1935; U.S. Egyptologist & historian

breast-feed (brest′fēd′) *vt.* **-fed′** (-fed′), **-feed′ing** to feed (a baby) milk from the breast; suckle; nurse

breast·pin (-pin′) *n.* ☆an ornamental pin or brooch worn on a dress, near the throat

breast·plate (-plāt′) *n.* **1.** a piece of armor for the breast **2.** in ancient times, an embroidered cloth worn on the breast of the Jewish high priest: it was set with twelve jewels representing the twelve tribes of Israel: also (RSV) **breast′piece′ 3.** a strap across the breast of a saddled horse

breast stroke a stroke in which the swimmer faces the water and extends both arms outward and sideways from a position close to the chest, at the same time drawing up the legs and then extending them quickly backward

breast·work (-wurk′) *n.* a low wall put up quickly as a defense in battle, esp. to protect gunners

breath (breth) *n.* [ME. *breth* < OE. *bræth,* odor, exhalation < IE. base *bher-,* to boil up, foam up (of water, etc.), whence FERMENT, BARM, BROOD] **1.** air taken into the lungs and then let out **2.** the act of breathing; respiration **3.** the power to breathe easily

BREAST STROKE

and naturally [to get one's *breath* back] **4.** life or spirit **5.** air or vapor given off from anything **6.** air carrying fragrance or odor **7.** a puff or whiff, as of air; slight breeze **8.** moisture produced by a condensing of the breath, as in cold air **9.** an utterance, esp. in a low voice; whisper or murmur **10.** the time taken by a single respiration; a moment **11.** a slight pause or rest **12.** a faint hint or indication **13.** *Phonet.* a voiceless exhalation of the air stream with relative stillness at the vocal bands, as in pronouncing (s) or (p) —**below** (or **under**) **one's breath** in a whisper or murmur —**catch one's breath 1.** to gasp or pant **2.** to pause or rest so as to regain a normal rhythm of breathing —**in the same breath** almost simultaneously —**out of breath** breathless from or as from exertion —**save one's breath** to refrain from talking when talk would be useless —**take one's breath away** strike one with wonder or awe; thrill

☆**Breath·a·lyz·er** (breth′ə līz′ər) [*breath* (*an*)*alyzer*] a trademark for a U.S. device that tests exhaled breath to measure the amount of alcohol in the body: **Breathalyser** is the spelling for a trademarked Brit. device with the same purpose —*n.* [b-] such a device

breathe (brēth) *vi., vt.* **breathed, breath′ing** [ME. *brethen* < *breth,* BREATH] **1.** to take (air) into the lungs and let it out again; inhale and exhale, esp. easily and naturally **2.** to live **3.** to give out (an odor) **4.** to give out or instill as if by breathing [to *breathe* confidence] **5.** to blow softly **6.** to speak or sing softly; whisper; murmur **7.** to give or take time to breathe; rest [to *breathe* a horse] **8.** to pant or cause to pant, as from exertion —**breathe again** (or **freely**) to have a feeling of relief or reassurance —**breathe one's last** to die —**breath′a·ble** (brēth′-) *adj.*

breathed (bretht; *also for 2* brēthd) *adj.* [BREATH + -ED] **1.** having a (specified kind of) breath: used in hyphenated compounds [foul-*breathed*] **2.** [pp. of BREATHE] *Phonet.* voiceless

breath·er (brē′thər) *n.* **1.** one who breathes in a certain way [a mouth *breather*] **2.** [Colloq.] a cause of panting or fast breathing, as brisk exercise **3.** a small vent, as for the release of moisture from an enclosed space **4.** [Colloq.] a pause as for rest

breath·ing (brē′thin) *adj.* that breathes; living; alive —*n.* **1.** respiration **2.** a single breath or the time taken by this **3.** a pause for rest **4.** aspiration; yearning **5.** the sound of the letter *h* in *hit, hope,* etc.; an aspirate: see also ROUGH BREATHING, SMOOTH BREATHING

breathing space 1. enough space or time to breathe freely **2.** a chance to rest or consider a situation

breath·less (breth'lis) *adj.* **1.** without breath **2.** no longer breathing; dead **3.** out of breath; panting or gasping **4.** unable to breathe easily because of excitement, fear, etc. **5.** still and heavy, as the air; stifling —**breath'less·ly** *adv.* —**breath'less·ness** *n.*

breath·tak·ing (-tāk'iŋ) *adj.* **1.** that takes one's breath away **2.** very exciting; thrilling —**breath'tak'ing·ly** *adv.*

breath·y (-ē) *adj.* characterized by an excessive and audible emission of breath *[a breathy voice, speaker, etc.]* —**breath'i·ly** *adv.* —**breath'i·ness** *n.*

brec·ci·a (brech'ē ə, bresh'-; bresh'shē ə) *n.* [It., fragments of stone < Fr. *brèche*: see BRASH²] rock consisting of sharp-cornered bits of fragmented rock, cemented together by sand, clay, or lime

brec·ci·ate (-āt') *vt.* **-at'ed, -at'ing** to form (rock fragments) into breccia —**brec'ci·a'tion** *n.*

Brecht (breHt; *E.* brekt), **Ber·tolt** (ber'tōlt) 1898–1956; Ger. playwright

Breck·in·ridge (brek'n rij'), **John Cabell** 1821–75; vice president of the U.S. (1857–61); Confederate general

Brec·on·shire (brek'ən shir, -shər) county of SE Wales: 733 sq. mi.; pop. 54,000: also called **Breck'nock·shire** (brek'näk-, -nak-), **Breck'nock**

bred (bred) *pt. & pp. of* BREED

Bre·da (brā dä') city in S Netherlands: pop. 116,000

brede (brēd) *n.* [var. of BRAID] [Archaic] braiding or embroidery

bree (brē) *n.* [ME. *bre* < OE. **breo*, var. of *briw*, akin to G. *brei*] [Scot.] thin, watery soup; broth

breech (brēch; *for vt. 1, usually* brich) *n.* [ME. *brech* < OE. *brec*, pl. of *broc* < IE. base **bhreg-*: see BREAK¹] **1.** the buttocks; rump **2.** the lower or back part of a thing; specif., *a)* the lower end of a pulley block *b)* the part of a gun behind the barrel See also BREECHES —*vt.* **1.** to clothe with breeches **2.** to provide (a gun) with a breech

breech·block (-bläk') *n.* the block in a breech-loading gun which when closed receives the force of the combustion of the charge

☆**breech·cloth** (-klôth') *n.* a cloth worn about the loins; loincloth: also **breech'clout'** (-klout')

breech delivery the delivery of a fetus presenting itself with its breech at the head of the birth canal

breech·es (brich'iz) *n.pl.* [see BREECH] **1.** trousers reaching to or just below the knees and often tapered to fit closely **2.** [Colloq.] any trousers —**too big for one's breeches** [Colloq.] too forward, presumptuous, etc. for one's position or status

breech·es buoy (brēch'iz, brich'-) a device for rescuing people at sea, consisting of a pair of short canvas breeches suspended from a life preserver that is run along a rope from ship to shore or to another ship

breech·ing (brich'iŋ, brēch'-) *n.* a harness strap around a horse's hindquarters to help him hold back on a down grade

breech·less (brēch'lis) *adj.* without a breech

breech·load·er (brēch'lō'dər) *n.* any gun loaded at the breech

breech-load·ing (-lō'diŋ) *adj.* loading at the breech instead of the muzzle, as many guns

breed (brēd) *vt.* **bred, breed'ing** [ME. *breden* < OE. *bredan* < *brod*, fetus, hatching: see BROOD] **1.** to bring forth (offspring) from the womb or hatch (young) from the egg **2.** to be the source of; produce *[ignorance breeds prejudice]* **3.** *a)* to cause to reproduce; raise, esp. by controlled mating *[to breed dogs]* *b)* to produce (plants) by selective pollination *c)* to mate with *d)* to develop (a stock or certain characteristics in it) by such mating or pollination **4.** to bring up, train, or educate *[bred to be a gentleman]* **5.** to produce (fissionable material) in a breeder reactor —*vi.* **1.** to be produced; originate *[crime breeds in slums]* **2.** to bring forth offspring; reproduce —*n.* **1.** a group, or stock, of animals or plants descended from common ancestors and having similar characteristics, esp. such a group cultivated by man **2.** a kind; sort; type *[men of the same breed]*

breed·er (-ər) *n.* **1.** an animal or plant that produces offspring **2.** a person who breeds animals or plants **3.** a cause; source **4.** *same as* BREEDER REACTOR

breeder reactor a nuclear reactor that, in addition to generating atomic energy, creates additional fuel by producing more fissionable material than it consumes

breed·ing (-iŋ) *n.* [see BREED] **1.** the producing of young **2.** the rearing of young; upbringing, education, or training, esp. in manners or social behavior **3.** good upbringing or training *[tolerance is a sign of breeding]* **4.** the producing of plants and animals, esp. for the purpose of developing new or better types

BREECHES

BREECHES BUOY

Breed's Hill (brēdz) hill near Bunker Hill in Boston, where the Battle of Bunker Hill was actually fought

breeks (brēks) *n.pl.* [Chiefly Scot.] *same as* BREECHES

☆**breen** (brēn) *n.* [BR(OWN) + (GR)EEN] a brownish-green color —*adj.* of a brownish-green color

breeze¹ (brēz) *n.* [16th-c. nautical term *brize* < Fr. *brise*, prob. < EFris. *brisen*, to blow fresh and strong] **1.** a light current of air; wind, esp. a gentle wind **2.** [Brit. Colloq.] commotion or disturbance ☆**3.** [Colloq.] a thing easy to do **4.** *Meteorol.* any wind ranging in speed from 4 to 31 miles per hour: see BEAUFORT SCALE —*vi.* **1.** to blow (often with *up*): said of a wind ☆**2.** [Slang] to move or go quickly, jauntily, easily, etc. —☆**in a breeze** [Colloq.] with little or no effort; easily —☆**shoot** (or **bat**) **the breeze** [Slang] to converse idly about trivial matters —*SYN.* see WIND²

breeze² (brēz) *n.* [Fr. *braise*, live coals: see BRAISE] a substance left when coke, coal, or charcoal is burned, used as a filler for concrete, etc.

☆**breeze·way** (-wā') *n.* a covered passageway, as between a house and garage, often enclosed on the sides

breez·y (-ē) *adj.* **breez'i·er, breez'i·est 1.** with breezes blowing; slightly windy *[a breezy day]* **2.** light and gay; lively and carefree *[breezy talk]* —**breez'i·ly** *adv.* —**breez'i·ness** *n.*

Bre·genz (brā'gents) city in westernmost Austria, on Lake Constance: pop. 21,000

breg·ma (breg'mə) *n., pl.* **breg'ma·ta** (-mə tə) [Gr.: see BRAIN] the part of the skull where the frontal bone and side bones come together —**breg·mat'ic** (-mat'ik) *adj.*

Bre·men (brem'ən; *G.* brā'mən) **1.** state of N West Germany, consisting of the cities of Bremen & Bremerhaven: 156 sq. mi.; pop. 733,000 **2.** capital of this state; seaport on the Weser River: pop. 588,000

Bre·mer·ha·ven (brem'ər hä'vən; *G.* brā'mər häf'ən) seaport at the mouth of the Weser River, in N West Germany: pop. 145,000

brems·strah·lung (brem'shträ loon) *n.* [G., lit., braked radiation < *bremse*, a brake + *strahlung*, radiation] the electromagnetic radiation given off by a high-energy particle, as an electron, when suddenly accelerated or retarded by another charged particle, as an atomic nucleus

Bren·da (bren'də) [prob. fem. of *Brand* < G. *brand* or ON. *brandr*, a sword: see BRAND] a feminine name

Bren (gun) (bren) [< *Br*no, Czechoslovakia, where first made + *En*field, England, where manufactured for the Brit. army] a light, fast, gas-operated machine gun used by the British army in World War II

Bren·nan (bren'ən), **William J(oseph), Jr.** 1906– ; associate justice, U.S. Supreme Court (1956–)

Bren·ner Pass (bren'ər) mountain pass across the Alps at the border between Italy & Austria: 4,495 ft. high

brent (brent) *n. same as* BRANT

☆**br'er** (brur) [South Dial.] brother: used before a name

Bre·scia (bre'shä) commune in N Italy, at the foot of the Alps: pop. 191,000

Bres·lau (bres'lou) *Ger. name of* WROCLAW

Brest (brest) **1.** seaport in W France, on the Atlantic: pop. 136,000 **2.** city in W Byelorussian S.S.R., on the Bug River: pop. 78,000: site of the signing of a Russo-German treaty (1918): before 1921 called **Brest-Li·tovsk** (brest'li tôfsk')

Bre·tagne (brə tän'y') *Fr. name of* BRITTANY

breth·ren (breth'rən, -ərn) *n.pl.* [ME. *bretheren*, pl.: see BROTHER] brothers: now chiefly in religious use

Bret·on (bret'n) *adj.* [Fr., ult. same word as BRITON] of Brittany, its people, or their language —*n.* **1.** a native or inhabitant of Brittany **2.** the Celtic language of the Bretons

Bre·ton (brə tōn'), **An·dré** (än drā') 1896–1966; Fr. poet & art critic: a founder of surrealism

Breton lace a delicate lace with a design of heavy thread embroidered on net

Bret·ton Woods (bret'n) [after *Bretton* Hall, Eng. country-seat of one of the founders] resort in the White Mountains, N.H.: site of a UN monetary and financial conference (1944)

Breu·ghel (brü'gəl) *occas.* broi'-) *same as* BRUEGEL

breve (brev, brēv) *n.* [It. < L. *brevis*, BRIEF] **1.** a mark (˘) put over a short vowel or short or unstressed syllable **2.** *Law* a judicial writ **3.** *Music* a note (⊏⊐) equal to two whole notes: now seldom used in notation

bre·vet (brə vet'; *chiefly Brit.* brev'it) *n.* [ME. < OFr., a note < ML. *breve*, letter (in LL., summary) < L. *brevis*, BRIEF] *Mil.* a commission nominally promoting an officer to a higher honorary rank without higher pay or greater authority —*adj.* held or given by brevet —*vt.* **-vet'ted** or **-vet'ed, -vet'ting** or **-vet'ing** to promote by brevet

bre·vet·cy (brə vet'sē) *n., pl.* **-cies** any honorary rank conferred by brevet

brev·i- (brev'ē) [< L. *brevis*, BRIEF] a combining form meaning short

bre·vi·ar·y (brē'vē er'ē, brēv'yər ē) *n., pl.* **-ar'ies** [ML. *breviarium* < L., an abridgment < *breviarius*, abridged <

brevis, BRIEF] **1.** a book containing the prayers, hymns, etc. that priests and certain other clerics of the Roman Catholic Church are required to recite daily **2.** a book like this used in the Orthodox Eastern Church

bre·vier (brə vir′) *n.* [OFr. < ML. *breviarium*: so called from use in breviaries] a size of type, 8 point

brev·i·rost·rate (brev′ə räs′trāt) *adj.* [BREVI- + ROSTRATE] having a short beak or bill: said of a bird

brev·i·ty (brev′ə tē) *n.* [L. *brevitas* < *brevis*, BRIEF] **1.** the quality of being brief; shortness of time **2.** the quality of being concise; terseness

brew (brōō) *vt.* [ME. *breuen* < OE. *breowan*, akin to G. *brauen*: for IE. base see BREAD] **1.** to make (beer, ale, etc.) from malt and hops by steeping, boiling, and fermenting **2.** to make (tea, coffee, etc.) by steeping or boiling **3.** to plan (mischief, trouble, etc.); plot; scheme —*vi.* **1.** to brew beer, ale, etc. **2.** to begin to form: said of a storm, trouble, etc. —*n.* **1.** a beverage that has been brewed **2.** an amount brewed **3.** the brewing process —**brew′er** *n.*

brew·age (-ij) *n.* **1.** anything brewed; esp., malt liquor **2.** the process of brewing

brewer's yeast a yeast (*Saccharomyces cerevisiae*) used in brewing beer **2.** the by-product yeast left after brewing, often used in medicine and foods

brew·er·y (brōō′ər ē, brōō′rē) *n., pl.* **-er·ies** an establishment where beer, ale, etc. are brewed

brew·ing (brōō′in) *n.* **1.** the preparation of a brew **2.** the amount of brew made at one time

brew·is (brōō′is) *n.* [ME. *broues* < OFr. *broez*, pl. of *broet*, beef broth, dim. of *bro*, broth < Gmc. base *brod-*, BROTH] [Dial.] **1.** beef broth **2.** bread soaked in beef broth

Brew·ster (brōō′stər), **William** 1567?–1644; Eng. Pilgrim who helped settle Plymouth Colony

Brezh·nev (brezh nyôf′; *E.* brezh′nef, -nev), **Le·o·nid I(lich)** (lā′ô nyēt′) 1906– ; general secretary of the Communist Party of the U.S.S.R. (1964– .)

Bri·an (brī′ən) [Celt., ? strong] a masculine name

Bri·an Bo·ru (brī′ən bə rōō′) 926?–1014: king of Ireland (1002–14): It. name **Brian Bo·ram·he** (brēn bô rō′)

Bri·and (brē än′), **A·ris·tide** (á rē stēd′) 1862–1932; Fr. statesman

bri·ar¹ (brī′ər) *n. same as* BRIER¹ —**bri′ar·y** *adj.*

bri·ar² (brī′ər) *n.* **1.** *same as* BRIER² **2.** a tobacco pipe made of brierroot

Bri·ar·e·us (brī ar′ē əs) [L. < Gr. *Briareōs* < *briaros*, strong] *Gr. Myth.* a hundred-handed giant who fought against the Titans —**Bri·ar′e·an** *adj.*

bri·ar·root (brī′ər rōōt′, -root′) *n. same as* BRIERROOT

bri·ar·wood (-wood′) *n. same as* BRIERWOOD

bribe (brīb) *n.* [ME. < OFr., morsel of bread given to beggars < *briber*, to beg] **1.** anything, esp. money, given or promised to induce a person to do something illegal or wrong **2.** anything given or promised to induce a person to do something against his wishes —*vt.* **bribed, brib′ing 1.** to offer or give a bribe to **2.** to get or influence by bribing —*vi.* to give a bribe or bribes —**brib′a·ble** *adj.* —**brib′er** *n.*

brib·er·y (brī′bər ē) *n., pl.* **-er·ies** [ME. & OFr. *briberie*, theft: see prec.] the giving, offering, or taking of bribes

bric-a-brac (brik′ə brak′) *n.* [Fr. *bric-à-brac* < phr. *à bric et à brac*, by hook or crook] **1.** small, rare, or artistic objects placed about a room for decoration **2.** knickknacks

brick (brik) *n.* [ME. *brike* < MDu. < *breken*, BREAK¹ (in sense "piece of baked clay") & < Fr. *brique*, of same orig.] **1.** a substance made from clay molded into oblong blocks and fired in a kiln or baked in the sun, used in building, paving, etc. **2.** one of these blocks, of any of various standard sizes **3.** bricks collectively **4.** anything shaped like a brick **5.** [Colloq.] a fine fellow —*adj.* **1.** built or paved with brick **2.** like brick [*brick* red] —*vt.* to build, line, or pave with brick —**brick up** (or **in**) to close or wall in with brick —✩**hit the bricks** [Slang] to go out on strike —**make bricks without straw** [from use of straw as binding agent in sun-baked bricks: cf. Ex. 5:7] to do something without the necessary material

brick·bat (-bat′) *n.* **1.** a piece of brick, esp. one used as a missile **2.** an unfavorable or critical remark

✩**brick cheese** a ripened, semihard American cheese shaped like a brick and containing many small holes

brick·lay·ing (-lā′in) *n.* the act or work of building or paving with bricks —**brick′lay′er** *n.*

brick·le (brik′l) *adj., n.* [ME. *brikel*, var. of *brokel*, brittle < base of OE. *brecan*, to break¹] [Dial.] brittle

brick red yellowish or brownish red —**brick′-red′** *adj.*

brick·work (-wurk′) *n.* **1.** a thing or part built of bricks **2.** bricklaying

✩**brick·yard** (-yärd′) *n.* a place where bricks are made or sold

bri·cole (bri kōl′, brik′l) *n.* [Fr. < Pr. *bricola*] **1.** a medieval catapult **2.** an indirect or oblique stroke, as a cushion shot in billiards

brid·al (brīd′l) *n.* [ME. *bridale* < OE. *bryd ealo*, bride ale, marriage feast < *bryd*, BRIDE¹ + *ealo*, ALE] a wedding —*adj.* **1.** of a bride **2.** of a wedding

bridal wreath ✩a cultivated shrub (*Spiraea prunifolia*) of the rose family, bearing numerous small, white double flowers in the spring

bride¹ (brīd) *n.* [ME. < OE. *bryd*, akin to G. *braut*, betrothed, fiancée] a woman who has just been married or is about to be married

bride² (brīd) *n.* [Fr. < OFr. < OHG. *britel*, akin to BRIDLE] in lace making and other needlework, a loop or tie that connects parts of a pattern

Bride (brīd), Saint *same as* BRIDGET (sense 2)

bride·groom (brīd′grōōm′, -groom′) *n.* [ME. *bridegome* < OE. *brydguma*, suitor < *bryd*, bride + *guma* (akin to L. *homo*), man; altered by folk-etym. after GROOM] a man who has just been married or is about to be married

brides·maid (brīdz′mād′) *n.* one of the young women who attend the bride at a wedding

bride·well (brīd′wel, -wəl) *n.* [after a former house of correction in London, orig. a royal palace, named from the nearby *St. Bride's Well*] a prison for minor offenses; jail; house of correction

bridge¹ (brij) *n.* [ME. *brigge* < OE. *brycge* < IE. base *bhrū*, log, beam, hence wooden causeway] **1.** a structure built over a river, railroad, highway, etc. to provide a way across for vehicles or pedestrians **2.** a thing that provides connection, contact, or transition [a common language is a *bridge* between cultures] **3.** *a)* the upper, bony part of the nose **b)** the curved bow of a pair of glasses fitting over the nose **4.** the thin arched piece over which the strings of a violin, cello, etc. are stretched **5.** an overhead framework across sets of railroad tracks, for carrying signals; gantry **6.** a platform above the main deck of a ship, from which it is controlled, as by the commanding officer **7.** a dividing partition for keeping fuel in place in a furnace or boiler **8.** *Billiards a)* the position in which the hand is placed to form a support for the cue in making a shot **b)** a notched piece of wood sometimes used for this purpose **9.** *Dentistry* a fixed or removable mounting for a false tooth or teeth, attached to a real tooth or teeth **10.** *Elec.* a device used primarily in measuring resistances, frequencies, etc., by comparing the effect of the unknown element with that of known or standard elements in the circuit **11.** *Music* a connecting passage between two sections of a composition —*vt.* **bridged, bridg′ing 1.** to build a bridge on or over **2.** to provide a bridge, connection, transition, etc. across or between —**burn one's bridges (behind one)** to commit oneself to a course from which there is no retreat —**bridge′a·ble** *adj.*

bridge² (brij) *n.* [earlier (1886) *biritch*, "Russian whist," altered after prec.; game and name ? of Russ. origin] any of various card games for two pairs of players, that developed from whist: see AUCTION BRIDGE, CONTRACT BRIDGE

bridge·board (-bôrd′) *n.* any of the notched boards holding the treads and risers of a staircase; string

bridge·head (-hed′) *n.* **1.** a fortified place or position established by an attacking force on the enemy's side of a bridge, river, defile, etc. **2.** *same as* BEACHHEAD (sense 2)

Bridge·port (brij′pôrt) [after the bridge across the Poquonock River] seaport in SW Conn., on Long Island Sound; pop. 157,000

Bridg·es (brij′əz) **1.** Harry, (born *Alfred Bryant Renton Bridges*) 1900– ; U.S. labor leader, born in Australia **2.** Robert (Seymour), 1844–1930; Eng. poet; poet laureate (1913–30)

Bridg·et (brij′it) [Ir. *Brighid*, lit., strong, lofty; akin to Sans. *bṛhati*, high, powerful] **1.** a feminine name: dim. *Biddy;* equiv. Fr. & Ger. *Brigitte* **2.** Saint, 451?–523 A.D.; Ir. abbess; a patron saint of Ireland: her day is Feb. 1 **3.** Saint, 1302?–73; Swed. nun: founder of the order of *Bri(d)gittines:* her day is Oct. 8

Bridge·town (brij′toun) capital & seaport of Barbados, West Indies: pop. 94,000

bridge·work (-wurk′) *n.* a dental bridge or bridges

bridg·ing (-in) *n.* braces used between timbers, as of a floor, for reinforcement and distribution of strain

bri·dle (brīd′l) *n.* [ME. & OE. *bridel* < *bregdan*, to pull, turn: see BRAID] **1.** a head harness for guiding a horse: it consists of headstall, bit, and reins **2.** a thing like a horse's bridle **3.** anything that controls or restrains **4.** *same as* FRENUM **5.** a connecting metal strip for limiting motion in machinery **6.** *Naut.* a cable with the ends fast and another cable attached to it between the ends for applying force —*vt.* **bri′dled, bri′dling 1.** to put a bridle on **2.** to curb or control with or as with a bridle —*vi.* **1.** to pull one's head back quickly with the chin drawn in as an expression of anger, scorn, pride, etc. **2.** to take offense (*at*) —*SYN.* see RESTRAIN

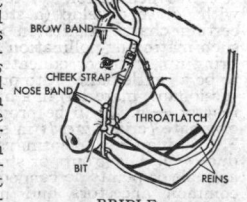

BRIDLE

bridle path a path for horseback riding

✩**bri·dle·wise** (-wīz′) *adj.* trained to obey the pressure of the reins on the neck instead of the pull on the bit

bri·doon (bri dōōn′) *n.* [Fr. *bridon* < *bride:* see BRIDE²] the snaffle bit and reins of a military bridle, used with or without curbs

Brie cheese (brē) [after *Brie*, region in France, east of Paris] a ripened soft, white cheese made in France, or a similar cheese made elsewhere

brief (brēf) *adj.* [ME. < OFr. *bref* < L. *brevis* < IE. base *mreghu-*, short, whence Gr. *brachys*, E. MERRY] **1.** of short duration or extent **2.** short in length **3.** using relatively

few words; concise **4.** curt or abrupt —*n.* [ME. *bref* < OFr. *bref* < L. *breve,* summary, short catalogue < the *adj.*] **1.** a summary or abstract **2.** a concise statement of the main points of a law case, usually filed by counsel for the information of the court **3.** *R.C.Ch.* a papal letter less formal than a bull **4.** [*pl.*] closefitting, legless underpants —*vt.* **1.** to make a summary of **2.** to supply with all the pertinent instructions or information *[to brief pilots before a flight]* **3.** [Brit.] *a)* to furnish with a legal brief *b)* to hire as counsel —**hold a brief for** to argue for or be in favor of —**in brief** in short; in a few words —**brief′ing** *n.*—**brief′ly** *adv.* —**brief′ness** *n.*

SYN.—brief and **short** are opposites of *long* in their application to duration *[a brief or short interval]*, although **brief** often emphasizes compactness, conciseness, etc. *[a brief review]* and **short** often implies incompleteness or curtailment *[a short measure, to make short work of it]*; **short** is usually used where linear extent is referred to *[a short man]* See also **abridgment** —*ANT.* **long, prolonged**

brief·case (-kās′) *n.* a flat, flexible case, usually of leather, for carrying papers, books, etc.

brief·less (-lis) *adj.* without clients: said of a lawyer

brief of title *Law* an abstract of all the legal documents, records, court proceedings, etc. affecting the title to a parcel of real property

bri·er¹ (brī′ər) *n.* [ME. *brere* (with vowel change as in FRIAR < ME. *frere*) < OE. *brer, brær*] **1.** any prickly or thorny bush, as a bramble, wild rose, etc. **2.** a growth of such bushes **3.** a twig of a brier —**bri′er·y** *adj.*

bri·er² (brī′ər) *n.* [Fr. *bruyère,* white heath < Gaul. **brucus,* heather, broom] **1.** a heath (genus *Erica*) native to S Europe: its root is used in making tobacco pipes **2.** this root or a tobacco pipe made from it: in this sense, usually sp. **bri′ar**

bri·er·root (brī′ər rōōt′, -root′) *n.* the root wood, esp. the root burl, of the brier, or a pipe made of this

bri·er·wood (-wood′) *n.* same as BRIERROOT

brig¹ (brig) *n.* [contr. < BRIGANTINE] a two-masted ship with square sails

☆**brig²** (brig) *n.* [< ?] **1.** the prison on a U.S. warship **2.** [Mil. Slang] the guardhouse; prison

bri·gade (bri gād′) *n.* [Fr.; < It. *brigata,* troop, company < *brigare,* to contend < *briga,* strife, quarrel] **1.** a large unit of soldiers **2.** formerly, a unit of the U.S. Army comprising two or more regiments; now, a military unit composed of two or more battalions with service and administrative units **3.** a group of people organized to function as a unit in some work *[a fire brigade]* —*vt.* **-gad′ed, -gad′ing** to organize into a brigade

brig·a·dier (brig′ə dir′) *n.* [Fr. < prec.] **1.** the commander of a brigade **2.** in the British and Canadian armies, an officer ranking above a colonel and below a major general

brigadier general *pl.* **brigadier generals** *U.S. Mil.* an officer ranking above a colonel and below a major general

brig·and (brig′ənd) *n.* [ME. *brigaunt* < OFr. < It. *brigante* < *brigare:* see BRIGADE] a bandit, usually one of a roving band

brig·and·age (-ən dij) *n.* [Fr. < prec.] **1.** plundering by brigands **2.** brigands collectively

brig·an·dine (brig′ən dēn′) *n.* [Fr. < It. *brigantina* < *brigare:* see BRIGADE] a flexible coat of armor made of small metal scales or rings fastened to leather or linen

brig·an·tine (brig′ən tēn′) *n.* [Fr. *brigantin* < It. *brigantino,* brigantine, pirate vessel: see BRIGAND] **1.** a two-masted ship with the foremast square-rigged and a fore-and-aft mainsail **2.** a hermaphrodite brig

Brig. Gen. Brigadier General

bright (brīt) *adj.* [ME. < OE. *bryht,* earlier *beorht* < IE. base **bhereg-,* to gleam, white, whence Goth. *bairhts,* E. BIRCH] **1.** shining with light that is radiated or reflected; full of light **2.** clear or brilliant in color or sound; vivid or intense **3.** lively; vivacious; cheerful *[a bright smile]* **4.** mentally quick; smart, clever, witty, etc. **5.** *a)* full of happiness or hope *[a bright outlook on life]* *b)* favorable; auspicious **6.** glorious or splendid; illustrious —*adv.* in a bright manner —*n.* [Poet.] brightness; splendor —**bright′ly** *adv.*

SYN.—bright, the most general term here, implies the giving forth or reflecting of light, or a being filled with light *[a bright day, star, shield, etc.]*; **radiant** emphasizes the actual or apparent emission of rays of light; **shining** implies a steady, continuous brightness *[the shining sun]*; **brilliant** implies intense or flashing brightness *[brilliant sunlight, diamonds, etc.]*; **luminous** is applied to objects that are full of light or give off reflected or phosphorescent light; **lustrous** is applied to objects whose surfaces gleam by reflected light and emphasizes gloss or sheen *[lustrous silk]* See also INTELLIGENT —*ANT.* **dull, dim, dark**

Bright (brīt), **John** 1811–89; Eng. statesman, political economist, & orator

bright·en (brīt′'n) *vt., vi.* [ME. < OE. *brihtan < beorht,* BRIGHT] **1.** to make or become bright or brighter **2.** to make or become happy or happier; gladden; cheer up

bright·ness (-nis) *n.* **1.** the quality or condition of being bright **2.** the luminous aspect of a color (as distinct from its hue) by which it is regarded as approaching the maxi-

mum luminance of pure white or the lack of luminance of pure black

Brigh·ton (brīt′'n) city in S England, on the English Channel: seaside resort: pop. 163,000

Bright's disease (brīts) [after Dr. Richard *Bright* (1798–1858), London physician who first diagnosed it] kidney disease characterized by the presence of albumin in the urine; nephritis

bright·work (brīt′wurk′) *n.* shiny metal trim or fittings

Brig·id (brij′id), Saint same as BRIDGET (sense 2)

brill (bril) *n., pl.* **brill, brills:** see PLURAL, II, D, 2 [< ? Corn. *brilli,* mackerel] an edible European flatfish (*Psetta laevis*) related to the turbot

Brill (bril), **A**(braham) **A**(rden) 1874–1948; U.S. psychoanalyst, born in Austria

Bril·lat-Sa·va·rin (brē yà′ så và ran′), **An·thelme** (än telm′) 1755–1826; Fr. expert on foods & cooking

bril·liance (bril′yəns) *n.* the fact of being brilliant; great brightness, radiance, intensity, splendor, intelligence, etc.: also **bril′lian·cy** (-yən sē)

bril·liant (-yənt) *adj.* [Fr. *brillant,* sparkling, prp. of *briller,* to sparkle, glitter < It. *brillare,* sparkle, whirl] **1.** shining brightly; sparkling **2.** vivid; intense **3.** very splendid or distinguished **4.** having or showing keen intelligence, great talent or skill, etc. —*n.* **1.** a gem, esp. a diamond, cut in a certain way with many facets to increase its sparkle **2.** *Printing* the smallest size of type in common use, 3 1/2 point —*SYN.* see BRIGHT, INTELLIGENT —**bril′liant·ly** *adv.*

☆**bril·lian·tine** (bril′yən tēn′) *n.* [Fr.: see prec. + -INE⁴] **1.** an oily dressing for grooming the hair **2.** a glossy cloth made of mohair and cotton

☆**Brill's disease** (brilz) [after N.E. *Brill* (1860–1925), U.S. physician] a form of epidemic typhus fever in which the disease recurs years after the original infection

brim (brim) *n.* [ME. < OE., sea, surf, edge of the sea: for IE. base see BRAMBLE] **1.** the topmost edge of a cup, glass, bowl, etc. **2.** [Archaic] *a)* a rim or edge around a body of water *b)* the water at such an edge **3.** a projecting rim or edge of anything *[the brim of a hat]* —*vt., vi.* **brimmed, brim′ming** to fill or be full to the brim —*SYN.* see BORDER —**brim′less** *adj.*

brim·ful (brim′fool′) *adj.* full to the brim

brim·mer (-ər) *n.* a cup or glass filled to the brim

brim·stone (-stōn′) *n.* [ME. *brimston* < OE. *brynstan:* see BURN¹ & STONE] same as SULFUR

Brin·di·si (brin′də zē; *It.* brēn′dē zē) seaport in SE Italy, on the Adriatic: pop. 70,000

brin·dle (brin′d'l) *adj.* [< ff.] same as BRINDLED —*n.* **1.** a brindled color **2.** a brindled animal

brin·dled (-d'ld) *adj.* [< earlier *brinded,* after *kindled;* prob. < ME. *brended < brennen,* BURN¹] having a gray or tawny coat streaked or spotted with a darker color *[a brindled cow]*

brine (brīn) *n.* [ME. & OE.; prob. < IE. base **bhrēi-,* to cut (whence L. *friare,* to crumble): orig. sense "cutting, sharp"] **1.** water full of salt; heavily saturated salt solution, as for use in pickling **2.** *a)* the water of the sea *b)* the sea; ocean —*vt.* **brined, brin′ing** to soak in or treat with brine

Bri·nell test (bri nel′) [after J. A. *Brinell* (1849–1925), Swed. engineer] a test for determining the relative hardness (**Brinell hardness**) of a metal by measuring the diameter of the indentation made when a hardened steel ball is forced into the metal under a given pressure: the measure of hardness (**Brinell number**) is equal to the load in kilograms divided by the surface area in square millimeters of the indentation

brine shrimp a small crustacean (*Artemia salina*) found in salt lakes and marshes and used as living food in aquariums

bring (briŋ) *vt.* **brought, bring′ing** [ME. *bringen* < OE. *bringan,* akin to G. *bringen* < IE. base **bhrenk-, *bronk-*] **1.** to carry or lead (a person or thing) to the place thought of as "here" or to a place where the speaker will be *[bring it to my house tomorrow]* **2.** to cause to be, happen, come, appear, have, etc. *[war brings death and famine, rest brings one health]* **3.** to lead, persuade, or influence along a course of action or belief **4.** to sell for *[eggs bring a high price today]* **5.** *Law a)* to present in a law court *[to bring charges]* *b)* to advance (evidence, etc.) —**bring about** to make happen; effect —**bring around (or round) 1.** to persuade by arguing, urging, etc. **2.** to put or coax into a good humor **3.** to bring back to consciousness or health —**bring down 1.** to cause to come down or fall **2.** to wound or kill —**bring forth 1.** *a)* to give birth to *b)* to produce (fruit, flowers, etc.) **2.** to make known; disclose —**bring forward 1.** to introduce; show **2.** *Bookkeeping* to carry over —**bring in 1.** to import **2.** *a)* to produce, as income or revenue ☆*b)* to cause (an oil well, etc.) to produce **3.** to give (a verdict or report) —**bring off** to succeed in doing; accomplish —**bring on** to cause to be, happen, or appear —**bring out 1.** to reveal; make clear or clearer **2.** to bring (a play, person, etc.) before the public, or to publish (a book, magazine, etc.) **3.** to cause to appear **4.** to introduce (a girl) formally to society —**bring over**

to convince or persuade —**bring to 1.** to revive (an unconscious person) **2.** to cause (a ship) to stop —**bring up 1.** to take care of during infancy and childhood; raise; rear **2.** to introduce, as into discussion **3.** a) to cough up b) to vomit **4.** to stop abruptly
SYN.—**bring** (in strict usage) implies a carrying or conducting to, and **take**, similar action away from, a specified or implied place [*bring* the book to me; I will *take* it back to the library]; **fetch** implies a going after something, getting it, and bringing it back
brink (briŋk) *n.* [ME. < MLowG. or Dan., shore, bank, grassy edge, prob. < IE. base *bhreng-*, var. of *bhren-*, project, edge, whence L. *frons*, FRONT] **1.** the edge, esp. at the top of a steep place; verge: often used figuratively [at the *brink* of war] **2.** the bank, esp. when steep, of a river or other body of water —**SYN.** see BORDER
☆**brink·man·ship** (-mən ship′) *n.* [BRINK + *-manship*, as in STATESMANSHIP] the policy of pursuing a hazardous course of action to the brink of catastrophe: also **brinks′-man·ship′** (briŋks′-)
brin·y (brīn′ē) *adj.* **brin′i·er, brin′i·est** of or like brine; very salty —**the briny** [Slang] the ocean; sea —**brin′i·ness** *n.*
bri·o (brē′ō) *n.* [It.] animation; vivacity; zest
bri·oche (brē ōsh′, -ōsh′; brē′ōsh, -ōsh) *n.* [Fr.] a light, rich roll made with flour, butter, eggs, and yeast
bri·o·lette (brē′ə let′) *n.* [Fr. < ? *brillant*, BRILLIANT] a teardrop diamond cut in triangular facets
bri·o·ny (brī′ə nē) *n., pl.* **-nies** *same as* BRYONY
bri·quette, bri·quet (bri ket′) *n.* [Fr. *briquette*, dim. of *brique*, BRICK] a brick made of compressed coal dust, sawdust, etc., used for fuel or kindling —*vt.* **-quet′ted, -quet′-ting** to form (ore particles, etc.) into briquettes
bri·sance (bri zäns′; Fr. brē zäns′) *n.* [Fr., lit., breaking, prp. of *briser*, to break] the shattering effect of the sudden release of energy, as in an explosion of nitroglycerin or in nuclear fission
Bris·bane (briz′bān, -bən) capital of Queensland, Australia, on the eastern coast: pop. (met. area) 664,000
Bri·se·is (brī sē′is) [L. < Gr. *Brisēis*] a pretty woman in the *Iliad*, seized by Agamemnon from Achilles, her captor
brisk (brisk) *adj.* [< ? Fr. *brusque*, BRUSQUE] **1.** quick in manner or movement; energetic [a *brisk* pace] **2.** cool, dry, and bracing [*brisk* air] **3.** pungent, keen, sharp, etc. [a *brisk* taste, a *brisk* tone of voice] **4.** active; busy [*brisk* trading] —*SYN.* see ACTIVE —**brisk′ly** *adv.* —**brisk′ness** *n.*
bris·ket (bris′kit) *n.* [ME. *brusket*, akin to Dan. *bryske*: for IE. base see BREAST] **1.** the breast of an animal **2.** meat cut from this part: see BEEF, illus.
bris·ling (bris′liŋ, briz′-) *n.* [Norw. dial. < older Dan. *bretling*] *same as* SPRAT (sense 1)
bris·tle (bris′'l) *n.* [ME. *bristel*, metathetic < OE. *byrst*, akin to G. *borste*, bristles < IE. base *bhares-, *bhores-*, point, sharp] **1.** any short, stiff, prickly hair of an animal or plant **2.** a) any of the hairs of a hog or of some other animals, used for brushes b) such a hair, or an artificial hair like it, in a brush —*vi.* **-tled, -tling 1.** to become stiff and erect, like bristles **2.** to have the bristles become erect, as in fear or irritation **3.** to become tense with fear, anger, etc.; be ready to fight back **4.** to be thickly covered (*with*) [the battlefield *bristled* with guns] —*vt.* **1.** to cause to stand up like bristles **2.** to put bristles on or in **3.** to make bristly
bris·tle-tail (-tāl′) *n.* any of several primitive, wingless insects (order Thysanura) with bristles at the posterior end, as the silverfish
bris·tly (bris′lē) *adj.* **-tli·er, -tli·est 1.** having bristles; rough with bristles **2.** bristlelike; stiff and short; prickly —**bris′tli·ness** *n.*
Bris·tol (bris′t'l) **1.** seaport in SW England: pop. 434,000 **2.** [after prec.] city in C Conn.: pop. 55,000
Bristol Bay arm of the Bering Sea between the SW Alaska mainland & the Alaska Peninsula
Bristol board [after BRISTOL, England] a fine, smooth pasteboard, used by artists, printers, etc.
Bristol Channel arm of the Atlantic, between S Wales & SW England: 85 mi. long
brit (brit) *n.pl., sing.* **brit** [Corn. < OCelt. *brith*, vari-colored; akin to Corn. *bruit*, speckled] **1.** the young of the herring and some other fishes **2.** small sea animals eaten by the whalebone whale; copepods
Brit. 1. Britain **2.** Britannia **3.** British
Brit·ain (brit′'n) *same as* GREAT BRITAIN
Bri·tan·ni·a (bri tan′yə, -tan′ē ə) **1.** Roman name for GREAT BRITAIN (sense 1), esp. the southern part **2.** British Empire —*n.* **1.** [Poet.] a female figure symbolizing Great Britain or the British Empire **2.** [b-] britannia metal
britannia metal [*also* B-] an alloy consisting chiefly of tin, copper, and antimony, used in making tableware: it resembles pewter but is harder
Bri·tan·nic (-ik) *adj.* [L. *Britannicus* < *Britannia*] of Britain or Great Britain; British
britch·es (brich′iz) *n.pl.* [Colloq.] *same as* BREECHES (sense 2)
☆**Brit·i·cism** (brit′ə siz'm) *n.* a word, phrase, or idiom peculiar to or characteristic of British English
Brit·ish (brit′ish) *adj.* [ME. *Brittish* < OE. *Bryttisc* < *Bret*, pl. *Bryttas*, name of the Celt. inhabitants of Britain; < Celt. origin] **1.** of Great Britain or its people **2.** of the British Commonwealth of Nations —*n.* **1.** the language of the ancient Britons; Cymric **2.** *same as* BRITISH ENGLISH

—**the British** the people of Great Britain: sometimes broadly applied to all the people of the British Commonwealth of Nations
British Columbia province of SW Canada, on the Pacific: 366,255 sq. mi.; pop. 1,874,000; cap. Victoria: abbrev. **B.C.**
British Commonwealth (of Nations) confederation of independent nations, with their dependencies, united under the British crown: it includes the United Kingdom, Australia, Barbados, Botswana, Canada, Ceylon, Cyprus, Fiji, Gambia, Ghana, Guyana, India, Jamaica, Kenya, Lesotho, Malawi, Malaysia, Malta, Mauritius, New Zealand, Nigeria, Pakistan, Sierra Leone, Singapore, Swaziland, Tanzania, Tonga, Trinidad & Tobago, Uganda, & Zambia: official name, **the Commonwealth**
British East Africa former Brit. territories of Kenya, Zanzibar, Tanganyika, & Uganda
British Empire formerly, the United Kingdom and the British dominions, colonies, etc.: the term is still sometimes used for the British Commonwealth of Nations
British English the English language as spoken and written in England and as distinguished esp. from AMERICAN ENGLISH
☆**Brit·ish·er** (-ər) *n.* a native of Great Britain, esp. an Englishman
British Guiana *former name of* GUYANA
British Honduras Brit. colony in Central America, on the Caribbean: 8,866 sq. mi.; pop. 122,000; cap. Belmopan
British India the part of India formerly under direct British rule
British Isles group of islands consisting of Great Britain, Ireland, & adjacent islands
Brit·ish·ism (-iz'm) *n. same as* BRITICISM
British Malaya former Brit. territories in the Malay Peninsula & the Malay Archipelago
British Museum famous museum in London, containing art treasures, one of the largest libraries in the world, a department of natural history, etc.
British Somaliland former Brit. protectorate in E Africa: merged with Italian Somaliland (1960) to form the independent republic of Somalia
British thermal unit a unit of heat equal to about 252 calories; quantity of heat required to raise the temperature of one pound of water at its maximum density one degree Fahrenheit
British West Africa former Brit. possessions in W Africa
British West Indies Brit. possessions in the West Indies, including the Bahamas, British Virgin Islands, and the Brit. colonies in the Leeward and Windward groups
Brit·on (brit′n) *n.* [ME. < OFr. *Breton* < L. *Brito, Britto*; of Celt. origin: see BRITISH] **1.** a member of an early Celtic people living in S Britain at the time of the Roman invasion **2.** a native or inhabitant of Great Britain, esp. an Englishman
Brit·ta·ny (brit′'n ē) peninsula & former province of NW France, between the English Channel & the Bay of Biscay: Fr. name, BRETAGNE
Brit·ten (brit′'n), (Edward) Benjamin 1913- ; Eng. composer
brit·tle (brit′'l) *adj.* [ME. *britel* < OE. *breotan*, to break to pieces] **1.** easily broken or shattered because it is hard and not flexible **2.** having a sharp, hard quality [*brittle* tones] **3.** stiff and unbending in manner —☆*n.* a brittle, crunchy candy with nuts in it [peanut *brittle*] —*SYN.* see FRAGILE —**brit′tle·ly, brit′tly** *adv.* —**brit′tle·ness** *n.*
Brit·ton·ic (bri tän′ik) *adj.* [< L. *Britto*, gen. *Brittonis* (var. of *Brito*: see BRITON) + -IC] *same as* BRYTHONIC
britz·ka, brits·ka (brits′kə) *n.* [Pol. *bryczka*, dim. of *bryka*, freight wagon] a long, spacious carriage with a folding top
Brix scale [after Adolf F. *Brix* (died 1870), Ger. chemist] a scale for measuring the density or concentration of sugar in solution
Br·no (bʉr′nō) city in C Czechoslovakia: former capital of Moravia: pop. 327,000
bro. *pl.* **bros.** brother
broach (brōch) *n.* [ME. *broche*, a pin, peg, spit < OFr. *broche, broc* < ML. *brocca*, a spike < L. *broccus*, with projecting teeth] **1.** a sharp-pointed rod used to hold roasting meat; spit **2.** a tapered bit pulled or pushed through a hole to make the hole larger or of a certain shape **3.** a device for tapping casks **4.** a hole made by a broach **5.** *same as* BROOCH —*vt.* **1.** to make a hole in so as to let out liquid; tap (a cask) **2.** to enlarge or shape (a hole) by reaming **3.** to start a discussion of; bring up; introduce —*SYN.* see UTTER² —**broach to** *Naut.* to turn or swing so that the beam faces the waves and wind and there is danger of swamping or capsizing —**broach′er** *n.*

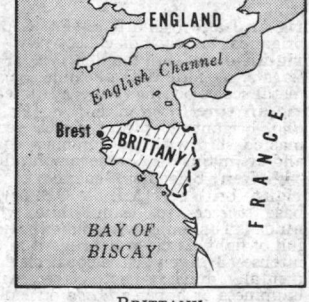

ENGLAND
English Channel
Brest
BRITTANY
FRANCE
BAY OF BISCAY

BRITTANY

broad (brôd) *adj.* [ME. *brod* < OE. *brad;* akin to G. *breit*] **1.** of large extent from side to side; wide **2.** having great extent or expanse; spacious [*broad* prairies] **3.** extending all about; clear; open; full [*broad* daylight] **4.** plain to the mind; not subtle; obvious [*a broad* hint] **5.** strongly marked: said of dialects or accents **6.** coarse or ribald [*a broad* joke] **7.** tolerant; liberal [to take a *broad* view of a matter] **8.** wide in range; not limited [*a broad* variety, a *broad* education] **9.** main or general; not detailed [in *broad* outline] **10.** *Phonet.* pronounced with the tongue held low and flat in the mouth; open, esp. as the (ä) of *father* —*adv.* in a broad manner; widely —*n.* **1.** the broad part of anything **2.** [Slang] a woman: a vulgar term of contempt —**broad′ly** *adv.* —**broad′ness** *n.*
SYN.—**broad** and **wide** both are applied to extent from side to side of surfaces having height or length, **wide** being preferred when the distance between limits is stressed [two feet *wide*, a *wide* aperture], and, **broad**, when the full extent of surface is considered [*broad* hips, *broad* plains]; **deep**, in this connection, refers to extent backward, as from the front, an opening, etc. [a *deep* lot, a *deep* cave] —**ANT. narrow**
broad arrow 1. an arrow with a broad, barbed head **2.** an identification mark in the form of a broad arrow that the British government puts on its property, as on prisoners' uniforms
broad·ax, broad·axe (-aks′) *n.* an ax with a broad blade, used as a weapon or for hewing timber
broad bean a plant (*Vicia faba*) of the legume family, bearing large, broad pods with flat, edible seeds, used chiefly for fodder

BROAD ARROW

broad·bill (-bil′) *n.* any of various birds with a broad bill, as the scaup and shoveler ducks, spoonbill, etc.
broad·cast (-kast′, -käst′) *vt.* -**cast′** or, in radio, occas. -**cast′ed**, -**cast′ing 1.** to scatter (seed) over a broad area rather than sow in drills **2.** to spread (information, gossip, etc.) widely **3.** to transmit by radio or television —*vi.* to broadcast radio or television programs —*adj.* **1.** widely scattered **2.** of, for, or by radio or television broadcasting —*n.* **1.** the act of broadcasting **2.** a radio or television program —*adv.* far and wide — **broad′cast′er** *n.*
Broad Church that party of the Anglican Church which, in matters of doctrine and communion, holds a position between the ritualism and formality of the High Church and the evangelism of the Low Church —**Broad′-Church′** *adj.* —**Broad′-Church′man** *n., pl.* -**men**
broad·cloth (-klôth′) *n.* **1.** a fine, smooth woolen cloth: so called because it originally was made on wide looms **2.** a fine, smooth cotton or silk cloth, used for shirts, pajamas, etc.
broad·en (-'n) *vt., vi.* to make or become broad or broader; widen; expand
broad gauge a width (between the rails of a railroad) greater than standard gauge or width (56 1/2 inches) —**broad′-gauge′, broad′-gauged′** *adj.*
broad hatchet a hatchet having a broad blade backed by a broad hammerhead
broad jump a jump for distance rather than height: a track and field event now officially called *long jump*
broad·leaf (-lēf′) *n.* ☆any of various tobaccos with broad leaves used for making cigars —*adj. same as* BROAD-LEAVED
broad-leaved (-lēvd′) *adj.* having broad leaves; specif., having flat rather than needlelike leaves, as some ever-green shrubs or trees
broad·loom (-lōōm′) *adj.* woven on a broad, or wide, loom, as in widths of 6, 9, 12, 15, or 18 feet [*broadloom* carpeting]
broad-mind·ed (-mīn′did) *adj.* tolerant of opinions and behavior which are unconventional or which differ from one's own; not bigoted; liberal —**broad′-mind′ed·ly** *adv.* —**broad′-mind′ed·ness** *n.*
broad seal the public seal of a state or nation
broad·side (-sīd′) *n.* **1.** the entire side of a ship above the waterline **2.** *a)* all the guns that can be fired from one side of a ship *b)* the simultaneous firing of these guns **3.** a vigorous or abusive attack in words, esp. in a newspaper **4.** the broad surface of any large object **5.** *a)* orig., a large sheet of paper printed on one side, as with a political message, or, in 17th-cent. England, a popular ballad: also **broad′sheet′** *b)* a large sheet of paper printed on one or both sides, as with advertising, and often folded —*adv.* **1.** with the length turned (*to* an object) [the ship came *broadside* to the dock] **2.** directly in the side [the train rammed the car *broadside*] **3.** indiscriminately [to level charges *broadside*]
broad-spec·trum (-spek′trəm) *adj.* effective against a wide variety of microorganisms [a *broad-spectrum* antibiotic]
broad·sword (-sôrd′) *n.* a sword with a broad blade, for slashing rather than thrusting
broad·tail (-tāl′) *n.* **1.** a thick-tailed sheep of C Asia; karakul **2.** the glossy, wavy pelt of its lamb, esp. of one prematurely born; astrakhan

Broad·way (brôd′wā′) [transl. of Du. *Breed Wegh*, broad way] **1.** street running north and south through New York City, known as the axis of the city's main theater and entertainment section **2.** the New York commercial theater or entertainment industry
Brob·ding·nag (bräb′diŋ nag′) in Swift's *Gulliver's Travels* a land inhabited by giants about 60 feet tall —**Brob′ding-nag′i·an** *adj., n.*
bro·cade (brō kād′) *n.* [Sp. *brocado* < It. *broccato*, orig. pp. of *broccare*, to prick, embroider < *brocco:* see BROACH] a rich cloth with a raised design, as of silk, velvet, gold, or silver, woven into it —*vt.* -**cad′ed**, -**cad′ing** to weave a raised design into (cloth)
broc·a·telle, broc·a·tel (bräk′ə tel′) *n.* [Fr. *brocatelle* < It. *broccatello*, dim. of *broccato:* see BROCADE] a heavy, figured cloth like brocade, usually of silk and linen, used in upholstery
broc·co·li (bräk′ə lē) *n.* [It., pl. of *broccolo*, a sprout, cabbage sprout, dim. of *brocco:* see BROACH] **1.** a plant (*Brassica oleracea italica*) related to the cauliflower but bearing tender shoots with greenish buds cooked as a vegetable **2.** any of several strains of cauliflower
bro·ché (brō shā′) *adj.* [Fr. < *brocher*, to stitch, brocade < *broche:* see BROACH] woven with a raised design
bro·chette (brō shet′) *n.* [Fr., dim. of *broche:* see BROACH] a skewer on which small pieces of meat and vegetables are fixed for broiling
bro·chure (brō shoor′, -shyoor′) *n.* [Fr. < *brocher*, to stitch: see BROACH] a pamphlet

BROCCOLI

brock (bräk) *n.* [ME. *brok* < OE. & Gael. *broc*] [Scot. or Brit. Dial.] a badger
Brock·en (bräk′ən) mountain in the Harz Mountains, C Germany: in German folklore, the meeting place of witches on Walpurgis Night: 3,747 ft.
brock·et (bräk′it) *n.* [ME. *broket* < NormFr. *broquet*, yearling (of roe deer) < OFr. *broc*, a spit, tine of a stag's horn: see BROACH] **1.** a male European red deer two years old **2.** any of various small S. American deer (genus *Mazama*) with short, unbranched horns
Brock·ton (bräk′tən) [after Sir Isaac *Brock* (1769–1812), Lt. Gov. of Canada] city in E Mass.: pop. 89,000
‡**bro·de·rie an·glaise** (brō drē än glez′) [Fr., lit., English embroidery] fine eyelet embroidery in floral or other designs, usually white, used on women's garments and on linens
bro·gan (brō′g'n) *n.* [Ir., dim. of *brōg*] a heavy work shoe, fitting high on the ankle
Bro·glie (brô glē′; *Fr.* brô′y′) a prominent Fr. family, including esp. **1. Achille Charles Léonce Victor,** Duc de, 1785–1870; statesman, under Napoleon I & Louis Philippe **2.** (**Louis César Victor**) **Maurice,** Duc de, 1875–   ; physicist: great-grandson of *prec.* **3. Louis Victor,** Prince de, 1892–   ; physicist: brother of *prec.*
brogue¹ (brōg) *n.* [prob. < Ir. *barróg*, a hold, grip (esp. on the tongue)] the pronunciation peculiar to a dialect, esp. that of English as spoken by the Irish
brogue² (brōg) *n.* [Gael. & Ir. *brōg*, a shoe] **1.** a coarse shoe of untanned leather, formerly worn in Ireland **2.** a man's heavy oxford shoe, usually a kind of blucher with decorative perforations and a wing tip
broi·der (broi′dər) *vt.* [altered (after *broid*, old var. of BRAID) < *brouder* < Fr. *broder* < OFr. *brosder* < Gmc. *bruzdan*, to embroider] [Archaic] to embroider —**broi′der·y** *n.*
broil¹ (broil) *vt.* [ME. *broilen* < OFr. *bruillir*, to broil, roast, prob. by confusion of *bruir*, to burn (< Gmc. *brojan*, to brew) & *usler* (Fr. *brûler*) < L. *ustulare*, to singe] **1.** to cook by exposing to a flame or other direct source of intense heat **2.** to expose directly to intense heat —*vi.* **1.** to become broiled **2.** to become heated or angry —*n.* **1.** the act or state of broiling **2.** anything broiled
broil² (broil) *n.* [ME. *broilen*, to quarrel, concoct lies < OFr. *brouillier*, to dirty, prob. ult. < Frank. *broth*, mud, froth] a noisy or violent quarrel; brawl —*vi.* to take part in a broil
broil·er (broil′ər) *n.* ☆**1.** a pan, grill, etc. for broiling **2.** the part of a stove designed for broiling **3.** a young chicken suitable for broiling
broke (brōk) *pt. & archaic pp.* of BREAK¹ —*adj.* [Colloq.] having little or no money; bankrupt —**go broke** [Colloq.] become penniless or bankrupt —**go for broke** [Slang] to risk everything on an uncertain undertaking
bro·ken (brō′k'n) [ME. < OE. *brocen*, pp. of *brecan*, BREAK¹] *pp.* of BREAK¹ —*adj.* **1.** split or cracked into pieces; splintered, fractured, burst, etc. **2.** not in working condition; out of order [a *broken* watch] **3.** not kept or observed; violated [a *broken* promise] **4.** disrupted as by divorce [a *broken* home] **5.** sick, weakened, or beaten [*broken* health, a *broken* spirit] **6.** bankrupt **7.** not even or continuous; interrupted [*broken* terrain, *broken* tones]

8. not complete [broken sizes] **9.** imperfectly spoken, esp. with reference to grammar and syntax [broken English] **10.** subdued and trained; tamed **11.** [Colloq.] demoted in rank For phrases, see BREAK¹ —**bro′ken·ly** adv. —**bro′ken·ness** n.

bro·ken-down (-doun′) adj. **1.** sick or worn out, as by old age or disease **2.** out of order; useless

bro·ken-heart·ed (-här′tid) adj. crushed by sorrow, grief, or disappointment; inconsolable

broken wind Vet. same as HEAVES

bro·ken-wind·ed (-win′did) adj. gasping with or as with the heaves

bro·ker (brō′kər) n. [ME. brokour < ONormFr. broceor < OFr. brokier, brochier, to BROACH, tap; orig. sense "wine dealer"] **1.** a person hired to act as an agent or intermediary in making contracts or sales **2.** same as STOCK-BROKER

bro·ker·age (-ij) n. **1.** the business or office of a broker **2.** a broker's fee

brol·ly (brŏl′i) n. [altered < (UM)BRELLA] [Brit. Colloq.] an umbrella

brom- (brōm-) same as BROMO-

bro·mal (brō′mal) n. [G. < brom, bromine + alkohol, alcohol] an oily, colorless, sharp-smelling liquid, CBr₃CHO, obtained by passing bromine through alcohol: used medicinally

bro·mate (-māt) n. [BROM- + -ATE²] a salt of bromic acid —vt. -mat·ed, -mat·ing to treat or combine with a bromate or with bromine

Brom·berg (bräm′bərg; G. brôm′berk) Ger. name of BYDGOSZCZ

brome (brōm) n. [L. bromos < Gr. bromos, oats] any of a large genus (Bromus) of grasses of the temperate zone, having closed sheaths and spikelets with awns: a few are crop plants but many are weeds: also **brome′grass′**

bro·me·li·ad (brō mē′lē ad′) n. [ModL. Bromelia, genus name (after 17th-c. Swed. botanist Olaf Bromel) + -(A)D¹] any member of the pineapple family of plants, usually having stiff, leathery leaves and spikes of bright flowers, as the pineapple and Spanish moss

bro·mic (brō′mik) adj. [BROM- + -IC] of or containing bromine, esp. bromine with a valence of five

bromic acid an acid, HBrO₃, of which bromates are salts: it cannot be prepared in the pure state, and is found only in dilute aqueous solutions

bro·mide (-mīd) n. [BROM- + -IDE] **1.** a compound of bromine with another element or with a radical **2.** potassium bromide, KBr, used in medicine as a sedative ☆**3.** a) [Old Slang] a person who says trite things b) a trite saying or statement —SYN. see PLATITUDE

☆**bro·mid·ic** (brō mid′ik) adj. [see BROMIDE] using or containing a trite remark or remarks; dull; tiresome

bro·mi·nate (brō′mi nāt′) vt. -nat·ed, -nat·ing Chem. to treat or combine with bromine —**bro′mi·na′tion** n.

bro·mine (brō′mēn) n. [Fr. brome < Gr. brōmos, stench + -INE⁴] a chemical element, usually in the form of a reddish-brown, corrosive liquid volatilizing to form a vapor that has an unpleasant odor and is very irritating to mucous membranes: used in making dyes, in photography, and, in the form of certain compounds, in antiknock motor fuel: symbol, Br; at. wt., 79.909; at. no., 35; sp. gr., 3.119 (4°C); melt. pt., -7.2°C; boil. pt., 58.78°C

bro·mism (-miz′m) n. Med. a condition caused by overuse of bromides

bro·mize (-mīz) vt. -mized, -miz·ing Chem. to treat with bromine or a bromide

Brom·ley (bräm′lē) city in SE England: pop. 69,000

bro·mo- (brō′mō) a combining form meaning bromine

Bro·mo Selt·zer (brō′mō selt′sər) [< BROMIDE + SELTZER] a trademark for a compound containing a bromide, sodium bicarbonate, etc., used to relieve headaches and upset stomachs, and as a sedative —n. [b- s-] this compound: also **bro′mo·selt′zer, bro′mo, Bro′mo**

☆**bronc** (bränk) n. [Colloq.] same as BRONCO

bronch- (bränk) same as BRONCHO-: used before a vowel

bron·chi (bräŋ′kī) n. pl. of BRONCHUS

bron·chi·al (-kē əl) adj. of or pertaining to the bronchi or bronchioles

bronchial tubes the bronchi and the tubes branching from them

bron·chi·ec·ta·sis (bräŋ′kē ek′tə sis) n. [ModL. < bronchus, BRONCHUS + Gr. ektasis, a stretching out < ekteinein, to stretch out < ek-, out + teinein, to stretch (see TEND²)] a chronic enlargement of certain of the bronchial tubes

bron·chi·ole (bräŋ′kē ōl′) n. [dim. of LL. bronchia, after ModL. diminutives ending in -iola] any of the small subdivisions of the bronchi

bron·chi·tis (bräŋ kīt′is) n. [BRONCH- + -ITIS] an inflammation of the mucous lining of the bronchial tubes — **bron·chit′ic** (-kit′ik) adj.

☆**bron·cho** (bräŋ′kō) n., pl. -chos same as BRONCO

bron·cho- (bräŋ′kō, -kə) [< Gr. bronchos, windpipe] a combining form meaning having to do with the bronchi [bronchoscope]

bron·cho·pneu·mo·nia (bräŋ′kō nōō mō′nyə, -nyōō-) n. inflammation of the bronchi accompanied by inflamed patches in the nearby lobules of the lungs

bron·cho·scope (bräŋ′kə skōp′) n. [BRONCHO- + -SCOPE] a slender, tubular instrument with a small electric light,

for examining or treating the inside of the windpipe or the bronchi, or for removing foreign bodies from them —**bron′cho·scop′ic** (-skäp′ik) adj. —**bron′cho·scop′i·cal·ly** adv. —**bron·chos′co·py** (-käs′kə pē) n.

bron·chus (bräŋ′kəs) n., pl. -chi (-kī) [ModL. < Gr. bronchos, windpipe] either of the two main branches of the trachea, or windpipe

☆**bron·co** (bräŋ′kō) n., pl. -cos [MexSp. < Sp., rough] **1.** a wild or only partially tamed horse or pony of the western U.S. plains **2.** [Canad.] an Englishman, esp. an immigrant

☆**bron·co·bust·er** (-bus′tər) n. [Colloq.] a cowboy who breaks, or tames, broncos —**bron′co·bust′ing** n.

Bron·të (brän′tē) name of three Eng. sisters: **1.** Anne, (pseud. Acton Bell) 1820–49; novelist **2.** Charlotte, (Mrs. Arthur Bell Nicholls; pseud. Currer Bell) 1816–55; novelist: author of Jane Eyre **3.** Emily Jane, (pseud. Ellis Bell) 1818–48; novelist & poet: author of Wuthering Heights

☆**bron·to·sau·rus** (brän′tə sôr′əs) n., pl. -sau′rus·es, -sau′ri (-ī) [ModL. < Gr. brontē, thunder + -SAURUS] a huge, plant-eating American dinosaur of the Jurassic Period, which had a long, slender neck and a thick, tapering tail, and weighed as much as 30 tons: also **bron′to·saur′** (-sôr′)

Bronx (bräŋks) [after Jonas Bronck, early N.Y. settler] northernmost borough of New York City, between the Harlem River & Long Island Sound: pop. 1,472,000

BRONTOSAURUS
(to 75 ft. long)

☆**Bronx cheer** [Slang] a noisy vibration of the lips and the extended tongue, to show derision or scorn

bronze (bränz) n. [Fr. < It. bronzo & ML. bronzium, associated with L. Brundisium, BRINDISI, but prob. ult. < Per. birinj, copper] **1.** a) an alloy consisting chiefly of copper and tin b) any of certain other alloys with a copper base **2.** an article, esp. a sculpture or other work of art, made of bronze **3.** a reddish-brown color like that of bronze —adj. of or like bronze —vt. bronzed, bronz′ing [Fr. bronzer < the n.] to make look like bronze; give a bronze color to —**bronz′y** adj.

Bronze Age a phase of human culture (c. 3500–1000 B.C.) characterized by bronze tools and weapons, usually regarded as between the Stone Age and the Iron Age

Bronze Star Medal a U.S. military decoration awarded for heroic or meritorious achievement or service in combat not involving aerial flight

brooch (brōch, brōōch) n. [ME. broche: see BROACH] a large ornamental pin with a clasp, worn usually at the bosom or neck of a woman's dress

brood (brōōd) n. [ME. & OE. brod, akin to G. brut, a hatching: for IE. base see BREATH] **1.** the offspring, or a family of offspring, of animals; esp., a group of birds or fowl hatched at one time and cared for together **2.** all the children in a family **3.** a group of a particular breed or kind [the new brood of poets] —vt. **1.** to sit on and hatch (eggs) **2.** to hover over or protect (offspring, etc.) with or as with wings **3.** to ponder in a troubled or morbid way [to brood revenge] —vi. **1.** to brood eggs or offspring **2.** to keep thinking about something in a distressed or troubled way; worry (often with on, over, or about) **3.** to hover or loom; hang low —adj. kept for breeding [a brood mare]

brood·er (-ər) n. **1.** a person or animal that broods ☆**2.** a heated shelter for raising young fowl

brood·y (-ē) adj. brood′i·er, brood′i·est **1.** ready to brood, as poultry **2.** inclined to brood, or dwell moodily on one's own thoughts —**brood′i·ly** adv. —**brood′i·ness** n.

brook¹ (brook) n. [ME. brok < OE. broc < ? base of BREAK¹ in the sense of "a stream bursting forth"] a small stream, usually not so large as a river

brook² (brook) vt. [ME. brouken, to use, enjoy < OE. brucan, akin to G. brauchen: for IE. base see FRUIT] to put up with; endure: usually in the negative [I will brook no interference] —SYN. see BEAR¹

Brooke (brook), Rupert 1887–1915; Eng. poet

Brook Farm a farm near West Roxbury (now part of Boston), Mass., where a group of U.S. writers & scholars set up an experimental communist community (1841–47)

brook·ite (brook′it) n. [after H. J. Brooke (1771–1857), Eng. mineralogist] a form of titanium dioxide, TiO₂, occurring in brown, semitransparent crystals

brook·let (-lit) n. a little brook

Brook·line (brook′līn) [orig. name of estate of Judge S. Sewall] suburb of Boston, in E Mass.: pop. 59,000

Brook·lyn (brook′lən) [< Du. Bruijkleen (or Breukelen) Colonie: cf. Breukelen, village near Utrecht, Neth.] borough of New York City, on W Long Island: pop. 2,602,000 —**Brook′lyn·ite′** (-lə nīt′) n.

Brooklyn Center [after prec.] city in E Minn., on the Mississippi: suburb of Minneapolis: pop. 35,000

Brooks (brooks) **1.** Phillips, 1835–93; U.S. clergyman & writer **2.** Van Wyck (van wik′), 1886–1963; U.S. critic & biographer

Brooks Range (brooks) [after A. H. Brooks (1871–1924),

Alas. geologist] mountain range extending across N Alas.: highest peak, 9,239 ft.

☆**brook trout** a mottled stream trout (*Salvelinus fontinalis*) native to NE N. America, but widely introduced elsewhere as a game fish

broom (brōōm, broom) n. [ME. & OE. *brom*, brushwood: for IE. base see BRAMBLE] **1.** any of a group of flowering shrubs (esp. genera *Cytisus, Genista,* and *Spartium*) of the legume family, often grown for their abundant, usually yellow, flowers **2.** a bundle of long, stiff fibers or straws (orig. twigs of broom) fastened to a long handle and used for sweeping —*vt.* to sweep as with a broom

☆**broom·corn** (-kôrn′) n. a cultivated variety of sorghum (*Sorghum vulgare*), the panicles of which are used in making brooms and brushes

broom·rape (-rāp′) n. [BROOM + RAPE², used as transl. of ML. *rapum genistae*, lit., broom tuber] any of a genus (*Orobanche*) of leafless, fleshy, parasitic plants growing on the roots of other plants —*adj.* designating a family (Orobanchaceae) of leafless plants, including beechdrops, broomrape, etc., parasitic on the roots of other plants

broom·stick (-stik′) n. the long handle of a broom

bros. brothers

brose (brōz) n. [Scot., alt. < ME. *broues,* BREWIS] a dish made by stirring boiling water or milk into oatmeal

broth (brôth) n. [ME. & OE., akin to OHG. *brod:* for IE. base see BREAD] a clear, thin soup made by boiling meat, or sometimes cereals or vegetables, in water

broth·el (brôth′əl, bräth′-) n. [ME., wretched person < OE. *brothen,* pp. of *broethan,* to waste away, go to ruin; confused with BORDEL] a house of prostitution

broth·er (bruth′ər) n., *pl.* **broth′ers;** chiefly religious, **breth′ren** [ME. < OE. *brothor* < IE. base **bhrāter,* whence Goth. *brothar,* L. *frater,* OIr. *brāthir,* Sans. *bhrātar*] **1.** a man or boy as he is related to the other children of his parents: sometimes also used of animals **2.** a man or boy related to one by having a parent in common; half brother **3.** a stepbrother **4.** a foster brother **5.** any male relative; kinsman **6.** a close friend who is like a brother **7.** a fellow man **8.** a fellow member of the same race, creed, profession, organization, etc. **9.** a lay member of a men's religious order —*vt.* to treat or address as a brother

broth·er·hood (-hood′) n. [ME. *brotherhede:* see BROTHER & -HOOD] **1.** the state of being a brother or brothers; bond between brothers **2.** an association of men united in a common interest, work, creed, etc., as a fraternity, religious order, or labor union

broth·er-in-law (-in lô′) n., *pl.* **broth′ers-in-law′ 1.** the brother of one's husband or wife **2.** the husband of one's sister **3.** the husband of the sister of one's wife or husband

Brother Jonathan [apparently first applied to New Eng. militia besieging Boston by Brit. soldiers evacuating the city (March, 1776)] a name formerly used to personify the United States or its people

broth·er·ly (-lē) adj. **1.** of, like, or befitting a brother or brothers **2.** friendly, kind, loyal, etc. —adv. [Archaic] as a brother —**broth′er·li·ness** n.

brougham (brōōm; brōō′əm, brō′-) n. [after Lord *Brougham* (1778–1868), Brit. political leader] **1.** a closed, four-wheeled carriage with the driver's seat outside **2.** any of certain early types of automobile; esp., *a*) an electrically powered automobile styled somewhat like a coupé *b*) a limousine with the driver's seat unenclosed

BROUGHAM

brought (brôt) [OE. *broht,* pt., (ge)broht, pp.] *pt. & pp.* of BRING

brou·ha·ha (brōō′hä hä′, brōō hä′hä) n. [Fr.] a noisy stir or wrangle; hubbub; uproar; commotion

Brou·wer (brou′ər), **A·dri·aen** (ä′drē än′) 1606?–38; Fl. painter

brow (brou) n. [ME. *broue* < OE. *bru* < IE. base **bhru-,* eyebrow, whence Sans. *bhrū-h,* ON. *brūn*] **1.** the eyebrow **2.** the forehead **3.** the facial expression [an angry *brow*] **4.** the projecting top edge of a steep hill or cliff

brow·beat (-bēt′) vt. **-beat′, -beat′en, -beat′ing** to intimidate with harsh, stern looks and talk; bully

brown (broun) adj. [ME. *broun* < OE. *brun* < IE. base **bhrou-no-* < **bher-,* light brown: see BEAR²] **1.** having the color of chocolate or coffee, a combination of red, black, and yellow **2.** having a naturally dark or tanned skin; dark-skinned —n. **1.** brown color **2.** brown pigment or dye —vt., vi. to make or become brown, esp. by exposure to sunlight, as in tanning, or heat, as in cooking —**be browned off** [Slang] to be angry, disgusted, resentful, etc.

Brown (broun) **1. Charles Brock·den** (bräk′dən), 1771–1810; U.S. novelist **2. John,** 1800–59; U.S. abolitionist: as part of a plan for a general uprising among the slaves, he led a raid on a U.S. arsenal at Harpers Ferry, and was hanged for treason

brown algae a group of large algae (Phaeophyta) found in cold seas, having a brown pigment that obscures the green color of the chlorophyll

brown bear any of various bears with brown fur, found in Europe, North America, etc.; esp., a color variety of the black bear

☆**brown bet·ty** (bet′ē) [also b- B-] a baked apple pudding made with butter, spices, sugar, and bread crumbs

brown bread 1. any bread made of dark flour **2.** same as BOSTON BROWN BREAD

brown coal same as LIGNITE

Browne (broun) **1. Charles Far·rar** (far′ər), see Artemus WARD **2. Sir Thomas,** 1605–82; Eng. physician & writer

brown fat a heat-producing tissue stored in certain areas of the body by a hibernating animal: it prevents freezing and helps to warm the awakening animal

Brown·i·an movement (broun′ē ən) [after Robert *Brown* (1773–1858), Brit. botanist who first described it] the constant, random, zigzag movement of small particles dispersed in a fluid medium, caused by collision with molecules of the fluid

brown·ie (broun′ē) n. **1.** a small, helpful, brown elf or goblin in folk tales, who does helpful tasks for people at night **2.** [B-] a member of the Girl Scouts in the youngest group, seven and eight years old ☆**3.** any of the small bars cut from a flat, moist, rich chocolate cake with nuts in it

Brown·ing (broun′iŋ) **1. Elizabeth Barrett,** 1806–61; Eng. poet: wife of *Robert* **2. John Moses,** 1855–1926; U.S. inventor of automatic firearms **3. Robert,** 1812–89; Eng. poet

brown·ish (-ish) adj. somewhat brown

brown·out (-out′) n. a partial elimination of lights in a city, as to save electric power during a shortage

brown rice rice that has not been polished

brown rot a disease of stone fruits and pome fruits, caused by a fungus (*Monilinia fructicola*) and marked by blight of flowers and twigs, by rotting, etc.

brown shirt 1. [often B- S-] a storm trooper in Nazi Germany **2.** any Nazi; Hitlerite

brown·stone (-stōn′) n. ☆**1.** a reddish-brown sandstone, used for building ☆**2.** a house with a façade of brownstone: also **brownstone front**

brown study [orig., somber thought < early sense of BROWN, somber, gloomy] a condition of being deeply absorbed in one's thoughts; reverie

brown sugar soft sugar prepared in such a way that the crystals retain a thin, brown coating of dark syrup

Browns·ville (brounz′vil) [< Fort *Brown,* after a Major J. *Brown,* killed there] seaport in S Tex., at the mouth of the Rio Grande: pop. 53,000

Brown Swiss a hardy breed of large, brown dairy cattle, first raised in Switzerland

brown-tail moth (-tāl′) a white moth (*Euproctis chrysorrhea*) with a tuft of reddish-brown hairs at the posterior end: its hairy larvae are harmful to trees and cause an irritating skin rash: also **brown′tail′** n.

☆**brown thrasher** an American songbird related to the mockingbird, brownish-red above and white below

brown trout a golden-brown European trout (*Salmo trutta*), widely stocked in N. America as a game fish

browse (brouz) n. [OFr. *brouz,* pl. of *broust,* a bud or shoot < OS. *brustian,* to sprout] **1.** leaves, twigs, and young shoots of trees or shrubs, which animals feed on **2.** the act of browsing —vt. **browsed, brows′ing** [ME. *brousen* < OFr. *brouster* < the n.] **1.** to nibble at (leaves, twigs, etc.) **2.** to graze on **3.** to examine in a casual way; skim —vi. **1.** to nibble at leaves, twigs, etc. **2.** *a*) to glance through a book, library, etc. in a casual way, reading passages here and there *b*) to look casually over articles for sale —**brows′er** n.

Bruce (brōōs) [Scot. < Fr. *Brieuse,* locality in France] **1.** a masculine name **2. Robert (the),** 1274–1329; as *Robert I,* king of Scotland (1306–29): won independence of Scotland from England **3. Stanley Melbourne,** 1st Viscount, 1883–1967; prime minister of Australia (1923–29)

bru·cel·lo·sis (brōō′sə lō′sis) n. [after Sir David *Bruce* (1855–1931), Scot. physician + -OSIS] a disease, esp. in man and cattle, caused by bacteria (genus *Brucella*): see UNDULANT FEVER

Bruch (brookh), **Max** 1838–1920; Ger. composer

bru·cine (brōō′sēn) n. [after James *Bruce* (1730–94), Scot. explorer] a bitter, poisonous, white alkaloid, $C_{23}H_{26}N_2O_4$, found in seeds of nux vomica and several other related plants: used in medicine and as a lubricant additive

Bruck·ner (brook′nər), **Anton** 1824–96; Austrian composer

Brue·gel, Brue·ghel (brü′gəl; occas. broi′-) **1. Jan** (yän), 1568–1625; Fl. painter: son of ff. **2. Pie·ter** (pē′tər), 1522?–69; Fl. painter of peasant life

Brug·ge (broog′ə) city in NW Belgium: pop. 52,000: Fr. name **Bruges** (brüzh)

Bru·in (brōō′ən) [Du., brown] the bear in the medieval beast epic *Reynard the Fox;* hence [also b-] a name for the bear in fable and folklore

bruise (brōōz) vt. **bruised, bruis′ing** [ME. *bruisen* < OE. *brysan,* to crush, pound < IE. base **bhreus-,* to smash, crush; ME. form & meaning infl. by OFr. *bruisier,* to break,

shatter < Gaul. *brus-* < same IE. base] **1.** to injure (body tissue), as by a blow, without breaking the skin but causing discoloration **2.** to injure the surface or outside of so that there is spoilage, abrasion, denting, etc. [*bruised* peaches, a *bruised* auto fender] **3.** to crush with or as with mortar and pestle **4.** to hurt (the feelings, spirit, etc.) —*vi.* **1.** to bruise tissue, a surface, etc. **2.** to be or become bruised —*n.* **1.** a bruised area of tissue, a surface, etc. **2.** an injury to one's feelings, spirit, etc.

bruis·er (brōōz'ər) *n.* a strong, pugnacious man; specif., a professional boxer

bruit (brōōt) *n.* [ME. < OFr., noise, uproar, rumor < *bruire*, to rumble, prob. < L. *rugire*, to roar; ? infl. by VL. *bragire*, to cry out] [Archaic] **1.** clamor **2.** rumor —*vt.* to spread a report of; rumor (often with *about*)

‡**Bru·maire** (brü mer') *n.* [Fr. < *brume*, fog, mist < L. *bruma:* see ff.] the second month (Oct. 22–Nov. 20) of the French Revolutionary Calendar

bru·mal (brōō'məl) *adj.* [L. *brumalis* < *bruma*, winter, shortest day of the year < **brevima* < *brevissima*, superl. of *brevis*, brief] [Archaic] of winter; wintry

brume (brōōm) *n.* [Fr. < L. *bruma:* see prec.] mist; fog; vapor —**bru·mous** (brōō'məs) *adj.*

brum·ma·gem (brum'ə jəm) *adj.* [local vulgar pronunciation of *Birmingham* (in ME., *Bremingeham*), England, where cheap jewelry and gift toys were manufactured] [Colloq.] cheap and gaudy —*n.* [Colloq.] anything cheap and gaudy, esp. imitation jewelry

Brummell, George Bryan see Beau Brummell

brunch (brunch) *n.* [BR(EAKFAST) + (L)UNCH] [Colloq.] a late first meal of the day that takes the place of both breakfast and lunch

Brun·dis·i·um (brən diz'ē əm) *L. name of* Brindisi

Bru·nei (broo nī') **1.** Brit. protected sultanate on the NW coast of Borneo, consisting of two enclaves in the state of Sarawak: 2,226 sq. mi.; pop. 101,000 **2.** its capital: pop. 47,000

Bru·nel·les·chi (brōō'nel les'kē), **Fi·lip·po** (fē lēp'pō) 1377–1446; Florentine architect

bru·net (brōō net') *adj.* [Fr. < OFr., dim. of *brun*, brown < OHG. *brun*, brown] **1.** having black or dark-brown hair, often along with dark eyes and a dark complexion **2.** having a dark color: said of hair, eyes, or skin —*n.* a brunet person

bru·nette (-net') *adj.* [Fr., fem. of prec.] *same as* brunet —*n.* a brunette woman or girl

Brun·hild (brōōn'hild; *G.* brōōn'hilt) [MHG. *Brünhild* < OHG. *brunna*, armor + *hilti*, fight; hence, fighter in armor] in the *Nibelungenlied*, a queen of Iceland whom Gunther, king of Burgundy, gets as his bride with the help of Siegfried's magic: see also Brünnhilde, Brynhild

☆**bru·ni·zem** (brōō'nə zem') *n.* [coined (1938) by F. F. Riecken and Guy Smith, U.S. agronomists < *bruni-*, brown (suggested by Fr. *brun:* see brunet) + Russ. (*cherno*)*zem*, (black) earth < IE. base **ghthem-*, earth, whence L. *humus*] any of several dark-brown prairie soils

Brünn (brün) *Ger. name of* Brno

Brünn·hil·de (broon hil'də; *G.* brün-) [G.: see Brunhild] in Wagner's *Die Walküre*, a Valkyrie whom Siegfried releases from enchantment: see also Brunhild, Brynhild

Bru·no (brōō'nō) [OHG. < *brun*, brown] **1.** a masculine name **2.** **Gior·da·no** (jôr dä'nō), 1548–1600; It. philosopher: burned at the stake by the Inquisition **3.** **Saint,** 1030?–1101; Ger. monk: founder of the Carthusian order: his day is Oct. 6: also **Saint Bruno of Cologne**

Bruns·wick (brunz'wik) **1.** former duchy, then state, of C Germany, now part of the West German state of Lower Saxony **2.** city in NC West Germany: formerly, cap. of *prec.*: pop. 239,000: Ger. name, Braunschweig

brunt (brunt) *n.* [ME. *bront* < ? ON. *bruni*, heat, fire] **1.** orig., a heavy blow or attack **2.** the shock (of an attack) or impact (of a blow) **3.** the heaviest or hardest part [to bear the *brunt* of the blame]

brush[1] (brush) *n.* [ME. *brushe* < OFr. *broce, brosse*, bush, brushwood < VL. *bruscia* < Gmc. **bruskaz*, underbrush < IE. base **breus-*, to sprout forth, underbrush] **1.** *same as* brushwood ☆**2.** sparsely settled country, covered with wild scrub growth **3.** *a)* a device having bristles, hairs, or wires fastened into a hard back, with or without a handle attached: brushes are used for cleaning, polishing, painting, smoothing the hair, etc. *b)* a device of wires attached in a fanlike spread to a handle, used as on drums or cymbals for a swishing or muted effect **4.** the act of brushing **5.** a light, grazing stroke [a *brush* of the hand] **6.** *same as* brushwork **7.** a bushy tail, esp. that of a fox ☆**8.** [Slang] *same as* brushoff **9.** *Elec. a)* a piece, plate, rod, or bundle of carbon, copper, etc. used as a conductor between an external circuit and a revolving part, as in a motor *b)* same as brush discharge —*vt.* **1.** to use a brush on; clean, polish, paint, smooth, etc. with a brush **2.** to apply, spread, remove, etc. with or as with a brush **3.** to go over lightly, as with a brush **4.** to touch or graze in passing —*vi.* to move so as to push lightly aside, skim, or graze past something —**brush aside** (or **away**) **1.** to sweep out of the way **2.** to dismiss from consideration —☆**brush off** [Slang] to dismiss or get rid of abruptly or rudely —**brush up 1.** to make neat or presentable; clean up **2.** to refresh one's memory or skill (often with *on*) [to *brush up on* one's chess]

brush[2] (brush) *vi.* [ME. *bruschen*, rush < ? OFr. *brosser*, to

travel (? through woods), beat underbrush for game: see brush[1]] to move with a rush; hurry —*n.* a short, quick fight or quarrel; skirmish

brush discharge a visible, brushlike electric discharge, as in the air surrounding a wire at high potential

brushed (brusht) *adj.* processed by brushing so as to raise the nap, as some fabrics or leather

☆**brush fire 1.** a fire in brushwood **2.** a sudden flare-up, as of a military nature, that threatens to spread or intensify unless brought under control

☆**brush-off** (-ôf') *n.* [Slang] an abrupt or rude dismissal: esp. in the phrase **give** (or **get**) **the brushoff**

brush·wood (-wood') *n.* **1.** chopped-off or broken-off tree branches **2.** a thick growth of small trees and shrubs; underbrush; brush

brush·work (-wurk') *n.* **1.** work done with a brush; painting **2.** a characteristic way of putting on paint with a brush [Renoir's *brushwork*]

brush·y (-ē) *adj.* **brush'i·er, brush'i·est 1.** rough and bristly; brushlike; bushy **2.** covered with brushwood or underbrush —**brush'i·ness** *n.*

brusque (brusk; *chiefly Brit.* broosk) *adj.* [Fr. < It. *brusco* < ML. *bruscus*, brushwood; prob. akin to brush[1], but infl. by It. *rusco* < L. *ruscum*, butcher's broom] rough and abrupt in manner or speech; curt: also **brusk** —SYN. see BLUNT —**brusque'ly** *adv.* —**brusque'ness** *n.*

‡**brus·que·rie** (brüs kə rē') *n.* [Fr. < *brusque:* see prec.] brusqueness; curtness

Brus·sels (brus'lz) capital of Belgium, in the C part: pop. (with suburbs) 1,058,000: Fl. name **Brus'sel** (brö'səl); Fr. name, Bruxelles

Brussels carpet [after Brussels, where it was made] a patterned carpeting made of small loops of colored woolen yarn in a linen warp

Brussels lace 1. orig., a bobbin or needlepoint lace with a raised design **2.** a machine-made lace with an appliquéd design

Brussels sprouts 1. a plant (*Brassica oleracea gemmifera*) of the mustard family that bears miniature cabbagelike heads on an erect stem **2.** these edible heads

BRUSSELS SPROUTS

‡**brut** (brüt) *adj.* [Fr.: see BRUTE] very dry: said esp. of champagne to which the minimum of sugar has been added

bru·tal (brōōt''l) *adj.* [ME. & OFr. < ML. *brutalis*] **1.** like a brute; cruel and unfeeling; savage, violent, ruthless, etc. **2.** very harsh or rigorous [a *brutal* winter] **3.** plain and direct, although distressing in effect [*brutal* facts] **4.** [Archaic] of or belonging to beasts; animal —SYN. see CRUEL —**bru'tal·ly** *adv.*

bru·tal·i·ty (brōō tal'ə tē) *n.* **1.** the condition or quality of being brutal **2.** *pl.* **-ties** a brutal or savage act, treatment, etc.

bru·tal·ize (brōōt''l īz') *vt.* **-ized', -iz'ing 1.** to make brutal **2.** to treat in a brutal way —*vi.* to become brutal —**bru'tal·i·za'tion** *n.*

brute (brōōt) *adj.* [ME. & OFr. *brut* < L. *brutus*, senseless, irrational] **1.** lacking the ability to reason [a *brute* beast] **2.** having no consciousness or feelings; insensate [the *brute* force of nature] **3.** of or like an animal; specif., brutal, cruel, gross, sensual, stupid, etc. —*n.* **1.** an animal **2.** the animal impulses in man; sensuality (with *the*) **3.** a person who is brutal or very stupid, gross, sensual, etc.

brut·ish (brōōt'ish) *adj.* of or like a brute; savage, gross, stupid, sensual, irrational, etc. —**brut'ish·ly** *adv.* —**brut'ish·ness** *n.*

Bru·tus (brōōt'əs), **(Marcus Junius)** 85?–42 B.C.; Roman statesman & general: one of the conspirators who murdered Julius Caesar

Bru·xelles (brü sel') *Fr. name of* Brussels

Bry·an (brī'ən) **1.** a masculine name: see BRIAN **2.** **William Jen·nings** (jen'inz), 1860–1925; U.S. politician & orator

Bry·ansk (brē änsk'; *Russ.* bryänsk) city in W European R.S.F.S.R.: pop. 267,000

Bry·ant (brī'ənt), **William Cul·len** (kul'ən) 1794–1878; U.S. poet & journalist

Bryce (bris), **Viscount James** 1838-1922; Eng. jurist, statesman, & historian, born in Ireland

Bryce Canyon National Park (bris) [after Ebenezer *Bryce*, an early settler] national park in SW Utah: 56 sq. mi.

Bryn·hild (brin'hild) [ON. *Brynhildr* < *brynja*, armor + *hildr*, fight] *Norse Myth.* a Valkyrie awakened from an enchanted sleep by Sigurd: deceived by him into marrying Gunnar, she brings about Sigurd's death and then kills herself: see also Brunhild, Brünnhilde

bry·ol·o·gy (brī äl'ə jē) *n.* [< Gr. *bryon*, moss, lichen + -LOGY] the branch of botany dealing with bryophytes —**bry'o·log'i·cal** (-ə läj'i k'l) *adj.* —**bry·ol'o·gist** *n.*

bry·o·ny (brī'ə nē) *n., pl.* **-nies** [L. *bryonia* < Gr. *bryōnia* < *bryein*, to swell, sprout] any of a genus (*Bryonia*) of perennial vines of the gourd family with large fleshy roots and greenish flowers

bry·o·phyte (-fīt′) *n.* [< Gr. *bryon*, moss + -PHYTE] any member of a division (Bryophyta) of the plant kingdom consisting of the mosses and liverworts —**bry′o·phyt′ic** (-fit′ik) *adj.*

bry·o·zo·an (brī′ə zō′ən) *n.* [ModL. *bryozoa* < Gr. *bryon*, moss + -ZO(A) + -AN] *same as* ECTOPROCT

Bryth·on (brith′ən) *n.* [W. < Celt. base of L. *Brito, Britto*: see BRITISH] 1. a member of an early Celtic people living in Britain 2. a speaker of Brythonic

Bry·thon·ic (brith′än′ik) *adj.* of the Brythons or their language —*n.* the Brythonic branch of the Celtic subfamily of Indo-European, comprising Cornish, Welsh, and Breton

B/s, b/s 1. bags 2. bales

B.S. Bachelor of Science

b.s. 1. balance sheet 2. bill of sale

B.S.A. 1. Bachelor of Science in Agriculture 2. Boy Scouts of America

B.Sc. [L. *Baccalaureus Scientiae*] Bachelor of Science

B.S.Ed. Bachelor of Science in Education

bskt. basket

Bs/L bills of lading

Bt. Baronet

B.Th., B.T. [L. *Baccalaureus Theologiae*] Bachelor of Theology

btry battery (of artillery)

B.t.u. British thermal unit (or units): also **B.T.U., b.t.u., Btu, btu**

bu. 1. bureau 2. bushel; bushels

☆**bub** (bub) *n.* [< G. *bube*, boy] [Colloq.] brother; boy; little fellow: used in direct address

bu·bal, bu·bale (byōō′bəl) *n.* [ModL. *bubalis* < Gr. *boubalis*, var. of ff.] any of several large, horned antelopes (esp. genus *Alcelaphus*) of Africa: also **bu′ba·lis**

bu·ba·line (byōō′bə lin′, -lin) *adj.* [L. *bubalinus* < *bubalus* < Gr. *boubalos*: see BUFFALO] 1. of the bubals 2. of or like a buffalo

bub·ble (bub′'l) *n.* [ME. *bobel*, of echoic orig., as in MDu. *bubbel*] 1. a very thin film of liquid forming a ball around air or gas [*soap bubbles*] 2. a tiny ball of air or gas in a liquid or solid, as in carbonated water, glass, etc. 3. anything shaped like a bubble, sphere, or hemisphere, as a plastic or glass dome 4. *a)* anything that is ephemeral or insubstantial *b)* any idea, scheme, etc. that seems plausible at first but quickly shows itself to be worthless or misleading 5. the act, process, or sound of bubbling —*vi.* -bled, -bling [ME. *bobelen*] 1. to make bubbles; rise in bubbles; boil; foam; effervesce 2. to make a boiling or gurgling sound —*vt.* 1. to form bubbles in; make bubble ☆2. to cause (a baby) to burp 3. [Archaic] to cheat; swindle —**bubble over** 1. to overflow, as boiling liquid 2. to be unrestrained in expressing one's enthusiasm, zest, etc.

bubble and squeak [Brit.] a dish of cabbage and potatoes, and sometimes meat, fried together

☆**bubble bath** 1. a bath perfumed and softened by a solution, crystals, or powder that forms surface bubbles 2. such a solution, powder, etc.

☆**bubble chamber** a container filled with a superheated, transparent liquid in which charged atomic particles and their collisions can be studied by photographing the bubbles and violent boiling that occur along their paths

☆**bubble gum** a kind of chewing gum that can be blown into large bubbles

bub·bler (bub′lər) *n.* ☆a drinking fountain in which water is forced up in a small arc from a nozzle

☆**bub·ble-top** (bub′'l täp′) *n.* a bulletproof, transparent dome, as over the rear section of an automobile

bub·bly bub′lē) *adj.* 1. full of, or giving off, bubbles 2. like a bubble —*n.* [Slang] champagne

Bu·ber (bōō′bər), **Martin** 1878–1965; Israeli Jewish theologian & philosopher, born in Austria

bu·bo (byōō′bō, bōō′-) *n., pl.* -**boes** [ME. < ML. < Gr. *boubōn*, groin, swollen gland] an inflamed swelling of a lymph gland, esp. in the armpit or groin —**bu·bon′ic** (-bän′ik) *adj.*

bubonic plague a contagious disease caused by a bacterium (*Pasteurella pestis*) and characterized by buboes, fever, prostration, and delirium: fleas from infected rats are the carriers

bu·bon·o·cele (byōō bän′ə sēl′, bōō-) *n.* [Gr. *boubōn*, groin + -CELE] an incomplete or partial inguinal hernia forming a swelling in the groin

Bu·ca·ra·man·ga (bōō′kä rä mäŋ′gä) city in NC Colombia: pop. 230,000

buc·cal (buk′'l) *adj.* [L. *bucca*, cheek, mouth cavity + -AL] 1. of the cheek or cheeks 2. of the mouth or mouth cavity

buc·ca·neer (buk′ə nir′) *n.* [Fr. *boucanier*, user of a *boucan*, native Brazilian grill for roasting meat; orig. applied to Fr. hunters of wild oxen in Haiti] a pirate, or sea robber, esp. one who raided along the Spanish coasts of America in the 17th and 18th cent.

buc·ci·na·tor (buk′sə nāt′ər) *n.* [L., trumpeter < pp. of *buccinare*, to blow a trumpet < *buccina*, a trumpet] the flat muscle of the cheek which compresses it and retracts the corners of the mouth

Bu·ceph·a·lus (byōō sef′ə ləs) [L., lit., ox-headed < Gr. *bous*, ox + *kephalē*, a head] the war horse of Alexander the Great

Buch·an (buk′ən), **Sir John**, 1st Baron Tweedsmuir, 1875–1940; Scot. statesman, novelist, & historian: governor general of Canada (1935–40)

Bu·chan·an (byōō kan′ən), **James** 1791–1868; 15th president of the U.S. (1857–61)

Bu·cha·rest (bōō′kə rest′, byōō′-) capital of Romania, in the S part: pop. 1,239,000: Romanian name, BUCUREŞTI

Buch·en·wald (bōō′k'n wôld′; *G.* bōōkh′ən vält′) village in C Germany, near Weimar; site of a notorious Nazi concentration camp and extermination center

buck[1] (buk) *n.* [ME. *bukke* < OE. *bucca*, male goat < IE. base *bhugo-*, whence G. *bock*, Du. *bok*, Ir. *boc*] 1. *pl.* **bucks, buck**: see PLURAL, II, D, 1 a male deer, antelope, goat, rabbit, etc. ☆2. the act of bucking 3. *same as* BUCKSKIN 4. [Colloq.] a young man, esp. one who is bold, lively, vigorous, etc.: sometimes a contemptuous or patronizing term as applied to a young male Negro or Indian 5. [Now Rare] a fop or dandy —*vi.* ☆1. to rear upward quickly and descend with the back arched and forelegs stiff, in an attempt to throw off a rider: said of a horse, mule, etc. 2. to plunge forward with lowered head, as a goat ☆3. [Colloq.] to resist something as if plunging against it ☆4. [Colloq.] to move jerkily, as a car —*vt.* ☆1. to charge against, esp. with the head down, as in football ☆2. to dislodge or throw by bucking ☆3. [Colloq.] to resist stubbornly —*adj.* 1. male ☆2. of the lowest military rating [*buck* private, *buck* sergeant] —☆**buck for** [Slang] to work eagerly, sometimes too obviously, for (a promotion, etc.) —☆**buck up** [Colloq.] to cheer up; brace up —**buck′er** *n.*

☆**buck**[2] (buk) *n.* [Du. *zaagbok*, sawbuck < *zaag*, saw + *bok*: see prec.] 1. a sawbuck; sawhorse 2. a gymnastic apparatus somewhat like a sawhorse, with a padded, leather-covered top, for vaulting over

☆**buck**[3] (buk) *n.* [prob. < BUCKHORN: a knife with a buckhorn handle was often used as a counter] 1. *Poker* a counter placed before a player to remind him that the next turn to deal is his or of his obligation, after he has won a jackpot, to order a new jackpot on his next turn to deal 2. [Slang] a dollar —☆**pass the buck** [Colloq.] to evade blame or responsibility by trying to pass it to someone else

Buck (buk), **Pearl** (born *Pearl Sydenstricker*) 1892– ; U.S. novelist

☆**buck and wing** a complicated, fast tap dance

☆**buck·a·roo** (buk′ə rōō′, buk′ə rōō′) *n., pl.* -**roos** [prob. < Gullah *buckra* (see BUCKRA), white man, boss, altered after Sp. *vaquero*, cowboy] a cowboy

buck·bean (-bēn′) *n.* [after Du. *boksboon*, lit., goat's bean] a bog plant (*Menyanthes trifoliata*) of the gentian family, with glossy leaves made up of three leaflets and white flowers with bearded petals

BUCKBOARD

☆**buck·board** (buk′bôrd′) *n.* [< ?] a four-wheeled, open carriage with the seat carried on a flooring of long, flexible boards whose ends rest directly on the axles

buck·et (buk′it) *n.* [ME. *boket* < Anglo-Fr. *buket*, dim. of OE. *buc*, pitcher, bulging vessel, orig., belly] 1. a deep, round container with a flat bottom and a curved handle, used to hold or carry water, coal, etc.; pail 2. the amount held by a bucket: also **buck′et·ful′**, *pl.* -**fuls′** 3. a thing like a bucket, as a scoop on a steam shovel, any of the cups on a water wheel, any of the curved vanes in the rotor of a turbine, etc. 4. [Slang] the rump; buttocks —*vt., vi.* 1. to carry, draw, or lift (water, etc.) in a bucket or buckets 2. to speculate (with) dishonestly as in a bucket shop 3. [Brit.] *a)* to ride (a horse) at a fast pace *b)* to move or drive rapidly or recklessly —**kick the bucket** [? < obs. *bucket*, beam on which a slaughtered pig was hung] [Slang] to die

BUCKET (sense 3)

bucket brigade a line of persons passing buckets of water along in trying to put out a fire

bucket seat a single contoured seat with a back that can be tipped forward, as in some sports cars

☆**bucket shop** an establishment ostensibly accepting orders to buy and sell stocks, bonds, and commodities, but actually engaged in gambling on the rise and fall of their prices, or in betting secretly against its customers, speculating with funds entrusted to it, etc.

☆**buck·eye** (buk′ī′) *n.* [BUCK[1] + EYE: from the appearance of the seed] **1.** any of various trees (genus *Aesculus*) of the horse-chestnut family with large, spiny capsules enclosing shiny brown seeds **2.** the seed of such a tree **3.** [B-] [Colloq.] a native or inhabitant of Ohio, called the **Buck-eye State**

☆**buck fever** [Colloq.] nervous excitement of novice hunters when they first see game

buck·horn (-hôrn′) *n.* **1.** the horn of a buck, used esp. for ornamentation, knife handles, etc. **2.** a common lawn weed (*Plantago lanceolata*) of the plantain family

buck·hound (-hound′) *n.* a dog somewhat like a greyhound, used for hunting deer

Buck·ing·ham (buk′iɳ əm) **1.** 1st Duke of, (born *George Villiers*) 1592–1628; Eng. statesman **2.** 2d Duke of, (born *George Villiers*) 1628–87; Eng. statesman & writer: son of *prec.*

Buckingham Palace the official residence in London of British sovereigns

Buck·ing·ham·shire (buk′iɳ əm shir′) county in SC England: 749 sq. mi.; pop. 516,000: also called **Buck′ing-ham**

buck·ish (buk′ish) *adj.* of or like a buck, or dandy; foppish —**buck′ish·ly** *adv.*

buck·le[1] (buk′'l) *n.* [ME. *bokel*, a buckle, boss of a shield < OFr. *bocle* < LL. *bucula*, beaver, shield < L. *buccula*, cheek strap of a helmet, dim. of *bucca*, cheek] **1.** a clasp on one end of a strap or belt for fastening the other end in place **2.** a clasplike ornament, as for shoes —*vt.* **-led, -ling** **1.** to fasten or join with a buckle **2.** to bring together; join —*vi.* **1.** to be fastened or joined by a buckle **2.** [Obs.] to engage in a struggle; grapple —☆**buckle down** to apply oneself energetically; set to work with effort

buck·le[2] (buk′'l) *vt., vi.* **-led, -ling** [prob. < Du. *bukken*, to bend, infl. by Fr. *boucler*, to bulge] to bend, warp, or crumple, as under pressure or in intense heat —*n.* a distortion caused by buckling; bend, bulge, kink, etc. —**buckle under** to give in; yield; submit

Buck·le (buk′'l), **Henry Thomas** 1821–62; Eng. historian

buck·ler (buk′lər) *n.* [ME. *bokeler* < OFr. *bocler:* see BUCKLE[1]] **1.** a small, round shield held by a handle or worn on the arm **2.** any protection or defense —*vt.* to protect by shielding; defend

buck·o (buk′ō) *n., pl.* **-oes** [< BUCK[1]] **1.** a blustering or swaggering fellow; bully **2.** a young man; fellow: an Irishism often used in familiar address

☆**buck-pass·er** (-pas′ər) *n.* [Colloq.] a person who regularly seeks to shift blame or responsibility to someone else —**buck′-pass′ing** *n.*

☆**buck·ra** (buk′rə) *n.* [< Ibibio & Efik (in Nigeria) *mbakara*, lit., he who surrounds or governs] a white man or boss: term used chiefly in the SE U.S. by Negroes

buck·ram (buk′rəm) *n.* [ME. *bokeram* < OFr. *bouquerant*, prob. < *Bokhara*, in Asia Minor] **1.** a coarse cotton or linen cloth stiffened with glue or other size, for use in bookbinding, for lining or stiffening clothes, etc. **2.** [Now Rare] stiffness or formality —*adj.* **1.** of or like buckram **2.** [Now Rare] stiff; formal —*vt.* to stiffen with buckram

☆**buck·saw** (buk′sô′) *n.* [BUCK[2] + SAW[1]] a saw set in a frame, held on one side with both hands in cutting wood on a saw-buck

buck·shee (buk′shē′) *n.* [< BAK-SHEESH] something free; gratuity

☆**buck·shot** (buk′shät′) *n.* a large lead shot for shooting deer and other large game

buck·skin (-skin′) *n.* **1.** the skin of a buck **2.** a soft, usually napped, yellowish-gray leather made from the skins of deer or sheep ☆**3.** a yellowish-gray horse **4.** [*pl.*] clothes or shoes made of buck-skin ☆**5.** [*often* B-] an American backwoodsman of earlier times —*adj.* made of buckskin

BUCKSAW

buck·thorn (-thôrn′) *n.* [BUCK[1] + THORN] **1.** any of a genus (*Rhamnus*) of thorny trees or shrubs of a family (Rhamnaceae), bearing small greenish flowers and purple drupes **2.** any of a genus (*Bumelia*) of trees of the sapodilla family, native to the southern U.S.

buck·tooth (-tōōth′) *n., pl.* **-teeth′** [BUCK[1] + TOOTH] a projecting front tooth —**buck′toothed′** (-tōōtht′) *adj.*

buck·wheat (-hwēt′, -wēt′) *n.* [< OE. *boc-*, BEECH + WHEAT, after MDu. *boecweit* or MLowG. *bokwete:* from the resemblance of the seeds to beechnuts] **1.** any of several plants (genus *Fagopyrum*) of the buckwheat family, grown for their black, tetrahedral grains **2.** the grain of this plant, from which a dark flour is made ☆**3.** this flour —*adj.* designating a family (Polygonaceae) of plants including rhubarb, dock, and sorrel

bu·col·ic (byōō käl′ik) *adj.* [L. *bucolicus* < Gr. *boukolikos* < *boukolos*, herdsman < *bous*, ox] **1.** of shepherds; pastoral **2.** of country life or farms; rustic —*n.* **1.** a pastoral poem **2.** a rustic; countrified person —*SYN.* see RURAL —**bu·col′i·cal·ly** *adv.*

Bu·co·vi·na (bōō′kə vē′nə) same as BUKOVINA

Bu·cu·reşti (bōō kōō resht′) *Romanian name of* BUCHA-REST

bud[1] (bud) *n.* [ME. *budde*, bud, seedpod, akin to G. (*hage*)*butte*, hip of the dog rose, *butzen*, seedpod] **1.** *a)* a small swelling or projection on a plant, from which a shoot, cluster of leaves, or flower develops *b)* a partly opened flower **2.** any undeveloped or immature person or thing **3.** an asexually produced swelling or projection on the body of some lower animals that develops into a new individual —*vi.* **bud′ded, bud′ding** [< the *n.*] **1.** to put forth buds **2.** to begin to develop **3.** to be young, promising, etc. —*vt.* **1.** to put forth as a bud or buds **2.** to cause to bud **3.** to graft by inserting a bud of (a plant) into the bark of another sort of plant —**in (the) bud 1.** in the time of budding **2.** in a budding condition —**bud′der** *n.* —**bud′like′** *adj.*

☆**bud**[2] (bud) *n.* [Slang] *short for* BUDDY: used in addressing a man or boy

Bu·da·pest (bōō′də pest′) capital of Hungary, in the NC part, on the Danube: pop. 1,900,000

Bud·dha (bōōd′ə, bōō′də) [Sans., the enlightened one; pp. of *budh*, to awake, know] Siddhartha Gautama, a religious philosopher and teacher who lived in India 563?–483? B.C. and was the founder of Buddhism: the name is a title applied by Buddhists to someone regarded as embodying divine wisdom and virtue —*n.* a statue or image of Buddha

Bud·dhism (bōōd′iz'm, bōō′diz'm) a religion and philosophic system of central and eastern Asia, founded in India in the 6th cent. B.C. by Buddha: it teaches that right thinking and self-denial will enable the soul to reach Nirvana, a divine state of release from misdirected desire which causes all bodily pain and sorrow —**Bud′dhist** *n., adj.* —**Bud′dhis′tic** *adj.*

bud·dle (bud′'l, bōōd′-) *n.* [< ?] *Mining* a shallow, inclined trough or drain for washing ore

bud·dle·ia (bad lē′ə, bud′lē ə) *n.* [ModL., after Adam *Buddle*, 18th-cent. Eng. botanist] any of a genus (*Buddleia*) of shrubs and trees of the logania family, native to the tropics but commonly grown in temperate regions for their blossoms of purple, yellow, etc.

☆**bud·dy** (bud′ē) *n., pl.* **-dies** [c. 1852 < ? Brit. dial. *butty*, companion, with weakening of stop consonant] [Colloq.] **1.** a close friend; companion; comrade; esp., a comrade in arms **2.** either of two persons paired off in a partnership arrangement (**buddy system**) for mutual help and protection, as in combat, children's camp activities, etc. —*vi.* **-died, -dy·ing** [Colloq.] to associate as a buddy or buddies

☆**bud·dy-bud·dy** (bud′ē bud′ē) *adj.* [Slang] friendly or chummy, often in an effusive or insincere way

budge[1] (buj) *vt., vi.* **budged, budg′ing** [Fr. *bouger*, to move < VL. *bullicare*, to boil < L. *bullire*, BOIL[1]] **1.** to move even a little [*unable to budge the boulder*] **2.** to yield or cause to yield

budge[2] (buj) *n.* [ME., a bag, bulge < OFr. *bouge*, a bag < L. *bulga*, leather bag < Gaul. *bulga*] lambskin dressed so that the wool is worn outward, esp. as a trimming on academic gowns of the past —*adj.* [Archaic] solemn or pompous

budg·er·i·gar (buj′ə ri gär′) *n.* [native name] an Australian parakeet (*Melopsittacus undulatus*) having a greenish-yellow body, marked with bright blue on the cheeks and tail feathers, and wings striped with brown

budg·et (buj′it) *n.* [ME. *bougette* < OFr., dim. of *bouge:* see BUDGE[2]] **1.** orig., a bag, pouch, or purse, or its contents **2.** a collection of items; stock **3.** a plan or schedule adjusting expenses during a certain period to the estimated or fixed income for that period **4.** the cost or estimated cost of living, operating, etc. **5.** the amount of money needed or allotted for a specific use —*vt.* **1.** to put on or in a budget; provide for in a budget **2.** to plan (expenditures or activities) according to a budget **3.** to plan in detail; schedule [*budget* your time] —*vi.* to make a budget —**budg·et·ar·y** (buj′ə ter′ē) *adj.* —**budg′et·er** *n.*

budg·ie (buj′ē) *n.* [Colloq.] *same as* BUDGERIGAR

bud scale any of the thin, papery or leathery structures covering certain plant buds in winter

Bud·weis (bōōt′vīs) *Ger. name of* ČESKÉ BUDĚJOVICE

Bue·na Park (bwā′nə pärk′) [Sp. *buena*, good + PARK] city in SW Calif.: suburb of Los Angeles: pop. 64,000

‡**bue·nas no·ches** (bwe′näs nô′ches) [Sp.] good night

Bue·na·ven·tu·ra (bwe′nä ven tōō′rä) seaport in W Colombia, on the Pacific: pop. 97,000

Bue·na Vis·ta (bwā′nə vis′tə, byōō′nə) village in NW Mexico: site of a battle in the Mexican War, in which U.S. forces defeated the Mexicans

Bue·nos Ai·res (bwā′nəs er′ēz, ī′rēz; bō′nəs; *Sp.* bwe′nôs ī′res) **1.** capital of Argentina: federal district and seaport on the Río de la Plata: 74 sq. mi.; pop. 3,876,000 **2.** province of E Argentina, on the Atlantic: 118,750 sq. mi.; pop. 5,458,000; cap. La Plata **3. Lake,** lake in the S Andes, on the Chile–Argentina border; 865 sq. mi.

‡**bue·nos di·as** (bwe′nôs dē′äs) [Sp.] good day; good morning

buff[1] (buf) *n.* [earlier *buffe*, buffalo < Fr. *buffle* < It. *bufalo*, BUFFALO] **1.** a heavy, soft, brownish-yellow leather made from the skin of the buffalo or from other animal hides **2.** a military coat made of this leather **3.** *a)* a stick or small block covered with leather or cloth, used for cleaning or shining *b)* same as BUFFING WHEEL **4.** a dull brownish yellow ☆**5.** [Colloq.] a devotee or enthusiast; fan [a jazz *buff*] —*adj.* **1.** made of buff **2.** of the color buff —*vt.* **1.** to

clean or shine with a buff **2.** to make smooth or soft like buff —*SYN.* see POLISH —**in the buff** naked; nude
buff[2] (buf) *n.* [ME. & OFr. *buffe:* see BUFFET[1]] a blow: now only in BLINDMAN'S BUFF —*vt.* to lessen the force of —*vi.* to serve as a buffer
Buf·fa·lo (buf'ə lō') [transl. of the name of a Seneca Indian who lived there] city in W N.Y., on Lake Erie: pop. 463,000 (met. area 1,349,000)
buf·fa·lo (buf'ə lō') *n., pl.* **-loes', -los', -lo':** see PLURAL, II, D, 1 [It. *bufalo* < LL. *bufalus,* var. of *bubalus,* wild ox < Gr. *boubalos,* buffalo, antelope < *bous,* ox: for IE. base see COW[1]] **1.** any of various wild oxen, sometimes domesticated, as the water buffalo of India, Cape buffalo of Africa, etc. ☆**2.** popularly, the American bison ☆**3.** a robe made of buffalo skin ☆**4.** *same as* BUFFALO FISH —☆*vt.* **-loed', -lo'ing** [Slang] to baffle, bewilder, bluff, or overawe
☆**buffalo berry 1.** a shrub (genus *Shepherdia*) of the oleaster family, native to western N. America, with silvery leaves **2.** its red, fleshy, edible berry

BUFFALO
(55–70 in. high
at shoulder)

Buffalo Bill *nickname of* William CODY
☆**buffalo bug** *same as* CARPET BEETLE
☆**buffalo fish** any of several large, humpbacked freshwater fishes (genus *Ictiobus*) of the sucker family
buffalo grass a low, creeping native range grass (*Buchloe dactyloides*) of the Great Plains, used for forage
☆**buffalo moth** the hairy larva of a carpet beetle (*Anthremus scrophulariae*), harmful to furs and woolens
☆**buffalo robe** a carriage robe or rug made of the skin of the bison, dressed with the hair on
buff·er[1] (buf'ər) *n.* [BUFF[1], *v.* + -ER] **1.** a person who buffs or polishes **2.** a buffing wheel or stick
buff·er[2] (buf'ər) *n.* [BUFF[2], *v.* + -ER] **1.** a device using padding, springs, hydraulic pressure, etc. to lessen or absorb the shock of collision or impact **2.** any person or thing that serves to lessen shock or prevent sharp impact, as between antagonistic forces **3.** any substance in a solution that tends to stabilize the hydrogen ion concentration by neutralizing any added acid or alkali —*vt.* to add a buffer to (a solution)
buffer state a small country located between two large, antagonistic powers and regarded as lessening the possibility of conflict between them
buf·fet[1] (buf'it) *n.* [ME. < OFr. < *buffe,* a blow: prob. echoic] **1.** a blow with the hand or fist **2.** any blow or shock [the *buffets* of fate] —*vt.* **1.** to hit with the hand or fist; punch; slap **2.** to beat back as by repeated blows; thrust about [the waves *buffeted* the boat] **3.** to struggle against —*vi.* to struggle or force a way by struggling
buf·fet[2] (bə fā', boo-; *Brit.* buf'it) *n.* [Fr. < OFr. *buffet,* bench (whence ME. *buffet,* stool)] **1.** a piece of furniture with drawers and cupboards for dishes, table linen, silver, etc.; sideboard **2.** *a)* a counter or table where refreshments are served *b)* a restaurant with such a counter or table **3.** a meal at which guests serve themselves from a buffet or table
buff·ing wheel (buf'iŋ) a wheel covered with leather, cloth, etc., for buffing, or polishing, metal
☆**buf·fle·head** (buf''l hed') *n.* [obs. *buffle,* buffalo, fool < Fr. (see BUFF[1]) + HEAD] a small North American duck (*Bucephala albeola*), black on top and white underneath
‡**buf·fo** (boof'fō; *E.* boo'fō) *n., pl.* **-fi** (-fē) [It., comic: see BUFFOON] an opera singer, generally a bass, who plays a comic role
Buf·fon (bü fōn'), **Georges Louis Le·clerc** (zhôrzh lwē lə kler'), **Comte de** 1707–88; Fr. naturalist
buf·foon (bə foon') *n.* [Fr. *bouffon* < It. *buffone,* jester < *buffare,* to jest, puff, of echoic orig.] a person who is always clowning and trying to be funny; clown —**buffoon'er·y** *n.* —**buf·foon'ish** *adj.*
bu·fo·ten·ine (byoo'fə ten'ēn) *n.* [< ModL. *Bufo* (genus name) + *-ten-* (< ?) + *-INE*[4]] a poisonous hallucinogenic alkaloid, $C_{12}H_{16}ON_2$, extracted from the skin glands of the common toad (*Bufo vulgaris*)
Bug (boog) **1.** river in the S Ukraine, flowing southeastward into the Black Sea: 530 mi.: also called **Southern Bug 2.** river in the W Ukraine flowing northwestward into the Vistula near Warsaw and forming part of the Poland–U.S.S.R. border: 500 mi.: also called **Western Bug**
bug[1] (bug) *n.* [prob. < ff.] **1.** any of an order (Hemiptera-Heteroptera) of insects with sucking mouthparts and with forewings thickened toward the base, as a water bug, squash bug, etc. **2.** any insect or small, insectlike animal, specif. one regarded as a pest, as a bedbug, louse, cockroach, etc. **3.** [Colloq.] any microscopic organism, esp. one causing disease; germ or virus ☆**4.** [Slang] a tiny microphone hidden to record conversation secretly ☆**5.** [Slang] a defect or imperfection, as in a machine ☆**6.** [Slang] *a)* an enthusiast or devotee: often used in combination [a *shutterbug* pursues photography as a hobby] *b)* a particular

enthusiasm or obsession ☆**7.** [Slang] a small, compact automobile —☆*vt.* **bugged, bug'ging** [Slang] **1.** to hide a microphone in (a room, etc.), as for recording conversation secretly **2.** *a)* to annoy, bother, anger, etc. *b)* to confuse or puzzle —*vi.* [Slang] to bulge or open wide, as in amazement: said of the eyes —☆**bug off** [Slang] to stop annoying someone and leave: also [Brit.] **bugger off** —☆**bug out** [Slang] to run away; desert
bug[2] (bug) *n.* [ME. *bugge,* prob. < W. *bwg, bwgan*] [Obs.] a bugbear; hobgoblin
bug·a·boo (bug'ə boo') *n., pl.* **-boos'** [prec. + BOO] a bugbear
bug·bane (-bān') *n.* any of a genus (*Cimicifuga*) of perennial plants of the buttercup family, with long spikes of small white flowers whose odor is supposed to repel insects
bug·bear (-ber') *n.* [BUG[2] + BEAR[2]] **1.** an imaginary hobgoblin or terror used to frighten children into good conduct **2.** anything causing seemingly needless or excessive fear or anxiety
☆**bug-eyed** (-īd') *adj.* [Slang] with bulging eyes
bug·ger (bug'ər) *n.* [ME. *bougre* < OFr. *bolgre* < ML. *Bulgarus,* lit., a Bulgarian; orig., 11th-c. Bulgarian heretic] **1.** a sodomite **2.** a contemptible person **3.** a fellow; chap; also, a rascal or scamp: often used humorously or affectionately —*vt.* to commit sodomy with
bug·ger·y (-ē) *n. same as* SODOMY
bug·gy[1] (bug'ē) *n., pl.* **-gies** [18th c.; < ?] **1.** a light carriage with four (or, in England, two) wheels and a single seat, usually drawn by one horse ☆**2.** a small perambulator or baby carriage **3.** [Slang] an automobile, esp. an old one
bug·gy[2] (bug'ē) *adj.* **-gi·er, -gi·est 1.** infested or swarming with bugs **2.** [Slang] mentally ill; insane
☆**bug·house** (-hous') *n.* [Slang] an insane asylum —*adj.* [Slang] mentally ill; insane
bu·gle[1] (byoo'g'l) *n.* [ME., wild ox, drinking horn, hunting horn < OFr. < L. *buculus,* heifer, young ox, dim. of *bos,* ox] a brass-wind instrument like a trumpet but smaller, and usually without keys or valves: used chiefly for military calls and signals —*vi., vt.* **-gled, -gling** to call or signal by or as by blowing a bugle —**bu'gler** *n.*
bu·gle[2] (byoo'g'l) *n.* [< ? prec. (from the appearance)] a long, tubular glass bead for trimming dresses, etc. —*adj.* trimmed with bugles: also **bu'gled**
bu·gle[3] (byoo'g'l) *n.* [ME. & OFr. < LL. *bugula,* for L. *bugillo,* a plant] any of a genus (*Ajuga*) of plants of the mint family, having spikes of white, pink, or blue flowers
bu·gle·weed (hyoo'g'l wēd') *n.* **1.** *same as* BUGLE[3] ☆**2.** any of a genus (*Lycopus*) of plants of the mint family, with tiny white or pale blue flowers
bu·gloss (byoo'gläs', -glôs') *n.* [ME. & OFr. *buglosse* < L. *buglossa* < Gr. *bouglossos,* oxtongue < *bous,* ox + *glōssa,* tongue] *same as* ALKANET (sense 1 *a* & 2)
☆**bugs** (bugz) *adj.* [Slang] mentally ill; insane
☆**bug·seed** (bug'sēd') *n.* [so named from appearance of the seeds] a branching, annual weed (*Corispermum hyssopifolium*) of the goosefoot family, with sprays of oval fruits
bug·shah (bug'shə, -shô) *n., pl.* **-shah, -shahs** a unit of money in Yemen, equal to 1/100 riyal
buhl (bool) *n.* [after Charles André *Boulle* (1642–1732), Fr. cabinetmaker] **1.** decoration of furniture with designs of tortoise shell, brass, silver, etc. inlaid in wood **2.** furniture so decorated Also **buhl'work**
buhr·stone (bur'stōn') *n.* [*buhr,* var. of BURR[3] + STONE] **1.** a hard siliceous rock used to make grinding stones **2.** a stone made of this: also **buhr**
build (bild) *vt.* **built** or archaic **build'ed, build'ing** [ME. *bilden* < OE. *byldan,* to build < base of *bold,* a house: for IE. base see BONDAGE] **1.** *a)* to make by putting together materials, parts, etc.; construct; erect *b)* to order, plan, or direct the construction of **2.** to make a basis for; establish [to *build* a theory on facts] **3.** to cause to be or grow; create or develop (often with *up*) [to *build* good will, to *build* up a business] —*vi.* **1.** *a)* to put up a building *b)* to have a house, etc. built **2.** to be in the business of building houses, etc. **3.** to increase in amount, force, etc.; grow or intensify (often with *up*) **4.** *Card Games* to form a sequence according to suit, number, etc. —*n.* the way a thing is built or shaped; form or figure [a stocky *build*] —**build up 1.** to make more desirable or attractive [to *build up* a product by advertising] **2.** to erect many buildings in (an area)
build·er (bil'dər) *n.* **1.** a person or animal that builds **2.** a person in the business of constructing buildings **3.** an ingredient added to soap or a detergent to increase its effectiveness
build·er's knot (bil'dərz) *same as* CLOVE HITCH
build·ing (-diŋ) *n.* **1.** anything that is built with walls and a roof, as a house, factory, etc.; structure **2.** the act, process, work, or business of constructing houses, ships, etc. *SYN.*—**building** is the general term applied to a fixed structure in which people dwell, work, etc.; **edifice** implies a large or stately building and is sometimes used figuratively [the *edifice* of democracy]; **structure** also suggests an imposing building, but has special application when the material of construction is being stressed [a steel *structure*]; **pile** is applied in poetry and lofty prose to a very large building or mass of buildings

☆**build·up, build-up** (bild′up′) *n.* [Colloq.] **1.** favorable publicity or praise, esp. when systematic and intended to make something popular, well-known, etc. **2.** a gradual increase in amount, power, influence, etc.; expansion [a military *buildup*]

built (bilt) *pt. & pp.* of BUILD

☆**built-in** (bilt′in′) *adj.* **1.** made as part of the structure; not movable or detachable [a *built-in* bathtub, *built-in* cabinets] **2.** intrinsic; inherent

built-up (-up′) *adj.* **1.** made higher, stronger, larger, etc. by the addition of parts [*built-up* heels] **2.** having many buildings on it: said of an area

Bu·jum·bu·ra (boo′joom boor′ə) capital of Burundi; port at the N end of Lake Tanganyika: pop. 70,000

Bu·kha·ra (boo khä′rä; *E.* boo kär′ə) **1.** region of the Uzbek S.S.R.: 49,600 sq. mi.; pop. 573,000 **2.** capital of this region: pop. 69,000

Bu·ko·vi·na (boo′kə vē′nə) region in C Europe, partly in N Romania & partly in the SW Ukraine

bul. bulletin

Bu·la·wa·yo (boo′lə wä′yō) city in SW Rhodesia: pop. (with suburbs) 214,000

bulb (bulb) *n.* [ME. < L. *bulbus* < Gr. *bolbos*] **1.** an underground bud that sends down roots and consists of a very short stem covered with leafy scales or layers, as in a lily, onion, hyacinth, etc. **2.** a corm, tuber, or tuberous root resembling a bulb, as in a crocus, dahlia, cyclamen, etc. **3.** any plant that grows from a bulb **4.** anything shaped like a bulb; rounded thing or enlarged part [an electric light *bulb*, the *bulb* of a syringe] **5.** *Anat.* a) an enlargement on some tissues and organs, as at the root of a hair b) *same as* MEDULLA OBLONGATA

bul·ba·ceous (bəl bā′shəs) *adj.* [L. *bulbaceus*] *Bot. same as* BULBOUS

bul·bar (bul′bər) *adj.* of a bulb; esp., having to do with the medulla oblongata

bulbed (bulbd) *adj.* having a bulb or bulbs

bul·bif·er·ous (bəl bif′ər əs) *adj.* producing bulbs

bul·bil (bul′bil) *n.* [ModL. *bulbillus*, dim. of L. *bulbus*, BULB] a small bulb or fleshy bud on a flower stalk, as in some onions, or in the axil of a leaf, as in a tiger lily

bul·bous (bul′bəs) *adj.* [L. *bulbosus*] **1.** of, shaped like, or having a bulb or bulbs **2.** growing from a bulb

bul·bul (bool′bool) *n.* [Per.: prob. echoic] **1.** a songbird referred to in Persian poetry, perhaps a nightingale **2.** any of various small, dull-colored songbirds (family Pycnonotidae) of Asia and Africa

Bul·finch (bool′finch′) **1. Charles,** 1763–1844; U.S. architect **2. Thomas,** 1796–1867; U.S. writer & mythologist: son of *prec.*

Bulg. 1. Bulgaria **2.** Bulgarian

Bul·gar (bul′gär, bool′-) *n., adj. same as* BULGARIAN

Bul·gar·i·a (bul ger′ē ə, bool-) country in SE Europe, on the Black Sea: 42,796 sq. mi.; pop. 8,230,000; cap. Sofia

Bul·gar·i·an (-ē ən) *adj.* of Bulgaria, its people, or their language —*n.* **1.** a native or inhabitant of Bulgaria **2.** the Slavic language of the Bulgarians

bulge (bulj) *n.* [ME., var. of *bouge:* see BUDGE²] **1.** an outward swelling; protuberance **2.** a projecting part, as a military salient ☆**3.** [Colloq.] a sudden increase in size, value, etc. ☆**4.** [Colloq.] advantage or margin of advantage —*vi., vt.* **bulged, bulg′ing** to swell or bend outward; protrude or project —*SYN.* see PROJECTION

bulg·y (-ē) *adj.* having a bulge or bulges —**bulg′i·ness** *n.*

bu·lim·i·a (byoo lim′ē ə) *n.* [ModL. < Gr. *boulimia* < *bous,* ox + *limos,* hunger] *Med.* a continuous, abnormal hunger —**bu·lim′ic** *adj.*

bulk¹ (bulk) *n.* [ME., heap, cargo < ON. *bulki,* a heap, ship's cargo; prob. < IE. base *bhel-:* see BALL¹] **1.** size, mass, or volume, esp. if great **2.** the main mass or body of something; largest part or portion [the *bulk* of one's fortune] **3.** soft, bulky matter of a kind that remains unabsorbed in the intestines and in the eliminative process **4.** a ship's hold or cargo —*vi.* **1.** to form into a mass **2.** to increase in size, importance, etc. **3.** to have size or importance [to *bulk* large in the mind] —*vt.* **1.** to make (something) form into a mass **2.** to make bulge; stuff **3.** to give greater bulk, or size, to —*adj.* **1.** total; aggregate **2.** not put up in individual packages —**in bulk 1.** not put up in individual packages **2.** in large amounts; in great volume *SYN.*—**bulk, mass,** and **volume** all refer to a quantity of matter or collection of units forming a body or whole, **bulk** implying a body of great size, weight, or numbers [the lumbering *bulk* of a hippopotamus, the *bulk* of humanity], **mass,** an aggregate, multitude, or expanse forming a cohesive, unified, or solid body [an egg-shaped *mass,* a *mass* of color, the *mass* of workers], and **volume,** a moving or flowing mass, often of a fluctuating nature [*volumes* of smoke, the *volume* of production]

bulk² (bulk) *n.* [ME. *balk* < ON. *balkr,* partition, wall, akin to BALK] [Archaic] a projecting framework or stall built as the front of a shop

bulk·head (bulk′hed′, bul′ked′) *n.* [prec. + HEAD] **1.** any

of the upright partitions separating parts of a ship, airplane, etc. as for protection against fire or leakage **2.** a wall or embankment for holding back earth, fire, water, etc. ☆**3.** a boxlike structure built over an opening, as at the head of a staircase, elevator shaft, etc.

bulk·y (bul′kē) *adj.* **bulk′i·er, bulk′i·est 1.** *a)* having great bulk; large; massive *b)* relatively large for its weight **2.** awkwardly large; big and clumsy —**bulk′i·ly** *adv.* —**bulk′i·ness** *n.*

bull¹ (bool) *n.* [ME. *bole* < OE. *bula,* a steer, akin to ON. *boli,* G. *bulle* < IE. base **bhel-,* to swell up: see BALL¹] **1.** the adult male of any bovine animal, as the ox, buffalo, etc. **2.** the adult male of certain other large animals, as the elephant, elk, moose, walrus, whale, etc. **3.** a person who buys stocks or securities in the expectation that their prices will rise, or who seeks to bring about such a rise, in order to sell them at a profit: opposed to BEAR² **4.** a person regarded as like a bull in size, strength, etc. **5.** a bulldog ☆**6.** [Slang] a policeman or detective ☆**7.** [clip of *bull* "dung" (a euphemism)] [Slang] foolish, insincere, exaggerated, or boastful talk; nonsense —[B-] Taurus, the constellation and second sign of the zodiac —*vt.* **1.** to seek to raise the price of (stocks) or prices in (a stock market) ☆**2.** to make (one's way) with driving force ☆**3.** [Slang] to bluff, as with insincere talk —*vi.* to go up in price, as stocks —*adj.* **1.** male **2.** like a bull in size, strength, etc. **3.** rising in price [a *bull* market] —☆**shoot the bull** [Slang] to talk or chat idly —**take the bull by the horns** to face and deal boldly with a danger or difficulty

bull² (bool) *n.* [ME. & OFr. *bulle* < LL. *bulla,* a seal (L., anything round, knob, bubble)] **1.** *same as* BULLA (sense 1) **2.** an official document, edict, or decree, esp. one from the Pope

bull³ (bool) *n.* [ME. *bul,* trickery, lie < OFr. *boule,* lie < L. *bulla:* see prec.] a ludicrously illogical or incongruous mistake in statement (Ex.: I'm glad I hate onions because if I liked onions, I'd eat them, and I can't stand onions)

bull- (bool) [< BULL¹] *a combining form meaning:* **1.** of a bull or bulls [*bullfight*] **2.** like a bull or bull's [*bullhead*] **3.** large or male [*bullfrog*]

bull. bulletin

Bull (bool), **O·le** (ō′lə) 1810–80; Norw. violinist

bul·la (bool′ə, bul′ə) *n., pl.* **-lae** (-ē) [LL.: see BULL²] **1.** a round lead seal attached to an official document from the Pope **2.** *Med.* a large blister or vesicle

bul·lace (bool′is) *n.* [ME. *bolas* < OFr. *beloce* < ML. **bullucea,* small plum] **1.** a variety of the common E European plum (*Prunus domestica*), having small purple fruit borne in clusters ☆**2.** *same as* MUSCADINE

bul·late (bool′it, bul′-) *adj.* [L. *bullatus* < *bulla,* a bubble] **1.** having blisters **2.** blistered or puckered in appearance, as some leaves **3.** inflated like a blister

bull-bait·ing (bool′bāt′in) *n.* the setting of dogs on a chained or confined bull, formerly a popular pastime in England

☆**bull·bat** (-bat′) *n.* [BULL- + BAT²] *same as* NIGHTHAWK (sense 1)

☆**bull·bri·er** (-brī′ər) *n.* any of several species of thorny woody vines (genus *Smilax*) of the lily family, common in the forests of southern U.S.

bull·dog (-dôg′, -däg′) *n.* [BULL- + DOG] **1.** a short-haired, square-jawed, heavily built dog noted for its strong stubborn grip **2.** a short-barreled revolver of large caliber **3.** [Brit.] a university attendant employed to enforce the rules of behavior for students —*adj.* like or characteristic of a bulldog; stubborn, unrelenting, etc. —☆*vt.* **-dogged′, -dog′ging** to throw (a steer) by taking hold of its horns and twisting its neck

☆**bulldog edition** the early edition of a morning newspaper, chiefly for out-of-town distribution

BULLDOG
(18 in. high
at shoulder)

☆**bull·doze** (-dōz′) *vt.* **-dozed′, -doz′ing** [< *bulldose, n.,* a severe beating < *bull* (Botany Bay slang), a flogging of 75 lashes + DOSE] **1.** [Colloq.] to force or frighten by threatening; intimidate; bully **2.** to move, make level, dig out, etc. with a bulldozer

☆**bull·doz·er** (-dō′zər) *n.* **1.** a person who bulldozes **2.** *a)* a large, shovellike blade on the front of a tractor, for pushing or moving earth, debris, etc. *b)* a tractor with such a blade

bul·let (bool′it) *n.* [Fr. *boulette,* dim. of *boule,* a ball < L. *bulla:* see BULL²] **1.** a small ball or cone-shaped missile of lead, metal alloy, etc., with a round or pointed end, to be shot from a firearm **2.** loosely, a bullet in its casing; cartridge **3.** anything like a bullet in shape, action, etc.

BULLDOZER

bul·le·tin (bool′ət 'n) *n.* [Fr. < It. *bulletino,* dim. of LL. *bulla:* see BULL²] **1.** a brief official statement about a

BULBS
(A, tulip; B, onion;
C, lily; D, narcissus)

matter of public concern **2.** a brief statement of the latest news, as in a newspaper or on radio or TV **3.** a regular publication, as for the members of some society —*vt.* to announce or publish in a bulletin

☆**bulletin board** a board or wall area on which bulletins, notices, or displays are put up

bul·let·proof (bool′it proof′) *adj.* that bullets cannot pierce —*vt.* to make bulletproof

☆**bull fiddle** [Colloq.] *same as* DOUBLE BASS

bull·fight (bool′fīt′) *n.* a public show in which a bull is first provoked in various ways and is then maneuvered into position by a matador, who usually kills it with a sword: popular in Spain and Spanish America —**bull′fight′er** *n.* —**bull′fight′ing** *n.*

bull·finch[1] (-finch′) *n.* [BULL- + FINCH] **1.** a European songbird (*Pyrrhula pyrrhula*) with a black head and white rump **2.** any of various other small songbirds of Europe, Asia, and North America

bull·finch[2] (-finch′) *n.* [< ? *bull fence*] a hedge too high for a horse and rider to jump

☆**bull·frog** (-frôg′, -frä̆g′) *n.* [BULL- + FROG] a large North American frog (*Rana catesbiana*) that has a deep, loud croak

bull·head (-hed′) *n.* [see BULL-] ☆**1.** any of various North American, spiny, scaleless freshwater fishes (genus *Ameiurus*), with a large head, barbels, and a forked tail **2.** any of various marine and freshwater fishes (family Cottidae) with a spiny head and wide mouth **3.** a bull-headed person

bull·head·ed (-hed′id) *adj.* blindly stubborn; headstrong —**bull′head′ed·ly** *adv.* —**bull′head′ed·ness** *n.*

☆**bull·horn** (-hôrn′) *n.* [BULL- + HORN] a portable electronic voice amplifier

bul·lion[1] (bool′yən) *n.* [ME. < Du. *bulioen* < OFr. *billon*, small coin, alloy of copper with silver < *bille*, a stick, bar: see BILLET[2]] **1.** gold and silver regarded as raw material **2.** ingots of gold or silver, as before coinage

bul·lion[2] (-yən) *n.* [infl. by prec. but prob. < Fr. *bouillon* < *bouille*, a seal on silk goods < Sp. *bolla*, duty on silk < L. *bulla*: see BULL[2]] a heavy fringe or lace of twisted gold or silver thread

bull·ish (bool′ish) *adj.* **1.** of or like a bull **2.** *a)* rising, or causing, expecting, etc. a rise, in price on the stock exchange; hence *b)* optimistic —**bull′ish·ly** *adv.* —**bull′ish·ness** *n.*

bull mastiff a very strong, active breed of dog produced by crossing mastiffs and bulldogs

Bull Moose a member of the Progressive Party led by Theodore Roosevelt in the presidential campaign of 1912: so called from the symbol of the party

☆**bull·neck** (-nek′) *n. local name for* any of various American wild ducks, as the canvasback, the ruddy duck, the ring-necked duck, etc.

bull-necked (-nekt′) *adj.* having a short, thick neck

bull nose a contagious disease of pigs, caused by a bacillus and characterized by a swelling of the snout and a sloughing off of the infected tissues

bull·ock (bool′ək) *n.* [ME. *bulloke* < OE. *bulluc*, dim. of *bula*: see BULL[1]] **1.** orig., a young bull **2.** a castrated bull; steer

☆**bull·pen** (-pen′) *n.* **1.** a fenced enclosure for bulls **2.** [Colloq.] a large room or enclosure for a number of people; specif., a barred enclosure in a jail, where prisoners are kept together temporarily, as between their arrest and the placing of charges **3.** *Baseball* an area near the playing field, where relief pitchers practice and warm up

☆**bull·pout** (-pout′) *n.* the common bullhead or horned pout of the eastern U.S.

bull·ring (-rin′) *n.* an arena for bullfighting

bull-roar·er (-rôr′ər) *n.* a flat piece of wood at the end of a string, which makes a roaring noise when whirled: used in religious ceremonies of some peoples

Bull Run [< ?] small stream in NE Va.: site of two Civil War battles (1861 & 1862) in which Union forces were defeated: see also MANASSAS

☆**bull session** [cf. BULL[1], *n.* 7] [Colloq.] an informal discussion or conversation among a small group

bull's-eye (boolz′ī′) *n.* [as in Fr. *oeil de boeuf*, Dan. *kooie*, cow eye, Sw. *oxoga*, ox eye, all applied to small, round windows] **1.** a thick, circular glass in a roof, ship's deck, etc., for admitting light **2.** any circular opening for light or air **3.** *a)* the circular central mark of a target *b)* a shot that hits this *c)* a direct hit *d)* the exact achievement of a goal aimed at **4.** *a)* a convex lens for concentrating light *b)* a lantern with such a lens **5.** a hard, round candy **6.** *Naut.* a small wooden pulley

☆**bull·shot** (bool′shät′) *n.* a cocktail made of gin or vodka and bouillon

☆**bull snake** **1.** any of several large, brownish, nonpoisonous North American snakes (genus *Pituophis*) feeding mainly on rodents **2.** *same as* INDIGO SNAKE (sense 1)

bull terrier any of a breed of strong, lean, active dog with a smooth, white coat, developed by crossing the bulldog and the terrier

☆**bull tongue** [so called from its shape] a simple, detachable

plowshare, used esp. for breaking hard virgin soil —**bull′-tongue′** *vt.*, *vi.* -**tongued′**, -**tongu′ing**

☆**bull·whip** (bool′hwip′, -wip′) *n.* [BULL- + WHIP] a long, heavy whip, formerly used by cattle drivers and teamsters —*vt.* -**whipped′**, -**whip′ping** to whip with a bullwhip

bul·ly[1] (bool′ē) *n.*, *pl.* -**lies** [orig., sweetheart < Du. *boel*, lover, brother < MHG. *buole* (G. *buhle*), lover; later infl. by BULL[1]] **1.** a person who hurts, frightens, or tyrannizes over those who are smaller or weaker **2.** [Brit. Dial.] a companion or comrade **3.** [Archaic] a pimp **4.** [Archaic] a hired cutthroat or thug **5.** [Archaic] a fine fellow —*vt.* -**lied**, -**ly·ing** to hurt, frighten, or tyrannize over, as a bully does; browbeat —*vi.* to behave like a bully —*adj.* **1.** dashing, hearty, or jolly [*my bully lad*] ☆**2.** [Colloq.] fine; very good —*interj.* [Colloq.] good! well done!

bul·ly[2] (bool′ē) *n.* [Fr. *bouilli*, boiled beef < *bouillir*, BOIL[1]] canned or corned beef: also **bully beef**

☆**bully boy** a man who uses force or violence in carrying out plans or policies; esp., a hired ruffian

bul·ly·rag (bool′ē rag′) *vt.* -**ragged′**, -**rag′ging** [see BULLY[1], *vt.* & RAG[2], *vt.*] [Dial. or Colloq.] to bully, intimidate, or browbeat

bully tree [altered < BALATA tree] any of several tropical American trees of the sapodilla family that yield balata

Bü·low (bü′lō), Prince **Bern·hard von** (bern′härt fōn) 1849–1929; Ger. statesman; chancellor (1900–09)

bul·rush (bool′rush′) *n.* [ME. *bulryshe* < OE. *bol*, BOLE[1] + *risc*, a RUSH[2]] **1.** any of a number of marsh plants (genus *Scirpus*) of the sedge family, having slender, round or triangular stems tipped with brown spikelets of minute flowers **2.** [Brit.] the cattail **3.** popularly, any aquatic plant resembling a bulrush, as the papyrus: cf. Ex. 2:3

Bult·mann (boolt′män), **Rudolf (Karl)** 1884– ; Ger. Protestant theologian

bul·wark (bool′wərk, bul′-) *n.* [ME. *bulwerk* < MDu. *bolwerc*: see BOLE[1] & WORK[1]] **1.** an earthwork or defensive wall; fortified rampart **2.** *same as* BREAKWATER **3.** a person or thing serving as a strong defense or protection **4.** [*usually pl.*] the extension of the ship's side above the deck —*vt.* **1.** to provide bulwarks for **2.** to be a bulwark to

Bul·wer (bool′wər), **Edward Robert** *see* Owen MEREDITH

Bul·wer-Lyt·ton (bool′wər lit′'n), **Edward George Earle Lytton**, 1st Baron Lytton, 1803–73; Eng. novelist & playwright; father of *prec.*

☆**bum**[1] (bum) *n.* [< *bummer*, prob. < G. *bummler*, loafer, habitually tardy person < *bummeln*, to go slowly, waste time] [Colloq.] **1.** a vagrant, hobo, tramp, or beggar; specif., a shabby, often drunken derelict **2.** any shiftless or irresponsible person, loafer, idler, etc. **3.** a devotee, as of golf or skiing, who devotes so much time to the sport as to disrupt his family life, career, etc. **4.** an incompetent person, esp. an athlete —*vi.* **bummed**, **bum′ming** [Colloq.] **1.** to live as a bum, or vagrant **2.** to live by begging, or sponging on people —*vt.* [Slang] to get by begging or sponging; cadge [to *bum* a cigarette] —*adj.* **bum′mer** **bum′mest** [Slang] **1.** poor in quality [*bum* cooking] **2.** false, erroneous, or invalid [a *bum* steer, a *bum* rap] **3.** lame or ailing [a *bum* leg] —*SYN.* see VAGRANT —**give (or get) the bum's rush** [Slang] to eject (or be ejected) forcibly —**on a bum** [Slang] on a drunken spree —**on the bum** [Colloq.] **1.** living the life of a vagrant **2.** out of repair; broken —**bum′mer** *n.*

bum[2] (bum) *n.* [ME. *bom* < ? *botem*, bottom, as Du. dial. *boem* < *bodem*, & obs. *bummery* for *bottomry*] [Brit. Slang] the buttocks

bum·bail·iff (bum′bāl′lif) *n.* [prec. + BAILIFF: ? because the officer was often close behind] [Brit.] a bailiff or sheriff's officer: a contemptuous usage

☆**bum·ber·shoot** (bum′bər shoot′) *n.* [jocular alteration and merging of UMBR(ELLA) & (PARA)CHUTE] [Slang] an umbrella

bum·ble·bee (bum′b'l bē′) *n.* [altered (after ME. *bomblen*, var. of *bomben*, to boom, buzz, of echoic orig.) < ME. *humbul-be* < *humbil*, bumble bee (akin to G. *hummel* < IE. base *kem-*, to hum, of echoic orig.) + *be*, BEE[1]] any of a number of related large, hairy, yellow-and-black social bees (esp. genus *Bombus*)

bum·bling (bum′blin) *adj.* [prp. of *bumble*, buzz: see prec.] self-important in a blundering sort of way

bum·boat (bum′bōt′) *n.* [BUM[2] + BOAT; orig. (17th c.), sailors' slang for garbage boat] a boat used in peddling provisions and other articles to ships

bumf, bumph (bumf) *n.* [contr. < *bumfodder*, lit., toilet paper < BUM[2] + FODDER] [Brit. Slang] official documents, regarded disparagingly

bum·kin (bum′k'n) *n. same as* BUMPKIN (sense 1)

bump (bump) *vt.* [echoic] **1.** to hit or knock against with a jolt; collide lightly with ☆**2.** [Slang] to displace, as from a job, plane reservation, etc. ☆**3.** [Slang] to raise (a price, a salary, a bet in poker, etc.) —*vi.* **1.** to hit or collide with a jolt **2.** to move with jerks or jolts —*n.* **1.** a knock or blow; light jolt **2.** a swelling, lump, or bulge, esp. one caused by a blow **3.** any of the protuberances of the skull as interpreted with reference to one's mental faculties in the pseudoscience of phrenology ☆**4.** [Slang] a thrusting movement forward of the lower part of the torso, as in striptease

dancing: see also GRIND (n. 5) —☆**bump into** [Colloq.] to meet unexpectedly —☆**bump off** [Slang] to murder; kill

bump·er[1] (bum'pər) n. ☆ a device for absorbing some of the shock of a collision; specif., a metal bar for this purpose across the front or back of an automobile

bump·er[2] (-pər) n. [prob. < obs. *bombard*, liquor jug, altered after BUMP] 1. a cup or glass filled to the brim 2. [Colloq.] anything unusually large of its kind —*adj.* unusually large or abundant [a *bumper* crop]

bump·kin (bump'k'n, bum'-) n. [prob. < Du. *boomkin*, short tree, dim. of *boom*, a tree] 1. a short, projecting boom on a ship, as at the stern of a yacht for securing a permanent backstay 2. [prob. < MDu. *bommekijn*, small cask < *bomme*, a cask + -*kijn*, dim. suffix] an awkward or simple person from the country

bump·tious (bump'shəs) *adj.* [prob. < BUMP, by analogy with FRACTIOUS, etc.] disagreeably conceited, arrogant, or forward —**bump'tious·ly** *adv.* —**bump'tious·ness** *n.*

bump·y (bump'pē) *adj.* **bump'i·er, bump'i·est** full of bumps; rough; jolting —**bump'i·ly** *adv.* —**bump'i·ness** *n.*

bun[1] (bun) n. [ME. *bunne*, wheat cake, bun, prob. < OFr. *buigne*, a boil, swelling (whence Fr. *beigne*, fruit fritter) < Gaul. **bunia*] 1. a small roll, usually somewhat sweetened and often spiced or enriched with raisins, etc. 2. hair worn in a roll or knot

☆**bun**[2] (bun) n. [prob. contr. < colloq. (Scot.) *bung*, drunk (short for *bung-full*, filled to the bung)] [Slang] a drunken spree —**get a bun on** [Slang] to become drunk

Bu·na (boo'nə, byoo'-) n. [*ta(dien)*, butadiene + *Na*, (symbol for) sodium] *a trademark for* synthetic rubber made by polymerizing butadiene —n. [**b**-] this substance

bunch (bunch) n. [ME. *bonche*, bundle, hump < Wal. *bouge* <Fl. *boudje*, dim. of *boud*, bundle] 1. a cluster or tuft of things growing together [a *bunch* of grapes] 2. a collection of things of the same kind fastened or grouped together, or regarded as belonging together [a *bunch* of keys] 3. [Colloq.] a group of people, esp. of the same kind 4. [Obs.] a hump, protuberance, or swelling —*vt., vi.* 1. to form or collect into a bunch or bunches; gather together in a mass (often with *up*) 2. to gather into loose folds or wads, as a dress, skirt, etc. —**bunch'i·ness** n. —**bunch'y** *adj.*

bunch·ber·ry (-ber'ē, -bər ē) n., *pl.* -**ries** ☆ a N. American dwarf plant (*Cornus canadensis*) of the dogwood family, growing in cool forests and having minute flowers surrounded by four large, white bracts and, in the fall, bearing bunches of bright-red berries

Bunche (bunch), **Ralph Johnson** 1904–   ; U.S. statesman & educator

bunch·er (bunch'ər) n. 1. one who bunches ☆2. a device that bunches; esp., *Electronics* the electrically resonant cavity in a klystron which forms the electron beam into bunches of electrons

☆**bunch·flow·er** (-flou'ər) n. a tall plant (*Melanthium virginicum*) of the lily family, growing in the E U.S. and having large clusters of white or greenish flowers

☆**bunch grass** any of various grasses that grow in tufts

☆**bun·co** (bun'kō) n., *pl.* -**cos** [c. 1875 < Sp. *banca*, card game < It. *banca*, BANK[1]] [Colloq.] a swindle, esp. one carried out with confederates, as at a card game, lottery, etc.; confidence game —*vt.* -**coed, -co·ing** [Colloq.] to swindle; cheat

☆**bun·combe** (bun'kəm) n. [< *Buncombe* county, N.C.: from the fact that the representative to Congress (1819–21) from the district including this county felt bound to "make a speech for Buncombe"] [Colloq.] talk that is empty, insincere, or merely for effect; humbug

bund[1], **Bund** (boond; G. boont) n., *pl.* **bunds** (boondz); G. **Bün'de** (bün'də) [G. < root of *binden*, BIND] 1. a league or confederation 2. a political organization; specif., the German-American Bund, a former pro-Nazi organization in the U.S. —**bund'ist** n.

bund[2] (bund) n. [Anglo-Ind. < Hind. *band*, embankment, dike < Per. *bändär*, harbor] in the Orient, an embankment or quay, or an embanked road along a waterfront

Bun·des·rat, Bun·des·rath (boon'däs rät') n. [G., gen. of *bund*, BUND[1] + *rat, rath*, council] the federal council in West Germany and in Austria

Bun·des·tag (boon'dəs täg') n. [G. < gen. of *bund*, federation, BUND[1] + *tag*, meeting (cf. REICHSTAG)] the federal diet, or assembly, of West Germany

bun·dle (bun'd'l) n. [ME. *bundel*, prob. < MDu. *bondel*, dim. < *bond* < *binden*, BIND] 1. a number of things tied, wrapped, or otherwise held together 2. a package or parcel 3. a bunch, collection, or group 4. [Slang] a large amount of money 5. *Biol.* a) any of the strands of specialized cells that conduct fluids or add strength in higher plants: in full, **vascular bundle** b) an anatomic unit consisting of a number of separate nerve fibers, muscles, etc. closely banded together —*vt.* -**dled, -dling** 1. to make into a bundle; wrap or tie together 2. to send hastily or without ceremony; hustle (*away, off, out,* or *into*) —*vi.* 1. to move or go hastily; bustle 2. to lie in the same bed with one's sweetheart without undressing: a former courting custom, esp. in New England —**bundle up** to put on plenty of warm clothing —**bun'dler** n.

SYN.—**bundle** refers to a number of things bound together for convenience in carrying, storing, etc. and does not in itself carry connotations as to size, compactness, etc. [a *bundle* of discarded clothing]; **bale** implies a standardized or uniform quantity of goods,

as raw cotton, hay, etc., compressed into a rectangular mass and tightly bound; **parcel** and **package** are applied to something wrapped or boxed for transportation, sale, etc. and imply moderateness of size and a compact or orderly arrangement; **pack** is applied to a package of a standard amount [a *pack* of cigarettes] or to a compact bundle carried on the back of a person or animal

bung (bun) n. [ME. *bunge* < MDu. *bonge*] 1. a cork or other stopper for the hole in a barrel, cask, or keg 2. a bunghole —*vt.* 1. to close (a bunghole) with a stopper 2. to close as with a bung; stop up 3. [prob. infl. by BANG[1]] [Slang] to bruise or damage, as in a fight (with *up*) 4. [Slang] to toss; fling; throw

bun·ga·low (bun'gə lō') n. [Anglo-Ind. < Hind. *bānglā*, thatched house, lit., Bengalese] 1. in India, a low, one-storied house, usually with a wide, sweeping porch or veranda 2. a small, low house or cottage, usually of one story and an attic

bung·hole (bun'hōl') n. a hole in a barrel or keg through which liquid can be poured in or drawn out

bun·gle (bun'g'l) *vt.* -**gled, -gling** [< ? Sw. *bangla*, to work ineffectually] to spoil by clumsy work or action; botch —*vi.* to do or make things badly or clumsily —n. 1. a bungling, or clumsy, act 2. a bungled piece of work —**bun'gler** n. —**bun'gling·ly** *adv.*

Bu·nin (boo'nyin), **I·van A·lek·se·ye·vich** (ē vän' ä'lyik sā'yi vich) 1870–1953; Russ. novelist & poet, in France after 1920

bun·ion (bun'yən) n. [prob. < ME. *boni*, < OFr. *buigne*: see BUN[1]] an inflammation and swelling of the bursa at the base of the big toe, with a thickening of the skin

bunk[1] (bunk) n. [prob. < Scand. cognate of BENCH] 1. a shelflike bed or berth built into or against a wall, as in a ship 2. [Colloq.] any sleeping place, esp. a narrow cot —*vi.* 1. to sleep in a bunk 2. [Colloq.] to use a makeshift sleeping place —*vt.* to provide a sleeping place for

☆**bunk**[2] (bunk) n. [< BUNCOMBE] [Slang] buncombe; nonsense

bunk bed a pair of twin beds linked one above the other and often provided with a detachable ladder

bunk·er (bun'kər) n. [Scot.; < ?] 1. a large bin or tank, as for a ship's coal or fuel oil 2. a protected weapon emplacement of steel and concrete in an underground fortification system 3. a sand trap or mound of earth serving as a hazard or obstacle on a golf course —*vt.* 1. to supply (a ship) with fuel 2. *Golf* to hit (a ball) into a bunker

Bun·ker Hill (bun'kər) hill in Boston, Mass.: the Battle of Bunker Hill (1775), in which American colonial forces were defeated by the British, was actually fought on nearby Breed's Hill

bunk·house (bunk'hous') n. a kind of barracks for ranch hands, migratory farm workers, etc.

☆**bunk·mate** (-māt') n. a person who sleeps in an adjoining bunk or in the same bunkhouse

☆**bun·ko** (bun'kō) n., *pl.* -**kos,** *vt.* -**koed, -ko·ing** same as BUNCO

bun·kum (bun'kəm) n. same as BUNCOMBE

bun·ny (bun'ē) n., *pl.* -**nies** [dim. of dial. *bun*, rabbit] a rabbit: pet name used by children

Bun·sen (bun's'n; G. boon'zən), **Robert Wilhelm** 1811–99; Ger. chemist; inventor of the spectroscope

Bunsen burner (bun's'n) [after *Bunsen*] a small, gas burner that produces a hot, blue flame, used in chemistry laboratories, etc.: it consists of a hollow metal tube with adjustable holes at the bottom for admitting air to be mixed with the gas

bunt[1] (bunt) *vt., vi.* [< ? base of Bret. *bounta*, to butt, via Corn.] 1. [Brit. Dial.] to strike or butt with or as with horns ☆2. *Baseball* to bat (a pitched ball) lightly without swinging so that it does not go beyond the infield, usually in attempting a sacrifice play —n. 1. a butt or shove ☆2. *Baseball* a) the act of bunting b) a bunted ball

bunt[2] (bunt) n. [< earlier dial., a puffball] a disease that destroys the grain of wheat and other grasses, caused by various fungi (genus *Tilletia*)

bunt[3] (bunt) n. [< ? MLowG. & MDu., a binding, bundle; akin to BIND] 1. the sagging part of a fish net 2. the bellying part of a square sail

bun·ting[1] (bun'tin) n. [< ? ME. *bonting*, gerund of *bonten*, to sift: hence, cloth used for sifting] 1. a thin cloth used in making flags, streamers, etc. 2. flags, or strips of cloth in the colors of the flag, used as holiday decorations ☆3. a baby's garment of soft, warm cloth made into a kind of hooded blanket that can be closed so that only the face is exposed

bun·ting[2] (bun'tin) n. [ME.; < ?] any of various small, brightly colored birds (families Thraupidae and Fringillidae, and esp. genus *Passerina*), having a short, stout bill

bunt·line (bunt'lin, -lin') n. [BUNT[3] + LINE[1]] one of the ropes attached to the foot of a square sail to prevent the sail from bellying when drawn up to be furled

bun·ya-bun·ya (bun'yə bun'yə) n. [< native name] an Australian coniferous tree (*Araucaria bidwillii*) with thick, flat, lanceolate needles and large, edible seeds

Bun·yan (bun'yən) 1. **John,** 1628–88; Eng. writer & preacher: wrote *Pilgrim's Progress* 2. see PAUL BUNYAN

Buo·na·par·te (bwô'nä pär'te) *It. sp. of* BONAPARTE

Buo·nar·ro·ti (bwô'när rô'tē), **Michelangelo** see MICHEL-ANGELO

‡**buon gior·no** (bôn jyôr′nô) [It.] good day; hello

buoy (boo′ē, boi; *for v., usually* boi) *n.* [ME. < (? via MDu. *boeie*) OFr. *buie*, chain < L. *boia*, pl. *boiae*, fetter, orig. neck collar: apparently first applied to the chain anchoring the float] 1. a floating object anchored in a lake, river, etc. to warn of rocks, shoals, etc. or to mark a channel, and often equipped with a bell or light 2. *same as* LIFE BUOY —*vt.* [< Sp. *boyar*, to float] 1. to mark or provide with a buoy 2. to keep afloat: usually with *up* 3. to lift up or keep up in spirits; encourage: usually with *up*

BUOYS
(A, lighted whistle; B, lighted; C, whistling; D, bell; E, nun; F, spar; G, can)

buoy·an·cy (boi′ən sē, boo′yən-) *n.* [< BUOYANT] 1. the ability or tendency to float or rise in liquid or air 2. the power to keep something afloat; upward pressure on a floating object 3. lightness or resilience of spirit; cheerfulness

buoy·ant (-ənt, -yənt) *adj.* [< ? Sp. *boyante* < *boyar*, to float] having or showing buoyancy —**buoy′ant·ly** *adv.*

bu·pres·tid (byoo pres′tid) *n.* [L. *buprestis* < Gr. *bouprēstis*, poisonous beetle which when eaten with fodder caused cattle to swell up and die < *bous*, ox + *prēthein*, to swell up] any of a family (Buprestidae) of beetles with a long, flat, metallic-colored body: the larvae are harmful to woody plants

bur (bur) *n.* [ME. *burre* < Scand.: Dan. *burre*, Sw. *borre*] 1. the rough, prickly seedcase or fruit of certain plants, as of the sticktight, cocklebur, etc. 2. a weed or other plant with burs 3. anything that clings like a bur 4. *Dentistry* a cutting or drilling bit 5. *same as* BURR¹ & BURR² —*vt.* **burred, bur′ring** 1. to remove burs from 2. to burr

Bur. Burma

bur. bureau

bu·ran (boo rän′) *n.* [Turk.] a strong windstorm from the steppes of Russia and Siberia, accompanied in winter with driving snow and in summer with hot dust

Bur·bage (bur′bij), **Richard** 1567?–1619; Eng. actor: associate of Shakespeare

Bur·bank (bur′bank) [after Dr. D. *Burbank*, one of the city planners] city in SW Calif.: suburb of Los Angeles: pop. 89,000

Bur·bank (bur′bank), **Luther** 1849–1928; U.S. horticulturist: bred numerous varieties of fruits, vegetables, & flowers

bur·ble (bur′b'l) *vi.* **-bled, -bling** [ME. *burbelen*, to bubble; of echoic orig.] 1. to make a gurgling or bubbling sound 2. to babble as a child does —*n. Aeron.* the separation and breakup of the streamline flow of air, esp. over the surface of a wing at too great an angle of attack, resulting in a loss of lift and an increase of drag —**bur′bler** *n.*

bur·bot (bur′bət) *n., pl.* **-bot, -bots:** see PLURAL, II, D, 2 [ME. < OFr. *borbote*, earlier *barbote* < *barbe* < L. *barba*, a beard] a freshwater fish (*Lota lota*) of the cod family, with a broad, flat head and barbels on the nose and chin; widely distributed in Europe, Asia, and N. America

Burck·hardt (boork′härt), **Jacob** 1818–97; Swiss art historian & critic

burd (burd) *n.* [ME. *burde, birde,* prob. var. of *birthe*, BIRTH, offspring; infl. by association with *bride*, BRIDE] [Obs.] a lady; young lady

bur·den¹ (burd′'n) *n.* [ME. *birthen* < OE. *byrthen* < base of *beran*: see BEAR¹] 1. anything that is carried; load 2. anything one has to bear or put up with; heavy load, as of work, duty, responsibility, sorrow, etc. 3. the carrying of loads [a beast of *burden*] 4. the carrying capacity of a ship, or the weight of its cargo —*vt.* to put a burden on; load; weigh down; oppress

bur·den² (burd′'n) *n.* [ME. *burdoun*, bass in music, refrain < OFr. *bourdon*, a humming, buzzing < ML. *burdo*, DRONE², wind instrument, bumblebee] 1. [Archaic] a bass accompaniment in music 2. a chorus or refrain of a song 3. the drone of a bagpipe 4. a repeated, central idea; theme [the *burden* of a speech]

burden of proof the obligation to prove what is asserted and in dispute

bur·den·some (-səm) *adj.* hard to bear; heavy; oppressive —*SYN.* see ONEROUS —**bur′den·some·ly** *adv.*

bur·dock (bur′däk′) *n.* [BUR + DOCK³] any of several plants (genus *Arctium*) of the composite family, with large basal leaves, and purple-flowered heads covered with hooked prickles

bu·reau (byoor′ō) *n., pl.* **-reaus, -reaux** (-ōz) [Fr., writing table or desk, office < OFr. *burel*, coarse cloth (as table cover) < VL. *bura* < LL. *burra*, ragged (woolen garment] 1. [Brit.] a writing table or desk, with drawers for papers ☆2. a chest of drawers, with or without a mirror, as for clothing 3. an agency for collecting and giving information or performing other services [a credit *bureau*, a travel *bureau*] ☆4. a government department, or a subdivision of a government department

bu·reau·cra·cy (byoo rä′krə sē) *n., pl.* **-cies** [Fr. *bureaucratie* < *bureau* + *-cratie*, -CRACY] 1. the administration of government through departments and subdivisions managed by sets of appointed officials following an inflexible routine 2. the officials collectively 3. governmental officialism or inflexible routine: see also RED TAPE 4. the concentration of authority in a complex structure of administrative bureaus

bu·reau·crat (byoor′ə krat′) *n.* an official in a bureaucracy, esp. one who follows a routine in a mechanical, unimaginative way, insisting on proper forms, petty rules, etc. —**bu′reau·crat′ic** *adj.* —**bu′reau·crat′i·cal·ly** *adv.*

bu·reau·cra·tize (byoo rä′krə tiz′) *vt., vi.* **-tized′, -tiz′ing** to develop into a bureaucracy; make or become bureaucratic —**bu·reau′cra·ti·za′tion** *n.*

bu·rette, bu·ret (byoo ret′) *n.* [Fr. < OFr. *buirette*, dim. of *buire*, flagon] a graduated glass tube with a stopcock at the bottom, used as by chemists for measuring small quantities of liquid or gas

burg (burg) *n.* [var. of BOROUGH; colloq. use < -BURG in place names] 1. orig., a fortified or walled town ☆2. [Colloq.] a city, town, or village, esp. one regarded as quiet, unexciting, etc.

-burg (burg) *a suffix meaning* burg or borough [*Vicksburg*]

bur·gage (bur′gij) *n.* [ME. < OFr. *bourgage* < ML. *burgagium* < LL. *burgus*, castle, fortress < Gmc. *burgs:* see BOROUGH] a former system of land or property tenure in towns, specif., in England, from an overlord for a yearly rental and, in Scotland, from the crown for watching and warding

Bur·gas (boor gäs′) seaport in SE Bulgaria, on the Black Sea: pop. 106,000

bur·gee (bur′jē) *n.* [< ?] an identifying or signaling flag of swallow-tailed or triangular form, used on ships

bur·geon (bur′jən) *vi.* [ME. *burjournen* < OFr. *burjoner* < *burjon*, a bud] 1. to put forth buds, shoots, etc.; sprout 2. to grow or develop rapidly; expand; proliferate; flourish [the *burgeoning* suburbs]

☆**-burg·er** (bur′gər) [< (HAM)BURGER] *a combining form meaning:* 1. sandwich of a patty of ground meat, fish, etc. [*turkeyburger*] 2. hamburger and [*cheeseburger*]

Bur·ger (bur′gər), **Warren Earl** 1907– ; U.S. jurist; chief justice of the U.S. (1969–)

bur·gess (bur′jis) *n.* [ME. & OFr. *burgeis:* see BOURGEOIS] 1. [Now Rare] a citizen or freeman of a British borough 2. formerly, a member of the British Parliament representing a borough, corporate town, or university ☆3. a member of the House of Burgesses, the lower house of the legislature of Md. or Va. before the American Revolution

Bur·gess (bur′jəs), **(Frank) Ge·lett** (jə let′) 1866–1951; U.S. humorist & illustrator

burgh (burg) *Scot.* bu′rə *n.* [ME.: Scot. var. of BOROUGH] 1. [Brit.] a borough 2. in Scotland, an incorporated or chartered town

-burgh (burg) *Scot.* bu′rə *same as* -BURG

burgh·er (bur′gər) *n.* [ME. < *burgh*, BOROUGH; in ModE. ? assimilated < G. *bürger* or Du. *burger*] an inhabitant of a borough or town: now used chiefly of a middle-class townsman, esp. of some European countries

Burgh·ley (bur′lē), **1st Baron** (born *William Cecil*) 1520–98; Eng. statesman; adviser to Elizabeth I

bur·glar (bur′glər) *n.* [Anglo-L. *burglator*, altered after L. *latro*, thief (orig., hired servant < Gr. *latris:* see -LATRY) < OFr. *burgeor*, burglar, ult. < LL. *burgus:* see BOURGEOIS] a person who commits burglary

bur·glar·i·ous (bər gler′ē əs) *adj.* of, constituting, or inclined to burglary —**bur·glar′i·ous·ly** *adv.*

☆**bur·gla·rize** (bur′glə rīz′) *vt.* **-rized′, -riz′ing** [Colloq.] to commit burglary in or upon

bur·gla·ry (bur′glər ē) *n., pl.* **-ries** [BURGLAR + -Y⁴] 1. the act of breaking into a house at night to commit theft or other felony 2. the act of breaking into any building at any time to commit theft, some other felony, or a misdemeanor —*SYN.* see THEFT

bur·gle (bur′g'l) *vt., vi.* **-gled, -gling** [< BURGLAR] [Colloq.] to burglarize or commit burglary

bur·go·mas·ter (bur′gə mas′tər, -mäs′-) *n.* [ME. *burghmaster* < MDu. *burgemeester* < *burg* (see BOROUGH) + *meester*, MASTER] the mayor or head magistrate of a city or town in the Netherlands, Flanders, Austria, or Germany

bur·go·net (bur′gə net′) *n.* [Fr. *bourguignotte*, orig. fem. of *Bourguignot*, Burgundian < *Bourgogne*, Burgundy] a lightweight helmet or steel cap, worn in the 16th cent.

bur·goo (bur′goo, bər goo′) *n.* [18th-c. nautical slang; early sp. also *burgoût*] 1. a thick oatmeal porridge or gruel ☆2. [Dial.] *a)* a highly seasoned soup of meat and vegetables *b)* a barbecue, picnic, etc. at which this is served

Bur·gos (boor′gōs) city in NC Spain, in Old Castile: pop. 89,000

Bur·goyne (bər goin′, bur′goin), **John** 1722–92; Brit. general in the American Revolution: defeated by colonial forces under Gates at Saratoga (1777)

bur·grave (bur′grāv) n. [G. *burggraf* < *burg* (see BOROUGH) + *graf*, a count] formerly, the lord of a German burg and its environs, originally appointed, later hereditary

Bur·gun·dy (bur′gən dē) region in SE France: formerly a kingdom, province, and duchy of varying extent —n. [*occas.* **b-**] *pl.* **-dies** *a*) a kind of wine, either red or white and sometimes effervescent, made in the Burgundy region *b*) a similar red wine made elsewhere — **Bur·gun·di·an** (bər-gun′dē ən) *adj., n.*

bur·i·al (ber′ē əl) n. [ME. *biriel*, false sing. < *berieles* < OE. *byrgels*, tomb < *byrgan*, BURY] the act of burying; esp., the burying of a dead body; interment —*adj.* of or connected with burial

BURGUNDY

burial ground a cemetery; graveyard

bur·i·er (-ər) n. a person or thing that buries

bu·rin (byoor′in) n. [Fr. < It. *burino, borino* < Lombard. *boro*, borer] a pointed cutting tool used by engravers or marble workers

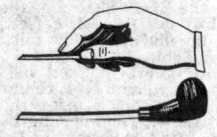

BURIN

burke (burk) vt. **burked, burk′ing** [after William *Burke*, executed for the act, in Edinburgh, 1829] 1. orig., to murder by suffocating so as to leave the body unmarked and fit to be sold for dissection 2. to get rid of quietly; evade or suppress, as a parliamentary bill, discussion, etc.

Burke (burk), **Edmund** 1729–97; Brit. statesman, orator, & writer, born in Ireland

burl (burl) n. [ME. *burle* < OFr. *bourle*, flocks or ends of threads < VL. *burrula*, small flock of wool < LL. *burra*, ragged garment] 1. a knot in wool, thread, yarn, etc. that gives a nubby appearance to cloth 2. a kind of knot on some tree trunks 3. veneer made from wood with burls in it —vt. to finish (cloth) by taking out the burls, loose threads, etc. —**burled** *adj.*

bur·lap (bur′lap) n. [17th c. *borelappe(s)* < ? ME. *borel*, coarse cloth (< OFr. *burel*: see BUREAU) + *lappa*, hanging part of a garment, LAP¹ (akin to G. *lappen*, Du. *lap*, rag)] a coarse cloth made of jute or hemp, used for making sacks, as a linoleum backing, etc.

Bur·leigh (bur′lē), 1st Baron, same as BURGHLEY

bur·lesque (bər lesk′) n. [Fr. < It. *burlesco* < *burla*, a jest, mockery] 1. any broadly comic or satirical imitation, as of a writing, play, etc.; derisive caricature; parody ☆2. (also, facetiously, bur′li kyoo′) a sort of vaudeville characterized by low comedy, striptease acts, etc. —*adj.* 1. derisively or comically imitating; parodying ☆2. of or connected with burlesque (vaudeville) —vt., vi. **-lesqued′, -lesqu′ing** to imitate derisively or comically; parody —SYN. see CARICATURE

☆**bur·ley** (bur′lē) n. [< ? a proper name] [*also* B-] a thin-leaved, light-colored tobacco grown in Kentucky and surrounding States

Bur·ling·ton (bur′liŋ tən) [< local pronun. of *Bridlington*, port in NE England] 1. city in NW Vt., on Lake Champlain: pop. 39,000 2. city in NC N.C.: pop. 36,000 3. town in SE Ontario, Canada, on Lake Ontario: pop. 66,000

bur·ly (bur′lē) *adj.* **-li·er, -li·est** [ME. *borlich*, excellent, noble, handsome < ? OE. *borlice*, very, excellently] 1. big and strong; heavy and muscular 2. rough and hearty in manner; bluff —**bur′li·ness** n.

Bur·ma (bur′mə) country in SE Asia, on the Indochinese peninsula: 261,789 sq. mi.; pop. 26,980,000; cap. Rangoon: officially, a federation of states called **Union of Burma**

☆**bur marigold** any of a genus (*Bidens*) of weedy plants of the composite family, having yellow-rayed flowers and barbed fruits

Burma Road road from Lashio, N Burma to Kunming, China: Allied supply route in World War II: c. 700 mi.

Bur·mese (bər mēz′) *adj.* of Burma, its people, or their language —n. 1. *pl.* **-mese** a native or inhabitant of Burma 2. the Tibeto-Burman language of the Burmese Also **Bur′man**

burn¹ (burn) vt. **burned** or **burnt, burn′ing** [ME. *brennen* < ON. & OE.: ON. *brenna*, burn, light; OE. *biernan*; both < IE. *bhre-n-u-* < base *bhereu-*, to boil forth, well up: cf.

BREAD] 1. to set on fire or subject to combustion, as in order to produce heat, light, or power 2. to destroy or consume by fire 3. to put to death by fire 4. to injure or damage by fire or something with the effect of fire, as intense heat, friction, or acid; scorch, singe, scald, etc. 5. to consume as fuel [to *burn* much gasoline] 6. to transform, as fat stored in the body, into energy by metabolism 7. to sunburn 8. to brand 9. to cauterize 10. to harden or glaze (bricks, pottery, etc.) by fire; fire 11. to cause by fire, heat, etc. [to *burn* a hole in a coat] 12. to cause a sensation of heat in [the horseradish *burns* the throat] 13. to use (candles, lights, heaters, etc.) ☆14. [Slang] to electrocute 15. [Slang] *a*) to cheat, swindle, or rob *b*) to cause to suffer through misplaced trust or confidence: usually used in the passive —vi. 1. to be on fire; flame; blaze 2. to undergo combustion 3. to give out light or heat; shine; glow 4. to be destroyed by fire or heat 5. to be injured or damaged by or as by fire or heat; become scorched, singed, etc. 6. to die by fire 7. to feel hot 8. to be excited or inflamed, as with desire, anger, etc. ☆9. [Slang] to be electrocuted —n. 1. an injury or damage caused by fire, heat, radiation, wind, caustics, etc.: in medicine, burns are classified as **first-degree**, reddening, **second-degree**, blistering, and **third-degree**, destructive of the skin and the tissues under it 2. the process or result of burning, as in brick making ☆3. a single firing of a rocket or thruster on a space vehicle —**burn down** to burn to the ground —**burn oneself out** to exhaust oneself by too much work or dissipation —**burn out** 1. to cease burning through lack of fuel 2. to disintegrate or wear out by heat from friction, etc. 3. to destroy the home, business, etc. of by fire —**burn up** 1. to burn completely ☆2. [Slang] to make or become angry SYN.—**burn** is the broadest term in this comparison, denoting injury to any extent by fire, intense heat, friction, acid, etc. [a *burnt* log, *sunburned, windburned*]; **scorch** and **singe** both imply superficial burning, **scorch** emphasizing discoloration or damaging of texture [to *scorch* a shirt in ironing], and **singe**, the burning off, often intentional, of bristles, feathers, the ends of hair, etc.; **sear** implies the burning of animal tissue and is applied specifically to the quick browning of the outside of roasts, etc. in cooking to seal in the juices; **char** implies a reduction by burning to charcoal or carbon All of these terms have figurative applications [a *burning* desire, a *scorching* tirade, a *singed* reputation, a soul-*searing* experience, *charred* hopes]

burn² (burn) n. [ME. *burne*, BOURN¹] [Scot.] a brook

burn·a·ble (-ə b'l) *adj.* that can be burned —n. something, especially refuse, that can be burned

Burne-Jones (burn′jōnz′), Sir **Edward Co·ley** (kō′lē) 1833–98; Eng. painter & designer

burn·er (bur′nər) n. 1. the part of a stove, furnace, etc. from which the flame comes 2. an apparatus for burning fuel or trash; furnace, incinerator, etc.

bur·net (bur′nit) n. [ME. < OFr. *brunet*: see BRUNET] any of a genus (*Sanguisorba*) of plants of the rose family, with white, red, purple, or greenish, apetalous flowers in thimble-shaped heads

Bur·nett (bər net′), **Frances Hodgson** 1849–1924; U.S. writer, esp. of children's books, born in England

Bur·ney (bur′nē), **Fanny** (born *Frances*; married name *Madame d'Arblay*) 1752–1840; Eng. novelist & diarist

burn·ing (bur′niŋ) *adj.* 1. that burns 2. of the utmost seriousness or importance [a *burning* issue]

burning bush [after the Biblical burning bush: cf. Ex. 3] ☆1. any of several American shrubs (genus *Euonymus*) of the staff-tree family, having brilliant red fruits or leaves 2. same as GAS PLANT

burning glass a convex lens for focusing the sun's rays so as to produce heat or set fire to something

bur·nish (bur′nish) vt., vi. [ME. *burnishen* < OFr. *burniss-*, extended stem of *brunir*, to make brown < *brun*: see BRUNET] to make or become shiny by rubbing; polish —n. a gloss or polish —SYN. see POLISH —**bur′nish·er** n.

Burn·ley (burn′lē) city in NW England, in Lancashire: pop. 80,000

bur·noose, bur·nous (bər noos′, bur′noos) n. [Fr. *burnous* < Ar. *burnus*, prob. < Gr. *birros*, a cloak] a long cloak with a hood, worn by Arabs and Moors

burn·out (burn′out′) n. 1. the point at which missile fuel is completely burned up and the missile enters its free-flight phase 2. damage caused by overheating

Burns (burnz), **Robert** 1759–96; Scot. poet

Burn·side (burn′sīd′), **Ambrose Everett** 1824–81; Union general in the Civil War

☆**burn·sides** (burn′sīdz′) *n.pl.* [after prec.] a style of beard with full side whiskers and mustache, but with the chin clean-shaven

burnt (burnt) *alt. pt. and pp.* of BURN¹ —*adj.* that has been burned

burnt offering an animal, food, etc. burned at an altar as an offering or sacrifice to a god

burnt sienna 1. a reddish-brown pigment made by burning raw sienna 2. a reddish brown

burnt umber 1. a dark-brown pigment made by burning raw umber 2. a dark brown

☆**bur oak** a N. American white oak (*Quercus macrocarpa*) having large acorns with fringed cups

☆**burp** (burp) n., vi. [echoic] [Colloq.] belch —vt. to cause (a baby) to relieve itself of stomach gas, as by patting its back

☆**burp gun** [echoic of the rapid bursts of fire] [Mil. Slang]

any of various automatic pistols or submachine guns introduced in World War II

burr[1] (bur) n. [var. of BUR] 1. a rough edge or ridge left on metal or other material by cutting or drilling 2. a washer on the small end of a rivet 3. same as BUR (senses 1, 2, 3) —vt. 1. to form a rough edge on 2. to remove burrs from (metal)

burr[2] (bur) n. [prob. echoic] 1. the trilling of *r*, with uvula or tongue, as in the dialectal speech of northern England and Scotland 2. a whirring sound —vi. 1. to speak with a burr 2. to make a whirring sound —vt. to pronounce with a burr

burr[3] (bur) n. same as BUHRSTONE

Burr (bur), **Aaron** 1756–1836; U.S. political leader; vice president of the U.S. (1801–05): killed Alexander Hamilton in a duel (1804)

bur reed any of a genus (*Sparganium*) of marsh or water plants of a family (Sparganiaceae), having grasslike leaves and hard, dry, prickly fruits

bur·ro (bur′ō, boor′ō; -ə) n., pl. -ros [Sp. < *burrico* < LL. *burricus*, small horse] a donkey, esp. one used as a pack animal in the southwestern U.S.

Bur·roughs (bur′ōz) 1. **Edgar Rice**, 1875–1950; U.S. writer, esp. of the Tarzan stories 2. **John**, 1837–1921; U.S. naturalist & writer

bur·row (bur′ō, -ə) n. [ME. *burgh* (see BOROUGH), infl. by *bergh*, hill, *berwen*, to defend, take refuge] 1. a hole or tunnel dug in the ground by an animal 2. any similar passage or hole for shelter, refuge, etc. —vi. 1. to make a burrow; dig (*in, into, under*, etc.) 2. to live or hide in or as in a burrow 3. to delve or search, as if by digging —vt. 1. to make burrows in (the ground) 2. to make by burrowing 3. to hide or shelter in or as in a burrow

☆**burrowing owl** a ground owl (*Speotyto cunicularia*) of the prairie regions of N. and S. America, having long legs and a small head: it makes its nest in abandoned burrows

burr·stone (bur′stōn′) n. same as BUHRSTONE

bur·ry[1] (bur′ē) adj. -ri·er, -ri·est 1. full of burs 2. like a bur or burs; prickly

bur·ry[2] (bur′ē) adj. -ri·er, -ri·est having a burr in speech

Bur·sa (boor sä′) city in NW Turkey: capital of the Ottoman Empire in 14th cent.: pop. 154,000

bur·sa (bur′sə) n., pl. -sae (-sē), -sas [ML., a purse, bag < Gr. *byrsa*, a hide] *Anat.* a sac or pouchlike cavity, esp. one containing a fluid that reduces friction, as between a tendon and bone —**bur′sal** adj.

bur·sar (bur′sər) n. [ML. *bursarius*, treasurer < *bursa*: see prec.] 1. a treasurer, as of a college or similar institution 2. in Scotland, a university student who has a scholarship

bur·sar·i·al (bər ser′ē əl) adj. of a bursar or bursary

bur·sa·ry (bur′sər ē) n., pl. -ries [ML. *bursaria* < *bursarius*: see BURSAR] 1. a treasury, esp. of a college 2. in Scotland, a university scholarship

burse (burs) n. [Fr. *bourse*: see BOURSE] 1. a purse 2. same as BURSARY (sense 2) 3. *R.C.Ch.* a flat, square, silk case for carrying the folded corporal to and from the altar

☆**bur·seed** (bur′sēd′) n. same as STICKSEED

bur·si·form (bur′sə fôrm′) adj. [< ML. *bursa* (see BURSA) + -FORM] *Anat.*, *Zool.* shaped like a bursa, or sac; pouchlike

bur·si·tis (bər sīt′is) n. [< BURSA + -ITIS] inflammation of a bursa, as near the shoulder or hip

burst (burst) vi. burst, burst′ing [ME. *bresten, bersten* < OE. *berstan* & ON. *bresta*, both < IE. base *bhres-*, to burst, break, crack] 1. to come apart suddenly and violently, as from internal pressure; fly into pieces; break open or out; explode 2. to give sudden expression to some feeling; break (*into* tears, laughter, a tirade, etc.) 3. to go, come, start, appear, etc. suddenly and with force [*he burst* into the room] 4. *a*) to be as full, crowded, or packed as possible *b*) to be filled (*with* anger, pride, energy, etc.) —vt. 1. to cause to burst; make explode 2. to fill or cause to swell to the bursting point —n. [ME. *burst, brist*, a damage, defect, injury < OE. *byrst*, loss] 1. the act of bursting; explosion, as of an artillery shell 2. the result of a bursting; break; rupture 3. a sudden, violent display of feeling 4. a sudden, forceful action or effort; spurt [*a burst* of speed] 5. a volley of shots, or a single series of shots from an automatic firearm —**burst′er** n.

bur·then (bur′thən) n., vt. [Archaic] same as BURDEN[1]

bur·ton (bur′tən) n. [< ?] a kind of tackle used with single or double pulley blocks for setting up or tightening rigging, or moving heavy articles

Bur·ton (bur′tən) 1. **Harold Hitz** (hits), 1888–1964; associate justice, U.S. Supreme Court (1945–1958) 2. **Sir Richard Francis**, 1821–90; Eng. writer & explorer 3. **Robert**, (pseud. *Democritus Junior*) 1577–1640; Eng. writer & clergyman: author of *The Anatomy of Melancholy*

Bu·ru (boo′roo) island of Indonesia, in the Molucca group: 3,668 sq. mi.

Bu·run·di (boo roon′dē, -run′-) country in EC Africa, east of Congo (sense 2): formerly part of UN trust territory of Ruanda-Urundi: 10,745 sq. mi.; pop. 2,800,000; cap. Bujumbura —**Bu·run′di·an** adj., n.

bur·weed (bur′wēd′) n. any of various plants with burs, as the burdock, bur marigold, cocklebur, etc.

bur·y (ber′ē) vt. bur′ied, bur′y·ing [ME. *birien* < OE. *byrgan*, akin to *beorgan* < IE. base *bhergh-*, protect, preserve, whence G. *bergen*, protect, Pol. *bróg*, barn] 1. to put (a dead body) into the earth, a tomb, the sea, etc., usually in a ceremonial manner; inter 2. *a*) to hide (something) in the ground *b*) to cover up so as to conceal [*she buried* her face in the pillow] 3. to put away, as from one's life, mind, etc. [*to bury* a feud] 4. to put (oneself) deeply into; plunge; immerse [*to bury* oneself in one's work] —SYN. see HIDE[1]

bus (bus) n., pl. bus′es, bus′ses [< (OMNI)BUS] 1. a large motor coach that can carry many passengers, usually along a regular route; omnibus 2. [Slang] an automobile 3. *Elec.* a conductor or group of conductors serving as a common connection for three or more circuits in the form of a bar, also called **bus′bar′** —vt. bused or bussed, bus′ing or bus′sing to transport by bus —vi. 1. to go by bus ☆2. to do the work of a busboy

bus. business

☆**bus·boy** (-boi′) n. a waiter's assistant who sets and clears tables, brings water, etc.

bus·by (buz′bē) n., pl. -bies [18th c., prob. < the name *Busby*] a tall fur hat worn as part of a full-dress uniform by hussars, guardsmen in the British army, etc.

BUSBY

bush[1] (boosh) n. [ME. < OE. *busc* (in place names) < WGmc. *busk-*; ME. forms *busk, bosk* < ML. *boscus* < Frank. *busc*, of same WGmc. orig.] 1. a woody plant having many stems branching out low instead of one main stem or trunk; shrub 2. a thicket of shrubs 3. anything resembling a bush; esp., *a*) a thickly furred tail *b*) [Slang] a beard ☆4. [< Colonial Du. *bosch*, bush] shrubby woodland or uncleared country, esp. wild or unsettled frontier country 5. *a*) a branch of ivy as a symbol for wine, formerly used on tavern signboards *b*) [Obs.] a tavern —vi. to grow thickly or spread out like a bush —vt. to decorate, cover, or surround with bushes —**beat around the bush** to talk around a subject without getting to the point; speak indirectly or hintingly —☆**the bushes** [Slang] rural or small-town districts

bush[2] (boosh) n. [MDu. *busse*, box < ML. *buxis*: see BOX[1]] same as BUSHING —vt. to fit with a bushing

Bush (boosh), **Van·ne·var** (və nē′vär) 1890– ; U.S. electrical engineer & administrator

bush baby any of various nocturnal lemurlike mammals (genus *Galago*) of African forests, with a long, bushy tail and large eyes

☆**bush bean** any of various low, erect, bushy forms of the common garden bean (*Phaseolus vulgaris*)

bush·buck (-buk′) n., pl. -buck, -bucks: see PLURAL, II, D, 2 a small striped antelope (*Tragelaphus scriptus*) of South Africa

bushed (boosht) adj. 1. bewildered, as by being lost in the bush ☆2. [Colloq.] very tired; exhausted

bush·el[1] (boosh′'l) n. [ME. *busshel* < OFr. *boissel* < *boisse*, grain measure < Gallic *bostia*, amount one can hold in one hand < *bosta*, palm of the hand] 1. a unit of dry measure for grain, fruit, etc., equal to 4 pecks or 8 gallons 2. a container holding one bushel 3. a weight taken as the equivalent of one bushel 4. [Colloq.] a large amount Abbrev. **bu.** —**bush′el·age** (-ij) n.

☆**bush·el**[2] (boosh′'l) vt., vi. -eled or -elled, -el·ing or -el·ling [< ? G. *bosseln*, to patch up, repair] to repair, renovate, or alter (esp. garments)

bush·el·bas·ket (boosh′'l bas′kit, -bäs′-) n. a rounded basket with a capacity of one bushel

☆**bush·el·er, bush·el·ler** (-ər) n. [see BUSHEL[2]] a person who alters or mends clothing, esp. a tailor's assistant; also **bush′el·man** (-mən), pl. -men (-mən)

☆**bush·ham·mer** (boosh′ham′ər) n. [prob. < G. *bossham·mer* < *bossen*, to beat, dress (stone) + *hammer*, hammer] a hammer whose face is cut up into projecting points, used for dressing stone

Bu·shi·do (boo′shē dō′) n. [Jap., way of the warrior] [*also* b-] the chivalric code of the samurai of feudal Japan, emphasizing loyalty and courage and preferring death to dishonor

bush·i·ness (boosh′ē nis) n. a bushy quality or state

bush·ing (boosh′iŋ) n. [< BUSH[2]] 1. a cylindrical metal sleeve inserted into a machine part or for reducing the effect of friction on moving parts or for decreasing the diameter of a hole 2. *Elec.* a similar insulating lining or part

bush·land (-land′) n. [Canad.] the unsettled forest lands of N Quebec, N Ontario, and the Prairie Provinces

☆**bush league** [Slang] *Baseball* a small or second-rate minor league —**bush′-league′** adj.

☆**bush leaguer** [Slang] 1. a baseball player in a bush league 2. an unimportant or second-rate performer in any sphere of activity Also **bush′er** n.

bush lot [Canad.] a tract of timberland

bush·man (boosh′mən) n., pl. -men (-mən) 1. a person who lives in the Australian bush 2. a backwoodsman 3.

[B-] [transl. of obs. Afrik. *boschjesman*] *a)* a member of a nomadic people living in the region of the Kalahari Desert in SW Africa *b)* their Khoisan language

bush·mas·ter (-mas′tər, -mäs′-) *n.* a large, poisonous snake, a pit viper (*Lachesis muta*) of Central and South America

bush·rang·er (-rān′jər) *n.* [< BUSH¹ (sense 4) + RANGER] **1.** a person who lives in the bush; backwoodsman **2.** in Australia, a person, esp. a highwayman, who makes the bush his hide-out

☆**bush·wa, bush·wah** (boosh′wä, boozh′-) *n.* [altered < *bull excrement* (euphemism)] [Slang] nonsense; bunk

☆**bush·whack** (boosh′hwak′, -wak′) *vi.* [prob. < BUSH¹ + WHACK] **1.** to beat or cut one's way through bushes **2.** to move a boat along a stream by pulling at the bushes on the bank **3.** to engage in guerrilla fighting, attacking from ambush —*vt.* to ambush —**bush′whack′er** *n.* —**bush′-whack′ing** *n.*

bush·y (boosh′ē) *adj.* **bush′i·er, bush′i·est 1.** covered or overgrown with bushes **2.** thick and spreading out like a bush [a *bushy* tail]

bus·i·ly (biz′ə lē) *adv.* in a busy manner

busi·ness (biz′nis) *n.* [ME. *bisinesse* < OE. *bisignes:* see BUSY & -NESS] **1.** one's work, occupation, or profession **2.** a special task, duty, or function **3.** rightful concern or responsibility [no one's *business* but his own] **4.** a matter, affair, activity, etc. [the *business* of packing for a trip] **5.** the buying and selling of commodities and services; commerce; trade **6.** a commercial or industrial establishment; store, factory, etc. **7.** the trade or patronage of customers **8.** commercial practice or policy **9.** action in a drama, esp. for a particular effect, to take up a pause in dialogue, etc. —*adj.* of or for business —**business is business** sentiment, friendship, etc. cannot be allowed to interfere with profit making —**do business with 1.** to engage in commerce with **2.** to have dealings with —☆**give (or get) the business** [Slang] to subject (or be subjected) to rough treatment, practical joking, etc. —**mean business** [Colloq.] to be in earnest

SYN.—**business,** in this comparison, refers generally to the buying and selling of commodities and services and connotes a profit motive; **commerce** and **trade** both refer to the distribution or exchange of commodities, esp. as this involves their transportation, but **commerce** generally implies such activity on a large scale between cities, countries, etc.; **industry** refers chiefly to the large-scale manufacture of commodities

☆**business college** (or **school**) a school offering instruction in secretarial skills, business administration, etc.

business cycle the regular alternation of periods of prosperity and periods of depression as characteristic of business and industry

busi·ness·like (-līk′) *adj.* having the qualities needed in business; efficient, methodical, etc.

busi·ness·man (-man′) *n., pl.* **-men′** (-men′) a man in business, esp. as an owner or executive —☆**busi′ness-wom′an** *n.fem., pl.* **-wom′en**

☆**business office** the office where the financial transactions, bookkeeping, etc. for a firm or institution are carried on

busk (busk) *vt.* [ME. *busken,* to prepare, adorn < ON. *buask,* to make oneself ready < *bua,* to prepare (cf. BONDAGE) + *sik,* reflexive pron.] [Scot. & North Eng. Dial.] **1.** to make ready **2.** to outfit

busk·er (bus′kər) *n.* [< Brit. slang *busk,* to be a strolling entertainer, orig., to seek < MFr. *busquer* < Sp. *buscar,* to seek, orig., prob. to gather wood < Goth. **buska,* a stick, log, akin to MHG. *bosch,* a club] [Brit.] a street singer or strolling entertainer, esp. on the streets of London —**busk′ing** *n.*

bus·kin (bus′kin) *n.* [< ? OFr. *broissequin* < MDu. *brosekin,* small leather boot] **1.** a boot reaching to the calf or knee, worn in ancient times; esp., the high, thick-soled, laced boot worn by actors in ancient Greek and Roman tragedy **2.** tragic drama; tragedy —**bus′kined** (-kind) *adj.*

bus·man (bus′mən) *n., pl.* **-men** (-mən) the operator of a bus

bus·man's holiday a holiday in which one's recreation is very similar to one's daily work

Bu·so·ni (boo zō′nē), **Fer·ruc·cio Ben·ve·nu·to** (fer root′chō ben′ve noo′tō) 1866-1924; It. composer

buss (bus) *n., vt., vi.* [? akin to G. (dial.) *bus,* kiss, or W. & Gael. *bus,* kiss, lip] [Archaic or Dial.] kiss, esp. in an unrestrained or playful manner

buss·bar (bus′bär′) *n. same as* BUSBAR: see BUS, *n.* 3

bus·ses (bus′iz) *n. alt. pl. of* BUS

bust¹ (bust) *n.* [Fr. *buste* < It. *busto*] **1.** a piece of sculpture representing the head, shoulders, and upper chest of a human body **2.** the human bosom; esp., the breasts of a woman —SYN. see BREAST

bust² (bust) *vt., vi.* [orig., dial. var. of BURST] [Slang] **1.** to burst or break **2.** to make or become penniless or bankrupt ☆**3.** to demote or become demoted in rank ☆**4.** to tame (esp. broncos) ☆**5.** to hit ☆**6.** to arrest —*n.* [Slang] ☆**1.** a person or thing that is a total failure ☆**2.** a financial collapse; economic crash ☆**3.** a punch ☆**4.** a spree ☆**5.** an arrest

bus·tard (bus′tərd) *n.* [ME. < OFr. *bistarde* (< OIt. *bistarda*) & *oustarde* (< Prov. *austarda*); both forms < L. *avis tarda,* lit., slow bird] any of a family (Otididae) of large, heavy, long-legged game birds of Europe, Asia, and Africa, related to the crane and the plover

bust·er (bus′tər) *n.* [BUST² + -ER] [Slang] **1.** something remarkably large, effective, destructive, etc. ☆**2.** *clipped form of* BRONCOBUSTER, TRUSTBUSTER, etc. ☆**3.** a spree ☆**4.** [also B-] boy; man; fellow: a mildly contemptuous or jocular term of direct address

☆**bus·tic** (bus′tik) *n.* [< ?] a tree (*Dipholis salicifolia*) of the sapodilla family, with hard, dark wood, native to S Florida

bus·tle¹ (bus′'l) *vi., vt.* **-tled, -tling** [for earlier *buskle* < ME. *busken:* see BUSK] to hurry busily or with much fuss and bother —*n.* busy and noisy activity; commotion —**bus′tling·ly** *adv.*

bus·tle² (bus′'l) *n.* [late 18th c. < ? G. *buschel,* a bunch, pad] a framework or padding worn at the back by women to puff out the skirt

bus·y (biz′ē) *adj.* **bus′i·er, bus′i·est** [ME. *busi* < OE. *bisig,* occupied, diligent; akin to Du. *bezig;* seen only in LG. & E.] **1.** occupied in some activity; at work; not idle **2.** full of activity; characterized by much action or motion **3.** *a)* in use at the moment, as a telephone line *b)* indicating such use [the *busy* signal] **4.** meddlesome **5.** having so much detail, variety of color, etc. as to create a confusing, displeasing effect —*vt.* **bus′ied, bus′y·ing** [ME. *busien* < OE. *bisgian,* to occupy, employ < *bisgu,* occupation, labor] to make or keep busy: often used reflexively

SYN.—**busy** suggests active employment in some task or activity, either temporarily or habitually [I'm *busy* just now]; **industrious** suggests habitual devotion to one's work or activity [an *industrious* salesclerk]; **diligent** implies unremitting attention, usually to a particular task, and connotes enjoyment in the task itself [a *diligent* student of music]; **assiduous** suggests painstaking, persevering preoccupation with some task [assiduous study]; **sedulous** implies unremitting devotion to a task until the goal is reached [a *sedulous* investigation of the crime] —ANT. idle, lazy, indolent

bus·y·bod·y (-bäd′ē) *n., pl.* **-ies** a person who mixes into other people's affairs; meddler or gossip

bus·y·ness (biz′ē nis) *n.* the quality or condition of being busy

☆**bus·y·work, bus·y-work** (-wurk′) *n.* an activity, often as assigned to a class in school, that has little purpose beyond keeping one occupied for a time

but¹ (but; *unstressed* bət) *prep.* [ME. < OE. *butan, buton,* without, outside < *be,* by + *utan,* out, from without < *ut,* out] **1.** with the exception of; excepting; save [nobody came *but* me]: earlier, and still sometimes, regarded as a conjunction and followed by the subjective case [nobody came *but* I (came)] **2.** except; other than: used with an infinitive as the object [we cannot choose *but* (to) stay] —*conj.* **1.** yet; still; however [he is a villain, *but* he has some virtues] **2.** on the contrary [I am old, *but* you are young] **3.** unless; if not [it never rains *but* it pours] **4.** that [I don't question *but* you're correct] **5.** that . . . not [I never think of summer *but* I think of childhood] —*adv.* **1.** only [if I had *but* known] **2.** merely; no more than; not otherwise than [he is *but* a child] **3.** just [I heard it *but* now] **4.** on the other hand; yet: used to introduce a sentence **5.** [Slang] absolutely; positively [do it *but* now!] —*pron.* who . . . not; which . . . not [not a man *but* felt it] —**but for** if it were not for —**but that 1.** about the fact that [I've no doubt *but* that he'll come] **2.** that there isn't some chance that [we can't be sure *but* that he's right] Also [Colloq.] **but what**

but² (but) *adj.* [akin to prec.] [Scot.] outside; outer —*n.* [Scot.] the outer room, esp. the kitchen of a cottage —**but and ben** [Scot.] the whole dwelling: orig., the outer and inner rooms of a two-room cottage

bu·ta·di·ene (byoot′ə dī′ēn, -dī ēn′) *n.* [BUTA(NE) + DI- + -ENE] a hydrocarbon, C_4H_6, obtained from petroleum or alcohol and used, after polymerization, to make buna

bu·tane (byoo′tān, byoo tān′) *n.* [BUT(YL) + -ANE] either of two hydrocarbons (normal butane, isobutane) in the methane series, having the same formula, C_4H_{10}, but different structures and used as a fuel, in organic synthesis, etc.

bu·ta·nol (byoo′tə nôl′, -nōl′) *n.* [BUTAN(E) + -OL¹] *same as* BUTYL ALCOHOL

bu·ta·none (byoo′tə nōn′) *n.* [BUTAN(E) + -ONE] a highly flammable liquid, C_4H_8O, that is a byproduct of acetone, used as a solvent

butch (booch) *adj.* [prob. < *Butch,* nickname for a boy, contr. < ? BUTCHER] [Slang] ☆**1.** designating or of a man's haircut in which the hair is cropped close to the head ☆**2.** masculine in appearance, manner, etc.: sometimes used specif. of a lesbian —*n.* [Slang] ☆a tough or rugged man or boy: used chiefly in direct address

butch·er (booch′ər) *n.* [ME. *bocher* < OFr. *bochier, bouchier,* one who kills and sells he-goats < *bouc,* he-goat < Frank.

BUSKINS

BUSTLE

bukk, akin to OE. *bucca:* see BUCK[1] **1.** a person whose work is killing animals or dressing their carcasses for meat **2.** a person who cuts up meat for sale **3.** anyone who kills as if slaughtering animals ☆**4.** a person who sells candy, drinks, etc. in theaters, trains, circuses, etc. —*vt.* **1.** to kill or dress (animals) for meat **2.** to kill (people, game, etc.) brutally, senselessly, or in large numbers; slaughter **3.** to mess up; botch —**butch′er·er** *n.* —**butch′er·ly** *adj.*

butch·er·bird (-burd′) *n.* any of various shrikes which, after killing prey, impale it on thorns

butch·er's-broom (booch′ərz broom′, -broom′) *n.* [? because formerly used to sweep butchers' shops] a shrubby plant (*Ruscus aculeatus*) of the lily family, with leathery, leaflike, flattened branches, clusters of small, white flowers, and large, red berries

butch·er·y (booch′ər ē) *n., pl.* **-er·ies** [ME. *bocherie* < OFr. *boucherie:* see BUTCHER] **1.** a place where animals are killed for meat; slaughterhouse **2.** the work or business of a butcher **3.** brutal bloodshed or slaughter **4.** the act or result of botching —*SYN.* see SLAUGHTER

Bute (byoot) **1.** island in the Firth of Clyde: 46 sq. mi. **2.** county of SW Scotland, consisting of this island, Arran, & several smaller ones: 218 sq. mi.; pop. 13,000: also **Bute′shire** (-shir)

bu·tene (byoo′tēn) *n.* same as BUTYLENE

bu·te·o (byoo′tē ō′) *n.* [ModL. < L.: see BUZZARD] any of a genus (*Buteo*) of large, broad-winged, soaring hawks that prey mainly on rodents

but·le (but′'l) *vi.* **-led, -ling** [< BUTLER] [Colloq.] to serve as a butler: a humorous usage

but·ler (but′lər) *n.* [ME. *boteler* < OFr. *bouteillier,* cupbearer < *bouteille,* BOTTLE[1]] a manservant, now usually the head servant of a household, in charge of wines, pantry, table silver, etc.

But·ler (but′lər) **1. Benjamin Franklin,** 1818–93; U.S. politician & Union general in the Civil War **2. Nicholas Murray,** 1862–1947; U.S. educator; president of Columbia University (1902–45) **3. Samuel,** *a*) 1612–80; Eng. satirical poet *b*) 1835–1902; Eng. novelist

butler's pantry a serving pantry between the kitchen and the dining room

but·ler·y (but′lər ē) *n., pl.* **-er·ies** [recoined < BUTLER + -y[1]; orig. ME. *botelerie* < OFr. *bouteillerie:* see BOTTLE[1]] the butler's pantry; buttery

Bu·ton (boo′tän) same as BUTUNG

butt[1] (but) *n.* [< several bases, variously confused in E. or Fr.: ME. *but, butte,* thick end, ? akin to ON. *būtr,* block of wood, Du. *bot,* stumpy, stocky, or ? < OFr. *bout,* end < *buter* (see BUTT[2]); ME. *but,* target, boundary < Fr. *but,* aim, goal < *abuter,* to arrive, aim (see ABUT) or < ? ON. *būtr*] **1.** the thick end of anything, as of a whip handle, rifle stock, etc. **2.** the remaining end of anything; stub; stump; specif., the stub of a partially smoked cigarette or cigar **3.** *a*) [? infl. by Fr. *butte,* mound < OFr. *buter*] a mound of earth, etc. behind a target, for receiving fired rounds *b*) a target *c*) [*pl.*] a target range **4.** a hole in the ground used as a blind by hunters of fowl **5.** an object of ridicule or criticism **6.** [Slang] a cigarette **7.** [Slang] the buttocks **8.** [Obs.] *a*) a limit *b*) a goal **9.** *Tanning* the part of a hide or pelt that covered the animal's backside —*vt., vi.* to join end to end

butt[2] (but) *vt.* [ME. *butten,* to drive, thrust < OFr. *buter* (< Frank. *botan*), to thrust against: for IE. base see BEAT] **1.** to strike or push with the head or horns; ram with the head **2.** to strike or bump against **3.** to abut on **4.** to make abut (*on, upon,* or *against*) —*vi.* **1.** to make a butting motion **2.** to move or drive headfirst **3.** to stick out; project **4.** to abut —*n.* [ME.; prob. < OFr. *buter,* or < the *v.*] **1.** a thrust with the head or horns **2.** a thrust in fencing —☆**butt in** (or **into**) [Slang] to mix into (another's business, a conversation, etc.)

butt[3] (but) *n.* [ME. *butte* < OFr. *botte* < ML. *butta* < LL. *bottis,* cask] **1.** a large barrel or cask, as for wine or beer **2.** a measure of liquid capacity equal to 126 gallons or two hogsheads

butt[4] (but) *n.* [ME. *butte, but* (also in tur*bot,* hali*but*); prob. < MLowG. *butte* (whence Sw. *butta,* Du. *bot,* G. *butte*) < *butte, adj.,* lumpy: akin to BUTT[2]] any of various flatfishes, as the halibut, turbot, etc.

Butte (byoot) [after the nearby *buttes*] city in SW Mont.: pop. 23,000

butte (byoot) *n.* [Fr., mound < OFr. *buter:* see BUTT[2]] a steep hill standing alone in a plain, esp. in the W U.S.; small mesa

but·ter (but′ər) *n.* [ME. *butere* < OE. *butere* < L. *butyrum* < Gr. *boutyron* < *bous,* ox, COW[1] + *tyros,* cheese] **1.** the thick, yellowish food product that results from churning cream or whole milk **2.** any of various substances somewhat like butter; specif., *a*) any of certain other spreads for bread [apple *butter,* peanut *butter*] *b*) any of certain vegetable oils having a solid consistency at ordinary temperatures [cocoa *butter*] *c*) any of certain metallic chlorides [*butter* of antimony] **3.** [Colloq.] flattery —*vt.* **1.** to spread with butter **2.** [Colloq.] to flatter so as to ingratiate oneself (often with *up*) —**look as if butter**

would not melt in one's mouth to look innocent or demure

but·ter-and-eggs (-'n egz′) *n.* a common, weedy plant (*Linaria vulgaris*) of the figwort family, with spurred orange and yellow flowers

☆**but·ter·ball** (-bôl′) *n.* **1.** same as BUFFLEHEAD **2.** [Colloq.] a fat person

butter bean any of various beans; specif., *a*) same as LIMA BEAN *b*) same as WAX BEAN

but·ter·bur (-bur′) *n.* any of several plants (genus *Petasites*) of the composite family, esp. a European plant (*Petasites hybridus*), with heads of purplish or whitish flowers and large, kidney-shaped basal leaves

☆**butter clam** any of a genus (*Saxidomus*) of large, edible clams found along the Pacific coast of N. America

but·ter·cup (-kup′) *adj.* designating a large, widespread family (Ranunculaceae) of flowering plants —*n.* any of a genus (*Ranunculus*) of yellow-flowered plants of this family, common in meadows and wet places

but·ter·fat (-fat′) *n.* the fatty part of milk, from which butter is made: it consists mainly of the glycerides of oleic, stearic, palmitic, and butyric acids

but·ter·fin·gers (-fin′gərz) *n.* a person who habitually fumbles or drops things, as if his fingers were buttery —**but′ter·fin′gered** *adj.*

but·ter·fish (-fish′) *n., pl.* **-fish′, -fish′es:** see FISH[2] any of various fishes (esp. family Stromateidae) with a slippery, protective covering of mucus, as the dollarfish, gunnel, etc.

but·ter·fly (-flī′) *n., pl.* **-flies′** [ME. *buterflie* < OE. *buttorfleoge* (see BUTTER & FLY[2]): ? first applied to a yellow species] **1.** any of a large group of insects (order Lepidoptera) active in the daytime, having a sucking mouthpart, slender body, ropelike, knobbed antennae, and four broad, usually brightly colored, membranous wings **2.** a person, esp. a woman, thought of as flitting about like a butterfly and being frivolous, fickle, etc. **3.** short for BUTTERFLY STROKE —*adj.* resembling a butterfly, esp. in having parts that are spread out like wings [*butterfly* chair, *butterfly* table]

butterfly bush same as BUDDLEIA

butterfly fish any of various fishes resembling butterflies in coloring or in having winglike fins, as the ocellated blenny; specif., any of a family (Chaetodontidae) of small, brightly colored, tropical reef fishes

butterfly orchid same as ONCIDIUM

butterfly stroke a swimming stroke performed face down, in which both arms are thrust out at the sides at the same time, then brought forward out of the water and down through the water in a circular motion

butterfly valve 1. a valve for a pipe, consisting of two clack valves hinged to a crossbar **2.** a disk-shaped valve turning on an axis along its diameter, serving esp. as a damper in a pipe

☆**butterfly weed** a widespread N. American wildflower (*Asclepias tuberosa*) of the milkweed family, with brilliant orange flowers

butter knife a small, dull-edged knife for cutting or spreading butter

but·ter·milk (but′ər milk′) *n.* the sour liquid left after churning butter from milk

☆**but·ter·nut** (-nut′) *n.* **1.** the oily, edible nut of the white walnut tree (*Juglans cinerea*) of eastern N. America **2.** this tree **3.** the souari nut **4.** [from the *butternut* bark dye used] [*pl.*] brown homespun overalls **5.** a Confederate soldier in the Civil War, esp. one from the backwoods wearing brown homespun clothes

☆**butternut squash** a small, bell-shaped, smooth winter squash, with yellowish flesh

but·ter·scotch (-skäch′) *n.* **1.** a hard, sticky candy made with brown sugar, butter, etc. **2.** a brown syrup with the flavor of butterscotch —*adj.* made of, or having the flavor of, butterscotch

butter tree any of several trees, as an Indian tree (*Bassia latifolia*), whose fatty seeds yield a butterlike substance

☆**but·ter·weed** (-wēd′) *n.* **1.** a plant (*Senecio glabellus*) of the composite family, with heads of minute yellow flowers **2.** same as HORSEWEED (sense 2)

but·ter·wort (-wurt′) *n.* any of a genus (*Pinguicula*) of small, stemless plants with flat, sticky leaves on which insects are trapped

but·ter·y[1] (but′ər ē, but′rē) *n., pl.* **-ter·ies** [ME. *boterie,* ale cellar, pantry < OFr. *boterie,* storage room for casks < ML. *buteria:* see BUTT[3]] **1.** a storeroom for wine and liquor **2.** a pantry **3.** a room in some English colleges where students can buy ale, wine, bread, etc.

but·ter·y[2] (but′ər ē) *adj.* **1.** like butter, as in consistency **2.** containing or spread with butter **3.** inclined to flattery; adulatory

butt hinge a hinge with one part set into the narrow edge of a door and the other into the facing edge of the jamb so that both parts meet when the door is closed

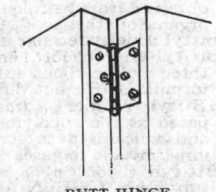

BUTT HINGE

butt joint any joint made by fastening plates or bars together end to end: it is sometimes strengthened with an additional plate or plates

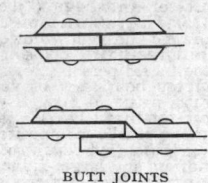

BUTT JOINTS

but·tock (but'ək) n. [ME. *buttok* < OE. *buttuc*, end, short piece of land, akin to BUTT¹] 1. either of the two fleshy, rounded parts at the back of the hips; either half of the rump 2. [pl.] the rump

but·ton (but'n) n. [ME. *botoun* < OFr. *boton*, a button, bud < *buter*: see BUTT¹] 1. any small disk, knob, etc. used as a fastening or ornament, as one put through a buttonhole on a garment 2. anything small and shaped like a button; specif., *a*) a small emblem of membership, distinction, etc., generally worn in the lapel *b*) a small knoblike part, as a bud on a plant or the end of a rattlesnake's rattles *c*) a small knob for operating a doorbell, electric lamp, etc. *d*) a guard on the tip of a fencing foil *e*) a small, immature mushroom ☆3. [Slang] the point of the chin 4. [pl.] [Slang] one's full senses or sanity [to have all of one's *buttons*] —vt., vi. 1. to fasten with or as with a button or buttons 2. to provide or be provided with a button or buttons —**button up (one's lip)** [Slang] to refrain from talking; esp., to keep a secret —☆**on the button** [Slang] exactly at the desired point, time, objective, etc. —**but'-ton·er** n. —**but'ton·like'** adj.

☆**but·ton·ball** (-bôl') n. 1. same as PLANE¹ 2. same as BUTTONBUSH

☆**but·ton·bush** (-boosh') n. a common N. American shrub (*Cephalanthus occidentalis*) of the madder family having whorled leaves and dense, round clusters of small white flowers

but·ton-down (-doun') adj. designating a collar, as on a shirt, having points fastened by small buttons to the front of the garment

but·ton·hole (-hōl') n. a slit or loop through which a button can be fastened —vt. **-holed', -hol'ing** 1. to make buttonholes in 2. to make with a buttonhole stitch 3. to make (a person) listen to one, as if by grasping his coat by a buttonhole —**but'ton·hol'er** n.

buttonhole stitch a closely worked loop stitch making a reinforced edge, as around a buttonhole

but·ton·hook (-hook') n. a small hook for pulling buttons through buttonholes, as in some former shoes

but·ton·mold (-mōld') n. a small disk of wood, metal, etc. covered as with cloth or leather to form a button

but·tons (but'nz) n.pl. [with sing. v.] [Chiefly Brit. Colloq.] a bellboy, hotel page, etc.

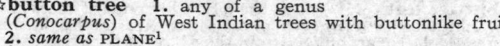

BUTTONHOLE STITCH

☆**button snakeroot** 1. same as BLAZING STAR (sense 1 *a*) 2. a perennial herb (*Eryngium yuccifolium*) of the parsley family, native to the E U.S.

☆**button tree** 1. any of a genus (*Conocarpus*) of West Indian trees with buttonlike fruit 2. same as PLANE¹

☆**but·ton·wood** (-wood') n. same as PLANE¹

but·ton·y (but'n ē) adj. 1. of or like a button 2. having or decorated with many buttons

but·tress (but'ris) n. [ME. *boteras* < OFr. *bouterez*, pl. of *bouteret*, flying buttress < *buter*: see BUTT²] 1. a projecting structure, generally of brick or stone, built against a wall to support or reinforce it 2. *a*) anything like a buttress in position, shape, or function *b*) a support or prop —vt. 1. to support or reinforce with a buttress 2. to prop up; bolster

butts and bounds *Law* same as METES AND BOUNDS

butt shaft a blunt, unbarbed arrow

butt weld a welded butt joint —**butt'-weld'** vt.

Bu·tung (boo'toon) island of Indonesia, SE of Celebes: c. 1,700 sq. mi.

bu·tyl (byoot'l) n. [< L. *butyrum* (see BUTTER) + -YL] any of the four organic radicals (normal butyl, secondary butyl, tertiary butyl, isobutyl) combined from the same elements in the same proportion by weight and having a valence of one, but differing in properties and structure; C_4H_9

butyl alcohol any of four isomeric alcohols, C_4H_9OH, obtained from petroleum products: used as solvents and in organic synthesis

butyl aldehyde same as BUTYRALDEHYDE

bu·tyl·ene (byoot'l ēn') n. [BUTYL + -ENE] any of the three hydrocarbons of the ethylene series having the same formula, C_4H_8, but differing properties and structures

☆**Butyl (rubber)** *a trademark for* a synthetic rubber prepared as the copolymer of butylene with isoprene, etc., and vulcanized to form a substance that is especially impermeable to gases

Bu·tyn (byoot'n) *a trademark for* a colorless crystalline substance, $(C_{18}H_{30}N_2)_2 \cdot H_2SO_4$, used as a local anesthetic, esp. on mucous membranes and in the eye —n. [b-] this anesthetic

bu·ty·ra·ceous (byoot'ə rā'shəs) adj. [L. *butyrum* (see BUTTER) + -ACEOUS] of, like, or producing butter

bu·tyr·al·de·hyde (byoot'ər al'də hīd') n. [< L. *butyrum* (see BUTTER) + ALDEHYDE] a clear liquid, $CH_3(CH_2)_2CHO$, with a characteristic aldehyde odor, important as an intermediate in the production of solvents, synthetic resins, plasticizers, etc.

bu·ty·rate (byoot'ə rāt') n. a salt or ester of butyric acid

bu·tyr·ic (byoo tir'ik) adj. [L. *butyrum* (see BUTTER) + -IC] 1. of or obtained from butter 2. of or pertaining to butyric acid

butyric acid a colorless, strong-smelling, fatty acid, $C_3H_7CO_2H$ found in rancid butter, perspiration, etc.

bu·ty·rin (byoot'ər in) n. [BUTYR(IC) + -IN¹] a glyceryl ester, $C_{15}H_{26}O_6$, of butyric acid

bux·om (buk'səm) adj. [ME., humble, obedient < base of *bouen*, to BOW¹ + -*sum*, -SOME¹] 1. healthy, comely, plump, jolly, etc.; specif. now, having a shapely, full-bosomed figure: said of a woman or girl 2. [Archaic] *a*) flexible; pliant *b*) obedient; obliging —**bux'om·ly** adv. —**bux'om·ness** n.

Bux·te·hu·de (book'stə hoo'də), **Did·er·ik** (dē'də rik) or G. **Diet·rich** (dēt'riH) 1637–1707; Dan. (perhaps born in Sweden) organist & composer, later in Germany

buy (bī) vt. **bought, buy'ing** [ME. *bien* < OE. *bycgan*, prob. < IE. base *bheug(h)*-, to bend, whence OE. *bugan*, BOW¹] 1. to get by paying or agreeing to pay money or some equivalent; purchase 2. to get as by an exchange [to *buy* time by negotiating] 3. to be the means of purchasing [all that money can *buy*] 4. to bribe or hire as by bribing ☆5. [Slang] to accept as true, valid, practical, agreeable, etc. [I can't *buy* his excuse] 6. *Theol.* [Archaic] to redeem —vi. 1. to buy something 2. to buy merchandise as a buyer —n. 1. the act of buying; a purchase 2. anything bought or buyable, esp. with reference to its worth as a bargain [a good (or bad) *buy*] ☆3. [Colloq.] something worth the price; bargain —**buy in** 1. to buy a share of or shares in 2. to buy back (an item) at an auction by a final, high bid when the other bids are much too low: said of the owner or his agent 3. [Slang] to pay money so as to become a participant, member, etc. Also, for senses 1 & 3, **buy into** —**buy off** to bribe —**buy out** to buy all the stock, business rights, etc. of —**buy up** to buy all of or all that is available of —**buy'a·ble** adj.

buy·er (-ər) n. 1. one who buys; consumer 2. a person whose work is to buy merchandise for a retail store

buzz (buz) vi. [echoic] 1. to make a sound like that of a prolonged *z*; hum like a bee 2. to talk excitedly or incessantly, esp. in low tones 3. to gossip 4. to move with a buzzing sound 5. to be filled with noisy activity or talk —vt. 1. to utter or tell (gossip, rumors, etc.) in a buzzing manner 2. to make (wings, etc.) buzz 3. to fly an airplane low over (a building, etc.), often as a signal 4. to signal (someone) with a buzzer 5. [Colloq.] to telephone —n. 1. a sound like that of a prolonged *z* or a bee's hum; buzzing 2. a confused sound, as of many excited voices 3. noisy activity; stir; agitation 4. a signal on a buzzer 5. [Colloq.] a telephone call —**buzz about (or around)** to scurry about —**buzz off** [Brit. Colloq.] to hurry away; leave

buz·zard (buz'ərd) n. [ME. *busard* < OFr. *busart* < *buse* (< L. *buteo*, kind of hawk) + -*art*, -ARD] 1. any of various hawks (esp. genus *Buteo*) that are slow and heavy in flight ☆2. same as TURKEY BUZZARD 3. a person regarded as mean, grasping, etc.

Buzzards Bay arm of the Atlantic, on the SE coast of Mass., at the base of Cape Cod peninsula

buzz bomb [Colloq.] a robot bomb, esp. as used against England by Germany in World War II

buzz·er (buz'ər) n. an electrical device that makes a buzzing sound as a signal

☆**buzz saw** a circular saw rotated by machinery

B.V.M. [L. *Beata Virgo Maria*] Blessed Virgin Mary

bvt. 1. brevet 2. brevetted

bwa·na (bwä'nə) n. [Swahili < Ar. *abūna*, our father < *abū*, father] [*often* B-] master; sir: native respectful term of address used in parts of Africa

B.W.I. British West Indies

bx. *pl.* **bxs.** box

by (bī) prep. [ME. *by*, *bi*, *be* < OE. *be* (unstressed), *bi* (stressed): cf. BY-, BE-; orig. adv. of place, meaning "beside, near," but already highly specialized prep. in OE.] 1. *expressing relation in space:* near or beside; at [stand *by* the wall] 2. *expressing relation in time: a*) in or during [to travel *by* night] *b*) for a fixed time [to work *by* the hour] *c*) not later than [be back *by* ten o'clock] 3. *expressing direction of movement: a*) through; via [to New Jersey *by* the Holland Tunnel] *b*) past; beyond [to march *by* the reviewing stand] *c*) toward [north *by* west] 4. *expressing direction of effort:* in behalf of [to do well *by* a friend] 5. *expressing means or agency:* through the means, work, or operations of [gained *by* fraud, made *by* hand, poems *by* Dryden] 6. *expressing manner or mode: a*) according to; with reference to [to go *by* the book] *b*) in [to grow dark *by* degrees] *c*) following in series [marching two *by* two] 7. *expressing permission, sanction,* etc.: with the authority or sanction of [*by* your leave] 8. *expressing measure or extent: a*) in or to the amount, extent, or degree of [apples *by* the peck] *b*) and in another dimension [two *by* four] *c*) using (the given number) as multiplier or divisor —adv. 1. close at hand; near [stand *by*] 2. away; aside [we have put money *by*] 3. close in passing; past

[the car sped *by*] ☆4. at the place specified or understood [stop *by* on your way home] —*adj.*, *n.* same as BYE —by and by 1. [Obs.] immediately 2. *a*) after a short while; soon *b*) sooner or later; eventually —by and large ☆on the whole; considering everything —by oneself 1. alone; solitary 2. without help; unaided —by the by incidentally; by the way

by- (bī) [< BY] *a prefix meaning*: 1. close by; near [*bystander*] 2. side [*bystreet*] 3. on the side; secondary; incidental to the main [*byproduct*]

by·and·by (bī'ən bī') *n.* a future time

by·bid·ding (bī'bid'iŋ) *n.* bidding by prearrangement with the auctioneer or owner so as to raise the price of the thing being sold at auction —by'·bid'der *n.*

by·blow (-blō') *n.* 1. an indirect blow or hit 2. a child born out of wedlock

Byd·goszcz (bid'gôshch) city in NC Poland: pop. 250,000

bye (bī) *n.* [see BY] 1. something incidental or secondary 2. a run made on a passed ball in the game of cricket 3. in sports tournaments, the status of the extra contestant after all others are paired: he automatically advances to the next round without playing —*adj.* of secondary importance; incidental —by the bye incidentally; by the way

bye-bye (bī'bī', bī'bī') *n., interj.* goodbye: orig., a child's word —go bye-bye to depart; leave: a child's term

by·e·lec·tion (bī'i lek'shən) *n.* a special election held in the interval between regular elections, esp. one held to fill a vacancy in the British House of Commons

Bye·lo·rus·sian Soviet Socialist Republic (bye'lō rush'ən) republic of the U.S.S.R., in the W European part: 80,154 sq. mi.; pop. 8,633,000; cap. Minsk: also Bye'lo·rus'sia *n.* —Bye'lo·rus'sian *adj., n.*

Bye·lo·stok (bye'lō stôk') *Russ. name of* BIALYSTOK

bye·low (bī'lō') *adv., interj.* hush: used in lullabies

by·gone (bī'gôn', -gän') *adj.* that has or have gone by; past; former —*n.* anything that is gone or past —let bygones be bygones to let past offenses or disagreements be forgotten

by·law (bī'lô') *n.* [ME. *bi-laue* < *bi*, village (< ON. *bȳr* < *būa*, to dwell: see BONDAGE) + *laue*, LAW: meaning infl. by BY] a secondary law or rule adopted by an organization or assembly for governing its own meetings or affairs

☆by·line (-līn') *n.* a line printed above a newspaper or magazine article, telling who wrote it

by·name (-nām') *n.* 1. a second name; surname 2. a nickname

Byng (biŋ), Julian Hedworth George (hed'wərth), 1st Viscount Byng of Vimy, 1862–1935; Brit. general & statesman; governor general of Canada (1921–26)

by·pass (bī'pas', -päs') *n.* 1. a way, path, etc. between two points that avoids or is auxiliary to the main way; detour 2. a pipe or channel providing an auxiliary passage for gas or liquid, as that leading to the pilot light in a gas stove 3. *Elec.* same as SHUNT (*n.* 3) —*vt.* 1. to go around instead of through; use a bypass to avoid 2. to furnish with a bypass 3. to ignore, fail to consult, etc.

bypass condenser *Radio* a low-impedance capacitor which provides an alternate path for alternating current while not passing any direct current

by·past (-past', -päst') *adj.* past; bygone

by·path, by·path (-path', -päth') *n.* a secluded path not used very much; byway

by·play (-plā') *n.* action, gestures, etc. going on aside from the main action or conversation, as in a play

by·prod·uct, by·prod·uct (-präd'əkt) *n.* anything produced, as from residues, in the course of making another thing; secondary or incidental product or result

Byrd (burd) 1. Richard Evelyn, 1888–1957; U.S. naval officer & antarctic explorer 2. William, 1543?–1623; Eng. composer

byre (bīr) *n.* [OE., hut, akin to BOWER¹] [Brit.] a cow barn

byr·nie (bur'nē) *n.* [ME. *brinie* < ON. *brynja*; akin to Goth. *brunjo*, prob. PrGmc. borrowing < Gaul. form of base appearing in OIr. *bruinne*, OCym. *broun*, breast: orig. breast protector] a coat of chain mail

by·road (bī'rōd') *n.* a road that is not a main road

By·ron (bī'rən) [Fr. *Biron*, orig. a family name < *Biron*, district in Périgord, France] 1. a masculine name 2. George Gordon, 6th Baron Byron, 1788–1824; Eng. poet

By·ron·ic (bī rän'ik) *adj.* of, like, or characteristic of Byron or his writings; romantic, passionate, cynical, ironic, etc. —By·ron'i·cal·ly *adv.*

bys·sus (bis'əs) *n., pl.* bys'sus·es, bys'si (-ī) [L. < Gr. *byssos*, fine linen or cotton < Heb. *būs* < Egypt.] 1. a fine fabric, esp. a linen cloth, used by the ancients, as in Egypt for mummy wrapping 2. *Zool.* a tuft of filaments, chemically similar to silk, occurring in certain mollusks and serving to attach them to an object

by·stand·er (bī'stan'dər) *n.* a person who stands near but does not participate; mere onlooker

by·street (-strēt') *n.* a side street off a main street

By·tom (bī'tôm) city in SW Poland: pop. 192,000

by·way (bī'wā') *n.* 1. a road or path other than the main one, esp. one not used very much; side road; bypath 2. a subsidiary activity, line of study, etc.

by·word (-wurd') *n.* [ME. & OE. *biword* < *bi* (see BY) + WORD: formed after L. *proverbium* (*pro* + *verbum*), PROVERB] 1. a familiar saying; proverb 2. a person or thing proverbial for some contemptible or ridiculous quality 3. [Rare] a nickname or epithet 4. a favorite or pet word or phrase

By·zan·tine (biz'n tēn', -tīn'; bi zan'tin) *adj.* [L. *Byzantinus*] 1. of or like Byzantium or the Byzantine Empire, its culture, etc. 2. of or pertaining to the Orthodox Eastern Church 3. *Archit.* designating or of a style developed in Byzantium and eastern Europe between the 4th and 15th cent., characterized by domes over square areas, round arches, elaborate mosaics, etc. 4. *Art* designating or of the decorative style of the mosaics, frescoes, etc. of the Byzantine Empire, characterized by lack of perspective, use of rich colors, esp. gold, and emphasis on religious symbolism —*n.* a native or inhabitant of Byzantium

Byzantine Empire empire (395–1453 A.D.) in SE Europe & SW Asia, formed by the division of the Roman Empire: cap. Constantinople: see also EASTERN ROMAN EMPIRE

By·zan·ti·um (bi zan'shē əm, -tē əm) *ancient name of* ISTANBUL (until 330 A.D.)

Bz. benzene

BYZANTINE EMPIRE (12th cent.)

C

C, c (sē) *n., pl.* C's, c's 1. the third letter of the English alphabet: from the Greek *gamma*, a borrowing from the Phoenician 2. a sound of *C* or *c*: it is usually a voiceless, alveolar fricative (s) before *e, i,* and *y,* and a voiceless velar stop (k) before *a, o,* and *u* 3. a type or impression for *C* or *c* 4. *a symbol for* the third in a sequence or group —*adj.* 1. of *C* or *c* 2. third in a sequence or group

C (sē) *n.* 1. an object shaped like *C* 2. a Roman numeral for 100: with a superior bar (C̄), 100,000 3. *Chem.* carbon ☆4. *Educ.* a grade indicating average work [a C in biology] 5. *Math. a symbol for* constant 6. *Music a*) the first tone or note in the scale of C major *b*) a key, string, etc. producing this tone *c*) the scale having this tone as the keynote *d*) the sign for 4/4 time 7. *a symbol for* heat capacity —*adj.*

1. shaped like *C* 2. average in quality

C- cargo transport

c *a symbol for* centi-

C, C. Celsius or centigrade

C. 1. Catholic 2. Celtic 3. Church 4. Congress 5. Consul 6. Corps 7. Court

C., c. 1. candle 2. canon 3. capacitance 4. capacity 5. carat 6. catcher 7. cathode 8. cent 9. centavo 10. center 11. centime 12. centimeter 13. century 14. *pl.* CC. chapter 15. circa 16. city 17. college 18. contralto 19. copyright 20. cup 21. current 22. cycle 23. [L. *centum*] hundredweight

ca' (kô) *vt.* [Scot.] to call, as in driving cattle

Ca *Chem.* calcium

ca. 1. cathode 2. centiare 3. circa 4. *Law* case; cases
C/A 1. capital account 2. credit account 3. current account
C.A. 1. Central America 2. Confederate Army
C.A., c.a. 1. chartered accountant 2. chief accountant 3. chronological age 4. commercial agent 5. consular agent 6. controller of accounts 7. crown agent
Caa·ba (kä′bə) *n. same as* KAABA
CAB Civil Aeronautics Board
cab[1] (kab) *n.* [< CABRIOLET] 1. a horse-drawn carriage, esp. one for public hire 2. a taxicab 3. the place in a locomotive, motor truck, crane, etc. where the operator sits
cab[2] (kab) *n.* [Heb. (II Kings 6:25) *qab,* hollow vessel < *qābab,* to hollow out] an ancient Hebrew dry measure, equal to about two quarts
ca·bal (kə bal′) *n.* [Fr., intrigue, society (popularized in England from the initials of the ministers of Charles II) < ML. *cabbala,* CABALA] 1. a small group of persons joined in a secret, often political intrigue; junto 2. the intrigues of such a group; plot —*vi.* -**balled′, -bal′ling** to join in a cabal; plot —*SYN.* see PLOT
cab·a·la (kab′ə lə, kə bäl′ə) *n.* [ML. *cabbala* < Heb. *qabbālāh,* received lore, tradition < *qābal,* to receive, take] 1. an occult religious philosophy developed by certain Jewish rabbis, esp. in the Middle Ages, based on a mystical interpretation of the Scriptures 2. any esoteric or secret doctrine; occultism
‡**ca·ba·let·ta** (kä′bä let′tä) *n.* [It., dim. of *cabala,* intrigue: see prec.] the last section of an aria or duet sung in rapid uniform rhythm
cab·a·lism (kab′ə liz′m) *n.* 1. occult doctrine based on the cabala 2. any occult doctrine —**cab′a·list** *n.* —**cab′a·lis′-tic** (-lis′tik) *adj.* —**cab′a·lis′ti·cal·ly** *adv.*
ca·bal·le·ro (kab′ə ler′ō, -əl yer′ō; *Sp.* kä′bä lye′rō) *n., pl.* **-ros** (-ōz; *Sp.* -rōs) [Sp. < LL. *caballarius* < L. *caballus,* horse: see CAVALIER] 1. a Spanish gentleman, cavalier, or knight ☆2. [Southwest] *a)* a horseman *b)* a lady's escort or admirer
☆**ca·ba·na** (kə bän′ə, -ban′ə, -bän′yə, -ban′yə) *n.* [Sp. *cabaña* < LL. *capanna,* hut] 1. a cabin or hut 2. a small shelter used as a bathhouse on the beach
cab·a·ret (kab′ə rā′, kab′ə rā′) *n.* [Fr., pothouse, < MDu. *cabret* < *cambret* < OFr. dial. *camberete,* dim. of *cambre,* CHAMBER] 1. a restaurant or café with dancing, singing, skits, etc. as entertainment 2. this kind of entertainment
cab·bage[1] (kab′ij) *n.* [ME. & OFr. *caboche,* earlier *caboce,* ult. < ? L. *caput,* the head] 1. a common vegetable (*Brassica oleracea capitata*) of the mustard family, with thick leaves formed into a round, compact head on a short, thick stalk 2. an edible bud at the end of the branch on some palm trees 3. [Slang] paper money
cab·bage[2] (kab′ij) *vt., vi.* -**baged, -bag·ing** [prob. < Fr. *cabasser,* to put into a basket, steal < *cabas,* basket < VL. *capacium,* reed basket] [Brit. Slang] to steal —*n.* [prob. < the *v.*] cloth snippets appropriated by a tailor when cutting out clothes
☆**cabbage bug** *same as* HARLEQUIN BUG
cabbage butterfly a common white butterfly (*Pieris rapae*), whose green larvae feed upon cabbage and other plants of the mustard family
cabbage palm 1. any of several palms with terminal buds used as a vegetable: also **cabbage tree** 2. *same as* PALMETTO (sense 1)
☆**cabbage palmetto** *same as* PALMETTO (sense 1)
cab·bage·worm (-wurm′) *n.* the larval stage of any insect that feeds on cabbage, as the caterpillar of the cabbage butterfly
cab·ba·la (kab′ə lə, kə bäl′ə) *n. same as* CABALA —**cab′-ba·lism** *n.* —**cab′ba·list** *n.* —**cab′ba·lis′tic** *adj.*
cab·driv·er (kab′drīv′ər) *n.* a person who drives a cab: also [Colloq.] **cab′by, cab′bie** (-ē), *pl.* **-bies**
Cab·ell (kab′′l), **James Branch** 1879-1958; U.S. novelist
ca·ber (kä′bər, kā′-) *n.* [Gael. *cabar*] a long, heavy pole thrown in a Gaelic game to test muscular strength
Ca·be·za de Va·ca (kä be′thä *the* vä′kä), **Ál·var Nú·ñez** (äl′vär nōō′nyeth) 1490?-1557?; Sp. explorer in the Americas
☆**ca·be·zon** (kab′ə zän′) *n.* [Sp. < *cabeza,* a head < L. *capitium,* covering for the head < *caput,* the HEAD] any of several fishes, esp. a large sculpin (*Scorpaenichthys marmoratus*) found in shallow waters along the Pacific Coast of N. America
cab·in (kab′′n) *n.* [ME. *caban* < OFr. *cabane* < Pr. *cabana* < LL. *capanna,* hut] 1. a small, one-story house built simply or crudely, as of logs ☆2. any simple, small structure designed for a brief stay, as for overnight [tourist *cabins*] 3. a private room on a ship, as a bedroom or office 4. a roofed section of a small boat, as a pleasure cruiser, for the passengers or crew 5. the enclosed section of an aircraft, where the passengers sit; also, the section housing the crew or used for cargo ☆6. the living quarters in a trailer —*vt.* to confine in or as in a cabin; cramp
cabin boy a boy whose work is to serve and run errands for the officers and passengers aboard a ship
cabin class a class of accommodations on a passenger ship, below first class and above tourist class
☆**cabin cruiser** a powerboat with a cabin and the necessary equipment for living on board
Ca·bin·da (kə bin′də) exclave of Angola, on the W coast of Africa: 2,800 sq. mi.; pop. 51,000

cab·i·net (kab′ə nit, kab′nit) *n.* [Fr., dim. of *cabine;* orig. obscure] 1. a case or cupboard with drawers or shelves for holding or storing things [a china *cabinet,* a medicine *cabinet*] 2. a boxlike enclosure, usually decorated, that houses all the assembled components of a record player, radio or television receiver, etc. 3. formerly, *a)* a private council room *b)* a meeting held there ☆4. [*often* C-] a body of official advisers to a president, king, governor, etc.: in the U.S., comprised of the heads of the various governmental departments 5. [Archaic] a small, private room —*adj.* 1. of a kind usually kept or displayed in cabinets [*cabinet* curios] 2. of or made by a cabinetmaker 3. of a political cabinet
cab·i·net·mak·er (-māk′ər) *n.* a workman who makes fine furniture, decorative moldings, etc. —**cab′i·net·mak′ing** *n.*
☆**cab·i·net·work** (-wurk′) *n.* 1. articles made by a cabinetmaker 2. the work or art of a cabinetmaker Also **cab′i·net·ry** (-rē)
ca·ble (kā′b′l) *n.* [ME. & OFr. < LL. *capulum,* a cable, rope < L. *capere,* to take hold] 1. a thick, heavy rope, now often of wire strands 2. the strong, heavy chain attached to a ship's anchor: anchor cables were formerly of rope 3. *same as* CABLE LENGTH 4. a bundle of insulated wires through which an electric current can be passed: telegraph or telephone cables are often laid under the ground or on the ocean floor ☆5. a cablegram —*vt.* **-bled, -bling** 1. to fasten or furnish with a cable or cables 2. to transmit by undersea cable 3. to send a cablegram to —*vi.* to send a cablegram
Ca·ble (kā′b′l), **George Washington** 1844-1925; U.S. novelist
☆**cable car** a car drawn by a moving cable, as across a canyon, up a steeply inclined street, etc.

CABLE

☆**ca·ble·gram** (-gram′) *n.* a message sent by undersea cable
ca·ble-laid (kā′b′l lād′) *adj.* made of three plain-laid ropes twisted together counterclockwise
cable length a unit of nautical measure variously equal to 720 feet (120 fathoms), 600 feet (100 fathoms), or, in the British navy, 607.6 feet (1/10 of a nautical mile): also **cable's length**
☆**cable railway** a street railway on which the cars are pulled by a continuously moving underground cable to which they are attached by a grip that can be released to halt the car
cable stitch a type of raised stitch used in knitting: it resembles ropes twisted together
☆**cable tools** a set of tools, including a heavy steel bit, attached to a cable in one system of drilling wells and alternately raised and dropped to cut through rock
ca·blet (kāb′lit) *n.* [CABL(E) + -ET] a cable-laid rope less than ten inches in circumference
cab·man (kab′mən) *n., pl.* **-men** (-mən) *same as* CABDRIVER
ca·bob (kə bäb′) *n.* [Ar. *kabāb*] *same as* KEBAB
ca·bo·chon (kab′ə shän′; *Fr.* kȧ bō shōn′) *n.* [Fr. < *caboche,* the head: see CABBAGE[1]] 1. any precious stone cut in convex shape, polished but not faceted 2. the style of cutting such a stone
ca·bom·ba (kə bäm′bə) *n.* [ModL. < Sp.] any of a genus (*Cabomba*) of plants of the waterlily family, esp. a water plant (*Cabomba caroliniana*) with submerged, finely divided leaves and rounded, floating ones: used in aquariums, garden pools, etc.
☆**ca·boo·dle** (kə bōō′d′l) *n.* [*ca-,* colloq. intens. prefix + BOODLE] [Colloq.] lot; group [the whole *caboodle*]
ca·boose (kə bōōs′) *n.* [MDu. *kabuys, kambuis* (of unc. orig.), cabin house, ship's galley] 1. [Brit.] a ship's galley or kitchen ☆2. the trainmen's car on a freight train, usually at the rear
Cab·ot (kab′ət) 1. **John,** (It. name *Giovanni Caboto*) 1450?-1498?; It. explorer in the service of England: discovered coast of N. America (1497) 2. **Sebastian,** 1476?-1557; Eng. cartographer & explorer: son of *prec.*
cab·o·tage (kab′ə tij, -täzh′) *n.* [Fr. < *caboter,* to sail along the coast < *cabo,* cape < Sp. < L. *caput,* HEAD] 1. coastal navigation and trade, esp. between ports within a country 2. air transport within a country 3. the right to engage in cabotage, esp. as granted to foreign carriers
ca·bret·ta (kə bret′ə) *adj.* [Sp. *cabra,* goat (< L. *caper,* he-goat: see CAPRIOLE) + It. dim. suffix *-etta*] designating or of a soft leather made from a special kind of sheep-skin
ca·bril·la (kə bril′ə, kə brē′yə) *n.* [Sp., prawn, dim. of *cabra,* goat] any of various edible, perchlike fishes (family Serranidae) found off Florida, the West Indies, etc.
Ca·bri·ni (kə brē′nē), **Saint Frances Xavier** (called *Mother Cabrini*) 1850-1917; U.S. nun, born in Italy: first U.S. citizen canonized: her day is Dec. 22
cab·ri·ole (kab′rē ōl′) *n.* [Fr.: see ff.] 1. a leg of a table, chair, etc. that curves outward and then tapers inward down to a clawlike foot grasping a ball 2. *Ballet* a leap in which one leg is extended horizontally and the feet are struck quickly together

CABRIOLE

cab·ri·o·let (kab′rē ə lā′, -let′) *n.* [Fr., dim. of *cabriole*, a leap, caper < It. *capriola*, CAPRIOLE] 1. a light two-wheeled carriage, usually with a hood that folds, drawn by one horse 2. a former style of automobile like a convertible coupe

cab·stand (kab′stand′) *n.* a place where cabs are stationed for hire

CABRIOLET

cac- (kak) same as CACO-: used before a vowel

ca′ canny see CANNY

ca·ca·o (kə kā′ō, -kā′-, -kou′) *n.*, *pl.* -os (-ōz) [Sp. < Nahuatl *cacauatl*, cacao seed] 1. a tropical American tree (*Theobroma cacao*) of the sterculia family, bearing large elliptical seed pods 2. the nutritious seeds (**cacao beans**) of this tree, from which cocoa and chocolate are made

cacao butter same as COCOA BUTTER

cac·ci·a·to·re (kach′ə tôr′ē; It. kät′chä tô′re) *adj.* [It., lit., a hunter < pp. of *cacciare*, to hunt, chase < VL. *captiare*, to CATCH] cooked in a casserole with olive oil and tomatoes, onions, spices, etc. [chicken *cacciatore*]

cach·a·lot (kash′ə lät′, -lō′) *n.* [Fr. < Sp. *cachalote* < ? Port. *cachola*, big head] same as SPERM WHALE

cache (kash) *n.* [Fr. < *cacher*, conceal < VL. *coacticare*, store up, collect, compress < L. *coactare*, constrain] 1. a place in which stores of food, supplies, etc. are hidden, as by explorers or trappers 2. a safe place for hiding or storing things 3. anything stored or hidden in such a place —*vt.*, *vi.* cached, cach′ing to hide or store in a cache —SYN. see HIDE[1]

cache·pot (kash′pät, -pō) *n.* [Fr., lit., hide-pot < *cacher*, to hide (see CACHE) + *pot*, POT] a decorative pot, jar, etc., used esp. for holding potted house plants: also **cache pot**

ca·chet (ka shā′, kash′ā) *n.* [Fr. < *cacher*: see CACHE] 1. a seal or stamp on an official letter or document: see also LETTRE DE CACHET 2. any sign of official approval 3. *a*) a mark or sign showing something is genuine, authentic, or of superior quality *b*) distinction; prestige 4. a commemorative design, slogan, advertisement, etc. stamped on mail, often as part of the cancellation 5. a little wafer enclosing a bad-tasting medicine

ca·chex·i·a (kə kek′sē ə) *n.* [ModL. < Gr. *kachexia*, bad habit of body < *kakos*, bad + *hexis*, habit < *echein*, to have] 1. a generally weakened, emaciated condition of the body, esp. as associated with a chronic illness 2. a general lack of mental vigor: also **ca·chex′y** (-sē) —**ca·chec′tic** (-kek′tik), **ca·chex′ic** (-kek′sik) *adj.*

cach·in·nate (kak′ə nāt′) *vi.* -nat′ed, -nat′ing [< L. *cachinnatus*, pp. of *cachinnare*, prob. of echoic origin] to laugh loudly or too much —**cach′in·na′tion** *n.*

ca·chou (ka shoo′) *n.* [Fr. < Malay *kachu*] 1. same as CATECHU 2. a lozenge for sweetening the breath

ca·chu·cha (kə choo′chə) *n.* [Sp.] 1. an Andalusian dance in 3/4 time, like the bolero 2. music for this

ca·cique (kə sēk′) *n.* [Sp. < Arawak word meaning "prince," "lord"] 1. *a*) in Spanish America, an Indian chief *b*) in Spanish America and Spain, a local political boss 2. any of several kinds of tropical American birds (family Icteridae) with conical bills —**ca·ciqu′ism** *n.*

cack·le (kak′'l) *vi.* -led, -ling [ME. *cakelen*; like Du. *kokkeln*, LowG. *kakkeln*, IE. base *kak-*, of echoic orig.] 1. to make the shrill, broken sounds of a hen 2. to laugh or chatter with similar sounds —*vt.* to utter in a cackling manner —*n.* 1. the act or sound of cackling 2. cackling laughter or chatter

caco- (kak′ə, -ō) [< Gr. *kakos*, bad, evil] *a combining form meaning* bad, poor, harsh [*cacography*]

cac·o·de·mon, cac·o·dae·mon (kak′ə dē′mən) *n.* [Gr. *kakodaimōn*: see CACO- & DEMON] an evil spirit or devil

cac·o·dyl (kak′ə dil) *n.* [< Gr. *kakōdēs*, bad-smelling < *kakos*, bad + *ozein*, to smell < -YL] *Chem.* 1. the radical As(CH₃)₂, composed of arsenic and methyl: its compounds are poisonous and bad-smelling 2. a poisonous, colorless liquid, As₂(CH₃)₄, with a bad smell: it is a polymer of this radical —**cac′o·dyl′ic** (-dil′ik) *adj.*

ca·co·ë·thes, ca·co·e·thes (kak′ō ē′thēz) *n.* [L. < Gr. *kakoēthēs* < *kakos*, bad + *ēthos*, habit, custom] an itch (to do something); mania

cac·o·gen·e·sis (kak′ə jen′ə sis) *n.* [ModL.: see CACO- & -GENESIS] the inability of two species to produce viable offspring

ca·cog·ra·phy (kə käg′rə fē) *n.* [CACO- + -GRAPHY] 1. bad handwriting 2. incorrect spelling —**cac·o·graph·ic** (kak′ə graf′ik) *adj.*

☆**cac·o·mis·tle** (kak′ə mis′'l) *n.* [AmSp. *cacomixtle* < Nahuatl *tlacomiztli*] 1. a slender, long-tailed, raccoonlike animal (*Bassariscus astutus*) of the southwestern U.S. and Mexico 2. its fur Also **cac′o·mix′le** (-mis′'l, -mik′sl)

ca·coph·o·ny (kə käf′ə nē) *n.*, *pl.* -nies [ModL. *cacophonia* < Gr. *kakophōnia* < *kakophōnos*, harsh-sounding < *kakos*, bad, evil + *phōnē*, voice] harsh, jarring sound; dissonance —**ca·coph′o·nous** (-nəs) *adj.* —**ca·coph′o·nous·ly** *adv.*

cac·tus (kak′təs) *n.*, *pl.* -tus·es, -ti (-tī) [L. < Gr. *kaktos*, kind of thistle, cardoon] any of a family (Cactaceae) of desert plants native to the New World, with fleshy stems, reduced or spinelike leaves, and often showy flowers

FISHHOOK CACTUS

ca·cu·mi·nal (kə kyoo′mə n'l) *adj.* [< L. *cacuminis*, gen. of L. *cacumen*, top + -AL] *Phonet.* pronounced with the tip of the tongue turned backward and upward against or toward the hard palate, as Swedish *d* or *t* after *r* —*n.* a cacuminal sound

cad (kad) *n.* [< CADDIE & CADET] a man or boy whose behavior is not gentlemanly: word originally applied to servants, then to town boys, by students at British universities and public schools

ca·das·tre, ca·das·ter (kə das′tər) *n.* [Fr. *catastre* < It. *catastro* < dial (Venetian) *catastico* < LGr. *katastichon*, register, list (lit., line by line): see CATA- & STICH] public record of the extent, value, and ownership of land within a district for purposes of taxation —**ca·das′tral** (-trəl) *adj.*

ca·dav·er (kə dav′ər) *n.* [L., prob. < *cadere*, to fall] a dead body, esp. of a person; corpse, as for dissection —**ca·dav′er·ic** *adj.* —SYN. see BODY

ca·dav·er·ine (-ər in, -ə rēn′) *n.* [CADAVER + -INE[2]] a colorless, bad-smelling, liquid ptomaine, NH₂(CH₂)₅NH₂, produced by the hydrolysis of proteins, as in putrefying flesh

ca·dav·er·ous (-ər əs) *adj.* [L. *cadaverosus*] of or like a cadaver; esp., pale, ghastly, or gaunt and haggard —**ca·dav′er·ous·ly** *adv.* —**ca·dav′er·ous·ness** *n.*

cad·die (kad′ē) *n.* [Scot. form of Fr. *cadet*: see CADET] 1. orig., an errand boy 2. a person who attends a golf player, carrying his clubs, etc. 3. a small, usually two-wheeled cart for carrying golf bags, heavy packages, etc. —*vi.* -died, -dy·ing to act as a caddie

cad·dis[1], cad·dice[1] (kad′is) *n.* [ME. & OFr. *cadas*, floss silk; confused with Fr. *cadis*, coarse serge] 1. a coarse woolen material; worsted yarn 2. a worsted ribbon

cad·dis[2], cad·dice[2] (kad′is) *n.* same as CADDIS WORM

caddis fly [see CADDIS WORM] a small, mothlike insect (order Trichoptera) with two pairs of wings, soft body, and long legs

cad·dish (kad′ish) *adj.* like or characteristic of a cad; ungentlemanly —**cad′dish·ly** *adv.* —**cad′dish·ness** *n.*

caddis worm [< OFr. *cadas*, floss silk (with reference to the case)] the wormlike larva of the caddis fly that usually lives in fresh water in an elongated case made of twigs, grains of sand, etc. cemented together with silk that it secretes: commonly used as bait by anglers

Cad·do (kad′ō) *n.*, *pl.* -does, -dos, -do [Caddo *Kädohädächo*, lit., real chiefs (self-designation of a leading subtribe)] 1. an Indian people consisting of several subtribes formerly living in Louisiana, Arkansas, and E Texas 2. a member of the Caddo people 3. their Caddoan language

Cad·do·an (-ən) *adj.* designating of or a family of N. American Indian languages spoken by the Caddo and various other tribes from Texas to N. Dakota, including the Pawnee —*n.* this family of languages

cad·dy[1] (kad′ē) *n.*, *pl.* -dies [< earlier *catty* < Malay *kati*, weight equivalent to a little more than a pound] 1. a small container used for tea 2. any of various devices for holding or storing certain articles, as phonograph records, ice-cube trays, etc.

cad·dy[2] (kad′ē) *n.*, *vi.* same as CADDIE

cade[1] (kād) *adj.* [LME., a pet] untended by its mother and brought up by a human being, often as a pet [a *cade* lamb]

cade[2] (kād) *n.* [Fr. < Pr. < LL. *catanus*] a bushy, Mediterranean juniper (*Juniperus oxycedrus*), whose tarlike oil distilled from the wood is used in the treatment of skin disorders

-cade (kād) [< (CAVAL)CADE] *a suffix meaning* procession, parade [*motorcade*]

ca·delle (kə del′) *n.* [Fr. < Pr. *cadello* < L. *catella*, fem. of *catellus*, puppy, whelp] the larva or adult of a small, shiny, black beetle (*Tenebroides mauritanicus*) harmful to grain

ca·dence (kād′'ns) *n.* [ME. < OFr. < It. *cadenza* or ML. *cadentia* < L. *cadens*, prp. of *cadere*, to fall] 1. fall of the voice in speaking 2. inflection or modulation in tone 3. any rhythmic flow of sound 4. measured movement, as in dancing or marching, or the beat of such movement 5. *Music* the harmonic ending, final trill, etc. of a phrase or movement Also **ca′den·cy** (-'n sē) —**ca′denced** (-'nst) *adj.*

ca·dent (-'nt) *adj.* 1. orig., falling 2. having cadence

ca·den·za (kə den′zə; It. kä dent′sä) *n.* [It.: see CADENCE] 1. an elaborate, often improvised musical passage played by an unaccompanied instrument in a concerto, usually near the end of the first movement 2. any brilliant flourish in an aria or solo passage

ca·det (kə det′) *n.* [Fr., younger son < Gascon *capdet*, captain, chief < Pr. *capdel* < LL. *capitellum*, dim. of L. *caput*: see CAPTAIN] 1. a younger son or brother 2. formerly, a younger son who became a gentleman volunteer in the army to offset his lack of patrimony 3. a student in

training at an armed forces academy **4.** a student at a military school ☆**5.** any trainee, as a practice teacher or a junior business associate **6.** [Old Slang] a pimp —**ca·det′·ship** n.

cadge (kaj) vt., vi. **cadged, cadg′ing** [ME. caggen, to tie; ? var. of cacchen, to catch] to beg or get by begging; sponge —**cadg′er** n.

cadg·y (kaj′ē) adj. [< ?] [Scot. & Brit. Dial.] **1.** lustful; lewd; wanton **2.** merry; cheerful

ca·di (kä′dē, kä′-) n. [Ar. qādi] a minor Moslem magistrate or judge

Ca·dil·lac (kä dē yäk′; E. kad′l ak′), sieur **An·toine de la Mothe** (än twän′ də lá môt′) 1656?–1730; Fr. explorer in America

Cá·diz (kə diz′, kā′diz; Sp. kä thēth′) seaport in SW Spain, on the Atlantic: pop. 128,000

Cad·man (kad′mən), **Charles Wake·field** (wāk′fēld′) 1881–1946; U.S. composer

Cad·me·an (kad mē′ən) adj. of or like Cadmus

Cadmean victory a victory won with great losses to the victors

cad·mi·um (kad′mē əm) n. [ModL. (so named by its discoverer, Strohmeyer, in 1817) < L. cadmia, zinc ore, calamine < Gr. kadmeia] a blue-white, malleable, ductile, metallic chemical element occurring as a sulfide or carbonate in zinc ores: it is used in some low-melting alloys, electroplating, etc.: symbol, Cd; at. wt., 112.40; at. no., 48; sp. gr., 8.642; melt. pt., 320.9°C; boil. pt., 765°C —**cad′·mic** (-mik) adj.

cadmium sulfide a pigment, CdS, varying from lemon yellow (**cadmium yellow**) to yellowish orange (**cadmium orange**)

Cad·mus (kad′məs) [Gr. Kadmos] Gr. Myth. a Phoenician prince who killed a dragon and sowed its teeth, from which many armed men rose and fought, five surviving to help him build the city of Thebes

ca·dre (kad′rē) n. [Fr., a frame < It. quadro < L. quadrum, a square] **1.** basic structure or framework **2.** an operational unit, as of staff officers or other key personnel, around which an expanded organization can be built **3.** a small, unified group organized to instruct or lead a larger group; nucleus

ca·du·ce·us (kə dōō′sē əs, -dyōō′-) n., pl. **-ce·i′** (-sē ī′) [L.] **1.** the staff of an ancient herald; esp., the winged staff carried by Mercury **2.** an emblematic staff like this with one or two serpents coiled about it, used as a symbol of the medical profession —**ca·du′ce·an** adj.

ca·du·ci·ty (kə dōō′sə tē, -dyōō′-) n. [Fr. caducité < LL. caducitas < L. caducus: see ff.] **1.** the quality or state of being perishable **2.** senility

ca·du·cous (-kəs) adj. [L. caducus, falling < cadere, to fall] **1.** dropping off **2.** fleeting; unenduring **3.** Bot. falling off early, as some leaves

cae·cil·i·an (sē sil′ē ən, -sil′yən) n. [< L. caecilia, kind of lizard < caecus: see CECUM] any of a family (Caeciliidae) of legless, tropical amphibians (order Gymnophiona) resembling worms

cae·cum (sē′kəm) n., pl. **-ca** (-kə) same as CECUM —**cae′cal** adj.

Caed·mon (kad′mən) fl. late 7th cent. A.D.; first Eng. poet whose name is known

Cae·li·an (sē′lē ən, sēl′yən) [< L. Caelius Mons, Caelian hill, named after the Tuscan Caeles Vibenna] see SEVEN HILLS OF ROME

Caen (kän) city in NW France: pop. 91,000

cae·no·gen·e·sis (sē′nə jen′ə sis, sen′ə-) n. same as CENOGENESIS

Caer·nar·von·shire (kär när′vən shir) county of NW Wales, on the Irish Sea: 569 sq. mi.; pop. 121,000: also **Car·nar′von**

Cae·sar (sē′zər), (**Gaius**) **Julius** [L. Caesar, said to be < caesus, pp. of caedere, to cut, but prob. of Etruscan orig.] 100?–44 B.C.; Roman general & statesman; dictator (49–44) of the Roman Empire —n. **1.** the title of the emperor of Rome from Augustus to Hadrian, or of the emperor of the Holy Roman Empire **2.** any emperor, dictator, or autocrat

Caes·a·re·a (ses′ə rē′ə, sez′-, sē′zə-) **1.** seaport in ancient Palestine, on the Mediterranean **2.** city in ancient Palestine, near Mt. Hermon: also **Caesarea Philippi 3.** ancient name of KAYSERI

Cae·sar·e·an, Cae·sar·i·an (si zer′ē ən) adj. of Julius Caesar or the Caesars —n. same as CAESAREAN SECTION

Caesarean section [from the ancient story (by association of the name Caesar with L. caedere: see CAESAR) that Caesar or an ancestor had been born in this manner] [also **c- s-**] a surgical operation for delivering a baby by cutting through the mother's abdominal and uterine walls

Cae·sar·ism (sē′zər iz′m) n. [also c-] absolutism in government; autocracy —**Cae′sar·ist** adj., n.

cae·si·um (sē′zē əm) n. same as CESIUM

caes·pi·tose (ses′pə tōs′) adj. same as CESPITOSE

cae·su·ra (si zhoor′ə, -zyoor′ə) n., pl. **-ras, -rae** (-ē) [L., a cutting < pp. of caedere, to cut] a break or pause in a line of verse: in Greek and Latin verse, the caesura falls within the metrical foot; in English verse, it is usually about the middle of the line and is shown in scanning by

the sign ‖ **2.** a pause showing rhythmic division of a melody —**cae·su′ral** adj.

C.A.F., c.a.f. cost and freight

‡**ca·fard** (ká fár′) n. [Fr., low spirits, lit., cockroach, orig., hypocrite, altered (with pejorative -ard) < MFr. caphars < Ar. kāfir, hypocrite, lit., infidel: see KAFFIR] boredom, melancholy, listlessness, etc.

ca·fé, ca·fe (ka fā′, kə-) n. [Fr., coffee, coffeehouse < It. caffè, COFFEE] **1.** coffee **2.** a coffeehouse **3.** a small restaurant, esp. one serving alcoholic drinks and sometimes providing entertainment **4.** a barroom

‡**ca·fé au lait** (kà fā ō lā′) [Fr.] **1.** coffee with an equal part of hot or scalded milk **2.** pale brown

café curtains short, straight curtains, esp. for covering the lower part of a window, hung from a rod by means of sliding rings

‡**ca·fé noir** (kà fā nwár′) [Fr.] black coffee

☆**caf·e·te·ri·a** (kaf′ə tir′ē ə) n. [AmSp., coffee store] a restaurant in which food, variously priced, is displayed on counters and patrons serve themselves

caf·feine, caf·fein (kaf′ēn, -ē in; ka fēn′) n. [G. kaffein (now coffein, after ModL. coffea, coffee), coined by F. F. Runge, Ger. chemist (1795–1867), its discoverer < kaffee, coffee (< Fr. café < It. caffè, COFFEE) + -in, -INE[4]] a bitter, crystalline alkaloid, $C_8H_{10}N_4O_2$, present in coffee, tea, and kola: it is a stimulant to the heart and central nervous system

caf·tan (kaf′tən, käf tän′) n. [Turk. qaftān] a long-sleeved robe with a girdle, worn in eastern Mediterranean countries

cage (kāj) n. [ME. & OFr. < L. cavea, hollow place, cage < cavus, hollow: see CAVE[1]] **1.** a box or enclosed structure made of wires, bars, etc., for confining birds or animals **2.** a fenced-in area as for confining prisoners of war **3.** any openwork structure or frame, as some elevator cars **4.** [Archaic] a jail ☆**5.** Baseball a partially enclosed backstop used in batting practice, etc.: in full, **batting cage** ☆**6.** Basketball the basket **7.** Hockey the network frame that is the goal —vt. **caged, cag′ing** to put or confine, as in a cage

CAFTAN

cage·ling (-lin) n. a bird kept in a cage

cag·er (-ər) n. [Slang] ☆a basketball player

☆**ca·gey, ca·gy** (kā′jē) adj. **ca′gi·er, ca′gi·est** [< ? CADGY] [Colloq.] **1.** sly; tricky; cunning **2.** careful not to get caught or fooled —**ca′gi·ly** adv. —**ca′gi·ness** n.

Ca·glia·ri (kä′lyä rē′) capital of Sardinia; seaport on the S coast: pop. 200,000

Ca·glia·ri (kä′lyä rē′), **Paolo** see Paolo VERONESE

Ca·glio·stro (kä lyô′strô), Count **A·les·san·dro di** (ä′les sän′drô dē) (born Giuseppe Balsamo) 1743–95; Sicilian alchemist & charlatan

Ca·guas (kä′gwäs) city in EC Puerto Rico: pop. 63,000

ca·hier (kä yā′) n. [Fr. < OFr. quaer: see QUIRE[2]] **1.** a notebook **2.** a report on policy or procedure

☆**ca·hoots** (kə hōōts′) n.pl. [< ?] [Slang] partnership; league —**go cahoots** [Slang] to share alike —**in cahoots** [Slang] in league: usually applied to questionable dealing or to conspiracy

Cai·a·phas (kā′ə fəs, kī′-) [Gr. Kaiaphas] Bible the high priest who presided at the trial that led to the condemnation of Jesus: Matt. 26:57–66

Cai·cos Islands (kā′kəs) group of islands in the West Indies: see TURKS & CAICOS ISLANDS

cai·man (kā′mən) n., pl. **-mans** [Sp. < Carib native name] any of a genus (Caiman) of Central and South American reptiles similar to alligators and crocodiles

Cain (kān) [Heb. qayin, lit., smith, craftsman] Bible the oldest son of Adam and Eve: he killed his brother Abel: Gen. 4 —n. any murderer, esp. of a brother —☆**raise Cain** [Slang] **1.** to create a great commotion **2.** to cause much trouble

Cai·no·zo·ic (kī′nə zō′ik, kā′-) adj. same as CENOZOIC

ca·ique, ca·ïque (kä ēk′) n. [Fr. < It. caicco < Turk. qayiq] **1.** a light rowboat used on the Bosporus **2.** a sailboat used esp. in the eastern Mediterranean

caird (kerd) n. [< ScotGael. ceard, a tinker < IE. base *kerd-, skillful, clever, whence Gr. kerdos, profit, L. cerdo, handicraftsman, ON. horskr, wise] [Scot.] a wandering tinker, vagrant, gypsy, etc.

cairn (kern) n. [Scot. < Gael. carn, an elevation < IE. base *ker-n-, highest part of the body, horn, hence tip, peak, whence L. cornu, horn, extremity, summit: see HORN] a conical heap of stones built as a monument or landmark —**cairned** (kernd) adj.

cairn·gorm (kern′gôrm) n. [after Cairngorm mountain and range in NE Scotland, where orig. found < Gael. carngorm < prec. + gorm, blue, azure] a yellow or brown variety of quartz, used as a gem

cairn terrier [said to be so named from its burrowing in cairns] a small, shaggy Scottish terrier

Cai·ro (kī′rō; for 2 ker′ō) **1.** capital of the United Arab Republic, at the head of the Nile delta: pop. 3,346,000 **2.** city in S Ill., at the confluence of the Ohio & Mississippi rivers: pop. 6,000

cais·son (kā′sän, kās′n) n. [Fr. < It. cassone < cassa, a chest < L. capsa, a box, CASE[2]] **1.** formerly, a box of explosives to be fired as a mine **2.** a chest for holding ammuni-

tion **3.** a two-wheeled wagon for transporting ammunition **4.** a watertight enclosure inside which men can do construction work under water **5.** a watertight box for raising sunken ships: after the box is sunk and attached, the water is forced out of it so that it floats **6.** a hollow, boat-shaped box, used as a floodgate at a dock or basin

☆**caisson disease** *same as* DECOMPRESSION SICKNESS

Caith·ness (kāth′nes, kāth nes′) county of NE Scotland: 685 sq. mi.; pop. 28,000: also **Caith′ness·shire** (-shir)

cai·tiff (kāt′if) n. [ME. < OFr. *caitif*, a captive, wretched man < L. *captivus*, CAPTIVE] a mean, evil, or cowardly person —adj. evil, mean, or cowardly

caj·e·put (kaj′ə pət) n. *same as* CAJUPUT

ca·jole (kə jōl′) vt., vi. **-joled′, -jol′ing** [Fr. *cajoler* < ? blend of *cage* (see CAGE) + *jaiole*, cage: see JAIL] to coax with flattery and insincere talk; wheedle —*SYN.* see COAX —**ca·jole′ment, ca·jol′er·y** n. —**ca·jol′er** n. —**ca·jol′ing·ly** adv.

☆**Ca·jun, Ca·jan** (kā′jən) n. [< ACADIAN] **1.** a native of Louisiana originally descended from Acadian French immigrants: sometimes used contemptuously **2.** the dialect of the Cajuns

caj·u·put (kaj′ə pət) n. [Malay *kāyūputīh* < *kāyū*, tree + *putih*, white] an Australian tree (*Melaleuca leucadendra*) of the myrtle family, with whitish flowers and thick bark, often grown in the extreme southern U.S.: its aromatic oil is used in medicine

cake (kāk) n. [ME. < ON. *kaka* < IE. base *gag-, *gog-*, something round, lump of something (orig. < baby talk), whence G. *kuchen*: not connected with COOK & L. *coquere*] **1.** a small, flat mass of dough or batter, or of some hashed food, that is baked or fried **2.** a mixture of flour, eggs, milk, sugar, etc. baked as in a loaf and often covered with icing **3.** a shaped, solid mass, as of soap, ice, etc. a hard crust or deposit —vt., vi. **caked, cak′ing** to form into a hard mass or a crust; solidify or encrust —**take the cake** [Slang] to win the prize; excel: often used ironically **cak′y** adj., **cak′i·er, cak′i·est**

cakes and ale the good things of life; worldly pleasures

☆**cake·walk** (-wôk′) n. **1.** an elaborate step or walk formerly performed by Negroes in the South competing for the prize of a cake **2.** a strutting dance developed from this — vi. to do a cakewalk —**cake′walk′er** n.

Cal. 1. California **2.** large calorie(s)

cal. 1. calendar **2.** caliber **3.** small calorie(s)

Cal·a·bar bean (kal′ə bär′, kal′ə bär′) [prob. after *Calabar*, name of a river & town in S Nigeria] the large, brown, poisonous seed of a woody tropical African vine (*Physostigma venenosum*) of the legume family, used in medicine as a source of physostigmine

cal·a·bash (kal′ə bash′) n. [Fr. *calebasse* < Sp. *calabaza* < ?] **1.** a tropical American tree (*Crescentia cujete*) of the bignonia family, or its large gourdlike fruit **2.** *a)* the bottle gourd (*Lagenaria siceraria*) of the gourd family, or its hard-rinded fruit *b)* a large smoking pipe made from the neck of this gourd **3.** the dried, hollow shell of a gourd or calabash, used as a bowl, cup, etc. **4.** any of various gourds

☆**cal·a·boose** (kal′ə boos′) n. [Sp. *calabozo*] [Slang] a prison; jail

Ca·la·bri·a (kə lā′brē ə; *It.* kä lä′bryä) **1.** region on the S coast of Italy, opposite Sicily: 5,823 sq. mi.; pop. 2,045,000 **2.** former region (until 11th cent.) constituting what is now S Apulia, in SE Italy

ca·la·di·um (kə lā′dē əm) n. [ModL. < Malay *kélády*, kind of plant] any of a genus (*Caladium*, esp. *Caladium bicolor*) of tropical American plants of the arum family, grown for ornament because of their brilliantly colored, variegated leaves

Cal·ais (ka lā′, kal′ā; *Brit. occas.* kal′is) **1.** seaport in N France, on the Strait of Dover: pop. 70,000 **2.** **Pas de** (pä′ də), *Fr.* name of Strait of DOVER

cal·a·man·co (kal′ə maŋ′kō) n., pl. **-coes, -cos** [Sp. *calamaco, calamanco*] a former kind of woolen cloth woven with a glossy, patterned face

cal·a·man·der (kal′ə man′dər) n. [< ? COROMANDEL (COAST)] the hard, heavy, black wood of an East Indian tree (genus *Diospyros*) of the ebony family, used in furniture

cal·a·mar·y (kal′ə mer′ē) n., pl. **-mar′ies** [L. *calamarius*, of a writing reed < *calamus*, a reed, pen: see CALAMUS] a squid: so called from its pen-shaped skeleton

cal·a·mine (kal′ə min′, -min) n. [Fr. < ML. *calamina* < L. *cadmia*, calamine: see CADMIUM] **1.** *same as* HEMIMORPHITE **2.** a pink powder consisting of zinc oxide mixed with a small amount of ferric oxide, used in skin lotions and ointments **3.** [Brit.] native zinc carbonate, $ZnCO_3$

cal·a·mint (kal′ə mint′) n. [ME. *calaminte* < OFr. *calamente* < ML. *calamentum* < L. *calaminthe* < Gr. *kalaminthē*] any of a genus (*Satureja*) of plants of the mint

family, esp. an aromatic species of savory (*Satureja calamintha*)

cal·a·mite (kal′ə mit′) n. [ModL. *Calamites*, genus name < Gr. *kalamitēs*, reedlike: see CALAMUS] an extinct paleozoic plant (order Calamitales) related to modern horsetails but growing to the size of a tree

ca·lam·i·tous (kə lam′ə təs) adj. [Fr. *calamiteux* < L. *calamitosus*] causing or bringing calamity —**ca·lam′i·tous·ly** adv. —**ca·lam′i·tous·ness** n.

ca·lam·i·ty (-tē) n., pl. **-ties** [Fr. *calamité* < L. *calamitas*: see CLASTIC] **1.** deep trouble or misery **2.** any extreme misfortune bringing great loss and sorrow; disaster —*SYN.* see DISASTER

Calamity Jane (nickname of *Martha Jane Burke*) 1852–1903; Am. frontier figure, noted for her marksmanship

cal·a·mon·din (kal′ə män′din) n. [Tag. *kalamunding*] a small, spicy orange (genus *Citrus*) of the Philippines

cal·a·mus (kal′ə məs) n., pl. **-mi** (-mi′) [L. < Gr. *kalamos*, a stalk, reed, stubble < IE. base *kolem-*, stalk, reed, whence G. *halm*, L. *culmus*] **1.** *same as* SWEETFLAG **2.** any of a genus (*Calamus*) of climbing palms of the Old World that yield rattan **3.** the quill of a feather

ca·lan·do (kä län′dō) adj., adv. [It., gerund of *calare*, to decrease < L. < Gr. *chalan*, to slacken] *Music* with gradually decreasing speed and volume; fading away

ca·lash (kə lash′) n. [Fr. *calèche* < G. *kalesche* < Czech *kolésa*, prob. < *kolo*, a wheel] **1.** a light, low-wheeled carriage, usually with a folding top **2.** a folding top of a carriage **3.** a folding hood or bonnet worn by women in the 18th cent.

cal·a·thus (kal′ə thəs) n., pl. **-thi′** (-thī′) [L. < Gr. *kalathos*] in ancient Greece, a basket for fruits: in art, a symbol of abundance and fruitfulness

☆**cal·a·ver·ite** (kal′ə ver′it) n. [< *Calaveras* County, Calif., where first discovered + -ITE¹] a native telluride of gold, AuTe₂, containing some silver

calc- (kalk) [G. *kalk*, lime < L. *calx* (gen. *calcis*), lime] a combining form meaning calcareous [*calcspar*]

cal·ca·ne·us (kal kā′nē əs) n., pl. **-ne·i** (-nē i′) [LL. < L. *calcaneum* < *calx*, the heel] **1.** the large tarsal bone that forms the heel in man; heel bone **2.** an analogous bone in other vertebrates Also **cal·ca′ne·um** (-əm), pl. **-ne·a** (-ə) —**cal·ca′ne·al** adj.

cal·car (kal′kär) n., pl. **cal·car′i·a** (-ker′ē·ə) [L., a spur < *calx* (gen. *calcis*), the heel] **1.** *Bot.* a hollow projection or nectar spur, as at the base of a corolla **2.** *Zool.* a spur on a bird's wing or leg —**cal·ca·rate′** (-kā·rāt′, -rit) adj.

cal·car·e·ous (kal ker′ē əs) adj. [L. *calcarius* < *calx*, lime] of, like, or containing calcium carbonate, calcium, or lime —**cal·car′e·ous·ness** n.

cal·ce·i·form (kal′sē ə fôrm′) adj. [< L. *calceus*, a shoe (< *calx*, heel) + -FORM] *same as* CALCEOLATE

cal·ce·o·la·ri·a (kal′sē ə ler′ē ə) n. [ModL. < L. *calceolarius*, shoemaker < *calceolus*, dim. of *calceus*: see prec.] any of a large genus (*Calceolaria*) of S. American plants of the figwort family, bearing colorful, slipper-shaped flowers

cal·ce·o·late (kal′sē ə lāt′) adj. [< L. *calceolus* (see prec.) + -ATE¹] *Bot.* shaped like a slipper, as the large, middle petal of an orchid

cal·ces (kal′sēz) n. *alt. pl.* of CALX

Cal·chas (kal′kəs) [L. < Gr. *Kalchas*] *Gr. Myth.* a priest of Apollo with the Greeks during the Trojan War

cal·ci- (kal′sə) [< L. *calx* (gen. *calcis*), lime] a combining form meaning calcium or lime [*calciferous, calcify*]

cal·cic (kal′sik) adj. of or containing calcium or lime

cal·ci·cole (kal′sə kōl′) n. [orig. adj. < Fr. < *calci-*, CALCI- + -*cole*, -colous < L. *colere*, to cultivate] a plant that grows in limy soils —**cal·cic·o·lous** (kal sik′ə ləs) adj.

cal·cif·er·ol (kal sif′ə rōl′, -rōl′) n. [CALCIF(EROUS) + (ERGOST)EROL] vitamin D₂: it is a crystalline alcohol, $C_{28}H_{43}OH$

cal·cif·er·ous (-ər əs) adj. [CALCI- + -FEROUS] producing or containing calcite

cal·cif·ic (kal sif′ik) adj. resulting from or undergoing calcification

cal·ci·fi·ca·tion (kal′sə fi kā′shən) n. **1.** a calcifying; specif., the deposition of calcium salts in body tissues **2.** a calcified substance or structure

cal·ci·fuge (kal′sə fyoōj′) n. [orig. adj., not growing in limy soil < Fr.: see CALCI- & -FUGE] a plant that grows in soils low in calcareous matter —**cal·cif·u·gous** (kal sif′yoo gəs) adj.

cal·ci·fy (kal′sə fi′) vt., vi. **-fied′, -fy′ing** [CALCI- + -FY] to change into a hard, stony substance by the deposit of lime or calcium salts

cal·ci·mine (-min′, -min) n. [< L. *calx* (gen. *calcis*), lime] a white or colored liquid of whiting or zinc white, glue, and water, used as a wash for plastered surfaces —vt. **-mined′, -min′ing** to cover with calcimine

cal·cine (kal′sin, kal sin′) vt., vi. **-cined, -cin·ing** [ME. *calcinen* < OFr. *calciner* < ML. *calcinare* (an alchemists' term)] **1.** to change to calx or powder by heat **2.** to burn to ashes or powder **3.** to oxidize —**cal·ci·na·tion** (kal′sə nā′shən) n.

cal·cite (kal′sit) n. [< L. *calx* (gen. *calcis*), lime + -ITE¹]

CALABASH

---

calcium carbonate, $CaCO_3$, with hexagonal crystallization, a mineral found in the form of limestone, chalk, and marble

cal·ci·um (kal′sē əm) *n.* [ModL. < L. *calx* (gen. *calcis*), lime] a soft, silver-white, metallic chemical element found in limestone, marble, chalk, etc., always in combination: symbol, Ca; at. wt., 40.08; at. no., 20; sp. gr., 1.55; melt. pt., 850°C; boil. pt., 1420°C

calcium arsenate a white compound, $Ca_3(AsO_4)_2$, used as an insecticide in the form of a spray or dust

calcium carbide a dark-gray, crystalline compound, CaC_2, used to produce acetylene and calcium cyanamide

calcium carbonate a white powder or colorless, crystalline compound, $CaCO_3$, found mainly in limestone, marble, and chalk, as calcite, aragonite, etc., and in bones, teeth, shells, and plant ash: used in making lime

calcium chloride a white, crystalline compound, $CaCl_2$, used in making ice, as a dehydrating agent, etc.

calcium cyanamide a white, crystalline compound, $CaCN_2$, used as a fertilizer and weed killer

calcium hydroxide slaked lime, $Ca(OH)_2$, a white, crystalline compound prepared by the action of water on calcium oxide, used in making alkalies, bleaching powder, etc.

calcium light *same as* LIMELIGHT (sense 1)

calcium oxide a white, soft, caustic solid, CaO, prepared by heating calcium carbonate; lime: used in making mortar and plaster, in ceramics, etc.

calcium phosphate any of a number of phosphates of calcium found in bones, teeth, and other animal tissues and used in medicine and in the manufacture of enamels, glass, cleaning agents, etc.

calc-sin·ter (kalk′sin′tər) *n.* [G. *kalksinter* < *kalk*, lime + *sinter*, slag] *same as* TRAVERTINE

calc·spar (-spär′) *n.* [G. *kalkspar* < *kalk*, lime + *spar*, SPAR²] *same as* CALCITE

calc-tu·fa (-tōō′fə, -tyōō′-) *n.* porous lime carbonate deposited by the waters of calcareous springs; calcareous tufa: also **calc′-tuff′** (-tuf′)

cal·cu·la·ble (kal′kyə lə b′l) *adj.* 1. that can be calculated 2. that can be relied on; dependable —**cal′cu·la·bil′i·ty** *n.* —**cal′cu·la·bly** *adv.*

cal·cu·late (kal′kyə lāt′) *vt.* -**lat′ed**, -**lat′ing** [< L. *calculatus*, pp. of *calculare*, to reckon < *calculus*, pebble used in doing arithmetic, dim. of *calx*, limestone] 1. to determine by using mathematics; compute 2. to reckon or determine by reasoning, evaluating, etc.; estimate; judge 3. to plan or intend for a purpose [a tale *calculated* to mislead us] ☆4. [Colloq.] to think, suppose, guess, etc. ☆5. [Dial.] to have in mind (*to* go, do, etc.); intend —*vi.* 1. to make a computation 2. to rely or depend (*on*)

SYN.—calculate refers to the mathematical determination of a quantity, amount, etc. and implies the use of higher mathematics [to *calculate* distances in astronomy]; **compute** suggests simpler mathematics and implies a determinable, hence precise, result [to *compute* the volume of a cylinder]; **estimate** implies the judging, usually in advance, of a quantity, cost, etc. and connotes an approximate result [to *estimate* the cost of building a house]; **reckon**, an informal substitute for **compute**, suggests the use of simple arithmetic such as can be performed mentally [to *reckon* the days before elections]

cal·cu·lat·ed (-lāt′id) *adj.* 1. done by mathematical calculation 2. undertaken or accepted after the probable results have been estimated [a *calculated* risk] 3. deliberately planned or intended [*calculated* cruelty] 4. apt or likely —**cal′cu·lat′ed·ly** *adv.*

cal·cu·lat·ing (-iŋ) *adj.* 1. shrewd or cunning, esp. in a selfish way; scheming 2. performing calculations

calculating machine a machine for doing rapid addition, subtraction, multiplication, and division

cal·cu·la·tion (kal′kyə lā′shən) *n.* [ME. *calculacioun*] 1. the act or process of calculating 2. something deduced by calculating; estimate; plan 3. careful planning or forethought, esp. with selfish motives —**cal′cu·la′tive** *adj.*

cal·cu·la·tor (kal′kyə lāt′ər) *n.* [L.] 1. a person who calculates 2. a book of tables for calculating 3. *same as* CALCULATING MACHINE

cal·cu·lous (kal′kyə ləs) *adj.* [L. *calculosus*] *Med.* caused by or having a calculus or calculi

cal·cu·lus (kal′kyə ləs) *n., pl.* -**li′** (-lī′), -**lus·es** [L.: see CALCULATE] 1. any abnormal stony mass or deposit formed in the body, as in a kidney or gallbladder 2. *Math.* *a)* a method of calculation using a special system of notation in symbols *b)* a system of mathematical analysis using the combined methods of DIFFERENTIAL CALCULUS and INTEGRAL CALCULUS

calculus of finite differences the branch of mathematics concerned with changes in a dependent variable due to discrete changes in the independent variable

calculus of variations the branch of mathematics which determines a curve so as to satisfy specified conditions and to maximize (or minimize) a quantity which depends on the curve

Cal·cut·ta (kal kut′ə) seaport in NE India, on the Hooghly River: capital of West Bengal state: pop. 2,927,000 (met. area 5,909,000)

cal·dar·i·um (kal der′ē əm) *n., pl.* -**i·a** (-ə) [L. < *caldarius*, pertaining to warming < *calidus*, warm, hot < IE. base *kel*-, warm, whence OE. *hlēowe*, warm] in ancient Roman baths, a room for taking hot baths

Cal·der (kôl′dər) 1. **Alexander**, 1898– ; U.S. abstract sculptor, esp. of mobiles and stabiles 2. **Alexander Stir·ling** (stur′liŋ), 1870–1945; U.S. sculptor: father of *prec.*

cal·de·ra (kal dir′ə) *n.* [Sp. < L. *caldarium*: see CALDARIUM] a broad, craterlike basin of a volcano, formed by an explosion or by collapse of the cone

Cal·de·rón de la Bar·ca (käl′the rôn′ *the* lä bär′kä), **Pe·dro** (pe′*th*rō) 1600–81; Sp. playwright

cal·dron (kôl′drən) *n.* [ME. & OFr. *caudron* < L. *caldaria*: see CALDARIUM] 1. a large kettle or boiler 2. a violently agitated condition like the boiling contents of a caldron

Cald·well (kôld′wel), **Ers·kine** (ur′skən) 1903– ; U.S. novelist

Ca·leb (kā′ləb) [Heb. *kāleb*, lit., dog: hence, faithful] 1. a masculine name 2. *Bible* a leader of the Israelites who, with Joshua, was permitted by God to enter Canaan: Num. 26:65; Deut. 1:36

ca·lèche, ca·leche (kə lesh′) *n.* [Fr. *calèche*: see CALASH] *same as* CALASH

Cal·e·do·ni·a (kal′ə dōn′yə, -dō′nē ə) [L.] *poet.* name for SCOTLAND —**Cal′e·do′ni·an** *adj., n.*

Caledonian Canal canal in N Scotland, extending northeastward from the Atlantic to the North Sea: 60-1/2 mi.

cal·e·fa·cient (kal′ə fā′shənt) *adj.* [L. *calefaciens*, prp. of *calefacere* < *calere*, to be warm (see CALDARIUM) + *facere*, to make] making warm; heating —*n. Med.* a substance applied to the body to give a sensation of heat

cal·e·fac·tion (kal′ə fak′shən) *n.* [L. *calefactio* < *calefacere*: see prec.] 1. the act of heating 2. the state of being made warm

cal·e·fac·to·ry (kal′ə fak′tər ē) *adj.* [LL. *calefactorius*] producing heat —*n., pl.* -**ries** [ML. *calefactorium*] a heated common room in a monastery

cal·en·dar (kal′ən dər) *n.* [ME. *calender* < L. *kalendarium*, account book < *kalendae*, CALENDS] 1. a system of determining the beginning, length, and divisions of a year and for arranging the year into days, weeks, and months 2. a table or chart that shows such an arrangement, usually for a single year 3. a list or schedule, as of pending court cases, bills coming before a legislature, planned social events, etc. —*adj.* such as that appearing on certain popular, conventional calendars [*calendar* art, a *calendar* girl] —*vt.* to enter in a calendar; specif., to schedule

calendar year the period of time from Jan. 1 through Dec. 31: distinguished from FISCAL YEAR

cal·en·der¹ (kal′ən dər) *n.* [Fr. *calendre* < ML. *calendra* < L. *cylindrus*, CYLINDER] a machine with rollers between which paper, cloth, etc. is run, as to give it a smooth or glossy finish —*vt.* [Fr. *calendrer* < the *n.*] to process (paper, cloth, etc.) in a calender —**cal′en·der·er** *n.*

cal·en·der² (kal′ən dər) *n.* [Per. *qalandar*] a member of an order of wandering dervishes among the Sufis

cal·ends (kal′əndz) *n.pl.* [often with sing. v.] [ME. *calendes* < OE. *calend*, beginning of a month < L. *kalendae*, the first of the month < *calare*, to announce solemnly < Gr. *kalein*, to proclaim] the first day of each month in the ancient Roman calendar

ca·len·du·la (kə len′jə lə) *n.* [ModL. < L. *kalendae*, calends: prob. because the plants flower in most months] any of a genus (*Calendula*) of plants of the composite family, with solitary yellow or orange flowers, esp. the pot marigold

cal·en·ture (kal′ən chər, -choor′) *n.* [Fr. < Sp. *calentura* < *calentar*, to heat < L. *calens*, prp. of *calere*, to be warm, glow] any fever caused, as in the tropics, by exposure to great heat

ca·les·cent (kə les′′nt) *adj.* [L. *calescens*, prp. of *calescere*, to grow warm < *calere*, to be warm or hot] increasing in warmth; getting hot —**ca·les′cence** *n.*

calf¹ (kaf, käf) *n., pl.* **calves**; esp. for 4, **calfs** [ME. < OE. *cealf* & ON. *kalfr* < IE. base *geleb(h)*-, to swell out (hence, swelling, fetus, offspring), whence L. *globus* & CALF², CLUB, KELP] 1. a young cow or bull 2. the young of some other large animals, as the elephant, whale, hippopotamus, seal, etc. 3. a large piece of ice broken off from an iceberg or coast glacier 4. leather from the hide of a calf; calfskin 5. [Colloq.] an awkward, callow, or silly youth —**kill the fatted calf** to make a feast of celebration or welcome: Luke 15:23

calf² (kaf, käf) *n., pl.* **calves** [ME. < ON. *kalfi*: see prec.] the fleshy back part of the leg below the knee

calf love [Colloq.] the immature love that a boy and girl may feel for each other; puppy love

calf's-foot jelly (kafs′foot′, käfs′-) an edible gelatin made by boiling calves' feet

calf·skin (kaf′skin′, käf′-) *n.* 1. the skin of a calf 2. a soft, flexible leather made from this

Cal·ga·ry (kal′gər ē) city in S Alberta, Canada: pop. 331,000

Cal·houn (kal hōōn′), **John Caldwell** 1782–1850; U.S. statesman; vice president (1825–32)

Ca·li (kä′lē) city in SW Colombia: pop. 638,000

Cal·i·ban (kal′ə ban′) [form of *canibal*, CANNIBAL, with interchanged *n* & *l*; *canibal* occurs in Hakluyt's *Voyages* (1598)] a deformed, savage creature, the slave of Prospero, in Shakespeare's *The Tempest*

cal·i·ber, cal·i·bre (kal′ə bər) *n.* [Fr. & Sp. *calibre* < *calibo* < Ar. *qālib*, a mold, last] 1. the size of a bullet or shell as measured by its diameter 2. the diameter of the bore of a gun measured in hundredths of inches or in

millimeters **3.** the diameter of a cylindrical body or of its hollowed interior **4.** degree of worth or value of a person or thing; quality or ability

cal·i·brate (kal′ə brāt′) *vt.* **-brat′ed, -brat′ing** **1.** to determine the caliber of **2.** to fix, check, or correct the graduations of (a measuring instrument, as a thermometer) —**cal′i·bra′tion** *n.* —**cal′i·bra′tor** *n.*

ca·li·ces (kā′lə sēz, kal′i-) *n. pl. of* CALIX

cal·i·che (kä lē′chē) *n.* [AmSp. < Sp. *cal*, lime < L. *calx*] **1.** impure sodium nitrate, NaNO₃, found in Chile and Peru **2.** crusted calcium carbonate formed on certain soils in dry regions by evaporation of rising solutions

cal·i·cle (kal′ə k'l) *n.* [L. *caliculus*, dim. of *calix*, a cup] *same as* CALYCULUS

cal·i·co (kal′ə kō′) *n., pl.* **-coes′, -cos′** [< CALICUT, where it was first obtained] **1.** orig., a cotton cloth from India **2.** any of several kinds of cotton cloth: in England, it is unprinted and uncolored, in the U.S., coarse and usually printed —*adj.* **1.** of calico **2.** spotted like calico [a calico cat]

☆**cal·i·co·back** (-bak′) *n. same as* HARLEQUIN BUG

☆**calico bass** *same as* CRAPPIE

☆**calico bush** *same as* MOUNTAIN LAUREL

Cal·i·cut (kal′ə kut′) *former name of* KOZHIKODE

ca·lif (kā′lif, kal′if) *n. same as* CALIPH —**cal·if·ate** (kal′ə fāt′, -fit) *n.*

Cal·i·for·ni·a (kal′ə fôr′nyə, -nē ə) [Sp., orig. name of a fabled island < ?] **1.** State of the SW U.S., on the Pacific coast: admitted, 1850; 158,693 sq. mi.; pop. 19,953,000; cap. Sacramento: abbrev. **Calif., CA** **2.** Gulf of, arm of the Pacific, between Baja California and the Mexican mainland —**Cal·i·for′ni·an** *adj., n.*

☆**California laurel** a Pacific coast shrub or tree (*Umbellularia californica*) of the laurel family, having aromatic evergreen leaves and hard wood

☆**California poppy** a plant (*Eschscholzia californica*) of the poppy family, with finely divided leaves and yellow to orange flowers

☆**California rosebay** a Pacific coast shrub or tree (*Rhododendron californicum*) of the heath family, with rosy or purplish flowers

☆**cal·i·for·ni·um** (kal′ə fôr′nē əm) *n.* [< University of CALIFORN(IA) + -IUM] a radioactive chemical element produced by intense neutron irradiation of plutonium or curium: symbol, Cf; at. wt., 251 (?); at. no., 98

ca·lig·i·nous (kə lij′ə nəs) *adj.* [L. *caliginosus* < *caligo*, darkness, gloom] [Archaic] dark; obscure

Ca·lig·u·la (kə lig′yoo lə) (born *Gaius Caesar*) 12–41 A.D.; Roman emperor (37–41 A.D.): noted for his cruelty

cal·i·pash (kal′ə pash′, kal′ə pash′) *n.* [WInd. < ? Sp. *carapacho* < *caparacho*, a shell] a greenish, jellylike, edible substance under the upper shell of a turtle

cal·i·pee (kal′ə pē′, kal′ə pē′) *n.* [var. of prec.] a yellowish, jellylike, edible substance inside the lower shell of a turtle

cal·i·per (kal′ə pər) *n.* [var. of CALIBER] **1.** [*usually pl.*] an instrument consisting of a pair of movable, curved legs fastened together at one end, used to measure the thickness or diameter of something: there are **inside calipers** and **outside calipers** **2.** *same as* CALIPER RULE **3.** thickness, as of paper or cardboard —*vt., vi.* to measure with calipers

caliper rule a graduated rule with one sliding jaw and one that is stationary

ca·liph (kā′lif, kal′if) *n.* [ME. & OFr. *calife* < Ar. *khalīfa*, caliph, successor < *khalafa*, to succeed] supreme ruler: the title taken by Mohammed's successors as secular and religious heads of Islam

cal·iph·ate (kal′ə fāt′, -fit) *n.* **1.** the rank or reign of a caliph **2.** the land ruled by a caliph

cal·i·say·a bark (kal′ə sā′ə) [AmSp. < ? Quechua] the bark of the yellow cinchona tree (*Cinchona calisaya*), from which quinine is obtained

cal·is·then·ics (kal′əs then′iks) *n.pl.* [< Gr. *kallos*, beauty + *sthenos*, strength] **1.** exercises, such as push-ups and sit-ups, to develop a strong, trim body; simple gymnastics **2.** [*with sing. v.*] the art of developing bodily strength and gracefulness by such exercises —**cal′is·then′ic, cal′is·then′i·cal** *adj.*

ca·lix (kā′liks, kal′iks) *n., pl.* **ca·li·ces** (kā′lə sēz′, kal′ə-) [L. < IE. base *kel(k)-*, cup, whence Gr. *kylix* & *kalyx*, Sans. *kalāśa-ḥ* (jug)] a cup; chalice

calk¹ (kôk) *vt. same as* CAULK —**calk′er** *n.*

calk² (kôk) *n.* [OE. *calc*, shoe, hoof < L. *calx*, a heel] **1.** the part of a horseshoe that projects downward to prevent slipping ☆**2.** a metal plate with spurs, fastened to the sole of a shoe to prevent slipping —*vt.* **1.** to fasten calks on **2.** to cut (its leg) accidentally with a calk: said of a horse

call (kôl) *vt.* [ME. *callen* < Late OE. *ceallian* & (or <) ON. *kalla* < IE. base *gal-*, to scream, shriek, whence Cym. *galw*, call, G. *klage* & (?) MIr. *gall*, swan] **1.** to say or read in a loud tone; shout; announce [to call the names of stations] **2.** to command or ask to come; summon [call him to supper] **3.** to summon to a specific duty, profession, etc. [the army called him] **4.** to convoke judicially or officially [to call a meeting] **5.** to give or apply a name to [call the baby Ann] **6.** to consider or describe as specified [I call it

silly] **7.** to awaken [call me at six] **8.** to communicate with by telephone **9.** to give orders for [to call a strike] ☆**10.** to stop or halt [game called because of rain] **11.** to demand or order payment of (a loan or bond issue) **12.** to utter or chant directions for (a square dance) ☆**13.** to imitate the sounds of in order to attract (a bird or animal) **14.** *a)* in pool, to describe (the shot one plans to make) *b)* to predict ☆**15.** *a)* Poker to require (a player) to show his hand by equaling his bet *b)* to challenge on, or force to account for, something said or done *c)* to expose (someone's bluff) by such action ☆**16.** *Sports* to declare officially to be [the umpire *called* him out] —*vi.* **1.** to speak in a loud tone; shout **2.** to utter its characteristic cry, as a bird or animal **3.** to visit for a short while **4.** to telephone ☆**5.** *Poker* to require a player to show his hand by equaling his bet —*n.* **1.** an act or instance of calling **2.** a loud utterance; shout **3.** *a)* the distinctive cry of an animal or bird *b)* a sound made in imitation of such a cry to attract an animal or bird *c)* a device that makes such a sound **4.** *a)* a summons to a meeting, rehearsal, etc. *b)* the calling up of a quota of men for military service **5.** a signal on a bugle, drum, etc. **6.** an economic demand, as for a product **7.** an inner urging toward a certain action or profession, esp. a religious vocation regarded as divinely inspired **8.** an invitation to accept a position as a minister, teacher, etc. **9.** power to attract or allure [the *call* of the wild] **10.** need; obligation; occasion [no *call* for tears] **11.** an order or demand for payment **12.** a market demand for a particular commodity **13.** a brief visit, esp. a formal or professional visit **14.** a direction given by a caller of square dances **15.** *same as* ROLL CALL **16.** an option permitting the holder to acquire a specified amount of stock or a commodity at a given price during a stated period: see also PUT **17.** *Bridge* a bid **18.** *Sports* an official's decision or ruling —**call back 1.** to ask or command to come back **2.** to telephone again or in return —**call down 1.** to invoke ☆**2.** [Colloq.] to scold sharply; rebuke —**call for 1.** to demand; require **2.** to come and get; stop for —**call forth** to bring into action or existence —**call in 1.** to summon for help or consultation **2.** to take out of circulation, as coin or bonds **3.** to ask for payment of —**call into question** to raise a question or doubt about —**call off 1.** to order away; divert **2.** to read aloud in order from a list **3.** to cancel (a scheduled event) —**call on** (or **upon**) **1.** to visit briefly **2.** to ask (a person) to speak, do something, etc. —**call out 1.** to speak aloud; shout **2.** to summon into action **3.** to summon (workers) to strike —**call time** *Sports* to suspend play temporarily —**call up 1.** to make one remember; recall **2.** to summon, esp. for military duty **3.** to telephone —**on call 1.** available when called for or summoned **2.** payable on demand —**within call** close enough to hear if called

SYN.—**call**, in this comparison, is the basic word signifying to request the presence of someone at some place [he *called* the waiter over]; **summon**, the more formal term, implies authority or peremptoriness in the request [to *summon* a witness]; **convoke** and **convene** refer to the summoning of a group to assemble as for deliberation or legislation, but **convoke** implies greater authority or formality [to *convene* a class, to *convoke* a congress]; **invite** suggests a courteous request for someone's presence, esp. as a guest or participant, and usually suggests that the decision to come rests with the invited

cal·la (kal′ə) *n.* [ModL. (so named by Linnaeus) < L., a plant (of unc. kind)] **1.** any of several plants (genus *Zantedeschia*) of the arum family, with a conspicuous white, yellow, or pink spathe surrounding a club-shaped yellow spadix **2.** the wild calla (*Calla palustris*), a bog plant of the arum family, having greenish-white spathes and bearing bright red berries Also **calla lily**

call·a·ble (kôl′ə b'l) *adj.* that can be called; specif., *a)* that must be paid upon demand, as a loan *b)* that must be presented for payment upon notice, as a bond

cal·lant (kāl′ənt) *n.* [Du. *kalant*, fellow, customer < dial. Fr. *calant*, for Fr. *chalant*, customer] [Scot.] a young fellow; boy; lad: also **cal′lan** (-ən)

Cal·la·o (kä yä′ō) seaport in W Peru: pop. 161,000

Cal·las (kal′əs, kä′läs), **Maria** (**Meneghini**) 1923– ; Gr. operatic soprano, born in the U.S.

☆**call·board** (kôl′bôrd′) *n. Theater* a bulletin board backstage for posting instructions, rehearsal times, etc.

call·boy (-boi′) *n.* **1.** a boy who calls actors when it is time for them to go on the stage **2.** a bellboy

call·er¹ (-ər) *n.* **1.** a person or thing that calls **2.** a person who makes a short visit —*SYN.* see VISITOR

cal·ler² (kal′ər, kä′lər) *adj.* [MScot.; ? var. of *calver*, fresh] [Scot.] **1.** fresh: said of food **2.** fresh and cool: said of the weather, a breeze, etc.

Cal·les (kä′yes), **Plu·tar·co E·lí·as** (plōō tär′kō e lē′äs) 1877–1945; Mex. general; president of Mexico (1924–28)

☆**call girl** a prostitute who is called by telephone to assignations

cal·lig·ra·phy (kə lig′rə fē) *n.* [Gr. *kalligraphia* < *kalligraphos* < *kallos*, beauty + *graphein*, to write] **1.** beautiful handwriting, esp. as an art **2.** handwriting; penmanship —**cal·lig′ra·pher** *n.* —**cal·lig′ra·phist** *n.* —**cal·li·graph·ic** (kal′ə graf′ik) *adj.*

call·ing (kôl′iŋ) n. **1.** the action of one that calls **2.** one's occupation, profession, or trade **3.** an inner urging toward some profession or activity; vocation

☆**calling card** a small card with one's name, and sometimes one's address, on it, used in making visits

Cal·li·o·pe (kə lī′ə pē′; for n., also kal′ē ōp′) [L. < Gr. Kalliopē, the beautiful-voiced < kallos, beauty + ops, voice] Gr. Myth. the Muse of eloquence and epic poetry —☆n. [c-] a keyboard instrument like an organ, having a series of steam whistles

cal·li·op·sis (kal′ē äp′sis) n. [ModL. < Gr. kallos, beauty + opsis, appearance] same as COREOPSIS

cal·li·per (kal′ə pər) n., vt. same as CALIPER

cal·li·pyg·i·an (kal′ə pij′ē ən) adj. [Gr. kallipygos < kallos, beauty + pygē, buttocks] having shapely buttocks

cal·lis·then·ics (kal′əs then′iks) n.pl. same as CALISTHENICS —**cal′lis·then′ic** adj.

Cal·lis·to (kə lis′tō) [L. < Gr. Kallistō] Gr. & Rom. Myth. **1.** a nymph loved by Zeus and changed into a bear by Hera **2.** the fifth satellite of Jupiter

call letters the letters, and sometimes the numbers, that identify a radio transmitting station

☆**call loan** a loan that must be repaid on demand

☆**call money 1.** money borrowed as a call loan **2.** money available for call loans

☆**call number** a group of numbers and letters placed on a book to indicate its location in a library

cal·lose (kal′ōs) n. [< L. callosus, CALLOUS] a carbohydrate in plant cells that plugs the sieve pores when the sieve tubes stop functioning

cal·los·i·ty (ka läs′ə tē, kə-) n. [ME. & OFr. calosite < L. callositas] **1.** the quality or state of being callous, hardened, or unfeeling **2.** pl. **-ties** a hardened, thickened place on skin or bark; callus

cal·lous (kal′əs) adj. [ME. < L. callosus < callum, hard skin] **1.** a) having calluses b) thick and hardened **2.** lacking pity, mercy, etc.; unfeeling; insensitive —vt., vi. to make or become callous —**cal′lous·ly** adv. —**cal′lous·ness** n.

cal·low (kal′ō) adj. [ME. calwe < OE. calu, bare, bald < IE. base *gal-, bald, naked, whence Czech holý, naked, G. kahl, bald] **1.** still lacking the feathers needed for flying; unfledged **2.** young and inexperienced; immature —**cal′low·ness** n.

☆**call rate** the rate of interest on call loans

☆**call slip** a form on which a library patron lists the title and call number of a desired book

call to quarters Mil. a bugle call shortly before taps, notifying soldiers to retire to their quarters

call-up (kôl′up′) n. Mil. an order, as to those in the reserves, to report for active duty

cal·lus (kal′əs) n., pl. **-lus·es** [L., var. of callum, hard skin] **1.** a hardened, thickened place on the skin **2.** the hard substance that forms at the break in a fractured bone and serves to reunite the parts **3.** a mass of undifferentiated cells that develops over cuts or wounds on plants as at the ends of stem or leaf cuttings —vi., vt. to develop or cause to develop a callus

calm (käm; occas. kälm) n. [ME. & OFr. calme < It. calma < LL. (Vulgate: Job 30:30) cauma, heat, heat of the day (hence, in It., time to rest, quiet: cf. SIESTA) < Gr. kauma, heat, esp. of the sun < kaiein, to burn; It. sp. infl. by L. calere, to be hot] **1.** lack of wind or motion; stillness **2.** lack of agitation or excitement; tranquillity; serenity **3.** Meteorol. a condition in which the air movement is less than one mile per hour: see BEAUFORT SCALE —adj. **1.** without wind or motion; still; quiet **2.** not agitated or excited; tranquil —vt., vi. to make or become calm (often with down) —**calm′ness** n.

SYN.—**calm**, basically applied to the weather, suggests a total absence of agitation or disturbance [a calm sea, mind, answer]; **tranquil** implies a more intrinsic or permanent peace and quiet than calm [they lead a tranquil life]; **serene** suggests an exalted tranquillity [he died with a serene smile on his lips]; **placid** implies an undisturbed or unruffled calm and is sometimes used in jocular disparagement to suggest dull equanimity [she's as placid as a cow]; **peaceful** suggests a lack of turbulence or disorder [a peaceful gathering] —ANT. **stormy, agitated, excited**

calm·a·tive (käm′ə tiv; occas. käl′mə-) adj. calming; soothing; sedative —n. a sedative medicine

calm·ly (käm′lē; occas. kälm′-) adv. **1.** in a calm manner; tranquilly **2.** in a cool, bold way; brazenly

cal·o·mel (kal′ə mel′, -məl) n. [Fr. < Gr. kalos, beautiful + melas, black] mercurous chloride, $HgCl$, a white, tasteless powder, formerly used as a cathartic, for intestinal worms, etc.

ca·lor·ic (kə lôr′ik, -lär′-) n. [Fr. calorique < L. calor, heat] **1.** an imagined substance to which the phenomena of burning and oxidation were formerly attributed **2.** [Archaic] heat —adj. **1.** of heat **2.** of or pertaining to calories —**ca·lor′i·cal·ly** adv.

cal·o·rie (kal′ə rē) n. [Fr. < L. calor, heat: for IE. base see CALDARIUM] **1.** the amount of heat needed to raise the temperature of one gram of water one degree centigrade: also **small calorie, gram calorie 2.** [occas. C-] the amount of heat needed to raise the temperature of one kilogram of water one degree centigrade: also **large calorie, great calorie, kilogram calorie 3.** a) a unit equal to the large calorie, used for measuring the energy produced by food

when oxidized in the body b) an amount of food able to produce one large calorie of energy

cal·o·rif·ic (kal′ə rif′ik) adj. [Fr. calorifique < L. calorificus < calor, heat + facere, to make, produce] producing heat

cal·o·rim·e·ter (kal′ə rim′ə tər) n. [< L. calor, heat + -METER] an apparatus for measuring amounts of heat, as in chemical combination, friction, etc.

cal·o·rim·e·try (kal′ə rim′ə trē) n. [< L. calor, heat + -METRY] measurement of the quantity of heat —**cal·o·ri·met·ric** (kə lôr′i met′rik, ka lōr′ə-), **cal′o·ri·met′ri·cal** adj.

cal·o·rize (kal′ə rīz′) vt. **-rized′, -riz′ing** [L. calor, heat + -IZE] Metallurgy to coat (steel) with aluminum by heating in a closed retort containing aluminum powder: the aluminum alloys with the steel surface and forms a protective coating against oxidation

cal·o·ry (kal′ə rē) n., pl. **-ries** same as CALORIE

ca·lotte (kə lät′) n. [Fr. < It. calotta < ? Gr. kalyptra, kind of hood < kalyptein, to cover] **1.** a small, brimless cap **2.** a skullcap worn by Roman Catholic clergymen

cal·o·yer (kal′ə yər, kə loi′ər) n. [Fr. < It. caloiero < ModGr. kalogēros, monk < kalos, beautiful + gēros, gēras, old age] a monk of the Orthodox Eastern Church

cal·pac, cal·pack (kal′pak) n. [Turk. qālpāk] a large cap made of felt or sheepskin, worn in some parts of the Near East

Cal·pe (käl′pā) ancient name of GIBRALTAR: see PILLARS OF HERCULES

calque (kalk) n. [Fr., an imitation, tracing < calquer, to trace < It. calcare, to press, trample < L., to tread: see CAULK] Linguis. **1.** a borrowing by which a specialized meaning of a word or phrase in one language is transferred to another language by a literal translation [masterpiece is a calque from German meisterstück] **2.** same as REDUPLICATION

cal·trop, cal·trap (kal′trəp) n. [ME. calketrappe < OE. calcatrippe, star thistle, caltrop: see CALK² & TRAP¹] **1.** an iron device with four spikes, placed on the ground so that one spike sticks up to hinder enemy cavalry **2.** a similar device used to puncture pneumatic tires **3.** any of a number of plants (family Zygophyllaceae) with spiny flowering parts or fruits, as the star thistle, the water chestnut, etc.

cal·u·met (kal′yə met′, -mit; kal′yə met′) n. [Fr., reed pipe, dim. of OFr. chalemel < LL. calamellus, dim. of L. calamus, a reed (see CALAMUS)] a long-stemmed ceremonial pipe, smoked by N. American Indians as a token of peace

CALUMET

ca·lum·ni·ate (kə lum′nē āt′) vt., vi. **-at′ed, -at′ing** [< L. calumniatus, pp. of calumniari, to slander < calumnia: see CALUMNY] to spread false and harmful statements about; slander —**ca·lum′ni·a′tion** n. —**ca·lum′ni·a′tor** n.

ca·lum·ni·ous (kə lum′nē əs) adj. [L. calumniosus, full of tricks, swindling] full of calumnies; slanderous —**ca·lum′ni·ous·ly** adv.

cal·um·ny (kal′əm nē) n., pl. **-nies** [Fr. calomnie < L. calumnia, trickery, slander < IE. base *kēl-, kol-, to deceive, confuse, whence OE. hol, guile] **1.** a false and malicious statement meant to hurt someone's reputation **2.** the uttering of such a statement; slander

☆**cal·u·tron** (kal′yə trän′) n. [CAL(IFORNIA) U(niversity), where developed + -TRON] a large, electromagnetic mass spectrometer used for separating isotopes in quantity

Cal·va·dos (kal′və dōs′, kal′və dōs′) n. [< Calvados, department in NW France, where chiefly distilled] [sometimes c-] a French brandy distilled from apple cider

cal·var·i·um (kal ver′ē əm) n., pl. **-var′i·a** (-ə) < ModL. < L. calvaria, skull] the upper, domed part of the skull: also **cal·var′i·a** —**cal·var′i·al, cal·var′i·an** adj.

Cal·va·ry (kal′vər ē) [LL. (Ecc.) Calvaria < L., skull; used to translate Gr. kranion, skull (cf. CRANIUM), used by the Evangelists to translate Aram. gulgulthā, Golgotha, lit., skull: so named prob. from the shape of the place] Bible the place near Jerusalem where the crucifixion of Jesus took place: Luke 23:33, Matt. 27:33 —n. [c-] pl. **-ries** a) an outdoor representation of the crucifixion of Jesus b) any experience involving intense pain or anguish

calve (kav, käv) vi., vt. **calved, calv′ing** [ME. calven < OE. cealfian < cealf, CALF¹] **1.** to give birth to (a calf) **2.** to release (a mass of ice): said of a glacier or an iceberg

Cal·vert (kal′vərt), **George** see Lord BALTIMORE

calves (kavz, kävz) n. pl. of CALF

Cal·vin (kal′vin) [ModL. Calvinus < Fr. Cauvin, Chauvin, prob. < L. calvus, bald] **1.** a masculine name **2. John,** (born Jean Caulvin or Cauvin or Chauvin) 1509–64; Fr. Protestant reformer

Cal·vin·ism (-iz′m) n. **1.** the theological system of John Calvin and his followers, which emphasizes the doctrines of predestination and salvation solely by God's grace **2.** belief and practice based on this system, associated with a stern moral code —**Cal′vin·ist** n., adj. —**Cal′vin·is·tic, Cal′vin·is′ti·cal** adj. —**Cal′vin·is′ti·cal·ly** adv.

cal·vi·ti·es (kal vish′i ēz′) *n.* [L. < *calvus*, bald] baldness

calx (kalks) *n., pl.* **calx′es, cal′ces** (kal′sēz) [L., small stone, lime] the ashy powder left after a metal or mineral has been calcined

ca·ly·ces (kā′lə sēz′, kal′ə-) *n. alt. pl.* of CALYX

ca·ly·cine (kā′lə sin, -sīn′; kal′ə-) *adj.* of or like a calyx: also **ca·lyc·i·nal** (kə lis′ə n′l)

ca·ly·cle (-k′l) *n.* [see CALYCULUS] *same as* EPICALYX

ca·lyc·u·lus (kə lik′yoo ləs) *n., pl.* **-li** (-lī′) [L., dim. of *calyx*, CALYX] *Anat., Zool.* a small, cuplike part, as a taste bud, or a cuplike depression, as in a coral skeleton

Cal·y·don (kal′ə dän′) ancient Greek city in S Aetolia —**Cal′y·do′ni·an** (-dō′nē ən, -dōn′yən) *adj.*

Calydonian boar *Gr. Myth.* a boar sent by Artemis to scourge the fields of Calydon and killed by Meleager

Ca·lyp·so (kə lip′sō) [L. < Gr. *Kalypsō*] in Homer's *Odyssey*, a sea nymph who kept Odysseus on her island for seven years —*n.* [c-] an orchid (*Calypso bulbosa*) growing in boggy regions of the Northern Hemisphere: its solitary white flower has purple or yellow markings

ca·lyp·so (kə lip′sō) *adj.* [< ? prec.] designating or of songs improvised and sung as originally by natives of Trinidad: they are satirical ballads, usually topical, characterized by wrenched syllabic stress and syncopated rhythms —*n.* a calypso song or calypso music

ca·lyp·tra (kə lip′trə) *n.* [ModL. < Gr. *kalyptra*, covering for the head, veil < *kalyptein*, to conceal, cover: for IE. base see CONCEAL] **1.** the remains of the female sex organ, or archegonium, of a moss, forming the caplike covering of the spore case **2.** any similar covering of a fruit or flower —**ca·lyp′trate** (-trāt) *adj.*

ca·lyp·tro·gen (kə lip′trə jən) *n.* [< prec. + -GEN] *Bot.* the layer of actively dividing cells at the tip of a root in many plants, as grasses, that produces the root cap cells

ca·lyx (kā′liks, kal′iks) *n., pl.* **ca·lyx·es, ca·ly·ces** (kā′lə sēz′, kal′ə-) [L., outer covering, pod < Gr. *kalyx:* for IE. base see CALIX] **1.** the outer whorl of protective leaves, or sepals, of a flower, usually green **2.** *Zool.* a cuplike part or cavity

cam (kam) *n.* [Du. *cam*, orig., a COMB[1]] a moving piece of machinery, such as a wheel, projection on a wheel, etc., which gives an eccentric rotation or a reciprocating motion to another wheel, a roller, shaft, etc., or receives such motion from it

Ca·ma·guëy (kä′mä gwä′) city in EC Cuba: pop. 191,000

ca·ma·ra·de·rie (käm′ə räd′ər ē, kam′-) *n.* [Fr. < *camarade:* see COMRADE] loyalty and warm, friendly feeling among comrades; comradeship

PLUNGER   PLUNGER   CAM   SHAFT   SHAFT   CAM   CAM

cam·a·ril·la (kam′ə ril′ə; *Sp.* kä′mä rēl′yä) *n.* [Sp., dim. of *camara*, chamber < L. *camera:* see CAMERA] **1.** a small meeting room **2.** a group of secret or confidential, esp. unofficial, advisers; cabal

☆**cam·ass, cam·as** (kam′əs) *n.* [AmInd. (Chinook) < *chamas*, sweet] any of a genus (*Camassia*) of N. American plants of the lily family, with sweet, edible bulbs and racemes of drooping, bluish flowers: see also DEATH CAMASS

cam·ber (kam′bər) *n.* [OFr., dial. var. of *chambre*, bent < L. *camur*, crooked, arched] **1.** a slight convex curve of a surface, as of a road, a ship's deck, a beam, etc. **2.** in automotive wheel alignment, a slight tilt given to each of a pair of wheels so that the bottoms are closer together than the tops **3.** *Aeron.* the arching curve of an airfoil from the leading edge to the trailing edge —*vt., vi.* [Fr. *cambrer*] to arch slightly; curve convexly

Cam·ber·well (kam′bər wel) metropolitan borough of London, south of the Thames: pop. 174,000

cam·bist (kam′bist) *n.* [Fr. *cambiste* < It. *cambista* < *cambiare*, to exchange < LL. *cambiare* < L. *cambire:* see CHANGE] **1.** a dealer in foreign bills of exchange **2.** a book that gives the rates of foreign exchange and equivalents of measure, weights, etc.

cam·bi·um (kam′bē əm) *n.* [LL., change: see prec.] a layer of formative cells between the wood and bark in woody plants: the cells increase by division and differentiate to form new wood and bark

Cam·bo·di·a (kam bō′dē ə) country in the S Indochinese peninsula: 69,884 sq. mi.; pop. 6,701,000; cap. Phnom Penh See INDOCHINA, map

Cam·bo·di·an *adj.* of Cambodia, its people, language, etc. —*n.* **1.** a native or inhabitant of Cambodia **2.** Khmer, the official language of Cambodia

cam·bo·gi·a (kam bō′jē ə) *n. same as* GAMBOGE

Cam·bri·a (kam′brē ə) [ML., var. of *Cumbria* < base of OCelt. *Combroges*, lit., co-landers, whence Celt. *Cymry*, Welshmen] *poet. name for* WALES

Cam·bri·an (-ən) *adj.* **1.** of Cambria; Welsh **2.** designating or of the first geological period in the Paleozoic Era, marked by a profusion of marine animals, esp. trilobites and brachiopods —*n.* a native or inhabitant of Cambria

Welshman —**the Cambrian** the Cambrian Period or its rocks: see GEOLOGY, chart

Cambrian Mountains mountain system of Wales

cam·bric (kām′brik) *n.* [< *Kambryk*, Fl. name of *Cambrai*, city in N France, where orig. made < L. *Camaracum*, name of the town] **1.** a very fine, thin linen **2.** a cotton cloth like this

☆**cambric tea** a hot drink of milk, sugar, and water or, often, weak tea

Cam·bridge (kām′brij) [ME. *Caumbrigge* < OE. *Grantanbrycge*, lit., bridge over the Granta (now called the Cam) River] **1.** city in EC England, in Cambridgeshire: pop. 96,000: site of Cambridge University **2.** *same as* CAMBRIDGESHIRE **3.** city in E Mass., across the Charles River from Boston: pop. 100,000

Cam·bridge·shire (-shir) **1.** county in EC England: 492 sq. mi.; pop. 195,000; county seat, Cambridge **2.** a region consisting of this county and Isle of Ely

Cam·by·ses (II) (kam bī′sēz) ?-522 B.C.; king of Persia: son of CYRUS (*the Great*)

Cam·den (kam′dən) [after Charles Pratt, Earl of *Camden* (1714–94)] city in SW N.J., on the Delaware River, opposite Philadelphia: pop. 103,000

came[1] (kām) *pt.* of COME

came[2] (kām) *n.* [< ? MDu. *kaam*] a grooved lead strip used to fasten together panes of glass, tile, etc.

cam·el (kam′'l) *n.* [ME. < OE. or OFr. < L. *camelus* < Gr. *kamēlos* < Heb. *gāmāl* (or) < Egypt. *kamāl*] **1.** either of two species of large, domesticated, cud-chewing mammals (genus *Camelus*) with a humped back, long neck, and large, cushioned feet: capable of storing water in its body tissue, the camel is the common beast of burden in Asian and African deserts: see BACTRIAN CAMEL and DROMEDARY **2.** a watertight cylinder used to raise sunken ships, wrecks, etc.: see CAISSON (sense 5) **3.** *Naut.* a wooden float serving as a fender alongside a dock —*adj.* of the tan color of camel's hair

cam·el·eer (kam′ə lir′) *n.* a camel driver

ca·mel·li·a (kə mēl′yə, -mēl′ē ə) *n.* [< *Camelli*, It. form of the name of G. J. *Kamel*, 18th-c. Moravian Jesuit missionary who brought specimens from Japan to London] **1.** any of a genus (*Camellia*) of Asiatic evergreen trees and shrubs of the tea family, with glossy evergreen leaves and waxy, roselike flowers **2.** the flower

ca·mel·o·pard (kə mel′ə pärd′) *n.* [LL. *camelopardus* < L. *camelopardalus* < Gr. *kamēlopardalis* < *kamēlos*, camel + *pardalis*, pard, leopard: so called from neck (like a camel's) and spots (like a pard's)] *early name for the* GIRAFFE —[C-] *same as* CAMELOPARDUS

Ca·mel·o·par·dus (kə mel′ə pär′dəs) [see prec.] a N constellation between Ursa Major and Cassiopeia: also **Ca·mel′o·par′da·lis** (-pär′də lis)

Cam·e·lot (kam′ə lät′) the legendary English town where King Arthur had his court and Round Table

camel's hair 1. the hair of the camel **2.** cloth made of this hair, sometimes mixed with wool, etc.: it is usually light tan and very soft —**cam′el's-hair′, cam′el-hair′** *adj.*

camel's-hair brush an artist's small brush, made of hair from a squirrel's tail

Cam·em·bert (cheese) (kam′əm ber′) [< *Camembert*, village in Normandy, where first made] a soft, creamy, rich cheese

Ca·me·nae (kə mē′nē) *n.pl. Rom. Myth.* nymphs with prophetic powers who inhabited springs and fountains: later identified with the Greek Muses

cam·e·o (kam′ē ō′, kam′yō) *n., pl.* **-os′** [It. *cammeo* < ML. *camaeus* < ?] **1.** a carving in relief on certain stratified gems (sardonyx, agate, etc.) or shells so that the raised design, often a head in profile, is usually in a layer of different color from its background: opposed to INTAGLIO **2.** a gem, shell, etc. so carved **3.** *a)* a minor, but well-defined role in a play, movie, etc., esp. when performed by a notable actor *b)* a fine bit of descriptive writing

cam·er·a (kam′ər ə, kam′rə) *n., pl.* **-er·as;** also for 1, **-er·ae′** (-ə rē′) [L. *camera, camara*, a vault < Gr. *kamara*, vaulted chamber] **1.** a chamber; specif., the private office of a judge **2.** *same as* CAMERA OBSCURA **3.** [< CAMERA OBSCURA] a device for taking photographs, consisting essentially of a closed box containing a sensitized plate or film on which an image is formed when light enters the box through a lens or hole **4.** *TV* that part of the transmitter which consists of a lens and a special cathode-ray tube containing a plate on which the image to be televised is projected for transformation into electrical signals —**in camera** in privacy or secrecy

cam·er·al (-ər əl) *adj.* [G. *kameral* < ML. *cameralis:* see CAMERA] of the chamber of a judge, legislature, etc.

camera lu·ci·da (loo′si də) [L., light chamber: see CAMERA & LUCID] an apparatus containing a prism or an arrangement of mirrors for reflecting an object on a surface so that its outline may be traced: often used with a microscope

cam·er·a·man (-man′, -mən) *n., pl.* **-men′** (-men′, -mən) an operator of a camera, esp. of a motion-picture or television camera

camera ob·scu·ra (äb skyoor′ə, əb-) [L., dark chamber:

see CAMERA & OBSCURE] a camera consisting of a dark chamber with a lens or opening through which an image is projected in natural colors onto an opposite surface

cam·er·a-shy (-shī') *adj.* unwilling to be photographed

cam·er·len·go (kam'ər leŋ'gō) *n.* [It. *camarlingo*, chamberlain < Gmc. *kamerlinc*: see CHAMBERLAIN] *R.C.Ch.* a cardinal who has charge of the papal treasury and accounts: also **cam'er·lin'go** (-liŋ'-)

Cam·er·on (kam'ər ən), **Richard** 1648?–80; Scot. minister & Covenanter whose followers formed the Reformed Presbyterian Church (1743)

Cam·e·roon (kam'ə rōōn') *same as* CAMEROUN

Cam·e·roons (-rōōnz') region in W Africa formerly consisting of two trust territories, **French Cameroons** (in 1960 forming the republic of CAMEROUN) and **British Cameroons** (in 1961 divided between Cameroun and Nigeria) —**Cam·e·roon'i·an** (-rōō'nē ən) *adj., n.*

Cam·e·roun (kam'ə rōōn'; *Fr.* kȧ mrōōn') 1. country in WC Africa, on the Gulf of Guinea: c. 183,000 sq. mi.; pop. 5,229,000; cap. Yaoundé: cf. CAMEROONS 2. mountain in W Cameroun: 13,350 ft. —**Cam'e·roun'i·an** *adj., n.*

cam gear a gear not centered on the shaft, used where discontinuous action is required

Ca·mil·la (kə mil'ə) a feminine name: see CAMILLE

Ca·mille (kə mēl') [Fr. < L. *camilla*, virgin of unblemished character] a feminine name: var. *Camilla*

cam·i·on (kam'ē ən; *Fr.* kȧ myōn') *n.* [Fr.] a motor truck or heavy dray wagon

cam·i·sa·do (kam'i sā'dō, -säd'ō) *n.* [Sp. *camisada* < *camisa*: see CHEMISE] [Archaic] an attack at night, orig. one in which shirts were worn over armor for identification: also **cam'i·sade'** (-sād')

ca·mise (kə mēs') *n.* [Ar. *qamis* < LL. *camisia*: see CHEMISE] a loose-fitting shirt, smock, or gown

cam·i·sole (kam'ə sōl') *n.* [Fr. < Sp. *camisola*, dim. of *camisa*: see CHEMISE] 1. formerly, a kind of jacket for men 2. a woman's sleeveless, often lace-trimmed underwaist, orig. a corset cover, now worn under a sheer blouse 3. a woman's short negligee

cam·let (kam'lit) *n.* [ME. *chamelet* < OFr. *chamelot*, prob. < Ar. *khamlat* < *khaml*, pile, plush] 1. formerly, an Oriental fabric of camel's hair or Angora wool 2. a satiny fabric of silk and wool or goat's hair 3. a garment made of either of these fabrics

Cam·maerts (käm'ärts), **É·mile** (**Léon**) (ā mēl') 1878–1953; Belgian poet in England

Ca·mões (kə moinsh'), **Lu·iz Vaz de** (lōō ēsh' vàzh də) 1524?–80; Port. epic poet: Eng. name **Cam·o·ëns** (kam'ō enz')

cam·o·mile (kam'ə mīl', -mēl') *n. same as* CHAMOMILE

Ca·mor·ra (kə môr'ə; *It.* kä mȯr'rä) *n.* [Sp., quarrel, dispute] 1. a secret society organized in Naples, Italy, c. 1820, which became notorious for terror, blackmail, and violence 2. [c-] any secret society like this —**Ca·mor'rist, ca·mor'rist n.**

cam·ou·flage (kam'ə fläzh', -fläj') *n.* [Fr. < *camoufler*, to disguise < *camouflet*, puff of smoke, smoke bomb < ? *ca-*, collective prefix + *moufler*, to muffle, cover up] 1. the disguising of troops, ships, guns, etc. to conceal them from the enemy, as by the use of paint, nets, leaves, etc. in patterns merging with the background 2. a disguise or concealment of this kind 3. any device or action used to conceal or mislead; deception —*vt., vi.* **-flaged', -flag'ing** to disguise (a thing or person) in order to conceal —**cam'ou·flag'er n.**

camp (kamp) *n.* [Fr. < It. *campo* < L. *campus*, a field: see CAMPUS] 1. *a*) a place where tents, huts, barracks, or other more or less temporary structures are put up, as for soldiers in training or in bivouac *b*) military life 2. *a*) a group of people who support or advance a common opinion, cause, etc. *b*) the position taken by such a group 3. a tent, cabin, etc., or a group of these, used for temporary lodging, as by hunters, fishermen, etc. 4. a place in the country for vacationers, esp. children, with outdoor recreation, often organized and supervised 5. the people living in a camp ☆6. [Slang] [orig., homosexual jargon] banality, mediocrity, artifice, ostentation, etc. so extreme as to amuse or have a perversely sophisticated appeal —☆*adj.* [Slang] characterized by camp (*n.* 6) —*vi.* 1. to set up a camp; encamp 2. to live or stay in or as if in a camp (often with *out*) —*vt.* 1. to put into a camp 2. to provide with accommodations — **break camp** to dismantle a camp; pack up camping equipment and go away —☆**camp it up** [Slang] to behave in a camp way

Camp (kamp), **Walter** (**Chauncey**) 1859–1925; U.S. football authority and coach

Cam·pa·gna di Ro·ma (käm pä'nyä dē rō'mä) plain in C Italy, around Rome: c. 800 sq. mi.

cam·paign (kam pān') *n.* [Fr. *campagne*, open country suited to military maneuvers; hence, military expedition < It. *campagna* < LL. *campania*, level country < L. *campus*, a field: see CAMPUS] 1. a series of military operations with a particular objective in a war 2. a series of organized, planned actions for a particular purpose, as for electing a candidate —*vi.* to participate in, or go on, a campaign —*SYN.* see BATTLE —**cam·paign'er n.**

Cam·pa·ni·a (kam pā'nē ə; *It.* käm pä'nyä) region in S Italy, on the Tyrrhenian Sea: 5,249 sq. mi.; pop. 4,756,000; chief city, Naples —**Cam·pa'ni·an** *adj., n.*

cam·pa·ni·le (kam'pə nē'lē) *n., pl.* **-les, -li** (-lē) [It. < LL. *campana*, a bell] a bell tower, esp. one that stands apart from any other building

cam·pa·nol·o·gy (kam'pə näl'ə jē) *n.* [< LL. *campana*, a bell + -LOGY] 1. the study of bells 2. the art of bell ringing —**cam'pa·nol'o·gist n.**

cam·pan·u·la (kam pan'yoo lə) *n.* [ModL. < LL., dim. of *campana*, a bell] any of a genus (*Campanula*) of plants of the bellflower family, as the Canterbury bell, harebell, etc.

cam·pan·u·late (kam pan'yoo lit, -lāt') *adj.* [< CAMPANULA + -ATE¹] shaped like a bell

Camp·bell (kam'b'l, -'l) 1. **Alexander**, 1788–1866; U.S. clergyman, born in Ireland: founder of the Disciples of Christ 2. Mrs. **Patrick**, (born *Beatrice Stella Tanner*) 1865–1940; Eng. actress 3. **Thomas**, 1777–1844; Scot. poet

Camp·bell-Ban·ner·man (-ban'ər mən), **Sir Henry** 1836–1908; Brit. statesman; prime minister (1905–08)

CAMPANILE

camp chair a lightweight folding chair

camp·craft (kamp'kraft', -kräft') *n.* the art or practice of camping outdoors

campeachy wood *same as* LOGWOOD (sense 1)

Cam·pe·che (kam pe'chē; *Sp.* käm pe'che) 1. state of SE Mexico, in the W Yucatán peninsula: 19,672 sq. mi.; pop. 186,000 2. capital of this state, a port on the Gulf of Campeche: pop. 44,000 3. **Gulf** (or **Bay**) **of**, arm of the Gulf of Mexico, west of the Yucatán peninsula

camp·er (kamp'ər) *n.* 1. a person who vacations at a camp ☆2. any of various motor vehicles or trailers equipped for camping out

‡**cam·pe·si·no** (käm'pe sē'nō) *n., pl.* **-nos** (-nōs) [Sp.] a peasant or farm worker

cam·pes·tral (kam pes'trəl) *adj.* [< L. *campester* (gen. *campestris*), of a level field < *campus*, field (see CAMPUS) + -AL] [Rare] of or having to do with fields or the countryside

camp·fire (kamp'fīr') *n.* 1. an outdoor fire at a camp 2. a social gathering around such a fire

☆**campfire girl** a member of the **Camp Fire Girls**, a girls' organization, founded in 1910, to promote a program of health and character-building activities

camp follower 1. a civilian who goes along with an army, esp. as a vendor of goods or services or as a prostitute 2. a nonmember who is associated with a certain group

☆**camp·ground** (-ground') *n.* 1. a place where a camp is set up 2. a place where a camp meeting or religious revival is held

cam·phene (kam'fēn, kam fēn') *n.* [CAMPH(OR) + -ENE] a colorless, crystalline compound, $C_{10}H_{16}$, prepared synthetically from pinene and used like camphor

cam·phire (kam'fīr) *n.* [var. of CAMPHOR: used in KJV (S. of Sol. 1:14) to transl. Heb. *kōpher*, henna plant] *same as* HENNA

cam·phol (kam'fōl) *n.* [CAMPH(OR) + -OL¹] *same as* BORNEOL

cam·phor (kam'fər) *n.* [ME. *camfre* < OFr. *camphre* < ML. *camfora* < Ar. *kāfūr* < Sans. *karpurah*, camphor tree] 1. a volatile, crystalline substance, $C_{10}H_{16}O$, with a strong characteristic odor, derived chiefly from the wood of the camphor tree: used to protect fabrics from moths, in manufacturing cellulose plastics, and in medicine as an irritant and stimulant 2. any of several derivatives of terpenes —**cam·phor'ic** (-fôr'ik) *adj.*

cam·phor·ate (kam'fə rāt') *vt.* **-rat'ed, -rat'ing** to put camphor in or on

camphorated oil a solution of camphor in cottonseed oil, used as a liniment

camphor ball *same as* MOTHBALL

☆**camphor ice** an ointment made of white wax, camphor, spermaceti, and castor oil, used for dry, chapped skin

camphor tree an evergreen tree (*Cinnamomum camphora*) of the laurel family, native to Japan and China: it is the source of camphor

Cam·pi·nas (käm pē'näs) city in SE Brazil, near São Paulo: pop. 156,000

cam·pi·on (kam'pē ən) *n.* [prob. ult. < L. *campus*, field] any of various flowering plants (genera *Lychnis* and *Silene*) of the pink family, with white or pink flowers

Cam·pi·on (kam'pē ən), **Thomas** 1567–1620; Eng. poet & composer of songs

☆**camp meeting** a religious gathering held outdoors or in a tent, etc., usually lasting several days

cam·po (käm'pō, kám'-) *n., pl.* **-pos** [Port. or Sp. < L. *campus*, field: see CAMPUS] a level, grassy plain in S. America, often with scattered plants and small trees

Cam·po·bel·lo (kam'pō bel'ō) island of New Brunswick, Canada, in the Bay of Fundy

☆**camp·o·ree** (kam'pə rē') *n.* [CAMP + (JAMB)OREE] a gathering or assembly of boy scouts on the regional or district level: distinguished from JAMBOREE

☆**cam·po san·to** (käm'pō san'tō) [Sp., lit., holy field] [Southwest] a cemetery

camp robber [Canad.] *same as* CANADA JAY

☆**camp·site** (kamp'sīt') *n.* 1. any site for a temporary camp 2. an area in a public or private park set aside for

camping, often equipped with water, toilets, picnic stoves, etc.

camp·stool (-stōōl′) *n.* a light folding stool

☆**cam·pus** (kam′pəs) *n., pl.* **-pus·es** [L., a field < IE. **kampos*, a corner, cove < base **kamp-*, to bend, whence Gr. *kampē*, a bending, curved part, Lith. *kampas*, corner, area] the grounds, sometimes including the buildings, of a school or college —*adj.* **1.** on or of the campus **2.** of a school or college [*campus* politics]

☆**camp·y** (kam′pē) *adj.* **camp′·i·er, camp′·i·est** [Slang] **1.** characterized by camp (n. 6) **2.** homosexual

cam·py·lot·ro·pous (kam′pi lä′trə pəs) *adj.* [< Gr. *kampylos*, curved (akin to *kampē*, a bend, curve: for IE. base see CAMPUS) + -TROPOUS] *Bot.* having the ovule bent so that its small exterior opening is near the base

cam·shaft (kam′shaft′, -shäft′) *n.* a shaft of which a cam is an essential part, or to which a cam is fastened

Ca·mus (kà mōō′; *Fr.* kà mü′), **Albert** 1913–60; *Fr.* writer, born in Algeria

can[1] (kan; *as an auxiliary, usually* kən, kin, ken, k'n) *vi. pt.* **could** [ME. < OE., 1st and 3d pers. sing., pres. indic., of *cunnan*, to know, have power to, be able; common Gmc. < IE. base **genē-*, seen also in KNOW, L. *gnosco*, etc.; orig. meaning "to be able mentally or spiritually," as distinguished from *may*, "to be able physically"] **1.** to know how to **2.** to be able to **3.** to be likely or at all likely to [*can* that be true?] **4.** to have the moral or legal right to **5.** [Colloq.] to be permitted to; may *Can* is used both as an auxiliary verb and as a substitution verb, and is followed by an infinitive without *to* —*vt.* [Obs.] to know —*can* but can only

SYN.—can, in informal usage, denotes ability, either physical or mental [*he can* walk, I *can* understand you]; **may** denotes possibility [*I may* go tomorrow]; or, in formal usage, permission [*you may* have another cooky]; in informal and colloquial usage, *can* is most frequently used to express permission, esp. in interrogative and negative statements [*can* I go? you *cannot!*].

can[2] (kan) *n.* [ME. & OE. *canne*, a cup, container; prob. < IE. base **gan(dh)*, container, whence MIr. *gann*, ON. *kani*] **1.** a container of various kinds, usually made of metal with a separate cover [a milk *can*, a garbage *can*, a *can* of shoe polish] ☆**2.** a container made of tinned iron or other metal, in which foods or other perishable products are sealed for preservation ☆**3.** the contents of a can; canful ☆**4.** [Slang] *a)* a prison *b)* the buttocks *c)* a toilet *d)* a destroyer (sense 2) —*vt.* **canned, can′ning 1.** to put up in airtight cans or jars for preservation **2.** [Slang] *a)* to dismiss; discharge *b)* to put an end to; stop *c)* to make a recording of

Can. 1. Canada **2.** Canadian **3.** Canon

Ca·na (kā′nə) village in Galilee, N Israel: scene of Jesus' first two miracles: John 2:1, 4:46

Ca·naan (kā′nən) [LL. (Vulgate, Gen. 10, ff.) *Chanaan* < Gr. *Chanan* < Heb. *kena′n*] Promised Land of the Israelites, a region between the Jordan and the Mediterranean

Ca·naan·ite (-īt′) *n.* **1.** one of the original inhabitants of Canaan **2.** the Semitic language spoken by the Canaanites **3.** a group of ancient Semitic languages, including Phoenician, Punic, and Hebrew —**Ca′naan·it′ish** (-īt′ish), **Ca′naan·it′ic** (-īt′ik) *adj.*

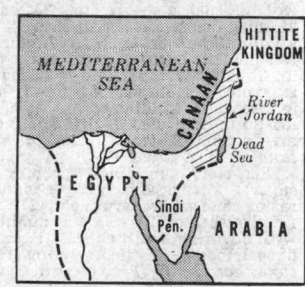

CANAAN

Canad. Canadian

Can·a·da (kan′ə də) [Fr. < Iroquoian (Huron) *kanáda*, village, settlement] country in N North America: a member of the Brit. Commonwealth: 3,852,000 sq. mi.; pop. 20,015,000; cap. Ottawa: abbrev. **Can.**

Canada balsam a thick, yellow, resinous fluid from the balsam fir, used as a transparent cement in microscopy

Canada goose the largest variety of wild goose (*Branta canadensis*) of Canada and the northern U.S.: it is brownish-gray, with black head and neck and a white patch on each side of the face

Canada jay a large N. American jay (*Perisoreus canadensis*) with gray and black feathers and no crest

☆**Canada lily** a wild lily (*Lilium canadense*) with small, funnel-shaped, orange-yellow or reddish flowers

☆**Canada lynx** a N. American lynx (*Lynx canadensis*) with tufted ears and a stubby tail, related to but larger than the bobcat

☆**Canada thistle** a prickly European weed (*Cirsium arvense*) of the composite family, with heads of purplish flowers and wavy leaves: now common as a fast-spreading, injurious weed throughout the U.S.

Ca·na·di·an (kə nā′dē ən) *adj.* of Canada, its people, or culture —*n.* a native or inhabitant of Canada

☆**Canadian bacon** cured, smoked pork taken from the loin in a boneless strip and having a hamlike flavor

Canadian English the English language as spoken and written in Canada

Canadian French the French language as spoken and written by French Canadians, mainly in Quebec and the Maritime Provinces

Ca·na·di·an·ism (kə nā′dē ən iz'm) *n.* **1.** a custom, characteristic, or belief of or originating in Canada **2.** a word or phrase originating in or peculiar to Canadian English

Canadian River river flowing eastward from N N.Mex. to the Arkansas River in E Okla.: 906 mi.

Canadian Shield an area of about 2,000,000 square miles of Precambrian strata, consisting largely of granite, gneiss, marble, and other igneous and metamorphic rocks that occupy most of eastern and central Canada: it has large deposits of copper, gold, and iron ore

ca·naille (kə näl′; *Fr.* kà nä′y′) *n.* [Fr., a mob, pack of dogs < It. *canaglia* < L. *canis*, dog] the mob; rabble

ca·nal (kə nal′) *n.* [ME., pipe or tube < OFr. < L. *canalis*, pipe, groove, channel < *canna*, reed: see CANE] **1.** an artificial waterway for transportation or irrigation **2.** a river artificially improved by locks, levees, etc. to permit navigation **3.** any of the long, narrow markings on the planet Mars **4.** *Anat.* any of various tubular passages or ducts —*vt.* **-nalled′** or **-naled′, -nal′ling** or **-nal′ing** to build a canal through or across

ca·nal·boat (-bōt′) *n.* a freight-carrying boat, usually long and narrow, used on canals: also **canal boat**

Ca·na·let·to (kä′nä let′tō), **An·to·ni·o** (än tō′nyō) (born *Antonio Canal* or *Canale*) 1697–1768; It. painter

can·a·lic·u·late (kan′ə lik′yoo lit, -lāt′) *adj.* [L. *canaliculatus*: see CANALICULUS] *Bot., Zool.* having a groove or grooves: also **can′a·lic′u·lat′ed** (-lāt′id), **can′a·lic′u·lar** (-lər)

can·a·lic·u·lus (-ləs) *n., pl.* **-li′** (-lī′) [L., dim. of *canalis*, a groove: see CANAL] *Anat., Bot., Zool.* a very small groove, as in bone

ca·nal·i·za·tion (kə nal′ə zā′shən, kan′'l ə-) *n.* **1.** the act of canalizing **2.** a system of canals or channels **3.** the formation of canals in the body tissues, naturally or artificially, as sometimes to drain wounds

ca·nal·ize (kə nal′īz, kan′ə līz′) *vt.* **-ized, -iz·ing 1.** to make a canal through **2.** to change into or make like a canal **3.** to provide an outlet for, esp. by directing into a specific channel or channels

canal rays *Physics* rays of positive ions passing through openings in the cathode of a vacuum tube

Canal Zone strip of land in Panama under perpetual lease to the U.S.: it extends about five miles on either side of the Panama Canal, excluding the cities of Panama and Colón: 362 sq. mi. (land area); pop. 45,000: abbrev. **CZ**

ca·na·pé (kan′ə pē, -pā′) *n.* [Fr.: see CANOPY; fig. application of Fr. sense: "upholstered divan"] a small piece of bread or toast or a cracker spread with spiced meat, fish, cheese, etc., served as an appetizer, often with drinks

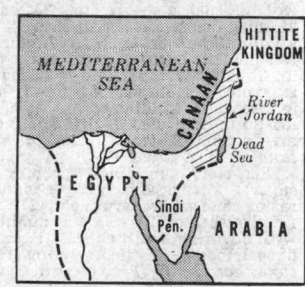

CANAL ZONE

ca·nard (kə närd′) *n.* [Fr., a duck, hoax, prob. < *can*, echoic for duck's quack + -*ard*, -ARD] **1.** a false, esp. malicious report, fabricated and spread as by a newspaper **2.** *a)* an airplane whose horizontal stabilizer is located forward of the wing or wings *b)* the horizontal control and stabilizing surfaces in such an aircraft

ca·nar·y (kə ner′ē) *n., pl.* **-nar′ies** [Fr. *canarie* < Sp. *canario* < L. *Canaria* (*insula*), Canary (island), lit., island of dogs < *canis*, a dog: so called from its large dogs] **1.** a small, yellow songbird (*Serinus canarius*) of the finch family, native to the Canary Islands, Madeira, and the Azores **2.** *same as* CANARY YELLOW **3.** a sweet wine like madeira, made in the Canary Islands **4.** a lively 16th-cent. Spanish or French dance

canary grass 1. an annual European grass (*Phalaris canariensis*) with thimble-shaped heads of seeds (**canary seed**) used as food for cage birds **2.** a perennial grass (*Phalaris arundinacea*), cultivated extensively for fodder: also called **reed canary grass**

Canary Islands group of islands in the Atlantic, off NW

Africa, forming two provinces of Spain: 2,808 sq. mi.; pop. 944,000: Sp. name **Is·las Ca·na·ri·as** (ēs'läs kä nä'rē äs)
canary yellow a light yellow
ca·nas·ta (kə nas'tə) *n.* [Sp., basket] a card game, a variation of rummy, for two to six players, using a double deck of cards and four jokers
Ca·na·ver·al (kə nav'ər əl), **Cape** [Sp. *cañaveral*, canebrake] *former name of* Cape KENNEDY
Can·ber·ra (kan'bər ə) capital of Australia, in the Australian Capital Territory: pop. 67,000
canc. 1. cancel 2. canceled 3. cancellation
can·can (kan'kan') *n.* [Fr. < ? children's name for duck (cf. CANARD), hence waddle] a gay dance with much high kicking performed by women entertainers, originally in Paris dance halls in the late 19th cent.
can·cel (kan's'l) *vt.* -celed or -celled, -cel·ing or -cel·ling [ME. *cancellen* < Anglo-Fr. *canceler* < L. *cancellare*, to make resemble a lattice (in LL., strike out, cancel) < *cancelli*, lattice, grating, pl. of *cancellus*, dim. of *cancer*, crossed bars, lattice] 1. to cross out with lines or mark over in some other way, as in deleting written matter or marking a postage stamp, check, etc. as used and cleared 2. to make invalid; annul 3. to do away with; wipe out; abolish, withdraw, etc. [to *cancel* an order or a ticket reservation] 4. to neutralize or balance in force or influence; offset (often with *out*) 5. *Math.* to remove (a common factor from both terms of a fraction, equivalents of opposite sign or on opposite sides of an equation, etc.) 6. *Printing* to delete or omit —*vi.* to offset or cancel each other (with *out*) —*n.* 1. the deletion or omission of matter in type or in print 2. *a*) the matter deleted or omitted *b*) the replacement for this —**can'cel·er, can'cel·ler** *n.*
can·cel·la·tion (kan'sə lā'shən) *n.* 1. the act of canceling 2. something canceled 3. the mark or marks showing that something is canceled
can·cel·lous (kan'sə ləs) *adj.* [< L. *cancelli*: see CANCEL] 1. *Anat.* having a porous or spongy structure: said of bones 2. *Bot.* having a close network of veins: said of certain leaves Also **can'cel·late** (-sə lit, -lāt'), **can'cel·lat·ed** (-lāt'id)
can·cer (kan'sər) [ME. & OE. < L., a crab; later, malignant tumor; by dissimilation (? already in IE.) < *carcro*- < IE. base *kar*-, redupl. *karkar*, hard, whence Sans. *karkara*, rough, hard, *karkata*, crab: see HARD] 1. [C-] a N constellation between Gemini and Leo, supposedly outlining a crab 2. [C-] the fourth sign of the zodiac (♋), which the sun enters about June 22: see ZODIAC, illus.—*n.* 1. a malignant new growth anywhere in the body of a person or animal; malignant tumor: cancers tend to spread locally and to distant parts of the body: see also CARCINOMA, SARCOMA 2. anything bad or harmful that spreads and destroys —**can'cer·ous** *adj.*
can·croid (kaŋ'kroid) *adj.* [< L. *cancer* (gen. *cancri*), CANCER + -OID] 1. like a crab 2. like cancer
can·de·la (kan dē'lə) *n.* [L., CANDLE] *see* CANDLE (*n.* 3 *a*)
can·de·la·brum (kan'də lä'brəm, -lab'rəm, -lā'brəm) *n.*, *pl.* **-bra** (-brə), **-brums** [L.: see CHANDELIER] a large branched candlestick or an electric lamp in imitation of this: also **can·de·la'bra**, *pl.* **-bras**
☆**can·de·lil·la** (kan'də lil'ə) *n.* [AmSp. < Sp., dim. of *candela* (< L.), a CANDLE] either of two shrubs (*Euphorbia anti-siphylitica* or *Pedilanthus pavonis*), of the spurge family, native to the Southwest and Mexico, which yield a wax used for polishes
can·dent (kan'dənt) *adj.* [L. *candens*, prp. of *candere*, to shine: see CANDESCENT] [Archaic] glowing with heat
can·des·cent (kan des''nt) *adj.* [L. *candescens*, prp. of *candescere*, inceptive form of *candere*, to shine < IE. base *kand*-, to glow, whence Sans. *candati*, gleams] glowing with intense heat; incandescent —**can·des'cence** *n.*
Can·di·a (kan'dē ə) 1. *former name of* CRETE 2. seaport and largest city in Crete, on the N coast: pop. 64,000: Gr. name, HERAKLION or IRAKLION
can·did (kan'did) *adj.* [L. *candidus*, white, pure, sincere < *candere*: see CANDESCENT] 1. free from prejudice or bias; fair; just; impartial 2. very honest or frank in what one says or writes 3. unposed and informal [a *candid* photograph] 4. [Archaic] *a*) white *b*) pure; innocent
☆**can·di·da·cy** (kan'də də sē) *n.*, *pl.* **-cies** the fact or state of being a candidate: also [Brit.] **can'di·da·ture** (-di chər, -dā'chər)
can·di·date (kan'də dāt', -dit) *n.* [L. *candidatus*, white-robed < *candidus* (see CANDID): office seekers in Rome wore white gowns] 1. a person who seeks, or who has been proposed for, an office, an award, etc. 2. a person apparently destined to come to a certain end [a *candidate* for greatness]
☆**candid camera** a camera, usually small, with a fast lens, used to take informal pictures, as of unposed subjects
can·died (kan'dēd) *adj.* 1. cooked in or with sugar or syrup, esp. to preserve, glaze, or encrust 2. crystallized into or like sugar 3. sugary in expression
Can·di·ot (kan'dē ät', -ət) *adj.* of Candia (Crete); Cretan —*n.* a Cretan Also **Can'di·ote'** (-ōt')

can·dle (kan'd'l) *n.* [ME. & OE. *candel* < L. *candela*, a light, torch < *candere*: see CANDESCENT] 1. a cylindrical mass of tallow or wax with a wick through its center, which gives light when burned 2. anything like a candle in form or use 3. *a*) a unit of luminous intensity equal to 1/60 of the luminous intensity of one square centimeter of a blackbody at the temperature of solidification of platinum: also called **candela, new candle** *b*) until 1940, a standard unit of luminous intensity equal to a certain fraction of the candle power of a group of 45 carbon-filament lamps kept at the National Bureau of Standards: also called **international candle** —*vt.* **-dled, -dling** to examine (eggs) for freshness, fertilization, etc. by holding in front of a light, originally that of a candle —**burn the candle at both ends** to work, or esp. play, too much so that one's energy is dissipated —**not hold a candle to** not be nearly so good as —(**a game**) **not worth the candle** 1. (a game) with stakes not sufficient to pay for the lights 2. (a thing) not worth doing —**can'dler** *n.*
☆**can·dle·ber·ry** (-ber'ē) *n.*, *pl.* **-ries** 1. *same as* BAYBERRY (sense 1) 2. *same as* CANDLENUT (senses 1 & 2)
can·dle·fish (-fish') *n.*, *pl.* **-fish', -fish'es:** see FISH² a small, oily, edible fish (*Thaleichthys pacificus*) related to the smelt, found in the N. Pacific: when dried it can be burned as a candle
can·dle·foot (-foot') *n. same as* FOOT-CANDLE
can·dle·hold·er (-hōl'dər) *n.* a candlestick
can·dle·light (-līt') *n.* 1. subdued light given by or as by candles 2. the time for lighting candles; twilight; evening
Can·dle·mas (kan'd'l məs) *n.* [ME. *candelmasse* < OE. *candelmæsse*: see CANDLE & MASS] a church feast, Feb. 2, commemorating the purification of the Virgin Mary: candles for sacred uses are blessed on this day: also **Candlemas Day**
can·dle·nut (kan'd'l nut') *n.* 1. the fruit of a tree (*Aleurites moluccana*) of the spurge family, growing in the Pacific Islands: the natives burn the fruit as candles and it is processed commercially for its oil 2. the tree
can·dle·pin (-pin') *n.* 1. a slender bowling pin shaped like a tapered candle 2. [*pl.*, *with sing. v.*] a game like tenpins played with such pins and a small ball
candle power the luminous intensity of a light source expressed in candles
can·dle·stick (-stik') *n.* a cupped or spiked holder for a candle or candles
can·dle·wick (-wik') *n.* 1. the wick of a candle 2. a thick, soft cotton yarn —*adj.* designating or of a muslin fabric, bedspread, etc. patterned with tufts of soft cotton yarn
can·dle·wood (-wood') *n.* [so called because it burns with a bright flame] 1. any of a genus (*Fouquieria*) of spiny desert shrubs or small trees with slender stems and clusters of brightly colored flowers, as the ocotillo 2. the wood of such a shrub, etc. ☆3. any resinous wood cut for kindling or used as for torches
can·dor (kan'dər) *n.* [L., whiteness, openness < *candere*, to shine: see CANDESCENT] 1. the quality of being fair and unprejudiced; impartiality 2. sharp honesty or frankness in expressing oneself 3. [Obs.] *a*) whiteness *b*) purity; innocence *c*) kindliness
can·dour (kan'dər) *n. Brit. sp.* of CANDOR
can·dy (kan'dē) *n.*, *pl.* **-dies** [< *sugar candy* < ME. *sugre candi* < OFr. *sucre candi* < It. *zucchero candi* < Ar. *qandi* < Per. *qand*, cane sugar; prob. < Sans. *khaṇḍa*, piece (of sugar)] 1. crystallized sugar made by boiling and evaporating cane sugar, syrup, etc. 2. *a*) a sweet food, usually in small pieces or bars, made mainly from sugar or syrup, with flavoring, fruit, chocolate, nuts, etc. added *b*) a piece of such food —*vt.* **-died, -dy·ing** [Fr. *candir* < It. *candire* < *candi*: see the *n.*] 1. to cook in or with sugar or syrup, esp. to preserve, glaze, or encrust 2. to crystallize into or like sugar 3. to sweeten; make pleasant —*vi.* to become candied (in senses 1 & 2)
can·dy-striped (-strīpt') *adj.* having diagonal, colored stripes like those on a certain kind of candy stick
can·dy·tuft (-tuft') *n.* [< CANDIA + TUFT] any of a genus (*Iberis*) of garden plants of the mustard family, with clusters of white, pink, or purplish flowers
cane (kān) *n.* [ME. & OFr. *canne* < It. *canna* < L. *canna*, a reed, cane < Gr. *kanna*, prob. < Assyr. *qanu* (or Heb. *qaneh*), tube, reed < Sumerian *gin*] 1. the slender, jointed, usually flexible stem of any of certain plants, as bamboo, rattan, etc. 2. any plant with such a stem, as sugar cane, sorghum, etc. 3. the woody stem of a small fruiting or flowering plant, as the blackberry, rose, etc. 4. any of a genus (*Arundinaria*) of tall grasses of the southern U.S. 5. a stick or rod used for flogging 6. *same as* WALKING STICK (sense 1) 7. split rattan, used in weaving chair seats, wickerwork, etc. —*vt.* **caned, can'ing** 1. to flog with a cane 2. to make or furnish (chairs, etc.) with cane —**can'er** *n.*
Ca·ne·a (kə nē'ə) capital of Crete, a seaport in the NW part: pop. 38,000: Gr. name, KHANIA
☆**cane·brake** (kān'brāk') *n.* [CANE + BRAKE³] 1. a dense growth of cane plants 2. an area overgrown with canes
ca·nel·la (kə nel'ə) *n.* [ML., dim. of L. *canna*: see CANE] the fragrant inner bark of a tropical American tree (*Canella winterana*), used as a spice and a tonic
ca·neph·o·ros (kə nef'ə räs') *n.*, *pl.* **-roe'** (-rē') [L. < Gr. *kanēphoros* < *kaneon*, a rush basket (< *kanna*: see CANE) + *pherein*, BEAR¹] 1. in ancient Greece, any of the maidens

who carried on the head a basket holding the sacred things used at feasts **2.** *Archit.* a representation of this, sometimes used as a caryatid Also **can·e·phor** (kan′ə fôr′)

ca·nes·cent (kə nes′'nt) *adj.* [L. *canescens*, prp. of *canescere*, to become white < *canere*, to be white < *canus*, white, hoary] **1.** becoming white or grayish **2.** covered with a white or grayish down, as some leaves

cane sugar sugar (*sucrose*) obtained from sugar cane

☆**can·field** (kan′fēld′) *n.* [after Richard A. *Canfield* (1855-1914), U.S. gambling house proprietor] a form of solitaire used as a gambling game

cangue (kaŋ) *n.* [Fr. < Port. *canga*, a yoke < Annamese *gong*] a large wooden yoke formerly fastened about the neck in China, as a punishment for petty crime

Ca·nic·u·la (kə nik′yoo lə) [L., dim. of *canis*, a dog] Sirius, the Dog Star

ca·nic·u·lar (-lər) *adj.* [ME. *caniculer* < L. *canicularis* < prec.] **1.** *a)* of the Dog Star *b)* measured by its rising **2.** of the dog days in July and August: see DOG DAYS

ca·nine (kā′nīn) *adj.* [L. *caninus* < *canis*, a dog < IE. base *kwon-*, dog, whence CYNIC, HOUND[1]] **1.** of or like a dog **2.** of the family (Canidae) of animals that includes dogs, wolves, jackals, and foxes —*n.* **1.** a dog or other canine animal **2.** a sharp-pointed tooth on either side of the upper jaw and lower jaw, between the incisors and the bicuspids; a cuspid or (in the upper jaw) eyetooth: in full **canine tooth**

Ca·nis Ma·jor (kā′nis mā′jər) [L., the Greater Dog] a S constellation southeast of Orion, containing the Dog Star, Sirius

Canis Mi·nor (mī′nər) [L., the Lesser Dog] a N constellation east of Orion, near Gemini, containing the bright star Procyon

can·is·ter (kan′is tər) *n.* [ME. < L. *canistrum*, wicker basket < Gr. *kanistron* < *kanna*, a reed: see CANE] **1.** a small box or can for coffee, tea, tobacco, etc. **2.** a boxlike vacuum cleaner **3.** *same as* CANISTER SHOT **4.** the part of a gas mask that contains the chemicals for filtering the air to be breathed

canister shot formerly, lead or iron shot in a container that scattered its contents when fired

can·ker (kaŋ′kər) *n.* [ME. < OFr. *cancre* < L. *cancer*: see CANCER] **1.** an ulcerlike sore, esp. in the mouth, that spreads **2.** *a)* a disease of plants that causes local decay of bark and wood *b)* a diseased area of woody tissues **3.** [Obs.] *same as* CANKERWORM **4.** anything that corrupts or gradually destroys **5.** [Now Dial.] the dog rose —*vt.* **1.** to attack or infect with canker **2.** to infect or debase with corruption —*vi.* to become cankered —**can′ker·ous** *adj.*

can·ker·worm (-wurm′) *n.* ☆any of several larvae of geometrid moths that are harmful to fruit and shade trees, esp. the spring cankerworm (*Paleacrita vernata*) that feeds on fruit and foliage

can·na (kan′ə) *n.* [L.: see CANE] any of a genus (*Canna*) of a family (Cannaceae) of broad-leaved tropical plants, often grown for ornament because of the striking foliage and brilliant flowers

can·na·bin (kan′ə bin) *n.* a poisonous, white crystalline resin extracted from cannabis

can·na·bis (-bis) *n.* [L., hemp < Gr. *kannabis*: for base see HEMP] **1.** *same as* HEMP **2.** the female flowering tops of the hemp

Can·nae (kan′ē) ancient town in SE Italy: site of a battle (216 B.C.) in which the Carthaginians under Hannibal defeated the Romans

☆**canned** (kand) *adj.* **1.** preserved in airtight cans or jars **2.** [Slang] *a)* recorded for reproduction, as on radio or TV [*canned* commercials] *b)* prepared for publication in a number of newspapers simultaneously [a *canned* editorial]

can·nel (**coal**) (kan′'l) [< ? *candle coal*] a variety of tough, lusterless bituminous coal that burns with a bright flame and has a high volatile content

can·nel·lo·ni (kan′ə lō′ne; *It.* kän′nel lô′nē) *n.pl.* [*usually with sing. v.*] [It., pl. of *cannellone*, a hollow noodle, lit., small tube, aug. of *cannello*, a tube, joint of cane, dim. of *canna*, CANE] tubular casings of dough filled with ground meat, baked, and served in a tomato sauce

☆**can·ner** (kan′ər) *n.* **1.** a person who cans foods **2.** an inferior animal fit only for canning as dog food

☆**can·ner·y** (kan′ər ē) *n.*, *pl.* **-ner·ies** a factory where foods are canned

Cannes (kan, kanz; *Fr.* kàn) city in SE France, on the Riviera: pop. 58,000

can·ni·bal (kan′ə b'l) *n.* [Sp. *canibal*, a savage, *cannibal* (term used by Columbus) < *Caniba*, a cannibal people, prob. < Carib *galibi*, lit., strong men] **1.** a person who eats human flesh **2.** an animal that eats its own kind —*adj.* of, resembling, or having the habits of cannibals —**can′ni·bal·ism** *n.* —**can′ni·bal·is′tic** (-bə lis′tik) *adj.*

☆**can·ni·bal·ize** (-īz′) *vt.*, *vi.* **-ized′, -iz′ing 1.** to strip (old or worn equipment) of parts for use in other units to help keep them in service **2.** to take any or all personnel or components from (one organization) for use in building up another **3.** to swallow up or devour (another of the same kind): used figuratively —**can′ni·bal·i·za′tion** *n.*

can·ni·kin (kan′ə k'n) *n.* [< CAN² + -KIN] **1.** a small can; cup **2.** [Dial.] a wooden bucket or pail

can·ni·ly (kan′'l ē) *adv.* in a canny manner

can·ni·ness (kan′ē nis) *n.* the quality of being canny

☆**can·ning** (kan′iŋ) *n.* the act, process, or work of putting foods in cans or jars for preservation

Can·ning (kan′iŋ), **George** 1770-1827; Brit. statesman; prime minister (1827)

can·non (kan′ən) *n.*, *pl.* **-nons, -non:** see PLURAL, II, D, 4 [ME. & OFr. *canon* < It. *cannone* < L. *canna:* see CANE; in n. 6 & v. 2, altered < CAROM] **1.** *a)* a large, mounted piece of artillery; sometimes, specif., a large gun with a relatively short barrel, as a howitzer *b)* an automatic gun, now usually of 20-mm. caliber, mounted on an aircraft **2.** a miniature gun like a cannon **3.** a part on a bell by which it is hung **4.** *same as* CANNON BONE **5.** *Mech.* a hollow tube within which a shaft revolves independently of the outer tube **6.** [Brit.] *Billiards* a carom —*vt.* **1.** to attack with cannon fire **2.** [Brit.] to cause to carom —*vi.* **1.** to fire cannon **2.** [Brit.] to make a carom

Can·non (kan′ən), **Joseph Gur·ney** (gur′nē) 1836-1926; U.S. congressman

can·non·ade (kan′ə nād′) *n.* [Fr. *canonnade* < *canon*, a CANNON] **1.** a continuous firing of artillery **2.** an attack with artillery —*vt.* **-ad′ed, -ad′ing** to attack or fire at with artillery —*vi.* to fire artillery

can·non·ball (kan′ən bôl′) *n.* **1.** a heavy ball, esp. of iron, formerly used as a projectile in cannon: also **cannon ball 2.** [Colloq.] *a)* a fast express train *b)* a hard, driving serve in tennis —*adj.* [Slang] fast; rapid —*vi.* [Slang] to move very rapidly

cannon bone the bone between hock or knee and fetlock in a four-legged, hoofed animal

can·non·eer (kan′ə nir′) *n.* [Fr. *canonnier* < *canon*, a CANNON] an artilleryman; gunner

cannon fodder soldiers, sailors, etc. thought of as being expended (i.e., killed or maimed) or expendable in war

can·non·ry (kan′ən rē) *n.*, *pl.* **-ries 1.** cannons collectively; artillery **2.** cannon fire

can·not (kan′ät, -ət; kə nät′) can not —**cannot but** have no choice but to; must

can·nu·la (kan′yoo lə) *n.*, *pl.* **-lae′** (-lē′), **-las** [L., dim. of *canna:* see CANE] a tube for insertion into body cavities or ducts, as for drainage

can·nu·lar (-lər) *adj.* tubular: also **can′nu·late** (-lit, -lāt′)

can·ny (kan′ē) *adj.* **-ni·er, -ni·est** [< CAN¹] **1.** careful and shrewd in one's actions and dealings; clever and cautious **2.** wise and well-informed **3.** careful with money; thrifty **4.** [Scot.] *a)* careful in action; gentle; easy; quiet *b)* artful or skillful **5.** [Brit. Dial.] comely; attractive —*adv.* [Scot.] in a canny or cautious manner —**ca′ canny** (kä, kô) **1.** [Scot.] call "canny"; hence, go cautiously **2.** [Brit.] slowing down at work [a *ca′ canny* policy]

ca·noe (kə noō′) *n.* [earlier *canoa* < Sp. *canoa* (term used by Columbus in 1493) < the Carib name] a narrow, light boat with its sides meeting in a sharp edge at each end: it is moved by one or more paddles —*vi.* **-noed′, -noe′ing** to paddle, or go in, a canoe —*vt.* to transport by canoe —**ca·noe′ist** *n.*

can·on¹ (kan′ən) *n.* [ME. < OE. & OFr. < L., measuring line, rule (hence, in ML.(Ec.), sacred writings admitted to the catalog according to the rule) < Gr. *kanōn*, rod, bar < *kanna:* see CANE] **1.** a law or body of laws of a church **2.** [Rare] any law or decree **3.** *a)* an established or basic rule or principle [the *canons* of good taste] *b)* a standard to judge by; criterion *c)* a body of rules, principles, criteria, etc. **4.** *a)* a list of books of the Bible officially accepted by a church or religious body as genuine *b)* a list of the genuine works of an author [the Shakespearean *canon*] **5.** *a)* [often C-] *Eccles.* the fundamental and essentially unvarying part of the Mass, between the Preface and the Communion, that centers on the consecration of the Host *b)* a list of recognized saints as in the Roman Catholic Church **6.** *Music* a polyphonic composition in which there are exact repetitions of a preceding part in the same or related keys —*SYN.* see LAW

can·on² (kan′ən) *n.* [ME. < OE. *canonic* & OFr. *chanoine*, both < LL.(Ec.) *canonicus*, a cleric, one living by the canon: see prec.] **1.** a member of a clerical group living according to a canon, or rule **2.** a clergyman serving in a cathedral or collegiate church **3.** *same as* CANON REGULAR

ca·ñon (kan′yən; *Sp.* kä nyôn′) *n.* a canyon

can·on·ess (kan′ən is) *n.* **1.** a woman member of a religious group living according to a canon, or rule, but not under an everlasting vow such as a nun takes **2.** a woman holding a canonry

ca·non·ic (kə nän′ik) *adj.* **1.** *same as* CANONICAL **2.** of a musical canon

ca·non·i·cal (kə nän′i k'l) *adj.* [ME. < ML.(Ec.) *canonicalis*] **1.** of, according to, or ordered by church canon **2.** authoritative; accepted **3.** belonging to the canon of the Bible **4.** of a canon (clergyman) —**ca·non′i·cal·ly** *adv.*

canonical hour any of the seven periods of the day assigned to prayer and worship: they are matins (with lauds), prime, terce, sext, none, vespers, and complin

ca·non·i·cals (-k'lz) *n.pl.* the clothes prescribed by canon for a clergyman when conducting services

ca·non·i·cate (-kāt', -kit) *n. same as* CANONRY (sense 1)

can·on·i·ci·ty (kan'ə nis'ə tē) *n.* [L. *canonicus,* according to rule (see CANON[1]) + -ITY] the fact or condition of being canonical

can·on·ist (kan'ən ist) *n.* an expert in canon law —**can'on·is'tic** *adj.*

can·on·ize (kan'ə nīz') *vt.* **-ized', -iz'ing** [ME. *canonizen* < LL.(Ec.) *canonizare:* see CANON[1] + -IZE] **1.** to declare (a dead person) a saint in formal church procedure **2.** to glorify **3.** to put in the Biblical canon **4.** to give church sanction or authorization to —**can'on·i·za'tion** *n.*

canon law the laws governing the ecclesiastical affairs of a Christian church

canon regular *pl.* **canons regular** *R.C.Ch.* a regular priest bound by religious vows and living under the rule of his institute

can·on·ry (kan'ən rē) *n., pl.* **-ries 1.** the benefice or position of a canon **2.** canons collectively

ca·noo·dle (kə nōō'd'l) *vt., vi.* **-dled, -dling** [G. *knudeln,* to cuddle < or akin to LowG. *knuddel,* a knot, clump, dim. of dial. *knude,* akin to OHG. *knodo,* OE. *cnotta,* KNOT[1]] [Old Slang] to caress or fondle in making love; pet; neck

ca·no·pic urn (kə nō'pik) [< L. *Canopicus,* of Canopus: see ff.] an urn used in ancient Egypt to hold and preserve the internal organs of the mummified dead: also **canopic jar** (or **vase**)

Ca·no·pus (-pəs) [L. < Gr. *Kanōpos*] **1.** the brightest star in southern skies, in the constellation Carina **2.** seaport in ancient Egypt, east of Alexandria, near the mouth of the Nile

can·o·py (kan'ə pē) *n., pl.* **-pies** [ME. *canape* < ML. *canapeum* < L. *conopeum* < Gr. *kōnōpeion,* couch with mosquito curtains, dim. of *kōnōps,* gnat] **1.** a drapery, awning, or other rooflike covering fastened above a bed, throne, etc., or held on poles over a person or sacred thing **2.** a structure of canvas on a framework sheltering an area or forming a sheltered walk to the entrance of a building **3.** anything that covers or seems to cover like a canopy, as the sky **4.** the transparent hood over an airplane cockpit **5.** the part of a parachute that opens up and catches the air **6.** a rooflike projection over a door, pulpit, etc. —*vt.* **-pied, -py·ing** to place or form a canopy over; cover; shelter

ca·no·rous (kə nôr'əs) *adj.* [L. *canorus* < *canor,* a tune < *canere,* to sing: see CHANT] pleasing in sound; melodious; musical —**ca·no'rous·ly** *adv.*

Ca·no·va (kä nō'vä), **An·to·nio** (än tō'nyō) 1757–1822; It. sculptor

canst (kanst; *unstressed* kənst) *archaic 2d pers. sing., pres. indic. of* CAN[1]: *used with* thou

cant[1] (kant) *n.* [< L. *cantus:* see CHANT] **1.** whining, singsong speech, esp. as used by beggars **2.** the secret slang of beggars, thieves, etc.; argot **3.** the special words and phrases used by those in a certain sect, occupation, etc.; jargon **4.** insincere or almost meaningless talk used merely from convention or habit **5.** religious phraseology used hypocritically; insincere, pious talk —*vi.* [< the *n.*] to use cant; speak in cant (in all senses of the *n.*) —*adj.* of, or having the nature of, cant —*SYN.* see DIALECT —**cant'er** *n.*

cant[2] (kant) *n.* [ME. & OFr. *cant,* a corner, edge, angle < L. *cant(h)us,* tire of a wheel (in LL., side, corner) < Celt., as in Cym. *cant,* rim of a wheel, edge < IE. base *kantho-,* corner, bend] **1.** a corner or outside angle, as of a building **2.** a sloping or slanting surface; beveled edge **3.** a sudden movement, toss, or pitch that causes tilting, turning, or overturning **4.** the tilt, turn, or slant thus caused —*vt.* **1.** to give a sloping edge to; bevel **2.** to tilt or overturn **3.** to throw off or out by tilting **4.** to throw with a jerk; pitch; toss —*vi.* **1.** to tilt or turn over **2.** to slant **3.** *Naut.* to change direction; turn —*adj.* **1.** with canted sides or corners **2.** slanting

cant[3] (kant) *adj.* [ME., bold, brave, prob. < or akin to MDu. *kant*] [Brit. Dial.] lusty; bold; hearty

can't (kant, känt) cannot

Cant. 1. Canterbury **2.** Canticles **3.** Cantonese

Cantab. Cantabrigian

can·ta·bi·le (kän tä'bi lā') *adj., adv.* [It. < *cantare,* to sing < L. *cantare:* see CHANT] *Music* in an easy, flowing manner; songlike —*n.* music in this style

Can·ta·brig·i·an (kan'tə brij'ē ən, -brij'ən) *adj.* [< ML. *Cantabrigia,* Cambridge] of Cambridge, England, or esp., of the University of Cambridge —*n.* **1.** a student or graduate of the University of Cambridge **2.** any inhabitant of Cambridge, England

can·ta·la (kan tä'lə) *n.* [< ?] a hard fiber derived from the leaves of an agave (*Agave cantala*): used in making twine

can·ta·loupe, can·ta·loup (kan'tə lōp') *n.* [Fr. < It. *cantalupo* < *Cantalupo,* former papal summer estate, near Rome, where the melon was first grown in Europe] **1.** a muskmelon (*Cucumis melo cantalupensis*) with a hard, rough rind and sweet, juicy, orange-colored flesh **2.** loosely, any muskmelon

can·tan·ker·ous (kan taŋ'kər əs) *adj.* [prob. < ME. *contakour,* a troublemaker < *contek,* strife, quarrel] + -OUS] bad-tempered; quarrelsome; perverse —**can·tan'ker·ous·ly** *adv.* —**can·tan'ker·ous·ness** *n.*

can·tar (kän tär') *n. same as* KANTAR

can·ta·ta (kən tät'ə) *n.* [It. < pp. of *cantare:* see CHANT] a musical composition consisting of vocal solos, choruses, etc., often with instrumental accompaniment, used as a setting for a story to be sung but not acted

‡can·ta·tri·ce (*It.* kän'tä trē'che; *Fr.* kän tä trēs') *n., pl.* It. **-tri'ci** (-chē); Fr. **-trices'** (-trēs') [Fr. & It. < L. *cantatrix,* fem. of *cantator,* singer < pp. of *cantare:* see CHANT] a woman professional singer

cant dog *same as* CANT HOOK

can·teen (kan tēn') *n.* [Fr. *cantine* < It. *cantina,* wine cellar, a vault < *canto,* an angle, corner: see CANT[2]] **1.** *same as* POST EXCHANGE **2.** a place outside a military camp where refreshments and entertainment are provided for members of the armed forces **3.** a recreation center, as for teen-agers **4.** a place where cooked food is dispensed to people in distress, as in a disaster area **5.** a small metal or plastic flask, usually encased in canvas, for carrying drinking water **6.** formerly, a military kit containing cooking equipment

can·ter (kan'tər) *n.* [contr. < *Canterbury gallop:* from pace at which the pilgrims rode to Canterbury] a smooth, easy pace like a moderate gallop —*vi., vt.* to ride or move at a canter

Can·ter·bur·y (kan'tər ber'ē, -bər ē) city in Kent, SE England: seat of a primate of the Church of England: pop. 31,000

Canterbury bells a cultivated bellflower (*Campanula medium*) with white, pink, or blue cuplike flowers

Canterbury Tales an unfinished literary work by Chaucer, largely in verse, consisting of stories told by pilgrims on their way to Canterbury

can·thar·i·des (kan thar'ə dēz') *n.pl.* [ME. *cantarides* < L. *cantharides,* pl. of *cantharis,* kind of beetle, Spanish fly < Gr. *kantharis,* blistering beetle] **1.** *pl. of* CANTHARIS **2.** [*with sing. or pl. v.*] a preparation of powdered, dried Spanish flies, formerly used internally as a diuretic and genitourinary stimulant, and externally as a skin irritant

can·tha·ris (kan'thər is) *n., pl.* **can·thar·i·des** (kan thar'ə dēz') *same as* SPANISH FLY (sense 1)

cant hook [see CANT[2]] a pole with a movable hooked arm at or near one end, for catching hold of logs and rolling them

can·thus (kan'thəs) *n., pl.* **-thi** (-thī) [ModL. < Gr. *kanthos:* for IE. base see CANT[2]] either corner of the eye, where the eyelids meet

can·ti·cle (kan'ti k'l) *n.* [ME. < L. *canticulum,* dim. of *canticum,* song < *cantus:* see CHANT] **1.** a song or chant **2.** a hymn whose words are taken from the Bible, used in certain church services

CANT HOOK

Can·ti·cles (-k'lz) *n.pl. same as* SONG OF SOLOMON: also (in the Douay Bible) **Canticle of Canticles**

can·ti·le·na (kan'tə lē'nə) *n.* [It. < L., a song < *cantare,* to sing: see CHANT] a smooth, flowing, lyrical passage of vocal, or sometimes instrumental, music

can·ti·le·ver (kan't'l ē'vər, -ev'ər) *n.* [as if < CANT[2] + LEVER, but of obscure orig.] **1.** a large bracket or block projecting from a wall to support a balcony, cornice, etc. **2.** a projecting beam or structure supported at only one end, which is anchored as to a pier or wall —*vt.* to support by means of cantilevers —**can'ti·le'vered** *adj.*

cantilever bridge a bridge whose span is formed by

CANTILEVER

two cantilevers projecting toward each other, sometimes with an extra section between them

can·til·la·tion (kan't'l ā'shən) *n.* [< *cantillate,* to chant (< L. *cantillatus,* pp. of *cantillare,* to hum, sing low < *cantare:* see CHANT) + -ION] in Jewish liturgy, a chanting or reciting with certain prescribed musical phrases indicated by notations —**can'til·late'** (-āt') *vt., vi.* **-lat'ed, -lat'ing**

☆**can·ti·na** (kan tē'nä) *n.* [Sp. < It.: see CANTEEN] [Southwest] saloon or barroom

can·tle (kan't'l) *n.* [ME. *cantel,* a corner, rim, piece < OFr. < ML. *cantellus,* dim. of L. *cantus:* see CANT[2]] **1.** a piece, esp. when cut off or out; slice **2.** the upward-curving rear part of a saddle

can·to (kan'tō) *n., pl.* **-tos** [It. < L. *cantus,* song: see CHANT] any of the main divisions of certain long poems, corresponding to the chapters of a book

Can·ton (kan tän'; *for b)* kän'tän) **1.** former name of *a)* KWANGCHOW *b)* CHU KIANG **2.** [< *Canton,* suburb of Boston < prec.] city in EC Ohio: pop. 110,000

can·ton (kan'tən, -tän; kan tän'; *for vt. 2* kan tän', -tōn') *n.* [Fr. < It. *cantone* < LL. *cantus,* corner: see CANT[2]] **1.** any of the political divisions of a country or territory; specif., *a)* any of the states in the Swiss Republic *b)* a division of an arrondissement in France **2.** *a) Heraldry* a small, square section of an escutcheon, usually in the upper right, or dexter, corner *b)* a rectangular section in a flag, in the upper corner nearest the staff —*vt.* **1.** to divide into cantons **2.**

to assign quarters to (troops, etc.); quarter —**can′ton·al** *adj.*

Can·ton crepe (kan′tän) a soft, crinkled silk or rayon fabric, like crepe de Chine but heavier

Can·ton·ese (kan′tə nēz′) *adj.* of Canton, China, or its people —*n.* **1.** *pl.* **Cantonese** a native or inhabitant of Canton **2.** the Chinese dialect of the Cantonese

Can·ton flannel (kan′tän) *same as* COTTON FLANNEL

can·ton·ment (kan tän′mənt, -tōn′-) *n.* [Fr. *cantonnement*: see CANTON] **1.** the assignment of troops to temporary quarters **2.** the quarters assigned

can·tor (kan′tər) *n.* [L., singer, poet, actor, in LL.(Ec.), precentor, < *canere*, to sing: see CHANT] **1.** a church choir leader; precentor **2.** a singer of liturgical solos in a synagogue, who leads the congregation in prayer; hazan —**can·to′ri·al** (-tôr′ē əl) *adj.*

can·trip (kan′trip) *n.* [< ?] [Chiefly Scot.] **1.** a magic spell **2.** a prank

can·tus (kan′təs) *n.*, *pl.* **can′tus** [L.: see CANTO] a melody; esp., the principal part of a polyphonic work

cantus fir·mus (fur′məs) [ML., lit., firm song] **1.** *same as* PLAINSONG **2.** a simple melody serving as the main theme in a contrapuntal work

cant·y (kan′tē) *adj.* [CANT³ + -Y²] [Scot. & Brit. Dial.] lively; cheerful

☆**Ca·nuck** (kə nuk′) *n.* [earlier *Kanuck*, apparently < Haw. *kanaka*, man] [Colloq.] **1.** a Canadian; sometimes specif., a French Canadian **2.** Canadian French —*adj.* [Colloq.] Canadian; sometimes specif., French Canadian

Ca·nute (kə nōōt′, -nyōōt′) 994?–1035; 1st Dan. king of England (1017–35) and king of Denmark (1018–35) and of Norway (1028–35): also called **Canute the Great**

can·vas (kan′vəs) *n.* [ME. & OFr. *canevas* < It. *canavaccio* < VL. *cannapaceum*, hempen cloth < L. *cannabis*, HEMP] **1.** a closely woven, coarse cloth of hemp, cotton, or linen, often unbleached, used for tents, sails, etc. **2.** a sail or set of sails **3.** *a*) a specially prepared piece of canvas on which an oil painting is made *b*) such a painting **4.** a tent or tents, esp. circus tents **5.** any coarse cloth of open mesh weave on which embroidery or tapestry is done —**the canvas** the canvas-covered floor of a boxing or wrestling ring —**under canvas 1.** in tents **2.** with sails unfurled **3.** by means of sails

☆**can·vas·back** (-bak′) *n.*, *pl.* **-backs′, -back′** see PLURAL, II, D, 1 [< the grayish, canvaslike appearance of the back] a large, N. American wild duck (*Aythya valisneria*) with a brownish-red head and dark back, hunted as a game bird

can·vass (kan′vəs) *vt.* [< *canvas:* ? because canvas was used for sifting] **1.** to examine or discuss in detail; look over carefully **2.** to go through (places) or among (people) asking for (votes, opinions, orders, etc.) **3.** [Obs.] to criticize severely —*vi.* to try to get votes, orders, etc.; solicit —*n.* the act of canvassing, esp. in an attempt to estimate the outcome of an election, sales campaign, etc. —**can′vass·er** *n.*

☆**can·yon** (kan′yən) *n.* [Sp. *cañón* < *caño*, a tube < L. *canna*, a reed: see CANE] a long, narrow valley between high cliffs, often with a stream flowing through it

Can·yon·lands National Park (kan′yən landz′) national park along the Green & Colorado rivers, in SE Utah: 403 sq. mi.

can·zo·ne (kän tsō′ne) *n.*, *pl.* **-ni** (-nē) [It. < L. *cantio*, song < *canere*, to sing: see CHANT] **1.** a lyric poem of Provençal or early Italian troubadours **2.** a musical setting for this, like a madrigal Also **can·zo′na** (-nä)

can·zo·net, can·zo·nette (kan′zə net′) *n.* [It. *canzonetta*, dim. of prec.] a short, sprightly song

caou·tchouc (kou chōōk′, kōō′chook) *n.* [Fr. < obs. Sp. *cauchuc* < Quechua *cauchuc*] rubber; esp., India rubber, or crude, natural rubber, obtained from latex

cap (kap) *n.* [ME. *cappe* < OE. *cæppe*, a cap, cape, hood < LL. *cappa, capa*, a cape, hooded cloak] **1.** any closefitting head covering, brimless or with only a front visor, and made of wool or cotton, as a baseball cap or overseas cap, or of muslin or lace, as a nurse's or baby's cap **2.** *a*) a special covering for the head, worn as a mark of occupation, rank, academic degree, etc. [a cardinal's *cap*, fool's *cap*] *b*) a mortarboard (sense 2) **3.** a caplike part or thing; cover or top, as the cap-shaped part of a mushroom, a small metal cover for a bottle, the cover over a camera lens or other projecting or end part, a kneecap, an artificial crown for a tooth, a mountain top, the capital of a column, etc. **4.** *same as* PERCUSSION CAP **5.** a little paper percussion cap for toy guns (**cap guns**) **6.** any of several sizes of writing paper: see LEGAL CAP, FOOLSCAP —*vt.* **capped, cap′ping 1.** *a*) to put a cap on *b*) to present ceremonially with a cap, as at a graduation [to *cap* a nurse] **2.** to cover (the top or end of); form a cap for [snow *capped* the hills] **3.** *a*) to do as well or better than; equal or excel *b*) to follow with another that is equivalent or better than; match [to *cap* a quotation] **4.** to bring to a high point, as of interest or excitement; climax —**cap in hand** in a humble or servile manner —☆**cap the climax** to be or do more than could be expected or believed —**set one's cap for** to try to win as a husband or lover

CAP, C.A.P. Civil Air Patrol

cap. 1. capacity **2.** *pl.* **caps.** capital **3.** capitalize **4.** capitalized **5.** captain **6.** [L. *capitulum*] chapter

ca·pa·bil·i·ty (kā′pə bil′ə tē) *n.*, *pl.* **-ties 1.** the quality of being capable; practical ability **2.** a capacity for being used or developed **3.** [*pl.*] abilities, features, etc. not yet developed or utilized

ca·pa·ble (kā′pə b'l) *adj.* [Fr. < LL. *capabilis* < L. *capere*, to take, seize] **1.** having ability; able to do things well; skilled; competent **2.** [Obs.] capacious or comprehensive —*SYN.* see ABLE —**capable of 1.** susceptible of; admitting of; open to **2.** having the ability or qualities necessary for **3.** able or ready to [*capable of* telling a lie] —**ca′pa·ble·ness** *n.* —**ca′pa·bly** *adv.*

ca·pa·cious (kə pā′shəs) *adj.* [< L. *capax* (gen. *capacis*), large < *capere*, to take, hold, contain + -OUS] able to contain or hold much; roomy; spacious —**ca·pa′cious·ly** *adv.* —**ca·pa′cious·ness** *n.*

ca·pac·i·tance (kə pas′ə təns) *n.* [CAPACIT(Y) + -ANCE] *Elec.* that property of a capacitor which determines how much charge can be stored in it for a given potential difference between its terminals, measured, in farads, by the ratio of the charge stored to the potential difference

ca·pac·i·tate (-tāt′) *vt.* **-tat′ed, -tat′ing** [CAPACIT(Y) + -ATE¹] [Rare] to prepare, fit, or qualify (*for*)

ca·pac·i·tive (-tiv) *adj.* of electrical capacitance

ca·pac·i·tor (-tər) *n. Elec.* a device consisting of two or more conducting plates separated from one another by an insulating material and used for storing an electric charge; condenser

ca·pac·i·tron (kə pas′ə trän′) *n.* [CAPACI(TOR) + -TRON] a type of mercury arc tube in which initiation of the arc is brought about by the sudden application of a high voltage between the cathode and an insulated starter electrode

ca·pac·i·ty (kə pas′ə tē) *n.*, *pl.* **-ties** [ME. & OFr. *capacite* < L. *capacitas* < *capax*: see CAPACIOUS] **1.** the ability to contain, absorb, or receive and hold **2.** *a*) the amount of space that can be filled; room for holding; content or volume [a tank with a *capacity* of 21 gallons] *b*) the point at which no more can be contained [filled to *capacity*] **3.** the power of receiving and holding knowledge, impressions, etc.; mental ability **4.** the ability or qualifications (*for*, or *to do*, something); aptitude **5.** maximum output or producing ability [operating at *capacity*] **6.** the quality of being adapted (*for* something) or susceptible (*of* something); capability; potentiality **7.** a condition of being qualified or authorized; position, function, status, etc. [acting in the *capacity* of an adviser] **8.** *Elec. same as* CAPACITANCE **9.** *Law* legal authority or competency —*SYN.* see FUNCTION

cap and bells a fool's cap with little bells on it, worn by court jesters

cap and gown a flat cap (MORTARBOARD) and a long robe, worn at some academic ceremonies, as commencement, and often used to symbolize the academic life

cap-a-pie, cap-à-pie (kap′ə pē′) *adv.* [OFr. *de cap a pie* < *cap*, head (< L. *caput*) + *pie*, foot < L. *pes*] from head to foot; entirely

ca·par·i·son (kə par′ə s'n) *n.* [Fr. *caparaçon* < Pr. *caparasso*, large hooded cloak < ff.] **1.** an ornamented covering for a horse; trappings **2.** clothing, equipment, and ornaments; outfit —*vt.* **1.** to cover (a horse) with trappings **2.** to adorn with rich clothing; deck out

cape¹ (kāp) *n.* [Fr. < Pr. *capa* < LL. *cappa*, mantle, cloak] a sleeveless garment fastened at the neck and hanging over the back and shoulders, worn separately or attached to a dress or cloak

cape² (kāp) *n.* [ME. & OFr. < ML. *caput*, headland < L., HEAD] a piece of land projecting into a body of water; promontory; headland —**the Cape 1.** Cape of Good Hope **2.** Cape of Good Hope Province **3.** Cape Cod

Cape Breton Island island constituting the NE part of Nova Scotia, Canada: 3,975 sq. mi.; pop. 166,000

Cape buffalo a large, black, nearly hairless, very fierce buffalo (*Syncerus caffer*) of S Africa, with horns joined at the bases to form a helmetlike structure

Cape Cod, Cape Charles, Cape Hatteras, etc. *see* COD, CHARLES, HATTERAS, etc.

☆**Cape Cod cottage** [after Cape COD] a rectangular house one or one-and-one-half stories high, with a gable roof

Cape Cod National Seashore national recreational area along the E shore of Cape Cod: c. 42 sq. mi.

Cape Colony *former name of* Cape of GOOD HOPE (sense 2)

Cape crawfish the spiny lobster (*Jasus lalandii*) of southern Africa: see LOBSTER TAIL

Cape Dutch *same as* AFRIKAANS

Ča·pek (chä′pek), **Ka·rel** (kär′əl) 1890–1938; Czech playwright and novelist

cap·e·lin (kap′ə lin) *n.*, *pl.* **-lin, -lins:** see PLURAL, II, D, 2 [Fr. *capelan*, a jocular use of Pr. *capelan*, chaplain] a small, slender, smeltlike fish (*Mallotus villosus*) of northern seas, used as food and esp. as bait

Ca·pel·la (kə pel′ə) [L., orig., she-goat, dim. of *capra*, she-goat] a yellow, giant, first-magnitude star, the brightest in the constellation Auriga

Cape Province *same as* Cape of GOOD HOPE (sense 2)

---

ca·per[1] (kā′pər) *vi.* [prob. < CAPRIOLE] to skip or jump about in a gay, playful manner; frisk; gambol —*n.* 1. a gay, playful jump or leap 2. a wild, foolish action or prank ☆3. [Slang] a criminal plan or act, esp. a robbery —**cut a caper** (or **capers**) 1. to caper 2. to frolic about; play silly tricks

ca·per[2] (kā′pər) *n.* [ME. *capar* < L. *capparis* < Gr. *kapparis*] 1. any of a genus (*Capparis*) of plants of the caper family, esp. a prickly, trailing Mediterranean bush (*Capparis spinosa*) whose tiny green flower buds are pickled and used to flavor sauces, etc. 2. any of these buds —*adj.* designating a family (Capparidaceae) of plants including bee plant, cleome, and caper

cap·er·cail·lie (kap′ər kāl′yē) *n.* [< Gael. *capull* (< L. *caballus,* a horse) *coille,* forest, hence lit., horse of the woods] the largest species of European grouse (*Tetrao urogallus*): also **cap′er·cail′zie** (-yē, -zē)

Ca·per·na·um (kə pʉr′nē əm) city in ancient Palestine, on the Sea of Galilee: cf. Matt. 4:12–17

cape·skin (kāp′skin′) *n.* [orig. made from the skin of goats from the *Cape* of Good Hope] fine leather made from goatskin or sheepskin, used esp. for gloves

Ca·pet (kā′pit, kap′it), **Hugh** 938?–996 A.D.; king of France (987–996)

Ca·pe·tian (kə pē′shən) *adj.* designating or of the French dynasty (987–1328 A.D.) founded by Hugh Capet —*n.* a member of the Capetian dynasty

Cape Town seaport & capital of Cape of Good Hope Province: seat of the legislature of South Africa: pop. 807,000: also, esp. formerly, **Cape′town′**

Cape York Peninsula large peninsula in NE Australia, part of Queensland

cap·ful (kap′fool′) *n., pl.* **-fuls′** as much as the cap of the bottle can hold

caph (käf) *n. same as* KAPH

Cap Haï·ti·en (kà pä ē syan′) seaport on the N coast of Haiti: pop. 30,000: also **Cap-Haï·ti·en**

ca·pi·as (kā′pē əs, kap′ē-) *n.* [ME. < ML. < L., 2d pers. sing., pres. subj., of *capere,* to take] *Law* a writ issued by a court directing an officer to arrest the person named

cap·il·la·ceous (kap′ə lā′shəs) *adj.* [L. *capillaceus,* hairlike < *capillus,* hair] 1. having hairlike filaments 2. like a hair or thread

cap·il·lar·i·ty (kap′ə ler′ə tē) *n.* [Fr. *capillarité* < L. *capillaris:* see ff.] 1. the state of being capillary 2. the property of exerting or having capillary attraction 3. *same as* CAPILLARY ATTRACTION

cap·il·lar·y (kap′ə ler′ē) *adj.* [L. *capillaris* < *capillus,* hair] 1. of or like a hair, esp. in being very slender 2. having a very small bore 3. in or of capillaries —*n., pl.* **-lar′ies** 1. a tube with a very small bore: also **capillary tube** 2. any of the tiny blood vessels connecting the arteries with the veins

capillary attraction a force that is the resultant of adhesion, cohesion, and surface tension in liquids which are in contact with solids, as in a capillary tube: when the cohesive force is greater, the surface of the liquid tends to rise in the tube; when the adhesive force is greater, the surface tends to be depressed in the tube: also **capillary action**

cap·i·tal[1] (kap′ə t'l) *adj.* [ME. & OFr. < L. *capitalis,* of the head < *caput,* the HEAD: see CHIEF] 1. involving or punishable by death (originally by decapitation) [a *capital* offense] 2. most important or most serious; principal; chief [a *capital* virtue] 3. of most political importance, as being the seat of government [a *capital* city] 4. of or having to do with capital, or wealth 5. first-rate; excellent [a *capital* idea] See also CAPITAL LETTER —*n.* 1. *same as* CAPITAL LETTER 2. a city or town that is the official seat of government of a state, nation, etc. 3. a city where a certain industry, activity, etc. is centered [the rubber *capital*] 4. wealth (money or property) owned or used in business by a person, corporation, etc. 5. an accumulated stock of such wealth or its value 6. wealth, in whatever form, used or capable of being used to produce more wealth 7. any source of benefit or assistance 8. [often C-] capitalists collectively: distinguished from LABOR 9. *Accounting a*) the net worth of a business; amount by which the assets exceed the liabilities *b*) the face value of all the stock issued or authorized by a corporation —*SYN.* see CHIEF —**make capital of** to get advantage from; make the most of; exploit

cap·i·tal[2] (kap′ə t'l) *n.* [ME. < OFr. *chapitel* < L. *capitellum,* dim. of *caput,* the HEAD] the top part of a column or pilaster

capital account 1. an account of the total capital invested in fixed assets by the owners of a business, including real estate, machinery, etc., but excluding current or operating expenses 2. *Accounting* the summed difference between the assets and liabilities of a business on any given date

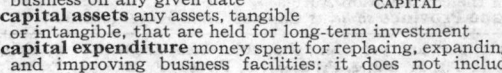

CAPITAL

capital assets any assets, tangible or intangible, that are held for long-term investment

capital expenditure money spent for replacing, expanding, and improving business facilities: it does not include operating expenses

capital gain profit resulting from the sale of capital investments, as stocks, real estate, etc., taxed at a lower rate than other income

capital goods commodities for use in production, as raw materials, machinery, buildings, etc.; producers' goods as distinguished from consumers' goods

cap·i·tal·ism (-iz'm) *n.* 1. the economic system in which all or most of the means of production and distribution, as land, factories, railroads, etc., are privately owned and operated for profit, originally under fully competitive conditions: it has been generally characterized by a tendency toward concentration of wealth, and, in its later phase, by the growth of great corporations, increased governmental control, etc. 2. the principles, methods, interests, power, influence, etc. of capitalists, especially of those with large holdings

cap·i·tal·ist (-ist) *n.* 1. a person who has capital; owner of wealth used in business 2. an upholder of capitalism 3. loosely, a wealthy person —*adj.* capitalistic

☆**cap·i·tal·is·tic** (kap′ə t'l is′tik) *adj.* 1. of or characteristic of capitalists or capitalism 2. upholding, preferring, or practicing capitalism —**cap′i·tal·is′ti·cal·ly** *adv.*

cap·i·tal·i·za·tion (-ə zā′shən) *n.* 1. *a*) the act or process of converting something into capital *b*) the amount or sum resulting from this 2. the total capital funds of a corporation, represented by stocks, bonds, undivided profit, surplus, etc. 3. the total par or stated value of the stocks and bonds outstanding of a corporation 4. *a*) the total invested in a business by the owner or owners *b*) the total corporate liability ☆5. the act or system of using capital letters in writing and printing

cap·i·tal·ize (kap′ə t'l īz′) *vt.* **-ized′, -iz′ing** 1. to use as capital; convert into capital 2. to calculate the present value of (a periodical payment, annuity, income, etc.); convert (an income, etc.) into one payment or sum equivalent to the computed present value 3. to establish the capital stock of (a business firm) at a certain figure 4. to convert (floating debt) into stock or shares 5. to supply capital to or for (an enterprise) ☆6. to print or write (a word or words) in capital letters ☆7. to begin (a word) with a capital letter 8. *Accounting* to set up (expenditures) as assets —**capitalize on (something)** to use (something) to one's own advantage or profit

capital letter the form of an alphabetical letter used to begin a sentence or proper name [A, B, C, etc. are *capital letters*]

capital levy a tax on individual or corporate capital levied at various times and in various countries in addition to an income tax

cap·i·tal·ly (kap′ə t'l ē) *adv.* in an excellent or admirable manner; very well

capital punishment penalty of death for a crime

capital ship formerly, an armored surface vessel of war, other than an aircraft carrier, carrying guns exceeding 8-inch caliber

capital stock 1. the capital of a corporation, divided into negotiable shares 2. the total par or stated value of the authorized and issued shares of stock

capital surplus 1. any surplus of a business firm not derived from direct earnings or profits 2. the excess of the amount of money received by a corporation for a stock issue over the stock's par or stated value

cap·i·tate (kap′ə tāt′) *adj.* [L. *capitatus,* having a head < *caput,* the HEAD] 1. enlarged at the head or tip 2. head-shaped, as some flowers

cap·i·ta·tion (kap′ə tā′shən) *n.* [LL. *capitatio* < L. *caput,* the HEAD] a tax or fee of so much per head; payment per capita: see also POLL TAX

Cap·i·tol (kap′ə t'l) [ME. & OFr. *capitolie* < L. *Capitolium,* temple of Jupiter in Rome, related by the ancients to *caput,* head, but of other, unknown orig.] 1. *a*) the temple of Jupiter on the Capitoline Hill in ancient Rome *b*) the hill itself ☆2. the building in which the U.S. Congress meets, at Washington, D.C. —*n.* ☆[*usually* c-] the building in which a State legislature meets

Cap·i·to·line (kap′ə t'l īn′) one of the SEVEN HILLS OF ROME —*adj.* 1. of or having to do with this hill 2. of the temple of Jupiter which stood there

ca·pit·u·lar (kə pich′ə lər) *adj.* [ME. *capituler* < ML. *capitularis* < L. *capitulum,* chapter, dim. of *caput,* the HEAD] of a chapter, esp. that of a religious order

ca·pit·u·lar·y (-ler′ē) *n., pl.* **-lar′ies** [ML. *capitularius* < prec.] an ordinance or a collection of ordinances, esp. as made formerly by Frankish kings

ca·pit·u·late (-lāt′) *vi.* **-lat′ed, -lat′ing** [< LL. *capitulatus,* pp. of *capitulare,* to draw up in heads or chapters, arrange conditions < L. *capitulum:* see CAPITULAR] 1. to give up (*to* an enemy) on prearranged conditions; surrender conditionally 2. to give up or give in; stop resisting —*SYN.* see YIELD

ca·pit·u·la·tion (kə pich′ə lā′shən) *n.* [Fr. < ML. *capitulatio:* see prec.] 1. a statement of the main parts of a subject 2. the act of capitulating; conditional surrender 3. a document containing terms of surrender, articles of concession, etc.; treaty; covenant

ca·pit·u·lum (kə pich′ə ləm) *n., pl.* **-la** (-lə) [L., dim. of *caput,* the HEAD: see CHIEF] 1. *Anat., Zool.* a knoblike part, as at the end of a bone in a joint 2. *Bot. same as* HEAD (*n.* 17 *a*)

ca·po (kä′pō) *n.*, *pl.* **-pos** [short for *capotasto* < It., lit., chief key < *capo*, chief, head (< L. *caput*, HEAD) + *tasto*, key < *tastare*, to touch < VL.: see TASTE] a device fastened over the fingerboard as of a guitar to shorten the strings uniformly and facilitate a change of key

ca·pon (kā′pän, -pən) *n.* [ME. *capoun* < OE. *capun* & OFr. *chapon* < L. *capo* < IE. base *(s)kep-, to cut, whence SHAFT] a castrated rooster, esp. one fattened for eating —**ca′pon·ize′** (-pə nīz′) *vt.* -**ized′**, -**iz′ing**

cap·o·ral[1] (kap′ər əl, kap′ə ral′) *n.* [Fr. < *tabac du caporal*, lit., corporal's tobacco (a better grade than *tabac du soldat*, soldier's tobacco) < It. *caporale*, CORPORAL[1]] a kind of tobacco

☆**cap·o·ral**[2] (kap′ə ral′, kä′pə räl′) *n.* [AmSp. < Sp., foreman < It. *caporale*, leader, CORPORAL[1]] [Southwest] the boss or an assistant boss of a ranch

Cap·o·ret·to (kap′ə ret′ō) It. village (now in Yugoslavia): scene of a severe Italian defeat (1917) by Austro-German forces Serbo-Croatian name, KOBARID

ca·pote (kə pōt′) *n.* [Fr., dim. of *cape*, CAPE[1]] a long cloak, usually with a hood

Cap·pa·do·ci·a (kap′ə dō′shē ə, -shə) ancient kingdom, later a Roman province, in E Asia Minor

cap·per (kap′ər) *n.* a person or device that caps or makes caps

‡**cap·puc·ci·no** (käp′pŌŌt chē′nō; E. kap′ə chē′nō) *n.*, *pl.* -**ni** (-nē) [It., lit., CAPUCHIN (in allusion to the brown habit worn by the friars)] espresso coffee served steaming hot with thick cream and variously flavored

cap·re·o·late (kap′rē ə lāt′, kə prē′ə lit) *adj.* [< L. *capreolus*, tendril, lit., wild goat + -ATE[1]] *Bot.* having tendrils

Ca·pri (ka prē′, kä′prē) island near the entrance to the Bay of Naples: 5 sq. mi.; pop. 6,000

cap·ric acid (kap′rik) [< L. *caper*, gen. *capris*, goat (see CAPRIOLE) + -IC: named from its goatlike smell] a fatty acid, $CH_3(CH_2)_8COOH$, occurring as a glyceride in natural fats and oils

ca·pric·ci·o (kə prē′chē ō; *It.* kä prēt′chō) *n.*, *pl.* -**ci·os**; *It.* -**pric′ci** (-chē) [It.; see CAPRICE] **1.** a prank; whim; caprice **2.** a musical composition of irregular form, usually lively and whimsical in spirit

ca·pric·ci·o·so (kə prē′chē ō′sō; *It.* kä′prēt chō′sō) *adj.*, *adv.* [It., CAPRICIOUS] *Music* in a light, free, whimsical style

ca·price (kə prēs′) *n.* [Fr. < It. *capriccio*, a shivering, whim < *capo* (< L. *caput*, head) + *riccio*, curl, frizzled, lit., hedgehog < L. *ericius:* see URCHIN] hence, orig., head with bristling hair, horripilation; meaning infl. by association with It. *capriola* (see CAPRIOLE) & *capra* < L. *capra*, she-goat] **1.** a sudden, impulsive change in the way one thinks or acts; freakish notion; whim **2.** a capricious quality or nature **3.** *Music* a capriccio

SYN.—**caprice** refers to a sudden, impulsive, apparently unmotivated turn of mind or emotion [discharged at the *caprice* of a foreman]; **whim** and **whimsy** both refer to an idle, quaint, or curious notion, but **whim** more often suggests willfulness and **whimsy** fancifulness [pursuing a *whim* he wrote a poem full of *whimsy*]; **vagary** suggests a highly unusual or extravagant notion [the *vagaries* in fashion in women's clothes]; **crotchet** implies great eccentricity and connotes stubbornness in opposition to prevailing thought, usually on some insignificant point [his *crotchets* concerning diet]

ca·pri·cious (kə prish′əs) *adj.* [Fr. *capricieux* < It. *capriccioso:* see prec.] **1.** subject to caprices; tending to change abruptly and without apparent reason; erratic; flighty **2.** [Obs.] showing wit or fancifulness —*SYN.* see INCONSTANT —**ca·pri′cious·ly** *adv.* —**ca·pri′cious·ness** *n.*

Cap·ri·corn (kap′rə kôrn′) [ME. < OFr. < L. *capricornus* < *caper*, goat + *cornu*, a HORN] **1.** a S constellation between Sagittarius and Aquarius, supposedly outlining a goat **2.** the tenth sign of the zodiac (♑), which the sun enters about Dec. 22: see ZODIAC, illus.

cap·ri·fi·ca·tion (kap′rə fi kā′shən) *n.* [L. *caprificatio*, ripening of figs by the stinging of the gall wasp < *caprificare*, to ripen figs (by this process) < *caprificus*, CAPRIFIG] the pollination of certain cultivated figs through the transfer to them of pollen from the wild fig by a gall wasp

cap·ri·fig (kap′rə fig′) *n.* [< L. *caprificus*, wild fig < *caper*, goat + *ficus*, fig] the wild fig (*Ficus carica sylvestris*) growing mainly in southern Europe and the Near East and used in caprification

cap·ri·ole (kap′rē ōl′) *n.* [Fr. < It. *capriola* < *capriolare*, to leap like a goat < *capriuolo*, doe, roe < L. *capreolus*, wild goat < *caper*, goat] **1.** a caper; leap **2.** an upward leap made by a horse without going forward —*vi.* -**oled′**, -**ol′ing** to make a capriole

ca·pri pants (ka prē′) [after CAPRI] [*also* C-] tightfitting trousers for women: also **ca·pris′** *n.pl.*

cap rock a relatively impervious rock layer immediately overlying a deposit of oil, gas, salt, etc.

ca·pro·ic acid (kə prō′ik) [*capro-* (for L. *caper*, goat) + -IC: so named from its smell] a colorless, liquid fatty acid, $CH_3(CH_2)_4COOH$, found in butter and other animal fats and used in the manufacture of esters

ca·pryl·ic acid (kə pril′ik) [CAPR(IC ACID) + -YL + -IC] a

fatty acid, $CH_3(CH_2)_6COOH$, with a rancid taste: used in the synthesis of dyes, drugs, perfumes, etc.

caps. capitals (capital letters)

cap·sa·i·cin (kap sā′ə s'n) *n.* [L. *capsa*, a box + -IC + -IN[1]] a bitter, strongly irritant, white crystalline alkaloid, $C_{18}H_{27}O_3N$, extracted from capsicum

cap screw a kind of bolt used in a tapped hole, usually without a nut, as for fastening cylinder covers, etc.

Cap·si·an (kap′sē ən) *adj.* [Fr. *capsien* < L. *Capsa*, ancient name of *Gafsa*, city in central Tunisia, near which artifacts were found] designating or of a paleolithic culture of North Africa characterized by backed blades, small hand tools, etc.

cap·si·cum (kap′sə kəm) *n.* [ModL. < L. *capsa*, a box: from the shape of the seedpods] **1.** any of several varieties of the red pepper (genus *Capsicum*), of the nightshade family, with pungent fleshy pods that are the chili peppers, cayenne peppers, bird peppers, etc. of commerce **2.** these pods variously prepared as condiments or, in medicine, as a gastric stimulant

cap·size (kap′sīz, kap sīz′) *vt.*, *vi.* -**sized**, -**siz·ing** [18th-c. naut. slang; ? altered (after dial. *cap*, to overtop + *side*) < Sp. *cabezar*, lit., to sink by the head (< *cabo*, *cabeza*, the head)] to overturn or upset: said esp. of a boat —*SYN.* see UPSET

cap·stan (kap′stən) *n.* [Fr. & Pr. *cabestan* < ? L. *capistrum*, halter, muzzle < *capere*, to take, hold] an apparatus, mainly on ships, around which cables or hawsers are wound for hoisting anchors, lifting weights, etc.: it consists of an upright, spool-shaped cylinder that is turned on an inner shafting by machinery or by hand

CAPSTAN

capstan bar any of the poles inserted in a capstan and used as levers in turning it by hand

cap·stone (kap′stōn′) *n.* **1.** the uppermost stone of a structure **2.** any of a series of slabs atop a wall; stone in a coping **3.** the highest point, as of achievement

cap·su·lar (kap′sə lər, -syoo-) *adj.* **1.** having the nature of a capsule **2.** of or in a capsule

cap·su·late (-lāt′, -lit) *adj.* contained in or formed into a capsule: also **cap′su·lat′ed**

cap·sule (kap′s'l, -syool) *n.* [Fr. < L. *capsula*, dim. of *capsa*, chest < base of *capere*, to take, contain] **1.** orig., a small case or sheath ☆**2.** a small, soluble gelatin container for enclosing a dose of medicine ☆**3.** *a)* an ejectable airplane cockpit *b)* a detachable, closed compartment designed to hold and protect men, instruments, etc. in a rocket: in full, **space capsule 4.** *Anat. a)* any sac or membrane enclosing an organ or part *b)* either of two layers of cerebral white matter **5.** *Bot.* a case, pod, or fruit, containing seeds, spores, or carpels, esp. one that bursts when ripe **6.** *Chem.* a shallow dish or tray for evaporating liquids —*adj.* in a concise or condensed form [a *capsule* biography] —*vt.* -**suled**, -**sul·ing** to condense

cap·sul·ize (-īz′) *vt.* -**ized′**, -**iz′ing 1.** to enclose in a capsule **2.** to express in a concise form; condense

Capt. Captain

cap·tain (kap′tən) *n.* [ME. *capitain* < OFr. *capitaine* < LL. *capitaneus*, chief in size < L. *caput*, the HEAD: cf. CHIEFTAIN] **1.** *a)* a chief or leader [*captains* of industry] *b)* an important military leader **2.** the head of a group or division; specif., *a)* U.S. *Mil.* an officer ranking above a first lieutenant and below a major *b)* U.S. *Navy* an officer ranking above a commander and below a rear admiral *c)* the commander or master of a ship *d)* the leader of a team or crew, as in sports ☆*e)* a precinct commander in a police or fire department ☆*f)* a district leader of a political party Abbrev. **Capt.** —*vt.* to be captain of; lead —**cap′tain·cy** (-sē), *pl.* -**cies, cap′tain·ship′** *n.*

captain's walk same as WIDOW'S WALK

cap·tion (kap′shən) *n.* [ME. *capcioun* < OFr. *capcion* < L. *captio* < pp. of *capere*, to seize, take] **1.** [Archaic] seizure **2.** *Law a)* a part of a legal instrument, such as an indictment, showing where, when, and by what authority it was executed *b)* a heading showing the names of the parties, court, and docket number in a pleading or deposition **3.** *a)* a heading or title, as of a newspaper article *b)* a descriptive title, or legend, as under an illustration **4.** *Motion Pictures* a subtitle —*vt.* to supply a caption for

cap·tious (-shəs) *adj.* [ME. *capcious* < L. *captiosus*: prec.] **1.** made only for the sake of argument or faultfinding; sophistical [*captious* criticism] **2.** fond of catching others in mistakes; quick to find fault; quibbling; carping —*SYN.* see CRITICAL —**cap′tious·ly** *adv.* —**cap′tious·ness** *n.*

cap·ti·vate (kap′tə vāt′) *vt.* -**vat′ed**, -**vat′ing** [< LL.(Ec.) *captivatus*, pp. of *captivare*, to take captive < L. *captivus*, CAPTIVE] **1.** orig., to take or hold captive **2.** to capture the attention or affection of, as by beauty, excellence, etc.; fascinate; charm —*SYN.* see ATTRACT —**cap′ti·vat′ing·ly** *adv.* —**cap′ti·va′tion** *n.* —**cap′ti·va′tor** *n.*

cap·tive (kap′tiv) *n.* [L. *captivus* < *captus*, pp. of *capere*, to take] **1.** a person caught and held prisoner, as in war **2.** a person who is captivated, as by beauty or love —*adj.* **1.** *a)* taken or held prisoner *b)* not able to act independently [a *captive* nation] ☆*c)* obliged or forced to listen, whether wanting to or not [a *captive* audience] **2.** captivated **3.** of captivity

cap·tiv·i·ty (kap tiv′ə tē) *n., pl.* **-ties** [ME. *captivite* < L. *captivitas*] the condition or time of being captive; imprisonment; bondage

cap·tor (kap′tər) *n.* [L.] a person who captures

cap·ture (-chər) *n.* [Fr. < L. *captura* < *captus*, pp. of *capere*, to take, seize: for IE. base see HAVE] **1.** a taking or being taken by force, surprise, or skill, as enemy troops, an opponent's piece in chess, etc. **2.** that which is thus taken or seized; specif., a prize or booty in war **3.** the absorption of a particle by an atomic nucleus; esp., the absorption of a neutron or an orbital electron that often results in the immediate emission of radiation —*vt.* **-tured, -tur·ing 1.** to take or seize by force, surprise, skill, etc. **2.** to represent (something transient, immaterial, etc.) in more or less permanent form [to *capture* her charm on canvas] **3.** to effect the capture of (a subatomic particle) —*SYN.* see CATCH

Cap·u·a (kap′yoo wə) **1.** ancient town in S Italy, near Naples **2.** modern town on a nearby site: pop. 13,000

ca·puche (kə pōōch′, -pōōsh′) *n.* [Fr. < *capuce* < It. *capuccio* < ML. *caputium*, cowl < LL. *cappa*, cloak, hooded cape] a long, pointed hood, as that worn by the Capuchins

Cap·u·chin (kap′yoo shin, -chin; kə pyōō′-) *n.* [Fr. *capucin*, monk who wears a cowl < prec.] **1.** a member of a branch (**Friars Minor Capuchin**) of the Franciscan order that adheres strictly to the original rule **2.** [c-] a woman's cloak with a hood **3.** [c-] any of a genus (*Cebus*) of New World monkeys with a nearly bare face and a hoodlike crown of hair

Cap·u·let (kap′yoo lit, -let′) the family name of Juliet in Shakespeare's *Romeo and Juliet*

cap·y·ba·ra (kap′ə bär′ə) *n.* [Port. *capibara* < Tupi *kapiwgara*, lit., one who eats grass] a tailless, partially web-footed, S. American animal (*Hydrochoerus capybara*) found in and around lakes and streams: the largest extant rodent, reaching a length of over four feet

car (kär) *n.* [ME. & ONornFr. *carre* < LL. *carrum* < L. *carrus*, orig., two-wheeled Celtic war chariot < Gaul. *carros* (OIr. *carr*) < ? IE. *$krsos$ < base *kers-*, to run, whence L. *currere*, to run (see COURSE)] **1.** any vehicle on wheels **2.** [Poet.] a chariot ☆**3.** a vehicle that moves on rails, as a streetcar **4.** an automobile ☆**5.** an elevator cage **6.** the part of a balloon or airship for carrying people and equipment

CAR, C.A.R. Civil Air Regulations

car. carat(s)

ca·ra·bao (kär′ə bou′) *n., pl.* **-baos, -bao:** see PLURAL, II, D, 1 [Sp. < Malay *karbau*] *same as* WATER BUFFALO

car·a·bid (kar′ə bid) *n.* [< ModL. *Carabidae*, name of the family < *Carabus*, the type genus < Gr. *karabos*, a horned beetle (cf. CARAVEL)] *same as* GROUND BEETLE

car·a·bi·neer, car·a·bi·nier (kar′ə bə nir′) *n.* [Fr. *carabinier*] a cavalryman armed with a carbine

‡**ca·ra·bi·nie·ri** (kä′rä bē nye′rē) *n.pl., sing.* **-nie′re** (-re) [It. < Fr. *carabinier*: see prec.] the Italian police

car·a·cal (ker′ə kal′) *n.* [Fr. < Turk. *qarah-qulaq* < *qara*, black + *qulaq*, ear] **1.** a reddish-brown lynx (*Felis caracal*) of SW Asia and E Africa, with black-tipped ears **2.** its fur

Car·a·cal·la (kar′ə kal′ə) (born *Marcus Aurelius Antoninus*) 188–217 A.D.; Roman emperor (211–217)

ca·ra·ca·ra (kär′ə kär′ə) *n.* [Sp. *caracara* < Tupi, of echoic orig.] any of a genus (*Caracara*) of large, vulturelike hawks of S. America

Ca·ra·cas (kə räk′əs, -rak′-; *Sp.* kä rä′käs) capital of Venezuela, in the NC part: pop. 787,000

car·a·cole (kar′ə kōl′) *n.* [Fr. < Wal. *caracoll*, lit., snail shell < Sp. *caracol* < Catal. *caragol* < Fr. *escargot*, snail] a half turn to the right or left made by a horse with a rider —*vi.* **-coled′, -col′ing** [Fr. *caracoler* < the *n.*] to make a caracole or caracoles

car·a·cul (kar′ə kəl) *n.* [see KARAKUL] *same as* KARAKUL, *esp. as a name for the fur*

ca·rafe (kə raf′, -räf′) *n.* [Fr. < It. *caraffa*, prob. < Ar. *gharrâf*, drinking cup < *gharafa*, to draw water] a bottle of glass or metal for water, coffee, etc.

ca·ra·ga·na (kar′ə gän′ə) *n.* [ModL., name of the genus < Kirghiz *karaghan*, the Siberian pea shrub] any of a genus (*Caragana*) of hardy shrubs of the legume family, grown for their showy golden flowers and often as windbreaks in dry climates

car·a·geen (kar′ə gēn′) *n. same as* CARRAGEEN

☆**ca·ram·ba** (kä räm′bä) *interj.* [AmSp. < Sp., euphemism for *carajo*, penis < VL. **caraculum*, small arrow] [Southwest] an exclamation of surprise, dismay, etc.

car·a·mel (kar′ə m'l, -mel′; kär′m'l) *n.* [Fr. < OFr. *calamele* < ML. *calamella*, var. of *canamella*, sugar cane < L. *canna mellis* < *canna* (see CANE) + *mellis*, honey] **1.** burnt sugar used to color or flavor food or beverages **2.** a chewy candy made from sugar, milk, etc.

car·a·mel·ize (kar′ə mə liz′, kär′mə liz′) *vt., vi.* **-ized′, -iz′ing** to turn into caramel

ca·ran·gid (kə ran′jid) *n.* [< ModL. *Carangidae*, name of the family < *Caranx*, type genus < Fr. *carangue*, horse mackerel, shad < Sp.] any of a family (Carangidae) of marine, game and food fishes, with a widely forked tail and, usually, bluish-silver markings, as the pompano —**ca·ran′-goid** (-raŋ′goid) *adj.*

car·a·pace (kar′ə pās′) *n.* [Fr. < Sp. *carapacho*] the horny, protective covering over all or part of the back of certain animals, as the upper shell of the turtle, armadillo, crab, etc.

car·at (kar′ət) *n.* [Fr. < It. *carato* < Ar. *qîrât*, pod, husk, weight of 4 grains < Gr. *keration*, little horn, carob seed, carat, dim. of *keras*, HORN] **1.** a unit of weight for precious stones and pearls, equal to 200 milligrams **2.** *same as* KARAT

Ca·ra·vag·gio (kä′rä väd′jō), **Mi·chel·an·ge·lo A·me·ri·ghi da** (mē′ke län′je lō ä′me rē′gē dä) (born *Michelangelo Merisi*) 1573–1610; It. painter

car·a·van (kar′ə van′) *n.* [Fr. *caravane* < OFr. *karouan* < Per. *kärwän*, caravan] **1.** a company of travelers, esp. of merchants or pilgrims traveling together for safety, as through a desert **2.** a number of vehicles traveling together **3.** a large covered vehicle for passengers, circus animals, gypsies, etc.; van **4.** [Brit.] a trailer (sense 3)

car·a·van·sa·ry (kar′ə van′sə rē) *n., pl.* **-ries** [Fr. *caravansérai* < Per. *kärwänsarāi* < *kärwän*, caravan + *sarāi*, palace, mansion, inn] in the Orient, a kind of inn with a large central court, where caravans stop for the night Also **car′a·van′se·rai** (-sə rī′, -sə rā′)

car·a·vel (kar′ə vel′) *n.* [Fr. *caravelle* < Port. *caravela*, dim. of *caravo*, small vessel < LL. *carabus* < Gr. *karabos*, kind of light ship, beetle, crayfish] any of several kinds of fast, small sailing ships, esp. one with a narrow, high poop and lateen sails, used by the Spaniards and Portuguese in the 16th cent.

car·a·way (kar′ə wā′) *n.* [ME. *carawai* < (? via ML. *carui*) Ar. *karawiyā′* < ? Gr. *karon*, caraway] **1.** a white-flowered biennial herb (*Carum carvi*) of the parsley family, with spicy, strong-smelling seeds **2.** the seeds, used as a flavoring for bread, cakes, cheese, etc., and as a carminative

carb- (kärb) *same as* CARBO-: used before vowels

car·ba·mate (kär′bə māt′, kär bam′āt) *n.* a salt or ester of carbamic acid

car·bam·ic acid (kär bam′ik) *adj.* [CARB- + AM(IDO) + -IC] an acid, NH_2COOH, known only by a number of salts and esters

car·ban·i·on (kär ban′i′än, -ən) *n.* [CARB- + ANION] a transient, negatively charged organic ion, as H_3C^-, R_3C^-, which has one more electron than the corresponding free radical

car·baz·ole (kär′bə zōl′) *n.* [CARB- + AZ- + -OLE] a white, crystalline substance, $(C_6H_4)_2NH$, occurring in crude anthracene: used in the manufacture of dyes, explosives, insecticides, etc.

car·bide (kär′bid) *n.* [CARB- + -IDE] a compound of an element, usually a metal, with carbon; esp., calcium carbide

car·bine (kär′bin, -bēn) *n.* [Fr. *carabine* < *carabin*, mounted rifleman < *escarrabin*, corpse bearer during the plague (lit., prob. "carrion beetle," used as epithet for archers from Flanders) < *scarabée*: see SCARAB] **1.** a rifle with a short barrel, orig. for use by cavalry ☆**2.** *U.S. Armed Forces* a light, semiautomatic or automatic .30-caliber rifle of relatively limited range

car·bi·neer (kär′bə nir′) *n. same as* CARABINEER

car·bi·nol (kär′bə nôl′, -nōl′) *n.* [*carbin* (name used by A. Kolbe, 19th-cent. G. chemist, for the methyl radical) + -OL] **1.** *same as* METHANOL **2.** any alcohol bearing a homologous relation to methanol, as diethyl carbinol $(CH_3·CH_2)_2CHOH$

car·bo- (kär′bə, -bō) *a combining form meaning* carbon [*carbohydrate*]

car·bo·cy·clic (kär′bə sī′klik) *adj.* [CARBO- + CYCLIC] designating an organic ring compound in which all the members of the ring are carbon atoms, as benzene or naphthalene

car·bo·hy·drate (kär′bə hī′drāt) *n.* [CARBO- + HYDRATE] any of certain organic compounds, including the sugars, starches, and celluloses, which have the general formula $C_x(H_2O)_y$: carbohydrates form an important class of foods in animal nutrition, supplying energy to the body

car·bo·lat·ed (kär′bə lāt′id) *adj.* containing or treated with carbolic acid

car·bol·ic acid (kär bäl′ik) *adj.* [CARB- + -OL[1] + -IC] *same as* PHENOL (sense 1)

car·bo·lize (kär′bə liz′) *vt.* **-lized′, -liz′ing** to treat or sterilize with phenol

car·bon (kär′bən) *n.* [Fr. *carbone* < L. *carbo* (gen. *carbonis*), coal] **1.** a nonmetallic chemical element found in many inorganic compounds and all organic compounds: diamond and graphite are pure carbon; carbon is also present, with other substances, in coal, coke, charcoal, soot, etc.: symbol, C; at. wt., 12.01115; at. no., 6; sp. gr., 2.25 (graphite); sublimes at 3652°C: a radioactive isotope of carbon (**carbon 14**) is used as a tracer in chemical and biochemical research, and, because of its presence in all carbon-containing matter, is the means of dating archaeological specimens, fossils, etc. **2.** a sheet of carbon paper **3.** *same as* CARBON COPY **4.** *Elec. a)* a stick of carbon used in an arc lamp *b)* a carbon plate or rod used in a battery —*adj.* of, like, or treated with carbon

car·bo·na·ceous (kär′bə nā′shəs) *adj.* of, consisting of, or containing carbon

car·bo·na·do (kär′bə nā′dō, -nä′-) *n., pl.* **-does, -dos** [Sp. *carbonada* < *carbon*, charcoal < L. *carbo*, coal] **1.** [Obs.] a piece of meat, often fish or fowl, scored and broiled **2.** [Port., carbonized] a massive form of diamond characterized by opacity and dark color, used for drills —*vt.* **-doed, -do·ing** [Obs.] **1.** to score and broil (meat) **2.** to cut gashes in; slash; hack

‡**Car·bo·na·ri** (kär′bo nä′rē) *n.pl., sing.* **-na·ro** (-rō) [It., pl. of *carbonaro*, charcoal burner < L. *carbonarius* < *carbo*, coal]: said to be so named from meeting among the charcoal burners and using their jargon] an Italian revolutionary group organized about 1811 to unify Italy and found a republic

car·bon·ate (kär′bə nit; *also, and for v. always,* -nāt′) *n.* [Fr.: see CARBON & -ATE²] a salt or ester of carbonic acid —*vt.* **-at′ed, -at′ing 1.** [Obs.] to burn to carbon; carbonize **2.** to charge with carbon dioxide [*carbonated* drinks] **3.** to form into a carbonate

car·bon·a·tion (kär′bə nā′shən) *n.* **1.** saturation with carbon dioxide, as in the manufacture of soda water: also **car′bon·a·ta′tion** (-nə tā′shən) **2.** the removal of lime, as in sugar refining, by precipitating it with carbon dioxide

carbon bisulfide *same as* CARBON DISULFIDE

carbon black finely divided carbon produced by the incomplete burning of oil or gas: used in rubber and ink manufacture

carbon copy 1. a copy, as of a letter, made with carbon paper **2.** any person or thing very much like another

carbon cycle 1. the cycle by which plants through photosynthesis use atmospheric carbon dioxide to produce carbohydrates, which are in turn metabolized by animals to decomposition products that return carbon dioxide to the atmosphere **2.** a cycle of thermonuclear processes in the interior of stars involving carbon and producing large quantities of energy by the transformation of hydrogen into helium

car·bon-date (-dāt′) *vt.* **-dat′ed, -dat′ing** to establish the approximate age of (fossil remains, archaeological specimens, etc.) by measuring the amount of radioactive carbon 14 remaining in them

carbon dioxide a colorless, odorless, incombustible gas, CO_2, somewhat heavier than air, that passes out of the lungs in respiration: produced commercially and used widely in fire extinguishers, carbonated beverages, etc.: in photosynthesis, carbon dioxide and water are absorbed by plants, which synthesize certain carbohydrates and release oxygen into the air

carbon disulfide a heavy, volatile, colorless liquid, CS_2, highly flammable and poisonous, used as a solvent, preservative, insecticide, etc.

car·bon·ic (kär bän′ik) *adj.* of, containing, or obtained from carbon or carbon dioxide

carbonic acid a weak, colorless acid, H_2CO_3, formed by the solution of carbon dioxide in water and existing only in solution

car·bon·ic-ac·id gas (kär bän′ik as′id) *same as* CARBON DIOXIDE

car·bon·if·er·ous (kär′bə nif′ər əs) *adj.* [< CARBON + -FEROUS] **1.** producing or containing carbon or coal **2.** [C-] designating or of a great coal-making period of the Paleozoic Era: the warm, damp climate produced great forests, which later formed rich coal seams —**the Carboniferous 1.** the Carboniferous Period **2.** the rock and coal strata formed during this period See GEOLOGY, chart

car·bon·i·um (kär bō′nē əm) *n.* [CARB- + (AMM)ONIUM] a transient, positively charged organic ion, as H_3C^+, R_3C^+, which has one less electron than the corresponding free radical

car·bon·ize (kär′bə nīz′) *vt.* **-ized′, -iz′ing 1.** to change into carbon, as by partial burning **2.** to treat, cover, or combine with carbon —*vi.* to become carbonized —**car′bon·i·za′tion** *n.*

carbon monoxide a colorless, odorless, highly poisonous gas, CO, produced by the incomplete combustion of carbonaceous material: it burns with a pale-blue flame

carbon paper 1. very thin paper coated on one side with a waxy, dark-colored preparation, as of carbon: it is placed between two sheets of paper so that the pressure of typing or writing on the upper sheet makes a copy on the lower **2.** paper used in the carbon process

carbon process a photographic printing process that uses paper coated with sensitized, pigmented gelatin which becomes progressively hardened and insoluble the more it is exposed to light

carbon tetrachloride a nonflammable, colorless, poisonous liquid, CCl_4, used in fire extinguishers, as a solvent for fats (in cleaning mixtures), etc.

car·bon·yl (kär′bə nil′) *n.* [CARBON + -YL] **1.** the bivalent radical CO **2.** any of a series of metal compounds containing this radical —**car′bon·yl′ic** (-nil′ik) *adj.*

carbonyl chloride *same as* PHOSGENE

☆**Car·bo·run·dum** (kär′bə run′dəm) [CARB(ON) + (C)O-RUNDUM] *a trademark for* a very hard abrasive substance,

esp. silicon carbide, used in grindstones, abrasives, etc. —*n.* [c-] such a substance

car·box·yl (kär bäk′s'l) *n.* [CARB- + OX(YGEN) + -YL] the univalent radical COOH, occurring in the fatty acids and most other organic acids —**car′box·yl′ic** (-sil′ik) *adj.*

car·box·yl·ase (kär bäk′sə lās′) *n.* [CARBOXYL + -ASE] an enzyme which is capable of removing carbon dioxide from alpha keto acids to produce aldehydes, as in the formation of acetaldehyde from pyruvic acid

car·box·yl·ate (kär bäk′sə lāt′) *n.* a salt or ester of a carboxylic acid —*vt.* **-at′ed, -at′ing** to form a carboxylic acid by introducing a carboxyl group into (a compound) —**car′box′yl·a′tion** *n.*

car·boy (kär′boi) *n.* [< Per. *qarābah*, large leather milk bottle] a large glass bottle enclosed for protection in basketwork or in a wooden crate: used esp. as a container for corrosive liquids

car·bun·cle (kär′buŋ k'l) *n.* [ME. < OFr. *carbuncle* < L. *carbunculus*, a little coal, gem < *carbo*, coal] **1.** *a*) formerly, any of certain deep-red gems *b*) a smooth, convex, deep-red garnet **2.** a painful, localized, pus-bearing inflammation of the tissue beneath the skin, more severe than a boil and having several openings —**car·bun′cu·lar** (-kyoo lər) *adj.*

car·bu·ret (kär′bə rāt′, -ret′; -byoo-) *vt.* **-ret′ed** or **-ret′ted, -ret′ing** or **-ret′ting** [CARB- + -URET] **1.** to combine chemically with carbon **2.** to mix or charge (gas or air) with volatile compounds of carbon in order to increase the potential heat energy —**car′bu·re′tion** (-rā′shən) *n.*

car·bu·ret·ant (-'nt) *n.* a substance, as gasoline or benzene, added to air or gas to carburet it

car·bu·ret·or (kär′bə rāt′ər, -byoo-) *n.* an apparatus for carbureting air or gas; esp., a device in which air is mixed with gasoline spray to make an explosive mixture in an internal-combustion engine: Brit. sp. **car·bu·ret·tor** (kär′byoo ret′ər)

car·bu·rize (-rīz′) *vt.* **-rized′, -riz′ing** [< Fr. *carbure*, carbide, hydrocarbon + -IZE] **1.** *same as* CARBURET (sense 2) **2.** to treat or combine with carbon; esp., to treat (iron) by heating in contact with carbon in making case-hardened steel —**car′bu·ri·za′tion** *n.*

car·byl·a·mine (kär′b'l ə mēn′) *n.* [CARB- + -YL + AMINE] any of a group of organic cyanides containing the radical NC

☆**car·ca·jou** (kär′kə jōō′, -zhōō′) *n.* [CanadFr. < Algonquian] *same as* WOLVERINE

car·ca·net (kär′kə net′) *n.* [dim. of Fr. *carcan*, iron collar, as on pillories < ML. *carcannum*; of Gmc. orig.] [Archaic] an ornamental collar, band, or necklace, usually of gold and often jeweled

car·cass (kär′kəs) *n.* [ME. *carcais* < OFr. *carcois* & < Fr. *carcasse* < ?] **1.** the dead body of an animal, often specif. of a slaughtered animal dressed as meat **2.** the human body, living or dead: scornful or humorous usage **3.** the worthless remains of something, esp. its outer shell **4.** the framework or base structure, as of a ship, tire, etc. Also, Brit. var., **car′case** (-kəs) —*SYN.* see BODY

Car·cas·sonne (kár kä sôn′) *n.* city in S France: site of a restored medieval walled city: pop. 41,000

car·cin·o·gen (kär sin′ə jən, -jen′) *n.* [< ff. + -GEN] any substance that produces cancer —**car·ci·no·gen·ic** (kär′sə nō jen′ik) *adj.* — **car′ci·no·gen′e·sis** (-jen′ə sis), **car′ci·no′ge·nic′i·ty** (-jə nis′ə tē) *n.*

car·ci·no·ma (kär′sə nō′mə) *n., pl.* **-mas, -ma·ta** (-mə tə) [L. < Gr. *karkinōma*, cancer < *karkinoun*, to affect with a cancer < *karkinos*, a crab, CANCER] any of several kinds of cancerous growths made up of epithelial cells —**car′ci·nom′a·tous** (-näm′ə təs, -nōm′ə-) *adj.*

car·ci·no·ma·to·sis (kär′sə nō′mə tō′sis) *n.* [see prec. & -OSIS] a condition in which epithelial cancer has spread extensively throughout the body

☆**car coat** a short overcoat, usually extending only to about the middle of the thigh

card¹ (kärd) *n.* [ME. *carde* < OFr. *carte* < ML. *carta*, a card, paper < L. *charta*, leaf of paper, tablet < Gr. *chartēs*, leaf of paper, layer of papyrus, prob. < Egypt.] **1.** a flat, stiff piece of thick paper or thin pasteboard, usually rectangular; specif., *a*) any of a pack of small, specially marked cards used in playing various games; playing card: see also CARDS *b*) the dial of a compass; compass card ☆*c*) a pasteboard with a number of small articles attached for sale [a *card* of thumbtacks] *d*) *same as* POST CARD *e*) *same as* CALLING CARD *f*) a card identifying a person as an agent, member, patron, etc. *g*) an illustrated or decorated card bearing a message or greeting for some occasion [a birthday *card*] *h*) a card to advertise or announce an event, product, etc. [a window *card*] *i*) any of a series of cards on which information is recorded [a library catalog *card*] ☆*j*) *same as* SCORE CARD (sense 1) ☆**2.** a series of events making up a program, as in boxing or racing **3.** an event or attraction as described in a printed program [drawing *card*] **4.** [Colloq.] a witty, comical, or clowning person —*vt.* **1.** to provide with a card **2.** to put on a card **3.** to list on cards for filing, cataloging, etc. **4.** to make as a score in golf —**card up one's sleeve** a plan or resource kept secret or

held in reserve —**in** (or **on**) **the cards** likely or seemingly destined to happen: from the use of cards in fortunetelling —**put** (or **lay**) **one's cards on the table** to reveal frankly one's intentions, schemes, resources, etc.

card[2] (kärd) *n.* [ME. & OFr. *carde* < Pr. *carda* < *cardar*, to card < VL. **caritare* < L. *carere*, to card; sp. infl. by association with ML. *cardus*, a card, thistle < L. *carduus*, thistle] **1.** a metal comb or wire brush for raising the nap on cloth or disentangling the fibers of wool, cotton, flax, etc. **2.** a machine with rollers covered with wire teeth, used to brush, clean, and straighten fibers of wool, cotton, etc. —*vt.* to use a card on (fibers of wool, cotton, etc.) in preparation for spinning —**card′er** *n.* —**card′ing** *n., adj.*

Card, Cardinal

car·da·mom (kär′də məm) *n.* [L. *cardamomum* < Gr. *kardamōmon* < *kardamon*, cress + *amōmon*, spice plant] **1.** an Asiatic plant (*Elettaria cardamomum*) of the ginger family **2.** its seed capsule or seed, used in medicine and as a spice Also **car′da·mon** (-mən)

card·board (kärd′bôrd′) *n.* a material made of paper pulp but thicker and stiffer than paper; pasteboard: it is used for making cards, boxes, etc. —*adj.* **1.** of or like cardboard **2.** flimsy, insubstantial, etc.

card-car·ry·ing (-kar′ē in) *adj.* **1.** owning a membership card in a specified organization **2.** [Colloq.] thorough, genuine, etc. [a *card-carrying* pacifist]

Cár·de·nas (kär′de näs′), **Lá·za·ro** (lä′sä rō′) 1895–1970; Mex. statesman & general; president of Mexico (1934–40)

☆**card file** a collection of cards containing data or records, arranged systematically, as in alphabetical order, in boxes or drawers: also **card catalog**

car·di- (kär′dē) *same as* CARDIO-: used before a vowel

car·di·ac (kär′dē ak′) *adj.* [Fr. *cardiaque* < L. *cardiacus* < Gr. *kardiakos* < *kardia*, the HEART] **1.** of, near, or affecting the heart **2.** relating to the part of the stomach connected with the esophagus —*n.* **1.** a medicine that stimulates cardiac action **2.** a person with a heart disorder

car·di·al·gi·a (kär′dē al′jē ə) *n.* [ModL. < Gr. *kardialgia* < *kardia*, HEART + *algos*, pain: so named because mistakenly thought to be located in the heart] **1.** a feeling of pain or discomfort in the region of the heart **2.** *same as* HEARTBURN (sense 1)

Car·diff (kär′dif) seaport in SE Wales, on the Bristol Channel; capital of Glamorganshire: pop. 261,000

Car·di·gan (kär′də gən) *same as* CARDIGANSHIRE —*n.* *see* WELSH CORGI

car·di·gan (kär′də gən) *n.* [after 7th Earl of *Cardigan* (1797–1868), Eng. general] a sweater or jacket, usually knitted, that opens down the front and is usually collarless and long-sleeved: also **cardigan sweater** (or **jacket**)

CARDIGAN

Cardigan Bay inlet of St. George's Channel, on the W coast of Wales

Car·di·gan·shire (-shir′) county of W Wales, on Cardigan Bay: 692 sq. mi.; pop. 53,000

car·di·nal (kärd′'n əl) *adj.* [ME. < OFr. < L. *cardinalis*, principal, chief < *cardo*, that on which something turns or depends, orig., door hinge] **1.** of main importance; principal; chief **2.** bright-red, like the robe of a cardinal —*n.* [ME. < LL.(Ec.) *cardinalis*, chief presbyter, cardinal < the L. *adj.*] **1.** one of the Roman Catholic officials appointed by the Pope to his council (COLLEGE OF CARDINALS) **2.** bright red **3.** a woman's short cloak, originally red and usually hooded, fashionable in the 18th cent. ☆**4.** [so named because colored like a cardinal's robe] a bright-red, crested American songbird (*Richmondena cardinalis*) related to the finch: in full, **cardinal bird 5.** *same as* CARDINAL NUMBER —**car′di·nal·ly** *adv.* —**car′di·nal·ship′** *n.*

car·di·nal·ate (-āt′) *n.* [< ML. *cardinalatus*] **1.** the position, dignity, or rank of a cardinal **2.** the Pope's council of cardinals

☆**cardinal flower 1.** the bright-red flower of a N. American plant (*Lobelia cardinalis*) of the bellflower family, that grows in damp, shady places or in shallow water **2.** this plant

cardinal number any number used in counting or in showing how many (e.g., two, forty, 627, etc.): distinguished from ORDINAL NUMBER

cardinal points the four principal points of the compass; north, south, east, and west

cardinal virtues the basic virtues of ancient Greek philosophy: justice, prudence, fortitude, and temperance: see also THEOLOGICAL VIRTUES

☆**card index** *same as* CARD FILE

car·di·o- (kär′dē ə, -ō) [< Gr. *kardia*, HEART] *a combining form meaning of the heart* [*cardiograph*]

car·di·o·gram (kär′dē ə gram′) *n. same as* ELECTROCARDIOGRAM —**car′di·o·graph′** (-graf′) *n.* —**car′di·og′ra·phy** (-äg′rə fē) *n.*

car·di·oid (kär′dē oid′) *n.* [Gr. *kardioeidēs*, heart-shaped < *kardia*, HEART + *eidos*, shape] *Math.* a curve more or less in the shape of a heart, traced by a point on the circumference of a circle that rolls around the circumference of another equal circle

car·di·ol·o·gy (kär′dē äl′ə jē) *n.* [CARDIO- + -LOGY] the branch of medicine dealing with the heart, its functions, and its diseases —**car′di·ol′o·gist** *n.*

car·di·o·ta·chom·e·ter (kär′dē ō′tə käm′ə tər) *n.* [CARDIO- + TACHOMETER] a device for counting the number of heartbeats over a given period of time

car·di·o·vas·cu·lar (-vas′kyoo lər) *adj.* [CARDIO- + VASCULAR] of the heart and the blood vessels as a unified body system

car·di·tis (kär dīt′is) *n.* [ModL. < Gr. *kardia*, HEART + -ITIS] inflammation of the heart

car·doon (kär dōōn′) *n.* [Fr. *cardon* < *carde*: see CHARD] a thistlelike, edible Mediterranean plant (*Cynara cardunculus*) of the composite family, closely related to the artichoke

Car·do·zo (kär dō′zō), **Benjamin Nathan** 1870–1938; U.S. jurist; associate justice, Supreme Court (1932–38)

cards (kärdz) *n.pl.* **1.** a game or games played with a deck of cards, as bridge, rummy, poker, pinochle, etc. **2.** the playing of such games; card playing

☆**cards and spades** [from the scoring, as in cassino, of both cards and spades] a generous handicap

☆**card shark** [Colloq.] **1.** an expert card player **2.** *same as* CARDSHARP

☆**card·sharp** (-shärp′) *n.* [Colloq.] a professional cheater at cards: also **card′sharp′er**

card table a table at which card games are played, esp. a small, square table with folding legs

care (ker) *n.* [ME. < OE. *caru*, sorrow < IE. base **gar-*, to cry out, scream, whence L. *garrulus*, garrulous, Goth. *kara*, care, G. *kar-*, in *karfreitag*, Good Friday] **1.** *a*) a troubled or burdened state of mind; worry; concern *b*) a cause of such a mental state **2.** close attention or careful heed [to drive with *care*] **3.** a liking or regard (*for*) [to show no *care* for others] **4.** charge; protection; custody [left in a friend's *care*] **5.** something to watch over or attend to; a responsibility —*vi.* **cared, car′ing 1.** to have objection, worry, regret, etc.; mind [do you *care* if I go?] **2.** to feel concern or interest [to *care* about others] **3.** to feel love or a liking (*for*) **4.** to take charge of; look after; provide (*for*) **5.** to wish (*for*); want [do you *care* for more pie?] —*vt.* **1.** to feel concern about or interest in [I don't *care* what you did] **2.** to wish or desire [do you *care* to eat now?] —**care of** in the charge of or at the address of —**have a care** to be careful or cautious: also **take care** —☆**take care of 1.** to have charge of or be responsible for; look after; attend to **2.** to provide for; protect against trouble, want, etc.

SYN.—**care** suggests a weighing down of the mind, as by dread, apprehension, or great responsibility [worn out by the *cares* of the day]; **concern** suggests mental uneasiness over someone or something in which one has an affectionate interest [I feel *concern* for their welfare]; **solicitude** implies thoughtfulness, often excessive apprehension, for the welfare, safety, or comfort of another [she stroked his head with great *solicitude*]; **worry** suggests mental distress or agitation over some problem [his chief *worry* was that he might fail]; **anxiety** suggests an apprehensive or uneasy feeling with less mental activity than **worry**, often over some indefinite but anticipated evil [he viewed the world situation with *anxiety*] —**ANT.** unconcern, indifference

☆**CARE** (ker) Cooperative for American Relief Everywhere, Inc.

ca·reen (kə rēn′) *vt.* [Fr. *carener*, to careen < *carène*, *carine* < It. *carena* < L. *carina*, keel of a ship] **1.** to cause (a ship) to lean or lie on one side, as for repairs **2.** to calk, clean, or repair (a ship in this position) **3.** to cause to lean sideways; tip; tilt —*vi.* **1.** to lean sideways, as a sailing ship before a high wind **2.** to lurch from side to side, esp. while moving rapidly —*n.* the act or position of careening

ca·reer (kə rir′) *n.* [Fr. *carrière*, road, racecourse < It. *carriera* < *carro*, CAR] **1.** orig., a racing course **2.** a swift course, as of the sun through the sky **3.** one's progress through life or in a particular vocation **4.** a profession or occupation which one trains for and pursues as a lifework —☆*adj.* pursuing a normally temporary activity as a lifework [a *career* soldier] —*vi.* to move at full speed; rush wildly —**in full career** at full speed

ca·reer·ist (kə rir′ist) *n.* a person interested chiefly in achieving his own professional ambitions, to the neglect of other things —**ca·reer′ism** *n.*

☆**career woman** (or **girl**) [Colloq.] a woman who follows a professional or business career, often to the exclusion of marriage

care·free (ker′frē′) *adj.* free from troubles, worry, or anxiety

care·ful (-fəl) *adj.* [ME. & OE.: see CARE & -FUL] **1.** acting or working in a thoughtful, painstaking way [a *careful* worker] **2.** cautious, wary, or guarded [a *careful* reply] **3.** accurately or thoroughly done or made; painstaking [a *careful* analysis] **4.** [Archaic] feeling or causing sorrow, worry, etc.; anxious —**care′ful·ly** *adv.* —**care′ful·ness** *n.*

SYN.—**careful** implies close attention to or great concern for whatever is one's work or responsibility, and usually connotes thoroughness, a guarding against error or injury, etc.; **meticulous** implies extreme, sometimes finicky, carefulness about details; **scrupulous** implies a conscientious adherence to what is considered right, true, accurate, etc.; **circumspect** implies a careful consideration of all circumstances to avoid error or unfavorable consequences; **cautious** implies a careful guarding against possible dangers or risks; **prudent** implies the exercise of both caution and circumspection, suggesting careful management in economic and practical

matters; **discreet** implies the exercise of discernment and judgment in the guidance of one's speech and action and suggests careful restraint; **wary** implies a cautiousness that is prompted by suspicion —ANT. **careless, negligent, lax**

care·less (-lis) *adj.* [ME. *careles* < OE. *carleas:* see CARE & -LESS] 1. without worry; carefree; untroubled 2. not paying enough attention; not thinking before one acts or speaks; neglectful; heedless; inconsiderate 3. done or made without enough attention, precision, etc.; not painstaking or thorough 4. artless; unstudied *[a careless grace]* —**careless of** indifferent to; untroubled by —**care′less·ly** *adv.* —**care′less·ness** *n.*

ca·ress (kə res′) *vt.* [Fr. *caresser* < It. *carezzare*, ult. < L. *carus*, dear] 1. to touch or stroke lovingly or gently; also, to embrace or kiss: often used figuratively, as of a voice, music, etc. 2. to treat kindly or affectionately —*n.* an affectionate touch or gesture, as a kiss, embrace, etc. —**ca·ress′er** *n.* —**ca·ress′ing·ly** *adv.* —**ca·res′sive** *adj.* —**ca·res′sive·ly** *adv.*

SYN.—**caress** refers to a display of affection by gentle stroking or patting; **fondle** implies a more demonstrative show of love or affection, as by hugging, kissing, etc.; **pet**, as applied generally, implies treatment with special affection and indulgence, including patting, fondling, etc., but informally it refers to indulgence, esp. by young couples, in hugging, kissing, and amorous caresses; **cuddle** implies affectionate handling, as of a small child by its mother, by pressing or drawing close within the arms; **dandle** implies a playful affection displayed toward a child by moving him up and down lightly on the knee

car·et (kar′it, ker′-) *n.* [L., there is lacking, 3d pers. sing. of *carere*, to lack] a mark (∧) used in writing or in correcting proof, to show where something is to be added

care·tak·er (ker′tāk′ər) *n.* 1. a person hired to take care of something or someone, esp. of a house, estate, etc. for an owner who is not always in residence; custodian 2. a person temporarily carrying out the duties as of an office

Ca·rew (kə rōō′, ker′ōō), **Thomas** 1595?-1639?; Eng. poet

care·worn (ker′wôrn′) *adj.* worn out by, or showing the effects of, troubles and worry; haggard

☆**car·fare** (kär′fer′) *n.* the price of a ride on a streetcar, bus, etc.

car·go (kär′gō) *n., pl.* -**goes**, -**gos** [Sp. *cargo*, burden, load < *cargar*, to load, impose taxes < VL. *carricare*: see CHARGE] the load of commodities carried by a ship, airplane, truck, etc.; freight

☆**car·hop** (kär′häp′) *n.* [CAR + (BELL)HOP] a waiter or, esp., a waitress who serves food to customers in cars at a drive-in restaurant

Car·i·a (ker′ē ə) ancient region in SW Asia Minor: chief city, Halicarnassus

Car·ib (kar′ib) *n.* [Sp. *caribe, caribal*, altered < *canibal:* see CANNIBAL] 1. a member of an Indian people who formerly inhabited the S West Indies and the N coast of S. America, where some still remain 2. the family of languages of the Caribs —**Car′ib·an** *adj., n.*

Car·ib·be·an (kar′ə bē′ən, kə rib′ē ən) *same as* CARIBBEAN SEA —*adj.* 1. of the Caribs, their language, culture, etc. 2. of the Caribbean Sea, its islands, etc. —*n. same as* CARIB (sense 1)

Caribbean Sea part of the Atlantic, bounded by the West Indies, Central America, and the N coast of S. America: c. 750,000 sq. mi.

ca·ri·be (kə rē′bā) *n.* [AmSp., lit., Carib (see CANNIBAL): so named from its voracity] *same as* PIRANHA

☆**car·i·bou** (kar′ə bōō′) *n., pl.* -**bous**, -**bou:** see PLURAL, II, D, 1 [CanadFr. < Algonquian name] any of several large, northern N. American deer (genus *Rangifer*) with branching antlers in both sexes: they are closely related to the reindeer

car·i·ca·ture (kar′ə kə chər, -choor′) *n.* [Fr. < It. *caricatura*, satirical picture, lit., an overloading < *caricare*, to load, exaggerate < VL. *carricare*, to load: see CHARGE] 1. a picture or imitation of a person, literary style, etc. in which certain features or mannerisms are exaggerated for satirical effect 2. the act or art of making such caricatures 3. a likeness or imitation that is so distorted or inferior as to seem ludicrous —*vt.* -**tured**, -**tur·ing** to depict in or as in a caricature —**car′i·ca·tur·ist** *n.*

CARIBOU
(40–55 in. high
at shoulder)

SYN.—**caricature** refers to an imitation or representation of a person or thing, in drawing, writing, or performance, that ludicrously exaggerates its distinguishing features; **burlesque** implies the handling of a serious subject lightly or flippantly, or of a trifling subject with mock seriousness; a **parody** ridicules a written work or writer by imitating the style closely, esp. so as to point up its peculiarities or affectations, and by distorting the content nonsensically or changing it to something absurdly incongruous; **travesty**, in contrast, implies that the subject matter is retained,

but that the style and language are changed so as to give a grotesquely absurd effect; **satire** refers to a literary composition in which follies, vices, stupidities, and abuses in life are held up to ridicule and contempt; **lampoon** refers to a piece of strongly satirical writing that uses broad humor in attacking and ridiculing the faults and weaknesses of an individual

car·ies (ker′ēz) *n.* [L., decay, prob. akin to Gr. *kēr*, death, destruction, Sans. *śr̥ṇāti*, he breaks, crushes] decay of bones or, esp., of teeth

car·il·lon (kar′ə län′; *occas.* kə ril′yən) *n.* [Fr., chime of bells (orig. composed of four) < OFr. *carrignon* < VL. *quaternio*, set of four, four-part sheet of paper (cf. QUIRE²) < L. *quattuor*, FOUR] 1. a set of stationary bells, each producing one tone of the chromatic scale, now usually sounded by means of a keyboard 2. a melody played on such bells 3. an organ stop producing a carillonlike sound

car·il·lon·neur (kar′ə lə nur′) *n.* [Fr.] a carillon player

Ca·ri·na (kə rī′nə, -rē′-) [L. *carina*, keel] a S constellation containing the bright star Canopus: one of the four separate parts into which the former constellation Argo has been divided

ca·ri·na (kə rī′nə, -rē′-) *n., pl.* -**nas**, -**nae** (-nē) [L., a keel: see CAREEN] *Biol.* a structure or part resembling a keel or ridge, as the projection on the breastbone of a bird —**ca·ri′nal** *adj.*

car·i·nate (kar′ə nāt′, -nit) *adj.* [L. *carinatus* < *carina*, a keel] *Biol.* having a ridge down the middle; keel-shaped: also **car′i·nat′ed**

Ca·rin·thi·a (kə rin′thē ə) province of S Austria: 3,680 sq. mi.; pop. 494,000; cap. Klagenfurt: Ger. name, KÄRNTEN

Car·i·o·ca (kar′ē ōk′ə) *n.* [Braz. Port. < Tupi, lit. white house] a native of Rio de Janeiro

car·i·ole (kar′ē ōl′) *n.* [Fr. *cariole* < It. *carriuolo*, dim. of *carro:* see CAR] 1. a small carriage drawn by one horse 2. a light, covered cart 3. [Canad.] a kind of dog sled

car·i·ous (kar′ē əs) *adj.* [L. *cariosus*] having caries; decayed —**car′i·os′i·ty** (-äs′ə tē) *n.*

cark (kärk) *vt., vi.* [ME. *carken* < ONormFr. *carkier*, var. of OFr. *chargier:* see CHARGE] [Archaic] to worry or be worried —*n.* [Archaic] distress; anxiety

Carl (kärl) a masculine name: see CHARLES

carl, carle (kärl) *n.* [ME. & OE. *curl* < ON. *karl*, a man, CHURL] 1. [Archaic or Obs.] a peasant, bondman, or villein 2. [Scot. or Archaic] an ill-bred fellow; churl 3. [Scot.] a sturdy fellow

car·line, car·lin (kär′lin) *n.* [ON. *kerling*, wife, old woman < *karl*, man, male + fem. suffix] [Scot.] 1. a woman, esp. an old woman 2. a hag; witch

car·ling (kär′lin) *n.* [Fr. *carlingue* < ON. *kerling*, lit., old woman: see prec.] any of the pieces of timber running fore and aft between two of the transverse beams supporting the deck of a ship

Car·lisle (kär līl′, kär′līl) city in NW England; county seat of Cumberland; pop. 71,000

Car·list (kär′list) *n.* [CARL(os) + -IST] a supporter of Don Carlos or of his heirs: see CARLOS —**Car′lism** *n.*

☆**car·load** (kär′lōd′) *n.* 1. a load that fills a car, esp. a freight car 2. the minimum weight of a specific commodity qualifying as a carload of that commodity in railroad shipping rates

☆**car·load·ings** (-inz) *n.pl.* the number of railroad carloads shipped in or out within a given period

☆**carload rate** a special low rate for shipment by carloads

Car·los (kär′ləs, -lōs), **Don** (born *Carlos Maria Isidro de Borbón*) 1788–1855; Sp. pretender to the throne

Car·lo·ta (kär lō′tä; E. kär lät′ə) (born *Marie Charlotte Amélie*) 1840–1927; empress of Mexico (1864–67): wife of MAXIMILIAN

Car·lot·ta (kär lät′ə) a feminine name: see CHARLOTTE

Car·lo·vin·gi·an (kär′lə vin′jē ən) *adj., n. same as* CAROLINGIAN

Carls·bad (kärlz′bad; G. kärls′bät) *former name of* KARLOVY VARY

Carls·bad Caverns National Park (kärlz′bad) national park in SE New Mexico, containing large limestone caverns with stalactites and stalagmites: 71 sq. mi.

Car·lyle (kär līl′, kär′līl), **Thomas** 1795–1881; Brit. writer, born in Scotland

car·ma·gnole (kär′mən yōl′) *n.* [Fr., altered (after *Carmagnola*, town in Piedmont, occupied by the revolutionaries in 1792) < older *carmignole*, kind of cap (dial. *carmignola*, jacket); prob. ult. < L. *carminare*, to card wool < *carmen*, a card < *carere:* see CARD²] 1. the short jacket with wide lapels, or the costume consisting of this jacket, black trousers, a red cap, and tricolored girdle, worn by French Revolutionaries (1792) 2. a lively song and street dance popular during the French Revolution

car·man (kär′mən) *n., pl.* -**men** (-mən) a streetcar conductor or motorman

Car·man (kär′mən), **(William) Bliss** (blis) 1861–1929; Canad. poet & journalist in the U.S.

Car·mar·then·shire (kär mär′thən shir) county of SW Wales, on the Bristol Channel: 919 sq. mi.; pop. 167,000: also **Car·mar′then**

fat, āpe, cär; ten, ēven; is, bīte; gō, hôrn, tōōl, look; oil, out; up, fur; get; joy; yet; chin; she; thin, then; zh, leisure; ŋ, ring; ə for *a* in *ago*, *e* in *agent*, *i* in *sanity*, *o* in *comply*, *u* in *focus*; ' as in *able* (ā′b'l); Fr. bál; ë, Fr. coeur; ö, Fr. feu; ô, Fr. mon; ô̆, Fr. coq; ü, Fr. duc; r, Fr. cri; H, G. ich; kh, G. doch. See inside front cover. ☆ Americanism; ‡foreign; *hypothetical; <derived from

Car·mel (kär′m'l), **Mount** mountain ridge in NW Israel, extending as a promontory into the Mediterranean: highest peak, c. 1,800 ft.

Car·mel·ite (kär′mə līt′) n. [Fr. < ML. Carmelita < LL.(Ec.) Carmelites, inhabitant of Mount CARMEL] 1. a mendicant friar of the order of Our Lady of Mount Carmel, founded in Syria about 1160 2. a nun of this order —adj. of this order

Car·mi·chael (kär′mi′k'l) [after the owner of the town site] suburb of Sacramento, in C Calif.: pop. 38,000

car·min·a·tive (kär min′ə tiv, kär′mə nāt′iv) adj. [ModL. carminativus < L. carminatus, pp. of carminare, to card, cleanse < carere, to card] causing gas to be expelled from the stomach and intestines —n. a carminative medicine

car·mine (kär′min, -min) n. [Fr. carmin < ML. carminium < Ar. qirmiz, crimson (< Sans. krimijā, insect-produced < krmi, worm, insect: the dye comes from crushed insects; cf. COCHINEAL); form infl. by L. minium, cinnabar red] 1. a red or purplish-red pigment obtained mainly from cochineal 2. its color —adj. red or purplish-red; crimson

car·nage (kär′nij) n. [Fr. < It. carnaggio, ult. < L. caro (gen. carnis), flesh < IE. base *(s)ker-, to cut, whence SHEAR, HARVEST] 1. bloody and extensive slaughter, esp. in battle; massacre; bloodshed 2. [Fr. < Pr. carnatge, flesh, CARRION < carn, flesh < L. caro] [Obs.] dead bodies, esp. on a battlefield —SYN. see SLAUGHTER

car·nal (-n'l) adj. [ME. & OFr. < LL.(Ec.) carnalis, fleshly (in contrast to spiritalis, SPIRITUAL) < L. caro: see prec.] 1. in or of the flesh; bodily; material or worldly, not spiritual 2. having to do with or preoccupied with bodily or sexual pleasures; sensual or sexual —have carnal knowledge of to have sexual intercourse with —car·nal·i·ty (kär nal′ə tē) n., pl. -ties —car′nal·ly adv.

SYN.—carnal implies relation to the body or flesh as the seat of basic physical appetites, now esp. sexual appetites, and usually stresses absence of intellectual or moral influence [carnal lust]; fleshly, expressing less censure, stresses these appetites and their gratification as natural to the flesh [fleshly frailty]; sensual stresses relation to or preoccupation with gratifying the bodily senses and usually implies grossness or lewdness [sensual lips]; animal is applied to the physical nature of man as distinguished from his intellectual and spiritual nature, and now rarely carries a derogatory implication [animal spirits]

car·nall·ite (kär′n'l īt′) n. [after Rudolf von Carnall (1804–74), Ger. mineralogist] a hydrous chloride of magnesium and potassium, MgCl₂·KCl·6H₂O: a major source of potassium

Car·nar·von·shire (kär när′vən shir) former sp. of CAERNARVONSHIRE

car·nas·si·al (kär nas′ē əl) adj. [< Fr. carnassier, carnivorous < Pr. carnasa, bad flesh < carn: see CARNAGE] designating or of teeth of a flesh-eating animal specialized for slicing or shearing rather than tearing, esp. the last premolars of the upper jaw and the first molars of the lower jaw —n. a carnassial tooth

Car·nat·ic (kär nat′ik) region in SE India, between the Coromandel Coast and the E Ghats

car·na·tion (kär nā′shən) n. [Fr. < LL. carnatio, fleshiness < caro: see CARNAGE] 1. formerly, flesh color or rosy pink; now, a deep red 2. a popular garden and greenhouse plant (Dianthus caryophyllus) of the pink family, with white, pink, or red, usually double flowers that smell like cloves

car·nau·ba (kär nô′bə, -nou′-) n. [Braz. Port. < Tupi native name] a Brazilian palm (Copernicia cerifera) that yields a hard wax used in making polishes, lipsticks, phonograph records, etc.

Car·ne·gie (kär′nə gē′; kär nā′gē, -neg′ē), **Andrew** 1835–1919; U.S. industrialist & philanthropist, born in Scotland

car·nel·ian (kär nēl′yən) n. [altered, after L. caro (gen. carnis), flesh (because of its color) < CORNELIAN] a red variety of chalcedony, used in jewelry

‡car·net (kär ne′) n. [Fr.] 1. an official certificate; esp., any of various customs documents required of motorists crossing European frontiers 2. a book of tickets for a bus, subway, etc.

car·ni·fy (kär′nə fī′) vt., vi. -fied′, -fy′ing [L. carnificare, to execute < caro (gen. carnis), flesh + facere, to make] to form into flesh or fleshlike tissue —car′ni·fi·ca′tion n.

car·ni·val (kär′nə vəl) n. [< Fr. carnaval (or) < It. carnevale < ML. carnelevarium < *carnem levare, to remove meat (see CARNAGE & LEVER); associated by folk etym. with ML. carne vale, "Flesh, farewell!" < L. caro (gen. carnis) + vale, farewell (see VALEDICTION)] 1. the period of feasting and revelry just before Lent, including Mardi gras 2. a reveling or time of revelry; festivity; merrymaking 3. a traveling commercial entertainment with side shows, rides, games, etc. 4. an organized program of festivities, contests, etc. [a winter sports carnival]

car·ni·vore (kär′nə vôr′) n. [Fr.: see ff.] 1. any of an order (Carnivora) of fanged, flesh-eating mammals, including the dog, wolf, cat, seal, etc.: opposed to HERBIVORE 2. a plant that ingests small animals, esp. insects

car·niv·o·rous (kär niv′ə rəs) adj. [L. carnivorus < caro (gen. carnis), flesh + vorare, to devour, eat] 1. a) flesh-eating: opposed to HERBIVOROUS b) insect-eating, as certain plants 2. of the carnivores —car·niv′o·rous·ly adv. —car·niv′o·rous·ness n.

Car·not (kär nō′) 1. La·zare (Nicolas Marguerite) (là zàr′), 1753–1823; Fr. soldier & statesman 2. Ni·co·las

Lé·o·nard Sa·di (nē kô lä′ lā ô nàr′ sà dē′), 1796–1832; Fr. physicist: son of prec. 3. (Marie François) Sadi, 1837–94; Fr. statesman; president (1887–94): grandson of Lazare

car·no·tite (kär′nə tīt′) n. [after A. Carnot (d. 1920), Fr. mine inspector] a yellow, radioactive mineral, K₂(UO₂)₂(VO₄)₂·3H₂O, an ore of uranium and vanadium

car·ny, car·ney, car·nie (kär′nē) n., pl. -nies [Slang] 1. a carnival (sense 3) 2. a person who works in such a carnival

car·ob (kar′əb) n. [Fr. caroube < It. carrubo < Ar. kharrub, bean pod < Aram. khārūbā < Assyr. kharūbu] 1. a leguminous tree (Ceratonia siliqua) of the E Mediterranean, bearing long, flat, leathery, brown pods with a sweet pulp 2. such a pod, used for fodder and sometimes human food

ca·roche (kə rōch′, -rōsh′) n. [MFr. carroche < It. carroccia < ML. *carrautium < carracutium < L. carrus: see CAR] a coach or carriage used for state occasions in the 17th cent.

CAROB

Car·ol (kar′əl) 1. a feminine name: see CAROLINE 2. [ML. Carolus: see CHARLES] a masculine name

car·ol (kar′əl) n. [ME. carole < OFr. carole, kind of dance, Christmas song < ML. choraula, a dance to the flute < L. choraules < Gr. choraulēs, flute player who accompanied the choral dance < choros, dance + aulein, to play the flute < aulos, flute] 1. [Obs.] a kind of circle dance 2. a song of joy or praise; esp., a Christmas song —vi. -oled or -olled, -ol·ing or -ol·ling 1. to sing, esp. in joy; warble 2. to sing carols, esp. Christmas carols, in chorus with others —vt. 1. to sing (a tune, etc.) 2. to praise or celebrate in song —car′ol·er, car′ol·ler n.

Car·o·li·na¹ (kar′ə li′nə) [L. fem. adj. of Carolus, in honor of CHARLES I] English colony (1663–1729) including what is now N.Carolina, S.Carolina, Ga., and N Fla. —the Carolinas N.Carolina and S.Carolina

Ca·ro·li·na² (kä′rô lē′nä) city in NE Puerto Rico, near San Juan: pop. 95,000

☆**Carolina allspice** any of a genus (Calycanthus) of plants bearing maroon flowers with the odor of strawberries

Car·o·line (kar′ə lin′, -lən) [G. & Fr. < It. Curolina, fem. < ML. Carolus, CHARLES] a feminine name: dim. Carrie; var. Carol —adj. of Charles I or Charles II of England, or the period in which they lived: also Car′o·le′an (-lē′ən)

Caroline Islands group of islands in Micronesia, in the W Pacific: see Trust Territory of the PACIFIC ISLANDS

Car·o·lin·gi·an (kar′ə lin jē′ən) adj. [ML. Carolingi, pl. of Carolingus < Carolus, Charles + Gmc. -ing, patronymic suffix + -AN] designating or of the second Frankish dynasty, founded (751 A.D.) by Pepin the Short, son of Charles Martel —n. a member of this dynasty

Car·o·lin·i·an (kar′ə lin′ē ən) adj. [< ML. Carolus, CHARLES] 1. of Charlemagne or his period 2. same as CAROLINE, adj. 3. [< Carolina] of North Carolina or South Carolina —n. a native or inhabitant of North Carolina or South Carolina

Car·o·lyn (kar′ə lin) same as CAROLINE

car·om (kar′əm) n. [< Fr. carambole < Sp. carambola] 1. Billiards a shot in which the cue ball successively hits the two object balls ☆2. a hitting and rebounding, as of a ball struck against a surface —☆vi. 1. to make a carom 2. to hit and rebound

car·o·tene (kar′ə tēn′) n. [< L. carota, CARROT + -ENE] any of three red or orange-colored isomeric hydrocarbons, C₄₀H₅₆, found in carrots and certain other vegetables, and changed into vitamin A in the body: also car′o·tin (-tin)

ca·rot·e·noid, ca·rot·i·noid (kə rät′ə noid′) n. any of several red and yellow plant and animal pigments related to and including carotene —adj. 1. of or like carotene 2. of the carotenoids

ca·rot·id (kə rät′id) adj. [Gr. karōtis, pl. karōtides, the two great arteries of the neck < karoun, to plunge into sleep or stupor: so called because compression of these causes unconsciousness] designating, of, or near either of the two principal arteries, one on each side of the neck, which convey the blood from the aorta to the head —n. a carotid artery

ca·rous·al (kə rou′zəl) n. same as CAROUSE (sense 1)

ca·rouse (kə rouz′) vi. -roused′, -rous′ing [Fr. carousse, carousal < G. gar aus, quite out < gar austrinken, to drink up entirely] to drink much alcoholic liquor, esp. along with others having a noisy, merry time; engage in a carousal —n. 1. a noisy, merry drinking party 2. [Obs.] a glassful drunk all at once, esp. as a toast

car·ou·sel (kar′ə sel′, -zel′) n. ☆same as CARROUSEL

carp¹ (kärp) n., pl. carp, carps: see PLURAL, II, D, 2 [ME. & OFr. carpe < Gmc. carpa] 1. any of a group of edible freshwater fishes (genus Cyprinus) living in ponds or other tranquil waters and widely cultivated in Europe and Asia for food 2. any of several other similar or related fishes (family Cyprinidae) as the goldfish

carp² (kärp) vi. [ME. carpen < ON. karpa, to brag; meaning infl. by L. carpere, to pluck, harass] to complain or find fault in a petty or nagging way —carp′er n.

-carp (kärp) [< Gr. karpos, fruit] a terminal combining form meaning fruit [endocarp]

car·pal (kär'pəl) *adj.* [ModL. *carpalis*] of the carpus —*n.* a bone of the carpus

car·pa·le (kär pā'lē) *n.*, *pl.* **-li·a** (-ə) [ModL., neut. of *carpalis*] *same as* CARPAL

Car·pa·thi·an Mountains (kär pā'thē ən) mountain system in C Europe, extending southeast from S Poland into NE Romania: highest peak, 8,737 ft.: also **Car·pa'thi·ans**

‡**car·pe di·em** (kär'pe dē'em, dī'-) [L., lit., seize the day] make the most of present opportunities

car·pel (kär'pəl) *n.* [ModL. dim. < Gr. *karpos*, fruit] **1.** a simple pistil, regarded as a single ovule-bearing leaf or modified leaflike structure **2.** any of the segments of a compound pistil, usually having a single stigma —**car'pel·lar'y** (-pə ler'ē) *adj.* —**car'pel·late'** (-pə lāt') *adj.*

(CARPEL)

Car·pen·tar·i·a (kär'pən ter'ē ə), **Gulf of** arm of the Arafura Sea, on the N coast of Australia: 480 mi. long; 420 mi. wide

car·pen·ter (kär'pən tər) *n.* [ME. & Anglo-Fr. < LL. *carpentarius*, a carpenter, wagon maker < L. *carpentum*, two-wheeled carriage, cart < Gaul.] a workman who builds and repairs wooden things, esp. the wooden parts of buildings, ships, etc. —*vi.* to do a carpenter's work —*vt.* to make or repair by or as if by carpentry

Car·pen·ter (kär'pən tər), **John Alden** 1876–1951; U.S. composer

carpenter bee any of several kinds of solitary bees (family Xylocopidae) that bore long tunnels in timber and lay eggs in them

car·pen·try (-trē) *n.* [ME. & OFr. *carpenterie*] the work or trade of a carpenter

car·pet (kär'pit) *n.* [ME. < OFr. *carpite*, a carpet, kind of cloth < ML. *carpita*, thick woolen cloth < pp. of L. *carpere*, to card, pluck: for IE. base see EXCERPT] **1.** a thick, heavy fabric of wool, cotton, or synthetic fibers for covering a floor, stairs, etc.: it is woven, usually with a pile, or felted **2.** a strip, or several joined strips, of such fabric **3.** anything laid down or spread like a carpet [a *carpet* of snow] —*vt.* to cover with or as with a carpet —**on the carpet 1.** under consideration **2.** being, or about to be, reprimanded

car·pet·bag (-bag') *n.* an old-fashioned type of traveling bag, made of carpeting —☆*adj.* of or having to do with carpetbaggers —☆*vi.* **-bagged'**, **-bag'ging** to act as a carpetbagger

☆**car·pet·bag·ger** (-bag'ər) *n.* **1.** any of the Northern politicians or adventurers who went South to take advantage of unsettled conditions after the Civil War: contemptuous term with reference to the luggage they used in traveling light **2.** any politician, promoter, etc. from the outside whose influence is resented

carpet beetle (or **bug**) any of a number of small beetles (family Dermestidae, esp. genus *Anthrenus*) whose larvae feed on furs and woolens, esp. carpets

car·pet·ing (-in) *n.* carpets or carpet fabric

carpet knight a knight or soldier who has never been in combat and lives in comfort: disparaging term

☆**carpet sweeper** a hand-operated device with a revolving brush to sweep up dirt from carpets and rugs

☆**car·pet·weed** (-wēd') *n.* a N. American annual weed (*Mollugo verticillata*) of the carpetweed family, that grows close to the ground, forming a mat —*adj.* designating a family (Aizoaceae) of plants growing chiefly on deserts and seashores in warm regions, including the fig marigolds, the mesembryanthemums, and the ice plant

car·pi (kär'pī) *n., pl. of* CARPUS

-car·pic (kär'pik) *same as* -CARPOUS

carp·ing (kär'pin) *adj.* tending to carp, or find fault; captious —*SYN.* see CRITICAL —**carp'ing·ly** *adv.*

car·po- (kär'pə, -pō) [< Gr. *karpos*, fruit] *a combining form meaning* fruit, seeds [*carpology*]

car·po·go·ni·um (kär'pə gō'nē əm) *n., pl.* **-ni·a** (-ə) [CARPO- + -GONIUM] the female reproductive organ in red algae

car·pol·o·gy (kär päl'ə jē) *n.* [CARPO- + -LOGY] the study of the structure of fruits and seeds

☆**car pool** an arrangement by a group to rotate the use of their cars, as for going to work

car·poph·a·gous (kär päf'ə gəs) *adj.* [Gr. *karpophagos* < *karpos*, fruit + *phagein*, to eat] fruit-eating

car·po·phore (kär'pə fôr') *n.* [CARPO- + -PHORE] *Bot.* **1.** the lengthened receptacle to which the carpels are attached **2.** any fruiting body or fruiting structure of a fungus

☆**car·port** (kär'pôrt') *n.* a shelter for an automobile, consisting of a roof extended from the side of a building, sometimes with an additional wall

car·po·spore (kär'pə spôr') *n.* a spore developed from the fertilized carpogonium in the red algae

-car·pous (kär'pəs) [< Gr. *karpos*, fruit] *a terminal combining form meaning* fruited; having (a certain number of) fruits or (a certain kind of) fruit [*monocarpous, apocarpous*]

car·pus (kär'pəs) *n., pl.* **-pi** (-pī) [ModL. < Gr. *karpos*, wrist] *Anat.* the wrist, or the wrist bones

car·rack (kar'ək) *n.* [ME. *carrack* < OFr. *caraque* < Sp. *carraca* < Ar. *qarāqīr*, pl. of *qurqūr*, merchant ship] *same as* GALLEON

car·ra·geen, car·ra·gheen (kar'ə gēn') *n.* [< *Carragheen*, near Waterford, Ireland] **1.** a purplish, edible seaweed (*Chondrus crispus*) of the red algae, found on rocky shores of N Europe and N. America: used in jellies, lotions, medicines, etc. **2.** a similar seaweed (*Gigartina mamillosa*) of the tropics

Car·ran·za (kär rän'zä), **Ve·nus·tia·no** (ve'nōōs tyä'nō) 1859–1920; Mex. revolutionist & statesman; president of Mexico (1917–20)

Car·ra·ra (kə rä'rə; *It.* kär rä'rä) commune in Tuscany, NW Italy: a fine, white marble (**Carrara marble**) is quarried in nearby mountains: pop. (with nearby Massa) 56,000

car·re·four (kár fōōr'; *E.* kar'ə fōōr') *n.* [Fr. < VL. *quadrifurcum, orig. neut. of *quadrifurcus, lit., four-forked, hence, where four roads meet < L. *quadri-* (see QUADRI-) + *furca*, FORK] **1.** a crossroads or intersection **2.** a public square or plaza

car·rel, car·rell (kar'əl) *n.* [ME. *caroll* < ML. *carula*, small study in a cloister] a small enclosure or space in the stack room of a library, designed for study or reading by individual patrons

Car·rel (kar'əl, kə rel'), **Alexis** 1873–1944; Fr. surgeon & biologist, in the U.S. (1905–39)

car·ri·age (kar'ij; *for 2, usually* kar'ē ij) *n.* [ME. *cariage* < Anglo-Fr. *cariage*, a cart, carriage < *carier*, CARRY] **1.** the act of carrying; transportation **2.** the cost of carrying; transportation charge **3.** [Archaic] *a)* management or handling *b)* conduct; behavior **4.** manner of carrying the head and body; posture; bearing **5.** *a)* a four-wheeled passenger vehicle, usually horse-drawn and often private *b)* a baby buggy **6.** [Brit.] a railroad passenger car; coach **7.** a wheeled frame or support for something heavy [a gun *carriage*] **8.** a moving part (of a machine) for supporting and shifting something [the *carriage* of a typewriter] —*SYN.* see BEARING

carriage dog *same as* DALMATIAN

☆**carriage trade** the wealthy patrons of a theater, store, etc., who formerly arrived in private carriages

car·rick bend (kar'ik) a kind of knot for joining two ropes: see KNOT, illus.

carrick bitt *Naut.* either of the two posts supporting a windlass

Car·rie (kar'ē) a feminine name: see CAROLINE

car·ri·er (kar'ē ər) *n.* [ME. *carier* < *carien*, CARRY] **1.** a person or thing that carries something, as a mailman, paperboy, etc. or a train, bus, etc. **2.** a person or company in the business of transporting goods or passengers **3.** a messenger or porter **4.** a container, support, or course in or on which something is carried or conducted, as a mechanical part or device, a water conduit, etc. ☆**5.** *same as* AIRCRAFT CARRIER **6.** a person or animal that carries and transmits disease germs, esp. a person who is immune to the germs he carries **7.** *Chem. a)* a catalytic agent that causes an element or radical to be transferred from one compound to another *b)* a body which supports the catalyst deposited in or on it *c)* a substance which when added to a small quantity of a similar substance will carry this minute amount **8.** *Electronics* the steady transmitted wave whose amplitude, frequency, or phase is modulated by the signal

carrier pigeon 1. a pigeon trained to fly over great distances back to a home point, carrying a written message fastened to its leg; homing pigeon **2.** any of a breed of large show pigeons with big wattles

car·ri·ole (kar'ē ōl') *n. same as* CARIOLE

car·ri·on (kar'ē ən) *n.* [ME. *carioun* < Anglo-Fr. *careine* < VL. *caronia, carcass < L. *caro*, flesh] **1.** the decaying flesh of a dead body, esp. when regarded as food for scavenging animals **2.** anything very disgusting or repulsive —*adj.* **1.** of or like carrion; rotten; vile **2.** feeding on carrion

carrion crow a common crow (*Corvus corone*) of Europe

carrion flower 1. a perennial vine (*Smilax herbacea*) of the lily family, with greenish, foul-smelling flowers **2.** *a common name for* STAPELIA

Car·roll (kar'əl) **1. Charles,** 1737–1832; Am. Revolutionary leader **2. Lewis,** (pseud. of *Charles Lutwidge Dodgson*) 1832–98; Eng. writer and mathematician: author of *Alice's Adventures in Wonderland*

car·rom (kar'əm) *n., vi. same as* CAROM

car·ron·ade (kar'ə nād') *n.* [< *Carron*, Scotland, where it was first made] an obsolete type of short, light cannon with a large bore, used at close range

car·rot (kar'ət) *n.* [Fr. *carotte* < L. *carota* < Gr. *karōton*, carrot] **1.** a biennial plant (*Daucus carota*) of the parsley family, with fernlike leaves and umbels of white flowers **2.** the fleshy, orange-red root of cultivated strains, eaten as a vegetable **3.** something offered as a tantalizing, but deceptive inducement, like a carrot dangled out of reach before a donkey's nose —**carrot and stick** pleasant promises coupled with threats

fat, āpe, cär; ten, ēven; is, bīte; gō, hôrn, tōōl, look; oil, out; up, fur; get; joy; yet; chin; she; thin, *th*en; zh, leisure; ŋ, ring; ə for *a* in *ago*, *e* in *agent*, *i* in *sanity*, *o* in *comply*, *u* in *focus*; ' as in *able* (ā'b'l); Fr. bål; ë, Fr. coeur; ö, Fr. feu; Fr. mon; ô, Fr. coq; ü, Fr. duc; r, Fr. cri; H, G. ich; kh, G. doch. See inside front cover. ☆ Americanism; ‡foreign; *hypothetical; <derived from

car·rot·y (-ē) *adj.* **1.** orange-red, like carrots [*carroty* hair] **2.** having red hair; redheaded

car·rou·sel (kar′ə sel′, -zel′) *n.* [Fr. < It. dial. (Naples) *carusiello*, kind of tournament in which players threw reed lances or balls of chalk at opponents, orig. lit. chalk ball < *caruso*, shaved head: form infl. by It. *carrozza*, stately carriage, prob. < *carro*: see CAR] ☆a merry-go-round

car·ry (kar′ē) *vt.* **-ried, -ry·ing** [ME. *carien* < Anglo-Fr. *carier* < VL. *carricare*: see CHARGE] **1.** to hold or support while moving [to *carry* a package] **2.** to take from one place to another; transport, as in a vehicle [to *carry* the mail] **3.** to hold, and direct the motion of; be a channel for; convey [a pipe *carrying* water] **4.** to cause to go; lead or impel [his ambition *carried* him to the top] **5.** to be a medium for the transmission of [air *carries* sounds] **6.** to transfer or extend [to *carry* a wall along a precipice] **7.** to transfer (a figure, entry, account, etc.) from one column, page, time, etc. to the next in order **8.** to bear the weight of [the balusters *carry* a railing] **9.** to be pregnant with **10.** *a)* to bear as a mark *b)* to have as a quality, characteristic, consequence, etc.; involve; imply [to *carry* a guarantee] **11.** to have on one's person or keep with one [to *carry* a watch, to *carry* memories] **12.** to hold or poise (oneself, one's weight, etc.) in a specified way **13.** to conduct (oneself) in a specified way ☆**14.** to include as part of its contents or program: said of a newspaper, radio or TV station, etc. **15.** to have or keep on a list or register [*carried* on the tax list] ☆**16.** to support financially **17.** to deal generously with (an opponent, a subordinate, etc.) **18.** to capture (a fortress, etc.) **19.** to win over, lead, or influence (a group) **20.** *a)* to gain support or victory for (a cause, point, etc.) *b)* to win (an election, argument, etc.) *c)* to gain a majority of the votes in (a district, state, etc.) **21.** to drink (liquor) without showing the effects **22.** [Archaic or Southern Dial.] to accompany; escort ☆**23.** *Commerce a)* to keep in stock; deal in [to *carry* leather goods] *b)* to keep on one's account books, etc. **24.** *Farming a)* to bear as a crop; produce *b)* to support (livestock) **25.** *Golf* to go past or beyond (an object or expanse) or cover (a distance) with one stroke **26.** *Hunting* to keep and follow (a scent) **27.** *Music* to sing the notes of (a melody or part) accurately —*vi.* **1.** to act as a bearer, conductor, etc. **2.** to have or cover a range [the shot *carried* to the next hill] **3.** to have the intended effect upon those watching or listening **4.** to hold the head, etc. in a specified way: said of a horse **5.** to win approval [the motion *carried*] —*n., pl.* **car′ries 1.** the range of, or distance covered by, a gun, golf ball, projectile, etc. ☆**2.** a portage between two navigable bodies of water **3.** the act or manner of carrying —**be** (or **get**) **carried away** to be moved to great or unreasoning emotion or enthusiasm —**carry forward 1.** to proceed or progress with **2.** *Bookkeeping* to transfer from one column, page, book, or account to another —**carry off 1.** to kill [the disease *carried off* thousands] **2.** to win (a prize, etc.) **3.** to handle (a delicate situation), esp. with success —**carry on 1.** to engage in; conduct **2.** to go on (*with*); continue as before, esp. in the face of difficulties **3.** [Colloq.] to behave in a wild, extravagant, or childish way **4.** [Colloq.] to engage in an illicit love affair —**carry out 1.** to put (plans, instructions, etc.) into practice **2.** to get done; bring to completion; accomplish —**carry over 1.** to have or be remaining **2.** to transfer, hold over for, or extend to another place or later time **3.** to postpone or allow to postpone; continue —**carry through 1.** to get done; bring to completion; accomplish **2.** to keep (a person) going, through trouble or difficulty; sustain

SYN.—**carry** means to take something from one place to another and implies a person as the agent or the use of a vehicle or other medium; **bear** emphasizes the support of the weight or the importance of that which is carried [borne on a sedan chair, to *bear* good tidings]; **convey**, often simply a formal equivalent of carry, is preferred where continuous movement is involved [boxes *conveyed* on a moving belt] or where passage by means of an agent or medium is implied [words *convey* ideas]; **transport** is applied to the movement of goods or people from one place to another, esp. over long distances; **transmit** stresses causal agency in connection with the sending or conducting of things [the telegrapher *transmitted* the message]

☆**car·ry·all**[1] (-ôl′) *n.* [< Fr. *carriole* (see CARIOLE); sp. infl. by CARRY & ALL] **1.** a light, covered carriage drawn by one horse and having seats for several people **2.** a moderately large, enclosed, trucklike vehicle with removable seats, for carrying passengers or merchandise

☆**car·ry·all**[2] (-ôl′) *n.* a large bag, basket, etc.

☆**carrying charge 1.** interest or other extra charge paid on the balance owed in installment buying **2.** the costs associated with ownership of property, as taxes, insurance, upkeep, etc.

car·ry·ings-on (kar′ē inz än′) *n.pl.* [Colloq.] wild, extravagant, or immoral behavior

☆**car·ry·out** (kar′ē out′) *adj.* designating a service, as of restaurants or taverns, by which prepared dishes, beverages, etc. may be taken out to be consumed elsewhere

car·ry·o·ver (kar′ē ō′vər) *n.* **1.** the act of carrying over **2.** something carried over; specif., *a)* a remainder, as of crops, goods, etc., held for future sale *b)* an amount carried forward in an account

☆**car·sick** (kär′sik′) *adj.* nauseated from riding in an automobile, bus, etc. —**car′sick′ness** *n.*

Car·son (kär′s'n) [after Kit CARSON] city in SW Calif.: suburb of Los Angeles: pop. 71,000

Car·son (kär′s'n) **1. Kit,** (born *Christopher Carson*) 1809–68; Am. frontiersman **2. Rachel (Louise),** 1907–64; U.S. biologist & science writer

Carson City [after Kit CARSON] capital of Nev., near Lake Tahoe: pop. 15,000

Car·stensz (kär′stənz), **Mount** mountain peak in West Irian, on New Guinea: c. 16,500 ft.

cart (kärt) *n.* [ME. < ON. *kartr* (akin to OE. *cræt*; orig., body of a cart made of wickerwork, hamper) < IE. base *ger-*, to twist, plait, whence CRADLE] **1.** any of various small, strong, two-wheeled vehicles drawn by a horse, ox, pony, etc. **2.** a light, uncovered wagon or carriage **3.** a small, wheeled vehicle, drawn or pushed by hand —*vt., vi.* to carry or deliver in or as in a cart, truck, etc.; transport —**put the cart before the horse** to deal with matters in reverse order, as because of illogical reasoning or erroneous anticipation —**cart′er** *n.*

cart·age (kär′tij) *n.* **1.** the act or work of carting **2.** the charge made for carting

Car·ta·ge·na (kär′tə jē′nə, -gā′-; *Sp.* kär′tä hā′nä) **1.** seaport in NW Colombia, on the Caribbean: pop. 242,000 **2.** seaport in SE Spain, on the Mediterranean: pop. 131,000

carte[1] (kärt) *n.* [Fr., CARD[1]] *same as* BILL OF FARE

carte[2] (kärt) *n. same as* QUARTE

Carte (kärt), **Richard D'Oy·ly** (doi′lē) 1844–1901; Eng. producer of Gilbert & Sullivan operas

carte blanche (kärt′ blänsh′, blänch′) *pl.* **cartes blanches** (kärts′ blänsh′, kärt blän′shəz) [Fr., white card, i.e., paper bearing only a person's signature, allowing the bearer to fill in conditions] **1.** full authority **2.** freedom to do as one thinks best

car·tel (kär tel′) *n.* [Fr. < It. *cartello*, dim. of *carta*, CARD[1]] **1.** a written challenge, as to a duel **2.** a written agreement between nations at war, esp. as to the exchange of prisoners **3.** [G. *kartell* < Fr. *cartel*] an association of industrialists, business firms, etc. for establishing a national or international monopoly by price fixing, ownership of controlling stock, etc.; trust **4.** [*often* C-] a political bloc in certain European countries —**SYN.** see MONOPOLY

Car·ter (kär′tər), **Nick 1.** a detective in a popular series of dime novels of the late 19th cent. **2.** the pseudonym of the several authors who wrote this series

Car·ter·et (kär′tər it), **John, 1st Earl Granville,** 1690–1763; Brit. statesman & diplomat

Car·te·sian (kär tē′zhən) *adj.* [< *Cartesius*, Latinized form of DESCARTES] of Descartes or his philosophical or mathematical ideas —*n.* a follower of Descartes' ideas or methods —**Car·te′sian·ism** *n.*

Cartesian coordinates *Geom.* **1.** a pair of numbers that locate a point by its distances from two intersecting, often perpendicular, lines in the same plane: each distance is measured along a parallel to the other line **2.** a triad of numbers which locate a point by its distance from three fixed planes that intersect one another at right angles

Car·thage (kär′thij) ancient city-state in N Africa, founded by the Phoenicians near the site of modern Tunis and destroyed by the Romans in 146 B.C. (see PUNIC WARS) —**Car·tha·gin·i·an** (kär′thə jin′ē ən) *adj., n.*

Car·thu·sian (kär thōō′zhən, -thyōō′-) *n.* [ML. *Cartusianus* < *Cartusia, Catorissium,* L. name for Chartreuse] a monk or nun of a very strict order founded at Chartreuse, France, in 1084, by Saint Bruno —*adj.* of or connected with the Carthusians

CARTHAGE (1st cent. B.C.)

Car·tier (kär tyā′), **Jacques** (zhàk) 1491–1557; Fr. explorer; discovered the St. Lawrence River

car·ti·lage (kärt′'l ij) *n.* [ME. & OFr. < L. *cartilago* < IE. base *kert-*, to twist together, plait, whence HURDLE] **1.** a tough, elastic, whitish animal tissue; gristle: the skeletons of embryos and young animals are composed largely of cartilage, most of which later turns to bone **2.** a part or structure consisting of cartilage

car·ti·lag·i·nous (kärt′'l aj′ə nəs) *adj.* [ME. & OFr. < L. *cartilaginosus*] **1.** of or like cartilage; gristly **2.** having a skeleton made up mainly of cartilage, as sharks

cart·load (kärt′lōd′) *n.* as much as a cart holds

car·to·gram (kär′tə gram′) *n.* [Fr. *cartogramme*: see CARD[1] & -GRAM] a map giving statistical data by means of lines, dots, shaded areas, etc.

car·tog·ra·pher (kär täg′rə fər) *n.* [see ff.] a person whose work is making maps or charts

car·tog·ra·phy (kär täg′rə fē) *n.* [< ML. *carta* (see CARD[1]) + -GRAPHY] the art or work of making maps or charts —**car·to·graph·ic** (kär′tə graf′ik), **car′to·graph′i·cal** *adj.*

car·ton (kärt′'n) *n.* [Fr. < It. *cartone* < *carta*: see CARD[1]] **1.** a cardboard box, esp. a large one, as for shipping mer-

chandise **2.** a boxlike container, as of stiff waxed paper, for liquids **3.** a full carton or its contents

car·toon (kär tōōn′) *n.* [Fr. *carton* < It. *cartone*, both in sense 2: see prec.] **1.** a drawing, as in a newspaper, caricaturing or symbolizing, often satirically, some event, situation, or person of topical interest **2.** a full-size preliminary sketch of a design or picture to be copied in a fresco, tapestry, etc. **3.** *a)* a humorous drawing, often with a caption *b)* *same as* COMIC STRIP **4.** *same as* ANIMATED CARTOON —*vt.* to draw a cartoon of —*vi.* to draw cartoons —**car·toon′ist** *n.*

car·touche, car·touch (kär tōōsh′) *n.* [Fr. < It. *cartoccio*, cartridge, roll of paper < *carta*, paper: see CARD[1]] **1.** a scroll-like ornament or tablet, esp. as an architectural feature **2.** on Egyptian monuments, an oval or oblong figure containing the name of a ruler or deity **3.** [Obs.] a paper cartridge (sense 1)

car·tridge (kär′trij) *n.* [altered < prec.] **1.** a cylindrical case of cardboard, metal, etc. containing the charge and primer, and usually the projectile, for a firearm **2.** any of various small containers, holding a supply of material for a larger device into which it is inserted *[an ink cartridge for a pen]* **3.** a protected roll of camera film **4.** a replaceable unit in the pickup of an electric phonograph, containing the stylus, or needle

cartridge clip a metal container for cartridges, inserted in certain types of firearms

car·tu·lar·y (kär′chə ler′ē) *n., pl.* **-ar′ies** [LL. *chartularium* < L. *chartula:* see CHARTER] a collection or register of charters, deeds, etc.

cart wheel 1. a kind of handspring performed sidewise ☆**2.** a large coin, esp. a silver dollar

Cart·wright (kärt′rīt) **1. Edmund,** 1743–1823; Eng. inventor, esp. of the power loom **2. John,** 1740–1824; Eng. political reformer: brother of *prec.*

car·un·cle (kar′əŋ k'l, kə ruŋ′k'l) *n.* [Fr. *caroncule* < L. *caruncula*, dim. of *caro*, flesh] **1.** an outgrowth of flesh, as the comb and wattles of a fowl **2.** a swelling at or near the hilum of a seed —**ca·run′cu·lar** (kə ruŋ′kyə lər), **ca·run′cu·lous** (-ləs), **ca·run′cu·late** (-lit) *adj.*

Ca·ru·so (kə rōō′sō; *It.* kä rōō′zō), **En·ri·co** (en rē′kō) 1873–1921; It. operatic tenor

car·va·crol (kär′və krôl′, -krōl′) *n.* [< Fr. *carvi*, caraway + L. *acer* (gen. *acris*), sharp + -OL[1]] a thick oily substance, (CH₃)₂CHC₆H₃(CH₃)(OH), extracted from oil of mint and other essential oils: used in perfumes, and as a fungicide and disinfectant

carve (kärv) *vt.* **carved, carv′ing** [ME. *kerven* < OE. *ceorfan* < IE. base *gerbh-*, to scratch, whence Gr. *graphein*, to draw, write, G. *kerben*, to notch] **1.** to make or shape by or as by cutting, chipping, hewing, etc. *[carve a statue out of wood or stone, carve a career]* **2.** to decorate the surface of with cut figures or designs **3.** to divide by cutting; slice *[to carve meat]* —*vi.* **1.** to carve statues or designs **2.** to carve meat —**carv′er** *n.*

car·vel (kär′vəl) *n. same as* CARAVEL

car·vel-built (-bilt′) *adj. Shipbuilding* with the hull planks laid edge to edge to form a smooth surface: distinguished from CLINKER-BUILT

carv·en (kär′v'n) *archaic pp.* of CARVE —*adj.* [Archaic or Poet.] carved

Car·ver (kär′vər) **1. George Washington,** 1864–1943, U.S. botanist & chemist **2. John,** 1575?–1621; Pilgrim leader: 1st governor of Plymouth Colony

carv·ing (kär′viŋ) *n.* **1.** the work or art of a person who carves **2.** a carved figure or design

carving fork a large, two-tined fork with a metal guard to protect the hand, used to hold meat being carved

carving knife a large knife for carving meat

☆**car·wash** (kär′wôsh′, -wäsh′) *n.* an establishment at which automobiles are washed and polished

Car·y (ker′ē), **(Arthur) Joyce (Lunel)** 1888–1957; Brit. novelist, born in Ireland

car·y·at·id (kar′ē at′id) *n., pl.* **-ids, -id·es′** (-ə dēz′) [< L. pl. *caryatides* < Gr. *karyatides*, priestesses of the temple of Diana at Karyai, in Macedonia] a supporting column that has the form of a draped female figure

car·y·o- (kar′ē ə, -ō) *same as* KARYO-

car·y·op·sis (kar′ē äp′sis) *n., pl.* **-op′ses** (-sēz), **-op′si·des** (-sə dēz′) [ModL.: see CARYO- & -OPSIS] a small, dry, one-seeded fruit in which the ovary wall remains joined with the seed in a single grain, as in barley, wheat, etc.

ca·sa·ba (kə sä′bə) *n.* [< *Kassaba*, town near Smyrna, Asia Minor, whence the melon came] any of a group of cultivated melons (*Cucumis melo inodorus*) with a hard, yellow rind and sweet, usually white flesh

Ca·sa·blan·ca (kas′ə blaŋ′kə, kä′sə bläŋ′kə) seaport in NW Morocco, on the Atlantic: pop. 1,085,000

Ca·sa·de·sus (kä sá dā süs′), **Ro·bert (Mar·cel)** (rô ber′) 1899– ; Fr. pianist

Ca·sa Gran·de (kas′ə gran′dē, kä′sə grän′dā) the main structure of a group of prehistoric Indian ruins in S Ariz., now constituting a national monument

Ca·sals (kə sälz′, -salz′; *Sp.* kä säls′) **Pa·blo** (päb′lō) (born *Pau Carlos Salvador Defillio de Casals*) 1876– ; Sp. cellist & composer in self-imposed exile

Ca·sa·no·va (kas′ə nō′və, kaz′ə-; *It.* kä′zä nô′vä), **Gio·van·ni Ja·co·po** (jō vän′nē yä′kō pō) 1725–98; It. adventurer, noted for his *Memoirs*

Ca·sau·bon (kə zô bôn′; *E.* kə sô′bən), **I·saac** (ē zäk′) 1559–1614; Fr. scholar & theologian, born in Switzerland

cas·bah (käz′bä, kas′-) *n.* [Fr. < Ar. dial. *qaṣba*, for Ar. *qaṣaba*, fortress] **1.** in N Africa, a fortress **2.** the old, crowded quarter of a N African city, esp. [C-] of Algiers

cas·ca·bel (kas′kə bel′) *n.* [Sp., a small bell, rattle, rattlesnake] a projecting part behind the breech of former muzzle-loading cannons

cas·cade (kas kād′) *n.* [Fr. < It. *cascata* < *cascare*, to fall < VL. *casicare* < pp. of L. *cadere*, to fall] **1.** a small, steep waterfall, esp. one of a series **2.** anything suggesting this, as a shower of sparks or an arrangement of lace or drapery in rippling folds **3.** a connected series, as of amplifiers for an increase in output —*vt., vi.* **-cad′ed, -cad′ing 1.** to fall or drop in a cascade **2.** to connect in a series

Cascade Range [referring to the cascades on the Columbia River] mountain range extending from N Calif., through W Oreg. and Wash., into S British Columbia: highest peak, Mt. RAINIER

☆**cas·car·a** (kas ker′ə) *n.* [Sp. *cáscara*, bark, prob. < *casca*, bark, husk, shell < *cascar:* see CASK] **1.** a small tree (*Rhamnus purshiana*) of the buckthorn family, growing on the Pacific coast of the U.S. and furnishing cascara sagrada **2.** *same as* CASCARA SAGRADA

☆**cascara sa·gra·da** (sə grä′də, -grä′-) [Sp., lit., sacred bark] **1.** a laxative made from cascara bark **2.** the bark

cas·ca·ril·la (kas′kə ril′ə) *n.* [Sp., dim. of *cáscara:* see CASCARA] **1.** a West Indian shrub (*Croton eluteria*) of the spurge family **2.** its aromatic bark, used as a tonic: also **cascarilla bark**

Cas·co Bay (kas′kō) bay on the SW coast of Maine, on which Portland is located

case[1] (kās) *n.* [ME. & OFr. *cas*, an event < L. *casus*, a falling, pp. of *cadere*, to fall < IE. base* *kad-*, to fall whence Sans. *śad-*, to fall off] **1.** an example, instance, or occurrence *[a case of carelessness, a case of measles]* **2.** a person being treated or helped, as by a doctor or social worker **3.** any individual or matter requiring or undergoing official or formal observation, study, investigation, etc. **4.** a statement of the facts or circumstances, as in a law court, esp. the argument of one side *[the case for the defendant]* **5.** supporting or convincing arguments or evidence; proper grounds for a statement or action *[he has no case]* **6.** a legal action or suit, esp. one studied or cited as a precedent ☆**7.** [Colloq.] a peculiar or eccentric person ☆**8.** [Colloq.] an infatuation; crush **9.** [so named because Latin cases were thought of as "falling away" from the nominative: cf. ACCIDENCE] *Gram. a)* any of the sets of forms for nouns, pronouns, and adjectives showing syntactic relationship in highly inflected languages such as Latin or German *b)* the form of a noun, pronoun, or adjective that shows such relationship *c)* the relationship shown by such inflection In English syntax the term is applied by analogy esp. to the subjective, objective, and possessive forms of pronouns and the possessive form of nouns —*vt.* **cased, cas′ing** ☆[Slang] to look over carefully, esp. in preparation for an intended robbery —*SYN.* see INSTANCE —**in any case** no matter what else may be true; anyhow —**in case** in the event that; if —**in case of** in the event of; if there should happen to be —**in no case** by no means; not under any circumstances; never

case[2] (kās) *n.* [ME. < ONormFr. *casse* < L. *capsa*, a box, chest < *capere*, to take, contain, hold] **1.** a container, as a box, crate, chest, sheath, folder, etc. **2.** a protective cover or covering part *[a watch case, seedcase]* **3.** a full box or its contents *[a case of beer]* **4.** a set or pair *[a case of pistols]* **5.** a frame as for a window or door **6.** *Bookbinding* the cover of a book before it is attached to the book **7.** *Printing* a shallow compartmental tray in which type is kept: the **upper case** is used for capitals and special characters, the **lower case** for small letters, figures, etc. —*vt.* **cased, cas′ing 1.** to put in a container **2.** to cover or enclose

ca·se·ase (kā′sē ās′) *n.* [CASE(IN) + -ASE] an enzyme made from bacterial cultures, which dissolves casein and albumin: used in the process of ripening cheese

ca·se·ate (-āt′) *vi.* **-at′ed, -at′ing** *Med.* to undergo caseation

ca·se·a·tion (kā′sē ā′shən) *n.* [< L. *caseatus*, mixed with cheese < *caseus*, CHEESE[1] + -ION] **1.** the precipitation of casein to form cheese **2.** *Med.* a degenerative process in which tissue changes into a dry, cheeselike substance, characteristically associated with tuberculosis

case·book (kās′book′) *n.* a book containing a selection of source materials on a certain subject used as a reference work or in teaching methods of research

ca·se·fy (kā′sə fī′) *vt., vi.* **-fied′, -fy′ing** [< L. *caseus*, CHEESE[1] + -FY] to make or become cheeselike

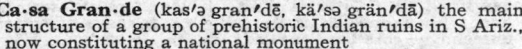

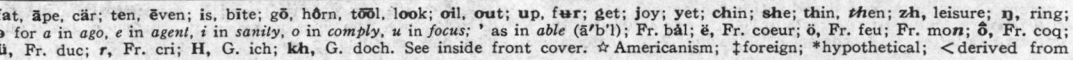

CARYATID

case·hard·en (kās′här′d'n) *vt.* **1.** *Metallurgy* to form a hard, thin surface on (an iron alloy) **2.** to make callous or unfeeling —**case′hard′ened** *adj.*

case history (or **study**) collected information about an individual or group, for use esp. in sociological, medical, or psychiatric studies

ca·se·in (kā′sē in, kā′sēn) *n.* [< L. *caseus*, CHEESE¹ + -IN¹] a phosphoprotein that is one of the chief constituents of milk and the basis of cheese: used in plastics, glues, etc.

ca·se·in·o·gen (kā′sē in′ə jən, kā sē′nə-) *n.* [< prec. + -GEN] that protein of milk which produces casein when acted upon by rennin

case knife 1. *same as* SHEATH KNIFE **2.** a table knife

case law law based on previous judicial decisions, or precedents: distinguished from STATUTE LAW

☆**case·load** (kās′lōd′) *n.* the number of cases being handled as by a court, social agency, or welfare department, or by a caseworker, probation officer, etc.

case·mate (kās′māt′) *n.* [Fr. < It. *casamatta* < Gr. *chasmata*, pl. of *chasma*, opening (see CHASM); altered after It. *casa*, a house, and *matto*, dim, dark] a shellproof or armored enclosure with openings for guns, as in a fortress wall or on a warship —**case′mat′ed** *adj.*

case·ment (kās′mənt) *n.* [ME., aphetic < OFr. *encassement*, a frame: see CASE²] **1.** a window frame that opens on hinges along the side: a **casement window** often has two such frames, opening like French doors **2.** a casing; covering —**case′ment·ed** *adj.*

Case·ment (kās′mənt), Sir **Roger David** 1864–1916; Ir. nationalist: hanged by the Brit. as a traitor in World War I

ca·se·ose (kā′sē ōs′) *n.* [CASE(IN) + -OSE¹] a soluble protein derivative formed during the digestion of casein

ca·se·ous (-əs) *adj.* [< L. *caseus*, CHEESE¹] of or like cheese

ca·sern, ca·serne (kə zurn′) *n.* [Fr. *caserne* < Pr. *cazerna*, small hut, orig., small room in fortress for a military night watch < LL. *quaterna*, four each < *quattuor*, FOUR] a military barracks in a fortified town

case shot a quantity of small projectiles enclosed in a single case, as a shrapnel shell, for firing from a gun

☆**case system** a method of training law students by analyzing and discussing selected cases and decisions rather than by systematic study of textbooks on law

case·work (kās′wurk′) *n.* social work in which the worker investigates a case of personal or family maladjustment and gives advice and guidance —**case′work′er** *n.*

case·worm (-wurm′) *n.* any of various insect larvae that build protective cases about their bodies

cash¹ (kash) *n.* [Fr. *caisse*, a box, money box, cash < Pr. *caissa* < L. *capsa*, a box: see CASE²] **1.** money that a person actually has, including money on deposit; esp., ready money **2.** bills and coins; currency **3.** money, a check, etc. paid at the time of purchase —*vt.* to give or get cash for [to *cash* a check] —*adj.* of, for, requiring, or made with cash [a *cash* sale] —☆**cash in 1.** to turn into cash; get money for **2.** [Slang] to die —☆**cash in on** to get profit or profitable use from

cash² (kash) *n., pl.* **cash** [Port. *caixa* < Tamil *kasu* < Sans. *karṣa*] any of several Chinese or Indian coins of small value; esp., a Chinese copper-alloy coin with a square perforation in the center

☆**cash-and-car·ry** (kash′ən kar′ē) *adj.* **1.** with cash payments and no deliveries **2.** operated on a cash-and-carry system

☆**ca·shaw** (kə shô′) *n. same as* CUSHAW

cash·book (kash′book′) *n.* a book in which all receipts and payments of money are entered

cash discount a discount from the purchase price allowed a purchaser paying within a specified period

cash·ew (kash′ōō, kə shōō′) *n.* [aphetic < Fr. *acajou* < Port. < Tupi *acajú*] **1.** a tropical evergreen tree (*Anacardium occidentale*) of the cashew family, bearing edible, kidney-shaped nuts, each at the end of an edible, pear-shaped receptacle and yielding a gum used in varnish **2.** the nut: also **cashew nut** —*adj.* designating a family (Anacardiaceae) of trees and shrubs including the pistachio, mango, and sumac

cash·ier¹ (ka shir′) *n.* [Fr. *caissier* < *caisse*: see CASH¹] **1.** a person hired to collect and keep a record of customers' payments, as in a store **2.** an officer in a bank or company responsible for receipts and disbursements

cash·ier² (ka shir′) *vt.* [MDu. *casseren*, to disband soldiers < Fr. *casser*, to break < LL. *cassare*, to nullify, destroy < L. *cassus*, empty, futile & *quassare*: see QUASH¹] **1.** to dismiss, esp. in dishonor, from a position of command, trust, etc. **2.** to discard or reject

☆**cashier's check** a check drawn by a bank on its own funds and signed by the cashier

Cash·mere (kash mir′, kash′mir) *former sp.* of KASHMIR

cash·mere (kazh′mir, kash′-) *n.* [< prec.] **1.** a fine carded wool obtained from goats of Kashmir and Tibet **2.** a soft, twilled cloth made of this or similar wool **3.** a cashmere shawl, sweater, coat, etc.

cash on delivery payment in cash when a purchase or shipment is delivered

☆**cash register** a business machine, usually with a money drawer, used to register visibly the amount of each sale: receipts may be recorded and totaled on tapes

cas·i·mere, cas·i·mire (kas′ə mir′) *n. same as* CASSIMERE

cas·ing (kās′iŋ) *n.* **1.** the act of encasing **2.** a protective covering; specif., ☆*a)* a cleaned intestine as of cattle, a plastic membrane, etc., used to encase processed meats ☆*b)* a pneumatic rubber tire exclusive of an inner tube and often of the tread ☆*c)* the steel pipe used to line an oil or gas well ☆**3.** a frame, as for a window or door opening

ca·si·no (kə sē′nō) *n., pl.* **-nos**; *for 1, also* **-ni** (-nē) [It., dim. of *casa*, house < L., cottage, hut, shed] **1.** in Italy, a small country house **2.** a public room or building for entertainments, dancing, or, now specif., gambling **3.** *same as* CASSINO

cask (kask, käsk) *n.* [ME. *caske* < Fr. *casque* < Sp. *casco*, potsherd, cask, helmet < *cascar*, to break < VL. *quassicare*, to break, freq. of L. *quassare*: see QUASH²] **1.** a barrel of any size made of staves, esp. one for liquids **2.** the contents of a full cask; barrelful

cas·ket (kas′kit, käs′-) *n.* [ME., prob. < OFr. *cassette*, dim. of *casse* (see CASE²); -*k* by analogy with prec.] **1.** a small box or chest, as for valuables ☆**2.** a coffin, esp. a costly one —*vt.* to put into a casket

Cas·lon (kaz′lən), **William** 1692–1766; Eng. type designer & founder

Cas·per (kas′pər) [earlier Fort Caspar, after Lt. *Caspar Collins*, killed there] city in C Wyo.: pop. 39,000

Cas·pi·an Sea (kas′pē ən) inland sea between Caucasia and Asiatic U.S.S.R.: 170,000 sq. mi. — **Cas′pi·an** *adj.*

casque (kask) *n.* [Fr.: see CASK] **1.** a helmet **2.** *Anat.* a helmetlike process or part —**casqued** (kaskt) *adj.*

Cass (kas), **Lewis** 1782–1866; U.S. statesman

cas·sa·ba (kə sä′bə) *n. same as* CASABA

Cas·san·dra (kə san′drə) [L. < Gr. *Kassandra*] *Gr. Myth.* the daughter of Priam and Hecuba: to win her love, Apollo gave her prophetic power, later, when thwarted, decreeing that no one should believe her prophecies —*n.* a person whose warnings of misfortune are disregarded

cas·sa·tion (ka sā′shən) *n.* [Fr. < *casser*: see CASHIER²] *Fr. Law* abrogation or annulment, as of a court decision, by a higher court

Cas·satt (kə sat′), **Mary** 1845–1926; U.S. painter

cas·sa·va (kə sä′və) *n.* [Fr. *cassave* < Sp. *casabe* (or) < Taino *casǎvi, cazǎbbi*] **1.** any of several tropical American plants (genus *Manihot*) of the spurge family, having edible starchy roots **2.** this root or a starch extracted from it, used in making bread and tapioca

Cas·sel (kas′'l; *Fr.* kà sel′) *same as* KASSEL

cas·se·role (kas′ə rōl′) *n.* [Fr., dim. of *casse*, a bowl, basin < Pr. *casa*, melting pan < VL. *cattia* < Gr. *kyathion*, dim. of *kyathos*, a bowl, pan] **1.** an earthenware or glass baking dish, usually with a cover, in which food can be cooked and then served **2.** the food baked and served in such a dish, usually rice, potatoes, or macaroni with meat or fish and vegetables **3.** *Chem.* a deep porcelain dish with a handle, used for heating or evaporating a substance

cas·sette (ka set′, kə-) *n.* [Fr., dim. < ONormFr. *casse*, a CASE²] **1.** a case with roll film in it, for loading a camera quickly and easily **2.** a similar case with magnetic tape, for use in a tape recorder

cas·sia (kash′ə) *n.* [ME. < L. < Gr. *kasia*, kind of cinnamon < Heb. *qeṣī′āh*] **1.** *a)* the bark of a tree (*Cinnamomum cassia*) of the laurel family, native to SE Asia; used as the source of a coarse variety of cinnamon: in full **cassia bark** *b)* this tree **2.** *a)* any of a genus (*Cassia*) of herbs, shrubs, and trees of the legume family, common in tropical countries: the pods (**cassia pods**) of some of these plants have a mildly laxative pulp (**cassia pulp**); from the leaves of others the cathartic drug senna is prepared *b)* cassia pods *c)* cassia pulp

cas·si·mere (kas′ə mir′) *n.* [var. of CASHMERE] a woolen cloth, twilled or plain, used for men's suits

Cas·si·no (kə sē′nō; *It.* käs sē′nō) town in SC Italy: scene of heavy fighting in World War II: pop. 8,000

cas·si·no (kə sē′nō) *n.* [see CASINO] a simple card game for two to four players

Cas·si·o·pe·ia (kas′ē ə pē′ə) [L. < Gr. *Kassiopeia*] **1.** *Gr. Myth.* the wife of Cepheus and mother of Andromeda **2.** a N constellation between Andromeda and Cepheus

Cassiopeia's Chair the five brightest stars in the constellation Cassiopeia, supposedly outlining a chair

Cas·si·rer (kä sē′rər), **Ernst** (ernst) 1874–1945; Ger. expatriate philosopher

cas·sis (ka sē′; *Fr.* kà sē′) *n.* [Fr., orig., black currant < L. *cassia*, CASSIA] the black currant was used as a substitute for cassia in medieval times] a liqueur made with black currants and frequently mixed with vermouth

cas·sit·er·ite (kə sit′ə rīt′) *n.* [Gr. *kassiteros*] native tin dioxide, SnO₂, the chief ore of tin: it is brown or black and very hard and heavy

Cas·si·us (Longinus) (kash′əs, kas′ē əs), **(Gaius)** ?–42 B.C.; Roman general & conspirator against Caesar

cas·sock (kas′ək) n. [Fr. *casaque* < Per. *kazhāghand*, a kind of jacket < *kazh*, raw silk] 1. a long, closefitting vestment, generally black, worn as an outer garment or under the surplice by clergymen, choristers, etc. 2. a clergyman or his position

cas·sou·let (kas′oo lā′) n. [Fr., akin to CASSEROLE] a casserole of beans slowly baked with various meats and poultries

cas·so·war·y (kas′ə wer′ē) n., pl. **-war′ies** [Malay *kasuārī*] any of a genus (*Casuarius*) of large, flightless birds of Australia and New Guinea, somewhat similar to the ostrich, but smaller and with a brightly colored neck and head

cast (kast, käst) vt. **cast, cast′ing** [ME. *casten* < ON. *kasta*, to throw] 1. a) to put, deposit, or throw with force or violence; fling; hurl b) to give vent to as if by throwing [to *cast* aspersions] 2. to deposit (a ballot or vote) 3. a) to cause to fall or turn; direct [to *cast* one's eyes or attention on a thing] b) to give forth; project [to *cast* light, gloom, etc.] 4. to throw out or drop (a net, anchor, etc.) at the end of a rope or cable 5. to throw out (a fly, etc.) at the end of a fishing line 6. to draw (lots) or shake (dice) out of a container 7. to drop (offspring) or bring forth (young), esp. prematurely 8. a) to throw off or away b) to shed; slough [the snake *casts* its skin] 9. to add up (accounts, a sum, etc.); calculate by arithmetic 10. to calculate (a horoscope, tides, etc.) 11. to arrange in some form or system; formulate 12. a) to form (molten metal, plastic, etc.) into a particular shape by pouring or pressing into a mold b) to make by such a method 13. a) to choose and assign actors for (a play or movie) b) to select (an actor) for (a role or part) 14. to twist; turn; warp 15. *Naut.* to veer 16. *Printing* to stereotype or electrotype —vi. 1. to throw dice 2. to throw out a fly, etc. at the end of a fishing line 3. [Brit. Dial.] to vomit 4. to turn; warp 5. to add up figures; calculate 6. to calculate horoscopes, tides, etc. 7. to be formed in a mold 8. [Obs.] a) to make a forecast; conjecture b) to deliberate; plan 9. *Hunting* to scatter in all directions in searching a lost scent 10. *Naut.* to veer —n. 1. the act of casting; a throw; also, a way of casting or distance thrown; specif., a) a throw of dice; also, the number thrown b) a stroke of fortune c) a turn of the eye; glance; look d) a throw of a fishing line, net, etc. e) an adding up; calculation f) a conjecture; forecast 2. a quantity or thing cast in a certain way, specif., a) some thing thrown up, off, or out, as bait on a line, a pair of hawks in falconry, the dirt thrown up by worms, the shed skin of an insect, etc. b) the amount of metal cast at one time c) something formed in or as in a mold, as a bronze or plaster reproduction of a statue modeled in clay; also, the mold d) a mold or impression taken of an object e) a plaster form for immobilizing a broken arm, leg, etc. f) the set of actors in a play or movie 3. the form or direction in which a thing is cast; specif., a) an arrangement b) an appearance or stamp, as of features c) kind; quality [of an aristocratic *cast*] d) a tinge; shade [a reddish *cast*] e) a trace or suggestion f) a turn or twist to one side; tendency; bent g) a slight turning in or out of the eye 4. *Hunting* a scattering of the hounds to find a lost scent 5. *Med.* a plastic substance formed in the cavities of some diseased organs [renal *casts*] —SYN. see THROW —**cast about** 1. to search; look (for) 2. to make plans; devise —**cast aside** (or **away**) to discard; abandon —**cast back** 1. to refer to something past 2. to resemble some distant ancestor —**cast down** 1. to turn downward 2. to sadden; depress; discourage —**cast off** 1. to discard; abandon; disown 2. to set free 3. to free a ship from a dock, quay, etc., as by releasing the lines 4. *Knitting* to make the last row of stitches —**cast on** *Knitting* to make the first row of stitches —**cast out** to force to get out or go away; expel —**cast up** 1. to throw up; vomit 2. to turn upward 3. to add up; total 4. to construct by digging [to *cast up* earthworks]

Cas·ta·li·a (kas tā′lē ə) [L. < Gr. *Kastalia*] spring on Mount Parnassus: in ancient times it was sacred to the Muses and was considered a source of poetic inspiration —**Cas·ta′li·an** adj.

cas·ta·nets (kas′tə nets′) n.pl. [Fr. *castagnette* (sing.) < Sp. *castañeta*, dim. < L. *castanea*, chestnut: so named from the shape] a pair of small, hollowed pieces of hard wood, ivory, etc., held in the hand by a connecting cord and clicked together with the fingers to beat time to music, esp. in Spanish dances

cast·a·way (kas′tə wā′, käs′-) n. 1. a person or thing cast out or off, esp. an outcast 2. a shipwrecked person —adj. 1. thrown away; discarded 2. cast adrift or stranded, as by shipwreck

caste (kast, käst) n. [Fr. < Port. *casta*, breed, race, caste < L. *castus*, pure, chaste, orig. cut off, separated: for IE. base see CASTRATE] 1. any of the

CASTANETS

distinct, hereditary Hindu social classes, each traditionally, but no longer officially, excluded from social dealings with the others 2. any exclusive and restrictive social or occupational class or group 3. rigid class distinction based on birth, wealth, etc., operating as a social system or principle 4. any of the differentiated types of individuals in a colony of social insects —**lose caste** to lose social status or position

cas·tel·lan (kas′tə lən) n. [ME. & Anglo-Fr. *castellain* < ML. *castellanus*, keeper of a castle (L., of a castle) < L. *castellum*, CASTLE] the warden or governor of a castle

cas·tel·la·ny (-lā′nē) n., pl. **-nies** 1. the office or position of a castellan 2. all the lands of a castle

cas·tel·lat·ed (-lāt′id) adj. [ML. *castellatus* < L. *castellum*, CASTLE] 1. built with turrets and battlements, like a castle 2. having many castles —**cas′tel·la′tion** n.

cast·er (kas′tər, käs′-) n. 1. a person or thing that casts 2. a) a small bottle or other container for serving vinegar, mustard, salt, etc. at the table ☆b) a stand for holding several such containers 3. a small wheel or freely rolling ball set in a swiveled frame and attached to each leg, bottom corner, etc. of a piece of furniture or other heavy object so that it can be moved easily

cas·ti·gate (kas′tə gāt′) vt. **-gat′ed, -gat′ing** [< L. *castigatus*, pp. of *castigare*, to purify, chastise < *castus*, pure] to punish or rebuke severely, esp. by harsh public criticism —SYN. see PUNISH —**cas′ti·ga′tion** n. —**cas′ti·ga′tor** n. —**cas′ti·ga·to′ry** (-gə tôr′ē) adj.

Cas·ti·glio·ne (käs′tē lyô′ne), Conte **Bal·das·sa·re** (bäl′däs sä′re) 1478–1529; It. writer & diplomat

Cas·tile (kas tēl′) region & former kingdom in N and C Spain, divided into Old Castile (to the north) and New Castile (to the south): Sp. name **Cas·til·la** (käs tēl′yä)

Castile soap [ME. *Castell sope* (< *Castile*, Spain, where first made)] [also c- s-] a fine, mild, hard soap prepared from olive oil and sodium hydroxide

Cas·til·ian (kas til′yən) adj of Castile, its people, language, or culture —n. 1. a native or inhabitant of Castile 2. the dialect of Spanish spoken in Castile, now the standard form of the language in Spain

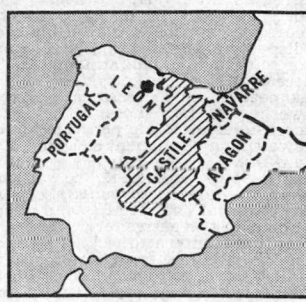

CASTILE (c. 12th cent.)

cast·ing (kas′tin, käs′-) n. 1. the action of a person or thing that casts (in various senses) 2. anything, esp. a metal piece, that has been cast in a mold 3. *Zool.* anything thrown off, ejected, or excreted, esp. the excrement of earthworms

casting vote (or **voice**) the deciding vote cast by the presiding officer when the voting on both sides is equal

cast-i·ron (kast′ī′ərn, käst′-) adj. 1. made of cast iron 2. very hard, rigid, strong, healthy, etc.

cast iron a hard, unmalleable alloy of iron made by casting: it contains a high proportion of carbon and silicon, has low tensile strength, and is very fluid and fusible when molten

cas·tle (kas′l, käs′-) n. [ME. < OE. & Anglo-Fr. *castel*, both < L. *castellum*, dim. of *castrum*, fort] 1. a large building or group of buildings fortified with thick walls, battlements, and often a moat: castles were the strongholds of noblemen in the Middle Ages 2. any massive dwelling somewhat like this 3. a safe, secure place; refuge 4. *Chess* same as ROOK[2] —vt. **-tled, -tling** 1. to put into, or furnish with, a castle 2. *Chess* to move (a king) two squares to either side and then, in the same move, set the castle in the square skipped by the king: permitted only when neither piece has been moved before and the spaces between them are not occupied —vi. *Chess* 1. to castle a king 2. to be castled: said of a king

cas·tled (-′ld) adj. same as CASTELLATED

castle in the air an imaginary scheme not likely to be realized; daydream: also **castle in Spain**

Cas·tle·reagh (kas′′l rā′, käs′-), Viscount, (*Robert Stewart*) 2d Marquis of Londonderry, 1769–1822; Brit. statesman, born in Ireland

cast·off (kast′ôf′, käst′-) adj. thrown away; discarded; abandoned —n. a person or thing cast off

Cas·tor (kas′tər, käs′-) [L. < Gr. *Kastōr*] 1. *Gr. & Rom. Myth.* the mortal twin of Pollux: see DIOSCURI 2. one of the two bright stars in the constellation Gemini: the brighter star is Pollux

cas·tor¹ (-tər) n. [Fr. < L. < Gr. *kastōr*, beaver < prec.] 1. [Rare] a beaver 2. a strong-smelling, oily substance obtained from sexual glands of the beaver, used as a scent in trapping and in making perfumes: also **cas·to-**

re·um (kas tôr′ē əm) **3.** a hat of beaver or rabbit fur

cas·tor² (-tər) *n. same as* CASTER (senses 2 & 3)

☆**castor bean 1.** the large, highly poisonous, beanlike seed of the castor-oil plant **2.** the plant itself

castor oil a colorless or yellowish oil from castor beans, used as a cathartic and as a lubricant

cas·tor-oil plant (kas′tər oil′, käs′-) a tropical plant (*Ricinus communis*) of the spurge family, with large, beanlike seeds from which castor oil is extracted

cas·trate (kas′trāt) *vt.* **-trat·ed, -trat·ing** [< L. *castratus*, pp. of *castrare*, to castrate, prune < IE. base *kes-, to cut, *kestrom*, knife, whence Sans. *śastrám*, a knife] **1.** *a)* to remove the testicles of; emasculate; geld *b)* [Rare] to remove the ovaries of; spay **2.** to deprive of essential vigor or significance by mutilating, expurgating, subjugating, etc.; emasculate **—cas·tra′tion** *n.*

cas·tra·to (käs trät′ō) *n., pl.* **-ti** (-ē) [It. < L. *castratus*, pp. of *castrare*, CASTRATE] formerly, esp. in the 18th cent., a singer castrated as a boy to preserve the soprano or contralto range of his voice

Cas·tro (kas′trō; *Sp.* käs′trô), **Fi·del** (fē del′) (*Fidel Castro Ruz*) 1927?– ; Cuban revolutionary leader; prime minister (1959–) **—Cas′tro·ism** *n.*

Cas·tro Valley (kas′trō) [after G. *Castro*, local rancher] suburb of Oakland, in W Calif.: pop. 45,000

cast steel steel formed by casting, as distinguished from rolling or forging **—cast′-steel′** *adj.*

cas·u·al (kazh′ōō wəl) *adj.* [ME. & OFr. *casuel* < LL. *casualis*, by chance < L. *casus*, chance, event: see CASE¹] **1.** happening or governed by chance; not planned; random; incidental [a *casual* visit] **2.** happening, active, etc. at irregular intervals; occasional [a *casual* worker] **3.** slight or superficial [a *casual* acquaintance] **4.** *a)* careless or cursory [far too *casual* in his methods] *b)* nonchalant; dispassionate [affecting *casual* unconcern] **5.** *a)* informal or relaxed [a *casual* atmosphere] *b)* designed for informal occasions or use [*casual* clothes] **—n. 1.** one who does something only occasionally or temporarily, esp. a casual worker **2.** [*pl.*] shoes, clothes, etc. designed for informal occasions **3.** *Mil.* a person temporarily attached to a unit, awaiting a permanent assignment **—SYN.** see ACCIDENTAL, RANDOM **—cas′u·al·ly** *adv.* **—cas′u·al·ness** *n.*

cas·u·al·ty (kazh′əl tē, -ōō wəl-) *n., pl.* **-ties** [ME. & OFr. *casuelte* < ML. *casualitas*: see CASUAL] **1.** an accident, esp. a fatal one **2.** *Mil. a)* a member of the armed forces who is lost to active service through being killed, wounded, captured, interned, sick, or missing *b)* [*pl.*] losses of personnel resulting from death, injury, etc. **3.** anyone hurt or killed in an accident **4.** anything lost, destroyed, or made useless by some unfortunate or unforeseen happening

ca·su·a·ri·na (kazh′ōō wə rē′nə) *n.* [ModL., name of the genus < Malay *kasuārī*, lit., CASSOWARY: so named because the twigs are similar to the bird's feathers] any of a genus (*Casuarina*) of trees native chiefly to Australia, esp. a species (*Casuarina equisetifolia*) with jointed, green branchlets that bear whorls of scalelike leaves

cas·u·ist (kazh′ōō wist) *n.* [Fr. *casuiste* < L. *casus*, CASE¹] a person expert in, or inclined to resort to, casuistry

cas·u·is·tic (kazh′ōō wis′tik) *adj.* **1.** of or having to do with casuistry or casuists **2.** quibbling; sophistical; specious Also **cas′u·is′ti·cal** **—cas′u·is·ti·cal·ly** *adv.*

cas·u·ist·ry (kazh′ōō wis trē) *n., pl.* **-ries** [CASUIST + -RY] **1.** the solving of specific cases of right and wrong in conduct by applying general principles of ethics **2.** subtle but misleading or false reasoning, esp. about moral issues; sophistry

‡**ca·sus bel·li** (kā′səs bel′ī) [L., an occurrence of war] an event or events provoking war or used as a pretext for making war

cat (kat) *n., pl.* **cats, cat:** see PLURAL, II, D, 1 [ME. & OE., akin to G. *katze* & LL. *cattus*] **1.** any of a family (Felidae) of flesh-eating, predaceous mammals, including the lion, tiger, cougar, leopard, lynx, etc.; specif., a small, lithe, soft-furred animal (*Felis catus*) of this family, domesticated since ancient times and often kept as a pet or for killing mice **2.** a person regarded as a cat in some way, esp. a woman who makes spiteful remarks **3.** *same as* CAT-O′-NINE-TAILS ☆**4.** a catfish **5.** a catboat **6.** *same as* TIPCAT ☆**7.** [C-] *same as* CATERPILLAR (tractor) ☆**8.** [Slang] *a)* a jazz musician or enthusiast *b)* any person, esp. a man **9.** *Naut.* tackle for hoisting an anchor to the cathead **—vt.** **cat′ted, cat′ting** to hoist (an anchor) to the cathead **—let the cat out of the bag** to let a secret be found out

CAT (kat) clear air turbulence

cat. 1. catalog **2.** catechism

cat·a- (kat′ə) [Gr. *kata-* < *kata*, down] *a prefix meaning:* **1.** down, downward [*catabolism*] **2.** away, completely [*catalysis*] **3.** against [*catapult*] **4.** through, throughout [*cataphoresis*] **5.** backward, in regression [*cataplasia*] Also, before a vowel, **cat-**

ca·tab·o·lism (kə tab′ə liz′m) *n.* [< CATA- + Gr. *bolē*, a throw < *ballein*, to throw + -ISM] the process in a plant or animal by which living tissue is changed into waste products of a simpler chemical composition; destructive metabolism: opposed to ANABOLISM **—cat·a·bol·ic** (kat′ə bäl′ik) *adj.* **—cat′a·bol′i·cal·ly** *adv.*

ca·tab·o·lite (-līt′) *n.* a waste product of catabolism

ca·tab·o·lize (-līz′) *vi., vt.* **-lized′, -liz′ing** to undergo or cause to undergo catabolism

cat·a·caus·tic (kat′ə kôs′tik) *adj.* [CATA- + CAUSTIC] designating or of a caustic curve or surface formed by reflection **—n.** a catacaustic curve or surface Opposed to DIACAUSTIC

cat·a·chre·sis (-krē′sis) *n., pl.* **-ses** (-sēz) [L. < Gr. *katachrēsis*, misuse of a word < *katachrēsthai* < *kata-*, against + *chrēsthai*, to use] **1.** incorrect use of a word or words, as by misapplication of terminology or by strained or mixed metaphor **2.** a change in the form of a word resulting from a misunderstanding of its etymology: cf. FOLK ETYMOLOGY **—cat′a·chres′tic** (-kres′tik), **cat′a·chres′ti·cal** *adj.* **—cat′a·chres′ti·cal·ly** *adv.*

cat·a·clas·tic (-klas′tik) *adj.* [< Gr. *kataklastos*, broken down < *kataklan*, to snap off, break down (see CATA- & CLASTIC) + -IC] of or pertaining to the deformation or fragmentation of metamorphic rock by extreme pressure

cat·a·cli·nal (-klī′n′l) *adj.* [CATA- + (IN)CLIN(E) + -AL] *Geol.* descending in the same direction as the dip of rock strata, as a stream bed or valley

cat·a·clysm (kat′ə kliz′m) *n.* [L. *cataclysmos* < Gr. *kataklysmos* < *kataklyzein* < *kata-*, down + *klyzein*, to wash] **1.** a great flood; deluge **2.** any great upheaval that causes sudden and violent changes, as an earthquake, war, etc. **—SYN.** see DISASTER **—cat·a·clys·mic** (kat′ə kliz′mik), **cat′a·clys′mal** *adj.*

cat·a·comb (kat′ə kōm′) *n.* [ME. *catacumb*, ult. < LL. *catacumba*, pl. *catacumbae*, region between 2d & 3d milestones of the Appian Way, Catacombs; prob. by dissimilation < L. *cata tumbas*, at the graves < *cata* (< Gr. *kata*, down), by + *tumbas*, acc. pl. of L. *tumba*, TOMB] any of a series of vaults or galleries in an underground burial place: *usually used in pl.*

ca·tad·ro·mous (kə tad′rə məs) *adj.* [< CATA- + -DROMOUS] going back to or toward the sea to spawn: said of certain freshwater fishes

cat·a·falque (kat′ə falk′, -fôlk′) *n.* [Fr. < It. *catafalco*, funeral canopy, stage; prob. < VL. *catafalicum*, scaffold < *cata-*, by, down (< Gr. *kata*, down) + *falicum* < L. *fala*, scaffolding, wooden tower] **1.** a temporary wooden framework, usually draped, on which the body in a coffin lies in state during an elaborate funeral **2.** *R.C.Ch.* a coffinlike structure used to represent the dead at a requiem Mass after the actual burial

Cat·a·lan (kat′l an′, -′l ən) *adj.* of Catalonia, its people, or their language **—n. 1.** a native or inhabitant of Catalonia **2.** the Romance language of Catalonia, closely akin to Provençal: it is spoken also in parts of SW France, Valencia, western Sardinia, and the Balearic Islands

cat·a·lase (kat′l ās′) *n.* [CATAL(YSIS) + -ASE] an enzyme found in blood and tissues, that decomposes hydrogen peroxide into water and free oxygen

cat·a·lec·tic (kat′l ek′tik) *adj.* [LL. *catalecticus* < Gr. *katalēktikos* < *kata-*, down + *lēgein*, to leave off, cease] *Prosody* lacking a syllable, esp. in the last foot

cat·a·lep·sy (kat′l ep′sē) *n.* [LL. *catalepsis* < Gr. *katalēpsis*, a seizing, grasping < *katalambanein* < *kata-*, down + *lambanein*, to take, seize] a condition in which consciousness and feeling are suddenly and temporarily lost, and the muscles become rigid: it may occur in epilepsy, schizophrenia, etc. **—cat′a·lep′tic** (-tik) *adj., n.*

Cat·a·li·na (Island) (kat′l ē′nə) [Sp., in honor of St. CATHERINE] *same as* SANTA CATALINA (ISLAND)

☆**cat·a·lo** (kat′l ō′) *n., pl.* **-loes′, -los′** [CAT(TLE) + (BUFF)A-LO] an animal developed from crossing the American buffalo, or bison, with domestic cattle

cat·a·log, cat·a·logue (kat′l ôg′, -äg′) *n.* [Fr. *catalogue* < LL. *catalogus* < Gr. *katalogos*, a list, register < *katalegein*, to reckon, list < *kata-*, down, completely + *legein*, to say, count] a complete list, esp. ☆*a)* an alphabetical card file, as of the books in a library *b)* a list of things exhibited, articles for sale, school courses offered, etc., usually with descriptive comments and often illustrations *c)* a book or pamphlet containing such a list **—vt., vi.** **-loged′** or **-logued′**, **-log′ing** or **-logu′ing 1.** to enter in a catalog **2.** to make a catalog of **—SYN.** see LIST¹ **—cat′a·log′er** or **cat′a·logu′er, cat′a·log′ist** or **cat′a·logu′ist** *n.*

‡**ca·ta·logue rai·son·né** (kå tå lôg′ re zô nā′) [Fr., lit., reasoned catalog] a catalog of books (esp. in a bibliography), pictures, etc. arranged by subjects and with explanatory notes

Cat·a·lo·ni·a (kat′l ō′nē ə) region in NE Spain, on the Mediterranean: Sp. name **Ca·ta·lu·ña** (kä′tä lōō′nyä) **— Cat′a·lo′ni·an** *adj., n.*

☆**ca·tal·pa** (kə tal′pə) *n.* [ModL. < AmInd. (Creek) *kutuhlpa*, lit., head with wings: so named because of its flowers] any of a genus (*Catalpa*) of hardy American and Asiatic trees of the bignonia family, with large, heart-shaped leaves, showy clusters of trumpet-shaped flowers, and slender beanlike pods

ca·tal·y·sis (kə tal′ə sis) *n., pl.* **-ses′** (-sēz′) [Gr. *katalysis*, dissolution < *kata-*, down + *lyein*, to LOOSE] the speeding up or, sometimes, slowing down of the rate of a chemical reaction by the addition of some substance which itself undergoes no permanent chemical change thereby

cat·a·lyst (kat′′l ist) *n.* **1.** any substance serving as the agent in catalysis **2.** a person or thing acting as the stimulus in bringing about or hastening a result

cat·a·lyt·ic (kat′′l it′ik) *adj.* of, in, or causing catalysis **—n.** a catalyst **—cat′a·lyt′i·cal·ly** *adv.*

catalytic cracker an apparatus used in the petroleum industry for the cracking of petroleum by catalysis

cat·a·lyze (kat′l īz′) *vt.* **-lyzed′, -lyz′ing** to change or bring about as a catalyst —**cat′a·lyz′er** *n.*

cat·a·ma·ran (kat′ə mə ran′) *n.* [Tamil *kaṭṭumaram* < *kaṭṭu,* tie + *maram,* log, tree] **1.** a narrow log raft or float propelled by sails or paddles **2.** a boat with two parallel hulls, built in the style of such a float **3.** [Canad.] a large sled, as for hauling wood

cat·a·me·ni·a (kat′ə mē′nē ə) *n.pl.* [Gr. *katamēnia,* neut. pl. of *katamēnios,* monthly < *kata-,* according to + *mēn,* month] [also with sing. *v.*] menstrual discharge; menstruation —**cat′a·me′ni·al** *adj.*

cat·a·mite (kat′ə mīt′) *n.* [L. *Catamitus,* altered < *Ganymedes* < Gr. *Ganymēdēs,* Ganymede] a boy used in pederasty

cat·a·mount (kat′ə mount′) *n.* [see ff.] any of various wild cats; esp., ☆*a*) the puma; cougar ☆*b*) the lynx

cat·a·moun·tain (kat′ə mount′n) *n.* [CAT + A² + MOUNTAIN] [Archaic] any of several wild cats, esp. the leopard or the European wildcat

Ca·ta·nia (kä tä′nyä; *E.* kə tän′yə) seaport on the E coast of Sicily: pop. 387,000

cat·a·pho·re·sis (kat′ə fə rē′sis) *n.* [ModL. < *cata-* + Gr. *phorēsis,* a bearing < *pherein,* to BEAR¹, carry] *same as* ELECTROPHORESIS

cat·a·phyll (kat′ə fil′) *n.* [CATA- + -PHYLL] *Bot.* any rudimentary leaf, as a bud scale, preceding the true foliage leaves

cat·a·pla·si·a (kat′ə plā′zhē ə, -zhə, -zē ə) *n., pl.* **-si·ae** (-zhē ē̆, -zē ē̆) [ModL.: see CATA- & PLASIA] *Biol.* a change in cells or tissues, characterized by reversion to an earlier stage —**cat′a·plas′tic** (-plas′tik) *adj.*

cat·a·plasm (kat′ə plaz′m) *n.* [Fr. < LL. *cataplasma* < Gr. *kataplasma:* see CATA & PLASMA] a poultice, often medicated

cat·a·pult (kat′ə pult′, -poolt′) *n.* [L. *catapulta* < Gr. *katapeltēs* < *kata-,* down + *pallein,* to toss, hurl] **1.** an ancient military contrivance for throwing or shooting stones, spears, etc. ☆**2.** a slingshot **3.** a device for launching an airplane, rocket missile, etc., as from a deck or ramp, at very high speed **4.** a device for ejecting a person from an airplane —*vt.* to shoot or launch from or as from a catapult; hurl —*vi.* to be catapulted; move quickly; leap

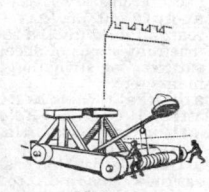

CATAMARAN

CATAPULT

cat·a·ract (kat′ə rakt′) *n.* [ME. *cataracte,* floodgate (of heaven), cataract (of the eye) < L. *cataracta,* a waterfall, portcullis < Gr. *katarraktēs* < *katarhēgnynai,* to break down < *kata-,* down + *rhēgnynai,* to break] **1.** a large waterfall **2.** any strong flood or rush of water; deluge **3.** *a*) an eye disease in which the crystalline lens or its capsule becomes opaque, causing partial or total blindness *b*) the opaque area

ca·tarrh (kə tär′) *n.* [ME. *catarre* < Fr. *catarrhe* < LL. *catarrhus* < Gr. *katarrhoos* < *katarrhein,* to flow down < *kata-,* down + *rhein,* to flow] inflammation of a mucous membrane, esp. of the nose or throat, causing an increased flow of mucus: earlier term no longer in use —**ca·tarrh′al** (-əl), **ca·tarrh′ous** (-əs) *adj.*

cat·ar·rhine (kat′ə rīn′, -rin) *adj.* [ModL. *catarrhinus* < Gr. *katarrin,* long-nosed < *kata-* (see CATA-) + *rhis* (gen. *rhinos*), nose: see RHINO-] having a slender nose with the nostrils spaced close together —*n.* a catarrhine creature, as man or certain other primates Distinguished from PLATYRRHINE

ca·tas·ta·sis (kə tas′tə sis) *n., pl.* **-ses′** (-sēz′) [Gr. *katastasis,* an arranging, setting forth < *kathistanai* < *kata-,* down + *histanai,* to set up, cause to STAND] the heightened part of the action in ancient drama, leading directly to the catastrophe

ca·tas·tro·phe (kə tas′trə fē) *n.* [L. *catastropha* < Gr. *katastrophē,* an overthrowing < *katastrephein,* to overturn < *kata-,* down + *strephein,* to turn] **1.** the culminating event of a drama, esp. of a tragedy, by which the plot is resolved; denouement **2.** a disastrous end, bringing overthrow or ruin **3.** any great and sudden calamity, disaster, or misfortune **4.** a total or ignominious failure **5.** *Geol.* a sudden, violent change, such as an earthquake —*SYN.* DISASTER —**cat·a·stroph·ic** (kat′ə sträf′ik) *adj.* —**cat′a·stroph′i·cal·ly** *adv.*

ca·tas·tro·phism (kə tas′trə fiz′m) *n.* **1.** the former theory that geological changes are caused in general by sudden upheavals rather than gradually **2.** an outlook envisioning imminent catastrophe —**ca·tas′tro·phist** *n., adj.*

cat·a·to·ni·a (kat′ə tō′nē ə) *n.* [< CATA- + Gr. *tonos,* tension] *Psychiatry* a syndrome, esp. of schizophrenia, marked by stupor or catalepsy, often alternating with phases of excitement —**cat′a·ton′ic** (-tän′ik) *adj., n.*

Ca·taw·ba (kə tô′bə) *n.* [< Choctaw *Katápa,* lit., separated, i.e., from other Siouan tribes] **1.** a member of a tribe of N. American Indians who formerly lived in S. Carolina **2.** their obsolete Siouan language **3.** [often c-] *a*) a cultivated variety of a native American reddish grape (*Vitis labruscanc*), widely grown in the E U.S. *b*) a wine made from this grape

☆**cat·bird** (kat′burd′) *n.* a slate-gray N. American songbird (*Dumetella carolinensis*) with a black crown and tail: it makes a mewing sound like that of a cat

☆**catbird seat** [prob. from the bird's habit of singing from a high perch] an enviable position, as of power

cat·boat (-bōt′) *n.* a catrigged sailboat, usually having a centerboard

☆**cat brier** any of several climbing woody vines (genus *Smilax*) of the lily family, with prickly stems, oval leaves, and black berries

cat burglar [Slang] a burglar who enters buildings by climbing up to openings in upper stories, roofs, etc.

cat·call (-kôl′) *n.* a shrill noise or whistle expressing derision or disapproval, as of a speaker, actor, etc. —*vt.* to deride with catcalls —*vi.* to make catcalls

catch (kach, kech) *vt.* **caught, catch′ing** [ME. *cacchen* < Anglo-Fr. *cachier* < VL. *captiare* < L. *captare,* to try to seize < pp. of *capere,* to take] **1.** to seize and hold, as after a chase; capture **2.** to seize or take by or as by a trap, snare, etc. **3.** to deceive; ensnare **4.** to discover by taking unawares; surprise in some act [to be *caught* stealing] **5.** to strike suddenly; hit [the blow *caught* him in the arm] **6.** to overtake or get to in time; be in time for [to *catch* a train] **7.** to intercept the motion or action of; lay hold of; grab or snatch [to *catch* a ball] **8.** *a*) to take or get as by chance or quickly [to *catch* one's attention, to *catch* a glimpse] *b*) [Colloq.] to manage to see, hear, find, etc. [to *catch* a radio program] **9.** to take or get passively; incur or contract without intention, as by exposure [to *catch* the mumps] **10.** *a*) to take in with one's mind or senses; understand; apprehend *b*) to show an understanding of by depicting [the statue *catches* her beauty] **11.** to captivate; charm **12.** to cause to be entangled or snagged [to *catch* one's heel in a rug] ☆**13.** *Baseball* to act as catcher for [a specified pitcher] —*vi.* **1.** to become held, fastened, or entangled [her sleeve *caught* on a nail] **2.** to take hold or spread, as fire **3.** to take fire; burn **4.** to take and keep hold, as a lock **5.** to act or serve as a catcher —*n.* **1.** the act of catching **2.** a thing that catches or holds **3.** the person or thing caught **4.** the amount caught **5.** a person worth catching, esp. as a husband or wife **6.** a snatch, scrap, or fragment [*catches* of old tunes] **7.** a break in the voice, caused by emotion ☆**8.** a simple game of throwing and catching a ball ☆**9.** [Colloq.] a hidden qualification; tricky condition [a *catch* in his offer] **10.** *Music* a round for three or more unaccompanied voices **11.** *Sports* a catching of a ball in a specified manner —*adj.* **1.** designed to trick; tricky [a *catch* question on an exam] **2.** attracting or meant to attract attention or interest —**catch as catch can** with any hold, approach, technique, etc.: originally said of a style of wrestling —**catch at 1.** to try to catch **2.** to reach for eagerly; seize desperately —**catch it** [Colloq.] to receive a scolding or other punishment —☆**catch on 1.** to grasp the meaning; understand **2.** to become fashionable, popular, etc. —**catch one's breath 1.** to return to normal breathing after exertion **2.** to rest or pause —**catch oneself** to hold oneself back abruptly from saying or doing something —**catch up 1.** to take or lift up suddenly; seize; snatch **2.** to show to be in error **3.** to heckle **4.** to come up even, as by hurrying or by extra work; overtake **5.** to fasten in loops —**catch up on** to engage in more (work, sleep, etc.) so as to compensate for earlier neglect

SYN.—**catch,** the most general term here, refers to a seizing or taking of a person or thing, whether by skill or cunning, and usually implies pursuit; **capture** implies a greater measure of resistance or elusiveness than **catch** and therefore stresses seizure by force or stratagem [to *capture* an outlaw]; **nab,** an informal word, specifically implies a sudden or quick taking into custody [the police *nabbed* the thief]; **trap** and **snare** both imply the literal or figurative use of a device for catching a person or animal and suggest a situation from which escape is difficult or impossible [to *trap* a bear, *snared* by her womanly wiles]

☆**catch-all** (-ôl′) *n.* a container or place for holding all sorts of things

catch basin a sievelike device at the entrance to a sewer to stop matter that could block up the sewer

catch crop a supplementary crop grown at a time when the ground would ordinarily lie fallow, as between the plantings of two principal crops

catch·er (-ər) *n.* **1.** a person or thing that catches ☆**2.** *Baseball* the player stationed behind home plate, who catches pitched balls not hit away by the batter

catch·fly (-flī′) *n., pl.* **-flies′** any of various plants (genus *Silene*) of the pink family, with sticky stems that can trap insects

catch·ing (-iŋ) *adj.* **1.** contagious; infectious **2.** attractive; catchy

catch·ment (-mənt) *n.* **1.** the catching or collecting of water, esp. rainfall **2.** a reservoir or other basin for catching water **3.** the water thus caught

catchment area (or **basin**) the area draining into a river, reservoir, etc.

catch·pen·ny (-pen′ē) *adj.* made merely to sell; cheap and flashy —*n., pl.* **-nies** a catchpenny commodity

catch phrase a phrase that catches or is meant to catch the popular attention

catch·pole, catch·poll (-pōl′) *n.* [ME. *cacchepol* & Late OE. *cæcepol*, tax gatherer < Anglo-Fr. *cache-pol*, lit., chicken chaser < ML. *cacepollus* < *cacere* (< VL. *captiare*: see CATCH) + L. *pullus*, fowl] formerly, a sheriff's officer who arrested nonpaying debtors

catch·up (kech′əp, kach′-) *n. same as* KETCHUP

catch·weight (kach′wāt′, kech′-) *adj., adv.* with no restrictions being set on the weight of the contestants [a *catchweight* wrestling match]

catch·word (-wurd′) *n.* **1.** orig., the first word of a printed page, repeated in the lower right-hand corner of the preceding page so as to catch the reader's eye **2.** a word placed to catch attention, as the first or last entry word of a page in a dictionary, encyclopedia, etc., printed at the top of the page as a guide **3.** an actor's cue **4.** a word or phrase repeated so often that it comes to epitomize a certain group, movement, etc.

catch·y (-ē) *adj.* **catch′i·er, catch′i·est 1.** catching attention; arousing interest **2.** easily caught up and remembered [a *catchy* tune] **3.** meant to trick; tricky **4.** spasmodic; fitful —**catch′i·ness** *n.*

cate (kāt) *n.* [< earlier *acate* < ME. *achat* < Anglo-Fr. *acat*, a purchase, thing bought < *acater*: see CATER] [Archaic] a choice food or delicacy; dainty

cat·e·che·sis (kat′ə kē′sis) *n., pl.* **-ses** (-sēz) [LL.(Ec.), religious instruction < Gr. *katēchēsis*, instruction < *katēchein*: see CATECHETICAL] oral instruction, esp. of catechumens

cat·e·chet·i·cal (kat′ə ket′i k′l) *adj.* [Gr.(Ec.) *katēchētikos* < *katēchētēs*, instructor < *katēchein*, to instruct by word of mouth (in NT., instruct in religion) < *kata-*, thoroughly + *ēchein*, to sound < *ēchē*, a sound] **1.** of, like, or conforming to catechesis or a catechism **2.** consisting of, or teaching by the method of, questions and answers Also **cat·e·chet′ic**

cat·e·chin (kat′ə chin, -kin) *n.* [< CATECH(U) + -IN¹] a yellow, powdery, acid compound, $C_{15}H_{14}O_6$, used in tanning, textile printing, etc.

cat·e·chism (kat′ə kiz′m) *n.* [LL.(Ec.) *catechismus* < Gr. *katēchismos* < *katēchizein*, to catechize < *katēchein*: see CATECHETICAL] **1.** a handbook of questions and answers for teaching the principles of a religion **2.** any similar handbook for teaching the fundamentals of a subject **3.** a formal series of questions; close questioning **4.** [Obs.] catechesis —**cat′e·chis′mal** *adj.* —**cat′e·chis′tic** (-kis′tik), **cat′e·chis′ti·cal** *adj.*

cat·e·chist (-kist) *n.* a person who catechizes, esp. one who instructs catechumens

cat·e·chize (-kīz′) *vt.* **-chized′, -chiz′ing** [ME. *catecizen* < LL.(Ec.) *catechizare* < Gr. *katēchizein*: see CATECHETICAL] **1.** to teach (esp. religion) by the method of questions and answers **2.** to question searchingly or fully Also sp. **cat′e·chise′** —*SYN.* see ASK —**cat′e·chi·za′tion** (-ki zā′shən) *n.* —**cat′e·chiz′er** *n.*

cat·e·chol (kat′ə chôl′, -chōl′, -kôl′, -kōl′) *n.* [CATECH(U) + -OL¹] *same as* PYROCATECHOL

cat·e·chu (kat′ə chōō′) *n.* [< Malay *kachu*] a hard, brown substance obtained from an Oriental acacia (*Acacia catechu*) and other Asiatic trees and shrubs: used as an astringent in medicine, and for dyeing, tanning, etc.

cat·e·chu·men (kat′ə kyōō′mən) *n.* [ME. *cathecumine* < LL.(Ec.) *catechumenus* < Gr. *katēchoumenos*, person instructed < *katēchein*: see CATECHETICAL] **1.** a person, esp. an adult, receiving instruction in the fundamentals of Christianity before baptism **2.** a person receiving instruction in the fundamentals of any subject

cat·e·gor·i·cal (kat′ə gôr′ə k′l, -gär′-) *adj.* [LL. *categoricus*: see CATEGORY & -ICAL] **1.** without qualifications or conditions; absolute; positive; direct; explicit: said of a statement, theory, etc. **2.** of, as, or in a category Also **cat′e·gor′ic** —**cat′e·gor′i·cal·ly** *adv.*

categorical imperative the Kantian doctrine that one's behavior should be governed by principles which one would have govern the behavior of all people

cat·e·go·rize (kat′ə ga riz′) *vt.* **-rized′, -riz′ing** to place in a category; classify —**cat′e·go·ri·za′tion** (-ri zā′shən) *n.*

cat·e·go·ry (kat′ə gôr′ē) *n., pl.* **-ries** [LL. *categoria* < Gr. *katēgoria* < *katēgorein*, to accuse, assert, predicate < *kata-*, down, against + *agoreuein*, to declaim, address an assembly < *agora*, assembly] **1.** a class or division in a scheme of classification **2.** *Logic* any of the various basic concepts into which all knowledge can be classified

ca·te·na (kə tē′nə) *n., pl.* **-nae** (-nē) [L.: see CHAIN] a linked or connected series, as of excerpted writings

cat·e·nane (kat′′n ān′) *n.* [< L. *catena*, CHAIN + -ANE] a compound having a chemical structure that consists of two

closed rings, chemically independent, which mechanically thread each other as the links in a chain

cat·e·nar·y (kat′′n er′ē; *chiefly Brit.* kə tē′nər ē) *n., pl.* **-nar′ies** [L. *catenarius* < *catena:* see CHAIN] the curve made by a flexible, uniform chain or cord freely suspended between two fixed points —*adj.* designating or of such a curve: also **cat′e·nar′i·an** (-er′ē ən)

cat·e·nate (kat′′n āt′) *vt.* **-nat·ed, -nat′ing** [< L. *catenatus*, pp. of *catenare* < *catena*, CHAIN] to form into a chain or linked series; link —**cat′e·na′tion** *n.*

ca·ten·u·late (kə ten′yoo lit, -lāt′) *adj.* [< LL. *catenula*, dim. of L. *catena*, CHAIN + -ATE¹] like or arranged like a chain

ca·ter (kā′tər) *vi.* [< obs. *cater*, buyer < ME. *catour*, aphetic for *achatour* < OFr. *achatour* < *achater*, to buy, provide < VL. *accaptare* < L. *ad-*, to + *captare* (intens. of *capere*, to take), to strive, seize] **1.** to provide food; serve as a caterer **2.** to take special pains in seeking to gratify another's needs or desires (with *to*) —*vt.* to serve as caterer for (a banquet, wedding, etc.)

cat·er·an (kat′ər ən) *n.* [Scot. *catherein* < Gael. *ceathairne*, common people] a Scottish Highlands robber

cat·er-cor·nered (kat′ē kôr′nərd, kat′ər-, kit′ē-) *adj.* [ME. *cater*, four (< OFr. *catre* < L. *quattuor*, FOUR) + CORNERED] diagonal —*adv.* diagonally or obliquely Also **cat′er-cor′ner**

ca·ter-cous·in (kāt′ər kuz′′n) *n.* [see prec. & COUSIN: orig., fourth-cousin] [Archaic] a close friend

ca·ter·er (kāt′ər ər) *n.* one who caters; esp., one whose business is providing food and service as for parties

cat·er·pil·lar (kat′ər pil′ər; kat′ə-) *n.* [ME. *catirpel* < ONormFr. *catepilose* (OFr. *chatepelose*), lit., hairy cat < L. *catta*, cat + *pilosus* < *pilus*, hair] the wormlike larva of various insects, esp. of a butterfly or moth —☆[C-] *a trademark for* a tractor equipped on each side with a continuous roller belt over cogged wheels, for moving over rough or muddy ground

cat·er·waul (kat′ər wôl′) *vi.* [ME. *caterwrawen, caterwawen* < *cater* (prob. < MDu. *kater*, tomcat) + *wrawlen, wawlen*, *v.*, prob. echoic] to make a shrill, howling sound like that of a cat at rutting time; screech; wail; scream —*n.* such a sound

cat·fall (-fôl′) *n. Naut.* a cable or chain for raising an anchor to the cathead

cat·fish (-fish′) *n., pl.* **-fish′, -fish′es:** see FISH² ☆any of a large group of scaleless fishes (family Ictaluridae) with long barbels, somewhat like a cat's whiskers, about the mouth and usually with sharp spines before the dorsal and pectoral fins

cat·gut (-gut′) *n.* [CAT + GUT (parallel with Du. *kattedarm*); reason for *cat* unc.] a tough string or thread made from the dried intestines of sheep, horses, etc. and used for surgical sutures, for stringing tennis rackets and musical instruments, etc.

cath- (kath) *same as* CATA-: used before an aspirate

Cath. **1.** Catholic **2.** [*also* c-] cathedral

Cath·a·rine (kath′rin, -ər in) a feminine name: see CATHERINE

ca·thar·sis (kə thär′sis) *n.* [ModL. < Gr. *katharsis*, purification < *kathairein*, to purify < *katharos*, pure] **1.** purgation, esp. of the bowels **2.** the purifying of the emotions or relieving of emotional tensions, esp. by art: applied originally by Aristotle to the purging of pity or terror by viewing a tragedy **3.** *Psychiatry* the alleviation of fears, problems, and complexes by bringing them to consciousness or giving them expression

ca·thar·tic (-tik) *adj.* [Gr. *kathartikos*] of or effecting catharsis; purging: also **ca·thar′ti·cal** —*n.* [LL. *catharticum*] a medicine for stimulating evacuation of the bowels; purgative —*SYN.* see PHYSIC

Ca·thay (ka thā′, kə-) [ML. *Cataya*, of Tatar origin] *poet.* or *archaic name of* CHINA

cat·head (kat′hed′) *n.* a projecting beam of iron or wood near the bow of a ship, to which the anchor is hoisted and fastened

ca·thect (ka thekt′) *vt.* [see CATHEXIS] *Psychoanalysis* to concentrate psychic energy on (some particular person, thing, or idea): also **ca·thec′ti·cize′** (-thek′tə siz′) **-cized′, -ciz′ing** —**ca·thec′tic** *adj.*

ca·the·dra (kə thē′drə, kath′i drə) *n.* [L., a chair, office of a teacher (in LL.(Ec.), of a bishop) < Gr. *kathedra*, a seat, bench < *kata-*, down + *hedra*, a seat < *hezesthai*, to sit] **1.** the throne of a bishop in a cathedral **2.** the episcopal see **3.** any seat of high authority See also EX CATHEDRA

ca·the·dral (kə thē′drəl) *n.* [ME. < OFr. < LL. *cathedralis* (*ecclesia*), (church) of a bishop's seat < L. *cathedra:* see prec.] **1.** the main church of a bishop's see, containing the cathedra **2.** loosely, any large, imposing church —*adj.* **1.** of, like, or containing a cathedra **2.** official; authoritative **3.** of or like a cathedral

ca·thep·sin (kə thep′sin) *n.* [< Gr. *kathepsein*, boil down, soften < *kata-*, down + *hepsein*, boil + -IN] any of several intracellular proteolytic enzymes that act as catalysts in the breakdown of protein

Cath·er (kath′ər), **Wil·la** (**Sibert**) (wil′ə) 1873–1947; U.S. writer

Cath·er·ine (kath′rin, -ər in) [Fr. < L. *Catharina, Ecaterina* < Gr. *Aikaterinē;* form and meaning infl. by *katharos*, pure, unsullied] **1.** a feminine name: dim. *Cathy, Kate, Kit, Kitty;* equiv. It. *Caterina*, Ir. *Kathleen*, Russ. *Ekaterina*, Scand.

Karen, Sp. *Catalina*, *Catarina* **2. Catherine I** (*Ekaterina Alekseevna*) 1684?–1727; wife of Peter the Great; empress of Russia (1725–27) **3. Catherine II** (*Ekaterina Alekseevna*) 1729–96; German-born empress of Russia (1762–96): called **Catherine the Great 4.** Saint, *a)* 4th cent. A.D.; Christian martyr of Alexandria: her day is Nov. 25 *b)* 1347–80; It. Dominican: her day is April 30: in full, Saint **Catherine of Siena**

Catherine de' Medici *see* Catherine de' MEDICI

Catherine of Aragon 1485–1536; 1st wife (1509–33) of Henry VIII of England

Catherine wheel [orig., a spiked wheel symbolizing the instrument of torture involved in the martyrdom of St. CATHERINE of Alexandria] [*also* c- w-] a firework like a pinwheel, that whirls and throws out colored lights

cath·e·ter (kath/ə tər) *n.* [LL. < Gr. *kathetēr* < *kathienai*, to let down, thrust in < *kata-*, down + *hienai*, to send] a slender tube, as of metal or rubber, inserted into a body passage, vessel, or cavity for passing fluids, making examinations, etc., esp. one for draining urine from the bladder

cath·e·ter·ize (-īz/) *vt.* **-ized', -iz'ing** to insert a catheter into —**cath'e·ter·i·za'tion** (-i zā/shən) *n.*

ca·thex·is (kə thek/sis) *n.* [ModL. < Gr. *kathexis*, a holding; transl. of G. *besetzung*, as used by Freud] *Psychoanalysis* concentration of psychic energy on some particular person, thing, idea, or aspect of the self

cath·ode (kath/ōd) *n.* [< Gr. *kathodos*, descent < *kata-*, down + *hodos*, way] **1.** in an electrolytic cell, the negative electrode, from which current flows **2.** in a vacuum tube, the negatively charged electron emitter **3.** the positive terminal of a battery —**ca·thod'ic** (ka thäd/ik) *adj.*

cathode rays streams of electrons projected from the surface of a cathode: cathode rays produce X-rays when they strike solids and visible fluorescence when they strike certain chemical salts

cathode-ray tube a vacuum tube in which the electrons streaming from the cathode are directed to strike a fluorescent screen and produce illuminated traces, visible from the exterior of the tube: such tubes are used as oscilloscopes, television picture tubes, etc.

cath·o·lic (kath/ə lik, kath/lik) *adj.* [ME. *catholik* < L. *catholicus*, universal, general (in LL.(Ec.) & ML., orthodox, Catholic) < Gr. *katholikos* < *kata-*, down, completely + *holos*, whole] **1.** of general scope or value; all-inclusive; universal **2.** broad in sympathies, tastes, or understanding; liberal **3.** [*often* C-] of the Christian church as a whole; specif., of the ancient, undivided Christian church **4.** [C-] of the Christian church headed by the Pope; Roman Catholic **5.** [C-] of any of the orthodox Christian churches, including the Roman, Greek Orthodox, Anglo-Catholic, etc., as distinguished from the Reformed or Protestant churches —*n.* **1.** [*often* C-] a member of the universal Christian church **2.** [C-] a member of any of the Catholic churches; esp., a Roman Catholic —**ca·thol'i·cal·ly** *adv.*

Ca·thol·i·cism (kə thäl/ə siz'm) *n.* the doctrine, faith, practice, and organization of a Catholic church, esp. the Roman Catholic Church

cath·o·lic·i·ty (kath/ə lis/ə tē) *n.* **1.** the quality or state of being catholic, as in taste, sympathy, or understanding; liberality, as of ideas **2.** comprehensive quality; universality **3.** [C-] Catholicism

ca·thol·i·cize (kə thäl/ə sīz/) *vt., vi.* **-cized', -ciz'ing 1.** to make or become catholic **2.** [C-] to convert or be converted to Catholicism

ca·thol·i·con (kə kän/, -ə kən) *n.* [ME. < ML. < Gr. *katholikon*, neut. of *katholikos*: see CATHOLIC] a supposed medicine to cure all diseases; panacea

☆**cat·house** (kat/hous/) *n.* [Slang] a house of prostitution

Cat·i·line (kat/'l īn/) (born *Lucius Sergius Catilina*) 108?–62 B.C.; Roman politician & conspirator

cat·i·on (kat/ī/ən) *n.* [coined by Faraday < Gr. *kation*, prp. of *katienai*, to go down < Gr. *kata*, downward + *ienai*, to go] a positively charged ion: in electrolysis, cations move toward the cathode under the influence of an applied potential difference: opposed to ANION —**cat·i·on·ic** (kat/ī än/ik) *adj.*

cat·kin (kat/kin) *n.* [Du. *katteken*, dim. of *katte*, cat: from resemblance to a cat's tail] a drooping, deciduous, scaly spike of unisexual flowers without petals, as on poplars, walnuts, and birches; ament

cat·like (-līk/) *adj.* like a cat or cat's; noiseless, stealthy, etc.

Cat·lin (kat/lən), **George** 1796–1872; U.S. ethnologist & artist

cat·mint (-mint/) *n. Brit. var. of* CATNIP

☆**cat·nap** (-nap/) *n.* a short, light sleep; doze —*vi.* **-napped', -nap'ping** to take a catnap

☆**cat·nip** (-nip/) *n.* [CAT + nip, dial. for *nep*, catnip < L. *nepeta*] a plant (*Nepeta cataria*) of the mint family, with downy leaves and spikes of bluish flowers: cats like its odor

CATKIN

Ca·to (kāt/ō) **1.** (Marcus Porcius), 234–149 B.C.; Roman

statesman: called *the Elder* or *the Censor* **2.** (**Marcus Porcius**), 95–46 B.C.; Roman statesman & Stoic philosopher: great-grandson of *prec.*: called *the Younger*

cat-o'-moun·tain (kat/ə moun/t'n) *n. same as* CATA-MOUNTAIN

cat-o'-nine-tails (kat/ə nīn/tālz/) *n., pl.* **-tails'** a whip made of nine knotted cords attached to a handle, formerly used for flogging

Ca·tons·ville (kāt/'nz vil/) [after Richard *Caton*, an early owner of the site] suburb of Baltimore, in N Md.: pop. 55,000

ca·top·trics (kə täp/triks) *n.pl.* [*with sing. v.*] [< Gr. *katoptrikos* < *katoptron*, a mirror < *kala-* (see CATA-) + *ops*, the EYE, face] the branch of optics dealing with the reflection of light from mirrors or mirrorlike surfaces —**ca·top'-tric**, **ca·top'tri·cal** *adj.*

cat rig a rig, esp. of a catboat, consisting of a single large sail on a mast well forward in the bow —**cat'rigged'** (-rigd/) *adj.*

cat's cradle a child's pastime in which a string looped over the fingers is transferred back and forth on the hands of the players so as to form different designs

cat's-eye (kats/ī/) *n.* any gem, stone, or piece of glass that reflects light in a way suggestive of a cat's eye, as a chrysoberyl, a child's marble, a reflector glass as on a road sign, etc.

Cats·kill Mountains (kat/skil/) [Du., cat stream; reason for name unknown] mountain range of the Appalachian system, in SE N.Y.: resort area: highest peak, c. 4,200 ft. Also **Cats/kills/**

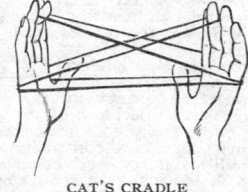

CAT'S CRADLE

cat's-paw (kats/pô/) *n.* **1.** a person used by another to do dangerous, distasteful, or unlawful work; dupe; tool: from the tale of the monkey who used the cat's foot to rake the chestnuts out of the fire **2.** a light breeze that ripples the surface of water **3.** a hitch in the loop of a rope that forms a second loop: it is used to hook a tackle: see KNOT[1], *illus.*

cat·sup (kech/əp, kach/-; kat/səp) *n. same as* KETCHUP

Catt (kat), **Carrie Chapman** 1859–1947; U.S. leader in the movement for women's suffrage

cat·tail (kat/tāl/) *n.* any of a genus (*Typha*) of a family (Typhaceae) of tall marsh plants with reedlike leaves and long, brown, fuzzy, cylindrical flower spikes; esp., either of two species (*Typha latifolia* and *Typha angustifolia*) whose long, flat leaves are used in making baskets and matting

☆**cat·ta·lo** (kat/'l ō) *n., pl.* **-loes, -los** *same as* CATALO

Cat·te·gat (kat/ə gat/) *same as* KATTEGAT

cat·tish (kat/ish) *adj.* **1.** like a cat; feline **2.** *same as* CATTY[1] —**cat'tish·ly** *adv.* —**cat'tish·ness** *n.*

cat·tle (kat/'l) *n.* [ME. & Anglo-Fr. *catel* (OFr. *chatel*) < ML. *captale*, property, stock < L. *capitalis*, principal, chief < *caput*, the head: orig. sense in var. CHATTEL: cf. CAPITAL[1]] **1.** [Archaic or Dial.] farm animals collectively; livestock **2.** domesticated bovine animals collectively; cows, bulls, steers, or oxen **3.** people in the mass: contemptuous term

☆**cat·tle·man** (-mən) *n., pl.* **-men** (-mən) a man who tends cattle or raises them for the market

cat·tle·ya (kat/lē ə; kat lē/ə, -lā/ə) *n.* [after Wm. *Cattley* (d. 1832), Brit. horticulturist] any of a genus (*Cattleya*) of tropical American orchids, often grown in greenhouses, with large, showy blossoms

Cat·ton (kat/'n), (**Charles**) **Bruce** 1899– ; U.S. historian

cat·ty[1] (kat/ē) *adj.* **-ti·er, -ti·est 1.** of or like a cat **2.** spiteful, mean, malicious, etc., as in the manner of an envious woman —*n. same as* TIPCAT —**cat'ti·ly** *adv.* —**cat'ti·ness** *n.*

cat·ty[2] (kat/ē) *n., pl.* **-ties** [Malay *kati*: see CADDY[1]] a unit of weight used in various countries of southeast Asia: in China it is equal to 500 grams, or 1.102 lb., but elsewhere it is equal to about 1-1/3 lb.

cat·ty-cor·nered (kat/ē kôr/nərd, kit/ē-) *adj., adv. same as* CATER-CORNERED: also **cat'ty-cor'ner**

Ca·tul·lus (kə tul/əs), (**Gaius Valerius**) 87?–55? B.C.; Roman lyric poet

CATV community antenna television

cat·walk (kat/wôk/) *n.* a narrow, elevated walk or platform, as one along the edge of a bridge or over the engine room of a ship

cat (or **cat's**) **whisker** *Radio* a thin wire that makes contact with a sensitive spot on the crystal in a crystal detector

Cau·ca (kou/kä) river in W Colombia, flowing north into the Magdalena River: c. 600 mi.

Cau·ca·sia (kô kā/zhə, -shə) *same as* CAUCASUS (sense 1)

Cau·ca·sian (kô kā/zhən) *adj.* **1.** of the Caucasus, its people, or their culture **2.** *same as* CAUCASOID **3.** designating or of the two independent families of languages spoken in the area of the Caucasus: North Caucasian includes Circassian, and South Caucasian includes Georgian Also **Cau·cas/ic** (-kas/ik) —*n.* **1.** a native of the Caucasus **2.**

same as CAUCASOID 3. the Caucasian languages; Circassian, Georgian, etc.

Cau·ca·soid (kôk'ə soid') *adj.* [from the erroneous notion that the original home of the hypothetical Indo-Europeans was the Caucasus] designating or of one of the major groups of mankind: it includes peoples of Europe, North Africa, the Near East, India, etc. and is loosely called the *white race* although it embraces many peoples of dark skin color —*n.* a member of the Caucasoid group

Cau·ca·sus (kô'kə səs) 1. region in SE European U.S.S.R., between the Black Sea and the Caspian: often called **the Caucasus** 2. mountain range in the Caucasus: highest peak, Mt. ELBRUS: in full, **Caucasus Mountains**

CAUCASUS

☆**cau·cus** (kôk'əs) *n.* [< ? *Caucus* Club, 18th-c. social and political club; ult. < MGr. *kaukos,* drinking cup] 1. a private meeting of leaders or a committee of a political party or faction to decide on policy, pick candidates, etc., esp. prior to a general, open meeting 2. a controlling organization within a British political party —*vi.* **-cused** or **-cussed, -cus·ing** or **-cus·sing** to hold, or take part in, a caucus

cau·dad (kô'dad) *adv.* [< L. *cauda,* tail + *ad,* toward] *Anat., Zool.* toward the tail or the caudal part of the body; posteriorly: opposed to CEPHALAD

cau·dal (kôd''l) *adj.* [< L. *cauda,* tail + -AL] 1. of or like a tail 2. at or near the tail —**cau'dal·ly** *adv.*

cau·date (kô'dāt) *adj.* [< L. *cauda,* tail + -ATE[1]] having a tail or taillike part: also **cau'dat·ed**

cau·dex (-deks) *n., pl.* **-di·ces'** (-di sēz'), **-dex·es** (-dek siz) [L., stem of a tree] 1. the persistent stem of a perennial plant 2. the axis or stem of a woody plant, esp. of a palm or tree fern

‡**cau·dil·lo** (kou *the̅*'lyō̅, -yō̅) *n., pl.* **-los** (-lyŏ̅s, -yŏ̅s) [Sp., akin to Pr. *capdel,* Gascon *capdet:* see CADET] a leader; esp., a military dictator

cau·dle (kôd''l) *n.* [ME. & Anglo-Fr. *caudel,* ult. < L. *calidus, caldus,* warm] a warm drink for invalids, esp. a spiced and sugared gruel with wine or ale added

caught (kôt) [ME. *cahte, cauhte*] *pt. & pp. of* CATCH

caul (kôl) *n.* [ME. *calle* < OE. *cawl,* basket, container, net] 1. the membrane enclosing a fetus; esp., a part of this membrane sometimes enveloping the head of a child at birth: thought by the superstitious to bring good luck 2. the part of the peritoneum that extends from the stomach to the large intestine; great omentum

caul·dron (kôl'drən) *n. same as* CALDRON

cau·les·cent (kô les''nt) *adj.* [< L. *caulis,* a stem + -ESCENT] *Bot.* having an obvious stem above the ground

cau·li·cle (kô'li k'l) *n.* [L. *cauliculus,* dim. of *caulis,* a stalk, stem] *Bot.* a small or rudimentary stem, as in an embryo

cau·li·flow·er (kôl'ə flou'ər, käl'-) *n.* [earlier *cole florye* (altered after COLE) < It. *cavolfiore* (< *cavolo,* cabbage + *fiore,* flower), whence Fr. *chou-fleur;* mod. sp. after L. *caulis,* a cabbage] 1. a variety of cabbage (*Brassica oleracea botrytis*) having a dense white mass of fleshy flower stalks that form the head 2. the head of this plant, eaten as a vegetable

☆**cauliflower ear** an ear permanently deformed as a result of injuries from repeated blows, as in boxing

cau·line (kô'līn, -lin) *adj.* [CAUL(IS) + -INE[1]] *Bot.* of or growing on a stem, esp. the upper part of a stem

cau·lis (-lis) *n., pl.* **-les** (-lēz) [L., akin to Gr. *kaulos:* for IE. base see HOLLOW] *Bot.* the main stem or stalk of a plant

caulk (kôk) *vt.* [ME. *cauken,* to tread < OFr. *cauquer,* to tread, tread in < L. *calcare,* to tread < *calx,* a heel] 1. to make (a boat, etc.) watertight by filling the seams or cracks with oakum, tar, etc. 2. to stop up (cracks of window frames, pipes, etc.) with a filler 3. to make (a joint of overlapping plates) tight by hammering the edge of one plate into the side of the other —**caulk'er** *n.*

caus. causative

caus·a·ble (kôz'ə b'l) *adj.* that can be caused

caus·al (-'l) *adj.* [ME. *causel* < LL. *causalis*] 1. of a cause or causes 2. being or involving a cause 3. relating to cause and effect 4. expressing a cause or reason —*n.* a word or connective expressing a cause, as *since, therefore, for* — **caus'al·ly** *adv.*

cau·sal·gi·a (kô zal'jə, -jē ə) *n.* [ModL. < Gr. *kausos,* fever, heat + -ALGIA] neuralgia characterized by a burning sensation

cau·sal·i·ty (kô zal'ə tē) *n., pl.* **-ties** 1. causal quality or agency 2. the interrelation of cause and effect; principle that nothing can exist or happen without a cause

cau·sa·tion (kô zā'shən) *n.* 1. the act of causing 2. a causal agency; anything producing an effect 3. causality

caus·a·tive (kôz'ə tiv) *adj.* [ME. & OFr. *causatif* < L.

causativus] 1. producing an effect; causing 2. expressing causation, as certain verbs [*fell* is a *causative* verb meaning "to cause to fall"] —*n.* a causative word or form — **caus'a·tive·ly** *adv.*

cause (kôz) *n.* [ME. < OFr. < L. *causa,* a cause, reason, judicial process, lawsuit: infl. (in senses 4, 5) by CASE[1]] 1. anything producing an effect or result 2. a person or thing acting voluntarily or involuntarily as the agent that brings about an effect or result [a woman was the *cause* of his downfall] 3. a reason, motive, or ground for some action, feeling, etc.; esp., sufficient reason [*cause* for complaint] 4. any objective or movement that a person or group is interested in and supports, esp. one involving social reform 5. *Law* an action or question to be resolved by a court of law —*vt.* **caused, caus'ing** to be the cause of; bring about; make happen; effect, induce, produce, compel, etc. —**make common cause with** to work together with toward the same objective; join forces —**cause'less** *adj.* —**caus'er** *n.* *SYN.*—**cause,** in its distinctive sense, refers to a situation, event, or agent that produces an effect or result [carelessness is often a *cause* of accident]; **reason** implies the mental activity of a rational being in explaining or justifying some act or thought [she had a *reason* for laughing]; a **motive** is an impulse, emotion, or desire that leads to action [the *motive* for a crime]; an **antecedent** is an event or thing that is the predecessor of, and is responsible for, a later event or thing [war always has its *antecedents*]; a **determinant** is a cause that helps to determine the character of an effect or result [ambition was a *determinant* in his success]

‡**cause cé·lè·bre** (kôz' sā leb'r'; *E.* kôz' sə leb') [Fr.] a celebrated law case, trial, or controversy

cause of action *Law* the right by which a party seeks a remedy against another in a court of law

cau·se·rie (kō'zə rē') *n.* [Fr. < *causer,* to chat < VL. *causare,* complain < L. *causari,* plead, dispute < *causa:* see CAUSE] 1. an informal talk or discussion; chat 2. a short piece of writing in a conversational style

cause·way (kôz'wā') *n.* [< CAUSEY + WAY] 1. a raised path or road, as across wet ground 2. a paved way or roadway; highway —*vt.* to furnish with a causeway

cau·sey (kô'zē) *n., pl.* **-seys** [ME. *cauce* < Anglo-Fr. *caucie* < VL. **calciata* < *calciare,* to make a road < L. *calx* (gen. *calcis*), lime] [Obs. or Brit. Dial.] a causeway

caus·tic (kôs'tik) *adj.* [ME. *caustik* < L. *causticus* < Gr. *kaustikos* < *kaustos,* burning < *kaiein,* to burn] 1. that can burn, eat away, or destroy tissue by chemical action; corrosive 2. cutting or sarcastic in utterance; biting 3. designating or of the curved radial surface, or a plane curve in this surface, formed by the reflection or refraction of rays from a curved solid surface —*n.* [L. *causticum* < the *adj.*] 1. any caustic substance 2. a caustic surface or curve — *SYN.* see SARCASTIC —**caus'ti·cal·ly** *adv.* —**caus·tic'i·ty** (-tis'ə tē) *n.*

caustic potash *same as* POTASSIUM HYDROXIDE

caustic soda *same as* SODIUM HYDROXIDE

cau·ter·ant (kôt'ər ənt) *adj.* that cauterizes —*n.* a substance or instrument that cauterizes

cau·ter·ize (kôt'ər īz') *vt.* **-ized', -iz'ing** [ME. *cauterizen* < LL. *cauterizare* < Gr. *kautēriazein* < *kautērion, kautēr,* burning or branding iron < *kaiein,* to burn] to burn with a hot iron or needle, or with a caustic substance, so as to destroy dead or unwanted tissue, prevent the spread of infection, etc. —**cau'ter·i·za'tion** *n.*

cau·ter·y (kôt'ər ē) *n., pl.* **-ter·ies** [ME. *cauterie* < L. *cauterium* < Gr. *kautērion*] 1. an instrument or substance for cauterizing 2. the act of cauterizing

cau·tion (kô'shən) *n.* [ME. *caucioun* < L. *cautio* < *same base as cavere,* to be on one's guard] 1. a warning; admonition 2. a word, sign, etc. by which warning is given 3. the act or practice of being cautious; wariness ☆4. [Colloq.] a person or thing provoking notice, comment, attention, etc. —*vt.* to urge to be cautious; warn; admonish —*SYN.* see ADVISE

cau·tion·ar·y (-er'ē) *adj.* urging caution or intended to warn; warning; admonishing

cau·tious (kô'shəs) *adj.* full of caution; careful to avoid danger; circumspect; wary —*SYN.* see CAREFUL —**cau'tious·ly** *adv.* —**cau'tious·ness** *n.*

Cau·ver·y (kô'vər ē) river in S India, flowing from the W Ghats southeastward into the Bay of Bengal: c. 475 mi.

cav. 1. cavalier 2. cavalry

cav·al·cade (kav''l kād', kav''l kād') *n.* [Fr. < It. *cavalcata* < *cavalcare,* to ride < VL. **caballicare* < L. *caballus,* horse] 1. a procession of horsemen or carriages 2. *a*) any procession *b*) a sequence or series, as of events

cav·a·lier (kav'ə lir') *n.* [Fr. < It. *cavaliere* < LL. *caballarius* < L. *caballus,* a horse] 1. an armed horseman; knight 2. a gallant or courteous gentleman, esp. one serving as a lady's escort 3. [C-] a partisan of Charles I of England in his struggles with Parliament (1641–1649): Royalist: opposed to ROUNDHEAD —*adj.* 1. [C-] *a*) of the Cavaliers *b*) associated with the court of Charles I of England [*Cavalier* poets] 2. *a*) free and easy; gay *b*) casual or indifferent toward matters of some importance *c*) haughty; arrogant; supercilious —**cav'a·lier'ly** *adv., adj.* —**cav'a·lier'ness** *n.*

ca·val·la (kə val'ə) *n., pl.* **-la, -las:** see PLURAL, II, D, 2 [Port. < *cavallo,* a horse < L. *caballa,* mare, fem. of *caballus,* a horse: the fishes mentioned below are sometimes called *horse mackerel* in England] *same as:* 1. CERO 2. CREVALLE

cav·al·ry (kav''l rē) *n., pl.* **-ries** [Fr. *cavalerie* < It. *cavalleria* < *cavaliere:* see CAVALIER] combat troops mounted originally on horses but now often on motorized armored vehicles, for greater mobility —**cav'al·ry·man** (-mən) *n., pl.* **-men** (-mən)

cav·a·ti·na (kav'ə tē'nə; *It.* kä'vä tē'nä) *n.* [It., dim. of *cavata,* a separate air] **1.** a short, simple solo song or melody that is usually part of a larger composition, such as an opera or oratorio **2.** loosely, an instrumental composition of lyric quality

cave¹ (kāv) *n.* [ME. & OFr. < L. *cava* < *cavus,* hollow < IE. base **keu-,* a swelling, arch, cavity] **1.** a hollow place inside the earth, usually an opening, as in a hillside, extending back horizontally; cavern **2.** [Brit. Slang] *a)* secession from a political party over an issue *b)* those seceding —*vt.* **caved, cav'ing** [< the *n.*] to hollow out; make a hollow in —*vi.* [Colloq.] **1.** to cave in **2.** to explore caves —**cave in 1.** to fall or sink in or down; collapse **2.** to make collapse; cause to fall or sink in or down **3.** [Colloq.] to give way; give in; yield —**cav'er** *n.*

‡**cave²** (käv) *n.* [Fr.] **1.** a wine cellar **2.** a small café with entertainment, typically in a cellar

ca·ve·at (kā'vē at', kav'ē-, kä'vē ät') *n.* [L., let him beware; 3d pers. sing., pres. subj., of *cavere,* to beware, take heed] **1.** *Law* a formal notice that an interested party files with the proper legal authorities directing them to stop or refrain from an action until he can be heard **2.** a warning

caveat emp·tor (emp'tôr) [L.] let the buyer beware (i.e., one buys at his own risk)

ca·ve·at·or (-ər) *n.* a person who files a caveat

‡**ca·ve ca·nem** (kä'vā kä'nəm) [L.] beware the dog

cave-in (kāv'in') *n.* **1.** an act or instance of caving in **2.** a place where the ground, a mine, etc. has caved in

Cav·ell (kav'əl), **Edith Louisa** 1865–1915; Eng. nurse executed by the Germans in World War I

cave man 1. a prehistoric human being of the Stone Age who lived in caves; also **cave dweller 2.** a man who is rough and crudely direct, esp. toward women

cav·en·dish (kav''n dish) *n.* [prob. after a proper name] leaf tobacco softened, sweetened as with molasses, and pressed into plugs or cakes

Cav·en·dish (kav''n dish), **Henry** 1731–1810; Eng. chemist & physicist

cav·ern (kav'ərn) *n.* [ME. & OFr. *caverne* < L. *caverna* < *cavus:* see CAVE¹] a cave, esp., a large cave —*vt.* **1.** to enclose in or as in a cavern **2.** to hollow (*out*)

cav·ern·ous (kav'ər nəs) *adj.* [ME. < L. *cavernosus*] **1.** full of caverns **2.** full of cavities; porous **3.** like or characteristic of a cavern; deep-set, hollow, etc. [a *cavernous* voice, *cavernous* cheeks] —**cav'ern·ous·ly** *adv.*

ca·vet·to (kə vet'ō) *n., pl.* **-vet'ti** (-vet'ē), **-vet'tos** [It., dim. of *cavo,* hollow < L. *cavus*] *Archit.* a concave molding with a curve of about 90°

cav·i·ar, cav·i·are (kav'ē är', käv'-; kav'ē är') *n.* [Fr. < It. *caviale* < Turk. *khāvyār* < Per. *khāviyār* < *khāya,* egg + *-dār,* bearing: orig., spawning fish, hence, roe] the salted eggs of sturgeon, salmon, etc. eaten as an appetizer —**caviar to the general** a thing appealing only to a highly cultivated taste: *Hamlet* II, ii

cav·i·corn (kav'ə kôrn') *adj.* [< L. *cavus,* hollow + *cornu,* a HORN] having hollow horns, as oxen, sheep, etc.

cav·il (kav''l) *vi.* **-iled** or **-illed, -il·ing** or **-il·ling** [OFr. *caviller* < L. *cavillari* < *cavilla,* a jest, quibbling] to object when there is little reason to do so; resort to trivial faultfinding; carp; quibble (*at* or *about*) —*vt.* [Rare] to cavil at —*n.* a trivial objection; quibble —**cav'il·er, cav'il·ler** *n.*

cav·i·ta·tion (kav'ə tā'shən) *n.* [< LL. *cavitas,* a hollow, CAVITY + -ATION] the formation of partial vacuums in a flowing liquid as a result of the separation of its parts: when these collapse, pitting or other damage is caused on metal surfaces in contact

Ca·vi·te (kä vē'te) seaport on the island of Luzon, in the Philippines: pop. 63,000

cav·i·ty (kav'ə tē) *n., pl.* **-ties** [Fr. *cavité* < LL. *cavitas* < L. *cavus,* hollow] **1.** a hole or hollow place **2.** a natural hollow place within the body [the abdominal *cavity*] **3.** a hollow place in a tooth, esp. when caused by decay **4.** *Electronics* a cylinder with a rod in the center enclosed by conducting walls and serving as a resonator for electromagnetic waves —*SYN.* see HOLE

☆**ca·vort** (kə vôrt') *vi.* [< ?] **1.** to leap about; prance or caper **2.** to romp about happily; frolic

Ca·vour (kä vōōr'), **Conte Ca·mil·lo Ben·so di** (kä mēl'lō ben'sō dē) 1810–61; It. statesman: a leader in the movement to unify Italy

CAVU *Aeron.* ceiling and visibility unlimited

ca·vy (kā'vē) *n., pl.* **-vies** [< ModL. *Cavia,* name of the genus < Galibi *cabiai*] any of several short-tailed S. American rodents (family Caviidae), as the guinea pig

caw (kô) *n.* [echoic] the harsh, strident cry of a crow or raven —*vi.* to make this sound

Cawn·pore (kôn pôr') former name of KANPUR

Cax·ton (kak'stən) *n.* **1.** any book printed by William Caxton **2.** black-letter type like that used by Caxton

Cax·ton (kak'stən), **William** 1422?–91; first Eng. printer

cay (kā, kē) *n.* [Sp. *cayo:* see KEY²] a low island, coral reef, or sandbank off a mainland

Cay·enne (kī en', kā-) chief town of French Guiana: seaport on the Atlantic: pop. 19,000

cay·enne (kī en', kā-) *n.* [< Tupi *kynnha;* popularly associated with prec.] **1.** a very hot red pepper made from the dried, pungent fruit of a pepper plant, esp. of the capsicum: also **cayenne pepper 2.** the fruit of a capsicum

cay·man (kā'mən) *n., pl.* **-mans** same as CAIMAN

Cay·man Islands (kā'mən, kī män') three Brit. islands south of Cuba: c. 100 sq. mi.; pop. c. 8,000

Ca·yu·ga (kā yōō'gə, kī-) *n., pl.* **-gas, -ga** [Iroquoian] **1.** any member of a tribe of Iroquoian Indians who lived around Cayuga Lake and Seneca Lake in N.Y.: see FIVE NATIONS **2.** their Iroquoian dialect

Cayuga Lake lake in WC N.Y., one of the Finger Lakes: 38 mi. long

Cay·use (kī'ōōs, kī ōōs') *n., pl.* **-us·es;** for 1 *a,* also **-use** [< *tribal name*] **1.** *a)* a member of a tribe of Oregonian Indians who lived in the Blue Mountains section of NE Oregon *b)* their language **2.** [c-] a horse, esp. a small Western horse used by cowboys

Cb *Chem.* columbium

CBC Canadian Broadcasting Corporation

CBS Columbia Broadcasting System

Cc cirrocumulus

cc. chapters

cc., c.c. cubic centimeter(s)

C.C., c.c. 1. carbon copy **2.** cashier's check **3.** chief clerk **4.** city council **5.** county clerk

CCC 1. Civilian Conservation Corps **2.** Commodity Credit Corporation

C.C.F. Cooperative Commonwealth Federation

C clef *Music* a sign on a staff indicating that C is the note on the third line (ALTO CLEF) or on the fourth line (TENOR CLEF): distinguished from TREBLE CLEF and BASS CLEF: see CLEF, illus.

Cd *Chem.* cadmium

CD, C.D. Civil Defense

cd. cord(s)

C/D, CD certificate of deposit

c.d. cash discount

CDR, Cdr. Commander

Ce *Chem.* cerium

C.E. 1. Chemical Engineer **2.** Chief Engineer **3.** Christian Endeavor **4.** Church of England **5.** Civil Engineer **6.** Common Era

Ce·a·rá (se'ä rä') **1.** state on the NE coast of Brazil: c. 57,000 sq. mi.; pop. 3,338,000; cap. Fortaleza **2.** same as FORTALEZA

cease (sēs) *vt., vi.* **ceased, ceas'ing** [ME. *cesen* < OFr. *cesser* < L. *cessare,* to loiter, be idle < pp. of *cedere,* to go away, yield, withdraw] to bring or come to an end; stop; discontinue —*n.* [ME. & OFr. *ces* < *v.*] a ceasing, as of some activity: chiefly in **without cease** —*SYN.* see STOP

cease-fire (sēs'fīr') *n.* a temporary cessation of warfare by mutual agreement of the participants; truce

cease·less (-lis) *adj.* unceasing; continual —**cease'less·ly** *adv.*

Ce·bu (sā bōō') **1.** island in the SC Philippines, between Negros & Leyte: 1,703 sq. mi. **2.** seaport & chief city on this island: pop. 290,000

Čech·y (chekh'ē) *Czech name of* BOHEMIA

Ce·cil (sēs''l; *esp.* for 2 ses''l) [L. *Caecilius,* name of a Roman gens; prob. < *caecus,* blind; hence, lit., dimsighted, blind] **1.** a masculine name: fem. Cecilia, Cecily **2. William,** see BURGHLEY, 1st Baron

Ce·cile (sə sēl') a feminine name: see CECILIA

Ce·cil·ia (sə sēl'yə) [L. *Caecilia,* fem. of *Caecilius:* see CECIL] **1.** a feminine name: dim. *Cis, Cissie;* var. *Cecile, Cecily, Cicely, Sheila* **2.** Saint, ?–230? A.D.; Christian martyr: patron saint of music: her day is Nov. 22

Cec·i·ly (ses''l ē) a feminine name: see CECILIA

☆**ce·cro·pi·a moth** (si krō'pē ə) [< ModL. *Cecropia,* name of a genus of mulberry trees < ff.] the largest moth (*Samia cecropia*) of the U.S., having wide wings, each with a crescent-shaped spot of white edged in red

Ce·crops (sē'kräps) [Gr. *Kekrops*] *Gr. Myth.* the first king of Attica and founder of Athens, represented as half man, half dragon

ce·cum (sē'kəm) *n., pl.* **-ca** (-kə) [L. *caecum* < *intestinum caecum,* blind intestine < *caecus,* blind < IE. base **kai-ka,* one-eyed, squinting, whence OIr. *caech,* one-eyed, blind, Goth. *haihs,* one-eyed] **1.** the pouch that is the beginning of the large intestine **2.** *Zool.* a cavity open at one end —**ce'cal** *adj.*

ce·dar (sē'dər) *n.* [ME. & OFr. *cedre* < L. *cedrus* < Gr. *kedros*] **1.** any of a genus (*Cedrus*) of widespreading coniferous trees of the pine family, having clusters of needlelike leaves, cones, and durable wood with a characteristic fragrance, as the cedar of Lebanon (*Cedrus libani*) **2.** any of various trees like this, as certain kinds of juniper, thuja, etc. **3.** same as SPANISH CEDAR **4.** the wood of any of these —*adj.* of cedar

☆**cedar chest** a chest made of cedar, in which woolens, furs, etc. are stored for protection against moths

ce·darn (sē′dərn) *adj.* [Poet.] of cedar or cedars

Cedar Rapids [after the rapids of the nearby Cedar River] city in EC Iowa: pop. 92,000

☆**cedar waxwing** a brownish-gray, crested American bird (*Bombycilla cedrorum*), with red, waxlike tips on its secondary wing feathers: also **ce′dar·bird′** *n.*

cede (sēd) *vt.* **ced′ed, ced′ing** [Fr. *céder* < L. *cedere*, to yield, orig., to go, leave < **ce-*, directive particle (< IE. **ke-*, this one, HERE) + **sed-*, akin to *sedere*, to SIT] **1.** to give up one's rights in; surrender formally **2.** to transfer the title or ownership of

ce·di (sā′dē) *n., pl.* **-dis** [< Akan *sedie*, cowrie, formerly used as money] the monetary unit of Ghana: see MONETARY UNITS, table

ce·dil·la (si dil′ə) *n.* [Fr. *cédille* < Sp. *cedilla*, dim. of *zeda* (< Gr. *zēta*, a zeta or z): so called because z was written after *c* to give the sound of the letter *s*] a hooklike mark put under *c* in some French words (Ex.: *façade*) to show that it is to be sounded like a voiceless *s* [IPA s]

Ced·ric (sed′rik, sē′drik) [< ? Celt.] a masculine name

ced·u·la (sej′ oo lə) *n.* [Sp. *cédula* < LL. *schedula:* see SCHEDULE] any of various certificates or documents issued in Spanish-speaking countries

cee (sē) *n.* the letter C, c —*adj.* shaped like a C

cei·ba (sā′bə; *also for 2* sī′bə) *n.* [Sp. < Arawakan name] **1.** any of various tropical trees of the bombax family, whose seed pods contain kapok; silk-cotton tree **2.** kapok; silk cotton

ceil (sēl) *vt.* [ME. *celen* < OFr. *celer*, to conceal < L. *celare*; prob. infl. by L. *caelum*, heaven & OFr. *celer* < L. *caelare*, to carve] **1.** to build a ceiling in or over **2.** to cover (the ceiling or walls of a room) with plaster or thin boards

ceil·ing (-iŋ) *n.* [< prec.] **1.** the inside top part or covering of a room, opposite the floor **2.** any overhanging expanse seen from below **3.** an upper limit set on anything, as by official regulation *[a ceiling on prices]* **4.** *Aeron.* a) a covering of clouds limiting vertical visibility b) the height of the lower surface of such a covering c) the maximum height at which an aircraft can fly under normal conditions —**hit the ceiling** [Slang] to become suddenly very angry; lose one's temper

☆**ceil·om·e·ter** (sē läm′ə tər) *n.* [CEIL(ING) + *-o-* + -METER] an automatic device used to determine the height of a cloud ceiling, as by means of a reflected light beam

cel·a·don (sel′ə dän′, -′d′n; *Fr.* sȧ lȧ dōn′) *n.* [Fr. *céladon*, a delicate green, earlier, a tender lover < *Céladon*, name of the hero in *Astrée*, romance by d'Urfe (1610) < L. *Celadon* (< Gr. *Keladōn*), a character in Ovid's *Metamorphoses*] a pale grayish green

cel·an·dine (sel′ən dīn′, -dēn′) *n.* [ME. & OFr. *celidoine* < ML. *celidonia* < L. *chelidonia* < Gr. *chelidonion*, swallowwort < *chelidōn*, a swallow] **1.** a weedy plant (*Chelidonium majus*) of the poppy family, with deeply divided leaves and yellow flowers and juice **2.** a perennial plant (*Ranunculus ficaria*) of the buttercup family, with yellow flowers: also called **lesser celandine**

-cele (sēl) [< Gr. *kēlē* < IE. base **kaulā*, whence OE. *heala*, hernia, rupture] **1.** *a combining form meaning* tumor, hernia, or swelling **2.** *same as* -COELE

Cel·e·bes (sel′ə bēz′, sə lē′bēz) island of Indonesia, east of Borneo: with small nearby islands, 72,986 sq. mi.; pop. 7,079,000: Indonesian name, SULAWESI

Celebes Sea part of the South Pacific Ocean, north of Celebes and south of the Philippines

cel·e·brant (sel′ə brənt) *n.* [< L. *celebrans*, prp. of *celebrare*: see ff.] **1.** a person who performs a religious rite, as the priest officiating at Mass **2.** any person who celebrates; celebrator

cel·e·brate (-brāt′) *vt.* **-brat′ed, -brat′ing** [ME. *celebraten* < L. *celebratus*, pp. of *celebrare*, to frequent, go in great numbers, honor < *celeber*, frequented, populous] **1.** to perform (a ritual, ceremony, etc.) publicly and formally; solemnize **2.** to commemorate (an anniversary, holiday, etc.) with ceremony or festivity **3.** to honor or praise publicly **4.** to mark (a happy occasion) by engaging in some pleasurable activity —*vi.* **1.** to observe a holiday, anniversary, etc. with festivities **2.** to perform a religious ceremony **3.** [Colloq.] to have a convivial good time —**cel′e·bra′tor** *n.* —**ce·leb·ra·to·ry** (sə leb′rə tôr′ē) *adj.*

SYN.—**celebrate** implies the marking of an occasion or event, esp. a joyous one, with ceremony or festivity *[let's celebrate his promotion]*; to **commemorate** is to honor the memory of some person or event by a ceremony *[to commemorate Lincoln's birthday]*; **solemnize** suggests the use of formal, grave ritual in signalizing an event, esp. a religious ceremony *[to solemnize a marriage]*; **observe** and the less formal **keep** suggest the respectful marking of a day or occasion in the prescribed or appropriate manner *[to observe, or keep, a religious holiday]*

cel·e·brat·ed (-id) *adj.* much spoken of; famous; renowned —*SYN.* see FAMOUS

cel·e·bra·tion (sel′ə brā′shən) *n.* [L. *celebratio*] **1.** the act or an instance of celebrating **2.** that which is done to celebrate

ce·leb·ri·ty (sə leb′rə tē) *n.* [ME. & OFr. *celebrite* < L. *celebritas*, multitude, fame < *celeber*, frequented, populous, famous] **1.** wide recognition; fame; renown **2.** *pl.* **-ties** a famous or well-publicized person

ce·le·ri·ac (sə ler′ē ak′) *n.* [altered < CELERY + ? obs. *ache*, an umbelliferous plant, wild celery, parsley < ME. < OFr. < L. *apium*, prob. < *apis*, bee] a variety of celery (*Apium graveolens rapaceum*) grown for its edible, turniplike root

ce·ler·i·ty (sə ler′ə tē) *n.* [Fr. *célérité* < L. *celeritas* < *celer*, swift] swiftness in acting or moving; speed

cel·e·ry (sel′ər ē, sel′rē) *n.* [Fr. *céleri* < It. *seleri* < L. *selinon* < Gr. *selinon*, parsley] a biennial plant (*Apium graveolens*) of the parsley family, whose long, crisp leafstalks are eaten as a vegetable

celery salt a seasoning made of celery seed and salt

ce·les·ta (sə les′tə) *n.* [Fr. *célesta* < *céleste*, celestial] a small keyboard instrument with hammers that strike small metal plates to produce bell-like tones

Ce·leste (sə lest′) [Fr. *Céleste:* see prec.] a feminine name: var. *Celestine*

ce·leste (sə lest′) *n. same as* CELESTA

ce·les·tial (sə les′chəl) *adj.* [ME. & OFr. < L. *caelestis* < *caelum*, heaven: for IE. base see CHINTZ] **1.** of the heavens; of the sky **2.** a) of heaven; divine *[celestial beings]* b) of the finest or highest kind; perfect *[celestial bliss]* **3.** [C-] of the former Chinese Empire —*n.* any being regarded as living in heaven —**ce·les′tial·ly** *adv.*

Celestial Empire [transl. of a former Chin. name for China] *same as* CHINESE EMPIRE

celestial equator the great circle of the celestial sphere formed on it by projecting the plane of the earth's equator

celestial globe a globe on which the stars, planets, etc. are depicted in their proper relative positions in the heavens

celestial latitude *Astron.* the angular distance of a heavenly body from the plane in which the earth moves around the sun

celestial longitude *Astron.* the arc of the ecliptic measured eastward from the vernal equinox to the point where the ecliptic is intersected by the great circle through the star, planet, etc. and the poles of the ecliptic

celestial navigation navigation based on observation of the sun, moon, stars, or planets to determine position and course

celestial pole either of the points in the celestial sphere where the earth's axis, if extended, would intersect

celestial sphere an imaginary sphere of infinite diameter containing the whole universe and on which all celestial bodies appear to be projected

Ce·les·tine (sə les′tēn) a feminine name: see CELESTE

cel·es·tine (sel′əs tin, -tin′; sə les′tin) *n.* [< L. *caelestis*, celestial + -INE⁴: from its blue color] *same as* CELESTITE

cel·es·tite (-tīt′) *n.* [altered (by J. D. Dana, 1813-95, U.S. mineralogist) < prec. + -ITE¹] *Mineralogy* strontium sulfate, SrSO₄, which occurs usually in white, crystalline form, but is sometimes blue: most strontium compounds are produced from it

Cel·ia (sēl′yə) [L. *Caelia*, fem. of *Caelius*, name of a Roman gens, of Etruscan orig., lit., prob. "September"] a feminine name

ce·li·ac (sē′lē ak′) *adj.* [L. *coeliacus* < Gr. *koiliakos* < *koilia:* see -COELE] of or in the abdominal cavity

celiac disease a deficiency disease of young children caused by faulty absorption of food in the intestines and characterized by diarrhea and malnutrition

cel·i·ba·cy (sel′ə bə sē) *n.* [< CELIBA(TE) + -CY] **1.** the state of being unmarried, esp. that of a person under a vow not to marry **2.** complete sexual abstinence

cel·i·bate (sel′ə bət, -bāt′) *n.* [L. *caelibatus* < *caelebs*, unmarried < IE. base **kaiwelo-*, alone + **lib(h)s-*, living (whence LIVE¹)] **1.** an unmarried person, esp. one under a vow to remain unmarried **2.** one who abstains from sexual intercourse —*n.* one in or a state of celibacy

cell (sel) *n.* [ME. < OE. < OFr. *celle* < L. *cella*, small room, hut, in LL.(Ec.), monastic cell, < IE. base **kel-*, to conceal, whence Goth. *halja*, HALL, HELL, HULL¹] **1.** a small convent or monastery attached to a larger one **2.** a hermit's hut **3.** a small room or cubicle, as in a convent or prison **4.** a very small hollow, cavity, or enclosed space; specif., a) any of the compartments in a honeycomb b) a small, hollow space in tissue, esp. in bone c) the space of an insect's wings enclosed by the veins d) any compartment of an ovary; also, a pollen sac or spore sac **5.** any of the smallest organizational units of a group or movement, as of a Communist party **6.** *Biol.* a very small, complex unit of protoplasm, usually with a nucleus, cytoplasm, and an enclosing membrane: all plants and animals are made up of one or more cells, usually very many **7.** *Elec.* a) a receptacle containing electrodes and an electrolyte, used either for generating electricity by chemical reactions or for decomposing compounds by electrolysis b) any compartment of a storage battery —**celled** (seld) *adj.*

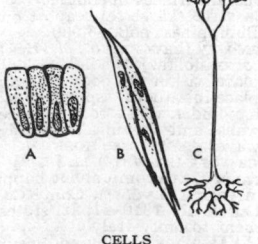

CELLS
(A, epithelial; B, smooth muscle; C, nerve)

cel·la (sel′ə) *n., pl.* **cel′lae** (-ē) [L.: see prec.] the inner part of an ancient Greek or Roman temple, housing the statue of a god or goddess

cel·lar (sel′ər) *n.* [ME. *celler* < OFr. *celier* < L. *cellarium*, pantry, storeroom < *cella:* see CELL] **1.** a room or group of rooms below the ground level and usually under a building, often used for storing fuel, provisions, wines, etc. **2.** a stock of wines kept in such a cellar —*vt.* to store in a cellar —☆**the cellar** [Colloq.] the lowest position, as in the relative standing of competing teams

cel·lar·age (-ij) *n.* **1.** space of or in a cellar **2.** cellars collectively **3.** the fee for storage in a cellar

cel·lar·er (-ər) *n.* a person in charge of a cellar or provisions, as in a monastery

cel·lar·et (sel′ə ret′) *n.* [CELLAR + -ET] a cabinet for bottles of wine or liquor, glasses, etc.

☆**cel·lar·way** (sel′ər wā′) *n.* an entrance to a cellar, esp. an outside stairwell leading down to a cellar

Cel·li·ni (chə lē′nē), **Ben·ve·nu·to** (ben′və nōō′tō) 1500-71; It. sculptor & goldsmith: also known for his autobiography

cel·list (chel′ist) *n.* a person who plays the cello; violoncellist: also sp. **'cel′list**

cell membrane *same as* PLASMA MEMBRANE

cel·lo (chel′ō) *n., pl.* **-los, -li** (-ē) [< VIOLONCELLO] an instrument of the violin family, between the viola and the double bass in size and pitch; violoncello: also sp. **'cel′lo**

cel·loi·din (sa loid′′n) *n.* [CELL + -OID + -IN¹] a concentrated solution of pyroxylin used in microscopy for embedding specimens that are to be cut into thin cross sections

cel·lo·phane (sel′ə fān′) *n.* [< CELLULOSE + -PHANE] a thin, transparent material made from cellulose, used as moistureproof wrapping for foods, tobacco, etc.

cel·lu·lar (sel′yoo lər) *adj.* **1.** of or like a cell **2.** consisting of or containing cells; porous —**cel′lu·lar′i·ty** (-lar′ə tē) *n.*

cel·lu·lase (-lās′, -lāz′) *n.* [CELLUL(OSE) + -ASE] an enzyme capable of hydrolyzing cellulose into smaller molecules: used in brewing, septic systems, and medicine

cel·lule (sel′yōōl) *n.* [L. *cellula*, dim. of *cella:* see CELL] a very small cell

cel·lu·li·tis (sel′yoo līt′is) *n.* [ModL. < prec. + -ITIS] an inflammation of connective tissue, esp. of subcutaneous tissue

☆**Cel·lu·loid** (sel′yoo loid′) [CELLUL(OSE) + -OID] *a trademark for* a flammable substance made from pyroxylin and camphor, used for toilet articles, novelties, etc. —*n.* [c-] **1.** this substance **2.** motion pictures: from use of celluloid, esp. formerly, for photographic films

cel·lu·lose (sel′yoo lōs′) *n.* [Fr. < L. *cellula* (see CELLULE) + -OSE, -OSE¹] the chief substance composing the cell walls or fibers of all plant tissue, a polymeric carbohydrate with the general formula $(C_6H_{10}O_5)_x$: it is used in the manufacture of paper, textiles, explosives, etc.

cellulose acetate any of several compounds produced by the action of acetic acid or acetic anhydride upon cellulose in the presence of concentrated sulfuric acid: used in making artificial silks, plastics, photographic films, etc.

cellulose nitrate *same as* NITROCELLULOSE

cel·lu·los·ic (sel′yoo lō′sik) *adj.* of or made from cellulose —*n.* a product or material made from cellulose

cel·lu·lous (sel′yoo las) *adj.* [Rare] consisting or full of cells

cell wall *Biol.* the covering or separating wall of a cell; esp., the relatively rigid covering of a plant cell, containing cellulose, hemicellulose, lignin, etc.

ce·lom (sē′ləm) *n. same as* COELOM

☆**Cel·o·tex** (sel′ə teks′) [arbitrary formation < ? CELLULOSE & TEXTURE] *a trademark for* a composition board made of sugar-cane residue, used for insulation in buildings —*n.* a sheet or sheets of this material

Cel·si·us (sel′sē əs) *adj.* [after Anders *Celsius* (1701-44), Swed. astronomer, the inventor] designating or of a thermometer on which, under laboratory conditions, 0° is the freezing point and 100° is the boiling point of water; centigrade: abbrev. C: the formula for converting a Celsius temperature to Fahrenheit is $C° = 5/9(F° − 32)$

Celt (selt, kelt) *n.* [Fr. *Celte,* orig., Breton < L. *Celta,* pl. *Celtae* (Gr. *Keltoi),* the Gauls] **1.** a person who speaks Celtic or a descendant of such a person: the Bretons, Irish, Welsh, and Highland Scots are Celts **2.** any of an ancient people in central and western Europe, reputedly including the Gauls and Britons

celt (selt) *n.* [< ML. *celtis* < LL. **celtis* inferred < Vulgate *vel celte sculpantur in silice* (Job 19:24); prob. ghost word (*certe* in other mss.) adopted as genuine by archaeologists] a prehistoric tool of stone or metal, resembling a chisel or ax head

Cel·tic (sel′tik, kel′-) *adj.* of the Celts, their languages, culture, characteristics, etc. —*n.* a subfamily of the Indo-European family of languages with a Goidelic branch (Irish Gaelic, Scottish Gaelic, Manx) in Ireland, the Scottish Highlands, and the Isle of Man, and a Brythonic branch (Welsh, Breton, and the extinct Cornish) in Wales and Brittany

Celtic cross a Latin cross having a wheellike circle around the intersection of the limbs

cem·ba·lo (chem′bə lō′) *n., pl.* **-li′** (-lē′), **-los′** [It., harpsichord, cymbal < L. *cymbalum,* CYMBAL] **1.** *same as* DULCIMER **2.** *same as* HARPSICHORD

ce·ment (si ment′) *n.* [ME. & OFr. *ciment,* rough stone, chippings < **caedimentum* < *caedere,* to cut] **1.** a powdered substance made of burned lime and clay, mixed with water and sand to make mortar or with water, sand, and gravel to make concrete: the mixture hardens like stone when it dries **2.** any soft substance that fastens things together firmly when it hardens, as glue **3.** a cement-like substance used in dentistry as to fill cavities **4.** anything that joins together or unites; bond **5.** *same as* CEMENTUM **6.** the fine-grained material that binds together the larger constituents in many kinds of sedimentary or clastic rock **7.** *Metallurgy* a dust or powder, as of charcoal or sand, or a finely divided metal, used in cementation —*vt.* **1.** to join or unite with or as with cement **2.** to spread or cover with cement —*vi.* to become cemented; stick —**ce·ment′er** *n.*

ce·men·ta·tion (sē′men tā′shən) *n.* **1.** a cementing or being cemented **2.** the process by which a solid surrounded by a metallurgic cement is heated intensely and made to combine chemically with the cement to produce a new product

ce·ment·ite (si men′tīt) *n.* [CEMENT + -ITE¹] the hard, brittle carbide of iron, Fe_3C, that occurs in and adds strength to steel, cast iron, and most other alloys of iron and carbon

ce·men·tum (-təm) *n.* [L. *caementum:* see CEMENT] the hard, bony tissue forming the outer layer of the root of a tooth

cem·e·ter·y (sem′ə ter′ē) *n., pl.* **-ter′ies** [LL.(Ec.) *coemeterium* < Gr. *koimētērion,* sleeping place (in LGr.(Ec.), cemetery) < *koiman,* to put to sleep] a place for the burial of the dead; graveyard

cen. **1.** central **2.** century

cen·a·cle (sen′ə k'l) *n.* [Fr. *cénacle* < L. *cenaculum,* a dining room < *cena,* dinner < OL. *cesnas* < IE. **(s)ker*- < base **(s)ker*-, to cut, whence SHEAR, SHORT] **1.** [C-] the room in which Jesus and his disciples ate the Last Supper **2.** a coterie, as of writers

-cene (sēn) [< Gr. *kainos,* recent] *a combining form meaning* recent, new, or, esp., designating a (specified) epoch in the Cenozoic Era [*Miocene*]

ce·nes·the·sia (sē′nis thē′zhə, -zhē ə; sen′is-) *n. same as* COENESTHESIA —**ce′nes·the′sis** *n.*

Ce·nis, Mont (mōn sə nē′) mountain and mountain pass in SE France, at the Italian border: a nearby railroad tunnel (8-1/2 mi. long) runs between Italy and France

ce·no- (sē′nə, -nō′; sen′ə) *same as* COENO-

cen·o·bite (sen′ə bīt′, sē′nə-) *n.* [ME. < LL.(Ec.) *coenobita* < *coenobium,* a cloister < Gr. *koinobion,* communal life, in LGr.(Ec.), monastery, neut. of *kuinobios* < *koinos,* common + *bios,* life] a member of a religious order living in a monastery or convent: distinguished from ANCHORITE —**cen′o·bit′ic** (-bit′ik), **cen′o·bit′i·cal** *adj.* —**cen′o·bit·ism** (-bit iz′m) *n.*

ce·no·gen·e·sis (sē′nə jen′ə sis, sen′ō-) *n.* [*ceno-* (< Gr. *kainos,* new) + -GENESIS] the development of structures in the embryonic or larval stage of an organism that are adaptive and do not appear in the evolutionary history of its group: cf. PALINGENESIS —**ce′no·ge·net′ic** (-jə net′ik) *adj.*

ce·no·spe·cies (sē′nə spē′shēz, sen′ə-) *n.* [CENO- + SPECIES] separate species of organisms that are related through their capability of interbreeding, as dogs and wolves

cen·o·taph (sen′ə taf′) *n.* [Fr. *cénotaphe* < L. *cenotaphium* < Gr. *kenotaphion* < *kenos,* empty + *taphos,* a tomb] a monument or empty tomb honoring a dead person whose body is somewhere else

ce·no·te (sə nōt′ē) *n.* [AmSp. < Maya *tzonot*] a deep natural well carved out of friable limestone

Ce·no·zo·ic (sē′nə zō′ik, sen′ə-) *adj.* [*ceno-* (< Gr. *kainos,* new, recent) + ZO- + -IC] designating or of the geologic era following the Mesozoic and including the present: it began about 65 million years ago and is characterized by the development of many varieties of mammals —**the Cenozoic** the Cenozoic Era or its rocks: see GEOLOGY, chart

cense (sens) *vt.* **censed, cens′ing** [ME. *censen,* aphetic < *encensen:* see INCENSE¹] **1.** to perfume with incense **2.** to burn incense to, as in worship

cen·ser (sen′sər) *n.* [ME. < OFr. *censier* < *encensier* < *encens:* see INCENSE¹] an ornamented container in which incense is burned, esp. in religious rites; thurible

cen·sor (sen′sər) *n.* [L. < *censere,* to tax, value, judge < IE.

base ***ƙens**, speak solemnly, announce, whence Sans. *śámsa*, praise, prayer of praise] **1.** one of two Roman magistrates appointed to take the census and, later, to supervise public morals **2.** an official with the power to examine publications, movies, television programs, etc. and to remove or prohibit anything considered obscene, libelous, politically objectionable, etc. **3.** an official in time of war who reads publications, mail, etc. to remove information that might be useful to the enemy **4.** in earlier psychoanalytic theory, and still popularly, a part of the unconscious that serves as the agent of censorship **5.** [Obs.] any faultfinder or adverse critic —*vt.* to subject (a book, letter, writer, etc.) to censorship —**cen·so·ri·al** (sen sôr′ē əl) *adj.*

cen·so·ri·ous (sen sôr′ē əs) *adj.* [L. *censorius*: see CENSOR] expressing censure; inclined to find fault; harshly critical —**cen·so′ri·ous·ly** *adv.* —**cen·so′ri·ous·ness** *n.*

cen·sor·ship (sen′sər ship′) *n.* **1.** the act or a system of censoring **2.** the work or position of a censor **3.** *Psychoanalysis* the agency by which unpleasant ideas, memories, etc. are kept from entering consciousness in their original form, as in dreams

cen·sur·a·ble (sen′shər ə b'l) *adj.* deserving, or liable to, censure; blameworthy —**cen′sur·a·bly** *adv.*

cen·sure (sen′shər) *n.* [L. *censura* < *censor*, CENSOR] **1.** a condemning as wrong; strong disapproval **2.** a judgment or resolution condemning a person for misconduct; specif., an official expression of disapproval passed by a legislature —*vt.* **-sured, -sur·ing** to express strong disapproval of; condemn as wrong —*SYN.* see CRITICIZE —**cen′sur·er** *n.*

cen·sus (sen′səs) *n.* [L., orig., pp. of *censere*, to assess: see CENSOR] **1.** in ancient Rome, the act of counting the people and evaluating their property for taxation **2.** an official, usually periodic, count of population and recording of economic status, age, sex, etc.

cent (sent) *n.* [ME. & OFr. < L. *centum* < IE. ****ƙm̥tóm***, hundred (< **(d)ƙm̥tom*, tenth ten < base **deƙm̥*, TEN, **deƙm̥tos*, tenth), whence Sans. *sátám*, Goth. *hunda*, Gr. *hekaton*, Cym. *cant*, HUNDRED] ☆**1.** a 100th part of a dollar, or a coin of this value; penny: symbol, *¢* **2.** a 100th part of certain other monetary units, as the gulden, rupee, piaster, etc., or a coin of this value

cent. **1.** centered **2.** centigrade **3.** centimeter **4.** central **5.** centum **6.** century

cen·tal (sen′t'l) *n.* [< L. *centum* (see CENT) + -AL, prob. after *quintal*] [Brit.] a unit of weight equal to 100 pounds avoirdupois, used for grain

cen·tare (sen′ter, -tär) *same as* CENTIARE

cen·taur (sen′tôr) *n.* [ME. < L. *Centaurus* < Gr. *Kentauros*] *Gr. Myth.* any of a race of monsters with a man's head, trunk, and arms, and a horse's body and legs —[**C-**] *same as* CENTAURUS

cen·tau·re·a (sen tôr′ē ə) *n.* [ModL. < ML. *centauria*, CENTAURY] any of a genus (*Centaurea*) of annual and perennial plants of the composite family, having funnel-shaped scaly or prickly basal leaves and variously colored flowers which often simulate ray flowers

Cen·tau·rus (sen tôr′əs) [L.: see CENTAUR] a S constellation between Hydra and the Southern Cross: its brightest star (**alpha Centauri**) is nearer the earth than any other known star

cen·tau·ry (sen′tôr ē) *n., pl.* **-ries** [ME. *centaurie* < ML. *centauria* < L. *centaureum* < Gr. *kentaureion* < *Kentauros*, centaur: the centaur Chiron was said to have discovered medicinal properties of the plant] any of a genus (*Centaurium*) of small plants of the gentian family, with flat clusters of red or rose flowers

cen·ta·vo (sen tä′vō) *n., pl.* **-vos** [Sp., a hundredth < L. *centum*, a hundred: see CENT] **1.** a unit of currency in the Philippines, Mexico, and certain S. American countries, equal to 1/100 peso **2.** a unit of currency equal to 1/100 of a Brazilian cruzeiro, a Guatemalan quetzal, a Portuguese escudo, etc. **3.** a coin of certain of these units

cen·te·nar·i·an (sen′tə ner′ē ən) *adj.* [< ff.] **1.** of 100 years; of a centenary **2.** of a centenarian; at least 100 years old —*n.* a person at least 100 years old

cen·te·nar·y (sen ten′ər ē; sen′tə ner′ē) *adj.* [L. *centenarius*, of a hundred < *centeni*, a hundred each < *centum*: see CENT] **1.** relating to a century; of a period of 100 years **2.** of a centennial —*n., pl.* **-nar·ies 1.** a century; period of 100 years **2.** a centennial

cen·ten·ni·al (sen ten′ē əl) *adj.* [< L. *centum*, a hundred (see CENT) + *annus*, year + -AL] **1.** of 100 years **2.** happening once in 100 years **3.** 100 years old **4.** of a 100th anniversary —*n.* a 100th anniversary or its celebration —**cen·ten′ni·al·ly** *adv.*

cen·ter (sen′tər) *n.* [ME. & OFr. *centre* < L. *centrum*, center, orig., that point of the compass around which the other describes the circle < Gr. *kentron*, sharp point, goad < *kentein*, to prick, goad < IE. base **kent-*, to prick, whence OHG. *hantag*, sharp, Goth. *handugs*, wise, ON. *hannarr*, skillful & (?) HANDY] **1.** a point equally distant from all points on the circumference of a circle or surface of a sphere **2.** the point around which anything revolves; pivot **3.** a place at which an activity or complex of activities is carried on [a shopping *center*], from which ideas, influences, etc. emanate [Paris, the fashion *center*], or to which many people are attracted [a *center* of interest] **4.** the approximate middle point, place, or part of anything **5.** a

group of nerve cells regulating a particular function [the vasomotor *centers*] **6.** *Football, Basketball, Hockey,* etc. a player whose position at the start of play is at the center of the line or playing area: the center often puts the ball or puck into play **7.** *Mechanics a)* one of two tapered or conical pins or rods, as on a lathe, for holding a piece of work in position *b)* an indentation in either end of such a piece in which the pin fits **8.** *Mil.* that part of an army situated between the flanks **9.** [*often* C-] *Politics* a position, party, or group between the left (radicals and liberals) and the right (conservatives and reactionaries): so called from the position of the seats occupied in some European legislatures —*vt.* **1.** to place in, at, or near the center **2.** to draw to one place; gather to a point **3.** to furnish with a center **4.** *Football* to pass (the ball) back to a player in the backfield: said of the center —*vi.* to be centered; be concentrated or focused —*SYN.* see MIDDLE

center bit a bit with a sharp, projecting center point and cutting wings on either side

☆**cen·ter·board** (-bôrd′) *n.* a movable board like a keel, that is lowered through a slot in the floor of a shallow-draft sailboat to prevent drifting to leeward

cen·tered (sen′tərd) *adj.* **1.** being at the center **2.** having (a specified thing) as the focus of interest or activity: used in hyphenated compounds [consumer-*centered*]

☆**center field** *Baseball* the middle part of the outfield

cen·ter·fire (-fir′) *adj.* designating a cartridge with the primer set in the center of the base: cf. RIMFIRE

cen·ter·ing (sen′tər iŋ, sen′triŋ) *n.* a temporary frame to support an arch or vault during construction

center of gravity that point in a body or system around which its weight is evenly distributed or balanced and may be assumed to act

center of mass the point in a body, or in a system of bodies, so situated that any plane drawn through it divides the body or system into parts having exactly equal masses: for bodies near the earth, this coincides with *center of gravity*

cen·ter·piece (sen′tər pēs′) *n.* an ornament, bowl of flowers, etc. for the center of a table

center punch a steel punch for marking a spot where a hole is to be drilled

cen·tes·i·mal (sen tes′ə məl) *adj.* [< L. *centesimus* < *centum* (see CENT) + -AL] **1.** hundredth **2.** of or divided into hundredths —**cen·tes′i·mal·ly** *adv.*

cen·tes·i·mo (sen tes′ə mō′; *It.* chen te′sē mô′; *Sp.* sen tes′ē mô′) *n., pl.* **-mos** (-mōz′; *Sp.* -môs′); *It.* **-mi** (-mē′) [It. & Sp. < L. *centesimus*: see prec.] **1.** a unit of currency equal to 1/100th of an Italian lira, a Uruguayan peso, a Panamanian balboa, or a Chilean escudo **2.** a coin of certain of these units

cen·ti- (sen′tə, -ti) [L. < *centum*: see CENT] *a combining form meaning:* **1.** hundred or hundredfold [*centipede*] **2.** a 100th part of; the factor 10⁻² [*centigram*]

cen·ti·are (sen′tē er′, -är′) *n.* [Fr.: see CENTI- & ARE²] a 100th part of an are; unit of land measure, equal to one square meter

cen·ti·grade (sen′tə grād′) *adj.* [Fr. < L. *centum* (see CENT) + *gradus*, a degree] **1.** consisting of or divided into 100 degrees **2.** *same as* CELSIUS: the preferred term in English until the adoption of *Celsius* in 1948 by an international conference on weights and measures: abbrev. **C**

cen·ti·gram (-gram′) *n.* [Fr. *centigramme*: see CENTI- & GRAM¹] a unit of weight, equal to 1/100 gram: also, chiefly Brit. sp., **cen′ti·gramme′**: abbrev. **cg., cgm.**

cen·tile (sen′til, -til) *n. same as* PERCENTILE

cen·ti·li·ter (sen′tə lēt′ər) *n.* [Fr. *centilitre*: see CENTI- & LITER] a unit of capacity, equal to 1/100 liter (.6102 cubic inch): also, chiefly Brit. sp., **cen′ti·li′tre**: abbrev. **cl.**

cen·time (sän′tēm; *Fr.* sän tēm′) *n.* [Fr. < OFr. *centisme*, the hundredth < L. *centesimus*: see CENTESIMAL] **1.** the 100th part of a franc, the Haitian gourde, the Algerian dinar, etc. **2.** a coin of this value

cen·ti·me·ter (sen′tə mēt′ər) *n.* [Fr. *centimètre*: see CENTI- & METER¹] a unit of measure, equal to 1/100 meter (.3937 inch): also, chiefly Brit. sp., **cen′ti·me′tre**: abbrev. **cm., c., C., cent.**

cen·ti·me·ter-gram-sec·ond (-gram′sek′ənd) *adj.* designating or of a system of measurement in which the centimeter, gram, and second are used as the units of length, mass, and time, respectively

cen·ti·mil·li- (sen′tə mil′i) [CENTI- + MILLI-] *a combining form meaning* the factor 10⁻⁵

cen·ti·mo (sen′tə mō′) *n., pl.* **-mos** [see CENTIME] **1.** the 100th part of a Spanish peseta, a Venezuelan bolívar, a Costa Rican colon, or a Paraguayan guarani **2.** a coin of certain of these units

cen·ti·pede (sen′tə pēd′) *n.* [Fr. < L. *centipeda < centum*, a hundred + *pes* (gen. *pedis*), a FOOT] any of a class (Chilopoda) of elongated, many-segmented, insect-eating arthropods with a pair of legs to each segment, the front pair being modified into poison claws

cen·ti·poise (sen′tə poiz′) *n.* [CENTI- + POISE²] a cgs unit of the measure of viscosity equal to 1/100 poise: the viscosity of water at 20°C is almost 1 centipoise

cen·ti·stere (-stir′) *n.* [Fr. *centistère*: see CENTI- & STERE] a unit of volume, equal to 1/100 cubic meter

cent·ner (sent′nər) *n.* [G. *centner, zentner* < ML. *centenarius*, weighing 100 pounds < L.: see CENTENARY] in some

European countries, a commercial weight roughly equal to the British hundredweight; specif., 50 kg. (110.23 lb.)

cen·to (sen'tō) *n.*, *pl.* **-tos** [L., patchwork garment < IE. base *kentho-*, rags, whence Sans. *kanthā*, patched garment, OHG. *hadara*, rag, patch] **1.** a literary or musical work made up of passages from other compositions **2.** anything made up of badly matched parts

centr- *same as* CENTRO-: used before vowels

cen·tra (sen'trə) *n. alt. pl. of* CENTRUM

cen·tral (sen'trəl) *adj.* [L. *centralis*] **1.** in, at, or near the center **2.** of or forming the center **3.** equally distant or accessible from various points **4.** most important; main; basic; principal **5.** of or having to do with a single source that controls all activity in an organization or system **6.** *a)* designating or of that part of the nervous system consisting of the brain and spinal cord (of a vertebrate) *b)* of the centrum of a vertebra **7.** *Phonet.* pronounced with the tongue in center position, as the vowel sound in *bud* —☆*n.* formerly, a telephone exchange, esp. the main one, or the telephone operator —**cen'tral·ly** *adv.*

Central African Republic country in C Africa, north of the Congo Republics: a member state of the French Community: formerly, the French territory UBANGI-SHARI: 238,224 sq. mi.; pop. 1,518,000; cap. Bangui

Central America part of N. America between Mexico and S. America: c. 230,-000 sq. mi.; pop. 14,342,000 —**Central American**

central city the principal municipality of a metropolitan area, surrounded by suburbs and smaller towns; esp., the crowded, industrial, often blighted area

Central Islip (ī'slip) [after its location in the township + *Islip*, village in C England] suburb of New York City, on E Long Island: pop. 36,000

CENTRAL AMERICA

cen·tral·ism (-iz'm) *n.* the principle or system of centralizing power or authority, as of a government —**cen'tral·ist** *adj.*, *n.* —**cen'tral·is'tic** *adj.*

cen·tral·i·ty (sen tral'ə tē) *n.* **1.** the quality, state, or fact of being central; center position **2.** the tendency to remain at or near the center

cen·tral·ize (sen'trə līz') *vt.* **-ized', -iz'ing 1.** to make central; bring to or focus on a center; gather together **2.** to organize under one control; concentrate the power or authority of in a central organization —*vi.* to become centralized —**cen'tral·i·za'tion** *n.* —**cen'tral·iz'er** *n.*

Central Powers in World War I, Germany and Austria-Hungary, and their allies, Turkey and Bulgaria

Central Provinces and Berar *former name of* MADHYA PRADESH

☆**Central Standard Time** a standard time used in a zone which includes the central States of the U.S., corresponding to the mean local time of the 90th meridian west of Greenwich, England: it is six hours behind Greenwich time: see TIME, chart

cen·tre (sen'tər) *n.*, *vt.*, *vi.* **-tred, -tring** *chiefly Brit. sp. of* CENTER

cen·tri- (sen'tri) *same as* CENTRO-

cen·tric (sen'trik) *adj.* [Gr. *kentrikos* < *kentron:* see CENTER] **1.** in, at, or near the center; central **2.** of or having a center Also **cen'tri·cal** —**cen'tri·cal·ly** *adv.* —**cen·tric'i·ty** (-tris'ə tē) *n.*

-cen·tric (sen'trik) *a combining form meaning:* **1.** having a center or centers (of a specified kind or number) [*unicentric*] **2.** having (a specified thing) as its center [*geocentric*]

cen·trif·u·gal (sen trif'yə gəl, -ə gəl) *adj.* [< ModL. *centrifugus* (coined by Newton < CENTRI- + L. *fugere*, to flee) + -AL] **1.** moving or tending to move away from a center **2.** using or acted on by centrifugal force **3.** *Bot.* developing from the center outward, as certain flower clusters **4.** *Physiol.* conveying away from a center; efferent —☆*n.* a machine that uses or causes centrifugal movement —**cen·trif'u·gal·ly** *adv.*

centrifugal force the force tending to pull a thing outward when it is rotating rapidly around a center

cen·trif·u·gal·ize (-īz') *vt.* **-ized', -iz'ing** to subject to or as to the action of a centrifuge —**cen·trif'u·gal·i·za'tion** *n.*

cen·trif·u·ga·tion (sen trif'yə gā'shən, -ə gā'-) *n.* a being subjected to centrifugal action, esp. in a centrifuge

cen·tri·fuge (sen'trə fyōōj') *n.* [Fr. < ModL. *centrifugus:* see CENTRIFUGAL] a machine using centrifugal force to separate particles of varying density, as cream from milk,

or to draw off moisture, as in a washing machine —*vt.* **-fuged', -fug'ing** to subject to the action of a centrifuge

cen·tri·ole (sen'trē ōl') *n.* [altered (after CENTRI-) < G. *zentriol* < *zentrum* (< L. *centrum*), CENTER + -*ol*, dim. suffix < Fr. -*ole* < L. -*olum*] a small, dense structure in the middle of the centrosome: it doubles before mitosis and each part forms the center of an aster at mitosis

cen·trip·e·tal (sen trip'ət 'l) *adj.* [ModL. *centripetus* (coined by Newton < CENTRI- + L. *petere*, to seek, move toward) + -AL] **1.** moving or tending to move toward a center **2.** using or acted on by centripetal force **3.** *Bot.* developing inward toward the center, as certain flower clusters **4.** *Physiol.* conveying toward a center; afferent —**cen·trip'e·tal·ly** *adv.*

centripetal force the force tending to pull a thing inward when it is rotating rapidly around a center

cen·trist (sen'trist) *n.* [Fr. *centriste:* see CENTER & -IST] a member of a political party of the center, as in some European legislatures

cen·tro- (sen'trō, -trə) [< L. *centrum*, CENTER] *a combining form meaning* center [*centrosome*]

cen·tro·bar·ic (sen'trə bar'ik) *adj.* [< CENTRO- + Gr. *baros*, weight + -IC] having to do with the center of gravity

cen·troid (sen'troid) *n. same as* CENTER OF MASS

cen·tro·mere (sen'trə mir') *n.* [CENTRO- + -MERE] a small, nonstaining structure, usually near the center of a chromosome to which the spindle fiber attaches at mitosis — **cen'tro·mer'ic** (-mer'ik, -mir'-) *adj.*

cen·tro·some (-sōm') *n.* [CENTRO- + -SOME³] a very small body near the nucleus in most animal cells, consisting of a centriole surrounded by a centrosphere: in mitosis it divides and the two parts move to opposite poles of the dividing cell —**cen'tro·som'ic** (-säm'ik, -sōm'-) *adj.*

cen·tro·sphere (-sfir') *n.* [CENTRO- + SPHERE] **1.** *Biol.* the portion of the centrosome surrounding the centriole; center of an aster **2.** *Geol.* the central part of the earth

cen·trum (sen'trəm) *n.*, *pl.* **-trums, -tra** (-trə) [L.] **1.** a center **2.** *Anat.* the body of a vertebra

cen·tum (ken'təm, -toom) *adj.* [L., HUNDRED: so named because the initial velar stop illustrates the typical development in this group from the IE. palatal stop (i.e., IE. *k̑* → centum k, satem sh)] designating ol of the group of Indo European languages, including Germanic, Italic, Hellenic, and Celtic, in which a complicated but systematic development of the Indo-European palatals and labiovelars sets the group apart from the satem group

cen·tu·ple (sen'too pəl, sen tōōp''l, -tyōōp'-) *adj.* [Fr. < LL.(Ec.) *centuplus:* see CENT & DOUBLE] a hundred times as much or as many; hundredfold —*vt.* **-pled, -pling** to make centuple; increase a hundredfold

cen·tu·pli·cate (sen tōō'plə kāt', -tyōō'-; *for adj. & n., usually* -kit) *vt.* **-cat'ed, -cat'ing** to increase a hundredfold; centuple —*adj.*, *n.* hundredfold

cen·tu·ri·al (sen tyoor'ē əl, -toor'-) *adj.* [L. *centurialis*] having to do with a century

cen·tu·ri·on (-ən) *n.* [ME. *centurioun* < L. *centurio* (gen. *centurionis*) < *centuria:* see CENTURY] the commanding officer of an ancient Roman century

cen·tu·ry (sen'chər ē) *n.*, *pl.* **-ries** [L. *centuria* < *centum*, a hundred: see CENT] **1.** any period of 100 years, as from 1620 to 1720 **2.** a period of 100 years reckoned from a certain time, esp. from the beginning of the Christian Era [1801 A.D. through 1900 A.D. is the 19th *century* A.D., 400 B.C. through 301 B.C. is the 4th *century* B.C.] **3.** in ancient Rome *a)* a military unit, originally made up of 100 men *b)* a subdivision of the people made for voting purposes **4.** a series, group, or amount of a hundred: now rare except [Slang] 100 dollars

☆**century plant** a tropical American agave (*Agave americana*) having fleshy leaves and a tall stalk that bears greenish flowers only once after 10 to 30 years and then dies: mistakenly thought to bloom only once a century

ceorl (cherl, che'ôrl) *n.* [OE.: see CHURL] in early English history, a freeman of the lowest class, ranking below a thane

ceph·al- (sef'əl) *same as* CEPHALO-: used before a vowel

ceph·a·lad (sef'ə lad') *adv.* [CEPHAL- + L. *ad*, to] *Anat.*, *Zool.* toward the head, or anterior part of the body: opposed to CAUDAD

ce·phal·ic (sə fal'ik) *adj.* [L. *cephalicus* < Gr. *kephalikos* < *kephalē*, the head < IE. base *ghebhel-*, head, peak, whence GABLE, MHG. *gebel*, skull] **1.** of the head, skull, or cranium **2.** in, on, near, or toward the head —**ce·phal'i·cal·ly** *adv.*

-ce·phal·ic (sə fal'ik) *a combining form meaning* head or skull [*dolichocephalic*]

cephalic index a measure of the human head computed by dividing its maximum breadth by its maximum length and multiplying by 100: see BRACHYCEPHALIC, DOLICHOCEPHALIC, MESOCEPHALIC

ceph·a·lin (sef'ə lin) *n.* [CEPHAL- + -IN¹ (after cognate earlier G. *kephalin*)] a group of fatty materials containing phosphorus, found esp. in brain and nerve tissue

ceph·a·li·za·tion (sef'ə li zā'shən) *n.* [CEPHAL- + -IZA-TION] the tendency in the evolution of animal life for sensory organs, the nervous system, etc. to become concentrated or centralized in or near the head

ceph·a·lo- (sef′ə lə, -lō) [see CEPHALIC] *a combining form meaning* the head, skull, or brain [*cephalopod*]

ceph·a·lo·chor·date (sef′ə lə kôr′dāt) *adj.* [< ModL. *Cephalochordata,* name of the subphylum: see prec. & CHORDATE] of a group of small, fishlike chordates, including the amphioxus, or lancelet, that have a permanent notochord extending from the anterior to the posterior end —*n.* any animal of this group

ceph·a·lom·e·ter (sef′ə läm′ə tər) *n.* an instrument for measuring the head or skull; craniometer —**ceph′a·lom′e·try** (-trē) *n.*

Ceph·a·lo·ni·a (sef′ə lō′nē ə) largest of the Ionian Islands, off the W coast of Greece: 289 sq. mi.; pop. (with nearby islands) 46,000: Gr. name, KEFALLINIA

ceph·a·lo·pod (sef′ə lə päd′) *n.* [CEPHALO- + -POD] any of the highest class (Cephalopoda) of mollusks, having a distinct head with a beak, and muscular tentacles about the mouth, usually with suckers on them: the octopus, squid, and cuttlefish are typical

ceph·a·lo·tho·rax (sef′ə lə thôr′aks) *n.* the head and thorax united as a single part, in certain crustaceans and arachnids

ceph·a·lous (sef′ə ləs) *adj.* [CEPHAL- + -OUS] having a head

-ceph·a·lous (sef′əl əs) [see CEPHALIC] *a combining form meaning* -headed [*microcephalous*]

ceph·e·id (variable) (sef′ē id, sē′fē-) [< ff. + -ID] any of a class of stars whose light varies in brightness in regular periods: from the period-luminosity relation the distance of such a star can be determined

Ce·pheus (sē′fyo͞os, -fē əs) [L. < Gr. *Kēpheus*] 1. *Gr. Myth.* the husband of Cassiopeia and father of Andromeda: he was placed among the stars after his death 2. a N constellation near the north celestial pole

cer- (sir) *same as* CERO-: used before a vowel

ce·ra·ceous (si rā′shəs) *adj.* [< L. *cera* (< Gr. *kēros*), wax + -ACEOUS] waxy; waxlike

Ce·ram (si ram′) one of the Molucca Islands, in Indonesia: 6,622 sq. mi.

ce·ram·al (sə ram′əl) *n.* [CERAM(IC) + AL(LOY)] *same as* CERMET

ce·ram·ic (sə ram′ik) *adj.* [Gr. *keramikos* < *keramos,* potter's clay, pottery] 1. of or relating to pottery, earthenware, tile, porcelain, etc. 2. of ceramics —*n.* 1. [*pl., with sing. v.*] the art or work of making objects of baked clay, as pottery, earthenware, etc. 2. an object made of such materials

ce·ram·ist (sə ram′ist, ser′ə mist) *n.* an expert in ceramics; ceramic artist: also **ce·ram′i·cist** (-ə sist)

ce·rar·gy·rite (sə rär′jə rīt′) *n.* [< Gr. *keras,* HORN + *argyros,* silver + -ITE¹] silver chloride, AgCl, a native ore of silver; horn silver

ce·ras·tes (sə ras′tēz) *n.* [L. < Gr. *kerastēs,* horned (serpent) < *keras,* HORN] any of a genus (*Cerastes*) of poisonous African snakes, esp. a viper (*Cerastes cornutus*) with a hornlike spine above each eye; horned viper

ce·rate (sir′āt) *n.* [L. *ceratus,* pp. of *cerare,* to wax < *cera,* wax < Gr. *kēros,* wax] a thick ointment consisting of a fat, as oil or lard, mixed with wax, resin, and other, often medicinal, ingredients

ce·rat·ed (sir′āt id) *adj.* [< prec. + -ED] covered with wax; waxed

cer·a·to- (ser′ə tō, -tə) [< Gr. *keras* (gen. *keratos*), HORN] *a combining form meaning* horn, horny [*ceratodus*]: also, before a vowel, **cer·at-**

ce·rat·o·dus (si rat′ə dəs, ser′ə tō′dəs) *n.* [ModL. < prec. + -ODUS] 1. any of a genus (*Ceratodus*) of extinct lungfishes 2. *same as* BARRAMUNDA

cer·a·toid (ser′ə toid′) *adj.* [Gr. *keratoeidēs:* see CERATO- & -OID] hornlike in shape or hardness; horny

Cer·ber·us (sur′bər əs) [L. < Gr. *Kerberos*] *Gr. & Rom. Myth.* the three-headed dog guarding the gate of Hades —**Cer·be·re·an** (sər bir′ē ən) *adj.*

cer·ca·ri·a (sər kar′ē ə) *n., pl.* **-ri·ae** (-i ē′) [ModL. < Gr. *kerkos,* tail] the free-swimming larva of a parasitic trematode worm, having a forked tail

cer·cis (sur′sis) *n.* [ModL., name of the genus < Gr. *kerkis,* the Judas tree, aspen, lit., weaver's shuttle (orig., prob. a staff, rod), dim. < *kerkos,* a tail] any of a genus (*Cercis*) of shrubs and small trees of the legume family, native to N. America and Eurasia

cer·cus (sur′kəs) *n., pl.* **cer′ci** (-sī) [ModL. < Gr. *kerkos,* tail] either of a pair of usually jointed, feelerlike appendages at the hind end of the abdomen of many insects

cere (sir) *n.* [Fr. *cire* < L. *cera,* wax < Gr. *kēros,* wax] a waxy, often brightly colored, fleshy area at the base of the beak of some birds, as the parrot, eagle, hawk, etc.: it contains the nostrils —*vt.* cered, cer′ing to wrap in or as in a cerecloth

ce·re·al (sir′ē əl) *adj.* [< L. *Cerealis,* of Ceres, goddess of agriculture < IE. base *ker-,* to grow, cause to grow, whence Arm. *ser,* descent, generation, OHG. *hirso,* millet] of grain or the grasses producing grain —*n.* 1. any grain used for food, as wheat, oats, rice, etc. 2. any grass producing such grain ☆3. food made from grain, esp. breakfast food, as oatmeal or corn flakes

cer·e·bel·lum (ser′ə bel′əm) *n., pl.* **-lums, -la** (-lə) [L., dim. of *cerebrum,* the brain < IE. *keres-* < base *ker-,* top of the head: see HORN] the section of the brain behind and below the cerebrum: it consists of two lateral lobes and a middle lobe and functions as the coordinating center for muscular movement

cer·e·bral (ser′ə brəl, sə rē′brəl) *adj.* [Fr. *cérébral* < L. *cerebrum:* see prec.] 1. of the brain or the cerebrum 2. of, appealing to, or conceived by the intellect rather than the emotions; intellectual 3. *Phonet. same as* CACUMINAL —*n. Phonet.* a cacuminal sound —**cer·e′bral·ly** *adv.*

cerebral accident a disturbance of the blood supply to parts of the brain, causing unconsciousness, paralysis, etc.; stroke

cerebral hemisphere either of the two lateral halves of the cerebrum

cerebral palsy any of several disorders of the central nervous system resulting from brain damage, esp. before or during birth, and characterized by spastic paralysis, defective motor ability, etc.

cer·e·brate (ser′ə brāt′) *vi.* **-brat′ed, -brat′ing** [< L. *cerebrum* (see CEREBELLUM) + -ATE¹] to use one's brain; think —**cer′e·bra′tion** *n.*

cer·e·bro- (ser′ə brō′, sə rē′brō) [< L. *cerebrum:* see CEREBELLUM] *a combining form meaning* the brain (and); cerebrum (and) [*cerebrospinal*] Also, before a vowel, **cer·e·br-**

cer·e·bro·side (ser′ə brō sīd′) *n.* [CEREBR(O)- + -OS(E)¹ + -IDE] a lipide that contains galactose and is found normally in brain and nerve tissue

cer·e·bro·spi·nal (ser′ə brō spī′n'l, sə rē′brō-) *adj.* 1. of or affecting the brain and the spinal cord 2. designating that part of the nervous system comprising the brain and the spinal cord together with their cranial and spinal nerves

cerebrospinal fluid the clear liquid surrounding the brain and spinal cord and filling the cavities of the brain

cerebrospinal meningitis an acute inflammation of the membranes of the brain and spinal cord, caused by various microorganisms and characterized by fever, skin eruptions, etc.

cer·e·brum (ser′ə brəm, sə rē′brəm) *n., pl.* **-brums, -bra** (-brə) [L.: see CEREBELLUM] the upper, main part of the brain of vertebrate animals, consisting of two equal hemispheres (left and right): in man it is the largest part of the brain and is believed to control conscious and voluntary processes

cere·cloth (sir′klôth′) *n.* [formerly *cered cloth:* see CERE] cloth treated with wax or a similar substance, esp. one used formerly to wrap a dead person for burial

cer·e·ment (ser′ə mənt, sir′mənt) *n.* [Fr. *cirement:* see CERE] 1. a cerecloth; shroud 2. [*usually pl.*] any burial clothes

cer·e·mo·ni·al (ser′ə mō′nē əl, -mō′nyəl) *adj.* of, for, or consisting of ceremony; ritual; formal —*n.* 1. an established system of rites or formal actions connected with an occasion, as in religion; ritual 2. a rite or ceremony —**cer′e·mo′ni·al·ism** *n.* —**cer′e·mo′ni·al·ist** *n.* —**cer′e·mo′·ni·al·ly** *adv.*

cer·e·mo·ni·ous (-nē əs, -nyəs) *adj.* [Fr. *cérémonieux*] 1. ceremonial 2. full of ceremony 3. characterized by conventional usages or formality; very polite —**cer′e·mo′ni·ous·ly** *adv.* —**cer′e·mo′ni·ous·ness** *n.*

cer·e·mo·ny (ser′ə mō′nē) *n., pl.* **-nies** [ME. *cerimonie* < L. *caerimonia,* awe, reverent rite, ceremony] 1. a formal act or set of formal acts established by custom or authority as proper to a special occasion, such as a wedding, religious rite, etc. 2. the service or function at which such acts are performed 3. a conventionally courteous or polite act 4. behavior that follows rigid etiquette or a prescribed form 5. *a)* formality or formalities *b)* empty or meaningless formality, or an act suggesting this 6. [Obs.] portent; omen —**stand on ceremony** to behave with or insist on formality *SYN.*—**ceremony** refers to a formal, usually solemn, act established as proper to some religious or state occasion [*the ceremony* of launching a ship/; **rite** refers to the prescribed form for a religious practice [*burial rites*]; **ritual** refers to rites or ceremonies collectively, esp. to the rites of a particular religion [*the ritual* of voodooism/; **formality** suggests a conventional, often meaningless, act or custom, usually one associated with social activity [*the formalities* of polite conversation/

Ce·ren·kov radiation (chə ren′kôf) [after P. A. *Cerenkov* (1904–   ), Russ. physicist] radiation emitted when a charged particle travels through a medium at a speed greater than the speed of light through that medium

Ce·res (sir′ēz) [L.: see CEREAL] 1. *Rom. Myth.* the goddess of agriculture, daughter of Ops and Saturn: identified by the Greeks with Demeter 2. *Astron.* the first asteroid discovered (1801), and the largest (c. 480 mi. in diameter)

ce·re·us (sir′ē əs) *n.* [L., wax taper < *cera,* wax: so named from the shape of certain varieties] any of a genus (*Cereus*) of cactus, including a number of night-blooming varieties, native to the SW U.S. and Mexico

ce·ri·a (sir′ē ə) *n.* [< CERIUM] cerium dioxide, CeO₂, a white compound used as in ceramics

ce·ric (sir′ik, ser′-) *adj.* of or containing cerium, esp. with a valence of plus four

ce·rif·er·ous (sə rif′ər əs) *adj.* [< L. *cera,* wax + -FEROUS] producing wax

Ce·ri·go (che′rē gō′) *It. name of* CYTHERA

ce·rise (sə rēs′, -rēz′) *n., adj.* [Fr.: see CHERRY] bright red; cherry red

ce·rite (sir′īt) *n.* [CER(IUM) + -ITE¹] a native hydrous silicate of cerium and other closely related metals

ce·ri·um (sir'ē əm) *n.* [named (1803) after the asteroid *Ceres*] a gray, metallic chemical element, the most abundant of the rare-earth group: symbol, Ce; at. wt., 140.12; at. no., 58; sp. gr., 6.90; melt. pt., 804°C; boil. pt., 3470°C

cerium metals a series of closely related metals belonging to the rare-earth group and having atomic numbers from 57 to 63; lanthanum, cerium, praseodymium, neodymium, promethium, samarium, and europium

cer·met (sur'met) *n.* [CER(AMIC) + MET(AL)] a bonded mixture of ceramic material and a metal, that is tough and heat-resistant: used in gas turbines, nuclear reactor mechanisms, rocket motors, etc.

CERN [*Conseil Européen pour la Recherche Nucléaire*] a cooperative European nuclear research organization centered in Geneva, Switzerland

Cer·nǎ·u·ți (chər nə ōōts') *Romanian name of* CHERNOVTSY

cer·nu·ous (sur'nyoo wəs) *adj.* [L. *cernuus,* stooping, head down: for IE. base see CEREBELLUM] bending or hanging downward, as a flower or bud

ce·ro (sir'ō) *n., pl.* -ro, -ros: see PLURAL, II, D, 2 [Sp. *sierra* < L. *serra,* a saw] a large mackerel (*Scomberomorus cavalla*) of the S Atlantic

ce·ro- (sir'ə, ser'-) [< L. *cera* < Gr. *kēros,* wax] *a combining form meaning* wax

ce·rog·ra·phy (si räg'rə fē) *n.* [CERO- + -GRAPHY] the process of engraving on a wax-covered metal plate from which a printing surface is prepared by electrotyping

ce·ro·plas·tic (sir'ə pläs'tik) *adj.* [Gr. *kēroplastikos* < *kēros,* wax + *plassein,* to mold] 1. having to do with wax modeling 2. modeled in wax

ce·ro·plas·tics (-tiks) *n.pl.* [*with sing. v.*] the art of modeling in wax

ce·rot·ic (sə rät'ik) *adj.* [< L. *cerotum,* a wax salve < Gr. *kēroton* < *kēros,* wax + -IC] designating or of either of two fatty acids, $C_{26}H_{52}O_2$ or $C_{27}H_{54}O_2$, esters of which are found in beeswax and other waxes and oils

ce·ro·type (sir'ə tīp') *n.* [CERO- + -TYPE] a printing plate or a print made by cerography: also **ce'ro·graph'**

ce·rous (sir'əs) *adj.* of or containing cerium with a valence of three

Cer·ro de Pas·co (ser'rō de päs'kō) mining town in the mountains of WC Peru: pop. 23,000

cert. 1. certificate 2. certificated 3. certified

cer·tain (surt'n) *adj.* [ME. & OFr. < VL. *certanus* < L. *certus,* determined, fixed, orig. pp. of *cernere,* to distinguish, decide, orig., to sift, separate < IE. base *(s)ker-,* to cut, separate, sift, whence CRITIC, RIDDLE², G. *rein,* pure] 1. fixed, settled, or determined 2. sure (to happen, etc.); inevitable 3. not to be doubted; unquestionable [*a certain evidence*] 4. not failing; reliable; dependable [*a certain cure*] 5. controlled; unerring [*his certain aim*] 6. without any doubt; assured; sure; positive [*certain of his innocence*] 7. not named or described, though definite and perhaps known [*a certain person*] 8. some, but not very much; appreciable [*to a certain extent*] —*pron.* [*with pl. v.*] a certain indefinite number; certain ones (*of*) —SYN. see SURE —**for certain** as a certainty; without doubt

cer·tain·ly (-lē) *adv.* beyond a doubt; surely

cer·tain·ty (-tē) *n.* [ME. *certeinte* < OFr. *certaineté*] 1. the quality, state, or fact of being certain 2. *pl.* -ties anything certain; definite fact —**of a certainty** [Archaic] without a doubt; certainly

SYN.—**certainty** suggests a firm, settled belief or positiveness in the truth of something; **certitude** is sometimes distinguished from the preceding as implying an absence of objective proof, hence suggesting unassailable blind faith; **assurance** suggests confidence, but not necessarily positiveness, usually in something that is yet to happen [I have *assurance* of his continuing support]; **conviction** suggests a being convinced because of satisfactory reasons or proof and sometimes implies earlier doubt —ANT. doubt, skepticism

cer·tes (sur'tēz) *adv.* [ME. & OFr. < VL. *certas,* for L. *certo,* surely < *certus*: see CERTAIN] [Archaic] certainly; verily

cer·ti·fi·a·ble (sur'tə fī'ə b'l) *adj.* that can be certified — **cer·ti·fi'a·bly** (-blē) *adv.*

cer·tif·i·cate (sur tif'ə kit; *for v.* -kāt') *n.* [ME. & OFr. *certificat* < ML. *certificatum* < LL. *certificatus,* pp. of *certificare,* CERTIFY] a written or printed statement by which a fact is formally or officially certified or attested; specif., *a*) a document certifying that one has met specified requirements, as for teaching *b*) a document certifying ownership, a promise to pay, etc. —*vt.* -cat'ed, -cat'ing to attest or authorize by a certificate; issue a certificate to —**cer·tif'i·ca·tor** (-kāt'ər) *n.* —**cer·tif'i·ca·to'ry** (-kə tôr'ē) *adj.*

certificate of deposit a bank certificate acknowledging the receipt of a specified large sum of money in a special kind of time deposit drawing interest and requiring written notice for withdrawal

certificate of incorporation a legal document stating the name and purpose of a proposed corporation, the names of its incorporators, its stock structure, etc.

certificate of origin a certificate submitted by an exporter to those countries requiring it, listing goods to be imported and stating their place of origin

certificate of stock a certificate issued by a corporation to a subscriber as written evidence of his ownership of shares of stock

cer·ti·fi·ca·tion (sur'tə fi kā'shən) *n.* [Fr.] 1. a certifying or being certified 2. a certified statement

cer·ti·fied (sur'tə fīd') *adj.* 1. vouched for; guaranteed 2. having, or attested to by, a certificate

☆**certified check** a check drawn by a depositor on his checking account, which his bank then certifies to be genuine and on which it guarantees payment

☆**certified mail** 1. a postal service which provides, for a fee, a receipt to the sender of first-class mail and a record of its delivery 2. mail sent by this service: it is not insurable

☆**certified milk** milk guaranteed to have been produced according to certain regulations of an authorized medical milk commission

☆**certified public accountant** a public accountant certified by a State examining board as having met the requirements of State law

cer·ti·fy (sur'tə fī') *vt.* -fied', -fy'ing [ME. *certifien* < OFr. *certifier* < LL. *certificare* < L. *certus,* CERTAIN + *facere,* to make] 1. to declare (a thing) true, accurate, certain, etc. by formal statement, often in writing; verify; attest 2. to declare officially insane and committable to a mental institution ☆3. to guarantee the quality or worth of (a check, document, etc.); vouch for 4. to issue a certificate or license to 5. [Archaic] to assure; make certain —*vi.* to testify (*to*) —SYN. see APPROVE —**cer'ti·fi'er** *n.*

cer·ti·o·ra·ri (sur'shē ə rer'ē, -rär'-) *n.* [ME. < LL., to be made more certain: a word in the writ] *Law* a discretionary writ from a higher court to a lower one, or to a board or official with some judicial power, requesting the record of a case for review

cer·ti·tude (sur'tə tōōd', -tyōōd') *n.* [ME. & OFr. < LL. *certitudo*] 1. a feeling of absolute sureness or conviction 2. sureness; inevitability —SYN. see CERTAINTY

ce·ru·le·an (sə rōō'lē ən) *adj.* [L. *caeruleus,* prob. < *caelulum,* dim. of *caelum,* heaven] sky-blue; azure

ce·ru·men (sə rōō'mən) *n.* [< L. *cera,* wax, after ALBUMEN] a yellowish, waxlike substance secreted by glands in the canal of the external ear; earwax —**ce·ru'mi·nous** (-mə nəs) *adj.*

ce·ruse (sir'ōōs, sə rōōs') *n.* [ME. & OFr. < L. *cerussa* < ? Gr. *kēroessa,* waxlike < *kēros,* wax] 1. *same as* WHITE LEAD 2. a former cosmetic containing white lead

ce·rus·site (ser'ə sīt', sə rus'īt) *n.* [< L. *cerussa* (see prec.) + -ITE¹] native lead carbonate, $PbCO_3$, widely distributed in crystalline or massive form

Cer·van·tes (Sa·a·ve·dra) (ther vän'tes sä'ä ved'rä; E. sər van'tēz), **Mi·guel de** (mē gel' *the*) 1547–1616; Sp. novelist, poet, & playwright: author of *Don Quixote*

cer·vi·cal (sur'vi kəl) *adj.* [< L. *cervix* (gen. *cervicis*), the neck + -AL] *Anat.* of the neck or a cervix

cer·vi·ces (sur'və sēz', sər vī'-) *n. alt. pl. of* CERVIX

cer·vi·ci·tis (sur'və sīt'əs) *n.* [see -ITIS] inflammation of the cervix of the uterus

cer·vi·co- (sur'və kō') [< L. *cervix* (gen. *cervicis*), the neck] *a combining form meaning* cervical (and) [*cervicodorsal*]: also, before a vowel, **cer'vic-**

cer·vid (sur'vid) *adj.* [< ModL. *Cervidae,* name of the family < *Cervus,* the type genus (< L., a stag, deer < IE. *kerewos,* horned, a horned animal < base *ker-,* horn, tip, whence HORN) + -*idae:* see -ID] of the deer family of ruminants, having typically (in the male) antlers of solid bone, and including deer, elk, moose, caribou, etc.

Cer·vin, Mont (môn ser van') *Fr. name of the* MATTERHORN

cer·vine (sur'vin, -vin) *adj.* [L. *cervinus* < *cervus,* deer < IE. base *kerewos,* having horns < *ker-:* see HORN] of or like a deer

cer·vix (sur'viks) *n., pl.* -vi·ces' (sur'və sēz', sər vī'-), -vix·es (L., the neck] 1. the neck, esp. the back of the neck 2. a necklike part, as of the uterus, urinary bladder, etc.

Ce·sar·e·an, Ce·sar·i·an (si zer'ē ən) *adj., n. same as* CAESAREAN

ce·si·um (sē'zē əm) *n.* [ModL., orig., neut. of L. *caesius,* bluish-gray] a soft, silver-white, ductile, metallic chemical element, the most electropositive of all the elements: it ignites in air, reacts vigorously with water, and is used in photoelectric cells: symbol, Cs; at. wt., 132.905; at. no., 55; sp. gr., 1.873; melt. pt., 28.5°C; boil. pt., 670°C: a radioactive isotope (**cesium 137**) with a half-life of 37 years is a fission product and is used in cancer research, radiation therapy, etc.

Čes·ké Bu·dě·jo·vi·ce (ches'ke bōō'de yō'vit sə) city in SW Czechoslovakia, on the Vlatava River: pop. 69,000

Čes·ko·slo·ven·sko (ches'kō slō ven'skō) *Czech name of* CZECHOSLOVAKIA

ces·pi·tose (ses'pi tōs') *adj.* [< L. *caespes,* turf, grassy field + -OSE²] growing in dense clumps and forming a thick, turflike carpet: said of mosses, etc.

cess (ses) *n.* [prob. < ASSESS] in Ireland, an assessment; tax: now used only in *bad cess to,* meaning "bad luck to"

ces·sa·tion (se sā'shən) *n.* [L. *cessatio* < pp. of *cessare,* CEASE] a ceasing, or stopping, either forever or for some time

ces·sion (sesh′ən) *n.* [ME. & OFr. < L. *cessio* < *cessus*, pp. of *cedere*, to yield] a ceding or giving up (of rights, property, territory, etc.) to another

ces·sion·ar·y (sesh′ə ner′ē) *n., pl.* **-ar′ies** *Law* same as ASSIGNEE

cess·pit (ses′pit′) *n.* [CESS(POOL) + PIT²] a pit for garbage, excrement, etc.

cess·pool (-pōōl′) *n.* [< It. *cesso*, privy < L. *secessus*, place of retirement (in LL., privy, drain): see SECEDE] **1.** a cistern or deep hole in the ground, usually covered, to receive drainage or sewage from the sinks, toilets, etc. of a house **2.** a center of moral filth and corruption

ces·ta (ses′tə) *n.* [Sp., basket] the narrow, curved, basket-like racket strapped to the forearm in jai alai

‡**c'est-à-dire** (se tà dēr′) [Fr.] that is to say; namely

‡**c'est la vie** (se là vē′) [Fr.] that's life; such is life

ces·tode (ses′tōd) *n.* [CEST(US)¹ + -ODE²] any of a class (Cestoda) of parasitic flatworms, with a ribbonlike body and no mouth or intestinal canal; tapeworm —*adj.* of such a worm

ces·toid (-toid) *adj.* ribbonlike, as a tapeworm

ces·tus¹ (-təs) *n.* [L. *cestus* < Gr. *kestos*, a girdle] in ancient times, a woman's belt or girdle

ces·tus² (-təs) *n.* [L. *caestus* < *caedere*, to strike, beat] a contrivance of leather straps, sometimes weighted with metal, worn on the hand by boxers in ancient Rome

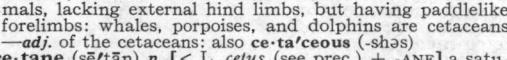

CESTUS

ce·su·ra (si zhoor′ə, -zyoor′ə) *n., pl.* **-ras, -rae** (-ē) *same as* CAESURA

ce·ta·cean (si tā′shən) *n.* [< L. *cetus*, large sea animal, whale < Gr. *kētos* + -ACE(A) + -AN] any of an order (Cetacea) of nearly hairless, fishlike water mammals, lacking external hind limbs, but having paddlelike forelimbs: whales, porpoises, and dolphins are cetaceans —*adj.* of the cetaceans: also **ce·ta′ceous** (-shəs)

ce·tane (sē′tān) *n.* [< L. *cetus* (see prec.) + -ANE] a saturated hydrocarbon of the methane series, $C_{16}H_{34}$, found as a colorless oil in petroleum

cetane number a number representing the ignition properties of diesel engine fuel oils, determined by the percentage of cetane that must be mixed with α- methylnaphthalene to produce the ignition quality of the fuel being tested: the higher the number, the better the ignition quality

‡**ce·te·ris pa·ri·bus** (set′ər is par′ə bəs, ket′-) [L., other things being equal] all else remaining the same

ce·tol·o·gy (si täl′ə jē) *n.* [< L. *cetus*, whale (see CETACEAN) + -LOGY] the branch of zoology that deals with whales — **ce·tol′o·gist** *n.* —**ce·to·log′i·cal** (sēt′ə läj′i k′l) *adj.*

Ce·tus (sēt′əs) [L., the whale] an equatorial constellation south of Pisces, containing the first known variable star, Mira

Ce·u·ta (thā′ōō tä; *E.* syoot′ə) Spanish seaport in NW Africa, an enclave in Morocco: pop. 76,000

Cé·vennes (sā ven′) mountain range in S France, west of the Rhone: highest peak, 5,755 ft.

ce·vi·tam·ic acid (sē′vī tam′ik, -vi-) [< C + VITAM(IN) + -IC] *same as* VITAMIN C

Cey·lon (sə län′, sā-, sē-) country on an island off the SE tip of India: a member of the Brit. Commonwealth: 25,332 sq. mi.; pop. 11,232,000; cap. Colombo —**Cey·lo·nese** (sel′ə nēz′, sā′lə-) *adj., n.*

Ceylon moss an East Indian seaweed (*Gracilaria lichenoides*) of the red algae, from which agar-agar is made

Cé·zanne (sā zàn′), **Paul** 1839–1906; Fr. impressionist & postimpressionist painter

Cf *Chem.* californium

cf. 1. *Bookbinding* calf **2.** *Baseball* center field; center fielder: also **cf 3.** [L. *confer*] compare

c/f *Bookkeeping* carried forward

C.F., c.f. cost and freight

C.F.I., c.f.i. cost, freight, and insurance

cfm, c.f.m. cubic feet per minute

cfs, c.f.s. cubic feet per second

CG, C.G. Coast Guard

cg, cg., cgm, cgm. centigram(s)

C.G., c.g. 1. center of gravity **2.** commanding general **3.** consul general

cgs, c.g.s., C.G.S. centimeter-gram-second

Ch. 1. Chaldean **2.** Chaldee **3.** China **4.** Chinese

Ch., ch. 1. chain **2.** champion **3.** chaplain **4.** chapter **5.** check **6.** chief **7.** child; children **8.** church

c.h., C.H. 1. courthouse **2.** customhouse

chab·a·zite (chab′ə zīt′) *n.* [Fr. *chabazie*, transliteration of a misspelling of Gr. *chalazie*, vocative of *chalazios*, a gem resembling a hailstone < *chalaza*, hailstone] *Mineralogy* a form of zeolite occurring in colorless to flesh-colored rhombohedral crystals

Cha·blis (shab′lē; *Fr.* shà blē′) *n.* a dry, white Burgundy wine, orig. from the region of Chablis, France

☆**cha-cha** (chä′chä) *n.* [AmSp., of echoic orig.] a modern ballroom dance of Latin-American origin, with a recurrent triplet beat —☆*vi.* to dance the cha-cha Also **cha′-cha′-cha′**

chac·ma (chak′mə) *n.* [< Hottentot *tchalikamma*] a large brownish-black baboon (*Papio comatus*) of South Africa

Cha·co (chä′kô) extensive lowland plain in Argentina, Paraguay, and Bolivia: c. 300,000 sq. mi.

CHACO

‡**cha·conne** (shä kôn′) *n.* [Fr. < Sp. *chacona*] **1.** a slow, solemn dance in 3/4 time, of Spanish or Moorish origin; later, a popular social dance in France in the 17th cent. and early 18th cent. **2.** music for this dance; later, either of two musical forms developed from it: *a)* a series of variations based on a short harmonic progression *b)* an expanded rondo form Both the dance and musical form are similar to the passacaglia

‡**cha·cun à son goût** (shà kën nà sôn gōō′) [Fr.] everyone to his own taste

Chad (chad) **1.** country in NC Africa, south of Libya: a member state of the French Community: c. 495,000 sq. mi.; pop. 3,307,000; cap. Fort Lamy **2. Lake**, lake at the juncture of the Chad, Niger, and Nigeria borders: 4,000– 8,000 sq. mi. (seasonal fluctuation) Fr. sp., TCHAD —*n.* a large group of Afro-Asiatic languages spoken in Nigeria and around Lake Chad, including Hausa —**Chad′i·an** *adj., n.*

cha·dor, cha·dar (chud′ər) *n. same as* CHUDDAR

Chad·wick (chad′wik) **1. George White·field** (hwīt′fēld′), 1854–1931; U.S. composer **2. Sir James**, 1891– ; Eng. physicist: discovered the neutron

Chaer·o·ne·a (ker′ə nē′ə) ancient Greek town in Boeotia: site of a battle (338 B.C.) that established Macedonian supremacy over the Greeks

chae·ta (kēt′ə) *n., pl.* **-tae** (-ē) [ModL. < Gr. *chaitē*, hair] a bristlelike projection, or seta, esp. on an annelid worm

chae·to- (kēt′ō, -ə) [< Gr. *chaitē*, hair] *a combining form meaning* hair or bristles: also, before a vowel, **chaet-**: see also SETI-

chae·tog·nath (kēt′əg nath′) *n.* [< ModL. *chaetognatha*, name of the group: see CHAETO- & -GNATHOUS] any of a small phylum (Chaetognatha) of very transparent, marine, wormlike animals having bristlelike jaws

chae·to·pod (kēt′ə päd′) *n.* [CHAETO- + -POD] *Zool.* any of a former class (Chaetopoda) of annelids, including the earthworms, leeches, etc.

chafe (chāf) *vt.* **chafed, chaf′ing** [ME. *chaufen* < OFr. *chaufer*, to warm < L. *calefacere*, to make warm < *calere*, to be warm + *facere*, to make] **1.** to rub so as to stimulate or make warm **2.** to wear away by rubbing **3.** to irritate or make sore by rubbing **4.** to annoy; irritate —*vi.* **1.** to rub (*on* or *against*) **2.** to be or become vexed, irritated, or impatient —*n.* **1.** an injury or irritation caused by rubbing **2.** [Archaic] a vexed or annoyed state —**chafe at the bit** to be impatient or vexed, as because of delay: originally said of horses

chaf·er (chāf′ər) *n.* [ME. < OE. *ceafor* (orig. sense prob. "devourer") < IE. base *ĝebh-*, jaw, mouth, devour, whence G. *kiefer*, jaw, Ir. *gob*, mouth, JOWL¹] any of various beetles (esp. family Scarabaeidae) that feed on plants, as the cockchafer, rose chafer, etc.

chaff (chaf, chäf) *n.* [ME. *chaf* < OE. *ceaf*; akin to MDu. *caf*, G. *kaff*] **1.** the husks of wheat or other grain separated in threshing or winnowing **2.** fine-cut hay or straw, used for fodder **3.** anything worthless **4.** tiny strips of metal foil dropped from aircraft in order to confuse enemy radar **5.** good-natured teasing or joking; banter **6.** *Bot.* the bracts that enclose the individual florets on the receptacles of certain composite heads —*vt., vi.* to tease or ridicule in a good-natured way

chaf·fer (chaf′ər) *n.* [ME. *chaffare*, merchandise, trade < OE. *ceap*, a purchase + *faru*, a journey: see CHEAP & FARE] **1.** [Obs.] trade; business **2.** [Archaic] a haggling over price or terms; bargaining —*vi.* **1.** [Now Rare] to haggle over price; bargain **2.** to chat idly —**chaf′fer·er** *n.*

chaf·finch (chaf′finch′) *n.* [OE. *ceaffinc*: see CHAFF & FINCH: it eats chaff and grain] a small European songbird (*Fringilla coelebs*), the male of which has a white patch on each shoulder: often kept in a cage as a pet

chaff·y (chaf′ē, chäf′-) *adj.* **chaff′i·er, chaff′i·est 1.** full of chaff **2.** like chaff; worthless

chaf·ing dish (chāf′in) [see CHAFE] a pan with a heating apparatus beneath it, to cook food at the table or to keep food hot

Cha·gall (shä gäl′), **Marc** 1887– ; Russ. painter in France and elsewhere

Cha·gas' disease (shäg′əs) [after Carlos *Chagas*, Braz. physician who identified it (1909)] a chronic wasting disease caused by a parasite (*Trypanosoma cruzi*) that is carried by insects: it affects large numbers of the rural population in Central and South America

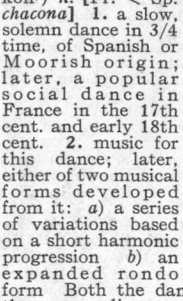

Cha·gres (chä′gres) river in Panama and the Canal Zone: a dam on this river forms Gatun Lake

cha·grin (shə grin′; *Brit.* -grēn′) *n.* [Fr., grief, sorrow, vexation, prob. < Norm. *chagreiner*, to become gloomy (said of the weather) < OFr. *graignier*, to sorrow < *graim*, sorrowful < Gmc. *gram*, sorrow, trouble] a feeling of embarrassment and annoyance because one has failed or been disappointed; mortification —*vt.* **-grined′**, **-grin′ing** [Fr. *chagriner*] to cause to feel chagrin; embarrass and annoy; mortify: usually in the passive voice

chain (chān) *n.* [ME. & OFr. *chaine* < L. *catena* < IE. base *kat-*, to twist, twine, whence prob. OE. *heathor*, confinement] **1.** a flexible series of joined links, usually of metal, used to pull, confine, etc. or to transmit power **2.** *same as* TIRE CHAIN **3.** [*pl.*] *a*) bonds, shackles, etc. *b*) anything that binds, ties, or restrains [*chains* of love] *c*) captivity; bondage **4.** any chainlike ornament, badge, etc. **5.** a chainlike measuring instrument, or its measure of length; specif., *a*) a surveyor's (or Gunter's) chain (100 links or 66 feet) *b*) an engineer's chain (100 links or 100 feet) **6.** a series of things connected causally, logically, physically, etc. [*chain* of events, mountain *chain*] ☆**7.** a number of stores, restaurants, etc. owned by one company **8.** *Chem.* a linkage of atoms in a molecule: see OPEN CHAIN, CLOSED CHAIN —*vt.* **1.** to fasten or shackle with chains **2.** to hold down, restrain, confine, etc. —*SYN.* see SERIES

☆**chain gang** a gang of prisoners chained together, as when working

chain letter a letter to be circulated among many people by being copied, or, sometimes, added to, and then passed to others with a request to do the same

☆**chain lightning** lightning that zigzags across the sky

chain mail flexible armor made of joined metal links

☆**chain·man** (-mən) *n.*, *pl.* **-men** (-mən) a surveyor's assistant who measures distances with a tape measure or surveyor's chain: chainmen work in pairs

chain-re·act (-rē akt′) *vi.* to be involved in or subjected to a chain reaction

☆**chain-re·act·ing pile** (-rē ak′tin) *same as* NUCLEAR REACTOR

chain reaction 1. a self-sustaining series of chemical or nuclear reactions in which the products of the reaction contribute directly to the propagation of the process: it can be started by light, an electric spark, sodium vapor, bombardment with alpha particles from radium, etc. **2.** any sequence of events, each of which results in, or has an effect on, the following

☆**chain saw** a portable power saw with an endless chain that carries cutting teeth

chain shot cannon shot consisting of two balls or half balls connected by a chain, formerly used in naval warfare to destroy masts, sails, etc.

chain-smoke (-smōk′) *vt.*, *vi.* **-smoked′**, **-smok′ing** to smoke (cigarettes) one right after the other, often using each to light the next —**chain smoker**, **chain′-smok′er** *n.*

chain stitch a fancy stitch in which the loops are connected in a chainlike way, as in crocheting —**chain′-stitch′** *vt.*

☆**chain store** any of a chain of retail stores

chair (cher) *n.* [ME. & OFr. *chaiere* < L. *cathedra*: see CATHEDRA] **1.** a piece of furniture for one person to sit on, having a back and, usually, four legs **2.** a seat of authority or dignity **3.** the position of a player in an instrumental section of a symphony orchestra **4.** an important or official position, as a professorship or chairmanship **5.** a person who presides over a meeting; chairman [address your remarks to the *chair*] **6.** *same as* SEDAN CHAIR ☆**7.** *same as* ELECTRIC CHAIR —*vt.* **1.** to place in a chair; seat **2.** to place in authority **3.** to preside over as chairman **4.** [Brit.] to carry (a person) in public triumph on, or as though on, a chair —**take the chair** to preside as chairman

☆**chair car** a railroad car with individual chairs; parlor car: distinguished from COACH, SLEEPING CAR, etc.

☆**chair·lift** (-lift′) *n.* a number of seats suspended from a power-driven endless cable, used esp. to carry skiers up a mountain slope

chair·man (-mən) *n.*, *pl.* **-men** (-mən) **1.** a person who presides at a meeting or heads a committee, board, etc. **2.** a man whose work is to carry or wheel people in a chair —*vt.* **-maned** or **-manned**, **-man·ing** or **-man·ning** to preside over as chairman —**chair′man·ship′** *n.* —**chair′wom′an** *n.fem.*, *pl.* **-wom′en**

chaise (shāz) *n.* [Fr., var. of *chaire*, CHAIR] **1.** any of several kinds of lightweight carriage, some with a collapsible top, having two or four wheels and drawn by one or two horses **2.** *same as* POST CHAISE **3.** *same as* CHAISE LONGUE

chaise longue (shāz′ lôɴ′; *often also* lounj′ —*see next entry*) *pl.* **chaise** (or **chaises**) **longues** (shāz′ lôɴz′; lounj′jəz) [Fr., lit., long chair] a couchlike chair with a support for the back of the sitter and a seat long enough to support his outstretched legs

chaise lounge (lounj) *pl.* **chaise lounges** [by folk etym. < prec.] *same as* CHAISE LONGUE

cha·la·za (kə lā′zə) *n.*, *pl.* **-zae** (-zē), **-zas** [ModL. < Gr. *chalaza*, hail < IE. base *gheled-*, ice, whence Per. *žāla*, hail, OSlav. *žlědica*, sleet] **1.** either of the spiral bands of dense

albumen extending from the yolk toward the lining membrane at each end of a bird's egg and serving to keep the yolk suspended near the center of the albumen **2.** *Bot.* the basal end of an ovule where the seed coats and the nucellus join —**cha·la′zal** *adj.*

chal·can·thite (kal kan′thīt) *n.* [< L. *chalcanthum* < Gr. *kalkanthon*, vitriol (< *kalkos*, copper + *anthos*, flower) + -ITE[1]] a native crystalline copper sulfate

Chal·ce·don (kal′sə dän′) ancient Greek city on the Bosporus, opposite Byzantium —**Chal′ce·do′ni·an** (-dō′nē ən) *adj.*

chal·ced·o·ny (kal sed′'n ē, kal′sə dō′nē) *n.*, *pl.* **-nies** [ME. & OFr. *calcedoine* < LL. (Vulgate) *calcedonius*, used to transl. Gr. *chalkēdōn* (only in Rev. 21:19), a precious stone < ?] a kind of quartz that has the luster of wax and is variously colored, usually grayish or milky: it comprises onyx, agate, sard, cat's-eye, jasper, carnelian, and chrysoprase

chal·cid (kal′sid) *n.* [< ModL. *Chalcis* (gen. *Chalcidis*), name of the typical genus < Gr. *chalkos*, copper: so named because of their metallic color] any of a large family (Chalcididae) of very small wasps, either four-winged or wingless, many of whose larvae are parasitic on the eggs, larvae, or pupae of other insects: also **chalcid fly**, **chalcid wasp** —*adj.* of these insects

Chal·cid·i·ce (kal sid′ə sē′) peninsula in NE Greece: Gr. name, KHALKIDIKI

Chal·cis (kal′sis) seaport in E Greece, on WC Evvoia island: pop. 24,000: Gr. name, KHALKIS: cf. NEGROPONTE

chal·co- (kal′kə, -kō) [< Gr. *chalkos*, copper, brass] a combining form meaning copper or brass [*chalcocite*]

chal·co·cite (kal′kə sīt′) *n.* [see prec.] native cuprous sulfide, Cu_2S, a dark-colored mineral with a metallic luster: it is an important copper ore

chal·cog·ra·phy (kal käg′rə fē) *n.* [ML. *chalcographia*, printing: see CHALCO- & -GRAPHY] the art of engraving on copper or brass —**chal′co·graph′ic** *adj.*

chal·co·py·rite (kal′kə pī′rīt) *n.* [CHALCO- + PYRITE] a yellow sulfide of copper and iron, $CuFeS_2$, an important copper ore

Chal·da·ic (kal dā′ik) *adj.*, *n.* *same as* CHALDEAN

Chal·de·a, Chal·dae·a (kal dē′ə) **1.** ancient province of Babylonia, in the region of the lower courses of the Tigris and Euphrates rivers **2.** Babylonia: so called during Chaldean supremacy, c. 6th cent. B.C.

CHALDEA

Chal·de·an, Chal·dae·an (-dē′ən) *adj.* [L. *Chaldaeus* < Gr. *Chaldaios*] **1.** of Chaldea, its people, their language, or culture **2.** [from the fact that astrology and magic flourished in Chaldea] having to do with astrology or occult lore —*n.* **1.** a native or inhabitant of Chaldea; member of a Semitic people related to the Babylonians **2.** an astrologer or sorcerer **3.** the Semitic language of the Chaldeans

Chal·dee (kal′dē, kal dē′) *adj.*, *n.* *same as* CHALDEAN

chal·dron (chôl′drən) *n.* [ME. < OFr. *chauderon*: see CALDRON] an old unit of dry measure variously equal to 32, 36, or more bushels, now used in England only for measuring coal or coke and equal to 36 bushels

cha·let (sha lā′, shal′ā) *n.* [Swiss-Fr., prob. dim. of OFr. *chasel*, farmhouse < VL. *casalis*, belonging to a house < L. *casa*, a house, cabin] **1.** a herdsman's hut or cabin in the Swiss Alps **2.** *a*) a type of Swiss house, built of wood with balconies and overhanging eaves *b*) any house, cottage, lodge, etc. built in this style

Cha·lia·pin (shä lyä′pin), **Feo·dor I·va·no·vich** (fyô′dôr ē vä′nō vich) 1873–1938; Russ. operatic basso

chal·ice (chal′is) *n.* [ME. & OFr. *chalice* < L. *calix*, a cup] **1.** a cup; goblet **2.** the cup for the wine of Holy Communion **3.** a cup-shaped flower

chal·iced (-ist) *adj.* cup-shaped: said of a flower

chalk (chôk) *n.* [ME. < OE. *cealc* < L. *calx* (gen. *calcis*) limestone, chalk] **1.** a white, gray, or yellowish limestone that is soft and easily pulverized: it is composed mainly of minute sea shells **2.** any substance like chalk in color, texture, etc. **3.** a piece of chalk, often colored, used for drawing, writing on a blackboard, etc. **4.** a mark or line made with chalk **5.** [Brit.] a score or tally, as in a game or as of credit given —*adj.* **1.** made or drawn with chalk ☆**2.** [Slang] *Horse Racing a*) favored to win *b*) betting on favorites only —*vt.* **1.** [Brit.] to treat with chalk; lime or fertilize (soil) **2.** to rub or smear with chalk; specif., to rub chalk on the tip of (a billiard cue) **3.** to make pale **4.** to write, draw, or mark with chalk —*vi.* to become chalky or powdery, as a

painted surface —**chalk out 1.** to mark out as with chalk
2. to outline; plan —**chalk up 1.** to score, get, or achieve
2. to charge or credit —**not by a long chalk** [Brit. Colloq.]
not by any means; not at all —**walk a chalk line** [Colloq.]
to behave with strict propriety or obedience

☆**chalk·board** (chôk′bôrd′) *n.* a blackboard, esp. a light-colored one

chalk·stone (-stōn′) *n. same as* TOPHUS

☆**chalk talk** a lecture accompanied with diagrams, illustrations, etc. drawn in chalk on a blackboard

chalk·y (-ē) *adj.* **chalk′i·er, chalk′i·est 1.** of, containing, or covered with chalk **2.** like chalk in color or texture —**chalk′i·ness** *n.*

chal·lah (hä′lə) *n. same as* HALLAH

chal·lenge (chal′ənj) *n.* [ME. & OFr. *chalenge,* accusation, claim, dispute < L. *calumnia,* false accusation: see CALUMNY] **1.** a demand for identification [a sentry gave the *challenge*] **2.** a calling into question; a demanding of proof, explanation, etc. [a *challenge* of the premises of an argument] **3.** a call or dare to take part in a duel, contest, etc. **4.** anything, as a demanding task, that calls for special effort or dedication ☆**5.** an exception to a vote or to someone's right to vote **6.** *Law* a formal objection or exception to a person who has been chosen as a prospective juror —*vt.* **-lenged, -leng·ing 1.** to call to a halt for identification **2.** *a*) to call to account *b*) to make objection to; call into question **3.** to call or dare to take part in a duel, contest, etc.; defy **4.** to call for; make demands on [to *challenge* the imagination] ☆**5.** to take exception to (a vote) as not valid or (a prospective voter) as not qualified to vote **6.** to take formal exception to (a prospective juror) —*vi.* to make, issue, or offer a challenge —**chal′lenge·a·ble** *adj.* —**chal′leng·er** *n.*

chal·lis, chal·lie (shal′ē) *n.* [< ?] a soft, lightweight fabric of wool, cotton, etc., usually printed with a design

chal·one (kal′ōn) *n.* [Gr. *chalōn,* prp. of *chalan,* to slacken] an internal secretion that reduces, restrains, or arrests the activity of various organs of the body

Châ·lons-sur-Marne (shä lōn′sür märn′) city in NE France, on the Marne River: scene of Attila's defeat (451 A.D.): pop. 42,000: also **Châ·lons′**

Cha·lon-sur-Saône (shä lōn′sür sōn′) city in EC France, on the Saône River: pop. 44,000: also **Cha·lon′**

chal·u·meau (shal′yoo mō′) *n.* [Fr. < OFr. *chalemel* < L. *calemellus,* dim. of *calamus,* reed: see CALAMUS] **1.** an obsolete single-reed wind instrument, forerunner of the clarinet **2.** the lowest register of the modern clarinet

cha·lutz (khä loots′) *n., pl.* **-lutz·im′** (-loot tsēm′) *same as* HALUTZ

cha·lyb·e·ate (kə lib′ē ət, -āt′) *adj.* [< L. *chalybs* < Gr. *chalybs,* steel < *Chalybes,* name of a people in Pontus, noted for their steel] **1.** containing salts of iron **2.** tasting like iron —*n.* a chalybeate liquid or medicine

cham (kam) *n. archaic var. of* KHAN[1]

cha·made (shə mäd′) *n.* [Fr. < Port. *chamada* < *chamar* < L. *clamare,* to shout] [Archaic] *Mil.* a signal for a parley or retreat, sounded on a drum or trumpet

Cha·mae·le·on (kə mēl′yən, -mē′lē ən) *n.* [L., see CHAMELEON] a S constellation near the south celestial pole

cham·ae·phyte (kam′ē fit′) *n.* [< ModL. *chamae-,* low, on the ground (< Gr. *chamai:* see CHAMELEON) + -PHYTE] a perennial plant whose winter buds are near the ground level

cham·ber (chām′bər) *n.* [ME. *chambre* < OFr. *chambre, cambre* < LL. *camera,* a chamber, room (in L., a vault): see CAMERA] **1.** *a*) a room in a house, esp. a bedroom *b*) a reception room in an official residence **2.** [*pl.*] [Brit.] a suite of rooms used by one person **3.** [*pl.*] a judge's office located near the courtroom **4.** an assembly hall **5.** a legislative or judicial body or division [the *Chamber* of Deputies] **6.** a council or board [a *chamber* of commerce] **7.** an enclosed space in the body of a plant or animal **8.** any enclosed space; compartment; specif., the part of a gun that holds the charge, or any of the compartments for cartridges in the cylinder of a revolver —*vt.* to provide a chamber or chambers for; put into a chamber —**cham′bered** *adj.*

chamber concert a concert of chamber music

cham·ber·lain (chām′bər lin) *n.* [ME. *chaumberlein* < OFr. *chamberlenc* < OHG. *chamarlinc* < *chamara, kamara* (< L. *camera*) + dim. suffix *-linc:* see CAMERA + -LING[1]] **1.** orig., the bedchamber attendant of a ruler or lord **2.** an officer in charge of the household of a ruler or lord; steward **3.** a high official in certain royal courts **4.** [Brit.] a treasurer, as of a municipality **5.** *R.C.Ch.* any of several high officials, as an honorary attendant on the Pope

Cham·ber·lain (chām′bər lin) **1. Sir (Joseph)** Austen, 1863–1937; Brit. statesman **2. Joseph,** 1836–1914; Brit. statesman: father of *prec.* & *ff.* **3. (Arthur) Neville,** 1869–1940; Brit. statesman; prime minister (1937–40)

Cham·ber·lin (chām′bər lin), **Thomas Chrow·der** (krou′dər) 1843–1928; U.S. geologist

cham·ber·maid (chām′bər mād′) *n.* a woman whose work is taking care of bedrooms, as in hotels

chamber music music for performance by a small group, as a string quartet, orig. for small audiences

chamber of commerce an association established to further the business interests of its community

chamber pot a portable container kept in a bedroom and used as a toilet

☆**cham·bray** (sham′brā) *n.* [var. of CAMBRIC] a smooth

fabric of cotton, made by weaving white or unbleached threads across a colored warp: used for dresses, shirts, etc.

cha·me·le·on (kə mēl′yən, -mē′lē ən) *n.* [ME. *camelioun* < L. *chamaeleon* < Gr. *chamaileōn* < *chamai,* on the ground + *leōn,* lion] **1.** any of various Old World lizards (family Chamaeleontidae), with an angular head, prehensile tail, eyes that move independently of each other, the ability to change skin color rapidly, and a long, agile tongue for catching prey **2.** any of various superficially similar lizards that can change the color of their skin, as the American chameleon (*Anolis carolinensis*) **3.** a changeable or fickle person—**cha·me·le·on·ic** (kə mē′lē än′ik) *adj.*

CHAMELEON
(to 24 in. long, including tail)

cham·fer (cham′fər) *n.* [Fr. *chanfrein* < OFr. *chanfraindre* < *chant fraindre* < L. *cantum frangere:* see CANT[2] & FRAGILE] a beveled edge or corner, esp. one cut at a 45° angle —*vt.* **1.** to cut a chamfer on; bevel **2.** to make a groove or fluting in

cham·fron, cham·frain (cham′frən) *n.* [Fr. *chanfrein* < OFr. *chaufrain,* snaffle, chamfron < *chafresner,* to fasten rein or bridle on a horse < L. *caput,* the HEAD + *frenum,* a bridle, reins] the headpiece of the armor worn by war horses in medieval times

cham·ois (sham′ē) *n., pl.* **cham′ois** [Fr. < VL. *camox* < a native Alpine word of IE. orig.] **1.** a small, goatlike antelope (*Rupicapra rupicapra*) of the mountains of Europe and the Caucasus, having straight horns with the tips bent backward **2.** *a*) a soft leather made from its skin or from the skin of sheep, deer, goats, etc. *b*) a piece of this leather, used as a polishing cloth: also **cham·my** (sham′ē) —*adj.* **1.** made of chamois **2.** yellowish-brown —*vt.* **cham′oised** (-ēd), **cham′ois·ing** (-ē in) to polish with a chamois skin

CHAMOIS
(30–32 in. high at shoulder)

cham·o·mile (kam′ə mīl′, -mēl′) *n.* [ME. *camomille* < OFr. *camemile* < L. *chamomilla* < Gr. *chamaimēlon,* earth apple < *chamai,* on the ground + *mēlon,* apple] any plant of two genera (*Anthemis* and *Matricaria*) of the composite family, with strong-smelling foliage; esp., a plant (*Anthemis nobilis*) whose dried, daisylike flower heads have been used in a medicinal tea

Cha·mo·nix (shä mō nē′) valley in E France, north of Mont Blanc: a resort area of the Fr. Alps

Cha·mor·ro (chä môr′ō) *n.* **1.** *pl.* **-ros** a member of one of the native tribes of Guam and the Mariana Islands **2.** their Indonesian language

champ[1] (champ) *vt.* [earlier *cham;* prob. echoic] **1.** to chew hard and noisily; munch **2.** [Scot.] to crush or mash —*n.* the act of champing —**champ at the bit 1.** to bite upon its bit repeatedly and restlessly: said of a horse **2.** to show impatience at restraint; be restless

☆**champ[2]** (champ) *n.* [Slang] a champion

cham·pac, cham·pak (cham′pak, chum′pək) *n.* [Hindi *champak* < Sans. *champaka*] an East Indian tree (*Michelia champaca*) of the magnolia family, with fragrant, yellow flowers

Cham·pagne (shän pän′y′; E. sham pān′) region and former province of NE France

cham·pagne (sham pān′) *n.* **1.** orig., any of various wines produced in Champagne, France **2.** *a*) now, any effervescent white wine made there or elsewhere: regarded as a symbol of luxurious living *b*) the typical color of such wine; pale, tawny yellow or greenish yellow

Cham·paign (sham pān′) [after a county in Ohio: so called from the level lands there: see ff.] city in EC Ill.: pop. 57,000

CHAMPAGNE

cham·paign (sham pān′) *n.* [ME. *champain* < OFr. *champaigne:* see CAMPAIGN] a broad plain; flat, open country —*adj.* of or like a champaign

cham·per·ty (cham′pər tē) *n., pl.* **-ties** [ME. *champartie* < OFr. *champart,* the lord's share in the crop of a tenant's land < L. *campi* pars < *campi,* gen. of *campus,* a field + *pars,* a part] *Law* an act by which a person not concerned in a lawsuit makes a bargain with one of the litigants to

help maintain the costs of the suit in return for a share of any proceeds: illegal in most States —**cham′per·tous** (-təs) *adj.*

cham·pi·gnon (sham pin′yən; *Fr.* shän pē nyôn′) *n.* [Fr., ult. < LL. *campania*, field: see CAMPAIGN] an edible mushroom, esp. the meadow mushroom

Cham·pi·gny-sur-Marne (shän pē nyē′sür märn′) city in N France, on the Marne: suburb of Paris: pop. 58,000

cham·pi·on (cham′pē ən) *n.* [ME. & OFr. (? via Gmc. *kampjo) < LL. *campio*, gladiator < L. *campus*, a field, place for games] 1. a valiant fighter 2. a person who fights for another or for a cause; defender; protector; supporter [a *champion* of the oppressed] 3. a winner of first place or first prize in a competition —*adj.* winning or capable of winning first place; excelling over all others —*vt.* 1. to fight for; defend; support 2. [Obs.] to challenge to a fight

cham·pi·on·ship (-ship′) *n.* 1. the act of championing; advocacy or defense 2. the position or title of a champion

Cham·plain (sham plān′), Lake [after the ff.] lake between N.Y. and Vt.: 125 mi. long

Cham·plain (sham plān′; *Fr.* shän plan′), **Samuel de** 1567–1635; Fr. explorer: founded Quebec (1608)

‡**champ·le·vé** (shän lə vā′) *adj.* [Fr.] designating or of a kind of enamel work in which furrows or hollows cut in a metal surface, usually copper, are filled with vitreous powders and then fired —*n.* champlevé enamel

Cham·pol·lion (shän pô lyôn′), **Jean Fran·çois** (zhän′ frän swä′) 1790–1832; Fr. Egyptologist

‡**Champs É·ly·sées** (shän zā lē zā′) [Fr., lit., Elysian fields] famous and fashionable avenue in Paris

Chan., Chanc. 1. Chancellor 2. Chancery

chan. channel

chance (chans, chäns) *n.* [ME. *chaunce* < OFr. *cheance* < ML. *cadentia*, that which falls out < L. *cadens*, prp. of *cadere*, to fall: see CASE¹] 1. the happening of events without apparent cause, or the apparent absence of cause or design; fortuity; luck [to leave things to *chance*] 2. an unpredictable event or accidental happening 3. a risk or gamble 4. a ticket in a lottery or raffle 5. an advantageous or opportune time or occasion; opportunity [you'll have a *chance* to go] 6. a possibility or probability [there is little *chance* of success] 7. [Archaic] a mishap, mischance ☆8. *Baseball* a fielding opportunity, esp. one on which a fielder is credited with a put-out or assist, or charged with an error —*adj.* happening by chance; accidental [a *chance* encounter] —*vi.* **chanced, chanc′ing** 1. to have the fortune, good or bad (to) 2. [Archaic] to happen by chance —*vt.* to leave to chance; risk [let's *chance* it] —SYN. see HAPPEN, RANDOM —**by chance** 1. as it may happen; perchance 2. accidentally —**chance on** (or **upon**) to find or meet by chance —**on the** (or **off**) **chance** relying on the (remote) possibility; in case

chance·ful (-fəl) *adj.* 1. eventful 2. [Archaic] *a*) dependent on chance *b*) risky

chan·cel (chan′s'l, chän′-) *n.* [ME. *chauncel* < OFr. *chancel* < LL. *cancellus* < L. *cancelli*, pl., lattices: see CANCEL] the part of a church around the altar, usually at the east end, reserved for the use of the clergy and the choir: it is sometimes set off by a railing or screen

chan·cel·ler·y (chan′sə lə rē, chän′-; -slə rē) *n., pl.* **-ler·ies** [ME. & OFr. *chancelerie* < ML. *cancellaria*] 1. the rank or position of a chancellor 2. a chancellor's office or the building that houses it 3. the office of an embassy or consulate Also sp. **chan′cel·lor·y**

chan·cel·lor (-lər) *n.* [ME. & OFr. *chanceler* < LL. *cancellarius*, keeper of the barrier, secretary: so called from the lattice behind which he worked: see CANCEL] 1. formerly, an official secretary to a nobleman or, esp., a king 2. [Rare] the chief secretary of an embassy or consulate 3. [*usually* C-] any of several high officials in the British government, sometimes with judicial powers 4. the title of the president or a high executive officer in some universities 5. the prime minister in certain countries ☆6. a chief judge of a court of chancery or equity in some States of the U.S. 7. *Anglican Church* an archdeacon or lay officer for legal affairs of a diocese 8. *R.C.Ch.* the title of the priest in charge of a diocesan chancery —**chan′cel·lor·ship′** *n.*

Chancellor of the Exchequer the minister of finance in the British government, a member of the Cabinet

Chan·cel·lors·ville (chan′sə lərz vil′) [after a family name] hamlet in NE Va.: site of a Civil War battle (May, 1863) won by Confederate forces

chance-med·ley (chans′med′lē, chäns′-) *n.* [lit., mixed chance: see CHANCE & MEDLEY] 1. accidental homicide; esp., a killing in self-defense during a sudden fight 2. haphazard action

chan·cer·y (chan′sər ē, chän′-) *n., pl.* **-cer·ies** [ME. *chancerie*, var. of *chancelerie*: see CHANCELLERY] 1. a division of the High Court of Justice in England and Wales, presided over by the Lord High Chancellor of England 2. a court of equity 3. the laws, practice, and proceedings of a court of equity; equity 4. a court of record; office of public archives 5. a chancellery (senses 2 & 3) 6. *R.C.Ch.* the diocesan office that has custody of certain documents, performs secretarial services for the bishop, etc. —**in chancery** 1. in process of litigation in a court of equity 2.

in an awkward or helpless situation 3. *Wrestling* with the head held firmly between an opponent's arm and his chest

chan·cre (shaŋ′kər) *n.* [Fr.: see CANCER] a venereal sore or ulcer; primary lesion of syphilis —**chan′crous** (-krəs) *adj.*

chan·croid (-kroid) *n.* [CHANCR(E) + -OID] a nonsyphilitic venereal ulcer, usually on or about the genitals, caused by a bacterium (*Hemophilus ducreyi*): also called **soft chancre**

chanc·y (chan′sē, chän′-) *adj.* **chanc′i·er, chanc′i·est** 1. risky; uncertain 2. [Scot.] bringing good luck

chan·de·lier (shan′də lir′) *n.* [Fr. < OFr. *chandelabre* < L. *candelabrum* < *candela*, CANDLE] a lighting fixture hanging from a ceiling, with branches for several candles, electric bulbs, etc.

chan·delle (shän del′) *n.* [Fr., lit., CANDLE] a quick, simultaneous climb and turn made by an airplane, in which the momentum of the airplane increases the rate of climb —*vi.* to make a chandelle

Chan·der·na·gor, Chan·der·na·gore (chun′dər nə gôr′) port in NE India, near Calcutta: former Fr. dependency: pop. 50,000: also **Chan·dar·na·gar** (chun′dər nug′ər)

Chan·di·garh (chun′dē gər) city (and a territory) in N India; capital of Punjab and interim capital of Hariana: pop. 89,000

chan·dler (chan′dlər, chän′-) *n.* [ME. *chandeler* < OFr. *chandelier* < *chandoile* (< L. *candela*), CANDLE] 1. a maker or seller of candles 2. a retailer of supplies, equipment, etc. of a certain kind [ship *chandler*]

chan·dler·y (-ē) *n., pl.* **-dler·ies** 1. a warehouse or storeroom for candles and other small wares 2. the merchandise, business, or warehouse of a chandler

Cha·nel (shə nel′) *adj.* [after Gabrielle *Chanel* (1883?–1971), Fr. fashion designer] designating or of a certain style of women's fashions, esp. of a straight-hanging, collarless jacket

Chang-chia-kou (chän′jyä′kō′) *same as* CHANGKIAKOW

Chang-chou (chan′chou′; *Chin.* jän′jō′) 1. city in Kiangsu province, E China, on the Grand Canal: pop. 300,000 2. city in Fukien province, SE China: pop. 81,000

Chang-chun (chän′choon′) city in NE China; capital of Kirin province: pop. 1,150,000

change (chānj) *vt.* **changed, chang′ing** [ME. *changen* < OFr. *changier* < LL. *cambiare* < L. *cambire*, to exchange, barter < Celt. (as in OIr. *camb*) < IE. base *kamb-, to bend, crook (whence W. *cam*, Bret. *kamm*, crooked)] 1. to put or take (a thing) in place of something else; substitute for, replace with, or transfer to another of a similar kind [to *change* one's clothes, to *change* jobs] 2. to give and receive reciprocally; exchange; switch [let's *change* seats] 3. *a*) to cause to become different; alter; transform; convert [success *changed* him] *b*) to undergo a variation of [leaves *change* color] 4. to give or receive the equivalent of (a coin or bank note) in currency of lower denominations or in foreign money 5. to substitute a fresh covering, as a diaper, bedclothes, etc., on —*vi.* 1. *a*) to become different; alter; vary [the scene *changes*] *b*) to undergo alteration or replacement 2. to pass from one phase to another, as the moon 3. to become lower in range: said specif. of the male voice at puberty 4. to leave one train, bus, etc. and board another 5. to put on other clothes 6. to make an exchange —*n.* 1. the act or process of substitution, alteration, or variation 2. absence of monotony; variety 3. something that is or may be substituted; something of the same kind but new or fresh 4. another set of clothes, esp. a fresh set to put on 5. *a*) money returned as the difference between the price of something bought and the bill or coin of larger denomination given in payment *b*) a number of coins or bills whose total value equals a single larger coin or bill *c*) small coins 6. a place where merchants meet to do business; exchange: also 'change 7. [*usually pl.*] *Bell Ringing* any pattern or order in which the bells may be rung —**change off** to take turns —**ring the changes** 1. to ring a set of bells with all possible variations 2. to do or say a thing in many and various ways

SYN.—**change** denotes a making or becoming distinctly different and implies either a radical transmutation of character or replacement with something else [I'll *change* my shoes/]; **alter** implies a partial change, as in appearance, so that the identity is preserved [to *alter* a garment]; **vary** suggests irregular or intermittent change [to *vary* one's reading/; **modify** implies minor change, often so as to limit or moderate [to *modify* the language of a report]; **transform** implies a change in form and now, usually, in nature or function [to *transform* matter into energy]; **convert** suggests more strongly change to suit a new function [to *convert* a dining room into a bedroom]

change·a·ble (chān′jə b'l) *adj.* [ME.] 1. that can change or be changed; likely or tending to change; variable; alterable; fickle 2. having a changing appearance or color, as some silk when looked at from different angles; iridescent —**change′a·bil′i·ty, change′a·ble·ness** *n.*—**change′a·bly** *adv.*

change·ful (chānj′f'l) *adj.* full of change; inconstant —**change′ful·ly** *adv.*—**change′ful·ness** *n.*

change·less (-lis) *adj.* unchanging; immutable —**change′·less·ly** *adv.*—**change′less·ness** *n.*

change·ling (-liŋ) *n.* 1. a child secretly put in the place of another; esp., in folk tales, one exchanged in this way by

fairies 2. [Archaic] a changeable person; turncoat 3. [Archaic] a feeble-minded person; idiot

change of life *same as* MENOPAUSE

change·o·ver (-ō'vər) *n.* a complete change, as in goods produced, methods of production, equipment, etc.

chang·er (-ər) *n.* a person or thing that changes something; esp., *short for* RECORD CHANGER

change ringing the art of ringing a series of unrepeated changes on a set of bells tuned together

☆**change-up** (-up') *n.* Baseball a change of pace: see PACE

Chang·kia·kow (chän'jyä'kō') city in NE China, in Hopeh province: pop. 630,000

Chang·sha (chän'shä') city in SE China; capital of Hunan province: pop. 709,000

Chang·teh, Chang·te (chän'du') city on the Yüan River, in Hunan province, China: pop. 95,000

Chan·kiang (chän'jyäŋ') city in S China, on the Luichow Peninsula, Kwangtung province: pop. 166,000

chan·nel¹ (chan'l) *n.* [ME. & OFr. *chanel, canel:* see CANAL] 1. the bed of a running stream, river, etc. 2. the deeper part of a river, harbor, etc. 3. a body of water joining two larger bodies of water 4. a tubelike passage for liquids 5. *a)* any means of passage *b)* a course through which something moves or is transmitted, conveyed, expressed, etc. 6. [*pl.*] the proper or official course of transmission of communications [to make a request through army *channels*] 7. a long groove or furrow 8. a rolled metal bar whose section is shaped thus ⌐: also **channel iron** (or **bar**) 9. *a)* a narrow band of frequencies within which a radio or television transmitting station must keep its signal to prevent interference with other transmitters *b)* the path followed by one type of signal, as in a radio receiver —*vt.* **-neled** or **-nelled**, **-nel·ing** or **-nel·ling** 1. to make a channel or channels in 2. to put grooves, or fluting, in (a pillar, column, etc.) 3. to send through a channel

chan·nel² (chan'l) *n.* [orig., *chain wale*] formerly, any of several metal ledges on the sides of a ship to secure the rigging and keep the ropes free of the gunwales

Channel Islands group of Brit. islands in the English Channel, off the coast of Normandy, including Jersey and Guernsey: 75 sq. mi.; pop. 104,000

chan·nel·ize (chan'l īz') *vt.* **-ized', -iz'ing** to provide a channel for —**chan'nel·i·za'tion** *n.*

Chan·ning (chan'iŋ), **William El·ler·y** (el'ər ē) 1780–1842; U.S. Unitarian leader & social critic

‡**chan·son** (shän sōn'; *E.* shan'sən) *n., pl.* **-sons** (-sōn'; *E.* -sənz) [Fr. < L. *cantio:* see CANZONE] a song

‡**chan·son de geste** (də zhest'; *E.* də jest') [Fr., song of heroic acts] any of the Old French epic poems of the 11th to 13th centuries, esp. of the type of the *Chanson de Roland* (*Song of Roland*)

chant (chant, chänt) *n.* [Fr. < L. *cantus,* song < the *v.*] 1. a song; melody 2. *a)* a simple liturgical song in which a string of syllables or words is sung to each tone *b)* words, as of a canticle or psalm, to be sung in this way 3. *a)* a monotonous tone of voice; singsong mode of speaking *b)* anything uttered in this way —*vi.* [ME. *chanten* < OFr. *chanter, canter* < L. *cantare,* freq. of *canere,* to sing < IE. base *kan-,* to sing, sound, whence Gr. *kanachē,* sound, noise, Bret. *cana,* sing, G. *hahn* & HEN] 1. to sing a chant; intone 2. to say something monotonously or repetitiously 3. [Poet.] to sing; warble —*vt.* 1. to sing 2. to celebrate in song 3. to utter, sing, or recite in the manner of a chant

chant·er (-ər) *n.* 1. one who chants or sings, esp. as in a choir; chorister 2. a priest who sang Masses in a chantry 3. that pipe of a bagpipe with finger holes on which the melody is played —**chant'ress** [Archaic] *n.fem.*

chan·te·relle (shan'tə rel', chan'-) *n.* [Fr., dim. < L. *cantharus,* drinking cup < Gr. *kantharos*] any of a genus (*Cantharellus*) of yellow or orange mushrooms with forking gills and funnel-shaped caps, esp. an edible species (*Cantharellus cibarius*)

chan·teuse (shan tooz'; *Fr.* shän töz') *n.* [Fr.: see CHANT] a woman singer, esp. of popular ballads

chan·tey (shan'tē, chan'tē) *n., pl.* **-teys** [< ? Fr. *chantez,* imperative of *chanter:* see CHANT] a song that sailors sing in rhythm with their motions while working: chanteys include **capstan chanteys** and **halyard** (i.e., hauling) **chanteys:** also **chan'ty,** *pl.* **-ties**

chan·ti·cleer (chan'tə klir') *n.* [ME. *chauntecler* < OFr. *chante-cler,* lit., sing loud, name of rooster in the medieval epic "Reynard the Fox": see CHANT & CLEAR] a rooster: used as a proper name

Chan·til·ly (shan til'ē; *Fr.* shän tē yē') town in N France: noted for a kind of lace (**Chantilly lace**) first made there: pop. 7,000

chan·try (chan'trē, chän'-) *n., pl.* **-tries** [ME. & OFr. *chanterie:* see CHANT] R.C.Ch. 1. an endowment to pay for the saying of Masses and prayers for the soul of a specified person, often the endower: an earlier term 2. a chapel or altar endowed, esp. in the Middle Ages, for this purpose

Cha·nu·kah (khä'noo kä') *same as* HANUKA

Chao·chow (chou'jō') city in Kwangtung province, SE China: pop. 101,000: former name **Chao'an'** (-än')

Chao Phra·ya (chou' prä yä') principal river of Thailand, in the W part, flowing into the Gulf of Siam: c. 160 mi. long: also called MENAM

cha·os (kā'äs) *n.* [L. < Gr. *chaos,* space, chaos (sense 1) < IE. base *ĝheu-,* to gape, whence ON. *gaula,* howl & GUM²]

1. the disorder of formless matter and infinite space, supposed to have existed before the ordered universe 2. extreme confusion or disorder 3. [Archaic] an abyss; chasm —*SYN.* see CONFUSION

cha·ot·ic (kā ät'ik) *adj.* in a state of chaos; in a completely confused or disordered condition —**cha·ot'i·cal·ly** *adv.*

chap¹ (chāp, chap) *n.* [prob. < ME. *cheppe* < ?] same as CHOP²

chap² (chap) *n.* [< CHAPMAN] 1. [Colloq.] a man or boy; fellow 2. [Brit. Dial.] a customer

chap³ (chap) *vt., vi.* **chapped** or **chapt, chap'ping** [ME. *chappen,* var. of *choppen* (see CHOP¹)] to crack open; split; roughen, as the skin from exposure to cold —*n.* a chapped place in the skin

chap. 1. chaplain 2. chapter

☆**cha·pa·re·jos, cha·pa·ra·jos** (chap'ə rā'hōs, shap'-) *n.pl.* [MexSp., altered < *chaparreras* (so named because worn to protect from *chaparro,* chaparral)] [Southwest] *same as* CHAPS¹

☆**chap·ar·ral** (chap'ə ral', shap'-) *n.* [Sp. < *chaparro,* evergreen oak < ? Basque *tšapar*] [Southwest] a dense thicket of shrubs, thorny bushes, etc., orig., of evergreen oaks

☆**chaparral cock** (or **bird**) *same as* ROAD RUNNER

☆**chaparral pea** a thorny evergreen shrub (*Pickeringia montana*) of the legume family, growing in chaparrals along the western coast of the U.S.

chap·book (chap'book') *n.* [*chap* (CHAPMAN) + BOOK: chapmen sold such books in the streets] a small book or pamphlet of poems, ballads, religious tracts, etc.

chape (chāp) *n.* [ME. < OFr., a cape < LL. *cappa:* see CAPE¹] a metal plate or mounting on a scabbard or sheath, esp. a protection for the point

cha·peau (sha pō'; *Fr.* -pō') *n., pl.* **-peaus, -peaux** (-pōz') [Fr. < OFr. *chapel* < VL. *cappellus,* dim. of *cappa:* see CAPE¹] a hat

chap·el (chap'l) *n.* [ME. & OFr. *chapelle* < ML. *capella, chapel* < VL. *cappella* (see prec.): orig., sanctuary in which the *cappa* or cope of St. Martin was preserved; then, any sanctuary] 1. a place of Christian worship subordinate to and smaller than a church 2. *a)* a room or building used as a place of worship, as in a hospital, school, or army post *b)* a room in a funeral home for funeral services 3. *a)* a room or recess in a church, set apart for special services and having its own altar *b)* a similar room in some Jewish synagogues 4. a service in a chapel, or any religious service, as at a school 5. the singers of a private chapel, collectively 6. an association of the workers in a printing office 7. in Great Britain, any place of worship for those who are not members of an established church

chap·er·on, chap·er·one (shap'ə rōn') *n.* [Fr. < OFr., head covering, hood (hence, protection, protector) < *chape:* see CHAPE] a person, esp. an older or married woman, who accompanies young unmarried people in public or is present at their parties, dances, etc. for the sake of propriety or to supervise their behavior —*vt., vi.* **-oned', -on'ing** to act as chaperon (to) —*SYN.* see ACCOMPANY —**chap'er·on'age** *n.*

chap·fall·en (chap'fô'lən, chap'-) *adj.* [CHAP¹ + FALLEN] 1. having the lower jaw hanging down, as from fatigue 2. disheartened, depressed, or humiliated

chap·i·ter (chap'i tər) *n.* [Fr. *chapitre:* see CHAPTER] *Archit.* the capital of a column

chap·lain (chap'lən) *n.* [ME. & OFr. *chapelain* < ML. *capellanus,* orig., custodian of St. Martin's cloak: see CHAPEL] 1. a clergyman attached to a chapel, as of a royal court 2. a minister, priest, or rabbi serving in a religious capacity with the armed forces, or in a prison, hospital, etc. 3. a clergyman, or sometimes a layman, appointed to perform religious functions in a public institution, club, etc. —**chap'lain·cy,** *pl.* **-cies, chap'lain·ship'** *n.*

chap·let (chap'lit) *n.* [ME. & OFr. *chapelet,* dim. of *chapel:* see CHAPEAU] 1. a wreath or garland for the head 2. *a)* a string of prayer beads one third the length of a full rosary *b)* the prayers said with such beads 3. any string of beads; necklace 4. *Archit.* a small convex molding somewhat resembling a string of beads

chap·let·ed (-id) *adj.* wearing a wreath or garland on the head

Chap·lin (chap'lin), **Charles Spencer** 1889– ; Eng. motion-picture actor & producer, in the U.S. (1910–52)

chap·man (chap'mən) *n., pl.* **-men** (-mən) [ME. *chapman* < OE. *ceapman,* trader < *ceap,* trade, a bargain (cf. CHEAP) + *man*] 1. [Brit.] a peddler; hawker 2. [Archaic] a trader; dealer

Chap·man (chap'mən), **George** 1559?–1634; Eng. poet, playwright, & translator of Homer

☆**chaps¹** (chaps, shaps) *n.pl.* [shortened from CHAPAREJOS] leather trousers without a seat, worn over ordinary trousers by cowboys to protect their legs

chaps² (chāps, chaps) *n.pl.* [see CHAP¹] *same as* CHOPS

chap·ter (chap'tər) *n.* [ME. & OFr. *chapitre, chapitle* < L. *capitulum,* head, capital (in LL., division of a writing; in ML., church division), dim. of *caput,* the head] 1. any of the main divisions of a book or other writing 2. a thing like a chapter; part; episode [a *chapter* of one's life] 3. *a)* [from meeting at which a *chapter* of monastic rule, etc. was read] a formal meeting of canons headed by a dean, or of the members of a religious order *b)* those assembled at such a meeting ☆4. a local branch of a club, fraternity, etc. —*vt.*

to divide (a book, etc.) into chapters —**chapter and verse** 1. the exact Scriptural reference 2. authority cited (for a statement, belief, etc.) 3. detailed information

chapter house 1. the place where a chapter, as of monks, meets: also **chapter room** ☆2. the house of a fraternity or sorority chapter

Cha·pul·te·pec (chə pool′tə pek′, -pul′-) [Nahuatl, lit., grasshopper hill] fortress near Mexico City: captured (Sept., 1847) by Gen. Winfield Scott in the Mexican War

char[1] (chär) *vt., vi.* **charred, char′ring** [back-formation < CHARCOAL] 1. to reduce to charcoal by burning; burn up 2. to burn slightly; scorch —*n.* anything charred; cinders; charcoal —*SYN.* see BURN[1]

char[2] (chär) *n.* [back-formation < CHARWOMAN] 1. *same as* CHARE 2. [Brit.] a charwoman —*vi.* **charred, char′ring** [Chiefly Brit.] to work as a charwoman

char[3] (chär) *n., pl.* **chars, char:** see PLURAL, II, D, 1 [< Gael. *ceara,* red < *cear,* blood] any of a genus (*Salvelinus*) of trouts with small scales and a red belly

char[4] (chär) *n.* [altered < *cha* < Chin. (Mandarin) *ch'a,* tea] [Brit. Slang] tea

char·a·banc, char·à·banc (shar′ə baŋk′, -baŋ′) *n.* [Fr. *char-à-banc,* lit., car with bench] [Brit.] an open sightseeing bus with transverse seats facing forward

char·a·cin (kar′ə sin) *n.* [ModL. *Characinidae* (the family) < Gr. *charax,* a kind of fish] any of a large family (Characinidae) of small, strong-jawed freshwater fishes of South and Central America and Africa

char·ac·ter (kar′ik tər) *n.* [ME. *carecter* < OFr. *caractere* < L. *character,* an engraving instrument < Gr. *charaktēr* < *charattein,* to engrave] 1. a distinctive mark 2. *a)* any letter, figure, or symbol used in writing and printing *b)* the letters of an alphabet, collectively 3. *a)* writing or printing *b)* style of printing or handwriting 4. *a)* a mystic symbol or magical emblem *b)* a code or cipher 5. a distinctive trait, quality, or attribute; characteristic 6. essential quality; nature; kind or sort 7. the pattern of behavior or personality found in an individual or group; moral constitution 8. moral strength; self-discipline, fortitude, etc. 9. *a)* reputation *b)* good reputation [left without a shred of *character*] 10. *same as* CHARACTER SKETCH (sense 1) 11. a statement about the behavior, qualities, etc. of a person, esp. as given by a former employer; reference 12. status; position 13. a personage [*great characters* in history] 14. *a)* a person in a play, story, novel, etc. *b)* a role as portrayed by an actor or actress 15. [Colloq.] an odd, eccentric, or noteworthy person 16. *Genetics* any attribute, as color, shape, etc., caused in an individual by the action of one or more genes —*vt.* 1. to write, print, or inscribe 2. to characterize 3. [Archaic] to represent; portray —*SYN.* see DISPOSITION, QUALITY —**in** (or **out of**) **character** consistent with (or inconsistent with) the role or general character

character actor an actor usually cast in the role of a person with pronounced or eccentric characteristics —**character actress** *fem.*

char·ac·ter·is·tic (kar′ik tə ris′tik) *adj.* [Gr. *charaktēristikos:* see CHARACTER] of or constituting the special character; typical; distinctive [the *characteristic* odor of cabbage] —*n.* 1. a distinguishing trait, feature, or quality; peculiarity 2. the whole number, or integral part, of a logarithm, as distinguished from the fractional remainder, or mantissa [4 is the *characteristic* of the logarithm 4.7193] —**char′ac·ter·is′ti·cal·ly** *adv.*

SYN.—**characteristic** suggests the indication of a quality that is peculiar to, and helps identify, something or someone [the *characteristic* taste of honey]; **individual** and **distinctive** refer to, or suggest the possession of, a quality or qualities that distinguish something from others of its class or kind, **distinctive** often implying a meritorious difference [an *individual,* or *distinctive,* literary style]

char·ac·ter·i·za·tion (kar′ik tər ə zā′shən) *n.* 1. the act of characterizing; description of characteristics 2. the delineation of character or creation of characters in a play, story, etc.

char·ac·ter·ize (kar′ik tə rīz′) *vt.* **-ized′, -iz′ing** [ML. *characterizare* < Gr. *charaktērizein:* see CHARACTER] 1. to describe or portray the particular qualities, features, or traits of 2. to be the distinctive character of; distinguish [a miser is *characterized* by greed]

char·ac·ter·o·log·i·cal (kar′ik tər ə läj′i k'l) *adj.* of or relating to character or the study of character

character sketch 1. a short piece of writing describing a person or type of person 2. a theatrical portrayal of a highly individualized character or role

char·ac·ter·y (kar′ək trē, -tər ē) *n., pl.* **-ter·ies** [see CHARACTER] [Chiefly Poet.] 1. the expression of thought by symbols 2. the symbols so used

cha·rade (shə rād′; *chiefly Brit.* -räd′) *n.* [Fr. < Pr. *charrada* < *charrar,* to gossip, chatter: orig. echoic] 1. [*often pl.*] a game in which a word or phrase to be guessed is acted out in pantomime, syllable by syllable or as a whole 2. such a word or phrase

char·coal (chär′kōl′) *n.* [ME. *char cole,* prob. < *charren,* to turn + *cole,* coal (hence, lit., wood turned to coal)] 1. an amorphous form of carbon produced by partially burning or oxidizing wood or other organic matter in large kilns or retorts from which air is excluded: used as a fuel, filter, gas absorbent, etc. 2. a pencil or crayon made of this substance 3. a drawing made with such a pencil or crayon 4. a very dark gray or brown, almost black —*vt.* to write or draw with charcoal

Char·cot (shär kō′), **Jean Mar·tin** (zhän mår tan′) 1825–93; Fr. neurologist

chard (chärd) *n.* [earlier *card* < Fr. *carde* < L. *carduus,* thistle, artichoke: sp. infl. by Fr. *chardon,* artichoke] a kind of beet (*Beta vulgaris cicla*) whose large leaves and thick stalks are used as food

Char·din (shår dan′) 1. **Jean** (**Baptiste**) **Si·mé·on** (zhän sē mä ôn′), 1699–1779; Fr. painter 2. **Teilhard de,** *see* TEILHARD DE CHARDIN

chare (cher) *n.* [ME. *char* < OE. *cierr,* a turn, job, piece of work < *cierran,* to turn] an odd job or household task; chore —*vi.* **chared, char′ing** 1. to do odd jobs or chores 2. *same as* CHAR[2]

charge (chärj) *vt.* **charged, charg′ing** [ME. *chargen* < OFr. *chargier* < VL. *carricare,* to load a wagon, cart < L. *carrus,* car, wagon: cf. CAR] 1. [Archaic] to put a load on or in 2. to load or fill to capacity or with the usual amount of required material 3. to load (a firearm, cannon, etc.) 4. to saturate (one substance) with another [air *charged* with steam] 5. to add carbon dioxide to (water, etc.) ☆6. to add an electrical charge to (a battery, etc.) II. 1. to load a burden on; give as a task, duty, etc. to; make responsible for [a nurse *charged* with the care of a child] 2. to give instructions to or command authoritatively [to *charge* a jury] 3. to accuse of wrongdoing; censure [he *charged* her with negligence] 4. *a)* to put liability on (a person) *b)* to make liable for (an error, etc.) 5. to ask as a price or fee [to *charge* a dollar for alterations] 6. *a)* to record as a debt against a person's name or account [to *charge* a purchase] ☆*b)* to make a record of (something borrowed) [to *charge* a library book] III. 1. to bear down on or set upon with force; attack vigorously 2. to bring (a gun or other weapon) to bear on; level; direct 3. *Heraldry* to place a bearing on —*vi.* 1. to crouch or squat when a command is given: said of dogs 2. to ask payment (*for*) [to *charge* for a service] 3. to attack vigorously or move forward as if attacking —*n.* I. 1. a load or burden 2. the maximum or necessary quantity, as of fuel, that a container or apparatus is built to hold; also, the actual quantity held 3. *a)* the amount of chemical energy stored in a battery and dischargeable as electrical energy *b)* the departure from electrical neutrality at a point, or in a region, as by the accumulation, or deficit, of electrical particles: more electrons than normal produce a negative charge; fewer, a positive charge 4. a cartridge or shell, or the amount of gunpowder needed to discharge a firearm or set off an explosive device ☆5. [Slang] pleasurable excitement; thrill II. 1. responsibility or duty (*of*) [to take *charge* of finances] 2. care, custody, or supervision (*of*) 3. a person or thing entrusted to someone's care 4. instruction or command, esp. instruction in points of law given by a judge to a jury 5. accusation; indictment [*charges* of cruelty] III. 1. the cost or price of an article, service, etc. 2. a liability to pay money; debt; expense 3. *a)* *same as* CHARGE ACCOUNT *b)* a debit entered in an account IV. 1. an attack with great force and speed; onslaught; onset 2. the signal for this 3. *Heraldry* a bearing —*SYN.* see ACCUSE, COMMAND —**charge off** 1. to treat or regard as a loss 2. to set down as belonging; ascribe —**in charge** 1. having the responsibility, control, or supervision 2. [Brit.] under arrest —**in charge of** 1. having the responsibility, control, or supervision of 2. under the control or supervision of; in the custody of: usually **in the charge of**

char·gé (shär zhā′) *n. same as* CHARGÉ D'AFFAIRES

charge·a·ble (chär′jə b'l) *adj.* 1. that can be, or is liable to be, charged 2. that may become a public charge

☆**charge account** a business arrangement by which a customer may buy things or services and pay for them within a specified future period

char·gé d'af·faires (shär zhā′ də fer′) *pl.* **chargés d'affaires** (shär zhāz′ də fer′, shär zhā′) [Fr., lit., entrusted with business] 1. a diplomatic official who temporarily takes the place of a minister or ambassador 2. a diplomatic officer sent to a foreign nation to represent his government, and ranking below an ambassador or minister

charge plate a metal or plastic plate embossed with the owner's name and address, used as a stamp on bills in making purchases on credit: also **charge′-a-plate′** (-ə plāt′) *n.*

charg·er[1] (chär′jər) *n.* 1. a person or thing that charges 2. a horse ridden in battle or on parade 3. an apparatus used to charge storage batteries

charg·er[2] (chär′jər) *n.* [ME. *chargeour*] [Archaic] a large, flat dish; platter

Cha·ri (shä′rē) *same as* SHARI

char·i·ly (cher′ə lē) *adv.* in a chary manner; cautiously

char·i·ness (-ē nis) *n.* the quality of being chary; cautiousness or frugality

Cha·ri-Nile (shä′rē nīl′) *n.* a subfamily of the Nilo-Saharan family of languages, including Sudanic, Dinka, Masai, etc.

char·i·ot (char′ē ət) n. [ME. < OFr. *charriote* < *charrier* < VL. *carricare*: see CHARGE] 1. a horse-drawn, two-wheeled cart used in ancient times for war, racing, parades, etc. 2. [Archaic] a light, four-wheeled carriage, used for pleasure or on some state occasions —vt., vi. to drive or ride in a chariot

CHARIOT

char·i·ot·eer (char′ē ə tir′) n. [ME. *charioter* < OFr. *charioteur*] a chariot driver —[C-] same as AURIGA

cha·ris·ma (kə riz′mə) n., pl. **-ma·ta** (-mə tə) [Gr.(Ec.), gift of God's grace < Gr., favor, grace < *charizesthai*, to show favor to < *charis*, grace, beauty, kindness < *chairein*, to rejoice at < IE. base **ĝher-*, to desire, like, whence YEARN] 1. *Christian Theol.* a divinely inspired gift, grace, or talent, as for prophesying, healing, etc. 2. a special quality of leadership that captures the popular imagination and inspires unswerving allegiance and devotion Also **char·ism** (kar′iz′m) —**char·is·mat·ic** (kar′iz mat′ik) adj.

char·i·ta·ble (char′i tə b'l) adj. [ME. & OFr.: see CHARITY] 1. kind and generous in giving money or other help to those in need 2. of or for charity 3. kind and forgiving in judging others; lenient —SYN. see PHILANTHROPIC —**char′i·ta·ble·ness** n. —**char′i·ta·bly** adv.

char·i·ty (char′ə tē) n., pl. **-ties** [ME. & OFr. *charite* < L. *caritas*, costliness, esteem, affection (in Vulgate, often used as transl. of LGr.(Ec.) *agapē*, AGAPE²) < *carus*, dear, valued < IE. base **kāro-*, to like, desire, whence Goth. *hors*, adulterer] 1. *Christian Theol.* the love of God for man or of man for his fellow men 2. an act of good will or affection 3. the feeling of good will; benevolence 4. kindness or leniency in judging others 5. a) a voluntary giving of money or other help to those in need b) money or help so given c) an institution or other recipient of such help 6. a welfare institution, organization, or fund —SYN. see MERCY

cha·ri·va·ri (shə riv′ə rē′, shiv′ə rē′; shiv′ə rē) n. [Fr. < LL. *caribaria*, headache < Gr. *karēbaria*, lit., heaviness in the head < *karē*, var. of *kara*, head (< IE. base **ker-*, head, horn, whence HORN) + *barys*, heavy] 1. same as SHIVAREE 2. a confusion of noises; din

char·kha, char·ka (chur′kə, chär′-) n. [Hind.] in India, a spinning wheel used esp. for cotton

char·la·dy (chär′lā′dē) n., pl. **-dies** [Brit.] a charwoman

char·la·tan (shär′lə t'n) n. [Fr. < It. *ciarlatano*, a quack < *cerretano*, one who cries out in the market place < LL. *cerretanus*, seller of papal indulgences at *Cerreto*, town in Italy: infl. by It. *ciarlare*, to prate] a person who pretends to have expert knowledge or skill that he does not have; fake; mountebank —SYN. see QUACK² —**char′la·tan·ism, char′la·tan·ry,** pl. **-ries** n.

Char·le·magne (shär′lə mān′) 742-814 A.D.; king of the Franks (768-814); emperor of the Western (or Holy) Roman Empire (800-814): also called **Charles I** or **Charles the Great**

Char·le·roi, Char·le·roy (shärl rwä′; E. shär′lə roi) city in SC Belgium: a coal & steel center: pop. 26,000 (met. area 284,000)

Charles¹ (chärlz) [Fr. < ML. *Carolus* (or) < Gmc. *Karl*; lit., full-grown; akin to OE. *ceorl* < *churl*)] 1. a masculine name: dim. *Charley, Charlie*; var. *Carl*; equiv. L. *Carolus*, G. *Carl, Karl*, It. *Carlo*, Sp. *Carlos*, Du. *Karel*; fem. *Charlotte, Caroline* 2. a) 823-877 A.D.; king of France (843-877) &, as **Charles II**, Holy Roman Emperor (875-877): called *the Bald* b) (*Charles Stuart*) 1600-49; king of England, Scotland, & Ireland (1625-49): beheaded c) (*Charles Francis Joseph*) 1887-1922; emperor of Austria &, as **Charles IV**, king of Hungary (1916-18): forced to abdicate d) same as CHARLEMAGNE 3. **Charles II** 1630-85; king of England, Scotland, & Ireland (1660-85) 4. **Charles IV** a) 1294-1328; king of France (1322-28): called *the Fair* b) 1748-1819; king of Spain (1788-1808): forced to abdicate by Napoleon I 5. **Charles V** a) 1337-80; king of France (1364-80): called *the Wise* b) 1500-58; Holy Roman Emperor (1519-56) &, as **Charles I**, king of Spain (1516-56): abdicated 6. **Charles VI** 1368-1422; king of France (1380-1422): called *the Well-Beloved* 7. **Charles VII** a) 1403-61; king of France (1422-61): called *the Victorious* b) (*Charles Albert; Charles of Bavaria*) 1697-1745; Holy Roman Emperor (1742-45) 8. **Charles XIV** (John): see BERNADOTTE

Charles² [after CHARLES I of England] 1. river in E Mass., flowing into Boston Bay: c. 60 mi. 2. **Cape**, cape in SE Va., at the mouth of Chesapeake Bay, forming the tip of Delmarva Peninsula See HAMPTON ROADS, map

Charles Edward Stuart see Charles Edward STUART

Charles Martel see Charles MARTEL

Charles's law (chärl′ziz) [after J. *Charles* (1746-1823), Fr. physicist who discovered it] the statement that for a body of ideal gas at constant pressure the volume is directly proportional to the absolute temperature

Charles's Wain (chärl′ziz) [OE. *Carles wægn*, wagon of *Carl* (Charlemagne): so named because of confusion between Charlemagne and King Arthur (L. *Arcturus*); orig., the wain of ARCTURUS] [Brit.] same as BIG DIPPER

Charles·ton (chärl′stən) [after CHARLES I of England] 1. capital of W.Va., in the W part: pop. 72,000 2. seaport in S.C.: pop. 67,000 —n. [< name of the seaport] a lively dance in 4/4 time, characterized by a twisting step and popular during the 1920's

Charles·town (chärl′stoun′) [see prec.] part of Boston, on the harbor: site of Bunker Hill

☆**char·ley horse** (chär′lē) [ballplayers' slang, c. 1888; prob. with reference to a lame racehorse] [Colloq.] a cramp in the leg or arm muscles, caused by strain

char·lock (chär′lək) n. [ME. *cherlok* < OE. *cerlic*] a weed (*Brassica kaber*) of the mustard family, with yellow flowers

Char·lotte (shär′lət) [Fr., fem. of *Charlot*, dim. of *Charles*] 1. a feminine name: dim. *Lotta, Lottie, Lotty*; equiv. It. *Carlotta* 2. [after Queen *Charlotte*, wife of GEORGE III] city in S N.C.: pop. 241,000

char·lotte (shär′lət) n. [Fr. < prec.] a dessert made of fruit, gelatin, custard, etc. in a mold lined with strips of bread, cake, etc.

Charlotte A·ma·lie (ə mäl′yə, ə mäl′ē) capital of the Virgin Islands of the U.S.; seaport on St. Thomas island: pop. 12,000

charlotte russe (rōōs) [Fr., lit., Russian charlotte] a dessert made of whipped cream, custard, etc. in a mold lined with spongecake

Char·lottes·ville (shär′ləts vil′) [cf. CHARLOTTE, N.C.] city in C Va.: pop. 39,000

Char·lotte·town (shär′lət toun′) capital of Prince Edward Island, Canada: pop. 18,000

charm¹ (chärm) n. [ME. & OFr. *charme* < L. *carmen*, song, verse, charm < *canmen < *canere*, to sing: see CHANT] 1. orig., a chanted word, phrase, or verse assumed to have magic power to help or hurt; incantation 2. any object assumed to have such power, as an amulet or talisman 3. any trinket worn as a decoration on a bracelet, necklace, watch chain, etc. 4. any action or gesture assumed to have magic power 5. a quality or feature in someone or something that attracts or delights people —vt. 1. to act on as though by magic; seemingly cast a spell on 2. to protect from harm as though by magic [a *charmed* life] 3. to attract or please greatly; enchant; allure; fascinate; delight —vi. 1. to practice magic 2. to be charming; please greatly —SYN. see ATTRACT

charm² (chärm) n. archaic var. of CHIRM

charm·er (-ər) n. [see CHARM¹] 1. a delightful, fascinating, or attractive person 2. a person who seemingly casts a spell; enchanter [a snake *charmer*]

char·meuse (shär mooz′) n. [Fr., fem. of *charmeur*, charmer] a soft, lightweight silk cloth with a finish like that of satin

charm·ing (chär′min) adj. attractive; fascinating; delightful —**charm′ing·ly** adv.

char·nel (chär′n'l) n. [ME. < OFr. *charnel* < LL. *carnale*, graveyard; neut. of *carnalis*, CARNAL] 1. [Obs.] a cemetery 2. a building or place where corpses or bones are deposited or piled up: in full, **charnel house** —adj. of, like, or fit for, a charnel house; deathlike

Cha·ron (ker′ən) [L. < Gr. *Charōn*] *Gr.Myth.* the boatman who ferried souls of the dead across the river Styx to Hades —n. a ferryman: humorous usage

Char·pen·tier (shär pän tyā′), **Gus·tave** (güs tàv′) 1860-1956; Fr. composer

char·poy (chär′poi) n. [Hind. *cārpāi* < Per. *čahār-pāi* < *čahār*, four + *pāi*, foot] a light bedstead or cot used in India: also **char′pai** (-pī)

char·qui (chär′kē) n. [Sp. *charquí, charqué* < Quechua *ch'arki*, dried meat] jerked or dried beef

charr (chär) n., pl. **charrs, charr;** see PLURAL, II, D, 1 same as CHAR³

‡**char·ro** (chär′rō) n. [AmSp. < Sp., ill-bred person < Basque *txar*, bad] a skilled Mexican horseman in a traditional, elaborate costume

char·ry (chär′ē) adj. **-ri·er, -ri·est** like charcoal

chart (chärt) n. [ME. < OFr. < ML. *carta*: see CARD¹] 1. a map, esp. one prepared for use in marine or air navigation 2. an outline map on which special information, as on weather conditions, economic resources, etc., is plotted geographically 3. a) a group of facts about something, set up in the form of a diagram, table, graph, etc. b) such a diagram or graph c) a sheet with such diagrams, graphs, etc. —vt. 1. to make a chart of; map; outline 2. to plot (a course) on, or by reference to, a chart or charts 3. to plan (a course of action) 4. to show by, on, or as by, a chart

char·ter (chär′tər) n. [ME. & OFr. *chartre* < L. *chartula*, dim. of *charta*: see CARD¹] 1. a franchise or written grant of specified rights made by a government or ruler to a person, corporation, etc. 2. a) a document setting forth the aims and principles of a united group, as of nations; specif., [C-] the Charter of the United Nations b) a document embodying the constitution of a city 3. a document by which a society authorizes the organization of a local chapter or lodge 4. a special privilege or exemption 5. a) the hire or lease of a ship, bus, airplane, etc. b) the agreement governing this: see also CHARTER PARTY 6. *Eng. Law* a deed, conveyance, or similar document —vt. 1. to grant a charter to 2. to hire or lease by charter or charter party 3. to hire for exclusive use —SYN. see HIRE —**char′ter·er** n.

chartered accountant in Great Britain, an accountant certified by the Institute of Accountants

Char·ter·house (chär′tər hous′) n. [ME., altered (by folk etym.) < OFr. *chartrouse*, Carthusian monastery] 1. [Archaic] a Carthusian monastery 2. a boys' school in

Surrey, England, orig. in London on the site of a Carthusian monastery

☆**charter member** any of the founders or original members of an organization, esp. of one with a charter

charter party [ME. *chartre parti* < OFr. *charte partie* < ML. *charta partita*, divided deed: so named because half was kept by each party to the transaction] **1.** an agreement between a shipowner and a carrier, merchant, etc. for the commercial lease of a ship or space on a ship for a particular voyage or period of time, esp. as recorded in a document **2.** the hiring or leasing of a vessel or space by such agreement

Chart·ism (chär'tiz'm) *n.* a movement for democratic social and political reform in England (1838–1848), or its principles set forth in the People's Charter (1838) —**Chart'-ist** *n.*, *adj.*

chart·ist (chär'tist) *n.* a person who compiles or uses charts, esp. one who consults charts in order to anticipate fluctuations in the stock market

chart·less (chärt'lis) *adj.* **1.** without a chart; unguided **2.** not mapped [*a chartless sea*]

char·tog·ra·phy (kär täg'rə fē) *n.* same as CARTOGRAPHY

Char·tres (shär'tr'; E. shärt) city in NC France, near Paris: site of a 13th-cent. Gothic cathedral: pop. 31,000

char·treuse (shär trööz', -trōōs'; Fr. shär tröz') *n.* [after *La Grande Chartreuse*, Carthusian monastery in France] **1.** a yellow, pale-green, or white liqueur made by the Carthusian monks **2.** pale, yellowish green

char·tu·lar·y (kär'chə ler'ē) *n.*, *pl.* **-lar'ies** same as CARTULARY

char·wom·an (chär'woom'ən) *n.*, *pl.* **-wom'en** [see CHARE, CHORE] a woman who does cleaning or scrubbing, as in office buildings: in England, also, one hired by the day to do rough housework

char·y (cher'ē, char'-) *adj.* **char'i·er**, **char'i·est** [ME. *chari*, concerned, sorrowful < OE. *cearig*, sorrowful < *cearu*, care; change of sense after *care*] **1.** not taking chances; careful; cautious [*to be chary of offending others*] **2.** not giving freely; sparing [*chary* of his hospitality]

Cha·ryb·dis (kə rib'dis) [L. < Gr.] whirlpool off the NE coast of Sicily, in the Strait of Messina: see SCYLLA

chase[1] (chās) *vt.* **chased**, **chas'ing** [ME. *chacen*, *cacchen* < OFr. *chacier*, *cachier*: see CATCH] **1.** to follow quickly or persistently in order to catch or harm **2.** to run after; follow; pursue **3.** to seek after **4.** to make run away; drive **5.** to hunt (game) **6.** [Slang] to court aggressively —*vi.* **1.** to go in pursuit; follow along [*chase* after him] **2.** [Colloq.] to go hurriedly; rush [to *chase* around town] —*n.* **1.** the act of chasing; pursuit **2.** *a)* the hunting of game for sport (often with *the*) *b)* anything hunted; quarry *c)* hunters collectively **3.** [Brit.] *a)* an unenclosed game preserve: distinguished from PARK *b)* a license to hunt over a specified area or to keep animals there as game —**give chase** to chase; pursue

chase[2] (chās) *n.* [ME. & OFr. *châsse*, a frame, shrine < *casse*: see CASE[2]] **1.** a groove; furrow **2.** the bore of a gun barrel **3.** a hollowed-out groove for drainpipes, in a wall, etc. **4.** a rectangular metal frame in which pages or columns of type are locked —*vt.* **chased**, **chas'ing** to make a groove or furrow in; indent

chase[3] (chās) *vt.* **chased**, **chas'ing** [< *enchase* < Fr. *enchâsser*, to enshrine < *châsse*, shrine: see prec.] to ornament (metal) by engraving, embossing, etc.

Chase (chās) **1.** Sal·mon Portland (sal'mən), 1808–73; U.S. jurist; chief justice of the U.S. (1864–73) **2.** Samuel, 1741–1811; Am. Revolutionary leader & U.S. jurist; associate justice, Supreme Court (1796–1811)

chas·er[1] (chā'sər) *n.* [CHASE[1] + -ER] **1.** a person or thing that chases or hunts; pursuer **2.** a gun on the stern or bow of a ship, used during pursuit of or by another ship ☆**3.** [Colloq.] a mild drink, as water, ginger ale, or beer, taken after or with whiskey, rum, etc.

chas·er[2] (chā'sər) *n.* [CHASE[2] + -ER] **1.** one that engraves or embosses metal **2.** a tool for threading screws

chasm (kaz'm) *n.* [L. & Gr. *chasma*, yawning hollow, gulf < Gr. *chainein*, to yawn, gape: for IE. base see CHAOS] **1.** a deep crack in the earth's surface; abyss; narrow gorge **2.** any break or gap **3.** a wide divergence of feelings, sentiments, interests, etc.; rift —**chas'mal** (-m'l), **chas'mic** (-mik) *adj.*

chas·sé (sha sā') *n.* [Fr., lit., a chasing, orig., pp. of *chasser*, CHASE[1]] a rapid, gliding dance step forward or sideways —*vi.* **-séd'**, **-sé'ing** to perform this step

chasse·pot (shás pō') *n.* [after the Fr. inventor, A. A. *Chassepot* (1833–1905)] a breech-loading rifle used by the French army between 1866 and 1874

chas·seur (sha sur') *n.* [Fr. < *chasser*, CHASE[1]] **1.** a hunter; huntsman **2.** a soldier, esp. one of certain French light infantry or cavalry troops, trained for rapid action **3.** a uniformed attendant

Chas·sid·im (has'i dim; *Heb.* khä sē'dim) *n.pl.*, *sing.* **Chas'sid** same as HASIDIM —**Chas·sid'ic** *adj.* —**Chas'sid-ism** *n.*

chas·sis (chas'ē, shas'-) *n.*, *pl.* **-sis** (-ēz) [Fr. *châssis*: see CHASE[2]] **1.** a frame on which the carriage of a cannon

moves back and forth **2.** the part of a motor vehicle that includes the frame, suspension system, wheels, steering mechanism, etc., but not the body and engine **3.** the frame supporting the body of an airplane **4.** *Radio & TV a)* the framework to which the parts of a receiving set, amplifier, etc. are attached *b)* the assembled frame and parts ☆**5.** [Slang] the body or figure, esp. of a woman

chaste (chāst) *adj.* [ME. & OFr. < L. *castus*, pure, chaste: see CASTE] **1.** not indulging in unlawful sexual activity; virtuous: said esp. of women **2.** sexually abstinent; celibate **3.** pure, decent, or modest in nature, behavior, etc. **4.** restrained and simple in style; not ornate —**chaste'ly** *adv.* —**chaste'ness** *n.*
SYN.—**chaste** and **virtuous**, in this connection, imply moral excellence manifested by forbearance from acts or thoughts that do not accord with virginity or strict marital fidelity; **pure** implies chastity through innocence and an absence of seductive influences rather than through self-restraint; **modest** and **decent** are both applied to propriety in behavior, dress, bearing, or speech as exhibiting morality or purity —*ANT.* **immoral, lewd, wanton**

chas·ten (chās'n) *vt.* [ME. *chastien* < OFr. *chastier* < L. *castigare*, to punish, chastise < *castus*, pure + *agere*, to lead, drive] **1.** to punish in order to correct or make better; chastise **2.** to restrain from excess; subdue **3.** to make purer in style; refine —*SYN.* see PUNISH —**chas'ten·er** *n.*

chas·tise (chas tīz', chas'tīz) *vt.* **-tised'**, **-tis'ing** [ME. *chastisen* < extended stem of OFr. *chastier*: see prec.] **1.** to punish, esp. by beating **2.** to scold or condemn sharply **3.** [Archaic] to chasten —*SYN.* see PUNISH —**chas·tise'ment** *n.* —**chas·tis'er** *n.*

chas·ti·ty (chas'tə tē) *n.* [ME. *chastite* < OFr. *chastete* < L. *castitas*: see CHASTE] the quality or state of being chaste; specif., *a)* virtuousness *b)* sexual abstinence; celibacy *c)* decency or modesty *d)* simplicity of style

chastity belt a beltlike device of metal, leather, etc. allegedly fastened on a woman in the Middle Ages to prevent sexual intercourse during the absence of her husband

chas·u·ble (chaz'yoo b'l, chas'-) *n.* [OFr. < ML. *casubla*, *casula*, hooded garment, prob. < L. *casula*, dim. of *casa*, a hut, cottage] a sleeveless outer vestment worn over the alb by priests at Mass

chat[1] (chat) *vi.* **chat'ted**, **chat'ting** [< CHATTER] to talk or converse in a light, easy, informal manner —*n.* **1.** light, easy, informal talk or conversation **2.** [Obs.] small talk; chitchat; chatter **3.** any of various birds with a chattering call; ☆esp., a large warbler (*Icteria virens*), olive green on top and yellow underneath: in full, American chat

CHASUBLE

chat[2] (chat) *n.* [Fr. < LL. *cattus*, CAT] **1.** an ament or catkin, as of a willow **2.** a samara, as of a maple **3.** a spike, as of plantain

châ·teau (sha tō') *n.*, *pl.* **-teaux'** (-tōz', -tō'), **-teaus'** [Fr. < OFr. *chustel*, *castel* < L. *castellum*, CASTLE] **1.** a French feudal castle **2.** a large country house and estate, esp. in France Also **cha·teau'**

Cha·teau·bri·and (sha tō brē än'), vicomte **Fran·çois Re·né** de (frän swä' rə nā' də) 1768–1848; Fr. statesman & man of letters —*n.* [c-] [after the prec.] a thick beef fillet cut from the center of the tenderloin, usually grilled and served with a sauce

Châ·teau-Thier·ry (sha tō tye rē') town in N France, on the Marne: scene of intensive fighting in World War I: pop. 10,000

Château wine any of certain wines made from grapes grown at some particular château in France, esp. in the region of Bordeaux

chat·e·lain (shat'l ān') *n.* [Fr. *châtelain*, CASTELLAN] the keeper of a castle; castellan

chat·e·laine (-ān') *n.* [Fr. *châtelaine*, fem. of prec.] **1.** *a)* the mistress of a castle or château *b)* the mistress of any large household **2.** a woman's ornamental chain or clasp, esp. one worn at the waist, with keys or a purse, watch, etc. fastened to it

Chat·ham (chat'əm) seaport in Kent, SE England: pop. 50,000

Chat·ham (chat'əm), 1st Earl of, see PITT

Chatham Islands group of islands off New Zealand, c. 500 mi. east of South Island: 372 sq. mi.; pop. 500

cha·toy·ant (sha toi'ənt) *adj.* [Fr., prp. of *chatoyer*, to change luster like the eye of a cat < *chat*, a cat] having a changeable color or luster [*chatoyant* silk] —*n.* a gem or polished stone, as the cat's-eye, with such luster —**cha·toy'ance**, **cha·toy'an·cy** *n.*

Chat·ta·hoo·chee (chat'ə hōō'chē) [< AmInd. (Creek), lit., pictured rocks] river in W Ga., flowing southward into the Apalachicola at the Fla. border: with the Apalachicola, 500 mi.

Chat·ta·noo·ga (chat'ə nōō'gə) [< AmInd. (Creek or Cherokee), meaning unc.] city in SE Tenn., on the Ga. border: pop. 119,000

chat·tel (chat′'l) *n*. [ME. & OFr. *chatel:* see CATTLE] **1.** *a*)a movable item of personal property, as a piece of furniture, an automobile, a head of livestock, etc.: in full, **chattel personal** *b*) any interest in real estate less than a freehold: in full, **chattel real 2.** [Archaic] a slave

chattel mortgage a mortgage on personal property

chat·ter (chat′ər) *vi*. [ME. *chateren:* orig. echoic] **1.** to make short, indistinct sounds in rapid succession, as birds, apes, etc. **2.** to talk fast, incessantly, and foolishly **3.** to click together rapidly, as the teeth do when the lower jaw trembles from fright or cold **4.** to rattle or vibrate [an improperly adjusted tool *chatters*] —*vt*. to utter with a chattering sound —*n*. **1.** the act or sound of chattering **2.** rapid, foolish talk —**chat′ter·er** *n*.

chat·ter·box (-bäks′) *n*. a person who talks incessantly

chatter mark 1. a mark left by a tool that chatters **2.** any of a series of small, curved abrasions on the surface of a glaciated rock, resulting from the vibrations of the glacier passing over

Chat·ter·ton (chat′ər tən), **Thomas** 1752–70; Eng. poet

chat·ty (chat′ē) *adj*. **-ti·er, -ti·est 1.** fond of chatting **2.** light, familiar, and informal: said of talk —**chat′ti·ly** (-'l ē) *adv*. —**chat′ti·ness** *n*.

Chau·cer (chô′sər), **Geoffrey** 1340?–1400; Eng. poet: author of *The Canterbury Tales* —**Chau·ce·ri·an** (-sir′ē ən) *adj*.

chauf·fer (chô′fər, shô′-) *n*. [var. of *chafer* (see CHAFE, to heat), altered after Fr. *chauffoir* < *chauffer*, to heat, warm] a small, portable stove or heater

chauf·feur (shō′fər, shō fur′) *n*. [Fr., lit., stoker (operator of a steam-driven car) < *chauffer*, to heat: see CHAFE] a person hired to drive a private automobile for someone else —*vt*. to act as chauffeur to

chaul·moo·gra (chôl mōō′grə) *n*. [Beng. *cāulmugrā*, East Indian tree] any of various SE Asian trees (genera *Taraktogenos* and *Hydnocarpus*),whose seeds yield a nonvolatile oil formerly much used to treat leprosy

Chaun·cey (chôn′sē, chän′-) [orig., a surname, prob. of Fr. orig.] a masculine name

chaunt (chônt) *n., vt., vi. archaic var. of* CHANT

chausses (shōs) *n.pl.* [OFr. *chauces* < L. *calcea*, stocking, fem. augmentative of *calceus:* see ff.] a tightfitting, medieval garment for the legs and feet, esp. such a garment of mail forming part of a knight's armor

‡**chaus·sure** (shō sür′) *n*. [Fr. < *chausser*, to shoe < OFr. *chaucier* < L. *calceare* < *calceus*, shoe < *calx*, the heel] an article of footwear; shoe, boot, slipper, etc.

☆**Chau·tau·qua** (shə tô′kwə) [< Seneca name, prob., lit., "one has taken out fish there"] **1.** lake in SW N.Y.: 18 mi. long **2.** town on this lake: pop. 4,000 —*n*. [c-] [< the summer schools inaugurated at Chautauqua in 1874] an educational and recreational assembly with a program that includes lectures, concerts, etc. —**Chau·tau′quan** *n., adj.*

chau·vin·ism (shō′və niz'm) *n*. [Fr. *chauvinisme* < Nicolas *Chauvin*, soldier of Napoleon I, notorious for his bellicose attachment to the lost imperial cause] **1.** militant, unreasoning, and boastful devotion to one's country; fanatical patriotism; jingoism **2.** unreasoning devotion to one's race, sex, etc. with contempt for other races, the opposite sex, etc. [male *chauvinism*] —**chau′vin·ist** *n., adj.* —**chau′vin·is′tic** *adj.* —**chau′vin·is′ti·cal·ly** *adv.*

Cha·vannes, Puvis de *see* PUVIS DE CHAVANNES

chaw (chô) *n., vt., vi.* [Now Dial.] chew

chay (chā, chī) *n.* [< Tamil *cāya*] **1.** the root of an Indian plant (*Oldenlandia umbellata*) of the madder family, from which a red dye is obtained **2.** this plant

☆**cha·yo·te** (chä yōt′ē) *n.* [Sp. < Nahuatl *chayotli*] a tropical American perennial (*Sechium edule*) vine of the gourd family, grown for its edible, fleshy, pear-shaped, singleseeded fruit

chaz·an, chaz·zan (hä′z'n; Heb. khä zän′) *n.* same as HAZAN

Ch.E. Chemical Engineer

cheap (chēp) *adj.* [< *good cheap*, favorable bargain < ME. *god chep* (used as transl. for OFr. *à bon marché*) < OE. *ceap*, a purchase, bargain, akin to G. *kaufen*, to buy, ult. < L. *caupo*, petty tradesman] **1.** low in price or cost; not expensive **2.** charging low prices [a chain of *cheap* stores] **3.** spending or able to spend little [a *cheaper* clientele] **4.** worth more than the price **5.** costing little labor or trouble; easily got [a *cheap* victory] **6.** of little value or poor quality; virtually worthless **7.** deserving of scorn; contemptible [made *cheap* by her own behavior] **8.** [Colloq.] stingy; niggardly **9.** *Econ.* lowered in exchange value or buying power; also, available at low interest rates: said of money —*adv.* at a low cost; cheaply —*n.* [OE. *ceap*, market, akin to Dan. *kjob* (ON. *kaup*) as in *Kjöbmavn* (Copenhagen)] **1.** a market: now only in place names [*Cheapside*] **2.** [Obs.] a bargain —**on the cheap** at very little cost; cheaply —**cheap′ly** *adv.* —**cheap′ness** *n.*

SYN.—**cheap** and **inexpensive** both mean low in cost or price, but **inexpensive** simply suggests value comparable to the price and **cheap**, in this sense, stresses a bargain; **cheap** may also imply inferior quality or value, tawdriness, contemptibleness, etc. [*cheap* jewelry, to feel *cheap*] —ANT. **costly, expensive, dear**

cheap·en (chēp′'n) *vt.* [ME. *chepen* < OE. *ceapian*, to trade, buy (pres. meaning < prec.)] **1.** to make cheap or cheaper **2.** to depreciate, belittle, or bring into contempt

3. [Archaic] to bargain for —*vi.* to become cheap or cheaper —**cheap′en·er** *n.*

cheap-jack (-jak′) *n.* [CHEAP (*adj.*) + JACK[1]] a peddler of cheap, inferior articles —*adj.* cheap, inferior, base, etc. Also **cheap′-john′** (-jän′)

Cheap·side (chēp′sīd′) street and district of London: in the Middle Ages it was a marketplace

☆**cheap·skate** (chēp′skāt′) *n.* [Slang] a person unwilling to give or spend money; miserly person

cheat (chēt) *n.* [ME. *chete* < *eschete:* see ESCHEAT] **1.** the act of deceiving or swindling; deception; fraud **2.** a person who defrauds, deceives, or tricks others; swindler **3.** *same as* CHESS[2] —*vt.* **1.** to deal with dishonestly for one's own gain; defraud; swindle **2.** to deceive by trickery; fool; mislead **3.** to foil or escape by tricks or by good luck [to *cheat* death] —*vi.* **1.** to practice fraud or deception; behave dishonestly, as at games ☆**2.** [Slang] to be sexually unfaithful (often with *on*) —**cheat′er** *n.* —**cheat′ing·ly** *adv.*

SYN.—**cheat,** the most general term in this comparison, implies dishonesty or deception in dealing with someone, to obtain some advantage or gain; **defraud,** chiefly a legal term, stresses the use of deliberate deception in criminally depriving a person of his rights, property, etc.; **swindle** stresses the winning of a person's confidence in order to cheat or defraud him of money, etc.; **trick** implies a deluding by means of a ruse, stratagem, etc., but does not always suggest fraudulence or a harmful motive; **dupe** stresses credulity in the person who is tricked or fooled; **hoax** implies a trick skillfully carried off simply to demonstrate the gullibility of the victim

☆**che·bec** (chi bek′) *n.* [echoic of the bird's note] *same as* LEAST FLYCATCHER

che·cha·ko (chē chä′kō) *n., pl.* **-kos** [Canad. & Alaskan slang < Chinook jargon] [Canad.] a tenderfoot, as in the Yukon

check (chek) *n.* [ME. *chek* < OFr. *eschec, eschac*, a check at chess, repulse < ML. *scaccus, scahus* < Per. *shāh*, king, principal piece in a game of chess (see SHAH); prob. sense development: king in danger—hostile action—restraining action—means of restraint or control] **1.** a sudden stop; abrupt halt **2.** any restraint or control put upon action **3.** a person or thing that restrains or controls **4.** a supervision of accuracy, efficiency, etc. **5.** *a*) a test, comparison, examination, etc. to determine if something is as it should be *b*) a standard or sample used in making such a determination **6.** a mark (√) to show approval or verification of something, or to call attention to it ☆**7.** an identification ticket or other token enabling one to claim an item left in a checkroom, etc. [a hat *check*] ☆**8.** one's bill at a restaurant or bar ☆**9.** [Now Rare] a gambling chip **10.** a written order to a bank to pay the stated amount of money from one's account **11.** *a*) a pattern of small squares like that of a chessboard *b*) one of these squares **12.** a fabric with such a pattern **13.** a small split, crack, or chink **14.** [Obs.] a rebuke; reprimand **15.** *Chess* the condition of a king that is in danger and must be put into a safe position **16.** *Hockey* a blocking of an opponent's play or movement —*interj.* **1.** [Colloq.] agreed! I understand! right! ok! **2.** *Chess* a call meaning that the opponent's king must be taken out of check —*vt.* **1.** to cause to stop suddenly; halt abruptly **2.** to hold back; restrain; control **3.** to rebuff, repulse, or rebuke **4.** to test, measure, verify, or control by investigation, comparison, or examination [check the accounts] **5.** to mark with a check (√) **6.** to mark with a pattern of squares ☆**7.** to deposit temporarily, as in a checkroom ☆**8.** to get (esp. luggage) cleared for shipment **9.** to make chinks or cracks in ☆**10.** *Agric.* to plant in checkrows **11.** *Chess* to place (an opponent's king) in check **12.** *Hockey* to block the play or movement of (an opponent) **13.** *Naut.* to reduce the strain on (a line) gradually —*vi.* ☆**1.** to agree with one another item for item [the accounts *check*] ☆**2.** to investigate in order to determine the condition, validity, etc. of something (often with *on*) ☆**3.** to draw a check on a bank account **4.** to crack in small checks [cheap paint may *check*] **5.** to stop or halt; specif., to pause, as a hunting dog, to pick up the scent **6.** *Chess* to place an opponent's king in check **7.** *Falconry* to turn away from the right game and follow lesser game (with *at*) ☆**8.** *Poker* to decline one's chance to open a round of betting —*adj.* **1.** used to check or verify [a *check* experiment] **2.** having a crisscross pattern; checked —SYN. see RESTRAIN —☆**check in 1.** to register at a hotel, convention, etc. **2.** [Colloq.] to report, as by presenting oneself [check in at the office] —☆**check off** to mark as verified, examined, etc. —☆**check out 1.** to settle one's bill and leave a hotel, etc. **2.** to add up the prices of purchases and collect the total: said of a cashier, as in a supermarket **3.** *a*) to examine and verify or approve *b*) to prove to be accurate, in sound condition, etc. upon examination **4.** to draw (money) from a bank by check **5.** [Slang] to die —☆**check up on** to examine the record, character, etc. of; investigate —**in check** in restraint; under control

☆**check·book** (-book′) *n.* a book containing detachable forms for writing checks on a bank

checked (chekt) *adj.* **1.** having a pattern of squares [a *checked* tablecloth] **2.** *Phonet. a*) ending in a consonant: said of a syllable *b*) sounded in such a syllable: said of a vowel

check·er[1] (chek′ər) *n.* [ME. *cheker*, chessboard, aphetic < *escheker* < OFr. *eschekier* < ML. *scaccarium:* see CHECK] **1.** a small square, as on a chessboard **2.** a pattern of such

squares **3.** *a*) [*pl.*, *with sing. v.*] a game played on a checker-board by two players, each with twelve round, flat pieces to move: Brit. name, DRAUGHTS *b*) any of these pieces **4.** *same as* SERVICE (TREE) —*vt.* **1.** to mark off in squares, or in patches of color **2.** to break the uniformity of, as with varied features or events, changes in fortune, etc.

check·er² (chek′ər) *n.* **1.** a person who examines or verifies ☆**2.** a person who checks hats, luggage, etc. **3.** a cashier, as in a supermarket

☆**check·er·ber·ry** (-ber′ē) *n.*, *pl.* **-ries 1.** *same as* WINTER-GREEN (sense 1 *a*) **2.** the edible, red, berrylike fruit of the wintergreen

check·er·bloom (-blōōm′) *n.* a California perennial plant (*Sidalcea malvaeflora*) of the mallow family, with rosy or purple flowers

check·er·board (-bôrd′) *n.* a board with 64 squares of two alternating colors, used in checkers and chess

check·ered (-ərd) *adj.* **1.** having a pattern of squares **2.** varied by the use of color and shading **3.** marked by diversified features or by varied events, some unpleasant [a *checkered* career]

☆**checking account** a bank account against which the depositor can draw checks at any time, without presenting a bankbook: it bears no interest

☆**check·list** (-list′) *n.* a list of things, names, etc. to be checked off or referred to for verifying, comparing, ordering, etc.: also **check list**

check·mate (-māt′) *n.* [ME. *chek mat* < OFr. *eschec mat*, ult. < Per. *shāh māt*, lit., the king is dead < *shāh*, king + *māt*, he is dead] **1.** *Chess a*) the move that wins the game by checking the opponent's king so that it cannot be put into safety *b*) the position of the king after such a move **2.** complete defeat, frustration, etc. —*interj. Chess* a call to indicate a checkmate —*vt.* **-mat′ed, -mat′ing 1.** to place in checkmate **2.** to defeat completely; frustrate; thwart

☆**check·off** (-ôf′) *n.* an arrangement by which dues of trade-union members are withheld from wages and turned over to the union by the employer

☆**check·out** (-out′) *n.* **1.** the act or place of checking out purchases, as in a supermarket **2.** the time by which one must check out of a hotel, etc. **3.** a testing, esp. of a machine, as for accuracy Also **check-out**

check·point (-point′) *n.* a place on a highway, a border between countries, etc. where traffic is stopped, as for inspection by authorities

check·rein (-rān′) *n.* **1.** a short rein attached to the bridle to keep a horse from lowering its head **2.** a branch rein connecting the driving rein of one of a team of horses to the bit of another Also called **check line**

☆**check·room** (-rōōm′, -room′) *n.* [see CHECK (*vt.* 7)] a room in which hats, coats, baggage, parcels, etc. may be left in safekeeping until called for

☆**check·row** (-rō′) *n.* any of a series of rows of plants crossing others at right angles to form a check pattern, so that the rows can be cultivated up and down or from side to side —*vt.* to plant (corn, etc.) in checkrows

☆**check·up** (-up′) *n.* an examination or investigation, esp. a general medical examination

Ched·dar (cheese) (ched′ər) [< *Cheddar*, Somersetshire, England, where orig. made] [*often* c-] a variety of hard, smooth cheese, mild to very sharp

‡**che·der** (khä′dər) *n. same as* HEDER

cheek (chēk) *n.* [ME. *cheke* < OE. *ceoke*, jaw, jawbone, akin to Du. *kaak*, LowG. *kâke*, jaw (only WGmc.)] **1.** either side of the face between the nose and ear, below the eye **2.** either of two sides of a thing, as the sides of a door jamb or the jaws of a vise: *usually used in pl.* **3.** either of the buttocks **4.** [Colloq.] disrespectful boldness; sauciness; effrontery; impudence —*vt.* [Brit. Colloq.] to speak insolently to —*SYN.* see TEMERITY —**cheek by jowl** close together; intimately —(**with**) **tongue in cheek** in a humorously ironic, mocking, or insincere way

cheek·bone (-bōn′) *n.* the bone of the upper cheek, just below the eye; zygomatic bone; malar

cheek pouch a pouchlike swelling in the cheek of certain rodents, monkeys, etc., used for holding food

cheek strap either of the side straps of a bridle, connecting the brow band with the bit: see BRIDLE, illus.

cheek·y (-ē) *adj.* **cheek′i·er, cheek′i·est** [CHEEK + -Y²] [Colloq.] saucy; impudent; insolent —**cheek′i·ly** *adv.* —**cheek′i·ness** *n.*

cheep (chēp) *n.* [echoic] the short, faint, shrill sound made by a young bird; peep; chirp —*vt., vi.* to make, or utter with, such a sound —**cheep′er** *n.*

cheer (chir) *n.* [ME. *chere*, the face, demeanor, bearing, mood < OFr. *chiere* < LL. *cara*, head < Gr. *kara* < IE. base **ker-*, head, whence HORN; modern senses < phr. good cheer (Fr. *bonne chère*)] **1.** state of mind or of feeling; mood; spirit: now usual only in such phrases as **be of good cheer, with good cheer 2.** gaiety; gladness; joy; encouragement **3.** festive food or entertainment **4.** anything that makes one happy; encouragement **5.** *a*) a glad, excited shout used to urge on, welcome, approve, etc. *b*) a jingle, rallying cry, etc. shouted in unison in rooting for a team

6. [Archaic] facial expression —*vt.* **1.** to fill with joy, good spirits, and hope; gladden; comfort (often with *up*) **2.** to urge on or encourage by cheers **3.** to greet or applaud with cheers —*vi.* **1.** to be or become cheerful; feel encouraged (usually with *up*) **2.** to shout cheers

cheer·ful (-fəl) *adj.* **1.** full of cheer; gay; joyful **2.** filling with cheer; bright and attractive [a *cheerful* room] **3.** willing; ready [a *cheerful* helper] —*SYN.* see HAPPY —**cheer′ful·ly** *adv.* —**cheer′ful·ness** *n.*

cheer·i·o (-ē ō′) *interj., n., pl.* **-os′** [Brit. Colloq.] **1.** goodbye **2.** good health: used as a toast

☆**cheer·lead·er** (-lē′dər) *n.* a person who leads others in cheering for a team, as at football games

cheer·less (-lis) *adj.* not cheerful; dismal; joyless; dreary —**cheer′less·ly** *adv.* —**cheer′less·ness** *n.*

cheer·ly (-lē) *adv.* [Archaic] cheerily; blithely

cheers (chirz) *interj.* [Chiefly Brit.] good health: used as a toast

cheer·y (-ē) *adj.* **cheer′i·er, cheer′i·est** cheerful; gay; lively; bright —**cheer′i·ly** *adv.* —**cheer′i·ness** *n.*

cheese¹ (chēz) *n.* [ME. *chese* < OE. *cyse* < Gmc. **kasjus* < IE. base **kwat-*, to ferment, become sour, whence also L. *caseus*, cheese] **1.** a food made from the curds of soured milk pressed together to form a solid that is usually allowed to ripen **2.** a shaped mass of this **3.** a thing like cheese in shape or consistency

cheese² (chēz) *n.* [Hind. *chīz*, a thing < Per. *čiz*, something] [Slang] an important person or thing

cheese·burg·er (chēz′bur′gər) *n.* [CHEESE¹ + -BURGER] a hamburger topped with a slice of melted cheese

cheese·cake (-kāk′) *n.* **1.** a kind of cake made of cottage cheese or cream cheese, eggs, sugar, etc., usually baked with a bottom crust of crumbs ☆**2.** [Slang] display of the figure, esp. the legs, of a pretty girl, as in some newspaper photographs

cheese·cloth (-klôth′) *n.* [from its use for wrapping cheese] a thin, cotton cloth with a very loose weave

cheese·par·ing (-per′iŋ) *n.* **1.** anything as worthless as a paring of cheese rind **2.** miserly handling of money or finances —*adj.* stingy; miserly

cheese·y (-ē) *adj.* **chees′i·er, chees′i·est 1.** like cheese in consistency, smell, etc. ☆**2.** [Slang] inferior; poor —**chees′i·ness** *n.*

chee·tah (chēt′ə) *n.* [Hind. *chītā*, leopard < Sans. *citra*, spotted: see CHINTZ] a swift, leopardlike animal (*Acinonyx jubatus*) of Africa and S Asia, with a small head, long legs, and a black-spotted, tawny coat: it can be trained to hunt

chef (shef) *n.* [Fr. < *chef de cuisine*, lit., head of the kitchen: see CHIEF] **1.** a man cook in charge of a kitchen, as of a restaurant; head cook **2.** any cook

‡**chef-d'oeu·vre** (she dë′vr′) *n., pl.* **chefs-d'oeu′vre** (she dë′vr′) [Fr., principal work] a masterpiece, as in art or literature

Che·foo (che′fōō′) *same as* YENTAI

chei·ro- (ki′rə, -rō) *same as* CHIRO-

Che·ju (chä′jōō′) island in the East China Sea; province of South Korea: c. 700 sq. mi.; pop. 293,000

Che·khov (chek′ôf; *Russ.* chekh′ôf), **An·ton Pa·vlo·vich** (än tōn′ pä vlô′vich) 1860–1904; Russ. dramatist & short-story writer: also sp. **Che′kov**

Che·kiang (che′kyan′; *Chin.* ju′jyän′) province of E China, on the East China Sea: 39,300 sq. mi.; pop. 25,280,000; cap. Hangchow

che·la (kē′lə) *n., pl.* **-lae** (-lē) [ModL. < Gr. *chēlē*, claw < IE. base **ghei*, to yawn, whence GAPE] a pincerlike claw of a crab, lobster, scorpion, etc.

che·late (kē′lāt) *adj.* resembling or having chelae —*n.* a chemical compound in which the central atom (usually a metal ion) is attached to neighboring atoms by at least two bonds in such a way as to form a ring structure —*vt.* **-lat·ed, -lat·ing** to cause (a metal ion) to react with another molecule to form a chelate —**che·la′tion** *n.* —**che′la·tor** *n.*

che·lic·er·a (kə lis′ə rə) *n., pl.* **-er·ae** (-ə rē′) [ModL. < Gr. *chēlē*, claw + *keras*, HORN] either of the first pair of appendages of spiders and other arachnids, used for grasping and crushing —**che·lic·er·ate** (-rāt′, -ə rit) *adj.*

che·lif·er·ous (ki lif′ər əs) *adj.* bearing chelae

che·li·form (kē′lə fôrm′) *adj.* having the form of a chela, or pincerlike claw

Chel·le·an (shel′ē ən) *adj.* [Fr. *chelléen* < *Chelles*, suburb of Paris, France, where the tools were found] *same as* ABBEVILLIAN

che·loid (kē′loid) *n. same as* KELOID

che·lo·ni·an (ki lō′nē ən) *adj.* [< ModL. *Chelonia* < Gr. *chelōnē* (< IE. base **ghelou-*, turtle) + -AN] of, like, or being a turtle or tortoise —*n.* a turtle or tortoise

Chel·sea (chel′sē) borough of London, on the N bank of the Thames: pop. 48,000

Chel·ten·ham (chelt′'n ham′; *Brit.* chelt′nəm, -'n əm) city in Gloucestershire, SW England: pop. 74,000

Chel·ya·binsk (chi lyä′binsk) city in the SW R.S.F.S.R., in the S Urals: pop. 805,000

Chel·yus·kin (chil yōōs′kin), **Cape** northernmost point of Asia, on the Taimyr Peninsula, Siberia

chem. 1. chemical; chemicals 2. chemist 3. chemistry
chem·ic (kem'ik) *adj.* 1. [Archaic] of alchemy; alchemical 2. [Now Poet.] chemical
chem·i·cal (kem'i k'l) *adj.* [prec. + -AL] 1. of or having to do with chemistry 2. made by or used in chemistry 3. operated or made by the use of chemicals —*n.* any substance used in or obtained by a chemical process —**chem'i·cal·ly** *adv.*
☆**chemical engineering** the science or profession of applying chemistry to industrial uses
chemical warfare warfare by means of chemicals and chemical devices such as poisonous gases, flame throwers, incendiary bombs, smoke screens, etc.
chem·i·lu·mi·nes·cence (kem'i loo'mə nes'ns) *n.* visible light produced by chemical action and not accompanied by heat —**chem'i·lu'mi·nes'cent** *adj.*
che·min de fer (shə man' də fer') [Fr., a railroad, lit., road of iron] a kind of baccarat, a gambling game
che·mise (shə mēz') *n.* [ME. < OFr. < VL. *camisia*, shirt, tunic, prob. via Gaul. < Gmc. **chamithja-* (whence OE. *hemethe*, G. *hemd*, shirt) < IE. base **kem-*, to cover, cloak, whence HEAVEN] 1. a woman's undergarment somewhat like a loose, short slip 2. a loose dress that hangs straight with no waistline; shift
chem·i·sette (shem'i zet') *n.* [Fr., dim. of prec.] a detachable shirt front formerly worn by women to fill in the neckline of a dress
chem·ism (kem'iz'm) *n.* [Fr. *chemisme:* see CHEMIST] [Rare] chemical force, action, or affinity
chem·i·sorb (kem'ə sôrb', -zôrb') *vt.* [CHEMI(CAL) + (AD)SORB] to bind (a substance) chemically onto the surface layer of an adsorbent —**chem'i·sorp'tion** *n.*
chem·ist (-ist) *n.* [aphetic < ALCHEMIST] 1. an expert or specialist in chemistry 2. [Brit.] a pharmacist, or druggist 3. [Obs.] an alchemist
chem·is·try (kem'is trē) *n.*, *pl.* **-tries** [prec. + -RY] 1. the science dealing with the composition and properties of substances, and with the reactions by which substances are produced from or converted into other substances 2. the application of this to a specified subject or field of activity 3. the chemical properties, composition, reactions, and uses of a substance 4. any process of synthesis or analysis similar to that used in chemistry [the *chemistry* of wit]
Chem·nitz (kem'nits) *former name of* KARL-MARX-STADT
chem·o- (kem'ō, -ə; kē'mō, -mə) *a combining form meaning* of, with, or by chemicals or chemistry [*chemotherapy*]
chem·o·au·to·tro·phic (kem'ō ôt'ə träf'ik, kē'mō-) *adj.* [CHEMO- + AUTOTROPHIC] producing organic matter by the use of energy obtained by oxidation of certain substances: said of some bacteria —**chem'o·au'to·tro'phi·cal·ly** *adv.* —**chem'o·au·tot'ro·phy** (-ō tät'rə fē) *n.*
chem·o·pro·phy·lax·is (-prō'fə lak'sis) *n.* the prevention of disease by the use of chemical drugs —**chem'o·pro'phy·lac'tic** (-lak'tik) *adj.*
chem·o·re·cep·tor (-ri sep'tər) *n.* a nerve ending, or sense organ, that can respond to chemical stimuli, as the taste and smell receptors —**chem'o·re·cep'tive** *adj.*
chem·os·mo·sis (kem'äs mō'sis) *n.* chemical action between substances that are separated by a semipermeable membrane —**chem'os·mot'ic** (-mät'ik) *adj.*
chem·o·sphere (kem'ə sfir', kē'mə-) *n.* an atmospheric zone about 20 to 50 mi. above the earth's surface, characterized by extensive photochemical activity
chem·o·ster·i·lant (kem'ō ster'ə lənt, kē'mō-) *n.* a chemical compound that can produce sterility, used esp. in insect control
chem·o·syn·the·sis (-sin'thə sis) *n.* the synthesis by certain bacteria of organic compounds from carbon dioxide and water by the use of energy obtained by the oxidation of certain chemicals, as hydrogen sulfide, ammonia, etc.: see also PHOTOSYNTHESIS —**chem'o·syn·thet'ic** (-sin thet'ik) *adj.* —**chem'o·syn·thet'i·cal·ly** *adv.*
chem·o·tax·is (-tak'sis) *n.* the property of certain living cells and organisms by which they are attracted to or repelled from chemical substances —**chem'o·tac'tic** (-tak'tik) *adj.* —**chem'o·tac'ti·cal·ly** *adv.*
chem·o·ther·a·py (-ther'ə pē) *n.* the prevention or treatment of infection by the systemic administration of chemical drugs: also **chem'o·ther'a·peu'tics** (-ther'ə pyoot'iks) —**chem'o·ther'a·peu'tic** *adj.* —**chem'o·ther'a·peu'ti·cal·ly** *adv.* —**chem'o·ther'a·pist** *n.*
chem·ot·ro·pism (kem ä'trə piz'm) *n.* [see CHEMO- & TROPISM] the tendency of certain plants or other organisms to turn or bend under the influence of chemical substances —**chem·o·trop·ic** (kem'ō träp'ik) *adj.*
chem·ur·gy (kem'ər jē) *n.* [CHEM(O)- + -URGY] the branch of chemistry dealing with the utilization of organic products, esp. from farms, in the manufacture of new products not classed as food or clothing (e.g., soybeans as a base for plastics) —**chem·ur'gic** (kem ur'jik) *adj.*
Che·nab (chi näb') river rising in Kashmir and flowing southwest into the Sutlej River in West Pakistan: c. 675 mi.
Chen·chiang (jen'jyäŋ') *same as* CHINKIANG
Cheng·chow, Cheng·chou (jen'jou') city in EC China; capital of Honan province: pop. 800,000
Cheng·tu (chun'doo') city in SC China; capital of Szechwan province: pop. 1,135,000
che·nille (shi nēl') *n.* [Fr., lit., hairy caterpillar < L.

canicula, dim. of *canis*, dog: from its hairy appearance] 1. a tufted, velvety yarn used for trimming, embroidery, etc. 2. a fabric filled or woven with such yarn, used for rugs, bedspreads, etc.
che·no·pod (kē'nə päd', ken'ə-) *n.* [< ModL. Chenopodium, name of the genus < Gr. *chēn* (gen. *chēnos*), goose + -PODIUM] any plant of the goosefoot family, as spinach, beets, etc.
che·ong·sam, che·ong-sam (che ôŋ'säm') *n.* [Chin.] a high-necked, closefitting dress with the skirt slit part way up the sides, traditionally worn by Chinese women
Che·ops (kē'äps) *Gr. name of* KHUFU
cheque (chek) *n. Brit. sp. of* CHECK (*n.* 10)
cheq·uer (chek'ər) *n., vt. Brit. sp. of* CHECKER[1]
Cher (sher) river in C France, flowing into the Loire near Tours: c. 200 mi.
Cher·bourg (sher'boorg; *Fr.* sher boor') seaport in NW France, on the English Channel: pop. 37,000
cher·ish (cher'ish) *vt.* [ME. *cherischen* < extended stem of OFr. *cherir* < *cher*, dear < L. *carus:* see CHARITY] 1. to hold dear; feel or show love for [to *cherish* one's family] 2. to take good care of; protect; foster [to *cherish* one's rights] 3. to cling to the idea or feeling of [to *cherish* a hope] —*SYN.* see APPRECIATE
Cher·nov·tsy (cher nôf'tsē) city in SW Ukrainian S.S.R.: pop. 172,000
cher·no·zem (cher'nə zem', -zyôm') *n.* [Russ. < *chernyi*, black + *zemlya*, earth, soil] a black topsoil, rich in humus and lime, found characteristically in the grasslands of C European Russia
Cher·o·kee (cher'ə kē') *n.* [< tribal name *Tsárǔgi*, prob. < Choctaw *chiluk-ki*, "cave people"] 1. *pl.* **-kees', -kee'** a member of a tribe of Iroquoian Indians most of whom were moved from the SE U.S. to Oklahoma 2. the Iroquoian language of these Indians
☆**Cherokee rose** an evergreen climbing rose (*Rosa laevigata*), with fragrant, large, white flowers and glossy leaves, native to China but now growing wild in the S U.S.
che·root (shə root') *n.* [< Tamil *churuṭṭu*, a roll] a cigar with both ends cut square
cher·ry (cher'ē) *n., pl.* **-ries** [ME. *cheri* < Anglo-Fr. *cherise* (taken as pl.) < OFr. *cerise* < VL. *ceresia* < Gr. *kerasion*, cherry < *kerasos*, cherry tree, prob. < IE. base **ker-*, whence CORNEL; derived by the ancients from *Cerasus*, city on the Black Sea: the city's name is itself from the cherries grown in the area] 1. a small, fleshy fruit containing a smooth, hard pit and ranging from yellow to very dark red 2. any of various trees (genus *Prunus*) of the rose family which bear this fruit 3. the wood of such a tree 4. the bright-red color of certain cherries 5. [Slang] ☆*a)* the hymen *b)* virginity —*adj.* 1. bright-red 2. made of cherry wood 3. made with cherries 4. having a flavor like that of cherries
cherry bomb a round, red, powerful firecracker
cherry laurel any of several shrubs (genus *Prunus*) of the rose family, with thick, glossy, evergreen leaves
☆**cherry picker** [Slang] an elevator tower mounted on a truck, with a platform from which spacecraft on launchers, raised electric power lines, etc. can be serviced
cherry plum a small tree (*Prunus cerasifera*) of the rose family, often used as a grafting stock for other varieties of plums
☆**cher·ry·stone** (cher'ē-stōn') *n.* a small quahog, a variety of clam: also **cherrystone clam**
cher·so·nese (kur'sə nēz') *n.* [L. *chersonesus* < Gr. *chersonēsos* < *chersos*, dry land + *nēsos*, island] a peninsula
chert (churt) *n.* [< ?] a very fine-grained, tough rock composed mainly of silica and occurring commonly in limestone beds —**chert'y** (-ē) *adj.* **chert'i·er, chert'i·est**
cher·ub (cher'əb) *n., pl.* **-ubs;** for 1, 2, & 3 usually **-u·bim** (-ə bim, -yoo bim) or (KJV) **-u·bims** [ME. < OE. *ceruphin* < LL.(Ec.) *cherub* < Heb. *kerūbh*] 1. *Bible* one of the winged heavenly beings that support the throne of God or act as guardian spirits: Ezek. 10; Ps. 80:1; Gen. 3:24 2. *Christian Theol.* any of the second order of angels, usually ranked just below the seraphim 3. a representation of one of the cherubim as, in early art, a winged angel clothed in red or, later, a chubby, rosy-faced child with wings 4. a person, esp. a child, with a sweet, chubby, innocent face —**che·ru·bic** (chə roo'bik) *adj.* —**che·ru'bi·cal·ly** *adv.*
Che·ru·bi·ni (ke'roo bē'nē), (Maria) **Lu·i·gi** (Carlo Zenobio Salvatore) (loo ē'jē) 1760–1842; It. composer
cher·vil (chur'vəl) *n.* [ME. *chervel* < OE. *cerfelle* < L. *chaerephyllum* < Gr. *chairephyllon* < *chairein*, to rejoice + *phyllon*, leaf] 1. an annual plant (*Anthriscus cerefolium*) of the parsley family, whose leaves are used for flavoring salads, soups, etc. 2. a similar plant (*Chaerophyllum bulbosum*) grown for its carrotlike root 3. *same as* SWEET CICELY
Ches·a·peake (ches'ə pēk') [see *ff.*] city in SE Va., at the base of Chesapeake Bay: pop. 90,000
Chesapeake Bay [*Chesapeake* < Algonquian, lit., country on a big river] arm of the Atlantic, extending north into Va. and Md.: c. 200 mi. long
Chesh·ire (chesh'ir, -ər) county of W England: 1,015 sq. mi.; pop. 1,410,000; county seat, Chester
Cheshire cat a proverbial grinning cat from Cheshire, England, esp. one described in Lewis Carroll's *Alice's Adventures in Wonderland*
Chesh·van (khesh'vän) *n. same as* HESHVAN

chess[1] (ches) *n.* [ME. *ches*, *chesse* < OFr. *esches*, pl. of *eschec*: see CHECK] a game of skill played on a chessboard by two players, each with 16 pieces limited in movement according to kind: the players make alternate moves until one wins by checkmating his opponent's king or until a stalemate or draw results

chess[2] (ches) *n.* [< ?] any of several varieties of brome grass, esp. a weedy kind (*Bromus secalinus*) found among wheat and other grains

chess·board (ches'bôrd') *n.* a board with 64 squares of two alternating colors, used in chess and checkers

chess·man (-man', -mən) *n., pl.* -men' (-men', -mən) [altered (after MAN) < ME. *ches-meyne*, lit., chess retinue: *meyne*, a household < OFr. *mesnie* < VL. *mansionata* < L. *mansio*: see MANSION] any of the pieces used in the game of chess: each player has 1 king, 1 queen, 2 rooks (or castles), 2 knights, 2 bishops, and 8 pawns

chest (chest) *n.* [ME. *chest*, *chiste* < OE., ON., or L.: OE. *cist* & ON. *kista* < L. *cista* < Gr. *kistē*, a box, basket, akin to OIr. *cess*, basket] 1. a box with a lid and, often, a lock, for storing or shipping things 2. [Rare] a place where money or funds are kept; treasury 3. a public fund (the community *chest*] 4. *same as* CHEST OF DRAWERS 5. a cabinet, as for holding medical supplies, toiletries, etc. 6. *a)* the part of the body enclosed by the ribs and breastbone; thorax *b)* the outside front part of this —**get (something) off one's chest** [Colloq.] to unburden oneself of (some trouble, annoyance, etc.) by talking about it

chest·ed (-id) *adj.* having a (specified kind of) chest, or thorax [hollow-*chested*]

Ches·ter (ches'tər) [OE. *Ceastre*, contr. < *Legacaestir*, for L. *legionum castra*, camp of the legions] 1. a masculine name 2. county seat of Cheshire, England: pop. 59,000 3. *former name of* CHESHIRE 4. [after prec.] seaport in SE Pa., near Philadelphia, on the Delaware River: pop. 56,000

Ches·ter·field (ches'tər fēld'), 4th Earl of, (*Philip Dormer Stanhope*) 1694–1773; Eng. statesman & writer on manners —**Ches'ter·field'i·an** (-ē ən) *adj.*

Ches·ter·field (-fēld') city in NC England, in Derbyshire: pop. 68,000 —*n.* [c-] [after a 19th-c. Earl of *Chesterfield*] 1. a single-breasted topcoat, usually with a fly front and a velvet collar 2. *a)* a kind of sofa, heavily stuffed and with upright ends *b)* [Canad.] any sofa

Ches·ter·ton (ches'tər tən), **G(ilbert) K(eith)** 1874–1936; Eng. writer

Chester White [after *Chester* County, Pa., where reputedly first bred] a variety of large, white hog

chest·nut (ches'nut', -nət) *n.* [< *chesten-nut* < ME. *chesteine* < OFr. *chastaigne* < L. *castanea* < Gr. *kastaneia*] 1. the smooth-shelled, sweet, edible nut of any of a genus (*Castanea*) of trees of the beech family 2. the tree that it grows on 3. the wood of this tree 4. *same as* HORSE CHESTNUT 5. reddish brown 6. a reddish-brown horse 7. the hard callus on the inner side of a horse's foreleg ☆8. [Colloq.] *a)* an old, stale joke or phrase; cliché *b)* a very familiar story, piece of music, etc. that is too often repeated —*adj.* reddish-brown —**pull someone's chestnuts out of the fire** [cf. CAT'S-PAW] to be persuaded or duped into doing a dangerous, hard, or unpleasant thing for someone else

CHESTNUTS

☆**chestnut blight** a disease of chestnut trees caused by a fungus (*Endothia parasitica*), that has virtually destroyed the American chestnut

chest of drawers an article of furniture, as for a bedroom, consisting of a frame containing a set of drawers, as for keeping clothing

☆**chest-on-chest** (chest'än chest') *n.* a chest of drawers fitted onto another, somewhat larger one, generally resting on short feet

chest register the lower register of the voice, in which the lower range of tones is produced

chest·y (ches'tē) *adj.* **chest'i·er, chest'i·est** [Colloq.] 1. *a)* having a large chest, or thorax *b)* bosomy ☆2. boastful, proud, or conceited

che·tah (chēt'ə) *n. same as* CHEETAH

cheth (khet) *n. same as* HET

che·val-de-frise (shə val'də frēz') *n., pl.* **che·vaux'-de-frise'** (shə vō'-) [Fr. < *cheval*, a horse + *de*, of + *Frise*, Friesland: first used by Frisians, who lacked cavalry, against Spaniards] 1. a piece of wood with projecting spikes, formerly used to hinder enemy horsemen 2. a row of spikes or jagged glass set into the masonry on top of a wall to prevent escape or trespassing

che·val glass (shə val') [Fr. *cheval*, horse, hence frame (cf. SAWHORSE) + GLASS] a full-length mirror mounted on swivels in a frame

chev·a·lier (shev'ə lir'; *for 1 & 3, often* shə val'yā') *n.* [ME. & Anglo-Fr. *chevaler* (Fr. *chevalier*) < LL. *caballarius*: see CAVALIER] 1. a member of the lowest rank of the French Legion of Honor 2. a chivalrous man; gallant; cavalier 3. formerly, a French noble of the lowest rank 4. [Archaic] a knight

‡**cheve·lure** (shəv lür') *n.* [Fr., head of hair < L. *capillatura*, the hair, a being hairy < *capillus*, hair: see CAPILLARY] a head of hair; specif., a coiffure

Chev·i·ot (chev'ē ət; *also, and for 2 always,* shev'ē ət) *n.* [after ff.] 1. any of a breed of sheep with short, dense wool 2. [*usually* c-] *a)* a rough wool fabric in a twill weave, formerly made from the wool of this sheep *b)* a cotton cloth resembling this

Cheviot Hills range of hills on the border between England & Scotland: highest peak, 2,676 ft.

chev·ron (shev'rən) *n.* [ME. *cheveroun* < OFr. *chevron*, rafter (from its shape) < *caprio* (gen. *caprionis*), ult. < L. *capra*, she-goat] an insignia consisting of a V-shaped bar or bars, worn on the sleeve as of a military or police uniform to show rank or service

chev·ro·tain (shev'rə tān', -tin) *n.* [Fr. *chevrotin*, orig., fawn during first half year < OFr. *chevrot*, dim. of *chèvre*, she-goat < L. *capra*, fem. of *caper*, goat] any of a family (Tragulidae) of small, hornless animals of SW Asia and W Africa, superficially resembling the deer

chev·y (chev'ē) *n., pl.* **chev'ies** [< hunting cry *chivy*, in the ballad of *Chevy Chase* < CHEVIOT (HILLS)] [Brit.] 1. a hunt; chase 2. *same as* PRISONER'S BASE —*vt., vi.* **chev'ied, chev'y·ing** 1. [Brit.] to hunt; chase; run about 2. to worry; fret; chivy

CHEVRON

chew (chōō) *vt.* [ME. *chewen* < OE. *ceowan*, to bite, chew < IE. base *gjeu-*, to chew, whence Per. *javidan*, G. *kauen*] 1. to bite and grind or crush with the teeth; masticate 2. *a)* to think over; consider *b)* to discuss at length ☆3. [Slang] to rebuke severely; reprimand (often with *out*) —*vi.* 1. to perform the act of chewing ☆2. [Colloq.] to chew tobacco —*n.* 1. the act of chewing 2. something chewed or for chewing; specif., a portion of tobacco for chewing —**chew the rag (or fat)** [Slang] to converse idly; chat —**chew'er** *n.*

☆**chew·ing gum** (chōō'iŋ) a gummy substance, such as chicle, flavored and sweetened for chewing

☆**che·wink** (chi wiŋk') *n.* [echoic of its note] the eastern towhee (*Pipilo erythrophthalmus*) of N. America, characterized by having the iris of the eye bright red

chew·y (chōō'ē) *adj.* **chew'i·er, chew'i·est** that needs much chewing [*chewy* candy]

Chey·enne[1] (shī en', -an') *n.* [AmInd. (Dakota) *shaiyena* < *shaia*, to speak unintelligibly] 1. *pl.* **-ennes', -enne'** a member of a tribe of Algonquian Indians who migrated from Minnesota to the headwaters of the Platte River and south into S Colorado and SW Kansas: they now live in Montana and Oklahoma 2. the Algonquian language of this tribe

Chey·enne[2] (shī an', -en') [< prec.] 1. capital of Wyo., in the SE part: pop. 41,000 2. river in E Wyo. and W S.Dak., flowing northeast into the Missouri: c. 300 mi.

‡**chez** (shā) *prep.* [Fr.] by; at; at the home of

chg. *pl.* **chgs.** charge

chgd. charged

chi (kī) *n.* [Gr.] the 22d letter of the Greek alphabet (X, χ)

Chi·an (kī'ən) *adj.* of Chios (Khios) —*n.* a native or inhabitant of Chios (Khios)

Chiang Kai-shek (chaŋ'kī shek', chyaŋ'-; *Chin.* jyäŋ'-) (born *Chiang Chung-chen*) 1888– ; Chin. generalissimo: head of Nationalist government on Taiwan (1950–)

Chiang Mai, Chiang·mai (jyäŋ'mī') city in NW Thailand, on a headstream of the Chao Phraya: pop. 66,000

Chi·an·ti (kē än'tē, -an'-) *n.* [It.] a dry, red wine, orig. made in Tuscany in the region of the Chianti mountains

Chi·a·pas (chē ä'päs) state of S Mexico, on the Guatemalan border: 28,732 sq. mi.; pop. 1,323,000

chi·a·ro·scu·ro (kē är'ə skyoor'ō) *n., pl.* **-ros** [It., lit., clear dark < L. *clarus*, clear + *obscurus*, dark] 1. the treatment of light and shade in a painting, drawing, etc., to produce the illusion of depth, a dramatic effect, etc. 2. a style of painting, drawing, etc. emphasizing such treatment 3. a painting, drawing, etc. in which chiaroscuro is used —**chi·a·ro·scu'rist** *n.*

chi·as·ma (kī az'mə) *n., pl.* **chi·as·ma·ta** (-tə) [ModL. < Gr. *chiasma*, a crosspiece < *chiasmos*, placing crosswise < *chiazein*, to mark with a *chi* (χ)] 1. a crossing or intersection of the optic nerves on the ventral surface of the brain 2. a point of contact between chromosomes during meiosis where two chromatids interchange corresponding segments 3. any crosswise fusion

chi·as·ma·typ·y (kī az'mə tī'pē) *n.* [CHIASMA + TYP(E) + -Y[3]] a twisting of homologous chromosomes about each other during one stage of meiosis, resulting in a possible interchange of genes by the chromosomes

chi·as·mus (kī az'məs) *n., pl.* **-as'mi** (-mī) [ModL. < Gr. *chiasmos*: see CHIASMA] *Rhetoric* inversion of the second of two parallel phrases, clauses, etc. (Ex.: she went to Paris; to New York went he) —**chi·as'tic** (-as'tik) *adj.*

chiaus (chous, choush) *n.* [Turk. *chaush*] a Turkish messenger, emissary, sergeant, etc.

Chi·ba (chē′bä) city on the E coast of Honshu, Japan, on Tokyo Bay, opposite Tokyo: pop. 301,000

Chib·cha (chib′chə) *n.* **1.** *pl.* **-chas, -cha** a member of a tribe of Chibchan Indians who lived in E Colombia and had a highly developed civilization **2.** their extinct language

Chib·chan (-chən) *adj.* designating or of various linguistic groups of South and Central American Indians: some of the languages are still extant

chi·bouk, chi·bouque (chi bōōk′, -book′) *n.* [Fr. *chibouque* < Turk. *chibūq*] a tobacco pipe with a long stem and a clay bowl

chic (shēk) *n.* [Fr., orig., subtlety < MLowG. *schick*, order, skill (or < cognate MHG. *schicken*, behavior, appearance)] smart elegance of style and manner: said esp. of women or their clothes —*adj.* **chic′quer** (shēk′ər), **chic′quest** (-ist) stylish in a smart, pleasing way

Chi·ca·go (shə kä′gō, -kô′-) [< Fr. < Algonquian, lit., place of the wild onion] city and port in NE Ill., on Lake Michigan: pop. 3,367,000 (met. area 6,979,000)

Chicago Heights city in NE Ill.: suburb of Chicago: pop. 41,000

☆**chi·ca·lo·te** (chik′ə lōt′ē) *n.* [AmSp., name used for various thorny plants < Nahuatl *chicalotl* < *chicaloyo*, thorny] the prickly poppy (*Argemone platyceras*) of Mexico and the SW U.S., with large, white or yellow flowers and prickly leaves

chi·cane (shi kān′, chi-) *n.* [Fr. < *chicaner*, to pettifog, quibble < MLowG. *schikken*, to arrange, bring about] *same as* CHICANERY —*vi.* **-caned′, -can′ing** to use chicanery —*vt.* **1.** to trick **2.** to get by chicanery

chi·can·er·y (-ər ē) *n.*, *pl.* **-er·ies** [Fr. *chicanerie* < prec.] **1.** the use of clever but tricky talk or action to deceive, evade, etc., as in legal dealings **2.** an instance of this —*SYN.* see DECEPTION

☆**Chi·ca·no** (chē kä′nō) *n.*, *pl.* **-nos** [< AmSp. (*Me*)*chicano*, phonetic misspelling of *Méjicano*, a Mexican] [*also* **c-**] a U.S. citizen or inhabitant of Mexican descent

Chi·chén It·zá (chē chen′ ēt sä′) ruined Mayan city in Yucatan, SE Mexico: fl. 10th–13th cent.

chi·chi, chi-chi (shē′shē, chē′chē) *adj.* [Fr.] extremely chic; very smart, elegant, or sophisticated: usually used in a somewhat derogatory sense, suggesting affectation, showiness, effeteness, etc. —*n.* a chichi quality, thing, or person

Chi·chi·haerh (chē′chē′här′) city in Heilungkiang province, NE China: pop. 704,000

chick (chik) *n.* [ME. *chike*, var. of *chiken*, CHICKEN] **1.** a young chicken **2.** any young bird **3.** a child: term of endearment ☆**4.** [Slang] a young woman

☆**chick·a·dee** (chik′ə dē′) *n.* [echoic of its note] any of various small birds (genera *Parus* and *Penthestes*), generally with black, gray, and white feathers, closely related to the titmice

Chick·a·mau·ga (chik′ə mô′gə) [AmInd. < ?] creek in NW Ga.: site of a Civil War battle (Sept., 1863)

☆**chick·a·ree** (chik′ə rē′) *n.* [echoic of its cry] a reddish squirrel (*Tamiasciurus fremonti* or *Tamiasciurus douglasi*) of the W U.S.

Chick·a·saw (chik′ə sô′) *n.* **1.** *pl.* **-saws′, -saw** a member of a tribe of Muskogean Indians who formerly lived in N Mississippi and part of Tennessee and now live in Oklahoma **2.** the dialect of the Muskogean language spoken by them

☆**chic·kee** (chik′ē, chə kē′) *n.* [< ? AmInd. (Creek)] a Seminole Indian house built on stilts, with open sides and a thatched roof of palm leaves

chick·en (chik′ən) *n.* [ME. *chiken* < OE. *cycen* (< *kukin*), lit., little cock < base of OE. *cocc* (see COCK[1]); akin to MLowG. *kûken* (Du. *kuiken, kieken*)] **1.** a common farm bird (*Gallus domesticus*) raised for its edible eggs or flesh; hen or rooster, esp. a young one **2.** the flesh of this bird **3.** a young bird of some other species **4.** a young or inexperienced person **5.** [Slang] a timid or cowardly person ☆**6.** [clipped form of "chicken excrement" (euphemism)] [Mil. Slang] petty insistence on rules —*adj.* **1.** made of chicken [*chicken* croquettes] **2.** small and tender [a *chicken* lobster] **3.** [Slang] timid or cowardly ☆**4.** [cf. *n.*, 6] [Mil. Slang] characterized by unnecessary discipline, pettiness, etc. —*vi.* [Slang] to lose courage and abandon a plan, action, etc. (usually with *out*) —**count one's chickens before they are hatched** to count on something that may not materialize —☆**play chicken** [Slang] to engage in mutual challenges or threats, hoping the opponent will withdraw before actual conflict or collision

chicken breast *same as* PIGEON BREAST

☆**chicken colonel** [from the eagle insignia worn on the shoulders] [Mil. Slang] a full colonel

☆**chicken feed** [Slang] an insignificant sum of money

☆**chicken hawk** any of various hawks that prey or are reputed to prey on barnyard fowl

chick·en-heart·ed (-här′tid) *adj.* cowardly; timid: also ☆**chick′en-liv′ered** (-liv′ərd)

chicken pox an acute, contagious virus disease, usually of young children, characterized by fever and eruptions

☆**chicken snake** any of a genus (*Elaphe*) of large, nonpoisonous N. American snakes, that feed chiefly on rodents

☆**chicken wire** light, pliable wire fencing, used esp. for enclosing chicken coops

chick·pea (chik′pē′) *n.* [for *chich pea* < ME. & OFr. *chiche* < L. *cicer*, pea] **1.** a bushy annual plant (*Cicer arietinum*) of the legume family, with short, hairy pods containing usually two seeds **2.** the edible seed

chick·weed (-wēd′) *n.* any of several low-growing plants (esp. genera *Cerastium* and *Stellaria*) of the pink family, often found as weeds in lawns and gardens

Chi·cla·yo (chē klä′yō) city in NW Peru: pop. 99,000

☆**chic·le** (chik′′l) *n.* [AmSp. < Nahuatl *chictli*] a gumlike substance made from the milky juice of the sapodilla tree and used in making chewing gum

☆**chi·co** (chē′kō) *n.*, *pl.* **-cos** [< AmSp. *chicalote*, CHICALOTE] *same as* GREASEWOOD (sense 1)

Chic·o·pee (chik′ə pē) [< AmInd., lit., swift river] city in SW Mass.: pop. 67,000: see SPRINGFIELD

chic·o·ry (chik′ə rē) *n.*, *pl.* **-ries** [ME. *cicory* < OFr. *cicorée* < L. *cichorium* < Gr. *kichora, kichoreia*, chicory, endive, succory] **1.** a perennial weedy plant (*Cichorium intybus*) of the composite family, with blue flowers: the young leaves are used as a salad **2.** its root, roasted and ground for mixing with coffee or for use as a coffee substitute

chide (chīd) *vt., vi.* **chid′ed** or **chid** (chid), **chid′ed** or **chid** or **chid·den** (chid′′n), **chid′ing** [ME. *chiden* < OE. *cidan*, *vi.*; not found outside OE.] to scold; now, usually, to reprove mildly —**chid′ing·ly** *adv.*

chief (chēf) *n.* [ME. & OFr. *chef, chief*, leader < VL. **capum* < L. *caput*, the head: for IE. base see HEAD] **1.** the head or leader of a group, organization, etc.; person of highest title or authority **2.** [Archaic] the most valuable or main part of anything **3.** *Heraldry* the upper third of a shield **4.** [*usually* C-] *Naut.* a chief engineer or chief petty officer —*adj.* **1.** highest, as in rank or office; foremost [the *chief* magistrate] **2.** most important or significant; main; principal [the *chief* advantages] —*adv.* [Archaic] chiefly —**in chief 1.** in the chief position; of highest title or authority [editor *in chief*] **2.** [Archaic] chiefly *SYN.*—**chief** is applied to the person or thing first in rank, authority, importance, etc., and usually connotes subordination of all others [his *chief* problem was getting a job]; **principal** is applied to the person who directs or controls others [a *principal* clerk] or to the thing or person having precedence over all others by reason of size, position, importance, etc. [the *principal* products of Africa]; **main**, in strict usage, is applied to the thing, often part of a system or an extensive whole, that is pre-eminent in size, power, importance, etc. [the *main* line of a railroad]; **leading** stresses capacity for guiding, conducting, or drawing others [a *leading* light, question, etc.]; **foremost** suggests a being first by having moved ahead to that position [the *foremost* statesman of our time]; **capital** is applied to that which is ranked at the head of its kind or class because of its importance or its special significance [the *capital* city] —*ANT.* **subordinate, subservient**

☆**Chief Executive** the President of the U.S.

chief justice the presiding judge of a court made up of several judges

Chief Justice of the United States the presiding judge of the U.S. Supreme Court

chief·ly (-lē) *adv.* **1.** most of all; above all **2.** mainly; mostly —*adj.* of or like a chief [a *chiefly* rank]

☆**chief master sergeant** *U.S. Air Force* a noncommissioned officer of the highest rank

chief of staff the head member of the staff officers of a division or higher unit in the armed forces, or of the Departments of the Army or Air Force

☆**chief petty officer** a noncommissioned officer of the highest rank of petty officers in the navy: abbrev. **CPO**

chief·tain (-tən) *n.* [ME. & OFr. *chevetaine* < LL. *capitaneus*, lit., pertaining to the head < L. *caput*, the HEAD: cf. CAPTAIN] a chief or leader, esp. of a clan or tribe —**chief′tain·cy**, *pl.* **-cies, chief′tain·ship′** *n.*

chiel (chēl) *n.* [Scot.] a young man; youth: also **chield** (chēld)

chiff·chaff (chif′chaf′) *n.* [echoic of its cry] a small, olive-green and brown European bird (*Phylloscopus collybita*) of the warbler family, feeding mainly on insects and spiders

chif·fon (shi fän′, shif′än) *n.* [Fr., dim. of *chiffe*, a rag, piece of cloth] **1.** a sheer, lightweight fabric of silk, nylon, etc. **2.** [*pl.*] ribbons, laces, etc. used as accessories to a woman's dress —*adj.* **1.** made of chiffon **2.** *Cooking* made light and porous as by the addition of stiffly beaten egg whites [lemon *chiffon* pie]

chif·fo·nier, chif·fon·nier (shif′ə nir′) *n.* [Fr., chest of drawers, orig., ragpicker < prec.] a narrow, high bureau or chest of drawers, often with a mirror

chig·ger (chig′ər) *n.* [of Afr. orig.] ☆**1.** the tiny, red larva of certain mites (family Trombiculidae), whose bite causes severe itching **2.** *same as* CHIGOE

chi·gnon (shēn′yän) *n.* [Fr., var. of *chainon*, link < OFr. *chaeignon*, chain, nape (of the neck) < VL. **catenio*, dim. < L. *catena*: see CHAIN] a knot or coil of hair usually worn at the back of the neck by women

chig·oe (chig′ō) *n.*, *pl.* **-oes** (-ōz) [? via Fr. *chique* < WInd. native name] a flea (*Tunga penetrans*) of tropical S. America and Africa: the female burrows into the skin, causing painful sores **2.** *same as* CHIGGER

Chih·li (chē′lē′) **1.** *former name of* HOPEI province, China **2.** Gulf of, *former name of* Po HAI

Chi·hua·hua (chi wä′wä) 1. state of N Mexico, on the U.S. border: 94,831 sq. mi.; pop. 1,374,000 2. capital of this state: pop. 198,000 —☆*n*. any of an ancient Mexican breed of very small dog with large, pointed ears

chil- *same as* CHILO-

chil·blain (chil′blān′) *n*. [CHIL(L) + blain < OE. *blegen*, a sore] a painful swelling or sore on the foot or hand, caused by exposure to cold —**chil′blained′** *adj*.

child (chīld) *n*., *pl.* **chil′dren** [ME., *pl. childre* (now dial. *childer; children* is double pl.) < OE. *cild*, pl. *cild, cildru* < IE. **gelt-*, a swelling up < base **gel-*, rounded (sense development: swelling—womb—fetus—offspring)] 1. an infant; baby 2. an unborn offspring 3. a boy or girl in the period before puberty 4. a son or daughter 5. a descendant 6. a person like a child in interests, judgment, etc., or one regarded as immature or childish 7. a person regarded as the product of a specified place, time, etc. [a *child* of the Renaissance] 8. a thing that springs from a specified source; product [a *child* of one's imagination] 9. [Archaic] *same as* CHILDE 10. [Brit. Dial.] a female infant —**with child** pregnant —**child′less** *adj*. —**child′less·ness** *n*.

Child (chīld), Francis James 1825–96; U.S. scholar and collector of English & Scottish ballads

child·bear·ing (-ber′iŋ) *n*. the act or process of giving birth to children; parturition

child·bed (-bed′) *n*. the condition of a woman who is giving birth to a child

child·birth (-barth′) *n*. the act of giving birth to a child

childe (chīld) *n*. [var. of CHILD] [Archaic] a young man of noble birth, esp. a candidate for knighthood

Chil·der·mas (chil′dər məs) *n*. [ME. *childermasse* < OE. *cildramæsse* < *cildra*, of infants + *mæsse*, Mass] *former name for* HOLY INNOCENTS′ DAY

child·hood (chīld′hood′) *n*. [ME. *childhod* < OE. *cildhad*: see CHILD & -HOOD] 1. the time or state of being a child; esp., the period from infancy to puberty 2. an early stage of development

child·ing (-iŋ) *adj*. [ME. < *childen*, to bear a child] [Archaic] 1. bearing a child; pregnant 2. bearing a cluster of newer blossoms around an older blossom

child·ish (-ish) *adj*. [ME. < OE. *cildisc*: see CHILD & -ISH] 1. of, like, or characteristic of a child 2. not fit for an adult; immature; silly —*SYN*. see CHILDLIKE —**child′ish·ly** *adv*. —**child′ish·ness** *n*.

child labor the regular, full-time employment of children under a legally defined age in factories, stores, offices, etc.: in the U.S., the minimum legal age under Federal law is 16 (in hazardous occupations, 18)

child·like (-līk′) *adj*. 1. belonging or suitable to a child 2. like or characteristic of a child; innocent, trusting, etc. —**child′like′ness** *n*.

SYN.—**childlike** and **childish** are both applied to persons of any age in referring to characteristics or qualities considered typical of a child, **childlike** suggesting the favorable qualities such as innocence, guilelessness, trustfulness, etc., and **childish**, the unfavorable, as immaturity, foolishness, petulance, etc.

child·ly (-lē) *adj*. [Rare] childlike; childish

chil·dren (chil′drən) *n*. [see CHILD] *pl.* of CHILD

children of Israel the Jews; Hebrews

child's play (chīldz) any very simple task

Chil·e (chil′ē; *Sp.* chē′le) country on the SW coast of S. America: 286,397 sq. mi.; pop. 9,566,000; cap. Santiago —**Chil′e·an** *adj*., *n*.

☆**chil·e** (chil′ē) *n*. *same as* CHILI

☆**chil·e con car·ne** (chil′ē kən kär′nē, kän′) *same as* CHILI CON CARNE

Chile saltpeter sodium nitrate, esp. as found naturally in Chile and Peru

☆**chil·i** (chil′ē) *n*., *pl.* **chil′ies** [MexSp. < Nahuatl *chilli*] 1. the dried pod of red pepper, a very hot seasoning 2. the tropical American plant (*Capsicum frutescens*) of the nightshade family, bearing this pod 3. *same as* CHILI CON CARNE

chil·i·ad (kil′ē ad′) *n*. [L. *chilias* (gen. *chiliadis*) < Gr. *chilias* < *chilioi*, a thousand] 1. a thousand; group of 1,000 2. a thousand years

chil·i·arch (-ärk′) *n*. [L. *chiliarches* < Gr. *chiliarchēs* < *chilioi*, a thousand + *archos*, leader] in ancient Greece, the military commander of 1,000 men

chil·i·asm (-az′m) *n*. [Gr. *chiliasmos* < *chilias*: see CHILIAD] belief in the coming of the millennium —**chil′i·ast′** (-ast′) *n*. —**chil′i·as′tic** *adj*.

☆**chil·i con car·ne** (chil′ē kən kär′nē, kän′) [< MexSp. *chile con carne*, lit., red pepper with meat] a spiced or highly seasoned dish with beef ground or in small pieces, chilies or chili powder, beans, and often tomatoes

☆**chili powder** a powder made of dried chili pods, herbs, etc., used as a seasoning

☆**chili sauce** a spiced sauce of chopped tomatoes, green and red sweet peppers, onions, etc.

Chil·koot Pass (chil′kōōt′) mountain pass in the N Rockies, leading to the Klondike; 3,500 ft. high

chill (chil) *n*. [ME. *chile* < OE. *ciele*, coldness < Gmc. base **kal-*, to be cold (cf. COLD); akin to L. *gel-* in *gelidus*, whence GELID] 1. a feeling of coldness that makes one shiver; uncomfortable coolness 2. a moderate coldness 3. a damper on enthusiasm; discouraging influence 4. a feeling of sudden fear, apprehension, etc. 5. coolness of manner; unfriendliness 6. *Metallurgy* a cooled iron mold placed in contact with that part of a casting which is to be cooled rapidly and thus hardened on the surface —*adj*. *same as* CHILLY — *vi*. 1. to become cool or cold 2. to be seized with a chill; shake or shiver, as with cold or fear 3. *Metallurgy* to become hardened on the surface by rapid cooling —*vt*. 1. to make cool or cold 2. to cause a chill in 3. to check (enthusiasm, etc.) 4. to depress; dispirit 5. *Metallurgy* to harden (metal) on the surface by rapid cooling —**chill′er** *n*. —**chill′ing·ly** *adv*. —**chill′ness** *n*.

Chi·llán (chē yän′) city in SC Chile: pop. 83,000

chill factor the effect of low temperatures and high winds on exposed skin, expressed as a loss of body heat

chil·li (chil′ē) *n*., *pl.* **-lies** *same as* CHILI

Chil·lum (chil′əm) [after *Chilham* Castle, Kent, England, seat of a 16th-c. Eng. family] suburb of Washington, D.C., in C Md.: pop. 36,000

chill·y (chil′ē) *adj*. **chill′i·er**, **chill′i·est** 1. moderately cold; uncomfortably cool 2. chilling; making cold 3. cool in manner; unfriendly 4. depressing; dispiriting —**chill′i·ly** *adv*. —**chill′i·ness** *n*.

chi·lo- (kī′lō, -lə) [< Gr. *cheilos*, lip] *a combining form meaning* lip

chi·lo·pod (kī′lə päd′) *n*. [< ModL. *chilopoda*: see CHILO- & -POD] *same as* CENTIPEDE

Chil·tern hundreds (chil′tərn) [from tract of crown lands in SC England, containing the Chiltern Hills] [Brit.] a purely nominal office held from the crown: appointment to it formally circumvents the rule against resigning for members of Parliament wishing to vacate their seats

Chi·lung (jē′loon′) seaport in N Taiwan: pop. 145,000

chi·mae·ra (ki mir′ə, kī-) *n*. [L.] 1. *same as* CHIMERA 2. any of a genus (*Chimaera*) of fishes related to the sharks, with a smooth skin and tapering body 3. any member of an order (Holocephali) of elasmobranch fishes

chim·ar (chim′ər) *n*. *same as* CHIMERE

chimb (chīm) *n*. *same as* CHIME²

Chim·bo·ra·zo (chim′bə rä′zō) peak of the Andes, in C Ecuador: c. 20,500 ft.

chime¹ (chīm) *n*. [ME. & OFr. *chimbe, cimble* < L. *cymbalum*, CYMBAL] 1. a contrivance for striking a bell or set of bells 2. [*usually pl.*] *a*) a set of bells tuned to a musical scale *b*) a similar set of metal tubes, hung vertically and struck with a hammer 3. a single bell rung by a hammer, as in a clock 4. [*usually pl.*] the musical sounds or harmony produced by or as by chimes 5. harmony; agreement -- *vi*. **chimed, chim′ing** 1. to ring out when struck; sound as a chime 2. to sound in harmony, as bells 3. to harmonize; agree —*vt*. 1. to ring, play, or strike (a bell, set of bells, etc.) 2. to make (music or sound) on chimes 3. to give (the time) by striking bells 4. to call, summon, etc. by sounding a chime —**chime in** 1. to join in or interrupt, as a conversation 2. to be in accord; agree —**chim′er** *n*.

chime² (chīm) *n*. [ME. *chimb* < OE. *cimb-* (only in compounds), akin to Du. *kim*, G. *kimme*, an edge & ? COMB¹] the extended rim at each end of a cask or barrel

Chi·me·ra (ki mir′ə, kī-) [ME. & OFr. < L. *chimaera* < Gr. *chimaira*, fabulous monster, orig., goat that has passed one winter < *cheima*, winter: for IE. base see HIBERNATE] *Gr. Myth.* a fire-breathing monster, usually represented as having a lion's head, a goat's body, and a serpent's tail —*n*. [c-] 1. any similar fabulous monster 2. an impossible or foolish fancy 3. *Biol.* a living structure or organism in which the tissues are of varied genetic origin, sometimes as the result of grafting

chi·mere (chi mir′, shi-) *n*. [ME. < OFr. *chamarre* < Sp. *zamarra* < Ar. *sammūr*, sable] a loose robe, sleeveless or with lawn sleeves attached, sometimes worn by Anglican bishops: also **chim′er** (chim′ər, shim′-)

chi·mer·i·cal (ki mir′i k'l, -mer′-; kī-) *adj*. [CHIMER(A) + -ICAL] 1. imaginary; fantastic; unreal 2. absurd; impossible 3. indulging in unrealistic fancies; visionary Also **chi·mer′ic** —**chi·mer′i·cal·ly** *adv*.

chim·ney (chim′nē) *n*., *pl.* -neys [ME. *chimene*, a fireplace < OFr. *cheminée* < LL. *caminata*, fireplace < L. *caminus*, furnace, flue < Gr. *kaminos*, oven, fireplace] 1. the passage through which smoke or fumes from a fire escape; flue 2. a structure containing a flue or flues and extending above the roof of a building 3. a glass tube, as that around the wick of an oil lamp, to shield the flame 4. something like a chimney; specif., *a*) a deep, narrow fissure in a cliff face ☆*b*) a vertical body of ore *c*) the vent of a volcano 5. [Chiefly Brit.] a smokestack 6. [Dial.] a fireplace or hearth

chimney corner 1. a large recess with seats at the sides of an old-fashioned fireplace 2. a place near the fire

chimney piece 1. the mantel of a fireplace; mantelpiece 2. [Obs.] a decoration put over a fireplace

chimney pot a short pipe fitted to the top of a chimney to carry the smoke away and increase the draft

chimney swallow ☆1. *same as* CHIMNEY SWIFT 2. the European barn swallow

chimney sweep a person whose work is cleaning the soot from chimneys

☆**chimney swift** a sooty-brown N. American bird (*Chaetura pelagica*) resembling the swallow: so called from its habit of making a nest in an unused chimney

chimp (chimp) *n*. [Colloq.] a chimpanzee

chim·pan·zee (chim'pan zē', chim pan'zē) *n*. [Fr. *chimpanzé* < Angola (West Africa) Bantu *kampenzi*] an anthropoid ape (genus *Pan*) of Africa, with black hair and large, outstanding ears: it is smaller and less fierce than a gorilla, and is noted for its intelligence

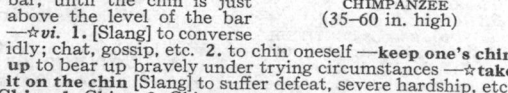
CHIMPANZEE
(35–60 in. high)

chin (chin) *n*. [ME. < OE. *cin* < IE. base *ĝenu-*, chin, jawbone, whence Goth. *kinnus*, cheek, L. *gena*, cheek, Gr. *genys*, chin] the part of the face below the lower lip; projecting part of the lower jaw —*vt*. **chinned, chin'ning** ☆*Gym*. to pull (oneself) up, while hanging by the hands from a horizontal bar, until the chin is just above the level of the bar —☆*vi*. **1.** [Slang] to converse idly; chat, gossip, etc. **2.** to chin oneself —**keep one's chin up** to bear up bravely under trying circumstances —☆**take it on the chin** [Slang] to suffer defeat, severe hardship, etc.

Chin. 1. China **2.** Chinese

Chi·na (chī'nə) country in E Asia, south and east of the U.S.S.R. and northeast of India: 3,691,000 sq. mi.; pop. 646,530,000; cap. Peking: see also TAIWAN

chi·na (chī'nə) *n*. **1.** *a*) porcelain, originally imported from China *b*) vitrified ceramic ware like porcelain **2.** dishes, ornaments, etc. made of china **3.** any earthenware dishes or crockery

China aster an annual garden flower (*Callistephus chinensis*) of the composite family, with large blooms of various colors: it is native to China and Japan

chi·na bark (kī'nə) [altered (after *China*) < Sp. *quina*: see QUININE] *same as* CINCHONA (sense 2)

☆**chi·na·ber·ry** (-ber'ē) *n*., *pl*. **-ries 1.** a tropical Asiatic tree (*Melia azederach*) of the mahogany family, bearing yellow, beadlike fruit: widely grown as a lawn tree throughout the S U.S. **2.** a tree (*Sapindus drummondi*) bearing orange-brown fruit rich in saponin and formerly used as soap: found in the dry areas of Mexico and the SW U.S. **3.** the fruit of either of these trees

Chi·na·man (-mən) *n*., *pl*. **-men** (-mən) a Chinese: now generally regarded as a contemptuous or patronizing term

Chi·nan (jē'nän') *same as* TSINAN

China rose 1. a cultivated rose (*Rosa chinensis*) of Chinese origin, ancestor of many modern roses **2.** a large hibiscus (*Hibiscus rosa-sinensis*) with showy flowers

China Sea *see* EAST CHINA SEA & SOUTH CHINA SEA

☆**Chi·na·town** (-toun') *n*. the Chinese quarter of any city outside of China

☆**China tree** *same as* CHINABERRY (sense 1)

chi·na·ware (-wer') *n*. *same as* CHINA

☆**chin·ca·pin** (chin'kə pin) *n*. *same as* CHINQUAPIN

chinch (chinch) *n*. [Sp. *chinche* < L. *cimex*, bug] **1.** *same as* BEDBUG **2.** *same as* CHINCH BUG

☆**chinch bug** a small, white-winged, black bug (*Blissus leucopterus*) that damages grain plants by sucking out the juices

chin·che·rin·chee (chin'chə rin'chē) *n*. [prob. echoic of stalks rubbing in the wind] a South African bulbous plant (*Ornithogalum thyrsoides*) of the lily family, with many spikes of white, long-lasting flowers

chin·chil·la (chin chil'ə) *n*. [Sp., prob. dim. of *chinche*: see CHINCH] **1.** a small rodent (*Chinchilla laniger*) found in the Andes, S. America, but bred extensively elsewhere for its fur **2.** the expensive, soft, pale-gray fur of this animal **3.** a breed of domestic cat with long, soft, silver-gray hair **4.** [prob. after *Chinchilla*, Spanish town where first made] a heavy cloth of wool, or wool and cotton, with a tufted, napped surface, used for making overcoats

CHINCHILLA
(11 1/2 to 21 in. long, including tail)

Chin·chow, Chin·chou (jin'jō') city in Liaoning province, NE China: pop. 400,000

Chin·dwin (chin'dwin) river in NW Burma; main tributary of the Irrawaddy: over 500 mi.

chine[1] (chīn) *n*. [ME. < OFr. *eschine* (Fr. *échine*) < Frank. *skina*, small bone, shin bone: cf. SHIN] **1.** the backbone; spine **2.** a cut of meat containing part of the backbone **3.** a ridge —*vt*. **chined, chin'ing** to cut along or across the backbone of (a carcass of meat)

chine[2] (chīn) *n*. [ME. < OE. *cine*, fissure, akin to *cinan* (Goth. *keinan*), to burst open < IE. base *ĝei-, *ĝi-*, to germinate, burst into bloom] [Brit. Dial.] a rocky ravine or deep fissure in a cliff

chine[3] (chīn) *n*. *same as* CHIME[2]

Chi·nese (chī nēz', -nēs'; *for adj., often* chī'nēz') *n*. [OFr. *Chineis* (Fr. *Chinois*)] **1.** *pl*. **Chi·nese**' a native of China or a descendant of the people of China **2.** the standard language of the Chinese, based on Peking speech; Mandarin **3.** any of the various languages of the Chinese **4.** a group of Sino-Tibetan languages comprising Mandarin and most of the other languages of China —*adj*. of China, its people, language, or culture

☆**Chinese cabbage** any of several vegetables (esp. *Brassica pekinensis*) of the mustard family, with long, narrow, blanched leaves growing in loose, cylindrical heads and tasting somewhat like cabbage

Chinese checkers [prob. so named from the characteristic ornamentation of the board] a game like checkers for two to six players, using marbles on a board with holes in a star-shaped pattern

Chinese Empire China from the founding of its first dynasty (c. 2200 B.C.) to the revolution of 1911

Chinese lantern a lantern made of brightly colored paper that can be folded up

Chi·nese-lan·tern plant (-lan'tərn) a perennial herb (*Physalis alkekengi*) of the nightshade family, grown for winter bouquets because of the inflated, bladderlike, red calyx that surrounds the small, tomatolike fruit

Chinese puzzle 1. an intricate puzzle **2.** anything intricate and hard to solve

Chinese red any of various shades of red, as chrome red or, esp., a brilliant orange-red

Chinese Revolution a revolution (1911) in which forces led by Sun Yat-sen overthrew the Manchu dynasty and set up a republic in China

Chinese Turkestan *former name of* the part of Sinkiang-Uighur region, China, south of the Tien Shan mountains

Chinese Wall *same as* GREAT WALL OF CHINA

Chinese white a dense white pigment made of zinc oxide, used esp. in white inks

Chinese windlass *same as* DIFFERENTIAL WINDLASS

Chinese wood oil *same as* TUNG OIL

Ching, Ch'ing (chiŋ) the Chinese dynasty (1644–1912) established by the Manchu; Manchu dynasty

Ching·hai (chiŋ'hī') *same as* TSINGHAI

Ching·tao (chiŋ'dou') *same as* TSINGTAO

Chin Hills mountain range in NW Burma, on the India border: highest peak, 10,018 ft.

chink[1] (chiŋk) *n*. [ME. *chine*, with unhistoric -*k*: see CHINE[2]] a narrow opening; crack; fissure; slit —*vt*. **1.** to close up the chinks in **2.** [Obs.] to form chinks in

chink[2] (chiŋk) *n*. [echoic] **1.** a sharp, clinking sound, as of coins striking together **2.** [Old Slang] coin or cash —*vt*., *vi*. to make or cause to make a sharp, clinking sound

☆**chin·ka·pin** (chiŋ'kə pin) *n*. *same as* CHINQUAPIN

Chin·kiang (chin'kyaŋ'; *Chin*. jin'jyän') city in Kiangsu province, E China: pop. 208,000

Chin·ling Shan (jē'liŋ' shän) *same as* TSINLING MOUNTAINS

Chin·men (jin'mun') *same as* QUEMOY

chi·no (chē'nō, shē'-) *n*. [< ?] **1.** a strong, twilled cotton cloth used for work clothes, uniforms, etc. **2.** [*pl*.] men's pants of chino for casual wear

Chi·no- (chī'nō) a combining form meaning Chinese and [*Chino-*Soviet]

chin·oise·rie (shin'wäz rē') *n*. [Fr. < *Chinois*, (< *Chine*, China) + -*erie*, -ERY] **1.** an ornate style of decoration for furniture, textiles, ceramics, etc., esp. in 18th-cent. Europe, based on Chinese motifs **2.** articles, designs, etc. in this style

Chi·nook (chi nook', -nook'; *for 4, usually* shi-) *n*., *pl*. **-nooks, -nook** [< *tsi-núk*, a Salish name for the Chinook tribe] **1.** any of a family of Indian tribes formerly inhabiting the Columbia River valley **2.** either of two languages, Lower Chinook, now extinct, and Upper Chinook, still spoken by certain tribes in Oregon and Washington **3.** *same as* CHINOOK JARGON **4.** [*usually* c-] a warm, moist SW wind blowing from the sea onto the coast of the NW U.S. and SW Canada in the winter and spring; also, a dry wind blowing down the E slope of the Rocky Mountains at recurring intervals: in full **chinook wind**

☆**Chi·nook·an** (-ən) *adj*. of the Chinook Indians, their culture, language, etc. —*n*. a Chinook Indian

☆**Chinook jargon** a pidgin language consisting of extremely simplified Chinook intermixed with words from English, French, and neighboring American Indian languages: it was formerly used among traders and Indians in the coastal areas of NW N. America

☆**chinook salmon** the largest species (*Oncorhynchus tschawytscha*) of Pacific salmon

☆**chin·qua·pin** (chiŋ'kə pin') *n*. [of Algonquian origin] **1.** any of several, usually bushlike, trees (genus *Castanea*) of the beech family, esp. the dwarf chestnut **2.** any of various species (genus *Castanopsis*) of evergreen trees of the beech family, found in W U.S. and Asia **3.** the edible nut of any of these trees

chintz (chints) *n*. [earlier *chints*, *pl*. of *chint* < Hind. *chhint*, chintz < Sans. *citra*, spotted, bright < IE. base *(s)kai-*, bright, whence -HOOD, OE. *hador*, bright, L. *caelum*, sky] a cotton cloth printed in colors with flower designs or other patterns and usually glazed

chintz·y (-ē) *adj*. **chintz'i·er, chintz'i·est** [prec. + -Y[2]: from the sleazy quality of some chintz fabrics] **1.** like

chintz 2. ☆[Colloq.] cheap, stingy, mean, petty, etc.

Chi·os (kī′äs) *same as* KHÍÓS

chip (chip) *vt.* **chipped, chip′ping** [ME. *chippen* < OE. **cippian* (cf. *cipp*, log); akin to Du. & G. *kippen*, to cut] **1.** [Rare] to cut or chop with an ax or other sharp tool **2.** *a)* to break or cut a small piece or thin slice from *b)* to break or cut off (a small piece or pieces) **3.** to shape by cutting or chopping [to *chip* a hole in the ice] —*vi.* **1.** to break off into small pieces **2.** *Golf* to make a chip shot —*n.* [ME. *chippe* < the *v.*] **1.** a small, thin piece of wood, stone, etc., cut or broken off **2.** a place where a small piece has been chipped off [a chip on the edge of a plate] **3.** wood, palm leaf, or straw split and woven into bonnets, hats, etc. ☆**4.** a fragment of dried animal dung, sometimes used for fuel ☆**5.** a worthless thing **6.** one of the small, round disks often used in poker and other gambling games as a token for money; counter **7.** *a)* a thin slice or shaving of food [a potato *chip*] *b)* [*pl.*] [Brit.] French fried potatoes **8.** *Electronics a)* a semiconductor body in which an integrated circuit is formed or is to be formed *b)* *same as* INTEGRATED CIRCUIT **9.** *Golf same as* CHIP SHOT —☆**cash in one's chips 1.** to turn in one's chips for their equivalent in money **2.** [Slang] to die —☆**chip in** [Colloq.] **1.** to share in giving money or help **2.** to add one's comments —**chip off the old block** a person much like his father in appearance or characteristics —☆**chip on one's shoulder** [Colloq.] an inclination to fight or quarrel —☆**in the chips** [Slang] rich; wealthy —**let the chips fall where they may** let the consequences be what they may —☆**when the chips are down** when something is really at stake; when one is put to the test; in a crisis

Chip·e·way·an (chip′ə wī′ən) *n.* [Cree *chipwayanawok*, lit., pointed skins (from their pointed parkas)] **1.** a member of a tribe of Athapascan Indians who live in northwest Canada **2.** their Northern Athapascan language Also sp. **Chip′e·way′an**

chip·munk (-muŋk′) *n.* [of Algonquian origin] any of a number of small N. American squirrels (genera *Eutamias* and *Tamias*) with striped markings on the head and back: it lives mainly on the ground

☆**chipped beef** dried or smoked beef sliced into shavings, usually served with a cream sauce

Chip·pen·dale (chip′'n dāl′) *adj.* [after Thomas *Chippendale* (1718?–79), Eng. cabinetmaker] designating or of an 18th-cent. Eng. style of furniture characterized by graceful lines and, often, rococo ornamentation

chip·per¹ (chip′ər) *adj.* [altered form of N Brit. *kipper*; ? akin to Du. *kipp*, quick, lively] [Colloq.] in good spirits; sprightly; lively

chip·per² (chip′ər) *n.* a person or thing that chips; esp., a tool for chipping

chip·per³ (chip′ər) *vi.* [echoic metathesis of CHIRRUP] **1.** to chirp or twitter: said of birds **2.** to chatter or prattle; babble

Chip·pe·wa (chip′ə wô′, -wä′, -wə, -wā′) *n., pl.* **-was, -wa** [var. of OJIBWA] *same as* OJIBWA: also **Chip′pe·way′** (-wā′)

☆**chip·ping sparrow** (chip′iŋ) [< *chip*, echoic of its cry] a small, N. American sparrow (*Spizella passerina*), with a reddish-brown crown and white breast

☆**chip·py, chip·pie** (chip′ē) *n., pl.* **-pies 1.** *same as* CHIPPING SPARROW **2.** a chipmunk **3.** [Slang] *a)* a promiscuous young woman *b)* a prostitute

chip shot *Golf* a short, lofted shot, made esp. from just off the green

Chi·ri·co (kē′rē kô), **Gior·gio de** (jôr′jô de) 1888– ; It. painter, born in Greece

chirk (churk) *vt., vi.* [ME. *chirken*, to twitter, var. of *churken* < OE. *cearcian*, to creak, gnash] [Colloq.] to cheer (*up*) —*adj.* [Colloq.] lively; cheerful

chirm (churm) *n.* [ME. < OE. *cierm*, noise] [Dial. or Rare] a twittering, warbling, or humming sound, as of birds, insects, a distant crowd, etc. —*vi.* [Dial. or Rare] to make this sound; twitter, hum, etc.

chi·ro- (kī′rə, -rō) [< Gr. *cheir*, the hand] *a combining form meaning* hand [*chiromancy*]

chi·rog·ra·phy (kī räg′rə fē) *n.* [CHIRO- + -GRAPHY] handwriting; penmanship —**chi·rog′ra·pher** *n.* —**chi·ro·graph·ic** (kī′rə graf′ik), **chi′ro·graph′i·cal** *adj.*

chi·ro·man·cy (kī′rə man′sē) *n.* [CHIRO- + -MANCY] *same as* PALMISTRY —**chi′ro·man′cer** *n.*

Chi·ron (kī′rän) [L. < Gr. *Cheirōn*] *Gr. Myth.* the wisest of all centaurs, famous for his knowledge of medicine: he taught Asclepius, Achilles, and Hercules

chi·rop·o·dy (kə räp′ə dē, ki-) *n.* [CHIRO- + -POD + -Y³] **1.** orig., treatment of diseases of the hands and feet **2.** *same as* PODIATRY —**chi·rop′o·dist** *n.*

☆**chi·ro·prac·tic** (kī′rə prak′tik, kī′rə prak′tik) *n.* [< CHIRO- + Gr. *praktikos*, practical] a method of treating disease based on the theory that disease is caused by interference with nerve function, and employing manipulation of the body joints, esp. of the spine, in seeking to restore normal nerve function —**chi′ro·prac′tor** *n.*

chi·rop·ter (kī räp′tər) *n.* [< CHIRO- + Gr. *pteron*, wing: see PTERO-] *same as* BAT² —**chi·rop′ter·an** *adj., n.*

chirp (churp) *vi.* [ME. *chirpen*, echoic var. of *chirken*,

CHIRK] **1.** to make the short, shrill sound of some birds or insects **2.** to speak in a lively, shrill way —*vt.* to utter in a sharp, shrill tone —*n.* a short, shrill sound —**chirp′er** *n.*

chirr (chur) *n.* [echoic] a shrill, trilled sound, as of some insects or birds —*vi.* to make such a sound

chir·rup (chur′əp, chir′-) *vi.* [var. of CHIRP] **1.** to chirp repeatedly **2.** to make a series of sharp, sucking sounds with the lips, as in urging a horse on —*n.* a chirruping sound —**chir′rup·y** *adj.*

chi·rur·geon (ki rur′jən) *n.* [altered, after L. forms < ME. *cirurgian* < OFr. *cirurgien* < ME. & OFr. *cirurgie*: see SURGERY] *archaic var. of* SURGEON —**chi·rur′ger·y** (-jər ē) *n.* —**chi·rur′gi·cal** (-jə k'l) *adj.*

chis·el (chiz′'l) *n.* [ME. & ONormFr. (OFr. *cisel*) < VL. *cisellum*, for L. **caesellum* < *caesus*, pp. of *caedere*, to cut] a sharp-edged tool for cutting or shaping wood, stone, or metal —*vi., vt.* **-eled** or **-elled, -el·ing** or **-el·ling 1.** to cut or shape with a chisel **2.** [Colloq.] *a)* to take advantage of by cheating, sponging, etc. *b)* to get (something) in this way —**chisel in** [Colloq.] to force oneself upon others without being asked or welcomed —**chis′el·er, chis′el·ler** *n.*

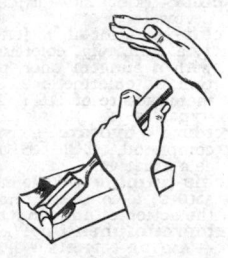

CHISEL

chis·eled, chis·elled (-'ld) *adj.* **1.** cut or shaped with a chisel **2.** finely wrought, as if shaped by a chisel

Chis·holm Trail (chiz′əm) [after Jesse *Chisholm* (1806?–68), Am. frontier scout] cattle trail from San Antonio, Tex., to Abilene, Kans.: important from 1865 until 1880's

chi-square (kī′skwer′) *n.* a statistical method used to test whether the classification of data can be ascribed to chance or to some underlying law

chit¹ (chit) *n.* [ME. *chitte*, prob. var. of *kitte*, for *kitten*] **1.** a child **2.** a young girl regarded as little better than a child: a mildly contemptuous term

chit² (chit) *n.* [< *chitty* < Hind. *ciṭṭhi*, letter, note < Sans. *citra*, spotted: see CHINTZ] **1.** [Chiefly Brit.] a short note or letter; memorandum **2.** a voucher of a small sum owed for drink, food, etc.

Chi·ta (chē tä′) city in SE R.S.F.S.R., near the Mongolian border: pop. 198,000

chit·chat (chit′chat′) *n.* [redupl. of CHAT¹] **1.** light, familiar, informal talk; chat; small talk **2.** gossip

chi·tin (kīt′n) *n.* [Fr. *chitine* < Gr. *chitōn*: see CHITON] a tough, horny polysaccharide secreted by the epidermis and forming the main bulk of the outer covering of insects, crustaceans, etc. —**chi′tin·ous** (-əs) *adj.*

chit·lins, chit·lings (chit′lənz) *n.pl. dial. var. of* CHITTERLINGS

chi·ton (kīt′n, kī′tän) *n.* [Gr. *chitōn*, garment, tunic, coat of mail < Sem., as in Heb. *ketōneth*, tunic coat] **1.** a loose garment of varying length, similar to a tunic, worn by both men and women in ancient Greece **2.** any of an order (Polyplacophora) of mostly small mollusks, with a long body and a calcareous dorsal shell of eight overlapping plates: a few species are edible

Chit·ta·gong (chit′ə gôŋ′, -gäŋ′) seaport in E East Pakistan, near the Bay of Bengal: pop. 364,000

chit·ter (chit′ər) *vi.* [ME. *chiteren*: orig. echoic] **1.** to twitter **2.** [Brit. Dial.] to shiver with cold

chit·ter·lings (chit′lənz; *now chiefly Brit.* chit′ər liŋz) *n.pl.* [ME. *chiterling*, entrails, souse < Gmc. base whence MLowG. *kūt*, soft parts of the body, G. *kutteln*, chitterlings, OE. *cyt-* in *cyt-wer*, rounded fish basket < IE. base **geu-*, to bend, curve, be rounded] the small intestines of pigs, used for food

chiv·al·ric (shi val′rik, shiv′'l rik) *adj.* **1.** of chivalry **2.** chivalrous

chiv·al·rous (shiv′'l rəs) *adj.* [ME. *chevalrous* < OFr. *chevalereus*: see CHIVALRY] **1.** having the noble qualities of an ideal knight; gallant, courteous, honorable, etc. **2.** of chivalry; chivalric —*SYN.* see CIVIL —**chiv′al·rous·ly** *adv.* —**chiv′al·rous·ness** *n.*

chiv·al·ry (-rē) *n.* [ME. & OFr. *chevalerie* < *chevaler*, a knight: doublet of CAVALRY] **1.** a group of knights or gallant gentlemen **2.** the medieval system of knighthood **3.** the noble qualities a knight was supposed to have, such as courage, honor, and a readiness to help the weak and protect women **4.** the demonstration of any of the knightly qualities **5.** [Obs.] the rank or position of a knight

chives (chivz) *n.pl.* [ME. & OFr. *cive* < L. *cepa*, onion] [*often with sing. v.*] a hardy plant (*Allium schoenoprasum*) of the lily family, with small, slender, hollow leaves having a mild onion odor: used to flavor soups, stews, etc.

chiv·y, chiv·vy (chiv′ē) *n., pl.* **chiv′ies** or **chiv′vies** *same as* CHEVY —*vt., vi.* **chiv′ied** or **chiv′vied, chiv′y·ing** or **chiv′vy·ing 1.** to fret; worry; nag **2.** to manipulate **3.** *same as* CHEVY

Chka·lov (chkä′lôf) *former name of* ORENBURG

chlam·y·date (klam'ə dāt') *adj.* [Gr. *chlamyd-*, base of *chlamys*, mantle + -ATE[1]] *Zool.* having a mantle, as certain mollusks

chla·myd·o·spore (klə mid'ə spôr') *n.* [< Gr. *chlamyd-*, base of *chlamys*, mantle + SPORE] an enlarged, thick-walled cell formed between the vegetative cells of a filamentous fungus as a resistant, resting spore

chla·mys (klā'məs, klam'əs) *n., pl.* **chla'mys·es, chlam·y·des** (klam'ə dēz') [L. < Gr. *chlamys*] a short mantle clasped at the shoulder, worn by men in ancient Greece

Chlo·e, Chlo·ë (klō'ē) [L. < Gr. *Chloē*, blooming, verdant] a feminine name: see also DAPHNIS AND CHLOE

chlor- (klôr) *same as* CHLORO-: used before a vowel

chlo·ral (klôr'əl) *n.* [CHLOR- + AL(COHOL)] 1. a thin, oily, colorless liquid, CCl₃CHO, with a pungent odor, prepared by the action of chlorine on alcohol: used in the manufacture of DDT 2. *same as* CHLORAL HYDRATE

chloral hydrate a colorless, crystalline compound, CCl₃·CH(OH)₂, used chiefly as a sedative

chlo·ra·mine (klôr'ə mēn') *n.* [CHLOR- + AMINE] a colorless, pungent liquid, NH₂Cl, obtained by the action of ammonia on some hypochlorite

chlor·am·phen·i·col (klôr'am fen'ə kôl', -kōl) *n.* [CHLOR- + AM(ID) + PHE(N)- + NI(TR)- + (GLY)COL] an antibiotic drug, C₁₁H₁₂Cl₂N₂O₅, prepared synthetically or isolated from a bacillus (*Streptomyces venezuelae*): it is used against a wide variety of bacterial and rickettsial diseases and against some viruses

chlo·rate (klôr'āt, -it) *n.* a salt of chloric acid

chlor·cy·cli·zine (klôr sī'klə zēn') *n.* [CHLOR- + CYCLIZINE] an antihistamine, C₁₈H₂₁ClN₂, used for treating allergies and insect bites

☆**chlor·dane** (klôr'dān) *n.* [CHLOR- + (*in*)*dane* a derivative of INDENE] a chlorinated, highly poisonous, volatile oil, C₁₀H₆Cl₈, used as an insecticide, esp. against soil grubs: also **chlor'dan** (-dan)

chlo·rel·la (klə rel'ə) *n.* [ModL. < CHLOR- + L. -*ella*, fem. of -*ellus*, dim. suffix] any of a genus (*Chlorella*) of small, unicellular, green algae with spherical cells: several species are rich sources of proteins, carbohydrates, and fats

chlo·ric (klôr'ik) *adj.* 1. of or containing chlorine with a higher valence than in the corresponding chlorous compounds 2. designating or of a colorless acid, HClO₃, whose salts are chlorates

chlo·ride (-īd) *n.* a compound in which chlorine is combined with another element or radical (e.g., a salt of hydrochloric acid)

chloride of lime a white powder with the approximate formula CaOCl₂, obtained by treating slaked lime with chlorine and used for disinfecting and bleaching

chlo·ri·nate (klôr'ə nāt') *vt.* -nat'ed, -nat'ing to treat or combine (a substance) with chlorine; esp., to pass chlorine into (water or sewage) for purification —**chlo'ri·nat'or** *n.* —**chlo'ri·na'tion** *n.*

chlo·rine (klôr'ēn, -in) *n.* [CHLOR- + -INE⁴] a greenish-yellow, poisonous, gaseous chemical element with a disagreeable odor, used as a bleaching agent, in water purification, in various industrial processes, etc.: symbol, Cl; at. wt., 35.453; at. no., 17; density, 3.214 g/l (0°C); melt. pt., -103°C; boil. pt., -34.6°C

chlo·rite¹ (-īt) *n.* a salt of chlorous acid

chlo·rite² (-īt) *n.* [L. *chloritis* < Gr. *chlōritis* < *chlōros*, pale green] a bright-green, complex silicate mineral, similar in structure to the micas —**chlo·rit'ic** (-rit'ik) *adj.*

chlo·ro- (klôr'ə, -ō) [< Gr. *chlōros*, pale green] *a combining form meaning:* 1. green [*chlorophyll, chlorosis*] 2. having chlorine in the molecule [*chloroform*]

chlo·ro·ben·zene (klôr'ə ben'zēn) *n.* [CHLORO- + BENZENE] a clear flammable liquid, C₆H₅Cl, used as a solvent for paints, lacquers, etc. and in organic synthesis

chlo·ro·form (klôr'ə fôrm') *n.* [Fr. *chloroforme*: see CHLORO- & FORMYL] a sweetish, colorless, volatile liquid, CHCl₃, used as a general anesthetic and as a solvent —*vt.* 1. to anesthetize with chloroform 2. to kill with chloroform

chlo·ro·hy·drin (klôr'ə hī'drin) *n.* [CHLORO- + HYDR- + -IN¹] 1. a colorless liquid, ClCH₂CHOHCH₂OH, prepared by the reaction of hydrochloric acid with glycerol and used in the manufacture of dyes and as a solvent 2. an organic compound in which a hydroxyl group of a polyhydroxy alcohol has been replaced by a chlorine atom

Chlo·ro·my·ce·tin (klôr'ə mī sēt'n) [CHLORO- + -MYCETE + -IN¹] *a trademark for* CHLORAMPHENICOL

chlo·ro·phyll, chlo·ro·phyl (klôr'ə fil') *n.* [Fr. *chlorophylle* < Gr. *chlōros*, green + *phyllon*, a leaf] the green pigment found in the chloroplasts of plant cells: it occurs in two forms (**chlorophyll a**), C₅₅H₇₂MgN₄O₅, and (**chlorophyll b**), C₅₅H₇₀MgN₄O₆: it is involved in the photosynthetic process and is used as a coloring agent, in topical medicines, etc. —**chlo'ro·phyl'lose** (-ōs), **chlo'ro·phyl'lous** (-əs) *adj.*

chlo·ro·pic·rin (klôr'ə pik'rən) *n.* [CHLORO- + PICR(IC) + -IN¹] a colorless liquid, CCl₃NO₂, prepared by treating chloroform with concentrated nitric acid, and used in

chemical warfare as a poison gas, and in insecticides, fungicides, etc.

chlo·ro·plast (klôr'ə plast') *n.* [CHLORO- + -PLAST] an oval, chlorophyll-bearing body found in the cytoplasm in cells of green plants

chlo·ro·prene (-prēn') *n.* [CHLORO- + (ISO)PRENE] a colorless liquid, CH₂:CHCCl:CH₂, made from acetylene: it can be polymerized to form a synthetic rubber (NEOPRENE)

chlo·ro·quine (klôr'ə kwin) *n.* [< CHLORO- + QUINOLINE] a synthetic drug used in treating malaria, and certain kinds of arthritis

chlo·ro·sis (klə rō'sis) *n.* [ModL.: see CHLORO- & -OSIS] 1. an abnormal condition of plants in which the green parts lose their color or turn yellow as a result of disease or lack of light 2. a kind of anemia sometimes affecting girls at puberty and causing the skin to turn a greenish color —**chlo·rot'ic** (-rät'ik) *adj.*

chlo·ro·thi·a·zide (klôr'ə thī'ə zīd') *n.* [CHLORO- + THI- + AZ- + -IDE] a synthetic drug used in treating hypertension and heart failure by removing extra salt and water through the kidneys

chlo·rous (klôr'əs) *adj.* 1. of or containing chlorine with a lower valence than that in corresponding chloric compounds 2. designating or of an unstable acid, HClO₂, a strong oxidizing agent which exists in solution only, and whose salts are known as chlorites

chlor·pic·rin (klôr pik'rən) *n. same as* CHLOROPICRIN

chlor·prom·a·zine (klôr präm'ə zēn') *n.* [CHLOR- + prom-azine, C₁₇H₂₀N₂S, contr. < *promethazine*, an antihistaminic drug < PRO(PYL) + (*di*)*meth*(*ylamine*), a gaseous compound, (CH₃)₂NH, + (*phenothi*)*azine*, C₁₂H₉NS < PHENO- + THIAZINE] a synthetic drug, C₁₇H₁₉N₂SCl, used as a tranquilizer in certain mental disorders and to control nausea and vomiting

☆**chlor·tet·ra·cy·cline** (-tet'rə sī'klēn, -klin) *n.* [CHLOR- + TETRACYCLINE] a yellow antibiotic, C₂₂H₂₃ClN₂O₈, isolated from a microorganism (*Streptomyces aureofaciens*): it is used against a wide variety of bacterial and rickettsial infections and certain viruses

chm., chmn. chairman

Choate (chōt), Rufus 1799–1859; U.S. lawyer

chock (chäk) *n.* [ONormFr. *choque*, a block < Gaul. *tsukka*, akin to PGmc. *stuk-*, a tree trunk, stump: for IE. base see STOCK] 1. a block or wedge placed under a wheel, barrel, etc. to prevent motion or used to fill in a space 2. *Naut.* a block with two hornlike projections curving inward, through which a rope may be run —*vt.* to provide or wedge fast with a chock or chocks —*adv.* as close or tight as can be

chock·a·block (-ə bläk') *adj.* [see CHOCK & BLOCK] 1. pulled so tight as to have the blocks touching: said of a hoisting tackle 2. crowded or jammed —*adv.* tightly together

chock-full (chäk'fool', chuk'-) *adj.* [ME. *chokkeful, chekefull* < *choke, cheke,* cheek + -*ful,* -FUL; now often associated with CHOCK, CHOKE] as full as possible; filled to capacity

choc·o·late (chôk'lət, chäk'-; -ə lət) *n.* [Fr. *chocolat* < Sp. *chocolate* < Nahuatl *chocolatl*] 1. a paste, powder, syrup, or bar made from cacao seeds that have been roasted and ground 2. a drink made of chocolate, hot milk or water, and sugar 3. a candy made of or coated with chocolate 4. reddish brown —*adj.* 1. made of or flavored with chocolate 2. reddish-brown

Choc·taw (chäk'tô) *n.* [< tribal name *Chata* < ?] 1. *pl.* -taws, -taw a member of a tribe of Muskogean Indians who lived in S Mississippi, Alabama, Georgia, and Louisiana and now live in Oklahoma 2. the dialect of the Muskogean language spoken by them 3. [Colloq.] strange, unintelligible talk or language; jargon

choice (chois) *n.* [ME. & OFr. *chois* < *choisir*, to choose < Goth. *kausjan*, to taste; cf. CHOOSE] 1. the act of choosing; selection 2. the right, power, or chance to choose; option 3. a person or thing chosen 4. the best or most preferable part 5. a variety from which to choose 6. a supply that is well chosen 7. an alternative 8. care in choosing —*adj.* **choic'er, choic'est** 1. of special excellence; select; superior 2. carefully chosen 3. designating or of a grade of government-classified meat between *prime* and *good* —**of choice** that is preferred [medically the treatment *of choice*] —**choice'ly** *adv.* —**choice'ness** *n.*

SYN.—**choice** implies the chance, right, or power to choose, usually by the free exercise of one's judgment [a bachelor *by choice*]; **option** suggests the privilege of choosing as granted by a person or group in authority that normally exercises the power [local *option* on liquor sales]; **alternative**, in strict usage, limits a choice to one of two possibilities [the *alternative* of paying a fine or serving 30 days]; **preference** suggests the determining of choice by predisposition or partiality [a *preference* for striped ties]; **selection** implies a wide choice and the exercise of careful discrimination [*selections* from the modern French poets]

choir (kwīr) *n.* [with sp. altered after L., < MF. *quere* < OFr. *cuer* < ML. *chorus*, choir < L.: see CHORUS] 1. a group of singers organized and trained to sing together, esp. in a church 2. the part of a church they occupy, as a chancel or choir loft 3. an instrumental section of an orchestra [the brass *choir*] 4. any organized group or band, as of dancers 5. *Theol.* any of the nine orders of angels —*vt., vi.* [Poet.] to sing in chorus

choir·boy (-boi') *n.* a boy who sings in a choir

choir loft the gallery occupied by the choir in a church

CHLAMYS

choir·mas·ter (-mas′tər, -mäs′-) *n.* the director, or conductor, of a choir

choke (chōk) *vt.* **choked, chok′ing** [ME. *choken*, aphetic < OE. *aceocian*, *vt.*, to choke, prob. < base of *ceace*, jawbone (cf. CHEEK)] **1.** to prevent from breathing by blocking the windpipe or squeezing the throat of; strangle; suffocate; smother; stifle **2.** to block up; obstruct by clogging **3.** to hinder the growth or action of; smother; suppress **4.** to fill up **5.** to cut off some air from the carburetor of (a gasoline engine) in order to make a richer gasoline mixture ☆**6.** to hold (a bat, golf club, etc.) away from the end of the handle and closer toward the middle —*vi.* **1.** to be suffocated; have difficulty in breathing **2.** to be blocked up; be obstructed **3.** to become strained with emotion [a *choking* voice] —*n.* **1.** the act of choking; strangulation **2.** a sound of choking **3.** the valve that chokes a carburetor **4.** a constriction, as in a chokebore —**choke back** to hold back (feelings, sobs, etc.) —**choke down** to swallow with difficulty —**choke off** to bring to an end; end the growth of —**choke up 1.** to block up; clog **2.** to fill too full ☆**3.** [Colloq.] to be unable to speak, act efficiently, etc., as because of fear, strong emotion, tension, etc.

☆**choke·ber·ry** (chōk′ber′ē) *n., pl.* **-ries 1.** the astringent berrylike fruit of certain N. American shrubs (genus *Aronia*) of the rose family **2.** such a shrub

choke·bore (-bôr′) *n.* **1.** a shotgun bore that tapers toward the muzzle to keep the shot closely bunched **2.** a gun with such a bore

☆**choke·cher·ry** (-cher′ē) *n., pl.* **-ries 1.** a N. American wild cherry tree (*Prunus virginiana*) **2.** its astringent fruit

choke coil a coil of wire with a core of iron or air, used for control of the alternating current in an electric circuit: it permits the passage of a direct-current component but has such a high reactance that little alternating current goes through: also **choking coil**

choke·damp (chōk′damp′) *n.* same as BLACKDAMP

choke·full (chōk′fool′) *adj.* same as CHOCK-FULL

chok·er (chōk′ər) *n.* **1.** a person or thing that chokes **2.** a necklace that fits closely around the neck **3.** a narrow fur piece worn around the neck **4.** formerly, a wide neckcloth or stiff collar worn tight around the neck

chok·y (-ē) *adj.* **chok′i·er, chok′i·est 1.** inclined to choke **2.** suffocating; stifling Also sp. **chok′ey**

cho·late (kō′lāt) *n.* a salt or ester of cholic acid

chol·e- (kät′ē, kō′lē) same as CHOLO-: also, before a vowel, **chol-**

chol·e·cyst (kät′ə sist, kō′lə-) *n.* [ModL. *cholecystis* < Gr. *cholē*, bile + *kystis*, bladder] the gallbladder

chol·e·cys·tec·to·my (kät′ə sis tek′tə mē, kō′lə-) *n., pl.* **-mies** [< prec. + -ECTOMY] the surgical removal of the gallbladder

chol·er (kät′ər) *n.* [altered (after L. forms) < ME. & OFr. *colre* < L. *cholera*: see ff.] **1.** [Obs.] bile: in medieval times yellow bile was considered one of the four humors of the body, and the source of anger and irritability **2.** [Now Rare] anger or ill humor

chol·er·a (kät′ər ə) *n.* [L., jaundice < Gr. *cholera*, cholera, nausea < *cholē*, gall bile < IE. base *ĝhel-*, yellow, green, whence GALL[1], GOLD] any of several intestinal diseases; esp., ASIATIC CHOLERA —**chol′e·ra′ic** (-ə rā′ik) *adj.*

cholera mor·bus (môr′bəs) [L., lit., the disease cholera] *earlier term for* GASTROENTERITIS

chol·er·ic (kät′ər ik, kə ler′ik) *adj.* [ME. *colerik*, having choler as the predominant humor, hence of bilious temperament < OFr. *colerique* < L. *cholericus* < Gr. *cholerikos*: see CHOLERA] **1.** having or showing a quick temper or irascible nature; easily angered **2.** [Obs.] bilious —*SYN.* see IRRITABLE

cho·les·ter·ol (kə les′tə rôl′, -rōl′) *n.* [< CHOLE- + Gr. *stereos*, solid, stiff + -OL[1]] a crystalline fatty alcohol, C₂₇H₄₅OH, found esp. in animal fats, blood, nerve tissue, and bile and thought to be a factor in atherosclerosis

cho·lic acid (kō′lik) [< Gr. *cholikos* < *cholē*, bile] an acid, C₂₄H₄₀O₅, found in the bile, generally in combination with amino acids

cho·line (kō′lēn, kät′ēn) *n.* [CHOL- + -INE[4]] a viscous liquid ptomaine, C₅H₁₅O₂N, found in many animal and vegetable tissues: a vitamin of the B complex

cho·lin·er·gic (kō′lə nur′jik, kät′ə-) *adj.* [< CHOLINE + Gr. *ergon*, work + -IC] **1.** having the properties of or resembling acetylcholine **2.** releasing or stimulated by acetylcholine

cho·lin·es·ter·ase (-nes′tə rās′) *n.* [< CHOLINE + ESTERASE] an enzyme which hydrolyzes acetylcholine into choline and acetic acid and is important in the functioning of the nervous system

☆**chol·la** (chō′yə) *n.* [Sp., lit., skull, head] a spiny cactus (genus *Opuntia*) with cylindrical stems, growing in the southwestern U.S. and Mexico

chol·o- (kät′ə, -ō) [Gr. < *cholē*, bile: see CHOLERA] a combining form meaning bile, gall [*chololith*]

chol·o·lith (kät′ə lith) *n.* [prec. + -LITH] same as GALLSTONE

Cho·lon (chə lun′, shə lōn′) city in S South Vietnam: part of the SAIGON urban area

Cho·lu·la (chə lōō′lə) town in C Mexico, near Puebla: site of Toltec and Aztec ruins

chomp (chämp) *vt., vi.* [dial. var. of CHAMP[1]] **1.** to chew hard and noisily; champ **2.** to bite down (*on*), repeatedly and restlessly [a cigar-*chomping* general] —*n.* the act or sound of chomping —**chomp′er** *n.*

chon (chän) *n., pl.* **chon** [Korean] a Korean unit of money, equal to 1/100 won

chon·dri·o·some (kän′drē ə sōm′) *n.* [< Gr. *chondrion*, dim. of *chondros*, cartilage + -SOME[3]] same as MITOCHONDRION

chon·drite (kän′drīt) *n.* [G. *chondrit* < *chondrum*, a chondrule (< Gr. *chondros*, grain, grit: see CHONDRO-) + -*it*, -ITE[1]] a stony meteorite that contains chondrules —**chon·drit·ic** (kän drit′ik) *adj.*

chon·dro- (kän′drō, -drə) [< Gr. *chondros*, cartilage, grain < IE. *ghren-* (whence GRIND), extension of base *gher-*, to rub, grind] a combining form meaning cartilage: also **chon′dri-** (-drē) or, before a vowel, **chon′dr-**

chon·dro·ma (kän drō′mə) *n., pl.* **-mas, -ma·ta** (-mə tə) [prec. + -OMA] a cartilaginous tumor

chon·drule (kän′drōōl) *n.* [< ModL. *chondrus*, chondrule (< Gr. *chondros*, grain: see CHONDRO-) + -ULE] a small rounded mass of various minerals, the size of a pea or smaller, contained in some stony meteorites

Chong·jin (chôn′jin′) seaport in NE North Korea, on the Sea of Japan: pop. 200,000

choo-choo (chōō′chōō′) *n.* [echoic] a railroad train or locomotive: a child's word

choose (chōōz) *vt.* **chose, cho′sen** or obs. **chose, choos′ing** [ME. *chesen, cheosen* < OE. *ceosan* < IE. base *ĝeus-*, to relish, enjoy by tasting, whence L. *gustare*, to taste, Goth. *kausjan*, to taste] **1.** to pick out by preference from what is available; take as a choice; select [to *choose* a book at the library] **2.** to decide or prefer; think proper (with an infinitive object) [to *choose* to remain] —*vi.* **1.** to make one's selection **2.** to have the desire or wish; please [do as you *choose*] —**cannot choose but** cannot do otherwise than; be compelled —**choose up** [Colloq.] to decide on the opposing players, as for an impromptu ball game —**choos′er** *n.* *SYN.*—**choose** implies the exercise of judgment in settling upon a thing or course from among those offered; **select**, and the more informal **pick**, imply a choosing by careful discrimination from a large number available, **pick** sometimes connoting random selection [*pick* a number from 1 to 10]; **elect** implies formal action in officially choosing a person or thing; **prefer** implies preconceived partiality for one thing over another but does not always connote the actual getting of what one chooses —*ANT.* reject

☆**choos·y, choos·ey** (chōō′zē) *adj.* **choos′i·er, choos′i·est** [Colloq.] very careful or fussy in choosing

chop[1] (chäp) *vt.* **chopped, chop′ping** [ME. *choppen*, prob. < a merging of northern OFr. *choper* (OFr. *coper*, Fr. *couper*, to cut, with MDu. *cappen* (Du. *kappen*), to chop off] **1.** to cut or make by blows with an ax or other sharp tool [to *chop* down a tree; to *chop* a hole] **2.** to cut into small bits; mince [*chopped* meat] **3.** to say in a jerky or abrupt way **4.** to hit with a short, sharp, downward stroke —*vi.* **1.** to make quick, cutting strokes with a sharp tool **2.** to do something with a quick, sharp, or jerky motion —*n.* **1.** the act of chopping **2.** a short, sharp, downward blow or stroke **3.** a piece chopped off **4.** a slice of lamb, pork, veal, etc. cut, along with a piece of bone, from the rib, loin, or shoulder **5.** a short, broken movement of waves

chop[2] (chäp) *n.* [var. of CHAP[1]] **1.** a jaw **2.** a cheek See CHOPS

chop[3] (chäp) *vi.* **chopped, chop′ping** [LME. *choppen*, var. of *chappen*, to barter < OE. *ceapian*, to bargain: see CHEAP] to shift or veer suddenly, as the wind; change direction —**chop and change** to change (one's plans, ideas, etc.) constantly —**chop logic** to argue, esp. in a hairsplitting way

chop[4] (chäp) *n.* [Hind. *chāp*] **1.** an official seal, stamp, permit, or license, as orig. in India and China **2.** a brand, or trademark **3.** [Colloq.] quality; grade; brand: *first chop* means "first-rate"

chop-chop (chäp′chäp′) *adv., interj.* [PidE.] quickly

chop·fall·en (-fô′lən) *adj.* same as CHAPFALLEN

chop·house[1] (-hous′) *n.* a restaurant that specializes in chops and steaks

chop·house[2] (-hous′) *n.* [see CHOP[4]] formerly, a Chinese customhouse

Cho·pin (shō′pan; Fr. shō pan′), **Fré·dé·ric Fran·çois** (frā dā rēk′ frän swä′) 1810–49; Pol. composer & pianist, in France after 1831

cho·pine (chō pēn′, chäp′in) *n.* [Sp. *chapin* < ? *chapa*, small leather strip] a woman's shoe with a very thick sole, as of cork, worn in the 16th and 17th centuries: also **chop·in** (chäp′in)

chop·per (chäp′ər) *n.* **1.** a person who chops **2.** a tool or machine for chopping, as an ax or cleaver **3.** [pl.] [Slang] a set of teeth, esp. false teeth ☆**4.** [Colloq.] a helicopter **5.** Electronics a) a device for modulating a direct-current signal to obtain an alternating-current signal, which is more easily amplified b) a device for interrupting a radio signal or beam of light automatically and periodically

chop·py[1] (-ē) *adj.* **-pi·er, -pi·est** [< CHOP[3] + -Y[2]] shifting constantly and abruptly, as the wind —**chop′pi·ness** *n.*

chop·py[2] (-ē) *adj.* **-pi·er, -pi·est** [< CHOP[1] + -Y[2]] **1.** rough with short, broken waves, as the sea **2.** making abrupt starts and stops; jerky; disjointed **—chop′pi·ly** *adv.* **—chop′pi·ness** *n.*

chops (chäps) *n.pl.* [see CHAP[1]] **1.** the jaws **2.** the mouth and lower cheeks

chop·sticks (-stiks′) *n.pl.* [PidE. for Chin. *k'wai-tsze,* the quick ones (see CHOP-CHOP)] **1.** two small sticks of wood or ivory, held together in one hand and used in some Asian countries to lift food to the mouth **2.** [*with sing. v.*] a short, choppy melody played on the piano with one finger of each hand

☆**chop su·ey** (chäp′ sōō′ē) [altered < Chin. *tsa-sui,* lit., various pieces] a Chinese-American dish consisting of meat, bean sprouts, celery, mushrooms, etc. cooked together in a sauce and served with rice

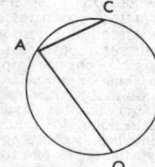

CHOPSTICKS

cho·ra·gus (kō rā′gəs, kə-) *n., pl.* **-gi** (-jī) [L. < Gr. *chorēgos < choros,* chorus + *agein,* to lead] **1.** the leader of the chorus in an ancient Greek play **2.** any leader of a chorus or band **—cho·rag′ic** (-raj′ik) *adj.*

cho·ral (kôr′əl) *adj.* [Fr.] of, for, sung by, or recited by a choir or chorus **—cho′ral·ly** *adv.*

cho·rale, cho·ral (kə ral′, kô-) *n.* [< Gr. *choral* (gesang), choral (song), hymn] **1.** a hymn tune, esp. in the Lutheran service, whose melody moves in an uncomplicated rhythm **2.** a choral composition based on such a tune **3.** a group of singers; choir or chorus

choral speaking recitation of poetry, dramatic pieces, etc. by a chorus of speakers

chord[1] (kôrd) *n.* [altered (after L. *chorda*) < CORD] **1.** [Poet.] the string of a musical instrument **2.** a feeling or emotion thought of as being played on like the string of a harp [to strike a sympathetic *chord*] **3.** *Aeron. a*) a straight line extending directly across an airfoil from the leading to the trailing edge *b*) the length of such a line **4.** *Anat.* same as CORD (sense 5) **5.** *Engineering* a principal horizontal member in a rigid framework, as of a bridge **6.** *Geom.* a straight line joining any two points on an arc, curve, or circumference

CHORDS (AC, AO)

chord[2] (kôrd) *n.* [altered (after L. *chorda*) < ME. *cord,* aphetic < *accord,* ACCORD] *Music* a combination of three or more tones sounded together in harmony **—vi., vt.** **1.** to harmonize **2.** to play chords on (a piano, guitar, etc.) **—chord′al** *adj.*

chor·date (kôr′dāt) *n.* [L. *chorda* (see CORD) + -ATE[1]] any of a phylum (Chordata) of animals having at some stage of development a notochord, gill slits, and a dorsal tubular nerve cord: the phylum includes the vertebrates, tunicates, and lancelets

chore (chôr) *n.* [ME. *cher, cherre:* see CHARE] **1.** a small routine task, as of a housekeeper or farmer; odd job: *often used in pl.* **2.** a hard or unpleasant task **—SYN.** see TASK

cho·re·a (kô rē′ə) *n.* [ModL. < L., a dance in a ring < Gr. *choreia,* choral dance] a disorder of the nervous system characterized by irregular, jerking movements caused by involuntary muscular contractions; St. Vitus's Dance

chor·e·o·graph (kôr′ē ə graf′) *vt., vi.* [back-formation < CHOREOGRAPHY] to design or plan the movements of (a dance, esp. a ballet) **—chor′e·og′ra·pher** (-äg′rə fər) *n.*

chor·e·og·ra·phy (kôr′ē äg′rə fē) *n.* [Gr. *choreia,* dance + -GRAPHY] **1.** dancing, esp. ballet dancing **2.** the arrangement or the written notation of the movements of a dance, esp. a ballet **3.** the art of devising dances, esp. ballets Also, rarely, **cho·reg′ra·phy** (kə reg′-) **—chor′e·o·graph′ic** (-ə graf′ik) *adj.* **—chor′e·o·graph′i·cal·ly** *adv.*

cho·ri·amb (kôr′ē am′, -amb′) *n.* [L. *choriambus* < Gr. *choriambos < choreios,* trochee, lit., pertaining to a chorus + *iambos,* iamb] a classical metrical foot of four syllables, the first and last long (or in English verse, stressed), the middle two short (or unstressed): also **cho′ri·am′bus** (-am′bəs), *pl.* **-bi** (-bī), **-bus·es** **—cho′ri·am′bic** (-am′bik) *adj.*

cho·ric (kôr′ik) *adj.* of, for, or in the manner of, a chorus, esp. in an ancient Greek play

☆**cho·rine** (kôr′ēn) *n.* [CHOR(US) + -INE[2]] [Colloq.] same as CHORUS GIRL

cho·ri·o·al·lan·to·is (kôr′ē ō′ə lan′tə wis) *n.* [ModL.: see CHORION & ALLANTOIS] an enveloping fetal membrane formed by the fusion of chorion and allantois in birds and some mammals: that of chicks is used as a culture medium for growing viruses **—cho′ri·o·al′lan·to′ic** (-al′ən tō′ik) *adj.*

cho·ri·oid (kôr′ē oid′) *adj., n.* same as CHOROID

cho·ri·on (kôr′ē än′) *n.* [ModL. < Gr. *chorion,* fetal membrane] the outermost of the two membranes that completely envelop a fetus **—cho′ri·on′ic** (-än′ik) *adj.*

cho·ri·pet·al·ous (kôr′i pet′'l əs) *adj.* [< Gr. *chōris,* apart, bereaved + PETALOUS] same as POLYPETALOUS

chor·is·ter (kôr′is tər) *n.* [altered (after CHORUS) < ME. *querister* < OFr. *cueristre:* see CHOIR] **1.** a member of a choir, esp. a boy singer ☆**2.** the leader of a choir

C-horizon *n.* the third soil zone, consisting of material essentially unaltered by weathering, solution, or the action of plant roots: see ABC SOIL

cho·rog·ra·phy (kō räg′rə fē, kə-) *n.* [L. *chorographia,* geography < Gr. *chōrographia < chōros,* open area + *graphein,* to write] **1.** the art of mapping or describing a region or district **2.** such a map or description **—cho·ro·graph·ic** (kôr′ə graf′ik) *adj.*

cho·roid (kôr′oid) *adj.* [Gr. *choroeidēs,* contr. < *chorioeidēs < chorion,* CHORION + *eidos,* form] designating or of the chorion or certain other vascular membranes **—n.** the dark, vascular membrane that forms the middle coat of the eye, between the sclera and the retina

chor·tle (chôr′t'l) *vi., vt.* **-tled, -tling** [coined by Lewis Carroll, in *Through the Looking Glass,* prob. < CHUCKLE + SNORT] to make, or utter with, a gleeful chuckling or snorting sound **—n.** such a sound **—chor′tler** *n.*

cho·rus (kôr′əs) *n.* [L., a dance, band of dancers or singers < Gr. *choros*] **1.** in ancient Greek drama, and drama like it, a company of performers whose singing, dancing, and narration provide explanation and elaboration of the main action **2.** in Elizabethan drama, a person who recites the prologue and epilogue **3.** a group of dancers and singers performing together in a modern musical show, opera, etc. **4.** the part of a drama, song, etc. performed by a chorus **5.** a group of people trained to sing or speak something together simultaneously **6.** a simultaneous utterance by many [*a chorus* of protest] **7.** that which is thus uttered **8.** music written for group singing **9.** that part of a musical composition in which the company joins the solo singer **10.** *a*) the refrain of a song or hymn following each verse *b*) the main tune, as of a jazz piece, following the introduction **—vt., vi.** to sing, speak, or say in unison **—in chorus** in unison

chorus girl (or **boy**) a woman (or man) singing or dancing in the chorus of a musical show

Cho·rzów (hô′zhoof) city in S Poland: pop. 153,000

chose[1] (chōz) *pt. & obs. pp.* of CHOOSE

chose[2] (shōz) *n.* [ME. < OFr., thing < L. *causa,* matter, affair] *Law* a piece of personal property; chattel

Cho·sen (chō′sen′) *Jap. name* of KOREA

cho·sen (chō′z'n) *pp.* of CHOOSE **—adj.** **1.** picked out by preference; selected **2.** *Theol.* elect; favored by God

chott (shät) *n.* same as SHOTT

Chou (jō) third Chinese dynasty (1122? to 256? B.C.)

Chou En-lai (jō′ en′lī′) 1898– ; Chin. Communist leader; prime minister (1949–)

chough (chuf) *n.* [ME. < IE. base *gou-, to cry, scream, whence MDu. *cauwe,* jackdaw, G. *kauz,* screech-owl] a European bird (*Pyrrhocorax pyrrhocorax*) of the crow family, with red legs and beak and glossy black feathers

chouse[1] (chous) *n.* [< CHIAUS: after a Turk. interpreter alleged to have swindled London merchants in 1609] [Chiefly Brit.] a swindle **—vt. choused, chous′ing** [Chiefly Brit.] to cheat; swindle

☆**chouse**[2] (chous) *vt.* [< ?] [Western] to herd (cattle) roughly

chow (chou) *n.* [< Chin. dial. form akin to Cantonese *kaú,* a dog] **1.** any of a breed of medium-sized dog, originally from China, with a compact, muscular body, a thick coat of brown or black, and a blue-black tongue: official name, **chow chow** ☆**2.** [Slang] food or mealtime

chow-chow (chou′chou′) *n.* [PidE. < Chin.] ☆**1.** chopped pickles in a highly seasoned mustard sauce **2.** a preserve of fruits, peels, and ginger, orig. Chinese

CHOW
(20 in. high)

☆**chow·der** (chou′dər) *n.* [Fr. *chaudière,* a pot < LL. *caldaria:* see CALDRON] a thick soup made variously, but usually containing onions, potatoes, and salt pork, sometimes corn, tomatoes, or other vegetables, and often, specif., clams and milk

☆**chow mein** (chou mān′) [Chin. *ch'ao,* to fry + *mien,* flour] a Chinese-American dish consisting of a thick stew of meat, celery, bean sprouts, etc., served with fried noodles and usually flavored with soy sauce

Chr. **1.** Christ **2.** Christian **3.** Chronicles

chres·tom·a·thy (kres täm′ə thē) *n., pl.* **-thies** [Gr. *chrēstomatheia < chrēstos,* useful + *mathein,* to learn] a collection of literary passages, esp. one used in studying a language

Chré·tien (or **Chres·tien**) **de Troyes** (krā tyan′ də trwä′) fl. 1165; Fr. poet

chrism (kriz′m) *n.* [ME. *crisme* < OE. *crisma* < LL.(Ec.) *chrisma,* an anointing, unction < Gr. *chrisma,* oil (in Ec. use, anointing) < *chriein,* to rub, anoint: see CHRIST] **1.** consecrated oil used in baptism and other sacraments in certain churches **2.** a sacramental anointing with such oil **—chris′mal** (-məl) *adj.*

chris·ma·to·ry (kriz′mə tôr′ē) *n., pl.* **-ries** [ML. *chrismatorium*] a container or receptacle for the chrism

chris·om (kriz′'m) *n.* [ME. *crisom* (var. of *crisme,* CHRISM),

orig., cloth to keep chrism off the face] **1.** a white cloth or robe formerly put on a baby at baptism as a symbol of innocence: it was used as a shroud if the child died within a month of birth **2.** [Archaic] an innocent baby; infant

Christ (krist) [ME. & OE. *Crist* < LL.(Ec.) *Christus* < Gr. *christos*, the anointed (in NT., MESSIAH) < *chriein*, to anoint < IE. base *ghrēi-*, to spread over, smear, whence GRIME] **1.** the Messiah whose appearance is prophesied in the Old Testament **2.** Jesus of Nazareth, regarded by Christians as the realization of the Messianic prophecy: originally a title (*Jesus the Christ*), later used as part of the name (*Jesus Christ*)

Chris·ta·bel (kris′tə bel′) [< L. *Christus* (see CHRIST) + *bella*, fem. of *bellus*, handsome] a feminine name

Christ·church (krist′church′) city on the E coast of South Island, New Zealand: pop. 159,000 (met. area 244,000)

christ·cross (kris′krôs′) n. [< ME. *Crist cros*, Christ's cross] **1.** [Obs.] the figure of a cross (✠) placed before the alphabet in hornbooks **2.** [Archaic] the mark of the cross (✕) used as a signature by a person who cannot write CROSS CRISSCROSS

chris·ten (kris′n) vt. [ME. *cristnen* < OE. *cristnian*: see CHRISTIAN] **1.** to take into a Christian church by baptism; baptize **2.** to give a name to at baptism **3.** to give a name to (a ship being launched, etc.) **4.** [Colloq.] to make use of for the first time

Chris·ten·dom (-dəm) n. [ME. & OE. *cristendom*, Christianity: see CHRISTIAN & -DOM] **1.** Christians collectively **2.** those parts of the world where most of the inhabitants profess the Christian faith

chris·ten·ing (kris′n iŋ, kris′niŋ) n. [ME. *cristninge*: see CHRISTEN] the Christian act or ceremony of baptizing and giving a name to an infant; baptism

Christ·hood (krist′hood′) n. [see -HOOD] the state or fact of being the Christ

Chris·tian (kris′chən) **1.** a masculine name: dim. *Chris, Christie*; fem. *Christina, Christine* **2.** the main character in Bunyan's *Pilgrim's Progress* —n. [ME. & OE. *cristen* < LL.(Ec.) *Christianus* < Gr. *christianos* < *christos* (see CHRIST); mod. sp. < L.] **1.** a person professing belief in Jesus as the Christ, or in the religion based on the teachings of Jesus **2.** [Colloq.] a decent, respectable person —adj. **1.** of Jesus Christ or his teachings **2.** of or professing the religion based on those teachings **3.** having the qualities demonstrated and taught by Jesus Christ, as love, kindness, humility, etc. **4.** of or representing Christians or Christianity **5.** [Colloq.] humane, decent, etc. —**Chris′tian·ly** adj., adv.

Christian X (born *Carl Frederick Albert Alexander Vilhelm*) 1870–1947; king of Denmark (1912–47)

Chris·ti·an·a (kris′tē an′ə) [LL., fem. of *Christianus*: see CHRISTIAN] a feminine name: dim. *Chrissie, Tina*; var. *Christina, Christine*

Christian Brothers a Roman Catholic lay order that undertakes the teaching of youth: in full, **Brothers of the Christian Schools**

Christian Era the era beginning with the year formerly thought to be that of the birth of Jesus Christ (but probably c. 8–4 B.C.): *A.D.* marks dates in this era, *B.C.* marks dates before it

Chris·ti·a·ni·a (kris′chē an′ē ə, -tē-; -än′-) former name of OSLO —n. [also c-] same as CHRISTIE

Chris·ti·an·i·ty (kris′chē an′ə tē) n. [ME. *cristianite* < OFr. *crestiente* < LL.(Ec.) *Christianitas* < *Christianus*, CHRISTIAN] **1.** Christians collectively; Christendom **2.** the Christian religion, based on the Old and New Testament **3.** a particular Christian religious system **4.** the state of being a Christian

Chris·tian·ize (kris′chə nīz′) vt. -ized′, -iz′ing [LL.(Ec.) *christianizare* < Gr.(Ec.) *christianizein*, to profess Christianity] **1.** to convert to Christianity **2.** to cause to conform with Christian character or precepts —vi. [Rare] to adopt Christianity —**Chris′tian·i·za′tion** n. —**Chris′tian·iz′er** n.

Christian name the baptismal name or given name, as distinguished from the surname or family name

Christian Science a religion and a system of healing founded by Mary Baker Eddy c. 1866, based on an interpretation of the Scriptures as upholding the idea that disease, sin, death, etc. are caused by mental error and have no real existence: official name, CHURCH OF CHRIST, SCIENTIST —**Chris′tian Sci′en·tist**

chris·tie, chris·ty (kris′tē) n., pl. -ties [< CHRISTIANIA] Skiing any of various high-speed turns to change direction, reduce speed, or stop, made by shifting weight, with the skis usually kept parallel

Chris·tie (kris′tē), **Agatha** (born *Agatha Mary Clarissa Miller*) 1891– ; Eng. writer of detective stories

Chris·ti·na (kris tē′nə) **1.** a feminine name: see CHRISTIANA **2.** 1626–89; queen of Sweden (1632–54)

Chris·tine (kris tēn′) a feminine name: see CHRISTIANA

Christ·like (krist′līk′) adj. like Jesus Christ, esp. in character or spirit —**Christ′like′ness** n.

Christ·ly (-lē) adj. of Jesus Christ; Christlike —**Christ′li·ness** n.

Christ·mas (kris′məs) n. [ME. *Cristemas* < OE. *Cristemæsse*: see CHRIST & MASS] **1.** a holiday on Dec. 25 celebrating the birth of Jesus Christ: also **Christmas Day 2.** same as CHRISTMASTIDE

Christmas Eve the evening before Christmas Day

Christmas Island 1. island in the Indian Ocean, south of Java: under Australian administration: 55 sq. mi.; pop. 3,000 **2.** Brit. island in C Pacific, in the Gilbert & Ellice Islands colony: 222 sq. mi.; pop. 300

Christ·mas·tide (-tīd′) n. Christmas time, from Christmas Eve through New Year's Day or to Epiphany (Jan. 6)

☆**Christmas tree** an evergreen or artificial tree hung with ornaments and lights at Christmas time

Chris·tol·o·gy (kris täl′ə jē) n. [< Gr. *christos* (see CHRIST) + -LOGY] the study of the work and person of Jesus Christ and of the literature that relates to him —**Chris′to·log′i·cal** (-tə läj′i k'l) adj.

Chris·tophe (krēs tôf′), **Hen·ri** (än rē′) 1767–1820; Haitian revolutionary leader; king of Haiti (1811–20)

Chris·to·pher (kris′tə fər) [ME. *Christofre* < LL.(Ec.) *Christophorus* < Gr.(Ec.) *Christophoros*, lit., bearing Christ < *christos* (see CHRIST) + *pherein*, to bear] **1.** a masculine name: dim. *Chris, Kit* **2.** Saint, 3d cent. A.D.; Christian martyr of Asia Minor: patron saint of travelers: his day is July 25

Christ's-thorn (krists′thôrn′) n. an Old World spiny shrub (*Paliurus spina-christi*) of the buckthorn family, supposed to have been used for Christ's crown of thorns

Chris·ty (kris′tē), **Howard Chandler** 1873–1952; U.S. painter & illustrator

chro·ma (krō′mə) n. [Gr. *chrōma*, color, orig. skin, color of the skin < IE. base *ghreu-*, to rub hard over, crumble, whence GRITS] [Chiefly Brit.] same as SATURATION (sense 2)

chro·mate (krō′māt) n. [CHROM(IUM) + -ATE²] a salt or ester of chromic acid

chro·mat·ic (krō mat′ik) adj. [LL. *chromaticus* < Gr. *chrōmatikos*, suited for color: see CHROMA] **1.** of color or having color or colors **2.** highly colored **3.** Biol. readily stained **4.** Music a) using or progressing by half tones [a *chromatic scale*] b) producing all the tones of such a scale [a *chromatic instrument*] c) using tones not in the key of a work [*chromatic harmony*] —n. Music a tone modified by an accidental —**chro·mat′i·cal·ly** adv. —**chro·mat′i·cism** (-ə siz′m) n.

chromatic aberration a property of lenses that causes the various colors in a beam of light to be focused at different points, thus causing a margin of colors to appear around the edges of the image

chro·ma·tic·i·ty (krō′mə tis′ə tē) n. the classification of a color with reference to its hue and its purity, i.e., its departure from white light

chro·mat·ics (krō mat′iks) n.pl. [with sing. v.] the scientific study of colors with reference to hue and saturation

chromatic scale the musical scale made up of thirteen successive half tones to the octave

chro·ma·tid (krō′mə tid) n. any of the usually four elongated structures containing the hereditary substance, and with a centromere, forming a chromosome

chro·ma·tin (-tin) n. [< Gr. *chrōma* (gen. *chrōmatos*), color + -IN¹] a protoplasmic substance in the nucleus of living cells that readily takes a deep stain: chromatin forms the chromosomes and contains the genes

chro·ma·tism (-tiz′m) n. [Gr. *chrōmatismos*: see prec. & -ISM] **1.** any abnormal coloring in parts of a plant ordinarily green **2.** same as CHROMATIC ABERRATION

chro·ma·to- (krō′mə tō, krō mat′ə) [< Gr. *chrōma* (gen. *chrōmatos*), color] a combining form meaning: **1.** color or pigmentation [*chromatography*] **2.** chromatin [*chromatolysis*] Also, before a vowel, **chromat-**

chro·mat·o·gram (krō mat′ə gram′) n. the arrangement of zones or bands resulting from a chromatographic separation

chro·mat·o·graph (-graf′) vt. to carry out a separation by chromatography —n. a display or record of the results of such a separation —**chro·mat′o·graph′ic** adj. —**chro·mat′o·graph′i·cal·ly** adv.

chro·ma·tog·ra·phy (krō′mə täg′rə fē) n. [CHROMATO- + -GRAPHY] the process of separating constituents of a mixture by permitting a solution of the mixture to flow through a column of adsorbent on which the different substances are selectively separated into distinct bands or spots

chro·ma·tol·y·sis (-täl′ə sis) n. [CHROMATO- + -LYSIS] Med. the disappearance of certain chromophil granules from nerve cells —**chro·mat·o·lyt·ic** (krō mat′ə lit′ik) adj.

chro·mat·o·phore (krō mat′ə fôr′, krō′mə tə fôr′) n. [CHROMATO- + -PHORE] **1.** a special animal cell, usually dermal, that contains pigment granules: it is often capable of expansion and contraction in such a manner that the skin color changes, as in the chameleon **2.** same as CHLOROPLAST

chrome (krōm) n. [Fr. < Gr. *chrōma*, color: so called because of the bright-colored compounds] **1.** chromium or chromium alloy, esp. as used for plating **2.** any of certain salts of chromium, used in dyeing and tanning **3.** a

chromium pigment —*vt.* **chromed, chrom′ing 1.** to plate with chromium **2.** to treat with a salt of chromium, as in dyeing

-chrome (krōm) [< Gr. *chrōma:* see CHROMA] *a suffix meaning:* **1.** color or coloring agent [*urochrome*] **2.** chromium [*ferrochrome*]

chrome alum an alum of which one of the components is chromium; esp., potassium chrome alum, $KCr(SO_4)_2 \cdot 12H_2O$, used in tanning and dyeing

chrome green 1. chromic oxide, Cr_2O_3, used as a green pigment **2.** in commercial use, a green pigment made by mixing chrome yellow and Prussian blue

chrome red any of various red pigments made from basic lead chromate, $PbCrO_4 \cdot PbO$

chrome steel *same as* CHROMIUM STEEL

chrome yellow neutral chromate of lead, $PbCrO_4$, used as a yellow pigment

chro·mic (krō′mik) *adj.* designating or of compounds containing trivalent chromium

chromic acid an acid, H_2CrO_4, existing only in solution or known in the form of its salts

chro·mide (krō′mid) *n. same as* CICHLID

chro·mi·nance (krō′mə nəns) *n.* [CHROM- + (LUM)INANCE] that attribute of light which produces the sensation of color apart from luminance; specif., color, in the form of hue and saturation, produced on a television receiver screen

chro·mite (krō′mit) *n.* a black mineral, $FeCr_2O_4$, with a metallic luster and an uneven fracture: it is the chief ore of chromium

chro·mi·um (-mē əm) *n.* [CHROM(E) + -IUM] a grayish-white, crystalline, very hard, metallic chemical element with a high resistance to corrosion: used in chromium electroplating, in alloy steel, and in alloys containing nickel, copper, manganese, and other metals: symbol, Cr; at. wt., 51.996; at. no., 24; sp. gr., 7.20; melt. pt., 1890°C; boil. pt., 2480°C

chromium steel a very strong, hard alloy steel containing chromium

☆**chro·mo** (krō′mō) *n., pl.* **-mos** a chromolithograph

chro·mo- (krō′mə, -mō) [< Gr. *chrōma:* see CHROMA] *a combining form meaning* color or pigment [*chromosome, chromolithograph*]: also, before a vowel, **chrom-**

chro·mo·gen (krō′mə jən) *n.* [prec. + -GEN] **1.** any substance that can become a pigment or coloring matter, as a substance in organic fluids that forms colored compounds when oxidized, or a compound, not itself a dye, that can become a dye **2.** any of certain bacteria that produce a pigment —**chro′mo·gen′ic** (-jen′ik) *adj.*

chro·mo·lith·o·graph (krō′mō lith′ə graf′) *n.* a colored picture printed by the lithographic process from a series of stone or metal plates, the impression from each plate being in a different color —**chro′mo·li·thog′ra·pher** (-li thäg′rə fər) *n.* —**chro′mo·lith′o·graph′ic** (-lith′ə graf′ik) *adj.* —**chro′mo·li·thog′ra·phy** *n.*

chro·mo·mere (krō′mə mir′) *n.* [CHROMO- + -MERE] any of the granules of chromatin arranged linearly on a chromosome —**chro′mo·mer′ic** (-mir′ik) *adj.*

chro·mo·ne·ma (krō′mə nē′mə) *n., pl.* **-ma·ta** (-tə) [< CHROMO- + Gr. *nēma,* thread (see NEMATO-)] a coiled, twisted, threadlike filament contained in a chromatid at all stages of mitosis —**chro′mo·ne′mal** *adj.*

chro·mo·phil (krō′mə fil) *adj.* [CHROMO- + -PHIL] readily stained with dyes —*n.* a chromophil cell or cell part

chro·mo·phore (krō′mə fôr′) *n.* [< CHROMO- + -PHORE] any chemical group, as the azo group, that produces color in a compound and unites with certain other groups to form dyes —**chro′mo·phor′ic** (-fôr′ik) *adj.*

chro·mo·plast (-plast′) *n.* [CHROMO- + -PLAST] a plastid containing a pigment other than green, usually yellow, orange, or red

chro·mo·pro·te·in (krō′mə prō′tēn, -prō′tē ən) *n.* a conjugated protein containing a pigment

chro·mo·some (krō′mə sōm′) *n.* [CHROMO- + -SOME³] any of the microscopic rod-shaped bodies into which the chromatin of a cell nucleus separates during mitosis: they carry the genes that convey hereditary characteristics, and are constant in number for each species —**chro′mo·so′mal** (-sō′məl) *adj.*

chro·mo·sphere (-sfir′) *n.* [CHROMO- + -SPHERE] the region around a star, esp. the sun, between the relatively cold, dense photosphere and the hot, tenuous corona —**chro′mo·spher′ic** (-sfir′ik, -sfer′-) *adj.*

chro·mous (krō′məs) *adj.* designating or of compounds containing divalent chromium

chro·myl (-mil) *n.* [CHROM- + -YL] the divalent radical $CrO_2 =$

chron- (krän) *same as* CHRONO-: used before a vowel

Chron. Chronicles

chron. 1. chronological **2.** chronology

chro·nax·ie, chro·nax·y (krō′nak sē) *n.* [< CHRON- + Gr. *axia,* value] the minimum time necessary to excite a tissue, such as muscle or nerve tissue, with an electric current of twice the minimum potential for stimulation

chron·ic (krän′ik) *adj.* [Fr. *chronique* < L. *chronicus* < Gr. *chronikos,* of time < *chronos,* time] **1.** lasting a long time or recurring often: said of a disease, and distinguished from ACUTE **2.** having had an ailment for a long time [a *chronic* patient] **3.** continuing indefinitely; perpetual; constant [a *chronic* worry] **4.** by habit, custom, etc.;

habitual; inveterate [a *chronic* complainer] —*n.* a chronic patient —**chron′i·cal·ly** *adv.* —**chro·nic·i·ty** (krə nis′ə tē) *n.*

SYN.—**chronic** suggests long duration or frequent recurrence and is used especially of diseases or habits that resist all efforts to eradicate them [*chronic* sinusitis/; **inveterate** implies firm establishment as a result of continued indulgence over a long period of time [an *inveterate* liar/; **confirmed** suggests fixedness in some condition or practice, often from a deep-seated aversion to change [a *confirmed* bachelor/; **hardened** implies fixed tendencies and a callous indifference to emotional or moral considerations [a *hardened* criminal/

chron·i·cle (krän′i k'l) *n.* [ME. & Anglo-Fr. *cronicle* < OFr. *chronique* < ML. *chronica* < L., pl., pertaining to time, chronicles < Gr. *chronika,* annals, pl. of *chronikos:* see CHRONIC] **1.** a historical record or register of facts or events arranged in the order in which they happened **2.** a narrative; history —*vt.* **-cled, -cling** to tell or write the history of; put into a chronicle; recount; record —**chron′i·cler** (-klər) *n.*

Chron·i·cles (-k'lz) either of two books of the Bible, I and II Chronicles

chro·no- (krän′ə, krō′nə) [Gr. < *chronos,* time] *a combining form meaning* time [*chronograph*]

chron·o·gram (krän′ə gram′, krō′nə-) *n.* [prec. + -GRAM] **1.** an inscription in which certain letters, made more prominent, express a date in Roman numerals (Ex.: MerCy MiXeD with LoVe In hIm—MCMXLVII=1947) **2.** a record kept by a chronograph

chron·o·graph (-graf′) *n.* [CHRONO- + -GRAPH] any of various instruments for measuring and recording brief, precisely spaced intervals of time, as a stopwatch —**chron′o·graph′ic** *adj.* —**chro·nog′ra·phy** (krə näg′rə fē) *n.*

chron·o·log·i·cal (krän′ə läj′i k'l) *adj.* [CHRONOLOG(Y) + -ICAL] **1.** arranged in the order of occurrence **2.** of chronology; esp., containing or relating to an account of events in the order of their occurrence Also **chron′o·log′ic** —**chron′o·log′i·cal·ly** *adv.*

chro·nol·o·gy (krə näl′ə jē) *n., pl.* **-gies** [CHRONO- + -LOGY] **1.** the science of measuring time in fixed periods and of dating events and epochs and arranging them in the order of occurrence **2.** the arrangement of events, dates, etc. in the order of occurrence **3.** a list or table of dates in their proper sequence —**chro·nol′o·gist, chro·nol′o·ger** *n.*

chro·nom·e·ter (-näm′ə tər) *n.* [CHRONO- + -METER] an instrument for measuring time precisely; highly accurate kind of clock or watch, as for scientific use

chron·o·met·ric (krän′ə met′rik, krō′nə-) *adj.* of a chronometer or chronometry: also **chron′o·met′ri·cal** —**chron′o·met′ri·cal·ly** *adv.*

chro·nom·e·try (krə näm′ə trē) *n.* the scientific measurement of time

chron·o·scope (krän′ə skōp′) *n.* [CHRONO- + -SCOPE] an instrument for measuring very small intervals of time

-chro·ous (krō əs) [Gr. *-chroos* < *chrōs, chroos,* color] *a terminal combining form meaning* colored [*isochrous*]

chrys·a·lid (kris′l id) *n. same as* CHRYSALIS —*adj.* of a chrysalis

chrys·a·lis (kris′l əs) *n., pl.* **chry·sal·i·des** (kri sal′ə dēz′), **chrys′a·lis·es** [L. *chrysallis* < Gr. *chrysallis,* golden-colored chrysalis of a butterfly < *chrysos,* gold: of Sem. origin, as in Heb. *hārūz,* gold, Aram. *harā,* yellow] **1.** the pupa of a butterfly, the form of the insect when between the larval and adult stages and in a case or cocoon **2.** the case or cocoon **3.** anything in a formative or undeveloped stage

chrys·an·the·mum (kri san′thə məm) *n.* [L. < Gr. *chrysanthemon,* marigold, lit., golden flower < *chrysos* (see prec.) + *anthemon,* a flower] **1.** any of a genus (*Chrysanthemum*) of plants of the composite family, cultivated for their showy flowers which bloom in late summer and fall in a variety of colors, most commonly yellow, white, red, or purple **2.** the flower

chrys·a·ro·bin (kris′ə rō′bən) *n.* [< Gr. *chrysos,* gold + ARAROBA + -IN¹] a yellow, crystalline substance, $C_{15}H_{12}O_3$, derived from Goa powder and used in the treatment of various skin disorders

Chry·se·is (kri sē′is) [L. < Gr. *Chrysēis*] in Homer's *Iliad,* the daughter of a priest of Apollo: seized by the Greeks during the Trojan War and given to Agamemnon, she was returned to her father only after Apollo caused a plague to fall on the Greek camp

chrys·el·e·phan·tine (kris′el ə fan′tēn, -tin) *adj.* [Gr. *chryselephantinos* < *chrysos* (see CHRYSALIS) + *elephantinos* (see ELEPHANT)] made of, or overlaid with, gold and ivory, as some ancient Greek statues

chrys·o- (kris′ə, -ō) [< Gr. *chrysos:* see CHRYSALIS] *a combining form meaning* golden, yellow [*chrysoberyl*]: also, before a vowel, **chrys-**

chrys·o·ber·yl (kris′ə ber′əl) *n.* [prec. + BERYL] beryllium aluminate, $BeAl_2O_4$, a yellowish or greenish mineral used as a semiprecious stone

chrys·o·lite (-lit′) *n.* [ME. & OFr. *crisolite* < L. *chrysolithos* < Gr. *chrysolithos,* topaz: see CHRYSO- & -LITE] *same as* OLIVINE

chrys·o·prase (-prāz′) *n.* [ME. & OFr. *crisopace* (& Late OE. *crisoprassus*) < L. *chrysoprasus* < Gr. *chrysoprasos* < *chrysos,* gold + *prason,* leek: so called from the color] a light-green variety of chalcedony sometimes used as a semiprecious stone

Chrys·os·tom (kris′əs təm, kri säs′təm), Saint **John** 347?–407 A.D.; Gr. church father; archbishop of Constantinople (398–404): his day is Jan. 27

chrys·o·tile (-til′) *n.* [< CHRYSO- + Gr. *tilos*, fiber] a fibrous variety of serpentine that is the principal source of asbestos

chs. chapters

chtho·ni·an (thō′nē ən) *adj.* [Gr. *chthonios*, in the earth < *chthōn*, the earth < IE. base *ǵhthom-*, whence L. *humus*, earth, L. *homo* & Goth. *guma*, man] *Gr. Myth.* designating or of the underworld of the dead and its gods or spirits

chthon·ic (thän′ik) *adj.* 1. *same as* CHTHONIAN 2. dark, primitive, and mysterious

chub (chub) *n., pl.* **chubs, chub**: see PLURAL, II, D,1 [Late ME. *chubbe*] ☆1. any of several small, freshwater fishes related to the minnows and carp: often used as bait 2. any of several herringlike, freshwater fishes (genus *Leucichthys*), found in cold northern waters 3. any of a number of saltwater scavenger fishes with a small mouth

chub·by (chub′ē) *adj.* **-bi·er, -bi·est** [< CHUB] round and plump [*chubby* cheeks] —**chub′bi·ness** *n.*

chuck¹ (chuk) *vt.* [< ? Fr. *choquer*, to shock, strike against] 1. to tap or pat gently, esp. under the chin, as a playful or affectionate gesture 2. to throw with a quick, short movement; pitch; toss 3. [Slang] *a)* to discard or eject; get rid of ☆*b)* to quit (as one's job) ☆*c)* to vomit (often with *up*) —*n.* 1. a light tap or squeeze under the chin 2. a toss; throw ☆3. [cf. *v.,* 2 & 3] [Chiefly Western] food

chuck² (chuk) *n.* [prob. var. of CHOCK] 1. a cut of beef including the parts around the neck and the shoulder blade: see BEEF, illus. 2. a clamplike device, as on a lathe, by which the tool or work to be turned is held 3. *same as* CHOCK

chuck³ (chuk) *vi., n.* [echoic] *same as* CLUCK

☆**chuck-a-luck** (chuk′ə luk′) *n.* [< CHUCK¹ + LUCK] a gambling game in which players bet on the throws of three dice: also called **chuck′-luck′**

chuck-full (chuk′fool′) *adj. same as* CHOCK-FULL

chuck·hole (chuk′hōl′) *n.* [< dial. *chock,* a bump in a road, orig., a stump, block (see CHOCK) + HOLE] a rough hole in pavement, made by wear and weathering

chuck·le (chuk′'l) *vi.* **-led, -ling** [prob. < CHUCK³ + freq. suffix *-le*] 1. to laugh softly in a low tone, as in mild amusement 2. to cluck, as a hen —*n.* a soft, low-toned laugh —*SYN.* see LAUGH —**chuck′ler** *n.*

chuck·le·head (-hed′) *n.* [< ? CHOCK + HEAD] [Colloq.] a stupid person; dolt —**chuck′le·head′ed** *adj.*

☆**chuck wagon** [CHUCK¹, *n.* 3 + WAGON] a wagon equipped as a kitchen for feeding cowboys or other outdoor workers

☆**chuck·wal·la** (chuk′wäl′ə) *n.* [MexSp. *chacahuala* < AmInd. (Cahuilla) *tcáxxwal*] any of several large, edible lizards (genus *Sauromalus*) living in NW Mexico and SW U.S.

☆**chuck-will's-wid·ow** (chuk′wilz′wid′ō) *n.* [echoic of its cry] a large goatsucker (*Caprimulgus carolinensis*) of the S U.S., a bird closely related to the whippoorwill

chud·dar, chud·der (chud′ər) *n.* [Hindi *chadar*] a large, square cloth worn as a shawl by women in India

Chud·sko·ye, Chud·sko·e (choot′skô yə) lake in W European U.S.S.R., on the E border of Estonian S.S.R.: c. 1,400 sq. mi. (with Lake Pskov)

chuff¹ (chuf) *n.* [ME. *chuffe*] a boor; churl

chuff² (chuf) *vi., n.* [echoic] *same as* CHUG

chuff·y (chuf′ē) *adj.* **chuff′i·er, chuff′i·est** [< obs. *chuff,* a fat cheek + -Y²] [Dial.] stocky or plump

☆**chug** (chug) *n.* [echoic] any of a series of abrupt, puffing or explosive sounds, as of a locomotive —*vi.* **chugged, chug′ging** to make, or move with, such sounds

☆**chug-a-lug** (chug′ə lug′) *adv.* [echoic] [Slang] in continuous gulps or in a single, long gulp —*vt., vi.* **-lugged′, -lug′ging** [Slang] to drink chug-a-lug; swill; guzzle

☆**chu·kar** (chə kär′) *n.* [Hindi *cakor* < Sans. *cakōra* < IE. echoic base *kāu-,* to scream, whence HOWL] an Asian and European partridge (*Alectoris graeca*), with red bill and feet, chestnut-colored above and white or gray below: introduced into several of the western States

Chuk·chee, Chuk·chi (chuk′chē) *n.* [< Russ. < Chukchee *tawtu,* keepers of the reindeer] 1. a member of a people now living in northeasternmost Siberia 2. their language, now nearly extinct

Chuk·chi Sea (chuk′chē) part of the Arctic Ocean, north of the Bering Strait

Chu Kiang (choo′ jyän′) river in SE China, forming an estuary between Macao & Hong Kong: c. 100 mi.

chuk·ka boot (chuk′ə) [altered < *chukker:* so named from resembling shoes worn for polo] a man's ankle-high shoe, usually with two or three pairs of eyelets and often fleece-lined

chuk·ker, chuk·kar (chuk′ər) *n.* [Hindi *chakar* < Sans. *cakra,* wheel] any of the periods of play, each lasting 7 1/2 minutes, into which a polo match is divided

Chu·la Vis·ta (choo′lə vis′tə) [AmSp., lit., beautiful view]
city in SW Calif.: suburb of San Diego: pop. 68,000

chum¹ (chum) *n.* [late 17th-c. slang; prob. altered sp. of *cham,* clipped form of *chamber (fellow), chamber (mate)*] [Colloq.] 1. orig., a roommate 2. a close friend —*vi.* **chummed, chum′ming** [Colloq.] 1. orig., to share the same room 2. to be close friends

☆**chum²** (chum) *n.* [< ? Scot. *chum,* food] bait, usually oily fish cut up into small pieces, scattered in the water to attract fish to the line

chum·my (chum′ē) *adj.* **-mi·er, -mi·est** [Colloq.] like a chum; intimate; friendly —**chum′mi·ly** *adv.* —**chum′mi·ness** *n.*

chump (chump) *n.* [< ? CHUCK² or CHUNK + LUMP¹] 1. a heavy block of wood 2. a thick, blunt end 3. [Colloq.] a foolish, stupid, or gullible person; dupe or fool —**off one's chump** [Earlier Slang] insane; crazy

Chung·king (choon′kin′, chun′-; *Chin.* joon′chin′) city in Szechwan province, SC China, on the Yangtze River: pop. 4,070,000: also **Chung·ching** (joon′chin′)

chunk (chunk) *n.* [< ? CHUCK²] 1. a short, thick piece, as of meat, wood, etc. 2. a considerable portion ☆3. a stocky animal, esp. a horse

chunk·y (chun′kē) *adj.* **chunk′i·er, chunk′i·est** 1. short and thick 2. stocky; thickset 3. containing chunks —**chunk′i·ness** *n.*

church (church) *n.* [ME. *chirche, kirke* < OE. *cirice* (& ON. *kirkja* < OE.) < Gmc. *kirika* < LGr.(Ec.) *kyrikē* < Gr. *kyriakē* (*oikia*), Lord's (house) < *kyriakos,* belonging to the Lord < *kyrios,* ruler < *kyros,* supreme power < IE. base *kewe-,* to swell, be strong, hero: cf. CAVE¹] 1. a building set apart or consecrated for public worship, esp. one for Christian worship 2. public worship; religious service 3. [*usually* C-] *a)* all Christians considered as a single body *b)* a particular sect or denomination of Christians 4. the ecclesiastical government of a particular religious group, or its power, as opposed to secular government 5. the profession of the clergy; clerical profession 6. a group of worshipers; congregation —*vt.* to bring (esp. a woman after childbirth) to church for special services —*adj.* 1. having to do with organized Christian worship 2. of or connected with a church

church·go·er (-gō′ər) *n.* a person who attends church, esp. regularly —**church′go′ing** *n., adj.*

Church·ill (chur′chil) river in Canada flowing through N Saskatchewan & N Manitoba into Hudson Bay: 1,000 mi.

Church·ill (chur′chil) 1. **John,** *see* Duke of MARLBOROUGH 2. Lord **Randolph (Henry Spencer),** 1849 95; Brit. statesman 3. **Win·ston** (win′stən), 1871–1947; U.S. novelist 4. Sir **Winston (Leonard Spencer),** 1874–1965; Brit. statesman & writer: prime minister (1940–45; 1951–55): son of Lord *Randolph*

church·less (-lis) *adj.* 1. having no church [a *churchless* village] 2. attending no church

church·ly (-lē) *adj.* 1. of or fit for a church 2. belonging to a church —**church′li·ness** *n.*

church·man (-mən) *n., pl.* **-men** (-mən) 1. a clergyman 2. a member of a church, esp. an active member

Church of Christ, Scientist *see* CHRISTIAN SCIENCE

Church of England the episcopal church of England; Anglican Church: it is an established church with the sovereign as its head

Church of Jesus Christ of Latter-day Saints *see* MORMON

Church of Rome the Roman Catholic Church

Church Slavic *see* OLD CHURCH SLAVIC

church text *same as* BLACK LETTER

church·ward·en (-wôr′d'n) *n.* [ME. *chirchewardein:* see CHURCH & WARDEN] 1. either of two lay officers chosen annually in every parish of the Church of England or of the Protestant Episcopal Church to usher at service and attend to certain secular matters 2. [Brit.] a clay tobacco pipe with a long stem

church·wom·an (-woom′ən) *n., pl.* **-wom′en** (-wim′in) a woman member of a church, esp. an active member

church·yard (-yärd′) *n.* the yard or ground adjoining a church, often used as a place of burial

churl (churl) *n.* [ME. *cherl* < OE. *ceorl,* peasant, freeman < IE. base *ǵer-,* to become ripe, grow old, whence Gr. *gerōn,* old man, L. *granum,* grain, CORN¹] 1. *same as* CEORL 2. a farm laborer; peasant 3. a surly, ill-bred person; boor 4. a miserly person; niggard

churl·ish (-ish) *adj.* 1. orig., of a churl or churls; rustic 2. like a churl; surly; boorish 3. miserly; stingy 4. hard to work or manage —**churl′ish·ly** *adv.* —**churl′ish·ness** *n.*

churn (churn) *n.* [ME. *chirne* < OE. *cyrne,* akin to *cyrnel,* kernel, grain (in reference to grainy appearance of churned cream): for IE. base, see CORN¹] 1. a container or contrivance in which milk or cream is beaten, stirred, and shaken to form butter 2. unusually strong activity or agitation —*vt.* [ME. *chirnen* < the *n.*] 1. to stir, beat, and shake (milk or cream) in a churn 2. to make (butter) in a churn 3. to stir up vigorously; shake violently 4. to produce (foam, etc.) by stirring vigorously —*vi.* 1. to use a churn in making butter 2. to move or stir as if in a churn; seethe [many ideas *churning* in his brain]

CHUCK
(of a drill)

churr (chᵘr) *n.* a low, trilled or whirring sound made by some birds —*vi.* to make such a sound

☆**chute¹** (sho͞ot) *n.* [Fr., a fall < OFr. *cheute* < *cheoite*, pp. of *cheoir*, to fall < L. *cadere*] 1. *a)* a waterfall *b)* rapids in a river 2. an inclined or vertical trough or passage down which something may be slid or dropped *[laundry chute]* 3. a steep slide, as for tobogganing

chute² (sho͞ot) *n.* [Colloq.] a parachute —**chut′ist** *n.*

☆**chute-the-chute** (sho͞ot′*thə* sho͞ot′) *n.* an amusement ride with a steep slide, often into a pool of water

chut·ney (chut′nē) *n., pl.* **-neys** [Hind. *chatni*] a relish made of fruits, spices, and herbs: also **chut′nee**

☆**chutz·pah, chutz·pa** (hoots′pə, khoots′-; -pä) *n.* [Heb. via Yid.] [Colloq.] shameless audacity; impudence; brass

chyle (kīl) *n.* [LL. *chylus* < Gr. *chylos*, juice, humor, chyle < *cheein*, to pour: see FOUND³] a milky fluid composed of lymph and emulsified fats: it is formed from chyme in the small intestine, is absorbed by the lacteals, and is passed into the blood through the thoracic duct —**chy·la·ceous** (kī lā′shəs), **chy·lous** (kī′ləs) *adj.*

chyme (kīm) *n.* [LL. *chymus* < Gr. *chymos*, juice < *cheein*, to pour: see FOUND³] the thick, semifluid mass resulting from gastric digestion of food: it passes from the stomach into the small intestine, where the chyle is formed from it —**chy·mous** (kī′məs) *adj.*

chym·ist (kim′ist) *n. obs. var. of* CHEMIST

chy·mo·tryp·sin (kī′mə trip′sin) *n.* [CHYM(E) + -o- + TRYPSIN] an enzyme that originates in the pancreas and is important in the digestion of proteins in the intestines

Ci. cirrus

C.I. Channel Islands

CIA, C.I.A. Central Intelligence Agency

Cia. [Sp. *Compañia*] Company

‡**ciao** (chou) *interj.* [It.] an informal expression of greeting or farewell

Cib·ber (sib′ər), **Col·ley** (käl′ē) 1671–1757; Eng. playwright & actor: poet laureate (1730–57)

ci·bo·ri·um (si bôr′ē əm) *n., pl.* **-ri·a** (-ə) [ML. < L., a cup < Gr. *kibōrion*, seed vessel of the Egyptian water lily, hence, a cup] 1. a canopy of wood, stone, etc. that rests on four columns, esp. one covering an altar; baldachin 2. a covered cup for holding the consecrated wafers of the Eucharist

ci·ca·da (si kā′də, -kä′-) *n., pl.* **-das, -dae** (-dē) [ME. < L.] any of a family (Cicadidae) of large flylike insects with transparent wings: the male makes a loud, shrill sound by vibrating a special organ on its undersurface

ci·ca·la (si käl′ə) *n.* [It. < L., var. of *cicada*] *poetic var. of* CICADA

cic·a·tri·cle (sik′ə trik′'l) *n.* [< L. *cicatricula*, dim. of *cicatrix*: see *fl.*] the protoplasmic disc in the yolk of an egg from which the embryo develops; germinal disc

cic·a·trix (sik′ə triks) *n., pl.* **ci·cat·ri·ces** (si kat′rə sēz′, sik′ə trī′sēz) [ME. & OFr. *cicatrice* < L. *cicatrix*, a scar] 1. *Med.* the contracted fibrous tissue at the place where a wound has healed; scar 2. *Bot. a)* the scar left on a stem where a branch, leaf, etc. was once attached *b)* the mark left where a wound has healed on a tree or plant *c) same as* HILUM (sense 2 *a)* Also **cic′a·trice** (-tris) —**cic′a·tri′cial** (-trish′əl) *adj.*

CICADA
(1 to 2 inches)

cic·a·trize (-trīz′) *vt., vi.* **-trized′, -triz′ing** [ME. *cicatrizen* < ML. *cicatrizare*: see CICATRIX] to heal with the formation of a scar —**cic′a·tri·za′tion** *n.*

Cic·e·ly (sis′'l ē) a feminine name: see CECILIA

cic·e·ly (sis′'l ē) *n., pl.* **-lies** [ME. *seseli* < L. *seselis* < Gr.] *same as* SWEET CICELY

Cic·er·o (sis′ə rō′) [after *fl.*] city in NE Ill.: suburb of Chicago: pop. 67,000

Cic·er·o (sis′ə rō′), **(Marcus Tullius)** 106–43 B.C.; Roman statesman, orator, & philosopher

ci·ce·ro·ne (sis′ə rō′nē; *It.* chē che rō′ne) *n., pl.* **-nes**; *It.* **-ni** (-nē) [It. < L. *Cicero*, the orator: ? from the usual loquacity of guides] a guide who explains the history and chief features of a place to sightseers

Cic·e·ro·ni·an (sis′ə rō′nē ən) *adj.* of or like Cicero or his polished literary style; eloquent

cich·lid (sik′lid) *n.* [< ModL. *Cichlidae*, name of the family < Gr. *kichlē*, a sea fish, wrasse] any of a family (Cichlidae) of tropical and subtropical freshwater fishes superficially similar to the American sunfishes —*adj.* of this family

‡**ci·cis·be·o** (si sis′bē ō′; *It.* chē′chēz bā′ō) *n., pl.* **-be′os**; *It.* **-be′i** (-ē) [It.] the lover of a married woman

Cid (sid; *Sp.* thēth), **the** [Sp. < Ar. *sayyid*, a lord] (born *Rodrigo*, or *Ruy*, *Díaz de Bivar*) 1040?–99; Sp. hero and soldier of fortune

C.I.D. Criminal Investigation Department

-cid·al (sīd′'l) [see -CIDE] *an adj.-forming suffix meaning:* **1.** of a killer or killing *[homicidal]* **2.** that can kill *[fungicidal]*

-cide (sīd) [< Fr. or L., Fr. *-cide* < L. *-cida* < *caedere*, to cut down, kill < IE. base *(s)k(h)ai-*, to strike, whence MDu. *heien*] *a n.-forming suffix meaning:* **1.** killer *[pesticide]* **2.** killing *[genocide]*

ci·der (sī′dər) *n.* [ME. *cidre, sider* < OFr. *sidre, cidere* < LL.(Ec.) *sicera* < Gr.(Ec.) *sikera*, an intoxicating drink, of Sem. origin, as in Akkadian *šikaru*, barley beer, Heb. *shēkār*, strong drink of grain and honey < *shākar*, to become intoxicated] the juice pressed from apples or, formerly, from other fruits, as cherries, used as a beverage or for making vinegar: **sweet cider** is unfermented, **hard cider** is fermented

cider press a machine that presses the juice out of apples, for making cider

‡**ci·de·vant** (sē də vän′) *adj.* [Fr., heretofore: applied in the Revolution to former nobles] former; recent

Cie [Fr. *compagnie*] Company

Cien·fue·gos (syen fwā′gōs) seaport on the S coast of Cuba: pop. 100,000

C.I.F., c.i.f. cost, insurance, and freight

ci·gar (si gär′) *n.* [Sp. *cigarro*, prob. < Maya *sicar*, to smoke rolled tobacco leaves < *sīč*, tobacco] a compact roll of tobacco leaves for smoking

cig·a·rette, cig·a·ret (sig′ə ret′, sig′ə ret′) *n.* [Fr. dim. of *cigare*, cigar] a small roll of finely cut tobacco wrapped in thin paper for smoking

cig·a·ril·lo (sig′ə ril′ō) *n., pl.* **-los** [Sp., dim. of *cigarro*, CIGAR] a small, thin cigar

cil·i·a (sil′ē ə) *n.pl., sing.* **-i·um** (-ē əm) [L., pl. of *cilium*, eyelid] 1. the eyelashes 2. *Bot.* small hairlike processes extending from certain plant cells and forming a fringe, as on the edges of some leaves 3. *Zool.* short, hairlike outgrowths of certain cells, capable of rhythmic beating that can produce locomotion, as in protozoans or small worms, or the movement of fluids, as in the ducts of higher forms

cil·i·ar·y (sil′ē er′ē) *adj.* 1. of, like, or having cilia 2. relating to the eyelashes 3. relating to certain fine structures of the eyeball

cil·i·ate (-it, -āt′) *adj. Bot., Zool.* having cilia: also **cil′i·at′ed** —*n.* any of a subphylum (Ciliophora) of microscopic protozoans characterized by cilia covering the body in whole or in part at some period of their life

cil·ice (sil′is) *n.* [Fr. < L. *cilicium* (whence OE. *cilic*), coarse covering of Cilician goats' hair, in LL.(Ec.), hair shirt < Gr. *kilikion*, garment of goats' hair < *Kilikia*, Cilicia, noted for its goats] a rough garment made of haircloth; hair shirt

Ci·li·cia (sə lish′ə) ancient region in SE Asia Minor, on the Mediterranean —**Ci·li′cian** *adj., n.*

Cilician Gates pass in the Taurus Mts., S Turkey

cil·i·o·late (sil′ē ə lāt′, -lit) *adj. Bot., Zool.* having very small cilia

cil·i·um (sil′ē əm) *n. sing. of* CILIA

Ci·ma·bu·e (chē′mä bo͞o′e), **Gio·van·ni** (jô vän′nē) (born *Cenni di Pepo*) 1240?–1302?; Florentine painter

Cim·ar·ron (sim′ə rōn′, -rän′) [AmSp. *cimarrón*, wild, unruly < ?] river flowing from NE N.Mex. eastward to the Arkansas River, near Tulsa, Okla.: 600 mi.

cim·ba·lom, cym·ba·lom (sim′bə ləm) *n.* [Hung. *czimbalom* < L. *cymbalum*, CYMBAL] a type of large dulcimer associated with Hungarian folk music

Cim·bri (sim′brī) *n.pl.* [L. < Gmc.: akin to G. *Kimbroi*] a Germanic people, supposedly from Jutland, who invaded N Italy and were defeated by the Romans (101 B.C.) —**Cim′bri·an** (-brē ən), **Cim′bric** (-brik) *adj.*

ci·mex (sī′meks) *n., pl.* **cim·i·ces** (sim′ə sēz′) [L., a bug] any of a genus (*Cimex*) of broad, flat, nearly wingless, bloodsucking bugs, including the common bedbug

Cim·me·ri·an (si mir′ē ən) *n.* [< L. *Cimmerius*, pertaining to the *Cimmerii*, Cimmerians < Gr. *Kimmerioi*] any of a mythical people whose land was described by Homer as a region of perpetual mist and darkness —*adj.* dark; gloomy

Ci·mon (sī′mən) 507?–449 B.C.; Athenian statesman & military leader

CINC, CinC, C. in C. Commander in Chief

☆**cinch** (sinch) *n.* [Sp. *cincha* < L. *cingulum*, a girdle < *cingere*, to surround, encircle < IE. base *kenk-*, to gird, encircle, whence Sans. *kāñcate*, he binds, Gr. *kakala*, walls] **1.** a saddle or pack girth **2.** [Colloq.] a firm grip **3.** [Slang] a thing easy to do or sure to happen —*vt.* **1.** to tighten a saddle girth on **2.** [Slang] *a)* to get a firm hold on *b)* to make sure of

cin·cho·na (sin kō′nə, siŋ-) *n.* [ModL., term coined by Linnaeus after the Countess del *Chinchón*, wife of a 17th-c. Peruv. viceroy, who was treated with the bark] **1.** any of a genus (*Cinchona*) of tropical S. American trees of the madder family, from the bark of which quinine and related medicinal alkaloids are obtained: the trees are widely cultivated in Asia and the East Indies **2.** the bitter bark of these trees —**cin·chon′ic** (-kän′ik) *adj.*

cin·cho·ni·dine (-kän′ə dēn′, -din) *n.* an alkaloid, $C_{19}H_{22}ON_2$, derived from cinchona bark and used in the treatment of malaria and to reduce fever

cin·cho·nine (sin′kə nēn′, siŋ′-; -nin) *n.* an alkaloid, $C_{19}H_{22}ON_2$, extracted from cinchona, closely related to quinine

cin·cho·nism (-niz'm) *n.* a pathological condition resulting from excessive use of cinchona bark or its derivatives, as quinine: it is characterized by headache, ringing in the ears, and deafness

cin·cho·nize (-nīz′) *vt.* **-nized′, -niz′ing** to treat with cinchona, quinine, etc.

Cin·cin·nat·i (sin′sə nat′ē, -ə) [< Society of the *Cincinnati*, formed (1783) by former Revolutionary officers, after

CINCINNATUS] city in SW Ohio, on the Ohio River: pop. 453,000 (met. area 1,385,000)

Cin·cin·na·tus (sin'sə nat'əs, -nāt'-), (**Lucius Quinctius**) 5th cent. B.C.; Roman statesman & general: dictator of Rome (458 & 439 B.C.)

cinc·ture (siŋk'chər) n. [L. *cinctura*, a girdle < *cingere*: see CINCH] 1. the act of encircling or girding 2. anything that encircles, as a belt or girdle —vt. -tured, -tur·ing to encircle with or as with a cincture

cin·der (sin'dər) n. [ME. & OE. *sinder*, dross of iron, slag < IE. base *sendhro-*, coagulating fluid, whence G. *sinter*, dross of iron, stalactite, *sintern*, to trickle, coagulate, Czech *śadra*, gypsum] 1. slag, as from the reduction of metallic ores 2. a rough piece of solid lava from a volcano 3. any matter, as coal or wood, burned out or partly burned, but not reduced to ashes 4. a minute piece of such matter 5. a coal that is still burning but not flaming 6. [pl.] ashes from coal or wood —vt. 1. [Rare] to burn to cinders 2. to cover with cinders —cin'der·y adj.

☆**cinder block** a building block, usually hollow, made of concrete and fine cinders

Cin·der·el·la (sin'də rel'ə) [CINDER + dim. suffix -ella: like Fr. *Cendrillon* (dim. < *cendre*, ashes), a partial transliteration of G. *Aschenbrödel*, lit., scullion (< *asche*, ASH[1] + *brodeln*, bubble up, BREW)] the title character of a fairy tale, a household drudge who, with the help of a fairy godmother, marries a prince —n. a person or thing whose merit, value, beauty, etc. is for a time unrecognized

cinder track a racing track covered with fine cinders

cin·e- (sin'ə) [< CINEMA] *a combining form meaning* motion picture [*cinecamera*]

‡**cin·é·aste** (sē nā äst', E. sin'ē ast') n. [Fr. < *cine(matographe)*, CINEMATOGRAPH + (*enthusi)aste*, enthusiast] 1. a person involved in motion-picture production 2. a devotee of motion pictures

cin·e·ma (sin'ə mə) n. [< CINEMATOGRAPH] [Chiefly Brit.] 1. a motion picture 2. a motion-picture theater —the cinema 1. the art or business of making motion pictures 2. motion pictures; the movies —cin'e·mat'ic (-mat'ik) adj. —cin'e·mat'i·cal·ly adv.

cin·e·mat·o·graph (sin'ə mat'ə graf') n. [Fr. *cinématographe* < Gr. *kinēma* (gen. *kinēmatos*), motion + *graphein*, to write] [Chiefly Brit.] a motion-picture projector, camera, theater, etc. —adj. [Chiefly Brit.] motion-picture

cin·e·ma·tog·ra·pher (sin'ə mə täg'rə fər) n. [Chiefly Brit.] a motion-picture cameraman

cin·e·ma·tog·ra·phy (-fē) n. the art of photography in making motion pictures —cin'e·mat'o·graph'ic (-mat'ə graf'ik), cin'e·mat'o·graph'i·cal adj. —cin'e·mat'o·graph'i·cal·ly adv.

‡**cin·é·ma vér·i·té** (sē nä mä' vā rē tā') [Fr., lit., truth cinema] a form of documentary film in which a small, hand-held camera and unobtrusive techniques are used to record scenes under the most natural conditions possible

cin·e·ole (sin'ē ōl') n. [< ModL. *oleum cinae* (oil of wormwood), with transposition of constituents] *same as* EUCALYPTOL

cin·e·rar·i·a (sin'ə rer'ē ə) n. [ModL. < L. *cinerarius*, pertaining to ashes < *cinis*, ashes (see ff.): so named from the ash-colored down on the leaves] a common hothouse plant (*Senecio cruentus*) of the composite family, with heart-shaped leaves and colorful flowers in shades of white, blue, pink, and purple-red

cin·e·rar·i·um (-ē əm) n., pl. -rar'i·a (-ə) [L. < *cinis*, ashes] a place to keep the ashes of cremated bodies —cin'e·rar'y adj.

cin·er·a·tor (sin'ə rāt'ər) n. [CINER(ARIUM) + -ATOR] a furnace for cremation; crematory

ci·ne·re·ous (si nir'ē əs) adj. [L. *cinerosus* < *cinis*, ashes] 1. of or like ashes 2. of the color of ashes; ash-gray Also **cin·er·i·tious** (sin'ə rish'əs)

cin·er·in (sin'ər in) n. [< L. *cinis* (gen. *cineris*: see INCINERATE) + -IN[1]] either of two compounds, $C_{20}H_{28}O_3$ and $C_{21}H_{28}O_5$, which occur in pyrethrum flowers and are used in insecticides

cin·gu·lum (siŋ'gyoo ləm) n., pl. -la (-lə) [L., girdle, belt < *cingere*, to encircle: see CINCH] Zool. a band or zone, as of color —cin'gu·late (-lit, -lāt'), cin'gu·lat'ed (-lāt'id) adj.

cin·na·bar (sin'ə bär') n. [ME. *cinabare* < L. *cinnabaris* < Gr. *kinnabari* < ? Ar. *zinjafr* < Per. *šangarf*, red lead, cinnabar] 1. mercuric sulfide, HgS, a heavy, bright-red mineral, the principal ore of mercury 2. artificial mercuric sulfide, used as a red pigment 3. brilliant red; vermilion

cin·nam·ic (si nam'ik) adj. 1. of or derived from cinnamon 2. designating a white, crystalline, organic acid, $C_6H_5·CH:CH·COOH$, produced from benzaldehyde: the corresponding aldehyde gives oil of cinnamon its characteristic flavor and odor

cin·na·mon (sin'ə mən) n. [ME. & OFr. *cinamome* < L. *cinnamomum* < Gr. *kinnamōmon* < Heb. *qinnāmōn*, cinnamon] 1. the yellowish-brown spice made from the dried inner bark of several trees or shrubs (genus *Cinnamomum*) of the laurel family, native to the East Indies and SE Asia 2. this bark 3. any tree or shrub from which this bark is

obtained 4. yellowish brown —adj. 1. yellowish-brown 2. made or flavored with cinnamon

cinnamon bear a reddish-brown variety of the American black bear

cinnamon stone *same as* ESSONITE

cin·quain (siŋ kān') n. [Fr. < *cinq*, five (see CINQUE) + (*quatr)ain*, QUATRAIN] a stanza of five lines

cinque (siŋk) n. [ME. *cink* < OFr. *cinc* (Fr. *cinq*) < L. *quinque*, five: for IE. base see FINGER] a five at dice or on a playing card

cin·que·cen·tist (chiŋ'kwə chen'tist) n. an Italian artist or writer of the cinquecento

cin·que·cen·to (-tō) n. [It., five hundred, short for *mille cinquecento*, one thousand five hundred] the 16th cent. as a period in Italian art and literature

cinque·foil (siŋk'foil') n. [ME. *cink foil* < OFr. *cinquefoil* < It. *cinquefoglie* < L. *quinque-folium*: see CINQUE & FOIL[2]] 1. any of a genus (*Potentilla*) of plants of the rose family, with white, yellow, or red flowers and fruit like a dry strawberry: some species have compound leaves arranged like the fingers on a hand 2. Archit. a circular design made up of five converging arcs

CINQUEFOIL

Cinque Ports (siŋk) group of towns (orig. five: Hastings, Romney, Hythe, Dover, and Sandwich) on the SE coast of England: they formerly received certain privileges in return for providing naval defense

CIO, C.I.O. Congress of Industrial Organizations: see AFL-CIO

ci·on (sī'ən) n. *same as* SCION (sense 1)

Ci·pan·go (si paŋ'gō) *old name for* JAPAN: used by Marco Polo & medieval geographers

ci·pher (sī'fər) n. [ME. *cifre* < OFr. *cyfre* < ML. *cifra* < Ar. *ṣifr*, *ṣefr*, a cipher, nothing < *ṣafara*, to be empty] 1. the symbol 0, indicating a value of naught; zero 2. a person or thing of no importance or value; nonentity 3. a) a system of secret writing based on a key, or set of predetermined rules or symbols b) a message in such writing c) the key to such a system: see also CODE 4. an intricate weaving together of letters, as a monogram 5. an Arabic numeral —vi. 1. [Now Rare] to solve arithmetical problems 2. to use secret writing —vt. 1. [Now Rare] to solve by arithmetic 2. to express in secret writing

cip·o·lin (sip'ə lin) n. [Fr. < It. *cipollino*, lit., little onion (ult. < L. *cepa*, onion): from its structure] a variety of Italian marble with alternating layers or streaks of color, esp. of white and green

cir., circ. 1. circa 2. circuit 3. circular 4. circulation 5. circumference

cir·ca (sur'kə) prep. [L.] about: used before an approximate date, figure, etc. [*circa* 1650]

cir·ca·di·an (sər kā'dē ən) adj. [coined < L. *circa*, about + *diem*, acc. sing. of *dies*, day] Biol. designating or of behavioral or physiological rhythms associated with the 24-hour cycles of the earth's rotation, as, in man, the regular metabolic, glandular, and sleep rhythms which may persist through a dislocation of day and night caused by high-speed travel

Cir·cas·si·a (sər kash'ə, -kash'ē ə) region of the U.S.S.R., in the NW Caucasus, on the Black Sea

Cir·cas·si·an (-ən, -ē ən) n. 1. any member of a group of Caucasian tribes of Circassia 2. an inhabitant of Circassia 3. the North Caucasian language of the Circassians —adj. of Circassia, its people, or their language

Circassian walnut the hard, heavy brown or purplish wood of the English walnut

Cir·ce (sur'sē) [L. < Gr. *Kirkē*] in Homer's *Odyssey*, an enchantress who turned men into swine —Cir·ce·an (sər sē'ən, sur'sē ən) adj.

cir·ci·nate (sur'sə nāt') adj. [L. *circinatus*, pp. of *circinare*, to make round < *circinus*, a pair of compasses < Gr. *kirkinos* < *kirkos*: see CIRCUS] rounded or circular; specif., rolled into a coil on its axis with the apex in the center, as the new fronds of a fern —cir'ci·nate'ly adv.

Cir·ci·nus (sur'sə nəs) n. [L., pair of compasses] a S constellation near Centaurus

cir·cle (sur'k'l) n. [ME. & OFr. *cercle* < L. *circulus*, a circle, dim. of *circus* < Gr. *kirkos*, a ring: see CIRCUS] 1. a plane figure bounded by a single curved line every point of which is equally distant from the point at the center of the figure 2. the line bounding such a figure; circumference 3. anything shaped like a circle, as a circular road, a ring, crown, halo, etc. 4. [Poet.] the orb of a heavenly body 5. the orbit of a heavenly body 6. a balcony or tier of seats as in a theater [the dress circle] 7. a complete or recurring series, usually ending as it began; cycle; period 8. a group of people bound together by common interests; group; coterie 9. formerly, a territorial division, esp. in Germany 10.

range or extent, as of influence or interest; scope 11. *a)* *same as* GREAT CIRCLE *b)* *same as* PARALLEL OF LATITUDE: see also ARCTIC CIRCLE, ANTARCTIC CIRCLE 12. an astronomical instrument with a part in the form of a calibrated circle 13. *Logic* a fault in reasoning in which the premise and conclusion are each in turn used to prove the other: see also VICIOUS CIRCLE —*vt.* -cled, -cling 1. to form a circle around; encompass; surround 2. to move around, as in a circle —*vi.* to go around in a circle; revolve —*SYN.* see COTERIE —**come full circle** to return to an original position or state after going through a series or cycle —**cir′cler** (-klər) *n.*

cir·clet (sur′klit) *n.* [ME. *cerclet* < OFr., dim. of *cercle*, CIRCLE] 1. a small circle 2. a ring or circular band worn as an ornament, esp. on the head

cir·cuit (sur′kit) *n.* [ME. < OFr. < L. *circuitus*, a going round, circuit < *circumire* < *circum-*, around + *ire*, to go] 1. the line or the length of the line forming the boundaries of an area 2. the area bounded 3. the act of going around something; course or journey around *(*the moon's *circuit* of the earth*)* 4. *a)* the regular journey of a person performing his duties, as of an itinerant preacher or a judge holding court at designated places *b)* the district periodically traveled through in the performance of such duties *c)* the route traveled ☆5. the judicial district of a U.S. Court of Appeals 6. *a)* a number of associated theaters at which plays, movies, etc. are shown in turn *b)* a group of nightclubs, resorts, etc. at which entertainers appear in turn ☆*c)* an association or league, as of athletic teams or of places at which series of contests or matches are held *(*the professional bowlers' *circuit]* 7. *a)* a complete or partial path over which current may flow *b)* any hookup, wiring, etc. that is connected into this path, as for radio, television, sound reproduction, etc. —*vi.* to go in a circuit —*vt.* to make a circuit about —*SYN.* see CIRCUMFERENCE —**cir′cuit·al** *adj.*

☆**circuit binding** a limp binding for books, as for Bibles, with covers that overlap the edges of the pages to protect them

☆**circuit breaker** a device that automatically interrupts the flow of an electric current, as when the current becomes excessive

☆**circuit court** 1. formerly, a Federal court of original jurisdiction presided over by a judge or judges who held court regularly at designated places in a district: abolished in 1911 2. a State court having original jurisdiction in several counties or a district

☆**circuit court of appeals** *same as* COURT OF APPEALS (sense 2)

cir·cu·i·tous (sər kyōō′ə təs) *adj.* [ML. *circuitosus* < L. *circuitus:* see CIRCUIT] roundabout; indirect; devious —**cir·cu′i·tous·ly** *adv.* —**cir·cu′i·tous·ness** *n.*

☆**circuit rider** a minister who travels from place to place in his circuit to preach

cir·cuit·ry (sur′kə trē) *n.* the scheme or system of an electric circuit, or the elements comprising such a circuit, as in a computer

cir·cu·i·ty (sər kyōō′ə tē) *n.*, *pl.* -ties [OFr. *circuité* < L. *circuitus]* the quality or state of being circuitous; devious procedure; indirection

cir·cu·lar (sur′kyə lər) *adj.* [ME. *circulare* < L. *circularis]* 1. in the shape of a circle; round 2. relating to a circle 3. moving in a circle or spiral 4. roundabout; circuitous 5. intended for circulation among a number of people —*n.* an advertisement, letter, etc., usually prepared in quantities for extensive circulation —*SYN.* see ROUND¹ —**cir′cu·lar′i·ty** (-ler′ə tē) *n.* —**cir′cu·lar·ly** *adv.* —**cir′cu·lar·ness** *n.*

cir·cu·lar·ize (-lə rīz′) *vt.* -ized′, -iz′ing 1. to make circular; make round 2. to send circulars to 3. to canvass for opinions, support, etc. —**cir′cu·lar·i·za′tion** *n.* —**cir′cu·lar·iz′er** *n.*

circular measure a system for measuring circles and angles: see TABLES OF WEIGHTS AND MEASURES in Supplements

circular mil a unit of measurement for the thickness of wires, equal to the area of a circle with a diameter of one mil

circular saw a saw in the form of a disk with a toothed edge, rotated at high speed as by a motor

cir·cu·late (sur′kyə lāt′) *vi.* -lat′ed, -lat′ing [< L. *circulatus*, pp. of *circulari*, to form a circle] 1. to move in a circle, circuit, or course and return to the same point, as blood through the body 2. to go from person to person or from place to place; specif., *a)* to move about freely, as air *b)* to move about in society, at a party, etc. *c)* to be made widely known, felt, existent, etc. *d)* to be distributed to a circle or mass of readers —*vt.* to cause to move around freely or go from one person or place to another; place in circulation —**cir′cu·la·to′ry** (-lə tôr′ē), **cir′cu·la′tive** (-lā′tiv) *adj.* —**cir′cu·lat′or** *n.*

circulating decimal *same as* REPEATING DECIMAL

circulating library a library from which books can be borrowed, sometimes for a small daily fee

circulating medium any medium of exchange that can be passed in ordinary commerce, as coin, currency, notes, checks, etc.

cir·cu·la·tion (sur′kyə lā′shən) *n.* [ME. *circulacioun* < L. *circulatio:* see CIRCULATE] 1. free movement around from place to place, as of air in ventilating 2. the act of moving

around in a complete circuit; specif., the movement of blood out of and back to the heart through the arteries and veins 3. the flow of sap in a plant 4. the passing of something, as money, news, etc., from person to person or place to place; dissemination 5. *a)* the distribution of newspapers, magazines, etc. among readers *b)* the extent to which something is circulated, as the average number of copies of a magazine sold in a given period

cir·cum- (sur′kəm, sər kum′) [< L. *circum*, around, about, adv. acc. of *circus:* see CIRCUS] *a prefix meaning* around, about, surrounding, on all sides *[circumnavigate, circumscribe, circumstance]*

cir·cum·am·bi·ent (sur′kəm am′bē ənt) *adj.* [CIRCUM- + AMBIENT] extending all around; surrounding —**cir′cum·am′bi·ence, cir′cum·am′bi·en·cy** *n.*

cir·cum·am·bu·late (sur′kəm am′byə lāt′) *vt.*, *vi.* -lat′ed, -lat′ing [< LL. *circumambulatus*, pp. of *circumambulare* < L. *circum-*, CIRCUM- + *ambulare:* see AMBULATE] to walk around —**cir′cum·am′bu·la′tion** *n.* —**cir′cum·am′bu·la·to′ry** (-lə tôr′ē) *adj.*

cir·cum·bend·i·bus (sur′kəm ben′di bəs) *n.* [jocular formation < CIRCUM- + BEND¹ + L. *-ibus*, ending of L. abl. pl.] [Now Rare] a roundabout way; circumlocution

cir·cum·cise (sur′kəm sīz′) *vt.* -cised′, -cis′ing [ME. *circumcisen* < OFr. *circonciser* < L. *circumcisus*, pp. of *circumcidere*, to cut around, in LL.(Ec.), to circumcise < *circum-*, around + *caedere*, to cut] 1. to cut off all or part of the foreskin of; also, in certain primitive rituals, to cut off the labia minora or clitoris of 2. [Archaic] to cleanse from sin; purify

cir·cum·ci·sion (sur′kəm sizh′ən) *n.* [ME. *circumcisioun* < LL.(Ec.) *circumcisio]* 1. a circumcising, or being circumcised, either as a religious rite of the Jews, Moslems, etc. (Gen. 17:10-14) or as a hygienic measure 2. [Archaic] a cleansing from sin 3. [C-] a festival on Jan. 1 commemorating the circumcision of Jesus

cir·cum·fer·ence (sər kum′fər əns, -frəns) *n.* [ME. < L. *circumferentia* < *circumferens*, prp. of *circumferre* < *circum-*, around + *ferre*, to carry] 1. the line bounding a circle, a rounded surface, or an area suggesting a circle 2. the distance measured by this line —**cir′cum·fer·en′tial** (-fə ren′shəl) *adj.* —**cir′cum·fer·en′tial·ly** *adv.*

SYN.—**circumference** refers to the line bounding a circle or any approximately circular or elliptical area; **perimeter** extends the meaning to a line bounding any area, as a triangle, square, or polygon; **periphery**, in its literal sense identical with **perimeter**, is more frequently used of the edge of a concrete object or in an extended metaphorical sense *[*the *periphery* of understanding*]*; **circuit** now usually refers to a traveling around a periphery *[*the moon's *circuit* of the earth*]*; **compass** refers literally to an area within specific limits but is often used figuratively *[*the *compass* of the city, the *compass* of freedom*]*

cir·cum·flex (sur′kəm fleks′) *n.* [L. *circumflexus*, pp. of *circumflectere* < *circum-*, around + *flectere*, to bend] a mark (^, ˆ, ˜) used over certain vowels in some languages to indicate a specific sound or quality of the vowel, or as a diacritical mark in some pronunciation systems: also **circumflex accent** —*adj.* 1. of, with, or marked by a circumflex 2. bending around; curved —*vt.* 1. to bend around; curve 2. to write with a circumflex —**cir′cum·flex′ion** (-flek′shən) *n.*

cir·cum·flu·ent (sər kum′floo wənt) *adj.* [L. *circumfluens*, prp. of *circumfluere*, to flow around < *circum-*, around + *fluere*, to flow] flowing around; surrounding; encompassing: also **cir·cum′flu·ous** (-floo wəs)

cir·cum·fuse (sur′kəm fyooz′) *vt.* -fused′, -fus′ing [< L. *circumfusus*, pp. of *circumfundere* < *circum-*, around + *fundere*, to pour] 1. to pour or spread (a fluid) around; diffuse 2. to surround *(with* a fluid); suffuse *(in)* —**cir′cum·fu′sion** *n.*

cir·cum·lo·cu·tion (sur′kəm lō kyoo′shən) *n.* [ME. *circumlocu-cioun* < L. *circumlocutio:* see CIRCUM- & LOCUTION] 1. a roundabout, indirect, or lengthy way of expressing something; periphrasis 2. an instance of this —**cir′cum·loc′u·to′ry** (-läk′yə tôr′ē) *adj.*

cir·cum·nav·i·gate (-nav′ə gāt′) *vt.* -gat′ed, -gat′ing [< L. *circumnavigatus*, pp. of *circumnavigare:* see CIRCUM- & NAVIGATE] to sail or fly around (the earth, an island, etc.) —**cir′cum·nav′i·ga′tion** *n.* —**cir′cum·nav′i·ga′tor** *n.*

cir·cum·nu·ta·tion (-nyoo tā′shən) *n.* [CIRCUM- + NUTATION] *Bot.* the irregular spiral or elliptical rotation of the apex of a growing stem, root, or shoot, caused by differences in the rate of growth of the opposite sides

cir·cum·po·lar (-pō′lər) *adj.* 1. surrounding or near either pole of the earth 2. *Astron.* moving around either of the celestial poles: said of stars always above the horizon

cir·cum·ro·tate (-rō′tāt) *vi.* -tat·ed, -tat·ing to turn like a wheel; rotate —**cir′cum·ro·ta′tion** *n.*

cir·cum·scis·sile (-sis′əl) *adj.* [CIRCUM- + SCISSILE] *Bot.* opening or splitting by a transverse fissure around the circumference, leaving an upper and lower half: said of certain seed pods or capsules

cir·cum·scribe (sur′kəm skrīb′, sur′kəm skrīb′) *vt.* -scribed′, -scrib′ing [ME. *circumscriben* < L. *circumscribere* < *circum-*, around + *scribere*, to write, draw] 1. to trace a line around; encircle; encompass 2. *a)* to set or mark off the limits of; limit; confine *b)* to restrict the action of; restrain 3. *Geom. a)* to draw a figure around (another

figure) so as to touch it at as many points as possible [circumscribe a triangle with a circle] b) to be thus drawn around [the hexagon circumscribed the square] —SYN. see LIMIT —**cir′cum·scrib′a·ble** adj. —**cir′cum·scrib′er** n.

cir·cum·scrip·tion (sur′kəm skrip′shən) n. [L. circumscriptio] 1. a circumscribing or being circumscribed 2. a boundary or outline 3. a limitation or restriction 4. a surrounding substance 5. a circumscribed space or area 6. an inscription around a coin, medal, etc. —**cir′cum·scrip′tive** adj.

cir·cum·spect (sur′kəm spekt′) adj. [ME. < L. circumspectus, pp. of circumspicere, to look about < circum-, around + specere, to look] careful to consider all related circumstances before acting, judging, deciding, etc.; cautious; careful —SYN. see CAREFUL —**cir′cum·spec′tion** n. —**cir′cum·spect′ly** adv.

cir·cum·stance (sur′kəm stans′, -stəns) n. [ME. & OFr. < L. circumstantia, a standing around, condition < circumstare < circum-, around + stare, to STAND] 1. a fact or event accompanying another, either incidentally or as an essential condition or determining factor [circumstances alter cases] 2. any happening or fact; event 3. [pl.] conditions surrounding and affecting a person, esp. financial conditions [in comfortable circumstances] 4. chance; luck [circumstance would have it so] 5. ceremony; show [pomp and circumstance] 6. a) accompanying or surrounding detail b) fullness of detail —vt. -stanced′, -stanc′ing to place in certain circumstances —SYN. see OCCURRENCE —under no circumstances under no conditions; never —under the circumstances conditions being what they are or were —**cir′cum·stanced′** adj.

cir·cum·stan·tial (sur′kəm stan′shəl) adj. 1. having to do with, or depending on, circumstances 2. not of primary importance; incidental 3. full or complete in detail 4. full of pomp or display; ceremonial —**cir′cum·stan′tial·ly** adv.

circumstantial evidence Law that evidence which is offered to prove certain attendant circumstances from which the existence of the fact at issue may be inferred; indirect evidence

cir·cum·stan·ti·al·i·ty (-stan′shē al′ə tē) n. 1. the quality of being circumstantial 2. pl. -ties particularity; detail

cir·cum·stan·ti·ate (-stan′shē āt′) vt. -at′ed, -at′ing to verify in every particular; give detailed proof or support of —**cir′cum·stan′ti·a′tion** n.

cir·cum·val·late (-val′āt) vt. -lat·ed, -lat·ing [< L. circumvallatus, pp. of circumvallare < circum-, around + vallare < vallum, rampart, WALL] to surround with or as with a wall or trench —adj. surrounded by or as by a wall or trench —**cir′cum·val·la′tion** n.

cir·cum·vent (sur′kəm vent′) vt. [< L. circumventus, pp. of circumvenire < circum-, around + venire, to COME] 1. to surround or circle around 2. to surround or encircle with evils, enmity, etc.; entrap 3. to get the better of or prevent from happening by craft or ingenuity —**cir′cum·ven′tion** n. —**cir′cum·ven′tive** adj.

cir·cum·vo·lu·tion (-və loo′shən) n. [ME. circumvolucioun < ML. circumvolutio < L. circumvolutus, pp. of circumvolvere: see ff.] 1. the act of rolling or turning around a center or axis 2. a fold, twist, or spiral 3. a circuitous course or form

cir·cum·volve (sur′kəm välv′) vt., vi. -volved′, -volv′ing [L. circumvolvere < circum-, around + volvere, to roll] to revolve

cir·cus (sur′kəs) n. [L., a circle, ring, racecourse < or akin to Gr. kirkos, a circle < IE. base *kirk- < *(s)ker-, to turn, bend, whence Gr. korōnos & L. curvus, curved] 1. in ancient Rome, an oval or oblong arena with tiers of seats around it, used for games, chariot races, etc. 2. a similar arena, often enclosed in a tent or building for a show of acrobats, trained animals, clowns, etc. 3. a traveling show of this sort or its personnel, equipment, etc. 4. the performance of such a show 5. [Brit.] a circular open place where many streets come together [Piccadilly Circus] ☆6. [Colloq.] any riotously entertaining person, thing, event, etc.

Circus Max·i·mus (mak′si məs) [L., lit., largest racecourse] a large amphitheater built in Rome c. 329 B.C., used for chariot races, games, etc.

ci·ré (sə rā′) adj. [Fr., lit., waxed, orig. pp. of cirer, to wax < cire, wax < L. cera < Gr. kēros] having a smooth, glossy finish imparted by treatment as with wax —n. a ciré silk, straw, etc.

Cir·e·na·i·ca (sir′ə nā′i kə; It. chē′re nä′ē kä) It. name for CYRENAICA (sense 1)

cirque (surk) n. [Fr. < L. circus: see CIRCUS] 1. a circular space or arrangement 2. [Poet.] a circle; ring 3. [Archaic] a circus 4. Geol. a steep, hollow excavation high on a mountainside, made by glacial erosion; natural amphitheater

cir·rate (sir′āt) adj. [L. cirratus < cirrus, a curl] Biol. having cirri

cir·rho·sis (sə rō′sis) n. [ModL. < Gr. kirrhos, tawny + -OSIS: so named by R. T. H. Laënnec (1781-1826) because of the orange-yellow appearance of the diseased liver] a degenerative disease in an organ of the body, esp. the liver, marked by excess formation of connective tissue

and the subsequent contraction of the organ —**cir·rhot′ic** (-rät′ik) adj.

cir·ri (sir′ī) n. pl. of CIRRUS

cir·ri- (sir′ə) [< L. cirrus] a combining form meaning curl, ringlet [cirriped]: also **cir′ro-, cir′rhi-, cir′rho-**

cir·ri·ped (sir′ə ped′) n. [< ModL. Cirripedia, name of the order < prec. + L. pes, pedis, FOOT] any of a subclass (Cirrepedia) of saltwater crustaceans that are attached or parasitic as adults, including the barnacles and the rhizocephalans

cir·ro·cu·mu·lus (sir′ō kyoo′myə ləs) n. a formation of clouds in small, white puffs, flakes, or streaks, at heights of and above 20,000 ft.; mackerel sky

cir·rose (sir′ōs) adj. [< L. cirrus, a curl + -OSE²] 1. Biol. a) having a cirrus or cirri b) resembling cirri 2. of or like cirrus clouds Also **cir′rous**

cir·ro·stra·tus (sir′ō strāt′əs, -strat′-) n. a formation of clouds in a thin, whitish veil, at heights above 20,000 ft.

cir·rus (sir′əs) n., pl. **cir′ri** (-ī) [L., a lock, curl, tendril] 1. Biol. a) a plant tendril b) a flexible, threadlike tentacle or appendage, as the feelers of certain organisms c) a cone-shaped cluster of fused cilia, occurring in many species of infusorians 2. Meteorol. a formation of clouds in detached, wispy filaments, or feathery tufts, at heights above 20,000 ft.

cir·soid (sur′soid) adj. [Gr. kirsoeidēs < kirsos, enlargement of a vein + -OID] like a varix, or enlarged blood vessel; varicose

cis- (sis) [< L. cis, on this side] a prefix meaning: 1. on this side of [cisalpine] 2. subsequent to

cis·al·pine (sis al′pin, -pin) adj. [L. cisalpinus: see CIS- & ALPINE] on this (the southern) side of the Alps: from the viewpoint of Rome

☆**cis·at·lan·tic** (-ət lan′tik) adj. on this (the speaker's) side of the Atlantic

☆**cis·co** (sis′kō) n., pl. **-co, -coes, -cos**: see PLURAL, II, D, 2 [< CanadFr. ciscovette < Algonquian] any of a number of fishes (genera Coregonus and Leucichthys) closely related to the whitefish and chub, found in the colder lakes of the NE U.S. and of Canada

cis·lu·nar (sis loo′nər) adj. [CIS- + LUNAR] on this side of the moon, between the moon and the earth

cis·mon·tane (sis män′tān) adj. [L. cismontanus] on this side of the mountains, esp. of the Alps

cis·pa·dane (sis′pə dān′, sis pā′dān) adj. [CIS- + L. Padanus, Po River] on this (the southern) side of the Po River: from the viewpoint of Rome

cis·soid (sis′oid) n. [Gr. kissoeidēs, ivylike < kissos, ivy + eidos, form] Math. a curve converging into an apex —adj. designating the angle formed by the concave sides of two intersecting curves: opposed to SISTROID

cist (sist; also for 1, kist) n. [L. cista < Gr. kistē (cf. CHEST); sense 1 via W. kist faen, lit., stone coffin] 1. a prehistoric tomb made of stone slabs or hollowed out of rock 2. in ancient times, a box or chest, esp. one containing sacred utensils

Cis·ter·cian (sis tur′shən) adj. [ME. & OFr. Cistercien < ML. Cistercium (now Cîteaux, France), original convent (1098) of the order] designating or of a monastic order following a strict interpretation of the Benedictine rule —n. a Cistercian monk or nun

cis·tern (sis′tərn) n. [ME. & OFr. cisterne < L. cisterna, reservoir for water < cista, CHEST] 1. a large receptacle for storing water; esp., a tank, usually underground, in which rain water is collected for use 2. Anat. a sac or cavity containing a natural body fluid

cis·ter·na (sis tur′nə) n., pl. **-nae** (-nē) [L.: see prec.] Anat. a cistern; specif., any of the enlarged spaces below the arachnoid —**cis·ter′nal** adj.

cis·tus (sis′təs) n. [ModL. < Gr. kistos, rockrose] any of a genus (Cistus) of low shrubs of the rockrose family, with white or purplish flowers resembling single roses: some species yield labdanum

cit. 1. citation 2. cited 3. citizen 4. citrate

cit·a·del (sit′ə d′l, -del′) n. [Fr. citadelle < It. cittadella, dim. of cittade, city < L. civitas, citizenship: see CITY] 1. a fortress on a commanding height for defense of a city 2. a fortified place; stronghold 3. a place of safety: refuge 4. the heavily armored central structure of earlier warships, on which the guns were mounted

ci·ta·tion (sī tā′shən) n. [ME. citacion < OFr. citation < L. citatio, a command (in LL., a summoning) < pp. of citare: see CITE] 1. a summons to appear before a court of law 2. the act of citing, or quoting 3. a passage cited; quotation 4. a reference to a legal statute, a previous law case, a written authority, etc., as precedent or justification ☆5. a) honorable mention in an official report for bravery or meritorious service in the armed forces b) a formal statement of the reasons for honoring a person in public with an award, degree, etc. —**ci′ta·tor** n. —**ci·ta·to·ry** (sit′ə tôr′ē) adj.

cite (sīt) vt. **cit′ed, cit′ing** [ME. citen < OFr. citer, to summon < L. citare, to arouse, summon < ciere, to put into motion, rouse < IE. base *kei-, whence OE. hatan, to command] 1. to summon to appear before a court of law

2. to quote (a passage, book, speech, writer, etc.) **3.** to refer to or mention by way of example, proof, precedent, etc. ☆**4.** to mention in a citation (sense 5) **5.** [Archaic] to stir to action; arouse —*n.* [Colloq.] a citation (sense 3) —**cit'a·ble, cite'a·ble** *adj.*

cith·a·ra (sith'ə rə) *n.* [L. < Gr. *kithara*] an ancient musical instrument somewhat resembling a lyre

cith·er (sith'ər) *n.* [Fr. *cithare* < prec.] *same as* CITTERN

cith·ern (sith'ərn) *n. same as* CITTERN

cit·ied (sit'ēd) *adj.* [Poet.] **1.** having a city or cities on it [the *citied* earth] **2.** like a city

☆**cit·i·fied** (sit'i fīd') *adj.* having the manners, dress, etc. attributed to city people

cit·i·zen (sit'ə zən) *n.* [ME. & Anglo-Fr. *citizein*, altered (? after *denizen*) < OFr. *citeain* (Fr. *citoyen*) < *cite*: see CITY; sense 3 infl. by use of Fr. *citoyen* during the Fr. Revolution] **1.** formerly, a native or inhabitant, esp. a freeman or burgess, of a town or city **2.** a native, inhabitant, or denizen of any place [*citizens* of the deep] **3.** a member of a state or nation, esp. one with a republican form of government, who owes allegiance to it by birth or naturalization and is entitled to full civil rights **4.** a civilian, as distinguished from a person in military service, a policeman, etc. **SYN.**—**citizen** refers to a member of a state or nation, esp. one with a republican government, who owes it allegiance and is entitled to full civil rights either by birth or naturalization; **subject** is the term used when the government is headed by a monarch or other sovereign; **national** is applied to a person residing away from the country of which he is, or once was, a citizen or subject, and is especially used of one another by fellow countrymen living abroad; **native** refers to one who was born in the country under question and is applied specifically to an original or indigenous inhabitant of the region —*ANT.* alien

cit·i·zen·ess (sit'ə zə nəs) *n.* [orig. transl. of Fr. *citoyenne* (Revolutionary term)] [Now Rare] a woman citizen

cit·i·zen·ry (sit'ə zən rē) *n.* all citizens as a group

citizen's arrest an arrest made under common law or statutory right by a citizen of a person he sees committing a felony

☆**citizens' band** either of two bands of short-wave radio frequencies set aside by the FCC for local use at low power by private persons or businesses

cit·i·zen·ship (-ship') *n.* **1.** the status or condition of a citizen **2.** the duties, rights, and privileges of this status **3.** a person's conduct as a citizen

citizenship papers the document stating that a naturalized person has been formally declared a citizen

Cit·lal·te·petl (sē'tläl tä'pet'l) *same as* ORIZABA

cit·ole (sit'ōl, si tōl') *n.* [ME. < OFr.: orig. dim. < L. *cithara*, CITHARA] *same as* CITTERN

cit·ral (si'trəl) *n.* [CITR- + AL(DEHYDE)] a liquid aldehyde, C₉H₁₅·CHO, with a pleasant odor, found in oil of lemon, oil of lime, etc. and used as a flavoring agent and in perfumes

cit·rate (si'trāt, sī'-) *n.* [CITR- + -ATE²] a salt or ester of citric acid

cit·re·ous (si'trē əs) *adj.* [L. *citreus*: see CITRUS] of the yellow color of a lemon

cit·ri- (si'trə) *a combining form meaning:* **1.** citrus, citrus fruits [*citriculture*] **2.** citric, citric acid [*citrate*] Also **cit'ro-** and, before a vowel, **citr-**

cit·ric (-trik) *adj.* [CITR- + -IC] **1.** of or from citrons, lemons, oranges, or similar fruits **2.** designating or of an acid, C₆H₈O₇, obtained from such fruits, used in making flavoring extracts, dyes, citrates, etc.

☆**cit·ri·cul·ture** (-trə kul'chər) *n.* the cultivation of citrus fruits

cit·rine (-trin, -trēn, -trīn) *adj.* [ME. < OFr. < ML. *citrinus* < L. *citrus*, CITRUS] of the yellow color of a lemon —*n.* **1.** lemon yellow **2.** a yellow, semiprecious variety of quartz resembling topaz

cit·ron (-trən) *n.* [Fr., lemon < It. *citrone* < L. *citrus*, CITRUS] **1.** a yellow, thick-skinned fruit resembling a lime or lemon but larger and less acid **2.** the semitropical tree (*Citrus medica*) of the rue family bearing this fruit **3.** the candied rind of this fruit, used as a confection, in fruitcake, etc. ☆**4.** *same as* CITRON MELON

cit·ron·el·la (si'trə nel'ə) *n.* [ModL. < *citron*: see CITRON] **1.** a volatile, sharp-smelling oil used in perfume, soap, insect repellents, etc.: also **citronella oil 2.** the southern Asiatic grass (*Cymbopogon nardus*) from which this oil is derived

cit·ron·el·lal (-al) *n.* [< prec. + -AL] a colorless liquid, C₁₀H₁₈O, with a very strong lemon odor, found in lemons, eucalyptus oil, etc. and used in perfumes and soaps

☆**citron melon** a kind of watermelon (*Citrullus vulgaris citroides*) with hard, white flesh: used only candied or preserved

cit·rus (si'trəs) *n.* [L., citron tree (whence Gr. *kitron*), prob. < base of Gr. *kedros*, juniper, cedar] **1.** any of a genus (*Citrus*) of trees and shrubs of the rue family, that bear oranges, lemons, limes, or other such fruit **2.** any such fruit —*adj.* of these trees and shrubs: also **cit'rous** (-trəs)

Cit·tà del Va·ti·ca·no (chēt tä' del vä'tē kä'nō) *It.* name of VATICAN CITY

cit·tern (sit'ərn) *n.* [< CITHER, prob. infl. by ME. *giterne* (see GITTERN)] a stringed instrument of the guitar family, pear-shaped with a flat back, popular from the 15th to the 18th cent.

cit·y (sit'ē) *n., pl.* **cit'ies** [ME. & OFr. *cite, citet* < L. *civitas*, citizenship, community of citizens, hence state, city < *civis*, citizen < IE. base *kei-*, to lie, camp, whence HOME] **1.** a center of population larger or more important than a town or village **2.** in the U.S., an incorporated municipality whose boundaries and powers of self-government are defined by a charter from the State in which it is located **3.** in Canada, any of various large urban municipalities within a province **4.** in Great Britain, a borough or town with a royal charter, usually a town that has been or is an episcopal see **5.** all of the people of a city **6.** in ancient Greece, a city-state —*adj.* of or in a city —**the City** the financial and commercial district of Greater London

☆**city chicken** pieces of pork or veal that are skewered and breaded, and cooked by braising or baking

☆**city editor** a newspaper editor who handles local news and distributes assignments to reporters

☆**city father** any of the important officials of a city; councilman, alderman, etc.

☆**cit·y·fied** (sit'i fīd') *adj. same as* CITIFIED

☆**city hall 1.** a building which houses the offices of a municipal government **2.** a municipal government —**to fight city hall** [Colloq.] to take up the apparently futile fight against petty or impersonal bureaucratic authority

☆**city manager** a person appointed as chief municipal administrator by a city council on a professional basis, with tenure free from public elections

City of God heaven: cf. Ps. 46:4

City of Seven Hills Rome

☆**cit·y·scape** (-skāp') *n.* [CITY + (LAND)SCAPE] **1.** a painting, photograph, etc. representing a view of a section of a city **2.** a view of a section of a city, esp. of buildings silhouetted against the horizon

☆**city slicker** [Colloq.] a city dweller regarded, esp. by rural people, as a smooth, tricky person

cit·y·state (-stāt') *n.* a state made up of an independent city and the territory directly controlled by it, as in ancient Greece

Ciu·dad Bol·í·var (syōō thäth' bō lē'vär) city in NE Venezuela, on the Orinoco: pop. 88,000

Ciudad Juá·rez (hwä'res) city in N Mexico, across the Rio Grande from El Paso, Tex.: pop. 385,000

civ. 1. civil **2.** civilian

civ·et (siv'it) *n.* [Fr. *civette* < It. *zibetto* < Ar. *zabād*] **1.** a yellowish, fatty substance with a musklike scent, secreted by a gland near the genitalia of the civet cat and used in making some perfumes **2.** the civet cat **3.** its fur

civet cat 1. any of several nocturnal, catlike, flesh-eating animals (family Viverridae) of Africa, India, Malaysia, and S China, with spotted, yellowish fur: valued for its civet ☆**2.** *same as* CACOMISTLE

civ·ic (siv'ik) *adj.* [L. *civicus*, civil < *civis*: see CITY] of a city, citizens, or citizenship —**civ'i·cal·ly** *adv.*

☆**civ·ics** (siv'iks) *n.pl.* [*with sing. v.*] the branch of political science that deals with civic affairs and the duties and rights of citizenship

civ·ies (siv'ēz) *n.pl.* [Slang] *same as* CIVVIES

civ·il (siv'l) *adj.* [ME. & OFr. < L. *civilis* < *civis*: see CITY] **1.** of a citizen or citizens [*civil* rights] **2.** of a community of citizens, their government, or their interrelations [*civil* service, *civil* war] **3.** cultured; civilized **4.** polite or courteous, esp. in a merely formal way **5.** of citizens in procedures or matters that are not military or religious [*civil* marriage] **6.** designating legally recognized divisions of time [a *civil* year] **7.** [*sometimes* **C-**] of or according to Roman civil law or modern civil law **8.** *Law* relating to the private rights of individuals and to legal actions involving these: distinguished from CRIMINAL, POLITICAL **SYN.**—**civil** implies merely a refraining from rudeness [keep a *civil* tongue in your head]; **polite** suggests a more positive observance of etiquette in social behavior [it is not *polite* to interrupt]; **courteous** suggests a still more positive and sincere consideration of others that springs from an inherent thoughtfulness [always *courteous* to strangers]; **chivalrous** implies disinterested devotion to the cause of the weak, esp. to helping women [quite *chivalrous* in her defense]; **gallant** suggests a dashing display of courtesy, esp. to women [her *gallant* tour] —*ANT.* rude

civil death *Law* deprivation of all civil rights as a result of being convicted of treason or, sometimes, of being declared an outlaw

civil defense a system of warning devices, fallout shelters, volunteer workers, etc. organized as a defense of the population, esp. against nuclear annihilation

civil disobedience nonviolent opposition to a government policy or law by refusing to comply with it, on the grounds of conscience: see also NONCOOPERATION, PASSIVE RESISTANCE

civil engineering the branch of engineering dealing with the design and construction of highways, bridges, tunnels, waterworks, harbors, etc. —**civil engineer**

ci·vil·ian (sə vil'yən) *n.* [ME. < OFr. *civilien* < L. *civilis*: see CIVIL] **1.** any person not an active member of the armed forces or of an official force having police power **2.** [Archaic] a specialist in civil or Roman law —*adj.* of or for civilians; nonmilitary

ci·vil·i·ty (-ə tē) *n., pl.* **-ties** [ME. & OFr. *civilite* < L. *civilitas* (< *civilis*, civil), politics, hence politic behavior, politeness] **1.** politeness, esp. in a merely formal way **2.** a civil, or polite, act or utterance

civ·i·li·za·tion (siv′ə lə zā′shən) *n.* [ML. *civilizatio*] **1.** the process of civilizing or becoming civilized **2.** the condition of being civilized; social organization of a high order, marked by the development and use of a written language and by advances in the arts and sciences, government, etc. **3.** the total culture of a particular people, nation, period, etc. **4.** the countries and peoples considered to have reached a high stage of social and cultural development **5.** intellectual and cultural refinement **6.** the amenities, esp. creature comforts of civilized life

civ·i·lize (siv′ə līz′) *vt., vi.* **-lized′, -liz′ing** [Fr. *civiliser* < L. *civilis*: see CIVIL & -IZE: lit. etym. sense, "to make citified"] **1.** to bring or come out of a primitive or savage condition and into a state of civilization **2.** to improve in habits or manners; refine —**civ′i·liz′a·ble** *adj.* —**civ′i·lized′** *adj.*

civil law 1. the body of codified law developed from Roman law and still in force in many European and American nations: distinguished from COMMON LAW **2.** the body of law that an individual nation or state has established for itself: distinguished from INTERNATIONAL LAW **3.** the body of law having to do with the private rights of individuals

civil liberties inalienable liberties guaranteed to the individual by law and by custom; rights of thinking, speaking, and acting as one likes without interference or restraint except in the interests of the public welfare

civil list in Great Britain, the amount fixed by Parliament for the personal and household expenses of the sovereign

civ·il·ly (siv′l ē) *adv.* **1.** with civility; politely **2.** in relation to civil law, civil rights, etc.

civil marriage a marriage performed by a justice of the peace, judge, or similar official, not by a clergyman

☆**civil rights** those rights guaranteed to the individual by the 13th, 14th, 15th, and 19th Amendments to the Constitution of the United States and by other acts of Congress; esp., the right to vote, exemption from involuntary servitude, and equal treatment of all people with respect to the enjoyment of life, liberty, and property and to the protection of law

civil servant a civil service employee

civil service [orig. applied to the civilian staff of the British East India Company] **1.** all those employed in government administration except in the army, navy, legislature, or judiciary **2.** any government service in which a position is secured through competitive public examination

civil war war between geographical sections or political factions of the same nation —**the Civil War** the war between the North (the Union) and the South (the Confederacy) in the U.S. (1861–1865)

civil year *same as* CALENDAR YEAR

civ·vies (siv′ēz) *n.pl.* [Colloq.] civilian clothes, as distinguished from a military uniform; mufti

C.J. Chief Justice

ck. *pl.* **cks. 1.** cask **2.** check

CL center line

Cl *Chem.* chlorine

cl. 1. centiliter(s) **2.** claim **3.** class **4.** clause **5.** clearance **6.** clerk **7.** clergyman **8.** cloth

c.l. 1. carload **2.** carload lots **3.** civil law

clab·ber (klab′ər) *n.* [Ir. *clabar*] [Dial.] thickly curdled sour milk; bonnyclabber —*vi., vt.* [Dial.] to curdle

clach·an (kläkh′ən) *n.* ScotGael., prob. < *clach*, stone] [Scot. or Irish] a hamlet

clack (klak) *vi.* [ME. *clacken*, prob. < ON. *klaka*, to chatter, of echoic orig.] **1.** to make a sudden, sharp sound, as by striking two hard substances together **2.** to talk fast, foolishly, etc.; chatter **3.** to cluck or cackle —*vt.* to cause to make a sudden, sharp sound —*n.* **1.** a sudden, sharp sound **2.** a clack valve or other device that makes such sounds **3.** chatter

Clack·man·nan (klak man′ən) county in EC Scotland, at the head of the Firth of Forth: 55 sq. mi.; pop. 42,000

clack valve a valve, often hinged at one side, which closes with a clacking sound and allows fluid to flow in only one direction

Clac·to·ni·an (klak tō′nē ən) *adj.* [< *Clacton*-on-Sea, England, where such tools were found] designating or of a lower paleolithic culture, characterized by chopping tools made by flaking

clad (klad) *alt. pt. & pp. of* CLOTHE —*adj.* **1.** clothed; dressed **2.** having a layer of some other metal or of an alloy bonded to it [*clad* steel]

clad·ding (-iŋ) *n.* [see prec.] **1.** a layer of some metal or alloy bonded to another metal **2.** the process of bonding such materials

cla·doc·er·an (klə däs′ər ən) *n.* [ModL. *Cladocera*, name of the order (< Gr. *klados*, a branch, shoot: see HOLT + Gr. *keras*, HORN) + -AN] any of an order (Cladocera) of crustaceans with a folded upper shell covering the body, as the water flea

clad·ode (klad′ōd) *n. same as* CLADOPHYLL

clad·o·phyll (klad′ə fil′) *n.* [< Gr. *klados*, a branch, shoot + *phyllon*, leaf] a flattened branch arising from the axil

of a leaf, with the shape and functions of a foliage leaf

claim (klām) *vt.* [ME. *claimen* < OFr. *claimer*, to call, claim < L. *clamare*, to cry out: for IE. base see CLAMOR] **1.** to demand or ask for as rightfully belonging or due to one; assert one's right to (a title, accomplishment, etc. that should be recognized) [to *claim* a record in the high jump] **2.** to call for; require; deserve [a problem that *claims* attention] ☆**3.** to state as a fact or as one's belief (something that may be called into question); assert —*n.* **1.** a demand for something rightfully or allegedly due **2.** a right or title to something [her sole *claim* to fame] **3.** something claimed, as a piece of land staked out by a settler or miner ☆**4.** a statement as a fact of something that may be called into question; assertion —**SYN.** see DEMAND —**lay claim to** to assert one's right or title to —**claim′a·ble** *adj.* —**claim′er** *n.*

claim·ant (klā′mənt) *n.* [ME. *claimand* < prp. of OFr. *claimer*: see prec.] a person who makes a claim

claiming race a horse race in which each entering horse is made available for purchase at a fixed price usually by an owner entering another horse in the meet

Claire (kler) a feminine name: see CLARA

clair·voy·ance (kler voi′əns) *n.* [Fr. < ff.] **1.** the supposed ability to perceive things that are not in sight or that cannot be seen **2.** keen perception or insight

clair·voy·ant (-ənt) *adj.* [Fr., lit., seeing clearly < *clair*, clear + *voyant*, seeing, prp. of *voir* < L. *videre*, to see] **1.** of clairvoyance **2.** apparently having clairvoyance **3.** having great insight; keenly perceptive —*n.* a clairvoyant person —**clair·voy′ant·ly** *adv.*

clam¹ (klam) *n., pl.* **clams, clam**: see PLURAL, II, D, 1 [< ff., in reference to the action of the shells] **1.** any of a large class (Pelecypoda) of hard-shelled, usually edible, bivalve mollusks, some of which live in the shallows of the sea, others in fresh water **2.** the soft, edible part of such a mollusk **3.** [Colloq.] a reticent or taciturn person ☆**4.** *same as* CLAMSHELL (sense 2) ☆**5.** [Slang] *a)* a dollar *b)* a mistake; error —*vi.* **clammed, clam′ming** to dig, or go digging, for clams —**clam up** [Colloq.] to keep silent or refuse to talk

clam² (klam) *n.* [ME. < OE. *clamm*, bond, fetter: for IE. base see CLIMB] [Now Rare] a clamp; vise

cla·mant (klā′mənt) *adj.* [L. *clamans* (gen. *clamantis*), prp. of *clamare*: see CLAMOR] **1.** clamorous, noisy **2.** demanding attention; urgent —**cla′mant·ly** *adv.*

clam·a·to·ri·al (klam′ə tôr′ē əl) *adj.* [< ModL. *Clamatores*, name of the suborder (< L., pl. of *clamator*, bawler < *clamare*: see CLAMOR) + -IAL] belonging to the flycatcher family of birds

☆**clam·bake** (klam′bāk′) *n.* **1.** a feast or picnic, orig. at the seashore, at which clams are steamed or baked with lobster, chicken, corn, etc., orig. on heated stones under a covering of seaweed **2.** the food so prepared **3.** [Colloq.] any large, noisy social gathering

clam·ber (klam′bər) *vi., vt.* [ME. *clambren*, akin to ON. *klembra*, CLIMB, G. (*sich*) *klammern*, to hook (oneself) on: for IE. base see CLIMB] to climb with effort or clumsily, esp. by using the hands as well as the feet —*n.* a clumsy or hard climb —**clam′ber·er** *n.*

clam·my (klam′ē) *adj.* **-mi·er, -mi·est** [ME. < *clam*, viscous, muddy, prob. < OE. *clam*, mud, clay: for IE. base see CLAY] unpleasantly moist, cold, and sticky to the touch —**clam′mi·ly** *adv.* —**clam′mi·ness** *n.*

clam·or (klam′ər) *n.* [ME. & OFr. *clamour* < L. *clamor* < *clamare*, to cry out < IE. base *kelā-* < base *kel-*, to call, yell, whence Gr. *kalein*, to call, name, OE. *hlowan*, to LOW²] **1.** a loud outcry; uproar **2.** a vehement, continued expression of the general feeling or of public opinion; loud demand or complaint **3.** a loud, sustained noise —*vi.* to make a clamor; cry out, demand, or complain noisily —*vt.* to express with, or bring about by, clamor Also, Brit. sp., **clam′our** —**SYN.** see NOISE —**clam′or·er** *n.*

clam·or·ous (-əs) *adj.* [ME. < ML. *clamorosus*: see prec.] **1.** loud and confused; noisy **2.** loudly demanding or complaining —**SYN.** see VOCIFEROUS —**clam′or·ous·ly** *adv.* —**clam′or·ous·ness** *n.*

clamp¹ (klamp) *n.* [ME. < MDu. *klampe*: for IE. base see CLIMB] any of various devices for clasping or fastening things together, or for bracing two parts; esp., an appliance with two parts that can be brought together, usually by screws, to grip something —*vt.* **1.** to grip, fasten, or brace with or as with a clamp ☆**2.** to put in effect forcefully; impose [to *clamp* a curfew on the town] —☆**clamp down** (on) to become more strict (with)

clamp² (klamp) *n.* [var. of CLUMP] the sound of heavy footsteps —*vi.* to tread heavily

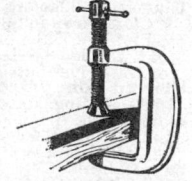

CLAMP

☆**clamp·down** (-doun′) *n.* a clamping down; repression or suppression, as in censoring

clam·shell (klam′shel′) *n.* **1.** the shell of a clam ☆**2.** a dredging bucket, hinged like the shell of a clam

clan (klan) *n.* [Gael. & Ir. *clann, cland,* offspring, tribe < L. *planta,* offshoot: see PLANT] **1.** an early form of social group, as in the Scottish Highlands, composed of several families claiming descent from a common ancestor, bearing the same family name, and following the same chieftain **2.** in certain primitive societies, a tribal division, usually exogamous, of matrilineal or patrilineal descent from a common ancestor **3.** a group of people with interests in common; clique; set **4.** [Colloq.] family (sense 3)

clan·des·tine (klan des′t'n) *adj.* [Fr. *clandestin* < L. *clandestinus,* secret, hidden < *clam,* secret < base of *celare,* to hide: see CONCEAL] kept secret or hidden, esp. for some illicit purpose; surreptitious; furtive —SYN. see SECRET —**clan·des′tine·ly** *adv.* —**clan·des′tine·ness** *n.*

clang (klaŋ) *vi.* [of echoic orig., but associated with L. *clangere,* also echoic] **1.** to make, or strike together with, a loud, sharp, ringing sound, as of metal being struck **2.** to move with such a sound **3.** to make a loud, harsh cry, as esp. the crane —*vt.* to cause to make a clanging sound —*n.* a clanging sound or cry

clang·er (klaŋ′ər) *n.* [see prec.] [Brit. Colloq.] a social blunder; faux pas

clan·gor (klaŋ′ər) *n.* [L. < *clangere:* see CLANG] a clanging sound, esp. a continued clanging —*vi.* to make a clangor Also, Brit. sps., **clan′gour** —**clan′gor·ous** *adj.* —**clan′gor·ous·ly** *adv.*

clank (klaŋk) *n.* [like Du. *klank,* MHG. *klanc,* of echoic orig.] a sharp, metallic sound, not so resonant as a clang and shorter in duration —*vi.* **1.** to make a clank **2.** to move with a clank —*vt.* to cause to clank

clan·nish (klan′ish) *adj.* **1.** of a clan **2.** tending to associate closely with one's own group and to avoid others —**clan′nish·ly** *adv.* —**clan′nish·ness** *n.*

clans·man (klanz′mən) *n., pl.* -**men** (-mən) a member of a clan —**clans′wom′an** *n.fem., pl.* -**wom′en**

clap[1] (klap) *vi.* **clapped** or archaic **clapt, clap′ping** [ME. *clappen* < OE. *clæppan,* to throb, beat; akin to ON. *klapp,* OHG. *klapf,* clap, crack: orig. echoic] **1.** to make a sudden, explosive sound, as of two flat surfaces being struck together **2.** to strike the palms of the hands together, as in applauding —*vt.* **1.** to strike together briskly and loudly **2.** [Rare] to applaud by clapping the hands **3.** to strike with an open hand, as in hearty greeting or encouragement **4.** to put, move, set, etc. swiftly *[clapped into jail]* **5.** to put together or contrive hastily *[to clap together a makeshift stage]* —*n.* **1.** a sudden, explosive sound, as of clapping *[a clap of thunder]* **2.** the act of striking the hands together, as in applauding **3.** a sharp slap, as in hearty greeting **4.** [Obs.] a sudden action or mishap —**clap eyes on** [Colloq.] to catch sight of; see

clap[2] (klap) *n.* [< ME. *claper,* brothel, orig. rabbit burrow < OFr. *clapier*] [Slang] gonorrhea: with *the*

clap·board (klab′ərd, klap′bôrd′) *n.* [partial transl. of MDu. *klapholt* < *klappen,* to fit + *holt,* wood, board] ☆a thin, narrow board with one edge thicker than the other, used as siding —☆*vt.* to cover with clapboards

clap·per (klap′ər) *n.* **1.** a person who claps **2.** a thing that makes a clapping sound, as the tongue of a bell or, facetiously, that of a garrulous person

clap·per·claw (-klô′) *vt.* [prob. < prec. + CLAW] [Archaic or Dial.] **1.** to claw or scratch with the hand and nails **2.** to revile or scold

clap·trap (klap′trap′) *n.* [CLAP[1] + TRAP[1]] showy, insincere, empty talk, expression, etc., intended only to get applause or notice —*adj.* showy and cheap

claque (klak) *n.* [Fr. < *claquer,* to clap: echoic] **1.** a group of people paid to go to a play, opera, etc. and applaud **2.** a group of admiring or fawning followers

clar. clarinet

Clar·a (klar′ə) [< L. *clara,* fem. of *clarus,* bright, CLEAR] a feminine name: var. *Clare, Clarice, Clarissa;* equiv. Fr. *Claire*

clar·a·bel·la (klar′ə bel′ə) *n.* [ModL. < L. *clarus,* clear + *bellus,* beautiful] an 8-foot organ stop producing a soft, velvety tone

Clare (kler) **1.** a masculine name: see CLARENCE **2.** a feminine name: see CLARA **3.** county in W Ireland, in Munster province: 1,231 sq. mi.; pop. 74,000

Clar·ence (klar′əns) [< name of Eng. dukedom of *Clarence* < *Clare,* town in Suffolk] a masculine name: var. *Clare* —*n.* [c-] [< the Duke of *Clarence,* later WILLIAM IV] a closed, four-wheeled carriage with seats for four inside and a seat for the driver outside

Clar·en·don (klar′ən dən), 1st Earl of, (*Edward Hyde*) 1609–74; Eng. statesman & historian

clar·et (klar′it) *n.* [ME. < OFr. (*vin*) *claret,* clear (wine); dim. of *cler,* clear < L. *clarus,* CLEAR] **1.** a dry red wine, esp. red Bordeaux **2.** purplish red: also **claret red** —*adj.* purplish-red

claret cup an iced drink of claret, lemon juice, brandy, sugar, and soda

Clar·ice (klar′is, klə rēs′) [Fr. *Clarisse*] a feminine name: see CLARA

clar·i·fy (klar′ə fī) *vt., vi.* -**fied′**, -**fy′ing** [ME. *clarifien* < OFr. *clarifier* < LL.(Ec.) *clarificare,* to make illustrious < *clarus,* clear, bright, famous + *facere,* to make] **1.** to make or become clear and free from impurities: said esp. of liquids **2.** to make or become easier to understand *[to clarify one's meaning]* —**clar′i·fi·ca′tion** *n.* —**clar′i·fi′er** *n.*

clar·i·net (klar′ə net′, klar′ə nit) *n.* [Fr. *clarinette,* dim. of *clarine,* little bell < ML. *clario:* see CLARION] a single-reed, woodwind instrument with a long wooden or metal tube and a flaring bell, played by means of holes and keys: also [Archaic] **clar′i·o·net′** (-ē ə net′) —**clar′i·net′ist, clar′i·net′-tist** *n.*

CLARINET

clar·i·on (klar′ē ən) *n.* [ME. *clarioun* < OFr. *clarion* < ML. *clario,* a trumpet < L. *clarus,* CLEAR] **1.** a trumpet of the Middle Ages producing clear, sharp, shrill tones **2.** [Poet.] the sound of a clarion, or a sound like this —*adj.* clear, sharp, and ringing *[a clarion call]* —*vt.* to announce forcefully or loudly

Cla·ris·sa (klə ris′ə) [It.] a feminine name: see CLARA

clar·i·ty (klar′ə tē) *n.* [ME. *clarite* < OFr. *clarte* < L. *claritas* < *clarus,* CLEAR] the quality or condition of being clear; clearness

Clark (klärk) **1. George Rogers,** 1752–1818; Am. frontiersman & Revolutionary War leader **2. Tom C**(ampbell), 1899– ; U.S. jurist; associate justice, Supreme Court (1949–67) **3. William** 1770–1838; Am. explorer: co-leader of the Lewis & Clark expedition: see Meriwether Lewis

Clark Fork river in W Mont. flowing northwest into Pend Oreille Lake, N Ida.: (with Pend Oreille River) 505 mi.

☆**clark·i·a** (klär′kē ə) *n.* [after Wm. CLARK] any of a genus (*Clarkia*) of W American wildflowers of the evening-primrose family, having rosy or purple flowers

cla·ro (klär′ō) *adj.* [Sp. < L. *clarus,* CLEAR] light-colored and mild: said of a cigar —*n., pl.* -**ros** a claro cigar

clar·y (kler′ē) *n., pl.* -**ies** [ME. *clare* < ML. *sclarea*] any of several plants (genus *Salvia*) of the mint family, esp. a species (*Salvia sclarea*) grown as an ornamental and sometimes used as an herb

clash (klash) *vi.* [echoic] **1.** to collide or strike together with a loud, harsh, metallic noise **2.** *a)* to come into conflict; disagree sharply *b)* to fail to harmonize *[clashing colors]* —*vt.* to strike together, shut, etc. with a loud, harsh, metallic noise —*n.* **1.** a loud, harsh noise, as of metallic objects colliding **2.** *a)* a sharp disagreement; conflict *b)* lack of harmony

clasp (klasp, klåsp) *n.* [ME. *claspe, clapse;* ? akin to OE. *clyppan,* clasp (see CLIP[2])] **1.** a fastening, as a hook, buckle, or catch, to hold two things or parts together **2.** the act of holding or grasping; embrace **3.** a grip of the hand **4.** a metal bar attached to the ribbon of a military decoration to show a subsequent award of the same medal or to specify the type or place of service —*vt.* [ME. *claspen* < the *n.*] **1.** to fasten with or as with a clasp **2.** to hold tightly with the arms or hands; grasp firmly; embrace **3.** to grip with the hand **4.** to entwine about; cling to —**clasp′er** *n.*

clasp knife a large pocketknife, esp. one with blades which, when open, can be secured by a catch

class (klas, kläs) *n.* [Fr. *classe* < L. *classis,* class or division of the Roman people, prob. akin to *calare,* to call] **1.** a number of people or things grouped together because of certain likenesses or common traits; kind; sort; category **2.** a group of people considered as a unit according to economic, occupational, or social status; esp., a social rank or caste *[the working class, the middle class]* **3.** high social rank or caste **4.** the division of society into ranks or castes ☆**5.** *a)* a group of students taught together according to standing, subject, etc. *b)* a meeting of such a group *c)* a group of students graduating together *[the class of 1970]* **6.** a division or grouping according to grade or quality **7.** conscripted troops, or men liable to conscription, all of whom were born in the same year *[to call up the class of 1947]* **8.** *same as* FORM CLASS **9.** [Slang] excellence, esp. of style or appearance **10.** *Biol.* a group of relatively closely related animals or plants having a common basic structure and ranking below a phylum or division and above an order —*vt.* to put in a class or arrange in classes; classify —*vi.* to be classed —**in a class by itself** (or **oneself**) unique **class. 1.** classic **2.** classical **3.** classification **4.** classified

☆**class book** a book published by members of a school or college class, containing pictures of students and teachers, an account of student activities, etc.

class consciousness an awareness of belonging to a class in the social order, with definite economic interests; sense of class solidarity —**class′-con′scious** *adj.*

☆**class day** the day on which special ceremonies are conducted by the senior class at a school or college, shortly before its graduation

clas·sic (klas′ik) *adj.* [L. *classicus,* relating to the (highest) classes of the Roman people, hence, superior < *classis,* CLASS] **1.** of the highest class; being a model of its kind; excellent; standard; authoritative; established *[a classic example of expressionism]* **2.** of the art, literature, and culture of the ancient Greeks and Romans, or their writers, artists, etc. **3.** characteristic of or derived from the literary and artistic standards, principles, and methods of the ancient Greeks and Romans **4.** of or having a style that is balanced, formal, objective, restrained, regular, simple,

etc.: a term variously interpreted, generally opposed to ROMANTIC **5.** famous or well-known, esp. as being traditional or typical [a *classic* court case] ☆**6.** [Colloq.] continuing in fashion because of its simple style: said of an article of apparel —*n.* **1.** a writer, artist, etc. or a literary or artistic work, generally recognized as excellent, authoritative, etc. ☆**2.** a famous traditional or typical event [the Kentucky Derby is a racing *classic*] ☆**3.** [Colloq.] a suit, dress, etc. that is classic (sense 6) ☆**4.** [Colloq.] an automobile of the period 1925–42 **5.** [Rare] a classicist —**the classics** the literature produced by outstanding writers, esp. of ancient Greece or Rome

clas·si·cal (-i k'l) *adj.* **1.** same as CLASSIC (senses 1, 2, 3, 4) **2.** well versed in or devoted to Greek and Roman culture, literature, etc. **3.** designating or of music that conforms to certain established standards of form, complexity, musical literacy, etc. [symphonies, concertos, sonatas, etc. are called *classical* music]: variously distinguished from POPULAR, ROMANTIC, MODERN **4.** designating or of a specified area or course of study that is or has been standard and traditionally authoritative, not new, recent, and experimental [*classical* political science] —**clas'si·cal·ly** *adv.*

clas·si·cal·ism (-iz'm) *n.* same as CLASSICISM

clas·si·cal·i·ty (klas'i kal'ə tē) *n.* **1.** the quality of being classical **2.** classical scholarship

clas·si·cism (klas'ə siz'm) *n.* **1.** the aesthetic principles or qualities regarded as characteristic of ancient Greece and Rome; objectivity, formality, balance, simplicity, restraint, etc.: generally contrasted with ROMANTICISM **2.** adherence to such principles **3.** knowledge of the literature and art of ancient Greece and Rome; classical scholarship **4.** a Greek or Latin idiom or expression

clas·si·cist (-sist) *n.* **1.** an advocate of the principles of classicism **2.** a student of or specialist in ancient Greek and Roman literature **3.** one who advocates the teaching of Greek and Latin in the schools

clas·si·cize (-sīz') *vt.* **-cized', -ciz'ing** to make classic —*vi.* to use or affect a classic style or form

clas·si·fi·ca·tion (klas'ə fi kā'shən) *n.* [Fr.] **1.** a classifying or being classified; arrangement according to some systematic division into classes or groups **2.** *a)* a system of such classes or groups *b)* such a class or group **3.** *Biol.* same as TAXONOMY —**clas·si·fi·ca·to·ry** (klas'ə fi kā'tər ē, -kə tôr'ē; klä sif'ə kə tôr'ē) *adj.*

☆**classified advertising** advertising compactly arranged, as in newspaper columns, according to subject, under such listings as *help wanted, lost and found*, etc.

clas·si·fy (klas'ə fī') *vt.* **-fied', -fy'ing** [< L. *classis* (see CLASS) + -FY] **1.** to arrange or group in classes according to some system or principle **2.** to place in a class or category **3.** to designate (governmental documents, reports, etc.) to be secret or confidential and available only to authorized persons —**clas'si·fi'a·ble** *adj.* —**clas'si·fi'er** *n.*

clas·sis (klas'is) *n., pl.* **clas'ses** (-ēz) [L., CLASS] **1.** a governing body in certain Reformed churches consisting of the ministers and representative elders from the churches in a district **2.** the district so governed

class·less (klas'lis) *adj.* having no distinct social or economic classes [a *classless* society]

☆**class·mate** (-māt') *n.* a member of the same class at a school or college

☆**class·room** (-rōōm') *n.* a room in a school or college in which classes are taught

class struggle in Marxism, the constant economic and political struggle held to exist between social classes regarded as exploiting and those regarded as exploited; specif., in capitalist countries, the struggle between capitalists (bourgeoisie) and workers (proletariat)

class·y (-ē) *adj.* **class'i·er, class'i·est** [Slang] first-class, esp. in style or manner; elegant; fine —**class'i·ness** *n.*

clas·tic (klas'tik) *adj.* [< Gr. *klastos*, broken < *klan*, to break (< IE. base *kla-*, var. of *kel-*, to strike, whence L. *calamitas*, calamity) + -IC] **1.** designating an anatomical model with removable sections to show internal structure **2.** *Geol.* consisting of fragments of older rocks

clath·rate (klath'rāt) *adj.* [L. *clathratus*, pp. of *clathrare*, to furnish with a lattice < L. *clathri*, lattice < Gr. *klēthra*] **1.** *Bot.* resembling latticework; reticulated **2.** *Chem.* of or pertaining to a mixture in which the molecules of one substance are completely entrapped in the crystal lattice or cell-like structure of the other

clat·ter (klat'ər) *vi.* [ME. *clateren* < OE. *clatrian* (akin to MDu. *klateren*) < IE. base *gal-*, to CALL, cry out] **1.** to make, or move with, a rapid succession of loud, sharp noises, as dishes rattling **2.** to chatter noisily —*vt.* to cause to clatter —*n.* [ME. *clater* < the *v.*] **1.** a rapid succession of loud, sharp noises; a tumult; hubbub **3.** noisy chatter —**clat'ter·er** *n.* —**clat'ter·ing·ly** *adv.*

Claude (klôd) [Fr. < L. *Claudius*, name of a Roman gens, prob. < *claudus*, lame] a masculine name: fem. *Claudia*

Clau·del (klō del'), **Paul (Louis Charles)** 1868–1955; Fr. poet, playwright, & diplomat

Claude Lor·rain (klôd lô ran') (born *Claude Gelée*) 1600–82; Fr. painter

Clau·di·a (klô'dē ə) [L.] a feminine name: see CLAUDE

clau·di·ca·tion (klô'də kā'shən) *n.* [L. *claudicatio* < *claudicatus*, pp. of *claudicare*, to limp < *claudus*, lame] the act of limping; lameness

Clau·di·us (klô'dē əs) **1. Claudius I** (*Tiberius Claudius Drusus Nero Germanicus*), 10 B.C.–54 A.D.; Roman emperor (41–54) **2. Claudius II** (*Marcus Aurelius Claudius*), 214–270 A.D.; Roman emperor (268–270)

claus·al (klô'z'l) *adj.* of or constituting a clause

clause (klôz) *n.* [ME. < OFr. < ML. *clausa*, for L. *clausula*, a closing (in legal use, section or clause) < *clausus*, pp. of *claudere*, to CLOSE[2]] **1.** a group of words containing a subject and finite verb, usually forming part of a compound or complex sentence: a dependent (subordinate) clause functions as a noun, adjective, or adverb; an independent (principal) clause can stand alone as a sentence: clauses may be joined by parataxis (The house is secluded; you will like it), by modified parataxis (The house is secluded, and you will like it), and by hypotaxis (Because the house is secluded, you will like it) **2.** a particular article, stipulation, or provision in a formal or legal document

Clau·se·witz (klou'zə vits), **Karl von** (kärl fōn) 1780–1831; Prussian army officer & writer on military strategy

claus·tral (klôs'trəl) *adj.* [ME. < LL. *claustralis* < L. *claustrum*: see CLOISTER] same as CLOISTRAL

claus·tro·pho·bi·a (klôs'trə fō'bē ə) *n.* [< L. *claustrum* (see CLOISTER) + -PHOBIA] an abnormal fear of being in an enclosed or confined place —**claus'tro·pho'bic** *adj.*

cla·vate (klā'vāt) *adj.* [< L. *clava*, a club + -ATE[1]] club-shaped —**cla'vate·ly** *adv.* —**cla·va'tion** *n.*

clave (klāv) *archaic pt. of* CLEAVE[1]

cla·ver (klā'vər) *vi.* [Scot., prob. < or akin to ScotGael. *clabaire*, babbler] [Scot.] to indulge in idle talk; gossip —*n.* [Scot.] gossip; chatter

clav·i·chord (klav'ə kôrd') *n.* [ME. *clavicord* < ML. *clavicordium* < L. *clavis*, a key + *chorda*, a string] a stringed musical instrument with a keyboard, predecessor of the piano: horizontal strings, generally of equal length, are struck at various points from below by metal wedges (*tangents*) at the end of each key, producing soft tones with limited dynamics: cf. HARPSICHORD

clav·i·cle (klav'ə k'l) *n.* [Fr. *clavicule* < L. *clavicula*, dim. of *clavis*, a key: see CLOSE[2]] a bone connecting the breastbone with the shoulder blade; collarbone: see SKELETON, illus. — **cla·vic·u·lar** (klə vik'yoo lər) *adj.*

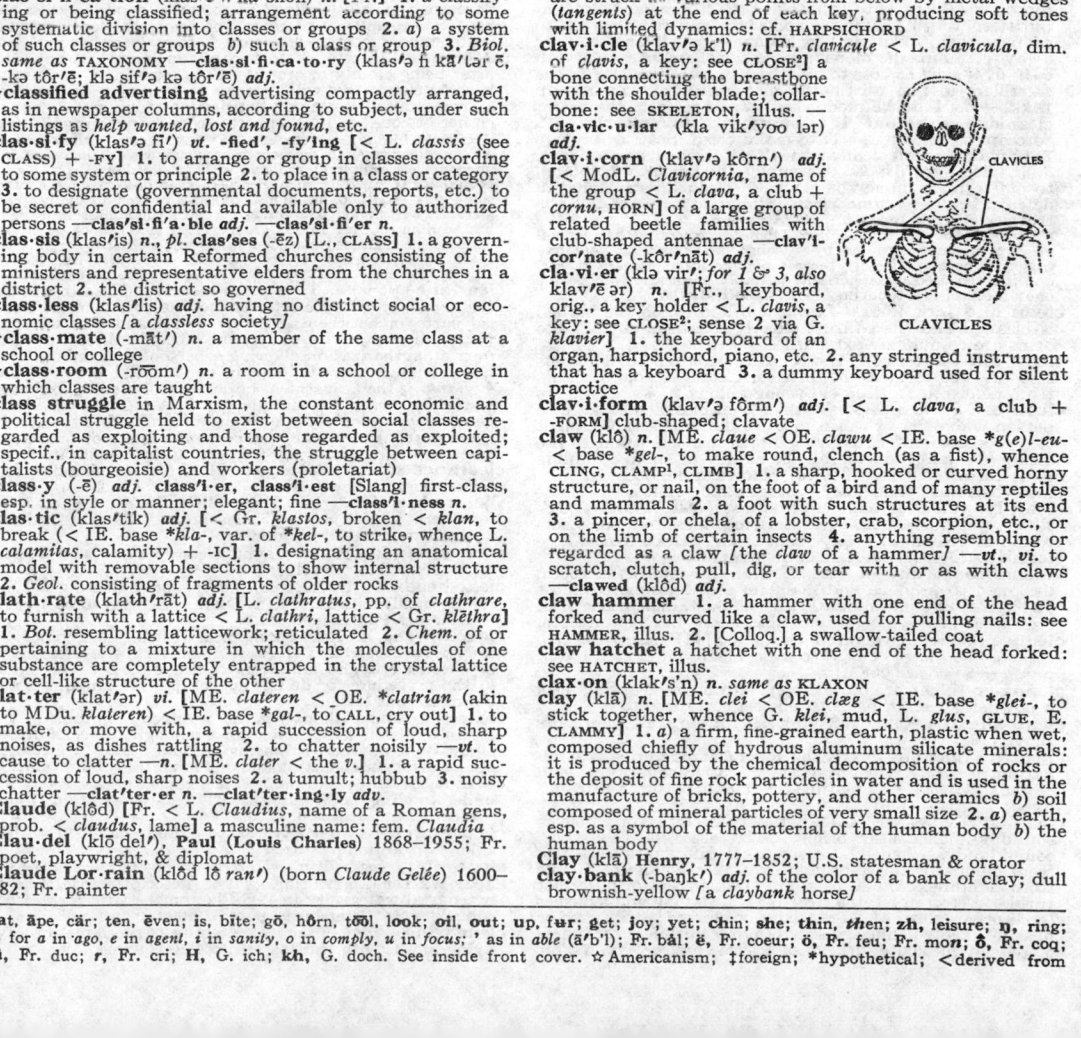

CLAVICLES

CLAVICLES

clav·i·corn (klav'ə kôrn') *adj.* [< ModL. *Clavicornia*, name of the group < L. *clava*, a club + *cornu*, HORN] of a large group of related beetle families with club-shaped antennae —**clav'i·cor'nate** (-kôr'nāt) *adj.*

cla·vi·er (klə vir'; *for 1 & 3, also* klav'ē ər) *n.* [Fr., keyboard, orig., a key holder < L. *clavis*, a key: see CLOSE[2]; sense 2 via G. *klavier*] **1.** the keyboard of an organ, harpsichord, piano, etc. **2.** any stringed instrument that has a keyboard **3.** a dummy keyboard used for silent practice

clav·i·form (klav'ə fôrm') *adj.* [< L. *clava*, a club + -FORM] club-shaped; clavate

claw (klô) *n.* [ME. *claue* < OE. *clawu* < IE. base *g(e)l-eu-* < base *gel-*, to make round, clench (as a fist), whence CLING, CLAMP[1], CLIMB] **1.** a sharp, hooked or curved horny structure, or nail, on the foot of a bird and of many reptiles and mammals **2.** a foot with such structures at its end **3.** a pincer, or chela, of a lobster, crab, scorpion, etc., or on the limb of certain insects **4.** anything resembling or regarded as a claw [the *claw* of a hammer] —*vt., vi.* to scratch, clutch, pull, dig, or tear with or as with claws —**clawed** (klôd) *adj.*

claw hammer 1. a hammer with one end of the head forked and curved like a claw, used for pulling nails: see HAMMER, illus. **2.** [Colloq.] a swallow-tailed coat

claw hatchet a hatchet with one end of the head forked: see HATCHET, illus.

clax·on (klak's'n) *n.* same as KLAXON

clay (klā) *n.* [ME. *clei* < OE. *clæg* < IE. base *glei-*, to stick together, whence G. *klei*, mud, L. *glus*, GLUE, E. CLAMMY] **1.** *a)* a firm, fine-grained earth, plastic when wet, composed chiefly of hydrous aluminum silicate minerals: it is produced by the chemical decomposition of rocks or the deposit of fine rock particles in water and is used in the manufacture of bricks, pottery, and other ceramics *b)* soil composed of mineral particles of very small size **2.** *a)* earth, esp. as a symbol of the material of the human body *b)* the human body

Clay (klā) **Henry,** 1777–1852; U.S. statesman & orator

clay·bank (-baŋk') *adj.* of the color of a bank of clay; dull brownish-yellow [a *claybank* horse]

clay·ey (-ē) *adj.* **clay′i·er, clay′i·est** **1.** of, smeared with, or full of clay **2.** like clay: also **clay′ish**

clay mineral any of a group of minerals, mainly hydrous aluminum silicates, occurring in very tiny crystals that readily adsorb water

clay·more (klā′môr′) *n.* [Gael. *claidheamhmor* < *claidheamh,* sword + *mor,* great] **1.** a large, two-edged broadsword formerly used by Scottish Highlanders **2.** a broadsword with a basket hilt worn by Highland regiments

clay pan a clay layer in the soil that restricts downward movement of water and root growth

☆**clay pigeon** a disk as of baked clay, tossed into the air from a trap as a target in trapshooting

clay stone **1.** rock consisting of hardened clay **2.** a hard concretionary body often found in clay deposits

☆**clay·to·ni·a** (kla tō′nē ə) *n.* [after the 18th-c. Am. botanist John *Clayton*] any of a genus (*Claytonia*) of small, spring-flowering plants of the purslane family, with white and rose-colored flowers

cld. 1. called **2.** cleared

clean (klēn) *adj.* [ME. *clene* < OE. *clæne,* clean, pure < IE. base *g̑(e)lēi- < g̑el-,* be gay, whence OIr. *gel,* gleaming, white, OHG. *kleini,* gleaming, bright, fine (whence G. *klein,* small)] **1.** free from dirt, contamination, or impurities; unsoiled; unstained ☆**2.** producing little immediate fallout: said of nuclear weapons **3.** recently laundered; fresh and unused **4.** *a)* morally pure; sinless *b)* not obscene or indecent [a *clean* joke] **5.** fair, sportsmanlike [a rough but *clean* contest] **6.** keeping oneself or one's surroundings clean; neat and tidy **7.** *a)* shapely; well-formed [a *clean* profile] *b)* trim; not ornate [*clean* architectural lines] **8.** skillful; deft [a *clean* stroke] **9.** having no obstructions, flaws, or roughnesses; clear; regular [a *clean* drain] **10.** entire; complete; thorough [a *clean* sweep] **11.** having few corrections; legible [*clean* copy for the printer] **12.** with nothing in it or on it [*clean* pockets, a *clean* sheet of paper] ☆**13.** [Slang] *a)* not carrying a weapon *b)* innocent of an alleged crime **14.** *Bible a)* free from ceremonial defilement *b)* fit for food: said of certain animals —*adv.* [OE. *clæne*] **1.** in a clean manner **2.** completely; wholly [*clean* forgotten] —*vt.* **1.** to make clean **2.** to remove (dirt, impurities, etc.) in making clean **3.** to empty or clear **4.** to prepare (fish, fowl, etc.) for cooking ☆**5.** [Slang] to take away or use up the money, possessions, etc. of (often with *out*) **6.** *Weight Lifting* to lift a barbell from the floor to the shoulders in one continuous movement: cf. CLEAN AND JERK —*vi.* **1.** to be made clean **2.** to perform the act of cleaning —**clean out 1.** to empty so as to make clean **2.** to empty —**clean up 1.** to make clean, neat, or orderly **2.** to make oneself clean and neat; get washed, combed, etc. **3.** [Colloq.] to dispose of completely; finish ☆**4.** [Slang] to make much money or profit —☆**clean up on** [Slang] to defeat; beat —☆**come clean** [Slang] to confess; tell the truth —**clean′a·ble** *adj.* —**clean′ness** *n.*
SYN.—**clean,** the broader term, denotes generally the removal of dirt or impurities, as by washing, brushing, etc.; **cleanse** suggests more specifically the use of chemicals, purgatives, etc. and is often used metaphorically to imply purification [to *cleanse* one's mind of evil thoughts] —**ANT. soil, dirty**

clean and jerk *Weight Lifting* a lift in which the barbell is cleaned and then thrust quickly overhead so that the arms are completely extended

clean-cut (-kut′) *adj.* **1.** with a clear, sharp edge or outline **2.** well-formed **3.** distinct; clear **4.** good-looking, trim, neat, etc. [a *clean-cut* young fellow]

clean·er (-ər) *n.* a person or thing that cleans; specif., *a)* a person who owns or works in a dry-cleaning establishment *b)* a preparation for removing dirt or grime —☆**take to the cleaners** [Slang] to take all the money of, as in gambling

clean·hand·ed (-han′did) *adj.* blameless; innocent

clean·limbed (-limd′) *adj.* having shapely limbs

clean·ly¹ (klēn′lē) *adj.* **-li·er, -li·est** [ME. *clenli* < OE. *clænlice* < *clæne,* CLEAN] **1.** keeping oneself or one's surroundings clean **2.** always kept clean —**clean′li·ness** *n.*

clean·ly² (klēn′lē) *adv.* in a clean manner

☆**clean room** any of various environments, as a room, designed to produce and maintain an atmosphere almost 100% free of contaminants, such as dust, pollen, bacteria, etc.: used in the assembly of spacecraft, in hospitals, etc.

cleanse (klenz) *vt.* **cleansed, cleans′ing** [ME. *clensen* < OE. *clænsian* < *clæne,* CLEAN] to make clean, pure, etc.; clean; purge —**SYN. see CLEAN**

cleans·er (klen′zər) *n.* any preparation for cleansing, esp. a powder for scouring pots, enamel surfaces, etc.

clean·shav·en (klēn′shā′v'n) *adj.* having all the hairs shaved off

clean·up (klēn′up′) *n.* **1.** the act of cleaning up ☆**2.** elimination of crime, vice, graft, etc. ☆**3.** [Slang] profit; gain —☆*adj. Baseball* designating the fourth batter in a team's lineup

clear (klir) *adj.* [ME. & OFr. *cler* < L. *clarus,* orig., clearsounding, hence clear, bright < IE. base *kel-,* to cry out, sound loudly, whence L. *calare,* to call out, CLAMOR] **1.** free from clouds or mist; bright; light [a *clear* day] **2.** free from cloudiness, muddiness, etc.; transparent or pure; not turbid [a *clear* crystal, a *clear* red] **3.** having no blemishes [a *clear* complexion] **4.** not faint or blurred; easily seen or heard; sharply defined; distinct [a *clear* outline, *clear* tones] **5.** perceiving acutely; keen or logical [a *clear* eye, a *clear*

mind] **6.** serene and calm [a *clear* countenance] **7.** free from confusion or ambiguity; not obscure; easily understood [the meaning is *clear*] **8.** obvious; unmistakable [a *clear* case of neglect] **9.** certain; positive [to be *clear* on a point] **10.** free from guilt or a charge of guilt; innocent [a *clear* conscience] **11.** free from charges or deductions; net [to earn a *clear* $10,000] **12.** free from debt or encumbrance [a *clear* title to the house] **13.** free from qualification; absolute; complete [a *clear* victory] **14.** free from contact; not entangled, confined, hindered, etc. [a style *clear* of cant] **15.** free from impediment or obstruction; open [keep the fire lanes *clear*] **16.** freed or emptied of freight or cargo —*adv.* **1.** in a clear manner; so as to be clear **2.** all the way; completely [it sank *clear* to the bottom] —*vt.* **1.** to make clear or bright **2.** to free from impurities, blemishes, cloudiness muddiness, etc. **3.** *a)* to make intelligible, plain, or lucid; clarify *b)* to decode or decipher **4.** to rid of obstructions, entanglements, or obstacles; open [to *clear* a path through snow] **5.** to get rid of; remove **6.** to empty or unload [to *clear* a freighter of cargo] **7.** to free (a person or thing) *of* or *from* something **8.** to free from a charge or a suspicion of guilt; prove the innocence of; acquit **9.** to pass or leap over, by, etc. **10.** to pass without contact [the tug *cleared* the bridge] **11.** to discharge (a debt) by paying it **12.** to give or get clearance for **13.** to be passed or approved by [the plan *cleared* the committee] **14.** to go through (a customs office) **15.** to handle and deal with (letters, files, etc.) properly **16.** to make (a given amount) as profit or earnings not subject to charges or deductions; net **17.** to make (the sight) clear or sharp **18.** *a)* to rid (the throat) of phlegm by hawking or coughing *b)* to rid (the voice) of hoarseness thus **19.** *Banking* to pass (a check, etc.) through a clearinghouse —*vi.* **1.** to become clear, unclouded, etc. **2.** to pass away; vanish **3.** to get clearance, as a ship leaving a port **4.** *Banking* to exchange checks and other banking paper, and balance accounts, through a clearinghouse —*n.* a clear space —**clear away 1.** to take away so as to leave a cleared space **2.** to go away; go out of sight —**clear off 1.** to clear away **2.** to remove something from in order to make clear —**clear out 1.** to clear by emptying ☆**2.** [Colloq.] to go away; depart —**clear the air** (or **atmosphere**) to get rid of emotional tensions, misunderstandings, etc. —**clear up 1.** to make or become clear **2.** to make orderly **3.** to become unclouded, sunny, etc. after being cloudy or stormy **4.** to explain **5.** to cure or become cured [this will *clear up* your cold] —**in the clear 1.** free from enclosing or limiting obstructions **2.** not in cipher or code **3.** [Colloq.] free from suspicion, guilt, etc. —**clear′a·ble** *adj.* —**clear′er** *n.* —**clear′ly** *adv.* —**clear′ness** *n.*
SYN.—**clear** suggests freedom from cloudiness, haziness, muddiness, etc., either literally or figuratively [a *clear* liquid, *clear* logic]; **transparent** suggests such clearness that objects on the other side (or by extension, meanings, etc.) may be seen distinctly [plate glass is *transparent*]; **translucent** implies the admission of light, but so diffused that objects on the other side cannot be clearly distinguished [stained glass is *translucent*]; **pellucid** suggests the sparkling clearness of crystal [a slab of *pellucid* ice, *pellucid* writing] See also EVIDENT —**ANT. opaque, cloudy, turbid**

clear·ance (-əns) *n.* **1.** an act or instance of clearing **2.** the clear space or distance between moving objects or mechanical parts, or between a moving object and that which it passes through, over, under, etc. **3.** official, esp. governmental, authorization allowing a person to examine classified documents, participate in confidential projects, etc. **4.** *Banking* the adjustment of debits and credits, exchange of checks, etc. in a clearinghouse **5.** *Naut. a)* a certificate from the collector of customs authorizing a ship to enter or leave port: also **clearance papers** *b)* the act or process of meeting the requirements for getting this certificate

clearance sale a sale to get rid of old merchandise and make room for new

Cle·ar·chus (klē är′kəs) ?–401 B.C.; Spartan general

clear-cut (-kut′) *adj.* **1.** clearly and sharply outlined **2.** distinct; definite; not doubtful

clear-eyed (-īd′) *adj.* **1.** having clear eyes or vision **2.** perceptive; thinking clearly

clear-head·ed (-hed′id) *adj.* having or indicating a clear mind; lucid; unconfused; rational —**clear′head′ed·ly** *adv.* —**clear′head′ed·ness** *n.*

clear·ing (-iŋ) *n.* **1.** a making clear or being cleared ☆**2.** an area of land cleared of trees **3.** *Banking a)* the exchanging of checks, etc. and balancing of accounts between banks *b)* the procedure for doing this *c)* [*pl.*] the amount of the balances thus settled

clear·ing·house (-hous′) *n.* **1.** an office maintained by a group of banks as a center for exchanging checks drawn against one another, balancing accounts, etc. **2.** a central office, as for the collection and dissemination of information

clear-sight·ed (-sīt′id) *adj.* **1.** seeing clearly **2.** perceiving, understanding, or thinking clearly —**clear′sight′ed·ly** *adv.* —**clear′sight′ed·ness** *n.*

clear-starch (-stärch′) *vt., vi.* to stiffen (laundry) with a colorless solution of starch

clear-sto·ry (-stôr′ē) *n., pl.* **-ries** *same as* CLERESTORY

Clear·wa·ter (klir′wôt′ər, -wät′-) [descriptive of the nearby coastal water] city in WC Fla., on the Gulf of Mexico: suburb of St. Petersburg: pop. 52,000

clear·wing (-wiŋ′) *n.* any of a family (Aegeriidae) of dayflying moths with transparent, scaleless wings

cleat (klēt) *n.* [ME. *clete* < OE. **cleat* (WGmc. **klaut*), a lump < IE. base **g(e)l-eu-* < **gel-:* see CLIMB] **1.** a piece of wood or metal, often wedge-shaped, fastened to something to strengthen it or give secure footing: cleats are used on gangways, under shelves, on the soles or heels of shoes, etc. **2.** *Naut.* a small piece of wood or metal with projecting ends on which a rope can be fastened —*vt.* to fasten to or with a cleat

cleav·age (klē′vij) *n.* **1.** a cleaving, splitting, or dividing **2.** the manner in which a thing splits **3.** a cleft; fissure; division **4.** the hollow between a woman's breasts, as made visible by a low-cut neckline **5.** *Biol. a)* cell division, esp. the series of mitotic cell divisions that transform the fertilized ovum into the earliest embryonic stage *b)* any single division in this series **6.** *Mineralogy* the tendency of some minerals to break in definite planes, producing smooth surfaces

cleave¹ (klēv) *vt.* **cleaved** or **cleft** or **clove, cleaved** or **cleft** or **clo′ven, cleav′ing** [ME. *cleven* < OE. *cleofan,* akin to G. *klieben* < IE. base **gleubh-,* to cut, slice, whence L. *glubere,* to flay] **1.** to divide by a blow, as with an ax; split **2.** to pierce **3.** to sever; disunite —*vi.* **1.** to split; separate; fall apart **2.** to make one's way by or as by cutting —**cleav′a·ble** *adj.*

cleave² (klēv) *vi.* **cleaved, cleav′ing** [ME. *cleven* < OE. *cleofian,* to adhere, akin to G. *kleben* < IE. base **gleibh-* < **glei-:* see CLAY] **1.** to adhere; cling (*to*) **2.** to be faithful (*to*) —*SYN.* see STICK

cleav·er (klēv′ər) *n.* [CLEAVE¹ + -ER] a heavy cutting tool with a broad blade, used by butchers

cleav·ers (-ərz) *n., pl.* **-ers** [< CLEAVE²] any of various plants (genus *Galium*) of the madder family, esp. a weedy species (*Galium aparine*), with stalkless leaves arranged in whorls, clusters of small, white or yellow flowers, and prickly stems

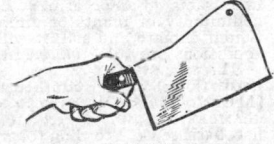

CLEATS

CLEAVER

cleek (klēk) *n.* [Scot. < ME. *cleke, cleche,* pastoral staff, crozier < *clechen,* to seize, catch < OE. **clæcan,* akin to *clyccan:* see CLUTCH¹] **1.** [Chiefly Scot.] a large hook **2.** *Golf a)* formerly, an iron with a narrow, slightly sloped face *b)* a wood with a small head and more loft than a spoon: now called *number 4 wood*

clef (klef) *n.* [Fr. < L. *clavis,* a key] a symbol used in music to indicate the pitch of the notes on the staff: there are three clefs: G (treble), F (bass), and C (tenor or alto)

cleft¹ (kleft) *n.* [ME. *clift* < OE. **clyft* < *cleofan:* see CLEAVE¹] **1.** an opening made by or as by cleaving; crack; crevice **2.** a hollow between two parts

cleft² (kleft) *alt. pt. & pp. of* CLEAVE¹ —*adj.* **1.** split; divided **2.** *Bot.* divided by one or more narrow fissures extending more than halfway to the midrib: said of leaves

cleft palate a cleft from front to back along the middle of the palate or roof of the mouth, caused by the failure of the two parts of the palate to join in prenatal development

Cleis·the·nes (klīs′thə nēz′) fl. c. 500 B.C.; Athenian statesman

cleis·tog·a·mous (klīs tä′gə məs) *adj.* [< Gr. *kleistos,* closed + -GAMOUS] *Bot.* having small, unopened, self-pollinating flowers, usually in addition to the showier flowers: also **cleis′to·gam′ic** (-tə gam′ik)

cleis·tog·a·my (-mē) *n.* [< Gr. *kleistos,* closed + -GAMY] *Bot.* self-pollination of certain unopened flowers

clem·a·tis (klem′ə tis, klə mat′is) *n.* [L. < Gr. *klēmatis,* brushwood, clematis < *klēma,* vine, twig] any of a genus (*Clematis*) of perennial plants and woody vines of the buttercup family, with bright-colored flowers of varying size and form

Clem·en·ceau (klā män sō′; E. klem′ən sō′), **Georges (Benjamin Eugéne)** (zhôrzh) 1841–1929; Fr. statesman; premier of France (1906–09; 1917–20)

clem·en·cy (klem′ən sē) *n., pl.* **-cies** [ME. *clemencie* < L. *clementia* < *clemens,* merciful] **1.** forbearance, leniency, or mercy, as toward an offender or enemy **2.** a merciful or lenient act **3.** mildness, as of weather —*SYN.* see MERCY

Clem·ens (klem′ənz), **Samuel Lang·horne** (laŋ′hôrn)

(pseud. *Mark Twain*) 1835–1910; U.S. writer & humorist

Clem·ent (klem′ənt) [L. *Clemens* < *clemens,* mild, gentle] **1.** a masculine name: dim. *Clem;* fem. *Clementine* **2.** Saint **Clement I** ?–97 A.D.; Pope (88–97), martyr & Apostolic Father: his day is Nov. 23 **3. Clement VII** (born *Giulio de′ Medici*) 1478–1534; Pope (1523–34): excommunicated Henry VIII

clem·ent (klem′ənt) *adj.* [L. *clemens*] **1.** forbearing; lenient; merciful **2.** mild, as weather —**clem′ent·ly** *adv.*

Clem·en·tine (klem′ən tin′, -tēn′) [Fr. < L. *Clemens:* see CLEMENT] a feminine name: also **Clem′en·ti′na** (-tē′nə)

Clement of Alexandria (*Titus Flavius Clemens*) 150?–215? A.D.; Gr. Christian theologian

clench (klench) *vt.* [ME. *clenchen* < OE. *-clencan* (in *be-clencan*), lit., to make cling, caus. of *clingan:* see CLING] **1.** to clinch (a nail, bolt, etc.) **2.** to bring together tightly; close (the teeth or fist) firmly **3.** to grip tightly —*n.* **1.** a firm grip **2.** a device that clenches —**clench′er** *n.*

cle·o·me (klē ō′mē) *n.* [ModL.] any of a large genus (*Cleome*) of mostly tropical plants of the caper family, with white, pink, yellow, green, or purple flowers having stalked petals and long stamens

Cle·om·e·nes (klē äm′ə nēz′) any of three Spartan kings of the 6th to the 3d centuries B.C.; esp., **Cleomenes III** (ruled 235?–220? B.C.), who sought to institute sweeping social reforms

Cle·on (klē′än) ?–422? B.C.; Athenian demagogue

Cle·o·pa·tra (klē′ə pat′rə, -pä′trə, -pä′trə) 69?–30 B.C.; queen of Egypt (51–49; 48–30): mistress of Julius Caesar & Mark Antony

Cleopatra's Needle either of two ancient Egyptian obelisks, one in London, the other in New York City

clepe (klēp) *vt.* [ME. *clepen* < OE. *cleopian, clipian*] **1.** [Obs.] to call or address (a person) **2.** [Archaic] to call by name; name: generally in the archaic past participle, *yclept, ycleped*

clep·sy·dra (klep′si drə) *n., pl.* **-dras** or **-drae** (-drē′) [L. < Gr. *klepsydra,* water clock < *kleptein,* to steal + *hydōr,* WATER] *same as* WATER CLOCK

clep·to·ma·ni·a (klep′tə mā′nē ə) *n.* *same as* KLEPTO-MANIA

clere·sto·ry (klir′stôr′ē) *n., pl.* **-ries** [ME. *clerestorie* < *cler,* CLEAR + *storie,* STORY²] **1.** the wall of a church rising above the roofs of the flanking aisles and containing windows for lighting the central part of the structure **2.** any similar windowed wall

cler·gy (klur′jē) *n., pl.* **-gies** [ME. & OFr. *clergie,* office or dignity of a clergyman < LL.(Ec.) *clericus:* see CLERK] men ordained for religious service, as ministers, priests, rabbis, etc., collectively

cler·gy·man (-mən) *n., pl.* **-men** (-mən) a member of the clergy; minister, priest, rabbi, etc.

Clergy Reserves [Canad.] tracts of land set aside in Upper and Lower Canada in 1791 for the support and maintenance of the Protestant clergy

cler·ic (kler′ik) *n.* [LL.(Ec.) *clericus:* see CLERK] a clergyman —*adj.* relating to a clergyman or the clergy

cler·i·cal (kler′i k'l) *adj.* [ME. < LL.(Ec.) *clericalis,* clerical, priestly < *clericus:* see CLERK] **1.** relating to a clergyman or the clergy **2.** relating to office clerks or their work **3.** favoring clericalism —*n.* **1.** a clergyman **2.** [*pl.*] clergymen's garments **3.** a person who favors clericalism —**cler′i·cal·ly** *adv.*

clerical collar a stiff, white collar buttoned at the back, worn by certain clergymen

cler·i·cal·ism (-iz'm) *n.* political influence or power of the clergy, or a policy or principles favoring this: generally a derogatory term —**cler′i·cal·ist** *n.*

cler·i·hew (kler′ə hyōō′) *n.* [after Edmund *Clerihew* Bentley (1875–1956), Eng. author] a humorous, quasi-biographical poem with four lines of varying length

cler·i·sy (kler′ə sē) *n.* [ME. *clericia* < LL.(Ec.) *clericus:* see CLERK] educated people as a class

clerk (klurk; *Brit.* klärk) *n.* [ME. < OFr. & OE. *clerc,* both < LL.(Ec.) *clericus,* a priest < Gr. *klērikos,* a cleric < *klēros,* lot, inheritance (later, from use in LXX, Deut. 18:2, of the Levites, hence the Christian clergy), orig., a shard used in casting lots < IE. **klaro-* < base **kel-,* to strike, break, whence OIr. *clar,* a board, tablet, L. *calamitas,* CALAMITY] **1.** a layman who has certain minor duties in a church **2.** an office worker who keeps records, types letters, does filing, etc. **3.** an official in charge of the records, accounts, etc. of a school board, court, town, etc. ☆**4.** a hotel employee who keeps the register, assigns guests to rooms, etc. ☆**5.** a person who sells in a store; salesclerk **6.** [Archaic] a clergyman **7.** [Archaic] a literate person; scholar —*vi.* ☆to work or be employed as a clerk, esp. a salesclerk —**clerk′ship** *n.*

clerk·ly (-lē) *adj.* **-li·er, -li·est 1.** of or like a clerk **2.** [Obs.] scholarly —*adv.* in a clerkly manner

Cler·mont-Fer·rand (kler mōn fe rän′) city in C France: pop. 128,000

cleve·ite (klē′vīt) *n.* [after P. T. *Cleve* (1840–1905), Swed. chemist] a radioactive crystalline variety of uraninite, found in Norway

Cleve·land (klēv'lənd) [after Moses *Cleaveland* (1754–1806), Connecticut surveyor] city and port in NE Ohio, on Lake Erie: pop. 751,000 (met. area 2,064,000)

Cleve·land (klēv'lənd), (Stephen) Gro·ver (grō'vər) 1837–1908; 22d and 24th president o. the U.S. (1885–89; 1893–97)

Cleveland Heights city in NE Ohio: suburb of Cleveland: pop. 61,000

clev·er (klev'ər) *adj.* [ME. *cliver*, prob. < EFris. *klüfer* or Norw. dial. *klöver*, ready, skillful; ? infl. by OE. *clifer*, claw, hand, in the sense, "adroit with the hand": for the latter sense development, cf. ADROIT, DEXTEROUS] **1.** skillful in doing something; adroit; dexterous **2.** quick in thinking or learning; intelligent, ingenious, quick-witted, witty, facile, etc. **3.** showing ingenuity or quick, sometimes superficial, intelligence [a *clever* book] **4.** [Dial.] *a)* amiable; good-natured *b)* handsome, convenient, nice, etc. —**clev'er·ly** *adv.* —**clev'er·ness** *n.*
SYN.—**clever**, in this comparison, implies quick-wittedness or adroitness, as in contriving the solution to a problem [a *clever* reply]; **cunning** suggests great skill or ingenuity, but often implies deception or craftiness [*cunning* as a fox]; **ingenious** stresses inventive skill, as in origination or fabrication [an *ingenious* explanation]; **shrewd** suggests cleverness accompanied by practicality [a *shrewd* understanding of the situation], sometimes verging on craftiness [a *shrewd* politician] See also INTELLIGENT

clev·is (klev'is) *n.* [ult. akin to CLEAVE²] a U-shaped piece of iron with holes in the ends through which a pin is run to attach one thing to another

clew (klōō) *n.* [ME. *cleue* < OE. *cliwen*, akin to Du. *klüwen* & dissimilated G. *knäuel* < IE. base *g(e)l-eu-:* see CLAW] **1.** a ball of thread or yarn: in Greek legend, a thread was used by Theseus as a guide out of the labyrinth **2.** something that leads out of a perplexity or helps to solve a problem: generally spelled **clue 3.** *Naut. a)* either of the lower corners of a square sail *b)* the after lower corner of a fore-and-aft sail *c)* a metal loop fastened in the corner of a sail *d)* [*pl.*] a combination of lines by which a hammock is hung —*vt.* **1.** to wind (*up*) into a ball **2.** *same as* CLUE —**clew down** (or **up**) to lower (or raise) a sail by the clews

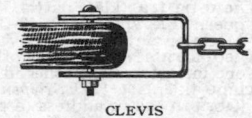
CLEVIS

clew lines the ropes connecting the clews of a sail with the yard, used in raising or lowering the sail

cli·ché (klē shā') *n.* [Fr. < *clicher*, to stereotype < G. *klitsch*, clump, claylike mass (hence, orig., to pattern in clay)] **1.** orig., a stereotype printing plate **2.** an expression or idea that has become trite —**SYN.** see PLATITUDE

Cli·chy (klē shē') city in N France, on the Seine: suburb of Paris: pop. 56,000

click (klik) *n.* [echoic, but associated with ME. *clike*, a locking latch (< OFr. *clique*) & *cliken*, to chatter (< OFr. *cliquer*)] **1.** a slight, sharp sound like that of a door latch snapping into place **2.** a mechanical device, as a catch or pawl, that clicks into position **3.** *Phonet.* any of a class of sounds, common in some African languages, made by drawing the breath into the mouth and explosively withdrawing the tongue from the roof of the mouth —*vi.* **1.** to make a click **2.** [Colloq.] *a)* to be suddenly clear or comprehensible *b)* to fit, work, or get along together successfully *c)* to be a success —*vt.* to cause to click —**click'er** *n.*

click beetle any of a family (Elateridae) of beetles that, when righting themselves after being on the back, make a clicking sound by the sudden release of a structure on the thorax

click·e·ty·clack (klik'ə tē klak') *n.* [echoic] a rhythmic, metallic sound, as that made by the wheels of a moving train —*vi.* to make this sound

cli·ent (klī'ənt) *n.* [ME. & OFr. < L. *cliens*, follower, retainer < IE. base *klei-*, to lean, incline, as in L. *clinare* (cf. INCLINE); basic sense, "one leaning on another (for protection)"] **1.** formerly, a person dependent on another, as for protection or patronage **2.** a person or company for whom a lawyer, accountant, advertising agency, etc. is acting **3.** a customer —**cli·en·tal** (klī en't'l) *adj.*

cli·en·tele (klī'ən tel'; *also, chiefly Brit.*, klē'än-) *n.* [Fr. *clientèle* < L. *clientela*, relation of patron and client, patronage: see CLIENT] all one's clients or customers, collectively: also **cli·ent·age** (klī'ən tij)

cliff (klif) *n.* [ME. & OE. *clif* < IE. base *gleibh-*, to adhere, be attached < *glei-* (see CLAY): basic sense prob. "slippery, smooth rock"] a high, steep face of rock, esp. one on a coast; precipice —**cliff'y** *adj.*

☆**cliff dweller 1.** a member of a race of ancient American Indians of the Southwest, who lived in hollows or caves in cliffs: they were ancestors of the Pueblo Indians **2.** [Colloq.] a person who lives in a large urban apartment house —**cliff'-dwell'ing** *adj.*

☆**cliff·hang·er, cliff-hang·er** (-haŋ'ər) *n.* **1.** an early type of serialized movie in which each episode ended with a suspenseful climax, as the hero hanging from a cliff **2.** any highly suspenseful story, situation, etc. —**cliff'hang'ing, cliff'-hang'ing** *adj.*

Clif·ford (klif'ərd) [< family or place name < CLIFF + FORD, hence, lit., ford at the cliff] a masculine name: dim. *Cliff*

☆**cliff swallow** a N. American swallow (*Petrochelidon pyrrhonota*) that builds its gourdlike nest of mud, grass, etc. against a cliff or under the eaves of a building

Clif·ton (klif'tən) [< CLIFF + *-ton*, town; hence, lit., town at a cliff] **1.** a masculine name **2.** [< its location under Weasel Mountain] city in NE N.J.: pop. 82,000 (met. area, with Paterson & Passaic, 1,359,000)

cli·mac·ter·ic (klī mak'tər ik, klī'mak ter'ik) *n.* [L. *climactericus* < Gr. *klimaktērikos* < *klimaktēr*, round of a ladder < *klimax*, ladder: see CLIMAX] **1.** a period in the life of a person when an important physiological change occurs, esp. the period of the menopause **2.** any crucial period or event —*adj.* of or resembling a climacteric; crucial: also **cli·mac·ter'i·cal**

cli·mac·tic (klī mak'tik) *adj.* of, constituting, or in the order of a climax: also **cli·mac'ti·cal** —**cli·mac'ti·cal·ly** *adv.*

cli·mate (klī'mət) *n.* [ME. & OFr. *climat* < L. *clima* < Gr. *klima*, region, zone < base of *klinein*, to slope (see INCLINE): orig., slope of the earth from the equator toward the poles] **1.** the prevailing or average weather conditions of a place, as determined by the temperature and meteorological changes over a period of years **2.** any prevailing conditions affecting life, activity, etc. [a favorable *climate* of opinion] **3.** a region with certain prevailing weather conditions [to move to a warmer *climate*] —**cli·mat·ic** (klī mat'ik) *adj.* —**cli·mat'i·cal·ly** *adv.*

cli·ma·tol·o·gy (klī'mə täl'ə jē) *n.* the science dealing with climate and climatic phenomena —**cli'ma·to·log'i·cal** (-tə läj'i k'l) *adj.* —**cli'ma·tol'o·gist** *n.*

cli·max (klī'maks) *n.* [L. < Gr. *klimax*, ladder < base of *klinein*, to slope: see INCLINE] **1.** formerly, a rhetorical series of ideas, images, etc. arranged progressively so that the most forceful is last **2.** the final, culminating element or event in a series; highest point, as of interest, excitement, etc.; specif., *a)* the decisive turning point of the action, as in a drama *b)* an orgasm **3.** *Ecol.* a final, self-perpetuating community of plants or animals that develops in a particular climate and soil: it will persist as long as the same conditions prevail —*vi., vt.* to reach, or bring to, a climax —**SYN.** see SUMMIT

climb (klīm) *vi., vt.* **climbed** or archaic **clomb, climb'ing** [ME. *climben* < OE. *climban* < IE. base *glembh-* (whence CLAMBER, CLUMP) < *gel-*, to make round, clench, as the fist: basic sense, "to cling to, grip"] **1.** to go up by using the feet and often the hands **2.** to rise or ascend gradually to a higher point; mount **3.** to move (*down, over, along,* etc.), using the hands and feet **4.** *Bot.* to grow upward on (a wall, trellis, etc.) by winding around or adhering with tendrils —*n.* **1.** an act or instance of climbing; rise; ascent **2.** a thing or place to be climbed —**climb'a·ble** *adj.*

climb·er (-ər) *n.* **1.** one that climbs ☆**2.** *same as* LINEMEN'S CLIMBER ☆**3.** [Colloq.] a person who constantly tries to advance himself socially or in business **3.** *Bot.* a climbing plant or vine

climbing iron *same as* LINEMEN'S CLIMBER

climbing perch any of a genus (*Anabas*) of freshwater, perchlike fishes of SE Asia that can live out of water for a few days and travel on the ground, and sometimes climb low tree branches

clime (klīm) *n.* [L. *clima*: see CLIMATE] [Poet.] a region or realm, esp. with reference to its climate

clin- (klīn) *same as* CLINO-: used before a vowel

cli·nan·dri·um (klī nan'drē əm) *n., pl.* **-dri·a** (-ə) [ModL. < Gr. *klinē*, bed + -ANDR(OUS) + -IUM] a cavity in the top of the column of an orchid, containing the anther

clinch (klinch) *vt.* [var. of CLENCH] **1.** to fasten (a nail, bolt, etc. that has been driven through something) by bending or flattening the projecting end **2.** to fasten firmly together by this means **3.** *a)* to settle (an argument, bargain, etc.) definitely *b)* to gain a victory in; win conclusively —*vi.* ☆**1.** *Boxing* to grip the opponent's body with the arms so as to hinder his punching ☆**2.** [Slang] to embrace —*n.* **1.** *a)* a fastening, as with a clinched nail *b)* a clinched nail, bolt, etc. *c)* the part clinched ☆**2.** *Boxing* an act of clinching ☆**3.** [Slang] an embrace **4.** *Naut.* a kind of knot or noose in a rope: see KNOT, illus.

clinch·er (-ər) *n.* a person or thing that clinches; specif., *a)* a tool for clinching nails *b)* a conclusive or decisive point, argument, act, etc.

cline (klīn) *n.* [prob. back-formation < INCLINE] a gradual change in a trait or in the frequency of a trait within a species over a geographical area —**cli'nal** *adj.*

cling (kliŋ) *vi.* **clung, cling'ing** [ME. *clingen* < OE. *clingan*, to adhere, stick together < IE. base *gel-g-* < *gel-* (see CLIMB), whence CLENCH] **1.** to hold fast by or by embracing, entwining, or sticking; adhere **2.** *a)* to be or stay near, as if holding fast *b)* to be emotionally attached —☆*adj., n. same as* CLINGSTONE —**SYN.** see STICK —**cling'er** *n.* —**cling'ing·ly** *adv.*

cling·fish (-fish') *n., pl.* **-fish'**, **-fish'es:** see FISH² any of various small, bony marine fishes (order Xenopterygii), having a sucking disc on the ventral surface near the head, with which they cling to rocks, etc.

☆**cling·ing vine** (kliŋ'iŋ) a woman inclined to be helpless and dependent in her relationship with a man

Cling·man's Dome (kliŋ'mənz) [after U.S. Senator T. L. *Clingman* (1812–97)] mountain on the Tenn.–N.C. border: highest peak of the Great Smoky Mountains, 6,642 ft.

☆**cling·stone** (kliŋ'stōn') *adj.* having a stone that clings to

the fleshy part: said of some peaches —*n.* a peach of this sort

clin·ic (klin′ik) *n.* [L. *clinicus*, physician who attends patients sick in bed < Gr. *klinikos*, of the bed < *klinē*, a bed] **1.** the teaching of medicine by examining and treating patients in the presence of students **2.** a class so taught **3.** a place where patients are studied or treated by specialist physicians practicing as a group **4.** a department of a hospital or medical school, where outpatients are treated, sometimes free or for a small fee **5.** an organization or institution that offers some kind of advice, treatment, or instruction [a maternal health *clinic*]

clin·i·cal (-i k′l) *adj.* **1.** of or connected with a clinic or a sickbed **2.** having to do with the direct treatment and observation of patients, as distinguished from experimental or laboratory study **3.** purely scientific; dispassionately curious; impersonal [to regard a problem with *clinical* detachment] **4.** austere, antiseptic, etc., like a medical clinic —**clin′i·cal·ly** *adv.*

clinical thermometer a thermometer with which the body temperature is measured

cli·ni·cian (kli nish′ən) *n.* an expert in or practitioner of clinical medicine, psychology, etc.

clink (kliŋk) *vi.*, *vt.* [ME. *clinken* < MDu. *klinken:* origin echoic] to make or cause to make a slight, sharp sound, as of glasses striking together —*n.* **1.** such a sound **2.** [< name of an 18th-c. prison in Southwark (London)] [Colloq.] a jail; prison

clink·er (-ər) *n.* [Du. *klinker*, vitrified brick that clinks when struck < *klinckaerd* < *klinken*, to ring] **1.** [Archaic] a very hard brick **2.** a hard mass of fused stony matter formed in a furnace, as from impurities in the coal **3.** [Slang] *a)* a mistake, or error; often, specif., a misplaced musical note *b)* a total failure —*vi.* to form clinkers in burning

clink·er-built (-bilt′) *adj.* [*clinker* < *clink*, dial. var. of CLENCH] built with overlapping boards or plates, as a boat

clink·stone (kliŋk′stōn′) *n. Mineralogy* any of various varieties of phonolite that make a clinking, metallic sound when struck

cli·no- (klī′nə, -nō) [< Gr. *klino-* < *klinein*, to slope (see INCLINE)] *a combining form meaning slope* [*clinometer*]

cli·nom·e·ter (kli näm′ə tər) *n.* [CLINO- + -METER] an instrument for measuring angles of slope or inclination —**cli·no·met·ric** (klī′nə met′rik), **cli′no·met′ri·cal** *adj.* —**cli·nom′e·try** (-ə trē) *n.*

clin·quant (kliŋ′kənt) *adj.* [Fr., prp. of earlier *clinquer*, to clink, glitter < MDu. *klinken* (cf. CLINK) [Archaic] glittering with or as with gold or silver; tinseled —*n.* [Archaic] imitation gold leaf; tinsel

Clin·ton (klin′t′n) [E. place name < ? ME. *clint*, cliff (< ON.) + OE. *tun*, enclosure, village: see TOWN] **1.** a masculine name **2.** [after De Witt CLINTON] city in E Iowa, on the Mississippi: pop. 35,000

Clin·ton (klin′t′n) **1. De Witt** (də wit′), 1769–1828; U.S. statesman; governor of N.Y. (1817–21; 1825–28) **2. George**, 1739–1812; vice president of the U.S. (1805–12): uncle of *prec.* **3. Sir Henry**, 1738?–95; Brit. general: commander of Brit. forces in N. America (1778–82)

☆clin·to·ni·a (klin tō′nē ə) *n.* [ModL., after De Witt CLINTON] any of a genus (*Clintonia*) of hardy plants of the lily family, with broad leaves, white or yellow flowers, and blue berries

Cli·o (klī′ō) [L. < Gr. *Kleiō* < *kleiein*, to celebrate < *kleos*, fame, glory] *Gr. Myth.* the Muse of history

clip¹ (klip) *vt.* **clipped**, **clip′ping** [ME. *clippen* < ON. *klippa*] **1.** to cut or cut off with shears or scissors **2.** to cut (an item) out of (a newspaper, magazine, etc.) **3.** *a)* to cut short *b)* to shorten by omitting syllables, letters, etc. **4.** to cut the hair of **5.** to cut off the edge of (coins, etc.) **6.** [Colloq.] to hit or punch with a quick, sharp blow **☆7.** [Slang] to cheat or swindle, esp. by overcharging —*vi.* **1.** to clip something **2.** to move rapidly —*n.* **1.** an act or instance of clipping **2.** a thing clipped; specif., *a)* the amount of wool clipped from sheep at one time or in one season *b)* a sequence clipped from a movie film **3.** a rapid pace **4.** [Colloq.] a quick, sharp punch or blow **5.** *same as* CLIPPED FORM

clip² (klip) *vi.*, *vt.* **clipped**, **clip′ping** [ME. *clippen* < OE. *clyppan*, to embrace < IE. **gleb-* (< base **gel-:* see CLIMB), whence L. *globus*, GLOBE, E. CALF²] **1.** to grip tightly; fasten **2.** [Archaic or Dial.] to hug; embrace closely **☆3.** *Football* to block (an opponent who is not carrying the ball) from behind: an illegal act —*n.* **1.** any of various devices that clip or fasten two or more things together **2.** *same as* CARTRIDGE CLIP **3.** [Obs.] an embrace **☆4.** *Football* an act of clipping

☆clip·board (-bôrd′) *n.* a portable writing board with a hinged clip at the top to hold papers

clip-fed (-fed′) *adj.* automatically loaded from a cartridge clip: said of certain repeating firearms

☆clip joint [Slang] a nightclub, restaurant, store, etc. that charges excessive prices

clipped form (or **word**) a shortened form of a word, as *pike* (for *turnpike*) or *fan* (for *fanatic*)

clip·per (klip′ər) *n.* [ME. < *clippen*, CLIP¹; senses 3 & 4 infl. (?) by MDu. *klepper*, orig., swift horse < LowG. *kleppen*, to sound like hoofbeats (echoic)] **1.** a person who cuts, trims, etc. **2.** [*usually pl.*] a tool for cutting or trimming [a barber's *clippers*] **3.** [for sense, cf. CUTTER ☆*a)* a sharp-bowed, narrow-beamed sailing ship (c. 1830–1854) built for great speed *b)* a modified form of this with less speed and greater cargo capacity **4.** a horse, sled, etc. regarded as very swift **5.** *Electronics* a circuit designed so that all voltages which would rise above or fall below a preset level are maintained at that level

CLIPPER SHIP

clip·ping (klip′in) *n.* [< CLIP¹] **1.** the act of cutting out or trimming off **2.** something cut out or trimmed off [hair *clippings*] **☆3.** a news story or other item clipped from a newspaper, magazine, etc.

clique (klēk, klik) *n.* [Fr. < *cliquer*, to make a noise: of echoic orig.] a small, exclusive circle of people; snobbish or narrow coterie —*SYN.* see COTERIE —**cliqu′ish** (-ish), **cliqu′ey**, **cliqu′y** (-ē) *adj.* —**cliqu′ish·ly** *adv.* —**cliqu′ish-ness** *n.*

Clis·the·nes (klis′thə nēz′) *same as* CLEISTHENES

clit·o·ris (klit′ər əs, klīt′-) *n.* [ModL. < Gr. *kleitoris* < *kleitys*, var. of *klitys*, hill, akin to *klinein*, to slope: see INCLINE] a small, sensitive, erectile organ at the upper end of the vulva: it corresponds to the penis of the male —**clit′o·ral** (-ər əl), **cli·tor·ic** (kli tôr′ik) *adj.*

Clive (klīv) [< the surname] **1.** a masculine name **2. Robert**, Baron Clive of Plassey, 1725–74; Brit. soldier & statesman: established Brit. control of India

clk. clerk

clo·a·ca (klō ā′kə) *n., pl.* **-cae** (-sē, -kē), **-cas** [L. < *cluere*, to cleanse < IE. base **klū-*, to rinse, clean, whence G. *lauter*, pure, E. CLYSTER] **1.** a sewer or cesspool **2.** *Zool. a)* the cavity into which both the intestinal and the genitourinary tracts empty in reptiles, birds, amphibians, and many fishes *b)* in some invertebrates, a similar cavity serving as an excretory, respiratory, and reproductive duct —**clo·a′cal** (-kəl) *adj.*

cloak (klōk) *n.* [ME. & OFr. *cloke*, a cloak < ML. *clocca* (see CLOCK¹), a bell, cloak: so called from its bell-like appearance] **1.** a loose, usually sleeveless outer garment **2.** something that covers or conceals; disguise —*vt.* **1.** to cover with or as with a cloak **2.** to conceal; hide

cloak-and-dag·ger (-ən dag′ər) *adj.* of or characteristic of the activities of spies and undercover agents, esp. as extravagantly depicted in fiction

cloak·room (-rōōm′) *n.* a room where hats, coats, umbrellas, etc. can be left temporarily

☆clob·ber (kläb′ər) *vt.* [< ?] [Slang] **1.** to beat or hit repeatedly; maul **2.** to defeat decisively

‡clo·chard (klō shär′) *n.* [Fr.] a tramp or vagrant

cloche (klōsh) *n.* [Fr. < ML. *clocca*, a bell: see ff.] **1.** a bell-shaped glass jar used to cover delicate plants **2.** a closefitting, bell-shaped hat for women

clock¹ (kläk) *n.* [ME. *clokke*, orig., clock with bells < ML. *clocca*, bell < Celt., as in OIr. *cloc* (whence OE. *clugge*, OHG. *glocka*), bell < ? IE. base **kel-*, to cry out, sound (cf. CLAMOR)] **1.** a device used for measuring and indicating time, usually by means of pointers moving over a dial: clocks, unlike watches, are not meant to be worn or carried about **☆2.** *same as* TIME CLOCK **☆3.** a measuring or recording device suggestive of a clock, as a taximeter —*vt.* **1.** to measure the speed or record the time of (a race, runner, motorist, etc.) with a stopwatch or other timing device **2.** to measure (work done, distance covered, etc.) with a registering device —**around the clock** day and night, without stopping

clock² (kläk) *n.* [< ? *prec.*, because of orig. bell shape] a woven or embroidered ornament on the side of a sock or stocking, going up from the ankle —**clocked** *adj.*

clock·like (-līk′) *adj.* as precise or regular as a clock

clock·mak·er (-māk′ər) *n.* a maker or repairer of clocks

☆clock radio a radio with a built-in clock that can be set to turn the radio on or off at any desired time

clock·wise (-wiz′) *adv., adj.* [CLOCK¹ + -WISE] in the direction in which the hands of a clock rotate

clock·work (-wurk′) *n.* **1.** the mechanism of a clock **2.** any similar mechanism, consisting of springs and geared wheels, as in some mechanical toys —**like clockwork** very regularly, precisely, and evenly

clod (kläd) *n.* [ME. & OE. < IE. base **g(e)l-eu-* < **gel-*, (see CLIMB), whence CLEAT, CLOT] **1.** a lump, esp. a lump of earth, clay, loam, etc. **2.** earth; soil **3.** a dull, stupid fellow; dolt **4.** the part of a neck of beef nearest the shoulder —**clod′dish** *adj.* —**clod′dish·ly** *adv.* —**clod′dish-ness** *n.* —**clod′dy** *adj.*

clod·hop·per (-häp′ər) *n.* [CLOD + HOPPER, ? after GRASS-

HOPPER] **1.** a plowman **2.** a clumsy, stupid fellow; lout **3.** a coarse, heavy shoe, like a plowman's

clod·pate (-pāt´) *n.* [CLOD + PATE] a stupid or foolish person; blockhead: also **clod′poll′** (-pōl′), **clod′pole′**

clog (kläg) *n.* [ME. *clogge*, a lump of wood < ? *clod* + *logge*, log] **1.** a weight fastened to the leg of an animal to hinder motion **2.** anything that hinders or obstructs; hindrance **3.** a shoe with a thick, usually wooden, sole: light clogs are used in clog dancing **4.** *same as* CLOG DANCE —*vt.* **clogged, clog′ging 1.** to hinder; impede **2.** to fill with obstructions or with thick, sticky matter; stop up; jam —*vi.* **1.** to become stopped up **2.** to become thick or sticky, so as to clog **3.** to do a clog dance —**clog′gi·ness** *n.* —**clog′gy** *adj.*

clog dance a dance in which clogs are worn to beat out the rhythm —**clog dancer** —**clog dancing**

cloi·son·né (kloi′zə nā′) *adj.* [Fr., lit., partitioned < *cloison*, partition < VL. **clausio* < L. *clausus:* see ff.] denoting a kind of enamel work in which the surface decoration is set in hollows formed by thin strips of wire welded to a metal plate in a complex pattern —*n.* cloisonné enamel

clois·ter (klois′tər) *n.* [ME. < OFr. *cloistre* & OE. *clauster*, both < L. *claustrum*, a bolt, place shut in, (in ML.(Ec.), that portion of a monastery closed off to the laity) < pp. of *claudere*, to close] **1.** a place of religious seclusion; monastery or convent **2.** monastic life **3.** any place where one may lead a secluded life **4.** an arched way or covered walk along the inside wall or walls of a monastery, convent, church, or college building, with a columned opening along one side leading to a courtyard or garden —*vt.* **1.** to seclude or confine in or as in a cloister **2.** to furnish or surround with a cloister —**clois′tered** *adj.*

SYN.—cloister is the general term for a place of religious seclusion, for either men or women, and emphasizes in connotation retirement from the world; **convent,** once a general term synonymous with **cloister,** is now usually restricted to such a place for women (nuns), formerly called a **nunnery; monastery** usually refers to a cloister for men (monks); an **abbey** is a cloister ruled by an abbot or abbess; a **priory** is a cloister ruled by a prior or prioress and is sometimes a subordinate branch of an abbey

clois·tral (-trəl) *adj.* **1.** of, like, or fit for a cloister **2.** as if confined in a cloister; secluded; retired

cloke (klōk) *n., vt.* **cloked, clok′ing** [Archaic] *same as* CLOAK

clomb (klōm) *archaic pt. & pp. of* CLIMB

clomp (klämp) *vi.* to walk heavily or noisily; clump

☆**clone** (klōn) *n.* [< Gr. *klon*, a twig] *Biol.* all the descendants derived asexually from a single individual, as by cuttings, bulbs, etc. or by fission, parthenogenesis, etc.: also **clon** (klōn, klän) —**clon′al** *adj.* —**clon′al·ly** *adv.*

clonk (kläŋk) *n., vi., vt.* [Colloq.] *same as* CLUNK

clo·nus (klō′nəs) *n.* [ModL. < Gr. *klonos*, turmoil] a series of spasms of a muscle or group of muscles, in certain nervous diseases —**clon·ic** (klän′ik) *adj.* —**clo·nic·i·ty** (klə nis′ə tē) *n.* —**clo′nism** *n.*

clop (kläp) *n.* [echoic] a sharp, clattering sound, like hoofbeats on a pavement —*vi.* **clopped, clop′ping** to make, or move with, such a sound

clo·qué (klō kā′) *n., pl.* **-qués** [Fr., lit., blistered, pp. of *cloquer*, to blister < *cloque*, a blister, bubble, dial. var. of *cloche*, a bell: see CLOCHE] a fabric with a raised or blisterlike design

close¹ (klōs) *adj.* **clos′er, clos′est** [ME. *clos* < OFr. < L. *clausus*, pp. of *claudere* (see ff.); senses under II from notion "with spaces or intervals closed up"] **I.** *denoting the fact or state of being closed or confined* **1.** shut; not open **2.** enclosed or enclosing; shut in **3.** confined or confining; narrow [*close* quarters] **4.** carefully guarded [*close* custody] **5.** shut away from observation; hidden; secluded **6.** secretive; reserved; reticent **7.** miserly; stingy **8.** restricted, as in membership **9.** oppressively warm and stuffy, as stale air **10.** not readily available [credit is *close*] **11.** *Phonet.* uttered with the tongue relatively near the palate: said of certain vowels, as the *a* in *ale* **II.** *denoting nearness* **1.** with little space between; with the intervening space closing or closed up; near together **2.** having parts or elements near together; compact; dense [*close* marching order, *close* weave] **3.** fitting tightly [a *close* coat] **4.** *a*) down or near to the surface on which something grows; very short [a *close* shave] *b*) not far away; nearby [a *close* neighbor] **5.** near in interests, affection, etc.; intimate; familiar [a *close* friend] **6.** varying little from the original or model [a *close* translation] **7.** strict; thorough; careful [a *close* search] **8.** compactly expressed; concise [a *close* description] **9.** accurate; logical; precise [*close* reasoning] **10.** nearly equal or alike [*close* in age] **11.** difficult to resolve or uncertain in outcome [a *close* decision, a *close* game] —*adv.* in a close manner —**close to the wind 1.** *Naut.* heading as closely as possible in the direction from which the wind blows **2.** barely avoiding what is unlawful —**close′ly** *adv.* —**close′ness** *n.*

SYN.—close suggests something whose parts or elements are near together with little space between [*close*-order drill]; **dense** suggests such a crowding together of elements or parts as to form an almost impervious mass [a *dense* fog]; **compact** suggests close and firm packing, esp. within a small space, and usually implies neatness and order in the arrangement of parts [a *compact* bundle]; **thick,** in this connection, suggests a great number of parts massed tightly together [*thick* fur] See also FAMILIAR, STINGY¹ —ANT. open, dispersed

close² (klōz) *vt.* **closed, clos′ing** [ME. *closen* < OFr. *clos-*, stem of *clore* < L. *claudere*, to close, block up < IE. base **klēu-, klāu-*, hook, crooked or forked branch, close with a hook or bar, whence L. *clavis*, key, OIr. *clo*, nail, & LOT, (with initial IE. *s-*) G. *schliessen*, to lock & SLOT¹] **1.** to move (a door, lid, etc.) to a position that covers the opening; shut **2.** to bar entrance to or exit from [to *close* a street] **3.** to fill up or stop (an opening) **4.** to draw the edges of together [to *close* an incision] **5.** to clench (a fist) **6.** to bind together; unite [to *close* forces] **7.** to bring to an end; finish **8.** to stop or suspend the operation of (a school, business, etc.) **9.** to complete or make final (a sale, agreement, etc.) **10.** to make stubbornly resistant [to *close* one's mind] —*vi.* **1.** to undergo shutting [the door *closes* quietly] **2.** to come to an end **3.** to end or suspend operations [the store *closes* at noon]; specif., in the stock exchange, to show an indicated price level at the day's end [steel *closed* high] **4.** to have its edges become joined together [the wound has *closed*] **5.** to come together **6.** to take hold [her hand *closed* on the package] **7.** to throng closely together [his friends *closed* about him] **8.** to lessen an intervening distance; gain [*closing* on the leading runner] **9.** to make contact or come close, as in order to begin fighting **10.** to arrive at an agreement —*n.* **1.** a closing or being closed **2.** the final part or conclusion; end **3.** [Archaic] a hand-to-hand encounter —**close down** ☆**1.** to shut or stop entirely ☆**2.** to settle down (*on*), as darkness or a fog —**close in** to draw near from various directions, cutting off escape on all sides; surround —☆**close out** to dispose of (goods) by sale, as in ending a business —**close round** to encircle; surround —**close up 1.** to draw nearer together **2.** to shut or stop up entirely **3.** to heal, as a wound does —**clos′er** *n.*

SYN.—close suggests a coming or bringing to a stop, as if by shutting something regarded as previously open [nominations are now *closed*]; **end** suggests the stopping of some process, whether or not it has been satisfactorily completed [let's *end* this argument]; to **conclude** is to bring or come to a formal termination, often by arriving at some decision [to *conclude* negotiations]; **finish** emphasizes the bringing to a desired end of that which one has set out to do, esp. by adding perfecting touches [to *finish* a painting]; **complete,** in its distinctive sense, suggests a finishing by filling in the missing or defective parts [the award will *complete* his happiness]; to **terminate** is to bring or come to an end regarded as a limit or boundary [to *terminate* a privilege] —ANT. begin, start, commence

close³ (klōs) *n.* [ME. & OFr. *clos* < L. *clausum*, orig., neut. pp. of *claudere:* see prec.] [Chiefly Brit.] **1.** an enclosed place, as a farmyard **2.** enclosed grounds around or beside a building [a cathedral *close*] **3.** a narrow street or passageway; also, a dead-end street

☆**close call** (klōs) [Colloq.] a narrow escape from danger

close corporation (klōs) a corporation in which a few persons hold all of the stock, which is rarely or never placed on the market: also **closed corporation**

closed (klōzd) *adj.* **1.** not open; shut [a *closed* door] **2.** covered over or enclosed [a *closed* wagon] **3.** functioning independently; self-sufficient [a *closed* economic system] **4.** not receptive to new or different ideas [a *closed* mind] **5.** not open to further analysis or debate [a *closed* question] **6.** restricted to certain individuals; exclusive [a *closed* society] **7.** *Math. a*) of or pertaining to a curve whose ends are joined *b*) of a surface whose plane sections are closed curves *c*) of a set in which an operation on pairs of its elements always produces an element of the set. **8.** *Phonet.* ending in a consonant sound: said of a syllable **9.** *Sports* designating a stance, as of a golfer, in which the front of the body is turned slightly toward the rear

closed chain the structural form of the molecule of certain chemical compounds, represented in models and formulas as a ring of atoms

closed circuit a system for transmitting a telecast over cables to a limited number of receivers connected to a circuit —**closed′-cir′cuit** *adj.*

closed-end (-end′) *adj.* of or pertaining to an investment company issuing a fixed number of shares which are traded on the open market by stockholders of record after the initial sale

☆**closed gentian** any of several N. American plants (genus *Gentiana*) with dark-blue, closed, tubular flowers, blooming in the fall

☆**closed primary** *see* DIRECT PRIMARY ELECTION

☆**closed rule** a parliamentary rule that bars amendments to a bill from the floor

☆**closed season** any of various annual periods during which it is illegal to kill or capture certain game or fish

☆**closed shop 1.** a factory, business, etc. operating under a contractual arrangement between a labor union and the employer by which only members of the union may be employed **2.** this arrangement

close·fist·ed (klōs′fis′tid) *adj.* stingy; miserly

close·fit·ting (-fit′iŋ) *adj.* fitting tightly, esp. in such a way as to show the contours of the body

close·grained (-grānd′) *adj.* having a fine, compact grain or texture, as certain woods

close harmony (klōs) *Music* harmony consisting primarily of chords having all four tones within the compass of an octave

close·hauled (klōs′hôld′) *adj.* having the sails adjusted (hauled close) for heading as nearly as possible into the wind

close·mouthed (-mou*th*d′, -moutht′) *adj.* not talking much; telling little; taciturn: also **close′lipped′** (-lipt′)

close order an arrangement of troops in compact units at close intervals and distances, as for marching

close punctuation punctuation characterized by the use of many commas and other marks

close quarters (klōs) 1. orig., an enclosed space on a ship, in which a last stand could be made against boarders 2. space that is narrow or crowded 3. hand-to-hand encounter with an enemy

☆**close shave** (klōs) [Colloq.] a narrow escape from danger

clos·et (kläz′it) *n.* [ME. & OFr., small enclosure, dim. of *clos:* see CLOSE³] 1. a small room or cupboard for clothes, household supplies, linens, etc. 2. a small, private room for reading, meditation, etc. 3. a monarch's private chamber as for prayer or conference 4. *same as* WATER CLOSET —*adj.* 1. private, secret, or clandestine *[closet* information*]* 2. marked by theorizing; speculative *[closet* thinking*]* —*vt.* to shut up in a private room for confidential discussion *[to closet* oneself with councilors*]*

closet drama drama written mainly to be read, not staged

☆**close-up** (klōs′up′) *n.* 1. a photograph or a movie or television shot made at very close range 2. a close or personal view or interpretation

clos·trid·i·um (kläs trid′ē əm, klōs-) *n.,* *pl.* -**trid′i·a** (-ə) [ModL. < Gr. *klōstēr,* a spindle + ModL. -*idium,* dim. suffix < Gr. -*idion:* so named from its shape] any of a large genus (*Clostridium*) of spore-forming, anaerobic, rod-shaped bacteria, including those causing tetanus and botulism —**clos·trid′i·al** *adj.*

clo·sure (klō′zhər) *n.* [ME. & OFr. < L. *clausura,* a closing < pp. of *claudere,* to CLOSE²] 1. a closing or being closed 2. a finish; end; conclusion 3. anything that closes or shuts 4. *same as* CLOTURE 5. *Geol.* the vertical distance between the highest point of an anticlinal structure and the lowest contour that encircles it 6. *Linguis.* the theoretical end point of a syntactic construction beyond which no further modification normally occurs 7. *Math.* the union of a set and all the points that limit a sequence of points of the given set 8. *Phonet.* a blocking of the air stream at some point in the oral cavity —*vt.* -**sured, -sur·ing** *same as* CLOTURE

clot (klät) *n.* [ME. & OE., akin to Du. *kloot,* ball, G. *klotz,* a block: for IE. base see CLOD, CLIMB] 1. a soft lump of earth, clay, etc.; clod 2. a soft, thickened area or lump formed on or within a liquid *[a* blood *clot]* 3. a thick or jumbled mass or cluster; agglomeration 4. [Brit. Slang] a stupid or silly person; fool —*vt., vi.* **clot′ted, clot′ting** to thicken or form into a clot or clots; coagulate

cloth (klôth, kläth) *n., pl.* **cloths** (klô*th*z, klä*th*z; *also* klôths, kläths *for* "*kinds of cloth*") [ME. < OE. *clath,* cloth, hence garment, akin to -*clithan,* to stick, *clitha,* poultice < IE. base *gleit-* (< *glei-,* to stick, adhere: see CLAY), whence G. *kleid,* dress] 1. a woven, knitted, or pressed fabric of fibrous material, as cotton, wool, silk, hair, synthetic fibers, etc. 2. a piece of such fabric for a specific use *[tablecloth, washcloth, loincloth]* 3. [Obs.] apparel; dress 4. *Naut.* canvas; sail —*adj.* made of cloth —**the cloth** 1. the usual or identifying dress of a profession, esp. of the clergy 2. the clergy collectively

cloth·bound (-bound′) *adj.* having a binding of stiff pasteboard covered with cloth: said of a book

clothe (klō*th*) *vt.* **clothed** *or* **clad, cloth′ing** [ME. *clothen* < OE. *clathian:* see CLOTH] 1. to put clothes on; dress 2. to provide with clothes 3. to cover over as if with a garment; provide or equip *[hills clothed* in snow*]*

clothes (klōz, klō*th*z) *n.pl.* [ME. < OE. *clathas,* clothes, pl. of *clath,* CLOTH] 1. articles, usually of cloth, designed to cover, protect, or adorn the body; wearing apparel; garments; attire 2. *same as* BEDCLOTHES

clothes·horse (-hôrs′) *n.* 1. a frame on which to hang clothes, etc. for airing or drying ☆2. [Slang] a person who pays too much attention to his clothes

clothes·line (-līn′) *n.* a rope or wire on which clothes are hung for drying or airing

clothes moth any of various small moths (family Tineidae) that lay their eggs in articles of wool, fur, etc. upon which the hatched larvae feed

☆**clothes·pin** (-pin′) *n.* a small clip, as a forked peg of wood or plastic, for fastening clothes on a line

☆**clothes·pole** (-pōl′) *n.* a pole for supporting a clothesline

clothes·press (-pres′) *n.* a closet, wardrobe, or chest in which to keep clothes

☆**clothes tree** an upright pole with branching hooks or pegs near the top to hold coats and hats

cloth·ier (klō*th*′yər, klō′*th*ē ər) *n.* [ME., one who makes or sells cloth] 1. a person who makes or sells clothes 2. a dealer in cloth

cloth·ing (klō′*th*in) *n.* [ME.: see CLOTH] 1. wearing apparel; clothes; garments 2. a covering

Clo·tho (klō′thō) [L. < Gr. *Klōthō* < *klōthein,* to spin] *Gr. Myth.* one of the three Fates, spinner of the thread of human life

cloth yard 1. a medieval unit of measure for cloth, fixed at 37 inches by Edward VI of England: also used as a length for longbow arrows 2. now, the standard yard (36 inches) as used in measuring cloth

clo·ture (klō′chər) *n.* [Fr. *clôture* < OFr. *closture* < ML. *clostura* (altered after L. *claustrum:* see CLOISTER) < L. *clausura:* see CLOSURE] the parliamentary procedure by which debate is closed and the measure under discussion put to an immediate vote —*vt.* -**tured, -tur·ing** to apply cloture to (a debate, bill, etc.)

cloud (kloud) *n.* [ME. *cloude, clude,* orig., mass of rock, hence, mass of cloud < OE. *clud,* mass of rock; for IE. base see CLOD, CLIMB] 1. a visible mass of condensed water vapor suspended in the atmosphere, consisting of minute droplets or ice crystals: clouds are commonly classified in four groups: *A* (high clouds above 20,000 ft.) CIRRUS, CIRROSTRATUS, CIRROCUMULUS; *B* (intermediate clouds, 6,500 to 20,000 ft.) ALTOSTRATUS, ALTOCUMULUS; *C* (low clouds, below 6,500 ft.) STRATUS, STRATOCUMULUS, NIMBO-STRATUS; *D* (clouds of great vertical continuity) CUMULUS, CUMULONIMBUS 2. a mass of smoke, dust, steam, etc. 3. a great number of things close together and in motion *[a cloud* of locusts*]* 4. an appearance of murkiness or dimness, as in a liquid 5. a dark marking, as in marble 6. anything that darkens, obscures, threatens, or makes gloomy —*vt.* 1. to cover or make dark as with clouds 2. to make muddy or foggy 3. to darken; obscure; threaten 4. to make gloomy or troubled 5. to cast slurs on; sully (a reputation, etc.) —*vi.* 1. to become cloudy 2. to become gloomy or troubled —**in the clouds** 1. high up in the sky 2. fanciful; impractical 3. in a reverie or daydream —**under a cloud** 1. under suspicion of wrongdoing 2. in a depressed or troubled state of mind

cloud·ber·ry (-ber′ē) *n., pl.* -**ries** a hardy wild raspberry (*Rubus chamaemorus*) with large yellowish fruit

☆**cloud·burst** (-burst′) *n.* a sudden, very heavy rain

cloud-capped (-kapt′) *adj.* having clouds around the top

cloud chamber an enclosed chamber supersaturated with water vapor for revealing the presence of moving charged particles by their ionization of the vapor

☆**cloud forest** a forest, usually near coastal mountain peaks in tropical regions, that has an almost constant cloud cover, even during the dry season

cloud·land (-land′) *n.* region of dreams, imagination, or impractical speculation; visionary realm

cloud·less (-lis) *adj.* free from clouds; clear; bright —**cloud′less·ly** *adv.* —**cloud′less·ness** *n.*

cloud·let (-lit) *n.* a small cloud

cloud nine [Slang] a condition of great joy or bliss; euphoric state

cloud·y (-ē) *adj.* **cloud′i·er, cloud′i·est** 1. covered with clouds; overcast 2. of or like clouds 3. variegated or streaked, as marble 4. opaque, muddy, or foggy *[a cloudy* liquid*]* 5. obscure; vague; not clear *[cloudy* ideas*]* 6. troubled; gloomy —**cloud′i·ly** *adv.* —**cloud′i·ness** *n.*

Clou·et (kloo ā′) 1. **Fran·cois** (fran swä′), 1516?–72; Fr. portrait painter: son of *ff.* 2. **Jean** (zhän), 1485?–1540?; Fr. portrait painter of Flemish descent

clough (kluf, klou) *n.* [ME. < OE. **cloh < *klanh,* akin to G. *klinge,* narrow gorge] [Rare] a narrow gorge

Clough (kluf), **Arthur Hugh** 1819–61; Eng. poet

clout (klout) *n.* [ME. *cloute* < OE. *clut* (akin to MLowG. *klūt,* clod of earth), orig., lump of something, hence, piece of cloth, patch: for IE. base see CLOD, CLIMB] 1. [Archaic or Dial.] *a)* a piece of cloth or leather for patching *b)* any piece of cloth, esp. one for cleaning; rag 2. a blow, with or as with the hand; rap ☆3. [Colloq.] *a)* a long hit in baseball *b)* power or influence; esp., political power 4. *Archery a)* a target of white cloth on a frame *b)* a shot that strikes the target —*vt.* **clutien** < the *n.*] 1. [Archaic or Dial.] to patch or mend coarsely 2. [Colloq.] to strike, as with the hand ☆3. [Slang] to hit (a ball) a far distance

clove¹ (klōv) *n.* [ME. *clowe* < OFr. *clou (de girofle),* lit., nail (of clove) < L. *clavus,* nail: so called from its shape] 1. the dried flower bud of a tropical evergreen tree (*Eugenia aromatica*) of the myrtle family, originally native to the East Indies: used as a pungent, fragrant spice 2. the tree

clove² (klōv) *n.* [ME. < OE. *clufu,* akin to *cleofan,* to split: see CLEAVE¹] a segment of a bulb, as of garlic

clove³ (klōv) *alt. pt. of* CLEAVE¹

clove hitch a kind of knot for fastening a rope around a spar, pole, or another rope: see KNOT, illus.

clo·ven (klō′v′n) *alt. pp. of* CLEAVE¹ —*adj.* divided; split

cloven foot (or **hoof**) a foot divided by a cleft, as in the ox, deer, and sheep: used as a symbol of the Devil, who is usually pictured with such hoofs —**clo′ven-foot′ed, clo′ven-hoofed′** (-hooft′) *adj.*

clove pink *same as* CARNATION (sense 2)

clo·ver (klō′vər) *n.* [ME. < OE. *clafre,* akin to MLowG. *klāver* < IE. base **glei-,* to stick, adhere (cf. CLAY, GLUE): so called ? from the sticky sap] 1. any of a genus (*Tri-folium*) of low-growing herbs of the legume family, with leaves of three leaflets and small flowers in dense heads, as **red clover,** used for forage, and **white clover,** common in lawn seed mixtures 2. any similar leguminous plant: cf. SWEET CLOVER —**in clover** living a life of ease and luxury, as cattle in good pasture

clo·ver·leaf (-lēf′) *n., pl.* **-leafs'** ☆a multiple highway interchange which, by means of an overpass with curving ramps that form the outline of a four-leaf clover and other connecting roads, permits traffic to move or turn in any of four directions with little interference —*adj.* in the shape or pattern of a leaf of clover

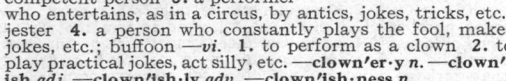

CLOVERLEAF

Clo·vis I (klō′vis) 466?–511 A.D.; founder of Frankish monarchy; king of the Franks (481–511)

clown (kloun) *n.* [altered < ? Fr. *colon*, farmer, orig. colonist, settler < L. *colonus:* see COLONY] 1. orig., a peasant or farmer; rustic 2. a clumsy, boorish, or incompetent person 3. a performer who entertains, as in a circus, by antics, jokes, tricks, etc.; jester 4. a person who constantly plays the fool, makes jokes, etc.; buffoon —*vi.* 1. to perform as a clown 2. to play practical jokes, act silly, etc. —**clown′·er·y** *n.* —**clown′·ish** *adj.* —**clown′ish·ly** *adv.* —**clown′ish·ness** *n.*

cloy (kloi) *vt., vi.* [aphetic < ME. *acloien*, to hamper, harm, obstruct < OFr. *encloyer*, to fasten with a nail, hinder < *clou*, a nail < L. *clavus*, a nail] to surfeit, or make weary of displeased, by too much of something, esp. something sweet, rich, etc. —*SYN.* see SATIATE —**cloy′ing·ly** *adv.*

C.L.U. Chartered Life Underwriter

club (klub) *n.* [ME. *clubbe* < ON. *klumba*, mass of something, CLUMP: for IE. base see CALF¹, GLOVE; sense 4 (17th c.) < ? basic meaning, as in *clump of trees*] 1. *a)* a heavy stick, usually thinner at one end, used as a weapon *b)* anything used to threaten or coerce 2. a variously shaped stick or bat used to strike the ball in certain games [a golf *club*] 3. same as INDIAN CLUB 4. a group of people associated for a common purpose or mutual advantage, usually in an organization that meets regularly: see also BOOK CLUB 5. the room, building, or facilities used by such a group 6. a nightclub 7. *a)* any of a suit of playing cards marked with a black figure like a clover leaf (♣) *b)* [*pl.*] this suit of cards —*vt.* **clubbed, club′bing** 1. to beat or strike as with a club 2. to combine or pool (resources, etc.) for a common purpose 3. to unite for a common purpose 4. to use (a rifle or the like) as a club by hitting with the butt end —*vi.* 1. to unite or combine for a common purpose 2. [Rare] to form into a clublike mass

club·ba·ble, club·a·ble (-ə b'l) *adj.* [Colloq.] suited to membership in a club; sociable

club·by (-ē) *adj.* **-bi·er, -bi·est** [Colloq.] 1. friendly or sociable, esp. in an effusive way 2. restricted, clannish, or exclusive, as some clubs are

☆**club car** a railroad lounge car, usually with a bar

club·foot (-foot′) *n.* 1. a congenital deformity of the foot, characterized by a misshapen or twisted, often clublike, appearance; talipes 2. *pl.* **-feet'** (-fēt′) a foot so deformed —**club′foot′ed** *adj.*

club·hand (-hand′) *n.* 1. a deformity of the hand analogous to clubfoot 2. a hand so deformed

club·haul (-hôl′) *vt.* [< nautical *club* (to drift with anchor dragging) + HAUL] to tack (a vessel in a precarious situation) by dropping the lee anchor as soon as the wind is out of the sails, then cutting the cable when the ship swings off onto the new tack

club·house (-hous′) *n.* 1. a building occupied by or used by a club ☆2. a locker room used by an athletic team

club·man (-mən, -man′) *n., pl.* **-men** (-mən, -men′) a man who is a member of, or spends much time at, a private club or clubs

club·moss (-môs′, -mäs′) *adj.* designating a family (Lycopodiaceae) of flowerless vascular plants, with small leaves, a mosslike appearance, and club-shaped cones containing spores

club moss any plant of an order (Lycopodiales) that includes many fossil forms; esp., any plant of two living genera (*Lycopodium* and *Selaginella*)

club·room (-rōōm′) *n.* a room used by a club as a meeting place, for social affairs, etc.

club root a disease of plants of the cabbage family, caused by a slime mold (*Plasmodiophora brassicae*) and characterized by swellings of the roots

☆**club sandwich** a sandwich of three or more slices of toast filled with layers of chicken, bacon, lettuce, mayonnaise, tomatoes, etc.

club soda same as SODA WATER

☆**club steak** a small beefsteak cut from the loin tip

☆**club·wom·an** (-woom′ən) *n., pl.* **-wom′en** (-wim′in) a woman member of a club or clubs; esp. one who devotes much time to club activities

cluck (kluk) *vi.* [ME. *clokken* < OE. *cloccian:* orig. echoic] to make a low, sharp, clicking sound, as of a hen calling her chickens or brooding —*vt.* to utter with such a sound [*to cluck* one's disapproval] —*n.* 1. the sound made by a hen clucking 2. a sound like this 3. [Slang] a dull, stupid person; dolt

clue (klōō) *n.* a clew; esp., a fact, object, etc. that helps to solve a mystery or problem —*vt.* **clued, clu′ing** 1. to indicate by or as by a clue ☆2. [Colloq.] to provide with the necessary information (often with *in*)

Cluj (klōōzh) city in Transylvania, NW Romania: pop. 167,000

clum·ber (spaniel) (klum′bər) [< *Clumber*, estate of the Duke of Newcastle] [also C-] a short-legged spaniel with a heavy body and a thick coat of straight, white hair marked with yellow or orange

clump (klump) *n.* [< Du. *klomp* or LowG. *klump:* for IE. base see CLIMB] 1. a lump; mass 2. a mass of bacteria 3. a cluster, as of shrubs or trees 4. the sound of heavy footsteps —*vi.* 1. to walk heavily; tramp 2. to form clumps —*vt.* 1. to plant in a clump; group together in a cluster 2. to cause to form clumps

clump·y (-ē) *adj.* **clump′i·er, clump′i·est** 1. full of or like clumps 2. heavy and clumsy: also **clump′ish**

clum·sy (klum′zē) *adj.* **-si·er, -si·est** [ME. *clumsid*, numb with cold, pp. of *clumsen*, to benumb < ON. base whence Sw. dial. *klummsen*, to benumb with the cold; base and basic sense as in CLAM²: see CLIMB] 1. lacking grace or skill, as in using one's hands or feet; awkward 2. awkwardly shaped or made; ill-constructed 3. badly contrived; inelegant [a *clumsy* style] —**clum′si·ly** *adv.* —**clum′si·ness** *n.* —*SYN.* see AWKWARD

clung (klun) *pt. & pp.* of CLING

clunk (klunk) *n.* [echoic] 1. a dull metallic sound 2. [Colloq.] a heavy blow 3. [Slang] a dull or stupid person —*vi., vt.* to move or strike with a clunk or clunks

clunk·er (-ər) *n.* [Slang] an old machine in poor repair; esp., a noisy, dilapidated automobile

Clu·ny (klōō′nē; Fr. klü nē′) town in EC France: site of a Benedictine monastery (910–1790): pop. 4,000

Cluny lace [after prec.] a heavy bobbin lace with an open design, made of silk and cotton thread

clu·pe·id (klōō′pē id) *n.* [< ModL. *Clupea*, name of the genus (< L. *clupea*, kind of small river fish) + -ID] any of a family (Clupeidae) of soft-finned fishes, as herring, sardines, etc. —*adj.* of this family of fishes

clu·pe·oid (-oid′) *adj.* [< ModL. *Clupea* (see prec.) + -OID] of or like the fish of the herring family —*n.* any fish of the herring family

clus·ter (klus′tər) *n.* [ME. < OE. *clyster*, cluster, akin to north G. dial. *kluster*, CLAW, CLOT] 1. a number of things of the same sort gathered together or growing together; bunch 2. a number of persons, animals, or things grouped together 3. *Linguis.* a group of nonsyllabic phonemes, esp. a group of two or more consecutive consonants —*vi., vt.* to gather or grow in a cluster or clusters —**clus′ter·y** *adj.*

clutch¹ (kluch) *vt.* [ME. *clucchen* < OE. *clyccan*, to clench (infl. in meaning by ME. *cloke*, a claw) < IE. base *glek- (< *gel-:* cf. CLIMB), whence CLING] 1. to grasp, seize, or snatch with a hand or claw 2. to grasp or hold eagerly or tightly —*vi.* to snatch or seize (*at*) —*n.* [ME. *clucche* < the v.] 1. a claw or hand in the act of seizing 2. [*usually pl.*] power; control 3. *a)* the act of clutching *b)* a grasp; grip 4. *a)* a mechanical device, as in an automobile, for engaging and disengaging the motor or engine *b)* the lever or pedal by which this device is operated 5. a device for gripping and holding, as in a crane 6. a woman's small handbag with no handle or strap, held in the hand: also **clutch bag** ☆7. [Colloq.] a critical situation or emergency [dependable in the *clutch*] —*SYN.* see TAKE

clutch² (kluch) *vt.* [dial. < ME. *clekken* (< ON. *klekja*), to hatch] [Rare] to hatch (chicks) —*n.* 1. a nest of eggs 2. a brood of chicks 3. a number of persons, animals, or things gathered together; cluster

clut·ter (klut′ər) *n.* [var. of *clotter* < CLOT] 1. a number of things scattered in disorder; jumble 2. [var. of CLATTER] [Dial.] same as CLATTER 3. the interfering traces on a radarscope caused by hills, buildings, etc. —*vt.* to put into disorder; jumble (often with *up*) —*vi.* [Dial.] to make a clatter; bustle —**clut′ter·y** *adj.*

Clyde (klīd) 1. a masculine name 2. river in S Scotland, flowing northwestward into the Firth of Clyde: 106 mi. 3. Firth of, estuary of the Clyde River: 64 mi.

Clyde·bank (-baŋk′) city in SW Scotland, on the Clyde River, near Glasgow: pop. 51,000

Clydes·dale (klīdz′dāl′) *n.* [after *Clydesdale*, the valley of the Clyde River, Scotland, where the breed originated] any of a breed of heavy, strong draft horse

clyp·e·ate (klip′ē it, -āt′) *adj.* [L. *clypeatus*, pp. of *clypeare*, to arm with a shield < *clypeus*, a shield] *Biol.* 1. shaped like a round shield 2. having a shieldlike process Also **clyp′e·at′ed**

clyp·e·us (-ē əs) *n., pl.* **clyp′e·i** (-ī′) [L., a shield] a median plate or shieldlike process on the anterior portion of the head of certain insects

clys·ter (klis′tər) *n.* [ME. *clister* < L. *clyster* < Gr. *klystēr* < *klyzein*, to wash < IE. base *klū-, to rinse: see CLOACA] an enema

Cly·tem·nes·tra, Cly·taem·nes·tra (klīt′əm nes′trə) *Gr. Myth.* the wife of Agamemnon: with the aid of her lover Aegisthus she murdered her husband and was in turn killed by their son Orestes

Cm *Chem.* curium

cm. centimeter; centimeters

c.m. 1. circular mil 2. common meter 3. corresponding member 4. countermarked 5. court-martial

cmd. command

cmdg. commanding

Cmdr. Commander

C.M.G. Companion (of the Order) of St. Michael and St. George

cml. commercial

C/N, CN 1. circular note 2. credit note

Cni·dus (nī'dəs) ancient city in SW Asia Minor

CNO Chief of Naval Operations

Cnos·sus (näs'əs) ancient city in N Crete, near modern Candia: center of ancient Minoan civilization

☆**C-note** (sē'nōt') *n.* [for CENTURY-note] [Slang] a one-hundred-dollar bill

C.N.S., CNS central nervous system

Cnut II (kə nōōt') *same as* CANUTE II

co- (kō) 1. *a prefix shortened from* COM-, *meaning a)* together with [*cooperation*] *b)* joint [*co-owner*] *c)* equally [*coextensive*] 2. *a prefix meaning* complement of [*cosine*]

Co *Chem.* cobalt

Co., co. *pl.* **Cos., cos.** 1. company 2. county

C/O cash order

C/O, c.o. 1. care of 2. carried over

C.O., CO 1. Commanding Officer 2. conscientious objector

co·ac·er·va·tion (kō as'ər vā'shən) *n.* [ME. *coacervacioun*, a heaping together < L. *coacervatio* < *coacervatus*, pp. of *coacervare*, to heap up < *co-* (see CO-) + *acervare*, to form a heap < *acervus*, a heap] the production of a liquid phase, usually in the form of liquid drops, in the coagulation of a lyophilic sol

coach (kōch) *n.* [Fr. *coche* < G. *kutsche* < Hung. *kocsi* (*szekér*), (carriage of) *Kócs*, village in Hungary where it was first used] 1. a large, covered, four-wheeled carriage with seats for passengers inside and an open, raised seat in front for the driver; stagecoach ☆2. a railroad passenger car furnishing the lowest-priced seating accommodations: distinguished from CHAIR CAR, SLEEPING CAR, etc. 3. the lowest-priced class of accommodations on some airlines 4. a bus (sense 1) 5. an enclosed automobile, usually a two-door sedan 6. [orig., university slang] a private tutor who prepares a student in a subject or for an examination 7. an instructor or trainer, as of athletes, actors, singers, etc. ☆8. *Baseball* a member of the team at bat stationed near first or third base to signal and direct the base runners and batters 9. *Sports* (exc. *Baseball*) the person who is in overall charge of a team and the strategy in games: cf. MANAGER —*vt.* 1. [Rare] to carry in a coach 2. to instruct in a subject, or prepare for an examination, by private tutoring 3. to instruct and train (athletes, actors, etc.) —*vi.* 1. to ride in a coach 2. to act as a coach

coach dog *same as* DALMATIAN

coach·man (-mən) *n., pl.* -**men** (-mən) 1. the driver of a coach or carriage 2. an artificial fly used in angling, with a spotted, green body and white wings

co·act (kō akt') *vi.* [CO- + ACT] to work or act together —**co·ac'tive** *adj.*

co·ac·tion[1] (kō ak'shən) *n.* [ME. *coaccioun* < ML. *coactio* < L. *coactare*, to constrain, force, freq. of *cogere*: see COGENT] coercion; force —**co·ac'tive** *adj.*

co·ac·tion[2] (-ak'shən) *n.* [CO- + ACTION] 1. cooperative action 2. *Ecology* any important interaction between two organisms, as in symbiosis, parasitism, etc.

coad. coadjutor

co·ad·ju·tant (-aj'ə tənt) *adj.* [COADJUT(OR) + -ANT] helping each other; cooperating —*n.* an assistant

co·ad·ju·tor (-aj'ə tər; *also, and for 2 usually*, kō'ə jōōt'ər) *n.* [ME. < OFr. *coadjuteur* < LL. *coadjutor* < L. *co-*, together + *adjutor*, assistant < *adjuvare*, to help < *ad-*, to + *juvare*, to assist] 1. an assistant; helper 2. a person, often another bishop, appointed to assist a bishop, usually becoming his successor

co·ad·u·nate (-aj'ə nit, -yōō nit; -nāt') *adj.* [LL. *coadunatus*, pp. of *coadunare*, to unite < L. *co-*, together + *adunare*, to join < *ad-*, to + *unare*, to unite < *unus*, ONE] 1. united; joined together. 2. *Bot., Zool.* grown together —**co·ad'u·na'tion** *n.*

co·ag·u·la·ble (kō ag'yōō lə b'l) *adj.* [ML. *coagulabilis*] that can be coagulated —**co·ag'u·la·bil'i·ty** *n.*

co·ag·u·lant (-lənt) *n.* [L. *coagulans*, prp. of *coagulare*] a substance that brings about coagulation

co·ag·u·lase (-lās') *n.* [COAGUL(ATE) + -ASE] an enzyme produced by certain bacteria, which causes coagulation of blood plasma

co·ag·u·late (-lāt') *vt.* -**lat'ed**, -**lat'ing** [ME. *coagulaten* < L. *coagulatus*, pp. of *coagulare*, to cause to curdle < *coagulum*: see COAGULUM] to cause (a liquid) to become a soft, semisolid mass; curdle; clot —*vi.* to become coagulated —**co·ag'u·la'tion** *n.* —**co·ag'u·la'tive** *adj.* —**co·ag'u·la'tor** *n.*

co·ag·u·lum (-ləm) *n., pl.* -**la** (-lə) [L. *coagulum*, means of coagulation, rennet < *cogere*, to curdle, bring together: see COGENT] a clot, curd, or coagulated albuminoid substance

Co·a·hui·la (kō'ä wē'lä) state of N Mexico, on the Tex. border: 58,068 sq. mi.; pop. 974,000; cap. Saltillo

coal (kōl) *n.* [ME. & OE. *col*, charcoal, live coal, akin to G. *kohle*, ON. *kol* < IE. base **g(e)u-lo-*, live coal, whence Ir. *gual*] 1. a black, combustible, mineral solid resulting from the partial decomposition of vegetable matter away from air and under varying degrees of increased temperature and pressure over a period of millions of years: used as a fuel and in the production of coke, coal gas, water gas, and many coal-tar compounds 2. a piece (or collectively, pieces) of this substance 3. a piece of glowing or charred wood, coal, or similar substance; ember 4. charcoal —*vt.* 1. to reduce (a substance) to charcoal by burning 2. to provide with coal —*vi.* to take in a supply of coal —**haul** (or **rake, drag, call**) **over the coals** to criticize sharply; censure; scold —**heap coals of fire on (someone's) head** to cause (someone) to feel remorse by returning good for his evil: Prov. 25:22

coal ball a concreted mass, commonly of calcite, found in some coal beds and containing preserved fragments of coal-forming plants

☆**coal car** 1. a railroad car designed for transporting coal, as from a mine 2. *same as* TENDER[3] (sense 4)

coal·er (-ər) *n.* a ship, railroad freight car, etc. that transports or supplies coal

co·a·lesce (kō'ə les') *vi.* -**lesced'**, -**lesc'ing** [L. *coalescere* < *co-*, together + *alescere*, to grow up] 1. to grow together, as the halves of a broken bone 2. to unite or merge into a single body, group, or mass —*SYN.* see MIX —**co'a·les'cence** *n.* —**co'a·les'cent** *adj.*

coal·fish (-fish') *n., pl.* -**fish'**, -**fish'es**: see FISH[2] 1. a dark-colored fish (*Pollachius virens*) of the cod family 2. any of various other dark-colored fishes

coal gas 1. a gas produced by the destructive distillation of bituminous coal: used for lighting and heating 2. a poisonous gas given off by burning coal

coal·i·fi·ca·tion (kōl'ə fi kā'shən) *n.* [COAL + -i- + -FICA-TION] the process by which vegetable matter is transformed into coal

coaling station a place, as a port or station, where ships or trains take on coal

co·a·li·tion (kō'ə lish'ən) *n.* [ML. *coalitio* < LL. *coalitus*, fellowship, orig. pp. of *coalescere*: see COALESCE] 1. a combination; union 2. a temporary alliance of factions, nations, etc., for some specific purpose, as of political parties in times of national emergency —*SYN.* see ALLI-ANCE —**co'a·li'tion·ist** *n.*

coal measures 1. coal beds or strata 2. sedimentary Carboniferous rocks that include coal-bearing strata

☆**coal oil** 1. kerosene or any other oil obtained by fractional distillation of petroleum 2. crude petroleum 3. unrefined oil, obtained by destructive distillation of coal: used as a lamp fuel

Coal·sack (-sak') *Astron.* either of two dark clouds in the Milky Way, esp. one located near the Southern Cross

coal tar a black, thick, opaque liquid obtained by the destructive distillation of bituminous coal: many synthetic compounds have been developed from it, including dyes, medicines, explosives, and perfumes

coal·y (kōl'ē) *adj.* **coal'i·er, coal'i·est** 1. full of coal 2. of or like coal; esp., black

coam·ing (kōm'miŋ) *n.* [17th c. < ?] a raised border around a hatchway, roof opening, etc., to keep out water

co·ap·ta·tion (kō'ap tā'shən) *n.* [LL.(Ec.) *coaptatio*, an accurate joining together < *coaptare*, to fit, adjust < L. *co-*, together + *aptare*, to fit, adapt, freq. of *apere*, to fasten, join: coined by Augustine to translate Gr. *harmonia* (see HARMONY)] the joining or adjusting of parts to each other, as of the ends of a broken bone

co·arc·tate (kō ärk'tāt) *adj.* [< L. *coarctatus*, pp. of *coarctare*, to press together < *co-*, together + *artare*, to press together < *artus*, fitted, narrow < *artus*, a joint, limb; sp. affected by assoc. with *arcere*, to enclose] *Biol.* 1. compressed or constricted 2. rigidly enclosed in the last larval skin: said of certain insect pupae —**co·arc'ta'tion** *n.*

coarse (kōrs) *adj.* [specialized var. of COURSE in sense of "ordinary or usual order" as in *of course*] 1. of inferior or poor quality; common [*coarse* fare] 2. consisting of rather large elements or particles [*coarse* sand] 3. not fine or delicate in texture, structure, form, etc.; rough; harsh [*coarse* features, *coarse* cloth] 4. for rough or crude work or results [a *coarse* file, *coarse* measurements] 5. lacking in refinement or good taste; vulgar; crude [a *coarse* joke] —**coarse'ly** *adv.* —**coarse'ness** *n.*

SYN.—**coarse,** in this comparison, implies such a lack of refinement in manners or speech as to be offensive to one's esthetic or moral sense [*coarse* laughter]; **gross** suggests a brutish crudeness or roughness [*gross* table manners]; **indelicate** suggests a verging on impropriety or immodesty [an *indelicate* remark]; **vulgar,** in this connection, emphasizes a lack of proper training, culture, or good taste [*the vulgar* ostentation of her home]; **obscene** is used of that which is offensive to decency or modesty and implies lewdness [*obscene* gestures]; **ribald** suggests such mild indecency or lewdness as might bring laughter from those who are not too squeamish [*ribald* jokes] —*ANT.* refined

coarse·grained (-grānd') *adj.* 1. having a coarse texture 2. lacking in refinement or delicacy; crude

coars·en (-'n) *vt., vi.* to make or become coarse

coast (kōst) *n.* [ME. *coste*, coast < OFr. *coste*, a rib, hill, shore, coast < L. *costa*, a rib, side] 1. land alongside the sea; seashore 2. [Obs.] frontier; borderland ☆3. [< CanadFr., hillside, slope] an incline down which a slide is

taken ☆**4.** a slide or ride, as on a sled going down an incline by the force of gravity —*vi.* **1.** to sail near or along a coast, esp. from port to port ☆**2.** to go down an incline on a sled ☆**3.** to continue in motion on momentum or by the force of gravity after propelling power has stopped ☆**4.** to continue without serious effort, letting one's past efforts carry one along —*vt.* **1.** [Obs.] to go along the side of **2.** to sail along or near the coast of —*SYN.* see SHORE[1] —**the Coast** [Colloq.] ☆in the U.S., the Pacific coast —**the coast is clear** there is no apparent danger or hindrance

coast·al (-'l) *adj.* of, at, near, or along a coast

coast artillery artillery used to defend a coast

coast·er (kōs'tər) *n.* **1.** a person or thing that coasts **2.** a ship that carries cargo or passengers from port to port along a coast ☆**3.** a sled or wagon for coasting **4.** [< obs. sense of *coast*, vi., "to pass close to or around"] formerly, a small tray, usually on wheels, for passing a wine decanter, etc. around a table ☆**5.** a small tray, mat, disk, etc. placed under a glass or bottle to protect a table or other surface

☆**coaster brake** a brake in the hub of the rear wheel of a bicycle, operated by reversing the pressure on the pedals: it also releases the wheel from the driving mechanism to permit free coasting

coast guard 1. a governmental force employed to defend a nation's coasts, prevent smuggling, aid vessels in distress, maintain lighthouses, etc.; specif. [C- G-], such a branch of the U.S. armed forces, under the control of the Department of Transportation or, in time of war, of the Department of the Navy **2.** a member of a coast guard —**coast guards'man, coast guard'man,** *pl.* **-men**

coast·land (kōst'land') *n.* land along a coast

coast·line (-līn') *n.* the contour or outline of a coast

Coast Mountains mountain range in W British Columbia & S Alas.: highest peak, 13,260 ft.

Coast Ranges series of mountain ranges along the W coast of N. America, extending from Alas. to Baja California: highest peak, Mount LOGAN

coast·ward (-wərd) *adj.*, *adv.* toward the coast: also **coast'wards** (-wərdz) *adv.*

coast·wise (-wīz') *adv.*, *adj.* along and near the coast: also **coast'ways'** (-wāz') *adv.*

coat (kōt) *n.* [ME. & OFr. *cote*, a coat < ML. *cota*, a tunic < Frank. *kotta*, coarse cloth (akin to G. *kotze*, shaggy overcoat)] **1.** a sleeved outer garment opening down the front and varying in length, as a suit jacket or a topcoat or overcoat **2.** a natural outer covering of an animal, as of skin, fur, wool, etc. **3.** the outer covering of a plant or of an animal structure or tissue **4.** a layer of some substance, as paint, over a surface **5.** [Dial.] a petticoat or skirt **6.** [Obs.] customary garb of a profession, class, etc. —*vt.* **1.** to provide or cover with a coat **2.** to cover with a layer of something —**coat'ed** *adj.*

coated paper a paper whose surface has been treated to take halftone impressions or color printing

Coates (kōts), **Eric** 1886–1958; Eng. composer

co·a·ti (kō ät'ē) *n.*, *pl.* **-tis** [Tupi < *cua*, a cincture + *tim*, the nose: so called from appearance of its snout] any of a genus (*Nasua*) of small, flesh-eating, tree-dwelling mammals found in Mexico and Central and South America: it is similar to the raccoon but with a long, flexible snout

co·a·ti·mun·di, co·a·ti·mon·di (-mun'dē) *n.* [Tupi < prec. + *mondi*, solitary] same as COATI

coat·ing (kōt'iŋ) *n.* **1.** a coat or layer over a surface [a *coating* of enamel] **2.** cloth for making coats

coat of arms [transl. of Fr. *cotte d'armes*, light garment worn over armor, generally blazoned with heraldic arms] a group of emblems and figures (heraldic bearings) usually arranged on and around a shield and serving as the special insignia of some person, family, or institution

coat of mail *pl.* **coats of mail** [after Fr. *cotte de mailles*, lit., coat of meshes] a suit of armor made of interlinked metal rings or overlapping plates

COAT OF ARMS

coat·tail (-tāl') *n.* the back part of a coat below the waist; esp., either half of this part when divided, as on a swallow-tailed coat —☆**ride** (or **hang,** etc.) **on** (**someone's**) **coattails** to have one's success dependent on that of someone else

co·au·thor (kō ô'thər) *n.* a joint author; collaborator

coax (kōks) *vt.* [orig. slang, "to make a *coax* of" < obs. slang *coax, cox, cokes,* a fool, ninny] **1.** to induce or try to induce to do something; (seek to) persuade by soothing words, agreeable manner, etc.; wheedle **2.** to get by coaxing —*vi.* to use gentle persuasion, urging, etc. —**coax'er** *n.* —**coax'ing·ly** *adv.*

SYN.—**coax** suggests repeated attempts to persuade someone to do something and implies the use of soothing words, an insinuating manner, etc.; **cajole** suggests the use of flattery or other blandishments; **wheedle** implies even more strongly the use of subtle flattery or seduction in gaining one's ends

co·ax·i·al (kō ak'sē əl) *adj.* [CO- + AXIAL] **1.** having a common axis: also **co·ax'al 2.** designating a compound loudspeaker consisting of a smaller unit mounted within and connected with a larger one on a common axis: the smaller unit reproduces the higher frequencies, beyond the range of

the larger ☆**3.** designating a high-frequency transmission line or cable in which a solid or stranded central conductor is surrounded by an insulating medium which, in turn, is surrounded by a solid or braided outside conductor in the form of a cylindrical shell: it is used for sending telephone, telegraph, television, etc. impulses

cob[1] (käb) *n.* [ME., prob. < LowG., as in Du. *kobbe* < Gmc. base *kubb-,* something rounded] **1.** [Brit. Dial.] *a*) a lump or small mass, as of coal *b*) a leader; chief ☆**2.** the central, kernel-bearing part of an ear of corn; corncob ☆**3.** a corncob pipe **4.** a male swan **5.** a short, thickset horse with a high gait

cob[2] (käb) *n.* [prob. < EFris. *kobbe*] the great, black-backed gull (*Larus marinus*), found in the northern Atlantic regions: also sp. **cobb**

co·balt (kō'bôlt) *n.* [G. *kobalt* < *kobold,* goblin, demon of the mines: term used by miners, who regarded it as worthless, from belief that goblins substituted it for silver] a hard, lustrous, steel-gray, ductile metallic chemical element, found in various ores: it is used in the preparation of alloys; its compounds are used in the production of inks, paints, and varnishes: symbol, Co; at. wt., 58.9332; at. no., 27; sp. gr., 8.71; melt. pt., 1495°C; boil. pt., 2900°C: a radioactive isotope (**cobalt 60**) is used in the treatment of cancer, in industrial radiography and research, etc.

cobalt blue 1. a dark blue pigment consisting of a mixture of cobalt and aluminum oxides **2.** dark blue

co·bal·tic (kō bôl'tik) *adj.* **1.** of cobalt **2.** designating or of compounds in which cobalt has a valence of three

co·balt·ite (kō'bôl tīt') *n.* cobalt sulfarsenide, CoAsS, a silver-white mineral: also **co'balt·ine'** (-tēn')

co·bal·tous (kō bôl'təs) *adj.* designating or of compounds in which cobalt has a valence of two

cob·ber (käb'ər) *n.* [prob. < Heb. (via Yid.) *chaver,* a comrade] [Australian Slang] a close companion; comrade

Cob·bett (käb'it), **William** (pseud. *Peter Porcupine*) 1762?–1835; Eng. journalist & political reformer

cob·ble[1] (käb''l) *vt.* **-bled, -bling** [ME., prob. akin to COB[1]] **1.** to mend or patch (shoes, etc.) **2.** to mend or put together clumsily or crudely

cob·ble[2] (käb''l) *n.* [prob. < COB[1]] **1.** a cobblestone **2.** [*pl.*] same as COB COAL —*vt.* **-bled, -bling** to pave with cobblestones

☆**cob·bler**[1] (käb'lər) *n.* [of U.S. orig. < ?] **1.** an iced drink containing wine, whiskey, or rum, an orange or lemon slice, sugar, and a sprig of mint **2.** a deep-dish fruit pie usually with a thick top crust of biscuit dough but no bottom crust

cob·bler[2] (käb'lər) *n.* [ME. *cobelere:* see COBBLE[1]] **1.** a person whose work is mending shoes **2.** [Archaic] a clumsy, bungling workman

cob·ble·stone (käb''l stōn') *n.* [ME. *cobel ston:* see COBBLE[2] + STONE] a rounded stone of a kind formerly much used for paving streets

cob coal [see COB[1]] coal in large rounded lumps

Cob·den (käb'dən), **Richard** 1804–65; Eng. political economist & statesman: advocate of free trade

co·bel·lig·er·ent (kō'bə lij'ər ənt) *n.* a nation associated but not formally allied with another or others in waging war

Cob·ham (käb'əm), **Lord** see OLDCASTLE

☆**co·bi·a** (kō'bē ə) *n.* [< ?] a large, voracious game fish (*Rachycentron canadus*) found in warm seas: it has a conspicuous black stripe along each side of the body

co·ble (kō'b'l, käb''l) *n.* [ME. *cobel* < OE. *cuopel,* prob. < Celt., as in W. *ceubal,* Bret. *caubal* (whence ? L. *caupulus*)] **1.** a small fishing boat with a lug sail, deep stem, large rudder, and flattish stern, used off the eastern coast of England **2.** in Scotland, a short, flat-bottomed rowboat

Co·blenz (kō'blents) same as KOBLENZ

cob·nut (käb'nut') *n.* [see COB[1]] same as FILBERT

co·bra (kō'brə) *n.* [< Port. *cobra* (de capello), serpent (of the hood) < L. *colubra,* a snake] **1.** any of a genus (*Naja*) of very poisonous snakes of Asia and Africa having around the neck loose skin which is expanded into a hood when the snake is excited **2.** leather made of the skin of this snake

cobra de ca·pel·lo (dē kə pel'ō) *pl.* **cobras de capello** [see prec.] a varicolored cobra (*Naja naja*), esp. of India, with a marking on the hood that looks like an eye

Co·burg (kō'bərg) city in N Bavaria, Germany: pop. 46,000

cob·web (käb'web') *n.* [ME. *copwebbe < coppe,* spider (< OE. *-coppe,* in *atorcoppe < ator,* poison + *-coppe,* spider) + WEB] **1.** a web spun by a spider **2.** a single thread of such a web **3.** anything flimsy, gauzy, or ensnaring, like the web of a spider —*vt.* **-webbed', -web'bing** to cover with or as with cobwebs —**cob'web'by** *adj.*

co·ca (kō'kə) *n.* [Quechuan *cuca*] **1.** any of a family of tropical S. American shrubs, esp. a species (*Erythroxylon coca*) whose dried leaves are the source of cocaine and some other alkaloids **2.** these dried leaves

INDIAN COBRA
(to 6 ft. long)

co·caine, co·cain (kō kān′, kō′kān) *n.* [COCA + -INE[4]] a crystalline alkaloid, $C_{17}H_{21}NO_4$, obtained from dried coca leaves: it is a narcotic and local anesthetic

co·cain·ism (kō kān′iz′m) *n.* a diseased condition resulting from excessive or habitual use of cocaine

co·cain·ize (kō kān′īz) *vt.* **-ized, -iz·ing** to anesthetize with cocaine

-coc·cal (käk′'l) *a combining form meaning* of or produced by a (specified kind of) coccus [staphylococcal]: also **-coc′cic** (-sik)

coc·ci (käk′sī) *pl. of* COCCUS

coc·cid (käk′sid) *n.* [< ModL. *Coccidae*, name of the family < Gr. *kokkis*, dim. of *kokkos*, berry] any of a family (*Coccidae*) of scale insects

coc·cid·i·oi·do·my·co·sis (käk sid′ē oi′dō mī kō′sis) *n.* [< ModL. *Coccidioid(es immitis)*, name of the genus + -o- + MYCOSIS] an infectious disease of man and animals, caused by a fungus (*Coccidioides immitis*) and characterized by respiratory difficulties, fever, and skin eruptions

coc·cid·i·o·sis (-ē ō′sis) *n.* [ModL. < *coccidium*, little berry + -OSIS] any of various diseases of domestic animals, birds, and, rarely, man, caused by members of an order (*Coccidia*) of sporozoans living as parasites in the intestines

coc·cif·er·ous (käk sif′ər əs) *adj.* [< L. *cocci*, pl. of *coccum* < Gr. *kokkos* (see COCCUS) + -FEROUS] producing berries

-coc·coid (käk′oid) *a combining form meaning* like a (specified kind of) coccus [staphylococcoid]

coc·co·lith (käk′ə lith′) *n.* [< ModL. *coccus* (see COCCUS) + -LITH] a minute calcareous plate covering the body of some floating marine organisms

coc·cus (käk′əs) *n.*, *pl.* **coc·ci** (käk′sī) [ModL. < Gr. *kokkos*, a kernel, seed, berry] **1.** a bacterium of a spherical shape **2.** any of the carpels into which compound fruits split when ripe: it contains a single seed —**coc′coid** *adj.*

-coc·cus (käk′əs) *a terminal combining form meaning* coccus: used in names of various bacteria [gonococcus]

coc·cyx (käk′siks) *n.*, *pl.* **coc·cy·ges** (käk sī′jēz) [L., cuckoo < Gr. *kokkyx*: so called because shaped like a cuckoo's beak] a small, triangular bone at the lower end of the vertebral column, formed by the fusion of four rudimentary vertebrae and articulating with the sacrum —**coc·cyg′e·al** (-sij′ē əl) *adj.*

Co·cha·bam·ba (kō′ohä bäm′bä) city in C. Bolivia: pop. 95,000

Co·chin (kō′chin; *for n.,* also käch′in) former native state of SW India: merged with Travancore, 1949 —*n.* [*also* c-] [< *Cochin China*, place of origin] any of an Asiatic breed of large domestic fowl with black, buff, white, or gray plumage and thickly feathered legs: also **Cochin China**

Cochin China, Cochin-China region & former Fr. colony in S Indochina: since 1949, a part of South Vietnam

coch·i·neal (käch′ə nēl′) *n.* [Fr. *cochenille* < It. *cocciniglia* < L. *coccinus*, scarlet-colored < *coccum*, a berry, scarlet: see COCCUS] a red dye made from the dried bodies of female cochineal insects: used, esp. formerly, in coloring foods and cosmetics and as a dye

cochineal insect a scale insect (*Dactylopius coccus*) having a brilliant red body fluid and feeding on opuntia cactus: found chiefly in Mexico and formerly much used as a source of cochineal

coch·le·a (käk′lē ə) *n.*, *pl.* **-le·ae** (-ē′), **-le·as** [L. < Gr. *kochlias*, snail, snail shell < *kochlos*, shellfish] the spiral-shaped part of the internal ear, containing the auditory nerve endings —**coch′le·ar** (-ər) *adj.*

coch·le·ate (-it, -āt′) *adj.* [L. *cochleatus*, spiral-shaped: see prec.] shaped like the shell of a snail: also **coch′le·at′ed**

cock[1] (käk) *n.* [ME. *cok* < OE. & OFr. *coc*, like Dan. *kok*, ON. *kokr*, of echoic orig.] **1.** *a)* the male of the chicken; rooster *b)* the male of certain other birds **2.** [Archaic] *a)* the crowing of a rooster, esp. at sunrise *b)* cockcrow **3.** a woodcock **4.** a weather vane in the shape of a rooster; weathercock **5.** a leader or chief, esp. one with some boldness or arrogance **6.** a faucet or valve for regulating the flow of a liquid or gas **7.** *a)* the hammer of a firearm *b)* the position of such a hammer when set for firing **8.** a tilting or turning upward, as of the eye **9.** a jaunty, erect position [the *cock* of a hat] —*vt.* **1.** to tilt or set (a hat, etc.) jauntily on one side **2.** to raise to an erect position [a dog *cocks* his ears] **3.** to turn (the eye or ear) toward something **4.** *a)* to set the hammer of (a gun) in firing position *b)* to set (a tripping device, as for the shutter of a camera) ready to be released **5.** to draw back (one's fist, arm, etc.) ready to strike —*vi.* **1.** to assume an erect or tilted position **2.** [Archaic] to behave in a cocky way; strut

cock[2] (käk) *n.* [ME. *cokke*, akin to ON. *køkkr*, Dan. *kok*, a pile < IE. base **guga*, a hump, ball: see COCKBOAT] a small, cone-shaped pile, as of hay —*vt.* to pile (hay, etc.) in cocks

cock·ade (kä kād′) *n.* [Fr. *cocarde* < *coq*, a cock: from resemblance to its comb] a rosette, knot of ribbon, etc., worn on the hat as a badge —**cock·ad′ed** *adj.*

cock-a-doo·dle-doo (käk′ə dōo′d'l dōo′) *n.* [echoic] a *conventionalized term* for the crow of a rooster

cock-a-hoop (käk′ə hōop′) *adj.* [Fr. *coq à huppe*, cock with a crest] **1.** in very high spirits; elated; exultant **2.** boastful; conceited

Cock·aigne (kä kān′) [ME. *cokaygne* < OFr. (*pais de*) *cocaigne*, (land of) sugar cake < MLowG. *kokenje*, sugar cake, cookie < *koke*, cake; akin to CAKE, G. *kuchen*, cake] an imaginary land of luxurious and idle living

cock-a-leek·ie (käk′ə lē′kē) *n.* [var. of *cocky-leeky* < *cocky*, dim. of COCK[1] + *leeky*, dim. of LEEK] [Scot.] a soup made by boiling chicken with leeks

cock·a·lo·rum (käk′ə lôr′əm) *n.* [pseudo L. extension of COCK[1]; infl. by Du. *kockeloeren*, to crow] **1.** a little man with an exaggerated idea of his own importance **2.** boastful talk; crowing

☆**cock·a·ma·mie** (käk′ə mā′mē) *adj.* [alteration of DECALCOMANIA, prob. infl. by *cock-a-nee-nee*, 19th-c. name in New York for a cheap molasses candy] [Slang] of poor quality; inferior: a generalized epithet of disapproval

cock-and-bull story (käk′'n bool′) [for earlier *cockalane* < Fr. *coq à l'âne*, lit., (to jump from) the cock to the donkey] an absurd, improbable story

cock·a·teel, cock·a·tiel (käk′ə tēl′) *n.* [Du. *kaketielje*, dim. of *kaketoc*: see ff.] a small, crested, Australian parrot (*Nymphicus hollandicus*) with a long tail and yellow head

cock·a·too (käk′ə tōo′, käk′ə tōo′) *n.*, *pl.* **-toos′** [Du. *kaketoe* < Malay *kakatua*; prob. echoic in origin, but < ? *kakak*, brother, sister + *tua*, old; sp. infl. by COCK[1]] any of a number of crested parrots (esp. genus *Kakatoe*) of Australia and the East Indies, usually with predominantly white plumage, often tinged with yellow or pink

cock·a·trice (käk′ə tris′) *n.* [ME. & OFr. *cocatrice* < L. **calcatrix* < L. *calcare*, to tread < *calx*, the heel] **1.** a fabulous serpent supposedly hatched from a cock's egg and having power to kill by a look **2.** *Bible* an unidentified deadly serpent

cock·boat (käk′bōt′) *n.* [ME. *cokbote* < *cok*, ship's boat (< Anglo-Fr. *coque* < or akin to MDu. *kogge*, ME. *cog*, OE. *cogg*[3] < IE. base **gugā*, a ball, rounded object < **gēu-*, to bend, arch, whence COCK[2], CUDGEL) + *bote*, BOAT] a small boat, esp. one used as a ship's tender

COCKATOO
(12–20 in. long)

cock·chaf·er (-chāf′ər) *n.* [COCK[1] (? because of size) + ME. *chafer*, a beetle < OE. *ceafor* < Gmc. base **kevra-*, gnawer (whence G. *käfer*) < IE. base **ĝebh-*, jaw, mouth, whence ON. *kjaptr*, CHAP[1], JOWL[1]] any of several large European beetles (family Melolonthidae) whose grubs live in the soil and feed on the roots of plants

Cock·croft (kō′krôft, käk′rôft), Sir **John Douglas** 1897– 1967; Eng. nuclear physicist

cock·crow (käk′krō′) *n.* the time when roosters begin to crow; early morning; dawn: also **cock′crow′ing**

cocked hat **1.** a three-cornered hat with a turned-up brim **2.** a hat pointed in front and in back and with the crown rising to a point —**knock into a cocked hat** [Slang] to damage or spoil completely; ruin

cock·er[1] (käk′ər) *n.* **1.** *same as* COCKER SPANIEL **2.** a person who breeds or trains fighting cocks

cock·er[2] (-ər) *vt.* [ME. *cokeren* < ?] to coddle; pamper

cock·er·el (käk′ər əl, käk′rəl) *n.* [dim. of COCK[1]] a young rooster, less than a year old

cocker spaniel [from its use in hunting woodcock] any of a breed of small spaniels with a compact body, short legs, long, silky hair, and long, drooping ears

cock·eye (-ī′) *n.* [COCK[1], *vi.* + EYE] a squinting eye

cock·eyed (-īd′) *adj.* **1.** cross-eyed **2.** [Slang] *a)* tilted to one side; crooked; awry *b)* silly; ridiculous; foolish *c)* drunk

cock·fight (-fīt′) *n.* a fight between gamecocks, usually wearing metal spurs on the legs, staged as a spectacle: illegal in the U.S. —**cock′fight′ing** *n.*

cock·horse (-hôrs′) *n.* [16th c., toy horse] *same as* ROCKING HORSE or HOBBYHORSE (sense 2)

cock·i·ly (käk′'l ē) *adv.* in a cocky manner

cock·i·ness (-ē nis) *n.* the quality of being cocky

cock·le[1] (käk′'l) *n.* [ME. *cokel* < OFr. *coquille*, a blister, shell, cockle, altered (after *coque*, COCK[1]) < L. *conchylium* < Gr. *konchylion*, shellfish < *konchē*: see CONCH] **1.** any of various shellfish with two heart-shaped, radially ridged shells, as the common, edible European species (*Cardium edule*) **2.** a cockleshell **3.** a wrinkle; pucker —*vi.*, *vt.* **-led, -ling** [Fr. *coquiller* < the *n.*] to wrinkle; pucker —**cockles of one's heart** [prob. < L. *coclea*, winding cavity, lit., snail: see COCHLEA] one's deepest feelings or emotions

cock·le[2] (käk′'l) *n.* [ME. *cokkel* < OE. *coccel*, darnel, tares] any of various weeds that grow in grainfields, as the corn cockle

☆**cock·le·bur** (-bur′) *n.* any of a genus (*Xanthium*) of coarse plants of the composite family, bearing closed burs and growing commonly as a weed

cock·le·shell (käk′'l shel′) *n.* **1.** the shell of a cockle **2.** loosely, a scallop shell, etc. **3.** a small, shallow, lightweight boat

cock·loft (käk′lôft′) *n.* [orig., lit. or fig., a loft where cocks roost] a small loft, attic, or garret

cock·ney (käk′nē) *n., pl.* **-neys** [ME. *cokenei*, spoiled child, milksop; understood as *coken-ey*, lit., cock's egg < *coken* (OE. *cocena*, gen. pl.), of cocks + *ey* (OE. *æg*), egg; ? infl. by Fr. *acquiné*, idle, spoiled (< *coquin*, rascal)] **1.** [*often* **C-**] a native of the East End of London, England, traditionally one born within sound of the bells of St. Mary-le-Bow (Bow Bells) and speaking a characteristic dialect **2.** this dialect, characterized by extreme diphthongization, loss of initial *h*, and use of an intrusive *r*: also **cock′ney·ese′** (-ēz′) **3.** loosely, any native or inhabitant of London: a humorous or disparaging usage —*adj.* of or like cockneys or their dialect —**cock′ney·ish** *adj.*

cock·ney·fy (käk′ni fi′) *vt.* **-fied′, -fy′ing** to give a cockney quality to (one's speech, manner, etc.)

cock·ney·ism (-nē iz'm) *n.* an idiom, pronunciation, quality, etc. characteristic of cockneys

cock of the walk a dominating person in any group, esp. an overbearing one

cock·pit (käk′pit′) *n.* **1.** an enclosed space for cockfighting **2.** a place where there have been many battles **3.** in small decked vessels, a sunken space toward the stern used by the steersman, etc. **4.** the space in a small airplane for the pilot and, sometimes, passengers, or in a large airplane for the pilot and copilot or crew **5.** formerly, the quarters of junior officers on a warship, used as a station for the wounded in battle **6.** [Obs.] the pit of a theater

cock·roach (-rōch′) *n.* [Sp. *cucaracha*, wood louse, cockroach, altered after COCK[1] + ROACH] any of an order (Blattaria) of insects with long feelers and a flat, soft body: some species are common household pests

cocks·comb (käks′kōm′) *n.* **1.** the red, fleshy growth on the head of a rooster **2.** *same as* COXCOMB **3.** an ornamental plant (*Celosia argentea*) of the amaranth family, with red or yellow flower heads somewhat like a rooster's crest

cock·shut (käk′shut′) *n.* [Obs. or Brit. Dial.] evening twilight

cock·shy (-shi′) *n., pl.* **-shies** [COCK[1] + SHY[2]] **1.** a throw at a mark **2.** the mark aimed at

COCKROACH
(to 1 1/2 in. long)

cock·spur (-spur′) *n.* **1.** the spur of a rooster **2.** a hawthorn (*Crataegus crusgalli*) of the rose family, having long thorns

cock·sure (-shoor′, -shur′) *adj.* [COCK[1] (cf. COCKY) + SURE] **1.** absolutely sure or certain **2.** sure or self-confident in a stubborn or overbearing way —**cock′sure′ness** *n.*

cock·swain (käk′s'n, -swān′) *n. same as* COXSWAIN

cock·tail (-tāl′) *n.* [< ?; various hypotheses in H. L. Mencken, *Am. Lang., Suppl. I,* p. 257; for senses 3 & 4, < COCK[1], *vi.* + TAIL[1]] ☆**1.** any of various alcoholic drinks made of a distilled liquor mixed with a wine, fruit juice, etc. and usually iced ☆**2.** an appetizer served at the beginning of a meal, as fruit juice, tomato juice, diced fruits, or seafood with a sharp sauce **3.** a horse with a docked tail **4.** a horse of impure breed

☆**cocktail table** a low table for serving refreshments, etc., esp. in a living room

cock·y (käk′ē) *adj.* **cock′i·er, cock′i·est** [< COCK[1] + -Y[2]] [Colloq.] jauntily conceited or overbearing; self-confident in an aggressive or swaggering way

co·co (kō′kō) *n., pl.* **-cos** [Sp. & Port. < L. *coccum*, a seed, kernel < Gr. *kokkos*, a berry] **1.** the coconut palm tree **2.** its fruit; coconut —*adj.* made of the fiber from coconut husks

co·coa (kō′kō) *n.* [Sp. & Port. *cacao* < Nahuatl *cacauatl*] **1.** powder made from cacao seeds that have been roasted and ground, with some of the fat removed; pulverized chocolate **2.** a drink made by adding sugar and hot water or milk to this powder **3.** a reddish-yellow brown

cocoa butter a yellowish-white fat prepared from cacao seeds: used in pharmacy and in making cosmetics

co·co·nut, co·coa·nut (kō′kə nut′) *n.* the fruit of the coconut palm, consisting of a thick, fibrous, brown, oval husk under which there is a thin, hard shell enclosing a layer of edible white meat: the hollow center is filled with a sweet, milky fluid called **coconut milk**

coconut oil oil obtained from the dried meat of coconuts, used for making soap, as an edible fat, etc.

coconut palm (or **tree**) a tall tree (*Cocos nucifera*) of the palm family, that bears coconuts and grows throughout the tropics: also **coco palm**

co·coon (kə kōōn′) *n.* [Fr. *cocon* < Pr. *coucoun*, egg shell, dim. < *coca*, shell-like container < ML. *coco*, shell, hull] **1.** the silky or fibrous case which the larvae of certain insects spin

COCONUT

about themselves to shelter them during the pupa stage **2.** any protective cover like this, as the egg capsule of certain spiders, leeches, etc. **3.** any cover used to waterproof or protect something, esp. military equipment for transport or storage

COCOON

Co·cos Islands (kō′kōs) group of small coral islands in the Indian Ocean, south of Sumatra: a territory administered by Australia: 5 1/2 sq. mi.; pop. 700

co·cotte (kō′kät′, kə kät′) *n.* [Fr., orig., hen < *coq*, cock] a woman who is sexually promiscuous

co·co·zel·le (kō′kə zel′ē, -zel′) *n.* [< It. dial. dim. of It. *cocuzza*, squash, gourd < LL. *cucutia*] a variety of summer squash similar to the zucchini, with club-shaped fruits

Coc·teau (kôk tō′), **Jean** (zhän) 1891–1963; Fr. poet, novelist, & playwright

Co·cy·tus (kō sīt′əs) [L. < Gr. *Kōkytos*, lit., a shrieking, wailing < *kōkyein*, to wail] *Gr. Myth.* the river of wailing, a tributary of the Acheron in Hades

cod[1] (käd) *n., pl.* **cod, cods:** see PLURAL, II, D, 2 [ME., < ? ff., in reference to shape] any of a family (Gadidae) of food fishes of northern seas, important as a source of cod-liver oil, esp. any of a genus (*Gadus*) with firm flesh and soft fins, found off the coast of Newfoundland and Norway

cod[2] (käd) *n.* [ME. < OE. *codd*, akin to ON. *koddi*, cushion < IE. base *geut- < *geu-*, to bend, arch, whence CUD, COT[2], L. *guttur*, throat] **1.** [Archaic] a bag **2.** [Dial.] a pod; husk **3.** [Obs.] the scrotum

Cod., cod. *pl.* **Codd., codd.** codex

C.O.D., c.o.d. **1.** cash on delivery **2.** collect on delivery

Cod (käd), **Cape** hook-shaped peninsula in E Mass., extending from Buzzards Bay to Provincetown: 65 mi. long

co·da (kō′də) *n.* [It. < L. *cauda*, a tail] *Music* a passage formally ending a composition or section

cod·dle (käd′'l) *vt.* **-dled, -dling** [prob. < CAUDLE] **1.** to cook (esp. eggs) gently by heating in water not quite at boiling temperature **2.** to treat (an invalid, baby, etc.) tenderly

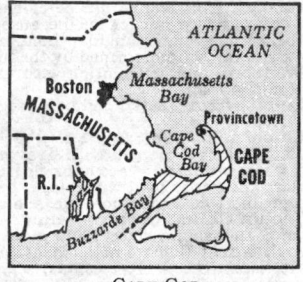
CAPE COD

code (kōd) *n.* [ME. & OFr. < L. *codex* (earlier *caudex*), wooden tablet for writing (hence, book: in LL.(Ec.), code of laws), orig., tree trunk, wood split into tablets, prob. < *cudere, *caudere,* to strike < IE. base,*kau-*, whence HEW] **1.** a body of laws, as of a nation, city, etc., arranged systematically for easy reference **2.** any set of principles or rules of conduct [a moral *code*] **3.** *a*) a set of signals representing letters or numerals, used in sending messages, as by telegraph, flags, heliograph, etc. *b*) a set of signals that determines the pattern of growth, behavior, etc. [the genetic *code* in DNA molecules] **4.** *a*) a system of symbols used in secret writing, information processing, etc., in which letters, figures, etc. are arbitrarily given certain meanings *b*) the symbols used in such a system —*vt.* **cod′ed, cod′ing** to put in the form or symbols of a code —**cod′er** *n.*

co·dec·li·na·tion (kō′dek li nā′shən) *n. Astron. same as* POLAR DISTANCE

co·de·fend·ant (kō′di fen′dənt) *n.* a joint defendant

co·deine (kō′dēn, -dē in) *n.* [< Gr. *kōdeia*, poppy head + -INE[4]] an alkaloid, $C_{18}H_{21}N \cdot H_2O$, derived from opium and resembling morphine, but milder in its action and less habit-forming: used for the relief of pain and in cough medicines: also **co′dein, co·de·ia** (kō dē′ə)

‡**Code Na·po·lé·on** (kōd nå pô lã ōn′) [Fr.] the Napoleonic code, the body of French civil law enacted in 1804: the model for the civil codes of many nations

co·dex (kō′deks) *n., pl.* **co·di·ces** (kō′də sēz′, käd′ə-) [L.: see CODE] **1.** orig., a code, or body of laws **2.** a manuscript volume, esp. of the Scriptures or of a classic text

Codex Ju·ris Ca·no·ni·ci (yoor′is kə nō′ni chē) [L., Code of Canon Law] the official body of laws governing the Roman Catholic Church since 1918: superseded the CORPUS JURIS CANONICI

cod·fish (käd′fish′) *n., pl.* **-fish′, -fish′es:** see FISH[2] same as COD[1]

codg·er (käj′ər) *n.* [prob. var. of CADGER] [Colloq.] a queer or eccentric, esp. elderly, fellow

cod·i·cil (käd′i s'l, -sil′) *n.* [ME. < L. *codicillus*, dim. of *codex*: see CODE] **1.** *Law* an addition to a will to change, explain, revoke, or add provisions **2.** an appendix or supplement —**cod′i·cil′la·ry** (-sil′ər ē) *adj.*

cod·i·fy (käd′ə fī′, kō′də-) *vt.* **-fied′, -fy′ing** [see CODE + -FY] to arrange (laws, rules, etc.) systematically —**cod′i·fi·ca′tion** (-fi kā′shən) *n.* —**cod′i·fi′er** (-fī′ər) *n.*

cod·ling[1] (käd′lin) *n., pl.* **-ling, -lings:** see PLURAL, II, D, 2 [COD[1] + -LING[1]] **1.** a young cod **2.** *same as* HAKE (sense 2)

cod·ling[2] (käd′lin) *n.* [earlier *querdling*, altered (after suffix -LING[1]) < Anglo-Fr. *querdelyon* < Fr. *coeur de lion*, lit., heart of lion] **1.** a variety of elongated apple **2.** a small, unripe apple Also **cod′lin** (-lin)

codling (or **codlin**) **moth** a nearly cosmopolitan small moth (*Carpocapsa pomonella*) whose larva bores into and destroys apples, pears, quinces, etc.

cod-liv·er oil (käd′liv′ər) oil obtained from the liver of the cod and related fishes: it is rich in vitamins A & D and is used in medicine to treat various diseases

☆**co·don** (kō′dän) *n.* [COD(E) + -*on*, as in PROTON] a small group of chemical units, believed to be a sequence of three nucleotides, which codes the incorporation of a specific amino acid into a protein molecule during the synthesis of the protein: codons are present in DNA and RNA

cod·piece (käd′pēs′) *n.* [COD[2] + PIECE] a bag or flap fastened over the front opening in the tight breeches worn by men in the 15th and 16th cent.

Co·dy (kō′dē), **William Frederick** 1846–1917; U.S. plainsman, frontier scout, & showman: called *Buffalo Bill*

☆**co·ed, co-ed** (kō′ed′) *n.* [Colloq.] a girl attending a coeducational college or university —*adj.* [Colloq.] **1.** coeducational **2.** of or having to do with a coed

☆**co·ed·u·ca·tion** (kō′ej ə kā′shən) *n.* [CO- + EDUCATION] the educational system in which students of both sexes are free to attend classes together —**co′ed·u·ca′tion·al** *adj.* —**co′ed·u·ca′tion·al·ly** *adv.*

coef., coeff. coefficient

co·ef·fi·cient (kō′ə fish′ənt) *n.* [CO- + EFFICIENT] **1.** a factor that contributes to produce a result **2.** *Math.* a number or algebraic symbol prefixed as a multiplier to a variable or unknown quantity [6 is a *coefficient* in 6*ab*, *x* is a *coefficient* in $x(y + z)$] **3.** *Physics* a number, constant for a given substance, used as a multiplier in measuring the change in some property of the substance under given conditions [the *coefficient* of expansion]

coe·la·canth (sē′lə kanth′) *n.* [ModL. *Coelacanthus*, name of the genus < Gr. *koilos* (see ff.) + *akantha*, thorn, point] any of an order (Coelacanthini) of primitive marine fishes, possibly ancestors to land animals: known only in fossil form until the discovery of a few living specimens in recent times

-coele, -coel (sēl) [< Gr. *koilia*, body cavity < *koilos*, hollow < IE. base see CAVE[1]] *a combining form meaning* cavity, chamber of the body, chamber of an organ [*blasto-coele*]

coe·len·ter·ate (si len′tə rāt′, -tər it) *n.* [< Gr. *Coelenterata*, name of the phylum < *coelenteron*: see ff.] any of a phylum (Coelenterata) of invertebrate animals, mainly marine, including the hydroids, jellyfishes, sea anemones, and corals, in which the characteristic structure is a cavity that functions in both digestion and circulation and has but a single opening

coe·len·ter·on (-tə rän′) *n., pl.* **-ter·a** (-rə) [ModL. < Gr. *koilos* (see -COELE) + *enteron*, intestine] the internal body cavity of coelenterates, flatworms, etc.

coe·li·ac (sē′lē ak′) *adj.* [L. *coeliacus* < Gr. *koiliakos* < *koilia*: see -COELE] *same as* CELIAC

coe·lom (sē′ləm) *n.* [Gr. *koiloma* < *koilos*: see -COELE] the main body cavity of most higher multicellular animals, in which the visceral organs are suspended

coe·lo·stat (sē′lə stat′) *n.* [< L. *caelum*, sky, heavens + -STAT] a moving mirror mounted on an axis parallel to the earth's axis of rotation and driven by clockwork so as to reflect the same portion of the sky continuously into a fixed telescope

coe·nes·the·sia (sē′nis thē′zhə, -zhē ə; sen′is-) *n.* [ModL. < Gr. *koinos*, common + *aisthēsis*, feeling] *Psychol.* the mass of undifferentiated sensations that make one aware of the body and its condition, as in the feeling of health, illness, discomfort, etc.: also **coe′nes·the′sis** (-sis)

coe·no- (sē′nə, sen′ə) [< Gr. *koinos*, common < *komios* < IE. base *kom*, with, beside, whence L. *cum*: cf. COMMON] *a combining form meaning* common [*coenocyte*]: also, before a vowel, **coen-**

coe·no·bite (sē′nə bīt′, sen′ə-) *n. same as* CENOBITE

coe·no·cyte (-sīt′) *n.* [COENO- + -CYTE] **1.** *same as* SYN-CYTIUM **2.** *a)* a mass of protoplasm containing several nuclei formed from an original cell with one nucleus *b)* an organism consisting of such a mass

coe·no·sarc (sē′nə särk′) *n.* [COENO- + Gr. *sarx* (gen. *sarkos*), flesh] the fleshy portion of the stalks and stolons of hydroids, which secretes the perisarc

coe·nu·rus (si nyoor′əs) *n., pl.* **-ri** (-ī) [ModL. < COEN- + -URUS] the compound larva of any of certain tapeworms, esp. one that attacks the brains of sheep, causing any of various diseases, as the staggers

co·en·zyme (kō en′zīm) *n.* an organic substance of low molecular weight that is not protein and that can unite with a given protein (*apoenzyme*) to form an active enzyme system

co·e·qual (-ē′kwəl) *adj., n.* equal —**co′e·qual′i·ty** (-i kwäl′ə tē) *n.* —**co·e′qual·ly** *adv.*

co·erce (kō urs′) *vt.* **-erced′, -erc′ing** [ME. *cohercen* < OFr. *cohercier* < L. *coercere*, to surround, restrain < *co-*, together + *arcere*, to confine] **1.** to restrain or constrain by force, esp. by legal authority; curb **2.** to force or compel to do something **3.** to bring about by using force; enforce — SYN. see FORCE —**co·er′ci·ble** *adj.* —**co·er′ci·bly** *adv.*

co·er·cion (kō ur′shən, -zhən) *n.* [L. *coercio*] **1.** the act or power of coercing **2.** government by force

co·er·cive (-siv) *adj.* of coercion or tending to coerce —**co·er′cive·ly** *adv.* —**co·er′cive·ness** *n.*

☆**coes·ite** (kō′sīt) *n.* [after Loring Coes, Jr. (1915–), U.S. chemist who synthesized it (c. 1957) + -ITE[1]] a dense variety of silica produced under very great pressure and found in the sandstone of large meteor craters

co·es·sen·tial (kō′i sen′shəl) *adj.* having one and the same essence or nature —**co′es·sen′tial·ly** *adv.*

co·e·ta·ne·ous (-i tā′nē əs) *adj.* [L. *coaetaneus* < *co-*, with + *aetas*, age] contemporary; coeval

co·e·ter·nal (-i tur′n'l) *adj.* existing together eternally — **co′e·ter′ni·ty** (-nə tē) *n.* —**co′e·ter′nal·ly** *adv.*

co·e·val (-ē′v'l) *adj.* [< LL.(Ec.) *coaevus* < L. *co-*, together + *aevum*, age + -AL] of the same age or period; contemporary —*n.* a contemporary —SYN. see CONTEMPORARY —**co′e′val·ly** *adv.*

co·ex·ec·u·tor (-ig zek′yoo tər) *n.* a person acting as executor jointly with another

co·ex·ist (-ig zist′) *vi.* **1.** to exist together, at the same time, or in the same place **2.** to live together without hostility or conflict despite differences, as in political systems —**co′ex·ist′ence** *n.* —**co′ex·ist′ent** *adj.*

co·ex·tend (-ik stend′) *vt., vi.* to extend equally in space or time —**co′ex·ten′sion** (-ik sten′shən) *n.*

co·ex·ten·sive (-ik sten′siv) *adj.* having the same extent in time or space —**co′ex·ten′sive·ly** *adv.*

C. of C. Chamber of Commerce

cof·fee (kôf′ē, käf′-) *n.* see PLURAL, II, D, 3 [It. *caffè* < Turk. *qahwe* < Ar. *qahwa*, coffee, orig., wine] **1.** a dark-brown aromatic drink made by brewing in water the roasted and ground beanlike seeds of a tall tropical shrub (genus *Coffea*) of the madder family **2.** these seeds, found in the red berries of the shrub: also **coffee beans 3.** the shrub itself **4.** the color of coffee containing milk or cream; brown

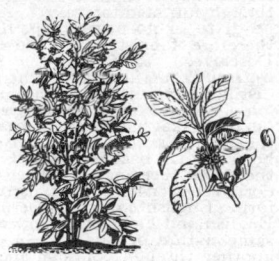

COFFEE
(plant, 5–10 ft. high; branch; berry)

☆**coffee break** a brief respite from work when coffee or other refreshment is usually taken

☆**cof·fee·cake** (-kāk′) *n.* a kind of cake or roll, often containing nuts, raisins, etc. or coated with sugar or icing, to be eaten with coffee or the like

cof·fee·house (-hous′) *n.* a place where coffee and other refreshments are served and people gather for conversation, entertainment, etc.

☆**coffee klatch** (or **klatsch**) *same as* KAFFEEKLATSCH

coffee mill a machine for grinding roasted coffee beans

☆**coffee nut 1.** *same as* KENTUCKY COFFEE TREE **2.** the fruit of this tree

cof·fee·pot (-pät′) *n.* a container with a lid and a spout, in which coffee is made or served

coffee shop an informal restaurant, as in a hotel, where light refreshments or meals are served

☆**coffee table** a low table, like a cocktail table, usually in a living room, for serving refreshments

coffee tree 1. any tree or shrub that produces coffee beans ☆**2.** *same as* KENTUCKY COFFEE TREE

cof·fer (kôf′ər, käf′-) *n.* [ME. < OFr. *cofre*, a chest < L. *cophinus*: see COFFIN] **1.** a chest or strongbox in which money or valuables are kept **2.** [*pl.*] a treasury; funds **3.** a decorative sunken panel in a vault, dome, ceiling, etc. **4.** a cofferdam **5.** a lock in a canal —*vt.* **1.** to enclose in a coffer or chest **2.** to furnish with decorative sunken panels

cof·fer·dam (-dam′) *n.* [prec. + DAM[1]] **1.** a watertight temporary structure in a river, lake, etc., for keeping the water from an enclosed area that has been pumped dry so that bridge foundations, dams, etc. may be constructed **2.** a watertight box or chamber attached to the side of a ship so that repairs can be made below the waterline

cof·fin (kôf′in, käf′-) *n.* [ME. & OFr. *cofin*, basket, coffer < L. *cophinus* < Gr. *kophinos*, a basket] **1.** the case or box in which a dead body is buried **2.** the horny part of a horse's hoof —*vt.* to put into or as if into a coffin

coffin bone the foot bone inside the hoof of a horse or other similar animal

☆**coffin corner** [radio slang, prob. with reference to the grave of the defending team's hopes] any of the corners of a football field formed by a goal line and side line: punts

are often directed to a coffin corner so that the ball will roll out of bounds near the opponent's goal line

☆**coffin nail** [Old Slang] a cigarette

cof·fle (kôf′'l, käf′-) *n.* [Ar. *qāfila,* caravan] a group of animals or slaves fastened together in a line, or driven along together —☆*vt.* **-fled, -fling** to fasten together in or as in a coffle

C. of S. Chief of Staff

cog[1] (käg) *n.* [ME. *cog, cogge* < Scand., as in Norw. *kug,* Sw. *kugge,* a cog, tooth] **1.** *a)* any of a series of teeth on the rim of a wheel, for transmitting or receiving motion by fitting between the teeth of another wheel; gear tooth *b)* a cogwheel ☆**2.** [Colloq.] a person or thing regarded as a minor part of the entire machinery of an activity, business, etc. —**cogged** *adj.*

cog[2] (käg) *n.* [altered (after prec.) < earlier *cock,* to secure, prob. ult. < It. *cocca,* a notch] a projection on a beam that fits into a corresponding groove or notch in another beam, making a joint —*vt., vi.* **cogged, cog′ging** to join by a cog or cogs

cog[3] (käg) *vt.* **cogged, cog′ging** [prob. slang extension of COG[1]] to manipulate (dice) in a fraudulent manner —*vi.* [Obs.] to cheat; swindle —*n.* [Obs.] a deception; trick

cog. cognate

co·gen·cy (kō′jən sē) *n.* [ML. *cogencia*] the quality or condition of being cogent; power to convince

co·gent (-jənt) *adj.* [L. *cogens,* prp. of *cogere,* to collect < *co-,* together + *agere,* to drive] forceful and to the point, as a reason or argument; compelling; convincing —*SYN.* see VALID —**co′gent·ly** *adv.*

cog·i·tate (käj′ə tāt′) *vi., vt.* **-tat′ed, -tat′ing** [< L. *cogitatus,* pp. of *cogitare* < **coagitare:* see CO- & AGITATE] to think seriously and deeply (about); ponder; meditate; consider —*SYN.* see THINK[1] —**cog′i·ta·ble** (-i tə b'l) *adj.* —**cog′i·ta′tion** *n.* —**cog′i·ta′tor** *n.*

cog·i·ta·tive (käj′ə tāt′iv) *adj.* [ME. *cogitatif* < LL. *cogitativus*] **1.** capable of cogitating **2.** tending to cogitate; thoughtful; meditative

‡**co·gi·to er·go sum** (käj′ə tō′ ɛr′gō sum′) [L.] I think, therefore I exist: the basic tenet of the philosophy of Descartes

co·gnac (kōn′yak, kän′-, kôn′-) *n.* [Fr.] **1.** a French brandy distilled from wine in the area of Cognac, France **2.** loosely, any French brandy or any brandy

cog·nate (käg′nāt) *adj.* [L. *cognatus,* related by birth < *co-,* together + *gnatus,* pp. of *gnasci,* older form of *nasci,* to be born: for IE. base see GENUS] **1.** related by family; having the same ancestor **2.** related through common ancestry, derivation, or borrowing; derived from a common original form [English *apple* and German *apfel* are *cognate* words, English and Flemish are *cognate* languages] **3.** having the same nature or quality —*n.* **1.** *a)* a person related to another through common ancestry *b)* a relative on the mother's side **2.** a cognate word, language, or thing —*SYN.* see RELATED

cog·na·tion (käg nā′shən) *n.* [ME. *cognacioun* < L. *cognatio:* see prec.] relationship by descent from the same ancestor or source

cog·ni·tion (käg nish′ən) *n.* [ME. *cognicioun* < L. *cognito,* knowledge < *cognitus,* pp. of *cognoscere,* to know < *co-,* together + *gnoscere,* KNOW] **1.** the process of knowing in the broadest sense, including perception, memory, judgment, etc. **2.** the result of such a process; perception, conception, etc. —**cog·ni′tion·al** *adj.* —**cog′ni·tive** (-nə tiv) *adj.*

cog·ni·za·ble (käg′ni zə b'l, käg ni′-; *occas.* kän′zə-) *adj.* [COGNIZ(E) + -ABLE] **1.** that can be known or perceived **2.** *Law* within the jurisdiction of a court

cog·ni·zance (käg′nə zəns; *occas.* kän′zə-) *n.* [ME. *cognisaunce* < OFr. *conoissance,* knowledge < *conoissant,* prp. of *conoistre,* to know < L. *cognoscere:* see COGNITION] **1.** perception or knowledge; esp., the range of knowledge possible through observation **2.** official observation of or authority over something **3.** *Heraldry* a distinguishing crest or mark **4.** *Law a)* the hearing of a case in court *b)* the right or power of dealing with a matter judicially; jurisdiction —**take cognizance of** to notice or recognize

cog·ni·zant (-zənt) *adj.* having cognizance; aware or informed (*of* something) —*SYN.* see AWARE

cog·nize (käg′nīz, käg nīz′) *vt.* **-nized, -niz·ing** [back-formation < COGNIZANCE] to take cognizance of; notice

cog·no·men (käg nō′mən) *n., pl.* **-no′mens, -nom′i·na** (-näm′i nə) [L. < *co-,* with + *nomen,* NAME: sp. infl. by assoc. with **gnomen* < Gr. *gnōma,* mark, token, akin to L. *gnoscere,* KNOW] **1.** the third or family name of an ancient Roman (Ex.: Marcus Tullius *Cicero*) **2.** any family name; surname; last name **3.** any name; esp., a nickname —**cog·nom′i·nal** (-näm′i n'l) *adj.*

co·gno·scen·te (kō′nyō shen′tā) *n., pl.* **-ti** (-tē) [It., orig. prp. of *conoscere,* to know < L. *cognoscere:* see COGNITION] a person with special knowledge in some field, esp. in the fine arts; expert

cog·nos·ci·ble (käg näs′ə b'l) *adj.* [LL. *cognoscibilis* < L. *cognoscere:* see COGNITION] [Rare] that can be known or perceived; cognizable

cog·no·vit (käg nō′vit) *n.* [short for L. *cognovit actionem,* lit., he has acknowledged the action] *Law* a written clause contained in a note or other instrument by which a debtor authorizes any attorney to enter judgment on the debt without a formal trial

co·gon (kə gōn′) *n.* [Sp. *cogón* < Tagalog name] any of several tall, coarse grasses (genus *Imperata*), esp. a grass (*Imperata cylindrica*) of the Philippines, used for forage and thatching

cog railway a railway for a very steep grade with traction supplied by a central cogged rail that meshes with a cog-wheel on the engine

cog·wheel (käg′hwēl′, -wēl′) *n.* a wheel with a rim notched into teeth, which mesh with those of another wheel or of a rack to transmit or receive motion

co·hab·it (kō hab′it) *vi.* [LL.(Ec.) *cohabitare* < L. *co-,* together + *habitare,* to dwell] **1.** to live together as husband and wife, esp. when not legally married **2.** [Archaic] to live together —**co·hab′i·ta′tion** *n.*

co·hab·it·ant (-i tənt) *n.* [< LL. *cohabitans,* prp. of prec.] a person living together with another or others

Co·han (kō han′; kō′han), **George M**(ichael) 1878-1942; U.S. actor, playwright, theatrical producer, & writer of popular songs

co·heir (kō′ɛr′) *n.* a person who inherits jointly with another or others —**co′heir′ess** *n.fem.*

Co·hen (kō′ən), **Morris Raphael** 1880-1947; U.S. philosopher, born in Russia

co·here (kō hir′) *vi.* **-hered′, -her′ing** [L. *cohaerere* < *co-,* together + *haerere,* to stick] **1.** *a)* to stick together, as parts of a mass *b)* to be united by molecular cohesion **2.** to be connected naturally or logically, as by a common principle; be consistent **3.** to become or stay united in action; be in accord —*SYN.* see STICK

co·her·ence (kō hir′əns) *n.* [Fr. < L. *cohaerentia* < *cohaerens,* prp. of prec.] **1.** the act or condition of cohering; cohesion **2.** the quality of being logically integrated, consistent, and intelligible; congruity [his story lacked *coherence*] **3.** *Physics* the mutual relationship between sets of electromagnetic or sound waves in which their amplitudes are exactly equivalent and rise and fall together Also **co·her′en·cy**

co·her·ent (-ənt) *adj.* [Fr. < L. *cohaerens,* prp.: see COHERE] **1.** sticking together; having cohesion **2.** having coherence; logically connected; consistent; clearly articulated **3.** capable of logical, intelligible speech, thought, etc. **4.** *Physics* exhibiting coherence —**co·her′ent·ly** *adv.*

co·he·sion (kō hē′zhən) *n.* [Fr. < L. *cohaesus,* pp. of *cohaerere:* see COHERE] **1.** the act or condition of cohering; tendency to stick together **2.** *Bot.* the union of like flower parts **3.** *Physics* the force by which the molecules of a substance are held together: distinguished from ADHESION

co·he·sive (-hēs′iv) *adj.* sticking together; causing or characterized by cohesion —**co·he′sive·ly** *adv.* —**co·he′-sive·ness** *n.*

Cohn (kōn), **Ferdinand Julius** 1828-98; Ger. botanist and early bacteriologist

co·ho (kō′hō) *n., pl.* **-ho, -hos:** see PLURAL, II, D, 2 [< ?] a comparatively small salmon (*Oncorhynchus kisutch*), native to the North Pacific Ocean and now widely introduced as a game fish into fresh waters of the N U.S.: also **coho salmon**

co·ho·bate (kō′hō bāt′) *vt.* **-bat′ed, -bat′ing** [< pp. of ModL. *cohobare,* orig. to give a darker color to (a distilled liquid) < Ar. *qohba,* brownish color] to redistill (a distillate) one or more times

co·hort (kō′hôrt) *n.* [ME. < L. *cohors,* enclosure, enclosed company, hence, retinue, crowd] **1.** an ancient Roman military unit of 300–600 men, constituting one tenth of a legion **2.** a band of soldiers **3.** any group or band **4.** an associate, colleague, or supporter [one of the mayor's *cohorts*]

☆**co·hosh** (kō′häsh, kə häsh′) *n.* [< Algonquian name] **1.** any of several American herbs of the buttercup family, as bugbane and baneberry **2.** a N. American herb (*Caulophyllum thalictroides*) of the barberry family, formerly used medicinally by the Indians

co·hune (kə hōōn′, kō-) *n.* [< Central AmInd. name *cóhuŋ*] a Central American palm (*Attalea cohune*) with featherlike leaves and large nuts that yield an edible oil

coif (koif; *for n. 5 & vt. 2, usually* kwäf) *n.* [ME. & OFr. *coife* < LL. *cofea,* a cap, hood < ? Gr. *skyphion,* skull] **1.** a cap that fits the head closely **2.** a white cap formerly worn by English lawyers, esp. by serjeants-at-law **3.** the rank of serjeant-at-law **4.** a thick skullcap formerly worn under a hood of mail **5.** [back-formation < COIFFURE] a style of arranging the hair —*vt.* **coifed, coif′ing;** also, and for 2 usually, **coiffed, coif′fing 1.** to cover with or as with a coif **2.** *a)* to style (the hair) *b)* to give a coiffure to

coif·feur (kwä fɛr′; Fr. kwä fër′) *n.* [Fr. < *coiffer,* to dress hair < prec.] a male hairdresser —**coif·feuse** (kwä fooz′; Fr. kwä föz′) *n.fem.*

coif·fure (kwä fyoor′, -fyɛr′; Fr. kwä für′) *n.* [Fr. < *coiffe,* COIF] **1.** a headdress **2.** a style of arranging the hair —*vt.* **-fured′, -fur′ing** to coif (sense 2)

coign of vantage [*coign,* archaic var. of *coin* (QUOIN)] an advantageous position for observation or action

coil[1] (koil) *vt.* [ME. *coilen,* to select, cull < OFr. *coillir,* to gather, pick < L. *colligere,* to gather together < *com-,*

COGWHEELS

together + *legere*, to gather] to wind or gather (rope, a hose, etc.) into a circular or spiral form —*vi.* 1. to wind around and around 2. to move in a winding course —*n.* 1. anything wound or gathered into a series of rings or a spiral 2. such a series of rings or a spiral 3. a single turn of a coiled figure 4. a series of connected pipes in rows or coils 5. *Elec.* a spiral or loop of wire or other conducting element used as an inductor, heating element, etc.

coil² (koil) *n.* [Early ModE. < ? OFr. *acueil*, collision] [Archaic] commotion; turmoil

Coim·ba·tore (koim′bə tôr′) city in S India, in Madras state: pop. 286,000

coin (koin) *n.* [ME. < OFr. *coin*, *coigne*, a wedge, stamp, corner < L. *cuneus*, a wedge < IE. base *kŭ-*, pointed, whence OIr. *cuil*, L. *culex*, gnat, Av. *sū-kā-*, needle] 1. *archaic var. of* QUOIN 2. *a)* a piece of metal with a distinctive stamp, and of a fixed value and weight, issued by a government and used as money *b)* such pieces collectively 3. [Slang] money —*vt.* 1. *a)* to make (coins) by stamping metal *b)* to make (metal) into coins 2. to make up; devise; invent (a new word, phrase, etc.) —*vi.* 1. to make coins 2. [Brit.] to make counterfeit money —**coin money** [Colloq.] to earn or accumulate wealth rapidly —**pay (a person) back in his own coin** to treat (a person) in the same way that he treated oneself or others —**coin′er** *n.*

coin·age (koi′nij) *n.* [ME. < OFr. *coignaige*] 1. the act or process of coining 2. metal money; coins 3. a system of money or metal currency 4. an invented word or expression *[laser is a recent coinage]*

co·in·cide (kō′in sid′) *vi.* **-cid′ed, -cid′ing** [Fr. *coincider* < ML. *coincidere* < L. *co-*, together + *incidere*, to fall upon: see INCIDENT] 1. to take up the same place in space; be exactly alike in shape, position, and area 2. to occur at the same time; take up the same period of time 3. to hold equivalent positions, as on a scale 4. to be identical; correspond exactly *[our interests coincide]* 5. to be in accord; agree —SYN. see AGREE

co·in·ci·dence (kō in′sə dəns) *n.* [Fr. < ML. *coincidentia*] 1. the fact or condition of coinciding 2. an accidental and remarkable occurrence of events, ideas, etc. at the same time, suggesting but lacking a causal relationship

co·in·ci·dent (-dənt) *adj* [Fr. < ML. *coincidens*, prp.] 1. occurring at the same time 2. taking up the same position in space at the same time 3. in agreement; similar or identical *[where desire and need are coincident]* —**co·in′ci·dent·ly** *adv.*

co·in·ci·den·tal (kō in′sə den′t'l) *adj.* characterized by coincidence —**co·in′ci·den′tal·ly** *adv.*

co·in·sur·ance (kō′in shoor′əns) *n.* 1. a form of property insurance in which the insured shares in losses proportionately to the extent that the amount of insurance falls short of a specified percentage of the value of the insured property 2. joint insurance by two or more insurers

☆**co·in·sure** (-in shoor′) *vt., vi.* **-sured′, -sur′ing** 1. to insure with coinsurance 2. to insure jointly with another or others —**co′in·sur′er** *n.*

Coin·treau (kwän trō′) *a trademark for* a sweet, orange-flavored, colorless liqueur —*n.* [c-] this liqueur

coir (koir) *n.* [Port. *cairo* < Malayalam *kayar*, a rope, cord < Tamil *kayaru*, to be twisted] the prepared fiber of the husks of coconuts, used to make rope, etc.

cois·trel, cois·tril (kois′trəl) *n.* [prob. < ME. *custrel*, a soldier (armed with a *custille*, two-edged dagger) < OFr. *coustellier*] [Archaic] 1. a groom in charge of a knight's horses 2. a knave; varlet; scoundrel

co·i·tion (kō ish′ən) *n.* [L. *coitio* < *coitus*, pp. of *coire* < *co-*, together + *ire*, to go] sexual intercourse

co·i·tus (kō′it əs, kō ēt′əs) *n.* [L.: see prec.] sexual intercourse —**co′i·tal** *adj.*

†**coitus in·ter·rup·tus** (in′tə rup′təs) [L.] *same as* ONANISM (sense 1)

coke¹ (kōk) *n.* [< ME. *colke*, core, charcoal (the unconsumed "core" of burned wood) < IE. base *gel-ĝ-*, rounded, ball-like, whence Gr. *gelgis*, clove of garlic: cf. CLING] 1. coal from which most of the gases have been removed by heating: it burns with intense heat and little smoke, and is used as an industrial fuel 2. a solid residue left after the distillation of petroleum or other liquid hydrocarbons —*vt., vi.* **coked, cok′ing** to change into coke

☆**coke²** (kōk) *n.* [short for COCAINE] [Slang] cocaine

Coke (kook), Sir **Edward** 1552–1634; Eng. jurist & statesman

coke oven an oven in which coke is made

col (käl) *n.* [Fr. < L. *collum*, the neck] 1. a gap between peaks in a mountain range, used as a pass 2. *Meteorol.* a low-pressure area between two anticyclones

col- (käl) *same as* COM-: used before *l*

Col. 1. Colombia 2. Colonel 3. Colorado 4. Colossians

col. 1. collected 2. collector 3. college 4. colonial 5. colony 6. color 7. colored 8. column

co·la¹ (kō′lə) *n.* [Latinized form of WAfr. name] 1. an African tree (*Cola acuminata*) of a family (Sterculiaceae) whose seeds, or nuts, contain caffeine and yield an extract used in soft drinks and medicines 2. a sweet, carbonated soft drink flavored with this extract

co·la² (kō′lə) *n.* 1. *pl. of* COLON¹ (sense 2) 2. *alt. pl. of* COLON²

col·an·der (kul′ən dər, käl′-) *n.* [prob. ult. < L. *colare*, to strain (< *colum*, strainer), as also in Sp. *colador* (ML. *colator*), strainer] a pan with a perforated bottom to drain off liquids, as in washing vegetables

co·lat·i·tude (kō lat′ə tōōd′, -tyōōd′) *n. Astron.* the complement of the latitude

Col·bert (kôl ber′), **Jean Bap·tiste** (zhän bá tēst′) 1619–83; Fr. statesman; minister of finance (1661–83)

col·can·non (kal kan′ən, käl-) *n.* [Ir. *cál ceannan* < *cál*, cabbage + *ceannan*, white-headed] an Irish dish made of potatoes and greens, esp. cabbage, boiled together and mashed

Col·ches·ter (kōl′ches′tər, -chis tər) city in SE England, in Essex: pop. 67,000

col·chi·cine (käl′chə sēn′, -ki sin) *n.* [< ff. + -INE⁴] a poisonous, yellow crystalline alkaloid, C₂₂H₂₅O₆N, extracted from the seeds or corms of a species of colchicum (*Colchicum autumnale*): used in the treatment of gout and to produce chromosome doubling in plants for greater growth and fertile hybrids

col·chi·cum (-kəm) *n.* [L. < Gr. *kolchikon*, plant with a poisonous root < *Kolchis*, Colchis, home of MEDEA] 1. any of a genus (*Colchicum*) of plants of the lily family, with crocuslike flowers usually blooming in the fall; autumn crocus 2. its dried seeds or corm: see COLCHICINE

Col·chis (käl′kis) ancient country south of the Caucasus Mountains, on the Black Sea, in what is now the Georgian S.S.R. —**Col′chi·an** (-kē ən) *adj., n.*

col·co·thar (käl′kə thər) *n.* [Sp. *colcotar* < Ar. *qulqutār* < Gr. *chalkanthos*, solution of blue vitriol (copper sulfate) < *chalkos*, copper + *anthos*, flower] a brownish-red oxide of iron, obtained by heating ferrous sulfate: it is used as a pigment, polishing agent, etc.

cold (kōld) *adj.* [ME. < OE. (Anglian) *cald*, akin to G. *kalt*, L. *gelidus* (cf. GELID): for IE. base see COOL] 1. of a temperature much lower than that of the human body; very chilly; frigid *[a cold wind]* 2. without the proper heat or warmth *[this soup is cold]* 3. dead 4. feeling chilled 5. without warmth of feeling; unfeeling; indifferent *[a cold personality]* 6. not cordial or kind; unfriendly *[a cold reception]* 7. sexually frigid 8. depressing or saddening; gloomy *[to realize the cold truth]* 9. not involving one's feelings; detached; objective *[cold logic]* 10. designating or having colors that suggest cold, as tones of blue, green, or gray 11. still far from what is being sought: said of the seeker 12. not strong or fresh; faint or stale *[a cold scent]* 13. [Colloq.] with little or no preparation *[to enter a game cold]* ☆14. [Slang] completely mastered *[the actor had his lines down cold]* ☆15. [Slang] unconscious *[the boxer was knocked cold]* —*n.* 1. *a)* absence of heat; lack of warmth: often thought of as an active force *b)* a low temperature; esp., one below freezing 2. the sensation produced by a loss or absence of heat 3. cold weather 4. an acute inflammation of the mucous membranes of the respiratory passages, esp. of the nose and throat, thought to be caused by several different viruses and characterized by a nasal discharge, malaise, etc. —**catch** (or **take**) **cold** to become ill with a cold —**cold comfort** little or no comfort at all —**have** (or **get**) **cold feet** [Colloq.] ☆to be (or become) timid or fearful —**in the cold** ignored; neglected —**throw cold water on** to be unenthusiastic about or toward; discourage —**cold′ly** *adv.* —**cold′ness** *n.*

cold·blood·ed (-blud′id) *adj.* 1. having a body temperature that fluctuates, approximating that of the surrounding air, land, or water *[fishes and reptiles are coldblooded animals]* 2. easily affected by cold 3. without normal human feelings of kindness and pity; cruel; callous —**cold′blood′ed·ly** *adv.* —**cold′blood′ed·ness** *n.*

cold chisel a hardened and tempered steel chisel without a handle, for cutting or chipping cold metal

☆**cold-cock** (-käk′) *vt.* [? < COLD + COCK¹ (in vulgar sense, penis)] [Slang] to strike so as to make unconscious

cold cream a creamy, soothing preparation of emulsified oil for softening and cleansing the skin

cold cuts a variety of sliced cold meats and, usually, cheeses

cold duck [transl. of G. *kalte ente* < ?] a drink made from equal parts of sparkling burgundy and champagne

☆**cold frame** an unheated, boxlike, glass-covered structure for protecting young plants

cold front *Meteorol.* the forward edge of a cold air mass advancing into a warmer air mass

cold-heart·ed (-här′tid) *adj.* lacking sympathy; unfeeling

cold light light not accompanied by the heat of combustion or incandescence, as phosphorescent light

cold pack 1. cold, wet blankets or sheets wrapped around a patient's body as a means of treatment 2. a process of canning foodstuffs in which the raw products are placed in jars fresh and then subjected to heat —**cold′-pack′** *vt.*

☆**cold rubber** a synthetic rubber formed by polymerizing and curing the starting materials, as butadiene-styrene, at a temperature of 41°F or lower: used in automobile tires because of its special resistance to abrasion

cold shoulder [Colloq.] deliberate indifference, coldness,

fat, āpe, cär; ten, ēven; is, bīte; gō, hôrn, tōōl, look; oil, out; up, fur; get; joy; yet; chin; she; thin, then; zh, leisure; ŋ, ring; ə for *a* in *ago*, *e* in *agent*, *i* in *sanity*, *o* in *comply*, *u* in *focus*; ' as in *able* (ā′b'l); Fr. bâl; ë, Fr. coeur; ö, Fr. feu; Fr. mon; ô, Fr. coq; ü, Fr. duc; r, Fr. cri; H, G. ich; kh, G. doch. See inside front cover. ☆ Americanism; ‡foreign; *hypothetical; <derived from

or neglect; a slight, rebuff, or snub: often used with *the* —**cold′-should′er** *vt.*

☆**cold snap** a sudden, brief spell of cold weather

cold sore a sore consisting of little blisters that often appear about the mouth during a cold or fever; herpes simplex

cold storage storage of perishable foods, furs, etc. in a very cold place, esp. in a refrigerating chamber

cold sweat perspiration accompanied by a cold, clammy feeling, as during fear or shock

☆**cold turkey** [COLD + TURKEY; reason for use obscure] [Slang] **1.** the abrupt and total withdrawal of drugs from an addict, as during an attempted cure **2.** in a frank, blunt, or matter-of-fact way *[to talk cold turkey about our chances]* **3.** without preparation or preliminaries *[to approach a sales prospect cold turkey]* —**cold′-tur′key** *adj.*

☆**cold war** hostility and sharp conflict in diplomacy, economics, etc. between states, without actual warfare

cold wave 1. a period of weather colder than is normal **2.** a permanent wave in which the hair is set with a liquid preparation instead of heat

cole (kōl) *n.* [ME. *col* < OE. *cal* < L. *caulis, colis,* a cabbage, stem: see CAULIS] any of a genus (*Brassica*) of plants of the mustard family; esp., rape

co·lec·to·my (kə lek′tə mē) *n., pl.* **-mies** [COL(ON)² + -ECTOMY] the surgical removal of all or part of the colon

☆**cole·man·ite** (kōl′mə nīt′) *n.* [after William T. *Coleman* (1824–93) U.S. manufacturer of borax] a white or colorless crystalline substance, $C_2B_6O_{11} \cdot 5H_2O$, a hydrous borate of calcium

co·le·op·ter·on (kō′lē äp′tər än′, käl′ē-) *n., pl.* **-ter·a** (-ə) [ModL.] any coleopterous insect: also **co′le·op′ter·an** (-ən)

co·le·op·ter·ous (-əs) *adj.* [ModL. *Coleoptera,* name of the order (< Gr. *koleopteros,* sheath-winged < *koleos,* sheath + *pteron,* wing) + -OUS] belonging to an order (Coleoptera) of insects, including beetles and weevils, with the front wings modified to form a horny covering for the hind wings, which are membranous and usually functional

co·le·op·tile (kō′lē äp′t'l, käl′ē-) *n.* [ModL. *coleoptilum* < Gr. *koleos,* sheath (see COLEUS) + *ptilon,* feather, prob. < IE. base *pti-,* var. of *pet-,* to rush upon, fly, whence FEATHER] the tubular protective sheath which surrounds the young shoot in the germinating grass seed

co·le·o·rhi·za (-ə rī′zə) *n., pl.* **-zae** (-zē) [ModL. < Gr. *koleos,* a sheath + *rhiza,* a root] a protective root sheath of grass seedlings through which the primary root emerges

Cole·ridge (kōl′rij, -ər ij), **Samuel Taylor** 1772–1834; Eng. poet & critic

☆**cole·slaw** (kōl′slô′) *n.* [< Du. *kool,* cabbage (akin to COLE) + *sla,* for *salade,* salad] a salad made of shredded raw cabbage, often mixed with salad dressing and seasoning: also **cole slaw**

Col·et (käl′it), **John** 1467?–1519; Eng. theologian & classical scholar

Co·lette (kô let′), (**Sidonie Gabrielle Claudine**) 1873–1954; Fr. novelist

co·le·us (kō′lē əs) *n.* [ModL. < Gr. *koleos,* a sheath: so named because of the way in which the stamens are joined] any of a genus (*Coleus*) of plants of the mint family, native to Africa and the East Indies, grown for their showy, bright-colored leaves

cole·wort (kōl′wurt′) *n.* [ME.: see COLE & WORT²] **1.** same as COLE **2.** any kind of cabbage, as kale, whose leaves do not form a compact head

Col·fax (kōl′faks), **Schuy·ler** (skī′lər) 1823–85; vice president of the U.S. (1869–73)

col·ic (käl′ik) *n.* [ME. *colik* < OFr. *colique* < L. *colicus,* pertaining to colic, sick with colic < Gr. *kōlikos* < *kōlon, kolon,* colon: from being seated in the colon and parts adjacent] acute abdominal pain caused by various abnormal conditions in the bowels —*adj.* **1.** of colic **2.** of or near the colon —**col′ick·y** (-i kē) *adj.*

☆**col·ic·root** (-rōōt′) *n.* **1.** a N. American bitter herb (*Aletris farinosa*) of the lily family, with white or yellow flowers **2.** any of a number of other plants, as the butterfly weed, supposed to cure colic

☆**col·ic·weed** (-wēd′) *n.* any of several N. American plants, as the Dutchman's-breeches

co·li·form (kō′lə fôrm′, käl′ə-) *adj.* designating, of, or like the aerobic bacillus normally found in the colon: a coliform count is often used as an indicator of fecal contamination of water supplies

Co·li·gny (kô lē nyē′), **Gas·pard de** (gȧs pȧr′ də) 1519–72; Fr. admiral & Huguenot leader

Co·li·ma (kô lē′mä) **1.** state of SW Mexico, on the Pacific: 2,010 sq. mi.; pop. 185,000 **2.** its capital: pop. 29,000 **3.** inactive volcano in Jalisco state, near Colima border: c. 14,240 ft. **4.** active volcano on the Jalisco-Colima border: c. 12,750 ft.

Co·lin (kō′lin, käl′in) [prob. < St. *Columba* (< L. *columba,* dove), patron saint of Cornish parishes] a masculine name

☆**col·in** (käl′in) *n.* [AmSp. < Nahuatl] the bobwhite or any related bird

col·i·se·um (käl′ə sē′əm) *n.* [ModL. < L. *colosseum*] **1.** [C-] the Colosseum **2.** a large building or stadium for sports events, shows, exhibitions, etc.

co·li·tis (kō līt′is) *n.* [ModL. < Gr. *kolon,* colon, large intestine + -ITIS] inflammation of the large intestine

coll. 1. colleague **2.** collect **3.** collection **4.** collector **5.** college **6.** colloquial

col·lab·o·rate (kə lab′ə rāt′) *vi.* **-rat′ed, -rat′ing** [< L. *collaboratus,* pp. of *collaborare,* to work together < *com-,* with + *laborare,* to work] **1.** to work together, esp. in some literary, artistic, or scientific undertaking **2.** to cooperate with the enemy; be a collaborationist —**col·lab′o·ra′tion** *n.* —**col·lab′o·ra′tive** *adj.* —**col·lab′o·ra′tor** *n.*

col·lab·o·ra·tion·ist (kə lab′ə rā′shən ist) *n.* a person who cooperates with an enemy invader of his country

col·lage (kə läzh′) *n.* [Fr., a pasting < *colle,* paste < Gr. *kolla,* glue] **1.** an art form in which bits of objects, as newspaper, cloth, pressed flowers, etc., are pasted together on a surface in incongruous relationship for their symbolic or suggestive effect **2.** a composition so made **3.** any collection of various unrelated bits and parts, as in a photomontage

col·la·gen (käl′ə jen′) *n.* [< Gr. *kolla,* glue + -GEN] a fibrous protein found in connective tissue, bone, and cartilage —**col′la·gen′ic** *adj.*

col·lapse (kə laps′) *vi.* **-lapsed′, -laps′ing** [< L. *collapsus,* pp. of *collabi* < *com-,* together + *labi,* to fall] **1.** to fall down or fall to pieces, as when supports or sides fail to hold; cave in; shrink together suddenly **2.** to break down suddenly; fail; give way *[the enemy's defense collapsed]* **3.** *a)* to break down or fail suddenly in health or physical strength *b)* to fall down, as from a blow or exhaustion *c)* to fall or drop drastically, as in value, force, etc. **4.** to fold or come together compactly —*vt.* to cause to collapse —*n.* the act of collapsing; a falling in or together; failure or breakdown, as in business, health, etc. —**col·laps′i·bil′i·ty** *n.* —**col·laps′i·ble** *adj.*

col·lar (käl′ər) *n.* [ME. *coler* < OFr. *colier* < L. *collare,* band or chain for the neck < *collum,* the neck < IE. base *kwel-,* to turn, whence WHEEL, G. *hals,* neck] **1.** the part of a garment that encircles the neck **2.** a cloth band or folded-over piece attached to the neck of a garment **3.** an ornamental band, chain, or circlet worn around the neck **4.** a band of leather or metal for the neck of a dog, cat, etc. **5.** the part of the harness which fits over the neck of a horse or other draft animal and against which the animal strains in pulling a load **6.** a ring or flange, as on rods or pipes, to prevent sideward motion, connect parts, etc. **7.** a distinctive band, as of a different color or texture, around the neck of an animal, bird, etc. **8.** the foam that forms on the top of a glass of beer ☆ **9.** [Slang] an arrest or capture —*vt.* **1.** to put a collar on ☆**2.** to seize by the collar **3.** [Colloq.] *a)* to take hold or control of; seize or capture *b)* to stop and delay by talking to

col·lar·bone (-bōn′) *n.* a flat, slender bone joining the breastbone to the shoulder blade; clavicle

☆**collar button** a small button or stud for fastening a collar to a shirt

col·lard (käl′ərd) *n.* [contr. < COLEWORT] a kind of kale (*Brassica oleracea acephala*) whose coarse leaves are borne in tufts

collat. collateral

col·late (kə lāt′, kə-; käl′āt) *vt.* **-lat′ed, -lat′ing** [< L. *collatus,* pp. of *conferre,* to bring together < *com-,* together + *ferre,* to BEAR¹] **1.** to compare (texts, data, etc.) critically in order to consolidate, note similarities and differences, etc. **2.** *a)* to gather (the sections of a book) together in proper order for binding *b)* to examine (such sections) to see that all pages, plates, etc. are present and in proper order **3.** to appoint (a clergyman) to a benefice —*SYN.* see COMPARE —**col·la′tor** *n.*

col·lat·er·al (kə lat′ər əl) *adj.* [ME. < ML. *collateralis* < L. *com-,* together + *lateralis,* LATERAL] **1.** side by side; parallel **2.** parallel in time, rank, importance, etc.; corresponding **3.** accompanying or existing in a subordinate, corroborative, or direct relationship **4.** descended from the same ancestors but in a different line **5.** *a)* designating or of security given as a pledge for the fulfillment of an obligation *b)* secured or guaranteed by property, as stocks, bonds, etc. *[a collateral loan]* —*n.* **1.** a collateral relative ☆**2.** anything, such as stocks or bonds, that secures or guarantees the discharge of an obligation —**col·lat′er·al·ly** *adv.*

col·la·tion (kä lā′shən, kə-) *n.* [ME. *collacioun* < OFr. *collacion,* discourse < L. *collatio:* see COLLATE] **1.** the act, process, or result of collating **2.** a conference or gathering, as of monks at the close of the day to listen to a reading from a religious book and to discuss it **3.** a light meal: originally such a meal was served in a monastery during the collation (sense 2) **4.** a description of the physical make-up of a book, including the size, number of pages, illustrations, etc.

col·league (käl′ēg) *n.* [Fr. *collègue* < L. *collega,* one chosen along with another < *com-,* with + *legare,* to appoint as deputy: cf. LEGATE] a fellow worker in the same profession; associate in office —*SYN.* see ASSOCIATE

col·lect¹ (kə lekt′) *vt.* [ME. *collecten* < OFr. *collecter* < L. *collectus:* see ff.] **1.** to gather together; assemble **2.** to gather (stamps, books, etc.) for a hobby **3.** to call for and receive (money) for rent, a fund, taxes, bills, etc.) **4.** to regain control of (oneself or one's wits); summon up (one's faculties or powers) —*vi.* **1.** to gather; assemble *[a crowd collected]* **2.** to accumulate *[water collects in the basement]* **3.** to collect payments, contributions, etc. —*adj., adv.* ☆with payment to be made by the receiver *[to telephone collect]* —*SYN.* see GATHER —**col·lect′a·ble, col·lect′i·ble** *adj.*

col·lect² (kəl′ekt) *n.* [ME. & OFr. *collecte* < LL. *collecta,* a gathering together of ideas from the day's reading < L. *collecta,* a gathering, contribution of money < *collectus,* pp. of *colligere* < *com-,* together + *legere,* to gather] [*also* C-] a short prayer suitable to the time or occasion, used in certain church services, as before the Epistle at Mass

col·lec·ta·ne·a (käl′ek tā′nē ə) *n.pl.* [neut. pl. of L. *collectaneus,* gathered together < *collectus:* see COLLECT²] a collection of writings of one or more authors; anthology; literary miscellany

col·lect·ed (kə lek′tid) *adj.* 1. gathered together; assembled [the *collected* works of Poe] 2. in control of oneself; calm and self-possessed; composed —*SYN.* see COOL —**col·lect′ed·ly** *adv.* —**col·lect′ed·ness** *n.*

col·lec·tion (-shən) *n.* [ME. *colleicioun* < L. *collectio*] 1. the act or process of collecting 2. things collected [a *collection* of stamps] 3. something that has gathered into a mass or pile; accumulation 4. money collected, as during a church service

col·lec·tive (-tiv) *adj.* [ME. & OFr. *collectif* < L. *collectivus*] 1. formed by collecting; gathered into a whole 2. of, as, or characteristic of a group; of or by all or many of the individuals in a group acting together [the *collective* effort of the students] 3. designating or of any enterprise in which people work together as a group, esp. under a system of collectivism [a *collective* farm] 4. *Gram.* designating a noun which is singular in form but denotes a collection of individuals (e.g., *army, orchestra, crowd*): it is treated as singular when the collection is thought of as a whole and as plural when the individual members are thought of as acting separately —*n.* 1. any collective enterprise; specif., a collective farm 2. the people who work together in such an enterprise 3. *Gram.* a collective noun —**col·lec′tive·ly** *adv.*

collective bargaining negotiation between organized workers and their employer or employers for reaching an agreement on wages, hours, and working conditions

collective fruit *same as* MULTIPLE FRUIT

collective security a system of international security in which the participating nations agree to take joint action against a nation that attacks any one of them

col·lec·tiv·ism (kə lek′tə viz′m) *n.* [Fr. *collectivisme* (c. 1880): see COLLECTIVE & -ISM] the ownership and control of the means of production and distribution by the people collectively; socialism —**col·lec′tiv·ist** *n., adj.* —**col·lec′tiv·is′tic** *adj.*

col·lec·tiv·i·ty (käl′ek tiv′ə tē, kə lek′-) *n.* 1. the quality or state of being collective 2. a collective whole 3. the people as a whole

col·lec·tiv·ize (kə lek′tə vīz′) *vt.* -ized′, -iz′ing to establish or organize under a system of collectivism —**col·lec′ti·vi·za′tion** *n.*

☆**collect on delivery** payment in cash when a purchase or shipment is delivered

col·lec·tor (kə lek′tər) *n.* [ME. *collectour* < ML. *collector*] a person or thing that collects; specif., *a*) a person whose work is collecting taxes, overdue bills, etc. *b*) a person who collects stamps, books, etc. as a hobby *c*) the output element of a transistor that, when properly biased, collects charge carriers

Col·leen (käl′ēn, kə lēn′) [Ir.: see ff.] a feminine name

col·leen (käl′ēn, kə lēn′) *n.* [Ir. *cailin,* dim. of *caile,* girl] [Irish] a girl

col·lege (käl′ij) *n.* [ME. & OFr. < L. *collegium,* community, society, guild, fraternity < *collega:* see COLLEAGUE] 1. an association of individuals having certain powers and duties, and engaged in some common pursuit [the electoral *college*] 2. [orig. with reference to the university communities of Oxford & Cambridge] an institution of higher education that grants degrees; university; specif., *a*) any of the schools of a university offering instruction and granting degrees in any of several specialized courses of study, as liberal arts, architecture, law, medicine, etc. *b*) the undergraduate division of a university, which offers a general four-year course leading to the bachelor's degree 3. a school offering specialized instruction in some profession or occupation [a secretarial *college*] 4. the students, faculty, or administrators of a college 5. a clerical group that has been given the legal status of an ecclesiastical corporation 6. the building or group of buildings of a college

College of Cardinals the cardinals of the Roman Catholic Church, serving as a privy council to the Pope: this College administers the Holy See in the absence of the Pope and elects his successor

col·le·gi·al (kə lē′jē əl) *adj.* [ME. < L. *collegialis*] 1. with authority or power shared equally among colleagues 2. *same as* COLLEGIATE

col·le·gi·al·i·ty (kə lē′jē al′ə tē) *n.* [see prec.] 1. the sharing of authority among colleagues 2. *R.C.Ch.* the principle that authority is shared by the Pope and the bishops

col·le·gian (kə lē′jən) *n.* [ME., member of a college < ML. *collegianus*] a college student

col·le·giate (-jət, -jē ət) *adj.* [ME. *collegiat* < LL. *colle-*

giatus, member of a college] 1. of the nature of a college 2. of or like a college 3. of, like, or for college students 4. of or like a collegiate church

collegiate church 1. a church with a chapter of canons although it is not a bishop's see 2. in Scotland, a church with two or more ministers serving jointly ☆3. in the U.S., a church associated with others under a joint body of pastors 4. such an association of churches

col·le·gi·um (kə lē′jē əm) *n., pl.* -gi·a (-ə), -gi·ums [L.] a group of individuals with equal power or authority; esp., an administrative board for a Soviet commissariat

col·lem·bo·lan (kə lem′bō lən) *n.* [< ModL. *Collembola,* name of the order (< Gr. *kolla,* glue + *embolon,* a peg, akin to *embolos,* a wedge: see EMBOLUS) + -AN] *same as* SPRINGTAIL

col·len·chy·ma (kə len′ki mə) *n.* [< Gr. *kolla,* glue + *enchyma,* a steeping, infusion] a type of plant tissue consisting of elongated cells thickened at the angles —**col·len·chym·a·tous** (käl′ən kim′ə təs) *adj.*

col·let (käl′it) *n.* [Fr., dim. of *col,* the neck < L. *collum:* see COLLAR] 1. a metal band or ring, such as is used in a watch to hold the end of a balance spring 2. the part of a ring in which the stone is set —*vt.* to set in, or furnish with, a collet

col·lide (kə līd′) *vi.* -lid′ed, -lid′ing [L. *collidere* < *com-,* together + *laedere,* to strike, injure] 1. to come into violent contact; strike violently against each other; crash 2. to come into conflict; clash

col·lie (käl′ē) *n.* [said to be < *coaly,* coal-black < the color of some of the breed] any of a breed of large, long-haired dog with a long, narrow head: first bred in Scotland for herding sheep

col·lier (käl′yər) *n.* [ME. *colyer:* see COAL + -IER] [Chiefly Brit.] 1. a coal miner 2. a ship for carrying coal, or any of its crew

col·lier·y (-ē) *n., pl.* -lier·ies [prec. + -Y⁴] [Chiefly Brit.] a coal mine and its buildings, equipment, etc.

COLLIE
(24–26 in. high
at shoulder)

col·li·gate (käl′ə gāt′) *vt.* -gat′ed, -gat′ing [< L. *colligatus,* pp. of *colligare,* to bind together < *com-,* together + *ligare,* to bind] 1. to bind together 2. *Logic* to relate (isolated facts) by some reasonable explanation, esp. so as to evolve a general principle —**col′li·ga′tion** *n.*

col·li·mate (käl′ə māt′) *vt.* -mat′ed, -mat′ing [< *collimare,* false reading of L. *collineare,* to direct in a straight line < *com-,* with + *lineare,* to make straight < *linea,* a line] 1. to make (light rays, etc.) parallel 2. to adjust the line of sight of (a telescope, surveyor's level, etc.) —**col′li·ma′tion** *n.*

col·li·ma·tor (-māt′ər) *n.* [see COLLIMATE] 1. a small telescope with cross hairs at its focus, fixed to another telescope, surveying instrument, etc. for adjusting the line of sight 2. the tube or lens of a spectroscope that receives the light and casts it upon the prism in parallel rays

col·lin·e·ar (kə lin′ē ər) *adj.* [COL- + LINEAR] in the same straight line

Col·lins (käl′inz) *n.* [supposedly after its inventor, a bartender named Tom *Collins*] ☆an iced drink made with gin (*Tom Collins*), or vodka, rum, whiskey, etc., mixed with soda water, lime or lemon juice, and sugar

Collins 1. **Michael,** 1890–1922; Ir. revolutionary leader 2. (**William**) **Wil·kie** (wil′kē), 1824–89; Eng. novelist 3. **William,** 1721–59; Eng. poet

☆**col·lin·si·a** (kə lin′zē ə, -sē ə) *n.* [ModL., after the U.S. botanist Z. *Collins* (1764–1831)] any of a genus (*Collinsia*) of hardy, low-growing plants of the figwort family, with flowers arranged in whorls

col·li·sion (kə lizh′ən) *n.* [ME. < LL. *collisio* < pp. of L. *collidere*] 1. the act of colliding, or coming together with sudden, violent force 2. a clash or conflict of opinions, interests, etc.

col·lo·cate (käl′ə kāt′) *vt.* -cat′ed, -cat′ing [< L. *collocatus,* pp. of *collocare,* to place together < *com-,* together + *locare:* see LOCATE] to arrange or place together, esp. side by side

col·lo·ca·tion (käl′ə kā′shən) *n.* [L. *collocatio*] a collocating or being collocated; specif., an arrangement, as of words in a sentence

☆**col·lo·di·on** (kə lō′dē ən) *n.* [< Gr. *kollōdēs,* gluelike < *kolla,* glue + *eidos,* form] a highly flammable, colorless or pale-yellow, viscous solution of nitrated cellulose in a mixture of alcohol and ether: it dries quickly, forming a tough, elastic film, and is used as a protective coating for wounds, in photographic films, etc.

col·logue (kə lōg′) *vi.* -logued′, -logu·ing [< Fr. *colloque,* conference < L. *colloquium* (see COLLOQUY); sp. altered after obs. *colleague,* to conspire] 1. to confer or converse privately 2. [Dial.] to intrigue or conspire

col·loid (käl′oid) *n.* [coined by Thomas Graham (1805–69), Scot. chemist < Gr. *kolla,* glue + -OID] 1. a) a solid, liquid,

or gaseous substance made up of very small, insoluble, nondiffusible particles (as single large molecules or masses of smaller molecules) that remain in suspension in a surrounding solid, liquid, or gaseous medium of different matter *b*) a state of matter consisting of such a substance dispersed in a surrounding medium *All living matter contains colloidal material, and a colloid has only a negligible effect on the freezing point, boiling point, or vapor tension of the surrounding medium* 2. the material within which the thyroid gland stores its hormones: it is a protein containing iodine

col·loi·dal (kə loi′d'l) *adj.* 1. of, like, or containing a colloid 2. of the nature, or in the form, of a colloid

col·lop (käl′əp) *n.* [ME. *colhoppe*, a dish of fried or roasted meat, a morsel < ? Scand., as in Sw. *kollops*, OSw. *kolhuppadher*, cooked on coal: first element prob. *kol*, COAL] 1. a portion or piece; esp., a small slice of meat 2. [Archaic] a fold of fatty flesh on the body

colloq. 1. colloquial 2. colloquialism 3. colloquially

col·lo·qui·al (kə lō′kwē əl) *adj.* [< L. *colloquium* (see COLLOQUY) + -AL] 1. having to do with or like conversation; conversational 2. designating or of the words, phrases, and idioms characteristic of informal speech and writing; informal: the label [Colloq.] is used throughout this dictionary in this sense, and does not indicate substandard or illiterate usage —**col′lo′qui·al·ly** *adv.*

col·lo·qui·al·ism (-iz'm) *n.* 1. colloquial quality, style, or usage 2. a colloquial word or expression 3. erroneously, a localism, or regionalism

col·lo·quist (käl′ə kwist) *n.* a participant in a colloquy

col·lo·qui·um (kə lō′kwē əm) *n., pl.* **-qui·a** (-ə), **-qui·ums** [L.: see ff.] an organized conference or seminar on some subject, involving a number of scholars or experts

col·lo·quy (käl′ə kwē) *n., pl.* **-quies** [L. *colloquium*, conversation < *com-*, together + *loqui*, to speak] 1. a conversation, esp. a formal discussion; conference 2. a literary work written as a dialogue or conversation

col·lo·type (käl′ə tīp′) *n.* [< Gr. *kolla*, glue + -TYPE] 1. a photomechanical process by which inked reproductions are transferred to paper directly from an image formed on a sheet of hardened gelatin 2. the printed reproduction

col·lude (kə lōōd′) *vi.* **-lud′ed, -lud′ing** [L. *colludere* < *com-*, with + *ludere*, to play] to act in collusion or conspire, esp. for a fraudulent purpose

col·lu·sion (kə lōō′zhən) *n.* [ME. < L. *collusio* < *collusus*, pp. of *colludere*: see COLLUDE] a secret agreement for fraudulent or illegal purpose; conspiracy —**col·lu′sive** (-siv) *adj.* —**col·lu′sive·ly** *adv.*

col·lu·vi·um (kə lōō′vē əm) *n., pl.* **-vi·a** (-ə), **-vi·ums** [ML., altered < L. *colluvies*, dregs, sweepings < *colluere*, to wash out < *col-*, COL- + *luere*, to wash, flow: for IE. base see LOSE] rock fragments, sand, etc. that accumulate on steep slopes or at the foot of cliffs

col·ly (käl′ē) *vt.* **-lied, -ly·ing** [< ME. *colwi*, sooty < *colwed*, blackened with coal, ult. < *col*, COAL] [Brit. Dial.] to blacken, as with soot or grime —*n.* [Brit. Dial.] soot; grime

col·lyr·i·um (kə lir′ē əm) *n., pl.* **-i·a** (-ə), **-i·ums** [L. < Gr. *kollyrion*, eye salve] any medicated preparation for the eyes; eyewash

col·ly·wob·bles (käl′ə wäb′'lz) *n.pl.* [*often with sing. v.*] [prob. < COLIC + WOBBLE] [Colloq.] pain in the abdomen; bellyache: usually with *the*

Col·mar (kôl′mär; *Fr.* kôl mår′) city in NE France, near the Rhine: pop. 52,000

Colo. Colorado

col·o·bus (käl′ə bəs) *n.* [ModL. < Gr. *kolobos*, curtailed, docked (akin to *kolos*, maimed: for IE. base see HALT²): so named prob. because of the absent or rudimentary thumbs] any of a genus (*Colobus*) of thumbless, long-haired, black and white African monkeys

co·lo·cate (kō lō′kāt′) *vt., vi.* **-cat′ed, -cat′ing** to locate or be located in the same place, as two or more military units —**co′·lo·ca′tion** *n.*

col·o·cynth (käl′ə sinth′) *n.* [L. *colocynthis* < Gr. *kolokynthis*] 1. an African and Asian perennial vine (*Citrullus colocynthis*) of the gourd family, whose small, dried fruits are used in making a strong cathartic 2. this fruit, or the cathartic prepared from it

Co·logne (kə lōn′) [Fr. < L. *Colonia* (*Agrippina*), the colony (of AGRIPPINA)] city in W West Germany, on the Rhine: pop. 848,000: Ger. name, KÖLN

co·logne (kə lōn′) *n. same as* EAU DE COLOGNE

Co·lom·bi·a (kə lum′bē ə; *Sp.* kô lôm′byä) country in NW S. America, on the Pacific Ocean & the Caribbean Sea: 455,335 sq. mi.; pop. 18,068,000; cap. Bogotá —**Co·lom′bi·an** *adj., n.*

Co·lom·bo (kə lum′bō) capital of Ceylon: seaport on the W coast: pop. 512,000

Co·lón (kə lōn′) [see COLON³] seaport in Panama, at the Caribbean end of the Panama Canal: pop. 60,000

co·lon¹ (kō′lən) *n.* [L. < Gr. *kōlon*, part of a verse, member, limb < IE. base *(s)kel-*, to bend, crooked, whence L. *coluber*, snake, *calx*, heel] 1. a mark of punctuation (:) used before an extended quotation, explanation, example, series, etc., and after the salutation of a formal letter 2. *pl.* **co′la** (-ə) *Gr. Prosody* a section of a prosodic period, consisting of a group of two to six feet forming a rhythmic unit with a principal accent

co·lon² (kō′lən) *n., pl.* **-lons, -la** (-lə) [L. < Gr. *kolon*] that part of the large intestine extending from the cecum to the rectum —**co·lon·ic** (kə län′ik) *adj.*

co·lon³ (kə lōn′; *Sp.* kô lôn′) *n., pl.* **-lons;** Sp. **-lon′es** (-lô′nes) [AmSp. *colón* < Sp. *Colón*, COLUMBUS] the monetary unit of Costa Rica and El Salvador: see MONETARY UNITS, table

‡**co·lon⁴** (kō lōn′; *E.* kə lōn′) *n.* [Fr.] a colonist, esp. one who owns a plantation

Co·lón (kō lôn′), **Ar·chi·pié·la·go de** (är′chē pyä′lä gō *the*) *same as* GALÁPAGOS ISLANDS

colo·nel (kur′n'l) *n.* [earlier *coronel* < Fr. *colonel*, *coronel* < It. *colonello* < *colonna*, (military) column < L. *columna*, COLUMN; Fr. & E. sp. modified after L. & It., but older pronun. kept in E.] 1. a military officer ranking above a lieutenant colonel and below a brigadier general, and corresponding to a captain in the navy ☆2. an honorary, nonmilitary title in some southern or western States —**colo′nel·cy** (-sē) *n., pl.* **-cies**

co·lo·ni·al (kə lō′nē əl) *adj.* 1. of or living in a colony or colonies 2. [*often* C-] of the thirteen British colonies that became the U.S., or characteristic of the styles of their period 3. made up of or having colonies —*n.* an inhabitant of a colony —**co·lo′ni·al·ly** *adv.*

colonial animal *same as* COMPOUND ANIMAL

co·lo·ni·al·ism (-iz'm) *n.* the system or policy by which a country maintains foreign colonies, esp. in order to exploit them economically —**co·lo′ni·al·ist** *n., adj.*

☆**col·o·nist** (käl′ə nist) *n.* 1. any of the original settlers or founders of a colony 2. an inhabitant of a colony

co·o·nize (käl′ə nīz′) *vt.* **-nized′, -niz′ing** 1. to found or establish a colony or colonies in 2. to settle (persons) in a colony ☆3. to place (voters) illegally in (a district) so as to influence an election —*vi.* 1. to found or establish a colony or colonies 2. to settle in a colony —**col′o·ni·za′tion** *n.* —**col′o·niz′er** *n.*

col·on·nade (käl′ə nād′) *n.* [Fr. < It. *colonnato* < *colonna* < L. *columna*, COLUMN] *Archit.* a series of columns set at regular intervals, usually supporting a roof or series of arches —**col′on·nad′ed** *adj.*

col·o·ny (käl′ə nē) *n., pl.* **-nies** [ME. *colonie* < L. *colonia* < *colonus*, farmer < *colere*, to cultivate] 1. *a*) a group of people who settle in a distant land but remain under the political jurisdiction of their native land *b*) the region thus settled 2. a territory distant from the state having jurisdiction or control over it 3. [C-] [*pl.*] the thirteen British colonies in N. America that won their independence in the Revolutionary War and became the U.S.: they were Va., N.Y., Mass., Conn., R.I., N.H., Md., N.J., N.C., S.C., Pa., Del., and Ga. 4. *a*) a community of people of the same nationality or pursuits concentrated in a particular district or place [the Hungarian *colony* of Cleveland, an artists' *colony*] *b*) such a district or place 5. *Bacteriology* a group of similar bacteria growing in or on a culture medium 6. *Biol.* a group of similar plants or animals living or growing together 7. *Zool.* a compound organism consisting of several to many incompletely separated individuals, as in corals, hydroids, etc.

col·o·phon (käl′ə fän′, -fən) *n.* [LL. < Gr. *kolophōn*, summit, top, end: for IE. base see COLUMN] 1. a notation often placed in a book, at the end, giving facts about its production 2. the distinctive emblem of the publisher, as on the title page or cover of a book

col·o·pho·ny (käl′ə fō′nē, kə läf′ə nē) *n.* [ME. *colofonie* < L. *colophonia* (*resina*) < Gr. *kolophōnia* (*rhētinē*), lit., Colophonian (resin) < *Kolophōn*, Colophon, ancient Ionian city; cf. prec.] *same as* ROSIN

col·or (kul′ər) *n.* [ME. & OFr. *colour.* < L. *color* < OL. *colos*, orig., a covering < IE. base **kel-*, to conceal, hide, whence HULL¹, HALL] 1. the sensation resulting from stimulation of the retina of the eye by light waves of certain lengths 2. the property of reflecting light of a particular wavelength: the distinct colors of the spectrum are red, orange, yellow, green, blue, indigo, and violet, each of these shading into the next; the *primary colors* of the spectrum are red, green, and blue, the light beams of which variously combined can produce any of the colors 3. any coloring matter; dye; pigment; paint: the *primary colors* of paints, pigments, etc. are red, yellow, and blue, which, when mixed in various ways, produce the *secondary colors* (green, orange, purple, etc.); black, white, and gray are often called colors (*achromatic colors*), although black is caused by the complete absorption of light rays, white by the reflection of all the rays that produce color, and gray by an imperfect absorption of all these rays 4. any color other than black, white, and gray; chromatic color: color is distinguished by the qualities of *hue* (as red, brown, yellow, etc.), *lightness* (for pigmented surfaces) or *brightness* (for light itself), and *saturation* (the degree of intensity of a hue) 5. color of the face; esp., a healthy rosiness or a blush 6. the color of a person's skin 7. the color of the skin of a Negro or other person not classified as Caucasian 8. [*pl.*] a colored badge, ribbon, costume, etc. that identifies the wearer 9. [*pl.*] *a*) a flag or banner of a country, regiment, etc. *b*) the armed forces of a country, symbolized by the flag [to serve with the *colors*] 10. [*pl.*] the side that a person is on; position or opinion [stick to your *colors*] 11. outward appearance or semblance; plausibility 12. appearance of truth, likelihood, validity, or right; justifica-

tion [the circumstances gave *color* to his contention] **13.** general nature; character [the *color* of his mind] **14.** vivid quality or character, as in a personality, literary work, etc.: see also LOCAL COLOR **15.** *Art* the way of using color, esp. to gain a total effect **16.** *Law* an apparent or prima-facie right ☆**17.** *Mining* a trace of gold found in panning **18.** *Music a)* timbre, as of a voice or instrument; tone color *b)* elaborate ornamentation —*vt.* **1.** to give color to; impregnate or cover with color, as with paint, stain, or dye **2.** to change the color of **3.** to give a pleasing, convincing, or reasonable appearance to; make plausible **4.** to alter or influence to some degree, as by distortion or exaggeration [prejudice *colored* his views] —*vi.* **1.** to become colored **2.** to change color, as ripening fruit **3.** to blush or flush —**call to the colors 1.** call or order to serve in the armed forces **2.** *Mil.* a bugle call for the daily flag-raising and flag-lowering ceremonies —**change color 1.** to become pale **2.** to blush or flush —**lose color** to become pale —**under color of** under the pretext or guise of —**col′or·er** *n.* **SYN.—color** is the general term, for which see the definition above; **shade** refers to any of the gradations of a color with reference to its degree of darkness [a light *shade* of green]; **hue**, often equivalent to **color**, is used specifically to indicate a modification of a basic color [orange of a reddish *hue*]; **tint** refers to a gradation of a color with reference to its degree of whiteness and suggests a paleness or delicacy of color [pastel *tints*]; **tinge** suggests the presence of a small amount of color, usually diffused throughout [white with a *tinge* of blue]

col·or·a·ble (-ə b'l) *adj.* [LL. *colorabilis*] **1.** capable of being colored **2.** apparently valid or plausible, but actually specious; deceptive —**col′or·a·bly** *adv.*

Col·o·rad·o (käl′ə rad′ō, -rä′dō) [< Sp. name of the river, *Río Colorado*, Red River] **1.** Mountain State of the W U.S.: admitted 1876; 104,247 sq. mi.; pop. 2,207,000; cap. Denver: abbrev. **Colo., CO 2.** river in SW U.S., flowing from N Colo. southwest through Utah & Ariz. into the Gulf of California: 1,450 mi. **3.** river in Tex., flowing from the NW part southeast into the Gulf of Mexico: 840 mi. —**Col′o·rad′an, Col′o·rad′o·an** *adj., n.*

col·o·rad·o (käl′ə rad′ō, -rä′dō) *adj.* [Sp., red, lit., colored, pp. of *colorar* < L. *colorare* < *color*: see COLOR] of medium strength and color: said of cigars

☆**Colorado beetle** a widely distributed black-and-yellow beetle (*Leptinotarsa decemlineata*) that is a destructive pest of potatoes and other plants

Colorado Desert desert in SE Calif., west of the Colorado River: c. 2,000 sq. mi.

Colorado Springs city in C Colo.: site of the U.S. Air Force Academy: pop. 135,000

☆**col·or·ant** (kul′ər ənt) *n.* [Fr. < prp. of *colorer*, to color] anything used to give color to something else; pigment, dye, etc.

col·or·a·tion (kul′ə rā′shən) *n.* **1.** the condition of being colored **2.** the way a thing is colored **3.** the technique of using colors, as in painting

col·o·ra·tu·ra (kul′ər ə toor′ə, -tyoor′-) *n.* [It. < L. *coloratus*, pp. of *colorare*: see COLOR] **1.** brilliant runs, trills, etc., used to display a singer's skill **2.** music containing such ornamentation **3.** a soprano capable of singing such music: in full **coloratura soprano**

color bar *same as* COLOR LINE

col·or·blind (-blīnd′) *adj.* unable to perceive colors or to distinguish between certain colors, as red and green —**col′or·blind′ness** *n.*

col·or·cast (-kast′, -käst′) *n.* [COLOR + (TELE)CAST] a television broadcast in color —*vt., vi.* **-cast′** or **-cast′ed, -cast′ing** to televise in color

col·ored (kul′ərd) *adj.* **1.** having color **2.** of a (specified) color **3.** of a group other than the Caucasoid; specif., Negro **4.** [C-] in South Africa, of racially mixed parentage: in this sense, usually **Coloured 5.** of or having to do with colored persons **6.** altered, influenced, distorted, or exaggerated to some degree [remarks *colored* by prejudice] —**the colored** (or **Coloured**) colored (or Coloured) persons

col·or·fast (-fast′, -fäst′) *adj.* that will keep its original color without fading or running —**col′or·fast′ness** *n.*

color filter a screen of colored glass, dyed gelatin, etc., used in photography to control or produce certain color or light effects

col·or·ful (kul′ər fəl) *adj.* **1.** full of color or of vivid colors **2.** full of interest or variety; picturesque; vivid —**col′or·ful·ly** *adv.* —**col′or·ful·ness** *n.*

☆**color guard** the persons carrying and escorting the colors (flag) in a parade, ceremony, etc.

col·or·if·ic (kul′ə rif′ik) *adj.* [Fr. *colorifique*: see COLOR & -FIC] **1.** producing or imparting color **2.** of color

col·or·im·e·ter (-rim′ə tər) *n.* [< COLOR + -METER] an instrument for determining the intensity and hue of a color, as of a solution in chemical analysis, by comparing it with standard colors

col·or·im·e·try (-rim′ə trē) *n.* the analysis or measurement of color by means of a colorimeter —**col·or·i·met′ric** (-ər ə me′trik) *adj.* —**col′or·i·met′ri·cal·ly** *adv.*

col·or·ing (kul′ər in) *n.* **1.** the act or art of applying colors **2.** anything applied to impart color; pigment, dye, stain,

etc. **3.** *a)* the way a thing is naturally colored; coloration *b)* the effect created by a particular use of color **4.** the complexion of the skin **5.** specious or false appearance **6.** alteration or influence

col·or·ist (-ist) *n.* **1.** a person who uses colors **2.** an artist skillful in using colors

col·or·is·tic (kul′ə ris′tik) *adj.* **1.** having to do with color or the use of color **2.** *Music* of or characterized by an emphasis on timbre or tonal effects —**col′or·is′tic·al·ly** *adv.*

col·or·less (-lis) *adj.* **1.** without color **2.** dull in color; gray or pallid **3.** lacking variety or interest; dull —**col′or·less·ly** *adv.* —**col′or·less·ness** *n.*

☆**color line** the barrier of social, political, and economic restrictions imposed on Negroes or other nonwhites —**draw the color line** to impose or accept the color line

color phase 1. a variant, atypical coloration of fur, feathers, skin, etc. occurring in an individual of an animal group **2.** a seasonal change in the coat or coloration of certain animals

color sergeant a sergeant detailed to carry the colors (flag), as in a color guard

Co·los·sae (kə läs′ē) city in ancient Phrygia, SW Asia Minor —**Co·los′sian** (-läsh′ən) *adj., n.*

co·los·sal (kə läs′'l) *adj.* **1.** like a colossus in size; huge; gigantic **2.** [Colloq.] astonishingly great; extraordinary [a *colossal* fool, a *colossal* production] —SYN. see ENORMOUS —**co·los′sal·ly** *adv.*

Col·os·se·um (käl′ə sē′əm) [L., orig., neut. of *colosseus*, gigantic < *colossus*, COLOSSUS] an amphitheater in Rome, built c. 75–80 A.D.: much of it is still standing —*n.* [c-] *same as* COLISEUM

Co·los·sians (kə läsh′ənz) a book of the New Testament which was an epistle from the Apostle Paul to the Christians of Colossae

co·los·sus (kə läs′əs) *n., pl.* -**los′si** (-ī), -**los′sus·es** [ME. < L. < Gr. *kolossos*] **1.** a gigantic statue; esp., [C-] that of Apollo set at the entrance to the harbor of Rhodes c. 280 B.C. and included among the seven wonders of the ancient world **2.** any huge or important person or thing

co·los·to·my (kə läs′tə mē) *n., pl.* -**mies** [COLO(N)² + -STOMY] the surgical operation of forming an artificial anal opening in the colon

co·los·trum (kə läs′trəm) *n.* [L., beestings] the first fluid, rich in protein, secreted by the mammary glands for several days after birth of the young

col·our (kul′ər) *n., vt., vi.* Brit. *sp.* of COLOR

-**co·lous** (kə ləs) [< base of L. *colere*, to cultivate, inhabit + -OUS] *a combining form meaning* growing (or living) in or among [*arenicolous*]

col·pi·tis (käl pīt′is) *n.* [< Gr. *kolpos*, womb + -ITIS] inflammation of the vagina; vaginitis

col·por·teur (käl′pôr′tər) *n.* [Fr., peddler; altered after *col*, the neck < OFr. *comporter*, to bring together: see COMPORT] a person who goes from place to place distributing or selling Bibles, religious tracts, etc. —**col′por′tage** (-tij) *n.*

colt (kōlt) *n.* [ME. & OE. < ? IE. *gel-d* < base *gel-*, to form a ball, rounded, whence CALF¹, CHILD] **1.** a young horse, donkey, zebra, etc.; specif., a male racehorse four years of age or under **2.** a young, inexperienced person **3.** *Naut.* a rope knotted at the end, formerly used for flogging

Colt (kōlt), **Samuel** 1814–62; U.S. inventor of a type of revolver

col·ter (kōl′tər) *n.* [ME. *culter* < OFr. *coltre* or OE. *culter*, both < L. *culter*, plowshare < IE. base *(s)kel-*, to cut, whence SHOULDER, SHIELD] a blade or disk on a plow, for making vertical cuts in the soil

colt·ish (kōl′tish) *adj.* of or like a colt; esp., frisky, frolicsome, gay. —**colt′ish·ly** *adv.*

colts·foot (kōlts′foot′) *n., pl.* -**foots** a plant (*Tussilago farfara*) of the composite family, with heads of small, yellow flowers and large leaves whose shape suggests the impression of a colt's foot

col·u·brine (käl′yoo brīn′, -brin) *adj.* [L. *colubrinus* < *coluber*, serpent: see COLON¹] **1.** of, characteristic of, or like a snake **2.** of any of a large, widespread family (Colubridae) of nonpoisonous snakes

co·lu·go (kə loō′gō) *n. same as* FLYING LEMUR

Col·um (käl′əm), **Pad·raic** (pô′thrig) 1881– ; Ir. poet and playwright, in the U.S.

Co·lum·ba (kə lum′bə), **Saint** 521–597 A.D.; Ir. missionary: converted Scotland to Christianity: his day is June 9

col·um·ba·ri·um (käl′əm ber′ē əm) *n., pl.* -**ri·a** (-ə) [L., lit., dovecote < *columba*, dove, orig., gray bird (< IE. base *kel-*, *kāl-*, grayish color); akin to Gr. *chelainos*, black] **1.** a vault with niches for urns containing the ashes of cremated bodies **2.** such a niche **3.** *same as* COLUMBARY

col·um·bar·y (käl′əm ber′ē) *n., pl.* -**bar′ies** [ME. *columbare* < L. *columbarium*: see prec.] a shelter for pigeons or doves; dovecote

☆**Co·lum·bi·a** (kə lum′bē ə, -byə) [after Christopher COLUMBUS] **1.** [Poet.] the U.S. personified as a woman **2.** capital of S.C., on the Congaree River: pop. 114,000 **3.** city in C Mo.: pop. 59,000 **4.** [after the name of the first ship to enter it (1792)] river flowing from SE British Columbia,

through Wash., & along the Wash.–Oreg. border into the Pacific: 1,214 mi.

☆**Co·lum·bi·an** (-bē ən, -byən) *adj.* **1.** of Columbia **2.** of Christopher Columbus

Col·um·bine (käl′əm bin′) [It. *Colombina* < L. *columbina*, fem. of *columbinus*, dovelike: see COLUMBARIUM] daughter of Pantaloon and sweetheart of Harlequin: a stock character in early pantomime

col·um·bine (käl′əm bin′) *n.* [ME. & OFr. < ML. *columbina* < L. *columbinus*, dovelike (see COLUMBARIUM): the flower is thought to resemble a flock of doves] any of a genus (*Aquilegia*) of plants of the buttercup family, with showy, spurred flowers of various colors —*adj.* [Rare] of or like a dove

co·lum·bite (kə lum′bit) *n.* [COLUMB(IUM) + -ITE¹] a black mineral of variable composition, mainly the oxide of iron and niobium

co·lum·bi·um (-bē əm) *n.* [ModL. < COLUMB(IA) + -IUM] *former name of* NIOBIUM

co·lum·bous (-bəs) *adj.* designating or of compounds containing columbium with a valence of three

Co·lum·bus (kə lum′bəs) [after ff.] **1.** capital of Ohio, in the C part: pop. 540,000 (met. area 916,000) **2.** city in W Ga., on the Chattahoochee River: pop. 154,000

Co·lum·bus (kə lum′bəs), **Christopher** (It. name *Cristoforo Colombo;* Sp. name *Cristóbal Colón*) 1451?–1506; It. explorer in the service of Spain: discovered America (1492)

Columbus Day a legal holiday in the U.S. commemorating the discovery of America by Columbus in 1492, observed on the second Monday in October

col·u·mel·la (käl′yoo mel′ə) *n., pl.* **-mel′lae** (-ē) [L., dim. of *columen:* see COLUMN] any of a number of columnlike structures in plants and animals, as a small bone in the middle ear of amphibians, reptiles, etc. —**col′u·mel′lar** *adj.* —**col′u·mel′late** (-āt) *adj.*

col·u·mel·li·form (-mel′ə fôrm′) *adj.* having the form or shape of a columella

col·umn (käl′əm; *now sometimes* -yəm) *n.* [ME. & OFr. *colomne* < L. *columna*, collateral form of *columen*, column, pillar < IE. base *kel-*, to project, whence Gr. *kolophōn*, E. HILL, HOLM¹] **1.** a slender upright structure, generally consisting of a cylindrical shaft, a base, and a capital; pillar: it is usually a supporting or ornamental member in a building **2.** anything like a column in shape or function *[a column of water, the spinal column]* **3.** a formation of troops, ships, etc. in a file or adjacent files **4.** any of the vertical sections of printed matter lying side by side on a page and separated by a rule or blank space **5.** a series of feature articles appearing regularly under a fixed title in a newspaper or magazine, written by a special writer or devoted to a certain subject —**col·um·nar** (kə lum′nər), **col′umned** (-əmd) *adj.*

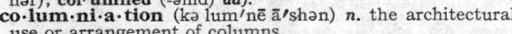

CAPITAL

SHAFT

BASE

COLUMN

co·lum·ni·a·tion (kə lum′nē ā′shən) *n.* the architectural use or arrangement of columns

☆**col·um·nist** (käl′əm nist, -ə mist; *now sometimes* käl′yəm ist) *n.* a person who writes or conducts a column, as in a newspaper

co·lure (kə loor′, kō′loor) *n.* [< L. *coluri* < Gr. *kolouroi*, the colures, lit., dock-tailed (ones), pl. of *kolouros < kolos*, docked + *oura*, tail: the "tail" (i.e., the lower part) is cut off from view by the horizon] *Astron.* either of two imaginary circles of the celestial sphere intersecting each other at right angles at the celestial poles: one passes through the ecliptic at the solstices (**solstitial colure**), the other at the equinoxes (**equinoctial colure**)

co·ly (kō′lē) *n., pl.* **-lies** [ModL. *colius* < Gr. *kolios*, green woodpecker] any of a group of small African birds (family Coliidae) with long tails and crested heads, that creep about on tree branches

col·za (käl′zə) *n.* [Fr. < Du. *koolzaad < kool*, a cabbage + *zaad*, a seed] **1.** any of several plants (genus *Brassica*) of the mustard family, esp. rape, whose seeds yield an oil used in lubricants, in the manufacture of synthetic rubber, etc. **2.** this oil: in full **colza oil**

com- (käm, kəm) [L. *com-* < OL. *com* (L. *cum*), with < IE. *kom*, closely along, next to, with, whence Gr. *koinos*, common] *a prefix meaning* with or together *[combine]:* also used as an intensive *[command]:* assimilated to *col-* before *l; cor-* before *r; con-* before *c, d, g, j, n, q, s, t,* and *v;* and *co-* before *h, w,* and all vowels

Com. **1.** Commander **2.** Commission **3.** Commissioner **4.** Committee

com. **1.** comedy **2.** comma **3.** commerce **4.** commercial **5.** common **6.** commonly **7.** communication

co·ma¹ (kō′mə) *n.* [ModL. < Gr. *kōma*, deep sleep < IE. base *ʰkeme-*, to grow tired, whence Sans. *śamitē* < *śam*, to work, prepare, Gr. *kamatos*, fatigue, effort] **1.** a state of deep and prolonged unconsciousness caused by injury or disease **2.** a condition of stupor or lethargy

co·ma² (kō′mə) *n., pl.* **-mae** (-mē) [L., hair of the head, foliage < Gr. *komē*, hair] **1.** *Astron.* a globular, cloudlike mass around the nucleus of a comet: the nucleus and coma together form the comet's head **2.** *a)* a bunch of branches, as on the top of some palm trees *b)* a terminal cluster of

bracts on a flowering stem, as in pineapples *c)* a tuft of hairs at the end of certain seeds **3.** *Photog.* a blur caused by the spherical aberration of oblique rays of light passing through a lens

Co·ma Ber·e·ni·ces (kō′mə ber′ə nī′sēz) [L., Berenice's Hair] a constellation in the N Hemisphere, north of Virgo: it contains the north galactic pole

co·make (kō′māk′) *vt.* **-made′**, **-mak′ing** *same as* COSIGN —**co′mak′er** *n.*

Co·man·che (kō man′chē) *n.* [MexSp. < Ute *komanchi*, stranger] **1.** *pl.* **-ches, -che** any member of a tribe of Uto-Aztecan Indians who formerly ranged from the Platte River to the Mexican border and now live in Oklahoma **2.** their Shoshonean dialect

☆**Co·man·che·an** (-chē ən) *adj.* [< *Comanche* County, Texas] designating or of a geologic epoch between the Jurassic and Cretaceous periods or its series of rocks, as typified by those found in the region of the Gulf of Mexico —**the Comanchean** the Comanchean Epoch or its series of rocks

co·mate (kō′māt) *adj.* [L. *comatus*, hairy < *coma*: see COMA²] *Bot.* hairy or tufted

co·ma·tose (kō′mə tōs′, käm′ə-) *adj.* [see COMA¹ & -OSE²] **1.** of, like, or in a coma or stupor **2.** as if in a coma; lethargic; torpid

co·mat·u·lid (kō mach′oo lid) *n.* [< ModL. *Comatulidae*, name of the family (< L. *comatulus*, having hair neatly curled, dim. of *comatus*, COMATE) + -ID] *same as* FEATHER STAR: also **co·mat′u·la** (-lə), *pl.* **-lae** (-lē′)

comb¹ (kōm) *n.* [ME. < OE. *camb*, comb, lit., toothed object, akin to G. *kamm* (OHG. *kamb*) < L. base *ʰgombho-s*, tooth, whence Sans. *jámbha-ḥ*, Gr. *gomphos*, tooth] **1.** a thin strip of hard rubber, plastic, metal, etc. with teeth, passed through the hair to arrange or clean it, or set in the hair to hold it in place or as an ornament **2.** anything like a comb in form, function, or location; specif., *a)* a currycomb *b)* an instrument used in cleaning and straightening wool, flax, etc. *c)* a red, fleshy outgrowth on the top of the head, as of a rooster *d)* a thing like a rooster's comb in position or appearance, as the crest of a helmet **3.** a honeycomb —*vt.* **1.** to clean, straighten out, or arrange with a comb **2.** to remove with or as with a comb; separate (often with *out*) **3.** to search thoroughly; look everywhere in *[to comb* a house for a missing book*]* —*vi.* to roll over; break: said of waves

comb² (kōōm, kōm) *n. same as* COOMB

comb. **1.** combination **2.** combining

com·bat (*for v.*, kəm bat′, käm′bat; *for n. & adj.*, käm′bat, kum′-) *vi.* **-bat′ed** *or* **-bat′ted, -bat′ing** *or* **-bat′ting** [Fr. *combattre* < VL. *combattere* < L. *com-*, with + *battuere*, to fight] to fight, contend, or struggle —*vt.* to fight or struggle against; oppose, resist, or seek to get rid of —*n.* [Fr. < the *v.*] **1.** armed fighting; battle **2.** any struggle or conflict; strife —*adj. Mil.* of or for combat —SYN. see BATTLE¹

com·bat·ant (käm′bə tənt, kəm bat′'nt) *adj.* [ME. < OFr., prp. of *combattre:* see prec.] **1.** fighting **2.** ready or prepared to fight —*n.* a person who engages in combat; fighter

combat fatigue a psychoneurotic condition characterized by anxiety, irritability, depression, etc., often occurring after prolonged combat in warfare

com·bat·ive (kəm bat′iv, käm′bə tiv) *adj.* fond of fighting or struggling; ready or eager to fight; pugnacious —**com·bat′ive·ly** *adv.* —**com·bat′ive·ness** *n.*

combe (kōōm, kōm) *n. same as* COOMB

comb·er (kō′mər) *n.* **1.** a person or thing that combs, as wool, flax, etc. **2.** ☆a large wave that rolls over or breaks on a beach, reef, etc.

com·bi·na·tion (käm bə nā′shən) *n.* [ME. *combinacioun* < LL. *combinatio*, a joining two by two] **1.** a combining or being combined **2.** a thing formed by combining **3.** an association of persons, firms, political parties, etc. for a common purpose **4.** *a)* the series of numbers or letters used in opening a combination lock *b)* the mechanism operating such a lock **5.** a one-piece undergarment combining an undershirt and drawers **6.** *Chem.* a uniting of substances to form a compound **7.** *Math.* any of the various groupings, or subsets, into which a number, or set, of units may be arranged without regard to order: dual combinations of 1, 2, 3, and 4 are 12, 13, 14, 23, 24, 34: cf. PERMUTATION —**com′bi·na′tion·al** *adj.*

☆**combination lock** a lock operated by a dial that is turned to a set series of numbers or letters to work the mechanism that opens it

com·bi·na·tive (käm′bə nāt′iv, kəm bī′nə tiv) *adj.* **1.** of or characterized by combination **2.** having the ability to combine **3.** resulting from combination

com·bine (kəm bin′; *for n. & v. 3*, käm′bin) *vt., vi.* **-bined′, -bin′ing** [ME. *combinen* < OFr. *combiner* < LL. *combinare*, to unite < L. *com-*, together + *bini*, two by two < base of *bis*: see BI-¹] **1.** to come or bring into union; act or mix together; unite; join **2.** to unite to form a chemical compound ☆**3.** [< *n.* 1] to harvest and thresh with a combine —*n.* ☆**1.** a machine for harvesting and threshing grain ☆**2.** an association of persons, corporations, etc. for commercial or political, often unethical, purposes —SYN. see JOIN —**com·bin′er** *n.*

comb·ings (kō′minz) *n.pl.* loose hair, wool, etc. removed in combing

combining form a word form that occurs only in compounds, or in compounds and derivatives, and that can combine with other such forms or with affixes to form a word (Ex.: *cardio-* and *-graph* in *cardiograph*, *odont-* in *odontoid*)

comb jelly same as CTENOPHORE

com·bo (käm′bō) *n., pl.* **-bos** [Colloq.] a combination; specif., a small jazz ensemble

com·bust (kəm bust′) *adj.* [ME. < L. *combustus,* pp. of *comburere,* to burn up: see COMBUSTION] *Astrol.* so close to the sun as to be obscured or, apparently, extinguished by its light: said of a star or planet —*vt., vi.* to undergo or cause to undergo combustion; burn

com·bus·ti·ble (kəm bus′tə b'l) *adj.* [Fr. < ML. *combustibilis:* see ff.] **1.** that catches fire and burns easily; flammable **2.** easily aroused; excitable; fiery —*n.* a flammable substance —**com·bus′ti·bil′i·ty** *n.* —**com·bus′ti·bly** *adv.*

com·bus·tion (-chən) *n.* [ME. < OFr. < LL. *combustio* < L. *combustus,* pp. of *comburere* (for **com-urere*), to burn < *com-,* intens. + **burere* (by faulty separation of *amburere,* to burn around < *ambi-,* AMBI- + *urere,* to burn, singe)] **1.** the act or process of burning **2.** rapid oxidation accompanied by heat and, usually, light **3.** slow oxidation accompanied by relatively little heat and no light **4.** violent excitement or agitation; tumult —**com·bus′tive** (-tiv) *adj.*

combustion furnace a furnace used in the laboratory to carry out elemental analysis of organic compounds

combustion tube a tube of heat-resistant glass in which a substance can be reduced by combustion, as in a furnace

☆**com·bus·tor** (-tər) *n.* the chamber in a jet engine, gas turbine, etc. in which combustion takes place

Comdr. Commander

Comdt. Commandant

come (kum) *vi.* **came, come, com′ing** [ME. *comen* < OE. *cuman,* akin to Goth. *qiman,* G. *kommen* < IE. base **gwem-, *gwā-,* to go, come, whence L. *venio,* I come, Gr. *bainein,* to go] **1.** to move from a place thought of as "there" or to or into a place thought of as "here": *a)* in the second person, with relation to the speaker [*come* to me, will you *come* to the dance tonight?] *b)* in the first person, with relation to the person addressed [I will *come* to see you] *c)* in the third person, with relation to the person or thing approached [he *came* into the room] **2.** to approach or reach by or as by moving toward **3.** to arrive or appear [help will *come*] **4.** to extend; reach [the bus line *comes* near the hotel] **5.** to happen; take place [success *came* to him early in life] **6.** to take form in the mind, as through recollection [her name finally *came* to him] **7.** to occur in a certain place or order [after 9 *comes* 10] **8.** *a)* to become actual; evolve; develop [peace will *come* in time] *b)* to proceed; progress; get (*along*) [how's your new book *coming* (along)?] **9.** *a)* to be derived [milk *comes* from cows] *b)* to be descended [he *comes* from an old family] *c)* to be a native, resident, or former resident (with *from*) **10.** to be caused; result [illness may *come* from a poor diet] ☆**11.** to be due or owed (*to*): used in the participle [to get what is *coming* to one] **12.** to pass by or as by inheritance [the house *came* to him on the death of his father] **13.** to enter into a certain state or condition [this word has *come* into use] **14.** to get to be; become [my shoe *came* loose] **15.** to be obtainable or available [this dress *comes* in four sizes] **16.** to amount; add up (*to*) **17.** [Colloq.] to have a sexual orgasm *Come* is often used in the subjunctive, with the subject inverted, to mean "when (a specified time or event) occurs" [*come* evening, he will return] —*interj.* look! see here! stop!: used to express irritation, impatience, remonstrance, etc. —**as good** (or **tough, strong,** etc.) **as they come** extremely good (or tough, strong, etc.) —**come about 1.** to happen; occur **2.** to turn about **3.** *Naut.* to change from one tack to another —**come across 1.** to meet by accident; find by chance **2.** [Colloq.] to be effective, readily understood, etc. ☆**3.** [Slang] to give, do, or say what is wanted —**come again?** ☆[Colloq.] what did you say? please repeat that! —**come along 1.** to appear or arrive **2.** to proceed or succeed —**come and get it!** [Colloq.] the meal is ready!: a summons to eat —**come around** (or **round) 1.** to revive; recover **2.** to make a turn or change in direction **3.** to concede or yield, as to a demand **4.** [Colloq.] to come to visit —**come at 1.** to reach; attain **2.** to approach angrily or swiftly, as in attacking —**come back 1.** to return ☆**2.** [Colloq.] to make a comeback —**come between** to cause estrangement between; divide —**come by 1.** to get; acquire; gain ☆**2.** to pay a visit —**come down** to suffer loss in status, wealth, etc. —**come down on** (or **upon)** to scold; criticize harshly —**come forward** to offer one's services; volunteer —**come in 1.** to enter **2.** to arrive **3.** to begin to be used; come into fashion ☆**4.** to start producing, as an oil well **5.** to finish in a competitive event [he *came* in fifth] **6.** *Radio* to answer a call or signal —**come in for** [Colloq.] to get or become eligible to get —**come into 1.** to enter into; join **2.** to inherit —**come off 1.** to become unfastened or detached **2.** to happen; occur **3.** to end up; emerge, as from a contest **4.** [Colloq.] to prove effective, successful, etc. [humor that

didn't *come off*] —☆**come off it!** [Slang] stop acting or talking in that way! —**come on 1.** to make progress **2.** to meet by accident; find **3.** to appear, begin to work, make an entrance, etc. —**come on!** [Colloq.] **1.** get started! hurry! **2.** stop behaving like that! Often used as a cajoling expression equivalent to *please* —**come one's way** to yield or become agreeable —**come out 1.** to be disclosed; become evident **2.** to be offered for public inspection, sale, etc. **3.** to be formally introduced to society; make a debut **4.** to end up; turn out [how did the election *come out*?] —**come out for** to announce one's approval of; endorse —**come out with 1.** to disclose **2.** to say; utter; publish **3.** to offer for public inspection, sale, etc. —**come over** to happen to; occur; seize [a strange feeling *came* over me] —**come through 1.** to wear through ☆**2.** to complete or endure something successfully ☆**3.** [Slang] to do what is wanted; provide (*with* what is needed) —**come to 1.** to recover consciousness **2.** *Naut. a)* to bring the ship's head nearer the wind *b)* to stop moving; anchor —**come up 1.** to arise; begin [a light breeze *came up*] **2.** to be mentioned, as in a discussion **3.** to rise or improve, as in status **4.** to be put forward, as for a vote **5.** [Brit.] to enter a university —**come upon 1.** to meet or encounter by accident **2.** to attack —**come up to 1.** to reach or extend to **2.** to equal —**come up with** to propose, produce, find, suggest, etc. —☆**how come?** [Colloq.] how does it come that? how is it that? why?

come·back (kum′bak′) *n.* [Colloq.] **1.** a return to a previous state or position, as of power, success, etc. ☆**2.** a witty answer; retort ☆**3.** ground for action or complaint; recourse

Com·e·con (käm′i kän′) Council for Mutual Economic Assistance: a trade organization of E European (Socialist) countries

co·me·di·an (kə·mē′dē ən) *n.* [Fr. *comédien:* see COMEDY] **1.** an actor who plays comic parts **2.** an entertainer who tells jokes, sings comic songs, etc. **3.** a person who amuses others by behaving in a comic way **4.** [Rare] a writer of comedy

co·me·dic (kə·mē′dik, -med′ik) *adj.* of or having to do with comedy

co·me·di·enne (kə·mē′dē en′) *n.* [Fr. *comédienne,* fem.] a woman comedian

com·e·do (käm′ə dō′) *n., pl.* **com′e·do′nes** (-dō′nēz), **com′e·dos′** [L., glutton < *comedere,* to eat up, devour < *com-,* intens. + *edere,* to EAT] a plug of dirt and fatty matter in a skin duct; blackhead

☆**come·down** (kum′doun′) *n.* a fall to a low or lower status or position, as of power, wealth, etc.

com·e·dy (käm′ə dē) *n., pl.* **-dies** [ME. & OFr. *comedie* < L. *comoedia* < Gr. *kōmōidia* < *kōmos,* banquet, festival + *aeidein,* to sing] **1.** orig., a drama or narrative with a happy ending or nontragic theme [Dante's *Divine Comedy*] **2.** *a)* any of various types of play or motion picture with a more or less humorous treatment of characters and situation and a happy ending: see also COMEDY OF MANNERS, FARCE, HIGH COMEDY, LOW COMEDY *b)* such plays collectively *c)* the branch of drama having to do with such plays *d)* the writing, acting, or theoretical principles of this kind of drama **3.** a novel or any narrative having a comic theme, tone, etc. **4.** the comic element in a literary work, or in life **5.** an amusing or comic event or sequence of events —**cut the comedy** [Slang] to stop joking; stop acting foolishly

comedy of manners a type of comedy depicting and satirizing the manners and customs of fashionable society: see also HIGH COMEDY

come-hith·er (kum′hith′ər) *adj.* [Colloq.] flirtatious or inviting [a come-hither look]

come·ly (kum′lē) *adj.* **-li·er, -li·est** [ME. *comli* < OE. *cymlic* < *cyme,* lovely, delicate, orig., feeble, akin to MHG. *kume,* weak (G. *kaum,* scarcely) < IE. base **gou-,* to cry out, whence Gr. *goaein,* to groan, bewail] **1.** pleasant to look at; attractive; fair **2.** [Archaic] seemly; decorous; proper —*SYN.* see BEAUTIFUL —**come′li·ness** *n.*

Co·me·ni·us (kō mē′nē əs), **John Amos** (born *Jan Amos Komensky*) 1592-1670; Moravian educational reformer & theologian

☆**come-on** (kum′än′) *n.* [Slang] **1.** an inviting look or gesture **2.** something offered as an inducement **3.** a swindler, esp. a shill

com·er (-ər) *n.* **1.** a person who comes [a contest open to all *comers*] ☆**2.** [Colloq.] a person or thing that shows promise of being a success

co·mes·ti·ble (kə mes′tə b'l) *adj.* [Fr. < L. *comestus, comesus,* pp. of *comedere,* to eat < *com-,* intens. + *edere,* to EAT] [Rare] eatable; edible —*n.* [*usually pl.*] food

com·et (käm′ət) *n.* [ME. *comete* < OE. *cometa* & OFr. *comete,* both < L. *cometa* < Gr. *kometēs* < *komē,* lit., hair of the head, fig., tail of a comet] a heavenly body in the solar system, having a starlike nucleus with a luminous mass (*coma*) around it, and, usually, a long, luminous tail that points away from the sun: comets follow an elliptical or parabolic orbit around the sun —**com′et·ar′y** (-ə ter′ē), **co·met·ic** (kä met′ik) *adj.*

co·meth·er (kō meth′ər) *n.* [dial. contr. < COME-HITHER] [Anglo-Ir. Dial.] **1.** an affair; circumstance **2.** friendship;

friendly relationship —**put the comether on** to use persuasion on; beguile

☆**come·up·pance** (kum'up'ns) *n.* [< COME + UP¹ + -ANCE] [Colloq.] deserved punishment; retribution

com·fit (kum'fit, käm'-) *n.* [ME. & OFr. *confit,* orig., pp. of *confire,* to preserve < L. *conficere:* see CONFECT] a candy or sweetmeat; esp., a candied fruit, nut, etc.

com·fort (kum'fart) *vt.* [ME. *comforten* < OFr. *conforter,* to comfort < LL. (esp. in Vulg. of OT.) *confortare,* to strengthen much < L. *com-,* intens. + *fortis,* strong] 1. to soothe in distress or sorrow; ease the misery or grief of; bring consolation or hope to 2. to give a sense of ease to 3. *Law* to help; aid —*n.* 1. aid; encouragement: now only in **aid and comfort** 2. relief from distress, grief, etc.; consolation 3. a person or thing that comforts 4. a state of ease and quiet enjoyment, free from worry, pain, etc. 5. anything that makes life easy or comfortable ☆6. a quilted bed covering; comforter —**com'fort·ing** *adj.* —**com'fort·less** *adj.*

SYN.—**comfort** suggests the lessening of misery or grief by cheering, calming, or inspiring with hope; **console** suggests like positive relief but implies a moderation of the sense of loss or disappointment [to *console* someone on the death of a parent]; **solace** suggests the relieving of melancholy, boredom, loneliness, etc. [he *solaced* himself by playing the flute]; **relieve** suggests the mitigation, often temporary, of misery or discomfort so as to make it bearable [to *relieve* the poor]; **soothe** implies the calming or allaying of pain or distress [she *soothed* the child with a lullaby] —*ANT.* afflict, distress

com·fort·a·ble (kumf'ar b'l, -tə b'l, kum'fər tə b'l) *adj.* [ME. < ML. *confortabilis*] 1. providing comfort or ease [*comfortable* shoes] 2. in a state of comfort; at ease in body or mind; contented 3. [Colloq.] sufficient to satisfy; adequate [a *comfortable* salary] —☆*n.* a quilted bed covering; comforter —**com'fort·a·ble·ness** *n.* —**com'fort·a·bly** *adv.*

SYN.—**comfortable** implies the absence of disturbing, painful, or distressing features and, in a positive sense, stresses ease, contentment, freedom from care, etc. [a *comfortable* climate]; **cozy** suggests such comfort as might be derived from shelter against storm, cold, hardship, etc. [a *cozy* nook by the fire]; **snug** is used of something that is small and compact, but just large enough to provide ease and comfort, and often carries additional connotations of coziness [a *snug* apartment]; **restful** applied to that which promotes relaxation, freedom from care, etc. [*restful* music] —*ANT.* miserable

com·fort·er (kum'fər tər, -fə tər) *n.* [ME. *comfortour* < OFr. *conforteor*] 1. a person or thing that comforts ☆2. a quilted bed covering 3. a long woolen scarf —**the Comforter** *Bible* the Holy Spirit: John 14:26

☆**comfort station** a public toilet or restroom

com·frey (kum'frē) *n., pl.* -**freys** [ME. & OFr. *confirie* < VL. *confervia,* comfrey, for L. *conferva,* a water plant < *confervere,* to heal, grow together, orig., to seethe, boil together < *com-,* with *fervere,* to boil: from use in medicine to congeal wounds] any of a genus (*Symphytum*) of European plants of the borage family, with rough, hairy leaves and small blue, purplish, or yellow flowers, sometimes used for forage

com·fy (kum'fē) *adj.* -**fi·er,** -**fi·est** [contr. < COMFORTABLE] [Colloq.] comfortable

com·ic (käm'ik) *adj.* [ME. *comice* < L. *comicus* < Gr. *kōmikos*] 1. of, like, or having to do with comedy 2. amusing or intended to be amusing; humorous; funny 3. of comic strips or cartoons —*n.* 1. a comedian 2. the humorous element in art or life ☆3. *a) same as* COMIC STRIP or COMIC BOOK *b)* [*pl.*] a section of comic strips, as in a newspaper —*SYN.* see FUNNY

com·i·cal (käm'i k'l) *adj.* 1. causing amusement; humorous; funny; droll 2. [Obs.] of or fit for comedy —*SYN.* see FUNNY —**com'i·cal·i·ty** (-kal'ə tē) *n.* —**com'i·cal·ly** *adv.*

☆**comic book** a paper booklet of extended comic strips, sometimes of a sensational or violent nature

comic opera opera with humorous situations, a story that ends happily, and, usually, some spoken dialogue

☆**comic strip** a series of cartoons, as in a newspaper, usually telling a humorous or adventurous story

Co·mines (kô mēn'), **Phi·lippe de** (fē lēp' də) 1445?-1509?; Fr. historian & diplomat

Com·in·form (käm'in fôrm') *n.* [< *Com(munist) Inform-(ation)*] the Communist Information Bureau, an association of various European Communist parties (1947–56)

com·ing (kum'iŋ) *adj.* 1. approaching; immediately next [this *coming* Tuesday] 2. showing promise of being successful, popular, important, etc. [a *coming* young actor, the *coming* thing] —*n.* arrival; approach; advent —☆**have (something) coming to one** to deserve or merit

Com·in·tern (käm'in turn') *n.* [< *Com(munist) · Inter-n(ational)*] the international organization (*Third International*) of Communist parties (1919–43)

co·mi·ti·a (kə mish'ē ə) *n.* [L., pl. of *comitium,* meeting place < *com-,* together + pp. stem of *ire,* to go] in ancient Rome, an assembly of citizens for electing officials, passing laws, etc. —**co·mi'ti·al** *adj.*

com·i·ty (käm'ə tē) *n., pl.* -**ties** [ME. *comite,* association < L. *comitas* < *comis,* polite, kind; earlier *cosmis,* prob. < *co-,* with + **smi-s* < IE. base **smei-,* to SMILE] 1. courteous behavior; politeness; civility 2. *same as* COMITY OF NATIONS 3. agreement among cooperating Christian denominations to avoid duplication of churches, missions,

etc. in specific areas 4. *Law* the principle by which the courts of one jurisdiction may give effect to the laws and decisions of another

comity of nations 1. the courtesy and respect of peaceful nations for each other's laws and institutions 2. loosely, the nations showing such courtesy and respect

comm. 1. commander 2. commentary 3. commerce 4. commissary 5. commission 6. committee 7. commonwealth 8. communication

com·ma (käm'ə) *n.* [L. < Gr. *komma,* clause in a sentence, that which is cut off < *koptein,* to cut off < IE. base **(s)kep-,* to cut, split, whence CAPON, SHAFT] 1. a mark of punctuation (,) used to indicate a slight separation of sentence elements, as in setting off nonrestrictive or parenthetical elements, quotations, items in a series, etc. 2. a slight pause

comma bacillus the bacillus (*Vibrio cholerae*) causing Asiatic cholera

com·mand (kə mand', -mänd') *vt.* [ME. *commanden* < OFr. *commander* < VL. *commandare* < L. *com-,* intens. + *mandare,* to commit, entrust: see MANDATE] 1. to give an order or orders to; direct with authority 2. to have authority or jurisdiction over; control 3. to have ready for use [to *command* a large vocabulary] 4. to deserve and get; require as due, proper, or becoming [to *command* respect] 5. to control or overlook from a higher position [the fort *commands* the entire valley] 6. [Obs.] to demand authoritatively —*vi.* 1. to exercise power or authority; be in control; act as a commander 2. to overlook, as from a height —*n.* 1. the act of commanding 2. an order; direction; mandate 3. authority to command 4. power to control or dominate by position 5. range of view 6. ability to have and use; mastery 7. *a)* a military or naval force, organization, or district, under a specified authority or jurisdiction *b) same as* AIR COMMAND 8. the post where the person in command is stationed

SYN.—**command,** when it refers to a giving of orders, implies the formal exercise of absolute authority, as by a sovereign, military leader, etc.; **order** often stresses peremptoriness, sometimes suggesting an arbitrary exercise of authority [I *ordered* him out of the house]; **direct** and **instruct** are both used in connection with supervision, as in business relations, **instruct** perhaps more often stressing explicitness of details in the directions given; **enjoin** suggests a directing with urgent admonition [he *enjoined* them to secrecy] and sometimes implies the legal prohibiting of an action; **charge** implies the imposition of a task as a duty, trust, or responsibility See also POWER

com·man·dant (käm'ən dant', -dänt') *n.* [Fr., orig. prp. of *commander:* see prec.] a commanding officer, specif. one in charge of a fort, service school, etc.

com·man·deer (käm'ən dir') *vt.* [Du. *kommandeeren,* to command, (esp. Afrik.) to commandeer < Fr. *commander,* COMMAND] 1. to force into military service 2. to seize (property) for military or governmental use 3. [Colloq.] to take forcibly

com·mand·er (kə man'dər, -män'-) *n.* [ME. *comaundour* < OFr. *comandeor*] 1. a person who commands; leader; specif., *a)* the chief officer of a unit in certain societies, fraternal orders, etc. *b) same as* COMMANDING OFFICER 2. a high-ranking member of an order of knighthood 3. *U.S. Navy* an officer ranking above a lieutenant commander and below a captain —**com·mand'er·ship'** *n.*

commander in chief *pl.* **commanders in chief** 1. the supreme commander of the armed forces of a nation, as, in the U.S., the President 2. an officer in command of all armed forces in a certain theater of war

com·mand·er·y (-ē) *n., pl.* -**er·ies** [ME. *comaundrie* < OFr. *comanderie* < ML. *commendaria* (< *commenda,* commendation, an entrusting < L. *commendare,* COMMEND), benefice entrusted to someone: sp. infl. by association with COMMAND] 1. the estate administered by a commander of an order of knights ☆2. a branch or lodge in certain societies, fraternal orders, etc.

commanding officer the officer in command of any of certain units or installations in the armed forces

com·mand·ment (kə mand'mənt, -mänd'-) *n.* [ME. & OFr. *comandement*] an authoritative command or order; mandate; precept; specif., any of the Ten Commandments: see TEN COMMANDMENTS

com·man·do (kə man'dō, -män'-) *n., pl.* -**dos,** -**does** [Afrik. < Port., lit., party commanded < *commandar,* to govern, command < VL. *commandare,* COMMAND] 1. *a)* orig., in South Africa, a force of Boer troops *b)* a raid or expedition made by such troops 2. *a)* a small raiding force trained to operate inside territory held by the enemy *b)* a member of such a group

command performance a performance, as of a play, put on as for a ruler by command or request

command post the field headquarters of a military unit, from which the commander directs operations

com·meas·ure (kə mezh'ər) *vt.* -**ured,** -**ur·ing** to equal in measure or extent —**com·meas'ur·a·ble** *adj.*

com·me·dia del·l'ar·te (kôm mä'dyä del lär'te) [It., lit., comedy of art] a type of Italian comedy developed in the 16th century and employing a stereotyped plot, improvised dialogue, and stock characters, as Pantaloon, Harlequin, Columbine, etc.

‡**comme il faut** (kô mēl fō') [Fr.] as it should be; proper; fitting

com·mem·o·rate (kə mem'ə rāt') *vt.* **-rat'ed, -rat'ing** [< L. *commemoratus*, pp. of *commemorare*, to call to mind < *com-*, intens. + *memorare*, to remind: see MEMORY] **1.** to honor the memory of, as by a ceremony **2.** to keep alive the memory of; serve as a memorial to —*SYN.* see CELEBRATE —**com·mem'o·ra'tor** *n.*

com·mem·o·ra·tion (kə mem'ə rā'shən) *n.* **1.** the act of commemorating **2.** a celebration in memory of someone or something —**in commemoration of** in honor of the memory of

com·mem·o·ra·tive (kə mem'ər ə tiv, -ə rāt'iv) *adj.* serving to commemorate: also **com·mem'o·ra·to'ry** (-tôr'ē) —*n.* anything that commemorates —**com·mem'o·ra·tive·ly** *adv.*

com·mence (kə mens') *vi., vt.* **-menced', -menc'ing** [ME. *commencen* < OFr. *comencier* < *cominitiare*, orig., to initiate as priest, consecrate < L. *com-*, together + *initiare*, to INITIATE] to begin; start; originate —*SYN.* see BEGIN —**com·menc'er** *n.*

com·mence·ment (-mənt) *n.* **1.** the act or time of commencing; beginning; start **2.** the ceremonies at which degrees or diplomas are conferred at a school or college **3.** the day when this takes place

com·mend (kə mend') *vt.* [ME. *commenden* < L. *commendare*, to entrust to, commend < *com-*, intens. + *mandare*, to commit to one's charge: see MANDATE] **1.** to put in the care of another; entrust **2.** to mention as worthy of attention; recommend **3.** to express approval of; praise **4.** [Archaic] to transmit the kind regards of —**com·mend'a·ble** *adj.* —**com·mend'a·bly** *adv.*

com·men·dam (kə men'dam) *n.* [< ML. *dare* in *commendam*, to give in trust: see COMMANDERY] **1.** formerly, the temporary holding of a benefice, with the right to its revenues, by a cleric or layman in the absence of a proper incumbent: he was said to hold the benefice *in commendam* **2.** a benefice held in this way

com·men·da·tion (käm'ən dā'shən) *n.* [ME. *commendacion* < L. *commendatio*] **1.** the act of commending; esp., recommendation or praise **2.** [*pl.*] [Archaic] greetings or regards, as to a friend

com·mend·a·to·ry (kə men'də tôr'ē) *adj.* [LL. *commendatorius* < L. *commendator*, one who commends] **1.** serving to commend; expressing praise or approval **2.** recommending

com·men·sal (kə men'sal) *n.* [ME. < ML. *commensalis* < L. *com-*, with + *mensa*, table] **1.** a companion at meals **2.** *Biol.* either of the organisms living in commensalism —*adj.* designating, of, or like a commensal —**com·men'sal·ly** *adv.*

com·men·sal·ism (-iz'm) *n. Biol.* a close association or union between two kinds of organisms, in which one is benefited by the relationship and the other is neither benefited nor harmed

com·men·su·ra·ble (kə men'shər ə b'l, -sər-) *adj.* [LL. *commensurabilis* < L. *com-*, together + *mensurare*, to measure < *mensura*, measurement] **1.** measurable by the same standard or measure; specif., designating two quantities having a common measure which is contained an integral number of times in each **2.** properly proportioned; proportionate —*SYN.* see PROPORTIONATE —**com·men'su·ra·bil'i·ty** *n.* —**com·men'su·ra·bly** *adv.*

com·men·su·rate (-shər it, -sər-) *adj.* [LL. *commensuratus* < *com-*, with + *mensuratus*, pp. of *mensurare*, to measure < L. *mensura*, MEASURE] **1.** equal in measure or size; coextensive **2.** corresponding in extent or degree; proportionate **3.** commensurable (sense 1) —*SYN.* see PROPORTIONATE —**com·men'su·rate·ly** *adv.*—**com·men'su·ra'tion** (-ā'shən) *n.*

com·ment (käm'ent) *n.* [ME. & OFr. < L. *commentum*, invention < *commentus*, pp. of *comminisci*, to contrive, devise < *com-*, intens. + base of *meminisse*, to remember, akin to *mens*, MIND] **1.** *a)* a note in explanation, criticism, or illustration of something written or said; annotation *b)* such notes collectively **2.** a remark or observation made in criticism or as an expression of opinion **3.** talk; chatter; gossip —*vi.* [ME. *commenten* < OFr. *commenter* < L. *commentari*, to consider thoroughly] to make a comment or comments (*on* or *upon*); make remarks —*vt.* [Rare] to make comments on; annotate —*SYN.* see REMARK

com·men·tar·y (käm'ən ter'ē) *n., pl.* **-tar'ies** [L. *commentarius*, notebook, annotation < *commentari*: see COMMENT] **1.** a series of explanatory notes or annotations, often forming a treatise on a text **2.** a series of remarks or observations, usually connected in a loose narrative **3.** something having the force of a comment, remark, or illustration **4.** [*usually pl.*] a historical narrative based on personal experience; memoir [*Caesar's Commentaries*] —*SYN.* see REMARK —**com'men·tar'i·al** *adj.*

com·men·tate (-tāt') *vt.* **-tat'ed, -tat'ing** [back-formation from ff.] to write or deliver a commentary on —*vi.* to perform as a commentator (sense 2)

com·men·ta·tor (-ər) *n.* [L., inventor, contriver (in LL., interpreter): see COMMENT] **1.** a person who writes or delivers a commentary **2.** a person who reports, analyzes, and evaluates news events, trends, etc., as on radio and television

com·merce (käm'ərs; *also, for v.,* kə murs') *n.* [Fr. < L. *commercium* < *com-*, together + *merx* (gen. *mercis*),

merchandise] **1.** the buying and selling of goods, esp. when done on a large scale between cities, states, or countries; trade **2.** social intercourse **3.** [Rare] sexual intercourse —*vi.* **-merced, -merc'ing** [Archaic] to have personal dealings (*with*) —*SYN.* see BUSINESS

com·mer·cial (kə mur'shəl) *adj.* **1.** of or connected with commerce or trade **2.** of or having to do with stores, office buildings, etc. [*commercial* property] **3.** of a lower grade, or for use in large quantities in industry [*commercial* sulfuric acid] **4.** *a)* made, done, or operating primarily for profit *b)* designed to have wide popular appeal **5.** offering training in business skills, methods, etc. **6.** *Radio & TV* paid for by sponsors —*n. Radio & TV* a paid advertisement —**com·mer'cial·ly** *adv.*

commercial bank a bank primarily concerned with accepting demand deposits, used as checking accounts

com·mer·cial·ism (-iz'm) *n.* the practices and spirit of commerce or business, often, specif., as showing an undue regard for profit —**com·mer'cial·ist** *n.* —**com·mer'cial·is'tic** *adj.*

com·mer·cial·ize (-īz') *vt.* **-ized', -iz'ing** **1.** to run as a business; apply commercial methods to **2.** to engage in or make use of mainly for profit, esp. at a sacrifice of other values **3.** to cause to be affected by commercialism —**com·mer'cial·i·za'tion** *n.*

☆**commercial paper** negotiable instruments, such as promissory notes and bills of exchange, calling for the payment of money and issued in the ordinary course of business

commercial traveler a traveling salesman

Com·mie (käm'ē) *adj., n.* [*sometimes* **c-**] [Colloq.] Communist

com·mi·na·tion (käm'ə nā'shən) *n.* [ME. *comminacioun* < L. *comminatio* < *comminatus*, pp. of *comminari*, to threaten < *com-*, intens. + *minari*, to MENACE] a threat or denunciation —**com·mi·na·to·ry** (käm'i nə tôr'ē, kə min'ə) *adj.*

Com·mines (kô mēn') *same as* COMINES

com·min·gle (kə miŋ'g'l) *vt., vi.* **-gled, -gling** to mingle together; intermix; blend

com·mi·nute (käm'ə nōōt', -nyōōt') *vt.* **-nut'ed, -nut'ing** [< L. *comminutus*, pp. of *comminuere*, to make small < *com-*, intens. + *minuere*, to make small: see MINUTE²] to reduce to small, fine particles; make into powder; pulverize —**com'mi·nu'tion** *n.*

com·mis·er·a·ble (kə miz'ər ə b'l) *adj.* worthy of commiseration; pitiable

com·mis·er·ate (kə miz'ə rāt') *vt.* **-at'ed, -at'ing** [< L. *commiseratus*, pp. of *commiserari*, to pity < *com-*, intens. + *miserari*, to pity: see MISERY] to feel or show sorrow or pity for —*vi.* to condole or sympathize (*with*) —**com·mis'er·a'tion** *n.* —**com·mis'er·a'tive** (-ə rāt'iv, -ər ə tiv) *adj.* —**com·mis'er·a'tive·ly** *adv.*

com·mis·sar (käm'ə sär') *n.* [Russ. *komissar* < ML. *commissarius*: see COMMISSARY] the head of any of the former commissariats in the U.S.S.R.: since 1946, called *minister*

com·mis·sar·i·at (käm'ə ser'ē ət) *n.* [Fr. < *commissaire*, commissary < ML. *commissarius:* see ff.] **1.** the branch of an army which provides food and supplies for the troops **2.** food supplies **3.** [Russ. *komissariat*] formerly, any of the government departments in the U.S.S.R.: since 1946, called *ministry*

com·mis·sar·y (käm'ə ser'ē) *n., pl.* **-sar'ies** [ME. *commissarie* < ML. *commissarius* < L. *commissus*, pp. of *committere*: see COMMIT] **1.** a person to whom some duty is given by authority; deputy; specif., *a)* in France, a police official *b)* a person representing a bishop in a part of his diocese **2.** formerly, an army officer in charge of providing soldiers with food and other supplies **3.** food supplies ☆**4.** a store in a lumber camp, army camp, etc. where food and supplies can be obtained ☆**5.** a restaurant in a motion-picture or television studio —**com'mis·sar'i·al** *adj.*

com·mis·sion (kə mish'ən) *n.* [ME. & OFr. < ML. *commissio*, delegation of business (in L., a bringing together in a contest) < L. *commissus*, pp. of *committere:* see COMMIT] **1.** *a)* an authorization to perform certain duties or tasks, or to take on certain powers *b)* a document giving such authorization **2.** authority to act in behalf of another **3.** that which a person is authorized to do for another **4.** the state of being authorized to perform certain duties or tasks **5.** an entrusting, as of power, authority, etc., to a person or body **6.** the act of committing or doing; perpetration, as of a crime **7.** *a)* a group of people officially appointed to perform specified duties *b)* an administrative agency of the government with quasi-judicial and quasi-legislative powers *c)* a type of municipal governing body: see COMMISSION PLAN **8.** a percentage of the money taken in on sales, given as pay to a salesclerk or agent, often in addition to salary or wages **9.** *Mil. a)* an official certificate conferring rank; specif., a document issued by the President, making one a commissioned officer in the U.S. armed forces *b)* the rank or authority conferred —*vt.* **1.** to give a commission to **2.** to give power or authority to; authorize **3.** to give an order for (a thing to be made or done) **4.** *Naut.* to put (a vessel)

into service —*SYN.* see AUTHORIZE —**in commission 1.** entrusted to commissioners **2.** in use **3.** in fit condition for use —**out of commission 1.** not in use **2.** not in fit condition for use

com·mis·sion·aire (kə mish′ə ner′) *n.* [Fr.] [Chiefly Brit. & Canad.] a person, esp. any of a group of pensioned service personnel, employed to do errands or small tasks, as a doorkeeper, messenger, etc.

commissioned officer an officer in the armed forces holding rank by a commission: the lowest rank in the U.S. Army, Air Force, and Marine Corps is second lieutenant; in the Navy and Coast Guard, ensign

com·mis·sion·er (kə mish′ə nər) *n.* **1.** a person authorized to do certain things by a commission or warrant **2.** a member of a commission (sense 7) **3.** an official in charge of a certain government bureau, commission, departmental office, etc. **4.** an official appointed to administer a territory, province, etc.: usually **high commissioner** ☆**5.** a man selected to regulate and control a professional sport —**com·mis′sion·er·ship′** *n.*

☆**commission house** a brokerage firm that buys and sells for customers on a commission basis

commission merchant a person who buys or sells goods for others on a commission basis

☆**commission plan** a form of municipal government in which all legislative and administrative powers are in the hands of an elected commission (usually five or six heads of various municipal departments) instead of a mayor and council

com·mis·sure (käm′ə shoor′) *n.* [ME. & OFr. < L. *commissura* < *commissus,* pp. of *committere:* see ff.] **1.** a line where two parts join or unite; joint; seam **2.** *Anat.* a band of fibers joining symmetrical parts, as of the right and left sides of the brain and spinal cord —**com·mis·su·ral** (kə mish′ər əl, käm′ə shoor′əl) *adj.*

com·mit (kə mit′) *vt.* **-mit′ted, -mit′ting** [ME. *committen* < L. *committere,* to bring together, commit < *com-,* together + *mittere,* to send] **1.** to give in charge or trust; deliver for safekeeping; entrust; consign [*we commit* his fame to posterity] **2.** to put officially in custody or confinement [*committed* to prison] **3.** to hand over or set apart to be disposed of or put to some purpose [to *commit* something to the trash heap] **4.** to do or perpetrate (an offense or crime) **5.** to bind as by a promise; pledge; engage [*committed* to the struggle] **6.** to make known the opinions or views of [to *commit* oneself on an issue] **7.** to refer (a bill, etc.) to a committee to be considered —**commit to memory** to learn by heart; memorize —**commit to paper** (or **writing**) to write down; record —**com·mit′ta·ble** *adj.* *SYN.*—**commit,** the basic term here, implies the delivery of a person or thing into the charge or keeping of another; **entrust** implies committal based on trust and confidence; **confide** stresses the private nature of information entrusted to another and usually connotes intimacy of relationship; **consign** suggests formal action in transferring something to another's possession or control; **relegate** implies a consigning to a specific class, sphere, place, etc., esp. one of inferiority, and usually suggests the literal or figurative removal of something undesirable

com·mit·ment (-mənt) *n.* **1.** a committing or being committed **2.** official consignment by court order of a person to prison, to a mental hospital, etc. **3.** a pledge or promise to do something **4.** a financial liability undertaken, as an agreement to buy or sell securities **5.** the act of sending proposed legislation to a committee

com·mit·tal (-′l) *n.* the act of committing; commitment

com·mit·tee (kə mit′ē) *n.* [ME. *committe,* a representative < Anglo-Fr. *comité,* pp. (for Fr. *commis*) of *commettre,* to commit < L. *committere:* see COMMIT] **1.** a group of people chosen, as from the members of a legislature or club, to consider, investigate, and report or act on some matter or on matters of a certain kind **2.** a group of people organized to support some cause **3.** [Archaic] someone into whose charge someone or something is committed —**in committee** under consideration by a committee, as a resolution or bill

com·mit·tee·man (-mən) *n., pl.* **-men** (-mən) **1.** a member of a committee ☆**2.** a ward or precinct leader for a political party —**com·mit′tee·wom′an** *n.fem., pl.* **-wom′en**

☆**committee of the whole** a committee comprising all the members of a legislative body, etc. under more informal rules than those used in a regular session

com·mix (kə miks′, kä-) *vt., vi.* [back-formation < ME. *commixt,* mixed together < L. *commixtus:* see ff.] [Archaic or Poet.] to mix together; blend

com·mix·ture (-chər) *n.* [L. *commixtura* < *commixtus,* pp. of *commiscere,* to mix together < *com-,* together + *miscere,* to MIX] a mixture

com·mode (kə mōd′) *n.* [Fr., chest of drawers, orig., convenient, suitable < L. *commodus,* suitable: see COM- & MODE] **1.** a high headdress worn by women around 1700 **2.** a chest of drawers **3.** a small, low table with drawers or cabinet space: also **commode table 4.** a movable washstand **5.** a kind of chair enclosing a chamber pot **6.** a toilet, or water closet

com·mo·di·ous (kə mō′dē əs) *adj.* [ME., convenient < ML. *commodiosus* < L. *commodus,* suitable: see COM- & MODE] offering plenty of room; spacious; roomy —**com·mo′di·ous·ly** *adv.* —**com·mo′di·ous·ness** *n.*

com·mod·i·ty (kə mäd′ə tē) *n., pl.* **-ties** [ME. & OFr. *commodite,* benefit, profit < L. *commoditas,* fitness, adapta-

tion < *commodus,* suitable: see COM- & MODE] **1.** any useful thing **2.** anything bought and sold; any article of commerce; often, specif., [*pl.*] basic items or staple products, as of agriculture **3.** [Archaic] personal advantage or convenience

☆**commodity dollar** the unit of a proposed system of currency, that would have a fluctuating gold value determined at regular intervals on the basis of an official index of the prices of key commodities

com·mo·dore (käm′ə dôr′) *n.* [earlier *commadore, commandore,* prob. via Du. *kommandeur* < Fr. *commandeur:* see COMMANDER] **1.** *U.S. Navy* an officer ranking above a captain and below a rear admiral: the rank was abolished in 1899 but temporarily restored in World War II **2.** *Brit. Navy* an unofficial title for a captain temporarily heading a squadron or division of a fleet **3.** a courtesy title given to the president of a yacht club, the senior captain of a merchant fleet, etc.

Com·mo·dus (käm′ə dəs), **Lu·cius Ae·li·us Au·re·li·us** (lōō′shəs ē′lē əs ô rē′lē əs) 161–192 A.D.; emperor of Rome (180–192)

com·mon (käm′ən) *adj.* [ME. *commun* < OFr. *comun* < L. *communis* (OL. *commoinos*), shared by all or many < IE. base **kom-moini-,* common (< **kom-,* COM- + **moini-,* achievement < **mei-,* to exchange, barter), whence OE. *gemæne,* public, general, G. *gemein:* cf. MEAN²] **1.** belonging equally to, or shared by, every one or all [the *common* interests of a group] **2.** belonging or relating to the community at large; public [*common* carriers] **3.** widely existing; general; prevalent [*common* knowledge] **4.** widely but unfavorably known [a *common* criminal] **5.** met with or occurring frequently; familiar; usual [a *common* sight] **6.** not of the upper classes; of the masses [the *common* man] **7.** having no rank [a *common* soldier] **8.** below ordinary; inferior [*common* ware] **9.** not refined; vulgar; low; coarse **10.** *Anat.* formed of or dividing into branches **11.** *Gram. a)* designating a noun that refers to any of a group or class, as book, apple, street: opposed to PROPER *b)* designating gender that is either masculine or feminine [the word *child* is of *common* gender] **12.** *Math.* belonging equally to two or more quantities [a *common* denominator] —*n.* ☆**1.** [*sometimes pl.*] land owned or used by all the inhabitants of a place; tract of open public land, esp. as a park in a city or town **2.** [*often C-*] *Eccles. a)* the office or service suitable for any of a class of festivals *b)* the ordinary of the Mass **3.** *Law* the right that a person has, in common with the owner or others, in the land or waters of another See also COMMONS —**in common** equally with, or shared by, another or all concerned —**com′mon·ness** *n.*

SYN.—**common** refers to that which is met with most frequently or is shared by all or most individuals in a group, body, etc., and may imply prevalence, usualness, or, in a depreciatory sense, inferiority [a *common* belief, a *common* hussy]; **general** implies connection with all or nearly all of a kind, class, or group and stresses extensiveness [*general* unrest among the people]; **ordinary** implies accordance with the regular or customary pattern, stressing commonplaceness and lack of special distinction [an *ordinary* workday]; **familiar** applies to that which is widely known and readily recognized [a *familiar* feeling]; **popular** and, in this connection, **vulgar** imply widespread currency, acceptance, or favor among the general public or the common people [a *popular* song, *Vulgar* Latin] See also MUTUAL —*ANT.* unusual, exceptional

com·mon·a·ble (-ə b′l) *adj.* [see COMMON, *n.,* 1] **1.** allowed to pasture on land owned by the village, town, etc. **2.** held in common: said of land

com·mon·age (-ij) *n.* [see COMMON, *n.,* 1 & -AGE] **1.** the right to pasture on land owned by the village, town, etc. **2.** the state of being held in common **3.** public or common land **4.** the common people; commonalty

com·mon·al·i·ty (käm′ə nal′ə tē) *n.* [ME. *communaltie* < OFr. *communallé:* see COMMUNAL & -TY] **1.** the common people; commonalty **2.** a sharing of common features, characteristics, etc.

com·mon·al·ty (käm′ən əl tē) *n., pl.* **-ties** [ME. & OFr. *communalte:* see COMMUNAL] **1.** the common people; people not of the upper classes **2.** a general body or group **3.** a corporation or its membership

common carrier a person or company in the business of transporting passengers or goods for a fee, at uniform rates available to all persons

common cold *same as* COLD (*n.* 4)

common denominator 1. a common multiple of the denominators of two or more fractions [10 is a *common* denominator of 1/2 and 3/5] **2.** a characteristic, element, etc. held in common

common divisor (or **factor**) a number or quantity that divides two or more numbers or quantities without a remainder; factor common to two or more numbers [6 is a *common divisor* of 6, 12, and 36]

com·mon·er (-ər) *n.* [ME. *comuner* < *comun,* COMMON] **1.** a person not of the nobility; member of the commonalty **2.** at Oxford University, a student who does not have a fellowship or scholarship, and therefore pays for his food (called *commons*)

Common Era *same as* CHRISTIAN ERA

common fraction a fraction with the numerator separated from the denominator by a diagonal or horizontal line, as 5/11 or 3/4: cf. DECIMAL (FRACTION)

common law the law of a country or state based on custom,

usage, and the decisions and opinions of law courts: distinguished from STATUTE LAW: it is now largely codified by legislative definition

com·mon-law marriage (käm'ən lô') *Law* a marriage not solemnized by religious or civil ceremony but effected by agreement to live together as husband and wife and, usually, by the fact of such cohabitation

common logarithm *Math.* a logarithm having 10 for its base

com·mon·ly (-lē) *adv.* **1.** in a common manner **2.** in the usual course of events; ordinarily

common market an association of countries formed to effect a closer economic union, esp. by means of mutual tariff concessions; specif., [C- M-] the European Economic Community

common measure *Music* same as COMMON TIME

common multiple *Math.* a multiple of each of two or more quantities [12 is a *common multiple* of 2, 3, 4, and 6]

com·mon·place (-plās') *n.* [lit. transl. of L. *locus communis*, Gr. *koinos topos*, general topic] **1.** orig., a passage marked for reference, or a number of such passages collected in a book (**commonplace book**) **2.** a trite or obvious remark; truism; platitude **3.** anything common or ordinary [travel is now a *commonplace*] —*adj.* neither new nor interesting; obvious or ordinary —*SYN.* see PLATITUDE, TRITE —**com'mon·place'ness** *n.*

common pleas *Law* ☆**1.** in some States, a court having general and original jurisdiction over civil and criminal trials **2.** in England, a former superior court with jurisdiction over civil suits

com·mons (käm'ənz) *n.pl.* [see COMMON] **1.** the common people; commonalty **2.** [often with sing. v.] *a)* the body politic that is made up of commoners *b)* [C-] same as HOUSE OF COMMONS **3.** [often with sing. v.] *a)* food provided for meals in common for all members of a group *b)* a room, building, table, or tables where such food is served, as at a college *c)* an allowance or ration of food

☆**common school** a public elementary school

common sense ordinary good sense or sound practical judgment —**com'mon-sense', com'mon-sen'si·cal** (-sen' si k'l) *adj.*

☆**common stock** ordinary capital stock in a company without a definite dividend rate or the privileges of preferred stock, but usually giving its owner a vote at shareholders' meetings in proportion to his holdings

common time *Music* a meter of four beats to the measure; 4/4 time

com·mon·weal (-wēl') *n.* [ME. *commun wele*: see COMMON & WEAL²] **1.** the public good; the general welfare **2.** [Archaic] a commonwealth

com·mon·wealth (-welth') *n.* [ME. *commun welthe*: see COMMON & WEALTH] **1.** the people of a nation or state; body politic **2.** *a)* a nation or state in which there is self-government; democracy or republic *b)* a federation of states [the *Commonwealth* of Australia] *Commonwealth* is also the official designation of Puerto Rico, in its special status under the U.S. government ☆**3.** loosely, any State of the U.S.; strictly, Ky., Mass., Pa., or Va., which were so designated in their first constitutions **4.** a group of people united by common interests **5.** [Obs.] the general welfare; commonweal —**the Commonwealth 1.** the government in England under the Cromwells and Parliament from 1649 to 1660: see also PROTECTORATE **2.** same as BRITISH COMMONWEALTH (OF NATIONS)

Commonwealth Day May 24, Queen Victoria's birthday, celebrated as a holiday in the British Commonwealth: cf. VICTORIA DAY

com·mo·tion (kə mō'shən) *n.* [L. *commotio* < *commotus*, pp. of *commovere*, to move, disturb < *com-*, together + *movere*, to MOVE] **1.** violent motion; turbulence **2.** a noisy rushing about; confusion; bustle **3.** [Archaic] a civil uprising; riot or insurrection **4.** [Archaic] mental agitation

com·move (kə mōōv') *vt.* **-moved', -mov'ing** [ME. *commoeven* < OFr. *commoveir* < L. *commovere*: see prec.] to move strongly; agitate; disturb; excite

com·mu·nal (käm'yoon 'l, kə myōōn''l) *adj.* [ME. & OFr. < LL. *communalis*] **1.** of a commune or communes **2.** of or belonging to the community; shared, or participated in, by all; public **3.** designating or of social or economic organization in which there is common ownership of property — **com·mu'nal·ly** *adv.*

com·mu·nal·ism (-iz'm) *n.* [Fr. *communalisme*] **1.** a theory or system of government in which communes or local communities, sometimes on an ethnic or religious basis, have virtual autonomy within a federated state **2.** the conflicting allegiance resulting from this **3.** communal organization; loosely, socialism —**com·mu'nal·ist** *n.*, *adj.* —**com·mu'nal·is'tic** *adj.*

com·mu·nal·ize (-īz') *vt.* **-ized', -iz'ing** to make communal; make public property of —**com·mu'nal·i·za'tion** *n.*

Com·mu·nard (käm'yoo närd') *n.* [Fr.] a person who supported or took part in the Commune of Paris (1871)

com·mune¹ (kə myōōn'; *for n.* käm'yōōn) *vi.* **-muned', -mun'ing** [ME. *communen* < OFr. *comuner*, to make common, share < *comun* (see COMMON); also < OFr. *communier*,

to administer the sacrament < L. *communicare*, to share, in LL.(Ec.), to receive the sacrament: see COMMUNICATE] **1.** *a)* to talk together intimately *b)* to be in close rapport [to *commune* with nature] **2.** to receive Holy Communion —*n.* [Poet.] intimate conversation —**commune with oneself** to think; ponder

com·mune² (käm'yōōn) *n.* [ME. & OFr. < ML. *communia*, orig. pl. of L. *commune*, lit., that which is common < *communis*, COMMON] **1.** [Archaic] the common people **2.** a community; specif., *a)* a local body for self-government, esp. in medieval towns *b)* formerly, a mir **3.** the smallest administrative district of local government in France, Belgium, and some other countries in Europe **4.** a strictly organized collective farm, as in China ☆**5.** a small group of people living communally and sharing in work, earnings, etc. —**the Commune 1.** the revolutionary government of Paris from 1792 to 1794 **2.** the revolutionary government established in Paris from March 18 to May 28, 1871

com·mu·ni·ca·ble (kə myōō'ni kə b'l) *adj.* [ME. < LL. *communicabilis*] **1.** that can be communicated, as an idea **2.** that can be transmitted, as a disease **3.** [Archaic] talkative —**com·mu'ni·ca·bil'i·ty** *n.* —**com·mu'ni·ca·bly** *adv.*

com·mu·ni·cant (-kənt) *n.* [< L. *communicans*, prp.: see ff.] **1.** a person who receives Holy Communion or belongs to a church that celebrates this sacrament **2.** [Rare] a person who communicates information; informant —*adj.* [Rare] communicating

com·mu·ni·cate (kə myōō'nə kāt') *vt.* **-cat'ed, -cat'ing** [< L. *communicatus*, pp. of *communicare*, to impart, share, lit., to make common < *communis*, COMMON] **1.** to pass along; impart; transmit (heat, motion, a disease, etc.) **2.** to make known; give (information, messages, etc.) —*vi.* **1.** to receive Holy Communion **2.** *a)* to give or exchange information, signals, or messages in any way, as by talk, gestures, writing, etc. *b)* to have a sympathetic or meaningful relationship **3.** to be connected [the living room *communicates* with the dining room] —**com·mu'ni·ca'tor** *n.*

com·mu·ni·ca·tion (kə myōō'nə kā'shən) *n.* **1.** the act of transmitting **2.** *a)* a giving or exchanging of information, signals, or messages by talk, gestures, writing, etc. *b)* the information, message, etc. **3.** close, sympathetic relationship **4.** a means of communicating; specif., *a)* [pl.] a system for sending and receiving messages, as by telephone, telegraph, radio, etc. *b)* [pl.] a system as of routes for moving troops and materiel *c)* a passage or way for getting from one place to another **5.** [often pl., with sing. v.] *a)* the art of expressing ideas, esp. in speech and writing *b)* the science of transmitting information, esp. in symbols

com·mu·ni·ca·tive (kə myōō'nə kāt'iv, -ni kə tiv) *adj.* **1.** giving information readily; talkative **2.** of communication —**com·mu'ni·ca'tive·ly** *adv.* —**com·mu'ni·ca'tive·ness** *n.*

com·mun·ion (kə myōōn'yən) *n.* [ME. *communioun* < OFr. *communion* < L. *communio*, a sharing (in LL.(Ec.), the sacrament of communion) < *communis*, COMMON] **1.** the act of sharing; possession in common; participation [a *communion* of interests] **2.** the act of sharing one's thoughts and emotions with another or others; intimate converse **3.** an intimate relationship with deep understanding **4.** a group of Christians professing the same faith and practicing the same rites; denomination **5.** [C-] a sharing in, or celebrating of, the Eucharist, or Holy Communion: see HOLY COMMUNION

com·mu·ni·qué (kə myōō'nə kā'; kə myōō'nə kā') *n.* [Fr., orig. pp. of *communiquer*, to communicate < L. *communicare*] an official communication or bulletin

com·mu·nism (käm'yə niz'm) *n.* [Fr. *communisme*: see COMMON + -ISM] **1.** any economic theory or system based on the ownership of all property by the community as a whole **2.** [often C-] *a)* a hypothetical stage of socialism, as formulated by Marx, Engels, Lenin, and others, to be characterized by a classless and stateless society and the equal distribution of economic goods and to be achieved by revolutionary and dictatorial, rather than gradualistic, means *b)* the form of government in the U.S.S.R., China, and other socialist states, professing to be working toward this stage by means of state planning and control of the economy, a one-party political structure, and an emphasis on the requirements of the state rather than on individual liberties: cf. SOCIALISM **3.** [often C-] *a)* a political movement for establishing a communist system *b)* the doctrines, methods, etc. of the Communist parties **4.** loosely, communalism

com·mu·nist (-nist) *n.* [Fr. *communiste*] **1.** an advocate or supporter of communism **2.** [C-] *a)* a member of a Communist Party *b)* loosely, a Communard —*adj.* **1.** of, characteristic of, or like communism or communists **2.** advocating or supporting communism **3.** [C-] of or having to do with a Communist Party —**com'mu·nis'tic** *adj.* —**com'mu·nis'ti·cal·ly** *adv.*

Communist Manifesto a pamphlet written in 1848 by Karl Marx and Friedrich Engels, summarizing their theory of, and program for, communism

Communist Party a political party based on the principles of communism as developed by Marx and Engels and

modified by Lenin, Stalin, and others, and dedicated to the establishment of communism

com·mu·ni·tar·i·an (kə myōō'nə ter'ē ən) *n.* a member or advocate of a communistic community

com·mu·ni·ty (kə myōō'nə tē) *n., pl.* **-ties** [ME. & OFr. *communite* < L. *communitas*, community, fellowship < *communis*, COMMON] **1.** *a)* all the people living in a particular district, city, etc. *b)* the district, city, etc. where they live **2.** a group of people living together as a smaller social unit within a larger one, and having interests, work, etc. in common [a college *community*] **3.** a group of nations loosely or closely associated because of common traditions or for political or economic advantage **4.** society in general; the public **5.** ownership or participation in common [*community* of goods] **6.** similarity; likeness [*community* of tastes] **7.** *a)* the condition of living with others *b)* friendly association; fellowship **8.** *Ecology* a group of animal and plant species living together and having close interactions, esp. through food relationships; biocenosis

☆**community center** a meeting place, often a complex of buildings, where the people of a community may carry on cultural, recreational, or social activities

☆**community chest** (or **fund**) a fund collected annually in many cities and towns by private contributions for certain local welfare agencies and institutions

☆**community college** a junior college established to serve a certain community and supported in part by it

☆**community property** in certain States of the U.S., property acquired by a husband or wife, or by both, during marriage and consequently owned in common by both

com·mu·nize (käm'yə nīz') *vt.* **-nized'**, **-niz'ing** **1.** to subject to communal ownership and control **2.** to cause to become communistic —**com'mu·ni·za'tion** *n.*

com·mut·a·ble (kə myōōt'ə b'l) *adj.* that can be commuted; interchangeable —**com·mut'a·bil'i·ty** *n.*

com·mu·tate (käm'yə tāt') *vt.* **-tat'ed**, **-tat'ing** [back-formation < ff.] to change the direction of (an electric current); esp., to change (alternating current) to direct current

com·mu·ta·tion (käm'yə tā'shən) *n.* [ME. & OFr. *com-mutacion* < L. *commutatio*, a changing < *commutatus*, pp. of *commutare*, COMMUTE] **1.** an exchange; substitution **2.** *a)* the substitution of one kind of payment for another *b)* the payment made ☆**3.** the act of traveling as a commuter, esp. by using a commutation ticket **4.** *Elec.* change of the direction of a current by a commutator **5.** *Law* a change of a sentence or punishment to one that is less severe

☆**commutation ticket** a ticket entitling the holder to travel over the same route, as on a railroad, a specified number of times at a reduced rate

com·mu·ta·tive (käm'yə tāt'iv, kə myōōt'ə tiv) *adj.* **1.** of commutation; involving exchange or replacement **2.** *Math.* of or pertaining to an operation in which the order of the elements does not affect the result, as, in addition, $3 + 2 = 2 + 3$ and in multiplication $2 \times 3 = 3 \times 2$

com·mu·ta·tor (käm'yə tāt'ər) *n.* [< L. *commutatus*, pp. of *commutare*, COMMUTE + -OR] **1.** a device for changing the direction of an electric current, esp. for changing alternating current to direct current **2.** in a dynamo or motor, a revolving part that collects the current from, or distributes it to, the brushes

com·mute (kə myōōt') *vt.* **-mut'ed**, **-mut'ing** [ME. *commuten* < L. *commutare*, to change < *com-*, intens. + *mutare*, to change] **1.** to change (one thing *for* or *into* another); exchange; substitute **2.** to change (an obligation, punishment, etc.) to one that is less severe —*vi.* **1.** *a)* to be a substitute *b)* make up; compensate **2.** to substitute payment in a lump sum, often reduced, for payment in installments ☆**3.** to travel as a commuter or by using a commutation ticket

☆**com·mut·er** (-ər) *n.* a person who travels daily or regularly, esp. by train, bus, etc., between two points at some distance

Com·my (käm'ē) *adj., n.* same as COMMIE

Com·ne·nus (käm nē'nəs) *pl.* **-ne·ni** (-nī) any member of a ruling family of the Byzantine Empire (1057–59; 1081–1185) and of the empire of Trebizond (1204–1461)

Co·mo (kō'mō) **1.** commune in N Italy, on Lake Como: pop. 82,000 **2. Lake,** lake in Lombardy, N Italy: 56 sq. mi.

Co·mo·do·ro Ri·va·da·via (kō'mō dō'rō rē'vä dä'vyä) seaport in S Argentina: pop. 75,000

Com·o·rin (käm'ə rin), **Cape** cape in Madras state, at the southernmost tip of India

Com·o·ro Islands (or **Archipelago**) (käm'ə rō') group of islands, a Fr. overseas territory, in the Indian Ocean, at the head of the Mozambique Channel: 838 sq. mi.; pop. 212,000; the Co·mores (kō mōr')

co·mose (kō'mōs) *adj.* [L. *comosus* < *coma*, hair] *Bot.* having a tuft of hairs; hairy

comp. 1. companion **2.** comparative **3.** compare **4.** comparison **5.** compilation **6.** compiled **7.** compiler **8.** composer **9.** composition **10.** compositor **11.** compound **12.** compounded **13.** comprising

com·pact (kəm pakt'; *also for adj., and for n. always,* käm'pakt) *adj.* [ME. < L. *compactus*, concentrated, pp. of *compingere*, to fasten together < *com-*, with, together + *pangere*, to fix, fasten: for IE. base see PEACE] **1.** closely and firmly packed or put together; dense; solid **2.** taking little space; arranged neatly in a small space **3.** not diffuse or wordy; terse **4.** made up or composed (*of*) ☆**5.** designating or of a relatively small, light, economical model of automobile —*vt.* **1.** to pack or join firmly together **2.** to make by joining or putting together **3.** to make more dense; compress; condense —*n.* **1.** [< the *adj.*, 2] a small cosmetic case, usually containing face powder and a mirror ☆**2.** a compact automobile **3.** [L. *compactum* < *compactus*, pp. of *compacisci*, to agree together < same base as *compingere*] an agreement between two or more individuals, states, etc.; covenant —*SYN.* see CLOSE¹ —**com·pact'ly** *adv.* —**com·pact'ness** *n.*

com·pac·tion (kəm pak'shən) *n.* a compacting or being compacted; compression

☆**com·pa·dre** (kəm pä'drā) *n.* [Sp., lit., godfather] [Southwest] a close friend; buddy

com·pan·ion¹ (kəm pan'yən) *n.* [ME. *compainoun* < OFr. *compaignon* < VL. *companio, lit., bread fellow, messmate < L. *com-*, with + *panis*, bread] **1.** a person who associates with or accompanies another or others; associate; comrade **2.** a person employed to live or travel with another **3.** [C-] a member of the lowest rank in an order of knighthood **4.** a thing that matches another in sort, color, etc.; one of a pair or set **5.** [Obs.] a scoundrel —*vt.* to be with as a companion; accompany —*SYN.* see ASSOCIATE

com·pan·ion² (kəm pan'yən) *n.* [Du. *kampanje*, quarterdeck < OFr. *compagne*, steward's room in a galley < It. (*camera della*) *compagna*, (room of the) company, crew: see COMPANY] *Naut.* **1.** the covering at the head of a companionway **2.** a companionway

com·pan·ion·a·ble (-ə b'l) *adj.* having the qualities of a good companion; sociable —**com·pan'ion·a·bil'i·ty** *n.* —**com·pan'ion·a·bly** *adv.*

com·pan·ion·ate (-it) *adj.* of or characteristic of companions

☆**companionate marriage** a proposed system of trial marriage in which the couple would postpone having children and could be divorced by mutual consent, until a final decision to stay married

com·pan·ion·ship (-ship') *n.* [COMPANION¹ + -SHIP] the relationship of companions; fellowship

com·pan·ion·way (-wā') *n.* [COMPANION² + WAY] **1.** a stairway leading from the deck of a ship to the cabins or space below **2.** the space for this stairway

com·pa·ny (kum'pə nē) *n., pl.* **-nies** [ME. & OFr. *com-paignie* < VL. *compania, lit., group sharing bread: see COMPANION¹] **1.** companionship; society [to enjoy another's *company*] **2.** a group of people; specif., *a)* a group gathered for social purposes *b)* a group associated for some purpose, as to form a commercial or industrial firm [a theatrical *company*, a business *company*] **3.** a trade guild in the Middle Ages **4.** the partners whose names are not given in the title of a firm [John Smith and *Company*] **5.** a guest or guests; visitor or visitors **6.** a habitual associate or associates [people are judged by the *company* they keep] **7.** *Mil.* a body of troops; specif., the lowest administrative unit, as of infantry, normally composed of two or more platoons and a headquarters **8.** *Naut.* the whole crew of a ship, including officers: in full, **ship's company** —*vt.* **-nied**, **-ny·ing** [Archaic] to go with as a companion; accompany —*vi.* [Archaic] to keep company: associate (*with*) —*SYN.* see TROOP —**bear company** to accompany —**keep company 1.** to associate (*with*) **2.** to go together; associate habitually: said esp. of a couple intending to marry —**keep (a person) company** to stay with (a person) so as to provide companionship —**part company 1.** to stop associating (*with*) **2.** to separate and go in different directions

☆**company union** an organization of workers in a single company, not affiliated with any group of labor unions: the term generally implies control by the employers

compar. 1. comparative **2.** comparison

com·pa·ra·ble (käm'pər ə b'l; *occas.* kəm par'ə b'l) *adj.* [ME. & OFr. < L. *comparabilis*] **1.** that can be compared; having characteristics in common **2.** worthy of comparison —**com'pa·ra·bil'i·ty**, **com'pa·ra·ble·ness** *n.* —**com'pa·ra·bly** *adv.*

com·par·a·tive (kəm par'ə tiv) *adj.* [ME. < L. *compara-tivus*] **1.** that compares; involving comparison as a method, esp. in a branch of study [*comparative* linguistics] **2.** estimated by comparison with something else; not absolute; relative [a *comparative* success] **3.** *Gram.* designating or of the second degree of comparison of adjectives and adverbs; expressing a greater degree of a quality or attribute than that expressed in the positive degree: usually indicated by the suffix *-er* (*harder*) or by the use of *more* with the positive form (*more* beautiful) —*n.* **1.** [Obs.] a competitor; rival **2.** *Gram. a)* the comparative degree *b)* a word or form in this degree —**com·par'a·tive·ness** *n.*

comparative literature the comparative study of various national literatures, stressing their mutual influences and their use of similar forms, themes, etc.

com·par·a·tive·ly (-lē) *adv.* **1.** in a comparative manner **2.** by comparison; relatively

com·pa·rat·or (käm'pə rāt'ər) *n.* any of various instruments for comparing some measurement, as of length, brightness, etc., with a fixed standard

com·pare (kəm per') *vt.* **-pared'**, **-par'ing** [ME. *comparen* < OFr. *comparer* < L. *comparare* < *com-*, with + *par*, equal] **1.** to regard as similar; liken (*to*) [to *compare* life to a river] **2.** to examine in order to observe or discover

similarities or differences (often followed by *with*) [*compare their voting records*] **3.** *Gram.* to form the positive, comparative, and superlative degrees of (an adjective or adverb) —*vi.* **1.** *a*) to be worthy of comparison (*with*) *b*) to be regarded as similar or equal **2.** to make comparisons —*n.* [Poet.] comparison —**beyond** (or **past** or **without**) **compare** without equal; incomparably good, bad, great, etc. *SYN.*—**compare** refers to a literal or figurative putting together in order to note points of resemblance and difference, and implies the weighing of parallel features for relative values [*to compare Shakespeare with Schiller*]; **contrast** implies a comparing for the purpose of emphasizing differences [*to contrast farm life with city life*]; **collate** implies detailed, critical comparison, specif. of different versions of the same text

com·par·i·son (kəm par′ə s'n) *n.* [ME. < OFr. *comparaison* < L. *comparatio* < pp. of prec.] **1.** a comparing or being compared; estimation of similarities and differences **2.** sufficient likeness to make meaningful comparison possible; possibility of comparison; similarity [*there is no comparison between the two singers*] **3.** *Gram.* the modification of an adjective or adverb to show the positive, comparative, and superlative degrees (Ex.: *long, longer, longest; good, better, best; slowly, more slowly, most slowly*) **4.** *Rhetoric* a figure of speech, as a simile, by which one thing is compared to another —**in comparison with** compared with

com·part (kəm pärt′) *vt.* [< OFr. *compartir* (or) < LL. *compartiri* < com-, intens. + *partiri, partire:* see PART, *v.*] to divide into parts; subdivide; partition

com·part·ment (-mənt) *n.* [Fr. *compartiment* < It. *compartimento* < *compartire*, COMPART] **1.** any of the divisions into which a space is partitioned off **2.** a separate section, part, division, or category —*vt.* same as COMPARTMENTALIZE —**com·part′men′tal** (-men′t′l) *adj.* —**com·part′ment·ed** *adj.*

com·part·men·tal·ize (kəm pärt′men′tə līz′) *vt.* -**ized**′, -**iz′ing** to put or separate into detached compartments, divisions, or categories —**com·part′men′tal·i·za′tion** *n.*

com·pass (kum′pəs) *vt.* [ME. *compassen* < OFr. *compasser*, to go around < VL. *compassare* < L. *com-*, together + *passus*, a step] **1.** to go round; make a circuit of **2.** to surround completely; form a circle around **3.** to grasp mentally; understand; comprehend **4.** to reach successfully; achieve; accomplish [*to compass one's ends*] **5.** to plot or contrive (something harmful) **6.** [Obs.] to curve —*n.* [ME. & OFr. *compas*, a circle, prob. < the *v*] **1.** [often *pl.*] an instrument consisting of two pointed legs connected at one end by a pivot, used for drawing arcs or circles or for taking measurements: also called **pair of compasses 2.** a boundary line; circumference **3.** an enclosed area **4.** full extent or range; reach; scope; specif., range of tones, as of a voice **5.** any of various instruments for showing direction, esp. one consisting of a magnetic needle swinging freely on a pivot and pointing to the magnetic north **6.** [Archaic] a circuit; course —*adj.* round; circular or semicircular —*SYN.* see RANGE —**com′pass·a·ble** *adj.*

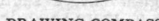

DRAWING COMPASS   COMPASS (SENSE 5)

compass card the circular card mounted on a free pivot inside a compass and marked with the points of direction and, often, the degrees of the circle

com·pas·sion (kəm pash′ən) *n.* [ME. & OFr. < LL.(Ec.) *compassio*, sympathy < *compassus*, pp. of *compati*, to feel pity < L. *com-*, together + *pati*, to suffer] sorrow for the sufferings or trouble of another or others, accompanied by an urge to help; deep sympathy; pity —*SYN.* see PITY

com·pas·sion·ate (-it; *for v.* -āt′) *adj.* feeling or showing compassion; sympathizing deeply; pitying —*vt.* -**at′ed**, -**at′ing** to pity —*SYN.* see TENDER[1] —**com·pas′sion·ate·ly** *adv.*

☆**compass plant 1.** a coarse plant (*Silphium laciniatum*) of the composite family, with large, bristly leaves and heads of yellow flowers, found on the prairies of central U.S.: the leaves reputedly point in a north-and-south direction **2.** any of various other plants whose leaves supposedly point to the north and south

compass saw a handsaw with a narrow, tapering blade for cutting curves

com·pat·i·ble (kəm pat′ə b'l) *adj.* [ME. < ML. *compatibilis* < LL. *compati:* see COMPASSION] **1.** capable of living together harmoniously or getting along well together; in agreement; congruous **2.** that can be mixed without react-

ing chemically or interfering with one another's action: said of drugs, insecticides, etc. **3.** *Bot.* that can be cross-fertilized or grafted readily **4.** *TV* designating or of a system of color transmission that produces satisfactory black and white pictures on a standard monochrome receiver —**com·pat′i·bil′i·ty, com·pat′i·ble·ness** *n.* —**com·pat′i·bly** *adv.*

com·pa·tri·ot (kəm pā′trē ət; *chiefly Brit.* -pat′rē-) *n.* [Fr. *compatriote* < LL. *compatriota:* see COM- & PATRIOT] **1.** a fellow countryman **2.** a colleague —*adj.* of the same country —**com·pa′tri·ot·ism** *n.*

compd. compound

com·peer (käm′pir, kəm pir′) *n.* [ME. & OFr. *compair* < L. *compar*, equal < *com-*, with + *par*, equal] **1.** a person of the same rank or status; equal; peer **2.** a companion; comrade —*vt.* [Obs.] to rival or match

com·pel (kəm pel′) *vt.* -**pelled**′, -**pel′ling** [ME. *compellen* < OFr. *compellir* < L. *compellere* < *com-*, together + *pellere*, to drive] **1.** to force or constrain, as to do something **2.** to get or bring about by force **3.** [Archaic or Poet.] to gather or drive together by force, as a flock —*SYN.* see FORCE —**com·pel′la·ble** *adj.* —**com·pel′ler** *n.* —**com·pel′ling·ly** *adv.*

com·pel·la·tion (käm′pə lā′shən) *n.* [L. *compellatio* < *compellare*, to accost, address] **1.** the act of addressing a person by a name or title **2.** the name or title so used; appellation

com·pend (käm′pend) *n. same as* COMPENDIUM

com·pen·di·ous (kəm pen′dē əs) *adj.* [ME. < L. *compendiosus*, short: see ff.] containing all the essentials in a brief form; concise but comprehensive —**com·pen′di·ous·ly** *adv.* —**com·pen′di·ous·ness** *n.*

com·pen·di·um (-əm) *n., pl.* -**di·ums, -di·a** (-ə) [L., a weighing together, abridgment < *compendere*, to weigh together < *com-*, together + *pendere*, to weigh] a summary or abstract containing the essential information in a brief form; concise but comprehensive treatise

com·pen·sa·ble (kəm pen′sə b'l) *adj.* [< ME. *compensen*, COMPENSATE + -ABLE] entitling to compensation

com·pen·sate (käm′pən sāt′) *vt.* -**sat′ed**, -**sat′ing** [< L. *compensatus*, pp. of *compensare*, to weigh one thing against another < *com-*, with + *pensare*, freq. of *pendere*, to weigh] **1.** to make up for; be a counterbalance to in weight, force, etc. **2.** to make equivalent or suitable return to; recompense; pay [*to compensate an owner for land taken by a city*] **3.** *Mech.* to counteract or make allowance for (a variation) —*vi.* **1.** to make or serve as compensation or amends (*for*) **2.** *Psychol.* to engage in compensation —*SYN.* see PAY[1] —**com·pen·sa·tive** (käm′pən sāt′iv, kəm pen′sə tiv) *adj.* —**com·pen·sa·to·ry** (kəm pen′sə tôr′ē) *adj.*

com·pen·sa·tion (käm′pən sā′shən) *n.* [ME. *compensacioun* < L. *compensatio*] **1.** a compensating or being compensated **2.** *a*) anything given as an equivalent, or to make amends for a loss, damage, unemployment, etc.; recompense *b*) payment for services; esp., wages or remuneration **3.** *Biol.* the counterbalancing of a defect in the structure or function of a part by a greater activity or development of another or other parts **4.** *Psychol.* a mechanism by which an individual seeks to make up for a real or imagined psychological defect by developing or exaggerating a psychological strength —**com′pen·sa′tion·al** *adj.*

com·pen·sa·tor (käm′pən sāt′ər) *n.* **1.** a person or thing that compensates **2.** any of various devices or circuits used to correct or offset some disturbing action, as speed deviations in a moving system, excessive current in a circuit, etc.

com·père (käm′per) *n.* [Fr., lit., godfather < ML.(Ec.) *compater*, orig., joint father (of the faithful) < L. *com-*, with (see COM-) + *pater*, FATHER] a master of ceremonies

com·pete (kəm pēt′) *vi.* -**pet′ed**, -**pet′ing** [L. *competere*, to strive together for, be qualified < *com-*, together + *petere*, to seek] to enter into or be in rivalry; contend; vie (*in* a contest, athletic meet, etc.)

com·pe·tence (käm′pə təns) *n.* [Fr. *compétence* < L. *competentia*, a meeting, agreement < *competens*, prp. of *competere*: see COMPETE] **1.** sufficient means for a modest livelihood **2.** condition or quality of being competent; ability; fitness; specif., legal capability, power, or jurisdiction Also **com′pe·ten·cy** (-tən sē)

com·pe·tent (-tənt) *adj.* [ME. < OFr. < L. *competens*, prp. of *competere*: see COMPETE] **1.** well qualified; capable; fit [*a competent doctor*] **2.** sufficient; adequate [*a competent understanding of law*] **3.** permissible or properly belonging (*with* to) **4.** *Law* legally qualified, authorized, or fit —*SYN.* see ABLE —**com′pe·tent·ly** *adv.*

com·pe·ti·tion (käm′pə tish′ən) *n.* [L. *competitio*] **1.** the act of competing; rivalry **2.** a contest, or match **3.** official participation in organized sport **4.** opposition, or effective opposition, in a contest or match **5.** rivalry in business, as for customers or markets **6.** the person or persons against whom one competes **7.** *Ecology* the struggle among individual organisms for food, water, space, etc. when the available supply is limited

SYN.—**competition** denotes a striving for the same object, position, prize, etc., usually in accordance with certain fixed rules; **rivalry** implies keen competition between opponents more or less evenly matched, and, unqualified, it often suggests unfriendliness or

even hostility; **emulation** implies endeavor to equal or surpass in achievement, character, etc. another, usually one greatly admired

com·pet·i·tive (kəm pet′ə tiv) *adj.* of, involving, or based on competition: also **com·pet′i·to′ry** (-tôr′ē) —**com·pet′i·tive·ly** *adv.* —**com·pet′i·tive·ness** *n.*

com·pet·i·tor (-tər) *n.* [L.] a person who competes, as a business rival

Com·piègne (kôⁿ pyen′y′) town in N France, on the Oise River: the armistices between the Allies & Germany (1918) & Germany & France (1940) were signed near here: pop. 24,000

com·pi·la·tion (käm′pə lā′shən) *n.* [ME. *compilacioun* < L. *compilatio*, a pillaging, hence collection of documents < *compilatus*, pp. of ff.] **1.** the act of compiling **2.** something compiled, as a book, report, etc.

com·pile (kəm pīl′) *vt.* **-piled′, -pil′ing** [ME. *compilen* < OFr. *compiler* < L. *compilare*, to snatch together, plunder < *com-*, together + *pilare*, to compress, ram down] **1.** to gather and put together (statistics, facts, etc.) in an orderly form **2.** to compose (a book, etc.) of materials gathered from various sources

com·pla·cen·cy (kəm plās′'n sē) *n.* [LL. *complacentia* < L. *complacens*: see ff.] quiet satisfaction; contentment; often, specif., self-satisfaction, or smugness: also **com·pla′cence** (-plās′'ns)

com·pla·cent (-'nt) *adj.* [L. *complacens*, prp. of *complacere*, to be very pleasing < *com-*, intens. + *placere*, to PLEASE] **1.** satisfied; esp., self-satisfied, or smug **2.** affable; complaisant —**com·pla′cent·ly** *adv.*

com·plain (kəm plān′) *vi.* [ME. *compleinen* < OFr. *complaindre* < VL. *complangere*, orig., to beat the breast < L. *com-*, intens. + *plangere*, to strike] **1.** to claim or express pain, displeasure, etc. **2.** to find fault; declare annoyance **3.** to make an accusation; bring a formal charge —**com·plain′er** *n.*

com·plain·ant (-ənt) *n.* [ME. *compleinaunt* < prp. of OFr. *complaindre*: see prec.] *Law* a person who files a charge or makes the complaint in court; plaintiff

com·plaint (kəm plānt′) *n.* [ME. & OFr. *complainte* < *complaindre*] **1.** the act of complaining; utterance of pain, displeasure, annoyance, etc. **2.** a subject or cause for complaining; grievance **3.** an illness; ailment **4.** *Law* a formal charge or accusation

com·plai·sance (kəm plā′z'ns, -s'ns; *chiefly Brit.* käm′pli zans′) *n.* [Fr. < ff.] **1.** willingness to please; disposition to be obliging and agreeable; affability **2.** an act or instance of this

com·plai·sant (kəm plā′z'nt, -s'nt; *chiefly Brit.* käm′pli zant′) *adj.* [Fr., prp. of *complaire* < L. *complacere*: see COMPLACENT] willing to please; affably agreeable; obliging —**com·plai′sant·ly** *adv.*

com·pleat (kəm plēt′) *adj. archaic sp.* of COMPLETE

com·plect (kəm plekt′) *vt.* [L. *complecti*: see COMPLEX] [Archaic] to twine together; interweave

☆**com·plect·ed** (-plek′tid) *adj.* [altered < COMPLEXIONED] [Dial. or Colloq.] *same as* COMPLEXIONED

com·ple·ment (käm′plə mənt; *for v.* -ment′) *n.* [ME. < L. *complementum*, that which fills up or completes < *complere*: see COMPLETE] **1.** that which completes or brings to perfection **2.** the amount or number needed to fill or complete **3.** a complete set; entirety **4.** something added to complete a whole; either of two parts that complete each other **5.** *Gram.* a word or group of words that, with the verb, complete the meaning and structure of the predicate (Ex.: *foreman* in *make him foreman, paid* in *he expects to get paid*) **6.** *Immunology* any of a group of heat-sensitive proteins in the blood plasma that act with specific antibodies to destroy corresponding antigens, as bacteria or foreign proteins **7.** *Math. a)* the number of degrees that must be added to a given angle or arc to make it equal 90 degrees *b)* the subset which must be added to any given subset to yield the original set **8.** *Music* the difference between a given interval and the complete octave **9.** *Naut.* the full crew of officers and men assigned to a ship —*vt.* to make complete; be a complement of

com·ple·men·tar·i·ty (käm′plə men ter′ə tē) *n.* [< ff. + -ITY] the state or fact of being complementary; necessary interrelationship or correspondence

com·ple·men·ta·ry (käm′plə men′tər ē) *adj.* **1.** acting as a complement; completing **2.** mutually making up what is lacking Also **com′ple·men′tal**

complementary angle either of two angles that together form a 90° angle

complementary colors any two colors of the spectrum that, combined in the right intensities, produce white or nearly white light

complement fixation *Immunology* the entering of complement into the product of an antigen–antibody reaction where it becomes inactive: used as an indicator in certain serological tests

com·plete (kəm plēt′) *adj.* [ME. & OFr. *complet* < L.

completus, pp. of *complere*, to fill up, complete < *com-*, intens. + *plere*, to fill: for IE. base see FULL¹] **1.** lacking no component part; full; whole; entire **2.** brought to a conclusion; ended; finished **3.** thorough; absolute /to have *complete* confidence in someone/ **4.** accomplished; skilled; consummate —*vt.* **-plet′ed, -plet′ing 1.** to end; finish; conclude **2.** to make whole, full, or perfect —**com·plete′ly** *adv.* —**com·plete′ness** *n.*

SYN.—**complete** implies inclusion of all that is needed for the integrity, perfection, or fulfillment of something [a *complete* set, *complete* control/; **full** implies the inclusion of all that is needed [a *full* dozen/ or all that can be held, achieved, etc. [in *full* bloom/; **total** implies an adding together of everything without exception [*total* number] and is, in general applications, equivalent to **complete** [*total* abstinence/; **whole** and **entire** imply unbroken unity, stressing that not a single part, individual, instance, etc. has been omitted or diminished [the *whole* student body, one's *entire* attention/; **intact** is applied to that which remains whole after passing through an experience that might have impaired it [the tornado left the barn *intact*/ See also CLOSE² —**ANT.** partial, defective

complete metamorphosis physical changes in the development of certain insects that include egg, larva, pupa, and adult stages, as in beetles, moths, bees, etc.

com·ple·tion (kəm plē′shən) *n.* [ME. < L. *completio*] **1.** the act of completing, or finishing **2.** the state of being completed

com·plex (kəm pleks′; *also, and for n. always,* käm′pleks) *adj.* [< L. *complexus*, pp. of *complecti*, to encircle, embrace < *com-*, with + *plectere*, to weave, braid] **1.** consisting of two or more related parts **2.** not simple; involved or complicated —*n.* **1.** a group of interrelated ideas, activities, etc. that form, or are viewed as forming, a single whole **2.** an assemblage of units, as buildings or roadways, that together form a single comprehensive group **3.** *Psychoanalysis a)* an integration of impulses, ideas, and emotions related to a particular object, activity, etc., largely unconscious, but strongly influencing the individual's attitudes and behavior *b)* popularly, an exaggerated dislike or fear; obsession —**com·plex′ly** *adv.*

SYN.—**complex** refers to that which is made up of many elaborately interrelated or interconnected parts, so that much study or knowledge is needed to understand or operate it [a *complex* mechanism/; **complicated** is applied to that which is highly complex and hence very difficult to analyze, solve, or understand [a *complicated* problem/; **intricate** specifically suggests a perplexingly elaborate interweaving of parts that is difficult to follow [an *intricate* maze/; **involved**, in this connection, is applied to situations, ideas, etc. whose parts are thought of as intertwining in complicated, often disordered, fashion [an *involved* argument/ —**ANT.** simple

complex fraction a fraction with a fraction in its numerator or denominator, or in both

com·plex·ion (kəm plek′shən) *n.* [ME. *complexioun* < OFr. *complexion*, combination of humors, hence temperament < L. *complexio*, combination < *complexus*: see COMPLEX] **1.** *a)* orig., the combination of the qualities of cold, heat, dryness, and moisture, or of the four humors, in certain proportions believed to determine the temperament and constitution of the body *b)* the temperament or constitution **2.** the color, texture, and general appearance of the skin, esp. of the face **3.** general appearance or nature; character; aspect —**com·plex′ion·al** *adj.*

com·plex·ioned (-shənd) *adj.* having a (specified) complexion [light-*complexioned*]

com·plex·i·ty (kəm plek′sə tē) *n.* **1.** the condition or quality of being complex **2.** *pl.* **-ties** anything complex or intricate; complication

complex number a number expressed as the formal sum of a real number and a multiple of the square root of –1 (Ex.: $a + b \sqrt{-1}$, when a and b are real)

complex sentence in traditional grammar, a sentence consisting of a main clause and one or more subordinate clauses

com·pli·a·ble (kəm plī′ə b'l) *adj.* [Archaic] compliant

com·pli·ance (-əns) *n.* **1.** a complying, or giving in to a request, wish, demand, etc.; acquiescence **2.** a tendency to give in readily to others Also **com·pli′an·cy** —**in compliance with** in accordance with

com·pli·ant (-ənt) *adj.* complying or tending to comply; yielding; submissive —**SYN.** see OBEDIENT —**com·pli′ant·ly** *adv.*

com·pli·ca·cy (käm′pli kə sē) *n.* **1.** the condition or quality of being complicated **2.** *pl.* **-cies** anything complicated; complication

com·pli·cate (käm′plə kāt′; *for adj.* -kit) *vt., vi.* **-cat′ed, -cat′ing** [< L. *complicatus*, pp. of *complicare*, to fold together < *com-*, together + *plicare*, to fold, weave < IE. base *plek-*, to braid (< *pel-*, to fold), whence FLAX] **1.** to make or become intricate, difficult, or involved **2.** [Obs.] to twist together —*adj.* **1.** [Archaic] complicated **2.** *Biol.* folded lengthwise, as some leaves or insects' wings

com·pli·cat·ed (-kāt′id) *adj.* made up of parts intricately involved; hard to untangle, solve, understand, analyze, etc. —**SYN.** see COMPLEX —**com′pli·cat′ed·ly** *adv.*

com·pli·ca·tion (käm′plə kā′shən) *n.* **1.** the act of complicating, or making involved **2.** a complicated condition or structure; complex, involved, or confused relationship of parts **3.** a complicating factor or occurrence as in the plot of a story or in the unfolding of events **4.** *Med.* a second disease or abnormal condition occurring during the course of a primary disease

COMPLEMENT
(arc YM, complement
of arc WY; angle
YXM, complement of
angle WXY)

com·plice (käm′plis) n. [ME. & OFr. < L. *complex*, a participant, confederate < *complicare:* see COMPLICATE] [Archaic] an accomplice or associate

com·plic·i·ty (kəm plis′ə tē) n., pl. -ties [Fr. *complicité* < L. *complex* (gen. *complicis*): see COMPLEX] 1. the fact or state of being an accomplice; partnership in wrongdoing 2. [Rare] complexity

com·pli·er (kəm plī′ər) n. a person who complies

com·pli·ment (käm′plə mənt; *for v.* -ment′) n. [Fr. < It. *complimento* < Sp. *cumplimiento* < *cumplir*, to fill up < VL. *complire*, for L. *complere*, to COMPLETE] 1. a formal act or expression of courtesy or respect 2. something said in admiration, praise, or flattery 3. [pl.] courteous greetings; respects [send with our *compliments*] 4. [Archaic or Dial.] a gift given for services; tip —vt. 1. to pay a compliment to; congratulate 2. to present something to (a person) as an act of politeness or respect

com·pli·men·ta·ry (käm′plə men′tər ē) adj. 1. paying or containing a compliment; expressing courtesy, respect, admiration, or praise 2. given free as a courtesy [a *complimentary* ticket] —com′pli·men·tar′i·ly (-men ter′ə lē, -men′tər ə lē) adv.

com·pline, com·plin (käm′plən) n. [ME. *compli(n)* < OFr. *complie* < ML.(Ec.) *completa (hora)*, completed (hour) < L. *completus:* see COMPLETE] *Eccles.* [often C-] the last of the seven canonical hours: also **com′plines, com′plins** (-plənz)

com·plot (käm′plät; *for v.* kəm plät′) n. [Fr. < OFr. *complote*, agreement (earlier, a crowd) < ? **compeloter*, to form into a ball < *com-*, together + *pelote*, a ball, ult. < L. *pila*, a ball] [Archaic] a plotting together; conspiracy —vt., vi. -plot′ted, -plot′ting [Archaic] to plot together; conspire

com·ply (kəm plī′) vi. -plied′, -ply′ing [ME. *complien* < OFr. *complir* < L. *complere:* see COMPLETE] 1. to act in accordance (*with* a request, order, rule, etc.) 2. [Obs.] to be formally polite

com·po (käm′pō) n., pl. -pos [< COMPO(SITION)] a composite substance, as mortar or plaster

com·po·nent (kəm pō′nənt) adj. [L. *componens*, prp. of *componere*, to compose < *com-*, together + *ponere*, to put] serving as one of the parts of a whole; constituent —n. 1. a) an element or ingredient b) any of the main constituent parts, as of a high-fidelity sound system 2. any of the elements into which a vector quantity, as force, velocity, etc., may be resolved on analysis —SYN. see ELEMENT

com·port (kəm pōrt′) vt. [ME. *comporten* < OFr. *comporter*, to allow, admit of < L. *comportare*, to bring together < *com-*, together + *portare*, to bring, carry] to behave or conduct (oneself) in a specified manner —vi. to agree or accord (*with*) —SYN. see BEHAVE

com·port·ment (-mənt) n. [Fr. *comportement:* see prec.] behavior or bearing; deportment

com·pose (kəm pōz′) vt. -posed′, -pos′ing [ME. *composen* < OFr. *composer* < *com-*, with + *poser*, to place; meaning infl. by L. *componere:* see COMPOSITE] 1. to form in combination; make up; constitute [mortar is *composed* of lime, sand, and water] 2. to put together; put in proper order or form 3. to create (a musical or literary work) 4. to adjust or settle; reconcile [to *compose* differences] 5. to put (oneself, one's mind, etc.) in a state of tranquillity or repose; calm; allay 6. *Printing* a) to set, or arrange (type) b) to set (a piece of writing) in type —vi. 1. to create musical or literary works 2. to set type

com·posed (-pōzd′) adj. [pp. of prec.] calm; tranquil; self-possessed —SYN. see COOL —com·pos′ed·ly (-pō′zid lē) adv. —com·pos′ed·ness n.

com·pos·er (-pō′zər) n. a person who composes, esp. one who composes music

composing room a room in which typesetting is done

composing stick a metal tray held in one hand by a compositor, in which he arranges the type into words

com·pos·ite (kəm päz′it) adj. [L. *compositus*, pp. of *componere*, to put together < *com-*, together + *ponere*, to put] 1. formed of distinct parts; compound 2. [C-] *Archit.* designating the classic order which combines the scroll-like ornaments of the Ionic capital with the acanthus design of the Corinthian 3. *Bot.* of a large family (Compositae) of dicotyledonous plants with flower heads composed of dense clusters of small flowers surrounded by a ring of small leaves or bracts: the daisy, thistle, artichoke, chrysanthemum, etc. belong to this family —n. 1. a thing of distinct parts; compound 2. *Bot.* a composite plant —com·pos′ite·ly adv.

COMPOSITE CAPITAL

composite number a number that can be divided without a remainder by some number other than itself or 1: distinguished from PRIME NUMBER

composite photograph a photograph made by superimposing one or more photographs on another

composite school [Canad.] a secondary school offering industrial and commercial, as well as academic, courses

com·po·si·tion (käm′pə zish′ən) n. [ME. *composicioun* < L. *compositio*, a putting together < *compositus:* see COMPOSITE] 1. the act of composing, or putting together a whole by combining parts; specif., a) the putting together of words; art of writing b) the creation of musical works 2. the makeup of a thing or person; aggregate of ingredients or qualities and manner of their combination; constitution 3. that which is composed; specif., a) a mixture of several parts or ingredients b) a work of music, literature, or art c) an exercise in writing done as school work 4. an arrangement of the parts of a work of art so as to form a unified, harmonious whole 5. an agreement, or settlement, often by compromise, as by the creditors of a potential bankrupt 6. the state or quality of being composite 7. *Linguis.* the device or process of forming compounds from two or more base morphemes: distinguished from AFFIXATION 8. *Printing* the work or skill of setting type —com′po·si′tion·al adj.

composition of forces *Mech.* the process of finding a force (the *resultant*) whose effect will equal that of two or more given forces (the *components*)

com·pos·i·tor (kəm päz′ə tər) n. [L., arranger, disposer: see COMPOSITE] a person who sets type; typesetter

com·pos men·tis (käm′pəs men′tis) [L.] *Law* of sound mind; sane

com·post (käm′pōst) n. [ME. < OFr. *composte*, condiment, pickle < L. *compositus:* see COMPOSITE] 1. a mixture; compound 2. a mixture of decomposing vegetable refuse, manure, etc. for fertilizing and conditioning the soil —vt. to convert (vegetable refuse) into compost

com·po·sure (kəm pō′zhər) n. [COMPOS(E) + -URE] calmness of mind or manner; tranquillity; self-possession —SYN. see EQUANIMITY

com·po·ta·tor (käm′pō tāt′ər) n. [LL. < *compotare* < *com-*, with + *potare*, to drink] [Rare] a drinking companion; fellow tippler —com′po·ta′tion n.

com·pote (käm′pōt) n. [Fr.: see COMPOST] 1. a dish of fruits stewed in a syrup ☆2. a long-stemmed dish for serving candy, fruit, nuts, etc.

com·pound¹ (käm pound′, kam-; *for adj. usually, and for n. always,* käm′pound) vt. [ME. *componen* < OFr. *compon(d)re*, to arrange, direct < L. *componere*, to put together < *com-*, together + *ponere*, to put, place] 1. to mix or combine 2. to make by combining parts or elements 3. to settle by mutual agreement; specif., to settle (a debt) by a compromise payment of less than the total claim 4. to compute (interest) on the sum of the principal and the accumulated interest which has accrued at regular intervals [interest *compounded* semiannually] 5. to increase or intensify by adding new elements [to *compound* a problem] —vi. 1. to agree 2. to compromise with a creditor 3. to combine and form a compound —adj. made up of two or more separate parts or elements —n. 1. a thing formed by the mixture or combination of two or more parts or elements 2. a substance containing two or more elements chemically combined in fixed proportions: distinguished from MIXTURE in that the constituents of a compound lose their individual characteristics and the compound has new characteristics 3. a word composed of two or more base morphemes, whether hyphenated or not: English compounds are usually distinguished from phrases by reduced stress on one of the elements and by changes in meaning (Ex.: *black′bird′*, *black′ bird′*; *grand′-aunt′*, *grand′ aunt′*) —**compound a felony** (or **crime**) [< vt.,] to agree, for a bribe or repayment, not to inform about or prosecute for a felony (or crime): it is an illegal act

com·pound² (käm′pound) n. [Anglo-Ind. < Malay *kampong*, enclosure] 1. in the Orient, an enclosed space with a building or group of buildings in it, esp. if occupied by foreigners 2. any similar enclosed space

compound animal any animal, such as most hydroids, corals, and bryozoans, composed of a number of individuals produced by budding from a single parent and usually so fused together that no demarcation is clearly distinguishable

compound engine an engine in which the steam is expanded under progressively lower pressures from cylinder to cylinder, to avoid excessive loss of steam by condensation

compound eye an eye made up of numerous simple eyes functioning collectively, as in insects

compound fraction same as COMPLEX FRACTION

compound fracture a bone fracture in which broken ends of bone have pierced the skin

compound interest interest paid on both the principal and the accumulated annual interest

compound leaf a leaf divided into two or more leaflets with a common leafstalk

compound meter *Music* any time signature in which the upper figure is a multiple of 3, as 6/8, 9/8, 12/8, etc.

compound microscope a microscope having a set of lenses built into the objective and another set in the eyepiece

compound number a quantity expressed in two or more sorts of related units (Ex.: 4 ft., 7 in.; 1 lb., 3 oz.)

compound sentence in traditional grammar, a sentence consisting of two or more independent, coordinate clauses

compound time any musical meter composed of multiples of two, three, or four beats to the measure, as 6/4, 9/8, etc.

---

fat, āpe, cär; ten, ēven; is, bīte; gō, hôrn, tōōl, look; oil, out; up, fur; get; joy; yet; chin; she; thin, then; zh, leisure; ŋ, ring; ə for *a* in *ago*, *e* in *agent*, *i* in *sanity*, *o* in *comply*, *u* in *focus*; ′ as in *able* (ā′b'l); Fr. bâl; ë, Fr. coeur; ö, Fr. feu; Fr. mon; ô, Fr. coq; ü, Fr. duc; r, Fr. cri; H, G. ich; kh, G. doch. See inside front cover. ☆ Americanism; ‡foreign; *hypothetical; < derived from

com·pra·dor, com·pra·dore (käm′prə dôr′) *n.* [Port., buyer < *comprar*, to buy < L. *comparare*, to procure, buy] formerly in China, a native agent for a foreign business, who had charge over the native workers, etc.

com·pre·hend (käm′prə hend′) *vt.* [ME. *comprehenden* < L. *comprehendere* < *com-*, with + *prehendere*, to catch hold of, seize: see PREHENSILE] **1.** to grasp mentally; understand **2.** to include; take in; comprise —*SYN.* see INCLUDE, UNDERSTAND —com′pre·hend′i·ble *adj.* —com′pre·hend′ing·ly *adv.*

com·pre·hen·si·ble (-hen′sə b'l) *adj.* [L. *comprehensibilis*] that can be comprehended; intelligible —com′pre·hen′si·bil′i·ty *n.* —com′pre·hen′si·bly *adv.*

com·pre·hen·sion (-hen′shən) *n.* [ME. *comprehensioun* < L. *comprehensio* < *comprehensus*, pp. of *comprehendere*: see COMPREHEND] **1.** the fact of including or comprising; inclusiveness **2.** *a)* the act of grasping with the mind *b)* knowledge that results from this **3.** the capacity for understanding ideas, facts, etc.

com·pre·hen·sive (-hen′siv) *adj.* [LL. *comprehensivus*] **1.** dealing with all or many of the relevant details; including much; inclusive [a *comprehensive* survey] **2.** able to comprehend fully [a *comprehensive* mind] —com′pre·hen′sive·ly *adv.* —com′pre·hen′sive·ness *n.*

com·press (kəm pres′; *for n.* käm′pres) *vt.* [ME. *compressen* < OFr. *compresser* < LL. *compressare* < L. *compressus*, pp. of *comprimere*, to squeeze < *com-*, together + *premere*, to PRESS¹] to press together; make more compact by or as by pressure —*n.* **1.** a pad of folded cloth, sometimes medicated or moistened, for applying pressure, heat, cold, etc. to some part of the body ☆**2.** a machine for compressing cotton bales —*SYN.* see CONTRACT —com·pres′si·bil′i·ty *n.* —com·pres′si·ble *adj.*

com·pressed (kəm prest′) *adj.* **1.** pressed together; made more compact by pressure **2.** *Bot.* flattened lengthwise, as the stalk of an aspen leaf **3.** *Zool.* flattened from side to side, as the body of the flounder or other flatfish

compressed air air reduced in volume by pressure and held in a container: the force with which it expands when released is used to operate machines

com·pres·sion (kəm presh′ən) *n.* [ME. < OFr. < L. *compressio*] **1.** a compressing or being compressed **2.** *Mech.* the compressing of a working fluid in an engine, as of the mixture in an internal-combustion engine just before ignition

com·pres·sive (-pres′iv) *adj.* compressing or tending to compress —com·pres′sive·ly *adv.*

com·pres·sor (-pres′ər) *n.* [L.] **1.** a person or thing that compresses **2.** a muscle that compresses a part **3.** a machine for compressing air, gas, etc.

com·prise (-prīz′) *vt.* **-prised′, -pris′ing** [ME. *comprisen* < OFr. *compris*, pp. of *comprendre*: see COMPREHEND] **1.** to include; contain **2.** to consist of; be composed of [a nation *comprising* thirteen States] **3.** to make up; form; constitute [a nation *comprised* of thirteen States]: in this sense regarded by some as a loose usage —*SYN.* see INCLUDE — com·pris′a·ble *adj.* —com·pris′al *n.*

com·pro·mise (käm′prə mīz′) *n.* [ME. & OFr. *compromis* < LL. *compromissum*, a compromise, mutual promise < L. *compromissus*, pp. of *compromittere*, to make a mutual promise to abide by an arbiter's decision < *com-*, together + *promittere*, to PROMISE] **1.** a settlement in which each side gives up some demands or makes concessions **2.** *a)* an adjustment of opposing principles, systems, etc. by modifying some aspects of each *b)* the result of such an adjustment **3.** something midway between two other things **4.** *a)* exposure, as of one's reputation, to danger, suspicion, or disrepute *b)* a weakening, as of one's principles —*vt.* **-mised′, -mis′ing 1.** to settle or adjust by concessions on both sides **2.** to lay open to danger, suspicion, or disrepute **3.** to weaken or give up (one's principles, ideals, etc.) as for reasons of expediency —*vi.* to make a compromise or compromises —com′pro·mis′er *n.*

☆**Comp·tom·e·ter** (kämp täm′ə tər) [*compto-* (< Fr. *compter* < L. *computare*: see COMPUTE) + -METER] *a trademark for* a calculating machine

Comp·ton (kämp′tən) [after G. D. *Compton,* a founder of the Univ. of S Calif.] city in SW Calif.: suburb of Los Angeles: pop. 79,000

Comp·ton (kämp′tən) **1. Arthur Hol·ly** (häl′ē), 1892-1962; U.S. physicist **2. Karl Taylor,** 1887-1954; U.S. physicist: brother of *prec.*

comp·trol·ler (kən trō′lər) *n.* [altered (after Fr. *compte,* an account) < CONTROLLER] *same as* CONTROLLER (sense 1, esp. in government usage) —comp·trol′ler·ship′ *n.*

com·pul·sion (kəm pul′shən) *n.* [ME. < LL. *compulsio* < L. *compulsus,* pp. of *compellere*] **1.** a compelling or being compelled; coercion; constraint **2.** that which compels; driving force **3.** *Psychol.* an irresistible, repeated, irrational impulse to perform some act

com·pul·sive (-siv) *adj.* [ML. *compulsivus*] of, having to do with, or resulting from compulsion —com·pul′sive·ly *adv.* —com·pul′sive·ness *n.*

com·pul·so·ry (-sər ē) *adj.* [ML. *compulsorius* < LL. *compulsor*, one who compels] **1.** that must be done, undergone, etc.; obligatory; required **2.** compelling; coercive — com·pul′so·ri·ly *adv.* —com·pul′so·ri·ness *n.*

com·punc·tion (kəm puŋk′shən) *n.* [ME. *compunccion* < OFr. *compunction* < LL. *compunctio,* a pricking (in LL.

(Ec.), the pricking of conscience) < L. *compunctus,* pp. of *compungere,* to prick, sting < *com-,* intens. + *pungere,* to prick] **1.** a sharp feeling of uneasiness brought on by a sense of guilt; twinge of conscience; remorse **2.** a feeling of slight regret for something done —*SYN.* see PENITENCE, QUALM —com·punc′tious *adj.* —com·punc′tious·ly *adv.*

com·pur·ga·tion (käm′pər gā′shən) *n.* [LL. *compurgatio,* a purifying < L. *compurgatus,* pp. of *compurgare,* to purge, purify < *com-,* intens. + *purgare,* to PURGE] formerly, the clearing of an accused person by the oaths of others testifying to his innocence

com·pur·ga·tor (käm′pər gāt′ər) *n.* [ML.: see prec.] formerly, one who testified in a compurgation

com·pu·ta·tion (käm′pyoo tā′shən) *n.* [ME. *computacioun* < L. *computatio*] **1.** the act of computing; calculation **2.** a method of computing **3.** a result obtained in computing; computed amount —com′pu·ta′tion·al *adj.*

com·pute (kəm pyoot′) *vt., vi.* **-put′ed, -put′ing** [L. *computare* < *com-,* with + *putare,* to reckon] to determine (a number, amount, etc.) by reckoning; calculate —*n.* computation: chiefly in the phrase **beyond compute** —*SYN.* see CALCULATE —com·put′a·bil′i·ty *n.* —com·put′a·ble *adj.*

com·put·er (kəm pyoot′ər) *n.* **1.** a person who computes **2.** a device used for computing; specif., an electronic machine which, by means of stored instructions and information, performs rapid, often complex calculations or compiles, correlates, and selects data: see also ANALOG COMPUTER, DIGITAL COMPUTER

☆**com·put·er·ize** (-īz′) *vt.* **-ized′, -iz′ing 1.** to equip with electronic computers so as to facilitate or automate procedures **2.** to operate, produce, regulate, compile, etc. by or as if by means of an electronic computer —com·put′er·i·za′tion *n.*

Comr. Commissioner

com·rade (käm′rad, -rəd) *n.* [Fr. *camarade* < Sp. *camarada,* chamber mate < L. *camera:* see CAMERA] **1.** a friend; close companion **2.** a person who shares interests and activities in common with others; partner; associate: used as a form of address, as in a Communist party **3.** [C-] [Colloq.] a Communist —*SYN.* see ASSOCIATE —com′rade·ly *adv.* — com′rade·ship′ *n.*

comrade in arms a fellow soldier

☆**com·rade·ry** (-rē) *n.* [altered (after COMRADE) < CAMARADERIE] *same as* CAMARADERIE

com·sat (käm′sat) *n.* [COM(MUNICATIONS) + SAT(ELLITE)] any of various communications satellites for relaying microwave transmissions, as of telephone, television, etc.

Com·stock·er·y (käm′stäk′ər ē) *n.* [after Anthony *Comstock* (1844-1915), U.S. self-appointed censor: prob. coined by G. B. SHAW] ruthless suppression of plays, books, etc. alleged to be offensive or dangerous to public morals

Com·stock Lode (käm′stäk′) [after H. T. *Comstock* (1820-70), who held first claim to it] rich deposits of silver & gold discovered in 1859 in W Nev.: virtually depleted by 1890

‡**comte** (kônt) *n.* [Fr.] *same as* COUNT² —com·tesse (kôn tes′) *n.fem.*

Comte (kônt; *E.* kômt), **(Isidore) Au·guste (Marie François Xavier)** (ô güst′) 1798-1857; Fr. philosopher: founder of positivism —Com·ti·an, Com·te·an (käm′tē ən, kôm′-) *adj.*

Comt·ism (käm′tiz'm, kôm′-) *n.* the philosophy of Auguste Comte; positivism —Comt′ist *adj., n.*

Co·mus (kō′məs) [L. < Gr. *kōmos,* festival] **1.** *Gr. & Rom. Myth.* a young god of festivity and revelry **2.** a masque (1634) by John Milton, praising chastity

con¹ (kän) *adv.* [contr. < L. *contra,* against] against; in opposition [to argue a matter pro and *con*] —*n.* a reason, vote, position, etc. in opposition

con² (kän) *vt.* **conned, con′ning** [ME. *connen,* to be able: see CAN¹] to peruse carefully; study; fix in the memory

con³ (kän) *vt., n. same as* CONN

☆**con⁴** (kän) *adj.* [Slang] confidence [a *con* man] —*vt.* **conned, con′ning** [Slang] **1.** to swindle (a victim) by first gaining his confidence **2.** to trick or fool, esp. by glib persuasion

☆**con⁵** (kän) *n.* [Slang] a convict

con- (kän, kən) *see* COM-

con. 1. [L. *contra*] against **2.** concerto **3.** conclusion **4.** connection **5.** consolidated **6.** consul **7.** continued **8.** [L. *conjunx*] wife

Co·na·kry (kän′ə krē′; *Fr.* kô nà krē′) capital of Guinea; seaport on the Atlantic: pop. 112,000

con a·mo·re (kän′ ə môr′ē; *It.* kôn′ ä mô′re) [It., lit., with love] **1.** tenderly **2.** with enthusiasm or devotion

Co·nan (kō′nən) [< Celt. base < ?] a masculine name

Conan Doyle, Sir **Arthur** *see* DOYLE

Co·nant (kō′nənt), **James Bryant** 1893- ; U.S. chemist & educator

co·na·tion (kō nā′shən) *n.* [L. *conatio,* an attempt < pp. of *conari,* to undertake, attempt < IE. base *ken-,* to strive: cf. DEACON] *Psychol.* the act or faculty of striving or making an effort —co·na′tion·al *adj.*

con·a·tive (kän′ə tiv, kō′nə-) *adj.* **1.** having to do with conation **2.** *Linguis.* expressing endeavor or effort: said of an aspect of certain verbs, as in Arabic

co·na·tus (kō nāt′əs) *n., pl.* **co·na′tus** [L. < *conari:* see CONATION] **1.** an effort or attempt; endeavor **2.** *Biol.* a natural active force, as of plants or animals, analogous to human effort

con bri·o (kän brē′ō, kōn) [It.] with spirit; spiritedly: a
direction to the performer in music

con·cat·e·nate (kän kat′′n āt′, kən-) *adj.* [LL. *con-
catenatus*, pp. of *concatenare*, to link together < L. *com-*,
together + *catenare* < *catena*, a chain] linked together;
connected —*vt.* **-nat′ed, -nat′ing** to link together or join,
as in a chain

con·cat·e·na·tion (kän kat′′n ā′shən, kən-) *n.* [LL. *con-
catenatio*: see prec.] **1.** a linking together or being linked
together in a series **2.** a series of things or events regarded
as causally or dependently connected

con·cave (kän kāv′; *also, and for n. usually,* kän′kāv) *adj.*
[ME. & OFr. < L. *concavus*, hollow < *com-*, intens. +
cavus, hollow: see CAVE[1]] hollow and curved like the inside
half of a hollow ball —*n.* a concave surface, line, object, etc.
—*vt.* **-caved′, -cav′ing** to make concave —**con·cave′ly** *adv.*
—**con·cave′ness** *n.*

con·cav·i·ty (kän kav′ə tē) *n.* [ME. & OFr. *concavite* < LL.
concavitas] **1.** the quality or condition of being concave **2.**
pl. **-ties** a concave surface, line, etc.

con·ca·vo-con·cave (kän kā′vō kän kāv′) *adj.* concave on
both sides, as some lenses

con·ca·vo-con·vex (-kän veks′) *adj.* **1.** concave on one side
and convex on the other **2.** *Optics* designating a lens whose
concave face has a greater degree of curvature than its
convex face, so that the lens is thinnest in the middle

con·ceal (kən sēl′) *vt.* [ME. *concelen* < OFr. *conceler* < L.
concelare, to hide < *com-*, together + *celare*, to hide < IE.
base *ʓkel*, to hide, conceal, whence HALL, HULL[1]] **1.** to put
out of sight; hide **2.** to keep from another's knowledge;
keep secret —*SYN.* see HIDE[1]

con·ceal·ment (-mənt) *n.* **1.** a concealing or being concealed **2.** a place or means of hiding

con·cede (kən sēd′) *vt.* **-ced′ed, -ced′ing** [L. *concedere* <
com-, with + *cedere*, to go, grant, CEDE] **1.** to admit as true
or valid; acknowledge [to *concede* a point in argument]
2. to admit as certain or proper [to *concede* victory to an
opponent] **3.** to grant as a right or privilege —*vi.* to make a
concession; specif., ☆to acknowledge defeat in an election
—**con·ced′er** *n.*

con·ceit (kən sēt′) *n.* [ME. *conceite* < *conceiven*, CONCEIVE]
1. *orig.*, *a)* an idea; thought; concept *b)* personal opinion
2. an exaggerated opinion of oneself, one's merits, etc.;
vanity **3.** [< It. *concetto*, of same ult. origin] *a)* an affectation in style or in expression of ideas; fanciful or witty
expression or notion; often, specif., a strained or bizarre
figure of speech *b)* the use of such figures in writing or
speaking **4.** a flight of imagination; fancy **5.** a small,
imaginatively designed item —*vt.* **1.** [Obs.] to think or
imagine **2.** [Dial.] to think well of; take a fancy to —*SYN.*
see PRIDE

con·ceit·ed (-id) *adj.* **1.** having an exaggerated opinion of
oneself, one's merits, etc.; vain **2.** [Obs.] whimsical;
fanciful —**con·ceit′ed·ly** *adv.* —**con·ceit′ed·ness** *n.*

con·ceiv·a·ble (kən sē′və b'l) *adj.* [ME.] that can be conceived, understood, imagined, or believed —**con·ceiv′a-
bil′i·ty** *n.* —**con·ceiv′a·bly** *adv.*

con·ceive (kən sēv′) *vt.* **-ceived′, -ceiv′ing** [ME. *conceiven*
< OFr. *conceveir* < L. *concipere*, to take in, receive < *com-*,
together + *capere*, to take] **1.** to become pregnant with;
cause to begin life in the womb **2.** to form or develop in
the mind **3.** to hold as one's conviction or opinion; think;
imagine **4.** to understand; apprehend **5.** to put in words;
couch; express —*vi.* **1.** to become pregnant **2.** to form a
concept or idea (*of*)

con·cel·e·brate (kän sel′ə brāt′) *vt.* **-brat′ed, -brat′ing** [<
L. *concelebratus*, pp. of *concelebrare*, to celebrate (a solemnity) in large numbers: see CON- & CELEBRATE] to celebrate
(the Eucharistic liturgy) jointly, the prayers being said in
unison by two or more of the officiating priests —**con′-
cel·e·bra′tion** *n.*

con·cent (kän sent′) *n.* [L. *concentus* < *concinere*, to sing
together < *com-*, with + *canere*, to sing] [Archaic] **1.**
musical harmony or concord **2.** agreement; accord

con·cen·ter (kän sen′tər) *vt., vi.* [Fr. *concentrer* < L. *com-*,
together + *centrum*, a CENTER] to bring or come to a common center; concentrate or converge

con·cen·trate (kän′sən trāt′) *vt.* **-trat′ed, -trat′ing** [<
prec. + -ATE[1]] **1.** to bring to, or direct toward, a common
center **2.** to collect or focus (one's thoughts, efforts, etc.)
3. to increase the strength, density, or intensity of **4.** to
mass (troops) in a place —*vi.* **1.** to come to or toward a
common center **2.** to direct one's thoughts or efforts; fix
one's attention (*on* or *upon*) **3.** to increase in strength,
density, or intensity —*n.* a substance that has been concentrated —*adj.* concentrated —**con′cen·tra′tor** *n.*

con·cen·tra·tion (kän′sən trā′shən) *n.* [ML. *concentratio*]
1. a concentrating or being concentrated **2.** close or fixed
attention **3.** strength or density, as of a solution **4.** a
concentrated substance

concentration camp a prison camp in which political
dissidents, members of minority ethnic groups, etc. are
confined

con·cen·tra·tive (kän′sən trāt′iv) *adj.* concentrating or
tending to concentrate

con·cen·tric (kən sen′trik) *adj.* [ME. *concentrik* < OFr.
concentrique < ML. *concentricus* < L.
com-, together + *centrum*, CENTER] having a center in common [*concentric*
circles]: also **con·cen′tri·cal** —**con·cen′-
tri·cal·ly** *adv.* —**con·cen·tric·i·ty** (kän′
sen tris′ə tē) *n.*

Con·cep·ción (kən sep′sē ōn′; *Sp.* kôn
sep′syôn′) city in SC Chile; seaport on a
river: pop. 167,000

CONCENTRIC
CIRCLES

con·cept (kän′sept) *n.* [L. *conceptus*, orig.
pp. of *concipere*: see CONCEIVE] an idea or
thought, esp. a generalized idea of a class
of objects; abstract notion —*SYN.* see IDEA

con·cep·ta·cle (kən sep′tə k'l) *n.* [L. *conceptaculum*,
receptacle < pp. of *concipere*: see CONCEIVE] *Bot.* a sac
opening outward and containing reproductive cells, found
in some brown algae

con·cep·tion (kən sep′shən) *n.* [ME. *concepcioun* < OFr.
conception < L. *conceptio*, a comprehending, conception <
conceptus: see CONCEIVE] **1.** a conceiving or being conceived
in the womb **2.** that which is so conceived; embryo or fetus
3. the beginning of some process, chain of events, etc. **4.**
the act, process, or power of conceiving mentally; formulation of ideas, esp. of abstractions **5.** a mental impression;
general notion; concept **6.** an original idea, design, plan,
etc. —*SYN.* see IDEA —**con·cep′tion·al** *adj.*

con·cep·tive (-tiv) *adj.* [L. *conceptivus*] having the power of
mental conception

con·cep·tu·al (kən sep′choo wəl) *adj.* [ML. *conceptualis*] of
conception or concepts —**con·cep′tu·al·ly** *adv.*

con·cep·tu·al·ism (-iz′m) *n.* the doctrine, intermediate
between nominalism and realism, that universals exist
explicitly in the mind as concepts, and implicitly in the
similarities shared by particular objects —**con·cep′tu·al-
ist** *n.* —**con·cep′tu·al·is′tic** *adj.*

con·cep·tu·al·ize (-īz′) *vt.* **-ized′, -iz′ing** to form a concept
or idea of; conceive —**con·cep′tu·al·i·za′tion** *n.*

con·cern (kən surn′) *vt.* [ME. *concernen* < ML. *concernere*,
to perceive, have regard to, fig. use of LL. *concernere*, to
sift, mix, as in a sieve < L. *com-*, with + *cernere*, to sift,
hence perceive, comprehend] **1.** to have a relation to or
bearing on; deal with **2.** to draw in; engage or involve; be a
proper affair of [that doesn't *concern* you] **3.** to cause to
feel uneasy or anxious —*n.* **1.** a matter of interest or
importance to one; that which relates to or affects one;
affair; matter; business **2.** interest in or regard for a person
or thing **3.** relation; reference **4.** worry; anxiety [to feel
concern over one's health] **5.** a business establishment;
company; firm —*SYN.* see CARE —**as concerns** in regard to;
with reference to; about —**concern oneself 1.** to busy
oneself (*with, about, over, in* something); take an interest
2. to be worried, anxious, or uneasy

con·cerned (kən surnd′) *adj.* **1.** involved or interested
(often with *in*) **2.** uneasy or anxious

con·cern·ing (-sur′niŋ) *prep.* relating to; having to do with;
in regard to; about

con·cern·ment (-surn′mənt) *n.* [Rare] concern; specif.,
a) an affair; matter *b)* importance *c)* worry; anxiety

con·cert (kän surt′; *for n. & adj.* kän′sərt) *vt., vi.* [Fr.
concerter < It. *concertare* < L. *concertare*, to contend, contest < *com-*, with + *certare*, to contend, strive: meanings
infl. by CONSORT & L. *conserere*, to join together] to arrange
or settle by mutual understanding; contrive or plan together; devise —*n.* [Fr. < It. *concerto*, agreement, union <
the *v.*] **1.** mutual agreement; concord; harmony of action
2. musical consonance **3.** a program of vocal or instrumental music, usually one in which a number of musicians
perform together —*adj.* of or for concerts —**in concert** in
unison; in agreement; together

con·cert·ed (kən sur′tid) *adj.* **1.** mutually arranged or
agreed upon; made or done together; combined **2.** *Music*
arranged in parts —**con·cert′ed·ly** *adv.*

concert grand (piano) the largest size of grand piano, for
concert performance

con·cer·ti·na (kän′sər tē′nə) *n.* [CONCERT + -INA: said to
have been coined by Sir Charles
Wheatstone (1802–75), Eng. physicist who invented it] a musical
instrument similar to an accordion
but smaller and with buttons instead of a keyboard

con·cer·ti·no (kän′cher tē′nō) *n.*
[It. dim.] **1.** a brief concerto, usually in a single movement **2.** the
solo group in a concerto grosso

con·cert·ize (kän′sər tīz′) *vi.* **-ized′,
-iz′ing** to perform as a soloist in
concerts; esp., to make concert
tours

CONCERTINA

con·cert·mas·ter (kän′sərt mas′
tər, -mäs′-) *n.* [transl. of G. *konzertmeister*] the leader of the
first violin section of a symphony orchestra, who plays the
solo passages and often serves as assistant to the conductor: also **con′cert·meis′ter** (-mīs′tər)

fat, āpe, cär; ten, ēven; is, bīte; gō, hôrn, tōōl, look; oil, out; up, fur; get; joy; yet; chin; she; thin, then; zh, leisure; ŋ, ring;
ə for a in ago, e in agent, i in sanity, o in comply, u in focus; ' as in able (ā′b'l); Fr. bal; ë, Fr. coeur; ö, Fr. feu; Fr. mon; ō, Fr. coq;
ü, Fr. duc; r, Fr. cri; H, G. ich; kh, G. doch. See inside front cover. ☆ Americanism; ‡foreign; *hypothetical; <derived from

con·cer·to (kən cher'tō) *n.*, *pl.* **-tos, -ti** (-tē) [It.: see CONCERT, *n.*] a musical composition for one, or two or three, solo instruments and an orchestra, usually in three movements of symphonic proportions

concerto gros·so (grō'sō) *pl.* **concerti gros'si** (-sē) [It., lit., big concerto] a concerto for a small group of solo instruments and a full orchestra

concert pitch *Music* **1.** a pitch, slightly higher than the usual pitch, to which concert instruments are sometimes tuned to achieve an increased brilliance of quality **2.** the standard pitch, in which A above middle C has a frequency of 440 vibrations a second **3.** the actual sound of a note written for a transposing instrument, as the trumpet

con·ces·sion (kən sesh'ən) *n.* [ME. & OFr. < L. *concessio* < *concessus*, pp. of *concedere*] **1.** an act or instance of conceding, granting, or yielding **2.** a thing conceded or granted; acknowledgment, as of an argument or claim **3.** a privilege granted by a government, company, etc.; esp., *a*) the right to use land, as for a specific purpose *b*) [Canad.] a government grant of land forming a subdivision of a township ☆*c*) the right or a lease to engage in a certain activity for profit on the lessor's premises [a refreshment or parking *concession*] ☆*d*) the land, space, etc. so granted or leased

con·ces·sion·aire (kən sesh'ə ner') *n.* [Fr. *concessionnaire*] the holder of a concession granted by a government, company, etc.: also ☆**con·ces'sion·er**

con·ces·sion·ar·y (kən sesh'ə ner'ē) *adj.* of a concession —*n.*, *pl.* **-ar'ies** a concessionaire

concession road [Canad.] any of the parallel roads of a township, about a mile apart, following closely the original survey lines

con·ces·sive (kən ses'iv) *adj.* [LL. *concessivus*] **1.** having the character of concession; conceding or tending to concede **2.** expressing concession [*though* is a *concessive* conjunction]

conch (käŋk, känch) *n.*, *pl.* **conchs** (käŋks), **conch·es** (kän'chəz) [ME. *conke* < L. *concha* < Gr. *konchē*, mussel, shell < IE. base *konkho-*, whence Sans. *śankhá-*, mussel] **1.** *a*) the large, spiral, one-piece shell of any of various sea mollusks *b*) such a mollusk, often edible **2.** *Rom. Myth.* such a shell used as a trumpet by the Tritons **3.** *same as* CONCHA (sense 1)

CONCH

conch. conchology

con·cha (käŋ'kə) *n.*, *pl.* **-chae** (-kē) [L.: see CONCH] **1.** *Anat.* any of several structures resembling a shell in form, as a thin, bony projection inside the nasal cavity, the largest hollow of the external ear, or the whole external ear **2.** *Archit.* the half dome covering an apse

con·chif·er·ous (käŋ kif'ər əs) *adj.* [< prec. + -FEROUS] having or bearing a shell

con·chi·o·lin (käŋ kī'ə lin, -kē'-) *n.* [< L. *concha*, a mussel (see CONCH) + -OL² + -IN¹] a protein of mollusks, forming the main portion of the organic matrix of the shell

con·choid (käŋ'koid) *n.* [< Gr. *konchoeidēs* (*grammē*), conchoid (line), lit., mussellike: see CONCH & -OID] a curve with a shell-like shape traced by an end point of a segment of constant length located on a straight line that revolves about a fixed point, while the other end point of this segment moves along a straight line that does not go through the fixed point

con·choi·dal (käŋ koi'd'l) *adj.* [< Gr. *konchoeidēs*, mussel-like (< *konchē*, CONCH) + -AL] *Mineralogy* producing smooth convexities or concavities, like those of a clamshell, when fractured: said of a brittle substance

con·chol·o·gy (-kä'lə jē) *n.* [see CONCH & -LOGY] the branch of zoology that deals with mollusks and shells —**con·chol'o·gist** *n.*

con·chy, con·chie (kän'chē, -shē) *n.*, *pl.* **-chies** [short for CONSCIENTIOUS] [Slang] a conscientious objector

con·ci·erge (kän'sē urzh'; *Fr.* kōn syerzh') *n.* [Fr., prob. ult. < VL. *conservius* < L. *conservus*, fellow slave < *com-*, with + *servus*, slave] **1.** a doorkeeper **2.** a custodian or head porter, as of an apartment house or hotel

con·cil·i·ar (kən sil'ē ər) *adj.* [< L. *concilium*, COUNCIL + -AR] of, from, or by means of a council

con·cil·i·ate (-āt') *vt.* **-at'ed, -at'ing** [< L. *conciliatus*, pp. of *conciliare*, to bring together, win over < *concilium*, COUNCIL] **1.** to win over; soothe the anger of; make friendly; placate **2.** to gain (regard, good will, etc.) by friendly acts **3.** [Archaic] to reconcile; make consistent —**SYN.** see PACIFY —**con·cil'i·a·ble** *adj.* —**con·cil'i·a'tion** *n.* —**con·cil'i·a'tor** *n.*

con·cil·i·a·to·ry (-ə tôr'ē) *adj.* tending to conciliate or reconcile: also **con·cil'i·a'tive** (-āt'iv)

con·cin·ni·ty (kən sin'ə tē) *n.*, *pl.* **-ties** [L. *concinnitas* < *concinnus*, skillfully joined, beautiful < **con-cid-nos*, cut together (so as to fit) < *com-*, with + base of *caedere*, to cut] a skillful arrangement of parts; harmony; elegance, esp. of literary style

con·cise (kən sīs') *adj.* [L. *concisus*, cut off, brief, pp. of *concidere*, to cut off < *com-*, intens. + *caedere*, to cut] brief and to the point; short and clear —**con·cise'ly** *adv.* —**con·cise'ness** *n.*

SYN.—concise implies the stating of much in few words, by removing all superfluous or expanded details [a *concise* summary]; **terse** adds to this the connotation of polished smoothness [a *terse* style]; **laconic**, on the other hand, suggests brevity to the point of curtness or ambiguity ["You'll see," was his *laconic* reply]; **succinct** implies clarity but compactness in the briefest possible number of words [he spoke in *succinct* phrases]; **pithy** suggests forcefulness and wit resulting from compactness [*pithy* axioms] —**ANT.** redundant, prolix

con·ci·sion (-sizh'ən) *n.* [L. *concisio*] **1.** orig., a cutting off; division **2.** concise quality; conciseness

con·clave (kän'klāv, käŋ'-) *n.* [ME. & OFr. < L., a room which may be locked < *com-*, with + *clavis*, a key] **1.** *R.C.Ch.* *a*) the private meeting of the cardinals to elect a pope *b*) the cardinals collectively **2.** any private or secret meeting

con·clude (kən klōōd') *vt.* **-clud'ed, -clud'ing** [ME. *concluden* < L. *concludere*, to conclude < *com-*, together + *claudere*, to shut] **1.** to bring to a close; end; finish **2.** to decide by reasoning; infer; deduce **3.** to decide (*to* do something); determine **4.** to arrange or settle; come to an agreement about [to *conclude* a pact] —*vi.* **1.** to come to a close; end; finish **2.** to come to an agreement —**SYN.** see CLOSE², DECIDE, INFER

con·clu·sion (kən klōō'zhən) *n.* [ME. & OFr. < L. *conclusio*, a closing, conclusion < pp. of prec.] **1.** the end or last part; as, *a*) the last division of a discourse, often containing a summary of what went before *b*) the last step in a reasoning process; judgment, decision, or opinion formed after investigation or thought *c*) the third and last part of a syllogism; inference *d*) the last of a chain of events; outcome **2.** an act or instance of concluding; final arrangement (*of* a pact, treaty, etc.) **3.** *Law a*) the formal closing of a plea or address to the court or a jury *b*) a binding act —**in conclusion** lastly; in closing —**try conclusions with** to engage in an argument, contest, etc. with

con·clu·sive (-siv) *adj.* [LL. *conclusivus* < pp. of L. *concludere*, CONCLUDE] that settles a question; final; decisive —**con·clu'sive·ly** *adv.* —**con·clu'sive·ness** *n.*

con·coct (kən käkt', kän-) *vt.* [< L. *concoctus*, pp. of *concoquere*, to boil together, prepare < *com-*, together + *coquere*, COOK] **1.** to make by combining various ingredients; compound **2.** to devise, invent, or plan —**con·coct'er** *n.* —**con·coc'tion** *n.* —**con·coc'tive** *adj.*

con·com·i·tance (-käm'ə təns) *n.* [ML. *concomitantia* < LL. *concomitans*, prp. of *concomitari*, to attend < L. *com-*, together + *comitari*, to accompany < *comes*, companion] the fact of being concomitant; accompaniment; existence in association: also **con·com'i·tan·cy**

con·com·i·tant (-käm'ə tənt) *adj.* [< LL. *concomitans*: see prec.] accompanying; attendant —*n.* an accompanying or attendant condition, circumstance, or thing —**con·com'i·tant·ly** *adv.*

Con·cord (kän'kôrd; *for 2 & 3 and for n.* käŋ'kərd) [prob. alluding to the amity hoped for among the inhabitants and their neighbors] **1.** city in W Calif., near Oakland: pop. 85,000 **2.** capital of N.H., on the Merrimack River: pop. 30,000 **3.** town in E Mass., near Boston: pop. 16,000: with Lexington, site of the first battles of the Revolutionary War (Apr. 19, 1775) —*n.* ☆**1.** a large, dark-blue variety of grape: in full, **Concord grape** ☆**2.** a wine made from this grape

con·cord (kän'kôrd, käŋ'-) *n.* [ME. & OFr. *concorde* < L. *concordia*, agreement, union < *concors* (gen. *concordis*), of the same mind < *com-*, together + *cor*, heart] **1.** agreement; harmony **2.** *a*) friendly and peaceful relations, as between nations *b*) a treaty establishing this **3.** *Gram. same as* AGREEMENT **4.** *Music* a combination of simultaneous and harmonious tones; consonance

con·cord·ance (kən kôr'd'ns, kän-) *n.* [ME. *concordaunce* < OFr. *concordance* < ML. *concordantia* < L. *concordans*, prp. of *concordare*, to agree < *concors*: see CONCORD] **1.** agreement; harmony **2.** an alphabetical list of the important words used in a book or by a particular writer, with references to the passages in which they occur

con·cord·ant (-d'nt) *adj.* [Fr. < L. *concordans*: see prec.] agreeing; consonant; harmonious —**con·cord'ant·ly** *adv.*

con·cor·dat (kən kôr'dat, kän-) *n.* [Fr. < ML. *concordatum*, agreement < L. *concordatus*, pp. of *concordare*: see CONCORDANCE] **1.** a compact; formal agreement; covenant **2.** an agreement between a pope and a government concerning the regulation of church affairs

☆**Concord coach** [after CONCORD, N.H., where the coaches were made] a 19th-cent. type of stagecoach used by early settlers of the western U.S.

con·course (kän'kôrs, käŋ'-) *n.* [ME. & OFr. *concours* < L. *concursus*, a running together < *concurrere*: see CONCUR] **1.** a coming or flowing together **2.** a crowd; throng; gathering **3.** a large open space where crowds gather, as in a park or railroad station **4.** a broad thoroughfare

con·cres·cence (kän kres''ns, kən-) *n.* [L. *concrescentia* < *concrescere*, to grow together < *com-*, together + *crescere*, to grow] *Biol.* a growing together of parts or cells, as of the lips of the blastopore along the dorsal side of the embryo during gastrulation

con·crete (kän krēt'; *also, and for n. & vt. 2 usually,* kän'krēt) *adj.* [ME. *concret* < L. *concretus*, pp. of *concrescere*: see CONCRESCENCE] **1.** formed into a solid mass; coalesced **2.** having a material, perceptible existence; of, belonging to, or characterized by things or events that can

be perceived by the senses; real; actual **3.** referring to a particular; specific, not general or abstract **4.** made of concrete **5.** designating a thing or class of things that can be perceived by the senses: opposed to ABSTRACT —*n.* **1.** a concrete thing, condition, idea, etc. **2.** a building material made of sand and gravel, bonded together with cement into a hard, compact substance and used in making bridges, dams, road surfaces, etc. —*vt.* **-cret'ed, -cret'ing 1.** to form into a mass; solidify **2.** to make of, or cover with, concrete —*vi.* to solidify —**con·crete'ly** *adv.* —**con·crete'ness** *n.*

concrete number a number telling how many or how much of a specific thing (Ex.: *seven* apples, *four* miles)

con·cre·tion (kän krē'shən, kən-) *n.* [L. *concretio:* see CONCRETE] **1.** a solidifying or being solidified **2.** an act or instance of concretizing **3.** a solidified mass; specif., *a) Geol.* an inclusion in sedimentary rock, usually rounded and harder than the surrounding rock, resulting from the formation of succeeding layers of mineral matter about some nucleus, as a grain of sand *b) Med.* a solidified mass, usually inorganic, deposited in a tissue or cavity of the body; calculus

con·cre·tion·ar·y (-er'ē) *adj.* **1.** of or formed by concretion **2.** containing concretions

con·cre·tize (kän'krə tīz', kän'-) *vt.* **-tized', -tiz'ing** to make (something) concrete; make specific; give definite form to —**con'cre·tiz'a·ble** *adj.*

con·cu·bi·nage (kän kyōō'bə nij) *n.* [ME. & OFr.] **1.** cohabitation without a legal marriage **2.** the state of being a concubine

con·cu·bi·nar·y (-ner'ē) *adj.* [ME. *concubinarius*] of, living in, or born from concubinage

con·cu·bine (kän'kyə bīn', kän'-) *n.* [ME. < OFr. *concubin(e)* < L. *concubina* (masc. *concubinus*) < *concumbere*, to lie with < *com-*, with + *cubare*, to lie down] **1.** a woman who cohabits with a man although not legally married to him **2.** in certain polygamous societies, a secondary wife, of inferior social and legal status

con·cu·pis·cence (kän kyōō'p'a s'ns) *n.* [ME. & OFr. < LL.(Ec.) *concupiscentia* < L. *concupiscens*, prp. of *concupiscere*, to desire eagerly < *com-*, intens. | *cupiscere*, to wish, desire < *cupere*, to desire] strong or abnormal desire or appetite, esp. sexual desire; lust —**con·cu'pis·cent** *adj.*

con·cur (kən kur') *vi.* **-curred', -cur'ring** [ME. *concurren* < L. *concurrere*, to run together < *com-*, together + *currere*, to run] **1.** to occur at the same time; happen together; coincide **2.** to combine in having an effect; act together [several events *concurred* to bring about this result] **3.** to agree (*with*); be in accord (*in* an opinion, etc.) —*SYN.* see CONSENT

con·cur·rence (-əns) *n.* [ME. < ML. *concurrentia* < L. *concurrens:* see ff.] **1.** a happening together in time or place **2.** a combining to produce or bring about something **3.** agreement; accord **4.** competition or rivalry: a Gallicism **5.** *Geom. a)* the point where three or more lines meet *b)* the junction of lines or surfaces **6.** *Law* a joint right or claim Also **con·cur'ren·cy**

con·cur·rent (-ənt) *adj.* [ME. < L. *concurrens*, prp. of *concurrere*, CONCUR] **1.** occurring at the same time; existing together **2.** meeting in or going toward the same point; converging **3.** acting together; cooperating **4.** in agreement; harmonious **5.** *Law* exercised equally over the same area [*concurrent* jurisdiction] —*n.* a concurrent circumstance, cause, etc. —**con·cur'rent·ly** *adv.*

☆**concurrent resolution** a resolution passed by one branch of a legislature and concurred in by the other, indicating the opinion of the legislature but not having the force of law: cf. JOINT RESOLUTION

con·cuss (kən kus') *vt.* [< L. *concussus*, pp. of *concutere:* see ff.] to cause to have a concussion

con·cus·sion (kən kush'ən) *n.* [ME. *concussioun* < L. *concussio* < pp. of *concutere*, shake violently < *com-*, together + *quatere*, to shake] **1.** a violent shaking; agitation; shock, as from impact **2.** *Med.* a condition of impaired functioning of some organ, esp. the brain, as a result of a violent blow or impact —**con·cus'sive** (-kus'iv) *adj.*

cond. 1. conducted **2.** conductivity **3.** conductor

Con·dé (kōn dā') , Prince de (*Louis II de Bourbon, duc d'Enghien*) 1621–86; Fr. general: called *the Great Condé*

con·demn (kən dem') *vt.* [ME. *condempnen* < OFr. *condemner* < L. *condemnare* < *com-*, intens. + *damnare*, to harm, condemn: cf. DAMN] **1.** to pass an adverse judgment on; disapprove of strongly; censure **2.** *a)* to declare to be guilty of wrongdoing; convict *b)* to pass judicial sentence on; inflict a penalty upon *c)* to doom ☆**3.** to declare (property) legally appropriated for public use **4.** to declare to be unfit for use or service [to *condemn* a slum tenement] —**con·demn'a·ble** (-dem'nə b'l, -ə b'l) *adj.* —**con·demn'er** (-dem'ər) *n.*

con·dem·na·tion (kän'dem nā'shən, -dəm-) *n.* [ME. *condempnacioun* < L. *condemnatio*] **1.** a condemning or being condemned **2.** a cause for condemning

con·dem·na·to·ry (kən dem'nə tôr'ē) *adj.* [< L. *condemnatus*, pp. of *condemnare* (see CONDEMN) + -ORY] condemning; expressing condemnation, explicitly or implicitly

con·den·sate (kän'dən sāt', kən den'sāt) *n.* a product of condensation

con·den·sa·tion (kän'dən sā'shən) *n.* [LL. *condensatio*] **1.** the act of condensing, as the reduction of a gas to a liquid or the abridgment of a piece of writing **2.** the product of such an act [to read a *condensation* of a novel] **3.** the condition of being condensed

con·dense (kən dens') *vt.* **-densed', -dens'ing** [Fr. *condenser* < L. *condensare* < *condensus*, very dense < *com-*, intens. + *densus*] **1.** to make more dense or compact; reduce the volume of; compress **2.** to express in fewer words; make concise; abridge **3.** to change (a substance) to a denser form, as from a gas to a liquid **4.** *Chem.* to cause molecules of (the same or different substances) to combine to form a more complex compound, often with elimination of a simple molecule, as water —*vi.* to become condensed —*SYN.* see CONTRACT —**con·dens'a·ble, con·dens'i·ble** *adj.* —**con·dens'a·bil'i·ty, con·dens'i·bil'i·ty** *n.*

☆**condensed milk** thick, sweetened milk made by evaporating part of the water from cow's milk and adding sugar: cf. EVAPORATED MILK

condensed type *Printing* a type face narrower than the standard type for the series

con·dens·er (kən den'sər) *n.* a person or thing that condenses; specif., *a)* an apparatus for converting gases or vapors to a liquid state *b)* a lens or series of lenses for concentrating light rays on an object or area *c) Elec.* same as CAPACITOR

con·de·scend (kän'də send') *vi.* [ME. *condescenden* < OFr. *condescendre* < LL.(Ec.) *condescendere*, to let oneself down, condescend < L. *com-*, together + *descendere*, DESCEND] **1.** to descend voluntarily to the level, regarded as lower, of the person that one is dealing with; be graciously willing to do something regarded as beneath one's dignity; deign **2.** to deal with others in a patronizing manner **3.** [Obs.] to make concessions; agree; assent —*SYN.* see STOOP

con·de·scend·ence (-sen'dəns) *n.* [ML. *condescentia*] **1.** condescension **2.** [Scot.] a listing of particulars

con·de·scend·ing (-sen'diŋ) *adj.* showing condescension; esp., patronizing —**con'de·scend'ing·ly** *adv.*

con·de·scen·sion (-sen'shən) *n.* [LL.(Ec.) *condescensio* < pp. of *condescendere*] **1.** act or instance of condescending **2.** a patronizing manner or behavior

con·dign (kən dīn') *adj.* [ME. & OFr. *condigne* < L. *condignus*, very worthy < *com-*, intens. + *dignus*, worthy] deserved; suitable: said esp. of punishment for wrongdoing —**con·dign'ly** *adv.*

Con·dil·lac (kōn dē yàk'), É·tienne Bon·not de (**Mably de**) (ä tyen' bô nō' də) 1715–80; Fr. philosopher

con·di·ment (kän'də mənt) *n.* [ME. & OFr. < L. *condimentum* < *condire*, to pickle, var. of *condere*, to put together < *com-*, together + *-dere*, to put, DO] a seasoning or relish for food, as pepper, mustard, sauces, etc.

con·di·tion (kən dish'ən) *n.* [ME. & OFr. *condicion* < L. *condicio*, agreement, situation < *condicere*, to speak with, agree < *com-*, together + *dicere*, to speak] **1.** anything called for as a requirement before the performance or completion of something else; provision; stipulation [to impose *conditions* by contract] **2.** anything essential to the existence or occurrence of something else; prerequisite [health is a *condition* of happiness] **3.** anything that modifies or restricts the nature, existence, or occurrence of something else; external circumstance or factor [conditions were favorable for business] **4.** manner or state of being **5.** *a)* state of health [what's the patient's *condition?*] *b)* [Colloq.] an illness; ailment [a lung *condition*] **6.** a proper or healthy state [athletes train to be in *condition*] **7.** social position; rank; station **8.** [Obs.] *a)* disposition of mind; character *b)* characteristic; trait ☆**9.** *Educ. a)* the requirement that a student make up deficiencies in a certain subject in order to pass it *b)* the grade stating this requirement **10.** *Gram.* a clause expressing a condition, as one beginning with *if* **11.** *Law* a clause in a contract, will, etc. that revokes, suspends, or modifies one or more of its stipulations upon the happening of an uncertain future event **12.** *Logic* a proposition on which the truth of another proposition depends —*vi.* [Archaic] to make conditions; bargain (*with*) —*vt.* **1.** to set as a condition or requirement; stipulate **2.** to impose a condition or conditions on **3.** to be a condition of; determine **4.** to affect, modify, or influence **5.** to bring into a proper or desired condition ☆**6.** *Educ.* to give a grade of condition to **7.** *a) Psychol.* to develop a conditioned reflex or behavior pattern in (a person or animal) *b)* to cause to become accustomed (*to* something) —*SYN.* see STATE —**on condition that** provided that; if —**con·di'tion·er** *n.*

con·di·tion·al (-'l) *adj.* **1.** containing, implying, or dependent on a condition or conditions; qualified; not absolute [a *conditional* award] **2.** expressing a condition [a *conditional* clause] —*n. Gram.* a word, clause, mood, or tense expressing a condition —**con·di'tion·al'i·ty** (-al'ə tē) *n.* —**con·di'tion·al·ly** *adv.*

con·di·tioned (kən dish'ənd) *adj.* **1.** in a (specified) condition **2.** subject to conditions; depending on certain conditions **3.** in a proper or desired condition **4.** *a)* having

fat, āpe, cär; ten, ēven; is, bīte; gō, hôrn, tōōl, look; oil, out; up, fur; get; joy; yet; chin; she; thin, *then*; zh, leisure; ŋ, ring; ə for *a* in *ago, e* in *agent, i* in *sanity, o* in *comply, u* in *focus;* ' as in *able* (ā'b'l); Fr. bål; ë, Fr. coeur; ö, Fr. feu; Fr. mon; ô, Fr. coq; ü, Fr. duc; r, Fr. cri; H, G. ich; kh, G. doch. See inside front cover. ☆ Americanism; ‡foreign; *hypothetical; <derived from

developed a conditioned reflex or behavior pattern   b) affected or influenced; esp., accustomed (to)

conditioned reflex a reflex in which the response (e.g., secretion of saliva in a dog) is occasioned by a secondary stimulus (e.g., the ringing of a bell) repeatedly associated with the primary stimulus (e.g., the sight of meat): also **conditioned response**

con·dole (kən dōl′) vi. **-doled′, -dol′ing** [LL.(Ec.) condolere, to suffer with < L. com-, with + dolere, to grieve] to express sympathy; mourn in sympathy; commiserate —vt. [Archaic] to show grief for —**con·do′la·to·ry** (-dō′lə tôr′ē) adj. —**con·dol′er** n.

con·do·lence (kən dō′ləns) n. [< LL.(Ec.) condolens: see prec.] [often pl.] expression of sympathy with another in grief: also **con·dole′ment** —SYN. see PITY

‡**con do·lo·re** (kôn dô lô′re) [It.] with grief; sadly: a direction to the performer in music

con·dom (kun′dəm, kän′-) n. [earlier cundum, supposedly after its inventor, a 17th-c. Brit. colonel] a thin protective sheath for the penis, generally of rubber, used to prevent venereal infection or as a contraceptive

con·do·min·i·um (kän′də min′ē əm) n. [ModL.: see COM- & DOMINIUM] **1.** a) joint rule by two or more states   b) the territory so ruled   ☆**2.** a) an arrangement under which a tenant in an apartment building or in a complex of multiple-unit dwellings holds full title to his unit and joint ownership in the common grounds   b) pl. **-i·ums, -i·a** (-ə) such a building or complex

Con·don (kän′dən), **Edward U(hler)** 1902– ; U.S. physicist

con·do·na·tion (kän′dō nā′shən, -də-) n. [L. condonatio < pp. of ff.] the act of condoning, esp. of implying forgiveness by overlooking an offense

con·done (kən dōn′) vt. **-doned′, -don′ing** [L. condonare < com-, intens. + donare, to give] to forgive, pardon, or overlook (an offense) —**con·don′a·ble** adj. —**con·don′er** n.

con·dor (kän′dər; for 3, Sp. kôn′dôr) n. [Sp. cóndor < Quechuan cuntur] **1.** a very large vulture (Vultur gryphus) of the S. American Andes, with black plumage, bare head and neck, and a ruff of downy white feathers at the base of the neck   **2.** a similar vulture (Gymnogyps californianus) of the mountains of S Calif.: it is now nearly extinct   **3.** pl. **con·do·res** (kôn dō′res) any of various S. American gold coins stamped with the figure of a condor

CONDOR
(wingspread to 12 ft.)

Con·dor·cet (kôn dôr sā′), Marquis de (born Marie Jean Antoine Nicolas Caritat) 1743–94; Fr. social philosopher, mathematician, and political leader

con·dot·tie·re (kän′də tyer′ē; It. kôn′dôt tye′re) n., pl. **-ri** (-ē; It. -rē) [It. < condotto, one hired < L. conductus, mercenary soldier < pp. of conducere, to hire, lead together (see ff.); infl. in It. by condotta, leadership < same L. source] in Europe from the 14th to the 16th cents., a captain of a band of mercenaries

con·duce (kən dōōs′, -dyōōs′) vi. **-duced′, -duc′ing** [ME. conducen < L. conducere, to lead together, conduce < com-, together + ducere, to lead] to tend or lead (to an effect); contribute

con·du·cive (-dōō′siv, -dyōō′-) adj. that conduces or contributes; tending or leading (to) —**con·du′cive·ness** n.

con·duct (kän′dukt′, -dəkt; for v. kən dukt′) n. [< L. conductus, pp. of conducere: see CONDUCE] **1.** [Rare] the act of leading; guidance   **2.** the process or way of managing or directing; management; handling   **3.** the way that one acts; behavior; deportment   **4.** [Obs.] an escort; convoy —vt. **1.** to show the way to; lead; guide; escort   **2.** to manage, control, or direct   **3.** to be the leader of; direct (an orchestra, choir, etc.)   **4.** to behave (oneself)   **5.** to be able to transmit or carry; convey [iron conducts electricity] —vi. **1.** to be or mark the way; lead   **2.** to act as a conductor —**con·duct′i·ble** adj. —**con·duct′i·bil′i·ty** n.

SYN.—conduct, in this comparison, implies a supervising by using one's executive skill, knowledge, wisdom, etc. [to conduct a sales campaign]; **direct** implies less supervision of actual details, but stresses the issuance of general orders or instructions [to direct the construction of a dam]; **manage** implies supervision that involves the personal handling of all details [to manage a department]; **control** implies firm direction by regulation or restraint and often connotes complete domination [the school board controls the system] See also BEHAVE

con·duct·ance (kən duk′təns) n. the ability of a component to conduct electricity, measured in a direct-current circuit by the ratio of the current to the applied electromotive force; the reciprocal of resistance

con·duc·tion (kən duk′shən) n. [L. conductio: see CONDUCT] **1.** a conveying, as of liquid through a channel   **2.** Physics a) a transmission (of electricity, heat, etc.) by the passage of energy from particle to particle   b) same as CONDUCTIVITY: see also CONVECTION, RADIATION   **3.** Physiol. the transmission of nerve impulses

con·duc·tive (-tiv) adj. **1.** having conductivity   **2.** having to do with conduction

con·duc·tiv·i·ty (kän′duk tiv′ə tē) n. **1.** the property of conducting or transmitting heat, electricity, etc.   **2.** Elec.

the current that will flow from one face of a unit cube of a given substance to the opposite face when a unit potential difference is maintained between these faces; reciprocal of resistivity

con·duc·tor (kən duk′tər) n. [L.] **1.** a person who conducts; leader; guide; manager   **2.** the director of an orchestra, choir, etc.   ☆**3.** the person who has charge of the passengers and collects fares on a train, streetcar, or bus   **4.** a substance or thing that conducts electricity, heat, sound, etc. —**con·duc·tor·i·al** (kən duk′tôr′ē əl) adj. —**con·duc′tor·ship′** n. —**con·duc′tress** n.fem.

con·duit (kän′dit, -doo wit) n. [ME. & OFr. < L. conductus, pp. of conducere: see CONDUCE] **1.** a pipe or channel for conveying fluids   **2.** a tube or protected trough for electric wires   **3.** [Archaic] a fountain

con·du·pli·cate (kän dōō′plə kit, -dyōō′-) adj. [L. conduplicatus, pp. of conduplicare < com-, with + duplicare: see DUPLICATE] folded lengthwise along the middle, as certain leaves and petals in the bud

con·dyle (kän′dil, -dil) n. [Fr. < L. condylus < Gr. kondylos, knuckle, orig., hard lump or knob] a rounded process at the end of a bone, forming a ball-and-socket joint with the hollow part of another bone —**con′dy·lar** (-də lər) adj.

con·dy·loid (-də loid) adj. of or like a condyle

con·dy·lo·ma (kän′də lō′mə) n., pl. **-ma·ta** (-mə tə) [L. < Gr. kondylōma < kondylos: see CONDYLE] a wartlike, inflammatory growth on the skin, usually occurring near the anus or genital organs

cone (kōn) n. [ME. < L. conus < Gr. kōnos, a wedge, peak, cone < IE. base kō(n)-, to sharpen, hone, whence L. cos, HONE[1]] **1.** a) a solid with a circle for its base and a curved surface tapering evenly to an apex so that any point on this surface is in a straight line between the circumference of the base and the apex   b) a solid described by the hypotenuse of a right triangle rotated about either of its legs as an axis   c) a surface described by a moving straight line passing through a fixed point (called the vertex) and tracing any fixed curve, as a circle, ellipse, etc., at another point   **2.** any object or mass shaped like a cone, as a crisp shell of pastry for holding a scoop of ice cream, the peak of a volcano, any of various machine parts, etc.   **3.** Bot. a) a reproductive structure of certain lower plants, consisting of an elongated central axis upon which are borne overlapping scales, bracts, sporophylls, etc., usually in a spiral fashion and in which are produced pollen, spores, or ovules; strobilus: cones are found in cycads, conifers, club mosses, horsetails, etc.   b) any similar structure, as the catkin of hops   **4.** Zool. a) any of the flask-shaped cells in the retina of most vertebrates, sensitive to bright light and color   b) same as CONE SHELL —vt. **coned, con′ing** to shape like a cone or a conical segment

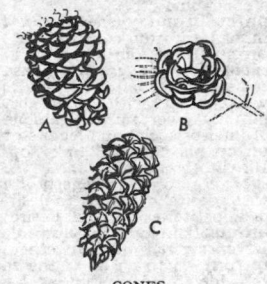

CONES
(A, longleaf pine; B, piñon; C, blue spruce)

☆**cone·flow·er** (-flou′ər) n. any of several genera (esp. Rudbeckia, Ratibida, Echinacea) of showy herbs of the composite family, having cone-shaped receptacles, as the black-eyed Susan

☆**CON·EL·RAD** (kän′'l rad′) [con(trol of) el(ectromagnetic) rad(iation)] a former system (from 1951 to 1963) of shifting broadcasting frequencies of AM stations to prevent possible use of their radio beams by enemy aircraft as a navigational aid

☆**cone·nose** (kōn′nōz′) n. any of several varieties of hemipteran insects (family Reduviidae) with a conelike base on the sucking beak, esp. a bloodsucking genus (Triatoma) that sometimes transmits parasites: found in the S U.S. and tropical America

cone shell any of a family (Conidae) of tropical, marine snails most species of which can inflict a very poisonous bite

☆**Con·es·to·ga wagon** (kän′ə stō′gə) [after Conestoga Valley, Lancaster County, Pa., where the wagons were made] a broad-wheeled covered wagon used by American pioneers crossing the prairies

co·ney (kō′nē) n., pl. **-neys, -nies** [ME. coni (taken as sing. of OFr. conis) < OFr. conin, conil (pl. conis) < L. cuniculus, rabbit] **1.** a rabbit, esp. the European rabbit   **2.** rabbit fur   **3.** a small animal mentioned in the Bible, probably the hyrax   **4.** same as PIKA   **5.** any of several unrelated marine fishes   **6.** [Obs.] a gullible person; dupe

Co·ney Island (kō′nē) [< Du. Konynen Eyland, rabbit island] beach & amusement park in Brooklyn, N.Y., on a peninsula, formerly an island, at the SW end of Long Island

conf. **1.** [L. confer] compare   **2.** conference   **3.** confessor

con·fab (kän′fab′; for v., usually kən fab′) n. [Colloq.] a confabulation; chat —vi. **-fabbed′, -fab′bing** [Colloq.] to confabulate; chat

con·fab·u·late (kən fab′yə lāt′) vi. **-lat′ed, -lat′ing** [< pp. of L. confabulari, to talk together < com-, together + fabulari, to converse: see FABLE] **1.** to talk together in an

informal way; chat **2.** *Psychol.* to fill in gaps in the memory with detailed, but more or less unconscious, accounts of fictitious events —**con·fab′u·la′tion** *n.*

con·far·re·a·tion (kän fär′ē ā′shən) *n.* [L. *confarreatio* < *confarreare*, to marry + *farreum*, spelt cake < *farreus*, spelt < *far*, kind of grain: cf. FARINA] in ancient Rome, the most solemn form of marriage, marked by the offering of a cake of spelt as a sacrifice to Jupiter

con·fect (kən fekt′) *vt.* [< L. *confectus*, pp. of *conficere*, to prepare < *com-*, with + *facere*, to make, DO¹] to prepare or make, esp. by mixing or combining

con·fec·tion (kən fek′shən) *n.* [ME. *confeccioun* < OFr. *confeccion* < L. *confectio*] **1.** the act or process of confecting **2.** any kind of candy or other sweet preparation, as ice cream, preserves, etc. **3.** a sweetened mixture of drugs; electuary **4.** a product or work having a frivolous, whimsical, or contrived effect **5.** a fancy, stylish article of women's clothing —*vt.* [Archaic] to prepare as a confection

con·fec·tion·ar·y (-er′ē) *adj.* **1.** of or like a confection **2.** of a confectioner or his work —*n.*, *pl.* **-ar′ies** ☆**1.** same as CONFECTIONERY (sense 3) **2.** a confection

con·fec·tion·er (-ər) *n.* a person whose work or business is making or selling confectionery

☆**confectioners′ sugar** sugar ground into a very fine powder so that it will dissolve more readily

con·fec·tion·er·y (-er′ē) *n.*, *pl.* **-er′ies 1.** confections or candy, collectively **2.** the business or work of a confectioner ☆**3.** a confectioner's shop; candy store

Confed. 1. Confederate **2.** Confederation

con·fed·er·a·cy (kən fed′ər ə sē, -fed′rə sē) *n.*, *pl.* **-cies** [ME. & OFr. *confederacie* < LL. *confoederatus*: see CONFEDERATE] **1.** people, groups, nations, or states united for some common purpose **2.** a league or alliance formed by such a union; federation or confederation **3.** people united for an unlawful purpose; conspiracy —*SYN.* see ALLIANCE —☆**the Confederacy** the league of Southern States that seceded from the U.S. in 1860 & 1861; Ala., Ark., Fla., Ga., La., Miss., N.C., S.C., Tenn., Tex., & Va.: official name, **Confederate States of America**

con·fed·er·al (kən fed′ər əl, -fed′rəl) *adj.* of or relating to a confederation

con·fed·er·ate (kən fed′ər it, -fed′rit; *for v.* -ə rāt′) *adj.* [ME. *confederat* < LL. *confoederatus*, pp. of *confoederare*, to unite by a league < *foedus*, a league: for IE. base see FIDELITY] **1.** united in a confederacy or league ☆**2.** [C-] of the Confederacy —*n.* **1.** a person, group, nation, or state united with another or others for a common purpose; ally; associate **2.** an associate in an unlawful act or plot; accomplice ☆**3.** [C-] any Southern supporter of the Confederacy —*vt.*, *vi.* **-at′ed, -at′ing** to unite in a confederacy; ally —*SYN.* see ASSOCIATE

con·fed·er·a·tion (kən fed′ə rā′shən) *n.* [ME. *confederacion* < LL. *confoederatio*: see prec.] **1.** a uniting or being united in a league or alliance **2.** a league or alliance; specif., independent nations or states joined in a league or confederacy whose central authority is usually confined to common defense or foreign relations —*SYN.* see ALLIANCE —☆**the Confederation 1.** the United States of America (1781–1789) under the Articles of Confederation **2.** the union of Ontario, Quebec, Nova Scotia, and New Brunswick in 1867 to form the Dominion of Canada

con·fed·er·a·tive (kən fed′ə rā′tiv, -ər ə tiv) *adj.* of confederates or a confederation

con·fer (kən fur′) *vt.* **-ferred′, -fer′ring** [L. *conferre*, to bring together, compare, confer < *com-*, together + *ferre*, to BEAR¹] **1.** to give, grant, or bestow **2.** [Obs.] to compare —*vi.* to have a conference or talk; meet for discussion; converse —*SYN.* see GIVE —**con·fer′ra·ble** *adj.* —**con·fer′rer** *n.*

con·fer·ee (kän′fə rē′) *n.* **1.** a participant in a conference **2.** a person on whom an honor, degree, favor, etc. is conferred

con·fer·ence (kän′fər əns, -frəns) *n.* [Fr. *conférence* < ML. *conferentia* < L. *conferens*, prp. of *conferre*: see CONFER] **1.** the act of conversing or consulting on a serious matter **2.** a formal meeting of a number of people for discussion or consultation **3.** a meeting of committees from both branches of a legislature to reconcile the differences between bills passed by both branches **4.** [often C-] the governing body of a religious denomination, such as the Methodists, on a national or district level **5.** a national or regional association, as of colleges or their athletic teams **6.** conferment; bestowal: also **con·fer·rence** (kən fur′əns) —**con·fer·en·tial** (kän′fə ren′shəl) *adj.*

con·fer·ment (kən fur′mənt) *n.* a conferring of an honor, degree, favor, etc.; bestowal: also **con·fer′ral**

con·fer·va (kən fur′və) *n.*, *pl.* **-vae** (-vē), **-vas** [L.: see COMFREY] *Bot.* a former name for any of various threadlike green algae, esp. a genus (*Tribonema*) found chiefly in fresh water —**con·fer′val, con·fer′void** *adj.*, *n.*

con·fess (kən fes′) *vt.* [ME. *confessen* < OFr. *confesser* < ML.(Ec.) *confessare* < L. *confessus*, pp. of *confiteri*, to acknowledge, confess < *com-*, together + *fateri*, to acknowledge] **1.** *a)* to admit (a fault, crime, etc.) *b)* to acknowledge (an opinion or view) **2.** to declare one's faith in **3.** [Poet.] to

be evidence of; reveal; manifest **4.** *Eccles. a)* to tell (one's sins) to God, esp. in public worship service or in private *b)* to hear the confession of (a person): said of a priest —*vi.* **1.** to admit a fault or crime; acknowledge one's guilt **2.** *Eccles. a)* to take part in public confession or make one's confession to a priest *b)* to hear confessions: said of a priest —*SYN.* see ACKNOWLEDGE —**confess to** to admit or admit having; acknowledge —**stand confessed as** to be revealed or admitted as

con·fess·ed·ly (-id lē) *adv.* by confession; admittedly

con·fes·sion (kən fesh′ən) *n.* **1.** the act of confessing; acknowledgment; specif., *a)* an admission of guilt, esp. formally in writing, as by a person charged with a crime *b)* the confessing of sins to a priest in the sacrament of penance *c)* a general acknowledgment of sin, or a form expressing this used in public worship **2.** something confessed **3.** *a)* a statement of religious beliefs, esp. as held by a Christian church, usually longer than a creed: in full, **confession of faith** *b)* a church having such a confession; communion **4.** the tomb or shrine of a martyr or confessor

con·fes·sion·al (-′l) *n.* [Fr., orig. (*chaire*) *confessionale*, (chair) for confession] **1.** a small, enclosed place in a church, where a priest hears confessions **2.** confession to a priest —*adj.* of, characterized by, or for a confession or confessions

con·fes·sor (kən fes′ər) *n.* **1.** a person who confesses **2.** a Christian who suffered for his faith; specif., *R.C.Ch.*, a male saint who was not a martyr **3.** a priest authorized to hear confessions

con·fet·ti (kən fet′ē) *n.pl.* [It., pl. of *confetto*, sweetmeat: see COMFIT] **1.** candies, or plaster imitations of candies, formerly scattered about at carnivals or other celebrations **2.** [*with sing. v.*] bits of colored paper now used in this way

con·fi·dant (kän′fə dant′, -dänt′; kän′fə dant′, -dänt′) *n.* [Fr. *confident* (fem. *confidente*) < L. *confidens*, prp. of *confidere*, CONFIDE] a close, trusted friend, to whom one confides intimate matters or secrets —**con′fi·dante′** *n.fem.*

con·fide (kən fīd′) *vi.* **-fid′ed, -fid′ing** [L. *confidere* < *com-*, intens. + *fidere*, to trust: see FIDELITY] to trust (*in* someone), esp. by sharing secrets or discussing private affairs —*vt.* **1.** to tell or talk about as a secret [to *confide* one's troubles to a friend] **2.** to entrust (a duty, object, person, etc. *to* someone) —*SYN.* see COMMIT —**con·fid′er** *n.*

con·fi·dence (kän′fə dəns) *n.* [ME. < L. *confidentia* < *confidens*, prp. of prec.] **1.** firm belief; trust; reliance **2.** the fact of being or feeling certain; assurance **3.** belief in one's own abilities; self-confidence **4.** a relationship as confidant [take me into your *confidence*] **5.** the belief that another will keep a secret; assurance of secrecy [told in strict *confidence*] **6.** something told as a secret **7.** [Rare] object of trust —☆*adj.* swindling or used to swindle

SYN.—**confidence**, in this comparison, implies belief in one's own abilities, or, esp. in the form **self-confidence**, reliance on one's own powers [he has *confidence* he will win]; **assurance**, in this connection, suggests an even stronger belief in one's ability, but in an unfavorable sense, it may connote (as may **confidence**) conceited or arrogant self-sufficiency; **self-possession** suggests that presence of mind which results from the ability to control one's feelings and behavior; **aplomb** refers, usually in a favorable sense, to an evident assurance of manner manifesting self-possession [he stood his ground with admirable *aplomb*] See also BELIEF, CERTAINTY —*ANT.* **diffidence, shyness**

☆**confidence game** a swindle effected by gaining the confidence of the victim

☆**confidence man** a swindler who tries to gain the confidence of his victim in order to defraud him

con·fi·dent (-dənt) *adj.* **1.** full of confidence; specif., *a)* assured; certain [*confident* of victory] *b)* sure of oneself; self-confident; bold [a *confident* manner] **2.** [Obs.] trustful; confiding —*n.* a confidant —*SYN.* see SURE —**con′fi·dent·ly** *adv.*

con·fi·den·tial (kän′fə den′shəl, -chəl) *adj.* **1.** told in confidence; imparted in secret **2.** of or showing trust in another; confiding **3.** entrusted with private or secret matters [a *confidential* agent] —*SYN.* see FAMILIAR —**con′fi·den′ti·al′i·ty** (-al′ə tē, -chē-), **con′fi·den′tial·ness** *n.* —**con′fi·den′tial·ly** *adv.*

con·fid·ing (kən fīd′iŋ) *adj.* trustful or inclined to trust —**con·fid′ing·ly** *adv.*

con·fig·u·ra·tion (kən fig′yə rā′shən) *n.* [L. *configuratio* < *configurare*, to form after < *com-*, together + *figurare*: see FIGURE] **1.** *a)* arrangement of parts *b)* form or figure as determined by the arrangement of parts; contour; outline **2.** *Chem.* the structure of a compound, esp. in the spatial relation of atoms in the molecule **3.** same as GESTALT —*SYN.* see FORM —**con·fig′u·ra′tion·al** *adj.* —**con·fig′u·ra′tive** *adj.*

con·fig·u·ra·tion·ism (-iz′m) *n.* same as GESTALT PSYCHOLOGY

con·fine (kən fīn′; *for n. 1* kän′fīn′) *n.* [ME. *confinies*, pl. < OFr. *confins*, pl., a border, boundary < L. *confinium* (pl. *confinia*), boundary, limit < *confinis*, bordering on < *com-*, with + *finis*, an end, limit] **1.** [*usually pl.*] a boundary or bounded region; border; limit **2.** [Poet.] confinement **3.** [Obs.] a place of confinement —*vi.* **-fined′, -fin′ing** [Fr.

confiner < the *n*.] [Rare] to border (*on*) or be contiguous (*with* or to another region) —*vt*. 1. to keep within limits; restrict [to *confine* a talk to ten minutes] 2. to keep shut up, as in prison, in bed because of illness, indoors, etc. —*SYN.* see LIMIT —**be confined** to be undergoing childbirth —**con·fin'a·ble, con·fine'a·ble** *adj.*

con·fine·ment (kən fīn'mənt) *n.* a confining or being confined; specif., *a*) imprisonment *b*) limitation; restriction; restraint *c*) childbirth; lying-in

con·firm (kən furm') *vt.* [ME. *confermen* < OFr. *confermer* < L. *confirmare* < *com-*, intens. + *firmare*, to strengthen < *firmus*] 1. to make firm; strengthen; establish; encourage 2. to make valid by formal approval; ratify 3. to prove the truth, validity, or authenticity of; verify 4. to cause to undergo the religious ceremony of confirmation —**con·firm'a·ble** *adj.*

SYN.—to **confirm** is to establish as true that which was doubtful or uncertain [to *confirm* a rumor]; **substantiate** suggests the producing of evidence that proves or tends to prove the validity of a previous assertion or claim [the census figures *substantiate* his charge]; **corroborate** suggests the strengthening of one statement or testimony by another [the witnesses *corroborated* her version of the event]; to **verify** is to prove to be true or correct by investigation, comparison with a standard, or reference to ascertainable facts [to *verify* an account]; **authenticate** implies proof of genuineness by an authority or expert [to *authenticate* a painting]; **validate** implies official confirmation of the validity of something [to *validate* a will] —ANT. **contradict, disprove**

con·fir·mand (kän'fər mand', kän'fər mand') *n.* a person who is to be confirmed in a religious ceremony

con·fir·ma·tion (kän'fər mā'shən) *n.* [ME. & OFr. *confirmacion* < L. *confirmatio* < pp. of *confirmare*] 1. a confirming or being confirmed; corroboration; ratification; verification 2. something that confirms or proves 3. *a*) a Christian ceremony in which a person is admitted to full membership in a church, having reaffirmed vows made at his baptism ☆*b*) a Jewish ceremony in which young people reaffirm their belief in the basic spiritual and ethical concepts of Judaism

con·firm·a·to·ry (kən furm'ə tôr'ē) *adj.* confirming or tending to confirm: also **con·firm'a·tive**

con·firmed (kən furmd') *adj.* 1. firmly established, as in a habit or condition; habitual [a *confirmed* bachelor] 2. chronic, as a disease 3. corroborated; proved 4. having gone through the religious ceremony of confirmation —*SYN.* see CHRONIC —**con·firm'ed·ly** *adv.*

con·fis·ca·ble (kən fis'kə b'l) *adj.* liable to be confiscated: also **con·fis·cat·a·ble** (kän'fə skät'ə b'l)

con·fis·cate (kän'fə skāt') *vt.* -**cat'ed, -cat'ing** [< L. *confiscatus*, pp. of *confiscare*, to lay up in a chest, confiscate < *com-*, together + *fiscus*, money basket or chest, public treasury] 1. to seize (private property) for the public treasury, usually as a penalty 2. to seize by or as by authority; appropriate —*adj.* 1. confiscated 2. having property confiscated —**con'fis·ca'tion** *n.* —**con'fis·ca'tor** *n.*

con·fis·ca·to·ry (kən fis'kə tôr'ē) *adj.* 1. of, constituting, or effecting confiscation [a *confiscatory* tax] 2. confiscating

con·fit·e·or (kən fit'ē ôr') *n.* [ME. < LL.(Ec.), I confess: see CONFESS] a formal prayer, as at the beginning of a Mass, in which sins are confessed

con·fi·ture (kän'fə choor) *n.* [ME. & Late OFr. < *confit*, COMFIT] a confection, sweetmeat, or preserve

con·fla·grant (kən flā'grənt) *adj.* [L. *conflagrans*, prp. of *conflagrare*: see ff.] burning; ablaze

con·fla·gra·tion (kän'flə grā'shən) *n.* [L. *conflagratio* < pp. of *conflagrare*, to burn < *com-*, intens. + *flagrare*, to burn (see BLACK)] a big, destructive fire

con·fla·tion (kən flā'shən) *n.* [ME. *conflacioun* < LL. *conflatio* < L. *conflare*, to blow together < *com-*, together + *flare*, to BLOW¹] a combining, as of two variant readings into a single text

con·flict (kən flikt'; *for n.*, kän'flikt) *vi.* [ME. *conflicten* < L. *conflictus*, pp. of *confligere*, to strike together < *com-*, together + *fligere*, to strike] 1. orig., to fight; battle; contend 2. to be antagonistic, incompatible, or contradictory; be in opposition; clash [ideas that *conflict*] —*n.* 1. a fight or struggle, esp. a protracted one; war 2. sharp disagreement or opposition, as of interests, ideas, etc.; clash 3. emotional disturbance resulting from a clash of opposing impulses or from an inability to reconcile impulses with realistic or moral considerations 4. [Rare] collision of moving bodies —**con·flic'tion** *n.* —**con·flic'tive** *adj.*

SYN.—**conflict** refers to a sharp disagreement or collision in interests, ideas, etc. and emphasizes the process rather than the end [the *conflict* over slavery]; **fight**, a rather general word for any contest, struggle, or quarrel, stresses physical or hand-to-hand combat; **struggle** implies great effort or violent exertion, physical or otherwise [the *struggle* for existence]; **contention** most frequently applies to heated verbal strife, or dispute [religious *contention* broke out]; **contest** refers to a struggle, either friendly or hostile, for supremacy in some matter [athletic *contests*, a *contest* of wits] —ANT. **accord, harmony**

conflict of interest a conflict between one's obligation to the public good and one's self-interest, as in the case of a public officeholder who owns stock in a company seeking government contracts

con·flu·ence (kän'floo əns) *n.* [ME. & OFr. < LL. *confluentia* < L. *confluens*, prp. of *confluere* < *com-*, together + *fluere*, to flow] 1. a flowing together, esp. of two or more

streams 2. the place where they join or a stream formed in this way 3. a coming together as of people; crowd; throng

con·flu·ent (-ənt) *adj.* [ME. < L. *confluens*: see prec.] 1. flowing or running together so as to form one [*confluent* streams] 2. *Med.* running together so as to form a merged mass, as sores, pimples, etc. —*n.* a stream uniting with another; loosely, a tributary

con·flux (kän'fluks) *n.* [< L. *confluxus*, pp. of *confluere*: see CONFLUENCE] *same as* CONFLUENCE

con·fo·cal (kän fō'k'l) *adj. Math.* having the same focus or foci

con·form (kən fôrm') *vt.* [ME. *conformen* < OFr. *conformer* < L. *conformare*, to fashion, form < *com-*, together + *formare*, to FORM] 1. to make the same or similar [to *conform* one's ideas to another's] 2. to bring into harmony or agreement; adapt: often used reflexively —*vi.* 1. to be or become the same or similar 2. to be in accord or agreement [the house *conforms* to specifications] 3. to behave in a conventional way, esp. in accepting without question customs, traditions, prevailing opinion, etc. 4. *Eng. History* to accept and adhere to the usages of the Established Church —*SYN.* see ADAPT, AGREE —**con·form'er** *n.* —**con·form'ism** *n.* —**con·form'ist** *n.*

con·form·a·ble (-fôr'mə b'l) *adj.* [ME.] 1. that conforms; specif., *a*) in harmony or agreement *c*) adapted; suited; corresponding 2. quick to conform; obedient; submissive; compliant 3. *Geol.* uninterruptedly parallel: said of sedimentary strata that show no disturbance at the time of deposition —**con·form'a·bil'i·ty** *n.* —**con·form'a·bly** *adv.*

con·for·mal (-fôr'm'l) *adj.* [< LL.(Ec.) *conformalis*, conformable, similar < L. *conformare*: see CONFORM] 1. *Math.* of a transformation in which corresponding angles are equal 2. designating or of a map projection in which shapes at any point are true, but areas become increasingly exaggerated

con·form·ance (-fôr'məns) *n. same as* CONFORMITY

con·for·ma·tion (kän'fôr mā'shən) *n.* [L. *conformatio* < pp. of *conformare*] 1. [Rare] a conforming or being conformed; adaptation 2. *a*) a completed or symmetrical formation and arrangement of the parts of a thing *b*) the structure or form of a thing as determined by such arrangements; specif., the shape or outline, as of an animal

con·form·i·ty (kən fôr'mə tē) *n., pl.* -**ties** [ME. & OFr. *conformite* < ML. **conformitas* < L. *conformare*: see CONFORM] 1. the condition or fact of being in harmony or agreement; correspondence; congruity; similarity 2. action in accordance with customs, rules, prevailing opinion, etc.; conventional behavior 3. *Eng. History* adherence to the usages of the Established Church

con·found (kən found', kän-; *for 3, usually* kän') *vt.* [ME. *confounden* < OFr. *confondre* < L. *confundere*, to pour together, confuse < *com-*, together + *fundere*, to pour: see FOUND³] 1. to mix up or lump together indiscriminately; confuse 2. to make feel confused; bewilder 3. to damn: used as a mild oath 4. [Archaic] to cause to fail; defeat or destroy 5. [Archaic] to make feel ashamed; abash —*SYN.* see PUZZLE

con·found·ed (-id) *adj.* 1. confused; bewildered 2. damned: a mild oath —**con·found'ed·ly** *adv.*

con·fra·ter·ni·ty (kän'frə tur'nə tē) *n., pl.* -**ties** [ME. *confraternite* < ML. *confraternitas*: see COM- & FRATERNITY] 1. fraternal bond; brotherhood 2. a group of men associated for some purpose or in a profession; esp., a religious society, usually of laymen, with a devotional or charitable purpose

con·frere (kän'frer, kōn'-) *n.* [ME. & OFr.: see COM- & FRÈRE] a fellow member or worker; colleague or associate, as in a profession

con·front (kən frunt') *vt.* [Fr. *confronter* < ML. *confrontare* < L. *com-*, together + *frons*, forehead: see FRONT] 1. to face; stand or meet face to face 2. to face or oppose boldly, defiantly, or antagonistically 3. to bring face to face (*with*) [to *confront* one with the facts] 4. to set side by side to compare —**con·fron·ta·tion** (kän'frən tā'shən), **con·front'al** *n.*

Con·fu·cian·ism (kən fyoo'shən iz'm) *n.* the ethical teachings formulated by Confucius and introduced into the Chinese religion, emphasizing devotion to parents, family, and friends, ancestor worship, and the maintenance of justice and peace —**Con·fu'cian·ist** *n., adj.*

Con·fu·cius (kən fyoo'shəs) (L. name of *K'ung Fu-tse*) 551?–479? B.C.; Chin. philosopher & teacher —**Con·fu'cian** (-shən) *adj., n.*

con·fuse (kən fyooz') *vt.* -**fused', -fus'ing** [ME. *confusen* < *confus*, perplexed < OFr. < L. *confusus*, pp. of *confundere*: see CONFOUND] 1. to mix up; jumble together; put into disorder 2. to mix up mentally; specif., *a*) to bewilder; perplex *b*) to embarrass; disconcert; abash *c*) to fail to distinguish between; mistake the identity of —*SYN.* see PUZZLE —**con·fus'ed·ly** (-fyooz'id lē) *adv.* —**con·fus'ed·ness** *n.* —**con·fus'ing·ly** *adv.*

con·fu·sion (kən fyoo'zhən) *n.* [ME. & OFr. < L. *confusio*] a confusing or being confused; specif., *a*) state of disorder *b*) bewilderment *c*) embarrassment *d*) failure to distinguish between things —**covered with confusion** greatly embarrassed —**con·fu'sion·al** *adj.*

SYN.—**confusion** suggests an indiscriminate mixing or putting together of things so that it is difficult to distinguish the individual

elements or parts [the hall was a *confusion* of languages]; **disorder** and **disarray** imply a disturbance of the proper order or arrangement of parts [the room was in *disorder*, her clothes were in *disarray*]; **chaos** implies total and apparently irremediable lack of organization [the troops are in a state of *chaos*]; **jumble** suggests a confused mixture of dissimilar things [his drawer was a *jumble* of clothing, books, etc.]; **muddle** implies a snarled confusion resulting from mismanagement or incompetency [they've made a *muddle* of the negotiations] —*ANT.* **order, system**

con·fu·ta·tion (kän′fyoo tā′shən) *n.* [L. *confutatio* < pp. of *confutare*] 1. the act of confuting 2. an argument, evidence, etc. that confutes —**con·fu·ta·tive** (kən fyoot′ə tiv) *adj.*

con·fute (kən fyoot′) *vt.* -fut′ed, -fut′ing [L. *confutare* < *com-*, intens. + **futare* < IE. base **bhau-t, *bhu-t,* to strike, BEAT] 1. to prove (a person, statement, etc.) to be in error or false; overcome by argument or proof 2. [Obs.] to make useless —*SYN.* see DISPROVE

Cong. 1. Congregational 2. Congregationalist 3. Congress 4. Congressional

cong. congius

☆**con·ga** (käŋ′gə) *n.* [AmSp., ult. < CONGO] 1. a ballroom dance of Latin American origin, in which the dancers form a winding line 2. music for this dance, in 4/4 syncopated time, with a heavy accent on the fourth beat 3. an elongated bass drum played with the hands —*vi.* to dance the conga

Con·ga·ree (käŋ′gər ē) river in S.C., joining the Wateree to form the Santee River: c. 55 mi.

con·gé (kän′zhā, -jā; *Fr.* kōn zhā′) *n.* [Fr., leave, departure < OFr. *congie* < L. *commeatus,* a going to and fro < *com-meare,* to come and go < *com-,* intens. + *meare,* to go] 1. a curt dismissal 2. permission to leave 3. a formal farewell 4. a bow, esp. at leave-taking 5. *Archit.* a concave molding

con·geal (kən jēl′) *vt., vi.* [ME. *congelen* < OFr. *congeler* < L. *congelare* < *com-,* together + *gelare,* to freeze: for IE. base see COOL] 1. to solidify or thicken by cooling or freezing 2. to thicken; coagulate; jell —**con·geal′a·ble** *adj.* —**con·geal′ment** *n.*

con·gee (kän′jē) *n.* [ME. *conge* < OFr. *congie*] [Now Rare] *same as* CONGÉ —*vi.* [Now Rare] to take formal leave; esp., to bow in leaving

con·ge·la·tion (kän′jə lā′shən) *n.* [ME. *congelacioun* < OFr. *congelation* < L. *congelatio* < pp. of *congelare*] 1. a congealing or being congealed 2. something congealed

con·gen·er (kän′jə nər) *n.* [L., of the same race or kind < *com-,* together + *genus* (gen. *generis*), race, kind] a person or thing of the same kind, class, race, or genus —**con′ge·ner′ic** (-jə ner′ik), **con·gen·er·ous** (kən jen′ər əs) *adj.*

con·gen·ial (kən jēn′yəl) *adj.* [see COM- & GENIAL[1]] 1. kindred; compatible [*congenial* tastes] 2. having the same tastes and temperament; friendly; sympathetic [*congenial* friends] 3. suited to one's needs or disposition; agreeable [*congenial* work] —**con·ge·ni·al·i·ty** (kən jēn′ē al′ə tē) *n.* —**con·gen′ial·ly** *adv.*

con·gen·i·tal (kən jen′ə t'l) *adj.* [< L. *congenitus,* born together with < *com-,* together + *genitus,* pp. of *gignere,* to bear + -AL] 1. existing as such at birth; resulting from or developing during one's prenatal environment [a *congenital* disease, a *congenital* idiot] 2. existing as if inborn; inherent [a *congenital* cheerfulness] —*SYN.* see INNATE —**con·gen′i·tal·ly** *adv.*

con·ger (eel) (käŋ′gər) *n.* [ME. < OFr. *congre* < LL. *congrus,* for L. *conger* < Gr. *gongros,* conger] any of a family (Congridae) of large saltwater eels with a long dorsal fin, sharp teeth, and powerful jaws; esp., any of an edible genus (*Conger*)

con·ge·ries (kän′jə rēz′, kän jir′ēz) *n., pl.* **con′ge·ries′** [L. < *congerere:* see ff.] a collection of things or parts massed together; heap; pile

con·gest (kən jest′) *vt.* [< L. *congestus,* pp. of *congerere,* to bring together, pile up < *com-,* together + *gerere,* to carry, perform] 1. to cause too much blood to accumulate in the vessels of (a part of the body) 2. to fill to excess; overcrowd; clog [a *congested* parking lot] —*vi.* to become congested —**con·ges′tion** (-jes′chən) *n.* —**con·ges′tive** (-tiv) *adj.*

con·gi·us (kän′jē əs) *n., pl.* -gi·i′ (-ī′) [ME. < L. < Gr. *konchos,* a measure, orig., CONCH] 1. an ancient Roman liquid measure equal to a little less than seven pints 2. *Pharmacy* a gallon

con·glo·bate (kän glō′bāt; kän′glō bāt′, käŋ′-) *vt., vi.* -bat·ed, -bat·ing [L. *conglobatus,* pp. of *conglobare* < *com-,* with + *globare,* to make into a globe < *globus,* GLOBE] to form or collect into a ball or rounded mass: also **con·globe** (kən glōb′) —*adj.* formed into a ball or rounded mass —**con′glo·ba′tion** *n.*

con·glom·er·ate (kən gläm′ə rāt′; *for adj. &* -ət, -ər it) *vt., vi.* -at·ed, -at·ing [< L. *conglomeratus,* pp. of *conglomerare,* to roll together < *com-,* together + *glomerare,* to gather into a ball < *glomus,* a ball < IE. base **glem-:* see CLIMB] to form or collect into a rounded or compact mass —*adj.* 1. formed or collected into a rounded or compact mass; clustered 2. made up of separate parts or substances collected together into a single mass 3. *Geol.* made up of

rock fragments or pebbles cemented together by clay, silica, etc.: also **con·glom′er·at′ic** (-ə rat′ik), **con·glom′-er·it′ic** (-ə rit′ik) —*n.* 1. a conglomerate mass; cluster ☆2. a large corporation formed by the merger of a number of companies in unrelated, widely diversified industries 3. *Geol.* a conglomerate rock

con·glom·er·a·tion (kən gläm′ə rā′shən) *n.* [LL. *conglomeratio*] 1. a conglomerating or being conglomerated 2. a collection, mixture, or mass of miscellaneous things

con·glu·ti·nant (kən gloot′'n ənt) *adj.* [< L. *conglutinans,* prp. of *conglutinare:* see ff.] 1. conglutinating 2. *Med.* promoting the healing or uniting of the edges of a wound

con·glu·ti·nate (-āt′) *adj.* [ME. *conglutinaten* < L. *conglutinatus,* pp. of *conglutinare,* to glue together < *com-,* together + *glutinare,* to glue < *gluten,* GLUE] glued or stuck together; adhering —*vt., vi.* -nat′ed, -nat′ing to stick together; unite by or as by adhesion —**con·glu′ti·na′tion** *n.* —**con·glu′ti·na′tive** *adj.*

Con·go (käŋ′gō) 1. river in C Africa flowing through Congo (sense 2) into the Atlantic: with LUALABA: c. 2,900 mi. 2. country in C Africa, on the equator: a former Belgian colony, 1908–60: 905,563 sq. mi.; pop. 15,986,000; cap. Kinshasa 3. country in WC Africa, west of Congo (sense 2): formerly, a territory (called MIDDLE CONGO) of French Equatorial Africa; since 1960, a member state of the French Community: 132,046 sq. mi.; pop. 826,000; cap. Brazzaville — **Con·go·lese** (käŋ′gə lēz′) *adj., n.*

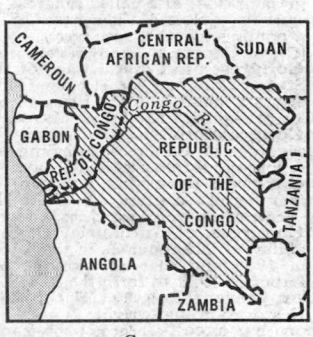
CONGO

con·go (käŋ′gō) *n. same as* CONGOU

Congo dye (or **color**) any of certain azo dyes, derived mainly from benzidine

☆**congo eel** an eellike amphibious animal (*Amphiuma means*) with two pairs of small, weak legs, found in the swamps of the SE U.S.: also called **congo snake**

Con·go-Kor·do·fan·i·an (-kôr′də fan′ē ən) *adj.* designating or of a large family of African languages comprising the Niger-Congo and the Kordofanian subfamilies

Congo red a sodium salt, $C_{32}H_{22}O_6N_6S_2Na_2$, used for dyeing wool and cotton and as an acid-base indicator: it becomes blue in an acid solution and remains red in an alkaline or neutral solution

con·gou (käŋ′goo) *n.* [Amoy *kang-hu-te,* lit., labor tea, tea on which work has been done < Chin. *kung-fu,* labor] a variety of black Chinese tea

con·grat·u·late (kən grach′ə lāt′) *vt.* -lat′ed, -lat′ing [< L. *congratulatus,* pp. of *congratulari* < *com-,* together + *gratulari,* to wish joy < *gratus,* agreeable] 1. to express to (a person) one's pleasure at his good fortune, success, etc.; felicitate [*congratulate* the winner] 2. [Obs.] to rejoice at; celebrate 3. [Obs.] to greet; hail —**con·grat′u·la′tor** *n.* —**con·grat′u·la·to′ry** (-lə tôr′ē) *adj.*

con·grat·u·la·tion (kən grach′ə lā′shən) *n.* [< L. *congratulatio*] 1. the act of congratulating 2. [pl.] expressions of pleasure and good wishes on the occasion of another's fortune or success

con·gre·gant (käŋ′grə gənt) *n.* one who congregates, as a member of a congregation, crowd, etc.

con·gre·gate (-gāt′; *for adj.* -git) *vt., vi.* -gat′ed, -gat′ing [< L. *congregatus,* pp. of *congregare,* to congregate < *com-,* together + *gregare,* to collect into a flock, gather < *grex* (gen. *gregis*), a flock] to gather into a mass or crowd; collect; assemble —*adj.* 1. assembled; collected 2. collective —**con′gre·ga′tive** *adj.* —**con′gre·ga′tor** *n.*

con·gre·ga·tion (käŋ′grə gā′shən) *n.* [ME. *congregacioun* < OFr. *congregation* or L. *congregatio,* an assembling in ML.(Ec.), religious community)] 1. a congregating or being congregated 2. a gathering of people or things; assemblage 3. an assembly of people for religious worship or teaching 4. the members of a particular place of worship ☆5. a settlement, town, or parish in the colonies of early New England where Congregationalism was established 6. *Bible* the whole body or assembly of Israelites 7. *R.C.Ch.* a) a religious community not necessarily under solemn vows but bound by a common rule b) a division of an order, made up of a group of monasteries c) a committee, as of cardinals, in charge of some department of church affairs

con·gre·ga·tion·al (-'l) *adj.* 1. of or like a congregation 2. [C-] of Congregationalism or Congregationalists

con·gre·ga·tion·al·ism (-'l iz'm) *n.* 1. a form of church organization in which each local congregation is self-

governing **2.** [**C-**] the faith and form of organization of a Protestant denomination in which each member church is self-governing: especially prominent in early New England and later marked by union with other Protestant bodies —**Con'gre·ga'tion·al·ist** *n.*, *adj.*

con·gress (käŋ'grəs) *n.* [ME. *congresse* < L. *congressus*, a meeting, hostile encounter, pp. of *congredi*, to come together < *com-*, together + *gradi*, to walk < *gradus*, a step] **1.** a coming together; meeting **2.** sexual intercourse **3.** social intercourse **4.** an association or society **5.** an assembly or conference; specif., a formal assembly of representatives from various nations, churches, etc., to discuss problems **6.** any of various legislatures, esp. the national legislature of a republic ☆**7.** [**C-**] *a)* the legislature of the U.S., consisting of the Senate and the House of Representatives *b)* a session of this legislature *c)* the body of Senators and Representatives during any of the two-year terms of Representatives

☆**congress boot** [*often* **C-**] a high shoe with an elastic insert in each side: also called **congress gaiter**, **congress shoe**

☆**con·gres·sion·al** (kən gresh'ən 'l) *adj.* [< L. *congressio*, a coming together (see prec.) + -AL] **1.** of a congress **2.** [**C-**] of Congress —**con·gres'sion·al·ly** *adv.*

☆**Congressional district** any of the districts into which a State is divided for electing Congressmen: each district elects a member of the House of Representatives

Congressional Medal *see* MEDAL OF HONOR

☆**Congressional Record** a daily publication of the proceedings of Congress, including a complete stenographic report of all remarks and debate

☆**con·gress·man** (käŋ'grəs mən) *n.*, *pl.* **-men** (-mən) a member of Congress, esp. of the House of Representatives —**con'gress·wom'an** *n.fem.* (a former usage)

☆**Congress of Industrial Organizations** a group of affiliated labor unions in the U.S. and Canada, founded in 1938 and merged with the American Federation of Labor in 1955 to form the AFL-CIO

Con·greve (käŋ'grēv, käŋ'-), **William** 1670–1729; Eng. Restoration playwright

con·gru·ence (käŋ'groo wəns, kən groo'əns) *n.* [ME. < L. *congruentia*: see CONGRUENT] **1.** the state or quality of being in agreement; correspondence; harmony **2.** *Math.* the relation between two numbers each of which, when divided by a third (called the *modulus*), leaves the same remainder Also **con'gru·en·cy**

con·gru·ent (-wənt, -ənt) *adj.* [ME. < L. *congruens*, prp. of *congruere*, to come together, correspond, agree < *com-*, with + IE. base *ghrĕu-*, to collapse, topple] **1.** in agreement; corresponding; harmonious **2.** *Geom.* of the same shape and size; congruent figures, if placed one upon another, coincide exactly in all their parts **3.** *Math.* in congruence [*congruent* numbers] —**con'gru·ent·ly** *adv.*

con·gru·i·ty (kən groo'ə tē) *n.*, *pl.* **-ties** [ME. & OFr. *congruite* < ML. *congruitas*] **1.** the condition or fact of being congruous or congruent; specif., *a)* agreement; harmony *b)* fitness; appropriateness *c)* *Geom.* exact coincidence (of two or more figures) **2.** an instance of agreement

con·gru·ous (käŋ'groo wəs) *adj.* [L. *congruus*] **1.** congruent **2.** corresponding to what is right, proper, or reasonable; fitting; suitable; appropriate —**con'gru·ous·ly** *adv.* —**con'gru·ous·ness** *n.*

con·ic (kän'ik) *adj.* [Gr. *kōnikos* < *kōnos*, a peak, CONE] conical —*n. same as* CONIC SECTION

con·i·cal (-i k'l) *adj.* **1.** of a cone **2.** resembling or shaped like a cone —**con'i·cal·ly** *adv.*

conic projection a type of map projection formed by projecting the earth's surface on the surface of a cone and unrolling this to a plane surface on which the parallels of latitude are then concentric circles and the meridians equally spaced radii

conic section 1. a curve, as an ellipse, circle, parabola, or hyperbola, produced by the intersection of a plane with a right circular cone **2.** [*pl.*, *with sing. v.*] the branch of geometry dealing with ellipses, circles, parabolas, and hyperbolas: also **con'ics** *n.*

co·nid·i·al (kə nid'ē əl) *adj.* **1.** of or like conidia **2.** producing conidia Also **co·nid'i·an**

co·nid·i·o·phore (kə nid'ē ə fôr') *n.* [< CONIDIUM + -PHORE] a specialized branch of the hypha in certain fungi, that bears conidia

co·nid·i·um (kə nid'ē əm) *n.*, *pl.* **-i·a** (-ə) [ModL. < Gr. *konis*, dust + -IUM] a small asexual spore abstricted from the tip of a conidiophore in certain fungi

co·ni·fer (kän'ə fər, kō'nə-) *n.* [L., cone-bearing < *conus*, CONE + *ferre*, to BEAR¹] any of an order (*Coniferales*) of cone-bearing trees and shrubs, mostly evergreens, as the pine, spruce, fir, cedar, yew, etc.

co·nif·er·ous (kə nif'ər əs) *adj.* **1.** bearing cones **2.** of conifers

co·ni·ine (kō'nē ēn', -in) *n.* [see ff. & -INE⁴] a very poisonous, oily alkaloid, C₈H₁₇N, extracted from the poison hemlock: also **co·nine** (kō'nēn, -nin)

co·ni·um (kō'nē əm) *n.* [L. < Gr. *kōneion*, hemlock] any of a small genus (*Conium*) of poisonous biennial herbs of the parsley family, with carrotlike leaves and rounded fruits, as the poison hemlock

conj. 1. conjugation **2.** conjunction **3.** conjunctive

con·jec·tur·al (kən jek'chər əl) *adj.* **1.** based on or involv-

ing conjecture **2.** inclined to make conjectures —**con·jec'-tur·al·ly** *adv.*

con·jec·ture (kən jek'chər) *n.* [ME. < L. *conjectura*, a putting together, guess, inference < *conjectus*, pp. of *conjicere*, to throw together, guess < *com-*, together + *jacere*, to throw] **1.** an inferring, theorizing, or predicting from incomplete or uncertain evidence; guesswork [an editorial full of *conjecture*] **2.** an inference, theory, or prediction based on guesswork; guess **3.** [Obs.] occult divination —*vt.* **-tured**, **-tur·ing** to arrive at or propose by conjecture; guess —*vi.* to make a conjecture —*SYN.* see GUESS —**con·jec'tur·a·ble** *adj.*

con·join (kən join') *vt.*, *vi.* [ME. *conjoinen* < OFr. *conjoindre* < L. *conjungere* < *com-*, together + *jungere*, JOIN] to join together; unite; combine

con·joint (-joint') *adj.* [ME. < OFr. < L. *conjunctus*, pp. of *conjungere*: see prec.] **1.** joined together; united; combined; associated **2.** of or involving two or more in association; joint —**con·joint'ly** *adv.*

con·ju·gal (kän'jə gəl, kən jōō'gəl) *adj.* [L. *conjugalis* < *conjunx*, *conjux*, husband or wife < *com-*, together + base akin to L. *jugum*, YOKE, *jungere*, JOIN] of marriage or the relation between husband and wife; matrimonial; connubial —**con'ju·gal'i·ty** (-jə gal'ə tē) *n.* —**con'ju·gal·ly** *adv.*

con·ju·gant (-jə gənt) *n.* either of a pair of one-celled organisms, or of gametes, in the process of conjugation

con·ju·gate (kän'jə gət; *also, and for v. always*, -gāt') *adj.* [ME. *conjugat* < L. *conjugatus*, pp. of *conjugare*, to join together < *com-*, together + *jugare*, to join < *jugum*, YOKE] **1.** joined together, esp. in a pair; coupled **2.** *Bot.* same as BIJUGATE **3.** *Chem.* *a)* related to each other by the difference of a proton: said of acids and bases *b)* of or pertaining to the alternation of single and double bonds in organic compounds **4.** *Gram.* derived from the same base and, usually, related in meaning: said of words **5.** *Math.* reciprocally related and interchangeable as to properties, as two points, lines, quantities, etc. —*n.* **1.** a conjugate word **2.** a conjugate point, line, quantity, etc. **3.** a chemically conjugated substance —*vt.* **-gat'ed**, **-gat'ing** **1.** [Archaic] to join together; unite; couple **2.** *Chem.* to join together so that the resulting substance can be readily reduced to its original components **3.** *Gram.* to inflect (a verb) systematically, giving its different forms according to voice, mood, tense, number, and person —*vi.* **1.** *Biol.* to unite in conjugation **2.** *Gram.* *a)* to conjugate a verb *b)* to be conjugated —**con'ju·ga'tor** *n.*

conjugated protein a protein containing one or more non-amino-acid radicals attached to the molecule, as in hemoglobin

con·ju·ga·tion (kän'jə gā'shən) *n.* [ME. *conjugacion* < L. *conjugatio*] **1.** a conjugating or being conjugated; union **2.** *Biol.* in the reproductive processes of simple forms *a)* the fusion of a male and female gamete, as in certain algae *b)* a temporary union of two one-celled organisms with an exchange of nuclear material, as in certain protozoans **3.** *Gram.* *a)* a methodical presentation or arrangement of the inflectional forms of a verb; paradigm *b)* a class of verbs with similar inflectional forms —**con'ju·ga'tion·al** *adj.* —**con'ju·ga'tion·al·ly** *adv.*

con·junct (kən juŋkt'; *also, and for n. always*, kän'juŋkt) *adj.* [ML. < L. *conjunctus*, pp. of *conjungere*: see CONJOIN] joined together; joint; associated —*n.* a person or thing joined or associated with another

con·junc·tion (kən juŋk'shən) *n.* [ME. *conjunccion* < OFr. *conjonction* < L. *conjunctio* < pp. of *conjungere*: see CONJOIN] **1.** a joining together or being joined together; union; association; combination **2.** an occurring together; coincidence [the *conjunction* of events] **3.** *Astrol.*, *Astron.* *a)* the apparent closeness of two or more heavenly bodies *b)* the condition of being in the same celestial longitude [planets in *conjunction*] **4.** *Gram.* an uninflected word used to connect words, phrases, clauses, or sentences; connective: conjunctions may be coordinating (e.g., *and*, *but*, or), subordinating (e.g., *if*, *when*, *as*, *because*, *though*, etc.), or correlative (e.g., *either* . . . *or*, *both* . . . *and*, etc.) —**con·junc'tion·al** *adj.* —**con·junc'tion·al·ly** *adv.*

con·junc·ti·va (kän'juŋk tī'və, kən juŋk'tī və) *n.*, *pl.* **-vas**, **-vae** (-vē) [ME. < ML. (*membrana*) *conjunctiva*, connecting (membrane): see CONJUNCTIVE] the mucous membrane lining the inner surface of the eyelids and covering the front part of the eyeball —**con'junc·ti'val** *adj.*

con·junc·tive (kən juŋk'tiv) *adj.* [ME. *conjunctif* < L. *conjunctivus*, connective (in LL., subjunctive mood) < *conjunctus*: see CONJOINT] **1.** serving to join together; connective **2.** united; combined; joint **3.** *Gram.* *a)* used as a conjunction [a *conjunctive* adverb] *b)* connecting both the meaning and the construction of sentence elements [and and *moreover* are *conjunctive*] *c)* always used in conjunction with the verb: said of unstressed forms of personal, reflexive, or reciprocal pronouns in some Romance languages (Ex.: *me* in French *il me faut*) —*n.* *Gram.* a conjunctive word, esp. a conjunction —**con·junc'tive·ly** *adv.*

con·junc·ti·vi·tis (kən juŋk'tə vīt'is) *n.* [ModL.: see CONJUNCTIVA & -ITIS] inflammation of the conjunctiva

con·junc·ture (kən juŋk'chər) *n.* [ML. *conjunctura*: see CONJOIN] **1.** [Rare] a joining together or being joined together **2.** a combination of events or circumstances, esp. one creating a critical situation; crisis

con·ju·ra·tion (kän'jə rā'shən) *n.* [ME. *conjuracioun* < L.

conjuratio] **1.** the act of conjuring; invocation **2.** a magic spell; incantation **3.** magic; sorcery **4.** [Archaic] a solemn entreaty; adjuration

con·jure (kän′jər, kun′-; *for vi. 1 & vt. 1* kən joor′) *vi.* **-jured, -jur·ing** [ME. *conjuren* < OFr. *conjurer* < L. *conjurare*, to swear together, conspire < *com-*, together + *jurare*, to swear] **1.** orig., to be sworn in a conspiracy **2.** in primitive or superstitious rites, to summon a demon, spirit, etc. by a magic spell **3.** to practice magic or legerdemain —*vt.* **1.** to call upon, appeal to, or entreat solemnly, esp. by some oath **2.** in primitive or superstitious rites, to summon (a devil, etc.) by a magic spell —☆*adj.* of or involved in conjuring [a *conjure* woman] —**conjure away** to cause to go away by or as by magic —**conjure up** *a*) to cause to be or appear by or as by magic *b*) to call to mind [the music *conjured up* memories]

con·jur·er, con·jur·or (kän′jər ər, kun′-; *for 1* kən joor′ər) *n.* [ME. *conjurour*: see prec.] **1.** a person who solemnly entreats or appeals to someone **2.** a magician; sorcerer **3.** a person skilled in legerdemain

conk¹ (käŋk, kôŋk) *n.* [< CONCH] [Slang] **1.** [Brit.] the nose **2.** the head **3.** a blow on the head —*vt.* [Slang] to hit on the head —**conk out** [Slang] **1.** to fail suddenly in operation, as a motor **2.** to become very tired and, usually, fall asleep **3.** to die

conk² (käŋk, kôŋk) *n.* [altered < ? CONCH] ☆a growth of fungus on certain trees, esp. the pine, or decay caused by it

conk·er (-ər) *n.* [Brit. dial., orig., a snail shell (< CONCH + -ER): the game (sense 2) was orig. played with shells] [Brit.] **1.** a horse chestnut **2.** [*pl., with sing. v.*] a child's game played with conkers tied to strings

☆**con man** [Slang] *same as* CONFIDENCE MAN

con mo·to (kän mō′tō; *It.* kôn mô′tō) [It.] *Music* with animated movement: a direction to the performer

conn (kän) *vt.* **conned, con′ning** [earlier *cond* < ME. *conduen*, to conduct < OFr. *conduire* < L. *conducere*: see CONDUCE] *Naut.* to direct the course of (a vessel) —*n. Naut.* **1.** the station of a person who conns **2.** the act of conning

Conn. Connecticut

Con·nacht (kän′ôt, -əkht) province of NW Ireland: 6,611 sq. mi.; pop. 419,000

con·nate (kän′āt) *adj.* [LL. *connatus*, pp. of *connasci*, to be born at the same time < L. *com-*, together + *nasci*, to be born] **1.** inborn; innate **2.** coexisting since birth or the beginning **3.** having the same origin or nature; related; cognate —**con′nate·ly** *adv.*

con·nat·u·ral (kə nach′ər əl) *adj.* [ML. *connaturalis*: see prec.] **1.** innate; natural **2.** related in nature; cognate —**con·nat′u·ral·ly** *adv.*

Con·naught (kän′ôt) *same as* CONNACHT

con·nect (kə nekt′) *vt.* [ME. *connecten* < L. *connectere*, to bind together < *com-*, together + *nectere*, to fasten] **1.** to join or fasten (two things together, or one thing *with* or *to* another); link; couple **2.** to show or think of as related; associate [to *connect* germs with disease] **3.** to provide with a circuit for communicating by telephone [connect me with Chicago] **4.** to plug into an electrical circuit —*vi.* **1.** to join or be joined ☆**2.** to meet so that passengers can transfer promptly: said of trains, buses, etc. **3.** to be related in some way or in a proper or logical way **4.** [Colloq.] to reach the thing aimed at; esp., *Sports* to hit a ball, target, etc. solidly —*SYN.* see JOIN —**con·nec′tor, con·nect′er** *n.*

Con·nect·i·cut (kə net′ə kət) [< Algonquian (Mahican), lit., place of the long river] **1.** New England State of the U.S.: one of the 13 original States; 5,009 sq. mi.; pop. 3,032,000; cap. Hartford: abbrev. **Conn., CT 2.** river in NE U.S., flowing from N N.H. across Mass. & Conn. into Long Island Sound: 407 mi.

connecting rod a rod connecting by reciprocating motion two or more moving parts of a machine, as the crankshaft and a piston of an automobile

con·nec·tion (kə nek′shən) *n.* [ME. *conneccioun* < L. *connexio* < *connexus*, pp. of *connectere*: see CONNECT] **1.** a joining or being joined; coupling; union **2.** a part or thing that joins; means of joining **3.** a relation; association; specif., *a*) the relation between things that depend on, involve, or follow each other; causal relationship *b*) the logical linking together of words or ideas; coherence *c*) the relation of a word, statement, etc. to the context, as it affects the meaning [in that *connection*, let me say this] *d*) relation by family ties, business, etc. **4.** *a*) a relative, esp. by marriage *b*) a business associate, acquaintance, etc., esp. an influential one through whom one can get special favors: *usually used in pl.* ☆**5.** [*usually pl.*] the act or means of transferring from one train, bus, etc. to another in the course of a journey **6.** a group of people associated together in politics, business, worship, etc. **7.** a religious sect or denomination ☆**8.** [Slang] a person who sells narcotics illicitly to addicts **9.** *Elec.* a circuit **10.** *Telephony, Telegraphy* a line of communication between points —**in connection with 1.** together with; in conjunction with **2.** with reference to —**con·nec′tion·al** *adj.*

con·nec·tive (kə nek′tiv) *adj.* connecting or serving to connect —*n.* **1.** something that connects, esp. a word that connects phrases, clauses, or other words, as a conjunction

or relative pronoun **2.** *Bot.* that part of a filament connecting the lobes of an anther —**con·nec′tive·ly** *adv.* —**con·nec·tiv·i·ty** (kän′ek tiv′ə tē) *n.*

connective tissue tissue found throughout the body, serving to bind together and support other tissues and organs: it is made up of various kinds of fibrils contained in a matrix of intercellular material

con·nex·ion (kə nek′shən) *n. Brit. sp. of* CONNECTION

conn·ing tower (kän′iŋ) [prp. of CONN] **1.** a heavily armored pilothouse on the deck of a warship **2.** a low observation tower on the deck of a submarine, serving also as an entrance to the interior

☆**con·nip·tion** (kə nip′shən) *n.* [arbitrary pseudo-Latin coinage] [Colloq.] [*often pl.*] a fit of anger, hysteria, etc.; tantrum: also **conniption fit**

con·niv·ance (kə nī′vəns) *n.* [Fr. *connivence* < L. *coniventia*, < prp. of *conivere*] the act of conniving; esp., passive cooperation, as by consent or pretended ignorance, esp. in wrongdoing

con·nive (kə nīv′) *vi.* **-nived′, -niv′ing** [< L. *conivere*, to wink, connive < *com-*, intens. + base akin to *nictare* < IE. base **knei-gwh-*, to bend, whence Goth. *hneiwan*, to bend, bow, OE. *hnigian*, to bow (the head)] **1.** to pretend not to see or look (*at* something wrong or evil), thus giving tacit consent or cooperation; feign ignorance of another's wrongdoing **2.** *a*) to cooperate secretly (*with* someone), esp. in wrongdoing; conspire *b*) to scheme in an underhanded way —**con·niv′er** *n.*

con·niv·ent (-nī′vənt) *adj.* [L. *conivens*, prp. of *conivere*: see CONNIVE] *Biol.* with the ends inclined toward each other, as wings, anthers, etc.

con·nois·seur (kän′ə sur′, -sōōr′) *n.* [Fr. (now *connaisseur*) < OFr. *conoisseor*, a judge, one well versed < *conoistre* < L. *cognoscere*, to know: see COGNITION] a person who has expert knowledge and keen discrimination in some field, esp. in the fine arts or in matters of taste —*SYN.* see AESTHETE —**con′nois·seur′ship** *n.*

con·no·ta·tion (kän′ə tā′shən) *n.* [ME. *connotacion* < ML. *connotatio*] **1.** the act or process of connoting **2.** something connoted; idea or notion suggested by or associated with a word, phrase, etc. in addition to its explicit meaning, or denotation ["politician" has different *connotations* from "statesman"] **3.** *Logic* the sum of all the attributes thought of as essential to the meaning of a term —**con·no·ta·tive** (kän′ə tāt′iv, kə nōt′ə tiv) *adj.* —**con′no·ta′tive·ly** *adv.*

con·note (kə nōt′) *vt.* **-not′ed, -not′ing** [ML. *connotare* < L. *com-*, together + *notare*, to mark: see NOTE] **1.** to suggest or convey (associations, overtones, etc.) in addition to the explicit, or denoted, meaning [the word "mother" means "female parent," but it generally *connotes* love, care, tenderness, etc.] **2.** to imply or involve as a result, accompaniment, etc.

con·nu·bi·al (kə nōō′bē əl, -nyōō′-) *adj.* [L. *conubialis* < *conubium*, marriage < *com-*, together + *nubere*, to marry: see NUBILE] of marriage or the state of being married; conjugal —**con·nu′bi·al′i·ty** (-bē al′ə tē) *n.* —**con·nu′bi·al·ly** *adv.*

co·no·dont (kō′nə dänt′, kän′ə-) *n.* [G. *konodont* < Gr. *kōnos*, a wedge, CONE + *odous* (gen. *odontos*), TOOTH] a very small, toothlike, Paleozoic fossil of uncertain identification zoologically

co·noid (kō′noid) *adj.* [Gr. *kōnoeidēs*: see CONE & -OID] cone-shaped: also **co·noi′dal** —*n.* **1.** a cone-shaped thing **2.** *Geom.* a solid described by a conic section revolving about its axis

con·quer (käŋ′kər) *vt.* [ME. *conqueren* < OFr. *conquerre* < VL. *conquaerere* (for L. *conquirere*), to search for, procure < L. *com-*, intens. + *quaerere*, to seek, acquire, hence lit., to get what one seeks] **1.** to get possession or control of by or as by winning a war **2.** to overcome by physical, mental, or moral force; get the better of; defeat —*vi.* to make conquests; be victorious; win —**con′quer·a·ble** *adj.* —**con′quer·or** *n.*

SYN.—**conquer** implies gaining mastery over someone or something by physical, mental, or moral force [to *conquer* bad habits]; **vanquish** implies a thorough overpowering or frustrating, often in a single conflict or battle [a *vanquished* army]; to **defeat** is to get the better of, often only for the time being [the *defeated* troops rallied and counterattacked]; **overcome** implies the overpowering of an antagonist or the surmounting of difficulties; to **subdue** is to defeat so as to break the spirit of resistance; to **subjugate** is to bring under complete subjection; **overthrow** implies a victory in which a prevailing power is dislodged by force; to **rout** is to defeat so overwhelmingly that the enemy is put to disorderly flight

con·quest (kän′kwest, käŋ′-) *n.* [ME. & OFr. *conqueste* < ML. *conquestus* < L. *conquisitus*, pp. of *conquirere*] **1.** the act or process of conquering **2.** something conquered; esp. land taken in war **3.** *a*) a winning of someone's affection or favor *b*) a person whose affection or favor has been won —*SYN.* see VICTORY —**the (Norman) Conquest** the conquering of England by the Normans under William the Conqueror in 1066

con·qui·an (käŋ′kē ən) *n.* [MexSp. *conquain* < *conquian* < *conquién* (< *con* + *quién*, lit., with whom] *same as* COON-CAN

con·quis·ta·dor (kän kwis′tə dôr′, -kēs′-; kän̠-) *n., pl.* **-dors, -dores** [Sp., conqueror < *conquistar* < pp. of VL. *conquaerere:* see CONQUER] any of the Spanish conquerors of Mexico, Peru, or other parts of America in the 16th century

Con·rad (kän′rad) [G. *Konrad* or Fr. *Conrade;* both < OHG. *Kuonrat, Chuonrat,* lit., bold or wise counselor < *kuon,* bold, wise (akin to KEEN¹) + *rat,* counsel < *ratan,* to advise (akin to READ¹)] **1.** a masculine name **2. Joseph,** (born *Józef Teodor Konrad Natecz Korzeniowski*) 1857–1924; Eng. novelist, born in Poland

cons. 1. consecrated **2.** consolidated **3.** consonant **4.** constitutional **5.** construction **6.** consulting

cons., Cons. 1. constable **2.** constitution **3.** consul

con·san·guin·e·ous (kän′saŋ gwin′ē əs, -san-) *adj.* [L. *consanguineus,* of the same blood: see COM- & SANGUINE] having the same ancestor; closely related: also **con·san′·guine** (-saŋ′gwin) —**con·san·guin′e·ous·ly** *adv.*

con·san·guin·i·ty (kän′saŋ gwin′ə tē, -san-) *n.* [ME. & OFr. *consanguinite* < L. *consanguinitas:* see CONSANGUINE-OUS] **1.** relationship by descent from the same ancestor; blood relationship **2.** close relationship; affinity

con·science (kän′shəns) *n.* [ME. & OFr. < L. *conscientia,* consciousness, moral sense < prp. of *conscire* < *com-,* with + *scire,* to know (replacing ME. *inwit,* knowledge within)] **1.** a knowledge or sense of right and wrong, with a compulsion to do right; moral judgment that opposes the violation of a previously recognized ethical principle and that leads to feelings of guilt if one violates such a principle **2.** [Obs.] *a)* consciousness *b)* inner thoughts or feelings —**in (all) conscience** in fairness; on any reasonable ground —**on one's conscience** causing one to feel guilty —**con′science·less** *adj.*

conscience clause a clause (in a law) exempting those whose religious or moral principles forbid compliance

conscience money money one pays to relieve one's conscience, as in compensation for some former dishonesty

con·science-strick·en (-strik′ən) *adj.* feeling guilty or remorseful because of having done some wrong

con·sci·en·tious (kän′shē en′shəs, -chəs) *adj.* [Fr. *conscientieux* < ML. *conscientiosus:* see CONSCIENCE & -OUS] **1.** governed by, or made or done according to, what one knows is right; scrupulous; honest **2.** showing care and precision; painstaking —**con′sci·en′tious·ly** *adv.* —**con′·sci·en′tious·ness** *n.*

conscientious objector ☆a person who refuses to take part in warfare because his conscience prohibits his participation in killing

con·scion·a·ble (kän′shə nə b'l) *adj.* [< CONSCIENCE + -ABLE] [Obs.] that agrees with one's ideas of right and wrong; just —**con′scion·a·bly** *adv.*

con·scious (kän′shəs) *adj.* [L. *conscius,* knowing, aware < *conscire:* see CONSCIENCE] **1.** having a feeling or knowledge (*of* one's own sensations, feelings, etc. or *of* external things); knowing or feeling (*that* something is or was happening or existing); aware; cognizant **2.** able to feel and think; in the normal waking state **3.** aware of oneself as a thinking being; knowing what one is doing and why **4.** *same as* SELF-CONSCIOUS **5.** accompanied by an awareness of what one is thinking, feeling, and doing; intentional [*conscious* humor] **6.** known to or felt by oneself [*conscious* guilt] —*SYN.* see AWARE —**the conscious** *Psychol.* that part of a person's mental activity of which he is fully aware at any given time: see also UNCONSCIOUS, PRECONSCIOUS —**con′scious·ly** *adv.*

con·scious·ness (-nis) *n.* **1.** the state of being conscious; awareness of one's own feelings, what is happening around one, etc. **2.** the totality of one's thoughts, feelings, and impressions; conscious mind

☆**con·script** (kən skript′; *for adj. & n.* kän′skript) *vt.* [< the *adj.*] **1.** to enroll for compulsory service in the armed forces; draft **2.** to force (labor, capital, etc.) into service for the government —*adj.* [L. *conscriptus,* pp. of *conscribere,* to enroll < *com-,* with + *scribere,* to write] conscripted —*n.* a conscripted person; draftee —**con·scrip′tion** *n.*

con·se·crate (kän′sə krāt′) *vt.* **-crat′ed, -crat′ing** [ME. *consecraten* < L. *consecratus,* pp. of *consecrare* < *com-,* together + *sacrare:* see SACRED] **1.** *a)* to set apart as holy; make or declare sacred for religious use [the priest *consecrated* the bread and wine] *b)* to make (someone) a bishop, ruler, etc. by a religious ceremony **2.** to devote entirely; dedicate [to *consecrate* one's life to art] **3.** to cause to be revered or honored; hallow [ground *consecrated* by their martyrdom] —*adj.* [L. *consecratus*] [Archaic] consecrated —*SYN.* see DEVOTE —**con′se·cra′tor** *n.* —**con′se·cra·to·ry** (-krə tôr′ē) *adj.*

con·se·cra·tion (kän′sə krā′shən) *n.* [ME. *consecracioun* < OFr. *consecration* < L. *consecratio*] **1.** a consecrating or being consecrated **2.** a ceremony for this

con·se·cu·tion (kän′sə kyōō′shən) *n.* [ME. *consecucioun* < L. *consecutio:* see ff.] **1.** logical sequence; chain of reasoning **2.** sequence; succession

con·sec·u·tive (kən sek′yə tiv) *adj.* [Fr. *consécutif* < ML. *consecutivus* < pp. of L. *consequi:* see CONSEQUENCE] **1.** following in order, without interruption; successive [for four *consecutive* days] **2.** proceeding from one part or idea to the next in logical order, as a story, reasoning, etc. —**con·sec′u·tive·ly** *adv.* —**con·sec′u·tive·ness** *n.*

Con·seil de l'En·tente (kôn̠ sā′y′ də län tänt′) [Council of the Entente] economic union (formed 1959) of the former French African colonies of Ivory Coast, Upper Volta,

Dahomey, & Niger, having special agreements with France

con·sen·su·al (kən sen′shoo wəl) *adj.* [< CONSENSUS + -AL] **1.** *Law* existing by mutual consent, as a contract **2.** *Physiol.* acting in sympathetic response to voluntary movements: said of involuntary movement —**con·sen′su·al·ly** *adv.*

con·sen·sus (kən sen′səs) *n.* [L. < pp. of *consentire:* see ff.] **1.** an opinion held by all or most **2.** general agreement, esp. in opinion

con·sent (kən sent′) *vi.* [ME. *consenten* < OFr. *consentir* < L. *consentire* < *com-,* with + *sentire,* to feel (see SENSE)] **1.** *a)* to agree (*to* do something) *b)* to give permission, approval, or assent (*to* something proposed or requested) **2.** [Obs.] to agree in opinion —*n.* **1.** permission, approval, or assent **2.** agreement in opinion or sentiment [by common *consent*] —**con·sent′er** *n.*
SYN.—**consent** implies compliance with something proposed or requested, stressing this as an act of the will; to **assent** is to express acceptance of or adherence to an opinion or proposition; **agree** implies accord reached by settling differences of opinion or overcoming resistance; **concur** implies agreement arrived at formally on a specific matter, often with regard to a line of action; to **accede** is to yield one's assent to a proposal; **acquiesce** implies tacit agreement or restraint of opposition in accepting something about which one has reservations —*ANT.* **dissent, refuse, deny**

con·sen·ta·ne·ous (kän′sen tā′nē əs) *adj.* [L. *consentaneus:* see CONSENT] [Rare] **1.** agreeing; suited (*to*); consistent (*with*) **2.** unanimous —**con′sen·ta′ne·ous·ly** *adv.*

con·sen·tient (kən sen′shənt) *adj.* [L. *consentiens,* prp. of *consentire:* see CONSENT] united in opinion; agreeing —**con·sen′tience** *n.*

con·se·quence (kän′sə kwens′, -kwəns) *n.* [ME. & OFr. < L. *consequentia* < *consequens,* prp. of *consequi,* to follow after < *com-,* with + *sequi,* to follow] **1.** a result of an action, process, etc.; outcome; effect **2.** a logical result or conclusion; inference **3.** the relation of effect to cause **4.** importance as a cause or influence [a matter of slight *consequence*] **5.** importance in rank; influence [a person of *consequence*] —*SYN.* see EFFECT, IMPORTANCE —**in consequence** as a result; therefore —**in consequence of** as a result of; because of —**take the consequences** to accept the results of one's actions

con·se·quent (-kwent′, -kwənt) *adj.* [ME. & OFr. < L. *consequens:* see prec.] **1.** following as a result; resulting **2.** proceeding in logical sequence —*n.* **1.** anything that follows **2.** *Logic a)* the second term of a conditional proposition *b)* an inference **3.** *Math.* the second term of a ratio: distinguished from ANTECEDENT —**consequent on** (or **upon**) **1.** following as a result of **2.** inferred from

con·se·quen·tial (kän′sə kwen′shəl) *adj.* [< L. *consequentia* (see CONSEQUENCE) + -AL] **1.** following as an effect or inference **2.** important **3.** [Rare] acting important; pompous —**con′se·quen′ti·al′i·ty** (-shē al′ə tē), **con′se·quen′tial·ness** *n.* —**con′se·quen′tial·ly** *adv.*

con·se·quent·ly (kän′sə kwent′lē, -kwənt-) *adv.* [ME.] as a result; by logical inference; therefore

con·ser·van·cy (kən sur′vən sē) *n.* **1.** conservation of natural resources **2.** [Brit.] a commission authorized to supervise a forest, river, or port —*adj.* organized or set apart for the protection of natural resources [a State *conservancy* district]

con·ser·va·tion (kän′sər vā′shən) *n.* [ME. *conservacioun* < OFr. *conservation* < L. *conservatio*] **1.** the act or practice of conserving; protection from loss, waste, etc.; preservation **2.** the official care and protection of natural resources, as forests —**con′ser·va′tion·al** *adj.*

con·ser·va·tion·ist (-ist) *n.* a person who advocates the conservation of natural resources

conservation of energy the principle that energy is never consumed but only changes form, and that the total energy in a physical system, such as the universe, cannot be increased or diminished

conservation of matter the principle that matter is neither created nor destroyed during any physical or chemical change: also **conservation of mass**

con·ser·va·tism (kən sur′və tiz′m) *n.* the principles and practices of a conservative person or party; tendency to oppose change in institutions and methods

con·ser·va·tive (-tiv) *adj.* [ME. & OFr. *conservatif* < LL. *conservativus*] **1.** conserving or tending to conserve; preservative **2.** tending to preserve established traditions or institutions and to resist or oppose any changes in these [*conservative* politics, *conservative* art] **3.** of or characteristic of a conservative **4.** [C-] designating or of the major right-wing political party of Great Britain or the similar one in Canada **5.** [C-] designating or of a movement in Judaism that accepts moderate adaptation of religious ritual and traditional forms to the framework of modern life **6.** moderate; cautious; safe [a *conservative* estimate] —*n.* **1.** [Rare] a preservative **2.** a conservative person **3.** [C-] a member of the Conservative Party of Great Britain or of the Progressive Conservative Party of Canada —**con·ser′va·tive·ly** *adv.* —**con·ser′va·tive·ness** *n.*

con·ser·va·toire (kən sur′və twär′, -sur′və twär′) *n.* [Fr. < It. *conservatorio* < LL. *conservatorium:* see CONSERVE] *same as* CONSERVATORY (*n.* 2)

con·ser·va·tor (kän′sər vāt′ər, kən sur′və tər) *n.* [ME. *conservatour* < L. *conservator* < pp. of *conservare:* see CONSERVE] a protector, guardian, or custodian

con·ser·va·to·ry (kən sʉr′və tôr′ē) *adj.* [LL. *conservatorium* < pp. of L. *conservare*: see CONSERVE] [Rare] that preserves —*n., pl.* **-ries** 1. a room enclosed in glass, for growing and showing plants; noncommercial greenhouse 2. a school, or academy, of music, art, etc.

con·serve (kən sʉrv′; *for n., usually* kän′sʉrv) *vt.* **-served′, -serv′ing** [ME. *conserven* < OFr. *conserver* < L. *conservare*, to keep, preserve < *com-*, with + *servare*: see OBSERVE] 1. to keep from being damaged, lost, or wasted; save 2. to make (fruit) into preserves —*n.* [*often pl.*] a kind of jam made of two or more fruits, often with nuts or raisins added —**con·serv′a·ble** *adj.* —**con·serv′er** *n.*

con·sid·er (kən sid′ər) *vt.* [ME. *consideren* < OFr. *considerer* < L. *considerare*, to look at closely, observe < *com-*, with + *sidus* (gen. *sideris*), a star] 1. orig., to look at carefully; examine 2. to think about in order to understand or decide; ponder [to *consider* a problem] 3. to keep in mind; take into account [her health is good if you *consider* her age] 4. to be thoughtful of (others, their feelings, etc.); show consideration for 5. to regard as; think to be [I *consider* him an expert] 6. to believe or conclude after thought [we *consider* that the plaintiff is not guilty] —*vi.* to think carefully or seriously; reflect

SYN.—**consider** basically denotes a directing of the mind to something in order to understand it or to make a decision about it; **study** implies more intense concentration of the mind and methodical attention to details; **contemplate** implies a deep, continued mental viewing of a thing, sometimes suggesting the use of intuitive powers in envisioning something or dwelling upon it; **weigh** suggests a balancing of contradictory information, conflicting opinions, or possible eventualities, in reaching a decision; **reflect**, suggesting a turning of one's thoughts back to something, implies quiet, earnest consideration

con·sid·er·a·ble (-ə b'l) *adj.* [ME.] 1. worth considering; important; noteworthy 2. much or large [*considerable* success] —*n.* ☆[Chiefly Dial.] a large amount or number; much: used chiefly in the phrases **a considerable of, by considerable** —**con·sid·er·a·bly** *adv.*

con·sid·er·ate (-it) *adj.* [ME. *consideratus* < L. *consideratus*, pp. of *considerare*: see CONSIDER] 1. having or showing regard for others and their feelings; thoughtful 2. [Obs.] well-considered; deliberate —*SYN.* see THOUGHTFUL —**con·sid·er·ate·ly** *adv.* —**con·sid·er·ate·ness** *n.*

con·sid·er·a·tion (kən sid′ə rā′shən) *n.* [ME. *consideracioun* < L. *consideratio*] 1. the act of considering; careful thought or attention; deliberation 2. thoughtful or sympathetic regard for others 3. something that is, or should be, considered, as in making a decision 4. a thought or opinion produced by considering 5. regard; esteem; importance 6. a recompense, as for a service rendered; fee; compensation 7. *Law* something of value given or done in exchange for something of value given or done by another, in order to make a binding contract; inducement for a contract —**in consideration of** 1. because of 2. in return for —**on no consideration** not for any reason; never —**take into consideration** to keep in mind; take into account; make allowance for —**under consideration** being thought over or discussed

con·sid·ered (kən sid′ərd) *adj.* 1. arrived at after careful thought; thought out 2. [Rare] respected

con·sid·er·ing (-ər iŋ) *prep.* in view of; taking into account —*adv.* [Colloq.] taking all circumstances into account; all things considered

con·sign (kən sīn′) *vt.* [L. *consignare*, to seal, register < *com-*, together + *signare*, to sign, mark < *signum*, SIGN] 1. to hand over; give up or deliver [*consigned* to jail] 2. to put in the care of another; entrust [*consign* the orphan to her uncle's care] 3. to assign to an undesirable position or place; relegate [*consigned* to oblivion] 4. to send or deliver, as goods to be sold —*vi.* [Obs.] to agree or submit —*SYN.* see COMMIT —**con·sign′a·ble** *adj.* —**con·sig·na·tion** (kän′sig nā′shən) *n.*

con·sign·ee (kän′sī nē′, kən sī′nē′) *n.* a person or agent to whom something, esp. goods, is consigned

con·sign·ment (kən sīn′mənt) *n.* 1. a consigning or being consigned 2. something consigned; esp., a shipment of goods sent to an agent for sale or safekeeping —**on consignment** shipped or turned over to an agent for sale, with payment to the shipper to follow sale

con·sign·or (kən sī′nər, kän′sī nôr′) *n.* a person or firm that consigns goods to an agent: also **con·sign′er**

con·sist (kən sist′) *vi.* [L. *consistere*, to stand together < *com-*, together + *sistere*, to stand, cause to stand, caus.-of *stare*, to STAND] 1. to be formed or composed (*of*) [water *consists* of hydrogen and oxygen] 2. to be contained or inherent (*in* something) as a cause, effect, or characteristic [wisdom does not *consist* only in knowing facts] 3. to exist in harmony (*with*); be consistent (*with*) 4. [Archaic] to hold together or be held together; exist (usually *by* some means or agent)

con·sis·ten·cy (-ən sē) *n., pl.* **-cies** [ML. *consistentia*: see ff.] 1. *a)* the condition of holding together; firmness or thickness, as of a liquid *b)* amount or degree of this [oil of the wrong *consistency*] 2. agreement; harmony; logical connection [arguments lacking *consistency*] 3. agreement with

what has already been done or expressed; conformity with previous practice Also **con·sis′tence**

con·sis·tent (-ənt) *adj.* [L. *consistens*, prp. of *consistere*: see CONSIST] 1. [Rare] holding together; firm; solid [*consistent* soil] 2. in agreement or harmony; in accord; compatible [deeds not *consistent* with his words] 3. holding always to the same principles or practice [*consistent* behavior] —**con·sis′tent·ly** *adv.*

con·sis·to·ry (kən sis′tər ē) *n., pl.* **-ries** [ME. & OFr. *consistorie* < L. *consistorium*, place of assembly, council < *consistere*: see CONSIST] 1. *a)* orig., a meeting place for a council or court *b)* the meeting of a council 2. *a)* a church council or court, as the papal senate, a council of deacons, etc. *b)* a session of such a body —**con·sis·to·ri·al** (kän′sis tôr′ē əl) *adj.*

con·so·ci·ate (kən sō′shē āt′; *also, for n.,* -it) *n.* [ME. *consociat* < L. *consociatus*, pp. of *consociare*, to share with, join < *com-*, with + *sociare*, to join: see SOCIAL] [Rare] an associate —*vt., vi.* **-at′ed, -at′ing** to join together; unite in association —**con·so′ci·a′tion** *n.*

con·sol (kän′säl, kən säl′) *n. sing. of* CONSOLS

con·so·la·tion (kän′sə lā′shən) *n.* [ME. *consolacioun* < OFr. *consolation* < L. *consolatio*] 1. a consoling or being consoled; comfort; solace 2. a person or thing that consoles

consolation prize a prize given to a contestant who does well but does not win, or who wins in a match for those previously defeated

con·sol·a·to·ry (kən sōl′ə tôr′ē, -säl′-) *adj.* [ME. *consolatorie* < L. *consolatorius* < pp. of *consolari*] consoling or tending to console; comforting

con·sole¹ (kən sōl′) *vt.* **-soled′, -sol′ing** [Fr. *consoler* < L. *consolari* < *com-*, with + *solari*, to solace, comfort] to make feel less sad or disappointed; comfort —*SYN.* see COMFORT —**con·sol′a·ble** *adj.* —**con·sol′ing·ly** *adv.*

con·sole² (kän′sōl) *n.* [Fr., prob. contr. < *consolateur*, lit., one who consoles (see prec.), name for carved figures supporting cornices or as rails in choir stalls (sense development analogous to MISERICORD, sense 2)] 1. an ornamental bracket for supporting a shelf, bust, cornice, etc. 2. same as CONSOLE TABLE 3. the desklike frame containing the keys, stops, pedals, and other controls of an organ 4. a radio, television, or phonograph cabinet designed to stand on the floor ☆5. an instrument panel or unit, containing the controls for operating aircraft, computers, and other electrical or electronic systems

CONSOLE (sense 3)

console table 1. formerly, a table supported by ornamental consoles 2. a small table with legs curved or carved to resemble consoles, placed against a wall

con·sol·i·date (kən säl′ə dāt′) *vt., vi.* **-dat′ed, -dat′ing** [< L. *consolidatus*, pp. of *consolidare* < *com-*, together + *solidare*, to make solid < *solidus*, solid] 1. to combine into a single whole; merge; unite 2. to make or become strong, stable, firmly established, etc. [the troops *consolidated* their position] 3. to make or become solid or compact —*adj.* [Archaic] consolidated —*SYN.* see JOIN —**con·sol′i·da′tor** *n.*

☆**consolidated school** a public school attended by pupils from several adjoining, esp. rural, districts

con·sol·i·da·tion (kən säl′ə dā′shən) *n.* a consolidating or being consolidated; specif., *a)* merger; union *b)* stabilization; strengthening *c)* solidification

con·sols (kän′sälz′, kän säls′) *n.pl.* [< *consolidated annuities*] British government stock, established in 1751 by consolidating various government securities

con·som·mé (kän′sə mā′) *n.* [Fr., orig. pp. of *consommer*, to CONSUMMATE, confused with *consumer*, to CONSUME] a clear soup made by boiling meat, and sometimes vegetables, in water and straining: it is served hot or as a cold jelly

con·so·nance (kän′sə nəns) *n.* [ME. & OFr. < L. *consonantia* < *consonans*, prp. of *consonare*, to sound together with < *com-*, with + *sonare* < *sonus*, a sound] 1. harmony or agreement of elements or parts; accord 2. a pleasing combination of simultaneous musical sounds; harmony of tones 3. *Prosody* a partial rhyme in which consonants in stressed syllables are repeated but vowels are not (Ex.: mocker, maker)

con·so·nan·cy (-nən sē) *n.* harmony; agreement

con·so·nant (kän′sə nənt) *adj.* [ME. & OFr. < L. *consonans:* see CONSONANCE] 1. in harmony or agreement; in accord 2. harmonious in tone: opposed to DISSONANT 3. *Prosody* having consonance 4. consonantal —*n.* 1. any speech sound produced by stopping and releasing the air stream (p, t, k, b, d, g), by stopping it at one point while it escapes at another (m, n, ŋ, l, r), by forcing it through a loosely closed or very narrow passage (f, v, s, z, sh, zh, th, th, H, kh, h, w, y), or by a combination of these means

(ch, j): cf. VOWEL 2. a letter or symbol representing such a sound 3. *Linguis.* any phoneme, esp. one produced as described above, that does not form the peak of a syllable —**con′so·nant·ly** *adv.*

con·so·nan·tal (kän′sə nant′'l) *adj.* 1. having the nature or function of a consonant 2. of or having a consonant or consonants

consonant shift a sound change or series of connected sound changes in the consonants of a language or family of languages, as a series of changes in the Indo-European stops that set Germanic apart from other Indo-European languages, or of changes in the Germanic stops that set High German apart from other Germanic languages

con·sort (kän′sôrt; *for v.* kən sôrt′) *n.* [ME. < OFr. < L. *consors* (gen. *consortis*), partner, neighbor < *com*-, with + *sors*, a share, lot] 1. orig., a partner; companion 2. a wife or husband; spouse, esp. of a reigning king or queen 3. a ship that travels along with another 4. [Obs. or Rare] *a)* [OFr. *consorte* < L. *consortium*, community of goods < *consors*] association; fellowship; company *b)* agreement; accord *c)* [altered < *concert*] harmony of sounds; also, an ensemble of musicians or musical instruments —*vi.* 1. to keep company; associate 2. to be in harmony or agreement; be in accord —*vt.* 1. to associate; join: usually reflexive 2. [Obs.] to accompany or escort

con·sor·ti·um (kən sôr′shē əm) *n., pl.* -ti·a (-ə) [L., community of goods: see prec.] 1. a partnership or association; as, *a)* a temporary alliance of two or more business firms in a common venture *b)* an international banking agreement or association 2. *Law* the companionship and support provided by marriage, including the right of each spouse to receive this from the other

con·spe·cif·ic (kän′spə sif′ik) *adj.* [< *conspecies*, fellow species (of a genus) < CON- + SPECIES, after SPECIFIC] belonging to the same species

con·spec·tus (kən spek′təs) *n.* [L., a view, range of sight, pp. of *conspicere:* see ff.] 1. a general view; survey 2. a summary; outline; synopsis; digest

con·spic·u·ous (kən spik′yoo wəs) *adj.* [L. *conspicuus,* open to view < *conspicere,* to look at, observe < *com*-, intens. + *specere,* see (see SPY)] 1. easy to see or perceive; obvious *[a conspicuous* billboard] 2. attracting attention by being unexpected, unusual, outstanding, or egregious; striking *[conspicuous* bravery, *conspicuous* folly] —SYN. see NOTICEABLE —**con·spic′u·ous·ly** *adv.* —**con·spic′u·ous·ness** *n.*

☆**conspicuous consumption** [coined by Thorstein VEBLEN in *The Theory of the Leisure Class*] showy extravagance in buying or using goods or services, meant to impress others with one's wealth, status, etc.

con·spir·a·cy (kən spir′ə sē) *n., pl.* -cies [ME. *conspiracie,* prob. < ML. *conspirancia* < L. *conspirare:* see CONSPIRE] 1. a planning and acting together secretly, esp. for an unlawful or harmful purpose, such as murder or treason 2. the plan agreed on; plot 3. the group taking part in such a plan 4. a combining or working together *[the conspiracy* of events] —SYN. see PLOT

con·spir·a·tor (-tər) *n.* [ME. & OFr. *conspiratour* < ML. *conspirator* < pp. of L. *conspirare:* see CONSPIRE] a person who takes part in a conspiracy

con·spir·a·to·ri·al (kən spir′ə tôr′ē əl) *adj.* 1. of or characteristic of a conspirator or conspiracy 2. conspiring or fond of conspiracy —**con·spir′a·to′ri·al·ly** *adv.*

con·spire (kən spir′) *vi.* -spired′, -spir′ing [ME. *conspiren* < OFr. *conspirer* < L. *conspirare,* to breathe together, agree, unite < *com*-, together + *spirare,* to breathe] 1. to plan and act together secretly, esp. in order to commit a crime 2. to combine or work together for any purpose or effect *[events conspired* to ruin him] —*vt.* [Rare] to plan or plot

con spi·ri·to (kän spir′i tō′) [It.] *Music* with spirit; with vigor: a direction to the performer

const., Const. 1. constable 2. constant 3. constitution

con·sta·ble (kän′stə b'l; *chiefly Brit.* kun′-) *n.* [ME. < OFr. *conestable* < LL. *comes stabuli,* lit., count of the stable, hence chief groom < L. *comes,* companion, fellow + *stabulum,* a stable] 1. in the Middle Ages, the highest ranking official of a royal household, court, etc. 2. the warden or keeper of a royal fortress or castle 3. a peace officer in a town or village, with powers and jurisdiction somewhat more limited than those of a sheriff 4. [Chiefly Brit.] a policeman

Con·sta·ble (kun′stə b'l, kän′-), **John** 1776–1837; Eng. landscape painter

con·stab·u·lar·y (kən stab′yə ler′ē) *n., pl.* -ies [ML. *constabularia*] 1. the territory under the jurisdiction of a constable 2. constables, collectively, as of a district 3. a police force characterized by a military organization but distinct from the regular army 4. the police: humorous usage —*adj.* of constables or a constabulary: also **con·stab′u·lar** (-lər)

Con·stance (kän′stəns) [Fr. < *Constantia,* lit., constancy] 1. a feminine name: dim. *Connie* 2. city in SW West Germany, on Lake Constance: pop. 50,000: Ger. name, KONSTANZ 3. **Lake (of),** lake bounded by Switzerland, West Germany, & Austria: 208 sq. mi.; c. 46 mi. long: Ger. name, BODENSEE

con·stan·cy (kän′stən sē) *n.* [L. *constantia* < *constans,* prp. of *constare* < *com*-, together + *stare,* to stand] the state or quality of being unchanging; specif., *a)* firmness of mind or purpose; resoluteness *b)* steadiness of affections or loyalties; faithfulness *c)* freedom from variation or change; regularity; stability

con·stant (kän′stənt) *adj.* [ME. & OFr. *constaunt* < L. *constans:* see prec.] 1. not changing; remaining the same; specif., *a)* remaining firm in purpose; resolute *b)* remaining steady in affections or loyalties; faithful *c)* remaining free from variation or change; regular; stable 2. going on all the time; continual; persistent *[constant* interruptions] —*n.* 1. anything that does not change or vary 2. *Math., Physics a)* a quantity (**absolute constant**) that always has the same value *b)* a quantity or factor (**arbitrary constant**) assumed to have one value throughout a particular discussion or investigation: symbol c (or k): opposed to VARIABLE — SYN. see CONTINUAL, FAITHFUL —**con′stant·ly** *adv.*

Con·stant (kôṅ stän′), **Benjamin** (*Henri Benjamin Constant de Rebecque*) 1767–1830; Fr. writer & politician, born in Switzerland

Con·stan·ta (kôn stän′tsä) seaport in SE Romania, on the Black Sea: pop. 121,000

con·stant·an (kän′stən tan′) *n.* [so named because of its CONSTANT-temperature coefficient of resistance] an alloy of copper (c. 55%) and nickel (c. 45%), used in pyrometers and thermocouples

Con·stan·tine¹ (kän′stən tēn′, -tin′) [L. *Constantinus* < *constans:* see CONSTANCY] 1. a masculine name 2. **Constantine I** (*Flavius Valerius Aurelius Constantinus*) 280?– 337 A.D.; emperor of Rome (306–337): converted to Christianity: called *the Great*

Con·stan·tine² (kän′stən tēn′; *Fr.* kôṅ stän tēn′) city in NE Algeria: pop. 223,000

Con·stan·ti·no·ple (kän′stan tə nō′p'l) *former name* (330 A.D.–1930) *of* ISTANBUL

con·stel·late (kän′stə lāt′) *vi., vt.* -lat′ed, -lat′ing [< LL. *constellatus:* see ff.] to unite in or as in a constellation; cluster

con·stel·la·tion (kän′stə lā′shən) *n.* [ME. & OFr. *constellacion* < LL. *constellatio* < *constellatus,* set with stars < L. *com*-, with + pp. of *stellare,* to shine < *stella,* a star: see STELLAR] 1. *a)* a number of fixed stars arbitrarily considered as a group, usually named after some object, animal, or mythological being that they supposedly suggest in outline *b)* the part of the heavens occupied by such a group 2. any brilliant cluster, gathering, or collection 3. *Astrol. a)* the grouping of the planets at any particular time, esp. at a person's birth *b)* one's disposition or fate as supposedly influenced by such a grouping 4. *Psychol.* a group of related thoughts or feelings regarded as clustered about one central idea —**con·stel·la·to·ry** (kən stel′tôr′ē) *adj.*

con·ster·nate (kän′stər nāt′) *vt.* -nat′ed, -nat′ing [L. *consternatus,* pp. of *consternare:* see ff.] to overcome with consternation; unnerve; dismay

con·ster·na·tion (kän′stər nā′shən) *n.* [L. *consternatio* < *consternare,* to terrify < *com*-, intens. + base akin to L. *sternax,* headstrong, restive < IE. base *ster-,* rigid, stiff, whence STARE, STRENUOUS] great fear or shock that makes one feel helpless or bewildered

con·sti·pate (kän′stə pāt′) *vt.* -pat′ed, -pat′ing [< L. *constipatus,* pp. of *constipare,* to press or crowd together < *com*-, together + *stipare,* to cram, pack] to cause constipation in

con·sti·pa·tion (kän′stə pā′shən) *n.* [ME. *constipacioun* < OFr. *constipation* < L. *constipatio:* see CONSTIPATE] a condition in which the feces are hard and elimination from the bowels is infrequent and difficult

con·stit·u·en·cy (kən stich′oo wən sē) *n., pl.* -cies [< CONSTITUENT + -CY] 1. all the people, esp. voters, served by a particular elected official, esp. a legislator 2. the district of such a group of voters, etc. 3. a group of clients, supporters, etc.

con·stit·u·ent (-oo wənt) *adj.* [< L. *constituens,* prp. of *constituere:* see ff.] 1. necessary in forming or making up a whole; component *[a constituent* part] 2. that can or does appoint or vote for a representative 3. authorized to make or revise a political constitution or establish a government *[a constituent* assembly] —*n.* 1. a person who appoints another as his agent or representative 2. a member of a constituency, esp. any of the voters represented by a particular official 3. a necessary part or element; component 4. *Linguis.* an element of a construction: in "they painted signs" the main elements *they* and *painted signs* are called *immediate constituents:* the further morphologically indivisible elements *they, paint, -ed, sign,* and *-s* are called *ultimate constituents* —SYN. see ELEMENT —**con·stit′u·ent·ly** *adv.*

con·sti·tute (kän′stə toot′, -tyoot′) *vt.* -tut′ed, -tut′ing [ME. *constituten* < L. *constitutus,* pp. of *constituere,* to set up, establish < *com*-, together + *statuere,* to set] 1. to set up (a law, government, institution, etc.); establish 2. to set up (an assembly, proceeding, etc.) in a legal or official form 3. to give a certain office or function to; appoint *[we constitute* you our spokesman] 4. to make up; be the components or elements of; form; compose *[twelve people constitute* a jury] 5. to be actually as designated *[such action constitutes* a felony]

con·sti·tu·tion (kän′stə too′shən, -tyoo′-) *n.* [ME. *constitucioun* < OFr. *constitution* < L. *constitutio:* see prec.]

1. the act of setting up or making up; establishment, appointment, or formation **2.** the way in which a thing is made up; structure; organization; makeup **3.** the physical, or rarely mental, makeup of a person *[a man of strong constitution]* **4.** the way in which a government, state, society, etc. is organized **5.** a decree, regulation, or custom **6.** *a)* the system of fundamental laws and principles of a government, state, society, corporation, etc., written or unwritten *b)* a document or set of documents in which these laws and principles are written down; specif., [C-] such a document of the U.S.: it consists of seven articles and twenty-five amendments, and has been the supreme law of the nation since its adoption in 1789

con·sti·tu·tion·al (-əl) *adj.* **1.** of or in the constitution of a person or thing; basic; essential **2.** for improving a person's constitution; good for one's health **3.** of, in, authorized by, subject to, dependent on, or in accordance with the constitution of a nation, state, or society *[constitutional rights, a constitutional monarchy]* **4.** upholding the constitution —*n.* a walk or other exercise taken for one's health

con·sti·tu·tion·al·ism (-əl iz'm) *n.* **1.** government according to a constitution **2.** adherence to constitutional principles or government —**con'sti·tu'tion·al·ist** *n.*

con·sti·tu·tion·al·i·ty (-tōō'shə nal'ə tē, -tyōō'-) *n.* the quality or condition of being constitutional; esp., accordance with a constitution of a nation

con·sti·tu·tion·al·ly (-tōō'shən əl ē, -tyōō'-) *adv.* **1.** in composition or physique *[constitutionally frail]* **2.** by nature or temperament *[constitutionally incapable of lying]* **3.** in accordance with the (or a) constitution

con·sti·tu·tive (kän'stə tōōt'iv, -tyōōt'-) *adj.* [LL. *constitutivus:* see CONSTITUTE] **1.** having power to establish, appoint, or enact **2.** making a thing what it is; basic **3.** forming a part (*of*); constituent; component —**con'sti·tu'tive·ly** *adv.*

constr. 1. construction **2.** construed

con·strain (kən strān') *vt.* [ME. *constreinen* < OFr. *constreindre* < L. *constringere*, to bind together, draw together < *com-*, together + *stringere*, to draw tight] **1.** to force into, or hold in, close bounds; confine **2.** to hold back (*from an action*) by force or strain; restrain **3.** to force; compel; oblige *[he was constrained to agree]* —*SYN.* see FORCE

con·strained (-strānd') *adj.* **1.** compelled; forced; obliged **2.** forced and unnatural *[a constrained laugh]* —**con·strain'ed·ly** (-strā'nid lē) *adv.*

con·straint (-strānt') *n.* [ME. & OFr. *constreinte:* see CONSTRAIN] **1.** a constraining or being constrained; specif., *a)* confinement or restriction *b)* compulsion or coercion **2.** *a)* repression of natural feelings or behavior *b)* forced, unnatural manner; awkwardness **3.** something that constrains

con·strict (kən strikt') *vt.* [< L. *constrictus*, pp. of *constringere:* see CONSTRAIN] **1.** to make smaller or narrower, esp. at one place, by binding, squeezing, or shrinking; contract; compress **2.** to hold in; limit; restrict —**con·stric'tive** *adj.*

con·stric·tion (-strik'shən) *n.* [ME. *constriccioun* < L. *constrictio*] **1.** a constricting or being constricted; contraction or restriction **2.** a feeling of tightness or pressure, as in the chest **3.** something that constricts **4.** a constricted part

con·stric·tor (-strik'tər) *n.* [ModL.] something that constricts; specif., *a)* a muscle that contracts a cavity or opening, or compresses an organ *b)* a snake that kills by coiling around its prey and squeezing

con·stringe (kən strinj') *vt.* **-stringed'**, **-string'ing** [L. *constringere:* see CONSTRAIN] [Rare] to cause to contract, constrict, or shrink —**con·strin'gen·cy** *n.* —**con·strin'gent** *adj.*

con·stru·a·ble (-strōō'ə b'l) *adj.* that can be construed

con·struct (kən strukt'; *for n.* kän'strukt) *vt.* [< L. *constructus*, pp. of *construere* < *com-*, together + *struere*, to pile up, build] **1.** to build, form, or devise by fitting parts or elements together systematically **2.** *Geom.* to draw (a figure) so as to meet the specified requirements —*n.* **1.** something built or put together systematically **2.** *a)* an idea or perception resulting from a synthesis of sense impressions, etc. *b)* a concept or theory devised to integrate in an orderly way the diverse data on a phenomenon: also **logical construct 3.** *Linguis.* a grammatical pattern consisting of two or more immediate constituents; construction —*SYN.* see MAKE —**con·struc'tor, con·struct'er** *n.*

con·struc·tion (kən struk'shən) *n.* [ME. *construccioun* < OFr. *construction* < L. *constructio*] **1.** the act or process of constructing **2.** the way in which something is constructed; manner or method of building **3.** something constructed; structure; building **4.** an explanation or interpretation *[to put the wrong construction on a statement]* **5.** the arrangement and relation of words in a phrase, clause, or sentence **6.** a three-dimensional work of art, usually nonrepresentational and constructed of more than one material —**con·struc'tion·al** *adj.* —**con·struc'tion·al·ly** *adv.*

con·struc·tion·ist (-ist) *n.* [see prec., sense 4] a person who interprets, or believes in interpreting, a law, document, etc. in a specified way

con·struc·tive (kən struk'tiv) *adj.* [ML. *constructivus*] **1.** helping to construct; leading to improvements or advances; formative; positive *[constructive criticism]* **2.** of construction or structure **3.** inferred or implied by legal or judicial interpretation *[constructive fraud]* —**con·struc'tive·ly** *adv.* —**con·struc'tive·ness** *n.*

con·struc·tiv·ism (-iz'm) *n.* a movement in sculpture, painting, architecture, etc., esp. in the Soviet Union during the 1920's, characterized by abstract and geometric design and massive structural form —**con·struc'tiv·ist** *adj., n.*

con·strue (kən strōō') *vt.* **-strued'**, **-stru'ing** [ME. *construen* < L. *construere:* see CONSTRUCT] **1.** to analyze (a sentence, clause, etc.) so as to show its syntactical construction and its meaning **2.** loosely, to translate (a passage) orally **3.** to explain or deduce the meaning of; interpret *[her silence was construed as agreement]* **4.** to infer or deduce **5.** *Gram.* to combine in syntax *[the verb "let," unlike "permit," is construed with an infinitive omitting the "to"]* —*vi.* **1.** to analyze sentence structure, esp. in translating **2.** to be construable, as a sentence **3.** [Obs.] to make deductions —*SYN.* see EXPLAIN

con·sub·stan·tial (kän'səb stan'shəl) *adj.* [ME. *consubstancial* < LL.(Ec.) *consubstantialis:* see COM- & SUBSTANTIAL] having the same substance or essential nature —**con'sub·stan'ti·al'i·ty** (-shē al'ə tē) *n.*

con·sub·stan·ti·ate (-stan'shē āt') *vt., vi.* **-at'ed**, **-at'ing** [< LL.(Ec.) *consubstantiatus*, pp. of *consubstantiare* < L. *com-*, with + *substantia:* see SUBSTANCE] to unite in one common substance or nature

con·sub·stan·ti·a·tion (-stan'shē ā'shən) *n.* [ML.(Ec.) *consubstantiatio* < LL.(Ec.) *consubstantiare* (see prec.), after *transubstantio* (see TRANSUBSTANTIATION)] *Theol.* the doctrine that the substance of the bread and wine of the Eucharist exists, after consecration, side by side with the substance of the body and blood of Christ but is not changed into it: cf. TRANSUBSTANTIATION

con·sue·tude (kän'swi tōōd', -tyōōd') *n.* [ME. < L. *consuetudo:* see CUSTOM] established custom or usage —**con'sue·tu'di·nar'y** (-tōō'də ner'ē, -tyōō'-) *adj.*

con·sul (kän's'l) *n.* [ME. < OFr. < L. < *consulere*, to deliberate, take counsel: cf. COUNSEL, CONSULT] **1.** either of the two chief magistrates of the ancient Roman republic **2.** one of the three highest officials of the French republic from 1799 to 1804: Napoleon Bonaparte was First Consul **3.** a person appointed by his government to live in a certain foreign city and serve his country's citizens and business interests there —**con'sul·ar** (-ər) *adj.* —**con'sul·ship'** *n.*

consular agent an official serving as a consul at a place of little commercial importance

con·sul·ate (-it) *n.* [ME. *consulat* < L. *consulatus*] **1.** the position, powers, and functions of a consul **2.** the office or residence of a consul **3.** the term of office of a consul; consulship **4.** a government by consuls —**the Consulate** [Fr. *Consulat*] the consular government of France from 1799 to 1804

consul general *pl.* **consuls general, consul generals** a consul stationed in a principal commercial city, who supervises other consuls within his district

con·sult (kən sult') *vi.* [L. *consultare* < pp. of *consulere*, to deliberate, consider, orig., prob., to call together, as in *consulere senatum*, to gather the senate, hence ask (it) for advice < *com-*, with + IE. base *sel-*, to take, seize, whence Gr. *helein*, to take, E. SELL] to talk things over in order to decide or plan something; confer —*vt.* **1.** *a)* to seek an opinion from; ask the advice of *[to consult a lawyer]* *b)* to refer to or turn to, esp. for information *[to consult a map]* **2.** to keep in mind while acting or deciding; show regard for; consider *[consult your own wishes in the matter]* **3.** [Obs.] *a)* to confer about *b)* to plan for —*n.* [Obs.] a consultation —**con·sult'er** *n.*

con·sult·ant (kən sul't'nt) *n.* [< L. *consultans*, prp. of *consultare*] **1.** a person who consults with another or others **2.** an expert who is called on for professional or technical advice or opinions

con·sul·ta·tion (kän'səl tā'shən) *n.* [L. *consultatio*] **1.** the act of consulting **2.** a meeting to discuss, decide, or plan something, as a meeting of several doctors to discuss the diagnosis and treatment of a case

con·sul·ta·tive (kən sul'tə tiv, kän's'l tā'-) *adj.* of or relating to consultation; advisory *[a consultative body]*: also **con·sul'ta·to'ry** (-tôr'ē)

con·sult·ing (-sul'tin) *adj.* consulted for professional or technical advice; advisory *[a consulting engineer]*

con·sul·tor (-sul'tər) *n.* a counselor or adviser; specif., *R.C.Ch.* one of a group of priests appointed to advise and assist a bishop

con·sume (kən sōōm', -syōōm') *vt.* **-sumed'**, **-sum'ing** [ME. *consumen* < OFr. *consumer* < L. *consumere*, to use up, eat, waste < *com-*, together + *sumere*, to take < *sub-*, under + *emere*, to buy, take] **1.** to destroy, as by fire; do away with **2.** to use up; spend wastefully; squander (time, energy, money, etc.) **3.** to eat or drink up; devour **4.** to absorb completely; engross or obsess *[consumed with envy, a consuming interest]* —*vi.* [Now Rare] to waste away; perish —**con·sum'a·ble** *adj.*

con·sum·ed·ly (-id lē) *adv.* extremely or excessively
con·sum·er (kən sōō′mər, -syōō′-) *n.* a person or thing that consumes; specif., a person who buys goods or services for his own needs and not for resale or to use in the production of other goods for resale: opposed to PRODUCER
☆**consumer credit** credit extended for buying goods and services for one's personal use through installment plans, charge accounts, short-term loans, etc.
consumer goods goods, such as food, clothing, etc., for satisfying people's needs rather than for producing other goods or services: also **consumers′ goods**
con·sum·er·ism (-iz′m) *n.* **1.** the practice and policies of protecting the consumer by making him aware of defective and unsafe products, misleading business practices, etc. **2.** the consumption of goods and services
con·sum·mate (kən sum′it; *for v.* kän′sə māt′) *adj.* [L. *consummatus,* pp. of *consummare,* to sum up, finish < *com-,* together + *summa,* a SUM] **1.** complete or perfect in every way; supreme [*consummate* happiness] **2.** very skillful; highly expert [a *consummate* liar] —*vt.* -**mat′ed,** -**mat′ing** [ME. *consummaten*] **1.** to bring to completion or fulfillment; finish; accomplish **2.** to make (a marriage) actual by sexual intercourse —**con·sum′mate·ly** *adv.* —**con·sum·ma·tive** (kän′sə māt′iv), **con·sum′ma·to·ry** (-ə tôr′ē) *adj.* —**con′sum·ma′tor** *n.*
con·sum·ma·tion (kän′sə mā′shən) *n.* [ME. *consummacioun* < OFr. *consumation* < L. *consummatio*] **1.** a consummating or being consummated; completion; fulfillment **2.** an end; conclusion; outcome
con·sump·tion (kən sump′shən) *n.* [ME. *consumpcioun* < OFr. *consomption* < L. *consumptio* < *consumptus,* pp. of *consumere*] **1.** *a*) a consuming or being consumed; specif., *Econ.* the using up of goods or services, either by consumers or in the production of other goods *b*) the amount consumed **2.** *a*) a wasting away of the body *b*) a disease causing this; esp., tuberculosis of the lungs
con·sump·tive (-tiv) *adj.* [ME. *consumpt* < L. *consumptus* (see prec.) + -IVE] **1.** consuming or tending to consume; destructive; wasteful **2.** *Med.* of, having, or relating to tuberculosis of the lungs —*n.* a person who has tuberculosis of the lungs —**con·sump′tive·ly** *adv.*
Cont. Continental
cont. **1.** containing **2.** contents **3.** continent **4.** continue **5.** continued **6.** contra **7.** contract **8.** control
con·tact (kän′takt) *n.* [L. *contactus,* pp. of *contingere,* to touch, seize < *com-,* together + *tangere,* to touch < IE. base *tag-,* to touch, whence Goth. *tekan,* to touch, OE. *thaccian,* to pat] **1.** the act or state of touching or meeting [two surfaces in *contact*] **2.** the state or fact of being in touch, communication, or association (*with*) [to come into *contact* with new ideas] ☆**3.** *a*) an acquaintance, esp. one who is influential *b*) a connection with such a person [his *contacts* at city hall] **4.** *Elec. a*) a connection or point of connection between two conductors in a circuit *b*) a device for opening and closing such a connection **5.** *Med.* a person who may have caught a disease from an infected person —*vt.* **1.** to place in contact **2.** to come into contact with ☆**3.** to get in touch or communication with —*adj.* of, involving, or relating to contact —*adv.* by means of contact flying —*vi.* to be in or come into contact
contact flying flying an airplane in conditions of good visibility so that the course and altitude can be determined by observing points or objects on the ground: distinguished from INSTRUMENT FLYING
contact lens a tiny, thin correctional lens of glass or plastic placed in the fluid over the cornea of the eye
con·tac·tor (-tak tər) *n. Elec.* a device for repeatedly making and breaking a circuit, usually automatically
contact potential an electric potential between two unlike metals in contact, resulting from the differing energy levels of the outer electrons in their atomic structures
contact print a photographic print made with the negative pressed against a photosensitive surface
con·ta·gion (kən tā′jən) *n.* [ME. *contagioun* < L. *contagio,* a touching < *contingere:* see CONTACT] **1.** the spreading of disease from one individual to another by direct or indirect contact **2.** any disease thus spread; contagious disease **3.** the causative agent of a communicable disease; germ, virus, etc. **4.** contagious quality **5.** *a*) the spreading of an emotion, idea, custom, etc. from person to person until many are affected [the *contagion* of mirth] *b*) the emotion, idea, etc. so spread **6.** a bad influence that tends to spread; corruption **7.** [Archaic or Poet.] a poison
con·ta·gious (-jəs) *adj.* [ME. < OFr. *contagieus* < LL. *contagiosus*] **1.** spread by direct or indirect contact; communicable: said of diseases **2.** carrying, or liable to transmit, the causative agent of a contagious disease **3.** for the care of contagious patients **4.** spreading or tending to spread from person to person [*contagious* laughter] —**con·ta′gious·ly** *adv.* —**con·ta′gious·ness** *n.*
con·ta·gi·um (-jē əm) *n., pl.* -**gi·a** (-jē ə) [L., a touching, var. of *contagio:* see CONTAGION] *same as* CONTAGION (sense 3)
con·tain (kən tān′) *vt.* [ME. *conteinen* < OFr. *contenir* < L. *continere,* to hold < *com-,* together + *tenere,* to hold: see TENANT] **1.** to have in it; hold, enclose, or include [the can *contains* tea, the list *contains* 50 items] **2.** to have the capacity for holding **3.** to be equivalent to [a gallon *contains* four quarts] **4.** to hold back or within fixed limits; specif., *a*) to restrain (one's feelings, oneself, etc.) *b*) to

check the power, expansion, or influence of **5.** to be divisible by, esp. without a remainder [10 *contains* 5 and 2] —*vi.* [Obs.] to restrain one's feelings —**con·tain′a·ble** *adj.*
SYN.—contain, in strict usage, signifies an enclosing within or including as a component, part, or fraction, and **hold,** the capacity for containing [the bottle *contains* two ounces of liquid, but it *holds* a pint]; to **accommodate** is to hold comfortably without crowding [an elevator built to *accommodate* twelve people]
con·tain·er (-ər) *n.* a thing that contains or can contain something; box, crate, can, jar, etc.
☆**con·tain·er·ize** (-īz′) *vt.* -**ized′, -iz′ing** to pack (general cargo) into huge, standardized containers for more efficient shipment, as in transferring from one mode of transportation to another —**con·tain′er·i·za′tion** *n.*
con·tain·ment (-mənt) *n.* a containing or being contained; specif., the policy of attempting to prevent the influence of an opposing nation or political system from spreading
con·tam·i·nant (kən tam′ə nənt) *n.* a substance that contaminates another substance, the air, water, etc.
con·tam·i·nate (-ə nāt′) *vt.* -**nat′ed, -nat′ing** [ME. *contaminaten* < L. *contaminatus,* pp. of *contaminare,* to defile < *contamen,* contact, contagion < *com-,* together + base of *tangere,* to touch: cf. CONTACT] to make impure, infected, corrupt, radioactive, etc. by contact with or addition of something; pollute; defile; sully; taint —**con·tam′i·na′tive** *adj.* —**con·tam′i·na′tor** *n.*
SYN.—contaminate refers to that which on coming into contact with something will make it impure, unclean, or unfit for use [fumes were *contaminating* the air]; **taint** emphasizes effect over cause and implies that some measure of decay or corruption has taken place [*tainted* food]; **pollute** implies complete befoulment, decay, or corruption through contamination; **defile** implies pollution or desecration of that which should be held sacred
con·tam·i·na·tion (kən tam′ə nā′shən) *n.* [ME. *contaminacioun* < L. *contaminatio*] **1.** a contaminating or being contaminated **2.** something that contaminates
contd. continued
conte[1] (kônt; *Fr.* kônt) *n., pl.* **contes** (kônts; *Fr.* kônt) [Fr. < *conter:* see COUNT[1]] a short fictional story, esp. a tale of adventure
‡**con·te**[2] (kôn′te) *n.* [It.] *same as* COUNT[2]
con·temn (kən tem′) *vt.* [ME. *contempnen* < OFr. *contemner* < L. *contemnere* < *com-,* intens. + *temnere,* to scorn] to treat or think of with contempt; scorn —*SYN.* see DESPISE —**con·temn′er, con·tem′nor** (-tem′ər, -tem′nər) *n.*
con·tem·plate (kän′təm plāt′) *vt.* -**plat′ed, -plat′ing** [< L. *contemplatus,* pp. of *contemplari,* to gaze attentively, observe (orig., in augury, to mark out space for observation) < *com-,* intens. + *templum,* TEMPLE[1]] **1.** to look at intently; gaze at **2.** to think about intently; study carefully; consider **3.** to have in mind as a possibility or plan; expect or intend —*vi.* to meditate or muse, sometimes specif. in a mystical or religious way —*SYN.* see CONSIDER —**con′tem·pla′tor** *n.*
con·tem·pla·tion (kän′təm plā′shən) *n.* [ME. & OFr. *contemplacion* < L. *contemplatio*] the act or fact of contemplating; specif., *a*) thoughtful inspection, study, etc. *b*) mystical meditation *c*) expectation or intention
con·tem·pla·tive (kən tem′plə tiv, kän′təm plāt′iv) *adj.* [ME. & OFr. *contemplatif* < L. *contemplativus*] of or inclined to contemplation; thoughtful; meditative —*n.* one who is dedicated to religious meditation, esp. in a religious order —*SYN.* see PENSIVE —**con·tem′pla·tive·ly** *adv.* —**con·tem′pla·tive·ness** *n.*
con·tem·po·ra·ne·ous (kən tem′pə rā′nē əs) *adj.* [L. *contemporaneus* < *com-,* with + *tempus* (gen. *temporis*), time] existing or happening in the same period of time —*SYN.* see CONTEMPORARY —**con·tem′po·ra′ne·i·ty** (-pər ə nē′ə tē), **con·tem′po·ra′ne·ous·ness** *n.* —**con·tem′po·ra′ne·ous·ly** *adv.*
con·tem·po·rar·y (kən tem′pə rer′ē) *adj.* [< L. *com-,* with + *temporarius,* of time < *tempus,* time: see TEMPER] **1.** living or happening in the same period of time **2.** of about the same age **3.** of or in the style of the present or recent times; modern: see MODERN —*n., pl.* -**ries 1.** a person living in the same period as another or others **2.** a person or thing of about the same age or date of origin as another
SYN.—contemporary and **contemporaneous** both mean existing or happening at the same period of time, **contemporary** (often applied to the present) referring more often to persons or their works, and **contemporaneous,** to events; **coeval** implies extension over the same period of time when a remote time or very long duration is involved; **synchronous** implies exact correspondence in time of occurrence or rate of movement; **simultaneous** implies occurrence at the same point or brief interval of time
con·tem·po·rize (kən tem′pə rīz′) *vt., vi.* -**rized′, -riz′ing** to make or be contemporary
con·tempt (kən tempt′) *n.* [ME. & OFr. < L. *contemptus,* scorn, pp. of *contemnere:* see CONTEMN] **1.** the feeling or actions of a person toward someone or something he considers low, worthless, or beneath notice; scorn **2.** the condition of being despised or scorned **3.** *Law* the punishable act of showing disrespect for the authority or dignity of a court (or legislature), as by disobedience, unruliness, etc.: in full, **contempt of court** (or **congress,** etc.)
con·tempt·i·ble (kən temp′tə b'l) *adj.* [ME. < L. *contemptibilis*] **1.** deserving of contempt or scorn; worthless; despicable **2.** [Obs.] contemptuous —**con·tempt′i·bil′i·ty, con·tempt′i·ble·ness** *n.* —**con·tempt′i·bly** *adv.*

con·temp·tu·ous (kən temp′choo wəs) *adj.* [ML. *contemptuosus*] full of contempt; scornful; disdainful —**con·temp′tu·ous·ly** *adv.* —**con·temp′tu·ous·ness** *n.*

con·tend (kən tend′) *vi.* [ME. *contendere*, to compete < L. *contendere*, to stretch out, strive after < *com-*, together + *tendere*, to extend] 1. to strive in combat or opposition; fight; struggle 2. to strive in debate or controversy; argue; dispute 3. to strive in competition; compete; vie [to *contend* for a prize] —*vt.* to hold to be a fact; assert [we *contend* that he is guilty] —**con·tend′er** *n.*

con·tent¹ (kən tent′) *adj.* [ME. < OFr. < L. *contentus*, pp. of *continere*: see CONTAIN] 1. happy enough with what one has or is; not desiring something more or different; satisfied 2. willing: used in the British House of Lords as an affirmative vote 3. [Archaic] pleased —*vt.* to make content; satisfy: often used reflexively —*n.* contentment —*SYN.* see SATISFY

con·tent² (kän′tent) *n.* [ME. < ML. *contentum* (pl. *contenta*), orig. neut. pp. of L. *continere:* see CONTAIN] 1. [*usually pl.*] *a*) all that is contained in something; everything inside [the *contents* of a jar, trunk, etc.] *b*) all that is contained or dealt with in a writing or speech [a table of *contents*] 2. *a*) all that is dealt with in a course or area of study, work of art, discussion, etc. *b*) essential meaning; substance [the *content* of a poem as distinguished from its form] 3. [Rare] *a*) holding power; capacity *b*) volume or area 4. the amount (of a specified substance) contained [iron with a high carbon *content*]

con·tent·ed (kən ten′tid) *adj.* having or showing no desire for something more or different; satisfied [a *contented* look] —**con·tent′ed·ly** *adv.* —**con·tent′ed·ness** *n.*

con·ten·tion (-ten′shən) *n.* [ME. *contencioun* < OFr. *contention* < L. *contentio* < pp. of *contendere:* see CONTEND] 1. the act of contending; strife, struggle, controversy, dispute, quarrel, etc. 2. a statement or point that one argues for as true or valid —*SYN.* see CONFLICT, DISCORD

con·ten·tious (-ten′shəs) *adj.* [ME. *contencios* < L. *contentiosus:* see prec.] 1. always ready to argue; quarrelsome 2. of, involving, or characterized by dispute; controversial —*SYN.* see BELLIGERENT —**con·ten′tious·ly** *adv.* —**con·ten′tious·ness** *n.*

con·tent·ment (kən tent′mənt) *n.* [ME. & OFr. *contentement*] 1. the state, quality, or fact of being contented 2. [Archaic] *a*) a satisfying or being satisfied *b*) something that satisfies

con·ter·mi·nous (kən tur′mə nəs, kän-) *adj.* [L. *conterminus*, bordering upon < *com-*, together + *terminus*, end] 1. having a common boundary; contiguous 2. contained within the same boundaries or limits [the *conterminous* U.S. includes all the States but Alaska and Hawaii] —**con·ter′mi·nous·ly** *adv.*

con·test (kən test′; *for n.* kän′test) *vt.* [Fr. *contester* < L. *contestari*, to call to witness, bring action < *com-*, together + *testari*, to bear witness < *testis*, a witness] 1. to try to disprove or invalidate (something) as by argument or legal action; dispute [to *contest* a will] 2. to fight for (ground, a military position, etc.); struggle to win or keep —*vi.* to contend; struggle (*with* or *against*) —*n.* 1. a fight, struggle, conflict, or controversy 2. any race, game, debate, etc. in which persons or teams compete with one another to determine the winner —*SYN.* see CONFLICT —**con·test′a·ble** *adj.* —**con·test′er** *n.*

con·test·ant (kən tes′tənt) *n.* [Fr.] 1. a person who competes in a contest 2. a person who contests a claim, decision, etc.

con·tes·ta·tion (kän′tes tā′shən) *n.* [Fr. < L. *contestatio* < *contestari*] the act of contesting; conflict

con·text (kän′tekst) *n.* [ME. < L. *contextus*, a joining together, orig., pp. of *contexere*, to weave together < *com-*, together + *texere*, to weave] 1. the parts of a sentence, paragraph, discourse, etc. immediately next to or surrounding a specified word or passage and determining its exact meaning [to quote a remark out of *context*] 2. the whole situation, background, or environment relevant to a particular event, personality, creation, etc.

con·tex·tu·al (kən teks′choo wəl) *adj.* of, depending on, or belonging to the context —**con·tex′tu·al·ly** *adv.*

con·tex·ture (-chər) *n.* [Fr. < L. *contextus:* see CONTEXT] 1. a weaving together; fabrication 2. an interwoven mass; fabric 3. the way in which a thing is put together; structure; composition 4. *same as* CONTEXT

contg. containing

con·ti·gu·i·ty (kän′tə gyōō′ə tē) *n.*, *pl.* -ties [Fr. *contiguité* < ML. *contiguitas:* see ff.] 1. the state of being contiguous; nearness or contact 2. [Rare] a continuous mass or unbroken series

con·tig·u·ous (kən tig′yoo wəs) *adj.* [L. *contiguus*, bordering upon < base of *contingere*, to touch upon: see CONTACT] 1. in physical contact; touching along all or most of one side 2. near, next, or adjacent —*SYN.* see ADJACENT —**con·tig′u·ous·ly** *adv.* —**con·tig′u·ous·ness** *n.*

con·ti·nence (känt′'n əns) *n.* [ME. < OFr. < L. *continentia* < prp. of *continere:* see CONTAIN] 1. self-restraint; moderation 2. self-restraint in sexual activity; esp., total abstinence Also [Rare] **con′ti·nen·cy**

con·ti·nent (-ənt) *adj.* [ME. < OFr. < L. *continens*, prp. of *continere:* see CONTAIN] 1. self-restrained; temperate 2. characterized by self-restraint, esp. by total abstinence, in sexual activity 3. [Obs.] restrictive —*n.* 1. [Rare] a thing that retains or contains something 2. the mainland: now rare except in **the Continent**, all of Europe except the British Isles 3. any of the main large land areas of the earth, conventionally regarded (with or without outlying islands) as units; Africa, Asia, Australia, Europe, N. America, S. America, and, sometimes, Antarctica —**con′ti·nent·ly** *adv.*

con·ti·nen·tal (känt′'n en′t'l) *adj.* 1. of a continent 2. [sometimes C-] of or characteristic of the Continent; European ☆3. [C-] of the American colonies at the time of the American Revolution, or of the States just after this —*n.* 1. [*usually* C-] a person living on the Continent; European ☆2. [C-] a soldier of the American army during the Revolution ☆3. a piece of paper money issued by the Continental Congress: it became almost worthless before the end of the war, hence the phrases **not care** (or **give**), or **not worth, a continental** —**con′ti·nen′tal·ly** *adv.*

continental code *see* MORSE (CODE)

Continental Congress either of two assemblies of representatives from the American colonies during the Revolutionary period: the first was held in 1774 to express grievances against British colonial policy; the second convened in 1775, created the Continental army, issued the Declaration of Independence (1776), and operated temporarily as the legislative body of the U.S.

Continental Divide ridge of the Rocky Mountains forming a N. American watershed that separates rivers flowing in an easterly direction from those flowing in a westerly direction

continental drift the theory that continents slowly shift their positions as a result of currents in the molten rocks of the earth's mantle

continental shelf the submerged shelf of land that slopes gradually from the exposed edge of a continent for a variable distance to the point where the steeper descent (**continental slope**) to the ocean bottom begins, commonly at a depth of about 600 feet

con·tin·gence (kən tin′jəns) *n.* [ME. & OFr. < ML. *contingentia* < L. *contingens*] 1. *same as* CONTINGENCY 2. tangency, or contact

con·tin·gen·cy (-jən sē) *n.*, *pl.* -cies [see prec.] 1. the quality or condition of being contingent; esp., dependence on chance or uncertain conditions 2. something whose occurrence depends on chance or uncertain conditions; a possible, unforeseen, or accidental occurrence [be prepared for any *contingency*] 3. some thing or event which depends on or is incidental to another —*SYN.* see EMERGENCY

con·tin·gent (-jənt) *adj.* [L. *contingens*, prp. of *contingere*, to touch: see CONTACT] 1. that may or may not happen; possible 2. happening by chance; accidental; fortuitous 3. unpredictable because dependent on chance 4. dependent (*on* or *upon* something uncertain); conditional 5. [Archaic] touching; tangential 6. *Logic* true only under certain conditions or in certain contexts; not always or necessarily true 7. *Philos.* not subject to determinism; free —*n.* 1. an accidental or chance happening 2. a share, proportion, or quota, as of troops, ships, laborers, delegates, etc. 3. a group forming part of a larger group, as of an assembly —**con·tin′gent·ly** *adv.*

con·tin·u·al (kən tin′yoo wəl) *adj.* [ME. & OFr. *continuel* < L. *continuus:* see CONTINUE] 1. happening over and over again; repeated often; going on in rapid succession 2. going on uninterruptedly; continuous —**con·tin′u·al·ly** *adv.*
SYN.—**continual** applies to that which recurs repeatedly or goes on unceasingly over a long period of time [*continual* arguments]; **continuous** applies to that which extends without interruption in either space or time [a *continuous* expanse]; **constant** stresses uniformity, steadiness, or regularity in occurrence or recurrence [the *constant* beat of the heart]; **incessant** implies unceasing or uninterrupted activity [*incessant* chatter]; **perpetual** applies to that which lasts or persists for an indefinitely long time [a *perpetual* nuisance]; **eternal** stresses endlessness or timelessness [the *eternal* verities] —*ANT.* **intermittent, interrupted**

con·tin·u·ance (-yoo wəns) *n.* [ME. & OFr.: see CONTINUE] 1. the act or process of continuing, or lasting 2. the time during which an action, process, or state lasts; duration 3. the fact of remaining (*in* a place or condition); stay 4. an unbroken succession 5. [Rare] continuation; sequel 6. *Law* the postponement or adjournment of proceedings to a later date

con·tin·u·ant (-yoo wənt) *n.* [ME. < L. *continuans*, prp.: see CONTINUE] a speech sound that can be prolonged as long as the breath lasts, with no significant change in the quality of the sound: continuants are called *fricatives* (s, f, th, etc.), *nasals* (m, n, ŋ), *liquids* (l, r), or *vowels:* distinguished from STOP

con·tin·u·ate (-yoo wət) *adj.* [Obs.] 1. continuous 2. continued; lasting

con·tin·u·a·tion (kən tin′yoo wā′shən) *n.* [ME. *continuacioun* < OFr. *continuation* < L. *continuatio* < pp. of *continuere:* see CONTINUE] 1. a keeping up or going on without interruption; continued and unbroken existence or

action **2.** a taking up or beginning again after an interruption; resumption **3.** a part or thing added to make something reach further or last longer; extension, supplement, sequel, etc.

con·tin·u·a·tive (kən tin′yoo wāt′iv, -wə tiv) *adj.* [LL. *continuativus*] **1.** continuing something **2.** *Gram.* expressing continuation, or sequel [a *continuative* clause]

con·tin·u·a·tor (-yoo wāt′ər) *n.* [ML.] a person who continues something, as work begun by another

con·tin·ue (kən tin′yōō, -yoo) *vi.* -**ued**, -**u·ing** [ME. *continuer* < OFr. *continuer* < L. *continuare*, to join, make continuous < *continuus*, continuous < *continere*: see CONTAIN] **1.** to remain in existence or effect; last; endure [the war *continued* for five years] **2.** to go on in a specified course of action or condition; persist [to *continue* to mourn] **3.** to go on or extend; stretch [the road *continues* to the highway] **4.** to remain in the same place or position; stay [to *continue* in office for another year] **5.** to go on again after an interruption; resume —*vt.* **1.** to go on with; carry on; keep up; persist in **2.** to carry farther; extend **3.** to go on with (an activity, story, etc.) again after an interruption; resume **4.** to cause to remain; keep; retain [to *continue* someone in office] **5.** *Law* to postpone or adjourn to a later date —**con·tin′u·a·ble** *adj.* —**con·tin′u·er** *n.*
SYN.—**continue** implies a going on in a specified course or condition and stresses uninterrupted existence rather than duration; **last** stresses duration, either for the specified time, or if unqualified, for a time beyond that which is usual; **endure** implies continued resistance to destructive influences or forces; **abide** is applied to that which remains stable and steadfast, esp. in contrast to that which is changing and transitory; **persist** implies continued existence beyond the expected or normal time —*ANT.* **stop, cease**

continued fraction a fraction whose denominator consists of a whole number plus a fraction whose denominator consists of a whole number plus a fraction, and so forth

continued proportion *same as* GEOMETRIC PROGRESSION

con·ti·nu·i·ty (kän′tə nōō′ə tē, -nyōō′-) *n.*, *pl.* -**ties** [ME. & OFr. *continuite* < L. *continuitas*] **1.** the state or quality of being continuous; connectedness; coherence **2.** a continuous flow, series, or succession; unbroken, coherent whole **3.** continuous duration ☆**4.** the script or scenario for a motion picture, radio or television program, etc.: cf. SHOOTING SCRIPT **5.** a series of comments or announcements connecting the parts of a radio or television program **6.** the script or story of a comic strip

con·tin·u·o (kən tin′yoo wō′) *n.* [It., orig., continuous < L. *continuus*: see ff.] a continuous bass accompaniment, indicated by a shorthand method in notation, and played as on a harpsichord or organ, esp. in baroque music: see also THOROUGH BASS

con·tin·u·ous (-yoo wəs) *adj.* [L. *continuus*: see CONTINUE] **1.** going on or extending without interruption or break; unbroken; connected **2.** *Math.* designating a function of points whose value at each point is approached by its values at neighboring points —*SYN.* see CONTINUAL —**con·tin′u·ous·ly** *adv.*

con·tin·u·um (-yoo wəm) *n.*, *pl.* -**u·a** (-wə), -**u·ums** [L., neut. of *continuus*] **1.** continuous whole, quantity, or series; thing whose parts cannot be separated or separately discerned **2.** *Math.* a connected set of points that has the same cardinal number as the set of all points on a straight line See also SPACE-TIME CONTINUUM

con·to (kän′tō) *n.*, *pl.* -**tos** [Port., lit., account, count < L. *computus*: see COUNT¹] a money of account equal in Portugal to 1,000 escudos and, unofficially, in Brazil to 1,000 cruzeiros

con·tort (kən tôrt′) *vt.*, *vi.* [< L. *contortus*, pp. of *contorquere*, to whirl, twist < *com-*, together + *torquere*, to twist] to twist or wrench out of its usual form into one that is grotesque; distort violently [a face *contorted* with pain] —*SYN.* see DEFORM

con·tor·tion (kən tôr′shən) *n.* [ME. *contorsioun*] **1.** a contorting or being contorted, esp. of the face or body **2.** a contorted condition or position —**con·tor′tive** *adj.*

con·tor·tion·ist (-ist) *n.* a person, as a circus acrobat, who can contort his body into unnatural positions

con·tour (kän′toor) *n.* [Fr. < It. *contorno* < LL. *contornare*, to go around < L. *com-*, intens. + *tornare*, to turn < *tornus*, a lathe < Gr. *tornos*, tool to make a circle with: see TURN] **1.** the outline of a figure, mass, land, etc. **2.** the representation of such an outline —*vt.* **1.** to make a contour or outline of **2.** to mark contour lines on **3.** to shape or mold to conform to the contour of something [a chair *contoured* to fit the body] **4.** to construct (a road, etc.) in accordance with natural contours —*adj.* **1.** made so as to conform to the shape or outline of something [*contour* sheets for a bed] **2.** characterized by the making of furrows along the natural contour lines so as to avoid erosion, as on a hillside [*contour* farming] —*SYN.* see OUTLINE

contour feathers feathers that form the surface plumage of a bird and determine the outer contour, apart from wings, tail, etc.

contour interval the difference in value between adjacent contour lines on a map or chart

contour line a line on a map or chart connecting all points of the same elevation (or depth) in a particular area

contour map a map showing contour lines

contr. 1. contract **2.** contracted **3.** contraction **4.** contralto **5.** contrary **6.** contrasted **7.** control

con·tra- (kän′trə) [< L. *contra*, against] *a prefix meaning:* **1.** against, opposite, opposed to, contrary [*contradict*, *contraceptive*] **2.** lower in musical pitch or register [*contrabassoon*]

con·tra·band (kän′trə band′) *n.* [Sp. *contrabanda*, a smuggling < It. *contrabando* < *contra-*, against + *bando* < VL. *bannum* (akin to BAN¹)] **1.** unlawful or prohibited trade **2.** goods forbidden by law to be imported and exported; smuggled merchandise **3.** *same as* CONTRABAND OF WAR ☆**4.** during the Civil War, a Negro slave who fled to, or was smuggled or found behind, the Union lines —*adj.* forbidden by law to be imported or exported

con·tra·band·ist (-ist) *n.* a person who trades in contraband goods; smuggler

contraband of war war materiel, as ammunition or weapons, which, by international law, may rightfully be intercepted and seized by a belligerent when shipped to the other one by a neutral country

con·tra·bass (kän′trə bās′) *adj.* [see CONTRA- & BASS¹] having its pitch an octave lower than the normal bass —*n.* *same as* DOUBLE BASS —**con′tra·bass′ist** *n.*

con·tra·bas·soon (kän′trə bə soon′) *n.* the double bassoon, which is larger than the ordinary bassoon and an octave lower in pitch

con·tra·cep·tion (kän′trə sep′shən) *n.* [CONTRA- + (CON)CEPTION] the intentional prevention of fertilization of the human ovum, as by special devices, drugs, etc.

con·tra·cep·tive (-tiv) *adj.* of or used for contraception —*n.* any contraceptive device or agent

con·tract (kän′trakt *for n. & usually for vt. 1 & vi. 1;* kən trakt′ *for v. generally*) *n.* [ME. & OFr. < L. *contractus*, pp. of *contrahere*, to draw together, make a bargain < *com-*, together + *trahere*, to DRAW] **1.** an agreement between two or more people to do something, esp. one formally set forth in writing and enforceable by law; compact; covenant **2.** a formal agreement of marriage or betrothal **3.** a document containing the terms of a contract **4.** the branch of law having to do with contracts **5.** *Bridge a)* the verbal agreement made by the highest bidder to make a number of tricks *b)* the number of tricks that he bids *c)* *same as* CONTRACT BRIDGE —*vt.* **1.** to enter upon, or undertake, by contract **2.** to get, acquire, or incur [to *contract* a disease, a debt, etc.] **3.** *a)* to reduce in size; draw together; narrow; shrink; shorten [cold *contracts* metals] *b)* to draw (the brow or brows) together; knit **4.** to narrow in scope; restrict **5.** [Rare] to betroth **6.** *Gram.* to shorten (a word or phrase) by the omission of a letter or sound, as in I'm, e'er, can't —*vi.* **1.** to make a contract; agree formally [to *contract* for a new car] **2.** to become reduced in size or bulk; draw together; shrink; narrow; shorten —**contract out 1.** to assign (a job) by contract **2.** [Chiefly Brit.] to withdraw from a contract or agreement —**con·tract′i·bil′i·ty** *n.* —**con·tract′i·ble** *adj.*
SYN.—**contract** implies a drawing together of surfaces or parts and a resultant decrease in size, bulk, or extent; to **shrink** is to contract so as to be short of the normal or required length, amount, extent, etc. [those shirts have *shrunk*]; **condense** suggests reduction of something into a more compact or more dense form without loss of essential content [*condensed* milk]; to **compress** is to press or squeeze into a more compact, orderly form [a lifetime's work *compressed* into one volume]; **deflate** implies a reduction in size or bulk by the removal of air, gas, or in extended use, anything insubstantial [to *deflate* a balloon, one's ego, etc.] —*ANT.* **expand, inflate**

con·tract bridge (kän′trakt) a form of auction bridge in which only the number of tricks named in the contract may be counted toward a game, additional tricks being counted as a bonus score

con·trac·tile (kən trak′t'l) *adj.* **1.** having the power of contracting **2.** producing contraction —**con·trac·til·i·ty** (kän′trak til′ə tē) *n.*

con·trac·tion (kən trak′shən) *n.* [ME. *contraccioun* < OFr. *contraction* < L. *contractio*] **1.** a contracting or being contracted **2.** the drawing up and thickening of a muscle fiber or a muscle in action **3.** *Gram.* a) the shortening of a word or phrase by the omission of one or more letters or sounds b) a word form resulting from this (Ex.: *aren't* for *are not*) **4.** *Econ.* a period of decrease in business activity —**con·trac′tion·al** *adj.*

con·trac·tive (-tiv) *adj.* [ML. *contractivus*] **1.** having the power of contracting **2.** producing or tending to produce contraction **3.** of contraction

con·trac·tor (kän′trak tər; *also, and for 3 usually*, kən trak′tər) *n.* [LL.] **1.** one of the parties to a contract **2.** a person who contracts to supply certain materials or do certain work for a stipulated sum; esp., one whose business is contracting work in any of the building trades **3.** a thing that contracts, narrows, or shortens; esp., a muscle that contracts

con·trac·tu·al (kən trak′choo wəl) *adj.* of, or having the nature of, a contract —**con·trac′tu·al·ly** *adv.*

con·trac·ture (kən trak′chər) *n.* a shortening or shrinkage of a muscle, tendon, etc., or the resulting persistent flexion or distortion at a joint

con·tra·dance (kän′trə dans′, -däns′) *n.* *same as* CONTREDANSE

con·tra·dict (kän′trə dikt′) *vt.* [< L. *contradictus*, pp. of *contradicere* < *contra-*, against + *dicere*, to speak] **1.** *a)* to assert the opposite of (what someone else has said) *b)* to

deny the statement of (a person) **2.** to declare (a statement, report, etc.) to be false or incorrect **3.** to be contrary or opposed to; go against [the facts *contradict* his theory] —*vi.* to speak in denial; oppose verbally —*SYN.* see DENY — **con′tra·dict′a·ble** *adj.* —**con′tra·dic′tor, con′tra·dict′er** *n.*

con·tra·dic·tion (-dik′shən) *n.* [ME. *contradiccioun* < OFr. *contradiction* < L. *contradictio*] **1.** a contradicting or being contradicted **2.** a statement in opposition to another; denial **3.** a condition in which things tend to be contrary to each other; inconsistency; discrepancy **4.** a person, thing, or statement having contradictory elements or qualities

con·tra·dic·tious (-dik′shəs) *adj.* **1.** inclined to contradict; contentious **2.** [Archaic] *a)* contradictory *b)* self-contradictory

con·tra·dic·to·ry (-dik′tər ē) *adj.* [ME. *contradictorie* < LL. *contradictorius*] **1.** involving a contradiction; inconsistent **2.** inclined to contradict or deny Also **con′tra·dic′tive** —*n., pl.* **-ries 1.** something that contradicts; an opposite **2.** *Logic* either of two propositions so related that if one is true the other must be false —**con′tra·dic′to·ri·ly** *adv.* —**con′tra·dic′to·ri·ness** *n.*

con·tra·dis·tinc·tion (-dis tiŋk′shən) *n.* distinction by contrast [tolerance in *contradistinction* to love] —**con′tra·dis·tinc′tive** (-tiv) *adj.* —**con′tra·dis·tinc′tive·ly** *adv.*

con·tra·dis·tin·guish (-dis tiŋ′gwish) *vt.* to distinguish (one thing from another) by contrasting

☆**con·trail** (kän′trāl′) *n.* [CON(DENSATION) + TRAIL] a white trail of condensed water vapor that sometimes forms in the wake of an aircraft

con·tra·in·di·cate (kän′trə in′də kāt′) *vt.* **-cat′ed, -cat′ing** *Med.* to make (the indicated, or expected, treatment or drug) inadvisable —**con′tra·in′di·ca′tion** *n.* —**con′tra·in·dic′a·tive** (-in dik′ə tiv) *adj.*

con·tral·to (kən tral′tō) *n., pl.* **-tos, -ti** (-tē) [It.: see CONTRA- & ALTO] **1.** the part sung by the lowest female voice or, formerly, the highest male voice **2.** a female voice of the lowest range **3.** a woman or girl who sings in this range —*adj.* of or for a contralto

con·tra·po·si·tion (kän′trə pə zish′ən) *n.* a placing opposite or over against; antithesis; contrast

con·trap·tion (kən trap′shən) *n.* [< ? CON(TRIVE) + TRAP¹, *n.* 2 + -TION] [Colloq.] a contrivance or gadget; device that one does not fully understand

con·tra·pun·tal (kän′trə pun′t'l) *adj.* [It. *contrapunto* (see COUNTERPOINT) + -AL] **1.** of or characterized by counterpoint **2.** according to the principles of counterpoint — **con′tra·pun′tal·ly** *adv.*

con·tra·pun·tist (-pun′tist) *n.* an expert in the principles and art of counterpoint

con·tra·ri·e·ty (kän′trə rī′ə tē) *n.* [ME. & OFr. *contrarieté* < LL. *contrarietas* < L. *contrarius*] **1.** the condition or quality of being contrary **2.** *pl.* **-ties** anything that is contrary; inconsistency or discrepancy

con·tra·ri·ous (kən trer′ē əs) *adj.* [ME. < ML. *contrariosus* < L. *contrarius*] [Rare] contrary; esp., perverse

con·tra·ri·wise (kän′trer ē wīz′; *for 3, often* kən trer′ē wīz′) *adv.* [ME.: see ff. + -WISE²] **1.** on the contrary; from the opposite point of view **2.** in the opposite way; in a reversed order, direction, etc. **3.** perversely

con·tra·ry (kän′trer ē; *for adj.* 4, *often* kən trer′ē) *adj.* [ME. *contrarie* < OFr. *contraire* < L. *contrarius*, opposite, opposed < *contra*, against] **1.** opposed; in opposition [*con-trary* to the rules] **2.** opposite in nature, order, direction, etc.; altogether different **3.** unfavorable [*contrary* winds] **4.** inclined to oppose or disagree stubbornly; perverse —*n., pl.* **-ries 1.** the opposite; thing that is the opposite of another **2.** *Logic* either of two propositions so related that both may be false but only one can be true —*adv.* in a contrary way; contrariwise —**by contraries** contrary to what is expected —**on the contrary** as opposed to what has been said —**to the contrary** to the opposite effect; in reversal of what is stated —**con·trar·i·ly** (kän′trer ə lē, kən trer′-) *adv.* —**con′trar·i·ness** *n.*

SYN.—**contrary**, in this comparison, implies a habitual disinclination to accept orders, advice, etc.; **perverse** implies an unreasonable obstinacy in deviating from what is considered right or acceptable; **restive** is applied to persons who are impatient under restraint or discipline and hence are hard to control or keep in order; **balky** implies a stopping short and stubbornly refusing to go on See also OPPOSITE

con·trast (kən trast′; *for n.* kän′trast) *vt.* [Fr. *contraster* < It. & VL. *contrastare*, to withstand < L. *contra*, against + *stare*, to STAND] to compare so as to point out the differences; set off against one another —*vi.* to show differences when compared; form a contrast —*n.* [Fr. *contraste* < It. *contrasto* < the *v.*] **1.** a contrasting or being contrasted **2.** a difference, esp. a striking difference, between things being compared **3.** a person or thing showing differences when compared with another **4.** the effect of a striking difference, as in color or tone, of adjacent parts of a painting, photograph, etc. —*SYN.* see COMPARE —**con·trast′a·ble** *adj.* —**con·trast′ive** *adj.*

con·trast·y (kän′tras tē, kən tras′tē) *adj. Photog.* showing sharp contrasts of tone, as between light and dark areas

con·tra·val·la·tion (kän′trə və lā′shən) *n.* [Fr. *contreval-lation* < L. *contra*, counter + *vallatio*, entrenchment < *vallum*, WALL] a fortification set up to protect a besieging force from attack by the defenders of the besieged place or by a relieving force from the outside

con·tra·vene (kän′trə vēn′) *vt.* **-vened′, -ven′ing** [Fr. *contrevenir* < LL. *contravenire* < L. *contra*, against + *venire*, to COME] **1.** to go against; oppose; conflict with; violate [practices *contravening* an ethical code] **2.** to disagree with in argument; contradict; dispute —**con′tra·ven′tion** (-ven′shən) *n.*

con·tre·coup (kän′trə kōō′, kōn′-) *n.* [Fr. < *contre* (L. *contra*), against + *coup*, a blow] an injury, as to the brain, resulting from a blow but produced in a part opposite to the part that received the blow, due to the impact of the organ against an unyielding surface

con·tre·danse (kän′trə dans′, kōn′trə däns′) *n.* [Fr., altered (after *contre*, opposite) < COUNTRY-DANCE] **1.** a folk dance in which the partners form two facing lines; country-dance **2.** music for this dance

con·tre·temps (kōn trə tän′; *often Anglicized to various hybrid forms, as* kän′trə tän′, kōn′-) *n., pl.* **-temps′** (-tän′) [Fr., altered (after *contre*, opposite & *temps*, time) < OFr. *contrestant*, prp. of *contrester*, to CONTRAST] an inopportune happening causing confusion or embarrassment; awkward mishap

con·trib·ute (kən trib′yōōt, -yoot) *vt., vi.* **-ut·ed, -ut·ing** [< L. *contributus*, pp. of *contribuere:* see COM- & TRIBUTE] **1.** to give or provide jointly with others; give to a common fund **2.** to write and give or sell (an article, story, poem, etc.) to a magazine, newspaper, etc. **3.** to give or furnish (knowledge, ideas, etc.) —**contribute to** to have a share in bringing about (a result); be partly responsible for [fatigue *contributed* to his defeat] —**con·trib′u·tive** *adj.* —**con·trib′u·tor** *n.*

con·tri·bu·tion (kän′trə byōō′shən) *n.* [ME. *contribucioun* < OFr. *contribution* < L. *contributio*] **1.** the act of contributing **2.** something contributed, as money to a charity or a poem to a magazine **3.** [Archaic] a special levy or tax, as for supporting an army in the field

con·trib·u·to·ry (kən trib′yoo tôr′ē) *adj.* [ME. *contribu-torie* < ML. *contributorius*] **1.** contributing, as to a common fund **2.** having a share in bringing about a result [*contributory* negligence] **3.** involving, or having the nature of, a contribution —*n., pl.* **-ries** a person or thing that contributes

con·trite (kən trīt′, kän′trīt) *adj.* [ME. & OFr. *contrit* < LL.(Ec.) *contritus*, lit., worn out, ground to pieces, pp. of L. *conterere*, to grind < *com-*, together + *terere*, to rub] **1.** feeling deep sorrow or remorse for having sinned or done wrong; penitent **2.** showing or resulting from remorse or guilt —**con·trite′ly** *adv.* —**con·trite′ness** *n.*

con·tri·tion (kən trish′ən) *n.* [ME. *contricioun* < OFr. *contrition* < LL.(Ec.) *contritio*, grief: see prec.] a feeling of remorse for sins or wrongdoing; earnest repentance —*SYN.* see PENITENCE

con·triv·ance (kən trī′vəns) *n.* **1.** the act, way, or power of contriving **2.** something contrived, as an invention, mechanical device, plan, etc.

con·trive (kən trīv′) *vt.* **-trived′, -triv′ing** [ME. *contreven* < OFr. *controver*, to find out, contrive, imagine < VL. *contropare*, to compare] **1.** to think up; devise; scheme; plan [to *contrive* a way to help] **2.** to construct skillfully or ingeniously; fabricate **3.** to bring about, as by a scheme; manage [he *contrived* to get in] —*vi.* to form plans; scheme —**con·triv′a·ble** *adj.* —**con·triv′er** *n.*

con·trived (-trīvd′) *adj.* too obviously the result of fore-thought and planning; not spontaneous or natural

con·trol (kən trōl′) *vt.* **-trolled′, -trol′ling** [ME. *countrollen* < Anglo-Fr. *contreroller* < Fr. *contrerole* < ML. *contrarotu-lus*, a counter, register < L. *contra*, against + *rotulus:* see ROLL] **1.** orig., to check or verify (payments, accounts, etc.) by comparison with a duplicate register **2.** to regulate (financial affairs) **3.** to verify (an experiment) by comparison with a standard or by other experiments **4.** to exercise authority over; direct; command **5.** to hold back; curb; restrain [control your grief] —*n.* [Fr. *contrôle* < OFr. *contrerole*] **1.** the act or fact of controlling; power to direct or regulate; ability to use effectively [her *control* over her passions, the violinist's *control* of his vibrato] **2.** the condition of being directed or restrained; restraint [the car went out of *control*] **3.** a means of controlling; check [wage and price *controls*] **4.** a standard of comparison for verifying or checking the findings of an experiment **5.** an instrument or apparatus to regulate a mechanism: *usually used in pl.* **6.** a spirit supposed to direct the actions and speech of a spiritualistic medium —*SYN.* see CONDUCT, POWER — **con·trol′la·bil′i·ty** *n.* —**con·trol′la·ble** *adj.*

control experiment an experiment in which the variable factors are controlled so as to make it possible to observe the results of varying one factor at a time

con·trol·ler (kən trōl′ər) *n.* [ME. *countrollour* < Anglo-Fr. *contrerollour* < OFr. *contreroller:* see CONTROL] **1.** a person in charge of expenditures or finances, as in a business, institution, government (usually sp. *comptroller*), etc.

2. a person or device that controls —**con·trol'ler·ship'** *n.*

control rod a rod or bar containing a neutron-absorbing material, used to regulate the fission chain reaction in a nuclear reactor

control stick the lever that controls the altitude and movement of an airplane

control tower a tower at an airport, from which air traffic is directed, chiefly by radio

con·tro·ver·sial (kän'trə vur'shəl) *adj.* [LL. *controversialis*] **1.** of, subject to, or stirring up controversy; debatable **2.** [Rare] liking to take part in controversy; disputatious —**con'tro·ver'sial·ly** *adv.*

con·tro·ver·sial·ist (-ist) *n.* a person who takes part in controversy or likes to do so

con·tro·ver·sy (kän'trə vur'sē) *n., pl.* **-sies** [ME. *controversie* < L. *controversia* < *controversus*, turned in an opposite direction < *contra*, against + *versus*, pp. of *vertere*, to turn] **1.** discussion of a question in which opposing opinions clash; debate; disputation **2.** a quarrel or dispute —*SYN.* see ARGUMENT

con·tro·vert (kän'trə vurt', kän'trə vurt') *vt.* [backformation < prec., after words ending in -*vert* (e.g., DIVERT, REVERT)] **1.** to argue or reason against; contradict; deny; dispute **2.** to argue about; debate; discuss —*SYN.* see DISPROVE —**con'tro·vert'i·ble** *adj.* —**con'tro·vert'i·bly** *adv.*

con·tu·ma·cious (kän'too mā'shəs, -tyoo-) *adj.* [< ff. + -OUS] obstinately resisting authority; insubordinate; disobedient —**con'tu·ma'cious·ly** *adv.*

con·tu·ma·cy (kän'too mə sē, -tyoo-; kən too'-) *n., pl.* **-cies** [ME. *contumacie* < L. *contumacia* < *contumax*, haughty, stubborn < *com-*, intens. + *tumere*, to swell up] stubborn refusal to submit to authority, esp. that of a law court; insubordination; disobedience

con·tu·me·li·ous (kän'too mē'lē əs, -tyoo-) *adj.* [ME. < OFr. *contumelieus* < L. *contumeliosus* < *contumelia*: see ff.] rude in a contemptuous way; insulting and humiliating —**con'tu·me'li·ous·ly** *adv.*

con·tu·me·ly (kän'too mə lē, -mē'-, -tyoo-; -toom lē, -tyoom-; kən too'mə lē; -tyoo'-; *etc.*) *n., pl.* **-lies** [ME. & OFr. *contumelie* < L. *contumelia*, a reproach, abuse; prob. akin to CONTUMACY] **1.** haughty and contemptuous rudeness; insulting and humiliating treatment or language **2.** an instance of this; scornful insult

con·tuse (kən tooz', -tyooz') *vt.* **-tused', -tus'ing** [ME. *contusen* < L. *contusus*, pp. of *contundere*, to beat, break to pieces < *com-*, intens. + *tundere*, to beat] to injure or bruise without breaking the skin

con·tu·sion (-too'zhən, -tyoo'-) *n.* [ME. *contusioun* < L. *contusio*: see prec.] **1.** a bruising or being bruised **2.** a bruise; injury in which the skin is not broken

co·nun·drum (kə nun'drəm) *n.* [16th-c. Oxford University L. slang for pedant, whim, etc.; early sp. *quonundrum*] **1.** a riddle whose answer contains a pun (Ex.: "What's the difference between a jeweler and a jailer?" "One sells watches and the other watches cells.") **2.** any puzzling question or problem —*SYN.* see MYSTERY

con·ur·ba·tion (kän'ər bā'shən) *n.* [< CON- + L. *urbs*, city + -ATION] an extremely large, densely populated urban area, usually a complex of suburbs and smaller towns together with the large city at their center

con·va·lesce (kän'və les') *vi.* **-lesced', -lesc'ing** [L. *convalescere*, to begin to grow strong < *com-*, intens. + *valescere*, to grow strong < *valere*, to be strong] to recover gradually from illness; regain strength and health

con·va·les·cence (-les''ns) *n.* [Fr. < L. *convalescens*, prp. of prec.] **1.** gradual recovery after illness **2.** the period of such recovery

con·va·les·cent (-les''nt) *adj.* [< L. *convalescens*] **1.** gradually recovering health after illness **2.** of or having to do with convalescence [*a convalescent diet*] —*n.* a person who is convalescing

con·vec·tion (kən vek'shən) *n.* [L. *convectio* < pp. of *convehere*, to bring together < *com-*, together + *vehere*, to carry, bear] **1.** a transmitting or conveying **2.** *a)* the mass movement of parts of a fluid within the fluid because of differences in the density, temperature, etc. of the parts *b)* the transference of heat by such movement, as by the upward movement of a warm, light air current —**con·vec'tion·al** *adj.* —**con·vec'tive** *adj.* —**con·vec'tive·ly** *adv.* —**con·vec'tor** *n.*

con·ve·nance (kän'və näns'; *Fr.* kōn v' näns') *n.* [Fr., fitness, propriety < *convenir*, to be in accord, fit < L. *convenire*, CONVENE] **1.** conventional social usage **2.** [*pl.*] the conventionalities

con·vene (kən vēn') *vi.* **-vened', -ven'ing** [ME. *convenen* < OFr. *convenir* < L. *convenire* < *com-*, together + *venire*, to COME] to meet together; assemble, esp. for a common purpose —*vt.* **1.** to cause to assemble, or meet together **2.** to summon before a court of law —*SYN.* see CALL —**con·ven'er** *n.*

con·ven·ience (kən vēn'yəns) *n.* [ME. < L. *convenientia* < *convenire*, CONVENE] **1.** the quality of being convenient; fitness or serviceableness **2.** personal well-being; comfort **3.** a condition personally favorable or suitable; advantage **4.** anything that adds to one's comfort or saves work; useful, handy or helpful device, article, service, etc. Also [Archaic] **con·ven'ien·cy** (-yən sē), *pl.* **-cies** —**at one's convenience** at a time, or in a place or manner, suitable to one

con·ven·ient (-yənt) *adj.* [ME. < L. *conveniens*, prp. of *convenire*, CONVENE] **1.** adding to one's comfort; easy to do, use, or get to; causing little trouble or work; handy **2.** [Obs.] appropriate; suitable **3.** [Colloq.] easily accessible (*to*); near (*to*) —**con·ven'ient·ly** *adv.*

con·vent (kän'vənt, -vent) *n.* [ME. & OFr. < L. *conventus*, assembly (in ML.(Ec.), religious house, convent), orig. pp. of *convenire*, CONVENE] **1.** a community of nuns or, sometimes, monks, living under strict religious vows **2.** the building or buildings occupied by such a group —*SYN.* see CLOISTER

con·ven·ti·cle (kən ven'ti k'l) *n.* [ME. < OFr. *conventicule* < L. *conventiculum*, dim. of prec.] **1.** an assembly, esp. a religious assembly, that is held illegally or secretly; specif., a prohibited meeting of any of certain Protestant sects that disputed the authority of the Church of England in the 16th and 17th cent. **2.** a place where such an assembly meets

con·ven·tion (kən ven'shən) *n.* [ME. *convencioun* < L. *conventio* < pp. of *convenire*, CONVENE] **1.** [Rare] a convening or being convened **2.** *a)* an assembly, often periodical, of members or delegates, as of a political, social, professional, or religious group *b)* the members or delegates at such an assembly **3.** *a)* an agreement between persons, nations, etc. [a copyright *convention;* the Geneva *Convention] b)* general agreement on the usages and practices of social life [bohemian revolt against *convention*] **4.** *a)* a customary practice, rule, method, etc.; usage [the soliloquy was an Elizabethan dramatic *convention] b)* Card Games a play or bid established as having a certain meaning between partners

con·ven·tion·al (-'l) *adj.* [LL. *conventionalis*] **1.** having to do with a convention or assembly **2.** of, sanctioned by, or growing out of custom or usage; customary **3.** *a)* depending on or conforming to formal or accepted standards or rules rather than nature; not natural, original, or spontaneous [*conventional* behavior] *b)* not unusual or extreme; ordinary **4.** stylized; conventionalized **5.** nonnuclear [*conventional* weapons] **6.** *Law* based on agreement between parties; contractual —**con·ven'tion·al·ism** *n.* —**con·ven'tion·al·ist** *n.* —**con·ven'tion·al·ly** *adv.*

con·ven·tion·al·i·ty (kən ven'shə nal'ə tē) *n., pl.* **-ties** **1.** the quality, fact, or condition of being conventional **2.** conventional behavior or act **3.** a conventional form, usage, or rule

con·ven·tion·al·ize (kən ven'shən 'l īz') *vt.* **-ized', -iz'ing** **1.** to make conventional **2.** *Art* to treat in a conventional manner —**con·ven'tion·al·i·za'tion** *n.*

☆**con·ven·tion·eer** (kən ven'shə nir') *n.* a delegate or member attending a convention

con·ven·tu·al (kən ven'choo wəl) *adj.* [ME. < ML. *conventualis*] of, like, or characteristic of, a convent —*n.* **1.** a member of a convent **2.** [C-] a member of a branch (**Friars Minor Conventual**) of the Franciscan order under a modified rule that permits the holding of property in common

con·verge (kən vurj') *vi.* **-verged', -verg'ing** [LL. *convergere* < L. *com-*, together + *vergere*, to turn, bend] **1.** to come together or tend to come together at a point **2.** to move or be directed toward each other or toward the same place, purpose, or result **3.** to approach a definite limit (as 2) in a progression of an infinite series of numbers (as $1 + 1/2 + 1/4 + 1/8 + 1/16 + 1/32 ...$) —*vt.* to cause to converge

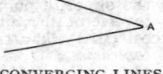

CONVERGING LINES (at point A)

con·ver·gence (kən vur'jəns) *n.* [< CONVERGENT] **1.** the act, fact, or condition of converging **2.** the point at which things converge **3.** *Biol.* the development of similarities in unrelated organisms living in the same environment Also **con·ver'gen·cy,** *pl.* **-cies** —**con·ver'gent** *adj.*

con·ver·sa·ble (kən vur'sə b'l) *adj.* [Fr. < ML. *conversabilis*] **1.** *a)* easy to talk to; affable *b)* liking to talk **2.** [Archaic] of or fit for conversation

con·ver·sant (kən vur's'nt, kän'vər-) *adj.* [ME. *conversaunt* < OFr. *conversant* < L. *conversans*, prp. of *conversari*: see CONVERSE[1]] familiar or acquainted (*with*), esp. as a result of study or experience; versed (*in*) —**con·ver'sance, con·ver'san·cy** *n.* —**con·ver'sant·ly** *adv.*

con·ver·sa·tion (kän'vər sā'shən) *n.* [ME. *conversacioun* < OFr. *conversation* < L. *conversatio* < pp. of *conversari*: see CONVERSE[1]] **1.** the act or an instance of talking together; specif., *a)* familiar talk; verbal exchange of ideas, opinions, etc. *b)* an informal conference on a problem or area of interest by representatives of governments, factions, etc. **2.** sexual intercourse: now only in the legal phrase *criminal conversation,* i.e., adultery as grounds for divorce or other action **3.** [Archaic] manner of living; behavior **4.** [Obs.] social intercourse **5.** [Obs.] familiarity based on study or use

con·ver·sa·tion·al (-'l) *adj.* **1.** of, like, or for conversation **2.** fond of or given to conversation; liking to converse —**con'ver·sa'tion·al·ly** *adv.*

con·ver·sa·tion·al·ist (-'l ist) *n.* a person who converses; esp., one who enjoys and is skilled at conversation: also **con'ver·sa'tion·ist**

conversation piece 1. a type of genre painting, popular in the 18th cent., which shows a group of people in an appropriate setting **2.** something, as an unusual article of furniture, that attracts attention or invites comment

‡con·ver·sa·zi·o·ne (kôn′ver sä tsyō′ne; *E.* kän′vər sät′se ō′nē) *n., pl.* **-o′ni** (-nē); *E.* **-o′nes** (-nēz) [It., lit., conversation] a social gathering for conversation about literature, the arts, etc.

con·verse[1] (kən vurs′; *for n.* kän′vərs) *vi.* **-versed′, -vers′-ing** [ME. *converser* < OFr. *converser* < L. *conversari,* to live with, keep company with, medial form of *conversare,* to turn around, freq. of *convertere:* see CONVERT] **1.** to hold a conversation; talk **2.** [Obs.] to consort; have social intercourse —*n.* **1.** informal talk; conversation **2.** [Obs.] social intercourse —*SYN.* see SPEAK —**con·vers′er** *n.*

con·verse[2] (kän′vərs; *also, for adj.,* kən vurs′) *adj.* [L. *conversus,* pp. of *convertere:* see CONVERT] reversed in position, order, action, etc.; opposite; contrary; turned about —*n.* **1.** a thing related in a converse way; the opposite **2.** *Logic* a proposition produced by conversion —**con·verse′ly** *adv.*

con·ver·sion (kən vur′zhən, -shən) *n.* [ME. *conversioun* < OFr. *conversion* < L. *conversio* < pp. of *convertere*] **1.** a converting or being converted; specif., *a)* a change from lack of faith to religious belief; adoption of a religion *b)* a change from one belief, religion, doctrine, opinion, etc. to another **2.** *Finance* a change of a security, currency, etc. from one form to another ☆**3.** *Football a)* a play in which a team that has just made a touchdown scores one or two extra points by a successful place kick, pass, or run *b)* the score so made **4.** *Law a)* unlawful appropriation and use of another's property *b)* the exchange of property from real property to personal, or the reverse **5.** *Logic* the transposition of the subject and predicate of a proposition, resulting in a new proposition **6.** *Math.* a change in the form of a quantity or an expression without a change in the value **7.** *Psychiatry* a mechanism by which emotional conflict is transformed into an apparent physical disability affecting the sensory or voluntary motor systems and having symbolic meaning: also **conversion reaction** and, formerly, **conversion hysteria** —**con·ver′sion·al, con·ver′sion·ar′y** (-cr′ē) *adj.*

con·vert (kən vurt′; *for n.* kän′vərt) *vt.* [ME. *converten* < OFr. *convertir* < L. *convertere* < *com-,* together + *vertere,* turn] **1.** to change from one form or use to another; transform [*convert* grain into flour] **2.** to cause to change from one religion, doctrine, course, etc. to another **3.** to exchange for something equal in value **4.** *Finance* to change into an equivalent of another form **5.** *Law a)* to appropriate and use (another's property) unlawfully *b)* to change (property) from real to personal, or the reverse **6.** *Logic* to change (a proposition) by transposing the subject and predicate —*vi.* **1.** to be converted ☆**2.** *Bowling* to knock down all of the standing pins on the second bowl, scoring a spare ☆**3.** *Football* to make a conversion —*n.* a person converted, as to a religion —*SYN.* see CHANGE, TRANSFORM

con·vert·er (kən vur′tər) *n.* a person or thing that converts; specif., *a)* a furnace for converting pig iron into steel in the Bessemer process *b)* an electrical device for converting alternating current into direct current: cf. INVERTER *c)* the part of a radio receiver that changes modulated high frequencies to lower frequencies *d)* any device for adapting a radio or television receiver to added frequencies or modulations Also sp. **con·ver′tor**

converter reactor a nuclear reactor that produces less fissionable material than it consumes, or one that produces a different fissionable material than it consumes

con·vert·i·ble (kən vur′tə b'l) *adj.* [ME. & OFr. < LL.(Ec.) *convertibilis*] that can be converted —*n.* **1.** a thing that can be converted ☆**2.** an automobile with a top, as of canvas, that can be folded back —**con·vert′i·bil′i·ty** *n.* —**con·vert′i·bly** *adv.*

☆con·vert·i·plane (kən vur′tə plän′) *n.* [CONVERTI(BLE) + (AIR)PLANE] an aircraft designed to take off and land vertically like a helicopter but to fly forward in level flight like a conventional airplane

con·vert·ite (kän′vər tīt′) *n.* [Archaic] a convert

con·vex (kän veks′, kən-; *also, and for n. usually,* kän′veks) *adj.* [L. *convexus,* vaulted, arched, pp. of *convehere,* to bring together < *com-,* together + *vehere,* to bring] curving outward like the surface of a sphere —*n.* a convex surface, line, object, etc. —**con·vex′ly** *adv.* —**con·vex′ness** *n.*

con·vex·i·ty (kən vek′sə tē, kän-) *n.* [L. *convexitas*] **1.** the quality or condition of being convex **2.** *pl.* **-ties** a convex surface, line, etc.

con·vex·o-con·cave (kän vek′sō kän kāv′) *adj.* **1.** convex on one side and concave on the other **2.** *Optics* designating a lens whose convex face has a greater degree of curvature than its concave face, so that the lens is thickest in the middle

con·vex·o-con·vex (-kän veks′) *adj.* convex on both sides, as some lenses

con·vex·o-plane (-plän′) *adj.* same as PLANO-CONVEX

CONVEX LENSES (A, plano-convex; B, convexo-concave; C, convexo-convex)

con·vey (kən vā′) *vt.* [ME. *conveien* < Anglo-Fr. *conveier* (OFr. *convoier*), to escort, convoy < VL. *conviare,* to accompany on the way < L. *com-,* together + *via,* way] **1.** to take from one place to another; transport; carry [a chimney *conveys* smoke to the outside] **2.** to serve as a channel or medium for; transmit **3.** to make known; communicate in words, actions, appearance, etc. **4.** to transfer, as property or title to property, from one person to another **5.** [Obs.] *a)* to take away secretly *b)* to steal —*SYN.* see CARRY —**con·vey′a·ble** *adj.*

con·vey·ance (-əns) *n.* [ME. *conveiaunce*] **1.** the act of conveying **2.** a means of conveying; carrying device, esp. a vehicle **3.** *a)* the transfer of the ownership of real property from one person to another *b)* the document by which this is effected; deed

con·vey·anc·ing (-ən siŋ) *n.* [< prec. + -ING] the act or work of drawing up documents for transferring the ownership of real property —**con·vey′anc·er** *n.*

con·vey·or, con·vey·er (-ər) *n.* one that conveys; esp., a mechanical contrivance, as a continuous chain or belt (**conveyor belt**), for conveying something

con·vict (kən vikt′; *for n.* kän′vikt) *vt.* [ME. *convicten* < L. *convictus,* pp. of *convincere:* see CONVINCE] **1.** to prove (a person) guilty [*convicted* by the evidence] **2.** to judge and find guilty of an offense charged [the jury *convicted* him of theft] **3.** to bring to a realization of one's guilt [*convicted* by his own conscience] —*n.* **1.** a person found guilty of a crime and sentenced by a court **2.** a person serving a sentence in prison

con·vic·tion (kən vik′shən) *n.* [ME. < LL.(Ec.) *convictio,* proof, demonstration] **1.** a convicting or being convicted **2.** [Rare] the act of convincing **3.** the state or appearance of being convinced, as of the truth of a belief [to speak with *conviction*] **4.** a strong belief —*SYN.* see CERTAINTY, OPINION

con·vic·tive (-tiv) *adj.* having power to convince or convict —**con·vic′tive·ly** *adv.*

con·vince (kən vins′) *vt.* **-vinced′, -vinc′ing** [L. *convincere,* to overcome, convict of error < *com-,* intens. + *vincere,* to conquer: see VICTOR] **1.** orig., to overcome, confute, or convict **2.** to overcome the doubts of; persuade by argument or evidence; make feel sure —**con·vinc′er** *n.* —**con·vin′ci·ble** *adj.*

con·vinc·ing (-vin′siŋ) *adj.* causing one to feel sure or to believe or agree; persuading as by evidence; cogent —*SYN.* see VALID —**con·vinc′ing·ly** *adv.*

con·viv·i·al (kən viv′ē əl) *adj.* [L. *convivialis* < *convivium,* a feast < *convivere,* to carouse together < *com-,* together + *vivere,* to live] **1.** having to do with a feast or festive activity **2.** fond of eating, drinking, and good company; sociable; jovial —**con·viv′i·al·ist** *n.* —**con·viv′i·al′i·ty** (-al′ə tē) *n.* —**con·viv′i·al·ly** *adv.*

con·vo·ca·tion (kän′və kā′shən) *n.* [ME. *convocacioun* < L. *convocatio*] **1.** the act of convoking **2.** a group that has been convoked; esp., an ecclesiastical or academic assembly —**con′vo·ca′tion·al** *adj.*

con·voke (kən vōk′) *vt.* **-voked′, -vok′ing** [Fr. *convoquer* < L. *convocare,* to call together < *com-,* together + *vocare,* to call] to call together for a meeting; summon to assemble; convene —*SYN.* see CALL

con·vo·lute (kän′və lōōt′) *adj.* [L. *convolutus,* pp. of *convolvere:* see CONVOLVE] rolled up in the form of a spiral with the coils falling one upon the other; coiled —*vt., vi.* **-lut′ed, -lut′ing** to wind around; coil —**con′vo·lute′ly** *adv.*

con·vo·lut·ed (-id) *adj.* **1.** having convolutions; coiled; spiraled **2.** extremely involved; intricate; complicated [a *convoluted* style]

con·vo·lu·tion (kän′və lōō′shən) *n.* [ML. *convolutio* < L. *convolutus,* pp. of *convolvere:* see CONVOLVE] **1.** a twisting, coiling, or winding together **2.** a convoluted condition **3.** a fold, twist, or coil of something convoluted; specif., any of the irregular folds or ridges on the surface of the brain

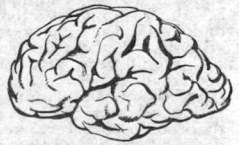

CONVOLUTIONS

con·volve (kən välv′) *vt., vi.* **-volved′, -volv′ing** [L. *convolvere,* to roll together < *com-,* together + *volvere,* to roll, turn] to roll, coil, or twist together

con·vol·vu·lus (kən väl′vyə ləs) *n., pl.* **-lus·es, -li′** (-lī′) [L., bindweed < *convolvere:* see CONVOLVE] any of a genus (*Convolvulus*) of trailing, twining, or erect plants of the morning-glory family, with funnel-shaped flowers and triangular leaves

con·voy (kän′voi; *also, for v.,* kən voi′) *vt.* [ME. *convoien* < OFr. *convoier* < VL. *conviare:* see CONVEY] to go along with as an escort, esp. in order to protect; escort —*n.* **1.** the act of convoying **2.** a protecting escort, as for ships or troops **3.** a group of ships, vehicles, etc. traveling together, as for mutual protection —*SYN.* see ACCOMPANY

con·vulse (kən vuls′) *vt.* **-vulsed′, -vuls′ing** [< L. *convulsus,* pp. of *convellere,* to tear loose < *com-,* together + *vellere,* to pluck] **1.** to shake or disturb violently; agitate **2.** to cause

convulsions, or spasms, in **3.** to cause to shake with laughter, rage, grief, etc.

con·vul·sion (kən vul′shən) *n.* [L. *convulsio < convulsus:* see prec.] **1.** a violent, involuntary contraction or spasm of the muscles: *often used in pl.* **2.** a violent fit of laughter **3.** any violent disturbance, as a social upheaval or an earthquake —**con·vul′sion·ar′y** *adj.*

con·vul·sive (-siv) *adj.* **1.** having the nature of a convulsion **2.** having, producing, or marked by convulsions —**con·vul′sive·ly** *adv.* —**con·vul′sive·ness** *n.*

co·ny (kō′nē) *n., pl.* **-nies** *same as* CONEY

coo (kōō) *vi.* [echoic] **1.** to make the soft, murmuring sound of pigeons or doves or a sound like this **2.** to speak gently and lovingly; utter with a coo: see BILL², *vi.* 2 —*vt.* to express gently and lovingly; utter with a coo —*n.* the sound made in cooing —*interj.* [Brit.] a lower-class expression of surprise, doubt, delight, etc. —**coo′ing·ly** *adv.*

☆**cooch** (kōōch) *n.* [< (HOOTCHY-)KOOTCH(Y)] [Slang] a female exhibition dance with sinuous hip movements, etc.; belly dance —**cooch dancer**

Cooch Be·har (kōōch′ bə här′) district in West Bengal, India, north of East Pakistan

coo·coo (kōō′kōō) *adj.* [Slang] *same as* CUCKOO

cook (kook) *n.* [ME. *cok < OE. coc < L. cocus < L. coquus < coquere,* to cook < IE. base *pekw-,* to cook, whence Sans. *pácate,* he cooks, OE. *afigen,* fried] a person who prepares food for eating —*vt.* [ME. *coken < the n.*] **1.** to prepare (food) for eating by subjecting to heat, as by boiling, baking, frying, etc. **2.** to subject to heat or to some treatment suggestive of a heating process **3.** [Brit. Colloq.] to tamper with; falsify **4.** [Slang] to spoil; ruin —*vi.* **1.** to act or serve as a cook **2.** to undergo the process of being cooked —**cook up** [Colloq.] to concoct; devise; invent *[to cook up* an alibi*]* —☆**what's cooking?** [Slang] what's happening? —**cook′er** *n.*

Cook, James 1728–79; Eng. naval officer & explorer: explored Australia, New Zealand, Antarctica, etc.

Cook, Mount mountain of the Southern Alps, New Zealand: highest peak in New Zealand: 12,349 ft.

☆**cook·book** (-book′) *n.* a book containing recipes and other information for the preparation of food

Cooke (kook), **Jay** 1821–1905; U.S. financier

cook·er·y (-ər ē) *n.* [ME. *cokerie*] [Chiefly Brit.] the art, practice, or work of cooking

cook·house (-hous′) *n.* a place for cooking, as an outdoor kitchen or a ship's galley

cook·ie (-ē) *n.* [prob. Du. *koekje,* dim. of *koek,* a cake, akin to CAKE, G. *kuchen*] ☆**1.** a small, sweet cake, usually flat **2.** [Scot.] a bun ☆**3.** [Slang] *a)* a person, esp. one qualified as "tough, smart, shrewd, etc." *b)* an attractive young woman

Cook Inlet arm of the Gulf of Alaska, in S Alas.: c. 200 mi. long

Cook Islands group of islands of New Zealand in the S Pacific, west of Society Islands: 93 sq. mi.; pop. 21,000

☆**cook·out** (-out′) *n.* a meal prepared on an outdoor grill, etc. and eaten outdoors, as at a picnic

Cook's tour [after Thomas *Cook* & Son, Brit. travel agents] any guided sightseeing or inspection tour: a humorous usage

☆**cook·stove** (-stōv′) *n.* a stove for cooking

Cook Strait strait between North Island & South Island, New Zealand: narrowest point, 16 mi.

cook·y (-ē) *n., pl.* **cook′ies** *same as* COOKIE

cool (kōōl) *adj.* [ME. & OE. *col < IE. base *gel-,* cold, to freeze, whence L. *gelu,* cold: cf. COLD, CHILL] **1.** moderately cold; neither warm nor very cold **2.** tending to reduce discomfort in warm or hot weather *[cool* clothes*]* **3.** *a)* not excited; calm; composed *[cool* in an emergency*]* ☆*b)* marked by control of the emotions; restrained *[cool* jazz*]* *c)* [Slang] emotionally uninvolved; uncommitted; dispassionate **4.** showing dislike or indifference; not cordial *[a cool* manner*]* **5.** calmly impudent or bold **6.** not suggesting warmth: said of colors in the blue-green end of the spectrum **7.** [Colloq.] without exaggeration *[he won a cool* thousand dollars*]* ☆**8.** [Slang] very good, pleasing, etc.; excellent —*adv.* in a cool manner —*n.* **1.** a cool place, time, thing, part, etc. *[the cool* of the evening*]* ☆**2.** [Slang] cool, dispassionate attitude or manner —*vi.* [ME. *colien < OE. colian,* to cool] to become cool —*vt.* to make cool —**cool off 1.** to calm down **2.** to lose enthusiasm, interest, etc. —☆**play it cool** [Slang] to exercise strict control over one's emotions; stay aloof, unenthusiastic, or uncommitted —**cool′ish** *adj.* —**cool′ly** *adv.* —**cool′ness** *n.*

SYN.—**cool,** in this comparison, implies freedom from the heat of emotion or excitement, suggesting a calm, dispassionate attitude or a controlled alertness in difficult circumstances; **composed** suggests readiness to meet a trying situation through self-possession or the disciplining of one's emotions; **collected** stresses a being in full command of one's faculties or emotions in a distracting situation; **unruffled** suggests the maintenance of poise or composure in the face of something that might agitate or embarrass one; **nonchalant** stresses a cool lack of concern or casual indifference —*ANT.* **excited, agitated**

cool·ant (-ənt) *n.* a substance, usually a fluid, used to remove heat, as from a nuclear reactor, an internal-combustion engine, molten metal, etc.

cool·er (-ər) *n.* **1.** a device, container, or room for cooling things or keeping them cool **2.** anything that cools, as a refreshing drink ☆**3.** [Slang] jail

cool·head·ed (-hed′id) *adj.* not easily flustered or confused; calm; imperturbable

Coo·lidge (kōō′lij), **(John) Calvin** 1872–1933; 30th president of the U.S. (1923–29)

coo·lie (kōō′lē) *n.* [Hind. *qŭlī,* hired servant, prob. < *kolī,* name of a tribe or caste of Gujarat] **1.** an unskilled native laborer, esp. formerly, in India, China, etc. **2.** a person doing heavy labor for little pay

coolth (kōōlth) *n.* [< COOL, after WARMTH] coolness: now chiefly a humorous usage

coomb (kōōm) *n.* [ME. < OE. *cumb < Celt. base *kumbos < IE. base *kumb-,* var. of *keu-,* bend: cf. COOP, CUP, HIVE] [Brit.] a deep, narrow valley; ravine

☆**coon** (kōōn) *n. clipped form of* RACCOON

☆**coon·can** (kōōn′kan′) *n.* [var. of CONQUIAN] a form of the card game rummy

☆**coon cat** [Colloq.] *same as* CACOMISTLE

☆**coon's age** (kōōnz) [fanciful & emphatic < RACCOON] [Colloq.] an indefinitely long time

☆**coon·skin** (kōōn′skin′) *n.* the skin of a raccoon, used as a fur —*adj.* made of coonskin

☆**coon·tie** (kōōn′tē) *n.* [Seminole *kunti,* coontie flour, starch] a tropical American cycad (*Zamia floridana*), with large, dark-green, leathery leaves and underground trunks that yield a starch

coop (kōōp) *n.* [ME. *coupe,* akin to MDu., MLowG. *kupe,* OHG. *kuofa < L. cupa,* tub, cask < IE. base *keup-,* bend, hollow, mound, whence HIVE: cf. CUP] **1.** a small cage, pen, or building for poultry, etc. **2.** any place of confinement; specif., [Slang] a jail —*vt.* to confine in or as in a coop (usually with *up* or *in*) —☆**fly the coop** [Slang] to escape, as from a jail

co-op (kō′äp, kō äp′) *n.* [Colloq.] a cooperative

co-op., coop. cooperative

coop·er (kōōp′ər, koop′-) *n.* [ME. *couper < MDu. cuper < LL. cuparius < L. cupa,* a cask: see COOP] a person whose work is making or repairing barrels and casks —*vt., vi.* to make or repair (barrels and casks)

Coop·er (kōōp′ər, koop′-) **1. James Fen·i·more** (fen′ə môr′), 1789–1851; U.S. novelist **2. Peter,** 1791–1883; U.S. inventor, industrialist, & philanthropist

coop·er·age (-ij) *n.* [ME. *couperage*] **1.** the workshop of a cooper **2.** *a)* the work of a cooper *b)* the price charged for such work

co·op·er·ate, co-op·er·ate (kō äp′ə rāt′) *vi.* -at′ed, -at′ing [< LL. *cooperatus,* pp. of *cooperari,* to work together < L. *co-,* with + *operari,* to work < *opus* (gen. *operis*), work] **1.** to act or work together with another or others for a common purpose **2.** to combine so as to produce an effect **3.** to engage in economic cooperation Also **co·öp′er·ate′** —**co·op′er·a′tor, co-op′er·a′tor** *n.*

co·op·er·a·tion, co-op·er·a·tion (kō äp′ə rā′shən) *n.* [LL. *cooperatio*] **1.** the act of cooperating; joint effort or operation **2.** the association of a number of people in an enterprise for mutual benefits or profits **3.** *Ecology* an interaction between organisms that is largely beneficial to all those participating Also **co·öp′er·a′tion**—**co·op′er·a′tion·ist, co-op′er·a′tion·ist** *n.*

co·op·er·a·tive, co-op·er·a·tive (kō äp′ər ə tiv, -ə rāt′iv; -äp′rə tiv) *adj.* **1.** cooperating or inclined to cooperate **2.** designating or of an organization (as for the production or marketing of goods), an apartment house, store, etc. owned collectively by members who share in its benefits —*n.* a cooperative society, store, etc. Also **co·öp′er·a·tive** —**co·op′er·a·tive·ly, co-op′er·a·tive·ly** *adv.* —**co·op′er·a·tive·ness, co-op′er·a·tive·ness** *n.*

☆**Coo·per's hawk** (kōō′pərz) [after Wm. *Cooper,* 19th-c. U.S. ornithologist] a relatively small hawk (*Accipiter cooperi*) with a long, rounded tail and short, rounded wings

coop·er·y (kōōp′ər ē, koop′-) *n., pl.* -er·ies [ME. *couperie*] the work, shop, or product of a cooper

co-opt (kō äpt′) *vt.* [L. *cooptare,* to choose, elect < *co-,* with + *optare,* to choose] **1.** to add (a person or persons) to a group by vote of those already members **2.** to appoint as an associate Also **co·öpt′** —**co′-op·ta′tion, co-op′tion** *n.* —**co-op′ta·tive** (-tə tiv), **co-op′tive** *adj.*

co·or·di·nate, co-or·di·nate (kō ôr′d'n it; *also, and for v. always,* -də nāt′) *adj.* [ML. *coordinatus,* pp. of *coordinare,* to set in order, arrange < L. *co-,* with + *ordinare,* to arrange < *ordo,* order] **1.** of the same order or importance; equal in rank **2.** of or involving coordination or coordinates **3.** *Gram.* being of equal structural rank *[coordinate* clauses*]* —*n.* **1.** a coordinate person or thing **2.** *Math.* any magnitude of a system of two or more magnitudes used to define the position of a point, line, curve, or plane —*vt.* -nat′ed, -nat′ing **1.** to place in the same order, rank, etc.; make coordinate **2.** to bring into proper order or relation; adjust (various parts) so as to have harmonious action; harmonize —*vi.* to become coordinate; function harmoniously Also **co·ör′di·nate** —**co·or′di·nate·ly, co·or′di·nate·ly** *adv.* —**co·or′di·na·tive, co·or′di·na·tive** (-nə tiv, -nāt′iv) *adj.* —**co·or′di·na′tor, co·or′di·na′tor** *n.*

coordinate bond a bond between an atom and another atom or group of atoms, in which the shared pair of electrons is supplied by only one of the atoms

coordinating conjunction a conjunction that connects coordinate words, phrases, or clauses (Ex.: *and, but, for, or, nor, yet*)

co·or·di·na·tion, co-or·di·na·tion (kō ôr′d'n ā′shən) *n.* [LL. *coordinatio*] **1.** a coordinating or being coordinated **2.** the state or relation of being coordinate; harmonious

adjustment or action, as of muscles in producing complex movements Also **co·ör′di·na′tion** n.

coordination complex one of a number of complex compounds in which an atom or group of atoms is bound to the central atom by a shared pair of electrons supplied by the coordinated group and not by the central atom: also called **coordinate valence**

Coorg (koorg) former state in SW India: since 1956, a district in the state of Mysore

Coos (kōōs) n. [< native name] 1. pl. **Coos** any member of an Indian people living in W Oregon 2. their Penutian language

coot (kōōt) n., pl. **coots**; also, for 1 & 2, **coot**: see PLURAL, II, D, 1 [ME. cote < ? MDu. koet] 1. any of various ducklike, fresh-water birds (genus Fulica) of the rail family, with long-lobed, un-webbed toes ☆2. same as SCOTER 3. [Colloq.] a foolish, stupid, or senile person

coot·ie (kōōt′ē) n. [Brit. World War I army slang, earlier a sea-man's term < Polynesian kutu, parasitic insect] [Slang] a louse

COOT
(to 16 in. long; wingspread to 28 in.)

cop¹ (käp) n. [ME. & OE. cop, prob. akin to G. kopf & Du. kop, head < LL. cuppa: see CUP] 1. [Obs. or Dial.] the top or crest, as of a hill 2. a cone-shaped roll of thread or yarn coiled round a spindle

cop² (käp) vt. **copped**, **cop′ping** [< north Brit. dial. form of obs. cap, to seize; prob. < OFr. caper < L. capere, to take] [Slang] to seize, capture, win, steal, etc. —☆n. [see COPPER²] [Slang] a policeman —☆**cop a plea** [Slang] to plead guilty to a criminal charge, esp. so as to get a lighter sentence —☆**cop out** [Slang] 1. to confess to the police, often implicating another 2. a) to go back (on a promise, commitment, etc.); back down; renege b) to give up; quit; surrender

co·pai·ba (kō pī′bə, -pā′-) n. [Sp. & Port. < Tupi cupaiba] 1. an aromatic resin obtained from certain S. American trees (genus Copaifera) of the legume family: formerly used in medicine 2. any of these trees

co·pal (kō′pəl, -pal) n. [Sp. < Nahuatl copalli, resin] fossil resin and other hard resins from tropical trees, used in varnishes and lacquers

☆**co·palm** (kō′päm′) n. [< ? CO(PAL) + PALM¹] 1. a brown-ish, aromatic resin obtained from the sweet gum tree 2. the tree

Co·pán (kō pän′) town in W Honduras: site of a ruined Mayan city of ? 7th-8th cent.: pop. 1,000

co·par·ce·nar·y (kō pär′sə ner′ē) n., pl. **-nar′ies** [CO- + PARCENARY] 1. Law joint heirship; partnership in inherit-ance 2. joint partnership or ownership —adj. of coparcenary or coparceners Also **co·par′ce·ny** (-sə nē), pl. **-nies**

co·par·ce·ner (-sə nər) n. [CO- + PARCENER] Law a person who shares jointly with others in an inheritance

co·part·ner (kō pärt′nər) n. a partner, or associate — **co·part′ner·ship′** n.

cope¹ (kōp) vi. **coped**, **cop′ing** [ME. coupen < OFr. couper, to slash, strike < coup, COUP] 1. to fight or contend (with) successfully or on equal terms 2. to deal with problems, troubles, etc. 3. [Archaic] to meet, encounter, or have to do (with) —vt. 1. [Archaic] to meet, as in contest; encounter 2. [Obs.] to match equally

cope² (kōp) n. [ME. < ML. capa, var. of cappa: see CAP] 1. a large, capelike vestment worn by priests at certain ceremonies 2. anything that covers like a cope, as a canopy, a vault, or the sky 3. same as COPING —vt. **coped**, **cop′ing** to cover or provide with a cope, coping, or something similar

cope³ (kōp) vt. **coped**, **cop′ing** [back-formation < COPING] to cut so as to fit over or against a coping or molding with curves, angles, etc.

co·peck (kō′pek) n. same as KOPECK

Co·pen·hag·en (kō′pən hā′gən, -hä′-; kōp′ən hā′gən) capital of Denmark: seaport on the E coast of Zealand: pop. 924,000 (met. area 1,348,000): Dan. name, KØBENHAVN

co·pe·pod (kō′pə päd′) n. [< Gr. kōpē, oar + -POD] any of a subclass (Copepoda) of small, sometimes parasitic, crusta-ceans living in either salt or fresh water

Copernican system the theory of Copernicus that the planets revolve around the sun and that the turning of the earth on its axis accounts for the apparent rising and setting of the stars: basis of modern astronomy

Co·per·ni·cus (kō pur′ni kəs), **Nic·o·la·us** (nik′ə lā′əs), (L. form of Mikołaj Kopernik) 1473–1543; Pol. astronomer —**Co·per′ni·can** adj., n.

cope·stone (kōp′stōn′) n. 1. a) the top stone of a wall or building b) a stone used in or for a coping 2. finishing stroke; culmination

cop·i·er (käp′ē ər) n. 1. a person who copies; specif., a) an imitator b) a transcriber 2. a duplicating machine

co·pi·lot (kō′pī′lət) n. the assistant pilot of an airplane, who aids or relieves the pilot

cop·ing (kō′piŋ) n. [< fig. use of COPE²] the top layer of a masonry wall, usually sloped to carry off water

coping saw a saw with a narrow blade in a U-shaped frame, esp. for cutting curved outlines

COPING SAW

co·pi·ous (kō′pē əs) adj. [ME. < L. copiosus < copia, abundance < co-, together + opes, wealth] 1. very plentiful; abundant 2. wordy; profuse or diffuse in language 3. full of information — SYN. see PLENTIFUL —co′pi·ous·ly adv. —co′pi·ous·ness n.

co·pla·nar (kō plā′nər) adj. Math. in the same plane: said of figures

Cop·land (kōp′lənd), **Aaron** 1900– ; U.S composer

Cop·ley (käp′lē), **John Singleton** 1738–1815; Am. painter, in England after 1775

co·pol·y·mer (kō pal′ə mər) n. Chem. a compound pro-duced by copolymerization —co·pol′y·mer′ic (-mer′ik) adj.

co·po·lym·er·i·za·tion (kō′pə lim′ə ri zā′shən, kō päl′ə mə ri-) n. a process resembling polymerization, in which unlike molecules unite in alternate sequences in a chain or in irregular or random alternations —co′po·lym′er·ize′ (-ə rīz′) vt., vi.

☆**cop-out** (käp′out′) n. [Slang] the act or an instance of copping out, as by confessing, reneging, quitting, etc.

cop·per¹ (käp′ər) n. [see PLURAL, II, D, 3 [ME. & OE. coper < LL. cuprum, contr. < Cyprium (aes), Cyprian (brass), copper < Gr. Kyprios, Cyprus, noted for its copper mines] 1. a reddish-brown, malleable, ductile, metallic element that is an excellent conductor of electricity and heat: symbol, Cu; at. wt., 63.546; at. no., 29; sp. gr., 8.93; melt. pt., 1083°C; boil. pt., 2336°C 2. [Now chiefly Brit.] a) a small coin of copper or bronze, as a penny b) a large metal container or boiler, orig. of copper 3. the color of copper; reddish brown ☆4. a small, copper-colored butterfly (Lycaena hypophloeas) found throughout the U.S. —adj. 1. of copper 2. copper-colored; reddish-brown —vt. 1. to cover or coat with copper ☆2. [from use of a copper coin to indicate such a bet in faro] [Slang] to bet against (an-other's bet) —cop′per·y adj.

cop·per² (käp′ər) n. [prob. < COP²] [Slang] a policeman

cop·per·as (käp′ər əs) n. [ME. & OFr. coperose < ML. (aqua) cuprosa, lit., copper (water)] ferrous sulfate, $FeSO_4 \cdot 7H_2O$, a green, crystalline compound used in dyeing, the making of ink, etc.

☆**cop·per·head** (käp′ər hed′) n. 1. a poisonous N. American pit viper (Agkistrodon contort-rix) with a copper-colored head and dark-brown cross bands 2. [C-] a Northerner who sympa-thized with the South at the time of the Civil War: so called in the North

COPPERHEAD
(to 40 in. long)

Cop·per·mine (käp′ər min′) river in Mackenzie District of Northwest Territories, Canada, flowing northwest into the Arctic Ocean: 525 mi.

cop·per·plate (-plāt′) n. 1. a flat piece of copper etched or engraved for printing 2. a print made from this 3. a printing or engraving process using copperplate

copper pyrites same as CHALCOPYRITE

cop·per·smith (-smith′) n. a man whose work is making utensils and other things out of copper

copper sulfate a blue, crystalline substance, $CuSO_4 \cdot 5H_2O$, which effloresces and turns white when heated: used in making pigments, germicides, batteries, etc.

cop·pice (käp′is) n. [ME. copis < OFr. copeis < couper, to cut: see COUP] same as COPSE

co·pra (kō′prə, käp′rə) n. [Port. < Malayalam koppara < Hind. khoprā] dried coconut meat, the source of coconut oil

cop·ro- (käp′rə, -rō) [< Gr. kopros, dung] a combining form meaning dung, excrement, feces [coprolite]: also, before a vowel, **copr-**

cop·ro·lite (käp′rə līt′) n. [prec. + -LITE] fossilized excre-ment of animals —cop′ro·lit′ic (-lit′ik) adj.

cop·rol·o·gy (kä präl′ə jē) n. [COPRO- + -LOGY] the study or treatment of scatological or pornographic subjects in art and literature

cop·roph·a·gous (kä präf′ə gəs) adj. [COPRO- + -PHAGOUS] feeding on dung, as some beetles —cop·roph′a·gy (-jē) n.

cop·ro·phil·i·a (käp′rə fil′ē ə) n. [COPRO- + -PHILIA] Psychol. an abnormal interest in feces

copse (käps) n. [< COPPICE] a thicket of small trees or shrubs; coppice

Copt (käpt) n. [ModL. Coptus: see COPTIC] 1. a native of Egypt descended from the ancient inhabitants of that country 2. a member of the Coptic Church

☆**cop·ter** (käp′tər) n. shortened form of HELICOPTER

Cop·tic (käp′tik) adj. [ModL. Copticus < Coptus, earlier Cophtus < Ar. Quft, Qift, the Copts < Coptic Gyptios < Gr. Aigyptios, Egyptian] 1. of the Copts, their language, culture, etc. 2. of the Coptic Church —n. the Afro-Asiatic language of the Copts, derived from ancient Egyptian and now used only in the ritual of the Coptic Church

Coptic Church the native Christian church of Egypt and of Ethiopia, Monophysitic in doctrine

cop·u·la (käp′yə lə) n., pl. **-las** [L., a band, link (earlier *co-apula*) < co-, together + apere, to join] something that connects or links together; specif. a) *Gram.* a weakened verbal form, esp. a form of *be* or any similar verb, as *seem, appear,* etc., which links a subject with a predicate complement; linking verb b) *Logic* the connecting link between the subject and predicate of a proposition —cop′u·lar adj.

cop·u·late (-lāt′) vi. **-lat′ed, -lat′ing** [ME. copulaten < L. copulatus, pp. of copulare, to unite, couple < copula: see COPULA] to have sexual intercourse —cop′u·la′tion n. —cop′u·la·to′ry (-lə tôr′ē) adj.

cop·u·la·tive (-lāt′iv, -lə tiv) adj. [ME. copulatif < LL. copulativus < L. copulatus: see COPULATE] 1. joining together; coupling 2. *Gram.* a) connecting coordinate words, phrases, or clauses [a copulative conjunction] b) involving connected words or clauses c) having the nature of a copula [a copulative verb] 3. of or for copulating —n. a copulative word —cop′u·la′tive·ly adv.

cop·y (käp′ē) n., pl. **cop′ies** [ME. & OFr. copie, abundance, full transcript < ML. copia, copious transcript < L. copia, plenty: see COPIOUS] 1. a thing made just like another; imitation of an original; full reproduction or transcription 2. [Now Rare] a model or pattern, as of penmanship, to be imitated or reproduced 3. any of a number of books, magazines, engravings, etc. printed from the same plates or having the same printed matter 4. matter, as a manuscript or illustration, to be set in type or put on a printing plate 5. anything that can provide subject matter for a journalist, novelist, etc. 6. the words of an advertisement, as distinct from the layout, pictures, music, etc. —vt., vi. **cop′ied, cop′y·ing** 1. to make a copy or copies of (a piece of writing, etc.); reproduce; transcribe 2. to make or do something in imitation of (some thing or person); imitate **SYN.**—copy, the broadest of these terms, refers to any imitation, often only approximate, of an original [a carbon copy]; **reproduction** implies a close imitation of the original, often, however, with differences, as of material, size, or quality [a reproduction of a painting]; a **facsimile** is an exact reproduction in appearance, sometimes, however, differing in scale [a photostated facsimile of a document]; a **duplicate** is a double, or counterpart, of something, serving all the purposes of the original [all the books of a single printing are duplicates]; a **replica** is an exact reproduction of a work of art, in strict usage, one made by the original artist See also IMITATE

cop·y·book (-book′) n. a book containing models of handwriting, formerly used in teaching penmanship —adj. ordinary; trite; commonplace [copybook maxims]

☆**copy boy** a messenger who runs errands and carries copy from desk to desk in a newspaper office

☆**cop·y·cat** (-kat′) n. a person who habitually imitates or mimics others: chiefly a child's term

☆**copy desk** the desk in a newspaper office where copy is edited and headlines are written

cop·y·hold (-hōld′) n. Eng. Law tenure of property less than a freehold proved by a written transcript or record in the rolls of a manorial court

cop·y·hold·er (-hōl′dər) n. ☆1. a person who reads copy aloud to a proofreader 2. a device for holding copy, as for a typesetter 3. Eng. Law a person who holds land by copyhold

cop·y·ist (-ist) n. 1. a person who makes written copies; transcriber 2. a person who imitates; copier

☆**cop·y·read·er** (-rē′dər) n. a person whose work is editing and correcting articles, stories, or other copy, as in a newspaper office or publishing house

cop·y·right (-rīt′) n. [COPY + RIGHT] the exclusive right to the publication, production, or sale of the rights to a literary, dramatic, musical, or artistic work, or to the use of a commercial print or label, granted by law for a specified period of time to an author, composer, artist, distributor, etc. —vt. to protect (a book, song, print, etc.) by copyright —adj. protected by copyright —cop′y·right′a·ble adj. —cop′y·right′er n.

cop·y·writ·er (-rīt′ər) n. a writer of copy for advertisements or promotional material

‡**coq au vin** (kôk ō van′) [Fr.] chicken sautéed and then stewed in wine

coq feather (kōk) [Fr., coq, a cock] the feather of a cock, or rooster

coque·li·cot (kō′klə kō′) n. [< Fr. coq, cock: applied to the poppy because of similarity of color to that of a cock's comb] same as CORN POPPY

Co·que·lin (kō klan′), **Be·noit Cons·tant** (bə nwả′ kôn stän′) 1841-1909; Fr. actor

co·quet (kō ket′) vi. **-quet′ted, -quet′ting** [Fr. coqueter, to flirt, lit., to strut like a rooster < coquet, dim. of coq, a rooster: see COCK[1]] 1. to behave as a coquette; flirt 2. to trifle or dally (with an idea, offer, etc.) —adj. coquettish —SYN. see TRIFLE

co·quet·ry (kōk′ə trē, kō ket′rē) n., pl. **-ries** [Fr. coqueterie < coqueter: see prec.] 1. the behavior or act of a coquette; flirting 2. the act of trifling or dallying

co·quette (kō ket′) n. [Fr. coquette, fem.: see COQUET] a girl or woman who merely from vanity tries to get men's attention and admiration —vi. **-quet′ted, -quet′ting** to behave as a coquette; flirt —co·quet′tish adj. —co·quet′-tish·ly adv. —co·quet′tish·ness n.

co·quil·la nut (kō kē′yə, -kēl′yə) [Sp. coquillo or Port. coquilho, dim. of coco, coconut] the fruit of a piassava palm (Attalea funifera) of Brazil: it yields palm oil and has a very hard, brown, ivorylike shell used in cabinetwork and by carvers

co·quille (kō kēl′; Fr. kō kē′y′) n. [Fr., a shell < OFr.: see COCKLE[1]] 1. a scallop shell or shell-shaped dish in which minced seafood, chicken, etc. is baked and served 2. any food so served

☆**co·qui·na** (kō kē′nə) n. [Sp., shellfish, dim. < dial. form of L. concha: see CONCH] 1. a soft, whitish limestone made up of broken sea shells and corals: used as a building material 2. any of a genus (Donax) of small, delicately colored saltwater clams

co·qui·to (kō kēt′ō) n., pl. **-tos** [Sp., dim. of coco, coco palm] a palm tree (Jubaea spectabilis) of Chile whose sweet sap and nuts are used for food

cor (kôr) interj. [earlier Gor < *Gord, altered < GOD] [Brit.] a lower-class exclamation of surprise, admiration, irritation, etc.

cor- (kôr) same as COM-: used before r

Cor. 1. Corinthians 2. Coroner 3. Corsica

cor. 1. corner 2. cornet 3. coroner 4. corpus 5. correct 6. correction 7. correlative 8. correspondence 9. correspondent 10. corresponding

Cor·a (kôr′ə) [L. < Gr. Korē, lit., maiden, name of Proserpina] a feminine name

cor·a·ci·i·form (kôr′ə sī′ə fôrm′, kə ras′ē ə fôrm′) adj. [< ModL. Coracii, name of the suborder < Gr. korax, raven + -FORM] of or belonging to an order (Coraciiformes) of birds with a strong, sharp bill and the third and fourth toes fused basally, as the kingfishers, bee eaters, hornbills, etc.

cor·a·cle (kôr′ə k'l, kär′-) n. [< W. corwgl < corwg, orig., leather-covered boat, akin to L. corium, hide: see CORIUM] a short, wide boat made of a waterproof material stretched over a wicker or wooden frame

cor·a·coid (kôr′ə koid′, kär′-) adj. [ModL. coracoides < Gr. korakoeidēs, like a raven < korax, raven + eidos, form] designating or of a rudimentary bony process on the shoulder blade in mammals, or a bone in many other vertebrates that extends from the shoulder blade to the breastbone —n. this bony process or bone

cor·al (kôr′əl, kär′-) n. [ME. & OFr. < L. coralium < Gr. korallion < ? Heb. gōrāl, pebble or Ar. garal, small stone] 1. the hard, stony skeleton secreted by certain marine polyps and often deposited in extensive masses forming reefs and atolls in tropical seas 2. any of a number of such polyps (esp. of the anthozoan order Madreporaria) living singly or in large colonies 3. a piece of coral, esp. the red kind used in jewelry 4. the mature ovaries of the lobster 5. a yellowish red or yellowish pink: also **coral red** or **coral pink** —adj. 1. made of coral 2. coral-red or coral-pink

☆**cor·al·bells** (-belz′) n., pl. **-bells′** a southwestern American plant (Heuchera sanguinea) of the saxifrage family, with racemes of drooping pink flowers

CORAL
(A, organ-pipe; B, reef; C, mushroom; D, Bermuda)

☆**cor·al·ber·ry** (-ber′ē) n., pl. **-ries** a small N. American plant (Symphoricarpos orbiculatus) of the honeysuckle family, with greenish or purplish flowers and pink or purple berries

Coral Gables [orig. the name of the founder's residence, built of coral rock with a colorful tile roof] city on the SE coast of Fla.: suburb of Miami: pop. 42,000

cor·al·line (kôr′ə lin′, kär′-; -lin) n. [ModL. corallina < the adj.] 1. any animal related to or resembling the corals 2. any of a family (Corallinaceae) of red algae that produce limestone —adj. [LL. corallinus, coral-red] 1. consisting of coral or corallines 2. resembling coral, esp. in color

cor·al·loid (-loid′) adj. resembling coral in appearance and form: also **cor′al·loi′dal**

coral reef a reef in relatively shallow, tropical seas composed chiefly of the skeletons of coral

cor·al·root (-root′, -root′) n. any of a genus (Corallorhiza) of brownish orchids with branched, corallike rootstocks and no leaves

Coral Sea part of the S Pacific, northeast of Australia & south of the Solomon Islands

coral snake ☆any of several small, poisonous, burrowing snakes (genera Micrurus and Micruroides), related to the cobra and found in the southern U.S. and subtropical America: it has coral-red, yellow, and black bands around its body

co·ran·to (kə ran′tō) n. [altered < COURANTE after It. & Sp. words ending in -o] same as COURANTE

cor·beil (kôr′bel, -bəl) n. [Fr. corbeille < LL. corbicula, dim. of L. corbis, a basket] a sculptured basket of fruit, flowers, etc., used in architectural design

cor·bel (kôr′bəl) *n.* [ME. & OFr., dim. of *corb*, raven < L. *corvus*, raven: so called from its beaked shape] **1.** a piece of stone, wood, or metal, often in the form of a bracket, projecting from the side of a wall and serving to support a cornice, the spring of an arch, etc. **2.** a short timber placed lengthwise under a beam or girder —*vt.* **-beled** or **-belled**, **-bel·ing** or **-bel·ling** to provide or support with a corbel or corbels

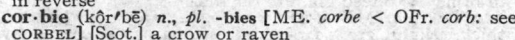

CORBEL

cor·bel·ing, **cor·bel·ling** (-iŋ) *n.* **1.** the fashioning of corbels **2.** courses of masonry, like steps in reverse

cor·bie (kôr′bē) *n., pl.* **-bies** [ME. *corbe* < OFr. *corb*: see CORBEL] [Scot.] a crow or raven

corbie gable a gable with corbiesteps

cor·bie-step (-step′) *n.* [CORBIE + STEP] one of a series of steps at the upper end wall of some gables

☆**cor·bi·na** (kôr bē′nə) *n. same as* CORVINA

Corbusier, **Le** *see* LE CORBUSIER

Cor·co·va·do (kôr′kō vä′thoo) mountain in SE Brazil, near Rio de Janeiro: 2,310 ft.

Cor·cy·ra (kôr sī′rə) *ancient name of* CORFU

cord (kôrd) *n.* [ME. & OFr. *corde* < L. *chorda* < Gr. *chordē*, catgut, chord, cord < IE. base *g̑her-, g̑horna*, intestine, whence L. *haru-* (in *haruspex*), entrails, ON. & G. *garn*, YARN] **1.** (a) thick string or thin rope **2.** any force acting as a tie or bond **3.** [from use of a cord in measuring] a measure of wood cut for fuel or pulpwood (128 cubic feet, as arranged in a pile 8 feet long, 4 feet high, and 4 feet wide) **4.** *a)* a rib on the surface of a fabric *b)* cloth with a ribbed surface; corduroy *c)* [*pl.*] corduroy trousers **5.** *Anat.* any part resembling a cord [the spinal *cord*, vocal *cords*, umbilical *cord*]: also CHORD **6.** *Elec.* a slender, flexible insulated cable fitted with a plug or plugs, as to connect a lamp to an outlet —*vt.* **1.** to fasten, connect, or provide with a cord or cords **2.** to stack (wood) in cords

cord·age (-ij) *n.* [Fr.: see CORD & -AGE] **1.** cords and ropes collectively, esp. the ropes in a ship's rigging **2.** the amount of wood, in cords, in a given area

cor·date (kôr′dāt) *adj.* [ModL. *cordatus* < *cor* (gen. *cordis*), heart] heart-shaped [*cordate* leaf] —**cor′date·ly** *adv.*

Cor·day (d'Armont) (kôr dā′), **(Marie Anne) Charlotte** 1768–93; Fr. Girondist: assassin of Marat

cord·ed (kôr′did) *adj.* **1.** fastened or tied with cords **2.** made of or provided with cords **3.** that looks like a tight cord, as a muscle **4.** having a ribbed or twilled surface, as corduroy **5.** stacked in cords, as wood

Cor·del·ia (kôr dēl′yə) [prob. ult. < Celt. *Creiryddlydd*, lit., daughter of the sea] **1.** a feminine name **2.** in Shakespeare's *King Lear*, the youngest of Lear's three daughters, and the only one faithful to him

Cor·de·lier (kôr′də lir′) *n.* [ME. & OFr. < *cordelle*, dim. of *corde* (see CORD): so named from the knotted cord worn as girdle] **1.** in France, a member of the Franciscan Observants **2.** [after the Church of the *Cordeliers*, Paris, where the meetings were held] a member of a radical French Revolutionary political club

☆**cor·delle** (kôr del′) *n.* [Fr., dim. of *corde*, rope: see CORD] a towing rope, esp. as formerly used on Mississippi flatboats and keelboats —*vt.* **-delled′**, **-dell′ing** to tow with or as with a cordelle

cor·dial (kôr′jəl; *Brit.* kôrd′yəl) *adj.* [ME. < ML. *cordialis* < L. *cor* (gen. *cordis*), heart] **1.** [Rare] stimulating the heart; invigorating; reviving **2.** *a)* warm and friendly; hearty [a *cordial* hello] *b)* sincere; deeply felt [a *cordial* distaste for formality] —*n.* **1.** [Rare] a medicine, food, or drink that stimulates the heart **2.** an aromatic, syrupy, alcoholic drink; liqueur —SYN. see AMIABLE —**cor′dial·ly** *adv.* —**cor′dial·ness** *n.*

cor·di·al·i·ty (kôr′jē al′ə tē, kôr jal′-; *Brit.* -dē al′-) *n.* **1.** cordial quality; warm, friendly feeling **2.** *pl.* **-ties** a warm, friendly act or remark

cor·di·er·ite (kôr′dē ə rīt′) *n.* [after P. L. A. *Cordier* (1777–1861), Fr. geologist] a bluish crystalline mineral, Mg₂Al₄Si₅O₁₈, a silicate of magnesium and aluminum, with some iron in it: used sometimes as a gemstone

cord·i·form (kôr′də fôrm′) *adj.* [< L. *cor* (gen. *cordis*), heart + -FORM] heart-shaped

cor·dil·le·ra (kôr′dil yer′ə, kôr dil′ər ə) *n.* [Sp. < *cordilla*, dim. of *cuerda*, rope, cord < L. *chorda*: see CORD] a system or chain of mountains; esp., the principal mountain range of a continent —**cor′dil·le′ran** *adj.*

Cor·dil·le·ras (kôr′dil yer′əz, kôr dil′ər əz) **1.** mountain system of W North America, including all mountains between the E Rockies & the Pacific coast **2.** mountain system of W South America; Andes

cord·ing (kôr′diŋ) *n.* the ribbed surface of corded cloth

cord·ite (-dīt) *n.* [CORD + -ITE¹: so called from its stringy appearance] a smokeless explosive containing nitroglycerin, guncotton, petroleum jelly, and acetone

☆**cord·less** (kôrd′lis) *adj.* **1.** lacking a cord **2.** operated only or optionally by batteries, unlike models operated only by current from an outlet [a *cordless* electric shaver]

Cór·do·ba (kôr′də bə, -və; *Sp.* kôr′thō bä) **1.** city in NC Argentina: pop. 589,000 **2.** city in S Spain, on the Guadalquivir River: pop. 215,000

cor·do·ba (kôr′də bə) *n.* [Sp. *córdoba*: named after F. Fernández de *Córdoba*, 16th-c. Sp. explorer] the monetary unit of Nicaragua: see MONETARY UNITS, table

cor·don (kôr′d'n) *n.* [ME. & OFr., dim. of *corde*: see CORD] **1.** a line or circle of police, soldiers, forts, ships, etc. stationed around an area to guard it **2.** a cord, ribbon, or braid worn as a decoration or badge **3.** a decorative, projecting band or molding, as of stone, along a wall; stringcourse —*vt.* to encircle or shut (*off*) with a cordon

‡**cor·don bleu** (kôr dōn blö′) [Fr.] **1.** the blue ribbon formerly worn as an emblem by Knights of the Order of the Holy Ghost, the highest order of knighthood in France under the Bourbon monarchy **2.** a very high distinction **3.** a person entitled to wear the cordon bleu **4.** any person highly distinguished in his field; specif., a very skilled chef

‡**cordon sa·ni·taire** (sȧ nē ter′) [Fr., lit., sanitary cordon] **1.** a barrier restraining free movement of people or goods, so as to keep a disease, infection, etc. from spreading from one locality into another **2.** a belt of countries serving to isolate another country and check its aggressiveness or lessen its influence

Cor·do·va (kôr′də və) *Eng. name of* CÓRDOBA

Cor·do·van (kôr′də vən) *adj.* [< Sp. *cordobán* < CÓRDOBA] **1.** of Córdoba **2.** [c-] made of cordovan —*n.* **1.** a native or inhabitant of Córdoba **2.** [c-] a fine-grained, colored leather, usually of split horsehide, but orig. made of goatskin at Córdoba, Spain **3.** [c-] [*pl.*] shoes made of this leather

cor·du·roy (kôr′də roi′) *n.* [prob. < *cord* + obs. *duroy*, a coarse fabric formerly produced in England: hence, corded duroy] **1.** a heavy cotton fabric with a piled, velvety surface, ribbed vertically **2.** [*pl.*] trousers made of this fabric —*adj.* **1.** made of, or ribbed like, corduroy ☆**2.** made of logs laid crosswise [a *corduroy* road]

cord·wain (kôrd′wān) *n.* [ME. & OFr. *cordewan* < Pr. *cordoan* < Sp. *cordobán*: see CORDOVAN] [Archaic] cordovan leather

cord·wain·er (-wān′ər) *n.* [ME. *cordwaner* < OFr. *cordouanier*: see prec.] [Archaic] a leatherworker who made things of cordovan, esp. shoes

cord·wood (-wood′) *n.* wood stacked or sold in cords

core (kôr) *n.* [ME. < OFr. *cor*, prob. < L. *cor*, heart] **1.** the hard, central part of an apple, pear, etc., that contains the seeds **2.** the central or innermost part of anything **3.** the most important part, as of a matter, discussion, etc.; essence; pith **4.** in foundry work, that part of a mold which forms the interior of a hollow casting **5.** a sample cylindrical section of the earth's strata beneath the surface of land or water, obtained with a hollow drill **6.** the region in the center of a nuclear reactor that contains the fissionable fuel **7.** the board to which outer layers of veneer are attached **8.** *Chem.* the nucleus together with the closed electron shells of an atom **9.** *Elec.* a mass of iron placed inside a wire coil, serving to channel and increase the strength of the magnetic field resulting from current in the coil —*vt.* **cored**, **cor′ing** to remove the core of

CORE (kôr) Congress of Racial Equality

co·re·la·tion (kō′ri lā′shən) *n. same as* CORRELATION —**co·rel′a·tive** (-rel′ə tiv) *adj.* —**co·rel′a·tive·ly** *adv.*

co·re·li·gion·ist (kō′ri lij′ə nist) *n.* a person of the same religion or religious denomination

Co·rel·li (kō rel′ē; *It.* kô rel′lē), **Arc·an·ge·lo** (är kän′je lô) 1653–1713; It. composer & violinist

☆**co·re·op·sis** (kôr′ē äp′sis) *n.* [ModL. < Gr. *koris*, bug + *opsis*, appearance: so named from the shape of the fruit] any of a genus (*Coreopsis*) of plants of the composite family, having showy heads with yellow, crimson, or maroon ray flowers

cor·er (kôr′ər) *n.* a cutting or piercing instrument for removing the cores of apples, pears, etc.

co·re·spond·ent (kō′ri spän′dənt) *n.* [CO- + RESPONDENT] *Law* a person charged with having committed adultery with the wife or husband from whom a divorce is being sought —**co′re·spond′en·cy** *n.*

corf (kôrf) *n., pl.* **corves** (kôrvz) [ME. < MDu. & MLowG. < L. *corbis*, a basket] [Brit.] a basket or small cart, as for carrying coal, ore, etc. in mines

☆**Cor·fam** (kôr′fam) [arbitrary coinage] *a trademark for* a leatherlike, porous synthetic material, used for shoe uppers —*n.* this material

Cor·fu (kôr′fōō; kôr fōō′, -fyōō′) **1.** one of the Ionian Islands, off the W coast of Greece: 229 sq. mi.; pop. (with small nearby islands) 102,000 **2.** its chief city, a seaport: pop. 27,000

cor·gi (kôr′gē) *n. same as* WELSH CORGI

co·ri·a·ceous (kôr′ē ā′shəs) *adj.* [LL. *coriaceus* < L. *corium*, hide: see CORIUM] of or like leather

co·ri·an·der (kôr′ē an′dər, kôr′ē an′dər) *n.* [ME. & OFr. *coriandre* < L. *coriandrum* < Gr. *koriandron*] **1.** a European annual herb (*Coriandrum sativum*) of the parsley family **2.**

its strong-smelling, seedlike fruit, used in flavoring food and liqueurs, and, formerly, in medicines

Co·rinne (kə rin', kôr ēn') [Fr. < L. *Corinna* < Gr. *Korinna*, ? dim. of *Korē*: see CORA] a feminine name

Cor·inth (kôr'inth, kär'-) **1.** ancient city in the NE Peloponnesus, at the head of the Gulf of Corinth, noted for its luxury: fl. 7th–2d cent. B.C. **2.** modern city near the site of ancient Corinth: pop. 18,000: Gr. name, KORINTHOS **3.** Gulf of, arm of the Ionian Sea, between the Peloponnesus & C Greece: 80 mi. long **4.** Isthmus of, land strip, joining the Peloponnesus with C Greece: 4–8 mi. wide See CRETE, map

Co·rin·thi·an (kə rin'thē ən) adj. **1.** of Corinth, its people, or culture **2.** dissolute and loving luxury, as the people of Corinth were said to be **3.** in the style of the art of Corinth; gracefully elaborate **4.** designating or of the most elaborate of the three orders of Greek architecture, distinguished by a slender, fluted column and a bell-shaped capital decorated with a design of acanthus leaves and volutes: cf. DORIC, IONIC —n. **1.** a native or inhabitant of Corinth **2.** a lover of elegantly luxurious living; sybarite **3.** a wealthy man-about-town **4.** [Archaic] a wealthy devotee of amateur sports ☆**5.** a yachtsman

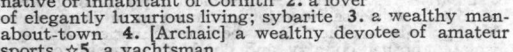
CORINTHIAN CAPITAL

Co·rin·thi·ans (-ənz) [with sing. v.] either of two books of the New Testament which were epistles from the Apostle Paul to the Christians of Corinth

Cor·i·o·la·nus (kôr'ē ə lā'nəs) a tragedy (c. 1608) by Shakespeare, based on the legend of Gaius Marcius Coriolanus, a Roman general of the 5th cent. B.C.

Cor·i·o·lis force (kôr'ē ō'lis) [after G. G. de *Coriolis*, 19th-c. Fr. mathematician] the inertial force caused by the earth's rotation that deflects a moving body to the right in the Northern Hemisphere and to the left in the Southern Hemisphere: this deflection (**Coriolis effect**) is produced by the acceleration of any body moving at a constant speed above the earth with respect to the surface of the rotating earth

co·ri·um (kôr'ē əm) n., pl. -ri·a (-ə) [L., skin, hide < IE. base *(s)ker-, to cut, whence SHEAR] **1.** same as DERMIS **2.** the elongated middle portion of the forewing of hemipterous insects

Cork (kôrk) **1.** county on the S coast of Ireland, in Munster province: 2,880 sq. mi.; pop. 330,000 **2.** its county seat, a seaport: pop. 78,000

cork (kôrk) n. [ME. < Sp. *corcho*, cork, ult. (via ? Ar.) < L. *quercus*, oak] **1.** the light, thick, elastic outer bark of an oak tree, the **cork oak** (*Quercus suber*) of the beech family, that grows in the Mediterranean area: used for floats, stoppers, linoleum, insulation, etc. **2.** a) a piece of cork or something made of cork; esp., a stopper for a bottle, cask, etc. b) a similar stopper made of rubber, glass, etc. **3.** Bot. the outer bark of the stems of woody plants —adj. made of cork —vt. **1.** to stop or seal with a cork **2.** to hold back; check **3.** to blacken with burnt cork

cork·age (-ij) n. [CORK + -AGE] a charge made at a tavern, restaurant, hotel, etc. for every bottle of wine or liquor uncorked and served, esp. for bottles bought elsewhere and brought in by guests

cork cambium Bot. the undifferentiated tissue between the cork and the cortex, from which the protective outer bark is formed; phellogen

cork·er (kôr'kər) n. [slang senses < CORK in sense "stopper"] **1.** a worker or device that corks bottles **2.** [Slang] a) a remarkable person or thing b) an argument, statement, or circumstance that appears conclusive c) a preposterous lie

cork·ing (-kiŋ) adj., adv., interj. [< CORK] [Chiefly Brit. Slang] very good; excellent

cork·screw (-skrōō') n. a device for pulling corks out of bottles, usually a spiral-shaped piece of steel with a point at one end and a handle at the other —adj. shaped like a corkscrew; spiral —vi., vt. to move in a winding or spiral course; twist

cork·wood (-wood') n. **1.** any of several trees whose wood is very light; specif., ☆a) a shrub or small tree (*Leitneria floridana*) of the SE U.S. b) the balsa **2.** the wood of any of these trees

cork·y (kôr'kē) adj. cork'i·er, cork'i·est **1.** of or like cork **2.** having the taste affected by the cork stopper: said esp. of wine

corm (kôrm) n. [< Gr. *kormos*, trunk of a tree with branches lopped off < *keirein*, to cut off] a fleshy, thickened, vertical, underground stem, usually having annual segments with a bud at the tip, thin external scale leaves, and roots at the base, as in the gladiolus: corms differ from bulbs in having much more stem tissue and fewer scale leaves

cor·mel (kôr'məl) n. [prec. + -el, dim. suffix < ME. < OFr. < L. -ellus (masc.), -ella (fem.), -ellum (neut.)] a new small corm arising from a mature corm

cor·mo·rant (kôr'mə rənt) n. [ME. cormoraunt < OFr. cormareng < corp marenc < L. corvus marinus < corvus, raven + marinus, MARINE] **1.** any of a number of large, voracious, diving birds (family Phalacrocoracidae) with webbed toes and a hooked beak: in the Orient, fishermen use leashed cormorants to catch fish **2.** a greedy person; glutton

corn[1] (kôrn) n. see PLURAL, II, D, 3 [ME. & OE. < IE. base *ger-, to ripen, mature, grow old, whence L. granum, GRAIN, CHURN, CHURL] **1.** [Now Dial.] a hard particle, as of salt or sand; granule; grain **2.** a small hard seed or seedlike fruit, esp. a seed or grain of a cereal grass; kernel: now chiefly in compounds, as *peppercorn*, *barleycorn* ☆**3.** a) a cultivated American cereal plant (*Zea mays*) of the grass family, with the grain borne on cobs enclosed in husks; maize; Indian corn b) the ears or kernels of this cereal plant **4.** [Brit.] a) the seeds of all cereal grasses, as wheat, rye, barley, etc.; grain b) any plant or plants producing grain **5.** the leading cereal crop in a particular place, as wheat in England or oats in Scotland and Ireland ☆**6.** [Colloq.] corn whiskey ☆**7.** [Slang] ideas, humor, music, etc. regarded as old-fashioned, trite, banal, or sentimental —vt. **1.** to form into granules **2.** to preserve or pickle with salt granules or in brine **3.** to feed grain to (animals)

corn[2] (kôrn) n. [ME. & OFr. corne < L. cornu, HORN] a hard, thick, painful growth of skin, esp. on a toe, caused by pressure or friction

☆**corn·ball** (kôrn'bôl') adj. [CORN[1], n. 7 + (SCREW)BALL] [Slang] unsophisticated, old-fashioned, banal, sentimental, etc.; corny —n. [Slang] a person or thing having or displaying these qualities

☆**Corn Belt** region in the NC plains area of the Middle West where much corn and cornfed livestock are raised: it extends from W Ohio to E Neb. and NE Kans.

☆**corn borer** the larva of a European moth (*Pyrausta nubilalis*), now a destructive pest in the U.S., feeding on corn and other plants

☆**corn bread** a baked or fried flat bread made with cornmeal and, variously, milk or water, flour, eggs, sugar, etc.

☆**corn·cake** (-kāk') n. same as JOHNNYCAKE

☆**corn·cob** (-käb') n. **1.** the woody core of an ear of corn, on which the kernels grow in rows **2.** a corncob pipe

☆**corncob pipe** a tobacco pipe with a bowl made of a hollowed piece of dried corncob

corn cockle a tall annual weed (*Agrostemma githago*) of the pink family, with flat, pink flowers and poisonous seeds, often found in grainfields

corn·crake (-krāk') n. [see CRAKE] a brown, short-billed N European rail (*Crex crex*), often found in grainfields

☆**corn·crib** (-krib') n. a small, ventilated structure for storing ears of corn

☆**corn·dodg·er** (-däj'ər) n. a small cake of cornmeal, baked or fried hard

cor·ne·a (kôr'nē ə) n. [ME. < ML. < L. cornea (tela), horny (web, tissue), fem. sing. of corneus < cornu, HORN] the transparent tissue forming the outer coat of the eyeball and covering the iris and pupil —cor'ne·al adj.

☆**corn ear·worm** (ir'wurm') the larva of a moth (*Heliothis obsoleta*), that feeds on corn ears and other crops

corned (kôrnd) adj. preserved with salt or brine [corned beef]

Cor·neille (kôr nā'y'), **Pierre** 1606–84; Fr. dramatist

cor·nel (kôr'n'l, -nel) n. [ME. & OFr. corneille < VL. cornea < L. cornus, akin to Gr. kranos, cornel tree] any of a genus (*Cornus*) of shrubs and small trees with very hard wood, including the dogwoods and the bunchberry

Cor·nel·ia (kôr nēl'yə) [L., fem. of Cornelius] **1.** a feminine name **2.** 2d cent. B.C.; mother of Gaius & Tiberius GRACCHUS

cor·nel·ian (kôr nēl'yən) n. [ME. & OFr. corneline, dim. < OFr. corneola, prob. (because of similarity of color) < VL. cornea: see CORNEL] same as CARNELIAN

Cor·nel·ius (kôr nēl'yəs) [L., name of a Roman gens] a masculine name

Cor·nell (kôr nel') **1.** Ezra, 1807–74; U.S. capitalist & philanthropist **2.** Katharine, 1898– ; U.S. actress

cor·ne·ous (kôr'nē əs) adj. [L. corneus < cornu, HORN] horny; hornlike

cor·ner (kôr'nər) n. [ME. < OFr. corniere < ML. cornerium < L. cornu, projecting point, HORN] **1.** the point or place where lines or surfaces join and form an angle **2.** the area or space within the angle formed at the joining of lines or surfaces [the corner of a room] **3.** the area at the tip of any of the angles formed at a street intersection **4.** something used to form, mark, protect, or decorate a corner **5.** a remote, secret, or secluded place [look in every nook and corner] **6.** region; quarter; part [every corner of America] **7.** an awkward position from which escape is difficult [driven into a corner] ☆**8.** a monopoly acquired on a stock or commodity so as to be able to raise the price —vt. ☆**1.** to drive or force into a corner or awkward position, so that escape is difficult ☆**2.** to get a monopoly on (a stock or commodity) —vi. **1.** to meet at or about (on) a corner: said of land, buildings, etc. **2.** to turn corners: said of a vehicle [this car corners easily] —adj. **1.** at or on a corner [a corner store] **2.** used in a corner [a corner table] —SYN. see MONOPOLY —**around the corner** in the immediate vicinity or future —☆**cut corners** **1.** to take a direct route by going across corners **2.** to cut down expenses, time, labor, etc. — **the (four) corners of the earth** the farthest parts of the earth —**turn the corner** to get safely past the critical point

cor·ner·back (-bak') n. Football either of two players of a defensive backfield whose position is between the line of scrimmage and the safety men

cor·nered (kôr'nərd) adj. having (a specified number or type of) corners [a three-cornered hat]

cor·ner·stone (kôr′nər stōn′) *n.* [ME.] **1.** a stone that forms part of the corner of a building; esp., a foundation stone of this kind, often inscribed, laid at a ceremony that marks the beginning of building **2.** the basic, essential, or most important part; foundation

cor·ner·wise (-wiz′) *adv.* **1.** with the corner to the front **2.** from one corner to an opposite corner; diagonally Also **cor′ner·ways′**

cor·net (kôr net′; *Brit.* kôr′nit) *n.* [ME. & OFr., dim. of *corn*, a horn < L. *cornu*, HORN] **1.** a brass-wind musical instrument of the trumpet class, having three valves worked by pistons **2.** *a)* a piece of paper twisted like a cone, for holding sugar, candy, etc. *b)* a cone-shaped piece of pastry, often filled as with whipped cream **3.** the spreading, white headdress that a Sister of Charity wears **4.** formerly, a British cavalry officer of the lowest rank, who carried his troop's flag

CORNET

cor·net·à·pis·tons (kôr net′ə pis′tənz; *Fr.* kôr nā á pē stōn′) *n., pl.* **cor·nets·à·pis·tons** (-nets′ə-; *Fr.* -nā zá-) *same as* CORNET (sense 1)

☆**cor·net·ist, cor·net·tist** (kôr net′ist) *n.* a cornet player

☆**corn·fed** (kôrn′fed′) *adj.* **1.** fed on corn **2.** [Slang] rustically robust and simple, unsophisticated, etc.

corn·field (-fēld′) *n.* a field in which corn is grown

☆**corn·flakes** (-flāks′) *n.pl.* a breakfast cereal of crisp flakes made from hulled corn and served cold, as with milk: also **corn flakes**

☆**corn flour** **1.** flour made from corn **2.** [Brit.] cornstarch

corn·flow·er (-flou′ər) *n.* an annual plant (*Centaurea cyanus*) of the composite family, with conspicuous white, pink, or blue false ray flowers

☆**corn·husk·ing** (kôrn′hus′kiŋ) *n.* **1.** the husking of corn **2.** a gathering of friends and neighbors for husking corn; husking bee: it is generally a festive event, followed by dancing, etc. —**corn′husk′er** *n.*

cor·nice (kôr′nis) *n.* [Fr. (now *corniche*) < It. < L. *coronis*, curved line, flourish in writing < Gr. *koronis*, a wreath] **1.** a horizontal molding projecting along the top of a wall, building, etc. **2.** the top part of an entablature **3.** a projecting, decorative strip above a window, designed to keep a curtain rod from showing —*vt.* **-niced, -nic·ing** to top as with a cornice

cor·niche (kôr′nish; *Fr.* kôr nēsh′) *n.* [Fr., lit., a cornice] a roadway that winds along a cliff or steep slope

cor·nic·u·late (kôr nik′yoo lit, -lāt′) *adj.* [L. *corniculatus* < *corniculus*, dim. of *cornu*, HORN] having horns or hornlike projections; horned

Cor·nish (kôr′nish) *adj.* of Cornwall, its people, or culture —*n.* **1.** the Brythonic Celtic language spoken by the people of Cornwall until c. 1800, closely related to Breton and Welsh **2.** *pl.* **Cor′nish** *a)* any of a British breed of chicken with meat of a particularly good quality *b)* any of a breed of miniature chicken crossbred from these chickens and Plymouth Rocks: popularly called **Cornish hens** or, in full, **Rock Cornish (hens)**

Cor·nish·man (-mən) *n., pl.* **-men** (-mən) a native or inhabitant of Cornwall

Corn Laws in England, certain laws imposing heavy duties on the importation of grain, repealed in 1846

corn·meal (kôrn′mēl′) *n.* ☆**1.** meal made from corn (maize) **2.** meal made from some other grain, as, in Scotland, oats: see CORN[1]

☆**corn picker** a machine for harvesting and husking corn

☆**corn pone** [Chiefly Southern] a kind of corn bread baked in pones

corn poppy a species of poppy (*Papaver rhoeas*), often found in grainfields of Europe and Asia

corn salad a European plant (*Valerianella olitoria*) of the valerian family, with rose, blue, or white flowers and leaves that are used in salads

☆**corn silk** the long, silky fibers that are the styles of an ear of corn: the longer fibers hang out of the husk in a tuft which catches pollen

☆**corn smut** a disease of corn caused by a smut fungus (*Ustilago zeae*), forming large black swellings on the ear and on other parts of the plant

corn snow snow that has alternately melted and frozen, as in the spring, to form coarse granules

☆**corn·stalk** (-stôk′) *n.* a stalk of corn (maize)

☆**corn·starch** (-stärch′) *n.* a fine, granular or powdery starch made from corn and used in cooking and to make corn sugar, corn syrup, etc.

☆**corn sugar** a dextrose made from cornstarch

corn syrup a sweet syrup made from cornstarch: it is a mixture of dextrose, maltose, and dextrins

cor·nu (kôr′noo, -noo) *n., pl.* **-nu·a** (-ə) [L., a HORN] *Anat.* any horn-shaped process or structure —**cor′nu·al** (-nyoo wəl) *adj.*

cor·nu·co·pi·a (kôr′nə kō′pē ə, -nyoo-) *n.* [L. *cornu copiae*, horn of plenty: see HORN & COPIOUS] **1.** *Gr. Myth.* a horn of the goat that suckled Zeus: it would become full of whatever its owner wanted **2.** a representation in painting, sculpture, etc. of a horn overflowing with fruits, flowers, and grain; horn of plenty **3.** an overflowing fullness; abundance **4.** any cone-shaped container

CORNUCOPIA

cor·nut·ed (kôr nyōōt′id, -nōōt′-) *adj.* [< L. *cornutus*, horned < *cornu*, HORN] **1.** having horns **2.** horn-shaped **3.** [Archaic] cuckolded

‡**cor·nu·to** (kôr nōō′tō) *n., pl.* **-nu′ti** (-tē) [It.: see prec.] a cuckold

Corn·wall (kôrn′wôl; *chiefly Brit.* -wəl) **1.** county at the SW tip of England: 1,357 sq. mi.; pop. 343,000 **2.** city in SE Ontario, on the St. Lawrence River: pop. 46,000

Corn·wal·lis (kôrn wôl′is, -wäl′-), **Charles,** 1st Marquis Cornwallis, 1738–1805; Eng. general & statesman: commanded Brit. forces during American Revolution

☆**corn whiskey** whiskey made from corn (maize)

corn·y[1] (kôr′nē) *adj.* **corn′i·er, corn′i·est** **1.** of or producing corn ☆**2.** [Colloq.] unsophisticated, old-fashioned, trite, banal, sentimental, etc.

corn·y[2] (kôr′nē) *adj.* **corn′i·er, corn′i·est** having or relating to corns on the feet

corol., coroll. corollary

co·rol·la (kə räl′ə) *n.* [L., dim. of *corona*, CROWN] the petals, or inner floral leaves, of a flower —**cor·ol·late** (kôr′ə lāt′, kär′-), **cor′ol·lat′ed** *adj.*

cor·ol·la·ceous (kôr′ə lā′shəs, kär′-) *adj.* **1.** having a corolla **2.** like a corolla

cor·ol·lar·y (kôr′ə ler′ē, kär′-; *Brit.* & *often Canad.*, kə räl′ər ē) *n., pl.* **-lar′ies** [ME. *corolarie* < LL. *corollarium*, a deduction < L., orig., money paid for a garland, hence gift, gratuity < *corolla*: see COROLLA] **1.** a proposition that follows from another that has been proved **2.** an inference or deduction **3.** anything that follows as a normal result

Cor·o·man·del Coast (kôr′ə man′d'l, kär′-) coastal region of SE India, extending inland to the Eastern Ghats

co·ro·na (kə rō′nə) *n., pl.* **-nas, -nae** (-nē) [L., CROWN] **1.** a crown or something resembling a crown **2.** a circular chandelier hanging from a church ceiling **3.** a cigar having a long, nontapering body and blunt ends **4.** *Anat. a)* a crownlike part *b)* the upper part of a tooth, of a skull, etc. **5.** *Archit.* the top projection of a cornice **6.** *Astron. a)* the outermost part of the sun's atmosphere, characterized by an extremely low density and an extremely high temperature: it can be seen during a total solar eclipse *b)* a ring of colored light seen around a luminous body, as the sun or moon, formed by the diffraction of light by drops of water or dust in the earth's atmosphere **7.** *Bot.* an extra whorl of flower parts between the corolla and the stamens, as in the daffodil, forming a crownlike or cuplike part **8.** *Elec.* a sometimes visible electric discharge resulting from a partial electric breakdown in a gas, as in the air surrounding a wire at high potential

Corona Aus·tra·lis (ôs trā′lis) [L., Southern Crown] a S constellation near Sagittarius

Corona Bo·re·a·lis (bôr′ē al′is) [L., Northern Crown] a N constellation between Hercules and Boötes, consisting of a semicircular group of seven stars

cor·o·nach (kôr′ə nəkh, kär′-) *n.* [Ir. *coranach* & ScotGael. *corranach* < *comh-*, together + *ranach*, outcry] **1.** [Scot.] a dirge, sung or played on bagpipes **2.** [Irish] a wailing lament for the dead

Co·ro·na·do (kôr′ə nä′dō; *Sp.* kō′rō nä′thō), **Fran·cis·co Vás·quez de** (frän thēs′kō väs′keth the) 1510?–54?; Sp. explorer of SW N. America

co·ro·na·graph (kə rō′nə graf′) *n.* [earlier *coronograph* < CORON(A) + -o- + -GRAPH] a telescope designed for observing the corona of the sun by means of devices that obstruct the light of the sun's disk

cor·o·nal (kôr′ə n'l; *for adj., usually* kə rō′n'l) *n.* [ME. < LL. *coronalis* < L. *corona*, CROWN] **1.** a circlet for the head; diadem; crown; coronet **2.** a wreath; garland —*adj.* **1.** of a crown, coronet, or halo **2.** *Anat. a)* of the corona of the skull *b)* designating, of, or lying in the direction of, the suture between the frontal and parietal bones of the skull

coronal suture *Anat.* a suture that extends across the skull between the frontal and parietal bones

cor·o·nar·y (kôr′ə ner′ē, kär′-) *adj.* [L. *coronarius:* see CROWN] **1.** of, or in the form of, a crown **2.** *Anat. a)* like a crown; encircling *b)* designating or relating to either of two arteries branching from the aorta and supplying blood directly to the heart muscle —☆*n., pl.* **-nar′ies** *same as* CORONARY THROMBOSIS

coronary insufficiency an inability of the coronary arteries to deliver an adequate blood supply to the myocardium, resulting in angina pectoris and heart failure

☆**coronary thrombosis** [coined (1912) by J. B. Halleck, U.S. physician] the formation of a clot in a branch of either

of the coronary arteries, resulting in obstruction of that artery: also called **coronary occlusion**

cor·o·na·tion (kôr/ə nā′shən, kär/-) n. [ME. & OFr. *coronacion* < L. *coronatus*, pp. of *coronare*, to crown < *corona*, CROWN] the act or ceremony of crowning a sovereign

cor·o·ner (kôr/ə nər, kär/-) n. [ME., officer of the crown < Anglo-Fr. *corouner* < *coroune*, *corone*, a crown < L. *corona*, CROWN] a public officer whose chief duty is to determine by inquest before a jury the causes of any deaths not obviously due to natural causes

cor·o·net (kôr/ə net′, kär′-, -nit) n. [ME. *corounet* < OFr. *coronete*, dim. of *corone* < L. *corona*, CROWN] 1. a small crown worn by princes and others of high rank 2. an ornamental band of precious metal, jewels, or flowers, worn around the head 3. the lowest part of a horse's pastern where it joins the hoof —**cor′o·net′ed**, **cor′o·net′ted** adj.

Co·rot (kə rō′; Fr. kô rō′), Jean Bap·tiste Ca·mille (zhän bä tēst′ kä mē′y′) 1796–1875; Fr. painter

Corp. Corporal

corp., corpn. corporation

cor·po·ra (kôr/pər ə) n. pl. of CORPUS

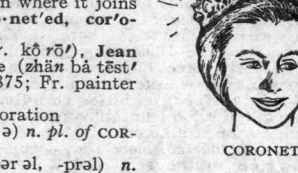

CORONET

cor·po·ral[1] (kôr/pər əl, -prəl) n. [< Fr. *caporal* < It. *caporale*, a corporal < *capo*, chief, head < L. *caput*, the head: sp. affected by association with *corps* or ff.] the lowest-ranking noncommissioned officer, just below a sergeant; specif., an enlisted man or woman in the fourth grade in the U.S. Army and Marine Corps —**cor′po·ral·cy**, pl. **-cies**, **cor′po·ral·ship**′ n.

cor·po·ral[2] (kôr/pər əl, -prəl) adj. [L. *corporalis* < *corpus* (gen. *corporis*), body: see CORPUS] 1. of the body; bodily 2. [Now Rare] personal 3. [Obs.] corporeal —SYN. see BODILY —**cor′po·ral·ly** adv.

cor·po·ral[3] (kôr/pər əl) n. [ME. & OFr. < ML. *corporale* < *corporalis* (*palla*), body (cloth): see prec.] *Eccles.* a small linen cloth put on the center of the altar, on which the bread and chalice are placed for the Eucharist

cor·po·ral·i·ty (kôr/pə ral/ə tē) n. [LL.(Ec.) *corporalitas*: see CORPORAL[2]] the state or quality of being material or having a body; bodily existence or substance

corporal punishment punishment inflicted directly on the body, as flogging: now usually distinguished from capital punishment, imprisonment, etc.

☆**corporal's guard** 1. a squad commanded by a corporal 2. any small group or gathering of people

cor·po·rate (kôr/pər it) adj. [ME. *corporat* < L. *corporatus*, pp. of *corporare*, to make into a body < *corpus*, body: see CORPUS] 1. [Archaic] united; combined 2. having the nature of, or acting by means of, a corporation; incorporated 3. of a corporation [*corporate* debts] 4. shared by all members of a unified group; common; joint [*corporate* responsibility] 5. same as CORPORATIVE (sense 2) —**cor′po·rate·ly** adv.

cor·po·ra·tion (kôr/pə rā′shən) n. [ME. *corporacioun* < LL.(Ec.) *corporatio*, assumption of a body, incarnation < pp. of L. *corporare*: see CORPORATE] 1. a group of people who get a charter granting them as a body certain of the legal powers, rights, privileges, and liabilities of an individual, distinct from those of the individuals making up the group: a corporation can buy, sell, and inherit property 2. a group of people, as the mayor and aldermen of an incorporated town, legally authorized to act as an individual 3. any of the political and economic bodies forming a corporative state, each being composed of the employers and employees in a certain industry, profession, etc. 4. [prob. from association with CORPULENT, etc.] [Colloq.] a large, prominent belly

cor·po·ra·tist (kôr/pər ə tist) adj. of or characteristic of a corporative state —**cor′po·ra·tism** n.

cor·po·ra·tive (-tiv) adj. [LL. *corporativus*] 1. of or connected with a corporation 2. designating or of a state, as theoretically Italy under Fascism (1924–1943), in which political and economic power is vested in an organization of corporations (sense 3)

cor·po·ra·tor (kôr/pə rā′tər) n. a member of a corporation

cor·po·re·al (kôr pôr/ē əl) adj. [< L. *corporeus* < *corpus*: see CORPUS] 1. of, for, or having the nature of, the body; bodily; not spiritual 2. of a material nature; physical; perceptible by the senses; tangible —SYN. see BODILY, MATERIAL —**cor·po′re·al·ly** adv.

cor·po·re·al·i·ty (kôr pôr/ē al′ə tē) n. the state or quality of being corporeal; bodily existence

cor·po·re·i·ty (kôr/pə rē′ə tē) n. [ML. *corporeitas* < L. *corporeus*] 1. same as CORPOREALITY 2. material or bodily substance

cor·po·sant (kôr/pə zant′) n. [Port. *corpo santo*, holy body < L. *corpus sanctum*, holy body] same as SAINT ELMO'S FIRE

corps (kôr) n., pl. **corps** (kôrz) [ME. < OFr. *corps*, *cors*, body < L. *corpus*, body: see CORPUS] 1. a body of people associated in some work, organization, etc. under common direction [a diplomatic *corps*] 2. *Mil.* a) a branch of the armed forces having some specialized function [the Signal *Corps*, the Marine *Corps*] b) a tactical subdivision of an

army, normally composed of two or more divisions, plus auxiliary service troops

corps de bal·let (kôr′ də ba lā′) [Fr.] the ensemble of a ballet company; esp., the ensemble apart from the featured dancers

corpse (kôrps) n. [var. of CORPS] 1. a dead body, esp. of a person 2. something once vigorous but now lifeless and of no use 3. [Obs.] a living body —SYN. see BODY

corps·man (kôr/mən) n., pl. **-men** (-mən) same as AIDMAN

cor·pu·lence (kôr/pyoo ləns) n. [ME. & OFr. < L. *corpulentia*: see CORPULENT] fatness or stoutness of body; obesity: also **cor′pu·len·cy**

cor·pu·lent (-lənt) adj. [ME. & MFr. < L. *corpulentus* < ff.] fat and fleshy; stout; obese —**cor′pu·lent·ly** adv.

cor·pus (kôr/pəs) n., pl. **cor′po·ra** (-pər ə) [L., body < IE. base *krep-, *krp-, body, form, whence Sans. *krp̄ā*, form, OHG. *href*, belly, womb, (MID)RIFF] 1. a human or animal body, esp. a dead one: now mainly a facetious usage 2. a complete or comprehensive collection, as of laws or writings of a specified type [the *corpus* of civil law] 3. the main body or substance of anything 4. the principal, as distinguished from the interest or income, of an estate, investment, etc. 5. *Anat.* the main part of an organ; also, a mass of tissue with a specialized function

corpus cal·lo·sum (kə lō′səm) pl. **corpora cal·lo′sa** (-sə) [ModL., lit., callous body] a mass of white, transverse fibers connecting the cerebral hemispheres in man and other higher mammals

Cor·pus Christ·i (kôr/pəs kris/tē) [L., Body of Christ] 1. *R.C.Ch.* a festival celebrated on the Thursday after Trinity Sunday, in honor of the Eucharist 2. city in SE Tex., on the Gulf of Mexico: pop. 205,000

cor·pus·cle (kôr/pəs 'l, -pus′'l) n. [L. *corpusculum*, dim. of *corpus*, body] 1. a very small particle 2. *Anat.* a protoplasmic particle with a special function; esp., any of the erythrocytes (**red corpuscles**) or leukocytes (**white corpuscles**) that float in the blood, lymph, etc. of vertebrates: see also ERYTHROCYTE, LEUKOCYTE Also **cor·pus·cule** (kôr pus/kyōōl) —**cor·pus·cu·lar** (kôr pus/kyoo lər) adj.

corpus de·lic·ti (di lik/tī, -tē) [ModL., lit., body of the crime] 1. the facts constituting or proving a crime; material substance or foundation of a crime: the corpus delicti in a murder case is not just the body of the victim, but the fact that he has been murdered 2. loosely, the body of the victim in a murder case

corpus ju·ris (joor/is, yoor/is) [L., a body of law] a collection of all the laws of a nation or district

Corpus Ju·ris Ca·no·ni·ci (yoor/is kə nō/ni chē′) [ML., lit., body of canon law] the body of laws governing the Roman Catholic Church up to 1918: superseded by the CODEX JURIS CANONICI

Corpus Juris Ci·vi·lis (si vī/lis, -vil/is) [L., lit., body of civil law] the body of civil, or Roman, law, compiled and issued during the reign of Justinian: it has been the basis of most European law

corpus lu·te·um (lōō/tē əm) pl. **corpora lu/te·a** (-ə) [ModL., lit., luteous body] 1. *Anat.* a mass of yellow tissue formed in the ovary by a ruptured Graafian follicle that has discharged its ovum: if the ovum is fertilized, this tissue secretes the hormone progesterone, needed to maintain pregnancy 2. a preparation containing this hormone, used in ovarian therapy

corpus stri·a·tum (strī ā/təm) pl. **corpora stri·a/ta** (-tə) [ModL., lit., striated body] *Anat.* either of two striated ganglia in front of the thalamus in each half of the brain

corr. 1. corrected 2. correction 3. correspondence 4. corresponding 5. corrugated 6. corruption

cor·rade (kə rād′) vt., vi. **-rad·ed**, **-rad′ing** [< L. *corradere*, to scrape together < *com-*, together + *radere*, to scrape] to erode by the abrasive action of running water or glacial ice containing sand, pebbles, and other debris —**cor·ra/sion** (-rā/zhən) n. —**cor·ra/sive** (-siv) adj.

☆**cor·ral** (kə ral′) n. [Sp. < *corro*, a circle, ring < L. *currere*, to run] 1. an enclosure for holding or capturing horses, cattle, or other animals; pen 2. a defensive area made by drawing up covered wagons to form an enclosing circle —vt. **-ralled′, -ral′ling** 1. to drive into or confine in a corral 2. to surround or capture; round up 3. to arrange (wagons) in the form of a corral 4. [Slang] to take possession of; lay hold of

cor·rect (kə rekt′) vt. [ME. *correcten* < L. *correctus*, pp. of *corrigere* < *com-*, together + *regere*, to lead straight, direct] 1. to make right; change from wrong to right; remove errors from 2. to point out or mark the errors or faults of 3. to make conform to a standard 4. to scold or punish so as to cause to rectify faults 5. to cure, remove, or counteract (a fault, disease, etc.) —vi. to make corrections; specif., to make an adjustment so as to compensate (for an error, counteracting force, etc.) —adj. 1. conforming or adhering to an established standard; proper [*correct* behavior] 2. conforming to fact or logic; true, accurate, right, or free from errors 3. equal to the required or established amount, number, price, etc. —**cor·rect/a·ble** adj. —**cor·rect/ly** adv. —**cor·rect/ness** n. —**cor·rec/tor** n.

SYN.—**correct** connotes little more than absence of error [a *correct* answer] or adherence to conventionality [*correct* behavior]; **accurate** implies a positive exercise of care to obtain conformity with fact or truth [an *accurate* account of the events]; **exact**

stresses perfect conformity to fact, truth, or some standard [the *exact* time, an *exact* quotation]; **precise** suggests minute accuracy of detail and often connotes a finicky or overly fastidious attitude [*precise* in all his habits] See also PUNISH —*ANT.* **wrong, false**

correcting lens (or **plate**) a thin lens used to correct spherical aberration introduced by the spherical mirror in certain optical systems

cor·rec·tion (kə rek′shən) *n.* [ME. *correccion* < OFr. *correction* < L. *correctio*] 1. a correcting or being corrected 2. a change that corrects a mistake; change from wrong to right, or from abnormal to normal; emendation; rectification 3. the amount of change made in correcting 4. punishment or scolding to correct faults —**cor·rec′tion·al** (-əl) *adj.*

cor·rect·i·tude (kə rek′tə tōōd′, -tyōōd′) *n.* [< CORRECT, after RECTITUDE] the quality of being correct, esp. in conduct; propriety

cor·rec·tive (-tiv) *adj.* [Fr. *correctif* < LL. *correctivus*] tending or meant to correct or improve; remedial —*n.* something corrective; remedy —**cor·rec′tive·ly** *adv.*

Cor·reg·gio (kə rej′ō), (**Antonio Allegri da**) 1494?-1534; It. painter

Cor·reg·i·dor (kə reg′ə dôr′) small fortified island in the Philippines, at the entrance to Manila Bay

correl. correlative

cor·re·late (kôr′ə lāt′, kär′-) *n.* [< COR- + L. *relatus:* see RELATE] either of two interrelated things, esp. if one implies the other —*adj.* closely and naturally related —*vi.* **-lat′ed, -lat′ing** to be mutually related (*to* or *with*) —*vt.* to bring (a thing) into mutual relation (*with* another thing); calculate or show the reciprocal relation between; specif., to bring (one of two related or interdependent quantities, sets of statistics, etc.) into contrast (*with* the other)

cor·re·la·tion (kôr′ə lā′shən, kär′-) *n.* [ML. *correlatio:* see COM- & RELATION] 1. mutual relationship or connection 2. the degree of relative correspondence, as between two sets of data [a *correlation* of 75 percent] 3. a correlating or being correlated —**cor′re·la′tion·al** *adj.*

correlation coefficient *Statistics* a descriptive index applied to two sets of numbers (x, y), the value of which serves to specify the overall dependence exhibited by the data between the variables x and y

cor·rel·a·tive (kə rel′ə tiv) *adj.* [ML. *correlativus*] 1. having or involving a mutual relationship; reciprocally dependent [*correlative* rights and duties] 2. *Gram.* expressing mutual relation and used in pairs [In "neither Tom nor I can go," "neither" and "nor" are *correlative* conjunctions] —*n.* 1. a thing closely related to something else 2. a correlative word —**cor·rel′a·tive·ly** *adv.* —**cor·rel′a·tiv′i·ty** *n.*

cor·re·spond (kôr′ə spänd′, kär′-) *vi.* [Fr. *correspondre* < ML. *correspondere* < L. *com-*, together + *respondere*, to answer] 1. to be in agreement (*with* something); conform (*to* something); tally; harmonize 2. to be similar, analogous, or equal (*to* something) 3. to communicate (*with* someone) by exchanging letters, esp. regularly —*SYN.* see AGREE — **cor·re·spond′ing·ly** *adv.*

cor·re·spond·ence (-spän′dəns) *n.* [ME. < ML. *correspondentia* < prp. of *correspondere:* see prec.] 1. agreement with something else or with one another; conformity 2. similarity; analogy 3. *a)* communication by exchange of letters *b)* the letters received or written

☆**correspondence school** a school that gives courses of instruction (**correspondence courses**) by mail, sending lessons and examinations to a student periodically, and correcting and grading the returned answers

cor·re·spond·en·cy (-spän′dən sē) *n., pl.* **-cies** same as CORRESPONDENCE (senses 1 and 2)

cor·re·spond·ent (kôr′ə spän′dənt, kär′-) *adj.* [ME. < ML. *correspondens,* prp. of *correspondere,* CORRESPOND] corresponding; agreeing; matching; analogous —*n.* 1. a thing that corresponds; correlate 2. *a)* a person who exchanges letters with another *b)* a person who writes to a magazine or newspaper, expressing an opinion, as on public affairs 3. a person hired by a magazine or newspaper to furnish news, articles, etc. of a certain type or from a distant place 4. a person or firm acting for, or having regular business relations with, another at a distance

cor·re·spon·sive (-siv) *adj.* [Archaic] corresponding

‡**cor·ri·da** (kô rē′thä; E. kə rēd′ə) *n.* [Sp. *corrida* (*de toros*), (bull-)baiting, lit., a running, race < fem. pp. of *correr,* to run < L. *currere:* see CURRENT] a bullfight or, esp., an entire program of bullfights

cor·ri·dor (kôr′ə dər, kär′-; -dôr′) *n.* [Fr. < It. *corridore,* a gallery, corridor, runner < *correre,* to run < L. *currere:* see CURRENT] 1. a long passageway or hall, esp. one onto which several rooms open 2. a strip of land forming a passageway through foreign-held land, as from a country to its seaport

cor·rie (kôr′ē, kär′ē) *n.* [< ScotGael. *coire,* cauldron + IE. base **kwer-,* pot, whence OE. *hwer,* kettle] [Scot.] a round hollow in a hillside

Cor·rie·dale (kôr′ē dāl′, kär′-) *n.* [< *Corriedale,* New Zealand] a breed of rather large, white-faced sheep, developed in New Zealand for their wool and meat

Cor·rien·tes (kôr ryen′tes) city in N Argentina, on the Paraná River; pop. 104,000

cor·ri·gen·dum (kôr′ə jen′dəm, kär′-) *n., pl.* **-gen′da** (-də) [L., gerundive of *corrigere:* see CORRECT] 1. an error to be corrected, esp. one in a printed work 2. [*pl.*] a list of such errors with their corrections, inserted in the published work

cor·ri·gi·ble (kôr′i jə b'l, kär′-) *adj.* [ME. < OFr. < ML. *corrigibilis* < L. *corrigere:* see CORRECT] capable of being corrected, improved, or reformed —**cor′ri·gi·bil′i·ty** (-bil′ə tē) *n.* —**cor′ri·gi·bly** *adv.*

cor·ri·val (kə rī′v'l) *n., adj.* [L. *corrivalis* < *com-*, with + *rivalis,* rival] same as RIVAL

cor·rob·o·rant (kə räb′ə rənt) *adj.* [L. *corroborans,* prp. of *corroborare:* see ff.] 1. corroborating 2. [Obs.] strengthening: said of a medicine or tonic —*n.* [Obs.] a tonic

cor·rob·o·rate (-rāt′) *vt.* **-rat′ed, -rat′ing** [< L. *corroboratus,* pp. of *corroborare,* to strengthen < *com-*, intens. + *roborare* < *robur,* strength] 1. orig., to strengthen 2. to make the validity of more certain; confirm; bolster; support [evidence to *corroborate* his testimony] —*SYN.* see CONFIRM —**cor·rob′o·ra′tion** *n.* —**cor·rob′o·ra′tor** *n.*

cor·rob·o·ra·tive (kə räb′ə rāt′iv, -ər ə tiv) *adj.* corroborating or tending to corroborate; confirmatory: also **cor·rob′o·ra·to′ry** (-ər ə tôr′ē)

cor·rob·o·ree (kə räb′ər ē) *n.* [< native *korobra,* dance] 1. a dance festival held at night by Australian aborigines to celebrate tribal victories and similar events 2. in Australia, *a)* a large or noisy festivity *b)* an uproar; tumult

cor·rode (kə rōd′) *vt.* **-rod′ed, -rod′ing** [ME. *corroden* < OFr. *corroder* < L. *corrodere,* to gnaw to pieces < *com-*, intens. + *rodere,* to gnaw] 1. to eat into or wear away gradually, as by rusting or by the action of chemicals 2. to work upon insidiously and cause to deteriorate [a heart corroded by *bitterness*] —*vi.* to become corroded —**cor·rod′i·ble** *adj.*

cor·ro·sion (kə rō′zhən) *n.* [ME. < OFr. *corrosion* < LL. *corrosio* < pp. of *corrodere:* see prec.] 1. a corroding or being corroded 2. a substance, as rust, formed by corroding

cor·ro·sive (kə rōs′iv) *adj.* [OFr. *corrosif* < ML. *corrosivus*] 1. corroding or causing corrosion 2. bitingly sarcastic; cutting —*n.* something causing corrosion —**cor·ro′sive·ly** *adv.* —**cor·ro′sive·ness** *n.*

corrosive sublimate same as MERCURIC CHLORIDE

cor·ru·gate (kôr′ə gāt′, kär′-; -yoo-) *vt., vi.* **-gat′ed, -gat′ing** [< L. *corrugatus,* pp. of *corrugare,* to wrinkle < *com-*, intens. + *rugare,* to wrinkle] to shape or contract into parallel grooves and ridges; make wrinkles in; furrow

CORRUGATED SURFACE

corrugated iron sheet iron or steel, usually galvanized, corrugated to give it added strength in construction

corrugated paper paper or pasteboard corrugated so as to be resilient, used for wrapping or packing

cor·ru·ga·tion (kôr′ə gā′shən, kär′-; -yoo-) *n.* [ML. *corrugatio*] 1. a corrugating or being corrugated 2. any of the parallel ridges or grooves of a corrugated surface

cor·rupt (kə rupt′) *adj.* [ME. < L. *corruptus,* pp. of *corrumpere,* to destroy, spoil, bribe < *com-*, together + *rumpere,* to break: see RUPTURE] 1. orig., changed from a sound condition to an unsound one; spoiled; contaminated; rotten 2. deteriorated from the normal or standard; specif., *a)* morally unsound or debased; perverted; evil; depraved *b)* taking bribes; venal *c)* containing alterations, errors, or admixtures of foreignisms: said of texts, languages, etc. —*vt., vi.* to make or become corrupt —*SYN.* see DEBASE — **cor·rupt′er, cor·rup′tor** *n.* —**cor·rupt′ly** *adv.* —**cor·rupt′ness** *n.*

cor·rupt·i·ble (kə rup′tə b'l) *adj.* [ME. < LL.(Ec.) *corruptibilis*] that can be corrupted, esp. morally —**cor·rupt′i·bil′i·ty** (-tə bil′ə tē) *n.* —**cor·rupt′i·bly** *adv.*

cor·rup·tion (kə rup′shən) *n.* [ME. *corruptioun* < OFr. *corruption* < L. *corruptio* < *corruptus,* CORRUPT] 1. the act or fact of making, becoming, or being corrupt 2. evil or wicked behavior; depravity 3. bribery or similar dishonest dealings 4. decay; putridity; rottenness 5. something corrupted, as an improperly altered word or text 6. [Rare] a corrupting influence

cor·rup·tion·ist (-ist) *n.* a person who engages in or upholds corrupt practices, esp. in public life

cor·rup·tive (kə rup′tiv) *adj.* [ME. *corruptif* < LL.(Ec.) *corruptivus*] tending to corrupt or produce corruption — **cor·rup′tive·ly** *adv.*

corrupt practices acts laws limiting contributions to and expenditures in election campaigns, illegalizing certain methods of influencing voters, etc.

cor·sage (kôr säzh′, -säj′) *n.* [Fr. < OFr. *cors:* see CORPS & -AGE] 1. the bodice of a dress ☆2. a small bouquet for a woman to wear, as at the waist or shoulder

cor·sair (kôr′ser) *n.* [Fr. *corsaire* < Pr. *corsar* < It. *corsaro* < VL. **cursarius,* running swiftly < L. *cursus,* COURSE] 1. a privateer, esp. of Barbary 2. a pirate 3. a pirate ship

Corse (kôrs) Fr. name of CORSICA

corse (kôrs) *n.* [Archaic or Poet.] a dead body; corpse

corse·let (kôrs′let) *n.* [Fr., dim. of OFr. *cors:* see CORPS, CORSET] **1.** a medieval piece of armor for the front and back of the body: also sp. **cors′let 2.** a woman's lightweight corset, usually without stays: also sp. **cor′se·lette′**

cor·set (kôr′sit) *n.* [ME. & OFr., dim. of *cors:* see CORPS] **1.** [*sometimes pl.*] a closefitting undergarment, often tightened with laces and reinforced with stays, worn, chiefly by women, to give support or a desired figure to the body from the hips to or including the breast **2.** *a)* a medieval, close-fitting, outer jacket; jerkin *b)* [Archaic] *same as* BODICE (sense 2) —*vt.* to dress in, or fit with, a corset

cor·se·tiere (kôr′sə tir′, -tyer′) *n.* [Fr. *corsetière,* fem. of *corsetier,* corset maker < *corset,* CORSET + *-ier* -ER] **1.** a person who fits clients for the correct size and type of corset, brassiere, etc. **2.** a manufacturer of or dealer in foundation garments

cor·set·ry (kôr′sə tre) *n.* **1.** the work or trade of making, selling, or fitting corsets, girdles, etc. **2.** corsets, girdles, etc., collectively

Cor·si·ca (kôr′si kə) Fr. island in the Mediterranean, north of Sardinia: 3,367 sq. mi.; pop. 275,000; cap. Ajaccio — **Cor′si·can** *adj., n.*

‡cor·so (kôr′sō; *E.* kôr′sō) *n.* [It.] **1.** a street, esp. a fashionable one **2.** a leisurely walk; promenade

cor·tege, cor·tège (kôr tezh′, -tāzh′) *n.* [Fr. *cortège* < It. *corteggio,* retinue < *corte* < L. *cohors:* see COURT] **1.** the group of attendants accompanying a person; retinue **2.** a ceremonial procession, as at a funeral

Cor·tes (kôr′tiz; *Sp.* kôr′tes) *n.* [Sp., pl. of *corte* < L. *cohors:* see COURT] the legislature of Spain

Cor·tés (kôr tez′; *Sp.* kôr tes′), **Her·nan·do** (hər nan′dō) or **Her·nán** (er nän′) 1485–1547; Sp. soldier & explorer: conqueror of Mexico: also sp. **Cor·tez′**

cor·tex (kôr′teks) *n., pl.* **-ti·ces′** (-tə sēz′) [L., bark of a tree: for IE. base see CORIUM] **1.** *a)* the outer part or external layers of an internal organ, as of the kidney or the adrenal glands *b)* the outer layer of gray matter over most of the brain **2.** *Bot. a)* a layer of tissue in the roots and stems of dicotyledonous plants located between the stele and epidermis *b)* loosely, any layer of stem tissue external to the xylem *c)* an outer layer of tissue in certain algae, lichens, and fungi **3.** *Pharmacy* the bark or rind of a plant

cor·ti·cal (kôr′ti k'l) *adj.* [ML. *corticalis* < L. *cortex* (gen. *corticis),* bark of a tree] **1.** of a cortex **2.** consisting of cortex **3.** involving, or in some way caused by, the brain cortex —**cor′ti·cal·ly** *adv.*

cor·ti·cate (-kit, -kāt′) *adj.* [L. *corticatus* < *cortex*] **1.** having a cortex **2.** covered with bark or a barklike substance Also **cor′ti·cat′ed** (-kāt′id), **cor′ti·cose′** (-kōs′)

cor·ti·co- (kôr′ti kō′) [< L. *cortex* (gen. *corticis),* bark] *a combining form meaning* cortex [*corticosteroid*]

cor·ti·coid (-koid′) *n. same as* CORTICOSTEROID

cor·ti·co·ste·roid (kôr′ti kō stir′oid, -käs′tə roid′) *n.* [CORTICO- + STEROID] any of the hormones secreted by the adrenal cortex, or any compound derived from these or prepared synthetically and having a similar structure

cor·ti·co·ste·rone (kôr′ti käs′tə rōn′) *n.* [CORTICO- + STER(OL) + -ONE] a crystalline steroid hormone, $C_{21}H_{30}O_4$, secreted by the adrenal cortex

cor·ti·co·tro·phin (kôr′ti kō trō′fin) *n.* [CORTICO- + -*troph(ic),* pertaining to nutrition (< -TROPHY + -IC) + -IN[1]] *same as* ACTH: also **cor′ti·co·tro′pin** (-pin)

cor·tin (kôrt′'n) *n.* [CORT(EX) + -IN[1]] *former term for the* secretions of the adrenal cortex

cor·ti·sol (kôr′tə sōl′) *n.* [CORTIS(ONE) + -OL] the principal carbohydrate-regulating corticosteroid, $C_{21}H_{30}O_5$, secreted by the human adrenal glands: its pharmacological use is similar to that of cortisone

☆cor·ti·sone (kôr′tə sōn′, -zōn′) *n.* [contr. < CORTICOSTERONE: so named by the inventor, Dr. Edward C. Kendall] a corticosteroid, $C_{21}H_{28}O_5$, used as a replacement in adrenal insufficiency and in the treatment of various inflammatory, allergic, and neoplastic diseases

Coruña, La LA CORUÑA

co·run·dum (kə run′dəm) *n.* [Tamil *kurundam* < Sans. *kuruvinda,* ruby] a common mineral, aluminum oxide, Al_2O_3, second only to the diamond in hardness: a dark, granular variety is used for grinding and polishing; pure, transparent varieties include the ruby and sapphire

Co·run·na (kə run′ə) *Eng. name of* LA CORUÑA

cor·us·cate (kôr′əs kāt′, kär′-) *vi.* **-cat′ed, -cat′ing** [< L. *coruscatus,* pp. of *coruscare,* to move quickly, glitter < *coruscus,* vibrating, shimmering] to give off flashes of light; glitter; sparkle —**cor·rus·cant** (kə rus′kənt) *adj.*

cor·us·ca·tion (kôr′əs kā′shən, kär′-) *n.* [L. *coruscatio*] **1.** a coruscating; sparkling **2.** a flash or gleam of light **3.** a sudden brilliant display, as of wit

Cor·val·lis (kôr val′əs) [< L. *cor,* heart + *vallis,* of the valley] city in W Oreg., on the Willamette River: pop. 35,000

cor·vée (kôr vā′) *n.* [Fr. < OFr. *corovee* < ML. *corrogata* (*opera*), required (work) < pp. of L. *corrogare,* to bring together (by entreaty) < *com-,* intens. + *rogare,* to ask] **1.** the enforced and unpaid labor of a peasant for his feudal lord **2.** forced labor exacted by a government, as for the construction of public works

corves (kôrvz) *n. pl. of* CORF

cor·vette (kôr vet′) *n.* [Fr., prob. ult. < L. *corbita (navis),* cargo (ship) < *corbis,* basket] **1.** formerly, a sailing warship larger than a sloop and smaller than a frigate, usually with one tier of guns **2.** a small, fast British warship of about 1,000 tons, used for anti-submarine and convoy duty

☆cor·vi·na (kôr vē′nə) *n.* [Sp., orig. fem. of *corvino,* raven-like (< L. *corvinus* < *corvus,* RAVEN[1]): so named because of its color] **1.** a gray ocean fish (*Menticirrhus undulatus*) found in the surf along the California coast **2.** any of several ocean fishes (esp. genera *Micropogon* and *Cynoscion*) valued for food and sport

cor·vine (kôr′vīn, -vin) *adj.* [L. *corvinus* < *corvus,* a raven] of or like a crow or raven

Cor·vus (kôr′vəs) [L., Raven] a small S constellation near Virgo

Cor·y·ate (kôr′ē ət), **Thomas** 1576?–1617; Eng. wit & travel writer: also sp. **Cor′y·at**

Cor·y·bant (kôr′ə bant′) *n., pl.* **-bants′, Cor′y·ban·tes** (-ban′tēz) **1.** *a)* *Gr. Myth.* any of the attendants who followed the Phrygian goddess Cybele with dancing and frenzied orgies *b)* a priest in the worship of Cybele **2.** [c-] a reveler —**Cor′y·ban′tic** (-ban′tik), **Cor′y·ban′tian** (-ban′shən) *adj.*

cor·yd·a·lis (kə rid′'l əs) *n.* [ModL. < Gr. *korydallis,* crested lark < *korys,* helmet] any of a genus (*Corydalis*) of plants of the fumitory family, with one-spurred yellow, rose, blue, or purple flowers

Cor·y·don (kôr′ə d'n, kär′-; -dän′) [L. < Gr. *Korydōn,* lit., a crested lark < *korys,* helmet] *traditional name for a* shepherd in a pastoral poem —*n.* a young country fellow

cor·ymb (kôr′im, -imb; kär′-) *n.* [Fr. *corymbe* < L. *corymbus,* cluster of fruit or flowers < Gr. *korymbos*] a broad, flat-topped cluster of flowers in which the outer flower stalks are long and those toward the center progressively shorter, as in the candytuft —**co·rym·bose** (kə rim′bōs), **cor·ym′bous** *adj.* —**co·rym′bose·ly** *adv.*

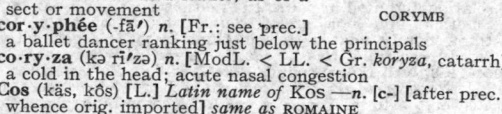

CORYMB

cor·y·phae·us (kôr′ə fē′əs, kär′-) *n., pl.* **-phae′i** (-ī) [L. < Gr. *koryphaios* < *koryphē,* head, top] **1.** the leader of the chorus in ancient Greek drama **2.** a leader, as of a sect or movement

cor·y·phée (-fā′) *n.* [Fr.: see prec.] a ballet dancer ranking just below the principals

co·ry·za (kə rī′zə) *n.* [ModL. < LL. < Gr. *koryza,* catarrh] a cold in the head; acute nasal congestion

Cos (käs, kôs) [L.] *Latin name of* KOS —*n.* [c-] [after prec., whence orig. imported] *same as* ROMAINE

cos cosine

Cos., cos. 1. companies **2.** counties

C.O.S., c.o.s. cash on shipment

cosec cosecant

co·se·cant (kō sē′kənt, -kant) *n.* [Fr. *cosécante,* for *co. secans,* short for ModL. *complementi secans,* lit., secant of the complement] *Trigonometry* the ratio between the hypotenuse and the side opposite a given acute angle in a right triangle; reciprocal of the sine of an angle or arc

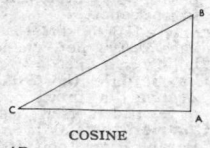

COSECANT

$\frac{R}{Y}$, cosecant of angle BAC)

co·seis·mal (kō sīz′m'l, -sīs′-) *adj.* [CO- + SEISMAL] of or designating points, or lines connecting such points, simultaneously affected by an earthquake shock: also **co·seis′mic** (-mik) —*n.* a coseismal line

co·sey, co·sie (kō′zē) *adj., n. same as* COZY

cosh (kôsh) *n.* [Brit. slang < Romany, contr. < *koshter,* skewer, stick] [Brit. Slang] a blackjack, bludgeon, or similar weapon —*vt.* [Brit. Slang] to strike with a cosh

cosh·er (käsh′ər) *vi.* [< Ir. *coisir,* a feast < ? IE. base **kois-,* to provide, whence L. *cura,* care] to be feasted, as at the dwelling of a vassal, tenant, etc. —*vt.* to pamper (sometimes with *up*)

co·sign (kō′sīn′) *vt., vi.* **1.** to sign (a promissory note) in addition to the maker, thus becoming responsible for the obligation if the maker should default **2.** to sign jointly —**co·sign·er** (kō′sī′nər) *n.*

co·sig·na·to·ry (kō sig′nə tôr′ē) *adj.* signing jointly —*n., pl.* **-ries** one of two or more joint signers, as of a treaty

co·sine (kō′sīn) *n.* [ModL. < *co. sinus,* short for *complementi sinus,* lit., sine of the complement] *Trigonometry* the ratio between the side adjacent to a given acute angle in a right triangle and the hypotenuse; reciprocal of the secant of an angle or arc

COSINE

$\frac{AB}{BC}$, cosine of angle ABC;
$\frac{AC}{BC}$, cosine of angle ACB)

cos·met·ic (käz met′ik) *adj.* [Gr. *kosmētikos,* skilled in arranging < *kosmein,* to arrange, adorn < *kosmos,* order] **1.** beautifying or designed to beautify the complexion, hair, etc. **2.** for improving the appearance by the re-

moval or correction of blemishes or deformities, esp. of the face —*n.* any cosmetic preparation for application to the skin, hair, etc., as rouge and powder —**cos·met′i·cal·ly** *adv.*

cos·me·ti·cian (käz′mə tish′ən) *n.* a person whose work is making, selling, or applying cosmetics

cos·me·tol·o·gy (-tä1′ə jē) *n.* the skill or work of applying cosmetics to women, as in a beauty shop; beauty culture —**cos′me·tol′o·gist** *n.*

cos·mic (käz′mik) *adj.* [Gr. *kosmikos* < *kosmos*, universe, order] **1.** of the cosmos; relating to the universe as an orderly whole **2.** of the universe exclusive of the earth [*cosmic* dust] **3.** vast; grandiose —**cos′mi·cal·ly** *adv.*

cosmic dust small particles, probably meteoric fragments, falling from interstellar space to the earth

☆**cosmic noise** interference caused by radio waves originating in sources beyond the earth

☆**cosmic rays** streams of highly penetrating charged particles, composed of protons, alpha particles, and a few heavier nuclei: these bombard the earth from outer space and, colliding at high speed in the upper atmosphere with atoms, penetrate their nuclei to produce mesons and various secondary nuclear particles

cos·mo- (käz′mə, -mö) [< Gr. *kosmos*, universe, world, order] *a combining form meaning* world, universe [*cosmopolitan, cosmology*]

cos·mo·drome (käz′mə dröm′) *n.* [Russ. *kosmodrom* < *kosmo-*, COSMO- + *-drom*, -DROME] any of the sites in the Soviet Union from which artificial satellites and spaceships are launched

cos·mog·o·ny (käz mäg′ə nē) *n.* [Gr. *kosmogonia*, creation of the world < *kosmogonos* < *kosmos*, universe + *-gonos* < base of *gignesthai*, to produce] **1.** the origin or generation of the universe **2.** *pl.* **-nies** a theory or account of this — **cos·mo·gon·ic** (käz′mə gän′ik), **cos′mo·gon′i·cal,** **cos·mog′o·nal** *adj.* —**cos·mog′o·nist** *n.*

cos·mog·ra·phy (-rə fē) *n.* [ME. *cosmographie* < LL. *cosmographia* < Gr. *kosmographia*, description of the world: see COSMO- & -GRAPHY] **1.** a general description of the world **2.** the science dealing with the structure of the universe as a whole and of its related parts: geology, geography, and astronomy are branches of cosmography — **cos·mog′ra·pher** *n.* —**cos·mo·graph·ic** (käz′mə graf′ik), **cos′mo·graph′i·cal** *adj.* —**cos′mo·graph′i·cal·ly** *adv.*

☆**Cos·mo·line** (käz′mə lēn′) [COSM(ETIC) + -OL + -INE⁴] *a trademark* for petrolatum of a heavy grade, used esp. as a protective coating for firearms, metals, etc. —*n.* [c-] this substance —*vt.* [c-] **-lined′, -lin′ing** to coat with this substance

cos·mol·o·gy (käz mäl′ə jē) *n.* [ML. *cosmologia:* see COSMO- & -LOGY] the branch of philosophy and science that deals with the study of the universe as a whole and of its form, nature, etc. as a physical system —**cos·mo·log·i·cal** (käz′mə läj′ə k'l) *adj.* —**cos′mo·log′i·cal·ly** *adv.* —**cos·mol′o·gist** *n.*

cos·mo·naut (käz′mə nôt′, -nät′) *n.* [Russ. *kosmonaut* < *kosmo-*, COSMO- + *-naut* < Gr. *nautēs*, sailor (see NAUTICAL)] a person trained to make rocket flights in outer space; astronaut

☆**cos·mop·o·lis** (käz mäp′ə lis) *n.* [COSMO(POLITAN) + (METRO)POLIS] a large city inhabited by people from many different nations

cos·mo·pol·i·tan (käz′mə päl′ə t'n) *adj.* [COSMOPOLIT(E) + -AN] **1.** common to or representative of all or many parts of the world; not national or local **2.** not bound by local or national habits or prejudices; at home in all countries or places **3.** having a worldwide distribution, as some plants or animals —*n.* a cosmopolitan person or thing; cosmopolite —**cos·mo·pol′i·tan·ism** *n.*

cos·mop·o·lite (käz mäp′ə līt′) *n.* [Gr. *kosmopolitēs* < *kosmos*, world + *politēs*, citizen < *polis*, city] **1.** a cosmopolitan person; citizen of the world **2.** a plant or animal common to all or most parts of the world —**cos·mop′o·lit′ism** *n.*

cos·mos (käz′məs; *for 1-3, also* -mōs, -mäs) *n.* [ME. < Gr. *kosmos*, universe, harmony] **1.** the universe considered as a harmonious and orderly system **2.** [Rare] harmony; order **3.** any complete and orderly system **4.** *pl.* **cos′mos** any of a genus (*Cosmos*) of tropical American plants of the composite family, with featherlike leaves and heads of white, pink, or purple flowers

☆**cos·mo·tron** (käz′mə trän′) *n.* [COSM(IC RAYS) + (CYCL)-OTRON] a high-energy proton accelerator

co·spon·sor (kō′spän′sər) *n.* a joint sponsor, as of a proposed piece of legislation —*vt.* to be a cosponsor of — **co′spon′sor·ship′** *n.*

Cos·sack (käs′ak, -ək; kô′sak) *n.* [Russ. *kozak* < Turk. *qazaq*, adventurer, guerrilla] a member of a people of southern Russia, famous as horsemen and cavalrymen — *adj.* of or characteristic of the Cossacks

cos·set (käs′it) *n.* [< ? OE. *cot-sæta*, cot dweller; similar in sense to It. *casiccio* (< *casa*, house), pet lamb] a pet lamb, or any small pet —*vt.* to make a pet of; fondle; pamper

cost (kôst) *vt.* **cost, cost′ing** [ME. *costen* < OFr. *coster* < ML. *costare* < L. *constare*, to stand together, stand at, cost

< *com-*, together + *stare*, to STAND] **1.** *a)* to be obtained or obtainable for (a certain price); be priced at *b)* to cause or require the expenditure, loss, or experience of [*victory cost* him his health] Orig. construed as a *vi.* with the apparent object an adverbial adjunct, and still felt as a *vi.* when used with an adverb [it *cost* him dearly] **2. cost′ed, cost′ing** *Business* to estimate the cost of making, producing, carrying out, etc., as a product or program (often with *out*) —*n.* **1.** *a)* the amount of money, etc. asked or paid for a thing; price *b)* the amount spent in producing or manufacturing a commodity *c)* the amount paid for something by a dealer, contractor, etc.: a markup is usually added to arrive at a selling price [stoves sold at *cost* in a sale] **2.** *a)* the amount of money, time, effort, etc. required to achieve an end *b)* loss; sacrifice; detriment **3.** [*pl.*] *Law* the expenses of a lawsuit, esp. those assessed by the court against the losing party —**at all costs** regardless of the cost or difficulty involved; by any means required: also **at any cost**

cos·ta (käs′tə) *n., pl.* **-tae** (-tē) [L., a rib] **1.** *Anat.* a rib **2.** a riblike part, as the thickened fore edge of an insect's wing or the central vein of a leaf

Cos·ta Bra·va (käs′tə brä′vä, kôs′-) coast of Catalonia, Spain: site of many resorts

cost accounting *Accounting* **1.** a system for recording, analyzing, and allocating production and distribution costs **2.** the keeping of such records —**cost accountant**

cos·tal (käs′t'l) *adj.* [Fr. < ML. *costalis* < L. *costa*, a rib] of or near a rib or the ribs

Cos·ta Me·sa (käs′tə mā′sə) [Sp. *costa mesa*, coast plateau] city in SW Calif., near Long Beach: pop. 73,000

co·star (kō′stär′; *for v., usually* kō′stär′) *n.* [CO- + STAR] any featured actor or actress given equal prominence with another or others in a motion picture, play, etc. —*vt., vi.* **-starred′, -star′ring** to present as or be a costar

cos·tard (käs′tərd, kôs′-) *n.* [ME., ribbed apple < OFr. *coste*, a rib + *-ard*, -ARD] **1.** a variety of large apple native to England **2.** [Archaic] a person's head: humorous or contemptuous usage

Cos·ta Ri·ca (käs′tə rē′kə, kôs′-, kōs′-) country in Central America, northwest of Panama: 19,575 sq. mi.; pop. 1,685,000; cap. San José —**Cos′ta Ri′can**

cos·tate (käs′tāt) *adj.* [L. *costatus* < *costa*, a rib] having ribs or riblike ridges

cos·ter·mon·ger (käs′tər muŋ′gər, kôs′-) *n.* [Early ModE. *costardmonger*, apple dealer: see COSTARD & MONGER] [Brit.] a person who sells fruit or vegetables from a cart or street stand: also **cos′ter**

cos·tive (käs′tiv, kôs′-) *adj.* [ME. < OFr. *costeve*, pp. of *costiver* < L. *constipare:* see CONSTIPATE] **1.** constipated or constipating **2.** [Obs.] *a)* uncommunicative *b)* stingy — **cos′tive·ly** *adv.* —**cos′tive·ness** *n.*

cost·ly (kôst′lē) *adj.* **-li·er, -li·est** [ME.: see COST & -LY] **1.** *a)* costing much; expensive; dear *b)* at the cost of great effort, damage, sacrifice, etc. [a *costly* victory] **2.** magnificent; sumptuous **3.** [Archaic] lavish; extravagant —**cost′-li·ness** *n.*

SYN.—costly refers to something that costs much and usually implies richness, magnificence, rareness, etc. [*costly* gems]: it is often applied to that which it would cost much in money or effort to correct or replace [a *costly* error]; **expensive** implies a price in excess of the article's worth or of the purchaser's ability to pay [an *expensive* hat]; **dear** implies an exorbitant price or one considerably beyond the normal or fair price [meat is so *dear* these days]; **valuable,** in this connection, implies such great value as to bring a high price [a *valuable* collection]; **invaluable** suggests value so great that it cannot be appraised in monetary terms [*invaluable* aid]—**ANT. cheap**

cost·mar·y (käst′mer′ē, kôst′-) *n.* [ME. *costmarye* < *cost* (< OE. < L. *costus* < Gr. *kostos*, costus root, an aromatic plant) + *Marie,* (St.) Mary] an herb (*Chrysanthemum balsamita*) of the composite family, with many small flowers and sweet-smelling leaves, used in flavoring

cost of living the average cost of the necessities of life, such as food, shelter, clothes, medical expenses, etc.

☆**cost-plus** (kôst′plus′) *adj.* with the price for goods or services set at the cost of materials, labor, etc. plus a specified percentage or amount of profit, as in some government contracts with industry

cos·trel (käs′trəl) *n.* [ME. < OFr. *costerel*, dim. of *costier*, something at the side < L. *costa*, a rib] [Archaic or Dial.] a large bottle or flask with loops by which it can be hung from the shoulders or waist

cos·tume (käs′tōōm, -tyōōm) *n.* [18th-c. art term < Fr. < It. < L. *consuetudo*, CUSTOM] **1.** *a)* the style of dress, including accessories, typical of a certain country, period, profession, etc. *b)* a set of clothes in such a style, as worn in a play or at a masquerade **2.** a set of outer clothes for some purpose or occasion, esp. one worn by a woman —*vt.* **-tumed, -tum·ing** to provide with a costume; put a costume on; dress —**cos′tume·ry** *n.*

costume jewelry jewelry made of relatively inexpensive materials or set with imitation gems

☆**cos·tum·er** (-ər) *n.* **1.** a person who makes, sells, or rents costumes, as for masquerades, theaters, etc. **2.** a clothes rack or hat tree

cos·tum·ier (käs tōōm′yər, -tyōōm′-; *Fr.* kôs tü myä′) *n.* [Fr.] *same as* COSTUMER (sense 1)

co·sy (kō′zē) *adj.* -si·er, -si·est & *n., pl.* -sies *same as* COZY —co′si·ly *adv.* —co′si·ness *n.*

cot[1] (kät) *n.* [Anglo-Ind. < Hind. *khāt* < Sans. *khaṭvā*] a narrow, collapsible bed, as one made of canvas or plastic sheeting on a frame that can be folded up

cot[2] (kät) *n.* [ME. & OE., cottage, hut, lit., covered place, akin to MDu. *kote*, ON. *kot* < IE. base *geu-*, to curve, bend, arch, whence COD[2], CUD] **1.** [Poet.] a cottage; small house **2.** a small shelter; cote **3.** a covering or sheath, as for a hurt finger

cot cotangent

co·tan·gent (kō tan′jənt) *n.* [ModL. *cotangens* < *co. tangens*, short for *complementi tangens*, lit., tangent of the complement] *Trigonometry* the ratio between the side adjacent to a given acute angle in a right triangle and the side opposite; reciprocal of the tangent of an angle or arc

cote[1] (kōt) *n.* [ME., COT[2]] **1.** a small shelter or shed for fowl, sheep, doves, etc. **2.** [Dial.] a cottage

COTANGENT ($\frac{x}{y}$, cotangent of angle BAC)

cote[2] (kōt) *vt.* cot′ed, cot′ing [< ? MFr. *cotoyer*, to go by the side of, coast along < OFr. *costeier* < *coste*, COAST] [Obs.] to pass by the side of; go around

Côte d'A·zur (kōt′ dà zür′) the part of the Riviera that is in France

co·tem·po·rar·y (kō tem′pə rer′ē) *adj., n. archaic var. of* CONTEMPORARY

co·ten·ant (kō ten′ənt) *n.* one of two or more tenants who share a place; joint tenant —co·ten′an·cy *n.*

co·te·rie (kōt′ər ē) *n.* [Fr., orig., organization of peasants holding land from a feudal lord < OFr. *cotier*, COTTER[1]] a close circle of friends who share a common interest or background; clique

SYN.—a **coterie** is a small, intimate, somewhat select group of people associated for social or other reasons [a literary *coterie*]; **circle** suggests any group of people having in common some particular interest or pursuit [in music *circles*]; **set** refers to a group, usually larger and, hence, less exclusive than a **coterie**, having a common background, interests, etc. [the sporting *set*]; **clique** refers to a small, highly exclusive group, often within a larger one, and implies snobbery, selfishness, or, sometimes, intrigue [a *clique* of obscurantist poets]

co·ter·mi·nous (kō tur′mə nəs) *adj. same as* CONTERMINOUS: also **co·ter′mi·nal** —**co·ter′mi·nous·ly** *adv.*

co·thur·nus (kō thur′nəs) *n., pl.* -ni (-nī) [L. < Gr. *kothornos*] **1.** a high, thick-soled boot or buskin worn by actors in ancient Greek and Roman tragedies **2.** tragedy or a lofty, tragic style in drama Also **co·thurn** (kō′thərn, kō thurn′)

co·tid·al (kō tīd′'l) *adj.* indicating the coincidence in time or extent of tides [*cotidal* lines on a map]

co·til·lion (kō til′yən, kə-) *n.* [Fr. *cotillon*, orig., petticoat < OFr. *cotte* < Frank. *kotta*: see COAT] **1.** *a)* a brisk, lively dance characterized by many intricate figures and the continual changing of partners *b)* music for such a dance **2.** a formal ball, esp. one at which debutantes are presented Also sp. **co·til′lon**

co·to·ne·as·ter (kə tō′nē as′tər) *n.* [ModL. < L. *cotonea*, QUINCE + -ASTER[2]] any of a genus (*Cotoneaster*) of shrubs of the rose family, grown for their attractive leaves, red or white flowers, and small, red or black fruits

Co·to·nou (kō tō nōō′) seaport and the principal city of Dahomey: pop. 85,000

Co·to·pax·i (kō′tə pak′sē; *Sp.* kô′tô pä′hē) volcanic mountain in the Andes, in N Ecuador: 19,344 ft.

cot·quean (kät′kwēn′) *n.* [COT[2] + QUEAN] [Archaic] **1.** a vulgar, scolding woman **2.** a man who does housework or other work regarded as women's

Cots·wold (käts′wōld, -wəld) *n.* any of a breed of sheep with long wool, orig. from the Cotswold Hills

Cotswold Hills a range of hills in SW England, mostly in Gloucestershire: also **Cots′wolds**

cot·ta (kät′ə) *n.* [ML. < Frank. *kotta*: see COAT] a short surplice

cot·tage (kät′ij) *n.* [ME. *cotage* < ML. *cotagium* < OFr. *cote* or ME. *cot*, COT[2]] **1.** a small, usually one-storied house, often one that is the dwelling of a peasant or farm laborer ☆**2.** a house at a resort or in the country, used for vacations or as a summer home ☆**3.** any of several separate dwelling units, as of an institution or camp, in which residents are housed in small groups

☆**cottage cheese** a soft, white cheese made by straining and seasoning the curds of sour milk

☆**cottage pudding** plain cake served with a sweet sauce on it

cot·tag·er (-ər) *n.* **1.** a person who lives or vacations in a cottage **2.** [Brit.] a farm laborer **3.** [Canad.] a summer resident

cot·ter[1] (kät′ər) *n.* [ME. < OFr. *cotier* < *cote*, cottage < OE. *cot* or MDu. *kote*), COT[2] a cottager; specif., *a)* [Scot.] a tenant farmer *b)* [Irish] a cottier Also sp. **cot′tar**

cot·ter[2] (kät′ər) *n.* [ME. *coter* < ?] **1.** a bolt or wedge put through a slot to hold together parts of machinery **2.** *same as* COTTER PIN

cotter pin a split pin used as a cotter, fastened in place by spreading apart its ends after it is inserted

COTTER PIN

Cot·ti·an Alps (kät′ē ən) (a division of the W Alps, between France & Italy: highest peak, c. 12,600 ft.

cot·ti·er (kät′ē ər) *n.* [ME. & OFr. *cotier*, COTTER[1]] **1.** in Great Britain and Ireland, a farmer who lives in a cottage **2.** formerly in Ireland, a peasant renting a small piece of land under a system (called **cottier tenure**) of renting land to the highest bidder

cot·ton (kät′'n) *n.* [ME. *cotoun* < OFr. *coton* < (? via It. *cotone*) Ar. *quṭun* < ? Egypt.] **1.** the soft, white seed hairs filling the seed pods of various shrubby plants (genus *Gossypium*) of the mallow family, originally native to the tropics **2.** a plant or plants producing this material **3.** the crop of such plants **4.** thread or cloth made of cotton **5.** a downy, cottonlike substance growing on other plants —*adj.* of cotton —**cotton to** [? < notion of cotton mixing well with wool, etc.] [Colloq.] **1.** to become drawn to; take a liking to **2.** to become aware of (a situation) —**cotton up to** [Colloq.] to try to ingratiate oneself, or make friends

COTTON BOLL

Cotton, John 1584–1652; Am. Puritan clergyman, born in England: grandfather of Cotton MATHER

☆**cotton batting** thin, pressed layers of fluffy, absorbent cotton, used for surgical dressing, quilting, etc.

☆**Cotton Belt** region in S and SE U.S. where much cotton is grown

cotton cake a mass of compressed cottonseed from which the oil has been extracted, used as feed

☆**cotton candy** a cottony candy consisting of threadlike fibers of melted sugar spun into a fluffy mass around a paper cone

cotton flannel a soft cotton cloth with a fleecy nap

☆**cotton gin** [see GIN[2]] a machine for separating cotton fibers from the seeds

cotton grass any of a genus (*Eriophorum*) of grasslike plants of the sedge family, with flower heads resembling tufts of cotton, common in northern bogs

☆**cotton gum** *same as* TUPELO

☆**cot·ton-mouth** (-mouth′) *n.* [from the whitish interior of its mouth] *same as* WATER MOCCASIN

☆**cotton picker 1.** a person or machine that picks cotton **2.** a machine for cleaning raw cotton

☆**cot·ton-pick·ing** (-pik′'n) *adj.* [Slang] worthless, damned, hateful, etc.: used as a general intensive of opprobrium

cot·ton·seed (-sēd′) *n.* the seed of the cotton plant, from which an oil (**cottonseed oil**) is pressed for use in margarine, cooking oil, soap, etc.

☆**cottonseed meal** hulled cottonseed ground up after the oil has been removed, used as fertilizer and fodder

☆**cotton stainer** any of several small red bugs (genus *Dysdercus*) that puncture cotton bolls and stain the fibers

☆**cot·ton·tail** (-tāl′) *n.* any of several common American rabbits (genus *Sylvilagus*) with a short, fluffy tail that is white underneath

cot·ton·weed (-wēd′) *n.* any of various wild plants with a cottony appearance, as the cudweed

☆**cot·ton·wood** (-wood′) *n.* **1.** any of several poplars that have seeds thickly covered with cottony or silky hairs, esp. a rapidly growing lowland tree (*Populus deltoides*) of E and C U.S. **2.** the wood of any of these trees

cotton wool 1. raw cotton **2.** *same as* COTTON BATTING

cot·ton·y (-ē) *adj.* **1.** of or like cotton; downy; fluffy **2.** covered with cottonlike hairs or fibers

cot·y·le·don (kät′'l ēd′'n) *n.* [L., kind of plant, navelwort < Gr. *kotylēdōn* < *kotylē*, a hollow, cavity] the first single leaf or one of the first pair of leaves produced by the embryo of a flowering plant, or any of various similar structures found in conifers —**cot′y·le·don·ous, cot′y·le′don·al** *adj.*

couch (kouch) *n.* [ME. & OFr. *couche*, a bed, lair: see the *v.*] **1.** an article of furniture on which one may sit or lie down; sofa; divan **2.** any resting place **3.** [Chiefly Poet.] a place for sleeping; bed **4.** [Obs.] an animal's lair or den **5.** *Brewing* a layer of grain spread to germinate **6.** *Fine Arts* a priming layer or coat, as of paint or varnish —*vt.* [ME. *couchen* < OFr. *couchier*, to lie down < L. *collocare*, to lay <*com*-, together + *locare*, to place] **1.** to lay or put on or as on a couch, as to sleep: now usually used reflexively or in the passive voice **2.** to lower or bring down; esp., to lower (a spear, lance, etc.) to an attacking position **3.** to put in words; phrase; express **4.** to embroider with thread laid flat and fastened down with fine stitches **5.** [Archaic] to put in a layer **6.** [Obs.] to hide **7.** *Brewing* to spread (grain) in a thin layer to germinate **8.** *Surgery* formerly, to remove (a cataract) by using a needle to push down the crystalline lens of the eye —*vi.* **1.** to lie down on a bed, as to sleep; recline **2.** to lie in hiding or in ambush **3.** to lie in a pile, as decomposing leaves

couch·ant (-ənt) *adj.* [Fr. *couchant*, prp. of *coucher*: see prec.] **1.** lying down: said esp. of animals **2.** *Heraldry*

lying down or crouching, but keeping the head up [a lion *couchant*]

couch grass (kouch) [var. of QUITCH] a weedy European perennial grass (*Agropyron repens*) that spreads rapidly by its underground stems and has become a common pest in N. America, where it is commonly called **quack grass**

cou·gar (kōō′gər, -gär) n., pl. **-gars, -gar**: see PLURAL, II, D, 1 [Fr. *couguar*, contr. (by Buffon) < *cuguacuara*, faulty transcription of Port. *çuçuarana*, for Tupi *susuarana*, lit., false deer < *suusú*, deer + *rana*, false: so named from its color] any of several large, tawny-brown animals (esp. *Felis concolor*) of the cat family, with a long, slender body and a long tail, found from Canada to Patagonia

COUGAR
(to 8 ft. long, including tail)

cough (kôf) vi. [ME. *coughen*, akin to MDu. *cuchen*, to cough, G. *keuchen*, to gasp] 1. to expel air suddenly and noisily from the lungs through the glottis, either as the result of an involuntary muscular spasm in the throat or to clear the air passages 2. to make a sound like this —vt. 1. to expel by coughing 2. to express or utter by coughing —n. 1. the act or sound of coughing 2. a condition, as of the lungs or throat, causing frequent coughing —**cough up** 1. to bring up or eject (phlegm, food, etc.) by coughing ☆2. [Slang] to hand over (money or the like) —**cough'er** n.
☆**cough drop** a small medicated tablet, often sweetened and flavored, for the relief of coughs, hoarseness, etc.

could (kood) v. [altered (after WOULD, SHOULD) < ME. *coud* < OE. *cuthe* (akin to Goth. *kuntha*, OHG. *konda*, ON. *kunna*), past tense of *cunnan*, to be able: see CAN¹] 1. pt. of CAN¹ [he did what he *could*] 2. an auxiliary in verbal phrases with present or future sense, generally equivalent to *can* in meaning and use, expressing esp. a shade of doubt or a smaller degree of ability or possibility [it *could* be so], permission [*could* I go?], the present conditional [it would help if he *could* wait], the past conditional [he would have left if he *could*], and suggesting politely less certainty than *can* [*could* you wait?]
could·n't (-'nt) could not
couldst (koodst) *archaic or poetic 2d pers. sing., past indic., of* CAN¹: *used with* thou
cou·lee (kōō′lē) n. [Fr. *coulée* < *couler*, to flow < L. *colare*, to strain, filter < *colum*, a strainer] 1. a stream of molten lava or a sheet of solidified lava ☆2. [Northwest] a deep gulch or ravine, usually dry in summer
cou·lisse (kōō lēs′) n. [Fr. < *couler*: see COULEE] 1. a grooved timber in which a sluice gate, etc. slides 2. a) any of the side flats of a theater stage b) the space between two such flats
cou·loir (kōōl wär′) n. [Fr. < *couler*: see COULEE] a deep mountain gorge or gully
cou·lomb (kōō läm′, kōō′läm) n. [after C. A. de *Coulomb* (1736-1806), Fr. physicist] the meter-kilogram-second unit of electric charge equal in magnitude to the charge of 6.25 × 10¹⁸ electrons; charge transported through a conductor by a current of one ampere flowing for one second
coul·ter (kōl′tər) n. same as COLTER
cou·ma·rin (kōō′mə rin) n. [Fr. *coumarine* < *coumarou*, tonka bean < Port. *cumaru* < Tupi *cumaru*] a white, crystalline substance, C₉H₆O₂, with the odor of vanilla, obtained from the tonka bean and certain plants or made synthetically: used in perfumes, soaps, etc.
cou·ma·rone (-rōn′) n. [G. *kumaron* < *kumarin* (< Fr. *coumarine*, COUMARIN) + *-on*, -one < Gr. *-ōnē*: see -ONE] a colorless liquid, C₈H₆O, derived from coal tar and combined with indene to produce synthetic resins used in paints, adhesives, etc.
coun·cil (koun′s'l) n. [ME. *counceil* < OFr. *concile* < L. *concilium*, group of people, meeting < *com-*, together + *calere*, to call (for IE. base see CLAMOR); confused in form and meaning in ME. with COUNSEL] 1. a group of people called together for consultation, discussion, advice, etc. 2. a group of people chosen as an administrative, advisory, or legislative assembly 3. the legislative body of a city or town 4. an assembly of church officials to discuss points of doctrine, etc. 5. a) a body of delegates from local units of a union, confederation, etc. b) an organization or society, or one of its levels of governing bodies 6. the discussion or deliberation in a council
Council Bluffs [scene of councils with the Indians by LEWIS & CLARK] city in SW Iowa, across the Missouri River from Omaha, Nebr.: pop. 60,000
council house [Brit.] any unit of a complex of dwelling units (**council estate**) built as a public housing project by a city or town
coun·cil·man (-mən) n., pl. **-men** (-mən) a member of a council, esp. of the governing body of a city or town — **coun'cil·man'ic** (-man′ik) adj.
council of ministers the highest administrative body of a nation, usually advisers to the chief executive
coun·ci·lor (koun′sə lər) n. [< COUNSELOR, by confusion

with COUNCIL] a member of a council: also [Chiefly Brit.] **coun'cil·lor** —**coun'ci·lor·ship'** n.
coun·sel (koun′s'l) n. [ME. & OFr. *counseil* < L. *consilium* (for base see CONSULT); confused in ME. with COUNCIL] 1. a mutual exchange of ideas, opinions, etc.; discussion and deliberation 2. a) advice resulting from such an exchange b) any advice 3. a) a lawyer or group of lawyers giving advice about legal matters and representing clients in court b) anyone whose advice is sought; consultant 4. [Archaic] intention or resolution; purpose 5. [Archaic] wisdom or judgment 6. [Obs.] a confidential idea, plan, etc.; secret —vt. **-seled** or **-selled, -sel·ing** or **-sel·ling** 1. to give advice to; advise 2. to urge the acceptance of (an action, plan, etc.); recommend —vi. to give or take advice —SYN. see ADVISE, LAWYER —**keep one's own counsel** to keep one's thoughts, plans, etc. to oneself —**take counsel** to discuss and deliberate; exchange advice, opinions, etc.
coun·se·lor, coun·sel·lor (-ər) n. [ME. *counseilere* < OFr. *conseillier* < L. *consiliator*] 1. a person who counsels; adviser 2. a legal adviser, as of an embassy or legation 3. a lawyer, esp. one who conducts cases in court: in full, **counselor-at-law** 4. a person in charge of a group of children at a camp —SYN. see LAWYER —**coun'se·lor·ship', coun'sel·lor·ship'** n.
count¹ (kount) vt. [ME. *counten* < OFr. *conter* (Fr. *compter*) < L. *computare*, COMPUTE] 1. to name numbers in regular order to (a certain number) [to *count* five] 2. to add up, one by one, by units or groups, so as to get a total [*count* the money] 3. to check by numbering off; inventory 4. to take account of; include [six, *counting* me] 5. to believe or take to be; consider [to *count* oneself fortunate] 6. [Archaic] to ascribe; attribute —vi. 1. to name numbers or add up items in order 2. to be taken into account; have importance, value, etc. [his opinions don't *count*] 3. to have a specified value (often with *for*) [a touchdown *counts* for six points] 4. to rely or depend (*on* or *upon*) 5. *Music* to keep time by counting the beats —n. 1. the act of counting; adding or numbering 2. the number reached by counting; total number or quantity 3. a reckoning or accounting 4. [Archaic] regard; notice; account 5. *Baseball* the number of balls and strikes that have been pitched to the batter 6. *Boxing* the counting of seconds up to ten, during which a boxer who has been knocked down must rise or lose the match 7. *Law* any of the charges in an indictment, each of which gives a reason and is sufficient for prosecution —SYN. see RELY —**count in** to include —**count off** to separate into equal divisions by counting —**count out** 1. to disregard; omit; exclude 2. [Brit.] to end a sitting of (Parliament) when the members present are not enough for a quorum 3. [Colloq.] to keep (a candidate) from office by counting the ballots incorrectly 4. *Boxing* to declare (a boxer) defeated when he has remained down for a count of ten —**count'a·ble** adj.
count² (kount) n. [ME. *counte* < OFr. *conte* < L. *comes* (gen. *comitis*), companion < *com-*, with + *ire*, to go] a nobleman in European countries, having a rank equivalent to that of an English earl
☆**count·down** (-doun′) n. the schedule of operations just before the firing of a rocket, the detonation of a nuclear explosion, etc.; also, the counting off, in reverse order, of units of time in such a schedule
coun·te·nance (koun′tə nəns) n. [ME. & OFr. *contenance*, bearing, conduct < L. *continentia*, lit., way one holds oneself, restraint < *continere*: see CONTAIN] 1. the look on a person's face that shows his nature or feelings 2. the face; facial features; visage 3. a) a look of approval on the face b) approval; support; sanction 4. calm control; composure 5. [Obs.] a) the way a thing looks; appearance b) false appearance —vt. **-nanced, -nanc·ing** to give support or sanction to; approve or tolerate —SYN. see FACE —**in countenance** calm; composed —**put out of countenance** to cause to lose composure; embarrass; disconcert
count·er¹ (koun′tər) n. [ME. *countour*: in senses 1 & 2 < OFr. *conteor* < L. *computator* < *computare*; in senses 3, 4, 5 < OFr. *contour*, counting room, table of a bank < ML. *computatorium* < L. *computare*: see COUNT¹] 1. a) a person or thing that counts; computer b) a device, as a tube containing two electrodes, for detecting and counting ionizing particles 2. an indicator on a machine, for keeping count of turns, strokes, etc. of the machine or its parts 3. a small piece of metal, wood, etc., used in playing some games, esp. for keeping score 4. an imitation coin, or token 5. a long table, board, cabinet top, etc., as in a store, lunchroom, or kitchen for the display and sale of goods, the serving or preparing of food, etc. —**over the counter** in direct trading between buyers and sellers: said of sales of stock not conducted through a stock exchange —**under the counter** in a surreptitious manner: said of sales, payments, etc. made illegally or unethically
count·er² (koun′tər) adv. [ME. *countre* < Fr. *contre* < L. *contra*, against, opposite] in a contrary direction, manner, etc.; in opposition; opposite —adj. that acts in opposition, tends in an opposite direction, or is opposite or contrary; opposed or opposing —n. 1. the opposite; contrary 2. an opposing or checking force or action 3. the part of a

horse's breast between the shoulders and under the neck **4.** a stiff leather piece around the heel of a shoe or boot **5.** the part of a ship's stern between the waterline and the arched or curved part **6.** a depression between the raised parts of a type face **7.** *Boxing a)* a blow given while receiving or parrying an opponent's blow *b)* the act of giving such a blow **8.** *Fencing* a circular parry of the foil —*vt., vi.* **1.** to act, do, move, etc. counter to (a person or thing); oppose or check **2.** to say or do (something) in reply, defense, or retaliation **3.** *Boxing* to attack or strike one's opponent while parrying (his blow)

coun·ter- (koun′tər) [ME. *countre-* < Fr. *contre-* < L. *contra-*, against] *a combining form meaning:* **1.** opposite, contrary to [*counterclockwise*] **2.** in retaliation or return [*counterplot*] **3.** complementary [*counterpart*]

coun·ter·act (koun′tər akt′) *vt.* to act directly against; check, neutralize, or undo the effect of with opposing action —**coun′ter·ac′tion** *n.* —**coun′ter·ac′tive** *adj., n.*

coun·ter·at·tack (koun′tər ə tak′; *for v., usually* koun′tər ə tak′) *n.* an attack made in opposition to, or in reprisal for, another attack —*vt., vi.* to attack in reprisal, or so as to offset the enemy's attack

coun·ter·bal·ance (koun′tər bal′əns; *for v., usually* koun′tər bal′əns) *n.* **1.** a weight used to balance another weight; counterpoise **2.** any force or influence that balances or offsets another —*vt.* **-anced, -anc·ing** to be a counterbalance to; offset

coun·ter·blow (-blō′) *n.* a blow given in return

coun·ter·change (koun′tər chānj′) *vt.* **-changed′, -chang′ing 1.** to transpose; interchange **2.** to checker; variegate

coun·ter·charge (koun′tər chärj′; *for v., usually* koun′tər chärj′) *n.* **1.** a charge in answer to another charge or against the accuser **2.** an attack in return —*vt.* **-charged′, -charg′ing 1.** to attack in return **2.** to accuse in return

coun·ter·check (-chek′; *for v., usually* -chek′) *n.* **1.** anything that checks, restrains, etc. **2.** a check upon a check; double check —*vt.* **1.** to check or restrain by a counteraction **2.** to check again; confirm by a second check

☆**counter check** a bank check kept on the counter for the use of depositors in making a withdrawal

coun·ter·claim (-klām′; *for v., usually* -klām′) *n.* an opposing claim; claim, as against the plaintiff in a lawsuit, to offset another claim —*vt., vi.* to present as, or make, a counterclaim —**coun′ter·claim′ant** *n.*

coun·ter·clock·wise (koun′tər kläk′wīz) *adj., adv.* in a direction opposite to that in which the hands of a clock move

coun·ter·cul·ture (koun′tər kul′chər) *n.* the culture of many young people of the 1960's and 1970's manifested by a life style that is opposed to the prevailing culture

coun·ter·es·pi·on·age (koun′tər es′pē ə näzh′, -näj′, -nij) *n.* actions to prevent or thwart enemy espionage

coun·ter·feit (koun′tər fit) *adj.* [ME. *countrefete* < OFr. *contrefait,* pp. of *contrefaire,* to make in opposition, imitate < *contre-,* counter- + *faire* < L. *facere,* to make] **1.** made in imitation of something genuine so as to deceive or defraud; forged [*counterfeit* money] **2.** pretended; sham; feigned [*counterfeit* sorrow] —*n.* **1.** *a)* an imitation made to deceive; forgery *b)* something that so closely resembles something else as to mislead **2.** [Obs.] an impostor; cheat —*vt., vi.* **1.** to make an imitation of (money, pictures, etc.), usually in order to deceive or defraud **2.** to pretend; feign **3.** to resemble (something) closely —*SYN.* see ARTIFICIAL, FALSE —**coun′ter·feit′er** *n.*

coun·ter·foil (-foil′) *n.* [COUNTER- + FOIL²] the stub of a check, postal money order, receipt, etc. kept by the issuer as a record of the transaction

coun·ter·force (-fôrs′) *n.* a force, action, etc. that counters or checks another; specif., the use of strategic air and missile nuclear forces to destroy the nuclear striking power of the enemy, esp. as an opening action in hostilities

coun·ter·in·sur·gen·cy (koun′tər in sur′jən sē) *n.* military and political action carried on to defeat an insurgency

coun·ter·in·tel·li·gence (-in tel′ə jəns) *n.* actions to counter enemy intelligence, espionage, sabotage, etc.

coun·ter·ir·ri·tant (-ir′ə tənt) *n.* anything used to produce a slight irritation, as of an area of the skin, in order to relieve more serious inflammation elsewhere

count·er·man (koun′tər man′, -mən) *n., pl.* **-men** (-men′, -mən) a man whose work is serving customers at the counter of a lunchroom or cafeteria

coun·ter·mand (koun′tər mand′; *also, and for n. always,* koun′tər mand′) *vt.* [ME. *contremaunden* < OFr. *contremander* < L. *contra,* against + *mandare:* see MANDATE] **1.** to cancel or revoke (a command or order) **2.** to call back or order back by a contrary order —*n.* a command or order canceling another

coun·ter·march (koun′tər märch′; *for v., also* koun′tər märch′) *n.* **1.** a march back or in the opposite direction **2.** a marching movement in which a file or column reverses its direction, the individuals remaining in the same order and position —*vi., vt.* to perform, or cause to perform, a countermarch

coun·ter·meas·ure (koun′tər mezh′ər, -mā′zhər) *n.* an action taken in opposition or retaliation

coun·ter·mine (koun′tər mīn′; *for v., also* koun′tər mīn′) *n.* [ME. *countremine:* see COUNTER- & MINE²] **1.** a military mine for intercepting or destroying an enemy mine **2.** same

as COUNTERPLOT —*vi., vt.* **-mined′, -min′ing 1.** to intercept (an enemy mine) with a countermine **2.** *same as* COUNTERPLOT

coun·ter·move (-mōōv′; *for v., also* -mōōv′) *n.* a move made in opposition or retaliation —*vi., vt.* **-moved′, -mov′ing** to move in opposition or retaliation

coun·ter·of·fen·sive (koun′tər ə fen′siv, koun′tər ə fen′siv) *n.* an attack in force by troops who have been defending a position

coun·ter·of·fer (-ôf′ər) *n.* an offer proposed in response to one that is unsatisfactory

coun·ter·pane (koun′tər pān′) *n.* [altered (after PANE) < ME. *countrepoint,* coverlet < OFr. *contre pointe,* earlier *cuilte pointe* < L. *culcita puncta,* lit., pricked (i.e., embroidered) quilt < *culcita* (see QUILT) + *puncta* (see POINT)] a bedspread; coverlet

coun·ter·part (-pärt′) *n.* [ME. *countrepart:* see COUNTER- & PART] **1.** a person or thing that corresponds to or closely resembles another, as in form or function **2.** a thing which, when added to another, completes or complements it **3.** a copy or duplicate, as of a lease

coun·ter·plot (-plät′; *for v., also* -plät′) *n.* a plot to defeat another plot —*vt., vi.* **-plot′ted, -plot′ting** to plot against (a plot); defeat (a plot) with another

coun·ter·point (-point′) *n.* [ME. < Fr. *contrepoint* < It. *contrappunto,* lit., pointed against: see COUNTER- & POINT, *n.*] **1.** a melody accompanying another melody note for note **2.** *a)* the art of adding a related but independent melody or melodies to a basic melody, in accordance with the fixed rules of harmony, to make a harmonic whole *b)* this kind of composition **3.** a thing set up in contrast or interaction with another

coun·ter·poise (-poiz′) *n.* [ME. & ONormFr. *countrepeis* (OFr. *contrepois):* see COUNTER² & POISE] **1.** a weight that balances another **2.** a force, influence, etc. that balances or neutralizes another **3.** a state of balance or equilibrium —*vt.* **-poised′, -pois′ing** same as COUNTERBALANCE

coun·ter·pro·duc·tive (-prə duk′tiv) *adj.* bringing about effects or results that are contrary to those intended

coun·ter·pro·po·sal (-prə pō′z'l) *n.* a proposal in response to one that is unsatisfactory

coun·ter·punch (-punch′) *n. Boxing* a punch delivered in countering an opponent's lead

coun·ter·ref·or·ma·tion (koun′tər ref′ər mā′shən) *n.* a reform movement to oppose a previous one

Counter-Reformation the reform movement in the Roman Catholic Church in the 16th cent., following the Protestant Reformation and in answer to it

coun·ter·rev·o·lu·tion (-rev′ə lōō′shən) *n.* **1.** a political movement or revolution against a government or social system set up by a previous revolution **2.** a movement to combat revolutionary tendencies —**coun′ter·rev′o·lu′tion·ar′y** *adj., n.* —**coun′ter·rev′o·lu′tion·ist** *n.*

coun·ter·scarp (koun′tər skärp′) *n.* [Fr. *contrescarpe:* see COUNTER- & SCARP] the outer slope or wall of a ditch, moat, etc. in a fortification

coun·ter·shaft (-shaft′, -shäft′) *n.* an intermediate shaft that transmits motion from the main shaft of a machine to a working part

coun·ter·sign (koun′tər sīn′; *for v., also* koun′tər sīn′) *n.* **1.** a signature added to a document previously signed by another, for authentication or confirmation **2.** a secret sign or signal in answer to another, as in a secret society **3.** *Mil.* a secret word or signal which must be given to a guard or sentry by someone wishing to pass; password —*vt.* to authenticate (a previously signed document) by adding one's own signature —**coun′ter·sig′na·ture** (-sig′nə chər) *n.*

coun·ter·sink (-siŋk′; *for v., also* -siŋk′) *vt.* **-sunk′, -sink′ing 1.** to enlarge the top part of (a hole in metal, wood, etc.) so that the head of a bolt, screw, etc. will fit flush with or below the surface **2.** to sink the head of (a bolt, screw, etc.) into such a hole —*n.* **1.** a tool for countersinking holes **2.** a countersunk hole

coun·ter·spy (-spī′) *n.* a spy used in counterespionage

coun·ter·ten·or (-ten′ər) *n.* [ME. *countretenour* < OFr. *contreteneur:* see COUNTER- & TENOR] **1.** the range of the highest mature male voice, above tenor **2.** a male voice or singer with such a range **3.** a part for such a voice

coun·ter·type (-tīp′) *n.* **1.** an opposite type **2.** a parallel, or corresponding, type

coun·ter·vail (koun′tər vāl′, koun′tər vāl′) *vt.* [ME. *countrevailen* < OFr. *contrevaloir* < *contre* (see COUNTER²) + *valoir,* to avail < L. *valere,* to be strong] **1.** to make up for; compensate **2.** to counteract; be successful, useful, etc. against; avail against **3.** [Archaic] to match or equal —*vi.* to avail (*against*)

coun·ter·weigh (-wā′) *vt. same as* COUNTERBALANCE

coun·ter·weight (koun′tər wāt′) *n.* a weight equal to another; counterbalance

counter word any word freely used as a general term of approval or disapproval without reference to its more exact meaning, as *nice, terrible, lousy, terrific*

coun·ter·work (-wurk′) *n.* anything made in opposition, as a fortification to oppose an enemy fortification

count·ess (koun′tis) *n.* [ME. *countesse* < OFr. *contesse* < ML. *cometissa:* see COUNT² & -ESS] **1.** the wife or widow of a count or earl **2.** a noblewoman whose rank is equal to that of a count or earl

count·ing·house (koun′tiŋ hous′) *n.* [Now Rare] a build-

ing or office in which a firm keeps records, handles correspondence, etc.: also called **counting room**

count·less (kount′lis) *adj.* too many to count; innumerable; myriad

count palatine 1. formerly, in Germany, a count granted certain powers from the emperor in his own territory 2. formerly, in England, an earl with supreme power in his county: also *earl palatine*

coun·tri·fied (kun′tri fīd′) *adj.* [< COUNTRY + -FY + -ED] 1. rural; rustic 2. having the appearance, actions, etc. attributed to country people

coun·try (kun′trē) *n., pl.* **-tries** [ME. *contre* < OFr. *contrée* < VL. *contrata*, region, that which is beyond < L. *contra*, opposite, over against] 1. an area of land; region [wooded *country*] 2. the whole land or territory of a nation or state 3. the people of a nation or state 4. the land of a person's birth or citizenship 5. land with farms and small towns; rural region, as distinguished from a city or town 6. *Law* a jury: in reference to the fact that the jury was originally a group of men from the vicinity; jury trial was called *trial by the country* —*adj.* 1. of, in, or from a rural district 2. characteristic of or like that of the country; rustic 3. [Obs. except Dial.] of one's own country; native —**go to the country** in Great Britain, to dissolve Parliament, as when it fails to support the Cabinet on an important issue, and call for the election of a new House of Commons

☆**country club** a social club, usually in the outskirts of a city, equipped with a clubhouse, golf course, etc.

country cousin a rural person not used to city life and confused or excited by it

coun·try-dance (-dans′, -däns′) *n.* an English folk dance, esp. one in which partners form two facing lines

coun·try·fied (-tri fīd′) *adj. same as* COUNTRIFIED

coun·try·man (-mən) *n., pl.* **-men** (-mən) 1. a man who lives in the country; rustic 2. a man of one's own country; compatriot —**coun′try·wom′an** *n.fem., pl.* **-wom′en**

☆**country mile** [Colloq.] a very long way or extent

country music rural folk music, esp. a commercialized variety deriving from the folk music of the Southern highlands and backwoods

country rock rock surrounding an ore body or invaded by igneous material

coun·try·seat (-sēt′) *n.* a rural mansion or estate

coun·try·side (-sīd′) *n.* a rural region or its inhabitants

coun·ty (koun′tē) *n., pl.* **-ties** [ME. *counte* < OFr. *conté* < ML. *comitatus*, jurisdiction of a count or earl < L. *comes*: see COUNT²] 1. a small administrative district of a country; esp., ☆*a*) the largest local administrative subdivision of most States *b*) any of the chief administrative, judicial, and political districts into which Great Britain and Ireland are divided 2. the people living in a county 3. [Obs.] the region governed by a count or earl

☆**county agent** a government-employed specialist assigned to inform farmers and rural families in a county of improved practices in agriculture and home economics

county borough a British borough (sense 3 *a*) with a population of 100,000 or more that ranks as a county

county commissioner ☆a member of an elected governing board in the counties of certain States

county palatine the land held by a count palatine

☆**county seat** a town or city that is the seat of government of a county

coup (kōō) *n., pl.* **coups** (kōōz; Fr. kōō) [ME. *coupe* & Fr. *coup*, both < OFr. *colp* < VL. *colpus, colapus* < L. *colaphus*, a cuff, blow on the ear < Gr. *kolaphos*] 1. literally, a blow 2. a sudden, successful move or action; brilliant stroke 3. *same as* COUP D'ÉTAT

‡**coup de fou·dre** (kōōt fōō′dr′) [Fr., lit., bolt of thunder] 1. a thunderbolt or something that strikes like a thunderbolt 2. a sudden, intense feeling of love

‡**coup de grâce** (kōō də gräs′) [Fr., lit., stroke of mercy] 1. the blow, shot, etc. that brings death to a sufferer; death blow 2. a finishing stroke

‡**coup de main** (man′) [Fr., lit., stroke of hand] a surprise attack or movement, as in war

‡**coup de maî·tre** (me′tr′) [Fr., lit., stroke of a master] a masterstroke; stroke of genius

‡**coup d'é·tat** (dā tä′) [Fr., lit., stroke of state] a sudden, forceful stroke in politics, esp. the sudden, forcible overthrow of a government, as by a cabal

‡**coup de thé·â·tre** (kōōt′ tā ä′tr′) [Fr., lit., stroke of theater] 1. a surprising or startling turn in a drama 2. an action for sensational effect; theatrical action

‡**coup d'oeil** (kōō dē′y′) [Fr., lit., stroke of eye] a rapid glance; quick view or survey

coupe (kōōp; *orig., but now rarely,* kōō pā′) *n.* [< ff.] a closed, two-door automobile with a body smaller than that of a sedan

cou·pé (kōō pā′) *n.* [Fr., orig. pp. of *couper*, to cut] 1. a closed carriage seating two passengers, with a seat outside for the driver 2. in British railway cars, a half-compartment at the end, with seats on only one side 3. *same as* COUPE

Cou·perin (kōō pran′), **Fran·çois** (frän swà′) 1668–1733; Fr. composer & organist

cou·ple (kup′'l) *n.* [ME. < OFr. *cople* < L. *copula*, a band, link: see COPULA] 1. anything joining two things together; bond; link 2. two things or persons of the same sort that are somehow associated 3. a man and woman who are engaged, married, or joined as partners in a dance, game, etc. 4. [Colloq.] a few; several [a *couple* of ideas]: now often used with adjectival force, omitting the *of* [a *couple* cups of coffee] 5. *Elec.* two metals in contact with each other to form a galvanic or thermoelectric current; voltaic couple 6. *Mech.* two equal forces producing rotation by moving in parallel but opposite directions —*vt.* **-pled, -pling** [ME. *couplen* < OFr. *copler* < L. *copulare* < *copula*] 1. to join together by fastening or by association; link; connect 2. [Archaic] to join in marriage 3. *Elec.* to join (two or more circuits) by a common magnetic or electric field or by direct connection —*vi.* 1. to come together; unite 2. to unite in sexual intercourse; copulate —*SYN.* see PAIR

cou·pler (kup′lər) *n.* a person or thing that couples; specif., *a*) a pneumatic device for coupling two railroad cars *b*) a device on an organ connecting two keyboards or keys an octave apart so that they can be played together

cou·plet (kup′lit) *n.* [Fr., dim. of *couple*, COUPLE] 1. two successive lines of poetry, esp. two of the same length that rhyme 2. [Rare] a couple; pair

cou·pling (kup′liŋ) *n.* 1. the act of joining together, pairing, copulating, etc. 2. a mechanical device or part for joining parts together 3. a device for joining two railroad cars together 4. the part of the body of a dog, horse, etc. joining the forequarters to the hindquarters 5. a method or device for joining two electric circuits for the transference of energy from one to the other

COUPLING

cou·pon (kōō′pän, kyōō′-) *n.* [Fr., remnant, coupon < *couper*, to cut] 1. a detachable printed statement on a bond, specifying the interest due at a given time: each coupon on a bond is presented for payment at the proper time 2. a certificate or ticket entitling the holder to a specified right, as redemption for cash or gifts, reduced purchase price, etc. 3. a part of a printed advertisement for use in ordering goods, samples, etc

cour·age (kur′ij) *n.* [ME. & OFr. *corage*, heart, spirit < L. *cor*, HEART] 1. the attitude of facing and dealing with anything recognized as dangerous, difficult, or painful, instead of withdrawing from it; quality of being fearless or brave; valor 2. [Obs.] mind; purpose; spirit —**the courage of one's convictions** the courage to do what one thinks is right

cou·ra·geous (kə rā′jəs) *adj.* having or showing courage; brave —*SYN.* see BRAVE —**cou·ra′geous·ly** *adv.* —**cou·ra′geous·ness** *n.*

cou·rante (kōō ränt′) *n.* [Fr. < *courant*, prp. of *courir*, to run, glide < L. *currere*, to run] 1. an old, lively French dance with gliding or running steps 2. the music for this dance Also **cou·rant′** (-ränt′)

Cour·bet (kōōr be′), **Gus·tave** (güs tàv′) 1819–77; Fr. painter

‡**cou·reur de bois** (kōō rēr də bwä′) *pl.* **cou·reurs de bois** (kōō rēr) [Fr., lit., runner of the woods] an unlicensed French or French-Indian fur trader or trapper roving the early frontiers of Canada

cou·ri·er (koor′ē ər, kur′-) *n.* [ME. *corour* (< OFr. *coreor* < LL. *curritor*) & *courier* (< OFr. *courrier* < It. *corriere*), both ult. < L. *currere*, to run] 1. a messenger sent in haste or on a regular schedule with important or urgent messages; specif., *a*) a member of the diplomatic corps charged with carrying messages *b*) a spy carrying secret information 2. a person hired to take care of hotel accommodations, luggage, etc. for a traveler

cour·lan (koor′lan) *n.* [Fr. < Galibi *kurlíri*, echoic of the cry] a tropical American marsh bird (*Aramus guarauna*), between the rails and the cranes in size

Cour·land (koor′land) region in W Latvian S.S.R.

course (kôrs) *n.* [ME. *cours* & Fr. *course*, both < OFr. *cours* < L. *cursus*, pp. of *currere*, to run: see CURRENT] 1. an onward movement; a going on from one point to the next; progress 2. the progress or duration of time [in the *course* of a week] 3. a way, path, or channel of movement; specif., *a*) [Brit.] *same as* RACECOURSE *b*) *same as* GOLF COURSE 4. the direction taken, esp. that taken or to be taken by a ship or plane, expressed in degrees measured clockwise from north or by points of the compass 5. *a*) a regular manner of procedure [the law must take its *course*] *b*) a way of behaving; mode of conduct [our wisest *course*] 6. *a*) a series of like things in some regular order *b*) a particular succession of events or actions 7. regular or natural order or development [the *course* of true love] 8. a part of a meal served at one time [the main *course* was roast beef] 9. an encounter of knights contesting in a tournament 10. a horizontal layer or row, as of bricks, in the face of a building 11. *Educ. a*) a complete series of studies leading to graduation, a degree, etc. *b*) any of the separate units of instruction in a subject, made up of recitations, lectures, etc. 12. *Naut.* a sail on any of the lowest yards of a square-rigged ship —*vt.* **coursed, cours′-**

fat, āpe, cär; ten, ēven; is, bīte; gō, hôrn, tōōl, look; oil, out; up, fur; get; joy; yet; chin; she; thin, *then*; zh, leisure; ŋ, ring; ə for *a* in *ago*, *e* in *agent*, *i* in *sanity*, *o* in *comply*, *u* in *focus*; ′ as in *able* (ā′b'l); Fr. bàl; ë, Fr. coeur; ö, Fr. feu; Fr. mon; ô, Fr. coq; ü, Fr. duc; r, Fr. cri; H, G. ich; kh, G. doch. See inside front cover. ☆ Americanism; ‡foreign; *hypothetical; < derived from

ing 1. to run or chase after; pursue **2.** to cause (esp. hunting hounds) to chase **3.** to run through or over; traverse —*vi.* **1.** to move swiftly; run or race **2.** to hunt with hounds —**in due course** in the usual or proper sequence (of events) —**in the course of** in the progress or process of; during —**of course 1.** as is or was to be expected; naturally **2.** certainly; without doubt —**on** (or **off**) **course** moving (or not moving) in the intended direction

cours·er¹ (kôr′sər) *n.* [ME. < OFr. *coursier* < *cours*, COURSE] [Poet.] **1.** a graceful, spirited or swift horse **2.** a war horse; charger

cours·er² (kôr′sər) *n.* [< ModL. *Cursorius*, name of the genus < LL., lit., pertaining to running: see CURSORY] any of various Asian and African swift-running birds (family Glareolidae) related to the plover

cours·er³ (kôr′sər) *n.* **1.** a person or thing that courses **2.** a dog for coursing

cours·ing (-siŋ) *n.* **1.** the action of a person or thing that courses **2.** hunting with hounds trained to follow game by sight rather than scent

court (kôrt) *n.* [ME. & OFr. < LL. *curtis* < L. *cohors* (gen. *cohortis*), enclosed place: see COHORT] **1.** *a)* an uncovered space wholly or partly surrounded by buildings or walls; courtyard *b)* a special section or area of a building, as a museum, somewhat like such a space but roofed as with a skylight **2.** a short street, often closed at one end **3.** *a)* a specially prepared space, usually quadrangular and often enclosed and roofed, for playing any of several ball games, as basketball, handball, tennis, squash, etc. *b)* any of the divisions of such a space **4.** formerly, a mansion or manor with a large, uncovered entrance area: now used occasionally in proper names [Hampton Court] ☆**5.** a motel: in full, **motor court 6.** *a)* the palace of a sovereign *b)* the family, advisers, and attendants of a sovereign, considered as a group *c)* a sovereign and his councilors, ministers, etc. as a governing body *d)* any formal gathering, reception, etc. held by a sovereign **7.** respectful or flattering attention paid to someone in order to get something **8.** courtship; wooing **9.** [Brit.] the board of directors of a corporation **10.** *a)* a person or persons appointed to try law cases, make investigations, etc.; judge or judges; law court *b)* a building or hall where trials are held, official investigations made, etc. *c)* a judicial assembly, whether civil, ecclesiastical, or military; also, a regular session of such an assembly —*vt.* **1.** to pay respectful or flattering attention to (a person) in order to get something **2.** to try to get the love of; seek as a mate; woo **3.** to try to get; seek [to *court* success] **4.** to make oneself open or liable to [to *court* insults] —*vi.* to carry on a courtship; woo —*adj.* of or fit for a court —**out of court 1.** without a trial in a law court **2.** not important enough for consideration or examination —**pay court to** to court, as for favor or love —**court′er** *n.*

court card [altered < *coat card* by association with prec.] [Brit.] *same as* FACE CARD

cour·te·ous (kur′tē əs) *adj.* [ME. *courteis* < OFr. *courteis* < *court:* see COURT & -EOUS] polite and gracious; considerate toward others; well-mannered —SYN. see CIVIL —**cour′te·ous·ly** *adv.* —**cour′te·ous·ness** *n.*

cour·te·san (kôr′tə z'n, kur′-) *n.* [Fr. *courtisane* < It. *cortigiana*, a prostitute, orig., court lady < *corte*, COURT] a prostitute; esp., formerly, a mistress of a king, nobleman, etc.: also **cour′te·zan**

cour·te·sy (kur′tə sē; *for 4,* kurt′sē) *n., pl.* -**sies** [ME. *courteisie* < OFr. *curteisie:* see COURTEOUS] **1.** courteous behavior; gracious politeness **2.** a polite, helpful, or considerate act or remark **3.** an act or usage intended to honor or compliment [a former legislator addressed as "Senator" by *courtesy*] **4.** [Obs.] a curtsy

☆**courtesy card** a card entitling the bearer to special privileges, as at a hotel, bank, etc.

court hand a kind of handwriting formerly used in English legal documents; Gothic handwriting

court·house (kôrt′hous′) *n.* **1.** a building in which law courts are held ☆**2.** a building that houses the offices of a county government ☆**3.** a county seat: used in names of towns or cities

cour·ti·er (kôr′tē ər, -tyər) *n.* [ME. *curteour* < OFr. *cortoier*, to frequent the court: see COURT] **1.** an attendant at a royal court **2.** a person who uses flattery to get something or to win favor

court·ly (kôrt′lē) *adj.* -**li·er**, -**li·est** [ME.] **1.** suitable for a king's court; dignified, polite, elegant, etc. [*courtly* manners] **2.** flattering, esp. in an obsequious way —*adv.* in a courtly manner —**court′li·ness** *n.*

court-mar·tial (kôrt′mär′shəl) *n., pl.* **courts′-mar′tial;** *for 2,* now often **court′-mar′tials 1.** a court of personnel in the armed forces for the trial of offenses against military law, or of army or navy personnel: see SUMMARY COURT-MARTIAL, SPECIAL COURT-MARTIAL, GENERAL COURT-MARTIAL **2.** a trial by a court-martial —*vt.* -**tialed** or -**tialled,** -**tial·ing** or -**tial·ling** to try by a court-martial

☆**court of appeals** [*often* C- A-] **1.** a State court to which appeals are taken from the trial courts: usually it is an intermediate appellate court, but in several States it is the final appellate court **2.** any of the Federal appellate courts, one in each of eleven judicial circuits, intermediate between the U.S. district courts and the Supreme Court

Court of St. James [after ST. JAMES'S PALACE] the British royal court

court plaster [so called from former use as beauty spots by court ladies] cloth covered with isinglass or some other adhesive material, formerly used for protecting minor cuts and scratches in the skin

Cour·trai (kōōr trā′) city in W Belgium, in West Flanders: pop. 44,000

court·room (kôrt′rōōm′) *n.* a room in which a law court is held

court·ship (-ship′) *n.* the act, process, or period of courting, or wooing

court tennis *see* TENNIS

court·yard (-yärd′) *n.* a space enclosed by walls, adjoining or in a castle or other large building

cous·cous (kōōs′kōōs, kōōs kōōs′) *n.* [Fr. < Berber *kuskus* < Ar. < *kaskasa*, to grind, pound] a N. African dish made with crushed grain, usually steamed and served with lamb, chicken, etc.

cous·in (kuz′'n) *n.* [ME. & OFr. *cosin* < L. *consobrinus*, orig., child of a mother's sister, also cousin, relation < *com-*, with + *sobrinus*, cousin on the mother's side < base of *soror*, sister: see SORORITY] **1.** orig., a collateral relative more distant than a brother or sister, descended from a common ancestor **2.** the son or daughter of one's uncle or aunt: also called *first* (or *full*) *cousin* or *cousin-german:* one's *second cousin* is a child of one's parent's first cousin; one's *first cousin once removed* is a child of one's first cousin **3.** loosely, any relative by blood or marriage **4.** a person or thing thought of as somehow related to another [the English and Australians are sometimes called *cousins*] **5.** a title of address used by a sovereign to another sovereign or to a nobleman ☆**6.** [Slang] a rival or competitor who unwittingly or unintentionally advances one's interests —**cous′in·ly** *adj., adv.* —**cous′in·ship′** *n.*

cous·in-ger·man (kuz′'n jur′mən) *n., pl.* **cous′ins-ger′-man** [Fr. *cousin germain:* see GERMAN²] a first cousin; child of one's uncle or aunt

cous·in·ry (-rē) *n., pl.* -**ries** cousins or other relatives, collectively

couth (kōōth) *obs. pt. and pp. of* CAN¹ —*adj.* [ME. *cuthe* < OE. *cuth* (see UNCOUTH); current use also back-formation < UNCOUTH] **1.** refined, polished, civilized, etc.: a humorous usage **2.** [Archaic] known; familiar

cou·ture (kōō tōor′) *n.* [Fr., sewing, seam < VL. *consutura, seam < L. *consulus*, pp. of *consuere*, to sew, stitch, join < *con-*, together (see COM-) + *suere*, to SEW] the work or business of designing new fashions in women's clothes; also, women's clothes in new or specially designed fashions

‡**cou·tu·rier** (kōō tü ryā′; *E.* kōō tōor′ē ā′) *n.* [Fr.] a designer of women's fashions, esp. one in the business of making and selling the clothes he has designed —**cou·tu·rière** (-ryer′; *E.* -ē er′) *n.fem.*

cou·vade (kōō väd′) *n.* [Fr. < *couver*, to hatch < OFr. *cover:* see COVEY] a custom of some primitive tribes, in which the father of a child just born engages in certain rites, such as resting in bed, as if he had borne the child

co·va·lence (kō vā′ləns) *n.* **1.** the number of pairs of electrons that an atom can share with its neighboring atoms **2.** the bond formed by a shared pair of electrons between two atoms —**co·va′lent** *adj.*

co·var·i·ance (kō ver′ē əns) *n. Statistics* a measure of the relationship between two variables whose values are observed at the same time; specif., the average value of the product of the two variables diminished by the product of their average values

cove¹ (kōv) *n.* [ME. < OE. *cofa*, cave, cell < IE. *gupā, den < base **geu-*, to bend, arch, whence COD², COOMB] **1.** a sheltered nook or recess, as in cliffs **2.** a small bay or inlet ☆**3.** a small valley or pass ☆**4.** a strip of open land extending into the woods **5.** *Archit. a)* a concave molding, esp. one where the wall meets the ceiling or floor *b)* a trough for concealed light fixtures on a wall near a ceiling *c)* a concave arch or vault —*vt., vi.* **coved, cov′ing** to form in a cove; curve concavely

cove² (kōv) *n.* [Romany *covo*, that man] [Brit. Slang] a boy or man; chap; fellow

cov·en (kuv′ən, kō′vən) *n.* [ME. *covin*, a group of confederates < OFr. *covine*, a band < VL. *convenium, an agreement < L. *convenire*, to come together, agree: see CONVENE] a gathering or meeting, esp. of witches

cov·e·nant (kuv′ə nənt) *n.* [ME. < OFr., agreement, orig., prp. of *covenir* < L. *convenire:* see CONVENE] **1.** a binding and solemn agreement made by two or more individuals, parties, etc. to do or keep from doing a specified thing; compact **2.** an agreement among members of a church to defend and maintain its doctrines, polity, faith, etc. **3.** [C-] an agreement of Presbyterians in Scotland in 1638 to oppose episcopacy: also called **National Covenant 4.** [C-] an agreement between the parliaments of Scotland and England in 1643 to extend and preserve Presbyterianism: also called **Solemn League and Covenant 5.** *Law a)* a formal, sealed contract *b)* a clause of such a contract *c)* a suit for damages for violation of such a contract **6.** *Theol.* the promises made by God to man, as recorded in the Bible —*vt.* to promise by a covenant —*vi.* to make a covenant —**cov′e·nan′tal** (-nan′t'l) *adj.*

cov·e·nan·tee (kuv′ə nan tē′) *n.* the party to whom the promises set down in a covenant are made

cov·e·nant·er (kuv′ə nən tər; *for 2, also* kuv′ə nan′tər) *n.* **1.** a person who enters into a covenant **2.** [C-] a person who

supported either of the Scottish Presbyterian Covenants (1638, 1643)

Covenant of the League of Nations the first section of the Treaty of Versailles (1919): it was the constitution of the League of Nations

cov·e·nan·tor (-nan tər) *n.* the party that has made the promises set down in a covenant

Cov·ent Garden (kuv′nt, käv′-) **1.** a market area in Westminster, London **2.** a theater, the Royal Opera House, in this area, first opened in 1732

Cov·en·try (kuv′ən trē, käv′-) city in Warwickshire, C England: industrial center; pop. 314,000 —*n.* [prob. 17th-c. Cavalier use: the town was strongly Roundhead] a state of banishment or exclusion from society; ostracism [to send someone to *Coventry*]

cov·er (kuv′ər) *vt.* [ME. *coveren* < OFr. *covrir* < L. *cooperire* < *co-*, intens. + *operire*, to hide] **1.** to place something on, over, or in front of, so as to conceal, protect, or close **2.** to extend over; overlay; blanket [snow *covered* the highway] **3.** to copulate with (the female): said chiefly of a stallion **4.** to clothe **5.** to coat, sprinkle, etc. thickly [*covered* with mud] **6.** to sit on (eggs); brood; incubate **7.** to conceal by hiding or screening **8.** to keep from harm or injury by shielding; protect by screening **9.** to include and provide for; take into account [the law *covers* such cases] **10.** *a*) to protect against financial loss or liability, as by insurance or reserve funds *b*) to make up for (a loss, injury, etc.) by insurance, reserve funds, etc. *c*) to be sufficient for payment of (expenses, a debt, etc.) **11.** to accept (a bet); stake the equivalent of (an opponent's stake) in a wager **12.** to travel over; go the length of [to *cover* a distance] **13.** to work in or be responsible for (a particular area or range of activity) [to *cover* a territory as a salesman] **14.** to deal with; treat of [to *cover* a subject] **15.** to bring upon (oneself) by one's actions [to *cover* oneself with glory] **16.** to point a firearm or similar weapon at; put or keep within the range and in the aim of a gun or the like **17.** *Card Games* to put a higher card on (a previously played card) ☆**18.** *Finance* to buy stock to replace (shares borrowed from a broker to effect a short sale) ☆**19.** *Journalism* to get news, pictures, etc. of [the reporter *covered* the train wreck] **20.** *Mil.* to keep (a man or men) within sight or contact so as to protect from enemy action ☆**21.** *Sports* to watch, guard, or obstruct (an opponent, position, etc.); specif., *Baseball* to be ready to receive a throw to (a particular base) —*vi.* **1.** to spread over a surface, as a liquid does **2.** to put on a cap, hat, etc. ☆**3.** to provide an alibi, excuse, or subterfuge (*for* another) —*n.* **1.** anything that covers, as a bookbinding, the front binding of a magazine, jar lid, box top, etc. **2.** a shelter for protection, as from gunfire **3.** a hiding place for game, as a thicket, underbrush, etc. **4.** [after Fr. *couvert*] a tablecloth and setting for a meal, esp. for one person ☆**5.** *same as* COVER CHARGE **6.** something used for hiding one's real actions, intentions, etc.; front **7.** *a*) an envelope, paper, wrapping, etc. for sending letters or other things by mail *b*) a stamped or franked envelope, postal card, etc. that has been postmarked for the collection of a philatelist —**break cover** to come out of protective shelter —**cover up 1.** to cover entirely; envelop; wrap **2.** to keep blunders, faults, crimes, etc. from being known or noticed —**take cover** to seek protective shelter —**under cover** in secrecy or concealment —**cov′er·er** *n.*

☆**cov·er·age** (-ij) *n.* **1.** the amount, extent, etc. covered by something **2.** *Insurance* all the risks covered by an insurance policy **3.** *Journalism* the extent to which a news story is covered

cov·er·all (-ôl′) *n.* [usually *pl.*] a one-piece, loosefitting, outer garment with sleeves and legs, worn, often over regular clothing, as to protect against dirt

☆**cover charge** [see COVER, *n.* 4] a fixed charge added to the cost of food and drink at a nightclub or restaurant, esp. at one offering entertainment

cover crop a crop, as vetch or clover, grown to protect soil from erosion and to keep it fertile

Cov·er·dale (kuv′ər dāl′), **Miles** 1488–1568; Eng. clergyman & translator of the Bible (1535)

☆**covered wagon** a large wagon with an arched cover of canvas, used by American pioneers

☆**cover girl** [Colloq.] a girl model whose picture is often put on magazine covers, etc.

cov·er·ing (kuv′ər in) *n.* anything that covers

covering letter (or **note**, etc.) a letter (or note, etc.) sent with a package, another letter, etc. as an explanation

cov·er·let (kuv′ər lit) *n.* [ME. *coverlite* < Anglo-Fr. *cuver-lit* < OFr. *covrir*, COVER + *lit*, bed < L. *lectus*] **1.** a bed covering; bedspread **2.** any covering

Cov·er·ley, **Sir Roger de** (də kuv′ər lē) **1.** an idealized country gentleman of the early 18th cent. in a series of sketches in the *Spectator* by Addison and Steele **2.** an old English country-dance

cov·er·lid (-lid) *n.* archaic or dial. var. of COVERLET

co·versed sine (kō′vərst) [*co-* (as in COSINE) + VERSED SINE] *Trigonometry* the versed sine of the complement of an angle or arc

cov·ert (kuv′ərt, kō′vərt) *adj.* [ME. & OFr., pp. of *covrir*, COVER] **1.** concealed, hidden, disguised, or surreptitious [a *covert* threat] **2.** [Archaic] sheltered; protected **3.** *Law* protected by a husband: said of a married woman —*n.* **1.** a covered or protected place; shelter **2.** a hiding place for game, as underbrush, a thicket, etc. **3.** *same as* COVERT CLOTH **4.** *Zool.* any of the small feathers covering the bases of the larger feathers of a bird's wing and tail —*SYN.* see SECRET —**cov′ert·ly** *adv.* —**cov′ert·ness** *n.*

covert cloth a smooth, twilled, lightweight cloth, usually of wool, used for suits, topcoats, etc.

cov·er·ture (kuv′ər chər) *n.* [ME. < OFr. < LL. **cooper-tura* < L.: see COVER] **1.** a covering **2.** a refuge **3.** a concealment or disguise **4.** *Law* the status of a married woman

☆**cov·er-up** (kuv′ər up′) *n.* something used for hiding one's real activities, intentions, etc.; front

cov·et (kuv′it) *vt., vi.* [ME. *coveiten* < OFr. *coveitier* < LL. **cupiditare* < L. *cupiditas*: see CUPIDITY] to want ardently (esp., something that another person has); long for with envy —*SYN.* see ENVY —**cov′et·er** *n.*

cov·et·ous (-əs) *adj.* [ME. & OFr. *coveitous*] tending to covet; greedy; avaricious —*SYN.* see GREEDY —**cov′et·ous·ly** *adv.* —**cov′et·ous·ness** *n.*

cov·ey (kuv′ē) *n., pl.* **-eys** [ME. *covey* < OFr. *covée*, a brood < *cover*, to sit on, hatch < L. *cubare*, to lie down] **1.** a small flock or brood of birds, esp. partridges or quail **2.** a small group of people or, sometimes, things —*SYN.* see GROUP

cov·in (kuv′in) *n.* [ME. & OFr. < LL. **convenium* < L. *convenire*, CONVENE] **1.** formerly, treachery, fraud, etc., or a group engaged in this **2.** *Law* a conspiracy of two or more people to defraud or injure another or others

cov·ing (kōv′in) *n.* a concave molding or arch; cove

Cov·ing·ton (kuv′in t'n) [after Gen. L. *Covington*, 1768–1813] city in N Ky., on the Ohio River: pop. 53,000

cow[1] (kou) *n., pl.* **cows**; archaic or poet. **kine** (kīn) [ME. *cou*, cow, pl. *kye* (southern doubled pl. *kyn*) < OE. *cu*, pl. *cy* < IE. base **gwou-*, cow, ox, whence Sans. *guuh*, Gr. *bous*, L. *bos*, OIr. *bo*, G. *kuh*] **1.** the mature female of domestic cattle (genus *Bos*), valued for its milk **2.** the mature female of certain other animals, as the buffalo, elephant, moose, whale, etc. The male of such animals is called a *bull* ☆**3.** [Western] a domestic bovine animal, whether a steer, bull, cow, or calf: *usually used in pl.*

cow[2] (kou) *vt.* [< ON. *kuga*, to subdue; meaning infl. by COW[1], COWARD] to make timid and submissive by filling with fear or awe; intimidate

cow·age (kou′ij) *n. same as* COWHAGE

cow·ard (kou′ərd) *n.* [ME. & OFr. *couard*, coward, lit., with tail between the legs < *coue*, *coe*, tail < L. *cauda*, tail] a person who lacks courage, esp. one who is shamefully unable to control his fear and so shrinks from danger or trouble —*adj.* cowardly

Cow·ard (kou′ərd), **Sir Noel (Pierce)** 1899– ; Eng. playwright, actor, and song writer

cow·ard·ice (-is) *n.* [ME. & OFr. *couardise* < *couard*: see COWARD] lack of courage; esp., shamefully excessive fear of danger, difficulty, suffering, etc.

cow·ard·ly (-lē) *adj.* of or typical of a coward; shamefully fearful —*adv.* in the manner of a coward —**cow′ard·li·ness** *n.* **SYN.**—**cowardly**, the general term, suggests a reprehensible lack of courage in the face of danger or pain [a *cowardly* deserter]; **craven** implies abject or fainthearted fear [a *craven* fear for one's life]; **pusillanimous** implies an ignoble, contemptible lack of courage or endurance [*pusillanimous* submission]; **dastardly** connotes a sneaking, malicious cowardice that is manifested in a despicable act [a *dastardly* informer] —*ANT.* brave

cow·bane (kou′bān′) *n.* [COW[1] + BANE] any of several plants (genus *Cicuta*) of the parsley family, with intensely poisonous roots and clusters of small white flowers

cow·bell (-bel′) *n.* a bell hung from a cow's neck to clank when she moves and thus indicate where she is

cow·ber·ry (kou′ber′ē) *n., pl.* **-ries 1.** a low creeping shrub (*Vaccinium vitis-idaea*) of the heath family, with white or pink flowers and dark-red, acid berries **2.** its berry

cow·bind (-bīnd′) *n.* either of two vines (*Bryonia alba* or *Bryonia dioica*) of the gourd family, with large, fleshy roots, greenish-white flowers, and red berries

☆**cow·bird** (-burd′) *n.* any of a number of small American blackbirds (esp. *Molothrus ater*) often seen near cattle: cowbirds lay eggs in other birds' nests

cow·boy (-boi′) *n.* ☆**1.** a ranch worker who rides horseback much of the time on his job of herding and tending cattle ☆**2.** a performer in a rodeo or Wild West show ☆**3.** a conventionalized character in novels, motion pictures, etc., typically an adventurous Westerner who rides horseback, carries pistols, sings ballads, etc. —☆**cow′girl′** *n.fem.*

☆**cow·catch·er** (-kach′ər, -kech′ər) *n.* a metal frame on the front of a locomotive or streetcar to remove obstructions from the tracks

Cow·ell (kou′əl), **Henry (Dixon)** 1897–1965; U.S. composer

cow·er (kou′ər) *vi.* [ME. *couren*, prob. < ON. base seen in Dan. *kűre*, Sw. *kura*, to squat, akin to G. *kauern* < IE. base **geu-*, to curve, bend, whence COD[2], CHICKEN] **1.** to crouch or huddle up, as from fear or cold **2.** to shrink and tremble, as from someone's anger, threats, or blows; cringe

---

fat, āpe, cär; ten, ēven; is, bīte; gō, hôrn, tōōl, look; oil, out; up, fur; get; joy; yet; chin; she; thin, *then*; zh, leisure; ŋ, ring; ə for *a* in *ago*, *e* in *agent*, *i* in *sanity*, *o* in *comply*, *u* in *focus*; ' as in *able* (ā′b'l); Fr. bál; ë, Fr. coeur; ö, Fr. feu; Fr. mon; δ, Fr. coq; ü, Fr. duc; r, Fr. cri; H, G. ich; kh, G. doch. See inside front cover. ☆ Americanism; ‡foreign; *hypothetical; < derived from

Cowes (kouz) resort town & yachting center on the N shore of the Isle of Wight: pop. 17,000

cow·fish (kou'fish') *n.*, *pl.* **-fish'**, **-fish'es**: see FISH[2] 1. any of several marine dolphins 2. any of the smaller marine mammals of the whale family, as the grampus 3. any of several trunkfishes (family Ostraciidae) with hornlike processes on the head 4. [Rare] a dugong or manatee

cow·hage (kou'ij) *n.* [altered after COW[1] < Hind. *kawānch*] a tropical vine (*Stizolobium pruriens*) of the legume family, bearing pods covered with fine barbed hairs that easily penetrate animal or human skin, causing intense itching: some strains are grown for forage

☆**cow·hand** (kou'hand') *n.* same as COWBOY (sense 1)

cow·herb (-urb') *n.* a pink-flowered annual plant (*Saponaria vaccaria*) of the pink family, sometimes growing as a weed in N. America

cow·herd (-hurd') *n.* a person who tends grazing cattle

cow·hide (-hid') *n.* 1. the hide of a cow 2. leather made from it ☆3. a whip made of this, often braided —*vt.* **-hid'ed**, **-hid'ing** to flog with a cowhide

☆**cow killer** a large, wingless, yellow and red wasp (*Dasymutilla occidentalis*) of the S U.S. that looks like a large ant and has a vicious sting

cowl[1] (koul) *n.* [ME. *coule* < OE. *cugle* < LL.(Ec.) *cuculla* < L. *cucullus*, cap, hood < ? IE. base (s)*keu-*, to cover, whence SKY] 1. *a)* a monk's hood *b)* a monk's cloak with a hood 2. something shaped like a cowl; esp., *a)* a hood-shaped, revolving metal cover for the top of a chimney, to increase the draft *b)* the top part at the front of an automobile body, to which the windshield and dashboard are fastened *c)* a cowling —*vt.* to put a cowl on; cover with or as with a cowl

COWL

cowl[2] (koul) *n.* [ME. *covel* < OFr. *cuvele* or OE. *cufel*, *cyfl*, both < LL. *cupella*, dim. of *cupa*, vat, cask] [Archaic] a large, two-handled tub for carrying water, usually borne on a pole

cowled (kould) *adj.* 1. wearing or having a cowl 2. hood-shaped; hooded

Cow·ley (kou'lē), **Abraham** 1618–67; Eng. poet & essayist

cow·lick (kou'lik) *n.* [from the notion that the hair looks as if it had been licked by a cow] a tuft of hair that cannot easily be combed flat

cowl·ing (kou'liŋ) *n.* [see COWL[1]] a detachable metal covering for an airplane engine, etc.

cowl·staff (koul'staf', -stäf'; kōl'-) *n.* [COWL[2] + STAFF] [Archaic] a pole run through the handles of a large tub so that it can be carried between two persons

☆**cow·man** (kou'mən) *n.*, *pl.* **-men** (-mən) 1. a man who owns or operates a cattle ranch 2. a man who tends cattle

co·work·er (kō'wur'kər) *n.* a fellow worker

cow parsnip any of several perennial plants (genus *Heracleum*) of the parsley family, with flattened clusters of white or purple flowers and thick, tubular stems

☆**cow·pea** (kou'pē') *n.* 1. a bushlike annual plant (*Vigna sinensis*) of the legume family, bearing seeds in slender pods: grown in S U.S. for forage, green manure, etc. 2. the edible seed of this plant, cooked as a vegetable

Cow·per (kōō'pər, koop'ər; *now occas.* kou'pər), **William** 1731–1800; Eng. poet

Cow·per's glands (kou'pərz, kōō'-) [after William *Cowper*, Eng. anatomist (1666–1709), who first described them] a pair of small glands with ducts opening into the male urethra: during sexual excitement they secrete a mucous substance

cow pilot same as PINTANO

☆**cow·poke** (kou'pōk') *n.* [cf. COWPUNCHER] [Colloq.] same as COWBOY

☆**cow pony** a pony used in herding cattle

cow·pox (kou'päks') *n.* a contagious disease of cows that causes pustules on the udders: people inoculated with a vaccine containing the virus of cowpox are temporarily immune to smallpox

☆**cow·punch·er** (-pun'chər) *n.* [so named from prodding the animals in herding] [Colloq.] same as COWBOY

cow·rie, **cow·ry** (kou'rē) *n.*, *pl.* **-ries** [Hind. *kaurī* < Sans. *kaparda*] 1. any of a number of gastropods (family Cypraeidae) having brightly colored, glossy shells and found in warm seas 2. the shell of any of these mollusks, esp. the shell of the **money cowrie** (*Cypraea moneta*), formerly used as currency in parts of Africa and S Asia

cow shark a large, dark-gray shark (*Hexanchus griseus*) of European and West Indian waters

cow·shed (kou'shed') *n.* a shelter for cows

cow·slip (-slip') *n.* [ME. *couslippe* < OE. *cuslyppe*, lit., cow dung < *cu*, cow + *slyppe*, paste (see SLIP[3])] 1. a European plant (*Primula veris*) of the primrose family, with yellow or purple flowers ☆2. same as MARSH MARIGOLD ☆3. same as SHOOTING STAR (sense 2) ☆4. same as VIRGINIA COWSLIP

cox (käks) *n.*, *pl.* **cox'es** [Colloq.] a coxswain —*vt.*, *vi.* to act as coxswain on (a boat) or to (a crew)

cox·a (käk'sə) *n.*, *pl.* **cox'ae** (-sē) [L., hip, angle < IE. base *koksā*, whence G. *hachse*, Achilles' tendon] 1. the hip or hip joint 2. the basal segment of the leg of an insect or other arthropod —**cox'al** *adj.*

cox·al·gi·a (käk sal'jē ə, -jə) *n.* [ModL.: see COXA & -ALGIA]

a pain in, or disease of, the hip or hip joint: also **cox·al'gy** (-jē) --**cox·al'gic** *adj.*

cox·comb (käks'kōm') *n.* [for *cock's comb*] 1. a cap topped with a notched strip of red cloth like a cock's comb, formerly worn by jesters 2. a silly, vain, foppish fellow; dandy —**cox·comb·i·cal** (käks kō'mi k'l, -käm'i-) *adj.* —**cox·comb'i·cal·ly** *adv.*

cox·comb·ry (-kōm'rē) *n.*, *pl.* **-ries** [see COXCOMB] 1. silly conceit or foppery 2. an instance of this

☆**Cox·sack·ie virus** (kook säk'ē) [so named because first found in a patient from *Coxsackie*, N.Y.] any of a group of viruses causing a variety of diseases, including some with symptoms similar to those of poliomyelitis

cox·swain (käk's'n, -swān') *n.* [< COCK(BOAT) + SWAIN] 1. a petty officer or other person in charge of a ship's boat and acting as its steersman 2. the man who steers a racing shell and calls out the rhythm of the oarsmen's stroke

coy (koi) *adj.* [ME., still, quiet < OFr. *coi*, earlier *quei* < LL. *quetus* < L. *quietus*: see QUIET] 1. orig., quiet; silent 2. *a)* shrinking from contact or familiarity with others; bashful; shy *b)* primly reserved; demure 3. affecting innocence or shyness, esp. in a playful or coquettish manner 4. reticent or evasive in making a commitment 5. [Archaic] inaccessible; secluded 6. [Obs.] disdainfully aloof —*vi.* [Archaic] to behave in a coy way —*vt.* [Obs.] to pet or caress —**coy'ly** *adv.* —**coy'ness** *n.*

☆**coy·o·te** (kī ōt'ē, kī'ōt) *n.*, *pl.* **coy·o'tes**, **coy·o'te**: see PLURAL, II, D, 1 [AmSp. < Nahuatl *coyotl*] a small wolf (*Canis latrans*) of the western prairies of N. America

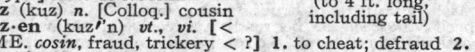

☆**coy·o·til·lo** (koi'ə tēl'yō, -til'ō; kī'-) *n.* [AmSp., dim. of prec.] a thorny, poisonous shrub (*Karwinskia humboldtiana*) of the buckthorn family, found in Mexico and the SW U.S.: its toxic berries produce paralysis

coy·pu (koi'pōō) *n.*, *pl.* **-pus**, **-pu**: see PLURAL, II, D, 1 [AmSp. *coipu* < Araucan *coypu*] same as NUTRIA

coz (kuz) *n.* [Colloq.] cousin

coz·en (kuz''n) *vt.*, *vi.* [< ME. *cosin*, fraud, trickery < ?] 1. to cheat; defraud 2. to deceive —**coz'en·age** *n.*

COYOTE
(to 4 ft. long, including tail)

co·zy (kō'zē) *adj.* **-zi·er**, **-zi·est** [Scot.; prob. < Scand., as in Norw. *kose sig*, to make oneself comfortable, *koselig*, snug] warm and comfortable; snug —*n.*, *pl.* **-zies** a knitted or padded cover placed over a teapot to keep the contents hot —*SYN.* see COMFORTABLE —☆**cozy up to** [Colloq.] to try to ingratiate oneself, or make friends, with —☆**play it cozy** [Slang] to act cautiously so as to avoid risk —**co'zi·ly** *adv.* —**co'zi·ness** *n.*

CP Command Post

cp, c.p. candlepower

cp. compare

C.P. 1. Cape Province 2. Chief Patriarch 3. Common Pleas 4. Common Prayer 5. Communist Party

c.p. chemically pure

CPA, C.P.A. Certified Public Accountant

C.P.C.U. Chartered Property Casualty Underwriter

cpd. compound

Cpl, Cpl. Corporal

cpm, c.p.m. cycles per minute

CPO, C.P.O. Chief Petty Officer

cps, c.p.s. cycles per second

cpt. counterpoint

CQ 1. a signal used by radio amateurs, inviting others to enter into communication 2. *Mil.* charge of quarters

Cr *Chem.* chromium

cr. 1. credit 2. creditor 3. crown

C.R. Costa Rica

crab[1] (krab) *n.* [ME. *crabbe* < OE. *crabba* < IE. base *grebh-*, *gerebh-*, to scratch, whence CARVE, OHG. *krebiz* (see CRAYFISH)] 1. any of various crustaceans (suborder Brachyura) with four pairs of legs, one pair of pincers, a flattish shell, and a short, broad abdomen folded under its thorax 2. any of several similar animals, as the hermit crab, king crab, etc. 3. same as CRAB LOUSE 4. any of various machines for hoisting heavy weights 5. [*pl.*] in the old game of hazard, the lowest throw of the dice, two aces 6. *Aeron.* the apparent sidewise motion of an aircraft with respect to the ground when headed into a cross wind —[C-] Cancer, the constellation and fourth sign of the zodiac —*vi.* **crabbed**, **crab'bing** to fish for crabs; catch crabs —*vt.* *Aeron.* to head (an aircraft) into a cross wind in order to counteract drift, thus causing apparent sidewise motion with respect to the ground —**catch a crab** *Rowing* to unbalance the boat by failing to clear the water in making the recovery stroke, or by missing the water in making a stroke —**crab'ber** *n.*

CRAB

crab[2] (krab) *n.* [ME. *crabbe*, akin ? to Scot. *scrabbe*, Sw. dial. *scrabba*, wild apple] **1.** *same as* CRAB APPLE **2.** a person who has a sour temper or is always complaining —*adj.* of a crab apple or the tree that it grows on —*vt.* **crabbed, crab′bing 1.** orig., *a*) to irritate; vex *b*) to sour; embitter **2.** [Rare] to find fault with; criticize —*vi.* [Colloq.] to complain peevishly; grumble —**crab one's act (the deal,** etc.) [Colloq.] to ruin or frustrate one's scheme (the deal, etc.) —**crab′ber** *n.*

crab apple 1. any of several species of small, very sour apples (genus *Malus*), growing wild or cultivated and used for making jellies and preserves **2.** a tree bearing crab apples: also **crab tree**

Crabbe (krab), **George** 1754-1832; Eng. poet

crab·bed (krab′id) *adj.* [< CRAB (APPLE)] **1.** peevish; morose; ill-tempered; cross **2.** hard to understand because intricate or complicated **3.** hard to read or make out because cramped or irregular [*crabbed* handwriting] —**crab′bed·ly** *adv.* —**crab′bed·ness** *n.*

crab·by (-ē) *adj.* [see prec.] **-bi·er, -bi·est** cross and complaining; peevish; ill-tempered —**crab′bi·ly** *adv.* —**crab′bi·ness** *n.*

☆**crab cactus** a common house plant (*Zygocactus truncatus*) with flat, jointed, fleshy stems and red flowers

crab grass [CRAB[1] + GRASS: so named from a fancied resemblance] ☆any of several weedy annual grasses (genus *Digitaria*) which spread rapidly because of their freely rooting stems, becoming a pest in lawns and gardens

crab louse a louse (*Phthirus pubis*) that infests the pubic regions, armpits, etc.: it somewhat resembles a crab in shape

Crab nebula a crab-shaped nebula in the constellation Taurus, believed to be the remnants of a supernova of 1054 A.D.: it is a very strong source of radio emission

crab's eyes *same as* JEQUIRITY

crab spider any of various webless spiders (family Thomisidae) that move sideways like crabs

crab·stick (-stik′) *n.* **1.** a stick, cane, or club made of the wood of the crab apple tree or some other wood **2.** [Archaic] an ill-tempered person

crack (krak) *vi.* [ME. *craken* < OE. *cracian*, to resound, akin to G. *krachen* < IE. base *ger-*, echoic of hoarse cry, whence Sans. *jarate*, (it) rustles] **1.** to make a sudden, sharp noise, as of something breaking **2.** to break or split, usually without complete separation of parts **3.** *a*) to become harsh or rasping, as the voice when hoarse *b*) to change suddenly from one register to another, as the voice of a boy in adolescence **4.** [Colloq.] to move with speed: now chiefly in phrase **get cracking,** to start moving with dispatch **5.** [Colloq.] to break down [to *crack* under a strain] **6.** [Scot.] to chat **7.** [Obs.] to brag —*vt.* **1.** to cause to make a sharp, sudden noise **2.** to cause to break or split, as by a sharp blow or by heavy pressure, intense heat, etc. **3.** to destroy or impair [to *crack* all opposition] **4.** to cause (the voice) to crack ☆**5.** to subject (as petroleum) to the process of cracking: see CRACKING[2] **6.** [Colloq.] to hit or strike with a sudden, sharp blow or impact **7.** to break through the difficulties of; manage to solve [to *crack* a secret code] **8.** [Colloq.] to manage to gain entrance, acceptance, etc. in **9.** [Colloq.] *a*) to break open or into; force open [to *crack* a safe] *b*) to open and consume the contents [to *crack* a bottle] *c*) to open and read or study [to *crack* a book] **10.** [Slang] to make (a joke) —*n.* **1.** a sudden, sharp noise, as of something breaking [the *crack* of a whip] **2.** *a*) a break, usually without complete separation of parts; fracture *b*) a slight defect; flaw [*cracks* in his composure] ☆**3.** a narrow opening as between boards; chink; fissure; crevice **4.** an abrupt, erratic shift of vocal tone, as from emotion or in adolescence **5.** a moment; instant [at the *crack* of dawn] **6.** [Colloq.] a sudden, sharp blow or impact **7.** [Colloq.] an attempt or try [to take a *crack* at working a puzzle] **8.** [Slang] a joke, gibe, or sharp remark **9.** [Old Slang] a burglar or burglary **10.** [Brit. Dial.] chatty talk; gossip **11.** [Brit. Dial.] a boasting or boast —*adj.* [Colloq.] excelling in skill or performance; first-rate [a *crack* shot, *crack* troops] —*SYN.* see BREAK[1] —**crack a smile** [Slang] to smile, esp. when not inclined to do so —☆**crack down (on)** to become strict or stricter (with) —☆**cracked up to be** [Colloq.] alleged or believed to be —**crack up 1.** to crash, as (in) an airplane **2.** [Colloq.] *a*) to break down physically or mentally *b*) to break into a fit of laughter or tears —☆**crack wise** [Old Slang] to joke or gibe

☆**crack·a·jack** (krak′ə jak′) *adj., n.* [Slang] *same as* CRACKERJACK

crack·brain (-brān′) *n.* a crackbrained person

crack·brained (-brānd′) *adj.* so senseless or unreasonable as to seem insane; crazy

☆**crack·down** (-doun′) *n.* a resorting to strict or stricter measures of discipline or punishment

cracked (krakt) *adj.* **1.** broken or fractured, usually without complete separation of parts; having a crack or cracks **2.** sounding harsh or strident [a *cracked* voice] **3.** [Colloq.] mentally unbalanced; crazy

cracked wheat coarsely milled wheat particles

crack·er (krak′ər) *n.* [< CRACK, *v.*; sense 5 < earlier sense "braggart, boaster"] **1.** a person or device that cracks **2.** a firecracker **3.** a little paper roll used as a favor at parties:

it contains candy, etc. and bursts with a popping noise when the ends are pulled **4.** a thin, crisp wafer or biscuit ☆**5.** *same as* POOR WHITE: contemptuous term

crack·er-bar·rel (-bar′əl) *adj.* [< the large barrel of soda crackers formerly found in general stores] [Colloq.] designating or typical of the informal discussions on all subjects by persons gathered at a country store [a *crackerbarrel* philosopher]

☆**Cracker Jack** a trademark for a confection of sweet, glazed popcorn and peanuts —*n.* this confection

☆**crack·er·jack** (krak′ər jak′) *adj.* [late 19th-c. slang: extension of CRACK, *adj.* + JACK[1] (nickname)] [Slang] outstanding, as in skill or ability; excellent —*n.* **1.** [Slang] a person or thing of recognized excellence **2.** [*also* C- *and occas. pl.*] *same as* CRACKER JACK

crack·ers (krak′ərz) *adj.* altered (after CRACKER) < CRACKED] [Chiefly Brit. Slang] crazy; insane

crack·ing (krak′iŋ) *adj.* [Colloq.] excellent; fine —*adv.* [Colloq.] very

crack·ing[2] (krak′iŋ) *n.* ☆the process of breaking down heavier hydrocarbons by heat and pressure or by catalysts into lighter hydrocarbons of lower molecular weight, as in producing gasoline from petroleum

crack·le (krak′'l) *vi.* **-led, -ling** [ME. *crakelen*, freq. of *craken*, CRACK] **1.** to make a succession of slight, sharp, popping sounds, as of dry wood burning **2.** to be bursting with energy, vivacity, etc. **3.** to develop a finely cracked surface —*vt.* **1.** to crush or break with crackling sounds **2.** to produce a finely cracked surface on —*n.* **1.** a succession of crackling sounds **2.** vivacity; animation **3.** the fine, irregular surface cracks on some pottery, porcelain, etc. or on old oil paintings **4.** *same as* CRACKLEWARE

crack·le·ware (krak′'l wer′) *n.* pottery, porcelain, etc. with a finely cracked surface

crack·ling (krak′liŋ; *for 2, usually* -lin) *n.* **1.** the producing of a succession of slight, sharp, popping sounds **2.** *a*) the browned, crisp rind of roast pork *b*) [*pl.*] the crisp part remaining after the lard has been removed from hog fat by frying

crack·ly (-lē) *adj.* crackling or tending to crackle

crack·nel (-n'l) *n.* [ME. *crakenelle*, altered < OFr. *craquelin* < MDu. *krakeling* < *kraken*, akin to CRACK] **1.** a variety of hard, crisp biscuit **2.** [*pl.*] small pieces of crisply fried fat pork **3.** [*pl.*] cracklings

crack of doom [phr. in *Macbeth*, IV, i] the signal for the beginning of Judgment Day

crack·pot (-pät′) *n.* [Colloq.] a mentally unbalanced or eccentric person —*adj.* [Colloq.] crazy or eccentric

cracks·man (kraks′mən) *n., pl.* **-men** (-mən) [< CRACK, *vt.* 8 + MAN] [Old Slang] a burglar or safecracker

crack-up (krak′up′) *n.* a cracking up; specif., *a*) a crash, as of an airplane or moving vehicle *b*) [Colloq.] a mental or physical breakdown; collapse

☆**crack·y** (-ē) *interj.* an exclamation used for emphasis: chiefly in the rustic phrase **by cracky**

Cra·cow (kra′kou, krä′-; -kō) *former sp. of* KRAKÓW

-cra·cy (krə sē) [Fr. *-cracie* < ML. *-cratia* < Gr. *-kratia*, rule < *kratos*, rule, power] a terminal combining form meaning a (specified) type of government; rule by [*autocracy, theocracy*]

cra·dle (krā′d'l) *n.* [ME. *cradel* < OE. *cradol* < **kradula*, little basket, akin to OHG. *kratto*, basket < IE. base **ger-*, to twist, turn, whence CART] **1.** a baby's small bed, usually on rockers **2.** the earliest period of one's life; infancy **3.** the place of a thing's beginning or early development [the *cradle* of civilization] **4.** [Poet.] a place of rest [rocked in the *cradle* of the deep] **5.** anything resembling a cradle or used somewhat like a cradle for holding, rocking, etc.; specif., *a*) a wooden or metal framework to support or lift a boat, ship, aircraft, etc. that is being built or repaired ☆*b*) *same as* CREEPER (sense 7) *c*) the support on which the handset of a telephone (**cradle telephone**) rests when not in use *d*) *Agric.* a frame fastened to a scythe (**cradle scythe**) so that the grain can be laid evenly as it is cut *e*) *Med.* a frame for keeping bedclothes raised over an injured limb, etc. ☆*f*) *Mining* a boxlike device on rockers, for washing the gold out of gold-bearing sand —*vt.* **-dled, -dling 1.** to place, rock, or hold in or as in a cradle **2.** to take care of in infancy; nurture **3.** to cut (grain) with a cradle scythe **4.** to support or lift (a boat, etc.) in or on a cradle ☆**5.** *Mining* to wash (gold-bearing sand) in a cradle —*vi.* [Obs.] to lie in or as in a cradle —**rob the cradle** to take as one's sweetheart or one's spouse a person much younger than oneself

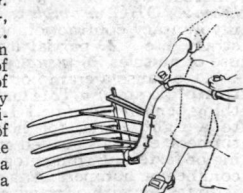

CRADLE SCYTHE

cra·dle·song (-sôŋ′) *n.* a lullaby

craft (kraft, kräft) *n.* [ME. < OE. *cræft*, strength, power, akin to G. *kraft*, strength, force (sense "skill" only in E.) < IE. **grep-* < base **ger-*, to twist, turn (whence CART, CRADLE): basic sense "cramping of muscles during exertion

of strength"] **1.** a special skill, art, or dexterity **2.** an occupation requiring special skill; esp., any of the manual arts **3.** the members of a skilled trade **4.** skill in deceiving or underhanded planning; guile; slyness **5.** *pl.* **craft** [prob. < phr. *vessels of small craft*, lit., of small power] a boat, ship, or aircraft —*vt.* to make with skill, artistry, or precision: usually in pp. —*SYN.* see ART[1]

-craft (kraft, kräft) [< prec.] *a terminal combining form meaning* the work, skill, or practice of [*handicraft*]

crafts·man (krafts′mən, kräfts′-) *n., pl.* **-men** (-mən) **1.** a worker in a skilled trade; artisan **2.** an artist: sometimes said of one skilled in the mechanics of his art, but lacking artistry —**crafts′man·ship′** *n.*

craft union a labor union to which only workers in a certain trade, craft, or occupation can belong: distinguished from INDUSTRIAL UNION

craft·y (kraf′tē, kräf′-) *adj.* **craft′i·er, craft′i·est** [ME. *crafti*, powerful, sly: see CRAFT & -Y[2]] subtly deceitful; sly; cunning; artful [*a crafty* rascal] —*SYN.* see SLY —**craft′i·ly** *adv.* —**craft′i·ness** *n.*

crag[1] (krag) *n.* [ME. < Celt., as in W. *craig*, Ir. *carraig*, Gael. *creag*] a steep, rugged rock that rises above others or projects from a rock mass

crag[2] (krag) *n.* [ME. *cragge* < MDu. *crage*: for IE. base see CRAW] [Chiefly Scot.] the neck, throat, or craw

crag·gy (-ē) *adj.* **-gi·er, -gi·est** having many crags; steep and rugged: also **crag′ged** (-id) —**crag′gi·ness** *n.*

crags·man (kragz′mən) *n., pl.* **-men** (-mən) an expert climber of crags

Crai·gie (krā′gē), Sir **William Alexander** 1867–1957; Eng. lexicographer, born in Scotland

Cra·io·va (krä yô′və) city in SW Romania: pop. 122,000

crake (krāk) *n., pl.* **crakes, crake:** see PLURAL, II, D, 1 [ME. *crak* < ON. *kraka*, crow: for IE. base see CRACK] any of several rails with long legs and a short bill; esp., the corn-crake

cram (kram) *vt.* **crammed, cram′ming** [ME. *crammen* < OE. *crammian*, to squeeze in, stuff, akin to MHG. *kram-men*, grip with claws < IE. base *grem-*, to press, compress (whence L. *gremium*, lap, bosom) < *ger-*, to hold, seize] **1.** to fill (a space, etc.) beyond normal capacity by pressing or squeezing; pack full or too full **2.** to stuff; force [*to cram* papers into a drawer] **3.** to feed to excess; stuff with food **4.** to prepare (a student) or review (a subject) for an examination in a hurried, intensive way —*vi.* **1.** to eat too much or too quickly **2.** to study or review a subject in a hurried, intensive way, as in preparation for an examination —*n.* **1.** a crowded condition; crush **2.** the act of cramming for an examination —**cram′mer** *n.*

Cram (kram), **Ralph Adams** 1863–1942; U.S. architect & writer

cram·bo (kram′bō) *n.* [< ? L. *crambe*, cabbage (as in *crambe repetita*, lit., cabbage repeatedly served, hence repeated story, old tale) < Gr. *krambē*] **1.** a game in which players find rhymes for words or lines of verse given by each other **2.** inferior poetry or rhyming

cram·oi·sy, cram·oi·sie (kram′ə zē) *adj.* [Fr. *cramoisi* < It. *cremesi* < Ar. *qirmizī*, scarlet-hued, ult. < Sans. *kṛmiga*, lit., worm-produced < *kṛmi*, worm] [Archaic] crimson —*n.* [Archaic] crimson cloth

cramp[1] (kramp) *n.* [ME. *crampe* < OFr. *crampe*, bent, twisted < Frank. *kramp*, akin to MDu. & MLowG. *krampe*, OHG. *kramph* & (?) CRAM] **1.** a sudden, painful, involuntary contraction of a muscle or muscles from chill, strain, etc. **2.** partial local paralysis, as from excessive use of muscles **3.** [*usually pl.*] abdominal spasms and pain —*vt.* to cause a cramp or cramps in: often in passive

cramp[2] (kramp) *n.* [MDu. *krampe*, lit., bent in, hence anything bent in: see prec.] **1.** a metal bar with both ends bent to a right angle, for holding together blocks of stone, timbers, etc.: also called **cramp iron 2.** a device for clasping or fastening things together; a clamp **3.** anything that confines or hampers **4.** a cramped condition or part —*vt.* **1.** to fasten with or as with a cramp **2.** to confine; hamper; restrain **3.** to turn (the front wheels of an automobile, etc.) sharply ·—*adj. same as* CRAMPED —☆**cramp one's style** [Slang] to hamper one's usual skill, confidence, etc. in doing something

cramped (krampt) *adj.* **1.** confined or restricted [*cramped* quarters] **2.** irregular and crowded, as some handwriting

cramp·fish (-fish′) *n., pl.* **-fish′, -fish′es:** see FISH *same as* ELECTRIC RAY

cram·pon (kram′pän, -pən) *n.* [Fr. < Frank. *krampo*, iron hook, akin to CRAMP[2]] **1.** either of a pair of iron hooks for raising heavy weights **2.** either of a pair of iron plates fastened on shoes to prevent slipping Also **cram·poon** (kram poon′)

Cra·nach (krä′näkh), **Lu·cas** (loo′käs) 1472–1553; Ger. painter & engraver

☆**cran·ber·ry** (kran′ber′ē, -bər i) *n., pl.* **-ries** [< Du. *kranebere*, LowG. *kraanbere*, lit., crane berry: name used by early Du. & G. settlers in U.S., replacing earlier Brit. *fen berry*] **1.** a firm, sour, edible, red berry, the fruit of any of several trailing evergreen shrubs (genus *Vaccinium*) of the heath family **2.** any of these shrubs

☆**cranberry bush** (or **tree**) a N. American shrub or small tree (*Viburnum trilobum*) of the honeysuckle family, bearing clusters of white flowers followed by acid red fruit, often used for preserves

crane (krān) *n.* [ME. *crane* < OE. *cran*: akin to Du. *kraan*, G. *kranich* < IE. *gr-on* < base *ger-*, to cry hoarsely, whence W. & Bret. *garan*, crane, CRAKE, CRACK] **1.** *pl.* **cranes, crane:** see PLURAL, II, D, 1 *a*) any of a family (Gruidae) of usually large wading birds with very long legs and neck, and a long straight bill *b*) popularly, any of various herons and storks **2.** any of various machines for lifting or moving heavy weights by means of a movable projecting arm or a horizontal beam traveling on an overhead support **3.** any device with a swinging arm fixed on a vertical axis [a fireplace *crane* is used for holding a kettle] —*vt., vi.* **craned, cran′ing 1.** to raise or move by or as by a crane **2.** to stretch (the neck) as a crane does, as in straining to see over something

SANDHILL CRANE (to 4 ft. high, wingspread to 7 ft.)

Crane (krān) **1.** (**Harold**) **Hart,** 1899–1932; U.S. poet **2. Stephen,** 1871–1900; U.S. novelist & short-story writer

crane fly any of various two-winged, slender flies (family Tipulidae) with very long legs: they look like large mosquitoes

cranes·bill, crane's-bill (krānz′bil′) *n.* [from the long beak of the seed capsule] *a popular name for* GERANIUM (sense 1)

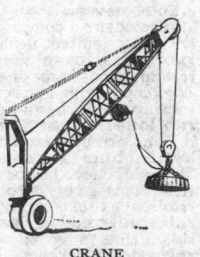

CRANE (sense 2)

cra·ni·al (krā′nē əl) *adj.* of or from the cranium —**cra′ni·al·ly** *adv.*

cranial index *Craniometry* the ratio of the greatest breadth of the human skull, multiplied by 100, to its greatest length from front to back

cranial nerve a peripheral nerve connected directly with the brain: there are twelve pairs of such nerves in man, including the olfactory, optic, trigeminal, facial, and auditory nerves

cra·ni·ate (krā′nē it, -āt′) *adj.* having a skull or cranium, as fishes, reptiles, birds, and mammals —*n.* a craniate animal

cra·ni·o- (krā′nē ō, -ə) [Gr. *kranio-* < *kranion:* see CRANIUM] *a combining form meaning* of the head, cranial [*craniology*]

cra·ni·ol·o·gy (krā′nē äl′ə jē) *n.* the scientific study of skulls, esp. human skulls, and their characteristics, including differences in size, shape, etc.

cra·ni·om·e·ter (-äm′ə tər) *n.* an instrument for measuring skulls

cra·ni·om·e·try (-äm′ə trē) *n.* the science of measuring skulls; cranial measurement

cra·ni·o·sa·cral (krā′nē ō sak′rəl, -sā′krəl) *adj.* **1.** of the cranium and sacrum **2.** *same as* PARASYMPATHETIC

cra·ni·ot·o·my (krā′nē ät′ə mē) *n., pl.* **-mies** the surgical operation of opening the skull, as for brain operations

cra·ni·um (krā′nē əm) *n., pl.* **-ni·ums, -ni·a** (-ə) [ML. < Gr. *kranion* < IE. base *ker-*, whence L. *cerebrum*, G. *hirn*, brain, HORN] **1.** the skull **2.** the bones forming the enclosure of the brain, excluding the lower jaw; brainpan

crank[1] (kraŋk) *n.* [ME. < OE. *cranc-*, as in *crancstæf*, yarn comb, CRINGE, CRINKLE: basic sense "something twisted" (fig. sense in G. *krank*, ill, lit., twisted by illness) < IE. base *ger-*, to twist, turn] **1.** a handle or arm bent at right angles and connected to a shaft of a machine, used to transmit motion or to change rotary motion into reciprocating motion, or vice versa **2.** [Colloq.] ☆a) a person who has odd, stubborn notions about something; eccentric *b*) an irritable, complaining person; cranky person **3.** [Archaic] a bend or turn **4.** [Rare] *a*) a fanciful or unusual turn of speech or thought; conceit *b*) a queer or fantastic action or idea; whim; caprice —*vt.* **1.** to form into the shape of a crank **2.** to start or operate by means of a crank **3.** [Rare] to provide with a crank —*vi.* **1.** to turn a crank, as in starting an engine or operating a device **2.** [Obs.] to wind and twist; zigzag —**crank up** [Colloq.] to get started or get moving faster

crank[2] (kraŋk) *adj.* [earlier *crank sided* < Du. or Fris. *krengd*, laid over (< *krengan*, to push over, lit., make cringe): assimilated in form to prec.] **1.** *Naut.* liable to lurch or capsize **2.** loose and shaky: said of machinery

crank[3] (kraŋk) *adj.* [LME. *cranke* < ?] [Now Dial.] **1.** high-spirited; lively **2.** cocky

crank·case (kraŋk′kās′) *n.* the metal casing that encloses the crankshaft of an internal-combustion engine

cran·kle (kraŋ′k'l) *vi., vt.* **-kled, -kling** & *n.* [freq. of CRANK[1]] [Archaic] bend, twist, or crinkle

crank·ous (kraŋ′kəs) *adj.* [Scot.] cranky; ill-tempered; irritable

crank·pin (kraŋk′pin′) *n.* the part, often a cylindrical bar or pin, of a crank or crankshaft to which a connecting rod is attached: also **crank pin**

crank·shaft (-shaft′, -shäft′) *n.* a shaft having one or more cranks for transmitting motion: in a gasoline engine the connecting rods transmit motion between the pistons and crankshaft

crank·y (kraŋ′kē) *adj.* **crank′i·er, crank′i·est** 1. out of order; shaky; loose 2. irritable; cross 3. queer; eccentric 4. [Rare] full of turns; crooked 5. *Naut.* liable to lurch or capsize; unsteady —*SYN.* see IRRITABLE —**crank′i·ly** *adv.* —**crank′i·ness** *n.*

CRANKSHAFT

Cran·mer (kran′mər), **Thomas** 1489–1556; Eng. churchman: archbishop of Canterbury (1533–56)

cran·nied (kran′ēd) *adj.* full of crannies or chinks

cran·nog (kran′əg) *n.* [Ir. < *crann*, a tree, mast, beam] an ancient Irish or Scottish lake dwelling, built on an artificial island or shallows

cran·ny (kran′ē) *n., pl.* **-nies** [ME. *crani* < OFr. *cran, cren,* a notch < OIt. *crena,* a groove < LL. *crena,* a notch, groove] a small, narrow opening; fissure; crevice; chink or crack, as in a wall

Cran·ston (kran′stən) [after Samuel *Cranston* (1698–1727), colonial governor] city in R.I.: suburb of Providence: pop. 73,000

☆**crap[1]** (krap) *n.* [see CRAPS] 1. *same as* CRAPS 2. any throw that causes the thrower to lose at craps —**crap out** 1. to lose at craps by throwing a two, three, or twelve on the first throw or a seven after the point has been established 2. [Slang] to fail, withdraw, give up, etc. because of exhaustion, cowardice, etc.

crap[2] (krap) *n.* [ME., chaff, siftings < OFr. *crape,* scale, ordure, prob. < Gmc. **krappa,* a hook, scale] [Vulgar Slang] ☆1. nonsense, falseness, insincerity, etc. ☆2. something useless, inferior, worthless, etc.; trash; junk —**crap′py** *adj.* **-pi·er, -pi·est**

crape (krāp) *n.* [Fr. *crêpe:* see CREPE] 1. *same as* CREPE (sense 1) 2. a piece of black crepe as a sign of mourning, often worn as a band around the arm —*vt.* **craped, crap′ing** [Rare] to cover or drape with black crepe

☆**crape·hang·er** (-haŋ′ər) *n.* [Slang] a pessimist or killjoy

☆**crape myrtle** [so named because of its crinkled, crepelike flowers] an ornamental shrub (*Lagerstroemia indica*) of the loosestrife family, having usually pink flowers with stalked petals, widely grown in the S U.S.

☆**crap·pie** (krap′ē) *n., pl.* **-pies, -pie:** see PLURAL, II, D, 1 [< ?] any of a genus (*Pomoxis*) of small N. American sunfish found in sluggish streams and ponds throughout E and C U.S.; specif., the **white crappie** (*Pomoxis annularis*) and the **black crappie** (*Pomoxis nigromaculatus*)

☆**craps** (kraps) *n.pl.* [*with sing. v.*] [Fr. *craps,* crabs < obs. E. *crabs,* lowest throw at hazard, two aces] a gambling game played with two dice: a first throw of seven or eleven wins, and a first throw of two, three, or twelve loses; any other first throw, to win, must be repeated before a seven is thrown

☆**crap·shoot·er** (krap′shoot′ər) *n.* a gambler at craps

crap·u·lence (krap′yoo ləns) *n.* [< CRAPULENT < LL. *crapulentus* < L. *crapula:* see CRAPULOUS] 1. sickness caused by excess in drinking or eating 2. gross intemperance, esp. in drinking; debauchery —**crap′u·lent** (-lənt) *adj.*

crap·u·lous (-ləs) *adj.* [LL. *crapulosus* < L. *crapula,* drunkenness < Gr. *kraipalē,* drunken headache, prob. < *kra(s)i-,* head (cf. CRANIUM) + *pallein,* to shake] 1. characterized by intemperance, esp. in drinking; debauched 2. sick from such intemperance

crash[1] (krash) *vi.* [ME. *crashen,* prob. echoic var. of *cracken* (see CRACK), akin to Dan. *krase,* to crackle, G. *krach,* crash, disaster < *krachen,* to crack] 1. to fall, collide, or break with force and with a loud, smashing noise 2. *a)* to make a sudden, loud noise, as of something falling and shattering *b)* to move or go with such a noise 3. to fall or land violently out of control so as to be damaged or smashed: said of aircraft 4. to come to sudden ruin; collapse; fail [their business *crashed*] —*vt.* 1. to break or dash into pieces; smash; shatter 2. to cause (a car, airplane, etc.) to crash 3. to cause to make a crashing sound 4. to force or impel with or as with a crashing noise (with *in, out, through,* etc.) ☆5. [Colloq.] to get into (a party, theater, etc.) without an invitation, ticket, etc. —*n.* 1. a loud, sudden noise, as of something falling and shattering 2. a breaking or smashing into pieces 3. a crashing, as of a car or an airplane 4. a sudden fall, collapse, or ruin, esp. of business or a business enterprise —*adj.* [Colloq.] characterized by the use of all possible resources, effort, and speed [a *crash* program to build highways] —*SYN.* see BREAK[1]

crash[2] (krash) *n.* [earlier *crasko, crasho,* "Russian linen," prob. a contr. < Russ. *krashenina,* colored linen] a coarse cotton or linen cloth with a plain loose weave, used for towels, curtains, clothes, etc.

Crash·aw (krash′ô), **Richard** 1613?–49; Eng. religious poet

crash dive a sudden submergence of a submarine to escape from a threatened attack —**crash′-dive′** *vi.* **-dived′, -div′ing**

crash helmet a thickly padded, protective helmet worn by racing-car drivers, motorcyclists, aviators, etc.

crash·ing (-iŋ) *adj.* [Colloq.] thorough; complete [a *crashing* bore]

crash-land (krash′land′) *vt., vi.* to bring (an airplane) down in a forced landing, esp. without use of the landing gear, so that some damage results —**crash landing**

crash pad ☆[Slang] a place to live or sleep temporarily

crass (kras) *adj.* [L. *crassus,* thick, gross, fat, akin ? to L. *cratis* (see CRATE)] 1. [Rare] gross; coarse; thick 2. grossly stupid, dull, or obtuse —**crass′ly** *adv.* —**crass′ness, cras′si·tude′** (-ə tood′, -ə tyood′) *n.*

Cras·sus (kras′əs), (**Marcus Licinius**) 115?–53 B.C.; Roman statesman & general

-crat (krat) [Fr. *-crate* < Gr. *-kratēs* < *kratos,* rule, power] a terminal combining form meaning participant in or supporter of (a specified kind of) government or ruling body [democrat, aristocrat]

cratch (krach) *n.* [ME. *cracche* < OFr. *creche,* crib: see CRÈCHE] [Brit. Dial.] a bin or rack for fodder

crate (krāt) *n.* [L. *cratis,* wickerwork, hurdle < IE. base **kert-,* to weave, whence HURDLE] 1. a large basket or hamper of wickerwork, or a box or case made of slats of wood, for packing things to be shipped or stored 2. [Slang] an old, decrepit automobile or airplane —☆*vt.* **crat′ed, crat′ing** to pack or enclose in a crate

cra·ter (krāt′ər) *n.* [L., mixing bowl, mouth of a volcano < Gr. *kratēr* < *kerannynai,* to mix: for IE. base see IDIOSYNCRASY] 1. in ancient Greece, a kind of bowl or jar 2. a bowl-shaped cavity, as at the mouth of a volcano or on the surface of the moon 3. a pit resembling this, as one made by an exploding bomb or fallen meteor —[C-] *Astron.* a S constellation north of Hydra

Crater Lake National Park national park in SW Oreg., containing a lake (**Crater Lake**), 6 mi. long, 5 mi. wide, c. 2,000 ft. deep, in the crater of an extinct volcano: area of the park, 250 sq. mi.

Crater Mound a huge, circular depression in C Ariz., believed to have been made by a meteorite: depth, 600 ft.; diameter, 3/4 mi.

craunch (krônch, kränch) *vt., vi., n.* [earlier form of CRUNCH: orig. echoic] *same as* CRUNCH

cra·vat (krə vat′) *n.* [Fr. *cravate* < *Cravate,* Croat, Croatian < G. *Krawat,* dial. form of *Krout* < Croatian *hrvat:* so applied in Fr. in reference to scarves worn by Croatian soldiers] 1. a neckcloth or scarf 2. a necktie

crave (krāv) *vt.* **craved, crav′ing** [ME. *craven* < OE. *crafian,* lit., to demand as right < base of *craft,* strength, might: see CRAFT] 1. to ask for earnestly; beg 2. to long for eagerly; desire strongly 3. to be in great need of —*vi.* to have an eager longing or strong desire (*for*) —*SYN.* see DESIRE —**crav′er** *n.*

cra·ven (krā′vən) *adj.* [ME. *cravant* < OFr. < *cravanté,* pp. of *cravanter,* to break < VL. **crepantare,* to cause to burst < L. *crepare,* to rattle, creak < IE. **krep-* (whence RAVEN) < base **ker-* (see CRACK)] very cowardly; abjectly afraid —*n.* a thorough coward —*SYN.* see COWARDLY —**cra′ven·ly** *adv.* —**cra′ven·ness** *n.*

crav·ing (krā′viŋ) *n.* an intense and prolonged desire; yearning or appetite, as for food, drink, etc.

craw (krô) *n.* [ME. *craue* < OE. **craga,* akin to MLowG. *krage,* MDu. *kraghe,* G. *kragen,* collar, orig., neck < ? IE. base **gwer-,* to swallow, whence L. *vorare,* to devour] 1. the crop of a bird or insect 2. the stomach of any animal —**to stick in the** (or one's) **craw** to be unacceptable or displeasing to one

☆**craw·dad** (krô′dad′) *n.* [fanciful alteration of CRAWFISH] [Dial.] *same as* CRAYFISH

craw·fish (-fish′) *n., pl.* **-fish′, -fish′es:** see FISH[2] *same as* CRAYFISH —*vi.* [Colloq.] to withdraw from a position; back down

crawl[1] (krôl) *vi.* [ME. *craulen* < ON. *krafla* < Gmc. base **krab-, *kreb-,* to scratch (whence G. *krabbeln*): for IE. base see CRAB[1]] 1. to move slowly by dragging the body along the ground, as a worm 2. to go on hands and knees; creep 3. to move or go slowly or feebly 4. to move or act in an abjectly servile manner 5. to swarm or teem (*with* crawling things) 6. to feel as if insects were crawling on the skin —*n.* 1. the act of crawling; slow movement 2. a swimming stroke in which one lies prone, with the face in the water except when turned briefly sideward for breathing, and uses alternate overarm strokes and a continuous flutter kick 3. [Brit. Slang] *same as* PUB-CRAWL —**crawl′er** *n.*

SYN.—**crawl,** in its strict usage, suggests movement by dragging the prone body along the ground [a snake *crawls*] and, figuratively, connotes abjectness or servility; **creep** suggests movement, often furtive, on all fours [a baby *creeps*] and, figuratively, connotes slow, stealthy, or insinuating progress

crawl[2] (krôl) *n.* [WIndDu. *kraal* < Sp. *corral:* see CORRAL] an enclosure made in shallow water for confining fish, turtles, etc.

☆**crawler tractor** a tractor equipped on each side with a continuous roller belt over cogged wheels, for moving over rough or muddy ground

☆**crawl space** a shallow or narrow space, as under a roof or floor, allowing access to wiring, plumbing, etc.

crawl·y (krôl′ē) *adj.* **-i·er, -i·est** *same as* CREEPY

cray·fish (krā′fish′) *n., pl.* **-fish′, -fish′es:** see FISH² [altered, after FISH² < ME. *crevise* < OFr. *crevice* (Fr. *écrevisse*) < OHG. *krebiz* (akin to OE. *crabba:* see CRAB¹] ☆1. any of a number of small freshwater crustaceans (genera *Astacus* and *Cambarus*) somewhat resembling little lobsters 2. same as SPINY LOBSTER

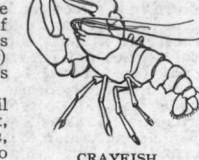

CRAYFISH
(to 5 in. long)

cray·on (krā′ən, -än′) *n.* [Fr., pencil < *craie*, chalk < L. *creta*, chalk, white earth, prob. < (*terra*) *creta*, sifted (earth) < pp. of *cernere*, to sift (cf. DISCERN)] 1. a small stick of chalk, charcoal, or colored wax, used for drawing, coloring, or writing 2. a drawing made with crayons —*vt.* to draw or color with crayons —**cray′on·ist** *n.*

craze (krāz) *vt.* **crazed, craz′ing** [ME. *crasen*, to crack, break < Scand., as in Dan. *krase*, to crackle, Sw. *krasa*, to break up: cf. CRASH¹] 1. to cause to become mentally ill; make insane 2. to produce a crackled surface or small cracks in the glaze of (pottery, porcelain, etc.) 3. [Obs.] to break or shatter —*vi.* 1. to become mentally ill 2. to become finely cracked, as the glaze of pottery 3. [Now Rare] to break, shatter, crack, etc. —*n.* 1. an exaggerated enthusiasm; mania 2. something that is currently the fashion; fad 3. a crack in glaze or enamel, as of pottery —*SYN.* see FASHION

cra·zy (krā′zē) *adj.* **-zi·er, -zi·est** [< CRAZE] 1. having flaws or cracks; shaky or rickety; unsound 2. *a)* unsound of mind; mentally unbalanced or deranged; psychopathic; insane *b)* of or for an insane person 3. temporarily unbalanced, as with great excitement, rage, etc. 4. [Colloq.] foolish, wild, fantastic, etc.; not sensible *[a crazy idea]* 5. [Colloq.] very enthusiastic or eager *[crazy* about the movies*]* ☆6. [Slang] excellent, wonderful, thrilling, etc. —**cra′zi·ly** *adv.* —**cra′zi·ness** *n.*

☆**crazy bone** same as FUNNY BONE

☆**crazy quilt** a quilt made of pieces of cloth of various colors, patterns, shapes, and sizes

☆**cra·zy·weed** (-wēd′) *n.* same as LOCOWEED

creak (krēk) *vi., vt.* [ME. *creken*, to make a sound like geese, crows, etc.; echoic var. of *croken:* see CROAK] to make, cause to make, or move with a harsh, shrill, grating, or squeaking sound, as rusted hinges or old floorboards —*n.* such a sound

creak·y (-ē) *adj.* **creak′i·er, creak′i·est** creaking or apt to creak —**creak′i·ly** *adv.* —**creak′i·ness** *n.*

cream (krēm) *n.* [ME. *creme* < OFr. *craime, cresme,* prob. a blend of LL. *chrisma* (see CHRISM) & VL. *crama* < Celt. base (as in Bret. *crammen,* skin, surface), ult. < IE. base *(s)ker-,* to cut, whence L. *corium,* hide] 1. the oily, yellowish part of milk, which rises to the top and which may be separated: commercial cream contains 18% or more butterfat 2. any of various foods made of cream or having a creamy consistency *[ice cream]* 3. a cosmetic or emulsion with a creamy consistency 4. a thick liqueur 5. the best or finest part *[the cream* of the crop*]* 6. the color of cream; yellowish white —*adj.* 1. containing cream; made of cream 2. having the consistency of cream; creamy 3. cream-colored —*vi.* 1. to form into cream or a foamy substance 2. to form cream or a creamy foam on top —*vt.* 1. to remove the cream from 2. to remove, use, etc. the best part of 3. to add cream to 4. to cook with cream or a cream sauce 5. to beat into a creamy consistency; make into a creamy mixture 6. to let (milk) form cream 7. to separate as cream ☆8. [Slang] to beat, thrash, or defeat soundly — **cream of** creamed purée or *[cream of* tomato soup*]*

cream cheese a soft, white cheese made of cream or of milk enriched with cream

cream-col·ored (-kul′ərd) *adj.* yellowish-white

☆**cream-cups** (-kups′) *n., pl.* **-cups′** an annual plant (*Platystemon californicus*) of the poppy family, with small, cream-colored flowers, native to the SW U.S.

cream·er (-ər) *n.* ☆1. a small pitcher for cream 2. a device for separating cream from milk

☆**cream·er·y** (-ər ē) *n., pl.* **-er·ies** [Fr. *crèmerie:* see CREAM & -ERY] 1. a place where milk and cream are pasteurized, separated, and bottled, and butter and cheese are made 2. a shop where dairy products are sold

cream of tartar a white, acid, crystalline substance, $KHC_4H_4O_6$, used in baking powder

☆**cream puff** 1. a round shell of pastry filled with whipped cream or custard 2. [Slang] a secondhand automobile in excellent condition: also **cream′puff′**

cream sauce a sauce made of butter and flour cooked together with milk or cream

☆**cream soda** soda pop, usually colorless, that is flavored with vanilla

cream·y (-ē) *adj.* **cream′i·er, cream′i·est** 1. full of cream; containing cream 2. like cream in consistency or color —**cream′i·ness** *n.*

crease¹ (krēs) *n.* [earlier *creaste,* lit., ridge < ME. *creste, crece,* crest, ridge (of a roof), fold in cloth < OFr. *creste:* see CREST] 1. a line, mark, or ridge made by folding and pressing cloth, paper, etc. *[the crease* in trousers*]* 2. a fold or wrinkle *[creases* in a jowl*]* 3. *Cricket* any of the lines that mark off the station of the batsman or of the bowler 4. *Hockey, Lacrosse* a rectangular area marked off by lines

in front of the goal cage, which cannot be entered by players on the offense except under certain conditions —*vt.* **creased, creas′ing** 1. to fold and make a crease in 2. to wrinkle; muss ☆3. to graze and injure slightly with a bullet —*vi.* to become creased —**crease′less** *adj.* —**creas′er** *n.* —**creas′y** *adj.*

crease² (krēs) *n.* same as CREESE

cre·ate (krē āt′) *vt.* **-at′ed, -at′ing** [ME. *createn* < L. *creatus,* pp. of *creare,* to create < IE. base **krē-,* to grow, cause to grow: cf. CEREAL] 1. to cause to come into existence; bring into being; make; originate; esp., to make or design (something requiring art, skill, invention, etc.) 2. to bring about; give rise to; cause *[new industries create* new jobs*]* 3. to invest with a new rank, function, etc. 4. to be the first to portray (a particular role in a play) —*adj.* [Archaic] created

cre·a·tine (krē′ə tēn′, -tin) *n.* [< Gr. *kreas,* flesh + -INE⁴] a white, crystalline substance, $C_4H_9N_3O_2$, an alkaloid or amino acid, present chiefly in the muscle tissue of vertebrates

cre·at·i·nine (krē at′ə nēn′, -nin) *n.* [G. *kreatinin* < *kreatin,* CREATINE + -in, -INE⁴] a nitrogen compound, $C_4H_7N_3O$, an anhydride of creatine, found in blood, muscle, and esp. urine, where measurement of its excretion is used to evaluate kidney function

cre·a·tion (krē ā′shən) *n.* [ME. *creacion* < L. *creatio*] 1. a creating or being created 2. the universe and everything in it; all the world 3. anything created; esp., something original created by the imagination; invention, design, work of art, etc. —**the Creation** *Theol.* God's creating of the world

cre·a·tion·ism (-iz'm) *n. Theol.* 1. the doctrine that God creates a new soul for every human being born: opposed to TRADUCIANISM 2. the doctrine that ascribes the origin of matter, species, etc. to acts of creation by God —**cre·a′tion·ist** *n.*

cre·a·tive (krē āt′iv) *adj.* [ML. *creativus*] 1. creating or able to create 2. productive (*of*) 3. having or showing imagination and artistic or intellectual inventiveness *[creative* writing*]* 4. stimulating the imagination and inventive powers *[creative* toys*]* —**cre·a′tive·ly** *adv.* — **cre·a′tive·ness** *n.*

cre·a·tiv·i·ty (krē′ā tiv′ə tē) *n.* creative ability; artistic or intellectual inventiveness

cre·a·tor (krē āt′ər) *n.* [ME. *creatour* < L. *creator*] 1. one who creates 2. [C-] God; the Supreme Being

crea·ture (krē′chər) *n.* [ME. < OFr. < L. *creatura*] 1. anything created, animate or inanimate 2. an animate or living being; esp., ☆*a)* a domestic animal, esp. [South] a horse *b)* a human being: often used in a patronizing, contemptuous, commiserating, or endearing sense *c)* a strange or imaginary being 3. a person completely dominated by, dependent on, or owing his success, position, etc. to, another —**the creature** whiskey or other intoxicating liquor: humorous usage —**crea′tur·al, crea′ture·ly** *adj.*

creature comfort anything providing bodily comfort, as food, clothing, or shelter

crèche (kresh, krāsh) *n.* [Fr. < Frank. **kripja* (G. *krippe*), crib < IE. **grebh-* < base **ger-,* to wind, turn, weave, whence CRADLE, CART] 1. a display of a stable with figures, as at Christmas, representing a scene at the birth of Jesus 2. an institution for foundlings 3. a day nursery: term applied to such an institution in England and European countries

Cré·cy (krā sē′; E. kres′ē) village in N France: scene of an English victory (1346) over the French: also **Cré·cy-en-Pon·thieu** (-än pōn tyē′)

cre·dal (krēd′l) *adj.* of a creed; creedal

cre·dence (krēd′ns) *n.* [ME. < OFr. < ML. *credentia* < L. *credens,* prp. of *credere:* see CREED] 1. belief, esp. in the reports or testimony of another *[to give credence* to rumors*]* 2. credentials: now only in the phrase, **letter of credence** 3. *Eccles.* a small table at the side of the communion table, on which the bread and wine are placed before consecration —*SYN.* see BELIEF

cre·den·da (kri den′də) *n.pl., sing.* **-den′dum** (-dəm) [L., pl. of gerundive of *credere:* see CREED] doctrines to be believed; matters of faith

cre·dent (krēd′nt) *adj.* 1. [Rare] giving credence; believing 2. [Obs.] credible

cre·den·tial (kri den′shəl, -chəl) *adj.* [ME. *credencial* < ML. *credentialis:* see CREDENCE] [Rare] entitling to credit, confidence, etc.; accrediting —*n.* 1. that which entitles to credit, confidence, etc. 2. [*usually pl.*] a letter or certificate given to a person to show that he has a right to confidence or to the exercise of a certain position or authority

cre·den·za (kri den′zə) *n.* [It., buffet holding foods to be tasted before serving, orig., faith, confidence (in *fare la credenza,* to make confidence, to taste) < ML. *credentia,* CREDENCE] a type of buffet, or sideboard

cred·i·ble (kred′ə b'l) *adj.* [ME. < L. *credibilis < credere:* see CREED] that can be believed; believable; reliable —*SYN.* see PLAUSIBLE —**cred′i·bil′i·ty, cred′i·ble·ness** *n.* — **cred′i·bly** *adv.*

cred·it (kred′it) *n.* [Fr. *crédit* < It. *credito* < L. *creditus,* pp. of *credere:* see CREED] 1. belief or trust; confidence; faith 2. [Rare] the quality of being credible or trustworthy 3. *a)* the favorable estimate of a person's character; reputation; good name *b)* one's influence based on one's reputation

4. praise or approval to which one is entitled; commendation [to deserve *credit* for trying] 5. a person or thing bringing approval or honor [a *credit* to the team] 6. acknowledgment of work done or assistance given; specif., [*pl.*] a list of such acknowledgments in a motion picture, television program, book, etc. 7. *a*) the amount of money remaining in a bank account, etc. *b*) a sum of money made available by a bank, on which a specified person or firm may draw 8. *Accounting a*) the acknowledgment of payment on a debt by entry of the amount in an account *b*) the right-hand side of an account, where such amounts are entered *c*) an entry on this side *d*) the sum of such entries *e*) a sum deducted (from an amount owed) or added (as to a bank account) in making an adjustment 9. *Business a*) trust in one's integrity in money matters and one's ability to meet payments when due *b*) one's financial reputation or status *c*) the time allowed for payment ☆10. *Educ. a*) the certification of a student's successful completion of a unit or course of study *b*) a unit of work so certified —*vt.* 1. to believe in the truth, reliability, etc. of; trust 2. to give credit to or deserved commendation for 3. to give credit in a bank account, charge account, etc. 4. [Rare] to bring honor to 5. *Accounting* to enter on the credit side ☆6. *Educ.* to enter a credit or credits on the record of (a student) —*SYN.* see ASCRIBE —**credit one with** to believe that one has or is responsible for; ascribe to one —**do credit to** to bring approval or honor to —**give credit to** 1. to have confidence or trust in; believe 2. to commend —**give one credit for** 1. to commend one for 2. to believe or recognize that one has —**on credit** with the agreement that payment will be made at a future date —**to one's credit** bringing approval or honor to one

cred·it·a·ble (-ə b'l) *adj.* 1. deserving some credit or praise 2. ascribable (*to*) 3. [Now Rare] credible 4. [Obs.] having good financial credit —**cred'it·a·bil'i·ty, cred'it·a·ble·ness** *n.* —**cred'it·a·bly** *adv.*

☆**credit bureau** an agency that is a clearinghouse for information on the credit rating of individuals or firms

☆**credit card** a card establishing the privilege of the person to whom it is issued to charge bills at certain restaurants, airlines, hotels, gas stations, etc.

☆**credit line** 1. an acknowledgment of work done or assistance given, as in a newspaper or motion picture 2. *same as* LINE OF CREDIT

cred·i·tor (-ər) *n.* [ME. < creditor < L. *creditor:* see CREDIT] a person who extends credit or to whom money is owed

☆**credit rating** the rating given to an individual or business firm as a credit risk, based on past records of debt repayment, financial status, etc.

☆**credit union** a cooperative association for pooling savings of members and making loans to them at a low rate of interest

cre·do (krē′dō, krā′-) *n., pl.* **-dos** [ME. < L., I believe: see CREED] 1. *same as* CREED 2. [*usually* C-] *a*) the Apostles' Creed or the Nicene Creed, both of which begin with *credo b*) a musical setting for either of these

cre·du·li·ty (krə dōō′lə tē, -dyōō′-) *n.* [ME. & OFr. *credulite* < L. *credulitas* < *credulus:* see CREDULOUS] a tendency to believe too readily, esp. with little or no proof; lack of doubt

cred·u·lous (krej′oo ləs) *adj.* [L. *credulus* < *credere:* see CREED] 1. tending to believe too readily; easily convinced 2. marked by credulity —**cred'u·lous·ly** *adv.* —**cred'u·lous·ness** *n.*

Cree (krē) *n.* [contr. & altered < Fr. *Kristinaux* < an unknown tribal name] 1. *pl.* **Crees, Cree** a member of a tribe of Algonquian Indians who live in an area extending from the southern end of Hudson Bay to northern Alberta, Canada 2. the Central Algonquian language of this tribe

creed (krēd) *n.* [ME. *crede* < OE. *creda* < L. *credo,* lit., I believe (< *credere,* to trust, believe < IE. base *kred-dhē-,* to attribute magic power to, believe): *credo* is the first word of the Apostles' and Nicene creeds] 1. a brief statement of religious belief; confession of faith 2. a specific statement of this kind, accepted as authoritative by a church 3. a statement of belief, principles, or opinions on any subject —**the Creed** the Apostles' Creed —**creed'al** *adj.*

Creek (krēk) *n.* [so named by frontiersmen because of the many creeks in the tribal territory] 1. an American Indian of any of several tribes, mainly Muskogean, formerly living in Georgia and Alabama in a tribal league (**Creek Confederacy**) and now living in Oklahoma 2. the Muskogean language of the Creeks

creek (krēk, krik) *n.* [ME. (rare) *creke* (whence mod. pronun. *krēk*), (common) *crike* (whence pronun. *krik*) < ON. *-kriki,* a winding, hence winding inlet, akin to OFris. *kreke,* winding brook, MDu. *creke,* inlet: for IE. base see CRANK¹] ☆1. a small stream, somewhat larger than a brook 2. [Now chiefly Brit.] a narrow inlet or bay 3. [Obs.] a narrow or winding passage —☆**up the creek** [Slang] in trouble

creel (krēl) *n.* [ME. *crel* < OFr. *grail:* see GRIDDLE] 1. a wicker basket for holding fish, often worn on the back by a fisherman 2. a basketlike cage for trapping fish, shellfish, etc. 3. a frame or rack for holding the bobbins or spools in spinning or weaving

creep (krēp) *vi.* **crept, creep′ing** [ME. *crepen* < OE. *creopan,* to creep, lit., go bent down, akin to Sw. *krypa* < IE. base **ger-,* to twist, turn, whence CART, CRIPPLE] 1. to move along with the body close to the ground, as on hands and knees 2. to move slowly, stealthily, timidly, or furtively 3. to come on gradually and almost unnoticed (often with *up*) 4. to cringe; fawn 5. to grow along the ground or a wall, as some plants 6. to slip slightly out of position ☆7. to change in shape as the result of constant stress, temperature, etc.: said of materials, metals, etc. —*n.* 1. the act of creeping 2. a creeping movement 3. the gradual deformation of a material, esp. a metal or alloy, due to constant stress, high temperature, etc. ☆4. [Slang] a person regarded as very annoying, disgusting, etc. 5. *Geol.* the slow movement of loose rock and soil down a slope —*SYN.* see CRAWL¹ —**make one's flesh (or skin) creep** to give one a feeling of fear, repugnance, etc. as if insects were creeping on one's skin —**the creeps** [Colloq.] a feeling of fear, repugnance, etc.

creep·age (-ij) *n.* a gradual creeping movement

creep·er (-ər) *n.* 1. a person, animal, or thing that creeps 2. any plant whose stem puts out tendrils or rootlets by which it can creep along a surface as it grows [the Virginia *creeper*] 3. any of various small birds that creep up on trees and bushes looking for insects, larvae, etc. to eat, as the American brown creeper (*Certhia familiaris*), certain warblers, etc. 4. a device with metal hooks for dragging the bottom of a lake, pond, etc.; grapnel ☆5. [*usually pl.*] a metal plate with spikes, fastened to a shoe to prevent slipping 6. any device for carrying material to or from a machine, or from one part of a machine to another ☆7. a low frame on wheels or casters for a mechanic to lie on when working under an automobile 8. the lowest gear in a truck, as for use on steep grades: in full, **creeper gear** ☆9. [*pl.*] a baby's one-piece garment, combining pants and shirt

creeping bent grass a low-growing grass (*Agrostis palustris*) which roots along the stem: see BENT²

creeping eruption a skin eruption with intense itching, caused by the burrowing of various larvae under the skin

creep·y (krēp′ē) *adj.* **creep'i·er, creep'i·est** 1. creeping; moving slowly 2. having or causing a feeling of fear or disgust, as if insects were creeping on one's skin —**creep'i·ly** *adv.* —**creep'i·ness** *n.*

creese (krēs) *n.* [Malay *keris*] *same as* KRIS

creesh (krēsh) *n., vt.* [< OFr. *cresse, n.* < L. *crassa,* fem. of *crassus:* see CRASS] [Scot.] grease

cre·mate (krē′māt, kri māt′) *vt.* **-mat·ed, -mat·ing** [< L. *crematus,* pp. of *cremare,* to burn < IE. base **ker-,* to burn, whence L. *carbo,* coal, HEARTH] to burn up, esp. to burn (a dead body) to ashes —**cre·ma'tion** *n.* —**cre'ma·tor** *n.*

cre·ma·to·ry (krē′mə tôr'ē; *chiefly Brit.* krem′ə-) *n., pl.* **-ries** [ModL. *crematorium*] 1. a furnace for cremating dead bodies 2. a building with such a furnace in it Also **cre'ma·to'ri·um** (-ē əm), *pl.* **-ri·ums, -ri·a** (-ə) —*adj.* of or for cremation: also **cre'ma·to'ri·al**

crème (krem, krēm) *n.* [Fr.] 1. cream 2. a thick liqueur

crème de ca·ca·o (də kə kä′ō, -kā′ō; də kōk′ō) [Fr., lit., cream of cocoa] a sweet liqueur, brown or colorless, with a chocolate flavor

‡**crème de la crème** (krem′ də lä krem′) [Fr., lit., cream of the cream] the very best

crème de menthe (krem də mänt′, menth′, mint′; krēm) [Fr., lit., cream of mint] a sweet liqueur, green or colorless, flavored with mint

Cre·mo·na (kri mō′nə; *It.* kre mō′nä) commune in Lombardy, N Italy, on the Po River: pop. 74,000 —*n.* any of the famous violins formerly made in Cremona, esp. by AMATI, STRADIVARI, or GUARNERI

cre·nate (krē′nāt) *adj.* [ModL. *crenatus* < VL. *crena,* a notch, groove] having a notched or scalloped edge, as certain leaves: also **cre'nat·ed** —**cre'nate·ly** *adv.*

cre·na·tion (kri nā′shən) *n.* 1. the condition of being crenate 2. a crenate formation; specif., *a*) a crenature (sense 1) *b*) the notched appearance of a red blood cell, as when exposed to salt

cren·a·ture (kren′ə chər, krē′nə-) *n.* [CRENAT(E) + -URE] 1. a rounded projection, as on the margin of a leaf, etc. 2. a notch between such projections

cren·el (kren′'l) *n.* [OFr., dim. < VL. *crena,* a notch, groove] any of the indentations or loopholes in the top of a battlement or wall; embrasure: also **cre·nelle** (kri nel′) —*vt.* -eled or -elled, -el·ing or -el·ling to crenelate

cren·el·ate, cren·el·late (kren′'l āt′) *vt.* **-el·at·ed or -el·lat·ed, -el·at·ing or -el·lat·ing** [Fr. *créneler* (< OFr. *crenel:* see CRENEL) + -ATE¹] to furnish with battlements or crenels, or with squared notches —**cren'el·a'tion, cren'el·la'tion** *n.*

cren·u·late (kren′yoo lit, -lāt′) *adj.* [ModL. *crenulatus* < *crenula,* dim. < VL. *crena,* a notch, groove] having tiny notches or scallops, as some leaves or shells: also **cren'u·lat·ed** (-lāt′id)

cren·u·la·tion (kren′yoo lā′-

CRENELATION

shən) *n.* [see CRENULATE] **1.** a tiny notch or scallop **2.** the condition of having tiny notches or scallops

cre·o·dont (krē′ə dänt′) *n.* [< ModL. *Creodonta*, pl. < Gr. *kreas*, flesh + *odous*, tooth] any of an extinct suborder (Creodonta) of small, primitive, flesh-eating mammals with small brains

Cre·ole, cre·ole (krē′ōl) *n.* [Fr. *créole* < Sp. *criollo* < Port. *crioulo*, native to the region, born at home < *criar*, to rear, nourish < L. *creare:* see CREATE] **1.** orig., a person of European parentage born in the West Indies, Central America, tropical South America, or the Gulf States **2.** a descendant of such persons; specif., ☆a) a person descended from the original French settlers of Louisiana, esp. of the New Orleans area ☆b) a person descended from the original Spanish settlers in the Gulf States, esp. Texas ☆c) a person of mixed Creole and Negro descent ☆**3.** French as spoken by Creoles, esp. in the New Orleans area: distinguished from CAJUN ☆**4.** loosely, anyone from Louisiana —*adj.* **1.** of or characteristic of the Creoles **2.** designating or of the languages of the Creoles ☆**3.** [*usually* c-] prepared with sautéed tomatoes, green peppers, onions, etc. and spices [*creole* sauce]

cre·ol·ized language (krē′ə līzd′) [< prec.] the form of language (e.g., Gullah) that develops when speakers of mutually unintelligible languages remain in persistent and long-lasting contact with each other, with one of the contributing languages typically dominant

Cre·on (krē′än) [Gr. *Kreōn*] *Gr. Legend* the King of Thebes who had his niece Antigone entombed alive because she defied him: see ANTIGONE

cre·o·sol (krē′ə sōl′, -sôl′) *n.* [CREOS(OTE) + -OL] a colorless, pungent, oily liquid, $CH_3OC_6H_3(CH_3)OH$, obtained from beechwood tar and the resin guaiacum: it is used as an antiseptic

cre·o·sote (krē′ə sōt′) *n.* [< Gr. *kreas* (gen. *kreōs*), flesh + *sōzein*, to save, preserve] a transparent, oily liquid with a pungent odor, obtained by the distillation of wood tar or coal tar: it is used as an antiseptic and as a preservative for wood —*vt.* -sot′ed, -sot′ing to treat (wood, etc.) with creosote

☆**creosote bush** an evergreen shrub (*Larrea divaricata*) of a family (Zygophyllaceae), with a pungent odor like that of creosote, found in N Mexico and the SW U.S.

crepe, crêpe (krāp; *for 3, also* krep) *n.* [Fr. *crêpe* < L. *crispa:* see CRISP] **1.** a thin, crinkled cloth of silk, rayon, cotton, wool, etc.; crape **2.** *same as* a) CRAPE (sense 2) b) CREPE PAPER c) CREPE RUBBER **3.** a very thin pancake, generally served rolled up or folded with a filling: usually **crêpe**

crepe de Chine (krāp′ də shēn′) [Fr., lit., crepe of China] a soft, rather thin crepe, usually of silk, used for women's blouses, lingerie, etc.

crepe paper thin paper crinkled like crepe

crepe rubber soft rubber in sheets with a wrinkled surface, used for shoe soles

crêpes su·zette (krāp′ soo zet′; *Fr.* krep′) [Fr. < *crêpe*, pancake, crepe (see CREPE) + *Suzette*, dim. of *Suzanne*] crêpes rolled or folded in a hot, orange-flavored sauce and usually served in flaming brandy

crep·i·tate (krep′ə tāt′) *vi.* -tat′ed, -tat′ing [< pp. of L. *crepitare*, freq. of *crepare:* see CRAVEN] to make slight, sharp, repeated crackling sounds; crackle —**crep′i·tant** *adj.* —**crep′i·ta′tion** *n.*

crept (krept) *pt. & pp. of* CREEP

cre·pus·cu·lar (kri pus′kyoo lər) *adj.* [see ff.] **1.** of or like twilight; dim **2.** active at twilight or just before sunrise [*crepuscular* insects]

cre·pus·cule (-kyool) *n.* [Fr. *crépuscule* < L. *crepusculum*, dim. < *creper*, dark] twilight; dusk: also **cre·pus′cle** (-′l)

cre·scen·do (krə shen′dō) *adj., adv.* [It., gerundive of *crescere:* see ff.] *Music* gradually increasing in loudness or intensity: indicated by the sign $<$ —*n., pl.* -dos *Music* **1.** a gradual increase in loudness or intensity **2.** a passage played crescendo —*vi.* -doed, -do·ing to increase gradually in loudness or intensity

cres·cent (kres′nt) *n.* [altered (after L.) < ME. *cressaunt* < OFr. *creissant*, prp. of *creistre*, to increase < L. *crescere*, to come forth, grow; akin to *creare:* see CREATE] **1.** the moon in its first or last quarter, when it appears to have one concave edge and one convex edge **2.** a figure of or like the moon in either of these phases **3.** anything shaped more or less like this, as a curved bun or roll **4.** [*also* C-] [< the Turkish crescent emblem] Turkish or Moslem power —*adj.* **1.** [Poet.] increasing; growing **2.** shaped like the moon in its first or last quarter —**cres·cen′tic** (krə sen′tik) *adj.*

cres·cive (-iv) *adj.* [< L. *crescere* (see prec.) + -IVE] [Rare] growing; increasing

cre·sol (krē′sōl, -sôl) *n.* [< CREOSOTE + -OL] any of three isomeric, colorless, oily liquids or solids with the formula $CH_3C_6H_4OH$, prepared by the fractional distillation of coal tar and used in the preparation of disinfectants, fumigating compounds, and dyestuffs

cress (kres) *n.* [ME. *cresse* < OE. *cressa*, akin to G. *kresse*, cress, lit. ? creeper < ? IE. base *gres-*, whence OHG. *kresan*, to creep] any of various plants of the mustard family, as water cress, the pungent leaves of which are used in salads and as garnishes

cres·set (kres′it) *n.* [ME. < OFr. *craisset* < *craisse:* see GREASE] a metal container for burning oil, wood, etc.,

fastened as to a pole or wall and used as a torch or lantern

Cres·si·da (kres′i də) *Medieval Legend* a Trojan woman who was unfaithful to her lover, Troilus

Cres·sy (kres′ē) *Eng. name for* CRÉCY

crest (krest) *n.* [ME. & OFr. *creste* < L. *crista*, prob. < IE. base *(s)kreis-*, to shake, whence MIr. *cressaim*, I shake, ON. *hrista*, to shake] **1.** any process or growth on the head of an animal, as a comb or feathered tuft on certain birds **2.** a plume or emblem formerly worn on a helmet **3.** a helmet or its apex **4.** a heraldic device placed above the shield in a coat of arms, or used separately on seals, silverware, note paper, etc. **5.** the top of anything, or the line or surface along the top; summit; ridge [the *crest* of a wave, a mountain *crest*] **6.** the highest point, level, degree, etc. **7.** a) the ridge of the neck of a horse, lion, etc. b) the mane growing on this **8.** *same as* CRESTING **9.** a projecting ridge, as along a bone —*vt.* **1.** to provide or decorate with a crest **2.** to lie at the top of; crown **3.** to reach the crest of —*vi.* **1.** to form a crest, as a wave **2.** to reach its highest level [the flooding river *crested* at 30 feet]

crest·ed (kres′tid) *adj.* having a crest

☆**crested flycatcher** any of various flycatchers (esp. genus *Myiarchus*) with a prominent crest

crest·fall·en (krest′fôl′ən) *adj.* **1.** with drooping crest or bowed head **2.** dejected, disheartened, or humbled

crest·ing (kres′tiŋ) *n.* an ornamental ridging on a wall, roof, etc.

cre·syl·ic (kri sil′ik) *adj.* [CRES(OL) + -YL + -IC] of or from cresol or creosote

cre·ta·ceous (kri tā′shəs) *adj.* [L. *cretaceus* < *creta:* see CRAYON] **1.** containing, composed of, or having the nature of, chalk **2.** [C-] designating or of the third and latest geological period of the Mesozoic Era: it is marked by the dying out of toothed birds, ammonites, and dinosaurs, the development of early mammals and flowering plants, and the deposit of chalk beds —**the Cretaceous** the Cretaceous Period or its rocks: see GEOLOGY, chart

Crete (krēt) **1.** Greek island in the E Mediterranean: 3,218 sq. mi.; pop. 483,000; cap. Canea: Gr. name, KRETE **2.** Sea of, S section of the Aegean Sea, between Crete and the Cyclades — **Cre·tan** (krēt′′n) *adj., n.*

CRETE

cre·tin (krēt′′n) *n.* [Fr. *crétin*, dial. form of *chrétien*; lit., Christian, hence human being (in contrast to brutes) < L. *Christianus* (see CHRISTIAN): sense development as in SILLY] a person suffering from cretinism —**cre′tin·ous** *adj.*

cre·tin·ism (-iz′m) *n.* [Fr. *crétinisme:* see prec.] a congenital deficiency of thyroid secretion with resulting deformity and idiocy

cre·tonne (krē′tän, kri tän′) *n.* [Fr. < *Creton*, village in Normandy, noted for its cloth since the 16th cent.] a heavy, unglazed, printed cotton or linen cloth, used for curtains, slipcovers, etc.

Cre·ü·sa (krē oo′sə) *Gr. & Rom. Myth.* **1.** the bride of Jason, killed by the sorcery of the jealous Medea **2.** the wife of Aeneas and daughter of Priam, lost in the flight from captured Troy

cre·val·le (krə val′ē) *n.* [altered < CAVALLA] a powerful, voracious game fish (*Caranx hippos*) with strong-smelling, oily flesh

cre·vasse (kri vas′) *n.* [Fr. < OFr. *crevace*, CREVICE] **1.** a deep crack or fissure, esp. in a glacier ☆**2.** a break in the levee of a river, dike, etc. —*vt.* -vassed′, -vas′sing to make a crevasse or crevasses in

Crève·coeur (krev kœr′; *Fr.* krev kër′), **Mi·chel Guillaume Jean de** (mē shel′ gē yōm′ zhän də) (pseud. *J. Hector St. John*) 1735–1813; Fr. essayist & agriculturist in America (1754–80; 1783–90)

crev·ice (krev′is) *n.* [ME. & OFr. *crevace* < VL. *crepacia, a crack < L. *crepare:* see CRAVEN] a narrow opening caused by a crack or split; fissure; cleft; chink —**crev′iced** *adj.*

crew[1] (kroo) *n.* [ME. & OFr. *creue*, increase, growth < pp. of *creistre*, to grow < L. *crescere* (see CRESCENT)] **1.** a group of people associating or classed together; company, set, gang, etc. **2.** a group of people working together, usually under the direction of a foreman or leader [a road *crew*, gun *crew*] **3.** all of a ship's personnel, usually excepting the officers **4.** all the men manning an aircraft; air crew: see also GROUND CREW **5.** a) a rowing team for a racing shell, usually of eight men b) the sport of rowing in races **6.** [Archaic] an organized band of armed men —*vt., vi.* to serve (on) as a member of a crew —**crew′man** (-mən), *pl.* -men

crew[2] (kroo) *alt. pt. of* CROW[2] (sense 1)

☆**crew cut** a style of man's haircut in which the hair is cropped close to the head

crew·el (kroo′əl) *n.* [LME. *crule* < ?] a loosely twisted, fine worsted yarn used in fancywork and embroidery —**crew′el·work′** *n.*

crew neck a round neckline, as on a sweater, fitting close around the base of the neck

crib (krib) *n.* [ME. & OE., ox stall, couch, akin to G. *krippe*, basic sense "what is woven or plaited, basket" (as CRÈCHE): senses of "steal," etc. < thieves' slang < orig. sense "to put in a basket"; *n.* 4 from Biblical application of sense 1] **1.** a rack, trough, or box for fodder; manger **2.** a stall for cattle, oxen, etc. **3.** a small, crude house or room **4.** a small bed with high sides, for a baby **5.** a framework of wooden or metal bars for support or strengthening, as in a mine **6.** a framework or enclosure as for storing grain ☆**7.** a structure anchored under water, serving as a pier, a water intake, etc. **8.** [Colloq.] *a*) a petty theft *b*) a plagiarism *c*) a translation of a foreign writing, notes, or other aids used, often dishonestly, in doing school work **9.** *Cribbage* the cards discarded by all the players and counted by the dealer as a second hand for points, but not played —*vt.* **cribbed, crib′bing 1.** to shut up in or as in a crib; confine **2.** to furnish with a crib or cribs **3.** [Colloq.] *a*) to steal *b*) to plagiarize —*vi.* **1.** to have the habit of crib biting **2.** [Colloq.] to do school work dishonestly, as by using a crib —**crib′ber** *n.*

crib·bage (krib′ij) *n.* [< prec. + -AGE] a card game for two, three, or four players, in which the object is to form various combinations that count for points: the score is kept on a small pegboard

crib·bing (-iŋ) *n.* **1.** the action of one that cribs **2.** something cribbed **3.** a framework of timber lining a shaft in a mine **4.** *same as* CRIB BITING

crib biting a habit that some horses have of biting the feeding trough and at the same time swallowing air — **crib′-bite′** *vi.* **-bit′, -bit′ten** or **-bit′, -bit′ing**

crib·ri·form (krib′rə fôrm′) *adj.* [< L. *cribrum*, sieve + -FORM] perforated like a sieve

crib·work (krib′wurk′) *n.* a supporting framework of beams, logs, etc. built in layers, each layer having its units at right angles to those of the layer below

cri·ce·tid (krī set′id, -set′-) *n.* [< ModL. *cricetidae*, name of the family < *cricetus*, type genus < Slav., as in Russ. *krisa*, rat, Czech *křeček*, hamster] any of a family (Cricetidae) of rodents, including the native American rats and mice

crick[1] (krik) *n.* [LME. *crykke* < ? ON., as in OIce. *kriki*, bend, Norw. *krykla*, twisted tree (basic sense: "twist"), akin to CREEK, CRUTCH] a painful muscle spasm or cramp in the neck, back, etc. —*vt.* to cause a crick in

crick[2] (krik) *n.* [Dial.] ☆*same as* CREEK (sense 1)

Crick (krik), **Francis H(arry) C(ompton)** 1916– ; Eng. scientist: helped determine the structure of DNA

crick·et[1] (krik′it) *n.* [ME. *criket* < OFr. *criquet* < *criquer*, to creak, of echoic origin] **1.** any of a large family (Gryllidae) of generally dark-colored, leaping insects related to the locusts and grasshoppers but usually having long antennae: the males produce a characteristic chirping noise by rubbing parts of the forewings together **2.** a small metal toy or signaling device that makes a clicking sound when pressed

crick·et[2] (krik′it) *n.* [OFr. *criquet*, a stake or bat in a ball game; prob. dim. of MDu. *cricke*, a stick, akin to CRUTCH] **1.** an outdoor game played by two teams of eleven men each, in which a ball, bats, and wickets are used; popular mainly in England **2.** [Colloq.] fair play; sportsmanship —*vi.* to play cricket —**crick′et·er** *n.*

CRICKET
(to 1 inch)

crick·et[3] (krik′it) *n.* [< ?] a wooden footstool

cri·coid (krī′koid) *adj.* [Gr. *krikoeidēs*, ring-shaped < *krikos*, ring + -*eidēs*, -OID] designating or of the ring-shaped cartilage forming the lower part of the larynx

‡**cri de coeur** (krē da kër′) [Fr., lit., cry from the heart] an impassioned protest, complaint, etc.

cried (krīd) *pt.* and *pp.* of CRY

cri·er (krī′ər) *n.* **1.** a person who cries **2.** *a*) an official who shouts out announcements, as in a court *b*) *same as* TOWN CRIER **3.** a person who shouts out announcements about his wares; huckster

Crile (krīl), **George Washington** 1864–1943; U.S. surgeon

crim. criminal

crim. con. criminal conversation

crime (krīm) *n.* [ME. & OFr. < L. *crimen*, verdict, object of reproach, offense, prob. < IE. base *(s)krei* (whence SCREAM), extension of *ker-*, echoic for hoarse, rough sounds (hence, ? orig., cry for help)] **1.** an act committed in violation of a law prohibiting it, or omitted in violation of a law ordering it; specif., any felony or misdemeanor except a petty violation of a local ordinance: crimes are variously punishable by death, imprisonment, or the imposition of certain fines or restrictions **2.** an offense against morality; sin **3.** criminal acts, collectively **4.** [Colloq.] something regrettable or deplorable; shame [it's a *crime* you didn't finish school]

Cri·me·a (krī mē′ə, krə-) peninsula in SW U.S.S.R., extending into the Black Sea, west of the Sea of Azov: c. 10,000 sq. mi.; pop. 1,202,000 —**Cri·me′an** *adj.*

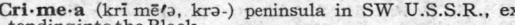

Crimean War a war (1854–1856) over the domination of SE Europe, in which England, France, Turkey, and Sardinia defeated Russia

CRIMEA

crim·i·nal (krim′ə n′l) *adj.* [ME. < OFr. *criminel* < L. *criminalis* < *crimen*: see CRIME] **1.** having the nature of crime; being a crime **2.** *a*) involving or relating to crime *b*) dealing with law cases involving crime **3.** guilty of crime **4.** [Colloq.] regrettable or deplorable —*n.* a person guilty of, or legally convicted of, a crime —**crim′i·nal·ly** *adv.*

criminal conversation *see* CONVERSATION (sense 2)

crim·i·nal·i·ty (krim′ə nal′ə tē) *n.* **1.** the quality, state, or fact of being criminal **2.** *pl.* **-ties** a criminal action

criminal law that area of law which deals in any way with crimes and their punishments

criminal lawyer a lawyer whose practice is largely devoted to the defense of those accused of crime

crim·i·nate (krim′ə nāt′) *vt.* **-nat′ed, -nat′ing** [< L. *criminatus*, pp. of *criminari* < *crimen*: see CRIME] **1.** to accuse of a crime or crimes **2.** to give proof of the guilt of; incriminate **3.** to condemn; censure —**crim′i·na′tion** *n.* —**crim′i·na′tive, crim′i·na·to′ry** (-nə tôr′ē) *adj.* —**crim′i·na′tor** *n.*

crim·i·nol·o·gy (krim′ə näl′ə jē) *n.* [< L. *crimen* (gen. *criminis*): see CRIME & -LOGY] the scientific study and investigation of crime and criminals —**crim′i·no·log′i·cal** (-nə läj′i k′l) *adj.* —**crim′i·no·log′i·cal·ly** *adv.* —**crim′i·nol′o·gist** *n.*

crim·mer (krim′ər) *n. same as* KRIMMER

crimp[1] (krimp) *vt.* [ME. *crimpen* < OE. *(ge)crympan*, to curl & MDu. *crimpen*, to draw together, wrinkle, both akin to CRAMP[1]] **1.** to press into narrow, regular folds; pleat or corrugate **2.** to make (hair, etc.) wavy or curly **3.** to gash (the flesh of a fish, etc.) so as to make the muscles contract and stay firm in cooking **4.** to mold or bend (leather for shoe uppers, etc.) into shape **5.** to pinch together or fold the edge of (one part) tightly over another ☆**6.** [Colloq.] to obstruct or hamper —*n.* **1.** the act of crimping **2.** a crimped pleat, fold, or part ☆**3.** [*usually pl.*] crimped hair ☆**4.** wavy condition; esp., the natural waviness of wool fiber —☆**put a crimp in** [Colloq.] to obstruct; hinder —**crimp′er** *n.*

crimp[2] (krimp) *n.* [< prec., prob. via 17th-c. game of cards] a person who gets men by force or trickery to serve as sailors or soldiers —*vt.* to decoy or force (men) into service as sailors or soldiers

crim·ple (krim′p′l) *vt., vi.* **-pled, -pling** [ME. *crimplen*, freq. of *crimpen*, CRIMP[1]] to wrinkle, crinkle, or crumple

crimp·y (krim′pē) *adj.* **crimp′i·er, crimp′i·est** [< CRIMP[1]] having small folds or waves; curly; wavy; frizzly [*crimpy* hair] —**crimp′i·ness** *n.*

crim·son (krim′z'n) *n.* [ME. *cremesin* < ML. *cremesinum*, ult. < Ar. *qirmiz*: see CARMINE] **1.** deep red **2.** deep-red coloring matter —*adj.* **1.** deep-red **2.** bloody —*vt., vi.* to make or become crimson

crimson clover an annual clover (*Trifolium incarnatum*) of the legume family, with elongated heads of deep red flowers, often grown in the southern U.S. as a cover or green manure crop

cringe (krinj) *vi.* **cringed, cring′ing** [ME. *crengen* (with nasalized vowel as in HINGE), caus. < OE. *cringan*, to fall (in battle): for IE. base see CRANK[1]] **1.** to draw back, bend, crouch, etc., as when afraid; shrink from something dangerous or painful; cower **2.** to act in a timid, servile manner; fawn —*n.* the act of cringing —**cring′er** *n.*

crin·gle (kriŋ′g'l) *n.* [ME. < ON. *kringla*, circle, or MDu. *kringel*, ring, both ult. < IE. base *ger-*: see CRANK[1]] a small ring or loop of rope or metal on the edge of a sail, through which a rope may be run for fastening the sail

cri·nite (krī′nīt) *adj.* [L. *crinitus*, pp. of *crinire*, to provide with hair < *crinis*, hair, akin to L. *crista* (see CREST)] **1.** hairy **2.** *Bot.* having hairy tufts

crin·kle (kriŋ′k'l) *vi., vt.* **-kled, -kling** [ME. *crenklen*, freq. < OE. *crincan*, var. of *cringan* (see CRINGE)] **1.** to be or cause to be full of wrinkles, twists, or ripples **2.** to rustle, as paper when crushed —*n.* **1.** a wrinkle, twist, or ripple **2.** a rustling sound —**crin′kly** *adj.* **-kli·er, -kli·est**

☆**crin·kle·root** (-rōōt′, -root′) *n.* a plant (*Dentaria diphylla*) of the mustard family, with small, white or lilac-colored flowers and a white, tuberous, pungent rootstock

crin·kum-cran·kum (kriŋ′kəm kraŋ′kəm) *n.* [redupl. of CRANK[1]] [Archaic] anything full of twists and turns

---

cri·noid (krī′noid, krin′oid) *adj.* [Gr. *krinoeidēs*, lilylike < *krinon*, lily + *eidēs*, -OID] 1. lily-shaped 2. designating or of a class (Crinoidea) of marine animals, some of which are flowerlike in form and are anchored by a stalk opposite the mouth, others of which are free-swimming —*n.* an animal of this class

crin·o·line (krin′′l in) *n.* [Fr. < It. *crinolino* < *crino*, horsehair (< L. *crinis:* see CRINITE) + *lino*, linen < L. *linum* (see LINE²)] 1. a coarse, stiff, heavily sized cloth used as a lining for stiffening garments: orig. made of horsehair and linen 2. a petticoat of this cloth, worn under a skirt to make it puff out 3. *same as* HOOP SKIRT

cri·num (krī′nəm) *n.* [ModL. < Gr. *krinon*, lily] any of a large genus (*Crinum*) of tropical bulbous plants of the amaryllis family, with thick, straplike leaves and large, tubular flowers of white, pink, or red

‡cri·o·llo (krē ð′yð) *n.* [Sp.: see CREOLE] 1. a person of Spanish or partly Spanish descent born in Latin America: see also CREOLE 2. any of various domestic animals bred in Latin America —*adj.* designating or of a criollo or criollos —**cri·o′lla** (-yä) *n.fem., adj.*

crip·ple (krip′′l) *n.* [ME. *cripel* < OE. *crypel* (akin to G. *krüppel*) < base of *creopan:* see CREEP] 1. a person or animal that is lame or otherwise disabled in a way that prevents normal motion of the limbs or body ☆2. [Dial.] thicketed, swampy or low, wet land —*vt.* -**pled**, -**pling** 1. to make a cripple of; lame 2. to make unable or unfit to act, function effectively, etc.; disable —*SYN.* see MAIM —**crip′pler** *n.*

Cri·sey·de (kri sā′də) Cressida: so spelled by Chaucer

cri·sis (krī′sis) *n., pl.* -**ses** (-sēz) [L. < Gr. *krisis* < *krinein*, to separate < IE. *(s)*krei*-, to sift, separate < base *(s)*ker*-, to cut, whence L. *cernere*, to separate, G. *rein*, pure] 1. *a*) the turning point in the course of a disease, when it becomes clear whether the patient will recover or die *b*) an intensely painful attack of a disease; paroxysm 2. a turning point in the course of anything; decisive or crucial time, stage, or event 3. a time of great danger or trouble, whose outcome decides whether possible bad consequences will follow [an economic *crisis*] —*SYN.* see EMERGENCY

crisp (krisp) *adj.* [ME. & OE. < L. *crispus*, curly, waving < IE. base *(s)*kreisp*-, to shake: cf. CREST] 1. stiff and brittle; easily broken, snapped, or crumbled [*crisp* bacon, pastry, etc.] 2. fresh and firm [*crisp* celery] 3. fresh and tidy [a *crisp* uniform] 4. sharp and clear [a *crisp* analysis] 5. lively; animated [*crisp* dialogue] 6. fresh and invigorating; bracing [*crisp* air] 7. closely curled and wiry [*crisp* hair] 8. rippled; wavy; wrinkled —*n.* something crisp or stiff and brittle —*vt., vi.* to make or become crisp —*SYN.* see FRAGILE —**crisp′ly** *adv.* —**crisp′ness** *n.*

cris·pate (kris′pāt) *adj.* [L. *crispatus*, pp. of *crispare:* see prec.] crisped; curled: also **cris′pat·ed**

cris·pa·tion (kris pā′shən) *n.* [< L. *crispare* (see CRISP) + -ATION] 1. a curling or being curled 2. a slight, involuntary contraction of the muscles or skin

crisp·er (kris′pər) *n.* one that makes or keeps things crisp, as a vegetable compartment in a refrigerator

Cri·spi (krē′spē), **Fran·ces·co** (frän ches′kð) 1819–1901; It. statesman; prime minister (1887–91; 1893–96)

Cris·pin (kris′pin) [L. *Crispinus* < *crispus*, curled (see CRISP), hence, lit., curly] 1. a masculine name 2. Saint, 3d cent. A.D.; Roman Christian martyr; patron saint of shoemakers: his day is Oct. 25

crisp·y (kris′pē) *adj.* **crisp′i·er, crisp′i·est** *same as* CRISP —**crisp′i·ness** *n.*

criss·cross (kris′krôs′) *n.* [ME. *Christcros*, Christ's cross, the cross at the head of an alphabet, for the symbol *X* (Gr. χ), abbrev. of Christ (*Christos*)] 1. a mark made of two crossed lines (X), often used as a signature by people who cannot write their names 2. a pattern made of crossed lines 3. a being confused or at cross-purposes —*adj.* marked with or moving in crossing lines —*vt.* 1. to mark or cover with crossing lines 2. to move to and fro across —*vi.* to move crosswise —*adv.* 1. crosswise 2. awry

cris·sum (kris′əm) *n., pl.* -**sa** (-ə) [ModL. < L. *crissare*, to move the haunches] 1. the area under the tail of a bird, around the cloacal opening 2. the feathers covering this area —**cris′sal** *adj.*

cris·ta (kris′tə) *n., pl.* -**tae** (-tē) [L., a crest, comb: see CREST] *Anat., Zool.* any of various crestlike structures, as a saclike projection extending into the interior from the inner membrane of mitochondria

cris·tate (kris′tāt) *adj.* [L. *cristatus* < *crista:* see CREST] crested, as some birds: also **cris′tat·ed**

Cris·to·bal (kris tō′bəl) seaport in the Canal Zone, at the Caribbean entrance to the canal: a part of the city of Colón, Panama: pop. 800

crit. 1. critical 2. criticism 3. criticized

cri·ter·i·on (krī tir′ē ən) *n., pl.* -**i·a** (-ē ə), -**i·ons** [< Gr. *kritērion*, means of judging < *kritēs*, judge: see ff.] a standard, rule, or test by which something can be judged; measure of value —*SYN.* see STANDARD

crit·ic (krit′ik) *n.* [L. *criticus* < Gr. *kritikos*, a critic, orig., critical, able to discern, akin to *krinein*, to discern, separate: see CRISIS] 1. *a*) a person who forms and expresses judgments of people or things according to certain standards or values *b*) such a person, whose profession is to write such judgments of books, music, paintings, sculpture, plays, motion pictures, television, etc., as for a newspaper or mag-

azine 2. a person who indulges in faultfinding and censure

crit·i·cal (krit′i k′l) *adj.* 1. tending to find fault; censorious 2. characterized by careful analysis and judgment [a sound *critical* estimate of the problem] 3. of critics or criticism 4. of or forming a crisis or turning point; decisive 5. dangerous or risky; causing anxiety [a *critical* situation in international relations] 6. of the crisis of a disease 7. designating or of important products or raw materials subject to increased production and restricted distribution under strict control, as in wartime 8. *a*) designating or of a point at which a change in character, property, or condition is effected *b*) designating or of the point at which a nuclear chain reaction becomes self-sustaining —**crit′i·cal·ly** *adv.* —**crit′i·cal′i·ty** (-kal′ə tē), **crit′i·cal·ness** *n.* *SYN.*—**critical**, in its strictest use, implies an attempt at objective judging so as to determine both merits and faults [a *critical* review], but it often and **hypercritical**, always) connotes emphasis on the faults or shortcomings; **faultfinding** implies a habitual or unreasonable emphasis on faults or defects; **captious** suggests a characteristic tendency to find fault with, or argue about, even the pettiest details [a *captious* critic]; **caviling** stresses the raising of quibbling objections on the most trivial points [a *caviling* gramarian]; **carping** suggests peevishness, perversity, or censoriousness in seeking out faults See also ACUTE

critical angle 1. *Optics* the smallest possible angle of incidence at which light rays are totally reflected 2. *Aeron.* that angle of attack at which the flow of air around an airfoil suddenly changes, with an abrupt reduction in lift and an increase of drag: see ANGLE OF ATTACK

critical constants the critical temperature, pressure, density, and volume of a substance

critical mass the minimum amount of fissionable material that can sustain a nuclear chain reaction under a given set of conditions

critical point the stage in temperature and pressure at which the liquid and vapor phases of a substance are in equilibrium with each other

critical pressure the minimum pressure necessary to liquefy a gas at its critical temperature

critical state that condition of a substance at its critical point when the liquid state and the vapor state have equal density

critical temperature that temperature above which a given gas cannot be liquefied, regardless of the pressure applied

crit·ic·as·ter (krit′i kas′tər) *n.* [CRITIC + -ASTER²] an incompetent, inferior critic

crit·i·cise (krit′ə sīz′) *vi., vt.* -**cised′**, -**cis′ing** *Brit. sp. of* CRITICIZE

crit·i·cism (krit′ə siz′m) *n.* 1. the act of making judgments; analysis of qualities and evaluation of comparative worth; esp., the critical consideration and judgment of literary or artistic work 2. a comment, review, article, etc. expressing such analysis and judgment 3. the act of finding fault; censuring; disapproval 4. the art, principles, or methods of a critic or critics 5. scientific investigation of literary documents to discover their origin, history, or original form: often called **textual criticism**

crit·i·cize (krit′ə sīz′) *vi., vt.* -**cized′**, -**ciz′ing** 1. to analyze and judge as a critic 2. to judge disapprovingly; find fault (with); censure —**crit′i·ciz′a·ble** *adj.* —**crit′i·ciz′er** *n.* *SYN.*—**criticize**, in this comparison, is the general term for finding fault with or disapproving of a person or thing; **reprehend** suggests sharp or severe disapproval, generally of faults, errors, etc. rather than of persons; **blame** stresses the fixing of responsibility for an error, fault, etc.; **censure** implies the expression of severe criticism or disapproval by a person in authority or in a position to pass judgment; **condemn** and **denounce** both imply an emphatic pronouncement of blame or guilt, **condemn** suggesting the rendering of a judicial decision, and **denounce**, public accusation against persons or their acts —*ANT.* praise

cri·tique (kri tēk′) *n.* [Fr. < Gr. *kritikē* (*technē*), critical (art) < *kritikos:* see CRITIC] 1. a critical analysis or evaluation of a subject, situation, literary work, etc. 2. the act or art of criticizing; criticism

crit·ter, crit·tur (krit′ər) *n.* [Dial.] *same as* CREATURE

croak (krōk) *vi.* [ME. *crouken* < OE. *cracian, inferred < *cræcettan*, to make sounds like a raven < IE. base *ger- (whence CRAKE, CRANE, CROW²), of echoic origin] 1. to make a deep, hoarse sound, as that of a frog or raven 2. to speak in deep, hoarse tones 3. to talk dismally; foretell evil or misfortune; grumble 4. [Slang] to die —*vt.* 1. to utter in deep, hoarse tones 2. [Slang] to kill —*n.* a croaking sound —**croak′y** (-ē) *adj.* **croak′i·er, croak′i·est**

croak·er (-ər) *n.* 1. an animal that croaks 2. any of various fishes (family Sciaenidae) that make croaking or grunting sounds 3. a person who talks dismally or foretells evil 4. [Slang] a doctor

Cro·at (krō′at, -ət; krōt) *n.* 1. a native or inhabitant of Croatia 2. *same as* CROATIAN (*n.* 2) —*adj. same as* CROATIAN

Cro·a·tia (krō ā′shə) republic of Yugoslavia, in the NW part: formerly, until 1918, a kingdom: 21,830 sq. mi.; pop. 4,160,000; cap. Zagreb

Cro·a·tian (krō ā′shən) *adj.* of Croatia, its people, language, or culture —*n.* 1. a Croat 2. the South Slavic language of the Croats: see SERBO-CROATIAN

Cro·ce (krō′che; *E.* krō′chē), **Be·ne·det·to** (be′ne det′tō) 1866–1952; It. philosopher and critic

cro·chet (krō shā′) *n.* [Fr., small hook: see CROTCHET] a kind of needlework in which loops of a thread or yarn are interwoven by means of a single hooked needle (**crochet hook**) —*vi.*, *vt.* **-cheted′** (-shād′), **-chet′ing** to do crochet or make by crochet —**cro·chet′er** *n.*

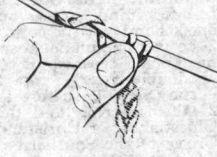

CROCHETING

cro·cid·o·lite (krə sid′′l it′) *n.* [< Gr. *krokis* (gen. *krokidos*), var. of *krokys*, nap on woolen cloth + -LITE] a fibrous, blue or bluish-green silicate of iron and sodium, one of the various forms of asbestos

crock[1] (kräk) *n.* [ME. *crokke* < OE. *crocca*, akin to G. *krug*, prob. < IE. base *ger-*, to turn, twist, whence CRIB] **1.** an earthenware pot or jar **2.** a broken piece of earthenware **3.** [clip of *a crock of "slops"* (a euphemism)] [Slang] something said or done that is absurd, insincere, exaggerated, etc.; nonsense

crock[2] (kräk) *n.* [Brit. dial. < ?] **1.** [Dial.] soot; smut **2.** coloring matter rubbed off from dyed fabric —*vt.* [Dial.] to soil with soot or smut —*vi.* to give off coloring matter: said of dyed fabric

crock[3] (kräk) *n.* [< ON. *kraki*, a weak, crippled person, orig., a bent object: for IE. base see CROOK] **1.** an old broken-down horse **2.** [Slang] anyone or anything worthless, useless, or worn-out, as from old age —*vi.*, *vt.* to make or become disabled; break down; collapse (often with *up*)

crocked (kräkt) *adj.* [pp. of *crock*, to disable, injure, prob. < or akin to CROCK[3]] ☆[Slang] drunk; intoxicated

crock·er·y (kräk′ər ē) *n.* [CROCK[1] + -ERY (sense 5)] earthenware pots, jars, dishes, etc.

crock·et (kräk′it) *n.* [ME. *croket* < ONormFr. *croquet* (OFr. *crochet*): see CROTCHET] a carved ornament, as of curved leaves or flowers, decorating the angles of roofs, gables, etc., esp. in Gothic architecture

Crock·ett (kräk′it), **David** (called *Davy Crockett*) 1786–1836; Am. frontiersman & politician

croc·o·dile (kräk′ə dīl′) *n.* [ME. *cocodril* < OFr. *cocodrille* < ML. *cocodrillus*, altered < L. *crocodilus* < Gr. *krokodilos*, lizard (hence, "lizard of the Nile," crocodile) < ? *krokē*, pebble, gravel + *drilos*, worm] **1.** any of a family (Crocodylidae) of large, flesh-eating lizard-like reptiles living in the water and on the muddy banks of tropical streams: crocodiles have a thick, horny skin composed of scales and plates, a long tail, and a long, narrow, triangular head with massive jaws and cone-shaped teeth **2.** leather made from a crocodile's hide

CROCODILE
(to 20 ft. long)

crocodile bird a small African bird (*Pluvianus aegyptius*) like the plover, which feeds on insects, often those that are parasites on the crocodile

Crocodile River *same as* LIMPOPO RIVER

crocodile tears insincere tears or a hypocritical show of grief: from an old belief that crocodiles shed tears while eating their prey

croc·o·dil·i·an (kräk′ə dil′ē ən) *adj.* **1.** of or like a crocodile **2.** a group of reptiles including the crocodile, alligator, cayman, and gavial —*n.* any reptile of this group

cro·co·ite (krō′kō īt′, krō′kə wīt′) *n.* [< Gr. *krokos*, saffron (see CROCUS) + -ITE[1]] native chromate of lead, PbCrO₄, a red or orange mineral: also **cro·co·i·site** (krō kō′ə sīt′, kräk′wə sīt′)

cro·cus (krō′kəs) *n.*, *pl.* **cro′cus·es**, **cro′ci** (-sī) [ME. < L. < Gr. *krokos*, saffron, via Sem. (as in Heb. *karkōm*, Ar. *kurkum*, Aram. *kūrkāmā*, saffron, crocus), ult. < Sans. *kuṅkuma*] **1.** any of a large genus (*Crocus*) of spring-blooming plants of the iris family, with fleshy corms, grass-like leaves, and a yellow, purple, or white flower **2.** an orange-yellow color; saffron **3.** powdered iron oxide used for polishing

Croe·sus (krē′səs) fl. 6th cent. B.C.; last king of Lydia (560–546), noted for his great wealth —*n.* a very rich man

croft (krôft) *n.* [ME. < OE., akin to MDu. *krocht*, hill, field among dunes < Gmc. *krufta*, lit., that which bends < IE. base *ger-*, to turn, whence CRANK[1] [Brit.] **1.** a small enclosed field **2.** a small farm, esp. one worked by a renter —**croft′er** *n.*

crois·sant (krə sänt′; Fr. krwä sän′) *n.* [Fr., lit., CRESCENT: used in 19th c. to translate G. *hörnchen* (lit., little horn); such rolls or cakes, shaped like the emblem of Turkey, were originated in Vienna to celebrate defeat of the Turks in 1689] a rich, flaky bread roll made in the shape of a crescent

‡**croix de guerre** (krwä də ger′) [Fr., cross of war] a French military decoration for bravery in action

☆**cro·ker sack** (krō′kər) [altered < *crocus sack* < *crocus*, a

---

coarse fabric (< ?) + SACK] [South] a bag made of burlap or similar material: also **crocus sack**

Cro-Ma·gnon (krō mag′nən, -man′yən) *adj.* [after the *Cro-Magnon* cave, Dordogne department, SW France, where remains were discovered] belonging to a prehistoric, caucasoid type of man who lived on the European continent, distinguished by tallness and erect stature, and the use of stone and bone implements, principally of Aurignacian culture —*n.* a member of this group

crom·lech (kräm′lek) *n.* [W. < *crom*, bent, crooked + *llech*, flat stone] **1.** *same as* DOLMEN **2.** an ancient monument of monoliths, arranged in a circle and surrounding a mound or dolmen

Cromp·ton (krämp′tən), **Samuel** 1753–1827; Eng. inventor of the spinning mule (1779)

Crom·well (kräm′wel, -wəl; krum′-) **1. Oliver,** 1599–1658; Eng. revolutionary leader & head (Lord Protector) of the Commonwealth (1653–58) **2. Richard,** 1626–1712; Lord Protector of the Commonwealth (1658–59): son of *prec.* **3. Thomas,** Earl of Essex, 1485?–1540; Eng. statesman

crone (krōn) *n.* [ME. term of abuse: beast, hag (revived by Scott in mod. sense) < Anglo-Fr. *carogne* (see CARRION) either directly or via MDu. *kronje* in sense "old ewe"] an ugly, withered old woman; hag

Cro·nus (krō′nəs) [L. < Gr. *Kronos*] *Gr. Myth.* a Titan who overthrew his father, Uranus, to become ruler of the universe and was himself overthrown by his son Zeus: identified by the Romans with Saturn

cro·ny (krō′nē) *n.*, *pl.* **-nies** [Brit. university slang < ? Gr. *chronios*, long-continued (hence taken as "old friend") < *chronos*, time] a close companion

crook (krook) *n.* [ME. *crok* < ON. *krōkr*, var. of *krākr*, a bending, hook, bay: for IE. base see CRANK[1]] **1.** a hooked, bent, or curved thing or part; hook **2.** *a)* a shepherd's staff, with a hook at one end *b)* a bishop's staff resembling this; crosier **3.** a bending or being bent **4.** a bend or curve ☆**5.** [Colloq.] a person who steals or cheats; swindler or thief **6.** [Scot.] a pothook —*vt.* **crooked** (krookt), **crook′ing 1.** to bend or curve **2.** [Slang] to steal —*vi.* to bend or curve

crook·back (-bak′) *n.* [Rare] a hunchback —**crook′backed′** *adj.*

crook·ed (krookt; *for 2 & 3* krook′id) *adj.* **1.** having a crook or hook **2.** not straight; bent; curved; askew ☆**3.** not straightforward; dishonest; swindling —**crook′ed·ly** *adv.* —**crook′ed·ness** *n.*

Crookes (krooks), **Sir William** 1832–1919; Eng. chemist & physicist

Crookes space [after prec.] a dark region near the cathode in the discharge column of certain low-pressure gas discharge tubes

Crookes tube a highly exhausted gas-discharge tube used by Sir William Crookes in the study of low-pressure electric discharges

☆**crook·neck** (krook′nek′) *n.* any of several varieties of squash with a long, tapering, curved neck

croon (kroon) *vi.*, *vt.* [ME. & MDu. *cronen*, akin to MLowG. *kronen*, to growl < IE. base *ger-*, echoic of hoarse cry] **1.** to sing or hum in a low, gentle tone ☆**2.** to sing (popular songs) in a soft, sentimental manner —*n.* a low, gentle singing or humming —**croon′er** *n.*

crop (kräp) *n.* [ME. *croppe* < OE. *croppa*, a cluster, flower, crop of bird, hence kidney, pebble; akin to Frank. *krupa*, G. *kropf*, a swelling, crop of bird (basic sense "something swelling out or swollen") < IE. *gr-eu-b-*, curving out < base *ger-*, to bend, curve, whence CRAMP[1], CRIB] **1.** a saclike enlargement of a bird's gullet or of a part of the digestive tract of earthworms and some insects, in which food is stored before digestion; craw **2.** any agricultural product, growing or harvested, or collected, as wheat, cotton, fruit, honey, etc. **3.** the yield of any product in one season or place **4.** a group or collection appearing together [a new *crop* of students] **5.** the entire tanned hide of an animal **6.** the handle or butt of a whip **7.** a whip with a looped lash and a short stock, used in horseback riding **8.** [< the *v.*] the act or result of cropping, esp. *a)* hair cut close to the head *b)* this style of haircut *c)* an earmark on an animal, made by clipping —*vt.* **cropped, crop′ping 1.** to cut off or bite off the tops or ends of [sheep *crop* grass] **2.** to grow or harvest as a crop **3.** to cause crops to grow on or in **4.** to cut (hair, etc.) short **5.** to cut short the ears, hair, etc. of —*vi.* **1.** to bear a crop or crops **2.** to plant or grow a crop **3.** to feed by cropping grass, etc.; graze —**crop out** (or **up**) **1.** to appear unexpectedly **2.** to appear at the surface, as a rock formation at the earth's surface

crop-dust·ing (-dust′iŋ) *n.* the process of spraying growing crops with pesticides from an airplane —**crop′-dust′** *vi.*, *vt.* —**crop′-dust′er** *n.*

crop-eared (-ird′) *adj.* **1.** having the ears cropped **2.** having the hair cut short, so that the ears show

crop·per (-ər) *n.* **1.** a person or thing that crops **2.** a machine or workman that cuts or shears leather, nap from cloth, etc. **3.** a sharecropper **4.** a plant that yields a crop **5.** [< ? phr. *neck and crop*] [Colloq.] *a)* a heavy or headlong

---

fall *b*) a disastrous occurrence; failure —**come a cropper** [Colloq.] 1. to fall heavily or headlong 2. to come to ruin; fail

☆**crop·pie** (kräp′ē) *n., pl.* **-pies, -pie:** see PLURAL, II, D, 1 *same as* CRAPPIE

crop rotation a system of growing successive crops that have different food requirements, to prevent soil depletion, break up a disease cycle, etc.

cropt (kräpt) *occas. pt. & pp. of* CROP

cro·quet (krō kā′; *Brit. & Canad.* krō′kā, -ki) *n.* [Fr., dial. form of *crochet:* see CROTCHET] 1. an outdoor game in which the players use mallets to drive a wooden ball through a series of hoops placed in the ground 2. the act of croqueting —*vt., vi.* **-queted′** (-kād′), **-quet′ing** in croquet, to drive away (an opponent's ball) by hitting one's own which has been placed in contact with it

cro·quette (krō ket′) *n.* [Fr. < *croquer,* to crunch, of echoic origin] a small, rounded or cone-shaped mass of chopped meat, fish, or vegetables, coated with beaten egg and crumbs and fried in deep fat

cro·quis (krō′kē) *n., pl.* **cro′quis** (-kē, -kēz) [Fr. < *croquer,* to sketch, draw hastily, earlier to know slightly, nibble, crunch < *croc,* a crackling noise, of echoic orig.] a simple, rough sketch, esp. one made by a designer of women's fashions

crore (krôr) *n., pl.* **crores, crore** [< Hind. *karor*] in India and Pakistan, one hundred lakhs, or the sum of ten million: said specif. of rupees

cro·sier (krō′zhər) *n.* [ME. *crocer* < OFr. *crocier,* bearer of a staff < *croce,* bishop's staff < ML. *crocia* < Frank. **krukja* (akin to CRUTCH), prob. infl. by association with OFr. *croc,* hook, hooked staff (< ON. *krōkr:* see CROOK)] 1. a staff with a crook at the top carried by or before a bishop or abbot as a symbol of his pastoral function 2. *Bot.* the coiled tip of a young fern frond

cross (krôs) *n.* [< ME. *cros & crois; cros* < OE. *cros* & ON. *kross,* both < OIr. *cros* < L. *crux* (gen. *crucis*), a cross < IE. **kreuk-,* extension of base **(s)ker-,* to turn, bend, whence L. *curvus;* ME. *crois* < OFr. *crois* < L. *crux*] 1. an upright post with a bar across it near the top, on which the ancient Romans fastened convicted persons to die 2. a representation or figure of a cross, used as a badge, decoration, etc.; also, such a badge, decoration, etc. [the Distinguished Service *Cross*] 3. a monument in the form of a cross, or with a cross on it, marking a crossroad, boundary, grave, etc. 4. a staff with a cross at the top, carried before an archbishop as a sign of his authority 5. *a*) a representation of a cross, in any of various recognized forms, as a symbol of the crucifixion of Jesus, and hence of the Christian religion *b*) a crucifix 6. *a*) the act of crossing, as from one side of a stage to the other *b*) the act of crossing oneself 7. any trouble or affliction that one has to bear; also, anything that thwarts or frustrates 8. any design, mark, or object made by two lines or surfaces that intersect one another 9. such a mark (X) made as a signature, as by a person who cannot write his name 10. *a*) a crossing, or mixing, of varieties or breeds; hybridization *b*) the result of such mixing; hybrid 11. something that combines the qualities of two different things or types 12. [Slang] a dishonest action, fixed contest or match, etc. 13. *Boxing* a blow delivered over and across the opponent's lead —*vt.* 1. to make the sign of the cross over or upon 2. to place across or crosswise [cross your fingers] 3. to lie or cut across; intersect [where two streets *cross* one another] 4. to draw or put a line or lines across [*cross* your t's] 5. to pass over; go from one side to the other of; go across [to *cross* the ocean] 6. to carry or lead across 7. to extend or reach across [the bridge *crosses* a river] 8. to meet and pass (each other) 9. to bring into contact, causing electrical interference [the wires were *crossed*] 10. to go counter to; thwart; oppose 11. to interbreed (animals or plants); breed (an individual of one type) with one of another; hybridize; cross-fertilize —*vi.* 1. to lie across; intersect 2. to go or extend from one side to the other: often with *over* 3. to pass each other while moving in opposite directions 4. to interbreed; hybridize; cross-fertilize —*adj.* 1. lying or passing across or through; transverse; crossing or crossed [*cross* street, *cross* ventilation] 2. going counter; contrary; opposed [at *cross* purposes] 3. ill-tempered; cranky; irritable 4. involving reciprocation 5. of mixed variety or breed; hybrid; crossbred 6. [Archaic] causing harm; unfavorable —*adv.* crosswise —*SYN.* see IRRITABLE —**cross off** (or **out**) to cancel by or as by drawing lines across —**cross oneself** to outline the form of a cross as a Christian religious act by moving the hand from the forehead to the breast and then from one shoulder to another —**cross one's fingers** to cross one finger over another of the same hand: superstitiously believed to bring good luck or mitigate the wrong of

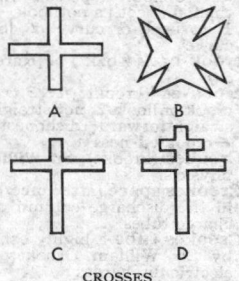

CROSSES
(A, Greek; B, Maltese;
C, Latin; D, Patriarchal)

telling a half-truth —**cross one's heart** to make the sign of the cross over one's heart as a token that one is telling the truth —**cross one's mind** to come suddenly or briefly to one's mind —**cross one's palm** 1. to make a cross on one's hand with a coin, specif. in paying a fortuneteller 2. to pay one money, esp. as a bribe —**cross one's path** to meet one —**cross up** 1. to confuse or disorder 2. to deceive, or double-cross —**take the cross** to become a crusader —**the Cross** 1. the cross on which Jesus was put to death 2. the suffering and death or Atonement of Jesus 3. Christianity or Christendom 4. *Astron. a*) the Northern Cross *b*) the Southern Cross —**cross′a·ble** *adj.* —**cross′ly** *adv.* —**cross′ness** *n.*

cross- (krôs) *a combining form meaning* cross (in various senses) [crossbow, crossbreed, crosswise]

cross·bar (krôs′bär′) *n.* a bar, line, or stripe placed crosswise, as a bar between football goal posts —*vt.* **-barred′, -bar′ring** to furnish or mark with crossbars

cross·beam (-bēm′) *n.* a beam placed across another or from one wall to another; transverse beam

cross·bed·ded (-bed′id) *adj. Geol.* having laminations oblique or transverse to the main beds of stratified rock

cross·bill (-bil′) *n.* any of a genus (*Loxia*) of finches having a bill with curving points that cross

cross·bones (-bōnz′) *n.* a representation of two thighbones placed across each other, usually under that of a skull, used as a symbol of death or danger

cross·bow (-bō′) *n.* a medieval weapon consisting of a bow set transversely on a wooden stock: the stock was grooved to direct a square-headed arrow (*quarrel*) or stone and notched to hold the bowstring, which was released by a trigger — **cross′bow′man** *n., pl.* **-men**

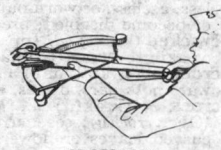

CROSSBOW

cross·bred (-bred′, -bred′) *adj.* produced by the interbreeding of different varieties or breeds —*n.* a crossbred plant or animal; hybrid; mongrel

cross·breed (-brēd′, -brēd′) *vt., vi.* **-bred** (-bred′, -bred′), **-breed′ing** *same as* HYBRIDIZE —*n. same as* HYBRID (sense 1)

cross-check (-chek′, -chek′) *vt., vi.* 1. to check or verify from various sources or points of view 2. *Hockey* to foul (an opponent) by touching or striking his body with one's stick held in both hands and lifted from the ice —*n.* the act of cross-checking

cross-coun·try (-kun′trē) *adj., adv.* 1. across open country or fields, not by roads 2. across a country [a *cross-country* flight] —*n.* a cross-country sport or sporting event; specif., cross-country footracing

cross·cur·rent (-kur′ənt) *n.* 1. a current flowing at an angle to the main current 2. a clashing or opposing opinion, influence, or tendency

cross·cut (-kut′) *adj.* 1. made or used for cutting across [a *crosscut* saw cuts wood across the grain] 2. cut across —*n.* 1. a cut across 2. something that cuts across 3. *Mining* a cutting made across a vein —*vt., vi.* **-cut′, -cut′ting** to cut across

crosse (krôs) *n.* [Fr.: see CROSIER] the long-handled, pouched racket used in playing lacrosse

cross-ex·am·ine (krôs′ig zam′in) *vt., vi.* **-ined, -in·ing** 1. to question closely 2. *Law* to question (a witness already questioned by the opposing side) in order to determine the validity of his testimony —**cross′-ex·am′i·na′tion** (-ə nā′shən) *n.* —**cross′-ex·am′in·er** *n.*

cross-eye (krôs′ī′) *n.* an abnormal condition in which the eyes are turned toward each other; convergent strabismus —**cross′-eyed′** (-īd′) *adj.*

cross-fer·tile (-furt′'l) *adj.* capable of cross-fertilization or of being cross-fertilized

cross-fer·ti·lize (-furt′'l īz′) *vt., vi.* **-lized′, -liz′ing** 1. to fertilize or be fertilized by pollen from another plant or variety of plant or from another species 2. *a*) to fertilize or be fertilized by a sperm (or male gamete) from another animal, as in the mutual exchange of sperm between individuals in a hermaphroditic species *b*) to fuse a male and female gamete derived from different varieties or species —**cross′-fer′ti·li·za′tion** (-furt′'l ə zā′shən) *n.*

cross-file (-fil′) *vi.* **-filed′, -fil′ing** ☆to file as a candidate in the primary elections of two or more parties

cross fire 1. *Mil.* fire directed at an objective from two or more positions so that the lines of fire cross 2. any complex of opposing forces, opinions, etc.

cross-grained (-grānd′) *adj.* 1. having an irregular or transverse grain: said of wood 2. cantankerous; contrary; perverse

cross hairs crossed lines, as of fine hair or cobweb, mounted on the front lens of a telescopic gun sight, surveyor's level, etc. to assist in precise aiming or centering of the instrument

cross·hatch (-hach′) *vt., vi.* to shade (a drawing) with two sets of parallel lines that cross each other

cross·head (-hed′) *n.* a bar joining a connecting rod with a piston rod

cross-in·dex (-in′deks) *vt., vi.* to provide (a reference book, index, etc.) with systematic cross-references

cross·ing (krôs′in) *n.* [see CROSS] 1. the act of passing across, thwarting, interbreeding, etc. 2. an intersection, as

of lines, streets, etc. **3.** a place where a street, river, etc. may be crossed

cross·ing·o·ver (-ō′vər) *n.* an exchange of equivalent genetic material between homologous chromatids during meiosis

cross-leg·ged (-leg′id, -legd′) *adj., adv.* **1.** with the ankles crossed and the knees spread apart **2.** with one leg crossed over the other

cross·let (-lit) *n.* [ME. *crosselet* < Anglo-Fr. *croiselete*, dim. of OFr. *crois*: see CROSS] *Heraldry* a small cross

cross-link (-link′) *n.* a crosswise connecting part; specif., an atom or group connecting parallel chains in a complex molecule —*vt.* to join crosswise

cros·sop·te·ryg·i·an (krə säp′tə rij′ē ən) *n.* [< ModL. *Crossopterygii*, name of the group (< Gr. *krossoi*, fringe + *pteryx*, fin) + -AN] any of a group of primitive bony fishes with rounded fins, extinct except for one species and regarded as precursors of amphibians

cross·o·ver (-ō′vər) *n.* **1.** the act, means, or place of crossing over from one part, side, etc. to another ☆**2.** a track by which a railroad train can be switched from one line to another **3.** *Biol. a)* same as CROSSING-OVER *b)* a character resulting from crossing-over

cross·patch (-pach′) *n.* [CROSS- + dial. *patch*, fool, childish person] [Colloq.] a cross, bad-tempered person

cross·piece (-pēs′) *n.* a piece lying across another

cross·pol·li·nate (krôs′päl′ə nāt′) *vt., vi.* -nat′ed, -nat′ing to subject or be subjected to cross-pollination

cross·pol·li·na·tion (-päl′ə nā′shən) *n.* the transfer of pollen from the anther of one flower to the stigma of another, as by the action of the wind or insects

cross·pur·pose (krôs′pur′pəs) *n.* a contrary or conflicting purpose —**at cross-purposes** having, or acting under, a misunderstanding as to each other's purposes

cross·ques·tion (-kwes′chən) *vt.* to cross-examine —*n.* a question asked in cross-examination

cross·re·fer (-ri fur′) *vt.* -ferred′, -fer′ring to refer from one part to another —*vi.* to make a cross-reference

cross·ref·er·ence (-ref′ər əns, -ref′rəns) *n.* a reference from one part of a book, catalog, index, etc. to another part, for additional information —*vt.* -enced, -enc·ing **1.** to provide (an index, reference book, etc.) with systematic cross-references **2.** same as CROSS-REFER

cross relation *Music* the appearance of a tone in one voice of a chord followed by a chromatic alteration of that tone in a different voice of the succeeding chord

cross·road (krôs′rōd′) *n.* **1.** a road that crosses another road **2.** a road that connects two or more main roads **3.** [usually pl.] *a)* the place where two or more roads intersect, often the site of a rural settlement *b)* any center of congregation, activity, etc. for a widespread area —**at the crossroads** at the point where one must choose between different courses of action

cross·ruff (-ruf′) *n.* [CROSS- + RUFF²] *Card Games* a sequence of plays in which a card is led from the hand of each of two partners in turn, which the other can trump

cross section 1. *a)* a cutting through something, esp. at right angles to its axis *b)* a piece so cut off *c)* a drawing or photograph of a plane surface exposed by such a cutting **2.** a sample that has enough of each kind in it to show what the whole is like **3.** *Nuclear Physics* a measure of the probability that a nuclear reaction will take place, under specified conditions, between two particles or a particle and another target: usually expressed in terms of the effective area a single target presents to the incoming particle: see BARN **4.** *Surveying* a vertical section of the ground surface taken at right angles to a survey line —**cross′-sec′tion** *vt.* —**cross′-sec′tion·al** *adj.*

cross·stitch (-stich′) *n.* **1.** a stitch made by crossing two stitches diagonally in the form of an X **2.** needlework made with this stitch —*vt., vi.* to sew or embroider with this stitch

cross talk *Radio, Telephony* interference in one channel from another or others

cross·tie (-tī′) *n.* a beam, post, rod, etc. placed crosswise to give support; ☆specif., any of the transverse timbers supporting the rails of a railroad track

☆**cross·town** (-toun′) *adj.* going across the main avenues or transportation lines of a city [a *cross-town* bus]

cross·trees (-trēz′) *n.pl.* two short, horizontal bars across a ship's masthead, which spread the rigging that supports the mast

☆**cross·walk** (-wôk′) *n.* a lane marked off for pedestrians to use in crossing a street

cross·way (-wā′) *n.* same as CROSSROAD (esp. sense 3)

cross·wind (-wind′) *n.* a wind blowing at right angles to the line of flight of an aircraft, the course of a ship, or any given course or direction

cross·wise (-wīz′) *adv.* **1.** [Archaic] in the form of a cross **2.** so as to cross; across Also **cross′ways** (-wāz′)

☆**cross·word puzzle** (-wurd′) an arrangement of numbered squares to be filled in with words, a letter to each square, so that a letter appearing in a word placed horizontally is usually also part of a word placed vertically: numbered synonyms, definitions, etc. are given as clues for the words

crotch (kräch) *n.* [ME. *croche*, var. of *crucche*, CRUTCH] **1.** a pole forked on top **2.** a forked place, as where a tree trunk divides into two branches **3.** the place where the legs fork from the human body **4.** the seam or place where the legs of a pair of pants, etc. meet —**crotched** *adj.*

crotch·et (kräch′it) *n.* [ME. & OFr. *crochet*, dim. < *croc*, hook: see CROSIER] **1.** [Archaic] *a)* a small hook *b)* a hooklike part or device **2.** [< sense "hooked, twisted"] a peculiar whim or stubborn notion **3.** *Music* [Brit.] a quarter note (♩) —SYN. see CAPRICE

crotch·et·y (-ē) *adj.* **1.** full of peculiar whims or stubborn notions; cantankerous; eccentric **2.** having the nature of a crotchet —**crotch′et·i·ness** *n.*

cro·ton (krōt′'n) *n.* [ModL. < Gr. *krotōn*, a tick, castor-oil tree or (in pl.) its ticklike seeds] **1.** any of a large, mostly tropical genus (*Croton*) of shrubs, trees, and rarely herbs of the spurge family: two species yield croton oil and cascarilla, formerly used in medicine, and other species are poisonous range weeds in the SW U.S. **2.** any of a genus (*Codiaeum*) of shrubs of the spurge family, grown for their ornamental, leathery leaves

☆**Croton bug** [< *Croton* Aqueduct (of the water-supply system of New York City): so named from becoming numerous in the city after the opening of the aqueduct] a small, winged cockroach (*Blatella germanica*)

cro·ton·ic acid (krō tän′ik) [CROTON + -IC] a colorless crystalline compound, $CH_2CH:CHCOOH$, existing in two isomeric forms: used in organic synthesis, the manufacture of resins, etc.

croton oil a thick, bitter oil obtained from croton seeds: it is used externally as a counterirritant and was formerly used internally as a strong cathartic

crouch (krouch) *vi.* [ME. *crouchen* < OFr. *crochir*, to be bent < *croc*, a hook: see CROSIER] **1.** to stoop or bend low with the limbs drawn close to the body, as an animal ready to spring or cowering in fear **2.** to cringe or bow in a servile manner —*vt.* [Archaic] to bow or bend low —*n.* the act or position of crouching

croup¹ (krōōp) *n.* [< obs. or dial. *croup*, to speak hoarsely, of echoic origin] an inflammation of the respiratory passages, with labored breathing, hoarse coughing, and laryngeal spasm —**croup′y** *adj.*

croup² (krōōp) *n.* [ME. & OFr. *croupe* < Frank. *hruppa*: see CROP] the rump of a horse, etc.

crou·pi·er (krōō′pē ā′, -ər; Fr. krōō pyā′) *n.* [Fr., orig., one who rides on the croup, hence an inferior assistant: see prec.] a person in charge of a gambling table, who rakes in and pays out the money

crouse (krōōs) *adj.* [ME. *crous*, fierce, grim, prob. < or akin to MLowG. *krus* (G. *kraus*), curly, tangled) [Scot. & Brit. Dial.] lively; pert; brisk

crou·ton (krōō′tän, krōō tän′) *n.* [Fr. *croûton* < *croûte*, a crust < L. *crusta*: see CRUST] any of the small, crisp pieces of toasted or fried bread often served in soup, salads, etc.

Crow (krō) *n.* [transl., via Fr. *gens de corbeaux*, of their native name, *Absaroke*, Crow people] **1.** *pl.* **Crows, Crow** a member of a tribe of Siouan Indians living in the upper basins of the Yellowstone and Bighorn rivers **2.** their Siouan language

crow¹ (krō) *n.* [ME. *croue* < OE. *crawa*, akin to G. *krähe* (& ff.) < IE. base *ger-*, echoic of hoarse cry, whence CRAKE, CRANE] **1.** any of several large, nonmigrating birds (esp. genus *Corvus*) with glossy black plumage and a typical harsh call: the raven, rook, and jackdaw are all crows **2.** [Rare] a crowbar —[C-] the S constellation Corvus —**as the crow flies** in a straight, direct line —☆**eat crow** [Colloq.] to undergo the humiliation of having to retract a statement, admit an error, etc.

crow² (krō) *vi.* **crowed** or, for 1, chiefly Brit., **crew** (krōō), **crowed, crow′ing** [ME. *crouen* < OE. *crawan*: for IE. base see prec.] **1.** to make the shrill cry of a rooster **2.** to boast in triumph; exult [to *crow* over a victory] **3.** to make a sound expressive of well-being or pleasure, as a baby does —*n.* a crowing sound, as one made by a rooster, or in triumph —SYN. see BOAST

crow·bar (krō′bär′) *n.* [from the end's resembling a crow's beak] a long metal bar, usually with a chisellike point at one end, used as a lever for prying, etc.

crow·ber·ry (-ber′ē) *adj.* [apparently transl. of G. *krähen-beere*] designating a family (Empetraceae) of shrubby evergreens —*n., pl.* -ries **1.** any of several hardy, low, evergreen shrubs (genus *Empetrum*) of the crowberry family, found in northern regions **2.** the black, edible berry of any of these shrubs

☆**crow blackbird** any of various N. American grackles

crowd¹ (kroud) *vi.* [ME. *crouden* < OE. *crudan*, to press, drive, akin to MHG. *kroten*, to oppress < IE. base *greut-*, to compel, press, whence Ir. *gruth*, curdled milk, CURD] **1.** to press, push, or squeeze **2.** to push one's way (*forward, into, through,* etc.) **3.** to come together in a large group; throng —*vt.* **1.** to press, push, or shove **2.** to press or force closely together; cram **3.** to fill too full; occupy to excess, as by pressing or thronging **4.** to be or press very near to; specif., ☆*Baseball* to stand very close to (the plate) when batting **5.** [Colloq.] to put (a person) under pressure or

stress, as by dunning or harassing —n. 1. a large number of people or things gathered closely together 2. the common people; the masses ☆3. [Colloq.] a group of people having something in common; set; clique —**crowd (on) sail** to put up more sails in order to increase the ship's speed —**crowd out** to exclude because of insufficient space or time —**crowd'ed** adj.

SYN.—**crowd** is applied to an assembly of persons or things in close proximity or densely packed together and may suggest lack of order, loss of personal identity, etc. [crowds lined the street]; **throng** specifically suggests a moving crowd of people pushing one another [throngs of celebrators at Times Square]; **multitude** stresses greatness of number in referring to persons or things assembled or considered together [a multitude arrayed against him]; **swarm** suggests a large, continuously moving group [a swarm of sightseers]; **mob**, properly applied to a disorderly or lawless crowd, is an abusive term when used to describe the masses or any specific group of people; **host** specifically suggests a large organized body marshaled together but may be used generally of any sizable group considered collectively [he has a host of friends]; **horde** specifically refers to any large predatory band [a horde of office seekers]

crowd² (kroud) n. [ME. croud < W. crwth, akin to Gael. cruinn, curved, round] 1. an obsolete Celtic musical instrument somewhat like a violin but with a shallow, broad body 2. [Brit. Dial.] a violin

crow·foot (krō′foot′) n., pl. for 1, -foots′; for 2 & 3, -feet′ 1. any of a number of plants of the buttercup family, characterized by simple or variously lobed leaves somewhat resembling a crow's foot, esp. any of a genus (Ranunculus) of chiefly yellow-flowered plants 2. same as CALTROP (sense 1) 3. Naut. an arrangement of small cords run through a block pulley to suspend an awning, etc.

crown (kroun) n. [ME. coroune < OFr. corone < L. corona, a garland, crown < Gr. korōnē, curved object, wreath < IE. base *(s)ker-, to turn, bend, whence L. curvus, crux] 1. a garland or wreath worn on the head as a sign of honor, victory, etc. 2. a reward or honor given for merit; specif., the position or title of a champion in a sport 3. a circlet or headdress of gold, jewels, etc., worn by a monarch as an emblem of sovereignty 4. [often C-] a) the position, power, or dominion of a monarch b) the monarch as head of the state 5. anything serving to adorn or honor like a crown 6. the figure of a crown or a thing like a crown in shape, position, etc. 7. a) orig., a coin stamped with the figure of a crown b) a British coin equal to five shillings c) any of various coins or monetary units whose name means crown: see KORUNA, KRONA, KRONE, etc. 8. the top part of the skull or head 9. the top part of a hat 10. the summit or highest point, as of a mountain, arch, etc. 11. the highest quality, point of development, state, etc. of anything 12. a) the enamel-covered part of a tooth, projecting beyond the gum line b) an artificial substitute for this, usually of porcelain or gold 13. the lowest point of an anchor, between the arms 14. a size of paper, usually 19 or 20 by 15 in. 15. Bot. a) same as CORONA (sense 7) b) the point at or just below the surface of the ground where the stem and the root join, esp. in perennial herbs c) the leafy head of a tree —vt. 1. a) to put a crown on the head of b) to make (a person) a monarch; enthrone 2. to honor or reward as with a crown 3. to be at the top of; surmount 4. to be the crown, highest part, or chief ornament of 5. to complete successfully; put the finishing touch on 6. to cover (a tooth) with an artificial crown 7. [Slang] to hit on the head 8. Checkers to make a king of —**crown'er** n.

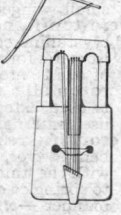

CROWD

☆**crown cap** a cork-lined metal stopper whose edges are crimped over the mouth of the bottle

crown colony a British colony directly under the control of the home government in London

crown·er (kroun′nər, krōō′-) n. [Archaic or Brit. Dial.] same as CORONER

crown glass 1. window glass made in flat, circular plates by blowing and whirling, with a small knot in the center left by the blower's rod 2. a very clear optical glass with a low index of refraction

crown land 1. land owned by the crown, the income from which (or, in Britain, a fixed payment by Parliament in place of it) goes to the reigning monarch 2. land under control of the government in certain countries and colonies of the British Commonwealth

crown lens a lens made of crown glass; specif., the convex member of an achromatic lens

Crown Point [mistranslation of Fr. name Pointe à la Chevelure, scalping point] town in NE N.Y., on Lake Champlain: site of a fort important in the French and Indian & the Revolutionary wars: pop. 1,900

crown prince the male heir apparent to a throne

crown princess 1. the wife of a crown prince 2. a female heir presumptive to a throne

crown saw a saw in the form of a hollow cylinder with teeth on the bottom edge, for cutting circles

crown vetch a European plant (Coronilla varia) of the legume family, with pink and white flowers: sometimes cultivated in the U.S. as a ground cover

crown wheel (or **gear**) a gearwheel with teeth set in the rim perpendicular to its plane

CROWN WHEEL

crow's-foot (krōz′foot′) n., pl. -feet′ 1. any of the wrinkles that often develop at the outer corners of the eyes of adults: usually used in pl. 2. a three-pointed, stitched design put on a garment, as at the end of a seam 3. same as CALTROP (sense 1) 4. Aeron. a way of rigging one rope to several ropes in order to distribute pull in handling balloons and airships: also **crows'foot'**

crow's-nest (-nest′) n. 1. a small, partly enclosed platform close to the top of a ship's mast, used by the lookout 2. any platform like this

Croy·don (kroid′'n) city in Surrey, England, just south of London: pop. 254,000

croze (krōz) n. [prob. < Fr. creux < OFr. croz, a groove] the groove at either end of the inside of a barrel or cask, in which the head is fixed

CROW'S-NEST

cro·zier (krō′zhər) n. same as CROSIER

crs. 1. creditors 2. credits

CRT cathode-ray tube

cru·ces (krōō′sēz) n. alt. pl. of CRUX

cru·cial (krōō′shəl) adj. [Fr. < L. crux (gen. crucis), CROSS] 1. of supreme importance; decisive; critical [a crucial decision] 2. extremely trying; severe; difficult 3. Med. having the form of a cross [a crucial incision] —SYN. see ACUTE —**cru′cial·ly** adv.

cru·ci·ate (krōō′shē it, -āt′) adj. [< ModL. cruciatus (in L., pp. of cruciare, to crucify) < L. crux, CROSS] 1. cross-shaped 2. Bot. having leaves or petals arranged in the form of a cross 3. Zool. crossing: said of wings

cru·ci·ble (krōō′sə b'l) n. [ML. crucibulum, lamp, crucible, prob. < Gmc., as in OE. cruce, pot, jug, MHG. kruse, earthen pot (cf. CRUSE) + L. suffix -ibulum (as in thuribulum, censer), but associated through folk etym. with L. crux (gen. crucis), CROSS, as if lamp burning before cross] 1. a container made of graphite, porcelain, platinum, or other substance that can resist great heat, for melting, fusing, or calcining ores, metals, etc. 2. the hollow at the bottom of an ore furnace, where the molten metal collects 3. a severe test or trial

crucible steel a high-grade steel made by melting special steel mixes in a crucible furnace or by fusing flux, wrought iron, and carbon: used for making knives, tools, etc.

cru·ci·fer (krōō′sə fər) n. [LL.(Ec.) < L. crux (gen. crucis), CROSS + ferre, to bear; sense 2 < arrangement of flower petals in the form of a cross] 1. a person who carries a cross, as in a church procession 2. Bot. any plant of the mustard family, including the cabbages, cresses, etc. —**cru·cif′er·ous** (-sif′ər əs) adj.

cru·ci·fix (krōō′sə fiks′) n. [ME. < OFr. or ML.; OFr. crucefix < ML.(Ec.) crucifixus, orig. pp. of LL.(Ec.) crucifigere: see CRUCIFY] 1. a Christian symbol consisting of a cross with the figure of Jesus crucified on it 2. the cross as a Christian symbol

cru·ci·fix·ion (krōō′sə fik′shən) n. 1. a crucifying or being crucified 2. [C-] the crucifying of Jesus, or a representation of this in painting, statuary, etc.

cru·ci·form (krōō′sə fôrm′) adj. [< L. crux (gen. crucis), CROSS + -FORM] cross-shaped —**cru′ci·form′ly** adv.

cru·ci·fy (krōō′sə fī′) vt. -fied′, -fy′ing [ME. crucifien < OFr. crucifier < LL.(Ec.) crucificare, for L. crucifigere < crux (gen. crucis), CROSS + figere (see FIX)] 1. to put to death by nailing or binding to a cross and leaving to die of exposure 2. to mortify or subdue (the flesh) as by asceticism 3. to be very cruel to; torment; torture —**cru′ci·fi′er** n.

crud¹ (krud) vt., vi. crud′ded, crud′ding [ME. crudden < crud: see CURD] [Dial.] to curdle —n. 1. [Dial.] a curd 2. [Slang] any coagulated substance, caked deposit, dregs, filth, etc. 3. [Slang] a worthless, disgusting, or contemptible person or thing —**crud′dy** adj. -di·er, -di·est

crud² (krud) n. [< ? W. cryd, fever, plague] [orig. Mil. Slang] an imaginary disease or vaguely identified disorder or ailment: with the

crude (krōōd) adj. [ME. < L. crudus, bleeding, raw, rough < IE. base *kreu-, congealed (blood), whence Gr. kryos, frost & kreas, flesh, L. crusta, cruor, MIr. cru, blood, E. RAW] 1. in a raw or natural condition, before being prepared for use; not refined or processed 2. lacking finish, grace, tact, taste, etc.; uncultured [a crude remark] 3. not carefully made or done; rough [crude woodwork] 4. stark and bare; undisguised or unadorned [crude reality] 5. [Archaic] not ripe; immature 6. Statistics untreated as by analysis, differentiation into groups, etc. —☆n. an unrefined or unprocessed substance; specif., crude petroleum —**crude′ly** adv. —**crude′ness** n.

cru·di·ty (krōō′də tē) n. [ME. & OFr. crudite < L. cruditas] 1. the condition or quality of being crude 2. pl. -ties a crude action, remark, etc.

cru·el (krōō′əl) adj. [ME. & OFr. < L. crudelis < crudus: see CRUDE] 1. deliberately seeking to inflict pain and suffering; enjoying others' suffering; without mercy or

pity **2.** causing, or of a kind to cause, pain, distress, etc. —**cru′el·ly** adv. —**cru′el·ness** n.

SYN.—**cruel** implies indifference to the suffering of others or a disposition to inflict it on others [cruel fate]; **brutal** implies an animallike or savage cruelty that is altogether unfeeling [a brutal prison guard]; **inhuman** stresses the complete absence of those qualities expected of a civilized human being, such as compassion, mercy, or benevolence; **pitiless** implies a callous refusal to be moved or influenced by the suffering of those one has wronged; **ruthless** implies a cruel and relentless disregard for the rights or welfare of others, while in pursuit of a goal —**ANT.** humane, kind

cru·el·ty (-tē) n. [ME. & OFr. cruelte < L. crudelitas < prec.] **1.** the quality or condition of being cruel; inhumanity; hardheartedness **2.** pl. **-ties** a cruel action, remark, etc. **3.** Law willful mistreatment seriously harmful to life or to physical or mental health

cru·et (kroo′it) n. [ME. < Anglo-Fr., dim. of OFr. crue, earthen pot < Gmc. *kruka (G. krug), whence CROCK¹] a small glass bottle, as for holding vinegar, oil, etc., for the table

Cruik·shank (krook′shank), **George** 1792–1878; Eng. caricaturist & illustrator

cruise (krooz) vi. **cruised, cruis′ing** [< Du. kruisen, to cross, cruise < kruis, cross < L. crux, CROSS] **1.** to sail from place to place, as for pleasure or in search of something **2.** to drive about in a similar manner [a taxi cruises to pick up passengers] ☆**3.** to go over a wooded area to estimate its lumber yield **4.** to move at the most efficient speed for sustained travel: said esp. of an aircraft —vt. **1.** to sail, journey, or move over or about ☆**2.** to make a cruising trip over (a wooded area) —n. the action of cruising; esp., a cruising voyage by ship

cruis·er (-ər) n. **1.** one that cruises, as a powerboat, airplane, squad car, etc. **2.** any of several types of fast and maneuverable warship somewhat smaller than a battleship and having less armor and fire power **3.** same as CABIN CRUISER

cruising radius the greatest distance that an aircraft or ship can cruise, usually from and back to a base, without refueling

☆**crul·ler** (krul′ər) n. [Du. < krullen, to CURL] **1.** a kind of twisted doughnut made with a rich dough **2.** [Now Dial.] any friedcake or doughnut

crumb (krum) n. [ME. crome < OE. cruma, lit., scraping from bread crust, akin to G. krume < IE. *gr-eu, to scratch, scrape (as in G. krauen, to scratch) < base *ger-, to turn, twist] **1.** a very small piece broken off something; small particle or bit, esp. of bread, cake, etc. **2.** any bit or scrap [crumbs of knowledge] **3.** the soft part of bread within the crust ☆**4.** [Slang] a worthless, disgusting, or despicable person: also **crum′bum′** —vt. **1.** [Rare] to crumble **2.** to clear (a table, etc.) of crumbs **3.** Cooking to cover or thicken with crumbs

crum·ble (krum′b′l) vt. **-bled, -bling** [freq. of prec.] to break into crumbs or small pieces —vi. to fall to pieces; disintegrate; decay —n. [Rare] a crumb or crumbling substance

crum·bly (-blē) adj. **-bli·er, -bli·est** apt to crumble; easily crumbled —**crum′bli·ness** n.

crum·by (krum′ē) adj. **-bi·er, -bi·est 1.** full of crumbs **2.** soft, as the inner part of bread ☆**3.** [Slang] same as CRUMMY² —**crum′bi·ness** n.

crum·mie, crum·my¹ (krum′ē) n., pl. **-mies** [via dial. < OE. crumb, crooked (akin to G. krumm & Du. krom) + -y²: for IE. base see CRAM] [Scot. & Brit. Dial.] a cow with crooked horns; also, occas., any cow

crum·my² (krum′ē) adj. **-mi·er, -mi·est** [< CRUM(B), with basic notion "brittle, friable, hence worthless" + -y²] [Slang] **1.** dirty, cheap, shabby, disgusting, etc. **2.** inferior, worthless, contemptible, etc. —**crum′mi·ness** n.

crump (krump) vt., vi. [echoic] [Chiefly Brit.] to strike or explode with a heavy thud —n. [Chiefly Brit.] **1.** the act or sound of crumping **2.** an exploding shell or bomb —adj. [< the v.] [Scot. or Brit. Dial.] brittle; crisp

crum·pet (krum′pit) n. [prob. < ME. crompid (cake) < OE. crompeht, flat cake, crumpet, lit., full of crumples, wrinkled, akin ? to ff.] a small, unsweetened batter cake baked on a griddle: it is usually toasted and buttered before serving

crum·ple (krum′p′l) vt. **-pled, -pling** [ME. crumplen, var. of crimplen, to wrinkle, freq. of crimpen, CRIMP¹] **1.** to crush together into creases or wrinkles **2.** to cause to collapse —vi. **1.** to become crumpled **2.** to fall or break down; collapse —n. a crease or wrinkle

crum·ply (-plē) adj. **-pli·er, -pli·est** apt to crumple; easily crumpled [crumply paper]

crunch (krunch) vi., vt. [earlier craunch, of echoic origin] **1.** to bite or chew with a noisy, crackling sound **2.** to press, grind, tread, fall, etc. with a noisy, crushing sound —n. **1.** the act or sound of crunching ☆**2.** [Slang] a) a showdown; test b) a tight situation; pinch

crunch·y (-ē) adj. **-i·er, -i·est** making a crunching sound, as when chewed —**crunch′i·ness** n.

cru·or (kroo′ôr) n. [L., blood (which flows from a wound): see CRUDE] coagulated blood; gore

crup·per (krup′ər, kroop′-) n. [ME. crouper < OFr. cropiere < crope, rump < Frank. *kruppa: see CROP] **1.** a leather strap attached to a saddle or harness and passed under the horse's tail **2.** the rump of a horse; croup **3.** [Colloq.] the buttocks

cru·ral (kroor′əl) adj. [L. cruralis < ff.] Anat. of or pertaining to the leg or thigh

crus (krus, kroos) n., pl. **cru·ra** (kroor′ə) [L., leg, shank] **1.** the part of a leg or hind limb between the knee and the ankle; shank **2.** any anatomical structure resembling a leg or (in the plural) a pair of legs, as the cerebral peduncles

cru·sade (kroo sād′) n. [< Sp. cruzada, altered after Fr. croisade, both < ML. cruciata < pp. of cruciare, to mark with a cross < L. crux, CROSS] **1.** [sometimes C-] any of the military expeditions which Christians undertook from the end of the 11th to the end of the 13th cent. to recover the Holy Land from the Moslems **2.** any church-sanctioned war or expedition like this **3.** vigorous, concerted action for some cause or idea, or against some abuse —vi. **-sad′ed, -sad′ing** to engage in a crusade —**cru·sad′er** (-ər) n.

cru·sa·do (kroo zā′dō, -sā′-) n., pl. **-does, -dos** [Port. cruzado, orig., pp. of cruzar < ML. cruciare: see CRUSADE] an obsolete Portuguese coin with the figure of a cross on it

cruse (krooz, kroos) n. [ME. crouse < OE. cruse, akin to MDu. cruyse, ON. krus, G. krause, pot with lid] a small container for water, oil, honey, etc.

crush (krush) vt. [ME. crushen < OFr. croisir, to gnash (teeth), crash, break < Frank. krostjan, to gnash, akin to OSw. krysta, Goth. kriustan] **1.** to press between two opposing forces so as to break or injure; put out of shape or condition by pressure; squeeze together; crumple **2.** to press, grind, or pound into small particles or into powder **3.** to subdue or suppress by or as by force; overwhelm **4.** to oppress harshly **5.** to extract by pressing or squeezing —vi. **1.** to be or become crushed **2.** to press forward; crowd (into, against, etc.) —n. **1.** the act of crushing; severe pressure **2.** a crowded mass, esp. of people **3.** a drink made from fruit juice [lemon crush] ☆**4.** [Colloq.] an infatuation —**SYN.** see BREAK¹ —**crush′a·ble** adj. —**crush′er** n.

Cru·soe (kroo′sō), **Robinson** see ROBINSON CRUSOE

crust (krust) n. [ME. cruste < OFr. or L.: OFr. crouste < L. crusta: for IE. base see CRUDE] **1.** a) the hard, crisp, outer part of bread b) a piece of this c) any dry, hard piece of bread **2.** the pastry shell of a pie **3.** any hard shell, covering, or surface layer, as of snow, soil, etc. **4.** a hard deposit formed by wine on the inside surface of a bottle **5.** [Slang] audacity; insolence; gall **6.** Geol. the solid, rocky, outer portion or shell of the earth; lithosphere **7.** Med. a dry, hard, outer layer of blood, pus, or other bodily secretion —vt., vi. **1.** to cover or become covered with a crust **2.** to form or harden into a crust

crus·ta·cean (krus tā′shən) n. [ModL. Crustacea, name of the class < crustaceus, having a crust or shell < L. crusta, CRUST] any of a class (Crustacea) of arthropods, including shrimps, crabs, barnacles, and lobsters, that usually live in the water and breathe through gills: they have a hard outer shell and jointed appendages and bodies —adj. of crustaceans

crus·ta·ceous (-shəs) adj. [ModL. crustaceus: see CRUSTACEAN] **1.** of or like a crust **2.** having a hard crust or shell **3.** Zool. same as CRUSTACEAN

crus·tal (krus′t′l) adj. of a crust, esp. the earth's crust

crust·y (-tē) adj. **crust′i·er, crust′i·est** [ME.] **1.** having, forming, or resembling a crust **2.** rudely abrupt or surly in speech and manner; bad-tempered —**crust′i·ly** adv. —**crust′i·ness** n.

crutch (kruch) n. [ME. crucche < OE. crycce, staff, akin to G. krücke < IE. base *ger-, to twist, turn, bend, whence CRANK¹, CROOK] **1.** any of various devices used, often in pairs, by lame people as an aid in walking; typically, a staff with a hand grip and a padded crosspiece on top that fits under the armpit **2.** anything one leans or relies on for support, help, etc.; prop **3.** any device that resembles a crutch, as a forked leg rest on a sidesaddle **4.** [Archaic] the crotch of the human body **5.** Naut. a forked support for a spar when the sail is furled —vt. to support with or as with a crutch or crutches; prop up

crux (kruks) n., pl. **crux′es, cru′ces** (kroo′sēz) [L., CROSS] **1.** Heraldry a cross **2.** a difficult problem; puzzling thing **3.** the essential or deciding point —[C-] the constellation Southern Cross

‡**crux an·sa·ta** (kruks′ an sāt′ə, -sät′ə) [L., lit., cross with a handle < crux, CROSS + fem. of ansatus < ansa, a handle] the ankh, an ancient Egyptian cross

cru·zei·ro (kroo zā′rō; Port. kroo zā′roo) n., pl. **-ros** [Port. < cruz, a cross < L. crux, CROSS] the monetary unit of Brazil: see MONETARY UNITS, table

crwth (krooth) n. [W.: see CROWD²] same as CROWD²

cry (krī) vi. **cried, cry′ing** [ME. crien < OFr. crier < L. quiritare, to wail, shriek (var. of quirritare, to squeal like a pig < *quis, echoic of a squeal); associated in ancient folk etym. with L. Quirites, Roman citizens (as if meaning "to call the Quirites," implore their help)] **1.** to make a loud vocal sound or utterance; call out, as for help; shout **2.** to sob and shed tears, in expressing sorrow, pain, etc.; weep

3. *a)* to plead or clamor (*for*) *b)* to show or suggest a great need (*for*) [problems *crying* for solution] **4.** to utter its characteristic call: said of an animal —*vt.* **1.** to plead or beg for [to *cry* quarter] **2.** to utter loudly; shout; exclaim **3.** to call out (wares for sale, services offered, etc.); announce publicly **4.** to bring into a specified condition by crying [to *cry* oneself asleep] —*n., pl.* **cries** [ME. & OFr. *cri* < the *v.*] **1.** a loud vocal sound expressing pain, anger, fright, joy, etc. **2.** any loud utterance; shout **3.** an announcement or advertisement called out publicly **4.** an urgent appeal; plea **5.** popular report; rumor; rallying call or battle cry; watchword **6.** the current opinion or fashion **7.** clamor of the people; public outcry **8.** a slogan **9.** a sobbing and shedding of tears; fit of weeping **10.** the characteristic vocal sound of an animal **11.** *a)* the baying of hounds in the chase *b)* a pack of hounds —**a far cry 1.** a great distance; long way **2.** a thing much different —**cry down** to belittle; disparage —**cry off** to withdraw from an agreement or undertaking —**cry one's eyes out** to weep much and bitterly —**cry out 1.** to shout; yell **2.** to complain loudly —**cry up** to shout praise of; praise highly —**in full cry** in eager pursuit: originally said of a pack of hounds **SYN.**—**cry** implies the expression of grief, sorrow, pain, or distress by making mournful, convulsive sounds and shedding tears; **weep** more specifically stresses the shedding of tears; to **sob** is to weep aloud with a catch in the voice and short, gasping breaths; **wail** implies the uttering of loud, prolonged, mournful cries in unsuppressed lamentation; **keen**, specifically an Irish term, signifies a wailing in lamentation for the dead; to **whimper** is to cry with subdued, whining, broken sounds, as a fretful or frightened child does; **moan** suggests the expression of sorrow or pain in a low, prolonged, mournful sound or sounds; **blubber**, a derisive term used chiefly of children, implies a contorting or swelling of the face with weeping, and broken, inarticulate speech

☆**cry·ba·by** (-bā'bē) *n.* **1.** a person, esp. a child, who cries often or with little cause **2.** a person who complains when he fails to win or get his own way

cry·ing (-iŋ) *adj.* **1.** that cries **2.** demanding immediate notice or remedy [a *crying* need] —**for crying out loud** [Slang] an exclamation of annoyance, surprise, etc.

cry·o- (krī'ə, -ō) [< Gr. *kryos*, cold, frost: see CRUDE] a *combining form meaning* cold or freezing [*cryogen*]

cry·o·bi·ol·o·gy (krī'ō bī äl'ə jē) *n.* [CRYO- + BIOLOGY] the science that deals with the study of organisms, esp. warm-blooded animals, at low temperatures —**cry'o·bi·ol'o·gist** *n.*

cry·o·gen (krī'ə jən) *n.* [CRYO- + -GEN] a refrigerant

cry·o·gen·ics (krī'ə jen'iks) *n.* [CRYOGEN + -ICS] the science that deals with the production of very low temperatures and their effect on the properties of matter

cry·o·hy·drate (-hī'drāt) *n.* [CRYO- + HYDRATE] a crystalline solid formed by the combination of some substance, as salt, with water to give a certain concentration which has a definite freezing point

cry·o·lite (krī'ə līt') *n.* [CRYO- + -LITE: with reference to its icy appearance] a fluoride of sodium and aluminum, Na₃AlF₆, found in Greenland and used in the molten state in the electrolytic production of aluminum

cry·om·e·ter (krī äm'ə tər) *n.* [CRYO- + -METER] a thermometer, usually filled with alcohol, for measuring lower temperatures than a mercury thermometer will register

cry·o·phyte (krī'ə fīt') *n.* [CRYO- + -PHYTE] a plant that grows on ice or snow

cry·o·probe (-prōb') *n.* [CRYO- + PROBE] a surgical instrument for conducting intense cold to small areas of body tissues in order to destroy those areas

cry·os·co·py (krī äs'kə pē) *n.* [CRYO- + -SCOPY] the science dealing with the determination of the freezing points of liquids

cry·o·stat (krī'ə stat') *n.* [CRYO- + -STAT] a regulator for maintaining a constant, low temperature

cry·o·sur·ger·y (krī'ə sur'jə rē) *n.* [CRYO- + SURGERY] surgery involving the selective destruction of tissues by freezing them, as with liquid nitrogen: also **cryogenic surgery** —**cry'o·sur'gi·cal** *adj.*

cry·o·ther·a·py (krī'ə ther'ə pē) *n.* [CRYO- + THERAPY] *Med.* treatment by the use of cold, as by the application of ice packs or by lowering the body temperature

crypt (kript) *n.* [ME. *cript* < L. *crypta* < Gr. *kryptē* < *kryptos*, hidden < *kryptein*, to hide < IE. *kru-bh-* < base *kru-*, to heap up, cover, whence OIr. *cráu*, hut] **1.** an underground chamber or vault, esp. one under the main floor of a church, often, esp. formerly, serving as a burial place **2.** *Anat.* any of various recesses, glandular cavities, or follicles in the body —**crypt·al** (krip't'l) *adj.*

crypt·a·nal·y·sis (krip'tə nal'ə sis) *n.* [CRYPT(OGRAM) + ANALYSIS] the act or science of deciphering a code or coded message without a prior knowledge of the key —**crypt·an'a·lyst** (-tan'ə list) *n.* —**crypt·an·a·lyt'ic** (-tan ə lit'ik) *adj.*

cryp·tic (krip'tik) *adj.* [LL. *crypticus* < Gr. *kryptikos* < *kryptos*: see CRYPT] **1.** *a)* having a hidden or ambiguous meaning; mysterious; baffling [a *cryptic* comment] *b)* obscure and curt in expression **2.** *Zool.* serving to conceal, as the form or coloring of certain animals Also **cryp'ti·cal** —*SYN.* see OBSCURE —**cryp'ti·cal·ly** *adv.*

cryp·to- (krip'tə, -tō) [< Gr. *kryptos*: see CRYPT] a *combining form meaning:* **1.** secret or hidden [*cryptogram*] **2.** being such secretly and not by public avowal [a *crypto*-Fascist] Also, before a vowel, **crypt-**

cryp·to·clas·tic (krip'tō klas'tik) *adj.* [CRYPTO- + CLASTIC] *Mineralogy* consisting of fragmental grains too small to be seen with the unaided eye

cryp·to·crys·tal·line (-kris't'l in) *adj. Mineralogy* having a crystalline structure consisting, however, of crystals too small to be seen even with a microscope

cryp·to·gam (krip'tə gam') *n.* [Fr. *cryptogame* < Gr. *kryptos* (see CRYPT) + *gamos*, marriage] a plant that bears no flowers or seeds but propagates by means of spores, as algae, mosses, ferns, etc. —**cryp'to·gam'ic, cryp·tog'a·mous** (-täg'ə məs) *adj.*

cryp·to·gen·ic (krip'tə jen'ik) *adj.* [CRYPTO- + -GENIC] of unknown or obscure origin: said of a disease

cryp·to·gram (krip'tə gram') *n.* [CRYPTO- + -GRAM] something written in code or cipher —**cryp'to·gram'mic** *adj.*

cryp·to·graph (-graf') *n.* **1.** *same as* CRYPTOGRAM **2.** a device for writing or solving cryptograms

cryp·tog·ra·phy (krip täg'rə fē) *n.* [CRYPTO- + -GRAPHY] **1.** the art of writing or deciphering messages in code **2.** the system used in a code or cipher —**cryp·tog'ra·pher, cryp·tog'ra·phist** *n.* —**cryp·to·graph·ic** (krip'tə graf'ik) *adj.* —**cryp'to·graph'i·cal·ly** *adv.*

cryp·to·me·ri·a (krip'tə mir'ē ə) *n.* [ModL. < Gr. *kryptos*, hidden (see CRYPT) + *meros*, a part (see MERIT) + ModL. *-ia* (see -IA): so named because the seeds are "hidden" within the scales of the cones] a cone-bearing Asiatic tree (*Cryptomeria japonica*) of the baldcypress family, with dark green needles

cryp·to·pine (krip'tə pēn', -pin) *n.* [CRYPT(O)- + OP(IUM) + -INE⁴] a poisonous alkaloid, C₂₁H₂₃NO₅, found in opium

cryp·to·xan·thin (krip'tō zan'thin) *n.* [CRYPTO- + XANTHIN] a carotenoid pigment, C₄₀H₅₆O, related to vitamin A and found in butter, eggs, and various plants

cryst. 1. crystalline **2.** crystallized **3.** crystallography

crys·tal (kris't'l) *n.* [altered (after L.) < ME. & OFr. *cristal*, OE. *cristalla* < L. *crystallum*, crystal, ice < Gr. *krystallos* < *kryos*: see CRUDE] **1.** *a)* a clear, transparent quartz *b)* a piece of this cut in the form of an ornament **2.** *a)* a very clear, brilliant glass *b)* an article or articles made of such glass, as goblets, bowls, etc. ☆**3.** the transparent protective covering over the face of a watch **4.** anything clear and transparent like crystal **5.** a solidified form of a substance in which the atoms or molecules are arranged in a definite pattern that is repeated regularly in three dimensions: crystals tend to develop forms bounded by definitely oriented plane surfaces that are harmonious with their internal structures **6.** *Radio, Elec.* a piezoelectric body or plate, as of quartz, used to control very precisely the frequency of an oscillator or as a circuit element in a crystal filter or a body, often of Rochelle salt, used in a transducer, as in a crystal pickup or microphone —*adj.* **1.** of or composed of crystal **2.** like crystal; clear and transparent **3.** *Radio* of or using a crystal

crystal detector *Radio* a semiconductor rectifier used for demodulation

crystal gazing the practice of gazing into a ball of rock crystal, or commonly glass, (**crystal ball**) and professing to see certain images, esp. of future events —**crystal gazer**

crys·tall- (kris't'l) *same as* CRYSTALLO-

crystal lattice the regular spaced pattern resulting when atoms, molecules, or ions are arranged to form a crystal

crys·tal·lif·er·ous (kris'tə lif'ər əs) *adj.* [< CRYSTALL- + -FEROUS] producing or containing crystals

crys·tal·line (kris'tə lin) *adj.* [ME. < OFr. & L.; OFr. *crystalin* < L. *crystallinus* < Gr. *krystallinos*: see CRYSTAL] **1.** consisting or made of crystal or crystals **2.** like crystal; clear and transparent **3.** having the character or structure of a crystal

crystalline lens the lens of the eye, a biconvex structure serving to focus light on the retina

crystalline system any of the six groups (isometric, hexagonal, tetragonal, orthorhombic, monoclinic, and triclinic) into which crystalline species are classified on the basis of the relationships of their crystallographic axes (imaginary lines of reference used to describe the crystal planes)

crys·tal·lite (kris'tə līt') *n.* [CRYSTALL- + -ITE¹] **1.** a tiny, embryonic crystal, too small to be identified with any mineral species **2.** a rock consisting mainly of such tiny crystals —**crys·tal·lit·ic** (kris'tə lit'ik) *adj.*

crys·tal·lize (kris'tə līz') *vt.* **-lized', -liz'ing 1.** to cause to form crystals or take on a crystalline structure **2.** to give a definite form to **3.** to coat with sugar —*vi.* **1.** to become crystalline in form **2.** to take on a definite form [their customs *crystallized* into law] —**crys'tal·liz'a·ble** *adj.* —**crys'tal·li·za'tion** *n.*

crys·tal·lo- (kris'tə lō) [< Gr. *krystallos*, CRYSTAL] a *combining form meaning* crystal [*crystallography*]

crys·tal·log·ra·phy (kris'tə läg'rə fē) *n.* [CRYSTALLO- + -GRAPHY] the science of the form, structure, properties, and classification of crystals —**crys·tal·lo·graph·ic** (kris'tə lə graf'ik), **crys·tal·lo·graph'i·cal** *adj.*

crys·tal·loid (kris'tə loid') *adj.* [CRYSTALL- + -OID] **1.** like a crystal **2.** having the nature of a crystalloid —*n.* **1.** a substance, usually crystallizable, which, when in solution, readily passes through vegetable and animal membranes **2.** a small crystalloid grain of protein found in some cells, seeds, etc. —**crys'tal·loi'dal** *adj.*

crystal pickup a piezoelectric vibration pickup or detector,

often used on electric phonographs: distinguished from MAGNETIC PICKUP

crystal set a primitive type of radio receiver with a crystal detector instead of an electron tube detector

crystal violet a rosaniline dye used as an antiseptic, an indicator, and in Gram's method for staining bacteria

Cs 1. *Chem.* cesium 2. *Meteorol.* cirrostratus

cs. case; cases

C.S. Christian Science; Christian Scientist

C.S., c.s. 1. capital stock 2. civil service

C.S.A. Confederate States of America

CSC Civil Service Commission

csc cosecant

csk. cask

C.S.O. Chief Signal Officer

CST, C.S.T. Central Standard Time

Ct. Connecticut

ct. 1. *pl.* **cts.** cent 2. county 3. court

cten·o- (ten′ə, tē′nə) [< Gr. *kteis* (gen. *ktenos*) < *pktenos*, akin to L. *pecten*, comb (see PECTINATE)] *a combining form meaning* ctenoid scales, teeth, etc. *[ctenophore]*: also, before a vowel, **cten-**

cte·noid (ten′oid, tē′noid) *adj.* [CTEN- + -OID] having an edge with projections like the teeth of a comb, as the scales and teeth of certain fishes

cte·noph·o·ran (ti näf′ə rən) *adj.* of a ctenophore —*n. same as* CTENOPHORE

cten·o·phore (ten′ə fôr′, tē′nə-) *n.* [CTENO- + -PHORE] any of a phylum (Ctenophora) of sea animals with an oval, transparent, jellylike body bearing eight rows of comblike plates that aid in swimming

Ctes·i·phon (tes′ə fän′) ancient ruined city on the Tigris, near Baghdad, in present-day Iraq

ctn. 1. carton 2. cotangent

ctr. center

cts. 1. centimes 2. cents

Cu [L. *cuprum*] *Chem.* copper

Cu., cu. cumulus

cu. cubic

cub (kub) *n.* [Early ModE. *cubbe*, young fox < ? OIr. *cuib*, whelp] 1. the young of certain mammals, as the fox, wolf, bear, lion, tiger, or whale 2. an inexperienced, awkward youth 3. a novice or beginner, esp. in newspaper reporting 4. [C-] *same as* CUB SCOUT —**cub′bish** *adj.* —**cub′bish·ness** *n.*

Cu·ba (kyōō′bə; *Sp.* kōō′bä) 1. island in the West Indies, south of Fla. 2. country comprising this island & several small nearby islands: 44,218 sq. mi.; pop. 7,833,000; cap. Havana —**Cu′ban** *adj., n.*

cub·age (kyōō′bij) *n.* [CUB(E) + -AGE] cubic content

Cu·ban·go (kōō vaŋ′gōō) *Port. name of* OKOVANGGO River

Cuban heel a heel of medium height and width used on some types of women's shoes

cu·ba·ture (kyōō′bə chər) *n.* [< L. *cubus*, CUBE¹, after (QUADR)ATURE] 1. the determination of the cubic content of a solid 2. cubic content; volume

cub·by·hole (kub′ē hōl′) *n.* [dim. < Brit. dial. *cub*, little shed < MHG. *kobe*, cage, stall: for IE. base see COVE¹) + HOLE] 1. a small, enclosed space or room that confines snugly or uncomfortably 2. a small, open compartment in a desk, etc.; pigeonhole Also **cub′by**

cube¹ (kyōōb) *n.* [Fr. < L. *cubus* < Gr. *kybos*, a cube, die, vertebra < IE. base *keu(b)*-, to bend, turn, whence HIP¹, HIVE, L. *cubare*, to lie down] 1. a solid with six equal, square sides 2. anything having more or less this shape [an *ice cube*] 3. the product obtained by multiplying a given number or quantity by its square; third power [the *cube* of 3 is 27 (3 × 3 × 3)] —*vt.* cubed, cub′ing 1. to raise to the third power; obtain the cube of (a number or quantity) 2. to cut or shape into cubes; dice [*cube* the vegetables] 3. to score (meat) in a crisscross pattern in order to tenderize it 4. to measure the cubic content of —**cub′er** *n.*

☆**cu·be²** (kyōō′bā, kōō′-) *n.* [< Sp. *quibey* < native name] a tropical American plant (*Lonchocarpus nicou*) of the legume family, whose roots yield rotenone

cu·beb (kyōō′beb) *n.* [ME. *quibibe* < OFr. *cubebe* < ML. *cubeba* < Ar. *kubāba*, var. of *kabāba*] 1. the small, spicy berry of an East Indian vine (*Piper cubeba*) of the pepper family ☆2. a cigarette made from the crushed dried berries, formerly smoked in treating catarrh

cube root the number or quantity of which a given number or quantity is the cube [the *cube root* of 8 is 2]

cu·bic (kyōō′bik) *adj.* [ME. *cubik* < OFr. *cubique* < L. *cubicus* < Gr. *kybikos*: see CUBE¹] 1. having the shape of a cube 2. having three dimensions, or having the volume of a cube whose length, width, and breadth each measure the given unit [a *cubic foot*] 3. designating a crystalline form that has three equal axes at right angles to one another 4. *Math.* of the third power or degree; relating to the cubes of numbers or quantities

cu·bi·cal (-bi k'l) *adj.* cubic; esp., cube-shaped —**cu′bi·cal·ly** *adv.*

cu·bi·cle (kyōō′bi k'l) *n.* [L. *cubiculum* < *cubare*, to lie down: see CUBE¹] 1. a small sleeping compartment, as in a dormitory 2. any small compartment, as for study

cubic measure a system of measuring volume in cubic units, esp. that in which 1,728 cubic inches = 1 cubic foot, and 1,000 cubic millimeters = 1 cubic centimeter: see TABLE OF WEIGHTS AND MEASURES in Supplement

cu·bic·u·lum (kyoo bik′yoo ləm) *n., pl.* -**u·la** (-lə) [L.: see CUBICLE] a burial chamber, as in catacombs

cu·bi·form (kyōō′bə fôrm′) *adj.* cube-shaped

cub·ism (kyōō′biz′m) *n.* a movement in art, esp. of the early 20th century, characterized by the use of cubes and other geometric forms in abstract arrangements rather than by a realistic representation of nature —**cub′ist** (-bist) *n., adj.* —**cu·bis′tic** (-bis′tik) *adj.*

cu·bit (kyōō′bit) *n.* [ME. & OE. < L. *cubitum*, the elbow, cubit: for IE. base see CUBE¹] an ancient measure of length, about 18–22 inches; orig., the length of the arm from the end of the middle finger to the elbow

cu·boid (kyōō′boid) *adj.* [Gr. *kyboeidēs*: see CUBE¹ & -OID] 1. shaped like a cube 2. designating a cubelike bone between the instep and the heel bone —*n.* 1. a six-sided figure each face of which is a rectangle 2. the cuboid bone —**cu·boi′dal** *adj.*

Cub Scout a member of a division of the Boy Scouts for boys eight through ten years old

‡**cu·ca·ra·cha** (kōō′kä rä′chä) *n.* [Sp.] a cockroach

Cu·chul·ain, Cu·chul·lin (kōō khool′in, -kul′in) [Ir.] *Ir. Legend* a heroic warrior who singlehandedly defended his country against invaders

cuck·ing stool (kuk′in) [ME. *coking-stole*, lit., toilet seat < ME. *coken* < ON. *kūka*, to defecate: the instrument was orig. made like a toilet seat to heighten the indignity] a chair in which disorderly women, scolds, cheats, etc. were fastened and exposed to public ridicule or sometimes ducked in water

cuck·old (kuk′'ld) *n.* [ME. *cokewold* < OFr. *cucuault* < *cucu* (see ff.): said to be in allusion to the female bird's habit of changing mates] a man whose wife has committed adultery —*vt.* to make a cuckold of —**cuck′old·ry** (-rē) *n.*

cuck·oo (kōō′kōō′, kook′ōō) *n.* [ME. < OFr. *coucou, cucu*, echoic of the bird's cry] 1. any of a family (Cuculidae) of birds with a long, slender body, grayish-brown on top and white below: many forms, including the European species (*Cuculus canorus*) lay eggs in the nests of other birds, but the American varieties hatch and rear their own young 2. the call of a cuckoo, which sounds somewhat like its name 3. an imitation of this call 4. [Slang] a crazy or foolish person —*vi.* to utter or imitate the call of a cuckoo —*vt.* to repeat continually, as the cuckoo does its call —*adj.* [Slang] crazy; foolish; silly

cuckoo clock a clock with a small toy figure of a cuckoo in it, which pops out at regular intervals, usually on the hour, to the accompaniment of a sound imitating the bird's call

cuck·oo·flow·er (-flou′ər) *n.* 1. a bitter cress (*Cardamine pratensis*) bearing white or rose flowers 2. *same as* RAGGED ROBIN

cuck·oo·pint (-pint′) *n.* a European wildflower (*Arum maculatum*) of the arum family, with large leaves and a spadix and spathe similar to those of the jack-in-the-pulpit

cuckoo spit (or **spittle**) 1. a frothy substance produced on plants by the nymphs of spittle insects to envelop their larvae 2. such an insect

cu·cu·li·form (kyoo kyōō′lə fôrm′, kə-) *adj.* [< L. *cuculus*, cuckoo + -FORM] of or like the cuckoos or the order (Cuculiformes) of birds to which they belong

cu·cul·late (kyōō′kə lāt′, kyoo kul′it) *adj.* [LL.(Ec.) *cucullatus* < *cuculla*, for L. *cucullus*, hood: for IE. base see CONCEAL] shaped like a hood; cowled, as the leaves of violets: also **cu′cul·lat′ed**

cu·cum·ber (kyōō′kum bər) *n.* [ME. *cucomer* < OFr. or L.; OFr. *concombre* < L. *cucumis* (gen. *cucumeris*)] 1. a trailing annual vine (*Cucumis sativus*) of the gourd family, grown for its edible fruit 2. the long fruit, with a green rind and firm, white flesh, gathered before fully mature and used in salads or preserved as pickles —**cool as a cucumber** 1. comfortably cool 2. calm and self-possessed

☆**cucumber tree** an American magnolia tree (*Magnolia acuminata*) with large, green flowers and fruit resembling a small cucumber

cu·cur·bit (kyoo kur′bit) *n.* [L. *cucurbita*] 1. any plant of the gourd family 2. [Fr. *cucurbite* < L. *cucurbita:* so called in allusion to its shape] a large, gourd-shaped flask with a wide mouth, formerly used in distillation

Cú·cu·ta (kōō′kōō tä) city in N Colombia: pop. 175,000

cud (kud) *n.* [ME. < OE. *cudu*, ball of cud, lit., what is rounded < IE. *geut-* < base *geu-*, to curve, bend, whence COD², COG³] a mouthful of previously swallowed food regurgitated from the first stomach of cattle and other ruminants back to the mouth, where it is chewed slowly a second time —**chew the cud** to recall and think over something; ruminate; ponder

cud·bear (kud′ber′) *n.* [coined < CUTHBERT by Dr. *Cuthbert* Gordon, 18th-cent. Brit. physician, who developed the dye] 1. a purple dye prepared from lichens 2. *same as* ARCHIL

cud·dle (kud′'l) *vt.* -**dled**, -**dling** [Early ModE., to make comfortable, prob. < ME. (northern dial.) *cudelen* for

*****couthelen** (for -d, cf. FIDDLE) < *couth*, known, hence acquainted with, comfortable with (cf. UNCOUTH) + *-le*, freq. suffix] to hold lovingly and gently in one's arms; embrace and fondle —*vi.* to lie close and snug; nestle —*n.* 1. a cuddling 2. an embrace; hug —*SYN.* see CARESS

cud·dle·some (-səm) *adj.* of such a kind as to invite cuddling; appealingly sweet; lovable

cud·dly (kud'lē) *adj.* -dli·er, -dli·est 1. *same as* CUDDLESOME 2. fond of cuddling

cud·dy[1] (kud'ē) *n., pl.* -dies [17th-c.: < ? MLowG. *kaiüte* < ONormFr. *cahutie*, ult. < MHG. *hütte*, HUT] 1. *a)* a small cabin on a ship *b)* the cook's galley on a small ship 2. any small room, cupboard, or closet

cud·dy[2] (kud'ē) *n., pl.* -dies [< ? *Cuddy*, dim. of CUTHBERT] [Chiefly Scot.] 1. a donkey 2. a fool

cudg·el (kuj'əl) *n.* [ME. (SW dial.) *kuggel* < OE. *cycgel*, lit., club with rounded head, akin to G. *kugel*, ball < IE. base *geu-*, to curve, bend, whence CUD] a short, thick stick or club —*vt.* -eled or -elled, -el·ing or -el·ling to beat with a cudgel —**cudgel one's brains** to think hard —**take up the cudgels (for)** to come to the defense (of)

cud·weed (kud'wēd') *n.* [prob. CUD + WEED: of uncertain allusion] any of several small plants (genus *Gnaphalium*) of the composite family, with cottony or woolly leaves

cue[1] (kyōō) *n.* [< *q*, *Q*, used in plays in 16th & 17th c. to indicate actors' entrances; prob. abbrev. of some L. word (as *quando*, when, *qualis*, in what manner)] 1. a bit of dialogue, action, or music that is a signal for an actor's entrance or speech, or for the working of curtains, lights, sound effects, etc. 2. the few notes or bars of music directly preceding an instrumentalist's or vocalist's part and serving as a signal to begin that part 3. anything serving as a signal to do something 4. an indirect suggestion; hint 5. [Now Rare] *a)* the role that one is assigned to play *b)* a necessary course of action 6. [Archaic] frame of mind; mood; temperament 7. *Psychol.* a secondary stimulus that guides behavior, often without entering consciousness —*vt.* cued, cu'ing or cue'ing to give a cue to —☆**cue in** to add (dialogue, music, etc.) at a particular point in a script

cue[2] (kyōō) *n.* [var. of QUEUE] 1. *same as* QUEUE 2. a long, tapering, tipped rod used in billiards, pool, etc. to strike the cue ball 3. a long, shovellike stick used in shuffleboard to push the disks —*vt.* cued, cu'ing or cue'ing 1. to braid (hair, etc.) 2. to strike (a cue ball, etc.) with a cue

cue ball the ball that a player strikes with his cue in billiards or pool: it is usually white or yellowish

cue card a card, unseen by the audience, carrying dialogue, lyrics, etc. as an aid to a television performer

Cuen·ca (kwen'kä) city in SC Ecuador: pop. 61,000

☆**cues·ta** (kwes'tə) *n.* [Sp. < L. *costa*, side, rib] [Southwest] a ridge or hill characterized by a steep incline on one side and a gentle slope on the other

cuff[1] (kuf) *n.* [by sense extension < ME. *cuffe*, *coffe*, hand covering, glove, prob. < ML. *cuffia*, head covering, parallel with OFr. *coiffe*: see COIF] 1. band or fold at the end of a sleeve, either sewed in or detachable 2. a turned-up fold at the bottom of a trouser leg 3. the part of a glove covering the wrist or forearm 4. a handcuff —*vt.* to put a cuff or cuffs on —☆**off the cuff** [Slang] in an offhand manner; extemporaneously —☆**on the cuff** [Slang] on credit —**shoot one's cuffs** to expose one's shirt cuffs beyond the coat sleeves

cuff[2] (kuf) *vt.* [Early ModE. < ? CUFF[1] (in orig. sense "glove")] to strike, esp. with the open hand; slap —*vi.* to fight or scuffle —*n.* a slap or blow

cuff link a pair of linked buttons or any similar small device for keeping a shirt cuff closed

Cu·fic (kyōōf'ik) *adj. same as* KUFIC

Cu·ia·bá (kōō'yä bä') city in W Brazil, capital of Mato Grosso state: pop. 58,000

‡**cui bo·no** (kwē bō'nō) [L., lit., to whom for a good] 1. for whose benefit? i.e., who stands to gain from this? 2. to what purpose? i.e., of what utility is this?

cui·rass (kwi ras') *n.* [Fr. *cuirasse* < It. *corazza* < VL. *coracea*, for L. (*vestis*) *coriacea*, leather (clothing) < *corium*, leather, hide: see CORIUM] 1. a piece of closefitting armor for protecting the breast and back, orig. made of leather 2. the breastplate of such armor 3. *Zool.* a protective structure of bony plates —*vt.* to cover with or as with a cuirass

cui·ras·sier (kwi'rə sir') *n.* [Fr.] a cavalryman wearing a cuirass

cui·sine (kwi zēn') *n.* [Fr. < L. *cocina*, var. of *coquina*, kitchen < *coquere*, to COOK] 1. the kitchen 2. the style of cooking; manner of preparing food 3. the food prepared, as at a restaurant

cuisse (kwis) *n.* [ME. *cuissues* < OFr. *cuisseaux*, pl. of *cuissel* < *cuisse*, thigh < L. *coxa*, hip: see COXA] a piece of armor to protect the thigh: also **cuish** (kwish)

Cul·bert·son (kul'bərt sən), E·ly (ē'lē) 1893-1955; U.S. authority on contract bridge, born in Romania

culch (kulch) *n. same as* CULTCH

cul-de-sac (kul'də sak', kool'-; *Fr.* küt såk') *n., pl.* **cul-de-sacs**; *Fr.* **culs-de-sac** (küt såk') [Fr., lit., bottom of a sack] 1. a passage or position with only one outlet; blind alley 2. a situation from which there is no escape 3. *Anat.* a blind pouch, as the cecum

-cule (kyōōl, kyool) [< Fr. or L.; Fr. *-cule* < L. *-culus*, *-cula*, *-culum*] a suffix meaning small [*animalcule*]

cu·let (kyōō'lit) *n.* [OFr., dim. of *cul*, posterior, bottom < L. *culus*, anus] the flat base of a diamond whose face is cut as a brilliant

cu·lex (kyōō'leks) *n.* [L., a gnat < IE. base *kū-*, sharp, pointed, whence OIr. *cuil*, gnat, Sans. *śula-*, spear] any of a large genus (*Culex*) of mosquitoes including many of the most common species found in N. America and Europe —**cu·li·cine** (kyōō'lə sin, -sīn') *adj., n.*

Cu·lia·cán (kōōl'yə kän') city in NW Mexico; capital of Sinaloa state: pop. 85,000

cu·lic·id (kyōō lis'id) *adj.* [< ModL. *Culicidae*, name of the family < L. *culex* (gen. *culicis*): see CULEX] of the mosquito family —*n.* a mosquito

cu·li·nar·y (kyōō'lə ner'ē, kul'ə-) *adj.* [LL. *culinarius* < L. *culina*, kitchen] 1. of the kitchen 2. of cooking 3. suitable for or used in cooking

cull (kul) *vt.* [ME. *cullen* < OFr. *coillir* < L. *colligere*: see COLLECT[2]] 1. to pick out; select 2. to select and gather (flowers, etc.); pick 3. to examine carefully so as to select or reject; pick over —*n.* something picked out; esp., something rejected as not being up to standard

Cul·len (kul'ən), **Coun·tee** (koun'tē) 1903-46; U.S. poet

cul·len·der (kul'ən dər) *n. same as* COLANDER

cul·let (kul'it) *n.* [< Fr. *collet*, dim. of *col*, neck, with reference to glass debris at the neck of a bottle in blowing] scraps of waste glass that can be remelted

cul·lion (kul'yən) *n.* [ME. *coillon*, wretch, lit., testicle < Fr. *couillon* < It. *coglione*, ult. < L. *coleus*, scrotum] [Obs.] a low, contemptible fellow

cul·lis (kul'is) *n.* [Fr. *coulisse*: see COULISSE] *Archit.* a gutter or groove

cul·ly (kul'ē) *n., pl.* -lies [17th-cent. thieves' slang; prob. contr. of CULLION] [Old Slang] 1. a dupe 2. a fellow; companion; mate —*vt.* -lied, -ly·ing [Old Slang] to trick; deceive; cheat

culm[1] (kulm) *n.* [northern Brit. dial. < ME. *colme*, *culme* < ? OE. *col*, COAL + ? suffix as in *fæthm*, FATHOM] 1. waste material from coal screenings or washings 2. [C-] *Geol.* a European Lower Carboniferous formation of shale or sandstone containing beds of impure anthracite: also **culm measures**

culm[2] (kulm) *n.* [L. *culmus*, a stalk, stem; akin to G. *halm*, blade (of grass), Gr. *calamos*, reed, cane] the jointed stem of various grasses, usually hollow —*vi.* to grow or develop into a culm

cul·mi·nant (kul'mə nənt) *adj.* [ML. *culminans*, prp.] 1. at the highest point or altitude 2. culminating

cul·mi·nate (-nāt') *vi.* -nat'ed, -nat'ing [< ML. *culminatus*, pp. of *culminare* < L. *culmen* (gen. *culminis*), peak, summit, contr. of *columen*: see COLUMN] 1. to reach its highest altitude: said of a celestial body 2. to reach its highest point or climax; result (*in*) —*vt.* to bring to its climax; cap

cul·mi·na·tion (kul'mə nā'shən) *n.* 1. a culminating; reaching of the highest altitude or point 2. the highest point; zenith; climax

cu·lotte (koo lät', kyōō-) *n.* [Fr. < *cul*, posterior < L. *culus*] [*often pl.*] a women's or girls' garment consisting of trousers made full in the legs to resemble a skirt

‡**cul·pa** (kool'pə, kul'-) *n.* [L.] 1. fault; guilt 2. *Law* neglect or fault; negligence

cul·pa·ble (kul'pə b'l) *adj.* [altered, after L. < ME. *coupable* < OFr. *coupable* < L. *culpabilis* < *culpa*, crime, fault, blame] deserving blame; blameworthy —**cul'pa·bil'i·ty** (-bil'ə tē) *n.* —**cul'pa·bly** (-blē) *adv.*

cul·prit (kul'prit) *n.* [< Anglo-Fr. *cul. prit*, contr. for phr. *culpable*, *prit* (*a averer nostre bille*), lit., guilty, ready (to prove our case): words used by prosecutor in opening case < *culpable* (see CULPABLE) + *prit*, for OFr. *prest* < LL. *praestus*, ready] 1. a person accused of a crime or offense, as in court; prisoner at the bar 2. a person guilty of a crime or offense; offender

cult (kult) *n.* [< L. *cultus*, care, cultivation, orig. pp. of *colere*, to till < IE. base *kwel-*, to turn, dwell, care for: cf. WHEEL, COLLAR] 1. a system of religious worship or ritual 2. *a)* devoted attachment to, or extravagant admiration for, a person, principle, etc., esp. when regarded as a fad [the cult of nudism] *b)* the object of such attachment 3. a group of followers; sect —**cult'ic** *adj.* —**cult'ism** *n.* —**cult'ist** *n.*

cultch (kulch) *n.* [< ? OFr. *culche*, *couche*, layer, deposit: see COUCH] 1. old shells, stones, etc., forming a spawning bed for oysters 2. [Dial.] rubbish

cul·ti·gen (kul'ti jən) *n.* [CULTI(VATED) + -GEN] a cultivated plant not known in a wild form and presumably originated in cultivation

cul·ti·va·ble (kul'tə və b'l) *adj.* [ML. *cultivabilis*] that can be cultivated: also **cul'ti·vat'a·ble** (-vāt'ə b'l) —**cul'ti·va·bil'i·ty** (-və bil'ə tē) *n.*

☆**cul·ti·var** (kul'ti vär', -ver') *n.* [CULTI(VATED) VAR(IETY)] a variety of a plant species originating and continuing in cultivation and given a name in a modern language

cul·ti·vate (kul'tə vāt') *vt.* -vat'ed, -vat'ing [< ML. *cultivatus*, pp. of *cultivare* < LL. *cultivus*, tilled < L. *cultus*: see CULT] 1. to prepare and use (soil, land, etc.) for growing crops; till 2. to break up the surface soil around (plants) in order to destroy weeds, prevent crusting, and preserve moisture 3. to grow (plants or crops) from seeds, bulbs, shoots, etc. 4. to improve or develop (plants) by various

horticultural techniques **5.** to improve by care, training, or study; refine [to *cultivate* one's mind] **6.** to promote the development or growth of; acquire and develop [to *cultivate* a taste for music] **7.** to seek to develop familiarity with; give one's attention to; pursue

cul·ti·vat·ed (-id) *adj.* **1.** prepared and used for growing crops; tilled [*cultivated* land] **2.** grown by cultivation: opposed to WILD **3.** trained and developed; refined; cultured [a *cultivated* person]

cul·ti·va·tion (kul'tə vā'shən) *n.* **1.** the act of cultivating (in various senses) **2.** refinement, or culture

cul·ti·va·tor (kul'tə vāt'ər) *n.* **1.** a person who cultivates **2.** an implement or machine for loosening the earth and destroying weeds around growing plants

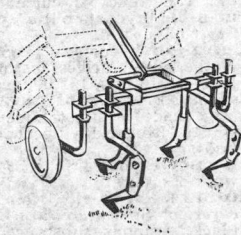

CULTIVATOR

cul·trate (kul'trāt) *adj.* [L. *cultratus*, knifelike < *culter*, a knife: cf. COLTER] sharp-edged and pointed

cul·tur·al (kul'chər əl) *adj.* **1.** of or pertaining to culture; specif., of the training and refinement of the mind, interests, tastes, skills, arts, etc. **2.** obtained by breeding or cultivation —**cul'tur·al·ly** *adv.*

cultural (or **culture**) **lag** the failure of one aspect of a cultural complex to keep pace with the changes in some other related aspect, as the failure of social institutions to keep pace with the rapid advances in science

cul·ture (kul'chər) *n.* [ME. < L. *cultura* < *colere*: see CULT] **1.** cultivation of the soil **2.** production, development, or improvement of a particular plant, animal, commodity, etc. **3.** *a)* the growth of bacteria or other microorganisms in a specially prepared nourishing substance, as agar *b)* a colony of microorganisms thus grown **4.** *a)* development, improvement, or refinement of the mind, emotions, interests, manners, taste, etc. *b)* the result of this; refined ways of thinking, talking, acting, etc. **5.** development or improvement of physical qualities by special training or care [body *culture*, voice *culture*] **6.** the ideas, customs, skills, arts, etc. of a given people in a given period; civilization —*vt.* **-tured, -tur·ing 1.** to cultivate **2.** to grow (microorganisms) in a specially prepared medium

cul·tured (-chərd) *adj.* **1.** produced or obtained by cultivation **2.** refined in speech, behavior, etc.

cultured pearl a pearl grown within a mollusk by controlled stimulation, as by insertion of a bead of mother-of-pearl

culture medium a nutrient substance sterilized and prepared for the controlled growth of microorganisms

cul·tur·ist (kul'chər ist) *n.* **1.** a person engaged in the culture of plants or animals **2.** one who advocates, or is devoted to, general cultural advancement

cul·tus (kul'təs) *n.* **1.** a cult, esp. a religious cult

cul·ver (kul'vər) *n.* [ME. < OE. *culfer, culufre* < VL. *columbra*, for L. *columbula*, dim. of *columba*: see COLUMBARIUM] a dove or pigeon

cul·ver·in (kul'vər in) *n.* [Fr. *coulevrine < couleuvre*, adder < VL. **culobra*, for L. *colubra*, a serpent, snake] **1.** a kind of musket used in the Middle Ages **2.** a long, heavy cannon of the 16th and 17th centuries

cul·vert (kul'vərt) *n.* [late 18th cent. < ?] a conduit, esp. a drain, as a pipelike construction of brick, stone, or concrete, that passes under a road, railroad track, footpath, etc. or through an embankment

cum (kum, kŏŏm) *prep.* [L.] with: used, chiefly in hyphenated compounds, with the general meaning "combined with," "plus" [vaude-ville-*cum*-burlesque]

CULVERT

Cu·mae (kyōō'mē) ancient Greek city in Campania, SW Italy, near Naples: thought to have been the first Greek colony in Italy, founded 9th or 8th cent. B.C.

Cu·mae·an (kyōō mē'ən) *adj.* **1.** of Cumae **2.** of a famous sibyl of Cumae: cf. SIBYLLINE BOOKS

Cu·ma·ná (kōō'mä nä') seaport in NE Venezuela, on the Caribbean: pop. 72,000

cum·ber (kum'bər) *vt.* [ME. *combren*, aphetic < *acombren* < OFr. *encombrer* < *en-* (see EN-[1]) + *combre*, obstruction, barrier < VL. **comboros*, something brought together, ult. (? via Gaul.) < IE. **kom* (see COM-) + base **bher-*, BEAR[1]] **1.** to hinder by obstruction or interference; hamper **2.** to burden in a troublesome way **3.** [Obs.] to perplex or distress —*n.* anything that cumbers

Cum·ber·land (kum'bər lənd) **1.** county in NW England, on the border of Scotland; 1,520 sq. mi.; pop. 296,000; county seat, Carlisle **2.** [after William Augustus, Duke

of Cumberland (1721–65), son of George II; Eng. general] river in S Ky. & N Tenn., flowing west into the Ohio at the S Ill. border: 687 mi.

Cumberland Gap pass in the Cumberland Plateau, at the juncture of the Va., Ky., & Tenn. borders: c. 1,700 ft. high

Cumberland Plateau (or **Mountains**) division of the W Appalachians, extending from S W.Va. to N Ala.: highest peak, 4,150 ft.

cum·ber·some (kum'bər səm) *adj.* hard to handle or deal with as because of size, weight, or many parts; burdensome; unwieldy; clumsy —*SYN.* see HEAVY —**cum'ber·some·ly** *adv.* —**cum'ber·some·ness** *n.*

cum·brance (kum'brəns) *n.* a troublesome burden

cum·brous (-brəs) *adj.* same as CUMBERSOME —**cum'brous·ly** *adv.* —**cum'brous·ness** *n.*

‡**cum gra·no sa·lis** (koom grä'nō sä'lis, kum grā'nō sā'lis) [ModL., lit., with a grain of salt] with due skepticism

cum·in (kum'in) *n.* [ME. < OFr. *cumin* < L. *cuminum* < Gr. *kyminon* < Sem., as in Heb. *kammōn*, Ar. *kammūn*: cf. KÜMMEL] **1.** a small plant (*Cuminum cyminum*) of the parsley family, bearing umbels of small, white or rose flowers **2.** its aromatic fruits, used for flavoring pickles, soups, etc. Also sp. **cum'min**

‡**cum lau·de** (koom lou'de, kum lô'dē) [L.] with praise: phrase used to signify graduation with honors from a college or university: cf. MAGNA CUM LAUDE, SUMMA CUM LAUDE

cum·mer (kum'ər) *n.* [ME. *commare* < OFr. *commere* < VL. *commater* + L. *com-*, with + *mater*, mother] [Scot.] **1.** a godmother **2.** a woman companion **3.** a woman or girl

cum·mer·bund (kum'ər bund') *n.* [Hind. & Per. *kamar-band*, loin band < Ar.-Per. *kamar*, loins + Per. *band*, band] a wide sash worn as a waistband, orig. by men in India, and adapted for wear with men's formal dress

Cum·mings (kum'iŋz), E(dward) E(stlin) 1894–1962; U.S. poet

cum·quat (kum'kwät) *n.* same as KUMQUAT

cum·shaw (kum'shô) *n.* [< dial. form of Chin. *kan hsieh*, grateful thanks] a tip or gratuity

cu·mu·late (kyōōm'yə lāt'; *for adj., usually* -lit) *vt., vi.* **-lat·ed, -lat·ing** [< L. *cumulatus*, pp. of *cumulare*, to heap up, amass < *cumulus*: see CUMULUS] to gather into a heap; accumulate —*adj.* gathered into a heap —**cu'mu·la'tion** *n.*

cu·mu·la·tive (kyōōm'yə lāt'iv, -lə tiv) *adj.* [see CUMULATE] **1.** increasing in effect, size, quantity, etc. by successive additions; accumulated [*cumulative* interest is interest that is added to the principal and draws additional interest] **2.** *Law* designating additional evidence that gives support to earlier evidence —**cu'mu·la'tive·ly** *adv.*

cumulative voting a system of voting for members of a legislature in which each voter is allowed as many votes as there are members to be elected: he may distribute his votes or give them all to one candidate

cu·mu·li·form (kyōōm'yoo lə fôrm') *adj.* [L. *cumuli*, pl. of *cumulus* + -FORM] designating, or having the form of, a cumulus (cloud)

cu·mu·lo·nim·bus (kyōōm'yoo lō nim'bəs) *n.* a dense cloud type towering to great heights, with the upper portion usually flattened, and commonly producing lightning and heavy showers

cu·mu·lous (kyōōm'yə ləs) *adj.* of, or having the form of, a cumulus (cloud), or consisting of cumuli

cu·mu·lus (-ləs) *n., pl.* **-li'** (-lī') [L., a heap < IE. **ku-me-los*, a swelling, increase < base **keu-*, to swell] **1.** a heap; mass; pile **2.** a thick cloud type, usually isolated, with a dark, nearly horizontal base and upper parts resembling domes or towers

Cu·nax·a (kyoo nak'sə) ancient town in Babylonia, near the Euphrates: site of a battle (401 B.C.) in which Cyrus the Younger was killed

CUMULUS CLOUDS

cunc·ta·tion (kəŋk tā'shən) *n.* [L. *cunctatio < cunctari*, to hesitate, linger] [Rare] a delaying or delay —**cunc·ta·tive** (kuŋk'tāt iv, -tə tiv) *adj.*

cu·ne·al (kyōō'nē əl) *adj.* [< L. *cuneus*, a wedge: for IE. base, see CULEX] wedge-shaped; esp., cuneiform: also **cu'ne·at'ic** (-nē ə'tik)

cu·ne·ate (kyōō'nē it, -āt') *adj.* [L. *cuneatus* < prec.] *Bot.* wedge-shaped; tapering, as some leaves: also **cu'ne·at'ed** (-āt'id) —**cu'ne·ate·ly** *adv.*

cu·ne·i·form (kyōō nē'ə fôrm', kyōō'nē ə-) *adj.* [< L. *cuneus* (see CUNEAL) + -FORM] wedge-shaped; esp., designating the characters used in ancient Akkadian, Assyrian, Babylonian, and Persian inscriptions, or such inscriptions —*n.* cuneiform characters or inscriptions

GOD   SUN   MAN

CUNEIFORM

cun·ner (kun'ər) n. [Brit. var. *conner* < ? CONN, in sense "directing fishing boats to herring shoals"] a small, edible, brownish-blue fish (*Tautogolabrus adspersus*) found along the Atlantic coast of N. America

cun·ni·lin·gus (kun'ə liŋ'gəs) n. [ModL. < L., lit., vulva-licker < *cunnus*, vulva + *lingere*, to LICK] a sexual activity involving oral contact with the female genitals

cun·ning (kun'iŋ) adj. [ME., having skill, knowing < prp. of *cunnen*, to know (see CAN¹): for sense, cf. KNOWING] 1. [Now Rare] skillful or clever 2. skillful in deception; sly; crafty 3. made or done with skill or ingenuity ☆4. attractive or pretty in a delicate way; cute —n. 1. [Now Rare] clever proficiency; skill 2. skill in deception; slyness; craftiness —SYN. see CLEVER, SLY —cun'ning·ly adv. —cun'ning·ness n.

cup (kup) n. [ME. & OE. *cuppe* < LL. *cuppa*, altered < L. *cupa*, tub < IE. base *geu-, to curve, bend, arch: cf. COOP, COOMB] 1. a small, open container for beverages, usually bowl-shaped and with a handle 2. the bowl part of a drinking vessel 3. a cup and its contents 4. the amount a cup holds; cupful: a standard measuring cup holds eight ounces 5. anything shaped like a cup 6. an ornamental cup with a stem and base given as a prize: it is usually of metal, esp. silver 7. *a)* the chalice containing the wine at Communion *b)* the wine 8. one's portion, share, or allotment *[his cup* of happiness was full*]* 9. something served as in a cup: see CLARET CUP, FRUIT CUP 10. *Biol.* any cuplike organ or structure 11. *Golf* the metal container set in the hole sunk into the green, into which the ball drops; hole 12. *Med.* a small glass bowl or similar object used in cupping —vt. **cupped, cup'ping** 1. to shape like a cup 2. to take in or put into a cup 3. *Med.* to treat with or subject to cupping —**in one's cups** drunk; intoxicated —**cup'like'** adj.

cup·bear·er (-ber'ər) n. a person who fills and serves the wine cups, as in a king's palace

cup·board (kub'ərd) n. [ME. *cuppebord*: see CUP & BOARD] a closet or cabinet with shelves for holding cups, plates, food, etc.

☆**cup·cake** (kup'kāk') n. a little cake for one person, baked in a small, cup-shaped mold and often iced

cu·pel (kyōō'pəl, kyōō pel') n. [Fr. *coupelle* < ML. *cupella*, dim. < L. *cupa*: see CUP] 1. a small, shallow, porous cup used in assaying gold, silver, etc. 2. a hearth for refining metals —vt. **-peled** or **-pelled, -pel·ing** or **-pel·ling** to assay or refine in a cupel —**cu'pel·la'tion** (-pə lā'shən) n.

cup·fer·ron (kup'fə rän', kōōp'-) n. [CUP(RIC) + FERR(O)- + -ON] a white crystalline material, C₆H₅N(NO)ONH₄, soluble in water: used as a precipitating reagent for copper, iron, aluminum, etc.

cup·ful (kup'fool') n., pl. **-fuls'** as much as a cup will hold: a standard measuring cup holds eight ounces

Cu·pid (kyōō'pid) [ME. & OFr. *Cupide* < L. *Cupido* < *cupido*, desire, passion < *cupidus*, eager, passionate < *cupere*, to desire < IE. base *kup-, to boil, smoke, be disturbed] *Rom. Myth.* the god of love, son of Venus: usually represented as a winged boy with bow and arrow and identified with the Greek god Eros —n. [c-] a representation of Cupid as a naked, winged cherub, as on a valentine

cu·pid·i·ty (kyōō pid'ə tē) n. [ME. & Anglo-Fr. *cupidite* < L. *cupiditas* < *cupidus*: see prec.] strong desire, esp. for wealth; avarice; greed

cu·pid's-bow (kyōō'pidz bō') adj. in the shape of the bow that Cupid is usually pictured as carrying *[a cupid's-bow mouth]*

cup of tea [Colloq.] a favorite thing, activity, etc. *[golf isn't his cup of tea]*

cu·po·la (kyōō'pə lə) n. [It. < L. *cupula*, dim. of *cupa*: see CUP] 1. a rounded roof or ceiling 2. a small dome or similar structure on a roof 3. a small furnace for melting metals 4. any of various dome-shaped structures or parts —**cu'po·laed** (-ləd) adj.

CUPOLA

cup·pa (kup'ə) n. [Brit. Colloq.] a cup of tea

cupped (kupt) adj. shaped like a cup; hollowed

cup·ping (-iŋ) n. the application to the skin of glass cups from which the air has been exhausted, in order to draw the blood to the surface: used, esp. formerly, to treat a variety of illnesses —**cup'per** n.

cu·pre·ous (kyōō'prē əs) adj. [L. *cupreus* < *cuprum*: see COPPER¹] 1. of or containing copper 2. copper-colored

cu·pri- (kyōō'pri) [see CUPRO-] a combining form meaning copper *[cupriferous]*

cu·pric (kyōō'prik) adj. [CUPR(O)- + -IC] *Chem.* of or containing copper with a valence of two

cu·prif·er·ous (kyōō prif'ər əs) adj. [CUPRI- + -FEROUS] containing copper

cu·prite (kyōō'prīt) n. cuprous oxide, Cu₂O, a dark-red ore of copper

cu·pro- (kyōō'prō) [< L. *cuprum*: see COPPER¹] a combining form meaning copper and: also, before a vowel, **cupr-**

cu·pro·nick·el (kyōō'prō nik'¹) n. an alloy of copper and nickel, used in the manufacture of hardware and in some coins

cu·prous (kyōō'prəs) adj. [CUPRO- + -OUS] *Chem.* of or containing copper with a valence of one

cu·prum (kyōō'prəm) n. [L.] copper: symbol, Cu

cu·pu·late (kyōō'pyə lāt') adj. [< ff. + -ATE¹] 1. shaped like a cupule or cup 2. having a cupule

cu·pule (kyōō'pyool) n. [ME. < L. *cupula*: see CUPOLA] *Biol.* a cuplike structure, as the part of an acorn that holds the nut

cur (kur) n. [ME. *curre*, earlier *kurdogge*, prob. < ON. or MLowG., as in Sw. dial. *kurre*, MLowG. *korre*, dog: basic sense "snarling, growling" < ON. *kurra* or MLowG. *korren*, to growl] 1. a dog of mixed breed; mongrel 2. a person who is mean, contemptible, cowardly, etc.

cur. 1. currency 2. current

cur·a·ble (kyoor'ə b'l) adj. that can be cured —**cur'a·bil'i·ty** (-bil'ə tē) n.

Cu·ra·çao (kyoor'ə sō', koor'ə sou') 1. largest island of the Netherlands Antilles, just north of the coast of Venezuela: 171 sq. mi.; pop. 132,000; cap. Willemstad 2. *former name of the* NETHERLANDS ANTILLES —n. [c-] [< prec., where orig. made] a sweet liqueur made by flavoring distilled spirits with the dried peel of bitter oranges: also **cu'ra·çoa'** (-sō')

cu·ra·cy (kyoor'ə sē) n., pl. **-cies** the position, office, or work of a curate

cu·ra·re, cu·ra·ri (kyoo rä'rē, koo-) n. [Port. *curare*, *curari* or Sp. *curaré*, *urarí* < native (Tupi) name] 1. a black, resinous substance prepared from the juices of certain S. American plants and used by some Indians for poisoning arrows: it causes motor paralysis when introduced into the bloodstream and is used in medicine to relax muscles, as during surgery 2. any of certain plants (esp. *Chondrodendron tomentosum*), from which curare is prepared

cu·ra·rine (-rin) n. any of a group of alkaloids derived from curare; esp., a toxic alkaloid, C₁₉H₂₆O N₂, used as a muscle relaxant

cu·ra·rize (kyoo rär'īz, kyoor'ə rīz') vt. **-rized, -riz·ing** to treat with curare —**cu·ra·ri·za·tion** (kyoo rär'i zā'shən, kyoor'ə ri-) n.

cu·ras·sow (kyoor'ə sō', kyoo ras'ō) n. [< CURAÇAO] any of several large, turkeylike game birds (esp. genera *Crax* and *Mitu*) of South and Central America, black or brown in color with an erectile crest

cu·rate (kyoor'it) n. [ME. *curat* < ML. *curatus*, one responsible for the care of souls < L. *curatus*: see ff.] 1. orig., any clergyman 2. a clergyman who assists a vicar or rector

cu·ra·tive (kyoor'ə tiv) adj. [ME. < OFr. *curatif* < ML. *curativus* < L. *curatus*, pp. of *curare*, to take care of < *cura*: see CURE] 1. of or for the curing of disease 2. curing, tending to cure, or having the power to cure —n. a thing that cures; remedy

cu·ra·tor (kyoo rāt'ər; kyoor'āt'ər, -ə tər) n. [ME. *curatour* < L. *curator* < *curare*: see prec.] 1. a person in charge of a museum, library, etc. 2. a guardian, as of a minor —**cu·ra·to·ri·al** (kyoor'ə tôr'ē əl) adj. —**cu·ra'tor·ship'** n.

curb (kurb) n. [ME. & OFr. *courbe*, curve, curb, orig., adj., curved, bent < L. *curvus*: see CURVE] 1. a chain or strap passed around a horse's lower jaw and attached to the bit: the curb checks the horse when the reins are pulled 2. anything that checks, restrains, or subdues 3. an enclosing framework 4. a raised margin around or along an edge, to strengthen or confine 5. the stone or concrete edging forming a gutter along a street 6. a market dealing in stocks and bonds not listed on the stock exchange: so called from the fact that early markets conducted their business on the street —vt. 1. to restrain; check; control *[to curb an impulse]* 2. to lead (a dog being walked) to the curb to pass its waste matter 3. to provide with a curb —SYN. see RESTRAIN

curb bit a horse's bit with a curb

curb·ing (-iŋ) n. 1. curbstones, collectively 2. material for a curb 3. a curb (sense 5)

curb roof same as MANSARD ROOF or GAMBREL ROOF

☆**curb service** service offered to customers who wish to remain in their cars, as at a drive-in restaurant

curb·stone (-stōn') n. any of the stones, or a row of stones, making up a curb

curch (kurch) n. [a sing. formed < *curches* < OFr. *couvrechés*, pl. of *couvrechef*: see KERCHIEF] [Scot.] a woman's kerchief for the head

cur·cu·li·o (kər kyōō'lē ō') n., pl. **-li·os'** [L., grain worm, weevil, akin to *circulus* (see CIRCLE)] any of a family (Curculionidae) of weevils characterized by heads extending into long snouts: some are harmful to fruit

cur·cu·ma (kur'kyoo mə) n. [ModL. < Ar. *kurkum*: see CROCUS] any of a genus (*Curcuma*) of tropical plants of the ginger family, with showy flowers and thick, tuberous rootstocks that yield starch: the turmeric (*Curcuma longa*) of India is used as a condiment and dye

curd (kurd) n. [15th-cent. form, metathesized < ME. *crud*, orig., any coagulated substance < IE. base *greut-, to press, coagulate, curd, whence CROWD¹] the coagulated part of milk, from which cheese is made: it is formed when milk sours and is distinguished from whey, the watery part —vt., vi. to form into curd; curdle

cur·dle (kur'd'l) vt., vi. **-dled, -dling** [CURD + -LE, sense 3]

to form into curd; coagulate; congeal —**curdle one's blood** to horrify or terrify one

curd·y (kur′dē) *adj.* 1. full of curd 2. like curd

cure (kyoor) *n.* [ME. & OFr. < L. *cura,* care, concern, trouble < OL. *coira* < IE. base **kois-,* be concerned] 1. a healing or being healed; restoration to health or a sound condition 2. a medicine or treatment for restoring health; remedy 3. a system, method, or course of treating a disease, ailment, etc. 4. spiritual charge of persons in a particular district; care of souls 5. the work or position of a curate; curacy 6. a process for curing meat, fish, tobacco, etc. —*vt.* **cured, cur′ing** 1. to restore to health or a sound condition; make well; heal 2. to get rid of or counteract (an ailment, evil, bad habit, etc.) 3. to get rid of a harmful or undesirable condition in (with *of*) [*cured* him of lying] 4. *a*) to preserve (meat, fish, etc.), as by salting or smoking *b*) to process (tobacco, leather, etc.), as by drying or aging —*vi.* 1. to bring about a cure 2. to undergo curing, preserving, or processing [tobacco *cures* in the sun] —**cure′less** *adj.* —**cur′er** *n.*

SYN.—**cure** and **heal** both imply a restoring to health or soundness, **cure** specifically suggesting the elimination of disease, distress, evil, etc., and **heal,** the making or becoming whole of a wound, sore, lesion, etc. or, figuratively, the mending of a breach; **remedy** stresses the use of medication or a specific corrective treatment in relieving disease, injury, distress, etc.

cu·ré (kyoo rā′, kyoor′ā) *n.* [Fr. < ML. *curatus:* see CURATE] in France, a parish priest

cure-all (kyoor′ôl′) *n.* ☆something supposed to cure all ailments or evils; panacea

cu·ret, cu·rette (kyoo ret′) *n.* [Fr. < *curer,* to cleanse: see CURE] a spoon-shaped surgical instrument for the removal of tissue from the walls of body cavities —*vt.* **-ret′ted, -ret′ting** to clean or scrape with a curet

cu·ret·tage (kyoor′ə tazh′, kyoo ret′ij) *n.* [Fr.: see prec.] the process of curetting

cur·few (kur′fyoo) *n.* [ME. *curfeu* < OFr. *covrefeu,* lit., cover fire < *covrir* (see COVER) + *feu,* fire < L. *focus,* fireplace (see FOCUS)] 1. *a*) in the Middle Ages, a regulation causing a bell to be rung every evening at a certain time as a signal for people to cover fires, put out lights, and retire *b*) the ringing of such a bell *c*) the time at which it was rung *d*) the bell 2. *a*) a time, generally in the evening, set as a deadline beyond which inhabitants of occupied cities in wartime, children under a specified age, etc. may not appear on the streets or in public places *b*) the regulation establishing this time

cu·ri·a (kyoor′ē ə) *n., pl.* **-ri·ae′** (-ē′) [L. (in ML., court) < **co-viria,* assembly of men < *co-,* together + **viro-,* man (see VIRILE)] 1. in ancient Rome, *a*) any of the ten political subdivisions into which the Latin, Sabine, and Etruscan tribes were each divided *b*) its meeting place *c*) the senate house at Rome 2. a medieval judicial council or court held in the king's name 3. [C-] the administrative body of the Roman Catholic Church, consisting of various departments, courts, officials, etc. functioning under the authority of the Pope: in full, **Curia Ro·ma·na** (rō mä′nə, -mä′-) —**cu′ri·al** *adj.*

Cu·rie (kyoo rē′, kyoor′ē; *Fr.* kü rē′) 1. **Marie,** (born *Marie Sklodowska*) 1867–1934; Pol. chemist & physicist in France: discovered polonium & radium (1898) in collaboration with her husband 2. **Pierre,** 1859–1906; Fr. physicist: husband of *prec.*

cu·rie (kyoor′ē, kyoo rē′) *n.* [after Marie CURIE] the unit used in measuring radioactivity, equal to the quantity of any radioactive material in which the number of disintegrations per second is 3.7×10^{10}

Curie point the temperature at which the magnetic properties of a substance change from ferromagnetic to paramagnetic, usually lower than the melting point of the substance: also **Curie temperature**

Curie's law [after Pierre CURIE] the law that the ratio of the magnetization of a paramagnetic substance to the magnetizing force is in inverse proportion to the absolute temperature

cu·ri·o (kyoor′ē ō′) *n., pl.* **-os′** [contr. of CURIOSITY] any unusual or rare article

cu·ri·o·sa (kyoor′ē ō′sə, -zə) *n.pl.* [L., lit., curious objects] curiosities; specif., books, etc. dealing with strange or unusual, often erotic, subjects

cu·ri·os·i·ty (kyoor′ē äs′ə tē) *n., pl.* **-ties** [ME. *curiousite* < OFr. *curiosité* < L. *curiositas* < *curiosus:* see CURIOUS] 1. a desire to learn or know 2. a desire to learn about things that do not properly concern one; inquisitiveness 3. anything curious, strange, rare, or novel 4. [Obs.] the quality of being careful, scrupulous, or fastidious

cu·ri·ous (kyoor′ē əs) *adj.* [ME. < OFr. *curios* < L. *curiosus,* careful, diligent, curious, akin to *cura,* care: see CURE] 1. eager to learn or know 2. unnecessarily inquisitive; prying 3. arousing attention or interest because unusual or strange; odd 4. [Rare] highly detailed, as in workmanship; elaborate 5. [Obs.] fastidious —**cu′ri·ous·ly** *adv.* —**cu′ri·ous·ness** *n.*

SYN.—**curious,** in this comparison, implies eagerness or anxiousness to find out things and may suggest a wholesome desire to be

informed; **inquisitive** implies a habitual tendency to be curious, esp. about matters that do not concern one, and an attempt to gain information by persistent questioning; **meddlesome** suggests unwelcome intrusion into the affairs of others; **prying** suggests an officious inquisitiveness and meddlesomeness that persist against resistance

Cu·ri·ti·ba (koo′rē tē′bə) city in S Brazil; capital of Paraná state: pop. 361,000

☆**cu·ri·um** (kyoor′ē əm) *n.* [ModL., after Pierre & Marie CURIE, by analogy with GADOLINIUM, which it resembles] an extremely radioactive actinide element generally produced by neutron irradiation of plutonium or americium: symbol, Cm; at. wt., 247(?); at. no., 96; sp. gr., 13.51; melt. pt., 1340°C

curl (kurl) *vt.* [ME. *curlen,* metathesized < *crullen,* to curl, bend, twist < *crul,* curly, akin to Du. *krul* (cf. CRULLER) < Gmc. **kruzla* < IE. **greu-s* < base **ger-,* to turn, twist] 1. to wind or twist (esp. hair) into ringlets or coils 2. to cause to roll over or bend around 3. to raise the upper corner of (the lip), as in showing contempt or scorn —*vi.* 1. to form curls; become curled 2. to assume a spiral or curved shape 3. to move in spirals; undulate 4. to play the game of curling —*n.* 1. a little coil of hair; ringlet 2. anything with a spiral or curled shape; any coil 3. a curling or being curled 4. any of various diseases of plants in which the leaves curl up —**curl up** 1. to gather into spirals or curls; roll up 2. to sit or lie with the legs drawn up 3. [Colloq.] to collapse; break down —**in curl** curled —**curl′er** *n.*

cur·lew (kur′loo, -lyoo) *n., pl.* **-lews, -lew:** see PLURAL, II, D, 1 [ME. *curlieu* < OFr. *corlieu,* of echoic origin, but infl. by association with *corlieu,* messenger, courier] any of a genus (*Numenius*) of large, brownish wading birds with long legs

CURLEW
(length to 19 in.; wingspread to 33 in.)

curl·i·cue (kur′li kyoo′) *n.* [< CURLY + CUE²] a fancy curve, flourish, etc., as in a design or in handwriting

curl·ing (kur′lin) *n.* [so named from the curving path of the stone when slid] a game played on ice by sliding a heavy, thick disk of stone or iron (**curling stone**) toward a target circle at the other end of the rink: players may sweep the ice before the moving disk to control its course

curling iron (or **irons**) an instrument for curling or waving the hair, generally a metal rod around which, after it is heated, a tress of hair is rolled into a ringlet

curl·pa·per (kurl′pā′pər) *n.* a piece of paper around which a tress of hair may be wrapped to make it curl

CURLING

curl·y (kur′lē) *adj.* **-i·er, -i·est** 1. curling or tending to curl 2. having curls 3. having an undulating grain, as certain woods do —**curl′i·ness** *n.*

cur·mudg·eon (kər muj′ən) *n.* [< ?] a surly, ill-mannered, bad-tempered person; cantankerous fellow —**cur·mudg′eon·ly** *adj.*

curn (kurn) *n.* [var. of CORN¹] [Scot.] 1. a single grain 2. a small number or quantity; few

curr (kur) *vi.* [< ON. *kurra,* to murmur, of echoic origin] [Rare] to make a murmuring, cooing sound

cur·rach, cur·ragh (kur′əkh, kur′ə) *n.* [Ir. & ScotGael. *curach,* akin to W. *corwg,* skin boat] [Ir. & Scot.] same as CORACLE

cur·ra·jong, cur·re·jong, cur·ri·jong (kur′ə jän′, -jôn′) *n.* same as KURRAJONG

cur·rant (kur′ənt) *n.* [ME. *corauns* < (*reisins of*) *Coraunce* < Anglo-Fr. (*raisins de*) *Corauntz,* (raisins of) Corinth: orig. imported from Corinth] 1. the dried fruit of a small, seedless grape (*Vitis vinifera,* cultivar) grown in the Mediterranean region, used in cooking 2. *a*) the small, sour, red, white, or black berry of several species of hardy shrubs (genus *Ribes*) of the saxifrage family, used for jellies and jams *b*) a shrub bearing this fruit

cur·ren·cy (kur′ən sē) *n., pl.* **-cies** [ML. *currentia,* a current < L. *currens:* see CURRENT] 1. a continual passing from hand to hand, as of a medium of exchange; circulation ☆2. the money in circulation in any country; often, specif., paper money 3. common acceptance; general use; prevalence [the *currency* of a pronunciation] 4. [Rare] the time during which anything is current

cur·rent (kur′ənt) *adj.* [altered (after L.) < ME. *curraunt* < OFr. *curant,* prp. of *courre* < L. *currere,* to run < IE. base **kers-,* to run, wagon, whence Gaul. *carros*] 1. orig., running or flowing 2. *a*) now going on; now in progress [the *current* month, his *current* job] *b*) at the present time; contemporary [*current* fashions] *c*) of most recent date

[the current edition] **3.** passing from person to person; circulating *[current money, current rumors]* **4.** commonly used, known, or accepted; prevalent *[a current term]* —*n.* **1.** a flow of water or air, esp. when strong or swift, in a definite direction; specif., such a flow within a larger body of water or mass of air **2.** a general tendency or drift; course **3.** *Elec.* the flow or rate of flow of electric charge in a conductor or medium between two points having a difference in potential, generally expressed in amperes —**cur′rent·ly** *adv.* —*SYN.* see PREVAILING, TENDENCY

current density the amount of electric current passing through a cross-sectional area (perpendicular to the direction of current) of a conductor in a given unit of time: commonly expressed in amperes per square centimeter or amperes per square inch

cur·ri·cle (kur′i k'l) *n.* [L. *curriculum:* see CURRICULUM] a light, two-wheeled carriage drawn by two horses side by side

cur·ric·u·lum (kə rik′yə ləm) *n., pl.* **-u·la** (-lə), **-u·lums** [L., lit., a running, course, race, career < *currere,* to run: see CURRENT] **1.** a fixed series of studies required, as in a college, for graduation, qualification in a major field of study, etc. **2.** all of the courses, collectively, offered in a school, college, etc., or in a particular subject —**cur·ric′u·lar** *adj.*

‡**curriculum vi·tae** (vīt′ē; vē′tī, wē′-) *pl.* **cur·ric′u·la** (-lə) **vi′tae** [L., course of life] a summary of one's personal history and professional qualifications, as that submitted by a job applicant; résumé

cur·ri·er (kur′ē ər) *n.* [ME. *curriour* < OFr. *corier* < L. *coriarius* < *corium,* hide (see CORIUM): infl. by association with CURRY[1]] **1.** a person who curries tanned leather **2.** a person who curries horses, etc.

Cur·ri·er and Ives (kur′ē ər ən īvz′) [after Nathaniel *Currier* (1813-88) & James M. *Ives* (1824-95), U.S. founders of the lithographing firm that published the prints] any of a 19th-cent. series of prints showing the manners, people, and events of the times

cur·rish (kur′ish) *adj.* of or resembling a cur; bad-tempered; mean; ill-bred —**cur′rish·ly** *adv.*

cur·ry[1] (kur′ē) *vt.* **-ried, -ry·ing** [ME. *curraien* < OFr. *correier, conreder,* to put in order < VL. **corredare* < L. *com-,* with + *-red-,* base appearing in **arredare:* see ARRAY] **1.** to rub down and clean the coat of (a horse, etc.) with a currycomb or brush **2.** to prepare (tanned leather) by soaking, scraping, cleaning, beating, etc. **3.** to beat or flog —**curry favor** [altered (after FAVOR) < ME. *curraien favel,* to flatter, lit., curry the chestnut horse; OFr. *favel,* chestnut horse (taken as symbol of duplicity) < dial. form of OHG. *falo,* pale, akin to OE. *fealu* (see FALLOW[2])] to try to win favor by flattery, fawning, etc.

cur·ry[2] (kur′ē) *n., pl.* **-ries** [Tamil *kari,* sauce] **1.** *same as* CURRY POWDER **2.** a sauce made with curry powder **3.** a kind of stew prepared with curry —*vt.* **-ried, -ry·ing** to prepare with curry powder

cur·ry·comb (kur′ē kōm′) *n.* [CURRY[1] + COMB] a comb with rows of teeth or ridges, for rubbing down and cleaning a horse's coat —*vt.* to use a currycomb on

curry powder a powder prepared from turmeric and various spices and herbs, used as a seasoning in cooking

CURRYCOMB

curse (kurs) *n.* [ME. & Late OE. *curs, n., cursian, v.:* basic sense, ? "wrath" < ? Anglo-Fr. *curuz,* wrath (OFr. *coroz*) + Anglo-Fr. *curcier* (OFr. *corocier*), to call down wrath upon < VL. **corruptiare:* see CORRUPT] **1.** a calling on God or the gods to send evil or injury down on some person or thing **2.** a profane, obscene, or blasphemous oath, imprecation, etc. expressing hatred, anger, vexation, etc. **3.** a person or thing that has been cursed **4.** evil or injury that seems to come in answer to a curse **5.** any cause of evil or injury —*vt.* **cursed** or **curst, curs′ing 1.** to call evil or injury down on; damn **2.** to swear at; use profane, blasphemous, or obscene language against **3.** to bring evil or injury on; afflict —*vi.* to utter a curse or curses; swear; blaspheme —**be cursed with** to be afflicted with; suffer from —**the curse** [Slang] menstruation, or a menstrual period

SYN.—**curse** is the general word for calling down evil or injury on someone or something; **damn** carries the same general meaning but, in strict usage, implies the use of the word "damn" in the curse *[he damned his enemies = he said, "Damn my enemies!"]*; **execrate** suggests cursing prompted by great anger or abhorrence; **imprecate** suggests the calling down of calamity on someone, esp. from a desire for revenge; **anathematize** strictly refers to the formal utterance of solemn condemnation by ecclesiastical authority, but in general use it is equivalent to **imprecate** —*ANT.* **bless**

curs·ed (kur′sid, kurst) *adj.* **1.** under a curse **2.** deserving to be cursed; specif., *a)* evil; wicked *b)* detestable; hateful *[this cursed cold]* **3.** [Archaic] malevolent; quarrelsome: usually sp. **curst**

cur·sive (kur′siv) *adj.* [ML. *cursivus* < L. *cursus:* see COURSE] flowing; not disconnected; specif., designating writing in which the strokes of the letters are joined in each word —*n.* **1.** a cursive character **2.** a manuscript in cursive

writing **3.** *Printing* a type face that looks like handwriting, but with unconnected letters

cur·so·ri·al (kər sôr′ē əl) *adj.* [< CURSORY + -AL] *Zool.* having legs or structural parts adapted for running

cur·so·ry (kur′sər ē) *adj.* [LL. *cursorius < cursor,* runner < *cursus:* see COURSE] hastily, often superficially, done; performed rapidly with little attention to detail —*SYN.* see SUPERFICIAL —**cur′so·ri·ly** *adv.* —**cur′so·ri·ness** *n.*

curt (kurt) *adj.* [L. *curtus:* for IE. base see SHORT] **1.** orig., short or shortened **2.** brief, esp. to the point of rudeness; terse or brusque *[a curt reply]* —*SYN.* see BLUNT —**curt′ly** *adv.* —**curt′ness** *n.*

cur·tail (kər tāl′) *vt.* [ME. *curtailen,* altered (after *taillen* < OFr. *taillier:* see TAILOR) < OFr. *curtald,* CURTAL] to cut short; reduce; abridge —*SYN.* see SHORTEN —**cur·tail′ment** *n.*

cur·tain (kur′t'n) *n.* [ME. & OFr. *cortine* < LL.(Ec.) *cortina,* lit. a cauldron, hence enclosing circle of a theater (< IE. base **(s)ker-,* to CURVE), used in Vulg. instead of L. *cors, cohors* (see COURT) to translate Gr. *aulaia,* curtain (esp. in a theater) < *aulē,* open court] **1.** a piece of cloth or other material, sometimes arranged so that it can be drawn up or sideways, hung for decoration, as at a window, or to cover, conceal, or shut off something **2.** anything that covers, conceals, or shuts off *[a curtain of fog]* **3.** that part of a rampart and parapet between two bastions or gates **4.** *Archit.* an enclosing wall that does not support a roof **5.** *Theater a)* the large drape or hanging screen at the front of the stage, which is drawn up or aside to reveal the stage *b)* the opening of the curtain at the beginning, or its closing at the end, of a play, act, or scene *c)* an effect, line, or situation in a play just before the curtain closes *d)* same as CURTAIN CALL ☆**6.** [*pl.*] [Slang] death; the end —*vt.* **1.** to provide or decorate with a curtain **2.** to cover, conceal, or shut off as with a curtain —**draw** (or **drop**) **the curtain 1.** to end **2.** to conceal —**lift** (or **raise**) **the curtain on 1.** to begin **2.** to reveal

curtain call 1. a call, usually by continued applause, for the performers to return to the stage at the end of a play, act, etc. **2.** such a return, acknowledging the applause

curtain lecture a private reprimand given by a wife to her husband: so called from the curtained beds in which such reproofs were conventionally given

curtain raiser 1. a short play or skit presented before a longer or more elaborate production **2.** any brief preliminary event, entertainment, etc.

curtain speech a speech delivered from in front of the curtain at the end of a theatrical performance

curtain wall an independently supported outer wall that carries only its own weight and is freely removable

cur·tal (kur′t'l) *adj.* [OFr. *curtald < court,* short < L. *curtus:* see CURT] [Obs.] shortened; curtailed —*n.* [Obs.] **1.** a horse with a docked tail **2.** anything cut short or shortened

curtal ax [altered < CUTLASS] [Archaic] a cutlass

cur·tate (kur′tāt) *adj.* [L. *curtatus,* pp. of *curtare,* to shorten < *curtus:* see CURT] shortened; abbreviated

cur·te·sy (kur′tə sē) *n., pl.* **-sies** [var. of COURTESY] *Law* the right that a husband has in the lands of his dead wife, provided they have had children capable of inheriting

cur·ti·lage (kur′t'l ij) *n.* [ME. < OFr. *cortillage < cortil,* dim. < ML. *cortis,* COURT] *Law* the fenced-in ground and buildings immediately surrounding a house or dwelling

Cur·tis (kur′tis) [< ONormFr. *curteis* (OFr. *corteis*): see COURTEOUS] a masculine name

Cur·tiss (kur′tis), **Glenn Hammond** 1878-1930; U.S. aviator & pioneer in aircraft construction

curt·sy (kurt′sē) *n., pl.* **-sies** [var. of COURTESY] a gesture of greeting, respect, etc. made, esp. formerly, by girls and women and characterized by a bending of the knees and a slight lowering of the body —*vi.* **-sied, -sy·ing** to make a curtsy Also sp. **curt′sey**

cu·rule (kyoor′ool) *adj.* [L. *curulis < currus,* chariot, akin to *currere,* to run: see CURRENT] **1.** designating a chair like an upholstered campstool with heavy curved legs, in which only the highest civil officers of Rome were privileged to sit **2.** privileged to sit in a curule chair; of the highest rank

cur·va·ceous (kər vā′shəs) *adj.* [CURV(E) + -ACEOUS] [Colloq.] having a full, shapely figure: said of a woman

cur·va·ture (kur′və chər) *n.* [ME. < L. *curvatura < curvare:* see CURVE] **1.** a curving or being curved **2.** a curve; curved part of anything **3.** *Geom.* the rate of deviation of a curve or curved surface from a straight line or plane surface tangent to it **4.** *Med.* an abnormal curving of a part *[curvature of the spine]*

curve (kurv) *adj.* [L. *curvus,* bent < IE. base **(s)ker-,* to turn, bend, whence Gr. *korōnos* (cf. CORONA), MIr. *cor,* circle] [Archaic] curved —*n.* **1.** a line having no straight part; bend having no angular part **2.** a thing or part having the shape of a curve **3.** the act of curving, or the extent of this **4.** [*pl.*] the pronounced curving outline of a shapely female figure ☆**5.** *Baseball* a pitched ball thrown with spin so that it curves to the opposite side before crossing the plate **6.** a curved line or similar graphic representation showing variations occurring or expected to occur in prices, business conditions, group achievements, etc. **7.** *Math.* a one-dimensional continuum of points in a space of two or more dimensions, such as a parabola in a plane or a helix in three-dimensional space —*vt., vi.* **curved, curv′ing 1.** to form a curve by bending **2.** to move in a curved path

SYN.—**curve** suggests a swerving or deflection in a line that follows or approximates the arc of a circle [he *curved* the next pitch]; **bend** refers to the curving of something that is normally straight but that yields to pressure or tension [to *bend* a wire]; **twist**, in this connection, implies greater resistance in the object to be bent and often connotes a wrenching out of the normal line [to *twist* one's arm]; **turn**, in this comparison often interchangeable with **bend**, is used specifically where the object is curved back upon itself [to *turn* a bed sheet]

cur·vet (kur′vit; *for v., usually* kər vet′) *n.* [It. *corvetta,* dim. < *corvo* < L. *curvus:* see CURVE] an upward leap made by a horse, in which the hind legs are raised from the ground just before the forelegs come down again —*vi.* -**vet′ted** or -**vet′ed, -vet′ting** *or* -**vet′ing** 1. to make a curvet 2. to leap; bound; frolic —*vt.* to cause to curvet

cur·vi- (kur′vɪ) [< L. *curvus,* curved] *a combining form meaning* curved or bent [*curvilinear*]

cur·vi·lin·e·ar (kur′və lin′ē ər) *adj.* consisting of or enclosed by a curved line or lines: also **cur′vi·lin′e·al** —**cur′vi·lin′e·ar·ly** *adv.*

curv·y (kur′vē) *adj.* **curv′i·er, curv′i·est** 1. having curves or a curve [a *curvy* road] 2. [Colloq.] curvaceous

Cur·zon (kur′z′n), **George Nathaniel,** 1st Marquis Curzon of Kedlestone, 1859–1925; Eng. statesman: viceroy of India (1899–1905)

Cus·co (kōōs′kō) *same as* CUZCO

cus·cus (kus′kus) *n.* [ModL. < native name in New Guinea] any of a genus (*Phalanger*) of sluggish, tree-dwelling marsupials, native to NE Australia and nearby islands, mostly vegetarian with foxlike ears and a prehensile tail

cu·sec (kyōō′sek′) *n.* [CU(BIC) + SEC(OND)] a unit for measuring volume of flow, equal to one cubic foot per second

Cush (kush) [Heb. *kūsh*] *Bible* 1. the oldest of Ham's sons 2. the land inhabited by his descendants, thought to be on the W shore of the Red Sea

cush·at (kush′ət, kōōsh′-) *n.* [N Brit. dial. < ME. *coushote* < OE. *cushote* as if < *cu-,* COO + base of *sceotan,* to shoot, dart (cf. SHOOT), in sense "cooing darter"] *same as* RING-DOVE (sense 1)

☆**cu·shaw** (kə shô′) *n.* [< AmInd. (Algonquian)] a variety of crookneck squash (*Cucurbita moschata*) of the gourd family

Cush·ing (kōōsh′in) 1. **Caleb,** 1800–79; U.S. diplomat: negotiated treaty (1845) opening Chinese ports to U.S. trade 2. **Harvey (Williams),** 1869–1939; U.S. neurosurgeon

Cush·ing's disease (kōōsh′inz) [after H. W. CUSHING] a disorder of the adrenal cortex, characterized by obesity, hypertension, diabetes mellitus, etc.

cush·ion (kōōsh′ən) *n.* [ME. *cuisshin* < OFr. *coissin* < ML. *coxinum,* altered (after L. *coxa,* hip) < Gallo-Roman **culcinum,* for L. *culcita,* cushion, QUILT] 1. a pillow or soft pad for sitting or kneeling on, or reclining against 2. a thing like a cushion in shape, softness, or use, as a small pillow used in lacemaking, padding of various sorts, etc. 3. a fatty or fibrous padlike part of the body 4. anything serving to absorb shock, as air or steam in some machines, the elastic inner rim of a billiard table, or a soft, padded insole 5. anything that moderates an adverse effect, relieves a distressing condition, provides comfort, etc. —*vt.* 1. to provide with a cushion or cushions 2. to scat or set on a cushion; prop up with cushions 3. to hide or suppress, as if under a cushion 4. to absorb (shock or noise) 5. to act as a cushion as in protecting from shock or injury, moderating ill effects, relieving distress, etc. [the bush *cushioned* his fall]

Cush·it·ic (kush it′ik, kōōsh-) *adj.* [< CUSH: cf. HAMITIC] designating or of a group of languages spoken in Ethiopia and E Africa, constituting a subfamily of the Afro-Asiatic family of languages —*n.* this group of languages

cush·y (kōōsh′ē) *adj.* **cush′i·er, cush′i·est** [orig. Brit. army slang < Hind. *khush,* pleasant < Per. *khūsh*] [Slang] easy; comfortable [a *cushy* job] —**cush′i·ness** *n.*

cusk (kusk) *n., pl.* **cusk, cusks:** see PLURAL, II, D, 2 [Brit. local name < ?] a large, edible sea fish (*Brosme brosme*) related to the cod, found in the N Atlantic ☆2. *same as* BURBOT

cusp (kusp) *n.* [L. *cuspis* (gen. *cuspidis*), point, pointed end, spear] 1. a point or pointed end; apex; peak 2. *Anat.* a) any of the elevations on the chewing surface of a tooth b) any of the triangular folds of a heart valve 3. *Archit.* a projecting point where two arcs meet, as in the internal curve of an arch 4. *Astron.* either horn of a crescent, as of the moon 5. *Geom.* a corner point formed by two tangent and oppositely directed branches of a curve

cus·pate (kus′pit, -pāt′) *adj. same as* CUSPIDATE: also **cus′pat′ed, cusped** (kuspt)

cus·pid (kus′pid) *n.* [L. *cuspis:* see CUSP] a tooth with one cusp; canine tooth —*adj. same as* CUSPIDATE

cus·pi·date (kus′pə dāt′) *adj.* [L. *cuspidatus,* pp. of *cuspidare,* to make pointed < *cuspis*] 1. having a cusp or cusps 2. having a short, abrupt point, as some leaves Also **cus′pi·dat′ed**

cus·pi·da·tion (kus′pə dā′shən) *n.* the use of cusps for decoration, as in architecture

☆**cus·pi·dor** (kus′pə dôr′) *n.* [Port. *cuspideira* < *cuspir,* to spit < L. *conspuere* < *com-,* intens. + *spuere,* to spit out] *same as* SPITTOON

cuss (kus) *n.* [< CURSE; *n.* 2 < ? CUSTOMER] [Colloq.] 1. a curse ☆2. a person or animal, esp. one regarded as queer or annoying: used humorously or contemptuously —*vt., vi.* [Colloq.] to curse —**cuss′er** *n.*

cuss·ed (kus′id) *adj.* [< prec. or CURSED] [Colloq.] 1. cursed 2. perverse; stubborn —**cuss′ed·ly** *adv.* —**cuss′ed·ness** *n.*

cus·tard (kus′tərd) *n.* [ME., altered < *crustade,* any dish baked in a crust, ult. (? via Pr. *crostado*) < L. *crusta,* CRUST] 1. a mixture of eggs, milk, sugar, and flavoring, either boiled or baked 2. a somewhat similar mixture frozen to the consistency of ice cream: in full, **frozen custard**

cus·tard-ap·ple (kus′tərd ap′'l) *adj.* [< prec., with references to the flavor and color] designating a family (Annonaceae) of tropical trees and shrubs, including the papaw, sweetsop, and soursop —*n.* 1. any of a genus (esp. *Annona reticulata*) of small trees of this family, grown for their large, edible, heart-shaped fruits 2. the fruit

Cus·ter (kus′tər), **George Armstrong** 1839–76; U.S. army officer: killed in a battle with the Sioux Indians on the Little Bighorn River

cus·to·di·al (kəs tō′dē əl) *adj.* of custody or custodians —*n.* a container for relics

cus·to·di·an (-dē ən) *n.* [< CUSTODY] 1. a person who has the custody or care of something, as of a private library; caretaker; keeper 2. a person responsible for the care and maintenance of a building; janitor —**cus·to′di·an·ship′** *n.*

cus·to·dy (kus′tə dē) *n., pl.* -**dies** [ME. *custodie* < L. *custodia* < *custos,* a guard, keeper < ? IE. base *(*s*)*keus-,* to cover, whence HOUSE] a guarding or keeping safe; care; protection; guardianship —**in custody** in the keeping of the police; under arrest —**take into custody** to arrest

cus·tom (kus′təm) *n.* [ME. < OFr. *costume* < L. *consuetudo* < *consuescere,* to accustom < *com-,* intens. + *suescere,* to become accustomed < *suus,* one's own] 1. a usual practice or habitual way of behaving; habit 2. *a)* a social convention carried on by tradition and enforced by social disapproval of any violation *b)* such practices, collectively 3. under feudalism, a service, rent, etc. regularly paid to a lord 4. [*pl.*] *a)* duties or taxes imposed by a government on imported and, occasionally, exported goods *b)* [*with sing. v.*] the government agency in charge of collecting these duties, or any of its offices 5. *a)* the regular support or patronage of a business establishment *b)* customers as a group 6. *Law* such usage as by common consent and long-established, uniform practice has taken on the force of law —*adj.* 1. made or done to order or, sometimes, made extra fine, as if to order 2. making things to order, or dealing in things made to order [a *custom* tailor] —**SYN.** see HABIT

cus·tom·a·ble (-ə b'l) *adj.* [Rare] subject to customs; taxable as imported

cus·tom·ar·i·ly (kus′tə mer′ə lē, kus′tə mer′ə lē) *adv.* according to custom; usually

cus·tom·ar·y (kus′tə mer′ē) *adj.* [ML. *customarius:* see CUSTOM] 1. in keeping with custom, or usage; usual; habitual 2. *Law* holding or held by custom —*n., pl.* -**ar′ies** a collection of the laws established by custom for a manor, region, etc.—*SYN.* see USUAL —**cus′tom·ar′i·ness** *n.*

☆**cus·tom-built** (-bilt′) *adj.* built to order, according to the customer's specifications

cus·tom·er (kus′tə mər) *n.* [ME. < OFr. *coustumier:* see CUSTOM] 1. a person who buys, esp. one who buys from, or patronizes, an establishment regularly 2. [Colloq.] any person with whom one has dealings [a rough *customer*]

cus·tom·house (kus′təm hous′) *n.* a building or office where customs or duties are paid, and ships are cleared for entering or leaving: also **cus′toms·house′**

☆**cus·tom·ize** (-īz′) *vt., vi.* -**ized′,** -**iz′ing** [CUSTOM + -IZE] to make or build according to personal or individual specifications —**cus′tom·iz′er** *n.*

☆**cus·tom-made** (-mād′) *adj.* made to order, according to the customer's specifications

customs union a union of nations that agree to eliminate customs restrictions among them and to follow a common tariff policy toward all others

cus·tu·mal (kus′tyoo məl) *n.* [ML. *custumalis*] *same as* CUSTOMARY

cut (kut) *vt.* **cut, cut′ting** [ME. *cutten, kytten* < Late OE. **cyttan* < Scand. base seen in Sw. dial. *kuta,* Ice. *kuta,* to cut with a knife: the word replaced OE. *ceorfan* (cf. CARVE), *snithan, sceran* (cf. SHEAR) as used in its basic senses] I. *denoting penetration or incision* 1. to make an opening in as with a sharp-edged instrument; pierce; incise; gash 2. to pierce, hit sharply, constrict, etc. so as to hurt 3. to hurt the feelings of 4. to grow (a new tooth making its way through the gum) II. *denoting separation, removal, or division* 1. to remove or divide into parts with a sharp-edged instrument; sever 2. to carve (meat) 3. to cause to fall by severing; fell; hew 4. to mow or reap with a scythe, sickle, etc. 5. to pass through or across; intersect; divide

[the path cuts the meadow diagonally*]* 6. *a*) to divide (a pack of cards) at random so as to rearrange the pack after shuffling or so as to show a card to determine the dealer, partners, etc. *b*) to select (a card) at random from a pack 7. to castrate; geld 8. [Colloq.] to pretend not to see or know (a person); snub 9. [Colloq.] to stay away from (a school class, etc.) without being excused 10. [Colloq.] to cause to stop operating *[cut* the engine*]* 11. to stop photographing (a motion-picture scene) ☆12. [Slang] to stop; discontinue *[cut* the noise*]* **III.** *denoting reduction* 1. to make less by or as by severing a part or parts; reduce; lessen; curtail *[to cut* salaries*]* 2. to make shorter by severing the ends of (hair, branches, fingernails, etc.); trim; shear; pare ☆3. to dilute (alcohol, etc.) 4. to dissolve or break up the fat globules of *[lye cuts* grease*]* **IV.** *denoting performance by incision, etc.* to make, do, form, or decorate by or as by cutting; specif., *a*) to make (an opening, clearing, channel, etc.) by incising, drilling, hacking, or excavating *b*) to engrave; inscribe *c*) to type or otherwise mark (a stencil) for mimeographing *d*) to cut cloth so as to form the parts for (a garment) *e*) to perform *[to cut* a caper*]* ☆*f*) to edit (motion-picture film) by deleting some scenes and assembling others in a desired sequence *g*) to hit, drive, or throw (a ball) so that it spins or is deflected *h*) to cause (a wheel) to turn sharply ☆*i*) to make a recording of (a speech, music, etc.) on (a phonograph record) —*vi.* 1. to do the work of a sharp-edged instrument; pierce, sever, gash, etc. 2. to do cutting; work as a cutter 3. to take cutting; be severed, etc. *[pine cuts* easily*]* 4. to use an instrument that cuts 5. to cause pain by or as by sharp, piercing or lashing strokes *[the wind cut* through his thin clothes*]* 6. to swing a bat, etc. (at a ball) 7. to change direction suddenly, as while running 8. to move swiftly 9. *Motion Pictures, Television, etc.* to make a sudden change, as from one scene or character to another —*adj.* 1. that has been cut 2. made, formed, or decorated by cutting 3. reduced; lessened 4. castrated 5. *Bot.* having an indented edge; incised, as some leaves or petals —*n.* 1. a cutting or being cut 2. a stroke or blow with a sharp-edged instrument, whip, etc. 3. a stroke taken at a ball, esp. one that causes it to spin 4. an opening, incision, wound, etc. made by a sharp-edged instrument 5. *a*) the omission of a part *b*) the part omitted 6. a piece or part cut off or out; specif., *a*) any of the segments of the carcass of a meat animal *b*) a slice from such a segment 7. the edge or outline of something cut 8. *a*) the amount cut, as of timber *b*) a reduction; lessening; decrease 9. a route that is the shortest distance across: usually **short cut** 10. a passage or channel cut or dug out or worn away 11. the style in which a thing is cut; fashion; form *[a* stylish *cut]* 12. an act, remark, etc. that hurts one's feelings 13. a block or plate engraved for printing or the impression made from it 14. [< ? W. *cwt, lot*] one of the bits of straw, stick, paper, etc. used in drawing lots to decide something 15. [Colloq.] the act of snubbing or ignoring ☆16. [Colloq.] an unauthorized absence from school, etc. ☆17. [Slang] a share, as of profits or loot —**a cut above** [Colloq.] somewhat better than —**cut across** to take a shorter course by going straight across as in a diagonal direction —**cut a figure** 1. to attract attention 2. to make a (specified kind of) showing or impression —**cut and dried** 1. prepared or arranged beforehand; routine 2. lifeless; dull; boring —**cut and run** 1. to cut the cable of a ship and set sail immediately 2. to get away quickly —**cut back** 1. to make shorter by cutting off the end 2. to reduce, decrease, or discontinue (production, personnel, etc.) ☆3. to go back to earlier narrative events, as in a novel or motion picture ☆4. to change direction suddenly, as a runner in football —**cut dead** [Colloq.] to snub completely —**cut down** 1. to cause to fall by cutting; fell 2. to kill, as by shooting 3. to reduce; lessen —**cut down to size** [Colloq.] to reduce the prestige or importance of —**cut in** 1. to move in suddenly, as into a small opening in a lane of traffic 2. to join in suddenly; break in on; interrupt ☆3. to interrupt a couple dancing in order to dance with one of them 4. to blend (shortening) into flour, etc. as with a knife 5. to put or bring in; introduce 6. to make a connection, as into an electrical circuit 7. to give a share to —**cut it fine** [Colloq.] 1. to make exact calculations 2. to make exact distinctions —**cut it out** [Colloq.] to stop doing what one is doing —**cut loose** 1. to cut a ship's moorings ☆2. [Colloq.] to act or speak without restraint —☆**cut no ice** [Colloq.] to make no impression —**cut off** 1. to separate from other parts by cutting; sever 2. to stop abruptly 3. to shut off 4. to break in on; interrupt 5. to intercept 6. to disinherit —**cut one's teeth on** to learn or use at an early age —**cut out** 1. to remove by cutting 2. to leave or take out; remove; omit; eliminate 3. to eliminate and take the place of (a rival) 4. to make or form by or as by cutting 5. [Colloq.] to stop running: said of an engine ☆6. [Colloq.] to discontinue; stop 7. [Slang] to leave abruptly —**cut out for** fitted for; suited for —**cut short** to stop abruptly before the end —**cut through** 1. to penetrate or go through by cutting 2. to go straight through —**cut up** 1. to cut into pieces 2. to inflict cuts or lacerations on 3. [Colloq.] *a*) to criticize harshly *b*) to cause to be dejected or distressed ☆4. [Slang] to clown, play practical jokes, etc. to attract attention

cu·ta·ne·ous (kyōō tā′nē əs) *adj.* [ML. *cutaneus* < L. *cutis:* see CUTICLE] of, on, or affecting the skin

cut·a·way (kut′ə wā′) *n.* a coat with the front of the skirt cut so as to curve back to the tails, worn by men for formal daytime occasions: also **cutaway coat** —*adj.* designating or of a diagram or model, showing in cross section, or with walls, etc. cut away, the parts or workings, as of a machine

CUTAWAY

cut·back (kut′bak′) *n.* the act or result of cutting back; specif., *a*) a reduction or discontinuance, as of production, personnel, etc. ☆*b*) a sequence of earlier events introduced at a later point in a novel, motion picture, etc.

cut·bank (-baŋk′) *n.* a steep stream bank, esp. one formed on the center curve of a meander by erosion

Cutch (kuch) *same as* KUTCH

cutch (kuch) *n. same as* CATECHU

☆**cute** (kyōōt) *adj.* **cut′er, cut′est** [aphetic < ACUTE] [Colloq.] 1. clever; sharp; shrewd 2. pretty or attractive, esp. in a delicate or dainty way 3. straining for effect; artificial —**cute′ly** *adv.* —**cute′ness** *n.*

cut glass glass, esp. flint glass, shaped or ornamented by grinding and polishing

cut-grass (kut′gras′, -gräs′) *n.* any grass (esp. *Leersia oryzoides*) having tiny hooks along the edges of the blades that cause scratches on the human skin

Cuth·bert (kuth′bərt) [OE. *Cuthbeorht*, lit., famously splendid < *cuth*, noted (pp. of *cunnan*, to know: see CAN¹) + *beorht* (see BRIGHT)] 1. a masculine name 2. Saint, 635?-687? A.D.; Eng. monk and bishop: his day is Mar. 20

cut·i·cle (kyōōt′i k'l) *n.* [L. *cuticula*, skin, dim. < *cutis*, skin < IE. base *(s)keu-t-*, to cover, whence HIDE²] 1. the outer layer of the skin; epidermis 2. hardened skin, such as accumulates at the base and sides of a fingernail 3. *Bot.* a delicate, waxy layer over the outer surface of the epidermis of plants: it contains cutin and protects against water loss and parasitic infections 4. *Zool.* the nonliving, thick or thin, tough outer structure secreted by the epidermis in many invertebrate organisms, as insects, crustaceans, earthworms, etc. —**cu·tic′u·lar** (kyōō tik′yə lər) *adj.*

cu·tic·u·la (kyōō tik′yə lə) *n., pl.* **-lae** (-lē′) [L.] *same as* CUTICLE (esp. sense 4)

☆**cu·tie** (kyōōt′ē) *n.* [CUT(E) + -IE] [Slang] 1. an attractive girl: also **cu′tie-pie′** (-pī′) 2. a shrewd or clever person, maneuver, etc.

cu·tin (kyōōt′'n) *n.* [< L. *cutis* (see CUTICLE) + -IN¹] *Bot.* a varnishlike material covering the epidermis of land plants and containing waxy and resinous materials, fatty acids, etc.

☆**cut-in** (kut′in′) *n.* something that is cut in, as a close-up of some object inserted into the sequence of a motion-picture scene

cu·tin·i·za·tion (kyōōt′'n ə zā′shən) *n. Bot.* a process in which the outermost plant cells become thickened and covered with cutin, making them waterproof —**cu′tin·ize′** (-īz′) *vi., vt.* **-ized′, -iz′ing**

cu·tis (kyōōt′is) *n.* [L.: see CUTICLE] 1. the vertebrate skin, including both of its layers, the dermis and the epidermis 2. the dermis only; corium

cut·lass, cut·las (kut′ləs) *n.* [Fr. *coutelas* < It. *coltellaccio* < *coltello*, knife < L. *cultellus*, dim. < *culter:* see COLTER] a short, thick, curving sword with a single cutting edge, formerly used esp. by sailors

cutlass fish any of a family (Trichiuridae) of very long, thin fishes with a long, sharply pointed tail and a wide, heavily toothed mouth, found near the surface in tropical seas

cut·ler (kut′lər) *n.* [ME. & Anglo-Fr. *cuteler* < OFr. *coutelier* < ML. *cultellarius*, one who makes knives < L. *cultellus:* see CUTLASS] a person who makes, sells, or repairs knives and other cutting tools

cut·ler·y (kut′lər ē) *n.* [ME. *cutellerie* < OFr. *coutellerie:* see prec.] 1. the work or business of a cutler 2. cutting implements, such as knives and scissors; often, specif., such implements used in preparing and eating food

cut·let (kut′lit) *n.* [altered (after CUT) < Fr. *côtelette*, dim. of OFr. *costel*, dim. of *coste*, rib < L. *costa:* see COAST] 1. a small slice of meat from the ribs or leg, for frying or broiling, often served breaded 2. a small, flat croquette of chopped meat or fish

cut·off (kut′ôf′) *n.* 1. the act of cutting off; esp., the limit or ending set for a process, activity, etc. 2. a road or passage that cuts across, shortening the distance ☆3. *a*) a new and shorter channel cut by a river across a bend, or dug out to straighten it *b*) the water thus cut off 4. the act of stopping steam, etc. from entering the cylinder of an engine 5. any device for cutting off the flow of a fluid, a connection, etc. —*adj.* of an arbitrary ending or limit *[cutoff* date*]*

cutoff frequency *Electronics* 1. the limits of the frequency band which a filter will pass without a significant weakening in the transmission 2. the lowest frequency that a waveguide can transmit without loss of strength

cut·out (-out′) *n.* 1. a switch or other device for breaking or closing an electric circuit 2. a device for letting the exhaust gases of an internal-combustion engine pass directly into the air instead of through a muffler 3. a design cut out of something, or to be cut out

☆**cut·o·ver** (-ō′vər) *adj.* cleared of trees —*n.* land cleared of trees

cut·purse (-purs′) *n.* **1.** orig., a thief who stole purses by cutting them from the belts or girdles to which they were attached **2.** a pickpocket

☆**cut-rate** (-rāt′) *adj.* **1.** available at a lower price or rate; cheap **2.** offering cut-rate goods or services

Cut·tack (kut′ək) city in E India, in Orissa state: pop. 146,000

☆**cut·tage** (kut′ij) *n.* the method of propagating plants by means of cuttings

cut·ter (kut′ər) *n.* **1.** a device, tool, or machine for cutting **2.** a person who cuts or whose work is cutting; specif., a person whose work is cutting to patterns the sections that form a garment **3.** any boat or small vessel that can cut swiftly through the water; specif., *a)* a boat carried aboard large ships as a communications tender: also **ship's cutter** *b)* an armed sailing vessel, formerly used by revenue authorities to pursue smugglers, etc.: also **revenue cutter** *c)* a small, armed, engine-powered ship, used by the Coast Guard for coastal or ocean patrol, etc.: also **Coast Guard cutter** *d)* a modern single-masted yacht or sailboat carrying two headsails under normal wind conditions ☆**4.** a small, light sleigh, usually drawn by one horse

cut·throat (kut′thrōt′) *n.* a person who cuts throats; murderer —*adj.* **1.** murderous **2.** merciless; ruthless ☆**3.** played by persons competing as individuals rather than with partners, as some forms of bridge or pinochle

cut time same as ALLA BREVE

cut·ting (kut′in) *n.* **1.** the act of one that cuts **2.** a piece cut off **3.** [Brit.] a clipping, as from a newspaper **4.** [Brit.] a passage for trains, cars, etc. cut through a hill or high ground; cut **5.** *Hort.* a slip or shoot cut away from a plant for rooting or grafting —*adj.* **1.** that cuts; for cutting; edged; sharp **2.** chilling or piercing [a *cutting* wind] **3.** wounding the feelings; sarcastic —*SYN.* see INCISIVE —**cut′ting·ly** *adv.*

cut·tle·bone (kut′'l bōn′) *n.* the internal shell of cuttlefish, used as a food supplement for caged birds and, when powdered, as a polishing agent

cut·tle·fish (-fish′) *n.*, *pl.* **-fish′**, **-fish′es:** see FISH² [ME. *codel* < OE. *cudele*, akin to Norw. dial. *kaule* (*kodle), OLowG. *cudele*, older Du. *kutlevisch*: sense "pouch fish": for IE. base see COD⁹] any of a genus (*Sepia*) of squidlike sea mollusks that have ten sucker-bearing arms and a hard internal shell: when in danger, some cuttlefishes eject a dark brown, inklike fluid: also **cuttle**

cut·ty (kut′ē) *adj.* [< CUT] [Scot. & Dial.] short —*n.*, *pl.* **-ties** a short pipe or spoon

CUTTLEFISH
(to 18 in. long)

cutty stool [Scot.] **1.** a low stool **2.** formerly, a seat in a church, in which offenders against chastity had to sit and be publicly rebuked by the minister

☆**cut·up** (kut′up′) *n.* [Colloq.] a person who clowns, plays practical jokes, etc. to attract attention

cut·wa·ter (-wôt′ər, -wät′ər) *n.* **1.** the fore part of a ship's stem **2.** the angular edge of the pier of a bridge, facing upstream

cut·work (-wurk′) *n.* openwork embroidery in which part of the cloth is cut away from the design

cut·worm (-wurm′) *n.* any of a number of soil-dwelling caterpillars (family Noctuidae) that feed on young plants of cabbage, corn, etc., cutting them off at ground level

cu·vette (kyōō vet′) *n.* [Fr., basin, dim. of *cuve*, vat] a small glass tube used in spectrometry and photometry

Cu·vier (kü vyā′; *E.* kōō′vē ā′), Baron **Georges (Léopold Chrétien Frédéric Dagobert)** 1769–1832; Fr. naturalist

Cuy·a·ho·ga Falls (kī′ə hō′gə, -hô′-, -hä′-; kə hô′gə) [after an Iroquois tribal name + *falls*, cascade] city in NE Ohio: suburb of Akron: pop. 50,000

Cuyp (koip), **Ael·bert** or **Aal·bert** (äl′bərt) 1620–91; Du. painter

Cuz·co (kōōs′kō) city in S Peru: cap. of the Inca empire, 12th–16th cent.; pop. 78,000

cwm (kōōm) *n.* [W. *cwmm*, COOMB] *Geol.* same as CIRQUE

CWO Chief Warrant Officer

C.W.O., c.w.o. cash with order

CWS Chemical Warfare Service

cwt. hundredweight

-cy (sē, si) [< ME. & OFr. *-cie*, L. *-cia*, *-tia*, Gr. *-kia*, *-keia*, *-tia*, *-teia*] a suffix meaning: **1.** quality, condition, state, or fact of being [*hesitancy*] **2.** position, rank, or office of [*captaincy*, *curacy*]

cy·an- (sī′ən) same as CYANO-

cy·an·am·ide (sī an′ə mīd′, -mid; *among chemists, often* sī′ə nam′īd, -id) *n.* [CYAN- + AMIDE] a white, crystalline compound, CN·NH₂, prepared by the reaction of carbon dioxide and hot sodium amide, and by other reactions: also **cy·an′am·id** (-mid, -id)

cy·a·nate (sī′ə nāt′) *n.* a salt or ester of cyanic acid

cy·an·ic (sī an′ik) *adj.* [CYAN- + -IC] **1.** of or containing cyanogen **2.** blue

cyanic acid a colorless, poisonous, unstable acid, HOCN, prepared by heating cyanuric acid

cy·a·nide (sī′ə nīd′, -nid) *n.* [CYAN- + -IDE] a substance composed of a cyanogen group in combination with some element or radical; esp., potassium cyanide, KCN, or sodium cyanide, NaCN, extremely poisonous, white, crystalline compounds with an odor of bitter almonds: used in extracting gold from low-grade ores, electroplating, casehardening of steel, and as a fluxing material —*vt.* **-nid′ed, -nid′ing** to treat with cyanide; esp., to caseharden (steel) in this way

cyanide process a process of extracting gold or silver from low-grade ores by treating them with a solution of sodium cyanide or potassium cyanide and then recovering the gold or silver by electrolysis

cy·a·nine (sī′ə nēn′, -nin) *n.* [CYAN- + -INE⁴] a soluble crystalline, blue dye, C₂₉H₃₅N₂I, derived from quinoline and used as a sensitizer in photography

cy·a·nite (-nīt′) *n.* [CYAN- + -ITE¹] a natural crystalline silicate of aluminum, Al₂SiO₅

cy·a·no- (sī′ə nō′, -nə; sī an′ə) [< Gr. *kyanos*, the color blue] *a combining form meaning:* **1.** dark-blue [*cyanosis*] **2.** *Chem.* of or containing the cyanogen group

cy·an·o·gen (sī an′ə jən) *n.* [CYANO- + -GEN] **1.** a colorless, poisonous, flammable gas, C₂N₂ **2.** the univalent radical –CN, occurring in cyanides

cy·a·no·hy·drin (sī′ə nō hī′drin) *n.* [CYANO- + HYDR(O)- + -IN¹] any of a class of organic chemical compounds containing both the –CN and –OH radicals

cy·a·no·sis (sī′ə nō′sis) *n.* [ModL. < Gr. *kyanōsis*, dark-blue color < *kyanos*, the color blue] a bluish coloration of the skin, caused by lack of oxygen in the blood —**cy·a·not′ic** (-nät′ik) *adj.*

cy·a·nu·rate (sī′ə nyoor′āt′, -it) *n.* [CYANUR(IC) + -ATE²] a salt or ester of cyanuric acid

cy·a·nu·ric acid (-ik) [CYAN- + URIC] a white, crystalline acid, C₃N₃(OH)₃, made by heating urea

Cyb·e·le (sib′ə lē′) [L. < Gr. *Kybelē*] a nature goddess of ancient Asia Minor: identified by the Greeks with Rhea

☆**cy·ber·cul·ture** (sī′bər kul′chər) *n.* [CYBER(NETICS) + CULTURE] the effect of cybernation upon social, political, cultural, and other institutions —**cy′ber·cul′tur·al** *adj.*

▲**cy·ber·nate** (-nāt′) *vt.* **-nat′ed, -nat′ing** to subject to cybernation

☆**cy·ber·na·tion** (sī′bər nā′shən) *n.* [CYBERN(ETICS) + -ATION: coined c. 1961 by D. N. Michael, of Peace Research Institute] the use of computers coupled with automatic machinery to control and carry out complex operations, as in manufacturing, to perform routine, repetitive tasks, as in government or business, etc.

☆**cy·ber·net·ics** (-net′iks) *n.pl.* [*with sing. v.*] [coined (1948) by Norbert WIENER < Gr. *kybernētēs*, helmsman + -ICS] a science dealing with the comparative study of the operations of complex electronic computers and the human nervous system —**cy′ber·net′ic** *adj.*

☆**cy·borg** (sī′bôrg) *n.* [*cyb(ernetic) org(anism)*] a hypothetical human being modified for life in a nonearth environment by the substitution of artificial organs and other body parts

cyc. **1.** cyclopedia **2.** cyclopedic

cy·cad (sī′kad) *n.* [ModL. *Cycas* (gen. *Cycadis*) < Gr. *kykas*, erroneous sp. for *koïkas*, acc. pl. of *koïx*, doum palm] any of an order (Cycadales) of tropical shrubs and trees resembling thick-stemmed palms, with crowns of leathery, fernlike leaves and large cones containing fleshy seeds

cy·cas (sī′kas) *n.* any of a genus (*Cycas*) of cycads with leathery, dark-green leaves and short, thick trunks, grown in warm climates for ornament

Cyc·la·des (sik′lə dēz′) group of islands of the S Aegean, forming a department of Greece: 995 sq. mi.; pop. 100,000

cy·cla·mate (sī′klə māt′, sik′lə-) *n.* [*cycl(ohexyl)*, C₆H₁₁, a univalent radical + (*sulf*)*amate*, ester of sulfamic acid, HSO₃NH₂] a salt of a complex organic acid, C₆H₁₁NHSO₃H, esp. the sodium or calcium salt with an extremely sweet taste

cy·cla·men (sī′klə mən, sik′lə-) *n.*, *pl.* **-mens** [ModL. < L. *cyclaminos* < Gr. *kyklaminos* < ? *kyklos*, a circle (with reference to the form of the roots)] any of a genus (*Cyclamen*) of plants of the primrose family, having heart-shaped leaves and white, pink, or red flowers with reflexed petals

cy·cla·zo·cine (sī′klə zō′sēn) *n.* [see CYCLO- & PENTAZOCINE] a pain-killing, nonaddictive, synthetic drug that blocks the effects of heroin or morphine

cy·cle (sī′k'l; *for n. 7 & vi. 2, also* sik′'l) *n.* [ME. *cicle* < LL. *cyclus* < Gr. *kyklos*, a circle, cycle < IE. **kwekwlo-*, redupl. of base **kwel-*, to turn, whence L. *colere*, cultivate, E. WHEEL] **1.** a recurring period of a definite number of years, used as a measure of time **2.** a period of time within which a round of regularly recurring events or phenomena is completed [the business *cycle*] **3.** a complete set of events or phenomena recurring in the same sequence **4.** a very long period of time; an age **5.** all of the traditional or

legendary poems, songs, etc. connected with a hero or an event [the Charlemagne *cycle*] **6.** a series of poems or songs on the same theme **7.** a bicycle, tricycle, or motorcycle **8.** *Astron.* the orbit of a heavenly body **9.** *Biol.* a recurring series of functional changes or events **10.** *Elec.* one complete period of the reversal of an alternating current from positive to negative and back again —*vi.* **-cled, -cling 1.** to occur or recur in cycles; pass through a cycle **2.** to ride a bicycle, tricycle, or motorcycle

cy·clic (sī′klik, sik′lik) *adj.* **1.** of, or having the nature of, a cycle; moving or occurring in cycles **2.** *Chem.* arranged in a ring or closed-chain structure: said of atoms Also **cy′cli·cal** —**cy′cli·cal·ly** *adv.*

cy·clist (sī′klist, sik′list) *n.* a person who rides a bicycle, motorcycle, etc.

cy·cli·zine (sī′klə zēn′) *n.* [CYCL(O)- + -*i*- + (PIPERA)ZINE] an antihistamine, $C_{18}H_{22}N_2$, used for treating nausea and motion sickness

cy·clo- (sī′klō, -klə; sik′lə) [< Gr. *kyklos*, a circle: see CYCLE] *a combining form meaning:* **1.** of a circle or wheel, circular [*cyclograph*] **2.** same as CYCLIC (sense 2) [*cycloparaffin*] Also, before a vowel, **cycl-**

cy·clo·hex·ane (sī′klō hek′sān) *n.* [CYCLO- + HEXANE] one of the saturated cyclic hydrocarbons, C_6H_{12}, present in petroleum: used as a solvent, paint remover, etc.

cy·cloid (sī′kloid) *n.* [Gr. *kykloeidēs*, circular < *kyklos* (see CYCLE) + *eidos*, form] *Geom.* a curve traced by any point on the circumference, or on a radius, of a circle which rolls without slipping through one complete revolution along a straight line in a single plane —*adj.* **1.** circular **2.** designating or having fish scales that are roundish in form with smooth edges **3.** designating or of a cyclothymic person —**cy·cloi·dal** (sī kloi′d'l) *adj.*

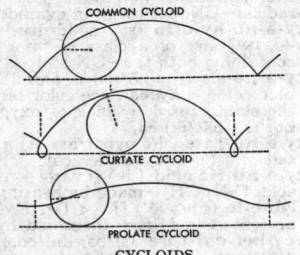
COMMON CYCLOID
CURTATE CYCLOID
PROLATE CYCLOID
CYCLOIDS

cy·clom·e·ter (sī kläm′ə tər) *n.* [CYCLO- + -METER] **1.** an instrument for measuring the arcs of circles **2.** an instrument for recording the revolutions of a wheel, used to measure the distance traveled by a vehicle

cy·clone (sī′klōn) *n.* [Gr. *kyklōn*, moving in a circle < *kykloein*, to circle around, whirl < *kyklos*: see CYCLE] **1.** loosely, a windstorm with a violent, whirling movement; tornado or hurricane **2.** *Meteorol.* a storm with strong winds rotating (clockwise in the S Hemisphere, counterclockwise in the N Hemisphere) about a moving center of low atmospheric pressure —**cy·clon·ic** (sī klän′ik) *adj.* —**cy·clon′i·cal·ly** *adv.*

☆**cyclone cellar** a deep cellar for shelter during heavy windstorms

cy·clo·nite (sī′klə nīt′) *n.* [contr. < *cyclo*(-*trimethylene-tri*)*nit*(*ramin*)*e*: intended to suggest CYCLONE & -ITE[1]] a high-melting, fairly insensitive, very powerful, chemical explosive, $C_3H_6N_6O_6$

cy·clo·par·af·fin (sī′klō par′ə fin) *n.* [CYCLO- + PARAFFIN] any of a series of saturated hydrocarbons of the general formula C_nH_{2n}, having a ring structure containing three or more carbon atoms

Cy·clo·pe·an (sī′klə pē′ən) *adj.* [< L. *Cyclopeus* < Gr. *Kyklōpeios* < *Kyklōps*, Cyclops + -AN] **1.** of the Cyclopes **2.** [c-] huge; gigantic; enormous; massive

cy·clo·pe·di·a, cy·clo·pae·di·a (sī′klə pē′dē ə) *n.* same as ENCYCLOPEDIA —**cy′clo·pe′dic, cy′clo·pae′dic** *adj.* —**cy′clo·pe′dist, cy′clo·pae′dist** *n.*

cy·clo·pen·tane (-pen′tān) *n.* [CYCLO- + PENTANE] a saturated, colorless liquid hydrocarbon, C_5H_{10}, derived from certain petroleums

cy·clo·ple·gi·a (-plē′jē ə) *n.* [ModL. < CYCLO- + -PLEGIA] paralysis of those muscles of the eye responsible for visual accommodation —**cy′clo·ple′gic** (-jik) *adj.*

cy·clo·pro·pane (-prō′pān) *n.* [CYCLO- + PROPANE] a colorless, flammable gas, C_3H_6, used as a general anesthetic

Cy·clops (sī′kläps) *n., pl.* **Cy·clo·pes** (sī klō′pēz) [L. < Gr. *Kyklōps*, lit., round-eyed < *kyklos* (see CYCLE) + *ōps*, EYE Gr. *Myth.* any of a race of giants who had only one eye, in the middle of the forehead

cy·clo·ra·ma (sī′klə ram′ə, -räm′-) *n.* [CYCLO- + Gr. *horama*, sight < *horan*, to see] **1.** a series of large pictures, as of a landscape, put on the wall of a circular room so as to appear in natural perspective to a spectator standing in the center **2.** a large, curved curtain or screen used as a background for stage settings —**cy′clo·ram′ic** *adj.*

cy·clo·sis (sī klō′sis) *n.* [ModL. < Gr. *kyklōsis*, an enveloping, surrounding < *kykloun*, to encircle < *kyklos*, a circle (see CYCLE)] a regular cyclic movement of protoplasm within a cell

cy·clo·sto·mate (sī kläs′tə māt′) *adj.* **1.** having a round mouth **2.** of a cyclostome or the cyclostomes Also **cy·clostom·a·tous** (sī′klə stäm′ə təs, -stō′mə-)

cy·clo·stome (sī′klə stōm′) *n.* [CYCLO- + -STOME] any of a subclass (Cyclostomata) of jawless parasitic fishes, including the lamprey and hagfish, with an eellike body and a circular, sucking mouth

cy·clo·thy·mi·a (sī′klə thī′mē ə) *n.* [ModL. < CYCLO- + Gr. *thymos*, spirit] an emotional condition characterized by alternate periods of elation and depression: in its more severe form, called *manic-depressive psychosis* —**cy′clo·thy′mic** *adj.*, *n.*

☆**cy·clo·tron** (sī′klə trän′) *n.* [CYCLO- + (ELEC)TRON] an apparatus for giving high energy to particles, usually protons, deuterons, and helium ions: through the combined action of a homogeneous magnetic field and an oscillating electrostatic field it causes a particle to move in a spiral path with increasing kinetic energy until the particle attains a velocity sufficiently high for the purpose intended, usually to initiate nuclear transformations upon collision with a suitable target

cy·der (sī′dər) *n. Brit. var. of* CIDER

cyg·net (sig′nət) *n.* [ME. *cignet*, dim. < Fr. *cygne*, swan < VL. *cicinus* < Gr. *kyknos*, swan, prob. echoic (as in Russ. *kyki*, swan's cry)] a young swan

Cyg·nus (sig′nəs) [L. < *cygnus*, swan < Gr. *kyknos*: see CYGNET] **1.** Gr. *Myth.* a mythical king of the Ligurians who was changed into a swan and placed among the stars **2.** a N constellation, the Swan, in the Milky Way

cyl. 1. cylinder **2.** cylindrical

cyl·in·der (sil′ən dər) *n.* [Fr. *cylindre* < L. *cylindrus* < Gr. *kylindros* < *kylindein*, to roll < IE. base *(s)kel-*, to bend, curved, whence L. *calx*, heel, *coluber*, snake] **1.** *Geom. a)* a solid figure described by the edge of a rectangle rotated around the parallel edge as axis: the ends of a cylinder are parallel and equal circles *b)* the surface generated by a line which always has a point in common with a given curve, and which moves so that it is always parallel with a given line not in the plane of the curve **2.** anything having the shape of a cylinder, whether hollow or solid; specif., *a)* the turning part of a revolver, containing chambers for cartridges *b)* the chamber in which the piston moves in a reciprocating engine *c)* the barrel of a pump *d)* on a printing press, a roller carrying the printing plates or the part receiving the impression *e)* a cylindrical stone with cuneiform inscriptions

cylinder head the closed end, usually detachable, of a cylinder in an internal-combustion engine

cy·lin·dri·cal (sə lin′dri k'l) *adj.* **1.** having the shape of a cylinder **2.** of a cylinder Also **cy·lin′dric** —**cy·lin′dri·cal′i·ty** (-kal′ə tē) *n.* —**cy·lin′dri·cal·ly** *adv.*

cy·lin·droid (sil′ən droid′) *n.* [Gr. *kylindroeidēs*: see CYLINDER & -OID] a solid body resembling a cylinder, but with elliptical ends —*adj.* resembling a cylinder

cy·lix (sī′liks, sil′iks) *n., pl.* **cyl·i·ces** (sil′ə sēz′) same as KYLIX

Cym. Cymric

cy·ma (sī′mə) *n., pl.* **-mae** (-mē) [ModL. < Gr. *kyma*: see CYME] *Archit.* a molding of a cornice, whose profile is a line partly convex and partly concave

cy·mar (si mär′) *n.* [Fr. *simarre*] same as SIMAR

cy·ma·ti·um (si mā′shē əm) *n., pl.* **-ti·a** (-ə) [L. < Gr. *kymation*, dim. of *kyma*, wave: see CYME] *Archit.* a cyma, esp. one topping an entablature

cym·bal (sim′b'l) *n.* [ME. < OFr. *cymble*, OE. *cymbal*, both < L. *cymbalum* < Gr. *kymbalon* < *kymbē*, hollow of a vessel < IE. **kumb-* (< base **keu-*, bend, arch), whence HUMP] a circular, slightly concave brass plate used as a percussion instrument producing a variety of metallic sounds: it is struck with a drumstick, brush, etc. or used in pairs which are struck together to produce a crashing, ringing sound —**cym′bal·ist** *n.*

cym·bid·i·um (sim bid′ē əm) *n.* [ModL. < L. *cymba*, a boat, skiff (< Gr. *kymbē*, a boat, hollow of a vessel, bowl: for IE. base see COOMB) + ModL. -*idium*, dim. suffix (< Gr. -*idion*)] any of a genus (*Cymbidium*) of tropical Asiatic orchids, producing sprays of moderate-sized flowers in shades of white, pink, cream, yellow, or maroon

CYMBALS

cyme (sīm) *n.* [L. *cyma*, young sprout of cabbage < Gr. *kyma*, cyme, wave, orig., something swollen < *kyein*, to be pregnant < IE. base **keu-*, to swell] a flat-topped flower cluster in which the central or uppermost flower blooms first, followed by the lower or outer ones

cy·mene (sī′mēn) *n.* [< Gr. *kyminon*: see CUMIN] a colorless hydrocarbon, $CH_3C_6H_4CH(CH_3)_2$, occurring in three isomeric forms (*orthocymene, metacymene,* and *paracymene*), derived from benzene: the most common form, paracymene, is found in the oil of certain plants, as cumin and wild thyme, and is used in paints and solvents

cy·mo- (sī′mō, -mō) [< Gr. *kymo-* < *kyma*: see CYME] *a combining form meaning* wave [*cymograph*]

cy·mo·gene (sī′mə jēn′) *n.* [< CYM(ENE) + -*gene*, var. of -GEN] a flammable distillate of petroleum, consisting mainly of butane, which, when condensed, is used as a freezing mixture

cy·mo·graph (sī′mə graf′) *n.* [CYMO- + -GRAPH] same as KYMOGRAPH

cy·moid (sī′moid) *adj.* resembling a cyma or cyme

cy·mo·phane (sī′mə fān′) *n.* [CYMO- + -PHANE] an opalescent variety of chrysoberyl

cy·mose (sī′mōs, sī mōs′) *adj.* [L. *cymosus < cyma*] 1. of or like a cyme 2. bearing a cyme or cymes Also **cy′mous** (-məs) —**cy·mose′ly** *adv.*

Cym·ric (kim′rik; *occas.*, sim′-) *adj.* [< *Cymri,* western Britons, Welsh < W. *Cymry,* pl. of *Cymro < Cymru,* Wales: see CAMBRIA] 1. of the Celtic people of Wales 2. of their language —*n.* Brythonic, the group of Celtic languages that includes Welsh, Breton, and extinct Cornish

Cym·ry (-rē) *n.pl.* the Cymric Celts; the Welsh

Cyn·e·wulf (kin′ə woolf′) fl. 8th cent. A.D.; Anglo-Saxon poet: also **Cyn·wulf** (kin′woolf)

cyn·ic (sin′ik) *n.* [L. *Cynicus:* see ff.] 1. [C-] a member of a school of ancient Greek philosophers who held virtue to be the only good, and stressed independence from worldly needs and pleasures: they became critical of the rest of society and its material interests 2. a cynical person —*adj.* 1. [C-] of or like the Cynics or their doctrines 2. cynical

cyn·i·cal (-i k'l) *adj.* [< L. *cynicus,* of the Cynics < Gr. *kynikos,* lit., canine, like a dog < *kyōn* (gen. *kynos),* dog: for IE. base see CANINE] 1. believing that people are motivated in all their actions only by selfishness; denying the sincerity of people's motives and actions, or the value of living 2. sarcastic, sneering, etc. 3. [C-] same as CYNIC —**cyn′i·cal·ly** *adv.*
SYN.—**cynical** implies a contemptuous disbelief in human goodness and sincerity *[he's cynical about recovering his lost watch];* **misanthropic** suggests a deep-seated hatred or distrust of people in general *[a misanthropic hermit];* **pessimistic** implies an attitude, often habitual, of expecting the worst to happen *[pessimistic about one's chances to win]* —**ANT. optimistic**

cyn·i·cism (sin′ə siz'm) *n.* 1. [C-] the philosophy of the Cynics 2. the attitude or beliefs of a cynic 3. a cynical remark, idea, or action

cy·no·sure (sī′nə shoor′, sin′ə-) [L. < Gr. *kynosoura,* dog's tail, constellation of Ursa Minor < *kyōn* (see CYNICAL) + *oura,* a tail] [C-] *an old name for* the constellation Ursa Minor or the North Star, in this constellation —*n.* any person or thing that is a center of attention or interest

Cyn·thi·a (sin′thē ə) [L. < Gr. *Kynthia,* epithet of Artemis, orig. fem. of *Kynthios,* lit., of or from *Kynthos,* Cynthus, mountain in Delos, celebrated as the birthplace of Apollo and Artemis] 1. a feminine name: dim. *Cindy* 2. Artemis (or Diana), goddess of the moon 3. the moon personified

CYO, C.Y.O. Catholic Youth Organization

cy·pher (sī′fər) *n., vt., vi.* Brit. var. of CIPHER

cy-pres (sē′prā′) *adj., adv.* [LAnglo-Fr. < OFr. *si pres,* so nearly] *Law* as near(ly) as possible: designating or according to an equitable doctrine applied to the interpretation of wills, as in cases of trusts when the terms cannot be carried out literally and an effort is made to adhere to the general intent of the testator or settlor —*n.* the cy-pres doctrine Also **cy pres**

cy·press¹ (sī′prəs) *adj.* [ME. & OFr. *cipres* < LL.(Ec.) *cypressus,* for L. *cupressus* < Gr. *kyparissos*] designating a family (Cupressaceae) of trees including the junipers —*n.* 1. any of a genus (*Cupressus*) of evergreen, cone-bearing trees of the cypress family, native to N. America, Europe, and Asia: they have dark foliage and a distinctive symmetrical form 2. any of a number of related trees, including the baldcypress and white cedar 3. the wood of any of these trees 4. the branches or sprigs of the cypress, used as a symbol of mourning

cy·press² (sī′pris) *n.* [ME. *cipres* < OFr. *Cipre,* Cyprus] [Obs.] any of various textile fabrics, originally made in Cyprus; specif., a fine, gauzelike lawn or silk: in black, it was often worn for mourning

☆**cypress vine** a tropical American, annual, twining vine (*Quamoclit pennata*) of the morning-glory family, with showy, trumpet-shaped, scarlet or white flowers

Cyp·ri·an¹ (sip′rē ən) *adj.* [< L. *Cyprius* < Gr. *Kyprios < Kypros,* Cyprus + -AN] 1. *same as* CYPRIOT 2. [Archaic] wanton; licentious: in reference to the worship of Aphrodite in Cyprus in ancient times —*n.* 1. *same as* CYPRIOT 2. [*also* c-] [Archaic] a prostitute

Cyp·ri·an² (sip′rē ən) Saint (born *Thascius Caecilius Cyprianus*) 200?-258 A.D.; Christian martyr; bishop of Carthage (248-258): his day is Sept. 16

cy·prin·o·dont (si prin′ə dänt′, si prī′nə-) *n.* [< Gr. *kyprinos,* carp + -ODONT] any of a family (Cyprinodontidae) of very small fishes with soft fins, including the killifishes, commonly used as bait

cyp·ri·noid (sip′rə noid′) *adj.* [< Gr. *kyprinos,* carp + -OID] of or like the fishes of the carp family —*n.* any of a family (Cyprinidae) of freshwater fishes, including the carps, minnows, dace, etc. Also **cyp′ri·nid** (-nid)

Cyp·ri·ot (sip′rē ət) *adj.* of Cyprus, its people, or its language —*n.* 1. a native or inhabitant of Cyprus 2. the Greek dialect of Cyprus Also **Cyp′ri·ote** (-ōt′)

cyp·ri·pe·di·um (sip′rə pē′dē əm) *n., pl.* **-di·ums, -di·a** (-ə) [ModL., lady's-slipper < Gr. *Kypris,* Venus + *podion,* slipper, dim. < *pous* (gen. *podis),* FOOT] 1. any of a genus (*Cypripedium*) of soil-rooted orchids of the North Tem-

perate Zone, with flat leaves and white, yellow, or rosy purple flowers having pouchlike lip petals; lady's-slipper 2. any of various cultivated species (genus *Paphiopedilum*) of tropical orchids with fleshy folded leaves and green, yellow, or brown-purple flowers of waxy texture

Cy·prus (sī′prəs) country that is an island at the E end of the Mediterranean, south of Turkey: member of the Brit. Commonwealth: 3,572 sq. mi.; pop. 603,000; cap. Nicosia

cyp·se·la (sip′sə lə) *n., pl.* **-lae** (-lē′) [ModL. < Gr. *kypselē,* a hollow vessel] an achene derived from an inferior ovary, as in plants of the composite family

Cyrano de Bergerac *see* BERGERAC

Cy·re·na·ic (sir′ə nā′ik, sī′rə-) *adj.* 1. of Cyrenaica or Cyrene 2. of the Greek school of philosophy founded by Aristippus of Cyrene, who considered individual sensual pleasure the greatest good —*n.* a philosopher of the Cyrenaic school

Cyr·e·na·i·ca (sir′ə nā′i kə, sī′rə-) 1. region, formerly a province, of E Libya: c. 330,000 sq. mi.; chief city, Benghazi 2. ancient Greek kingdom (7th-4th cent. B.C.) in the same general region, dominated by the city of Cyrene

Cy·re·ne (sī rē′nē) ancient Greek city in N Africa, near the Mediterranean; capital of Cyrenaica

Cy·ril (sir′əl) [LL. *Cyrillus* < Gr. *Kyrillos,* lit., lordly < *kyrios,* a lord] 1. a masculine name 2. Saint, a (died 376?-444 A.D.; Christian theologian; archbishop of Alexandria (412-444): his day is Feb. 9 b) (born *Constantine*) 827-869 A.D.; Gr. prelate & missionary; apostle to the Slavs: his day is July 7

Cy·ril·lic (sə ril′ik) *adj.* designating or of the Slavic alphabet attributed to Saint Cyril, 9th-cent. apostle to the Slavs: in modified form, it is still used in Russia, Bulgaria, and other Slavic countries

Cy·rus (sī′rəs) [L. < Gr. *Kyros* < OPer. *Kūrush*] 1. a masculine name: dim. *Cy* 2. ?-529 B.C.; king of the Medes & Persians: founder of the Persian Empire: called *the Great* 3. 424?-401B.C.; Persian prince: called *the Younger:* see CUNAXA

cyst (sist) *n.* [ModL. *cystis* < Gr. *kystis,* sac, bladder, akin to L. *cutis:* see CUTICLE] 1. any of certain saclike structures in plants or animals; specif., such a structure or pocket in the body when abnormal and filled with fluid or diseased matter 2. a spherical, usually thick membrane, resistant to freezing, drying, etc., with which certain organisms are surrounded when in a resting stage

cyst- (sist) *same as* CYSTO-: used before a vowel

-cyst (sist) [< Gr. *kystis:* see CYST] *a suffix meaning* sac, pouch, bladder *[encyst]*

cys·tec·to·my (sis tek′tə mē) *n., pl.* **-mies** [CYST- + -ECTOMY] 1. the surgical removal of a cyst 2. the surgical removal of the gall bladder or of part of the urinary bladder

cys·te·ine (sis′tē in, -ti ēn′) *n.* an amino acid, HSCH₂-CH(NH₂)COOH, derived from cystine and produced by the acid hydrolysis of proteins in digestion

cys·ti- (sis′tē) *same as* CYSTO-

cyst·ic (sis′tik) *adj.* [ModL. *cysticus*] 1. of or like a cyst 2. having or containing a cyst or cysts 3. enclosed in a cyst 4. *Anat.* of the gall bladder or the urinary bladder

cys·ti·cer·coid (sis′tə sur′koid) *adj.* of or like a cysticercus —*n.* the larva of certain tapeworms, similar to a cysticercus but having a much smaller bladder

cys·ti·cer·cus (-kəs) *n., pl.* **-cer′ci** (-sī) [ModL. < CYSTI- + Gr. *kerkos,* tail] the larva of certain tapeworms, parasitic in an intermediate host, in which the head and neck are partly enclosed in a bladderlike cyst

cystic fibrosis a congenital disease of children, characterized by fibrosis and malfunctioning of the pancreas, and frequent respiratory infections

cys·tine (sis′tēn, -tin) *n.* [CYST- + -INE⁴: so named from having been found first in urinary calculi] a crystalline amino acid, C₄H₆(NH₂)₂S₂(COOH)₂, produced in the digestion of proteins

cys·ti·tis (sis tīt′is) *n.* [CYST- + -ITIS] an inflammation of the urinary bladder

cys·to- (sis′tə, -tō) [< Gr. *kystis,* bladder, sac: see CYST] *a combining form meaning* of or like a bladder or sac *[cystocele]*

cys·to·carp (sis′tə kärp′) *n.* [CYSTO- + -CARP] a fruitlike structure (*sporocarp*) developed after fertilization in the red algae

cys·to·cele (-sēl′) *n.* [CYSTO- + -CELE] a hernia of the urinary bladder into the vagina

cyst·oid (sis′toid) *adj.* like a cyst or bladder —*n.* a cystlike formation

cys·to·lith (sis′tə lith′) *n.* [CYSTO- + -LITH] *Bot.* a crystalline deposit of calcium carbonate occurring as a knob on the end of a stalk within a plant cell

cys·to·scope (sis′tə skōp′) *n.* [CYSTO- + -SCOPE] an instrument for visually examining the interior of the urinary bladder —*vt.* **-scoped′, -scop′ing** to examine with a cystoscope —**cys·to·scop′ic** (-skäp′ik) *adj.*

cys·tos·co·py (sis täs′kə pē) *n., pl.* **-pies** examination of the urinary bladder with the aid of a cystoscope

cys·tot·o·my (sis tät′ə mē) *n., pl.* **-mies** [CYSTO- + -TOMY] the surgical operation of making an incision into the urinary bladder

-cyte (sīt) [< Gr. *kytos*, a hollow, akin to L. *cutis:* see CUTICLE] *a terminal combining form meaning* a cell *[lymphocyte]*

Cy·the·ra (si thir′ə) [L. < Gr. *Kythera*] Greek island just south of the Peloponnesus, near which Aphrodite is fabled to have arisen full-grown from the sea

Cyth·e·re·a (sith′ə rē′ə) [L. < Gr. *Kythereia* < *Kythera:* see prec.] *same as* APHRODITE —**Cyth′e·re′an** *adj.*

cy·to- (sīt′ə, -ō) [< Gr. *kytos*, a hollow: see -CYTE] *a combining form meaning* of a cell or cells *[cytology, cytoplasm]:* also, before a vowel, **cyt-**

cy·to·chem·is·try (sīt′ə kem′is trē) *n.* the study of the chemical constituents of tissues and cells, as with a microscope

cy·to·chrome (sīt′ə krōm′) *n.* [CYTO- + -CHROME] any of several iron-containing enzymes found in almost all animal and plant cells, very important in cell respiration

cy·to·ge·net·ics (sīt′ō jə net′iks) *n.pl.* [*with sing. v.*] the science correlating cytology and genetics as they relate to the behavior of chromosomes and genes in cells with regard to heredity and variation —**cy′to·ge·net′ic, cy′to·ge·net′i·cal** *adj.* —**cy′to·ge·net′i·cal·ly** *adv.* —**cy′to·ge·net′i·cist** (-ə sist) *n.*

cy·to·ki·ne·sis (-ki nē′sis) *n.* [CYTO- + Gr. *kinēsis*, motion] the cytoplasmic changes occurring in a cell during mitosis, meiosis, and fertilization —**cy′to·ki·net′ic** (-net′ik) *adj.*

cy·tol·o·gy (sī täl′ə jē) *n.* [CYTO- + -LOGY] the branch of biology dealing with the structure, function, pathology, and life history of cells —**cy·to·log·ic** (sī′tə läj′ik), **cy′to·log′i·cal** *adj.* —**cy′to·log′i·cal·ly** *adv.* —**cy·tol′o·gist** *n.*

cy·tol·y·sin (-ə sin) *n.* a substance or antibody that produces cytolysis

cy·tol·y·sis (-ə sis) *n.* [CYTO- + -LYSIS] *Biol.* the disintegration or dissolution of cells —**cy·to·lyt·ic** (sī′tə lit′ik) *adj.*

cy·to·plasm (sīt′ə plaz′m) *n.* [CYTO- + -PLASM] the protoplasm of a cell, exclusive of the nucleus —**cy′to·plas′mic** *adj.*

cy·to·plast (-plast′) *n. same as* CYTOPLASM —**cy′to·plas′tic** *adj.*

cy·to·sine (sīt′ə sēn′) *n.* [G. *zytosin* < *zyt-*, CYTO- + *-os*, -OSE¹ + *-in*, -INE⁴] a nitrogenous base, C₄H₅N₃O, a constituent of various nucleic acids, and one of the substances constituting the genetic code in DNA molecules

cy·to·tax·on·o·my (sīt′ō tak sän′ə mē) *n.* the branch of taxonomy that uses cytological structures, esp. the chromosomes, as an aid in classifying organisms —**cy′to·tax′o·nom′ic** (-sə näm′ik) *adj.* —**cy′to·tax′o·nom′i·cal·ly** *adv.*

cy·to·troph·o·blast (sīt′ō träf′ə blast′) *n.* [CYTO- + TROPHOBLAST] the thickened, inner part of the mammalian placenta nearest to the fetus, covering the chorion and chorionic villi during early pregnancy —**cy′to·troph′o·blas′tic** *adj.*

Cyz·i·cus (siz′i kəs) ancient Greek city in NW Asia Minor, on the S shore of the Sea of Marmara: near here, the Spartan fleet was defeated (410 B.C.) by the Athenians

C.Z. Canal Zone

czar (zär) *n.* [Russ. *tsar′*, contr. of *tsesar* < OSlav. *cēsarĭ*; prob. via Goth. *kaisar* < L. *Caesar:* see CAESAR] 1. an emperor: title of any of the former emperors of Russia and, at various times, the sovereigns of other Slavic nations ☆2. any person having great or unlimited power over others; autocrat —**czar′dom** *n.*

czar·das (chär′dəsh, -däsh) *n.* [Hung. *csárdás*] 1. a Hungarian dance consisting of a slow section followed by a fast one 2. music for this dance

czar·e·vitch (zär′ə vich′) *n.* [Russ. *tsarevich*, son of a czar] the eldest son of a czar of Russia

cza·ri·na (zä rē′nə) *n.* [G. *zarin, czarin*, fem. of *zar, czar* (< Russ.), for Russ. *tsaritsa*] the wife of a czar; empress of Russia: also **cza·rit′za** (-rit′sə)

czar·ism (zär′iz′m) *n.* 1. the Russian government under the czars 2. absolute rule; autocracy; despotism —**czar′ist** *adj., n.*

Czech (chek) *n.* 1. a Bohemian, Moravian, or Silesian Slav of Czechoslovakia 2. the West Slavic language of the Czechs —*adj.* of Czechoslovakia, its people, or their language: also **Czech′ish**

Czech·o·slo·vak (chek′ə slō′väk) *adj.* of Czechoslovakia or its people. *n.* a Czech or Slovak living in Czechoslovakia Also **Czech′o·slo·vak′i·an** (-slō vä′kē ən)

Czech·o·slo·va·ki·a (chek′ə slō vä′kē ə) country in C Europe, south of Poland and east of Germany: formed (1918) by the merger of Bohemia, Moravia, and parts of Silesia and Slovakia: 49,367 sq. mi.; pop. 14,194,000; cap. Prague: Czech name, CESKOSLOVENSKO

Czer·ny (cher′nē) Karl 1791–1857; Austrian pianist & composer

Czę·sto·cho·wa (chən′stō Hō′vä) city in S Poland, on the Warta River: pop. 173,000

D

D, d (dē) *n., pl.* **D's, d's** 1. the fourth letter of the English alphabet: from the Greek *delta*, a borrowing from the Phoenician 2. the sound of *D* or *d*, normally a voiced alveolar stop 3. a type or impression for *D* or *d* 4. a symbol *for* the fourth in a sequence or group —*adj.* 1. of *D* or *d* 2. fourth in a sequence or group

D (dē) *n.* 1. an object shaped like *D* 2. a Roman numeral for 500; with a superior bar (D̄), 500,000 or, less often, 5,000 3. *Chem.* deuterium ☆4. *Educ.* a grade indicating below average work, or merely passing 5. *Music a)* the second tone or note in the ascending scale of C major *b)* a key, string, etc. producing this tone *c)* the scale having this tone as the keynote 6. *Physics the symbol for* density —*adj.* 1. shaped like *D* 2. below average in quality

D- (dē) *a prefix meaning* having a spatial arrangement of atoms around an asymmetric carbon atom similar to that of d-glyceraldehyde, the arbitrary standard of comparison *[D-glucose]*

d- (dē) *a prefix meaning* dextrorotatory *[d-limonene]*

D. 1. December 2. Democrat 3. Democratic 4. Department (of the U.S. Army) 5. Doctor 6. Don 7. Duchess 8. Duke 9. Dutch 10. [L. *Deus*] God 11. [L. *Dominus*] Lord

d. 1. dam (in pedigrees) 2. date 3. daughter 4. day; days 5. dead 6. degree 7. delete 8. density 9. deputy 10. deserter 11. diameter 12. died 13. dime 14. dinar 15. director 16. dividend 17. dollar 18. dorsal 19. dose 20. drachma 21. dyne 22. [L. *denarius*, pl. *denarii*] penny; pence

†da (dä) *adv.* [Russ.] yes

da. 1. daughter 2. day; days

D.A. 1. Dictionary of Americanisms: also **DA** 2. District Attorney

dab¹ (dab) *vt., vi.* **dabbed, dab′bing** [ME. *dabben*, to strike, akin to MDu. *dabben* & Norw. *dabba* < ? IE. base **dhabh-*, to strike] 1. to touch or stroke lightly and quickly 2. to pat with something soft or moist 3. to put on (paint, etc.) with light, quick strokes —*n.* 1. a light, quick stroke; tap; pat 2. a small, soft, or moist bit of something *[a dab of rouge]*

dab² (dab) *n.* [ME. *dabbe* < ?] 1. any of several flounders (genus *Limanda*) found in coastal waters 2. any small flatfish

dab³ (dab) *n.* [contr. < Brit. *dab-hand:* see DAB¹, *v.*, 3 & DABSTER] [Brit. Colloq.] an expert

D.A.B., DAB Dictionary of American Biography

dab·ber (dab′ər) *n.* 1. a person or thing that dabs 2. a pad for inking type or engravings by hand

dab·ble (dab′'l) *vt.* **-bled, -bling** [Du. *dabbelen*, freq. of *dabben*, to strike, DAB] 1. to dip lightly in and out of a liquid 2. to wet by dipping, splashing, or sprinkling —*vi.* 1. to play in water, as with the hands 2. to do something superficially, not seriously (with *in* or *at*) *[to dabble in art]* —**dab′bler** *n.*

dab·chick (dab′chik′) *n.* [DAB¹ + CHICK: from the manner of diving] 1. the European little grebe (*Podiceps ruficollis*), a small diving bird ☆2. the pied-billed grebe (*Podilymbus podiceps*) of N. and S. America

dab·ster (dab′stər) *n.* [DAB¹ + -STER] 1. [Brit. Colloq.] an expert 2. [Colloq.] an amateurish worker; dabbler

†da ca·po (dä kä′pō) [It., from (the) head] *Music* from the beginning: a direction to the performer to repeat a passage

Dac·ca (dak′ə, däk′-) capital of the province of East Pakistan, in the central part: pop. 557,000

dace (dās) *n., pl.* **dace, dac′es:** see PLURAL, II, D, 2 [ME., dial. form (with *-r-* loss as in BASS²) of *dars* < OFr. *dars* < VL. *darsus*, of Gaul. origin] 1. a small freshwater fish (*Leuciscus vulgaris*) of the carp family, found in Europe ☆2. any of a number of small N. American fishes (as genera *Rhinichthys* and *Chrosomus*) of the carp family, found in freshwater streams

†da·cha (dä′chə) *n.* [Russ., orig. a giving, gift < *datya*, verbal noun < *dat′*, to give, akin to Sans. *dāti-*, Gr. *dosis*, gift] a country house or cottage used as a summer home

Da·chau (dä′khou) city in S Germany: pop. 26,000: site of a Nazi concentration camp & extermination center

dachs·hund (däks′hoond, -hoont; dash′hund) *n.* [G. < *dachs*, badger + *hund*, dog] a small dog of German breed, with a long body, short legs, and drooping ears

DACHSHUND
(8–10 in. high at shoulder)

Da·cia (dā′shə) ancient kingdom, later a Roman province, in SE Europe, corresponding approximately to modern Romania —**Da′cian** *adj., n.*

da·coit (də koit′) *n.* [Hind. *dākāit*, robber < *dākā*, attack by robbers] a member of a gang of robbers in India or Burma

da·coit·y (-ē) *n., pl.* **-coit′ies** [Hind. *dākāitī*: see DACOIT] robbery by dacoits

☆**Da·cron** (dā′krän, dak′rän) [arbitrary formation, with *-on* as in NYLON, RAYON] *a trademark for* a synthetic polyester fiber or a washable, wrinkle-resistant fabric made from it —*n.* [*also* d-] this fiber or fabric

dac·ry·o- (dak′rē ō, -ə) [< Gr. *dakryon*, tear] *a combining form meaning* a tear, or having to do with tears or the lacrimal apparatus: also, before a vowel, **dac′ry-**

dac·tyl (dak′t'l) *n.* [ME. *dactil* < L. *dactylus* < Gr. *daktylos*, a finger or (by analogy with the three joints of a finger) a dactyl] **1.** a metrical foot of three syllables, the first accented and the others unaccented, as in English verse, or the first long and the others short, as in Greek and Latin verse (Ex.: "táke hĕr úp|téndĕrlý″) **2.** *Zool.* a finger or toe

dac·tyl·ic (dak til′ik) *adj.* of or made up of dactyls —*n.* a dactylic verse

dac·tyl·o- (dak′tə lō′, dak til′ə) [< Gr. *daktylos*, a finger] *a combining form meaning* finger, toe, digit [*dactylogram*]: also, before a vowel, **dac′tyl-**

dac·tyl·o·gram (dak til′ə gram′) *n.* [DACTYLO- + -GRAM] a fingerprint

dac·ty·log·ra·phy (dak′tə läg′rə fē) *n.* [DACTYLO- + -GRAPHY] the study of fingerprints as a means of identification

dac·ty·lol·o·gy (-läl′ə jē) *n.* [DACTYLO- + -LOGY] the use of a finger alphabet, as among deaf-mutes

☆**dac·ty·los·co·py** (dak′tə läs′kə pē) *n.* [DACTYLO- + -SCOPY] the examination or classification of fingerprints

-dac·ty·lous (dak′t'l əs) [see ff.] *a combining form meaning* having fingers, toes, etc. of a specified kind or number

-dac·ty·ly (dak′t'l ē) [< Gr. *daktylos*, a finger] *a combining form meaning* a (specified) condition of the fingers, toes, etc.: also **dac′ty·li·a**

dad (dad) *n.* [< child's cry *dada*] [Colloq.] father

da·da (dä′dä, -də) *n.* [Fr., lit. hobbyhorse (< baby talk, altered < ? *dia dia*, giddap), selected by Tristan TZARA, leader of the cult, because of its resemblance to meaningless babble, as symbolic of the movement] [*also* D-] a cult (1916–1922) in painting, sculpture, and literature characterized by fantastic, abstract, or incongruous creations, by rejection of all accepted conventions, and by nihilistic satire: also **da′da·ism** —**da′da·ist** *adj., n.* —**da′da·is′tic** *adj.*

dad·dy (dad′ē) *n., pl.* **-dies** [see DAD] **1.** [Colloq.] father; dad **2.** [Slang] *same as* SUGAR DADDY

dad·dy-long·legs (dad′ē lôŋ′legz′) *n., pl.* **-long·legs 1.** *same as* HARVESTMAN (sense 2) **2.** *same as* CRANE FLY

da·do (dā′dō) *n., pl.* **-does** [It., a die, die-shaped part of pedestal, hence pedestal < L. *datum*, a die, lit., what is given: see DATE[1]] **1.** part of a pedestal between the cap and the base **2.** the lower part of the wall of a room if decorated differently from the upper part, as with panels or an ornamental border **3.** *a)* a rectangular groove cut in the side of one board so that another board may be fitted into it, usually at right angles *b)* the joint thus made: in full, **dado joint** —*vt.* **-doed, -do·ing 1.** to furnish with a dado **2.** to fit into a dado groove

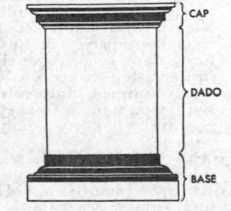

CAP
DADO
BASE

Da·dra and Na·gar Ha·vel·i (də drä′ ənd nə gur′ hä′vel ē) territory of India, on the S coast of Gujarat state: 189 sq. mi.; pop. 58,000

D.A.E., DAE Dictionary of American English

dae·dal (dē′d'l) *adj.* [L. *daedalus* < Gr. *daidalos* < *daidallein*, to work artfully] [Chiefly Poet.] **1.** skillfully made; ingenious **2.** highly wrought; intricate

Dae·da·li·an, Dae·da·le·an (di dāl′yən, -ē ən) *adj.* **1.** of Daedalus **2.** [d-] *same as* DAEDAL

Daed·a·lus (ded′'l əs, dēd′-) [L. < Gr. *Daidalos*, lit., the artful craftsman < *daidalos*: see DAEDAL] *Gr. Myth.* the skillful artist and builder of the Labyrinth in Crete, and fabricator of wings used by him and his son Icarus to escape from imprisonment in the Labyrinth

dae·mon (dē′mən) *n.* [L., a spirit (in LL.(Ec.), evil spirit, demon) < Gr. *daimōn*, divine power, fate, god, in LGr.(Ec.), evil spirit] **1.** *Gr. Myth.* any of the secondary divinities ranking between the gods and men **2.** a guardian spirit; inspiring or inner spirit **3.** *same as* DEMON —**dae·mon·ic** (di män′ik) *adj.*

daff[1] (daf) *vi.* [< ME. *daffe*, fool < *dafte*, DAFT] [Scot.] to act the part of a fool; behave playfully

daff[2] (daf) *vt.* [var. of DOFF] **1.** [Archaic] to turn or thrust aside **2.** [Obs.] to take off (clothes, etc.); doff

daf·fa·down·dil·ly, daf·fy·down·dil·ly (daf′ə doun dil′ē) *n., pl.* **-lies** [Poet. or Dial.] a daffodil: also **daf′fo·dil′ly, daf′fa·dil′ly**

daf·fo·dil (daf′ə dil′) *n.* [ME. *affodille* < ML. *affodillus* < L. *asphodelus* < Gr. *asphodelos*: initial *d-* < ?] **1.** any of various plants (genus *Narcissus*) of the amaryllis family, with a typically yellow flower having a large, trumpetlike corona **2.** the flower

daf·fy (daf′ē) *adj.* **-fi·er, -fi·est** [DAFF[1] + -Y[2]] [Colloq.] **1.** crazy; foolish; silly **2.** frolicsome in a giddy way — **daf′fi·ness** *n.*

daft (daft) *adj.* [ME. *dafte* < OE. *(ge)dæfte*, mild, gentle: for the sense development, see CRETIN, SILLY] **1.** silly; foolish **2.** insane; crazy **3.** [Scot.] gay or frolicsome in a giddy way —**daft′ly** *adv.* —**daft′ness** *n.*

dag (dag) *n.* [ME. *dagge*] **1.** *same as* DAGLOCK **2.** [Obs.] a hanging, usually pointed, end

da Gam·a (də gam′ə; *Port.* dä gä′mä), **Vas·co** (väs′kō) 1469?–1524; Port. navigator: discovered the sea route around Africa to India

Da·gan (dä′gän) [Assyr.-Babylonian *Dagān*] *Babylonian Myth.* the god of the earth

Dag·en·ham (dag′ən əm) city in Essex, SE England: suburb of London: pop. 109,000

dag·ga (dag′ə) *n.* [Afrik., hemp, prob. < Hottentot *daga-b*] *same as* MARIJUANA

dag·ger (dag′ər) *n.* [ME. *daggere* < ML. *daggarius* < ? Gael. *dag*] **1.** a weapon with a short, pointed blade, used for stabbing **2.** *Printing* a reference mark (†) shaped like a dagger: *cf.* DOUBLE DAGGER —*vt.* **1.** to stab with a dagger **2.** to mark with a dagger —**look daggers at** to look at with anger or hatred

dag·gle (dag′'l) *vt., vi.* **-gled, -gling** [< dial. *dag*, to besprinkle, make muddy, prob. < ON. *döggva*, to bedew, besprinkle < *dögg* (gen. *doggvar*), DEW + -LE] [Rare or Dial.] to soil by trailing through mud

dag·lock (dag′läk′) *n.* [< ME. *dagge*, a loose, hanging end (< ?) + LOCK[2]] a lock of wool matted with dirt, dung, etc.

Dag·mar (dag′mär) [Dan. < Gmc. *dag-*, DAY, brightness + *-mar*, akin to OE. *mære*, splendid] a feminine name

Da·gon (dā′gän) [ME. < LL.(Ec.) < LGr.(Ec.) < Heb. < ? *dāgān*, grain (hence ? god of agriculture)] the main god of the ancient Philistines and later of the Phoenicians, represented as half man and half fish

☆**da·guerre·o·type** (də ger′ə tīp′) *n.* [after Louis J. M. *Daguerre* (1789–1851), Fr. painter who developed the method] **1.** a photograph made by an early method on a plate of chemically treated metal or glass **2.** this method —*vt.* **-typed′, -typ′ing** to photograph by this method — **da·guerre′o·typ′y** *n.*

da·ha·be·ah, da·ha·bee·yah, da·ha·bi·ah (dä′hə bē′ə) *n.* [Ar. *dhahabiya*, lit., golden one < *dhabab*, golden] a large passenger boat used on the Nile, orig. equipped with lateen sails, now generally powered by a steam or gasoline engine

dahl·ia (dal′yə, däl′-; *chiefly Canad. & Brit.*, dāl′-) *n.* [after A. *Dahl*, 18th-c. Swed. botanist] **1.** any of a genus (*Dahlia*) of perennial plants of the composite family, with tuberous roots and large, showy flower heads in various bright colors, native to Mexico and Central America **2.** the flower of this plant

Da·ho·mey (də hō′mē; *Fr.* dà ô mā′) country in WC Africa, on the Gulf of Guinea: former French colony: 44,696 sq. mi.; pop. 2,300,000; cap. Porto Novo —**Da·ho′·man** (-mən), **Da·ho′me·an, Da·ho′me·yan** (-mē ən) *adj., n.*

☆**da·hoon** (də hōon′) *n.* [< ?] an evergreen tree or shrub (*Ilex cassine*) of the holly family, native to S U.S. and used for hedges

Dail Eir·eann (dôl′er′ən) [Ir. *dáil*, a gathering, assembly + *Eireann*, gen. of *Eire*, Ireland] the lower house of the legislature of Ireland

dai·ly (dā′lē) *adj.* [ME. *dayly* < OE. *dæglic* < *dæg*, DAY] **1.** relating to, done, happening, or published every day or every weekday **2.** calculated by the day [*daily rate*] —☆*n., pl.* **-lies** a daily newspaper —*adv.* every day; day after day

daily double a betting procedure or bet, the success of which depends on choosing both winners in two specified races on the same program

☆**daily dozen** [Colloq.] gymnastic setting-up exercises (originally twelve) done daily

dai·mio (dī′myō) *n., pl.* **-mio, -mios** [Jap. < Chin. *dai*, great + *mio*, name] formerly, a hereditary feudal nobleman of Japan: also sp. **dai′myo**

dai·mon (dī′mōn) *n.* [see DAEMON] *same as* DAEMON — **dai·mon′ic** (-män′ik) *adj.*

dain·ty (dān′tē) *n., pl.* **-ties** [ME. *deinte*, a feeling of esteem,

pleasure < OFr. *deinté*, worth, value, delicacy < L. *dignitas*, worth, DIGNITY] a choice food; delicacy —*adj.* [< the *n.*] **1.** delicious and choice [a *dainty* morsel] **2.** delicately pretty or lovely **3.** *a)* of, having, or showing delicate and refined taste; fastidious *b)* overly or affectedly fastidious; squeamish —**dain′ti·ly** *adv.* —**dain′ti·ness** *n.*
SYN.—dainty, in this comparison, suggests delicate taste and implies a tendency to reject that which does not fully accord with one's refined sensibilities [a *dainty* appetite]; **nice** suggests fine or subtle discriminative powers, esp. in intellectual matters [a *nice* distinction in definition]; **particular** implies dissatisfaction with anything that fails to conform in detail with one's standards [*particular* in one's choice of friends]; **fastidious** implies adherence to such high standards as to be disdainfully critical of even minor nonconformities [a *fastidious* taste in literature]; **squeamish** suggests such extreme sensitiveness to what is unpleasant, or such prudishness, as to result in disgust or nausea [not too *squeamish* in his business dealings]
☆**dai·qui·ri** (dak′ər ē, dīk′-) *n.* [after *Daiquirí*, village in E Cuba, source of the rum first used in this drink] a cocktail made of rum, sugar, and lime or lemon juice
Dai·ren (dī′ren′) *former name of* TALIEN
dair·y (der′ē) *n., pl.* **-ies** [ME. *daierie* < *daie*, dairymaid < OE. *dæge*, (female) breadmaker < *dag*, DOUGH + *-erie*, -ERY] **1.** a building, room, etc. where milk and cream are kept and butter, cheese, etc. are made **2.** *same as* DAIRY FARM **3.** *a)* a commercial establishment that processes and distributes milk and milk products *b)* a retail store where these are sold —*adj.* of milk, cream, butter, cheese, etc.
dairy cattle cows raised mainly for their milk
dairy farm a farm in the business of producing milk and milk products —**dairy farming**
dair·y·ing (-iŋ) *n.* the business of producing, making, or selling dairy products
dair·y·maid (-mād′) *n.* a girl or woman who milks cows or works in a dairy
dair·y·man (-mən) *n., pl.* **-men** (-mən) a man who works in or for a dairy or who owns or manages a dairy
da·is (dā′is, dī′-) *n., pl.* **da′is·es** [ME. & OFr. *deis*, high table in a hall < ML. *discus*, table < L., quoit, DISCUS] a platform raised above the floor at one end of a hall or room, as for a throne, seats of honor, a speaker's stand, etc.
Dai·sy (dā′zē) [< ff.] a feminine name
dai·sy (dā′zē) *n., pl.* **-sies** [ME. *daies ie* < OE. *dæges eage*, lit., day's eye < *dæges*, gen. of *dæg* + *eage*, EYE] ☆**1.** a common plant (*Chrysanthemum leucanthemum*) of the composite family, bearing flowers with white rays around a yellow disk: also called *oxeye daisy* **2.** any similar member of the composite family; esp., the ENGLISH DAISY **3.** the flower of any of these plants **4.** [Old Slang] something excellent, choice, etc. —**push up (the) daisies** [Slang] to be dead and buried
daisy chain 1. a garland or string of interlinked daisies ☆**2.** any interlinked series
Da·kar (dä kär′, dak′är) seaport and capital of Senegal, on Cape Verde: pop. 380,000
☆**Da·kin's solution** (dā′kinz) [after Henry D. *Dakin* (1880-1952), Eng. chemist in America, who first used it] a weak, mildly alkaline solution of sodium hypochlorite, used as an antiseptic in the treatment of wounds
Da·ko·ta (də kō′tə) *n.* [< Dakota *dakóta*, allies < *da*, to think of as + *koda*, friend] **1.** *pl.* **-tas, -ta** a member of a group of Indian tribes (also called *Sioux*) of the northern plains of the U.S. and adjacent S Canada **2.** their Siouan language **3.** a former territory of the U.S. (organized 1861) from which North Dakota and South Dakota were formed as States in 1889 —*adj.* **1.** of the Dakota Indians or their language **2.** of North Dakota, South Dakota, or both —**the Dakotas** North Dakota and South Dakota —**Da·ko′tan** *adj., n.*
Da·lai La·ma (dä lī′ lä′mə) [Mongol. *dalai*, ocean + *blama*: see LAMA] the traditional high priest of the Lamaist religion: see LAMAISM
Dalcroze, Émile Jaques *see* JAQUES-DALCROZE
dale (dāl) *n.* [ME. < OE. *dæl* (pl. *dalu*), infl. by ON. *dalr* < IE. base *dhel*, a hollow] a valley
Dale (dāl), **Sir Thomas** ?-1619; Eng. colonial governor of Virginia (1611; 1614-16)
d'A·lem·bert (dà län ber′), **Jean le Rond** (zhän lə rōn′) 1717-83; Fr. philosopher & encyclopedist
dales·man (dālz′mən) *n., pl.* **-men** (-mən) a person living in a dale, specif. in northern England
da·leth, da·ledh (däl′et, däl′əd) *n.* [Heb., door] the fourth letter of the Hebrew alphabet (ד)
Dal·hou·sie (dal hōō′zē, -hou′-) **1. Earl of,** (*George Ramsay*) 1770-1838; Brit. general, born in Scotland; governor of the Brit. colonies in Canada (1819-28) **2. Marquis of,** (*James Andrew Broun-Ramsay*) 1812-60; Brit. statesman, born in Scotland; governor general of India (1847-59): son of *prec.*
Da·li (dä′lē), **Sal·va·dor** (sal′və dôr′) 1904- ; Sp. surrealist painter, in U.S. since 1940
Dal·las (dal′əs) [after G. M. *Dallas* (1792-1864), U.S. vice president (1845-49)] city in NE Tex.: pop. 844,000 (met. area 1,556,000)
☆**dalles** (dalz) *n.pl.* [Fr. *dalle*, water trough, conduit, ult. < ON. *dæla*, drain gutter (on a ship's deck), akin to *dalr*: see DALE] the rapids of a river between the steep, rocky walls of a narrow canyon

dal·li·ance (dal′ē əns) *n.* [ME. *daliaunce* < *dalien*] the act of dallying; flirting, toying, trifling, etc.
☆**Dal·lis grass** (dal′əs) [< ?] a tall, succulent, forage grass (*Paspalum dilatatum*), with hairy spikelets, much grown in the S U.S.
dal·ly (dal′ē) *vi.* **-lied, -ly·ing** [ME. *dalien* < OFr. *dalier*, to converse, trifle] **1.** to make love in a playful way **2.** to deal lightly or carelessly (*with*); trifle; toy **3.** to waste time; loiter —*SYN.* see LOITER, TRIFLE —**dally away** to waste (time) in trifling activities —**dal′li·er** (-yər, -ē ər) *n.*
Dal·ma·tia (dal mā′shə) region along the Adriatic coast of Yugoslavia: part of the republic of Croatia

DALMATIA

Dal·ma·tian (-shən) *adj.* of Dalmatia or its people —*n.* **1.** a native or inhabitant of Dalmatia, esp. a Slavic-speaking native **2.** a Romance language formerly spoken in Dalmatia **3.** a large, short-haired dog with dark spots on a white coat, of a breed supposed to have originated in Dalmatia; coach dog
dal·mat·ic (dal mat′ik) *n.* [ME. *dalmatik* < OFr. *dalmatique* < LL.(Ec.) *dalmatica* (*vestis*), Dalmatian (garment) < *Dalmatia*: orig. made of Dalmatian wool] **1.** a loose outer garment with short, wide sleeves and open sides, worn by a deacon, or by a cardinal, bishop, or abbot under the chasuble at Mass **2.** a similar robe worn by an English king at his coronation

DALMATIAN
(19-23 in. high at shoulder)

‡**dal se·gno** (däl se′nyō) [It.] *Music* from the sign: a direction to return and repeat from the sign 𝄋
Dal·ton (dôl′t'n), **John** 1766-1844; Eng. chemist & physicist —**Dal·to·ni·an** (dôl tō′nē ən) *adj.*
Dal·ton·ism (dôl′tən iz′m) *n.* [after John DALTON, who had color blindness and investigated it scientifically] color blindness, esp. red-green blindness
Da·ly (dā′lē), **John Au·gus·tin** (ô gus′tin) 1838-99; U.S. playwright and theatrical manager
Da·ly City (dā′lē) [after a prominent citizen, John *Daly*] city in W Calif.: suburb of San Francisco: pop. 67,000
dam¹ (dam) *n.* [ME. < Gmc. base seen in MLowG., MDu. *dam*, ON. *dammr*, MHG. *tam*, Goth. *faur-dammjan*, to stop up < IE. base *dhē*, to set, put in place] **1.** a barrier built to hold back flowing water **2.** the water thus kept back **3.** any barrier like a dam, as a rubber sheet used in dentistry to keep a tooth dry —*vt.* **dammed, dam′ming 1.** to build a dam in **2.** to keep back or confine by or as by a dam (usually with *up*)

DAM

dam² (dam) *n.* [ME., var. of *dame*, DAME] **1.** the female parent of any four-legged animal **2.** [Archaic] a mother
dam·age (dam′ij) *n.* [ME. < OFr. < *dam* < L. *damnum*, loss, injury: see DAMN] **1.** injury or harm to a person or thing, resulting in a loss in soundness, value, etc. **2.** [*pl.*] *Law* money claimed by, or ordered paid to, a person to compensate for injury, loss, etc., caused by the wrong of the opposite party or parties **3.** [Colloq.] cost or expense —*vt.* **-aged, -ag·ing** to do damage to —*vi.* to incur damage —*SYN.* see INJURE —**dam′age·a·ble** *adj.*
Da·man (də män′) small region on the coast of Gujarat state, NW India: formerly part of Portuguese India, since 1962 it has been part of the territory of Goa, Daman, & Diu: see GOA
dam·an (dam′ən) *n.* [Ar. *damān Isrā′īl*, sheep of Israel] *same as* HYRAX
Da·man·hûr (dä′män hōōr′) city in N Egypt: pop. 126,000
Da·mão (də moun′) *Port. name of* DAMAN
dam·ar (dam′ər) *n. same as* DAMMAR
Dam·a·scene (dam′ə sēn′, dam′ə sēn′) *adj.* [L. *Damascenus*, of Damascus] **1.** of Damascus, its people, etc. **2.** [d-] of damascening or damask —*n.* **1.** a native or inhabitant of Damascus **2.** [d-] damascened work **3.** [d-] a small plum: see DAMSON —*vt.* **-scened′, -scen′ing** [d-] to decorate (iron, steel, etc.) with wavy markings or with inlaid patterns of gold or silver

Da·mas·cus (də mas′kəs) capital of Syria, a very ancient city in the SC part: pop. 508,000

Damascus steel 1. a hard, flexible steel decorated with wavy lines, orig. made in Damascus and used for sword blades 2. any steel like this

dam·ask (dam′əsk) n. [It. damasco < L. Damascus (the city)] 1. a durable, lustrous, reversible fabric as of silk or linen, in figured weave, used for table linen, upholstery, etc. 2. a) same as DAMASCUS STEEL b) the wavy markings of such steel 3. deep pink or rose —adj. 1. orig., of or from Damascus 2. made of damask 3. like damask 4. deep-pink or rose —vt. 1. to ornament with flowered designs or wavy lines 2. to make deep-pink or rose

damask rose a very fragrant cultivated rose (Rosa damascena), with clusters of white to red flowers, important as a source of attar of roses: an ancestor of hybrid roses

damask steel same as DAMASCUS STEEL

Dam·a·vand (dä′mə vänd′) same as DEMAVEND

dame (dām) n. [ME. < OFr. < L. domina, lady, fem. of dominus, a lord: see DOMINATE] 1. [D-] orig., a title given to a woman in authority or the mistress of a household: now only in personifications [Dame Care] 2. a lady: now only in the names of various organizations 3. an elderly or matronly woman 4. [D-] in Great Britain a) the legal title of the wife of a knight or baronet b) the title of a woman who has received an order of knighthood: used always with the given name 5. [Slang] a woman or girl

dame's violet (dāmz) [transl. of ModL. viola matronalis] an old-fashioned garden flower (Hesperis matronalis) of the mustard family, with white or purple, fragrant flowers in spring and early summer: also **dame's rocket**

Da·mi·en (de Veuster) (dā′mē ən; Fr. dá myaṅ′), Father (Joseph) 1840–89; Belgian Roman Catholic priest & missionary to the leper colony on Molokai

Dam·i·et·ta (dam′ē et′ə) city in N Egypt, in the E Nile delta: pop. 72,000

dam·mar, dam·mer (dam′ər) n. [Malay dāmar] 1. any of various resins from evergreen trees (genus Agathis) of Australia, New Zealand, and the East Indies, used in making varnish, lacquers, etc. 2. any of various natural resins from trees (esp. genera Shorea and Balanocarpus) native to SE Asia and the East Indies, used in varnishes and paints requiring high resistance to wear

damn (dam) vt. damned, damn′ing [ME. damnen < OFr. damner < L. damnare, to condemn, fine < damnum, loss, injury, akin to Gr. dapanē, cost < IE. *depno-, sacrificial feast < base *dā-, to divide, whence DEAL] 1. a) orig., to condemn as guilty b) to condemn to an unhappy fate; doom c) Theol. to condemn to endless punishment 2. to condemn as bad, inferior, etc.: often used in the imperative as a curse 3. to criticize adversely 4. to cause the ruin of; make fail 5. to swear at by saying "damn" —vi. to swear or curse; say "damn," etc. —n. the saying of "damn" as a curse —adj., adv. [Colloq.] clipped form of DAMNED —interj. an expression of anger, annoyance, disappointment, etc. —SYN. see CURSE —**damn with faint praise** to praise with so little enthusiasm as, in effect, to condemn —**not give (or care) a damn** [Colloq.] not care at all —**not worth a damn** [Colloq.] worthless

dam·na·ble (dam′nə b'l) adj. [ME. < OFr. < LL. damnabilis < L. damnare: see DAMN] 1. deserving damnation 2. deserving to be sworn at; outrageous; execrable — **dam′na·bly** adv.

dam·na·tion (dam nā′shən) n. [ME. damnacioun < OFr. damnation < LL.(Ec.) damnatio, the displeasure of God < L., condemnation] a damning or being damned —interj. an expression of anger, annoyance, etc.

dam·na·to·ry (dam′nə tôr′ē) adj. [L. damnatorius] 1. threatening with damnation; damning 2. condemning [damnatory evidence]

damned (damd; also, in oratory or poetry, dam′nid) adj. 1. condemned or deserving condemnation 2. [Colloq.] deserving cursing; outrageous: now often a mere intensive [a damned shame] —adv. [Colloq.] very [a damned good job] —**do (or try) one's damnedest (or damndest)** [Colloq.] to do or try one's utmost —**the damned** Theol. souls doomed to eternal punishment

dam·ni·fy (dam′nə fī′) vt. -fied′, -fy′ing [Early ModE. < OFr. damnifier < LL.(Ec.) damnificare, to harm < L. damnum (see DAMN) + facere, to make] Law to cause injury, damage, or loss to

Dam·o·cles (dam′ə klēz′) [L. < Gr. Damoklēs] a courtier of ancient Syracuse who, according to legend, was given a lesson in the perils to a ruler's life when the king seated him at a feast under a sword hanging by a single hair —**sword of Damocles** any imminent danger

dam·oi·selle, dam·o·sel, dam·o·zel (dam′ə zel′) n. [Archaic or Poet.] a damsel

Da·mon and Pyth·i·as (dā′mən ən pith′ē əs) Classical Legend friends so devoted to each other that when Pythias, who had been condemned to death, wanted time to arrange his affairs, Damon pledged his life that his friend would return

damp (damp) n. [MDu., vapor, steam, akin to OHG., MHG., G. dampf < IE. base *dhem-, to smoke, mist, whence DANK] 1. a slight wetness; moisture 2. a harmful gas sometimes found in mines; firedamp; chokedamp 3. [Archaic] a dejected or depressed state —adj. 1. somewhat moist or wet; humid 2. dejected; depressed —vt. 1. to make damp; moisten 2. to slow the combustion of (a fire) by cutting off most of the air supply; bank (usually with down) 3. to check or reduce (energy, action, etc.) 4. to check or deaden the vibration of (a piano string, drum membrane, etc.) 5. to reduce the amplitude of (oscillations, waves, etc.) —SYN. see WET —**damp off** to wither and die because of mildew, as seedlings, plant shoots, etc. —**damp′ish** adj. —**damp′ly** adv. —**damp′ness** n.

☆**damp-dry** (-drī′) vt. -dried′, -dry′ing to dry (laundry) so that some moisture is retained —adj. designating or of laundry so treated

damp·en (dam′pən) vt. 1. to make damp; moisten 2. to deaden, depress, reduce, or lessen —vi. to become damp —**damp′en·er** n.

damp·er (-pər) n. [see DAMP] 1. anything that deadens or depresses 2. a movable plate or valve in the flue of a stove or furnace, for controlling the draft 3. a device to check vibration in the strings of a stringed keyboard instrument 4. a device for lessening the oscillation of a magnetic needle, a moving coil, etc.

DAMPER

Dam·pier (dam′pyer, -pē ər, -pir), **William** 1652–1715; Eng. explorer & pirate

Dam·rosch (dam′räsh), **Walter (Johannes)** 1862–1950; U.S. conductor & composer, born in Germany

dam·sel (dam′z'l) n. [ME. damesele < OFr. dameisele < VL. *dominicella, dim. of L. domina: see DAME] [Archaic or Poet.] a girl; maiden

dam·sel·fly (-flī′) n., pl. -flies′ any of various slow-flying, usually brightly colored dragonflies (suborder Zygoptera) with long wings held vertically when at rest

dam·son (dam′z'n, -s'n) n. [ME. damasin < OFr. damascene, plum of Damascus < L. Damascenus, lit., of Damascus] 1. a variety of small, purple plum; bullace 2. the tree (Prunus domestica insititia) of the rose family on which it grows

Dan¹ (dan) [Heb. dān, a judge] 1. Bible a) the fifth son of Jacob b) the tribe of Israel descended from him, which settled in N Palestine 2. village in NE Israel (formed 1939): site of an ancient town at the northernmost extremity of Israelite territory

Dan² (dan) n. [ME. < OFr. < L. dominus, a master, lord] [Archaic] master; sir: a title [Dan Cupid]

Dan. 1. Daniel 2. Danish

Da·na (dā′nə) 1. Charles Anderson, 1819–97; U.S. newspaper editor 2. James Dwight, 1813–95; U.S. geologist & mineralogist 3. Richard Henry, 1815–82; U.S. writer & lawyer

Dan·a·e, Dan·a·ë (dan′ə ē′) [Gr. Danaē] Gr. Myth. the mother of Perseus: he was conceived when Zeus visited her in the form of a shower of gold

Da·na·i·des, Da·na·i·des (də nā′ə dēz′) n.pl., sing. **Dan·a·id, Dan·a·id** (dan′ē id) [Gr.] Gr. Myth. the fifty daughters of Danaus, a king of Argos: forty-nine murdered their husbands at their father's command and were condemned in Hades to draw water forever with a sieve

Da Nang (dä′ näŋ′) seaport in N South Vietnam, on the South China Sea: pop. 121,000: also sp. **Da′nang′**

Dan·a·us (dan′ē əs) see DANAIDES

Dan·bur·y (dan′ber′ē, -bər ē) [after Danbury (orig. Danebury, "camp of the Danes"), town in SE England] city in SW Conn., near Bridgeport: pop. 51,000

dance (dans, däns) vi. danced, danc′ing [ME. dauncen < OFr. danser < ? Frank. *dintjan, to tremble, move back and forth] 1. to move the body and feet in rhythm, ordinarily to music 2. to move lightly and gaily; caper 3. to bob up and down 4. to be stirred into rapid movement, as leaves in a wind —vt. 1. to take part in or perform (a dance) 2. a) to cause to dance b) to cause to move lightly, to bob up and down, etc. —n. 1. rhythmic movement of the body and feet, ordinarily to music 2. a particular kind of dance, as the waltz, tango, etc. 3. the art of dancing 4. one round of a dance 5. a party to which people come to dance 6. a piece of music for dancing 7. rapid, lively movement —**dance attendance on** to be always near so as to wait on, lavish attentions on, etc. —**dance to another tune** to alter one's actions or opinions as a result of changed conditions —**danc′er** n.

dance of death a symbolic portrayal, esp. in medieval art, of Death whirling persons away in a dance as each dies

D and C dilatation (of the cervix) and curettage (of the uterus)

dan·de·li·on (dan′də lī′ən, -dē-) n. [ME. dentdelyon < OFr. dent de lion, lit., tooth of the lion < L. dens (gen. dentis), TOOTH + de, of + leo, lion: so called from the outline of the leaves] any of several plants (genus Taraxacum) of

fat, āpe, cär; ten, ēven; is, bīte; gō, hôrn, tōōl, look; oil, out; up, fur; get; joy; yet; chin; she; thin, then; zh, leisure; ŋ, ring; ə for a in ago, e in agent, i in sanity, o in comply, u in focus; ' as in able (ā′b'l); Fr. bâl; ë, Fr. coeur; ö, Fr. feu; Fr. mon; ö̃, Fr. coq; ü, Fr. duc; r, Fr. cri; H, G. ich; kh, G. doch. See inside front cover. ☆ Americanism; ‡foreign; *hypothetical; <derived from

the composite family, common lawn weeds with jagged leaves, often used as greens, and yellow flowers

dan·der (dan'dər) *n.* [< ?] 1. tiny particles, as from feathers, skin, or hair, that may cause allergies 2. [Colloq.] anger or temper —**get one's dander up** [Colloq.] to become or make angry; lose, or make lose, one's temper

Dan·die Din·mont terrier (dan'dē din'mänt) [after *Dandie* (Andrew) *Dinmont,* character in Scott's *Guy Mannering*] a small, active dog with drooping ears, short legs, and a rough coat, usually gray or tan, of a breed originated in Scotland

dan·di·fy (dan'də fī') *vt.* **-fied', -fy'ing** to make look like a dandy; dress up —**dan'di·fi·ca'tion** *n.*

dan·dle (dan'd'l) *vt.* **-dled, -dling** [< ? or akin to OIt. *dandolare,* (later) *dondolare,* to swing up and down, dally, trifle] 1. to dance (a child, etc.) up and down on the knee or in the arms 2. to fondle; pet —*SYN.* see CARESS

dan·druff (dan'drəf) *n.* [< earlier *dandro, dander* (< ?) + dial. *hurf, scab* < ON. *hrufa*] little scales or flakes of dead skin formed on the scalp —**dan'druff·y** *adj.*

dan·dy (dan'dē) *n., pl.* **-dies** [< ? playful Scot. form of *Andy* < *Andrew* (see MERRY-ANDREW)] 1. a man who pays too much attention to his clothes and appearance; fop; coxcomb 2. a kind of sloop or yawl 3. [Colloq.] something very good or first-rate —*adj.* **-di·er, -di·est** 1. [Rare] of or for a dandy; foppish 2. [Colloq.] very good; first-rate —**dan'dy·ish** *adj.* —**dan'dy·ism** *n.*

dandy roll [< ?] *Papermaking* a cylinder covered with wire gauze that puts on the watermark

Dane (dān) *n.* [< ME. *Danes* (pl.) < OE. *Dene,* the Danes, orig., name of a continental Anglian people] a native or inhabitant of Denmark

Dane·geld (-geld') *n.* [ME. < ON. *Danagiald* < *Dana,* gen. pl. of *Danr,* Dane + *gjald,* payment, penalty, akin to OE. *gieldan:* see YIELD] an Anglo-Saxon tax supposedly first levied to support forces resisting the Danes invading England and later continued as a land tax

Dane·law, Dane·lagh (-lô') *n.* [ME. *Danelagh* < OE. *Dena lagu,* Danes' law] 1. the code of laws established in E and N England by Danish invaders and settlers in the 9th and 10th cent. A.D. 2. the E and N section of England that was under this code

dan·ger (dān'jər) *n.* [ME. *daunger,* power, domination, arrogance < OFr. *danger,* absolute power of an overlord < VL. **dom(i)narium* < L. *dominium,* lordship < *dominus,* a master] 1. liability to injury, damage, loss, or pain; peril 2. a thing that may cause injury, pain, etc. 3. [Obs.] power of a lord, esp. to harm

SYN.—**danger** is the general term for liability to injury or evil, of whatever degree or likelihood of occurrence [the *danger* of falling on icy walks]; **peril** suggests great and imminent danger [the burning house put them in *peril* of death]; **jeopardy** emphasizes exposure to extreme danger [liberty is in *jeopardy* under tyrants]; **hazard** implies a foreseeable but uncontrollable possibility of danger, but stresses the element of chance [the *hazards* of hunting big game]; **risk** implies the voluntary taking of a dangerous chance [he jumped at the *risk* of his life] —*ANT.* safety, security

dan·ger·ous (-əs) *adj.* [ME. < OFr. *dangereus*] full of danger; likely to cause injury, pain, etc.; unsafe; perilous —**dan'ger·ous·ly** *adv.* —**dan'ger·ous·ness** *n.*

dan·gle (dan'g'l) *vi.* **-gled, -gling** [< Scand., as in Dan. *dangle,* Ice. *dingla,* to dangle] 1. to hang swinging loosely 2. to be a hanger-on; follow (*after*) 3. *Gram.* to lack clear connection in modifying another element in the same sentence [in "After marrying him, her trouble began," the participle "marrying" *dangles*] —*vt.* to hold (something) so that it hangs and swings loosely; cause to dangle —*n.* [Rare] the act of dangling —**dan'gler** *n.*

☆**dan·gle·ber·ry** (-ber'ē) *n., pl.* **-ries** [DANGLE + BERRY] a species of huckleberry (*Gaylussacia frondosa*) of the heath family, native to E N. America

Dan·iel (dan'yəl) [Heb. *dāni'ēl,* lit., God is my judge] 1. a masculine name: dim. *Dan* 2. *Bible a*) a Hebrew prophet whose faith saved him in the lions' den: Dan. 6:16–27 *b*) the book containing his story and prophecies 3. **Samuel,** 1562–1619; Eng. poet

Dan·iels (dan'yəlz) **Josephus** 1862–1948; U.S. statesman & journalist; secretary of the navy (1913–21)

da·ni·o (dā'nē ō') *n., pl.* **-os** [ModL., old name of a genus < native name in East India] any of several brightly colored, tropical, Asiatic aquarium fishes (family Cyprinidae)

Dan·ish (dā'nish) *adj.* [ME. < OE. *Denisc:* see DANE] of Denmark, the Danes, or their language —*n.* 1. the N. Germanic language of the Danes 2. [*also* d-] *clipped form of* DANISH PASTRY

Danish pastry [*also* d- p-] (a) rich, flaky pastry of raised dough filled with fruit, cheese, etc. and usually topped with icing

Danish West Indies *former name of the* VIRGIN ISLANDS OF THE UNITED STATES

Dan·ite (dan'īt) *adj.* of the Hebrew tribe of Dan —*n.* 1. a member of this tribe: Judg. 13:2 ☆2. a member of an alleged secret Mormon organization, supposed to have been formed about 1838

dank (dank) *adj.* [ME., akin to ON. *døkk,* marshy area, Sw. dial. *dunken,* moist < IE. **dhengwo-* < base **dhem:* see DAMP¹] disagreeably damp; moist and chilly —*SYN.* see WET —**dank'ly** *adv.* —**dank'ness** *n.*

Danl. Daniel

Dan·mark (dan'märk) *Dan. name for* DENMARK

D'An·nun·zio (dä nōōn'tsyô), **Ga·bri·e·le** (gä'brē e'le) 1863–1938; It. poet, writer, & political adventurer

‡**danse du ventre** (däns dü vän'tr') [Fr.] *same as* BELLY DANCE

‡**danse ma·ca·bre** (däns mà kà'br') [Fr.] *same as* DANCE OF DEATH

‡**dan·seur no·ble** (dän sër' nô'bl') [Fr., lit., noble dancer] a male ballet dancer

dan·seuse (dän sooz'; *Fr.* dän söz') *n., pl.* **-seus·es** (-sooz'əz; *Fr.* -söz') [Fr., fem. of *danseur,* dancer] a girl or woman dancer, esp. a ballet dancer

Dan·te (Alighieri) (dän'tā, -tē; *It.* dän'te) (born *Durante Alighieri*) 1265–1321; It. poet: wrote *The Divine Comedy* —**Dan'te·an** *adj., n.* —**Dan·tesque'** (-tesk') *adj.*

Dan·ton (dän tōn'), **Georges Jacques** (zhôrzh zhäk) 1759–94; Fr. Revolutionary leader

Dan·ube (dan'yōōb) river in S Europe, flowing from SW Germany eastward into the Black Sea: c. 1,770 mi.: Ger. name **Donau,** Hung. name **Duna,** Romanian name **Dunărea** —**Da·nu'bi·an** *adj.*

Dan·ville (dan'vil, -vəl) 1. [after *Dan* River (in allusion to the Biblical town of DAN¹), on which the city is located + -VILLE] city in S Va.: pop. 46,000 2. [after *Dan* Beckwith, an early trader] city in E Ill.: pop. 43,000

Dan·zig (dan'sig; *G.* dän'tsiH) 1. *Ger. name of* GDAŃSK 2. Free city of, former autonomous state (1920–39) under League of Nations protection, including the city of Danzig and its surrounding area: annexed by Germany, 1939–45

dap (dap) *vi.* **dapped, dap'ping** [var. of DAB¹, ? infl. by DIP] 1. to fish by dropping the bait gently on the water 2. to dip lightly and suddenly into water, as a bird 3. to bounce or skip, as a stone thrown along the surface of water

Daph·ne (daf'nē) [L. < Gr. *daphnē,* the laurel or bay tree] 1. a feminine name 2. *Gr. Myth.* a nymph who escaped from Apollo by becoming a laurel tree —*n.* [d-] any of a genus (*Daphne*) of small evergreen shrubs of the mezereum family, with fragrant flowers

Daph·nis and Chlo·e (or **Chlo·ë**) (daf'nis ən klō'ē) two lovers in an old Greek pastoral romance of the same name, attributed to Longus (? 3d cent. A.D.)

Da Pon·te (dä pōn'tā), **Lorenzo** (born *Emanuele Coneglia-no*) 1749–1838; It. poet & librettist

dap·per (dap'ər) *adj.* [ME. *daper,* agile, trim < ? MDu. *dapper,* nimble, powerful, akin to G. *tapfer,* brave, ON. *dapr,* heavy < IE. base **dheb-,* thick, solid, stocky: the sense development is from "heavy, powerful" to "nimble" to "trim, neat"] 1. small and active 2. trim, neat, or smart in dress or appearance —**dap'per·ly** *adv.* —**dap'per·ness** *n.*

dap·ple (dap''l) *adj.* [ME. in comp. *dappel-grai,* dapple-gray < ON. *depill,* a spot, dot, splash of water < *dapi,* a pool] marked or variegated with spots; mottled: also **dap'pled** —*n.* 1. a spotted condition 2. an animal whose skin is spotted —*vt., vi.* **-pled, -pling** to cover or become covered with spots, as of a different color

dap·ple-gray (-grā') *adj.* gray spotted with darker gray —*n.* a dapple-gray horse

DAR, D.A.R. Daughters of the American Revolution

☆**darb** (därb) *n.* [prob. contr. < obs. slang *darby,* ready money, orig., a strict usurer's bond, short for *Father Darby's bonds* < surname *Darby* or *Derby*] [Slang] a person or thing regarded as remarkable or excellent

d'Ar·blay (där'blā), **Madame** *see* BURNEY

Dar·by and Joan (där'bē ən jōn') [< an 18th-cent. song] an old married couple much devoted to each other

d'Arc, Jeanne (zhän därk') *see* JOAN OF ARC

Dard (därd) *n.* a group of Indo-European languages spoken in NE Afghanistan, NW Pakistan, and Kashmir: also **Dar'dic**

Dar·da·nelles (där'də nelz') strait joining the Sea of Marmara and the Aegean Sea: c. 40 mi. long; 1–4 mi. wide

Dar·da·ni·an (där dā'nē ən) *adj., n.* [L. *Dardanius* < Gr. *Dardanios* < *Darda-nos,* son of Zeus, pl. *Dardanoi,* a people allied with the Tro-jans in the Trojan War, later identified with them] *same as* TROJAN; also **Dar'-dan** (-dən)

DARDANELLES

dare (der, dar) *vi.* **dared** *or archaic* **durst** (durst), **dared, dar'ing**; 3d pers. sing., pres. indic., **dare, dares** [ME. *dar, der* < OE. *dear, dearr,* 1st pers. sing., pres. indic. of *durran,* to dare < IE. base **dhers-,* to dare, be bold, whence Gr. *thersos,* courage] to have enough courage or audacity for some act; be fearless; venture —*vt.* 1. to have courage for; venture upon [will he *dare* the journey?] 2. to oppose and defy; face [he *dared* the wrath of the tyrant] 3. to challenge (someone) to do something hard or dangerous as a test of courage —*n.* a challenge to do a hard, dangerous, or rash thing, esp. as a test of courage —**dare say** to think likely; suppose [I *dare say* you're right] —**dar'er** *n.*

Dare (der), **Virginia** 1587–?; 1st child born in America of Eng. parents

dare·dev·il (-dev′'l) *adj.* bold and reckless —*n.* a bold, reckless person —**dare′dev′il·ry, dare′dev′il·try** *n.*

Dar es Sa·laam (där′ es sə läm′) capital of Tanzania; seaport on the Indian Ocean: pop. 150,000

Dar·fur (där foor′) province in W Sudan: 191,650 sq. mi.; pop. 1,539,000

Dar·i·en (der′ē ən, dar′-; der′ē en′, dar′-; *Sp.* dä ryen′) **1. Gulf of,** wedge-shaped extension of the Caribbean, between N Colombia & E Panama **2. Isthmus of,** *a) former name of* Isthmus of PANAMA *b)* isthmus across E Panama, between the Gulf of Darien on the east & an inlet of the Pacific on the west

dar·ing (der′iŋ, dar′-) *adj.* having, showing, or requiring a bold willingness to take risks, violate conventions, etc.; fearless [a *daring* book, a *daring* enterprise] —*n.* bold courage —**dar′ing·ly** *adv.*

Da·ri·us I (də rī′əs) 550?–486? B.C.; king of Persia (521–486?): called *the Great:* also **Darius Hys·tas·pis** (his tas′pis)

Dar·jee·ling (där jē′liŋ) *n.* [< *Darjeeling,* district in NE India] a fine variety of tea grown in the mountainous regions around Darjeeling

dark (därk) *adj.* [ME. *derk* < OE. *deorc,* gloomy, cheerless < IE. **dherg-* < base **dher-,* dirty, somber, whence MHG. *terken,* to sully] **1.** *a)* entirely or partly without light *b)* neither giving nor receiving light ☆2. giving no performance; closed [this theater is *dark* tonight] **3.** *a)* almost black *b)* not light in color; deep in shade **4.** not fair in complexion; brunet or swarthy **5.** hidden; secret **6.** not easily understood; hard to make clear; obscure **7.** gloomy; hopeless; dismal **8.** angry or sullen [a *dark* countenance] **9.** evil; sinister **10.** ignorant; unenlightened **11.** deep and rich, with a melancholy sound **12.** *Phonet.* back: said of vowels —*n.* **1.** the state of being dark **2.** night; nightfall **3.** a dark color or shade —*vt., vi.* [Obs. or Poet.] to darken —**in the dark** uninformed; ignorant —**keep dark** to keep secret or hidden —**dark′ish** *adj.* —**dark′ly** *adv.* —**dark′ness** *n.*
SYN.—dark, the general word in this comparison, denotes an absence of light, entirely or partly [a *dark* night]; **dim** implies so little light that objects can be seen only indistinctly; **dusky** suggests the grayish, shadowy light of twilight [a *dusky* winter evening]; **murky** now usually suggests the thick, heavy darkness of fog or smoke-filled air [the *murky* ruins of a temple]; **gloomy** suggests a cloudy, cheerless darkness [a *gloomy* forest] —ANT. **light, bright**

dark adaptation the adaptation of the eye to vision in the dark by dilation of the pupil, retinal adjustment, etc. — **dark′-a·dapt′ed** *adj.*

Dark Ages, dark ages 1. the Middle Ages; esp., the earlier part from about 476 A.D. to about the end of the 10th cent.: so called from the idea that this period in Europe was characterized by intellectual stagnation, widespread ignorance and poverty, cultural decline, etc. **2.** any period like this

Dark Continent Africa: so called because it was little known until the late 19th cent.

dark·en (där′kən) *vi.* to become dark or darker —*vt.* **1.** to make dark or darker **2.** to make blind —**not darken one's door** (or **doorway**) not come to one's home —**dark′en·er** *n.*

dark-field illumination the illumination of the field of a microscope by directing a beam of light from the side so that the specimen is seen against a dark background

dark-field microscope *same as* ULTRAMICROSCOPE

dark horse [Colloq.] **1.** an unexpected winner in a horse race, previously supposed to have little chance **2.** an almost unknown contestant regarded by few as a likely winner ☆3. *Politics* a person who gets or may get the nomination unexpectedly, often by a compromise

dark lantern a lantern with a shutter that can hide the light

dar·kle (där′k'l) *vi.* **-kled, -kling** [< ff.] **1.** to appear dark or unclear **2.** to grow dark, gloomy, etc.

dark·ling (där′kliŋ) *adv.* [ME. *derkeling:* see DARK & -LING²] [Poet.] in the dark —*adj.* [Poet.] **1.** in or happening in darkness **2.** dark, dim, obscure, etc.

darkling beetle a sluggish, dark beetle (family Tenebrionidae) that feeds on plants at night

dark·room (-rōōm′) *n.* a room from which all actinic rays are excluded, so that photographs can be developed in it

dark·some (-səm) *adj.* [Poet.] **1.** dark; darkish **2.** dismal

Dar·ling (där′liŋ) river in SE Australia, flowing southwest into the Murray River: 1,760 mi.

dar·ling (där′liŋ) *n.* [ME. *dereling* < OE. *deorling,* dim. of *deor,* DEAR] **1.** a person much loved by another: often a term of affectionate address **2.** a favorite **3.** a sweet, lovable, or gracious person —*adj.* **1.** very dear; beloved **2.** [Rare] cherished; yearned for **3.** [Colloq.] cute; attractive [a *darling* dress]

Dar·ling·ton (där′liŋ tən) city in Durham, N England: pop. 84,000

Darm·stadt (därm′stat; *G.* därm′shtät) city in SW West Germany, in the state of Hesse: pop. 139,000

darn¹ (därn) *vt., vi.* [< MFr. dial. *darner,* to piece together, mend < Bret. *darn,* a piece < IE. base **der-,* to pull off,

split apart, whence TEAR¹] to mend (cloth, etc.) or repair (a hole or tear in cloth) by sewing a network of stitches across the gap —*n.* a darned place in fabric —*SYN.* see MEND —**darn′er** *n.*

darn² (därn) *vt., n., adj., adv., interj.* [Colloq.] *a euphemism for* DAMN (the curse) —**darned** *adj., adv.*

dar·nel (där′n'l) *n.* [ME. < Fr. dial. *darnelle,* prob. < OFr. dial. *darnu,* stupefied < Frank. **darn,* stupefied + OFr. *niella* < VL. *nigella,* black caraway < L. *niger,* black: so called from its supposed stupefying qualities] a weedy rye grass (*Lolium temulentum*) often occurring in grainfields: when its seeds are infested with a certain fungus, they become poisonous

darn·ing (där′niŋ) *n.* **1.** a mending with interlaced stitches **2.** things to be darned

darning needle 1. a large needle for darning **2.** *same as* DRAGONFLY

Darn·ley (därn′lē), **Lord** (*Henry Stewart* or *Stuart*) 1545–67; 2d husband of Mary, Queen of Scots: father of JAMES I

Dar·row (dar′ō), **Clarence** (**Seward**) 1857–1938; U.S. lawyer

dar·shan (dur′shən, där′-) *n.* [Hind. *darśan* < Sans. *darśana,* a seeing, akin to d*ŕ*ś, sight < IE. base **derk-,* to see, whence Gr. *derkomai,* I see, OE. *torht,* bright] the virtue, uplift, blessing, etc. which, many Hindus believe, one gets in the presence of a great man

dart (därt) *n.* [ME. < OFr. < Frank. **darod* (akin to OE. *daroth*), spear] **1.** a small, pointed missile for throwing or shooting **2.** anything resembling this **3.** a sudden, quick movement **4.** a short, tapered seam to make a garment fit more closely **5.** [*pl., with sing. v.*] a game in which a number of small, pointed missiles are thrown at a target —*vt., vi.* **1.** to throw, shoot, send out, etc. suddenly and fast **2.** to move suddenly and fast

dart·er (-ər) *n.* **1.** a thing or animal that darts ☆2. a swimming and diving bird (*Anhinga anhinga*) of tropical and subtropical America, with a slender head, long, sharp-pointed bill, and long neck ☆3. any of various small, fresh-water, brightly colored fishes (family Percidae) of N. America

dar·tle (-'l) *vt., vi.* **-tled, -tling** [DART + -LE, sense 3] to dart again and again; dart about

Dart·moor (därt′moor, -mōr) **1.** mountainous wasteland in Devonshire, SW England **2.** a prison in this region

Dart·mouth (därt′məth) city in S Nova Scotia, Canada, near Halifax: pop. 59,000

☆**Dar·von** (där′vän) *a trademark for* a pain-killing drug that contains phenacetin, aspirin, caffeine, and an analgesic (C₂₂H₂₉NO₂·HCl) related to methadone

Dar·win (där′win) capital of Northern Territory, Australia; seaport on the Timor Sea: pop. 15,000

Dar·win (där′win) **1. Charles Robert,** 1809–82; Eng. naturalist: originated theory of evolution by natural selection **2. Erasmus,** 1731–1802; Eng. naturalist, physician, & poet: grandfather of *prec.* —**Dar·win′i·an** (-win′ē ən) *adj., n.*

Darwinian theory Darwin's theory of evolution, which holds that all species of plants and animals developed from earlier forms by hereditary transmission of slight variations in successive generations, those forms surviving which are best adapted to the environment (*natural selection*)

Dar·win·ism (där′win iz'm) *n.* **1.** the Darwinian theory **2.** adherence to the Darwinian theory —**Dar′win·ist** *adj., n.* —**Dar′win·is′tic** *adj.*

dash (dash) *vt.* [ME. *dashen,* to strike, rush < Scand., as in Sw. *daska,* Dan. *daske,* slap, prob. of echoic origin] **1.** to throw so as to break; smash **2.** to strike violently (*against*) **3.** to throw, knock, or thrust (with *away, down,* etc.) **4.** to splash or spatter (liquid) on (someone or something) **5.** to mix with a little of another substance **6.** to destroy; frustrate [to *dash* one's hopes] **7.** to depress; discourage **8.** to put to shame; abash **9.** [euphemism for DAMN] [Colloq.] to damn: usually in the imperative as a mild curse —*vi.* **1.** to strike violently (*against* or *on*) **2.** to move swiftly or impetuously; rush —*n.* **1.** the effect or sound of smashing or splashing **2.** a bit of something added **3.** a sudden, swift movement; rush ☆4. a short, fast run or race **5.** spirited quality; vigor; verve **6.** striking or showy appearance or display **7.** *short for* DASHBOARD (sense 2) **8.** a hasty stroke with pen or brush **9.** the mark (—), used in printing and writing to indicate a break in a sentence, a parenthetical element, an omission, etc. **10.** *Telegraphy* a long sound or signal, as in Morse code: cf. DOT —**cut a dash** [Colloq.] to make a striking appearance or impression —**dash off 1.** to do, write, etc. hastily **2.** to rush away

dash·board (dash′bôrd′) *n.* **1.** a screen at the front or side of a carriage, boat, etc., for protection against splashing **2.** a panel with instruments and gauges on it, as in an automobile

da·sheen (da·shēn′) *n.* [< ? Fr. *de,* of + *Chine,* China] *same as* TARO

dash·er (dash′ər) *n.* **1.** a person or thing that dashes **2.** a rotating device for whipping cream, as in a churn, etc. **3.** [Colloq.] a person full of dash or spirit

☆**da·shi·ki** (dä shē′kē) *n.* [coined (1967) by J. Benning, its U.S. manufacturer] a loose-fitting, usually brightly colored, robe or tunic modeled after an African tribal garment

dash·ing (-iŋ) *adj.* 1. full of dash or spirit; bold and lively 2. showy; striking; stylish —**dash′ing·ly** *adv.*

dash light a light to illuminate a dashboard (sense 2)

Dasht-i-Ka·vir, Dasht-e-Ka·vir (däsh′tē kä vir′) salt desert of C Iran: N section of the Dasht-i-Lut

Dasht-i-Lut, Dasht-e-Lut (-loot′) vast desert region of central and SE Iran: c. 800 mi. long

das·sie (däs′ē) *n.* [Afrik.] any of several hyraxes (family Procaviidae) of Africa and the Middle East

das·tard (das′tərd) *n.* [ME., a craven, prob. < Scand. base, as in ON. *dasast*, to become exhausted (cf. DAZE) + ME. *-ard*, -ARD] a sneaky, cowardly evildoer

das·tard·ly (-lē) *adj.* of, like, or fit for a dastard; mean, cowardly, etc. —*SYN.* see COWARDLY —**das′tard·li·ness** *n.*

da·sym·e·ter (da sim′ə tər, də-) *n.* [< Gr. *dasys*, dense + -METER] a device for measuring the density of gases

das·y·ure (das′ē yoor′) *n.* [ModL. *dasyurus* < Gr. *dasys*, thick, hairy + *oura*, tail] any of a family (Dasyuridae) of small Australian marsupials that feed on flesh or insects; esp., any of a genus (*Dasyurus*) that live in trees

dat. dative

da·ta (dāt′ə, dat′-, dät′-) *n.pl.* [*often with sing. v.*] [see DATUM] things known or assumed; facts or figures from which conclusions can be inferred; information

data processing the recording and handling of information by means of mechanical or electronic equipment

da·ta·ry (dāt′ə rē) *n.*, *pl.* -ries [ML. *datarius*, official of the Roman chancery < L., to be given away < *datus*, pp. of *dare*, to give] *R.C.Ch.* 1. the office of the Curia that examines candidates for papal benefices and handles the claims of those with rights to pensions 2. the cardinal in charge of this office

date[1] (dāt) *n.* [ME. < OFr. < L. *data*, fem. of *datus*, pp. of *dare*, to give; the first word in Roman letters, giving the place and time of writing, as *data Romae*, lit., given at Rome] 1. a statement on a writing, coin, etc. of when it was made 2. the time at which a thing happens or is done 3. the time that anything lasts or goes on 4. [Rare] a season or period of time 5. the day of the month ☆6. *a*) an appointment for a set time, esp. one for a social engagement with a person of the opposite sex *b*) such an engagement *c*) a person of the opposite sex with whom one has such an engagement —*vt.* **dat′ed, dat′ing** 1. to mark (a letter, etc.) with a date 2. to find out, determine, set, or record the date of 3. to assign a date to 4. *a*) to show or reveal as typical of a certain period or age *b*) to make seem old-fashioned or out of date 5. to reckon by dates ☆6. to have a social engagement or engagements with —*vi.* 1. to belong to, or have origin in, a definite period in the past (usually with *from*) ☆2. to have social engagements with persons of the opposite sex —**out of date** old-fashioned; no longer in use —**to date** until now; as yet —**up to date** now fashionable; keeping up with the latest ideas, styles, etc.; modern —**dat′a·ble, date′a·ble** *adj.* —**dat′er** *n.*

date[2] (dāt) *n.* [ME. < OFr. < L. *dactylus* < Gr. *daktylos*, a date, lit., a finger: so named from its shape] 1. the sweet, fleshy fruit of the date palm, having a large, hard seed 2. *same as* DATE PALM

date·less (-lis) *adj.* 1. without a date 2. without limit or end 3. too old for its date to be fixed 4. still good or interesting though old

date·line (-līn′) *n.* ☆1. the date and place of writing or issue, as given in a line in a letter, a newspaper, a dispatch, etc. 2. *same as* DATE LINE —☆*vt.* **-lined′, -lin′ing** to furnish with a dateline

date line an imaginary line drawn north and south through the Pacific Ocean, largely along the 180th meridian: at this line, by international agreement, each calendar day begins at midnight, so that when it is Sunday just west of the line, it is Saturday just east of it

date palm a cultivated desert palm (*Phoenix dactylifera*) with a stout trunk and large leaves and bearing dates

da·tive (dāt′iv) *adj.* [ME. < L. *dativus*, relating to giving < *datus*, pp. of *dare*, to give; its grammatical use in LL. (*casus*) *dativus*, dative (case), translates Gr. *dotikē*] designating, of, or in that case of a noun, pronoun, or adjective which expresses the indirect object of a verb and, in many

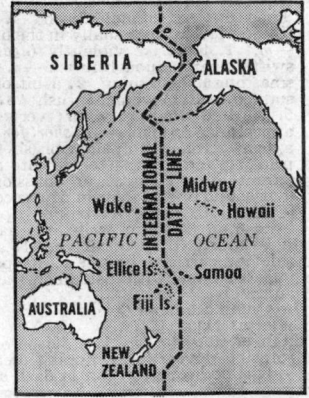

INTERNATIONAL DATE LINE

languages, approach toward something —*n.* 1. the dative case: in English, the dative is expressed analytically by *to* or by word order (Ex.: I gave the book *to Jack*; I gave *him* the book) 2. a word or phrase in the dative case —**da·ti·val** (dā tī′v′l) *adj.* —**da′tive·ly** *adv.*

da·to, dat·to (dä′tō) *n.*, *pl.* **-tos** [< Malay *datóq*] the chief of a Moslem Moro tribe in the Philippine Islands

da·tum (dāt′əm, dat′-, dät′-) *n.*, *pl.* **da′ta** (-ə); *for 2* **da′tums** [L., what is given, neut. of *datus*: see DATIVE] 1. something known or assumed; fact from which conclusions can be inferred: see also DATA 2. a real or assumed thing, used as a basis for calculations or measurements, as a level (also **datum plane**) from which elevations and depths are measured in surveying

da·tu·ra (də tyoor′ə) *n.* [Hind. *dhatūrā* < Sans. *dhattūra*] 1. any of a genus (*Datura*) of herbs, shrubs, or trees of the nightshade family, which are poisonous and have an unpleasant odor 2. the flower of any of these

daub (dôb) *vt.*, *vi.* [ME. *dauben* < OFr. *dauber*, to whiten, whitewash < L. *dealbare*, to whiten, whitewash < *de-*, intens. + *albus*, white] 1. to cover or smear with sticky, soft matter, such as plaster, grease, etc. 2. to smear on (plaster, grease, etc.) 3. to paint coarsely or unskillfully —*n.* 1. anything daubed on 2. a daubing stroke or splash 3. a poorly painted picture —**daub′er** *n.*

daub·er·y (-ər ē) *n.* painting done in an inartistic or unskillful manner: also **daub′ry**

Dau·bi·gny (dō bē nyē′,) **Charles Fran·cois** (shàrl frän swä′) 1817–78; Fr. landscape painter

Dau·det (dō dā′) 1. **Al·phonse** (ál fōns′), 1840–97; Fr. novelist 2. **Lé·on** (lā ōn′), 1867–1942; Fr. politician & journalist: son of *prec.*

Dau·ga·va (dou′gä vä) *Lettish name of the* DVINA *River*

Dau·gav·pils (dou′gäf pēls′) city in SE Latvian S.S.R., on the Daugava (Dvina) River: pop. 84,000

daugh·ter (dôt′ər) *n.* [ME. *doughter* < OE. *dohtor*, akin to Goth. *dauhtar*, G. *tochter* < IE. base *dhugheter*, whence Sans. *duhitár*, Gr. *thugatēr*] 1. a girl or woman as she is related to either or both parents: sometimes also used of animals 2. a female descendant 3. *a*) a daughter-in-law *b*) a stepdaughter 4. a female thought of as if in the relation of child to parent [a *daughter* of France] 5. anything thought of as like a daughter in relation to its source or origin [the colonies are the *daughters* of the mother country] 6. *Physics* an element that results immediately from the disintegration of a radioactive element

daughter cell *Biol.* either of the two cells that result from the division of a cell, as in mitosis

daugh·ter-in-law (-in lô′) *n.*, *pl.* **daugh′ters-in-law′** the wife of one's son

daugh·ter·ly (-lē) *adj.* of, like, or proper to a daughter

Dau·mier (dō myā′), **Ho·no·ré** (ô nô rā′) 1809–79; Fr. painter, lithographer, & caricaturist

daunt (dônt, dänt) *vt.* [ME. *daunten* < OFr. *danter*, *donter*, to daunt, subdue < L. *domitare*, to tame, break in < *domare*, TAME] to make afraid or discouraged; intimidate; dishearten —*SYN.* see DISMAY

daunt·less (-lis) *adj.* that cannot be daunted or intimidated; fearless —**daunt′less·ly** *adv.* —**daunt′less·ness** *n.*

dau·phin (dô′fən; *Fr.* dō faṇ′) *n.* [Fr., lit., DOLPHIN: used as a proper name by the counts of Vienne, and hence as a title by the oldest son of the king after the province of Dauphiné (comprising Vienne and Auvergne) was ceded to the crown] the eldest son of the king of France: a title used from 1349 to 1830

dau·phine (dō′fēn; *Fr.* dō fēn′) *n.* [Fr., fem. of *dauphin*] the wife of a dauphin: also **dau′phin·ess** (dô′fən is)

Dau·phi·né (dō fē nā′) region, formerly a province, of SE France, on the Italian border, north of Provence

daut (dôt, dät) *vt.* [Scot.] to fondle; pet; caress

Da·vao (dä vou′) seaport in the Philippines, on SE coast of Mindanao: pop. 260,000

D'Av·e·nant, Dav·e·nant (dav′ə nənt), **Sir William** 1606–68; Eng. poet & playwright

Dav·en·port (dav′ən pôrt′) [after Col. G. *Davenport*, 19th cent. fur trader] city in E Iowa, on the Mississippi: pop. 98,000

dav·en·port (dav′ən pôrt′) *n.* [< ?] ☆1. a large couch or sofa, sometimes convertible into a bed 2. [Brit.] a small writing desk with a hinged lid

Da·vid (dā′vid) [Heb. *dāvid*, lit., beloved] 1. a masculine name: dim. *Dave, Davy, Davey;* fem. *Davida, Vida* 2. *Bible* the second king of Israel and Judah, succeeding Saul and followed by his son Solomon: the reputed writer of the Psalms 3. Saint, 6th cent. A.D.; Welsh bishop: patron saint of Wales: his day is March 1 (dä vēd′), **Jacques Lou·is** (zhäk lwē), 1748–1825; Fr. neoclassical painter

David I 1084?–1153; king of Scotland (1124–53)

Da·vid d'An·gers (dä vēd′ dän zhā′) (born *Pierre Jean David*) 1789–1856; Fr. sculptor

Da·vid·son (dā′vid s′n), **Jo(seph)** 1883–1952; U.S. sculptor

da Vin·ci (də vin′chē; *It.* dä vēn′chē), **Le·o·nar·do** (lē′ə när′dō; *It.* le′ō när′dō) 1452–1519; It. painter, sculptor, architect, engineer, & scientist

Da·vis (dā′vis) 1. **Jefferson**, 1808–89; U.S. statesman; president of the Confederacy (1861–65) 2. **Richard Harding**, 1864–1916; U.S. journalist, novelist, & editor

Davis Strait arm of the Atlantic between Baffin Island, Canada, and W Greenland: c. 200–400 mi. wide

dav·it (dav′it) *n.* [ME. & OFr. *daviot*, dim. of *David*, prob. with reference to the slaying of Goliath (see GOLIATH)] **1.** either of a pair of curved uprights projecting over the side of a ship for suspending or lowering a small boat **2.** formerly, a crane in a ship's bow, used to raise or lower the anchor

Da·vy (dā′vē), Sir **Humphry** 1778–1829; Eng. chemist

Da·vy Jones (dā′vē jōnz′) the spirit of the sea: humorous name given by sailors

Davy Jones's locker (jōn′ziz, jōnz) the bottom of the sea; grave of those drowned at sea or buried there

Davy lamp [after Sir Humphry DAVY, its inventor] an early safety lamp for miners, in which the flame was enclosed by wire gauze as a protection against firedamp

DAVIT

daw[1] (dô) *n.* [ME. *dawe*, akin to OHG. *taha*, G. *dohle* < PGmc. *dhakw-*, echoic of its cry] *same as* JACKDAW

daw[2] (dô) *vi.* [Scot.] to dawn

daw·dle (dôd′'l) *vi.*, *vt.* **-dled**, **-dling** [< ? or akin to ME. *dadel*(ing), chattering (of birds), *dadelar*, glib talker, prob. of echoic origin] to waste (time) in trifling or by being slow; idle (often with *away*) —*SYN.* see LOITER —**daw′dler** *n.*

dawn (dôn) *vi.* [ME. *daunen*, back-formation < *dauninge*, daybreak, prob. altered (after ON. *dagan*, dawn) < OE. *dagung* < *dagian*, to become day < *dæg*, DAY] **1.** to begin to be day; grow light **2.** to begin to appear, develop, etc. **3.** to begin to be understood or felt (usually with *on* or *upon*) [the meaning suddenly *dawned* on me] —*n.* **1.** daybreak **2.** the beginning (of something) [the *dawn* of the Space Age]

dawn redwood a coniferous Chinese tree (*Metasequoia glyptostroboides*) of the baldcypress family, resembling the coastal redwood of California but having deciduous twigs and needles: it is now propagated in the U.S.

Daw·son (dô′s'n) [after G. M. *Dawson* (1849–1901), Canad. geologist] city in W Yukon Territory, Canada, on Yukon River: former gold-mining center: pop. 900

Daw·son (dô′s'n), Sir **John William** 1820–99; Canad. geologist, naturalist, & educator

Dawson Creek city in E British Columbia, Canada: S terminus of the Alaska Highway: pop. 12,000

dawt (dôt, dät) *vt.* *same as* DAUT

day (dā) *n.* [ME. *dai* < OE. *dæg* (pl. *dagas*), akin to ON. *dagr*, Goth. *dags*, OHG. *tag* < PGmc. *dōgaz-*, bright part of the day < IE. base *dhegwh-*, to burn, shine] **1.** *a)* the period of light between sunrise and sunset *b)* daylight *c)* sunshine **2.** *a)* the time (24 hours) that it takes the earth to revolve once on its axis: the civil or legal day is from midnight to midnight, the astronomical day from noon to noon *b)* *Astron.* the time that it takes any celestial body to revolve once on its axis **3.** [often D-] a particular or specified day [Memorial Day] **4.** [also *pl.*] a period or time; era; age [the best writer of his *day*, in *days* of old] **5.** a time of flourishing, power, glory, success, etc. [he has had his *day*] **6.** the struggle or contest occurring on a certain day [they won the *day*] **7.** the time one works each day [an eight-hour *day*] **8.** an unspecified past or future time [one of these *days*] **9.** [pl.] one's lifetime; life [to spend one's *days* in study] —**call it a day** [Colloq.] to stop working for the day —**day after day** every day —**day by day** each day —**day in, day out** every day —**from day to day 1.** from one day to the next **2.** without particular concern about the future

Day·ak (dī′ak) *n. same as* DYAK

day·bed (dā′bed′) *n.* a couch that can also be used as a bed

day·book (-book′) *n.* **1.** a diary or journal **2.** *Bookkeeping* a book used for recording the transactions of each day as they occur

day·break (-brāk′) *n.* the time in the morning when light first appears; dawn

day-care center (-ker′) *same as* DAY NURSERY

day·dream (-drēm′) *n.* **1.** a pleasant, dreamlike thinking or wishing; reverie **2.** a pleasing but visionary notion or scheme —*vi.* to have daydreams —**day′dream′er** *n.*

☆**day·flow·er** (-flou′ər) *n.* **1.** any of a genus (*Commelina*) of plants of the spiderwort family, with creeping stems, pointed leaves, and usually blue flowers **2.** the flower

day·fly (-flī′) *n.*, *pl.* **-flies**′ *same as* MAYFLY

☆**Day-Glo** (dā′glō′) *a trademark for* a coloring agent added to pigments, dyes, etc. to produce any of a variety of brilliant fluorescent colors —*adj.* designating, of, or like such a color or colors

☆**day in court 1.** a day on which one may present his case or claim in court **2.** an opportunity to present one's side of a matter; hearing

day laborer an unskilled worker paid by the day

☆**day letter** a telegram with a minimum charge for fifty words or fewer, sent in the daytime: it is cheaper but slower than a regular telegram

Day Lewis, C(ecil) 1904–   ; Brit. poet & (under pseud. *Nicholas Blake*) novelist, born in Ireland; poet laureate (1968–   )

day·light (-līt′) *n.* **1.** the light of day; sunlight **2.** dawn; daybreak **3.** daytime **4.** full understanding or knowledge of something hidden or obscure **5.** the approaching end of a task or an ordeal [to see *daylight* ahead] **6.** [*pl.*] [Slang] orig., the eyes; hence, consciousness: often used hyperbolically, as in **scare** (or **beat, knock**, etc.) **the daylights out of**

day·light-sav·ing time (-sā′viŋ) time that is one hour later than standard time, generally used in the summer to give an hour more of daylight at the end of the usual working day

day lily 1. any of a genus (*Hemerocallis*) of plants of the lily family, with showy trumpet-shaped flowers, usually opening for a single day **2.** *same as* PLANTAIN LILY

day·long (dā′lôŋ′) *adj.*, *adv.* through the entire day; all day

day-neu·tral (-nōō′trəl) *adj.* maturing and blooming whether exposed to long or short periods of daylight

☆**day nursery** a nursery school for the daytime care and training of preschool children, as of working mothers

Day of Atonement *same as* YOM KIPPUR

Day of Judgment *same as* JUDGMENT DAY

day room a room for recreation, reading, etc., as in a barracks, institution, or the like

days (dāz) *adv.* on every day or most days

day school 1. a school that has classes only in the daytime **2.** a private school whose students live at home and attend classes daily: cf. BOARDING SCHOOL

days·man (dāz′mən) *n.*, *pl.* **-men** (-mən) [Archaic] an arbiter or umpire: see Job 9:33

days of grace extra time allowed, as for payment of a note, insurance premium, etc. after it is due

day·spring (dā′spriŋ′) *n.* [ME. *daies* spring (< *daies*, gen. of *dai*): see DAY & SPRING] [Poet.] the dawn

day·star (-stär′) *n.* [ME. *daisterre*: see DAY & STAR] **1.** the morning star **2.** [Poet.] the sun

day student a college student who does not reside in a facility provided by the college

day·time (-tīm′) *n.* the time of daylight, between dawn and sunset

day-to-day (dā′tə dā′) *adj.* everyday; daily; routine

Day·ton (dāt′'n) [after Gen. Elias *Dayton* (1737–1807)] city in SW Ohio: pop. 244,000 (met. area 850,000)

Day·to·na Beach (dā tō′nə) [after Mathias *Day*, the founder] resort city in NE Fla., on the Atlantic: pop. 45,000

day·work (dā′wurk′) *n.* work done, esp. by a domestic worker, and paid for on a daily basis

daze (dāz) *vt.* **dazed**, **daz′ing** [ME. *dasen* < ON. *dasa-*, refl. *dasast*, to become weary < *dasi*, lazy, tired < IE. base *dhē-*, to wear away: cf. FATIGUE] **1.** to stupefy, stun, or bewilder, as by a shock or blow **2.** to dazzle —*n.* a dazed condition; bewilderment —**daz′ed·ly** *adv.*

daz·zle (daz′'l) *vt.* **daz′zled**, **daz′zling** [freq. of DAZE] **1.** to overpower or dim the vision of with very bright light or moving lights **2.** to confuse, surprise, or overpower with brilliant qualities, display, etc. —*vi.* **1.** to be overpowered by glare **2.** to arouse admiration by brilliant display —*n.* **1.** the act of dazzling **2.** something that dazzles —**daz′-zle·ment** *n.* —**daz′zling·ly** *adv.*

db decibel; decibels

dba, d.b.a. doing business as

D.B.E. Dame Commander of the Order of the British Empire

D.B.H., d.b.h. *Forestry* diameter at breast height

D.Bib. Douay Bible

dbl. double

DC, D.C., d.c. direct current

D.C. 1. District of Columbia **2.** Doctor of Chiropractic **3.** *da capo*

D.C.L. Doctor of Civil Law

dd., d/d delivered

D.D. 1. demand draft: also **D/D 2.** [L. *Divinitatis Doctor*] Doctor of Divinity

D-day (dē′dā′) *n.* [*D*, the first letter of DAY] the day, sometimes unspecified, on which a military attack or other important operation is to take place; specif., June 6, 1944, the day of the invasion of W Europe by Allied forces in World War II

☆**DDD** [d(ichloro)d(iphenyl)d(ichloroethane)] a colorless, crystalline insecticide, (ClC₆H₄)₂CHCHCl₂, closely related to DDT but considered to be less toxic to animals

D.D.S. Doctor of Dental Surgery

DDT [d(ichloro)d(iphenyl)t(richloroethane)] a powerful insecticide, (ClC₆H₄)₂CHCCl₃, effective upon contact

de, De (də, dē) *prep.* [Fr. < L. *de*: see DE-] **1.** of **2.** from: in French family names, it indicates place of origin

de- (di, də; *with some slight stress*, dē) [L., a prefix signifying separation, cessation, intensification, or contraction; also < Fr. *dé-* (< L. *de*) or OFr. *des-* (< L. *dis-*): see DIS-] *a prefix meaning:* **1.** away from, off [*depilate, derail*] **2.** down [*depress, decline*] **3.** wholly, entirely [*defunct*] **4.** reverse the action of; undo [*defrost, decode*]

DE Destroyer Escort

dea·con (dēk′'n) *n.* [ME. *deken* < OE. *deacon* < LL.(Ec.) *diaconus*, a servant of the church, deacon < Gr. *diakonos*, servant, messenger (in NT., deacon)] **1.** a cleric ranking

just below a priest in the Roman Catholic and Anglican churches 2. in certain other Christian churches, a church officer who helps the minister, esp. in matters not having to do with worship —*vt.* ☆1. [Colloq.] to read (a verse) aloud before it is sung by the congregation (usually with *off*) ☆2. [Old Slang] *a)* to pack (fruit, etc.) so that only the best shows *b)* to practice trickery on or with *c)* to adulterate

dea·con·ess (dē̄k′n is) *n.* [ME. *dekenesse* < LL. *diaconissa,* fem. of *diaconus:* see DEACON + -ESS] a woman appointed as an assistant in a church, as for helping with the care of the sick and poor of a parish

de·ac·ti·vate (dē ak′tə vāt′) *vt.* **-vat′ed, -vat′ing** 1. to make (an explosive, chemical, etc.) inactive or inoperative 2. *Mil.* to place (a division, regiment, etc.) on a nonactive status; demobilize —**de·ac′ti·va′tion** *n.*

dead (ded) *adj.* [ME. *ded* < OE. *dead,* akin to ON. *dauthr,* OHG. *tot,* Goth. *dauths:* orig. pp. of an old v. base appearing in ON. *deyja,* OS. *dojan,* OHG. *touwen,* all < IE. base *dheu-,* to become senseless, die] 1. no longer living; having died 2. naturally without life; inanimate [*dead* stones] 3. such as to suggest death; deathlike [a *dead* faint] 4. lacking positive qualities, as of warmth, vitality, interest, brightness, brilliance, etc. [a *dead* handshake, a *dead* party, a *dead* white] 5. wholly indifferent; insensible [*dead* to love] 6. without feeling, motion, or power [his arm hung *dead* at his side] 7. *a)* not burning; extinguished [*dead* coals] *b)* extinct [a *dead* volcano] 8. characterized by little or no activity; slack, stagnant, etc. 9. not working, moving, or turning [a *dead* axle] 10. having lost resiliency or elasticity [a *dead* tennis ball] 11. no longer used or significant; obsolete [*dead* languages, *dead* laws] 12. *a)* not fertile; barren [*dead* soil] *b)* not yielding a return; unproductive [*dead* capital] 13. certain as death; unerring; sure [a *dead* shot] 14. exact; precise [in *dead* center] 15. complete; total; absolute [a *dead* stop] 16. unvarying; undeviating [*dead* level] 17. [Colloq.] very tired; exhausted 18. *Elec. a)* having no current passing through [a *dead* wire] *b)* having lost its charge [a *dead* battery] 19. *Printing a)* prepared or set up, but not to be used *b)* already used [*dead* type] 20. *Sports a)* no longer in play [a *dead* ball] *b)* barred by a game's rules from making a particular play —*n.* the time of greatest darkness, most intense cold, etc. [the *dead* of night, the *dead* of winter] —*adv.* 1. completely; absolutely [*dead* right] 2. directly [*dead* ahead] —**the dead** those who have died

SYN.—**dead** is the general word for someone or something that was alive but is no longer so; **deceased** and **departed** are both euphemistic, esp. for one who has recently died, but the former is largely a legal, and the latter a religious, usage; **late** always precedes the name or title of one who has recently died [the *late* Mr. Green] or of one who preceded the incumbent in some office or function [his *late* employer]; **defunct,** applied to a person, is now somewhat rhetorical or jocular, but it is also commonly used of something that because of failure no longer exists or functions [a *defunct* government]; **extinct** is applied to a species, race, etc. that has no living member; **inanimate** refers to that which has never had life [*inanimate* rocks]; **lifeless** is equivalent to either **dead** or **inanimate** [her *lifeless* body, *lifeless* blocks] —ANT. **alive, living**

dead·beat (-bēt′) *adj.* 1. making a beat without recoil [a *deadbeat* clock escapement] 2. not oscillating: said of an indicator on a meter, etc. —☆*n.* [Slang] 1. a person who tries to evade paying for things; sponger 2. a lazy, idle person

dead center 1. that position of a crank and a connecting rod in which both are in the same straight line, so that no force is exerted 2. a nonrevolving center, as of a lathe spindle 3. the exact center

dead duck (or **pigeon**) ☆[Slang] a person or thing that is ruined or certain to suffer ruin, failure, or death; goner

dead·en (ded′'n) *vt.* [DEAD + -EN, replacing ME. *deden*] 1. to lessen the vigor, intensity, or liveliness of; dull 2. to take away the sensitivity of; make numb 3. to treat (a wall, floor, or ceiling) so as to keep sounds from going through; make soundproof —*vi.* to become as if dead; lose vigor, intensity, etc.

dead-end (-end′) *adj.* 1. having only one exit or outlet [a *dead-end* street] 2. giving no opportunity for progress or advancement [a *dead-end* plan] ☆3. [Colloq.] [< *Dead End,* a play (1935) by Sidney Kingsley about New York slum life] of or characteristic of slums or slum life

dead end 1. an end of a street, alley, etc. that has no regular exit 2. an impasse

dead·en·ing (ded′'n in) *n.* 1. material used to make rooms soundproof 2. coating used to reduce gloss

dead·eye (-ī′) *n.* 1. a round, flat block of wood with three holes in it for the lanyard, used on a ship to fasten the shrouds 2. [Slang] an accurate marksman

dead·fall (-fôl′) *n.* 1. a trap arranged so that a heavy weight is dropped on the prey, killing or disabling it ☆2. a tangled mass of fallen trees and brush

dead hand *same as* MORTMAIN

dead·head (-hed′) *n.* ☆1. a person using a free ticket to get into a show, ride a train, etc. ☆2. a vehicle traveling, as to a terminal, without cargo or passengers 3. *same as* BOLLARD ☆4. a floating log, almost submerged ☆5. [Slang] a stupid or boring person —☆*vt.* to drive (a vehicle) as a deadhead —☆*vi.* 1. to use free tickets 2. to make a trip

without passengers or cargo —☆*adv.* without passengers or cargo

dead heat a race in which two or more contestants reach the finish line at exactly the same time; tie

dead letter 1. a law, practice, etc. no longer enforced or operative but not formally done away with 2. a letter that cannot be delivered or returned, as because of incorrect addressing on the envelope

dead-let·ter office (ded′let′ər) the postal department to which dead letters are sent to be opened and returned to the writer, if possible, or destroyed

dead lift 1. a direct lifting without any mechanical assistance, as of a dead weight 2. [Archaic] a difficult task requiring all one's powers

dead·light (-līt′) *n.* 1. a strong cover placed over a ship's porthole or cabin window in stormy weather 2. a window of heavy glass in the deck or side of a ship 3. a skylight made so as not to be opened

dead·line (-līn′) *n.* ☆1. orig., a line around a prison beyond which a prisoner could go only at the risk of being shot by a guard ☆2. a boundary which it is forbidden to cross ☆3. the latest time by which something must be done or completed [a *deadline* for payment, publication, etc.]

dead load *Engineering* the uniform pressure or weight inherent in any structure: opposed to LIVE LOAD

dead·lock (-läk′) *n.* 1. a standstill resulting from the action of equal and opposed forces; stalemate 2. a tie between opposing sides in the course of a contest 3. a springless lock with a bolt moved only by turning the key or knob —*vt., vi.* to bring or come to a deadlock

dead·ly (-lē) *adj.* **-li·er, -li·est** [ME. *dedlich* < OE. *deadlic:* see DEAD & -LY¹] 1. causing death or likely to cause death [a *deadly* poison] 2. to the death; mortal or implacable [*deadly* enemies, *deadly* combat] 3. typical of death [*deadly* pallor] 4. very harmful; destructive 5. *a)* extreme or excessive [*deadly* silence] *b)* out-and-out; utter [with *deadly* gravity] 6. oppressively tiresome [a *deadly* bore] 7. perfectly accurate [*deadly* aim] 8. *Theol.* causing spiritual death [the seven *deadly* sins] —*adv.* 1. in a way suggestive of death [to lie *deadly* still] 2. extremely or excessively [*deadly* serious] —SYN. see FATAL —**dead′li·ness** *n.*

deadly nightshade *same as* BELLADONNA (sense 1)

deadly sins *Theol.* the seven capital sins (pride, covetousness, lust, anger, gluttony, envy, and sloth): so called because regarded as causing spiritual death

dead march solemn funeral music in slow march tempo; esp., a military funeral march

☆**dead·pan** (-pan′) *n.* [Slang] 1. an expressionless face 2. a person, as an actor, who has or assumes such a face —*adj., adv.* [Slang] without expression or show of emotion; blank(ly)

dead point *same as* DEAD CENTER

dead reckoning [< ? *ded* (for *deduced*) *reckoning*] the finding of a ship's location by using compass readings and other data recorded in the log, as speed and distance traveled, rather than astronomical observations: used in fog, etc.

Dead Sea inland body of salt water between Israel and Jordan: c. 370 sq. mi.; c. 1,290 ft. below sea level

Dead Sea Scrolls a number of scrolls dating from about 100 B.C. to about 70 A.D., discovered at various times since 1947 in caves near the Dead Sea: they contain Jewish Scriptural writings and religious writings of an Esselenelike community

dead set 1. the motionless stance of a hunting dog in pointing game 2. a resolute attack or effort

☆**dead soldier** [Slang] an emptied liquor bottle

dead weight 1. the weight of an inert person or thing 2. a heavy or oppressive burden 3. the weight of a vehicle without a load 4. *same as* DEAD LOAD 5. freight for which charge is made by weight instead of bulk

dead·wood (-wood′) *n.* 1. dead wood on trees ☆2. a useless or burdensome person or thing 3. the timbers or planks just above the keel of a ship, esp. at the stern

deaf (def) *adj.* [ME. *def* < OE. *deaf,* akin to G. *taub, taubs* < IE. *dheubh-,* misty, obscured < base *dheu-,* to rise up as mist] 1. totally or partially unable to hear 2. unwilling to hear or listen; giving no heed [*deaf* to her pleas] —**deaf′ly** *adv.* —**deaf′ness** *n.*

deaf-and-dumb (-'n dum′) *adj.* 1. deaf-mute 2. of or for deaf-mutes Now regarded as opprobrious

deaf·en (-'n) *vt.* 1. to make deaf 2. to overwhelm with noise 3. to soundproof with insulation 4. [Archaic] to drown out (a sound) with a louder sound —**deaf′en·ing** *adj., n.* —**deaf′en·ing·ly** *adv.*

deaf-mute (-myo͞ot′) *n.* a person who is deaf, esp. from birth, and therefore unable to speak: most deaf-mutes, having the necessary vocal organs, can be taught to speak —*adj.* of or being a deaf-mute

deal¹ (dēl) *vt.* **dealt** (delt), **deal′ing** [ME. *delen* < OE. *dælen,* to divide, share, akin to G. *teilen:* see ff.] 1. to portion out or distribute 2. to give; administer [to *deal* someone a blow] —*vi.* 1. to have to do (*with*); concern oneself or itself [*science deals* with facts] 2. to act or conduct oneself (followed by *with*) [*deal* fairly with others] 3. to consider or attend to; handle; cope (*with*) [to *deal* with a problem] 4. to do business; trade (*with* or *in*) [to *deal* with the corner grocer, to *deal* in cutlery] 5. to distribute playing cards to the players —*n.* 1. *a)* the act of

distributing playing cards *b*) cards dealt *c*) a player's turn or right to deal *d*) the playing of one deal of cards **2.** a business transaction ☆**3.** a bargain or agreement, esp. when secret or underhanded ☆**4.** *a*) [Colloq.] a particular kind of behavior or conduct toward another; treatment [a square *deal*] *b*) a particular plan, policy, or administration, usually involving some sort of distribution [the New *Deal*] —**big deal** [Colloq.] ☆**1.** a very important or impressive person or thing ☆**2.** an exclamation of mock wonderment, admiration, joy, etc. —☆**make a big deal out of** [Colloq.] to attach extreme importance to; make a big fuss about

deal² (dēl) *n.* [ME. *del* < OE. *dæl*, a part, share, akin to G. *teil*, Goth. *dails* < IE. base *dhai-*, ? var. of *dāi*, to part, cut up, rend] **1.** an indefinite amount or degree **2.** a considerable amount or extent [a *deal* of difference] —**a good** (or **great**) **deal 1.** a large amount or degree **2.** very much

deal³ (dēl) *n.* [ME. & MDu. *dele* < PGmc. *thela-* (whence OE. *thille*, thin board) < IE. base *telo-*, flat surface, board] **1.** a fir or pine board of any of several sizes **2.** fir or pine wood —*adj.* made of deal

de·a·late (dē ā′lāt) *adj.* [DE- + ALATE] having lost its wings: said of ants and other insects whose wings are shed after the mating flight: also **de′a·lat′ed** —**de′a·la′tion** *n.*

deal·er (dēl′ər) *n.* **1.** a person who deals; specif., *a*) one who distributes, as cards in a card game *b*) a buyer and seller; person engaged in trading [a *dealer* in furs] **2.** a person who acts in a specified way [a plain *dealer*]

☆**deal·er·ship** (-ship′) *n.* a franchise to market a product in a specified area, or a distributor holding such a franchise

deal·fish (dēl′fish′) *n.*, *pl.* **-fish′, -fish′es:** see FISH¹ *same as* RIBBONFISH

deal·ing (dēl′iŋ) *n.* **1.** the act of one who deals; distribution **2.** way of acting toward others **3.** [*usually pl.*] transactions or relations, usually of business

dealt (delt) *pt.* and *pp.* *of* DEAL

de·am·i·nate (dē am′ə nāt′) *vt.* **-nat′ed, -nat′ing** to remove the amino group, –NH₂, from a molecule, usually by hydrolysis, oxidation, or reduction, with the accompanying formation of ammonia —**de′am·i·na′tion** *n.*

de·am·i·nize (-nīz′) *vt.* **-nized′, -niz′ing** *same as* DEAMINATE —**de·am′i·ni·za′tion** *n.*

dean (dēn) *n.* [ME. *den* < OFr. *deien*, dean < LL. *decanus*, chief of ten soldiers, in LL.(Ec.), monk, < L. *decem*, TEN] **1.** *a*) the presiding official of a cathedral or collegiate church *b*) R.C.Ch. a priest chosen by his bishop to supervise a number of parishes within the diocese ☆**2.** a member of a college or university administration in charge of a school, faculty, special section of students, or of the whole body of students **3.** *a*) the senior member of a particular group *b*) an experienced and preeminent member of a group [the *dean* of American poets] —**dean′ship′** *n.*

Deane (dēn), **Silas** 1737–89; Am. Revolutionary patriot & diplomat

dean·er·y (dēn′ər ē) *n.*, *pl.* **-er·ies 1.** the position, authority, or jurisdiction of a dean **2.** the official residence of a dean

☆**dean's list** a list of students achieving the highest grades, periodically issued at certain colleges

dear (dir) *adj.* [ME. *dere* < OE. *deore*, precious, costly, beloved, akin to Du. *duur*, G. *teuer*] **1.** much loved; beloved **2.** much valued; highly thought of; esteemed: used with a title or name as a polite form of address, as in writing letters [*Dear* Sir] **3.** *a*) high-priced; costly *b*) charging high prices **4.** earnest; fervent [our *dearest* wish] —*adv.* **1.** with deep affection **2.** at a high cost —*n.* **1.** a loved person; darling: often a term of affectionate address **2.** an endearing person; one who arouses gentle affection, tenderness, or gratitude —*interj.* an expression of distress, surprise, pity, etc., often in such phrases as **dear me! dear God!** etc. —*SYN.* see COSTLY —**dear′ly** *adv.* —**dear′ness** *n.*

Dear·born (dir′bərn, -bôrn′) [after Gen. Henry *Dearborn*, U.S. Secretary of War (1801–09)] city in SE Michigan: suburb of Detroit: pop. 104,000

Dearborn Heights [see prec.] city in SE Michigan: suburb of Detroit: pop. 80,000

☆**Dear John (letter)** [Colloq.] **1.** a letter from one's fiancée or sweetheart breaking off an engagement or love affair **2.** any letter breaking off a close relationship

dearth (durth) *n.* [ME. *derth* < *dere*: see DEAR & -TH¹] **1.** orig., costliness; dearness **2.** scarcity of food supply; famine **3.** any scarcity or lack

dear·y, dear·ie (dir′ē) *n.*, *pl.* **-ies** [Colloq.] dear; darling: now often ironic or humorous

death (deth) *n.* [ME. *deth* < OE. *death*, akin to OS. *doth*, OHG. *tod*, ON. *dauthi*: see DEAD] **1.** the act or fact of dying; permanent ending of all life in a person, animal, or plant **2.** [D-] the personification of death, usually pictured as a skeleton in a black robe, holding a scythe **3.** the state of being dead **4.** any ending resembling dying; total destruction [the *death* of our hopes] **5.** any condition or experience thought of as like dying or being dead **6.** the cause of death [cancer was his *death*] **7.** murder or bloodshed **8.** [Obs.] pestilence [the Black *Death*] —**at death's door** nearly dead —**be death on** to deal with in a devastat-

ing manner —**do to death** [Archaic] to kill —**in at the death 1.** present at the killing of the quarry by the hounds **2.** present at the end or culmination —**put to death** to kill or cause to be killed; execute —**to death** to the extreme; very much [he worries me *to death*] —**to the death 1.** to the very end (of a struggle, quarrel, etc.) **2.** to the end of life; always —**death′like′** *adj.*

death·bed (-bed′) *n.* **1.** the bed on which a person dies **2.** the last hours of a person's life —*adj.* done or made in the last hours of life [a *deathbed* will]

death bell a bell tolled to announce a death

death·blow (-blō′) *n.* **1.** a blow that causes death **2.** a thing or event destructive or fatal (*to* something)

☆**death camass** (or **camas**) any of various plants (genus *Zigadenus*) of the lily family, with grasslike basal leaves and clusters of greenish or white flowers: often poisonous to sheep in the W U.S.

death chamber 1. a room in which someone has died **2.** a room in which condemned prisoners are executed

death cup a deadly mushroom (*Amanita phalloides*) with a white, scaly cap and a cuplike structure enveloping the base of the stalk

death duty [Brit.] *same as* INHERITANCE TAX

death·ful (deth′fəl) *adj.* **1.** deathlike; deathly **2.** [Archaic] deadly; murderous **3.** [Archaic] mortal

☆**death house** a place, as a cell block, where prisoners condemned to die are kept until the time of execution

death·less (-lis) *adj.* that cannot die; living forever; immortal —**death′less·ly** *adv.* —**death′less·ness** *n.*

death·ly (-lē) *adj.* [ME. *dethlich* < OE. *deathlic*] **1.** causing death; deadly **2.** like or characteristic of death **3.** [Poet.] of death —*adv.* **1.** in a deathlike way; to a deadly degree **2.** extremely [*deathly* ill]

death mask a cast of a person's face, taken soon after his death

death rate the number of deaths per year per thousand of population in a given community, area, or group: sometimes other units of time or population are used

death rattle a sound that sometimes comes from the throat of a dying person, caused by breath passing through mucus

☆**death row** *same as* DEATH HOUSE

death's-head (deths′hed′) *n.* a human skull or a representation of it, symbolizing death

death's-head moth a large, dark colored, European hawk moth (*Acherontia atropos*) with markings on its back that resemble a human skull

deaths·man (-mən) *n.*, *pl.* **-men** (-mən) [Archaic] an executioner

death tax *same as* INHERITANCE TAX

☆**death·trap** (deth′trap′) *n.* **1.** an unsafe building, vehicle, etc. **2.** any very dangerous place or situation

Death Valley dry, hot desert basin in E Calif. & S Nev.: contains lowest point in Western Hemisphere, 282 ft. below sea level

death warrant 1. an official order to put a person to death **2.** anything that makes inevitable the destruction or end of a person or thing

death·watch (-wäch′, -wôch′) *n.* **1.** a vigil kept beside a dead or dying person **2.** a guard set over a person soon to be executed **3.** any of various insects, esp. certain wood-burrowing beetles (family Anobiidae) whose heads make a tapping sound superstitiously regarded as an omen of death

death wish *Psychiatry* a conscious or unconscious desire for the death of another or for one's own death

Deau·ville (dō′vil; *Fr.* dō vēl′) resort town in NW France, on the English Channel: pop. 5,200

☆**deb** (deb) *n.* [Colloq.] *short for* DEBUTANTE

deb. debenture

de·ba·cle (di bäk′'l, -bak′-; -dä-) *n.* [Fr. *débâcle*, breakup, overthrow < *débâcler*, to break up < *dé-*, DE-, + *bâcler*, to bar, prob. < VL. *bacculare* < *bacculum*, var. of L. *baculum*, staff] **1.** a breaking up of ice in a river, etc. **2.** a rush of debris-filled waters **3.** an overwhelming defeat or rout **4.** a stunning, ruinous collapse or failure, often ludicrously calamitous

de·bar (dē bär′) *vt.* **-barred′, -bar′ring** [ME. *debarren* < Anglo-Fr. *debarrer*: see DE- & BAR¹] **1.** to keep (*from* some right or privilege); exclude; bar **2.** to prevent, hinder, or prohibit —*SYN.* see EXCLUDE —**de·bar′ment** *n.*

de·bark (di bärk′) *vt.*, *vi.* [Fr. *débarquer*: see DE- & BARK³] to unload from or leave a ship or aircraft —**de·bar·ka·tion** (dē′bär kā′shən) *n.*

de·base (di bās′) *vt.* **-based′, -bas′ing** [DE- + *base*, aphetic < ABASE] to make lower in value, quality, character, dignity, etc.; cheapen —**de·base′ment** *n.* —**de·bas′er** *n.* *SYN.*—**debase** implies generally a lowering in quality, value, dignity, etc. [greed had *debased* his character]; **deprave** suggests gross degeneration, esp. with reference to morals [a mind *depraved* by crime]; **corrupt** implies a deterioration or loss of soundness by some destructive or contaminating influence [a government *corrupted* by bribery]; **debauch** implies a loss of moral purity or integrity as through dissipation or intemperate indulgence [*debauched* young profligates]; **pervert** suggests a distorting of or departure from what is considered right, natural, or true [a

perverted sense of humor*]* See also DEGRADE —*ANT.* elevate, improve

de·bat·a·ble (di bāt′ə b'l) *adj.* **1.** lending itself to formal debate; having strong points on both sides **2.** that can be questioned or disputed; questionable **3.** in dispute, as land claimed by two countries

de·bate (di bāt′) *vi.* **-bat′ed, -bat′ing** [ME. *debaten* < OFr. *debatre,* to fight, contend, debate: see DE- & BATTER¹] **1.** to discuss opposing reasons; argue **2.** to take part in a formal discussion or a contest in which opposing sides of a question are argued **3.** to deliberate (*with* oneself or *in* one's own mind) **4.** [Obs.] to fight or quarrel —*vt.* **1.** to dispute about, esp. in a meeting or legislature **2.** to argue (a question) or argue with (a person) formally **3.** to consider reasons for and against (*with* oneself or *in* one's own mind) —*n.* [ME. & OFr. *debat* < the *v.*] **1.** discussion or consideration of opposing reasons; argument about or deliberation on a question **2.** a formal contest of skill in reasoned argument, with two teams taking opposite sides of a specified question **3.** the art or study of formal debate —*SYN.* see DISCUSS —**de·bat′er** *n.*

de·bauch (di bôch′) *vt.* [Fr. *débaucher* < OFr. *desbaucher,* to seduce, orig., to separate (branches from trunk) < *des-,* away from + *bauch,* beam, tree trunk < Frank. **balko,* beam: see BALK] to lead astray morally; corrupt; deprave —*vi.* to indulge in debauchery; dissipate —*n.* [Fr. *débauche* < the *v.*] **1.** debauchery **2.** an orgy —*SYN.* see DEBASE —**de·bauch′ed·ly** (-id lē) *adv.* —**de·bauch′er** *n.* —**debauch′ment** *n.*

deb·au·chee (di bôch′ē′; deb′ô chē′, -shē′) *n.* [Fr. *débauché,* pp. of *débaucher:* see DEBAUCH] a person who indulges in debauchery; dissipated person

de·bauch·er·y (di bôch′ər ē) *n., pl.* **-er·ies** [DEBAUCH + -ERY] **1.** extreme indulgence of one's appetites, esp. for sensual pleasure; dissipation **2.** [*pl.*] orgies **3.** a leading astray morally

de·ben·ture (di ben′chər) *n.* [ME. *debentur* < ML. < L., 3d pers. pl., pres. indic., of *debere:* see DEBT: so called from receipts beginning with the Latin words *debentur mihi,* there are owing to me] **1.** a voucher or certificate acknowledging that a debt is owed by the signer **2.** a customhouse order for payment of a drawback, as to an importer **3.** an interest-bearing bond issued against the general credit of a corporation or governmental unit, often with no specific pledge of assets

de Bergerac, Cyrano *see* BERGERAC

de·bil·i·tate (di bil′ə tāt′) *vt.* **-tat′ed, -tat′ing** [< L. *debilitatus,* pp. of *debilitare,* to weaken < *debilis,* weak, not strong < *de-* (see DE-) + deriv. of IE. base **bel-,* strong] to make weak or feeble; enervate —*SYN.* see WEAKEN —**de·bil′i·ta′tion** *n.*

de·bil·i·ty (-tē) *n., pl.* **-ties** [ME. *debilite* < OFr. *débilité* < L. *debilitas,* weakness < *debilis:* see DEBILITATE] weakness, esp. of the body; feebleness

deb·it (deb′it) *n.* [LME. & OFr. *debite* < L. *debitum,* what is owing, debt; neut. pp. of *debere:* see DEBT] **1.** an entry on the left-hand side of an account, giving rise to an increase in an asset account or decrease in a liability or net worth account **2.** the total of such entries —*vt.* **1.** to enter as a debit or debits; enter on the left-hand side of an account

deb·o·nair, deb·o·naire (deb′ə ner′) *adj.* [ME. *debonaire* < OFr. < *de bon aire,* lit., of good breed or race: see AERIE] **1.** pleasant and friendly in a cheerful way; genial; affable **2.** easy and carefree in manner; jaunty; sprightly —**deb′o·nair′ly** *adv.*

Deb·o·rah (deb′ə rə, deb′rə) [Heb. *debôrāh,* lit., a bee] **1.** a feminine name: dim. *Debby* **2.** *Bible* a prophetess and one of the judges of Israel: Judg. 4 & 5

de·bouch (di bōōsh′) *vi.* [Fr. *déboucher,* to emerge from < *dé-* (see DE-) + *bouche,* mouth, opening < L. *bucca,* cheek] **1.** *Mil.* to come forth from a narrow or shut-in place into open country **2.** to come forth; emerge —*vt.* to cause to come forth —*n.* a débouché

‡dé·bou·ché (dā bōō shā′) *n.* [Fr., pp.: see prec.] an outlet, as for troops to debouch through

de·bouch·ment (di bōōsh′mənt) *n.* [Fr. *débouchement*] **1.** the act of debouching **2.** a mouth, as of a river; outlet: also **de·bou·chure** (dā′bōō shoor′, di bōō′-)

De·bre·cen (de′bre tsen′) city in E Hungary: pop. 137,000

dé·bride·ment (di brēd′mənt; *Fr.* dā brēd mäṅ′) *n.* [Fr. < *débrider,* to cut away tissue, lit., to unbridle < *de-* (see DE-) + *bride,* bridle < ME. *bridel*] *Surgery* the cutting away of dead or contaminated tissue from a wound to prevent infection

de·brief (dē brēf′) *vt.* [DE- + BRIEF] to receive information from (a pilot, emissary, etc.) concerning a flight or mission just completed and, often, to instruct as to restrictions in making this information public —**de·brief′ing** *n.*

de·bris, dé·bris (də brē′; *also, esp. Brit. & Canad.* de′brē, dā′-) *n.* [Fr. *débris* < OFr. *desbrisier,* to break apart: see DE- & BRUISE] **1.** rough, broken bits and pieces of stone, wood, glass, etc., as after destruction; rubble **2.** bits and pieces of rubbish; litter **3.** a heap of rock fragments, as that deposited by a glacier

‡dé·brouil·lard (dā brōō yär′) *n., adj.* [Fr.] (one) skilled or resourceful at handling any difficulty

Debs (debz), **Eugene Victor** 1855–1926; U.S. labor leader & Socialist candidate for president

debt (det) *n.* [altered (after L.) < ME. & OFr. *dette* < L.

debitum, neut. pp. of *debere,* to owe < *de-,* from + *habere,* to have: see HABIT] **1.** something owed by one person to another or others **2.** an obligation or liability to pay or return something **3.** the condition of owing [to be in *debt*] **4.** *Theol.* a sin

debt of honor a debt contracted in gambling or betting: not legally enforceable

debt·or (-ər) *n.* [altered (after L.) < ME. *dettur* < OFr. *detor* < L. *debitor* < *debitus,* pp. of *debere:* see DEBT] a person, company, nation, etc. that owes something to another or others

☆**de·bug** (dē bug′) *vt.* **-bugged′, -bug′ging** [DE- + BUG¹] **1.** to remove insects from **2.** [Slang] to find and correct the defects, errors, malfunctioning parts, etc. in **3.** [Slang] to find and remove hidden electronic listening devices from (a room, building, etc.)

☆**de·bunk** (di buŋk′) *vt.* [DE- + BUNK²] [Colloq.] to expose the false or exaggerated claims, pretensions, glamour, etc. of

De·bus·sy (də bü sē′; *E.* deb′yoo sē′, də byōō′sē), (**Achille**) **Claude** 1862–1918; Fr. composer

de·but, dé·but (di byōō′, dā-; dā′byōō) *n.* [Fr. *début* < *débuter,* to play first, lead off < (*jouer*) *de but,* (to play) for the mark: see DE- & BUTT¹] **1.** a first appearance before the public, as of an actor **2.** the formal introduction of a girl into society **3.** the beginning of a career, course, etc.

deb·u·tant (deb′yoo tänt′, deb′yoo tänt′) *n.* [Fr. *débutant,* prp. of *débuter:* see prec.] a person making a debut

deb·u·tante (-tänt′, -tänt′) *n.* [Fr., fem. of prec.] a girl or woman making a debut, esp. into society

De·bye (də bī′), **Peter J(oseph) W(illiam)** 1884–1966; U.S. physicist & chemist, born in the Netherlands

Dec. December

dec. 1. deceased **2.** decimeter **3.** declaration **4.** declension **5.** declination **6.** decrease

dec·a- (dek′ə) [< Gr. *deka,* TEN] *a combining form meaning* ten, the factor 10¹ [*decagon, decameter*]: also, before a vowel, **dec-** (dek)

dec·ade (dek′ād, de kād′; *for 3, usually* dek′əd) *n.* [LME. < OFr. < L. *decas* (gen. *decadis*) < Gr. *dekas* < *deka,* TEN] **1.** a group of ten **2.** a period of ten years **3.** a division of the rosary consisting of one large bead and ten small beads

dec·a·dence (dek′ə dəns, di kād′'ns) *n.* [Fr. *décadence,* a falling away < ML. *decadentia* < prp. of VL. *decadere,* to fall away < L. *de-,* from + *cadere,* to fall] a process, condition, or period of decline, as in morals, art, literature, etc.; deterioration; decay: also **dec′a·den·cy** (-dən sē)

dec·a·dent (-dənt) *adj.* [Fr. *décadent:* see prec.] in a state of decline; characterized by decadence —*n.* a decadent person, esp. a decadent writer or artist —**dec′a·dent′ly** *adv.*

dec·a·gon (dek′ə gän′) *n.* [ML. *decagonum:* see DECA- & -GON] a plane figure with ten sides and ten angles —**de·cag·o·nal** (di kag′ə nəl) *adj.*

dec·a·gram (-gram′) *n.* [Fr. *décagramme:* see DECA- & GRAM] a measure of weight equal to 10 grams (0.3527 oz.): also, chiefly Brit., **dec′a·gramme′** (-gram′)

dec·a·he·dron (dek′ə hē′drən) *n., pl.* **-drons, -dra** (-drə) [ModL.: see DECA- & -HEDRON] a solid figure with ten plane surfaces —**dec′a·he′dral** (-drəl) *adj.*

de·cal (di kal′, dē′kal) *n. same as* DECALCOMANIA

de·cal·ci·fy (dē kal′sə fī′) *vt.* **-fied′, -fy′ing** to remove calcium or lime from (bones, teeth, etc.) —**de·cal′ci·fi·ca′tion** *n.* —**de·cal′ci·fi′er** *n.*

de·cal·co·ma·ni·a (di kal′kə mā′nē ə) *n.* [Fr. *décalcomanie* < *décalquer,* to trace, copy (< *dé-,* DE- + *calquer,* to copy < It. *calcare,* to press, trample < L. *calcare:* see CALK¹) + *manie* < Gr. *mania,* madness] **1.** the process of transferring to glass, wood, etc. decorative pictures or designs printed on specially prepared paper. **2.** a picture or design of this kind

de·ca·les·cence (dē′kə les′'ns) *n.* [< L. *decalescens,* prp. of *decalescere,* to become warm < *de-,* intens. + *calescere,* to grow hot < *calere,* to be warm] a sudden decrease in the rate of temperature rise of heated metal after a certain temperature has been reached (795°C for iron) due to greater absorption of heat —**de·ca·les′cent** *adj.*

dec·a·li·ter (dek′ə lēt′ər) *n.* [Fr. *décalitre:* see DECA- & LITER] a measure of capacity, equal to 10 liters (2.64 gal. liquid measure or 9.08 qt. dry measure): also, chiefly Brit., **dec′a·li′tre** (-lēt′ər)

Dec·a·logue, Dec·a·log (dek′ə lôg′, -läg′) *n.* [ME. *decaloge* < LL.(Ec.) *decalogus* < Gr.(Ec.) *dekalogos:* see DECA- & -LOGUE] [*sometimes* **d-**] *same as* TEN COMMANDMENTS

De·cam·er·on (di kam′ər ən) *n.* [It. *Decamerone* < Gr. *deka,* ten + *hēmera,* day] a collection of a hundred tales by Boccaccio (pub. 1353): so called because described as told by a group of Florentines to while away ten days during a plague

dec·a·me·ter (dek′ə mēt′ər) *n.* [Fr. *décamètre:* see DECA- & METER] a measure of length, equal to 10 meters (32.808 ft.): also, chiefly Brit., **dec′a·me′tre** (-mēt′ər)

de·camp (di kamp′) *vi.* [Fr. *décamper,* to break camp: see DE- & CAMP] **1.** to break or leave camp **2.** to go away suddenly and secretly; run away —**de·camp′ment** *n.*

dec·a·nal (dek′ə n'l, di kā′n'l) *adj.* [< LL.(Ec.) *decanus* (see DEAN) + -AL] of a dean or deanery

dec·ane (dek′ān) *n.* [DEC- + -ANE] any of the isomeric hydrocarbons having the formula $C_{10}H_{22}$ and belonging to the methane series, present in petroleum or in certain petroleum products, such as kerosene

de·cant (di kant′) *vt.* [Fr. *décanter* < ML. *decanthare* < L. *de-*, from + *canthus*: see CANT²] **1.** to pour off (a liquid) gently without stirring up the sediment **2.** to pour from one container into another —**de·can·ta·tion** (dē′kan tā′shən) *n.*

de·cant·er (-ər) *n.* a decorative glass bottle, generally with a stopper, used for serving wine, etc.

de·cap·i·tate (di kap′ə tāt′) *vt.* -tat′ed, -tat′ing [Fr. *décapiter* < ML. *decapitatus*, pp. of *decapitare* < L. *de-*, off + *caput*, the HEAD] to cut off the head of; behead —**de·cap′i·ta′tion** *n.* —**de·cap′i·ta′tor** *n.*

dec·a·pod (dek′ə päd′) *adj.* [< ModL. *Decapoda*, name of the order: see DECA- & -POD] ten-legged —*n.* **1.** any crustacean with ten legs, as a lobster, shrimp, crab, etc. **2.** any cephalopod with ten arms, as a squid —**de·cap·o·dal** (di kap′ə d'l), **de·cap′o·dous** (-dəs) *adj.* —**de·cap′o·dan** (-dən) *adj.*, *n.*

De·cap·o·lis (di kap′ə lis) ancient region of NE Palestine, mostly east of the Jordan

DECANTER

de·car·bon·ate (dē kär′bə nāt′) *vt.* -at′ed, -at′ing to remove carbon dioxide or carbonic acid from

de·car·bon·ize (-nīz′) *vt.* -ized′, -iz′ing to remove carbon from —**de·car′bon·i·za′tion** *n.*

de·car·boxy·la·tion (dē′kär bäk′sə lā′shən) *n.* [DE- + CARBOXYL + -ATION] **1.** the removal of one or more carboxyl groups from an organic compound, usually by eliminating carbon dioxide **2.** the removal of a molecule of carbon dioxide from amino acids and proteins by bacterial action, with the resultant formation of amines —**de′car·box′y·late** *vt.*, *vi.* -lat′ed, -lat′ing

de·car·bu·rize (dē kär′byə rīz′, -bə-) *vt.* -rized′, -riz′ing *same as* DECARBONIZE —**de·car′bu·ri·za′tion** *n.*

dec·are (dek′er) *n.* [Fr.: see DECA- & ARE²] a metric unit of surface measure equal to 10 ares (0.2471 acre)

dec·a·stere (dek′ə stir′) *n.* [Fr. *décastère*: see DECA- & STERE] a metric measure of volume, equal to 10 cubic meters (13.08 cu. yd.)

dec·a·syl·la·ble (dek′ə sil′ə b'l) *n.* a line of verse having ten syllables —**dec′a·syl·lab′ic** (-si lab′ik) *adj.*, *n.*

de·cath·lon (di kath′län, -lən) *n.* [DEC- + Gr. *athlon*, a contest] an athletic contest in which each contestant takes part in ten events (100-meter dash, 400-meter dash, long jump, 16-pound shot-put, high jump, 110-meter hurdles, discus throw, pole vault, javelin throw, and 1500-meter run): the winner is the contestant receiving the highest total of points

De·ca·tur (di kāt′ər) [after ff.] **1.** city in C Ill.: pop. 90,000 **2.** city in N Ala., on the Tennessee River: pop. 38,000

De·ca·tur (di kāt′ər), **Stephen** 1779-1820; U.S. naval officer

de·cay (di kā′) *vi.* [ME. *decaien* < Anglo-Fr. & OFr. *decäir* < VL. *decadere*: see DECADENCE] **1.** to lose strength, soundness, health, beauty, prosperity, etc. gradually; waste away; deteriorate **2.** to rot or decompose **3.** to undergo radioactive disintegration spontaneously —*vt.* to cause to decay —*n.* **1.** a gradual decline; deterioration **2.** a wasting away **3.** a rotting or decomposing, as of vegetable matter **4.** *a)* rottenness *b)* decayed or rotted matter **5.** *a)* the spontaneous disintegration of radioactive atoms with a resulting decrease in their number *b)* the spontaneous disintegration of a particle or nucleus, as a meson, baryon, etc., with the formation of a more stable state **SYN.**—**decay** implies gradual, often natural, deterioration from a normal or sound condition [his teeth have begun to *decay*]; **rot** refers to the decay of organic, esp. vegetable, matter, caused by bacteria, fungi, etc. [*rotting* apples]; **putrefy** suggests the offensive, foul-smelling rotting of animal matter [bodies *putrefying* in the fields]; **spoil** is the common informal word for the decay of foods [fish *spoils* quickly in summer]; **molder** suggests a slow, progressive, crumbling decay [old buildings *molder* away]; **disintegrate** implies the breaking up of something into parts or fragments so that the wholeness of the original is destroyed [the *disintegration* of rocks]; **decompose** suggests the breaking up or separation of something into its component elements [a *decomposing* chemical compound]: it is also a somewhat euphemistic substitute for **rot** and **putrefy**

Dec·can Plateau (dek′ən) triangular tableland occupying most of the peninsula of India, between the Eastern Ghats & Western Ghats & south of the Narbada River

decd. deceased

de·cease (di sēs′) *n.* [ME. & OFr. *deces* < L. *decessus*, lit., departure, pp. of *decedere*, to depart, go away < *de-*, from + *cedere*, to go, move] death —*vi.* -ceased′, -ceas′ing to die —*SYN.* see DIE¹

de·ceased (di sēst′) *adj.* dead —*SYN.* see DEAD —**the deceased** the dead person or persons

de·ce·dent (di sēd′'nt) *n.* [L. *decedens*, prp. of *decedere*: see DECEASE] *Law* a deceased person

de·ceit (di sēt′) *n.* [ME. < OFr. *deceite* < pp. of *deceveir*: see DECEIVE] **1.** the act of representing as true what is known to be false; a deceiving or lying **2.** a dishonest action or trick; fraud or lie **3.** the quality of being deceitful

de·ceit·ful (-fəl) *adj.* **1.** tending to deceive; apt to lie or

cheat **2.** intended to deceive; deceptive; false —*SYN.* see DISHONEST —**de·ceit′ful·ly** *adv.* —**de·ceit′ful·ness** *n.*

de·ceive (di sēv′) *vt.* -ceived′, -ceiv′ing [ME. *deceiven* < OFr. *deceveir* < L. *decipere*, to ensnare, deceive < *de-*, from + *capere*, to take] **1.** to make (a person) believe what is not true; delude; mislead **2.** [Archaic] to be false to; betray **3.** [Archaic] to while away (time) —*vi.* to use deceit; lie —**de·ceiv′a·ble** *adj.* —**de·ceiv′er** *n.* —**de·ceiv′ing·ly** *adv.* **SYN.**—**deceive** implies deliberate misrepresentation of facts by words, actions, etc., generally to further one's ends [*deceived* into buying fraudulent stocks]; to **mislead** is to cause to follow the wrong course or to err in conduct or action, although not always by deliberate deception [*misled* by the sign into going to the wrong floor]; **beguile** implies the use of wiles and enticing prospects in deceiving or misleading [*beguiled* by promises of a fortune]; to **delude** is to fool someone so completely that he accepts what is false as true; **betray** implies a breaking of faith while appearing to be loyal

de·cel·er·ate (dē sel′ə rāt′) *vt.*, *vi.* -at′ed, -at′ing [DE- + (AC)CELERATE] to reduce the speed (of); slow down —**de·cel′er·a′tion** *n.* —**de·cel′er·a′tor** *n.*

de·cel·er·on (dē sel′ə rän′) *n.* [DECELER(ATE) + (AILER)ON] an aerodynamic surface used to slow down an aircraft in flight

De·cem·ber (di sem′bər) *n.* [ME. & OFr. *Decembre* < L. *December* < *decem*, TEN (+ -*ber* < ?): so named as the tenth month of the ancient Roman year, which began with March] the twelfth and last month of the year, having 31 days: abbrev. **Dec., D.**

De·cem·brist (-brist) *n.* any of the conspirators against Czar Nicholas I of Russia, in December, 1825

de·cem·vir (di sem′vər) *n.*, *pl.* -virs, -vir·i′ (-və rī′) [L., sing. of *decemviri* < *decem*, TEN + *vir*, a man] **1.** a member of a council of ten magistrates in ancient Rome: in 451-450 B.C. this body drew up the first Roman code of laws **2.** a member of any authoritative group of ten men — **de·cem′vir·al** (-və rəl) *adj.*

de·cem·vi·rate (-və rit, -rāt′) *n.* [see prec. & -ATE²] **1.** a body of decemvirs **2.** the position or term of such a group

de·cen·cy (dē′s'n sē) *n.*, *pl.* -cies [L. *decentia* < *decens*: see DECENT] **1.** the quality or condition of being decent; propriety of conduct and speech; proper behavior, modesty, courtesy, good taste, etc. **2.** [*pl.*] socially proper actions; the proprieties **3.** [*pl.*] things needed for a proper or comfortable standard of living —*SYN.* see DECORUM

de·cen·na·ry (di sen′ər ē) *n.*, *pl.* -ries [< L. *decennis*, lasting ten years < *decem*, TEN + *annus*, year + -ARY] a period of ten years —*adj.* ten-year; decennial

de·cen·ni·al (-ē əl) *adj.* [< L. *decennium* (see ff.) + -AL] **1.** of or lasting ten years **2.** occurring every ten years —☆*n.* a tenth anniversary or its celebration —**de·cen′ni·al·ly** *adv.*

de·cen·ni·um (-ē əm) *n.*, *pl.* -ni·ums, -ni·a (-ə) [L. < *decennis*: see DECENNARY] a period of ten years; decade

de·cent (dē′s'nt) *adj.* [MFr. *décent* < L. *decens* (gen. *decentis*), prp. of *decere*, to befit < IE. base **dek-*, to receive, greet, be suitable, whence Sans. *dấkšati*, (he) is helpful, Gr. *dekomai*, I accept] **1.** proper and fitting [a *decent* burial] **2.** not immodest; not obscene; chaste [*decent* language] **3.** conforming to approved social standards; respectable [*decent* apparel] **4.** reasonably good; adequate [*decent* wages] **5.** fair and kind [*decent* treatment] **6.** [Colloq.] adequately clothed for propriety —*SYN.* see CHASTE —**de′cent·ly** *adv.*

de·cen·tral·ize (dē sen′trə līz′) *vt.* -ized′, -iz′ing to break up a concentration of (governmental authority, industry, population, etc.) in a main center and distribute more widely —**de·cen′tral·i·za′tion** *n.*

de·cep·tion (di sep′shən) *n.* [ME. *decepcioun* < OFr. *deception* < L. *deceptio* < pp. of *decipere*: see DECEIVE] **1.** the act or practice of deceiving **2.** the fact or condition of being deceived **3.** something that deceives, as an illusion, or is meant to deceive, as a fraud or imposture **SYN.**—**deception** is applied to anything that deceives, whether by design or illusion; **fraud** suggests deliberate deception in dishonestly depriving a person of property, rights, etc.; **subterfuge** suggests an artifice or stratagem used to deceive others in evading something or gaining some end; **trickery** implies the use of tricks or ruses in fraudulently deceiving others; **chicanery** implies the use of petty trickery and subterfuge, esp. in legal actions

de·cep·tive (-tiv) *adj.* [Fr. *déceptif* < LL. *deceptivus*: see DECEIVE & -IVE] deceiving or intended to deceive —**de·cep′tive·ly** *adv.* —**de·cep′tive·ness** *n.*

de·cern (di surn′) *vt.* [ME. *decernen* < OFr. *decerner* < L. *decernere*, to decide, judge < *de-*, DE- + *cernere*, to separate, sift] **1.** [Rare] *same as* DISCERN **2.** *Scot. Law* to decree by judicial sentence

dec·i- (des′i, -ə) [Fr. *deci-* < L. *decimus*, tenth < *decem*, TEN] *a combining form meaning* one tenth; the factor 10⁻¹ [*decigram*]

dec·i·are (des′ē er′) *n.* [Fr.: see DECI- & ARE²] a metric measure of surface equal to 1/10 are (10 square meters or 11.96 square yards)

dec·i·bel (des′ə bel′, -b'l) *n.* [DECI- + BEL] **1.** *Acoustics* a numerical expression of the relative loudness of a sound: the difference in decibels of two sounds is ten times the

common logarithm of the ratio of their power levels **2.** *Electronics, Radio* a numerical expression of the relative differences in power levels of electrical signals equal to ten times the common logarithm of the ratio of the two signal powers Sometimes an absolute reference is used in the power ratio (10^{-16} watt per sq. cm. in acoustics, one milliwatt in electronics and radio)

de·cide (di sīd′) *vt.* **-cid′ed, -cid′ing** [ME. *deciden* < L. *decidere*, to cut off, decide < *de-*, off, from + *caedere*, to cut] **1.** to end (a contest, dispute, etc.) by giving one side the victory or by passing judgment **2.** to make up one's mind, or reach a decision, about; determine [to *decide* which tie to wear] **3.** to cause to reach a decision —*vi.* to arrive at a judgment, choice, or decision —**de·cid′a·ble** *adj.* —**de·cid′er** *n.*

SYN.—**decide** implies the bringing to an end of vacillation, doubt, dispute, etc. by making up one's mind as to an action, course, or judgment; **determine** in addition suggests that the form, character, functions, scope, etc. of something are precisely fixed [the club *decided* on a lecture series and appointed a committee to *determine* the speakers, the dates, etc.]; **settle** stresses finality in a decision, often one arrived at by arbitration, and implies the termination of all doubt or controversy; to **conclude** is to decide after careful investigation or reasoning; **resolve** implies firmness of intention to carry through a decision [he *resolved* to go to bed early every night]

de·cid·ed (di sīd′id) *adj.* **1.** definite and unmistakable; clear-cut [a *decided* change] **2.** unhesitating; determined —**de·cid′ed·ly** *adv.*

de·cid·u·a (di sij′ōō wə) *n.* [ModL. (*membrana*) *decidua*, deciduous (membrane), orig. fem. of L. *deciduus:* see DECIDUOUS] a membrane lining the uterus during pregnancy, cast off at childbirth —**de·cid′u·al** *adj.*

de·cid·u·ous (-ōō wəs) *adj.* [L. *deciduus* < *decidere*, to fall off < *de-*, off, down + *cadere*, to fall] **1.** falling off at a certain season or stage of growth, as some leaves, antlers, insect wings, etc. **2.** shedding leaves annually: opposed to EVERGREEN **3.** short-lived; temporary —**de·cid′u·ous·ly** *adv.* —**de·cid′u·ous·ness** *n.*

dec·i·gram (des′ə gram′) *n.* [Fr.: see DECI- & GRAM] a metric weight, equal to 1/10 gram (1.5432 grains or .003527 oz.): also, chiefly Brit., **dec′i·gramme′** (-gram′)

dec·ile (des′īl, -il) *n.* [DEC- + -ILE] *Statistics* any of the values in a series dividing the distribution of the individuals in the series into ten groups of equal frequency; also, any of these groups

dec·i·li·ter (des′ə lēt′ər) *n.* [Fr. *décilitre:* see DECI- & LITER] a metric measure of volume, equal to 1/10 liter (3.38 fluid oz. or 6.1025 cubic in.): also, chiefly Brit., **dec′i·li′tre** (-lēt′ər)

de·cil·lion (di sil′yən) *n.* [DEC- + (M)ILLION] **1.** in the U.S. and France, the number written as 1 followed by 33 zeros **2.** in England and Germany, the number written as 1 followed by 60 zeros —*adj.* amounting to one decillion in number

dec·i·mal (des′ə m'l) *adj.* [OFr. < ML. *decimalis* < L. *decimus*, tenth < *decem*, TEN] of or based on the number 10; progressing by tens —*n.* a fraction with an unwritten denominator of 10 or some power of 10, indicated by a point (**decimal point**) before the numerator (Ex.: .5 = 5/10): in full, **decimal fraction**

☆**decimal classification** a system of classifying books in libraries by the use of numbers with decimals

dec·i·mal·ize (des′ə m'l īz′) *vt.* **-ized′, -iz′ing 1.** to adopt a decimal system for (currency, etc.) **2.** to change into a decimal or decimals —**dec′i·mal·i·za′tion** *n.*

dec·i·mal·ly (-ē) *adv.* **1.** by tens **2.** in decimals

decimal system 1. a system of computation based on the number ten ☆**2.** *same as* DECIMAL CLASSIFICATION

dec·i·mate (des′ə māt′) *vt.* **-mat′ed, -mat′ing** [< L. *decimatus*, pp. of *decimare* < *decem*, TEN] **1.** orig., to select by lot and kill every tenth one of **2.** to destroy or kill a large part of [famine *decimated* the population] **3.** [Obs.] to take a tenth part of; tithe —**dec′i·ma′tion** *n.* —**dec′i·ma′tor** *n.*

dec·i·me·ter (des′ə mēt′ər) *n.* [Fr.: see DECI- & METER] a metric measure of length, equal to 1/10 meter (3.937 inches): also, chiefly Brit., **dec′i·me′tre** (-mēt′ər)

dec·i·mil·li- (des′ə mil′ē) [DECI- + MILLI-] a *combining form meaning* the factor 10^{-4}

de·ci·pher (di sī′fər) *vt.* [DE- + CIPHER] **1.** to translate (a message in cipher or code) into ordinary, understandable language; decode **2.** to make out the meaning of (ancient inscriptions, illegible writing, etc.) —**de·ci′pher·a·ble** *adj.* —**de·ci′pher·ment** *n.*

de·ci·sion (di sizh′ən) *n.* [ME. *decisioun* < OFr. *decision* < L. *decisio*, a cutting short, decision < *decisus*, pp. of *decidere*, DECIDE] **1.** the act of deciding or settling a dispute or question by giving a judgment **2.** the act of making up one's mind **3.** a judgment or conclusion reached or given **4.** determination; firmness of mind [a man of *decision*] **5.** *Boxing* a victory on points instead of by a knockout —**de·ci′sion·al** *adj.*

de·ci·sive (di sī′siv) *adj.* [ML. *decisivus* < L. *decisus:* see prec.] **1.** that settles or can settle a dispute, question, etc.: conclusive [*decisive* evidence] **2.** determining or clearly affecting what comes next; critically important; crucial [a *decisive* moment in his career] **3.** having the quality of decision; showing determination or firmness [a *decisive* tone of voice] —**de·ci′sive·ly** *adv.* —**de·ci′sive·ness** *n.*

dec·i·stere (des′ə stir′) *n.* [Fr.: see DECI- & STERE] a metric measure of volume, equal to 1/10 cubic meter (3.53 cu. ft.)

deck[1] (dek) *n.* [prob. aphetic < MLowG. *verdeck* (< *ver-*, prefix of indefinite force + *decken*, to cover, akin to THATCH), transl. of It. *coperta*, cover] **1.** a platform or roof over a section of a ship's hold, serving as a floor **2.** any platform, floor, shelf, etc. resembling a ship's deck **3.** a pack of playing cards ☆**4.** [Slang] a packet containing a narcotic, as heroin —*vt.* ☆[Slang] to knock down; floor —**clear the decks 1.** to remove unnecessary things from the decks of a ship, as for combat **2.** to get ready for action —☆**hit the deck** [Slang] **1.** to get out of bed; get up **2.** to get ready for action **3.** to throw oneself to the floor, ground, etc., as to avoid injury **4.** to be knocked down —☆**on deck** [Colloq.] **1.** ready; on hand **2.** waiting to take one's turn, as at batting in baseball

deck[2] (dek) *vt.* [MDu. *decken*, to hide, cover] **1.** to cover or clothe with finery or ornaments; adorn; trim **2.** to furnish (a ship, etc.) with a deck **3.** [Archaic] to cover

deck chair a lightweight folding chair, usually with arms and a leg rest, used on ship decks, etc.

-deck·er (dek′ər) *a combining form meaning* having (a specified number of) decks, layers, etc. [two-*decker*]

Decker, Thomas *see* DEKKER

☆**deck·hand** (dek′hand′) *n.* a common sailor

deck·house (-hous′) *n.* a small cabinlike structure built onto the upper deck of a ship

deck·le (dek′'l) *n.* [Gr. *deckel*, dim. of *decke*, a cover: see DECK] **1.** a removable wooden frame used as an edging for the four sides of a sheet mold in making paper by hand **2.** either of the two edgings used for controlling the width of a sheet of paper in a papermaking machine

deckle edge 1. the rough, irregular edge of a sheet of paper after it leaves the deckle and before it is trimmed: such edges are often favored as decorative **2.** an imitation of this, produced in a trimmed sheet of paper by sawing, tearing, etc. —**deck′le-edged′** *adj.*

deck tennis a game somewhat like tennis, in which a small ring of rope, etc. is tossed back and forth over a net: so called because often played on passenger liners

de·claim (di klām′) *vi.* [ME. *declamen* < L. *declamare* < *de-*, intens. + *clamare*, to cry, shout] **1.** to recite a speech, poem, etc. with studied or artificial eloquence **2.** *a)* to speak in a dramatic, pompous, or blustering way *b)* to make an impassioned verbal attack; deliver a tirade; inveigh —*vt.* **1.** to recite (a poem, speech, etc.) **2.** to utter with feeling, pomposity, etc. —**de·claim′er** *n.*

dec·la·ma·tion (dek′lə mā′shən) *n.* [ME. *declamacioun* < L. *declamatio* < pp. of prec.] **1.** the act or art of declaiming **2.** a speech, poem, etc. that is or can be declaimed

de·clam·a·to·ry (di klam′ə tôr′ē) *adj.* [L. *declamatorius*] **1.** of, characterized by, or fit for declaiming **2.** marked by passion or pomposity; bombastic

de·clar·a·ble (di klar′ə b'l, -kler′-) *adj.* that can be or must be declared for taxation

dec·la·ra·tion (dek′lə rā′shən) *n.* [ME. *declaracioun* < OFr. *declaration* < L. *declaratio*] **1.** the act of declaring; announcement **2.** a thing declared **3.** a formal statement; proclamation **4.** a statement of taxable goods [a *declaration* at the customs office] **5.** *Card Games a) same as* MELD[1] *b)* the winning bid in bridge **6.** *Law a)* a statement of the plaintiff's cause for complaint in a court action *b)* a witness's unsworn statement, made out of court, which may be admissible in evidence under certain circumstances: distinguished from OATH

Declaration of Independence the formal statement, written by Thomas Jefferson and adopted July 4, 1776, by the Second Continental Congress, declaring the thirteen American colonies free and independent of Great Britain: there were fifty-six signers

de·clar·a·tive (di klar′ə tiv, -kler′-) *adj.* [LL. *declarativus:* see DECLARE] making a statement or assertion [a *declarative* sentence] —**de·clar′a·tive·ly** *adv.*

de·clar·a·to·ry (-ə tôr′ē) *adj.* [ME. *declaratorie* < ML. *declaratorius] same as* DECLARATIVE

de·clare (di kler′) *vt.* **-clared′, -clar′ing** [ME. *declaren* < OFr. *declarer* < L. *declarare* < *de-*, intens. + *clarare*, to make clear < *clarus*, CLEAR] **1.** to make clearly known; state or announce openly, formally, etc. **2.** to show or reveal **3.** to say positively or emphatically **4.** to make a statement, or account, of (taxable goods), as at customs **5.** to authorize the payment or distribution of (a dividend, etc.) **6.** *Card Games a)* to meld *b)* to establish (trump or no-trump) by a successful bid —*vi.* **1.** to make a declaration **2.** to state openly a choice, opinion, etc. (*for* or *against*) —**declare oneself 1.** to state strongly one's opinion **2.** to reveal one's true character, identity, etc. —**I declare!** I am surprised, startled, etc. —**de·clar′er** *n.*

SYN.—**declare** implies a making known openly by an explicit or clear statement, often one expressed formally [he *declared* his intention to run for office]; to **announce** is to make something of interest known publicly or officially, esp. something of the nature of news [to *announce* a sale]; to **publish** is to make known through a medium that reaches the general public, now esp. the medium of printing; **proclaim** implies official, formal announcement, made with the greatest possible publicity, of something of great moment or significance ["*Proclaim* liberty throughout all the land . . ."] See also **assert**

de·clar·ed·ly (-id lē) *adv.* openly or admittedly

dé·clas·sé (dā′klä sā′, -kla-) *adj.* [Fr., pp. of *déclasser*, to cause to lose class: see DE- & CLASS] having lost class; lowered in social status

de·clas·si·fy (dē klas′ə fī′) *vt.* **-fied′, -fy′ing** ☆to remove (governmental documents, reports, etc.) from secret or restricted classifications and make available to the public —**de·clas′si·fi·ca′tion** *n.*

de·clen·sion (di klen′shən) *n.* [ME. *declenson* < OFr. *declinaison* < L. *declinatio*, a bending aside, inflection (< pp. of *declinare*: see DECLINE): ME. form infl. by association with L. *descensio*, a descending (see DESCEND)] **1.** a bending or sloping downward; slope; descent **2.** a falling off or away; decline, deterioration **3.** [see CASE[1] *Gram. a*) a class of nouns, pronouns, or adjectives having the same or a similar system of inflections to show case *b*) the inflection of such words

de·clen·sion·al (-əl) *adj. Gram.* of declension

de·clin·a·ble (di klīn′ə b'l) *adj. Gram.* that can be declined; having case inflections

dec·li·na·tion (dek′lə nā′shən) *n.* [ME. *declinacioun* < L. *declinatio*: see DECLENSION] **1.** a bending or sloping downward; deviation from the horizontal or vertical **2.** an oblique variation from some definite direction **3.** the angle formed by a magnetic needle with the line pointing to true north **4.** a polite declining or refusal **5.** [Archaic] decline; deterioration; decay **6.** *Astron.* the angular distance of a heavenly body north or south from the celestial equator

DECLINATION (CP, celestial poles; CE, celestial equator; O, observer, or center of earth; DS, or angle DOS, declination of star S)

de·cline (di klīn′) *vi.* **-clined′, -clin′-ing** [ME. *declinen* < OFr. *decliner*, to bend, turn aside < L. *declinare*, to bend from, inflect < *de-*, from + *-clinare*, to bend: for IE. base see DECLIVITY] **1.** to bend, turn, or slope downward or aside **2.** *a*) to sink, as the setting sun *b*) to approach the end; wane [the day is *declining*] **3.** to lessen in force, health, value, etc.; deteriorate; decay **4.** to descend to behavior that is base or immoral **5.** to refuse to accept or do something, esp. in a way that is formally polite *vt.* **1.** to cause to bend or slope downward or aside **2.** to refuse, esp. in a formally polite way [I must *decline* your offer] **3.** *Gram.* to give the inflected forms of (a noun, pronoun, or adjective) —*n.* **1.** the act of declining, or becoming less, smaller, lower, etc.; deterioration; decay **2.** a failing of health, etc. **3.** a period of decline **4.** the last part [the *decline* of life] **5.** a wasting disease, esp. tuberculosis of the lungs **6.** a downward slope —**de·clin′er** *n.*

SYN.—**decline** implies courtesy in expressing one's nonacceptance of an invitation, proposal, etc. [he *declined* the nomination]; **refuse** is a more direct, sometimes even blunt term, implying an emphatic denial of a request, demand, etc. [to *refuse* a person money]; **reject** stresses a negative or antagonistic attitude and implies positive refusal to accept, use, believe, etc. [they *rejected* the damaged goods]; **repudiate** implies the disowning, disavowal, or casting off with condemnation of a person or thing as having no authority, worth, validity, truth, etc. [to *repudiate* the claims of faith healers]; to **spurn** is to refuse or reject with contempt or disdain [she *spurned* his attentions] —*ANT.* accept

de·cliv·i·tous (di kliv′ə təs) *adj.* [L. *declivitas* (see ff.) + -OUS] fairly steep

de·cliv·i·ty (-tē) *n., pl.* **-ties** [L. *declivitas* < *declivis*, a sloping downward < *de-*, down + *clivus*, a slope < IE. *kloiwos* < base *klei-*, LEAN[1], whence L. *-clinare*, to bend; OE. *hlaw*, grave mound] a downward slope or sloping, as of a hill: opposed to ACCLIVITY

de·coct (di käkt′) *vt.* [ME. *decocten* < pp. of L. *decoquere*, to boil down < *de-*, down + *coquere*, COOK] to extract the essence, flavor, etc. of by boiling

de·coc·tion (di käk′shən) *n.* **1.** a decocting or being decocted **2.** an extract produced by decocting

de·code (dē kōd′) *vt.* **-cod′ed, -cod′ing** to translate (a coded message) into ordinary, understandable language

de·cod·er (-ər) *n.* **1.** a person who decodes messages **2.** a device that decodes scrambled messages sent by telephone **3.** in an electronic digital computer, a circuit device that determines the content of a given instruction or performs digital-to-analog conversion

de·col·late (di käl′āt) *vt.* **-lat′ed, -lat′ing** [< L. *decollatus*, pp. of *decollare*, to behead < *de-*, from + *collum*, neck] to behead —**de·col·la·tion** (dē′kä lā′shən) *n.*

dé·col·le·tage (dā käl′ə tàzh′; Fr. dā kôl tàzh′) *n.* [Fr. *décolletage*: see ff.] **1.** the neckline or top of a dress cut low so as to bare the neck and shoulders **2.** a décolleté dress, etc.

dé·col·le·té (dā käl′ə tā′; Fr. dā kôl tā′) *adj.* [Fr., pp. of *décolleter*, to bare the neck and shoulders < *dé-* (L. *de*), from + *collet*, dim. of *col* (< L. *collum*), neck] **1.** cut low so as to bare the neck and shoulders, as some dresses **2.** wearing a décolleté dress, etc.

de·col·o·ni·za·tion (dē käl′ə nə zā′shən) *n.* the act or process of eliminating colonialism or freeing from colonial status: also **de·co·lo·ni·al·i·za·tion** (dē′kə lō′nē əl ə zā′ shən) —**de·col′o·nize′** (-ə nīz′) *vt., vi.* **-nized′, -niz′ing**

de·col·or (dē kul′ər) *vt. same as* DECOLORIZE —**de′col·or·a′-tion** (-ā′shən) *n.*

de·col·or·ant (-ənt) *adj.* decolorizing; bleaching —*n.* a substance that decolorizes

de·col·or·ize (-īz′) *vt.* **-ized′, -iz′ing** to take the color out of, as by bleaching —**de′col′or·i·za′tion** *n.*

de·com·pen·sa·tion (dē käm′pən sā′shən) *n.* failure of the heart muscle to compensate for a valvular or myocardial defect; heart failure

de·com·pose (dē′kəm pōz′) *vt., vi.* **-posed′, -pos′ing** [Fr. *décomposer*: see DE- & COMPOSE] **1.** to break up or separate into basic components or parts **2.** to rot —**de′com·pos′a·ble** *adj.* —**de·com·po·si·tion** (dē′käm pə zish′ən) *n.*

de·com·pound (dē′kəm pound′; *also, and for n. always,* dē käm′pound) *vt.* **1.** orig., to compound (things already compounded) **2.** to break up (a compound) into its parts; decompose —*adj.* **1.** compounded of substances already compounded **2.** *Bot.* made up of parts that are themselves compound, as some leaves —*n.* a compound containing some other compound or compounds

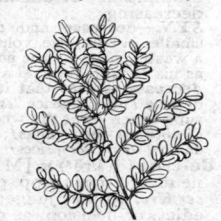

DECOMPOUND LEAF

de·com·press (dē′kəm pres′) *vt.* **1.** to free from pressure **2.** to free (a deep-sea diver, tunnel worker, etc.) from compression or air pressure by means of an air lock

de·com·pres·sion (-presh′ən) *n.* **1.** a decompressing or being decompressed **2.** a surgical operation to relieve excessive pressure, as in the cranium, a body cavity, etc.

☆**decompression sickness** a condition caused by the formation of nitrogen bubbles in the blood or body tissues as the result of a sudden lowering of atmospheric pressure, as in deep-sea divers returning to the surface too quickly: it is characterized by tightness in the chest, by pains in the joints, and by convulsions and collapse in severe cases

de·con·gest·ant (dē′kən jes′tənt) *n.* a medication or treatment that relieves congestion, as in the nasal passages

de·con·tam·i·nate (-tam′ə nāt′) *vt.* **-nat′ed, -nat′ing** to rid of a polluting or harmful substance, as poison gas, radioactive products, etc. —**de′con·tam′i·na′tion** *n.*

de·con·trol (-trōl′) *vt.* **-trolled′, -trol′ling** to free from controls —*n.* withdrawal of controls

dé·cor, de·cor (dā kôr′, dā′kôr) *n.* [Fr. < L. *decor*, beauty, elegance < *decere*, to befit, be suitable: see ff.] **1.** decoration **2.** the decorative scheme of a room, stage set, etc.

dec·o·rate (dek′ə rāt′) *vt.* **-rat′ed, -rat′ing** [< L. *decoratus*, pp. of *decorare*, to decorate < *decus*, an ornament < IE. base *dek-*, to take, accept, do what is suitable, whence L. *dignus*, worthy, *docere*, to teach] **1.** to add something to so as to make more attractive; adorn; ornament **2.** to plan and arrange the colors, furnishings, etc. of **3.** to paint or wallpaper [to *decorate* a room] **4.** to give a medal or similar token of honor to —*SYN.* see ADORN

dec·o·ra·tion (dek′ə rā′shən) *n.* [ME. *decoracioun* < OFr. *decoration* < ML. *decoratio*] **1.** the act of decorating **2.** anything used for decorating; ornament **3.** a medal, badge, or similar token of honor

☆**Decoration Day** *same as* MEMORIAL DAY

dec·o·ra·tive (dek′ər ə tiv, -ə rāt′iv; dek′rə-) *adj.* that serves to decorate; ornamental —**dec′o·ra·tive·ly** *adv.* —**dec′o·ra·tive·ness** *n.*

dec·o·ra·tor (dek′ə rāt′ər) *n.* a person who decorates; specif., a specialist in interior decoration

dec·o·rous (dek′ər əs, di kôr′əs) *adj.* [L. *decorus*, becoming < *decor*: see DECORATE] characterized by or showing decorum, propriety, good taste, etc. —**dec′o·rous·ly** *adv.* —**dec′o·rous·ness** *n.*

de·cor·ti·cate (di kôr′tə kāt′) *vt.* **-cat′ed, -cat′ing** [< L. *decorticatus*, pp. of *decorticare* < *de-*, from + *cortex*, bark] to remove the bark, husk, or peel from —**de·cor′ti·ca′tion** *n.* —**de·cor′ti·ca′tor** *n.*

de·co·rum (di kôr′əm) *n.* [L., neut. of *decorus*, fit, proper < *decor*: see DECORATE] **1.** whatever is suitable or proper; propriety; fitness **2.** propriety and good taste in behavior, speech, dress, etc. **3.** an act or requirement of polite behavior: *often used in pl.*

SYN.—**decorum** implies stiffness or formality in rules of conduct or behavior established as suitable to the circumstances [levity not in keeping with *decorum*]; **decency** implies observance of the requirements of modesty, good taste, etc. [have the *decency* to thank her]; **propriety** suggests conformity with conventional standards of proper or correct behavior, manners, etc. [his offensive language oversteps the bounds of *propriety*]; **dignity**, in this connection, implies conduct in keeping with one's position or one's self-respect; **etiquette** refers to the forms established by convention or prescribed by social arbiters for behavior in polite society

de·cou·page, dé·cou·page (dā′kōō pàzh′) *n.* [Fr., the act of cutting up or carving] **1.** the art of cutting out designs or

illustrations from paper, foil, etc. and mounting them on a surface in a decorative arrangement 2. work done by decoupage

de·coy (di koi′; *for n., also* dē′koi) *n.* [< Du. *de kooi*, the cage < *de*, def. art. (akin to THE) + *kooi*, cage < WGmc. **kawia* < L. *cavea*, CAGE] 1. a place into which wild ducks, etc. are lured for capture 2. an artificial bird or animal, or sometimes a trained live one, used to lure game to a place where it can be shot 3. a thing or person used to lure or tempt into danger or a trap [a police *decoy*] —*vt., vi.* to lure or be lured into a trap, danger, etc. —*SYN.* see LURE

de·crease (di krēs′; *also, & for n. usually*, dē′krēs) *vi., vt.* -creased′, -creas′ing [ME. *decresen* < OFr. *decreistre* < L. *decrescere* < *de*-, from, away + *crescere*, to grow: see CREATE] to become or cause to become gradually less, smaller, etc.; diminish —*n.* [ME. *decres*] 1. a decreasing; lessening; diminution 2. amount of decreasing —**on the decrease** decreasing

SYN.—**decrease** and **dwindle** suggest a growing gradually smaller in bulk, size, volume, or number, but **dwindle** emphasizes a wasting away to the point of disappearance [his hopes *decreased* as his fortune *dwindled* away to nothing]; **lessen** is equivalent to **decrease**, except that it does not imply any particular rate of decline [his influence *lessened* overnight]; **diminish** emphasizes subtraction from the whole by some external agent [disease had *diminished* their ranks]; **reduce** implies a lowering, or bringing down [to *reduce* prices] —*ANT.* increase

de·cree (di krē′) *n.* [ME. *decre* < OFr. *decret* < L. *decretum*, neut. of *decretus*, pp. of *decernere*, to decree < *de*-, from + *cernere*, to see, judge: see CERTAIN] 1. an official order, edict, or decision, as of a church, government, court, etc. 2. something that is or seems to be foreordained —*vt.* -creed′, -cree′ing to order, decide, or appoint by decree or officially —*vi.* to issue a decree; ordain

dec·re·ment (dek′rə mənt) *n.* [L. *decrementum* < *decrescere*: see DECREASE] 1. a decreasing or decrease; loss; waste 2. amount lost by decrease or waste 3. *Math.* the quantity by which a variable decreases or is decreased: a negative decrement results in an increase

de·crep·it (di krep′it) *adj.* [ME. & OFr. < L. *decrepitus* < *de*-, intens. + *crepitus*, pp. of *crepare*, to creak, rattle (in LL., to burst, die) < IE. **krep*- (< base **ker*-, echoic of hoarse cry), whence RAVEN] broken down or worn out by old age, illness, or long use —*SYN.* see WEAK —**de·crep′it·ly** *adv.*

de·crep·i·tate (di krep′ə tāt′) *vt.* -tat′ed, -tat′ing [< ModL. **decrepitatus*, pp. of **decrepitare* < L. *de*-, intens. + *crepitare*, to crackle, rattle < *crepare*: see DECREPIT] to roast or calcine (salts, minerals, etc.) until a crackling sound is caused or until this sound stops —*vi.* to crackle when exposed to heat —**de·crep′i·ta′tion** *n.*

de·crep·i·tude (-tōōd′, -tyōōd′) *n.* [Fr. *décrépitude*] the condition of being decrepit; feebleness or infirmity

de·cre·scen·do (dē′krə shen′dō, dā′-) *adj., adv.* [It., prp. of *decrescere* < L., DECREASE] *Music* with a gradual decrease in loudness or intensity; diminuendo: symbol > —*n., pl.* -dos *Music* 1. a gradual decrease in loudness or intensity 2. a passage played or sung decrescendo

de·cres·cent (di kres′'nt) *adj.* [L. *decrescens*, prp. of *decrescere*, DECREASE] decreasing; lessening; waning: said esp. of the moon in its final quarter

de·cre·tal (di krēt′'l) *adj.* [ME. < LL. *decretalis*] of or containing a decree —*n.* 1. a decree 2. *R.C.Ch. a)* a decree issued by the Pope on some matter of ecclesiastical discipline *b)* [usually *pl.*] any collection of such decrees, formerly a part of canon law

dec·re·to·ry (dek′rə tôr′ē) *adj.* [L. *decretorius*] 1. settled by a decree 2. having the nature or force of a decree: also **de·cre·tive** (di krēt′iv)

de·cry (di krī′) *vt.* -cried′, -cry′ing [Fr. *décrier* < OFr. *descrier*: see DE- & CRY] 1. to speak out against strongly and openly; denounce [to *decry* religious intolerance] 2. to depreciate (money, etc.) officially —**de·cri′al** *n.* —*SYN.* see DISPARAGE

☆**de·crypt** (di kript′) *vt.* [DE- + CRYPT(OGRAM)] to decode or decipher

de·cum·bent (di kum′bənt) *adj.* [L. *decumbens*, prp. of *decumbere*, to lie down < *de*-, down + -*cumbere*, *cubare*, to recline, lie down] 1. lying down 2. *Bot.* trailing on the ground and rising at the tip, as some stems —**de·cum′-ben·cy** (-bən sē) *n.*

dec·u·ple (dek′yoo p'l) *adj.* [ME. < L. *decuplus* < *decem*, TEN + -*plus*, -FOLD] ten times as large; tenfold 2. in tens —*n.* a number or quantity ten times as large as another one, or repeated ten times —*vt.* -pled, -pling to make tenfold; multiply by ten

de·cu·ri·on (di kyoor′ē ən) *n.* [ME. *decurioun* < L. *decurio* < *decuria*, company of ten men < *decem*, TEN] *Rom. History* 1. an officer having charge of ten men 2. a member of a municipal or colonial senate

de·cur·rent (di kur′ənt) *adj.* [L. *decurrens*, prp. of *decurrere* < *de*-, down + *currere*, to run] *Bot.* extending down along the stem, as the base of some leaves

de·curved (di kurvd′) *adj.* [transl. of LL. *decurvatus* < L. *de*-, DE- + *curvatus*, pp. of *curvare*, to CURVE] *Zool.* curved or bent downward

dec·u·ry (dek′yoo rē) *n., pl.* -ries [L. *decuria*, a group of ten] *Rom. History* 1. the group commanded by a decurion 2. a division or class, as of the judges, the curiae, etc.

de·cus·sate (di kus′āt, dek′ə sāt′; *for adj., usually* di kus′it) *vt., vi.* -sat·ed, -sat·ing [< L. *decussatus*, pp. of *decussare*, to cross in the form of an X < *decussis*, the figure ten (X) < *decem*, TEN) to cross or cut so as to form an X; intersect —*adj.* 1. forming an X; decussated 2. *Bot.* arranged in pairs growing at right angles to those above and below: said of leaves or branches —**de·cus′sate·ly** *adv.*

de·cus·sa·tion (dē′kə sā′shən, dek′ə-) *n.* [L. *decussatio*] 1. a decussating or being decussated 2. an intersection forming an X 3. *Anat.* a crossing of bands of nerve fibers in the central nervous system or spinal cord

DECUSSATE LEAVES

de·dal (dē′d'l) *adj. same as* DAEDAL

De·da·li·an (di dāl′yan, -ē ən) *adj. same as* DAEDALIAN

de·dans (də dän′; Fr. -dän′) *n., pl.* de·dans′ (-dänz′; Fr. -dän′) [Fr., lit., the interior] *Court Tennis* 1. a gallery for spectators in the end wall of a court 2. the spectators at a match in court tennis

ded·i·cate (ded′ə kit; *for v.*, -kāt′) *adj.* [ME. *dedicat* < L. *dedicatus*, pp. of *dedicare*, to consecrate, declare < *de*-, intens. + *dicare*, to proclaim < *dicere*, to say] [Poet. or Archaic] dedicated —*vt.* -cat′ed, -cat′ing [ME. *dedicaten* < the *adj.*] 1. to set apart for worship of a deity or devote to a sacred purpose 2. to set apart seriously for a special purpose; devote to some work, duty, etc. 3. to address or inscribe (a book, artistic performance, etc.) to someone or something as a sign of honor or affection ☆4. to open formally (a public building, fair, etc.) 5. *Law* to devote (land, etc.) to public use —*SYN.* see DEVOTE —**ded′i·ca′tor** *n.*

ded·i·ca·tion (ded′ə kā′shən) *n.* [ME. *dedicacioun* < L. *dedicatio*] 1. a dedicating or being dedicated 2. an inscription, as in a book, dedicating it to a person, cause, etc. 3. wholehearted devotion

ded·i·ca·to·ry (ded′i kə tôr′ē) *adj.* of or as a dedication: also **ded·i·ca·tive** (-kāt′iv, -kə tiv)

de·dif·fer·en·ti·a·tion (dē dif′ə ren′shē ā′shən) *n.* a reversal of cell development, esp. in plants, so that the differentiation that had occurred previously is lost and the cell becomes more generalized in structure and in developmental potential

de·duce (di dōōs′, -dyōōs′) *vt.* -duced′, -duc′ing [ME. *deducen* < L. *deducere*, to lead down, bring away < *de*-, down + *ducere*, to lead] 1. to trace the course or derivation of 2. to infer by logical reasoning; reason out or conclude from known facts or general principles —*SYN.* see INFER —**de·duc′i·ble** *adj.*

de·duct (di dukt′) *vt.* [ME. *deducten* < L. *deductus*, pp. of *deducere*: see DEDUCE] to take away or subtract (a quantity)

de·duct·i·ble (-ə b'l) *adj.* 1. that can be deducted 2. that is allowed as a deduction in computing income tax [deductible expenses] —**de·duct′i·bil′i·ty** *n.*

de·duc·tion (di duk′shən) *n.* [ME. *deduccioun* < L. *deductio*] 1. a deducting or being deducted; subtraction 2. a sum or amount deducted or allowed to be deducted 3. *Logic* the act or process of deducing; reasoning from a known principle to an unknown, from the general to the specific, or from a premise to a logical conclusion; also, a conclusion so deduced: opposed to INDUCTION —**de·duc′-tive** *adj.* —**de·duc′tive·ly** *adv.*

Dee (dē) 1. river in NE Scotland, flowing east into the North Sea: 90 mi. 2. river in N Wales and W England, flowing northeast into the Irish Sea: 70 mi.

deed (dēd) *n.* [ME. *dede* < OE. *dæd, dæd*, akin to G. *tat*, ODu. *dede*, ON. *dath*, Goth. *deds*: for IE. base see DO[1]] 1. a thing done; act 2. a feat of courage, skill, etc. 3. action; actual performance [honest in word and *deed*] 4. *Law* a document under seal which, when delivered, transfers a present interest in property —☆*vt.* to transfer (property) by such a document —**in deed** in fact; really

☆**dee·jay** (dē′jā′) *n.* [D(ISC) J(OCKEY)] [Colloq.] *same as* DISC JOCKEY

deem (dēm) *vt., vi.* [ME. *demen* < OE. *deman*, to judge, decree < base of *dom*, DOOM] to think, believe, or judge

de·em·pha·size (dē em′fə sīz′) *vt.* -sized′, -siz′ing to remove emphasis from; lessen the importance or prominence of —**de·em′pha·sis** (-sis) *n.*

deep (dēp) *adj.* [ME. *dep* < OE. *deop*, akin to G. *tief*, Goth. *diups* < IE. base **dheub*-, deep, hollow, whence DIP, DUMP[1]] 1. extending far downward from the top or top edges, inward from the surface, backward from the front, or far to the sides or edge [a *deep* cut, a *deep* lake, a *deep* drawer] 2. extending thus for a specified length or distance [eight feet *deep*] 3. *a)* located far down or back [*deep* in the outfield] *b)* coming from or going far down or back [a *deep* breath] 4. far off in time or space [the *deep* past] 5. hard to understand; abstruse [a *deep* book] 6. extremely grave or serious [in *deep* trouble] 7. strongly felt [*deep* love] 8. intellectually profound [a *deep* discussion] 9. *a)* tricky and sly; devious [*deep* dealings] *b)* carefully guarded [a *deep* secret] 10. dark and rich [a *deep* red] 11. sunk in or absorbed by (with *in*) [*deep* in thought] 12. *a)* great in degree; intense [*deep* joy] *b)* heavy and unbroken [a *deep* sleep] 13. much involved [*deep* in debt]

14. of low pitch or range [a *deep* voice] —n. [ME. *dep* < OE. *deop*] **1.** a deep place or any of the deepest parts, as in water or earth **2.** the extent of encompassing space or time, of the unknown, etc. **3.** the middle part; part that is darkest, most silent, etc. [in the *deep* of night] **4.** *Naut.* any of the unmarked fathom points between those marked on a sounding line —adv. [ME. *depe* < OE. *deope*] in a deep way or to a deep extent; far down, far in, far back, far on, etc. [to dig *deep*] —*SYN.* see BROAD —**go off the deep end 1.** to dive or jump into deep water **2.** [Colloq.] to plunge rashly into an enterprise **3.** [Colloq.] to become angry or excited —**in deep water** in trouble or difficulty —**the deep** [Poet.] the sea or ocean —**deep'ly** adv. —**deep'ness** n.

deep-chest·ed (-ches'tid) adj. having, or coming as from, a thick chest [a *deep-chested* roar]

☆**deep-dish pie** (-dish') a pie, usually of fruit, baked in a deep dish and having only a top crust

deep-dyed (-dīd') adj. **1.** stained throughout **2.** thoroughgoing; unmitigated [a *deep-dyed* villain]

deep·en (-'n) vt., vi. to make or become deep or deeper

☆**Deep-freeze** (-frēz') [< DEEP + FREEZE] a trademark for a deep freezer —n. [d-] **1.** a deep freezer **2.** storage in or as in a deep freezer **3.** a condition of suspended activity, dealings, etc. —vt. [d-] -froze' or -freezed', -fro'zen or -freezed', -freez'ing **1.** to subject (foods) to sudden freezing so as to preserve and store **2.** to store in a deep freezer

☆**deep freezer** any freezer for quick-freezing and storing food

deep-fry (-frī') vt. -fried', -fry'ing to fry in a deep pan of boiling fat or oil

deep-laid (-lād') adj. carefully worked out and kept secret [*deep-laid* plans]

deep-root·ed (-root'id, -root'id) adj. **1.** having deep roots **2.** firmly fixed; hard to remove [*deep-rooted* bias]

deep scattering layer any of the zones of unknown composition registering sonic reverberation at depths of several hundred fathoms over much of the deep ocean: they are thought to consist of concentrations of marine animal life

deep-sea (-sē') adj. in or of the deeper parts of the sea [*deep-sea* fishing]

deep-seat·ed (-sēt'id) adj. **1.** placed or originating far beneath the surface **2.** *same as* DEEP-ROOTED (sense 2)

deep-set (-sct') adj. **1.** deeply set **2.** firmly fixed

☆**deep South** that area of the U.S. regarded as most typically Southern and conservative, including the southernmost parts of Ga., Ala., Miss., and La.

deep space *same as* OUTER SPACE

deer (dir) n., pl. **deer**, occas. **deers** [ME. *der* < OE. *deor*, wild animal, akin to G. *tier* < IE. base *dheues-*, *dheus-*, to stir up, blow, breathe: for sense development cf. ANIMAL] **1.** any of a family (Cervidae) of hoofed, cud-chewing animals, including the mule deer, moose, reindeer, caribou, etc., the males of which usually bear antlers that are shed annually: popularly used only of the smaller species of this family **2.** [Obs.] any animal; beast

☆**deer·fly** (-flī') n., pl. -**flies'** any of a genus (*Chrysops*) of bloodsucking flies related to the horsefly, but smaller and with banded wings

deer·hound (-hound') n. any of a Scottish breed of large, shaggy-haired dog, orig. used in hunting deer

☆**deer lick** a salt lick where deer come

☆**deer mouse 1.** a white-footed mouse (*Peromyscus maniculatus*) of N. America **2.** a light-brown mouse (*Peromyscus boylii*) of the SW U.S. and Mexico

deer·skin (-skin') n. **1.** the hide of a deer **2.** leather or a garment made from this —adj. made of deerskin

deer·stalk·er (-stôk'ər) n. **1.** a hunter who stalks deer **2.** a hunter's tightfitting cap with a low crown, and a visor in front and in back

☆**de-es·ca·late** (dē es'kə lāt') vi., vt. -lat'ed, -lat'ing to reverse the effect of escalation on (something); reduce or lessen in scope, magnitude, etc. —**de-es'ca·la'tion** n.

def. 1. defendant **2.** defense **3.** deferred **4.** defined **5.** definite **6.** definition

de·face (di fās') vt. -faced', -fac'ing [ME. *defacen* < OFr. *desfacier*: see DE- & FACE] **1.** to spoil the appearance of; disfigure; mar **2.** to make illegible by injuring the surface of —**de·face'ment** n. —**de·fac'er** n.

de fac·to (di fak'tō, dā) [L.] existing or being such in actual fact though not by legal establishment, official recognition, etc. [a *de facto* government]: distinguished from DE JURE

de·fal·cate (di fal'kāt, -fôl'-) vi. -cat·ed, -cat·ing [< ML. *defalcatus*, pp. of *defalcare*, to cut off < L. *de-*, from + *falx* (gen. *falcis*), a sickle] to steal or misuse funds entrusted to one's care; embezzle —**de·fal'ca·tor** n.

de·fal·ca·tion (dē'fal kā'shən, -fôl'-) n. [ML. *defalcatio*: see prec.] **1.** embezzlement **2.** the amount embezzled

def·a·ma·tion (def'ə mā'shən) n. [ME. *defamacioun* < OFr. *difamacion* < LL. *diffamatio*] a defaming or being defamed; detraction, slander, or libel

de·fam·a·to·ry (di fam'ə tôr'ē) adj. [ML. *diffamatorius*] defaming or tending to defame; slanderous

de·fame (di fām') vt. -famed', -fam'ing [ME. *defamen*,

dif·famen < OFr. *diffamer* or ML. *defamere*, both < L. *diffamare* < *dis-*, from + *fama*: see FAME] **1.** to attack or injure the reputation or honor of by false and malicious statements; malign, slander, or libel **2.** [Archaic] to bring infamy on; disgrace **3.** [Obs.] to accuse —**de·fam'er** n.

de·fault (di fôlt') n. [ME. < OFr. *defaute* < VL. *defallita*, pp. of *defallere*, to lack < L. *de-*, away + *fallere*, to fail, deceive] **1.** failure to do something or be somewhere when required or expected; specif., *a)* failure to pay money due *b)* failure to appear in court to defend or prosecute a case *c)* failure to take part in or finish a contest **2.** [Obs.] a fault, lack, or want —vi. [ME. *defauten* < OFr. *defauter*] **1.** to fail to do something or be somewhere when required or expected; specif., *a)* to fail to make payment when due *b)* to fail to appear in court when required *c)* to fail to take part in or finish a contest **2.** to lose by default —vt. to fail to do, pay, finish, etc. (something) when required **2.** to lose (a contest, etc.) by default; forfeit —**in default of** in the absence of; through lack of —**de·fault'er** n.

de·fea·sance (di fē'z'ns) n. [ME. & Anglo-Fr. *defesaunce* < OFr. *defesance* < *defesant*, prp. of *defaire*, *desfaire*: see DEFEAT] **1.** the annulment of a contract or deed **2.** a clause stating a condition the fulfillment of which makes the deed, contract, etc. void in whole or in part

de·fea·si·ble (di fē'zə b'l) adj. [see DEFEASANCE & -IBLE] that can be undone or made void

de·feat (di fēt') vt. [ME. *defeten* < *defet*, disfigured, null and void < OFr. *desfait*, pp. of *desfaire*, to undo < ML. *disfacere*, to deface, ruin < L. *dis-*, from + *facere*, to DO] **1.** to win victory over; overcome; beat **2.** to bring to nothing; frustrate [*defeating* our plans] **3.** to make null and void **4.** [Obs.] to undo; destroy —n. [ME. *defet*] **1.** the act of defeating, or gaining victory **2.** the fact of being defeated; failure to win or succeed **3.** frustration **4.** nullification —*SYN.* see CONQUER

de·feat·ist (-ist) n. [Fr. *défaitiste*] a person who too readily accepts or expects defeat —adj. of or characteristic of a defeatist —**de·feat'ism** n.

de·fea·ture (di fē'chər) n. [altered (after DE- & FEATURE) < ME. *defaiture* < OFr. *desfaiture* < *desfaire*: see DEFEAT] **1.** [Archaic] disfigurement **2.** [Obs.] defeat

def·e·cate (def'ə kāt') vt. -cat'ed, -cat'ing [< L. *defaecatus*, pp. of *defaecare*, to cleanse from dregs, strain < *de-*, from + *faex* (gen. *faecis*), grounds, dregs] to remove impurities from; refine (sugar, wine, etc.) —vi. **1.** to become free from impurities **2.** to excrete waste matter from the bowels —**def'e·ca'tion** n. —**def'e·ca'tor** n.

de·fect (dē'fekt; also, and for v. always, di fekt') n. [ME. < L. *defectus* < *deficere*, to undo, fail < *de-*, from + *facere*, to DO] **1.** lack of something necessary for completeness; deficiency; shortcoming **2.** an imperfection or weakness; fault; flaw; blemish —vi. to forsake a party, cause, etc., esp. so as to join the opposition —**de·fec'tor** n.

SYN.—**defect** implies a lack of something essential to completeness or perfection [a *defect* in vision]; an **imperfection** is any faulty detail that detracts from perfection [minor *imperfections* of style]; a **blemish** is a superficial or surface imperfection that mars the appearance [skin *blemishes*]; a **flaw** is an imperfection in structure or substance, such as a crack or gap, that mars the wholeness or continuity [a *flaw* in a metal bar]

de·fec·tion (di fek'shən) n. [L. *defectio* < *defectus*: see prec.] **1.** abandonment of loyalty, duty, principle, etc.; desertion **2.** a failing or failure

de·fec·tive (-tiv) adj. [ME. & OFr. *defectif* < LL. *defectivus*] **1.** having a defect or defects; imperfect; faulty **2.** *Gram.* lacking some of the usual grammatical forms ["ought" is a *defective* verb] **3.** subnormal in intelligence —n. ☆**1.** a person with some bodily or mental defect **2.** *Gram.* a defective word —**de·fec'tive·ly** adv. —**de·fec'tive·ness** n.

de·fence (di fens') n. Brit. sp. of DEFENSE

de·fend (di fend') vt. [ME. *defenden* < OFr. *defendre* < L. *defendere*, to ward off, repel < *de-*, away, from + *fendere*, to strike < IE. base *gwhen-*, to strike, whence Sans. *hanti*, he strikes, OE. *guth*, combat] **1.** *a)* to guard from attack; keep from harm or danger; protect *b)* to protect (a goal, etc.) against scoring by an opponent **2.** to support, maintain, or justify [*defend* one's conduct] **3.** *Law a)* to oppose (an action, etc.) *b)* to plead (one's cause) in defense *c)* to act as lawyer for (an accused) —vi. to make a defense —**de·fend'a·ble** adj. —**de·fend'er** n.

SYN.—**defend** implies an active effort to repel an actual attack or invasion [to *defend* oneself in court]; **guard** suggests a watching over to keep safe from any potential attack or harm [to *guard* a coastline]; **protect** and **shield** imply a keeping safe from harm or injury by interposing a barrier [he built a fence to *protect* his garden], but **shield** also connotes a present or imminent attack or harmful agency [to *shield* one's eyes against a glare]; **preserve** implies a keeping safe from encroaching deterioration or decay [to *preserve* civil liberties]—ANT. attack

de·fend·ant (di fen'dənt) adj. [ME. *defendaunt* < OFr. *defendant*, prp. of *defendre*] defending —n. *Law* the defending party; person sued or accused: opposed to PLAINTIFF

Defender of the Faith a title used by English sovereigns, orig. conferred upon Henry VIII by Pope Leo X

de·fen·es·tra·tion (dē fen'ə strā'shən) n. [DE- + L.

fenestra, window + -TION] a tossing out through a window

de·fense (di fens', dē'fens) n. [ME. < OFr. < LL. *defensa* < fem. of L. *defensus*, pp. of *defendere*] 1. the act or power of defending, or guarding against attack, harm, or danger 2. the fact or state of being defended 3. *a)* something that defends; means of or resources for protection *b)* a plan or system for defending 4. justification or support by speech or writing; vindication 5. self-protection, as by boxing 6. the side that is defending in any contest 7. *a)* the arguments of the defendant or his lawyer in contesting a case ☆*b)* the defendant and his lawyer or lawyers, collectively —*vt.* **-fensed', -fens'ing** [Colloq.] to plan a defense against (an offensive maneuver) in a game or sport

de·fense·less (-lis) *adj.* lacking defense; unable to defend oneself; open to attack; helpless; unprotected —**de·fense'-less·ly** *adv.* —**de·fense'less·ness** *n.*

defense mechanism 1. any self-protective physiological reaction of an organism 2. *Psychiatry* any behavior or thought process unconsciously brought into use by an individual to protect himself against painful or anxiety-provoking feelings, impulses, perceptions, etc.

de·fen·si·ble (di fen'sə b'l) *adj.* [ME. & OFr. *defensable* < L. *defensabilis* < *defensare*, intens. < *defendere:* see DEFEND] that can be defended, protected, or justified —**de·fen'si·bil'i·ty** *n.* —**de·fen'si·bly** *adv.*

de·fen·sive (-siv) *adj.* [ME. & OFr. *defensif* < ML. *defensivus* < L. *defensus:* see DEFENSE] 1. defending 2. of or for defense 3. *Psychol.* constantly feeling under attack and hence quick to justify one's actions —*n.* 1. orig., something that defends 2. a position of defense: chiefly in the phrase **on the defensive,** in a position that makes defense necessary —**de·fen'sive·ly** *adv.* —**de·fen'sive·ness** *n.*

de·fer¹ (di fur') *vt., vi.* **-ferred', -fer'ring** [ME. *differren* < OFr. *differer:* see DIFFER] 1. to put off to a future time; postpone; delay 2. to postpone the induction of (a person) into the armed forces —**de·fer'rer** *n.*

de·fer² (di fur') *vi.* **-ferred', -fer'ring** [ME. *deferen* < OFr. *deferer*, to yield, pay deference to < L. *deferre*, to bring down < *de-*, down + *ferre*, to BEAR¹] to give in to the wish or judgment of another, as in showing respect; yield with courtesy (*to*) —*SYN.* see YIELD

def·er·ence (def'ər əns) n. [Fr. *déférence* < L. *deferens*, prp. of prec.] 1. a yielding in opinion, judgment, wishes, etc. 2. courteous regard or respect —*SYN.* see HONOR —**in deference to** out of regard or respect for (a person, his wishes, etc.)

def·er·ent¹ (-ənt) *adj.* same as DEFERENTIAL

def·er·ent² (-ənt) *adj.* [Fr. *déférent* < L. *deferens*, prp. of *deferre:* see DEFER²] 1. carrying down or out 2. *Anat.* of or relating to the vas deferens

def·er·en·tial (def'ə ren'shəl) *adj.* showing deference; very respectful —**def'er·en'tial·ly** *adv.*

de·fer·ment (di fur'mənt) *n.* [see DEFER¹] a deferring or being deferred; postponement: also **de·fer'ral**

de·ferred (di furd') *adj.* [pp. of DEFER¹] 1. postponed 2. having the rights, interest, etc. withheld until a certain date [a *deferred* annuity]

de·fer·ves·cence (dē'fər ves''ns, def'ər-) *n.* [G. *defervescenz* (first used by K. A. Wunderlich, 1815–1877, Ger. physician) < L. *defervescens*, prp. of *defervescere*, to cool off, orig. stop boiling < *de-*, down, DE- + *fervescere*, to grow hot: see EFFERVESCE] the abating or disappearance of a fever

de·fi·ance (di fī'əns) *n.* [ME. *defiaunce* < OFr. *defiance* < *defier*, DEFY] 1. the act of defying; open, bold resistance to authority or opposition 2. a challenge —**bid defiance to** to defy —**in defiance of** 1. defying 2. in spite of

de·fi·ant (-ənt) *adj.* [Fr. *défiant*, prp. of *défier*] full of defiance; openly and boldly resisting —**de·fi'ant·ly** *adv.*

de·fib·ril·late (di fib'rə lāt', -fī'brə-) *vt.* **-lat'ed, -lat'ing** to stop fibrillation of the heart, as by the use of electric current —**de·fib'ril·la'tion** *n.* —**de·fib'ril·la'tor** *n.*

de·fi·cien·cy (di fish'ən sē) *n.* [ME. *deficience* < LL. *deficientia* < L. *deficiens*, prp. of *deficere*, to lack, fail < *de-*, from + *facere*, to DO] 1. the quality or state of being deficient; absence of something essential; incompleteness 2. *pl.* **-cies** *a)* a shortage *b)* the amount of shortage; deficit

deficiency disease a disease, as rickets or pellagra, caused by a lack of vitamins, minerals, etc. in the diet

deficiency judgment *Law* a judgment in favor of a mortgagee for the remainder of a debt not completely cleared by foreclosure and sale of the mortgaged property

de·fi·cient (di fish'ənt) *adj.* [L. *deficiens:* see DEFICIENCY] 1. lacking in some essential; incomplete; defective 2. inadequate in amount, quality, degree, etc.; not sufficient —*n.* a deficient person or thing —**de·fi'cient·ly** *adv.*

def·i·cit (def'ə sit) *n.* [L., there is lacking, 3d pers. sing., pres. indic., of *deficere* (see DEFICIENCY): from use as first word in inventory clauses] the amount by which a sum of money is less than the required amount; specif., an excess of liabilities over assets, of losses over profits, or of expenditure over income

deficit financing *Econ.* the theory or practice of seeking to increase a nation's productivity and consumption by governmental expenditures financed by borrowing (**deficit spending**)

‡**de fi·de** (dā fē'dā) [L.] *R.C.Ch.* of faith: used to designate doctrines held to be revealed by God and so requiring the unconditional assent of faith by all

de·fi·er (di fī'ər) *n.* a person who defies

def·i·lade (def'ə lād', def'ə lād') *vt., vi.* **-lad'ed, -lad'ing** [< Fr. *défilade*, a filing off, succession < *défiler:* see DEFILE²] to arrange (troops and fortifications) so that the terrain will protect them, esp. from gunfire against either flank —*n.* 1. the act of defilading 2. the protection afforded by defilading

de·file¹ (di fīl') *vt.* **-filed', -fil'ing** [ME. *defilen*, altered (after *filen*, to make foul < OE. *fylan* < *ful*, FOUL) < *defoulen* < OFr. *defouler*, to tread underfoot, insult < *de-*, intens. + *fouler* < VL. **fullare*, to tread, FULL²] 1. to make filthy or dirty; pollute 2. to make ceremonially unclean 3. to corrupt 4. to profane or sully, as a person's name 5. [Archaic] to violate the chastity of; deflower —*SYN.* see CONTAMINATE —**de·file'ment** *n.* —**de·fil'er** *n.*

de·file² (di fīl', dē'fīl) *vi.* **-filed', -fil'ing** [Fr. *défiler*, to file off, unravel < *dé-* (L. *de*), from + *filer*, to form a line < *fil*, thread: see FILE¹] to march in single file or by files —*n.* [Fr. *défilé* < the *v.*] 1. a narrow passage through which troops must defile 2. any narrow valley or mountain pass 3. a march in single file or by files

de·fine (di fīn') *vt.* **-fined', -fin'ing** [ME. *diffinen* < OFr. *definer* & ML. *diffinire*, both < L. *definire*, to limit, define < *de-*, from + *finire*, to set a limit to, bound < *finis*, boundary] 1. *a)* to determine or set down the boundaries of *b)* to trace the precise outlines of; delineate 2. to determine or state the extent and nature of; describe exactly [*define* your duties] 3. *a)* to give the distinguishing characteristics of *b)* to constitute the distinction of; differentiate [reason *defines* man] 4. to state the meaning or meanings of (a word, etc.) —*vi.* to prepare definitions, as of words —**de·fin'a·ble** *adj.* —**de·fin'er** *n.*

def·i·nite (def'ə nit) *adj.* [L. *definitus*, pp. of *definire:* see prec.] 1. having exact limits 2. precise and clear in meaning; explicit 3. certain; positive [it's *definite* that he'll go] 4. *Gram.* limiting or specifying ["the" is the *definite* article] 5. *Bot.* having a constant number of stamens, etc., less than 20 but always a multiple of the number of petals —*SYN.* see EXPLICIT —**def'i·nite·ly** *adv.* —**def'i·nite·ness** *n.*

definite integral *Math.* an integral in which the range of integration is specified

def·i·ni·tion (def'ə nish'ən) *n.* [ME. *diffinicioun* < OFr. *definicion* & ML. *diffinitio*, both < L. *definitio*] 1. a defining or being defined 2. a statement of what a thing is 3. a statement of the meaning of a word, phrase, etc. 4. *a)* a putting or being in clear, sharp outline *b)* a making or being definite, explicit, clear, etc. 5. the power of a lens to show (an object) in clear, sharp outline 6. the degree of distinctness of a photograph, etc. 7. the clearness with which recorded or broadcast sounds or televised images are reproduced; absence of fuzziness —**def'i·ni'tion·al** *adj.*

de·fin·i·tive (di fin'ə tiv) *adj.* [ME. *diffinitif* < OFr. *definitif* < L. *definitivus* < pp. of *definire*, DEFINE] 1. that decides or settles in a final way; decisive; conclusive [a *definitive* answer] 2. most nearly complete and accurate [a *definitive* biography] 3. serving to define; limiting or distinguishing precisely [*definitive* details] 4. *Biol.* fully developed, as a structure or part —**de·fin'i·tive·ly** *adv.* —**de·fin'i·tive·ness** *n.*

definitive host the organism on or in which a parasite lives in the adult stage

de·fin·i·tude (di fin'ə tōōd', -tyōōd') *n.* [< L. *definitus* (see DEFINITE), after FINITUDE] the quality of being definite; precision

def·la·grate (def'lə grāt') *vt., vi.* **-grat'ed, -grat'ing** [< L. *deflagratus*, pp. of *deflagrare*, to burn, consume < *de-*, intens. + *flagrare*, to burn] to burn rapidly, with intense heat and dazzling light —**def'la·gra'tion** *n.*

de·flate (di flāt') *vt., vi.* **-flat'ed, -flat'ing** [DE- + (IN)FLATE] 1. to collapse by letting out air or gas [to *deflate* a tire] 2. to make smaller or less important 3. to cause deflation of (currency, prices, etc.) Opposed to INFLATE —*SYN.* see CONTRACT —**de·fla'tor** *n.*

de·fla·tion (di flā'shən) *n.* 1. a deflating or being deflated 2. a lessening of the amount of money in circulation, resulting in a relatively sharp and sudden rise in its value and fall in prices 3. *Geol.* erosion by the wind See INFLATION —**de·fla'tion·ar'y** *adj.*

de·flect (di flekt') *vt., vi.* [L. *deflectere* < *de-*, from + *flectere*, to bend] to turn or make go to one side; bend; swerve —**de·flec'tive** *adj.* —**de·flec'tor** *n.*

de·flec·tion (di flek'shən) *n.* [LL. *deflexio* < L. *deflexus*, pp. of prec.] 1. *a)* a deflecting or being deflected; a turning aside, bending, or deviation *b)* the amount of this 2. the deviation from the zero mark of the needle or pointer of a measuring instrument

de·flexed (di flekst') *adj.* [earlier *deflex* (< L. *deflexus*, pp. of *deflectere*, DEFLECT) + -ED] bent downward, as branches, leaves, or hairs

de·flex·ion (di flek'shən) *n.* Brit. sp. of DEFLECTION

def·lo·ra·tion (def'lə rā'shən) *n.* [ME. *defloracioun* < OFr. *desfloracion* < LL.] the act of deflowering

de·flow·er (di flou'ər) *vt.* [ME. *deflouren* < OFr. *desflorer* < L. *deflorare* < *de-*, from + *flos* (gen. *floris*), FLOWER] 1. to make (a woman) no longer a virgin 2. to ravage or spoil 3. to remove flowers from (a plant)

De·foe (di fō'), **Daniel** 1660?–1731; Eng. writer

☆**de·fo·li·ant** (dē fō'lē ənt) *n.* a chemical spray that strips growing plants of their leaves

de·fo·li·ate (-āt') *vt.* **-at'ed, -at'ing** [< LL. *defoliatus*, pp.

of *defoliare* < L. *de-*, from + *folium*, a leaf] **1.** to strip (trees, etc.) of leaves ☆**2.** to use a defoliant on —**de·fo'li·a'-tion** *n.* —**de·fo'li·a'tor** *n.*

de·force (dē fôrs') *vt.* **-forced', -forc'ing** [ME. *deforcen* < Anglo-Fr. *deforcier* < OFr. *de-*, from + *forcier*, to FORCE] *Law* **1.** to keep (property, etc.) from the rightful owner by force **2.** to keep (a person) from rightful possession by force —**de·force'ment** *n.*

de·for·ciant (-fôr'shənt) *n.* [ME. *deforciaunt*] *Law* a person who deforces another or another's property

de·for·est (dē fôr'ist, -fär'-) *vt.* to clear (land) of forests or trees —☆**de·for'est·a'tion** *n.*

De For·est (di fôr'ist, fär'-), Lee 1873–1961; U.S. inventor of telegraphic, telephonic, & radio apparatus

de·form (di fôrm') *vt.* [ME. *deformen* < OFr. *deformer* < L. *deformare* < *de-*, from + *forma*, form] **1.** to impair the form or shape of **2.** to make ugly; disfigure **3.** *Physics* to change the shape of by pressure or stress —*vi.* to become deformed **SYN.**—**deform** implies a marring of form, appearance, or character, as if by pressure or stress [a body *deformed* by disease]; **distort** implies a twisting or wrenching out of the normal or proper shape or form [a mind *distorted* by fear]; **contort** suggests an even more violent wrenching out of shape so as to produce a grotesque or unpleasant result [a face *contorted* by pain]; **warp** implies a bending out of shape, as of wood in drying, and, hence, suggests a turning aside from the true or right course [judgment *warped* by prejudice]

de·for·ma·tion (dē'fôr mā'shən, def'ər-) *n.* [ME. *defor·macioun* < L. *deformatio*] **1.** a deforming or being deformed **2.** the result of deforming; disfigurement **3.** a change in form for the worse **4.** *Physics* a) the changing of form or shape, as by stress b) the changed form that results

de·formed (di fôrmd') *adj.* changed as in form or shape, esp. so as to be misshapen, ugly, etc.

de·form·i·ty (di fôr'mə tē) *n., pl.* **-ties** [ME. *deformite* < OFr. *deformité* < L. *deformitas* < *deformis*, misshapen < *de-*, from + *forma*, form] **1.** the condition of being deformed **2.** *a*) abnormal bodily formation b) a deformed or disfigured part of the body **3.** ugliness or depravity **4.** anything deformed or disfigured

de·fraud (di frôd') *vt.* [ME. *defrauden* < OFr. *defrauder* < L. *defraudare* < *de-*, from + *fraudare*, to cheat < *fraus*, FRAUD] to take away or hold back property, rights, etc. from by fraud; cheat —**SYN.** see CHEAT —**de·frau·da·tion** (dē'frô dā'shən) *n.* —**de·fraud'er** *n.*

de·fray (di frā') *vt.* [Fr. *défrayer* < OFr¹. *desruier* < *de-* (L. *de*), from, off + **frai* (Fr. *frais*, pl.), expense, cost, "damages," prob. < L. *fractum*, neut. pp. of *frangere*, to BREAK¹] to pay or furnish the money for (the cost or expenses) —**de·fray'a·ble** *adj.* —**de·fray'al, de·fray'ment** *n.*

de·frock (dē fräk') *vt.* same as UNFROCK (sense 2)

de·frost (di frôst') *vt.* **1.** to remove frost or ice from by thawing **2.** to cause (frozen foods) to become unfrozen —*vi.* to become defrosted

de·frost·er (-ər) *n.* any device for melting ice and frost or preventing their formation, as on a windshield

deft (deft) *adj.* [ME. *defte, dafte*: see DAFT] skillful in a quick, sure, and easy way; dexterous —**SYN.** see DEXTEROUS —**deft'ly** *adv.* —**deft'ness** *n.*

de·funct (di funkt') *adj.* [L. *defunctus*, pp. of *defungi*, to do, finish, die < *de-*, from, off + *fungi*, to perform: see FUNCTION] no longer living or existing; dead or extinct —**SYN.** see DEAD

de·fuse, de·fuze (dē fyōoz') *vt.* **-fused', -fus'ing 1.** to remove the fuse from (a bomb or the like) **2.** to render harmless

de·fy (di fī'; *also, for n.,* dē'fī) *vt.* **-fied', -fy'ing** [ME. *defien* < OFr. *defier*, to distrust, repudiate, defy < LL. *disfidare* < *dis-*, from + **fidare*, to trust < *fidus*, faithful] **1.** to resist or oppose boldly or openly **2.** to resist completely in a baffling way [the puzzle *defied* solution] **3.** to dare (someone) to do or prove something **4.** [Archaic] to challenge (someone) to fight —☆*n., pl.* **-fies** [substantival use of the *v.*] [Colloq.] a defiance or challenge

deg. degree; degrees

dé·ga·gé (dā'gä zhā') *adj.* [Fr., pp. of *dégager*, to disengage] **1.** free and easy or unconstrained in manner, attitude, etc. **2.** uncommitted, uninvolved, detached, etc.

de·gas (dē gas') *vt.* **-gassed', -gas'sing** to remove gas from

De·gas (də gä'), **(Hilaire Germain) Ed·gar** (ed gär') 1834–1917; Fr. painter

de Gaulle (də gôl'; Fr. gōl'), **Charles (André Joseph Marie)** 1890–1970; Fr. general & statesman; president of France (1959–69)

de·gauss (di gous') *vt.* [DE- + GAUSS] to demagnetize (as a ship for protection against magnetic mines) by passing an electric current through a coil or coils along or around the edge in order to neutralize the surrounding magnetic field —**de·gauss'er** *n.*

de·gen·er·a·cy (di jen'ər ə sē) *n.* **1.** the state of being degenerate **2.** the process of degenerating **3.** degenerate behavior

de·gen·er·ate (-ər it; *for v.,* -ə rāt') *adj.* [L. *degeneratus*, pp. of *degenerare*, to become unlike one's race, degenerate < *degener*, not genuine, base < *de-*, from + *genus*, race,

kind: see GENUS] **1.** having sunk below a former or normal condition, character, etc.; deteriorated **2.** morally corrupt; depraved —*n.* a degenerate person, esp. one who is morally depraved or sexually perverted —*vi.* **-at'ed, -at'ing 1.** to lose former, normal, or higher qualities **2.** to decline or become debased morally, culturally, etc. **3.** *Biol.* to undergo degeneration; deteriorate —**de·gen'er·ate·ly** *adv.* —**de·gen'er·ate·ness** *n.*

de·gen·er·a·tion (di jen'ə rā'shən, dē'-) *n.* [LL. *degeneratio*] **1.** the process of degenerating **2.** a degenerate condition **3.** *Biol.* deterioration or loss of a function or structure in the course of evolution, as in the vestigial eyes of many cave animals **4.** *Med.* deterioration in structure or function of cells, tissues, or organs, as in disease or aging

de·gen·er·a·tive (di jen'ər ə tiv, -ə rāt'iv) *adj.* **1.** of, showing, or causing degeneration **2.** tending to degenerate —**de·gen'er·a·tive·ly** *adv.*

de·glu·ti·nate (dē glōōt'n āt') *vt.* **-nat'ed, -nat'ing** [< L. *deglutinatus*, pp. of *deglutinare*, to unglue < *de-*, from + *glutinare*, to glue < *gluten*, GLUE] to extract gluten from (wheat, etc.) —**de·glu'ti·na'tion** *n.*

de·glu·ti·tion (dē'glōō tish'ən) *n.* [Fr. *déglutition* < pp. of LL. *deglutire*, to swallow down < L. *de-*, from, down + *glutire*, to swallow] the act, process, or power of swallowing

deg·ra·da·tion (deg'rə dā'shən) *n.* [Fr. *dégradation* < LL. *degradatio* < *degradare*: see ff.] **1.** a degrading or being degraded in rank, status, condition, etc. **2.** a degraded condition **3.** *Geol.* the lowering of land surfaces by erosion **4.** *R.C.Ch.* a punishment whereby a priest is permanently deprived of the rights of his office

de·grade (di grād', dē-) *vt.* **-grad'ed, -grad'ing** [ME. *degraden* < OFr. *degrader* < LL. *degradare*, to reduce in rank < L. *de-*, down + *gradus*: see GRADE] **1.** to lower in rank or status, as in punishing; demote **2.** to lower or corrupt in quality, moral character, value, etc.; debase **3.** to bring into dishonor or contempt **4.** *Chem.* to convert (an organic compound) into a simpler compound by removal of one or more parts of the molecule; decompose **5.** *Geol.* to lower (a land surface) by erosion —*vi.* [Rare] to sink to a lower grade or type; degenerate —**de·grad'a·ble** *adj.* —**de·grad'er** *n.*

SYN.—**degrade** literally means to lower in grade or rank, but it commonly implies a lowering or corrupting of moral character, self-respect, etc.; **abase** suggests a loss, often merely temporary and self-imposed, of dignity, respect, etc. [he *abased* himself before his employer]; **debase** implies a decline in value, quality, character, etc. [a *debased* mind]; to **humble** is to lower the pride or increase the humility, esp. of another, and, unqualified, suggests that such lowering is deserved [*humbled* by the frightening experience]; to **humiliate** is to humble or shame (another) painfully and in public [*humiliated* by their laughter] —**ANT.** exalt, dignify

de·grad·ed (-id) *adj.* disgraced, debased, depraved, etc.

de·grad·ing (-iŋ) *adj.* that degrades; debasing —**SYN.** see BASE² —**de·grad'ing·ly** *adv.*

de·gree (di grē') *n.* [ME. *degre* < OFr. *degré*, degree, step, rank < VL. **degradus* < *degradare*: see DEGRADE] **1.** any of the successive steps or stages in a process or series **2.** a step in the direct line of descent [a cousin in the second *degree*] **3.** social or official rank, position, or class [a man of low *degree*] **4.** relative condition; manner, respect, or relation [each contributing to victory in his *degree*] **5.** extent, amount, or relative intensity [hungry to a slight *degree*, burns of the third *degree*] **6.** *Algebra* rank as determined by the sum of a term's exponents [a^3c^2 and x^5 are each of the fifth *degree*] **7.** *Educ.* a rank given by a college or university to a student who has completed a required course of study, or to a distinguished person as an honor **8.** *Gram.* a grade of comparison of adjectives and adverbs [the positive *degree* is "good," the comparative *degree* is "better," and the superlative *degree* is "best"] ☆**9.** *Law* the seriousness of a crime [murder in the first *degree*] **10.** *Math., Astron., Geog., etc.* a unit of measure for angles or arcs, one 360th part of the circumference of a circle: the measure of an angle is the number of degrees between its sides considered as radii of a circle (Ex.: a right angle has 90 *degrees*) **11.** *Music* a) a line or space on the staff b) an interval between two such lines or spaces **12.** *Physics* a) a unit of measure on a scale, as for temperature b) a line marking a degree, as on a thermometer —**by degrees** step by step; gradually —**to a degree 1.** [Chiefly Brit.] to a great extent **2.** somewhat

de·gree-day (-dā') *n.* a unit representing one degree of declination from a standard temperature in the average temperature of one day, used in determining fuel requirements

degrees of freedom *Statistics* the number of unrestricted and independent deviations entering into some measure of dispersion

de·gres·sion (di gresh'ən) *n.* [ML. *degressio* < L. *degressus*, pp. of *degredi*, to go down < *de*, down + *gredi*, to go] a going down; descent or decrease; specif., a gradual decrease in the rate of taxation on sums below a specified amount —**de·gres'sive** *adj.*

de·gust (di gust') *vt., vi.* [< L. *degustare* < *de-*, from + *gustare*, to taste: see GUSTO] [Rare] to taste, esp. to taste

attentively so as to perceive the flavor —**de·gus·ta·tion** (dē'gəs tā'shən) *n.*

‡de gus·ti·bus non dis·pu·tan·dum (est) (di gus'ti bəs nän dis/pyo͞o tan/dəm est) [L.] there is no disputing about tastes

de·hisce (di his') *vi.* **-hisced'**, **-hisc'ing** [L. *dehiscere* < *de-*, off + *hiscere*, to gape, yawn] to burst or split open, as a seed pod

de·his·cence (-his'ns) *n.* [L. *dehiscens*, prp. of *dehiscere*: see prec.] a bursting or splitting open, as of a pod, anther, etc. to discharge its contents —**de·his'cent** *adj.*

☆de·horn (dē hôrn') *vt.* to remove the horns from

de·hu·man·ize (dē hyo͞o'mə nīz') *vt.* **-ized'**, **-iz'ing** to deprive of human qualities, as pity, kindness, individuality, creativity, etc.; make inhuman or machinelike —**de·hu'·man·i·za'tion** *n.*

de·hu·mid·i·fy (dē'hyo͞o mid'ə fī') *vt.* **-fied'**, **-fy'ing** to remove moisture from (the air, etc.) —**de'hu·mid'i·fi·ca'tion** *n.* —**de'hu·mid'i·fi'er** *n.*

de·hy·drate (dē hī'drāt) *vt.* **-drat·ed**, **-drat·ing** [DE- + HYDRATE] to remove water from (a compound, substance, body tissues, etc.); dry *[foods are dehydrated to conserve them for future use]* —*vi.* to lose water; become dry —**de'hy·dra'tion** *n.* —**de·hy'dra·tor** *n.*

☆de·hy·dro·gen·ase (dē hī'drə jə nās', dē'hī dräj'ə nās') *n.* [DE- + HYDROGEN + -ASE] any of a class of enzymes found in animal and plant tissues, which induce oxidation in a number of compounds by removing hydrogen

de·hy·dro·gen·ate (-nāt') *vt.* **-at'ed**, **-at'ing** to remove hydrogen from: also **de·hy'dro·gen·ize'** (-nīz') **-ized'**, **-iz'ing** —**de·hy·dro·gen·a'tion** *n.*

de·hyp·no·tize (dē hip'nə tīz') *vt.* **-tized'**, **-tiz'ing** to arouse from a hypnotic trance

de·ice (dē īs') *vt.* **-iced'**, **-ic'ing** to melt ice from or keep free of ice —**de·ic'er** *n.*

de·i·cide (dē'ə sīd') *n.* **1.** [LL.(Ec.) *deicida* + L. *deus*, god + *caedere*, to kill] the killer of a god **2.** [< L. *deus*, god + -CIDE] the killing of a god

deic·tic (dīk'tik) *adj.* [Gr. *deiktikos* < *deiktos*, capable of proof < *deiknynai*, to prove] [Rare] directly pointing out or proving

de·if·ic (dē if'ik) *adj.* [LL. *deificus*] **1.** deifying or making divine **2.** godlike; divine

de·i·fi·ca·tion (dē'ə fi kā'shən) *n.* [ME. *deificacioun* < LL.(Ec.) *deificalio*] **1.** the act of deifying **2.** the state of being deified **3.** a deified embodiment

de·i·fy (dē'ə fī') *vt.* **-fied'**, **-fy'ing** [ME. *deifien* < OFr. *deifier* < LL.(Ec.) *deificare*, to make divine < L. *deus*, god + *facere*, to make] **1.** to make a god of; rank among the gods **2.** to look upon or worship as a god **3.** to glorify, exalt, or adore in an extreme way; idolize

deign (dān) *vi.* [ME. *deignen* < OFr. *deignier* < L. *dignare*, *dignari*, to deem worthy < *dignus*, worthy] to think it not beneath one's dignity *(to do something)*; condescend —*vt.* **1.** to condescend to give; vouchsafe *[will you deign* no answer?*]* **2.** [Obs.] to condescend to accept —*SYN.* see STOOP

deil (dēl) *n.* [ME. *deile*, var. of *devel*, DEVIL] [Scot.] **1.** the devil **2.** a mischievous person

de·i·on·ize (dē ī'ə nīz') *vt.* **-ized'**, **-iz'ing** **1.** to remove ions from (water) by the use of cation and anion exchangers **2.** to restore (gas that has become ionized) to its former condition

Deir·dre (dir'drə) [OIr. *Derdriu*, prob. akin to MIr. *der*, young girl] *Irish Legend* a princess of Ulster who eloped to Scotland with her lover: when he was treacherously killed, she committed suicide

Deir ez Zor (der' ez zôr') city in E Syria, on the Euphrates: pop. 60,000

de·ism (dē'iz'm) *n.* [Fr. *déisme* < L. *deus*, god] belief in the existence of a God on purely rational grounds without reliance on revelation or authority; esp., the 17th- and 18th-cent. doctrine that God created the world and its natural laws, but takes no further part in its functioning

de·ist (dē'ist) *n.* [Fr. *déiste*] a believer in deism —*SYN.* see ATHEIST —**de·is'tic**, **de·is'ti·cal** *adj.* —**de·is'ti·cal·ly** *adv.*

de·i·ty (dē'ə tē) *n.*, *pl.* **-ties** [ME. *deite* < OFr. *deité* < LL.(Ec.) *deitas*, divinity (after L. *divinitas*) < L. *deus*, god < IE. *deiwos*, god < base *dei-*, to gleam, shine, whence L. *dies*, day] **1.** the state of being a god; divine nature; godhood **2.** a god or goddess —**the Deity** God

‡dé·jà vu (dā zhà vü') [Fr., lit., already seen] *Psychol.* the illusion that one has previously had an experience that is actually new to one

de·ject (di jekt') *vt.* [ME. *dejecten* < L. *dejectus*, pp. of *dejicere* < *de-*, down + *jacere*, to throw: see JET¹] to cast down in spirit; dishearten; depress —*adj.* [Archaic] dejected

de·jec·ta (di jek'tə) *n.pl.* [ModL., neut. pl. of L. *dejectus*: see prec.] feces; excrement

de·ject·ed (-tid) *adj.* in low spirits; depressed; disheartened; downcast —*SYN.* see SAD —**de·ject'ed·ly** *adv.* —**de·ject'·ed·ness** *n.*

de·jec·tion (di jek'shən) *n.* [ME. *dejeccioun* < L. *dejectio*: see DEJECT] **1.** lowness of spirits; depression **2.** *Med.* *a)* defecation *b)* feces; excrement

‡dé·jeu·ner (dā'zhē nā') *n.* [Fr. < OFr. *desjeuner* < VL. *disjejunare*: see DINE] a late breakfast, or luncheon

de ju·re (di joor'ē, dā) [L.] by right or legal establishment *[de jure* government*]*: cf. DE FACTO

dek·a- (dek'ə) *same as* DECA-: also, before a vowel, **dek-**

De Kalb (də kalb'; *G.* kälp'), **Jo·hann** (yō'hän) (born *Johann Kalb*) 1721–81; Fr. general, born in Germany, who served in the Am. Revolutionary army: called *Baron De Kalb*

Dek·ker (dek'ər), **Thomas** 1570?–1641?; Eng. playwright

dek·ko (dek'ō) *n.* [Hind. *dekho*, pl. imper. of *dekhnā*, to see, akin to Sans. *dŕś*, sight: see DARSHAN] [Brit. Colloq.] a look; glance

de Koon·ing (də kō'niŋ), **Wil·lem** (wil'əm) 1904– ; U.S. painter, born in the Netherlands

de Kruif (də krīf), **Paul (Henry)** 1890– ; U.S. bacteriologist & writer

Del. Delaware

del. 1. delegate **2.** delegation **3.** delete **4.** [L. *delineavit*] he (or she) drew it: formerly used after the artist's signature on a painting

De·la·croix (də là krwà'), **(Ferdinand Victor) Eu·gène** (ö zhen') 1798–1863; Fr. painter

Del·a·go·a Bay (del'ə gō'ə) inlet of the Indian Ocean, on the SE coast of Mozambique: 55 mi. long

de·laine (də lān') *n.* [for *muslin de laine* < Fr. *de laine*, of wool < L. *de-*, of, from + *lana*, wool] **1.** formerly, a lightweight fabric of wool or wool and cotton **2.** a kind of wool, used esp. in fine worsteds

de la Mare (del'ə mer', mar'), **Walter (John)** 1873–1956; Eng. poet & novelist

de·lam·i·nate (dē lam'ə nāt') *vt.*, *vi.* **-nat'ed**, **-nat'ing** [DE- + LAMINATE] to separate into layers

de·lam·i·na·tion (dē lam'ə nā'shən) *n.* separation into layers; specif., *Embryology* the formation of endoderm by the splitting of the blastoderm into two layers of cells

De·la·roche (də là rōsh'), **(Hippolyte) Paul** 1797–1856; Fr. painter

de·late (di lāt') *vt.* **-lat'ed**, **-lat'ing** [< L. *delatus*, pp. of *deferre*: see DEFER²] **1.** [Chiefly Scot.] to accuse or inform against **2.** [Archaic] to relate; announce; make public —**de·la'tion** *n.* —**de·la'tor** *n.*

De·la·vigne (də là vēn'y'), **(Jean François) Cas·i·mir** (kà zē mir') 1793–1843; Fr. poet & playwright

Del·a·ware (del'ə wer', -war') [after Baron DE LA WARR] **1.** Eastern State of the U.S., on the Atlantic: one of the 13 original States; 2,057 sq. mi.; pop. 548,000; cap. Dover: abbrev. **Del.**, **DE 2.** river flowing from S N.Y. along the Pa. -N.Y. and Pa.-N.J. borders into Delaware Bay: c. 300 mi. —*n.* **1.** *pl.* **-wares'**, **-ware'** a member of a tribe of Indians who lived in the Delaware River valley **2.** their Algonquian language **3.** a small, sweet, reddish American grape —**Del'a·war'e·an** *adj.*, *n.*

Delaware Bay estuary of the Delaware River, between SW N.J. and E Del.: c. 55 mi. long

De La Warr (del'ə wer', war'), **Baron** (*Thomas West*) 1577–1618; 1st Eng. colonial governor of Virginia (1610–11): called *Lord Delaware*

de·lay (di lā') *vt.* [ME. *delaien* < OFr. *delaier* < *de-*, intens. + *laier*, to leave, let, altered (? after conjugation of *faire*) < *laissier* < L. *laxare*: see RELAX] **1.** to put off to a future time; postpone **2.** to make late; slow up; detain —*vi.* to stop for a while; linger —*n.* **1.** a delaying or being delayed **2.** the period of time for which something is delayed —**de·lay'er** *n.*

SYN.—**delay** implies the interference of something that causes a detainment or postponement *[I was delayed by the storm]*; **retard** implies the action of something in causing a slowing down of movement or progress *[the advancing army had been retarded]*; **slacken** suggests a slowing down by relaxation of activity or intensity *[trade had slackened somewhat]*; **impede** implies interference with movement or progress by some obstruction *[the muddy roads impeded our journey]*; **hinder** suggests a holding back or restraining of movement or action, often of that which has not yet begun *[the search was hindered by his arrival]* —*ANT.* hasten, expedite

delayed neutron a neutron emitted from short half-life products formed as a result of nuclear fission, important in the control of nuclear reactors

delaying action maneuvers to cover a retreat, gain time, etc.

de·le (dē'lē) *vt.* **-led**, **-le·ing** [L., imperative sing. of *delere*: see DELETE] *Printing* to take out (a letter, word, etc.); delete: usually in the imperative and expressed by the mark (φ), indicating the matter to be deleted —*n.* this mark

de·lec·ta·ble (di lek'tə b'l) *adj.* [ME. & OFr. < L. *delectabilis* < *delectare*: see DELIGHT] very pleasing; delightful; now, esp., pleasing to the taste; delicious; luscious —**de·lec'ta·bil'i·ty** *n.* —**de·lec'ta·bly** *adv.*

de·lec·ta·tion (dē lek tā'shən, di lek'-) *n.* [ME. *delectacioun* < OFr. *delectation* < L. *delectatio* < *delectare*: see DELIGHT] delight; enjoyment; entertainment

del·e·ga·cy (del'ə gə sē) *n.*, *pl.* **-cies 1.** a delegating or being delegated **2.** a delegation

del·e·gate (del'ə git'; *also, for n.*, -git) *n.* [ME. *delegat* < ML. *delegatus* < pp. of L. *delegare*, to send from one place to another, appoint, assign < *de-*, from + *legare*, to send, appoint] **1.** a person authorized or sent to speak and act for others; representative, as at a convention **☆2.** formerly, a representative of a U.S. Territory in the House of Representatives, with the right to speak but not to vote **☆3.** a member of a House of Delegates —*vt.* **-gat'ed**, **-gat'ing 1.**

to send or appoint as a representative or deputy **2.** to entrust (authority, power, etc.) to a person acting as one's agent or representative

del·e·ga·tion (del′ə gā′shən) *n.* [L. *delegatio*] **1.** a delegating or being delegated **2.** a body of delegates

de·lete (di lēt′) *vt.* **-let′ed, -let′ing** [< L. *deletus,* pp. of *delere,* to blot out, destroy < *de-,* from + base of *linere,* to daub, rub over (writing on a wax tablet with the blunt end of the style) < IE. base *lei-,* viscous, smooth (whence LIME¹)] to take out (a printed or written letter, word, etc.); cross out —SYN. see ERASE

del·e·te·ri·ous (del′ə tir′ē əs) *adj.* [Gr. *dēlētērios* < *dēlētēr,* a destroyer < *dēleisthai,* to injure] harmful to health, well-being, etc.; injurious —SYN. see PERNICIOUS —del′e·te′ri·ous·ly *adv.* —del′e·te′ri·ous·ness *n.*

de·le·tion (di lē′shən) *n.* [L. *deletio*] **1.** a deleting or being deleted **2.** a deleted word, passage, etc. **3.** *Genetics* the absence of some normal portion of a chromosome

Delft (delft) city in W Netherlands: pop. 77,000

delft·ware (delft′wer′) *n.* **1.** glazed earthenware, usually blue and white, which originated in Delft **2.** any similar ware Also **delft, delf** (delf)

Del·hi (del′ē) **1.** territory in N India: 573 sq. mi.; pop. 2,659,000 **2.** city in this territory, on the Jumna River: pop. 2,062,000: also called **Old Delhi:** see also NEW DELHI

Del·ia (dēl′yə) [L., fem. of *Delius,* of Delos] a feminine name

De·li·an (dē′lē ən) *adj.* of or having to do with Delos —*n.* a native or inhabitant of Delos

de·lib·er·ate (di lib′ər it; *for v.,* -āt′) *adj.* [ME. < L. *deliberatus,* pp. of *deliberare,* to consider, weigh well < *de-,* intens. + *librare,* to weigh < *libra,* a scales] **1.** carefully thought out and formed, or done on purpose; premeditated **2.** careful in considering, judging, or deciding; not rash or hasty **3.** unhurried and methodical [take *deliberate* aim] —*vi.* -at′ed, -at′ing to think or consider carefully and fully; esp., to consider reasons for and against a thing in order to make up one's mind [a jury *deliberates*] —*vt.* to consider carefully —SYN. see THINK¹, VOLUNTARY —de·lib′er·ate·ly *adv.* —de·lib′er·ate·ness *n.* —de·lib′er·a′tor *n.*

de·lib·er·a·tion (di lib′ə rā′shən) *n.* [ME. *deliberacioun* < OFr. *deliberation* < L. *deliberatio*] **1.** a deliberating, or considering carefully **2.** [*often pl.*] consideration and discussion of alternatives before reaching a decision [the *deliberations* of statesmen] **3.** the quality of being deliberate; carefulness; slowness

de·lib·er·a·tive (di lib′ə rāt′iv, -ər ə tiv) *adj.* [L. *deliberativus*] **1.** of or for deliberating [a *deliberative* assembly] **2.** characterized by or resulting from deliberation —de·lib′er·a′tive·ly *adv.*

De·libes (də lēb′), (Clément Philibert) Lé·o (lā ō′) 1836-91; Fr. composer

del·i·ca·cy (del′i kə sē) *n., pl.* **-cies** [ME. *delicacie* < ML. *delicacia* < L. *delicatus:* see DELICATE] **1.** the quality of being delicate in taste, odor, texture, etc. **2.** fragile beauty or graceful slightness, softness, etc.; fineness [the *delicacy* of a petal, of spun glass, or of a child's face] **3.** weakness of constitution or health; frailty **4.** the quality or condition of needing careful and deft handling [negotiations of great *delicacy*] **5.** fineness of feeling, observation, or appreciation [*delicacy* of musical taste] **6.** sensitiveness of response [the *delicacy* of a compass] **7.** fineness of touch, skill, etc. **8.** a fine regard for the feelings of others **9.** a sensitive or, sometimes, finical distaste for what is considered improper or offensive **10.** a choice food [caviar and other *delicacies*] **11.** [Obs.] luxuriousness or voluptuousness

del·i·cate (del′i kit) *adj.* [ME. *delicat* < L. *delicatus,* giving pleasure, delightful < *delicare,* for OL. *delicere,* to allure, entice < *de-,* intens. + *lacere:* see DELIGHT] **1.** pleasing in its lightness, mildness, subtlety, etc. [a *delicate* flavor, odor, color, etc.] **2.** beautifully fine in texture, quality, workmanship, etc. [*delicate* linen, *delicate* skin] **3.** slight and subtle [a *delicate* difference] **4.** easily damaged, spoiled, disordered, etc. [a *delicate* vase, a *delicate* stomach] **5.** frail in health [a *delicate* child] **6.** *a)* needing careful handling, tact, etc. [a *delicate* situation] *b)* showing tact, consideration, etc. **7.** finely sensitive in feeling, understanding, discriminating, or responding [a *delicate* ear for music, a *delicate* gauge] **8.** finely skilled **9.** having or showing a sensitive or, sometimes, finical distaste for what is considered offensive or improper —*n.* [Archaic or Poet.] a delicacy; dainty —del′i·cate·ly *adv.* —del′i·cate·ness *n.* SYN.—**delicate** and **dainty** are both used to describe things that are pleasing to highly refined tastes or sensibilities, **delicate** implying fragility, subtlety, or fineness, and **dainty,** smallness, fastidiousness, or gracefulness; **exquisite** is applied to something so delicately wrought or subtly refined as to be appreciated by only the most keenly discriminating or fastidious —ANT. **gross, crude, coarse**

☆**del·i·ca·tes·sen** (del′i kə tes′n) *n.* [G. *delikatessen,* derived by folk etym. < *delikat* (< Fr. *délicat*) + *essen,* food, but actually *pl.* of *delikatesse* < Fr. *délicatesse,* delicacy (< *délicat:* see prec.) after It. *delicatezza,* ult. of same origin] **1.** prepared cooked meats, smoked fish, cheeses,

salads, relishes, etc., collectively **2.** a shop where such foods are sold

de·li·cious (di lish′əs) *adj.* [ME. < OFr. *delicieus* < L. *deliciosus* < *deliciae,* delight < *delicere:* see DELICATE] **1.** very enjoyable; delightful [a *delicious* bit of gossip] **2.** very pleasing, esp. to taste or smell —☆*n.* [D-] a variety of sweet, red winter apple —de·li′cious·ly *adv.* —de·li′cious·ness *n.*

de·lict (di likt′) *n.* [L. *delictum,* a fault < pp. of *delinquere,* to leave undone: see DELINQUENCY] *Law* an offense; wrong or injury

de·light (di līt′) *vt.* [ME. *deliten* < OFr. *delitier* < L. *delectare,* to delight, freq. of *delicere* < *de-,* from + *lacere,* to entice, lit., to ensnare < IE. base *lek-,* twig, snare, whence OE. *læl,* whip: sp. infl. by LIGHT²] to give great joy or pleasure to —*vi.* **1.** to give great joy or pleasure **2.** to be highly pleased; rejoice (usually with *in* or an infinitive) —*n.* [ME. & OFr. *delit* < the *v.*] **1.** great joy or pleasure **2.** something giving great joy or pleasure **3.** [Poet.] the power of pleasing greatly —SYN. see PLEASURE

de·light·ed (-id) *adj.* **1.** highly pleased; happy **2.** [Obs.] delightful —de·light′ed·ly *adv.*

de·light·ful (-fəl) *adj.* giving delight; very pleasing; charming: also [Archaic] **de·light′some** (-səm) —de·light′ful·ly *adv.* —de·light′ful·ness *n.*

De·li·lah (di lī′lə) [Heb. *delilāh,* lit., delicate] *Bible* the mistress of Samson, who betrayed him to the Philistines: Judg. 16 —*n.* a seductive, treacherous woman; temptress

de·lim·it (dē lim′it) *vt.* [Fr. *délimiter* < L. *delimitare* < *de-,* from + *limitare*] to fix the limits of; mark the boundaries of: also **de·lim′i·tate** (-ə tāt′) -tat′ed, -tat′ing —de·lim′i·ta′tion *n.* —de·lim′i·ta′tive *adj.*

de·lin·e·ate (di lin′ē āt′) *vt.* -at′ed, -at′ing [< L. *delineatus,* pp. of *delineare,* to mark out, sketch < *de-,* from + *linea,* LINE¹] **1.** to trace the outline of; sketch out **2.** to draw; depict **3.** to depict in words; describe —de·lin′e·a′tion *n.* —de·lin′e·a′tive *adj.* —de·lin′e·a′tor *n.*

de·lin·quen·cy (di liŋ′kwən sē) *n., pl.* **-cies** [LL. *delinquentia* < L. *delinquens,* prp. of *delinquere,* to leave undone, commit a fault < *de-,* from + *linquere,* to leave < IE. base *leikw-,* to leave, whence Gr. *leipein,* to leave, OE. *læn,* LOAN] **1.** failure or neglect to do what duty or law requires ☆**2.** an overdue debt, tax, etc. **3.** a fault; misdeed ☆**4.** behavior, esp. by the young, that is antisocial or in violation of the law: see JUVENILE DELINQUENCY

de·lin·quent (-kwənt) *adj.* [L. *delinquens:* see prec.] **1.** failing or neglecting to do what duty or law requires ☆**2.** past the time for payment; overdue [*delinquent* taxes] —*n.* a delinquent person; esp., a juvenile delinquent —de·lin′quent·ly *adv.*

del·i·quesce (del′ə kwes′) *vi.* -quesced′, -quesc′ing [L. *deliquescere* < *de-,* from + *liquescere,* to melt < *liquere,* to be liquid] **1.** to melt away **2.** *Biol. a)* to melt away in the course of growth or decay, as parts of certain fungi *b)* to branch into many fine divisions, as leaf veins **3.** *Chem.* to become liquid by absorbing moisture from the air —del′i·ques′cence *n.* —del′i·ques′cent *adj.*

del·i·ra·tion (del′ə rā′shən) *n.* [L. *deliratio:* see DELIRIUM] [Rare] mental aberration; delirium; madness

de·lir·i·ous (di lir′ē əs) *adj.* [L. *deliriosus:* see ff. & -OUS] **1.** in a state of delirium; raving incoherently **2.** of, characteristic of, or caused by delirium **3.** wildly excited [*delirious* with joy] —de·lir′i·ous·ly *adv.* —de·lir′i·ous·ness *n.*

de·lir·i·um (-ē əm) *n., pl.* **-i·ums, -i·a** (-ə) [L., madness < *delirare,* to rave, lit., to turn the furrow awry in plowing < *de-,* from + *lira,* a line, furrow] **1.** a temporary state of extreme mental excitement, marked by restlessness, confused speech, and hallucinations: it sometimes occurs during a fever, in some forms of insanity, etc. **2.** uncontrollably wild excitement or emotion [a *delirium* of joy] —SYN. see MANIA

delirium tre·mens (trē′mənz) [ModL. (1813), lit., trembling delirium] a violent delirium resulting chiefly from excessive drinking of alcoholic liquor, and characterized by sweating, trembling, anxiety, and frightening hallucinations

del·i·tes·cent (del′ə tes′nt) *adj.* [L. *delitescens,* prp. of *delitescere,* to hide away < *de-,* from + *latescere,* to hide oneself < *latere,* to lurk: see LATENT] [Rare] lying hidden; latent or inactive —del′i·tes′cence *n.*

De·li·us (dē′lē əs, dēl′yəs), Frederick 1862-1934; Eng. composer

de·liv·er (di liv′ər) *vt.* [ME. *deliveren* < OFr. *délivrer* < VL. *deliberare,* to liberate < L. *de-,* from + *liberare,* to set free < *liber,* free] **1.** to set free or save from evil, danger, etc. [*delivered* from bondage] **2.** to assist (a female) at the birth of (offspring) [to *deliver* a woman of twins, to *deliver* a baby] **3.** to give forth, or express, in words; make (a speech, pronouncement, etc.); utter **4.** to give or hand over; transfer **5.** to carry to and leave at the proper place or places; distribute [*deliver* the mail] **6.** to give or send forth; discharge; emit [the oil well *delivered* 20 barrels a day] **7.** to strike (a blow) **8.** to throw or toss [the

pitcher *delivered* a curve] ☆9. [Colloq.] to cause (votes, a political delegation, etc.) to go to the support of a particular candidate or cause —*vi.* 1. to give birth to a child 2. to make deliveries, as of merchandise —*SYN.* see RESCUE —**be delivered of** to give birth to —**deliver oneself of** to express; utter —**de·liv'er·a·ble** *adj.* —**de·liv'er·er** *n.*

de·liv·er·ance (-əns) *n.* [ME. *deliveraunce:* see prec. & -ANCE] 1. a setting free; rescue or release 2. the fact or state of being freed 3. an opinion, judgment, etc. formally or publicly expressed

de·liv·er·y (-ē) *n., pl.* **-er·ies** [ME. *deliveri* < OFr. *delivré,* pp. of *délivrer:* see DELIVER] 1. a giving or handing over; transfer 2. a distributing, as of goods or mail 3. a giving birth; childbirth 4. any giving or sending forth 5. the act or manner of giving a speech, striking a blow, throwing a ball, etc. 6. something delivered or to be delivered, as mail, goods, a pitched ball, etc. 7. [Now Rare] a setting free, or rescuing 8. *Law a)* the irrevocable transfer of a deed or other instrument of conveyance *b)* the transfer of goods or interest in goods from one person to another ☆**de·liv·er·y·man** (-man', -mən) *n., pl.* **-men** (-mən) a man whose work is delivering goods to purchasers

dell (del) *n.* [ME. & OE. *del* < IE. base **dhel-*, cavity, hollow, whence DALE, W. *dol,* valley, Du. *dal,* dale] a small, secluded valley or glen, usually a wooded one

del·la Rob·bia (del'lä rôb'byä; *E.* del'ə rō'bē ə) Florentine family of sculptors & workers in enameled terra cotta; esp., Lu·ca (loo'kä), 1400?–82

☆**dells** (delz) *n.pl. same as* DALLES

Del·mar·va Peninsula (del mär'və) peninsula in the E U.S., between Chesapeake Bay and the Atlantic: it consists of Del. & parts of Md. & Va.: c. 180 mi. long

De·lorme, de l'Orme (də lôrm'), **Phi·li·bert** (fē lē ber') 1510?–70; Fr. Renaissance architect

De·los (dē'läs) small island of the Cyclades in the Aegean: legendary birthplace of Artemis & Apollo

de·louse (dē lous', -louz') *vt.* **-loused', -lous'ing** to rid of lice —**de·lous'er** *n.*

Del·phi (del'fī) ancient city in Phocis, on the slopes of Mount Parnassus See GREECE, map

Del·phic (-fik) *adj.* 1. of Delphi 2. designating or of the oracle of Apollo at Delphi in ancient times 3. obscure in meaning; ambiguous; oracular Also **Del'phi·an** (-fē ən)

del·phi·nine (del'fə nēn', -nin) *n.* [DELPHIN(IUM) + -INE[4]] a poisonous, white, crystalline alkaloid, $C_{34}H_{47}NO_9$, found in the seeds of certain larkspurs

del·phin·i·um (del fin'ē əm) *n.* [ModL. < Gr. *delphinion,* larkspur < Gr. *delphis, delphin,* dolphin: from some resemblance of the nectary to a dolphin] any of a genus (*Delphinium*) of plants of the buttercup family, bearing spikes of spurred, irregular flowers, usually blue, on tall stalks: several species are poisonous

Del·phi·nus (del fī'nəs) [L., lit., dolphin: see prec.] a small N constellation between Pegasus and Aquila

Del·sarte system (del särt') [after François *Delsarte* (1811–71), Fr. teacher of singing & dramatics] a system of calisthenics combined with singing, declamation, and dancing to develop bodily grace and poise

del·ta (del'tə) *n.* [L. < Gr. *delta,* of Sem. orig., as in Heb. *dāleth,* 4th letter of the alphabet, lit., door] 1. the fourth letter of the Greek alphabet (Δ, δ) 2. something in the shape of a delta (Δ); specif., a deposit of sand and soil, usually triangular, formed at the mouth of some rivers, as of the Nile —*adj. Chem.* see ALPHA —**del·ta·ic** (del tā'ik) *adj.*

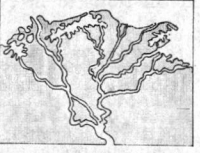

DELTA

delta ray any particles ejected by primary ionizing particles passing through matter

delta wing the triangular structure of certain jet aircraft —**del'ta-wing', del'ta-winged'** *adj.*

del·toid (del'toid) *adj.* [Gr. *deltoeidēs* < *delta* (Δ) + *eidos,* form] 1. shaped like a delta; triangular 2. designating or of a large, triangular muscle of the shoulder, which raises the arm away from the side —*n.* the deltoid muscle

de·lude (di lood') *vt.* **-lud'ed, -lud'ing** [ME. *deluden* < L. *deludere* < *de-*, from + *ludere,* to play, sport] 1. to fool, as by false promises, wrong notions, etc.; mislead; deceive; trick 2. [Obs.] to elude or frustrate —*SYN.* see DECEIVE

del·uge (del'yōoj) *n.* [ME. < OFr. < L. *diluvium < diluere,* to wash away < *dis-*, off, from + *lavere,* to wash: see LATHER] 1. a great flood 2. a heavy rainfall 3. an overwhelming, floodlike rush of anything [a *deluge* of visitors] —*vt.* **-uged, -ug·ing** 1. to flood; inundate 2. to overwhelm as with a flood —**the Deluge** *Bible* the great flood in Noah's time: Gen. 7

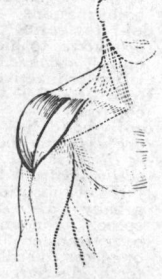

DELTOID MUSCLE

de·lu·sion (di loo'zhən) *n.* [ME. *delusioun* < LL. *delusio* < *delusus,* pp. of *deludere*] 1. a deluding or being deluded

2. a false belief or opinion 3. *Psychiatry* a false, persistent belief not substantiated by sensory or objective evidence —**de·lu'sion·al** *adj.*

SYN.—**delusion** implies belief in something that is contrary to fact or reality, resulting from deception, a misconception, or a mental disorder [to have *delusions* of grandeur]; **illusion** suggests the false perception or interpretation of something that has objective existence [perspective in drawing gives the *illusion* of depth]; **hallucination** implies the apparent perception, in a nervous or mental disorder, of something external that is actually not present; **mirage** refers to an optical illusion caused by atmospheric conditions, and, in figurative use, implies an unrealizable hope or aspiration

de·lu·sive (di loo'siv) *adj.* [L. *delusus* (see prec.) + -IVE] 1. tending to delude; misleading 2. of or like a delusion; unreal Also **de·lu'so·ry** (-loo'sə rē) —**de·lu'sive·ly** *adv.* —**de·lu'sive·ness** *n.*

de·luxe (di luks', -looks, -looks') *adj.* [Fr., lit., of luxury] of extra fine quality; luxurious; sumptuous; elegant —*adv.* in a deluxe manner

delve (delv) *vi.* **delved, delv'ing** [ME. *delven* < OE. *delfan,* to dig, akin to OHG. *telban,* Du. *delven* < IE. base **dhelbh-*, to dig out, whence Czech *dlubu,* to hollow out] 1. [Archaic or Brit. Dial.] to dig with a spade 2. to investigate for information; search (*into* books, the past, etc.) —*vt.* [Archaic or Brit. Dial.] to dig or turn up (ground) —*n.* [Obs.] a den or pit dug out —**delv'er** *n.*

Dem. 1. Democrat 2. Democratic

de·mag·net·ize (dē mag'nə tīz') *vt.* **-ized', -iz'ing** to deprive of magnetism or magnetic properties —**de·mag'net·i·za'tion** *n.* —**de·mag'net·iz'er** *n.*

dem·a·gog·ic (dem'ə gäj'ik, -gäg'-, -gō'jik) *adj.* [Gr. *dēmagōgikos:* see DEMAGOGUE] of, like, or characteristic of a demagogue or demagogy —**dem'a·gog'i·cal** *adj.* —**dem'·a·gog'i·cal·ly** *adv.*

dem·a·gog·ism, dem·a·gogu·ism (dem'ə gäg'iz'm, -gôg'-) *n.* the methods or practices of a demagogue

dem·a·gogue, dem·a·gog (dem'ə gäg', -gôg') *n.* [< Gr. *dēmagōgos,* leader of the people < *dēmos,* the people + *agōgos,* leader < *agein,* to lead] 1. orig., a leader of the common people 2. a person who tries to stir up the people by appeals to emotion, prejudice, etc. in order to win them over quickly and so gain power —*vi.* **-gogued'** or **-goged',** **-gogu'ing** or **-gog'ing** to behave as a demagogue

dem·a·gog·y (dem'ə gō'jē, -gäg'ē, -gôg'ē) *n.* [Gr. *dēmagōgia,* control of the people] the methods or practices of a demagogue: also ☆**dem'a·gog'uer·y** (-gäg'ər ē, -gôg'-) *n.*

de·mand (di mand', -mänd') *vt.* [ME. *demaunden* < OFr. *demander,* to demand < L. *demandare,* to give in charge < *de-*, away, from + *mandare,* to entrust: see MANDATE] 1. to ask for boldly or urgently 2. to ask for as a right or with authority 3. to order to appear; summon 4. to ask to know or be informed of 5. to call for as necessary; require; need [the work *demands* patience] 6. *Law* to ask relief in court for (what is due one) —*vi.* to make a demand —*n.* 1. the act of demanding 2. a thing demanded 3. a strong or authoritative request 4. an urgent requirement or claim 5. [Obs.] a question; query 6. *Econ.* the desire for a commodity together with ability to pay for it; also, the amount people are ready and able to buy at a certain price: opposed to SUPPLY 7. *Law* a peremptory claim which presupposes no doubt of the claimant's rights —**in demand** wanted or sought —**on demand** when presented for payment

SYN.—**demand** implies a calling for as owing or necessary, connoting a peremptory exercise of authority or an imperative need [to *demand* obedience]; **claim** implies a demanding of something as allegedly belonging to one [to *claim* a throne]; **require** suggests a pressing need, often one inherent in the nature of a thing, or the binding power of rules or laws [aliens are *required* to register]; **exact** implies a demanding and the enforcing of the demand at the same time [an *exacting* foreman]

de·mand·ant (-ənt) *n. Law same as* PLAINTIFF

demand bill a bill payable on demand

demand deposit *Banking* a deposit that may be withdrawn on demand, without advance notice

de·mand·ing (-iŋ) *adj.* making difficult or irksome demands on one's resources, patience, energy, etc. —**de·mand'ing·ly** *adv.*

demand loan *same as* CALL LOAN

demand note a promissory note payable on demand

de·man·toid (di man'toid) *n.* [G. < *demant,* diamond (< MHG. *diemant* < OHG. *diamant,* DIAMOND) + *-oid,* -OID] a transparent green variety of andradite, used as a semiprecious gem

de·mar·cate (di mär'kāt, dē'mär kāt') *vt.* **-cat·ed, -cat·ing** [< ff.] 1. to set or mark the limits of; delimit 2. to mark the differences between; distinguish; separate Also **de·mark'**

de·mar·ca·tion, de·mar·ka·tion (dē'mär kā'shən) *n.* [Sp. *demarcación* (in *linea de demarcación,* 1493) < *de-* (L. *de*), from + *marcar,* to mark boundaries < Gmc. *marka,* a boundary, MARK[1]] 1. the act of setting and marking limits or boundaries 2. a limit or boundary 3. a separation or distinction

dé·marche (dā märsh') *n.* [Fr. < *démarcher* < OFr. *demarchier,* orig., to trample under foot: see DE- & MARCH[1]] a line of action; move or countermove; maneuver, esp. in diplomatic settings

de·ma·te·ri·al·ize (dē'mə tir'ē ə līz') *vi., vt.* **-ized', -iz'ing** to lose or cause to lose material form

Dem·a·vend (dem′ə vend′), **Mount** highest peak of the Elburz Mountains, N Iran: 18,934 ft.

deme (dēm) *n*. [Gr. *dēmos*, deme, people, district: see DEMOCRACY] 1. any of the hundred townships into which ancient Attica was divided 2. *Biol.* a particular interbreeding population within a species, having clearly definable characters, etc.

de·mean[1] (di mēn′) *vt*. [DE- + MEAN², after DEBASE] to lower in status or character; degrade; humble [to *demean* oneself by taking a bribe]

de·mean[2] (di mēn′) *vt*. [see ff.] to behave, conduct, or comport (oneself) —*SYN*. see BEHAVE

de·mean·or (-ər) *n*. [ME. *demenure* < *demenen*, to rule, govern oneself, behave < OFr. *demener*, to lead < *de-* (L. *de*), from + *mener*, to lead < LL. *minare*, to drive, conduct < L. *minari*, to threaten] outward behavior; conduct; deportment —*SYN*. see BEARING

de·mean·our (-ər) *n*. *Brit. sp.* of DEMEANOR

de·ment (di ment′) *vt*. [< L. *dementare* < *demens* (gen. *dementis*), mad, out of one's mind < *de-*, out from + *mens*, MIND] [Rare] to make insane

de·ment·ed (-id) *adj*. [pp. of prec.] mentally deranged; insane; mad —*de·ment′ed·ly adv*.

de·men·tia (di men′shə) *n*. [L., insanity < *demens*: see DEMENT] 1. orig. insanity; madness 2. *Psychiatry* loss or impairment of mental powers due to organic causes: distinguished from AMENTIA —*SYN*. see INSANITY

dementia prae·cox (prē′käks, prā′-) [ModL.: see PRECOCIOUS & DEMENTIA] *obs. term for* SCHIZOPHRENIA

de·mer·it (di mer′it) *n*. [ME. & OFr. *demerite* < ML. *demeritum*, fault < pp. of *demerere*, to forfeit, not merit, with meaning altered (*de-* taken in negative sense) < L. *demerere*, to merit < *de-*, intens. + *merere*, to deserve] 1. a quality deserving blame, fault; defect 2. lack of merit ☆3. a mark recorded against a student, trainee, etc. for poor conduct or work

☆**Dem·e·rol** (dem′ə rōl′, -rôl′) *a trademark for* MEPERIDENE

de·mer·sal (di mur′s'l) *adj*. [< L. *demersus*, pp. of *demergere*, to submerge < *de-*, down, DE- + *mergere*, to immerse (see MERGE) + AL] found on or near the bottom of a sea, lake, etc.

de·mesne (di mān′, -mēn′) *n*. [ME. & OFr. *demeine* < L. *dominium* (see DOMAIN); sp. altered after OFr. *mesnee*, household < L. *mansio* (see MANSION)] 1. *Law* possession (of real estate) in one's own right 2. formerly, the land or estate belonging to a lord and not rented or let but kept in his hands 3. the land around a mansion; lands of an estate 4. a region or domain: also used figuratively

De·me·ter (di mēt′ər) [Gr. *Dēmētēr* < Doric Gr. *Damatēr*] *Gr. Myth.* the goddess of agriculture and fertility: identified with the Roman goddess Ceres

dem·i- (dem′ē, -i) [ME. & OFr. < *demi*, half < L. *dimidius*, half, back-formation < *dimidiatus*, halved, ult. < *dis-*, apart + *medius*, middle] *a prefix meaning*: 1. half [*demisemiquaver, demivolt*] 2. less than usual in size, power, etc. [*demigod, demitasse*]

dem·i·god (dem′ē gäd′) *n*. 1. *Myth. a*) a lesser god; minor deity *b*) the offspring of a human being and a god or goddess 2. a godlike person

dem·i·john (-jän′) *n*. [Fr. *dame-jeanne*, demijohn, lit. Dame Jeanne: prob. orig. a fanciful name for the bottle] a large bottle of glass or earthenware, with a narrow neck and a wicker casing and handle

de·mil·i·ta·rize (dē mil′ə tə rīz′) *vt*. **-rized′, -riz′ing** 1. to free from organized military control 2. to take away the military power or character of —*de·mil′i·ta·ri·za′tion n*.

De Mille (də mil′) 1. **Agnes (George)**, 1905?– ; U.S. dancer & choreographer: niece of *ff*. 2. **Cecil B(lount)**, 1881–1959; U.S. motion-picture producer

dem·i·mon·daine (dem′ē män dān′) *n*. [Fr.] a woman of the demimonde

dem·i·monde (dem′ē mänd′, dem′ē mänd′) *n*. [Fr. < *demi-* (see DEMI-) + *monde*, world, society < L. *mundus*, world] 1. the class of women who have lost social standing because of sexual promiscuity 2. a demimondaine 3. prostitutes as a group 4. any group whose activities are ethically questionable

dem·i·re·lief (dem′ē ri lēf′) *n*. [DEMI- + RELIEF, sense 6] *same as* MEZZO-RELIEVO

dem·i·rep (dem′ē rep′) *n*. [DEMI- + REP(UTATION)] a woman of poor reputation, suspected of sexual promiscuity

de·mise (di mīz′) *n*. [Fr. *démise*, fem. pp. of *démettre*, to dismiss, put away < L. *demittere*: see DEMIT] 1. *Law* a transfer of an estate by lease, esp. for a fixed period 2. the transfer of sovereignty by death or abdication 3. a ceasing to exist; death —*vt*. **-mised′, -mis′ing** 1. to grant or transfer (an estate) by lease, esp. for a fixed period 2. to transfer (sovereignty) by death or abdication

dem·i·sem·i·qua·ver (dem′ē sem′ē kwä′vər) *n*. [Chiefly Brit.] *Music* a thirty-second note

de·mis·sion (di mish′ən) *n*. [Fr. *démission* < L. *demissio*, a letting down < *demissus*, pp. of *demittere*] a demitting; resignation or abdication (of an office)

de·mit (di mit′) *vt*. **-mit′ted, -mit′ting** [L. *demittere*, to send down, let fall < *de-*, down + *mittere*, to send: see

MISSION] 1. to resign (a position or office) 2. [Archaic] to dismiss —*vi*. to resign

dem·i·tasse (dem′ē tas′, -täs′) *n*. [Fr. < *demi* (see DEMI-) + *tasse*, a cup: see TASS] a small cup of or for black coffee served following dinner

dem·i·urge (dem′ē urj′) *n*. [Gr. *dēmiourgos*, one who works for the people, skilled workman, creator < *dēmios*, belonging to the people (< *dēmos*, the people) + *-ergos*, worker (see ERG)] 1. [*often* D-] *a*) in Plato's philosophy, the deity as creator of the material world *b*) in Gnostic philosophy, a deity subordinate to the supreme deity, sometimes considered the creator of evil 2. *Gr. History* a magistrate in certain states 3. a ruling force or creative power —*dem′i·ur′gic* (-ur′jik), **dem′i·ur′gi·cal** *adj*. —**dem′i·ur′gi·cal·ly** *adv*.

dem·i·volt (dem′ē vōlt′) *n*. [Fr. *demi-volte* < *demi-* (see DEMI-) + *volte*, a leap] in horseback riding, a half turn with the forelegs of the horse raised

de·mob (dē mäb′) *vt*. **-mobbed′, -mob′bing** [Brit. Colloq.] to demobilize —*n*. [Brit. Colloq.] demobilization

de·mo·bi·lize (dē mō′bə līz′) *vt*. **-lized, -liz′ing** 1. to disband (troops) 2. to discharge (a person) from the armed forces —*de·mo′bi·li·za′tion n*.

de·moc·ra·cy (di mäk′rə sē) *n., pl.* **-cies** [Fr. *démocratie* < ML. *democratia* < Gr. *dēmokratia* < *dēmos*, the people (< IE. *damos*, a division of the people < base *da-*, to cut, divide: cf. TIDE¹) + *kratein*, to rule] 1. government in which the people hold the ruling power either directly or through elected representatives; rule by the ruled 2. a country, state, etc. with such government 3. majority rule 4. the principle of equality of rights, opportunity, and treatment, or the practice of this principle 5. the common people, esp. as the wielders of political power ☆6. [D-] [Now Rare] the principles of the Democratic Party of the U.S.

dem·o·crat (dem′ə krat′) *n*. [Fr. *démocrate* < *démocratie*: see prec.] 1. a person who believes in and upholds government by the people; advocate of rule by the majority 2. a person who believes in and practices the principle of equality of rights, opportunity, and treatment ☆3. [D-] a member of the Democratic Party

dem·o·crat·ic (dem′ə krat′ik) *adj*. [Fr. *démocratique* < ML. *democraticus* < Gr. *dēmokratikos*] 1. of, belonging to, or upholding democracy or a democracy 2. of, for, or popular with all or most people [a *democratic* art form] 3. treating persons of all classes in the same way; not snobbish ☆4. [D-] of, belonging to, or characteristic of the Democratic Party —**dem′o·crat′i·cal·ly** *adv*.

☆**Democratic Party** one of the two major political parties in the U.S.: it descended from the Democratic-Republican Party (c. 1830), developed from the Republican Party led by Thomas Jefferson

de·moc·ra·tism (di mäk′rə tiz'm) *n*. the principles of democracy —*de·moc′ra·tist adj., n*.

de·moc·ra·tize (-tīz′) *vt., vi*. **-tized′, -tiz′ing** [Fr. *démocratiser* < ML. *democratizare* < Gr. *dēmokratizein*] to make or become democratic —*de·moc′ra·ti·za′tion n*.

De·moc·ri·tus (di mäk′rə təs) 460?–370? B.C.; Gr. philosopher; exponent of atomism

‡**dé·mo·dé** (dā mô dā′) *adj*. [Fr.] out-of-date; old-fashioned

de·mod·u·late (dē mäj′oo lāt′) *vt*. **-lat′ed, -lat′ing** to cause to undergo demodulation

de·mod·u·la·tion (dē mäj′oo lā′shən) *n*. *Radio* the process of recovering at the receiver a signal that has been modulated on a carrier wave; detection

de·mod·u·la·tor (dē mäj′oo lāt′ər) *n*. *Radio* a device used in demodulation

De·mo·gor·gon (dē′mə gôr′gən) [LL.: prob. of oriental origin, but infl. by L. *daemon* (see DAEMON) + *Gorgo* (see GORGON)] a terrifying and mysterious god or demon of the underworld in ancient mythology

de·mog·ra·phy (di mäg′rə fē) *n*. [< Gr. *dēmos*, the people + -GRAPHY] the statistical science dealing with the distribution, density, vital statistics, etc. of populations —*de·mog′ra·pher n*. —**de·mo·graph·ic** (dē′mə graf′ik, dem′ə-) *adj*. —**de′mo·graph′i·cal·ly** *adv*.

dem·oi·selle (dem′wə zel′) *n*. [Fr. < OFr. *dameisele*] 1. a damsel 2. a small crane (*Anthropoides virgo*) of Africa, Asia, and Europe 3. *same as* DAMSELFLY ☆4. any of a family (Pomacentridae) of rough-scaled, brightly colored tropical reef fishes

de·mol·ish (di mäl′ish) *vt*. [< extended stem of Fr. *démolir* < L. *demoliri*, to pull down, destroy < *de-*, down + *moliri*, to build, construct < *moles*, a mass] 1. to pull down, tear down, or smash to pieces (a building, etc.) 2. to destroy; ruin; bring to naught —*SYN*. see DESTROY —*de·mol′ish·er n*. —*de·mol′ish·ment n*.

dem·o·li·tion (dem′ə lish′ən, dē′mə-) *n*. [Fr. *démolition* < L. *demolitio*] a demolishing or being demolished; often, specif., destruction by explosives

de·mon (dē′mən) *n*. [ME. < L.: see DAEMON] 1. *same as* DAEMON 2. a devil; evil spirit 3. a person or thing regarded as evil, cruel, etc. [the *demon* of jealousy] 4. a person who has great energy or skill [a *demon* at golf] —*de·mon·ic* (di män′ik) *adj*. —*de·mon′i·cal·ly adv*.

de·mon·e·tize (dē män′ə tīz′) *vt.* **-tized′, -tiz′ing 1.** to deprive (currency) of its standard value **2.** to stop using (silver or gold) as a monetary standard —**de·mon′e·ti·za′·tion** *n.*

de·mo·ni·ac (di mō′nē ak′) *adj.* [ME. *demoniak* < LL. (Ec.) *daemoniacus* < Gr. *daimoniakos*] **1.** possessed or influenced by a demon **2.** of a demon or demons **3.** like or characteristic of a demon; fiendish; frenzied Also **de·mo·ni·a·cal** (dē′mə nī′ə k'l) —*n.* a person supposedly possessed by a demon —**de′mo·ni′a·cal·ly** *adv.*

de·mon·ism (dē′mən iz'm) *n.* **1.** belief in the existence and powers of demons **2.** *same as* DEMONOLATRY —**de′mon·ist** *n.*

de·mon·ize (-īz′) *vt.* **-ized′, -iz′ing 1.** to make into a demon **2.** to bring under the influence of demons

de·mon·o- (dē′mən ō) [Gr. *daimono-* < *daimōn*: see DAEMON] *a combining form meaning* demon [*demonology*]: also, before a vowel, **demon-**

de·mon·ol·a·try (dē′mə näl′ə trē) *n.* [DEMONO- + -LATRY] the worship of demons —**de′mon·ol′a·ter** *n.*

de·mon·ol·o·gy (-jē) *n.* the study of demons or of beliefs about them —**de′mon·ol′o·gist** *n.*

de·mon·stra·ble (di män′strə b'l, dem′ən-) *adj.* [ME. & OFr. < L. *demonstrabilis*] that can be demonstrated, or proved —**de·mon′stra·bil′i·ty, de·mon′stra·ble·ness** *n.* —**de·mon′stra·bly** *adv.*

dem·on·strate (dem′ən strāt′) *vt.* **-strat′ed, -strat′ing** [< L. *demonstratus*, pp. of *demonstrare*, to point out, show < *de-*, out, from + *monstrare*, to show] **1.** to show by reasoning; prove **2.** to explain or make clear by using examples, experiments, etc. **3.** to show the operation or working of; specif., to show (a product) in use in an effort to sell it **4.** to show (feelings) plainly —*vi.* **1.** to show one's feelings or views by taking part in a public meeting, parade, etc. **2.** to show military power or preparedness

dem·on·stra·tion (dem′ən strā′shən) *n.* [ME. *demonstracion* < L. *demonstratio* < *demonstrare*: see prec.] **1.** the act, process, or means of making evident or proving **2.** an explanation by example, experiment, etc. **3.** a practical showing of how something works or is used; specif., such a showing of a product in an effort to sell it **4.** a display or outward show [a *demonstration* of grief] **5.** a public show of feeling or opinion, as by a mass meeting or parade **6.** a show of military force or preparedness **7.** a logical proof in which certain results follow from certain premises

de·mon·stra·tive (di män′strə tiv) *adj.* [ME. & OFr. *demonstratif* < L. *demonstrativus*: see DEMONSTRATE] **1.** that demonstrates or shows; illustrative **2.** giving convincing evidence or conclusive proof (usually with *of*) **3.** having to do with demonstration **4.** showing feelings openly and frankly **5.** *Gram.* pointing out [''this'' is a *demonstrative* pronoun] —*n. Gram.* a demonstrative pronoun or adjective —**de·mon′stra·tive·ly** *adv.* —**de·mon′stra·tive·ness** *n.*

dem·on·stra·tor (dem′ən strāt′ər) *n.* [L.] **1.** one that demonstrates; specif., *a)* a person who takes part in a public demonstration ☆*b)* a person who demonstrates a product ☆**2.** a product, as an automobile, used in demonstrations

☆**de·mor·al·ize** (di môr′ə līz′, -mär′-) *vt.* **-ized′, -iz′ing** [coined by Noah Webster < DE- + MORALIZE] **1.** [Now Rare] to corrupt the morals of; deprave **2.** to lower the morale of; weaken the spirit, courage, discipline, or staying power of **3.** to throw into confusion —**de·mor′al·i·za′·tion** *n.* —**de·mor′al·iz′er** *n.*

‡**de mor·tu·is nil ni·si bo·num** (dē môr′choo̅ wis nil ni′si bō′nəm) [L.] of the dead (say) nothing but good

de·mos (dē′mäs) *n.* [Gr. *dēmos*: see DEMOCRACY] **1.** the people or commonalty of an ancient Greek state **2.** the common people; the people; the masses

De·mos·the·nes (di mäs′thə nēz′) 384?–322 B.C.; Athenian orator & statesman

☆**de·mote** (di mōt′) *vt.* **-mot′ed, -mot′ing** [DE- + (PRO)MOTE] to reduce to a lower grade; lower in rank: opposed to PROMOTE —**de·mo′tion** *n.*

de·mot·ic (di mät′ik) *adj.* [ML. *demoticus* < Gr. *dēmotikos* < *dēmotes*, one of the people < *dēmos*: see DEMOCRACY] **1.** of the people; popular; specif., vernacular (sense 2) **2.** designating or of a simplified system of ancient Egyptian writing: distinguished from HIERATIC —*n.* [D-] *same as* ROMAIC

de·mount (dē mount′) *vt.* to remove from a mounting [to *demount* a motor] —**de·mount′a·ble** *adj.*

Demp·sey (demp′sē), **Jack** (born *William Harrison Dempsey*) 1895– ; U.S. prize fighter

de·mul·cent (di mul′s'nt) *adj.* [L. *demulcens*, prp. of *demulcere*, to stroke down, soften < *de-*, down + *mulcere*, to stroke] soothing —*n.* a medicine or ointment that soothes irritated or inflamed mucous membrane

de·mur (di mur′) *vi.* **-murred′, -mur′ring** [ME. *demuren* < OFr. *demorer* < L. *demorari*, to delay < *de-*, from + *morari*, to delay < *mora*, a delay < IE. base *(s)mer-*, to remember, whence MEMORY] **1.** to hesitate because of one's doubts or objections; have scruples; object **2.** *Law* to enter a demurrer —*n.* **1.** an act or instance of demurring **2.** an objection raised or exception taken Also **de·mur′ral** *n.* —*SYN.* see OBJECT

de·mure (di myoor′) *adj.* [ME. *demur* < *de-* (prob. intens.) + *mur* < OFr. *mëur*, ripe, mature < L. *maturus*, MATURE]

1. decorous; modest; reserved **2.** affectedly modest or shy; coy —*SYN.* see SHY¹ —**de·mure′ly** *adv.* —**de·mure′ness** *n.*

de·mur·rage (di mur′ij) *n.* [OFr. *demorage*, a delay < *demorer*: see DEMUR] **1.** the delaying of a ship, freight car, etc., as by the freighter's failure to load, unload, or sail within the time allowed **2.** the compensation paid for this as damages

de·mur·rer (-ər) *n.* [OFr. *demorer*, to DEMUR: inf. used as *n.*] **1.** a plea for the dismissal of a pleading on the grounds that even if the statements of the opposing party are true, they do not sustain the claim because they are insufficient or otherwise legally defective **2.** an objection; demur **3.** a person who demurs

de·my (di mī′) *n., pl.* **-mies** [ME.: see DEMI-] any of several sizes of writing and printing paper, averaging from 15 1/2 by 20 to 18 by 23 inches

de·my·e·lin·ate (dē mī′ə li nāt′) *vt.* **-at′ed, -at′ing** to destroy or damage the myelin sheath of (nerves) —**de·my′·e·li·na′tion** *n.*

☆**de·my·thol·o·gize** (dē′mi thäl′ə jīz′) *vt.* **-gized′, -giz′ing** *Theol.* to discount mythological elements in (the Bible, a Christian doctrine, etc.) in order to facilitate understanding and acceptance

den (den) *n.* [ME. < OE. *denn*, lair, pasture, akin to G. dial. *denn*, place where grass is trodden down, lair < IE. base *dhen-*, flattened place] **1.** the cave or other lair of a wild animal **2.** a retreat or headquarters, as of thieves; haunt **3.** a small, squalid room **4.** a small, cozy room where one can be alone to read, work, etc. —*vi.* denned, den′ning to live or hide in or as in a den

Den. Denmark

de·nar·i·us (di nar′ē əs, -ner′-) *n., pl.* **-nar′i·i** (-ē ī′) [ME. < L., orig., adj., containing ten < *deni*, by tens < *decem*, TEN] **1.** an ancient Roman silver coin, the penny of the New Testament: the initial letter is now the symbol (*d*) for British pence **2.** an ancient Roman gold coin, worth 25 silver denarii

den·a·ry (den′ər ē, dē′nər ē) *adj.* [see prec.] having to do with the number ten; tenfold; decimal

de·na·tion·al·ize (dē nash′ə n'l iz′) *vt.* **-ized′, -iz′ing** [Fr. *dénationaliser*: see DE- & NATIONALIZE] **1.** to deprive of national rights or status **2.** to place (an industry owned or controlled by the government) under private ownership —**de·na′tion·al·i·za′tion** *n.*

de·nat·u·ral·ize (dē nach′ər ə liz′) *vt.* **1.** to make unnatural **2.** to take citizenship away from —**de·nat′u·ral·i·za′tion** *n.*

de·na·ture (dē nā′chər) *vt.* **-tured, -tur·ing** [ML. *denaturare*: see DE- & NATURE] **1.** to change the nature of; take natural qualities away from **2.** to make (alcohol, etc.) unfit for human consumption without spoiling for other uses **3.** to change the structure of (a protein) by heat, acids, alkalis, etc., so that the original properties are greatly changed or eliminated **4.** to add a nonfissionable isotope to (a fissionable isotope) so that the mixture cannot be used in nuclear bombs but can still be used as fuel material —**de·na′tur·ant** *n.* —**de·na′tur·a′tion** *n.*

de·na·zi·fy (dē nät′sə fī′) *vt.* **-fied′, -fy′ing** to rid of Nazi elements or influences —**de·na′zi·fi·ca′tion** *n.*

Den·bigh·shire (den′bi shir) county of N Wales, on the Irish Sea: 669 sq. mi.; pop. 175,000: also **Den′bigh**

den·dri- (den′drə, -dri) *same as* DENDRO-

den·dri·form (-fôrm′) *adj.* shaped like a tree

den·drite (den′drīt) *n.* [< Gr. *dendritēs*, of a tree < *dendron*, a tree: see DENDRO-] **1.** a branching, treelike mark made by one mineral crystallizing in another **2.** a stone or mineral with such a mark **3.** the branched part of a nerve cell that carries impulses toward the cell body **4.** [*pl.*] the protoplasmic filaments of a nerve cell body —**den·drit·ic** (den drit′ik), **den·drit′i·cal** *adj.* —**den·drit′i·cal·ly** *adv.*

den·dro- (den′drō, -drə) [< Gr. *dendron*, earlier *dendreon*, a tree, a reduplicated form < IE. base *drewo-*, TREE] *a combining form meaning* tree [*dendrology*]: also, before a vowel, **dendr-**

☆**den·dro·chron·ol·o·gy** (-krə näl′ə jē) *n.* the science of dating past events or climatic changes by a comparative study of growth rings in tree trunks —**den′dro·chron′o·log′i·cal** (-krän′ə läj′i k'l) *adj.*

den·droid (den′droid) *adj.* [Gr. *dendroeidēs*: see DENDRO- & -OID] treelike in form

den·drol·o·gy (den dräl′ə jē) *n.* [DENDRO- + -LOGY] the scientific study of trees —**den′dro·log′ic** (-drə läj′ik), **den′dro·log′i·cal** *adj.* —**den·drol′o·gist** *n.*

-den·dron (den′drən) [< Gr. *dendron*, a tree: see DENDRO-] *a combining form meaning* tree or treelike structure [*rhododendron*]

dene (dēn) *n.* [akin to DUNE] [Brit.] a low dune or sandy tract near a seashore

Den·eb (den′eb) [Ar. *dhanab*, short for *dhanab aldajāja*, tail of the hen] a first-magnitude star in the constellation Cygnus (Swan)

den·e·ga·tion (den′i gā′shən) *n.* [Fr. *dénégation* < VL. *denegatio* < L. *denegare*: see DENY] a denying or statement of denial

☆**den·gue** (den′gē, -gā) *n.* [WInd. Sp. < Swahili *dinga*, cramplike attack, confused with Sp. *dengue*, affected contortion] an infectious tropical disease transmitted by mosquitoes and characterized by severe pains in the joints and back, fever, and rash

Den Hel·der (dən hel'dər) seaport in NW Netherlands, on the North Sea: pop. 54,000

de·ni·a·ble (di nī'ə b'l) *adj.* that can be denied

de·ni·al (di nī'əl) *n.* 1. the act of denying; a saying "no" (to a request, etc.) 2. a statement in opposition to another; contradiction *[the denial of a rumor]* 3. the act of disowning; repudiation *[the denial of one's family]* 4. a refusal to believe or accept (a doctrine, etc.) 5. *same as* SELF-DENIAL 6. *Law* the opposing by a defendant of a claim or charge against him

de·nic·o·tin·ize (dē nik'ə ti nīz') *vt.* -ized', -iz'ing [DE- + NICOTIN(E) + -IZE] to remove nicotine from (tobacco) —de·nic'o·tin'i·za'tion *n.*

de·nier[1] (də nir'; *for 2,* den'yər) *n.* [ME. *dener* < OFr. (Fr. *denier*) < L. *denarius,* DENARIUS] 1. a small, obsolete French coin of little value 2. a unit of weight for measuring the fineness of threads of silk, rayon, nylon, etc., equal to .05 gram per 450 meters

de·ni·er[2] (di nī'ər) *n.* a person who denies

den·i·grate (den'ə grāt') *vt.* -grat'ed, -grat'ing [< L. *denigratus,* pp. of *denigrare,* to blacken < *de-,* intens. + *nigrare,* to blacken < *niger,* black] 1. to blacken 2. to disparage the character or reputation of; defame —den'i·gra'tion *n.* —den'i·gra'tor *n.* —den'i·gra·to'ry (-grə tôr'ē) *adj.*

den·im (den'əm) *n.* [< Fr. (serge) *de Nîmes,* (serge) of NÎMES, where first made] a coarse, twilled, sturdy cotton cloth used for overalls, uniforms, etc.

Den·is (den'is) [Fr. < L. *Dionysius*] 1. a masculine name 2. Saint, 3d cent. A.D.; patron saint of France: his day is Oct. 9

de·ni·trate (dē nī'trāt) *vt.* -trat·ed, -trat·ing to remove nitric acid, the nitrate radical, the nitro group, or nitrogen oxide from —de'ni·tra'tion *n.*

de·ni·tri·fy (-trə fī') *vt.* -fied', -fy'ing 1. to remove nitrogen or its compounds from 2. to reduce (nitro groups, nitrates, or nitrites) to compounds of lower oxidation —de·ni'tri·fi·ca'tion *n.*

den·i·zen (den'i zən) *n.* [ME. *denisein* < Anglo-Fr. *deinzein* < OFr. *denzein,* native inhabitant < *denz,* within < VL. *deintus* < L. *de intus,* from within] 1. *a)* an inhabitant or occupant *b)* a frequenter of a particular place 2. [Brit.] an alien granted specified rights of citizenship 3. an animal, plant, foreign word, etc. that has become naturalized —*vt.* [Brit.] to naturalize

Den·mark (den'märk) country in Europe, occupying most of the peninsula of Jutland and several nearby islands in the North and Baltic seas: 16,615 sq. mi.; pop. 4,758,000; cap. Copenhagen: Dan. name, DANMARK

Denmark Strait strait between SE Greenland & Iceland: c. 180 mi. wide

☆**den mother** a woman who supervises meetings of a small group (**den**) of Cub Scouts

Den·nis (den'is) a masculine name: *var. of* DENIS

de·nom·i·nate (di näm'ə nāt'; *for adj., usually* -nit) *vt.* -nat'ed, -nat'ing [< L. *denominatus,* pp. of *denominare,* to name < *de-,* intens. + *nominare:* see NOMINATE] to give a specified name to; call —*adj.* designating a number that represents a unit of measure *[3 lb. and 15 ft. are denominate numbers]*

de·nom·i·na·tion (di näm'ə nā'shən) *n.* [ME. *denominacioun* < OFr. < L. *denominatio:* see prec.] 1. the act of denominating 2. a name; esp., the name of a class of things 3. a class or kind (esp. of units in a system) having a specific name or value *[coins of different denominations]* 4. a particular religious sect or body, with a specific name, organization, etc.

de·nom·i·na·tion·al (-'l) *adj.* of, sponsored by, or under the control of, a religious denomination; sectarian —de·nom'i·na'tion·al·ly *adv.*

de·nom·i·na·tion·al·ism (-'l iz'm) *n.* 1. denominational principles 2. a denominational system 3. acceptance or support of such principles or system 4. division into denominations

de·nom·i·na·tive (di näm'ə nə tiv, -nāt'iv) *adj.* [LL. *denominativus*] 1. denominating; naming 2. *Gram.* formed from a noun or adjective stem *[to eye is a denominative verb]* —*n.* a denominative word, esp. a verb

de·nom·i·na·tor (-nāt'ər) *n.* [ML.] 1. [Now Rare] a person or thing that denominates 2. a shared characteristic 3. the usual level; standard 4. *Math.* the term below or to the right of the line in a fraction; the term that divides the numerator *[7 is the denominator of 6/7]*

de·no·ta·tion (dē'nō tā'shən) *n.* [LL. *denotatio*] 1. the act of denoting 2. the direct, explicit meaning or reference of a word or term: cf. CONNOTATION 3. an indication or sign 4. [Rare] a distinguishing name; designation 5. *Logic* all the individuals or objects to which a given term applies

de·no·ta·tive (dē'nō tāt'iv, di nōt'ə tiv) *adj.* 1. denoting; indicative 2. of denotation —de'no·ta'tive·ly *adv.*

de·note (di nōt') *vt.* -not'ed, -not'ing [Fr. *dénoter* < L. *denotare,* to mark out, denote < *de-,* down + *notare,* to mark < *nota,* NOTE] 1. to be a sign of; indicate *[dark clouds denote rain]* 2. to signify or refer to explicitly; stand for; mean: said of words, signs, or symbols, and distinguished from CONNOTE 3. *Logic* to be the name for (individuals of a class) —de·not'a·ble *adj.*

de·noue·ment, dé·noue·ment (dā nōō'män; Fr. dā nōō män') *n.* [Fr. < *dénouer,* to untie < *dé-* (L. *dis-*), from, out + *nouer,* to tie < L. *nodare,* to knot < *nodus,* a knot: see NODE] 1. the outcome, solution, unraveling, or clarification of a plot in a drama, story, etc. 2. the point in the plot where this occurs 3. any final revelation or outcome

de·nounce (di nouns') *vt.* -nounced', -nounc'ing [ME. *denouncen* < OFr. *denoncier* < L. *denuntiare:* see DENUNCI-ATION] 1. to accuse publicly; inform against *[to denounce an accomplice in crime]* 2. to condemn strongly as evil 3. to give formal notice of the ending of (a treaty, armistice, etc.) 4. [Obs.] to announce, esp. in a menacing way —*SYN.* see CRITICIZE —de·nounce'ment *n.* —de·nounc'er *n.*

‡**de no·vo** (dē nō'vō) [L.] once more; anew; again

dens. density

dense (dens) *adj.* [ME. < L. *densus,* compact < IE. base **dens-,* thick, whence Gr. *dasys,* thick (used of hair), Hittite *dassuš,* strong] 1. having the parts crowded together; packed tightly together; compact 2. difficult to get through, penetrate, etc. *[a dense fog, dense ignorance]* 3. slow to understand; stupid 4. *Photog.* opaque, with good contrast in light and shade: said of a negative —*SYN.* see CLOSE[1], STUPID —dense'ly *adv.* —dense'ness *n.*

den·sim·e·ter (den sim'ə tər) *n.* [< L. *densus,* DENSE + -METER] any instrument for measuring density or specific gravity

den·si·tom·e·ter (den'sə täm'ə tər) *n.* [< ff. + -METER] 1. a device for measuring the optical density of a photographic negative 2. *same as* DENSIMETER

den·si·ty (den'sə tē) *n., pl.* -ties [Fr. *densité* < L. *densitas*] 1. the quality or condition of being dense; specif., *a)* thickness; compactness *b)* stupidity *c)* *Photog.* degree of opacity of a negative 2. quantity or number per unit, or of area *[the density of population]* 3. *Elec. same as* CURRENT DENSITY 4. *Physics* the ratio of the mass of an object to its volume

dent[1] (dent) *n.* [ME., var. of DINT] 1. a slight hollow made in a surface by a blow or pressure 2. an appreciable effect or impression, as by lessening —*vt.* to make a dent in —*vi.* to become dented

dent[2] (dent) *n.* [Fr. < L. *dens:* see DENTAL] a toothlike projection as in a gearwheel, lock, etc.

dent. 1. dental 2. dentist 3. dentistry

den·tal (den't'l) *adj.* [ModL. *dentalis* < L. *dens* (gen. *dentis*), a tooth, akin to Cym. *dant,* OHG. *zan,* OS. *tand,* ON. *tönn,* Goth. *tunthus,* Pre-OE. **tanth,* OE. *toth,* TOOTH] 1. of or for the teeth or dentistry 2. *Phonet.* formed by placing the tip of the tongue against or near the upper front teeth —*n. Phonet.* a dental consonant (th, *th*) —den'tal·ly *adv.*

☆**dental floss** thin, strong thread for removing food particles from between the teeth

☆**dental hygienist** a dentist's assistant, who cleans teeth, takes dental X-rays, etc.

den·ta·li·um (den tā'lē əm) *n., pl.* -li·a (-ə) [ModL., the type genus (< L. *dentalis,* DENTAL) + -IUM] any of a genus (*Dentalium*) of marine mollusks

den·tate (den'tāt) *adj.* [ME. *dentat* < L. *dentatus* < *dens:* see DENTAL] 1. having teeth or toothlike projections; toothed or notched 2. *Bot.* having a toothed margin, as some leaves —den'tate·ly *adv.*

den·ta·tion (den tā'shən) *n.* 1. the quality or state of being dentate 2. a toothlike projection, as on a leaf

☆**dent corn** a strain of Indian corn in which the mature kernel develops a hollow at the tip

den·ti- (den'tə, -ti) [< L. *dens:* see DENTAL] *a combining form meaning* tooth or teeth *[dentiform]:* also, before a vowel, **dent-**

den·ti·cle (den'ti k'l) *n.* [L. *denticulus,* dim. of *dens:* see DENTAL] a small tooth or toothlike projection

den·tic·u·late (den tik'yoo lit, -lāt') *adj.* [L. *denticulatus*] 1. having denticles 2. having dentils 3. *Bot.* finely dentate Also **den·tic'u·lat'ed** —den·tic'u·late·ly *adv.*

den·tic·u·la·tion (den tik'yoo lā'shən) *n.* 1. the quality or condition of being denticulate 2. a denticle

den·ti·form (den'tə fôrm') *adj.* [DENTI- + -FORM] tooth-shaped

den·ti·frice (-fris') *n.* [ME. *dentifricie* < L. *dentifricium,* tooth powder < *dens* (see DENTAL) + *fricare,* to rub] any preparation for cleaning teeth, as a powder, paste, or liquid

den·tig·er·ous (den tij'ər əs) *adj.* bearing teeth

den·til (den'til) *n.* [MFr. *dentille,* dim. of *dent* < L. *dens:* see DENTAL] *Archit.* any of a series of small rectangular blocks projecting like teeth, as from under a cornice

den·tin (den'tin) *n.* [< L. *dens* (gen. *dentis*): see DENTAL & -INE[4]] the hard, dense, calcareous tissue forming the body of a tooth, under the enamel: also **den'tine** (-tēn, -tin)

den·tist (den'tist) *n.* [Fr. *dentiste* < ML. *dentista* < L. *dens:* see DENTAL] a person whose profession is the care of teeth and the surrounding tissues, including the prevention and elimination of decay, the replacement of missing teeth with artificial ones, the correction of malocclusion, etc.

den·tist·ry (-rē) *n.* the profession or work of a dentist

den·ti·tion (den tish′ən) *n.* [L. *dentitio*, a teething < *dentire*, to cut teeth < *dens:* see DENTAL] 1. the teething process 2. the number and kind of teeth and their arrangement in the mouth

den·to- (den′tō, -tə) 1. *same as* DENTI- 2. *a combining form meaning* dental or dental and [*dentosurgical*]

den·toid (den′toid) *adj.* [DENT- + -OID] tooth-shaped

Den·ton (den′tən) [after Rev. John B. Denton, a pioneer] city in N Tex., near Fort Worth: pop. 40,000

den·to·sur·gi·cal (den′tō sur′ji k′l) *adj.* relating to or used in both dentistry and surgery

D'En·tre·cas·teaux Islands (dän tr′ kas tō′) group of islands off SE New Guinea: part of the Australian territory of Papua: c. 1,200 sq. mi.

den·ture (den′chər) *n.* [Fr. < *dent*, tooth < L. *dens:* see DENTAL] 1. a set of teeth 2. a fitting for the mouth, with artificial teeth, often a full set

de·nu·cle·ar·ize (dē nōō′klē ə rīz′, -nyōō′-) *vt.* -ized′, -iz′ing to prohibit or prevent the possession of nuclear weapons and launching devices in (an area or nation) — **de·nu′cle·ar·i·za′tion** *n.*

de·nu·date (di nōō′dāt, -nyōō′-; den′yoo dāt′) *vt.* -dat·ed, -dat·ing [< L. *denudatus*, pp. of *denudare*, to strip off < *de-*, off + *nudare*, to strip: see NUDE] *same as* DENUDE — **de·nu·da·tion** (dē′nōō dā′shən, -nyōō-; den′yoo-) *n.*

de·nude (di nōōd′, -nyōōd′) *vt.* -nud′ed, -nud′ing [L. *denudare:* see DENUDATE] to make bare or naked; strip; specif., *a)* to destroy all plant and animal life in (an area) *b) Geol.* to lay bare as by erosion —*SYN.* see STRIP[1]

de·nu·mer·a·ble (di nōō′mər ə b′l, -nyōō′-) *adj.* [DE- + NUMERABLE] countable: said of a set whose elements can be put in one-to-one correspondence with the natural integers

de·nun·ci·ate (di nun′sē āt′) *vt.* -at′ed, -at′ing [< L. *denuntiatus:* see ff.] *same as* DENOUNCE —**de·nun′ci·a′tor** *n.*

de·nun·ci·a·tion (di nun′sē ā′shən) *n.* [ME. *denunciacioun* < L. *denuntiatio* < *denuntiatus*, pp. of *denuntiare*, to announce, denounce < *de-*, intens. + *nuntiare*, ANNOUNCE] the act of denouncing —**de·nun′ci·a·to·ry** (-ə tôr′ē), **de·nun′ci·a′tive** (-āt′iv) *adj.*

Den·ver (den′vər) [after J. W. *Denver* (1817–94), governor of Kans.] capital of Colo., in the NC part: pop. 515,000 (met. area 1,228,000)

de·ny (di nī′) *vt.* -nied′, -ny′ing [ME. *denien* < OFr. *denier* < L. *denegare* < *de-*, intens. + *negare*, to deny: see NEGATION] 1. to declare (a statement) untrue; contradict 2. to refuse to accept as true or right; reject as unfounded, unreal, etc. 3. to refuse to acknowledge as one's own; disown; repudiate 4. to refuse the use of or access to 5. to refuse to grant or give 6. to refuse the request of (a person) 7. [Obs.] to forbid —**deny oneself** 1. to do without desired things 2. to abstain from
SYN.—**deny** implies a refusal to accept as true, real, valid, existent, or tenable [he *denied* the charge]; to **gainsay** is to dispute what a person says or to challenge the person saying it [facts that cannot be *gainsaid*]; **contradict** not only implies emphatic denial, but, in addition, often suggests belief or evidence that the opposite or contrary is true; **impugn** implies a direct, forceful attack against that which one calls into question [she *impugned* his motives]

De·nys (den′is; *Fr.* də nē′), *Saint same as* DENIS

de·o·dand (dē′ə dand′) *n.* [Anglo-Fr. *deodande* < ML.(Ec.) *deodandum* < *Deo dandum*, lit., to be given to God < L. *Deo*, dat. of *Deus*, God + *dandum*, gerundive of *dare*, to give] *Eng. Law* formerly, any property instrumental in a person's death, and consequently forfeited to the crown to be used for some pious purpose

de·o·dar (dē′ə där′) *n.* [Hind. *dēodār* < Sans. *dēvadāru*, lit., tree of the gods < *dēva-h*, god (akin to L. *deus*) + *daru*, wood] 1. the Himalayan cedar (*Cedrus deodara*) of the pine family, with drooping branches and fragrant, durable, light-red wood 2. the wood

de·o·dor·ant (dē ō′dər ənt) *adj.* [< DE- + L. *odorans*, prp. of *odorare*, to smell < *odor*, a smell] having the power of preventing, destroying, or masking undesired odors —*n.* any deodorant preparation; esp., a deodorant salve or liquid used on the body

de·o·dor·ize (dē ō′də rīz′) *vt.* -ized′, -iz′ing to remove or mask the odor of or in —**de·o′dor·i·za′tion** *n.*

de·o·dor·iz·er (-rīz′ər) *n.* any substance or device used in deodorizing something; esp., a spray or the like used to mask odors, as in a room

de·on·tol·o·gy (dē′än täl′ə jē) *n.* [< Gr. *deon* (gen. *deontos*), that which is binding, necessity < *dein*, to bind + -LOGY] the theory of duty or moral obligation; ethics — **de·on·to·log·i·cal** (dē än′tə läj′ə k′l) *adj.*

‡De·o vo·len·te (dē′ō vō len′tē, dā′-) [LL.(Ec.)] (if) God is willing

de·ox·i·dize (dē äk′sə dīz′) *vt.* -dized′, -diz′ing to remove oxygen, esp. chemically combined oxygen, from

de·ox·y- (dē äk′sē) *a combining form meaning* containing less oxygen than its parent compound [*deoxyribonucleic* acid]

de·ox·y·cor·ti·cos·ter·one (dē äk′si kôr′tə käs′tə rōn′) *n.* a minor hormone, $C_{21}H_{30}O_3$, of the adrenal cortex, that can be synthesized: used in treating adrenal insufficiency

de·ox·y·gen·ate (dē äk′sə jə nāt′) *vt.* -at′ed, -at′ing to remove oxygen, esp. free oxygen, from (water, air, etc.)

de·ox·y·ri·bo·nu·cle·ic acid (-si rī′bō nōō klē′ik, -nyōō-) an essential component of all living matter and a basic

material in the chromosomes of the cell nucleus: it contains the genetic code and transmits the hereditary pattern

dep. 1. department 2. departs 3. departure 4. deponent 5. deposed 6. deposit 7. depot 8. deputy

de·part (di pärt′) *vi.* [ME. *departen* < OFr. *departir* < VL. *dispartire*, to divide, separate < L. *dis-*, apart + *partire*, to divide < *pars* (see PART): orig. *vt.*, to divide] 1. to go away (*from*); leave 2. to set out; start 3. to die 4. to turn aside (*from* something) [*to depart* from custom] —*vt.* to leave: now only in **depart this life**, to die —*n.* [Obs.] a departure —*SYN.* see GO[1]

de·part·ed (-id) *adj.* 1. gone away; past; bygone 2. dead —*SYN.* see DEAD —**the departed** the dead person or dead persons

de·part·ment (-mənt) *n.* [ME. & OFr. *departement* < *departir:* see DEPART] 1. a separate part, division, or branch, as of a government, business, or school [the police *department*, the accounting *department*, the history *department*] 2. a field of knowledge or activity [rewriting is his *department*] ☆3. a specialized column or section appearing regularly in a periodical 4. an administrative district in France or in certain Latin American countries

de·part·men·tal (di pärt′men′t'l, dē′pärt-) *adj.* 1. having to do with a department or departments 2. arranged into departments —**de·part′men′tal·ly** *adv.*

de·part·men·tal·ism (-iz′m) *n.* strict or excessive adherence to departmental organization, rules, etc.

de·part·men·tal·ize (di pärt′men′tə liz′, dē′pärt-) *vt.* -ized′, -iz′ing to organize into departments; subdivide — **de·part′men′tal·i·za′tion** *n.*

☆**department store** a large retail store for the sale of many kinds of goods arranged in departments

de·par·ture (di pär′chər) *n.* [ME. < OFr. *departeure*] 1. a departing, or going away 2. a starting out, as on a trip or new course of action 3. a deviation or turning aside (*from* something) 4. [Archaic] death 5. *Naut. a)* the distance of a ship due east or west from the meridian of its starting point *b)* a ship's position in latitude and longitude at the start of a voyage, from which the dead reckoning is begun

de·pas·ture (di pas′chər, -päs′-) *vt.* -tured, -tur·ing [Archaic] 1. to consume the herbage of (a piece of land) by grazing 2. to pasture (cattle, etc.) —*vi.* [Archaic] to graze

de·pend (di pend′) *vi.* [ME. *dependen* < OFr. *dependre* < L. *dependere*, to hang down from < *de-*, down + *pendere*, to hang] 1. to be influenced or determined by something else; be contingent (*on*) 2. to be sure of; rely (*on*) 3. to rely (*on*) for support or aid 4. [Archaic] to hang down 5. *Law* to be undecided or pending —*SYN.* see RELY

de·pend·a·ble (di pen′də b'l) *adj.* that can be depended on; trustworthy; reliable —*SYN.* see RELIABLE —**de·pend′a·bil′i·ty, de·pend′a·ble·ness** *n.* —**de·pend′a·bly** *adv.*

de·pend·ence (-dəns) *n.* [ME. *dependaunce* < OFr. *dependance* or ML. *dependentia* < L. *dependens:* see DEPENDENT] 1. the condition or fact of being dependent; specif., *a)* a being contingent upon or influenced, controlled, or determined by something else *b)* reliance (*on* another) for support or aid *c)* subordination 2. reliance; trust 3. [Rare] a person or thing relied on 4. [Archaic] anything suspended Also sp. **de·pend′ance**

de·pend·en·cy (-dən sē) *n., pl.* -cies 1. dependence 2. something dependent or subordinate 3. a land or territory geographically distinct from the country governing it, and held in trust or as a possession, etc. in a subordinate status

de·pend·ent (-dənt) *adj.* [ME. < OFr. *dependant* < L. *dependens*, prp. of *dependere:* see DEPEND] 1. hanging down 2. influenced, controlled, or determined by something else; contingent 3. relying (*on* another) for support or aid 4. subordinate —*n.* 1. a person who depends on someone else for existence, support, etc. 2. [Obs.] a subordinate part Also, esp. for *n.*, **de·pend′ant** —**de·pend′ent·ly** *adv.*

dependent clause *same as* SUBORDINATE CLAUSE

dependent variable a variable whose value is determined by the value of another variable

de·per·son·al·ize (dē pur′s'n ə liz′) *vt.* -ized′, -iz′ing 1. to deprive of individuality; treat in an impersonal way 2. to cause to lose one's sense of personal identity —**de·per′son·al·i·za′tion** *n.*

de·pict (di pikt′) *vt.* [ME. *depicten* < L. *depictus*, pp. of *depingere* < *de-*, intens. + *pingere*, to PAINT] 1. to represent in a drawing, painting, sculpture, etc.; portray; picture 2. to picture in words; describe —**de·pic·tion** (-pik′shən) *n.* —**de·pic′tor** *n.*

de·pic·ture (-pik′chər) *vt.* -tured, -tur·ing to depict

de·pig·men·ta·tion (dē′pig mən tā′shən, -men-) *n.* loss of, or deficiency in, pigmentation

dep·i·late (dep′ə lāt′) *vt.* -lat′ed, -lat′ing [< L. *depilatus*, pp. of *depilare*, to deprive of hair < *de-*, from + *pilus*, hair] to remove hair from (a part of the body) —**dep′i·la′tion** *n.* —**dep′i·la′tor** *n.*

de·pil·a·to·ry (di pil′ə tôr′ē) *adj.* serving to remove unwanted hair —*n., pl.* -ries a depilatory cream or other substance or device

de·plane (dē plān′) *vi.* -planed′, -plan′ing to get out of an airplane after it lands

de·plete (di plēt′) *vt.* -plet′ed, -plet′ing [< L. *depletus*, pp. of *deplere*, to empty < *de-*, from + *plere*, to fill] 1. *a)* to make less by gradually using up (resources, funds, strength, etc.) *b)* to use up gradually the resources, strength, etc. of 2. to empty wholly or partly —**de·ple′tive** *adj.*

de·ple·tion (di plē'shən) n. 1. a depleting or being depleted 2. the gradual using up or destruction of capital assets, esp. of natural resources

de·plor·a·ble (di plôr'ə b'l) adj. 1. that can or should be deplored; lamentable; regrettable 2. very bad; wretched —**de·plor'a·bly** adv.

de·plore (di plôr') vt. -plored', -plor'ing [Fr. déplorer < L. deplorare < de-, intens. + plorare, to weep] 1. to be regretful or sorry about; lament 2. to regard as unfortunate or wretched —**de·plor'er** n.

de·ploy (dē ploi') vt. [Fr. déployer, to unfold, display < OFr. desployer, to unfold < L. displicare, to scatter (in ML., to unfold): see DISPLAY] 1. Mil. a) to spread out (troops, etc.) so as to form a wider front b) to station or place (forces, equipment, etc.) in accordance with a plan 2. to spread out or place like military troops —vi. to be deployed —**de·ploy'ment** n.

de·plume (dē plōom') vt. -plumed', -plum'ing [ME. deplumen < ML. deplumare: see DE- & PLUME] 1. to pull or pluck the feathers from 2. to strip of honor, riches, etc. —**de'plu·ma'tion** n.

de·po·lar·ize (dē pō'lə rīz') vt. -ized', -iz'ing to destroy or counteract the polarity or polarization of —**de·po'lar·i·za'tion** n. —**de·po'lar·iz'er** n.

de·po·lit·i·cize (dē'pə lit'ə sīz') vt. -cized', -ciz'ing to remove from political influence: also **de'po·lit'i·cal·ize'** -ized', -iz'ing

de·pone (di pōn') vt., vi. -poned', -pon'ing [L. deponere, to put down (in ML., testify): see DEPOSE] [Archaic] to declare under oath, esp. in writing; testify

de·pon·ent (di pō'nənt) adj. [L. deponens, prp. of deponere, to lay down, set down: see DEPOSE] L. & Gr. Gram. denoting a verb with a passive or middle voice form and an active meaning —n. 1. L. & Gr. Gram. a deponent verb 2. Law a) a person who makes an affidavit b) a person who gives written testimony under oath as to the truth of certain facts

de·pop·u·late (dē päp'yə lāt') vt. -lat'ed, -lat'ing [< L. depopulatus, pp. of depopulari, to lay waste < de-, from + populari, to ravage, ruin < populus, PEOPLE] to reduce the population of, esp. by violence, pestilence, etc. —**de·pop'·u·la'tion** n. —**de·pop'u·la'tor** n.

de·port (di pôrt') vt. [OFr. deporter < de- (L. de), intens. + porter < L. portare, to carry, bear: see PORT³] 1. to behave or conduct (oneself) in a specified way 2. [Fr. déporter < L. deportare, to carry away, banish < de-, from | portare] to carry or send away; specif., to force (an alien) to leave a country by official order; expel —n. [Obs.] deportment —SYN. see BANISH, BEHAVE

de·port·a·ble (-ə b'l) adj. 1. liable to deportation 2. punishable by deportation

de·por·ta·tion (dē'pôr tā'shən) n. [Fr. déportation < L. deportatio] a deporting or being deported; expulsion, as of an undesirable alien, from a country

de·por·tee (dē'pôr tē') n. [DEPORT + -EE¹] a deported person or one sentenced to deportation

de·port·ment (di pôrt'mənt) n. [OFr. deportement: see DEPORT] the manner of conducting or bearing oneself; behavior; demeanor —SYN. see BEARING

de·pos·al (di pō'z'l) n. the act of deposing from office; deposition

de·pose (di pōz') vt. -posed', -pos'ing [ME. deposen, to deprive of office, testify < OFr. deposer, to set down < de- (L. de), from, away + poser (< L. pausare: see POSE¹), to cease, lie down; confused in sense and form with L. deponere (pp. depositus), to lay down, lay aside (in ML., testify): see DEPOSIT] 1. to remove from office or a position of power, esp. from a throne; oust 2. [Archaic] to lay down 3. Law to state or testify under oath but out of court —vi. to bear witness —**de·pos'a·ble** adj.

de·pos·it (di päz'it) vt. [< L. depositus, pp. of deponere, to put down < de-, down + ponere, to put: see POSITION] 1. to place or entrust for safekeeping 2. to put (money) in a bank, as for safekeeping or to earn interest 3. to put down as a pledge or partial payment 4. to put, lay, or set down 5. to leave lying, as sediment —n. [L. depositum < depositus: see the v.] 1. something placed or entrusted for safekeeping; specif., money put in a bank 2. a pledge or part payment 3. the act of depositing 4. a depository 5. something deposited or left lying; specif., Geol., Mining sand, clay, mineral masses, etc. deposited by the action of wind, water, volcanic eruption, or ice —**on deposit** placed or entrusted for safekeeping

de·pos·i·tar·y (di päz'ə ter'ē) n., pl. -tar'ies [LL. depositarius < L. depositum: see prec.] 1. a person, firm, etc. entrusted with something for safekeeping; trustee 2. a storehouse; depository

dep·o·si·tion (dep'ə zish'ən, dē'pə-) n. [ME. & OFr. < L. depositio, a laying or putting down < L. depositus: see DEPOSIT] 1. a deposing or being deposed; removal from office or position of power 2. the act of testifying 3. a depositing or being deposited 4. something deposited or left lying 5. Law the testimony of a witness, made under oath but not in open court, and written down to be used when the case comes to trial

de·pos·i·tor (di päz'ə tər) n. [LL.] a person who deposits something, esp. money in a bank

de·pos·i·to·ry (di päz'ə tôr'ē) n., pl. -ries [LL. depositorium: see DEPOSIT] 1. a place where things are put for safekeeping; storehouse 2. a trustee; depositary

de·pot (dē'pō; military & Brit. dep'ō) n. [Fr. dépôt, a deposit, storehouse < L. depositum: see DEPOSIT] 1. a storehouse; warehouse ☆2. a railroad or bus station: orig. used of a freight station 3. Mil. a) a storage place for supplies b) a station for assembling either recruits for training or combat replacements for assignment to a unit

dep·ra·va·tion (dep'rə vā'shən) n. [L. depravatio < pp. of depravare] 1. a depraving or becoming depraved 2. a depraved condition; depravity

de·prave (di prāv') vt. -praved', -prav'ing [ME. depraven < OFr. depraver < L. depravare, to make crooked < de-, intens. + pravus, crooked] 1. to lead into bad habits; make morally bad; corrupt; pervert 2. [Obs.] to defame or slander —SYN. see DEBASE —**de·prav'er** n.

de·praved (-prāvd') adj. morally bad; corrupt; perverted —**de·prav'ed·ly** (-prā'vid lē) adv.

de·prav·i·ty (-prav'ə tē) n. [altered (after DEPRAVE) < obs. pravity < L. pravitas, crookedness] 1. a depraved condition; corruption; wickedness 2. pl. -ties a depraved act or practice

dep·re·cate (dep'rə kāt') vt. -cat'ed, -cat'ing [< L. deprecatus, pp. of deprecari, to ward off by intercession < de-, off, from + precari, PRAY] 1. to feel and express disapproval of; plead against 2. to depreciate; belittle 3. [Archaic] to try to avert by prayer —**dep're·cat'ing·ly** adv. —**dep're·ca'tion** n. —**dep're·ca'tor** n.

dep·re·ca·to·ry (-kə tôr'ē) adj. [LL.(Ec.) deprecatorius] 1. deprecating 2. apologetic or belittling Also **dep're·ca'tive**

de·pre·ci·a·ble (di prē'shē ə b'l, -shə b'l) adj. that can be depreciated, or lessened in value

de·pre·ci·ate (di prē'shē āt') vt. -at'ed, -at'ing [ME. depreciaten < L. depreciatus, pp. of depretiare, to lower the price of (in LL.(Ec.), to make light of) < de-, from + pretiare, to value < pretium, PRICE] 1. to reduce in value or price 2. to make seem less important; belittle —vi. to drop in value or price —SYN. see DISPARAGE —**de·pre'ci·a'tor** n. —**de·pre'ci·a·to'ry** (-shē ə tôr'ē, -shə tôr'ē), **de·pre'ci·a'tive** (-shē āt'iv, -shə tiv) adj.

de·pre·ci·a·tion (di prē'shē ā'shən) n. [see prec.] ☆1. a) a decrease in value of property through wear, deterioration, or obsolescence b) the allowance made for this in bookkeeping, accounting, etc. ☆2. a decrease in the purchasing power of money 3. a making seem less important; disparagement

dep·re·date (dep'rə dāt') vt., vi. -dat'ed, -dat'ing [LL. depraedatus, pp. of depraedari < L. de-, intens. + praedari, to plunder < praeda, booty, PREY] [Archaic] to plunder —**dep're·da'tor** n. —**de·pre·da·to·ry** (di pred'ə tôr'ē, dep'rə də-) adj.

dep·re·da·tion (dep'rə dā'shən) n. [LL. depraedatio: see prec.] the act or an instance of robbing, plundering, or laying waste

de·press (di pres') vt. [ME. depressen < OFr. depresser < L. depressus, pp. of deprimere, to press down, sink < de-, down + premere, to PRESS¹] 1. to press down; push or pull down; lower 2. to lower in spirits; make gloomy; discourage; sadden 3. to decrease the force or activity of; weaken 4. to lower in value, price, or amount 5. [Obs.] to suppress 6. Music to lower the pitch of —**de·press'ing** adj. —**de·press'ing·ly** adv.

de·pres·sant (-ənt) adj. [prec. + -ANT] lowering the rate of muscular or nervous activity —n. a depressant medicine, drug, etc.; sedative

de·pressed (di prest') adj. 1. pressed down 2. lowered in position, intensity, amount, or degree 3. flattened or hollowed, as if pressed down 4. gloomy; dejected; sad 5. characterized by widespread unemployment, poverty, lack of opportunity, etc.; impoverished [a depressed area] 6. Bot. flattened vertically, as if from downward pressure 7. Zool. having the horizontal diameter longer than the vertical; broad —SYN. see SAD

de·pres·si·ble (-pres'ə b'l) adj. that can be depressed

de·pres·sion (-presh'ən) n. [ME. depressioun < OFr. depression < L. depressio: see DEPRESS] 1. a depressing or being depressed 2. a depressed part or place; hollow or low place on a surface 3. low spirits; gloominess; dejection; sadness 4. a decrease in force, activity, amount, etc. 5. Astron. the angular distance of a heavenly body below the horizon ☆6. Econ. a period marked by slackening of business activity, widespread unemployment, falling prices and wages, etc. 7. Med. a decrease in functional activity 8. Meteorol. a) a lowering of the atmospheric pressure indicated by the fall of mercury in a barometer b) an area of relatively low barometric pressure; low 9. Psychol. an emotional condition, either neurotic or psychotic, characterized by feelings of hopelessness, inadequacy, etc. 10. Surveying the angular distance of an object below the horizontal plane

de·pres·sive (-pres'iv) adj. 1. tending to depress 2. charac-

terized by psychological depression —de·pres'sive·ly adv. —de·pres'sive·ness n.

de·pres·so·mo·tor (di pres'ō mōt'ər) adj. slowing down or decreasing motor activity —n. any depressomotor drug or other agent

de·pres·sor (di pres'ər) n. 1. a person or thing that depresses 2. any of various muscles that draw down a part of the body 3. a nerve which when stimulated decreases the activity of a part of the body 4. an instrument that presses a protruding part out of the way during a medical examination or operation [a tongue depressor]

dep·ri·va·tion (dep'rə vā'shən) n. [ME. deprivacioun] 1. a depriving or being deprived 2. a loss Also [Rare] de·priv·al (di prī'v'l) —dep'ri·va'tion·al adj.

de·prive (di prīv') vt. -prived', -priv'ing [ME. depriven < ML. deprivare < L. de-, intens. + privare, to deprive, separate: see PRIVATE] 1. to take something away from forcibly; dispossess [to deprive someone of his property] 2. to keep from having, using, or enjoying [to be deprived of one's rights] 3. to remove from office, esp. ecclesiastical office —de·priv'a·ble adj.

de·prived (-prīvd') adj. that has undergone deprivation; specif., of or from a poor or depressed area; underprivileged

‡de pro·fun·dis (dē' prō fun'dis, dā') [LL.(Ec.), out of the depths] 1. from the deepest sorrow or misery 2. [D- P-] Psalm 130 (in the Douay version, Psalm 129): from the first words of the Latin version

dep·side (dep'sīd, -sid) n. [< Gr. depsein, to tan + -IDE] any of a class of anhydrides of phenol carboxylic acids, similar to esters

dept. 1. department 2. deponent 3. deputy

Dept·ford (det'fərd) metropolitan borough of London, on the S bank of the Thames: pop. 68,000

depth (depth) n. [ME. depthe < dep: see DEEP & -TH¹] 1. a) the distance from the top downward, from the surface inward, or from front to back b) perspective, as in a painting 2. the quality or condition of being deep; deepness; specif., a) intensity, as of colors, silence, emotion, etc. b) profundity of thought c) lowness of pitch 3. the middle part [the depth of winter] 4. [usually pl.] the far inner or inmost part [the depths of a wood] 5. [usually pl.] the deep or deepest part, as of the sea 6. [usually pl.] the most extreme degree, as of despair 7. reserve strength, as of suitable substitute players for a team —in depth in a thorough and comprehensive way [analysis in depth] —out of (or beyond) one's depth 1. in water too deep for one 2. past one's ability or understanding

depth charge a powerful explosive charge timed to explode at a certain depth, and used against submarines or other underwater targets: also called depth bomb

depth perception the ability to perceive objects in perspective

depth psychology any system of psychology, as psychoanalysis, dealing with the processes of the unconscious

dep·u·rate (dep'yoo rāt') vt. -rat'ed, -rat'ing [< ML. depuratus, pp. of depurare, to purify < L. de-, intens. + purare, to purify < purus, PURE] to purify —dep'u·ra'tion n. —de·pu'ra·tive adj., n.

dep·u·ta·tion (dep'yoo tā'shən) n. [ME. deputacioun < LL. deputatio] 1. a deputing or being deputed 2. a group of persons, or a single person, appointed to represent others; delegation

de·pute (di pyoot') vt. -put'ed, -put'ing [ME. deputen < OFr. deputer < L. deputare, to cut off, detach, hence depute < de-, from + putare, lit., to cleanse, hence lop off, count, consider] 1. to give (authority, functions, etc.) to someone else as deputy 2. to appoint as one's substitute, agent, or representative

dep·u·tize (dep'yə tīz') vt. -tized', -tiz'ing to appoint as deputy —vi. to act as deputy

dep·u·ty (dep'yə tē) n., pl. -ties [ME. depute < Anglo-Fr. deputé, pp. of deputer: see DEPUTE] 1. a person appointed to act as a substitute for, or as an assistant to, another 2. a member of a legislature called a Chamber of Deputies, as the lower house of the Italian legislature —adj. acting as deputy —SYN. see AGENT

De Quin·cey (də kwin'sē), Thomas 1785–1859; Eng. essayist & critic

der. 1. derivation 2. derivative 3. derived

de·rac·i·nate (di ras'ə nāt') vt. -nat'ed, -nat'ing [Fr. déraciner < dé- (L. dis-), from + racine, a root < LL. radicina < L. radix (gen. radicis), ROOT] to pull up by or as by the roots; uproot; eradicate; extirpate —de·rac'i·na'tion n.

de·raign (di rān') vt. [ME. dereinen < OFr. deraisnier, to plead, vindicate < de- (L. de), from + raisnier < LL. *rationare < L. ratio, REASON] Law formerly, to determine (an issue), esp. by personal combat between the litigants

de·rail (di rāl') vt. [Fr. dérailler < dé- (L. de-), from + rail < RAIL¹] to cause (a train, etc.) to go off the rails —vi. to go off the rails —de·rail'ment n.

De·rain (də ran'), An·dré (än drā') 1880–1954; Fr. painter

de·range (di rānj') vt. -ranged', -rang'ing [Fr. déranger < OFr. desrengier < des- (L. dis-), apart + rengier (Fr. ranger): see RANGE] 1. to upset the arrangement, order, or operation of; unsettle; disorder 2. to make insane —de·ranged' adj. —de·range'ment n.

de·ray (di rā') n. [ME. deraie < OFr. desrei: see DIS- & ARRAY] [Obs.] disorder; esp., disorderly revelry

Der·bent (der bent') city in SW U.S.S.R., on the W shore of the Caspian: pop. 50,000

Der·by (dur'bē; chiefly Brit., där'bē) 1. city in Derbyshire, England: pop. 132,000 2. same as DERBYSHIRE —n. 1. [after the twelfth Earl of Derby, who founded the race in 1780] a race for three-year-old horses, run annually at Epsom Downs in Surrey 2. any similar horse race; esp., the Kentucky Derby ☆3. [d-] a stiff felt hat with a round crown and curved brim; bowler

Der·by·shire (dur'bi shir; chiefly Brit., där'-) county in C England: 1,006 sq. mi.; pop. 898,000

DERBY

de·re·ism (dē rē'iz'm) n. [L. de re, unreal, lit., away from fact < de-, DE- + res, thing (see REAL¹) + -ISM] a mental condition in which there is a loss of interest in external reality and deviation from normal logic —de're·is'tic adj.

der·e·lict (der'ə likt') adj. [L. derelictus, pp. of derelinquere, to forsake utterly, abandon < de-, intens. + relinquere: see RELINQUISH] 1. deserted by the owner; abandoned; forsaken ☆2. neglectful of duty; remiss; negligent —n. 1. a property abandoned by the owner; esp., a ship deserted at sea 2. a destitute person, without a home or regular job and rejected by society 3. land exposed by the receding of water —SYN. see REMISS

der·e·lic·tion (der'ə lik'shən) n. [L. derelictio: see prec.] 1. an abandoning or forsaking 2. the state of being abandoned or forsaken 3. a neglect of, or failure in, duty; a being remiss 4. Law a) the gaining of land from water by the gradual retreat of the sea below the usual watermark b) the land so exposed

de·ride (di rīd') vt. -rid'ed, -rid'ing [L. deridere < de-, pejorative + ridere, to laugh: see RIDICULE] to laugh at in contempt or scorn; make fun of; ridicule —SYN. see RIDICULE —de·rid'er n. —de·rid'ing·ly adv.

‡de ri·gueur (də rē gër') [Fr.] 1. required by etiquette; according to good form 2. fashionable or faddish

de·ris·i·ble (di riz'ə b'l) adj. [ML. derisibilis: see ff. & -ABLE] deserving to be derided

de·ri·sion (di rizh'ən) n. [ME. < LL. derisio < L. derisus, pp. of deridere] 1. a deriding or being derided; contempt or ridicule 2. [Rare] a person or thing derided

de·ri·sive (di rī'siv) adj. [ML. derisivus: see prec. & -IVE] 1. showing derision; ridiculing 2. provoking derision; ridiculous Also de·ri'so·ry (-sə rē) —de·ri'sive·ly adv. —de·ri'sive·ness n.

deriv. 1. derivation 2. derivative 3. derived

de·riv·a·ble (de rī'və b'l) adj. that can be derived

der·i·va·tion (der'ə vā'shən) n. [ME. derivacioun < L. derivatio < pp. of derivare] 1. a deriving or being derived 2. descent or origination 3. something derived; a derivative 4. the source or origin of something 5. a) the origin and development of a word; etymology b) the process of tracing this 6. the process of forming words from bases by the addition of affixes other than inflectional endings, by internal phonetic change, etc. [the derivation of "warmth" from "warm"] —der'i·va'tion·al adj.

de·riv·a·tive (də riv'ə tiv) adj. [ME. derivatif < LL. derivativus < L. derivatus, pp. of derivare: see ff.] 1. derived 2. using or taken from other sources; not original 3. of derivation —n. 1. something derived 2. Chem. a substance derived from, or of such composition and properties that it may be considered as derived from, another substance by chemical change, esp. by the substitution of one or more elements or radicals 3. Linguis. a word formed from another or others by derivation 4. Math. the limiting value of a rate of change of a function with respect to the variable —de·riv'a·tive·ly adv.

de·rive (di rīv') vt. -rived', -riv'ing [ME. deriven < OFr. deriver < L. derivare, to divert, orig., to turn a stream from its channel < de-, from + rivus, a stream] 1. to get or receive (from a source) 2. to get by reasoning; deduce or infer 3. to trace from or to a source; show the derivation of 4. Chem. to obtain or produce (a compound) from another compound by replacing one element with one or more other elements —vi. to come (from a source); be derived; originate —SYN. see RISE —de·riv'er n.

derm- (durm) same as DERMO-: used before a vowel

-derm (durm) [see ff.] a suffix meaning skin or covering [blastoderm, endoderm]

der·ma¹ (dur'mə) n. [ModL. < Gr. derma] same as DERMIS

der·ma² (dur'mə) n. [Yid. derme, pl. of darm, gut < MHG. < OHG. daram < IE. *tormo-s, hole < base *ter-, to rub, bore, whence THROW, Gr. tormos, hole] beef casing stuffed with a filling of bread crumbs, seasoning, etc. and roasted

der·mal (-m'l) adj. of the skin or the dermis

der·map·ter·an (dər map'tər ən) n. [< ModL. dermaptera, name of the order < derma (see DERMA¹) + -ptera < Gr. -ptera, neut. pl. of -pteros, winged < pteron, wing (see FEATHER) + -AN] any of an order (Dermaptera) of small, nocturnal insects with a pair of terminal pincers, including the earwigs —der·map'ter·ous adj.

der·ma·ti·tis (dur'mə tīt'is) n. [ff. + -ITIS] inflammation of the skin

der·ma·to- (dur'mə tō; dər mat'ō, -ə) [Gr. dermato- < derma (gen. dermatos), skin, hide < IE. base *der-, to skin,

split off, whence TEAR[1]] *a combining form meaning* skin or hide [*dermatology*]: also, before a vowel, **dermat-**

der·mat·o·gen (dər mat'ə jən) n. [DERMATO- + -GEN] *Bot.* a layer of dividing cells from which the epidermis is formed

der·ma·tol·o·gy (dur'mə täl'ə jē) n. [DERMATO- + -LOGY] the branch of medicine dealing with the skin and its diseases —**der'ma·to·log'i·cal** (-tə läj'ə k'l) adj. —**der'ma·tol'o·gist** n.

der·ma·tome (dur'mə tōm') n. [DERMA[1] + -TOME] any of the segmentally arranged mesodermal masses in a vertebrate embryo, destined to form dermis

der·ma·to·phyte (dur'mə tō fit', dər mat'ə-) n. [DERMATO- + -PHYTE] any plant parasitic on the skin, as the fungus that causes ringworm

der·ma·to·plas·ty (-plas'tē) n. [DERMATO- + -PLASTY] plastic surgery of the skin, as by skin grafts

der·ma·to·sis (dur'mə tō'sis) n., pl. **-to·ses** (-sēz) [DERMAT(O)- + -OSIS] any disorder of the skin

der·mes·tid (dər mes'tid) n. [< ModL. *Dermestidae*, name of the family < *Dermestes*, type genus < Gr. *dermēstēs*, a leather-eating worm < *derma*, skin (see DERMA[1]) + *esthiein*, to eat < *esthi*, imper. of *edmenai*, to eat < IE. base *ed-*, to EAT] any of a family (Dermestidae) of small, drab-colored beetles, whose larvae and adults are destructive to hides, furs, woolens, cereals, etc.

der·mic (dur'mik) adj. same as DERMAL

der·mis (dur'mis) n. [ModL. < LL. *epidermis*, EPIDERMIS] the layer of skin just below the epidermis

der·mo- (dur'mō, -mə) [< Gr. *derma*, the skin] same as DERMATO-

der·moid (dur'moid) adj. [DERM- + -OID] 1. consisting of tissues of ectodermal origin, such as skin, hair, and teeth, as found in certain tumors 2. skinlike

der·mop·ter·an (dər mäp'tər ən) n. [< ModL. *dermoptera*, name of the order < *dermo-* (see DERMO-) + *-ptera* (see DERMAPTERAN) + -AN] any of an order (Dermoptera) of gliding mammals of SE Asia, including the flying lemurs

‡**der·nier cri** (der nyā krē') [Fr., lit., the latest cry] the latest fashion; last word

der·o·gate (der'ə gāt') vt. -gat'ed, -gat'ing [ME. *derogaten* < L. *derogatus*, pp. of *derogare*, to repeal part of (a law). detract from < *de-*, from + *rogare*, to ask] 1. [Archaic] to take away (*from*) so as to impair 2. [Rare] to lower in esteem; disparage —vi. 1. to take something desirable away; detract 2. to lower oneself; lose face

der·o·ga·tion (der'ə gā'shən) n. [ME. *derogacioun* < OFr. *derogation* < L. *derogatio*: see prec.] 1. a lessening or weakening (*of* power, authority, position, etc.) 2. disparagement; detraction 3. a lowering of oneself; loss of rank

de·rog·a·to·ry (di räg'ə tôr'ē) adj. [L. *derogatorius*: see DEROGATE] 1. tending to lessen or impair; detracting 2. disparaging; belittling Also **de·rog'a·tive** —**de·rog'a·to'ri·ly** adv.

der·rick (der'ik) n. [after Thos. *Derrick*, London hangman of the early 17th c.: orig. applied to a gallows] 1. a large apparatus for lifting and moving heavy objects: it consists of a long beam pivoted at the base of a vertical, stationary beam and moved by ropes running on pulleys ☆2. a tall, tapering framework, as over an oil well, to support drilling machinery, etc.

der·ri·ère (der'ē er') n. [Fr., back part, rear, orig. adv., behind < LL. *deretro* < L. *de retro* < *de*, from + *retro*, back] the buttocks

der·ring-do (der'iŋ dōō') n. [ME. *derrynge do, durring don*, lit., daring to do; misunderstood as abstract *n.* by Spenser and thence popularized by Scott (*Ivanhoe*)] daring action; reckless courage

☆**der·rin·ger** (der'in jər) n. [after Henry *Deringer* (1806-68), U.S. gunsmith] a small, short-barreled pistol of large caliber

der·ris (der'is) n. [ModL. < Gr. *derris*, hide < IE. base *der-*: see DERMATO-] any of a genus (*Derris*) of woody, leguminous plants of the East Indies, from whose roots rotenone is extracted

Der·ry (der'ē) same as LONDONDERRY

der·ry (der'ē) n., pl. **-ries** 1. a meaningless word in the refrains of some old ballads 2. a ballad

der·vish (dur'vish) n. [Turk. *dervish* < Per. *darvesh*, beggar] a member of any of various Moslem orders, dedicated to a life of poverty and chastity: some dervishes practice whirling, howling, etc. as religious acts

☆**de·sal·i·na·tion** (dē sal'ə nā'shən, -sā'lə-) n. [DE- + SALIN(E) + -ATION] the removal of salt, esp. from sea water to make it drinkable: also **de·sal'i·ni·za'tion** —**de·sal'i·nate'** -nat'ed, -nat'ing or **de·sal'i·nize'** -nized', -niz'ing vt.

☆**de·salt** (dē sôlt') vt. to remove salt from (esp. sea water)

desc. descendant

des·cant (des'kant; for vi., esp. 1, also des kant') n. [ME. < Anglo-Fr. *deschaunt* & ML. *discantus* < L. *dis-*, from apart + *cantus*, song: see CHANT] 1. *Medieval Music* a) two-part

singing in which there is a fixed, known melody and a subordinate melody added above b) this added upper melody c) the highest voice in polyphonic singing, as the treble or soprano In these senses, many musicologists prefer DISCANT 2. a varied song or melody 3. [< the *v.*] a comment; criticism; discourse —vi. [ME. *discanten* < the *n.*] 1. to talk or write at length; comment expansively; discourse (*on* or *upon*) 2. to sing or play a descant to the main melody 3. to sing

Des·cartes (dā kärt') **Re·né** (rə nā') 1596-1650; Fr. philosopher & mathematician

de·scend (di send') vi. [ME. *descenden* < OFr. *descendre* < L. *descendere*, to climb down, fall < *de-*, down + *scandere*, to climb < IE. base whence Gr. *skandalon* (see SCANDAL), Sans. *skandati*, (he) leaps] 1. to move from a higher to a lower place; come down or go down 2. to pass from an earlier to a later time, from greater to less, from general to particular, etc. 3. to slope or extend downward 4. to come down (*from* a source, as *from* an ancestor): usually with auxiliary *be* [he is descended from pioneers] 5. to pass by inheritance or heredity [the estate descended to the nephew] 6. to lower oneself or stoop (*to* some act) 7. to make a sudden attack, raid, or visit (*on* or *upon*) 8. *Astron.* to move toward the south or the horizon 9. *Music* to move down the scale —vt. to move down, down along, or through —**de·scend'i·ble** adj.

de·scend·ant (-ənt) adj. [ME. *descendaunt* < OFr. *descendant* < L. *descendens*, prp. of *descendere*: see DESCEND] descending: also **de·scend'ent** —n. 1. a person who is an offspring, however remote, of a certain ancestor, family, group, etc. 2. something that derives from an earlier form

de·scend·er (-ər) n. 1. a person or thing that descends 2. *Typography* a) the part of a letter, such as *g* or *y*, that extends below the line b) such a letter

de·scent (di sent') n. [ME. *descent* < OFr. *descente* < *descendre*: see DESCEND] 1. a descending; coming down or going down 2. lineage; ancestry 3. one generation (in a specified lineage) 4. a downward slope 5. a way down or downward 6. a sudden attack, raid, or invasion (*on* or *upon*) 7. a decline; fall 8. a stooping (*to* an act) 9. *Law* transference (of property) to heirs or offspring by inheritance

Des·chutes (dā shōōt') [< Fr. *rivière des chutes*, river of the falls] river in C and N Oreg., flowing north into the Columbia River: c. 250 mi.

de·scribe (di skrīb') vt. -scribed', -scrib'ing [ME. *descriven* < OFr. *descrivre* < L. *describere*, to copy down, transcribe < *de-*, from + *scribere*, to write: see SCRIBE] 1. to tell or write about; give a detailed account of 2. to picture in words 3. to trace the outline of [his arm described an arc in the air] 4. [Obs.] to descry; so used through confusion —**de·scrib'a·ble** adj. —**de·scrib'er** n.

de·scrip·tion (di skrip'shən) n. [ME. *descripcioun* < OFr. *description* < L. *descriptio*, a marking out, delineation < pp. of *describere*] 1. the act, process, art, or technique of describing, or picturing in words 2. a statement or passage that describes 3. sort, kind, or variety [books of every description] 4. the act of tracing or outlining [the description of a circle]

de·scrip·tive (-tiv) adj. describing; of or characterized by description; specif., a) designating or of a branch of a science in which its data or materials are described and classified [descriptive anatomy] b) *Gram.* designating an adjective that indicates a quality or condition of the word it modifies ["big" in "big barn" is a *descriptive* adjective] —**de·scrip'tive·ly** adv. —**de·scrip'tive·ness** n.

descriptive geometry the system of geometry that uses plane projections and perspective drawings of solid figures, usually in order to describe and analyze their properties for engineering and manufacturing purposes

descriptive linguistics the branch of linguistics which describes the structure of a language or languages as they exist, without reference to their histories or to comparison with other languages

de·scry (di skrī') vt. -scried', -scry'ing [ME. *descrien* < OFr. *descrier*, to proclaim < *des-*, from + *crier*: see CRY] 1. to catch sight of; discern (distant or obscure objects) 2. to look for and discover; detect —SYN. see SEE[1]

Des·de·mo·na (dez'də mō'nə) in Shakespeare's *Othello*, the wife of Othello, whom he smothers to death

des·e·crate (des'ə krāt') vt. -crat'ed, -crat'ing [< DE- + (CON)SECRATE] to take away the sacredness of; treat as not sacred; profane —**des'e·crat'er, des'e·cra'tor** n.

des·e·cra·tion (des'ə krā'shən) n. a desecrating or being desecrated —SYN. see SACRILEGE

de·seg·re·gate (dē seg'rə gāt') vt., vi. -gat'ed, -gat'ing to abolish the segregation of races in (public schools, etc.) —**de·seg're·ga'tion** n.

de·sen·si·tize (dē sen'sə tīz') vt. -tized', -tiz'ing 1. to take away the sensitivity of; make less sensitive 2. to make (a photographic plate or film) less sensitive to light, so that it may be developed in a brighter light than ordinarily 3. *Med.* to make (a person, animal, or tissue) nonreactive or nonallergic to a substance by removing the antibodies from sensitized cells —**de·sen'si·ti·za'tion** n. —**de·sen'si·tiz'er** n.

---

de·sert[1] (di zʉrt′) *vt.* [Fr. *déserter* < LL. *desertare* < *desertus*, pp. of L. *deserere*, to desert, lit., to disjoin < *de-*, from + *serere*, to join < IE. base *ser-*, to join, place in a row, whence Gr. *eirein*, to fasten in rows, L. *series*] **1.** to forsake (someone or something that one ought not to leave); abandon **2.** to leave (one's post, military service, etc.) without permission **3.** to fail (someone) when most needed —*vi.* to leave one's post, military duty, etc. without permission and with no intent to return, or, in time of war, in order to avoid hazardous duty —*SYN.* see ABANDON —**de·sert′er** *n.*

des·ert[2] (dez′ərt) *n.* [ME. < OFr. < LL.(Ec.) *desertum*, a desert, neut. of *desertus*: see prec.] **1.** an uncultivated region without inhabitants; wilderness **2.** a dry, barren, sandy region, naturally incapable of supporting almost any plant or animal life —*adj.* **1.** of a desert or deserts **2.** wild and uninhabited [a desert island] —*SYN.* see WASTE

de·sert[3] (di zʉrt′) *n.* [ME. & OFr. *deserte* < *deservir*: see DESERVE] **1.** the fact of deserving reward or punishment **2.** [often *pl.*] deserved reward or punishment [to get one's just *deserts*] **3.** the quality of deserving reward; merit

de·ser·tion (di zʉr′shən) *n.* [ME. *desercioun* < OFr. *desertion* < L. *desertio*] a deserting or being deserted; specif., *Law* the willful abandonment of cohabitation with one's spouse or of the duties of parenthood

☆**desert varnish** a dark, glistening coating of iron or manganese oxide, found on rock surfaces in deserts

de·serve (di zʉrv′) *vt.* -**served′**, -**serv′ing** [ME. *deserven* < OFr. *deservir*, to deserve < L. *deservire*, to serve diligently < *de-*, intens. + *servire*, SERVE] to have a right to because of acts or qualities; be worthy of (reward, punishment, etc.) —*vi.* to be worthy; merit

de·served (di zʉrvd′) *adj.* rightfully earned or merited; just —**de·serv′ed·ly** (-zʉr′vid lē) *adv.*

de·serv·ing (-zʉr′viŋ) *adj.* that deserves; worthy (*of* help, reward, etc.) —*n.* desert; merit or demerit

de Se·ver·sky (də sə ver′skē), **Alexander P**(rocofieff) 1894– ; U.S. aeronautical engineer, born in Russia

de·sex (dē seks′) *vt.* **1.** to remove the sex organs of **2.** to suppress or lessen the sexual characteristics of

de·sex·u·al·ize (dē sek′shoo wəl iz′) *vt.* -**ized′**, -**iz′ing** *same as* DESEX —**de·sex′u·al·i·za′tion** *n.*

des·ha·bille (dez′ə bēl′, -bil′) *n. same as* DISHABILLE

des·ic·cant (des′i kənt) *adj.* [L. *desiccans*, prp. of *desiccare*: see ff.] drying —*n.* a substance having a great affinity for water and used as a drying agent

des·ic·cate (-kāt′) *vt.* -**cat′ed**, -**cat′ing** [< L. *desiccatus*, pp. of *desiccare*, to dry up completely < *de-*, intens. + *siccare*, to dry < *siccus*, dry < IE. base *seikw-*, to drip, pour out, whence OE. *seon*, to trickle, *sic*, small stream] **1.** to dry completely **2.** to preserve (food) by drying —*vi.* to become completely dry —**des′ic·ca′tion** *n.* —**des′ic·ca′tive** *adj.*, *n.*

des·ic·ca·tor (-ər) *n.* **1.** an apparatus for drying foods, etc., esp. by heat **2.** a chemist's device containing a water-absorbing material, used to dry or store substances

de·sid·er·ate (di sid′ə rāt′) *vt.* -**at′ed**, -**at′ing** [< L. *desideratus*, pp. of *desiderare*: see DESIRE] to feel the lack of and desire for; want; miss; need —**de·sid′er·a′tion** *n.* —**de·sid′er·a′tive** *adj.*

de·sid·er·a·tum (di sid′ə rāt′əm, -zid′-; -rät′-) *n.*, *pl.* -**ta** (-ə) [L., neut. of *desideratus*, pp. of *desiderare*: see DESIRE] something needed and wanted

de·sign (di zīn′) *vt.* [ME. *designen* < L. *designare*, to mark out, define < *de-*, out, from + *signare*, to mark < *signum*, a mark, SIGN] **1.** to make preliminary sketches of; sketch a pattern or outline for; plan **2.** to plan and carry out, esp. by artistic arrangement or in a skillful way **3.** to form (plans, etc.) in the mind; contrive **4.** to plan to do; purpose; intend **5.** to intend or set apart for some purpose —*vi.* **1.** to make designs **2.** to make original plans, sketches, patterns, etc.; work as a designer —*n.* [Fr. *dessein* < It. *disegno* < *disignare* < L. *designare*] **1.** a plan; scheme; project **2.** purpose; intention; aim **3.** a thing planned for or outcome aimed at **4.** a working out by plan, or development according to a plan [to find a *design* in history] **5.** [*pl.*] a secret, usually dishonest or selfish scheme (often with *on* or *upon*) [to have *designs* on another's property] **6.** a plan or sketch to work from; pattern [a *design* for a house] **7.** the art of making designs or patterns **8.** the arrangement of parts, details, form, color, etc. so as to produce a complete and artistic unit; artistic or skillful invention [the *design* of a rug] **9.** a finished artistic work or decoration —*SYN.* see INTEND, PLAN —**by design** with deliberate intent; purposely

des·ig·nate (dez′ig nāt′; *for adj., also* -nit) *adj.* [ME. < L. *designatus*, pp. of *designare*: see prec.] named for an office, etc. but not yet in it [ambassador *designate*] —*vt.* -**nat′ed**, -**nat′ing** **1.** to point out; mark out; indicate; specify **2.** to refer to by a distinguishing name, title, etc.; name **3.** to name for an office or duty; appoint —**des′ig·na′tive** *adj.* —**des′ig·na′tor** *n.*

des·ig·na·tion (dez′ig nā′shən) *n.* [ME. *designacioun* < L. *designatio*: see prec.] **1.** a pointing out or marking out; indication **2.** a naming or being named for an office, post, etc. **3.** a distinguishing name, title, etc.

de·sign·ed·ly (di zīn′id lē) *adv.* by design; purposely

des·ig·nee (dez′ig nē′) *n.* a person designated

de·sign·er (di zī′nər) *n.* a person who designs; specif., one

who makes original sketches, patterns, etc. [a scene *designer*]

de·sign·ing (-niŋ) *adj.* **1.** that designs, or makes plans, patterns, etc. **2.** scheming; crafty; artful —*n.* the art or work of creating designs, patterns, etc.

des·i·nence (des′i nəns) *n.* [Fr. *désinence* < ML. *desinentia* < L. *desinens*, prp. of *desinere*, to leave off < *de-*, from + *sinere*, to let, allow] [Rare] a termination or ending; specif., a suffix

de·sir·a·ble (di zīr′ə b'l) *adj.* [ME. < OFr.: see DESIRE & -ABLE] worth wanting or having; pleasing, attractive, worthwhile, excellent, etc. —*n.* a desirable person or thing —**de·sir′a·bil′i·ty, de·sir′a·ble·ness** *n.* —**de·sir′a·bly** *adv.*

de·sire (di zīr′) *vt.* -**sired′**, -**sir′ing** [ME. *desiren* < OFr. *desirer* < L. *desiderare*, orig., prob., to await from the stars < *de-*, from + *sidus* (gen. *sideris*), a star: cf. CONSIDER] **1.** to wish or long for; crave; covet **2.** to ask for; request **3.** to want sexually —*vi.* to have or feel a desire —*n.* **1.** a strong wish or craving **2.** sexual appetite; lust **3.** an asking for something; request **4.** a thing or person desired —*SYN.*—desire, generally interchangeable with the other words here in the sense of "to long for," stresses intensity or ardor [to *desire* success]; wish is not so strong a term as desire and has special application when an unrealizable longing is meant [he *wished* summer were here]; want, specifically suggesting a longing for something lacking or needed, generally is a weaker and more formal equivalent of wish [she *wants*, or *wishes*, to go with us]; crave suggests desire to gratify a physical appetite or an urgent need [to *crave* affection]

de·sir·ous (di zīr′əs) *adj.* [ME. < OFr. *desireus* < VL. *desiderosus* < L. *desiderare*: see DESIRE] desiring; having or characterized by desire

de·sist (di zist′) *vi.* [LME. *desisten* < OFr. *desister* < L. *desistere* < *de-*, from + *sistere*, to cause to stand < *stare*, to STAND] to cease (*from* an action); stop; abstain [desist from fighting] —*SYN.* see STOP —**de·sis′tance** *n.*

desk (desk) *n.* [ME. *deske* < ML. *desca*, a table, ult. < L. *discus*: see DISCUS] **1.** a kind of table equipped with drawers, compartments, etc., and a flat or sloping top for writing, drawing, or reading **2.** a lectern **3.** *a)* the post of a clerk, official, etc. in a department or office *b)* the place in a hotel where guests are registered, mail is picked up, etc. *c)* a division of a newspaper office [the city *desk*] **4.** a musician's stand in an orchestra

des·man (des′mən, dez′-) *n.*, *pl.* -**mans** [< Sw. *desman* (*rätta*), musk (rat)] a molelike, insect-eating, aquatic mammal with webbed feet and a long, flexible snout: one species (*Desmana moschata*) is found in Russia and the other (*Galemys pyrenaicus*) in the Pyrenees

des·mid (-mid) *n.* [ModL. *desmidium*, dim. < Gr. *desmos*, a chain] any of a group of microscopic, freshwater green algae (Chlorophyta) having single cells composed of two identical half-cells with the nucleus located between them: also **des·mid′i·an**

des·moid (-moid) *adj.* [< Gr. *desmos*, a band, ligament + -OID] **1.** like a ligament **2.** of fibrous texture, as certain tumors

Des Moines (də moin′) [Fr., lit., of the monks] **1.** capital of Iowa, in the C part on the Des Moines River: pop. 201,000 **2.** river in Iowa, flowing southeast into the Mississippi; c. 325 mi.

Des·mou·lins (dā mōō lan′), (**Lucie Simplice**) **Ca·mille** (**Benoît**) (kȧ mē′y′) 1760–94; Fr. Revolutionary journalist & pamphleteer

des·o·late (des′ə lit; *for v.* -lāt′) *adj.* [ME. *desolat* < L. *desolatus*, pp. of *desolare*, to leave alone, forsake, strip of inhabitants < *de-*, intens. + *solare*, to make lonely < *solus*, alone] **1.** left alone; lonely; solitary **2.** uninhabited; deserted **3.** made uninhabitable; laid waste; in a ruinous state **4.** forlorn; wretched —*vt.* -**lat′ed**, -**lat′ing** [ME. *desolaten* < the *adj.*] **1.** to make desolate; rid of inhabitants **2.** to make uninhabitable; lay waste; devastate **3.** to forsake; abandon **4.** to make forlorn, wretched, etc. —**des′o·late·ly** *adv.* —**des′o·late·ness** *n.* —**des′o·la′tor, des′o·lat′er** *n.*

des·o·la·tion (des′ə lā′shən) *n.* [ME. *desolacioun* < OFr. *desolation* < LL.(Ec.) *desolatio*] **1.** a making desolate; laying waste **2.** a desolate condition; ruin; waste **3.** lonely grief; misery **4.** loneliness **5.** a desolate place

de·sorb (dē sôrb′) *vt.* [DE- + (AB)SORB] to remove (an adsorbed or absorbed material) by a chemical or physical process —**de·sorp′tion** (-sôrp′shən) *n.*

De So·to (di sōt′ō), **Her·nan·do** (hər nan′dō) 1500?–42; Sp. explorer in America: discovered the Mississippi River (1541): also **de Soto**

des·ox·y- (des äk′sē) *same as* DEOXY-

de·spair (di sper′) *vi.* [ME. *despeiren* < OFr. *desperer* < L. *desperare*, to be without hope < *de-*, without + *sperare*, to hope < *spes*, hope] to lose or give up hope; be without hope (usually with *of*) —*vt.* [Archaic] to give up hope of —*n.* **1.** a despairing; loss of hope **2.** a person or thing despaired of or causing despair

de·spair·ing (-in) *adj.* feeling or showing despair; hopeless —*SYN.* see HOPELESS —**de·spair′ing·ly** *adv.*

des·patch (di spach′) *vt., n. same as* DISPATCH

des·per·a·do (des′pə rä′dō, -rā′-) *n.*, *pl.* -**does**, -**dos** [OSp. pp. of *desperar* < L. *desperare*: see DESPAIR] a dangerous, reckless criminal; bold outlaw

des·per·ate (des′pər it, -prit) *adj.* [ME. *desperat* < L.

desperatus, pp. of *desperare:* see DESPAIR] **1.** *a)* driven to or resulting from loss of hope; rash or violent because of despair *[a desperate* criminal*] b)* having a very great desire, need, etc. *[desperate* for affection*]* **2.** offering so little chance, as for improvement, as to cause despair; extremely dangerous or serious *[a desperate* illness*]* **3.** extreme; drastic *[in desperate* need*]* **4.** [Archaic] despairing; without hope —*SYN.* see HOPELESS —**des'per·ate·ly** *adv.* —**des'per·ate·ness** *n.*

des·per·a·tion (des'pə rā'shən) *n.* [ME. *desperacioun* < L. *desperatio*] **1.** the state of being desperate **2.** recklessness resulting from despair

des·pi·ca·ble (des'pik ə b'l, di spik'ə b'l) *adj.* [LL. *despicabilis:* see DESPISE] deserving to be despised; contemptible —**des'pi·ca·ble·ness** *n.* —**des'pi·ca·bly** *adv.*

de·spise (di spīz') *vt.* **-spised', -spis'ing** [ME. *despisen* < OFr. *despis-*, stem of *despirer* < L. *despicere*, to look down upon, despise < *de*, down, from + *specere*, to look at: see SPECTACLE] **1.** to look down on with contempt and scorn **2.** to regard with dislike or repugnance
SYN. —**despise** implies a strong emotional response toward that which one looks down upon with contempt or aversion *[to despise* a hypocrite*];* to **scorn** is to feel indignation toward or deep contempt for *[to scorn* the offer of a bribe*];* **disdain** implies a haughty or arrogant contempt for what one considers beneath his dignity *[to disdain* flattery*];* **contemn**, chiefly a literary word, implies a vehement disapproval of a person or thing as base, vile, despicable, etc. See also HATE

de·spite (di spīt') *n.* [ME. & OFr. *despit* < L. *despectus*, a looking down upon, despising < *despicere:* see prec.] **1.** a contemptuous act; insult; injury **2.** malice; spite **3.** [Archaic] contempt; scorn —*prep.* in spite of; notwithstanding —*vt.* [Archaic] to scorn —**in despite of 1.** in defiance of **2.** in spite of

de·spite·ful (-fəl) *adj.* [ME. *despitful:* see DESPITE & FUL] [Archaic] spiteful; malicious —**de·spite'ful·ly** *adv.*

de·spit·e·ous (dis pit'ē əs) *adj.* [ME. < OFr. *despiteus:* see DESPITE & -OUS] [Archaic] spiteful; malicious

Des Plaines (des plānz') [< ?; prob. in allusion to the sugar maples *(plaines* in Miss. Valley F₁.) once there] city in NE Ill.: suburb of Chicago: pop. 57,000

de·spoil (di spoil') *vt.* [ME. *despoilen* < OFr. *despoiller* < L. *despoliare* < *de-*, intens. + *spoliare*, to strip, rob: see SPOIL] to deprive *(of* something) by force; rob; plunder —*SYN.* see RAVAGE —**de·spoil'ment** *n.*

de·spo·li·a·tion (di spō'lē ā'shən) *n.* [LL. *despoliatio:* see DESPOIL] a despoiling or being despoiled; pillage

de·spond (di spänd') *vi.* [L. *despondere*, to lose courage, yield < *de-*, from + *spondere*, to promise] to lose courage or hope; become disheartened; be depressed —*n.* despondency: now chiefly in **slough of despond**

de·spond·en·cy (-spän'dən sē) *n.* [see ff.] loss of courage or hope; dejection: also **de·spond'ence**

de·spond·ent (-dənt) *adj.* [L. *despondens*, prp. of *despondere:* see DESPOND] filled with despondency; dejected —*SYN.* see HOPELESS —**de·spond'ent·ly** *adv.*

des·pot (des'pət, -pät) *n.* [OFr. *despote* < Gr. *despotēs*, a master, lord < IE. **dems-potis*, lit., house master < **dem-*, house (whence TIMBER, L. *domus*) + **potis*, master, husband (whence L. *potis*, POTENT, Goth. *-faths*, husband)] **1.** orig., a title meaning "master," applied to certain classes of rulers, as Byzantine emperors, bishops of the Greek church, etc. **2.** an absolute ruler; king with unlimited powers; autocrat **3.** anyone in charge who acts like a tyrant

des·pot·ic (de spät'ik, di-) *adj.* [Fr. *despotique* < Gr. *despotikos*] of or like a despot; autocratic; tyrannical: also **des·pot'i·cal** —**des·pot'i·cal·ly** *adv.*

des·pot·ism (des'pə tiz'm) *n.* [Fr. *despotisme*] **1.** rule or government by a despot; autocracy **2.** the methods or acts of a despot; tyranny **3.** a government, political system, or state dominated by a despot

de·spu·mate (di spyoo'māt, des'pyoo māt') *vt.* **-mat·ed, -mat·ing** [< L. *despumatus*, pp. of *despumare*, to skim off < *de-*, off, from + *spumare*, to foam < *spuma*, foam] **1.** to take the scum off; skim **2.** to throw off as froth —*vi.* to become rid of scum —**des'pu·ma'tion** *n.*

des·qua·mate (des'kwə māt') *vi.* **-mat'ed, -mat'ing** [< L. *desquamatus*, pp. of *desquamare*, to scale off < *de-*, off + *squama*, a scale, SQUAMA] to fall off in scales; peel off —**des'qua·ma'tion** *n.*

Des·sau (des'ou) city in C East Germany: pop. 94,000

des·sert (di zurt') *n.* [ME. < OFr. < *desservir*, to clear the table < *des-* (L. *de*), from + *servir* < L. *servire*, SERVE] ☆**1.** a usually sweet course, as of pudding, pie, cake, etc. served at the end of a meal **2.** [Brit.] uncooked fruit and ♯nuts served after the sweet course

des·sert·spoon (-spoon') *n.* a spoon between a teaspoon and tablespoon in size, used for eating dessert

des·sia·tine (des'yə tēn') *n.* [Russ. *dyesyatina*, lit., tithe < *dyesyat'*, ten] a Russian unit of land measure equal to about 2.7 acres

Des·sye (des'yā) city in NC Ethiopia: pop. 53,000

de·sta·bi·lize (dē stā' bə liz') *vt.* **-lized', -liz'ing** to upset the stability or equilibrium of; unbalance

de Staël, Madame *see* STAËL

de·stain (dē stān') *vt.* to remove stain from (a specimen or part of a specimen) to facilitate microscopic study

de·Stal·i·ni·za·tion (dē stäl'i na zā'shən) *n.* the progressive elimination by the Soviet government of political methods or influences derived from Stalin

de·ster·i·lize (dē ster'ə liz') *vt.* **-lized', -liz'ing** to bring back from a sterile state; specif., to release (gold) from a neutralized position into an active position in the monetary system where it can support credit and monetary issues

‡**de Stijl** (də stil') *n.* [Du., lit., the Style, name of a journal founded in 1917 in Holland by MONDRIAN and Theodore van Doesburg] an abstract art movement marked by the use of rectangular forms and by emphasis on primary colors or grays and blacks

des·ti·na·tion (des'tə nā'shən) *n.* [ME. *destinacioun* < L. *destinatio*, settlement, appointment < *destinare*] **1.** [Rare] a destining or being destined **2.** the end for which something or someone is destined **3.** the place toward which someone or something is going or sent

des·tine (des'tin) *vt.* **-tined, -tin·ing** [ME. *destinen* < OFr. *destiner* < L. *destinare*, to fasten down, secure < *de-*, intens. + **stanare* < base of *stare*, STAND] **1.** to predetermine, as by fate: usually in the passive **2.** to set apart for a certain purpose; intend —**destined for 1.** headed for; bound for **2.** intended for *[destined for* leadership*]*

des·tin·y (des'tə nē) *n., pl.* **-ies** [ME. *destine* < OFr. *destinee*, fem. pp. of *destiner:* see prec.] **1.** the seemingly inevitable or necessary succession of events **2.** what will necessarily happen to any person or thing; (one's) fate **3.** that which determines events: said of either a supernatural agency or necessity—*SYN.* see FATE

des·ti·tute (des'tə toot', -tyoot') *adj.* [ME. < L. *destitutus*, pp. of *destituere*, to forsake, abandon < *de-*, down, away + *statuere*, to set, place: see STATUTE] **1.** not having; being without; lacking (with *of) [destitute* of trees*]* **2.** lacking the necessities of life; living in complete poverty **3.** [Obs.] abandoned —*vt.* **-tut'ed, -tut'ing** [Rare] **1.** to deprive **2.** to make destitute —*SYN.* see POOR

des·ti·tu·tion (des'tə tōō'shən, -tyōō'-) *n.* [ME. *destitucioun* < L. *destitutio*] the state of being destitute; esp., abject poverty —*SYN.* see POVERTY

des·tri·er (des'trē ər, des'trē ər) *n.* [ME. *destrer* < OFr. *destrier* < ML. *dextrarius* < VL. **dextrare*, to lead (by the right hand) < *dextra*, right hand] [Archaic] a war horse; charger

de·stroy (di stroi') *vt.* [ME. *destroien* < OFr. *destruire* < L. *destruere* < *de-*, down + *struere*, to build: see STRUCTURE] **1.** to tear down; demolish **2.** to break up or spoil completely; ruin **3.** to bring to total defeat; crush **4.** to put an end to; do away with **5.** to kill **6.** to neutralize the effect of **7.** to make useless —*vi.* to bring about destruction
SYN. —**destroy** implies a tearing down or bringing to an end by wrecking, ruining, killing, eradicating, etc. and is the term of broadest application here *[to destroy* a city, one's influence, etc.*];* **demolish** implies such destructive force as to completely smash to pieces *[the bombs demolished* the factories*];* **raze** means to level to the ground, either destructively or by systematic wrecking with a salvaging of useful parts; to **annihilate** is to destroy so completely as to blot out of existence *[rights that cannot be annihilated]*

de·stroy·er (-ər) *n.* **1.** a person or thing that destroys **2.** [orig. *torpedo-boat destroyer]* a small, fast, highly maneuverable warship armed with 3-inch or 5-inch guns, depth charges, torpedoes, etc.

☆**destroyer escort** a warship smaller and slower than a destroyer, used mainly to escort shipping

destroying angel *same as* DEATH CUP

☆**de·struct** (di strukt', dē'strukt') *n.* [back-formation < DESTRUCTION] the deliberate destruction of a malfunctioning missile, rocket, etc. after its launch —*vi.* to be automatically destroyed

de·struct·i·ble (di strukt'ə b'l) *adj.* [LL. *destructibilis*] that can be destroyed; subject to destruction —**de·struct'·i·bil'i·ty** *n.*

de·struc·tion (di struk'shən) *n.* [ME. *destruccioun* < OFr. *destruction* < L. *destructio* < *destructus*, pp. of *destruere:* see DESTROY] **1.** the act or process of destroying; demolition or slaughter **2.** the fact or state of being destroyed **3.** the cause or means of destroying —*SYN.* see RUIN

de·struc·tion·ist (-ist) *n.* a person who believes in or favors destruction, as of an existing social order

de·struc·tive (di struk'tiv) *adj.* [OFr. *destructif* < LL. *destructivus*] **1.** tending or likely to cause destruction **2.** causing or producing destruction; destroying **3.** merely negative; not helpful *[destructive* criticism*]* —**de·struc'tive·ly** *adv.* —**de·struc'tive·ness, de·struc'tiv'i·ty** *n.*

destructive distillation the decomposition of a material, as coal, wood, etc., by heat in the absence of air, followed by the recovery of volatile products of the decomposition by condensation or other means

de·struc·tor (di struk'tər) *n.* [LL. < *destructus:* see DESTRUCTION] **1.** [Brit.] an incinerator for rubbish ☆**2.** an explosive device for bringing about a destruct

des·ue·tude (des'wi tood', -tyood') *n.* [ME. < L. *desuetudo* < *desuetus*, pp. of *desuescere*, to disuse < *de-*, from + *suescere*, to be accustomed: for IE. base see ETHICAL] the

condition of not being used any more; disuse /laws fallen into *desuetude/*

de·sul·fur·ize (dē sul'fə rīz') *vt.* **-ized', -iz'ing** to remove sulfur from: also **de·sul'fur** —**de·sul'fur·i·za'tion** *n.* —**de·sul'fur·iz'er** *n.*

des·ul·to·ry (des'l tôr'ē) *adj.* [L. *desultorius* < *desultor,* vaulter < *desultus,* pp. of *desilire,* to leap down < *de-,* down, from + *salire,* to leap: see SALIENT] 1. passing from one thing to another in an aimless way; disconnected; not methodical /a *desultory* conversation/ 2. lacking direct relevancy; random; incidental /a *desultory* observation/ —*SYN.* see RANDOM —**des'ul·to'ri·ly** *adv.* —**des'ul·to'ri·ness** *n.*

det. 1. detachment 2. detail

de·tach (di tach') *vt.* [Fr. *détacher* < OFr. *detachier, destachier* < *de-,* DE- + *estachier,* to ATTACH] 1. to unfasten or separate and remove; disconnect; disengage 2. to send (troops, ships, etc.) on a special mission —**de·tach'a·bil'i·ty** *n.* —**de·tach'a·ble** *adj.*

de·tached (di tacht') *adj.* 1. not connected; separate 2. not involved by emotion, interests, etc.; aloof; impartial —*SYN.* see INDIFFERENT —**de·tach'ed·ly** (-tach'id lē) *adv.* —**de·tach'ed·ness** *n.*

de·tach·ment (di tach'mənt) *n.* [Fr. *détachement]* 1. a detaching; separation 2. *a)* the sending of troops or ships on special service *b)* a unit of troops separated from a larger unit for special duty *c)* a small permanent unit organized for special service 3. the state of being disinterested, impartial, or aloof

de·tail (di tāl', dē'tāl) *n.* [Fr. *détail* < the *v.*] 1. the act of dealing with things item by item /the *detail* of business/ 2. a minute account; circumstantial story /to go into *detail* about a trip/ 3. any of the small parts that go to make up something; item; particular /the *details* of a plan/ 4. *a)* small secondary or accessory part or parts of a picture, statue, building, etc. *b)* a small segment as of a painting, reproduced separately for detailed study 5. *a)* one or more soldiers, sailors, etc. chosen for a particular task *b)* the task itself —*vt.* [Fr. *detailler,* to cut up, tell in particulars < *dé-* (L. *de*), from + *tailler,* to cut: see TAILOR] 1. to give the particulars of; tell item by item 2. to choose for a particular task /detail a man for sentry duty/ —*SYN.* see ITEM —**in detail** item by item; with particulars

detail drawing a separate drawing of a small part or section, as of a machine, showing the details

de·tailed (di tāld', dē'tāld) *adj.* marked by careful attention to detail /a *detailed* plan/

☆**detail man** a salesman for a pharmaceutical firm who visits doctors, dentists, etc. in a certain district to describe and promote the sales of new drugs

de·tain (di tān') *vt.* [ME. *deteinen* < OFr. *detenir* < L. *detinere,* to hold down or off, keep back, detain < *de-,* off, from + *tenere,* to hold] 1. to keep in custody; confine 2. to keep from going on; hold back 3. [Obs.] to withhold —**de·tain'ment** *n.*

de·tain·er (-ər) *n.* 1. a person or thing that detains 2. [Anglo-Fr. *detener,* inf. used as *n.* < OFr. *detenir:* see prec.] *Law a)* the unlawful withholding of land or goods from the rightful owner *b)* the detention of a person without his consent *c)* a writ for continuing to hold a person already in custody

de·tas·sel (dē tas'l) *vt.* **-seled** or **-selled, -sel·ing** or **-sel·ling** to remove tassels from (corn), thus forcing cross-pollination

de·tect (di tekt') *vt.* [ME. *detecten* < L. *detectus,* pp. of *detegere,* to uncover < *de-,* from + *tegere,* to cover] 1. to catch or discover, as in a misdeed 2. to discover or manage to perceive (something hidden or not easily noticed) /to *detect* a flaw in an argument/ 3. *Radio a)* same as RECTIFY *b)* same as DEMODULATE 4. [Obs.] to uncover; reveal —**de·tect'a·ble, de·tect'i·ble** *adj.*

☆**de·tec·ta·phone** (di tek'tə fōn') *n.* [DETECT + *-a-* + (TELE)PHONE] a device for listening secretly to others' telephone conversations

de·tec·tion (-shən) *n.* [ME. < LL. *detectio:* see DETECT] 1. a finding out or being found out: said esp. of what tends to elude notice 2. same as DEMODULATION

de·tec·tive (-tiv) *adj.* 1. of or for detection 2. of detectives and their work —*n.* [short for *detective policeman*] a person, usually on a police force, whose work is investigating and trying to solve crimes, getting secret information, etc.

de·tec·tor (-tər) *n.* [LL.] 1. a person or thing that detects 2. an apparatus or device for indicating the presence of something, as electric waves 3. same as DEMODULATOR

de·tent (di tent', dē'tent) *n.* [Fr. *détente* < *détendre,* to relax, unbend < *dé-* (L. *dis-*), from + *tendre,* to stretch < L. *tendere,* to stretch out: for IE. base see THIN] *Mech.* a part that stops or releases a movement, as a catch for controlling the striking of a clock

dé·tente, de·tente (dā tänt') *n.* [Fr.: see prec.] a lessening of tension or hostility, esp. between nations, as through treaties, trade agreements, etc.

de·ten·tion (di ten'shən) *n.* [ME. *detencioun* < OFr. *detention* < L. *detentio* < *detentus,* pp. of *detinere*] a detaining or being detained; specif., *a)* a keeping in custody; confinement *b)* an enforced delay

☆**detention home** a place where juvenile offenders or delinquents are held in custody, esp. temporarily pending disposition of their cases by the juvenile court

de·ter (di tur') *vt.* **-terred', -ter'ring** [L. *deterrere* < *de-,* from + *terrere,* to frighten: see TERROR] to keep or discourage (a person) from doing something by instilling fear, anxiety, doubt, etc.

de·terge (di turj') *vt.* **-terged', -terg'ing** [L. *detergere,* to wipe off < *de-,* off, from + *tergere,* to wipe, cleanse < IE. **terg-* < base **ter-:* see THROW] to cleanse, as a wound

de·ter·gen·cy (-tur'jən sē) *n.* the quality or power of cleansing Also **de·ter'gence**

de·ter·gent (-jənt) *adj.* [L. *detergens,* prp. of *detergere:* see DETERGE] cleansing —*n.* a cleansing substance; specif., a surface-active chemical preparation that is, like soap, capable of emulsifying dirt but is made from the alkyl benzene sulfonates, the alkyl sulfates, etc. and not from fats and lye

de·te·ri·o·rate (di tir'ēə rāt') *vt., vi.* **-rat'ed, -rat'ing** [< LL. *deterioratus,* pp. of *deteriorare,* to make worse < L. *deterior,* worse, inferior < **deter,* below] to make or become worse; lower in quality or value; depreciate —**de·te'ri·o·ra'tion** *n.*

de·te·ri·o·ra·tive (-rāt'iv) *adj.* tending to deteriorate

de·ter·ment (di tur'mənt) *n.* 1. a deterring 2. a thing that deters

de·ter·mi·na·ble (di tur'mi nə b'l) *adj.* [ME. < OFr. < LL. *determinabilis*] 1. that can be determined 2. that can be ended; terminable —**de·ter'mi·na·bil'i·ty** *n.* —**de·ter'mi·na·bly** *adv.*

de·ter·mi·na·cy (-nə sē) *n.* 1. the state or quality of being determinate 2. the condition of being determined, as in being caused or in having predictable results

de·ter·mi·nant (-nənt) *adj.* [L. *determinans,* prp. of *determinare*] determining —*n.* 1. a thing or factor that determines 2. *Math.* the sum of the products formed, in accordance with certain laws, from a series of quantities arranged in an equal number of rows and columns —*SYN.* see CAUSE

de·ter·mi·nate (-nit) *adj.* [ME. < L. *determinatus,* pp. of *determinare:* see DETERMINE] 1. having exact limits; definite; distinct; fixed 2. settled or decided; conclusive 3. resolute; determined 4. *Bot.* having a flower at the end of the primary axis and of each secondary axis; cymose 5. *Math. a)* having a fixed value *b)* of problems, having sufficient conditions stated for a solution to exist and be unique —**de·ter'mi·nate·ly** *adv.* —**de·ter'mi·nate·ness** *n.*

determinate cleavage cell division in a fertilized or unfertilized egg resulting in daughter cells no longer able to produce by themselves a complete embryo

☆**determinate growth** 1. growth of a plant stem that is terminated early by the formation of a bud 2. naturally self-limited growth, resulting in a plant of a definite maximum size

de·ter·mi·na·tion (di tur'mə nā'shən) *n.* [L. *determinatio*] 1. a determining or being determined (in all senses of the verb) 2. a firm intention 3. the quality of being resolute; firmness of purpose 4. *Law* the ending of an estate or of an interest or right in property

de·ter·mi·na·tive (di tur'mə nā'tiv, -nə tiv) *adj.* [Fr. *déterminatif*] determining or serving to determine —*n.* a thing or factor that determines —**de·ter'mi·na'tive·ly** *adv.* —**de·ter'mi·na·tive·ness** *n.*

de·ter·mi·na·tor (-nāt'ər) *n.* same as DETERMINER

de·ter·mine (di tur'mən) *vt.* **-mined, -min·ing** [ME. *determinen* < OFr. *determiner* < L. *determinare,* to bound, limit < *de-,* from + *terminare,* to set bounds < *terminus,* an end: for IE. base see TERM] 1. to set limits to; bound; define 2. to settle (a dispute, question, etc.) conclusively; decide 3. to reach a decision about after thought and investigation; decide upon 4. to establish or affect the nature, kind, or quality of; fix /genes *determine* heredity/ 5. to find out exactly; calculate precisely; ascertain /to *determine* a ship's position/ 6. to give a definite aim or direction to; direct /a decision that *determines* the future/ 7. *Law* to end; terminate —*vi.* 1. to decide; resolve 2. *Law* to come to an end —*SYN.* see DECIDE, LEARN

de·ter·mined (-mənd) *adj.* 1. having one's mind made up; decided; resolved 2. resolute; unwavering —**de·ter'mined·ly** *adv.* —**de·ter'mined·ness** *n.*

de·ter·min·er (-mən ər) *n.* anything that determines, as, specif., a word, such as *the, a, an, this,* etc., that determines the use of a noun without significantly modifying it

de·ter·min·ism (-mə niz'm) *n.* the doctrine that everything, esp. one's choice of action, is determined by a sequence of causes independent of one's will —**de·ter'min·ist** *n., adj.* —**de·ter'min·is'tic** *adj.* —**de·ter'min·is'ti·cal·ly** *adv.*

de·ter·rence (di tur'əns) *n.* the act of deterring

de·ter·rent (-ənt) *adj.* [L. *deterrens,* prp. of *deterrere*] deterring or tending to deter —*n.* a thing or factor that deters; hindrance

de·ter·sive (di tur'siv) *adj., n.* [Fr. *détersif* < L. *detersus,* pp. of *detergere:* see DETERGE] detergent

de·test (di test') *vt.* [Fr. *détester* < L. *detestari,* to curse by calling the gods to witness, execrate, detest < *de-,* down + *testari,* to witness < *testis,* a witness: see TESTIFY] to dislike intensely; hate; abhor —*SYN.* see HATE —**de·test'er** *n.*

de·test·a·ble (di tes'tə b'l) *adj.* [ME. & OFr. < L. *detestabilis*] that is or should be detested; hateful; execrable; odious —*SYN.* see HATEFUL —**de·test'a·bil'i·ty, de·test'a·ble·ness** *n.* —**de·test'a·bly** *adv.*

de·tes·ta·tion (dē'tes tā'shən) *n.* [ME. *detestacioun* < OFr.

detestation < L. *detestatio:* see DETEST] **1.** intense dislike or hatred; loathing **2.** a detested person or thing

de·throne (dē thrōn′) *vt.* **-throned′, -thron′ing 1.** to remove from a throne; depose **2.** to oust from any high position —**de·throne′ment** *n.* —**de·thron′er** *n.*

det·i·nue (det′n yōō′, -i nōō′) *n.* [ME. < OFr., fem. pp. of *detenir:* see DETAIN] *Law* **1.** the unlawful detention of personal property which originally was rightfully acquired **2.** an action or writ for the recovery of property unlawfully detained, as in a pawnshop

det·o·nate (det′n āt′) *vi.* **-nat′ed, -nat′ing** [< L. *detonatus,* pp. of *detonare,* to thunder < *de-,* intens. + *tonare,* THUNDER] to explode violently and noisily —*vt.* to cause (a bomb, dynamite, etc.) to explode —**det′o·na′tion** *n.*

det·o·na·tor (-āt′ər) *n.* [see DETONATE] **1.** a fuse, percussion cap, etc. for setting off explosives **2.** an explosive

de·tour (dē′toor, di toor′) *n.* [Fr. *détour,* a turning, evasion < *détourner,* to turn aside < OFr. *destourner* < *des-* (L. *dis-*) + *tourner:* see TURN] **1.** a roundabout way; deviation from a direct way **2.** a route used when the direct or regular route is closed to traffic —*vi., vt.* to go or cause to go by way of a detour

de·tox·i·fy (dē tāk′sə fī′) *vt.* **-fied′, -fy′ing** [DE- + TOXI(N) + -FY] to remove a poison or a poisonous effect from —**de·tox′i·fi·ca′tion** *n.*

de·tract (di trakt′) *vt.* [ME. *detracten* < L. *detractare,* to decline, depreciate < *detractus,* pp. of *detrahere,* to draw away < *de-,* from + *trahere,* to DRAW] **1.** to take or draw away **2.** [Now Rare] to belittle; disparage —*vi.* to take something desirable away (*from*) [frowning *detracts* from her beauty] —**de·trac′tor** *n.*

de·trac·tion (-trak′shən) *n.* [ME. *detraccioun*] **1.** [Rare] a taking away; detracting **2.** a malicious discrediting of someone's character, accomplishments, etc., as by revealing hidden faults or by slander; defamation —**de·trac′·tive** *adj.*

de·train (dē trān′) *vi., vt.* to get off or remove from a railroad train —**de·train′ment** *n.*

de·trib·a·lize (dē trī′bə līz′) *vi., vt.* **-lized′, -liz′ing** [DE- + TRIBAL + -IZE] to abandon or cause to abandon tribal organization —**de·trib′al·i·za′tion** *n.*

det·ri·ment (det′rə mənt) *n.* [ME. & OFr. < L. *detrimentum,* a rubbing off, damage < *detritus,* pp. of *deterere,* to rub off, wear away < *de-,* off, from + *terere,* to rub, wear: for IE. base see THROW] **1.** damage; injury; harm **2.** anything that causes damage or injury

det·ri·men·tal (det′rə men′t'l) *adj.* [see prec.] causing damage; harmful —*SYN.* see PERNICIOUS —**det′ri·men′tal·ly** *adv.*

de·tri·tion (di trish′ən) *n.* [ML. *detritio:* see DETRIMENT + -ION] a wearing away or down by friction

de·tri·tus (di trīt′əs) *n.* [L., a rubbing away: see DETRIMENT] **1.** fragments of rock produced by disintegration or wearing away **2.** any accumulation of disintegrated material, or debris —**de·tri′tal** (-′l) *adj.*

De·troit (di troit′) [< Fr. *détroit,* strait: first applied to the river] **1.** city in SE Mich., on the Detroit River: pop. 1,511,000 (met. area 4,200,000) **2.** river flowing south from Lake St. Clair into Lake Erie: c. 31 mi.

‡**de trop** (də trō′) [Fr.] **1.** too much; too many **2.** unwanted; superfluous; in the way

de·trude (di trōōd′) *vt.* **-trud′ed, -trud′ing** [L. *detrudere* < *de-,* down + *trudere,* THRUST] **1.** to press down with force **2.** to thrust away or out —**de·tru′sion** *n.*

de·trun·cate (di trun′kāt) *vt.* **-cat·ed, -cat·ing** [< L. *detruncatus,* pp. of *detruncare:* see DE- & TRUNCATE] to shorten by cutting off a part

de·tu·mes·cence (dē′too mes′ns, -tyōō-) *n.* [< L. *detumescens,* prp. of *detumescere,* to stop swelling, subside: see DE- & TUMESCENCE] a subsidence, or lessening, of a swelling —**de′tu·mes′cent** *adj.*

Deu·ca·lion (dōō kāl′yən, dyōō-) [L. < Gr. *Deukaliōn*] *Gr. Myth.* a son of Prometheus and husband of Pyrrha, with whom he survived a great flood sent by Zeus and became the ancestor of all succeeding mankind

deuce[1] (dōōs, dyōōs) *n.* [ME. & OFr. *deus* < L. *duos,* acc. of *duo,* TWO] **1.** a playing card with two spots **2.** the side of a die bearing two spots, or a throw of the dice totaling two **3.** [< Fr. *à deux de jeu*] *Tennis* a score of 40 each (or five games each) after which one player or side must get two successive points (or games) to win the game (or set)

deuce[2] (dōōs, dyōōs) *n., interj.* [ME. *dewes,* God < OFr. *dieu* & L. *deus* (see DEITY): associated with DEUCE[1], in reference to low score at dice] bad luck, the devil, etc.: a mild oath or exclamation of annoyance, surprise, etc.

deu·ced (dōō′sid, dyōō′-; dōōst, dyōōst) *adj.* [see prec.] **1.** devilish; confounded **2.** extreme Used in mild oaths or exclamations —*adv.* extremely; very: also **deu′ced·ly**

Deur·ne (dër′nə) city in N Belgium: suburb of Antwerp: pop. 72,000

‡**De·us** (dā′oos, dē′əs) [L.] God

‡**de·us ex ma·chi·na** (eks′ mak′i nə) [L., god from a machine] **1.** in ancient Greek and Roman plays, a deity brought in by stage machinery to intervene in the action **2.** any unconvincing character or event brought artificially into the plot of a story, play, etc. to settle an involved situation **3.** anyone who unexpectedly intervenes to change the course of events

Deut. Deuteronomy

deu·ter·ag·o·nist (dōōt′ə rag′ə nist, dyōōt′-) *n.* [Gr. *deuteragōnistēs:* see DEUTERO- & AGONIZE] *Ancient Gr. Drama* the character second in importance to the protagonist

deu·ter·an·ope (dōōt′ər ə nōp′, dyōōt′-) *n.* a person who has deuteranopia

deu·ter·an·o·pi·a (dōōt′ər ə nō′pē ə, dyōōt′-) *n.* [DEUTER- + AN-[1] + -OPIA] defective color vision in the red-yellow-green part of the spectrum

deu·ter·at·ed (dōōt′ər āt′id, dyōōt′-) *adj.* **1.** designating or of a substance, compound, or organism in which part or all of the normal hydrogen atoms are replaced with deuterium **2.** containing deuterium

☆**deu·ter·ide** (dōōt′ə rīd′, dyōōt′-) *n.* [DEUTER(IUM) + -IDE] a compound analogous to a hydride, in which ordinary hydrogen is replaced by deuterium

☆**deu·te·ri·um** (dōō tir′ē əm, dyōō-) *n.* [ModL.: see DEUTERO- & -IUM] the hydrogen isotope having an atomic weight of 2.0141 and boiling point of −249.7°C; heavy hydrogen: symbol, D: with oxygen it forms deuterium oxide, D_2O (heavy water)

deu·ter·o-, deu·ter- (dōōt′ər ō, dyōōt′-) [< Gr. *deuteros,* second, orig., farther from, a compar. form < base of *deuein,* dial. var. of *dein,* to lack, be far from < IE. base *deu-,* to move away, distance, whence Sans. *dūráḥ,* remote, L. *durare,* to last] *a combining form meaning* second, secondary [*deuteroplasm*]

deu·ter·o·ca·non·i·cal (dōōt′ər ō′kə nän′ə k'l, dyōōt′-) *adj.* [prec. + CANONICAL] of or constituting a second or subsequent canon; specif., designating certain Biblical books accepted as canonical in the R.C.Church, but held by Protestants to be apocryphal

deu·ter·og·a·my (dōōt′ə räg′ə mē, dyōōt′-) *n.* [ML. *deuterogamia* < Gr. < *deuteros,* second + *gamos,* marriage] a marriage after the death or divorce of the first spouse

☆**deu·ter·on** (dōōt′ər än′, dyōōt′-) *n.* [ModL.: see DEUTERIUM] the nucleus of an atom of deuterium containing one proton and one neutron

Deu·ter·on·o·my (dōōt′ər än′ə mē, dyōōt′-) *n.* [LL.(Ec.) *Deuteronomium* < Gr. *Deuteronomion:* see DEUTERO- & -NOMY] the fifth book of the Pentateuch in the Bible, in which the law of Moses is set down in full for the second time

deu·to- (dōōt′ə, dyōōt′-) *same as* DEUTERO-: also, before a vowel, **deut-**

deu·to·plasm (-plaz′m) *n.* [DEUTO- + -PLASM] the yolky substance in eggs or ova that provides food for the developing embryo: also **deu′ter·o·plasm′** —**deu′to·plas′mic** (-plaz′mik) *adj.*

deut·sche mark (doi′chə märk′) *pl.* **mark′, marks′** the monetary unit of West Germany; abbrev. **DM** See MONETARY UNITS, table

Deutsch·land (doich′länt′) [G. < *Deutsch,* German (< OHG. *diutisc,* of the people < OHG. *thioda,* akin to OE. *theod,* people < IE. *teutā-,* crowd < *teu-,* to swell, whence L. *tumere,* to swell, E. THUMB, THOUSAND) + OHG. *-isc, -ISH* + G. *land,* LAND] Ger. *name of* GERMANY

deut·zi·a (dōōt′sē ə, dyōōt′-, doit′-) *n.* [ModL., after Jean *Deutz,* 18th-c. Du. flower fancier] any of a genus (*Deutzia*) of small shrubs of the saxifrage family, bearing many white flowers in the spring

de·va ((dā′və) *n.* [Sans., god: see DEITY] *Hindu Myth.* a god or good spirit

De Va·ler·a (dev′ə ler′ə, -lir′ə), **Ea·mon** (ā′mən) 1882– ; Ir. statesman, born in U.S.; prime minister of Ireland (1937–48; 1951–54; 1957–59); president of Ireland (1959–)

de·val·u·a·tion (dē val′yoo wā′shən) *n.* **1.** *a*) a reduction in the amount or fineness of a metal, esp. gold, officially designated as the standard of value of a monetary unit *b*) an official lowering of the exchange value of a currency with reference to other currencies **2.** a lessening in value, importance, etc.

de·val·ue (dē val′yōō) *vt.* **-ued, -u·ing 1.** to lessen or, sometimes, annul the value, importance, etc. of **2.** to subject (a monetary unit or a currency) to devaluation Also **de·val′u·ate′** (-yoo wāt′) **-at′ed, -at′ing**

De·va·na·ga·ri (dā′və nä′gər ē) *n.* [Sans. *devanāgarī,* city (writing) of the gods < *deva,* god (see DEITY) + *nāgara,* city] the alphabet in which Sanskrit and most northern Indic languages are written

dev·as·tate (dev′ə stāt′) *vt.* **-tat′ed, -tat′ing** [< L. *devastatus,* pp. of *devastare,* to lay waste < *de-,* intens. + *vastare,* to make empty < *vastus,* empty: see VAST] **1.** to lay waste; make desolate; ravage; destroy **2.** to make helpless; overwhelm [a *devastating* remark] —**dev′as·tat′ing·ly** *adv.* —**dev′as·ta′tor** *n.*

dev·as·ta·tion (dev′ə stā′shən) *n.* a devastating or being devastated; destruction; desolation

dev·el (dev′'l) *n.* [< ?] [Scot.] a heavy or stunning blow —*vt.* [Scot.] to strike with such a blow

de·vel·op (di vel′əp) *vt.* [Fr. *développer* < *de-* (L. *dis-*),

apart + OFr. *voloper*, to wrap: see ENVELOP] **I.** to cause to grow gradually in some way; cause to become gradually fuller, larger, better, etc.; esp., **1.** to build up or expand (a business, industry, etc.) **2.** to make stronger or more effective; strengthen (muscles) **3.** to bring (something latent or hypothetical) into activity or reality **4.** to cause (one's personality, a bud, etc.) to unfold or evolve gradually **5.** to make (housing, highways, etc.) more available or extensive **6.** *Music* to elaborate (a theme) as by rhythmic or melodic changes **7.** *Photog. a)* to put (an exposed film, plate, or printing paper) in various chemical solutions in order to make the picture visible *b)* to make (a picture) visible by doing this **II.** to show or work out by degrees; reveal; disclose; esp., **1.** to make (a theme or plot) known gradually **2.** to explain more clearly; enlarge upon **3.** *Geom.* to change the form of (a surface); esp., to flatten out (a curved surface) **4.** *Math.* to work out in detail or expand (a function or expression) —*vi.* **1.** to come into being or activity; occur or happen **2.** to become larger, fuller, better, etc.; grow or evolve, esp. by natural processes **3.** to become known or apparent; be disclosed **4.** to progress economically, socially, and politically after emergence into statehood /the *developing* nations/ —**de·vel'op·a·ble** *adj.*

de·vel·op·er (-ər) *n.* a person or thing that develops; specif., *a)* a person who develops real estate on a speculative basis *b)* *Photog.* a chemical used to develop film, plates, etc.

de·vel·op·ment (-mənt) *n.* [Fr. *développement*] **1.** a developing or being developed **2.** a step or stage in growth, advancement, etc. **3.** an event or happening **4.** a thing that is developed; specif., a number of structures on a large tract of land, built by a real-estate developer —**de·vel'op·men'tal** (-men't'l) *adj.* —**de·vel'op·men'tal·ly** *adv.*

De·ven·ter (dā'vən tər) city in E Netherlands: medieval commercial & educational center: pop. 59,000

de·verb·a·tive (di vur'bə tiv) *adj.* [DE- + VERB + -ATIVE] formed from a verb or indicating derivation from a verb —*n.* a deverbative word

Dev·e·reux (dev'ə rōō', -rooks'), **Robert** *see* ESSEX²

de·vest (di vest') *vt.* [OFr. *devester* < L. *devestire*, to undress < *dis-*, from + *vestire*, to dress < *vestis*, a dress: see VEST] **1.** orig., to undress; strip **2.** *Law a)* to take away (a right, property, etc.) *b)* [Archaic] to strip (of a title, etc.)

De·vi (dā'vē) [Sans., fem. of *deva*, god: see DEITY] a Hindu goddess, the consort of Siva

de·vi·ant (dē'vē ənt) *adj.* [< LL. *devians*, prp. of *deviare*: see ff.] deviating, esp. from what is considered normal in a group or for a society —*n.* a person whose behavior is deviant —**de'vi·an·cy, de'vi·ance** *n.*

de·vi·ate (dē'vē āt'; *for adj. &* n., -it) *vi.* **-at'ed, -at'ing** [< LL. *deviatus*, pp. of *deviare*, to turn aside < *de-*, from + *via*, road: see VIA] to turn aside (*from* a course, direction, standard, doctrine, etc.); diverge; digress —*vt.* to cause to deviate —*adj. same as* DEVIANT —*n.* a deviant; esp., one whose sexual behavior is deviant —**de'vi·a'tor** *n.*

SYN.—**deviate** suggests a turning aside, often to only a slight degree, from the correct or prescribed course, standard, doctrine, etc. /to *deviate* from the truth/; **swerve** implies a sudden or sharp turning from a path, course, etc. /the car *swerved* to avoid hitting us/; **veer**, originally used of ships and wind, suggests a turning or series of turnings so as to change direction; **diverge** suggests the branching off of a single path or course into two courses constantly leading away from each other /the sides of an angle *diverge* from a single point/; **digress** suggests a wandering, often deliberate and temporary, from the main topic in speaking or writing

de·vi·a·tion (dē'vē ā'shən) *n.* [ME. *deviacion* < LL. *deviatio*] the act or an instance of deviating; specif., *a)* sharp divergence from normal behavior *b)* divergence from the official ideology or policies of a political party *c)* the deflection of a compass needle due to magnetic influences, as in a ship *d)* *Statistics* a measure of the way items are distributed in a frequency distribution: see MEAN DEVIATION, STANDARD DEVIATION

de·vi·a·tion·ism (-iz'm) *n.* the practice or advocacy of deviation in politics —**de'vi·a'tion·ist** *adj., n.*

de·vice (di vīs') *n.* [ME. & OFr. *devis*, division, will < *diviser*: see DEVISE] **1.** a thing devised; plan; scheme; esp., a sly or underhanded scheme; trick **2.** a mechanical invention or contrivance for some specific purpose **3.** something used to gain an artistic effect /rhetorical *devices*/ **4.** an ornamental figure or design **5.** a design, often with a motto, on a coat of arms; heraldic emblem **6.** any motto or emblem **7.** [Archaic] the act or power of devising —**leave to one's own devices** to allow to do as one wishes

dev·il (dev''l) *n.* [ME. *devel* < OE. *deofol* < LL.(Ec.) *diabolus* < Gr. *diabolos*, slanderous (in LXX, Satan; in NT., devil) < *diaballein*, to slander, lit., throw across < *dia-*, across + *ballein*, to throw] **1.** [*often* D-] *Theol. a)* the chief evil spirit, a supernatural being subordinate to, and the foe of, God and the tempter of man; Satan (with *the*): he is typically depicted as a man with horns, a tail, and cloven feet *b)* any of such subordinate beings who reside in hell; demon **2.** a very wicked or malevolent person **3.** a person who is mischievous, energetic, reckless, etc. **4.** an unlucky, unhappy person /that poor devil/ **5.** anything difficult, hard to operate, control, understand, etc. **6.** [orig. *printer's devil* (17th c.)] a printer's errand boy or apprentice **7.** any of various machines for tearing things,

as paper or rags, to bits —*vt.* **-iled** or **-illed, -il·ing** or **-il·ling 1.** [from the notion of heat] to prepare (food, often finely chopped food) with hot seasoning /*deviled* ham/ **2.** to tear up (rags, etc.) with a special machine ☆**3.** to annoy; torment; tease —**a devil of** a an extreme example of a —**between the devil and the deep (blue) sea** between equally unpleasant alternatives —**give the devil his due** to acknowledge the ability or success of even a wicked or unpleasant person —**go to the devil** to fall into bad habits; degenerate morally: used also in the imperative as an expression of anger, annoyance, etc. —**play the devil with** [Colloq.] to cause to go awry; upset —**raise the devil 1.** to conjure up the devil **2.** [Colloq.] to make a commotion or have a boisterous good time —**the devil!** [Colloq.] an exclamation of anger, surprise, negation, etc.: often in such phrases as **the devil you did!**, meaning "did you really?" —**the devil take the hindmost** leave the last, slowest, or least able to his fate without bothering about him —**the devil to pay** trouble as a consequence

dev·il·fish (-fish') *n., pl.* -fish', -fish'es: see FISH² **1.** any of several large rays (genus *Manta*) of warm seas: so called because its pectoral fins are hornlike when rolled up **2.** any large cephalopod, esp. the octopus

DEVILFISH
(to 20 ft. across)

dev·il·ish (dev''l ish, dev'lish) *adj.* [ME. *develish*] **1.** of, like, or characteristic of a devil or devils; wicked; cruel; diabolical **2.** mischievous; energetic; reckless **3.** [Colloq.] extremely bad **4.** [Colloq.] very great; extreme —*adv.* [Colloq.] extremely; excessively; very —**dev'il·ish·ly** *adv.* —**dev'il·ish·ness** *n.*

dev·il·kin (-kin) *n.* [DEVIL + -KIN] a little devil; imp

dev·il-may-care (dev''l mā ker') *adj.* reckless or careless; happy-go-lucky

dev·il·ment (dev''l mənt) *n.* **1.** [Archaic] evil behavior or action **2.** mischief or mischievous action

dev·il·ry (-rē) *n., pl.* -ries [ME. *develri*] [Chiefly Brit.] **1.** black magic; witchcraft **2.** evil or diabolical behavior; great wickedness or cruelty **3.** *same as* DEVILTRY

devil's advocate [transl. of ML. *advocatus diaboli*] **1.** *R.C.Ch.* an official selected to examine critically the facts and raise objections in the case of a dead person named for beatification or canonization **2.** a person who upholds the wrong side or an indefensible cause, perversely or for argument's sake

dev·il's-darn·ing-nee·dle (dev''lz där'niŋ nē'd'l) *n.* **1.** *same as* DRAGONFLY **2.** *same as* DAMSELFLY

☆**dev·il's-food cake** (dev''lz food') a rich cake made with chocolate or cocoa and baking soda

Devil's Island Fr. island off the coast of French Guiana: site of a former penal colony (1851-1951): Fr. name, ÎLE DU DIABLE

☆**devil's paintbrush** a perennial European plant (*Hieracium aurantiacum*) of the composite family, with naked flower stalks bearing a cluster of orange-red heads: now a common weed in N U.S. and Canada

devil's tattoo a rapid or nervous drumming with the fingers or feet

dev·il's walk·ing-stick (dev''lz wôk'iŋ stik') ☆*same as* HERCULES'-CLUB (sense 1)

dev·il·try (-trē) *n., pl.* -tries [altered < DEVILRY] **1.** reckless mischief, fun, etc. **2.** *same as* DEVILRY

☆**dev·il·wood** (-wood') *n.* a small evergreen tree (*Osmanthus americanus*) of the olive family, with whitish bark, glossy leaves, greenish flowers, and hard wood, found in SE U.S.

de·vi·ous (dē'vē əs) *adj.* [L. *devius* < *de-*, off, from + *via*, road: see VIA] **1.** not in a straight path; roundabout; winding **2.** deviating from the proper or usual course; going astray **3.** not straightforward or frank; deceiving —**de'vi·ous·ly** *adv.* —**de'vi·ous·ness** *n.*

de·vis·al (di vī'z'l) *n.* the act of devising

de·vise (di vīz') *vt., vi.* **-vised', -vis'ing** [ME. *devisen* < OFr. *deviser*, to distribute, direct, regulate, talk < VL. *divisare* < L. *divisus*, pp. of *dividere*: see DIVIDE] **1.** to work out or create (something) by thinking; contrive; plan; invent **2.** *Law* to bequeath (real property) by will **3.** [Archaic] to make secret plans for; plot **4.** [Obs.] to guess or imagine —*n. Law* **1.** a gift of real property by will **2.** a will, or clause in a will, granting such a gift **3.** the property so granted —**de·vis'a·ble** *adj.* —**de·vis'er** *n.*

dev·i·see (dev'ə zē', di vī'zē') *n.* [< DEVISE + -EE¹] *Law* the person to whom real property has been devised

de·vi·sor (dev'ə zôr', di vī'zôr) *n.* [Anglo-Fr. *devisour*] *Law* a person who devises property; testator

de·vi·tal·ize (dē vīt''l īz') *vt.* **-ized', -iz'ing 1.** to make lifeless; kill **2.** to lower the vitality of; weaken —**de·vi'tal·i·za'tion** *n.*

de·vit·ri·fy (dē vit'rə fī') *vt.* **-fied', -fy'ing** [Fr. *dévitrifier*: see DE- & VITRIFY] **1.** to take away or destroy the glassy qualities of **2.** to make (glass, etc.) opaque, hard, and crystalline, as by prolonged heating —**de·vit'ri·fi·ca'tion** *n.*

de·voice (dē vois') *vt.* **-voiced', -voic'ing** *same as* UNVOICE: also **de·vo'cal·ize'** (-vō'k'l īz') **-lzed', -iz'ing**

de·void (di void') *adj.* [ME., orig. pp. of *devoiden*, to put away < OFr. *desvuidier* < *des-* (L. *dis-*), from + *vuidier*: see VOID] completely without; empty or destitute (*of*)

de·voir (də vwär′, dev′wär) n. [ME.< OFr., to owe < L. *debere*, to owe: see DEBT] 1. duty 2. [*pl.*] acts or expressions of due respect or courtesy as in greeting

dev·o·lu·tion (dev′ə lōō′shən) n. [ML. *devolutio*, a rolling back < L. *devolutus*, pp. of *devolvere:* see ff.] 1. orig., a rolling down or falling 2. a passing down from stage to stage 3. the passing (of property, rights, authority, etc.) from one person to another 4. a delegating (of duties) to a substitute or subordinate 5. a delegating (of power or authority) by a central government to local governing units 6. *Biol.* evolution of structures toward greater simplicity or disappearance; degeneration —**dev′o·lu′tion·ar′y** adj. —**dev′o·lu′tion·ist** n.

de·volve (di välv′) vt., vi. -**volved′**, -**volv′ing** [ME. *devolven* < L. *devolvere*, to roll down < *de-*, down + *volvere*, to roll: see WALK] 1. orig., to roll down or onward 2. to pass (on) to another or others: said of duties, responsibilities, etc. —**de·volve′ment** n.

Dev·on (dev′ən) 1. Canadian island in the Arctic Ocean, north of Baffin Island: 20,861 sq. mi. 2. *same as* DEVONSHIRE —n. any of a breed of small, hardy cattle, originally raised in Devonshire

De·vo·ni·an (di vō′nē ən) adj. 1. of Devon or Devonshire 2. *Geol.* designating or of the period after the Silurian and before the Carboniferous in the Paleozoic Era, marked by an abundance of fishes and the appearance of the first authentic land plants and amphibians: so called because its rocks were first studied in Devonshire —n. a native or inhabitant of Devon or Devonshire —**the Devonian** the Devonian Period or its rocks: see GEOLOGY, chart

Dev·on·shire (dev′ən shir′) county of SW England, on the English Channel: 2,612 sq. mi.; pop. 833,000; county seat, Exeter

de·vote (di vōt′) vt. -**vot′ed**, -**vot′ing** [< L. *devotus*, pp. of *devovere*, to dedicate by vow < *de-*, from + *vovere*, to vow: see VOTE] 1. to set apart for a special use or service; dedicate 2. to give up (oneself or one's time, energy, etc.) to some purpose, activity, or person 3. [Archaic] curse or doom —**de·vote′ment** n.

SYN.—**devote** suggests the giving up or applying of oneself or something with the seriousness or earnestness evoked by a formal vow [to *devote* one's life to a cause]; to **dedicate** is to set apart or assign (something), as in a formal rite, to some serious, often sacred, purpose [to *dedicate* a temple]; to **consecrate** is to set apart for some religious or holy use [to *consecrate* ground for a church]; **hallow**, a stronger word, suggests an intrinsic holiness in the thing set apart [to *hallow* the Sabbath]

de·vot·ed (-id) adj. 1. dedicated; consecrated 2. very loving, loyal, or faithful 3. [Archaic] doomed —**de·vot′ed·ly** adv. —**de·vot′ed·ness** n.

dev·o·tee (dev′ə tē′, -tā′) n. 1. a person strongly devoted to something or someone [a *devotee* of the ballet] 2. a person extremely devoted to religion; zealot

de·vo·tion (di vō′shən) n. [ME. *devociun* < OFr. *devotion* < L. *devotio*] 1. the fact, quality, or state of being devoted 2. piety; devoutness 3. religious worship 4. [*pl.*] prayers, esp. as used in private 5. loyalty or deep affection 6. the act of devoting

de·vo·tion·al (-'l) adj. of or characterized by devotion —☆n. a brief worship service —**de·vo′tion·al·ly** adv.

de·vour (di vour′) vt. [ME. *devouren* < OFr. *devorer* < L. *devorare* < *de-*, intens. + *vorare*, to swallow whole: see VORACIOUS] 1. to eat or eat up hungrily, greedily, or voraciously 2. to consume or destroy with devastating force 3. to take in greedily with the eyes, ears, or mind [the child *devours* fairy tales] 4. to absorb completely; engross [*devoured* by curiosity] 5. to swallow up; engulf —**de·vour′er** n.

de·vout (di vout′) adj. [ME. < OFr. *devot* < L. *devotus*, devoted (in LL.(Ec.), devout): see DEVOTE] 1. very religious; pious 2. showing reverence 3. earnest; sincere; heartfelt —**de·vout′ly** adv. —**de·vout′ness** n.

SYN.—**devout** implies sincere, worshipful devotion to one's faith or religion; **pious** suggests scrupulous adherence to the forms of one's religion but may, in derogatory usage, connote hypocrisy [the *pious* burghers who defraud their tenants]; **religious** stresses faith in a particular religion and constant adherence to its tenets [to lead a *religious* life]; **sanctimonious** in current usage implies a hypocritical pretense of piety or devoutness and often connotes smugness or haughtiness [his *sanctimonious* disapproval of dancing] —ANT. impious

De Vries (də vrēs′), Hugo 1848–1935; Du. botanist

dew (dōō, dyōō) n. [ME. < OE. *deaw*, akin to G. *tau* < IE. base **dheu-*, to run, whence Sans. *dhāvati*, a spring, brook] 1. the moisture that condenses after a warm day and appears during the night in little drops on cool surfaces 2. anything regarded as refreshing, gently falling, pure, etc., like dew 3. any moisture in small drops [the *dew* of his brow] —vt. [Poet.] to wet with or as with drops of dew; bedew

de·wan (di wän′) n. [Hind. *dīwān* < Per.: see DIVAN] in India, any of various high officials

Dew·ar (flask) (dyōō′ər, dōō′-) [after Sir James *Dewar* (1842–1923), Scot. chemist & physicist who invented it] a double-walled flask with a vacuum between the walls that are silvered on the inside, used esp. for storage of liquefied gases: also sp. **dew′ar**

dew·ber·ry (dōō′ber′ē, dyōō′-) n., *pl.* -**ries** 1. any of various trailing blackberry plants (genus *Rubus*) of the rose family 2. the fruit of any of these plants

dew·claw (-klô′) n. 1. a functionless digit on the foot of some animals, as on the inner side of a dog's leg or above the true hoof in cattle, deer, etc. 2. the claw or hoof at the end of such a digit

dew·drop (-dräp′) n. a drop of dew

Dew·ey (dōō′ē, dyōō′-) 1. George, 1837–1917; U.S. admiral in the Spanish-American War 2. John, 1859–1952; U.S. philosopher & educator: exponent of pragmatism 3. Melvil, (born *Melville Louis Kossuth Dewey*) 1851–1931; U.S. librarian & educator: originator of a system (**Dewey Decimal System**) for book classification in libraries, using three-digit numbers, further extended beyond a decimal point for subclasses

dew·fall (-fôl′) n. 1. the formation of dew 2. the time of the evening when this begins

dew·lap (-lap′) n. [ME. *dewlappe:* see DEW & LAP[1]] a loose fold of skin hanging from the throat of cattle and certain other animals, or a similar loose fold under the chin of an elderly person —**dew′lapped′** (-lapt′) adj.

☆**DEW line** (dōō, dyōō) [*Distant Early Warning*] a line of radar stations near the 70th parallel in North America

dew point the temperature at which dew starts to form or vapor to condense into liquid

dew-point spread (dōō′point′, dyōō′-) the degrees of difference between the air temperature and the dew point: also called **dew-point deficit, dew-point depression**

dew worm *same as* NIGHT CRAWLER

dew·y (-ē) adj. **dew′i·er, dew′i·est** [ME. *deui* < OE. *deawig*] 1. wet or damp with dew 2. of dew 3. [Poet.] dewlike; refreshing, gentle, etc. [*dewy* slumber] —**dew′i·ly** adv. —**dew′i·ness** n.

☆**Dex·e·drine** (dek′sə drēn′, -drin) [DEX(TRO-) + (EPH)-EDRINE] a trademark for dextroamphetamine

dex·i·o·trop·ic (dek′sē ō träp′ik) adj. [< Gr. *dexios*, on or toward the right (for IE. base see DEXTER) + -TROPIC] turning from left to right, as the whorls in most gastropod shells

Dex·ter (dek′stər) [L.: see ff.] a masculine name

dex·ter (dek′stər) adj. [L. *dextor*, right, to the right < IE. **deks-* < base **dek-*, to take: see DECENT] 1. of or on the right-hand side 2. [Obs.] auspicious because seen on the right 3. *Heraldry* on the right-hand side of a shield (the left of the viewer): opposed to SINISTER

dex·ter·i·ty (dek ster′ə tē) n. [L. *dexteritas*, skillfulness, handiness < *dexter:* see prec.] 1. skill in using one's hands or body; adroitness 2. skill in using one's mind; cleverness 3. [Rare] right-handedness

dex·ter·ous (dek′strəs, -stər əs) adj. [L. *dexter* (see DEXTER) + -OUS] 1. having or showing skill in the use of the hands or body 2. having or showing mental skill 3. [Rare] right-handed —**dex′ter·ous·ly** adv. —**dex′ter·ous·ness** n.
SYN.—**dexterous** implies an expertness, natural or acquired, demonstrated in the ability to do things with skill and precision [a *dexterous* mechanic]; **adroit** adds to this a connotation of cleverness and resourcefulness and is now generally used of mental facility [an *adroit* evasion]; **deft** suggests a nimbleness and sureness of touch [a *deft* seamstress]; **handy** suggests skill, usually without training, at a variety of small tasks [a *handy* man around the house] —ANT. clumsy, awkward, inept

dextr- *same as* DEXTRO-: used before a vowel

dex·tral (dek′strəl) adj. [< L. *dextra*, right-hand side (see DEXTER) + -AL] 1. on the right-hand side; right 2. right-handed 3. having whorls that rise to the apex in counter-clockwise spirals: said of the shells of certain mollusks with the apex toward the viewer Opposed to SINISTRAL —**dex·tral′i·ty** (-stral′ə tē) n. —**dex′tral·ly** adv.

dex·tran (dek′stran, -strən) n. [DEXTR- + -AN] a chainlike polymer of glucose produced by certain strains of bacteria acting on sucrose, as in sugar refinery tanks or in various fermentation processes: it is used as a substitute or expander for blood plasma, in confections, as an emulsifying agent, etc.

dex·trin (dek′strin) n. [Fr. *dextrine* (see DEXTER & -IN[1]): so called because it rotates the plane of polarization to the right] any of a number of water-soluble, gummy, dextrorotatory polysaccharides obtained from the breakdown of starch and used as adhesives, as sizes, in certain foods, etc.: also **dex′trine** (-strēn, -strən)

dex·tro (dek′strō) adj. Chem. *same as* DEXTROROTATORY

dex·tro- (dek′strə, -strō) [< L. *dexter:* see DEXTER] a combining form meaning: 1. toward or on the right-hand side [*dextrorotatory*] 2. Chem. dextrorotatory

dex·tro·am·phet·a·mine (dek′strō am fet′ə mēn′) n. [DEXTRO- + AMPHETAMINE] a drug used as a central nervous system stimulant and appetite depressant

dex·tro·glu·cose (-glōō′kōs) n. *same as* DEXTROSE

dex·tro·gy·rate (-jī′rāt) adj. [DEXTRO- + GYRATE] *same as* DEXTROROTATORY

dex·tro·ro·ta·tion (-rō tā′shən) n. dextrorotatory direction or movement

fat, āpe, cär; ten, ēven; is, bīte; gō, hôrn, tōōl, look; oil, out; up, fur; get; joy; yet; chin; she; thin, *th*en; zh, leisure; ŋ, ring; ə for a in ago, e in agent, i in sanity, o in comply, u in focus; ′ as in able (ā′b'l); Fr. bāl; ë, Fr. coeur; ö, Fr. feu; ô, Fr. mon; ö, Fr. coq; ü, Fr. duc; r, Fr. cri; H, G. ich; kh, G. doch. See inside front cover. ☆ Americanism; ‡foreign; *hypothetical; <derived from

dex·tro·ro·ta·to·ry (-rōt′ə tôr′ē) *adj.* **1.** turning or circling to the right, in a clockwise direction **2.** that turns the plane of polarized light clockwise: said of certain crystals, etc. Also **dex′tro·ro′ta·ry** (-rōt′ər ē)

dex·trorse (dek′strôrs) *adj.* [L. *dextrorsus*, toward the right < *dexter* (see DEXTER) + *versus*, to turn: see VERSE] *Bot.* twining upward to the right, as the stem of the hop: opposed to SINISTRORSE—**dex′trorse·ly** *adv.*

dex·trose (dek′strōs) *n.* [DEXTR- + -OSE] a crystalline, dextrorotatory glucose, $C_6H_{12}O_6$, found in plants and animals and in the human blood, and made by the hydrolysis of starch with acids or enzymes

dex·trous (-strəs) *adj. same as* DEX-TEROUS

DEXTRORSE VINE

dey (dā) *n.* [Fr. *dey* < Turk. *dāi*, maternal uncle: orig., friendly title given to an older person] **1.** the former title of the governor of Algiers **2.** a pasha in the former Barbary States of Tunis or Tripoli

Dezh·nev (dyezh′nyev), **Cape** cape at the northeastern-most point of Asia, in the R.S.F.S.R., projecting into Bering Strait: also **Cape Dezh′nev·a** (-nye və)

DF, D/F, D.F. *Radio* **1.** direction finder **2.** direction-finding

D.F. 1. [L. *Defensor Fidei*] Defender of the Faith **2.** [Sp. *Distrito Federal*] Federal District (in Mexico)

D.F.A. Doctor of Fine Arts

D.F.C., DFC Distinguished Flying Cross

dg. decigram; decigrams

d.h. [G. *das heisst*] that is; namely; i.e.

‡**dhar·ma** (dur′mə, där′-) *n.* [Sans., law, custom < IE. base *dher-, to hold, support, whence L. *firmus*, OHG. *tarnen*, to conceal] *Hinduism, Buddhism* **1.** cosmic order or law, including the natural and moral principles that apply to all beings and things **2.** dutiful observance of this law in one's life; right conduct

‡**dhar·na** (-nə) *n.* [Hind. *dharnā*, persistence, a holding firm: for IE. base see prec.] in India, a method of seeking justice by sitting at the door of one's debtor or wrongdoer and fasting to death if necessary

Dhau·la·gi·ri (dou′lə gir′ē) mountain of the Himalayas, in NC Nepal: 26,810 ft.

‡**dho·bi** (dō′bē) *n.* [Hind. < *dhob*, washing, akin to Sans. *dhāvati*, (he) cleans, *dhavala*, shining white < IE. base *dheu-, gleaming] in India, a person who does laundry

dhole (dōl) *n., pl.* **dholes, dhole:** see PLURAL, II, D, 1 [native name] a red-colored, wild dog (*Cuon alpinus*) of Central and E Asia, that hunts in packs, attacking even large game

D-horizon *n.* a stratum, as of rock, sometimes underlying the C-horizon

dho·ti (dō′tē) *n.* [Hind. *dhotī*] a loincloth worn by Hindu men, or the cloth used for it: also **dhoo′ti** (dōō′-)

dhow (dou) *n.* [< Ar. *dāwa*] a single-masted ship with a lateen sail, sharp prow, and raised deck at the stern, used in the Indian Ocean, esp. along coasts

dhur·na (dur′nə) *n. same as* DHARNA

di-[1] (dī) [Gr. *di-* < *dis*, twice < IE. *dwis* (whence L. *bis*, MHG. *zwis*) < base *dwo*, TWO] *a prefix meaning:* **1.** twice, double, twofold [*dichroism, dicotyledon*] **2.** *Chem.* having two atoms, molecules, radicals, etc. [*diacid*] Also **dis-**

di-[2] (di) *same as* DIS-

di-[3] (dī) *same as* DIA-

di., dia. diameter

di·a- (dī′ə) [ME. < OFr. < L. < Gr. *dia*, through, across < *disa*, in two, apart < IE. *dis-* < base *dwo*, TWO] *a prefix meaning:* **1.** through, throughout, across [*diaphragm, diagonal*] **2.** apart, between [*diagnose, diacritical*]

di·a·base (dī′ə bās′) *n.* [Fr. < Gr. *diabasis*, a crossing over < *dia-*, through + *bainein*, to go, COME] **1.** formerly, diorite **2.** a finely crystalline basaltic rock made up mainly of plagioclase feldspar and pyroxene **3.** [Brit.] altered dolerite—**di′a·bas′ic** (-bā′sik) *adj.*

di·a·be·tes (dī′ə bēt′is, -ēz) *n.* [ME. *diabete* < L. *diabetes*, siphon (in LL., diabetes) < Gr. *diabētēs* < *diabainein*, to pass through < *dia-*, through + *bainein*, to go, COME] any of various diseases characterized by an excessive discharge of urine; esp., DIABETES MELLITUS

diabetes in·sip·i·dus (in sip′i dəs) [ModL., lit., insipid diabetes] a disorder caused by a pituitary deficiency and characterized by the heavy discharge of urine and intense thirst

diabetes mel·li·tus (mə līt′is) [ModL., lit., honey diabetes < L. *mellitus*, honeysweet < *mel*, honey] a chronic form of diabetes involving an insulin deficiency and characterized by excess of sugar in the blood and urine, hunger, thirst, and gradual loss of weight

di·a·bet·ic (dī′ə bet′ik) *adj.* of or having diabetes —*n.* a person who has diabetes

di·a·ble·rie (dē ä′blər ē) *n.* [Fr. < OFr. < *diable*, devil < LL.(Ec.) *diabolus:* see DEVIL] **1.** *a)* a supposed dealing with devils, as by sorcery or witchcraft *b)* diabolical behavior; great wickedness **2.** lore about devils, diabolism, etc. **3.** deviltry; mischief

di·a·bol·ic (dī′ə bäl′ik) *adj.* [Fr. *diabolique* < LL.(Ec.) *diabolicus* < *diabolus:* see DEVIL] **1.** of the Devil or devils

2. very wicked or cruel; fiendish Also **di′a·bol′i·cal** —**di′a·bol′i·cal·ly** *adv.*

di·ab·o·lism (dī ab′ə liz′m) *n.* [< LL.(Ec.) *diabolus* (see DEVIL) + -ISM] **1.** supposed dealings with the Devil or devils, as by sorcery or witchcraft **2.** belief in or worship of the Devil or devils **3.** diabolical action or behavior **4.** the character or condition of the Devil or a devil —**di·ab′o·list** (-list) *n.*

di·ab·o·lize (-līz′) *vt.* **-lized′, -liz′ing** **1.** to make diabolical **2.** to portray as diabolical

di·ab·o·lo (dē ab′ə lō′) *n.* [c. 1907; prob. < Gr. *dia-*, across + *bolē*, a throw < *ballein*, to throw, but associated with It. *diavolo*, a devil] a toy consisting of a wooden spool which is whirled and tossed on a string tied to two sticks held one in each hand

DIABOLO

di·a·caus·tic (dī′ə kôs′tik) *adj.* [DIA- + CAUSTIC] designating or of a caustic curve or surface formed by refraction —*n.* a diacaustic curve or surface

di·a·chron·ic (-krän′ik) *adj.* [DIA- + CHRONIC] of or concerned with the study of changes occurring over a period of time, as in language, mores, etc. —**di′a·chron′i·cal·ly** *adv.*

di·ac·id (dī as′id) *adj.* **1.** containing in each molecule two atoms of hydrogen replaceable by basic atoms or radicals: usually said of acids and acid salts **2.** capable of forming a salt or ester by reacting with one molecule of a diacid, or two of a monoacid: usually said of bases and alcohols —*n.* an acid having in each molecule two hydrogen atoms which can be replaced by a metal or react with basic substances

di·ac·o·nal (dī ak′ə n'l) *adj.* [LL.(Ec.) *diaconalis*] of a deacon or deacons

di·ac·o·nate (-nit) *n.* [LL.(Ec.) *diaconatus*] **1.** the rank, office, or tenure of a deacon **2.** a group or board of deacons

di·a·crit·ic (dī′ə krit′ik) *adj.* [Gr. *diakritikos* < *diakrinein*, to distinguish < *dia-*, across + *krinein*, to separate: see CRITIC] *same as* DIACRITICAL —*n.* a diacritical mark

di·a·crit·i·cal (-i k'l) *adj.* **1.** serving to distinguish; distinguishing **2.** able to distinguish —**di′a·crit′i·cal·ly** *adv.*

diacritical mark a mark, such as a macron or a cedilla, added to a letter or symbol to show its pronunciation or to distinguish it in some way

di·ac·tin·ic (dī′ak tin′ik) *adj.* capable of transmitting actinic rays of light —**di·ac′tin·ism** *n.*

di·a·del·phous (dī′ə del′fəs) *adj.* [< DI-[1] + Gr. *adelphos*, brother + -OUS] **1.** arranged in two bundles or sets by the fusion of the filaments: said of stamens **2.** having the stamens so arranged, as in the sweet pea

di·a·dem (dī′ə dem′, -dəm) *n.* [ME. & OFr. *diademe* < L. *diadema* < Gr. *diadēma*, a band, fillet < *dia-*, through + IE. *demn*, a band < base *de-*, to bind, whence Gr. *dein*] **1.** a crown **2.** an ornamental cloth headband worn as a crown **3.** royal power, authority, or dignity —*vt.* to put a diadem on; crown

DIADELPHOUS STAMENS (of pea)

di·ad·ro·mous (dī ad′rə məs) *adj.* [DIA- + -DROMOUS] **1.** *Bot.* with leaf veins radiating in a fanlike arrangement **2.** *Zool.* migrating between fresh and salt water: said of certain fishes

di·aer·e·sis (dī er′ə sis) *n. same as* DIERESIS

diag. 1. diagonal **2.** diagram

di·a·gen·e·sis (dī′ə jen′ə sis) *n.* [ModL.: see DIA- & -GENE-SIS] *Geol.* the physical and chemical changes occurring in sediments during and after the period of deposition up until the time of consolidation

di·a·ge·o·tro·pism (dī′ə jē ät′rə piz′m) *n.* [DIA- + GEOT-ROPISM] the tendency of the stems, branches, rhizomes, etc. of certain plants to grow in a direction horizontal to the surface of the earth —**di′a·ge′o·trop′ic** (-jē′ə träp′ik) *adj.*

Dia·ghi·lev (dyä′gi lyef; *E.* -lef), **Ser·gei Pav·lo·vich** (syer gyä′i päv lô′vich) 1872–1929; Russ. ballet producer & choreographer

di·ag·nose (dī′əg nōs′, -nōz′) *vt., vi.* **-nosed′, -nos′ing** [< DIAGNOSIS] to make a diagnosis of (a disease, a problem, etc.) —**di′ag·nos′a·ble** *adj.*

di·ag·no·sis (dī′əg nō′sis) *n., pl.* **-ses** (-sēz) [ModL. < Gr. *diagnōsis*, a distinguishing < *diagignōskein*, to distinguish < *dia-*, through, between + *gignōskein*, KNOW] **1.** the act or process of deciding the nature of a diseased condition by examination of the symptoms **2.** a careful examination and analysis of the facts in an attempt to understand or explain something [*a diagnosis of the economy*] **3.** a decision or opinion based on such examination **4.** *Biol.* a short scientific description for taxonomic classification

di·ag·nos·tic (-näs′tik) *adj.* [ML. *diagnosticus* < Gr. *diagnōstikos*] **1.** of or constituting a diagnosis **2.** of value for a diagnosis; specif., characteristic —*n.* **1.** [*usually pl., with sing. v.*] the art, science, or method of diagnosis, esp. medical diagnosis **2.** a distinguishing sign or symptom; characteristic —**di′ag·nos′ti·cal·ly** *adv.*

di·ag·nos·ti·cian (dī′əg näs tish′ən) *n.* a person who makes diagnoses; specif., a specialist in diagnostics

di·ag·o·nal (dī ag′ə n'l) *adj.* [L. *diagonalis* < Gr. *diagōnios* < *dia-*, through + *gōnia*, an angle, corner: for IE. base see KNEE] **1.** extending between the vertices of any two nonadjacent angles in a polygonal figure or between any two vertices not in the same face in a polyhedral figure; extending slantingly between opposite corners **2.** moving or extending obliquely, esp. at a 45° angle; slanting **3.** having slanting markings, lines, etc. —*n.* **1.** *a*) a diagonal line or plane *b*) *same as* VIRGULE **2.** any diagonal course, row, order, or part **3.** cloth woven with diagonal lines; twill —**di·ag′o·nal·ly** *adv.*

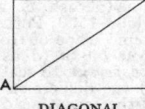

DIAGONAL

di·a·gram (dī′ə gram′) *n.* [Gr. *diagramma* < *diagraphein*, to mark out by lines, draw < *dia-*, through, across + *graphein*, to write: see GRAPHIC] **1.** a geometrical figure, often used to illustrate a theorem **2.** a sketch, drawing, or plan that explains a thing by outlining its parts and their relationships, workings, etc. **3.** a chart or graph explaining or illustrating ideas, statistics, etc. —*vt.* **-gramed′** or **-grammed′, -gram′ing** or **-gram′ming** to show or represent by a diagram; make a diagram of —**di′a·gram·mat′ic** (-grə mat′ik), **di′a·gram·mat′i·cal** *adj.* —**di′a·gram·mat′i·cal·ly** *adv.*

di·a·ki·ne·sis (dī′ə ki nē′sis) *n.* [ModL. < DIA- + Gr. *kinēsis*, motion: see KINEMATICS] in the meiosis of germ cells, a stage in which the maternal and paternal chromosomes have paired within the nucleus —**di′a·ki·net′ic** (-net′ik) *adj.*

di·al (dī′əl, dīl) *n.* [ME. < ML. *dialis*, daily < L. *dies*, day: see DEITY] **1.** a sundial **2.** the face of a watch or clock **3.** the face of a meter, gauge, compass, etc. on which a pointer or the like indicates an amount, degree, direction, etc. **4.** a graduated disk on a radio, or television set, esp. one for tuning in stations or channels ☆**5.** a rotating disk on a telephone, used in making connections automatically —*vt.,* *vi.* **-aled** or **-alled, -al·ing** or **-al·ling 1.** to measure with or as with a dial **2.** to show on a dial **3.** to tune in (a radio station, television channel, program, etc.) ☆**4.** to call on a telephone by using a dial

dial. **1.** dialect(al) **2.** dialectic(al)

di·a·lect (dī′ə lekt′) *n.* [L. *dialectus* < Gr. *dialektos*, discourse, discussion, dialect < *dialegesthai*, to discourse, talk < *dia-*, between + *legein*, to choose, talk: see LOGIC] **1.** the sum total of local characteristics of speech **2.** the sum total of an individual's characteristics of speech; idiolect **3.** any form of speech considered as deviating from a real or imaginary standard speech **4.** the form or variety of a spoken language peculiar to a region, community, social group, occupational group, etc.: in this sense, *dialects* are regarded as being, to some degree, mutually intelligible while *languages* are not mutually intelligible **5.** any language as a member of a group or family of languages [English is a West Germanic *dialect*] —*adj.* of or in dialect [*dialect* ballads] —**di′a·lec′tal** *adj.* —**di′a·lec′tal·ly** *adv.*

SYN.—**dialect**, in this comparison, refers to a form of a language peculiar to a locality or group and differing from the standard language in matters of pronunciation, syntax, etc.; **vernacular** today commonly refers to the informal or colloquial variety of a language as distinguished from the formal or literary variety; **cant**, in this connection, refers to the distinctive stock words and phrases used by a particular sect, class, etc. [clergymen's *cant*]; **jargon** is used of the special vocabulary and idioms of a particular class, occupational group, etc., esp. by one who is unfamiliar with these; **argot** refers esp. to the secret jargon of thieves and tramps; **lingo** is a humorous or mildly contemptuous term applied to any language, dialect, or jargon by one to whom it is unintelligible

dialect atlas *same as* LINGUISTIC ATLAS

dialect geography *same as* LINGUISTIC GEOGRAPHY

di·a·lec·tic (dī′ə lek′tik) *n.* [ME. *dialetik* < OFr. *dialetique* < L. *dialectica* (*ars*) < Gr. *dialektikē* (*technē*) the dialectic (art) < *dialektikos*: see DIALECT] **1.** [*often pl.*] the art or practice of examining opinions or ideas logically, often by the method of question and answer, so as to determine their validity **2.** logical argumentation **3.** [*often pl.*] *a*) the method of logic used by Hegel and adapted by Marx to observable social and economic processes: it is based on the principle that an idea or event (*thesis*) generates its opposite (*antithesis*) leading to a reconciliation of opposites (*synthesis*) *b*) the general application of this principle in analysis, criticism, exposition, etc. —*adj.* same as DIALECTICAL

di·a·lec·ti·cal (-ti k'l) *adj.* **1.** of or using dialectic or dialectics **2.** of or characteristic of a dialect; dialectal —**di′a·lec′ti·cal·ly** *adv.*

dialectical materialism the philosophy stemming from Marx and Engels which applies Hegel's dialectical method to observable social processes and to nature

di·a·lec·ti·cian (dī′ə lek tish′ən) *n.* [Fr. *dialecticien*] **1.** an expert in dialectics; logician **2.** a specialist in dialects

di·a·lec·tol·o·gy (-täl′ə jē) *n.* the scientific study of dialects —**di′a·lec·tol′o·gist** *n.* —**di′a·lec′to·log′i·cal** (-tə läj′i k'l) *adj.* —**di′a·lec′to·log′i·cal·ly** *adv.*

di·al·lage (dī′ə lij) *n.* [Fr. < Gr. *diallagē*, change, interchange < *diallassein*, to interchange < *dia*, through + *allassein*, to alter < *allos*, other (see ELSE): so named from having unlike fracture planes] a dark-green mineral that is a laminated variety of pyroxene

di·a·log (dī′ə lôg′, -läg′) *n., v. same as* DIALOGUE

di·a·log·i·cal (dī′ə läj′i k'l) *adj.* of or marked by dialogue: also **di′a·log′ic** —**di′a·log′i·cal·ly** *adv.*

di·al·o·gist (dī al′ə jist, dī′ə lôg′ist, -läg′-) *n.* **1.** a writer of dialogue **2.** a person who takes part in a dialogue —**di·al·o·gis·tic** (dī′ə lō jis′tik) *adj.*

di·a·logue (dī′ə lôg′, -läg′) *n.* [ME. *dialog* < OFr. *dialogue* < L. *dialogus* < Gr. *dialogos* < *dialegesthai*: see DIALECT] **1.** a talking together; conversation **2.** interchange and discussion of ideas, esp. when open and frank, as in seeking mutual understanding or harmony **3.** a written work in the form of a conversation **4.** the passages of talk in a play, story, radio act, etc. —*vi.* **-logued′, -logu′ing** to hold a conversation —*vt.* to express in dialogue

Dialogue Mass *R.C.Ch.* a Low Mass at which the congregation, following an earlier custom now revived, makes the responses aloud and in unison

☆**dial tone** a low buzzing sound indicating to the user of a dial telephone that the line is open and a number may be dialed

di·al·y·sis (dī al′ə sis) *n., pl.* **-ses′** (-sēz′) [L. < Gr., separation, dissolution < *dialyein*, to separate, dissolve < *dia-*, apart + *lyein*, LOOSE] the separation of crystalloids or dissolved substances from colloids in solution by the greater diffusibility of the smaller molecules through a semipermeable membrane: used as in the mechanical elimination of impurities from the blood during kidney failure —**di·a·lyt·ic** (dī′ə lit′ik) *adj.* —**di′a·lyt′i·cal·ly** *adv.*

di·a·lyze (dī′ə līz′) *vt.* **-lyzed′, -lyz′ing** to apply dialysis to or separate by dialysis —*vi.* to undergo dialysis

di·a·lyz·er (-lī′zər) *n.* an apparatus for dialyzing, esp. one used as an artificial kidney

diam. diameter

di·a·mag·net·ic (dī′ə mag net′ik) *adj.* having or relating to diamagnetism —*n.* a diamagnetic substance, as bismuth or zinc: also **di′a·mag′net**

di·a·mag·net·ism (-mag′nə tiz′m) *n.* **1.** the property that certain substances have of being repelled by both poles of a magnet and hence taking a position at right angles to the magnet's line of influence **2.** diamagnetic force **3.** diamagnetic phenomena **4.** the science that deals with such phenomena and substances

di·a·man·té (dē′ə män tā′, -män′tä; *Fr.* dyä män tā′) *adj.* [Fr. < pp. of *diamanter*, to tinsel, lit., set with diamonds < *diamant*, DIAMOND] decorated with rhinestones or with other brightly glittering bits of material [*diamanté* sandals] —*n.* glittering ornamentation

di·am·e·ter (dī am′ət ər) *n.* [ME. & OFr. *diametre* < ML. *diametra* < L. *diametros* < Gr. *diametros* < *dia-*, through + *metron*, a measure: see METER¹] **1.** a straight line passing through the center of a circle, sphere, etc. from one side to the other **2.** the length of such a line; width or thickness of a circular, or somewhat circular, figure or object **3.** *Optics* the unit of measure of the magnifying power of a lens

di·a·met·ri·cal (dī′ə met′ri k'l) *adj.* **1.** of or along a diameter: also **di·am·e·tral** (dī am′ə trəl) **2.** designating an opposite, a contrary, a difference, etc. that is wholly so; complete [*diametrical* opposites]: also **di′a·met′ric** —**di′a·met′ri·cal·ly** *adv.*

di·am·ine (dī am′ēn, -in; dī′ə mēn′) *n.* any of a group of chemical compounds containing two NH_2 radicals; double amine

di·a·mond (dī′mənd, -ə mənd) *n.* [ME. *diamaunt* < OFr. *diamant* < ML. *diamas* (gen. *diamantis*), for L. *adamas* < Gr. *adamas*, adamant, diamond] **1.** a mineral consisting of nearly pure carbon in crystalline form, usually colorless, the hardest natural substance known: transparent, unflawed stones are cut into precious gems of great brilliance; less perfect forms are used for cutting tools, abrasives, phonograph-needle tips, etc. **2.** a gem or other piece cut from this mineral **3.** *a*) a lozenge-shaped plane figure (◊) *b*) a red mark like this, used for one of the four suits of playing cards *c*) [*pl.*] this suit *d*) a card of this suit ☆**4.** *Baseball a*) the infield *b*) the whole playing field —*adj.* of, like, or set with a diamond or diamonds —*vt.* to adorn with or as with diamonds —**diamond in the rough 1.** a diamond in its natural state **2.** a person or thing of fine quality but lacking polish

diamond anniversary the sixtieth, or sometimes seventy-fifth, anniversary of an event

di·a·mond·back (-bak′) *adj.* having diamond-shaped markings on the back —*n.* ☆**1.** a large, poisonous rattlesnake (*Crotalus adamanteus*) with diamond-shaped markings on its back, native to the S U.S. ☆**2.** an edible turtle (*Malaclemys terrapin*) with diamond-shaped markings on its shell, found in coastal salt marshes from Cape Cod to Mexico: in full, **diamondback terrapin 3.** a small, brown and white cosmopolitan moth (*Plutella maculipennis*) whose wings, when folded, form a diamond

Diamond Head promontory in Honolulu, Hawaii

diamond jubilee *same as* DIAMOND ANNIVERSARY

diamond wedding a sixtieth, or sometimes seventy-fifth, wedding anniversary

Di·an·a (dī anʹə) [ML. < L. < *Diviana < divus, dius, divine: see DEITY] 1. a feminine name: Fr. Diane 2. Rom. Myth. the virgin goddess of the moon and of hunting: identified with Artemis

di·an·drous (dī anʹdrəs) adj. [DI-¹ + -ANDROUS] having two stamens

di·a·no·et·ic (dīʹə nō etʹik) adj. [< Gr. dianoētikos < dia-, through + noein, to think over] of or proceeding from logical reasoning rather than intuition

di·an·thus (dī anʹthəs) n. [ModL. < Gr. dios, divine (see DEITY) + anthos, a flower] any of a genus (Dianthus) of plants of the pink family, as the carnation, sweet William, etc.

di·a·pa·son (dīʹə pāzʹ'n, -pāsʹ-) n. [ME. diapasoun < L. diapason < Gr. diapasōn, contr. < hē dia pasōn chordōn symphōnia, concord through all of the notes < dia, through + pasōn, gen. pl. of pas, all] 1. a) the entire range of a musical instrument or voice b) the entire range of some activity, emotion, etc. 2. one of the principal stops of an organ covering the instrument's complete range and producing its characteristic tone quality 3. a swelling burst of harmony 4. a standard of musical pitch 5. a tuning fork 6. [Obs.] the interval of an octave 7. [Obs.] complete harmony

☆**di·a·pause** (dīʹə pôzʹ) n. [Gr. diapausis, a pause < dia-pauein, to bring to an end, pause: see DIA- & PAUSE] a period of delayed development or growth accompanied by reduced metabolism and inactivity, esp. in certain insects, snails, etc.

di·a·pe·de·sis (dīʹə pə dēʹsəs) n. [ModL. < Gr. diapēdēsis, lit., a leaping through < dia-, through + pēdan, to leap < IE. base *pēd-, FOOT] the migration of blood cells, esp. erythrocytes, through intact capillary walls into the tissues —**di'a·pe·det'ic** (-detʹik) adj.

di·a·per (dīʹpər, dīʹə pər) n. [ME. < OFr. diapre, diaspre, kind of ornamented cloth < ML. diasprum, flowered cloth, altered (after dia-, DIA-, because of ML. pronun. of initial j-) < jaspis < L. iaspis, JASPER] 1. a) orig., cloth or fabric with a pattern of repeated small figures, such as diamonds b) a napkin, towel, etc. of such cloth c) such a pattern, as in art 2. a soft, absorbent cloth folded and arranged between the legs and around the waist of a baby —vt. 1. to give a diaper design to 2. to put a fresh diaper on (a baby)

di·aph·a·nous (dī afʹə nəs) adj. [ML. diaphanus < Gr. diaphanēs, transparent < diaphainein, to shine through < dia-, through + phainein, to show] 1. so fine or gauzy in texture as to be transparent or translucent [diaphanous cloth] 2. vague or indistinct; airy —**di·aph'a·nous·ly** adv. —**di·aph'a·nous·ness** n.

di·a·phone (dīʹə fōnʹ) n. [DIA- + -PHONE] a group of sounds popularly recognized as being the same although pronounced with slight differences by various speakers: see PHONEME

di·a·pho·re·sis (dīʹə fə rēʹsis) n. [LL. < Gr. diaphorēsis, a carrying away, perspiration < diaphorein < dia-, through + pherein, BEAR] perspiration, esp. when profuse

di·a·pho·ret·ic (-retʹik) adj. [ME. diaforetic < LL. diaphoreticus: see prec.] producing or increasing perspiration —n. a diaphoretic medicine, treatment, etc.

di·a·phragm (dīʹə framʹ) n. [ME. diafragma < LL. diaphragma < Gr. < dia-, through + phragma, a fence < phrassein, to enclose] 1. the partition of muscles and tendons between the chest cavity and the abdominal cavity; midriff 2. a) any membrane or partition that separates one thing from another b) a dividing wall at the node of a plant stem 3. a device to regulate the amount of light entering the lens of a camera, microscope, etc. ☆4. a kind of contraceptive pessary 5. a thin, flexible disk or cone that vibrates in response to sound waves to produce electrical signals, as in a microphone, or that vibrates in response to electrical signals to produce sound waves, as in a loudspeaker —**di'a·phrag·mat'ic** (-frag matʹik) adj. —**di'a·phrag·mat'i·cal·ly** adv.

di·aph·y·sis (dī afʹə sis) n., pl. -ses' (-sēzʹ) [ModL. < Gr., line of separation, spinous process of the tibia < diaphyein, to grow through < dia-, through + phyein, to bring forth, produce] the shaft of a long bone, as distinguished from the growing ends —**di·a·phys·e·al, di·a·phys·i·al** (dīʹə fizʹē əl) adj.

di·a·poph·y·sis (dīʹə päfʹə sis) n., pl. -ses' (-sēzʹ) [ModL.: see DIA- & APOPHYSIS] the transverse process of a vertebra —**di·ap·o·phys·i·al** (dīʹap ə fizʹē əl) adj.

di·ar·chy (dīʹär kē) n., pl. -chies [DI-¹ + -ARCHY] government shared by two rulers, powers, etc.

di·a·rist (dīʹə rist) n. a person who keeps a diary

di·ar·rhe·a, di·ar·rhoe·a (dīʹə rēʹə) n. [ME. diarea < OFr. diarrie & LL. diarrhoea < Gr. diarrhoia < dia-, through + rhein, to flow] excessive frequency and looseness of bowel movements —**di'ar·rhe'al, di'ar·rhe'ic** adj.

di·ar·thro·sis (dīʹär thrōʹsis) n., pl. -ses' (-sēzʹ) [ModL. < Gr. diarthrōsis < diarthroun, to divide by joints, articulate < dia-, through + arthroun, to connect by a joint < arthron, a joint: see ARTHRO-] Anat. any articulation, as of the hip, permitting free movement in any direction

di·a·ry (dīʹə rē) n., pl. -ries [L. diarium, daily allowance (of food or pay); hence, record of this < dies, day: see DEITY]

1. a daily written record, esp. of the writer's own experiences, thoughts, etc. 2. a book for keeping such a record

Di·as (dēʹəsh; E. -əs), **Bar·tho·lo·me·u** (bärʹtoo loo meʹoo) 1450?–1500; Port. navigator & explorer; first European to round Cape of Good Hope (1486)

Di·as·po·ra (dī asʹpə rə) n. [Gr. diaspora, a scattering < diasperein, to scatter < dia-, across + speirein, to sow] 1. a) the dispersion of the Jews after the Babylonian exile b) the Jews thus dispersed c) the places where they settled 2. [d-] any scattering of people with a common origin, background, beliefs, etc.

di·a·spore (dīʹə spôrʹ) n. [< Gr. diaspora: see prec.] a native hydrate of aluminum, Al₂O₃·H₂O, which crackles and disperses when heated

di·a·stase (dīʹə stāsʹ) n. [Fr. < Gr. diastasis, a separation < dia, apart + histanai, to STAND] a vegetable amylase enzyme, occurring in the seed of grains and malt, that is capable of changing starches into maltose and later into dextrose —**di·a·stat·ic** (dīʹə statʹik) adj.

di·a·stem (dīʹə stemʹ) n. [LL. diastema < Gr. diastēma, an interval < diistanai, to set apart < dia-, apart + histanai, to cause to stand, STAND] a minor interruption in the deposition of sedimentary material

di·a·ste·ma (dīʹə stēʹmə) n., pl. -ste'ma·ta (-tə) [Gr. diastēma: see prec.] a marked gap between two teeth, esp. of the upper jaw —**di'a·ste·mat'ic** (-sti matʹik) adj.

di·as·ter (dī asʹtər) n. [DI-¹ + -ASTER¹] the stage of mitosis, just preceding the formation of the two new nuclei, in which there is a set of chromosomes near each pole of the spindle —**di·as'tral** adj.

di·as·to·le (dī asʹtə lēʹ) n. [LL. < Gr. diastolē, expansion, dilatation < diastellein, to separate, dilate < dia-, apart + stellein, to put: see LOCUS] 1. the usual rhythmic dilatation of the heart, esp. of the ventricles, following each contraction (systole), during which the heart muscle relaxes and the chambers fill with blood 2. Gr. & Latin Prosody the lengthening of a short syllable —**di·a·stol·ic** (dīʹə stälʹik) adj.

di·as·tro·phism (dī asʹtrə fiz'm) n. [< Gr. diastrophē, distortion < diastrephein, to turn aside, distort < dia-, aside + strephein, to turn + -ISM] 1. the process by which the earth's surface is reshaped through rock movements and displacements 2. formations so made —**di·a·stroph·ic** (dīʹə sträfʹik) adj.

di·a·tes·sa·ron (dīʹə tesʹə ränʹ) n. [L.(Ec.), in Tatian 2d c. A.D. (in L., a medicine made of four drugs) < Gr. dia, through + tessarōn, gen. of tessares, four] the four Gospels combined into a single account

di·a·ther·man·cy (dīʹə thurʹmən sē) n. [Fr. diathermansie < Gr. dia-, through + thermansis, a heating] the property of transmitting infrared or heat rays —**di'a·ther'ma·nous** adj.

di·a·ther·mic (-mik) adj. [Fr. diathermique] 1. relating to diathermy 2. letting heat rays pass through freely

di·a·ther·my (dīʹə thurʹmē) n. [ModL. diathermia < Gr. dia-, through + thermē, heat] medical treatment in which heat is produced in the tissues beneath the skin by a high-frequency electric current

di·ath·e·sis (dī athʹə sis) n., pl. -ses' (-sēzʹ) [LL. < Gr. diathesis, arrangement < diatithenai, to arrange < dia-, apart + tithenai, to put] a predisposition to certain diseases —**di·a·thet·ic** (dīʹə thetʹik) adj.

di·a·tom (dīʹə tämʹ, -ət əm) n. [ModL. diatoma < Gr. diatomos, cut in two < diatemnein, to cut through < dia-, through + temnein, to cut] any of a number of related microscopic algae (phylum Chrysophyta), one-celled or in colonies, whose cell walls consist of two boxlike parts or valves and contain silica: diatoms are a source of food for all kinds of marine life —**di·a·to·ma·ceous** (dīʹət ə māʹshəs, dī atʹə-) adj.

di·a·tom·ic (dīʹə tämʹik) adj. [DI-¹ + ATOMIC] 1. having two atoms in the molecule 2. having two replaceable atoms or radicals in the molecule

di·at·om·ite (dī atʹə mītʹ) n. an earthy deposit formed mainly of the siliceous shells of diatoms and used in a finely pulverized state as an abrasive, absorbent, filter, etc.: also **diatomaceous earth**

di·a·ton·ic (dīʹə tänʹik) adj. [Fr. diatonique < LL. diatonicus < Gr. diatonikos, stretched through (the notes) < dia-, through + teinein, to stretch] Music designating, of, or using any standard major or minor scale of eight tones without the chromatic intervals —**di·a·ton'i·cal·ly** adv. —**di'a·ton'i·cism** (-ə sizʹm) n.

di·a·tribe (dīʹə trībʹ) n. [Fr. < L. diatriba, learned discussion < Gr. diatribē, a wearing away < diatribein < dia-, through + tribein, to rub, akin to L. terere, to rub: see THROW] a bitter, abusive criticism or denunciation

di·at·ro·pism (dī atʹrə piz'm) n. [DIA- + TROPISM] Bot. the tendency of some plant parts to place themselves crosswise to the line of force of a stimulus —**di·a·tro·pic** (dīʹə träpʹik) adj.

Diaz, Bartholomeu *same as* Bartholomeu DIAS

Dí·az (dēʹäs), **(José de la Cruz) Por·fi·ri·o** (pôr fēʹrē ô) 1830–1915; Mex. general & statesman; president of Mexico (1877–80; 1884–1911)

Dí·az del Cas·til·lo (dēʹäth del käs tēlʹyô), **Ber·nal** (ber nälʹ) 1492?–1581?; Sp. historian & soldier with Cortés

di·a·zine (dīʹə zēnʹ, dī azʹin) n. [DI-¹ + AZ- + -INE²] any chemical compound with a molecular structure consisting

of four atoms of carbon and two of nitrogen, arranged in a ring; esp., any of the three isomeric compounds having the formula $C_4H_4N_2$

di·az·i·non (dī az′ə nän) *n.* [DIAZIN(E) + -ON(E)] a colorless liquid, $C_{12}H_{21}N_2O_3PS$, used as an insecticide, especially against flies

di·a·zo (dī az′ō, -ā′zō) *adj.* [DI-[1] + AZO] 1. having a group of two nitrogen atoms combined directly with one hydrocarbon radical 2. designating or of a paper sensitive to ultraviolet light or a copying machine or process using this paper

di·az·o- (dī az′ō, -ā′zō) *a combining form meaning* diazo: also, before a vowel, **diaz-**

di·az·o·am·i·no (dī az′ō ə mē′nō, dī ā′zō-) *adj.* denoting or of a diazo compound in which the group —N:N·NH— is attached to the nitrogen atom of an amino radical, replacing one of the atoms normally present

diazo dye any of a class of intensely colored azo compounds containing the —N₂— group in the molecule, used for dyeing cotton and rayon

di·a·zole (dī′ə zōl′, dī az′ōl) *n.* [DIAZ(O)- + -OLE] 1. any chemical compound with a molecular structure consisting of three atoms of carbon and two of nitrogen, arranged in a ring 2. a derivative of such a compound

di·a·zo·ni·um (dī′ə zō′nē əm) *adj.* [DIAZ(O)- + (AMM)-ONIUM] designating or containing the bivalent organic radical =N:N in which one nitrogen atom can be considered to have a formal valence of three and the other a valence of five: it occurs in a series of aromatic compounds

di·az·o·tize (dī az′ə tīz′) *vt.* **-tized′, -tiz′ing** [< Fr. *diazoter* (see DI-[1] & AZOTE) + -IZE] to convert chemically into a diazo compound

dib (dib) *vi.* **dibbed, dib′bing** [ME. *dibben*, to dip, prob. akin to DIP] *same as* DIBBLE (*vi.* 2)

di·bas·ic (dī bās′ik) *adj.* 1. denoting or of an acid with two hydrogen atoms either or both of which may be replaced by basic radicals or atoms to form a salt 2. having two atoms of a univalent metal

dib·ble (dib′'l) *n.* [ME. *dibbel*, prob. < *dibben*: see DIB] a pointed tool used to make holes in the soil for seeds, bulbs, or young plants: also called **dib′ber** —*vt.* **-bled, -bling** 1. to make a hole in (the soil) with a dibble 2. to plant with a dibble —*vi.* 1. to use a dibble 2. to dip bait gently into the water

dib·buk (dib′ək) *n. same as* DYBBUK

d'I·ber·ville (dē ber vēl′), sieur (born *Pierre Le Moyne*) 1661–1706; Fr. explorer in N. America: brother of sieur de BIENVILLE

di·bran·chi·ate (dī bran′kē it) *adj.* [< ModL. *dibranchia*, name of the order < Gr. *di-*, two + *branchia*, gills of fish] of or belonging to an order (Dibranchia) of cephalopod mollusks, as the squids and octopuses, having two gills, two auricles, two nephridia, many armlike appendages, and a sac for ejecting an inky liquid

dibs (dibz) *n.pl.* [pl. of *dib*, contr. < *dibstone*, a knucklebone or jack in a children's game < *dib* (< ?) + STONE] ☆[Colloq.] a claim to a share of, or rights in, something wanted —☆*interj.* an exclamation announcing such a claim: chiefly a child's term

di·cast (dī′kast, dik′ast) *n.* [Gr. *dikastēs* < *dikazein*, to pass judgment < *dikē*, right, law, justice, akin to L. *dicere*: see DICTION] in ancient Athens, any of a large group of citizens chosen annually to serve as a court hearing cases

dice (dīs) *n.pl., sing.* **die** or **dice** [ME. *dis*, pl.: see DIE[2]] 1. small cubes of bone, plastic, etc. marked on each side with a different number of spots (from one to six) and used, usually in pairs, in games of chance 2. [*with sing. v.*] a gambling game played with dice 3. any small cubes —*vi.* **diced, dic′ing** to play or gamble with dice, by throwing them to see what the spots on the upturned faces total —*vt.* 1. to lose by gambling with dice 2. to cut (vegetables, etc.) into small cubes 3. to mark with a pattern of cubes or squares; checker —**no dice** [from a call in craps disallowing a throw] [Colloq.] 1. no: used in refusing a request 2. no success, luck, etc. —**dic′er** *n.*

di·cen·tra (dī sen′trə) *n.* [ModL. < DI-[1] + Gr. *kentron*, a spur: see CENTER] any of a genus (*Dicentra*) of plants of the fumitory family, with finely cut leaves and heart-shaped flowers of white, rose, etc., as the bleeding heart or Dutchman's-breeches

di·ceph·a·lous (dī sef′l əs) *adj.* [Gr. *dikephalos* < *di-* (see DI-[1]) + *kephalē*, a head: see CEPHALIC] having two heads, as certain fetal monsters

dic·ey (dī′sē) *adj.* [DICE + -Y[2]] [Chiefly Brit. Colloq.] hazardous; risky; chancy

di·cha·si·um (dī kā′zē əm, -zhē-) *n., pl.* **-si·a** (-ə) [ModL. < Gr. *dichasis*, a division < *dichazein*, to divide into two < *dicha*: see DICHO-] *Bot.* a cyme in which two opposite branches arise below each terminal flower

di·chlo·ride (dī klōr′īd, -id) *n.* any chemical compound in

which two atoms of chlorine are combined with an element or radical

di·chlo·ro·phe·nox·y·a·ce·tic acid (dī klōr′ō fi näk′sē ə set′ik) a chlorine derivative of phenol and acetic acid, $C_6H_3Cl_2OCH_2COOH$, used to destroy broad-leaved weeds without injuring grass: also called 2,4-D

di·cho- (dī′kō) [Gr. *dicho-* < *dicha*, in two, asunder, akin to *dis*: see DI-[1]] *a combining form meaning* in two, asunder [*dichotomy*]: also, before a vowel, **dich-**

di·chog·a·my (dī käg′ə mē) *n.* [DICHO- + -GAMY] *Bot.* the maturing of pistils and stamens at different times, preventing self-pollination —**di·chog′a·mous, di·cho·gam·ic** (dī′kə gam′ik) *adj.*

di·chon·dra (dī kän′drə) *n.* [ModL. < *di-* (see DI-[1]) + Gr. *chondros*, grain (see CHONDRO-)] any of a genus (*Dichondra*) of creeping vines of the morning-glory family, sometimes cultivated in warm climates as ground cover

di·chot·o·mize (dī kät′ə mīz′) *vt.* **-mized′, -miz′ing** [see ff. & -IZE] to divide or separate into two parts —*vi.* to undergo or exhibit dichotomy —**di·chot′o·mist** (-mist) *n.* —**di·chot′o·mi·za′tion** *n.*

di·chot·o·my (-mē) *n., pl.* **-mies** [Gr. *dichotomia*: see DICHO- & -TOMY] 1. division into two parts, groups, or classes, esp. when these are sharply distinguished or opposed 2. *Astron.* the phase of the moon or of a planet in which just half of its surface facing the earth seems illuminated 3. *Biol., Bot.* a dividing or branching into two parts, esp. when repeated —**di·chot′o·mous** (-məs) *adj.* —**di·chot′o·mous·ly** *adv.*

di·chro·ic (dī krō′ik) *adj.* having or showing dichroism or dichromatism: also **di′chro·it′ic** (-it′ik)

di·chro·ism (dī′krō iz′m) *n.* [< Gr. *dichroos*, of two colors < *di-*, two + *chrōs*, skin, complexion, color + -ISM] 1. the property that doubly refracting crystals have of transmitting light of different colors when looked at from different angles 2. the property of a substance of transmitting light of different colors depending on its thickness or on its concentration in solution 3. the property of a substance of having one color when it reflects light and another when it transmits light

di·chro·mate (dī krō′māt) *adj.* [< DI-[1] + CHROMATE] any salt of dichromic acid

di·chro·mat·ic (dī′krō mat′ik) *adj.* [DI-[1] + CHROMATIC] 1. having two colors 2. of or characterized by dichromatism 3. *Biol.* having two varieties of coloration that are independent of sex or age, as certain species of insects, owls, parrots, etc.

di·chro·ma·tism (dī krō′mə tiz′m) *n.* 1. the quality or condition of being dichromatic 2. color blindness in which a person can see only two of the three primary colors (red, green, and blue) 3. *same as* DICHROISM

di·chro·mic (dī krō′mik) *adj.* 1. *same as* DICHROMATIC 2. *Chem. a)* having two atoms of chromium per molecule *b)* designating a hypothetical acid, $H_2Cr_2O_7$, from which dichromates are formed

di·chro·scope (dī′krə skōp′) *n.* [< Gr. *dichroos* (see DICHROISM) + -SCOPE] an instrument for studying dichroism: also **di·chro·o·scope** (dī krō′ə skōp′)

Dick (dik) a nickname for Richard —*n.* [contr. < DETECTIVE] [d-] [Slang] a detective

☆**dick·cis·sel** (dik sis′'l) *n.* [echoic of its cry] an American bunting (*Spiza americana*) with a black throat and yellow breast, living in prairie regions of Canada and the U.S. and migrating to N S. America

dick·ens (dik′'nz) *interj.* [prob. < *Dickon*, nickname for RICHARD] [Colloq.] devil; deuce: used in mild oaths

Dick·ens (dik′'nz), **Charles (John Huffam)** (pseud. *Boz*) 1812–70; Eng. novelist —**Dick·en·si·an** (di ken′zē ən) *adj.*

☆**dick·er** (dik′ər) *vi., vt.* [< *dicker*, ten, ten hides (as a unit of barter) < ME. *dycer*, akin to Du. *daker*, G. *decher*, Dan. *deger*, ult. < L. *decuria*, a division of ten < *decem*, TEN] to trade by bargaining, esp. on a small or petty scale; barter or haggle —*n.* [< the *v.*] the act of bargaining or haggling

dick·ey[1] (dik′ē) *n., pl.* **-eys** [< the nickname DICK] 1. a man's detachable, or false, shirt front 2. a woman's detachable collar or blouse front 3. a child's bib or pinafore 4. a small bird: also **dickey bird** 5. *a)* the driver's seat in a carriage: also **dickey box** *b)* a seat at the back of a carriage, as for servants 6. [Brit.] a donkey

dick·ey[2] (dik′ē) *adj.* [Brit.] *same as* DICKY[2]

Dick·in·son (dik′in s'n) 1. **Emily (Elizabeth)**, 1830–86; U.S. poet 2. **John**, 1732–1808; Am. statesman

☆**Dick test** [after George F. *Dick* (1881–1967) & his wife, Gladys *Dick* (1881–), U.S. physicians who devised it] a skin test formerly used for determining susceptibility or immunity to scarlet fever

dick·y[1] (dik′ē) *n., pl.* **dick′ies** *same as* DICKEY[1]

dick·y[2] (dik′ē) *adj.* **dick′i·er, dick′i·est** [late 18th-c. Brit. slang < ?] [Brit. Colloq.] diseased; unsound [a *dicky* heart]

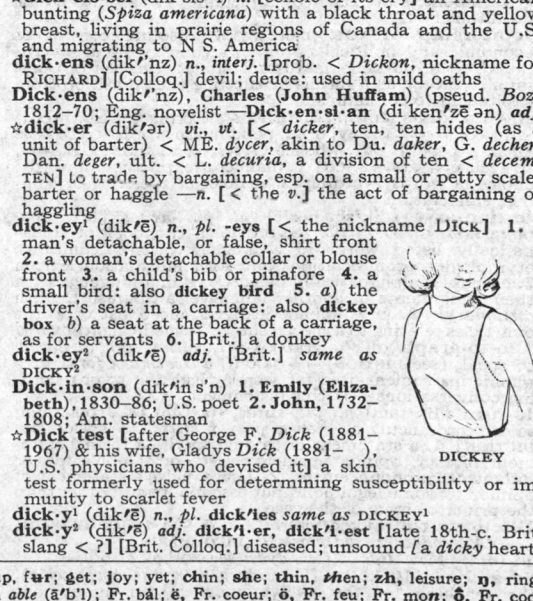

DIBBLE

DICKEY

di·cli·nous (dī klī'nəs) *adj.* [< DI-¹ + Gr. *klinē*, bed + -OUS] *Bot.* having the stamens and pistils in separate flowers —**di·cli·nism** (dī'klī niz'm), **di'cli·ny** (-nē) *n.*

di·cot (dī'kät') *n. clipped form of* DICOTYLEDON

di·cot·y·le·don (dī'kät 'l ēd'n, dī kät''l-) *n.* a flowering plant with two seed leaves (cotyledons); *specif.*, any plant belonging to that one (Dicotyledoneae) of the two subclasses of flowering plants which is characterized by embryos with two cotyledons, net-veined leaves, flower parts in fours or fives, and the presence of cambium —**di'cot·y·le'don·ous** *adj.*

☆**di·cou·ma·rin** (dī kōō'mər in) [DI-¹ + COUMARIN: a clip for the full name *bishydroxycoumarin*] a chemical compound, C₁₉H₁₂O₆, extracted from spoiled sweet clover or prepared synthetically, used in medicine to retard the formation of blood clots

di·crot·ic (dī krät'ik) *adj.* [< Gr. *dikrotos*, double-beating (< *di-*, DI-¹ + *krotos*, rattling noise) + -IC] of or having a double pulse beat with each heart beat [a *dicrotic* artery] —**di'cro·tism** (-krə tiz'm) *n.*

dict. 1. dictator 2. dictionary

dic·ta (dik'tə) *n. alt. pl. of* DICTUM

☆**Dic·ta·phone** (dik'tə fōn') [DICTA(TE) + -PHONE] *a trademark for* a machine that records spoken words so that they can be played back later for typed transcripts, etc. —*n.* this machine

dic·tate (dik'tāt; *also, for v.* dik tāt') *vt., vi.* **-tat·ed, -tat·ing** [< L. *dictatus*, pp. of *dictare*, freq. of *dicere*, to speak: see DICTION] 1. to speak or read (something) aloud for someone else to write down 2. to command expressly 3. to impose or give (orders) with or as with authority 4. to give (orders or instructions) arbitrarily —*n.* 1. an authoritative command 2. a guiding principle or requirement [the *dictates* of conscience]

dic·ta·tion (dik tā'shən) *n.* [LL. *dictatio*: see prec.] 1. the dictating of words for another to write down 2. the words so spoken or read 3. the giving of authoritative orders or commands —**dic·ta'tion·al** *adj.*

dic·ta·tor (dik'tāt ər, dik tāt'ər) *n.* [ME. *dictatour* < L. *dictator*: see DICTATE] 1. in ancient Rome, a magistrate with supreme authority, appointed in times of emergency 2. a ruler with absolute power and authority, esp. one who exercises it tyrannically 3. a person who orders others about domineeringly, or one whose pronouncements on some subject are meant to be taken as the final word 4. a person who dictates words for another to write down

dic·ta·to·ri·al (dik'tə tôr'ē əl) *adj.* of, like, or characteristic of a dictator; autocratic; tyrannical; domineering —**dic'ta·to'ri·al·ly** *adv.*

SYN.—**dictatorial** implies the domineering, autocratic methods or manner of a dictator [the *dictatorial* enunciation of his opinions]; **arbitrary** suggests the unreasoned, unpredictable use of one's power or authority in accord only with one's own will or desire [an *arbitrary* decision]; **dogmatic** suggests the attitude of a religious teacher in asserting certain doctrines as absolute truths not open to dispute [the scientific method is not *dogmatic*]; **doctrinaire** implies a rigid adherence to abstract doctrines or theories, without regard to their practical application

dic·ta·tor·ship (dik tāt'ər ship', dik'tāt ər-) *n.* 1. the position or office of a dictator 2. a dictator's tenure of office; time that a dictator's rule lasts 3. a dictatorial government; state ruled by a dictator 4. absolute power or authority

dictatorship of the proletariat absolute control of economic and political power in a country by a government of the working class (proletariat): regarded in Communist theory as a means of effecting the transition from capitalism to communism

dic·tion (dik'shən) *n.* [L. *dictio*, a speaking (in LL., word) < *pp.* of *dicere*, to say, orig., point out in words < IE. base *deik-*, to point out, whence G. *zeigen*, to show, OE. *teon*, to accuse, *tæcan*, TEACH] 1. manner of expression in words; choice of words; wording 2. manner of speaking or singing; enunciation

dic·tion·ar·y (dik'shə ner'ē) *n., pl.* **-ar·ies** [ML. *dictionarium* < LL. *dictio*: see DICTION] 1. a book of alphabetically listed words in a language, with definitions, etymologies, pronunciations, and other information; lexicon 2. a book of alphabetically listed words in a language with their equivalents in another language [a Spanish-English *dictionary*] 3. any alphabetically arranged list of words or articles relating to a special subject [a medical *dictionary*]

☆**Dic·to·graph** (dik'tə graf') [< L. *dictus*, pp. of *dicere*, to speak (see DICTION) + -GRAPH] *a trademark for* a telephonic instrument used for secretly listening to or recording conversations —*n.* this instrument

dic·tum (dik'təm) *n., pl.* **-tums, -ta** (-tə) [L., something said, word, neut. of *dictus*, pp. of *dicere*, to speak: see DICTION] 1. a statement or saying; *specif.*, a formal statement of fact, opinion, principle, etc., or of one's will or judgment; pronouncement 2. *Law* a judge's statement of opinion on some legal point not essential to and other than the principal issue of the case

☆**di·cu·ma·rol** (dī kōō'mə rôl', -kyōō'-) [< DICOUMAR(IN) + -OL] *a collective trademark for* DICOUMARIN

did (did) [ME. *dide* < OE. *dyde*: see DO¹] *pt. of* DO¹

Did·a·che (did'ə kē') *n.* [Gr. *didachē* (*tōn dōdeka apostolōn*), the teaching (of the twelve apostles)] an anonymous Christian treatise of the early 2d cent.

☆**di·dact** (dī'dakt) *n.* [back-formation < ff.] a didactic person

di·dac·tic (dī dak'tik) *adj.* [Gr. *didaktikos*, apt at teaching < *didaskein*, to teach, prob. reduplicated < IE. base *dens-*, wisdom, to teach, learn, whence Av. *didainghē*, I am taught] 1. used or intended for teaching or instruction 2. morally instructive, or intended to be so 3. too much inclined to teach others; boringly pedantic or moralistic Also **di·dac'ti·cal** —**di·dac'ti·cal·ly** *adv.* —**di·dac'ti·cism** (-tə siz'm) *n.*

di·dac·tics (-tiks) *n.pl.* [*usually with sing. v.*] the art or science of teaching; pedagogy

di·dap·per (dī'dap'ər) *n.* [ME. *didopper* < OE. *dufedoppa* < *dufan*, to dive + *-doppa* < base of *dyppan*: see DIP] *same as* DABCHICK

did·dle¹ (did'l) *vi., vt.* **-dled, -dling** [E. dial. *duddle, diddle*, to totter, akin to DODDER¹] [Colloq.] to move back and forth jerkily; jiggle —**did'dler** (-lər) *n.*

did·dle² (did'l) *vt., vi.* **-dled, -dling** [< ? Jeremy *Diddler*, character in the play *Raising the Wind* (1803), by James Kenney: name prob. < dial. *duddle*, to trick, ult. < OE. *dyderian*, to fool] [Colloq.] 1. to cheat, swindle, or victimize 2. to waste (time) in trifling —**did'dler** (-lər) *n.*

Di·de·rot (dēd'ə rō'; *Fr.* dē drō'), **Denis** 1713–84; Fr. encyclopedist & philosopher

did·n't (did'nt) did not

Di·do (dī'dō) [L. < Gr. *Didō*] *Rom. Myth.* founder and queen of Carthage: in the *Aeneid* she falls in love with Aeneas and kills herself when he leaves her

di·do (dī'dō) *n., pl.* **-does, -dos** [< ? prec.: cf. the story that Dido, on purchasing as much land as might be covered with the hide of a bull, ordered the hide cut into thin strips, with which she surrounded a large area] [Colloq.] a mischievous trick; prank; caper

Did·rik·son (did'rik s'n), **Mildred (Babe)** (married name *Zaharias*) 1913–56; U.S. athlete in many sports

didst (ditst) *archaic 2d pers. sing., past indic.,* of DO¹: used *with* thou

di·dy (dī'dē) *n., pl.* **-dies** [< nursery alteration of DIAPER] [Colloq.] a diaper (sense 2)

di·dym·i·um (dī dim'ē əm) *n.* [ModL. < Gr. *didymos*, twin (with lanthanum)] a rare metal, formerly considered an element but later found to be a mixture of rare-earth elements neodymium and praseodymium, often found associated with cerium and lanthanum: symbol, Di

did·y·mous (did'ə məs) *adj.* [< Gr. *didymos*, twin, double < *dyo*, TWO] *Bot., Zool.* growing in pairs; twin

di·dyn·a·mous (dī din'ə məs) *adj.* [< ModL. *didynamia*, name coined (1735) by Linnaeus < Gr. *di-* (see DI-¹) + *dynamis*, power (see DYNAMIC), for a class of plants, in reference to the two stamens of greater length + -OUS] of or having four stamens occurring in pairs of unequal length

die¹ (dī) *vi.* **died, dy'ing** [ME. *dien* < ON. *deyja* < IE. base *dheu-*, to pass away, become senseless, whence OS. *doian*, to die, OE. *dead*, OHG. *tot*, dead] 1. to stop living; become dead 2. to suffer the agony of death or an agony regarded as like it 3. *a)* to cease existing; end *b)* to stop functioning 4. to lose force or activity; become weak, faint, unimportant, etc. 5. to fade or wither away 6. to become alien or indifferent (*to*), as if dead 7. to pine away, as with desire 8. [Colloq.] to wish with extreme intensity; yearn [she's *dying* to learn the secret] 9. *Theol.* to suffer spiritual death —**die away** to become weaker and cease gradually: also **die down** —**die back** to wither to the roots or woody part: also **die down** —**die hard** to cling to life, a cause, etc.; resist to the last —**die off** to die one by one until all are gone —**die out** to go out of existence

SYN.—**die** is the basic, simple, direct word meaning to stop living or to become dead; **decease, expire,** and **pass away** are all euphemisms, **decease** being also the legal term, **expire** meaning literally to breathe one's last breath, and **pass away** suggesting a coming to an end; **perish** implies death by a violent means or under difficult circumstances

die² (dī) *n., pl.,* for 1 & 2, **dice** (dīs); for 3 & 4, **dies** (dīz) [ME. *de* (pl. *dis*) < OFr. *de* < VL. *datum*, orig. neut. of L. *datus*, pp. of *dare*, to give] 1. a small, marked cube used in games of chance: see also DICE 2. any small cube resembling this 3. *Archit.* a dado of a pedestal 4. *Mech.* any of various tools or devices, originally cubical in form, for molding, stamping, cutting, or shaping; *specif., a)* a piece of engraved metal used for stamping money, medals, etc. *b)* the stationary part of a machine for shaping or punching holes in sheet metal, etc.; matrix: distinguished from PUNCH¹ *c)* the punch and matrix as a unit *d)* a tool used for cutting threads, as of screws or bolts *e)* a piece of metal with a hole through it, used in drawing wire, extruding rods, etc. —*vt.* **died, die'ing** to mold, stamp, cut, or shape with a die —**the die is cast** [after L. *jacta est alea*, ascribed to Caesar at the Rubicon] the irrevocable decision has been made

☆**die·back** (dī'bak') *n.* a disease of vascular plants characterized by a dying backward from the tip of twigs and branches and caused by parasites, insufficient moisture, etc.

die casting 1. the process of making a casting by forcing molten metal into a metallic mold, or die, under great pressure 2. a casting so made —**die caster**

Die·fen·bak·er (dēf'n bā'kər), **John G(eorge)** 1895– ; prime minister of Canada (1957–63)

dief·fen·bach·i·a (dēf'n bak'ē ə) n. [ModL. < Ernst *Dieffenbach*, 19th-c. Ger. botanist + *-ia*, -IA] any of a genus (*Dieffenbachia*) of tropical plants of the arum family, with thick, fleshy jointed stems and large leaves, dark green and often splashed with white: grown as house plants, though poisonous

die-hard, die·hard (dī'härd') adj. extremely stubborn in resistance; unwilling to give in —n. a stubborn or resistant person, esp. an extreme conservative

☆**diel·drin** (dēl'drin) n. [*Diel*(s-Al)*d*(e)*r* (reaction) + -IN[1]] a highly toxic, long-lasting insecticide, $C_{12}H_8OCl_6$

di·e·lec·tric (dī'ə lek'trik) n. [< DIA- + ELECTRIC: so called because it permits the passage of the lines of force of an electrostatic field but does not conduct the current] a material, as rubber, glass, etc., or a medium, as a vacuum, gas, etc., that does not conduct electricity and that can sustain an electric field: dielectrics are used in capacitors, between adjacent wires in a cable, etc. —adj. having the properties or function of a dielectric

☆**dielectric heating** the heating of dielectric materials by subjecting them to a high-frequency, alternating electric field, used in the bonding, drying, etc. of materials, as plastics and plywoods

Dien Bien Phu (dyen' byen' foo') village in NW North Vietnam: besieged & captured by Vietminh forces (1954) marking the end of French occupation of Indochina

di·en·ceph·a·lon (dī'en sef'ə län') n. [ModL. < DIA- + ENCEPHALON] the posterior end of the prosencephalon, or forebrain, in vertebrates —**di'en·ce·phal'ic** (-sə fal'ik) adj.

Di·eppe (dē ep'; Fr. dyep) city in N France, on the English Channel: pop. 30,000

di·er·e·sis (dī ėr'ə sis) n., pl. **-ses** (-sēz') [LL. *diaeresis* < Gr. *diairesis*, division < *diairein*, to divide, separate < *dia-*, apart + *hairein*, to take] 1. the separation of two consecutive vowels, esp. of a diphthong, into two syllables 2. a mark (¨) placed over the second of two consecutive vowels to show that it is pronounced in a separate syllable: the dieresis is now usually replaced by a hyphen (*reënter*, *re-enter*), or simply omitted (*cooperate, naive*) The mark is also used, as in this dictionary, to show a certain pronunciation of a vowel (ä, ë, ö, ü) 3. *Prosody* a slight break or pause in a line of verse, resulting when the end of a metric foot coincides with the end of a word —**di·e·ret·ic** (dī'ə ret'ik) adj.

die·sel (dē'z'l, -s'l) n. [after Rudolf *Diesel* (1858–1913), Ger. inventor] [often D-] 1. a type of internal-combustion engine that burns fuel oil: the ignition is brought about by heat resulting from air compression, instead of by an electric spark as in a gasoline engine: also **diesel engine** (or **motor**) 2. a locomotive, truck, etc. powered by such an engine

die·sink·er (dī'siŋ'kər) n. a maker of dies used in stamping or shaping —**die'sink'ing** n.

‡**Di·es I·rae** (dē'ez ir'ā, dē'ās; ir'ē) [L., Day of Wrath] a medieval Latin hymn about Judgment Day, beginning *Dies Irae*, a part of the Requiem Mass

di·e·sis (dī'ə sis) n., pl. **-ses** (-sēz') [L. < Gr. *diesis* < *diienai*, to send through < *dia-*, through + *hienai*, to send: for IE. base, see JET[1]] a reference mark (‡) used in printing: also called DOUBLE DAGGER

‡**di·es non** (dī'ēz nän', dē'ās nōn') [L. *dies non* (*juridicus*) not a (court) day] *Law* a day on which courts are not in session, as a legal holiday

die·stock (dī'stäk') n. a frame to hold dies for cutting threads on water pipes, screws, bolts, etc.

di·es·trum (dī es'trəm) n. [ModL. < DI-[1] + (O)ESTRUM] the quiescent interval between successive periods of sexual heat in female mammals Also **di·es'trus** —**di·es'trous** (-trəs) adj.

di·et[1] (dī'ət) n. [ME. *diete* < OFr. < ML. *dieta*, diet, daily food allowance (meaning infl. by ff.) < L. *diaeta* < Gr. *diaita*, way of life, regimen < *dia-*, through + root of *aisa*, fate < IE. *aito-*, share < base *ai-*, to give, allot] 1. a) what a person or animal usually eats and drinks; daily fare b) figuratively, what a person regularly reads, listens to, does, etc. 2. a regimen of special or limited food and drink, chosen or prescribed for health or to gain or lose weight —vi., vt. [ME. *dieten* < ML. *dietare*] to eat or cause to eat special or limited food, esp. for losing weight —**di'et·er** n.

di·et[2] (dī'ət) n. [ME. *diete* < OFr. < ML. *dieta* < L. *dies*, day: see DEITY] 1. [Scot.] a day's session of an assembly 2. a formal assembly, as formerly of princes, electors, etc. of the Holy Roman Empire 3. in some countries, a national or local legislative assembly

di·e·tar·y (dī'ə ter'ē) n., pl. **-ies** [ME. *dietarie* < ML. *dietarium*] 1. a system of diet 2. daily food allowance or ration —adj. 1. of diet 2. of a dietary

di·e·tet·ic (dī'ə tet'ik) adj. [L. *diaeteticus* <Gr. *diaitētikos*] of, relating to, or designed for a particular diet of food and drink: also **di'e·tet'i·cal** —**di'e·tet'i·cal·ly** adv.

di·e·tet·ics (-iks) n.pl. [with sing. v.] the study of the kinds and quantities of food needed for health

di·eth·yl·bar·bi·tu·ric acid (dī eth'1 bär'bə tyoor'ik, -toor'-) same as BARBITAL

di·eth·yl ether (dī eth'1) same as ETHER (sense 4 b)

di·eth·yl·stil·bes·trol (-stil bes'trōl, -trōl) n. [*diethyl-* (< DI-[1] + ETHYL) + STILBESTROL] a nonsteroidal synthetic estrogen, $C_{18}H_{20}O_2$, used as a substitute for natural estrogens

☆**di·e·ti·tian, di·e·ti·cian** (dī'ə tish'ən) n. an expert in dietetics; specialist in planning meals or diets

‡**Dieu et mon droit** (dyō' ā mōn drwä') [Fr.] God and my right: motto of British royalty

dif- (dif) same as DIS-: used before f

dif·fer (dif'ər) vi. [ME. *differen* < OFr. *differer* < L. *differre*, to carry apart, differ < *dis-*, apart + *ferre*, to bring, BEAR[1]] 1. to be unlike; be not the same (often with *from*) 2. to be of opposite or unlike opinions; disagree 3. [Archaic] to quarrel (*with*)

dif·fer·ence (dif'ər əns, dif'rəns) n. [ME. < OFr. < L. *differentia* < *differens*, prp. of *differre*: see DIFFER] 1. condition, quality, fact, or instance of being different 2. the way in which people or things are different; esp., a determining point or factor that makes for a distinct change or contrast 3. the state of holding a differing opinion; disagreement; also, the point at issue; point of disagreement 4. a dispute; quarrel 5. a discrimination or distinction 6. *Math.* the amount by which one quantity is greater or less than another; remainder left after subtraction —vt. **-enced', -enc'ing** [Rare] to distinguish as or make different —**make a difference** 1. to have an effect; matter 2. to change the outlook or situation 3. to discriminate or differentiate; give different treatment —**split the difference** 1. to share equally what is left over 2. to make a compromise —**what's the difference?** [Colloq.] what does it matter?

dif·fer·ent (dif'ər ənt, dif'rənt) adj. [ME. < OFr. < L. *differens*: see prec.] 1. not alike; dissimilar (with *from*, or, esp. colloquially, *than*, and, in Brit. usage, *to*) 2. not the same; distinct; separate; other 3. various 4. unlike most others; unusual —**dif'fer·ent·ly** adv. —**dif'fer·ent·ness** n.

SYN.—**different**, applied to things that are not alike, implies individuality [three *different* doctors/ or contrast [the twins wore *different* hats/; **diverse** more emphatically sets apart the things referred to, suggesting a conspicuous difference [*diverse* interests/; **divergent** suggests a branching off in different directions with an ever-widening distance between, and stresses irreconcilability [*divergent* schools of thought/; **distinct**, as applied to two or more things, stresses that each has a different identity and is unmistakably separate from the others, whether or not they are similar in kind, class, etc. [charged with two *distinct* offenses/; **dissimilar** stresses absence of similarity in appearance, properties, or nature [*dissimilar* techniques/; **disparate** implies essential or thoroughgoing difference, often stressing an absence of any relationship between things [*disparate* concepts/; **various** emphasizes the number and diversity of kinds, types, etc. [*various* gifts/.—ANT. alike, similar

dif·fer·en·ti·a (dif'ə ren'shē ə, -shə) n., pl. **-ti·ae** (-shi ē') [L.: see DIFFERENCE] *Logic* a distinguishing characteristic, esp. one that distinguishes one species from another of the same genus

dif·fer·en·ti·a·ble (-shē ə b'l, -shə-) adj. 1. open to differentiation 2. *Math.* designating or of a function which has a derivative at the point in question —**dif'fer·en'ti·a·bil'i·ty** n.

dif·fer·en·tial (-shəl) adj. [ML. *differentialis* < L. *differentia*: see DIFFERENCE] 1. of, showing, or depending on a difference or differences [*differential* rates/ 2. constituting or making a specific difference; distinguishing [*differential* qualities/ 3. having different effects or results; making use of differences [a *differential* gear] 4. *Math.* of or involving differentials —n. 1. a differentiating amount, degree, factor, etc. [*differentials* in salary] 2. *Math.* a) an infinitesimal difference between two consecutive values of a variable quantity b) the derivative of a function multiplied by the increment of the independent variable 3. *Mech.* a differential gear ☆4. *Railroading* a difference in rates, as between different routes —**dif'fer·en'tial·ly** adv.

differential calculus the branch of higher mathematics which deals with derivatives and their applications: cf. INTEGRAL CALCULUS

differential coefficient same as DERIVATIVE (n. 4)

differential compaction *Geol.* the compaction of porous sediments deposited on an uneven surface so that a nearly horizontal upper layer partially reproduces the underlying topographical features as a result of the greater compression of the thick deposits over the lowlands in comparison with the thinner ones over the heights

differential equation *Math.* an equation containing two variables and the first, often higher, derivatives of one variable with respect to the other

differential gear (or **gearing**) a certain arrangement of gears (*epicyclic train*) connecting two axles in the same line and dividing the driving force between them, but allowing one axle to turn faster than the other: it is used in the rear axles of automobiles to permit a difference in axle speeds while turning curves

differential windlass a windlass with two drums of different diameters to increase the lifting power

dif·fer·en·ti·ate (dif'ə ren'shē āt') *vt.* **-at'ed, -at'ing** [< ML. *differentiatus,* pp. of *differentiare* < L. *differentia:* see DIFFERENCE] **1.** to constitute a difference in or between **2.** to make unlike; develop specialized differences in **3.** to perceive or express the difference in; distinguish between; discriminate **4.** *Math.* to work out the differential or derivative of —*vi.* **1.** to become different or differentiated; develop new characteristics **2.** to perceive or express a difference **3.** *Biol.* to undergo differentiation —*SYN.* see DISTINGUISH

dif·fer·en·ti·a·tion (-ren'shē ā'shən) *n.* **1.** a differentiating or being differentiated **2.** *Biol.* the modification of tissues, organs, etc. in structure or function during the course of development **3.** *Math.* the working out of the differential or derivative

dif·fi·cile (dif'ə sēl') *adj.* [MFr. < L. *difficilis,* difficult: reintroduced < ModFr.] hard or difficult; esp., hard to deal with, please, etc.

dif·fi·cult (dif'i kəlt, -kult') *adj.* [ME., back-formation < ff.] **1.** hard to do, make, manage, understand, etc.; involving trouble or requiring extra effort, skill, or thought **2.** hard to satisfy, persuade, please, etc. —*SYN.* see HARD —**dif'fi·cult·ly** *adv.*

dif·fi·cul·ty (dif'i kul'tē, -kəl-) *n., pl.* **-ties** [ME. & OFr. *difficulte* < L. *difficultas* < *difficilis,* difficult < *dis-,* not + *facilis,* easy: see FACILE] **1.** the condition or fact of being difficult **2.** something that is difficult, as a hard problem or an obstacle or objection **3.** trouble, distress, etc., or a cause of this **4.** a disagreement or quarrel —**in difficulties** in distress, esp. financially

SYN.—**difficulty** is applied to anything hard to contend with, without restriction as to nature, intensity, etc. [a slight *difficulty,* great *difficulty*]; **hardship,** stronger in connotation, suggests suffering, privation, or trouble that is extremely hard to bear [the *hardships* of poverty]; **rigor** suggests severe hardship but further connotes that it is imposed by external, impersonal circumstances beyond one's control [the *rigors* of winter]; **vicissitude,** a bookish word, suggests a difficulty that is likely to occur in the course of something, often one inherent in a situation [the *vicissitudes* of political life]

dif·fi·dence (dif'ə dəns) *n.* [ME. < L. *diffidentia* < *diffidens,* prp. of *diffidere,* to distrust < *dis-,* not + *fidere,* to trust: see FIDELITY] lack of confidence in oneself, marked by a hesitancy to assert oneself; shyness

dif·fi·dent (-dənt) *adj.* [L. *diffidens:* see prec.] full of diffidence; lacking self-confidence; timid; shy —*SYN.* see SHY —**dif'fi·dent·ly** *adv.*

dif·fract (di frakt') *vt.* [< L. *diffractus,* pp. of *diffringere,* to break in pieces < *dis-,* apart + *frangere,* BREAK¹] to break into parts; specif., to subject to diffraction

dif·frac·tion (di frak'shən) *n.* [ModL. *diffractio* < L. *diffractus:* see prec.] **1.** the breaking up of a ray of light into dark and light bands or into the colors of the spectrum, caused by the interference of one part of a beam with another, as when the ray is deflected at the edge of an opaque object or passes through a narrow slit **2.** a similar breaking up of other kinds of wave motion, as of sound or electricity —**dif·frac'tive** (-tiv) *adj.* —**dif·frac'tive·ly** *adv.*

diffraction grating *Optics* a plate of glass or polished metal ruled with a series of very close, equidistant, parallel lines, used to produce a spectrum by the diffraction of reflected or transmitted light

dif·fuse (di fyoos'; *for v.* -fyooz') *adj.* [ME. < L. *diffusus,* pp. of *diffundere,* to pour in different directions < *dis-,* apart + *fundere,* to pour: see FOUND³] **1.** spread out or dispersed; not concentrated **2.** using more words than are needed; long-winded; wordy —*vt., vi.* **-fused', -fus'ing 1.** to pour, spread out, or disperse in every direction; spread or scatter widely **2.** *Physics* to mix by diffusion, as gases, liquids, etc. —*SYN.* see WORDY —**dif·fuse'ly** *adv.* —**dif·fuse'ness** *n.*

dif·fus·er, dif·fus·or (di fyoo'zər) *n.* [LL. *diffusor*] a person or thing that diffuses, as a device for distributing light evenly

dif·fus·i·ble (di fyoo'zə b'l) *adj.* that can be diffused —**dif·fus'i·bil'i·ty** *n.*

dif·fu·sion (-zhən) *n.* [ME. *diffusioun* < L. *diffusio*] **1.** a diffusing or being diffused; specif., *a)* a dissemination, as of news, cultures, etc. *b)* a scattering of light rays, as by reflection; also, the dispersion and softening of light, as by using frosted glass *c)* an intermingling of the molecules of liquids, gases, etc. **2.** wordiness; diffuseness

dif·fu·sive (-siv) *adj.* [ML. *diffusivus*] **1.** tending to diffuse **2.** characterized by diffusion **3.** diffuse —**dif·fu'sive·ly** *adv.* —**dif·fu'sive·ness** *n.*

dig (dig) *vt.* dug *or archaic & poet.* **digged, dig'ging** [ME. *diggen* < Anglo-Fr. **diguer* < OFr. *digue,* dike < Du. *dijk:* see DIKE¹] **1.** to break and turn up or remove (ground, etc.) with a spade or other tool, or with hands, claws, snout, etc.

2. to make (a hole, cellar, one's way, etc.) by or as by doing this **3.** to uncover and get from the ground in this way [to *dig* potatoes] ☆**4.** to find out, as by careful study or investigation; unearth (usually with *up* or *out*) [to *dig* out the truth] **5.** to thrust, jab, or prod [to *dig* an elbow into someone's ribs] ☆**6.** [Slang] *a)* to understand *b)* to approve of or like —*vi.* **1.** to dig the ground or any surface **2.** to make a way by or as by digging (*through, into, under*) ☆**3.** [Colloq.] to work or study hard —*n.* **1.** the act of digging **2.** [Colloq.] a thrust, poke, nudge, etc. **3.** [Colloq.] a sarcastic comment; taunt; gibe **4.** an archeological excavation or its site **5.** [*pl., often with sing. v.*] [Colloq.] living quarters; lodgings; diggings —**dig in 1.** to dig trenches or foxholes for cover **2.** to entrench oneself **3.** [Colloq.] *a)* to begin to work intensively *b)* to begin eating —**dig into 1.** to penetrate by or as by digging **2.** [Colloq.] to work hard at

dig. digest

di·gam·ma (dī gam'ə) *n.* [Gr. < *di-,* two + *gamma:* so called because it resembles two gammas (Γ) in form] the sixth letter (F, F) of the early Greek alphabet, derived from the Semitic *vav* and having the sound of English *w:* it was replaced in the Latin alphabet by F

dig·a·my (dig'ə mē) *n.* [LL. & Gr. *digamia* < *di-,* two, twice + *gamos,* marriage] a second legal marriage; marriage after the death or divorce of the first spouse —**dig'a·mous** (-məs) *adj.*

di·gas·tric (dī gas'trik) *adj.* [ModL. *digastricus* < Gr. *di-,* two + Gr. *gastēr,* belly] designating of or a muscle that bellies out from both sides of its tendon and functions to depress the lower jaw and indirectly move the tongue

di·gen·e·sis (dī jen'ə sis) *n.* [ModL.: see DI-¹ + GENESIS] *Biol.* successive reproduction by two processes, sexual in one generation and asexual in the next —**di·ge·net·ic** (dī'jə net'ik) *adj.*

di·gest (dī'jest; *for v.* di jest', dī-) *n.* [ME. < L. *digesta* (in LL., a collection of writings), orig. pl. of *digestus,* pp. of *digerere,* to separate, explain < *di-,* apart + *gerere,* to bear, carry] **1.** a collection of condensed, comprehensive, systematic information; summary or synopsis, as of scientific, legal, or literary material **2.** a book, periodical, etc. consisting chiefly of such summaries or synopses or of articles, etc. condensed from other publications **3.** [D-] [*often pl.*] *Rom. Law* the Pandects of the Emperor Justinian —*vt.* [ME. *digesten* < L. *digestus:* see the *n.*] **1.** *a)* to arrange or classify systematically, usually in condensed form *b)* to condense (a piece of writing) by briefly summarizing or abridging its contents **2.** to change (food), esp. in the mouth, stomach, and intestines by the action of gastric and intestinal juices, enzymes, and bacteria, into a form that can be absorbed by the body **3.** to aid the digestion of (food) **4.** to think over and absorb **5.** to tolerate or accept **6.** to soften, disintegrate, dissolve soluble materials in, etc. by heating, esp. with water or other liquid and, sometimes, under pressure —*vi.* **1.** to be digested **2.** to digest food —*SYN.* see ABRIDGMENT

di·gest·er (di jes'tər, dī-) *n.* **1.** a person who makes a digest **2.** a heavy metal container in which substances are heated or cooked to soften them or extract soluble elements from them **3.** *same as* AUTOCLAVE

di·gest·i·ble (-tə b'l) *adj.* [ME. < OFr. < LL. *digestibilis*] that can be digested —**di·gest'i·bil'i·ty** *n.* —**di·gest'i·bly** *adv.*

di·ges·tion (-chən) *n.* [ME. *digestioun* < OFr. *digestion* < L. *digestio*] **1.** the act or process of digesting food **2.** the ability to digest food **3.** the absorption of ideas **4.** decomposition of sewage by bacteria

di·ges·tive (-tiv) *adj.* [ME. & OFr. *digestif* < L. *digestivus*] of, for, or aiding digestion —*n.* any substance or drink that aids digestion —**di·ges'tive·ly** *adv.* —**di·ges'tive·ness** *n.*

digged (digd) *archaic or poet. pt. & pp.* of DIG

dig·ger (dig'ər) *n.* **1.** a person or thing that digs; specif., any tool or machine for digging ☆**2.** [D-] a member of any of several tribes of Indians in the W U.S. who dug roots for food **3.** *same as* DIGGER WASP **4.** [D-] [Slang] an Australian or New Zealander

digger wasp any of various wasps (esp. superfamily Sphecoidea) that lay eggs on caterpillars, spiders, etc. that they have paralyzed and entombed in nests dug in the ground

dig·gings (dig'inz) *n.pl.* **1.** materials dug out **2.** [*often with sing. v.*] a place where digging or mining, esp. gold mining, is carried on **3.** [Slang] orig., a gold miner's camp; hence, one's lodgings or quarters

dight (dīt) *vt.* dight *or* dight'ed, dight'ing [ME. *dihten* < OE. *dihtan,* to arrange, dispose, make < L. *dictare,* to say: see DICTATE] [Archaic or Poet.] **1.** to adorn **2.** to equip Now chiefly in past participle

dig·it (dij'it) *n.* [ME. < L. *digitus,* a finger, toe, inch < IE. base **deik-,* to show, point, whence L. *dicere,* to say, TEACH] **1.** a finger or toe **2.** a measure of length, equal to 3/4 inch, based on the breadth of a finger **3.** any numeral from 0 to 9: so called because originally counted on the fingers

dig·it·al (-'l) *adj.* [ME. < L. *digitalis*] **1.** of, like, or constituting a digit, esp. a finger **2.** having digits **3.** performed with the finger **4.** using numbers that are digits to represent all the variables involved in calculation —*n.* **1.** a finger **2.** a key played with a finger, as on the piano —**dig'it·al·ly** *adv.*

☆**digital computer** a computer that uses numbers to perform logical and numerical calculations, usually in a binary system

dig·i·tal·in (dij′ə tal′in; *chiefly Brit.* -tā′lin) *n.* [< ff. + -IN¹] a poisonous crystalline glucoside, $C_{36}H_{56}O_{14}$, obtained from the seed of the digitalis

dig·i·tal·is (-tal′is; *chiefly Brit.* -tā′lis) *n.* [ModL., foxglove < L. *digitalis*, belonging to the finger < *digitus*, a finger, DIGIT: so named by Fuchs (1542) from its thimblelike flowers, after the G. name *fingerhut*, thimble] **1.** any of a genus (*Digitalis*) of plants of the figwort family, with long spikes of thimblelike flowers **2.** the dried leaves of the purple foxglove (*Digitalis purpurea*) **3.** a medicine made from these leaves, used as a heart stimulant

dig·i·tal·ize (dij′it ′l īz′) *vt.* **-ized′, -iz′ing** to treat with sufficient digitalis drugs to achieve the desired therapeutic effect —**dig′i·tal·i·za′tion** *n.*

dig·i·tate (dij′ə tāt′) *adj.* [L. *digitatus*: see DIGIT] **1.** having separate fingers or toes **2.** like a digit; fingerlike **3.** *Bot.* having fingerlike divisions, as some leaves Also **dig′i·tat′ed** —**dig′i·tate′ly** *adv.* —**dig′i·ta′tion** *n.*

dig·i·ti- (dij′it ə) [Fr. < L. *digitus:* see DIGIT] *a combining form meaning* of the fingers or toes, fingerlike [*digitigrade*]

dig·i·ti·form (dij′i tə fôrm′) *adj.* shaped like a finger

dig·i·ti·grade (-grād′) *adj.* [Fr.: see DIGITI- & -GRADE] walking on the toes with the heels not touching the ground, as cats, dogs, horses, etc. —*n.* any animal that walks in this manner

DIGITATE LEAF

dig·i·tize (dij′ə tīz′) *vt.* **-tized′, -tiz′ing** to translate an analogue measurement of (data) into a numerical description expressed in digits in a scale of notation

dig·i·tox·in (dij′ə tӓk′s'n) *n.* [DIGI(TALIS) + TOXIN] a glucoside, $C_{41}H_{64}O_{13}$, extracted from digitalis leaves, like digitalis in physiological action, but more potent

di·glot (dī′glӓt) *adj.* [Gr. *diglōttos*, speaking two languages < *di-*, two + *glōtta, glossa*, the tongue: see GLOSS²] bilingual —*n.* a bilingual edition of a book

dig·ni·fied (dig′nə fīd′) *adj.* having or showing dignity or stateliness —**dig′ni·fied′ly** *adv.*

dig·ni·fy (dig′nə fī′) *vt.* **-fied′, -fy′ing** [ME. *dignifien* < OFr. *dignifier* < ML. *dignificare* < L. *dignus*, worthy + *-ficare < facere*, to make, DO¹] **1.** to give dignity to; make worthy of esteem; honor, exalt, or ennoble **2.** to make seem worthy or noble, as by giving a high-sounding name to [to *dignify* cowardice by calling it prudence]

dig·ni·tar·y (-ter′ē) *n., pl.* **-tar′ies** [< L. *dignitas*, dignity + -ARY] a person holding a high, dignified position or office —*adj.* of or like a dignitary

dig·ni·ty (-tē) *n., pl.* **-ties** [ME. & OFr. *dignite* < L. *dignitas*, worth, merit < *dignus*, worthy < IE. base *dek-*, to receive, be fitting: cf. DECOR, DOCILE] **1.** the quality of being worthy of esteem or honor; worthiness **2.** high repute; honor **3.** the degree of worth, repute, or honor **4.** a high position, rank, or title **5.** loftiness of appearance or manner; stateliness **6.** proper pride and self-respect **7.** [Archaic] a dignitary —*SYN.* see DECORUM

di·graph (dī′graf) *n.* [DI-¹ + -GRAPH] a combination of two letters to express a simple sound (Ex.: r*ea*d, *sh*ow, gra*ph*ic) —**di·graph′ic** *adj.* —**di·graph′i·cal·ly** *adv.*

di·gress (di gres′, dī-) *vi.* [< L. *digressus*, pp. of *digredi*, to go apart < *dis-*, apart + *gradi*, to go, step: see GRADE] to turn aside; esp., to depart temporarily from the main subject in talking or writing; ramble —*SYN.* see DEVIATE

di·gres·sion (-gresh′ən) *n.* [ME. < L. *digressio*] an act or instance of digressing; a wandering from the main subject in talking or writing —**di·gres′sion·al** *adj.*

di·gres·sive (-gres′iv) *adj.* [LL. *digressivus*] digressing or given to digression —**di·gres′sive·ly** *adv.* —**di·gres′sive·ness** *n.*

di·he·drai (dī hē′drəl) *adj.* [< DI-¹ + Gr. *hedra*, a seat, base + -AL] **1.** having or formed by two intersecting plane faces [a *dihedral* angle] **2.** *a*) having wings that form a dihedral angle with each other, as some airplanes *b*) being inclined to each other at a dihedral angle: said of airplane wing pairs —*n.* **1.** a dihedral angle **2.** the angle between either wing of an airplane and the horizontal plane of its transverse axis

di·hy·brid (dī hī′brid) *n.* [DI-¹ + HYBRID] *Genetics* an offspring of parents differing from one another in two pairs of alleles

DIHEDRAL ANGLE (angle formed by planes MWON and MWXY)

di·hy·dro·chlo·ride (dī hī′drə klôr′īd) *n.* a compound containing two molecules of hydrochloric acid

Di·jon (dē zhôn′) city in EC France: pop. 136,000

dik·dik (dik′dik′) *n.* [< the Ethiopian native name] any of several very small antelopes (genera *Madoqua* and *Rhynchotragus*) found in E Africa

dike¹ (dīk) *n.* [ME. < OE. *dic* & ON. *diki*, akin to DITCH, Du. *dijk*, G. *deich* < IE. base **dheigw-*, to pierce, fasten, whence L. *figere*, FIX] **1.** [Obs. exc. Brit. Dial.] *a*) a ditch or watercourse *b*) the bank of earth thrown up in digging a ditch **2.** an embankment or dam made to prevent flooding by the sea or by a river **3.** a protective barrier or obstacle **4.** [Scot. or Brit. Dial.] a low dividing wall of earth or stone **5.** [Archaic] a raised causeway **6.** *Geol.* igneous rock that solidified as a tabular body in a more or less vertical fissure —*vt.* **diked, dik′ing 1.** to provide, protect, or enclose with a dike or dikes **2.** to drain by a ditch

dike² (dīk) *n. same as* DYKE² —**dik′ey** *adj.*

‡**dik·tat** (dik tӓt′) *n.* [G.] an authoritarian decree, order, or policy

di·lac·er·ate (di las′ə rāt′) *vt.* **-at′ed, -at′ing** [DI-² + LACERATE] to tear to pieces; rip apart

☆**Di·lan·tin** (di lan′tin, dī-) [< *di(pheny)l(hyd)ant(o)in*] *a trademark for* a drug, $C_{15}H_{11}N_2O_2Na$, used in the treatment of epileptic attacks: in full **Dilantin Sodium** —*n.* [d-] this substance

di·lap·i·date (di lap′ə dāt′) *vi., vt.* **-dat′ed, -dat′ing** [< L. *dilapidatus*, pp. of *dilapidare*, to squander, demolish < *dis-*, apart + *lapidare*, to throw stones at < *lapis*, a stone, akin to Gr. *lepas*, bare rock < ? IE. base **lep-*, rock] to become or cause to become partially ruined and in need of repairs, as through neglect

di·lap·i·dat·ed (-id) *adj.* falling to pieces or into disrepair; broken down; shabby and neglected

di·lap·i·da·tion (di lap′ə dā′shən) *n.* [ME. *dilapidacioun* < LL. *dilapidatio*] **1.** a dilapidating or becoming dilapidated **2.** a dilapidated condition —*SYN.* see RUIN

di·lat·ant (dī lāt′'nt, di-) *adj.* [L. *dilatans*, prp. of *dilatare*] **1.** dilating or tending to dilate **2.** expanding in bulk when the shape is changed: said of masses of certain granular substances **3.** becoming solid, or setting, under pressure, as certain colloidal solutions —*n.* a thing that can dilate —**di·lat′an·cy** *n.*

dil·a·ta·tion (dil′ə tā′shən, dī′lə-) *n.* [ME. *dilatacioun* < OFr. *dilatation* < LL. *dilatatio*] **1.** *same as* DILATION **2.** *Med.* enlargement of an organ, cavity, duct, or opening of the body beyond normal size or breadth —**dil′a·ta′tion·al** *adj.*

di·late (dī lāt′, di-; dī′lāt) *vt.* **-lat′ed, -lat′ing** [ME. *dilaten* < L. *dilatare* < *dis-*, apart + *latus*, wide: see LATERAL] to make wider or larger; cause to expand or swell; stretch —*vi.* **1.** to become wider or larger; swell **2.** to speak or write in detail (*on* or *upon* a subject) —*SYN.* see EXPAND —**di·lat′a·bil′i·ty** *n.* —**di·lat′a·ble** *adj.* —**di·lat′ive** *adj.*

di·la·tion (dī lā′shən, di-) *n.* **1.** a dilating or being dilated **2.** a dilated part

dil·a·tom·e·ter (dil′ə täm′ə tər) *n.* an instrument for measuring volume changes in order to determine the transition points between liquid and solid phases

di·la·tor (dī lāt′ər, di-; dī′lāt ər) *n.* a person or thing that dilates; specif., *a*) any muscle that dilates a part of the body *b*) a surgical instrument for dilating an opening, wound, etc.

dil·a·to·ry (dil′ə tôr′ē) *adj.* [ME. *dilatorie* < LL. *dilatorius* < L. *dilator*, dilatory person < *dilatus*, pp. of *differre*, DEFER¹] **1.** causing or tending to cause delay; meant to gain time, defer action, etc. **2.** inclined to delay; slow or late in doing things —**dil′a·to′ri·ly** *adv.* —**dil′a·to′ri·ness** *n.*

di·lem·ma (di lem′ə) *n.* [LL. < LGr.(Ec.) *dilēmma < di-*, two + *lēmma*, proposition: see LEMMA¹] **1.** an argument necessitating a choice between equally unfavorable or disagreeable alternatives **2.** any situation in which one must choose between unpleasant alternatives; difficult choice —*SYN.* see PREDICAMENT —**dil·em·mat·ic** (dil′ə mat′ik) *adj.*

dil·et·tante (dil′ə tänt′, -tän′tē, -tan′tē; dil′ə tänt′) *n., pl.* **-tantes, -tan·ti** (-tän′tē, -tan′tē) [It. < prp. of *dilettare*, to delight < L. *delectare*, to charm, DELIGHT] **1.** a person who loves the fine arts **2.** a person who follows an art or science only for amusement and in a superficial way; dabbler —*adj.* of or characteristic of a dilettante —*SYN.* see AESTHETE, AMATEUR —**dil′et·tant′ish** *adj.* —**dil′et·tant′ism, dil′et·tan′te·ism** *n.*

dil·i·gence¹ (dil′ə jəns) *n.* [ME. < OFr. < L. *diligentia* < *diligens*, prp. of *diligere*, to esteem highly, select < *di-*, apart + *legere*, to choose: for IE. base see LOGIC] **1.** the quality of being diligent; constant, careful effort; perseverance; industry **2.** [Obs.] speed; haste **3.** *Law* the degree of attention or care expected of a person in a given situation

dil·i·gence² (dil′ə jəns; *Fr.* dē lē zhäns′) *n.* [Fr. < *carrosse de diligence*, lit., coach of diligence, i.e., fast coach < *faire diligence*, to hurry] a public stagecoach, esp. as formerly used in France

dil·i·gent (dil′ə jənt) *adj.* [ME. < OFr. < L. *diligens*: see DILIGENCE¹] **1.** persevering and careful in work; hardworking; industrious **2.** done with careful, steady effort; painstaking —*SYN.* see BUSY —**dil′i·gent·ly** *adv.*

dill (dil) *n.* [ME. & OE. *dile*, akin to OS. *dille*, OHG. *tilli*] 1. any of a genus (*Anethum*) of plants of the parsley family, esp. a European herb (*Anethum graveolens*) with bitter seeds and aromatic leaves, used to flavor pickles, soups, etc. 2. the seeds or leaves

☆**dill pickle** a cucumber pickle flavored with dill

☆**dil·ly** (dil′ē) *n., pl.* **-lies** [orig. adj., prob. altered & contr. < DEL(IGHT-FUL) + -Y[1]] [Slang] a surprising or remarkable person, thing, event, etc.

dil·ly·dal·ly (dil′ē dal′ē) *vi.* **-lied, -ly·ing** [redupl. form of DALLY] to waste time in hesitation or vacillation; loiter or dawdle

dil·u·ent (dil′yoo wənt) *adj.* [L. *diluens,* prp. of *diluere*] diluting —*n.* a thing that dilutes another thing

di·lute (di loot′, di-) *vt.* **-lut′ed, -lut′ing** [< L. *dilutus,* pp. of *diluere,* to wash away < *dis-,* off, from + -*luere* < *lavere,* to wash: see LATHER] 1. to thin down or weaken as by mixing with water or other liquid 2. to change or weaken (in brilliance, force, effect, etc.) by mixing with something else —*vi.* to become diluted —*adj.* diluted —**di·lute′ness** *n.* —**di·lut′er, di·lu′tor** *n.*

di·lu·tion (-loo′shən) *n.* 1. a diluting or being diluted 2. something diluted

di·lu·vi·al (di loo′vē əl) *adj.* [LL. *diluvialis* < L. *diluvium:* see DILUVIUM] 1. of or caused by a flood, esp. the Deluge 2. of debris left by a flood or glacier Also **di·lu′vi·an**

di·lu·vi·um (-əm) *n., pl.* **-vi·ums, -vi·a** (-ə) [L., a deluge < *diluere:* see DILUTE] *Geol. an old term for* glacial drift, specif. as believed to have resulted from a great flood, esp. the Biblical Deluge

dim (dim) *adj.* **dim′mer, dim′mest** [ME. < OE., akin to ON. *dimmr,* dark < IE. base **dhem-,* to be dusty, misty, whence DAMP, G. *dunkel,* dark] 1. not bright; somewhat dark 2. not clear or distinct in character; lacking definition, distinction, strength, etc. 3. without luster; dull 4. not clearly seen, heard, perceived, or understood; vague 5. not clearly seeing, hearing, understanding, etc. 6. not likely to turn out well [*dim* prospects] —*vt., vi.* **dimmed, dim′ming** 1. to make or grow dim 2. to make seem dim, as by comparison —*n.* 1. [Archaic or Poet.] dim light; dimness; dusk 2. a dim headlight on an automobile —*SYN.* see DARK —**take a dim view of** to view skeptically, pessimistically, without enthusiasm, etc. —**dim′ly** *adv.* —**dim′ness** *n.*

dim. 1. dimension 2. diminuendo 3. diminutive

Di·mashq (dē mäshk′) *Arabic name of* DAMASCUS

dime (dim) *n.* [ME. < OFr. *disme,* tithe, tenth < L. *decima* (*pars*), tenth (part), fem. of *decimus* < *decem,* TEN] ☆a coin of the U.S. and of Canada equal to ten cents; tenth of a dollar: the U.S. dime is made of cupronickel —☆**a dime a dozen** [Colloq.] abundant and easily obtained; cheap

di·men·hy·dri·nate (di′men hi′drə nāt′) *n.* [*dime*(*thyl*) + (AMI)N(E) + (*diphen*)*hydr*(*am*)*in*(*e*) + -ATE[2]] a white crystalline solid, C₂₄H₂₈ClN₅O₃, used to control nausea and vomiting, as in motion sickness

☆**dime novel** a cheap, melodramatic novel without literary worth, originally costing a dime

di·men·sion (də men′shən) *n.* [ME. *dimensioun* < L. *dimensio,* a measuring < *dimensus,* pp. of *dimetiri,* to measure off < *dis-,* off, from + *metiri,* to MEASURE] 1. any measurable extent, as length, width, depth, etc.: see also FOURTH DIMENSION 2. [*pl.*] measurements in length and width, and often depth 3. [*often pl.*] *a)* extent, size, or degree *b)* scope or importance 4. the nature and relationship of the units entering into some physical quantity [the *dimension* for speed is length divided by time] 5. [*often pl.*] [Obs.] bodily form —*adj.* designating lumber, stone, etc. cut to specified dimensions —*vt.* to shape to or mark with specified dimensions: usually in past participle —**di·men′sion·less** *adj.*

di·men·sion·al (-′l) *adj.* 1. of dimension or dimensions 2. having (a specified number of) dimensions [a three-*dimensional* figure] —**di·men′sion·al′i·ty** (-al′ə tē) *n.* —**di·men′sion·al·ly** *adv.*

di·mer (di′mər) *n.* [DI-[1] + (POLY)MER] a compound formed by the combination of two identical molecules —**di·mer′ic** (-mer′ik) *adj.*

dim·er·ous (dim′ər əs) *adj.* [ModL. *dimerus:* see DI-[1] & -MEROUS] having two parts; specif., *a)* having two members in each whorl: said of flowers *b)* having two-jointed tarsi: said of insects

☆**dime store** *same as* FIVE-AND-TEN-CENT STORE

dim·e·ter (dim′ə tər) *n.* [LL. < Gr. *dimetros* < *di-,* two + *metron,* a MEASURE] 1. a line of verse containing two metrical feet or measures 2. verse consisting of dimeters —*adj.* having two metrical feet or measures

di·meth·yl (di meth′′l) *adj.* containing two methyl radicals, (CH₃)₂

di·meth·yl sulf·ox·ide (sulf äk′sid) *same as* DMSO

dimi- *same as* DECIMILLI-

di·mid·i·ate (di mid′ē āt′, -di-) *adj.* [< L. *dimidiatus,* pp. of *dimidiare,* to divide into halves < *dimidium,* a half <

dis-, apart, from + *medius,* MID[1]] 1. halved 2. *Biol.* having only one half developed 3. *Bot.* split on one side, as the calyptra of mosses —*vt.* **-at′ed, -at′ing** [Archaic] to halve

dimin. 1. diminuendo 2. diminutive

di·min·ish (də min′ish) *vt.* [ME. *diminishen,* a blend of *diminuen,* to reduce (< OFr. *diminuer* < L. *diminuere,* var. of *deminuere* < *de-,* from + *minuere,* to lessen < *minus,* small) & *minishen,* to make smaller < OFr. *menusier* < VL. *minutiare* < L. *minutus,* MINUTE[2]] 1. to make, or make seem, smaller; reduce in size, degree, importance, etc.; lessen 2. *Archit.* to cause to taper 3. *Music* to reduce (a minor interval) by a half step —*vi.* 1. to become smaller or less 2. *Archit.* to taper —*SYN.* see DECREASE —**di·min′ish·a·ble** *adj.*

di·min·ished (-isht) *adj.* 1. made smaller; lessened; reduced 2. *Music* lessened by a half step: said of intervals or of chords formed with such an interval

di·min·ish·ing returns (-ish iŋ) *Econ.* the proportionately smaller increase in productivity observed after a certain point in the increase of capital, labor, etc.

di·min·u·en·do (di min′yoo wen′dō) *adj., adv., n., pl.* **-dos** [It. < *diminuere:* see DIMINISH] *same as* DECRESCENDO

dim·i·nu·tion (dim′ə nyoo′shən, -noo′-) *n.* [ME. < OFr. < LL. *deminutio*] 1. a diminishing or being diminished; lessening; decrease 2. *Music* the recurrence of a theme in notes of one half or one quarter the length of those in the original

di·min·u·tive (də min′yoo tiv) *adj.* [ME. & OFr. *diminutif* < LL. *diminutivus* < pp. of L. *deminuere,* DIMINISH] 1. much smaller than ordinary or average; very small; tiny 2. *Gram.* expressing smallness or diminution [a *diminutive* suffix] —*n.* 1. a very small person or thing 2. *a)* a word or name formed from another by the addition of a suffix expressing smallness in size and, sometimes, endearment or condescension, as *ringlet* (*ring* + -*let*), *Jackie* (*Jack* + -*ie*), *lambkin* (*lamb* + -*kin*) *b)* such a suffix —*SYN.* see SMALL —**di·min′u·tive·ly** *adv.* —**di·min′u·tive·ness** *n.*

Di·mi·trov·grad (di mē′trôf gräd′) city in SC Bulgaria: pop. 45,000

dim·i·ty (dim′ə tē) *n., pl.* **-ties** [ME. *demit* < ML. *dimitum* < MGr. *dimitos,* double-threaded < *dis-,* two + *mitos,* a thread: cf. TWILL] a thin, strong, corded cotton cloth, often figured, used for curtains, dresses, etc.

dim·mer (-ər) *n.* 1. a person that dims 2. a device for dimming an electric light, as in automobile headlights or theater stage lights

di·mor·phism (di môr′fiz′m) *n.* [< Gr. *dimorphos,* having two forms (< *di-,* two + *morphē,* form) + -ISM] 1. *Bot.* the state of having two different kinds of leaves, flowers, stamens, etc. on the same plant or in the same species 2. *Mineralogy* the property of crystallizing in two forms 3. *Zool.* the occurrence of two types of individuals in the same species, distinct in coloring, size, etc. —**di·mor′phic** (-fik), **di·mor′phous** (-fəs) *adj.*

dim·out (dim′out′) *n.* a dimming or reduction of the night lighting in a city, etc. to make it less easily visible, as to enemy aircraft; incomplete blackout

dim·ple (dim′p′l) *n.* [ME. *dimpel,* akin to MHG. *tumpfel,* G. *tümpel,* deep hole in water < IE. base **dheub-, *dheup-,* hollow and deep, whence DEEP, DIP] 1. a small, natural hollow on the surface of the body, as on the cheek or chin 2. any little hollow, as on water —*vt.* **-pled, -pling** to make dimples in —*vi.* to show or form dimples; become dimpled —**dim′ply** (-plē) *adj.*

dim·wit (dim′wit′) *n.* [Slang] a stupid person; simpleton —**dim′wit′ted** *adj.* —**dim′wit′ted·ly** *adv.* —**dim′wit′ted·ness** *n.*

din (din) *n.* [ME. *dine* < OE. *dyne,* akin to ON. *dynr* < IE. base **dhwen-, *dhun-,* to sound, boom, whence Sans. *dhvani-,* sound, noise, thunder, word] a loud, continuous noise; confused clamor or uproar —*vt.* **dinned, din′ning** 1. to beset with a din 2. to repeat insistently or noisily [to *din* an idea into one's ears] —*vi.* to make a din —*SYN.* see NOISE

Di·nah (di′nə) [Heb. *dināh,* lit., judged] a feminine name

di·nar (di när′) *n.* [Ar. *dinār* < LGr. *dēnarion* < L. *denarius:* see DENARIUS] 1. an ancient gold coin, used in some Moslem countries 2. the monetary unit of Algeria, Iraq, Jordan, Kuwait, Southern Yemen, Tunisia, and Yugoslavia: see MONETARY UNITS, table 3. an Iranian coin equal to 1/100 rial

Di·nar·ic Alps (di nar′ik) range of the E Alps, along the Adriatic coast of Yugoslavia: highest peak, 7,800 ft.

din·dle (din′d′l, din′′l) *vt., vi.* **-died, -dling** [ME. *dindelen,* prob. < *dine* (see DIN), with intrusive *-d-* and freq. suffix] [Scot. & Brit. Dial.] to tingle or vibrate, as with or from a loud sound, shock, etc. —*n.* [Scot. & Brit. Dial.] a tingling; thrill

d'In·dy (dan dē′), (Paul Marie Théodore) **Vin·cent** (Fr. van săn′) 1851–1931; Fr. composer

dine (din) *vi.* **dined, din′ing** [ME. *dinen* < OFr. *disner* < VL. **disjejunare* < *dis-,* away + LL. *jejunare,* to fast < L. *jejunus,* fasting] to eat dinner —*vt.* to provide a dinner for, or entertain at dinner —*n.* [Obs.] dinner —**dine out** to eat dinner away from home

din·er (di′nər) *n.* 1. a person eating dinner ☆2. *same as* DINING CAR ☆3. a small restaurant built to look like a dining car

di·ner·ic (di ner′ik) *adj.* [< DI-[1] + Gr. *nēron, nēros,* water +

-ic] *Physics* constituting, or having to do with, the surface of contact of two immiscible liquids in a container

☆di·ner·o (di ner′ō) *n.* [Sp.] [Southwest Colloq.] money

Din·e·sen (dē′nə sən, din′ə-), I·sak (ē′säk) (pseud. of Baroness *Karen Blixen-Finecke*) 1885–1962; Dan. author

☆din·ette (dī net′) *n.* [see DINE & -ETTE] 1. an alcove or small, partitioned space used as a dining room 2. a set of table and chairs for such a space

ding (diŋ) *vi.* [ME. *dingen*, to strike, beat < Scand. (as in ON. *dengja*, to hammer): for IE. base see DINT] 1. to make a sound like that of a bell; ring 2. [Colloq.] to speak repetitiously and tiresomely —*vt.* 1. to make ring 2. [Colloq.] to repeat insistently or tiresomely; din —*n.* the sound of a bell

☆ding-a-ling (diŋ′ə liŋ′) *n.* [< the ringing in the head of a punch-drunk boxer] [Slang] a crazy or unbalanced person

☆ding·bat (-bat′) *n.* [< DING, in obs. sense "to fling" + BAT¹] [Colloq.] 1. a stone, stick, or other object suitable for throwing 2. *same as* DINGUS 3. *Printing* a decorative mark, as at the beginning of a paragraph

ding-dong (-dôŋ′, -däŋ′) *n.* [echoic] the sound of a bell struck repeatedly —*adj.* [Colloq.] carried out, as a contest, fight, etc., with continual, successive changes in the lead or advantage; vigorously contested —*vi.* to sound with a ding-dong —*vt.* to impress by repeating

din·ghy (diŋ′gē, diŋ′ē) *n., pl.* -ghies [Hind. *ḍiṅgī*] 1. orig., a rowboat used on the rivers of India 2. a small boat carried on a warship 3. a small boat, orig. a rowboat, used as a tender to a yacht, motor cruiser, etc. 4. a small, undecked, single-masted racing boat 5. an inflatable, pneumatic life raft Also sp. din′gey

din·gle (diŋ′g'l) *n.* [ME. *dingel*, abyss, deep hollow, prob. akin to OE. *ding*, dungeon: ult. < IE. base *dhengh-*, to press, cover: see DUNG] a small, deep, wooded valley; dell

din·go (diŋ′gō) *n., pl.* -goes [native name] the Australian wild dog (*Canis dingo*), usually tawny in color, with short, pointed ears and a bushy tail

ding·us (diŋ′əs) *n.* [Du. *dinges* (or G. *dings*), thingumbob, orig. gen. of *ding*, THING¹] [Colloq.] any device; contrivance; gadget: humorous substitute for a name not known or temporarily forgotten

din·gy (din′jē) *adj.* -gi·er, -gi·est [orig. dial. var. of DUNGY] 1. dirty-colored; not bright or clean; grimy 2. dismal; shabby —din′gi·ly *adv.* —din′gi·ness *n.*

☆dining car a railroad car equipped to serve meals to passengers

dining room a room where meals are eaten

di·ni·tro- (di ni′trō, -tra) *a combining form meaning* having two nitro groups per molecule [*dinitrobenzene*]

di·ni·tro·ben·zene (di ni′trō ben′zēn) *n.* any of three isomeric compounds, the C₆H₄(NO₂)₂, formed by the reaction of nitric acid and benzene or nitrobenzene: used in dyes, organic synthesis, etc.

dink (diŋk) *adj.* [< ?] [Scot.] dressed in fine array; trim —*vt.* [Scot.] to dress (oneself) in fine array

Din·ka (diŋ′kä) *n.* 1. a member of a group of Sudanic Negroid tribes living in S Sudan (sense 2) 2. the language of the Dinkas, a branch of the Chari-Nile subfamily

din·key (diŋ′kē) *n.* [prob. < DINKY] [Colloq.] ☆1. a small locomotive for hauling cars, shunting, etc. in a railroad yard 2. a small trolley car

din·kum (diŋ′kəm) *adj.* [< dial. (Lincolnshire), a fair share of work < ?] [Austral. Slang] genuine; true; real —*n.* [Austral. Slang] the truth

din·ky (diŋ′kē) *adj.* -ki·er, -ki·est [< DINK + -Y²] [Colloq.] small and unimportant; of no consequence —*n., pl.* -kies *same as* DINKEY

din·ner (din′ər) *n.* [ME. *diner* < OFr. *disner*, inf. used as *n.*: see DINE] 1. the chief meal of the day, whether eaten in the evening or about noon 2. a banquet in honor of some person or event 3. a complete meal at a set price with no course omitted; table d'hôte

dinner jacket a tuxedo jacket

☆dinner ring a ring with a large setting, worn on formal occasions

din·ner·ware (-wer′) *n.* 1. plates, cups, saucers, etc., collectively 2. a set of such dishes

di·no- (dī′nə, -nō) [< Gr. *deinos*, terrible < IE. base *dwei-*, to fear, whence L. *dirus*, dreadful, DIRE] *a combining form meaning* terrible, dreadful [*dinosaur*]

di·no·flag·el·late (dī′nə flaj′ə lit, -lāt′) *n.* [< ModL. *dinoflagellata*, name of the order < Gr. *dinos*, rotation (< IE. base *deye-*, to swing, whirl, whence OIr. *dian*, swift) + ModL. *flagellum* (see FLAGELLUM) + *-ata* < L., neut. pl. of *-atus*: see -ATE¹] any of an order (Dinoflagellata) of single-celled organisms, mainly marine and often with a cellulose shell: some species are luminescent and some cause the red tides that are extremely toxic to marine life

di·no·saur (dī′nə sôr′) *n.* [< DINO- + Gr. *sauros*, lizard: cf. -SAURUS] any of a large group of extinct, mostly land-dwelling, four-limbed reptiles of the Mesozoic Era, including some almost 100 ft. long: the flesh-eaters usually walked on their hind limbs, the plant-eaters on all fours —di′no·sau′ri·an (-sôr′ē ən) *adj.*

di·no·there (dī′nə thir′) *n.* [< DINO- + Gr. *thēr*, wild

beast: for IE. base see FIERCE] any of a genus (*Dinotherium*) of extinct elephantlike animals of the Miocene Epoch with tusks curving downward from the lower jaw

dint (dint) *n.* [ME. < OE. *dynt* < IE. base *dhen-*, to strike, whence DING] 1. force; exertion: now chiefly in by dint of 2. a dent 3. [Archaic] a blow —*vt.* 1. to dent 2. to drive in with force

Din·wid·die (din wid′ē, din′wid ē), Robert 1693–1770; Brit. lieutenant governor of Va. (1751–58)

dioc. 1. diocesan 2. diocese

di·oc·e·san (dī äs′ə s'n) *adj.* [ME. < ML. *diocesanus*] of a diocese —*n.* the bishop of a diocese

di·o·cese (dī′ə sis, -sēs′) *n.* [ME. & OFr. *diocise* < L. *diocesis*, district, government, in LL.(Ec.), diocese < Gr. *dioikēsis*, administration < *dioikein*, to keep house < *dia-*, through + *oikos*, a house] the district under a bishop's jurisdiction

Di·o·cle·tian (dī′ə klē′shən) (L. name *Gaius Aurelius Valerius Diocletianus*) 245–313 A.D.; Rom. emperor (284–305)

di·ode (dī′ōd) *n.* [DI-¹ + -ODE¹] 1. *a)* an electron tube of the high-vacuum type with a cold anode and a heated cathode, used as a rectifier of alternating current, a demodulator, etc. *b)* a low-pressure, gas-filled electron tube used as a rectifier 2. a semiconductor device used in a similar manner

di·oe·cious (dī ē′shəs) *adj.* [< DI-¹ + Gr. *oikos*, a house + -OUS] *Biol.* having the male reproductive organs in one individual and the female organs in another; having separate sexes —di·oe′cious·ly *adv.* —di·oe′cism (-siz′m) *n.*

di·oes·trum (dī es′tram, -ēs′-) *n. same as* DIESTRUM

Di·og·e·nes (dī äj′ə nēz′) 412?–323? B.C.; Gr. Cynic philosopher: noted for his asceticism

Di·o·mede Islands (dī′ə mēd′) island group in the Bering Strait, between Siberia & Alaska: U.S.-U.S.S.R. boundary passes between the two main islands, Big Diomede (U.S.S.R.) and Little Diomede (U.S.)

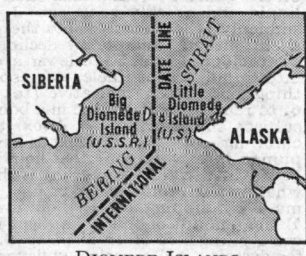

DIOMEDE ISLANDS

Di·o·me·des (dī′ə mē′dēz) *Gr. Legend* a Greek warrior at the siege of Troy, who helped Odysseus steal the statue of Athena: also Di′o·med′ (-med′), Di′o·mede′ (-mēd′)

Di·o·ny·si·a (dī′ə nish′ē ə) *n.pl.* [L. < Gr. *Dionysia* (*hiera*), (rites) of Dionysus] any of the various Greek festivals in honor of Dionysus, esp. those at Athens from which the Greek drama originated

Di·o·nys·i·ac (-nis′ē ak′, -ni′sē ak′) *adj.* [L. *Dionysiacus* < Gr. *Dionysiakos*] 1. of Dionysus or the Dionysia 2. *same as* DIONYSIAN (sense 2)

Di·o·ny·sian (-nish′ən, -nis′ē ən, -ni′sē ən) *adj.* 1. Dionysiac 2. of the orgiastic nature of the Dionysia; wild, frenzied, and sensuous 3. of any of several historical figures named Dionysius

Di·o·ny·si·us (-nish′əs, -nis′ē əs, -ni′sē əs) 1. 430?–367 B.C.; Gr. tyrant of ancient Syracuse (405–367): called the *Elder* 2. 395?–340? B.C.; Gr. tyrant of Syracuse (367–356; 347–343): son of *prec.*: called the *Younger*

Dionysius Ex·ig·u·us (ig zig′yoo wəs, -sig′-) 6th cent. A.D.; Roman monk & Christian theologian, born in Scythia: believed to have introduced the current system of numbering years on the basis of the Christian Era

Dionysius of Halicarnassus 1st cent. B.C.; Gr. critic & historian in Rome

Di·o·ny·sus, Di·o·ny·sos (dī′ə nī′səs) [L. < Gr. *Dionysos*] *Gr. Myth.* the god of wine and revelry: identified by the Romans with Bacchus

di·op·side (dī äp′sid) *n.* [Fr. < *di-* (see DI-²) + Gr. *opsis*, appearance, sight; associated in meaning with Gr. *diopsis*, transparency < *dia-*, through + *opsis*] *Mineralogy* a kind of pyroxene, usually greenish

di·op·tase (-tās) *n.* [Fr. < Gr. *dia-*, through + *optazein*, to see] a hydrous silicate of copper which occurs as green, glassy prisms

di·op·ter, di·op·tre (dī äp′tər) *n.* [Fr. *dioptre* < L. *dioptra* < Gr. *dioptra*, instrument for leveling, etc. < *dia-*, through + base of *opsis*, sight] a unit of measure of the refractive power of a lens, equal to the power of a lens with a focal distance of one meter —di·op′tral *adj.*

di·op·tom·e·ter (dī′äp täm′ə tər) *n.* [DI-² + OPTOMETER] an instrument for testing the refraction of the eye —di′op·tom′e·try *n.*

di·op·tric (dī äp′trik) *adj.* [Gr. *dioptrikos*, relating to the DIOPTER] 1. of optical lenses or the method of numbering them according to their refractive powers; dioptral 2. of dioptrics; refractive 3. helping the sight by refractive correction Also di·op′tri·cal

di·op·trics (-triks) *n.pl.* [with *sing. v.*] [< DIOPTRIC]

[Archaic] the branch of optics dealing with the refraction of light through lenses

di·o·ra·ma (dī′ə ram′ə, -räm′-) *n.* [DI(A)- + (PAN)ORAMA] **1.** a picture painted on a set of transparent cloth curtains and looked at through a small opening **2.** a miniature scene, wholly or partially three-dimensional, depicting figures in a naturalistic setting **3.** a museum display of a preserved or reconstructed specimen, as of wildlife in a simulation of its habitat

di·o·rite (dī′ə rīt′) *n.* [Fr. < Gr. *diorizein,* to divide < *dia-,* through + *horizein,* to separate (see HORIZON)] a dark-gray or greenish igneous rock, consisting chiefly of feldspar and hornblende

Di·os·cu·ri (dī′ə skyoor′ī, dī äs′kyoo rī′) [Gr. *Dioskouroi* < *Dios* (gen. of *Zeus*) + *kouroi,* pl. of *kouros,* boy, son] *Gr. Myth.* Castor and Pollux, twin sons of Zeus: identified as stars in the constellation Gemini

di·ox·ane (dī äk′sān) *n.* [DI-¹ + OX- + -ANE] an ether, $C_4H_8O_2$, prepared from ethylene oxide or glycol and used as a solvent for fats, greases, etc. and in cosmetics, deodorants, etc.

di·ox·ide (dī äk′sīd) *n.* an oxide containing two atoms of oxygen per molecule

dip (dip) *vt.* **dipped** or, occas., **dipt, dip′ping** [ME. *dippen* < OE. *dyppan,* to immerse: for IE. base see DIMPLE] **1.** to put into or under liquid for a moment and then quickly take out; immerse **2.** to dye in this way **3.** to baptize by immersion **4.** to clean (sheep or hogs) by bathing in disinfectant **5.** to make (a candle) by putting a wick repeatedly in melted tallow or wax **6.** to coat, plate, or galvanize by immersion **7.** to get or take out by, or as if by, scooping up with a container, the hand, etc. **8.** to lower and immediately raise again [*dip* the flag in salute] ☆**9.** to put (snuff) on the gums, as with a snuff stick —*vi.* **1.** to plunge into a liquid and quickly come out **2.** to sink or seem to sink suddenly [the sun *dips* into the ocean] **3.** to undergo a slight, usually temporary decline [sales *dipped* in May] **4.** to slope down **5.** to lower a container, the hand, etc. into liquid, a receptacle, etc., esp. in order to take something out: often figurative [to *dip* into one's savings] **6.** to read here and there in a book, etc., or inquire into a subject superficially **7.** *Aeron.* to drop suddenly before climbing —*n.* **1.** a dipping or being dipped **2.** *a)* a brief plunge into water or other liquid *b)* a brief swim **3.** a liquid into which something is dipped, as for dyeing **4.** whatever is removed by or used in dipping **5.** a candle made by dipping **6.** *a)* a downward slope or inclination *b)* the amount of this **7.** a slight hollow **8.** a short downward plunge, as of an airplane **9.** *a)* a sweet liquid sauce for desserts ☆*b)* a variously flavored, thick, creamy sauce, in which crackers, etc. are dipped to be eaten as appetizers **10.** [Slang] a pickpocket **11.** *Geol., Mining* the downward inclination of a stratum or vein, with reference to a horizontal plane **12.** *Gym.* the act of lowering oneself by the arms between parallel bars until the chin reaches the bar level, and then raising oneself by straightening the arms **13.** *Physics a)* the deviation of a dip needle from the horizontal *b)* the amount of such deviation **14.** *Surveying* the angular amount by which the horizon is below eye level

di·pet·al·ous (dī pet′l əs) *adj. same as* BIPETALOUS

di·phase (dī′fāz′) *adj.* [DI-¹ + PHASE] having two phases: also **di·pha′sic** (-fā′zik)

di·phen·yl (dī fen′'l, -fēn′-) *n.* **1.** a chemical compound, $(C_6H_5)_2$, the molecule of which consists of two chemically combined phenyl groups **2.** containing two phenyl groups as part of each molecule

di·phen·yl·a·mine (dī fen′'l ə mēn′, -fēn′-; -am′ēn) *n.* [prec. + AMINE] a colorless, crystalline chemical compound, $(C_6H_5)_2NH$, used as a stabilizer of explosives, as a test for nitric acid, and in making dyes

di·phos·gene (dī fäs′jēn, -fäz′-) *n.* a poisonous liquid compound, $ClCO_2CCl_3$, related to phosgene and used as a lung-irritant gas in chemical warfare

diph·the·ri·a (dif thir′ē ə, dip-) *n.* [ModL. < Fr. *diphthérie* (so named by Trousseau in 1855, replacing earlier *diphtérite,* name first used in 1821 by Bretonneau) < Gr. *diphthera,* leather < *dephein,* to tan hides] an acute infectious disease caused by a bacterium (*Corynebacterium diphtheriae*) and characterized by weakness, high fever, and the formation in the air passages of a tough, membrane-like obstruction to breathing —**diph·the′ri·al** *adj.*

diph·the·rit·ic (dif′thə rit′ik, dip′-) *adj.* [< Fr. *diphthérite* (see DIPHTHERIA) + -IC] **1.** of, characteristic of, or like diphtheria **2.** having diphtheria Also **diph·ther′ic**

diph·thong (dif′thôŋ, dip′-) *n.* [ME. *diptonge* < LL. *diphthongus* < Gr. *diphthongos* < *di-,* two + *phthongos,* voice, sound < *phthengesthai,* to utter] *Phonet.* **1.** a complex vowel sound made by gliding continuously from the position for one vowel to that for another within the same syllable, as (ou) in *down;* (ī), IPA [aɪ], in *ride;* (oi) in *boy* **2.** *Printing* either of the ligatures æ or œ, pronounced as diphthongs in classical Latin —**diph·thon′gal** (-thôŋ′g'l) *adj.*

diph·thong·ize (-īz′) *vt.* **-ized′, -iz′ing** to pronounce (a simple vowel) as a diphthong —*vi.* to become a diphthong —**diph′thong·i·za′tion** *n.*

diph·y·cer·cal (dif′i sur′k'l) *adj.* [< Gr. *diphyēs,* twofold (< *di-,* DI-¹ + *phyein,* to bear, bring forth: see BE) + *kerkos,* tail + -AL] designating, of, or having a tail fin in which

the upper and lower lobes taper symmetrically to a point to which the spinal column extends

di·phy·let·ic (dī′fī let′ik) *adj.* [DI-¹ + PHYLETIC] having two ancestral lines of descent

di·phyl·lous (dī fil′əs) *adj.* [DI-¹ + -PHYLLOUS] having two leaves or sepals

di·phy·o·dont (dī fī′ə dänt′, dif′ē ə-) *adj.* [< Gr. *diphyēs* (see DIPHYCERCAL) + -ODONT] developing two consecutive sets of teeth, as in man

dipl. 1. diplomat **2.** diplomatic

di·ple·gi·a (dī plē′jē ə) *n.* [ModL.: see DI-¹ & -PLEGIA] paralysis of similar parts on both sides of the body; bilateral paralysis

di·plex (dī′pleks) *adj.* [altered (after DI-¹) < DUPLEX] using a single circuit or transmission link for the simultaneous transmission or reception of two signals

dip·lo- (dip′lə, -lō) [< Gr. *diploos,* DOUBLE] *a combining form meaning* two, double, twin [*diplococcus*]: also, before a vowel, **dipl-**

dip·lo·blas·tic (dip′lə blas′tik) *adj. Zool.* of or pertaining to a body with only two cellular layers, the ectoderm and the endoderm

dip·lo·coc·cus (-käk′əs) *n., pl.* **-coc′ci** (-käk′sī) any of a group of parasitic bacteria occurring in pairs, as the pneumococcus that causes lobar pneumonia —**dip′lo·coc′-cal** (-käk′'l), **dip′lo·coc′cic** (-käk′sik) *adj.*

☆**di·plod·o·cus** (di pläd′ə kəs) *n.* [ModL. < DIPLO- + Gr. *dokos,* main supporting beam: coined (1878) by O. C. Marsh, U.S. paleontologist] any of a genus (*Diplodocus*) of huge, plant-eating dinosaurs of the Upper Jurassic of W N. America

dip·lo·e (dip′lə wē′) *n.* [ModL. < Gr. *diploē,* lit., a fold, doubling < *diploos,* DOUBLE] the spongy bone between the two dense inner and outer layers of the skull bones —**di·plo·ic** (di plō′ik) *adj.*

dip·loid (dip′loid) *adj.* [DIPL- + -OID] **1.** twofold or double **2.** *Biol.* having twice the number of chromosomes normally occurring in a mature germ cell: most somatic cells are diploid —*n.* a diploid cell —**dip·loi′dy** (-loi′dē) *n.*

di·plo·ma (di plō′mə) *n., pl.* **-mas;** for sense 1, also **-ma·ta** (-mə tə) [L., state letter of recommendation < Gr. *diplōma,* folded letter < *diploun,* to double < *diploos,* DOUBLE] **1.** an official state document or historical document; charter **2.** a certificate conferring honors, privileges, etc. **3.** a certificate issued to a student by a school, college, or university, indicating graduation from the institution or conferring a degree

di·plo·ma·cy (di plō′mə sē) *n., pl.* **-cies** [Fr. *diplomatie* < *diplomate:* see DIPLOMAT] **1.** the conducting of relations between nations, as in building up trade, making treaties, etc. **2.** skill in doing this **3.** skill in dealing with people; tact —*SYN.* see TACT

☆**diploma mill** [Colloq.] an unaccredited school or college that grants relatively worthless diplomas, as for a fee

dip·lo·mat (dip′lə mat′) *n.* [Fr. *diplomate,* back-formation < *diplomatique* (after nouns ending in -ate, as *aristocrate*), DIPLOMATIC] **1.** a representative of a government who conducts relations with another government in the interests of his own country; person whose career or profession is diplomacy **2.** a person skilled in dealing with other people; tactful person Also **di·plo·ma·tist** (di plō′mə tist)

dip·lo·mate (-māt′) *n.* [DIPLOM(A) + -ATE²] a doctor who is certified as a specialist by an examining board in a particular branch of medicine

dip·lo·mat·ic (dip′lə mat′ik) *adj.* [Fr. *diplomatique* < ModL. *diplomaticus* < L. *diploma* (gen. *diplomatis*), DIPLOMA] **1.** *a)* of official or original documents *b)* designating or of a copy or edition exactly reproducing an original document or manuscript **2.** of or connected with diplomacy **3.** tactful and adroit in dealing with people —*SYN.* see SUAVE —**dip′lo·mat′i·cal·ly** *adv.*

diplomatic immunity exemption from local taxation, court action, etc. in a foreign country, granted by international law to all members of a diplomatic service

dip·lont (dip′länt) *n.* [DIPL- + -ont, a cell, organism (< Gr. *ontos:* see ONTO-)] an animal or plant whose somatic nuclei are diploid

di·plo·pi·a (di plō′pē ə) *n.* [ModL. < Gr. *diploos,* double + *ōps* (gen. *ōpos*), EYE] an eye symptom in which a single object appears double; double vision —**di·plo′pic** (-plō′pik, -pläp′ik) *adj.*

dip·lo·pod (dip′lə päd′) *n.* [< ModL. *diplopoda,* name of the class: see DIPLO- & -POD] *same as* MILLIPEDE

di·plo·sis (di plō′sis) *n.* [ModL. < Gr. *diplōsis,* a doubling] doubling of the number of chromosomes through the fusion of two haploid sets in the union of gametes, resulting in the formation of the somatic chromosome number

dip needle a magnetic needle vertically suspended and freely moving, used to indicate the direction of the earth's magnetism: it is horizontal at the magnetic equator (*aclinic line*) but vertical at the magnetic poles

dip·no·an (dip′nō ən) *adj.* [< Gr. *dipnoos,* double-breathed < DI-¹ + *pnoē,* breath (see PNEUMA)] of or belonging to a group (Dipnoi) of fishes that can respire by lungs as well as by gills —*n.* a dipnoan fish

dip·o·dy (dip′ə dē) *n., pl.* **-dies** [LL. *dipodia* < Gr. *dipodia* < *di-,* twice + *pous* (gen. *podos*), FOOT] *Prosody* a single measure consisting of two feet —**di·pod·ic** (di päd′ik) *adj.*

di·pole (dī′pōl′) *n.* **1.** *Physics* any system having two

equal but opposite electric charges or magnetic poles separated by a very small distance **2.** *Chem.* a molecule in which the centers of positive and negative charge are separated **3.** a radio or television antenna that is a single linear conductor (commonly equal in length to one half the wavelength at the frequency employed) separated at the center by a transmission line feed or other source or receiver of radio signals: in full, **dipole antenna** —di·po′lar (-pō′lər) *adj.*

dip·per (dip′ər) *n.* **1.** a person whose work is dipping something in liquid **2.** a long-handled cup or similar container for dipping ☆**3.** [D-] either of two groups of stars in the shape of a dipper, one (BIG DIPPER) in Ursa Major, the other (LITTLE DIPPER) in Ursa Minor **4.** any of a genus (*Cinclus*) of songbirds, as the water ouzel, living near swift streams into which they wade and submerge in search of insects, larvae, etc. —dip′per·ful′ *n.*, *pl.* -fuls′

dip·py (dip′ē) *adj.* -pi·er, -pi·est [Slang] crazy; insane

di·pro·pel·lant (dī′prə pel′ənt) *n. same as* BIPROPELLANT

dip·so·ma·ni·a (dip′sō mā′nē ə, -nyə) *n.* [ModL. < Gr. *dipsa,* thirst + -MANIA] an abnormal and insatiable craving for alcoholic drink —dip′so·ma′ni·ac′ (-ak′) *n.* —dip′so·ma·ni′a·cal (-mə nī′ə k′l) *adj.*

dip·stick (dip′stik′) *n.* **1.** a graduated metal rod for measuring the quantity or depth of a substance in its container, as of oil in an automobile crankcase ☆**2.** *same as* SNUFF STICK

dipt (dipt) *occas. pt. & pp. of* DIP

dip·ter·al (dip′tər əl) *adj. Archit.* surrounded by a double row of columns

dip·ter·an (-ən) *n.* [< ModL. *Diptera,* name of the order < neut. pl. of Gr. *dipteros:* see DIPTEROUS] any of a large order (Diptera) of insects, including the housefly, mosquito, gnat, etc., having one pair of functional, membranous wings and usually a vestigial second pair

dip·ter·ous (-əs) *adj.* [ModL. *dipterus* < Gr. *dipteros:* see DI-¹ & PTERO- & -OUS] **1.** having two wings, as some insects, or two winglike appendages, as some seeds **2.** of the dipterans

dip·tych (dip′tik) *n.* [LL. *diptycha,* writing tablet of two leaves < Gr. *diptycha,* neut. pl. of *diptychos,* folded < *di-,* twice + *ptychē,* a fold < *ptyssein,* to fold] **1.** an ancient writing tablet made up of a hinged pair of wooden or ivory pieces folding to protect the inner waxed writing surfaces **2.** a picture painted or carved on two hinged tablets **3.** anything consisting of two parallel or contrasting parts

Di·rac (di rak′), **Paul Adrien Maurice** 1902- ; Eng. mathematician & nuclear physicist

dir·dum (dir′dəm, dur′-) *n.* [ME. *durdom* < Celt., as in Ir. *deardan,* tempest < ? IE. base **dheur-,* to storm] [Scot. & Brit. Dial.] an uproar, act of censure

dire (dīr) *adj.* **dir′er, dir′est** [L. *dirus,* fearful < IE. base **dwei-,* to fear, whence Gr. *deinos,* fearful] **1.** arousing terror or causing extreme distress; dreadful; terrible **2.** calling for quick action; urgent [a *dire* need] —dire′ly *adv.* —dire′ness *n.*

di·rect (də rekt′, dī-) *adj.* [ME. < L. *directus,* pp. of *dirigere,* to lay straight, direct < *di-,* apart, from + *regere,* to keep straight, rule: for IE. base see REGAL] **1.** by the shortest way, without turning or stopping; not roundabout; not interrupted; straight [a *direct* route] **2.** honest and to the point; straightforward; frank [a *direct* answer] **3.** with nothing or no one between; immediate; close, first-hand, or personal [*direct* contact, *direct* knowledge] **4.** in an unbroken line of descent; lineal **5.** exact; complete; absolute [the *direct* opposite] **6.** in the exact words of the speaker [a *direct* quotation] **7.** not needing a mordant: said of certain dyes **8.** by or of action of the people through popular vote instead of through representatives or delegates **9.** *Astron.* from west to east: opposed to RETROGRADE **10.** *Math.* designating or of a relation between variables in which one increases or decreases with the other [a *direct* proportion]: opposed to INVERSE —*vt.* **1.** to manage the affairs, course, or action of; guide; conduct; regulate **2.** to order or command with authority **3.** to turn or point (a person or thing) toward an object or goal; aim; head **4.** to tell (a person) the way to a place **5.** to address (words, remarks, etc.) to a specific person or persons, or in a specific direction **6.** to write the name and address on (a letter, etc.) **7.** *a)* to plan the action and effects of (a play, motion picture, etc.) and to supervise and instruct (the actors and technicians) in the carrying out of such a plan *b)* to rehearse and conduct the performance of (a choir, band, etc.) —*vi.* **1.** to give directions; make a practice of directing **2.** to be a director, as of a group of performers —*adv.* in a direct manner; directly —*SYN.* see COMMAND, CONDUCT —di·rect′ness *n.*

direct action action aimed directly at achieving an objective; esp., the use of strikes, demonstrations, civil disobedience, etc. in disputes or struggles for rights

direct current an electric current flowing in one direction

di·rect·ed (də rek′tid, dī-) *adj.* indicated as being positive or negative, as a number, angle, or line segment

di·rec·tion (də rek′shən, dī-) *n.* [ME. *direccioun* < L. *directio*] **1.** the act of directing; management; supervision

2. [*usually pl.*] instructions for doing, operating, using, preparing, etc. **3.** an authoritative order or command **4.** the point toward which something faces or the line along which something moves or lies [north, "up," "forward," and "left" are *directions*] **5.** an aspect, line of development, way, trend, etc. [research in new *directions*] **6.** *Theater a)* the director's plan for achieving certain effects, as of acting, lighting, etc. *b)* his instructions to the actors, etc. **7.** *Music a)* a word, phrase, or sign showing how a note, passage, etc. is to be played *b)* the work or art of directing a choir, band, etc.

di·rec·tion·al (-'l) *adj.* **1.** of, aimed at, or indicating (a specific) direction **2.** designed for radiating or receiving radio signals most effectively in one or more particular directions [a *directional* antenna] **3.** designed to pick up or send out sound most efficiently in one direction —di·rec′tion·al′i·ty *n.* —di·rec′tion·al·ly *adv.*

direction finder a device for finding out the direction from which radio waves or signals are coming, as a loop antenna that can be rotated freely on a vertical axis

di·rec·tive (də rek′tiv, dī-) *adj.* **1.** directing; tending or intended to direct **2.** indicating direction —*n.* a general instruction or order issued authoritatively

di·rect·ly (də rekt′lē, dī-) *adv.* **1.** in a direct way or line; straight **2.** without a person or thing coming between; immediately [*directly* responsible] **3.** exactly; completely [*directly* opposite] **4.** instantly; right away —*conj.* [Chiefly Brit.] as soon as

☆**direct mail** mail sent directly to a large number of individuals, advertising or promoting a product, institution, etc., and soliciting orders, donations, or the like

direct object the word or words denoting the thing or person that receives the action of a transitive verb; goal or result of a verbal action (Ex.: *ball in hit the ball*)

Di·rec·toire (di rek twär′) *n.* [Fr. < ML. *directorium:* see DIRECTORY] an executive body of five men in the First Republic in France, given office October 27, 1795, and ousted November 9, 1799 —*adj.* of or characteristic of the simple, neoclassical lines of the period of the Directoire: said of furniture, dress, etc.

di·rec·tor (də rek′tər) *n.* [Anglo-Fr. *directour* < LL. *director*] a person or thing that directs or controls; specif., *a)* the head of a project, bureau, school, etc.; supervisor *b)* a member of a board chosen to direct the affairs of a corporation or institution ☆*c)* a person who directs the production of a play, motion picture, etc. *d) Music* a conductor —di·rec′tor·ship′ *n.* —di·rec′tress (-tris) *n.fem.*

di·rec·tor·ate (-it) *n.* **1.** the position of director **2.** a board of directors

di·rec·to·ri·al (də rek′tôr′ē əl, dī-) *adj.* **1.** of a director or directorate **2.** of directing or management

di·rec·to·ry (də rek′tə rē, dī-) *adj.* [LL. *directorius*] directing, guiding, or advising —*n.,* *pl.* -ries [ML. *directorium* < LL. *directorius*] **1.** a book of directions, as for church service **2.** a book listing the names, addresses, etc. of a specific group of persons [a telephone *directory*] **3.** a directorate **4.** [D-] *same as* DIRECTOIRE

☆**direct primary election** a preliminary election at which candidates for public office are chosen by direct vote of the people instead of by delegates at a convention: **closed primary elections** are those in which voters must declare party affiliation and may vote only for candidates of their party

di·rec·trix (də rek′triks, dī-) *n.,* *pl.* -trix·es, -tri·ces (dī′rek trī′sēz) **1.** [Rare] a woman director **2.** *Geom.* a fixed line associated with an ellipse, parabola, or hyperbola, such that for any point on the curve the ratio of the distance from the focus to the distance from the fixed line is a constant

direct tax a tax levied directly on the person by whom it is to be paid, as an income tax or property tax

dire·ful (dīr′fəl) *adj.* dreadful; terrible —dire′ful·ly *adv.*

dirge (durj) *n.* [ME. < L. *dirige,* imperative of *dirigere,* to direct, the first word of an antiphon (Psalm 5:8) in the Office for the Burial of the Dead] **1.** a funeral hymn **2.** a slow, sad song, poem, or musical composition expressing grief or mourning; lament

dir·ham (dir ham′) *n.* [Ar. < L. *drachma,* DRACHMA] **1.** the standard monetary unit of Morocco: see MONETARY UNITS, table **2.** a monetary unit of Qatar equal to 1/100 of a riyal

dir·i·gi·ble (dir′i jə b'l, də rij′ə-) *adj.* [ML. *dirigibilis:* see DIRECT & -IBLE] that can be directed or steered —*n. same as* AIRSHIP

dir·i·ment (dir′ə mənt) *adj.* [< L. *dirimens,* prp. of *dirimere,* to interrupt < *dis-,* apart + *emere,* to take < IE. base **em,* whence Lith. *imù*] making absolutely void; nullifying —**diriment impediment** *R.C.Ch.* any obstacle that automatically annuls a marriage

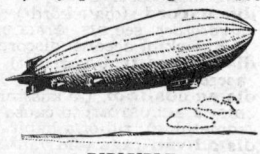

DIRIGIBLE

dirk (durk) n. [so spelled by Dr. Johnson; earlier *dork, durk* < ?] a short straight dagger —vt. to stab with a dirk

dirl (dirl, durl) vt., vi. [var. of Scot. *thirl,* to pierce < ME. *thirlen, thrillen;* cf. THRILL] [Scot. & North Eng. Dial.] to vibrate or tingle

dirn·dl (durn'd'l) n. [G. *dirndl(kleid),* orig., (peasant) girl's (dress), dial. dim. of *dirne,* maid, girl < OHG. *diorna,* servant girl, akin to OE. *theow,* servant, slave] 1. a kind of dress with a full skirt, gathered waist, and closefitting bodice 2. a full skirt with a gathered waist: also **dirndl skirt**

dirt (durt) n. [ME., by metathesis < *drit* < ON. *dritr,* excrement, akin to OE. *dritan,* to excrete < IE. base **dher-,* whence L. *forire,* defecate] 1. any unclean or soiling matter, as mud, dust, dung, trash, etc.; filth 2. earth or garden soil 3. anything common, filthy, or contemptible 4. dirtiness, nastiness, corruption, etc. ☆5. obscene writing, speech, etc.; pornography ☆6. malicious talk or gossip ☆7. *Gold Mining* the gravel, soil, etc. from which gold is separated by washing or panning —adj. ☆having a surface of compacted earth [a *dirt* road] —☆**do one dirt** [Slang] to do harm to one, as by deception or malicious gossip —**hit the dirt** [Slang] to drop to the ground

dirt-cheap (-chēp') adj., adv. [Colloq.] as cheap as dirt; very inexpensive

☆**dirt farmer** [Colloq.] a farmer who works his own land

dirt·y (-ē) adj. **dirt'i·er, dirt'i·est** [ME. *dritti*] 1. soiled or soiling with dirt; unclean 2. causing one to be soiled with dirt [a *dirty* occupation] 3. grayish, muddy, or clouded [a *dirty* green] 4. obscene; pornographic [*dirty* jokes] 5. disagreeable or contemptible; mean; nasty [a *dirty* coward] 6. unfair; dishonest; unsportsmanlike [a *dirty* player] 7. unkind; malicious or malevolent [*dirty* remarks] ☆8. producing much fallout: said of nuclear weapons 9. revealing anger or irritation [a *dirty* look] ☆10. [Slang] rasping, reedy, ragged, or robust in tone [a *dirty* trumpet] 11. *Naut.* squally; rough [*dirty* weather] —vt., vi. **dirt'ied, dirt'y·ing** to make or become dirty; soil; tarnish; stain —**a dirty shame** a very unfortunate circumstance —**dirty linen (or wash)** secrets or problems, esp. those that could cause gossip —☆**dirty pool** [Slang] unfair or dishonest tactics — **dirt'i·ly** adv. —**dirt'i·ness** n.

SYN. —**dirty** is applied to that which is covered or filled with any kind of dirt and is the broadest of these terms [a *dirty* face, a *dirty* room]; **soiled** generally suggests the presence of superficial dirt in an amount sufficient to impair cleanness or freshness [a *soiled* shirt]; **grimy** suggests soot or granular dirt deposited on or ingrained in a surface [a miner with a *grimy* face]; **filthy** is applied to that which is disgustingly dirty [*filthy* as a pigpen]; **foul** implies extreme filth that is grossly offensive or loathsome because of its stench, putridity, or corruption [*foul* air] —ANT. clean

Dis (dis) [L.] *Rom. Myth.* 1. the god of the lower world: identified by the Greeks with Pluto 2. Hades

dis- (dis; *in some words,* diz) [< ME. or OFr. or L.; OFr. *des-* < L. *dis-* (*di-* before *b, d, g, l, v, m, n, l, r; dif-* before *f*) < IE. **dis-* (< **dwis-,* twice, in two: cf. BI-[1], TWO), whence also OE. *te-,* OHG. *zi-,* Goth. *dis-:* cf. DE-] 1. *a v.-forming prefix meaning: a)* away, apart [*dismiss, disperse*] *b)* deprive of, expel from [*disfrock, disbar*] *c)* cause to be the opposite of [*disable*] *d)* fail, cease, refuse to [*dissatisfy, disappear, disallow*] or do the opposite of [*disjoin, disintegrate*]: also used as an intensive [*disannul*] 2. *an adj.-forming prefix meaning* not, un-, the opposite of [*dishonest, dissatisfied, displeasing*] 3. *a n.-forming prefix meaning* opposite of, lack of [*disease, disunion*]

dis. 1. discount 2. distance 3. distant 4. distribute

dis·a·bil·i·ty (dis'ə bil'ə tē) n., pl. **-ties** 1. a disabled condition 2. that which disables, as an illness or injury 3. a legal disqualification or incapacity 4. something that restricts; limitation; disadvantage

disability clause a clause in an insurance contract entitling a policyholder who becomes permanently disabled to cease premium payments without loss of life insurance, and sometimes to receive a specified indemnity

dis·a·ble (dis ā'b'l) vt. **-bled, -bling** 1. to make unable, unfit, or ineffective; cripple; incapacitate 2. to make legally incapable; disqualify legally —SYN. see MAIM —**dis·a'ble·ment** n.

dis·a·buse (dis'ə byōōz') vt. **-bused', -bus'ing** to rid of false ideas; undeceive

di·sac·cha·ride (dī sak'ə rīd') n. [DI-[1] + SACCHARIDE] any of a group of sugars with a common formula, $C_{12}H_{22}O_{11}$, as sucrose, maltose, and lactose, which on hydrolysis yield two monosaccharides

dis·ac·cord (dis'ə kôrd') vi. [ME. *disacorden* < OFr. *desacorder:* see DIS- & ACCORD] to refuse to agree; disagree —n. lack of accord; discord; disagreement

dis·ac·cred·it (-ə kred'it) vt. to cause to be no longer accredited, or authorized

dis·ac·cus·tom (-ə kus'təm) vt. [OFr. *desacostumer:* see DIS- & ACCUSTOM] to cause to be no longer accustomed (*to* something); rid of a habit

dis·ad·van·tage (-əd van'tij, -vän'-) n. [ME. *disavauntage* < OFr. *desavantage:* see DIS- & ADVANTAGE] 1. an unfavorable situation or circumstance; drawback; handicap 2. loss or injury, as to reputation or credit; detriment —vt. **-taged, -tag'ing** to act to the disadvantage of —**at a disadvantage** in an unfavorable situation (for doing something)

dis·ad·van·taged (-tijd) adj. deprived of a decent standard of living, education, etc. by poverty and a lack of opportunity; underprivileged

dis·ad·van·ta·geous (dis ad'vən tā'jəs) adj. causing or characterized by disadvantage; unfavorable; adverse; detrimental —**dis·ad'van·ta'geous·ly** adv.

dis·af·fect (dis'ə fekt') vt. to cause to lose affection for; make unfriendly, discontented, or disloyal, esp. toward the government —**dis'af·fect'ed** adj. —**dis'af·fec'tion** n.

dis·af·fil·i·ate (-ə fil'ē āt') vt., vi. **-at'ed, -at'ing** to end an affiliation (with) —**dis'af·fil'i·a'tion** n.

dis·af·firm (-ə furm') vt. 1. to deny or contradict (a former statement) 2. *Law a)* to refuse to abide by (a contract, agreement, etc.); repudiate *b)* to reverse or set aside (a former decision) —**dis'af·firm'ance, dis'af·fir·ma'tion** (-af ər mā'shən) n.

dis·af·for·est (-ə fôr'ist, -fär'-) vt. [ML. *disafforestare:* see DIS- & AFFOREST] *Eng. Law* to reduce from the legal status of a forest to that of ordinary land

dis·a·gree (-ə grē') vi. [LME. *disagre* < OFr. *desagreer:* see DIS- & AGREE] 1. to fail to agree; be different; differ 2. to differ in opinion; often, specif., to quarrel or dispute 3. to be harmful or give distress (followed by *with*) [apples *disagree* with me]

dis·a·gree·a·ble (-ə b'l) adj. [ME. *disagreeable* < OFr. *desagreable:* see prec. & -ABLE] 1. not to one's taste; unpleasant; offensive 2. hard to get along with; quarrelsome —**dis'a·gree'a·ble·ness** n. —**dis'a·gree'a·bly** adv.

dis·a·gree·ment (-mənt) n. 1. refusal to agree or comply 2. failure to agree; difference; incongruity; discrepancy [a *disagreement* between accounts] 3. difference of opinion 4. a quarrel or dispute

dis·al·low (dis'ə lou') vt. [ME. *disalouen* < Anglo-Fr. *desalouer,* to blame, disapprove of: see DIS- & ALLOW] to refuse to allow; reject as untrue, invalid, or illegal —**dis'-al·low'ance** n.

dis·an·nul (-ə nul') vt. to cancel completely; annul

dis·a·noint (-ə noint') vt. to annul the anointing of

dis·ap·pear (-ə pir') vi. [ME. *disaperen:* see DIS- & APPEAR] 1. to cease to be seen; go out of sight 2. to cease being; go out of existence, use, etc.; become lost or extinct —SYN. see VANISH —**dis'ap·pear'ance** n.

dis·ap·point (-ə point') vt. [ME. *disapointen* < OFr. *desapointer:* see DIS- & APPOINT] 1. to fail to satisfy the hopes or expectations of; leave unsatisfied 2. to undo or frustrate (a plan, intention, etc.); balk; thwart —**dis'ap·point'ing·ly** adv.

dis·ap·point·ment (-mənt) n. 1. a disappointing or being disappointed 2. a person or thing that disappoints

dis·ap·pro·ba·tion (dis ap'rə bā'shən) n. disapproval

dis·ap·prov·al (dis'ə prōōv''l) n. 1. failure or refusal to approve; rejection 2. unfavorable opinion; condemnation

dis·ap·prove (dis'ə prōōv') vt. **-proved', -prov'ing** 1. to have or express an unfavorable opinion of; consider (something) wrong; condemn 2. to refuse to approve; reject —vi. to have or express disapproval (*of*) —**dis'ap·prov'ing·ly** adv.

dis·arm (dis ärm') vt. [ME. *disarmen* < OFr. *desarmer:* see DIS- & ARM[2]] 1. to take away weapons or armaments from 2. to deprive of the ability to hurt; make harmless 3. to overcome the hostility of; make friendly —vi. 1. to lay down arms 2. to reduce or do away with armed forces and armaments

dis·ar·ma·ment (-är'mə mənt) n. 1. the act of disarming 2. the reduction of armed forces and armaments, as to a limitation set by treaty

dis·arm·ing (-är'miŋ) adj. removing or allaying suspicions, fears, or hostility —**dis·arm'ing·ly** adv.

dis·ar·range (dis'ə rānj') vt. **-ranged', -rang'ing** to undo the order or arrangement of; make less neat; disorder — **dis'ar·range'ment** n.

dis·ar·ray (-ə rā') vt. [ME. *disaraien* < OFr. *desareer:* see DIS- & ARRAY] 1. to throw into disorder or confusion; upset 2. [Archaic] to undress —n. [ME. *disarai* < OFr. *desarroi*] 1. an untidy condition; disorder; confusion 2. a state of disorderly or insufficient dress —SYN. see CONFUSION

dis·ar·tic·u·late (-är tik'yoo lāt') vt. **-lat'ed, -lat'ing** to separate at the joints; disjoint —vi. to become disjointed —**dis'ar·tic'u·la'tion** n.

dis·as·sem·ble (-ə sem'b'l) vt. **-bled, -bling** ☆to take apart —☆**dis'as·sem'bly** (-blē) n.

dis·as·so·ci·ate (-ə sō'shē āt', -sē-) vt. **-at'ed, -at'ing** to sever association with; separate; dissociate —**dis'as·so'ci·a'tion** n.

dis·as·ter (di zas'tər, -zäs'-) n. [OFr. *desastre* < It. *disastro* < L. *dis-* + *astrum* < Gr. *astron* (see ASTRAL), a star: from astrological notions: cf. ILL-STARRED] any happening that causes great harm or damage; serious or sudden misfortune; calamity

SYN. —**disaster** implies great or sudden misfortune that results in loss of life, property, etc. or that is ruinous to an undertaking; **calamity** suggests a grave misfortune that brings deep distress or sorrow to an individual or to the people at large; **catastrophe** is specifically applied to a disastrous end or outcome; **cataclysm** suggests a great upheaval, esp. a political or social one, that causes sudden and violent change with attending distress, suffering, etc.

dis·as·trous (-trəs) adj. [Fr. *désastreux*] of the nature of a disaster; causing great harm, damage, grief, etc.; calamitous —**dis·as'trous·ly** adv.

dis·a·vow (dis′ə vou′) *vt.* [ME. *disavouen* < OFr. *desavoer:* see DIS- & AVOW] to deny any knowledge or approval of, or responsibility for; disclaim; disown; repudiate — **dis′a·vow′al** *n.*

dis·band (dis band′) *vt.* [MFr. *desbander:* see DIS- & BAND¹] 1. to break up (an association or organization) 2. to dismiss (a military force) from service —*vi.* to cease to exist or function as an organization; scatter; disperse — **dis·band′ment** *n.*

dis·bar (-bär′) *vt.* **-barred′, -bar′ring** to expel (a lawyer) from the bar; deprive of the right to practice law —SYN. see EXCLUDE —**dis·bar′ment** *n.*

dis·be·lief (dis′bə lēf′) *n.* refusal to believe; absence of belief —SYN. see UNBELIEF

dis·be·lieve (-lēv′) *vt.* **-lieved′, -liev′ing** to refuse to believe; reject as untrue —*vi.* to refuse to believe (*in*) —**dis′be·liev′er** *n.*

dis·branch (dis branch′, -bränch′) *vt.* 1. to break or cut off (a branch) 2. to cut branches from; prune

dis·bur·den (-bur′d'n) *vt.* 1. to relieve of a burden or of anything burdensome 2. to get rid of (a burden); unload —*vi.* to get rid of a burden —**dis·bur′den·ment** *n.*

dis·burse (-burs′) *vt.* **-bursed′, -burs′ing** [OFr. *desbourser:* see DIS- & BOURSE] to pay out; expend —**dis·burs′a·ble** *adj.* —**dis·burs′er** *n.*

dis·burse·ment (-burs′mənt) *n.* 1. the act of disbursing 2. money disbursed; expenditure

disc (disk) *n.* 1. *same as* DISK 2. a phonograph record ☆3. any of the sharp, circular blades on a disc harrow 4. *Biol.* any disk-shaped part or structure: cf. DISK

disc. 1. discount 2. discovered

dis·calced (dis kalst′) *adj.* [< L. *discalceatus,* unshod < *dis-,* not + *calceatus,* a sandal, shoe < pp. of *calceare,* to provide with shoes < *calceus,* a shoe < *culx,* a heel: akin to CALK²] barefooted, as members of certain religious orders

dis·cant (dis′kant; *for vi.,* also dis kant′) *n., vi. same as* DESCANT

dis·card (dis kärd′; *for n.* dis′kärd) *vt.* [OFr. *doscarter,* prob. < *des-* + *carte:* see DIS- & CARD¹] 1. *Card Games* a) to remove (a card or cards) from the hand that one has been dealt b) to play (a card not a trump and not in the suit led) 2. to throw away, abandon, or get rid of as no longer valuable or useful —*vi. Card Games* to make a discard —*n.* 1. a discarding or being discarded 2. something discarded 3. *Card Games* the card or cards discarded

disc brake a brake, as on an automobile, that functions by causing two friction pads to press on either side of a disc rotating along with the wheel

dis·cern (di surn′, -zurn′) *vt.* [ME. *discernen* < OFr. *discerner* < L. *discernere* < *dis-,* apart + *cernere,* to separate: see CERTAIN] 1. to separate (a thing) mentally from another or others; recognize as separate or different 2. to perceive or recognize; make out clearly —*vi.* to perceive or recognize the difference —**dis·cern′er** *n.* —**dis·cern′i·ble** *adj.* —**dis·cern′i·bly** *adv.*

SYN. —**discern** implies a making out or recognizing of something visually or mentally [to *discern* one's motives]; **perceive** implies recognition by means of any of the senses, and, with reference to mental apprehension, often implies keen understanding or insight [to *perceive* a change in attitude]; **distinguish,** in this connection, implies a perceiving clearly or distinctly by sight, hearing, etc. [he *distinguished* the voices of men down the hall]; **observe** and **notice** both connote some measure of attentiveness, and usually suggest use of the sense of sight [to *observe* an eclipse, to *notice* a sign]

dis·cern·ing (-iŋ) *adj.* having or showing good judgment or understanding; astute —**dis·cern′ing·ly** *adv.*

dis·cern·ment (-mənt) *n.* 1. an act or instance of discerning 2. the power of discerning; keen perception or judgment; insight; acumen

dis·cerp·ti·ble (di surp′tə b'l) *adj.* [< L. *discerptus,* pp. of *discerpere,* to pluck to pieces (< *dis-,* apart + *carpere,* to pluck) + -IBLE: for IE. base see EXCERPT] [Rare] that can be torn apart or divided; separable

dis·charge (dis chärj′; *for n., usually* dis′chärj) *vt.* **-charged′, -charg′ing** [ME. *dischargen* < OFr. *descharger* < VL. *discarricare,* to unload < L. *dis-,* from + *carrus,* wagon, CAR] 1. to relieve of or release from something that burdens or confines; specif., *a*) to remove the cargo of (a ship); unload *b*) to release the charge of (a gun); fire *c*) to release (a soldier, jury, etc.) from duty *d*) to dismiss (a special committee) after it has reported to the legislature of which it is a part *e*) to dismiss from employment *f*) to release (a prisoner) from jail, (a defendant) from suspicion, (a patient) as cured, (a debtor or bankrupt) from obligations, etc. 2. to release or remove (that by which one is burdened or confined); specif., *a*) to unload (a cargo) *b*) to shoot (a projectile) *c*) to remove (dye) from cloth 3. to relieve oneself or itself of (a burden, load, etc.); specif., *a*) to throw off; send forth; emit [to *discharge* pus] *b*) to get rid of; acquit oneself of; pay (a debt) or perform (a duty) 4. *Archit. a*) to relieve (a wall, etc.) of excess pressure by distribution of weight *b*) to distribute (weight) evenly over a supporting part ☆5. *Elec.* to

remove stored energy from (a battery or capacitor) —*vi.* 1. to get rid of a burden, load, etc. 2. to be released or thrown off 3. to fire; go off: said of a gun, etc. 4. to emit waste matter: said of a wound, etc. 5. to run: said of a dye —*n.* [OFr. *descharge* < the *v.*] 1. a discharging or being discharged (in all senses) 2. that which discharges, as a legal order for release, a certificate of dismissal from military service, etc. 3. that which is discharged, as pus from a sore 4. a flow of electric current across a gap, as in a spark or arc —SYN. see FREE —**dis·charge′a·ble** *adj.* —**dis·charg′er** *n.*

discharge tube a device in which a gas or metal vapor conducting an electric discharge is the source of light, as in a mercury-vapor lamp

☆**disc harrow** a harrow with sharp, revolving circular blades used to break up the soil for sowing

dis·ci·ple (di sī′p'l) *n.* [ME. < OFr. *desciple* & OE. *discipul,* both < L. *discipulus,* learner, pupil, in LL.(Ec.), a disciple of Jesus < **discipere,* to comprehend < *dis-* + *capere,* to hold: infl. by *discere,* to learn] 1. a pupil or follower of any teacher or school of religion, learning, art, etc. 2. an early follower of Jesus, esp. one of the Apostles ☆3. [D-] a member of the Disciples of Christ —SYN. see FOLLOWER —**dis·ci′ple·ship′** *n.*

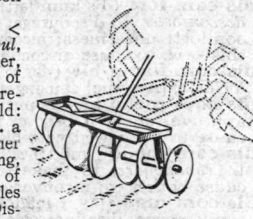

DISC HARROW

☆**Disciples of Christ** a Christian denomination, organized in 1809, that makes the Bible the only basis for faith and practice and baptizes by immersion

dis·ci·plin·ant (dis′ə plin ənt) *n.* a person who disciplines himself; specif., [D-] any member of a former Christian sect in Spain who flagellated and otherwise tortured themselves publicly as a means of discipline

dis·ci·pli·nar·i·an (dis′ə pli ner′ē ən) *n.* a person who believes in or enforces strict discipline

dis·ci·pli·nar·y (dis′ə pli ner′ē) *adj.* 1. of or having to do with discipline 2. that enforces discipline by punishing or correcting

dis·ci·pline (dis′ə plin) *n.* [ME. < OFr. *descepline* < L. *disciplina* < *discipulus:* see DISCIPLE] 1. a branch of knowledge or learning 2. *a*) training that develops self-control, character, or orderliness and efficiency *b*) strict control to enforce obedience 3. the result of such training or control; specif., *a*) self-control or orderly conduct *b*) acceptance of or submission to authority and control 4. a system of rules, as for the conduct of members of a monastic order 5. treatment that corrects or punishes —*vt.* **-plined, -plin·ing** 1. to subject to discipline; train; control 2. to punish —SYN. see PUNISH —**dis′ci·plin·a·ble** *adj.* —**dis′ci·plin·al** *adj.* —**dis′ci·plin·er** *n.*

☆**disc jockey** a person who conducts a radio program of recorded music, interspersed with chatter, commercials, etc.

dis·claim (dis klām′) *vt.* [ME. *disclaimen* < Anglo-Fr. *disclaimer:* see DIS- & CLAIM] 1. to give up or renounce any claim to or connection with 2. to refuse to acknowledge or admit; deny; repudiate —*vi.* to make a disclaimer

dis·claim·er (-ər) *n.* [Anglo-Fr. *desclamer,* inf. used as n.] 1. a disclaiming; denial or renunciation, as of a claim, title, etc. 2. a refusal to accept responsibility for something; disavowal

dis·cla·ma·tion (dis′klə mā′shən) *n.* an act of disclaiming; renunciation; repudiation

dis·cli·max (dis klī′maks) *n. Ecol.* a climax community disrupted and changed by continuous disturbance, esp. by man or domestic animals

dis·close (-klōz′) *vt.* **-closed′, -clos′ing** [ME. *disclosen* < base of OFr. *desclore:* see DIS- & CLOSE²] 1. to bring into view; uncover 2. to reveal; make known —*n.* [Obs.] disclosure —SYN. see REVEAL —**dis·clos′er** *n.*

dis·clo·sure (-klō′zhər) *n.* 1. a disclosing or being disclosed 2. a thing disclosed; revelation

dis·co- (dis′kō, -kə) [< L. *discus:* see DISK] *a prefix meaning:* 1. disk-shaped; discoid 2. phonograph record [*discography*]

dis·co·bo·lus (dis käb′ə ləs) *n.* [L. < Gr. *diskobolos* < *diskos,* discus + *ballein,* to throw] a discus thrower

dis·cog·ra·phy (dis käg′rə fē) *n., pl.* **-phies** [DISCO- + (BIBLIO)GRAPHY] 1. the systematic study and cataloging of phonograph records 2. a list of the recordings of a particular performer, composer, composition, etc. —**dis·cog′ra·pher** *n.*

dis·coid (dis′koid) *adj.* [LL. *discoides* < Gr. *diskoeidēs,* disk-shaped < *diskos,* a disk + *eidos,* form] 1. shaped like a disk 2. *Bot.* lacking ray flowers and having only tubular florets, as a composite flower head Also **dis·coi′dal** —*n.* anything shaped like a disk

dis·col·or (dis′kul′ər) *vt., vi.* [ME. *discolouren* < OFr. *descolourer* < ML. *discolorare* < L. *discolor,* of another color: see DIS- & COLOR] to change in color by fading, streaking, or staining

dis·col·or·a·tion (-kul'ə rā'shən) *n.* **1.** a discoloring or being discolored **2.** a discolored spot or mark

dis·col·our (-kul'ər) *vt.*, *vi. Brit. sp.* of DISCOLOR

☆**dis·com·bob·u·late** (dis'kəm bäb'yoo lāt') *vt.* **-lat'ed**, **-lat'ing** [whimsical alteration and extension, prob. of DISCOMFIT] [Colloq.] to upset the composure of; disconcert; confuse

dis·com·fit (dis kum'fit) *vt.* [ME. *discomfiten* < OFr. *desconfit*, pp. of *desconfire* < VL. **disconficere* < L. *dis-* + *conficere*: see CONFECT] **1.** orig., to defeat; overthrow; put to flight **2.** to frustrate the plans or expectations of; thwart **3.** to make uneasy; confuse; disconcert —*SYN.* see EMBARRASS

dis·com·fi·ture (-fi chər) *n.* [ME. < OFr. *desconfiture*] a discomfiting or being discomfited; frustration, confusion, etc.

dis·com·fort (dis kum'fərt) *n.* [ME. < OFr. *desconfort* < *desconforter*, to discourage: see DIS- & COMFORT] **1.** lack of comfort; uneasiness; inconvenience **2.** anything causing this —*vt.* to cause discomfort to; distress

dis·com·fort·a·ble (-fər tə b'l) *adj.* [ME. < OFr. *desconfortable*] [Archaic] causing discomfort

dis·com·mend (dis'kə mend') *vt.* **1.** [Rare] to express disapproval of **2.** [Obs.] *a)* to speak of dissuasively *b)* to cause to be viewed with disfavor

dis·com·mode (-mōd') *vt.* **-mod'ed**, **-mod'ing** [< DIS- + L. *commodare*, to make suitable: see ACCOMMODATE] to cause bother to; inconvenience

dis·com·mod·i·ty (-mäd'ə tē) *n.*, *pl.* **-ties** [Archaic] inconvenience; disadvantage

dis·com·pose (-kəm pōz') *vt.* **-posed'**, **-pos'ing** **1.** to disturb the calm or poise of; fluster; disconcert **2.** [Now Rare] to disturb the order of; disarrange —*SYN.* see DISTURB —**dis'com·po'sure** (-pō'zhər) *n.*

dis·con·cert (-kən surt') *vt.* [OFr. *desconcerter*: see DIS- & CONCERT] **1.** to upset or frustrate (plans, etc.) **2.** to upset the composure or self-possession of; embarrass; confuse —*SYN.* see EMBARRASS —**dis'con·cert'ing** *adj.* —**dis'con·cert'ing·ly** *adv.*

dis·con·form·i·ty (-kən fôr'mə tē) *n.* [ML. *disconformitas*: see DIS- & CONFORMITY] **1.** [Archaic] lack of conformity **2.** *Geol.* an unconformity separating parallel strata

dis·con·nect (-kə nekt') *vt.* to break or undo the connection of; separate, detach, unplug, etc. —**dis'con·nec'tion** *n.*

dis·con·nect·ed (-kə nek'tid) *adj.* **1.** separated, detached, unplugged, etc. **2.** broken up into unrelated parts; incoherent —**dis'con·nect'ed·ly** *adv.* —**dis'con·nect'ed·ness** *n.*

dis·con·so·late (dis kän'sə lit) *adj.* [ME. < ML. *disconsolatus* < L. *dis-* + *consolatus*, pp. of *consolari*: see DIS- & CONSOLE¹] **1.** so unhappy that nothing will comfort; inconsolable; dejected **2.** causing or suggesting dejection; cheerless —**dis'con'so·late·ly** *adv.* —**dis'con'so·late·ness**, **dis·con'so·la'tion** (-lā'shən) *n.*

dis·con·tent (dis'kən tent') *adj.* [ME.] *same as* DISCONTENTED —*n.* lack of contentment; dissatisfaction; restless desire for something more or different: also **dis'con·tent'ment** —*vt.* to make discontented

dis·con·tent·ed (-id) *adj.* not contented; wanting something more or different —**dis'con·tent'ed·ly** *adv.* —**dis'con·tent'ed·ness** *n.*

dis·con·tin·u·ance (dis'kən tin'yoo wəns) *n.* [ME. < Anglo-Fr.: see DISCONTINUE & -ANCE] **1.** a stopping or being stopped; cessation or interruption **2.** *Law* the stopping of a legal action prior to trial, either voluntarily by the plaintiff or by order of the court

dis·con·tin·u·a·tion (-tin'yoo wā'shən) *n.* [Fr. < ML. *discontinuatio*] *same as* DISCONTINUANCE (sense 1)

dis·con·tin·ue (-tin'yoo) *vt.* **-ued**, **-u·ing** [ME. *discontinuen* < OFr. *discontinuer* < ML. *discontinuare*: see DIS- & CONTINUE] **1.** to stop using, doing, etc.; cease; give up **2.** *Law* to effect a discontinuance of (a suit) —*vi.* to stop; end —*SYN.* see STOP

dis·con·ti·nu·i·ty (dis kän'tə noo'ə tē, dis'kän-; -nyoo'-) *n.*, *pl.* **-ties** [ML. *discontinuitas*: see prec. & -ITY] **1.** lack of continuity, or logical sequence **2.** a gap or break **3.** *Math.* a value of the argument x of a mathematical function f(x) at which this function is not continuous

dis·con·tin·u·ous (dis'kən tin'yoo wəs) *adj.* not continuous; broken up by interruptions or gaps; intermittent —**dis'con·tin'u·ous·ly** *adv.*

dis·co·phile (dis'kə fil') *n.* [DISCO- + -PHILE] an expert on, or collector of, phonograph records

dis·cord (dis'kôrd; *for v., usually* dis kôrd') *n.* [ME. < OFr. *descorde* < L. *discordia* < *discors* (gen. *discordis*), discordant < *dis-*, apart + *cor*, HEART] **1.** lack of concord; disagreement; dissension; conflict **2.** a harsh or confused noise, as the sound of battle; clash; din **3.** *Music* a lack of harmony in tones sounded together; inharmonious combination of tones; dissonance —*vi.* to disagree; be in harmonious; clash

SYN.—**discord** denotes disagreement or lack of concord and may imply quarreling between persons, clashing qualities in things, dissonance in sound, etc.; **strife** stresses the struggle to win out where there is a conflict or disagreement; **contention** suggests verbal strife as expressed in argument, controversy, dispute, etc.; **dissension** implies difference of opinion, usually suggesting contention between opposing groups in a body —*ANT.* harmony, agreement

dis·cord·ant (dis kôr'd'nt) *adj.* [ME. *discordaunt* < OFr.

descordant, prp. of *descorder*: see DISCORD] **1.** not in accord; disagreeing; conflicting **2.** not in harmony; dissonant; clashing —**dis·cord'ance**, **dis·cord'an·cy** *n.* —**dis·cord'ant·ly** *adv.*

☆**dis·co·thèque** (dis'kə tek) *n.* [Fr. < *disque*, disk, record (< L. *discus*: see DISCUS) + *bibliothèque*, library < L. *bibliotheca*: see BIBLIOTHECA] a nightclub or other public place for dancing to recorded popular music

dis·count (dis'kount; *for v., also* dis kount') *n.* [< OFr. *desconter*, to count off < ML. *discomputare*: see DIS- & COMPUTE] **1.** *a)* a reduction from a usual or list price *b)* a deduction from a debt, allowed for paying promptly or in cash **2.** the interest deducted in advance by one who buys, or lends money on, a bill of exchange, promissory note, etc. **3.** the rate of interest charged for discounting a bill, note, etc.: also called **discount rate** **4.** a discounting, as of a bill, note, etc. —*vt.* **1.** to pay or receive the present value of (a bill of exchange, promissory note, etc.), minus a deduction to cover interest for the purchaser **2.** to deduct an amount or percent from (a bill, price, etc.) **3.** to sell at less than the regular price **4.** *a)* to take (a story, statement, opinion, etc.) at less than face value, allowing for exaggeration, bias, etc. *b)* to disbelieve or disregard entirely; set aside as inaccurate or irrelevant **5.** to lessen the effect of by anticipating; reckon with in advance —*vi.* to lend or sell with discounts —**at a discount** **1.** below the regular price; below face value **2.** worth little; unwanted and easily obtained

dis·coun·te·nance (dis koun'tə nəns) *vt.* [DIS- + COUNTENANCE] **1.** to make ashamed or embarrassed; disconcert **2.** to refuse approval or support to; discourage

☆**discount house** (or **store**) a retail store that sells its goods for less than the regular or list prices

dis·cour·age (dis kur'ij) *vt.* **-aged**, **-ag·ing** [ME. *discoragen* < OFr. *descoragier*: see DIS- & COURAGE] **1.** to deprive of courage, hope, or confidence; dishearten **2.** to advise or persuade (a person) to refrain **3.** to prevent or try to prevent by disapproving or raising objections or obstacles —*vi.* to become discouraged

dis·cour·age·ment (-mənt) *n.* [OFr. *descoragement*] **1.** a discouraging **2.** the fact, state, or feeling of being discouraged **3.** anything that discourages

dis·cour·ag·ing (-iŋ) *adj.* that discourages; disheartening; depressing —**dis·cour'ag·ing·ly** *adv.*

dis·course (dis'kôrs; *also, and for v. usually,* dis kôrs') *n.* [ME. & OFr. *discours* < L. *discursus*, discourse < pp. of *discurrere*, to run to and fro < *dis-*, from, apart + *currere*, to run: see CURRENT] **1.** communication of ideas, information, etc., esp. by talking; conversation **2.** a long and formal treatment of a subject, in speech or writing; lecture; treatise; dissertation **3.** [Archaic] ability to reason; rationality —*vi.* **-coursed'**, **-cours'ing** **1.** to carry on conversation; talk; confer **2.** to speak or write (*on* or *upon* a subject) formally and at some length —*vt.* [Archaic] to utter or tell —*SYN.* see SPEAK —**dis·cours'er** *n.*

dis·cour·te·ous (dis kur'tē əs) *adj.* not courteous; impolite; rude; ill-mannered —*SYN.* see RUDE —**dis·cour'te·ous·ly** *adv.* —**dis·cour'te·ous·ness** *n.*

dis·cour·te·sy (-tə sē) *n.* **1.** lack of courtesy; impoliteness; bad manners; rudeness **2.** *pl.* **-sies** a rude or impolite act or remark

dis·cov·er (dis kuv'ər) *vt.* [ME. *discoveren* < OFr. *descovrir* < LL. *discooperire*, to discover, reveal: see DIS- & COVER] **1.** to be the first to find out, see, or know about **2.** to find out; learn of the existence of; realize **3.** *a)* [Now Rare] to reveal; disclose; expose *b)* [Archaic] to uncover —*SYN.* see LEARN —**dis·cov'er·a·ble** *adj.* —**dis·cov'er·er** *n.*

dis·cov·ert (-ərt) *adj.* [ME. < OFr. *descovert*, lit., not covered, hence not protected: see DIS- & COVER] *Law* having no husband: said of a spinster, widow, or divorcée —**dis·cov'er·ture** (-ər chər) *n.*

dis·cov·er·y (-ər ē) *n.*, *pl.* **-er·ies** **1.** the act of discovering **2.** anything discovered **3.** [Archaic] the act of revealing; disclosure **4.** *Law* any disclosure that a defendant is compelled to make, as of facts or documents

☆**Discovery Day** *same as* COLUMBUS DAY

dis·cred·it (dis kred'it) *vt.* **1.** to reject as untrue; disbelieve **2.** to show or be a reason for disbelief or distrust; cast doubt on **3.** to damage the credit or reputation of; disgrace —*n.* **1.** absence or loss of belief or trust; disbelief; doubt **2.** damage to one's reputation; loss of respect or status; disgrace; dishonor **3.** something that causes disgrace or loss of status

dis·cred·it·a·ble (-ə b'l) *adj.* damaging to one's reputation or status; disgraceful —**dis·cred'it·a·bly** *adv.*

dis·creet (dis krēt') *adj.* [ME. & OFr. *discret* < L. *descretus*, pp. of *discernere*: see DISCERN] careful about what one says or does; prudent; esp., keeping silent or preserving confidences when necessary —*SYN.* see CAREFUL —**dis·creet'ly** *adv.* —**dis·creet'ness** *n.*

dis·crep·an·cy (dis krep'ən sē) *n.*, *pl.* **-cies** [ME. *discrepauns* < OFr. *discrepance* < L. *discrepantia* < *discrepans*, prp. of *discrepare*, to sound differently < *dis-*, from + *crepare*, to rattle: see CRAVEN] lack of agreement, or an instance of this; difference; inconsistency

dis·crep·ant (-ənt) *adj.* [ME. *discrepante* < L. *discrepans*] lacking agreement; differing; at variance; inconsistent —**dis·crep'ant·ly** *adv.*

dis·crete (dis krēt') *adj.* [ME. *discret*: see DISCREET] **1.** separate and distinct; not attached to others; unrelated

2. made up of distinct parts; discontinuous —**dis·crete′ly** adv. —**dis·crete′ness** n.

dis·cre·tion (dis kresh′ən) n. [ME. discrecioun < OFr. discrecion < L. discretio, separation (in LL., discernment) < discretus: see DISCREET] **1.** the freedom or authority to make decisions and choices; power to judge or act **2.** the quality of being discreet, or careful about what one does and says; prudence **3.** [Archaic] the action or power of discerning; judgment —**at one's discretion** as one wishes

dis·cre·tion·ar·y (-er′ē) adj. left to one's discretion; regulated by one's own choice: also **dis·cre′tion·al**

dis·crim·i·na·ble (dis krim′ə nə b'l) adj. that can be discriminated or distinguished

dis·crim·i·nant (-nənt) n. Math. an expression whose sign serves to classify observations into two separate classes

dis·crim·i·nate (dis krim′ə nāt′; for adj. -nit) vt. -nat′ed, -nat′ing [< L. discriminatus, pp. of discriminare, to divide, distinguish < discrimen, division, distinction < discernere: see DISCERN] **1.** to constitute a difference between; differentiate **2.** to recognize the difference between; distinguish —vi. **1.** to see the difference (between things); distinguish **2.** to be discerning **3.** to make distinctions in treatment; show partiality (in favor of) or prejudice (against) —adj. **1.** involving discrimination; distinguishing carefully **2.** [Archaic] distinct; distinguished —SYN. see DISTINGUISH

dis·crim·i·nat·ing (-nāt′iŋ) adj. **1.** that discriminates; distinguishing **2.** able to make or see fine distinctions; discerning **3.** same as DISCRIMINATORY Also **dis·crim′i·na′tive** (-nāt′iv, -nə tiv)

dis·crim·i·na·tion (dis krim′ə nā′shən) n. [L. discriminatio] **1.** the act of discriminating, or distinguishing differences **2.** the ability to make or perceive distinctions; perception; discernment **3.** a showing of partiality or prejudice in treatment; specif., action or policies directed against the welfare of minority groups

dis·crim·i·na·tor (-krim′ə nāt′ər) n. [LL.] one that discriminates; specif., Radio a circuit for demodulating frequency-modulated or phase-modulated carrier waves

dis·crim·i·na·to·ry (-nə tôr′ē) adj. **1.** practicing discrimination, or showing prejudice **2.** discriminating, or distinguishing

dis·cur·sion (dis kur′zhən, -shən) n. [LL. discursio, a running different ways, scattering < L. discursus: see DISCOURSE] **1.** rambling discourse; digression **2.** discursive reasoning

dis·cur·sive (-siv) adj. [ML. discursivus < L. discursus: see DISCOURSE] **1.** wandering from one topic to another; skimming over many apparently unconnected subjects; rambling; desultory; digressive **2.** Philos. going from premises to conclusions in a series of logical steps: distinguished from INTUITIVE —**dis·cur′sive·ly** adv. —**dis·cur′sive·ness** n.

dis·cus (dis′kəs) n., pl. **dis′cus·es, dis·ci** (dis′ī) [L. < Gr. diskos < base of dikein, to throw, akin to deiknynai, to show, point out < IE. base *deik-, whence L. dicere] **1.** a heavy disk of metal and wood, orig. often of stone, thrown for distance as a test of strength and skill **2.** the throwing of the discus as a field event in track and field meets: in full, **discus throw**

dis·cuss (dis kus′) vt. [ME. discussen, to examine, scatter < L. discussus, pp. of discutire, to strike asunder, scatter < dis-, apart + quatere, to shake, beat: see QUASH²] **1.** to talk or write about; take up in conversation or in a discourse; consider and argue the pros and cons of **2.** [Old Colloq.] to eat or drink (something) with enjoyment **3.** [Obs.] to disperse; dispel **4.** [Obs.] to make known; reveal —**dis·cuss′a·ble, dis·cuss′i·ble** adj. —**dis·cuss′er** n.

SYN. —**discuss** implies a talking about something in a deliberative fashion, with varying opinions offered constructively and, usually amicably, so as to settle an issue, decide on a course of action, etc.; **argue** implies the citing of reasons or evidence to support or refute an assertion, belief, proposition, etc.; **debate** implies a formal argument, usually on public questions, in contests between opposing groups; **dispute** implies argument in which there is a clash of opposing opinions, often presented in an angry or heated manner

☆**dis·cuss·ant** (-ənt) n. a person taking part in an organized discussion

dis·cus·sion (dis kush′ən) n. [ME. discussioun < LL. discussio] the act of discussing; talk or writing in which the pros and cons or various aspects of a subject are considered —**under discussion** being discussed

dis·dain (dis dān′) vt. [ME. disdeinen < OFr. desdaignier < VL. *disdignari < L. dis-, not + dignari, DEIGN] to regard or treat as unworthy or beneath one's dignity; specif., to refuse or reject with aloof contempt or scorn —n. the

DISCUS THROWER

feeling, attitude, or expression of disdaining; aloof contempt or scorn —SYN. see DESPISE

dis·dain·ful (-fəl) adj. feeling or expressing disdain; scornful and aloof —SYN. see PROUD —**dis·dain′ful·ly** adv. —**dis·dain′ful·ness** n.

dis·ease (di zēz′) n. [ME. disese, inconvenience, trouble, sickness < OFr. desaise, discomfort < des-, DIS- + aise, EASE] **1.** any departure from health; illness in general **2.** a particular destructive process in an organ or organism, with a specific cause and characteristic symptoms; specif., an illness; ailment **3.** any harmful or destructive condition, as of society —vt. -eased′, -eas′ing [ME. disesen < OFr. desaaisier < the n.] to cause disease in; infect or derange: usually in pp. —**dis·eased′** adj.

SYN. —**disease** may apply generally to any deviation of the body from its normal or healthy state or it may refer to a particular disorder with a specific cause and characteristic symptoms; **affection** refers to a disorder of a specific organ or part [an affection of the spleen]; **malady** usually refers to a deep-seated chronic disease, frequently one that is ultimately fatal; **ailment** refers to a chronic, annoying disorder of whatever degree of seriousness [the minor ailments of the aged]

dis·em·bark (dis′im bärk′) vt. [Fr. désembarquer: see DIS- & EMBARK] to unload (passengers or goods) from a ship, aircraft, etc. —vi. to go ashore from a ship or leave an aircraft or other means of transportation —**dis·em·bar·ka·tion** (dis′em bär kā′shən, dis em′-) n.

dis·em·bar·rass (-im bar′əs, -ber′-) vt. to rid or relieve of something embarrassing, annoying, entangling, perplexing, or burdensome

dis·em·bod·y (-im bäd′ē) vt. -bod′ied, -bod′y·ing to free from bodily existence; make incorporeal —**dis′em·bod′ied** adj. —**dis′em·bod′i·ment** n.

dis·em·bogue (-im bōg′) vt., vi. -bogued′, -bogu′ing [Sp. desembocar, to come out of the mouth of a river or haven < des- (L. dis-), apart + embocar, to enter by the mouth < L. in, in + bucca, cheek] to pour out (its waters) at the mouth; empty (itself): said of a stream, etc.

dis·em·bos·om (-im booz′m, -booz′-) vt., vi. to reveal (a secret, etc.); unbosom (oneself)

dis·em·bow·el (-im bou′əl) vt. -eled or -elled, -el·ing or -el·ling to take out the bowels, or entrails, of; eviscerate —**dis′em·bow′el·ment** n.

dis·em·ployed (-im ploid′) adj. out of work, esp. because of lack of skill, training, or education, rather than because work is unavailable —**dis′em·ploy′ment** n.

dis·en·a·ble (-in ā′b'l) vt. -bled, -bling to cause to become unable or incapable; prevent or disable

dis·en·chant (-in chant′, -chänt′) vt. [Fr. désenchanter: see DIS- & ENCHANT] to set free from an enchantment or illusion —**dis′en·chant′ment** n.

dis·en·cum·ber (dis′in kum′bər) vt. [OFr. desencombrer: see DIS- & ENCUMBER] to relieve of a burden; free from a hindrance or annoyance

dis·en·dow (-in dou′) vt. to deprive of an endowment —**dis′en·dow′ment** n.

dis·en·fran·chise (-in fran′chīz) vt. -chised, -chis·ing same as DISFRANCHISE —**dis′en·fran′chise·ment** n.

dis·en·gage (-in gāj′) vt. -gaged′, -gag′ing [OFr. desengagier: see DIS- & ENGAGE] to release or loosen from something that binds, holds, entangles, or interlocks; unfasten; detach; disentangle; free —vi. to release oneself or itself; become disengaged

dis·en·gaged (-in gājd′) adj. **1.** having no engagements; at leisure **2.** set loose; detached **3.** not in gear

dis·en·gage·ment (-in gāj′mənt) n. **1.** a disengaging or being disengaged **2.** freedom from obligation, occupation, etc.; ease; leisure **3.** withdrawal from a stated policy, previous involvement or position, etc.

disengaging action a voluntary tactical withdrawal of troops in a critical situation: sometimes a euphemism for RETREAT

dis·en·tail (-in tāl′) vt. Law to free from entail

dis·en·tan·gle (-in taŋ′g'l) vt. -gled, -gling **1.** to free from something that entangles, confuses, etc.; extricate; disengage **2.** to straighten out (anything tangled, confused, etc.); unravel; untangle —vi. to get free from a tangle —**dis′en·tan′gle·ment** n.

dis·en·thrall, dis·en·thral (-in thrôl′) vt. to free from bondage or slavery; liberate

dis·en·throne (dis′in thrōn′) vt. -throned′, -thron′ing to dethrone; depose —**dis′en·throne′ment** n.

dis·en·ti·tle (-in tīt′'l) vt. -tled, -tling to deprive of a right, title, or claim

dis·en·tomb (-in toom′) vt. to take from a tomb; disinter

dis·en·twine (-in twīn′) vt., vi. -twined′, -twin′ing to disentangle; untwine; unwind

di·sep·al·ous (dī sep′'l əs) adj. Bot. having two sepals

dis·e·quil·i·brate (dis′i kwil′ə brāt′) vt. -brat′ed, -brat′ing to destroy the equilibrium in or of; throw out of balance —**dis′e·quil′i·bra′tion** n.

dis·e·qui·lib·ri·um (dis ē′kwə lib′rē əm) n., pl. -ri·ums, -ri·a (-ə) lack or destruction of equilibrium, esp. in the economy

dis·es·tab·lish (dis′ə stab′lish) vt. **1.** to deprive of the

status of being established **2.** to deprive (a state church) of official sanction and support by the government —**dis'·es·tab'lish·ment** n.

dis·es·teem (-ə stēm') vt. to hold in low esteem; dislike; despise; slight —n. lack of esteem; disfavor

‡**di·seuse** (dē zēz') n. [Fr., fem. of diseur, speaker < base dis- of dire (L. dicere), to say, speak] a woman entertainer who performs monologues, dramatic impersonations, etc.

dis·fa·vor (dis fā'vər) n. **1.** an unfavorable opinion; dislike; disapproval **2.** the state of being disliked or disapproved of; disesteem [he fell into disfavor with his patron] **3.** an unkind or harmful act; disservice —vt. to regard or treat unfavorably; slight

dis·fea·ture (-fē'chər) vt. -tured, -tur·ing to impair the features of; disfigure

dis·fig·ure (-fig'yər) vt. -ured, -ur·ing [ME. disfiguren < OFr. desfigurer < des-, DIS- + figurer < L. figurare, to fashion, form < figura, FIGURE] to hurt the appearance or attractiveness of; deform; deface; mar

dis·fig·ure·ment (-mənt) n. **1.** a disfiguring or being disfigured **2.** anything that disfigures; blemish; defect; deformity Also **dis·fig'u·ra'tion** (-yə rā'shən)

dis·fran·chise (-fran'chīz) vt. -chised, -chis·ing **1.** to deprive of the rights of citizenship, esp. of the right to vote **2.** to deprive of a privilege, right, or power —**dis·fran'chise·ment** (-chiz mənt, -chiz-) n.

dis·frock (-fräk') vt. same as UNFROCK

dis·gorge (-gôrj') vt., vi. -gorged', -gorg'ing [OFr. desgorger: see DIS- & GORGE] **1.** to force (something swallowed) out through the throat; vomit **2.** to give up (something) against one's will **3.** to pour forth (its contents); empty (itself)

dis·grace (-grās') n. [Fr. disgrâce < It. disgrazia < dis- (L. dis-), not + grazia, favor < L. gratia: see GRACE] **1.** the state of being in disfavor as because of bad conduct; loss of favor or respect; public dishonor; ignominy; disrepute; shame **3.** a person or thing that brings shame, dishonor, or reproach (to one, etc.) —vt. -graced', -grac'ing [Fr. disgracier < It. disgraziare < the n.] **1.** to bring shame or dishonor upon; be a discredit to; be unworthy of [to disgrace one's family] **2.** to dismiss from a position of favor; punish by degrading; humiliate

SYN. —**disgrace** refers to a loss of favor or respect and a sense of humiliation brought on by one's own or another's actions [I felt disgrace at his expulsion]; **dishonor** implies a loss of honor or self-respect brought on by one's own actions; **shame** emphasizes the humiliation felt at a loss of esteem [his guilt brought him no shame]; **infamy** stresses the notoriety occasioned by a great disgrace; **ignominy** stresses the contemptible nature of that which causes disgrace; **odium** refers to the disgrace or infamy brought on by hateful action; **scandal**, in this connection, stresses the severe criticism, gossip, etc. brought on by a shameful or infamous act —ANT. honor, respect, esteem

dis·grace·ful (-grās'fəl) adj. causing or characterized by disgrace; shameful —**dis·grace'ful·ly** adv. —**dis·grace'ful·ness** n.

dis·grun·tle (-grun't'l) vt. -tled, -tling [DIS- + obs. gruntle, freq. of GRUNT] to make peevishly discontented; displease and make sulky —**dis·grun'tle·ment** n.

dis·guise (-gīz') vt. -guised', -guis'ing [ME. disgisen < OFr. desguiser, to change costume: see DIS- & GUISE] **1.** to make appear, sound, etc. different from usual so as to be unrecognizable [to disguise one's voice] **2.** to hide or obscure the existence or real nature of [to disguise an emotion] **3.** [Obs.] to alter or disfigure —n. **1.** any clothes, equipment, manner, etc. used for disguising **2.** the state of being disguised **3.** the act or practice of disguising —**dis·guis'ed·ly** (-gīz'id lē) adv. —**dis·guise'ment** n. —**dis·guis'er** n.

dis·gust (dis gust') n. [MFr. desgoust, distaste < des- (see DIS-) + L. gustus, a taste, relish: see GUSTO] a sickening distaste or dislike: deep aversion; repugnance —vt. [MFr. desgouster < des- (see DIS-) + L. gustare, to taste] to cause to feel disgust; be sickening, repulsive, or very distasteful to —vi. to arouse disgust —**dis·gust'ed** adj. —**dis·gust'ed·ly** adv. —**dis·gust'ing** adj. —**dis·gust'ing·ly** adv.

dis·gust·ful (-fəl) adj. **1.** causing disgust; disgusting **2.** full of disgust —**dis·gust'ful·ly** adv.

dish n. [ME. < OE. disc, disc, plate < PGmc. *diskuz < L. discus: see DISCUS] **1.** a) any container, generally shallow and concave and of porcelain, earthenware, glass, plastic, etc. for serving or holding food b) [pl.] plates, bowls, saucers, cups, etc., collectively **2.** a) the food in a dish b) a particular kind of food [one's favorite dish] **3.** a dishful **4.** a dish-shaped object, as the reflector of a dish antenna **5.** a dishlike concavity, or the amount of this ☆**6.** [Slang] a) a pretty girl or woman b) a favorite thing; preference: also **dish of tea** —vt. **1.** to serve (food) in a dish (usually with up or out) **2.** to shape (an object, surface, or hole) like a dish; make concave (usually with out) **3.** [Slang, chiefly Brit.] to cheat or outwit; frustrate —vi. to be or become dish-shaped; cave in —☆**dish it out** [Slang] to scold, punish, harass, etc.

dis·ha·bille (dis'ə bēl') n. [Fr. déshabillé, pp. of déshabiller, to undress < dés- (see DIS-) + habiller, to dress, altered (after HABIT) < OFr. abillier, to prepare, orig., to dress a log < bille, log: see BILLET²] **1.** the state of being dressed only partially or in night clothes **2.** [Now Rare] clothing worn in this state

dish antenna a radio transmitting or receiving antenna consisting of a dish-shaped reflector and one or more leads

dis·har·mo·nize (dis här'mə nīz') vt., vi. -nized', -niz'ing to put or be out of harmony

dis·har·mo·ny (-nē) n. absence of harmony; discord —**dis'har·mo'ni·ous** (-här mō'nē əs) adj.

dish·cloth (-klôth', -kläth') n. a cloth for washing dishes

☆**dishcloth gourd** **1.** any of a genus (Luffa) of tropical vines of the gourd family, having thin-shelled, large, cylindrical fruits with dense fibrous interior tissues used for dishcloths or filters **2.** this fruit

dis·heart·en (dis härt'n) vt. to deprive of courage or enthusiasm; discourage; depress —**dis·heart'en·ing** adj. —**dis·heart'en·ing·ly** adv. —**dis·heart'en·ment** n.

dished (disht) adj. **1.** dish-shaped; concave **2.** farther apart at the top than at the bottom: said of a pair of wheels on the same axle

di·shev·el (di shev'l) vt. -eled or -elled, -el·ing or -el·ling [back-formation < ff.] **1.** to cause (hair, clothing, etc.) to become disarranged and untidy, as by pulling or loosening, etc.; tousle or rumple **2.** to cause the hair or clothes of (a person) to become thus disarranged —**di·shev'el·ment** n.

di·shev·eled, di·shev·elled (-'ld) adj. [ME. discheveled < OFr. deschevelé (pp. of descheveler, to tousle < des-, DIS- + chevel, hair < L. capillus) + -ed, -ED] **1.** disarranged and untidy; tousled; rumpled: said of hair, clothing, etc. **2.** having disheveled hair or clothing

dish·ful (dish'fool') n., pl. -fuls as much as a dish holds

dis·hon·est (dis än'ist) adj. [ME. < OFr. deshoneste, altered (after des-, DIS-) < L. dehonestus: see DE- & HONEST] not honest; lying, cheating, etc. —**dis·hon'est·ly** adv.

SYN. —**dishonest** implies the act or practice of telling a lie, or of cheating, deceiving, stealing, etc. [a dishonest official]; **deceitful** implies an intent to make someone believe what is not true, as by giving a false appearance, using fraud, etc. [a deceitful advertisement]; **lying** suggests only the act of telling a falsehood [curb your lying tongue]; **untruthful** is used as a somewhat softened substitute for lying, esp. with reference to statements, reports, etc. [an untruthful account] —ANT. honest

dis·hon·es·ty (-ē) n. [ME. dishoneste < OFr. deshonesté] **1.** the quality of being dishonest; dishonest behavior; deceiving, stealing, etc. **2.** pl. -ties a dishonest act or statement; fraud, lie, etc.

dis·hon·or (dis än'ər) n. [ME. deshonour < OFr. deshonor: see DIS- & HONOR] **1.** a) loss of honor, respect, or reputation b) state of shame; disgrace; ignominy **2.** a person, thing, or action that brings dishonor; discredit **3.** the act of refusing or failing to pay a check, draft, bill of exchange, etc. —vt. **1.** to treat disrespectfully; insult **2.** to bring shame or discredit upon; disgrace **3.** to violate the virginity or chastity of **4.** to refuse or fail to pay (a check, draft, bill of exchange, etc.) —SYN. see DISGRACE —**dis·hon'or·er** n.

dis·hon·or·a·ble (-ə b'l) adj. causing or deserving dishonor; not honorable; shameful; disgraceful —**dis·hon'or·a·ble·ness** n. —**dis·hon'or·a·bly** adv.

☆**dish·pan** (dish'pan') n. a pan in which dishes, cooking utensils, etc. are washed

☆**dish·rag** (-rag') n. same as DISHCLOTH

☆**dish towel** a towel for drying dishes

☆**dish·wash·er** (-wôsh'ər, -wäsh'-) n. **1.** a machine for washing dishes, cooking utensils, etc. **2.** a person, esp. an employee so of a restaurant, who washes dishes, etc.

dish·wa·ter (-wôt'ər, -wät'-) n. water in which dishes, cooking utensils, etc. are, or have been, washed

dis·il·lu·sion (dis'i loo'zhən) vt. **1.** to free from illusion or false ideas; disenchant **2.** to take away the ideals or idealism of and make disappointed, bitter, etc. —n. same as DISILLUSIONMENT

dis·il·lu·sion·ment (-mənt) n. **1.** an act of disillusioning **2.** the fact or state of being disillusioned

dis·in·cen·tive (dis'in sen'tiv) n. a thing or factor that keeps one from doing something; deterrent

dis·in·cli·na·tion (dis in'klə nā'shən, dis'in-) n. a dislike or lack of desire; aversion; reluctance

dis·in·cline (dis'in klīn') vt. -clined', -clin'ing to make unwilling

dis·in·clined (-klīnd') adj. unwilling; reluctant —SYN. see RELUCTANT

dis·in·fect (dis'in fekt') vt. [Fr. désinfecter: see DIS- & INFECT] to destroy the harmful bacteria, viruses, etc. in; sterilize —**dis'in·fec'tion** n.

dis·in·fect·ant (-ənt) adj. [Fr. désinfectant] disinfecting —n. anything that disinfects; means for destroying harmful bacteria, viruses, etc.

dis·in·fest (dis'in fest') vt. to remove insects, small rodents, or other pests from —**dis·in·fes·ta·tion** (dis in' fes tā'shən, dis'in-) n.

dis·in·fla·tion (-in flā'shən) n. Econ. a reduction of the general level of prices, planned to increase purchasing power but control deflation —**dis'in·fla'tion·ar'y** adj.

dis·in·gen·u·ous (-in jen'yoo wəs) adj. not straightforward; not candid or frank; insincere —**dis'in·gen'u·ous·ly** adv. —**dis'in·gen'u·ous·ness** n.

dis·in·her·it (-in her'it) vt. [altered (after INHERIT) < earlier disherit] **1.** to deprive of an inheritance or the right to inherit **2.** to deprive of any right or established privilege —**dis'in·her'it·ance** n.

dis·in·te·grate (dis in'tə grāt') vt., vi. -grat'ed, -grat'ing **1.** to separate into parts or fragments; break up; dis-

unite **2.** to undergo or cause to undergo a nuclear transformation as a result of radioactive decay or a nuclear reaction —*SYN.* see DECAY —**dis·in'te·gra'tion** n. —**dis·in'te·gra'tive** adj. —**dis·in'te·gra'tor** n.

dis·in·ter (dis'in tur') vt. -**terred'**, -**ter'ring** [Fr. *désenterrer*: see DIS- & INTER] **1.** to remove from a grave, tomb, etc.; dig up; exhume **2.** to bring (something hidden) to light —**dis'in·ter'ment** n.

dis·in·ter·est (dis in'trist, -tər ist) n. **1.** lack of personal or selfish interest; disinterestedness **2.** lack of interest or concern; indifference

dis·in·ter·est·ed (-id) adj. **1.** not influenced by personal interest or selfish motives; impartial; unbiased **2.** uninterested; indifferent: in this usage, a revival of an obsolete meaning —*SYN.* see INDIFFERENT —**dis·in'ter·est·ed·ly** adv. —**dis·in'ter·est·ed·ness** n.

dis·in·vest·ment (dis'in vest'mənt) n. a diminution or expenditure of capital investment, as in the failure to replenish inventories or in the sale of a capital item

‡**dis·jec·ta mem·bra** (dis jek'tə mem'brə) [L.] scattered parts or fragments, as of an author's writings

dis·join (dis join') vt. [ME. *disjoinen* < OFr. *desjoindre* < L. *disjungere*: see DIS- & JOIN] to undo the joining of; separate; detach —vi. [Obs.] to become separated

dis·joint (dis joint') adj. [ME. < OFr. *desjoint*, pp. of *desjoindre*: see prec.] [Obs.] disjointed —vt. [< the adj.] **1.** to put out of joint; dislocate **2.** to take apart joint by joint; dismember **3.** to destroy the unity, connections, or orderliness of —vi. to come apart at the joints; go out of joint

dis·joint·ed (-id) adj. **1.** out of joint **2.** dismembered **3.** disconnected; without unity or coherence —**dis·joint'ed·ly** adv. —**dis·joint'ed·ness** n.

dis·junct (dis junkt') adj. [L. *disjunctus*, pp. of *disjungere*: see DISJOIN] **1.** disjoined; separated **2.** *Music* having to do with the use of intervals larger than a major second **3.** *Zool.* having the body sharply divided by deep furrows, as in the divisions into head, thorax, and abdomen in most insects

dis·junc·tion (dis junk'shən) n. [ME. *disjunccioun* < L. *disjunctio*] **1.** a disjoining or being disjoined; separation: also **dis·junc'ture** (-chər) **2.** *Logic* a) the relation between two or more alternatives of a compound proposition b) a disjunctive proposition

dis·junc·tive (-tiv) adj. [ME. *disjunctif* < L. *disjunctivus*] **1.** disjoining; separating or causing to separate **2.** having to do with disjunction **3.** *Gram.* indicating a contrast or an alternative between words, clauses, etc. [in "John or Bob may go, but their sister may not," "or" and "but" are *disjunctive* conjunctions] **4.** *Logic* presenting alternatives [a *disjunctive* proposition] —n. **1.** *Gram.* a disjunctive conjunction **2.** *Logic* a disjunctive proposition —**dis·junc'tive·ly** adv.

disk (disk) n. [L. *discus*: see DISCUS] **1.** a thin, flat, circular thing of any material **2.** anything like this in form [the moon's *disk*] **3.** same as DISC; specif., a) the disk-shaped center of certain composite flowers b) a layer of fibrous connective tissue with small masses of cartilage among the fibers, occurring between adjacent vertebrae **4.** [Obs.] same as DISCUS

disk flower any of the tubular flowers that make up the central disk of the flower head of a composite plant

☆**disk harrow** same as DISC HARROW

☆**disk jockey** same as DISC JOCKEY

disk wheel a wheel made solid from rim to hub instead of having spokes

dis·like (dis līk') vt. -**liked'**, -**lik'ing** to have a feeling of not liking; feel aversion to; have objections to —n. a feeling of not liking; distaste; aversion; antipathy —**dis·lik'a·ble**, **dis·like'a·ble** adj.

dis·limn (-lim') vt. [Obs. or Poet.] to obliterate or efface the outlines of (a picture, etc.); blot out

dis·lo·cate (dis'lō kāt', dis lō'kāt) vt. -**cat'ed**, -**cat'ing** [< ML. *dislocatus*, pp. of *dislocare*: see DIS- & LOCATE] **1.** to put out of place; specif., to displace (a bone) from its proper position at a joint **2.** to upset the order of; disarrange; disrupt

dis·lo·ca·tion (dis'lō kā'shən) n. **1.** a dislocating or being dislocated **2.** an imperfection in the atomic structure of a crystal, usually consisting of a row of disordered atoms in the crystal lattice

dis·lodge (dis läj') vt. -**lodged'**, -**lodg'ing** [ME. *disloggen* < OFr. *deslogier*: see DIS- & LODGE] to force from a position or place where lodged, hiding, etc.; drive out —vi. to leave a lodging place —**dis·lodg'ment** n.

dis·loy·al (-loi'əl) adj. [OFr. *desloial*: see DIS- & LOYAL] not loyal or faithful; faithless —*SYN.* see FAITHLESS —**dis·loy'al·ly** adv.

dis·loy·al·ty (-tē) n. **1.** the quality of being disloyal **2.** pl. -**ties** a disloyal act

dis·mal (diz'm'l) adj. [ME., orig. n., evil days of the medieval calendar] < OFr. *dis mal* < ML. *dies mali*, evil days] **1.** causing gloom or misery; depressing **2.** dark and gloomy; bleak; dreary **3.** depressed; miserable —**dis'mal·ly** adv.

Dismal Swamp marshy region between Norfolk, Va. & Albemarle Sound, N.C.: 20 to 30 mi. long

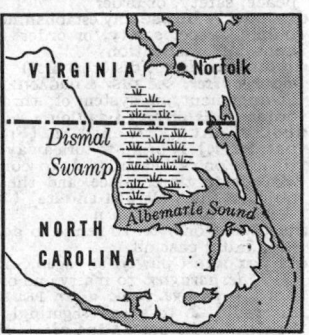

DISMAL SWAMP

dis·man·tle (dis man't'l) vt. -**tled**, -**tling** [OFr. *desmanteller*, to take off one's cloak: see DIS- & MANTLE] **1.** to strip of covering **2.** to strip (a house, ship, etc.) of furniture, equipment, means of defense, etc. **3.** to take apart; disassemble —*SYN.* see STRIP¹ —**dis·man'tle·ment** n.

dis·mast (-mast', -mäst') vt. to remove or destroy the mast or masts of

dis·may (-mā') vt. [ME. *dismayen* < Anglo-Fr. *desmaier* < *des-*, intens. + OFr. *esmayer*, to deprive of power < VL. *exmagare* < L. *ex-*, from + Gmc. base *mag*, power: see MAIN¹] to make afraid or discouraged at the prospect of trouble or danger; fill with apprehension or alarm; daunt —n. a loss of courage or confidence at the prospect of trouble or danger; consternation

SYN. —**dismay** suggests fear or, esp. in modern usage, discouragement at the prospect of some difficulty or problem which one does not quite know how to resolve [dismayed at his lack of understanding]; **appall** suggests terror or (now more commonly) dismay at a shocking but apparently unalterable situation [an appalling death rate]; **horrify** suggests horror or loathing (or, in a weakened sense, irritation) at that which shocks or offends one [horrified at the suggestion]; **daunt** implies a becoming disheartened in the performance of an act that requires some courage [never daunted by adversity]

dis·mem·ber (-mem'bər) vt. [ME. *dismembren* < OFr. *desmembrer*: see DIS- & MEMBER] **1.** to remove the limbs of by cutting or tearing **2.** to pull or cut to pieces; separate into parts; divide up or mutilate —**dis·mem'ber·ment** n.

dis·miss (-mis') vt. [ME. *dismissen* < ML. *dismissus*, pp. of *dismittere*, for L. *dimittere*, to send away < *dis-*, from + *mittere*, to send] **1.** to send away; cause or allow to leave **2.** to remove or discharge from a duty, office, position, or employment **3.** to put out of one's mind [to dismiss one's fears] **4.** *Law* to discontinue or reject (a claim or action) —*SYN.* see EJECT —**dis·miss'i·ble** adj.

dis·miss·al (-mis''l) n. **1.** a dismissing or being dismissed **2.** an order for the dismissing of someone Also [Archaic] **dis·mis'sion** (-mish'ən)

dis·mis·sive (-mis'iv) adj. **1.** [Rare] dismissing or expressing dismissal **2.** haughty or contemptuous

dis·mount (-mount') vi. to get off or down, as from a horse, bicycle, etc.; alight —vt. **1.** to remove (a thing) from its mounting or setting **2.** to cause to dismount, as from a horse **3.** to take apart; dismantle —n. the act of dismounting

dis·na·ture (-nā'chər) vt. -**tured**, -**tur·ing** to make lose its natural quality, looks, etc.; make unnatural

Dis·ney (diz'nē), **Walt(er Elias)** 1901-66; U.S. motion-picture producer, esp. of animated cartoons

☆**Dis·ney·land** (diz'nē land) n. [after an amusement center near Los Angeles, created by Walt DISNEY] a place or condition of unreality, fantasy, incongruity, etc.

dis·o·be·di·ence (dis'ə bē'dē əns) n. [ME. < OFr. *desobedience*: see DIS- & OBEDIENCE] refusal to obey; failure to follow commands; insubordination

dis·o·be·di·ent (-ənt) adj. [ME. < OFr. *desobedient*] not obedient; refusing or failing to obey; insubordinate; refractory —**dis'o·be'di·ent·ly** adv.

dis·o·bey (dis'ə bā') vt., vi. [ME. *disobeien* < OFr. *desobeir*: see DIS- & OBEY] to refuse or fail to obey

dis·o·blige (-ə blīj') vt. -**bliged'**, -**blig'ing** [Fr. *désobliger*: see DIS- & OBLIGE] **1.** to refuse to oblige; not do for (another) what he wants done **2.** to slight; offend —**dis'o·blig'ing** adj. —**dis'o·blig'ing·ly** adv.

dis·op·er·a·tion (dis'äp ə rā'shən) n. a coaction that is harmful to the organisms involved

dis·or·der (dis ôr'dər) n. [prob. < Fr. *désordre*] **1.** a lack of order; confusion; jumble **2.** a breach of public peace; riot **3.** a disregard of system; irregularity **4.** an upset of normal function; ailment —vt. **1.** to throw into disorder; disarrange **2.** to upset the normal functions or health of —*SYN.* see CONFUSION

dis·or·dered (-dərd) adj. **1.** put out of order; jumbled **2.** not normal in health or function; ill

dis·or·der·ly (-dər lē) adj. **1.** not orderly; untidy; unsystematic **2.** causing a disturbance; unruly; riotous **3.** *Law* violating public peace, safety, or order —adv. [Archaic] in a disorderly manner —**dis·or'der·li·ness** n.

disorderly conduct *Law* any petty offense against public peace, safety, or order

disorderly house any establishment where offenses against public peace, safety, or order habitually occur; esp., a house of prostitution

dis·or·gan·ize (dis ôr′gə nīz′) *vt.* -ized′, -iz′ing [Fr. *désorganiser:* see DIS- & ORGANIZE] to break up the order, arrangement, or system of; throw into confusion or disorder —**dis·or′gan·i·za′tion** *n.*

dis·o·ri·ent (-ôr′ē ent′) *vt.* [Fr. *désorienter:* see DIS- & ORIENT, *v.*] 1. orig., to turn away from the east 2. to cause to lose one's bearings 3. to confuse mentally, esp. with respect to time, place, and the identity of persons and objects Also **dis·o′ri·en·tate′** (-ən tāt′) -tat′ed, -tat′ing —**dis·o′ri·en·ta′tion** *n.*

dis·own (-ōn′) *vt.* to refuse to acknowledge as one's own; repudiate; cast off

dis·par·age (-par′ij) *vt.* -aged, -ag·ing [ME. *disparagen* < OFr. *desparagier,* to marry one of inferior rank < *des-* (see DIS-) + *parage,* rank < *per,* PEER[1]] 1. to lower in esteem; discredit 2. to speak slightingly of; show disrespect for; belittle —**dis·par′ag·ing** *adj.* —**dis·par′ag·ing·ly** *adv.* *SYN.* —to **disparage** is to attempt to lower in esteem, as by insinuation, invidious comparison, faint praise, etc.; to **depreciate** is to lessen (something) in value as by implying that it has less worth than is usually attributed to it [*he depreciated* her generosity]; **decry** implies vigorous public denunciation, often from the best of motives [to *decry* corruption in government]; **belittle** is equivalent to **depreciate,** but stresses a contemptuous attitude in the subject; **minimize** suggests an ascription of the least possible value or importance [don't *minimize* your own efforts] —*ANT.* extol, praise, magnify

dis·par·age·ment (-mənt) *n.* 1. a disparaging or being disparaged; detraction 2. anything that discredits

dis·pa·rate (dis′pər it) *adj.* [L. *disparatus,* pp. of *disparare,* to separate < *dis-,* apart, not + *parare,* to make equal < *par,* equal: see PAR] essentially not alike; distinct or different in kind; unequal —*SYN.* see DIFFERENT —**dis′pa·rate·ly** *adv.* —**dis′pa·rate·ness** *n.*

dis·par·i·ty (dis par′ə tē) *n., pl.* -ties [Fr. *disparité* < ML. *disparitas* < L. *dispar,* unequal: see DIS- & PAR] 1. inequality or difference, as in rank, amount, quality, etc. 2. unlikeness; incongruity

dis·part (-pärt′) *vt., vi.* [prob. < It. *dispartire* < L., to divide < *dis-,* apart, from + *partire,* to part, divide < *pars* (gen. *partis*), a part] [Archaic] to divide into parts; separate

dis·pas·sion·ate (-pash′ən it) *adj.* free from passion, emotion, or bias; calm; impartial —*SYN.* see FAIR[1] —**dis·pas′sion** *n.* —**dis·pas′sion·ate·ly** *adv.*

dis·patch (-pach′) *vt.* [Sp. *despachar* & It. *dispacciare,* to send off, lit., to remove impediments, hence facilitate < OFr. *despeechier* < *des-* (see DIS-) + (*em*)*peechier,* to impede < LL. *impedicare,* to entangle < L. *in-,* in + *pedica,* a shackle < *pes,* FOOT] 1. to send off or out promptly, usually on a specific errand or official business 2. to put an end to; kill 3. to finish quickly or promptly 4. [Colloq.] to eat up quickly —*n.* 1. a dispatching; sending out or off 2. an act of killing 3. efficient speed; promptness 4. a message, esp. an official message 5. a news story sent to a newspaper, radio station, etc., as by a special reporter or news agency —*SYN.* see HASTE, KILL[1]

dis·patch·er (-ər) *n.* 1. a person who dispatches ☆2. a transportation worker who sends out trains, buses, trucks, etc. according to a schedule

dis·pel (dis pel′) *vt.* -pelled′, -pel′ling [ME. *dispellen* < L. *dispellere* < *dis-,* apart + *pellere,* to drive < IE. base **pel-,* whence FELT[1]] to scatter and drive away; cause to vanish; disperse —*SYN.* see SCATTER

dis·pen·sa·ble (dis pen′sə b'l) *adj.* [ML.(Ec.) *dispensabilis*] 1. that can be dispensed, dealt out, or administered 2. that can be dispensed with; not important 3. *R.C.Ch.* that can be permitted by dispensation —**dis·pen′sa·bil′i·ty** *n.*

dis·pen·sa·ry (-sə rē) *n., pl.* -ries [< ML. *dispensarius,* one who dispenses, steward] a room or place, as in a school, camp, or factory, where medicines and first-aid treatment are available

dis·pen·sa·tion (dis′pən sā′shən, -pen-) *n.* [ME. *dispensacioun* < OFr. *despensation* < L. *dispensatio,* management, charge < pp. of *dispensare*] 1. a dispensing, or giving out; distribution 2. anything dispensed or distributed 3. the system by which anything is administered; management 4. any release or exemption from an obligation 5. *Law* the suspension of a statute in a specific case for extenuating reasons 6. *R.C.Ch.* an exemption or release from the provisions of a specific church law 7. *Theol. a)* the ordering of events under divine authority *b)* any religious system —**dis′pen·sa′tion·al** *adj.*

dis·pen·sa·tor (dis′pen sāt′ər) *n.* [ME. *dispensatour* < L. *dispensator,* manager < pp. of *dispensare*] [Obs.] one who dispenses; distributor or administrator

dis·pen·sa·to·ry (dis pen′sə tôr′ē) *n., pl.* -ries [ML. *dispensatorium* < LL. *dispensatorius,* of management or control < L. *dispensare:* see ff.] 1. a handbook on the preparation and use of medicines; pharmacopoeia 2. [Obs.] a dispensary

dis·pense (-pens′) *vt.* -pensed′, -pens′ing [ME. *dispensen* < OFr. *despenser* < L. *dispensare,* to pay out < pp. of *dispendere,* to weigh out < *dis-,* out + *pendere,* to weigh: see PEND] 1. to give or deal out; distribute 2. to prepare and give out (medicines, prescriptions, etc.) 3. to administer [to *dispense* the law justly] 4. to exempt; excuse —*SYN.* see DISTRIBUTE —**dispense with** 1. to get rid of; do away with 2. to do without; manage without

dis·pen·ser (-pen′sər) *n.* a person or thing that dispenses; specif., a container designed to dispense its contents in handy units or portions

dis·peo·ple (-pēp′'l) *vt.* -pled, -pling *same as* DEPOPULATE

di·sper·mous (dī spur′məs) *adj.* [DI-[1] + SPERMOUS] *Bot.* having two seeds

dis·per·sal (dis pur′s'l) *n.* a dispersing or being dispersed; distribution

dis·perse (-purs′) *vt.* -persed′, -pers′ing [ME. *dispersen* < L. *dispersus,* pp. of *dispergere,* to scatter abroad < *dis-,* out + *spargere,* to scatter, strew: for IE. base see SPROUT] 1. to break up and scatter in all directions; spread about; distribute widely 2. to dispel (mist, etc.) 3. to break up (light) into its component colored rays —*vi.* to break up and move in different directions; scatter —*SYN.* see SCATTER —**dis·pers′er** *n.* —**dis·pers′i·ble** *adj.*

disperse system a two-phase colloidal system consisting of the colloidal particles (**disperse phase**) and the medium in which they are suspended (**disperse medium**)

dis·per·sion (dis pur′zhən, -shən) *n.* [ME. *dispersioun* < OFr. *dispersion* < L. *dispersio*] 1. a dispersing or being dispersed 2. the breaking up of light into component colored rays, as by means of a prism 3. the resolution of a complex electromagnetic radiation into components in accordance with some characteristic, as wavelength 4. the variation or scattering of data around a median value 5. a colloidal system with its dispersed particles and the medium in which these are suspended 6. [D-] *same as* DIASPORA

dis·per·sive (-siv) *adj.* dispersing or tending to disperse —**dis·per′sive·ly** *adv.*

dis·per·soid (-soid) *n.* a colloidal system, as an emulsion, in which the colloidal particles are quite small and well suspended in the disperse medium

dis·pir·it (di spir′it) *vt.* to lower the spirits of; make sad, discouraged, or apathetic; depress; deject —**dis·pir′it·ed** *adj.* —**dis·pir′it·ed·ly** *adv.*

dis·pit·e·ous (dis pit′ē əs) *adj.* [var. of DESPITEOUS] [Archaic] without pity or mercy; ruthless

dis·place (-plās′) *vt.* -placed′, -plac′ing [OFr. *desplacer:* see DIS- & PLACE] 1. to move from its usual or proper place 2. to remove from office; discharge 3. to take the place of; replace [a ship *displaces* a certain amount of water] —*SYN.* see REPLACE

displaced person a person forced from his country, esp. as a result of war, and left homeless elsewhere

dis·place·ment (-mənt) *n.* 1. a displacing or being displaced 2. *a)* the weight or volume of a fluid displaced by a floating object; specif., the weight of water, in long tons, displaced by a ship *b)* the volume displaced by a stroke of a piston 3. the difference between a later position of a thing and its original position 4. *Geol.* a fault 5. *Psychiatry* a defense mechanism in which an emotion is transferred to another, more acceptable object

dis·plant (dis plant′, -plänt′) *vt.* [Obs.] to transplant, dislodge, or displace

dis·play (-plā′) *vt.* [ME. *displeien* < OFr. *despleier* < L. *displicare,* to scatter, unfold < *dis-,* apart + *plicare,* to fold: for IE. base see FLAX] 1. to unfold; spread out; unfurl 2. to unfold to the eye; put or spread out so as to be seen; exhibit 3. to unfold to the mind; disclose; reveal 4. to print conspicuously, as in large or fancy type —*n.* 1. a displaying; exhibition 2. anything displayed; exhibit 3. showy exhibition; ostentation 4. *a)* a manifestation [a *display* of courage] *b)* a mere show of something that is not genuine [a *display* of sympathy] —*adj.* designating printing type in larger sizes, used for headings, advertisement, etc. —*SYN.* see SHOW

dis·please (-plēz′) *vt., vi.* -pleased′, -pleas′ing [ME. *displesen* < OFr. *desplaisir* < VL. **displacere,* for L. *displicere* < *dis-,* not + *placere:* see PLEASE] to fail to please or to be disagreeable (to); annoy; offend; irritate

dis·pleas·ure (-plezh′ər) *n.* [ME. *displesir* < OFr. *desplaisir,* inf. used as n.: see prec.] 1. the fact or feeling of being displeased; dissatisfaction, disapproval, annoyance, etc. 2. [Archaic] discomfort, sorrow, trouble, etc. —*SYN.* see OFFENSE

dis·plode (-plōd′) *vt., vi.* -plod′ed, -plod′ing [L. *displodere* < *dis-,* apart + *plaudere,* to applaud] [Obs.] *same as* EXPLODE —**dis·plo′sion** (-plō′zhən) *n.*

dis·plume (-ploōm′) *vt.* -plumed′, -plum′ing [Rare] *same as* DEPLUME

dis·port (-pôrt′) *vi.* [ME. *disporten,* to bear, support < OFr. *desporter* < *des-* (see DIS-) + *porter* < L. *portare,* to carry: see PORT[3]] to indulge in amusement; play; frolic —*vt.* to amuse or divert (oneself) —*n.* [Archaic] a disporting; amusement; play

dis·pos·a·ble (-pō′zə b'l) *adj.* 1. that can be thrown away after use [*disposable* bottles] 2. that can be disposed; not restricted to any specific use

dis·pos·al (-pō′z'l) *n.* 1. the act of disposing; specif., *a)* arrangement in a particular order [the *disposal* of furniture in a room] *b)* a dealing with matters or settling of affairs *c)* a giving away; transfer; bestowal *d)* a getting rid of 2. the power to dispose of 3. *same as* DISPOSER

(sense 2) —**at one's disposal** available to be used as one wishes

dis·pose (-pōz′) *vt.* **-posed′, -pos′ing** [ME. *disposen* < OFr. *disposer*, to put apart, hence arrange < perf. stem of L. *disponere*, to arrange: see DIS- & POSITION] **1.** to place in a certain order or arrangement **2.** to arrange (matters); settle or regulate (affairs) **3.** to make willing; incline **4.** to make susceptible or liable —*vi.* to have the power to arrange or settle affairs —**dispose of 1.** to deal with conclusively; settle **2.** to give away or sell **3.** to get rid of; throw away **4.** to eat or drink up; consume

dis·posed (-pōzd′) *adj.* inclined; having a certain tendency: often preceded by an adverb [to feel well-*disposed* toward someone]

dis·pos·er (-pō′zər) *n.* **1.** one that disposes ☆**2.** a device installed in the drain of a kitchen sink to grind up garbage that is then flushed down the drain

dis·po·si·tion (dis′pə zish′ən) *n.* [ME. *disposicioun* < OFr. *disposition* < L. *dispositio* < *dispositus*, pp. of *disponere*, to arrange: see DIS- & POSITION] **1.** a putting in order or being put in order; arrangement [the *disposition* of the troops] **2.** management or settlement of affairs **3.** a selling or giving away, as of property **4.** a getting rid of something [the *disposition* of wastes] **5.** the power or authority to arrange, settle, or manage; control **6.** an inclination or tendency [a *disposition* to quarrel] **7.** [from astrological use as applied to planets] one's customary frame of mind; one's nature or temperament

SYN. —**disposition** refers to the normal or prevailing aspect of one's nature [a genial *disposition*]; **temperament** refers to the balance of traits that are manifested in one's behavior or thinking [an artistic *temperament*]; **temper** refers to one's basic emotional nature, esp. as regards relative quickness to anger [a hot *temper*, an even *temper*]; **character** is applied to the sum of moral qualities associated with a distinctive individual [a weak *character*] and, unqualified, suggests moral strength, self-discipline, etc. [a man of *character*]; **personality** is applied to the sum of physical, mental, and emotional qualities that distinguish one as a person [a negative *personality*] and, unqualified, suggests attractiveness or charm [a girl with *personality*]

dis·pos·sess (-pə zes′) *vt.* to deprive of the possession of something, esp. land, a house, etc.; oust —**dis′pos·ses′sion** (-zesh′ən) *n.* —**dis′pos·ses′sor** *n.*

dis·po·sure (dis pō′zhər) *n.* [Archaic] disposition or disposal (in various senses)

dis·praise (-prāz′) *vt.* **-praised′, -prais′ing** [ME. *dispreisen* < OFr. *despreisier*, to blame: see DIS- & PRAISE] to speak of with disapproval or disparagement; censure —*n.* a dispraising; blame —**dis·prais′ing·ly** *adv.*

dis·prize (-prīz′) *vt.* **-prized′, -priz′ing** [ME. *disprisen* < OFr. *despriser*, var. of *despreisier*: see DISPRAISE] [Archaic] to regard as of low value; not prize

dis·proof (-prōōf′) *n.* **1.** the act of disproving; refutation **2.** evidence that disproves

dis·pro·por·tion (dis′prə pôr′shən) *n.* a lack of proportion; lack of symmetry; disparity —*vt.* to cause to be disproportionate —**dis′pro·por′tion·al** *adj.* —**dis′pro·por′tion·al·ly** *adv.*

dis·pro·por·tion·ate (-it) *adj.* not proportionate; not in proportion —**dis′pro·por′tion·ate·ly** *adv.*

dis·prove (dis prōōv′) *vt.* **-proved′, -prov′ing** [ME. *disproven* < OFr. *desprover*: see DIS- + PROVE] to prove to be false or in error; refute —**dis·prov′a·ble** *adj.*

SYN. —**disprove** implies the presenting of evidence or reasoned arguments that demonstrate an assertion, etc. to be false or erroneous; **refute** implies a more thorough assembly of evidence and a more careful development of argument and hence suggests conclusiveness of proof against; **confute** suggests the overwhelming or silencing of a person by argument or proof; **controvert** implies a disputing or denying of statements, arguments, etc. in an endeavor to refute them; **rebut** stresses formality in refuting an argument, such as is observed in debate, court procedure, etc.

dis·pu·ta·ble (dis pyōōt′ə b'l, dis′pyoot-) *adj.* [L. *disputabilis*] that can be disputed; debatable —**dis·pu′ta·bil′i·ty** *n.* —**dis·pu′ta·bly** *adv.*

dis·pu·tant (dis pyōōt′'nt, dis′pyoo tənt) *adj.* [L. *disputans*, prp. of *disputare*] disputing —*n.* a person who disputes, or debates

dis·pu·ta·tion (dis′pyoo tā′shən) *n.* [ME. *disputacioun* < L. *disputatio*] **1.** the act of disputing; dispute **2.** discussion marked by formal debate, often as an exercise

dis·pu·ta·tious (-shəs) *adj.* inclined to dispute; fond of arguing; contentious: also **dis·pu·ta·tive** (dis pyōōt′ə tiv) —**dis′pu·ta′tious·ly** *adv.* —**dis′pu·ta′tious·ness** *n.*

dis·pute (dis pyōōt′) *vi.* **-put′ed, -put′ing** [ME. *disputen* < OFr. *desputer* < L. *disputare*, lit., to compute, discuss, hence argue about < *dis-*, apart + *putare*, to think: see PUTATIVE] **1.** to argue; debate **2.** to quarrel —*vt.* **1.** to argue or debate (a question); discuss pro and con **2.** to question the truth of; doubt **3.** to oppose in any way; resist **4.** to fight for; contest [to *dispute* every foot of ground] —*n.* **1.** a disputing; argument; debate **2.** a quarrel **3.** [Obs.] a fight —SYN. see ARGUMENT, DISCUSS —**beyond dispute 1.** not open to dispute or question; settled **2.** indisputably —**in dispute** still being argued about; not settled

dis·qual·i·fy (dis kwäl′ə fī′) *vt.* **-fied′, -fy′ing 1.** to make unfit or unqualified; incapacitate **2.** to make or declare ineligible; take a right or privilege away from, as of further participation in a sport, for breaking rules —**dis·qual′i·fi·ca′tion** (-fi kā′shən) *n.*

dis·qui·et (-kwī′ət) *vt.* to make anxious, uneasy, or restless; disturb; fret —*n.* a disturbed or uneasy feeling; anxiety; restlessness **2.** [Archaic] restless; uneasy —**dis·qui′et·ing** *adj.* —**dis·qui′et·ing·ly** *adv.*

dis·qui·e·tude (-kwī′ə tōōd′, -tyōōd′) *n.* a disturbed or uneasy condition; restlessness; anxiety

dis·qui·si·tion (dis′kwə zish′ən) *n.* [L. *disquisitio* < *disquisitus*, pp. of *disquirere*, to investigate < *dis-*, apart + *quaerere*, to seek] a formal discussion of some subject, often in writing; discourse or treatise

Dis·rae·li (diz rā′lē), **Benjamin, 1st Earl of Beaconsfield, 1804–81; Eng. statesman & writer; prime minister (1868; 1874–80)**

dis·rate (dis rāt′) *vt.* **-rat′ed, -rat′ing** to lower in rating, or rank; demote

dis·re·gard (dis′ri gärd′) *vt.* **1.** to pay little or no attention to **2.** to treat without due respect; slight —*n.* **1.** lack of attention; neglect **2.** lack of due regard or respect —SYN. see NEGLECT —**dis′re·gard′ful** *adj.*

dis·rel·ish (dis rel′ish) *n., vt.* dislike

dis·re·mem·ber (dis′ri mem′bər) *vt.* [Dial. or Colloq.] to forget; be unable to remember

dis·re·pair (-ri per′) *n.* the condition of needing repairs; state of neglect; dilapidation

dis·rep·u·ta·ble (dis rep′yoo tə b'l) *adj.* **1.** not reputable; having or causing a bad reputation; discreditable **2.** not fit to be seen; dirty, shabby, etc. —**dis·rep′u·ta·bly** *adv.*

dis·re·pute (dis′ri pyōōt′) *n.* lack or loss of repute; bad reputation; disgrace; disfavor

dis·re·spect (-ri spekt′) *n.* lack of respect or esteem; discourtesy —*vt.* to have or show lack of respect for

dis·re·spect·a·ble (-ə b'l) *adj.* not respectable

dis·re·spect·ful (-fəl) *adj.* having or showing lack of respect; discourteous; impolite; rude —**dis′re·spect′ful·ly** *adv.* —**dis′re·spect′ful·ness** *n.*

dis·robe (dis rōb′) *vt., vi.* **-robed′, -rob′ing** [DIS- + ROBE] to undress

dis·root (dis rōōt′, -root′) *vt.* same as UPROOT

dis·rupt (-rupt′) *vt., vi.* [< L. *disruptus*, pp. of *disrumpere*, to break apart < *dis-*, apart + *rumpere*, to break: see RUPTURE] **1.** to break apart; split up; rend asunder **2.** to disturb or interrupt the orderly course of (a social affair, meeting, etc.) —**dis·rupt′er, dis·rup′tor** *n.* —**dis·rup′tion** *n.*

dis·rup·tive (-rup′tiv) *adj.* **1.** causing disruption **2.** produced by disruption —**dis·rup′tive·ly** *adv.*

disruptive discharge a sudden and large increase in electric current through an insulating medium, caused by failure of the medium under stress

dis·sat·is·fac·tion (dis sat′is fak′shən) *n.* **1.** the condition of being dissatisfied or displeased; discontent **2.** anything that dissatisfies

dis·sat·is·fac·to·ry (-tə rē) *adj.* not satisfactory

dis·sat·is·fied (dis sat′is fīd′) *adj.* **1.** not satisfied; displeased **2.** showing dissatisfaction

dis·sat·is·fy (-fī′) *vt.* **-fied′, -fy′ing** to fail to satisfy; discontent; displease

dis·seat (dis sēt′) *vt.* [Archaic] same as UNSEAT

dis·sect (di sekt′, dī-) *vt.* [< L. *dissectus*, pp. of *dissecare*, to cut apart < *dis-*, apart + *secare*, to cut: for IE. base see SAW] **1.** to cut apart piece by piece; separate into parts, as a body for purposes of study; anatomize **2.** to examine or analyze closely

dis·sect·ed (-id) *adj.* **1.** cut up into parts **2.** *Bot.* consisting of many lobes or segments, as some leaves **3.** *Geol.* cut by erosion into valleys and hills

dis·sec·tion (di sek′shən, dī-) *n.* [LL. *dissectio*] **1.** a dissecting or being dissected **2.** anything dissected, as a plant or animal for study **3.** analysis part by part; detailed examination

dis·sec·tor (-tər) *n.* **1.** a person who dissects **2.** an instrument used in dissecting

dis·seize (dis sēz′) *vt.* **-seized′, -seiz′ing** [ME. *disseisen* < Anglo-Fr. *disseisir* < OFr. *dessaisir*: see DIS- & SEIZE] *Law* to deprive wrongfully of real property; dispossess unlawfully: also sp. **dis·seise′**

dis·sei·zee, dis·sei·see (dis′sē zē′, dis sē′zē′) *n. Law* a disseized person

dis·sei·zin, dis·sei·sin (dis sē′zin) *n.* [ME. *disseisine* < OFr. *dessaisine* < *dessaisir*] *Law* a disseizing or being disseized; unlawful dispossession from real property

dis·sei·zor, dis·sei·sor (-zər, -zôr) *n.* [ME. *disseisour*] *Law* a person who disseizes

dis·sem·ble (di sem′b'l) *vt.* **-bled, -bling** [ME. *dissemblen* < OFr. *dessembler* < *des-*, DIS- + *sembler* < L. *simulare*: see SIMULATE] **1.** to conceal under a false appearance; disguise [to *dissemble* fear by smiling] **2.** to pretend to be in a state of; simulate; feign [to *dissemble* innocence] **3.** [Obs.] to pretend not to notice; ignore —*vi.* to conceal the truth, or one's true feelings, motives, etc., by pretense; behave hypocritically —**dis·sem′blance** *n.* —**dis·sem′bler** *n.*

dis·sem·i·nate (di sem'ə nāt') vt. -nat'ed, -nat'ing [< L. disseminatus, pp. of disseminare, lit., to scatter seed, hence disseminate < dis-, apart + seminare, to sow < semen, seed] to scatter far and wide; spread abroad, as if sowing; promulgate widely —**dis·sem'i·na'tion** n. —**dis·sem'i·na'tive** adj. —**dis·sem'i·na'tor** n.

dis·sem·i·nule (-nyōōl') n. [DISSEMIN(ATE) + -ULE] Biol. a detachable plant organ or structure of an organism capable of being dispersed and of propagating, as a seed, resting egg, etc.

dis·sen·sion (di sen'shən) n. [ME. dissencion < OFr. dissension < L. dissensio < dissensus, pp. of dissentire: see ff.] a difference of opinion; disagreement or, esp., violent quarreling or wrangling —SYN. see DISCORD

dis·sent (di sent') vi. [ME. dissenten < L. dissentire < dis-, apart + sentire, to feel, think: see SEND¹] 1. to differ in belief or opinion; disagree (often with from) 2. to reject the doctrines and forms of an established church —n. the act of dissenting; specif., a) the rendering of a minority opinion in the decision of a law case b) religious nonconformity —**dis·sent'ing** adj. —**dis·sent'ing·ly** adv.

dis·sent·er (-ər) n. a person who dissents; specif., [D-] a Protestant who refuses to accept the doctrines and forms of the Established Church in England or Scotland

dis·sen·tient (di sen'shənt) adj. [L. dissentiens, prp. of dissentire] dissenting, esp. from the majority opinion —n. a person who dissents; dissenter

dis·sen·tious (-shəs) adj. of or inclined to dissension; quarrelsome; contentious

dis·sep·i·ment (di sep'ə mənt) n. [L. dissaepimentum < dis-, from + saepire, to fence in: see SEPTUM] Biol. a separating membrane or partition, as that between adjacent carpels of a compound ovary

dis·ser·tate (dis'ər tāt') vi. -tat'ed, -tat'ing [< L. dissertatus, pp. of dissertare, to discuss, argue, freq. of disserere < dis-, apart + serere, to join: see SERIES] [Rare] to discuss a subject formally; discourse: also **dis·sert** (di surt') —**dis'ser·ta'tor** n.

dis·ser·ta·tion (dis'ər tā'shən) n. [LL. dissertatio: see prec.] a formal and lengthy discourse or treatise on some subject, esp. one written as partial fulfillment of requirements for the degree of doctor; thesis

dis·serve (dis surv') vt. -served', -serv'ing [Rare] to do a disservice to; harm

dis·serv·ice (-sur'vis) n. [DIS- + SERVICE¹] harmful action; injury

dis·sev·er (di sev'ər) vt. [ME. disseveren < OFr. dessevrer < LL. disseparare < L. dis-, intens. + separare, to SEPARATE] 1. to cause to part; sever; separate 2. to divide into parts —vi. to separate or part; disunite —**dis·sev'er·ance**, **dis·sev'er·ment** n.

dis·si·dence (dis'ə dəns) n. [L. dissidentia < dissidens, prp. of dissidere, to disagree < dis-, apart + sidere, SIT¹] disagreement; dissent

dis·si·dent (-dənt) adj. [L. dissidens: see prec.] not agreeing; dissenting —n. a dissident person; dissenter —**dis'si·dent·ly** adv.

dis·sil·i·ent (di sil'ē ənt) adj. [L. dissiliens, prp. of dissilire, to leap or burst apart < dis-, apart + salire, to leap: see SALIENT] springing or bursting apart, as some plant capsules or pods

dis·sim·i·lar (di sim'ə lər) adj. not similar or alike; different —SYN. see DIFFERENT —**dis·sim'i·lar·ly** adv.

dis·sim·i·lar·i·ty (di sim'ə lar'ə tē) n. 1. absence of similarity; unlikeness; difference 2. pl. -ties an instance or point of difference, or unlikeness

dis·sim·i·late (di sim'ə lāt') vt. -lat'ed, -lat'ing [DIS- + (AS)SIMILATE] 1. to make dissimilar 2. to cause to undergo dissimilation —vi. to become dissimilar —**dis·sim'i·la'tive** adj.

dis·sim·i·la·tion (di sim'ə lā'shən) n. 1. a making or becoming dissimilar 2. a process of linguistic change in which one of two identical phonemes within a form becomes unlike the other or disappears (Ex.: Eng. marble < OFr. marbre, It. pellegrino < L. peregrinus)

dis·si·mil·i·tude (dis'si mil'ə tōōd', -tyōōd') n. [ME. < L. dissimilitudo < dissimilis, unlike < dis-, not + similis, like] dissimilarity; difference

dis·sim·u·late (di sim'yə lāt') vt., vi. -lat'ed, -lat'ing [ME. dissimulaten < pp. of L. dissimulare: see DIS- & SIMULATE] to hide (one's feelings, motives, etc.) by pretense; dissemble —**dis·sim'u·la'tion** n. —**dis·sim'u·la'tor** n.

dis·si·pate (dis'ə pāt') vt. -pat'ed, -pat'ing [ME. dissipaten < L. dissipatus, pp. of dissipare, to scatter < dis-, apart + supare, to throw < IE. base *swep-, whence Sans. svapū, broom, LowG. swabbeln, to SWAB] 1. to break up and scatter; dispel; disperse 2. to drive completely away; make disappear 3. to waste or squander —vi. 1. to be dissipated; disperse or vanish 2. to spend much time and energy on indulgence in pleasure, esp. drinking, gambling, etc., to the point of harming oneself —SYN. see SCATTER —**dis'si·pat'er**, **dis'si·pa'tor** n. —**dis'si·pa'tive** adj.

dis·si·pat·ed (-id) adj. 1. scattered 2. squandered or wasted 3. characterized by, or showing the harmful effects of, dissipation

dis·si·pa·tion (dis'ə pā'shən) n. [ME. dissipacioun < L. dissipatio: see DISSIPATE] 1. a scattering or being scattered; dispersion 2. a wasting or squandering 3. an idle or

frivolous amusement or diversion 4. indulgence in pleasure to the point of harming oneself; intemperance; dissoluteness

dis·so·ci·a·ble (di sō'shə b'l, -shē ə-) adj. [Fr. < L. dissociabilis] 1. that can be dissociated; separable; distinguishable 2. ill-matched; incongruous 3. [DIS- + SOCIABLE] unsociable —**dis·so'ci·a·bil'i·ty** n.

dis·so·cial (di sō'shəl) adj. unsocial or unsociable

dis·so·ci·ate (di sō'shē āt', -sē-) vt. -at'ed, -at'ing [< L. dissociatus, pp. of dissociare < dis-, apart + sociare, to join < socius, companion: see SOCIAL] 1. to break the ties or connection between; sever association with; separate; disunite 2. to cause to undergo dissociation —vi. 1. to part company 2. to undergo dissociation —**dissociate oneself from** to deny or repudiate any connection with

dis·so·ci·a·tion (di sō'sē ā'shən, -shē-) n. [L. dissociatio] 1. a dissociating or being dissociated; separation 2. Chem. the breaking up of a compound into simpler components, frequently in a reversible manner so that the components may recombine 3. Psychol. a) a split in the conscious process in which a group of mental activities breaks away from the main stream of consciousness and functions as a separate unit, as if belonging to another person b) the abnormal separation of related ideas, thoughts, or emotions —**dis·so'ci·a·tive** adj.

dis·sol·u·ble (di säl'yoo b'l) adj. [L. dissolubilis < dissolvere: see DISSOLVE] that can be dissolved —**dis·sol'u·bil'i·ty** n.

dis·so·lute (dis'ə loot') adj. [L. dissolutus, loosened, lax, unrestrained; pp. of dissolvere: see DISSOLVE] dissipated and immoral; profligate; debauched —**dis'so·lute'ly** adv. —**dis'so·lute'ness** n.

dis·so·lu·tion (dis'ə loo'shən) n. [ME. dissolucioun < L. dissolutio] a dissolving or being dissolved; specif., a) a breaking up or into parts; disintegration b) the termination, as of a business, association, or union c) the ending of life; death d) the dismissal of an assembly or adjournment of a meeting

dis·solve (di zälv', -zôlv') vt., vi. -solved', -solv'ing [ME. dissolven < L. dissolvere, to loosen < dis-, apart + solvere, to loosen: see SOLVE] 1. to make or become liquid; liquefy; melt 2. to merge with a liquid; pass or make pass into solution 3. to break up; disunite; decompose; disintegrate 4. to end by or as by breaking up; terminate 5. to disappear or make disappear ☆6. Motion Pictures & TV to fade or make fade into or out of view —☆n. Motion Pictures & TV a fade-in or fade-out —SYN. see ADJOURN, MELT —**dissolved in tears** weeping —**dis·solv'a·ble** adj.

dis·sol·vent (-ənt) adj. [L. dissolvens, prp. of dissolvere] that can dissolve other substances —n. a dissolvent substance; solvent

dis·so·nance (dis'ə nəns) n. [ME. dissonaunce < LL. dissonantia < L. dissonans, prp. of dissonare, to be discordant < dis-, apart + sonus, a sound¹] 1. an inharmonious sound or combination of sounds; discord 2. any lack of harmony or agreement; incongruity 3. Music a chord that sounds incomplete or unfulfilled until resolved to a harmonious chord

dis·so·nant (-nənt) adj. 1. characterized by or constituting a dissonance; discordant 2. opposing in opinion, temperament, etc.; incompatible; incongruous —**dis'so·nant·ly** adv.

dis·suade (di swād') vt. -suad'ed, -suad'ing [L. dissuadere < dis-, away, from + suadere, to persuade: see SWEET] 1. to turn (a person) aside (from a course, etc.) by persuasion or advice 2. [Obs.] to advise against (an action) —**dis·suad'er** n.

dis·sua·sion (di swā'zhən) n. [ME. dissuasioun < L. dissuasio] the act of dissuading

dis·sua·sive (-siv) adj. trying or meant to dissuade —**dis·sua'sive·ly** adv.

dis·syl·la·ble (dis'sil'ə b'l) n. same as DISYLLABLE —**dis·syl·lab·ic** (dis'si lab'ik) adj.

dis·sym·me·try (dis sim'ə trē) n., pl. -tries 1. a lack of deficiency of symmetry 2. symmetry in opposite directions, as of a person's hands —**dis·sym·met·ri·cal** (dis'si met'ri k'l), **dis·sym·met'ric** adj.

dist. 1. distance 2. distant 3. distinguish 4. distinguished 5. district

dis·taff (dis'taf, -täf) n. [ME. distaf < OE. distæf < dis-, flax (see DIZEN) + stæf, STAFF¹] 1. a staff on which flax, wool, etc. is wound for use in spinning 2. woman's work or concerns 3. woman, or women in general —adj. female; specif., designating the maternal side of a family

dis·tain (dis tān') vt. [ME. disteinen < OFr. desteindre < L. dis- + tingere, to wet, TINGE] [Archaic] 1. to discolor; stain 2. to stain the honor of; disgrace

dis·tal (dis't'l) adj. [DIST(ANT) + -AL: formed in contrast to PROXIMAL] Anat. farthest from the center or the point of attachment or origin; terminal: opposed to PROXIMAL —**dis'tal·ly** adv.

dis·tance (dis'təns) n. [ME. distaunce < OFr. distance < L. distantia < distans, prp. of distare, to stand apart < dis-, apart + stare, STAND] 1. the fact or condition of being separated or removed in space or time; remoteness 2. a gap, space, or

DISTAFF

interval between two points, lines, objects, etc. **3.** an interval between two points in time **4.** the length of a line between two points [the *distance* between Paris and Rome] **5.** a remoteness in relationship; dissimilarity; disparity [the *distance* between wealth and poverty] **6.** a remoteness in behavior; coolness of manner; reserve **7.** a remote point in space [away in the *distance*] **8.** a faraway point of time [at this *distance* we cannot know Neanderthal man] **9.** *Painting* the depicting of distance, as in a landscape **10.** *Racing* a space that is a certain distance back from the finish line: in order to be qualified for future heats, a horse must have reached this space by the time the winner has completed the course —*vt.* -tanced, -tanc-ing **1.** to place or hold at some distance **2.** to do better or more than; leave behind; outdo; outdistance —**go the distance** to last through an activity; specif., to pitch an entire baseball game without being replaced —**keep at a distance** to be reserved or cool toward; treat aloofly —**keep one's distance** to be or remain aloof or reserved

dis·tant (-tənt) *adj.* [ME. *distaunt* < L. *distans*: see prec.] **1.** having a gap or space between; separated **2.** widely separated; far apart or far away in space or time **3.** at a measured interval; away [a town 100 miles *distant*] **4.** far apart in relationship; remote [a *distant* cousin] **5.** cool in manner; aloof; reserved **6.** from or at a distance [a *distant* sound] **7.** faraway or dreamy [a *distant* look] —*SYN.* see FAR —**dis'tant·ly** *adv.*

dis·taste (dis tāst') *n.* dislike or aversion (*for*) —*vt.* -tast'ed, -tast'ing [Archaic] **1.** to have a distaste for; dislike **2.** to displease, offend —*vi.* [Obs.] to be distasteful

dis·taste·ful (-fəl) *adj.* **1.** unpleasant to taste **2.** causing distaste; unpleasant; disagreeable —**dis·taste'ful·ly** *adv.* —**dis·taste'ful·ness** *n.*

Dist. Atty. District Attorney

dis·tem·per¹ (dis tem'pər) *vt.* [ME. *distemperen* < OFr. *destemprer* or ML. *distemperare*, to disorder (esp. the "tempers," or four humors) < L. *dis-*, apart + *temperare*, to mix in proportion: see TEMPER] **1.** [Archaic] to make bad-tempered; disturb; ruffle **2.** to upset or unbalance the functions of; derange; disorder —*n.* **1.** a mental or physical derangement or disorder; disease **2.** any of several infectious diseases of animals, characterized by rhinitis, fever, etc.; specif., *a)* an infectious virus disease of young dogs *b)* strangles, a disease of horses **3.** civil disorder or turmoil

dis·tem·per² (-pər) *vt.* [OFr. *destemprer* < ML. *distemperare*, to mix, dilute < L. *dis-*, intens. + *temperare*: see prec.] **1.** to mix (colors or pigments) with water and egg yolks or with size or some other binding medium **2.** to paint with such a mixture —*n.* **1.** a method of painting using distempered pigment, as in murals; tempera **2.** a painting done in this way **3.** distempered paint **4.** any of various water-based paints, as whitewash

dis·tem·per·a·ture (-prə chər, -pər ə chər) *n.* [< DIS-TEMPER¹, after TEMPERATURE] [Archaic] a disordered condition, esp. of the body or the mind

dis·tend (dis tend') *vt., vi.* [ME *distenden* < L. *distendere* < *dis-*, apart + *tendere*, to stretch: see TEND²] **1.** to stretch out **2.** to expand, as by pressure from within; make or become swollen —*SYN.* see EXPAND

dis·ten·si·ble (-tenˈsə b'l) *adj.* [< LL. *distensus* (L. *distentus*), pp. of *distendere*] that can be distended

dis·tent (-tent') *adj.* [Poet.] distended; swollen

dis·ten·tion, dis·ten·sion (-tenˈshən) *n.* [L. *distentio*] a distending or being distended; inflation; expansion

dis·tich (disˈtik) *n.* [L. *distichon* < Gr. *distichon* < *dis-*, two + *stichos*, a row, verse < base of *steichein*, to step: see STILE¹] two successive lines of verse regarded as a unit; couplet

dis·tich·ous (disˈti kəs) *adj.* [< LL. *distichus* < Gr. *distichos*: see prec. + -OUS] *Bot.* arranged in two vertical rows, as leaves on opposite sides of a stem —**dis'tich·ous·ly** *adv.*

dis·till, dis·til (dis til') *vi.* -tilled', -till'ing [ME. *distillen* < OFr. *distiller* < L. *destillare*, to trickle down < *de-*, down + *stillare*, to drop < *stilla*, a drop, dim. < *stiria*, a frozen drop, icicle: for IE. base see STONE] **1.** to fall in drops; trickle; drip **2.** to undergo distillation **3.** to be produced as the essence of something —*vt.* **1.** to cause or allow to fall in drops **2.** to subject to, or purify or refine by, distillation [to *distill* water] **3.** to remove, extract, or produce by distillation [to *distill* whiskey] **4.** to purify, refine, or concentrate as if by distillation [to *distill* one's style] **5.** to draw out or obtain the part that is essential, pure, etc. [to *distill* the meaning of a poem]

dis·til·late (dis'tə lāt', -t'l it) *n.* [< L. *distillatus*, pp. of *distillare*] **1.** a product of distillation; liquid obtained by distilling **2.** the essence of anything

dis·til·la·tion (dis'tə lāˈshən) *n.* [ME. *distillacioun* < L. *destillatio*] **1.** a distilling; specif., the process of first heating a mixture to separate the more volatile from the less volatile parts, and then cooling and condensing the resulting vapor so as to produce a more nearly pure or refined substance **2.** anything distilled; distillate

dis·tilled (dis tild') *adj.* produced by distillation

dis·till·er (-til'ər) *n.* **1.** a person or apparatus that distills **2.** a person, company, etc. in the business of making alcoholic liquors produced by distillation

dis·till·er·y (-til'ər ē) *n., pl.* -er·ies a place where distilling is carried on; specif., an establishment where alcoholic liquors are distilled

dis·till·ment, dis·til·ment (-til'mənt) *n.* [Archaic] distillation or a distillate

dis·tinct (-tiŋkt') *adj.* [ME. & OFr. < L. *distinctus*, pp. of *distinguere*: see DISTINGUISH] **1.** not alike; different **2.** not the same; separate; individual **3.** clearly perceived or marked off; clear; plain [a *distinct* image] **4.** well-defined; unmistakable; definite [a *distinct* success] **5.** [Poet.] decorated or variegated —*SYN.* see DIFFERENT —**dis·tinct'ly** *adv.* —**dis·tinct'ness** *n.*

dis·tinc·tion (-tiŋkˈshən) *n.* [ME. *distinccioun* < OFr. *distinction* < L. *distinctio* < pp. of *distinguere*: see DIS-TINGUISH] **1.** the act of making or keeping distinct; differentiation between or among things **2.** the condition of being different; difference **3.** that which makes or keeps distinct; quality, mark, or feature that differentiates **4.** the state of getting special recognition or honor; fame; eminence [a singer of *distinction*] **5.** the quality that makes one seem superior or worthy of special recognition [to serve with *distinction*] **6.** a mark or sign of special recognition or honor

dis·tinc·tive (-tiŋkˈtiv) *adj.* [ME. < ML. *distinctivus*] making distinct; distinguishing from others; characteristic —*SYN.* see CHARACTERISTIC —**dis·tinc'tive·ly** *adv.* —**dis·tinc'tive·ness** *n.*

dis·tin·gué (dē taŋ gā') *adj.* having an air of distinction; distinguished: also, sometimes, **dis·tin·guée'** *fem.*

dis·tin·guish (dis tiŋ'gwish) *vt.* [< L. *distinguere*, to separate, discriminate < *dis-*, apart + *-stinguere*, to prick < IE. base *steig-*, to prick, pierce, whence STICK, G. *stichen*, to embroider, Gr. *stigma*: see -ISH, 2] **1.** to separate or mark off by differences; perceive or show the difference in; differentiate **2.** to be an essential characteristic of; characterize **3.** to perceive clearly; recognize plainly by any of the senses **4.** to separate and classify **5.** to make famous or eminent; give distinction to [to *distinguish* oneself in battle] —*vi.* to make a distinction (*between* or *among*) —**dis·tin'guish·a·ble** *adj.* —**dis·tin'guish·a·bly** *adv.*

SYN.—**distinguish** implies a recognizing or marking apart from others by special features or characteristic qualities [to *distinguish* good from evil]; **discriminate**, in this connection, suggests a distinguishing of minute or subtle differences between similar things [to *discriminate* scents]; **differentiate** suggests the noting or ascertaining of specific differences between things by comparing in detail their distinguishing qualities or features See also DISCERN

dis·tin·guished (-gwisht) *adj.* **1.** celebrated; eminent **2.** having an air of distinction —*SYN.* see FAMOUS

Distinguished Flying Cross☆ **1.** a decoration awarded to members of the U. S. armed forces for heroism or extraordinary achievement while participating in aerial flight **2.** a British Royal Air Force decoration awarded for gallantry while flying in combat

Distinguished Service Cross☆ **1.** a decoration awarded to members of the U.S. Army or Air Force for extraordinary heroism in combat **2.** a British Royal Navy decoration awarded for distinguished service against the enemy

Distinguished Service Medal☆ **1.** a decoration awarded to members of the U.S. armed forces for exceptionally meritorious service to the government in a duty of great responsibility **2.** a British decoration awarded to personnel of the Royal Navy or Marines for distinguished service in time of war

Distinguished Service Order a British military decoration awarded in recognition of special services in action

dis·tome (di'stōm') *n.* [< ModL. *distoma*, name of the type genus: see DI-¹ & STOMA] any of various digenetic flukes, with an anterior oral sucker and the posterior sucker located on the ventral surface

dis·tort (dis tôrt') *vt.* [< L. *distortus*, pp. of *distorquere*, distort < *dis-*, intens. + *torquere*, to twist: see TORT] **1.** to twist out of shape; change the usual or normal shape, form, or appearance of **2.** to misrepresent; misstate; pervert [to *distort* the facts] **3.** to modify (a wave, sound, signal, etc.) so as to produce an unfaithful reproduction —*SYN.* see DEFORM —**dis·tort'er** *n.*

dis·tor·tion (-tôr'shən) *n.* [L. *distortio*] **1.** a distorting or being distorted **2.** anything distorted —**dis·tor'tion·al** *adj.*

distr. **1.** distributed **2.** distribution **3.** distributor

dis·tract (dis trakt') *vt.* [ME. *distracten* < L. *distractus*, pp. of *distrahere*, to draw apart < *dis-*, apart + *trahere*, DRAW] **1.** to draw (the mind, attention, etc.) away in another direction; divert **2.** to draw in conflicting directions; create conflict or confusion in **3.** [Obs.] to drive insane; craze —**dis·tract'ed** *adj.* —**dis·tract'ed·ly** *adv.* —**dis·tract'i·ble** *adj.* —**dis·tract'ing** *adj.* —**dis·tract'ing·ly** *adv.*

dis·trac·tion (-trak'shən) *n.* [ME. *distraccioun* < L. *distractio*] **1.** a distracting or being distracted; confusion **2.** anything that distracts; specif., *a)* a mental intrusion

or cause of confusion *b*) anything that gives mental relaxation; amusement; diversion **3.** great mental disturbance or distress —**dis·trac′tive** *adj.*

dis·train (dis trān′) *vt., vi.* [ME. *distreinen* < OFr. *destreindre* < ML. *distringere*, to force by seizure of goods < L., to pull asunder, detain < *dis-*, apart + *stringere*, to draw tight, stretch: see STRICT] *Law* to seize and hold (property) as security or indemnity for a debt —**dis·train′a·ble** *adj.* —**dis·train′er, dis·trai′nor** *n.*

dis·train·ee (dis′trā nē′, dis trā′-) *n.* [prec. + -EE[1]] a person whose property has been distrained

dis·traint (dis trānt′) *n.* [ME. *distreint* < OFr. *destreinte*] *Law* the action of distraining; seizure

dis·trait (-trā′) *adj.* [ME. < OFr. *destrait*, pp. of *distraire* < L. *distrahere*: see DISTRACT] absent-minded; inattentive —*SYN.* see ABSENT-MINDED

dis·traught (-trôt′) *adj.* [ME., var. of prec.] **1.** extremely troubled; mentally confused; distracted; harassed **2.** driven mad; crazed —*SYN.* see ABSENT-MINDED

dis·tress (dis tres′) *vt.* [ME. *distressen* < OFr. *destrecier*, orig., to constrain (to do something) < *destrece*, constraint < ML. *destrescia* < L. *districtus*, pp. of *distringere*: see DISTRAIN] **1.** to cause sorrow, misery, or suffering to; pain; trouble **2.** to exhaust or weaken with strain of any sort **3.** [Archaic] to constrain (to do something) **4.** *Law* to distrain —*n.* **1.** the state of being distressed; pain, suffering, etc. **2.** anything that distresses; affliction **3.** a state of danger or trouble; bad straits **4.** *Law a*) distraint *b*) the property distrained —**dis·tress′ing** *adj.* —**dis·tress′ing·ly** *adv.*

SYN.—**distress** implies mental or physical strain imposed by pain, trouble, worry, or the like and usually suggests a state or situation that can be relieved [*distress* caused by famine]; **suffering** stresses the actual enduring of pain, distress, or tribulation [the *suffering* of the wounded]; **agony** suggests mental or physical torment so excruciating that the body or mind is convulsed with the force of it [in mortal *agony*]; **anguish** has equal force but is more often applied to acute mental suffering [the *anguish* of despair]

dis·tressed (-trest′) *adj.* **1.** full of distress; anxious, suffering, troubled, etc. **2.** given the appearance of being antique, as by having the finish marred [*distressed* walnut] **3.** designating or of an area in which there is widespread unemployment, poverty, etc. **4.** designating or of repossessed goods sold at low prices

dis·tress·ful (-tres′fal) *adj.* **1.** causing distress; painful; grievous **2.** feeling, expressing, or full of distress

dis·trib·u·tar·y (dis trib′yoo ter′ē) *n., pl.* **-tar′ies** [< DISTRIBUTE, after TRIBUTARY] any branch of a river that flows away from the main stream and does not rejoin it: opposed to TRIBUTARY

dis·trib·ute (dis trib′yoot) *vt.* **-ut·ed, -ut·ing** [ME. *distributen* < L. *distributus*, pp. of *distribuere*, to distribute < *dis-*, apart + *tribuere*, to allot: see TRIBUTE] **1.** to divide and give out in shares; allot **2.** to scatter or spread out, as over a surface **3.** to divide and arrange according to a classification; classify **4.** to put (things) in various distinct places; specif., *Printing* to break up (type) and put the letters back in the proper boxes **5.** [Obs.] to administer, as justice **6.** *Law* to apportion (an intestate's property) to those entitled to it **7.** *Logic* to use (a term) in its full or extended meaning, so as to refer to every individual denoted —**dis·trib′ut·a·ble** *adj.*

SYN.—**distribute** implies a dealing out of portions or a spreading about of units among a number of recipients [to *distribute* leaflets]; **dispense** suggests the careful measuring out of that which is distributed [to *dispense* drugs]; **divide** suggests separation of a whole into parts to be shared [an inheritance *divided* among five children]; **dole** implies a distributing of money, food, etc. in charity or in a sparing or niggardly manner

☆**dis·trib·u·tee** (dis trib′yoo tē′) *n. Law* one of those to whom an intestate's property is to be apportioned

dis·tri·bu·tion (dis′tra byoo′shan) *n.* [ME. *distribucioun* < L. *distributio*] **1.** a distributing or being distributed; specif., *a*) apportionment by law (*of* funds, property, etc.) *b*) the process by which commodities get to final consumers, including storing, selling, shipping, and advertising *c*) frequency of occurrence or extent of existence **2.** anything distributed; portion; share **3.** *Statistics* the arrangement of a set of numbers classified according to some property, as frequency, or to some other criterion, as time or location —**dis′tri·bu′tion·al** *adj.*

distribution class *same as* FORM CLASS

distribution ratio *Chem.* the ratio of concentrations of a solute distributed between two immiscible phases in contact with each other

dis·trib·u·tive (dis trib′yoo tiv) *adj.* [ME. & OFr. *distributif* < LL. *distributivus*] **1.** distributing or tending to distribute **2.** relating to distribution **3.** *Gram.* referring to each member of a group regarded individually ["each" and "either" are *distributive* words] **4.** *Logic* distributed in a given proposition: said of a term **5.** *Math.* of the principle in multiplication that allows the multiplier to be used separately with each term of the multiplicand —*n.* a distributive word or expression —**dis·trib′u·tive·ly** *adv.*

dis·trib·u·tor (-tar) *n.* [L.] a person or thing that distributes; specif., ☆*a*) an agent or business firm that distributes goods to consumers or dealers ☆*b*) a device for distributing electric current to the spark plugs of a gasoline engine so that they fire in proper order —**dis·trib′u·tor·ship′** *n.*

dis·trict (dis′trikt) *n.* [Fr. < ML. *districtus*, orig., control; hence in feudal law, a territory within which a lord had jurisdiction < L. *districtus*, pp. of *distringere*: see DISTRAIN] **1.** a geographical or political division made for a specific purpose [a school *district*] **2.** any region; part of a country, city, etc. [the business *district*] —☆*vt.* to divide into districts

☆**district attorney** a lawyer serving in a specified judicial district as prosecutor for the State or for the Federal government in criminal cases

☆**district court 1.** the Federal trial court sitting in each district of the U.S. **2.** in some States, the court of general jurisdiction in each judicial district

District of Columbia [after Christopher COLUMBUS] federal district of the U.S., on the N bank of the Potomac River: 69 sq. mi.; pop. 757,000; coextensive with the city of Washington: abbrev. D.C., DC

dis·trust (dis trust′) *n.* a lack of trust, of faith, or of confidence; doubt; suspicion —*vt.* to have no trust, faith, or confidence in; doubt; suspect

dis·trust·ful (-fal) *adj.* distrusting; doubting —**distrustful of** suspicious of; having no confidence in —**dis·trust′ful·ly** *adv.* —**dis·trust′ful·ness** *n.*

dis·turb (dis turb′) *vt.* [ME. *distourben* < OFr. *distourber* < L. *disturbare*, to drive asunder < *dis-*, intens. + *turbare*, to disorder < *turba*, a mob: see TURBID] **1.** to break up the quiet or serenity of; agitate (what is quiet or still) **2.** to upset mentally or emotionally; make uneasy or anxious **3.** to break up the settled order or orderly working of [to *disturb* the books on a shelf] **4.** to break in on; interrupt; interfere with **5.** to inconvenience [don't *disturb* yourself] —**dis·turb′er** *n.*

SYN.—**disturb** implies the unsettling of normal mental calm or powers of concentration by worry, interruption, etc. [to *disturb* one's train of thought]; **discompose** implies the upsetting of one's self-possession [her sudden outburst *discomposed* him]; to **perturb** is to cause to have a troubled or alarmed feeling [the bad news *perturbed* him]; **agitate** suggests an arousing of intense mental or emotional excitement [he was so *agitated*, he could not answer]

dis·turb·ance (-ans) *n.* [ME. < OFr. *destourbance*] **1.** *a*) a disturbing or being disturbed *b*) any departure from normal **2.** anything that disturbs **3.** the state of being worried, troubled, or anxious **4.** commotion; disorder

di·sul·fate (dī sul′fāt) *n.* **1.** a salt of pyrosulfuric acid **2.** a chemical compound containing two sulfate groups per molecule **3.** a bisulfate

di·sul·fide (-fīd) *n.* **1.** a chemical compound in which two sulfur atoms are united with a single radical or with a single atom of an element **2.** an organic compound in which the –SS– group is attached to two different carbon atoms

di·sul·fu·ric acid (dī′sul fyoor′ik) *same as* PYROSULFURIC ACID

dis·un·ion (dis yoon′yan) *n.* **1.** the breaking up or ending of union; separation **2.** lack of unity; discord

dis·un·ion·ist (-ist) *n.* **1.** a person who advocates or tries to cause disunion ☆**2.** a person favoring secession, as in the Civil War; secessionist —**dis·un′ion·ism** *n.*

dis·u·nite (dis′yoo nīt′) *vt.* **-nit′ed, -nit′ing** to destroy or take away the unity of; divide or separate —*vi.* to become separated or divided

dis·u·ni·ty (dis yoo′na tē) *n.* lack of unity

dis·use (-yooz′; *for n.* -yoos′) *vt.* **-used′, -us′ing** to stop using —*n.* the fact or state of being or becoming unused; lack of use

dis·u·til·i·ty (dis′yoo til′a tē) *n.* a lack of utility; quality of being harmful, inconvenient, etc.

dis·val·ue (dis val′yoo) *vt.* **-val′ued, -val′u·ing** to regard as of little or no value; depreciate —*n.* negative value

di·syl·la·ble (dī sil′a b'l, di-; dī′sil′-) *n.* [altered, after SYLLABLE, < Fr. *dissyllabe* < L. *disyllabus* < Gr. *disyllabos*, of two syllables < *di-*, two + *syllabē*, SYLLABLE] a word of two syllables —**di·syl·lab·ic** (dī′si lab′ik, di′-) *adj.*

☆**dit** (dit) *n.* [echoic] the dot character in the Morse code

ditch (dich) *n.* [ME. *dich* < OE. *dic*, a ditch, drain: see DIKE[1]] a long, narrow channel dug into the earth, as a trough for drainage or irrigation of the soil —*vt.* **1.** to border with a ditch **2.** to make a ditch or ditches in ☆**3.** *a*) to cause (a car, wagon, etc.) to go into a ditch *b*) to derail (a train) **4.** to set (a disabled aircraft) down on water and abandon it ☆**5.** [Slang] *a*) to get rid of *b*) to get away from (an unwanted companion, etc.) —*vi.* **1.** to dig a ditch or ditches **2.** to ditch a disabled plane

di·the·ism (dī′thē iz'm) *n.* [DI-[1] + THEISM] belief in two supreme gods; dualism

dith·er (dith′ər) *vi.* [ME. *dideren*, prob. akin to *daderen*, DODDER[1]] to be nervously excited or confused —*n.* a nervously excited or confused condition

di·thi·on·ic acid (dī′thī än′ik) [DI-[1] + THIONIC] an acid, $H_2S_2O_6$, having two sulfur atoms in each molecule and existing only in salts or solutions

dith·y·ramb (dith′a ram′, -ramb′) *n.* [L. *dithyrambus* < Gr. *dithyrambos*] **1.** in ancient Greece, a wild, emotional choric hymn in honor of Dionysus **2.** any wildly emotional speech or writing —**dith′y·ram′bic** (-bik) *adj., n.*

Dit·mars (dit′märz), **Raymond Lee** 1876–1942; U.S. naturalist & zoo curator

dit·ta·ny (dit′'n ē) *n., pl.* **-nies** [ME. *ditane* < OFr. *ditan* < L. *dictamnum* < Gr. *diktamnon* < ? *Diktē*, Mount Dicte, in Crete, where it grew] **1.** a creeping, woolly herb (*Amaracus dictamnus*) of the mint family, native to Greece **2.** *same as* GAS PLANT ☆**3.** a small perennial herb (*Cunila origanoides*) of the mint family, found in E U.S.

dit·to (dit'ō) *n., pl.* **-tos** [It. < L. *dictum*, a saying: see DICTUM] **1.** the same (as something said or appearing above or before) **2.** a duplicate; another of the same **3.** *same as* DITTO MARK —*adv.* as said above; as before; likewise —*vt.* **-toed, -to·ing 1.** to duplicate or make copies of **2.** to indicate repetition of, by using ditto marks **3.** to do again; repeat

dit·tog·ra·phy (di täg'rə fē) *n.* [< Gr. *dittos*, var. of *dissos*, double (< *dis-*: see DIS- + -GRAPHY] accidental repetition of a letter or letters in writing or copying

ditto mark a mark (") used in itemized lists or tables to show that a word, figure, or passage above is to be repeated (Ex.: 4 hrs. overtime Sat.
    2 " " Mon.)

dit·ty (dit'ē) *n., pl.* **-ties** [ME. *dite* < OFr. *dité* < L. *dictatum*, thing dictated, neut. pp. of *dictare*: see DICTATE] a short, simple song

ditty bag (or **box**) [< ? obs. *dutty*, coarse calico, orig. Anglo-Ind., prob. < Hind. *dhōtī*, loincloth] a small bag (or box) used as by sailors for carrying sewing equipment, toilet articles, etc.

Di·u (dē'ōo) small island just off the coast of Gujarat state, NW India: formerly, with a section of the mainland, part of Portuguese India; since 1962 part of the territory of Goa, Daman, and Diu: see GOA

di·u·re·sis (dī'yoo rē'sis) *n.* [ModL. < Gr. *diourein* < *dia-*, through + *ourein*, to urinate < *ouron*, URINE] an increased or excessive secretion or flow of urine

di·u·ret·ic (-ret'ik) *adj.* [ME. *diuretik* < LL. *diureticus* < Gr. *diourētikos* < *diourein*: see prec.] increasing the secretion and flow of urine —*n.* a diuretic drug or other substance —**di·u·ret'i·cal·ly** *adv.*

di·ur·nal (dī ur'n'l) *adj.* [ME. < L. *diurnalis* < *diurnus*, daily < *dies*, day: see DEITY] **1.** happening each day; daily **2.** of or in the daytime: opposed to NOCTURNAL **3.** *a*) *Bot.* opening in the daytime and closing at night: said of a flower *b*) *Zool.* active in the daytime —*n.* **1.** [Archaic] *a*) a diary *b*) a daily newspaper **2.** *Eccles.* a service book containing prayers for the daytime canonical hours —**di·ur'nal·ly** *adv.*

di·va (dē'və) *n., pl.* **-vas**; It. **-ve** (-ve) [It. < L., goddess, fem. of *divus*, god: see DEITY] a leading woman singer, esp. in grand opera; prima donna

di·va·gate (dī'və gāt') *vi.* **-gat'ed, -gat'ing** [< pp. of LL. *divagari*, to wander about < L. *dis-*, from + *vagari*, to wander: see VAGABOND] **1.** to wander about **2.** to stray from the subject; digress —**di'va·ga'tion** *n.*

di·va·lent (di vā'lənt) *adj. Chem. same as* BIVALENT

di·van (di van', -vän' *for 1 & 4*; dī'van, di van' *for 2 & 3*) *n.* [Turk. *dīwan* < Per., orig., bundle of written sheets, hence accounts, customhouse, council room, appropriate furniture] **1.** in Oriental countries, a royal council or council room **2.** a large, low couch or sofa, usually without armrests or back **3.** a coffee room, café, or smoking room **4.** a group of poems, as in Persian, by a single poet

di·var·i·cate (dī vär'ə kāt', di-) *vi., vt.* **-cat'ed, -cat'ing** [< L. *divaricatus*, pp. of *divaricare*, to spread apart < *dis-*, apart + *varicare*, to straddle: see PREVARICATE] to spread widely apart; separate into diverging parts or branches; fork; branch —*adj.* spreading or branching far apart; widely diverging

di·var·i·ca·tion (dī vär'ə kā'shən, di-) *n.* **1.** a divaricating, or branching **2.** a difference of opinion

di·var·i·ca·tor (dī vär'ə kāt'ər, di-) *n.* the muscle that stretches apart the shells of a bivalve

dive (dīv) *vi.* **dived** or **dove, dived, div'ing** [ME. *diven* < OE. *dyfan*, to immerse, caus. of *dufan* to dive, akin to ON. *dȳfa*, to plunge, *dūfa*, a wave < IE. base *dheup-*, deep and hollow: cf. DIP] **1.** to plunge head first into water **2.** to go under water; submerge, as a submarine or skin diver **3.** to plunge the hand or body suddenly into something [to *dive* into a foxhole] **4.** to bring oneself zestfully or with abandon into something [to *dive* into one's work] **5.** to make a steep, sudden descent or take a sudden drop, as an airplane —*vt.* **1.** to cause to dive; specif., to send (one's airplane) into a dive **2.** [Archaic] to explore or penetrate by or as by diving —*n.* **1.** a plunge into water head first; esp., any of various formalized plunges performed as in a competition **2.** any sudden plunge or submersion **3.** a sharp descent or sudden drop, as of an airplane ☆**4.** [Colloq.] a cheap, disreputable saloon, gambling place, etc. —☆**take a dive** [Slang] to lose a prizefight purposely by pretending to get knocked out

dive bomber an airplane designed to release bombs while diving steeply at a target —**dive'bomb'** *vt., vi.*

div·er (dīv'ər) *n.* one that dives; specif., *a*) a person who works or explores under water, usually breathing air supplied through a special mask or helmet *b*) any of several diving water birds, esp. the loon

di·verge (də vurj', dī-) *vi.* **-verged', -verg'ing** [ML. *divergere* (for LL. *devergere*) < L. *dis-*, apart + *vergere*, to turn: see VERGE²] **1.** to go or move in different directions from a common point or from each other; branch off [paths that *diverge*] **2.** to take on gradually a different form or become a different kind [*diverging* customs] **3.** to depart from a

given viewpoint, practice, etc.; differ [*diverging* opinions] —*vt.* to make diverge

di·ver·gence (-vur'jəns) *n.* [ML. *divergentia*] **1.** a diverging, separating, or branching off **2.** a becoming different in form or kind **3.** departure from a particular viewpoint, practice, etc. **4.** difference of opinion; disagreement Also **di·ver'gen·cy,** *pl.* **-cies**

di·ver·gent (-vur'jənt) *adj.* [ML. *divergens*, prp. of *divergere*] **1.** diverging **2.** varying from one another or from a norm; deviating; different **3.** causing divergence **4.** not convergent, as a mathematical sequence —*SYN.* see DIFFERENT —**di·ver'gent·ly** *adv.*

di·vers (dī'vərz) *adj.* [ME. & OFr. *divers(e)*: see ff.] **1.** several; various **2.** [Archaic] diverse

di·verse (di vurs', də-; dī'vurs) *adj.* [ME. & OFr. < L. *diversus*, pp. of *divertere*, to turn aside < *dis-*, apart + *vertere*, to turn: see VERSE] **1.** different; dissimilar **2.** varied; diversified —*SYN.* see DIFFERENT —**di·verse'ly** *adv.* —**di·verse'ness** *n.*

di·ver·si·fied (də vur'sə fīd', di-) *adj.* varied

di·ver·si·form (-fôrm') *adj.* [see DIVERSE & -FORM] having various forms or shapes

di·ver·si·fy (-fī') *vt.* **-fied', -fy'ing** [ME. *diversifien* < OFr. *diversifier* < ML. *diversificare*, to make different < L. *diversus* (see DIVERSE) + *facere*, DO¹] **1.** to make diverse; give variety to; vary **2.** to divide up (investments, liabilities, etc.) among different companies, securities, etc. **3.** to expand (a business, line of products, etc.) by increasing the variety of things produced or of operations undertaken —*vi.* to undertake expansion of a line of products or otherwise multiply business operations —**di·ver'si·fi·ca'tion** *n.*

di·ver·sion (də vur'zhən, dī-) *n.* [ME. *diversioun* < ML. *diversio* (for LL. *deversio*)] **1.** a diverting, or turning aside (*from*) [*diversion* of funds from the treasury] **2.** distraction of attention [*diversion* of the enemy] **3.** anything that diverts or distracts the attention; specif., a pastime or amusement

di·ver·sion·ar·y (-er'ē) *adj.* having the nature of a diversion; specif., *Mil.* serving to distract the enemy from the main point of attack [*diversionary* tactics]

di·ver·sion·ist (-ist) *n.* a person engaged in diversionary activity or tactics

di·ver·si·ty (də vur'sə tē, dī-) *n., pl.* **-ties** [ME. *diversite* < OFr. *diverseté*] **1.** quality, state, fact, or instance of being diverse; difference **2.** variety

di·vert (-vurt') *vt.* [ME. *diverten* < OFr. *divertir* < L. *divertere*: see DIVERSE] **1.** to turn (a person or thing) aside (*from* a course, direction, etc.); deflect **2.** to distract the attention of **3.** to amuse; entertain —*SYN.* see AMUSE

di·ver·tic·u·li·tis (dī'vər tik'yoo līt'əs) *n.* [see -ITIS] inflammation of a diverticulum

di·ver·tic·u·lo·sis (-lō'sis) *n.* [see -OSIS] the abnormal condition of having a number of diverticula protruding from the wall of the intestinal tract

di·ver·tic·u·lum (dī'vər tik'yoo ləm) *n., pl.* **-la** [L. *diverticulum*, var. of *deverticulum*, a bypath < *devertere*, to turn aside < *de-*, from + *vertere*, to turn] *Anat.* a normal or abnormal pouch or sac opening out from a tubular organ or main cavity

di·ver·ti·men·to (di ver'ti men'tō) *n., pl.* **-ti** (-tē), **-tos** [It.: see DIVERT] any of various light, melodic instrumental compositions in several movements

di·vert·ing (də vurt'iŋ, dī-) *adj.* that diverts; esp., amusing or entertaining —**di·vert'ing·ly** *adv.*

‡**di·ver·tisse·ment** (dē ver tēs män', E. di vurt'is mənt) *n.* [Fr.: see DIVERT] **1.** a diversion; amusement **2.** a short ballet, etc. performed between the acts of a play or opera; entr'acte **3.** *same as* DIVERTIMENTO

Di·ves (dī'vēz) [ME.: so named < use of L. *dives*, rich, in the parable in the Vulgate] *Bible* the rich man in a parable: Luke 16:19-31 —*n.* any rich man

di·vest (də vest', dī-) *vt.* [altered < DEVEST] **1.** to strip (*of* clothing, equipment, etc.) **2.** to deprive or dispossess (*of* rank, rights, etc.) **3.** to disencumber or rid (*of* something unwanted) **4.** *Law same as* DEVEST

di·vest·i·ture (-ə chər) *n.* a divesting or being divested: also **di·vest'ment, di·ves'ture**

di·vide (də vīd') *vt.* **-vid'ed, -vid'ing** [ME. *dividen* < L. *dividere*, to separate, divide, distribute < *ai-* (< *dis-*, apart) + base seen in *vidua*, WIDOW < IE. base *weidh-*, to separate (prob. < *wi-*, apart + *dhē-*, set, DO¹)] **1.** to separate into parts; split up; sever **2.** to separate into groups; classify **3.** to make or keep separate by or as by a boundary or partition **4.** to give out in shares; apportion; distribute **5.** to cause disagreement between or among; alienate **6.** to separate (a legislature) into groups in voting on a question **7.** *Math. a*) to separate into equal parts by a divisor *b*) to function as a divisor of **8.** *Mech.* to mark off the divisions of; graduate; gradate —*vi.* **1.** to be or become separate; part **2.** to differ in opinion; disagree **3.** to separate into groups in voting on a question **4.** to share **5.** *Math.* to do division —*n.* **1.** the act of dividing ☆**2.** a ridge that divides two drainage areas; watershed —*SYN.* see DISTRIBUTE, SEPARATE —**di·vid'a·ble** *adj.*

di·vid·ed (-id) *adj.* **1.** *a)* separated into parts; parted *b)* having a center strip, as of turf, separating traffic moving in opposite directions [a *divided* highway] *c)* having distinct indentations or notches reaching to the base or midrib, as in certain compound leaves **2.** disagreeing or differing in opinion

div·i·dend (div'ə dend, -dənd) *n.* [< L. *dividendum*, that which is to be divided < *dividendus*, gerundive of *dividere*] **1.** the number or quantity to be divided **2.** *a)* a sum or quantity, usually of money, to be divided among stockholders, creditors, members of a cooperative, etc. *b)* an individual's share of such a sum or quantity **3.** a gift of something extra; bonus **4.** the refund made under some insurance policies to the insured from the year's surplus profit

di·vid·er (də vīd'ər) *n.* a person or thing that divides; specif., *a)* [*pl.*] an instrument for dividing lines, measuring or marking off distances, etc.; compasses *b)* a screen, set of shelves, etc. used to separate a room into distinct areas

div·i·div·i (div'ē div'ē) *n.* [Sp. < Caribbean word] **1.** a small tropical American tree (*Caesalpinia coriaria*) of the legume family **2.** its curled, astringent pods, which yield tannin used in dyeing and tanning

di·vid·u·al (də vij'oo wəl) *adj.* [< L. *dividuus* + -AL] [Archaic] **1.** divided; separate **2.** divisible; separable **3.** distributed; shared —**di·vid'u·al·ly** *adv.*

div·i·na·tion (div'ə nā'shən) *n.* [ME. *divinacioun* < L. *divinatio* < *divinatus*, pp. of *divinare*: see DIVINE] **1.** the act or practice of trying to foretell the future or the unknown by occult means **2.** a prophecy; augury **3.** a successful guess; clever conjecture —**di·vin·a·to·ry** (də vin'ə tôr'ē) *adj.*

di·vine (də vīn') *adj.* [ME. & OFr. < L. *divinus* < *divus*, god, DEITY] **1.** of or like God or a god **2.** given or inspired by God; holy; sacred **3.** devoted to God; religious; sacrosanct **4.** having to do with theology **5.** supremely great, good, etc. **6.** [Colloq.] very pleasing, attractive, etc.: a feminine intensive —*n.* **1.** a clergyman **2.** a theologian —*vt.* -vined', -vin'ing [ME. *devinen* < OFr. *deviner* < *divinare* < *divinus*] **1.** to prophesy **2.** to guess; conjecture **3.** to find out by intuition —*vi.* **1.** to engage in divination **2.** to make a conjecture **3.** to use a divining rod —*SYN.* see HOLY —**di·vine'ly** *adv.* —**di·vin'er** *n.*

Divine Comedy an elaborate narrative poem in Italian, written (c. 1307–1321) by Dante Alighieri: it deals with the author's imaginary journey through Hell, Purgatory, and Paradise

Divine Liturgy the Eucharistic rite of the Orthodox Eastern Church

Divine Office the prayers assigned to each of the canonical hours

divine right of kings the supposedly God-given right of kings to rule, as formerly believed

div·ing bell (div'iŋ) a large, hollow, bell-shaped apparatus in which divers can work under water: air is pumped into it through a hose

☆**diving board** a springboard projecting over a swimming pool, lake, etc., for use as a takeoff in diving

diving duck any of various ducks that dive for food or protection, as the redhead

diving suit a heavy, waterproof garment covering the body, worn by divers working under water: it has a detachable helmet into which air is pumped through a hose

divining rod a forked branch or stick alleged to reveal hidden water or minerals by dipping downward

di·vin·i·ty (də vin'ə tē) *n.*, *pl.* -ties [ME. & OFr. *divinite* < L. *divinitas* < *divinus*] **1.** the quality or condition of being divine **2.** a divine being; a god; deity **3.** a divine power, virtue, etc. **4.** the study of religion; theology ☆**5.** a soft, creamy kind of candy —**the Divinity** God

☆**divinity circuit** *same as* CIRCUIT BINDING

div·i·nize (div'ə nīz') *vt.* -nized', -niz'ing to make or regard as divine; deify —**div'i·ni·za'tion** *n.*

di·vi·nyl·ben·zene (dī vī'n'l ben zēn') *n.* [DI-¹ + VINYL + BENZENE] an unsaturated aromatic hydrocarbon, $C_6H_4$$(CH:CH_2)_2$, existing in three isomeric forms: used to produce special synthetic rubbers, ion-exchange resins, etc.

di·vis·i·ble (də viz'ə b'l) *adj.* [ME. < LL. *divisibilis*] that can be divided; dividable, esp. without leaving a remainder —**di·vis'i·bil'i·ty** *n.*

di·vi·sion (də vizh'ən) *n.* [ME. *divisioun* < L. *divisio* < *divisus*, pp. of *dividere*] **1.** a dividing or being divided; separation **2.** a sharing or apportioning; distribution **3.** a difference of opinion; disagreement **4.** a separation into groups in voting **5.** anything that divides; partition; boundary **6.** anything separated or distinguished from the whole or from the larger unit of which it is a part; as, *a)* a particular section of a country, state, etc. divided off as for administration *b)* a particular department of a government, business, school, or other organization *c)* an administrative or operational part or unit of an airline, train system, etc. *d)* a particular rank or kind, as of students or athletes, based on achievement, age, sex, etc. *e)* a segment, as of the body **7.** *Bot.* any of the major groups into which the plant kingdom is divided in some systems of classification **8.** *Hort.* a form of plant propagation in which new plants are grown from segments detached from the parent plant **9.** *Math.* the process of finding how many times a number (the *divisor*) is contained in

another number (the *dividend*): the number of times constitutes the *quotient* **10.** *Mil.* a major tactical or administrative unit that can act independently and is under one command; specif., *a)* an army unit larger than a regiment and smaller than a corps, to which various numbers and types of battalions can be attached as required *b)* a naval unit of several ships, usually four *c)* an air force unit of two or more combat wings —*SYN.* see PART —**di·vi'sion·al** *adj.*

di·vi·sion·ism (-iz'm) *n. same as* POINTILLISM —**di·vi'sion·ist** *n.*, *adj.*

division sign (or **mark**) the symbol (÷), indicating that the preceding number is to be divided by the following number (Ex.: $8 \div 4 = 2$)

di·vi·sive (də vī'siv, -vis'iv) *adj.* [LL. *divisivus*] causing division; esp., causing disagreement or dissension —**di·vi'sive·ly** *adv.* —**di·vi'sive·ness** *n.*

di·vi·sor (də vī'zər) *n.* [L.] **1.** the number or quantity by which the dividend is divided to produce the quotient **2.** *same as* COMMON DIVISOR

di·vorce (də vôrs') *n.* [ME. & OFr. < L. *divortium* < *divertere*, earlier *divortere*, to turn different ways: see DIVERSE] **1.** legal and formal dissolution of a marriage **2.** any complete separation or disunion —*vt.* -vorced', -vorc'ing **1.** to dissolve legally a marriage between; separate by divorce **2.** to dissolve the marriage with (one's spouse) by divorce **3.** to separate; disunite —*vi.* to get a divorce

☆**di·vor·cé** (də vôr'sā', -sē'; -vôr'sā, -sē) *n.* [Fr., orig. pp. of *divorcer*] a divorced man

☆**di·vor·cée, di·vor·cee** (-vôr'sā', -sē'; -vôr'sā, -sē) *n.* [Fr., fem. of prec.] a divorced woman

di·vorce·ment (də vôrs'mənt) *n.* divorce

div·ot (div'ət) *n.* [Scot. dial. < ?] **1.** [Scot.] a thin slice of turf used as for roofing **2.** *Golf* a lump of turf dislodged by a player's club in making a stroke

di·vul·gate (də vul'gāt) *vt.* -gat·ed, -gat·ing [< L. *divulgatus*, pp. of *divulgare*] [Rare] *same as* DIVULGE

di·vulge (-vulj') *vt.* -vulged', -vulg'ing [ME. *divulgen* < L. *divulgare* < *di-* (< *dis-*), apart + *vulgare*, to make public < *vulgus*, the common people: see VULGAR] to make known; disclose; reveal —*SYN.* see REVEAL

di·vul·gence (-vul'jəns) *n.* a divulging or being divulged; disclosure: also **di·vulge'ment**

di·vul·sion (-vul'shən) *n.* [< L. *divulsio* < *divulsus*, pp. of *divellere*, to rend asunder < *di-* (< *dis-*), apart + *vellere*, to pull out < IE. base *wel-*, to tear, wound, whence L. *vulnus*, wound] a tearing or being torn apart; violent rending or separation

div·vy (div'ē) *vt.*, *vi.* -vied, -vy·ing [clipped form of DIVIDE] [Slang] to share; divide (*up*) —*n.* [Slang] a division

di·wan (di wän', -wôn') *n. same as* DEWAN

Dix·ie (dik'sē) *n.* [< *Dixie* (earlier, *Dixie's Land*), title of song (1859) by Daniel D. Emmett (1815–1904), U.S. song writer, after *Dixie*, orig. name of a Negro character in a minstrel play (1850)] the Southern States of the U.S., collectively; Dixieland

☆**Dix·ie·crat** (-krat') *n.* [prec. + (DEMO)CRAT] a member of the States' Rights Party organized in 1948 by Southern Democrats in opposition to the civil rights platform of the regular Democratic Party

☆**Dixie Cup** *a trademark for* a small, paper drinking cup —[d- c-] such a cup

Dix·ie·land (-land') *adj.* in, of, or like a style of jazz as modified by white New Orleans musicians, characterized by a fast, ragtime tempo and a strict beat —*n.* **1.** the South; Dixie: also **Dixie Land 2.** Dixieland jazz

dix·it (dik'sit) *n.* [L., 3d pers. sing., perf. indic., of *dicere*: see DICTION] an arbitrary or dogmatic statement

Di·yar·ba·kir (dē yär'bä kir') city in SE Turkey, on the Tigris: pop. 80,000

diz·en (diz'n, dī'z'n) *vt.* [MDu. *disen*, to put flax on a distaff < LG. *diesse*, bunch of flax, akin to OE. *dis-*: see DISTAFF] [Archaic or Poet.] *same as* BEDIZEN

diz·zy (diz'ē) *adj.* -zi·er, -zi·est [ME. *disi*, *dusi* < OE. *dysig*, foolish < IE. base *dheues-*, to eddy, whirl, whence DOZE, DUSK, L. *furere*, to rage: cf. DEER] **1.** feeling giddy or unsteady **2.** causing or likely to cause giddiness [dizzy heights] **3.** confused; bewildered **4.** [Colloq.] silly; foolish; harebrained —*vt.* -zied, -zy·ing to make dizzy —**diz'zi·ly** *adv.* —**diz'zi·ness** *n.*

Dja·kar·ta (jə kär'tə) *same as* JAKARTA

Dja·wa (jä'vä) *Indonesian name of* JAVA

djeb·el (jeb'əl) *n.* [Fr. < Ar. *jebel*] *same as* JEBEL

djel·la·ba, djel·la·bah (jə lä'bə) *n.* [Ar. *jallabah*] a long, loose outer garment worn by both men and women in some Moslem countries

Dji·bou·ti (ji boot'ē) capital of French Somaliland: seaport on the Gulf of Aden: pop. 41,000

djin·ni (ji nē') *n.*, *pl.* **djinn** *same as* JINNI

Djok·ja·kar·ta (jōk'yə kär'tə) *former name of* JOGJAKARTA

dkg. decagram; decagrams

dkl. decaliter; decaliters

dkm. decameter; decameters

D/L demand loan

dl. deciliter; deciliters

D layer the lowest layer of the ionosphere, existing only in the daytime: it begins at an altitude of about 40 miles and merges with the E layer

D.Lit., D.Litt. [L. *Doctor Lit(t)erarum*] Doctor of Letters
D.L.S. Doctor of Library Science
dlvy. delivery
DM, Dm deutsche mark
dm. decimeter; decimeters
DMSO [*d(i)m(ethyl) s(ulf)o(xide)*] a colorless liquid, (CH₃)₂SO, that diffuses very rapidly through the skin: used as a solvent, and experimentally in medicine
☆**DMT** [*d(i)m(ethyl)t(ryptamine)*] a synthetic, hallucinogenic drug, similar to LSD in its effects, which are, however, more rapid in onset and shorter in duration
D.Mus. Doctor of Music
DMZ demilitarized zone
DNA deoxyribonucleic acid
D.N.B. Dictionary of National Biography (British)
Dne·pr (nĕ′pər; *Russ.* dnye′pər) river in W U.S.S.R., flowing south and southwest into the Black Sea; 1,420 mi.
Dne·pro·dzer·zhinsk (dnye′prŏ dzer zhinsk′) city in the Ukrainian S.S.R., on the Dnepr just west of Dnepropetrovsk: pop. 218,000
Dne·pro·pe·trovsk (-pye trŏfsk′) city in the Ukrainian S.S.R., on the Dnepr: pop. 774,000
Dnes·tr (nĕs′tər; *Russ.* dnyes′tər) river in SW U.S.S.R., flowing southeast into the Black Sea: c. 850 mi
Dnie·per (nē′pər) *same as* DNEPR
Dnies·ter (nēs′tər) *same as* DNESTR
do¹ (dōō) *vt.* **did, done, do′ing** [ME. & OE. *don*, akin to G. *tun*, OS. *duan* < IE. base **dhē-*, to put, place, set, whence Sans. *dadhāmi*, Gr. *tithenai*, to place, put, L. *-dere* (as in *condere*, to set down), *facere*, to do, make] **1.** *a)* to perform (an action, etc.) [*do great deeds*] *b)* to carry out; fulfill [*do what I tell you*] *2.* to bring to completion; finish [*dinner has been done for an hour*] *3.* to bring about; cause; produce [*it does no harm, who did this to you?*] *4.* to exert (efforts, etc.) [*do your best*] *5.* to deal with as is required; attend to [*do the ironing, do one's nails or hair*] *6.* to have as one's work or occupation; work at or on [*what does he do for a living?*] *7.* to work out; solve [*do a problem*] *8.* to produce or appear in (a play, etc.) [*we did Hamlet*] *9.* to play the role of [*I did Polonius*] *10.* to write or publish (a book), compose (a musical score), etc. *11.* *a)* to cover (distance) [*to do a mile in four minutes*] *b)* to move along at a speed of [*to do 100 miles an hour*] *12.* to visit as a sightseer; tour [*they did Europe in two months*] *13.* to translate [*to do Horace into English*] *14.* to give; render [*to do honor to the dead*] *15.* to suit; be convenient to [*this will do me very well*] *16.* [Colloq.] to cheat; swindle [*you've been done*] *17.* [Colloq.] to serve (a jail term) —*vi.* **1.** to act in a specified way; behave [*he does well when treated well*] *2.* to be active; work [*do; don't merely talk*] *3.* to finish; used in the perfect tenses [*have done with dreaming*] *4.* to get along; fare [*mother and child are doing well*] *5.* to be adequate or suitable; serve the purpose [*the black dress will do*] *6.* to take place; go on [*anything doing tonight?*] Auxiliary uses of *do:* **1.** to give emphasis, or as a legal convention [*do stay a while, do hereby enjoin*] *2.* to ask a question [*did you write?*] *3.* to serve as part of a negative command or statement [*do not go, they do not like it*] *4.* to serve as a substitute verb [*love me as I do (love) you*] *5.* to form inverted constructions after some adverbs [*little did he realize*] —*n., pl.* **do's** *or* **dos** **1.** [Chiefly Brit. Colloq.] a hoax; swindle **2.** [Colloq.] a party or social event **3.** something to be done, or an order to do it —**do by** to act toward or for; behave in respect to or in behalf of —**do for** [Colloq.] to ruin; destroy —**do in** [Slang] to kill —**do oneself well** (or **proud**) [after G. *sich gütlich tun*] to achieve success for oneself —**do over** [Colloq.] to redecorate —**do up** [Colloq.] **1.** to clean and prepare (laundry, etc.) **2.** to wrap up; tie up **3.** to arrange (the hair) so that it is off the neck and shoulders **4.** to tire out; exhaust —**do up right** (or **brown**) [Colloq.] to do carefully or thoroughly —**do with** to make use of; find helpful —**do without** to get along without; dispense with —**have to do with 1.** to be related to or connected with **2.** to be associated with; deal with —**make do** to get along, or manage, with what is available —**to do 1.** for keeping one occupied **2.** that needs to be done
do² (dō) *n.* [It. < ? *dominus*, first word of a Latin hymn]: used instead of earlier UT: see GAMUT] *Music* a syllable representing the first or last tone of the diatonic scale: see SOLFEGGIO
DO defense order
D/O, d.o. delivery order
do. ditto
D.O. Doctor of Osteopathy
DOA, D.O.A. dead on arrival
do·a·ble (dōō′ə b'l) *adj.* that can be done
☆**dob·ber** (däb′ər) *n.* [< Du. *dobber*] [Dial.] the float on a fisherman's line
dob·bin (däb′in) *n.* [< *Dobbin*, nickname for ROBIN, ROBERT] a horse, esp. a plodding, patient one
dob·by weave (däb′ē) [< *Dobbie*, dim. of *Dob, Dobbin*: see prec.] a weave with small, geometric patterns
Do·bell's solution (dō belz′) [after H. B. *Dobell* (1828–1917), Eng. physician] a solution of sodium borate, formerly used as a wash for skin inflammations

Do·ber·man pin·scher (dō′bər mən pin′shər) [G. *Dobermann pinscher* < L. *Dobermann*, 19th-c. breeder + *pinscher*, terrier < ? *Pinzgau*, area in N Austria known for breeding of dogs and horses] a breed of large dog, with short, smooth, dark hair and tan markings
Do·bie (dō′bē), **J**(ames) **Frank** 1888–1964; U.S. scholar & writer, esp. on the folklore of the Southwest
do·bla (dō′blä) *n.* [Sp. < *doble* < L. *duplus*, DOUBLE] an obsolete gold coin of Spain
do·bra (-bra) *n.* [Port. < *dobre* < L. *duplus*, DOUBLE: so named because double the value of another coin] any of several obsolete gold coins of Portugal
Do·bru·ja (dō′brōō ja) region in SE Europe, on the Black Sea: divided, since 1940, between Romania & Bulgaria: also sp. **Dobrudja**
Dob·son (däb′s'n), **(Henry) Austin** 1840–1921; Eng. poet & man of letters
☆**dob·son** (däb′s'n) *n.* [fisherman's term < ? the name *Dobson*] the larva of the dobsonfly; hellgrammite
☆**dob·son·fly** (-flī′) *n., pl.* **-flies′** any of a number of large insects (family Corydalidae) whose larvae live in water and the male of which, in some species, develop enormous mandibles
☆**do·by** (dō′bē) *n., pl.* **-bies** [Colloq.] adobe
Dob·zhan·sky (däb zhan′skē), **Theodosius (Grigorievich)** 1900– ; U.S. geneticist, born in Russia
☆**doc** (däk) *n.* [Slang] doctor: often used as a general term of address like *Mac, Bud, Jack,* etc.
doc. document
☆**do·cent** (dō′s'nt; *G.* dō tsent′) *n.* [G., earlier sp. of *dozent*, teacher, lecturer < L. *docens*, prp. of *docere*, to teach: see DOCTOR] in some American universities, a teacher or lecturer not on the regular faculty
Do·ce·tism (dō sēt′iz'm, dō′sə tiz'm) *n.* [< Gr.(Ec.) *Dokētai*, name of the sect < *dokein*, to seem, believe (see DOGMA) + -ISM] a doctrine of certain early Christian sects who held that Christ merely seemed to have a human body —**Do·ce′tist** *n.*
doc·ile (däs′'l; *Brit. & Canad., usually* dō′sīl) *adj.* [Fr. < L. *docilis*, easily taught < *docere*, to teach: see DOCTOR] **1.** easy to teach; teachable **2.** easy to manage or discipline; tractable —SYN. see OBEDIENT —**doc′ile·ly** *adv.* —**do·cil·i·ty** (dä sil′ə tē, dō-) *n.*
dock¹ (däk) *n.* [orig., mud channel made by a vessel's bottom at low tide: hence, dock < MDu. *docke*, channel < It. *doccia*, conduit, canal: see DOUCHE] **1.** a large excavated basin equipped with floodgates, used for receiving ships between voyages ☆**2.** a landing pier; wharf **3.** the area of water between two landing piers ☆**4.** a platform at which trucks or freight cars are loaded and unloaded ☆**5.** a building, platform, or area for servicing aircraft —*vt.* **1.** to bring or pilot (a ship) to a dock ☆**2.** to join (vehicles) together in outer space —*vi.* **1.** to come into a dock ☆**2.** to join up with another vehicle in outer space
dock² (däk) *n.* [< Fl. *docke, dok*, hutch, pen, cage] the place where the accused stands or sits in court
dock³ (däk) *n.* [ME. *dokke* < OE. *docce*, akin to MHG. *tocke*, bundle, tuft] any of a genus (*Rumex*) of the buckwheat family of coarse weeds, with stout taproots, small green or brown flowers, and large leaves
dock⁴ (däk) *n.* [ME. *dok* < OE. *-docca* or ON. *dockr*, a short, stumpy tail, akin to prec.] **1.** the solid part of an animal's tail, excluding the hair **2.** an animal's bobbed tail —*vt.* [ME. *dokken* < the *n.*] **1.** to cut off the end of (a tail, etc.); clip or bob **2.** to shorten the tail of by cutting **3.** to deduct a part from (wages, etc.) **4.** to deduct a part from the wages of **5.** to remove part of
dock·age¹ (däk′ij) *n.* [DOCK¹ + -AGE] **1.** the fee charged for the use of a dock **2.** docking accommodations **3.** the docking of ships
dock·age² (-ij) *n.* [DOCK⁴ + -AGE] a cutting off or down; curtailment; deduction
dock·er¹ (-ər) *n.* a dock worker; longshoreman
dock·er² (-ər) *n.* a person or thing that docks
dock·et (däk′it) *n.* [earlier *doggette*, abstract, register < ? It. *doghetta*, small heraldic bend] **1.** a summary, as of a legal proceeding, or a list of legal decisions ☆**2.** a list of cases to be tried by a law court **3.** any list or summary of things to be done; agenda **4.** a label listing the contents of a package, directions, etc. —*vt.* ☆**1.** to enter in a docket **2.** to put a docket, or label, on; ticket
☆**dock·mack·ie** (däk′mak′ē) *n.* [? via Du. < AmInd. (Lenape) *dogekumak*] a shrub (*Viburnum acerifolium*) of the honeysuckle family, with maplelike leaves, small clusters of yellow-white flowers, and dark berries
dock·side (däk′sīd′) *n.* the area alongside a dock
☆**dock·wal·lop·er** (-wäl′əp ər) *n.* [DOCK¹ + WALLOPER] a dock worker; longshoreman

DOBERMAN PINSCHER
(26–28 in. high at shoulder)

dock·yard (-yärd′) *n.* **1.** a place with docks, machinery, and supplies for repairing or building ships **2.** [Brit.] *same as* NAVY YARD

doc·tor (däk′tər) *n.* [ME. *doctour*, teacher, learned man < OFr. or < L. *doctor*, teacher < pp. of *docere*, to teach < IE. base *dek-*, to receive, do what is suitable, teach, whence L. *decere*, Gr. *dokein*: cf. DECENT] **1.** orig., a teacher or learned man **2.** a person on whom a university or college has conferred one of its highest degrees, either after he has fulfilled certain academic requirements or as an honorary title **3.** a physician or surgeon (M.D.) **4.** a person licensed to practice any of the healing arts, as an osteopath, dentist, veterinarian, etc. **5.** a witch doctor or medicine man **6.** a makeshift device, apparatus, etc., for emergency use **7.** a bright-colored artificial fly used in fishing —*vt.* [Colloq.] **1.** to try to heal; apply medicine to **2.** to repair; mend **3.** to tamper with or change in order to deceive [to *doctor* accounts] —*vi.* [Colloq.] **1.** to practice medicine ☆**2.** to undergo medical treatment, take medicine, etc. —**doc′tor·al** (-əl) *adj.*

doc·tor·ate (-it) *n.* [ML. *doctoratus*] the degree or status of doctor conferred by a university or college

doc·tri·naire (däk′trə ner′) *n.* [Fr. < *doctrine*, DOCTRINE] a person who dogmatically seeks to apply theories regardless of the practical problems involved —*adj.* adhering to a doctrine or theory in an unyielding, dogmatic way —*SYN.* see DICTATORIAL —**doc′tri·nair′ism** *n.*

doc·trine (däk′trən) *n.* [ME. < L. *doctrina* < *doctor*: see DOCTOR] **1.** something taught; teachings **2.** something taught as the principles or creed of a religion, political party, etc.; tenet or tenets; belief; dogma **3.** a rule, theory, or principle of law ☆**4.** an official statement of a nation's policy, esp. toward other nations [the Monroe *Doctrine*] —**doc′tri·nal** (-trə nəl) *adj.* —**doc′tri·nal·ly** *adv.*
SYN.—**doctrine** refers to a theory based on carefully worked out principles and taught or advocated by its adherents [scientific or social *doctrines*]; **dogma** refers to a belief or doctrine that is handed down by authority as true and indisputable, and often connotes arbitrariness, arrogance, etc. [religious *dogma*]; **tenet** emphasizes the maintenance or defense, rather than the teaching, of a theory or principle [the *tenets* of a political party]; **precept** refers to an injunction or dogma intended as a rule of action or conduct [to teach by example rather than by *precept*]

doc·u·ment (däk′yə mənt; *for v.* -ment′) *n.* [ME. & OFr. < L. *documentum*, lesson, example, proof < *docere*, to teach: see DOCTOR] **1.** anything printed, written, etc., relied upon to record or prove something **2.** anything serving as proof —*vt.* **1.** to provide with a document or documents **2.** to provide (a book, pamphlet, etc.) with references as proof or support of things said **3.** to prove or support, as by reference to documents —**doc′u·men′tal** (-men′t'l) *adj.*

doc·u·men·ta·ry (däk′yə men′tə rē) *adj.* **1.** consisting of, supported by, contained in, or serving as a document or documents **2.** designating or of a motion picture, television program, etc. that dramatically shows or analyzes news events, social conditions, etc., with little or no fictionalization —*n., pl.* **-ries** a documentary film, television show, etc.

doc·u·men·ta·tion (-mən tā′shən, -men-) *n.* **1.** the supplying of documents or supporting references; use of documentary evidence **2.** the documents or references thus supplied **3.** the collecting, abstracting, and coding of printed or written information for future reference

dod·der¹ (däd′ər) *vi.* [ME. *daderen*, akin to OE. *dyderian*, to confuse, delude, MDu. *doten*, DOTE < IE. base *dheudh-*, to whirl in confusion, shake, whence Gr. *thysanos*, fringe] **1.** to shake or tremble, as from old age **2.** to be unsteady or move unsteadily; totter

dod·der² (däd′ər) *n.* [ME. *doder* < Late OE. *dodder* < same base as prec.: akin to dial. *dodder*, quaking-grass & G. *dotter*, egg yolk] any of a genus (*Cuscuta*) of parasitic plants of the morning-glory family, lacking leaves, roots, and chlorophyll, but having special suckers for drawing nourishment from the host

dod·dered (-ərd) *adj.* [prob. < ME. *dodden*, to cut off; ? infl. by DODDER¹] having lost its branches or top because of age, decay, etc.: said of a tree

dod·der·ing (-ər in) *adj.* shaky, tottering, or senile

do·dec·a- (dō dek′ə) [< Gr. *dōdeka*, twelve < *dō-*, two < *dwo-* < IE. *dwō-*, TWO + Gr. *deka*, ten (see DECA-)] a prefix meaning twelve [*dodecagon*]: also, before a vowel, **do·dec-**

do·dec·a·gon (dō dek′ə gän′) *n.* [Gr. *dōdekagōnon*: see DODECA- & -GON] a plane figure with twelve angles and twelve sides

do·dec·a·he·dron (dō′dek ə hē′drən) *n., pl.* **-drons, -dra** (-drə) [Gr. *dōdekaedron*: see DODECA- & -HEDRON] a solid figure with twelve plane faces —**do′dec·a·he′dral** (-drəl) *adj.*

Do·dec·a·nese (dō dek′ə nēz′, -nēs′) group of Greek islands in the Aegean, off the SW coast of Turkey: 1,050 sq. mi.; pop. 122,000; cap. Rhodes —**Do·dec′a·ne′sian** *adj., n.*

do·dec·a·phon·ic (-fän′ik) *adj.* [DODECA- + -PHON(E) + -IC] *same as* TWELVE-TONE —**do·dec′a·pho′nist** (-fō′nist) *n.* —**do·dec′a·pho′ny** (-fō′nē), **do·dec′a·pho′nism** *n.*

DODECAHEDRON

dodge (däj) *vi.* **dodged, dodg′ing** [? akin to Scot. *dod*, to jog: for the base, see DODDER¹] **1.** to move or twist quickly aside; shift suddenly, as to avoid a blow **2.** to use tricks, deceits, or evasions; be shifty —*vt.* **1.** to avoid (a blow, etc.) by moving or shifting quickly aside **2.** to evade (a question, charge, etc.) by trickery, cleverness, etc. **3.** to avoid meeting **4.** *Photog.* to achieve an effect of shading in (a print) —*n.* **1.** a dodging **2.** a trick used in evading or cheating **3.** a clever or resourceful device, plan, etc.

☆**dodg·em** (däj′əm) *n.* [DODG(E) + (TH)EM] an amusement-park ride consisting of small electrically powered vehicles, whose drivers move them about erratically within an enclosed area, frequently bumping one another

dodg·er (-ər) *n.* **1.** a person who dodges **2.** a tricky, dishonest person; shifty rascal ☆**3.** a bread or cake made of cornmeal ☆**4.** a small handbill **5.** *Photog.* a device used to achieve shading effects in a print

dodg·er·y (-ər ē) *n.* trickery, evasiveness, etc.

Dodg·son (däj′s'n), **Charles Lut·widge** (lut′wij) *see* Lewis CARROLL

dodg·y (däj′ē) *adj.* **dodg′i·er, dodg′i·est** tricky, evasive, etc.

do·do (dō′dō) *n., pl.* **-dos, -does** [Port. *doudo*, lit., foolish, stupid] **1.** a large bird (*Raphus cucullatus*), now extinct, that had a hooked bill, short neck and legs, and rudimentary wings useless for flying: formerly found on Mauritius **2.** an old-fashioned person; fogy

Doe (dō) [same word as *doe*; John Doe and Richard Roe were orig. fictitious plaintiff and defendant in a form of ejection action] a name (*John Doe, Jane Doe*) used in law courts, legal papers, etc. to refer to any person whose name is unknown

doe (dō) *n., pl.* **does, doe:** see PLURAL, II, D, 1 [ME. *do* < OE. *da*, akin to Alemannic *te* < IE. base *dome-*, TAME, whence OIr. *dam*, ox] the female of the deer, or of the antelope, rabbit, or almost any other animal the male of which is called a buck

DODO
(2 ft. high)

do·er (dōō′ər) *n.* **1.** a person who does something or acts in a specified manner [a *doer* of good] **2.** a person who gets things done; active or energetic person

does (duz) *3d pers. sing., pres. indic.,* of DO¹

doe·skin (dō′skin′) *n.* **1.** the skin of a female deer **2.** leather made from this or, now usually, from lambskin **3.** a fine, soft, smooth woolen cloth with a slight nap, used for suits, sportswear, etc.

does·n't (duz′'nt) does not

do·est (dōō′ist) *archaic 2d pers. sing., pres. indic.,* of DO¹: *used with* thou

do·eth (-ith) *archaic 3d pers. sing., pres. indic.,* of DO¹: *used with* thou

doff (däf, dôf) *vt.* [ME. *doffen* < *don of*: see DO¹ & OFF] **1.** to take off (clothes, etc.) **2.** to remove or lift (one's hat), as in greeting **3.** to put aside or discard

dog (dôg, däg) *n., pl.* **dogs, dog:** see PLURAL, II, D, 1 [ME., generalized in sense < late, rare OE. *docga* (usual *hund*: see HOUND¹) < ?] **1.** *a)* any of a large and varied group of domesticated animals (*Canis familiaris*) related to the fox, wolf, and jackal *b)* any of a family (Canidae) to which it and other, wild animals belong **2.** the male of any of these animals **3.** a mean, contemptible fellow **4.** a prairie dog, dogfish, or other animal thought to resemble a dog **5.** [< its orig. shape: cf. Fr. *chenet*] an andiron; firedog **6.** [Colloq.] a boy or man [lucky *dog*, gay *dog*] ☆**7.** [*pl.*] [Slang] feet **8.** [Slang] *a)* an unattractive or unpopular person ☆*b)* an unsatisfactory thing or unsuccessful venture **9.** [D-] *Astron.* either of two constellations near Orion; the Great Dog (CANIS MAJOR) or the Little Dog (CANIS MINOR) **10.** *Mech.* any of several devices for holding or grappling **11.** *Meteorol. a)* a parhelion; sundog *b)* a fogdog —*vt.* **dogged, dog′ging** **1.** to follow, hunt, or track down as a dog does ☆**2.** to hold down with a mechanical dog —*adv.* very; completely: used in combination [*dog*-tired] —**a dog's age** [Colloq.] a long time —**a dog's life** a wretched existence —**dog eat dog** ruthless and savage competition —**dog in the manger** a person who keeps others from using something which he has but cannot or will not use: from the fable of the dog that kept the ox from eating the hay —**every dog has his day** something good or lucky happens to everyone at one time or another —**go to the dogs** [Colloq.] to deteriorate; degenerate —**let sleeping dogs lie** to let well enough alone; not disturb things as they are for fear of something worse —☆**put on the dog** [Slang] to make a show of being very elegant, wealthy, etc. —**teach an old dog new tricks** to induce a person of settled habits to adopt new methods or ideas

dog·bane (-bān′) *adj.* [so named because said to be poisonous to dogs] designating a family (Apocynaceae) of herbs, shrubs, and trees including dogbane, frangipani, and periwinkle —*n.* any of a genus (*Apocynum*) of sometimes poisonous plants of the dogbane family, with opposite entire leaves, small white or pink flowers, and milky juice

dog·ber·ry (-ber′ē) *n., pl.* **-ries** **1.** the berry or fruit of any of various plants, as the mountain ash **2.** any of these plants

dog biscuit **1.** a hard biscuit containing ground bones, meat, etc., for feeding dogs ☆**2.** [Slang] an army field-ration biscuit

dog·cart (-kärt′) *n.* **1.** a small, light cart drawn by dogs **2.** a small, light, open carriage, usually with two wheels, having two seats arranged back to back: it originally had a box under the seat for a sportsman's dog

☆**dog·catch·er** (-kach′ər) *n.* a local official whose work is catching and impounding stray or unlicensed animals

dog collar **1.** a collar to be worn by a dog **2.** *same as* CLERICAL COLLAR

dog days the hot, uncomfortable days in July and August: so called because during that period the Dog Star rises and sets with the sun

doge (dōj) *n.* [It. < L. *dux,* leader < *ducere,* to lead: see DUKE] the chief magistrate of either of the former republics of Venice and Genoa

dog·ear (dôg′ir′, däg′-) *n.* a turned-down corner of the leaf of a book —*vt.* to turn down the corner or corners of (a leaf in a book) —**dog′eared** *adj.*

☆**dog·face** (-fās′) *n.* [Slang] an enlisted man in the army, esp. an infantryman

dog fennel **1.** an annual weed (*Anthemis cotula*) of the composite family, having daisylike flower heads with white rays and yellow centers, and an offensive smell ☆**2.** a tall, annual weed (*Eupatorium capillifolium*) of the composite family, with finely divided leaves and a terminal cluster of tiny rayless flower heads

dog·fight (-fit′) *n.* a rough, violent fight between, or as between, dogs; specif., *Mil.* combat as between fighter planes at close quarters

dog·fish (-fish′) *n., pl.* **-fish′, -fish′es:** see FISH² **1.** any of various small sharks (esp. family Squalidae) with a single spine in front of each of the two dorsal fins **2.** any of several other fishes, as the bowfin

dog·ged (dôg′id, däg′-) *adj.* [ME. < *dogge,* DOG] not giving in readily; persistent; stubborn —SYN. see STUBBORN —**dog′ged·ly** *adv.* —**dog′ged·ness** *n.*

dog·ger (-ər) *n.* [ME. < MDu. < ?] a two-masted boat with a broad beam, used by fishermen in the North Sea

Dog·ger Bank (-ər) extensive sand bank in the C North Sea, between England & Denmark, at a depth of 60–120 ft.

dog·ger·el (-ər əl) *n.* [ME. *dogerel* (Chaucer), prob. < It. *doga,* barrel stave, but infl. by *dog* as in DOG LATIN: parallel with G. *knüttelvers,* lit., cudgel verse, Pr. *bastonnet,* little stick, type of verse] trivial, poorly constructed verse, usually of a burlesque or comic sort; jingle —*adj.* designating or of such verse Also **dog′grel** (-rəl)

dog·ger·y (-ər ē) *n., pl.* **-ger·ies** **1.** mean or surly behavior like that of a snappish dog **2.** dogs collectively **3.** the rabble· riffraff

☆**dog·gie bag** (-ē) a bag supplied to a patron of a restaurant, in which he may place leftovers as to take out to his dog or other pet

dog·gish (-ish) *adj.* **1.** of or like a dog; snarling or snapping **2.** [Colloq.] stylish and showy —**dog′gish·ly** *adv.* —**dog′gish·ness** *n.*

dog·go (-ō) *adv.* [< DOG + -*o*] [Slang] out of sight: in the phrase **lie doggo** to stay hidden; lie low

dog·gone (-gôn′, däg′gän′) *interj.* [euphemism for *God damn*] damn! darn!: an exclamation used variously to express anger, irritation, surprise, pleasure, etc. —*vt.* **-goned′, -gon′ing** [Colloq.] to damn —*n.* [Colloq.] a damn —*adj.* [Colloq.] damned: also **dog′goned′**

dog·gy (-ē) *n., pl.* **-gies** of a dog: a child's word: also **dog′gie** —*adj.* **-gi·er, -gi·est** **1.** of or like a dog ☆**2.** [Colloq.] stylish and showy

dog·hole (-hōl′) *n.* **1.** a small, miserable place or building ☆**2.** [Slang] a small, unsafe coal mine

dog·house (-hous′) *n.* a dog's shelter; kennel —☆**in the doghouse** [Slang] in disfavor

☆**dog·gie** (dō′gē) *n.* [< ?] in the western U.S., a stray or motherless calf

dog Latin incorrect or ungrammatical Latin

dog·leg (-leg′) *n.* a sharp angle or bend like that formed by a dog's hind leg, as in a golf fairway —*vi.* **-legged′, -leg′ging** to go or lie in one direction and then angle off in another —*adj.* of, or having the form of, a dogleg: also **dog′legged′**

dog·ma (dôg′mə, däg′-) *n., pl.* **-mas, -ma·ta** (-mə tə) [L., an opinion, that which one believes, in LL.(Ec.), a decree, order < Gr. *dogma,* opinion, judgment < *dokein,* to seem: see DOCTOR] **1.** a doctrine; tenet; belief **2.** doctrines, tenets, or beliefs, collectively **3.** a positive, arrogant assertion of opinion **4.** *Theol.* a doctrine or body of doctrines formally and authoritatively affirmed —SYN. see DOCTRINE

dog·mat·ic (dôg mat′ik, däg′-) *adj.* [L. *dogmaticus* < Gr. *dogmatikos*] **1.** of or like dogma; doctrinal **2.** asserted a priori or without proof **3.** stating opinion in a positive or arrogant manner: also **dog·mat′i·cal** —SYN. see DICTATORIAL —**dog·mat′i·cal·ly** *adv.*

dog·mat·ics (-iks) *n.pl.* [*with sing. v.*] the study of religious dogmas, esp. those of Christianity

dog·ma·tism (dôg′mə tiz′m, däg′-) *n.* [Fr. *dogmatisme* < ML. *dogmatismus* < Gr. *dogmatizein,* to lay down a decree: see DOGMA] dogmatic assertion of opinion, usually without reference to evidence —**dog′ma·tist** *n.*

dog·ma·tize (-tiz′) *vi.* **-tized′, -tiz′ing** [Fr. *dogmatiser* < ML. *dogmatizare* < Gr. *dogmatizein*] to speak or write dogmatically —*vt.* to formulate or express as dogma —**dog′ma·tiz′er** *n.*

☆**dog·nap** (-nap′) *vt.* **-naped′** or **-napped′, -nap′ing** or **-nap′ping** [DOG + (KID)NAP] to steal (a dog), esp. in order to sell it to a medical research laboratory —**dog′nap′er, dog′nap′per** *n.*

☆**do-good·er** (dōō′good′ər) *n.* [Colloq.] a person who seeks to correct social ills in an idealistic, but usually impractical or superficial way —**do′-good′, do′-good′ing** *adj.* —**do′-good′ism** *n.*

dog paddle a simple swimming stroke in which the body is kept nearly upright, the arms paddle, and the legs move up and down as in running

☆**dog·rob·ber** (-räb′ər) *n.* [DOG + ROBBER] [Mil. Slang] an officer's orderly

dog rose [transl. of the taxonomic name] a European wild rose (*Rosa canina*), with single, pink flowers and hooked spincs

☆**dog salmon** a large salmon (*Oncorhynchus keta*) with pale flesh, found on the NW Pacific coast of the U.S. and in Japan

dog sled (or **sledge**) a sled (or sledge) drawn by dogs

dog's-tail (dôgz′tāl′, dägz′-) *n.* any of a genus (*Cynosurus*) of perennial grasses, esp. the **crested dog's-tail** (*Cynosurus cristatus*) with a slender spike resembling that of timothy: also **dog's-tail grass**

Dog Star **1.** Sirius, the brightest star in the constellation Canis Major **2.** Procyon, a bright star in the constellation Canis Minor

dog's-tongue (-tuŋ′) *n. same as* HOUND'S-TONGUE

dog tag **1.** an identification tag or license tag for a dog ☆**2.** [Slang] a military identification tag worn about the neck

dog·tooth (-tōōth′) *n., pl.* **-teeth** **1.** a canine tooth; eyetooth **2.** an ornamental molding in some medieval buildings, consisting of a series of toothlike projections **3.** *same as* HOUNDSTOOTH CHECK

dogtooth violet ☆**1.** any of a genus (*Erythronium*) of small American plants of the lily family, esp. an early spring flower (*Erythronium americanum*) with two mottled leaves and a yellow or white flower **2.** a European plant (*Erythronium denscanis*) with a purple or rose flower Also **dog's-tooth violet**

dog·trot (-trät′) *n.* **1.** a slow, easy trot, like a dog's ☆**2.** a covered passageway between two parts of a building

dog·watch (-wäch′, -wôch′) *n. Naut.* either of two duty periods (from 4 to 6 P.M. and from 6 to 8 P.M.) half the length of the normal period

dog·wood (-wood′) *adj.* [shortened < *dogberry wood, dogberry tree*] designating a family (Cornaceae) of small trees and shrubs —*n.* **1.** any of a genus (*Cornus*) of trees and shrubs of the dogwood family, esp. the **flowering dogwood** (*Cornus florida*), a small tree of E U.S., with groups of small flowers surrounded by four large white or pink bracts **2.** its hard, closegrained wood

☆**do·gy** (dō′gē) *n., pl.* **-gies** *same as* DOGIE

Do·ha (dō′ha) capital of Qatar, on the Persian Gulf: pop. 45,000

Doh·ná·nyi (dô′nän yē), Er·nö (er′nö) (Ger. name *Ernst von Dohnanyi*) 1877–1960; Hung. composer & pianist

doi·ly (doi′lē) *n., pl.* **-lies** [after a 17th-c. London draper named *Doily* or *Doyley*] **1.** a small napkin **2.** a small mat, as of lace or paper, put under a dish, vase, or the like, as a decoration or to protect a surface

do·ings (dōō′iŋz) *n.pl.* things done; actions, events, etc.

doit (doit) *n.* [Du. *duit,* akin to ON. *thveiti,* a small weight of silver: for IE. base, see WHITTLE] **1.** a small, obsolete Dutch coin of little value **2.** anything of trifling value

doit·ed (doit′id) *adj.* [prob. var. of *doted:* cf. DOTE] [Scot.] foolish, as from old age; senile

☆**do-it-your·self** (dōō′it yoor self′) *n.* the practice of constructing, repairing, redecorating, etc. by oneself instead of hiring another to do it —*adj.* of, used for, or engaged in do-it-yourself

dol. **1.** *Music dolce* **2.** *pl.* **dols.** dollar

do·lab·ri·form (dō lab′ri fôrm′) *adj.* [< L. *dolabra,* pickax (< *dolare,* to chip < IE. base *del-,* to cut) + -FORM] shaped like the head of an ax, as certain leaves

‡**dol·ce** (dôl′che; E. dōl′chā) *adj.* [It., sweet] **1.** sweet and soft **2.** *Music* smooth in performance

‡**dolce far nien·te** (fär nyen′te) [It., (it is) sweet doing nothing] pleasant idleness or inactivity

‡**dolce vi·ta** (vē′tä) [It., lit., (the) sweet life] a casual way of life, characterized by dissipation and promiscuity

dol·drums (däl′drəmz, dōl′-) *n.pl.* [< ? ME. *dul* (see DULL), after TANTRUM] **1.** *a)* low spirits; dull, gloomy, listless feeling *b)* sluggishness or complete inactivity; stagnation

2. *a)* equatorial ocean regions noted for dead calms and light fluctuating winds *b)* such calms and winds

dole[1] (dōl) *n.* [ME. *dol* < OE. *dal*, a share, parallel to *dæl*: see DEAL[2]] **1.** a giving out of money or food to those in great need; relief **2.** that which is thus given out **3.** anything given out sparingly **4.** a form of payment by a government to the unemployed, as in England **5.** [Archaic] one's destiny or lot —*vt.* **doled, dol'ing** to give sparingly or as a dole (usually with *out*) —*SYN.* see DISTRIBUTE —**on the dole** receiving government relief funds

dole[2] (dōl) *n.* [see ff.] [Archaic] sorrow; dolor

dole·ful (dōl'fəl) *adj.* [ME. *dolful* < *dol*, grief (< OFr. *doel* < VL. *dolus*, grief, pain < L. *dolere*, to suffer, prob. < IE. base *del-*, *dol-*, to split, cut) + *-ful*, -FUL] full of or causing sorrow or sadness; mournful; melancholy: also [Rare] **dole'some** —*SYN.* see SAD —**dole'ful·ly** *adv.* —**dole'ful·ness** *n.*

dol·er·ite (däl'ə rīt') *n.* [Fr. *dolérite* < Gr. *doleros*, deceptive < *dolos*, deceit (for IE. base, see TALE): from its close resemblance to diorite] **1.** a coarse, crystalline variety of basalt **2.** loosely, diabase or any of various other igneous rocks whose composition cannot be analyzed without microscopic examination

dol·i·cho·ce·phal·ic (däl'i kō'sə fal'ik) *adj.* [< Gr. *dolichos*, LONG[1] + -CEPHALIC] having a relatively long head; having a head whose width is less than 76 percent of its length: also **dol'i·cho·ceph'a·lous** (-sef'ə ləs): see also CEPHALIC INDEX —**dol'i·cho·ceph'a·ly** (-sef'ə lē) *n.*

dol·i·cho·cra·ni·al (-krā'nē əl) *adj.* [< Gr. *dolichos*, LONG[1] + -CRANIAL] long-skulled, with a cranial index of 76 or less: also **dol'i·cho·cra'nic** (-nik) —**dol'i·cho·cra'ny** (-nē) *n.*

doll (däl) *n.* [< *Doll*, nickname for DOROTHY] **1.** a child's toy made to resemble a human being **2.** a pretty but frivolous or silly young woman **3.** a pretty child **4.** [Slang] any girl or young woman **5.** [Slang] any attractive or lovable person —*vt.*, *vi.* [Colloq.] to dress carefully and stylishly or showily (with *up*)

dol·lar (däl'ər) *n.* [LowG. & Early ModDu. *daler* < G. *thaler* (now *taler*), contr. < *Joachimsthaler*, coin made (orig. in 1519) at (St.) *Joachimstal*, Bohemia < (St.) *Joachim* + *thal*, *tal*, valley (see DALE)] ☆**1.** the monetary unit of the U.S., equal to 100 cents: symbol, $, as, $1.00 **2.** the standard monetary unit of various other countries, as of Canada, Australia, Liberia, Ethiopia, etc.: see MONETARY UNITS, table **3.** the Mexican peso **4.** any of several monetary units used only in trade, as the British Hong Kong dollar, the Straits Settlements dollar, etc. **5.** a coin or piece of paper money of the value of a dollar **6.** [Obs.] a Spanish coin (piece of eight) used in American Revolutionary times

☆**dollar diplomacy** the policy of using the economic power or influence of a government to promote in other countries the business interests of its private citizens, corporations, etc.

☆**dol·lar·fish** (-fish') *n.*, *pl.* **-fish'**, **-fish'es**: see FISH[2] a saltwater food fish (*Poronotus triacanthus*) with a short, compressed body and small, smooth scales, occurring along the Atlantic coast of the U.S.

☆**dollar sign, dollar mark** a symbol, $, for dollar(s)

dol·lop (däl'əp) *n.* [< ?] **1.** a soft mass or blob, as of some food; lump **2.** a small quantity of liquid; splash, jigger, dash, etc. **3.** a measure or amount [a *dollop* of wit]

dol·ly (däl'ē) *n.*, *pl.* **-lies** [dim. of DOLL] **1.** a doll: child's word **2.** a tool used to hold a rivet at one end while a head is hammered out of the other end **3.** [Dial.] a stick or board for stirring, as in laundering clothes or washing ore; dasher ☆**4.** any of several kinds of low, flat, wheeled frames for transporting heavy objects, as in a factory ☆**5.** a narrow-gauge locomotive for railroad yard work ☆**6.** *Motion Pictures & TV* a low, wheeled platform on which the camera is mounted for moving it about the set —☆*vi.* **-lied, -ly·ing** to move a dolly forward (*in*), backward (*out*), etc. in photographing or televising the action —☆*vt.* to move (a camera, load, etc.) on a dolly

Dolly Var·den (vär'd'n) [after the character in Dickens' *Barnaby Rudge*] **1.** a dress of sheer figured muslin worn over a bright-colored petticoat **2.** a woman's flower-trimmed hat with a large brim ☆**3.** a kind of red-spotted trout (*Salvelinus malma*) found in streams west of the Rocky Mountains and in E Asia

dol·man (däl'mən, dōl'-) *n.*, *pl.* **-mans** [Fr., earlier *doloman* < Turk. *dolama*, parade attire of the Janizaries] **1.** a long Turkish robe **2.** a hussar's showy, gold-braided jacket worn like a cape with the sleeves hanging free **3.** a woman's coat or wrap with dolman sleeves

dolman sleeve a kind of sleeve for a woman's coat or dress, tapering from a wide opening at the armhole to a narrow one at the wrist

dol·men (däl'mən, dōl'-) *n.* [Fr. < Bret. *taol*, table + *men*, stone] a prehistoric tomb or monument consisting of a large, flat stone laid across upright stones; cromlech

DOLMEN

do·lo·mite (dō'lə mīt', däl'ə-) *n.* [after the Fr. geologist Déodat de *Dolomieu* (1750–1801)] **1.** a common rock-forming mineral, $CaMg(CO_3)_2$,

often occurring in extensive beds **2.** any of several rocks similar to dolomite in composition

Dol·o·mites (dō'lə mīts', däl'ə-) division of the E Alps, in N Italy: highest peak, 10,965 ft.: also **Dolomite Alps**

do·lor (dō'lər) *n.* [ME. & OFr. *dolour* < L. *dolor* < *dolere*, to suffer: see DOLEFUL] [Poet.] sorrow; grief

Do·lor·es (də lôr'əs) [Sp. < *Maria de los Dolores*, lit., Mary of the sorrows] a feminine name

‡**do·lo·ro·so** (dō'lō rō'sō; *E.* dō'lə rō'sō) *adj.*, *adv.* [It.] *Music* with a sorrowful or plaintive quality

do·lor·ous (dō'lər əs, däl'ər-) *adj.* [OFr. *dolerous* < LL. *dolorosus*: see DOLOR] **1.** very sorrowful or sad; mournful **2.** painful —**do'lor·ous·ly** *adv.*

do·lour (dō'lər) *n.* *Brit. sp.* of DOLOR

dol·phin (däl'fən, dôl'-) *n.* [ME. & OFr. *dolfin* < OFr. *dalphin* < VL. *dalfinus*, for L. *delphinus* < Gr. *delphinos*, gen. of *delphis*, akin to *delphys*, womb < IE. base *gwelbh-*, whence Av. *garewa-*] **1.** any of several water-dwelling mammals (family Delphinidae), with numerous teeth and often a beaklike snout, common in warm seas **2.** either of two swift marine game fishes (genus *Coryphaena*), with colors that brighten and change when the fish is taken out of the water **3.** *Naut.* a buoy or spar for mooring a boat —[D-] *Astron.* same as DELPHINUS

BOTTLE-NOSED DOLPHIN (70–160 in. long)

dolphin striker a small spar under the bowsprit of a vessel, helping to form a truss which supports the jib boom; martingale

dolt (dōlt) *n.* [prob. < ME. *dolte*, pp. of *dullen*: see DULL, *v.*] a stupid, slow-witted person; blockhead —**dolt'ish** *adj.* —**dolt'ish·ly** *adv.* —**dolt'ish·ness** *n.*

Dom (däm) *n.* [Port. < L. *dominus*, a lord, master] **1.** a title given to certain monks and clerics **2.** a title of respect formerly given to gentlemen of Brazil and Portugal: used with the given name

-dom (dəm) [ME. & OE. *dom*, state, condition, power: see DOOM[1]] *a n.-forming suffix meaning:* **1.** rank or position of, domain or dominion of [*kingdom*, *earldom*] **2.** fact or state of being [*wisdom*, *martyrdom*] **3.** a total of all who are [*officialdom*]

dom. **1.** domestic **2.** dominion

do·main (dō mān', də-) *n.* [ME. *domein* < MFr. *domaine* < L. *dominium*, right of ownership, dominion < *dominus*, a lord: see DOMINATE] **1.** territory under one government or ruler; dominion **2.** land belonging to one person; estate **3.** supreme ownership: see also EMINENT DOMAIN, PUBLIC DOMAIN **4.** field or sphere of activity or influence [the *domain* of science] **5.** *Math.* *a)* the set of those values of a variable which can be used as arguments for a given function *b)* the set of all integers, or a set of elements whose combinative properties are the same as those of the integers

do·mal (dō'm'l) *adj.* same as CACUMINAL

dome (dōm) *n.* [sense 1 < L. *domus*, house (< IE. *domu-* < base *dem-*, to build); others < Fr. *dôme* < Pr. *doma* < LL.(Ec.), roof, building, cathedral < Gr. *dōma*, housetop, house, temple < same IE. base: cf. TIMBER, DOMINATE] **1.** [Poet.] a mansion or stately building **2.** a hemispherical roof or one formed by a series of rounded arches or vaults on a round or many-sided base; cupola **3.** any dome-shaped structure or object **4.** [Slang] the head **5.** *Geol.* *a)* an anticlinal structure of circular or broadly elliptical form *b)* a form produced by a pair of corresponding planes parallel to one crystal axis but inclined to the other two —*vt.* **domed, dom'ing** **1.** to cover with or as with a dome **2.** to form into a dome —*vi.* to swell out into a dome

domes·day (dōōmz'dā', dōmz'-) *n.* same as DOOMSDAY

Domesday Book [said to be so named because it judged all men without bias, like the Last Judgment] the record of a survey of England made under William the Conqueror in 1086, listing all landowners and showing the value and extent of their holdings

do·mes·tic (də mes'tik) *adj.* [ME. < OFr. *domestique* < L. *domesticus* < *domus*: see DOME] **1.** having to do with the home or housekeeping; of the house or family [*domestic* joys] **2.** of one's own country or the country referred to [Canada's *domestic* affairs] **3.** made or produced in the home country; native [*domestic* wine] **4.** domesticated; tame: said of animals **5.** enjoying and attentive to the home and family life —*n.* **1.** a servant for the home, as a maid or cook **2.** [*pl.*] native products —**do·mes'ti·cal·ly** *adv.*

do·mes·ti·cate (də mes'tə kāt') *vt.* **-cat'ed, -cat'ing** [< ML. *domesticatus*, pp. of *domesticare*, to tame, live in a family < L. *domesticus* < *domus*: see DOME] **1.** to accustom to home life; make domestic **2.** *a)* to tame (wild animals) and breed for many purposes of man *b)* to adapt (wild plants) to home cultivation *c)* to introduce (foreign animals or plants) into another region or country; naturalize **3.** to bring (a foreign custom, word, etc.) into a region or country and make it acceptable —*vi.* to become domestic —**do·mes'ti·ca'tion** *n.*

do·mes·tic·i·ty (dō'mes tis'ə tē) *n.*, *pl.* **-ties** **1.** home life; family life **2.** devotion to home and family life **3.** [*pl.*] household affairs or duties

☆**domestic relations court** in some states, a court with jurisdiction over matters involving relations within the family or household, as between husband and wife or parent and child

☆**domestic science** *same as* HOME ECONOMICS

dom·i·cal (dōm′i k'l, dām′-) *adj.* **1.** of or like a dome **2.** having a dome, domes, or domelike structure

dom·i·cile (däm′ə sil′, -sil; dō′mə-) *n.* [ME. *domicelle* < OFr. *domicile* < L. *domicilium*, a dwelling, home < *domus*: see DOME] **1.** a customary dwelling place; home; residence **2.** *Law* one's fixed place of dwelling, where one intends to reside more or less permanently —*vt.* -ciled′, -cil′ing to establish (oneself or another) in a domicile —**dom′i·cil′i·ar′y** (-sil′ē er′ē) *adj.*

dom·i·cil·i·ate (däm′ə sil′ē āt′, dō′mə-) *vt.* -at′ed, -at′ing to establish in a domicile —**dom′i·cil′i·a′tion** *n.*

dom·i·nance (däm′ə nəns) *n.* a dominating, or being dominant; control; authority: also **dom′i·nan·cy**

dom·i·nant (-nənt) *adj.* [L. *dominans*, prp. of *dominari*: see DOMINATE] **1.** exercising authority or influence; dominating; ruling; prevailing **2.** *Genetics* designating or relating to that one of any pair of allelic hereditary factors which, when both are present in the germ plasm, dominates over the other and appears in the organism: opposed to RECESSIVE: see MENDEL'S LAWS **3.** *Music* of or based upon the fifth tone of a diatonic scale —*n.* **1.** *Ecology* that species of plant or animal most numerous in a community or exercising control over the other organisms by its influence upon the environment **2.** *Genetics* *a)* a dominant character or factor *b)* an organism having such characters **3.** *Music* the fifth note of a diatonic scale —**dom′i·nant·ly** *adv.*

SYN.—**dominant** refers to that which dominates or controls, or has the greatest effect [*dominant* characteristics in genetics]; **predominant** refers to that which is at the moment uppermost in importance or influence [the *predominant* reason for his refusal]; **paramount** is applied to that which ranks first in importance, authority, etc. [of *paramount* interest to me]; **preeminent** implies prominence because of surpassing excellence [the *preeminent* writer of his time]; **preponderant** implies superiority in amount, weight, power, importance, etc. [the *preponderant* religion of a country]

dom·i·nate (-nāt′) *vt.*, *vi.* -nat′ed, -nat′ing [< L. *dominatus*, pp. of *dominari*, to rule < *dominus*, a master < *domonos* < base of *domus*: see DOME] **1.** to rule or control by superior power or influence [to *dominate* a group] **2.** to tower over (other things); rise high above (the surroundings, etc.) [a building that *dominates* the city] **3.** to have foremost place in [to *dominate* a baseball league] —**dom′i·na′tive** (-tiv) *adj.* —**dom′i·na′tor** *n.*

dom·i·na·tion (däm′ə nā′shən) *n.* [ME. *dominacioun* < OFr. *domination* < L. *dominatio*] a dominating or being dominated; rule; control; ascendancy

dom·i·neer (däm′ə nir′) *vi.*, *vt.* [Du. *domineren* < Fr. *dominer* < L. *dominari*: see DOMINATE] to rule (*over*) in a harsh or arrogant way; tyrannize; bully

dom·i·neer·ing (-in) *adj.* arrogant; overbearing; tyrannical —*SYN.* see MASTERFUL —**dom′i·neer′ing·ly** *adv.*

Dom·i·nic (däm′ə nik) [L. *Dominicus*, lit., belonging to a lord < *dominus*, a master: see DOMINATE] **1.** a masculine name: var. *Dominick* **2.** Saint, 1170–1221; Sp. priest: founder of the Dominican order: his day is Aug. 4

Dom·i·ni·ca (däm′ə nē′kə, də min′i kə) self-governing island of the Windward group in the West Indies, under Brit. protection: 290 sq. mi.; pop. 69,000

do·min·i·cal (də min′i k'l) *adj.* [ME. < ML.(Ec.) *dominicalis* < LL.(Ec.) *Dominicus*, of the Lord < L. of a lord < *dominus*, a lord, in LL.(Ec.), Christ: see DOMINATE] **1.** having to do with Jesus as the Lord **2.** having to do with the Lord's Day (Sunday)

dominical letter any of the first seven letters in the alphabet as used in church calendars to indicate Sundays: the letters are assigned to the first seven days of January, and the letter falling to Sunday is the arbitrary symbol for Sunday the rest of the year

Do·min·i·can (-kən) *adj.* **1.** of Saint Dominic **2.** designating or of a mendicant order founded by him **3.** of the Dominican Republic —*n.* **1.** a member of a mendicant order of friars or nuns founded in 1215 by Saint Dominic **2.** a native or inhabitant of the Dominican Republic

Dominican Republic country occupying the E part of the island of Hispaniola, in the West Indies: 18,816 sq. mi.; pop. 4,012,000; cap. Santo Domingo

Dom·i·nick (däm′ə nik) a masculine name: see DOMINIC —*n. same as* DOMINIQUE

dom·i·nie (däm′ə nē; *for 2, usually* dō′mə-) *n.* [< voc. (*domine*) of L. *dominus*: see DOMINATE] **1.** in Scotland, a schoolmaster ☆**2.** in the U.S., a pastor of the Dutch Reformed Church **3.** [Colloq.] any pastor or clergyman

do·min·ion (də min′yən) *n.* [ME. *dominioun* < ML. *dominio* < L. *dominus*: see DOMINATE] **1.** rule or power to rule; sovereign authority; sovereignty **2.** a governed territory or country **3.** [D-] formerly, any of certain self-governing member nations of the British Commonwealth of Nations **4.** *Law* ownership; dominium —*SYN.* see POWER

Dominion Day in Canada, July 1, a legal holiday commemorating the anniversary of the proclamation in 1867 of the establishment of the Dominion of Canada

☆**Dom·i·nique** (däm′ə nēk′) *n.* [Fr., DOMINICA] one of an American breed of domestic chickens with yellow legs and gray, barred plumage

do·min·i·um (dō min′ē əm) *n.* [L.: see DOMAIN] *Law* the right of property and its ownership and control

dom·i·no (däm′ə nō′) *n.*, *pl.* -noes′, -nos′ [Fr. & It., hooded cloak (worn by cathedral canons) < dat. of L. *dominus*, a lord, master] **1.** a loose cloak or robe with wide sleeves, hood, and mask, worn at masquerades **2.** a small mask, generally black, for the eyes; half mask **3.** a person dressed in such a cloak or mask **4.** [Fr. < Sp.: in reference to the blackness of the piece] a small, oblong piece of wood, plastic, etc. marked into halves, each half being blank or having from one to six dots marked on it **5.** [*pl.*, *with sing. v.*] a game played with twenty-eight such pieces, which the players must match according to the dots on each half

☆**domino theory** a postulation that if one country, as in SE Asia, should come under Communist control, others would quickly follow, as a row of dominoes standing on edge would fall if the first were pushed

‡**Do·mi·nus** (dō′mē noos, däm′ə nəs) *n.* [L.] the Lord

‡**Dominus vo·bis·cum** (vō bis′koom, -kəm) [L.] the Lord be with you

Do·mi·tian (də mish′ən) (L. name *Titus Flavius Domitianus Augustus*), 51–96 A.D.; Rom. emperor (81–96)

Dom·ré·my (dōn rā mē′) village in NE France: birthplace of Joan of Arc: now called **Dom·ré·my-la-Pu·celle** (-lä pü sel′)

Dom. Rep. Dominican Republic

Don (dän; *Russ.* dôn) river of the C European R.S.F.S.R., flowing south into the Sea of Azov: c. 1,200 mi.

don[1] (dän) *n.* [Sp. < L. *dominus*, master: see DOMINATE] **1.** [D-] Sir; Mr.: a Spanish title of respect, used with the given name [*Don* Pedro]: abbrev. **D.** **2.** a Spanish nobleman or gentleman **3.** a distinguished man **4.** [Colloq.] a head, tutor, or fellow of any college of Oxford or Cambridge

don[2] (dän) *vt.* **donned, don′ning** [contr. of *do on*] to put on (a garment, etc.); dress in (a certain color or material)

‡**Do·ña** (dō′nyä) *n.* [Sp. < L. *domina*, mistress, lady] **1.** Lady; Madam: a Spanish title of respect, used with the given name **2.** [d-] a Spanish lady

‡**Do·na** (dō′nə) *n.* [Port.: see DOÑA] **1.** Lady; Madam: a Portuguese title of respect, used with the given name **2.** [d-] a Portuguese lady

Don·ald (dän′'ld) [Ir. *Donghal*, lit., brown stranger (or ? Gael. *Domhnall*, lit., world ruler)] a masculine name: dim. *Don*

Do·nar (dō′när) [OHG.: see THUNDER] *Germanic Myth.* the god of thunder

☆**do·nate** (dō′nāt, dō nāt′) *vt.*, *vi.* -nat·ed, -nat·ing [prob. back-formation < DONATION] to give, esp. to some philanthropic or religious cause; contribute —*SYN.* see GIVE —**do′na·tor** *n.*

Do·na·tel·lo (dō′nä tel′lō; *E.* dän′ə tel′ō) (born *Donato di Niccolò di Betto Bardi*) 1386?–1466; It. sculptor

do·na·tion (dō nā′shən) *n.* [ME. *donacioun* < L. *donatio* < *donatus*, pp. of *donare* < *donum*, gift < IE. *do-* < base *do-*, give] **1.** the act of donating **2.** a gift or contribution, as to a charitable organization —*SYN.* see PRESENT

Don·a·tist (dän′ə tist) *n.* [ML. *Donatista* < *Donatus*, Bishop of Casae Nigrae, founder of the sect] a member of a North African Christian sect formed in the 4th cent., holding extremely rigorous views concerning purity and sanctity —**Don′a·tism** *n.*

do·na·tive (dō′nə tiv, dän′ə-) *n.* [ME. *donatif* < L. *donativum* < *donativus*] a donation; gift

Do·nau (dō′nou) Ger. name of the DANUBE

Don·bas, Don·bass (dôn bäs′) *same as* DONETS BASIN

Don·cas·ter (dän′kas tər, -kəs-) city in NC England, in West Riding of Yorkshire: pop. 87,000

Don Cossack a member of the eastern branch of the Cossacks, living along the Don

done (dun) *pp.* of DO[1] —*adj.* **1.** completed; ended **2.** sufficiently cooked **3.** socially acceptable —**done in** (or **up**) [Colloq.] exhausted; worn out —**done (for)** [Colloq.] **1.** dead, ruined, etc. **2.** discarded or dismissed as a failure

do·nee (dō nē′) *n.* [DON(OR) + -EE[1]] a person who receives a gift or donation

Don·e·gal (dän′ə gôl′; *Ir.* dun′ə gôl′) northernmost county of Ireland, in Ulster province: 1,865 sq. mi.; pop. 114,000

Do·nets (də nets′; *Russ.* dô nyets′) river in SW European U.S.S.R., flowing southeast into the Don: c. 650 mi.

Donets Basin major industrial and coal-producing region in the lower valley of the Donets River

Do·netsk (dō nyetsk′) city in SE Ukrainian S.S.R., in the Donets Basin: pop. 809,000

dong[1] (dôŋ, däŋ) *n.* [echoic] a sound imitating or representing that of a large bell

dong[2] (däŋ) *n.* the monetary unit of North Vietnam: see MONETARY UNITS, table

don·ga (dôŋ′gə, däŋ′-) *n.* [Afrik. < Zulu *udonga*] in South Africa, a gully in a veld

Do·ni·zet·ti (dän'ə zet'ē; *It.* dō'nē dzet'tē), **Ga·e·ta·no** (gä'e tä'nō) 1797–1848; It. composer of operas

don·jon (dun'jən, dän'-) n. [old sp. of DUNGEON] the heavily fortified inner tower or keep of a castle

Don Ju·an (dän' jōō'ən, dän' wän'; *Sp.* dōn Hwän') 1. *Sp. Legend* a dissolute nobleman and seducer of women, the hero of many poems, plays, and operas 2. any man who seduces women or has one love affair after another; libertine; philanderer; rake

don·key (dän'kē, dôn'-, duŋ'-) n., pl. **-keys** [also earlier *donky:* late slang, rhyming with and patterned after MONKEY: < ? DUNCAN or < ? DUN¹] 1. a domesticated ass: see ASS¹ 2. a person regarded as stupid, foolish, or obstinate 3. *same as* DONKEY ENGINE

donkey engine 1. a small steam engine, esp. one used on a ship to lift cargo, etc. ☆2. a small locomotive

Don·na (dän'ə) [It. < L. *domina*, fem. of *dominus:* see DOMINATE] a feminine name —n. (*It.* dōn'nä) 1. Lady; Madam: an Italian title of respect, used with the given name 2. [d-] an Italian lady

don·née (dô nā') n. [Fr. < fem. pp. of *donner*, to give < L. *donare:* see DONATION] the main premise or complex of events and forces used as the basis for the development of the plot in a novel, play, etc.

Donne (dun), **John** 1573–1631; Eng. metaphysical poet & clergyman

don·nered, don·nard (dän'ərd) adj. [< Scot. dial. *donner*, to stun, akin to THUNDER] [Scot.] dazed

Don·ner Pass (dän'ər) [after the ill-fated *Donner* party who wintered there 1846–47] mountain pass in E Calif., in the Sierra Nevada: 7,135 ft. high

don·nish (dän'ish) adj. of or like a university don —**don'-nish·ly** adv. —**don'nish·ness** n.

don·ny·brook (dän'ē brook') n. [< *Donnybrook* Fair] [Colloq.] a rough, rowdy fight or free-for-all

Don·ny·brook Fair (dän'ē brook') a yearly fair formerly held at Donnybrook, near Dublin, Ireland, during which there was much brawling and rowdiness

do·nor (dō'nər) n. [ME. & Anglo-Fr. *donour* < L. *donator*] 1. a person who donates; giver, esp. to a philanthropic cause 2. one from whom blood for transfusion, tissue for grafting, etc. is taken

do·noth·ing (dōō'nuth'iŋ) n. a person without ambition or initiative; idler —adj. showing no ambition or initiative; complacent; unenterprising

Don Qui·xo·te (dän' kē hōt'ē, dän' kwik'sət; *Sp.* dōn' kē Hō'te) 1. a satirical romance by Cervantes, published in two parts (1605, 1615) 2. the hero of this romance, who tries in a chivalrous but unrealistic way to rescue the oppressed and fight evil

don't (dōnt) 1. do not 2. does not: in this sense now generally considered a substandard usage

do·nut (dō'nut') n. *an informal spelling for* DOUGHNUT

☆**doo·dad** (dōō'dad') n. [see DOOHICKEY] [Colloq.] 1. a trinket; bauble 2. any small object or device whose name does not readily occur to one

doo·dle (dōōd'l) vi. **-dled, -dling** [G. *dudeln*, to play (the bagpipe), hence to trifle, dawdle (< Pol. *dudlić* < *dudy*, a bagpipe < Turk. *duduk*, a flute); reinforced by echoic TOOTLE & DAWDLE] 1. to move aimlessly or foolishly; dawdle ☆2. to scribble or draw aimlessly or nervously, esp. when the attention is elsewhere; make doodles ☆3. [Colloq.] to play music in a casual, informal way —n. ☆a mark, design, figure, etc. made in doodling —**doo'dler** n.

☆**doo·dle·bug** (-bug') n. [DOODLE + BUG¹] 1. *same as* ANT LION (sense 1) 2. [Colloq.] a) a short-line train; shuttle b) a small car, truck, plane, etc. 3. [Colloq.] a divining rod or other device used unscientifically in trying to locate something underground

☆**doo·hick·ey** (dōō'hik'ē) n. [fanciful extension of DO¹ as also in DOODAD] [Colloq.] any small object or device whose name is not known or temporarily forgotten

☆**doo·lie** (dōō'lē) n. [< ? DULY (in official statement of appointment, "*You are duly appointed . . .*")] [Colloq.] a freshman at the U.S. Air Force Academy

doom¹ (dōōm) n. [ME. & OE. *dom*, lit., what is laid down, decree, akin to Goth. *doms*, judgment < IE. base *dhē-:* see DO¹] 1. orig., a statute; decree 2. a judgment; esp., a sentence of condemnation 3. destiny; fate 4. tragic fate; ruin or death 5. Judgment Day —vt. 1. to pronounce judgment on; condemn; sentence 2. to destine to a tragic fate 3. to ordain as a penalty —SYN. see FATE

doom² (dōōm) n. *same as* DOUM

dooms·day (dōōmz'dā') n. [ME. & OE. *domes dæg < domes*, gen. of *dom*, DAY] 1. *same as* JUDGMENT DAY 2. any day of judgment

Doomsday Book *same as* DOMESDAY BOOK

Doon (dōōn) river in SW Scotland, flowing north into the Firth of Clyde: c. 27 mi.

door (dôr) n. [ME. *dure, dor* < OE. *duru* fem. (orig., pair of doors), *dor* neut., akin to G. *tür*, door, *tor*, gate < IE. base *dhwer-*, *dhwor-*, door, whence L. *fores* (pl. of *foris*), two-leaved door, Gr. *thyra*, door (in pl., double door)] 1. a) a movable structure for opening or closing an entrance, as to a building or room, or giving access to a closet, cupboard, etc.: most doors turn on hinges, slide in grooves, or revolve on an axis b) *same as* AIR CURTAIN 2. the room or building to which a particular door belongs [two *doors* down the hall] 3. any opening with a door in it; doorway

4. any way to go in or out; passage; access —**lay at the door of** to blame (a person) for —**lie at one's door** to be imputable or chargeable to one —**out of doors** outside a house, building, etc.; outdoors —**show (someone) the door** to ask or command (someone) to leave one's house, room, etc.

door·bell (dôr'bel') n. a bell rung by someone wishing to enter a building or room

do-or-die (dōō'ər dī') adj. showing or involving a desperate effort or need to succeed

door·jamb (dôr'jam') n. a vertical piece of wood, etc. constituting the side of a doorway

door·keep·er (-kēp'ər) n. a person guarding the entrance of a house, hotel, etc.; porter

door·knob (-näb') n. a small knob or lever on a door, usually for releasing the latch

door·man (-man', -mən) n., pl. **-men** (-men', -mən) a man whose work is opening the door of a building for those who enter or leave, hailing taxicabs, etc.

door·mat (-mat') n. a mat for people to wipe their shoes on before entering a house, room, etc.

door·nail (-nāl') n. a large-headed nail used as studding on some doors —**dead as a doornail** dead beyond a doubt

door·plate (-plāt') n. a plate on an entrance door, bearing the number, occupant's name, etc.

door·post (-pōst') n. *same as* DOORJAMB

☆**door prize** a prize given by lottery to one or more of those attending some public function

door·sill (-sil') n. a length of wood, masonry, etc. along the bottom of a doorway; threshold

door·step (-step') n. a step that leads from an outer door to a path, lawn, etc.

door·stop (-stäp') n. 1. a device used to hold a door open at a desired position or prevent it from closing too forcibly or slamming against a wall 2. a thin wooden strip affixed to the frame of a doorway, against which the door closes

☆**door-to-door** (-tə dôr') adj., adv. from one home to the next, calling on each in turn [*door-to-door* selling]

door·way (-wā') n. 1. an opening in a wall that can be closed by a door; portal 2. any means of access

☆**door·yard** (-yärd') n. a yard onto which a door of a house opens

☆**doo·zy** (dōō'zē) n., pl. **-zies** [< ?] [Slang] anything outstanding of its kind

☆**do·pa·mine** (dō'pə mēn', -min) n. [*d(ihydr)o(xy)p(henyl)* + AMINE] an amine essential to normal nerve activity in the brain, an intermediate biochemical product in the synthesis of norepinephrine and melanin

dop·ant (dōp'ənt) n. [DOPE + -ANT] an impurity added to a substance to produce a deliberate change

☆**dope** (dōp) n. [Du. *doop*, sauce, dip, baptism < *doopen*, to dip, akin to G. *taufen:* see DIP] 1. any thick liquid or pasty substance, or other material, used to lubricate or absorb something 2. a) a dressing, varnish, or filler, as for protecting the cloth covering of airplane wings b) any additive, as a food preservative 3. a drug used to stimulate race horses 4. [Slang] any drug or narcotic 5. a slow-witted, stupid, or lethargic person 6. [Slang] a) advance information on a race horse's condition b) any information, esp. advance information for prediction 7. *Photog.* a developer —vt. **doped, dop'ing** 1. to give dope to; treat with dope 2. to drug or stupefy 3. to introduce an adulterant, additive, or impurity into (another substance) in order to produce a deliberate change —**dope out** [Colloq.] to figure out or work out; solve

☆**dope fiend** [Old Slang] a drug addict

☆**dope·ster** (dōp'stər) n. [DOPE (OUT) + -STER] [Colloq.] one who analyzes or predicts trends as in politics or sports

☆**do·pey, do·py** (dō'pē) adj. **-pi·er, -pi·est** [Slang] 1. under the influence of a narcotic 2. mentally slow or confused; lethargic or stupid —**do'pi·ness** n.

dop·pel·gäng·er (däp''l gaŋ'ər; G. dō'p'l gaŋ'ər) n. [G. < *doppel*, double + *gänger*, goer: see GANG²] the supposed ghostly double or wraith of a living person

Dop·pler effect (däp'lər) [after Christian *Doppler* (1803–53), Austrian mathematician and physicist] the apparent change of frequency of sound waves or light waves, varying with the relative velocity of the source and the observer: if the source and observer are drawing closer together, the observed frequency is higher than the emitted frequency

Dor·a (dôr'ə) a feminine name: see DOROTHEA, THEODORA

do·ra·do (də rä'dō) n. [Sp., lit., gilded, pp. of *dorar* < LL. *deaurare:* see DORY²] *same as* DOLPHIN (sense 2) —[D-] a S constellation, near the south celestial pole, including most of the large Magellanic cloud

dor·bee·tle (dôr'bēt''l) n. [< ME. *dore* (< OE. *dora*, a beetle < IE. base *dher-*, to buzz, whence Gr. *thrylein*, to murmur, babble) + BEETLE¹] 1. any of several European dung beetles (family Scarabaeidae) 2. any beetle that flies with a buzzing sound Also **dor**

Dor·cas (dôr'kəs) [L. < Gr. *Dorkas*, lit., gazelle] 1. a feminine name 2. *Bible* a woman who spent her life making clothes for the poor: Acts 9:36–41

Dor·dogne (dôr dōn'y') river in SW France, uniting with the Garonne to form the Gironde estuary: c. 300 mi.

Dor·drecht (dôr'dreHt) city in SW Netherlands, on the Maas (Meuse) delta: pop. 88,000

Do·ré (dô rā'), **(Paul) Gus·tave** (güs täv') 1832?–83; Fr. book illustrator & painter

do·ré (dô rā′) *adj.* [Fr.: see DORY²] coated with gold or a gold color; gilded [bronze *doré*]

dor·hawk (dôr′hôk′) *n.* [*dor*, a buzzing insect + HAWK¹; so named from eating such insects] *same as* NIGHTJAR

Do·ri·an (dôr′ē ən) *adj.* [< L. *Dorius* < Gr. *Dōrios* < *Doris*] *same as* DORIC —*n.* a native of Doris; member of a race that formed one of the four main divisions of the ancient Greeks

Dor·ic (dôr′ik, där′-) *adj.* [L. *Doricus* < Gr. *Dōrikos*] 1. of Doris, its people, their language, or culture 2. designating or relating to the classic order of architecture characterized by simplicity of form, esp. by fluted, heavy columns with simple capitals: cf. CORINTHIAN, IONIC —*n.* 1. the Greek dialect of Doris 2. a rustic English dialect as contrasted with Standard English

Dor·is (-is) [L. < Gr. *Dōris*] 1. a feminine name 2. ancient mountainous region in what is now WC Greece: regarded as the home of the Dorians: see GREECE, map

DORIC CAPITAL

Dor·king (dôr′kin) *n.* [< *Dorking*, town in Surrey, England] one of the oldest breeds of domestic fowl, having a large, heavy body, short legs, five-toed feet, and plumage of varying colors

☆**dorm** (dôrm) *n.* [Colloq.] *same as* DORMITORY

dor·man·cy (dôr′mən sē) *n.* the state of being dormant

dor·mant (-mənt) *adj.* [ME. < OFr. prp. of *dormir* < L. *dormire* < IE. base *dre-*, to sleep, whence Sans. *ni-dra*, sleep] 1. sleeping 2. as if asleep; quiet; still 3. inoperative; inactive 4. *Biol. a)* torpid in winter; in a state of suspended animation *b)* live, but not actively growing 5. *Heraldry* lying down in a sleeping position [a lion *dormant*]: cf. COUCHANT —*SYN.* see LATENT

dor·mer (dôr′mər) *n.* [OFr. *dormeour* < L. *dormitorium*: see DORMITORY] 1. a window set upright in a sloping roof 2. the roofed projection in which this window is set Also **dormer window**

dor·mie, dor·my (dôr′mē) *adj.* [< ? Fr. *dormi*, asleep] *Golf* ahead of an opponent by as many holes as are yet to be played

dor·mi·to·ry (dôr′mə tôr′ē) *n., pl.* **-ries** [ME. *dormitorie* < L. *dormitorium*, place for sleeping < *dormitorius*, of or for sleeping < pp. of *dormire*: see DORMANT] 1. a room, building, or part of a building with sleeping accommodations for a number of people 2. a building with many rooms that provide sleeping and living accommodations for a number of people, as at college 3. [Chiefly Brit.] a suburb of a large city, esp. one that lacks recreational and cultural activities of its own: in full **dormitory suburb** (or **town**)

DORMER

dor·mouse (dôr′mous′) *n., pl.* **-mice** (-mīs′) [ME. *dormous*; altered by folk etym. (after *mous*, MOUSE) < OFr. *dormeuse*, sleepy, sluggish < *dormir*: see DORMANT] any of several small, furry-tailed, mostly tree-dwelling old-world rodents (family Gliridae) that somewhat resemble squirrels

dor·nick¹ (dôr′nik) *n.* [< *Doornik*, Fl. name of Tournai, Belgium, where it was originally made] a heavy damask formerly used for hangings, vestments, etc.

☆**dor·nick²** (dôr′nik) *n.* [Ir. Gael. *dornóg*, ScotGael. *doirneag* < *dorn*, hand] a stone of a size suitable for throwing

Dor·o·the·a (dôr′ə thē′ə, där′-) [L. < Gr. *Dōrothea*, lit., gift of God < *dōron*, gift + *theos*, God] a feminine name: var. **Dorothy**; dim. **Dolly, Doll, Dora, Dot, Dotty**

Dor·o·thy (dôr′ə thē, där′-; dôr′thē) a feminine name: see DOROTHEA

dorp (dôrp) *n.* [Du., akin to G. *dorf*, THORP] [Obs.] a village; hamlet

dor·sad (dôr′sad′) *adv.* [< L. *dorsum*, the back + -AD²] toward the back or posterior part of the body

dor·sal¹ (dôr′s'l) *adj.* [ME. < ML. *dorsalis* < L. *dorsualis* < *dorsum*, the back] 1. of, on, or near the back 2. *Bot.* on or of the underside of a surface —**dor′sal·ly** *adv.*

dor·sal², dor·sel (-s'l) *n. same as* DOSSAL

dorsal lip that part of the rim of the blastopore that lies on the future dorsal side of the embryo: in vertebrates it contains the organizer that determines the position of the future nerve cord

dorsal root the more posterior of the two roots that merge to form each spinal nerve: it contains the nerve fibers that transmit sensation

Dor·set Horn (dôr′sət) any of a breed of large-horned sheep with wool of medium length: orig. from Dorsetshire

Dor·set·shire (-shir) county in SW England, on the English Channel: 974 sq. mi.; pop. 322,000: also **Dor′set**

dor·si- (dôr′si) [see DORSO] *a combining form meaning:* 1. of, on, or along the back *same as* DORSO-

dor·si·ven·tral (dôr′si ven′trəl) *adj.* 1. *Bot.* having both dorsal and ventral surfaces 2. *Zool. same as* DORSOVENTRAL

dor·so- (dôr′sō) [< L. *dorsum*, the back] *a combining form meaning:* 1. the back and 2. *same as* DORSI-

dor·so·ven·tral (dôr′sō ven′trəl) *adj.* 1. *Bot. same as* DORSIVENTRAL 2. *Zool.* extending from the dorsal to the ventral side

dor·sum (dôr′səm) *n., pl.* **-sa** (-sə) [L.] 1. the back (of an animal) 2. any part corresponding to or like the back [the *dorsum* of the hand]

Dort (dôrt) *same as* DORDRECHT

Dort·mund (dôrt′moont; *E.* dôrt′mənd) city in W West Germany, in North Rhine—Westphalia: pop. 655,000

dort·y (dôr′tē) *adj.* [< Scot. dial. *dort*, to sulk (< Scot-Gael., prob. ult. < IE. *dord-*, partial redupl. of base *der-*, to grumble, whence Gr. *darda*, a bee) + -Y²] [Scot.] bad-tempered; sullen

do·ry¹ (dôr′ē) *n., pl.* **-ries** [AmInd. (Central America) *dori, duri*, a dugout] a small, flat-bottomed fishing boat with high, outward curving sides

do·ry² (dôr′ē) *n., pl.* **-ries** [ME. *dorre* < MFr. *dorée*, lit., gilt, fem. of *doré*, pp. of *dorer* < LL. *deaurare* < L. *de-*, intens. + *aurare*, to gild < *aurum*, gold: see AUROUS] 1. *same as* JOHN DORY 2. *same as* WALLEYED PIKE

dos-à-dos (dō′zä dō′; *for 2* dō′sē-) *adv.* [Fr.] back to back —*n., pl.* **dos′-à-dos′** (-dōz′) 1. any seat, carriage, etc. in which the occupants sit back to back 2. a movement in various folk dances, in which two dancers approach each other, pass back to back, and return to their original positions: often written **do-si-do** (dō′sē-)

dos·age (dōs′ij) *n.* 1. a dosing or being dosed 2. the system to be followed in taking doses, as of medicine [the prescribed *dosage* is 1/2 teaspoon every hour] 3. the amount used in a dose 4. the adding of an ingredient to wine, esp. to champagne, to flavor or strengthen it

dose (dōs) *n.* [ME. < OFr. < ML. *dosis* < Gr. *dosis*, orig., a giving < *didonai*, to give] 1. exact amount of a medicine or extent of some other treatment to be given or taken at one time or at stated intervals 2. amount of a punishment or other unpleasant experience undergone at one time 3. the amount of radiation delivered to a particular area or to a given part of the body 4. any ingredient added to wine, esp. champagne, to flavor or strengthen it 5. [Slang] a venereal infection, esp. gonorrhea —*vt.* **dosed, dos′ing** [< the *n.*] 1. to give a dose or doses to 2. to give (medicine, etc.) in doses 3. to add something to (wine) for increasing flavor or strength —*vi.* to take a dose or doses of medicine

do·sim·e·ter (dō sim′ə tər) *n.* [see DOSE & -METER] a small device for measuring the number of roentgens absorbed in a single exposure to radiation —**do′si·met′ric** (-sə met′rik) *adj.* —**do·sim′e·try** (-sim′ə trē) *n.*

Dos Pas·sos (dəs pas′əs), **John** (**Roderigo**) 1896–1970; U.S. writer

doss (däs) *n.* [< Fr. *dos*, a back < VL. *dossum* < L. *dorsum*: see DORSAL¹] [Brit. Slang] a bed or bunk, esp. in a cheap lodging house —*vi.* [Brit. Slang] to sleep

dos·sal, dos·sel (däs′'l) *n.* [ML. *dossale*, var. of *dorsale* < *dorsalis*: see DORSAL¹] 1. formerly, an ornamental upholstery at the back of a chair, throne, etc. 2. an ornamental cloth hung behind an altar, at the back of a chancel, etc.

dos·ser (-ər) *n.* [ME. < OFr. *dossier* < *dos*, the back: see DOSS] 1. *same as* PANNIER (sense 1) 2. *same as* DOSSAL

doss house [see DOSS] [Brit. Slang] a place where a night's lodging can be had very cheaply

dos·si·er (däs′ē ā′, dôs′-) *n.* [Fr. < *dos* (see DOSS): so named because labeled on the back] a collection of documents concerning a particular person or matter

dos·sil (däs′'l) *n.* [ME. *dosel*, a barrel spigot < OFr. *doisil* < VL. *duciculus*, dim. < L. *ducere*, to lead, draw] a plug, wad, or fold of cotton or cloth, as for a wound

dost (dust) *archaic 2d pers. sing., pres. indic., of* DO¹: *used with* thou (chiefly as an auxiliary)

Dos·to·ev·ski (dôs′tô yef′skē), **Feo·dor Mi·khai·lo·vich** (fyô′dôr mi khī′lô vich) 1821–81; Russ. novelist: also sp. **Dos′to·yev′sky**

DOT Department of Transportation

dot¹ (dät) *n.* [OE. *dott*, head of boil: prob. reinforced (16th c.) by Du. *dot*, akin to G. *dütte*, nipple, Du. *dodde*, a plug, Norw., LowG. *dott*, little heap or swelling] 1. a tiny spot, speck, or mark, esp. one made with or as with a pointed object; as, *a)* the mark placed above an *i* or *j* in writing or printing *b) Math.* a decimal point; also, a point used as a symbol of multiplication *c) Music* a point after a note or rest, increasing its time value by one half; also, a point put above or below a note to show that it is staccato 2. any small, round spot [polka *dot*] 3. *Telegraphy* a short sound or click as in Morse code: cf. DASH —*vt.* **dot′ted, dot′ting** 1. to mark with or as with a dot 2. to make or form with dots [a *dotted* line] 3. to cover with or as with dots; appear as dotlike parts in [gas stations *dotted* the landscape] —*vi.* to make a dot or dots —**dot one's i's and cross one's t's** to be minutely correct or detailed in doing or saying something —**on the dot** [Colloq.] at the exact time or point —**dot′ter** *n.*

dot² (dät) *n.* [Fr. < L. *dos* (gen. *dotis*) < *dare*, to give] a woman's marriage dowry —**do·tal** (dōt′'l) *adj.*

dot·age (dōt′ij) *n.* [ME. < *doten*, DOTE] 1. feeble and childish state due to old age; senility 2. a doting; foolish or excessive affection

dot·ard (-ərd) *n.* [ME. < *doten*, DOTE] a person in his dotage; foolish and doddering old person

do·ta·tion (dō tā′shən) *n.* [ME. *dotacioun* < OFr. *dotation* < ML. *dotatio* < L. *dotare*, to endow: cf. DOT²] an endowing or endowment

dote (dōt) *vi.* **dot′ed, dot′ing** [ME. *doten*, akin to MDu. *doten*, to dote & *dotten*, to be insane: for IE. base, see DODDER¹] 1. to be foolish or weak-minded, esp. because of old age 2. to be excessively or foolishly fond (with *on* or *upon*) —**dot′er** *n.*

doth (duth) [cf. DOETH] *archaic 3d pers. sing., pres. indic.,* of DO¹ (chiefly in auxiliary uses)

Do·than (dō′thən) [after *Dothan*, city in ancient Palestine (see Gen. 37:17)] city in SE Ala.: pop. 37,000

dot·ing (dōt′in) *adj.* foolishly or excessively fond —**dot′ing·ly** *adv.*

☆**dotted swiss** a type of fine, sheer, crisp fabric, as of cotton, with dots woven or applied to the surface: it is used for blouses, curtains, etc.

dot·ter·el (dät′ər əl) *n., pl.* **-els,** for 1 **-el:** see PLURAL, II, D, 1 [ME. *doterel* < *doten*, DOTE: so called because regarded as stupid and easy to catch] 1. a European and Asian plover (*Charadrius morinellus*) with a short bill 2. [Brit. Dial.] an easy dupe

dot·tle, dot·tel (dät′'l) *n.* [ME. *dotelle*, irreg. var. of *dosel*, DOSSIL] the tobacco plug left in the bowl of a pipe after it has been smoked

dot·ty (dät′ē) *adj.* **-ti·er, -ti·est** [< DOT¹ + -Y²] 1. covered with dots; dotted 2. [Colloq.] feeble; unsteady; shaky 3. [Colloq.] feeble-minded or crazy

Dou (dou), **Ge·rard** (gā′rärt) 1613–75; Du. painter: also sp. **Douw, Dow**

Dou·ai (dōō ā′) city in N France: pop. 48,000: formerly sp. **Dou·ay′**

Dou·a·la (dōō ä′lə) seaport in Cameroun: pop. 150,000

Douay Bible an English version of the Bible translated from the Latin Vulgate edition for the use of Roman Catholics: the New Testament was orig. published at Reims (1582) and the Old Testament at Douai (1609–1610): also called **Douay Version**

dou·ble (dub′'l) *adj.* [ME. < OFr. < L. *duplus*, lit., twofold (akin to Gr. *diploos*) < *duo*, TWO + *-plus* < IE. *pel-*, to fold, whence L. *plicare*, to fold: cf. SIMPLE, HAPLO-, FOLD¹] 1. two combined; twofold; duplex 2. having two layers; folded in two 3. having two of one kind; paired; repeated [a *double* consonant] 4. being of two kinds; dual [a *double* standard] 5. having two meanings; ambiguous 6. twice as much, as many, as large, etc. [pay *double* fare] 7. of extra size, value, strength, or quantity 8. designed or made for two [a *double* bed] 9. characterized by duplicity; two-faced; deceiving [leading a *double* life] 10. having a tone an octave lower [*double* bass] 11. *Bot.* having more than one set of petals —*adv.* 1. to twice the extent or degree; twofold 2. two together; in or by pairs [to ride *double*] —*n.* 1. anything twice as much, as many, or as large as normal 2. a person or thing looking very much like another; duplicate; counterpart 3. a substitute actor or singer 4. a stand-in or substitute, as in motion pictures 5. a fold; second ply 6. a sharp turn or shift of direction 7. a trick; shift 8. [*pl.*] a game of tennis, handball, etc. with two players on each side ☆9. *Baseball* a hit on which the batter reaches second base 10. *Bridge a)* the doubling of an opponent's bid *b)* a hand that makes this possible —*vt.* **-bled, -bling** 1. to make double; make twice as much or as many; multiply by two 2. to fold; add another ply to [*double* the bandage] 3. to repeat or duplicate 4. to be the double of ☆5. *Baseball a)* to put out (the second runner) in executing a double play *b)* to advance (a runner) by hitting a double 6. *Bridge* to increase the point value or penalty of (an opponent's bid) 7. *Music* to supply the upper or lower octave to (another part or voice) [*double* the tenor in brass] 8. *Naut.* to sail around [they *doubled* Cape Horn] —*vi.* 1. to become double; increase twofold 2. to bend or turn sharply backward [the animal *doubled* on its tracks] 3. to serve as a double 4. to serve an additional purpose ☆5. [Colloq.] to double-date ☆6. *Baseball* to hit a double —**double back** 1. to fold back 2. to turn and go back in the direction from which one came —☆**double in brass** [Slang] 1. to be capable of playing another (esp., brass-wind) instrument in addition to one's usual instrument 2. to do or be capable of doing something additional to one's specialty —**double up** 1. to fold completely; clench (one's fist) 2. to bend over, as in laughter or pain 3. to share a room, etc. with someone —**on** (or **at**) **the double** [Colloq.] 1. in double time 2. quickly

double agent a spy who infiltrates an enemy espionage organization in order to betray it

double bar *Music* two parallel vertical lines drawn through the staff to indicate the end of a movement

dou·ble-bar·reled (-bar′əld) *adj.* 1. having two barrels, as a kind of shotgun 2. having two purposes 3. that can be taken in two ways; ambiguous

double bass (bās′) the largest and deepest-toned instru-

ment of the violin family (orig. of the viol family), with a range of approximately three octaves

double bassoon *same as* CONTRABASSOON

DOUBLE BASS

double (Blackwall) hitch a kind of knot: see KNOT, illus.

☆**dou·ble-blind** (-blind′) *adj.* designating or of a technique or method of evaluating the effects of a drug, course of treatment, etc. in which neither the subjects nor the researchers know who specifically is receiving the drug or treatment under study

☆**double boiler** a cooking utensil consisting of two pans, one of which fits over the other: the heat from water boiling in the lower one cooks the food in the upper without scorching

double bond *Chem.* the sharing of two pairs of electrons between two atoms, usually represented in structural formulas by $-C=C-$

dou·ble-breast·ed (-bres′tid) *adj.* overlapping so as to provide a double thickness of material across the breast, and having a double row of buttons, as a coat

☆**dou·ble-check** (-chek′) *vt., vi.* to check again; verify —*n.* the act of double-checking

double chin a fold of excess flesh beneath the chin

double counterpoint a type of counterpoint in which either part may be made the higher or the lower part

dou·ble-cross (-krôs′) *vt.* [Colloq.] to betray (a person) by doing the opposite of, or intentionally failing to do, what one has promised —**dou′ble-cross′er** *n.*

double cross 1. a hybrid produced by crossing two pairs of inbred lines and then intercrossing the offspring of these crosses, as in producing seed corn 2. [Colloq.] a double-crossing; treachery

double dagger a mark (‡) used in printing and writing to indicate a note or cross reference; diesis

☆**dou·ble-date** (-dāt′) *vi., vt.* **-dat′ed, -dat′ing** [Colloq.] to go out on a double date (with)

☆**double date** [Colloq.] a social engagement shared by two couples

Dou·ble·day (dub′'l dā′), **Abner** 1819–93; U.S. army officer: traditional inventor of baseball

dou·ble-deal·ing (dub′'l dēl′in) *n.* the act of doing the opposite of what one pretends to do; duplicity; deceit —**dou′ble-deal′er** *n.*

dou·ble-deck·er (-dek′ər) *n.* 1. any structure or vehicle with an upper deck or floor ☆2. [Colloq.] a sandwich with two layers of filling and three slices of bread

☆**double eagle** a former U.S. gold coin with a face value of $20

dou·ble-edged (-ejd′) *adj.* 1. having two cutting edges 2. applicable against as well as for: said of an argument, remark, etc.

dou·ble-en·ten·dre (dōō′blän tän′drə, dub′'l än-) *n.* [Fr. (now obs.), double meaning] 1. a term with two meanings, esp. when one of them has a risqué or indecorous connotation 2. the use of such a term or terms; ambiguity

double entry a system of bookkeeping in which every transaction is entered as both a debit and a credit in conformity with the underlying accounting equation which states that assets equal liabilities plus net worth

double exposure *Photog.* 1. the making of two exposures on the same film or plate, either by mistake or for a composite photograph 2. such a photograph

dou·ble-faced (dub′'l fāst′) *adj.* 1. having two faces or aspects 2. having a finished nap on both sides: said of cloth 3. hypocritical; insincere; two-faced

☆**double feature** two full-length motion pictures on the same program

double flat a symbol (♭♭) placed before a note to show that it is to be lowered two halftones

dou·ble-gang·er (-gaŋ′ər) *n.* [partial transl. and modification of DOPPELGÄNGER] *same as* DOPPELGÄNGER

☆**dou·ble-head·er** (-hed′ər) *n.* 1. a train pulled by two locomotives 2. two games played in succession on the same day, usually by the same two teams

double indemnity a clause in life insurance policies providing for the payment of twice the face value of the contract in the case of accidental death

☆**double jeopardy** *Law* the jeopardy in which a defendant is placed by a second prosecution for the same offense or crime: prohibited by the U.S. Constitution

dou·ble-joint·ed (-join′tid) *adj.* having joints that permit limbs, fingers, etc. to bend at other than the usual angles

dou·ble-knit (-nit′) *adj.* knit with a double stitch, which gives extra thickness to the fabric

dou·ble-mind·ed (-min′did) *adj.* undecided in mind; vacillating

double negative the use of two negatives in a single statement having a negative force (Ex.: "I didn't hear nothing"): now generally regarded as substandard

☆**dou·ble-park** (-pärk′) *vt., vi.* to park (a vehicle) parallel to another parked vehicle alongside a curb

☆**double play** *Baseball* a single play in which two players are put out

double pneumonia pneumonia of both lungs

dou·ble-quick (-kwik′) *adj.* very quick —*n.* a very quick marching pace; specif., *same as* DOUBLE TIME (sense 2) —☆*vi., vt.* to march at such a pace —*adv.* at this pace

dou·ble-reed (-rēd′) *adj.* designating or of any of a group of woodwind instruments, as the oboe or bassoon, having two reeds that are separated by a narrow opening and vibrated against each other by the breath —*n.* a double-reed instrument

double refraction *same as* BIREFRINGENCE

double salt *Chem.* 1. a salt, as sodium potassium tartrate, which in solution produces two different cations or anions 2. any compound that may be regarded as a combination of two different salts

double sharp a symbol (✕ or ⁑) placed before a note to show that it is to be raised two halftones

dou·ble-space (-spās′) *vt., vi.* **-spaced′, -spac′ing** to type (copy) so as to leave a full space between lines

double standard a system, code, criterion, etc. applied unequally; specif., a code of behavior that is stricter for women than for men, esp. in matters of sex

double star 1. *same as* BINARY STAR 2. two stars at widely different distances from the earth, whose directions make them appear close together

dou·ble-stop (-stäp′) *vi.* to produce two tones simultaneously on a stringed instrument by drawing the bow over two strings at the same time —*n.* 1. the two tones thus produced 2. the notes showing these

dou·blet (dub′lit) *n.* [ME. < OFr., dim. of *double*, orig., something folded, a kind of material: see DOUBLE] 1. a man's closefitting jacket with or without sleeves, worn chiefly from the 14th to the 16th cent. 2. either of a pair of similar things 3. a pair; couple 4. [*pl.*] a pair of thrown dice with identical sides uppermost 5. a simulated gem produced by cementing two crystals together with a layer of colored glass between them 6. *Linguis.* either of two words that derive ultimately from the same source but have changed in form (e.g., *card, chart; regal, royal*) 7. *Radio same as* DIPOLE (ANTENNA)

double tackle a pulley block with two grooved wheels

DOUBLET

☆**double take** a delayed reaction to some remark, situation, etc., in which there is at first unthinking acceptance and then startled surprise on a second glance as the real meaning or actual situation suddenly becomes clear: often used as a comic device in acting

double talk 1. ambiguous and deceptive talk 2. deliberately confusing or unintelligible talk made up of a mixture of real words and meaningless syllables

dou·ble-think, dou·ble·think (-thiŋk′) *n.* [coined (1949) by Geo. ORWELL, in *1984*] illogical or deliberately perverse thinking in terms that distort or reverse the truth to make it more acceptable

double time ☆1. a rate of payment twice as high as usual, as for work on Sundays 2. a marching cadence of 180 three-foot steps a minute: normal cadence is 120 steps a minute 3. *Music* duple time

dou·ble-tongue (-tuŋ′) *vi.* **-tongued′, -tongu′ing** to alternate quickly and regularly the use of the tip and base of the tongue in playing a flute, trumpet, etc. to facilitate rapid articulation

dou·ble-tongued (-tuŋd′) *adj.* deceitful

☆**dou·ble·tree** (dub′l trē′) *n.* [DOUBLE + (SINGLE)TREE] a crossbar on a wagon, carriage, plow, etc., to each end of which the singletrees are attached when two horses are harnessed abreast

dou·bloon (du blōōn′) *n.* [Fr. *doublon* < Sp. *doblón* < *dobla*, DOBLA] an obsolete Spanish gold coin which varied in value from about $5 to about $16

‡**dou·blure** (dōō blür′) *n.* [Fr., lining < *double*, DOUBLE] an ornamental lining, as of leather, on the inner side of a book cover

dou·bly (dub′lē) *adv.* 1. twice; to twice the degree or quantity 2. two at a time

Doubs (dōō) river in E France, flowing into the Saône: c. 270 mi.

doubt (dout) *vi.* [ME. *douten* < OFr. *douter* < L. *dubitare*, to waver in opinion (see DUBIOUS); *-b-* reintroduced, after L., in 16th cent.] 1. to be uncertain in opinion or belief; be undecided 2. to be inclined to disbelief 3. [Archaic] to hesitate —*vt.* 1. to be uncertain about; question; feel distrust of 2. to be inclined to disbelieve; be skeptical of 3. [Archaic] to be fearful or suspicious of —*n.* 1. *a)* a wavering of opinion or belief; lack of conviction; uncertainty *b)* lack of trust or confidence 2. a condition of uncertainty [the outcome was in *doubt*] 3. an unsettled point or matter; difficulty 4. [Obs.] apprehension or fear —SYN. see UNCERTAINTY —**beyond** (or **without**) **doubt** certainly —**no doubt** 1. certainly 2. very likely; probably —**doubt′a·ble** *adj.* —**doubt′er** *n.* —**doubt′ing·ly** *adv.*

doubt·ful (-fəl) *adj.* [ME. *doutefull*] 1. in doubt; not clear or definite; ambiguous; not clearly predictable; uncertain; unsure 3. giving rise to doubt or suspicion; questionable, as in reputation 4. feeling doubt; unsettled in opinion or belief —**doubt′ful·ly** *adv.* —**doubt′ful·ness** *n.* SYN.—**doubtful** implies strong uncertainty as to the probability, value, honesty, validity, etc. of something [a *doubtful* remedy]; **dubious** is less strong, suggesting merely vague suspicion or hesitancy [*dubious* about the future]; **questionable** strictly suggests only that there is some reason for doubt, but it is often used as a euphemism to imply strong suspicion, almost amounting to certainty, of immorality, dishonesty, etc. [a *questionable* reputation]; **problematical** implies only uncertainty with no suggestion of a moral question [a *problematical* success] —ANT. **certain, sure**

doubt·ing Thomas (dout′iŋ) [after the apostle THOMAS] a person who habitually doubts; chronic skeptic

doubt·less (-lis) *adj.* [ME. *douteles*] [Rare] free from doubt; sure —*adv.* 1. without doubt; certainly 2. probably —**doubt′less·ly** *adv.* —**doubt′less·ness** *n.*

douce (dōōs) *adj.* [ME. < OFr., fem. of *douz* < L. *dulcis*: see DULCET] [Scot.] pleasant or hospitable

‡**dou·ceur** (dōō sër′) *n.* [Fr., lit., sweetness: see prec.] [Archaic] 1. gentleness 2. a gratuity; tip

douche (dōōsh) *n.* [Fr. < It. *doccia*, shower bath, orig., conduit, back-formation < *doccione*, water pipe < L. *ductio*, a leading away < *ductus*, pp. of *ducere*, to lead, bring] 1. a jet of liquid applied externally or internally to some part of the body, esp. as a bath or treatment 2. a bath or treatment of this kind 3. a device for douching —*vt., vi.* **douched, douch′ing** to apply a douche to (some part of the body, esp. the vagina)

dough (dō) *n.* [ME. < OE. *dag*, akin to Goth. *daigs*, G. *teig* < IE. base *dheigh-*, to knead, form, whence Gr. *teichos*, wall, L. *fingere*, to form: cf. FIGURE] 1. a mixture of flour, liquid, and other ingredients, worked into a soft, thick mass for baking into bread, pastry, etc. 2. any pasty mass like this ☆3. [Slang] money

dough·boy (-boi′) *n.* 1. a boiled dumpling ☆2. [Colloq.] a U.S. infantryman, esp. of World War I

☆**dough·face** (-fās′) *n.* [DOUGH + FACE] in the Civil War, a Northerner who sided with the South on the slavery issue

dough·nut (-nut′) *n.* a small, usually ring-shaped cake of sweetened, leavened dough, fried in deep fat

dough·ty (dout′ē) *adj.* **-ti·er, -ti·est** [ME. < OE. *dohtig*, altered < *dyhtig* (after cognate *dohte*, past tense of *dugan*, to avail), akin to G. *tüchtig*, fit, good, excellent < IE. base *dheugh-*, to press, give abundantly] valiant; brave: now used humorously with a somewhat archaic flavor —**dough′-ti·ly** *adv.* —**dough′ti·ness** *n.*

Dough·ty (dout′ē), C(harles) M(ontagu) 1843–1926; Eng. travel writer & poet

dough·y (dō′ē) *adj.* **dough′i·er, dough′i·est** of or like dough; soft, pasty, flabby, etc. —**dough′i·ness** *n.*

Doug·las[1] (dug′ləs) [< Gael., lit., black stream] 1. a masculine name: dim. **Doug** 2. a prominent Scottish noble family, including esp. Sir James, *a)* 1286?–1330; military leader: called *Black Douglas b)* 1358?–88; military leader 3. (George) Norman, 1868–1952; Brit. novelist & essayist 4. Stephen A(rnold), 1813–61; U.S. politician: noted for his debates with Lincoln in Illinois senatorial campaign (1858) 5. William O(rville), 1898– ; associate justice, U.S. Supreme Court (1939–)

Doug·las[2] (dug′ləs) capital of the Isle of Man: pop. 19,000

Douglas fir (or **spruce, pine, hemlock**) [after David *Douglas* (1798–1834), Scot. botanist in U.S.] a tall evergreen tree (*Pseudotsuga taxifolia*) of the pine family, found in W N. America and valued for its wood

Doug·lass (dug′ləs), **Frederick** (born *Frederick Augustus Washington Bailey*) 1817?–95; U.S. Negro leader, journalist, & statesman

Dou·kho·bors (dōō′kə bôrz′) *n.pl. same as* DUKHOBORS

doum (dōōm) *n.* [Fr. < Ar. *dawm*] an African palm tree (*Hyphæne thebaica*) bearing an edible fruit about as large as an apple, that tastes somewhat like gingerbread

doup·pi·o·ni, dou·pi·o·ni (dōō′pē ō′nē) *n.* [It. *doppioni*, pl. of *doppione*, a double cocoon, lit., a double < *doppio*, double < L. *duplus*, DOUBLE: sp. infl. by Fr. *doupion* < It.] a thick, silk yarn of irregular ply used chiefly for suit fabrics

dour (door, dōōr, dour) *adj.* [ME. < L. *durus*: see DURABLE] 1. [Scot.] hard; unbending; stern; severe 2. [Scot.] obstinate 3. sullen; gloomy; forbidding —**dour′ly** *adv.* —**dour′ness** *n.*

dou·rine (dōō rēn′) *n.* [Fr.] a disease of horses and mules, caused by a protozoan (*Trypanosoma equiperdum*) and transmitted in copulation

Dou·ro (dō′rōō) river flowing from NC Spain across N Portugal into the Atlantic: c. 500 mi.; Sp. name, DUERO

douse[1] (dous) *vt.* **doused, dous′ing** [16th-c. slang, ? akin to MDu. *dossen*, to beat noisily] 1. orig., to hit forcefully 2. *Naut.* to lower (sails) quickly 3. [Colloq.] to pull off (shoes, clothes, etc.) 4. [Colloq.] to put out (a light or fire) quickly; extinguish

douse[2] (dous) *vt.* **doused, dous′ing** [< ? prec.] 1. to plunge or thrust suddenly into liquid 2. to drench; pour liquid over —*vi.* to get immersed or drenched —*n.* an immersion or drenching

douse³ (douz) *vi.* **doused, dous'ing** *same as* DOWSE²

douze·pers (dōōz'perz') *n.pl.* [ME. *dousse pers* < OFr. *douze pers*, lit., twelve peers] **1.** *Fr. History* the twelve great peers of the realm **2.** *Medieval Romance* the twelve great paladins or knights of Charlemagne

dove¹ (duv) *n.* [ME. *douve* < OE. *dūfe* or ON. *dūfa*, akin to Goth. *dubō*, G. *taube* < IE. base *dheubh-*, smoky, misty, dark (of color), whence DEAF, DUMB] **1.** a bird of the pigeon family (Columbidae), esp. the smaller species, with a full-breasted body, short legs, and a typical cooing cry: it is often used as a symbol of peace ☆**2.** an advocate of measures in international affairs designed to avoid or reduce open hostilities: cf. HAWK¹ **3.** a person regarded as gentle, innocent, or beloved —**dov'ish** *adj.*

dove² (dōv) *alt. pt. of* DIVE

dove·cote (duv'kōt', -kät') *n.* [ME. *douvecote:* see DOVE¹ & COT²] a small house or box with compartments for nesting pigeons, usually on a pole, etc. above the ground: also **dove'cot'** (-kät')

dove·kie, dove·key (duv'kē) *n.* [DOVE¹ + -kie, -key, dim. suffix] **1.** a small auk (*Plautus alle*) of the Arctic and N Atlantic coasts **2.** *same as* BLACK GUILLEMOT

Do·ver (dō'vər) **1.** seaport in Kent, SE England, on the Strait of Dover: pop. 36,000 **2.** capital of Del., in the C part: pop. 17,000 **3. Strait** (or **Straits**) **of,** strait between France and England, joining the North Sea and the English Channel: narrowest point, 21 mi.

Do·ver's powder (dō'vərz) [after Thomas *Dover* (1660–1742), Brit. physician] a preparation of opium, ipecac, etc., formerly used to relieve pain and induce perspiration

dove·tail (duv'tāl') *n.* **1.** a part or thing shaped like a dove's tail; specif., a projecting, wedge-shaped part (*tenon*) that fits into a corresponding cut-out space (*mortise*) to form an interlocking joint **2.** a joint thus formed —*vt.* **1.** to join or fasten together by means of dovetails **2.** to piece together (facts, etc.) so as to make a logically connected whole —*vi.* to fit together closely or logically

DOVETAIL

Dow (dou), **Gerard** *see* DOU

dow·a·ger (dou'ə jər) *n.* [OFr. *douagiere* < *douage,* dowry < *douer,* to give a dowry < L. *dotare,* to endow < *dos:* see DOT²] **1.** a widow with a title or property derived from her dead husband: often used in combination with the title [queen *dowager,* *dowager* duchess] **2.** an elderly woman of wealth and dignity

Dow·den (dou'd'n), **Edward** 1843–1913; Ir. critic, biographer, & Shakespearean scholar

dow·dy (dou'dē) *adj.* **-di·er, -di·est** [< ME. *doude,* an unattractive woman + -Y²] not neat, fashionable, or smart in dress or appearance; shabby; slovenly —*n., pl.* **-dies 1.** a dowdy woman ☆**2.** *same as* PANDOWDY —**dow'di·ly** *adv.* —**dow'di·ness** *n.* —**dow'di·ish** *adj.*

dow·el (dou'əl) *n.* [ME. *doule,* prob. akin to MLowG. *dövel,* G. *döbel,* a plug < ? IE. base *dheubh-*, a peg, wooden pin: cf. DUB¹] a peg or pin of wood, metal, etc., usually fitted into corresponding holes in two pieces to fasten them together —*vt.* **-eled** or **-elled, -el·ing** or **-el·ling** to fasten or furnish with dowels

DOWEL

dow·er (dou'ər) *n.* [ME. *douere* < OFr. *douaire* < ML. *dotarium* < L. *dos:* see DOT²] **1.** that part of a man's property which his widow inherits for life **2.** a dowry **3.** a natural talent, gift, or endowment —*vt.* **1.** to give a dower to **2.** to endow (*with*)

dow·er·y (-ē) *n., pl.* **-er·ies** *same as* DOWRY

☆**dow·itch·er** (dou'ə chər) *n., pl.* **-ers, -er:** see PLURAL, II, D, 1 [< AmInd. (Iroquoian) native name] a medium-sized, long-legged shore bird (*Limnodromus griseus*) of N. America

Dow·land (dou'lənd), **John** 1563?–1626; Eng. lutanist & composer of songs

Down (doun) county in SE Northern Ireland, on the Irish Sea: 952 sq. mi.; pop. 277,000

down¹ (doun) *adv.* [ME. *doun* < *adune,* adown < OE. *adune, ofdune,* from the hill < a-, of-, off, from + *dune,* dat. of *dun,* hill: see DOWN³] **1.** from a higher to a lower place; toward the ground **2.** in or on a lower position or level; specif., to a sitting or reclining position **3.** *a)* in or to a place thought of as lower or below; often, specif., southward [to go *down* to Florida] *b)* out of one's hands [put it *down*] **4.** below the horizon **5.** from an earlier to a later period or person [*down* through the years] **6.** into a low or dejected emotional condition **7.** into a low or prostrate physical condition [to come *down* with a cold] **8.** in or into an inferior position or condition [held *down* by harsh laws] **9.** to a lower amount, value, or bulk [to come *down* in price] **10.** to a less excited or active condition; into a tranquil or quiet state [to settle *down*] **11.** in a serious or earnest manner [to get *down* to work] **12.** completely; to the full extent [loaded *down*] **13.** in cash or when bought [five dollars *down* and the remainder in installments] **14.** in writing; on record [take *down* his name] —*adj.* **1.** descending; directed toward a lower position **2.** in a lower place; on the ground **3.** gone, brought, pulled, etc. down **4.** dejected; discouraged **5.** prostrate; ill **6.** completed; finished [four *down,* six to go]

☆**7.** in cash, as part of the purchase price [a *down* payment] **8.** *Sports* ☆*a)* no longer in play: said of a football *b)* trailing an opponent by a specified number of points, strokes, etc. ☆*c)* *Baseball* put out —*prep.* down toward, along, through, into, or upon —*vt.* **1.** *a)* to put, bring, get, throw, or knock down *b)* to defeat, as in a game **2.** to gulp or eat rapidly —*vi.* [Rare] to go, come, or get down —*n.* **1.** a downward movement or depressed condition; defeat, misfortune, etc.: chiefly in the phrase UPS AND DOWNS ☆**2.** *Football a)* one of four consecutive plays in which a team, in order to keep possession of the ball, must either score or advance the ball at least ten yards *b)* the declaring of the ball as down, or no longer in play —☆**down and out 1.** *Boxing* knocked out **2.** in the state of being penniless, friendless, ill, etc. —**down on** [Colloq.] hostile to; angry or annoyed with —**down to the ground** thoroughly; completely —**down with 1.** put down **2.** overthrow; do away with: an expression of disfavor See also phrases under BREAK¹, PUT, TRACK, etc.

down² (doun) *n.* [ME. *doun* < ON. *dūnn,* akin to Goth. *dauns,* fume < IE. base *dheu-,* to fly like dust, whence L. *fumus* (cf. FUME)] **1.** soft, fine feathers, as on young birds **2.** soft, fine hair or hairy growth

down³ (doun) *n.* [ME. *doun* < OE. *dun,* a hill, akin to ODu. *duna,* LowG. *düne,* sandhill (see DUNE)] **1.** an expanse of open, high, grassy land: *usually used in pl.* **2.** [confused with DUNE] [Archaic] a sandy mound formed by the wind —**the Downs 1.** two ranges of low, grassy hills (**North Downs & South Downs**) in SE England, extending from Hampshire east to the English Channel **2.** roadstead in the Strait of Dover, off the coast of Kent, England

down- (doun) *a combining form meaning* down [*downhill*]

down·beat (-bēt') *n. Music* the downward stroke of the conductor's hand or baton indicating the first beat of each measure —☆*adj.* [Colloq.] grimly realistic; depressing

down·bow (-bō') *n.* a stroke on a violin, etc. in which the bow is drawn across the strings from the handle to the tip: symbol, ⌐

down·cast (-kast', -käst') *adj.* **1.** directed downward **2.** very unhappy or discouraged; sad; dejected —*n. Mining* a ventilating shaft

down·come (-kum') *n.* a comedown; downfall; humiliation

☆**Down East** [Colloq.] New England, esp. Maine: also **down east** —**down'-east'** *adj.* —**down'-east'er** *n.*

down·er (-ər) *n.* [Slang] any depressant or sedative, as a tranquilizer, barbiturate, alcoholic drink, etc.

Dow·ney (dou'nē) [after John G. *Downey,* governor of Calif., 1860–62] city in SW Calif.: suburb of Los Angeles: pop. 88,000

down·fall (doun'fôl') *n.* **1.** *a)* a sudden fall, as from prosperity or power *b)* the cause of such a fall **2.** a sudden, heavy fall, as of snow

down·fall·en (-fôl'n) *adj.* fallen; ruined

☆**down·grade** (-grād') *n.* a downward slope, esp. in a road —*adv.,* downhill; downward —*vt.* **-grad'ed, -grad'ing 1.** to demote to a less skilled job at lower pay **2.** to lower in importance, value, esteem, etc. **3.** to refer to disparagingly; belittle —**on the downgrade** losing status, influence, health, etc.; declining

down·haul (-hôl') *n.* a rope or series of ropes for hauling down a sail

down·heart·ed (-här'tid) *adj.* in low spirits; discouraged; dejected —**down'heart'ed·ly** *adv.*

down·hill (-hil') *adv.* **1.** toward the bottom of a hill; downward **2.** to a poorer condition, status, etc. —*adj.* **1.** sloping or going downward **2.** of or having to do with skiing downhill

down·i·ness (doun'ē nis) *n.* the quality of being downy

Down·ing Street (doun'iŋ) [after Sir George *Downing* (1623–84), who owned property there] **1.** street in the West End of London, location of some of the principal government offices, including the official residence of the prime minister (No. 10) **2.** the British government

down·pour (doun'pôr') *n.* a heavy rain

☆**down·range** (-rānj') *adv., adj.* along the course away from the launching site

down·right (-rīt') *adv.* [ME. *doun riht:* see DOWN¹ & RIGHT] **1.** thoroughly; utterly; really **2.** [Archaic] straight down —*adj.* **1.** absolute; thoroughgoing; utter [a *downright* insult] **2.** straightforward; plain; frank [a *downright* fellow] **3.** [Archaic] going straight downward

☆**down·spout** (-spout') *n.* a vertical pipe for carrying rain water from a roof gutter to ground level

Down's syndrome (dounz) [after J. L. H. *Down* (1828–96), Eng. physician who first described it] *see* MONGOLISM

down·stage (doun'stāj') *adv.* toward the front of the stage —*adj.* having to do with the front of the stage

down·stairs (-sterz') *adv.* **1.** down the stairs **2.** on or to a lower floor —*adj.* situated on a lower floor —*n.* a lower floor or floors

☆**down·state** (-stāt') *n.* that part of a State farther to the south —*adj., adv.* in, to, or from downstate —**down'-stat'er** *n.*

down·stream (-strēm') *adv., adj.* in the direction of the current of a stream

down·swing (-swiŋ') *n.* **1.** the downward part of a swing, as of a golf club **2.** a downward trend, as in business

down·throw (-thrō') *n. Geol.* that side of a fault which has moved downward relative to the other side

down·time (-tīm′) *n.* the time during which a machine, factory, etc. is shut down for repairs or the like
down-to-earth (-tə urth′) *adj.* realistic or practical
☆**down·town** (-toun′) *adj., adv.* of, in, like, to, or toward the lower or main business section of a city or town —*n.* the downtown section of a city or town
down·trod·den (-träd′'n) *adj.* 1. trampled on or down 2. oppressed; subjugated; tyrannized over
down·turn (-turn′) *n.* a downward trend, as in business activity
down under [Colloq.] Australia or New Zealand
down·ward *adv., adj.* [ME. *dounward* < OE. *aduneweard:* see DOWN¹ & -WARD] 1. toward a lower place, position, state, etc. 2. from an earlier to a later time Also **down′wards** *adv.* —**down′ward·ly** *adv.*
down·wash (-wôsh′, -wäsh′) *n.* the downward deflection of air as by an airplane wing
down·wind (-wind′) *adv., adj.* in the direction in which the wind is blowing or usually blows
down·y (-ē) *adj.* **down′i·er, down′i·est** 1. of or covered with soft, fine feathers or hair 2. soft and fluffy, like down
☆**downy mildew** a disease of angiosperms characterized by the appearance of whitish or downy patches of fungus threads on the surfaces of plant parts, caused by various fungi (family Peronosporaceae)
dow·ry (dou′rē) *n., pl.* **-ries** [ME. *douerie* < Anglo-Fr. & OFr. *douarie:* see DOWER] 1. the property that a woman brings to her husband at marriage 2. a natural talent, gift, or endowment 3. [Archaic] a widow's dower 4. [Archaic] a gift by a man to his bride
dowse¹ (dous) *vt.* **dowsed, dows′ing** *same as* DOUSE¹
dowse² (douz) *vi.* **dowsed, dows′ing** [< ? ME. *dushen,* to push down] to search for a source of water or minerals with a divining rod —**dows′er** *n.*
Dow·son (dou′s'n), **Ernest (Christopher)** 1867–1900; Eng. lyric poet
dox·ol·o·gy (däk säl′ə jē) *n., pl.* **-gies** [ML.(Ec.) *doxologia* < Gr.(Ec.) *doxologia,* a praising < *doxologos,* giving praise < *doxa,* praise, opinion < *dokein,* to seem (see DOCTOR) + -*logia,* -LOGY] any of several hymns of praise to God; specif., **a)** the **greater doxology,** which begins *Gloria in excelsis Deo* (glory to God in the highest) **b)** the **lesser doxology,** which begins *Gloria Patri* (glory to the Father) **c)** a hymn beginning "Praise God from whom all blessings flow"
dox·y¹ (däk′sē) *n., pl.* **dox′ies** [< (ORTHO)DOXY, etc.] [Colloq.] a doctrine or creed, esp. in religion
dox·y² (däk′sē) *n., pl.* **dox′ies** [< ? obs. *docke,* rump, or archaic Du. *docke,* doll] [Old Brit. Slang] a woman of low morals; specif., a prostitute or mistress
‡**doy·en** (dwä yan′; E. doi′ən) *n.* [Fr.: see DEAN] the senior member, or dean, of a group —**doy·enne′** (-yen′; E. -en′) *n.fem.*
Doyle (doil), Sir **Arthur Co·nan** (kō′nən) 1859–1930; Eng. physician & novelist: known for his *Sherlock Holmes* stories
doy·ley, doy·ly (doi′lē) *n. same as* DOILY
D'Oyly Carte, Richard *see* CARTE
doz. dozen; dozens
doze (dōz) *vi.* **dozed, doz′ing** [prob. < Scand., as in Ice. (& Sw. dial.) *dusa:* for IE. base, see DIZZY] to sleep lightly or fitfully; nap; be half asleep —*vt.* to spend (time) in dozing (usually with *away*) —*n.* a light sleep; nap —**doze off** to fall into a light sleep —**doz′er** *n.*
doz·en (duz′'n) *n., pl.* **-ens** or, esp. after a number, **-en** [ME. *dozeine* < OFr. *dozaine* < *douze,* twelve < L. *duodecim,* twelve < *duo,* TWO + *decem,* TEN] a set of twelve: see also BAKER's DOZEN —**doz′enth** *adj.*
doz·y (dō′zē) *adj.* **doz′i·er, doz′i·est** [see DOZE] sleepy; drowsy —**doz′i·ly** *adv.* —**doz′i·ness** *n.*
DP, D.P. 1. degree of polymerization 2. diametrical pitch 3. displaced person
D.Ph., D.Phil. Doctor of Philosophy
D.P.H. Doctor of Public Health
dpt. 1. department 2. deponent
Dr. 1. Doctor 2. Drive
dr. 1. debit 2. debtor 3. drachma(s) 4. dram(s)
D.R., D/R, d.r. 1. dead reckoning 2. deposit receipt
drab¹ (drab) *n.* [< Fr. *drap,* cloth < VL. *drappus,* ult. < ? same IE. base as DRAFF] 1. a kind of cloth, esp. a yellowish-brown wool 2. a dull yellowish brown —*adj.* **drab′ber, drab′best** 1. of a dull yellowish-brown color 2. not bright, lively, etc.; dull, dreary, or monotonous —**drab′ly** *adv.* —**drab′ness** *n.*
drab² (drab) *n.* [< Celt., as in Ir. *drabog,* Gael. *drabag,* slattern] 1. a slovenly woman; slattern 2. a prostitute —*vi.* **drabbed, drab′bing** [< the *n.*] to fornicate with prostitutes
drab·bet (drab′it) *n.* [< DRAB¹] [Brit.] a coarse, unbleached linen
drab·ble (drab′'l) *vt.* **-bled, -bling** [ME. *drabelen,* akin to (or < ?) LowG. *drabbeln,* to walk in mud or water] to make wet and dirty by dragging in mud and water; draggle —*vi.* to become drabbled
dra·cae·na (drə sē′nə) *n.* [ModL. < LL., she-dragon < Gr. *drakaina,* fem. of *drakōn,* DRAGON] any of a genus (*Dracaena*)

of tropical shrubs and trees of the agave family, including the dragon tree
drachm (dram) *n.* [ME. *dragme* < OFr. *dragme* < L. *drachma* < Gr.] 1. *same as* DRACHMA 2. *same as* DRAM
drach·ma (drak′mə) *n., pl.* **-mas, -mae** (-mē), **-mai** (-mī) [L. < Gr. *drachmē,* lit., a handful < *drassesthai,* to grasp, take by handfuls < IE. base *dergh-,* to grasp, whence TARGE] 1. an ancient Greek silver coin 2. an ancient Greek unit of weight approximately equal to the weight of this coin 3. any of several modern weights or measures: see DRAM 4. the monetary unit of modern Greece: see MONETARY UNITS, table
Dra·co (drā′kō) 1. 7th cent. B.C.; Athenian statesman & lawgiver: also **Dra′con** (-kän) 2. [L.: see DRAGON] *Astron.* a large N constellation containing the north pole of the ecliptic
Dra·co·ni·an (drā kō′nē ən, drə-) *adj.* 1. of Draco or the very harsh code of laws attributed to him 2. [*sometimes* d-] extremely severe or cruel
dra·con·ic (-kän′ik) *adj.* [< L. *draco:* see DRAGON] 1. of or like a dragon 2. [*usually* D-] Draconian
draff (draf) *n.* [ME. *draf* < ON., akin to G. dial. *treber* (pl.), dregs < IE. *dhrābh-* < base *dher-,* dark refuse, somber] refuse or dregs, esp. of malt after brewing
draft (draft, dräft) *n.* [ME. *draught,* a drawing, pulling, stroke < base of OE. *dragan,* DRAW] 1. **a)** a drawing or pulling, as of a vehicle or load **b)** the thing, quantity, or load pulled 2. **a)** a drawing in of a fish net **b)** the amount of fish caught in one draw 3. **a)** a taking of liquid into the mouth; drinking **b)** the amount taken at one drink 4. **a)** a portion of liquid for drinking; specif., a dose of medicine **b)** [Colloq.] a portion of beer, ale, etc. drawn from a cask 5. **a)** a drawing into the lungs, as of air or tobacco smoke **b)** the amount of air, smoke, etc. drawn in 6. a rough or preliminary sketch of a piece of writing 7. a plan or drawing of a work to be done 8. a current of air, as in a room, heating system, etc. 9. a device for regulating the current of air in a heating system 10. a written order issued by one person, bank, firm, etc., directing the payment of money to another; check 11. a demand or drain made on something 12. **a)** the choosing or taking of an individual or individuals from a group for some special purpose, esp. for compulsory military service **b)** the condition of being so taken ☆**c)** a group of those so taken 13. *Commerce* a deduction allowed for waste or loss in weight 14. *Hydraulics* the size of an opening for the flow of water 15. *Masonry* a narrow border along the edge or across the face of a stone, serving as a guide in leveling the surface 16. *Mechanics* the taper given to a pattern or die so that the work can be removed easily 17. *Naut.* the depth of water that a ship draws, or displaces, esp. when loaded ☆18. *Sports* a system by which a league of professional teams allots to each team exclusive rights to specified individuals in a group of new players —*vt.* 1. to choose or take for some special purpose, as compulsory military service, by drawing from a group 2. to draw off or away 3. to make a preliminary sketch of or working plans for —*adj.* 1. used for pulling loads [*draft* animals] 2. drawn from a cask on order [*draft* beer] 3. in a preliminary or rough form [a *draft* resolution] —**on draft** ready to be drawn directly from the cask —**draft′a·ble** *adj.* —**draft′er** *n.*
draft animal an animal used for pulling heavy loads
☆**draft board** an official board of civilians designated to select qualified persons for compulsory service in the U.S. armed forces
draft dodger ☆a person who avoids or tries to avoid being drafted into the armed forces
☆**draft·ee** (draf tē′, dräf-) *n.* a person drafted, esp. one drafted for service in the armed forces
drafts·man (drafts′mən, dräfts′-) *n., pl.* **-men** (-mən) 1. a person who draws plans of structures or machinery 2. a person who draws up legal documents, speeches, etc. 3. an artist skillful in drawing —**drafts′man·ship′** *n.*
draft·y (draf′tē, dräf′-) *adj.* **draft′i·er, draft′i·est** letting in, having, or exposed to a draft or drafts of air —**draft′i·ly** *adv.* —**draft′i·ness** *n.*
drag (drag) *vt.* **dragged, drag′ging** [ME. *draggen* < ON. *draga* (or OE. *dragan*): see DRAW] 1. to pull or draw with force or effort, esp. along the ground; haul 2. **a)** to move (oneself) with effort **b)** to force into some situation, action, etc. 3. to pull a grapnel, net, etc. over the bottom of (a river, lake, etc.) in searching for something; dredge 4. to draw a harrow over (land) 5. to draw (something) out over a period of time; protract tediously or painfully 6. to bring (a subject) into conversation, a piece of writing, etc. unnecessarily or as if by force ☆7. *Baseball* to hit (a bunt) very lightly —*vi.* 1. to be dragged; be pulled along the ground or other surface; trail 2. to lag behind 3. to be prolonged tediously; move or pass too slowly 4. to search a body of water with a grapnel, net, etc. 5. to cause the sensation of dragging or tugging [a *dragging* fear] 6. [Slang] to draw deeply (on a cigarette, pipe, etc.) —*n.* 1. something dragged or pulled along the ground; specif., **a)** a harrow used for breaking ground **b)** a heavy sledge, or

sled *c*) a large, heavy coach with seats inside and on top **2.** a device used to catch and haul up something under water; grapnel, dragnet, etc. **3.** a thing that checks motion, as in a brake on the wheel of a carriage **4.** anything that hinders or obstructs [a *drag* on his resources] **5.** the amount by which anything drags **6.** the act of dragging; slow, cumbersome movement ☆**7.** [Slang] influence that gains special or undeserved favors; pull ☆**8.** [Slang] *a*) a deep puff of a cigarette, pipe, etc. *b*) a swallow of liquid ☆**9.** [Slang] a dance **10.** [Slang] street; road [the main *drag*] ☆**11.** [Slang] *same as* DRAG RACE ☆**12.** [Slang] a dull or boring person, situation, etc. **13.** [Slang] clothing of the opposite sex, esp. as worn by a male homosexual **14.** *Aeron.* a resisting force exerted on an aircraft parallel to its air stream and opposite in direction to its motion **15.** *Hunting a*) a trail of scent left by an animal *b*) something dragged over the ground to leave a trail of scent *c*) a hunt over such a trail: in full, **drag hunt** —*SYN.* see PULL —**drag on** (or **out**) to prolong or be prolonged tediously —**drag one's feet** (or **heels**) [Slang] to act with deliberate slowness or obvious reluctance; be uncooperative —**drag'ger** *n.*

‡**dra·gée** (drả zhā′) *n.* [Fr.] a sugar-coated candy, nut, or pill

drag·gle (drag′'l) *vt.* **-gled, -gling** [freq. of DRAG] to make wet and dirty by dragging in mud or water —*vi.* **1.** to be or become draggled; trail on the ground **2.** to lag behind; straggle

drag·gle·tail (-tāl′) *n.* a slovenly woman, as one with draggled skirts; slattern —**drag'gle·tailed'** *adj.*

drag·gy (drag′ē) *adj.* **-gi·er, -gi·est** that drags; slow-moving, lethargic, dull, boring, etc.

drag·line (-līn′) *n.* **1.** *same as* DRAGROPE **2.** a machine for excavating

drag link a link connecting the cranks of two engine shafts

drag·net (-net′) *n.* **1.** a net dragged along the bottom of a river, lake, etc. for catching fish **2.** a net for catching small game ☆**3.** an organized system or network for gathering in or catching criminals or others wanted by the authorities

drag·o·man (drag′ə·mən) *n., pl.* **-mans, -men** (-mən) [ME. *drogeman* < OFr. < It. *dragomanno* < MGr. *dragomanos* < Ar. *targumān* < Aram. *tūrgĕmānā* < Assyr. *targūmanu*, akin to *ragāmu*, to speak] in the Near East, an interpreter or professional guide for travelers

drag·on (drag′ən) *n.* [ME. *dragoun* < OFr. *dragon* < L. *draco* < Gr. *drakōn*, dragon, serpent, lit., the seeing one < *derkesthai*, to see < IE. base *derk-, to see, whence OIr. *derc*, eye] **1.** a mythical monster, usually represented as a large reptile with wings and claws, breathing out fire and smoke **2.** a fierce person; esp., a fiercely watchful female guardian; strict chaperon **3.** *a*) formerly, a short musket fastened to a soldier's belt *b*) a soldier armed with such a musket: see DRAGOON **4.** [Archaic] a large serpent or snake **5.** *Bible* (*KJV*) a word used to translate several Hebrew words now understood to mean *serpent, jackal, Old Serpent* (Satan), etc. **6.** *Zool.* any of a number of small tree lizards (genus *Draco*) of SE Asia, with winglike membranes used in gliding from tree to tree —[D-] *Astron.* Draco

drag·on·et (drag′ə nit, drag′ə net′) *n.* [ME. < OFr., dim. of prec.] **1.** a small dragon **2.** any of a family (Callionymidae) of small, brightly colored, scaleless sea fishes related to the goby

drag·on·fly (drag′ən flī′) *n., pl.* **-flies'** any of an order (Odonata) of large insects, harmless to man, having narrow, transparent, net-veined wings and feeding mostly on flies, mosquitoes, etc. while in flight

drag·on·head (-hed′) *n.* any of a genus (*Dracocephalum*) of plants of the mint family, with dense spikes of white or bluish flowers: also **drag'on's-head'**

DRAGONFLY
(to 5 in. long)

drag·on·nade (drag′ə nād′) *n.* [Fr. < *dragon*, DRAGOON] **1.** the persecution of the French Protestants by the troops of Louis XIV, esp. by the dragoons **2.** any persecution or raid in which troops are used

dragon's blood any of several red, resinous substances obtained from various tropical plants and trees, esp. a Malaysian palm (*Daemonorops draco*), and used for coloring varnishes and in photoengraving

dragon tree a tree (*Dracaena draco*) of the agave family, native to the Canary Islands, having variegated foliage and yielding dragon's blood

dra·goon (drə gōōn′) *n.* [Fr. *dragon*: see DRAGON] **1.** formerly, a soldier armed with a short musket, capable of fighting on horseback or on foot; mounted infantryman **2.** a heavily armed cavalryman **3.** [Obs.] a short musket —*vt.* **1.** to harass or persecute by dragoons **2.** to force (*into* doing something); coerce

☆**drag race** [Slang] a race between hot-rod cars (**dragsters**) to test their rates of acceleration from a complete stop, generally held on a short, straight course (**drag strip**) —**drag'-race'** *vi.* **-raced', -rac'ing**

drag·rope (drag′rōp′) *n.* **1.** a rope for dragging something, as a cannon **2.** a rope hung from a balloon or dirigible for use as a variable ballast or mooring line

drag sail (or **sheet**) a sea anchor made from a sail

drain (drān) *vt.* [ME. *dreinen* < OE. *dreahnian*, to strain off, lit., to dry out < base of *dryge*, DRY] **1.** to draw off (liquid, etc.) gradually **2.** to draw water or any liquid from gradually so as to dry or empty [to *drain* swamps] **3.** to receive the waters of [the St. Lawrence *drains* the Great Lakes] **4.** to drink all the liquid from (a cup, glass, etc.) **5.** to exhaust (strength, emotions, or resources) gradually **6.** [Obs.] to filter —*vi.* **1.** to flow off or trickle through gradually **2.** to become dry by the drawing or flowing off of liquid **3.** to disappear gradually; fade [his courage *drained* away] **4.** to discharge its waters [central Europe *drains* into the Danube] —*n.* **1.** a channel or pipe for carrying off water, sewage, etc. **2.** a draining or exhausting **3.** that which gradually exhausts strength, resources, etc. **4.** *Surgery* a tube or other device for drawing off discharge, as from an abscess —**down the drain** lost in a wasteful, heedless way —**drain'er** *n.*

drain·age (-ij) *n.* **1.** the act, process, or method of draining **2.** a system of drains; arrangement of pipes, etc. for carrying off waste matter **3.** that which is drained off **4.** a region or area drained, as by a river

☆**drainage basin** the land drained by a river system

drain·pipe (-pīp′) *n.* a large pipe used to carry off water, sewage, etc.

drake[1] (drāk) *n.* [ME. < WGmc. *drako*, male, as in OHG. *anutrehho*, lit., duck-male] a male duck

drake[2] (drāk) *n.* [ME., dragon < OE. *draca* < L. *draco*, DRAGON] **1.** a small cannon of the 17th and 18th cent. **2.** *an angler's term for* MAYFLY **3.** [Obs.] a dragon

Drake (drāk), **Sir Francis** 1540?–96; Eng. admiral & buccaneer; 1st Englishman to sail around the world

Dra·kens·berg (drä′kənz bᵘrg′) mountain range in E South Africa, extending *c*. 700 mi. from S Cape Province to E Transvaal: highest peak, 11,425 ft.

Drake Passage strait between Cape Horn & the South Shetland Islands: *c*. 400 mi. wide

dram (dram) *n.* [ME. < OFr. *dragme* < ML. *dragma* < L. *drachma*: see DRACHMA] **1.** *Apothecaries' Weight* a unit equal to 60 grains (1/8 ounce): symbol, ʒ **2.** *Avoirdupois Weight* a unit equal to 27.34 grains (1/16 ounce) **3.** *same as* FLUID DRAM **4.** a small drink of alcoholic liquor **5.** a small amount of anything

dra·ma (drä′mə, dram′ə) *n.* [LL. < Gr., a deed, drama, tragedy < *dran*, to do < IE. base *drā-, to work, whence Lett. *darît*, to do] **1.** a literary composition that tells a story, usually of human conflict, by means of dialogue and action, to be performed by actors; play; now often specif., any play that is not a comedy **2.** the art or profession of writing, acting, or producing plays; institution of the theater (often with *the*) **3.** plays collectively [Elizabethan *drama*] **4.** a series of events so interesting, vivid, etc. as to resemble those of a play **5.** the quality of being dramatic

☆**Dram·a·mine** (dram′ə mēn′) *a trademark for* DIMENHYDRINATE —*n.* [d-] a tablet of this substance

dra·mat·ic (drə mat′ik) *adj.* [LL. *dramaticus* < Gr. *dramatikos*] **1.** of or connected with drama **2.** *a*) having the characteristics of a drama, esp. conflict; like a play *b*) filled with action, emotion, or exciting qualities; vivid, striking, etc. Also [Archaic] **dra·mat'i·cal** —**dra·mat'i·cal·ly** *adv.*

dra·mat·ics (-iks) *n.pl.* **1.** [*usually with sing. v.*] the art of performing or producing plays **2.** plays performed and produced by amateurs **3.** dramatic effect; esp., exaggerated emotionalism

dram·a·tis per·so·nae (dram′ə tis pər sō′nē) [ModL. < LL. *dramatis*, gen. of *drama*, DRAMA + L. *personae*, pl. of *persona*, character, PERSON] the characters in a play, or a list of these

dram·a·tist (dram′ə tist) *n.* [see DRAMA] a playwright

dram·a·ti·za·tion (dram′ə ti zā′shən) *n.* **1.** the act of dramatizing **2.** a dramatized version, as of a novel

dram·a·tize (dram′ə tīz′) *vt.* **-tized', -tiz'ing** [< LL. *drama* (gen. *dramatis*), DRAMA + -IZE] **1.** to make into a drama; adapt (a story, events, etc.) for performance on the stage, in a movie, etc. **2.** to regard or present (actions, oneself, etc.) as though in a play; give dramatic quality to —*vi.* **1.** to be capable of being dramatized **2.** to dramatize oneself

dram·a·tur·gy (dram′ə tᵘr′jē) *n.* [G. *dramaturgie* < Gr. *dramatourgia* < *dramatourgos*, dramatist, orig., contriver < *drama* (see DRAMA) + *ergon*, WORK] the art of writing plays or producing them —**dram'a·tur'gic, dram'a·tur'gi·cal** *adj.* —**dram'a·tur'gi·cal·ly** *adv.* —**dram'a·tur'gist, dram'a·turge'** *n.*

dram. pers. dramatis personae

dram·shop (dram′shäp′) *n.* [Brit. Rare] a bar; saloon

Dran·cy (drän sē′) city in NC France: suburb of Paris: pop. 66,000

drank (draŋk) *pt. & often colloq. pp. of* DRINK

drape (drāp) *vt.* **draped, drap'ing** [ME. *drapen*, to weave into cloth, drape < OFr. *draper* < *drap*: see DRAB[1]] **1.** to cover, hang, or decorate with or as with cloth or clothes in loose folds **2.** to arrange (a garment, cloth, etc.) artistically in folds or hangings —*vi.* to hang or fall in folds, as a garment, cloth, etc. —*n.* [Fr. *drap*, cloth] **1.** cloth hanging in loose folds; esp., drapery; curtain: *usually used in pl.* **2.** the manner in which cloth hangs or is cut to hang, as in a garment

drap·er (drā′pər) *n.* [ME. < OFr. *drapier*: see prec.]

1. orig., a maker of cloth **2.** [Brit.] a dealer in cloth and dry goods

Dra·per (drā′pər) **1.** Henry, 1837–82; U.S. astronomer **2.** John William, 1811–82; U.S. historian & scientist, born in England: father of *prec.*

dra·per·y (drā′pər ē) n., pl. -per·ies [ME. & OFr. *draperie:* see DRAPE & -ERY] **1.** [Brit.] *same as* DRY GOODS **2.** [Brit.] the business of a draper **3.** a) hangings, covering, or clothing arranged in loose folds b) an artistic arrangement of such hangings, etc., esp. as represented in sculpture, painting, etc. **4.** [pl.] curtains of heavy material

dras·tic (dras′tik) adj. [Gr. *drastikos,* active < *dran,* to do: see DRAMA] acting with force; having a strong or violent effect; severe; harsh; extreme —**dras′ti·cal·ly** adv.

drat (drat) interj. [aphetic < ′*od rot* < *God rot*] confound! darn!: a mild oath expressing annoyance

drat·ted (drat′id) adj. [cf. DRAT] [Colloq.] darned

Drau (drou) Ger. *name of the* DRAVA

draught (draft, dräft) n., vt., adj. now chiefly Brit. sp. of DRAFT

draughts (drafts, dräfts) n.pl. [Brit.] the game of checkers

draughts·man (-mən) n., pl. -men (-mən) **1.** Brit. sp. of DRAFTSMAN **2.** [Brit.] any of the pieces used in playing draughts —**draughts′man·ship′** n.

draught·y (draf′tē, dräf′-) adj. Brit. sp. of DRAFTY —**draught′i·ly** adv. —**draught′i·ness** n.

Dra·va (drä′vä) river in SC Europe flowing from S Austria into the Danube in N Yugoslavia: c. 450 mi.

drave (drāv) archaic pt. of DRIVE

Dra·vid·i·an (drə vid′ē ən) n. [< Sans. *Drāviḍa,* name of district in southern India] **1.** any of a group of intermixed races chiefly in S India and N Ceylon **2.** the family of non-Indo-European languages spoken by these races, including Tamil, Malayalam, etc. —adj. of the Dravidians or their languages: also **Dra·vid′ic**

draw (drô) vt. drew, drawn, draw′ing [ME. *drawen* < OE. *dragan,* akin to ON. *draga,* to drag, G. *tragen,* to bear, carry < IE. base *dheragh-,* to pull, draw along, whence L. *trahere,* to pull, draw (cf. TRACTION)] **I.** indicating traction **1.** to make move toward one or along with one by or as by exerting force; pull; haul; drag [a horse *draws* the cart] **2.** a) to pull up (a sail, drawbridge, etc.) b) to pull down (a window shade, etc.) c) to pull in (a dragnet, etc.) d) to pull aside or together (a curtain, etc.) e) to pull across, as a violin bow over strings **3.** to pull back the bowstring of (an archer's bow) **4.** to need (a specified depth of water) to float in: said of a ship **5.** *Billiards* to give backspin to (the cue ball) **6.** *Cricket* to deflect (the ball) to the side of the field on which the batsman stands, by a slight turn of the bat **II.** indicating attraction **1.** a) to attract; charm; entice b) to attract (audiences of a specified size or kind) **2.** to take (air, smoke, etc.) into the mouth or lungs; breathe in, inhale, etc. **3.** to bring forth; elicit [his challenge *drew* no reply] **4.** to bring about as a result; bring on; provoke [to *draw* the enemy's fire] **5.** *Med.* to cause a flow of (blood, pus, etc.) to some part **III.** indicating extraction **1.** to pull out; take out; remove; extract, as a tooth, cork, weapon, etc. **2.** a) to remove (a liquid, etc.) by sucking, draining, distilling, seeping, etc. b) to bring up, as water from a well c) to cause (liquid) to flow from an opening, tap, etc. [to *draw* a bath, to *draw* blood] **3.** to take out the viscera of; disembowel **4.** to get or receive from some source [to *draw* a good salary] **5.** to withdraw (money) held in an account **6.** to have accruing to it [savings that *draw* interest] **7.** to write (a check or draft) **8.** to reach (a conclusion or inference); deduce **9.** to get or pick (a number, straw, prize, etc.) at random, as in a lottery **10.** to bring (a contest or game) to a tie **11.** *Card Games* a) to take or get (cards) b) to cause (a card or cards) to be played out [*draw* your opponent's trump] **IV.** indicating tension **1.** to pull out to its fullest extent; make tense; stretch; extend [to *draw* a rope tight] **2.** to pull out of shape; distort **3.** to stretch, flatten, or shape (metal) by die stamping, hammering, etc. **4.** to make metal into (wire) by pulling it through holes **V.** indicating delineation **1.** to "pull" across paper, etc.] **1.** to make (lines, figures, pictures, etc.), as with a pencil, pen, brush, or stylus; sketch; diagram **2.** to describe in words **3.** to make (comparisons, etc.); formulate —vi. **1.** to draw something (in various senses of the vt.) **2.** to be drawn or have a drawing effect **3.** to come; move; approach [to *draw* nearer] **4.** to shrink or contract **5.** to allow a draft of air, smoke, etc. to move through [the chimney *draws* well] **6.** to suck (on a tobacco pipe, etc.) **7.** to attract audiences **8.** to become filled with wind: said of sails **9.** to steep: said of tea **10.** to make a demand or demands (on or upon) **11.** *Hunting* a) to track game by following its scent b) to move slowly toward the game after pointing: said of hounds —n. **1.** a drawing or being drawn (in various senses) **2.** the result of drawing **3.** a thing drawn **4.** the cards dealt as replacements in draw poker **5.** [from the former withdrawal of stakes in case of a tie] stalemate [the game ended in a *draw*] **6.** a thing that attracts interest, audiences, etc. ☆**7.** the movable part of a drawbridge **8.** a gully or ravine that water drains into or through —SYN. see PULL —☆**beat to the draw** to be quicker than (another) in doing something, as in drawing one's weapon —**draw and quarter** *Medieval History* **1.** to execute by tying each arm and leg to a different horse, and then driving the horses in four different directions **2.** to eviscerate and cut into pieces after hanging —**draw away** to move away or ahead —**draw on** (or **nigh**) to approach —**draw oneself up 1.** to assume a straighter posture; stand or sit straight **2.** to bridle —**draw out 1.** to extend; lengthen; prolong **2.** to take out; extract **3.** to get (a person) to answer or talk —**draw up 1.** to arrange in order; marshal **2.** to compose (a document) in proper form; draft **3.** to bring or come to a stop

draw·back (-bak′) n. ☆**1.** money paid back from a charge previously paid; refund, esp. of import duties when the taxed commodities are later exported **2.** anything that prevents or lessens full satisfaction; shortcoming; detriment; disadvantage

☆**draw·bar** (-bär′) n. a coupling used to connect railroad cars, or a bar at the rear of a tractor for attaching a plow, harrow, etc.

draw·bore (-bôr′) n. a hole bored through a mortise-and-tenon joint so that a pin driven into it will force the tenon more securely into the mortise

draw·bridge (-brij′) n. a bridge that can be raised, lowered, or drawn aside

draw·ee (drô′ē′) n. the party that the drawer directs, by means of a bill of exchange, order, draft, etc., to pay money over to a third party (called *payee*)

draw·er (drô′ər; for 5, drôr) n. **1.** a person or thing that draws **2.** a person who draws liquor, as at a bar **3.** a person who draws an order for the payment of money **4.** a draftsman **5.** a sliding box in a table, bureau, chest, etc., that can be drawn out and then pushed back into place

draw·ers (drôrz) n.pl. [< DRAW, because drawn on] an undergarment, long or short, for the lower part of the body, with a separate opening for each leg; underpants

draw·ing (drô′iŋ) n. **1.** the act of one that draws; specif., the art of representing something by lines made on a surface with a pencil, pen, etc. **2.** a picture, design, sketch, etc. thus made **3.** a lottery

drawing account an account of or for money paid for expenses or as advances on salary, commissions, etc., as to a salesman

drawing board a flat, smooth board on which paper, canvas, etc. is fastened for making drawings —**on the drawing board** in the planning stage

☆**drawing card** an entertainer, speaker, show, etc. that normally can be expected to draw a large audience

drawing room [< *withdrawing room:* orig. name for room to which guests withdrew after dinner] **1.** a room where guests are received or entertained; living room or parlor: term no longer much used **2.** a formal reception ☆**3.** a private compartment on a railroad sleeping car, with accommodations for several people

draw·knife (drô′nīf′) n., pl. -knives′ (-nīvz′) a knife with a handle at each end, usually at right angles to the blade, which is drawn toward the user in shaving a surface: also **drawing knife**

drawl (drôl) vt., vi. [prob. freq. of DRAW] to speak slowly, prolonging the vowels —n. a manner of speech characterized by slowness and prolongation of vowels —**drawl′er** n. —**drawl′ing·ly** adv.

DRAWKNIFE

drawn (drôn) pp. of DRAW —adj. **1.** pulled out of the sheath **2.** with neither side winning or losing; even; tied **3.** disemboweled; eviscerated **4.** tense; haggard

☆**drawn butter** melted butter, sometimes thickened and seasoned, used as a sauce

drawn·work (-wurk′) n. ornamental work done on textiles by pulling out threads to produce a lacelike design

draw·plate (drô′plāt′) n. a metal plate with holes through which wire is drawn to get the desired thickness

☆**draw poker** a form of poker in which each player is dealt five cards face down, and may be dealt replacements for any unwanted cards (usually not more than three)

draw·shave (-shāv′) n. same as DRAWKNIFE

draw·string (-striŋ′) n. a string drawn through a hem, as in the waist of a garment or mouth of a bag, to tighten or close it by taking up the fullness

draw·tube (-tōōb′, -tyōōb′) n. a tube sliding within another tube, as in the eyepiece of a microscope

dray (drā) n. [ME. *dreye,* orig., a drag, sled < OE. *dræge,* lit., something drawn, dragnet < *dragan,* to DRAW] a low, sturdily built cart with detachable sides, for carrying heavy loads —vt. to carry or haul on a dray —vi. to drive a dray

dray·age (-ij) n. **1.** the hauling of a load by dray ☆**2.** the charge made for this

dray·man (-mən) n., pl. -men (-mən) a man who drives a dray

Dray·ton (drāt′n), Michael 1563–1631; Eng. poet

dread (dred) vt. [ME. *dreden* < Late OE. *drædan,* aphetic for *ondrædan* (akin to OS. *andradan,* OHG.

intraten) < *ond-*, in, on, against + base < ?] **1.** to anticipate with fear, misgiving, or distaste; fear intensely **2.** [Archaic] to regard with awe —*vi.* [Archaic] to be very fearful —*n.* **1.** intense fear, esp. of something which may happen **2.** fear mixed with awe or reverence **3.** something dreaded —*adj.* **1.** dreaded or dreadful **2.** inspiring awe or reverence; awesome —*SYN.* see AWE, FEAR

dread·ful (-fəl) *adj.* [ME. *dredeful*] **1.** inspiring dread; terrible or awesome **2.** [Colloq.] very bad, offensive, disagreeable, etc. —**dread′ful·ness** *n.*

dread·ful·ly (-fəl ē) *adv.* **1.** in a dreadful manner **2.** [Colloq.] very; extremely [*dreadfully* tired]

dread·nought, dread·naught (-nôt′, -nät′) *n.* **1.** *a)* a coat made of a thick woolen cloth *b)* the cloth **2.** [< *Dreadnought*, the first of such a class of British battleships, built in 1906] any large, heavily armored battleship with many powerful guns

dream (drēm) *n.* [ME. *dream, dreme:* form < OE. *dream,* joy, music < IE. base *dher-,* echoic of a humming (cf. DORBEETLE); sense < ON. *draumr,* akin to G. *traum,* Du. *droom* < IE. base *dhreugh-,* to deceive] **1.** a sequence of sensations, images, thoughts, etc. passing through a sleeping person's mind **2.** a fanciful vision of the conscious mind; daydream; fantasy; reverie **3.** the state, as of abstraction or reverie, in which such a daydream occurs **4.** a fond hope or aspiration **5.** anything so lovely, charming, transitory, etc. as to seem dreamlike —*vi.* **dreamed** (drēmd, dremt) or **dreamt** (dremt), **dream′ing 1.** to have a dream or dreams **2.** to have daydreams **3.** to think (*of*) as at all possible, desirable, etc. [I wouldn't *dream* of going] —*vt.* **1.** *a)* to have (a dream or dreams) *b)* to have a dream of **2.** to spend in dreaming (with *away* or *out*) **3.** to imagine as possible; fancy; suppose —*adj.* that realizes one's fondest hopes; ideal [her *dream* house] —**dream up** *vt.* [Colloq.] to conceive of, imagine, or devise, as by giving free rein to the imagination —**dream′ful** *adj.* —**dream′less** *adj.* —**dream′like′** *adj.*

☆**dream·boat** (-bōt′) *n.* [Slang] a person or thing that seems ideal to one or attracts one strongly

dream·er (-ər) *n.* **1.** a person who dreams **2.** a person given to daydreaming **3.** a person who has ideas or schemes considered impractical; visionary

dream·land (-land′) *n.* **1.** any lovely but imaginary place, as one seen in a dream **2.** sleep

dream world 1. *same as* DREAMLAND **2.** the realm of fantasy; world as seen by one full of illusions about life

dream·y (drē′mē) *adj.* **dream′i·er, dream′i·est 1.** filled with dreams **2.** fond of daydreaming; given to reverie; visionary; impractical **3.** like something in a dream; not sharply defined; misty, vague, etc. **4.** having a soft, soothing quality [*dreamy* music] ☆**5.** [Slang] excellent, wonderful, delightful, etc.: a generalized term of approval —**dream′i·ly** *adv.* —**dream′i·ness** *n.*

drear (drir) *adj.* [Poet.] dreary; melancholy

drear·y (-ē) *adj.* **drear′i·er, drear′i·est** [ME. *dreri* < OE. *dreorig,* sad, orig., bloody, gory < *dreor,* blood < base of *dreosan,* to drip, hence akin to G. *trauern,* to sorrow] **1.** gloomy; cheerless; depressing; dismal; dull **2.** [Archaic] sad —**drear′i·ly** *adv.* —**drear′i·ness** *n.*

dredge¹ (drej) *n.* [prob. < MDu. *dregge,* akin to DRAG] **1.** a device consisting of a net attached to a frame, dragged along the bottom of a river, bay, etc. to gather shellfish, marine plant specimens, etc. **2.** an apparatus for scooping or sucking up mud, sand, rocks, etc., as in deepening or clearing channels, harbors, etc. **3.** a barge or other boat equipped with a dredge — *vt.* **dredged, dredg′ing 1.** to search for or gather (*up*) with or as with a dredge **2.** to enlarge or clean out (a river channel, harbor, etc.) with a dredge —*vi.* **1.** to use a dredge **2.** to search as with a dredge —**dredg′er** *n.*

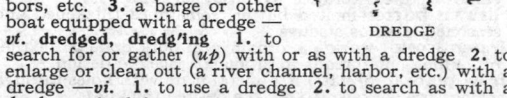

DREDGE

dredge² (drej) *vt.* **dredged, dredg′ing** [< ME. *dragge,* sweetmeat < OFr. *dragie* < ML. *dragium,* earlier *dragetum* < L. *tragemata* < Gr. *tragēmata,* pl. of *tragēma,* dried fruit, dessert < *trōgein,* to gnaw < IE. *trog-* < base *ter-,* to rub: see THROW] **1.** to coat (food) with flour or the like, as by sprinkling **2.** to sprinkle (flour, etc.) —**dredg′er** *n.*

dree (drē) *vt.* **dreed, dree′ing** [ME. *drien* < OE. *dreogan* < IE. *dhereugh* < base *dher-,* to hold firm: see FIRM¹] [Scot. or Archaic] to endure; suffer —*adj.* [Scot. or Archaic] dreary; tedious

dreg·gy (dreg′ē) *adj.* **-gi·er, -gi·est** full of, or having the nature of, dregs; foul —**dreg′gi·ness** *n.*

D region the lowest atmospheric zone within the ionosphere, at an altitude of about 25 to 60 miles, in which the D layer forms

dregs (dregz) *n.pl.* [ME. *dregges,* pl. of *dregge* < ON. *dregg,* barm, lees < IE. *dherēgh,* residue (< base *dher-,* dark, dirty): see DARK, DRAB¹] **1.** the particles of solid matter that settle at the bottom in a liquid; lees **2.** the most worthless part [the *dregs* of society] **3.** [*sing.*] a small amount remaining; residue

Drei·ser (drī′sər, -zər), **Theodore (Herman Albert)** 1871– 1945; U.S. novelist

drench (drench) *vt.* [ME. *drenchen* < OE. *drencan,* to make

drink, drown, caus. of *drincan,* to drink < Gmc. **drank-,* preterit stem of **drinkan,* DRINK + *-jan,* caus. suffix] **1.** to make (a horse, cow, etc.) swallow a medicinal liquid **2.** to make wet all over; soak or saturate in liquid —*n.* **1.** a large liquid dose, esp. for a sick animal **2.** a drenching or soaking **3.** a thing that drenches; solution for soaking —*SYN.* see SOAK

Dres·den (drez′dən) city in SC East Germany, on the Elbe: pop. 504,000 —*n.* a fine, decorated porcelain or chinaware made near Dresden —*adj.* designating or of such porcelain or chinaware

dress (dres) *vt.* **dressed** or **drest, dress′ing** [ME. *dressen,* to make straight, direct < OFr. *drecier,* to set up, arrange < VL. **directiare* < L. *directus:* see DIRECT] **1.** to put clothes on; clothe **2.** to provide with clothing **3.** to decorate; trim; adorn **4.** to arrange a display in [to *dress* a store window] **5.** to arrange or do up (the hair) **6.** to arrange (troops, etc.) in a straight line or lines **7.** to apply medicines and bandages to (a wound, sore, etc.) **8.** to treat as required in preparing for use, grooming, etc.; *a)* to clean and eviscerate (a fowl, deer, etc.) *b)* to till, cultivate, or fertilize (fields or plants) *c)* to curry (a horse, leather, etc.) *d)* to smooth and polish (stone, wood, etc.) —*vi.* **1.** to put on clothes; wear clothes **2.** to dress in formal clothes **3.** to get into a straight line or proper alignment: said of soldiers —*n.* **1.** clothes, clothing, or apparel, esp. as suitable for certain occasions [casual *dress*] or for a certain place or time [modern *dress*] **2.** the usual outer garment worn by women, generally of one piece with a skirt **3.** formal clothes **4.** external covering or appearance —*adj.* **1.** of or for dresses [*dress* material] **2.** worn on formal occasions [a *dress* suit] **3.** requiring formal clothes [a *dress* occasion] —**dress down** to scold severely; reprimand —**dress ship** to raise the ensign at each masthead and the flagstaff and, often, string signal flags over the mastheads —**dress up 1.** to dress in formal clothes, or in clothes more elegant, showy, etc. than one usually wears **2.** to improve the appearance of, as by decorating **3.** to arrange in a straight line, as troops

dres·sage (drə säzh′) *n.* [Fr., training < *dresser,* to arrange, train: see DRESS] exhibition riding or horsemanship in which the horse is controlled in certain difficult steps and gaits by very slight movements of the rider

dress circle a section of seats in a theater or concert hall, usually a tier partly encircling and above the orchestra: formal dress was formerly customary there

dress·er¹ (dres′ər) *n.* **1.** a person who dresses another; esp., one who helps actors and actresses put on their costumes **2.** a person who dresses something, as store windows, leather, wounds, etc. **3.** a tool used for dressing stone, metal, etc. **4.** a person who dresses elegantly or in a certain way [a fancy *dresser*]

dress·er² (-ər) *n.* [ME. *dressour* < OFr. *dreceur:* see DRESS] **1.** formerly, a table or sideboard on which food was prepared for serving **2.** a cupboard for dishes and kitchen utensils ☆**3.** a chest of drawers for clothes, usually with a mirror; bureau

dress·i·ly (-′l ē) *adv.* in a dressy manner

dress·i·ness (-ē nis) *n.* the quality of being dressy

dress·ing (-iŋ) *n.* **1.** the act of one that dresses **2.** that which is used to dress something (as manure applied to soil, medicines and bandages applied to wounds, etc.) **3.** a substance used to stiffen fabric during manufacture **4.** a sauce added to salads and other dishes **5.** a mixture as of bread and seasoning, for stuffing roast fowl or other meat

dress·ing-down (-doun′) *n.* a sound scolding

dressing gown a loose robe for wear when one is not fully clothed, as before dressing or when lounging

dressing room a room for getting dressed in; esp., a room backstage where actors dress and put on makeup

dressing station a military station near a combat area for receiving the wounded and giving first aid

dressing table a low table with a mirror, for use while putting on cosmetics, grooming the hair, etc.

dress·mak·er (dres′māk′ər) *n.* a person who makes dresses and other clothes for women —☆*adj.* designating or of a woman's suit, coat, etc. not cut on severe, mannish lines: cf. TAILORED —**dress′mak′ing** *n.*

☆**dress parade** a military parade in dress uniform

dress rehearsal a final rehearsal, as of a play or ceremony, performed exactly as it is to take place

dress shield a pad worn at the armpit to protect a garment from perspiration

dress suit a man's formal suit for evening wear

dress uniform a military uniform worn on formal occasions

dress·y (-ē) *adj.* **dress′i·er, dress′i·est 1.** showy or elaborate in dress or appearance **2.** stylish, elegant, smart, etc.

drest (drest) *alt. pt. & pp. of* DRESS

drew (drōō) *pt. of* DRAW

Drew (drōō), **John** 1853–1927; U.S. actor

Drey·fus (drā′fəs, drī′-; *Fr.* dre füs′), **Alfred** 1859–1935; Fr. army officer convicted of treason & imprisoned but later exonerated when proved to be the victim of anti-Semitism & conspiracy

drib (drib) *vi., vt.* **dribbed, drib′bing** [< DRIP] [Obs.] to fall, or let fall, in or as in driblets —**dribs and drabs** [< N. Eng. dial. *drib,* driblet, droplet + *drab* for *drap,* dial. form of DROP] small amounts

drib·ble (-'l) *vi.*, *vt.* **-bled, -bling** [freq. of DRIB] **1.** to flow, or let flow, in drops or driblets; trickle **2.** to come forth or let out a little at a time **3.** to let (saliva) drip from the mouth; drool **4.** to keep (a ball or puck) in motion or move (it) forward by a rapid succession of bounces (in basketball), short kicks (in soccer), or light taps with a stick (in hockey) —*n.* **1.** a small drop, or a flowing in small drops **2.** a very small amount **3.** the act of dribbling a ball or puck **4.** a drizzling rain —**drib′bler** *n.*

drib·let (-lit) *n.* [dim. of prec.] a small amount; bit [to pay one's debts in *driblets*]

dried (drīd) *pt. & pp.* of DRY

driegh (drēkh) *adj.* [Scot.] same as DREE

dri·er (drī′ər) *n.* **1.** a substance added to paint, varnish, etc. to make it dry fast **2.** same as DRYER —*adj. compar.* of DRY

dri·est (-ist) *adj. superl.* of DRY

drift (drift) *n.* [ME. (akin to ON. & MDu. *drift*, OHG. *trift*) < OE. *drīfan*, DRIVE] **1.** an act or instance of being driven or carried along, as by a current of air or water or by circumstances **2.** the course on which something is directed or driven **3.** the deviation of a ship, airplane, rocket, etc. from its path, caused by side currents or winds **4.** *a)* the velocity of a current of water *b)* a slow ocean current **5.** *a)* a gradual shifting in position *b)* a random course, variation, or deviation **6.** a gradual movement or change in some direction or toward some end or purpose; trend; tendency **7.** general meaning of what is said or done; intent; tenor **8.** *a)* something driven, as rain, snow, or smoke driven before the wind, or floating matter driven by water currents *b)* a heap of snow, sand, etc. piled up by the wind, or floating matter washed ashore **9.** *Electronics* a deviation or variation of a quantity, as voltage, from its assigned value **10.** *Geol.* sand, gravel, boulders, etc. moved and deposited by a glacier or by water arising from its melting ice **11.** *Linguis.* a gradual change along a certain line of development in the various elements of a language **12.** *Mech. a)* a tool used for ramming or driving down a heavy object *b)* a tool for enlarging or shaping holes **13.** *Mining a)* a horizontal passageway driven into or along the path of a vein or rock layer *b)* a small tunnel connecting two larger shafts —*vi.* **1.** to be carried along by or as by a current **2.** to be carried along by circumstances; go along aimlessly **3.** to wander about from place to place, from job to job, etc. **4.** to accumulate in heaps by force of wind or water **5.** to become heaped with drifting snow, sand, etc. **6.** to move easily or gradually or away from a set position ✰**7.** [Western] to range far afield in a drove, as in seeking pasture or escaping a storm: said of cattle —*vt.* **1.** to cause to drift **2.** to cover with drifts —*SYN.* see TENDENCY, WASH —**drift′er** *n.*

drift·age (-ij) *n.* **1.** the action of something that drifts **2.** the deviation caused by drifting **3.** that which has drifted or has washed ashore

drift anchor same as SEA ANCHOR

drift·wood (-wood′) *n.* wood drifting in the water, or that has been washed ashore

drift·y (drif′tē) *adj.* **drift′i·er, drift′i·est** having drifts or a tendency to form drifts

drill¹ (dril) *n.* [Du. *dril* < *drillen*, to bore, ult. < IE. base *ter*, to rub (esp. with turning motion), whence L. *terere*: cf. THROW] **1.** a tool or apparatus for boring holes in wood, metal, stone, teeth, etc. **2.** the sound of drilling or boring ✰**3.** any of a genus (*Urosalpinx*) of snails, esp. a marine species (*Urosalpinx cinerea*), that bores through the shells of oysters and other shellfish and consumes their flesh **4.** *a)* military or physical training, esp. of a group, as in marching, the manual of arms, or gymnastic exercises *b)* a single exercise in such training **5.** *a)* the process of training or teaching by the continued repetition of an exercise *b)* a single exercise in such training or teaching **6.** the method or style of drilling —*vt.* [Du. *drillen*] **1.** to bore (a hole) in (something) with or as with a drill **2.** to train in military or physical exercises; specif., to exercise (troops) in close-order drill **3.** to teach or train by having do repeated exercises **4.** to instill (ideas, facts, etc.) *into* by repeated exercises ✰**5.** [Colloq.] to cause to move swiftly and in a direct line [he *drilled* the ball past the pitcher] ✰**6.** [Slang] to penetrate with bullets —*vi.* **1.** to bore a hole or holes **2.** to engage in, or be put through, military, physical, or mental exercises —*SYN.* see PRACTICE —**drill′er** *n.*

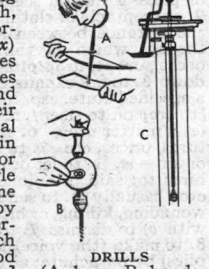

DRILLS
(A, bow; B, hand; C, rotary oil)

drill² (dril) *n.* [< ? prec.] **1.** a furrow in which seeds are planted **2.** a row of planted seeds **3.** a machine for making holes or furrows, dropping seeds into them, and covering

them —*vt.* **1.** to sow (seeds) in rows **2.** to plant (a field) in drills

drill³ (dril) *n.* [< earlier *drilling* < Gr. *drillich* < OHG. *drilich*, made of three threads < L. *trilix* (gen. *trilicis*) < *tri-*, TRI- + *licium*, thread] a coarse linen or cotton cloth with a diagonal weave, used for work clothes, linings, uniforms, etc.

drill⁴ (dril) *n.* [< ? Fr. *drille*, orig. argot term, vagabond soldier, cunning fellow] a short-tailed, bright-cheeked monkey (*Mandrillus leucophaeus*) native to W Africa, resembling the mandrill but smaller

✰**drilling mud** a suspension of fine-grained mineral matter, usually in water, circulated in oil-well drilling to counterbalance the pressure of oil, gas, etc., plug up porous surfaces, etc.

drill·mas·ter (-mas′tər, -mäs′-) *n.* **1.** an instructor in military drill, esp. in close-order drill **2.** a person who teaches by drilling and strict discipline

drill press a machine tool for drilling holes in metal, etc.

drill·stock (-stäk′) *n.* that part of a drilling machine or tool which holds the shank of a drill or bit

dri·ly (drī′lē) *adv.* same as DRYLY

drink (driŋk) *vt.* **drank** or archaic **drunk** (druŋk), **drunk** or now colloq. **drank** or archaic **drunk′en, drink′ing** [ME. *drinken* < OE. *drincan*, akin to OHG. *trinkan*, Goth. *drigkan* < ? IE. base **dhreĝ-*, to draw, whence Sans. *dhrājas-*, draft] **1.** to take (liquid) into the mouth and swallow it **2.** to absorb (liquid or moisture) **3.** to swallow the contents of **4.** to propose or take part in (a toast) **5.** to bring (oneself) into a specified condition by drinking **6.** to use (*up*) or spend by drinking alcoholic liquor —*vi.* **1.** to take liquid into the mouth and swallow it **2.** to absorb anything as if in drinking **3.** to drink alcoholic liquor, sometimes specif. as a matter of habit or to excess —*n.* **1.** any liquid for drinking; beverage **2.** alcoholic liquor **3.** habitual or excessive use of alcoholic liquor **4.** a portion of liquid drunk or for drinking —**drink deep (of)** to take in a large amount (of) by or as by drinking —**drink in** to take in with the senses or the mind, esp. in an eager manner —**drink to** to drink in honor of; drink a toast to —✰**the drink** [Colloq.] any body of water, esp. the ocean

drink·a·ble (-ə b'l) *adj.* fit for drinking —*n.* a liquid fit for drinking; beverage: *usually used in pl.*

drink·er (-ər) *n.* **1.** a person who drinks **2.** a person who drinks alcoholic liquor habitually or excessively

drinking fountain a device for providing a jet or flow of drinking water as in a public place

drinking song a song celebrating the pleasures of drinking alcoholic liquors; song for a drinking party

drip (drip) *vi.* **dripped** or **dript, drip′ping** [ME. *dryppen* < OE. *dryppan*, intens. form (< Gmc. **drupjan*), akin to *dreopan* (G. *triefen*), to drop, drip < IE. base **dhreub-*, to break away, crumble] **1.** to fall in or as in drops **2.** to let drops of liquid fall **3.** to be so soaked or filled with liquid as to have some trickle down or over —*vt.* to let fall in drops —*n.* **1.** a falling in drops; trickling **2.** moisture or liquid falling in drops **3.** the sound made by liquid falling in drops **4.** a projecting part of a sill, cornice, etc. that sheds rain water **5.** [Slang] a person regarded as unpleasant or insipid **6.** *Med.* a continuous giving of a solution of salt, sugar, etc., esp. intravenously —**drip′per** *n.*

✰**drip-dry** (-drī′) *adj.* designating or of fabrics or garments that dry quickly when hung soaking wet and require little or no ironing —*vi.* **-dried′, -dry′ing** to launder as a drip-dry fabric does

✰**drip grind** a fine grind of coffee, for use in a Dripolator

✰**Drip·o·la·tor** (drip′ə lāt′ər) [DRIP + (PERC)OLATOR] *a trademark for* a kind of coffeepot in which boiling water poured into the top section seeps slowly through finely ground coffee in the perforated middle section, and then drips into the one below

drip·ping (drip′iŋ) *adv.* so as to drip; thoroughly [*dripping* wet] —*n.* **1.** a falling of liquid drop by drop **2.** [*usually pl.*] anything that drips, esp. the fat and juices that drip from roasting meat

dripping pan a pan to catch drippings: also **drip pan**

drip·py (drip′ē) *adj.* **-pi·er, -pi·est** **1.** characterized by dripping water, rain, etc. [a *drippy* faucet] **2.** [Slang] overly sentimental, stupid, etc.

drip·stone (-stōn′) *n.* **1.** a projecting part of a sill, cornice, etc. that sheds rain water **2.** calcium carbonate, $CaCO_3$, deposited by dripping water in the form of stalactites or stalagmites

dript (dript) *alt. pt. & pp.* of DRIP

drive (drīv) *vt.* **drove, driv′en, driv′ing** [ME. *driven* < OE. *drīfan*, akin to Goth. *dreiban*, G. *treiben*, ON. *drīfa* < IE. base **dhreibh-*, to push] **1.** to force to go; urge onward; push forward **2.** to force into or from a state or act [*driven* mad] **3.** to force to work, usually to excess **4.** *a)* to force by or as by a blow, thrust, or stroke *b)* to throw, hit, or cast hard and swiftly; specif., *Golf* to hit from the tee, usually with a driver **5.** to cause to go through; make penetrate **6.** to make or produce by penetrating [to *drive* a hole through metal] **7.** to control the movement or direct the course of (an automobile, horse and wagon, locomotive,

etc.) **8.** to transport in an automobile or other vehicle **9.** to impel or propel as motive power; set or keep going; cause to function [a gasoline engine *drives* the motorboat] **10.** to carry on with vigor; push (a bargain, etc.) through **11.** *Hunting a)* to chase (game) from thickets into the clear or into nets, traps, etc. *b)* to cover (an area) in this way —*vi.* **1.** to advance violently; dash **2.** to work or try hard, as to reach a goal **3.** to drive a blow, ball, missile, etc. **4.** to be driven; operate: said of a motor vehicle **5.** to go or be conveyed in a vehicle **6.** to operate a motor vehicle —*n.* **1.** the act of driving **2.** a trip in a vehicle **3.** *a)* a road for automobiles, etc. *b)* a driveway ☆**4.** *a)* a rounding up or moving of animals on foot for branding, slaughter, etc. *b)* the animals rounded up or moved **5.** a hard, swift blow, thrust, etc., as of a ball in a game; specif., *Golf* a shot from the tee, usually with a driver **6.** the manner in which a ball, etc. is driven ☆**7.** *a)* an organized movement to achieve some purpose; campaign *b)* a large-scale military offensive to gain an objective ☆**8.** the power or energy to get things done; enthusiastic or aggressive vigor **9.** that which is urgent or pressing; pressure ☆**10.** a collection of logs being floated down a river to a sawmill **11.** *a)* the apparatus controlling the propulsion of a motor vehicle [a gear *drive*] *b)* that arrangement in an automatic transmission of a motor vehicle which allows movement forward at varying speeds **12.** a device that communicates motion to a machine or machine part **13.** *Psychol.* any of the basic biological impulses or urges, such as self-preservation, hunger, sex, etc. —**drive at** **1.** to aim at **2.** to mean; intend —**drive in** **1.** to force in, as by a blow ☆**2.** *Baseball* to cause (a runner) to score or (a run) to be scored, as by getting a hit —**let drive** to hit or aim

☆**drive-in** (drīv'in′) *adj.* designating or of a restaurant, movie theater, bank, etc. designed to render its services to persons who drive up and remain seated in their cars —*n.* such a restaurant, theater, etc.

driv-el (driv'l) *vi.* **-eled** or **-elled, -el-ing** or **-el-ling** [ME *drivelen* < OE. *dreflian*, to slobber: for IE. base see DRAFF] **1.** to let saliva flow from one's mouth; drool; slobber **2.** to speak in a silly or stupid manner; talk childish nonsense —*vt.* to say in a silly, stupid, or nonsensical manner —*n.* **1.** [Now Rare] saliva running from the mouth **2.** silly, stupid talk; childish nonsense; twaddle —**driv'el-er, driv'el-ler** *n.*

driv-en (driv'n) *pp.* of DRIVE —*adj.* **1.** moved along and piled up by the wind [*driven* snow] **2.** forced into a (specified) condition [*driven* mad]

driv-er (drī'vər) *n.* **1.** a person who drives; specif., *a)* one who drives an automobile, team of horses, etc. *b)* one who herds cattle *c)* one who makes his subordinates work hard **2.** a thing that drives; specif., *a)* a mallet, hammer, etc. *b)* a golf club with a wooden head and little loft, used in hitting the ball from the tee: also called *number 1 wood c)* any machine part that communicates motion to another part —**the driver's seat** the position of control or dominance

driver ant *same as* ARMY ANT; specif., any of several related genera (family Dorylidae) of such ants

drive shaft a shaft that transmits motion or power, as from the transmission to the rear axle in an automobile

☆**drive-way** (drīv'wā′) *n.* a path for cars, leading from a street or road to a garage, house, etc.

driv-ing (drī'viŋ) *adj.* **1.** transmitting force or motion **2.** moving with force and violence [a *driving* rain] **3.** vigorous; energetic [a *driving* jazz solo] —*n.* the way one drives an automobile, etc.

driving wheel a wheel that transmits motion, as one of the large wheels of a locomotive which receive power from the engine by means of the connecting rod

driz-zle (driz'l) *vi., vt.* **-zled, -zling** [prob. freq. of ME. *drisnen* (found only as ger. *drisning*), to fall as dew, akin to Norw. dial. *drysja*, to drizzle & OE. *dreosan*: see DREARY] to rain or let fall in fine, mistlike drops —*n.* a fine, mistlike rain —**driz'zly** *adj.*

Dro-ghe-da (drô′ə də) seaport in E Ireland, at the mouth of the Boyne River: captured (1649) by Cromwell, who massacred its people: pop. 17,000

drogue (drōg) *n.* [prob. altered < Scot. *drug*, dial. var. of DRAG] **1.** *same as* SEA ANCHOR **2.** a funnel-shaped device towed behind an aircraft for its drag effect (also **drogue parachute**), or as a target, for use in certain refueling operations, etc.

droit (droit; *Fr.* drwä) *n.* [ME. < OFr. < ML. *directum*, right, justice < L. *directus*: see DIRECT] **1.** a legal right **2.** that to which one has legal claim

‡**droit du sei-gneur** (drwä dü sān yĕr′) [Fr., right of the lord] **1.** the right, purportedly claimed by some feudal lords, to the first night with brides in their domains **2.** any assumption of a right considered like this in its extreme arrogance

droll (drōl) *adj.* [Fr. *drôle*, orig. n., buffoon, jester < MDu. *drol*, short, stout fellow, lit., bowling pin] amusing in an odd or wry way —*n.* [Now Rare] a droll person; jester —*vi.* [Now Rare] to joke; play the jester —*SYN.* see FUNNY —**droll'ness** *n.* —**drol'ly** *adv.*

droll-er-y (-ər ē) *n., pl.* **-er-ies** **1.** a droll act, remark, picture, story, etc. **2.** the act of joking **3.** a droll quality; quaint or wry humor

-drome (drōm) [< Gr. *dromos*, a running race, racecourse] *a suffix meaning* running, racecourse [*motordrome*]

drom-e-dar-y (dräm′ə der′ē) *n., pl.* **-dar'ies** [ME. *dromedarie* < OFr. *dromadaire* < LL.(Ec.) *dromedarius* (*camelus*), dromedary (camel) < L. *dromas*, dromedary (+ *-arius*, -ARY) < Gr. *dromas*, a runner, running < *dramein*, to run < IE. base *drem-*, *dreb-*, to run, whence Sans. *drâmati*, (he) runs, TRAMP] the one-humped, or Arabian camel (*Camelus dromedarius*), occurring from N Africa to India and trained especially for fast riding

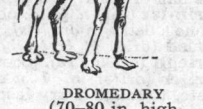

DROMEDARY (70–80 in. high at shoulder)

drom-ond (dräm′ənd, drum′-) *n.* [ME. < OFr. *dromont*, swift ship < LL. *dromo* (gen. *dromonis*) < LGr. *dromōn*, runner: see prec.] a large, medieval, swift-sailing ship

-dro-mous (drə məs) [< Gr. *-dromos:* see DROMEDARY] *a suffix meaning* running, moving [*catadromous*]

drone¹ (drōn) *n.* [ME. < OE. *dran*, akin to OS. *dran*, MLowG. *drone* < IE. *dhren-* < base *dher-*, to buzz, hum, whence DOR(BEETLE)] **1.** a male bee, as a male honeybee, which serves only in a reproductive capacity, has no sting, and does no work **2.** an idle person who lives by the work of others; parasite; loafer **3.** a pilotless airplane that is directed in flight by remote control —*vi.* droned, dron'ing to live in idleness; loaf

drone² (drōn) *vi.* droned, dron'ing [LME. *dronen* < prec.] **1.** to make a continuous and monotonous humming or buzzing sound **2.** to talk on and on in a dull, monotonous way —*vt.* to utter in a dull, monotonous tone —*n.* **1.** a continuous and monotonous humming or buzzing sound **2.** *a)* a bagpipe *b)* any of the pipes of fixed tone in a bagpipe **3.** *a)* a bass voice or part, sustaining a single low tone *b)* such a tone

drool (drōōl) *vi.* [< DRIVEL] **1.** to let saliva flow from one's mouth; drivel **2.** to flow from the mouth, as saliva **3.** [Slang] to speak in a silly or stupid way **4.** [Slang] to be overly enthusiastic, eager, etc. —*vt.* **1.** to let drivel from the mouth **2.** [Slang] to say in a silly or stupid way —*n.* **1.** saliva running from the mouth **2.** [Slang] silly, stupid talk; nonsense

droop (drōōp) *vi.* [ME. *droupen* < ON. *drūpa:* for IE. base see DROP] **1.** to sink down; hang or bend down **2.** to lose vitality or strength; become weakened; languish **3.** to become dejected or dispirited —*vt.* to let sink or hang down —*n.* an act or instance of drooping

droop-y (-ē) *adj.* **droop'i-er, droop'i-est** **1.** drooping or tending to droop **2.** [Colloq.] tired or dejected —**droop'i-ly** *adv.* —**droop'i-ness** *n.*

drop (dräp) *n.* [ME. *drope* < OE. *dropa*, akin to ON. *drūpa*, DROOP, G. *triefen* < IE. base *dhreub-:* cf. DRIP] **1.** a small quantity of liquid that is somewhat spherical or pear-shaped, as when falling **2.** a very small quantity of liquid **3.** [*pl.*] liquid medicine taken in drops **4.** a very small quantity of anything **5.** a thing like a drop in shape, size, etc., as a pendent earring or a small piece of candy **6.** the act or fact of dropping; sudden fall, descent, slump, or decrease [a *drop* in prices] **7.** the dropping of troops or supplies by parachute; airdrop **8.** anything that drops or is used for dropping or covering something, as a drop curtain or piece of theater scenery, a drop hammer, or a trap door **9.** a receptacle or slot into which something is dropped **10.** the distance between a higher and lower level; distance through which anything falls or sinks —*vi.* **dropped** or, occas., **dropt, drop'ping** **1.** to fall in drops **2.** to fall; come down **3.** to fall exhausted, wounded, or dead **4.** to pass into a specified state, esp. into a less active or less desirable one [to *drop* off to sleep] **5.** to come to an end or to nothing [to let a matter *drop*] **6.** to become lower or less, as temperatures, prices, etc. **7.** to move down with a current of water or air —*vt.* **1.** to let or make fall; release hold of **2.** to give birth to: said of animals **3.** to utter (a suggestion, hint, etc.) casually **4.** to send (a letter) **5.** to cause to fall, as by wounding, killing, or hitting **6.** *a)* to stop, end, or have done with *b)* to dismiss **7.** to make lower or less; lower or lessen **8.** to make (the voice) less loud **9.** to drop (troops or supplies) by parachute; airdrop **10.** to omit (a letter or sound) in a word **11.** [Colloq.] to leave (a person or thing) at a specified place **12.** [Slang] to lose (money or a game) —**a drop in the bucket** [Colloq.] an insufficient or trifling amount —☆**at the drop of a hat** immediately; at the slightest provocation —**drop back** **1.** to move back; retreat **2.** *same as* DROP BEHIND —**drop behind** to be outdistanced; fall behind —**drop in** (or over, by, etc.) to pay a casual or unexpected visit —**drop off** **1.** to become fewer or less; decline; decrease **2.** [Colloq.] to fall asleep —**drop out** to stop being a member or participant —☆**get** (or **have**) **the drop on** [Slang] **1.** to draw and aim one's gun at (another) more quickly than he can draw and aim at one **2.** to get (or have) any advantage over

☆**drop-cloth** (-klôth′, -kläth′) *n.* a large piece of cloth, plastic, etc. for protection against dripping paint

☆**drop cookie** any of various cookies made from batter which is dropped onto a baking sheet as by teaspoonfuls

drop curtain a theater curtain that is lowered and raised rather than drawn

drop·forge (-fôrj′) *vt.* **-forged′, -forg′ing** to pound or shape (heated metal) between dies with a drop hammer or a press —**drop′-forg′er** *n.*

drop forging a product made by drop-forging

☆**drop hammer** **1.** a machine for pounding metal into shape, with a heavy weight that is raised and then dropped on the metal **2.** this weight

drop kick *Football* a kick in which the ball is dropped and kicked just as it rebounds from the ground —**drop′-kick′** *vt., vi.* —**drop′-kick′er** *n.*

☆**drop leaf** a hinged board attached to the side or end of a table as an extension of the surface: it hangs down when not in use —**drop′-leaf′** *adj.*

drop·let (-lit) *n.* a very small drop

droplet infection disease spread by dispersion into the air of droplets from an infected respiratory tract

☆**drop letter** a letter posted at and delivered from the same office

☆**drop·light** (-līt′) *n.* a light so suspended from a fixture that it can be raised or lowered as desired

drop-off (-ôf′) *n.* **1.** a very steep drop **2.** a decline or decrease, as in sales, prices, etc.

☆**drop·out** (-out′) *n.* a student who withdraws from school, esp. high school, before graduating

drop·per (-ər) *n.* **1.** a person or thing that drops ☆**2.** a small glass tube usually capped by a hollow rubber bulb at one end, used to measure out a liquid in drops

drop·ping (-iŋ) *n.* **1.** the act of a person or thing that drops **2.** that which drops or falls in drops **3.** [*pl.*] dung of animals

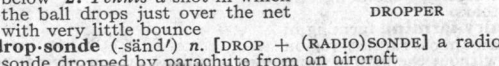

DROPPER

☆**drop press** same as DROP HAMMER

drop shot **1.** shot made by letting molten metal fall in drops to solidify in a container of water below **2.** *Tennis* a shot in which the ball drops just over the net with very little bounce

drop·sonde (-sänd′) *n.* [DROP + (RADIO)SONDE] a radio-sonde dropped by parachute from an aircraft

drop·sy (dräp′sē) *n.* [ME. *dropesie* < *ydropesie* < OFr. *idropisie* < L. *hydropisis* < Gr. *hydrōps*, dropsy < *hydōr*, WATER] *an earlier term for* EDEMA —**drop′si·cal** (-si k′l), **drop′sied** (-sēd) *adj.* —**drop′si·cal·ly** *adv.*

dropt (dräpt) *occas. pt. & pp.* of DROP

drop·wort (dräp′wurt′) *n.* a tall plant (*Filipendula hexapetala*) of the rose family, with fernlike leaves and white or reddish flowers: it resembles the meadowsweet

dros·er·a (dräs′ər ə) *n.* [ModL. < Gr. *droserē*, fem. of *droseros*, dewy < *drosos*, dew] any of a genus (*Drosera*) of small plants of the sundew family, having leaves covered with adhesive hairs that trap insects which are digested by the plant

drosh·ky (dräsh′kē, drôsh′-) *n., pl.* **-kies** [Russ. *drozhki*, dim. of *drogi*, a wagon < *droga*, a bar between front and back axles] **1.** a low, open, four-wheeled Russian carriage with a long, narrow bench which the passengers straddle **2.** any of various other carriages Also **dros′ky** (dräs′-, drôs′-)

DROSHKY

dro·soph·i·la (drə säf′ə lə, drō-) *n., pl.* **-lae** (-lē′) [ModL. < Gr. *drosos*, dew + *phila*, fem. of *philos*, loving] any of a genus (*Drosophila*) of small flies used in laboratory experiments in heredity because of their short life cycle and great reproductivity; fruit fly

dross (drôs, dräs) *n.* [ME. & OE. *dros*, dregs, akin to *dærst* & ON. *dregg*, DREGS] **1.** a scum formed on the surface of molten metal **2.** waste matter; worthless stuff; rubbish — **dross′i·ness** *n.* —**dross′y** *adj.,* **dross′i·er, dross′i·est**

drought (drout, drouth) *n.* [ME. < OE. *drugoth*, dryness < *drugian*, to dry up, akin to *dryge*, DRY] **1.** a prolonged period of dry weather; lack of rain **2.** a prolonged or serious shortage or deficiency **3.** [Archaic] thirst —**drought′y** *adj.,* **drought′i·er, drought′i·est**

drouth (drouth, drouth) *n.* same as DROUGHT

drove[1] (drōv) *n.* [ME. < OE. *draf* < *drifan,* DRIVE] **1.** a number of cattle, hogs, sheep, etc. driven or moving along as a group; flock; herd **2.** a moving crowd of people **3.** *a)* a broad-faced chisel for grooving or dressing stone: also **drove chisel** *b)* a grooved surface made with this chisel: also **drove work** —*vt., vi.* droved, drov′ing to finish (stone) with a drove chisel —SYN. see GROUP

drove[2] (drōv) *pt.* of DRIVE

dro·ver (drō′vər) *n.* a person who herds droves of animals, esp. to market

drown (droun) *vi.* [ME. *drounen,* prob. < var. of ON. *drukna,* drown, akin to OE. *druncnian,* to become drunk, be drowned < *druncen,* pp. of *drincan,* DRINK] to die by suffocation in water or other liquid —*vt.* **1.** to kill by suffocation in water or other liquid **2.** *a)* to cover with

water; flood; inundate *b)* to overwhelm **3.** to be so loud as to overcome (another sound): usually with *out* **4.** to cause to disappear; get rid of [to *drown* one's worries in drink]

drowse (drouz) *vi.* drowsed, drows′ing [< OE. *drusian,* to become sluggish < base of *dreosan,* to fall: see DREARY] to sleep lightly; be half asleep; doze —*vt.* **1.** [Rare] to make sleepy or sluggish **2.** to spend (time) in drowsing —*n.* the act or an instance of drowsing; doze

drow·sy (drou′zē) *adj.* **-si·er, -si·est** **1.** *a)* sleepy or half asleep; lethargic *b)* making drowsy; soporific **2.** brought on by sleepiness **3.** peacefully quiet or inactive [a *drowsy* village] —SYN. see SLEEPY —**drow′si·ly** *adv.* —**drow′si·ness** *n.*

drub (drub) *vt.* drubbed, drub′bing [< ? Turk. *durb* < Ar. *darb,* a beating < *daraba,* to cudgel, bastinado] **1.** to beat as with a stick or club; cudgel; thrash **2.** to defeat soundly in a fight, contest, etc. —*vi.* to drum or tap —*n.* a blow as with a club; thump —**drub′ber** *n.*

drub·bing (-iŋ) *n.* a thorough beating or defeat

drudge (druj) *n.* [ME. *druggen,* prob. < OE. *dreogan:* see DREE] a person who does hard, menial, or tedious work —*vi.* drudged, drudg′ing to do such work

drudg·er·y (druj′ər ē) *n., pl.* **-er·ies** [see DRUDGE] work that is hard, menial, or tiresome

drug (drug) *n.* [ME. *drogge* < OFr. *drogue* < ? LowG. *drooge* (*fat*), dry (cask), the adj. mistaken as the name of the contents: see DRY] **1.** any substance used as a medicine or as an ingredient in a medicine **2.** formerly, any substance used in chemistry, dyeing, etc. **3.** a narcotic, hallucinogen, etc., esp. one that is habit-forming —*vt.* **drugged, drug′ging** **1.** to put a harmful drug in (a food, drink, etc.) **2.** to administer a drug to **3.** to stupefy with or as with a drug —**drug on the market** a commodity for which there is little or no demand because the supply is so plentiful

drug addict a habitual user of narcotics

drug·get (-it) *n.* [Fr. *drouguet,* dim. of *drogue,* stuff, trash, prob. of same origin as DRUG] **1.** formerly, a woolen or part-woolen material used for clothing **2.** a coarse fabric used as a floor covering, carpet lining, etc. **3.** a coarse rug from India made of jute or cotton and hair

drug·gist (-ist) *n.* [Fr. *droguiste* < *drogue,* DRUG] **1.** a dealer in drugs, medical equipment, etc. **2.** a person authorized to fill prescriptions; pharmacist ☆**3.** an owner or manager of a drugstore

☆**drug·store** (-stôr′) *n.* a store where medical prescriptions are filled and drugs and medical supplies are sold: most drugstores now also sell a wide variety of merchandise

dru·id (drōō′id) *n.* [Fr. *druide* < L. *druides,* pl. < Celt., as in OIr. *drūi* < IE. **dru-wid-,* lit., oak-wise (< base **dereu-,* oak, TREE + **wid-,* know, WISE!)] [*often* D-] a member of a Celtic religious order of priests, soothsayers, judges, poets, etc. in ancient Britain, Ireland, and France —**dru·id·ic** (drōō id′ik), **dru·id′i·cal** *adj.*

dru·id·ism (-iz′m) *n.* the religious and philosophic system of the druids

drum[1] (drum) *n.* [< Du. *trom,* akin to MLowG. *trumme,* drum, OHG. *trumba:* see TRUMPET] **1.** a percussion instrument consisting of a hollow cylinder or hemisphere with a membrane stretched tightly over the end or ends, played by beating with the hands, sticks, etc. **2.** the sound produced by beating a drum, or any sound like this **3.** any of various drumlike cylindrical objects; specif., *a)* a metal spool or cylinder around which cable, etc. is wound in a machine *b)* a barrellike metal container for oil, etc. *c)* any of the cylindrical blocks making up the shaft of a stone column *d)* the circular or polygonal wall supporting a dome ☆**4.** any of various saltwater and freshwater fishes (family Sciaenidae) that make a drumming sound **5.** *Anat. a)* same as MIDDLE EAR *b)* same as EARDRUM —*vi.* **drummed, drum′ming** **1.** to beat a drum **2.** to beat or tap continually or rhythmically, as with the fingers ☆**3.** to make a loud, reverberating sound by quivering the wings: said of the ruffed grouse, etc. —*vt.* **1.** to play (a tune, rhythm, etc.) on or as on a drum **2.** to beat or tap continually **3.** to assemble by beating a drum **4.** to instill (ideas, facts, etc. *into*) by continued repetition —**beat the drum for** [Colloq.] to seek to arouse interest in or enthusiasm for —**drum out of** **1.** orig., to expel from (the army) with drums beating **2.** to expel from in disgrace —**drum up** **1.** to summon by or as by beating a drum **2.** to get (business, etc.) by canvassing or soliciting

drum[2] (drum) *n.* [see DRUMLIN] [Scot. & Irish] **1.** a narrow hill or ridge **2.** same as DRUMLIN

drum·beat (-bēt′) *n.* a sound made by beating a drum

drum·beat·er (-bēt′ər) *n.* ☆[Colloq.] one who actively publicizes or campaigns for something, as a press agent —**drum′beat′ing** *n.*

drum·fire (drum′fīr′) *n.* heavy and continuous gunfire, thought of as resembling rapid drumbeats

☆**drum·fish** (-fish′) *n., pl.* **-fish′, -fish′es:** see FISH same as DRUM (*n.* 4)

drum·head (-hed′) *n.* **1.** the membrane stretched over the open end or ends of a drum **2.** the top of a capstan, into which bars are inserted for leverage in turning it

drumhead court-martial [from the former use of a drum as the judges' table] a summary court-martial held in the field for trial of offenses committed during military operations or troop movements

drum·lin (drum′lin) *n.* [< Ir. *druim*, narrow ridge + *-lin*, dim. suffix < *-LING*[1]] a long ridge or oval-shaped hill formed of glacial drift

drum major a person who leads a marching band, or one who precedes it, often twirling a baton and prancing — ☆**drum ma·jor·ette** (mā′jə ret′) *fem.*

drum·mer (drum′ər) *n.* 1. a drum player 2. any of various animals that make a drumming sound 3. [see DRUM, phr. *drum up*] [Colloq.] a traveling salesman

drum·stick (-stik′) *n.* 1. a stick for beating a drum 2. the lower half of the leg of a cooked fowl

drunk (druŋk) [ME. *dronke* < *drunken*: see DRUNKEN] *pp. & archaic pt. of* DRINK —*adj.* [*usually used in the predicate*] 1. overcome by alcoholic liquor to the point of losing control over one's faculties; intoxicated 2. overcome by any powerful emotion [*drunk* with joy] 3. [Colloq.] *same as* DRUNKEN (sense 2) —*n.* [Slang] 1. a drunken person 2. a drinking spree

SYN.—**drunk** is the simple, direct word, usually used in the predicate, for one who is overcome by alcoholic liquor [he is *drunk*]; **drunken**, usually used attributively, is equivalent to **drunk** but sometimes implies habitual, intemperate drinking of liquor [a *drunken* bum]; **intoxicated** and **inebriated** are euphemisms, the former often expressing slight drunkenness and the latter, a state of drunken exhilaration; there are many euphemistic and slang terms in English expressing varying degrees of drunkenness: e.g., **tipsy** (slight), **tight** (moderate, but without great loss of muscular coordination), **blind** (great), **blotto** (to the point of unconsciousness), etc. —*ANT.* **sober**

drunk·ard (druŋ′kərd) *n.* [DRUNK + -ARD: ? after Du. *dronkaard*] a person who often gets drunk; inebriate

drunk·en (-kən) [ME. *dronken* < OE. *druncen*, pp. of *drincan*, to DRINK] *archaic pp. of* DRINK —*adj.* [*used before the noun*] 1. intoxicated or habitually intoxicated; drunk 2. caused by, characterized by, or occurring during intoxication [*drunken* driving] —*SYN.* see DRUNK —**drunk′en·ly** *adv.* —**drunk′en·ness** *n.*

☆**drunk·o·me·ter** (drəŋ käm′ə tər, druŋ′kə mēt′ər) *n.* [DRUNK + -*o*- + -METER] a device for testing a sample of exhaled breath to measure the amount of alcohol in the body

drupe (drōōp) *n.* [ModL. *drupa* < L. *drupa* (*oliva*), over-ripe (olive) < Gr. *dryppa*, olive] any fruit with a soft, fleshy part (*mesocarp*) covered by a skinlike outer layer (*exocarp*, or *epicarp*) and surrounding an inner stone (*endocarp*) that contains the seed, as an apricot, cherry, plum, etc. —**dru·pa·ceous** (drōō pā′shəs) *adj.*

drupe·let (-lit) *n.* a small drupe: a single blackberry consists of many drupelets

DRUPE

Dru·ry Lane (drōōr′ē) street and district in London, famous in the 17th and 18th cent. for its theaters

Druse, Druze (drōōz) *n.* [Ar. *Durūz*, pl. < Ismail al-*Darazī* (lit., tailor), the founder (11th c.)] a member of a secret religious sect in Syria and Lebanon whose creed is basically Moslem —**Dru′si·an** or **Dru′zi·an, Dru′se·an** or **Dru′ze·an** (drōō′zē ən) *adj.*

druse (drōōz) *n.* [G. < MHG. *druos*, a boil, swelling, gland ' < OHG., akin to Du. *droes*, goiter] a crystalline crust, usually quartz, lining the sides of a small rock cavity

Dru·sus (drōō′səs), **(Nero Claudius)** 38-9 B.C.; Rom. general

druth·ers (druth′ərz) *n.* [contr. < *I'd rather*, with sound infl. by OTHER] ☆[Dial. or Colloq.] a choice or preference [if I had my *druthers*]

dry (drī) *adj.* **dri′er, dri′est** [ME. *drie* < OE. *dryge*, akin to G. *trocken*, Du. *droog* < IE. **dhereugh*, fast, firm, solid (< base **dher-*, to hold out, hold fast, whence FIRM[1]] 1. not watery; not under water [*dry* land] 2. having no moisture; not wet or damp 3. not shedding tears 4. lacking rain or water [a *dry* summer] 5. having lost liquid or moisture; specif., *a*) arid; withered *b*) empty of water or other liquid *c*) dehydrated 6. needing water or drink; thirsty 7. not yielding milk [a *dry* cow] 8. without butter, jam, etc. on it [*dry* toast] 9. solid; not liquid 10. not sweet; unsweetened; sec [*dry* wine] 11. having no mucous or watery discharge [a *dry* cough] ☆12. prohibiting or opposed to the use or sale of alcoholic liquors [a *dry* town] 13. not colored by emotion, prejudice, etc.; plain; matter-of-fact [*dry* facts] 14. clever and shrewd but ironic or subtle [*dry* wit] 15. not producing results; unfruitful [a *dry* interview] 16. boring, dull, or tedious [a *dry* lecture] 17. [Obs.] without bleeding [a *dry* death] —*n.* 1. dryness or drought 2. a dry place ☆3. *pl.* **drys** [Colloq.] a prohibitionist —*vt., vi.* **dried, dry′ing** to make or become dry —**dry out** 1. to make or become thoroughly dry 2. [Slang] to withdraw from addiction to alcohol or a narcotic —**dry up** 1. to make or become thoroughly dry; parch or wither 2. to make or become unproductive, uncreative, etc. ☆3. [Slang] to stop talking —**not dry behind the ears** [Colloq.] immature; inexperienced; naive

SYN.—**dry** suggests a lack or insufficiency of moisture, in either a favorable or unfavorable sense [a *dry* climate, a *dry* river bed]; **arid** implies an abnormal, intense dryness, esp. with reference to a region or climate, and connotes barrenness or lifelessness [an *arid* waste] —*ANT.* **wet, moist**

dry·ad (drī′əd, -ad) *n., pl.* **-ads, -ad·es** (-ə dēz′) [L. *dryas* (gen. *dryadis*) < Gr. *dryas* < *drys*, an oak, tree: for IE. base see DRUID] *Gr. & Rom. Myth.* [*also* D-] any nymph living in a tree; wood nymph —**dry·ad·ic** (drī ad′ik) *adj.*

dry·as·dust (drī′əz dust′) *n.* a dull, pedantic person —*adj.* dull and boring

dry battery 1. an electric battery made up of several connected dry cells 2. a dry cell

dry-bulb thermometer (drī′bulb′) *see* WET-BULB THERMOMETER

dry cell a voltaic cell in which the electrolyte is in the form of a paste or is treated with an absorbent so that its contents cannot spill

dry-clean (drī′klēn′) *vt.* to clean (garments, etc.) with some solvent other than water, as naphtha, gasoline, carbon tetrachloride, etc. —**dry cleaner** —**dry cleaning**

Dry·den (drī′d'n), **John** 1631-1700; Eng. poet, critic, & playwright: poet laureate (1670-88)

dry-dock (-däk′) *vt., vi.* to place or go into a dry dock

dry dock a dock from which the water can be emptied, used for building and repairing ships

dry·er (-ər) *n.* 1. a person or thing that dries; specif., *a*) a frame or rack for drying clothes, etc. *b*) an apparatus for drying by heating or blowing air, esp. an appliance for drying clothes 2. *same as* DRIER

dry-eyed (-īd′) *adj.* not weeping; shedding no tears

☆**dry farming** farming in an almost rainless region without the help of irrigation: it is done by conserving the natural moisture of the soil and by planting crops that can resist drought —**dry′-farm′** *vt., vi.* —**dry farmer**

DRY DOCK

dry fly *see* FLY[2], sense 2

dry gangrene gangrene in which the involved body part does not become infected, but mummifies

dry goods cloth, cloth products, thread, etc.

☆**Dry Ice** *a trademark for* carbon dioxide solidified and compressed into snowlike cakes that vaporize at −78.5°C without passing through a liquid state: used as a refrigerant —[d- i-] such cakes of carbon dioxide

drying oil an organic oil that, when applied in a thin film, dries to form a hard, but elastic solid: widely used in paints and varnishes

dry kiln an enclosed place in which lumber is dried and seasoned by artificial heat

dry·ly (-lē) *adv.* in a dry manner; matter-of-factly

dry measure a system of measuring the volume of dry things, such as grain, vegetables, etc.; esp., the system in which 2 pints = 1 quart, 8 quarts = 1 peck, and 4 pecks = 1 bushel: see TABLE OF WEIGHTS AND MEASURES in Supplement

dry·ness (-nis) *n.* the quality or state of being dry

dry nurse a nurse who takes care of a baby but does not breast-feed it: cf. WET NURSE —**dry′-nurse′** *vt.*, **-nursed′, -nurs′ing**

dry·o·pith·e·cine (drī′ō pith′ə sēn′, -sīn′) *adj.* [< ModL. *dryopithecinae*, name of the subfamily < *Dryopithecus*, type genus < Gr. *drys*, TREE + ModL. *-pithecus*, ape (see PITHECANTHROPUS) + -*inae*, suffix for members of a subfamily < L., fem. pl. of -*inus*, -INE[1]] of or belonging to a genus (*Dryopithecus*) of fossil manlike apes —*n.* a dryopithecine ape

dry point 1. a fine, hard needle for engraving lines on a copper plate without using acid 2. a picture printed from such a plate 3. this way of engraving

dry rot 1. a fungous decay causing seasoned timber to become brittle and crumble to powder 2. a similar fungous disease of plants, fruits, and vegetables 3. any of various fungi causing such decay 4. any internal moral or social decay, generally resulting from lack of new or progressive influences —**dry′-rot′** *vi., vt.*, **-rot′ted, -rot′ting**

☆**dry run** 1. [Mil. Slang] practice in firing without using live ammunition 2. [Slang] a simulated or practice performance; rehearsal

dry-salt (drī′sôlt′) *vt.* to salt and dry (meat, etc.) in order to preserve it

dry-salt·er (-ər) *n.* [Brit.] a dealer in chemical products, dyes, etc. or, formerly, in dried or salted foods

dry-salt·er·y (-ər ē) *n., pl.* **-er·ies** [Brit.] the stock, shop, or trade of a drysalter

dry-shod (-shäd′) *adj.* without having wet shoes or feet

dry socket a tooth socket in which the blood clot has either broken down after extraction of a tooth or has never formed, resulting in very painful healing

Dry Tor·tu·gas (tôr tōō′gəz) group of small islands of Fla. in the Gulf of Mexico, west of Key West

dry wall 1. a wall of rocks or stones with no mortar or

cement ☆2. a wall constructed of wallboard, plasterboard, etc. without using wet plaster —**dry′wall′** *adj.*

☆**dry wash** laundry washed and dried but not ironed

D.S., d.s. [It. *dal segno*] (repeat) from this sign

d.s. 1. daylight saving   2. *Commerce* days after sight   3. detached service

D.S., D.Sc. Doctor of Science

D.S.C., DSC 1. Distinguished Service Cross   2. Doctor of Surgical Chiropody

D.S.M., DSM Distinguished Service Medal

D.S.O. Distinguished Service Order

D.S.T., DST Daylight Saving Time

d.t. 1. delirium tremens   2. double time

D.Th., D.Theol. Doctor of Theology

D.T.'s (dē′tēz′) [Slang] *same as* DELIRIUM TREMENS

Du. 1. Duke   2. Dutch

du·ad (dōō′ad, dyōō′-) *n.* [var. of DYAD] two together; pair; couple

du·al (-əl) *adj.* [L. *dualis* < *duo*, TWO] 1. of two   2. having or composed of two parts or kinds, like or unlike; double; twofold *[a dual nature]* —*n.* Linguis. 1. *same as* DUAL NUMBER   2. a word having dual number —**du·al·i·ty** (dōō al′ə tē, dyōō-) *n.* —**du′al·ly** *adv.*

du·al·ism (-iz′m) *n.* 1. the state of being dual; duality   2. *Philos.* the theory that the world is ultimately composed of, or explicable in terms of, two basic entities, as mind and matter   3. *Theol. a)* the doctrine that there are two mutually antagonistic principles in the universe, good and evil   *b)* the doctrine that man has two natures, physical and spiritual —**du′al·ist** *n.*

du·al·is·tic (dōō′ə lis′tik, dyōō′-) *adj.* 1. of or based on dualism   2. dual —**du′al·is′ti·cal·ly** *adv.*

du·al·ize (dōō′əl īz′, dyōō′-) *vt.* **-ized′, -iz′ing** to make, or consider as, dual

dual number in some languages, a grammatical number indicating *two, a pair*: distinguished by inflection from *singular* and *plural*

du·al-pur·pose (dōō′əl pur′pəs, dyōō′-) *adj.* having, or meant to have, two uses

dub¹ (dub) *vt.* **dubbed, dub′bing** [ME. *dubben* < OE. *dubbian*, to strike (akin to DOWEL, ON. *dubba*, to dub, EFris. *dubhen*, push) < IE. base *dheubh, a club, wooden pin] 1. to hit; strike; thrust; poke   2. to beat (a drum)   3. to confer knighthood on by tapping on the shoulder with a sword   4. *a)* to confer a title or rank upon   *b)* to call, name, or nickname   5. to make (wood, etc.) smooth, as by hammering or scraping   6. to dress (leather) by rubbing   7. [Slang] to bungle (a golf stroke, etc.) —*vi.* to thrust or poke (*at*) —*n.* 1. a drumbeat   ☆2. [Slang] a clumsy, unskillful performer or person —**dub′ber** *n.*

☆**dub²** (dub) *vt.* **dubbed, dub′bing** (contr. < DOUBLE) 1. to re-record the sound from (an old recording): distinguished from RE-PRESS   2. to provide with a sound track —*n.* dialogue, music, etc. inserted in a sound track, as of a motion picture —**dub** *in Motion Pictures, Radio & TV* 1. to insert (dialogue, music, etc.) in the sound track   2. to insert (synchronized dialogue in another language) in place of the original dialogue —**dub′ber** *n.*

dub³ (dub) *n.* [Scot. & N. Eng. dial., prob. < Scand., akin to Norw. *dobbe*, swampy land, MDu. *doppe*, shell, MLowG. *dobbe*, pool: for IE. base see DIMPLE] [Scot.] a small pool or puddle

du Bar·ry (dōō bar′ē; *Fr.* dü bä rē′), comtesse (born *Marie Jeanne Bécu*) 1743?–93; mistress of Louis XV of France

dub·bin (dub′n) *n.* [< *dubbing*: see DUB¹, *v.* 6] a greasy preparation for softening and waterproofing leather: also **dub′bing**

du·bi·e·ty (dōō bī′ə tē, dyōō-) *n.* [LL. *dubietas*] 1. the quality of being dubious; doubtfulness   2. *pl.* **-ties** a doubtful thing —*SYN.* see UNCERTAINTY

du·bi·os·i·ty (dōō′bē äs′ə tē, dyōō′-) *n., pl.* **-ties** vague doubt or uncertainty —*SYN.* see UNCERTAINTY

du·bi·ous (dōō′bē əs, dyōō′-) *adj.* [L. *aubiosus* < *dubius*, doubting, uncertain < *du-* < or akin to *duo*, TWO + IE. base **hhu-*, to be] 1. causing doubt; ambiguous; vague *[a dubious remark]*   2. feeling doubt; hesitating; skeptical   3. with the outcome undecided or hanging in the balance *[dubious battle]*   4. rousing suspicion; questionable; shady *[a dubious character]* —*SYN.* see DOUBTFUL —**du′bi·ous·ly** *adv.* —**du′bi·ous·ness** *n.*

du·bi·ta·ble (dōō′bi tə b'l, dyōō′-) *adj.* [L. *dubitabilis*] to be doubted; uncertain —**du′bi·ta·bly** *adv.*

du·bi·ta·tion (dōō′bə tā′shən, dyōō′-) *n.* [ME. *dubita-cioun* < L. *dubitatio*] [Rare] doubt —**du·bi·ta·tive** (dōō′bə tā′tiv, dyōō′-) *adj.*

Dub·lin (dub′lən) 1. capital of Ireland: seaport on the Irish Sea: pop. 537,000   2. county in E Ireland, on the Irish Sea: 356 sq. mi.; pop. 718,000; county seat, Dublin

du Bois (dü bwä′), **Guy Pène** (gē pen) 1884–1958; U.S. painter & art critic

Du Bois (dōō bois′), **W(illiam) E(dward) B(urghardt)** 1868–1963; U.S. historian, educator, & Negro leader

Du·brov·nik (dōō′brôv nik) seaport in SW Yugoslavia, on the Adriatic: pop. 23,000: It. name, RAGUSA

Du·buque (də byōōk′) [after Julien *Dubuque*, early lead miner] city in E Iowa, on the Mississippi: pop. 62,000

du·cal (dōō′k'l, dyōō′-) *adj.* [OFr. < LL. *ducalis*, of a leader < L. *dux*] of a duke or dukedom —**du′cal·ly** *adv.*

duc·at (duk′ət) *n.* [ME. & OFr. < It. *ducato*, ducat, coin bearing image of a duke < LL. *ducatus*: see DUCHY] 1. any of several gold or silver coins formerly used in some European countries   2. [Slang] a piece of money   3. [Slang] a ticket, esp. an admission ticket

‡**du·ce** (dōō′che) *n.* [It. < L. *dux* (gen. *ducis*): see DUKE] chief; leader: title (*Il Duce*) assumed by Benito Mussolini, Fascist head of Italy (1922–43)

Du·champ (dü shän′), **Mar·cel** (mär sel′) 1887–1968; U.S. painter, born in France

duch·ess (duch′is) *n.* [ME. & OFr. *duchesse*, fem. of *duc*, DUKE] 1. the wife or widow of a duke   2. a woman who has the rank of a duke and rules a duchy

duch·y (-ē) *n., pl.* **duch′ies** [ME. & OFr. *duchee* < LL. *ducatus*, military command, territory of a duke < L. *dux*: see DUKE] the territory ruled by a duke or duchess; dukedom

duck¹ (duk) *n.* [ME. *doke* < OE. *duce*, lit., diver, ducker < base of ff.; replaces OE. *ened* (G. *ente*), common Gmc. word for the bird] *pl.* **ducks, duck**: see PLURAL, II, D, 1 1. any of a large number of relatively small swimming fowl (family Anatidae) with a flat bill, short neck and legs, and webbed feet   2. a female duck: opposed to DRAKE¹ 3. the flesh of a duck as food   4. [Chiefly Brit. Colloq.] a darling; dear ☆5. [Slang] a person, esp. one qualified as being "odd," "harmless," "funny," etc. —**like water off a duck's back** with no effect or reaction

duck² (duk) *vt., vi.* [ME. *douken* < OE. *ducan, to plunge, dive, akin to OHG. *tūhan* (G. *tauchen*), MLowG. *dūken*, Du. *duiken*, to dive] 1. to plunge or dip under water for a moment   2. to lower, turn, or bend (the head, body, etc.) suddenly, as in avoiding a blow or in hiding   3. [Colloq.] to avoid (a task, person, etc.)   4. [Slang] to move (*in* or *out*) quickly —*n.* the act of ducking —**duck′er** *n.*

duck³ (duk) *n.* [Du. *doek*, akin to G. *tuch*, cloth] 1. a cotton or linen cloth somewhat like canvas but finer and lighter in weight   2. [*pl.*] clothes, esp. white trousers, made of this cloth

duck⁴ (duk) *n.* [altered (after DUCK¹) < *DUKW*, military code name] [Mil. Slang] an amphibious motor vehicle

duck-bill (duk′bil′) *n. same as* PLATYPUS

duck-board (-hôrd′) *n.* a board or boards forming a slightly raised surface or flooring on a muddy road, wet place, etc.

duck-foot·ed (-foot′id) *adj.* having the hind toe pointing forward, as on a duck's foot: said of fowl

duck hawk ☆a N. American falcon (*Falco peregrinus*) with a slaty back and a barred belly

ducking stool a chair at the end of a plank, in which a culprit was tied and then ducked into water: a form of punishment formerly used, as in New England, esp. for quarrelsome women

DUCKING STOOL

duck·ling (-liŋ) *n.* a young duck

duck·pins (-pinz′) *n.pl.* 1. [*with sing. v.*] a game like bowling or ten-pins, played with smaller pins and balls   2. the pins used in this game

ducks and drakes the game of throwing a small, flat stone so that it will skim or skip along the surface of water —**make ducks and drakes of** to deal with recklessly or squander: also **play ducks and drakes with**

☆**duck sickness** a disease of wild ducks associated with the consumption of decaying algae, and variously considered to be the result of algal toxins or of botulism

☆**duck soup** [Slang] something that is easy to do; cinch

duck·weed (duk′wēd′) *n.* any of a family (Lemnaceae) of minute flowering plants that float on ponds and sluggish streams and reproduce by a kind of budding: so called because eaten by ducks

duck·y (duk′ē) *adj.* **duck′i·er, duck′i·est** [early 19th-c. term of endearment < DUCK¹ + -Y²] [Slang] pleasing, delightful, darling, etc.: often used ironically

duct (dukt) *n.* [ML. *ducta*, conduit < L. *ductus*, a leading, conducting, pp. of *ducere*, to lead: see DUKE] 1. a tube, channel, or canal through which a gas or liquid moves   2. a tube in the body for the passage of excretions or secretions *[a tear duct, bile duct]*   3. a conducting tubule in plant tissues, esp. one containing resin, latex, etc.   4. a pipe or conduit through which wires or cables are run —**duct′less** *adj.*

duc·tile (duk′t'l) *adj.* [ME. *ductil* < L. *ductilis* < *ductus*: see prec.] 1. that can be stretched, drawn, or hammered thin without breaking; not brittle: said of metals   2. easily molded; plastic; pliant   3. easily led; tractable —*SYN.* see PLIABLE —**duc·til·i·ty** (duk til′ə tē) *n.*

ductless gland an endocrine gland

duct·ule (duk′tyool) *n.* a small duct

dud (dud) *n.* [prob. < Du. *dood*, dead] [Colloq.] 1. a bomb or shell that fails to explode 2. a person or thing that fails or is ineffectual —*adj.* [Colloq.] worthless

dud·dy, dud·die (dud′ē) *adj.* [< dial. *dud*, coarse cloak (see DUDS) + -Y²] [Scot.] ragged; tattered

☆**dude** (dōōd) *n.* [< ?] 1. a man too much concerned with his clothes and appearance; dandy; fop 2. [Western Slang] a city fellow or tourist, esp. an Easterner who is vacationing on a ranch —**dud′ish** *adj.*

du·deen (dōō dēn′) *n.* [< Ir. *dúidín*, a little pipe < *dúd*, a pipe] [Irish] a short-stemmed clay tobacco pipe

☆**dude ranch** a ranch or farm operated as a vacation resort, with horseback riding and similar sports

Dude·vant (düd vän′), Baronne *see* George SAND

dudg·eon¹ (duj′ən) *n.* [16th-c. (*take*) *in dudgeon*, also *endugine*, prob. Anglo-Fr. *en digeon*, with reference to the hand on the dagger hilt: see ?] anger or resentment: now chiefly in the phrase **in high dudgeon**, very angry, offended, or resentful

dudg·eon² (duj′ən) *n.* [ME. *dogeon*, Anglo-Fr. *digeon*] [Obs.] 1. a wood, perhaps boxwood, used for dagger hilts 2. a hilt of this wood or a dagger hilted with it

Dud·ley¹ (dud′lē) [< the family (earlier place) name, orig. "Dudda's lea"] 1. a masculine name 2. **Robert**, *see* Earl of LEICESTER

Dud·ley² (dud′lē) city in Worcestershire, WC England, near Birmingham: pop. 64,000

duds (dudz) *n.pl.* [ME. *dudde*, cloth, cloak, prob. < or akin to ON. *duthi*, swaddling clothes < *dutha*, to swathe] [Colloq.] 1. clothes 2. trappings; belongings

due (dōō, dyōō) *adj.* [ME. < OFr. *deu*, pp. of *devoir*, to owe < L. *debere*, to owe: see DEBT] 1. owed or owing as a debt, right, etc.; payable [the first payment is *due*] 2. suitable; fitting; proper [with all *due* respect] 3. as much as is required; enough; adequate [*due* care, in *due* time] 4. expected or scheduled to arrive or be ready; timed for a certain hour or date [the plane is *due* at 6:30 P.M.] —*adv.* exactly; directly [*due* west] —*n.* anything due or owed: specif., *a)* deserved recognition [to give a man his *due*] *b)* [*pl.*] fees, taxes, or other charges [membership *dues*] —**become** (or **fall**) **due** to become payable as previously arranged —☆**due to** 1. caused by; resulting from [an omission *due to* oversight] 2. [Colloq.] because of [the name was omitted *due to* oversight]: widely so used despite objections by some grammarians

☆**due bill** a written acknowledgment of a debt to a person named, but neither payable to his order nor transferable by endorsement; often, such an acknowledgment exchangeable for merchandise or services only

du·el (dōō′əl, dyōō′-) *n.* [ME. *duelle* < ML. *duellum* < OL. *dvellum* (L. *bellum*), war < IE. base *dāu-*, *deu-*, to injure, destroy, burn, whence Sans. *dū*, pain, OE. *teona*, harm] 1. a formal fight between two persons armed with deadly weapons: it is prearranged and witnessed by two others, called *seconds*, one for each combatant 2. any contest or encounter suggesting such a fight, usually between two persons [a verbal *duel*] —*vi.*, *vt.* **-eled** or **-elled**, **-el·ing** or **-el·ling** to fight a duel with (a person or persons) —**du′el·ist** or **du′el·list, du′el·er** or **du′el·ler** *n.*

du·el·lo (dōō el′ō, dyōō-) *n.*, *pl.* **-los** [It. < ML. *duellum*, DUEL] 1. the art, rules, or code of dueling 2. [Obs.] a duel

du·en·na (-en′ə) *n.* [Sp. *dueña* < L. *domina*, mistress: see DAME] 1. an elderly woman who has charge of the girls and young unmarried women of a Spanish or Portuguese family 2. a chaperon or governess

due process (of law) the course of legal proceedings established by the legal system of a nation or state to protect individual rights and liberties

Due·ro (dwe′rō) Sp. name of DOURO River

du·et (dōō et′, dyōō-) *n.* [It. *duetto*, dim. of *duo*, duet < L. *duo*, TWO] *Music* 1. a composition for two voices or two instruments 2. the two performers of such a composition; duo

duff¹ (duf) *n.* [dial. var. of DOUGH, with *ff* for ME. *-gh* (cf. LAUGH), orig. pronounced (kh); sense 2 & 3 < ?] 1. a thick flour pudding boiled in a cloth bag 2. decaying vegetable matter on the ground in a forest 3. coal dust or slack

☆**duff**² (duf) *n.* [< ?] [Slang] the buttocks

duf·fel, duf·fle (duf′'l) *n.* [Du. < *Duffel*, town in N Belgium] 1. a coarse woolen cloth with a thick nap ☆2. essential clothing and equipment carried by a sportsman, camper, soldier, etc. ☆3. *same as* DUFFEL BAG 4. *same as* DUFFEL COAT

☆**duffel** (or **duffle**) **bag** a large, cylindrical cloth bag, esp. of waterproof canvas or duck, for carrying clothing and personal belongings

duffel (or **duffle**) **coat** a knee-length coat made of duffel or other wool cloth, usually with a hood

duf·fer (duf′ər) *n.* [< thieves' slang *duff*, to counterfeit, fake] [Slang] 1. formerly, a peddler of cheap jewelry, etc. 2. anything counterfeit or worthless 3. an incompetent, awkward, or stupid person; specif., a relatively unskilled golfer

Du·fy (dü fē′), **Ra·oul** (Ernest Joseph) (rä ōōl′) 1877–1953; Fr. painter

dug¹ (dug) *pt. & pp.* of DIG

dug² (dug) *n.* [< same base as Dan. *dægge*, to suckle, caus. of Dan. *die*, to suck < IE. base *dhē-*: see FEMALE] a nipple, teat, or udder

du·gong (dōō′gôn, -gän) *n.* [Malay *dūyung*] any of a genus (*Dugong*) of large, somewhat whalelike, tropical mammals that live along the shores of the Indian Ocean and Red Sea and feed mostly on seaweed

DUGONG
(to 8 ft. long)

☆**dug·out** (dug′out′) *n.* 1. a boat or canoe hollowed out of a log 2. a shelter, as in warfare, dug in the ground or in a hillside and often covered or reinforced with logs, beams, etc. 3. *Baseball* a covered shelter near the diamond for the players to sit in when not at bat or in the field

Du·ha·mel (dü ȧ mel′), **Georges** (zhôrzh) 1884– ; Fr. novelist, poet, & dramatist

dui·ker (dīk′ər) *n.*, *pl.* **-kers, -ker**: see PLURAL, II, D, 1 [Du. *duiker*, lit., a diver < *duiken*, to DUCK²] any of several small, African antelopes (as genera *Cephalophus* and *Sylvicapra*) common south of the Sahara

Duis·burg (düs′boork) city in W West Germany, at the junction of the Rhine & Ruhr rivers: pop. 492,000

duke (dōōk, dyōōk) *n.* [ME. *duk* < OFr. *duc* < L. *dux*, leader < *ducere*, to lead < IE. base *deuk-*, to pull, whence TEAM, TUG] 1. a prince who rules an independent duchy 2. a nobleman of the highest hereditary rank below that of prince —**duke′dom** (-dəm) *n.*

dukes (dōōks, dyōōks) *n.pl.* [< *duke*, short for *Duke of York*, used in 19th-c. E. rhyming slang for *fork*, hence fingers, hence fist] [Slang] the fists or hands

Du·kho·bors (dōō′kə bôrz′) *n.pl.* [Russ. *dukhobortsy*, lit., spirit wrestlers < *dukh*, spirit + *bortsy*, wrestlers] a Russian religious sect separated from the Orthodox Church in 1785: many Dukhobors emigrated to W Canada in the 1890's to escape persecution: also **Du·kho·bor·tsy** (dōō′khȧ bôr′tsē)

dul·cet (dul′sit) *adj.* [ME. *doucet* < OFr., dim. of *douz, sweet* < ? IE. base *dlku-*, sweet, whence Gr. *glykys*] 1. soothing or pleasant to hear; sweet-sounding; melodious 2. [Archaic] sweet to taste or smell —*n.* an organ stop like the dulciana, but one octave higher in pitch —**dul′cet·ly** *adv.*

dul·ci·an·a (dul′sē an′ə) *n.* [ML. < L. *dulcis*, see prec.] an organ stop with a sweet, mellow tone like that of a stringed instrument

dul·ci·fy (dul′sə fī′) *vt.* **-fied, -fy′ing** [< L. *dulcis* (see DULCET) + -FY] [Rare] 1. to sweeten 2. to make pleasant or agreeable; mollify

dul·ci·mer (dul′sə mər) *n.* [ME. *doucemer* < OFr. *doulcemer* < Sp. *dulcemele* < L. *dulce melos* < *dulce*, neut. of *dulcis*, sweet + *melos* < Gr. *melos*, a song, strain] 1. a musical instrument with metal strings, which are struck with two small hammers by the player ☆2. a violin-shaped stringed instrument of the southern Appalachians, played by plucking with a wooden plectrum or goose quill: also **dul′ci·more′** (-môr′, -mər) 3. *Bible* a musical instrument, variously interpreted to be a kind of harp, bagpipe, etc.: see Dan. 3:5

DULCIMER

Dul·ci·ne·a (dul′sə nē′ə, dul sin′ē ə) [Sp. < *dulce*, sweet < L. *dulcis*: see DULCET] the plain peasant girl whom Don Quixote imagines to be a beautiful lady and falls in love with —*n.* any idealized sweetheart

du·li·a (dōō lī′ə, dyōō-) *n.* [ME. < ML. < Gr. *douleia*, service < *doulos*, a slave] *R.C.Ch.* the homage paid to angels and saints: distinguished from LATRIA

dull (dul) *adj.* [ME. *dul* < OE. *dol*, stupid, akin to G. *toll* < IE. *dh(e)wel-* < base *dheu-*, smoke, dark, turbid, whence DUMB, DWELL, OIr. *dall*, blind] 1. mentally slow; stupid 2. lacking sensitivity; blunted in feeling or perception [*dull* to grief] 3. physically slow; slow-moving; sluggish 4. lacking spirit, zest, etc.; not lively; listless, insipid, etc. 5. not active or busy; slack [a *dull* period for sales] 6. causing boredom; tedious [a *dull* party] 7. not pointed or sharp; blunt; not keen [a *dull* blade] 8. not felt keenly; not acute [a *dull* headache] 9. *a)* not vivid; not brilliant; dim [a *dull* color] *b)* not shiny or glossy; lusterless [a *dull* finish] 10. not distinct, resonant, etc.; muffled [a *dull* thud] 11. gloomy; cloudy [*dull* weather] —*vt.*, *vi.* to make or become dull —**dull′ish** *adj.* —**dull′ness, dul′ness** *n.* —**dul′ly** *adv.*

SYN.—**dull** is specifically applied to a point or edge that has lost its previous sharpness [a *dull* knife] and generally connotes a lack of keenness, zest, spirit, intensity, etc. [a *dull* book, pain, etc.]; **blunt** is often equivalent to **dull**, but specifically refers to a point or edge that is intentionally not sharp [a *blunt* fencing saber]; **obtuse** literally applies to a pointed end whose sides form an angle greater than 90°, and figuratively connotes great dullness of understanding or lack of sensitivity [too *obtuse* to comprehend] See also STUPID —**ANT.** sharp, keen

dull·ard (-ərd) *n.* [ME.: see DULL & -ARD] a stupid person

dulse (duls) *n.* [Ir. & Gael. *duileasg*] any of several edible marine algae (esp. *Rhodymenia palmata*) with large, red, wedge-shaped fronds

Du·luth (də lōōth′) [after Daniel G. *Du Lhut* (or *Du Luth*) 1636?–1709?, Fr. explorer] city and port in NE Minn., on Lake Superior: pop. 101,000

du·ly (dōō′lē, dyōō′-) *adv.* in a due manner; specif., *a)* as due; rightfully *b)* when due; at the right time; on time *c)* as required; sufficiently

Du·ma (dōō′mä) *n.* [Russ. < Gmc., as in Goth. *doms*, ON. *domr*, OE. *dom*, judgment: see DOOM¹] the parliament of czarist Russia (1905–17)

Du·mas (dü mä′; *E.* dōō′mä) **1.** Alexandre, 1802–70; Fr. novelist & playwright: called *Dumas père* **2.** Alexandre, 1824–95; Fr. playwright & novelist: son of *prec.:* called *Dumas fils*

du Mau·ri·er (dōō môr′ē ā′, dyōō), George (Louis Pal-mella Busson) 1834–96; Eng. illustrator & novelist, born in France

dumb (dum) *adj.* [ME. & OE., akin to G. *dumm* (Goth. *dumbs*), mute, stupid < nasalized var. of IE. *dheubh-:* see DULL] **1.** lacking the power of speech; mute **2.** unwilling to talk; silent; reticent **3.** not accompanied by speech **4.** temporarily speechless, as from fear, grief, etc. **5.** producing no sound **6.** lacking some normal part, characteristic, or quality ☆**7.** [G. *dumm*] [Colloq.] stupid; moronic; unintelligent —*SYN.* see VOICELESS —**dumb′ly** *adv.* —**dumb′ness** *n.*

Dum·bar·ton (dum bär′t'n) **1.** city in W Scotland, on the Clyde River; county seat of Dunbarton: pop. 26,000 **2.** *same as* DUNBARTON

dumb·bell (dum′bel′) *n.* [DUMB + BELL¹: from orig. shape] **1.** a device usually used in pairs, consisting of round weights joined by a short bar, by which it is lifted or swung about in the hand for muscular exercise ☆**2.** [cf. DUMB, sense 7] [Slang] a stupid person

dumb cane *a common name for* DIEFFENBACHIA

DUMBBELL

dumb·found, dum·found (dum′found′) *vt.* [DUMB + (CON)FOUND] to make speechless by shocking; amaze; astonish —*SYN.* see PUZZLE

dumb show 1. formerly, a part of a play done in pantomime **2.** gestures without speech

dumb·struck (dum′struk′) *adj.* so shocked as to be speechless: also **dumb′strick·en** (-strik′ən)

dumb·wait·er (-wāt′ər) *n.* **1.** a small, portable stand for serving food, often with shelves ☆**2.** a small elevator for sending food, trash, etc. from one floor to another

dum·dum (bullet) (dum′dum′) [< *Dumdum*, arsenal near Calcutta, India < Hindi *damdama*, hill, fortification] a soft-nosed bullet that expands when it hits, inflicting a large, jagged wound

Dum·fries (dum frēs′) **1.** county of S Scotland, on Solway Firth; 1,075 sq. mi.; pop. 88,000: also **Dum·fries·shire** (dum frē′shir) **2.** its county seat: pop. 27,000

dum·my (dum′ē) *n., pl.* **-mies** [< DUMB + -Y²] **1.** a person unable to talk; mute: now vulgar in this sense **2.** a figure made in human form, as for displaying clothing, practicing tackling in football, etc. **3.** an imitation or sham; substitute for the real thing, as an empty container or false drawer **4.** a person secretly acting for another while apparently representing his own interests **5.** [Slang] a stupid person **6.** *Bridge, Whist,* etc. *a)* the declarer's partner, whose hand is exposed on the board and played by the declarer *b)* the hand thus exposed **7.** *Printing* the skeleton copy, as of a magazine or book, upon which the format is planned and laid out —*adj.* **1.** imitation; sham; fictitious **2.** secretly acting as a front for another [*a dummy corporation*] **3.** *Bridge,* etc. played with a dummy — **dummy up, -mied, -my·ing** [Slang] to refuse to talk or tell what one knows

dump¹ (dump) *vt.* [ME. *dompen,* to plunge, throw down; prob. < Dan. *dumpe,* Sw. *dompa:* for IE. base see DEEP] **1.** to throw down or out roughly; empty out or unload as in a heap or mass **2.** *a)* to throw away (garbage, rubbish, etc.) esp. in a place set apart for the purpose *b)* to get rid of in an abrupt, rough, or careless manner **3.** to sell (a commodity) in a large quantity at a very low price, esp. abroad so as to maintain a higher domestic market price —*vi.* **1.** to fall in a heap or mass **2.** to unload rubbish **3.** to dump commodities —*n.* **1.** a rubbish pile ☆**2.** a place for dumping rubbish, etc. **3.** *Mil.* a temporary storage center in the field, as of ammunition, food, or clothing ☆**4.** [Slang] a place that is unpleasant, ugly, rundown, etc. —**dump′er** *n.*

dump² (dump) *n.* [prob. < Du. *domp,* haze, dullness, akin to DAMP] [Obs.] **1.** a sad tune or song **2.** any tune or song —**(down) in the dumps** in low spirits; depressed

dump³ (dump) *n.* [< ? DUMPY¹] [Brit.] a small, shapeless lump or chunk, as of lead

dump·ish (-ish) *adj.* [see DUMP²] [Rare] gloomy; depressed

dump·ling (dump′lin) *n.* [< ? DUMP³ + -LING] **1.** a small piece of dough, steamed or boiled and served with meat or soup **2.** a crust of dough filled with fruit and steamed or baked **3.** [Colloq.] a short, fat person or animal

☆**dump truck** a truck whose contents are unloaded by tilting the truck bed backward with the tailgate open

dump·y¹ (dum′pē) *adj.* **dump′i·er, dump′i·est** [prob. < DUMP¹] **1.** short and thick; squat; stumpy **2.** [Slang] ugly, rundown, etc. —**dump′i·ly** *adv.* —**dump′i·ness** *n.*

dump·y² (dum′pē) *adj.* **dump′i·er, dump′i·est** [see DUMP²] melancholy; depressed

dumpy level a surveyor's level consisting of a telescope mounted exactly level on a three- or four-legged stand and rotating only horizontally

Dum·yât (doom yät′) *Arabic name of* DAMIETTA

dun¹ (dun) *adj.* [ME. & OE., akin to OS. *dun,* chestnut-brown, ult. (? via Celt.) < IE. *dhus-no* < *dhus,* dust-colored, mist-gray, whence DUSK, DUST] dull grayish-brown —*n.* **1.** a dull grayish brown **2.** a dun horse **3.** an artificial fishing fly of this color: also **dun fly 4.** *same as* MAY FLY —**dun′ness** *n.*

dun² (dun) *vt., vi.* **dunned, dun′ning** [? dial. var. of DIN] **1.** to ask (a debtor) insistently or repeatedly for payment **2.** to annoy constantly —*n.* **1.** a person who duns **2.** an insistent demand, esp. for payment of a debt

Du·na (dōō′nä) *Hung. name of the* DANUBE

☆**Dun and Brad·street** (dun′ ən brad′strēt′) an agency that furnishes subscribers with information as to the financial standing and credit rating of businesses

Du·nant (dü nän′), Jean Hen·ri (zhän än rē′) 1828–1910; Swiss philanthropist: founder of the Red Cross society

Du·nă·rea (dōō′nər yä) *Romanian name of the* DANUBE

Dun·bar (dun′bär) **1.** Paul Laurence, 1872–1906; U.S. poet **2.** William, 1460?–1520?; Scot. poet

Dun·bar·ton (dun bär′t'n) county of W Scotland, on the Clyde River: 241 sq. mi.; pop. 23,000; county seat, Dumbarton: also **Dun·bar′ton·shire′** (-shir′)

Dun·can (dun′kən) [Gael. *Donnchadh,* lit., brown warrior] **1.** a masculine name **2.** in Shakespeare's *Macbeth,* the aged king of Scotland, murdered by Macbeth **3.** Isadora, 1878–1927; U.S. dancer

Duncan Phyfe designating or of furniture in a modified Empire and Directoire style designed by Duncan PHYFE

dunce (duns) *n.* [< John DUNS SCOTUS: his followers, called *Dunsmen, Dunses, Dunces,* were regarded as foes of Renaissance humanism] **1.** a dull, ignorant person **2.** a person who learns more slowly than others

dunce cap a cone-shaped hat that children slow at learning were formerly forced to wear in school

Dun·dalk (dun′dôk) suburb of Baltimore, in C Md.: pop. 85,000

Dun·dee (dun dē′) seaport in Angus, E Scotland, on the Firth of Tay: pop. 185,000

dun·der·head (dun′dər hed′) *n.* [< Du. *donder,* thunder, associated by rhyme with BLUNDER (cf. BLUNDERBUSS) + HEAD] a stupid person; dunce —**dun′der·head′ed** *adj.*

dune (dōōn, dyōōn) *n.* [Fr. < ODu. *duna:* for IE. base see DOWN²] a rounded hill or ridge of sand heaped up by the action of the wind

☆**dune buggy** a small, light automobile generally made from a standard, compact, rear-engine chassis and a prefabricated, often fiberglass body: orig. equipped with wide, low-pressure tires for driving on sand dunes

Dun·e·din (də nē′d'n) city on the SE coast of South Island, New Zealand: pop. (with suburbs) 109,000

Dun·ferm·line (dən furm′lin) city in Fife, E Scotland, near the Firth of Forth: pop. 50,000

dung (dun) *n.* [ME. & OE., prob. identical with *dung,* a prison, orig., cellar covered with dung for warmth, as in OS. *dung,* OHG. *tung,* cellar where women weave < IE. base *dheng-,* to cover, covering layer] **1.** animal excrement; manure **2.** filth —*vt.* to spread or cover with dung, as in fertilizing

dun·ga·ree (dun′gə rē′) *n.* [Hind. *dungri*] **1.** a coarse cotton cloth; specif., blue denim **2.** [*pl.*] work trousers or overalls made of this cloth

dung beetle any of various beetles (family Scarabaeidae) that breed in dung and feed on it

dun·geon (dun′jən) *n.* [ME. *dongoun* < OFr. *donjon,* prob. < Frank. *dungjo,* earth-covered cellar for storing fruits: see DUNG] **1.** *same as* DONJON **2.** a dark underground cell, vault, or prison —*vt.* [Rare] to confine in a dungeon

dung·hill (dun′hil′) *n.* **1.** a heap of dung **2.** anything vile or filthy

dung·y (-ē) *adj.* **dung′i·er, dung′i·est** of, like, or soiled with dung; filthy; vile

dun·ite (dun′īt) *n.* [< Mt. *Dun,* in New Zealand + -ITE²] a dense, igneous rock consisting largely of olivine and, usually, chromite

☆**dunk** (dunk) *vt.* [G. *tunken,* to steep, dip, soak < OHG. *dunchôn:* for IE. base see TINGE] **1.** to dip (bread, cake, etc.) into coffee or other liquid before eating it **2.** to immerse in a liquid for a short time

Dun·kerque (dön kerk′) *Fr. name of* DUNKIRK

☆**Dunk·ers** (dun′kərz) *n.pl.* [G. *tunker,* dipper < *tunken* (see DUNK): so named from practice of immersion] a sect of German-American Baptists opposed to military service

---

fat, āpe, cär; ten, ēven; is, bīte; gō, hôrn, tōōl, look; oil, out; up, fur; get; joy; yet; chin; she; thin, *then;* zh, leisure; ŋ, ring; ə for *a* in *ago, e* in *agent, i* in *sanity, o* in *comply, u* in *focus;* ' as in *able* (ā′b'l); Fr. bäl; ë, Fr. coeur; ö, Fr. feu; Fr. mon; ô, Fr. coq; ü, Fr. duc; r, Fr. cri; H, G. ich; kh, G. doch. See inside front cover. ☆ Americanism; ‡foreign; *hypothetical; < derived from

and the taking of oaths: also called **Dunk′ards** (-ərdz), but properly called **Church of the Brethren**

Dun·kirk (dun′kərk) seaport in N France, on the North Sea: scene of the evacuation of Allied troops under fire (1940): pop. 28,000

dun·lin (dun′lin) *n., pl.* **-lins, -lin:** see PLURAL, II, D, 1 [< *dunling* < DUN¹ + -LING¹] a small sandpiper (*Erolia alpina*) with a reddish back, a black patch on its belly, and a striped breast during breeding season

dun·nage (dun′ij) *n.* [ME. *dunnage* < ML. *dennagium* < ?] 1. a loose packing of any bulky material put around cargo for protection 2. personal baggage or belongings

Dunne (dun), **Finley Peter** 1867–1936; U.S. humorist & journalist

☆**dun·nite** (dun′īt) *n.* [after B. W. *Dunn* (1860–1936), U.S. army officer who invented it] a high explosive, C₆H₂(NO₂)₃-ONH₄, used esp. in armor-piercing shells because of its relative insensitivity to shock

Dun·sa·ny (dən sā′nē), **Lord** (born *Edward John Moreton Drax Plunkett*), 18th Baron Dunsany, 1878–1957; Ir. playwright & poet, born in London

Dun·si·nane (dun′sə nān′) hill in Perthshire, C Scotland: ruined fortress at its summit is the reputed site of Macbeth's defeat as related in Shakespeare's play

Duns Sco·tus (dunz skŏt′əs), **John** (or **Johannes**) 1265?–1308; Scot. scholastic philosopher and theologian: see SCOTISM

Duns·tan (dun′stən), **Saint** 924?–988 A.D.; Eng. prelate: archbishop of Canterbury (961–988): his day is May 19

dunt (dunt, doont) *n.* [ME., var. of *dint*, a blow: see DINT] [Scot. & Brit. Dial.] 1. a heavy, dull-sounding blow 2. a wound caused by such a blow —*vt., vi.* [Scot. & Brit. Dial.] to strike with such a blow

du·o (dōō′ō, dyōō′-) *n., pl.* **du′os, du′i** (-ē) [It.] 1. *same as* DUET (esp. sense 2) 2. a pair; couple

du·o- (-ə) [< L. *duo*, TWO] a combining form meaning two, double [*duotype*]

du·o·dec·i·mal (dōō′ə des′ə m′l, dyōō′-) *adj.* [< L. *duodecim*, twelve (< *duo*, TWO + *decem*, TEN) + -AL] 1. relating to twelve or twelfths 2. consisting of or counting by twelves or powers of twelve —*n.* 1. one twelfth 2. [*pl.*] *Math.* a system of numeration with twelve as its base, rather than ten as in the decimal system

du·o·dec·i·mo (-mō′) *n., pl.* **-mos′** [short for L. *in duodecimo*, in twelve: see prec.] 1. the page size of a book made up of printer's sheets folded into twelve leaves, each leaf being approximately 5 by 7 1/2 inches 2. a book consisting of pages of this size Also called *twelvemo*, and written *12mo* or *12°* —*adj.* consisting of pages of this size

du·o·de·nal (dōō′ə dē′nəl, dyōō′-; dōō äd′′n əl) *adj.* in or of the duodenum

du·o·de·ni·tis (dōō′ə də nīt′is, dyōō′-; dōō äd′′n īt′is) *n.* [< ff. + -ITIS] inflammation of the duodenum

du·o·de·num (dōō′ə dē′nəm, dyōō′-; dōō äd′′n əm) *n., pl.* **-de′na** (-nə), **-de′nums** [ME. < ML. < L. *duodeni*, twelve each: its length is about twelve fingers' breadth] the first section of the small intestine, between the stomach and the jejunum

du·o·logue (dōō′ə lôg′, -läg′; dyōō′-) *n.* [DUO- + (MONO)LOGUE] a conversation between two people, esp. in a dramatic performance

‡**duo·mo** (dwô′mō) *n., pl.* **-mi** (-mē) [It.: see DOME] a cathedral

du·op·o·ly (dōō äp′ə lē, dyōō-) *n.* [DUO- + (MONO)POLY] control of a commodity or service in a given market by only two producers or suppliers

du·o·tone (dōō′ə tōn′, dyōō′-) *adj.* showing a two-tone color effect —*n.* a picture having such an effect

☆**du·o·type** (-tīp′) *n.* an illustration printed from a pair of half-tone plates etched separately from a single negative

dup. duplicate

dupe (dōōp, dyōōp) *n.* [Fr. < OFr. *duppe* < L. *upupa*, hoopoe, stupid bird] a person easily tricked or fooled —*vt.* **duped, dup′ing** [Fr. *duper* < the *n.*] to deceive by trickery; fool or cheat —SYN. see CHEAT —**dup′a·ble** *adj.* —**dup′er** *n.*

dup·er·y (dōō′pər ē, dyōō′-) *n., pl.* **-ies** a duping or being duped; deception

du·pi·o·ni (dōō′pē ō′nē) *n. same as* DOUPPIONI

du·ple (dōō′p′l, dyōō′-) *adj.* [L. *duplus:* see DOUBLE] 1. double; twofold 2. *Music* containing two (or a multiple of two) beats to the measure [*duple time*]

Du·ples·sis-Mor·nay (dü ple sē′môr nā′) *see* MORNAY

du·plex (dōō′pleks, dyōō′-) *adj.* [L., consisting of two leaves, double < *duo*, TWO + -*plex*, -fold, akin to *plaga*, region, area < IE. base *plak-*, *plag-*, whence Gr. *plax*, surface, FLAG²: infl. by early association with *duplus*, DOUBLE] 1. double; twofold 2. designating or of a system of telegraphy in which two messages may be sent simultaneously in opposite directions over a single circuit 3. *Machinery* having two units operating in the same way or simultaneously —*n. same as* DUPLEX HOUSE or DUPLEX APARTMENT —**du·plex′i·ty** *n.*

☆**duplex apartment** an apartment with rooms on two floors and a private inner stairway

☆**duplex house** a house consisting of two separate family units

du·pli·cate (dōō′plə kit, dyōō′-; *for v.* -kāt′) *adj.* [ME. *duplicaten* < L. *duplicatus*, pp. of *duplicare*, to double: see DUPLEX] 1. double 2. having two similar parts 3. corre-

sponding exactly 4. designating a way of playing bridge, etc., in which, for comparative scoring, the same hands are played off again by players who did not hold them originally —*n.* 1. an exact copy or reproduction; replica; facsimile 2. a counterpart or double 3. a duplicate game of bridge, etc. ☆4. *same as* TAX DUPLICATE —*vt.* **-cat′ed, -cat′ing** 1. to make double or twofold 2. to make an exact copy or copies of 3. to make, do, or cause to happen again —SYN. see COPY —**in duplicate** in two precisely similar forms —**du′pli·ca·ble** (-kə b′l), **du′pli·cat′a·ble** *adj.*

duplicating machine a machine for making exact copies of a letter, photograph, drawing, etc.

du·pli·ca·tion (dōō′plə kā′shən, dyōō′-) *n.* [ME. *duplicacioun* < L. *duplicatio*] 1. a duplicating or being duplicated 2. a copy; replica —**du′pli·ca′tive** *adj.*

du·pli·ca·tor (dōō′plə kāt′ər, dyōō′-) *n.* [LL., doubler < *duplicare*, DUPLICATE] *same as* DUPLICATING MACHINE

du·plic·i·ty (dōō plis′ə tē, dyōō-) *n., pl.* **-ties** [ME. *duplicite* < OFr. *duplicité* < LL. *duplicitas:* see DUPLEX] hypocritical cunning or deception; double-dealing

du Pont (dōō pänt′, dōō′pänt; dyōō-; *Fr.* dü pōn′), **É·leu·thère I·ré·née** (*Fr.* ā lē ter′ ē rā nā′) 1771–1834; U.S. industrialist, born in France

Dur. Durham

du·ra (door′ə, dyoor′-) *n. same as* DURA MATER

du·ra·ble (door′ə b′l, dyoor′-) *adj.* [ME. & OFr. < L. *durabilis* < *durare*, to last, harden < IE. **duros*, long < base **deu-*, to move forward (whence TIRE¹): meaning infl. in L. by *durus*, hard (see DURESS)] 1. lasting in spite of hard wear or frequent use 2. continuing to exist; stable —*n.* [*pl.*] *same as* DURABLE GOODS —**du′ra·bil′i·ty** *n.* —**du′ra·bly** *adv.*

durable goods goods that remain usable for a relatively long period of time, as machinery, automobiles, or household appliances

du·ral (door′əl, dyoor′-) *adj.* of the dura mater

du·ral·u·min (doo ral′yoo m′n, dyoo-) *n.* [DUR(ABLE) + ALUMIN(UM)] a strong, lightweight, corrosion-resistant alloy of aluminum with copper, manganese, magnesium, and silicon

du·ra ma·ter (door′ə māt′ər, dyoor′-) [ME. < ML., lit., hard mother, transl. of an Ar. term] the outermost, toughest, and most fibrous of the three membranes covering the brain and spinal cord

du·ra·men (doo rā′mən, dyoo-) *n.* [L., hardness < *durare:* see DURABLE] *same as* HEARTWOOD

dur·ance (door′əns, dyoor′-) *n.* [ME. *duraunce* < OFr. < L. *durans*, prp. of *durare*, to last: see DURABLE] imprisonment, esp. when long continued: mainly in **in durance vile**

Du·ran·go (doo ran′gō; *E.* də raŋ′gō) 1. state of NW Mexico: 47,691 sq. mi.; pop. 806,000 2. its capital: pop. 59,000

du·ra·tion (doo rā′shən, dyoo-) *n.* [ME. *duracioun* < ML. *duratio* < pp. of L. *durare:* see DURABLE] 1. continuance in time 2. the time that a thing continues or lasts

Dur·ban (dur′bən) seaport in Natal, on the E coast of South Africa: pop. 681,000

dur·bar (dur′bär) *n.* [Hindi < *darbār* < Per., a ruler's court < *dar*, portal + *bār*, court] 1. formerly in India or Africa, an official reception or audience held by a native prince, or by a British ruler or governor 2. the place or hall where this was held

dure (door, dyoor) *adj.* [ME. & OFr. *dur* < L. *durus:* see DURESS] [Obs.] hard; stern —*vi., vt.* **dured, dur′ing** [ME. *duren* < L. *durare:* see DURABLE] [Obs. or Dial.] to last; continue; endure

Dü·rer (dü′rər; *E.* dyoor′ər), **Al·brecht** (äl′breHt) 1471–1528; Ger. painter & wood engraver

du·ress (doo res′, dyoo-; door′is, dyoor′-) *n.* [ME. *dures* < OFr. *durece* < L. *duritia*, hardness, harshness < *durus*, hard < IE. base **deru-*, tree, oak (orig. ? hard), whence TREE] 1. imprisonment 2. the use of force or threats; compulsion [a confession signed under *duress*]

Dur·ham (dur′əm) 1. county of N England, on the North Sea: 1,015 sq. mi.; pop. 1,535,000 2. its county seat: pop. 23,000 3. city in NC N.C.: pop. 95,000 —*n.* one of a breed of short-horned beef cattle, orig. bred in Durham County

du·ri·an, du·ri·on (door′ē ən) *n.* [Malay < *duri*, thorn, prickle] 1. the oval, spiny, edible fruit of an East Indian tree (*Durio zibethinus*) of the bombax family 2. the tree

dur·ing (door′iŋ, dyoor′-) *prep.* [ME. *duringe*, prep., orig. prp. of *duren*, DURE, v.] 1. throughout the entire time of; all through [food was scarce *during* the war] 2. at some point in the entire time of; in the course of [he left *during* the lecture]

dur·mast (dur′mast, -mäst) *n.* [apparently for *dun mast* oak, dark acorned oak: see DUN¹ & MAST²] any of several European oaks (genus *Quercus*) valued for their heavy, tough wood

durn (durn) *vt., n., adj., adv., interj.* [Colloq.] *same as* DARN²

du·ro (door′ō) *n., pl.* **-ros** [Sp., for *peso duro*, lit., hard peso] the silver peso, or dollar, of Spain and Spanish America

☆**Du·roc-Jer·sey** (door′äk jur′zē, dyoor′-) *n.* [< *Duroc*, name of progenitor boar (named after famous 19th-c. Am. stallion) + *Jersey* (Red), breed of swine] any of a breed of large, red hog: also **Du′roc**

dur·ra (door′ə) *n.* [Ar. *dhurah*] a variety of grain-producing sorghum (*Sorghum vulgare*), widely grown in Asia and Africa

Dur·rës (door′əs) seaport in W Albania, on the Adriatic: as *Epidamnus*, chief port of ancient Illyria: pop. 46,000

durst (durst) *archaic pt. of* DARE

du·rum (door′əm, dyoor′-) *n.* [ModL. < L., neut. of *durus*, hard: see DURESS] a hard wheat (*Triticum durum*) that yields flour and semolina used in macaroni, spaghetti, etc.

Du·se (dōō′ze), **E·le·o·no·ra** (e′le ô nô′rä) 1859–1924; It. actress

Du·shan·be (dōō shän′be) capital of the Tadzhik S.S.R., in the W part: pop. 316,000: former name, STALINABAD

dusk (dusk) *adj.* [ME., by metathesis < OE. *dox*, dark-colored: see DUN¹] [Poet.] dark in color; dusky; shadowy —*n.* 1. the beginning of darkness in the evening; dim part of twilight 2. gloom; dusky quality —*vt., vi.* to make or become dusky or shadowy

dusk·y (dus′kē) *adj.* **dusk′i·er, dusk′i·est** [DUSK + -Y²] 1. somewhat dark in color; esp., swarthy 2. lacking light; dim; shadowy 3. gloomy; melancholy —**dusk′i·ly** *adv.* —**dusk′i·ness** *n.*

SYN.—**dusky** suggests a darkness of color or an absence of light, verging on blackness [*dusky* twilight]; **swarthy** and **tawny** both refer only to color, **swarthy** suggesting a dark brown verging on black [a *swarthy* complexion] and **tawny**, a yellowish-brown, or tan [*tawny* hair] See also DARK

Düs·sel·dorf (düs′əl dôrf′) city in W West Germany, on the Rhine; capital of North Rhine–Westphalia: pop. 699,000

dust (dust) *n.* [ME. < OE., akin to MLowG. *dust*: for IE. base see DUN¹] 1. powdery earth or other matter in bits fine enough to be easily suspended in air 2. a cloud of such matter 3. confusion; turmoil 4. a) earth, esp. as the place of burial b) mortal remains disintegrated or thought of as disintegrating to earth or dust 5. a humble or abject condition 6. anything worthless 7. [Brit.] ashes, rubbish, etc. 8. pollen ☆9. *same as* GOLD DUST 10. [Archaic] a particle —*vt.* 1. to sprinkle with dust or a fine powdery substance [to *dust* crops with an insecticide] 2. to sprinkle (powder, etc.) on 3. to rid of dust, as by brushing, shaking, or wiping (often with *off*) 4. [Archaic] to make dusty —*vi.* 1. to remove dust, esp. from furniture, floors, etc. 2. to bathe in dust: said of a bird —**bite the dust** to be killed, esp. in battle —**dust off** 1. [Colloq.] to prepare to use ☆2. [Slang] to pitch a baseball deliberately close to (the batter) —**lick the dust** 1. to act energetically 2. to move swiftly —**make the dust fly** 1. to be very busy —**shake the dust off one's feet** to leave with disdain or contempt: cf. Matt. 10:14 —**throw dust in (someone's) eyes** to mislead or deceive (someone)

dust·bin (-bin′) *n.* [Brit.] a container for dust, rubbish, etc.; ashes

☆**dust bowl** a region where eroded topsoil is blown away by winds during drought so that a desert area results

dust devil a small whirlwind that raises dust and litter in a narrow column

dust·er (-ər) *n.* 1. a person or thing that dusts 2. a brush or cloth for removing dust from furniture, etc. 3. a device for sprinkling on a powder, as for applying an insecticide ☆4. a lightweight coat worn to protect the clothes from dust, as formerly in open automobiles ☆5. a short, loose, lightweight housecoat

dust jacket a detachable paper cover for protecting the binding of a book, usually designed to display the book effectively and advertise its contents

dust·less (-lis) *adj.* having or causing no dust

dust·man (-mən) *n., pl.* **-men** (-mən) [Brit.] a man whose work is removing rubbish, ashes, garbage, etc.

dust·pan (-pan′) *n.* a shovellike receptacle into which dust or debris is swept from a floor

dust·proof (-prōōf′) *adj.* keeping out dust

☆**dust storm** a windstorm that sweeps up clouds of dust when passing over an arid region

dust-up (-up′) *n.* [Slang] a commotion, quarrel, or fight

dust·y (-ē) *adj.* **dust′i·er, dust′i·est** [ME. *dusti* < OE. *dustig*] 1. covered with dust; full of dust 2. like dust; powdery 3. of the color of dust

dusty miller any of various garden plants having white, woolly foliage

Dutch (duch) *adj.* [ME. *Duch* < MDu. *Duutsch*, Dutch, German: see DEUTSCHLAND] 1. of the Netherlands, its people, language, or culture ☆2. of the Pennsylvania Dutch 3. [Obs. exc. Slang] German —*n.* 1. the language of the Netherlands 2. [Obs. exc. Slang] German —**beat the Dutch** [Colloq.] to be very unusual or extraordinary —☆**go Dutch** [Colloq.] to have every participant pay his own expenses —☆**in Dutch** [Colloq.] in trouble or disfavor —**the Dutch** 1. the people of the Netherlands ☆2. the Pennsylvania Dutch 3. [Obs.] the German people

Dutch Belted any of a breed of dairy cattle that are black with a broad white stripe around the body

☆**Dutch bob** a style of haircut with bangs and a straight, even bob that covers the ears

Dutch Borneo formerly, the part of Borneo that belonged to the Netherlands

Dutch courage [Colloq.] 1. courage stimulated by drinking alcoholic liquor 2. alcoholic liquor

Dutch door a door with upper and lower halves that can be opened separately

Dutch East Indies *same as* NETHERLANDS (EAST) INDIES

☆**Dutch elm disease** [from its first appearance in the Netherlands] a virulent and widespread disease of elms caused by a fungus (*Ceratocystis ulmi*) that produces wilting and drying of the leaves and, ultimately, death of the tree

DUTCH DOOR

Dutch Guiana *former name of* SURINAM

Dutch·man (-mən) *n., pl.* **-men** (-mən) 1. a native or inhabitant of the Netherlands; Hollander 2. a Dutch ship 3. [Obs. exc. Slang] a German

Dutch·man's-breech·es (-brich′iz) *n.sing. & pl.* a spring wildflower (*Dicentra cucullaria*) of the fumitory family, with finely divided basal leaves and pinkish, double-spurred flowers, found in E U.S.

☆**Dutch·man's-pipe** (-pīp′) *n.* [from the resemblance of the blossom to a pipe bowl] a hardy, woody vine (*Aristolochia durior*) with U-shaped flowers having a flaring mouth

Dutch metal tombac, an alloy of copper and zinc

Dutch New Guinea *same as* NETHERLANDS NEW GUINEA

Dutch oven 1. a heavy metal or enamelware pot with a high, arched lid, for cooking pot roasts, etc. 2. a metal container for roasting meats, etc., with an open side placed so that it is toward the fire 3. a brick oven whose walls are preheated for cooking

☆**Dutch treat** [Colloq.] any entertainment, party, etc. at which each participant pays his own expenses

Dutch uncle [Colloq.] a person who bluntly and sternly lectures or scolds someone else

Dutch West Indies *former name of* NETHERLANDS ANTILLES

du·te·ous (dōōt′ē əs, dyōōt′-) *adj.* dutiful; obedient —**du′te·ous·ly** *adv.* —**du′te·ous·ness** *n.*

du·ti·a·ble (dōōt′ē ə b'l, dyōōt′-) *adj.* necessitating payment of a duty or tax, as imported goods

du·ti·ful (-ə fəl) *adj.* 1. showing, or resulting from, a sense of duty 2. having a proper sense of duty; obedient —**du′ti·ful·ly** *adv.* —**du′ti·ful·ness** *n.*

du·ty (dōōt′ē, dyōōt′-) *n., pl.* **-ties** [ME. *duete* < Anglo-Fr. *dueté*, what is due (owing): see DUE & -TY¹] 1. the obedience or respect that one should show toward one's parents, older people, etc. 2. conduct based on moral or legal obligation or a sense of propriety [one's *duty* to vote] 3. any action, task, etc. required by or relating to one's occupation or position [the *duties* of a secretary] 4. a sense or feeling of obligation [*duty* calls] 5. service, esp. military service [overseas *duty*] 6. a payment due to the government, esp. a tax imposed on imports, exports, or manufactured goods 7. [Brit.] the performance of a machine as measured by the output of work per unit of fuel 8. the amount of work that a machine is meant to do; rated efficiency under specified conditions ☆9. *Agriculture* the amount of water needed for irrigation per acre per crop: also **duty of water** —**do duty for** to be a substitute for; serve as —**on** (or **off**) **duty** at (or temporarily relieved from) one's assigned work, duty, etc.

SYN.—**duty** refers to the general conduct required by one's sense of justice, morality, etc. or by the dictates of one's conscience [*duty* to one's fellow men]; **obligation** refers to what one is bound to do to fulfill a particular contract, promise, social requirement, etc. [you are under *obligation* to care for her]; **responsibility** refers to a particular task, trust, etc. for which one is accountable or answerable [the garden is her *responsibility*] See also FUNCTION

du·ty-free (-frē′) *adj., adv.* with no payment of a duty or tax required

du·um·vir (dōō um′vər, dyōō-) *n., pl.* **-virs, -vi·ri′** (-və rī′) [L., earlier *duovir*, sing. of *duoviri*, lit., two men < *duo*, two + *vir*, a man] 1. either of two magistrates in ancient Rome who held office jointly 2. either member of any duumvirate

du·um·vi·rate (-və rit) *n.* [L. *duumviratus*: see prec. & -ATE²] 1. governmental position or authority held jointly by two men 2. two men jointly holding such position or authority

du·ve·tyne, du·ve·tyn (dōō′və tēn′) *n.* [Fr. *duvetine* < *duvet*, eiderdown < MFr., altered < *dumet* < OFr. *dum*, *dun*, altered (? after *plume*) < ON. *dunn*, DOWN²] a soft textile with a short, velvety nap, originally made of cotton with a spun-silk filling

D.V. 1. Douay Version (of the Bible) 2. [L. *Deo volente*] God willing

Dvi·na (dvē nä′) 1. river in the R.S.F.S.R. and Latvian S.S.R., flowing northwest into the Gulf of Riga: c. 600 mi.: also called **Western Dvina** 2. river in R.S.F.S.R., flowing northwest into Dvina Bay near Archangel: c. 450 mi.: often called **Northern Dvina**

Dvina Bay arm of the White Sea, in the NW R.S.F.S.R.: c. 65 mi. long

Dvinsk (dvēnsk) *Russ. name of* DAUGAVPILS

D.V.M. Doctor of Veterinary Medicine

Dvo·rák (dvôr′zhäk, -zhak), **An·ton** (än′tôn) 1841–1904; Czech composer

D/W dock warrant

dwarf (dwôrf) *n.*, *pl.* **dwarfs**, **dwarves** (dwôrvz) [ME. *dwerf*, *dwergh* < OE. *dweorg*, akin to G. *zwerg* < IE. **dhwergh-*, prob. < base **dhwer-*, to trick, injure, whence Sans. *dhvarati*, (he) injures] **1.** any human being, animal, or plant that is much smaller than the usual one of its species **2.** *Folklore* a little being, usually ugly or malformed, to whom magic powers are attributed **3.** a star of relatively small size or mass and low luminosity: in full **dwarf star** —*vt.* **1.** to keep from growing to full natural size; stunt the growth of **2.** to make small or insignificant **3.** to make seem small in comparison; tower over —*vi.* to become stunted or dwarfed —*adj.* much smaller than the normal size; undersized; stunted —**dwarf′ish** *adj.* —**dwarf′ish·ness** *n.* —**dwarf′ism** *n.*

SYN.—**dwarf** refers to any individual that is considerably smaller than the average for the species and sometimes implies malformation or disproportion of parts; **midget** refers to a normally formed and proportioned, but diminutive, human being; **Pygmy** strictly refers to a member of any of several small-sized African or Asiatic peoples, but it is sometimes used (written **pygmy**) as a synonym for **dwarf** or **midget**

☆**dwarf chestnut 1.** any of a species (*Castanea pumila*) of chinquapin **2.** its edible nut

dwell (dwel) *vi.* **dwelt** or **dwelled**, **dwell′ing** [ME. *dwellen* < OE. *dwellan*, to lead astray, hinder, akin to ON. *dvelja*, to deceive < IE. base **dh(e)wel-*, to obscure, make dull: cf. DULL] to make one's home; reside; live —**dwell on** (or **upon**) to linger over in thought or speech; think about or discuss at length —**dwell′er** *n.*

dwell·ing (-iŋ) *n.* [ME.: see DWELL] a place to live in; residence; house; abode: also **dwelling place**

Dwight (dwīt) [orig. a surname < ?] a masculine name

dwin·dle (dwin′d'l) *vi.*, *vt.* **-dled**, **-dling** [freq. of ff.] to keep on becoming or making smaller or less; diminish; shrink —*SYN.* see DECREASE

dwine (dwīn) *vi.* **dwined**, **dwin′ing** [ME. *dwinen* < OE. *dwinan*, akin to ON. *dvina* < IE. base **dheu-*, to vanish, die, whence DEAD] [Archaic or Brit. Dial.] to pine away; languish; fade; wither

dwt. [D(ENARIUS) W(EIGH)T] pennyweight(s)

DX, D.X. *Radio* **1.** distance **2.** distant

Dy *Chem.* dysprosium

dy·ad (dī′ad) *n.* [LL. *dyas* (gen. *dyadis*) < Gr. *dyas* < *dyo*, TWO] **1.** two units regarded as one; pair **2.** *Biol.* a double chromosome resulting from the division of a tetrad in meiosis; half of a tetrad **3.** *Chem.* an atom, element, or radical with a valence of two —*adj.* consisting of two —**dy·ad′ic** *adj.*

Dy·ak (dī′ak) *n.* [Malay *dayak*, savage] **1.** a member of an aboriginal people living in the interior of Borneo **2.** the Indonesian language of this people

dy·ar·chy (dī′är kē) *n.*, *pl.* **-chies** [< Gr. *dyo*, two + -ARCHY] government shared by two rulers, powers, etc.

dyb·buk (dib′ək) *n.* [Heb. *dibbûq* < *dābhaq*, to cleave, hold to] *Jewish Folklore* the spirit of a dead person that enters the body of a living person and possesses it

dye (dī) *n.* [ME. *dee* < OE. *deag*, akin to OHG. *tougal*, dark, secret < IE. **dhwek-*, dark color, secret < base **dheu-*: cf. DULL] **1.** color produced in a substance by saturating it with a coloring agent; tint; hue **2.** any substance used to give color to fabric, hair, etc.; coloring matter or a solution containing it —*vt.* **dyed**, **dye′ing** [ME. *deien* < OE. *deagian*] to color with or as with a dye —*vi.* to take on color in dyeing —**of (the) deepest dye** of the most marked, esp. worst sort —**dy′er** *n.*

dyed-in-the-wool (dīd′'n *thə* wool′) *adj.* **1.** dyed before being woven ☆**2.** thoroughgoing; unchanging

dye·ing (dī′iŋ) *prp.* of DYE —*n.* the process or work of coloring fabrics with dyes

dy·er's-broom (dī′ərz broom′) *n.* same as WOADWAXEN: also called **dy′er's green′weed′**

dy·er's-weed (-wēd′) *n.* any of a number of plants that yield a dyestuff, as woadwaxen or dyer's woad

dyer's woad a biennial plant (*Isatis tinctoria*) with yellow flowers: its leaves yield a blue dye used by the ancient Britons

dye·stuff (dī′stuf′) *n.* any substance constituting or yielding a dye

dye·wood (-wood′) *n.* any wood yielding a dye

dy·ing (dī′iŋ) *prp.* of DIE[1] —*adj.* **1.** about to die or come to an end **2.** of or at the time of death *[his dying words]* —*n.* a ceasing to live or exist; death

dyke[1] (dīk) *n.*, *vt.* same as DIKE[1]

dyke[2] (dīk) *n.* [short for *bull-dike*, a female pervert] [Slang] a lesbian, esp. one with pronounced masculine characteristics —**dyk′ey** *adj.*

dyn., dynam. dynamics

dy·na- (dī′nə) [< Gr. *dynamis*, power: see DYNAMIC] a combining form meaning power *[dynameter]*: also, before a vowel, **dyn-**

dy·nam- (dī nam′) same as DYNAMO-: used before a vowel

dy·nam·e·ter (dī nam′ə tər) *n.* [DYNA- + -METER] an instrument for finding the magnifying power of a telescope

dy·nam·ic (dī nam′ik) *adj.* [Fr. *dynamique* < Gr. *dynamikos* < *dynamis*, power, strength < *dynasthai*, to be able] **1.** relating to energy or physical force in motion: opposed to STATIC **2.** relating to dynamics **3.** energetic; vigorous; forceful **4.** relating to or tending toward change or productive activity Also **dy·nam′i·cal** —*n.* **1.** a force producing motion or change **2.** same as DYNAMICS (sense 2 *a*) —**dy·nam′i·cal·ly** *adv.*

dy·nam·ics (-iks) *n.pl.* [with sing. v. for 1, 2 c, & 3] **1.** the branch of mechanics dealing with the motions of material bodies under the action of given forces; kinetics **2.** *a*) the various forces, physical, moral, economic, etc., operating in any field *b*) the way such forces shift or change in relation to one another *c*) the study of such forces **3.** the effect of varying degrees of loudness or softness in the performance of music

dy·na·mism (dī′nə miz'm) *n.* [DYNAM- + -ISM] **1.** the theory that force or energy, rather than mass or motion, is the basic principle of all phenomena **2.** the quality of being energetic, vigorous, etc. —**dy′na·mis′tic** *adj.*

dy·na·mite (dī′nə mīt′) *n.* [coined (1866 or 1867) by Alfred NOBEL < Gr. *dynamis*: see DYNAMIC] **1.** a powerful explosive made by soaking nitroglycerin into some absorbent, such as sodium nitrate and wood pulp **2.** [Colloq.] anything potentially dangerous —*vt.* **-mit′ed**, **-mit′ing** to blow up or destroy with dynamite —**dy′na·mit′er** *n.*

dy·na·mo (dī′nə mō′) *n.*, *pl.* **-mos** [< *dynamoelectric machine*] **1.** *earlier term for* GENERATOR (sense 1 *b*) **2.** a forceful, dynamic person

dy·na·mo- (dī′nə mō) [< Gr. *dynamis*: see DYNAMIC] *a combining form meaning power [dynamoelectric]*

dy·na·mo·e·lec·tric (dī′nə mō i lek′trik) *adj.* having to do with the production of electrical energy from mechanical energy, or of mechanical energy from electrical energy: also **dy′na·mo·e·lec′tri·cal**

dy·na·mom·e·ter (dī′nə mäm′ə tər) *n.* [Fr. *dynamomètre*: see DYNAMO- & -METER] an apparatus for measuring force or power; esp., one for measuring mechanical power, as of an engine

dy·na·mom·e·try (-trē) *n.* [DYNAMO- + -METRY] the process of measuring forces at work —**dy′na·mo·met′ric** (-mō met′rik) *adj.*

dy·na·mo·tor (dī′nə mōt′ər) *n.* an electrical machine combining generator and motor, for transforming current of one voltage to that of another voltage

dy·nast (dī′nast, -nəst) *n.* [L. *dynastes* < Gr. *dynastēs* < *dynasthai*, to be able or strong] a ruler, esp. a hereditary ruler

dy·nas·ty (dī′nəs tē) *n.*, *pl.* **-ties** [ME. *dinastie* < ML. *dynastia* < Gr. *dynasteia*, lordship, rule < *dynastēs*: see DYNAST] **1.** a succession of rulers who are members of the same family **2.** the period during which a certain family reigns —**dy·nas′tic** (dī nas′tik), **dy·nas′ti·cal** *adj.* —**dy·nas′ti·cal·ly** *adv.*

dy·na·tron (dī′nə trän′) *n.* [DYNA- + (ELEC)TRON] a four-electrode electron tube in which the anode functions as a dynode

dyne (dīn) *n.* [Fr. < Gr. *dynamis*, power] the amount of force that imparts to a mass of one gram an acceleration of one centimeter per second per second: the unit of force in the cgs system

☆**Dy·nel** (dī nel′) *a trademark for* a synthetic fiber made from vinyl chloride and acrylonitrile —*n.* [**d-**] a fabric or yarn made from this fiber, usually with a texture like hair or fur

dy·node (dī′nōd) *n.* [< Gr. *dyn*(*amis*), power (see DYNAMIC) + -ODE[1]] an electrode in an electron tube designed so that each impinging electron causes the emission of two or more secondary electrons

dys- (dis) [Gr. < IE. base **dus-*, bad, ill, whence Goth. *tuz-*, OHG. *zur-* (G. *zer-*), Sans. *duṣ-*] *a prefix meaning* bad, ill, abnormal, impaired, difficult, etc. *[dysgenic]*

dys·cra·si·a (dis krā′zhə, -zhē ə, -zē ə) *n.* [ModL. < ML., distemper, disease < Gr. *dyskrasia*, bad temperament < *dys-*, bad (see DYS-) + *krasis*, a mixing < *kerannynai*, to mix: see IDIOSYNCRASY] an abnormality of some part of the body, as of the formed elements of the blood

dys·en·ter·y (dis′'n ter′ē) *n.* [ME. *dissenterie* < OFr. < L. *dysenteria* < Gr. *dysenteria* < *dys-*, bad + *enteron*, pl. *entera*, bowels: see INTER-] any of various intestinal inflammations characterized by abdominal pain and intense diarrhea with bloody, mucous feces —**dys′en·ter′ic** *adj.*

dys·func·tion (dis funk′shən) *n.* abnormal, impaired, or incomplete functioning, as of a body organ or part —**dys·func′tion·al** *adj.*

dys·gen·ic (dis jen′ik) *adj.* causing deterioration of hereditary qualities of a stock

dys·gen·ics (-iks) *n.pl.* [with sing. v.] the study of dysgenic trends in a population

dys·lex·i·a (dis lek′sē ə) *n.* [ModL. < Gr. *dys-*, bad + *lexis*, speech < *legein*, to speak] impairment of the ability to read, often as the result of genetic defect or brain injury —**dys·lex′ic** *adj.*

dys·lo·gis·tic (dis′lə jis′tik) *adj.* [DYS- + (EU)LOGISTIC] not favorable; opprobrious: opposed to EULOGISTIC

dys·men·or·rhe·a (dis′men ə rē′ə) *n.* [ModL. < DYS- + Gr. *mēn*, MONTH + *rhoia*, a flowing] painful or difficult menstruation

dys·pep·si·a (dis pep′shə, -sē ə) *n.* [L. < Gr. *dyspepsia* < *dys-* + *pepsis*, cooking, digestion < *peptein*, to soften, cook, digest: for IE. base see COOK] impaired digestion; indigestion: also [Dial.] **dys·pep′sy** (-sē)

dys·pep·tic (-pep′tik) *adj.* [< Gr. *dyspeptos* (see DYSPEPSIA) + -IC] **1.** of, causing, or having dyspepsia **2.** gloomy; grouchy —*n.* a person who suffers from dyspepsia — **dys·pep′ti·cal·ly** *adv.*

dys·pha·gi·a (-fā′jē ə) *n.* [ModL. < DYS- + -PHAGIA] *Med.* difficulty in swallowing —**dys·phag′ic** (-faj′ik) *adj.*

dys·pha·si·a (-fā′zhə, -fā′zhē ə) *n.* [ModL. < DYS- + -PHASIA] impairment of the ability to speak or, sometimes, to understand language, as the result of brain injury —**dys·pha′sic** (-fā′zik) *adj., n.*

dys·pho·ni·a (-fō′nē ə) *n.* [ModL. < Gr. *dysphōnia* < *dys-*, bad + *phōnē*, voice] any difficulty in producing speech sounds —**dys·phon′ic** (-fän′ik) *adj.*

dys·pho·ri·a (-fôr′ē ə) *n.* [ModL. < Gr. *dysphoria* < *dys-*, hard + *pherein*, to BEAR[1]] *Psychol.* a generalized feeling of ill-being; esp., an abnormal feeling of anxiety, discontent, physical discomfort, etc.: opposed to EUPHORIA —**dys·phor′ic** (-fôr′ik) *adj.*

dys·pla·si·a (-plā′zhē ə, -plā′zhə) *n.* [ModL.: see DYS- & -PLASIA] a disordered growth or faulty development of various tissues or body parts —**dys·plas′tic** (-plas′tik) *adj.*

dysp·ne·a (disp′nē ə, disp nē′ə) *n.* [L. *dispnoea* < Gr. *dyspnoia* < *dys-*, hard + *pnoē*, breathing < *pnein*, to breathe] difficult or painful breathing —**dysp·ne′al, dysp·ne′ic** *adj.*

dys·pro·si·um (dis prō′sē əm, -zē-, -shē-) *n.* [ModL. < Gr. *dysprositos*, difficult of access < *dys-*, hard + *prositos*, approachable < *prosienai*, come to < *pros*, toward + *ienai*, to go] a chemical element of the rare-earth group: symbol, Dy; at. wt. 162.50; at. no., 66; sp. gr., 8.556; melt. pt., 1407°C; boil. pt., 2564°C: it is one of the most magnetic of all known substances

dys·tro·phic (dis träf′ik, -trō′fik) *adj.* **1.** of or caused by dystrophy **2.** of a lake or pond derived from a bog and characterized by brown, humic matter, high acidity, and poorly developed fauna and flora

dys·tro·phy (dis′trə fē) *n.* [ModL. *dystrophia*: see DYS- & -TROPHY] **1.** faulty nutrition **2.** faulty development, or degeneration: cf. MUSCULAR DYSTROPHY

dys·u·ri·a (dis yoor′ē ə) *n.* [LL. < Gr. *dysouria* < *dys-*, hard + *ouron*, urine] difficult or painful urination

dz. dozen; dozens

Dzer·zhinsk (dzir zhinsk′) city in C European R.S.F.S.R., near Gorky: pop. 193,000

Dzun·ga·ri·a (zoon ger′ē ə) region of N Sinkiang province, China

E

E, e (ē) *n., pl.* **E's, e's 1.** the fifth letter of the English alphabet: from the Greek *epsilon*, a borrowing from the Phoenician **2.** a sound of E or *e*: in English, usually the mid-front, lax, unrounded vowel (e) of *bed*, or the high-front, tense, unrounded vowel (ē); also used in written diphthongs (*ea, ei, ie*, etc.) and as a silent final letter (orig., a vocalized inflectional ending in Middle English) to indicate a so-called "long vowel" quality in the preceding vowel, as in *fate, site, note*, etc. **3.** a type or impression for E or e **4.** *a symbol for* the fifth in a sequence or group —*adj.* **1.** of E or e **2.** fifth in a sequence or group

E (ē) *n.* **1.** an object shaped like E **2.** *Chem.* einsteinium **3.** *Educ. a)* a grade indicating below average work, often equivalent to *condition b)* sometimes, a grade indicating excellence **4.** *Music a)* the third tone or note in the ascending scale of C major *b)* a key, string, etc. producing this tone *c)* the scale having this tone as the keynote **5.** *Physics the symbol for a)* energy *b)* the modulus of elasticity *c)* electromotive force —*adj.* shaped like E

e- (ē; *unstressed*, i, ə) *a prefix meaning* out, out of, from, without [*eject, egress*]: see EX-[1]

e 1. *Physics* erg **2.** *Math.* the number used as the base of the system of natural logarithms, approximately 2.71828: written *e*

E, E., e, e. 1. east **2.** eastern

E. 1. Earl **2.** Easter **3.** English

E., e. 1. earth **2.** *Physics* electromotive force **3.** engineer(ing) **4.** *Baseball* errors

ea. each

E.A., EA *Psychol.* Educational Age

each (ēch) *adj., pron.* [ME. *ech, elc*, each, every < OE. *ælc* < *agilic*, akin to OHG. *iogilih* (G. *jeglich*) < PGmc. *aiw-galic*: see AYE[1] & ALIKE] every one of two or more considered separately —*adv.* apiece [give them two apples *each*] —**each other** each one the other; one another: some speakers use *each other* only of two individuals and *one another* only of more than two, but most speakers use either phrase in referring to two or more [we help *each other*]

Eads (ēdz), **James Buchanan** 1820–87; U.S. engineer: noted for bridge construction & river control

ea·ger[1] (ē′gər) *adj.* [ME. *egre* < OFr. *aigre* < L. *acer*, sharp, acute, ardent, eager: see ACID] **1.** feeling or showing keen desire; impatient or anxious to do or get; ardent **2.** [Archaic] sharp; keen —**ea′ger·ly** *adv.* —**ea′ger·ness** *n.* SYN.—*eager* implies great enthusiasm, zeal, or sometimes impatience, in the desire for or pursuit of something [*eager* to begin work]; *avid* suggests an intense, sometimes greedy, desire to enjoy or possess something [*avid* for power]; *keen* implies deep interest and a spirited readiness to achieve something [the team was *keen* on winning]; *anxious*, in this connection, suggests an eagerness that is accompanied with some uneasiness over the outcome [*anxious* to do his best]

ea·ger[2] (ē′gər, ā′-) *n.* same as EAGRE

☆**eager beaver** [Slang] a person characterized by much, or too much, industry, initiative, or enthusiasm

ea·gle (ē′g'l) *n.* [ME. *egle* < OFr. *aigle* < L. *aquila*, eagle] **1.** any of a number of large, strong, flesh-eating birds of prey belonging to the falcon family, noted for their sharp vision and powerful wings, as the bald eagle **2.** a representation of the eagle, used as a symbol or emblem of a nation, etc., esp., *a)* the military standard of the Roman Empire ☆*b)* the national emblem of the U.S., or the seal bearing this emblem ☆*c)* the military insigne of a colonel in the U.S. armed forces (captain in the U.S. Navy) ☆**3.** a former U.S. gold coin with a face value of $10 **4.** *Golf* a score of two under par on any hole —[E-] the constellation Aquila

ea·gle-eyed (-īd′) *adj.* having keen vision

☆**Eagle Scout** a boy scout in the highest rank

ea·glet (ē′glit) *n.* [Fr. *aiglette*, dim. of *aigle*] a young eagle

ea·gre (ē′gər, ā′-) *n.* [Brit. eastern dial. form, prob. ult. < OE. *eagor*, flood, high tide, akin to ON. *ægir*, ocean < IE. base *ekw-*, var. of *akwa-*, water, whence L. *aqua*] a high tidal wave in an estuary; bore

Ea·kins (ā′kinz), **Thomas** 1844–1916; U.S. painter & sculptor

eal·dor·man (ôl′dər mən) *n. Anglo-Saxon History* the chief officer in a shire; alderman

Ea·ling (ē′liŋ) city in Middlesex, SE England: suburb of London: pop. 183,000

-e·an (ē′ən) [< L. *-ae-, -e-, -i-* & Gr. *-ai-, -ei-* (stem endings of nouns and adjectives) + -AN] *a suffix meaning* of, belonging to, like [*European, Aegean*]

E. & O.E. errors and omissions excepted

E. and P. Extraordinary and Plenipotentiary

ear[1] (ir) *n.* [ME. *ere* < OE. *eare*, akin to Goth. *ausō*, G. *ohr* < IE. base *ous-*, ear, whence L. *auris*, Gr. *ous*, OIr. *au*] **1.** the part of the body specialized for the perception of sound; organ of hearing: the human ear consists of *a)* the external ear (pinna and external auditory canal); *b)* the inner ear (labyrinth), containing the cochlea and semicircular canals; and *c)* the middle ear (tympanum), a cavity connected to the external ear by the tympanic membrane, to the pharynx by the Eustachian tube, and to the inner ear by a series of three small bones called the *hammer, anvil*, and *stirrup* **2.** the visible, external part of the ear **3.** the sense of hearing **4.** the

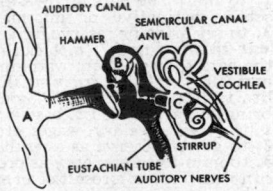

HUMAN EAR
(A, external ear;
B, middle ear;
C, inner ear)

ability to recognize slight differences in sound, esp. in the pitch, rhythm, etc. of musical tones **5.** anything shaped or placed like an ear, as the handle of a pitcher or a small box in the upper corner of a newspaper page —**be all ears** to be listening attentively or eagerly —☆**bend someone's ear** [Slang] to talk excessively to someone —**fall on deaf ears** to be ignored or unheeded —**give (or lend) ear** to give attention, esp. favorable attention; listen; heed —☆**have (or keep) an ear to the ground** to give careful attention to the trends of public opinion —**have the ear of** to be in a favorable position to talk to and influence; be heeded by —**in one ear and out the other** heard but without effect —**play by ear** to play (a musical instrument or piece) without the use of notation, improvising an arrangement —**play it by ear** [Colloq.] to act as the situation demands, without a preconceived plan; improvise —**set on its ear** [Colloq.] to cause excitement, upheaval, etc. in —**turn a deaf ear** to be unwilling to listen or heed

ear² (ir) n. [ME. er < OE. ær, akin to G. ähre, Goth. ahs < IE. *aces (< base *ak, sharp), whence L. acus, chaff] the grain-bearing spike of a cereal plant, as of corn, or maize —vi. to sprout ears; form ears

ear·ache (ir′āk′) n. an ache or pain in the (middle or inner) ear; otalgia

ear·drop (-dräp′) n. **1.** an earring or hanging ornament for the ear **2.** [pl.] any of various liquid medicines put into the ear in drops

ear·drum (-drum′) n. **1.** same as TYMPANIC MEMBRANE **2.** same as TYMPANUM (sense 1)

eared (ird) adj. having ears: often used in hyphenated compounds meaning having (a specified kind of) ears [long-eared]

eared seal any of a family (Otariidae) of fur seals, with distinct external ears and hind limbs used in locomotion: cf. EARLESS SEAL

ear·flap (ir′flap′) n. either of a pair of cloth or fur flaps on a cap, turned down to protect the ears from cold

☆**ear·ful** (-fool′) n. [Colloq.] **1.** enough or too much of what is heard **2.** important or startling news or gossip **3.** a scolding

Ear·hart (er′härt′), **Amelia** (Mrs. George Palmer Putnam) 1898–1937; U.S. pioneer aviator

ear·ing (ir′in) n. [< EAR¹, sense 5] a small rope for attaching the upper corner of a sail to the yard or gaff

Earl, Earle (url) [see ff.] a masculine name

earl (url) n. [ME. erl, nobleman, count < OE. eorl, warrior, akin to ON. jarl, leader, noble < ? IE. base *er-, eagle] a British nobleman ranking above a viscount and below a marquess: the wife or widow of an earl is called a countess —earl′dom n.

ear·lap (ir′lap′) n. ☆**1.** same as EARFLAP **2.** the ear lobe **3.** the external ear

ear·less seal (ir′lis) any of a family (Phocidae) of seals, with inconspicuous ears and rudimentary hind limbs: cf. EARED SEAL

Earl Marshal a high officer of state in England, marshal of state ceremonies and head of the Heralds' College

ear·ly (url′lē) adv., adj. -li·er, -li·est [ME. erli < OE. ærlice, adv. (whence ærlic, adj.) < ær, before (see ERE) + -lice, adv. suffix see -LY², LIKE¹] **1.** near the beginning of a given period of time or of a series, as of events; soon after the start **2.** before the expected or customary time **3.** in the far distant past; in ancient or remote times **4.** in the near future; before much time has passed —ear′li·ness n.

Ear·ly (url′lē), **Jubal Anderson** 1816–94; Confederate general in the Civil War

early bird [Colloq.] a person who arrives early, or one who gets up early in the morning

Early Modern English the English language as spoken and written from about the mid-15th cent. to about the mid-18th cent.

ear·mark (ir′märk′) n. **1.** an identification mark or brand put on the ear of a domestic animal to show ownership **2.** an identifying mark or feature; characteristic; sign —vt. **1.** to mark the ears of (livestock) for identification **2.** to set a distinctive or informative mark upon; identify **3.** to set aside or reserve for a special purpose or recipient

☆**ear·muffs** (-mufs′) n.pl. cloth or fur coverings worn over the ears to keep them warm in cold weather

earn (urn) vt. [ME. ernen < OE. earnian, to gain, labor for, lit., to harvest, akin to G. ernte, harvest, OHG. arnōn, to bring to harvest < IE. base *es-en, summer, harvest time] **1.** to receive (salary, wages, etc.) for one's labor or service **2.** to get or deserve as a result of something one has done **3.** to gain (interest, etc.) as profit ☆**4.** Baseball to score (a run which is not a result of an error) against a pitcher: used only in the pp. —earn′er n.

Ear·nest (ur′nist) a masculine name: see ERNEST

ear·nest¹ (ur′nist) adj. [ME. ernest < OE. eornoste < eornost, earnestness, zeal, akin to G. ernst, seriousness (OHG. ernust) < IE. base *er-, to set oneself in motion, arouse, whence RUN] **1.** serious and intense; not joking or playful; zealous and sincere **2.** not petty or trivial; important —SYN. see SERIOUS —**in earnest 1.** serious; not joking **2.** in a serious or determined manner —ear′nest·ly adv. —ear′nest·ness n.

ear·nest² (ur′nist) n. [altered (after prec.) < ME. ernes < OFr. erres < L. arrae, pl. of arra, arrabo, earnest money < Gr. arrabōn < Heb. 'ērābōn] **1.** money given as a part

payment and pledge in binding a bargain: in full, **earnest money 2.** something given or done as an indication or assurance of what is to come; token —SYN. see PLEDGE

earn·ings (ur′ninz) n.pl. **1.** money, etc. earned by labor or service; wages or other recompense **2.** money made by an investment or an enterprise; profits

ear·phone (ir′fōn′) n. a receiver for radio, telephone, or a hearing aid, etc., either held to the ear or put into the ear

ear·plug (-plug′) n. a plug inserted in the outer ear, as to keep out sound when sleeping or water when swimming

ear·ring (-rin′) n. a ring or other small ornament for the lobe of the ear, either passed through a hole pierced in the lobe or fastened with a screw or clip

ear shell 1. same as ABALONE **2.** the shell of the abalone, shaped somewhat like the human ear

ear·shot (-shät′) n. [by analogy with BOWSHOT] the distance within which a sound, esp. that of the unaided human voice, can be heard; range of hearing

ear·split·ting (-split′in) adj. so loud as to hurt the ears; very loud; deafening

ear·stone (-stōn′) n. same as OTOLITH (sense 1)

earth (urth) n. [ME. erthe < OE. eorthe, akin to G. erde < IE. base *er-, whence Gr. era, earth, Corn. erw, field, Du. aarde, earth] **1.** the planet that we live on; terrestrial globe: it is the fifth largest planet of the solar system and the third in distance from the sun: diameter, 7,927 mi.: symbol, ⊕ **2.** this world, as distinguished from heaven and hell **3.** all the people on the earth **4.** land, as distinguished from sea or sky; the ground **5.** the soft, granular or crumbly part of land; soil; ground **6.** [Poet.] a) the substance of the human body b) the human body c) the concerns, interests, etc. of human life; worldly matters **7.** the hole of a burrowing animal; lair **8.** [Obs.] a land or country **9.** Chem. any of the metallic oxides, formerly classed as elements, which are reduced with difficulty, as alumina, zirconia, strontia, etc. **10.** Elec. [Brit.] same as GROUND¹ —vt. **1.** to cover (up) with soil for protection, as seeds or plants **2.** to chase (an animal) into a hole or burrow —vi. to hide in a burrow: said of a fox, etc. —**come back (or down) to earth** to stop being impractical; return to reality —**down to earth** practical; realistic —**on earth** of all things: an intensive used mainly after interrogative pronouns [what on earth do you mean?] —**run to earth** [< use in fox hunting] **1.** to hunt down **2.** to find by search

SYN.—**earth** is applied to the globe or planet we live on, but in religious use is opposed to heaven or hell; **universe** refers to the whole system of planets, stars, space, etc. and to everything that exists in it; **world** is equivalent to **earth**, esp. in its relation to man and his activities, but it is sometimes a generalized synonym for **universe**

earth·born (-bôrn′) adj. **1.** born on or springing from the earth **2.** human; mortal

earth·bound (-bound′) adj. **1.** confined to or by the earth or earthly things **2.** headed for the earth

earth·en (ur′thən) adj. **1.** made of earth or of baked clay **2.** earthly

earth·en·ware (-wer′) n. the coarser sort of containers, tableware, etc. made of baked clay

earth·i·ness (ur′thē nis) n. an earthy quality or state

earth·light (urth′līt′) n. same as EARTHSHINE

earth·ling (-lin) n. **1.** a person who lives on the earth; human being **2.** a worldly person; worldling

earth·ly (-lē) adj. [ME. ertheli < OE. eorthlic] **1.** of the earth; specif., a) terrestrial b) worldly c) temporal or secular **2.** conceivable; possible [a thing of no earthly good] —earth′li·ness n.

SYN.—**earthly** is applied to that which belongs to the earth or to the present life and is chiefly contrasted with heavenly [earthly pleasures]; **terrestrial**, having as its opposite celestial (both Latin-derived parallels of the preceding terms), has special application in formal and scientific usage [terrestrial magnetism]; **worldly** implies reference to the material concerns or pursuits of mankind and is chiefly contrasted with spiritual [worldly wisdom]; **mundane**, although often used as a close synonym of **worldly**, now esp. stresses the commonplace or practical aspects of life [to return to mundane matters after a flight of fancy]

☆**earth·man** (-man′) n., pl. -men (-men′) a human being on or from the planet earth, as in science fiction

☆**earth·mov·er** (-mōōv′ər) n. a bulldozer or other large machine for excavating or moving large quantities of earth

earth·nut (-nut′) n. **1.** the root, tuber, or underground pod of various plants, as the peanut **2.** an edible underground fungus; truffle

earth·quake (-kwāk′) n. a shaking or trembling of the crust of the earth, caused by underground volcanic forces or by breaking and shifting of rock beneath the surface: also used figuratively

earth·shak·ing (-shā′kin) adj. profound or basic in significance, effect, or influence; momentous

earth·shine (-shin′) n. the faint illumination of the dark part of the moon by sunlight reflected from the earth

earth·star (-stär′) n. any of a genus (Geaster) of puffball fungi, in which the outer wall of the spore fruit splits into a starlike form surrounding the spore sac

earth·ward (-wərd) adv., adj. toward the earth

earth·wards (-wərdz) adv. same as EARTHWARD

earth·work (-wurk′) n. **1.** an embankment made by piling up earth, esp. as a fortification **2.** Engineering the work of excavating and building embankments

earth·worm (-wurm′) *n.* any of a number of round, segmented worms (class Oligochaeta) that burrow in the soil, esp. any of a genus (*Lumbricus*) very important in aerating and fertilizing the soil

earth·y (ur′thē) *adj.* **earth′i·er, earth′i·est** **1.** of or like earth or soil **2.** [Archaic] worldly **3.** *a)* coarse; unrefined *b)* simple and natural; hearty

ear trumpet a trumpet-shaped tube formerly used as a hearing aid by the partially deaf

ear·wax (ir′waks′) *n.* the yellowish, waxlike secretion found in the canal of the outer ear; cerumen

ear·wig (-wig′) *n.* [ME. *erwig* < OE. *earwicga* < *eare*, EAR¹ + *wicga*, beetle, worm < IE. base *weik-*, to wind, bend, whence L. *vicia*, VETCH: so called from the baseless notion that it particularly seeks out the human ear to crawl into] any of an order (Dermaptera) of widely distributed insects with short, horny forewings, a pair of forceps at the terminal end of the abdomen, and biting mouthparts

ease (ēz) *n.* [ME. *ese* < OFr. *aise* < VL. **adjaces* < L. *adjacens*, lying nearby, hence easy to reach: see ADJACENT] **1.** freedom from pain, worry, or trouble; comfort **2.** freedom from stiffness, formality, or awkwardness; natural, easy manner; poise **3.** freedom from difficulty; facility; adroitness [to write with *ease*] **4.** freedom from poverty; state of being financially secure; affluence **5.** rest; leisure; relaxation —*vt.* **eased, eas′ing 1.** to free from pain, worry, or trouble; comfort **2.** to lessen or alleviate (pain, anxiety, etc.) **3.** to make easier; facilitate **4.** to reduce the strain, tension, or pressure of or on; loosen; slacken: often with *away, down, up,* or *off* **5.** to fit or move by careful shifting, slow pressure, etc. [to *ease* a piano into place] —*vi.* **1.** to move or be moved by careful shifting, slow pressure, etc. **2.** to lessen in tension, speed, pain, etc. —**at ease 1.** having no anxiety, pain, or discomfort **2.** *Mil. a)* in a relaxed position but maintaining silence and staying in place *b)* a command to take such a position —**ease the rudder** (or **helm**) *Naut.* to reduce the angle the rudder makes with the fore-and-aft line —**take one's ease** to relax and be comfortable

ease·ful (-f'l) *adj.* characterized by, promoting, or full of ease —**ease′ful·ly** *adv.*

ea·sel (ē′z'l) *n.* [17th c. < Du. *ezel* (G. *esel*), ass, ult. < L. *asellus*, dim. of *asinus*, ASS¹: for sense, cf. Fr. *chevalet*, easel, lit., little horse & see SAWHORSE, CHEVAL GLASS] an upright frame or tripod to hold an artist's canvas, a picture on display, etc.

ease·ment (ēz′mənt) *n.* [ME. *esement* < OFr. *aisement*] **1.** an easing or being eased **2.** something that gives ease; a comfort, relief, or convenience **3.** *Law* a right or privilege that a person may have in another's land, as the right of way

EASEL

eas·i·ly (ē′z'l ē) *adv.* [ME. *esili*] **1.** in an easy manner; with little or no difficulty, discomfort, awkwardness, etc. **2.** without a doubt; by far [*easily* the best of the lot] **3.** very likely [the train may *easily* be late]

eas·i·ness (ē′zē nis) *n.* the quality or state of being easy to do or get, or of being at ease

east (ēst) *n.* [ME. *est* < OE. *east*, akin to G. *osten*, ON. *austr* < Gmc. base **aust-*, dawn < IE. **aues-*, to shine, dawn, whence L. *aurora*, dawn (cf. AURORA) & *aurum*, gold (cf. AUREATE)] **1.** the direction to the right of a person facing north; direction in which sunrise occurs: it is properly the point on the horizon at which the center of the sun rises at the equinox **2.** the point on a compass at 90°, directly opposite west **3.** a region or district in or toward this direction **4.** [E-] the eastern part of the earth, esp. Asia and the nearby islands; Orient —*adj.* **1.** in, of, to, toward, or facing the east **2.** from the east [an *east* wind] **3.** [E-] designating the eastern part of a continent, country, etc. [*East* Pakistan] **4.** in, of, or toward the altar of a church —*adv.* in or toward the east; in an easterly direction —☆**the East** the eastern part of the U.S.; specif., *a)* the part east of the Allegheny Mountains, from Maine through Maryland *b)* the part east of the Mississippi and north of the Ohio

East Anglia 1. region in E England comprising the counties of Norfolk and Suffolk **2.** ancient Anglo-Saxon kingdom of this region: one of the HEPTARCHY

East Bengal *former name of* EAST PAKISTAN

East Berlin capital of the German Democratic Republic: pop. 1,071,000: see BERLIN

☆**east·bound** (-bound′) *adj.* bound east; going eastward

East·bourne (-bôrn′) city in Sussex, SE England, on the English Channel: pop. 62,000

east by north the direction, or the point on a mariner's compass, halfway between due east and east-northeast; 11° 15′ north of due east

east by south the direction, or the point on a mariner's compass, halfway between due east and east-southeast; 11° 15′ south of due east

East Chicago city and port in NW Ind., on Lake Michigan, near Chicago: pop. 47,000: see GARY

East China Sea part of the Pacific Ocean east of China and west of Kyushu, Japan, and the Ryukyu Islands: c. 480,000 sq. mi.

East Cleveland city in NE Ohio: suburb of Cleveland: pop. 40,000

East Detroit city in SE Mich.: suburb of Detroit: pop. 46,000

East·er (ēs′tər) *n.* [ME. *ester* < OE. *eastre*, pl. *eastron*, spring, Easter; orig., name of pagan vernal festival almost coincident in date with paschal festival of the church < *Eastre*, dawn goddess < PGmc. **Austro* (whence G. *Ostern*): see EAST] **1.** an annual Christian festival celebrating the resurrection of Jesus, held on the first Sunday after the date of the first full moon that occurs on or after March 21 **2.** the Sunday of this festival: also **Easter Sunday**

Easter egg a colored egg or an egg-shaped piece of candy, etc., used as an Easter gift or ornament

Easter Island [from the fact that it was discovered *Easter* day, 1722] Chilean island in the South Pacific, c. 2,000 mi. west of Chile: 64 sq. mi.; pop. c. 850: native name RAPA NUI

Easter lily any of several species of white-flowered lilies (esp. *Lilium longiflorum*), commonly grown for Easter display

east·er·ly (ēs′tər lē) *adj.* **1.** in, of, or toward the east **2.** from the east [an *easterly* wind] —*adv.* **1.** toward the east **2.** from the east

east·ern (-tərn) *adj.* [ME. *esterne* < OE. *easterne*] **1.** in, of, toward, or facing the east **2.** from the east [an *eastern* wind] **3.** [E-] of or characteristic of the East

Eastern Church 1. orig., the Christian Church in the Eastern Roman Empire, consisting of the four patriarchates in eastern Europe, western Asia, and Egypt, headed by the Bishops of Constantinople, Alexandria, Antioch, and Jerusalem: distinguished from the WESTERN CHURCH **2.** *same as* ORTHODOX EASTERN CHURCH **3.** all Uniates, collectively

east·ern·er (-ər) *n.* **1.** a native or inhabitant of the east ☆**2.** [E-] a native or inhabitant of the eastern part of the U.S.

Eastern Hemisphere that half of the earth which includes Europe, Africa, Asia, and Australia

east·ern·most (-mōst′) *adj.* farthest east

Eastern Orthodox Church *same as* ORTHODOX EASTERN CHURCH

Eastern Roman Empire Byzantine Empire, esp. so called from 395 A.D., when the Roman Empire was divided, until 476 A.D., when the Western Roman emperor was deposed

Eastern Shore E shore of Chesapeake Bay, including all of Md. and Va. east of the Bay

☆**Eastern Standard Time** a standard time used in a zone which includes the Eastern States of the U.S., corresponding to the mean local time of the 75th meridian west of Greenwich, England: it is five hours behind Greenwich time: see TIME, chart

East·er·tide (ēs′tər tīd′) *n.* [EASTER + TIDE¹] the period after Easter, extending in various churches to Ascension Day, Whitsunday, or Trinity Sunday

East Flanders province of NW Belgium: 1,147 sq. mi.; pop. 1,289,000; cap. Ghent

East Germany German Democratic Republic: see GERMANY

East Ham city in Essex, SE England, on the Thames: suburb of London: pop. 105,000

East Hartford suburb of Hartford, in C Conn., on the Connecticut River: pop. 58,000

East India Company any of several European companies from the 16th to the 19th cent. for carrying on trade with the East Indies; esp., such an English company, chartered in 1600 and dissolved in 1874

East Indies 1. Malay Archipelago; esp., the islands of Indonesia (formerly, the Netherlands Indies) **2.** formerly, India, the Indochinese peninsula, the Malay Peninsula, and the Malay Archipelago: also **East India** —**East Indian**

east·ing (ēs′tin) *n.* **1.** *Naut.* the distance covered sailing in an easterly direction **2.** movement in an easterly direction

East Lansing city in SC Mich.: suburb of Lansing: pop. 48,000

East London seaport on the SE coast of South Africa, on the Indian Ocean: pop. 116,000

East Los Angeles suburb of Los Angeles, in SW Calif.: pop. 105,000

East Lo·thi·an (lō′*th*ē ən) county of SE Scotland, on the Firth of Forth: 267 sq. mi.; pop. 53,000

East·man (ēst′mən), **George** 1854–1932; U.S. industrialist & inventor of photographic equipment

East Meadow suburb of New York City, on W Long Island: pop. 46,000

east-north·east (ēst′nôrth′ēst′; *in naut. usage,* -nôr′-) *n.* the direction, or the point on a mariner's compass, halfway between due east and northeast; 22°30′ north of due east —*adj., adv.* **1.** in or toward this direction **2.** from this direction [an *east-northeast* wind]

East Orange city in NE N.J., adjoining Newark: pop. 75,000

East Pakistan one of the two provinces of Pakistan, at the head of the Bay of Bengal: formed from the partition of the former Indian province of Bengal and a part of Assam: 55,134 sq. mi.; pop. 50,840,000; cap. Dacca

East Point city in NC Ga.: suburb of Atlanta: pop. 39,000

East Providence city in E R.I.: suburb of Providence: pop. 48,000

East Prussia former province of NE Germany, on the Baltic Sea, separated from Prussia proper by the Polish Corridor: since 1945, in Poland & the U.S.S.R.

East Riding administrative division of Yorkshire county, NE England: 1,172 sq. mi.; pop. 533,000

East River strait in SE N.Y., connecting Long Island Sound and upper New York Bay and separating Manhattan Island from Long Island: c. 16 mi. long

East Siberian Sea part of the Arctic Ocean, off the NE coast of the U.S.S.R., between the New Siberian Islands & Wrangel Island

east-south-east (ēst′south′ēst′; *in naut. usage*, -sou′-) *n.* the direction, or the point on a mariner's compass, halfway between due east and southeast; 22° 30′ south of due east —*adj.*, *adv.* **1.** in or toward this direction **2.** from this direction [an *east-southeast* wind]

East St. Louis city in SW Ill., on the Mississippi, opposite St. Louis: pop. 70,000

East Suffolk *see* SUFFOLK

East Sussex *see* SUSSEX

east-ward (ēst′wərd) *adv.*, *adj.* toward the east —*n.* an eastward direction, point, or region

east-ward-ly (-lē) *adv.*, *adj.* **1.** toward the east **2.** from the east [an *eastwardly* wind]

east-wards (-wərdz) *adv.* same as EASTWARD

eas-y (ē′zē) *adj.* **eas′i-er, eas′i-est** [ME. *esi* < OFr. *aisé*, pp. of *aisier* (& *aaisie*, pp. of *aaisier* < *a-* + *aisier*) < *aise*: see EASE] **1.** that can be done, got, mastered, endured, etc. with ease; not difficult; not exacting **2.** free from trouble, anxiety, pain, etc. [an *easy* life] **3.** conducive to comfort or rest; comfortable [an *easy* chair] **4.** fond of comfort, ease, or idleness **5.** free from constraint; not stiff, awkward, or embarrassed [an *easy* manner] **6.** not strict, harsh, or severe; lenient [*easy* terms] **7.** readily influenced; compliant or credulous [an *easy* mark] **8.** *a)* unhurried; not fast [an *easy* pace] *b)* not steep; gradual [an *easy* descent] **9.** *Business a)* in little demand: said of a commodity *b)* lacking firmness in prices: said of a market *c)* with funds plentiful and interest rates low: said of a money market Opposed to TIGHT —*adv.* [Colloq.] **1.** easily **2.** slowly and carefully —**easy come—easy go** got and spent or lost with equal ease: implying a carefree attitude toward money —**easy does it** be careful, go slowly, etc. —**easy on the eyes** [Colloq.] pleasant to look at; attractive —☆**go easy on** [Colloq.] **1.** to use or consume with restraint [go *easy on* the paper] **2.** to deal with leniently [to go *easy* on traffic violators] —☆**on easy street** well-to-do; in easy circumstances —**take it easy** [Colloq.] **1.** to refrain from anger, violence, haste, etc. **2.** to refrain from hard work; relax; rest Sometimes used as a farewell

SYN.—**easy** is the broadest term here in its application to that which demands little effort or presents little difficulty [*easy* work]; **facile** means occurring, moving, working, etc. easily and quickly, sometimes unfavorably suggesting a lack of thoroughness or depth [a *facile* style]; **effortless**, in contrast, favorably suggests expert skill or knowledge as responsible for performance that seems to require no effort [the *effortless* grace of the skater]; **smooth** suggests freedom from or riddance of irregularities, obstacles, or difficulties as bringing ease of movement [a *smooth* path to success]; **simple**, in this connection, suggests freedom from complication, elaboration, or involvement, as making something easy to understand [a *simple* explanation] —ANT. **hard, difficult**

easy chair a stuffed or padded armchair

eas-y-go-ing (-gō′iŋ) *adj.* **1.** dealing with things in a relaxed, unworried manner; not hurried or agitated **2.** not strict about things; lenient or lackadaisical

☆**easy mark** [Colloq.] a person easily duped, tricked, or taken advantage of

eat (ēt) *vt.* **ate** (āt; Brit. et) or archaic & dial. **eat** (et, ēt), **eat-en** (ēt′'n) or archaic **eat** (et, ēt), **eat′ing** [ME. *eten* < OE. *etan*, akin to G. *essen* < IE. base *ed-*, to eat, whence L. *edere*, Gr. *edmenai*] **1.** to put (food) in the mouth, chew, and swallow **2.** to use up, devour, destroy, or waste as by eating; consume or ravage (usually with *away* or *up*) **3.** to penetrate and destroy, as acid does; corrode **4.** to make by or as by eating [the acid *ate* holes in the cloth] **5.** to bring into a specified condition by eating [to *eat* oneself sick] ☆**6.** [Slang] to worry or bother [what's *eating* him?] —*vi.* **1.** to eat food; have a meal or meals **2.** to destroy or use up something gradually (often with *into*) —**eat one's words** to retract something said earlier —**eat′er** *n.*

eat-a-ble (-ə b'l) *adj.* fit to be eaten; edible —*n.* a thing fit to be eaten; food: *usually used in pl.*

☆**eat-er-y** (-ər ē) *n.*, *pl.* **-er-ies** [EAT + -ERY] [Colloq.] a restaurant

eat-ing (-iŋ) *n.* **1.** the action of a person or thing that eats **2.** something edible, with reference to its quality as food —*adj.* **1.** that eats or consumes **2.** good for eating uncooked [*eating* apples]

Ea-ton (ēt′'n), **Cyrus S(tephen)** 1883– ; U.S. industrialist & financier, born in Canada

☆**eats** (ēts) *n.pl.* [Colloq.] food; meals

‡**eau** (ō) *n.*, *pl.* **eaux** (ō) [Fr. < L. *aqua*, water] water

Eau Claire (ō′ kler′) [Fr., clear water] city in WC Wis.: pop. 45,000

eau de Co-logne (də kə lōn′) [Fr., lit., water of Cologne: orig. made at Cologne, Germany] a perfumed toilet water made of alcohol and aromatic oils; cologne

‡**eau de vie** (ōd vē′) [Fr., lit., water of life] brandy

eaves (ēvz) *n.pl.*, *mod. sing.* **eave** [orig. sing., ME. *eves* (pl. *evesen*) < OE. *efes*, edge, border, eaves, akin to ON. *ups*, church porch, OHG. *obiza*, porch < IE. *upes-* < base *upo-*, up from behind, whence UP[1], L. *summus*] the lower edge or edges of a roof, usually projecting beyond the sides of a building

eaves-drop (-dräp′) *n.* [ME. *evesdrop*, altered (after *drop*, DROP) < OE. *yfesdrype* (see EAVES & DRIP)] [Rare] water that drips from the eaves, or the ground on which it drips —*vi.* **-dropped′**, **-drop′ping** [prob. back-formation < *eavesdropper*, lit., one who stands on the eavesdrop to listen] to listen secretly to the private conversation of others —**eaves′drop′per** *n.*

ebb (eb) *n.* [ME. *ebbe* < OE. *ebba* (common LowG., as in MLowG. *ebbe*, whence G. *ebbe*, OFris. *ebba*) < Gmc. *abjan*, a going back < IE. base *apo-*, from, away from, whence OFF] **1.** the flow of water back toward the sea, as the tide falls **2.** a weakening or lessening; decline [the *ebb* of one's hopes] —*vi.* [ME. *ebben* < OE. *ebbian*] **1.** to flow back or out; recede, as the tide **2.** to weaken or lessen; decline —SYN. see WANE

ebb tide the outgoing or falling tide: opposed to FLOOD TIDE

Eb-en-e-zer (eb′ə nē′zər) [Heb. *eben-ha-'ēzer*, lit., stone of help: see I Sam. 7:12] a masculine name

Eb-lis (eb′lis) [Ar. *Iblīs*] *Moslem Myth.* Satan

EbN east by north

eb-on (eb′ən) *adj.*, *n.* [ME. *eban* < L. *ebenus, hebenus* < Gr. *ebenos* < Egypt. *hbnj* (whence Heb. *hobnīm*)] [Poet.] same as EBONY

eb-on-ite (-īt′) *n.* [EBON(Y) + -ITE[1]] same as VULCANITE

eb-on-ize (-īz′) *vt.* **-ized′, -iz′ing** to finish (wood, etc.) to look like ebony

eb-on-y (-ē) *n.*, *pl.* **-on-ies** [ME. *ebenif* < LL.(Ec.) *ebenius* < *ebenus*: see EBON] **1.** the hard, heavy, dark, durable wood of any of various trees, esp. of a group of persimmons (genus *Diospyros*) native to tropical Africa, Asia, and Ceylon: it is used for furniture and decorative woodwork **2.** any tree that yields this wood —*adj.* **1.** made of ebony **2.** like ebony, esp. in color; dark; black **3.** designating a family (Ebenaceae) of tropical trees and shrubs including the calamander and persimmon

E-bo-ra-cum (i bôr′ə kəm) *ancient name of* YORK: chief city of the Roman province of Britain

E-bro (ā′brō; E. ē′brō) river in N Spain, flowing into the Mediterranean: c. 575 mi.

e-bul-lient (i bool′yənt, -bul′-) *adj.* [L. *ebulliens*, prp. of *ebullire*, to boil up < *e-*, out + *bullire*, BOIL[1]] **1.** bubbling; boiling **2.** overflowing with enthusiasm, high spirits, etc.; exuberant —**e-bul′lience, e-bul′lien-cy** *n.* —**e-bul′-lient-ly** *adv.*

e-bul-li-tion (eb′ə lish′ən) *n.* [ME. *ebullitioun* < LL. *ebullitio* < pp. of *ebullire*: see prec.] **1.** a boiling or bubbling up; effervescence **2.** a sudden outburst, as of some emotion

e-bur-na-tion (ē′bər nā′shən, eb′ər-) *n.* [< L. *eburnus*, of ivory (< *ebur*, IVORY) + -ATION] an abnormal condition of bone or cartilage in which it becomes hard like ivory

é-car-té (ā′kär tā′) *n.* [Fr., pp. of *écarter*, to discard: any or all of the cards dealt may be discarded and replaced from the pack] a card game for two persons played with thirty-two cards (sevens up through aces)

Ec-bat-a-na (ek bat′'n ə) capital of ancient Media, on the site of modern HAMADAN

ec-bol-ic (ek bäl′ik) *adj.* [Gr. *ekbolē*, a throwing out < *ek-*, out + *ballein*, to throw (see BALL[2]) + -IC] helping to bring forth the fetus in birth, or causing abortion, by contracting the uterus: said of certain drugs —*n.* an ecbolic drug

‡**ec-ce** (ek′ā, ek′sē; *Eccles.* e′chā) *interj.* [L.] behold! lo! see!

‡**ecce homo** [L.] **1.** behold the man: the Vulgate version of Pilate's words when he presented Jesus to the populace before the crucifixion: John 19:5 **2.** a picture or statue of Jesus wearing the crown of thorns

ec-cen-tric (ek sen′trik) *adj.* [ME. *eccentrik* < ML. *eccentricus* < LL. *eccentros*, out of the center, eccentric < Gr. *ekkentros* < *ek-*, out of (see EX-[1]) + *kentron*, CENTER] **1.** not having the same center, as two circles one inside the other: opposed to CONCENTRIC **2.** not having the axis exactly in the center; off-center [an *eccentric* wheel] **3.** not exactly circular in shape or motion **4.** deviating from the norm, as in conduct; out of the ordinary; odd; unconventional —*n.* **1.** a disk set off center on a shaft and revolving inside a strap attached to one end of a rod, thereby converting the circular motion of the shaft into back-and-forth motion of the rod **2.** an odd or unconventional person —**ec-cen′tri-cal-ly** *adv.*

ECCENTRIC CIRCLES AND WHEEL

ec·cen·tric·i·ty (ek'sen tris'ə tē, -sən-) *n.*, *pl.* **-ties** [see ECCENTRIC] **1.** the state, quality, or amount of being eccentric **2.** deviation from what is ordinary or customary, as in conduct or manner; oddity; unconventionality **3.** *Math.* the ratio of the distances from any point on a curve of a conic section to the focus and to the directrix **4.** *Mech.* the distance between the center (as of an eccentric wheel) and the axis; throw —*SYN.* see IDIOSYNCRASY

ec·chy·mo·sis (ek'i mō'sis) *n.* [ModL. < Gr. *ekchymōsis* < *ekchymousthai*, to pour out, extravasate < *ek-*, out of (see EX-¹) + *chein*, to pour] *Med.* **1.** an oozing of blood from a blood vessel into the tissues as the result of a bruise **2.** a black-and-blue or yellowish mark caused by this —**ec'-chy·mot'ic** (-mät'ik) *adj.*

eccl., eccles. 1. ecclesiastic **2.** ecclesiastical

Eccles., Eccl. Ecclesiastes

ec·cle·si·a (i klē'zhē ə, -zē-) *n.*, *pl.* **-si·ae** (-ē') [L., assembly, in LL.(Ec.), assembly of Christians < Gr. *ekklēsia*, assembly (in NT., the church as a body of Christians) < *ekklētos*, summoned < *ekkalein*, to summon < *ek-*, out + *kalein*, to call: see CLAMOR] **1.** in ancient Greek states, a political assembly of citizens **2.** *Eccles.* a) the members of a church *b)* a church building

Ec·cle·si·as·tes (i klē'zē as'tēz) [LL.(Ec.) < Gr. *ekklēsiastēs*, member of an ecclesia (see prec.): used in Septuagint for Heb. *qōhēleth*, he who calls together an assembly] a book of the Bible, written as though by Solomon

ec·cle·si·as·tic (-tik) *adj.* [LL.(Ec.) *ecclesiasticus* < Gr. *ekklēsiastikos*: see ECCLESIA] *same as* ECCLESIASTICAL —*n.* a clergyman

ec·cle·si·as·ti·cal (-ti k'l) *adj.* [ME.: see prec. & -AL] **1.** of the church, the organization of the church, or the clergy **2.** used chiefly in early writings relating to Christianity [*ecclesiastical* Latin or Greek] —**ec·cle'si·as'ti·cal·ly** *adv.*

ec·cle·si·as·ti·cism (-tə siz'm) *n.* **1.** ecclesiastical principles, rituals, customs, etc. **2.** strong attachment to these things

Ec·cle·si·as·ti·cus (-ti kəs) [LL.(Ec.), short for *ecclesiasticus liber*, lit., the church book (see ECCLESIASTIC): from its frequent use for catechetical teaching] a book of proverbs in the Apocrypha, included as canonical in the Douay Bible: abbrev. **Ecclus.**

ec·cle·si·ol·o·gy (i klē'zē äl'ə jē) *n.* [< ECCLESIA + -LOGY] the study of church architecture, art, etc.

ec·crine (ek'rin, -rin) *adj.* [< Gr. *ekkrinein*, to separate, secrete: see EX-¹ & ENDOCRINE] designating or of the common sweat glands of the human body that secrete the clear, watery sweat important in heat regulation

☆**ec·dys·i·ast** (ek diz'ē ast) *n.* [coined (1940) by H. L. MENCKEN < ff. + -*ast*, one occupied with (< ME. *-aste* < L. *-astes* < Gr. *-astēs*)] a stripteaser

ec·dy·sis (ek'də sis) *n.* [ModL. < Gr. *ekdysis*, a getting out, stripping < *ekdyein*, to strip off < *ek-*, out of + *dyein*, to enter] *Zool.* the shedding of an outer layer of skin or integument, as by snakes, insects, etc.

ec·dy·sone (-sōn') *n.* [ECDYS(IS) + -ONE] a hormone produced in the prothoracic glands of insects and stimulating the shedding of the exoskeleton

e·ce·sis (i sē'sis) *n.* [< Gr. *oikēsis*, act of dwelling, residence < *oikein*, to inhabit < *oikos*, house (see ECONOMY) + *-sis*, fem. suffix of action] the successful establishment of a plant or animal in a new locality

ECG electrocardiogram

ech·e·lon (esh'ə län') *n.* [Fr. *échelon*, ladder rung < *échelle* < OFr. *eschelle* < L. *scala*, ladder: see SCALE¹] **1.** a) a steplike formation of ships or troops, in which each unit is slightly to the left or right of the one preceding it *b)* a similar formation of aircraft with each step at a higher or lower level **2.** any of the units in such a formation **3.** a subdivision of a military force, according to position [*rear echelon*] or to function [*command echelon*] **4.** a) any of the levels of responsibility or importance in an organization *b)* the persons at one of these levels —*vt.*, *vi.* to assemble, or assume position, in echelon

ech·e·ve·ri·a (ech'ə ver'ē ə, ek'-) *n.* [ModL., after *Echeveri*, Mex. illustrator of 19th-c. botanical works] any of a large genus (*Echeveria*) of tropical American plants of the orpine family, with dense rosettes of thick fleshy leaves

e·chid·na (i kid'nə) *n.* [ModL. < L., adder, viper < Gr., ult. < IE. base **ĕghi-*, snake, whence G. *egel*, leech] any of several small, egg-laying, toothless Australasian mammals (order Monotremata) with a long, tapering snout and a sticky, extensible tongue: they feed on ants and are covered with spines

ech·i·nate (ek'ə nāt', ə ki'nit) *adj.* [L. *echinatus*: see ECHINUS] covered with prickles; prickly; bristling, as a porcupine: also **ech'i·nat'ed**

e·chi·no- (i ki'nə, ek'ə nō) [< Gr. *echinos*, sea urchin, hedgehog, akin to OE. *igil*: for IE. base, see ECHIDNA] *a combining form* meaning prickly, spiny [*echinoderm*]: also, before a vowel, **e·chin-**

ECHIDNA
(14–21 in. long)

e·chi·no·coc·cus (i ki'nə käk'əs, ek'ə nō-) *n.* [prec. + -COCCUS] any of a genus (*Echinococcus*) of animal tapeworms that in the larval stage can cause human disease, if ingested by man

e·chi·no·derm (i ki'nə durm', ek'ə nə-) *n.* [< ModL. *echinodermata*, name of the class: see ECHINO- & DERMATO-] any of a phylum (Echinodermata) of marine animals with a water vascular system, and usually with a hard, spiny skeleton and radial body, including the starfishes, sea urchins, etc. —**e·chi'no·der'ma·tous** (-dur'mə təs) *adj.*

e·chi·noid (i ki'noid, ek'ə-) *adj.* [ECHIN(O)- + -OID] of or like a sea urchin —*n.* any of a class (Echinoidea) of marine animals, as the sea urchins, sand dollars, etc.

e·chi·nus (i ki'nəs) *n.*, *pl.* **e·chi'ni** (-ni) [L. < Gr. *echinos*: see ECHINO-] **1.** *same as* SEA URCHIN **2.** *Archit.* a) molding under the abacus of the capital of a Doric column *b)* any of several similar moldings

ech·o (ek'ō) *n.*, *pl.* **-oes** [ME. *ecco* < L. *echo* < Gr. *ēchō* < IE. base **(s)wagh-*, var. of **wag-*, to cry out, whence L. *vagire*, OE. *swogan*, to sound, roar] **1.** a) the repetition of a sound by reflection of sound waves from a surface *b)* a sound so produced **2.** a) any repetition or imitation of the words, style, ideas, etc. of another *b)* a person who thus repeats or imitates **3.** sympathetic response **4.** *Bridge* the play of first a high and then a low card in a suit as a signal to one's partner to lead the suit **5.** *Electronics* a radar wave reflected from an object, appearing as a spot of light on a radarscope **6.** *Music* a) a soft repetition of a phrase *b)* an organ stop for producing the effect of echo **7.** *Radio & TV* the reception of two similar and almost simultaneous signals due to the reflection of one of them from the Heaviside layer in transmission —[E-] *Gr. Myth.* a nymph who, because of her unreturned love for Narcissus, pined away until only her voice remained —*vi.* **-oed, -o·ing 1.** to resound with an echo; reverberate **2.** to be repeated as or like an echo —*vt.* **1.** a) to repeat (another's words, ideas, etc.) *b)* to repeat the words, etc. of (another person) **2.** to repeat or reflect (sound) from a surface

echo chamber a room used in recording and broadcasting to increase resonance, produce echo effects, etc.

☆**ech·o·gram** (-gram') *n.* [ECHO + -GRAM] a record of abnormal tissue, as a neoplasm, produced on an oscilloscope screen by a difference in the reflection of ultrasonic waves from diseased and normal tissue

e·cho·ic (e kō'ik) *adj.* **1.** having the nature of an echo **2.** imitative in sound; onomatopoeic: a term in linguistics used, as in the etymologies of this dictionary, to indicate that a word (e.g., *tinkle*) is formed in approximate imitation of some sound —**ech'o·ism** *n.*

ech·o·la·li·a (ek'ō lā'lē ə) *n.* [ModL. < *echo* (see ECHO) + *-lalia*, speech defect < Gr. *lalia*, speech < *lalein*, to talk, prattle < redupl. of IE. echoic **la-* (as in L. *lallare*, G. *lallen*, to lull)] the automatic repetition by someone of words spoken in his presence, esp. as a symptom of mental disorder

ech·o·lo·ca·tion (-lō kā'shən) *n.* the determination, as by a bat, of the position of an object by the emission of sound waves which are reflected back to the sender as echoes —**ech'o·lo'cate** *vt.*, *vi.* **-cat·ed, -cat·ing**

echo sounding the determining of depth of water or distances under water by means of a device (**echo sounder**) that measures the time it takes for a sound wave to be reflected from the bottom or from an underwater object

‡**echt** (eHt) *adj.* [G.] genuine; real; authentic

Eck (ek), **Jo·hann Mai·er von** (yō'hän mi'ər fōn) 1486–1543; Ger. Catholic theologian

Eck·hart (ek'härt), **Jo·han·nes** (yō hän'əs) 1260?–1327?; Ger. theologian & mystic: called **Meister Eckhart**

é·clair (ā kler', ē-, i-) *n.* [Fr., lit., a flash, lightning] a small, oblong pastry shell filled with flavored custard or whipped cream and covered with frosting

‡**é·clair·cisse·ment** (ā kler sēs män') *n.* [Fr. < *éclaircir*, to clear up < OFr. *esclarcir* < VL. **exclaricire* < L. *ex-*, intens. + *claricare*, to gleam < *clarus*, CLEAR] **1.** a clearing up, as of a disputed or difficult point; clarification **2.** [E-] the Enlightenment

ec·lamp·si·a (e klamp'sē ə) *n.* [ModL. < Gr. *eklampsis*, a shining forth < *ek-*, out + *lampein*, to shine: see LAMP] an attack of convulsions; specif., a disorder occurring late in pregnancy and characterized by convulsions, edema, and elevated blood pressure

é·clat (ā klä', i-) *n.* [Fr., noise, clap, splendor < *éclater*, to burst (out), shine, prob. < Gmc. base seen in OHG. & Lombard *slaitan*, to tear, split, akin to SLIT] **1.** brilliant or conspicuous success **2.** dazzling display; striking effect **3.** approval; acclaim **4.** fame; renown

ec·lec·tic (i klek'tik, e-) *adj.* [Gr. *eklektikos* < *eklegein*, to select, pick out < *ek-*, out + *legein*, to choose, pick: see LOGIC] **1.** selecting from various systems, doctrines, or sources **2.** composed of material gathered from various sources, systems, etc. —*n.* a person who uses eclectic methods in philosophy, science, or art —**ec·lec'ti·cal·ly** *adv.*

ec·lec·ti·cism (-tə siz'm) *n.* **1.** an eclectic method or system of thought **2.** the using or upholding of such a method or system

e·clipse (i klips′, ē-) *n.* [ME. < OFr. < L. *eclipsis* < Gr. *ekleipsis*, an abandoning, eclipse < *ekleipein*, to leave out, fail < *ek-*, out + *leipein*, to leave < IE. base **leikw-*, to leave, whence L. *linquere* & LOAN] **1.** the partial or total obscuring of the sun when the moon comes between it and the earth (called **solar eclipse**), or of the moon when the earth's shadow is cast upon it (called **lunar eclipse**) **2.** any overshadowing or cutting off of light **3.** a dimming or extinction, as of fame, glory, etc. —*vt.* **e·clipsed′, e·clips′ing** [ME. *eclipsen*] **1.** to cause an eclipse of; darken or obscure **2.** to make seem less brilliant, famous, etc.; overshadow; outshine; surpass

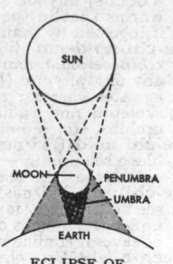

ECLIPSE OF THE SUN

e·clip·tic (i klip′tik, ē-) *n.* [ME. *ecliptik* < ML. *ecliptica* < LL. *(linea) ecliptica* < Gr. *ekleiptikos*, of an eclipse] **1.** the apparent annual path of the sun on the celestial sphere: it is a great circle inclined about 23 1/2° to the celestial equator **2.** a great circle on the celestial sphere formed by the intersection of an infinite plane through the earth's orbit with the celestial sphere —*adj.* of eclipses or the ecliptic

ec·lo·gite (ek′lə jīt′) *n.* [< Gr. *eklogē*, selection (see ff.) + -ITE¹] a metamorphic rock consisting mainly of a green pyroxene, red garnet, and other minerals

ec·logue (ek′lôg, -läg) *n.* [ME. *eclog* < L. *ecloga*, a short poem (esp. one of the *Eclogae*, bucolic poems of Virgil) < Gr. *eklogē*, selection, esp. of poems < *eklegein*: see ECLECTIC] a short pastoral poem, usually in the form of a dialogue between two shepherds

e·clo·sion (i klō′zhən) *n.* [Fr. *éclosion* < *éclore*, to hatch, be hatched < OFr. *esclore* < VL. **excludere*, to hatch out, altered (as if < L. *ex-* + *claudere*, to CLOSE²) < L. *excludere*, to hatch, drive out, EXCLUDE] the emergence of an insect from its egg or from the pupal case

e·co- (ē′kō, ek′ō) [LL. *oeco-* < Gr. *oiko-* < *oikos*, house: see ECONOMY] *a combining form meaning* environment or habitat [*ecotype*]

ecol. **1.** ecological **2.** ecology

‡é·cole (ā kôl′) *n.* [Fr. < L. *schola*] school

ec·o·log·i·cal (ek′ə läj′i k'l, ē′kə-) *adj.* of or by ecology: also **ec′o·log′ic** —**ec′o·log′i·cal·ly** *adv.*

e·col·o·gy (ē käl′ə jē) *n.* [G. *ökologie* < Gr. *oikos*, house + *-logia*, -LOGY] **1.** *a)* the branch of biology that deals with the relations between living organisms and their environment *b)* the complex of relations between a specific organism and its environment **2.** *Sociology* the study of the relationship and adjustment of human groups to their geographical environment —**e·col′o·gist** *n.*

econ. **1.** economic **2.** economics **3.** economy

e·con·o·met·rics (i kän′ə met′riks) *n.pl.* [*with sing. v.*] [ECONO(MY) + METRICS] the use of mathematical and statistical methods in the field of economics to verify and develop economic theories —**e·con′o·met′ric** *adj.* —**e·con′-o·me·tri′cian** (-mə trish′ən) *n.*

e·co·nom·ic (ē′kə näm′ik, ek′ə-) *adj.* [L. *oeconomicus* < Gr. *oikonomikos* < *oikonomia*: see ECONOMY] **1.** of or having to do with the management of the income, expenditures, etc. of a household, private business, community, or government **2.** of or having to do with the production, distribution, and consumption of wealth **3.** of or having to do with economics **4.** of or having to do with the satisfaction of the material needs of people [*economic biology*] **5.** [Archaic] economical

e·co·nom·i·cal (-i k'l) *adj.* **1.** not wasting money, time, fuel, etc.; thrifty [an *economical* person, an *economical* stove] **2.** expressed or done with economy, using few lines, words, etc. [an *economical* style] **3.** of economics; economic —*SYN.* see THRIFTY —**e′co·nom′i·cal·ly** *adv.*

economic geography the branch of geography that deals with the relation of economic conditions to physical geography and natural resources

e·co·nom·ics (-iks) *n.pl.* [*with sing. v.*] **1.** the science that deals with the production, distribution, and consumption of wealth, and with the various related problems of labor, finance, taxation, etc.; political economy **2.** economic factors or relationships

e·con·o·mist (i kän′ə mist) *n.* **1.** a specialist in economics **2.** [Archaic] an economizer or thrifty person

e·con·o·mize (-mīz′) *vi.* **-mized′, -miz′ing** to avoid waste or needless expenditure; reduce expenses —*vt.* to manage or use with thrift —**e·con′o·miz′er** *n.*

e·con·o·my (-mē) *n., pl.* **-mies** [L. *oeconomia* < Gr. *oikonomia*, management of a household or state, public revenue < *oikonomos*, manager < *oikos*, house (< IE. **woiko-*, *weik-*, whence L. *vicus*, group of houses, village, whence OE. *wic*, house, village) + *nomos*, managing < *nemein*, to distribute, manage (akin to OE. *niman*, to take)] **1.** the management of the income, expenditures, etc. of a household, private business, community, or government **2.** *a)* careful management of wealth, resources, etc.; avoidance of waste by careful planning and use; thrift or thrifty use *b)* restrained or efficient use of one's materials, technique, etc., esp. by an artist *c)* an instance of such management or use, or a way of economizing **3.** an orderly

management or arrangement of parts; organization or system [the *economy* of the human body] **4.** *a)* a system of producing, distributing, and consuming wealth *b)* the condition of such a system; relative prosperity of a country, industry, era, etc.

ECOSOL Economic and Social Council (of the UN)

e·co·spe·cies (ē′kō spē′shēz, ek′ō-) *n.* [ECO- + SPECIES] a biological species, distinguished from its close relatives, with which it can interbreed, by its adaptations to its particular environment —**e′co·spe·cif′ic** (-spə sif′ik) *adj.*

e·co·sys·tem (-sis′təm) *n.* [ECO- + SYSTEM] a system made up of a community of animals, plants, and bacteria and the physical and chemical environment with which it is interrelated

☆e·co·tone (-tōn′) *n.* [< ECO- + Gr. *tonos*, a stretching: see TONE] a transitional zone between two adjacent communities, containing species characteristic of both as well as other species occurring only within the zone

e·co·type (-tīp′) *n.* [ECO- + TYPE] a group of physiological or morphological variants within a biological species, adapted to particular environmental conditions —**e′co·typ′ic** (-tip′ik) *adj.* —**e′co·typ′i·cal·ly** *adv.*

‡é·cra·seur (ā krä zēr′) *n.* [Fr. < *écraser*, to crush] a surgical instrument consisting of a looped wire or cord, gradually tightened about a part so as to cut it off

ec·ru (ek′rōō, ā′krōō, ā krōō′) *adj., n.* [Fr. *écru*, unbleached, raw < OFr. *escru* < *es-* (L. *ex-*), intens. + *cru*, raw < L. *crudus* (see CRUDE): in reference to the color of unbleached linen] light tan; beige

ec·sta·sy (ek′stə sē) *n., pl.* **-sies** [ME. & OFr. *extasie* < LL.(Ec.) *ecstasis* < Gr. *ekstasis*, a being put out of its place, distraction, trance < *ek-*, out + *histanai*, to place] **1.** a state of being overpowered by emotion, as by joy, grief, passion, etc. [an *ecstasy* of delight] **2.** a feeling of overpowering joy; great delight; rapture **3.** a trance, esp. one resulting from religious fervor

SYN.—**ecstasy** implies extreme emotional exaltation, now usually intense delight, that overpowers the senses and lifts one into a trancelike state; **bliss** implies a state of great happiness and contentment, often literally or figuratively suggesting heavenly joy; **rapture** now generally suggests the mental exaltation experienced when one's entire attention is captured by something that evokes great joy or pleasure; **transport** implies a being carried away by any powerful emotion

ec·stat·ic (ik stat′ik, ek-) *adj.* [ML. *ecstaticus* < Gr. *ekstatikos*] **1.** of, having the nature of, or characterized by ecstasy **2.** causing, or caused by, ecstasy **3.** subject to ecstasy —**ec·stat′i·cal·ly** *adv.*

ec·to- (ek′tə, -tō) [ModL. < Gr. *ektos*, outside < IE. **eghstos* < base **eghs-*, out, whence L. *ex*] *a combining form meaning* outside, external [*ectoderm*]: also, before a vowel, **ect-**

ec·to·blast (ek′tə blast′) *n.* [ECTO- + BLAST] *same as* EPIBLAST —**ec′to·blas′tic** *adj.*

ec·to·com·men·sal (-kə men′s'l) *n.* a commensal living on the outer surface of the host organism

ec·to·derm (ek′tə dʉrm′) *n.* [ECTO- + -DERM] **1.** the outer layer of cells of an animal embryo, from which the nervous system, skin, hair, teeth, etc. are developed **2.** the layer or layers of cells composing the skin, nervous system, etc. in animals from coelenterates to chordates, but excluding protozoans and sponges —**ec′to·der′mal, ec′to·der′mic** *adj.*

ec·tog·e·nous (ek täj′ə nəs) *adj.* that can develop outside the host: said of certain parasitic bacteria: also **ec·to·gen·ic** (ek′tə jen′ik)

ec·to·mere (ek′tə mir′) *n.* [ECTO- + -MERE] any of the early cells that form the ectoderm of an embryo —**ec′to·mer′ic** (-mer′ik, -mir′ik) *adj.*

ec·to·morph (ek′tə môrf′) *n.* an ectomorphic individual

ec·to·mor·phic (ek′tə môr′fik) *adj.* [ECTO- + -MORPHIC] designating or of the slender physical type, characterized by predominance of the structures developed from the ectodermal layer of the embryo, as skin, nerves, brain, and sense organs; asthenic: cf. ENDOMORPHIC & MESOMORPHIC —**ec′to·mor′phi·cal·ly** *adv.* —**ec′to·mor′phy** (-fē) *n.*

-ec·to·my (ek′tə mē) [< Gr. *ektomē*, a cutting out < *ek-*, out + *temnein*, to cut < IE. base **tem-*: cf. ESTIMATE] *a combining form meaning* a surgical excision of [*appendectomy, tonsillectomy*]

ec·to·par·a·site (ek′tō par′ə sīt′) *n.* any parasite that lives on the outer surface of an animal: opposed to ENDO-PARASITE —**ec′to·par′a·sit′ic** (-sit′ik) *adj.*

ec·to·pi·a (ek tō′pē ə) *n.* [ModL. < Gr. *ektopos*, away from a place < *ek-*, out of (see EX-¹) + *topos*, a place (see TOPIC) + ModL. *-ia*, -IA] an abnormal position of a body part or organ —**ec·top·ic** (ek täp′ik) *adj.*

ec·to·plasm (ek′tə plaz′m) *n.* [ECTO- + -PLASM] **1.** the outer layer of the cytoplasm of a cell **2.** the vaporous, luminous substance supposed to emanate from the medium's body during a spiritualistic trance —**ec′to·plas′mic** *adj.*

ec·to·proct (-präkt′) *n.* [< ModL. *Ectoprocta* < *ecto-* (see ECTO-) + Gr. *prōktos*, anus] any of a phylum (Ectoprocta) of minute water animals that form fixed, branching, mosslike colonies and reproduce by budding —**ec′to·proc′tan** *adj.*

ec·to·sarc (-särk′) *n.* [< ECTO- + Gr. *sarx* (gen. *sarkos*), flesh] the ectoplasm of one-celled animals

ec·type (ek′tīp′) *n.* [L. *ectypus* < Gr. *ektypos*, engraved in

relief < *ek-*, out + *typos*, a figure: see TYPE] a reproduction of an original; copy

‡é·cu (ā kü′) n., pl. -cus (-kü′) [Fr. < OFr. *escu* < L. *scutum*, a shield] any of various French silver or gold coins, esp. a silver crown of the 17th–18th cent.

Ec·ua·dor (ek′wə dôr′) country on the NW coast of S. America: 104,506 sq. mi.; pop. 5,890,000; cap. Quito — Ec′ua·do′re·an, Ec′ua·do′ri·an, Ec′ua·dor′an adj., n.

ec·u·men·i·cal (ek′yoo men′i k'l) adj. [LL. *oecumenicus* < Gr. *oikoumenikos*, of or from the whole world < *oikoumenē* (*gē*), the inhabited (world) < *oikein*, to dwell, inhabit < *oikos*: see ECONOMY] 1. general, or universal; esp., of or concerning the Christian church as a whole 2. a) furthering or /intended to further the unity or oneness of Christian churches b) of or having to do with ecumenism Also ec′u·men′ic —ec′u·men′i·cal·ism n. —ec′u·men′i·cal·ly adv.

ec·u·men·i·cism (-i siz'm) n. same as ECUMENISM

ec·u·men·ism (ek′yoo mə niz'm, e kyoo′-) n. 1. the ecumenical movement among Christian churches 2. the principles or practice of promoting cooperation or better understanding among differing religious faiths Also ec·u·me·nic·i·ty (ek′yoo mə nis′ə tē) —ec′u·men·ist n.

ec·ze·ma (ek′sə mə, eg′-; ig zē′mə) n. [ModL. < Gr. *ekzema* < *ek-*, out + *zein*, to boil: see YEAST] a disease of the skin characterized by inflammation, itching, and the formation of scales —ec·zem·a·tous (ig zem′ə təs, -zē′mə-) adj.

-ed (id, əd *as a separate syllable, esp. after t or d; d after a voiced sound in the same syllable; t after a voiceless sound in the same syllable*) 1. [as ending of past tense < ME. < OE. -*ede*, -*ode*, -*ade*, -*de*; as ending of past participles and analogous forms < ME. < OE. -*ed*, -*od*, -*ad*] *a suffix used:* a) to form the past tense and past participle of weak verbs [*walked, wanted*] b) to form adjectives from nouns or verbs [*cultured, versed*] or from other adjectives ending in -*ate* [*echinated*] 2. [< OE. -*ede*] *a suffix added to nouns, meaning:* having, provided with, characterized by [*bearded, sugared, small-mouthed*]

ed. 1. edited 2. pl. eds. a) edition b) editor 3. education

e·da·cious (i dā′shəs) adj. [< L. *edax* (gen. *edacis*) < *edere*, EAT + -IOUS] voracious; consuming, devouring

e·dac·i·ty (i das′ə tē) n. [L. *edacitas*] the state of being edacious; huge capacity for eating: now humorous

E·dam (cheese) (ē′dəm, -dam) [< *Edam*, town in NW Netherlands, where orig. made] a mild yellow cheese, made in a round mold, usually with a red paraffin coating

e·daph·ic (i daf′ik) adj. [< Gr. *edaphos*, soil, earth, bottom (prob. < or akin to *hedos*, seat, chair < IE. *sedos-* < base *sed-*, SIT) + -IC] *Ecol.* pertaining to the chemical and physical characteristics of the soil or water environment, without reference to climate

Ed.B. Bachelor of Education

Ed.D. Doctor of Education

Ed·da (ed′ə) [ON.] either of two early Icelandic literary works: a) the Prose, or Younger, Edda (c. 1230), a summary of Norse mythology with two treatises on skaldic poetry, attributed to Snorri Sturluson b) the Poetic, or Elder, Edda (c. 1200), a collection of Old Norse poetry — Ed·dic (ed′ik), Ed·da·ic (i dā′ik) adj.

Ed·ding·ton (ed′iŋ tən), Sir Arthur Stanley, 1882–1944; Eng. astronomer & astrophysicist

ed·do (ed′ō) n., pl. -does [prob. < native name in W Africa] the edible corm of the taro

ed·dy (ed′ē) n., pl. -dies [ME. *ydy*, prob. < ON. *itha*, an eddy, whirlpool < IE. base *eti*, furthermore, and, whence L. *et*] 1. a current of air, water, etc. moving against the main current and with a circular motion; little whirlpool or whirlwind 2. a contrary movement or trend, limited in importance or effect —vi. -died, -dy·ing to move with a circular motion against the main current; move in an eddy

Ed·dy (ed′ē), Mary Baker (born *Mary Morse Baker*) 1821–1910; U.S. founder of Christian Science

Ed·dy·stone Light (ed′i stən) lighthouse on dangerous rocks (Eddystone Rocks) just off the SE coast of Cornwall, in the English Channel

E·de (ā′də) city in Gelderland province, C Netherlands: pop. 65,000

e·del·weiss (ā′d'l vīs′) n. [G. < *edel*, noble, precious + *weiss*, white] a small, flowering plant (*Leontopodium alpinum*) of the composite family, native to the high mountains of Europe and C Asia, esp. the Alps, with leaves and petallike bracts that are white and woolly

e·de·ma (i dē′mə) n., pl. -mas, -ma·ta (-mə tə) [ModL. < Gr. *oidēma*, a swelling, tumor < IE. base *oid-*, to swell, whence OE. *ator*, poison] 1. an abnormal accumulation of fluid in cells, tissues, or cavities of the body, resulting in swelling 2. a similar swelling in plant cells or tissues — e·dem·a·tous (i dem′ə təs, i dē′mə-) adj.

E·den (ē′d'n) [LL. < Heb. *'ēdhen*, lit., delight] *Bible* the garden where Adam and Eve first lived; Paradise —n. any delightful place or state; a paradise

E·den (ē′d'n), Sir (Robert) Anthony, 1897– ; Brit. statesman; prime minister (1955–57)

e·den·tate (ē den′tāt) adj. [L. *edentatus*, pp. of *edentare*, to render toothless < *e-*, out + *dens* (gen. *dentis*), TOOTH] 1. without teeth 2. of the edentates —n. any of an order (Edentata) of mammals having only molars or no teeth at all, as the sloths, armadillos, and anteaters

e·den·tu·lous (ē den′choo ləs) adj. without teeth

E·des·sa (i des′ə) ancient city in NW Mesopotamia, on the site of modern URFA

Ed·gar (ed′gər) [OE. *Eadgar* < *ead*, riches, prosperity, happiness < Gmc. **autha-*, whence Goth. *audags*, fortunate, OHG. *ot*, wealth) + *gar*, a spear (see GORE³)] a masculine name: dim. *Ed, Ned*

edge (ej) n. [ME. *egge* < OE. *ecg*, akin to ON. *egg*, G. *ecke*, corner < IE. base **ak-*, sharp, pointed, whence also L. *acer*, sharp (cf. ACRID)] 1. the thin, sharp, cutting part of a blade 2. the quality of being sharp or keen 3. the projecting ledge or brink, as of a cliff 4. the part farthest from the middle; line where something begins or ends; border, or part nearest the border; margin 5. the verge or brink, as of a condition 6. *Geom.* a line at which two surfaces of a solid meet ☆7. [Colloq.] advantage [you have the *edge* on me] —vt. edged, edg′ing 1. a) to form or put an edge on; provide an edge for b) to trim the edge of 2. to make (one's way) sideways, as through a crowd 3. to move gradually or cautiously 4. [Colloq.] to defeat in a contest by a narrow margin (often with *out*) ☆5. *Skiing* to tilt (a ski) so that one edge bites into the snow, as in traversing a slope —vi. 1. to move sideways 2. to move gradually or cautiously [to *edge* away from danger] —SYN. see BORDER —on edge 1. so tense or nervous as to be easily upset; irritable 2. eager; impatient —set one's teeth on edge 1. to give a sensation of tingling discomfort, as the sound of a fingernail scraped on a slate 2. to irritate; provoke —take the edge off to dull the intensity, force, or pleasure of —edg′er n.

edge species *Ecol.* a species of animal or plant living primarily in an ecotone

edge tool a chisel or similar tool with a cutting edge

edge·ways (-wāz′) adv. with the edge foremost; on, by, with, or toward the edge: also edge′wise′ (-wīz′) —get a word in edgeways to manage to say something in a conversation being monopolized by another or others

Edge·worth (ej′wərth), Maria 1767–1849; Eng. novelist in Ireland

edg·ing (ej′iŋ) n. something forming an edge or placed along the edge; fringe, trimming, etc. for a border

edg·y (ej′ē) adj. edg′i·er, edg′i·est 1. having an edge or edges; sharp 2. irritable; on edge 3. having outlines that are too sharp: said of drawings, paintings, etc. —edg′i·ly adv. —edg′i·ness n.

edh (eth) n. a letter of the Old English alphabet (ð, Ð), a modification of Latin *d, D*, used to represent the voiced or voiceless dental fricative *th*, which replaced it in Middle English: in some phonetic alphabets it stands for the voiced dental fricative

ed·i·ble (ed′ə b'l) adj. [LL. *edibilis* < L. *edere*, EAT] fit to be eaten; eatable —n. anything fit to be eaten; food: *usually used in pl.* —ed′i·bil′i·ty (-bil′ə tē), ed′i·ble·ness n.

e·dict (ē′dikt) n. [L. *edictum*, neut. pp. of *edicere*, to proclaim < *e-*, out + *dicere*, to speak: see DICTION] an official public proclamation or order issued by authority; decree —e·dic·tal (ē dik′t'l) adj.

ed·i·fi·ca·tion (ed′ə fi kā′shən) n. [ME. *edificacioun* < LL.(Ec.) *aedificatio* < L., act of building] an edifying or being edified; instruction; esp., moral or spiritual instruction or improvement

ed·i·fice (ed′ə fis) n. [ME. < OFr. < L. *aedificium*, a building < *aedificare*: see EDIFY] 1. a building, esp. a large, imposing one 2. any elaborately constructed institution, organization, etc. —SYN. see BUILDING

ed·i·fy (ed′ə fī′) vt. -fied′, -fy′ing [ME. *edifien* < OFr. *edifier* < L. *aedificare*, to build, construct (in LL.(Ec.), to edify) < *aedes*, a dwelling, house, temple, orig., hearth, fireplace < IE. base **ai-dh-*, to burn (whence Gr. *aithein*, to burn, OE. *ad*, pyre) + -*ficare* < *facere*, to make] 1. to instruct; esp., to instruct or improve morally or spiritually; enlighten 2. [Archaic] to build; establish —ed′i·fi′er n.

c·dile (ē′dīl) n. same as AEDILE

E·di·na (e dē′nə) [coined by Scot. settlers after *ff.*] village in E Minn.; suburb of Minneapolis: pop. 44,000

Ed·in·burgh (ed′'n bur'ə, -ō) capital of Scotland and county seat of Midlothian, on the Firth of Forth: pop. 472,000

E·dir·ne (e dir′ne) city in NW European Turkey, near the Greek border, on the site of ancient ADRIANOPLE

Ed·i·son (ed′ə s'n), Thomas Alva 1847–1931; U.S. inventor, esp. of electrical & communication devices, including the incandescent lamp, phonograph, & microphone

ed·it (ed′it) vt. [back-formation < EDITOR] 1. to prepare (an author's works, journals, letters, etc.) for publication, by selection, arrangement, and annotation 2. to revise and make ready (a manuscript) for publication 3. to supervise the publication of and set the policy for (a newspaper or periodical) ☆4. to prepare (a film, tape, or recording) for presentation by cutting and splicing, dubbing, rearranging, etc. —☆edit out to delete in editing

edit. 1. edited 2. edition 3. editor

E·dith (ē′dith) [OE. *Eadgyth* < *ead* (see EDGAR) + *guth*, combat, battle, war] a feminine name

e·di·tion (i dish′ən) *n.* [ME. *edicion* < L. *editio*, a bringing forth, publishing < *edere*: see EDITOR] **1.** the size, style, or form in which a book is published [a pocket *edition*] **2.** *a)* the total number of copies of a book or the like printed from the same plates, type, etc. and published at about the same time *b)* a single copy of such a printing **3.** the issue of a well-known work distinguished by its editor, publisher, etc. [the Skeat *edition* of Chaucer] **4.** any of the various regular issues of a newspaper [the Sunday *edition*]

ed·i·tor (ed′i tər) *n.* [L. < *editus*, pp. of *edere*, to give out, publish < *e-*, out + *dare*, to give: see DATIVE] **1.** a person who edits **2.** a writer of editorials **3.** the head of a department of a newspaper, magazine, etc. ☆**4.** a device for editing motion-picture film, video tape, etc. as by viewing, cutting, and splicing —**ed′i·tor·ship′** *n.*

ed·i·to·ri·al (ed′ə tôr′ē əl) *adj.* **1.** of or by an editor or of or for editing **2.** characteristic of an editor or editorial; expressing opinion in the manner of an editor [an *editorial* comment] —☆*n.* an article in a newspaper, etc. explicitly stating opinions of the editor or publisher —**ed′i·to′ri·al·ly** *adv.*

☆**ed·i·to·ri·al·ist** (-ist) *n.* a writer of editorials

☆**ed·i·to·ri·al·ize** (-īz′) *vt., vi.* **-ized′, -iz′ing 1.** to express editorial opinions about (something) **2.** to put editorial opinions into (a newspaper article, etc.) —**ed′i·to′ri·al·i·za′tion** *n.* —**ed′i·to′ri·al·iz′er** *n.*

editor in chief *pl.* **editors in chief** the editor who heads or supervises the editorial staff of a publication

Ed.M. Master of Education

Ed·mon·ton (ed′mən tən) **1.** capital of Alberta, Canada, in the C part: pop. 377,000 **2.** city in Middlesex, SE England: suburb of London: pop. 91,000

Ed·mund, Ed·mond (ed′mənd) [OE. *Eadmund* < *ead* (see EDGAR) + *mund*, hand, protection, akin to L. *manus* (see MANUAL): hence, wealthy protector] a masculine name: dim. *Ed, Ned*

Ed·na (ed′nə) [Gr. *Edna* < Heb. *'ēdnāh*, rejuvenation] a feminine name

E·do (ē′dō) *n.* **1.** any of a people living in the Benin province of S Nigeria **2.** their Kwa language

E·dom (ē′dəm) **1.** *Bible* Esau, Jacob's brother **2.** ancient kingdom in SW Asia, between the Dead Sea and the Gulf of Aqaba

E·dom·ite (-īt′) *n. Bible* a descendant of Edom, or Esau; inhabitant of Edom: Gen. 36 —**E′dom·it′ish** *adj.*

EDP electronic data processing

educ. 1. education **2.** educational

ed·u·ca·ble (ej′ə kə b'l) *adj.* that can be educated or trained —**ed′u·ca·bil′i·ty** *n.*

ed·u·cate (ej′ə kāt′) *vt.* **-cat′ed, -cat′ing** [ME. *educaten* < L. *educatus*, pp. of *educare*, to bring up, rear, or train < *educere* < *e-*, out + *ducere*, to lead, draw, bring: see DUKE] **1.** to train or develop the knowledge, skill, mind, or character of, esp. by formal schooling or study; teach; instruct **2.** to form and develop (one's taste, etc.) **3.** to pay for the schooling of (a person) —*SYN.* see TEACH

ed·u·cat·ed (-kāt′id) *adj.* **1.** having, or showing the results of, much education ☆**2.** based on knowledge or experience [an *educated* guess]

ed·u·ca·tion (ej′ə kā′shən) *n.* [L. *educatio*: see prec.] **1.** the process of training and developing the knowledge, skill, mind, character, etc., esp. by formal schooling; teaching; training **2.** knowledge, ability, etc. thus developed **3.** *a)* formal schooling at an institution of learning *b)* a stage of this [a high-school *education*] **4.** systematic study of the methods and theories of teaching and learning

ed·u·ca·tion·al (-'l) *adj.* **1.** relating to education **2.** giving instruction or information; educating [an *educational* film] —**ed′u·ca′tion·al·ly** *adv.*

☆**educational park** a centralized, integrated educational facility in a metropolitan area, designed for students from widespread areas throughout the community and consisting variously of schools from kindergarten through college in a parklike setting

ed·u·ca·tion·ist (-ist) *n.* an educator; esp., an authority on educational theory: often a disparaging term with varying connotations of inflexibility, antitraditionalism, intellectual limitations, etc.: also **ed′u·ca′tion·al·ist**

ed·u·ca·tive (ej′ə kāt′iv) *adj.* **1.** educating or tending to educate; instructive **2.** of education; educational

ed·u·ca·tor (ej′ə kāt′ər) *n.* [L.] **1.** a person whose work is to educate others; teacher **2.** a specialist in the theories and methods of education

e·duce (i dōos′, ē-; -dyōos′) *vt.* **-duced′, -duc′ing** [L. *educere*: see EDUCATE] **1.** to draw out; elicit **2.** to infer from data; deduce —*SYN.* see EXTRACT —**e·duc′i·ble** *adj.* —**e·duc·tion** (i duk′shən, ē-) *n.*

e·duct (ē′dukt) *n.* [L. *eductum*, neut. pp. of *educere*] **1.** something educed **2.** a substance separated unchanged from another substance: distinguished from PRODUCT

Ed·ward (ed′wərd) [OE. *Eadweard* < *ead* (see EDGAR) + *weard*, guardian, protector (see WARD): hence, wealthy (or fortunate) guardian] **1.** a masculine name: dim. *Ed, Ned;* equiv. Fr. *Édouard,* G. *Eduard,* It. & Sp. *Eduardo,* Scand. *Edvard* **2.** 1330–76; Prince of Wales: son of EDWARD III: called the *Black Prince* **3.** name of eight kings of England: *a)* **Edward I** 1239–1307; king (1272–1307) *b)* **Edward II**

1284–1327; king (1307–27) *c)* **Edward III** 1312–77; king (1327–77) *d)* **Edward IV** 1442–83; king (1461–70; 1471–83) *e)* **Edward V** 1470–83; king (1483): murdered reputedly by order of his uncle, RICHARD III *f)* **Edward VI** 1537–53; king (1547–53): son of HENRY VIII & Jane SEYMOUR *g)* **Edward VII** (born *Albert Edward*) 1841–1910; king (1901–10): son of Queen VICTORIA *h)* **Edward VIII** *see* Duke of WINDSOR

Edward, Lake lake in EC Africa, between the Congo (sense 2) and Uganda: 830 sq. mi.

Ed·ward·i·an (ed wär′dē ən, -wôr′-) *adj.* designating or of the reigns of any of the English kings named Edward; specif., *a)* designating, or in the style of, the architecture of the period of the first three Edwards *b)* of or characteristic of the time of Edward VII, esp. with reference to literature and art

Ed·wards (ed′wərdz), **Jonathan** 1703–58; Am. theologian

Edward the Confessor 1004?–66; king of England (1042–66): canonized; his day is Oct. 13

Ed·win (ed′win) [OE. *Eadwine* < *ead* (see EDGAR) + *wine*, friend < Gmc. **weniz* < IE. base **wen-*, to strive, desire, love (whence WIN(SOME), WISH, L. *Venus*): lit., rich friend] a masculine name: dim. *Ed;* fem. *Edwina*

Ed·win·a (ed wē′nə, -win′ə; ed′wə nə) [fem. of prec.] a feminine name

-ee¹ (ē) [< Anglo-Fr. & OFr. *-é*, orig. masc. ending of pp. of verbs in *-er* < L. *-atus:* see *-ATE*²] *a n.-forming suffix designating:* **1.** the recipient of a specified action, grant, or benefit [*appointee, selectee, mortgagee*] **2.** a person in a specified condition [*absentee, employee*] **3.** a person or thing associated in some way with another [*bargee, goatee*]

-ee² (ē) *a suffix forming nonstandard singulars from nouns ending in -ese* [*Chinee, Portugee*]

E.E. Electrical Engineer

e.e. errors excepted

E.E.C. European Economic Community: see COMMON MARKET

EEG electroencephalogram

eel (ēl) *n., pl.* **eels, eel:** see PLURAL, II, D, 1 [ME. *ele* < OE. *æl*, akin to G. *aal* < ? IE. base **elo-*, furrow, streak] **1.** any of a large variety of fishes (order Apodes) with long, slippery, snakelike bodies and no pelvic fins **2.** any of various other snakelike fishes, including the electric eel and lamprey —**eel′y** (-ē) *adj.*

☆**eel·grass** (-gras′, -gräs′) *n.* **1.** a flowering plant (*Zostera marina*) of the pondweed family, that grows under water and has long, grasslike leaves **2.** *same as* TAPE GRASS

EEL
(to 5 ft. long)

eel·pout (-pout′) *n., pl.* **-pout′, -pouts′:** see PLURAL, II, D, 2 [OE. *ælepute:* see EEL & POUT²] **1.** any of a group of saltwater fishes (family Zoarcidae) resembling the blenny **2.** *same as* BURBOT

eel·worm (-wurm′) *n.* any of a large number of nematode worms that are free-living or parasitic on plants

e'en (ēn) *adv.* [Poet.] even —*n.* [Poet. or Dial.] even(ing)

e'er (er, ar) *adv.* [Poet.] ever

-eer (ir) [Fr. *-ier* < L. *-arius*] *a suffix used to form:* **1.** *nouns meaning* a person or thing that has to do with [*auctioneer, engineer, mountaineer*] or a person who writes, makes, etc. [*pamphleteer, profiteer*]: sometimes used derogatorily **2.** *verbs meaning* to have to do with [*electioneer*]

ee·rie, ee·ry (ir′ē) *adj.* **-ri·er, -ri·est** [N. Eng. dial. & Scot. < ME. *eri*, filled with dread, prob. var. of *erg*, cowardly, timid < OE. *earg*, akin to G. *arg*, bad, wicked: for IE. base, see ORCHESTRA] **1.** orig., timid or frightened; uneasy because of superstitious fear **2.** mysterious, uncanny, or weird, esp. in such a way as to frighten or make uneasy —*SYN.* see WEIRD —**ee′ri·ly** *adv.* —**ee′ri·ness** *n.*

ef- (ef, if, əf) *same as* EX-¹: used before *f*

cf·face (i fās′, e-) *vt.* **-faced′, -fac′ing** [Fr. *effacer* < *e-* (L. *ex*, out) + *face:* see FACE] **1.** to rub out, as from a surface; erase; wipe out; obliterate [time *effaced* the memory] **2.** to make (oneself) inconspicuous; withdraw (oneself) from notice —*SYN.* see ERASE —**ef·face′a·ble** *adj.* —**ef·face′ment** *n.* —**ef·fac′er** *n.*

ef·fect (ə fekt′, i-) *n.* [ME. < OFr. (& L.) < L. *effectus*, orig., pp. of *efficere*, to bring to pass, accomplish < *ex-*, out + *facere*, DO¹] **1.** anything brought about by a cause or agent; result **2.** the power or ability to bring about results; efficacy [a law of little *effect*] **3.** influence or action on something [the drug had a cathartic *effect*] **4.** general meaning; purport [he spoke to this *effect*] **5.** *a)* the impression produced on the mind of the observer or hearer, as by artistic design or manner of speaking, acting, etc. [to do something just for *effect*] *b)* something, as a design, aspect of nature, etc., that produces a particular impression [striking cloud *effects*] **6.** the condition or fact of being operative or in force [the law goes into *effect* today] **7.** [*pl.*] belongings; property [household *effects*] —*vt.* to bring about; produce as a result; cause; accomplish [to *effect* a compromise] —**give effect to** to put into practice; make operative —**in effect 1.** in result; actually; in fact **2.** in essence; virtually **3.** in operation; in force —**take effect** to begin to produce results; become operative —**to the effect** with the purport or meaning —**ef·fect′er** *n.*

SYN.—**effect** is applied to that which is directly produced by an action, process, or agent and is the exact correlative of *cause;* **consequence** suggests that which follows something else on which it is dependent in some way, but does not connote as direct a connection with *cause;* **result** stresses that which is finally brought about by the effects or consequences of an action, process, etc.; **issue**, in this connection, suggests a result in which there is emergence from difficulties or conflict; **outcome** refers to the result of something that was in doubt See also PERFORM —*ANT.* cause

ef·fec·tive (ə fek′tiv, i-) *adj.* [ME. & OFr. *effectif* < L. *effectivus*] 1. having an effect; producing a result 2. producing a definite or desired result; efficient 3. in effect; operative; active 4. actual, not merely potential or theoretical 5. making a striking impression; impressive 6. equipped and ready for combat —*n.* a soldier, unit, etc. equipped and ready for combat: *usually used in pl.* —**ef·fec′tive·ly** *adv.* —**ef·fec′tive·ness** *n.*
SYN.—**effective** is applied to that which produces a definite effect or result [an *effective* speaker]; **efficacious** refers to that which is capable of producing the desired effect or result [an *efficacious* remedy]; **effectual** specifically implies the production of the desired effect or result in a decisive manner [an *effectual* reply to his charge]; **efficient** implies skill and economy of energy in producing the desired result and is often applied to persons [an *efficient* worker] —*ANT.* futile

ef·fec·tor (-tər) *n.* [L., a producer < *effectus:* see EFFECT] 1. a muscle, gland, etc. capable of responding to a stimulus, esp. to a nerve impulse 2. that part of a nerve which transmits an impulse to an organ of response

ef·fec·tu·al (ə fek′choo wəl, i-) *adj.* [ME. < OFr. *effectuel* < ML. *effectualis*] 1. producing, or able to produce, the desired effect 2. having legal force; valid —*SYN.* see EFFECTIVE —**ef·fec′tu·al′i·ty** (-wal′ə tē) *n.*

ef·fec·tu·al·ly (-wə lē) *adv.* with the desired effect; completely; effectively

ef·fec·tu·ate (-wāt′) *vt.* -**at′ed**, -**at′ing** [< Fr. *effectuer* (< L. *effectus:* see EFFECT), with ending after verbs in -*ate* (e.g., ACTUATE)] to bring about; cause to happen; effect —**ef·fec′tu·a′tion** *n.*

ef·fem·i·na·cy (i fem′ə nə sē) *n.* the quality or state of being effeminate

ef·fem·i·nate (-ə nit) *adj.* [ME. *effeminat* < L. *effeminatus,* pp. of *effeminare,* to make womanish < *ex-,* out + *femina,* a woman: see FEMALE] 1. having the qualities generally attributed to women, as weakness, timidity, delicacy, etc.; unmanly; not virile 2. characterized by such qualities; weak; soft, decadent, etc. [*effeminate* art] —*SYN.* see FEMALE —**ef·fem′i·nate·ly** *adv.*

ef·fen·di (i fen′dē) *n., pl.* -**dis** [Turk. *efendi* < ModGr. *aphentēs* < Gr. *authentēs,* a master: see AUTHENTIC] Sir; Master: a Turkish title of respect, abolished as an official title in 1934

ef·fer·ent (ef′ər ənt) *adj.* [< L. *efferens,* prp. of *efferre,* to carry out < *ex-,* out + *ferre,* BEAR[1]] *Physiol.* carrying away from a central part; specif., designating nerves that carry impulses away from a nerve center: opposed to AFFERENT —*n.* an efferent nerve, duct, etc.

ef·fer·vesce (ef′ər ves′) *vi.* -**vesced′**, -**vesc′ing** [L. *effervescere,* to boil up, foam up < *ex-,* out + *fervescere,* to begin to boil < *fervere,* to boil: see FERVENT] 1. to give off gas bubbles, as carbonated beverages; bubble; foam 2. to rise and come out in bubbles, as gas in a liquid 3. to be lively and high-spirited

ef·fer·ves·cent (-ves′'nt) *adj.* [L. *effervescens,* prp.: see EFFERVESCE] 1. giving off gas bubbles; bubbling up; foaming 2. lively and high-spirited; vivacious —**ef′fer·ves′cence** *n.* —**ef′fer·ves′cent·ly** *adv.*

ef·fete (e fēt′, i-) *adj.* [L. *effetus,* that has brought forth offspring, exhausted < *ex-,* out + *fetus,* productive: for IE. base, see FEMALE] 1. no longer capable of producing; spent and sterile 2. lacking vigor, force of character, moral stamina, etc.; decadent, soft, overrefined, etc. —**ef·fete′ly** *adv.* —**ef·fete′ness** *n.*

ef·fi·ca·cious (ef′ə kā′shəs) *adj.* [L. *efficax* (gen. *efficacis*) < *efficere,* to bring to pass, accomplish (see EFFECT) + -OUS] producing or capable of producing the desired effect; having the intended result; effective [an *efficacious* drug] —*SYN.* see EFFECTIVE —**ef′fi·ca′cious·ly** *adv.* —**ef′fi·ca′cious·ness** *n.*

ef·fi·ca·cy (ef′i kə sē) *n., pl.* -**cies** [ME. & OFr. *efficace* < L. *efficacia* < *efficax:* see prec.] power to produce effects or intended results; effectiveness

ef·fi·cien·cy (ə fish′ən sē, i-) *n., pl.* -**cies** [L. *efficientia:* see EFFICIENT] 1. ability to produce a desired effect, product, etc. with a minimum of effort, expense, or waste; quality or fact of being efficient 2. the ratio of effective work to the energy expended in producing it, as of a machine; output divided by input ☆3. *same as* EFFICIENCY APARTMENT

☆**efficiency apartment** a small apartment consisting basically, apart from bathroom, of a single room with a kitchenette

☆**efficiency engineer** (or **expert**) a person whose work is to increase the productive efficiency of a business or industry by finding better methods of performing various operations, reducing waste and costs, etc.

ef·fi·cient (-ənt) *adj.* [ME. & OFr. < L. *efficiens,* prp. of *efficere:* see EFFECT] 1. directly producing an effect or result; causative; effective [the *efficient* cause] 2. producing a desired effect, product, etc. with a minimum of effort, expense, or waste; working well —*SYN.* see EFFECTIVE —**ef·fi′cient·ly** *adv.*

ef·fi·gy (ef′ə jē) *n., pl.* -**gies** [Fr. *effigie* < L. *effigies,* a copy, image < *effingere* < *ex-,* out + *fingere,* to form: see FIGURE] a portrait, statue, or the like, esp. of a person; likeness; often, a crude representation of a despised person —**burn** (or **hang**) **in effigy** to burn (or hang) an image of a person, as in a demonstration of public protest against him

ef·flo·resce (ef′lô res′, -lə-) *vi.* -**resced′**, -**resc′ing** [L. *efflorescere,* to blossom, flourish < *ex-,* out + *florescere,* to begin to blossom < *florere,* to blossom < *flos* (gen. *floris*), a flower] 1. to blossom out; flower; bloom 2. *Chem. a)* to change from a crystalline to a powdery state through loss of the water of crystallization when exposed to air *b)* to develop a powdery crust as a result of evaporation or chemical change

ef·flo·res·cence (-res′'ns) *n.* [Fr. < L. *efflorescens,* prp. of *efflorescere:* see prec.] 1. a flowering; blooming 2. the time of flowering 3. the peak or fulfillment, as of a career 4. *Chem. a)* the changing of certain crystalline compounds to a whitish powder or powdery crust through loss of their water of crystallization *b)* the powder or crust thus formed 5. *Med.* an eruption on the skin; rash or other skin lesion —**ef′flo·res′cent** *adj.*

ef·flu·ence (ef′loo wəns) *n.* [ME. < ML. *effluentia* < L. *effluens,* prp. of *effluere,* to flow out < *ex-,* out + *fluere,* to flow: see FLUENT] 1. a flowing out or forth 2. a thing that flows out or forth; emanation

ef·flu·ent (-wənt) *adj.* [ME. < L. *effluens:* see prec.] flowing out or forth —*n.* a thing that flows out or forth; specif., *a)* a stream flowing out of a body of water *b)* the outflow of a sewer, septic tank, etc.

ef·flu·vi·um (e floo′vē əm, i-) *n., pl.* -**vi·a** (-ə), -**vi·ums** [L., a flowing out, outlet: see EFFLUENCE] 1. a real or supposed outflow in the form of a vapor or stream of invisible particles; aura 2. a disagreeable or noxious vapor or odor —**ef·flu′vi·al** *adj.*

ef·flux (ef′luks) *n.* [< L. *effluxus,* pp. of *effluere:* see EFFLUENCE] 1. a flowing out, or emanating 2. a thing that flows out; outflow; emanation 3. an ending; expiration Also **ef·flux·ion** (e fluk′shən)

ef·fort (et′ərt) *n.* [Fr. < OFr. *esforz < esforcier,* to make an effort < VL. **exfortiare < ex-,* intens. + **fortiare:* see FORCE] 1. the using of energy to get something done; exertion of strength or mental power 2. a try, esp. a hard try; attempt; endeavor 3. a product or result of working or trying; achievement
SYN.—**effort** implies a conscious attempt to achieve a particular end [make some *effort* to be friendly]; **exertion** implies an energetic, even violent, use of power, strength, etc., often without reference to any particular end [she feels faint after any *exertion*]; **endeavor** suggests an earnest, sustained attempt to accomplish a particular, usually meritorious, end [a life spent in the *endeavor* to do good]; **pains** suggests a laborious, diligent attempt [to take *pains* with one's work] —*ANT.* ease

ef·fort·less (-lis) *adj.* making, requiring, or showing virtually no effort —*SYN.* see EASY —**ef′fort·less·ly** *adv.* —**ef′fort·less·ness** *n.*

ef·fron·ter·y (e frun′tər ē, i-) *n., pl.* -**ter·ies** [Fr. *effronterie* < *effronté,* shameless, bold < L. *effrons,* barefaced, shameless < *ex-,* from + *frons,* forehead: see FRONT] unashamed boldness; impudence; audacity; presumption —*SYN.* see TEMERITY

ef·fulge (e fulj′, i-) *vt., vi.* -**fulged′**, -**fulg′ing** [L. *effulgere:* see ff.] [Now Rare] to shine or flash out

ef·ful·gence (-ful′jəns) *n.* [< L. *effulgens,* prp. of *effulgere* < *ex-,* forth + *fulgere,* to shine: see FLAGRANT] great brightness; radiance; brilliance —**ef·ful′gent** *adj.*

ef·fuse (e fyooz′, i-; *for adj.* -fyoos′) *vt., vi.* -**fused′**, -**fus′ing** [< L. *effusus,* pp. of *effundere,* to pour forth < *ex-,* out + *fundere,* to pour: see FOUND[3]] 1. to pour out or forth 2. to spread out; diffuse; radiate —*adj.* 1. [Obs.] poured or spread out freely 2. *Bot.* spread out loosely and flat, without form

ef·fu·sion (e fyoo′zhən, i-) *n.* [ME. & OFr. < L. *effusio:* see prec.] 1. a pouring forth 2. unrestrained or emotional expression in speaking or writing 3. *a)* an escape of fluid that is bloody, serous, etc. into body cavities or tissues *b)* the fluid thus escaping 4. the passage of a gas under pressure through an orifice whose size is smaller than the mean free path of the gas molecules, as in measuring low vapor pressures

ef·fu·sive (-siv) *adj.* 1. formerly, pouring out or forth; overflowing 2. expressing excessive emotion in an unrestrained manner; too demonstrative 3. designating or of igneous rocks formed from lava that has flowed out on the earth's surface —**ef·fu′sive·ly** *adv.* —**ef·fu′sive·ness** *n.*

Ef·ik (ef′ik) *n., pl.* **Ef′iks**, **Ef′ik** 1. an agricultural people of SE Nigeria 2. a member of the Efik people 3. the language of the Efiks, belonging to the Niger-Congo subfamily of the Congo-Kordofanian family of languages

eft[1] (eft) *n.* [ME. *euete* < OE. *efeta*, older, dial., & literary form of NEWT] *same as* NEWT
eft[2] (eft) *adv.* [ME. < OE., orig. compar. (Gmc. *aftis*) of AFT] [Obs.] **1.** again **2.** afterwards
eft·soon (eft sōōn′) *adv.* [ME. *eftsone* < OE. *eftsona* < prec. + *sona* (see SOON)] **1.** [Archaic] *a)* soon afterward *b)* forthwith **2.** [Obs.] at frequent intervals; often **3.** [Obs.] again Also **eft·soons′** (-sōōnz′)
Eg. 1. Egypt **2.** Egyptian **3.** Egyptology
e.g. [L. *exempli gratia*] for the sake of example; for example
e·gad (i gad′, ē-) *interj.* [prob. < *oh God*] a softened or euphemistic oath
e·gal·i·tar·i·an (i gal′ə ter′ē ən, ē-) *adj.* [< Fr. *égalitaire* < *égalité* < OFr. *equalité* (see EQUALITY) + -IAN] of, advocating, or characterized by the belief that all men should have equal political, social, and economic rights —*n.* a person who advocates or supports this belief —**e·gal′i·tar′i·an·ism** *n.*
‡**é·ga·li·té** (ā gà lē tā′) *n.* [Fr.] equality
Eg·bert (eg′bərt) [OE. *Ecgbeorht* < *ecg* (see EDGE) + *beorht* (see BRIGHT): hence, bright sword] **1.** a masculine name **2.** 775?–839 A.D.; king of the West Saxons (802–839) & first king of all England (829–839)
E·ge·ri·a (i jir′ē ə, ē jir′-) [L. < Gr. *Ēgeria*] *Rom. Myth.* a nymph who advised Numa, second king of Rome —*n.* any woman who acts as an adviser
e·gest (ē jest′) *vt.* [< L. *egestus*, pp. of *egerere*, to bear out, discharge < *e-*, out + *gerere*, to bear] to pass off (perspiration, excrement, etc.); excrete —**e·ges′tion** *n.* —**e·ges′tive** *adj.*
e·ges·ta (ē jes′tə) *n.pl.* [ModL. < L., neut. pl. of *egestus*: see prec.] egested matter; feces, perspiration, etc.
egg[1] (eg) *n.* [ME. < ON., replacing cognate native *ey* < OE. *æg*, akin to G. *ei* (pl. *eier*), prob. < IE. base *owjom-*, *ojom-*, of a bird (whence L. *ovum*, Gr. *ōion*) < ? *awei-*, bird, whence L. *avis*] **1.** the oval or round body laid by a female bird, fish, reptile, insect, etc., containing the germ of a new individual along with food for its development, and having an enclosing shell or membrane **2.** a reproductive cell produced by the female; ovum: also called **egg cell 3.** a hen's egg, raw or cooked in any way **4.** a thing resembling a hen's egg **5.** [Slang] a person /he's a good *egg*/ —*vt.* **1.** to mix or cover with the yolk or white of eggs, as in cooking ☆**2.** [Colloq.] to throw eggs at —☆**lay an egg** [Slang] to fail completely: said of a joke, theatrical performance, etc. —**put** (or **have**) **all one's eggs in one basket** to risk all that one has on a single venture, method, etc.

HEN'S EGG
(A, yolk; B, air space; C, white; D, outer shell membrane; E, inner shell membrane; F, chalaza-bearing membrane; G, chalaza; H, shell)

egg[2] (eg) *vt.* [ME. *eggen* < ON. *eggja*, lit., to give edge to < *egg*, EDGE] to urge or incite (with *on*)
egg and dart a decorative molding used in architecture and cabinetwork, consisting of an egg-shaped form alternating with a form shaped like an arrow, anchor, or tongue: also **egg and anchor, egg and tongue**
☆**egg·beat·er** (-bēt′ər) *n.* **1.** a kitchen utensil, esp. one with rotary blades, for beating eggs, cream, etc. **2.** [Slang] a helicopter
egg coal a size of anthracite coal about 2 to 4 inches in diameter
egg·er (-ər) *n.* [prob. < EGG[1] + -ER: from its egg-shaped cocoon] any of a family (Lasiocampidae) of moths whose larvae feed on the leaves of trees
☆**egg foo yong** (or **young**) (eg′ fōō yuŋ′) a Chinese-American dish consisting of eggs beaten and cooked with bean sprouts, onions, minced pork or shrimp, etc.
☆**egg·head** (-hed′) *n.* [Slang] an intellectual: usually a term of derision as used by anti-intellectuals
Eg·gles·ton (eg′'l stən) **Edward** 1837–1902; U.S. novelist & historian
☆**egg·nog** (-näg′, -nôg′) *n.* [EGG[1] + NOG[2]] a thick drink made of beaten eggs, milk, sugar, and nutmeg, often containing whiskey, rum, wine, etc.
egg·plant (-plant′, -plänt′) *n.* **1.** a perennial plant (*Solanum melongena*) of the nightshade family, with a large, ovoid, usually purple-skinned fruit, which is eaten as a vegetable **2.** the fruit
☆**egg roll** thin, flat egg dough wrapped around minced vegetables, meat, shrimp, etc. in a small roll and fried in deep fat: a Chinese-American dish
egg·shell (-shel′) *n.* the hard, brittle covering of a bird's egg —*adj.* **1.** fragile and thin, like an eggshell **2.** yellowish-white
e·gis (ē′jis) *n. same as* AEGIS
eg·lan·tine (eg′lən tīn′, -tēn′) *n.* [Fr. *églantine* < OFr. *aiglent* < LL. **aculentus* < L. *aculeus*, a sting, prickle, dim. of *acus*, a point, sting: see ACUITY] a European rose (*Rosa eglanteria*) with hooked spines, sweet-scented leaves, and usually pink flowers; sweetbrier
Eg·mont (eg′mänt; *Du.* ekh′mônt), **Count of** (born *Lamoral Egmont*) 1522–68; Fl. statesman & general
e·go (ē′gō; *chiefly Brit.*, eg′ō) *n.*, *pl.* **e′gos** [L.: see I[2]] **1.** the

self; the individual as aware of himself **2.** egotism; conceit **3.** *Philos.* the self, variously conceived as a spiritual substance on which experience is superimposed, the series of acts and mental states introspectively recognized, etc. **4.** *Psychoanalysis* that part of the psyche which experiences the external world through the senses, organizes the thought processes rationally, and governs action: it mediates between the instinctual impulses of the id, the demands of the environment, and the standards of the superego
e·go·cen·tric (ē′gō sen′trik; *chiefly Brit.*, eg′ō-) *adj.* **1.** viewing everything in relation to oneself; self-centered **2.** *Philos.* existing only as conceived in the individual mind: said of the world —*n.* an egocentric person —**e′go·cen′tri·cal·ly** *adv.* —**e′go·cen·tric′i·ty** (-tris′ə tē) *n.* —**e′go·cen′trism** (-triz′m) *n.*
ego ideal *Psychoanalysis* the ego's conception of a better or more successful future self, usually but not always integrated with the superego
e·go·ism (ē′gō iz′m; *chiefly Brit.*, eg′ō-) *n.* [Fr. *égoïsme* < L. *ego:* see I[2]] **1.** the tendency to be self-centered, or to consider only oneself and one's own interests; selfishness **2.** egotism; conceit **3.** the doctrine that self-interest is the proper goal of all human actions: opposed to ALTRUISM
e·go·ist (-ist) *n.* [Fr. *égoïste* < L. *ego:* see I[2]] **1.** a person who is self-centered or selfish **2.** a conceited person; egotist **3.** a person who accepts the doctrine of egoism
e·go·is·tic (ē′gō is′tik; *chiefly Brit.*, eg′ō-) *adj.* **1.** self-centered or selfish **2.** egotistic; conceited **3.** of an egoist or egoism Also **e′go·is′ti·cal** —**e′go·is′ti·cal·ly** *adv.*
e·go·ma·ni·a (-mā′nē ə, -mān′yə) *n.* [EGO + -MANIA] abnormally excessive egotism —**e′go·ma′ni·ac′** (-ak′) *n.* —**e′go·ma·ni′a·cal** (-mə nī′ə k'l) *adj.*
ego psychology the study of the adaptive and mediating functions of the ego and their role in personality development and emotional disorder
e·go·tism (ē′gə tiz′m; *chiefly Brit.*, eg′ə-) *n.* [L. *ego*, I[2] + -*tism* (for -ISM), as in NEPOTISM] **1.** constant, excessive reference to oneself in speaking or writing **2.** self-conceit **3.** selfishness *Egoism* and *egotism* are sometimes used interchangeably, but *egotism* is generally considered the more opprobrious term
e·go·tist (-tist) *n.* a person characterized by egotism —**e′go·tis′tic, e′go·tis′ti·cal** *adj.* —**e′go·tis′ti·cal·ly** *adv.*
e·gre·gious (i grē′jəs, -jē əs) *adj.* [L. *egregius*, separated from the herd, hence select < *e-*, out + *grex* (gen. *gregis*), a herd: see GREGARIOUS] **1.** outstanding for undesirable qualities; remarkably bad; flagrant /an *egregious* error/ **2.** [Archaic] outstanding; remarkable —**e·gre′gious·ly** *adv.* —**e·gre′gious·ness** *n.*
e·gress (ē′gres) *n.* [L. *egressus* < pp. of *egredi*, to go out < *e-*, out + *gradi*, to step, go: see GRADE] **1.** the act of going out or forth; emergence: also **e·gres·sion** (i gresh′ən) **2.** the right to go out **3.** a way out; exit
e·gret (ē′grit, eg′rit) *n.* [ME. < OFr. *aigrette*, kind of heron, tuft of feathers < Pr. *aigreta* < *aigron* < Frank. **haigiro:* see HERON] **1.** *pl.* **-grets, -gret** [see PLURAL, II, D] any of several heronlike wading birds, usually with long, white plumes, esp. the **American egret** (*Casmerodius albus*) of temperate and tropical America **2.** *same as* AIGRETTE (sense 1)
E·gypt (ē′jipt) country in NE Africa, on the Mediterranean and Red seas: ancient Egyptian dynasties may date back as far as 4500 B.C.: c. 386,000 sq. mi.; pop. 32,501,000; cap. Cairo: see also the UNITED ARAB REPUBLIC

EGYPT

Egypt. Egyptian
E·gyp·tian (i jip′shən, ē-) *adj.* **1.** of Egypt, its people, or their culture **2.** of the language of the ancient Egyptians **3.** [Obs.] gypsy —*n.* **1.** a native or inhabitant of Egypt **2.** the language of the ancient Egyptians, constituting a subfamily of the Afro-Asiatic family of languages **3.** [Obs.] a gypsy
E·gyp·tol·o·gy (ē′jip täl′ə jē) *n.* the science or study of ancient Egyptian architecture, inscriptions, language, customs, etc. —**E′gyp·tol′o·gist** *n.*
eh (ā, e, en) *interj.* a sound expressing: **1.** surprise **2.** doubt or inquiry: equivalent to *a)* "What did you say?" *b)* "Don't you agree?"
EHF extremely high frequency
Ehr·en·burg (er′ən berg; *Russ.* ā′rən boorkh′), **Il·ya** (ēl′yä) (**Grigorievich**) 1891–1967; Soviet writer
Ehr·lich (er′lik; *G.* er′liH), **Paul** 1854–1915; Ger. bacteriologist: pioneer in immunology & chemotherapy
ei·der (ī′dər) *n.* [ult. < ON. *æthar*, gen. of *æthr*, eider duck] **1.** *pl.* **-ders, -der:** see PLURAL, II, D] any of several large sea ducks (genus *Somateria*) that live in northern regions of

Europe, Asia, and N. America: often **eider duck** **2.** *same as* EIDERDOWN

ei·der·down (-doun′) *n.* [< ON. *æthar-dūn:* see prec. & DOWN²] **1.** the soft, fine breast feathers, or down, of the eider duck, used as a stuffing for quilts, pillows, etc. **2.** a bed quilt stuffed with such feathers

ei·det·ic (ī det′ik) *adj.* [Gr. *eidētikos,* constituting a figure < *eidos,* what is seen, shape < IE. *weidos-* < *wedi-,* to see, whence L. *videre:* see VISION] designating or of mental images that are unusually vivid and almost photographically exact —**ei·det′i·cal·ly** *adv.*

ei·do·lon (ī dō′lən) *n., pl.* **-lons, -la** (-lə) [Gr. *eidōlon,* an image: see IDOL] **1.** an image without real existence; phantom; apparition ☆**2.** an ideal person or thing — **ei·do′lic** *adj.*

Eif·fel Tower (ī′f'l) [after A. G. *Eiffel* (1832–1923), Fr. engineer who designed it] tower of iron framework in Paris, built for the International Exposition of 1889: 984 ft. high

eight (āt) *adj.* [ME. *eighte* < OE. *eahta,* akin to G. *acht* < IE. base *oktō(u)-,* whence L. *octo,* OIr. *ocht*] totaling one more than seven —*n.* **1.** the cardinal number between seven and nine; 8; VIII **2.** any group of eight people or things, as a crew of eight oarsmen **3.** *a)* something numbered eight or having eight units, as a playing card, throw of dice, etc. *b)* an engine or automobile having eight cylinders **4.** anything shaped like an eight, as a figure in skating

☆**eight ball** a black ball with the number eight on it, used in playing pool: in one form of the game, if a player pockets the eight ball before all the other balls are pocketed, he immediately loses the game —**behind the eight ball** [Slang] in a very unfavorable position: from having the eight ball lie so that the shooter runs the risk of pocketing it

eight·een (ā′tēn′) *adj.* [ME. *eightetene* < OE. *eahtatiene:* see EIGHT & -TEEN] eight more than ten —*n.* the cardinal number between seventeen and nineteen; 18; XVIII

eight·een·mo (-mō′) *n., pl.* **-mos** [prec. + *-mo,* as in OCTODECIMO] **1.** the page size of a book made up of printer's sheets folded into eighteen leaves, each leaf being approximately 4 by 6 1/2 in. **2.** a book consisting of pages of this size Usually written *18mo* or *18°* —*adj.* consisting of pages of this size

eight·eenth (ā′tēnth′) *adj.* [ME. *eihtetenthe:* see EIGHTEEN & -TH²] **1.** preceded by seventeen others in a series; 18th **2.** designating any of the eighteen equal parts of something —*n.* **1.** the one following the seventeenth **2.** any of the eighteen equal parts of something; 1/18

eight·fold (āt′fōld′) *adj.* [see -FOLD] **1.** having eight parts **2.** having eight times as much or as many —*adv.* eight times as much or as many

eighth (ātth, āth) *adj.* [ME. *eightethe* < OE. *eahtothe* < *eahta:* see EIGHT & -TH] **1.** preceded by seven others in a series; 8th **2.** designating any of the eight equal parts of something —*n.* **1.** the one following the seventh **2.** any of the eight equal parts of something; 1/8 **3.** *Music* the interval of an octave —**eighth′ly** *adv.*

eighth note *Music* a note having one eighth the duration of a whole note: see NOTE, illus.

eight·i·eth (āt′ē ith) *adj.* [ME. *eightelithe:* see EIGHTY & -TH²] **1.** preceded by seventy-nine others in a series; 80th **2.** designating any of the eighty equal parts of something —*n.* **1.** the one following the seventy-ninth **2.** any of the eighty equal parts of something; 1/80

eight·y (āt′ē) *adj.* [ME. *eighteti* < OE. *(hund)eahtatig:* see EIGHT & -TY²] eight times ten —*n., pl.* **eight′ies** the cardinal number between seventy-nine and eighty-one; 80; LXXX —**the eighties** the numbers or years, as of a century, from eighty through eighty-nine

ei·kon (ī′kän) *n. same as* ICON

Ei·leen (ī lēn′, ā-) [Ir. *Eibhlin*] a feminine name

-ein, -eine (ēn, ē in) [altered < *-IN*¹ & *-INE*⁴] *Chem.* a suffix used: **1.** to differentiate a compound that could be confused with another spelled similarly but with the suffix *-in* or *-ine* **2.** to indicate a compound containing an internal anhydride

EInd. East Indian

Eind·ho·ven (int′hō′vən) city in North Brabant province, S Netherlands: pop. 178,000

Ein·stein (īn′stīn), **Albert** 1879–1955; U.S. physicist, born in Germany: formulated theory of relativity —**Ein·stein′i·an** (-stī′nē ən) *adj.*

☆**ein·stein·i·um** (īn stī′nē əm) *n.* [after prec.] a radioactive element discovered in the debris of the first thermonuclear explosion, but now produced by irradiating plutonium with neutrons: symbol, Es; at. wt., 252(?); at. no., 99

Eir·e (er′ə) *Gaelic name of* IRELAND (the country); also, its former official name (1937–49)

Ei·sen·how·er (ī′z'n hou′ər), **Dwight David** 1890–1969; U.S. general & 34th president of the U.S. (1953–61); commander of Allied forces in Europe (1943–45; 1951–52)

Ei·sen·stein (ī′z'n stīn′; *Russ.* -shtīn′), **Ser·gei Mik·hai·lo·vich** (syer gyā′ mē khī′lō vich′) 1898–1948; Russ. motion-picture director & producer

eis·tedd·fod (ī steth′vōd, -väd′) *n., pl.* **-fods**; Welsh **eis·tedd·fod·au** (ī′steth vō′dī) [W., a sitting, session <

eistedd, to sit (< *eitsedd* < IE. *aty-en-sed-,* hence akin to L. *sedere,* SIT¹) + *bod,* being < IE. *bhut-* < base *bheu-:* see BE] a yearly meeting in Wales of poets, musicians, etc., at which prizes are given for compositions and performances: 19th-cent. revival of an old Welsh custom

ei·ther (ē′thər, ī′-) *adj.* [ME. < OE. *æghwæther* < *a* (æ), always (see AY) + *gehwæther,* each of two (cf. WHETHER): akin to, and of same formation as, OHG. *eogihwedar*] **1.** one or the other (of two) /use *either* hand/ **2.** each (of two); the one and the other /he had a tool in *either* hand/ —*pron.* one or the other (of two) —*conj.* the first element of the pair of disjunctive correlatives *either . . . or,* implying a choice of alternatives /*either* go or stay/ —*adv.* **1.** any more than the other; also (following negative expressions) /if you don't go, I won't *either*/ **2.** [Colloq.] an intensifier in a negative statement /"It's mine." "It isn't *either!*"; he has no family, or friends *either*/

ei·ther-or *adj.* designating a proposition, situation, etc. limited to only two alternatives

e·jac·u·late (i jak′yə lāt′) *vt., vi.* **-lat′ed, -lat′ing** [< L. *ejaculatus,* pp. of *ejaculari,* to throw out < *e-,* out + *jaculari,* to throw < *jaculum,* a dart, missile < *jacere,* to throw] **1.** to eject or discharge (esp. semen) **2.** to utter suddenly and vehemently; exclaim —**e·jac′u·la′tive** (-lāt′iv, -lə tiv) *adj.* —**e·jac′u·la′tor** *n.*

e·jac·u·la·tion (i jak′yə lā′shən) *n.* [see EJACULATE] **1.** a sudden ejection of fluid, esp. of semen, from the body **2.** a sudden vehement utterance; exclamation **3.** *R.C.Ch.* any very brief private prayer

e·jac·u·la·to·ry (i jak′yə lə tôr′ē) *adj.* **1.** ejaculating; of or for ejaculation /an *ejaculatory* duct/ **2.** of the nature of an ejaculation; exclamatory /*ejaculatory* words/

e·ject (i jekt′, ē-) *vt.* [< L. *ejectus,* pp. of *ejicere,* to throw out < *e-,* out + *jacere,* to throw: see JET¹] **1.** to throw out; cast out; expel; emit; discharge /the chimney *ejects* smoke/ **2.** to drive out; evict /to *eject* a heckler/ —**e·jec′ta·ble** *adj.* —**e·jec′tion** *n.* —**e·jec′tive** *adj.* —**e·jec′tor** *n.* **SYN.—eject,** the term of broadest application here, implies generally a throwing or casting out from within /to *eject* saliva from the mouth/; **expel** suggests a driving out, as by force, specif. a forcing out of a country, organization, etc., often in disgrace /*expelled* from school/; **evict** refers to the forcing out, as of a tenant, by legal procedure; **dismiss,** in this connection, refers to the removal of an employee, etc. but does not in itself suggest the reason for the separation /*dismissed* for incompetence/; **oust** implies the getting rid of something undesirable, as by force or the action of law /to *oust* corrupt officials/

e·jec·ta (i jek′tə) *n.pl.* [with sing. or pl. v.] [ModL. < neut. pl. of *ejectus*] ejected matter

ejection seat a seat designed to be ejected with its occupant from an aircraft in an emergency and parachuted to the ground

e·ject·ment (i jekt′mənt) *n.* **1.** an ejecting or ousting; eviction **2.** *Law* an action to secure or recover possession of real property by the true owner

‡**e·ji·do** (e hē′dō) *n., pl.* **-dos** [Sp.] in Mexico, the communal farmland of a village, usually assigned in small parcels to the villagers to be farmed under a federally supported system of communal land tenure

eke¹ (ēk) *vt.* **eked, ek′ing** [ME. *eken,* to increase < OE. *eacan & eacian* < IE. base *aweg-:* see AUGMENT, WAX²] [Archaic or Dial.] to make larger or longer; increase —**eke out 1.** to add to so as to make sufficient; supplement /to *eke out* an income with a second job/ **2.** to manage to make (a living) with difficulty **3.** to use (a supply) frugally

eke² (ēk) *adv., conj.* [ME. < OE. *eac,* akin to G. *auch* < IE. base *au-,* again, on the other hand, whence L. *aut,* Gr. *au,* on the other hand] [Archaic] also

EKG electrocardiogram

☆**e·kis·tics** (i kis′tiks) *n.pl.* [with sing. v.] [< Gr. *oikos,* house + -ICS] the science of city and area planning, dealing with the integration of the basic needs of both the individual and the entire community, as transportation, communication, education, entertainment, etc. —**e·kis′ti·cal** *adj.*

el (el) *n.* **1.** *same as* ELL¹ (sense 1) ☆**2.** [< EL(EVATED)] [Colloq.] an elevated railway

e·lab·o·rate (i lab′ər it; *for v.* -ə rāt′) *adj.* [L. *elaboratus,* pp. of *elaborare,* to work out, labor greatly < *e-,* out + *laborare* < *labor,* LABOR] **1.** worked out carefully; developed in great detail **2.** highly wrought or ornamented; complicated **3.** painstaking —*vt.* **-rat′ed, -rat′ing 1.** to produce by effort; develop by labor **2.** to work out carefully; develop in great detail **3.** to change (food or substances in the body) into compounds that can be assimilated, excreted, etc. —*vi.* to state something in detail or add more details (usually with *on* or *upon*) —**e·lab′o·rate′ly** *adv.* —**e·lab′o·rate′ness** *n.* —**e·lab′o·ra′tion** *n.* —**e·lab′o·ra′tive** *adj.* —**e·lab′o·ra′tor** *n.*

el·ae·op·tene (el′ē äp′tēn) *n. same as* ELEOPTENE

El·a·gab·a·lus (el′ə gab′ə ləs) (born *Varius Avitus Bassianus*) 205?–222 A.D.; Roman emperor (218–222)

E·laine (i lān′, ē-) [OFr.] a feminine name: see HELEN **2.** *Arthurian Legend a)* a woman of Astolat, who loved Sir Lancelot *b)* the mother of Sir Galahad

E·lam (ē′ləm) ancient kingdom of SW Asia, at the head of the Persian Gulf

E·lam·ite (-īt′) *n.* **1.** a native or inhabitant of Elam **2.** the dead language of the Elamites: it had no known relationship with any other language —*adj.* of Elam, the Elamites, or their language

E·lam·it·ic (ē′lə mit′ik) *n.* same as ELAMITE (*n.* 2) —*adj.* same as ELAMITE

é·lan (ā län′; *Fr.* -län′) *n.* [Fr., a start, outburst, impetuosity < *élancer*, to dart, throw < *é-*, out + *lancer*, to throw a lance, hence throw < LL.(Ec.) *lanceare* < *lancea*, LANCE] spirited self-assurance; verve; dash

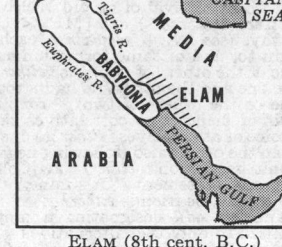

ELAM (8th cent. B.C.)

e·land (ē′lənd) *n.*, *pl.* **e′land, e′lands**: see PLURAL, II, D, 2 [Afrik. < Du., elk < obs. G. *elen*(d) < Lith. *élnis*: see ELK] either of two large, oxlike African antelopes (genus *Taurotragus*) with spirally twisted horns

‡é·lan vi·tal (ā län vē tál′) [Fr., lit., vital force] in Bergsonian philosophy, the original vital impulse which is the substance of consciousness and nature

el·a·pine (el′ə pīn′) *adj.* [< ModL. *Elapinae*, name of the subfamily < *Elaps*, a genus of venomous snakes (< MGr. *elaps*, serpent, fish, altered < Gr. *ellops*) + *-inae*, -INAE] of or pertaining to a family (Elapidae) of poisonous snakes with small, erect fangs, including the cobras and coral snakes —**el′a·pid** (-pid) *n.*

e·lapse (i laps′) *vi.* **e·lapsed′, e·laps′ing** [< L. *elapsus*, pp. of *elabi*, to glide away < *e-*, out + *labi*, to glide, fall: see LABOR] to slip by; pass: said of time

e·las·mo·branch (i laz′mə braŋk′, -las′-) *adj.* [< ModL. *elasmobranchii* < Gr. *elasmos*, beaten metal (akin to ff.) + L. *branchia*, gills] designating or of a class (Chondrichthyes) of fishes characterized by cartilaginous skeletons, placoid scales, and lack of air bladders —*n.* any fish of this class, as the shark, skate, ray, etc.

e·las·tic (i las′tik) *adj.* [ModL. *elasticus* < LGr. *elastikos* < Gr. *elaunein*, to set in motion, beat out < IE. base *el-*, to drive, move, go, whence (prob.) LANE¹] **1.** having the property of immediately returning to its original size, shape, or position after being stretched, squeezed, flexed, expanded, etc.; flexible; springy **2.** having the ability to recover easily from dejection, fatigue, etc.; buoyant [an *elastic* temperament] **3.** readily changed or changing to suit circumstances; adaptable [*elastic* regulations] —*n.* **1.** a loosely woven fabric made flexible by strands of rubber or a rubberlike synthetic running through it **2.** a band, garter, etc. of this material **3.** a rubber band —**e·las′ti·cal·ly** *adv.*

SYN.—**elastic** implies ability to return without permanent injury to the original size or shape after being stretched, expanded, etc. [an *elastic* garter]; **resilient** implies ability to spring back quickly into shape after being deformed, esp. by compression [a healthy, *resilient* skin]; **flexible** refers to anything that can be bent without breaking, whether or not it returns to its original form [a *flexible* wire]; **supple** is applied to that which is easily bent, twisted, or folded without breaking, cracking, etc. [kidskin is *supple*]—**ANT. rigid, stiff**

e·las·tic·i·ty (i las′tis′ə tē, ē′las-) *n.*, *pl.* **-ties** the quality or condition of being elastic; specif., *a)* springiness; flexibility; resilience *b)* buoyancy of spirit *c)* adaptability

e·las·ti·cize (i las′tə sīz′) *vt.* **-cized′, -ciz′ing** to make (fabric) elastic, as by interweaving with rubber strands

elastic tissue a connective tissue consisting largely of yellow, elastic fibers, occurring especially in the walls of arteries and veins

e·las·tin (i las′tin) *n.* [see ELASTIC & -IN¹] a protein that is the basic constituent of elastic tissue, characterized by its elasticity when moist

☆**e·las·to·mer** (i las′tə mər) *n.* [< ELAST(IC) + (POLY)MER] a rubberlike synthetic polymer, as silicone rubber —**e·las′to·mer′ic** (-mer′ik) *adj.*

e·late (i lāt′, ē-) *vt.* **-lat′ed, -lat′ing** [< L. *elatus*, pp. of *efferre*, to bring out, lift up < *ex-*, out + *ferre*, BEAR¹] to raise the spirits of; make very proud, happy, or joyful —*adj.* [Poet.] filled with elation —**e·lat′ed·ly** *adv.* —**e·lat′ed·ness** *n.*

e·la·ter (el′ə tər) *n.* [ModL. < Gr. *elatēr*, driver < *elaunein*: see ELASTIC] **1.** an elastic filament that scatters the ripe spores, found in certain plants, as in the capsule of liverwort **2.** same as CLICK BEETLE

e·lat·er·id (i lat′ər id) *n.* same as CLICK BEETLE —*adj.* of the family of click beetles

e·lat·er·in (-in) *n.* [ELATER(IUM) + -IN¹] a white, crystalline substance, $C_{20}H_{28}O_5$, the active principle of elaterium, used as a cathartic

e·lat·er·ite (-īt′) *n.* [ELATER, sense 1 + -ITE¹] a dark-brown, rubberlike, elastic mineral hydrocarbon

e·la·te·ri·um (el′ə tir′ē əm) *n.* [L. < Gr. *elatērion*, neut. of *elatērios*, driving < *elaunein*: see ELASTIC] a cathartic

and diuretic obtained from the dried juice of the wild cucumber (*Ecballium elaterium*)

e·la·tion (i lā′shən, ē-) *n.* [L. *elatio:* see ELATE] a feeling of exultant joy or pride; high spirits

E layer a layer of the ionosphere at an altitude of about 60 miles that can reflect radio waves

El·ba (el′bə) It. island in the Tyrrhenian Sea, between Corsica & Italy: site of Napoleon's first exile (1814–15): 86 sq. mi.

El·be (el′bə, elb) river in C Europe, flowing from NW Czechoslovakia through Germany into the North Sea: c. 720 mi.

El·bert (el′bərt) a masculine name: see ALBERT

ELBA

Elbert, Mount [after Gov. S. H. *Elbert* (1873–74)] mountain in C Colo.; highest peak of the Sawatch Range: 14,431 ft.

El·bląg (el′blôṅ) city in N Poland: pop. 82,000: Ger. name **El·bing** (el′biṅ)

el·bow (el′bō) *n.* [ME. *elbowe* < OE. *elboga* < PGmc. *alino-bogus* (whence G. *ellenbogen*): see ELL² & BOW²] **1.** *a)* the joint between the upper and lower arm; esp., the outer part of the angle made by a bent arm *b)* the joint corresponding to this in the forelimb of quadrupeds **2.** anything bent like an elbow, as a pipe used in plumbing —*vt.* **1.** to shove or jostle with or as with elbows **2.** to push (one's way) with the elbows or rudely —*vi.* **1.** to make one's way by shoving or jostling **2.** to form an angle —**at one's elbow** very close to one; easy to reach —**out at (the) elbows** shabby; poverty-stricken —**rub elbows with** to associate or mingle with (famous or prominent people, etc.) —**up to the elbows** deeply engaged (*in* work, etc.)

elbow grease [Colloq.] vigorous physical effort

el·bow·room (-rōōm′, -room′) *n.* room enough to move or work in; ample space or scope

El·brus (el′brōōs, -brōōz), **Mount** mountain of the Caucasus range, in the Georgian S.S.R.: highest peak in Europe, 18,481 ft.: also sp. **El′brus**

El·burz Mountains (el boorz′) mountains in N Iran, along the Caspian Sea: highest peak, Mount DEMAVEND

El Ca·jon (el kə hōn′) [Sp., the box: the city is boxed in by hills] city in S Calif.: suburb of San Diego: pop. 52,000

eld (eld) *n.* [ME. *elde* < OE. *eldo* < base of *ald*, *eald* (see OLD)] [Archaic] **1.** old age **2.** ancient times; antiquity; days of yore

eld·er¹ (el′dər) *adj.* [ME. < OE. (Mercian) *eldra*, *ældra*, compar. < base of *ald*, *eald* (see OLD); akin to OHG. *eltiro* (G. *älter*), Goth. *althiza*] **1.** born or brought forth earlier than another or others; exceeding another in age; senior; older **2.** of longer standing or superior rank, position, validity, etc. **3.** earlier; former; ancient —*n.* **1.** an older person **2.** an aged person **3.** a forefather; ancestor; predecessor **4.** an older person with some authority or dignity in a tribe or community **5.** *a)* an officer in an early Christian church *b)* in some Protestant churches, a minister; also, a member appointed to the ruling body who may also assist at Communion ☆*c)* a member of the Melchizedek priesthood in the Mormon Church

eld·er² (el′dər) *n.* [ME. *ellerne* & (with intrusive *-d-* as in ALDER) *eldore* < OE. *ellern*, *ellen*, akin to MLowG. *ellern*, *eldern* < IE. base *el-*, whence ELM, ALDER, L. *alnus*, elder] **1.** any of a genus (*Sambucus*) of shrubs and small trees of the honeysuckle family, with compound leaves and flat-topped clusters of small white flowers followed by red or purple berries **2.** any of various unrelated plants, as the box elder or the marsh elder

el·der·ber·ry (-ber′ē) *n.*, *pl.* **-ries** **1.** same as ELDER² (sense 1) **2.** its berry, or drupe, used for making wines, jelly, etc.

eld·er·ly (-lē) *adj.* somewhat old; past middle age; approaching old age —**eld′er·li·ness** *n.*

eld·er·ship (-ship′) *n.* [ELDER¹ + -SHIP] **1.** the position or duties of an elder in a church **2.** a group of elders; presbytery

elder statesman 1. formerly, in Japan, any of a number of retired statesmen who served informally as a group of advisers to the emperor **2.** any elderly retired statesman who continues to be consulted unofficially on governmental matters

eld·est (el′dist) *adj.* [ME. < OE. *eldest*(a), *ieldest*(a), superl. of *ald*, *eald* (see OLD)] oldest; esp., first-born or oldest surviving

El Do·ra·do, El·do·ra·do (el′də rä′dō, -rā′dō, -rad′ō) *pl.* **-dos** [Sp., the gilded; *dorado*, pp. of *dorar*, to gild < LL. *deaurare*, to gild + L. *de-*, intens. + *aurum*, gold] **1.** a legendary country in S. America, supposed to be rich in

gold and precious stones and sought by early Spanish explorers ☆**2.** any place that is, or is supposed to be, rich in gold, opportunity, etc.

el·dritch (el′drich) *adj.* [Early ModE. *elrich*, prob. (as Scot. *elphrish*) < ME. *elf, elve, elf*] weird; eerie

El·ea·nor (el′ə nər, -nôr′) [OFr. *Elienor:* see HELEN] a feminine name: dim. *Ella, Nell, Nora:* var. *Leonora*

Eleanor of Aquitaine 1122–1204; queen of France (1137–52) as the wife of Louis VII & queen of England (1154–89) as the wife of Henry II

El·e·at·ic (el′ē at′ik) *adj.* [L. *Eleaticus* < *Elea* (Velia), ancient Gr. colony in Italy] designating or of an ancient Greek school of philosophy, centering in Elea during the 5th and 6th cent. B.C., which held that the singular and unchangeable "Being" was the only reality and that plurality, change, and motion were only illusory: Parmenides and Zeno were its outstanding adherents —*n.* an Eleatic philosopher —**El′e·at′i·cism** (-ə siz′m) *n.*

El·e·a·zar, El·e·a·zer (el′ē ā′zər) [LL.(Ec.) *Eleazar* < Gr.(Ec.) *Eleazar* < Heb. *el′āzār*, lit., God has helped] *Bible* Aaron's son and successor as high priest of Israel: Num. 20:28

elec., elect. 1. electric **2.** electrical **3.** electricity

el·e·cam·pane (el′i kam pān′) *n.* [ME. *elena campana*, altered < ML. *enula campana* < L. *inula* (altered by metathesis < Gr. *helenion*, prob. < *Helenē*, daughter of Zeus) + *campana* (< *campus*, field: see CAMPUS)] a tall, hairy European perennial plant (*Inula helenium*) of the composite family, having flower heads with many slender yellow rays: naturalized in the U.S.

e·lect (i lekt′) *adj.* [ME. < L. *electus*, pp. of *eligere*, to pick out, choose < *e-*, out + *legere*, to pick, choose: see LOGIC] **1.** chosen; given preference **2.** elected but not yet installed in office *[the mayor-elect]* **3.** *Theol.* chosen by God for salvation and eternal life —*n.* a person who is elect —*vt.* **1.** to select for some office by voting **2.** to choose; select *[we elected to stay]* **3.** *Theol.* to choose for eternal salvation: only in the passive, with *God* as the implied subject —*vi.* to make a choice; choose —*SYN.* see CHOOSE —**the elect 1.** persons belonging to a specially privileged group **2.** *Theol.* those chosen by God for salvation and eternal life

e·lec·tion (i lek′shən) *n.* [ME. *eleccioun* < OFr. *election* < L. *electio*, a choice, in LL.(Ec.), the election of believers: see prec.] **1.** a choosing or choice **2.** a choosing or being chosen for office by vote **3.** *Theol.* the selection by God of certain people for salvation and eternal life

e·lec·tion·eer (i lek′shə nir′) *vi.* to canvass votes for, or otherwise work for the success of, a candidate, political party, etc. in an election

e·lec·tive (i lek′tiv) *adj.* [ME. < LL. *electivus*] **1.** *a)* filled by election *[an elective office] b)* chosen by election; elected **2.** of or based on election **3.** having the power to choose **4.** that may be chosen but is not required; optional **5.** [Now Rare] having or referring to a tendency to attract or combine with certain substances in preference to others —☆*n.* an optional course or subject in a school or college curriculum —**e·lec′tive·ly** *adv.*

e·lec·tor (-tər) *n.* [ME. *electour* < L. *elector*] **1.** a person who elects; specif., a qualified voter **2.** a member of the electoral college **3.** [*usually* E-] [transl. of G. *kurfürst*, lit., choosing prince] any of the German princes of the Holy Roman Empire who took part in the election of the emperor

e·lec·tor·al (-tər əl, -trəl) *adj.* **1.** of an election or electors **2.** made up of electors

electoral college ☆an assembly elected by the voters to perform the formal duty of electing the president and the vice president of the United States: the electors of each State, equal in number to its members in Congress, are expected to cast their votes for the candidates selected by the popular vote in their State

e·lec·tor·ate (-tər it) *n.* [ML. *electoratus*] **1.** all those qualified to vote in an election **2.** the rank or territory of an elector in the Holy Roman Empire

E·lec·tra (i lek′trə) [L. < Gr. *Ēlektra*, lit., shining one: cf. ELECTRIC] *Gr. Myth.* the daughter of Agamemnon and Clytemnestra: she encouraged her brother, Orestes, to kill their mother and their mother's lover, who together had murdered Agamemnon

Electra complex *Psychoanalysis* the unconscious tendency of a daughter to be attached to her father and hostile toward her mother: an obsolescent term: cf. OEDIPUS COMPLEX

e·lec·tric (i lek′trik) *adj.* [ModL. *electricus*, orig., produced from amber by rubbing < ML., of amber < L. *electrum*, amber, electrum < Gr. *ēlektron*, akin to *ēlektōr*, shining, the sun < ?] **1.** of, charged with, or conveying electricity *[an electric wire]* **2.** producing, or produced by, electricity *[an electric generator]* **3.** operated by electricity *[an electric iron]* **4.** very tense or exciting; electrifying —*n.* **1.** [Archaic] a substance which does not conduct electricity but can be used to store or excite an electrical charge ☆**2.** a train, car, etc. operated by electricity

e·lec·tri·cal (-tri k'l) *adj.* **1.** same as ELECTRIC **2.** connected with the science or use of electricity *[an electrical engineer]*

e·lec·tri·cal·ly (-trik lē, -tri k'l ē) *adv.* by or with electricity

electrical transcription *same as* TRANSCRIPTION (sense 2 *c*)

electric blue a bright, metallic blue

☆**electric chair 1.** an apparatus in the form of a chair, used in electrocuting persons sentenced to death **2.** the death sentence by electrocution

electric eel a large eel-shaped fish (*Electrophorus electricus*) of N. S. America, having special organs that can give severe electric shocks

☆**electric eye** *same as* PHOTOELECTRIC CELL

electric field a region at every point within which there is a force on an electric charge

electric furnace a furnace heated to high temperatures by an electric current, used in smelting, melting metals, manufacturing carbides, etc.

☆**electric guitar** a kind of guitar whose tones are transmitted to an amplifier and loudspeaker through an electrical pickup attached to the instrument

☆**e·lec·tri·cian** (i lek′trish′ən, ē′lek-) *n.* a person whose work is the construction, repair, or installation of electric apparatus

e·lec·tric·i·ty (-tris′ə tē) *n.* [see ELECTRIC] **1.** a property of certain fundamental particles of all matter, as electrons (negative charges) and protons or positrons (positive charges) that have a force field associated with them and that can be separated by the expenditure of energy: electrical charge can be generated by friction, induction, or chemical change and is manifested by an accumulation of electrons on an atom or body, constituting a negative charge, and a loss of electrons, constituting a corresponding positive charge **2.** *a)* an electric current: see CURRENT (*n.* 3) *b)* an electric charge: see CHARGE (*n.* I, 3) **3.** the branch of physics dealing with electricity **4.** electric current supplied as a public utility for lighting, heating, etc. **5.** strong emotional tension, excitement, etc.

electric needle a high-frequency electrode in the form of a needle, used in surgery to cut through tissue, searing it at the same time to prevent bleeding

electric ray any of a genus (*Torpedo*) of cartilaginous fishes (family *Torpedinidae*) with electric organs that can stun enemies or prey

e·lec·tri·fy (i lek′trə fī′) *vt.* **-fied′, -fy′ing 1.** to charge with electricity **2.** to give an electric shock to **3.** to give a shock of excitement to; thrill **4.** to equip for the use of electricity; provide with electric power —**e·lec′tri·fi′a·ble** *adj.* —**e·lec′tri·fi·ca′tion** *n.* —**e·lec′tri·fi′er** *n.*

e·lec·tro (i lek′trō) *n., pl.* **-tros** *short for:* **1.** ELECTROTYPE **2.** ELECTROPLATE

e·lec·tro- (i lek′trō) *n.* [< Gr. *ēlektron* (with sense of ModL. *electricus*): see ELECTRIC] *a combining form meaning:* **1.** electric *[electromagnet]* **2.** electrically *[electrocute]* **3.** electricity *[electrostatics]* **4.** electrolysis *[electrodeposit]*

e·lec·tro·a·nal·y·sis (i lek′trō ə nal′ə sis) *n.* analysis of a substance by means of electrolysis —**e·lec′tro·an′a·lyt′ic** (-an′ə lit′ik), **e·lec′tro·an′a·lyt′i·cal** *adj.*

e·lec·tro·car·di·o·gram (-kär′dē ə gram′) *n.* a tracing showing the changes in electric potential produced by the contractions of the heart and used in the diagnosis of heart disease

e·lec·tro·car·di·o·graph (-kär′dē ə graf′, -gräf′) *n.* an instrument for making an electrocardiogram —**e·lec′tro·car′di·o·graph′ic** *adj.* —**e·lec′tro·car′di·o·graph′i·cal·ly** *adv.* —**e·lec′tro·car′di·og′ra·phy** (-äg′rə fē) *n.*

e·lec·tro·chem·is·try (-kem′is trē) *n.* the science that deals with the use of electrical energy to bring about a chemical reaction or with the generation of electrical energy by means of chemical action —**e·lec′tro·chem′i·cal** *adj.* —**e·lec′tro·chem′i·cal·ly** *adv.*

e·lec·tro·con·vul·sive therapy (-kən vul′siv) *see* SHOCK THERAPY

☆**e·lec·tro·cute** (i lek′trə kyōōt′) *vt.* **-cut′ed, -cut′ing** [ELECTRO- + (EXE)CUTE] to kill with a charge of electricity; specif., to execute in the electric chair —**e·lec′tro·cu′tion** *n.*

e·lec·trode (i lek′trōd) *n.* [ELECTR(O)- + -ODE¹] any terminal that conducts an electric current into or away from various conducting substances in a circuit, as the anode or cathode in a battery or the carbons in an arc lamp, or that emits, collects, or controls the flow of electrons in an electron tube, as the cathode, plate, or grid

e·lec·tro·de·pos·it (i lek′trō ō pāz′it) *vt.* to deposit (a metal, etc.) electrolytically —*n.* a deposit made by an electric current, as in electroplating —**e·lec′tro·dep′o·si′tion** (-dep′ə zish′ən) *n.*

e·lec·tro·di·al·y·sis (-dī al′ə sis) *n.* the rapid removal of undesired ions from solution by the application of a direct current to electrodes inserted into a dialysis system

e·lec·tro·dy·nam·ics (-dī nam′iks) *n.pl.* [*with sing. v.*] the branch of physics dealing with the phenomena of electric currents and associated magnetic forces —**e·lec′tro·dy·nam′ic** *adj.* —**e·lec′tro·dy·nam′i·cal·ly** *adv.*

e·lec·tro·dy·na·mom·e·ter (-dī′nə mäm′ə tər) *n.* an instrument in which the magnetic forces between two parts of the same circuit are used for detecting or measuring an electric current

e·lec·tro·en·ceph·a·lo·gram (-en sef′ə lə gram′) *n.* a

tracing showing the changes in electric potential produced by the brain

e·lec·tro·en·ceph·a·lo·graph (-en sef′ə lə graf′, -gräf′) *n.* an instrument for making electroencephalograms —**e·lec′tro·en·ceph′a·lo·graph′ic** *adj.* —**e·lec′tro·en·ceph′a·log′ra·phy** (-ə läg′rə fē) *n.*

☆**e·lec·tro·form·ing** (i lek′trə fôrm′iŋ) *n.* the production or reproduction of articles by the electrolytic deposition of a metal on a conducting mold

e·lec·tro·graph (-graf′, -gräf′) *n.* **1.** an electrical device for etching or engraving plates **2.** a telegraphic instrument for transmitting photographs, drawings, etc.

e·lec·tro·jet (-jet′) *n.* a narrow, high-velocity stream of electric energy that girdles the earth in the ionosphere above the magnetic equator

e·lec·tro·ki·net·ics (i lek′trō ki net′iks) *n.pl.* [*with sing. v.*] the branch of electrodynamics dealing with electricity in motion, or electric currents: cf. ELECTROSTATICS

e·lec·tro·lu·mi·nes·cence (-lōō′mə nes′′ns) *n.* the emission of nonincandescent light by certain substances when acted upon by an alternating electric field —**e·lec′tro·lu′mi·nes′cent** *adj.*

e·lec·trol·y·sis (i lek′träl′ə sis) *n.* [ELECTRO- + -LYSIS] **1.** the decomposition of an electrolyte by the action of an electric current passing through it **2.** the removal of unwanted hair from the body by destroying the hair roots with an electrified needle

e·lec·tro·lyte (i lek′trə līt′) *n.* [ELECTRO- + -LYTE¹] any substance which in solution or in a liquid form is capable of conducting an electric current by the movement of its dissociated positive and negative ions to the electrodes of opposite charge, where the ions are deposited as a coating, liberated as a gas, etc.

e·lec·tro·lyt·ic (i lek′trə lit′ik) *adj.* **1.** of or produced by electrolysis **2.** of or containing an electrolyte —**e·lec′tro·lyt′i·cal·ly** *adv.*

e·lec·tro·lyze (i lek′trə līz′) *vt.* **-lyzed′, -lyz′ing** to subject to, or decompose by, electrolysis

e·lec·tro·mag·net (i lek′trō mag′nit) *n.* a soft iron core surrounded by a coil of wire, that temporarily becomes a magnet when an electric current flows through the wire

e·lec·tro·mag·net·ic (-mag net′ik) *adj.* of, produced by, or having to do with electromagnetism or an electromagnet —**e·lec′tro·mag·net′i·cal·ly** *adv.*

electromagnetic spectrum the complete range of frequencies of electromagnetic waves from the lowest to the highest frequency, including, in order, radio, infrared, visible light, ultraviolet, X-ray, gamma ray, and cosmic ray waves

electromagnetic wave a wave propagated through space or matter by the oscillating electric and magnetic field generated by an oscillating electric charge

e·lec·tro·mag·net·ism (-mag′nə tiz′m) *n.* **1.** magnetism produced by an electric current **2.** the branch of physics that deals with the relations between electricity and magnetism

e·lec·tro·me·chan·i·cal (-mə kan′i k′l) *adj.* designating or of a mechanical device or operation that is activated or regulated by electricity

e·lec·tro·met·al·lur·gy (-met′′l ur′jē) *n.* the branch of metallurgy having to do with the use of electricity, as for producing heat in smelting, refining, etc., or for refining, plating, or depositing metals by electrolysis

e·lec·trom·e·ter (i lek′träm′ə tər, ē′lek-) *n.* **1.** a device for detecting or measuring differences of potential by means of electrostatic forces **2.** an active circuit arrangement for measuring differences of potential without drawing appreciable current from the source of the potential differences

e·lec·tro·mo·tive (i lek′trə mōt′iv) *adj.* **1.** producing an electric current through differences in potential **2.** relating to electromotive force

electromotive force the force or electric pressure that causes or tends to cause a current to flow in a circuit, equivalent to the potential difference between the terminals and commonly measured in volts

e·lec·tron (i lek′trän) *n.* [coined (1891) by George J. Stoney, Ir. physicist < ELECTR(IC) + -ON] any of the negatively charged particles that form a part of all atoms, each carrying a negative charge of 1.602×10^{-19} coulomb: the mass of an electron is about 1/1836 of that of a proton with a rest mass of 9.10904×10^{-28} gram, and the number of electrons circulating around a nucleus is equal to the number of positive charges on the nucleus

electron camera same as CAMERA (sense 4)

e·lec·tro·neg·a·tive (i lek′trō neg′ə tiv) *adj.* **1.** having a negative electrical charge; tending to move to the positive electrode, or anode, in electrolysis **2.** having the ability to attract electrons, esp. in forming a chemical bond, as the atoms of nonmetallic, acid-forming chemical elements —*n.* an electronegative substance

electron gun the part of a cathode-ray tube that collects, focuses, and emits the electrons

e·lec·tron·ic (i lek′trän′ik, ē′lek-) *adj.* **1.** of an electron or electrons **2.** operating, produced, or done by the action of electrons or by devices dependent on such action —**e·lec′tron′i·cal·ly** *adv.*

electronic data processing data processing by means of electronic equipment, esp. computers

electronic music music in which the sounds are originated, organized, or altered by electronic devices, and arranged and recorded on tape for presentation

☆**electronic organ** a musical instrument with a console like that of a pipe organ, but producing tones by means of electronic devices instead of pipes

e·lec·tron·ics (-iks) *n.pl.* [*with sing. v.*] the science that deals with the behavior and control of electrons in vacuums and gases, and with the use of electron tubes, photoelectric cells, transistors, etc.

electron lens a configuration of electric or magnetic fields, or a combination of both, that serves to focus or deflect an electron beam, as in an electron microscope

electron microscope an instrument for focusing a beam of electrons, using electric or magnetic fields, to form an enlarged image of an object on a fluorescent screen or photographic plate: it is much more powerful than any optical microscope

electron multiplier a device that amplifies the stream of electrons emitted from the cathode by accelerating the secondary electrons

electron optics the branch of electronics having to do with the focusing and deflection of beams of electrons by means of electric and magnetic fields, which act upon the beams in the same way that lenses act on light rays

electron telescope an instrument using a cathode-ray tube to form a visible image of infrared rays brought into focus from a distant object by optical lenses

electron tube a sealed glass or metal tube completely evacuated or filled with gas at low pressure, used to control the flow of electrons

e·lec·tron-volt (-vōlt′) *n.* a unit of energy equal to that attained by an electron falling unimpeded through a potential difference of one volt; 1.602×10^{-12} erg

e·lec·tro·op·tics (i lek′trō äp′tiks) *n.pl.* [*with sing. v.*] the branch of optics dealing with the relations between an electric field and light —**e·lec′tro·op′tic, e·lec′tro·op′ti·cal** *adj.* —**e·lec′tro·op′ti·cal·ly** *adv.*

e·lec·tro·phile (i lek′trə fīl′) *n.* [ELECTRO(N) + -PHILE] a molecule, ion, group, or radical that has a strong affinity for electrons —**e·lec′tro·phil′ic** (-fil′ik) *adj.*

e·lec·tro·pho·re·sis (i lek′trō fə rē′sis) *n.* [ModL. < ELECTRO- + (CATA)PHORESIS] the movement of colloidal particles suspended in a fluid toward the electrodes in the fluid, through which an electric current is passed, with the resulting collection of the particles at the electrodes —**e·lec′tro·pho·ret′ic** (-fə ret′ik) *adj.*

e·lec·troph·o·rus (i lek′träf′ər əs) *n., pl.* **-ri** (-ī′) [ModL. < ELECTRO- + Gr. *-phoros*, bearing < *pherein*, BEAR¹] an apparatus consisting of an insulated disk of resin, shellac, etc. and a metal plate, used in generating static electricity by induction

e·lec·tro·phys·i·ol·o·gy (i lek′trō fiz′ē äl′ə jē) *n.* **1.** the study of the electrical properties of living cells **2.** the study of the production of electric currents by living organisms —**e·lec′tro·phys′i·o·log′i·cal** (-ə läj′i k′l) *adj.* —**e·lec′tro·phys′i·ol′o·gist** *n.*

e·lec·tro·plate (i lek′trə plāt′) *vt.* **-plat′ed, -plat′ing** to deposit a coating of metal on by electrolysis —*n.* anything so plated

e·lec·tro·pos·i·tive (i lek′trə päz′ə tiv) *adj.* **1.** having a positive electrical charge; tending to move toward the negative electrode, or cathode, in electrolysis **2.** having the ability to give up electrons, esp. in forming a chemical bond, as the atoms of chemical elements that are light metals —*n.* an electropositive substance

e·lec·tro·scope (i lek′trə skōp′) *n.* [ELECTRO- + -SCOPE] an instrument for detecting very small charges of electricity, and indicating whether they are positive or negative, as by the divergence of electrically charged strips of gold leaf: when fitted with optical means for quantitative observation of the divergence, an electroscope serves as an electrometer —**e·lec′tro·scop′ic** (-skäp′ik) *adj.*

GOLD LEAF

ELECTROSCOPE

e·lec·tro·shock therapy (-shäk′) *see* SHOCK THERAPY

electrostatic generator a generator of electricity which produces electrical discharges of high voltage: sometimes used to accelerate charged particles in the production of nuclear reactions

e·lec·tro·stat·ics (i lek′trə stat′iks) *n.pl.* [*with sing. v.*] the branch of electrodynamics dealing with the phenomena accompanying electric charges at rest, or static electricity: cf. ELECTROKINETICS —**e·lec′tro·stat′ic** *adj.* —**e·lec′tro·stat′i·cal·ly** *adv.*

electrostatic unit any of several units in the particular cgs unit system which assigns the value of unity to the dielectric constant of a vacuum and measures electric energy in ergs

e·lec·tro·sur·ger·y (-sur′jər ē) *n.* the use of electricity in surgery, as in cauterizing

e·lec·tro·syn·the·sis (-sin′thə sis) *n. Chem.* synthesis produced by means of an electric current

e·lec·tro·ther·a·py (-ther′ə pē) *n.* the treatment of dis-

ease by means of electricity, as by diathermy —e·lec'tro-ther'a·pist *n.*

e·lec·tro·ther·mal (-thʉr'm'l) *adj.* using, relating to, or generating heat from electric energy

e·lec·tro·ther·mics (-thʉr'miks) *n.pl.* [*with sing. v.*] the branch of science which deals with the direct transformations of electric energy and heat, as in the heating chamber of certain rockets —e·lec'tro·ther'mic *adj.*

e·lec·trot·o·nus (i lek'trät'n əs) *n.* [ModL.: see ELECTRO- & TONE] the changed state of a nerve or muscle when an electric current is passed through any part of it —e·lec'tro·ton'ic (-trə tän'ik) *adj.*

e·lec·tro·type (i lek'trə tīp') *n. Printing* 1. a facsimile plate made by electroplating a wax or plastic impression of the page of type or surface to be reproduced with a thin layer of copper that is backed with type metal after separation from the impression 2. a print made from such a plate 3. *same as* ELECTROTYPY —*vt., vi.* -typed', -typ'ing to make an electrotype or electrotypes (of) —e·lec'tro·typ'er *n.* —e·lec'tro·typ'ic (-tip'ik) *adj.*

e·lec·tro·typ·y (-tī'pē) *n.* the process of making electrotypes

e·lec·tro·va·lence (i lek'trō vā'ləns) *n.* 1. a chemical bond between two oppositely charged ions formed when one atom transfers electrons to another atom, as in the formation of sodium chloride when sodium reacts with chlorine 2. the number of electrons an atom gains or loses in forming a compound during a chemical reaction

e·lec·trum (i lek'trəm) *n.* [L. < Gr. *ēlektron:* see ELECTRIC] a light-yellow alloy of gold and silver

e·lec·tu·ar·y (i lek'choo wer'ē) *n., pl.* -ar'ies [ME. *electuarie* < LL. *electuarium* < Gr. *ekleikton* < *ekleichein,* to lick out < *ek-,* out + *leichein,* to LICK] a medicine made by mixing drugs with honey or syrup to form a paste

el·ee·mos·y·nar·y (el'i mäs'ə ner'ē, el'ē ə-) *adj.* [ML. *eleemosynarius* < LL.(Ec.) *eleemosyna,* alms < Gr. *eleēmosynē,* pity, mercy (in LXX & NT., charity, alms) < *eleēmōn,* merciful < *eleos,* mercy] 1. of or for charity or alms; charitable 2. supported by or dependent on charity 3. given as charity; free

el·e·gance (el'ə gəns) *n.* [Fr. *élégance* < L. *elegantia*] 1. the quality of being elegant; specif., *a)* dignified richness and grace, as of design *b)* polished fastidiousness or refined grace, as in manners 2. anything elegant Also, esp. for sense 2, el'e·gan·cy, *pl.* -cies

el·e·gant (-gənt) *adj.* [Fr. *élégant* < L. *elegans,* prp. of **elegare* < *e-,* out + *legare,* var. of *legere,* to choose: see LOGIC] 1. characterized by dignified richness and grace, as of design, dress, style, etc.; luxurious or opulent in a restrained, tasteful manner 2. characterized by a sense of propriety or refinement; impressively fastidious in manners and tastes 3. [Colloq.] excellent; fine; first-rate —el'e·gant·ly *adv.*

el·e·gi·ac (el'ə jī'ak, i lē'jē ak') *adj.* [L. *elegiacus* < Gr. *elegeiakos* < *elegeion:* see ELEGY] 1. *Gr. & Rom. Prosody* of or composed in dactylic hexameter couplets, the second line (sometimes called a pentameter) having only an accented syllable in the third and sixth feet: the form was used for elegies and various other lyric poems 2. of, like, or fit for an elegy 3. sad; mournful; plaintive 4. writing or having written elegiacs or elegies Also el'e·gi'a·cal —*n.* 1. an elegiac couplet 2. [*pl.*] a series of such couplets; poem or poems written in such couplets

el·e·gist (el'ə jist) *n.* a writer of an elegy or elegies

e·le·git (i lē'jit) *n.* [L., 3d pers. sing., perf. indic., of *eligere,* to choose: see ELECT] *Law* a writ of execution by which a plaintiff is given possession of the defendant's goods until his claim is satisfied

el·e·gize (el'ə jīz') *vi.* -gized', -giz'ing to write elegies —*vt.* to commemorate or lament as in an elegy

el·e·gy (-jē) *n., pl.* -gies [Fr. *élégie* < L. *elegia* < Gr. *elegeia* < *elegos,* a lament] 1. a poem or song of lament and praise for the dead, as Shelley's "Adonais" 2. any poem in elegiac verse 3. any poem, song, etc. in a mournfully contemplative tone [Gray's "Elegy in a Country Churchyard"]

elem. 1. element(s) 2. elementary

el·e·ment (el'ə mənt) *n.* [ME. < OFr. < L. *elementum,* first principle, element] 1. any of the four substances —earth, air, fire, water—formerly believed to constitute all physical matter 2. any of these four substances thought of as the natural environment of a class of living beings 3. the natural or suitable environment, situation, etc. for a person or thing 4. *a)* a component part or quality, often one that is basic or essential [a good story has an *element* of suspense] *b)* a constituent group of a specified kind [the criminal *element* in a city] *c)* a determining factor *d)* any of the data needed or used to make certain calculations, solve a particular problem, etc. 5. *Chem.* any substance that cannot be separated into different substances by ordinary chemical methods: all matter is composed of such substances: elements can be transformed into other elements by radioactive decay or by nuclear reactions 6. [*pl.*] *Eccles.* the bread and wine of Communion 7. *Elec. a)* any device with terminals at

which it can be connected with other electrical devices *b)* the wire coil that becomes glowing hot, as in an electric oven 8. *Math. a)* an infinitesimal part of any magnitude; differential *b)* the point, line, etc. that generates a line, surface, etc. *c)* a part of a configuration, as a side of a triangle or a number in a matrix 9. *Mil.* a subdivision of a unit or formation —**the elements** 1. the first or basic principles; rudiments 2. wind, rain, etc.; forces of the atmosphere See table of CHEMICAL ELEMENTS on next page SYN.—**element,** in its general use, is the broadest term for any of the basic, irreducible parts or principles of anything, concrete or abstract [the *elements* of a science]; **component** and **constituent** both refer to any of the simple or compound parts of some complex thing or concept, but **constituent** also implies that the part is essential to the complex [hemoglobin is a *constituent* of blood]; **ingredient** refers to any of the substances (sometimes nonessential) that are mixed together in preparing a food, medicine, etc. [the *ingredients* of a cocktail]; **factor** applies to any of the component parts that are instrumental in determining the nature of the complex [luck was a *factor* in his success]

el·e·men·tal (el'ə men't'l) *adj.* [ME. < ML. *elementalis*] 1. of any or all of the four elements (sense 1) 2. of or like natural forces; characteristic of the physical universe 3. basic and powerful; not subtle or refined; primal [hunger and sex are *elemental* drives] 4. *same as* ELEMENTARY (sense 2 *a*) 5. being an essential or basic part or parts 6. being a chemical element in uncombined form —*n.* a basic principle; rudiment: *usually used in pl.* —el'e·men'tal·ly *adv.*

el·e·men·ta·ry (el'ə men'tər ē, -trē) *adj.* [ME. *elementare* < *elementarius*] 1. *same as* ELEMENTAL 2. *a)* of first principles, rudiments, or fundamentals; introductory; basic; simple *b)* of or having to do with the formal instruction of children in basic subjects —el'e·men'ta·ri·ly *adv.* —el'e·men'ta·ri·ness *n.*

elementary particle a subatomic particle which is not a composite of other particles but is capable of independent existence, as a neutron, proton, electron, meson, etc.

elementary school a school of the first six grades (sometimes, first eight grades), where basic subjects are taught

el·e·mi (el'ə mē) *n.* [Fr. *élémi* < Ar. *al-lāmī*] any of various resins from tropical trees (family Burseraceae), used esp. in varnishes, ointments, and inks

e·len·chus (i leŋ'kəs) *n., pl.* -chi (-kī) [L. < Gr. *elenchos,* cross-examination, refutation < *elenchein,* to shame, refute] *Logic* a syllogism that refutes a proposition by proving the direct contrary of its conclusion —e·lenc'tic, e·lench'tic (-leŋk'tik) *adj.*

el·e·op·tene (el'ē äp'tēn) *n.* [< Gr. *elaion,* olive oil, OIL + *ptēnos,* winged] that part of an essential oil which does not become solid: cf. STEAROPTENE

el·e·phant (el'ə fənt) *n., pl.* -phants, -phant: see PLURAL, II, D, 1 [ME. *elefaunt* < L. *elephantus* < Gr. *elephas* (gen. *elephantos*), elephant, ivory] a huge, thick-skinned, almost hairless mammal, the largest of extant four-footed animals, with a long, flexible snout (called a *trunk*) and, usually, two ivory tusks growing out of the upper jaw: the two existing species are the Asian (or **Indian**) elephant (*Elephas maximus*), which is commonly domesticated, and the **African** elephant (*Loxodonta africana*), which has a flatter head and larger ears

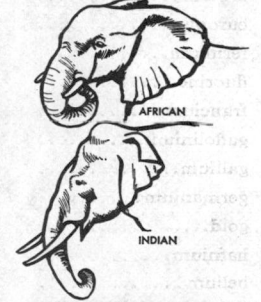

ELEPHANTS
(shoulder height: African, 10–13 ft.; Indian, 8 1/2–10 ft.)

el·e·phan·ti·a·sis (el'ə fən ti'ə sis) *n.* [L. < Gr. *elephantiasis* < *elephas,* elephant: from resemblance of the skin to the elephant's hide] a chronic disease of the skin characterized by the enlargement of certain parts of the body, esp. the legs and genitals, and by the hardening and ulceration of the surrounding skin: it is caused by obstruction of the lymphatic vessels, often due to infestation by filarial worms

El·e·phan·ti·ne (el'ə fan ti'nē, -tē'-) small island in the Nile, opposite Aswan: site of ancient ruins

el·e·phan·tine (el'ə fan'tēn, -tīn, -tin) *adj.* [L. *elephantinus* < Gr. *elephantinos*] 1. of an elephant or elephants 2. like an elephant in size or gait; huge, heavy, slow, clumsy, ungainly, etc.

el·e·phant's-ear (el'ə fənts ir') *n.* 1. any of several plants (genus *Colocasia*) of the arum family, esp. an ornamental taro (*Colocasia antiquorum*) having enormous heart-shaped leaves 2. any of various cultivated begonias with large, showy leaves

El·eu·sin·i·an (el'yōō sin'ē ən) *adj.* 1. of Eleusis 2. designating or of the secret religious rites (**Eleusinian mysteries**) celebrated at the ancient Greek city of Eleusis in honor of Demeter and Persephone

---

fat, āpe, cär; ten, ēven; is, bīte; gō, hôrn, tōōl, look; oil, out; up, fʉr; get; joy; yet; chin; she; thin, then; zh, leisure; ŋ, ring; ə for a in ago, e in agent, i in sanity, o in comply, u in focus; ' as in able (ā'b'l); Fr. bāl; ë, Fr. coeur; ö, Fr. feu; Fr. mon; ō̃, Fr. coq; ü, Fr. duc; r, Fr. cri; H, G. ich; kh, G. doch. See inside front cover. ☆ Americanism; ‡foreign; *hypothetical; <derived from

CHEMICAL ELEMENTS

With International Atomic Weights. Carbon at 12 is the standard.

	Symbol	Atomic Number	Atomic Weight		Symbol	Atomic Number	Atomic Weight
actinium.............	Ac	89	227(?)	mercury.............	Hg	80	200.59
aluminum...........	Al	13	26.9815	molybdenum........	Mo	42	95.94
americium...........	Am	95	243.13	neodymium.........	Nd	60	144.24
antimony...........	Sb	51	121.75	neon...............	Ne	10	20.183
argon..............	Ar	18	39.948	neptunium..........	Np	93	237.00
arsenic.............	As	33	74.9216	nickel.............	Ni	28	58.71
astatine............	At	85	210(?)	niobium............	Nb	41	92.906
barium.............	Ba	56	137.34	nitrogen...........	N	7	14.0067
berkelium...........	Bk	97	248(?)	nobelium...........	No	102	255(?)
beryllium...........	Be	4	9.0122	osmium............	Os	76	190.2
bismuth............	Bi	83	208.980	oxygen............	O	8	15.9994
boron..............	B	5	10.811	palladium...........	Pd	46	106.4
bromine............	Br	35	79.909	phosphorus.........	P	15	30.9738
cadmium...........	Cd	48	112.40	platinum...........	Pt	78	195.09
calcium............	Ca	20	40.08	plutonium..........	Pu	94	239.05
californium.........	Cf	98	251(?)	polonium..........	Po	84	210.05
carbon.............	C	6	12.01115	potassium..........	K	19	39.102
cerium.............	Ce	58	140.12	praseodymium......	Pr	59	140.907
cesium.............	Cs	55	132.905	promethium.........	Pm	61	145(?)
chlorine............	Cl	17	35.453	protactinium........	Pa	91	231.10
chromium...........	Cr	24	51.996	radium............	Ra	88	226.00
cobalt..............	Co	27	58.9332	radon.............	Rn	86	222.00
copper.............	Cu	29	63.546	rhenium...........	Re	75	186.2
curium.............	Cm	96	247(?)	rhodium...........	Rh	45	102.905
dysprosium.........	Dy	66	162.50	rubidium..........	Rb	37	85.47
einsteinium.........	Es	99	252(?)	ruthenium..........	Ru	44	101.07
erbium.............	Er	68	167.28	samarium...........	Sm	62	150.35
europium...........	Eu	63	151.96	scandium..........	Sc	21	44.956
fermium............	Fm	100	257(?)	selenium...........	Se	34	78.96
fluorine............	F	9	18.9984	silicon.............	Si	14	28.086
francium...........	Fr	87	223(?)	silver..............	Ag	47	107.868
gadolinium..........	Gd	64	157.25	sodium............	Na	11	22.9898
gallium.............	Ga	31	69.72	strontium...........	Sr	38	87.62
germanium.........	Ge	32	72.59	sulfur..............	S	16	32.064
gold...............	Au	79	196.967	tantalum...........	Ta	73	180.948
hafnium............	Hf	72	178.49	technetium.........	Tc	43	97(?)
helium.............	He	2	4.0026	tellurium..........	Te	52	127.60
holmium...........	Ho	67	164.930	terbium...........	Tb	65	158.924
hydrogen...........	H	1	1.00797	thallium...........	Tl	81	204.37
indium.............	In	49	114.82	thorium...........	Th	90	232.038
iodine..............	I	53	126.9044	thulium...........	Tm	69	168.934
iridium.............	Ir	77	192.2	tin.................	Sn	50	118.69
iron................	Fe	26	55.847	titanium...........	Ti	22	47.90
krypton............	Kr	36	83.80	tungsten..........	W	74	183.85
lanthanum..........	La	57	138.91	uranium...........	U	92	238.03
lawrencium.........	Lr	103	256(?)	vanadium...........	V	23	50.942
lead................	Pb	82	207.19	xenon..............	Xe	54	131.30
lithium.............	Li	3	6.939	ytterbium..........	Yb	70	173.04
lutetium............	Lu	71	174.97	yttrium............	Y	39	88.905
magnesium..........	Mg	12	24.312	zinc................	Zn	30	65.37
manganese..........	Mn	25	54.9380	zirconium...........	Zr	40	91.22
mendelevium........	Md	101	258(?)				

E·leu·sis (e lōō′sis) town in Greece, northwest of Athens: site of an ancient Greek city

elev. elevation

el·e·vate (el′ə vāt′) *vt.* **-vat′ed, -vat′ing** [ME. *elevaten* < L. *elevatus*, pp. of *elevare*, to raise < *e-*, out + *levare*, to make light, lift < *levis*, light: see LEVER] **1.** to lift up; raise **2.** to raise the pitch or volume of (esp. the voice) **3.** to raise (a person) in rank or position **4.** to raise to a higher intellectual or moral level **5.** to raise the spirits of; elate; exhilarate —*adj.* [Archaic] elevated —*SYN.* see LIFT

el·e·vat·ed (-vāt′id) *adj.* **1.** lifted up; raised; high **2.** exalted; dignified; lofty **3.** high-spirited; exhilarated —☆*n. same as* ELEVATED RAILWAY

☆**elevated railway** (or **railroad**) a railway elevated above a street on a framework so that the street is left free for other traffic

el·e·va·tion (el′ə vā′shən) *n.* [ME. *elevacioun* < OFr. *elevacion* < L. *elevatio*] **1.** an elevating or being elevated **2.** a high place or position **3.** height above the surface of the earth **4.** the execution of a leap, esp. by a dancer **5.** dignity; eminence; loftiness **6.** a flat scale drawing of the front, rear, or side of a building, etc. **7.** *Astron.* the angular altitude of any heavenly body above the horizon **8.** *Geog.* height above sea level; altitude **9.** *Mil.* angular distance of the muzzle of a gun above the horizontal —*SYN.* see HEIGHT

el·e·va·tor (el′ə vāt′ər) *n.* [LL.(Ec.): see ELEVATE] **1.** a person or thing that raises or lifts up ☆**2.** a suspended cage or car for hoisting or lowering people or things, as in a building or mine, attached by cables to a machine that moves it ☆**3.** a machine, usually consisting of buckets or scoops fastened to an endless belt or chain, for hoisting grain, etc., as in a warehouse ☆**4.** a warehouse, often cylindrical, for storing, hoisting, and discharging grain **5.** a movable airfoil like a horizontal rudder, usually hinged to the tail section of an aircraft, for making the craft go up or down

e·lev·en (i lev′ən) *adj.* [ME. *elleven* < OE. *endleofan*, akin to OFris. *andlofa*, OHG. *einlif* (G. *elf*) < Gmc. **ainlif*, lit., one left over (after ten) < **ain-* (OE. *an*; cf. A¹, AN¹) + *-lif*, left over, prob. < IE. base **leikw-*, to leave behind, whence LOAN] totaling one more than ten —*n.* **1.** the cardinal number between ten and twelve; 11; XI **2.** any group of eleven people or things; esp., a football or cricket team **3.** something numbered eleven or having eleven units, as a throw of dice

e·lev·en-plus (-plus′) *n.* [Brit.] an examination given in school, esp. formerly, at about the age of eleven to determine whether a pupil will go to a vocational or academic secondary school

e·lev·ens·es (-ən ziz) *n.pl.* [pl. of *elevens*, luncheon, pl. of ELEVEN: orig. an eleven-o'clock meal] [Brit. Colloq.] tea, a light snack, etc. served in the late morning

e·lev·enth (-ənth) *adj.* [ME. *elleventhe* < OE. *endlyfta*: see ELEVEN & -TH²] **1.** preceded by ten others in a series; 11th **2.** designating any of the eleven equal parts of something —*n.* **1.** the one following the tenth **2.** any of the eleven equal parts of something; 1/11 —**at the eleventh hour** [< Matt. 20:1–16] at the last possible time; just before it is too late

el·e·von (el′ə vän′) *n.* [ELEV(ATOR) + (AILER)ON] a movable hinged section of the wing of a tailless airplane, that serves as both an elevator and aileron

elf (elf) *n., pl.* **elves** (elvz) [ME. < OE. *ælf*, akin to OHG. *alb* (G. *alb*, nightmare), prob. < IE. base **albho-*, white, whence L. *albus*, white: prob. basic sense "whitish figure" (in the mist)] **1.** *Folklore* a tiny, often prankish fairy, supposedly exercising magic powers and haunting woods and hills; sprite **2.** a small child or being, esp. a mischievous one —**elf′like′** *adj.*

El Faiyûm *same as* FAIYÛM

El Fer·rol (el fə rōl′) seaport in NW Spain, on the Atlantic: pop. 80,000: official name *El Ferrol del Caudillo*

elf·in (el′fin) *adj.* [prob. < ME. *elvene*, gen. pl.: see ELF] of, appropriate to, or like an elf; fairylike; tiny, delicate, etc. —*n.* an elf

elf·ish (-fish) *adj.* like or characteristic of an elf; elfin or prankish —**elf′ish·ly** *adv.* —**elf′ish·ness** *n.*

elf·lock (-läk′) *n.* a lock of hair tangled as if by elves

El·gar (el′gər, -gär), Sir **Edward (William)** 1857–1934; Eng. composer

El·gin (el′jin) [after *Elgin*, city in Scotland] city in NE Ill., near Chicago: pop. 56,000

El·gin marbles (el′gən) [after 7th Earl of *Elgin* (1766–1841) who brought them to England] a collection of ancient Athenian sculptures in the British Museum

El Gîzah, El Gîzeh *same as* GÎZA

El·gon (el′gän) extinct volcano on the border of Kenya & Uganda: 14,178 ft.; crater, 5 mi. wide

El Gre·co (el grek′ō) (born *Domenikos Theotokopoulos* 1541?–1614?; painter in Italy (c. 1560–75) & Spain, born in Crete

E·li (ē′lī) [Heb. *'ēlī*, lit., high] **1.** a masculine name **2.** *Bible* a high priest of Israel and teacher of Samuel: I Sam. 3

E·li·a (ē′lē ə, ēl′yə) *see* Charles LAMB

E·li·as (i lī′əs) [L. < Gr. *Ēlias* < Heb.: see ELIJAH] **1.** a masculine name **2.** *Bible* Elijah: spelling used in the New Testament (KJV) and in the Douay Version

e·lic·it (i lis′it) *vt.* [< L. *elicitus*, pp. of *elicere*, to draw out < *e-*, out + *lacere*, to entice, akin to *laqueus*: see LACE] **1.** to draw forth; evoke [to *elicit* an angry reply] **2.** to cause to be revealed [to *elicit* facts] —*SYN.* see EXTRACT —**e·lic′i·ta′tion** *n.* —**e·lic′i·tor** *n.*

e·lide (i līd′) *vt.* **e·lid′ed, e·lid′ing** [L. *elidere*, to strike out < *e-*, out + *laedere*, to hurt] **1.** to leave out; suppress, omit, or ignore **2.** to leave out or slur over (a vowel, syllable, etc.) in pronunciation —**e·lid′i·ble** *adj.*

el·i·gi·ble (el′i jə b'l) *adj.* [ME. < ML. *eligibilis* < L. *eligere*: see ELECT] **1.** fit to be chosen; legally or morally qualified **2.** suitable or desirable, esp. for marriage —*n.* an eligible person —**el′i·gi·bil′i·ty** *n.* —**el′i·gi·bly** *adv.*

E·li·hu (el′ə hyōō′, ə lī′hyōō) [Heb. *elīhū*, lit., my God is he] **1.** a masculine name **2.** *Bible* one of Job's visitors in his affliction: Job 32–37

E·li·jah (i lī′jə) [Heb. *'ēliyāhū*, lit., Jehovah is God] **1.** a masculine name: dim. *Lige*; var. *Elias* **2.** *Bible* a prophet of Israel in the 9th century B.C.: I Kings 17–19; II Kings 2:1–11

e·lim·i·nate (i lim′ə nāt′) *vt.* **-nat′ed, -nat′ing** [< L. *eliminatus*, pp. of *eliminare*, to turn out of doors, banish < *e-*, out + *limen*, threshold, prob. akin to *limes*, boundary: see LIMES] **1.** to take out; remove; get rid of **2.** to leave out of consideration; reject; omit **3.** to drop (a person, team, etc. losing a round or match in a contest) from further competition **4.** *Algebra* to get rid of (an unknown quantity) by combining equations **5.** *Physiol.* to expel (waste products) from the body; excrete —*SYN.* see EXCLUDE —**e·lim′i·na′tion** *n.* —**e·lim′i·na′tive** *adj.* —**e·lim′i·na′tor** *n.* —**e·lim′i·na·to′ry** (-nə tôr′ē) *adj.*

E·li·nor (el′ə nər, -nôr′) *same as* ELEANOR

El·i·ot (el′ē ət, el′yət) [dim. of ELLIS] **1.** a masculine name **2. Charles William,** 1834–1926; U.S. educator; president of Harvard U. (1869–1909) **3. George,** (pseud. of *Mary Ann Evans*) 1819–80; Eng. novelist **4. John,** 1604–90; Am. clergyman, born in England; known for missionary work among the Am. Indians **5. T(homas) S(tearns),** 1888–1965; Brit. poet & critic, born in the U.S.

E·lis (ē′lis) ancient country in the W Peloponnesus, in which Olympia was located: see GREECE, map

E·lis·a·beth (i liz′ə bəth) *var. of* ELIZABETH¹

E·lis·a·beth·ville (-vil′) *former name of* LUBUMBASHI

E·li·sha (i lī′shə) [Heb. *elishā'*, lit., God is salvation] **1.** a masculine name: dim. *Lish*; var. *Ellis* **2.** *Bible* a prophet of Israel, ordained by Elijah as his successor: I Kings 19:16, 19; II Kings 2

e·li·sion (i lizh′ən) *n.* [L. *elisio*, a striking out (in LL., elision) < pp. of *elidere*: see ELIDE] **1.** the omission, assimilation, or slurring over of a vowel, syllable, etc. in pronunciation: often used in poetry to preserve meter, as when a word ends with a vowel before another word beginning with a vowel (Ex.: "th' inevitable hour") **2.** any act or instance of leaving out or omitting a part or parts

e·lite, é·lite (i lēt′, ā-) *n.* [Fr. *élite* < OFr. *eslite*, fem. pp. of *eslire*, to choose < VL. **exligere*, for L. *eligere*: see ELECT] **1.** [also used with *pl. v.*] the group or part of a group selected or regarded as the finest, best, most distinguished, most powerful, etc. **2.** a size of type for typewriters, measuring twelve characters to the linear inch —*adj.* of, forming, or suitable for an elite

e·lit·ism (-iz′m) *n.* **1.** government or control by an elite **2.** advocacy of such control —**e·lit′ist** *adj., n.*

e·lix·ir (i lik′sər) *n.* [ME. < ML. < Ar. *al-iksir* < *al*, the + *iksir*, philosopher's stone, prob. < Gr. *xērion*, powder for drying wounds < *xēros*, dry: see XERO-] **1.** a hypothetical substance sought for by medieval alchemists to change base metals into gold or (in full, **elixir of life**) to prolong life indefinitely **2.** [Rare] the quintessence; underlying principle **3.** a supposed remedy for all ailments; panacea **4.** *Pharmacy* a medicine made of drugs in alcoholic solution, usually sweetened

Eliz. **1.** Elizabeth **2.** Elizabethan

E·li·za (i lī′zə) a feminine name: dim. *Liza*: see ff.

E·liz·a·beth¹ (i liz′ə bəth) [LL.(Ec.) *Elizabetha* < Gr.(Ec.) *Elisabet* < Heb. *elīsheba'*, lit., God is (my) oath] **1.** a feminine name: dim. *Bess, Bessie, Beth, Betsey, Betty, Elsie, Libby, Lizzie*; var. *Elisabeth, Eliza* **2.** *Bible* the mother of John the Baptist and a kinswoman of Mary: Luke 1 **3.** *see* ELIZABETH PETROVNA **4. Elizabeth I** 1533–1603; queen of England (1558–1603): daughter of HENRY VIII & Anne BOLEYN **5. Elizabeth II** 1926– ; queen of England (1952–): daughter of GEORGE VI

Elizabeth² [after the wife of Sir George Carteret, proprietor] city in NE N.J., adjacent to Newark: pop. 113,000

E·liz·a·be·than (i liz′ə bē′thən, -be·th′ən) *adj.* of or characteristic of the time when Elizabeth I was queen of England —*n.* an English person, esp. a writer, of the time of Queen Elizabeth I

Elizabethan sonnet *same as* SHAKESPEAREAN SONNET

Elizabeth Pe·trov·na (pə trôv′nə) 1709–62; empress of Russia (1741–62): daughter of PETER I

elk (elk) *n., pl.* **elk, elks:** see PLURAL, II, D, 2 [ME., irreg. development (with *-k*) < OE. *eolh,* akin to G. *elch,* ON. *elgr* < Gmc. base **alchis* < IE. base **el-,* stag, hart, whence W. *elain,* doe, Lith. *élnis,* Gr. *elaphos,* deer] **1.** a large, mooselike deer (*Alces alces*) of N Europe and Asia, with broad antlers ☆**2.** *same as* WAPITI **3.** a light, flexible leather of cowhide or calfskin

ELK
(54–60 in. high
at shoulder)

Elk·hart (elk′kärt) [after the nearby *Elkhart* River, transl. of Indian name, allegedly given because of an island at its mouth shaped like an elk's heart] city in N Ind.: pop. 43,000

elk·hound (elk′hound′) *n. same as* NORWEGIAN ELKHOUND

ell[1] (el) *n.* ☆**1.** an extension or wing at right angles to the main structure **2.** an L-shaped joint of piping or tubing

ell[2] (el) *n.* [ME. *elle, elne* < OE. *eln,* akin to G. *elle* < Gmc. **alinō,* lit., arm, hence arm's length < IE. base **elei-,* to bend, **olina,* elbow, whence L. *ulna,* arm, elbow, Gr. *ōlenē,* elbow] a former English measure of length, mainly for cloth, equal to 45 in., or any of various other European measures of different lengths

El·la (el′ə) a feminine name: see ELEANOR

El·len (el′ən) a feminine name: see HELEN

Elles·mere Island (elz′mir) island in the Arctic Ocean, Northwest Territories, Canada, west of NW Greenland: 82,119 sq. mi.

El·lice Islands (el′is) group of islands in the South Pacific, between the Gilbert & Fiji islands: part of the Brit. colony of GILBERT AND ELLICE ISLANDS: 9 1/2 sq. mi.: pop. 7,000

El·ling·ton (el′iŋ tən), **Duke** (born *Edward Kennedy Ellington*) 1899– ; U.S. jazz musician and composer

El·li·ot, El·li·ott (el′ē ət) a masculine name: see ELIOT

el·lipse (i lips′, ə-) *n., pl.* **-lip′ses** (-siz) [ModL. *ellipsis* < Gr. *elleipsis,* a defect, ellipse < *elleipein,* to fall short < *en-,* in + *leipein,* to leave (see LOAN): so named from falling short of a perfect circle] *Geom.* the path of a point that moves so that the sum of its distances from two fixed points (called *foci*) is constant; closed curve produced when a cone is cut by a plane inclined obliquely to the axis and not touching the base

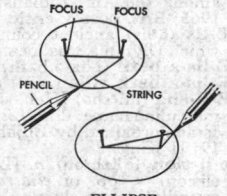

FOCUS   FOCUS

PENCIL   STRING

ELLIPSE

el·lip·sis (i lip′sis, ə-) *n., pl.* **-ses** (-sēz) [L. < Gr. *elleipsis:* see prec.] **1.** *Gram.* the omission of a word or words necessary for complete grammatical construction but understood in the context (Ex.: "if possible" for "if it is possible") **2.** *Writing & Printing a*) a mark (. . . or formerly * * *) indicating an intentional omission of words or letters or an abrupt change of thought, lapse of time, incomplete statement, etc. *b*) the use of such marks

el·lip·soid (-soid) *n.* [Fr. *ellipsoïde:* see ELLIPSE & -OID] *Geom.* **1.** a solid whose plane sections are all ellipses or circles **2.** the surface of such a solid —*adj.* of or shaped like an ellipsoid: also **el·lip′soi′dal**

el·lip·ti·cal (i lip′ti k'l, ə-) *adj.* [< Gr. *elleiptikos* (see ELLIPSE) + -AL] **1.** of, or having the form of, an ellipse, as some leaves **2.** of or characterized by ellipsis; with a word or words omitted, with obscure, incomplete constructions, etc. Also **el·lip′tic** —**el·lip′ti·cal·ly** *adv.*

el·lip·tic·i·ty (i lip′tis′ə tē, ə-) *n.* **1.** the condition of being elliptical; elliptical form **2.** the degree of deviation of an ellipse, elliptical orbit, etc. from circular form, or of a spheroid from spherical form

El·lis (el′is) **1.** a masculine name: see ELISHA **2.** (**Henry**) **Have·lock** (hav′läk, -lək), 1859–1939; Eng. psychologist & writer, esp. on human sexual behavior

Ellis Island [after Sam. *Ellis,* a former owner] small island in Upper New York Bay: former (1892–1943) examination center for immigrants seeking to enter the U.S.

Ellis·worth (elz′wərth) **1. Lincoln,** 1880–1951; U.S. polar explorer **2. Oliver,** 1745–1807; U.S. jurist: chief justice of the U.S. (1796–99)

elm (elm) *adj.* [ME. & OE., akin to OHG. *elm:* see ELDER[2]] designating a family (Ulmaceae) of trees growing largely in the N. Temperate Zone —*n.* **1.** any of a genus (*Ulmus*) of tall, hardy shade trees of the elm family, once widely planted as a lawn tree: see DUTCH ELM DISEASE **2.** the hard, heavy wood of this tree

El·man (el′mən), **Mi·scha** (mish′ə) 1891–1967; U.S. violinist, born in Russia

☆**elm bark beetle** the bark-boring beetle (*Scolytus multistriatus*) that feeds on the bark of elm trees and carries Dutch elm disease

El·mer (el′mər) [ult. < ? OE. *Æthelmær* (< *æthel,* noble + *mære,* famous), or < ? *Egilmær* (< *egil-* < *ege,* awe, dread + *mære*)] a masculine name

Elm·hurst (elm′hurst′) [after the many *elms* set out there

+ *hurst,* a grove] city in NE Ill.: suburb of Chicago: pop. 51,000

El·mi·ra (el mī′rə) [after *Elmira* Teall, child of an early settler] city in SC N.Y.: pop. 40,000

El Mis·ti (el mēs′tē) volcano in S Peru: c. 19,200 ft.

El Mon·te (el män′tē) [Sp., the thicket: after a dense clump of willows there] city in SW Calif.: suburb of Los Angeles: pop. 70,000

El O·beid (el ō bād′) city in C Sudan: pop. 60,000

el·o·cu·tion (el′ə kyōō′shən) *n.* [ME. ellocucioun < L. *elocutio* < pp. of *eloqui:* see ELOQUENT] **1.** style or manner of speaking or reading in public **2.** the art of public speaking or declaiming: now often associated with a studied or artificial style of speaking —**el′o·cu′tion·ar′y** *adj.* —**el′o·cu′tion·ist** *n.*

e·lo·de·a (i lō′dē ə) *n.* [ModL., name of the genus < Gr. *helōdēs,* swampy < *helos,* a swamp < IE. **selos-,* whence Sans. *sáras-,* a lake, pool] any of a genus (*Elodea*) of submerged water plants of the frog's-bit family, with whorls of short, strap-shaped leaves and white floating flowers: often grown as aquarium plants

E·lo·him (e lō′him; Heb. e lō hēm′) [Heb. *elōhīm,* pl. of *elōah,* God] God: name used in parts of the Hebrew scriptures: see JEHOVAH

E·lo·hist (e lō′hist) the unknown author of those parts of the Hebrew scriptures in which the name *Elohim,* instead of *Yahweh* (Jehovah), is used for God: see YAHWIST —**El·o·his·tic** (el′ō his′tik) *adj.*

e·loign, e·loin (i loin′) *vt.* [ME. *eloinen* < OFr. *esloignier* < *es-* (L. *ex-*) + L. *longe,* far (*adv.*): see LONG[1]] **1.** [Archaic] to take (oneself) away; seclude (oneself) **2.** to carry away (property) **3.** *Law* to remove (private property) beyond the jurisdiction of a sheriff, etc. —*n.* a return by a sheriff stating that goods to be seized to satisfy a just debt have been removed from the jurisdiction —**e·loign′ment, e·loin′ment** *n.*

El·o·ise (el′ə wēz′, el′ə wēz′) a feminine name: equiv. Fr. *Héloïse:* see LOUISE

e·lon·gate (i lôŋ′gāt) *vt., vi.* **-gat·ed, -gat·ing** [< LL. *elongatus,* pp. of *elongare,* to prolong < L. *e-,* out + *longus,* LONG[1]] to make or become longer; stretch —*adj.* **1.** lengthened; stretched **2.** *Bot.* long and narrow, as certain leaves —*SYN.* see EXTEND

e·lon·ga·tion (i lôŋ′gā′shən, ē′lôŋ-) *n.* [ME. *elongacioun* < ML. *elongatio*] **1.** an elongating or being elongated; lengthening; extension **2.** something elongated; lengthened part; continuation **3.** the angular distance in degrees of a planet or the moon from the sun, as viewed from the earth

e·lope (i lōp′, ə-) *vi.* **e·loped′, e·lop′ing** [Anglo-Fr. *aloper,* prob. < ME. **aleapen,* to leap up, run away < OE. *ahleapan* (infl. ? by cognate ON. *hlaupa,* to run, whence LOPE) < *a-,* away + *hleapan,* to run, LEAP] **1.** to run away secretly, esp. in order to get married **2.** to run away; escape; abscond —**e·lope′ment** *n.* —**e·lop′er** *n.*

el·o·quence (el′ə kwəns) *n.* [ME. & OFr. < L. *eloquentia:* see ff.] **1.** speech or writing that is vivid, forceful, fluent, graceful, and persuasive **2.** the art or manner of such speech or writing **3.** persuasive power

el·o·quent (-kwənt) *adj.* [ME. & OFr. < L. *eloquens,* prp. of *eloqui,* to speak out, utter < *e-,* out + *loqui,* to speak] **1.** having, or characterized by, eloquence; fluent, forceful, and persuasive **2.** vividly expressive [an *eloquent* sigh] —**el′o·quent·ly** *adv.*

El Pas·o (el pas′ō) [Sp., earlier *El Paso del Norte,* ford (of the river) of the north] city in westernmost Tex., on the Rio Grande: pop. 322,000

El·sa (el′sə) [G. < ?] a feminine name

El Sal·va·dor (el sal′və dôr′; *Sp.* säl′vä thôr′) country in Central America, southwest of Honduras, on the Pacific: 8,260 sq. mi.; pop. 3,390,000; cap. San Salvador

else (els) *adj.* [ME. & OE. *elles,* adv. gen. of n. base *el-,* other (as in OE. *el-land,* foreign land), akin to Goth. *aljis,* OHG. *elles,* of same formation < IE. base **al-,* that, yonder one, whence L. *alius,* another, *alienus,* belonging to another, Gr. *allos,* other] **1.** different; other [somebody *else*] **2.** in addition; more [is there anything *else?*] *Else* follows the word modified and after a pronoun takes the possessive inflection [anybody *else's*] —*adv.* **1.** in a different or additional time, place, or manner; differently; otherwise [where *else* can I go?] **2.** if not [study, (or) *else* you will fail]

else·where (-hwer′, -wer′) *adv.* [ME. *elleswher* < OE. *elleshwær*] in or to some other place; somewhere else

El·sie (el′sē) a feminine name: see ALICE, ELIZABETH[1], ELSA

El·si·nore (el′sə nôr′) *Eng. name of* HELSINGØR, Denmark, as in Shakespeare's *Hamlet*

É·lu·ard (ā lü ár′), **Paul** (pôl) (pseud. of *Eugène Grindel*) 1895–1952; Fr. poet

el·u·ate (el′yoo wit, -wāt′) *n.* the solution that results from eluting

e·lu·ci·date (i lōō′sə dāt′, ə-) *vt., vi.* **-dat·ed, -dat·ing** [< LL. *elucidatus,* pp. of *elucidare,* to make light or clear < L. *e-,* out + *lucidus,* light, clear < *lux,* LIGHT[1]] to make clear (esp. something abstruse); explain —*SYN.* see EXPLAIN —**e·lu′ci·da′tion** *n.* —**e·lu′ci·da′tive** *adj.* —**e·lu′ci·da′tor** *n.*

e·lu·cu·bra·tion (i lōō′kə brā′shən) *n. same as* LUCUBRATION

e·lude (i lood′) *vt.* **e·lud′ed, e·lud′ing** [L. *eludere*, to finish play, parry a blow, frustrate < *e-*, out + *ludere*, to play] **1.** to avoid or escape from by quickness, cunning, etc.; evade **2.** to escape detection, notice, or understanding by [*his name eludes me*] —*SYN.* see ESCAPE

El·ul (el′ool) *n.* [Heb. *elūl*] the twelfth month of the Jewish year: see JEWISH CALENDAR

e·lu·sion (i loo′zhən, ə-) *n.* [LL. *elusio* < L. *elusus*, pp. of *eludere*] an eluding; escape or avoidance by quickness or cunning; evasion

e·lu·sive (-siv) *adj.* [< L. *elusus* (see ELUSION) + -IVE] **1.** tending to elude **2.** hard to grasp or retain mentally; baffling Also, rarely, **e·lu′so·ry** (-sə rē) —**e·lu′sive·ly** *adv.* —**e·lu′sive·ness** *n.*

e·lute (i loot′) *vt.* **e·lut′ed, e·lut′ing** [< L. *elutus*, pp. of *eluere*, to wash out: see ELUTRIATE] to remove (adsorbed material) by use of a solvent —**e·lu′tion** *n.*

e·lu·tri·ate (i loo′trē āt′) *vt.* **-at′ed, -at′ing** [< L. *elutriatus*, pp. of *elutriare*, to wash out, rack off < *eluere* < *e-*, out + *luere*, to wash: see LAVE¹] to purify by washing and straining or by decanting —**e·lu′tri·a′tion** *n.*

e·lu·vi·al (i loo′vē əl) *adj.* of or relating to eluvium or to eluviation

e·lu·vi·ate (-āt′) *vi.* **-at′ed, -at′ing** to be subjected to eluviation

e·lu·vi·a·tion (i loo′vē ā′shən) *n.* [see ff. & -ATION] the weathering of rocks in place and the movement of soil material in solution or in suspension downward or sidewise by water

e·lu·vi·um (i loo′vē əm) *n.* [ModL. < L. *eluere* (see ELUTRIATE), after L. *alluvium*: see ALLUVIUM] an accumulation of dust and soil particles caused by the weathering and disintegration of rocks in place, or deposited by drifting winds: distinguished from ALLUVIUM

el·ver (el′vər) *n.* [for *eelfare*, the passage of young eels up a stream] a young eel, esp. a young freshwater eel that has migrated from saltwater, where it first develops by metamorphosis from the larval stage

elves (elvz) *n. pl.* of ELF

El·vi·ra (el vī′rə, -vir′ə) [Sp., prob. < Goth.] a feminine name

elv·ish (el′vish) *adj. same as* ELFISH —**elv′ish·ly** *adv.*

E·ly (ē′lē) **1.** urban district in the Isle of Ely: pop. 10,000 **2. Isle of,** county in EC England: 375 sq. mi.; pop. 90,000: see also CAMBRIDGESHIRE

El·y·ot (el′ē ət, el′yət), Sir **Thomas** 1490?–1546; Eng. writer & diplomat

E·lyr·i·a (i lir′ē ə, ə-) [after Justin *Ely*, proprietor, and M*aria*, his wife; ? infl. by ILLYRIA] city in N Ohio, near Cleveland: pop. 53,000

E·ly·sian (i lizh′ən, -ē ən) *adj.* **1.** in or like Elysium **2.** happy; blissful; delightful

E·ly·si·um (i lizh′ē əm, -liz′-) [L. < Gr. *Ēlysion* (*pedion*), Elysian (plain), plain of the departed] *Gr. Myth.* the dwelling place of virtuous people after death —*n.* any place or condition of ideal bliss or complete happiness; paradise Also **Elysian fields**

el·y·troid (el′ə troid′) *adj.* like an elytron

el·y·tron (-trän′) *n., pl.* **-tra** (-trə) [ModL. < Gr. *elytron*, a covering, sheath < IE. *welutrom* < base *wel-*, to roll: cf. WALK] either of the front pair of modified, usually thickened, wings in beetles, which act as protective covering for the rear wings: also **el′y·trum** (-trəm), *pl.* **-tra** (-trə)

El·ze·vir (el′zə vir′) family of Du. printers & publishers of the 16th & 17th cent., esp. **1. Bon·a·ven·ture** (bän′ə ven′chər), 1583–1652: son of *ff.* **2. Louis,** 1540?–1617; founder of his family's printing tradition

em (em) *n.* **1.** the letter M, m **2.** *Printing* formerly, the letter M of any given font, now a square of any type body, used as a unit of measure, as of column width; esp., an em pica, equal to about 1/6 of an inch

'em (əm, 'm) *pron.* [taken as corruption of THEM, but also < ME. *hem*, dat. pl. of 3d pers. pron. used as acc. & later replaced by THEM] [Colloq.] them

em- (im, em) *same as* EN-¹, used before bilabial consonants *p, b, m*

EM 1. electromagnetic **2.** engineer of mines: also **E.M. 3.** enlisted man (or men)

Em *Chem. symbol for* EMANATION (sense 3 *a*)

e·ma·ci·ate (i mā′shē āt′, -sē-) *vt.* **-at′ed, -at′ing** [< L. *emaciatus*, pp. of *emaciare*, to make lean < *e₂*, out + *macies*, leanness < *macer*, lean < IE. base *mak-*, whence OE. *mæger*, lean] to cause to become abnormally lean; cause to lose much flesh or weight, as by starvation or disease — **e·ma′ci·a′tion** *n.*

em·a·nate (em′ə nāt′) *vi.* **-nat′ed, -nat′ing** [< L. *emanatus*, pp. of *emanare*, to flow out, arise < *e-*, out + *manare*, to flow] to come forth; issue, as from a source —*vt.* [Rare] to send forth; emit —*SYN.* see RISE

em·a·na·tion (em′ə nā′shən) *n.* [LL. *emanatio*] **1.** the act of emanating **2.** something that comes forth from a source; thing emitted **3.** *Chem. a) same as* RADON *b)* a gaseous radioactive species liberated by several natural and artificial radioactive series —**em′a·na′tive** *adj.*

e·man·ci·pate (i man′sə pāt′) *vt.* **-pat′ed, -pat′ing** [< L.

emancipatus, pp. of *emancipare* < *e-*, out + *mancipare*, to deliver up or make over as property < *manceps*, purchaser < *manus*, the hand + *capere*, to take] **1.** to set free (a slave, etc.); release from bondage, servitude, or serfdom **2.** to free from restraint or influence, as of convention **3.** *Law* to release (a child) from parental control and supervision —*SYN.* see FREE —**e·man′ci·pa′tion** *n.* —**e·man′ci·pa′tive, e·man′ci·pa·to′ry** (-pə tôr′ē) *adj.* —**e·man′ci·pa′tor** *n.*

☆**Emancipation Proclamation** a proclamation issued by President Lincoln in September, 1862, effective January 1, 1863, freeing the slaves in all territory still at war with the Union

E·man·u·el (i man′yoo wəl, -wel′) *var.* of EMMANUEL

e·mar·gi·nate (i mär′jə nit, -nāt′) *adj.* [L. *emarginatus*, pp. of *emarginare*, to deprive of its edge: see E- & MARGINATE] having a notched margin or tip, as some leaves or wings: also **e·mar′gi·nat′ed**

e·mas·cu·late (i mas′kyə lāt′; *for adj.* -lit) *vt.* **-lat′ed, -lat′ing** [< L. *emasculatus*, pp. of *emasculare* < *e-*, out + *masculus*, MASCULINE] **1.** to deprive (a male) of the power to reproduce, as by removing the testicles; castrate; geld **2.** to destroy the strength or force of; weaken [a novel *emasculated* by censorship] —*adj.* deprived of virility, strength, or vigor; effeminate —**e·mas′cu·la′tion** *n.* — **e·mas′cu·la′tive, e·mas′cu·la·to′ry** (-lə tôr′ē) *adj.* — **e·mas′cu·la′tor** *n.*

em·balm (im bäm′) *vt.* [ME. *embaumen* < OFr. *embaumer:* see EN-¹ & BALM] **1.** to treat (a dead body) with various chemicals, usually after removing the viscera, etc., to keep it from decaying rapidly **2.** to preserve in memory **3.** to make fragrant; perfume —**em·balm′er** *n.* —**em·balm′ment** *n.*

em·bank (im bank′) *vt.* to protect, support, or enclose with a bank or banks of earth, rubble, etc.

em·bank·ment (-mənt) *n.* **1.** the act or process of embanking **2.** a bank of earth, rubble, etc. used to keep back water, hold up a roadway, or the like

☆**em·bar·ca·der·o** (em bär′kə der′ō) *n., pl.* **-der′os** [Sp. < pp. of *embarcar*, EMBARK] a wharf, dock, or pier

em·bar·go (im bär′gō) *n., pl.* **-goes** [Sp. < *embargar* < VL. *imbarricare* < L. *in-*, in, on + ML. *barra*, BAR¹] **1.** a government order prohibiting the entry or departure of commercial ships at its ports, esp. as a war measure **2.** any restriction or restraint, esp. one imposed on commerce by law; specif., *a)* a prohibition of trade in a particular commodity *b)* a prohibition or restriction of freight transportation —*vt.* **-goed, -go·ing** to put an embargo upon

em·bark (-bärk′) *vt.* [Fr. *embarquer* < Sp. or OPr. *embarcar* < *em-* (L. *in-*) + L. *barca*, BARK³] **1.** to put or take (passengers or goods) aboard a ship, airplane, etc. **2.** to engage (a person) or invest (money, etc.) in an enterprise —*vi.* **1.** to go aboard a ship, airplane, etc. **2.** to begin a journey **3.** to engage in an enterprise —**em·bar·ka′tion, em·bar·ca′tion** (em′bär kā′shən), **em·bark′ment** *n.*

‡**em·bar·ras de ri·chesses** (än bà rä′ də rē shes′) [Fr.] literally, an embarrassment of wealth (of good things); hence, too much to choose from

em·bar·rass (im ber′əs) *vt.* [Fr. *embarrasser*, lit., to encumber, obstruct < Sp. *embarazar* < It. *imbarrazzare* < *imbarrare*, to bar, impede < *in-* (L. *in-*) + *barra*, BAR¹] **1.** to cause to feel self-conscious, confused, and ill at ease; disconcert; fluster **2.** to cause difficulties to; hinder; impede **3.** to cause to be in debt; cause financial difficulties to **4.** to make more difficult; complicate —**em·bar′rass·ing** *adj.* —**em·bar′rass·ing·ly** *adv.* —**em·bar′rass·ment** *n.* *SYN.*—to **embarrass** is to cause to feel ill at ease so as to result in a loss of composure [*embarrassed* by their compliments]; **abash** implies a sudden loss of self-confidence and a growing feeling of shame or inadequacy [I stood *abashed* at his rebukes]; **discomfit** implies a frustration of plans or expectations and often connotes a resultant feeling of discomposure or humiliation; to **disconcert** is to cause to lose quickly one's self-possession so as to result in confusion or mental disorganization [his interruptions were *disconcerting*]; **rattle** and **faze** are colloquial equivalents for **disconcert**, but the former emphasizes emotional agitation, and the latter is most commonly used in negative constructions [danger does not *faze* him] —*ANT.* compose, assure

em·bas·sa·dor (im bas′ə dər) *n. same as* AMBASSADOR

em·bas·sage (em′bə sij) *n. archaic var.* of EMBASSY

em·bas·sy (em′bə sē) *n., pl.* **-sies** [earlier *ambassy* < MFr. *ambassée* < OIt. *ambasciata* < Pr. *ambaisada* < *ambaissa:* see AMBASSADOR] **1.** the position, functions, or business of an ambassador **2.** the official residence or offices of an ambassador in a foreign country **3.** an ambassador and his staff **4.** a person or group sent on an official mission to a foreign government **5.** any important or official mission, errand, or message

em·bat·tle¹ (im bat′'l) *vt.* **-tled, -tling** [ME. *embataillen:* see EN-¹ & BATTLEMENT] to provide with battlements; build battlements on

em·bat·tle² (-bat′'l) *vt.* **-tled, -tling** [ME. *embatailen* < OFr. *embataillier* < *en-* (L. *in-*), in + *bataille:* see BATTLE¹] **1.** [Rare, except in pp.] to prepare, array, or set in line for battle **2.** to fortify

em·bay (im bā′) *vt.* **1.** to put or force (a boat, etc.) into a

bay for protection or shelter **2.** to shut in; enclose or surround, as in a bay

em·bay·ment (-mənt) *n.* **1.** a forming into a bay **2.** a bay or a formation resembling a bay

em·bed (im bed′) *vt.* **-bed′ded, -bed′ding 1.** to set (flowers, etc.) in earth **2.** to set or fix firmly in a surrounding mass *[to embed tiles in cement]* **3.** to fix in the mind, memory, etc. **—em·bed′ment** *n.*

em·bel·lish (im bel′ish) *vt.* [ME. *embelishen* < extended stem of OFr. *embelir* < *em-* (L. *in*) + *bel* < L. *bellus,* beautiful] **1.** to decorate or improve by adding detail; ornament; adorn **2.** to add grace notes, syncopated accents, trills, etc. to (a melody, etc.) **3.** to improve (a story, etc.) by adding details, often of a fictitious kind; touch up **—SYN.** see ADORN

em·bel·lish·ment (-mənt) *n.* **1.** an embellishing or being embellished; ornamentation **2.** something that embellishes, as an ornament, a fictitious touch added to a story, a grace note, etc.

em·ber[1] (em′bər) *n.* [ME. *eymere* & (with intrusive -*b*) *eymbre* < OE. *æmerge* (& cognate ON. *eimyrja*) < *æm-* (akin to ON. *eimr,* steam) + -*yrge* (akin to ON. *ysja,* fire) < IE. base **eus-,* to burn, whence L. *urere,* to burn] **1.** a glowing piece of coal, wood, etc. from a fire; esp., such a piece smoldering among ashes **2.** *[pl.]* the smoldering remains of a fire

em·ber[2] (em′bər) *adj.* [ME. (SE dial.) *embyr-,* as in *embyr-dayes* < OE. *ymbren,* lit., a coming around < *ymbryne,* circuit, revolution < *ymb,* round (akin to AMBI-) + *ryne,* a running (< base of RUN)] *[often* E-] designating or of three days (Wednesday, Friday, and Saturday) set aside for prayer and fasting in a specified week of each of the four seasons of the year: observed in the Roman Catholic and certain other churches

em·bez·zle (im bez′'l) *vt.* **-zled, -zling** [ME. *embesilen* < Anglo-Fr. *enbesiler* < OFr. *embesillier* < *en-* (see EN-[1]) + *besillier,* to destroy] to steal (money, etc. entrusted to one's care); take by fraud for one's own use **—em·bez′zle·ment** *n.* **—em·bez′zler** *n.*

em·bit·ter (-bit′ər) *vt.* **1.** to make bitter; make resentful or morose **2.** to make more bitter; exacerbate; aggravate **—em·bit′ter·ment** *n.*

em·blaze[1] (-blāz′) *vt.* **-blazed′, -blaz′ing** [EM- + BLAZE[1]] [Archaic] **1.** to light up; illuminate **2.** to set on fire; kindle

em·blaze[2] (-blāz′) *vt.* **-blazed′, -blaz′ing** [EM- + BLAZE[3]] *archaic var. of* EMBLAZON

em·bla·zon (im blā′z'n) *vt.* [see BLAZON] **1.** to decorate or adorn *(with* coats of arms, etc.) **2.** to display brilliantly; decorate with bright colors **3.** to spread the fame of; praise; celebrate **—em·bla′zon·ment** *n.*

em·bla·zon·ry (-rē) *n., pl.* **-ries 1.** heraldic decoration **2.** any brilliant decoration or display

em·blem (em′bləm) *n.* [orig., inlaid work < L. *emblema* < Gr. *emblēma,* insertion < *emballein* < *en-,* in + *ballein,* to throw, put: see BALL[2]] **1.** formerly, a picture with a motto or verses, allegorically suggesting some moral truth, etc. **2.** a visible symbol of a thing, idea, class of people, etc.; object or representation that stands for or suggests something else *[the cross is an emblem of Christianity]* **3.** a sign, badge, or device **—** *vt.* [Rare] to emblematize

em·blem·at·ic (em′blə mat′ik) *adj.* of, containing, or serving as an emblem; symbolic: also **em′blem·at′i·cal** **—em′blem·at′i·cal·ly** *adv.*

em·blem·a·tize (em blem′ə tīz′) *vt.* **-tized′, -tiz′ing 1.** to be an emblem of; symbolize **2.** to represent by or as by an emblem Also **em′blem·ize′, -ized′, -iz′ing**

em·ble·ments (em′blə mənts) *n.pl.* [ME. *enblaymentez* < OFr. *emblaement* (sing.) < *emblaer* < *en-* (L. *in-*) + *blee,* grain < WGmc. base akin to G. *blatt,* leaf, MDu. *blat,* BLADE] *Law* **1.** cultivated growing crops which are produced annually **2.** the profits from such crops

em·bod·i·ment (im bäd′ē mənt) *n.* **1.** an embodying or being embodied **2.** that in which something is embodied; concrete expression of some idea, quality, etc. *[she is the embodiment of virtue]*

em·bod·y (-bäd′ē) *vt.* **-bod′ied, -bod′y·ing 1.** to give bodily form to; make corporeal; incarnate **2.** to give definite, tangible, or visible form to; make concrete *[a speech embodying democratic ideals]* **3.** to bring together into an organized whole *[the laws embodied in a legal code]* **4.** to make part of an organized whole; incorporate *[the latest findings embodied in the new book]*

em·bold·en (-bōl′d'n) *vt.* [EM- + BOLD + -EN] to give courage to; cause to be bold or bolder

em·bo·lec·to·my (em′bə lek′tə mē) *n.* [EMBOL(US) + -ECTOMY] the surgical removal of an embolus

em·bol·ic (em bäl′ik) *adj.* **1.** of or caused by embolism or an embolus **2.** of or during emboly

em·bo·lism (em′bə liz′m) *n.* [ME. *embolisme* < LL. *embolismus* < Gr. *embolismos,* intercalary < *embolos:* see ff.] **1.** the intercalation of a day, month, etc. into a calendar, as in leap year **2.** the time intercalated **3.** *Med.* **a)** the obstruction of a blood vessel by an embolus too large to pass through it **b)** loosely, an embolus

em·bo·lus (-ləs) *n., pl.* **-li** (-lī) [ModL. < Gr. *embolos,* anything put in, wedge < *emballein* < *en-,* in + *ballein,* to throw: see BALL[2]] any foreign matter, as a blood clot or air bubble, carried in the bloodstream

em·bo·ly (-lē) *n.* [< Gr. *embolē,* insertion, lit., a putting in

< *emballein:* see EMBOLUS] *Embryology* the process by which cells move inward during gastrulation to form the archenteron

‡em·bon·point (äⁿ bôⁿ pwaⁿ′) *n.* [Fr. < OFr. *en bon point,* lit., in good condition] plumpness; corpulence

em·bos·om (im booz′əm, -bōō′zəm) *vt.* **1.** to take to one's bosom; embrace; cherish **2.** to enclose protectively; surround; shelter

em·boss (-bôs′, -bäs′) *vt.* [ME. *embocen* < OFr. *embocer:* see EN-[1] & BOSS[2]] **1.** to decorate or cover with designs, patterns, etc. raised above the surface **2.** to carve, raise, or print (a design, etc.) so that it is raised above the surface; raise in relief **3.** to embellish; ornament **—em·boss′er** *n.* **—em·boss′ment** *n.*

em·bou·chure (äm′boo shoor′, äm′boo shoor′) *n.* [Fr. < *emboucher,* to put into the mouth < VL. **imbuccare* < L. *in,* in + *bucca,* the cheek] **1.** the mouth of a river **2.** *Music* **a)** the mouthpiece of a wind instrument **b)** the method of applying the lips and tongue to the mouthpiece of a wind instrument

em·bow (im bō′) *vt.* [ME. *embouen:* see EM- & BOW[2]] [Archaic except in pp.] to bend into the form of an arch or bow *[a dolphin embowed on the shield]*

em·bow·el (-bou′əl, -boul′) *vt.* **-eled** or **-elled, -el·ing** or **-el·ling** [OFr. *enboweler,* altered < *esbouler* < *es-* (L. *ex*), out of + *bouel,* BOWEL] **1.** *rare var. of* DISEMBOWEL **2.** [EM- + BOWEL] [Obs.] to embed deeply

em·bow·er (-bou′ər) *vt.* to enclose or shelter in or as in a bower

em·brace[1] (-brās′) *vt.* **-braced′, -brac′ing** [ME. *embracen* < OFr. *embracier* < VL. **imbrachiare* < L. *im-,* in + *brachium,* an arm: see BRACE[1]] **1.** to clasp in the arms, usually as an expression of affection or desire; hug **2.** to accept readily; avail oneself of *[to embrace an opportunity]* **3.** to take up or adopt, esp. eagerly or seriously *[to embrace a new profession]* **4.** to encircle; surround; enclose *[an isle embraced by the sea]* **5.** to include; contain *[biology embraces botany and zoology]* **6.** to take in mentally; perceive *[his glance embraced the scene]* **—vi.** to clasp or hug each other in the arms **—n.** an embracing; hug **—SYN.** see INCLUDE **—em·brace′a·ble** *adj.* **—em·brace′ment** *n.* **—em·brac′er** *n.*

em·brace[2] (-brās′) *vt.* **-braced′, -brac′ing** [ME. *embrasen* < OFr. *embraser,* to set on fire, incite < *en-,* in + *braise,* live coals: see BRAISE] *Law* to try illegally to influence or instruct (a jury)

em·bra·ceor, em·bra·cer (-brā′sər) *n.* [ME. *embracer* < OFr. *embraseor:* see prec.] *Law* a person guilty of embracery

em·brac·er·y (-brā′sər ē) *n.* [ME. *embracerie:* see EM-BRACE[2]] *Law* an illegal attempt to influence or instruct a jury

em·branch·ment (-branch′mənt, -bränch′-) *n.* a branching out or off, as of a river, etc.; ramification

em·bran·gle (-braŋ′g'l) *vt.* **-gled, -gling** [EM- + dial. *brangle,* to wrangle, prob. var. of WRANGLE, infl. ? by Fr. *branler,* to confuse] to entangle; mix up; confuse; perplex **—em·bran′gle·ment** *n.*

em·bra·sure (im brā′zhər) *n.* [Fr. < obs. *embraser,* to widen an opening < *em-* (L. *in*), in + ? *braser,* akin to BRAISE] **1.** an opening (for a door, window, etc.), esp. one with the sides slanted so that it is wider on the inside than on the outside **2.** an opening (in a wall or parapet) with the sides slanting outward to increase the angle of fire of a gun

em·bro·cate (em′brō kāt′, -brə-) *vt.* **-cat′ed, -cat′ing** [< LL. *embrocatus,* pp. of *embrocare,* to foment < L. *embrocha,* wet poultice < Gr. *embrochē* < *embrechein* < *en-,* in + *brechein,* to wet < IE. base **meregh-,* whence Czech *mrholiti,* to drizzle] to moisten and rub (a part of the body) with an oil, liniment, etc.

em·bro·ca·tion (em′brō kā′shən, -brə-) *n.* **1.** an embrocating **2.** a liquid used in embrocating; liniment, etc.

em·broi·der (im broi′dər) *vt.* [ME. *embrouderen* < OFr. *embroder:* see EN-[1] & BROIDER] **1.** to ornament (fabric) with a design in needlework **2.** to make (a design, etc.) on fabric with needlework **3.** to embellish (a story, etc.); add fanciful details to; exaggerate **—vi. 1.** to do embroidery **2.** to exaggerate **—em·broi′der·er** *n.*

em·broi·der·y (-ē) *n., pl.* **-der·ies** [ME. *embrouderie:* see prec. & -ERY] **1.** the art or work of ornamenting fabric with needlework; embroidering **2.** embroidered work or fabric; ornamental needlework **3.** embellishment, as of a story **4.** something superficial or unnecessary that attractive or desirable

em·broil (im broil′) *vt.* [Fr. *embrouiller:* see EN-[1] & BROIL[2]] **1.** to confuse (affairs, etc.); mix up; muddle **2.** to draw into a conflict or fight; involve in trouble **—em·broil′ment** *n.*

em·brown (-broun′) *vt.* to make darker in color; esp., to make brown or tan

em·brue (-broo′) *vt.* **-brued′, -bru′ing** *same as* IMBRUE

em·bry·ec·to·my (em′brē ek′tə mē) *n., pl.* **-ec·to·mies** [EMBRY(O)- + -ECTOMY] the surgical removal of an embryo, esp. in cases of pregnancy outside of the uterus

em·bry·o (em′brē ō′) *n., pl.* **-os′** [ME. *embrio* < ML. *embryo* < Gr. *embryon,* embryo, fetus, thing newly born, neut. of *embryos,* growing in < *en-* + *bryein,* to swell, be full] **1.** an animal in the earliest stages of its development in the uterus: the human organism up to the third month after conception is called an *embryo,* thereafter a *fetus* **2.**

a) an early or undeveloped stage of something *b*) anything in such a stage **3.** the rudimentary plant contained in a seed, usually made up of hypocotyl, radicle, plumule, and cotyledons —*adj. same as* EMBRYONIC

em·bry·o- (em′brē ō) *a combining form meaning* embryo, embryonic *[embryology]:* also, before a vowel, **em′bry-**

em·bry·og·e·ny (em′brē äj′ə nē) *n.* [EMBRYO- + -GENY] the formation and development of the embryo: also **em′bry·o·gen′e·sis** (-ō jen′ə sis) —**em′bry·o·gen′ic** (-jen′ik), **em′bry·o·ge·net′ic** (-jə net′ik) *adj.*

em·bry·ol·o·gy (-äl′ə jē) *n.* [EMBRYO- + -LOGY] the branch of biology dealing with the formation and development of embryos —**em′bry·o·log′ic** (-ə läj′ik), **em′bry·o·log′i·cal** *adj.* —**em′bry·o·log′i·cal·ly** *adv.* —**em′bry·ol′o·gist** *n.*

em·bry·on·ic (-än′ik) *adj.* **1.** of or like an embryo: also **em·bry·o·nal** (em′brē ə n′l) **2.** in an early stage; undeveloped; rudimentary

embryonic membrane any of several living membranes enclosing or closely associated with the developing vertebrate embryo, as the allantois, amnion, yolk sac, etc.

embryo sac *Bot.* the female gametophyte of a flowering plant, consisting typically of a microscopic lozenge-shaped sac in the center of the immature seed, containing eight nuclei in seven cells: it gives rise to the embryo and endosperm of the seed after fertilization

☆**em·cee** (em′sē′) *vt., vi.* **-ceed′, -cee′ing** [< M.C., sense 2] [Colloq.] to act as master of ceremonies (for) —*n.* [Colloq.] a master of ceremonies

Em·den (em′dən) seaport in NW West Germany, on the Ems River estuary: pop. 43,000

e·meer (ə mir′) *n. same as* EMIR —**e·meer′ate** (-it) *n.*

Em·e·line (em′ə lin′, -lēn′) a feminine name: see EMILY

e·mend (i mend′) *vt.* [ME. *emenden* < L. *emendare,* AMEND] **1.** [Rare] to correct or improve **2.** to make scholarly corrections or improvements in (a text)

e·men·date (ē′mən dāt′) *vt.* **-dat′ed, -dat′ing** [< L. *emendatus,* pp. of *emendare*] *same as* EMEND, sense 2 —**e′men·da′tor** *n.* —**e·men·da·to·ry** (i men′də tôr′ē) *adj.*

e·men·da·tion (ē′mən dā′shən, em′ən-) *n.* [ME. *emenda cioun* < L. *emendatio*] **1.** the act of emending **2.** correction or change made in a text, as in an attempt to restore the original reading

em·er·ald (em′ər əld, em′rəld) *n.* [ME. & OFr. *emeralde* < VL. *smaraldus,* for L. *smaragdus* < Gr. *smaragdos,* of Oriental orig.] **1.** a bright-green, transparent precious stone; green variety of beryl **2.** a similar variety of corundum **3.** bright green **4.** *Printing* a size of type between minion and nonpareil, about 6 1/2 point —*adj.* **1.** bright-green **2.** made of or with an emerald or emeralds **3.** designating or of a cut of gem in a rectangular style used esp. with emeralds

Emerald Isle [after its green landscape] Ireland

e·merge (i murj′) *vi.* **e·merged′, e·merg′ing** [L. *emergere* < *e-,* out + *mergere,* to dip, immerse] **1.** to rise from or as from a surrounding fluid **2.** *a*) to come forth into view; become visible *b*) to become apparent or known **3.** to develop or evolve as something new, improved, etc. *[a strong breed emerged]*

e·mer·gence (i mur′jəns) *n.* [< L. *emergens,* prp. of *emergere*] **1.** an emerging **2.** an outgrowth from beneath the outer layer of a plant, as a rose thorn

e·mer·gen·cy (-jən sē) *n., pl.* **-cies** [orig. sense, emergence: see prec.] a sudden, generally unexpected occurrence or set of circumstances demanding immediate action —*adj.* for use in case of sudden necessity *[an emergency brake]*
SYN.—emergency refers to any sudden or unforeseen situation that requires immediate action *[the flood had created an emergency]*; **exigency** may refer either to such a situation or to the need or urgency arising from it *[the exigencies of the moment require drastic action]*; **contingency** is used of an emergency regarded as remotely possible in the future *[prepare for any contingency]*; **crisis** refers to an event regarded as a turning point which will decisively determine an outcome *[an economic crisis]*; **strait** (or **straits**) refers to a trying situation from which it is difficult to extricate oneself *[the loss left them in dire straits]*

e·mer·gent (-jənt) *adj.* [< L. *emergens,* prp. of *emergere*] **1.** emerging **2.** arising unexpectedly or as a new or improved development

e·mer·i·tus (i mer′ə təs) *adj.* [L., pp. of *emereri,* to serve out one's time < *e-,* out + *mereri,* to serve, earn, MERIT] retired from active service, usually for age, but retaining one's rank or title *[professor emeritus]* —*n., pl.* **-ti** (-tī′) a person with such status

e·mersed (ē murst′) *adj.* [< L. *emersus* (pp. of *emergere,* EMERGE) + -ED] having emerged above the surface; specif., standing out above the water, as the leaves of certain aquatic plants

e·mer·sion (ē mur′zhən, -shən) *n.* [< L. *emersus:* see prec.] an emerging; emergence

Em·er·son (em′ər sən), **Ralph Waldo** 1803–82; U.S. essayist, philosopher, & poet

Em·er·y (em′ər ē) [prob. by way of OFr. *Aimeri* < OHG. *Amalrich,* lit., work ruler < **amal-,* work (in battle) + **rich,* ruler (akin to L. *rex,* king)] a masculine name: equiv. L. *Almericus,* Ger. *Emmerich,* It. *Amerigo*

em·er·y (em′ər ē, em′rē) *n.* [Fr. *émeri* < OFr. *emeril* < It. *smeriglio* < MedGr. *smeri,* for Gr. *smyris,* emery < IE. base **smer-,* SMEAR] a dark, very hard, coarse variety of corundum used for grinding, polishing, etc.

emery board a small, flat stick coated with powdered emery, used as a manicuring instrument

emery cloth cloth coated with a mixture of powdered emery and glue, used for polishing and cleaning metal

emery wheel a wheel composed of emery or surfaced with emery, used in grinding, polishing, cutting, etc.

em·e·sis (em′ə sis) *n.* [ModL. < Gr. *emesis:* see ff.] vomiting

e·met·ic (i met′ik) *adj.* [L. *emeticus* < Gr. *emetikos* < *emein,* to vomit < IE. base **wemē-,* VOMIT] causing vomiting —*n.* an emetic medicine or other substance

em·e·tine (em′ə tēn′, -tin) *n.* [EMET(IC) + -INE⁴] an emetic alkaloid, $C_{29}H_{40}N_2O_4$, obtained from ipecac root, used chiefly in the treatment of amebiasis

e·meu (ē′myoō) *n. same as* EMU

‡**é·meute** (ā mōt′) *n.* [Fr. < pp. of *émouvoir,* to agitate: see EMOTION] a popular uprising; riot

E.M.F., e.m.f., EMF, emf electromotive force

-e·mi·a (ēm′ē ə, ēm′yə) [ModL. < Gr. *-aimia* < *haima,* blood] *a suffix meaning* a (specified) condition or disease of the blood *[leukemia]*

em·i·grant (em′ə grənt) *adj.* [L. *emigrans,* prp. of *emigrare*] **1.** emigrating **2.** of emigrants or emigration —*n.* a person who emigrates

em·i·grate (em′ə grāt′) *vi.* **-grat′ed, -grat′ing** [< L. *emigratus,* pp. of *emigrare,* to move away < *e-,* out + *migrare,* to move, MIGRATE] to leave one country or region to settle in another —*SYN.* see MIGRATE

em·i·gra·tion (em′ə grā′shən) *n.* [LL. *emigratio*] **1.** the act of emigrating **2.** emigrants collectively

é·mi·gré, e·mi·gré (em′ə grā′, ā′mə grā′) *n.* [Fr. < pp. of *émigrer* < L. *emigrare:* see EMIGRATE] **1.** an emigrant **2.** a person forced to flee his country for political reasons, as a Royalist during the French Revolution —*SYN.* see ALIEN

E·mil (ā′m′l, ē′-; em′l) [G. < Fr. *Émile* < L. *Aemilius,* name of a Roman gens < L. *aemulus:* see EMULATE] a masculine name: fem. *Emily*

E·mil·i·a (i mil′yə, -ē ə) a feminine name: see EMILY

E·mil·ia-Ro·ma·gna (ā mēl′yä rō mä′nyä) region in NC Italy, near the mouth of the Adriatic: 8,542 sq. mi.; pop. 3,647,000; cap. Bologna

Em·i·ly (em′′l ē) [Fr. *Émilie* < L. *Aemilia,* fem. of *Aemilius:* see EMIL] a feminine name: var. *Emilia, Emeline, Emmeline*

em·i·nence (em′ə nəns) *n.* [ME. < OFr. < L. *eminentia* < *eminens,* excellent, prominent, prp. of *eminere,* to stand out < *e-,* out + **minere,* to project: see MENACE] **1.** a high or lofty place, thing, etc., as a hill **2.** *a*) superiority in rank, position, character, achievement, etc.; greatness; celebrity *b*) a person of eminence **3.** [E-] *R.C.Ch.* a title of honor used in speaking to or of a cardinal, preceded by *His* or *Your* **4.** *Anat.* a raised area, usually on the surface of a bone

‡**ém·i·nence grise** (ā mē näns grēz′) [Fr., lit., gray eminence, nickname of François Leclerc du Tremblay (1577–1638), Fr. monk and confidential agent of, and an assumed influence over, Richelieu: so named from the color of his habit] a person who wields great power and influence, but secretly or unofficially

em·i·nen·cy (em′ə nən sē) *n., pl.* **-cies** **1.** formerly, eminence **2.** prominence; importance

em·i·nent (em′ə nənt) *adj.* [ME. < L. *eminens:* see EMINENCE] **1.** rising above other things or places; high; lofty **2.** projecting; prominent; protruding **3.** standing high by comparison with others, as in rank or achievement; renowned; exalted; distinguished **4.** outstanding; remarkable; noteworthy *[a man of eminent courage]* —*SYN.* see FAMOUS —**em′i·nent·ly** *adv.*

eminent domain *Law* ☆the right of a government to take, or to authorize the taking of, private property for public use, just compensation usually being given to the owner

e·mir (i mir′) *n.* [Ar. *amir* < *amara,* to command] **1.** in certain Moslem countries, a ruler, prince, or commander **2.** a title given Mohammed's descendants through his daughter Fatima —**e·mir′ate** (-it, -āt) *n.*

em·is·sar·y (em′ə ser′ē) *n., pl.* **-sar′ies** [L. *emissarius* < pp. of *emittere:* see EMIT] a person or agent, esp. a secret agent, sent on a specific mission —*adj.* of, or serving as, an emissary or emissaries

e·mis·sion (i mish′ən) *n.* [L. *emissio* < pp. of *emittere*] **1.** the act of emitting; issuance; specif., *a*) the transmission of radio waves *b*) the ejection of electrons from a surface by heat, radiation, etc. *c*) a discharge of fluid from the body; esp., an involuntary discharge of semen **2.** something emitted; discharge

e·mis·sive (i mis′iv) *adj.* [ML. *emissivus* < L. *emissus,* pp. of *emittere*] emitting or able to emit

em·is·siv·i·ty (em′ə siv′ə tē) *n.* the relative ability of a surface to radiate energy as compared with that of an ideally black surface under the same conditions

e·mit (i mit′) *vt.* **e·mit′ted, e·mit′ting** [L. *emittere* < *e-*, out + *mittere*, to send: see MISSION¹] **1.** to send out; give forth; discharge [*geysers emit* water] **2.** to utter (sounds, etc.) **3.** to transmit (a signal) as by radio waves **4.** to give off (electrons) under the influence of heat, radiation, etc. **5.** to issue (paper money, etc.); put into circulation

e·mit·ter (-ər) *n.* **1.** one that emits; specif., a substance that emits particles [a beta *emitter*] **2.** in a transistor, the region or layer of semiconductor material from which a flow of electrons or holes is injected into the base region

Em·ma (em′ə) [G. < *Erma* < names beginning with *Erm-* (e.g., *Ermenhilde*): see IRMA] a feminine name

Em·man·u·el (i man′yoo wəl) [Gr. *Emmanouēl* < Heb. *'immānūēl*, lit., God with us] **1.** a masculine name: var. *Emanuel, Immanuel, Manuel* **2.** the Messiah: see IMMANUEL

Em·me·line (em′ə lin′, -lēn′) a feminine name: var. *Emeline:* see EMILY

Em·men (em′ən) city in NE Netherlands: pop. 73,000

em·men·a·gogue (i men′ə gäg′, -gôg′; i mē′nə-) *n.* [< Gr. *emmēna, n.pl.,* menses (< *en-*, in + *mēn*, month) + -AGOGUE] anything used to stimulate the menstrual flow

em·mer (em′ər) *n.* [G. < OHG. *amaro:* cf. YELLOWHAMMER] a species (*Triticum dicoccum*) of wheat having a spike broken up into segments and grains that do not thresh free of the chaff: one of the tetraploid wheats

em·met (em′it) *n.* [see ANT] [Dial. or Archaic] an ant

Em·met (em′it), **Robert** 1778–1803; Ir. patriot: hanged by the British after he led an abortive revolt

em·me·tro·pi·a (em′ə trō′pē ə) *n.* [ModL. < Gr. *emmetros,* in measure, fit < *en-*, in + *metron,* measure + -OPIA] the condition of normal refraction of light in the eye, in which vision is perfect —**em′me·trop′ic** (-träp′ik) *adj.*

Em·my (em′ē) *n., pl.* **-mys** [altered < *Immy,* engineering slang for the image-orthicon camera: name proposed (1948) in contrast to OSCAR by Harry R. Lubcke, U.S. TV engineer] ☆[Slang] any of the statuettes awarded annually in the U.S. for special achievement in television programming, acting, etc.

EmnE., EMnE. Early Modern English

e·mol·li·ent (i mäl′yənt, -ē ənt) *adj.* [L. *emolliens,* prp. of *emollire,* to soften < *e-*, out + *mollire,* to soften < *mollis,* soft: see MILL¹] softening; soothing —*n.* something that has a softening or soothing effect; esp., an emollient preparation or medicine applied to surface tissues of the body

e·mol·u·ment (-yoo mənt) *n.* [ME. < L. *emolumentum,* the result of exertion, gain, profit < *emolere,* to grind out < *e-*, out + *molere,* to grind: see MILL¹] gain from employment or position; payment received for work; salary, wages, fees, etc. —*SYN.* see WAGE

Em·or·y (em′ər ē) a masculine name: see EMERY

☆**e·mote** (i mōt′) *vi.* **e·mot′ed, e·mot′ing** [< ff., by analogy with DEVOTE] [Colloq.] to act in an emotional or theatrical manner while, or as though, playing a role in a drama: often used humorously

e·mo·tion (i mō′shən) *n.* [Fr. (prob. after *motion*) < *émouvoir,* to agitate, stir up < VL. **exmovere,* for L. *emovere* < *e-*, out + *movere,* MOVE] **1.** *a)* strong feeling; excitement *b)* the state or capability of having the feelings aroused to the point of awareness **2.** any specific feeling; any of various complex reactions with both mental and physical manifestations, as love, hate, fear, anger, etc. —*SYN.* see FEELING —**e·mo′tion·less** *adj.*

e·mo·tion·al (-′l) *adj.* **1.** of or having to do with emotion or the emotions **2.** showing emotion, esp. strong emotion **3.** easily aroused to emotion; quick to weep, be angry, etc. **4.** appealing to the emotions; moving people to tears, anger, etc. —**e·mo′tion·al·ly** *adv.*

e·mo·tion·al·ism (-′l iz′m) *n.* **1.** the tendency to be emotional or to show emotion quickly and easily **2.** display of emotion **3.** an appeal to emotion, esp. to sway an audience to some belief

e·mo·tion·al·ist (-′l ist) *n.* **1.** a very emotional person **2.** a person who uses or relies on emotion or emotional effects, as in oratory, art, etc.

e·mo·tion·al·i·ty (i mō′shə nal′ə tē) *n.* the quality or state of being emotional

e·mo·tion·al·ize (i mō′shən ′l īz′) *vt.* **-ized′, -iz′ing** to treat, present, or interpret in an emotional way —**e·mo′tion·al·i·za′tion** *n.*

e·mo·tive (i mōt′iv) *adj.* **1.** characterized by, expressing, or producing emotion **2.** relating to the emotions —**e·mo′tive·ly** *adv.*

Emp. 1. Emperor **2.** Empire **3.** Empress

em·pale (im pāl′) *vt.* **-paled′, -pal′ing** *same as* IMPALE

em·pan·el (-pan′′l) *vt.* **-eled** or **-elled, -el·ing** or **-el·ling** *same as* IMPANEL

em·path·ic (im path′ik) *adj.* of or characterized by empathy: also **em·pa·thet·ic** (em′pə thet′ik)

em·pa·thize (em′pə thīz′) *vi.* **-thized′, -thiz′ing** [< ff., after SYMPATHIZE] to undergo or feel empathy (*with* another or others)

em·pa·thy (-thē) *n.* [< Gr. *empatheia,* affection, passion < *en-*, in + *pathos,* feeling: used to translate G. *einfühlung* (< *ein-*, in + *fühlung,* feeling)] **1.** the projection of one's own personality into the personality of another in order to understand him better; ability to share in another's emotions or feelings **2.** the projection of one's own per-

sonality into an object, with the attribution to the object of one's own emotions, responses, etc.

Em·ped·o·cles (em ped′ə klēz′) 495?–435? B.C.; Gr. philosopher & poet

em·pen·nage (em′pə näzh′, em′pə nij′; Fr. än pe nåzh′) [Fr. < *empenner,* to feather an arrow < *em-*, in + *penne,* a feather: see PEN²] the tail assembly of an airplane, consisting of vertical and horizontal stabilizers, and including the fin, rudder, and elevators

em·per·or (em′pər ər, -prər) *n.* [ME. *emperour* < OFr. *empereor,* ruler (of the Holy Roman Empire) < L. *imperator,* commander in chief < pp. of *imperare,* to command < *in-*, in + *parare,* to set in order, PREPARE] the supreme ruler of an empire —**em′per·or·ship′** *n.*

emperor butterfly any of several obscurely colored tawny or brownish butterflies, such as the **tawny emperor** (*Asterocampa clyton*) of the S U.S.

emperor penguin the largest of the extant penguins (*Apotenodytes forsteri*), found only in Antarctica and growing to four feet in height

em·per·y (em′pər ē) *n., pl.* **-per·ies** [ME. & OFr. *emperie* < L. *imperium < imperare:* see EMPEROR] [Poet.] **1.** the sovereignty of an emperor; empire **2.** broad dominion or authority

em·pha·sis (em′fə sis) *n., pl.* **-ses′** (-sēz′) [L. < Gr. *emphasis,* an appearing in, outward appearance < *emphainein,* to indicate < *en-*, in + *phainein,* to show < IE. base **bha-,* to shine, whence OE. *bonian,* to ornament] **1.** force of expression, thought, feeling, action, etc. **2.** special stress given to a syllable, word, phrase, etc. in speaking **3.** special attention given to something so as to make it stand out; importance; stress; weight [to put less *emphasis* on athletics]

em·pha·size (-sīz′) *vt.* **-sized′, -siz′ing** to give emphasis to; give special force or prominence to; stress

em·phat·ic (im fat′ik) *adj.* [Gr. *emphatikos*] **1.** expressed, felt, or done with emphasis **2.** using emphasis in speaking, expressing, etc. **3.** very striking; forcible; definite [an *emphatic* defeat] **4.** *Gram.* designating or of a present tense or past tense in which a form of *do* is used as an auxiliary for emphasis (Ex.: I *do* care, we *did* go) —**em·phat′i·cal·ly** *adv.*

em·phy·se·ma (em′fə sē′mə) *n.* [ModL. < Gr. *emphysēma,* inflation < *emphyseein,* to inflate, blow in < *en-*, in + *physaein,* to blow] **1.** an abnormal swelling of body tissues caused by the accumulation of air; esp., such a swelling of the alveoli or of the tissue connecting the alveoli in the lungs, accompanied by atrophy of the tissues and impairment in breathing **2.** *same as* HEAVES —**em′phy·se′ma·tous** (-sem′ə təs, -sē′mə təs) *adj.*

em·pire (em′pīr; *for adj., usually* äm pir′) *n.* [ME. & OFr. < L. *imperium < imperare:* see EMPEROR] **1.** supreme rule; absolute power or authority; dominion **2.** *a)* government by an emperor or empress *b)* the period during which such government prevails **3.** *a)* a group of states or territories under the sovereign power of an emperor or empress *b)* a state uniting many territories and peoples under one ruler **4.** an extensive social or economic organization under the control of a single person, family, or corporation —*adj.* [E-] of or characteristic of the first French Empire (1804–15) under Napoleon; specif., *a)* designating a style of furniture of this period, characterized by massiveness and the use of heavy textiles and bronze ornamentation *b)* designating a gown in the style of the period, with a short waist, décolleté bodice, flowing skirt, and short, puffed sleeves

Empire Day *former name for* COMMONWEALTH DAY

☆**Empire State** *nickname of* NEW YORK (State)

em·pir·ic (em pir′ik) *n.* [L. *empiricus* < Gr. *empeirikos,* experienced < *empeiria,* experience < *en-*, in + *peira,* a trial, experiment: for IE. base see FARE] **1.** a person who relies solely on practical experience rather than on scientific principles **2.** [Archaic] a practitioner without proper qualifications and regular training; charlatan; quack —*adj.* empirical

em·pir·i·cal (-i k′l) *adj.* [prec. + -AL] **1.** relying or based solely on experiment and observation rather than theory [the *empirical* method] **2.** relying or based on practical experience without reference to scientific principles [an *empirical* remedy] —**em·pir′i·cal·ly** *adv.*

empirical formula a chemical formula which gives the composition of elements in a molecule in their lowest relative proportions but does not specify the structural arrangement or true molecular weight (Ex.: CH for benzene)

em·pir·i·cism (-ə siz′m) *n.* **1.** experimental method; search for knowledge by observation and experiment **2.** *a)* a disregarding of scientific methods and relying solely on experience *b)* quackery **3.** *Philos.* the theory that experience is the only source of knowledge —**em·pir′i·cist** *n.*

em·place (im plās′) *vt.* **-placed′, -plac′ing** [back-formation < ff.] to place in position

em·place·ment (-mənt) *n.* [Fr. < *emplacer,* to put in position: see EN-¹ + PLACE] **1.** the act of emplacing; placement **2.** the position in which something is placed; specif., *Mil.,* the prepared position from which a heavy gun or guns are fired

em·plane (em plān′) *vi.* **-planed′, -plan′ing** *same as* ENPLANE

em·ploy (im ploi′) *vt.* [ME. *emploien* < OFr. *emploier* < L. *implicare*, to enfold, engage: see IMPLY] **1.** to make use of; use **2.** to keep busy or occupied; take up the attention, time, etc. of; devote [to *employ* oneself in study] **3.** to provide work and pay for [mining *employs* fewer men now] **4.** to engage the services or labor of for pay; hire —*n.* **1.** the state of being employed, esp. for pay; paid service; employment **2.** [Now Poet.] work or occupation —*SYN.* see USE

em·ploy·a·ble (-ə b'l) *adj.* that can be employed; specif., *a)* physically or mentally fit to be hired for work *b)* meeting the minimum requirements for a specified kind of work or position of employment —**em·ploy′a·bil′i·ty** (-ə bil′ə tē) *n.*

em·ploy·ee, em·ploy·e (im ploi′ē, -ploi′ē′; em′ploi ē′) *n.* [Fr. *employé* (fem. *employée*), pp. of *employer*: see EMPLOY] a person hired by another, or by a business firm, etc., to work for wages or salary

em·ploy·er (im ploi′ər) *n.* one who employs, esp. a person, business firm, etc. that hires one or more persons to work for wages or salary

em·ploy·ment (-mənt) *n.* **1.** an employing or being employed **2.** the thing at which one is employed; work; occupation; profession; job **3.** the number or percentage of persons gainfully employed **4.** [Archaic] purpose to which something is put

em·poi·son (im poi′z'n) *vt.* [ME. *empoisounen* < OFr. *empoisoner*: see EN-[1] & POISON] **1.** [Archaic] to make poisonous; taint or corrupt **2.** to embitter; envenom

em·po·ri·um (em pôr′ē əm) *n., pl.* -ri·ums, -ri·a (-ə) [L. < Gr. *emporion*, trading place, mart < *emporios*, pertaining to trade, commerce < *emporos*, traveler < *en-*, in + *poros*, way: for IE. base see FARE] **1.** a place of commerce; trading center; marketplace **2.** a large store with a wide variety of things for sale

em·pow·er (im pou′ər) *vt.* **1.** to give power or authority to; authorize [Congress is *empowered* to levy taxes] **2.** to give ability to; enable; permit

em·press (em′pris) *n.* [ME. *emperesse* < OFr., fem. of *empereor*, EMPEROR] **1.** the wife of an emperor **2.** a woman ruler of an empire **3.** a woman with great power or influence [the *empress* of his heart]

‡em·presse·ment (än pres män′) *n.* [Fr., eagerness < *s'empresser*, to be eager, hasten: see IMPRESS[2]] effusive regard or cordiality

em·prise, em·prize (em prīz′) *n.* [ME. *emprise* < OFr. < pp. of *emprendre*, to undertake < VL. **imprehendere* < L. *im-*, in + *prehendere*, to take: see PREHENSILE] [Archaic] **1.** an enterprise or adventure **2.** prowess or daring [knights of great *emprise*]

emp·ty (emp′tē) *adj.* **-ti·er, -ti·est** [ME. *emti* & (with intrusive -*p*-) *empti* < OE. *æmettig*, unoccupied, lit., at leisure < *æmetta*, leisure (< *æ*-, without + base of *motan*, to have to: see MUST[1]) + -*ig*, -Y[2]] **1.** containing nothing; having nothing in it **2.** having no one in it; unoccupied; vacant [an *empty* house] **3.** carrying or bearing nothing; bare **4.** having no worth or purpose; useless or unsatisfying [*empty* pleasure] **5.** without meaning or force; insincere; vain [*empty* promises] **6.** [Colloq.] hungry —*vt.* **-tied, -ty·ing 1.** to make empty **2.** *a)* to pour out or remove (the contents) of something *b)* to transfer (the contents) into, onto, or on something else **3.** to unburden or discharge (oneself or itself) —*vi.* **1.** to become empty **2.** to pour out; discharge [the river *empties* into the sea] —*n., pl.* **-ties** an empty freight car, truck, bottle, etc. —**empty of** lacking; without; devoid of —**emp′ti·ly** *adv.* —**emp′ti·ness** *n.*
SYN.—*empty* means having nothing in it [an *empty* box, street, stomach, etc.]; *vacant* means lacking that which appropriately or customarily occupies or fills it [a *vacant* apartment, position, etc.]; *void*, as discriminated here, specifically stresses complete or vast emptiness [*void* of judgment]; *vacuous*, now rare in its physical sense, suggests the emptiness of a vacuum See also VAIN —*ANT.* full

emp·ty-hand·ed (-han′did) *adj.* bringing or carrying away nothing

emp·ty-head·ed (-hed′id) *adj.* frivolous and stupid; silly and ignorant

Empty Quarter *Eng. name of* RUB′ AL KHALI

em·pur·ple (im pur′p'l) *vt., vi.* **-pled, -pling** to make or become purple

em·py·e·ma (em′pī ē′mə, -pē-) *n., pl.* -ma·ta (-mə tə) [altered (after Gr.) < ME. *empima* < ML. *empyema* < Gr. *empyēma* < *empyein*, to suppurate < *en-*, in + *pyon*, PUS] the accumulation of pus in a body cavity, esp. in the pleural cavity —**em′py·e′ma·tous** (-mə təs), **em′py·e′mic** (-mik) *adj.*

em·pyr·e·al (em pir′ē əl; em′pī rē′əl, -pə-) *adj.* [LL. *empyrius, empyreus* < Gr. *empyrios*, in fire < *en-*, in + *pyr*, FIRE] of the empyrean; heavenly; sublime

em·py·re·an (em′pī rē′ən, -pə-; em pir′ē ən) *n.* [see prec. & -AN] **1.** the highest heaven; specif., *a)* among the ancients, the sphere of pure light or fire *b)* among Christian poets, the abode of God **2.** the sky; the celestial vault; firmament —*adj. same as* EMPYREAL

Ems (emz) river in NW Germany, flowing into the North Sea: c. 200 mi.

e·mu (ē′myo͞o) *n.* [prob. < Port. *ema*, a crane] a large, nonflying Australian bird (*Dromiceius novae-hollandiae*), similar to the ostrich but somewhat smaller

E.M.U., e.m.u., emu electromagnetic units

em·u·late (em′yə lāt′; *for adj.* -lit) *vt.* **-lat′ed, -lat′ing** [< L. *aemulatus*, pp. of *aemulari* < *aemulus*, trying to equal or excel < IE. base **ai*-, to give, accept, take, whence Gr. *ainymai*, take] **1.** to try to equal or surpass; esp., to imitate or copy with a view to equaling or surpassing **2.** to rival successfully —*adj.* [Obs.] ambitious —**em′u·la′tor** *n.*

EMU
(5 ft. high)

em·u·la·tion (em′yə lā′shən) *n.* [L. *aemulatio*] **1.** the act of emulating **2.** desire or ambition to equal or surpass **3.** [Obs.] *a)* ambitious rivalry *b)* envious dislike —*SYN.* see COMPETITION —**em′u·la′tive** *adj.* —**em′u·la′tive·ly** *adv.*

em·u·lous (em′yə ləs) *adj.* [L. *aemulus*: see EMULATE] **1.** desirous of equaling or surpassing **2.** characterized or caused by emulation **3.** [Obs.] jealous; envious *SYN.* see AMBITIOUS —**em′u·lous·ly** *adv.* —**em′u·lous·ness** *n.*

e·mul·si·fi·a·ble (i mul′sə fī′ə b'l) *adj.* that can be emulsified: also **e·mul′si·ble** (-sə b'l)

e·mul·si·fy (-fī′) *vt., vi.* **-fied′, -fy′ing** to form into an emulsion —**e·mul′si·fi·ca′tion** *n.* —**e·mul′si·fi′er** *n.*

e·mul·sion (i mul′shən) *n.* [ModL. *emulsio* < L. *emulsus*, pp. of *emulgere*, to milk or drain out < *e-*, out + *mulgere*, to MILK] a fluid, as milk, formed by the suspension of a very finely divided oily or resinous liquid in another liquid; specif., *a) Pharmacy* a preparation of an oily substance held in suspension in a watery liquid by means of a gummy substance [an *emulsion* of cod-liver oil] *b) Photog.* a suspension of a salt of silver in gelatin or collodion, used to coat plates and film —**e·mul′sive** (-siv) *adj.*

e·mul·soid (-soid′) *n.* a lyophilic sol

e·munc·to·ry (i munk′tər ē) *n., pl.* **-ries** [ModL. *emunctorium* < pp. of L. *emungere*, to blow the nose, cleanse < *e-*, out + *mungere*, to blow the nose: for IE. base see MUCUS] any organ or part of the body that gives off waste products, as the kidneys, lungs, or skin —*adj.* giving off waste products; excretory

en (en) *n.* **1.** the letter N, n **2.** *Printing* a space half the width of an em

en-[1] (in, en) [ME. < OFr. < L. *in-* < *in*, IN] *a v.-forming prefix of various uses and meanings:* **1.** *prefixed to nouns and meaning: a)* to put or get into or on [*enthrone, entrain*] *b)* to cover or wrap with [*enrobe*] **2.** *prefixed to nouns or adjectives and meaning* to make, make into or like, cause to be [*endanger, enfeeble*] **3.** *prefixed to verbs and meaning* in or into [*enclose*] **4.** *used as an intensifier* [*encourage*] Many words beginning *en-* are also spelled *in-* (Ex.: *enquire, inquire*)

en-[2] (in, en) [Gr. *en-* < *en*, IN] *a prefix meaning* in [*endemic*]: used chiefly in Greek derivatives

-en (ən, 'n) *the common form taken by several suffixes, variously used:* **1.** [ME. *-en, -ien* < OE. *-nian*] *to form verbs, usually transitive, meaning: a)* when added to adjectives to become or cause to be [*darken, weaken*] *b)* when added to nouns to come to have, cause to have [*heighten, hearten, strengthen*] **2.** [ME. & OE., akin to L. *-inus*, Gr. *-inos*] *to form adjectives from concrete nouns, meaning* made of [*wooden, woolen*] **3.** [ME. & OE.] *to form the pp. of strong verbs* [*risen, written*] **4.** [OE. *-an*] *to form plurals* [*children, brethren*] **5.** [OE.] *to form feminines of nouns* [*vixen*] **6.** [OE.] *to form diminutives* [*chicken*]

en·a·ble (in ā′b'l) *vt.* **-bled, -bling 1.** to make able; provide with means, opportunity, power, or authority (*to* do something) **2.** to make possible or effective

en·act (in akt′) *vt.* **1.** to make (a bill, etc.) into a law; pass (a law); decree; ordain **2.** to represent or perform in or as in a play; act out —**en·ac′tor** *n.*

en·ac·tive (in ak′tiv) *adj.* enacting or having the power to enact

en·act·ment (-akt′mənt) *n.* **1.** an enacting or being enacted **2.** something enacted, as a law or decree

en·am·el (i nam′'l) *n.* [ME. < the *v.*] **1.** a glassy, colored, opaque substance fused to surfaces of metals, glass, and pottery as an ornamental or protective coating **2.** any smooth, hard, glossy coating or surface like enamel **3.** the hard, white, glossy coating of the crown of a tooth **4.** anything enameled; enameled ware or a piece of jewelry, etc. produced in enamel **5.** paint or varnish that produces a smooth, hard, glossy surface when it dries —*vt.* **-eled** or **-elled, -el·ing** or **-el·ling** [ME. *enamelen* < Anglo-Fr. *enamayller* < *en-* (see EN-[1]) + *amayl* < OFr. *esmail*, enamel < Gmc. **smalts*, a glaze, melted substance: see SMELT[2]] **1.** to inlay or cover with enamel **2.** to decorate in various colors, as if with enamel **3.** to form an enamellike surface on

en·am·el·er, en·am·el·ler (-ər) *n.* **1.** a person whose work is applying enamel, as to metal surfaces **2.** an artist who designs and produces jewelry and other fine objects in

enamel: in this sense, now usually **en·am′el·ist** or **en·am′el·list**

en·am·el·ware (-wer′) *n.* kitchen utensils, etc. made of enameled metal

en·am·or (in am′ər) *vt.* [ME. *enamouren* < OFr. *enamourer* < *en-*, in + *amour* < L. *amor*, love] to fill with love and desire; charm; captivate: now mainly in the passive voice, with *of* [much *enamored* of her]

en·an·ti·o·morph (in an′tē ə môrf′) *n.* [G. < Gr. *enantios*, opposite (< *en-*, IN + *anti*, against, ANTI-) + G. *-morph*, -MORPH] either of two crystals that are mirror images of each other: they are usually optically active, one form is dextrorotatory and the other levorotatory —**en·an′ti·o·mor′phic** *adj.* —**en·an′ti·o·mor′phism** *n.*

‡**en ar·rière** (än nå ryer′) [Fr.] 1. in the rear; behind 2. in arrears

en·ar·thro·sis (en′är thrō′sis) *n.* [ModL. < Gr. *enarthrōsis* < *enarthros*, jointed < *en-*, in + *arthron*, a joint: see ARTHRO-] *same as* BALL-AND-SOCKET JOINT

‡**en a·vant** (än nå vän′) [Fr.] forward; onward

en bloc (en bläk′; *Fr.* än blôk′) [Fr., lit., in a block] in one lump; as a whole; all together

‡**en bro·chette** (än brô shet′) [Fr.] broiled on small spits or skewers

‡**en brosse** (än brôs′) [Fr., lit., like a brush] cut short so as to stand up like brush bristles: said of hair

enc. enclosure

en·cae·ni·a (en sē′nē ə, -sēn′yə) *n.pl.* [often with sing. *v.*] [altered (after L.) < ME. *encennia* < L. *encaenia* < Gr. *enkainia* < *en-*, in + *kainos*, new] a festival commemorating the founding of a city, church, university, etc.; esp., [E-] the annual ceremony commemorating the founding of Oxford University

en·cage (in kāj′) *vt.* **-caged′**, **-cag′ing** to shut up in a cage; confine

en·camp (in kamp′) *vi.* to set up a camp —*vt.* 1. to put in a camp 2. to form into a camp

en·camp·ment (-mənt) *n.* 1. an encamping or being encamped 2. a camp or campsite

en·cap·su·late (in kap′sə lāt′, -syoo-) *vt.* **-lat′ed**, **-lat′ing** 1. to enclose in or as if in a capsule 2. to put in concise form; condense Also **en·cap′sule** (-s′l, -syool), **-suled**, **-sul·ing** —**en·cap′su·la′tion** *n.*

en·car·nal·ize (in kär′nə līz′) *vt.* **-ized′**, **-iz′ing** 1. to incarnate 2. to make carnal; make sensual

en·case (in kās′) *vt.* **-cased′**, **-cas′ing** 1. to cover completely; enclose 2. to put into a case or cases —**en·case′ment** *n.*

en cas·se·role (en kas′ə rōl′; *Fr.* än kås rôl′) [Fr.] (baked and served) in a casserole

en·caus·tic (en kôs′tik) *adj.* [L. *encausticus* < Gr. *enkaustikos* < *enkaustos*, burnt in < *enkaiein*, to burn in < *en-*, in + *kaiein*, to burn] done by a process of burning in or applying heat [encaustic tile] —*n.* a method of painting in which colors in wax are fused to a surface with hot irons —**en·caus′ti·cal·ly** *adv.*

-ence (əns, 'ns) [ME. < OFr. *-ence* & L. *-entia* < *-ent-* (see -ENT) + *-ia*, n. ending] *a n.-forming suffix meaning* act, fact, quality, state, result, or degree [conference, excellence]

‡**en·ceinte**[1] (än sant′; *E.* än sānt′) *n.* [Fr. < pp. of *enceindre* < L. *incingere*, to gird about < *in-*, in + *cingere*, surround] 1. the line of works enclosing a fortified place 2. the space so enclosed

‡**en·ceinte**[2] (än sant′; *E.* än sānt′) *adj.* [Fr. < VL. *incincta*, orig. fem. of *incinctus*, ungirt < L. *in-*, not + *cinctus*, pp. of *cingere*, to gird, surround] pregnant; with child

En·cel·a·dus (en sel′ə dəs) [L. < Gr. *Enkelados*] *Gr. Myth.* a giant with a hundred arms, who fought against the gods

en·ce·phal·ic (en′sə fal′ik) *adj.* [ENCEPHAL(O)- + -IC] of or near the brain

en·ceph·a·li·tis (en sef′ə līt′is, en′sef-) *n.* [ENCEPHAL(O)- + -ITIS] inflammation of the brain —**en·ceph′a·lit′ic** (-lit′ik) *adj.*

encephalitis le·thar·gi·ca (li thär′ji kə) a form of encephalitis epidemic in the period from 1915 to 1926; sleeping sickness

en·ceph·a·lo- (en sef′ə lō) [< Gr. *enkephalos*: see ENCEPHALON] *a combining form meaning* of the brain: also, before a vowel, **en·ceph′al-**

en·ceph·a·lo·gram (-gram′) *n.* shortened form of *a*) ELECTROENCEPHALOGRAM *b*) PNEUMOENCEPHALOGRAM

en·ceph·a·lo·my·e·li·tis (en sef′ə lō mī′ə līt′əs) *n.* [ENCEPHALO- + MYELITIS] inflammation of the brain and spinal cord; specif., a virus disease of horses and other animals sometimes communicable to man

en·ceph·a·lon (en sef′ə län′) *n.*, *pl.* **-la** (-la) [ModL. < Gr. *enkephalos*, (what is) in the head < *en-*, in + *kephalē*, the head: see CEPHALIC] *Anat.* the brain

en·chain (in chān′) *vt.* [ME. *encheinen* < OFr. *enchainer*: see EN-[1] & CHAIN] 1. to bind or hold with chains; fetter 2. to hold fast; captivate —**en·chain′ment** *n.*

en·chant (in chant′, -chänt′) *vt.* [ME. *enchanten* < OFr. *enchanter* < L. *incantare*, to bewitch: see INCANTATION] 1. to cast a spell over, as by magic; bewitch 2. to charm greatly; delight —*SYN.* see ATTRACT —**en·chant′er** *n.*

en·chant·ing (-in) *adj.* 1. charming; delightful 2. bewitching; fascinating —**en·chant′ing·ly** *adv.*

en·chant·ment (-mənt) *n.* [ME. & OFr. *enchantement*: see ENCHANT & -MENT] 1. an enchanting or being enchanted 2. a magic spell or charm 3. something that charms or delights greatly 4. great delight or pleasure

en·chant·ress (-ris) *n.* [ME. & OFr. *enchanteresse*: see ENCHANT] 1. a sorceress; witch 2. a fascinating or charming woman

en·chase (in chās′) *vt.* **-chased′**, **-chas′ing** [ME. **enchasen* < OFr. *enchasser* < *en-*, in + *châsse*: see CHASE[2]] 1. to put in a setting or serve as a setting for 2. to ornament by engraving, embossing, or inlaying with gems, etc. 3. to engrave or carve (designs, etc.)

☆**en·chi·la·da** (en′chə lä′də) *n.* [AmSp. < *en-* (see EN-[1]) + *chile* (see CHILI) + *-ada* (see -ADE)] a tortilla usually rolled with meat inside and served with a chili-flavored sauce

en·chi·rid·i·on (en′kī rid′ē ən, -kə-) *n.* [LL. < Gr. *encheiridion* < *en-*, in + *cheir*, hand + *-idion*, dim. suffix] a handbook; manual

en·chon·dro·ma (en′kän drō′mə) *n.*, *pl.* **-ma·ta** (-mə tə), **-mas** [ModL. < Gr. *en*, in + *chondros*, cartilage + -OMA] a cartilaginous tumor —**en′chon·drom′a·tous** (-dräm′ə təs, -drō′mə təs) *adj.*

en·cho·ri·al (en kôr′ē əl) *adj.* [< Gr. *enchōrios*, native (< *en-*, in + *chōra*, country, place) + -AL] of or used in a particular country; native; popular; esp., demotic (sense 1)

☆**en·ci·na** (en sē′nə) *n.* [Sp. < VL. *ilicina*, holm oak < L. *ilex*, ILEX] *same as* LIVE OAK; esp., the live oak of California (*Quercus agrifolia*)

en·ci·pher (in sī′fər) *vt.* to convert (a message, etc.) from ordinary language into cipher or code

en·cir·cle (-sur′k'l) *vt.* **-cled**, **-cling** 1. to make a circle around; enclose within a circle; surround 2. to move in a circle around —**en·cir′cle·ment** *n.*

encl. enclosure

en·clasp (-klasp′, -kläsp′) *vt.* to hold in a clasp; embrace

en·clave (en′klāv) *n.* [Fr. < OFr. < *enclaver*, to enclose, lock in < VL. **inclavare* < L. *in*, in + *clavis*, a key: for IE. base see LOT] 1. a territory surrounded or nearly surrounded by the territory of another country 2. a minority culture group living as an entity within a larger group

en·clit·ic (en klit′ik) *adj.* [LL. *encliticus* < Gr. *enklitikos* < *enklinein*, to lean toward, incline < *en-*, in + *klinein*, to lean: see INCLINE] *Gram.* dependent for its stress on the preceding word: said of a word that has lost its stress in combination (Ex.: *man* in *layman*) —*n.* any such word or particle

en·close (in klōz′) *vt.* **-closed′**, **-clos′ing** [ME. *enclosen*, prob. < *enclos*, an enclosure < OFr., orig. pp. of *enclore*, to enclose < VL. **inclaudere*, for L. *includere*, INCLUDE] 1. to shut in all around; hem in; fence in; surround 2. to insert in an envelope, wrapper, etc., often along with something else [to *enclose* a check with one's order] 3. to contain

en·clo·sure (-klō′zhər) *n.* [ME. & OE.: see prec. & -URE] 1. an enclosing or being enclosed 2. something that encloses, as a fence, wall, etc. 3. something enclosed; specif., *a*) an enclosed place or area *b*) a document, money, etc. enclosed as with a letter

en·code (in kōd′) *vt.* **-cod′ed**, **-cod′ing** to put (a message, information, etc.) into code —**en·cod′er** *n.*

en·co·mi·ast (en kō′mē ast′) *n.* [Gr. *enkōmiastēs* < *enkōmiazein*, to praise < *enkōmion*] a person who speaks or writes encomiums; eulogist

en·co·mi·as·tic (en kō′mē as′tik) *adj.* 1. of an encomiast 2. of or like an encomium; eulogistic

en·co·mi·um (en kō′mē əm) *n.*, *pl.* **-mi·ums**, **-mi·a** (-ə) [L. < Gr. *enkōmion*, hymn to a victor, neut. of *enkōmios* < *en-*, in + *kōmos*, a revel] a formal expression of high praise; eulogy; panegyric —*SYN.* see TRIBUTE

en·com·pass (in kum′pəs) *vt.* 1. to shut in all around; surround; encircle 2. to contain; include 3. to bring about; achieve; contrive [to *encompass* its destruction] —**en·com′pass·ment** *n.*

en·core (äŋ′kôr, än kôr′) *interj.* [Fr., again, still < OFr. *ancor*, prob. < L. (*hinc*) *hac hora*, (from that time) to the present hour] again; once more: cf. BIS —*n.* 1. a demand by the audience, shown by continued applause, for the repetition of a piece of music, etc., or for another appearance of the performer or performers 2. the repetition, further performance, etc. in answer to such a demand 3. the piece of music, etc. performed in answer to such a demand —*vt.* **-cored**, **-cor·ing** to demand a repetition of (a piece of music, etc.) or from (a performer) by applauding

en·coun·ter (in koun′tər) *vt.* [ME. *encontren* < OFr. *encontrer* < *encontre*, against < VL. **incontra* < L. *in*, in + *contra*, against] 1. to meet unexpectedly; come upon 2. to meet in conflict or battle 3. to meet with; face (difficulties, trouble, etc.) —*vi.* to meet accidentally or in opposition —*n.* 1. a direct meeting, as in conflict or battle 2. a meeting with another, esp. when unexpected or by chance —*adj.* designating or of a small group that meets for a kind of therapy in personal interrelationship, involving a release of inhibitions, an open exchange of intimate feelings, etc. —*SYN.* see BATTLE[1]

en·cour·age (in kur′ij) *vt.* **-aged**, **-ag·ing** [ME. *encouragen* < OFr. *encoragier*: see EN-[1] & COURAGE] 1. to give courage, hope, or confidence to; embolden; hearten 2. to give support to; be favorable to; foster; help

en·cour·age·ment (-mənt) *n.* 1. an encouraging or being encouraged 2. something that encourages

en·cour·ag·ing (-iŋ) *adj.* giving courage, hope, or confidence —**en·cour'ag·ing·ly** *adv.*

en·crim·son (in krim′z'n) *vt.* to make crimson

en·cri·nite (en′krə nīt′) *n.* [ModL. *encrinites* < Gr. *en*, in + *krinon*, lily] a fossil crinoid (genus *Encrinus*), a spiny sea invertebrate

en·croach (in krōch′) *vi.* [ME. *encrochen* < OFr. *encrochier*, to seize upon, take < *en-*, in + *croc*, *croche*, a hook: cf. CROCHET] 1. to trespass or intrude (*on* or *upon* the rights, property, etc. of another), esp. in a gradual or sneaking way 2. to advance beyond the proper, original, or customary limits; make inroads (*on* or *upon*) —*SYN.* see TRESPASS —**en·croach'ment** *n.*

en·crust (in krust′) *vt., vi.* same as INCRUST —**en·crus·ta'tion** *n.*

en·crypt (en kript′) *vt.* [< EN-1 + CRYPT(OGRAM)] to encode or encipher

en·cul·tu·rate (in kul′chə rāt′) *vt.* -rat'ed, -rat'ing to cause to adapt to the prevailing cultural patterns of one's society —**en·cul'tu·ra'tion** *n.*

en·cum·ber (in kum′bər) *vt.* [ME. *encombren* < OFr. *encombrer*: see EN-1 & CUMBER] 1. to hold back the motion or action of, as with a burden; hinder; hamper 2. to fill in such a way as to obstruct; block up; obstruct 3. to load or weigh down, as with claims, debts, etc.; burden

en·cum·brance (-brəns) *n.* [ME. & OFr. *encombraunce*] 1. something that encumbers; hindrance; obstruction; burden 2. [Rare] a dependent, esp. a child 3. *Law* same as INCUMBRANCE

-en·cy (ən sē, 'n sē) [L. *-entia*] a *n.*-forming suffix meaning act, fact, quality, state, result, or degree [*dependency*, *emergency*, *efficiency*]

ency., encyc., encycl. encyclopedia

en·cyc·li·cal (in sik′li k'l, -sī′kli-) *adj.* [LL. *encyclicus* < Gr. *enkyklios*, in a circle, general, common < *en-*, in + *kyklos*, a circle: see CYCLE] for general circulation: also **en·cyc'lic** —*n.* R.C.Ch. a letter from the Pope to the bishops of the church, usually dealing with doctrinal matters

en·cy·clo·pe·di·a, en·cy·clo·pae·di·a (in sī′klə pē′dē ə) *n.* [ModL. (1508) *encyclopaedia* < Gr. *enkyklopaideia*, false reading for *enkyklios paideia*, instruction in the circle of the arts and sciences < *enkyklios* (*en-*, in + *kyklos*, a circle: see CYCLE), in a circle, general + *paideia*, education < *puileuein*, to educate, bring up a child < *pais* (gen. *paidos*), child: see PEDO-1] 1. a book or set of books giving information on all or many branches of knowledge, generally in articles alphabetically arranged 2. a similar work giving information in a particular field of knowledge

en·cy·clo·pe·dic, en·cy·clo·pae·dic (-pē′dik) *adj.* of or like an encyclopedia; esp., giving information about many subjects; comprehensive in scope —**en·cy'clo·pe'di·cal·ly, en·cy'clo·pae'di·cal·ly** *adv.*

en·cy·clo·pe·dism, en·cy·clo·pae·dism (-pē′diz'm) *n.* encyclopedic knowledge or learning

en·cy·clo·pe·dist, en·cy·clo·pae·dist (-pē′dist) *n.* 1. a person who compiles or helps compile an encyclopedia 2. [E-] [*pl.*] the writers of the French Encyclopedia (1751-1772) edited by Diderot and d'Alembert, which contained the advanced ideas of the period

en·cyst (en sist′) *vt., vi.* to enclose or become enclosed in a cyst, capsule, or sac —**en·cyst'ment, en'cys·ta'tion** (-sis tā′shən) *n.*

end (end) *n.* [ME. & OE. *ende*, akin to Gr. *ende*, Goth. *andeis* < IE. *antyos, opposite, lying ahead < base **anti-*, opposite, facing (< *ants, front, forehead) whence Gr. *anti*, L. *ante*] 1. a limit or limiting part; point of beginning or stopping; boundary 2. the last part of anything; final point; finish; completion; conclusion [the *end* of the day] 3. *a)* a ceasing to exist; death or destruction *b)* the cause or manner of this 4. the part at, toward, or near either of the extremities of anything; tip 5. *a)* an outer district or region [the west *end* of town] *b)* a division, as of an organization 6. what is desired or hoped for; object; purpose; intention 7. an outcome; result; upshot; consequence 8. a piece left over; fragment; remnant [odds and *ends*] 9. the reason for being; final cause ☆10. *Football a)* a player at either end of the line *b)* his position —*vt.* [ME. *enden* < OE. *endian*] 1. to bring to an end; finish; stop; conclude 2. to be or form the end of —*vi.* 1. to come to an end; terminate: often with *up* 2. to die —*adj.* at the end; final [*end* man, *end* product] —*SYN.* see CLOSE², INTENTION —**end for end** with the ends, or the position, reversed —**ends of the earth** remote regions —**end to end** in a line so that the ends touch or meet —**keep one's end up** [Colloq.] to do one's share —**make an end of** 1. to finish; stop 2. to do away with —**make (both) ends meet** [cf. Fr. *joindre les deux bouts*] to manage to keep one's expenses within one's income —**no end** [Colloq.] extremely; very much or many —**on end** 1. in an upright position 2. without interruption or pause [for days *on end*] —**put an end to** 1. to stop; finish 2. to do away with —**to end** that surpasses or exceeds [a trip *to end* all trips]

end-all (end′ôl′) *n.* see BE-ALL AND END-ALL

en·dam·age (in dam′ij) *vt.* -aged, -ag·ing to cause damage or injury to

en·da·moe·ba (en′də mē′bə) *n.* [see ENDO- & AMOEBA] any of a genus (*Endamoeba*) of amoebas parasitic in the digestive tract of cockroaches and termites and of certain vertebrates; often, specif., the species (*Endamoeba histolytica*) that causes amoebic dysentery in man: also sp. **en'da·me'ba** —**en'da·moe'bic** *adj.*

en·dan·ger (in dān′jər) *vt.* to expose to danger, harm, or loss; imperil —**en·dan'ger·ment** *n.*

en·darch (en′därk) *adj.* [< END(O)- + Gr. *archē*, beginning] *Bot.* having the primary xylem maturing from the center of the stem toward the outside

end·brain (end′brān′) *n.* same as TELENCEPHALON

en·dear (in dir′) *vt.* to make dear, beloved, or well liked [to *endear* oneself by acts of generosity]

en·dear·ing (-iŋ) *adj.* 1. that makes dear or well liked 2. expressing affection [*endearing* tones]

en·dear·ment (-mənt) *n.* 1. an endearing or being endeared; affection 2. a word or act expressing affection

en·deav·or (in dev′ər) *vi.* [ME. *endever* < *en-* (see EN-1) + *dever* < OFr. *deveir* (Fr. *devoir*), duty, as in *se mettre en devoir*, to try to do: see DEVOIR] to make an earnest attempt —*vt.* 1. [Archaic] to try to achieve 2. to try (*to* do something) —*n.* an earnest attempt or effort Also, Brit. sp., **en·deav'our** —*SYN.* see EFFORT, TRY

En·de·cott (en′di kät′, -kət), **John** 1588?-1665; English Puritan; 1st governor of Massachusetts Bay colony: also sp. **En'di·cott**

en·dem·ic (en dem′ik) *adj.* [Fr. *endémique* < *endémie*, endemic disease < Gr. *endēmia*, a dwelling in < *endēmos*, native < *en-*, in + *dēmos*, the people] 1. native to a particular country, nation, or region: said of plants, animals, and, sometimes, customs, etc. 2. restricted to and constantly present in a particular country or locality: said of a disease: also **en·dem'i·cal** —*n.* 1. an endemic plant or animal 2. an endemic disease —*SYN.* see NATIVE —**en·dem'i·cal·ly** *adv.* —**en·de·mic·i·ty** (en′də mis′ə tē), **en·dem'ism** *n.*

En·der·by Land (en′dər bē) region of Antarctica, opposite the Southern tip of Africa: discovered 1831

en·der·mic (en dur′mik) *adj.* [< Gr. *en*, in + *derma*, the skin + -IC] *Med.* applied to the skin and acting by absorption through it —**en·der'mi·cal·ly** *adv.*

En·ders (en′dərz), **John F(ranklin)** 1897- ; U.S. bacteriologist

end·ing (en′diŋ) *n.* [OE. *endung*: see END] 1. an end; specif., *a)* the last part; finish; conclusion *b)* death 2. *Gram.* the letter or letters added to the end of a word or word base to make a derivative or an inflectional form [-ed is the *ending* in *wanted*]

en·dive (en′dīv, än′dēv) *n.* [ME. & OFr. < ML. *endivia* < MGr. *endivi* < L. *intibus* < Gr. *entybon*, prob. < Egypt. *tybi*, January (when it is said to grow in Egypt)] 1. *a)* a cultivated plant (*Cichorium endivia*) of the composite family, similar to the dandelion: its curled, narrow leaves are cooked or blanched and used for salads *b)* another form of this vegetable with wide, smooth leaves, used as a potherb or in salads 2. the young leaves of chicory (sense 1) blanched for salads

end·less (end′lis) *adj.* [ME. *endeles* < OE. *endeleas* (see END & -LESS)] 1. having no end; going on forever; eternal; infinite 2. lasting too long; interminable [an *endless* speech] 3. continual [*endless* interruptions] 4. with the ends joined to form a closed unit that can move continuously over wheels, etc. [an *endless* chain] —**end'less·ly** *adv.* —**end'less·ness** *n.*

end·long (-lôŋ′) *adv.* [Archaic] 1. lengthwise 2. on end

end man 1. a man at the end of a row ☆2. in a minstrel show, the comic performer at each end of the first row, for whom the interlocutor serves as a foil

end·most (-mōst′) *adj.* at or nearest to the end; farthest; most remote; last

en·do- (en′dō, -də) [< Gr. *endon*, within < *en*, in + (?) *dom, locative of base seen in L. *domus*, house: hence, orig., in the house] *a combining form meaning* within, inner [*endoderm*]: also, before a vowel, **end-**

en·do·bi·ot·ic (en′dō bī ät′ik) *adj.* [ENDO- + BIOTIC] living within the tissues of a host organism, as the malaria parasite

en·do·blast (en′də blast′) *n.* [ENDO- + -BLAST] same as ENDODERM

en·do·car·di·al (en′də kär′dē əl) *adj.* 1. within the heart 2. of the endocardium

en·do·car·di·tis (en′dō kär dīt′is) *n.* [ModL.: see -ITIS] inflammation of the endocardium

en·do·car·di·um (en′də kär′dē əm) *n.* [ModL. < ENDO- + Gr. *kardia*, HEART] the thin endothelial membrane lining the cavities of the heart

en·do·carp (en′də kärp′) *n.* [ENDO- + -CARP] the inner layer of the wall of a ripened ovary or fruit, as the pit surrounding the seed of a plum

en·do·cen·tric (en′də sen′trik) *adj.* *Linguis.* designating or of a construction which in its totality has the same syntactic function as one or more of its constituents (Ex.:

the phrase *ham and eggs* has the same syntactic function as *ham* or *eggs*): cf. EXOCENTRIC

en·do·com·men·sal (en'dō kə men's'l) *n.* a commensal living within the body of the host organism

en·do·cra·ni·um (en'də krā'nē əm) *n.*, *pl.* **-ni·a** (-ə), **-ni·ums** 1. *same as* DURA MATER 2. the processes supporting the brain in the head capsule of an insect

en·do·crine (en'də krin, -krīn', -krēn') *adj.* [ENDO- + Gr. *krinein*, to separate: see CRISIS] 1. designating or of any gland producing one or more internal secretions that are introduced directly into the bloodstream and carried to other parts of the body whose functions they regulate or control 2. designating or of such a secretion —*n.* any such gland or its secretion: the thyroid, adrenal, and pituitary glands are endocrines

en·do·cri·nol·o·gy (en'dō kri näl'ə jē, -krī-) *n.* the branch of medicine dealing with the endocrine glands and the internal secretions of the body —**en'do·cri'no·log'i·cal** (-nə läj'i k'l) *adj.* —**en'do·cri·nol'o·gist** *n.*

en·do·derm (en'də durm') *n.* [ENDO- + -DERM] the inner layer of cells of the embryo, from which is formed the lining of the digestive tract, of other internal organs, and of certain glands —**en'do·der'mal, en'do·der'mic** *adj.*

en·do·der·mis (en'də dur'mis) *n.* the specialized innermost layer of cells of the cortex, found in roots and in many stems

☆**en·do·don·tics** (-dän'tiks) *n.pl.* [END(O)- + -ODONT + -ICS] [*with sing. v.*] the branch of dentistry that treats disorders of the pulp; root-canal therapy: also **en'do·don'tia** (-shə) —**en'do·don'tic** *adj.* —**en'do·don'tist** *n.*

en·do·en·zyme (en'dō en'zīm) *n.* an enzyme that functions within the cell

en·dog·a·my (en däg'ə mē) *n.* [ENDO- + -GAMY] 1. the custom of marrying only within one's own tribe, clan, etc.; inbreeding: opposed to EXOGAMY 2. cross-pollination among flowers of the same plant —**en·dog'a·mous, en·do·gam·ic** (en'də gam'ik) *adj.*

en·do·gen (en'də jən) *n.* [Fr. *endogène* (see ENDO- & -GEN): the stems were formerly believed to grow from within] *former term for* MONOCOTYLEDON

en·dog·e·nous (en däj'ə nəs) *adj.* [prec. + -OUS] 1. developing from within; originating internally 2. *Biol.* growing or developing from or on the inside 3. *Physiol.*, *Biochem.* of the anabolism of cells

en·dog·e·ny (-nē) *n.* [ENDO- + -GENY] *Biol.* growth from within; endogenous formation of cells

en·do·lymph (en'də limf') *n.* [ENDO- + LYMPH] *Anat.* the fluid in the membranous labyrinth of the ear

en·do·me·tri·o·sis (en'dō mē'trē ō'sis) *n.* [see ff. & -OSIS] the growth of endometrial tissue in abnormal locations, as on the ovaries or within the peritoneal cavity

en·do·me·tri·um (-mē'trē əm) *n.* [ENDO- + Gr. *mētra*, uterus] the inner lining of the uterus —**en'do·me'tri·al** *adj.*

en·do·mix·is (en'də mik'sis) *n.* [ENDO- + ModL. -*mixis*, a mixing < Gr. *mixis* < base of *mygnynai*, to MIX] a rejuvenating nuclear reorganization within the cell of certain ciliates, not involving nuclear fusion: cf. CONJUGATION —**en'do·mic'tic** (-mik'tik) *adj.*

en·do·morph (en'də môrf') *n.* [ENDO- + -MORPH] 1. a mineral, esp. a crystal, enclosed within another 2. a person of the endomorphic physical type

en·do·mor·phic (en'də môr'fik) *adj.* 1. of an endomorph 2. of or caused by endomorphism 3. designating or of the abdominal physical type, characterized by predominance of the structures developed from the endodermal layer of the embryo (i.e., the internal organs): cf. ECTOMORPHIC & MESOMORPHIC —**en'do·mor'phy** (-fē) *n.*

en·do·mor·phism (-môr'fiz'm) *n.* structural change caused in an intrusive igneous rock by the action of the surrounding rock

en·do·par·a·site (-par'ə sīt') *n.* a parasite that inhabits the internal organs or tissues of an animal or plant; hookworm, tapeworm, endamoeba, etc.

en·do·pep·ti·dase (-pep'tə dās') *n.* any enzyme that hydrolyzes peptide bonds in the interior of a peptide chain

en·doph·a·gous (en däf'ə gəs) *n.* [ENDO- + -PHAGOUS] feeding from the inside of an animal or plant: said of certain parasitic insects

en·do·phyte (en'də fīt') *n.* [ENDO- + -PHYTE] any plant that grows within another plant, as certain parasitic fungi or algae —**en'do·phyt'ic** (-fit'ik) *adj.*

en·do·plasm (en'də plaz'm) *n.* [ENDO- + -PLASM] the inner part of the cytoplasm of a cell: distinguished from ECTOPLASM —**en'do·plas'mic** *adj.*

en·do·proct (en'də präkt') *n.* [ENDO- + Gr. *prōktos*, anus] any of a phylum (Endoprocta) of small, mosslike organisms with a complete digestive tract and an anus opening near the mouth and within the circlet of oral tentacles: also **en'to·proct'** (-tə-)

end organ any specialized structure at the peripheral end of nerve fibers having either sensory or motor functions

en·dorse (in dôrs') *vt.* **-dorsed', -dors'ing** [altered (after L.) < ME. *endosen* < OFr. *endosser* < ML. *indorsare* < L. *in*, on, upon + *dorsum*, the back] 1. to write on the back of (a document); specif., a) to sign (one's name) as payee on the back of (a check, money order, etc.) b) to make (a check, etc.) payable to another person by thus signing one's name and specifying the payee 2. to write a note, title, etc. on (a document) 3. a) to give approval to; support; sanction [to

endorse a candidate*]* b) to state, as in an advertisement, that one approves of (a product, service, etc.), often in return for a fee —*SYN.* see APPROVE —**en·dors'a·ble** *adj.* —**en·dors'er** *n.*

en·dor·see (in dôr'sē', en'-) *n.* the person to whom a check, note, etc. is made over by endorsement

en·dorse·ment (in dôrs'mənt) *n.* [ME. *endosement*] 1. the act of endorsing something 2. something written in endorsing; specif., a) the signature of a payee on the back of a check, note, etc. b) a change, as of coverage or beneficiary, written on or added to an insurance policy, and signed by an agent of the insurer c) a statement endorsing a person, product, etc., as in an advertisement

en·do·scope (en'də skōp') *n.* [ENDO- + -SCOPE] an instrument for examining visually the inside of a hollow organ of the body, as the bladder or rectum —**en'do·scop'ic** (-skäp'ik) *adj.* —**en·dos·co·py** (en däs'kə pē) *n.*

en·do·skel·e·ton (en'də skel'ə t'n) *n.* the internal bony, cartilaginous, or chitinous supporting structure in vertebrates, echinoderms, etc.: distinguished from EXOSKELETON —**en'do·skel'e·tal** *adj.*

en·dos·mo·sis (en'däs mō'sis, -däz-) *n.* [altered (after OSMOSIS) < Fr. *endosmose* < *endo-*, ENDO- + Gr. *ōsmos*: see OSMOSIS] in osmosis, the more rapid diffusion of the less dense fluid through the semipermeable membrane to mingle with the more dense: opposed to EXOSMOSIS —**en'dos·mot'ic** (-mät'ik) *adj.*

en·do·sperm (en'də spurm') *n.* [ENDO- + SPERM¹] a tissue which surrounds the developing embryo of a seed and provides food for its growth; albumen —**en'do·sper'mic** *adj.* —**en'do·sper'mous** *adj.*

en·do·spore (-spôr') *n.* 1. an asexual spore formed within the cell wall of the parent cell, as in certain bacteria, fungi, and algae 2. the inner wall of a spore or pollen grain; intine: also **en'do·spo'ri·um** (-spôr'ē əm), *pl.* **-ri·a** (-ə) —**en'do·spor'ic** *adj.*

en·dos·te·um (en däs'tē əm) *n.*, *pl.* **-te·a** (-ə) [ModL. < END(O)- + Gr. *osteon*, a bone] the vascular connective tissue lining the marrow cavities of bones —**en·dos'te·al** *adj.*

en·dos·to·sis (en'däs tō'sis) *n.* [ModL. < END(O)- + OSTOSIS] the formation of bone within cartilage

en·do·the·ci·um (en'də thē'sē əm) *n.*, *pl.* **-ci·a** (-ə) [ENDO- + ModL. -*thecium*, a fine enclosing structure < Gr. *thēkion*, a small case, dim. of *thēkē*: see THECA] an inner layer, as the inner wall of a pollen grain or the inner layer of a moss capsule

en·do·the·li·um (en'də thē'lē əm) *n.*, *pl.* **-li·a** (-ə) [ModL. < ENDO- + (EPI)THELIUM] the layer of cells lining the inside of blood and lymph vessels, of the heart, and of some other closed cavities —**en'do·the'li·al** *adj.* —**en'do·the'li·oid', en·doth·e·loid** (en däth'ə loid') *adj.*

en·do·ther·mic (en'də thur'mik) *adj.* [ENDO- + THERMIC] designating, of, or produced by a chemical change in which there is an absorption of heat: also **en'do·ther'mal**

en·do·tox·in (en'də täk'sən) *n.* [ENDO- + TOXIN] a toxic substance found in certain disease-producing bacteria and liberated by the disintegration of the bacterial cell: they harm certain tissue cells

en·do·tra·che·al (-trā'kē əl) *adj.* within the trachea: said of devices thus placed for administering anesthetic gases, for examination, etc.

en·dow (in dou') *vt.* [ME. *endouen* < Anglo-Fr. *endouer* < OFr. *en-*, in + *douer* < L. *dotare*, to endow: cf. DOT²] 1. to provide with some talent, quality, etc. [*endowed* with courage*]* 2. to think of as having some quality or characteristic [*to endow* gods with human traits*]* 3. to give money or property so as to provide an income for the support of (a college, hospital, etc.) 4. [Obs.] to provide with a dower

en·dow·ment (-mənt) *n.* [ME. *endouement*] 1. the act of endowing 2. that with which something is endowed; specif., any bequest or gift that provides an income for an institution or person 3. a gift of nature; inherent talent, ability, quality, etc.

☆**endowment policy** an insurance policy by which a stated amount is paid to the insured after the period of time specified in the contract, or to the beneficiaries in case the insured dies within the time specified

end·pa·per (end'pā'pər) *n.* a folded sheet of paper one half of which is pasted to the inside of either cover of a book, the other half to the inside edge of the first (or last) page of the book

end plate the area of specialized tissue that forms the junction between an individual muscle fiber and its motor nerve

end product the final result of any series of changes, processes, or chemical reactions

☆**en·drin** (en'drin) *n.* [< ? EN-¹ + (AL)DRIN] a synthetic insecticide, $C_{12}H_8OCl_6$

☆**end table** a small table to be placed at either end of a sofa, beside a chair, etc.

en·due (in dōō', -dyōō') *vt.* **-dued', -du'ing** [ME. *endeuen* < OFr. *enduire* < L. *inducere*, to lead in (see INDUCE): form and sense infl. by L. *induere* (see INDUE) & ENDOW] 1. [Rare] to put on (a garment) 2. to provide (with something); specif., to endow (*with* qualities, talents, etc.)

en·dur·a·ble (in door'ə b'l, -dyoor'-) *adj.* that can be endured; bearable —**en·dur'a·bly** *adv.*

en·dur·ance (-əns) *n.* **1.** the act of enduring **2.** the power of enduring; specif., *a)* ability to last, continue, or remain *b)* ability to stand pain, distress, fatigue, etc.; fortitude **3.** duration **4.** [Rare] that which is endured; hardship —*SYN.* see PATIENCE

en·dure (in door', -dyoor') *vt.* -dured', -dur'ing [ME. *enduren* < OFr. *endurer* < LL.(Ec.) *indurare*, to harden the heart < L., to harden < *in-*, in + *durare*, to last, hold out, last < *durus*, hard: see DURABLE] **1.** to hold up under (pain, fatigue, etc.); stand; bear; undergo **2.** to put up with; tolerate —*vi.* **1.** to continue in existence; last; remain **2.** to bear pain, etc. without flinching; hold out —*SYN.* see BEAR[1], CONTINUE

en·dur·ing (-iŋ) *adj.* lasting; permanent; durable —**en·dur'ing·ly** *adv.*

end·ways (end'wāz') *adv.* **1.** on end; upright **2.** with the end foremost **3.** lengthwise **4.** end to end Also **end'wise'** (-wīz')

En·dym·i·on (en dim'ē ən) [L. < Gr. *Endymiōn*] *Gr. Myth.* a beautiful young shepherd loved by Selene

☆**end zone** *Football* the area between the goal line and the end boundary (**end line**) ten yards behind it, at each end of the playing field

-ene (ēn) [after L. *-enus*, Gr. *-enos*, adj. suffix] *a suffix used:* **1.** *Chem.* to form the names of unsaturated compounds containing at least one double bond, esp. open chain hydrocarbons containing only one double bond *[propylene, benzene]* **2.** to form some commercial names

ENE, E.N.E., e.n.e. east-northeast

en·e·ma (en'ə mə) *n.* [LL. < Gr. *enema*, injection < *enienai*, to send in < *en-*, in + *hienai*, to send] **1.** a liquid injected into the colon through the anus, as a purgative, medicine, etc.; clyster **2.** the injection of such a liquid

en·e·my (en'ə mē) *n., pl.* -mies [ME. & OFr. *enemi* < L. *inimicus*, unfriendly, enemy < *in-*, not + *amicus*, friend: see AMIABLE] **1.** a person who hates another, and wishes or tries to injure him; foe **2.** *a)* a nation or force hostile to another *b)* troops, fleet, ship, member, etc. of a hostile nation **3.** a person hostile to an idea, cause, etc. **4.** anything injurious or harmful —*adj.* **1.** of an enemy; of a hostile nation **2.** [Obs.] hostile —*SYN.* see OPPONENT

enemy alien an alien residing or interned in a country with which his own country is at war

en·er·get·ic (en'ər jet'ik) *adj.* [Gr. *energētikos*] of, having, or showing energy; vigorous; forceful —*SYN.* see ACTIVE —**en'er·get'i·cal·ly** *adv.*

en·er·get·ics (-iks) *n.pl.* [*with sing. v.*] the science that deals with the laws of energy and its transformations

en·er·gid (en'ər jid) *n.* [G. < Gr. *energos*, active (see ENERGY) + G. *-id*, -ID] the nucleus of a cell together with the mass of protoplasm around it

en·er·gism (-jiz'm) *n. Ethics* the view that the supreme good is activation of human powers rather than pleasure or happiness

en·er·gize (-jīz') *vt.* -gized', -giz'ing **1.** to give energy to; activate; invigorate **2.** *Elec.* to apply a source of electromotive force or current to (a circuit, system of conductors, etc.) —*vi.* to show energy; be active —**en'er·giz'er** *n.*

en·er·gu·men (en'ər gyōō'mən) *n.* [LL.(Ec.) *energumenos* < Gr. *energoumenos*, prp. pass. of *energein*, to work on: see ff.] **1.** a person supposedly possessed by an evil spirit; demoniac **2.** a fanatic; enthusiast

en·er·gy (en'ər jē) *n., pl.* -gies [LL. *energia* < Gr. *energeia* < *energēs*, active, at work < *en-*, in + *ergon*, WORK] **1.** force of expression or utterance **2.** *a)* potential forces; inherent power; capacity for vigorous action *b)* [*often pl.*] such forces or power, esp. in action *[to apply all one's energies]* **3.** strength or power efficiently exerted **4.** *Physics* the capacity for doing work and overcoming resistance: see MATTER (sense 2) —*SYN.* see STRENGTH

energy level a stable state in which the energy of a physical system remains constant

en·er·vate (en'ər vāt'; *for adj.* i nur'vit) *vt.* -vat'ed, -vat'ing [< L. *enervatus*, pp. of *enervare* < *enervis*, nerveless, weak < *e-*, out + *nervus*, NERVE] to deprive of strength, force, vigor, etc.; weaken physically, mentally, or morally; devitalize; debilitate —*adj.* enervated; weakened —*SYN.* see UNNERVE, WEAKEN —**en'er·va'tion** *n.* —**en'er·va'tor** *n.*

E·nes·co (i nes'kō), **Georges** (zhôrzh) 1881-1955; Romanian violinist, composer, & conductor

en·face (en fās') *vt.* -faced', -fac'ing [Brit.] to write or print on the face of (a document, check, etc.) —**en·face'·ment** *n.*

‡**en fa·mille** (än fà mē'y) [Fr., lit., in (one's) family] **1.** with one's family; at home **2.** in an informal way

‡**en·fant ter·ri·ble** (än fän te rē'bl') [Fr., lit., terrible child] **1.** an unmanageable, mischievous child **2.** a person who causes trouble or embarrassment by his imprudent remarks or actions

en·fee·ble (in fē'b'l) *vt.* -fee'bled, -fee'bling [ME. *enfeblen* < OFr. *enfeblir*] to make feeble —**en·fee'ble·ment** *n.*

en·feoff (en fef', -fēf') *vt.* [ME. *enfeffen* (Anglo-Fr. *enfeoffer*) < OFr. *enfeffer*: see EN-[1] & FIEF] *Law* to invest with an estate held in fee —**en·feoff'ment** *n.*

en·fet·ter (in fet'ər) *vt.* to bind in or as in fetters

En·field (en'fēld') **1.** city in Middlesex, England, near London: pop. 110,000 **2.** [after prec.] suburb of Hartford, in N Conn., on the Connecticut River: pop. 46,000

en·fi·lade (en'fə lād', en'fə lād') *n.* [Fr. < *enfiler*, to thread, string, rake with fire < OFr. < *en-* (L. *in*), in + *fil* (L. *filum*, a thread)] **1.** gunfire directed from either flank along the length of a column or line of troops **2.** a disposition or placement of troops that makes them vulnerable to such fire —*vt.* -lad'ed, -lad'ing to direct such gunfire at (a column, etc.)

‡**en·fleu·rage** (än flē räzh') *n.* [Fr. < *en-*, in + *fleur*, a flower] a process of extracting perfumes by having odorless fats absorb the exhalations of certain flowers

en·fold (in fōld') *vt.* **1.** to wrap in folds; wrap up; envelop **2.** to embrace

en·force (in fôrs') *vt.* -forced', -forc'ing [ME. *enforcen* < OFr. *enforcier* < *en-*, in + *force*, FORCE] **1.** to give force to; urge *[to enforce an argument by analogies]* **2.** to bring about or impose by force *[to enforce one's will on a child]* **3.** to compel observance of (a law, etc.) —**en·force'a·ble** *adj.* —**en·force'ment** *n.* —**en·forc'er** *n.*

en·fran·chise (in fran'chīz) *vt.* -chised, -chis·ing [ME. *enfranchisen* < OFr. *enfranchiss-*, stem of *enfranchir*, to set free, enfranchise < *en-*, in + *franchir*, to set free < *franc*: see FRANK[1]] **1.** to free from slavery, bondage, legal obligation, etc. **2.** to give a franchise to; specif., to admit to citizenship, esp. to the right to vote —**en·fran'chise·ment** (-chīz mənt, -chiz-) *n.*

Eng. 1. England **2.** English

eng. 1. engine **2.** engineer **3.** engineering **4.** engraved **5.** engraver **6.** engraving

En·ga·dine (eŋ'gə dēn) valley of the Inn River, E Switzerland: site of many resorts: c. 60 mi. long

en·gage (in gāj') *vt.* -gaged', -gag'ing [ME. *engagen* < OFr. *engagier*: see EN-[1] & GAGE[1]] **1.** orig., to give or assign as security for a debt, etc. **2.** to bind (oneself) by a promise; pledge; specif. (now only in the passive), to bind by a promise of marriage; betroth *[he is engaged to Ann]* **3.** to arrange for the services of; hire; employ *[to engage a lawyer]* **4.** to arrange for the use of; reserve *[to engage a hotel room]* **5.** to draw into; involve *[engage him in conversation]* **6.** to attract and hold (the attention, etc.) **7.** to employ or keep busy; occupy *[reading engages his spare time]* **8.** to enter into conflict with (the enemy) **9.** to interlock with; mesh together *[engage the gears]* **10.** [Obs.] to entangle; ensnare —*vi.* **1.** to pledge oneself; promise; undertake; agree *[to engage to do something]* **2.** to occupy or involve oneself; take part; be active *[to engage in dramatics]* **3.** to enter into conflict **4.** to interlock; mesh

‡**en·ga·gé** (än gà zhā') *adj.* [Fr.] committed to, or actively supporting, a political or social cause

en·gaged (in gājd') *adj.* **1.** pledged; esp., pledged in marriage; betrothed **2.** not at leisure; occupied; employed; busy **3.** *a)* involved in combat, as troops *b)* voluntarily committed or personally involved: cf. ENGAGÉ **4.** attached to or partly set into a wall, etc. *[engaged columns]* **5.** in gear; interlocked; meshed

en·gage·ment (-gāj'mənt) *n.* **1.** an engaging or being engaged; specif., *a)* a promise; pledge *b)* a promise of marriage; betrothal *c)* an arrangement to go somewhere, do something, meet someone, etc.; appointment *d)* employment or period of employment, esp. in the performing arts *e)* a conflict; battle *f)* [*usually pl.*] financial obligations; commitments *g)* state of being in gear **2.** something that engages —*SYN.* see BATTLE[1]

en·gag·ing (-gāj'iŋ) *adj.* attractive; pleasant; winning; charming —**en·gag'ing·ly** *adv.*

‡**en garde** (än gàrd') [Fr.] *Fencing* on guard: the opening position in which the fencer is prepared either to attack or defend

en·gar·land (in gär'lənd) *vt.* [Poet.] to put a garland or garlands on or around

En·gels (eŋ'gəlz; G. eŋ'əls), **Frie·drich** (frē'driH) 1820-95; Ger. socialist leader & writer, in England after 1850: close associate of Karl Marx

en·gen·der (in jen'dər) *vt.* [ME. *engendren* < OFr. *engendrer* < L. *ingenerare*, to beget < *in-*, in + *generare*: see GENERATE] **1.** [Rare] to beget **2.** to bring into being; bring about; cause; produce *[pity engendered love]* —*vi.* [Obs.] to be produced; originate

engin. 1. engineer **2.** engineering

en·gine (en'jən) *n.* [ME. *engin*, native talent, hence something produced by this < OFr. *engin* < L. *ingenium*, natural ability, genius < *in-*, in & base of *gignere*, to produce: see GENUS] **1.** any machine that uses energy to develop mechanical power; esp., a machine for starting motion in some other machine **2.** a railroad locomotive **3.** any instrument or machine; apparatus *[engines of warfare, engines of torture]* **4.** *same as* FIRE ENGINE **5.** [Archaic] any means, agent, or device

en·gi·neer (en'jə nir') *n.* [earlier *enginer* < ME. *enginour* < OFr. *engineur*] **1.** [Rare] a person who makes engines **2.** a person skilled or occupied in some branch of engineering *[a mechanical engineer]* **3.** *a)* a person who operates or supervises the operation of engines or technical equipment

fat, āpe, cär; ten, ēven; is, bīte; gō, hôrn, tōōl, look; oil, out; up, fur; get; joy; yet; chin, she; thin, then; zh, leisure; ŋ, ring; ə for *a* in *ago, e* in *agent, i* in *sanity, o* in *comply, u* in *focus;* ' as in *able* (ā'b'l); Fr. bal; ë, Fr. coeur; ö, Fr. feu; Fr. mon; ô, Fr. coq; ü, Fr. duc; r, Fr. cri; H, G. ich; kh, G. doch. See inside front cover. ☆ Americanism; ‡ foreign; *hypothetical; < derived from

*[a locomotive *engineer*, radio *engineer*]* b) a specialist in planning and directing operations in some technical field **4.** a skillful or clever manager **5.** *Mil.* a member of that branch of the army concerned with engineering problems, as the construction and demolition of bridges, roads, etc. —*vt.* ☆**1.** to plan, construct, or manage as an engineer ☆**2.** to plan and direct skillfully; superintend; guide (a measure, action, etc. *through*)

en·gi·neer·ing (-iŋ) *n.* **1.** *a)* the science concerned with putting scientific knowledge to practical uses, divided into different branches, as civil, electrical, mechanical, or chemical engineering *b)* the planning, designing, construction, or management of machinery, roads, bridges, buildings, waterways, etc. **2.** the act of maneuvering or managing

☆**engine house** a building in which engines, as fire engines, railroad locomotives, etc., are housed

en·gine·ry (en′jən rē) *n.* **1.** [Rare] engines or machinery collectively; esp., instruments of war **2.** [Obs.] the art of making military instruments or works

en·gird (en gurd′) *vt.* -**girt′** or -**gird′ed**, -**gird′ing** to encircle; encompass; gird: also **en·gir′dle** (-′l)

en·gla·cial (en glā′shəl) *adj.* within a glacier

Eng·land (iŋ′glənd) [ME. *Englonde, Yngelonde* (with vowel change as in WING < ME. *weng*) < OE. *Engla land*, lit., land of the Angles (as opposed to the Saxons), hence England: cf. ANGLES] **1.** division of the United Kingdom of Great Britain & Northern Ireland, occupying most of the southern half of the island of Great Britain: 50,331 sq. mi.; pop. 47,023,000; cap. London **2.** England & Wales, considered an administrative unit **3.** *same as* UNITED KINGDOM

Eng·land·er (-ər) *n.* a native of England

Eng·lish (iŋ′glish) *adj.* [ME. < OE. *Englisc*, lit., of the Angles: see ANGLES & -ISH] **1.** of England, its people, their culture, etc. **2.** of their language —*n.* **1.** the language of the people of England, the official language of the British Commonwealth, the U.S., Liberia, etc. **2.** the English language of a specific period or place: see AMERICAN ENGLISH, BRITISH ENGLISH, OLD ENGLISH, MIDDLE ENGLISH, MODERN ENGLISH **3.** a characteristic way of using this language *[broken English]* **4.** the equivalent in the English language; English translation **5.** a school course or class in the English language or its literature ☆**6.** *[sometimes e-]* *Billiards, Bowling*, etc. a spinning motion given to a ball, as by striking it on one side **7.** *Printing* a size of type, 14 point —*vt.* **1.** to translate into English **2.** to apply the principles of English pronunciation, spelling, etc. to; Anglicize (a foreign word) ☆**3.** *[sometimes e-]* *Billiards, Bowling*, etc. to give English to (a ball) —**the English** the people of England

English Channel arm of the Atlantic, between England & France: 21-150 mi. wide; c. 350 mi. long

☆**English daisy** a small perennial herb (*Bellis perennis*) of the composite family, having single stalked heads with white or pink ray flowers

English horn a double-reed instrument of the woodwind family, similar to the oboe but larger and a fifth lower in pitch

Eng·lish·ism (-iz′m) *n.* **1.** *same as* BRITICISM **2.** an attachment to English ways and things

☆**English ivy** *same as* IVY (sense 1)

Eng·lish·man (-mən) *n.*, *pl.* -**men** (-mən) **1.** a native or inhabitant of England, esp. a man **2.** an English ship

Englishman's tie a kind of knot: see KNOT, illus.

☆**English muffin** a large, somewhat flat yeast roll, often baked on a griddle, and served split and toasted

Eng·lish·ry (-rē) *n.* [ME. *Englishrie:* see ENGLISH & -ERY] **1.** [Now Rare] a group of people of English descent; specif., the English population of Ireland **2.** the fact or state of being English by birth

ENGLISH HORN

English setter any of a breed of setter having a flat, white, long-haired coat with black, yellow, or orange spots, and feathery hair on the legs and tail

English sonnet *see* SHAKESPEAREAN SONNET

☆**English sparrow** the common street sparrow (*Passer domesticus*), a small brownish-gray European finch now found extensively in N. America

English springer spaniel any of a breed of springer spaniel with a long, glossy, liver-and-white or black-and-white coat and feathery hair on the legs and tail

English toy spaniel any of a breed of toy spaniel with a compact body, a soft, wavy coat, and long ears

☆**English walnut 1.** an Asiatic walnut tree (*Juglans regia*) now grown in Europe and N. America **2.** its nut

Eng·lish·wom·an (-woom′ən) *n.*, *pl.* -**wom·en** (-wim′ən) a woman who is a native or inhabitant of England

en·glut (in glut′) *vt.* -**glut′ted**, -**glut′ting** [OFr. *englotir* < LL. *ingluttire:* see EN-¹ & GLUT] [Archaic or Poet.] **1.** to gulp down; swallow **2.** to glut

en·gorge (-gôrj′) *vt.* -**gorged′**, -**gorg′ing** [Fr. *engorger* < OFr.: *en-*, in + *gorge*, throat] **1.** to gorge **2.** to devour greedily **3.** *Med.* to congest (a blood vessel, tissue, etc.) with blood or other fluid —*vi.* to eat greedily; feed ravenously —**en·gorge′ment** *n.*

engr. 1. engineer **2.** engineering **3.** engraved **4.** engraver **5.** engraving

en·graft (in graft′, -gräft′) *vt.* **1.** to graft (a shoot, etc.) from one plant onto another **2.** to establish firmly; implant

en·grail (-grāl′) *vt.* [ME. *engrelen* (only in pp.) < OFr. *engresler* < *en-*, in + *gresle*, slender < L. *gracilis*: see GRACILE] **1.** to indent (an edge or rim) with concave, curved notches **2.** to ornament the edge of with such a pattern —**en·grailed′** *adj.* —**en·grail′ment** *n.*

en·grain (-grān′) *vt.* [ME. *engreinen* < OFr. *engrainer*, to dye scarlet < *en-* (see EN-¹) + *graine*, seed, cochineal dye; associated in both Fr. & E. with *grain* (texture): see GRAIN] **1.** *same as* INGRAIN **2.** to grain in imitation of wood

en·gram (en′gram) *n.* [EN-¹ + -GRAM] **1.** *Biol.* a hypothetical permanent change produced by a stimulus in the protoplasm of a tissue **2.** *Psychol.* a permanent effect produced in the psyche by stimulation, assumed in explaining persistence of memory —**en·gram′mic** *adj.*

en·grave (in grāv′) *vt.* -**graved′**, -**grav′ing** [Fr. *engraver* < *en-*, in + *graver*, to incise < OFr. *grafe*, stylus < L. *graphium* < Gr. *graphion*, graving tool < *graphein*: see GRAPHIC] **1.** to cut or etch letters, designs, etc. in or on (a surface) **2.** to impress deeply or permanently on the mind or memory, as though by engraving **3.** to cut or etch (a picture, letters, etc.) into a metal plate, wooden block, etc. for printing **4.** to print by means of such a plate, block, etc. —**en·grav′er** *n.*

en·grav·ing (-iŋ) *n.* **1.** the act, process, or art of one who engraves **2.** an engraved plate, design, etc. **3.** any printed impression made from an engraved surface

en·gross (in grōs′) *vt.* [ME. *engrossen* < OFr. *engrosser*, to acquire in large quantity (< *en-*, in + *gros*, large < L. *grossus*) & *engroissier*, to become thick < *en-* + *groisse*, thickness < VL. **grossia* < L. *grossus:* see GROSS] **1.** *a)* to write out in large letters of a kind once used for legal documents *b)* to make a final fair copy of (esp. a legislative bill) **2.** to express formally or in legal form **3.** to take the entire attention of; occupy wholly; absorb *[engrossed in a book]* **4.** *a)* [Archaic] to buy all of so as to monopolize *b)* to take or require all of —**en·gross′er** *n.* —**en·gross′ment** *n.*

en·gross·ing (-iŋ) *adj.* taking one's entire attention; very interesting; absorbing

en·gulf (in gulf′) *vt.* [EN-¹ + GULF] **1.** to swallow up; overwhelm **2.** to plunge, as into a gulf

en·hance (-hans′, -häns′) *vt.* -**hanced′**, -**hanc′ing** [ME. *enhauncen* < Anglo-Fr. *enhauncer* < OFr. *enhaucier* < VL. **inaltiare* < *in-*, in + **altiare*, to raise < L. *altus*, high] to make greater, as in cost, value, attractiveness, etc.; heighten, improve, augment, etc. —*vi.* to increase, as in value or price —*SYN.* see INTENSIFY —**en·hance′ment** *n.* —**en·hanc′er** *n.*

en·har·mon·ic (en′här män′ik) *adj.* [L. *enharmonicus* < Gr. *enarmonikos:* see EN-¹ & HARMONY] *Music* **1.** *a)* designating or of an interval less than a half step *b)* designating a quarter step in early Greek music **2.** designating a scale containing such intervals **3.** *a)* relating to tones that are nearly identical in absolute pitch, as E♭ and D♯, and that on a keyed instrument tuned to equal temperament are made identical *b)* designating a change of notation without change in sound of such a tone —**en′har·mon′i·cal·ly** *adv.*

E·nid¹ (ē′nid) [prob. < OW. *enaid*, soul, used as term of endearment] **1.** a feminine name **2.** *Arthurian Legend* the wife of Geraint, a model of constancy

E·nid² (ē′nid) [after prec. (sense 1)] city in NC Okla.: pop. 44,000

e·nig·ma (ə nig′mə) *n.*, *pl.* -**mas** [L. *aenigma* < Gr. *ainigma < ainissesthai*, to speak in riddles < *ainos*, tale, story] **1.** a perplexing, usually ambiguous, statement; riddle **2.** a perplexing, baffling, or seemingly inexplicable matter, person, etc. —*SYN.* see MYSTERY

e·nig·mat·ic (en′ig mat′ik, ē′nig-) *adj.* [Fr. *énigmatique* < LL. *aenigmaticus*] of or like an enigma; perplexing; baffling: also **e′nig·mat′i·cal** —*SYN.* see OBSCURE —**e′nig·mat′i·cal·ly** *adv.*

en·isle (in īl′) *vt.* -**isled′**, -**isl′ing** [Poet.] **1.** to make (something) into or like an island **2.** to place on or as on an island; isolate

E·ni·we·tok (en′ə wē′täk) atoll in the Marshall Islands: site of U.S. atomic & hydrogen bomb tests

en·jamb·ment, en·jambe·ment (in jam′mənt; *Fr.* än zhänb män′) *n.* [Fr. *enjambement* < *enjamber*, to encroach < *en-* (see EN-¹) + *jambe*, leg: see JAMB] *Prosody* the running on of a sentence from one line or couplet to the next, with little or no pause

en·join (in join′) *vt.* [ME. *enjoinen* < OFr. *enjoindre* < L. *injungere*, to join into, put upon < *in-*, in + *jungere*, JOIN] **1.** to urge or impose with authority; order; enforce *[enjoin* silence on a class*]* **2.** to prohibit, esp. by legal injunction; forbid *[the company was *enjoined* from using false advertising]* **3.** to order (someone) authoritatively to do something, esp. by legal injunction —*SYN.* see COMMAND, FORBID

en·joy (in joi′) *vt.* [ME. *enjoien* < OFr. *enjoir* < *en-*, in + *joir*, to rejoice < L. *gaudere*, to be glad: see JOY] **1.** to have or experience with joy; get pleasure from; relish **2.** to have the use or benefit of; have as one's lot or advantage *[the book *enjoyed* large sales]* —**enjoy oneself** to have a good time; have pleasure

en·joy·a·ble (-ə b'l) *adj.* giving or capable of giving enjoyment; pleasurable —*SYN.* see PLEASANT —**en·joy'a·ble·ness** *n.* —**en·joy'a·bly** *adv.*

en·joy·ment (-mənt) *n.* **1.** the act or state of enjoying; specif., *a)* the possession, use, or benefit of something *b)* a pleasurable experiencing of something **2.** something enjoyed **3.** pleasure; gratification; joy —*SYN.* see PLEASURE

en·kin·dle (en kin'd'l) *vt.* -**dled,** -**dling 1.** to set on fire; make blaze up **2.** to stir up; arouse; excite

enl. 1. enlarge **2.** enlarged **3.** enlisted

en·lace (in lās') *vt.* -**laced,** -**lac'ing** [ME. *enlacen* < OFr. *enlacer* < *en-,* in + *lacer,* to tie, tangle < L. *laqueare* < *laqueus,* a noose: see LACE] **1.** to wind about as with a lace or laces; encircle; enfold **2.** to entangle; interlace **3.** to cover as with lace or netting —**en·lace'ment** *n.*

en·large (in lärj') *vt.* -**larged,** -**larg'ing** [ME. *enlargen* < OFr. *enlargier:* see EN-[1] & LARGE] **1.** to make larger; increase in size, volume, extent, etc.; broaden; expand **2.** *Photog.* to reproduce on a larger scale **3.** [Archaic] to release from imprisonment —*vi.* **1.** to become larger; increase in size, extent, etc.; expand **2.** to speak or write at greater length or in greater detail; expatiate (*on* or *upon*) —*SYN.* see INCREASE —**en·larg'er** *n.*

en·large·ment (-mənt) *n.* **1.** an enlarging or being enlarged **2.** something that enlarges by being added **3.** a reproduction, as of a photograph, on a larger scale

en·light·en (in līt'n) *vt.* **1.** to give the light of fact and knowledge to; reveal truths to; free from ignorance, prejudice, or superstition **2.** to give clarification to (a person) as to meanings, intentions, etc.; inform **3.** [Archaic] to light up —**en·light'en·er** *n.*

en·light·en·ment (-mənt) *n.* an enlightening or being enlightened —**the Enlightenment** an 18th-cent. European philosophical movement characterized by rationalism, an impetus toward learning, and a spirit of skepticism and empiricism in social and political thought

en·list (in list') *vt.* **1.** to enroll for service in some branch of the armed forces **2.** to win the support of; get the help or services of [to *enlist* men in a cause] **3.** to get (another's help, support, aid, etc.) —*vi.* **1.** to join some branch of the armed forces **2.** to join or support a cause or movement (with *in*) —**en·list'ee'** *n.*

enlisted man any man in the armed forces who is not a commissioned officer or warrant officer

en·list·ment (-mənt) *n.* **1.** an enlisting or being enlisted ☆**2.** the period of time for which one enlists

en·liv·en (in līv'n) *vt.* to make active, vivacious, interesting, or cheerful; liven up or brighten —**en·liv'en·er** *n.* —**en·liv'en·ment** *n.*

en masse (en mas'; *Fr.* än mås') [Fr., lit., in mass] in a group; as a whole; altogether

en·mesh (en mesh') *vt.* to catch in or as in the meshes of a net; entangle

en·mi·ty (en'mə tē) *n., pl.* -**ties** [ME. *enemite* < OFr. *enemistie* < VL. **inimicitas* < L. *inimicus:* see ENEMY] the bitter attitude or feelings of an enemy or of mutual enemies; hostility; antagonism

SYN.—**enmity** denotes a strong, settled feeling of hatred, whether concealed, displayed, or latent; **hostility** usually suggests enmity expressed in active opposition, attacks, etc.; **animosity** suggests bitterness of feeling that tends to break out in open hostility; **antagonism** stresses the mutual hostility or enmity of persons, forces, etc.

en·ne·ad (en'ē ad') *n.* [Gr. *enneas* (gen. *enneados*) < *ennea,* NINE] a group or set of nine (books, gods, etc.)

en·no·ble (i no'b'l) *vt.* -**bled,** -**bling** [ME. *ennoblen* (only in pp.) < Fr. *ennoblir:* see EN-[1] & NOBLE] **1.** to raise to the rank of nobleman **2.** to give a noble quality to; dignify —**en·no'ble·ment** *n.* —**en·no'bler** *n.*

en·nui (än'wē; *Fr.* än nwē') *n.* [Fr.: see ANNOY] weariness and dissatisfaction resulting from inactivity or lack of interest; boredom

E·noch (ē'nək) [Gr. *Enōch* < Heb. *ḥănōkh,* lit., dedicated] **1.** a masculine name **2.** *Bible a)* the eldest son of Cain: Gen. 4:17 *b)* the father of Methuselah: Gen. 5:21

e·nol (ē'nôl, -nōl) *n.* [< -ENE + -OL[1]] the tautomeric form of a compound that contains the >C:C(OH)– group —**e·nol'ic** (-näl'ik, -nō'lik) *adj.*

e·nol·o·gy (ē näl'ə jē) *n.* [< Gr. *oinos,* wine + -LOGY] the science or study of wines and wine making —**e·nol'o·gist** *n.*

e·nor·mi·ty (i nôr'mə tē) *n., pl.* -**ties** [Fr. *enormité* < L. *enormitas* < *enormis,* irregular, immoderate, immense < *e-,* out + *norma,* rule: see NORM] **1.** great wickedness [the *enormity* of a crime] **2.** a monstrous or outrageous act; very wicked crime **3.** enormous size or extent; vastness: in modern use, generally considered a loose usage

e·nor·mous (i nôr'məs) *adj.* [ME. *enormyouse* < L. *enormis* (see prec.) + -OUS] **1.** very much exceeding the usual size, number, or degree; of great size; huge; vast; immense **2.** [Archaic] very wicked; outrageous —**e·nor'mous·ly** *adv.* —**e·nor'mous·ness** *n.*

SYN.—**enormous** implies an exceeding by far what is normal in size, amount, or degree [an *enormous* nose, *enormous* expenses]; **immense,** basically implying immeasurableness, suggests size beyond the regular run of measurements but does not connote abnormality in that which is very large [redwoods are *immense* trees]; **huge** usually suggests an immense mass or bulk [a *huge* building, *huge* profits]; **gigantic, colossal,** and **mammoth** basically imply a likeness to specific objects of great size (respectively, a giant, the Colossus of Rhodes, and the huge, extinct elephant) and therefore emphasize the idea of great magnitude, force, importance, etc., now often hyperbolically; **tremendous,** literally suggesting that which inspires awe or amazement because of its great size, is also used loosely as an intensive term

E·nos (ē'nəs) [Gr. *Enōs* < Heb. *enōsh,* lit., man] **1.** a masculine name **2.** *Bible* a son of Seth: Gen. 4:26

e·nough (i nuf') *adj.* [ME. *inough* < OE. *genoh* < Gmc. compound (seen also in G. *genug-,* ON. *gnogr,* Goth. *ganohs*) < *ga-,* intens. + **noh,* enough < IE. base **enek-, *nek-,* to attain, achieve, whence L. *nactus,* attained, Sans. *nākṣati,* (he) attains] as much or as many as necessary, desirable, or tolerable; sufficient —*n.* the amount or number needed, desired, or allowed; sufficiency —*adv.* **1.** as much or as often as necessary; to the required degree or amount; sufficiently **2.** fully; quite [oddly *enough*] **3.** just adequately; tolerably; fairly [he played well *enough*] —*SYN.* see SUFFICIENT

e·nounce (ē nouns') *vt.* **e·nounced', e·nounc'ing** [Fr. *énoncer* < L. *enuntiare*] same as ENUNCIATE

☆**E·no·vid** (ē'nə vid) [arbitrary coinage, based on EN-[1] & OVI- & -ID] *a trademark for* a hormonal compound used to regulate the menstrual cycle and as an oral contraceptive

e·now (i nou') *adj., n., adv.* [ME. *ynoghe, inou* < OE. *genog,* early form of *genoh* (see ENOUGH): considered in Scot. dial. as pl.] [Archaic] enough

‡**en pas·sant** (än pä sän') [Fr.] in passing; by the way: used, in chess, of the capture of a pawn, which has taken a first move of two squares, passing an opponent's pawn that dominates the first of those squares

en·phy·tot·ic (en'fī tät'ik) *adj.* [< *en-* + Gr. *phyton,* a plant (see -PHYTE) + -IC] affecting certain plants of an area at regular intervals: said of various diseases

en·plane (en plān') *vi.* -**planed', -plan'ing** [EN-[1] + PLANE[4], after ENTRAIN] to board an airplane

en·quire (in kwir') *vt., vi.* -**quired', -quir'ing** same as INQUIRE —**en·quir'y** *n., pl.* -**quir'ies**

en·rage (in rāj') *vt.* -**raged', -rag'ing** [OFr. *enrager*] to put into a rage; make very angry; infuriate

‡**en rap·port** (än rà pôr') [Fr.] in harmony; in sympathy; in accord

en·rapt (in rapt') *adj.* enraptured; rapt

en·rap·ture (-rap'chər) *vt.* -**tured, -tur·ing** to fill with great pleasure or delight; entrance; enchant: also **en·rav'ish**

en·reg·is·ter (-rej'is tər) *vt.* [Fr. *enregistrer*] to enter in a register; enroll; record

‡**en rè·gle** (än reg'l') [Fr.] according to rule; in order

en·rich (in rich') *vt.* [ME. *enrichen* < OFr. *enrichier*] to make rich or richer; specif., *a)* to give more wealth to *b)* to give greater value, importance, effectiveness, etc. to [to *enrich* a curriculum] *c)* to decorate; adorn *d)* to fertilize (soil) *e)* to add vitamins, minerals, etc. to (bread, flour, etc.) so as to increase the food value —**en·rich'ment** *n.*

en·robe (in rōb') *vt.* -**robed', -rob'ing** to dress in or as in a robe

en·roll, en·rol (in rōl') *vt.* -**rolled', -roll'ing** [ME. *enrollen* < OFr. *enroller:* see EN-[1] & ROLL] **1.** to record in a list **2.** to enlist **3.** to accept as or cause to be a member **4.** [Rare] to roll up; wrap up ☆**5.** to make a final fair copy of (a bill passed by a legislature) —*vi.* **1.** to enroll oneself or become enrolled; register; enlist; become a member

en·roll·ee (in rōl'ē') *n.* a person who is enrolled

en·roll·ment, en·rol·ment (in rōl'mənt) *n.* **1.** an enrolling or being enrolled **2.** a list of those enrolled **3.** the number of those enrolled

en·root (in rōōt', -root') *vt.* [EN-[1] + ROOT[1]] to implant firmly or deeply: used chiefly in the passive

en route (än rōōt', en) [Fr.] on the way; along the way

‡**ens** (enz) *n.* [LL. *ens* (gen. *entis*), a being < prp. of *esse,* to be] *Philos.* abstract being; existence, in the most general sense

Ens. Ensign

en·sam·ple (en sam'p'l, -säm'-) *n.* [ME. *ensaumple* < OFr. *ensample, essample:* see EXAMPLE] [Archaic] same as EXAMPLE

en·san·guine (in saŋ'gwən) *vt.* -**guined, -guin·ing** [EN-[1] + SANGUINE] to stain with blood; make bloody

en·sate (en'sāt) *adj.* [< L. *ensis,* sword (see ENSIFORM) + -ATE[1]] same as ENSIFORM

En·sche·de (en'skhə dā') city in E Netherlands, near the German border: pop. 134,000

en·sconce (in skäns') *vt.* -**sconced', -sconc'ing** [EN-[1] + SCONCE] **1.** [Now Rare] to hide; conceal; shelter **2.** to place or settle comfortably, snugly, or securely [to *ensconce* oneself in an armchair]

en·sem·ble (än säm'b'l) *n.* [Fr. < OFr., together < L. *insimul,* at the same time < *in-* + *simul,* at the same time: see SAME] **1.** all the parts considered as a whole; total effect **2.** a whole costume, esp. one of matching or complementary articles of dress **3.** *a)* a company of actors, dancers, etc., or all but the featured stars *b)* their per-

formance together **4.** *Music a)* a small group of musicians playing or singing together *b)* the instruments or voices constituting such a group *c)* the performance together of such a group, or of an orchestra, chorus, etc.

en·sep·ul·cher, en·sep·ul·chre (in sep′'l kər) *vt.* **-chered** or **-chred, -cher·ing** or **-chring** to put into a sepulcher; entomb

en·sheathe (-shē*th*′) *vt.* **-sheathed′, -sheath′ing** to put in or cover with or as with a sheath

en·shrine (-shrīn′) *vt.* **-shrined′, -shrin′ing 1.** to enclose in or as in a shrine **2.** to hold as sacred; cherish [*enshrined* in memory] **—en·shrine′ment** *n.*

en·shroud (-shroud′) *vt.* to cover as if with a shroud; hide; veil; obscure

en·si·form (en′sə fôrm′) *adj.* [< L. *ensis*, sword (< IE. *nsi-s, whence Sans. *así-*) + -FORM] sword-shaped, as an iris leaf; xiphoid

en·sign (en′sīn; *also, and for 4 always,* -s′n) *n.* [ME. & OFr. *enseigne* < L. *insignia:* see INSIGNIA] **1.** a badge, symbol, or token of office or authority **2.** a flag or banner; specif., a national flag, as one displayed on a ship **3.** *Brit. Army* formerly, a commissioned officer who served as standard-bearer ☆**4.** [after Fr. *enseigne de vaisseau*, ship's ensign, midshipman] *U.S. Navy* a commissioned officer of the lowest rank, ranking below a lieutenant junior grade: abbrev. **Ens. —en′sign·ship′, en′sign·cy** *n.*

en·si·lage (en′s'l ij) *n.* [Fr. < *ensiler*, to preserve in an underground granary < *en-*, in + *silo:* see SILO] **1.** the preserving of green fodder by storage in a silo **2.** green fodder so preserved; silage **—***vt.* **-laged, -lag·ing** *same as* ENSILE

en·sile (en sīl′, en′sīl) *vt.* **-siled′, -sil′ing** [Fr. *ensiler:* see prec.] to store (green fodder) in a silo, or orig. a pit, for preservation

en·slave (in slāv′) *vt.* **-slaved′, -slav′ing 1.** to put into slavery; make a slave of **2.** to dominate; subjugate **—en·slave′ment** *n.* **—en·slav′er** *n.*

en·snare (-sner′) *vt.* **-snared′, -snar′ing** to catch in or as in a snare; trap **—en·snare′ment** *n.*

en·snarl (-snärl′) *vt.* to draw into a snarl or tangle

en·sor·cell, en·sor·cel (in sôr′s'l) *vt.* **-celled** or **-celed, -cell·ing** or **-cel·ing** [OFr. *ensorceler*, for **ensorcerer:* see EN-¹ & SORCERY] [Archaic] to bewitch

en·soul (en sōl′) *vt.* **1.** to take or put into the soul **2.** to endow with a soul

en·sphere (en sfir′) *vt.* **-sphered′, -spher′ing** to enclose in or as in a sphere

en·sta·tite (en′stə tīt′) *n.* [G. *enstatit* < Gr. *enstatēs*, opponent + G. *-it*, -ITE¹: from its refractory nature] a mineral, MgSiO₃, of the pyroxene group, occurring in orthorhombic form

en·sue (in sōō′, -syōō′) *vi.* **-sued′, -su′ing** [ME. *ensuen* < stem of OFr. *ensuivre* < VL. *insequere < L. *insequi* < *in-* + *sequi*, to follow] **1.** to come afterward; follow immediately **2.** to happen as a consequence; result **—***vt.* [Archaic] to strive for; follow; pursue **—***SYN.* see FOLLOW

☆**en suite** (än swēt′) [Fr.] in a series; in a set; following one another in order

en·sure (in shoor′) *vt.* **-sured′, -sur′ing** [ME. *ensuren* < Anglo-Fr. *ensurer* (for OFr. *asseurer:* see ASSURE) < *en-* (see EN-¹) + *seur*, SURE] **1.** to make sure or certain; guarantee; secure [*measures to ensure* accuracy] **2.** to make safe; protect [*safety devices to ensure* workers against accidents] **3.** *obs. var. of* INSURE (sense 1)

en·swathe (-swā*th*′, -swä*th*′) *vt.* **-swathed′, -swath′ing** to wrap or bind in or as in a bandage; swathe

ent- (ent) *same as* ENTO-: used before a vowel

-ent (ənt, 'nt) [< Fr. *-ent*, L. *-ens* (gen. *-entis*), stem ending of certain present participles] **1.** *an adj.-forming suffix meaning* that has, shows, or does [*insistent*] **2.** *a n.-forming suffix meaning* a person or thing that [*superintendent, solvent*] See also -ANT

en·tab·la·ture (en tab′lə chər) *n.* [MFr. < It. *intavolatura* < *intavolare* < *in-*, in + *tavola*, table, base < L. *tabula:* see TABLE] *Archit.* **1.** a horizontal superstructure supported by columns and composed of architrave, frieze, and cornice **2.** any structure like this

en·ta·ble·ment (en tā′b'l mənt) *n.* [Fr. < OFr. < *entabler:* see EN-¹, TABLE, & -MENT] **1.** *obs. var. of* ENTABLATURE **2.** the platform or series of platforms directly beneath a statue and on top of the dado and the base

en·tail (in tāl′) *vt.* [ME. *entailen* < *en-*, in + *taile, talie*, an agreement < OFr. *taillié*, pp. of *taillier*, to cut: see TAILOR] **1.** *Law* to limit the inheritance of (real property) to a specific line or class of heirs **2.** to cause or require as a necessary consequence; involve; necessitate [the plan *entails* work] **—***n.* **1.** an entailing or being entailed **2.** that which is entailed, as an estate **3.** necessary sequence, as the order of descent for an entailed inheritance **—en·tail′ment** *n.*

en·ta·moe·ba (en′tə mē′bə) *n.*, *pl.* **-bae** (-bē), **-bas** (-bəz) *same as* ENDAMOEBA

en·tan·gle (in taŋ′g'l) *vt.* **-gled, -gling 1.** to involve in or as in a tangle; catch, as in a net, vine, etc., so that escape is difficult; ensnare **2.** to involve in difficulty **3.** to confuse mentally; perplex **4.** to cause to be tangled; complicate **—en·tan′gle·ment** *n.*

en·ta·sis (en′tə sis) *n.*, *pl.* **-ses′** (-sēz′) [ModL. < Gr. *entasis*, lit., a stretching < *enteinein*, to stretch tight < *en-*,

in + *teinein:* see THIN] *Archit.* a slight, convex swelling in the shaft of a column: it prevents the illusion of concavity produced by a perfectly straight shaft

En·teb·be (en teb′ə) city in S Uganda, on Lake Victoria: former cap. of Uganda: pop. 11,000

en·tel·e·chy (en tel′ə kē) *n.*, *pl.* **-chies** [ME. *entelechia* < L. < Gr. *entelecheia*, actuality < *en telei echein* < *en*, in + *telei*, dat. of *telos*, end, completion + *echein*, to hold] **1.** in Aristotelian philosophy, the actualization of potentiality or of true existence **2.** in vitalism, the immanent force which controls and directs life and its development

en·tel·lus (en tel′əs) *n.*, *pl.* **-lus·es** [after *Entellus*, ancient Sicilian athletic hero] *same as* HANUMAN

en·tente (än tänt′) *n.* [Fr. < OFr. < *entendre*, to understand: see INTENT] **1.** an understanding or agreement, as between nations **2.** the parties to this

en·ter (en′tər) *vt.* [ME. *entren* < OFr. *entrer* < L. *intrare* < *intra*, within, inside: see INTRA-] **1.** to come or go in or into **2.** to force a way into; penetrate; pierce [the bullet *entered* his body] **3.** to put into; insert **4.** to write down in a record, list, diary, etc.; make an entry of **5.** *a)* to list as a participant in a competition, race, etc. *b)* to become a participant in (a contest) **6.** to join; become a part or member of (a political party, school, club, etc.) **7.** to get (a person, etc.) admitted **8.** to start upon; begin [to *enter* a career] **9.** to present for consideration; submit, esp. formally or officially [to *enter* a protest] **10.** to register (a ship or cargo) at a customhouse **11.** *Law a)* to place on record before a court *b)* to go upon or into (land or property) and take possession; also, to file a claim for (a parcel of public land) **—***vi.* **1.** to come or go into some place; make an entrance **2.** to pierce; penetrate **—enter into 1.** to engage in; take part in [to *enter into* a conversation] **2.** to form a part or component of; be or become a factor in **3.** to deal with; discuss **4.** to sympathize with; appreciate and share [to *enter into* the spirit of an occasion] **—enter on** (or **upon) 1.** to begin; set out on; start **2.** to begin to possess or enjoy; take possession of

en·ter·ic (en ter′ik) *adj.* intestinal; of the enteron: also **en·ter·al** (en′tər əl)

enteric fever *old term for* TYPHOID FEVER: see TYPHOID

en·ter·i·tis (en′tə rīt′is) *n.* [ENTER- + -ITIS] inflammation of the intestine, esp. the small intestine

en·ter·o- (en′tə rō′) [< Gr. *enteron*, intestine < IE. **entero-*, inner < base **en-*, in: cf. INTER] *a combining form meaning* intestine [*enterocolitis*]: also, before a vowel, **enter-**

en·ter·o·bi·a·sis (-ō bī′ə sis) *n.* [ModL. < *Enterobius*, name of the genus (< ENTERO- + Gr. *bios*, life: see BIO-) + -IASIS] infestation with pinworms

en·ter·o·coc·cus (-käk′əs) *n.*, *pl.* **-coc′ci** (-käk′sī) [ENTERO- + -COCCUS] a streptococcus normally present in the intestinal tract but often a cause of disease when found elsewhere **—en′ter·o·coc′cal** (-käk′əl) *adj.*

en·ter·o·coele, en·ter·o·coel (en′tə rō sēl′) *n.* [ENTERO- + -COELE] the coelomic cavity formed by pouchlike outfoldings of the wall of the archenteron

en·ter·o·co·li·tis (en′tə rō′kə līt′is) *n.* [ModL. < ENTERO- + COLITIS] inflammation of the colon and the small intestine

en·ter·o·gas·trone (-gas′trōn) *n.* [ENTERO- + GASTR- + -ONE] a hormone secreted by the intestinal mucosa, that inhibits the secretion of gastric juice and stomach movements

en·ter·o·ki·nase (-kī′nās, -kin′ās) *n.* [G. < *entero-*, ENTERO- + *kinase* < *kin(etisch)*, KINETIC + -ase, -ASE] an enzyme produced by the small intestine that transforms trypsinogen into trypsin

en·ter·on (en′tə rän′) *n.* [Gr. *enteron:* see ENTERO-] the alimentary canal

en·ter·os·to·my (en′tə räs′tə mē) *n.*, *pl.* **-mies** [ENTERO- + -STOMY] the surgical operation of making an artificial opening into the intestine through the abdominal wall, as for drainage

en·ter·prise (en′tər prīz′) *n.* [ME. < OFr. *entreprise* < fem. pp. of *entreprendre*, to undertake < *entre-* (L. *inter*), in, between + *prendre* < L. *prehendere:* see PREHENSILE] **1.** an undertaking; project; specif., *a)* a bold, difficult, dangerous, or important undertaking *b)* a business venture or company **2.** willingness to undertake new or risky projects; energy and initiative **3.** active participation in projects

en·ter·pris·er (-prī′zər) *n.* *same as* ENTREPRENEUR

en·ter·pris·ing (-prī′ziŋ) *adj.* [< archaic v. *enterprise*, to undertake < the *n.*] showing enterprise; full of energy and initiative; willing to undertake new projects **—***SYN.* see AMBITIOUS **—en′ter·pris′ing·ly** *adv.*

en·ter·tain (en′tər tān′) *vt.* [ME. *entretinen* < OFr. *entretenir*, to maintain, hold together < *entre* (L. *inter*), between + *tenir* (L. *tenere*), to hold] **1.** to keep the interest of and give pleasure to; divert; amuse **2.** to give hospitality to; have as a guest **3.** to allow oneself to think about; have in mind; consider [to *entertain* an idea] **4.** [Archaic] to keep up; maintain **—***vi.* to give hospitality to guests **—***SYN.* see AMUSE

en·ter·tain·er (-ər) *n.* a person who entertains; esp., a popular singer, dancer, comedian, etc.

en·ter·tain·ing (-iŋ) *adj.* interesting and pleasurable; diverting; amusing **—en′ter·tain′ing·ly** *adv.*

en·ter·tain·ment (-mənt) *n.* [ME. & OFr. *entretenement*] **1.** an entertaining or being entertained **2.** something that entertains; interesting, diverting, or amusing thing; esp., a show or performance

en·thal·py (en thal′pē, en′thal pē) *n.* < [Gr. *enthalpein*, to warm in (< *en-*, EN²- < *en*, IN + *thalpein*, to heat) + -y³] a measure of the energy content of a system per unit mass

en·thrall, en·thral (in thrôl′) *vt.* **-thralled′**, **-thrall′ing** [ME. *enthrallen*: see EN-¹ & THRALL] **1.** [Now Rare] to make a slave of; enslave **2.** to hold as if in a spell; captivate; fascinate —**en·thrall′ment, en·thral′ment** *n.*

en·throne (-thrōn′) *vt.* **-throned′, -thron′ing 1.** to place on a throne; make a king or bishop of **2.** to accord the highest place to; exalt —**en·throne′ment** *n.*

☆**en·thuse** (-thōōz′) *vi.* **-thused′, -thus′ing** [back-formation < ff.] [Colloq.] to express enthusiasm —*vt.* [Colloq.] to make enthusiastic

en·thu·si·asm (in thōō′zē az′m, -thyōō′-) *n.* [Gr. *enthousiasmos* < *enthousiazein*, to be inspired, be possessed by a god, inspire < *enthous, entheos,* possessed by a god < *en-*, in + *theos*, god] **1.** orig., supernatural inspiration or possession; inspired prophetic or poetic ecstasy **2.** intense or eager interest; zeal; fervor **3.** something arousing such interest or zeal **4.** [Archaic] religious fanaticism —*SYN.* SEE PASSION

en·thu·si·ast (-ast′) *n.* [Gr. *enthousiastēs*] a person full of enthusiasm; specif., *a)* an ardent supporter *b)* a religious fanatic or zealot —*SYN.* SEE ZEALOT

en·thu·si·as·tic (in thōō′zē as′tik, -thyōō′-) *adj.* [Gr. *enthousiastikos*] **1.** having or showing enthusiasm; ardent **2.** of, or having the nature of, enthusiasm —**en·thu′si·as′ti·cal·ly** *adv.*

en·thy·meme (en′thə mēm′) *n.* [L. *enthymema* < Gr. *enthymēma* < *enthymeisthai,* to consider, reflect upon < *en-*, in + *thymos*, mind < IE. *dhūmos < base **dheu-*, to blow (as dust), be in motion, whence DUMB, DOWN³] **1.** in Aristotle, a rhetorical argument from probabilities **2.** *Logic* an argument in which one of the premises or, sometimes, the conclusion is not expressed but implied —**en′thy·mem′ic** *adj.*

en·tice (in tīs′) *vt.* **-ticed′, -tic′ing** [ME. *enticen* < OFr. *enticier*, to set afire, rouse, excite, entice, prob. < VL. *intitiare < L. *in*, in + *titio*, a burning brand] to attract by offering hope of reward or pleasure; tempt; allure —*SYN.* SEE LURE —**en·tice′ment** *n.* —**on·tic′ing·ly** *adv.*

en·tire (in tīr′) *adj.* [ME. *enter* < OFr. *entier* < L. *integer,* whole, untouched, undiminished: see INTEGER] **1.** *a)* not lacking any of the parts; whole *b)* complete; thorough; absolute [*entire* confidence] **2.** unbroken; intact **3.** being wholly of one piece; undivided; continuous **4.** not castrated **5.** [Obs.] not mixed or alloyed; pure **6.** *Bot.* having an unbroken margin, without notches or indentations, as some leaves —*n.* **1.** [Rare] the whole; entirety **2.** a stallion —*SYN.* SEE COMPLETE —**en·tire′ness** *n.*

en·tire·ly (-lē) *adv.* **1.** wholly; completely; totally; fully **2.** solely; only

en·tire·ty (-tē) *n., pl.* **-ties** [ME. *enterete* < OFr. *entiereté*] **1.** the state or fact of being entire; wholeness; completeness **2.** an entire thing; whole; total **3.** *Law* undivided or sole possession —**in its entirety** as a whole; completely

en·ti·tle (in tīt′l) *vt.* **-tled, -tling** [ME. *enlitlen* < OFr. *entituler* < LL. *intitulare* < L. *in*, in + *titulus*, TITLE] **1.** to give a title or name to **2.** to honor or dignify by a title **3.** to give a right or legal title to; qualify (a person *to do* something) —**en·ti′tle·ment** *n.*

en·ti·ty (en′tə tē) *n., pl.* **-ties** [< Fr. *entité* or ML. *entitas* < L. *ens* (gen. *entis*), prp. of *esse*, to be] **1.** *a)* being; existence *b)* the essence of something apart from its accidental properties **2.** a thing that has definite, individual existence in reality or in the mind; anything real in itself

en·to- (en′tə) [ModL. < Gr. *entos*, within < IE. *entos < base **en-*, in] *a combining form meaning within or inner* [*entophyte*]

en·to·blast (en′tə blast′) *n.* [ENTO- + BLAST] *same as* ENDODERM; also **en′to·derm′** (-durm′)

en·toil (in toil′) *vt.* [Archaic or Poet.] to trap in toils or snares; ensnare

entom., entomol. 1. entomological **2.** entomology

en·tomb (in tōōm′) *vt.* [ME. *entoumben* < OFr. *entoumber:* see EN-¹ & TOMB] **1.** to place in a tomb or grave; bury **2.** to be a tomb for —**en·tomb′ment** *n.*

en·to·mo- (en′tə mə) [Fr. < Gr. *entoma* (zōa), notched (animals), insects < *entomos,* cut, notched (< *en-*, in + *temnein*, to cut): so named from their structure (cf. INSECT)] *a combining form meaning* insect or insects [*entomology*]: also, before a vowel, **entom-**

en·to·mol·o·gy (en′tə mäl′ə jē) *n.* [Fr. *entomologie:* see ENTOMO- & -LOGY] the branch of zoology that deals with insects —**en′to·mo·log′i·cal** (-mə läl′i k′l), **en′to·mo·log′ic** *adj.* —**en′to·mo·log′i·cal·ly** *adv.* —**en′to·mol′o·gist** *n.*

en·to·moph·a·gous (-mäf′ə gəs) *adj.* [ENTOMO- + -PHA-GOUS] feeding on insects

en·to·moph·i·lous (-mäf′ə ləs) *adj.* [ENTOMO- + -PHILOUS] pollinated by insects

en·to·mos·tra·can (-mäs′trə kən) *n.* [< ModL. *entomos-*

traca, name of the subclass < *entomo-* (see ENTOMO-) + Gr. *ostrakon,* a shell (see OSTRACIZE) + -AN] any of a large variety of small crustaceans, as the cladocerans, copepods, barnacles, etc., formerly constituting a subclass (Entomostraca)

en·to·phyte (en′tə fīt′) *n.* [ENTO- + -PHYTE] *same as* ENDOPHYTE —**en′to·phyt′ic** (-fit′ik) *adj.*

en·to·proct (-präkt′) *n. same as* ENDOPROCT

en·tou·rage (än′tōō räzh′) *n.* [Fr. < *entourer,* to surround < *en tour,* around < *en,* in + *tour,* round] **1.** [Now Rare] surroundings; environment **2.** a group of associates or attendants; retinue

en·to·zo·on (en′tə zō′än) *n., pl.* **-zo′a** (-ə) [ENTO- + Gr. *zōion,* animal] an internal animal parasite, esp. a parasitic worm infesting the intestines, muscles, etc. —**en′to·zo′al** (-əl), **en′to·zo′ic** (-ik) *adj.*

en·tr'acte (än trakt′, än′trakt) *n.* [Fr. < *entre-*, between + *acte*, an act] **1.** the interval between two acts of a play, opera, etc.; intermission **2.** a musical selection, dance, etc. performed during this interval

en·trails (en′trālz, -trəlz) *n.pl.* [ME. & OFr. *entrailles* < ML. *intralia* < L. *interanea*, pl. of *interaneum,* intestine < *interaneus*, internal < *inter,* between: see INTER-] **1.** the inner organs of men or animals; specif., the intestines; viscera; guts **2.** the inner parts of a thing

en·train¹ (in trān′) *vt.* [coined after EMBARK] to put (troops, etc.) aboard a train —*vi.* to go aboard a train

en·train² (-trān′) *vt.* [< Fr. *entraîner* < *en-* (< L. *inde*), away + *traîner,* to drag: see TRAIN] **1.** [Rare] to drag along after oneself **2.** *Chem.* to suspend (a liquid in the form of fine droplets) in a vapor, so that the vapor will carry the liquid away, as during distillation or evaporation —**en·train′ment** *n.*

en·trance¹ (en′trəns) *n.* [ME. *entraunce* < OFr. *entrant*, prp. of *entrer:* see ENTER] **1.** the act or point of entering [to make an *entrance*] **2.** a place for entering; door, gate, etc. **3.** permission, right, or power to enter; admission

en·trance² (in trans′, -träns′) *vt.* **-tranced′, -tranc′ing 1.** to put into a trance **2.** to fill with rapture or delight; enchant; charm; enrapture —**en·trance′ment** *n.* —**en·tranc′ing·ly** *adv.*

en·trant (en′trənt) *n.* [Fr. < OFr.: see ENTRANCE¹] a person who enters, esp. one who enters a contest

en·trap (in trap′) *vt.* **-trapped′, -trap′ping** [OFr. *entraper*] **1.** to catch in or as in a trap **2.** to deceive or trick into difficulty, as into incriminating oneself —**en·trap′-ment** *n.*

en·treat (-trēt′) *vt.* [ME. *entreten,* to treat, deal with, beseech < Anglo-Fr. *entretier* < OFr. *entraiter* < *en-*, in + *traiter:* see TREAT] **1.** to ask earnestly; beg; beseech; implore **2.** [Archaic] to behave toward; treat —*vi.* **1.** to make an earnest appeal; plead **2.** [Obs.] to speak or write (*of*) —*SYN.* SEE BEG —**en·treat′ing·ly** *adv.* —**en·treat′-ment** *n.*

en·treat·y (-ē) *n., pl.* **-treat′ies** [ME. *entrete:* see prec.] an earnest request; supplication; prayer

en·tre·chat (än′trə shä′) *n.* [Fr. < It. (*capriola*) *intrecciata,* intricate (leap) < *intrecciare* < *in-*, in + *treccia*, a pleat: see TRESS] *Ballet* a leap straight upward during which the dancer crosses his legs or strikes his heels together a number of times

‡**en·tre·côte** (än trə kôt′) *n.* [Fr.] boned rib steak

en·tree, en·trée (än′trā; *Fr.* än trā′) *n.* [Fr. *entrée* < OFr. < fem. pp. of *entrer,* ENTER] **1.** *a)* the act of entering *b)* right, permission, or freedom to enter, use, or take part in; access **2.** *a)* the main course of a meal *b)* formerly, and still in some countries, a dish served before the roast or between the main courses, as between the fish and the meat

en·tre·mets (än′trə mā′; *Fr.* än trə me′) *n., pl.* **en′tre·mets′** (-māz′; *Fr.* -me′) [ME. *entermes* < OFr. *entre,* between (< L. *inter*) + *mes,* a dish: see MESS] a dish served between the main courses or as a side dish

en·trench (in trench′) *vt.* [EN-¹ + TRENCH] **1.** to surround or fortify with a trench or trenches **2.** to establish securely: used in the passive voice or with a reflexive pronoun [an official *entrenched* in office] **3.** to cut down into, as by erosion, so as to form a trough or trench —*vi.* to encroach or infringe (*on* or *upon*) —**en·trench′ment** *n.*

‡**en·tre nous** (än trə nōō′) [Fr., lit., between us] between ourselves; confidentially

en·tre·pôt (än′trə pō′; *Fr.* än trə pō′) *n.* [Fr. < *entreposer:* see INTERPOSE] **1.** a place for the storage of goods; warehouse **2.** a distributing center for goods

en·tre·pre·neur (än′trə prə nur′, -noor′, -nyoor′) *n.* [Fr. < OFr. *entreprendre:* see ENTERPRISE] a person who organizes and manages a business undertaking, assuming the risk for the sake of the profit —**en′tre·pre·neur′i·al** *adj.* —**en′tre·pre·neur′ship** *n.*

en·tre·sol (än′tər säl′; *Fr.* än trə sôl′) *n.* [Fr. < *entre-*, between + *sol*, ground < L. *solum*, whence SOIL¹] a low story or floor just above the street floor; mezzanine

en·tro·py (en′trə pē) *n.* [G. *entropie,* arbitrary use (by R.J.E. *Clausius,* 1822–88, Ger. physicist) of Gr. *entropē,* a turning toward, as if < *en*(*ergie*), ENERGY + Gr. *tropē,* a

turning: see TROPE] **1.** a thermodynamic measure of the amount of energy unavailable for useful work in a system undergoing change **2.** a measure of the degree of disorder in a substance or a system: entropy always increases and available energy diminishes in a closed system, as the universe **3.** in information theory and computer science, a measure of the information content of a message evaluated as to its uncertainty

en·trust (in trust′) *vt.* **1.** to charge or invest with a trust or duty [*entrust* a lawyer with records] **2.** to assign the care of; turn over for safekeeping [*entrust* the key to me] —SYN. see COMMIT —**en·trust′ment** *n.*

en·try (en′trē) *n., pl.* **-tries** [ME. < OFr. *entree* < fem. pp. of *entrer*: see ENTER] **1.** *a)* the act of entering; entrance *b)* the right or freedom to enter; entree **2.** a way or passage by which to enter; door, hall, etc.; entryway **3.** *a)* the recording of an item, note, etc. in a list, journal, etc. *b)* an item thus recorded **4.** *a)* the registration of a ship or cargo at a customhouse *b)* the documents involved in this transaction *c)* the actual movement of goods through customs **5.** one entered in a race, competition, etc.; entrant **6.** *Law a)* the taking possession of buildings, land, etc. by entering or setting foot upon them *b)* the entering upon premises with the intention of committing burglary or some other crime

☆**en·try·way** (-wā′) *n.* a way or passage by which to enter

en·twine (in twīn′) *vt., vi.* **-twined′, -twin′ing** to twine, weave, or twist together or around

en·twist (in twist′) *vt.* **1.** to twist together or in (*with*) **2.** to make into a twist

e·nu·cle·ate (i nōō′klē āt′, -nyōō′-; *for adj.* -it) *vt.* **-at′ed, -at′ing** [< L. *enucleatus*, pp. of *enucleare*, to remove kernels < *e-*, out + *nucleus*: see NUCLEUS] **1.** [Archaic] to make clear; explain **2.** *Biol.* to remove the nucleus from (a cell) **3.** *Surgery* to remove (a tumor, organ, etc.) as a whole from its enclosing sac —*adj.* enucleated —**e·nu′cle·a′tion** *n.*

e·nu·mer·ate (i nōō′mə rāt′, -nyōō′-) *vt.* **-at′ed, -at′ing** [< L. *enumeratus*, pp. of *enumerare* < *e-*, out + *numerare*, to count < *numerus*, NUMBER] **1.** to determine the number of; count **2.** to name one by one; specify, as in a list —**e·nu′mer·a′tion** *n.* —**e·nu′mer·a′tive** *adj.* —**e·nu′mer·a′tor** *n.*

e·nun·ci·a·ble (i nun′sē ə b′l, -shē-) *adj.* [ML. *enuntiabilis*] that can be enunciated

e·nun·ci·ate (-āt′) *vt.* **-at′ed, -at′ing** [< L. *enuntiatus*, pp. of *enuntiare* < *e-*, out + *nuntiare*, to announce < *nuntius*, a messenger] **1.** to state definitely; express in a systematic way [to *enunciate* a theory] **2.** to announce; proclaim **3.** to pronounce (words), esp. clearly and distinctly —*vi.* to pronounce words, esp. clearly and distinctly; articulate —SYN. see UTTER² —**e·nun′ci·a′tion** *n.* —**e·nun′ci·a′tive** (-āt′iv, -ə tiv) *adj.* —**e·nun′ci·a′tor** *n.*

en·ure (in yoor′) *vt., vi. -ured′, -ur′ing same as* INURE

en·u·re·sis (en′yoo rē′sis) *n.* [ModL. < Gr. *enourein*, to urinate in: see EN-¹ & URINE] inability to control urination; esp., involuntary bed-wetting —**en′u·ret′ic** (-ret′ik) *adj.*

env. envelope

en·vel·op (in vel′əp) *vt.* [ME. *envolupen* < OFr. *envoluper*: see EN-¹ & DEVELOP] **1.** to wrap up; cover completely **2.** to surround **3.** to conceal; hide; obscure —**en·vel′opment** *n.*

en·ve·lope (en′və lōp′, än′-) *n.* [Fr. & OFr. *enveloppe* < OFr. *envoluper*: see prec.] **1.** a thing that envelops; wrapper; covering **2.** a folded paper container for letters, etc., usually with a gummed flap for sealing **3.** *a)* the outer covering of a dirigible or balloon *b)* the bag that contains the gas in a dirigible or balloon **4.** the set of limitations, as for a particular aircraft, system, etc., within the boundaries of which it can operate safely and efficiently **5.** *Astron.* a cloudy mass surrounding the nucleus of a comet; coma **6.** *Biol.* any enclosing membrane, skin, shell, etc. **7.** *Math.* a curve that is tangent to every one of a family of curves, or a surface that is tangent to every one of a family of surfaces

en·ven·om (in ven′əm) *vt.* [ME. *envenimen* < OFr. *envenimer*] **1.** to put venom or poison on or into; make poisonous **2.** to fill with hate; embitter

en·vi·a·ble (en′vē ə b′l) *adj.* good enough to be envied or desired —**en′vi·a·bly** *adv.*

en·vi·er (en′vē ər) *n.* a person who envies

en·vi·ous (en′vē əs) *adj.* [ME. < OFr. *envieus* < L. *invidiosus* < *invidia*, ENVY] **1.** characterized by envy; feeling, showing, or resulting from envy **2.** [Obs.] *a)* emulous *b)* spiteful *c)* enviable —**en′vi·ous·ly** *adv.* —**en′vi·ous·ness** *n.*

en·vi·ron (in vī′rən) *vt.* [ME. *envirounen* < OFr. *environner* < *environ*, about: see ENVIRONS] to form a ring about; surround; encircle

en·vi·ron·ment (in vī′rən mənt, -ərn mənt) *n.* [prec. + -MENT] **1.** [Rare] a surrounding or being surrounded **2.** something that surrounds; surroundings **3.** all the conditions, circumstances, and influences surrounding, and affecting the development of, an organism or group of organisms —**en·vi′ron·men′tal** (-men′t′l) *adj.* —**en·vi′ron·men′tal·ly** *adv.*

en·vi·rons (in vī′rənz, -ərnz; en′vər ənz) *n.pl.* [ME. *environ* (sing.) < OFr. *environ*, orig. adv., around < *en*, in + *viron*, a circuit < *virer*, to turn: see VEER²] **1.** the districts surrounding a town or city; suburbs or outskirts **2.** surrounding area; vicinity

en·vis·age (en viz′ij) *vt.* **-aged, -ag·ing** [Fr. *envisager*: see EN-¹ & VISAGE] **1.** [Rare] to face; confront **2.** to form an image of in the mind; visualize; imagine

en·vi·sion (en vizh′ən) *vt.* [EN-¹ + VISION] to imagine (something not yet in existence); picture in the mind

en·voi (en′voi, än′-) *n.* [Fr.] **1.** *same as* ENVOY² **2.** something said or done in farewell or conclusion

en·voy¹ (en′voi, än′-) *n.* [Fr. *envoyé* < pp. of *envoyer*, to send < OFr. *envoier* < *en-* (L. *in*), in + *voie* (L. *via*), way] **1.** a messenger; agent **2.** an agent sent by a government or ruler to transact diplomatic business; specif., a diplomat of second rank (in full, **envoy extraordinary**) just below an ambassador

en·voy² (en′voi, än′-) *n.* [ME. *envoye* < OFr. *envoy*, lit., a sending < *envoier*: see prec.] a postscript to a poem, essay, or book, containing a dedication, climactic summary, explanation, etc.; specif., a short, concluding stanza of this kind added to a ballade and some other verse forms

en·vy (en′vē) *n., pl.* **-vies** [ME. & OFr. *envie* < L. *invidia* < *invidus*, having hatred or ill will < *invidere*, to look askance at < *in-*, in, upon + *videre*, to look: see WISE²] **1.** a feeling of discontent and ill will because of another's advantages, possessions, etc.; resentful dislike of another who has something that one desires **2.** desire for some advantage, quality, etc. that another has **3.** an object of envious feeling **4.** [Obs.] ill will; spite —*vt.* **-vied, -vy·ing** to feel envy toward, at, or because of; regard with envy —*vi.* [Obs.] to feel or show envy —**en′vy·ing·ly** *adv.*
SYN. —to **envy** another is to feel ill will, jealousy, or discontent at his possession of something that one keenly desires to have or achieve oneself; **begrudge** implies an unwillingness that someone should possess or enjoy something that he needs or deserves; to **covet** is to long ardently and wrongfully for something that belongs to another

en·wind (en wīnd′) *vt.* **-wound′, -wind′ing** to wind about or around

en·womb (-wōōm′) *vt.* to enclose in or as in a womb

en·wrap (-rap′) *vt.* **-wrapped′, -wrap′ping** to wrap; envelop

en·wreathe (-rēth′) *vt.* **-wreathed′, -wreath′ing** to encircle or surround with or as with a wreath

en·zo·ot·ic (en′zō ät′ik) *adj.* [< Gr. *en-*, in + *zōion*, animal + *-otic*, as in EPIZOOTIC] affecting animals in a certain area, climate, or season: said of diseases: cf. ENDEMIC —*n.* an enzootic disease

en·zyme (en′zīm) *n.* [G. *enzym* < LGr. *enzymos*, leavened < Gr. *en-*, in + *zymē*, leaven] any of various proteinlike substances, formed in plant and animal cells, that act as organic catalysts in initiating or speeding up specific chemical reactions and that usually become inactive or unstable at high temperatures —**en′zy·mat′ic** (-zī mat′ik, -zī-), **en·zy′mic** *adj.*

en·zy·mol·o·gy (en′zī māl′ə jē, -zī-) *n.* the science dealing with the structure and properties of enzymes and the chemical reactions they catalyze —**en′zy·mol′o·gist** *n.*

e·o- (ē′ə, -ō) [< Gr. *ēōs*, dawn < IE. base *awes-*, to shine, whence L. *aurora*, EASTER] *a prefix meaning* early, early part of a period [*Eocene, eolithic*]

e·o·bi·ont (ē′ō bī′änt) *n.* [coined by J. D. Bernal (1901–), F.R.S. Brit. physicist < EO- + Gr. *biounti-*, stem of *biōn*, living, prp. of *bioun*, to live < *bios*, life: see BIO-] a hypothetical precursor of living organisms in the chemical evolution preceding the occurrence of life

E·o·cene (ē′ə sēn′) *adj.* [EO- + Gr. *kainos*, new] designating or of the second and longest epoch of the Tertiary Period in the Cenozoic Era, during which mammals became the dominant animals —**the Eocene** the Eocene Epoch or its rocks: see GEOLOGY, chart

e·o·hip·pus (ē′ō hip′əs) *n.* [ModL. < EO- + Gr. *hippos*, horse] any of a genus (*Eohippus*) of extinct progenitors of the modern horse, found in the Lower Eocene of W U.S.: it was about the size of a fox and had four toes on the front feet and three on the hind

E·o·li·an (ē ō′lē ən) *adj., n. same as* AEOLIAN

E·ol·ic (ē äl′ik) *adj., n. same as* AEOLIC

e·o·lith (ē′ə lith′) *n.* [EO- + -LITH] any of the crude stone tools used in the early part of the Stone Age

e·o·lith·ic (ē′ə lith′ik) *adj.* [see prec. & -IC] designating or of the early part of the Stone Age, during which crude stone tools were first used

e.o.m. end of (the) month

e·on (ē′ən, ē′än) *n.* [LL. < Gr. *aiōn*, an age, lifetime, eternity < IE. base *aiw-*, vitality: see AYE¹] an extremely long, indefinite period of time; thousands and thousands of years —SYN. see PERIOD

e·o·ni·an (ē ō′nē ən) *adj. same as* AEONIAN

E·os (ē′äs) [L. < Gr. *Ēōs*: see EO-] *Gr. Myth.* the goddess of dawn: identified with the Roman Aurora

e·o·sin (ē′ə sin) *n.* [< Gr. *ēōs*, dawn + -IN¹] **1.** *a)* a rose-colored dye, $C_{20}H_8O_5Br_4$, prepared by brominating fluorescein and used to color inks, fabrics, etc. and to stain tissues *b)* its sodium or potassium salt, used as a reddish dye and as a stain in microscopy **2.** any of various other red dyes obtained from coal tar Also **e′o·sine** (-sin, -sēn′) —**e′o·sin′ic** *adj.*

e·o·sin·o·phil (ē′ō sin′ə fil′) *n.* [prec. + -o- + -PHIL] *Biol.* any of the white blood cells that are readily stainable with eosin and that increase greatly in number in certain allergic and parasitic diseases: also **e′o·sin′o·phile′** (-fīl′) —**e′o·sin′o·phil′ic** (-fil′ik) *adj.*

e·o·sin·o·phile (-fīl′) *adj.* [see prec.] *Chem.* easily stained by eosin: also **e′o·sin′o·phil′** (-fīl′)

-e·ous (ē əs) [< L. *-eus* + *-ous*] *an adj.-forming suffix meaning* having the nature of, like [*beauteous*]

E·o·zo·ic (ē′ə zō′ik) *adj.* [EO- + ZO- + -IC] *former name for* PRECAMBRIAN

ep- (ep) *same as* EPI-: used before a vowel

e·pact (ē′pakt) *n.* [Fr. *épacte* < LL. *epactae* < Gr. *epaktai* (*hemerai*), intercalary (days) < *epagein*, to bring in, intercalate < *epi-*, on, in + *agein*, to bring, lead] **1.** the period of about eleven days by which the solar year exceeds the lunar year of twelve months **2.** the age, in days, of the calendar moon on the first of the year

E·pam·i·non·das (i pam′ə nän′dəs) 418?–362 B.C.; Theban (Gr.) general & statesman

ep·arch (ep′ärk) *n.* [Gr. *eparchos* < *epi-*, over + *archos*, ruler: see -ARCH] **1.** the governor of an eparchy **2.** *Orthodox Eastern Ch.* a metropolitan, or bishop

ep·arch·y (ep′är kē) *n.,* *pl.* **-arch·ies** [Gr. *eparchia* < *eparchos*: see EPARCH] **1.** a political subdivision of a province of Greece **2.** *Orthodox Eastern Ch.* a diocese —**ep·ar′chi·al** (-kē əl) *adj.*

‡é·pa·ter (ā pä tā′) *vt.* [Fr.] to startle or shock, as out of complacency, conventionality, etc.

ep·au·let, ep·au·lette (ep′ə let′) *n.* [Fr. *épaulette*, dim. of *épaule*, the shoulder < OFr. *espale* < L. *spatula*: see SPATULA] **1.** a shoulder ornament for certain uniforms, esp. military uniforms **2.** any similar ornament, as on a woman's dress

EPAULETS

e·pee, é·pée (e pā′, ā-) *n.* [Fr. *épée* < OFr. *espee* < L. *spatha*, broad, two-edged sword without a point < Gr. *spathē*, any broad blade: see SPADE[1]] a sword, esp. a thin, pointed sword without a cutting edge, like a foil but heavier and more rigid, used in fencing —**e·pee′ist, é·pée′ist** n.

ep·ei·rog·e·ny (ep′ī räj′ə nē) *n.* [< Gr. *ēpeiros*, mainland + -GENY] movements of uplift or depression affecting large areas of the earth's crust and producing continents, ocean basins, etc. —**e·pei·ro·gen·ic** (e pī′rə jen′ik), **e·pei′ro·ge·net′ic** (-jə net′ik) *adj.*

ep·en·ceph·a·lon (ep′en sef′ə län′) *n.* [ModL. < EP- + ENCEPHALON] **1.** the front part of the most posterior primary vesicle of an embryo's brain: it develops into the pons and part of the cerebellum **2.** [Rare] the cerebellum

ep·en·dy·ma (e pen′di mə) *n.* [ModL., arbitrary use (by Rudolf VIRCHOW) of Gr. *ependyma*, an upper garment < *ependyein*, to put on over < *epi-*, over + *endyein* < *en-*, on + *dyein*, to put] the membrane lining the central cavities of the brain and spinal cord

ep·en·the·sis (pen′thə sis) *n.,* *pl.* **-ses** (-sēz) [LL. < Gr. *epenthesis* < *epi-*, upon + *en-* in + *thesis*, a placing] **1.** a phonetic change which involves the insertion of an unhistorical sound or syllable in a word, as the *b* in *mumble* or the extra syllable in the pronunciation (ath′ə lēt′) for *athlete* **2.** a sound or letter so occurring —**ep·en·thet·ic** (ep′ən thet′ik) *adj.*

e·pergne (i purn′, ā pern′) *n.* [prob. < Fr. *épargne*, a saving < *épargner*, to save < Frank. *sparanjan*, akin to G. *sparen*, to save] an ornamental dish or stand with several compartments for fruit, candy, flowers, etc., used as a centerpiece for a dining table

ep·ex·e·ge·sis (ep ek′sə jē′sis) *n.* [Gr. *epexēgēsis*, detailed account < *epexē-geisthai*, to recount in detail < *epi-*, on, in + *exēgeisthai*, to point out: see EXEGESIS] additional explanation; further clarification, as by the addition of a word or words —**ep·ex·e·get′i·cal** (-jet′i k′l), **ep·ex·e·get′ic** *adj.*

EPERGNE

eph- (ef) *same as* EPI-

Eph. Ephesians: also **Ephes.**

e·phah, e·pha (ē′fə) *n.* [ME. *ephi* < LL.(Ec.) < Heb. *'ēphāh*] an ancient Hebrew dry measure, estimated at from 1/3 bushel to a little over one bushel

e·phebe (i fēb′, ef′ēb) *n.* [< L. *ephebus*, EPHEBUS] a young man; specif., an ephebus

e·phe·bus (e fē′bəs) *n.,* *pl.* **-bi** (-bī) [L. < Gr. *ephēbos* < *epi-*, at, upon + *hēbē*, early manhood] in ancient Athens, a young citizen (18 to 20 years) undergoing physical and military training: also **e·phebe** (ef′ēb, e fēb′) —**e·phe′bic** *adj.*

e·phed·rine (i fed′rin; *chiefly Brit.,* ef′ə drēn′) *n.* [< ModL. *Ephedra*, genus name < L., the plant horsetail < Gr. *ephedra*, sitting by < *epi-*, on, near + *hedra*, a seat: cf. SIT] an alkaloid, $C_{10}H_{15}NO$, derived from certain Asiatic plants (genus *Ephedra*) or synthesized, and used to relieve nasal congestion and asthma and to constrict blood vessels

e·phem·er·a (i fem′ər ə) *n.,* *pl.* **-er·as, -er·ae** (-ē′) [ModL., name of the genus < Gr. *ephēmeron:* see EPHEMERON] **1.** *same as* MAYFLY **2.** an ephemeral thing

e·phem·er·al (-əl) *adj.* [< Gr. *ephēmeros* (see EPHEMERON) + -AL] **1.** lasting only one day **2.** short-lived; transitory [*ephemeral glory*] —*n.* an ephemeral thing; specif., a plant with a brief life cycle —*SYN.* see TRANSIENT —**e·phem′er·al·ly** *adv.*

e·phem·er·id (-id) *n.* [EPHEMER(A) + -ID] *same as* MAYFLY

e·phem·er·is (-is) *n.,* *pl.* **eph·e·mer·i·des** (ef′ə mer′ə dēz′) [L. < Gr. *ephēmeris*, diary, calendar < *ephēmeros:* see ff.] **1.** a table giving the computed positions of a heavenly body for every day of a given period **2.** an astronomical almanac containing such tables **3.** [Obs.] a calendar or diary

e·phem·er·on (-än′) *n.,* *pl.* **-er·a** (-ə), **-er·ons** [Gr. *ephēmeron*, short-lived insect < *ephēmeros*, for the day, short-lived < *epi-*, upon + *hēmera*, day] *same as* MAYFLY

E·phe·sian (i fē′zhən) *adj.* of Ephesus or its people —*n.* a native or inhabitant of Ephesus

E·phe·sians (-zhənz) a book of the New Testament which was an epistle of the Apostle Paul to the Christians of Ephesus

Eph·e·sus (ef′ə səs) ancient Greek city in W Asia Minor: site of a large ancient temple of Artemis

eph·od (ef′äd, -əd) *n.* [ME. < LL.(Ec.) < Heb. *ēphōd* < *āphad*, to put on] a richly embroidered outer vestment worn by Jewish priests in ancient times

eph·or (ef′ôr, -ər′) *n.,* *pl.* **-ors, -or·i′** (-ə rī′) [L. *ephorus* < Gr. *ephoros*, overseer < *ephoran* < *epi-*, over + *horan*, to see] in ancient Sparta, any of a body of five magistrates annually elected by the people of Sparta

E·phra·im (ē′frē əm) [LL.(Ec.) < Gr.(Ec.) < Heb. *ephrayim*, lit., very fruitful] **1.** a masculine name **2.** *Bible* a) the younger son of Joseph b) the tribe of Israel descended from this son c) the kingdom of Israel

E·phra·im·ite (-īt′) *n.* a descendant of Ephraim; member of the tribe of Ephraim

epi- (ep′ə, -i) [< Gr. *epi*, at, on, upon, over, besides < IE. base *epi*, whence Sans. *ápi*, L. *ob*] a *prefix meaning* on, upon, over, on the outside, anterior, beside, besides, among [*epiglottis, epidemic, epidermis*]: it becomes **ep-** before a vowel [*eparch*] and **eph-** in an aspirated word [*ephemeral*]

ep·i·ben·thos (ep′ə ben′thəs) *n.* [EPI- + BENTHOS] the animals and plants living on the sea bottom between the low tide level and a depth of 100 fathoms

ep·i·blast (ep′ə blast′) *n.* [EPI- + -BLAST] the outer layer of cells of an embryo

e·pib·o·ly (i pib′ə lē) *n.* [Gr. *epibolē*, a throwing upon < *epiballein*, to throw upon < *epi-*, on, upon + *ballein*, to throw: see BALL[2]] *Embryology* the growth of a group of cells around another group, resulting from the more rapid division of the former —**ep·i·bol·ic** (ep′ə bäl′ik) *adj.*

ep·ic (ep′ik) *n.* [L. *epicus* < Gr. *epikos*, epic] *adj.* < *epos*, a word, speech, song, epic < IE. *wekwos*-, word < base *wekw*-, to speak, whence L. *vox*, OE. *woma*, noise] **1.** a long narrative poem in a dignified style about the deeds of a traditional or historical hero or heroes; typically, *a*) a poem like the *Iliad* and *Odyssey*, with certain formal characteristics of structure (beginning *in medius res*, catalog passages, invocations of the muse, etc.): called **classical epic** *b*) a poem like Milton's *Paradise Lost*, in which such structural characteristics are applied to later or different materials: called **art epic, literary epic** *c*) a poem like *Beowulf*, considered as expressing the early ideals and traditions of a people or nation: called **folk epic, national epic 2.** any long narrative poem regarded as having the style, structure, and importance of an epic, as Dante's *Divine Comedy* **3.** a prose narrative, play, movie, etc. regarded as having the qualities of an epic **4.** a series of events regarded as a proper subject for an epic —*adj.* **1.** of an epic **2.** having the nature of an epic; specif., *a*) heroic; grand; majestic; imposing *b*) dealing with or characterized by events of historical or legendary importance: also **ep′i·cal** —**ep′i·cal·ly** *adv.*

EPICALYX

ep·i·ca·lyx (ep′ə kā′liks, -kal′iks) *n.,* *pl.* **-lyx·es, -ly·ces′** (-lə sēz′) [EPI- + CALYX] a ring of small leaves (called *bracts*) at the base of certain flowers, resembling an extra outer calyx, as in the mallows

ep·i·can·thus (-kan′thəs) *n.* [EPI- + CANTHUS] a small fold of skin sometimes covering the inner corner of the eye, as in many Asian peoples —**ep′i·can′thic** *adj.*

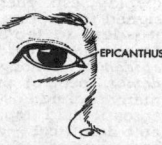

EPICANTHUS

ep·i·car·di·um (-kär′dē əm) *n.,* *pl.* **-di·a** (-ə) [ModL. < EPI- + Gr. *kardia*, HEART] the innermost layer of the pericardium —**ep′i·car′di·al** *adj.*

ep·i·carp (ep′ə kärp′) *n.* [EPI- + -CARP] *same as* EXOCARP

ep·i·ce·di·um (ep′ə sē′dē əm) *n.,* *pl.*

-**di·a** (-ə) [L. < Gr. *epikēdeion* < *epikēdeios*, funereal < *epi-*, in, on + *kēdos*, grief, funeral rites: see HATE] a funeral ode or hymn; dirge

ep·i·cene (ep′ə sēn′) *adj.* [ME. < L. *epicoenus* < Gr. *epikoinos*, common < *epi-*, upon, to + *koinos*, common: see COM-] 1. designating a noun, as in Latin or Greek, having only one grammatical form to denote an individual of either sex 2. belonging to one sex but having characteristics of the other, or of neither; specif., effeminate; unmanly —*n.* an epicene person

ep·i·cen·ter (-sen′tər) *n.* [< ModL. *epicentrum* < EPI- + L. *centrum*, CENTER] 1. the area of the earth's surface directly above the place of origin, or focus, of an earthquake: also **ep′i·cen′trum** (-trəm), *pl.* -**tra** (-trə) 2. a focal or central point —**ep′i·cen′tral** *adj.*

ep·i·cot·yl (ep′ə kät′'l) *n.* [< EPI- + COTYLEDON] *Bot.* that part of the stem of a seedling or embryo just above the cotyledons —**ep′i·cot′yl·e′don·ar′y** (-ē′d'n er′ē) *adj.*

ep·i·cra·ni·um (-krā′nē əm) *n., pl.* -**ni·a** (-ə) 1. *Anat.* the structures covering the cranium 2. *Entomology* the upper portion of the head of an insect between the frons and the neck —**ep′i·cra′ni·al** *adj.*

ep·i·crit·ic (-krit′ik) *adj.* [Gr. *epikritikos*, determinative < *epikrisis*, judgment < *epikrinein*, to judge < *epi-*, upon + *krinein*, to judge: see CRISIS] designating or of the nerve fibers in the skin that transmit the finer sensations of touch and temperature

Ep·ic·te·tus (ep′ik tēt′əs) 50?-135? A.D.; Gr. Stoic philosopher in Rome & Epirus

ep·i·cure (ep′i kyoor′) *n.* [< L. *Epicurus* < Gr. *Epikouros*: see EPICURUS] 1. a person who enjoys and has a discriminating taste for fine foods and drinks 2. [Archaic] a person who is especially fond of luxury and sensuous pleasure
SYN.—an **epicure** is a person who has a highly refined taste for fine foods and drinks and takes great pleasure in indulging it; a **gourmet** is a connoisseur in eating and drinking who discriminatingly appreciates differences in flavor or quality; **gourmand**, occasionally equivalent to **gourmet**, is more often applied to a person who has a hearty liking for good food or one who is inclined to eat to excess; a **gastronome** is an expert in all phases of the art or science of good eating; a **glutton** is a greedy, voracious eater and drinker

Ep·i·cu·re·an (ep′i kyoo rē′ən, -kyoor′ē ən) *adj.* [ME. *Epicurien* < L. *Epicureus* < Gr. *Epikoureios* < *Epikouros*] 1. of Epicurus or his philosophy 2. [e-] *a)* fond of luxury and sensuous pleasure, esp. that of eating and drinking *b)* suited to or characteristic of an epicure —*n.* 1. a follower of Epicurus or his philosophy 2. [e-] an epicure —*SYN.* see SENSUOUS

Ep·i·cu·re·an·ism (-iz′m) *n.* 1. the philosophy of Epicurus or his school 2. adherence to or practice of this philosophy 3. [e-] *same as* EPICURISM

ep·i·cur·ism (ep′i kyoor iz′m) *n.* 1. the tastes, habits, or pursuits of an epicure 2. [E-] *same as* EPICUREANISM

Ep·i·cu·rus (ep′ə kyoor′əs) 341?-270 B.C.; Gr. philosopher: founder of the Epicurean school, which held that the goal of man should be a life of calm pleasure regulated by morality, temperance, serenity, and cultural development

ep·i·cy·cle (ep′ə sī′k'l) *n.* [ME. *epicicle* < LL. *epicyclus* < Gr. *epikyklos* < *epi-*, upon + *kyklos*, a circle: see CYCLE] 1. a circle whose center moves along the circumference of another, larger circle: term used to describe planetary motions in the Ptolemaic system 2. *Geom.* a circle which, by rolling around the interior or exterior of another circle, generates a hypocycloid or epicycloid respectively —**ep′i·cy′clic** (-sī′klik, -sik′lik), **ep′i·cy′cli·cal** *adj.*

epicyclic train a system of cogwheels, belt pulleys, etc., in which at least one wheel axis moves around the circumference of another fixed or moving axis, permitting an unusual velocity ratio with relative simplicity of parts

ep·i·cy·cloid (ep′ə sī′kloid) *n.* [EPICYCL(E) + -OID] *Geom.* the curve traced by a point on the circumference of a circle that rolls around the outside of a fixed circle —**ep′i·cy·cloi′dal** (-kloi′d'l) *adj.*

epicycloidal wheel a wheel of an epicyclic train

Ep·i·dam·nus (ep′ə dam′nəs) *see* DURRËS

ep·i·deic·tic (ep′ə dīk′tik) *adj.* [Gr. *epideiktikos*, declamatory < *epideikti(os)*, verbal adj. (< *epideiknynai*, to display < *epi-*: see EPI- + *deiknynai*, to show: for IE. base see DICTION) + *-ikos*, -IC] intended for display, esp. rhetorical display; designed to impress

ep·i·dem·ic (ep′ə dem′ik) *adj.* [Fr. *épidémique* < *épidémie* < ML. *epidemia* < Gr. *epidēmia* < *epidēmios*, among the people, general < *epi-*, among + *dēmos*, people] prevalent and spreading rapidly among many individuals in a community at the same time; widespread: said esp. of a human contagious disease Also **ep′i·dem′i·cal** —*n.* 1. an epidemic disease 2. the rapid spreading of such a disease 3. the rapid, widespread occurrence of a fad, fashion, etc. —**ep′i·dem′i·cal·ly** *adv.*

epidemic encephalitis encephalitis caused by a variety of viruses

ep·i·de·mi·ol·o·gy (-dē′mē äl′ə jē, -dem′ē-) *n.* [Gr.

epidēmios (see EPIDEMIC) + -LOGY] 1. the branch of medicine that investigates the causes and control of epidemics 2. all the elements contributing to the occurrence or non-occurrence of a disease in a population; ecology of a disease —**ep′i·de′mi·o·log′ic** (-ə läj′ik), **ep′i·de′mi·o·log′i·cal** *adj.* —**ep′i·de′mi·ol′o·gist** *n.*

ep·i·den·drum (ep′ə den′drəm) *n.* [ModL. < EPI- + Gr. *dendron*, tree: see DENDRO-] any of a genus (*Epidendrum*) of small-flowered, chiefly tropical American, epiphytic orchids

ep·i·der·mis (-dur′mis) *n.* [LL. *epidermis* < Gr. *epidermis* < *epi-*, upon + *derma*, the skin] 1. the outermost layer of the skin in vertebrates, having no blood vessels and consisting of several layers of cells, covering the dermis 2. the outermost layer of cells covering seed plants and ferns 3. any of various other integuments —**ep′i·der′mal**, **ep′i·der′mic** *adj.*

ep·i·der·moid (-dur′moid) *adj.* like, or having the nature of, epidermis: also **ep′i·der·moi′dal** *adj.*

ep·i·di·a·scope (ep′ə dī′ə skōp′) *n.* [EPI- + DIA- + -SCOPE] an optical device for projecting on a screen a magnified image of an opaque or transparent object

ep·i·did·y·mis (-did′i məs) *n., pl.* **ep′i·di·dym′i·des′** (-di dim′ə dēz′) [ModL. < Gr. *epididymis* < *epi-*, upon + *didymoi*, testicles, orig. pl. of *didymos*, double, redupl. of *duo*, TWO] a long, oval-shaped structure attached to the rear upper surface of each testicle, consisting mainly of the excretory ducts of the testicles —**ep′i·did′y·mal** *adj.*

ep·i·dote (ep′ə dōt′) *n.* [Fr. *épidote* < Gr. *epididonai*, to give besides, increase < *epi-*, over + *didonai*, to give (for IE. base see DONATION): from the enlarged base of some of the crystal forms] a hydrous silicate of calcium, aluminum, and iron, $Ca_2(Al, Fe)_3(SiO_4)_3OH$, yellowish-green to black in color, found in the form of monoclinic crystals, grains, or fibers —**ep′i·dot′ic** (-dät′ik) *adj.*

ep·i·fo·cal (ep′ə fō′k'l) *adj.* over the focus, or center of disturbance, of an earthquake; epicentral

ep·i·gas·tric (-gas′trik) *adj.* 1. of or located within the epigastrium 2. of or pertaining to the front walls of the abdomen

ep·i·gas·tri·um (-gas′trē əm) *n., pl.* -**tri·a** (-ə) [ModL. < Gr. *epigastrion*, neut. of *epigastrios*, over the stomach < *epi-*, upon + *gastēr*, the stomach: see GASTRO-] *Anat.* the upper middle portion of the abdomen, including the area over and in front of the stomach; epigastric region

ep·i·ge·al (-jē′al) *adj.* [Gr. *epigeios*, on the earth (< *epi-*, upon + *gē*, the earth) + -AL] 1. *Bot. a)* growing on or close to the ground *b)* directed above the ground after germination: said of cotyledons 2. *Zool.* living or developing on the exposed surface of the earth or in shallow water Also **ep′i·ge′an**

ep·i·gene (ep′ə jēn′) *adj.* [Fr. *épigène* < Gr. *epigenēs*, born late: see EPI- & -GEN] *Geol.* produced or formed on or near the earth's surface [*epigene* rocks]

ep·i·gen·e·sis (ep′ə jen′ə sis) *n.* [ModL.: see EPI- & -GENESIS] 1. *Biol.* the theory that the germ cell is structureless and that the embryo develops as a new creation through the action of the environment on the protoplasm 2. *Geol.* metamorphism 3. *Med. a)* the appearing of secondary symptoms *b)* a secondary symptom

ep·i·ge·net·ic (-jə net′ik) *adj.* 1. of, or having the nature of, epigenesis 2. *Geol. a)* produced on or near the surface of the earth *b)* formed or deposited later than the enclosing rocks: said of ore deposits, structures, etc.

ep·i·ge·nous (e pij′ə nəs) *adj.* [EPI- + -GENOUS] *Bot.* growing on the surface of a leaf or other plant part, esp. on the upper surface, as some fungi

ep·i·ge·ous (ep′ə jē′əs) *adj. same as* EPIGEAL

ep·i·glot·tis (-glät′is) *n.* [ModL. < Gr. *epiglōttis*: see EPI- & GLOTTIS] the thin, triangular, lidlike piece of cartilage that folds back over the opening of the windpipe during swallowing, thus preventing food, etc. from entering the lungs —**ep′i·glot′tal**, **ep′i·glot′tic** *adj.*

ep·i·gone (ep′ə gōn′) *n., pl.* -**gones′**, **e·pig′o·ni** (e pig′ə nī′) [G., sing. of *epigonen* < Gr. (*hoi*) *Epigonoi*, lit., (the) Afterborn, epithet of the sons of the chiefs who fell in the first war against Thebes, pl. of *epigonos*, orig. adj., born after: see EPI- & GONO-] a descendant less gifted than his ancestors, or any inferior follower or imitator

ep·i·gram (-gram′) *n.* [ME. < OFr. *epigramme* < L. *epigramma* < Gr. *epigramma*, inscription, epigram < *epigraphein* < *epi-*, upon + *graphein*, to write: see GRAPHIC] 1. a short poem with a witty or satirical point 2. any terse, witty, pointed statement, often antithetical (Ex.: "Experience is the name everyone gives to his mistakes") 3. the use of epigrams —*SYN.* see SAYING

ep·i·gram·mat·ic (ep′i gram mat′ik) *adj.* [L. *epigrammaticus* < Gr. *epigrammatikos*] 1. of or full of epigram or epigrams 2. having the nature of an epigram; terse, witty, etc. Also **ep′i·gram·mat′i·cal** —**ep′i·gram·mat′i·cal·ly** *adv.*

ep·i·gram·ma·tism (ep′ə gram′ə tiz′m) *n.* the use of epigrams, or a style characterized by epigram —**ep′i·gram′ma·tist** *n.*

ep·i·gram·ma·tize (-tīz′) *vt., vi.* -**tized′**, -**tiz′ing** to express (something) epigrammatically; make epigrams (about)

ep·i·graph (ep′ə graf′, -gräf′) *n.* [Gr. *epigraphē*, inscription < *epigraphein*: see EPIGRAM] 1. an inscription on a building, monument, etc. 2. a motto or quotation at the beginning of a book, chapter, etc.

ROTATING CIRCLE

EPICYCLOID

FIXED CIRCLE

EPICYCLOID
(P, point of rotating circle)

ep·i·graph·ic (ep'ə graf'ik) *adj.* of or having to do with an epigraph or epigraphy: also **ep'i·graph'i·cal** —**ep'i·graph'i·cal·ly** *adv.*

e·pig·ra·phist (i pig'rə fist) *n.* a specialist in epigraphy: also **e·pig'ra·pher**

e·pig·ra·phy (-fē) *n.* **1.** inscriptions collectively **2.** the study that deals with deciphering, interpreting, and classifying inscriptions, esp. ancient inscriptions

e·pig·y·nous (i pij'ə nəs) *adj.* [EPI- + -GYNOUS] designating petals, sepals, and stamens that are attached to the top of the ovary: opposed to HYPOGYNOUS —**e·pig'y·ny** *n.*

ep·i·lep·sy (ep'ə lep'sē) *n.* [OFr. *epilepsie* < LL. *epilepsia* < Gr. *epilēpsia, epilēpsis,* lit., a seizure, hence epilepsy < *epilambanein,* to seize upon < *epi-,* upon + *lambanein,* to seize < IE. base *(s)lagw-,* to seize, whence LATCH] a chronic disease of the nervous system, characterized by convulsions and, often, unconsciousness: see GRAND MAL, PETIT MAL

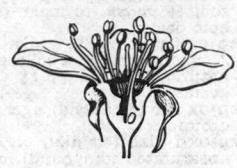
EPIGYNOUS BLOSSOM
(of pear)

ep·i·lep·tic (ep'ə lep'tik) *adj.* [Fr. *épileptique* < L. *epilepticus* < Gr. *epilēptikos*] **1.** of, like, or having the nature of, epilepsy **2.** having epilepsy —*n.* a person who has epilepsy —**ep'i·lep'ti·cal·ly** *adv.*

ep·i·lep·toid (-toid) *adj.* resembling epilepsy: also **ep'i·lep'ti·form'** (-tə fôrm')

ep·i·lim·ni·on (ep'ə lim'nē ən) *n.* [ModL. < EPI- + Gr. *limnion,* dim. of *limnē,* marshy lake, prob. < IE. base *lei-,* to bend, whence LIMB¹] the upper layer of warm water in a lake, containing more oxygen than the lower layers

ep·i·logue, ep·i·log (ep'ə lôg', -läg') *n.* [ME. *epiloge* < OFr. *epilogue* < L. *epilogus* < Gr. *epilogos,* conclusion, epilogue < *epilegein,* to say in addition, add < *epi-,* upon + *legein,* to say, speak: see LOGIC] **1.** a closing section added to a novel, play, etc., providing further comment, interpretation, or information **2.** a short speech or poem spoken to the audience by one of the actors at the end of a play **3.** the actor or actors who speak this

ep·i·mere (ep'ə mir) *n.* [EPI- + -MERE] the dorsal portion of the mesodermal mass in the early development of chordate embryos that gives rise to the skeletal muscles

ep·i·my·si·um (-mis'ē əm, -miz'-) *n.* [ModL. < EPI- + Gr. *mys,* muscle (see MYO-) + ModL. *-ium* (see -IUM)] the sheath of connective tissue surrounding a muscle

ep·i·nas·ty (ep'ə nas'tē) *n.* [EPI- + -NASTY] *Bot.* the condition in which an organ, as a leaf, turns downward because of the more rapid growth of the upper layers of cells: opposed to HYPONASTY —**ep'i·nas'tic** *adj.*

ep·i·neph·rine (ep'ə nef'rin, -rēn) *n.* [EPI- + NEPHR- + -INE⁴] a hormone, C₉H₁₃NO₃, secreted by the medulla of the adrenal gland, that stimulates the heart, increases muscular strength and endurance, etc.: it is extracted from animal adrenals or prepared synthetically for therapeutic use

ep·i·neu·ri·um (-noor'ē əm, -nyoor'-) *n.* [ModL. < EPI- + Gr. *neuron,* a nerve] the layer of connective tissue surrounding a peripheral nerve

E·piph·a·ny (i pif'ə nē) *n., pl.* **-nies** [ME. & OFr. *epiphanie* < LL.(Ec.) *epiphania* < Gr. *epiphaneia,* appearance < Gr. *epiphainein,* to show forth, manifest < *epi-,* upon + *phainein,* to show: see FANTASY] **1.** [e-] an appearance or manifestation of a god or other supernatural being **2.** in many Christian churches, a yearly festival, held January 6, commemorating the revealing of Jesus as the Christ to the Gentiles in the persons of the Magi or the baptism of Jesus: also called TWELFTH DAY

ep·i·phe·nom·e·nal·ism (ep'i fə näm'ə nəl iz'm) *n.* the theory that mental or conscious processes simply accompany certain neural processes as epiphenomena

ep·i·phe·nom·e·non (-fə näm'ə nän') *n., pl.* **-na** (-nə) [EPI- + PHENOMENON] **1.** a phenomenon that occurs with and seems to result from another but which has no effect or subsequent influence on the process **2.** *Med.* a secondary or additional occurrence in the course of a disease —**ep'i·phe·nom'e·nal** *adj.* —**ep'i·phe·nom'e·nal·ly** *adv.*

e·piph·y·sis (i pif'ə sis) *n., pl.* **-ses'** (-sēz') [ModL. < Gr. *epiphysis,* a growth upon, excrescence < *epiphyein,* to grow upon < *epi-,* upon + *phyein,* to grow: see BONDAGE] **1.** the end part of a long bone which is at first separated from the main part by cartilage, but later fuses with it by ossification **2.** the pineal body: in full, **epiphysis cer·e·bri** (ser'ə brī') —**ep·i·phys·e·al, ep·i·phys·i·al** (ep'ə fiz'ē əl) *adj.*

ep·i·phyte (ep'ə fīt') *n.* [EPI- + -PHYTE] **1.** a plant that grows on another plant but is not a parasite and produces its own food by photosynthesis, as certain orchids, mosses, and lichens; air plant **2.** a plant parasitic on the external surface of an animal body —**ep'i·phyt'ic** (-fit'ik) *adj.* —**ep'i·phyt'i·cal·ly** *adv.*

ep·i·phy·tol·o·gy (ep'ə fī täl'ə jē) *n.* [< prec. + -LOGY] the study of epidemic plant diseases

ep·i·phy·tot·ic (-fī tät'ik) *adj.* [< EPI- + Gr. *phyton,* a plant + -OTIC] epidemic among plants —*n.* an epiphytotic disease

ep·i·rog·e·ny (ep'i räj'ə nē) *n.* same as EPEIROGENY —**e·pi·ro·gen·ic** (i pi'rə jen'ik) *adj.*

E·pi·rus (i pi'rəs) **1.** ancient kingdom on the E coast of the Ionian Sea, in what is now S Albania & NW Greece **2.** division of NW Greece: 3,511 sq. mi.; pop. 353,000 See GREECE, map

Epis. Epistle

Epis., Episc. **1.** Episcopal **2.** Episcopalian

e·pi·sci·a (i pish'ə, -ē ə) *n.* [ModL. < Gr. *episkia,* fem. of *episkios,* shaded < *epi-,* EPI- + *skia,* shadow < IE. *skiya-,* var. of base *skāi-,* to gleam softly, whence SHINE] any of a genus (*Episcia*) of tropical American plants with elliptical, hairy leaves and white to red flowers, related to the African violet

e·pis·co·pa·cy (i pis'kə pə sē) *n., pl.* **-cies** [< LL.(Ec.) *episcopatus,* office of a bishop < *episcopus,* BISHOP] **1.** the system of church government by bishops **2.** *same as* EPISCOPATE

e·pis·co·pal (-kə pəl) *adj.* [ME. < LL.(Ec.) *episcopalis*] **1.** of or governed by bishops **2.** [E-] designating or of any of various churches governed by bishops, as the Protestant Episcopal or the Anglican Church —**e·pis'co·pal·ly** *adv.*

E·pis·co·pa·li·an (i pis'kə pāl'yən, -pā'lē ən) *adj.* [prec. + -IAN] **1.** [e-] of church government by bishops **2.** *same as* EPISCOPAL —*n.* **1.** [e-] a member of an episcopal church or a person believing in episcopal government ☆**2.** a member of the Protestant Episcopal Church —**E·pis'co·pa'li·an·ism** *n.*

e·pis·co·pal·ism (i pis'kə pəl iz'm) *n.* the theory or doctrine that the authority to govern a church rests in a body of bishops and not in any individual

e·pis·co·pate (-pit, -pāt') *n.* [see EPISCOPACY] **1.** the position, rank, or term of office of a bishop **2.** a bishop's see **3.** bishops collectively

e·pi·si·ot·o·my (i pē'zē ät'ə mē) *n., pl.* **-mies** [< Gr. *epision,* pubic region + -TOMY] an incision of the perineum, often performed during childbirth to prevent injury to the vagina

ep·i·sode (ep'ə sōd') *n.* [Gr. *epeisodion,* addition, episode, orig. neut. of *epeisodios,* following upon the entrance < *epi-,* upon + *eisodos,* an entrance < *eis-,* into + *hodos,* way, road < IE. base *sed-,* to go, whence (?) L. *cedere*] **1.** the part of an ancient Greek tragedy between two choric songs: it corresponds to an act **2.** in a novel, poem, etc., any part of the story, or a narrative digression, that is complete in itself; incident **3.** any event or series of events complete in itself but forming part of a larger one [an *episode* in the war] **4.** any installment of a serialized story or drama **5.** *Music a)* in a strict fugue, any section that does not contain the principal subject in its entirety *b)* any incidental passage in a composition not derived from a principal theme —*SYN.* see OCCURRENCE

ep·i·sod·ic (ep'ə säd'ik) *adj.* **1.** having the nature of an episode; incidental **2.** divided into episodes, often not closely related or well integrated Also **ep·i·sod'i·cal** —**ep·i·sod'i·cal·ly** *adv.*

ep·i·some (ep'ə sōm') *n.* [EPI- + -SOME³] a small genetic element or unit of DNA that is not essential to the life of the cell and that can, therefore, be lost or transferred

e·pis·ta·sis (i pis'tə sis) *n.* [ModL. < Gr. *epistasis,* a stopping < *ephistanai,* to stop, orig. to place upon < *epi-,* EPI- + *histanai,* to STAND] *Genetics* the suppression of gene expression by one or more other genes

ep·i·stax·is (ep'ə stak'sis) *n.* [ModL. < Gr. *epistazein,* to bleed at the nose < *epi-,* upon + *stazein,* to fall in drops: for IE. base see STAGNATE] *Med.* nosebleed; nasal hemorrhage

ep·i·ste·mic (ep'ə stē'mik) *adj.* [< Gr. *epistēmē* (see ff.) + -IC] of or having to do with knowledge —**ep'i·ste'mi·cal·ly** *adv.*

e·pis·te·mol·o·gy (i pis'tə mäl'ə jē) *n., pl.* **-gies** [< Gr. *epistēmē,* knowledge < *epistanai,* to understand, believe (< *epi-* + *histanai,* orig., to stand before, confront: see STAND) + -LOGY] the study or theory of the origin, nature, methods, and limits of knowledge —**e·pis'te·mo·log'i·cal** (-mə läj'i k'l) *adj.* —**e·pis'te·mo·log'i·cal·ly** *adv.* —**e·pis'te·mol'o·gist** *n.*

ep·i·ster·num (ep'ə stur'nəm) *n., pl.* **-na** (-nə) [ModL.: see EPI- & STERNUM] **1.** the most anterior part of the sternum in amphibians and mammals **2.** in some lizards, a dermal bone lying ventral to the sternum —**ep'i·ster'nal** *adj.*

e·pis·tle (i pis''l) *n.* [ME. *epistel* < OFr. *epistle* (& OE. *epistol*) < L. *epistola, epistula* < Gr. *epistolē,* a letter, message < *epistellein,* to send to < *epi-,* + *stellein,* to send, summon: see STALK²] **1.** a letter, esp. a long, formal, instructive letter: now generally a facetious use **2.** [E-] *a)* any of the letters in the New Testament written by an Apostle *b)* a selection, usually from these Epistles, read as part of Mass, Communion, etc. in various churches

e·pis·tler (-'l ər, -lər) *n.* **1.** a letter writer **2.** [*usually* E-]

the person who reads the Epistle during Mass, etc.: also **e·pis'to·ler** (-tə lər)

e·pis·to·lar·y (-tə ler'ē) *adj.* [Fr. *épistolaire* < L. *epistolaris* < *epistola*, EPISTLE] **1.** of or suitable to letters or letter writing **2.** contained in or conducted by letters **3.** composed as a series of letters, as certain novels of the 18th cent.

ep·i·style (ep'ə stīl') *n.* [L. *epistylium* < Gr. *epistylion* < *epi-*, upon + *stylos*, column: see STYLITE] *same as* ARCHITRAVE (sense 1)

ep·i·taph (-taf', -täf') *n.* [ME. & OFr. *epitaphe* < L. *epitaphium*, eulogy < Gr. *epitaphion* < *epi*, upon, at + *taphos*, tomb < *thaptein*, to bury] **1.** an inscription on a tomb or gravestone in memory of the person buried there **2.** a short composition in prose or verse, written as a tribute to a dead person —**ep'i·taph'ic, ep'i·taph'i·al** *adj.*

e·pit·a·sis (i pit'ə sis) *n.* [ModL. < Gr. *epitasis*, a stretching, intensity < *epiteinein*, to stretch, intensify < *epi-*, EPI- + *teinein*, to stretch: see TEND²] that part of a play, esp. in classical drama, between the protasis, or exposition, and the catastrophe or denouement

ep·i·tax·y (ep'ə tak'sē) *n.* [EPI- + -TAXY] the overgrowth in layers of a crystalline substance deposited in a definite orientation on a base or substratum composed of different crystals —**ep'i·tax'i·al, ep'i·tax'ic** *adj.*

ep·i·tha·la·mi·um (ep'ə thə lā'mē əm) *n.,* *pl.* **-mi·ums, -mi·a** (-ə) [L. < Gr. *epithalamion* < *epithalamios*, nuptial < *epi-*, at + *thalamos*, bridal chamber] a song or poem in honor of a bride or bridegroom, or of both; nuptial song: also **ep'i·tha·la'mi·on** (-ən), *pl.* **-mi·a** (-ə)

ep·i·the·li·al (ep'ə thē'lē əl) *adj.* of, or having the nature of, epithelium

ep·i·the·li·oid (-oid') *adj.* resembling epithelium

ep·i·the·li·o·ma (ep'ə thē'lē ō'mə) *n.,* *pl.* **-ma·ta** (-mə tə), **-mas** [ModL. < ff. + -OMA] a benign tumor composed mostly of epithelial cells: a former term for a malignant tumor of the skin

ep·i·the·li·um (-thē'lē əm) *n.,* *pl.* **-li·ums, -li·a** (-ə) [ModL. < Gr. *epi-*, upon + *thēlē*, nipple: see FEMALE] cellular tissue covering surfaces, forming glands, and lining most cavities of the body: it consists of one or more layers of cells with only little intercellular material

ep·i·the·lize (-thē'līz) *vt.* **-lized, -liz·ing** to cover with epithelium, as in the healing of an ulcer: also **ep'i·the'li·al·ize', -ized', -iz'ing**

ep·i·thet (ep'ə thet', -thət) *n.* [L. *epitheton* < Gr. *epitheton*, lit., that which is added < *epitithenai*, to put on, add < *epi-*, on + *tithenai*, to put, DO¹] **1.** an adjective, noun, or phrase used to characterize some person or thing, often specif. a disparaging one (Ex.: "egghead" for an intellectual) **2.** a descriptive name or title (Ex.: Philip the Fair; America the Beautiful) —**ep'i·thet'i·cal, ep'i·thet'ic** *adj.*

e·pit·o·me (i pit'ə mē) *n.,* *pl.* **-mes** [L. < Gr. *epitomē*, abridgment < *epitemnein*, to cut short < *epi-*, upon + *temnein*, to cut: see -TOMY] **1.** a short statement of the main points of a book, report, incident, etc.; abstract; summary **2.** a person or thing that is representative or typical of the characteristics or general quality of a whole class —*SYN.* see ABRIDGMENT

e·pit·o·mize (-mīz') *vt.* **-mized', -miz'ing** to make or be an epitome of —**e·pit'o·miz'er** *n.*

ep·i·zo·ic (ep'ə zō'ik) *adj.* living on or attached to the external surface of an animal, but not parasitic —**ep'i·zo'ite** (-īt)

ep·i·zo·on (-zō'än) *n.,* *pl.* **-zo'a** (-ə) [ModL. < EPI- + Gr. *zōion*, animal] a parasite or commensal living on the outside of an animal's body

ep·i·zo·ot·ic (-zō ät'ik) *adj.* [Fr. *épizootique* < *épizootie*, epizooty, formed by analogy with *épidémie* (see EPIDEMIC) < Gr. *epi*, upon + *zōion*, animal] epidemic among animals —*n.* an epizootic disease

ep·i·zo·ot·i·ol·o·gy (-zō ät'ē äl'ə jē) *n.* [< prec. + -LOGY] the study of epidemic animal diseases

‡e plu·ri·bus u·num (ē' ploor'ə bəs yōō'nəm) [L.] out of many, one: a motto of the U.S.

ep·och (ep'ək; *Brit. & Canad., usually* ē'päk) *n.* [ML. *epocha* < Gr. *epochē*, a check, cessation < *epechein*, to hold in, check < *epi-*, upon + *echein*, to hold < IE. base *seĝh-*, to hold fast, whence Sans. *sáhas-*, victory, G. *sieg*: cf. SCHOOL¹] **1.** the beginning of a new and important period in the history of anything [the first earth satellite marked a new *epoch* in the study of the universe] **2.** a period of time considered in terms of noteworthy and characteristic events, developments, persons, etc. [an *epoch* of social revolution] **3.** a point in time or a precise date: now rare, except specif., *Astron.* the time at which observations are made, as of the positions of planets or stars **4.** *Geol.* a subdivision of a geologic period [the Eocene *Epoch*]: see also ERA, PERIOD, AGE —*SYN.* see PERIOD —**ep'och·al** *adj.* —**ep'och·al·ly** *adv.*

ep·ode (ep'ōd) *n.* [MFr. *épode* < L. *epodos* < Gr. *epōidos*, aftersong, lit., singing, or sung, to music < *epaeidein*, to sing to accompaniment < *epi-*, upon + *aeidein*, to sing: see ODE] **1.** a form of lyric poem, as of Horace, in which a short line follows a longer one **2.** the final stanza of a Pindaric or ancient Greek ode: it follows the strophe and antistrophe

ep·o·nym (ep'ə nim') *n.* [< Gr. *epōnymos*, eponymous < *epi-*, upon + *onyma*, NAME] **1.** a real or mythical person from whose name the name of a nation, institution, etc. is derived or is supposed to have been derived [William *Penn* is the *eponym* of *Pennsylvania*] **2.** a person whose name has become identified with some period, movement, theory, etc. —**e·pon·y·mous** (i pän'ə məs), **ep'o·nym'ic** (-nim'ik) *adj.*

e·pon·y·my (i pän'ə mē) *n.* the derivation, often conjectural, of the name of a people, nation, etc. from the name of a real or mythical person

ep·o·pee (ep'ə pē', ep'ə pē') *n.* [Fr. *épopée* < Gr. *epopoiia*, the making of epics < *epopoios*, epic poet < *epos* (see EPIC) song + *poiein*, to make (see POET)] **1.** an epic poem **2.** epic poetry

ep·os (ep'äs) *n.* [L. < Gr. *epos*: see EPIC] **1.** an epic poem **2.** epic poetry **3.** a collection of poems of a primitive epic nature, handed down by word of mouth **4.** a series of epic events

ep·ox·ide (ē päk'sīd) *n.* a compound containing the epoxy group

ep·ox·i·dize (-sə dīz') *vt.* **-dized', -diz'ing** to convert (an unsaturated compound) into an epoxide

ep·ox·y (e päk'sē) *adj.* [EP- + OXY(GEN)] designating or of a compound in which an oxygen atom is joined to two carbon atoms in a chain to form a bridge; specif., designating a resin, containing epoxy groups, that polymerizes spontaneously when mixed with a diphenol, forming a strong, hard, resistant adhesive used in glues, enamel coatings, etc. —*n.,* *pl.* **-ox·ies** an epoxy resin

ep·si·lon (ep'sə län', -lən) *n.* [LGr. *e psilon*, lit., plain *e*: so named to distinguish it from *ai*, which had come to have the same pronunciation] the fifth letter of the Greek alphabet (Ε, ε)

Ep·som (ep'səm) town in Surrey, England, southwest of London: site of **Epsom Downs**, where the Derby is run: now part of the borough of **Epsom and Ewell**, pop. 71,000

Epsom salts (or **salt**) [< *Epsom*, England, famous for its mineral waters] a white, crystalline salt, magnesium sulfate, $MgSO_4·7H_2O$, used as a cathartic

Ep·stein (ep'stīn), Sir **Jacob** 1880–1959; Brit. sculptor, born in the U.S.

eq. **1.** equal **2.** equalizer **3.** equation **4.** equator **5.** equivalent

eq·ua·ble (ek'wə b'l, ē'kwə-) *adj.* [L. *aequabilis* < *aequare*, to make equal < *aequus*, EQUAL] **1.** not varying or fluctuating much; steady; uniform [an *equable* temperature] **2.** not readily upset; even; tranquil; serene [an *equable* temperament] —*SYN.* see STEADY —**eq'ua·bil'i·ty** (-bil'ə-tē) *n.* —**eq'ua·bly** *adv.*

e·qual (ē'kwəl) *adj.* [ME. < L. *aequalis*, equal < *aequus*, plain, even, flat] **1.** of the same quantity, size, number, value, degree, intensity, quality, etc. **2.** having the same rights, privileges, ability, rank, etc. **3.** evenly proportioned; balanced or uniform in effect or operation **4.** having the necessary ability, strength, power, capacity, or courage (with *to*) [*equal* to the challenge] **5.** [Archaic] fair; just; impartial **6.** [Archaic] smooth and flat; level **7.** [Archaic] equable —*n.* any thing or person that is equal [to be the *equal* of another] —*vt.* **e'qualed** or **e'qualled, e'qual·ing** or **e'qual·ling 1.** to be equal to; match in value **2.** to do or make something equal to [to *equal* a record] **3.** [Archaic] to make equal; equalize **4.** [Obs.] to recompense in full —*SYN.* see SAME

e·qual-ar·e·a (ē'kwəl er'ē ə) *adj.* designating any of several map projections in which areas enclosed between corresponding meridians and parallels are proportionally equal to areas on the earth's surface, but distances and directions are distorted

e·qual·i·tar·i·an (i kwäl'ə ter'ē ən, -kwôl'-) *adj., n. same as* EGALITARIAN —**e·qual'i·tar'i·an·ism** *n.*

e·qual·i·ty (i kwäl'ə tē, -kwôl'-) *n.,* *pl.* **-ties** [ME. *equalite* < OFr. *equalité* < L. *aequalitas*] state or instance of being equal

e·qual·ize (ē'kwə līz') *vt.* **-ized', -iz'ing 1.** to make equal **2.** to make uniform —**e'qual·i·za'tion** *n.*

e·qual·iz·er (-ər) *n.* **1.** a person who equalizes **2.** a thing that equalizes, as a group of components inserted in a circuit so as to change the frequency response in a predetermined manner

e·qual·ly (ē'kwə lē) *adv.* in an equal manner; in or to an equal extent or degree; uniformly, impartially, etc.

equal sign (or **mark**) the arithmetical sign (=), indicating that the terms on either side of it are equal

e·qua·nim·i·ty (ek'wə nim'ə tē, ē'kwə-) *n.* [L. *aequanimitas* < *aequanimus* < *aequus*, even, plain + *animus*, mind] the quality of remaining calm and undisturbed; evenness of mind or temper; composure

SYN.—**equanimity** implies an inherent evenness of temper or disposition that is not easily disturbed; **composure** implies the disciplining of one's emotions in a trying situation or habitual self-possession in the face of excitement; **serenity** implies a lofty, clear peace of mind that is not easily clouded by ordinary stresses or excitements; **nonchalance** implies a casual indifference to or a cool detachment from situations that might be expected to disturb one emotionally; **sang-froid** implies great coolness and presence of mind in dangerous or trying circumstances

e·quate (i kwāt') *vt.* **e·quat'ed, e·quat'ing** [ME. *equaten* < L. *aequatus*, pp. of *aequare*, to make equal < *aequus*, plain, even] **1.** *a)* to make equal or equivalent; equalize *b)* to treat, regard, or express as equal, equivalent, identical, or closely related [to *equate* wealth with happiness] **2.** *Math.*

equation 473 **equivalency**

to state or express the equality of; put in the form of an equation —*vi.* [Rare] to be equal —**e·quat′a·ble** *adj.*

e·qua·tion (i kwā′zhən) *n.* [ME. *equacioun* < L. *aequatio*] **1.** the act of equating; equalization **2.** the state of being equated; equality, equivalence, or balance; also, identification or association **3.** *a)* a complex whole *[the human equation] b)* an element in a complex whole: see also PERSONAL EQUATION **4.** a statement of equality between two quantities, as shown by the equal sign (=) *[a quadratic equation]* **5.** an expression in which symbols and formulas are used to represent a chemical reaction (Ex.: $H_2SO_4 + 2NaCl = 2HCl + Na_2SO_4$) —**e·qua′tion·al** *adj.*

equation of time *Astron.* the difference between apparent and mean solar time, varying throughout the year and amounting at its maximum to about sixteen minutes

e·qua·tor (i kwāt′ər) *n.* [ME. < ML. < LL. *aequator*, lit., one who makes equal: see EQUATE] **1.** an imaginary circle around the earth, equally distant at all points from both the North Pole and the South Pole: it divides the earth's surface into the Northern Hemisphere and the Southern Hemisphere **2.** a circle like this around any heavenly body **3.** any circle that divides a sphere or other body into two equal and symmetrical parts **4.** *same as* CELESTIAL EQUATOR

e·qua·to·ri·al (ē′kwə tôr′ē əl, ek′wə-) *adj.* **1.** of or near the earth's equator **2.** of any equator **3.** like or characteristic of conditions near the earth's equator *[equatorial heat]* **4.** designating or of a telescope mounted in such a way as to have two axes of motion, one (called *polar axis*) parallel to the earth's axis, the other (called *declination axis*) perpendicular to it: by rotation about the polar axis it can follow the apparent motion of a heavenly body —*n.* an equatorial telescope

Equatorial Guinea country in C Africa, consisting of the provinces of Río Muni & Fernando Póo: formerly (until 1968) a Sp. possession: 10,832 sq. mi.; pop. 246,000; cap. Santa Isabel

eq·uer·ry (ek′wər ē; *also, esp. Brit.*, i kwer′ē) *n., pl.* **-ries** [altered (after L. *equus*, horse) < Fr. *écurie* < OFr. *escuerie*, status of a squire: see ESQUIRE] **1.** formerly, an officer in charge of the horses of a royal or noble household **2.** an officer who is a personal attendant on some member of a royal family

e·ques·tri·an (i kwes′trē ən) *adj.* [< L. *equestris* (< *eques*, horseman < *equus*, horse < IE. base *ekwos*, whence Gr. *hippos*, OE. *eoh*) + -AN] **1.** of horses, horsemen, horseback riding, or horsemanship **2.** on horseback, or so represented *[an equestrian statue]* **3.** *a)* of the ancient Roman equites *b)* of or made up of knights —*n.* a rider on horseback, esp. one performing acrobatics on horseback, as in a circus —**e·ques′tri·an·ism** *n.* —**e·ques′tri·enne′** (-trē en′) *n.fem.*

e·qui- (ē′kwə, ek′wə) [< L. *aequus*, equal] *a combining form meaning* equal, equally *[equivalent, equidistant]*

e·qui·an·gu·lar (ē′kwə aŋ′gyə lər) *adj.* having all angles equal

e·qui·dis·tant (ē′kwə dis′tənt) *adj.* equally distant —**e′qui·dis′tance** *n.* —**e′qui·dis′tant·ly** *adv.*

e·qui·lat·er·al (-lat′ər əl) *adj.* [LL. *aequilateralis* < L. *aequus*, equal + *latus*, side (see LATERAL)] having all sides equal *[an equilateral triangle]* —*n.* **1.** a figure having equal sides **2.** a side exactly equal to another or others

e·quil·i·brant (i kwil′ə brənt) *n.* [Fr. *équilibrant*, prp. of *équilibrer*, to equilibrate < *équilibre*, equilibrium < L. *aequilibrium*, EQUILIBRIUM] *Physics* a force or combination of forces that can balance another force or forces

e·quil·i·brate (i kwil′ə brāt′, ē′kwə lī′brāt) *vt., vi.* **-brat′ed, -brat′ing** [< LL. *aequilibratus*, in equilibrium, level, pp. of *aequilibrare*] to bring into or be in equilibrium; balance or counterbalance —**e·quil′i·bra′tion** *n.* —**e·quil′i·bra′tor** *n.*

e·quil·i·brist (i kwil′ə brist) *n.* [Fr. *équilibriste* < *équilibre*: see EQUILIBRANT] a performer who does tricks of balancing, as a tightrope walker

e·qui·lib·ri·um (ē′kwə lib′rē əm) *n., pl.* **-ri·ums, -ri·a** (-ə) [L. *aequilibrium* < *aequilibris*, evenly balanced < *aequus*, even, equal + *libra*, a balance] **1.** a state of balance or equality between opposing forces **2.** a state of balance or adjustment of conflicting desires, interests, etc. **3.** *a)* the ability of the animal body to keep itself properly oriented or positioned; bodily stability or balance *b)* mental or emotional stability or balance; poise **4.** the condition in a reversible chemical reaction in which the products of the forward or direct reaction are consumed by the reverse reaction at the same rate as they are formed and there is no net change in the concentrations of the products or the reactants **5.** the stage of a radioactive material at which the rate of disintegration and the rate of formation are equal

e·qui·mo·lal (-mō′ləl) *adj.* having the same molal concentration of solute in a solvent

e·qui·mo·lar (-mō′lər) *adj.* **1.** having the same molar concentration of solute in a solvent **2.** having the same number of moles of a given substance

e·qui·mo·lec·u·lar (-mə lek′yə lər) *adj.* having an equal number of molecules

e·quine (ē′kwin, ek′wīn) *adj.* [L. *equinus* < *equus*: see

EQUESTRIAN] of, like, or characteristic of a horse —*n.* a horse

e·qui·noc·tial (ē′kwə näk′shəl) *adj.* [ME. & OFr. *equinoxial* < L. *aequinoctialis*] **1.** relating to either of the equinoxes **2.** occurring at or about the time of an equinox, when night and day are equal in length **3.** equatorial —*n.* **1.** *same as* CELESTIAL EQUATOR **2.** a storm occurring at or about the time of an equinox

equinoctial circle (or **line**) *same as* CELESTIAL EQUATOR

e·qui·nox (ē′kwə näks′) *n.* [ME. < OFr. *equinoxe* < ML. *aequinoxium* < L. *aequinoctium* < *aequus*, equal + *nox*, NIGHT] **1.** the time when the sun crosses the equator, making night and day of equal length in all parts of the earth: the **vernal equinox** occurs about March 21, the **autumnal equinox** about September 22 **2.** either of the two points on the celestial equator where the sun crosses it on these dates: also called **equinoctial point**

e·quip (i kwip′) *vt.* **e·quipped′, e·quip′ping** [Fr. *équiper* < OFr. *esquiper*, to embark, put out to sea, prob. < OE. *scipian*, to embark < *scip* (see SHIP); or < ? ON. *skipa*, to arrange, make ready] **1.** to provide with what is needed; outfit *[troops equipped for battle]* **2.** to prepare by training, instruction, etc. **3.** to dress (oneself) for a certain purpose —*SYN.* see FURNISH

eq·ui·page (ek′wə pij) *n.* [MFr. < *esquiper*: see prec.] **1.** the furnishings, accessories, or outfit of a ship, army, expedition, etc.; equipment **2.** a carriage, esp. one with horses and liveried servants **3.** [Archaic] *a)* toilet articles *b)* a case for these **4.** [Archaic] retinue; body of attendants

e·quip·ment (i kwip′mənt) *n.* **1.** an equipping or being equipped **2.** whatever a person, group, or thing is equipped with; the special things needed for some purpose; supplies, furnishings, apparatus, etc. **3.** goods used in providing service, esp. in transportation, as the rolling stock of a railroad **4.** one's abilities, knowledge, etc.

e·qui·poise (ek′wə poiz′, ē′kwə-) *n.* [EQUI- + POISE[1]] **1.** equal distribution of weight; state of balance, or equilibrium **2.** a weight or force that balances another; counterbalance

e·qui·pol·lent (ē′kwə päl′ənt) *adj.* [ME. & OFr. *equipolent* < L. *aequipollens* < *aequus*, equal + *pollens*, prp. of *pollere*, to be strong] **1.** equal in force, weight, validity, etc. **2.** equivalent in meaning or result —*n.* something equipollent —**e′qui·pol′lence, e′qui·pol′len·cy** *n.*

e·qui·pon·der·ant (-pän′dər ənt) *adj.* [ML. *aequiponderans*, prp. of *aequiponderare* < L. *aequus*, equal + *ponderare*, to weigh: see PONDER] of the same weight; evenly balanced —**e′qui·pon′der·ance** *n.*

e·qui·pon·der·ate (-pän′də rāt′) *vt.* **-at·ed, -at′ing** [< pp. of ML. *aequiponderare*: see prec.] **1.** to counterbalance **2.** to make evenly balanced

e·qui·po·ten·tial (-pə ten′shəl) *adj.* **1.** having equal potentiality or power **2.** *Physics* of the same potential at all points

eq·ui·se·tum (ek′wə sēt′əm) *n., pl.* **-tums, -ta** (-tə) [ModL. < L. *equisaetum*, the plant horsetail < *equus*, horse + *saeta*, bristle: see SINEW] *same as* HORSETAIL

eq·ui·ta·ble (ek′wit ə b'l) *adj.* [Fr. *équitable* < *équité*] **1.** characterized by equity; fair; just: said of actions, results of actions, etc. **2.** *Law a)* having to do with equity, as distinguished from common or statute law *b)* valid in equity —**eq′ui·ta·ble·ness** *n.* —**eq′ui·ta·bly** *adv.*

eq·ui·tant (-wi tənt) *adj.* [L. *equitans*, prp. of *equitare*: see ff.] *Bot.* overlapping: said of a leaf whose base overlaps and covers partly the leaf above it, as in the iris

eq·ui·ta·tion (ek′wə tā′shən) *n.* [L. *equitatio* < *equitatus*, pp. of *equitare*, to ride < *eques*: see EQUESTRIAN] the art of riding on horseback; horsemanship

eq·ui·tes (ek′wət ēz′) *n.pl.* [L., pl. of *eques*: see EQUESTRIAN] members of a specially privileged class of citizens in ancient Rome, from which the cavalry was formed; equestrian order of knights

eq·ui·ty (ek′wət ē) *n., pl.* **-ties** [ME. *equite* < OFr. *equité* < L. *aequitas*, equality < *aequus*, equal] **1.** fairness; impartiality; justice **2.** anything that is fair or equitable ☆**3.** the value of property beyond the total amount owed on it in mortgages, liens, etc. **4.** *Law a)* resort to general principles of fairness and justice whenever existing law is inadequate *b)* a system of rules and doctrines, as in the U.S., supplementing common and statute law and superseding such law when it proves inadequate for just settlement *c)* a right or claim recognized in a court of equity *d) same as* EQUITY OF REDEMPTION

☆**equity capital** **1.** funds contributed by the owners of a business **2.** assets minus liabilities; net worth

equity of redemption the right of a mortgagor to redeem his forfeited estate by payment of capital and interest within a reasonable time: it is granted by a court of equity

equiv. equivalent

e·quiv·a·lence (i kwiv′ə ləns) *n.* [Fr. *équivalence* < ML. *aequivalentia*] **1.** the condition of being equivalent; equality of quantity, value, force, meaning, etc. **2.** *Chem.* equality of combining capacity; the principle that different weights of different substances are equivalent in chemical reactions Also **e·quiv′a·len·cy**

e·quiv·a·lent (-lənt) *adj.* [ME. < OFr. < LL. *aequivalens*, prp. of *aequivalere*, to have equal power < L. *aequus*, equal + *valere*, to be strong: see VALUE] **1.** equal in quantity, value, force, meaning, etc. **2.** *Chem.* having the same valence **3.** *Geom.* equal in area, volume, etc., but not of the same shape —*n.* **1.** an equivalent thing **2.** *Chem. a)* the quantity by weight (of a substance) that combines with one gram of hydrogen or eight grams of oxygen *b)* the weight obtained by dividing the atomic weight by the valence —*SYN.* see SAME —[e·quiv′a·lent·ly *adv.*

e·quiv·o·cal (i kwiv′ə k'l) *adj.* [< LL. *aequivocus* (see EQUIVOCATE) + -AL] **1.** that can have more than one interpretation; having two or more meanings; purposely vague, misleading, or ambiguous [an *equivocal* reply] **2.** uncertain; undecided; doubtful [an *equivocal* outcome] **3.** suspicious; questionable [*equivocal* conduct] —*SYN.* see OBSCURE —e·quiv′o·cal′i·ty (-kal′ə tē), e·quiv′o·cal·ness *n.* —e·quiv′o·cal·ly *adv.*

e·quiv·o·cate (-kāt′) *vi.* -cat′ed, -cat′ing [ME. *equivocaten* < ML. *aequivocatus*, pp. of *aequivocari*, to have the same sound < LL. *aequivocus*, of like sound < L. *aequus*, equal + *vox*, VOICE] to use equivocal terms in order to deceive, mislead, hedge, etc.; be deliberately ambiguous —*SYN.* see LIE² —e·quiv′o·ca′tion *n.* —e·quiv′o·ca′tor *n.*

eq·ui·voque, eq·ui·voke (ek′wə vōk′) *n.* [Fr., orig. adj., equivocal < LL. *aequivocus:* see prec.] [Now Rare] **1.** an ambiguous expression or term **2.** a pun or punning **3.** verbal ambiguity; double meaning

E·quu·le·us (i kwōō′lē əs) [L., dim. of *equus*, horse] a very small constellation on the equator

er (*variously* u, ə, ä, *etc.*; ʉr, ər *are spelling pronunciations*) *interj.* a conventionalized representation of a sound often made by a speaker when hesitating briefly; vocalized pause

-er (ər) *a suffix of various origins, functions, and meanings:* **1.** [ME. -er(e) < OE. -ere < WGmc. *-arj, *-ārj < or akin to, and reinforced by, L. -*arius*, -*arium*, agentive suffixes, (Anglo-Fr. -*er*, -*ier*), L. -*ar* (OFr. -*er*), L. -*atur* (OFr. -*eure*), L. -*atorium* (OFr. -*eor*, Fr. -*oir*), L. -*ator* (OFr. -*eor*)] *a)* added to nouns, meaning a person having to do with, esp. as an occupation or profession [*hatter*, *geographer*]: see also -IER, -YER *b)* added to place names or nouns, meaning a person living in [*New Yorker*, *cottager*] *c)* added to nouns, noun compounds, and noun phrases, meaning a thing or action connected with [*diner*] *d)* added to verbs, meaning a person or thing that [*sprayer*, *roller*]: see also -AR, -OR **2.** [ME. -*re*, -*er* < OE. -*ra*] added to many adjectives and adverbs to form the comparative degree [*later*, *greater*] **3.** [ME. < Anglo-Fr. inf. suffix] added to verb bases in legal language, meaning the action of ——ing [*demurrer*, *waiver*] **4.** [ME. -*ren*, -*rien* < OE. -*rian*, freq. suffix] added to verbs and verb bases, meaning repeatedly [*flicker*, *patter*]

Er *Chem.* erbium

e·ra (ir′ə; *now often* er′ə) *n.* [LL. *aera*, era, earlier senses, "counters," "items of account" < pl. of L. *aes* (gen. *aeris*), brass: see ORE] **1.** a system of reckoning time by numbering the years from some important occurrence or given point of time [the Christian *Era*] **2.** an event or date that marks the beginning of a new or important period in the history of something **3.** a period of time measured from some important occurrence or date **4.** a period of time considered in terms of noteworthy and characteristic events, developments, men, etc. [an *era* of progress] **5.** any of the five main divisions of geologic time [the Paleozoic *Era*]: see also EPOCH, PERIOD, AGE —*SYN.* see PERIOD

ERA *Baseball* earned run average

e·ra·di·ate (ē rā′dē āt′) *vi.*, *vt.* -at′ed, -at′ing to shoot out, as light rays; radiate —e·ra′di·a′tion *n.*

e·rad·i·cate (i rad′ə kāt′) *vt.* -cat′ed, -cat′ing [ME. *eradicaten* < L. *eradicatus*, pp. of *eradicare*, to root out < *e-*, out + *radix* (gen. *radicis*), ROOT¹] **1.** to tear out by the roots; uproot **2.** to get rid of; wipe out; destroy —*SYN.* see EXTERMINATE —e·rad′i·ca·ble (-kə b'l) *adj.* —e·rad′i·ca′-tion *n.* —e·rad′i·ca′tive *adj.* —e·rad′i·ca′tor *n.*

e·rase (i rās′) *vt.* e·rased′, e·ras′ing [< L. *erasus*, pp. of *eradere*, to scratch out < *e-*, out + *radere*, to scrape, scratch: see RAZE] **1.** to rub, scrape, or wipe out (esp. written or engraved letters); efface; expunge **2.** to remove (something recorded) from (magnetic tape) **3.** to remove any sign of; obliterate, as from the mind **4.** [Slang] to kill —e·ras′a·ble *adj.*

SYN.—**erase** implies a scraping or rubbing out of something written or drawn, or figuratively, the removal of an impression; to **expunge** is to wipe or rub out completely; **efface** implies a rubbing out from a surface, and, in extended use, suggests a destroying of the distinguishing marks, or even of the very existence, of something; **obliterate** implies a thorough blotting out of something so that all visible traces of it are removed; **delete** implies the marking of written or printed matter for removal, or the removal of the matter itself

e·ras·er (i rā′sər) *n.* a thing that erases; specif., a device made of rubber for erasing ink or pencil marks, or a pad of felt or cloth for removing chalk marks from a blackboard

e·ra·sion (-zhən) *n.* [ML. *erasio*] **1.** the act of erasing **2.** *Surgery* the removal of diseased tissue by scraping, as with a curet

E·ras·mus (i raz′məs) [ML. < Gr. *Erasmios*, lit., lovely < *eran*, to love, akin to *erōs*, love] **1.** a masculine name **2. Des·i·der·i·us** (des′ə dir′ē əs), (born *Gerhard Gerhards*)

1466?–1536; Du. humanist, scholar, & theologian — E·ras′mi·an (-mē ən) *adj.*, *n.*

E·ras·tian (i ras′chən, -tē ən) *adj.* **1.** of or supporting Thomas Erastus or his doctrines **2.** advocating the supreme authority of the state in church matters —*n.* a follower of Erastus or his doctrines —E·ras′tian·ism *n.*

E·ras·tus (i ras′təs) [L. < Gr. *Erastos*, lit., beloved, lovely < *eran*, to love] **1.** a masculine name **2. Thomas**, (born *Thomas Liebler* or *Lieber*) 1524–83; Ger. theologian & physician

e·ra·sure (i rā′shər; *chiefly Brit.*, -zhər) *n.* **1.** the act of erasing **2.** an erased word, mark, etc. **3.** the place on a surface where something has been erased

Er·a·to (er′ə tō′) [L. < Gr. *Eratō*] *Gr. Myth.* the Muse of erotic lyric poetry

Er·a·tos·the·nes (er′ə täs′thə nēz′) 275?–195? B.C.; Gr. geographer, astronomer, & mathematician

Er·bil (er′bil) city in N Iraq: pop. 34,000: ancient name, ARBELA

er·bi·um (ʉr′bē əm) *n.* [ModL. < (*Ytt*)*erby*, town in Sweden, where first found] a trivalent metallic chemical element of the rare-earth group: symbol, Er; at. wt., 167.28; at. no., 68; sp. gr., 9.164; melt. pt., 1497°C; boil. pt., 2900°C

ere (er) *prep.* [ME. *er* < OE. *ær*, adv., prep., conj., akin to G. *eher*, *ehe*, orig. compar. as seen in cognate Goth. *airis*, earlier < *air*, early < IE. *aier*-, dawn < base *ai-*, to burn, shine] [Archaic or Poet.] before (in time) —*conj.* [Archaic or Poet.] **1.** before **2.** sooner than; rather than

Er·e·bus (er′ə bəs) [L. < Gr. *Erebos*] **1.** *Gr. Myth.* the dark place under the earth through which the dead passed before entering Hades **2. Mount**, volcanic mountain on Ross Island, just off the coast of Victoria Land, Antarctica: over 13,000 ft.

Er·ech·the·um (er′ek thē′əm) [Gr. *Erechtheion* < *Erechtheus*, lit., the render, a mythical king of Athens supposedly entombed there < *erechthein*, to rend, break < IE. base *rekth-*, to harm, whence Sans. *rákṣas-*, torment] temple on the Acropolis in Athens, built 5th cent. B.C.: it contains famous examples of Ionic architecture

e·rect (i rekt′) *adj.* [ME. < L. *erectus*, pp. of *erigere*, to set up < *e-*, out, up + *regere*, to make straight: see RIGHT] **1.** not bending or leaning; straight up; upright; vertical **2.** sticking out or up; bristling; stiff **3.** [Archaic] *a)* not depressed; uplifted *b)* alert —*vt.* **1.** to raise or construct (a building, etc.) **2.** to set up; cause to arise [to *erect* arbitrary social barriers] **3.** to set in an upright position; raise **4.** to set up; assemble **5.** [Archaic] to establish; found **6.** *Geom.* to construct or draw (a perpendicular, figure, etc.) upon a base line **7.** *Physiol.* to cause to become swollen and rigid by being filled with blood —e·rect′ly *adv.* —e·rect′ness *n.*

e·rec·tile (i rek′t'l; *chiefly Brit.*, -tīl′) *adj.* [Fr. < L. *erectus*] that can become erect: used esp. to designate tissue, as in the penis, that becomes swollen and rigid when filled with blood —e·rec·til·i·ty (i rek/til′ə tē) *n.*

e·rec·tion (i rek′shən) *n.* **1.** an erecting or being erected **2.** something erected; structure, building, etc. **3.** *Physiol.* a being or becoming rigid and erect by filling with blood; specif., such a condition of the penis

e·rec·tor (-tər) *n.* a person or thing that erects; specif., a muscle that causes erection

E region the atmospheric zone within the ionosphere between about 60 and 75 miles above the earth, where the E layer is found

ere·long (er′lôŋ′) *adv.* [Archaic or Poet.] before long; soon

er·e·mite (er′ə mīt′) *n.* [ME. < OFr. or LL.; OFr. *ermite*, *hermite*: see HERMIT] a religious recluse; hermit —er′e·mit′ic (-mit′ik), er′e·mit′i·cal *adj.*

er·em·u·rus (er′ə myoor′əs) *n.*, *pl.* -u·ri (-ī) [ModL. < Gr. *erēmos*, lonely + ModL. -*urus* < Gr. *oura*, tail: see URO-²] any of a genus (*Eremurus*) of perennial plants of the lily family, cultivated for their tall spikes of small, white or colored flowers

ere·now (er′nou′) *adv.* [Archaic or Poet.] before now; heretofore

e·rep·sin (i rep′sin) *n.* [G. < L. *ereptus*, pp. of *eripere*, to snatch away (< *e*, out + *rapere*, to snatch: see RAPE¹) + G. *pepsin*, PEPSIN] an enzyme mixture secreted by the intestine and involved in the breaking down of proteins into their component amino acids

er·e·thism (er′ə thiz′m) *n.* [Fr. *éréthisme* < Gr. *erethismos*, irritation < *erethizein*, to irritate < IE. base *er-*, whence RISE, RUN] [Rare] *Physiol.* extreme irritability or sensitivity (of an organ, tissue, etc.)

ere·while (er′hwīl′) *adv.* [ME. *er whil*] [Archaic] a short while before; a short time ago: also **ere′whiles′**

Er·furt (er′foort) city in SW East Germany: pop. 190,000

erg (ʉrg) *n.* [< Gr. *ergon*, WORK] *Physics* the unit of work or energy in the cgs (metric) system, being the amount of work done by one dyne acting through a distance of one centimeter

†er·go (ʉr′gō, er′-) *conj.*, *adv.* [L.] therefore; hence

er·go·graph (ʉr′gə graf′, -gräf′) *n.* [< Gr. *ergon*, WORK + -GRAPH] an instrument for measuring and recording the amount of work that a muscle is capable of doing

er·gom·e·ter (ər gäm′ə tər) *n.* [< Gr. *ergon*, WORK + -METER] an instrument for measuring the amount of work done by a muscle or muscles over a period of time — **er·gom′e·try** (-trē) *n.*

er·go·nom·ics (ur'gə näm'iks) *n.pl.* [*with sing. v.*] [ERG + (EC)ONOMICS] the study of the problems of people in adjusting to their environment; esp., the science that seeks to adapt work or working conditions to suit the worker —**er·go·nom'i·cal** *adj.* —**er·gon'o·mist** (-gän'ə məst) *n.*

☆**er·go·no·vine** (ur'gə nō'vēn) *n.* [*ergo*- (< Fr. < *ergot*, ERGOT) + *nov*- (< L. *novus*, NEW) + -INE⁴] a water-soluble alkaloid of ergot, C₁₉H₂₃N₃O₂, used to increase contraction of the uterus during childbirth and prevent uterine hemorrhage

er·gos·ter·ol (ər gäs'tə rōl') *n.* [< ff. + STEROL] a crystalline steroid alcohol, C₂₈H₄₄O, of high molecular weight, formerly prepared from ergot but now chiefly from yeast: when exposed to ultraviolet rays it produces a vitamin (D₂) used to prevent or cure rickets

er·got (ur'gət) *n.* [Fr. < OFr. *argot*, a rooster's spur, hence (from the shape) the disease growth in the plant] **1.** the hard, reddish-brown or black grainlike masses (*sclerotia*) of certain parasitic fungi (esp. genus *Claviceps*) that replace the kernels of rye, or of other cereal plants **2.** the disease in which this occurs; specif., the disease of rye caused by a species (*Claviceps purpurea*) of this fungus **3.** the dried sclerotia of the rye fungus from which several alkaloids are extracted that have the ability to contract blood vessels and smooth muscle tissue **4.** any of these alkaloids —**er·got·ic** (ər gät'ik) *adj.*

er·got·a·mine (ər gät'ə mēn') *n.* [ERGOT + AMINE] an alkaloid, C₃₃H₃₅O₅N₅, isolated from ergot and used esp. in the treatment of migraine headaches

er·got·ism (ur'gət iz'm) *n.* a diseased condition resulting from the excessive or improper use of ergot or the eating of grain or grain products infested with ergot fungus

Er·ic (er'ik) [Scand. < ON. *Eiríkr* < Gmc. *aizo*, honor (akin to G. *ehre*, honor) + base akin to L. *rex* (see RICH): hence, lit., honorable ruler] a masculine name

Er·ics·son (er'ik sən) **1.** *Leif*, fl. 1000; Norw. explorer & adventurer: discovered VINLAND, believed to be part of N. America: son of ERIC THE RED: also sp. **Er'ic·son 2.** *John*, 1803–89; U.S. naval engineer & inventor, born in Sweden: builder of the *Monitor*

Eric the Red fl. 10th cent.; Norw. explorer & adventurer: discovered & colonized Greenland

E·rid·a·nus (i rid'ə nəs) [L., poetic name of the Po River] a long S constellation, extending southward from the equator

Er·ie (ir'ē) *n.*, *pl.* **Er'ies, Er'ie** [AmFr. < Huron *yěñresh*, wildcat, lit., it is long-tailed + -'e, at the place of] a member of a tribe of Iroquoian Indians who lived in an area east and southeast of Lake Erie —**1.** port on Lake Erie, in NW Pa.: pop. 129,000 **2. Lake**, one of the Great Lakes, between Lake Huron & Lake Ontario: 9,914 sq. mi.; 241 mi. long

Erie Canal barge canal between Buffalo, on Lake Erie, and Albany, on the Hudson, completed in 1825: c. 350 mi. long: now part of New York State Barge Canal

ERIE CANAL

E·rig·e·na (i rij'ə nə), *Jo·han·nes Sco·tus* (jō hän'əs skōt'əs) 815?–880?; Ir. theologian & philosopher in France

e·rig·er·on (i rij'ə rän') *n.* [L., groundsel < Gr. *ērigerōn* < *ēri*, early + *gerōn*, old man: from the hoary down on some varieties] any of a genus (*Erigeron*) of plants of the composite family having asterlike flower heads with white, rose, or violet rays

Er·in (er'in) [OIr. *Ērinn*, dat. of *Ēriu*, Eire] *poet.* name for IRELAND

E·rin·y·es (i rin'ē ēz') *n.pl.*, *sing.* **E·rin'ys** (i rin'is, -rī'nis) [L. < Gr. *Erinys*] *Gr. Myth.* same as FURIES

E·ris (ir'is, er'-) [L. < Gr. *Eris* (see ff.)] *Gr. Myth.* the goddess of strife and discord

er·is·tic (i ris'tik) *adj.* [Gr. *eristikos* < *erizein*, to strive, dispute < *eris*, strife] of or provoking controversy or given to sophistical argument and specious reasoning —*n.* **1.** eristic discourse; sophistical argument **2.** a person who engages in such discourse or argument

Er·i·tre·a (er'ə trē'ə) province of Ethiopia, on the Red Sea: 45,000 sq. mi.; pop. 1,200,000; cap. Asmara —**Er'i·tre'an** *adj., n.*

Er·i·van (er'ə vän') *Eng.* name of YEREVAN

Er·len·mey·er flask (ur'lən mī'ər, er'-) [after Emil *Erlenmeyer* (1825–1909), Ger. chemist] [*also* e-] a conical-based laboratory flask with a flat bottom and a short, straight neck

erl·king (url'kiŋ') *n.* [after G. *erlkönig*, lit., alder king < misunderstanding by Herder (1779) of Dan. *ellerkonge*,

var. of *elverkonge*, king of the elves] *Germanic Folklore* a spirit who does mischief and evil, esp. to children

er·mine (ur'mən) *n.*, *pl.* **-mines, -mine**: see PLURAL, II, D, 1 [ME. & OFr. *ermin*; OFr. *ermine, hermine*, prob. < MHG. *hermin*, erminelike < *harme*, ermine < OHG. *harmo*, weasel (OE. *hearma*): infl. by folk-etymological association with L. (*mus*) *Armenius*, Armenian (mouse)] **1.** any of several weasels of northern regions, specif., in Europe, the stoat (*Mustela erminea*), whose fur is brown in summer but white with a black-tipped tail

ERMINE
(body 5–10 in. long; tail 1–6 in. long)

in winter **2.** the soft, white fur of this animal, used for women's coats, trimming, etc. **3.** the position, rank, or functions of some European judges or peers, whose state robe is trimmed with ermine **4.** *Heraldry* the representation of fur, consisting of a white field with black spots

er·mined (-mənd) *adj.* wearing or trimmed with ermine

erne, ern (urn) *n.* [ME. *ern* < OE. *earn*, akin to MLowG. *arn* < IE. base *er-, *or-*, great bird, eagle, whence G. *aar*, eagle & Gr. *ornis*, bird] the European white-tailed eagle (*Haliaeetus albicilla*) which lives near the sea

Er·nest (ur'nəst) [G. *Ernst* < OHG. *Ernust, Ernost*, lit., resolute < *ernust*: see EARNEST¹] a masculine name: dim. *Ernie*; var. *Earnest*; equiv. It. & Sp. *Ernesto*, Ger. *Ernst*; fem. *Ernestine*

Er·nes·tine (ur'nəs tēn') [G., fem. < *Ernst*: see prec.] a feminine name

Ernst (ernst), **Max** (mäks) 1891– ; Ger. surrealist painter, in France & the U.S.

e·rode (i rōd') *vt.* **e·rod'ed, e·rod'ing** [Fr. *éroder* < L. *erodere* < *e-*, out, off + *rodere*, to gnaw: see RAZE] **1.** to eat into; wear away; disintegrate [acid *erodes* metal] **2.** to form by wearing away gradually [the running water *eroded* a gully] **3.** to cause to deteriorate, decay, or vanish —*vi.* to become eroded —**e·rod'i·ble** *adj.*

e·rog·e·nous (i räj'ə nəs) *adj.* [< Gr. *erōs*, love + -GENOUS] same as EROTOGENIC: also **e·ro·gen·ic** (er'ə jen'ik)

☆**er·oo** (ə rōō') [prob. < BUCKAROO] a humorous slang suffix added to nouns

E·ros (er'äs, ir'-) [L. < Gr. *Erōs* < *erōs*, love] *Gr. Myth.* the god of love, son of Aphrodite: identified by the Romans with Cupid —*n.* [e-] **1.** sexual love or desire **2.** *Psychoanalysis* libido or the psychic energy associated with it

e·rose (i rōs') *adj.* [L. *erosus*, pp. of *erodere*: see ERODE] **1.** irregular, as if gnawed away **2.** *Bot.* having an irregularly notched edge, as some leaves —**e·rose'ly** *adv.*

e·ro·sion (i rō'zhən) *n.* [L. *erosio* < *erosus*, pp. of *erodere*] an eroding or being eroded —**e·ro'sion·al** *adj.*

e·ro·sive (i rō'siv) *adj.* causing erosion; eroding

e·rot·ic (i rät'ik) *adj.* [Gr. *erōtikos* < *erōs* (gen. *erōtos*), love] **1.** of or arousing sexual feelings or desires; having to do with sexual love; amatory **2.** highly susceptible to sexual stimulation —*n.* an erotic person —**e·rot'i·cal·ly** *adv.*

e·rot·i·ca (-i kə) *n.pl.* [*often with sing. v.*] [ModL. < Gr. *erōtika*, neut. pl.] erotic books, pictures, etc.

e·rot·i·cism (-ə siz'm) *n.* **1.** erotic quality or character **2.** *a)* sexual instincts or desire *b)* sexual excitement or behavior **3.** preoccupation with sex Also, and for 2 now usually, **er·o·tism** (er'ə tiz'm)

e·ro·to·gen·ic (i rät'ə jen'ik, -rō'tə-; er'ə tə-) *adj.* [*eroto*-, sexual desire (< Gr. *erōto*- < stem of *erōs*: see EROS) + -GENIC] designating or of those areas of the body, as the genital, oral, and anal zones, that are particularly sensitive to sexual stimulation

e·ro·to·ma·ni·a (-mā'nē ə) *n.* [ModL.: see prec. & -MANIA] abnormally strong sexual desire

err (ur, er) *vi.* [ME. *erren* < OFr. *errer* < L. *errare*, to wander, go astray, err < IE. base *eres-*, whence RACE¹, G. *irren*, to err] **1.** to be wrong or mistaken; fall into error **2.** to deviate from the established moral code; do wrong **3.** [Obs.] to go astray; wander

er·ran·cy (er'ən sē) *n.*, *pl.* **-cies** [L. *errantia* < *errans*: see ERRANT] **1.** the state or an instance of erring **2.** a tendency to err

er·rand (er'ənd) *n.* [ME. *erende* < OE. *ærende*, message, mission, news, lit., that delivered by messenger < base of *ar*, messenger, akin to OS. *ārundi*, OHG. *ārunti*] **1.** a trip to carry a message or do a definite thing, often esp. for someone else **2.** the thing to be done on such a trip; purpose or object for which one goes or is sent

er·rant (er'ənt) *adj.* [ME. *erraunt* < OFr. *errant*, prp. of *errer* < ML. *iterare*, to travel < L. *iter*, a journey: cf. ERR] **1.** roving or wandering, esp. in search of adventure; itinerant [a knight-*errant*] **2.** *a)* [OFr., prp. of *errer* (see ERR), confused with *errer*, to rove, travel] erring or straying from what is right or the right course *b)* shifting about [an *errant* wind] **3.** *obs. sp.* of ARRANT (sense 1) —**er'rant·ly** *adv.*

er·rant·ry (-rē) *n.* the condition or behavior of a knight-errant; spirit or deeds of chivalry

er·ra·ta (e rät′ə, -rāt′-, -rat′-) *n.* **1.** *pl.* of ERRATUM **2.** a list of errors with their corrections, inserted on a separate page (**errata page**) of a published work

er·rat·ic (i rat′ik) *adj.* [ME. *erratik* < OFr. *erratique* < L. *erraticus*, wandering < pp. of *errare:* see ERR] **1.** having no fixed course or purpose; irregular; random; wandering **2.** deviating from the normal, conventional, or customary course; eccentric; queer **3.** *Geol.* designating a boulder or rock formation transported some distance from its original source, as by a glacier —*n.* an erratic person —**er·rat′i·cal·ly** *adv.*

er·ra·tum (e rät′əm, -rāt′-, -rat′-) *n.*, *pl.* -ta (-tə) [L., neut. of *erratus* < pp. of *errare:* see ERR] an error in printing or writing: see ERRATA

er·ro·ne·ous (ə rō′nē əs, e-) *adj.* [ME. < L. *erroneus*, wandering about < *errare:* see ERR] containing or based on error; mistaken; wrong —**er·ro′ne·ous·ly** *adv.*

er·ror (er′ər) *n.* [ME. & OFr. *errour* < L. *error* < L. *errare:* see ERR] **1.** the state of believing what is untrue, incorrect, or wrong **2.** a wrong belief; incorrect opinion **3.** something incorrectly done through ignorance or carelessness; mistake **4.** a departure from the accepted moral code; transgression; wrongdoing; sin **5.** *a)* the difference between a computed or estimated result and the actual value, as in mathematics *b)* the amount something deviates from what is required ☆**6.** *Baseball* any misplay in fielding a ball which, properly played, should have resulted in an out, or one which permits a runner to advance **7.** *Law* a mistake in judgment or proceedings of a court of record, usually prejudicial to the complainant —**er′ror·less** *adj.* *SYN.*—**error** implies deviation from truth, accuracy, correctness, right, etc. and is the broadest term in this comparison [*an error in judgment, in computation, etc.*]; **mistake** suggests an error resulting from carelessness, inattention, misunderstanding, etc. and does not in itself carry a strong implication of criticism [*a mistake in reading a blueprint*]; **blunder** implies stupidity, clumsiness, inefficiency, etc. and carries a suggestion of more severe criticism [*a tactical blunder cost them the war*]; **a slip** is a mistake, usually slight, made inadvertently in speaking or writing; **a faux pas** is a social blunder or error in etiquette that causes embarrassment; **boner** and **booboo**, slang terms, are applied to a silly or ridiculous blunder

er·satz (ur′zäts, er′-; *G.* er zäts′) *n.*, *adj.* [G., lit., replacement < *ersetzen*, to replace < *er-* + *setzen*, to place, SET] substitute or synthetic: the word usually suggests inferior quality —*SYN.* see ARTIFICIAL

Erse (urs) *adj.*, *n.* [ME. *Erish*, var. of *Irisc*, IRISH] same as GAELIC, *adj.* 2 & *n.* 2

Er·skine (ur′skin) **1.** John, 1509–91; Scot. religious reformer: called **Erskine of Dun 2.** John, 1695–1768; Scot. jurist: called **Erskine of Carnock 3.** John, 1879–1951; U.S. educator & writer

erst (urst) *adv.* [ME. *erest* < OE. *ærest*, superl. of *ær:* see ERE] **1.** [Obs.] at first; originally **2.** [Archaic] formerly —*adj.* [Obs.] first

erst·while (-hwīl′) *adv.* [Archaic] some time ago; formerly —*adj.* of an earlier time; former [*my erstwhile friend*]

e·ruct (i rukt′) *vt.*, *vi.* [L. *eructare* < *e-*, out + *ructare*, to belch < IE. base **reug-*, whence OE. *rocettan*] to belch: also **e·ruc′tate** (-tāt), -**tat·ed**, -**tat·ing** —**e·ruc·ta·tion** (i ruk′tā′shən, ē′ruk-) *n.*

er·u·dite (er′yoo dīt′, -oo-) *adj.* [ME. *erudit* < L. *eruditus*, pp. of *erudire*, to instruct < *e-*, out + *rudis*, RUDE] having or showing a wide knowledge gained from reading; learned; scholarly —**er′u·dite′ly** *adv.*

er·u·di·tion (er′yoo dish′ən, -oo-) *n.* [ME. *erudicioun* < L. *eruditio:* see prec.] learning acquired by reading and study; scholarship —*SYN.* see INFORMATION

e·rum·pent (i rum′pənt) *adj.* [< L. *erumpens*, prp. of *erumpere*, to burst forth: see ERUPT] *Bot.* bursting out, as certain spores, seeds, etc.

e·rupt (i rupt′) *vi.* [< L. *eruptus*, pp. of *erumpere*, to break out, burst forth < *e-*, out + *rumpere*, to break: see RUPTURE] **1.** to burst forth or out, as from some restraint [*erupting lava, a riot erupted*] **2.** to throw forth lava, water, steam, etc., as a volcano **3.** to break out in a rash **4.** to break through the gums and become visible: said of new teeth —*vt.* to cause to burst forth; throw forth; eject —**e·rupt′i·ble** *adj.*

e·rup·tion (i rup′shən) *n.* [ME. *erupcioun* < L. *eruptio:* see ERUPT] **1.** a bursting forth or out, as of lava from a volcano **2.** a throwing forth of lava, water, steam, etc. **3.** a sudden outburst, as of emotion or social discontent **4.** *Med.* *a)* a breaking out in a rash *b)* a rash

e·rup·tive (-tiv) *adj.* **1.** erupting or tending to erupt **2.** of, produced by, or formed by eruption [*eruptive rock*] **3.** *Med.* causing or characterized by a skin eruption —*n.* *Geol.* a rock thrown out by volcanic eruption —**e·rup′tive·ly** *adv.*

Er·vine (ur′vin), **St. John** (Greer) (sin′jən) 1883–1971; Brit. playwright & novelist, born in Ireland

Er·win (ur′win) [*G. Erwin*, earlier *Herwin* < OHG. *hari*, host, crowd (akin to OE. *here:* see HARRY) + *wini*, wine (see EDWIN)] a masculine name: var. *Irwin*

-er·y (ər ē) [ME. *-erie* < OFr. *-erie* < LL. *-aria*, or by addition of *-ie* (L. *-ia*) to OFr. nouns of agency in *-ier*] a *n.-forming suffix meaning:* **1.** a place to [*tannery, brewery*] **2.** a place for [*nunnery, vinery*] **3.** the practice, act, or occupation of [*surgery, robbery*] **4.** the product or goods of [*pottery, millinery*] **5.** a collection of [*greenery, crockery*] **6.** the state or condition of [*drudgery, slavery*] **7.** the behavior or qualities of [*tomfoolery*]

Er·y·man·thus (er′ə man′thəs), **Mount** mountain in the NW Peloponnesus, Greece: 7,297 ft.: in Greek mythology, haunt of a savage boar captured by Hercules —**Er′y·man′·thi·an** (-thē ən) *adj.*

e·ryn·go (i riŋ′gō) *n.*, *pl.* -**goes** [ult. < Gr. *ēryngos*] **1.** any of a genus (*Eryngium*) of plants of the parsley family, with flowers in dense heads and usually stiff, spiny leaves **2.** [Obs.] the candied root of the sea holly, formerly used as an aphrodisiac

e·ry·sip·e·las (er′ə sip′′l əs, ir′-) *n.* [ME. *erisipela* < L. *erysipelas* < Gr. *erysipelas* < base of *erythros*, RED[1] + *-pelas*, akin to L. *pellis:* see FELL[4]] an acute infectious disease of the skin or mucous membranes caused by a streptococcus and characterized by local inflammation and fever —**er′y·si·pel′a·tous** (-si pel′ə təs) *adj.*

e·ry·sip·e·loid (-oid) *n.* [see prec. & -OID] an infectious skin disease caused by an organism (*Erysipelothrix rhusiopathiae*), and characterized by red-colored lesions

er·y·the·ma (er′ə thē′mə) *n.* [ModL. < Gr. *erythēma* < *erythainein*, to redden, blush < *erythros*, RED[1]] an abnormal redness of the skin resulting from irritation and dilation of the capillaries —**er′y·the′mic** (-mik), **er′y·them′a·tous** (-them′ə təs, -thē′mə-) *adj.*

er·y·thrism (i rith′riz m, er′ə thriz′m) *n.* [ERYTHR(O)- + -ISM] unusual redness, esp. of the hair of mammals or the feathers of birds —**er′y·thris·mal** (er′ə thriz′məl) *adj.* —**er′y·thris′tic** (-thris′tik) *adj.*

er·y·thrite (-rīt′, -thrit′) *n.* [ERYTHR(O)- + -ITE[1]] **1.** same as ERYTHRITOL **2.** a hydrous cobalt arsenate, $CO_2(ASO_4)_2\cdot8H_2O$, usually rose-colored

e·ryth·ri·tol (-rə tōl′) *n.* [< prec. + -OL[1]] a sweet, colorless crystalline compound, $C_4H_{10}O_4$, an alcohol, obtained from some lichens and algae and by synthesis

e·ryth·ro- (i rith′rə, -rō) [< Gr. *erythros*, RED[1]] *a combining form meaning:* **1.** red [*erythrocyte*] **2.** erythrocyte [*erythroblast*] Also, before a vowel, **erythr-**

e·ryth·ro·blast (-blast′) *n.* [ERYTHRO- + -BLAST] any of the small nucleated cells, found normally in the marrow of bones, from which the erythrocytes develop —**e·ryth′ro·blas′tic** *adj.*

e·ryth·ro·blas·to·sis (i rith′rō blas tō′sis) *n.* **1.** an increase in erythroblasts in the bone marrow, often with the appearance of immature red blood cells in the circulating blood **2.** a disease of the developing fetus and newborn infant, characterized by a hemolytic anemia and jaundice and caused by an incompatibility of blood types between mother and fetus, usually involving the Rh factor

e·ryth·ro·cyte (i rith′rə sīt′) *n.* [ERYTHRO- + -CYTE] a red blood corpuscle: it is a very small, circular disk with both faces concave, and contains hemoglobin, which carries oxygen to the body tissues —**e·ryth′ro·cyt′ic** (-sit′ik) *adj.*

er·y·throid (er′ə throid′) *adj.* [ERYTHR(O)- + -OID] **1.** reddish in color **2.** pertaining to erythrocytes or the primitive cells from which they develop

☆**e·ryth·ro·my·cin** (i rith′rə mī′sin) *n.* [ERYTHRO- + -MYCIN] an antibiotic isolated from a soil bacterium (*Streptomyces erythreus*), used in treating various bacterial diseases

er·y·thron (er′ə thrän′) *n.* [ModL. < Gr. *erythron*, neut. of *erythros*, RED[1]] the red blood cell system as an organic unit, comprising the erythrocytes, their sources of production and destruction, etc.

e·ryth·ro·poi·e·sis (i rith′rō poi ē′sis) *n.* [ModL. < ERYTHRO- + Gr. *poiēsis*, a making: see POESY] the body process of developing red blood cells —**e·ryth′ro·poi·et′ic** (-poi et′ik) *adj.*

e·ryth·ro·sin (i rith′rə sin) *n.* [ERYTHRO- + (EO)SIN] a sodium or potassium salt formed from an iodine derivative of fluorescein and used in making food colors and biological stains: also **e·ryth′ro·sine′** (-sēn′)

Erz·ge·bir·ge (erts′gə bir′gə) mountain range between East Germany & Czechoslovakia: highest peak, 4,080 ft.

Er·zu·rum (er′zə room′) city in NE Turkey: pop. 90,000

Es *Chem.* einsteinium

-es (iz, əz, z) *a suffix used:* **1.** [ME. < OE. *-as*, pl. inflection of masc. nouns] to form the plural of some nouns, as in *fishes:* see PLURAL, I, A & B; II, A; VI **2.** [ME. < Northumbrian OE. *-s*, 3d pers. sing., pres. tense inflection of verbs] to form the third person singular, present indicative, of verbs, as in (he) *drives:* cf. -S

E·sau (ē′sô) [L. < Gr. *Esau* < Heb. *'ēsāw*, lit., hairy] *Bible* the son of Isaac and Rebekah, who sold his birthright to his younger twin brother, Jacob: Gen. 25: 21–34, 27

Es·bjerg (es′byer) seaport in SW Jutland, Denmark, on the North Sea: pop. 55,000

es·ca·drille (es′kə dril′; *Fr.* es kà drē′y′) *n.* [Fr. < Sp. *escudrilla*, dim. of *escuadra*, squad, orig., square < VL. **exquadra:* see SQUARE] a squadron of airplanes, usually six, with their men and equipment, as in the French armed forces of World War I

es·ca·lade (es′kə lād′, es′kə lād′) *n.* [Fr. < It. *scalata* < *scalare*, to climb < L. *scala*, ladder: see SCALE[1]] the act of scaling or climbing the walls of a fortified place by ladders —*vt.* -**lad′ed**, -**lad′ing** to climb (a wall, etc.) or enter (a fortified place) by ladders

☆**es·ca·late** (es'kə lāt') *vi.* **-lat'ed, -lat'ing** [back-formation < ESCALATOR] **1.** to rise on or as on an escalator **2.** to expand step by step, as from a limited or local conflict into a general, esp. nuclear, war **3.** to grow or increase rapidly, often to the point of becoming unmanageable, as prices or wages —*vt.* to cause to escalate —**es'ca·la'tion** *n.*

☆**es·ca·la·tor** (es'kə lāt'ər) *n.* [coined as a trademark (1895) < ESCALA(DE) + -*tor*, as in (ELEVA)TOR] **1.** a moving stairway consisting of treads linked in an endless belt, used in department stores, subway stations, etc. **2.** *same as* ESCALATOR CLAUSE

☆**escalator clause** a clause in a contract providing for increases or decreases in wages, prices, etc. based on fluctuations in the cost of living, production costs, etc.

es·cal·lo·ni·a (es'kə lō'nē ə) *n.* [ModL. < *Escallon*, name of a Spanish traveler who discovered the shrub in Colombia] any of a genus (*Escallonia*) of shrubs of the saxifrage family, with white, pink, or red flowers

es·cal·lop, es·cal·op (e skäl'əp, -skal'-) *n., vt.* [OFr. *escalope*, a shell: see SCALLOP] *same as* SCALLOP

es·ca·pade (es'kə pād') *n.* [Fr. < Sp. *escapada* < *escapar*, to escape, flee < LL. *excappare: see ESCAPE] **1.** [Archaic] the act of escaping or breaking loose from restraint or confinement **2.** a reckless adventure or prank

es·cape (ə skāp', e-) *vi.* **-caped', -cap'ing** [ME. *escapen* < ONormFr. *escaper*, var. of *eschaper* < VL. *excappare < L. *ex-*, out of + *cappa*, cloak (i.e., leave one's cloak behind)] **1.** to get free; get away; get out; break loose, as from a prison **2.** to avoid an illness, accident, pain, etc. [two were injured, but he *escaped*] **3.** to flow, drain, or leak away [gas *escaping* from a pipe] **4.** to slip away; disappear [the image *escaped* from her memory] **5.** *Bot.* to grow wild, as a plant running from cultivation —*vt.* **1.** to get away from; flee from [to *escape* pursuers] **2.** to manage to keep away from; avoid [to *escape* punishment] **3.** to come from involuntarily or unintentionally [a scream *escaped* her lips] **4.** to slip away from; be missed, unperceived, or forgotten by [his name *escapes* me] —*n.* [ME. *escap*] **1.** an act or instance of escaping **2.** the state of having escaped **3.** a means or way of escape **4.** an outward flow or leakage **5.** a temporary mental release from reality [movies are her *escape*] **6.** *Bot.* a garden plant growing wild —*adj.* **1.** giving temporary mental release from reality **2.** *a)* making escape possible [an *escape* hatch] *b)* giving a basis for evading or circumventing a claim, responsibility, etc. [an *escape* clause] —**es·cap'a·ble** *adj.* —**es·cap'er** *n.*

SYN.—**escape**, as compared here, implies a getting out of, a keeping away from, or simply a remaining unaffected by an impending or present danger, evil, confinement, etc. [to *escape* death, criticism, etc.]; **avoid** suggests the display of conscious effort in keeping clear of something undesirable or harmful [to *avoid* crowds during a flu epidemic]; to **evade** is to escape or avoid by artifice, cunning, adroitness, etc. [to *evade* pursuit, one's duty, etc.]; to **elude** is to escape the grasp of someone or something by artful or slippery dodges or because of a baffling quality [the criminal *eluded* the police, the meaning *eluded* him]

escape artist an entertainer, as in vaudeville, who is skilled at escaping from shackles or other confinement

es·cap·ee (ə skā'pē', e-) *n.* a person who has escaped, esp. from confinement

escape mechanism *popular term for* DEFENSE MECHANISM (sense 2)

es·cape·ment (ə skāp'mənt, e-) *n.* [ESCAPE + -MENT, after Fr. *échappement*] **1.** [Rare] the action of escaping or a means of escape **2.** the part in a clock or watch that controls the speed and regularity of the balance wheel or pendulum, and thereby of the entire mechanism, by the movement of a notched wheel (**escape wheel**), one tooth of which is permitted to escape from the detaining catch at a time **3.** a ratchet mechanism, esp. one in typewriters that regulates the horizontal movement of the carriage

ESCAPEMENT

escape velocity the minimum speed required for a particle, space vehicle, or other body to escape permanently from the gravitational field of a planet, star, etc.: it is approximately seven miles per second for escape from the earth

es·cap·ism (ə skāp'iz'm, e-) *n.* **1.** a tendency to escape from reality, the responsibilities and routine of real life, etc., esp. by unrealistic imaginative activity **2.** behavior characterized by this tendency

es·cap·ist (-ist) *adj.* characterized by, expressing, or catering to escapism —*n.* a person whose behavior, writing, etc. is escapist

‡**es·car·got** (es kàr gō') *n.* [Fr.] a snail, esp. an edible variety

es·ca·role (es'kə rōl') *n.* [Fr. < ML. *escariola* < L. *escarius*, pertaining to food < *esca*, food (see ESCULENT)] *same as* ENDIVE (sense 1)

es·carp (e skärp') *n., vt.* [Fr. *escarpe*, *n.* < It. *scarpa*: see SCARP] *same as* SCARP

es·carp·ment (-mənt) *n.* [Fr. *escarpement*: see prec.] **1.** a steep slope or cliff formed by erosion or, less often, by

faulting **2.** ground formed into a steep slope on the exterior of a fortification   See also SCARP

Es·caut (es kō') *Fr. name of the* SCHELDT River

-es·cence (es'ns) [L. *-escentia* < *-escens*: see ff.] *a n.-forming suffix corresponding to the adjective suffix* -ESCENT [*obsolescence*]

-es·cent (es'nt) [L. *-escens* (gen. *-escentis*), prp. ending of inceptive or inchoative verbs in *-escere*] *an adj.-forming suffix meaning:* **1.** in process of ____ing, starting to be, being, or becoming (as indicated) [*convalescent*] **2.** giving off or reflecting light, or exhibiting a play of color (as indicated) [*phosphorescent*]

esch·a·lot (esh'ə lät') *n.* [Fr. *eschallotte*: see SHALLOT] *same as* SHALLOT

es·char (es'kär) *n.* [altered (after L.) < ME. *escare* < OFr. *escare* < L. *eschara*: see SCAR¹] a dry scab that forms as a result of a burn or of corrosive action

es·cha·rot·ic (es'kə rät'ik) *adj.* [LL. *escharoticus* < Gr. *escharōtikos*] producing or tending to produce an eschar; corrosive; caustic —*n.* a corrosive or caustic substance

es·cha·tol·o·gy (es'kə täl'ə jē) *n.* [< Gr. *eschatos*, furthest (< *ex-*, out < IE. base *eǵhs, whence L. *ex*) + -LOGY] the branch of theology, or doctrines, dealing with death, resurrection, judgment, immortality, etc. —**es·cha·to·log·i·cal** (es'kə tə läj'i k'l, e skat'ə-) *adj.* —**es'cha·to·log'i·cal·ly** *adv.*

es·cheat (es chēt') *n.* [ME. *eschete* < OFr., lit., that which falls to one < pp. of *escheoir*, to fall to one's share < VL. *excadere*, to fall upon < L. *ex-*, out + *cadere*, to fall] *Law* **1.** the reverting of property to the lord of the manor (in feudal law), to the crown (in England), or to the government (in the U.S.) when there are no legal heirs **2.** property so reverting **3.** *same as* ESCHEATAGE —*vt.* to cause to escheat; confiscate —*vi.* to revert or go by escheat —**es·cheat'a·ble** *adj.*

es·cheat·age (-ij) *n.* the right to take by escheat

es·chew (es chōō') *vt.* [ME. *eschewen* < Anglo-Fr. *eschuer* < OFr. *eschiver* < OHG. *sciuhan*, to fear, akin to SHY¹] to keep away from (something harmful or disliked); shun; avoid; abstain from —**es·chew'al** *n.*

Es·cof·fier (es kô fyā'), **Au·guste** (ō güst') 1847–1935; Fr. chef & writer on cooking

☆**es·co·lar** (es'kə lär') *n.* [Sp., lit., scholar (< LL. *scholaris*: see SCHOLAR): so named because the rings around the eyes resemble spectacles] an oily, deep-water, mackerellike food fish (*Ruvettus pretiosus*) of the tropical Atlantic Ocean

Es·con·di·do (es'kän dē'dō) [Sp., hidden: after nearby *Escondido* Creek, whose source was difficult to find] city in S Calif., near San Diego: pop. 37,000

Es·cor·i·al (es kôr'ē əl; *Sp.* es kō ryäl') [Sp. *escorial*, lit., place where a mine has been exhausted < *escoria* < L. *scoria*, dross < Gr. *skōria*, SCORIA] huge granite structure near Madrid, built (16th cent.) by Philip II of Spain: it encloses a palace, church, monastery, etc.

es·cort (es'kôrt; *for v.* i skôrt') *n.* [Fr. *escorte* < It. *scorta* < *scorgere*, to perceive, lead < LL. *excorrigere < L. *ex-*, out + *corrigere*, to set right, CORRECT] **1.** one or more persons (or cars, ships, airplanes, etc.) accompanying another or others to give protection or show honor **2.** a man or boy accompanying a woman or girl, as to a party **3.** accompaniment by an escort —*vt.* [Fr. *escorter* < It. *scortare*] to go with as an escort; accompany to protect or show honor or courtesy to —*SYN.* see ACCOMPANY

es·cri·toire (es'krə twär') *n.* [OFr. *escriptoire* (Fr. *écritoire*) < LL. *scriptorium*, metallic style for writing on wax tablets < pp. of L. *scribere*, to write: see SCRIBE] a writing desk or table; secretary

es·crow (es'krō; *chiefly Brit.*, es krō') *n.* [OFr. *escroue*, roll of writings, bond: see SCROLL] *Law* a written agreement, as a bond or deed, put in the care of a third party and not delivered or put into effect until certain conditions are fulfilled —☆**in escrow** *Law* put in the care of a third party until certain conditions are fulfilled, as a bond, deed, etc.

es·cu·do (es kōō'dō; *Sp.* es kōō'thō; *Port.* ish kōō'dōō) *n., pl.* **-dos** (-dōz; *Sp.* -*thōs*; *Port.* -dōōsh) [Sp., a shield, gold coin < L. *scutum*, a shield] **1.** any of several obsolete coins of Spain, Portugal, and their former colonies **2.** the monetary unit of Chile and Portugal: see MONETARY UNITS, table

es·cu·lent (es'kyoo lənt) *adj.* [L. *esculentus* < *esca*, food < IE. **edes-* < base **ed-*, to eat, whence L. *edere*, EAT] fit for food; edible —*n.* something fit for food, esp. a vegetable

Es·cu·ri·al (es kyoor'ē əl) *n. same as* ESCORIAL

es·cutch·eon (i skuch'ən) *n.* [ONormFr. *escuchon* < VL. *scutio < L. *scutum*, shield] **1.** a shield or shield-shaped surface on which a coat of arms is displayed **2.** something shaped like an escutcheon; specif., *a)* an ornamental shield or plate, as that around a keyhole *b)* the space on a ship's stern bearing the name —**a blot on one's escutcheon** a stain on one's honor; disgrace to one's reputation

ESCUTCHEON

Es·dra·e·lon (ez'drə ē'lən, es'-) plain in N Israel, extending from the Jordan

River valley to Mt. Carmel: also, & in the Bible always, called JEZREEL

Es·dras (ez′drəs) [Gr. *Esdras*, Ezra] *Douay Bible name for* EZRA

-ese (ēz, ēs) [OFr. *-eis*, It. *-ese* < L. *-ensis*] 1. *an adj.-forming suffix meaning: a)* of a country or place *[Javanese] b)* in the language or dialect of *[Cantonese] c)* in the style of *[Carlylese]* 2. *a n.-forming suffix meaning: a) pl.* -ese a native or inhabitant of *[Portuguese] b)* the language or dialect of *[Brooklynese] c)* the style of *[journalese]*

ESE, E.S.E., e.s.e. east-southeast

es·er·ine (es′ə rēn′) n. [Fr. *ésérine* < *esér-* (prob. < an African native term) + *-ine*, -INE[1]] *same as* PHYSOSTIGMINE

Es·fa·hán (es′fä hän′) city in WC Iran: cap. of Persia in the 17th cent.: pop. 340,000

Esk. Eskimo

es·ker, es·kar (es′kər) n. [Ir. *eiscir*, a ridge] a winding, narrow ridge of sand or gravel, probably deposited by a stream flowing in or under glacial ice

Es·ki·mo (es′kə mō′) n. [< Fr. < Algonquian; cf. Abnaki *esquimantsic*, Ojibwa *ashkimeq*, lit., eaters of raw flesh] 1. *pl.* -mos′, -mo′ a member of a group of native N. American people thinly scattered in areas extending from Greenland across N Canada and Alaska through the NE tip of Asia 2. either of the two languages of the Eskimos, belonging to the Eskimo-Aleut language family —*adj.* of the Eskimos, their language, or their culture — **Es′ki·mo′an** *adj.*

Eskimo dog a strong breed of dog native to Greenland and Labrador, with a bushy tail and gray-ish, shaggy fur: it is used by the Eskimos to pull sleds

Es·ki·şe·hir (es kē′she hir′) city in WC Turkey: pop. 153,000

e·soph·a·gus (i säf′ə gəs) n., *pl.* -a·gi′ (-jī′) [altered (after ML.) < ME. *ysophagus*, OFr. *ysofague* < ML. *oesophagus* < Gr. *oisophagos*, lit., passage for food < *oisein*, fut. inf. of *pherein*, to carry (see BEAR[1]) + *phagein*, to eat: see -PHAGOUS] the tube through which food passes from the pharynx to the stomach; gullet —**e·soph·a·ge·al** (i säf′ə jē′əl, ē′sə faj′ē əl) *adj.*

ESKIMO DOG
(2 ft. high at shoulder)

es·o·ter·ic (es′ə ter′ik) *adj.* [Gr. *esōterikos* < *esōteros*, inner, compar. of *esō*, within < *es, eis*, into] 1. *a)* intended for or understood by only a chosen few, as an inner group of disciples or initiates: said of ideas, doctrines, literature, etc. *b)* beyond the understanding or knowledge of most people; recondite; abstruse 2. confidential; private; withheld *[an esoteric plan]* —**es′o·ter′i·cal·ly** *adv.*

es·o·ter·i·ca (-i kə) *n.pl.* esoteric facts or things

es·o·tro·pi·a (es′ə trō′pē ə) n. [ModL. < Gr. *esō*, within + ModL. *-tropia*, -TROPY] a condition in which only one eye fixes on an object while the other turns inward, producing the appearance of cross-eye

ESP extrasensory perception

esp., espec. especially

es·pa·drille (es′pə dril′) n. [Fr., altered by metathesis < *espardille* < dial. (Gascon) *espartilho*, dim. < Sp. *esparto*, ESPARTO] a kind of shoe for casual wear, with a canvas upper and a sole of twisted rope or, now often, rubber, etc.

es·pal·ier (es pal′yər) n. [Fr. < It. *spalliera*, support for the shoulders < *spalla*, the shoulder < L. *spatula*: see SPATULA] 1. a lattice or trellis on which trees and shrubs are trained to grow flat 2. a plant, tree, etc. so trained —*vt.* 1. to train as or on an espalier 2. to provide with an espalier

Es·pa·ña (es pä′nyä) *Sp. name of* SPAIN

es·par·to (es pär′tō) n. [Sp. < L. *spartum* < Gr. *sparton, spartos* < IE. base *sper-*, to twist: cf. SPIRAL] either of two kinds of long, coarse grass (*Stipa tenacissima* or *Lygeum spartum*) growing in Spain and N Africa, used to make cordage, baskets, shoes, and paper: also **esparto grass**

es·pe·cial (ə spesh′əl, es pesh′-) *adj.* [ME. & OFr. < L. *specialis*] special; particular; outstanding; exceptional —*SYN.* see SPECIAL

es·pe·cial·ly (-ē) *adv.* particularly; mainly; to a marked degree; unusually

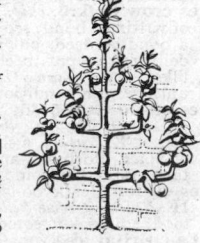
ESPALIER

Es·pe·ran·to (es′pə rän′tō, -ran′-) n. [after pseudonym of Dr. L. L. Zamenhof, Russ. physician who invented the language (1887), lit. (in Esperanto), one who hopes < prp. of *esperi*, to hope < Romance forms (Fr. *esperer*, Sp. *esperar*, etc.) < L. *sperare*, to hope] an artificial language for international (chiefly European) use, based on word bases common to the main European languages: it has self-evident parts of speech (all nouns end in *-o*, all adjectives in *-a*, etc.), a single and regular conjugation of verbs, a few simplified inflections, etc.

es·pi·al (ə spī′əl, es pī′-) n. [ME. *espiaille* < OFr. < *espier*:

see SPY] 1. an espying or being espied; observation 2. discovery 3. [Obs.] a spy

es·pi·o·nage (es′pē ə näzh′, -nij′) n. [Fr. *espionnage* < *espionner*, to spy < *espion* < It. *spione* < *spia*, SPY] 1. the act of spying 2. the use of spies by a government to learn the military secrets of other nations

Es·pí·ri·to San·to (i spē′rē too sän′too) state of E Brazil, on the Atlantic: 15,200 sq. mi.; pop. 1,189,000; cap. Vitória

es·pla·nade (es′plə näd′, -näd′) n. [Fr. < It. *spianata* < *spianare*, to level < L. *explanare*, to level: see EXPLAIN] a level, open space of ground; esp., a public walk or roadway, often along a shore; promenade

es·pous·al (e spou′z′l) n. [ME. *espousaile* < OFr. *espousailles (pl.)* < L. *sponsalia* < *sponsus* (fem. *sponsa*): see SPOUSE] 1. [*often pl.*] *a)* a betrothal or betrothal ceremony *b)* a marriage or wedding 2. an espousing (of some cause, idea, etc.); advocacy

es·pouse (e spouz′) vt. -poused′, -pous′ing [ME. *espousen* < OFr. *espouser* < LL. *sponsare* < L. *sponsus*: see SPOUSE] 1. to take as a spouse, esp. as a wife; marry 2. to give in marriage 3. to take up, support, or advocate (some cause, idea, etc.) —**es·pous′er** n.

es·pres·so (es pres′ō) n., *pl.* -sos [It. (*caffè*) *espresso*, pressed-out (coffee), pp. of *esprimere*, to press out, express < L. *exprimere*: see EXPRESS] coffee prepared in a special machine from finely ground coffee beans, through which steam under high pressure is forced

es·prit (es prē′) n. [Fr.] 1. spirit 2. lively intelligence or wit

es·prit de corps (es prē′ də kôr′) [Fr., lit., spirit of a body (of persons)] group spirit; sense of pride, honor, etc. shared by those in the same group or undertaking

es·py (ə spī′, es pī′) vt. -pied′, -py′ing [ME. *espien* < OFr. *espier*: see SPY] to catch sight of; make out; spy; descry —*SYN.* see SEE[1]

Esq., Esqr. Esquire

-esque (esk) [Fr. < It. *-esco* < Gmc. suffix akin to OHG. *-isc*, -ISH] *an adj.-forming suffix meaning:* 1. in the manner or style of *[Romanesque]* 2. having the quality of, like *[picturesque]*

Es·qui·line (es′kwə līn′) [L. (Mons) *esquilinus* < *Esquiliae*, name of the hill < base akin to *colere*, to till (see CULT)] *see* SEVEN HILLS OF ROME

Es·qui·mau (es′kwə mō′) n., *pl.* -maux′ (-mō′, -mōz′), -mau′ [Fr.] *same as* ESKIMO

es·quire (es′kwir, ə skwir′) n. [ME. *esquier* < OFr. *escuier* < LL. *scutarius*, a squire, shield-bearer < L. *scutum*, a shield, prob. < IE. base *skeit-*, to cut, split, whence OIr. *sciath*, shield, SKI, SKID] 1. formerly, a candidate for knighthood, acting as attendant and shield-bearer for a knight; squire 2. in England, a member of the gentry ranking just below a knight 3. [E-] a title of courtesy, usually abbreviated *Esq., Esqr.*, placed after a man's surname and corresponding, more ceremoniously, to *Mr.* 4. [Archaic] a landed country gentleman; squire

ess (es) n., *pl.* **ess′es** 1. the letter S, s 2. something shaped like an S

-ess (is, əs; *occas.* es) [ME. *-esse, -isse* < OFr. *-esse* < LL. *-issa* < Gr. *-issa*] *a suffix meaning* female *[lioness]* In nouns of agent ending in *-tor* or *-ter*, the vowel is usually dropped before adding *-ess* (Ex.: *actress*): as applied to persons (*poetess, Negress*, etc.), now often avoided as patronizing or discriminating

ESSA Environmental Science Services Administration (a former U.S. agency incorporating the Weather Bureau)

es·say (e sā′; *for n. 1 usually, and for n. 2 always*, es′ā) vt. [OFr. *essayer* < VL. **exagiare* < L. *exagium*, a weight, weighing < *ex-*, out of + *agere*, to do: see ACT] 1. to test the nature or quality of; try out 2. to try; attempt —n. [OFr. *essai* < LL. *exagium*] 1. *a)* a trying or testing *b)* an attempt; trial 2. a short literary composition of an analytical or interpretive kind, dealing with its subject usually from a personal point of view or in a limited way —*SYN.* see TRY —**es·say′er** n.

es·say·ist (es′ā ist) n. one who writes essays

†es·se (es′ē) n. [L., to be] being; existence; essence

Es·sen (es′n) city in W West Germany, in the Ruhr valley of North Rhine–Westphalia: pop. 728,000

es·sence (es′ns) n. [ME. < OFr. & < L. *essentia < esse*, to be: for IE. base see IS] 1. something that is, or exists; entity 2. that which makes something what it is; intrinsic, fundamental nature or most important quality (of something); essential being 3. *a)* a substance that keeps, in concentrated form, the flavor, fragrance, or other properties of the plant, drug, food, etc. from which it is extracted; essential oil *b)* a solution of such a substance or oil in alcohol *c)* a perfume 4. *Philos. a)* the inward nature of anything, underlying its manifestations; true substance *b)* the indispensable conceptual characteristics and relations of anything

Es·sene (es′ēn, ə sēn′) n. [L. *Esseni* < Gr. *Essēnoi*, said (by Philo) to be < *hosios*, holy, pious, but prob. < Sem. (< ? East Aram. *hasēn*, pious)] a member of an ancient Jewish sect of ascetics and mystics, which existed from the 2d century B.C. to the 2d century A.D. —**Es·se·ni·an** (es ē′nē ən), **Es·sen′ic** (-en′ik) *adj.*

es·sen·tial (ə sen′shəl) *adj.* [ME. *essencial* < LL. *essentialis*: see ESSENCE] 1. of or constituting the intrinsic,

fundamental nature of something; basic; inherent /an *essential* difference/ 2. absolute; complete; perfect 3. absolutely necessary; indispensable; requisite 4. containing, or having the properties of, a concentrated extract of a plant, drug, food, etc. /an *essential* oil/ —n. something necessary or fundamental; indispensable, inherent or basic feature or principle —**es·sen′tial·ly** *adv.*
SYN.—**essential**, in strict usage, is applicable to that which constitutes the absolute essence or the fundamental nature of a thing and therefore must be present for the thing to exist, function, etc. /food is *essential* to life/; an **indispensable** person or thing cannot be done without if the specified or implied purpose is to be achieved; **requisite** is applied to that which is required by the circumstances or for the purpose and generally suggests a requirement that is imposed externally rather than an inherent need /the *requisite* experience for a position/; **necessary** implies a pressing need but does not always connote absolute indispensability
es·sen·tial·ism (-iz′m) *n.* *Philos.* a theory which stresses essence as opposed to existence —**es·sen′tial·ist** *n.*
es·sen·ti·al·i·ty (i sen′shē al′ə tē) *n., pl.* **-ties** [ME. *essencialite* < ML. *essentialitas*] essential quality, fact, or thing
essential oil any volatile oil that gives distinctive odor, flavor, etc. to a plant, flower, or fruit
Es·se·qui·bo (es′ə kē′bō) river in Guyana, flowing northward to the Atlantic: c. 600 mi.
Es·sex[1] (es′iks) 1. former East Saxon kingdom in E England 2. county of SE England, on the North Sea: 1,528 sq. mi.; pop. 2,347,000 3. [after prec.] suburb of Baltimore, in N Md.: pop. 38,000
Essex[2], 2d Earl of, (*Robert Devereux*) 1566–1601; Eng. soldier & courtier: executed for treason
es·so·nite (es′ə nit′) *n.* [< Gr. *hēssōn*, inferior (i.e., to real hyacinth) + -ITE[1]] a dark-brown kind of garnet
-est (ist, əst) *a suffix used to form:* 1. [ME. < OE. -*est*, -*ost*, -*ast*, superl. suffix of adjectives & adverbs, akin to OIIG. -*isto* < IE. *-*istho*- (whence Gr. -*isto*-, Sans. -*ištha*-)] the superlative degree of most adjectives and adverbs of one or two syllables /*greatest*, *soonest*/ 2. [ME. < OE. -*est*, -*ast*, 2d pers. sing., pres. tense inflection < IE. *-*si*, *-*s* + initial dental of enclitic pronoun (эсс TIIOU)] the archaic 2d pers. sing., pres. indic., of verbs /*goest*/
EST, E.S.T. Eastern Standard Time
est. 1. established 2. estimate 3. estimated
es·tab·lish (ə stab′lish) *vt.* [ME. *establissen* < extended stem of OFr. *establir* < L. *stabilire* < *stabilis*, STABLE[1]] 1. to make stable; make firm; settle /to *establish* a habit/ 2. to order, ordain, or enact (a law, statute, etc.) permanently 3. to set up (a government, nation, business, etc.); found; institute 4. to cause to be or happen; bring about /efforts to *establish* a friendship/ 5. to settle in an office or position, or set up as in business or a profession 6. to make a state institution of (a church) 7. to set up (a precedent, theory, reputation, etc.) permanently; cause to be accepted or recognized 8. to prove; demonstrate /to *establish* one's case at law/ 9. *Card Games* to win control of (a suit) so that one is sure of taking all the remaining tricks in it —**es·tab′lish·er** *n.*
established church a church officially recognized by the government and supported as a national institution; specif., [E- C-] the Church of England
es·tab·lish·ment (-mənt) *n.* 1. an establishing or being established 2. a thing established, as a business, military organization, household, etc. —**the Establishment** 1. the Church of England 2. the Presbyterian Church of Scotland 3. in England, a complex consisting of the church, the royal family, and the plutocracy, regarded as holding the chief measure of power and influence 4. the ruling inner circle of any nation, institution, etc.
‡es·ta·mi·net (es tå mē nā′) *n.* [Fr.] a café
‡es·tan·cia (es tän′syä) *n.* [Sp., orig., a stop, stopping place] a large estate, esp. a cattle ranch, in Spanish America
es·tate (ə stāt′) *n.* [ME. & OFr. *estat*, STATE] 1. *a*) state or condition /to restore the theater to its former *estate*/ *b*) a condition or stage of life /to come to man's *estate*/ *c*) status or rank 2. formerly, esp. in feudal times, any of the three social classes having specific political powers: the first estate was the Lords Spiritual (clergy), the second estate the Lords Temporal (nobility), and the third estate the Commons (bourgeoisie) 3. property; possessions; capital; fortune 4. the assets and liabilities of a dead or bankrupt person 5. landed property; individually owned piece of land containing a residence, esp. one that is large and maintained by great wealth 6. [Archaic] display of wealth; pomp 7. *Law a*) the degree, nature, extent, and quality of interest or ownership that one has in land, or other property *b*) all the property, real or personal, owned by one —**the fourth estate** [cf. sense 2] [often F- E-] journalism or journalists
Es·tates-Gen·er·al (ə stāts′jen′ər əl) *n. same as* STATES-GENERAL (sense 1)
es·teem (ə stēm′) *vt.* [ME. *estemen* < OFr. *estimer* < L. *aestimare*, to value, appraise, estimate; prob. < *ais-temos, one who cuts copper, mints money < IE. *ayos- (L. *aes*),

brass, copper (see ORE) + *tem-, to cut: cf. -TOMY] 1. to have great regard for; value highly; respect 2. to hold to be; consider; regard /we *esteem* it an honor to be invited/ —n. 1. favorable opinion; high regard; respect /to be held in high *esteem*/ 2. [Archaic] an opinion; estimation —*SYN.* see APPRECIATE, REGARD
Es·tel·la (e stel′ə) [Sp. < L. *Stella*, lit., star: see STELLAR] a feminine name: var. *Estelle, Stella*
Es·telle (es tel′) [Fr.] a feminine name: see ESTELLA
es·ter (es′tər) *n.* [G., contr. < *essigäther* < *essig*, vinegar + *äther*, ETHER] an organic compound, comparable to an inorganic salt, formed by the reaction of an acid and an alcohol, or a phenol, with the elimination of water: the organic radical of the alcohol or phenol replaces the acid hydrogen of the acid
es·ter·ase (-ās′) *n.* [ESTER + -ASE] any of a group of enzymes by whose action the hydrolysis or, sometimes, synthesis of esters is accelerated
es·ter·i·fy (es ter′ə fi′) *vt., vi.* -**fied′**, -**fy′ing** to change into an ester —**es·ter′i·fi·ca′tion** *n.*
Es·tes Park (es′tēz) [after Joel Estes, first settler (c. 1859)] resort town in N Colo., at the entrance to Rocky Mountain National Park: pop. 1,600
Es·ther (es′tər) [LL.(Ec.) *Esthera* < Gr.(Ec.) *Esthēr* < Heb. *estēr*, prob. < Bab. *Ishtar*, Ishtar] 1. a feminine name: var. *Hester, Hesther* 2. *Bible a*) the Jewish wife of the Persian king Ahasuerus: she saved her people from slaughter by Haman *b*) the book telling her story: abbrev. **Esth.**
es·the·si·a (es thē′zhə, -zhē ə, -zē ə) *n.* [ModL. < Gr. *aisthēsis*, perception, sense-impression < *aisthanesthai*: see AESTHETIC] the ability to feel sensations
es·the·si·om·e·ter (es thē′zē äm′ə tər) *n.* [< ModL. *aesthesia*, AESTHESIA + -METER] an instrument for measuring the sensitivity of the sense of touch, esp. one for testing how far apart two points pressed against the skin have to be for the points to be felt as separate
es·thete (es′thēt′) *n. same as* AESTHETE
es·thet·ic (es thet′ik) *adj.* [see AESTHETIC] 1. *same as* AESTHETIC 2. of esthesia; having to do with sensation —**es·thet′i·cal·ly** *adv.*
es·the·ti·cian (es′thə tish′ən) *n. same as* AESTHETICIAN
es·thet·i·cism (es thet′ə siz′m) *n. same as* AESTHETICISM
es·thet·ics (es thet′iks) *n.pl. same as* AESTHETICS
Es·tho·ni·a (es tō′nē ə, -thō′-) *former sp. of* ESTONIA — **Es·tho′ni·an** *adj., n.*
Es·tienne (es tyen′) (L. name *Stephanus*) Fr. family of printers and publishers, esp. 1. **Hen·ri** (än rē′), *a*) 1460?–1520; founder of the family's printing business *b*) 1528–98; son of *ff*. 2. **Ro·bert** (rō ber′), 1503–59; son of Henri (1, *a*)
es·ti·ma·ble (es′tə mə b'l) *adj.* [ME. & OFr. < L. *aestimabilis* < *aestimare*: see ESTEEM] 1. [Obs.] that can be estimated or evaluated; calculable 2. worthy of esteem; deserving to be respected or valued highly —**es′ti·ma·bly** *adv.*
es·ti·mate (es′tə māt′; *for n.* -mit) *vt.* -**mat′ed**, -**mat′ing** [< L. *aestimatus*, pp. of *aestimare*: see ESTEEM] 1. to form an opinion or judgment about 2. to judge or determine generally but carefully (size, value, cost, requirements, etc.); calculate approximately —*vi.* to make an estimate or estimates —n. 1. a general calculation of size, value, etc.; esp., an approximate computation of the probable cost of a piece of work made by a person undertaking to do the work 2. an opinion or judgment —**es′ti·ma′tive** *adj.*, —**es′ti·ma′tor** *n.*
SYN.—**estimate**, in this comparison, refers broadly to the forming of a personal opinion or judgment; **appraise** implies the aim of giving an accurate or expert judgment, as of value or worth /to *appraise* a new house/; **evaluate** also connotes an attempt at an exact judgment, but rarely with reference to value in terms of money /let us *evaluate* the evidence/; **rate** implies assignment of comparative value, quality, etc. /he is *rated* the best in his field/ See also CALCULATE
es·ti·ma·tion (es′tə mā′shən) *n.* [ME. *estimacioun* < OFr. *estimacion* < L. *aestimatio*] 1. the act of estimating 2. an estimate, opinion, or judgment 3. esteem; regard
es·ti·val (es′tə v'l, es tī′v'l) *adj.* [L. *aestivalis* < *aestivus* < *aestas*, summer < IE. base *aidh-, to burn: see EDIFY] of or for summer
es·ti·vate (es′tə vāt′) *vi.* -**vat′ed**, -**vat′ing** [< L. *aestivatus*, pp. of *aestivare* < *aestas*: see AESTIVAL] 1. to spend the summer 2. to pass the summer in a dormant state, as snails: opposed to HIBERNATE
es·ti·va·tion (es′tə vā′shən) *n.* 1. *Zool.* the state of an estivating creature 2. *Bot.* the arrangement of petals in a flower bud before it opens
Es·to·ni·a (es tō′nē ə) republic (**Estonian Soviet Socialist Republic**) of the U.S.S.R., in NE Europe, on the Baltic Sea: 17,410 sq. mi.; pop. 1,300,000; cap. Tallinn
Es·to·ni·an (-nē ən, -nyən) *adj.* of Estonia, its people, their language, or culture —n. 1. a native or inhabitant of Estonia 2. the Finno–Ugric language of the Estonians
es·top (e stäp′) *vt.* -**topped′**, -**top′ping** [ME. *estoppen* < Anglo-Fr. & OFr. *estoper* < VL. *stuppare, to stop with

tow: see STOP] **1.** orig., to stop up **2.** [Rare] to stop; prevent; bar **3.** *Law* to bar or prevent by estoppel

es·top·pel (-'l) *n.* [OFr. *estoupail*, stopper, bung < *estoper*: see ESTOP] *Law* the prevention of a person from making an affirmation or denial because it is contrary to a previous affirmation or denial that he has made

es·to·vers (e stō'vərz) *n.pl.* [ME. < OFr. *estovoir*, to be necessary: inf. used as n.] certain reasonable necessaries allowed by law, as wood given to a tenant for fuel or repairs, alimony for a divorced wife, etc.

es·tra·di·ol (es'trə dī'ōl, -ôl) *n.* [ESTR(ONE) + -a- + DI-¹ + -OL¹] a female sex hormone, $C_{18}H_{24}O_2$, used in correcting female hormone deficiency and in the treatment of cancers in males and females

es·trange (ə strānj') *vt.* **-tranged', -trang'ing** [OFr. *estranger*, to remove < ML. *extraneare*, to treat as a stranger < L. *extraneus*, STRANGE] **1.** to remove, as from usual surroundings or associates; keep apart or away **2.** to turn (a person) from an affectionate or friendly attitude to an indifferent, unfriendly, or hostile one; alienate the affections of —**es·trange'ment** *n.*

es·tray (e strā') *n.* [Anglo-Fr. < *estraier*: see STRAY] **1.** any person or thing out of its usual place **2.** *Law* a stray and unclaimed domestic animal —*vi.* [Archaic] to stray

es·treat (e strēt') *n.* [ME. & Anglo-Fr. *estrete* < OFr. *estraite* < ML. *extracta* < pp. of L. *extrahere*: see EXTRACT] a true copy or extract of an original record entered in a law court, as of fines —*vt.* **1.** to take from the records of a law court for purposes of prosecution **2.** to take as a levy, fine, etc.

Es·tre·ma·dur·a (es'trə mə door'ə; *Sp.* es'tre mä thōō'rä; *Port.* esh'trə mə dōō'rə) **1.** region & former province in WC Spain, on the Portuguese border **2.** region & former province in C Portugal, on the Atlantic

es·tri·ol (es'trī ōl', -ôl') *n.* [ES(TRUS) + TRI- + -OL¹] a female sex hormone, $C_{18}H_{24}O_3$

es·tro·gen (es'trə jən) *n.* [< ESTRUS + -GEN] any of several female sex hormones or synthetic compounds having similar composition or effect

es·tro·gen·ic (es'trə jen'ik) *adj.* **1.** of estrogen **2.** of or producing estrus

es·trone (es'trōn) *n.* [ESTR(US) + -ONE] a female sex hormone, $C_{18}H_{22}O_2$

es·trous (es'trəs, ēs'-) *adj.* of, or having the characteristics of, estrus

estrous cycle the regular female reproductive cycle of most placental mammals that is under hormonal control and includes a period of heat, followed by ovulation and complex changes of the uterine lining

es·trus (-trəs) *n.* [ModL. < L. *oestrus*, gadfly, horsefly, frenzy < Gr. *oistros*, gadfly, sting, frenzy < IE. base *eis-*, to move violently, whence ON. *eisa*, to rush on, L. *ira*, ire, Lith. *aistra*, violent passion] **1.** the periodic sexual excitement of most female placental mammals, corresponding to *rut* in males; heat **2.** the period of this when the female will accept mating with the male, characterized by changes in the sex organs Also **es'trum** (-trəm)

es·tu·ar·ine (es'choo wər in, -in') *adj.* **1.** of an estuary **2.** formed or deposited in an estuary

es·tu·ar·y (es'choo wer'ē) *n.,* pl. **-ar'ies** [L. *aestuarium* < *aestus*, the tide, orig., a boiling, akin to *aestas*, summer heat: see AESTIVAL] an inlet or arm of the sea; esp., the wide mouth of a river, where the tide meets the current —**es'tu·ar'i·al** *adj.*

e.s.u., esu electrostatic unit(s)

e·su·ri·ent (i soor'ē ənt, -syoor'-) *adj.* [< L. *esuriens*, prp. of *esurire*, to be hungry < pp. of *edere*, EAT] hungry; voracious; greedy —**e·su'ri·ence, e·su'ri·en·cy** *n.* —**e·su'ri·ent·ly** *adv.*

†et (et; *Fr.* ā) [L., or Fr. < L.] and

-et (it, ət) [ME. *-et* < OFr. *-et*, masc., *-ete* (Fr. *-ette*), fem. < LL. *-itus, -ita*] a suffix added to nouns, meaning little [*islet, eaglet*]

Et, et *Chem. symbol for* ETHYL

e·ta (āt'ə, ēt'ə) *n.* [LL. < Gr. *ēta* < Sem., as in Heb. *ḥēth*] the seventh letter of the Greek alphabet (Η,η): in English transliteration, as in the etymologies of this dictionary, it is shown as ē

ETA, E.T.A. estimated time of arrival

†é·ta·gère (ā tä zher') *n.* [Fr.] a stand with open shelves like a whatnot, for displaying small art objects, ornaments, etc.

et al. **1.** [L. *et alibi*] and elsewhere **2.** [L. *et alii*] and others

et·a·mine (et'ə mēn) *n.* [Fr. *étamine* < VL. *staminea* < L. *stamineus*, full of threads < *stamen*, thread] a loosely woven cotton or worsted cloth, similar to bunting or voile, used for dresses, curtains, etc.

etaoin shrdlu two sequences of letters forming the two left-hand vertical rows of a linotype keyboard: if a linotyper makes an error in setting, he often fills out the line by running a finger down these rows, and *etaoin shrdlu* may thus accidentally appear in print

etc. et cetera

et cet·er·a (et set'ər ə, ˌset'rə) [L.] and others; and the like; and the rest; and so forth

et·cet·er·as (-əz, -rəz) *n.pl.* additional things or persons; customary extras

etch (ech) *vt.* [Du. *etsen* < G. *ätzen*, to corrode < MHG. *etzen*, to cause to eat, caus. of *ezzen* (G. *essen*), EAT] **1.** to

make (a drawing, design, etc.) on metal, glass, etc. by the action of an acid, esp. by coating the surface with wax and letting acid eat into the lines or areas laid bare with a special needle **2.** to engrave (a metal plate, glass, etc.) in this way, for use in printing such drawings or designs **3.** to depict or impress sharply and distinctly —*vi.* to make etchings —**etch'er** *n.*

etch·ant (ech'ənt) *n.* a substance, as an acid, used in etching

etch·ing (-iŋ) *n.* **1.** the art, process, or act of producing drawings or designs on plates of metal, glass, etc. by the action of acid **2.** an etched plate, drawing, or design **3.** a print made from an etched plate

ETD, E.T.D. estimated time of departure

E·te·o·cles (i tē'ə klēz') *n.* [L. < Gr. *Eteoklēs*] *Gr. Myth.* a son of Oedipus and Jocasta: see SEVEN AGAINST THEBES

e·ter·nal (i tur'n'l) *adj.* [ME. < OFr. < LL. *aeternalis* < L. *aeternus* < *aevum*, an age < IE. base *aiw-*, **āju-*, a life, lifetime, whence OE. *a*, always] **1.** without beginning or end; existing through all time; everlasting **2.** of eternity **3.** forever the same; always true or valid; unchanging [the *eternal* verities] **4.** always going on; never stopping; perpetual [*eternal* rest] **5.** seeming never to stop; happening very often [her *eternal* complaints] **6.** *Philos., Theol.* outside or beyond time or time relationships; timeless —*SYN.* see CONTINUAL —**the Eternal** God —**e·ter'nal·ly** *adv.* —**e·ter'nal·ness** *n.*

e·terne (i turn') *adj.* [Archaic or Poet.] eternal

e·ter·ni·ty (i tur'nə tē) *n.,* pl. **-ties** [ME. *eternite* < OFr. *eternité* < L. *aeternitas*] **1.** the quality, state, or fact of being eternal; eternal existence or duration; continuance without end **2.** infinite time; time without beginning or end **3.** a long period of time that seems endless [an *eternity* of waiting] **4.** the endless time after death

e·ter·nize (-nīz) *vt.* **-nized, -niz·ing** [Fr. *éterniser* < ML. *aeternizare* < L. *aeternus*] **1.** to make eternal; cause to last forever **2.** to make famous forever; immortalize Also **e·ter'nal·ize' -ized', -iz'ing** —**e·ter'ni·za'tion** *n.*

e·te·sian (i tē'zhən) *adj.* [L. *etesius* < Gr. *etēsios* < *etos*, year < IE. base *wet-*, whence L. *vetus*, old, Goth. *withrus*, yearling lamb] annual: said of certain Mediterranean winds that blow from the northwest for several weeks every summer

eth (eth) *n. same as* EDH

-eth¹ (əth, ith) [expanded form < ME. *-the*] a suffix used in forming ordinal numerals from bases ending in a vowel [*fortieth*]: see also -TH²

-eth² (ith, əth) [ME. *-(e)th* < OE. *-(a)th* (ult. < IE. *-t-*, whence L. *-(i)t*, Sans. *-ti*)] archaic ending of the third person singular, present indicative, of verbs [*asketh, bringeth*]: see also -TH³

Eth. 1. Ethiopia **2.** Ethiopian **3.** Ethiopic

E·than (ē'thən) [LL.(Ec.) < Heb. *ēthān*, strength, firmness] a masculine name

eth·ane (eth'ān) *n.* [ETH(YL) + -ANE] an odorless, colorless, gaseous hydrocarbon, CH_3CH_3, of the methane series: it is found in natural gas and illuminating gas, and is used as a refrigerant and fuel

eth·a·nol (eth'ə nōl', -nôl') *n.* [ETHAN(E) + -OL¹] *same as* ALCOHOL (sense 1)

Eth·el (eth'əl) [OE. *Æthelu* < *æthel*, noble, akin to G. *adel*: see ADELAIDE] a feminine name

Eth·el·bert (eth'əl bərt) [OE. *Æthelbryht*, lit., noble bright < *æthele*, noble + *beorht*, bright: cf. ALBERT] **1.** a masculine name **2.** 552?–616 A.D.; king of Kent (560–616)

Eth·el·red II (eth'əl red') 968–1016; king of England (978–1016): called *the Unready*

eth·ene (eth'ēn) *n. same as* ETHYLENE

e·ther (ē'thər) *n.* [ME. < L. *aether* < Gr. *aithēr* < *aithein*, to kindle, burn < IE. base *aidh-*, whence L. *aestus*, summer, OE. *ǣlan*, to burn] **1.** an imaginary substance regarded by the ancients as filling all space beyond the sphere of the moon, and making up the stars and planets **2.** the upper regions of space; clear sky **3.** [Rare] the air **4.** *Chem.* a) any of a series of organic compounds the molecules of which have an oxygen atom attached to two carbon atoms in hydrocarbon radicals b) a volatile, colorless, highly flammable liquid, $(C_2H_5)_2O$, belonging to this series and prepared by the reaction of sulfuric acid and ethyl alcohol: it is used as an anesthetic and a solvent for resins and fats **5.** *Physics* a hypothetical invisible substance postulated (in older theory) as pervading space and serving as the medium for the transmission of light waves and other forms of radiant energy

e·the·re·al (i thir'ē əl) *adj.* [< L. *aetherius* < Gr. *aitherios* + -AL] **1.** of or like the ether, or upper regions of space **2.** very light; airy; delicate [*ethereal* music] **3.** not earthly; heavenly; celestial **4.** *Chem.* of, like, or containing ether —**e·the're·al'i·ty** (-al'ə tē), **e·the're·al·ness** *n.* —**e·the're·al·ly** *adv.*

e·the·re·al·ize (-ə līz') *vt.* **-ized', -iz'ing** to make, or treat as being, ethereal: also, chiefly Brit. sp., **e·the're·al·ise'** —**e·the're·al·i·za'tion** *n.*

Eth·er·ege (eth'ər ij), Sir George 1635?–91; Eng. playwright of the Restoration

e·ther·i·fy (i ther'ə fī') *vt.* **-fied', -fy'ing** to change (an alcohol) into ether —**e·ther'i·fi·ca'tion** *n.*

e·ther·ize (ē'thə rīz') *vt.* **-ized', -iz'ing** ☆to anesthetize by or as by causing to inhale ether fumes —**e'ther·i·za'tion** *n.*

eth·ic (eth′ik) *n.* [ME. *ethik* < OFr. *ethique* < L. *ethica* < Gr. *ēthikē* (*technē*), ethical (art): see ff.] **1.** ethics or a system of ethics [the humanist *ethic*] **2.** any single element in a system of ethics —*adj. same as* ETHICAL

eth·i·cal (-i k′l) *adj.* [ME. *ethik* (< L. *ethicus* < Gr. *ēthikos* < *ēthos*, character, custom < IE. base *swedh-*, essential quality, own character, whence Goth. *swes*, L. *suus*, one's own & L. *suescere*, to become accustomed) + -AL] **1.** having to do with ethics or morality; of or conforming to moral standards **2.** conforming to the standards of conduct of a given profession or group **3.** designating or of a drug obtainable only on a doctor's prescription —*SYN.* see MORAL —**eth′i·cal′i·ty** (-kal′ə tē), **eth′i·cal·ness** *n.* —**eth′i·cal·ly** *adv.*

☆**Ethical Culture** a movement, founded by Felix Adler in New York in 1876, whose members accept as supreme the ethical aim in all relations of life apart from any theological or metaphysical considerations

eth·i·cist (eth′ə sist) *n.* a person versed in ethics or devoted to ethical ideals: also **eth·i·cian** (e thish′ən)

eth·i·cize (eth′ə siz′) *vt.* -**cized′**, -**ciz′ing** to make, or regard as, ethical

eth·ics (eth′iks) *n.pl.* [*with sing. v. in* 1 *&* 2, *and occas.* 3] **1.** the study of standards of conduct and moral judgment; moral philosophy **2.** a treatise on this study **3.** the system or code of morals of a particular person, religion, group, profession, etc.

E·thi·op (ē′thē äp′) *n., adj.* [Archaic or Poet.] *same as* ETHIOPIAN: also **E′thi·ope′** (-ōp′)

E·thi·o·pi·a (ē′thē ō′pē ə) **1.** ancient kingdom in NE Africa, on the Red Sea, corresponding to modern Sudan & N Ethiopia (sense 2): cf. CUSH **2.** country in E Africa, on the Red Sea: 457,000 sq. mi.; pop. 23,000,000; cap. Addis Ababa

E·thi·o·pi·an (-ō′pē ən) *adj.* **1.** of Ethiopia, its people, or culture **2.** [Archaic] Negro —*n.* **1.** a native or inhabitant of Ethiopia **2.** [Archaic] a Negro

E·thi·op·ic (-äp′ik, -ō′pik) *adj.* **1.** *same as* ETHIOPIAN **2.** of the Semitic languages of the Ethiopians —*n.* **1.** the classical Semitic language of Ethiopia, still used as the liturgical language of the Christian church in Ethiopia **2.** the group of languages spoken by Ethiopians, belonging to the Semitic branch of the Afro-Asiatic language family

eth·moid (eth′moid) *adj.* [Gr. *ēthmoeidēs* < *ēthmos*, strainer, sieve (< *ēthein*, to strain) + *eidos*, form] designating or of the perforated bone or bones of the skull that form part of the septum and walls of the nasal cavity: the olfactory nerves pass through the perforations —*n.* an ethmoid bone

eth·nic (eth′nik) *adj.* [ME. *ethnik* < LL.(Ec.) *ethnicus*, pagan < Gr. *ethnikos*, national, in LGr.(Ec.), gentile, heathen, < *ethnos*, nation, people, *ta ethnē*, nations (in LXX, non-Jews, in NT., gentile Christians): akin to *ēthos* (see ETHICAL)] **1.** [Now Rare] of nations or groups neither Christian nor Jewish; heathen **2.** designating or of any of the basic groups or divisions of mankind or of a heterogeneous population, as distinguished by customs, characteristics, language, common history, etc.; ethnological Also **eth′ni·cal** —**eth′ni·cal·ly** *adv.*

eth·nic·i·ty (eth nis′ə tē) *n.* [ETHNIC + -ITY] ethnic classification or affiliation

eth·no- (eth′nə, -nō) [Fr. < Gr. *ethnos*: see ETHNIC] a combining form meaning ethnic group or division; people or peoples [*ethnology*]: also, before a vowel, **ethn-**

eth·no·cen·trism (eth′nə sen′triz′m) *n.* [ETHNO- + CENTR- + -ISM] the emotional attitude that one's own ethnic group, nation, or culture is superior to all others —**eth′no·cen′tric** *adj.* —**eth′no·cen′tri·cal·ly** *adv.*

eth·nog·ra·phy (eth näg′rə fē) *n.* [Fr. *ethnographie*: see ETHNO- & -GRAPHY] the branch of anthropology that deals descriptively with specific cultures, esp. those of nonliterate peoples or groups —**eth·nog′ra·pher** *n.* —**eth′no·graph′ic** (-nə graf′ik), **eth′no·graph′i·cal** *adj.* —**eth′no·graph′i·cal·ly** *adv.*

eth·nol·o·gy (eth näl′ə jē) *n.* [ETHNO- + -LOGY] the branch of anthropology that deals with the comparative cultures of various peoples, including their distribution, characteristics, folkways, etc. —**eth′no·log′i·cal** (eth′nə läj′i k′l), **eth′no·log′ic** *adj.* —**eth′no·log′i·cal·ly** *adv.* —**eth·nol′o·gist** *n.*

e·thol·o·gy (e thäl′ə jē, ē-) *n.* [L. *ethologia*, character portrayal < Gr. *ēthologia*: see ETHOS & -LOGY] *Biol.* the scientific study of the characteristic behavior patterns of animals —**e·tho·log·i·cal** (eth′ə läj′i k′l, ē′thə-) *adj.* —**e·thol′o·gist** *n.*

e·thos (ē′thäs) *n.* [Gr. *ēthos*, disposition, character: see ETHICAL] the characteristic and distinguishing attitudes, habits, beliefs, etc. of an individual or of an ethnic, political, occupational, or other group

eth·yl (eth′′l) *n.* [ETH(ER) + -YL] the monovalent hydrocarbon radical, C_2H_5, which forms the base of common alcohol, ether, and many other compounds —**eth·yl·ic** (i thil′ik) *adj.*

ethyl acetate a colorless liquid with a characteristic fruity odor, $CH_3COOC_2H_5$, formed from acetic acid and ethyl alcohol and used as a solvent, in flavoring, in the manufacture of synthetic resins, etc.

ethyl alcohol *same as* ALCOHOL (sense 1)

eth·yl·ate (eth′ə lāt′; *for n.* -lit) *vt.* -**at′ed**, -**at′ing** to compound with one or more ethyl groups —*n.* a compound formed by the replacement of the hydrogen atom in the hydroxyl group of ethyl alcohol by an active metal —**eth′y·la′tion** *n.*

ethyl cellulose a cellulose ether obtained as a white granular solid by treating alkali cellulose with ethyl chloride: used in adhesives, plastics, insulation, etc.

ethyl chloride a colorless liquid, C_2H_5Cl, prepared by heating ethyl alcohol with hydrogen chloride in the presence of zinc chloride: used in preparing lead tetraethyl and ethyl cellulose, and as a local anesthetic

eth·yl·ene (eth′ə lēn′) *n.* [ETHYL + -ENE] a colorless, flammable, gaseous hydrocarbon of the olefin series, $CH_2:CH_2$, with a disagreeable odor: it is obtained from natural or coal gas, by cracking petroleum, by the action of sulfuric or phosphoric acid on alcohol, etc., and is used as a fuel and anesthetic, in hastening the ripening of fruits, and to form polyethylene

ethylene glycol a colorless, viscous liquid, the simplest polyhydric alcohol, $HOCH_2CH_2OH$, used as an antifreeze, solvent, in resins, etc.

ethyl ether *same as* ETHER (sense 4 *b*)

É·tienne (ā tyen′) *same as* ESTIENNE

e·ti·o·late (ēt′ē ə lāt′) *vt.* -**lat′ed**, -**lat′ing** [Fr. *étioler* < dial. var. of *éteule*, stubble, straw < OFr. *estouble*: see STUBBLE] **1.** to cause to be pale and unhealthy **2.** to deprive of strength; weaken **3.** *Bot.* to blanch or bleach by depriving of sunlight —**e′ti·o·la′tion** *n.*

e·ti·ol·o·gy (ēt′ē äl′ə jē) *n., pl.* -**gies** [LL. *aetiologia* < Gr. *aitiologia* < *aitia*, cause + *logia*, description (see -LOGY)] **1.** the assignment of a cause, or the cause assigned [the *etiology* of a folkway] **2.** the science of causes or origins **3.** *a*) the science of the causes or origins of disease *b*) the causes of a specific disease —**e′ti·o·log′ic** (-ə läj′ik), **e′ti·o·log′i·cal** *adj.* —**e′ti·o·log′i·cal·ly** *adv.*

et·i·quette (et′i kət, -ket′) *n.* [Fr. *étiquette*, TICKET] **1.** the forms, manners, and ceremonies established by convention as acceptable or required in social relations, in a profession, or in official life **2.** the rules for such forms, manners, and ceremonies —*SYN.* see DECORUM

Et·na (et′nə) volcanic mountain in E Sicily: 10,705 ft. —*n.* [e-] a former kind of alcohol lamp for heating or vaporizing liquids

ETO, E.T.O. European Theater of Operations

E·ton (ēt′′n) town in Buckinghamshire, on the Thames, near London: pop. 5,000: site of a private preparatory school for boys (**Eton College**)

Eton collar a broad, white linen collar worn with an Eton jacket, or a collar resembling this

E·to·ni·an (ē tō′nē ən) *adj.* of Eton —*n.* a student or former student at Eton College

Eton jacket (or **coat**) a black waist-length jacket with broad lapels, left open in front, as that worn by students at Eton College

E·tru·ri·a (i troor′ē ə) ancient country occupying what is now Tuscany & part of Umbria in WC Italy

E·trus·can (i trus′kən) *adj.* of Etruria, its people, their language, or culture —*n.* **1.** a native or inhabitant of Etruria **2.** the language of the ancient Etruscans: it had no established relationship to any other language Also **E·tru′ri·an** (i troor′ē ən)

ETRURIA (8th cent. B.C.)

et seq. **1.** [L. *et sequens*] and the following **2.** [L. *et sequentes* or *et sequentia*] and those that follow

Et·ta (et′ə) a feminine name: see HENRIETTA

-**ette** (et) [Fr.: see -ET] a *n.-forming suffix meaning:* **1.** little [*statuette*] **2.** female [*majorette*] **3.** a substitute for [*leatherette*]

‡**et tu, Bru·te!** (et tōō′ brōō′te) [L.] and you (too), Brutus!: said to be Julius Caesar's reproach on seeing his friend Brutus among his assassins

é·tude (ā′tōōd, -tyōōd; *Fr.* ā tüd′) *n.* [Fr., STUDY] a musical composition for a solo instrument, designed to give practice in some special point of technique, but often performed for its artistic worth

e·tui, e·twee (ā twē′, e-; et′wē) *n.* [Fr. *étui* ≍ OFr. *estui* < *estuier*, to place in a cover, enclose < LL. **studiare*, to treat with care < L. *studium*: see STUDY] an ornamental case for small articles, as needles

ETV educational television

ety., etym., etymol. 1. etymological 2. etymology

et·y·mo·log·i·cal (et′ə mə lăj′ə k′l) *adj.* [< L. *etymologicus* < Gr. *etymologikos* + -AL] of or according to the etymology, or to the principles of etymology —**et′y·mo·log′i·cal·ly** *adv.*

et·y·mol·o·gist (et′ə mäl′ə jist) *n.* an expert in etymology

et·y·mol·o·gize (-jīz′) *vt., vi.* -gized′, -giz′ing to trace the etymology of, or give or suggest an etymology for (a word or words)

et·y·mol·o·gy (-jē) *n., pl.* -gies [ME. & OFr. *ethimologie* < L. *etymologia* < Gr. *etymologia:* see ff. & -LOGY] 1. the origin and development of a word, affix, phrase, etc.; the tracing of a word or other form back as far as possible in its own language and to its source in contemporary or earlier languages: in this dictionary etymologies are given in brackets following the part-of-speech label 2. the branch of linguistics that deals with the origin and development of words

et·y·mon (et′ə män′) *n., pl.* -mons′, -ma (-mə) [L. < Gr. *etymon,* literal sense of a word, etymology, neut. of *etymos,* true < IE. *seto-* < base *es-,* to be (whence L. *sum, est,* E. IS)] 1. the original form of a word, as at an earlier period in the development of a language, or as it appeared in some allied or foreign language 2. a word or morpheme from which derivatives or compounds have developed

eu- (yŌŌ, yoo) [Fr. < Gr. *eu-,* good, well < IE. base *esu-,* good] *a prefix meaning* good, well [*eulogy, euphony*]: opposed to DYS-, CACO-

Eu *Chem.* europium

Eu·boe·a (yŌŌ bē′ə) *former name of* EVVOIA

eu·caine (yŌŌ kān′, yŌŌ′kān) *n.* [EU- + (CO)CAINE] either of two synthetic alkaloids, **alpha-eucaine**, $C_{19}H_{27}NO_4$, or **beta-eucaine**, $C_{18}H_{21}NO_2$, made from piperidine: the hydrochloride of beta-eucaine is used as a local anesthetic

eu·ca·lyp·tol, eu·ca·lyp·tole (yŌŌ′kə lip′tōl, -tôl) *n.* [EUCALYPT(US) + -OL¹, -OLE] a liquid, $C_{10}H_{18}O$, with a camphorlike odor and spicy taste, present in turpentine and many essential oils: used in medicines, in perfumes, and for flavoring

eu·ca·lyp·tus (-təs) *n., pl.* -tus·es, -ti (-tī) [ModL. < EU- + Gr. *kalyptos,* covered (from the covering of the buds) < *kalyptein,* to cover, conceal < IE. base *kel-,* whence HALL] any of a genus (*Eucalyptus*) of tall, aromatic, chiefly Australian evergreen trees of the myrtle family, bearing pendent leaves and umbels of white or pink flowers and valued for their timber, gum, and oil: also **eu′ca·lypt′**

eucalyptus oil an essential oil derived from eucalyptus leaves, used as an antiseptic and expectorant

eu·cha·ris (yŌŌ′kə ris) *n.* [ModL. < Gr. *eucharis,* charming, gracious < *eu-,* well (see EU-) + *charis,* favor (see ff.)] any of a genus (*Eucharis*) of S. American plants of the amaryllis family, with white, fragrant flowers

Eu·cha·rist (-rist) *n.* [ME. *eukarist* < OFr. *eucariste* < LL.(Ec.) *eucharistia* < Gr. *eucharistia,* gratitude (in NT., the Eucharist) < *eucharistos,* grateful < *eu-,* well + *charizesthai,* to show favor to < *charis,* favor < IE. base *gher-,* to desire, like, whence YEARN] 1. *same as* HOLY COMMUNION 2. the consecrated bread and wine used in Holy Communion —**Eu′cha·ris′tic** *adj.*

☆**eu·chre** (yŌŌ′kər) *n.* [earlier also *yuker, uker* < ?] 1. a card game basically for two, three, or four persons, played with thirty-two cards, all the cards below seven except the ace being removed 2. a euchring or being euchred —*vt.* -chred, -chring 1. to prevent (the trump-declaring opponent at euchre) from taking the required three tricks 2. [Colloq.] to outwit or cheat (often with *out*)

eu·chro·ma·tin (yŌŌ krō′mə tin) *n.* [G.: see EU- & CHROMATIN] *Biol.* the portion of the chromosome containing most of the genetic material and staining less densely than the heterochromatin

eu·cil·i·ate (yŌŌ sil′ē it) *n.* [EU- + CILIATE] any of a subclass (Euciliata) of ciliated protozoans in which cilia are present for the entire life cycle

eu·clase (yŌŌ′klās) *n.* [Fr. < *eu-,* EU- + Gr. *klasis,* a breaking < *klan,* to break (see CLASTIC): so named from breaking easily] a green or blue crystalline silicate of aluminum and beryllium, HBeAlSiO₄, used as a gem

Eu·clid¹ (yŌŌ′klid) [L. *Euclides* < Gr. *Eukleidēs*] fl. 300 B.C.; Gr. mathematician; author of a basic work in geometry —**Eu·clid′e·an, Eu·clid′i·an** (-ē ən) *adj.*

Eu·clid² (yŌŌ′klid) [so named (after prec.) by its surveyors] city in NE Ohio: suburb of Cleveland: pop. 72,000

eu·dae·mo·ni·a, eu·de·mo·ni·a (yŌŌ′di mō′nē ə) *n.* [Gr. *eudaimonia,* happiness < *eudaimōn,* blessed with a good genius, fortunate < *eu-,* good + *daimōn:* see DEMON] happiness; specif., in Aristotle's philosophy, happiness, the main universal goal, derived from a life of activity governed by reason

eu·dae·mon·ic, eu·de·mon·ic (-män′ik) *adj.* [Gr. *eudaimonikos:* see prec.] conducive to happiness: also **eu′dae·mon′i·cal, eu′de·mon′i·cal**

eu·dae·mon·ism (yŌŌ dē′mən iz′m) *n.* [Gr. *eudaimonismos,* a calling happy < *eudaimonizein,* to call happy < *eudaimōn:* see EUDAEMONIA] the system of ethics that considers the moral value of actions in terms of their ability to produce personal happiness: also **eu·de·mon′ism** —**eu·dae′mon·ist** *n., adj.* —**eu·dae′mon·is′tic** *adj.*

eu·di·om·e·ter (yŌŌ′dē äm′ə tər) *n.* [< Gr. *eudios,* clear, fair (< *eudia,* fair weather < *eu-,* good + *dia,* day < IE. base *diw-,* glowing day < *dei-,* to shine: cf. DIVINE) +

-METER] 1. orig., an instrument for measuring the amount of oxygen in the air 2. an instrument for measuring and analyzing gases volumetrically —**eu′di·o·met′ric** (-ə met′rik), **eu′di·o·met′ri·cal** *adj.* —**eu′di·o·met′ri·cal·ly** *adv.* —**eu′di·om′e·try** *n.*

Eu·gene¹ (yŌŌ jēn′, yŌŌ′jēn; *for 2,* Fr. ö zhen′) [Fr. *Eugène* < L. *Eugenius* < Gr. *Eugenios* < *eugenēs,* well-born: cf. EUGENIC] 1. a masculine name: dim. *Gene;* fem. *Eugenia* 2. Prince, (*François Eugène de Savoie-Carignan*) 1663–1736; Austrian general, born in France

Eu·gene² (yŌŌ jēn′) [after *Eugene* Skinner, early settler] city in W Oreg.: pop. 76,000

Eu·ge·ni·a (yŌŌ jē′nē ə, -jēn′yə) [L. < Gr. *Eugenia:* see EUGENE¹] a feminine name: dim. *Genie*

eu·gen·ic (yŌŌ jen′ik) *adj.* [Gr. *eugenēs,* well-born: see EU- & GENESIS] 1. relating to the bearing of sound offspring 2. of, relating to, or improved by eugenics Also **eu·gen′i·cal** —**eu·gen′i·cal·ly** *adv.*

eu·gen·i·cist (-ə sist) *n.* a specialist in or advocate of eugenics: also **eu·gen·ist** (yŌŌ′jə nist, yoo jen′ist)

eu·gen·ics (yŌŌ jen′iks) *n.pl.* [*with sing. v.*] [< Gr. *eugenēs* (see EUGENIC) + -ICS] the movement devoted to improving the human species through the control of hereditary factors in mating

Eu·gé·nie (yŌŌ jē′nē; Fr. ö zhā nē′), Empress (*Eugénie Marie de Montijo de Guzmán*) 1826–1920; wife of Louis Napoleon & empress of France (1853–71), born in Spain

eu·ge·nol (yŌŌ′jə nōl′, -nôl′) *n.* [< ModL. *Eugenia,* a genus of tropical trees + -OL¹] a colorless, aromatic liquid phenol, $C_{10}H_{12}O_2$, found in oil of cloves and used in perfumes, as an antiseptic in dentistry, etc.

eu·gle·na (yŌŌ glē′nə) *n.* [< EU- + Gr. *glēnē,* pupil of the eye < IE. base *ĝel-,* *ĝlē-,* to gleam, be gay: cf. CLEAN] any of a genus (*Euglena*) of green protozoans with a single flagellum and a characteristic red pigment spot

eu·gle·noid movement (-noid) a wormlike, wriggling, usually nonlocomotive movement, as in certain protozoans, consisting of a progressive expansion and contraction of the cell body

eu·he·mer·ism (yoo hē′mər iz′m, -hem′ər-) *n.* [< L. *Euhemerus* (< Gr. *Euhēmeros*) + -ISM] the theory of the Greek writer Euhemerus (4th cent. B.C.) that the gods of mythology were deified human beings; theory that myths are based on traditional accounts of real people and events —**eu·he′mer·ist** *n., adj.* —**eu·he′mer·is′tic** *adj.* —**eu·he′mer·is′ti·cal·ly** *adv.*

eu·he·mer·ize (-īz′) *vt.* -ized′, -iz′ing to interpret (myths, etc.) by euhemerism

☆**eu·la·chon** (yŌŌ′lə kän′) *n.* [Chinook jargon *ulâkân*] *same as* CANDLEFISH

Eu·la·li·a (yŌŌ lā′lē ə, -lāl′yə) [L. < Gr. *Eulalia,* lit., fair (in) speech < *eu-,* well + *lalein,* to talk] a feminine name

eu·la·mel·li·branch (yŌŌ′lə mel′ə braŋk′) *n.* [< ModL. *Eulamellibranchia,* name of the order: see EU- & LAMELLIBRANCH] any of an order (Eulamellibranchia) of bivalve mollusks having two pairs of V-shaped gills and two well-developed adductor muscles —**eu′la·mel′li·bran′chi·ate** (-braŋ′kē it) *n., adj.*

Eu·ler (oi′lər), **Le·on·hard** (lā′ŏn härt′) 1707–83; Swiss mathematician

eu·lo·gi·a (yŌŌ lō′jē ə) *n.* [ML., food, blessing (in eccles. use, the Eucharist): see EULOGY] 1. orig., the Eucharist 2. bread blessed but not consecrated, and given in small pieces to the noncommunicants at Mass, esp. in the Orthodox Eastern Church

eu·lo·gis·tic (yŌŌ′lə jis′tik) *adj.* of or expressing eulogy; praising highly; laudatory —**eu′lo·gis′ti·cal·ly** *adv.*

eu·lo·gi·um (yŌŌ lō′jē əm) *n., pl.* -gi·ums, -gi·a (-ə) [ML.] *same as* EULOGY

eu·lo·gize (yŌŌ′lə jīz′) *vt.* -gized′, -giz′ing to praise highly; compose a eulogy about; extol —*SYN.* see PRAISE —**eu′lo·gist, eu′lo·giz′er** *n.*

eu·lo·gy (-jē) *n., pl.* -gies [ME. *euloge* < ML. *eulogia* < Gr. *eulogia,* praise, lit., fine language (in LXX & NT., blessing) < *eulegein,* to speak well of, bless: see EU- & -LOGY] 1. speech or writing in praise of a person, event, or thing; esp., a formal speech praising a person who has recently died 2. high praise; commendation —*SYN.* see TRIBUTE

Eu·men·i·des (yoo men′ə dēz′) *n.pl.* [L. < Gr. *Eumenides,* lit., the gracious ones < *eumenēs,* well-disposed, gracious < *eu-,* well + *menos,* the mind, temper: a propitiatory euphemism] *same as* the FURIES

Eu·nice (yŌŌ′nis) [LL.(Ec.) < Gr. *Eunikē,* lit., good victory < *eu-,* well + *nikē,* victory] a feminine name

eu·nuch (yŌŌ′nək) *n.* [ME. *eunuk* < L. *eunuchus* < Gr. *eunouchos,* guardian of the bed, chamberlain, eunuch < *eunē,* bed + *echein,* to have, hold: for IE. base see SCHEME] 1. a castrated man in charge of an Oriental harem or employed as a chamberlain or high officer by an Oriental potentate 2. any man or boy lacking normal function of the testes, as through castration or disease

eu·on·y·mus (yoo än′ə məs) *n.* [ModL., name of the genus < L., the spindle tree < Gr. *euōnymos* < *eu-,* good + *onyma,* dial. form of *onoma,* NAME] any of a genus (*Euonymus*) of deciduous or evergreen shrubs and woody vines of the staff-tree family, with colorful seeds and pods

eu·pa·to·ri·um (yŌŌ′pə tôr′ē əm) *n.* [ModL. < Gr. *eupatorion,* hemp agrimony, named in honor of Mithridates *Eupatōr,* king of Pontus] any of a genus (*Eupatorium*) of

plants of the composite family, including the mistflower, joe-pye weed, boneset, etc.

eu·pat·rid (yoo pat'rid, yoo'pə trid') *n.*, *pl.* **-rid·ae** (-rə dē'), **-rids** [Gr. *eupatridēs* < *eu-*, well, good + *patēr*, FATHER] [*also* E-] any of the hereditary aristocrats of ancient Athens or other Greek states

eu·pep·si·a (yoo pep'shə, -sē ə) *n.* [ModL. < Gr. *eupepsia*, digestibility: see EU- & DYSPEPSIA] good digestion

eu·pep·tic (-tik) *adj.* [< Gr. *eupeptos* (< *eu-*, well + *peptein*, to digest: see COOK) + -IC] **1.** of or having good digestion **2.** healthy and happy; cheerful

eu·phau·si·id (yoo fô'zē id) *n.* [< ModL. *Euphausia*, name of the genus < ? Gr. *eu-*, EU- + *pha(inein)*, to show (see -PHANE) + *ousia*, substance (cf. HOMOIOUSIAN) + -ID] any of an order (Euphausiacea) of shrimplike animals with thoracic appendages that have two branches: important as food, esp. for certain whales: also **eu·phau'sid** (-zid)

eu·phe·mism (yoo'fə miz'm) *n.* [Gr. *euphēmismos* < *euphēmizein*, to use words of good omen < *euphēmos*, of good sound or omen < *eu-*, good + *phēmē*, voice < *phanai*, to speak < IE. base *bha-*, to speak, whence BAN¹] **1.** the use of a word or phrase that is less expressive or direct than considered less distasteful, less offensive, etc. than another **2.** a word or phrase so substituted (Ex.: *remains* for *corpse*) —**eu'phe·mist** *n.* —**eu'phe·mis'tic**, **eu'phe·mis'ti·cal** *adj.* —**eu'phe·mis'ti·cal·ly** *adv.*

eu·phe·mize (-mīz') *vt.*, *vi.* **-mized'**, **-miz'ing** to speak or write (of) euphemistically

☆**eu·phen·ics** (yoo fen'iks) *n.pl.* [*with sing. v.*] [coined (1963) by Joshua Lederberg, U.S. geneticist < EU- + *phen-* (as in PHENOTYPE) + -ICS, after EUGENICS] a movement seeking to improve the human species by modifying the biological development of the individual, as through the prenatal manipulation of genes with chemical agents

eu·phon·ic (yoo fän'ik) *adj.* [ML. *euphonicus*] **1.** of or having to do with euphony **2.** euphonious Also **eu·phon'i·cal** —**eu·phon'i·cal·ly** *adv.*

eu·pho·ni·ous (yoo fō'nē əs) *adj.* characterized by euphony; having a pleasant sound; harmonious —**eu·pho'ni·ous·ly** *adv.*

eu·pho·ni·um (-əm) *n.* [< Gr. *euphōnos* (see EUPHONY) + (HARMON)IUM] a brass-wind instrument like the baritone but having a more mellow tone

eu·pho·nize (yoo'fə nīz') *vt.* **-nized'**, **-niz'ing** to make euphonious

eu·pho·ny (-nē) *n.*, *pl.* **-nies** [Fr. *euphonie* < LL. *euphonia* < Gr. *euphōnia* < *euphōnos*, sweet-voiced, musical < *eu-*, well + *phōnē*, voice: see PHONE¹] the quality of having a pleasing sound; pleasant effect of a combination of agreeable sounds in spoken words; also, such a combination of words

eu·phor·bi·a (yoo fôr'bē ə) *n.* [ME. *euforbia* < L. *euphorbea*, said to be named after *Euphorbus*, physician of 1st cent. A.D., who used it medically] *same as* SPURGE

eu·pho·ri·a (yoo fôr'ē ə) *n.* [ModL. < Gr. *euphoria*, power of bearing easily < *euphoros*, bearing well < *eu-*, well + *pherein*, BEAR¹] a feeling of vigor, well-being, or high spirits, specif., *Psychol.* one that is exaggerated and without an obvious cause —**eu·phor'ic** (-fôr'ik, -fär'-) *adj.*

eu·pho·ri·ant (-ənt) *n. Med.* a drug or other agent that produces euphoria

eu·pho·tic (yoo fōt'ik) *adj.* [EU- + PHOTIC] *Ecol.* of or pertaining to the uppermost portion of a body of water, into which light enters to a degree sufficient for photosynthesis and the consequent growth of plants

eu·phra·sy (yoo'frə sē) *n.*, *pl.* **-sies** [ME. *eufrasie* < ML. *euphrasia* < Gr. *euphrasia* < *euphrainein*, to cheer < *eu-*, well + *phren*, mind: see PHRENO-] *same as* EYEBRIGHT

Eu·phra·tes (yoo frāt'ēz) river flowing from EC Turkey through Syria & Iraq, joining the Tigris to form the Shatt al Arab: c. 1,700 mi.

eu·phroe (yoo'frō, -vrō) *n.* [< Du. *juffrouw*, lit., young woman < *jong*, young + *vrouw*, woman] a long, perforated, cylindrical block to fasten and tighten the ropes supporting an awning on shipboard, a tent, etc.

Eu·phros·y·ne (yoo fräs'ə nē', -fräz'-) [L. < Gr. *Euphrosynē* < *euphrōn*, cheerful] *Gr. Myth.* Joy, one of the three Graces

eu·phu·ism (yoo'fyoo wiz'm) *n.* [< *Euphues*, fictitious character in two prose romances by John LYLY < Gr. *euphyēs*, shapely, graceful < *eu-*, well + *phyē*, growth < *phyein*, to grow: see BONDAGE] **1.** the artificial, affected, high-flown style of speaking or writing used by John Lyly and his imitators, characterized by alliteration, balanced sentences, farfetched figures of speech, etc. **2.** any artificial, high-flown style of speech or writing **3.** an instance of this —**eu'phu·ist** *n.*

eu·phu·is·tic (yoo'fyoo wis'tik) *adj.* of, having the nature of, or characterized by euphuism; high-flown, affected, etc. —*SYN.* see BOMBASTIC —**eu'phu·is'ti·cal** *adj.* —**eu'phu·is'ti·cal·ly** *adv.*

eu·plas·tic (yoo plas'tik) *adj.* [EU- + PLASTIC] *Physiol.* easily formed into or adapted to the formation of tissue —*n.* a euplastic material

eu·ploid (yoo'ploid) *adj.* [EU- + -PLOID] with the complement of chromosomes being an exact multiple of the haploid number, as diploid, triploid, etc. —**eu'ploi'dy** (-ploi'dē) *n.*

eup·ne·a, eup·noe·a (yoop'nē ə, yoop nē'ə) *n.* [ModL. < Gr. *eupnoia* < *eu-*, well + *pnoē*, breathing < *pnein*, to breathe: see PNEUMA] [Obs.] normal breathing

Eur. **1.** Europe **2.** European

Eur·a·sia (yoo rā'zhə; *chiefly Brit.*, -shə) land mass made up of the continents of Europe & Asia

Eur·a·sian (-zhən; *chiefly Brit.*, -shən) *adj.* **1.** of Eurasia **2.** of mixed European and Asian descent —*n.* **1.** a person who has one European parent and one Asian parent, or a person who is generally of mixed European and Asian descent **2.** a member of a people of both Europe and Asia

Eur·a·tom (yoor'ə täm') European Atomic Energy Community, the agency for the joint development of nuclear energy by the countries of the European Economic Community

eu·re·ka (yoo rē'kə) *interj.* [Gr. *heurēka*, 1st pers., perf. indic. act., of *heuriskein*, to find, discover < IE. base *wer-*, to find, take, whence Arm. *gerem*, (I) capture, OIr. *fūar*, I have found] I have found (it): exclamation supposedly uttered by Archimedes when he discovered a way to determine the purity of gold by applying the principle of specific gravity

eu·rhyth·mics (yoo ri*th*'miks) *n.pl. same as* EURYTHMICS —**eu·rhyth'mic** *adj.* —**eu·rhyth'my** *n.*

Eu·rip·i·des (yoo rip'ə dēz') 479?-406? B.C.; Gr. writer of tragedies —**Eu·rip'i·de'an** (-dē'ən) *adj.*

eu·ri·pus (yoo rī'pəs) *n.*, *pl.* **-pi** (-pī) [L. < Gr. *euripos* < *eu-*, well + *rhipē*, rush, impetus, orig., turning motion < IE. base *wrei-*, to turn, whence Gr. *reiben*, to grate] a strait or channel with a violent and unpredictable current or tide

Eu·ro- (yoor'ō, -ə) *a combining form meaning:* **1.** Europe, European [*Euromart*] **2.** Europe and, European and [*Euro-American*] Also, before a vowel, **Eur-** [*Eurasia*]

Eu·roc·ly·don (yoo räk'lə dän') *n.* [Gr. *euroklydōn* (as if < *euros*, east wind + *klydōn*, wave, billow), var. of *eurakyton*, a northeast wind < *euros* (see EURUS) + L. *aquilo*, the north (or north-by-east) wind < *aquilus*, dark, stormy, orig., watery < *aqua*, water] **1.** *Bible* a stormy northeast wind of the Mediterranean, referred to in the account of Paul's voyage to Rome: Acts 27:14 **2.** any stormy wind

Eu·ro·crat (yoor'ə krat') *n.* [EURO- + -CRAT, with an implied pun on BUREAUCRAT] any of the officials or employees of the European Economic Community

Eu·ro·dol·lars (-däl'ərz) *n.pl.* U.S. dollars circulated among European banks and lending institutions, usually in short-term trade financing

eu·ro·ky (yoo rō'kē) *n.* [contr. < *euryoky* < EURY- + -oky < Gr. *oikia*, a dwelling, akin to *oikos*, house: see VICINITY] *Biol.* the ability of an organism to live under variable environmental conditions: opposed to STENOKY: also **eu·ry·o·ky** (yoo're ō'kē) —**eu·ro'kous** (-kəs), **eu'ry·o'kous** *adj.*

Eu·ro·mart (yoor'ə märt') *n. same as* EUROPEAN ECONOMIC COMMUNITY: also **Eu'ro·mar'ket** (-mär'kit)

Eu·ro·pa (yoo rō'pə) [L. < Gr. *Europē*] **1.** *Gr. Myth.* a Phoenician princess loved by Zeus: disguised as a white bull, he carried her off across the sea to Crete **2.** the third satellite of Jupiter

Eu·rope (yoor'əp) [L. *Europa* < Gr. *Europē*] continent between Asia & the Atlantic Ocean: the Ural Mountains are generally considered the E boundary: c. 3,750,000 sq. mi.; pop. c. 620,000,000

Eu·ro·pe·an (yoor'ə pē'ən) *adj.* of Europe, its people, their culture, etc. —*n.* **1.** a native or inhabitant of Europe **2.** in Africa and Asia, any Caucasian, or white person

European Economic Community the European common market formed in 1958 by Belgium, France, West Germany, Italy, Luxembourg, and the Netherlands: see COMMON MARKET

Eu·ro·pe·an·ize (-īz') *vt.* **-ized'**, **-iz'ing** **1.** to make European in habits, dress, culture, scope, etc. **2.** to integrate (the economy of a European nation) with that of other European nations —**Eu'ro·pe'an·i·za'tion** *n.*

☆**European plan** a system of hotel operation in which the rate charged to guests covers rooms and service but not meals: distinguished from AMERICAN PLAN

eu·ro·pi·um (yoo rō'pē əm) *n.* [ModL. < EUROPE + -IUM] a chemical element of the rare-earth group: symbol, Eu; at. wt., 151.96; at. no., 63; sp. gr., 5.24; melt. pt., 826°C; boil. pt., 1430°C

Eu·rus (yoor'əs) [ME. < L. *euros*, prob. ult. < IE. base *eus-*, to burn, whence L. *urere*, to burn] *Gr. Myth.* the god of the east wind or southeast wind

eu·ry- (yoor'i) [ModL. < Gr. *eury-* < *eurys*, wide, broad < IE. base *wer-*, broad, whence Sans. *uru*] *a combining form meaning* wide, broad [*euryhaline*]

eu·ry·bath (yoor'i bath') *n.* [EURY- + Gr. *bathos*, depth] *Biol.* an organism that can live in a wide range of water depths: opposed to STENOBATH —**eu'ry·bath'ic** *adj.*

Eu·ryd·i·ce (yoo rid'ə sē') [L. < Gr. *Eurydikē*] *Gr. Myth.* the wife of Orpheus: see ORPHEUS

---

eu·ry·ha·line (yoor'i hā'lǐn, -hal'ǐn) *adj.* [G. *euryhalin* < *eury-*, EURY- + Gr. *halinos*, saline < *hals*, SALT] *Biol.* able to exist in waters with wide variations in their salt content: opposed to STENOHALINE

eu·ry·hy·gric (-hī'grǐk) *adj.* [EURY- + HYGR- + -IC] *Biol.* able to withstand a wide range of humidity: opposed to STENOHYGRIC

eu·ryph·a·gous (yoo rǐf'ə gəs) *adj.* [EURY- + -PHAGOUS] *Biol.* eating a wide variety of foods: opposed to STENOPHAGOUS

eu·ryp·ter·id (yoo rǐp'tə rǐd') *n.* [< ModL. *Eurypterida* (pl.), name of the order < Gr. *eurys*, broad + *pteron*, feather, wing: so named from a pair of broad swimming appendages] any of an order (Eurypterida) of large, aquatic, scorpionlike arthropods of the Paleozoic Era, related to the horseshoe crab and sometimes reaching a length of 6 ft.

eu·ry·therm (yoor'i thurm') *n.* [G., independent of temperature variations: see EURY- & THERM] an organism that can live in a wide range of temperatures: opposed to STENOTHERM —**eu'ry·ther'mal** (-thur'm'l), **eu'ry·ther'mous** (-məs), **eu'ry·ther'mic** (-mǐk) *adj.*

eu·ryth·mic (yoo rǐth'mǐk) *adj.* 1. characterized by perfect proportion and harmony, or by movement in rhythm 2. of eurythmics Also **eu·ryth'mi·cal**

eu·ryth·mics (-mǐks) *n.pl.* [*with sing. v.*] [< ff. + -ICS] the art of performing various bodily movements in rhythm, usually to musical accompaniment

eu·ryth·my (-mē) *n.* [L. *eurythmia* < Gr. *eurythmia* < *eurythmos*, rhythmical < *eu-*, well + *rhythmos*, RHYTHM] 1. rhythmical movement 2. harmonious proportion

eu·ry·top·ic (yoor'i täp'ǐk) *adj.* [< G. *eurytop*, widely distributed (< *eury-*, EURY- + -*top* < Gr. *topos*, place: see TOPIC) + -IC] *Biol.* able to withstand a wide range of environmental conditions: opposed to STENOTOPIC — **eu'ry·to·pic'i·ty** (-tō pǐs'ə tē) *n.*

Eu·se·bi·us (Pam·phi·li) (yōo sē'bē əs pam'fə lī') 264?–340 A.D.; Gr. ecclesiastical historian

Eus·tace (yōōs'təs) [OFr. *Eustace* < L. *Eustachius* < Gr. *Eustachios* < *eustachys*, rich in corn, fruitful < *eu-*, well + *stachys*, ear of grain] a masculine name

Eu·sta·chi·an tube (yoo stā'shən, -shē ən, -kē ən) [after Bartolommeo *Eustachio* (1520–74), It. anatomist] a slender tube between the middle ear and the pharynx, which serves to equalize air pressure on both sides of the eardrum: see EAR, illus.

eu·stat·ic (yoo stat'ǐk) *adj.* [EU- + STATIC] of or pertaining to changes in sea level throughout the world, as because of extensive formation or melting of icecaps

eu·stele (yōo'stēl, yoo stē'lē) *n.* [EU- + STELE] the typical vascular cylinder of a dicotyledonous plant, consisting of a ring of collateral bundles of xylem, cambium, and phloem

eu·tec·tic (yoo tek'tǐk) *adj.* [< Gr. *eutēkos*, easily fused < *eu-*, well + *tēkein*, to melt + -IC] fusing at the lowest possible temperature; specif., designating or of a mixture or alloy with a melting point lower than that of any other combination of the same components —*n.* a eutectic mixture or alloy —**eu·tec'toid** *adj., n.*

Eu·ter·pe (yoo tur'pē) [L. < Gr. *Euterpē* < *euterpēs*, charming < *eu-*, well + *terpein*, to delight, charm] *Gr. Myth.* the Muse of music and lyric poetry

eu·tha·na·si·a (yōo'thə nā'zhə, -zhē ə) *n.* [Gr. *euthanasia*, painless, happy death < *eu-*, well + *thanatos*, death: see THANATO-] 1. an easy and painless death 2. act or method of causing death painlessly, so as to end suffering: advocated by some as a way to deal with persons dying of incurable, painful diseases

☆eu·then·ics (yoo then'ǐks) *n.pl.* [*with sing. v.*] [< Gr. *euthēnein*, to flourish (< *eu-*, well + IE. base *gwhen-*, to swell, whence Per. *āganiš*, full) + -ICS] the movement devoted to improving species and breeds, esp. the human species, through control of environmental factors

eu·troph·ic (-träf'ǐk, -trō'fǐk) *adj.* [EU- + TROPHIC] designating or of a lake, pond, etc. rich in plant nutrient minerals and organisms but often deficient in oxygen in midsummer —**eu'troph·i·ca'tion** *n.*

eux·e·nite (yōok'sə nīt') *n.* [G. *euxenit* < Gr. *euxenos*, hospitable (< *eu-*, well + *xenos*, stranger, guest + -ITE¹: so named from containing several rare elements] a lustrous, brown-black mineral containing columbium, titanium, yttrium, erbium, cerium, and uranium

Eux·ine Sea (yōok'sən, -sǐn) [L. *Pontus Euxinus*] ancient name of the BLACK SEA

ev, EV electron-volt

EVA extravehicular activity

E·va (ē'və, ev'ə) a feminine name: see EVE

e·vac·u·ant (i vak'yoo wənt) *adj.* [L. *evacuans*, prp. of *evacuare*: see ff.] causing evacuation, esp. of the bowels; cathartic or emetic —*n.* an evacuant medicine

e·vac·u·ate (-wāt') *vt.* -at'ed, -at'ing [< L. *evacuatus*, pp. of *evacuare* < *e-*, out + *vacuare*, to make empty < *vacuus*, empty] 1. to make empty; remove the contents of; specif., to remove air from so as to make a vacuum 2. to discharge (bodily waste, esp. feces) 3. to remove (inhabitants, troops, etc.) from (a place or area), as for protective or strategic purposes; withdraw from —*vi.* 1. to withdraw, as from a besieged town or area of danger 2. to discharge bodily waste, esp. feces —**e·vac'u·a'tive** *adj.* —**e·vac'u·a'tor** *n.*

e·vac·u·a·tion (i vak'yoo wā'shən) *n.* [ME. *evacuacioun* < L. *evacuatio*] 1. an evacuating or being evacuated 2. something evacuated; specif., feces

e·vac·u·ee (i vak'yoo wē', i vak'yoo wē') *n.* a person evacuated from an area of danger

e·vade (i vād') *vi.* e·vad'ed, e·vad'ing [Fr. *évader* < L. *evadere* < *e-*, out, from + *vadere*, to go < IE. base *wādh-*, whence WADE] 1. [Rare] to escape; get away 2. to be deceitful or clever in avoiding or escaping something; use evasion —*vt.* 1. to avoid or escape from by deceit or cleverness; elude [to evade a pursuer] 2. to avoid doing or answering directly; get around; get out of [to evade a question, to evade payment of a tax] —SYN. see ESCAPE —**e·vad'a·ble** *adj.* —**e·vad'er** *n.*

e·vag·i·nate (i vaj'ə nāt') *vt.* -nat'ed, -nat'ing [< L. *evaginatus*, pp. of *evaginare*, to unsheath < *e-*, from + *vagina*, a sheath] 1. to turn inside out 2. to cause to protrude by turning inside out —**e·vag'i·na'tion** *n.*

e·val·u·ate (i val'yoo wāt') *vt.* -at'ed, -at'ing [back-formation < *evaluation* < Fr. *évaluation* < *évaluer* < *é-* (L. *ex-*), out + *valuer*, to VALUE] 1. to find the value or amount of 2. to judge or determine the worth or quality of; appraise 3. *Math.* to find the numerical value of; express in numbers —SYN. see ESTIMATE —**e·val'u·a'tion** *n.* —**e·val'u·a'tive** *adj.*

Ev·an (ev'ən) [W., var. of JOHN] a masculine name

ev·a·nesce (ev'ə nes') *vi.* -nesced', -nesc'ing [L. *evanescere* < *e-*, out + *vanescere*, to vanish < *vanus*, VAIN] to fade from sight like mist or smoke; disappear; vanish

ev·a·nes·cence (-nes'ns) *n.* [ML. *evanescentia*: see ff.] 1. a fading from sight; vanishing 2. a tendency to fade from sight; evanescent quality; transitoriness

ev·a·nes·cent (-nes'nt) *adj.* [< L. *evanescens*, prp.: see EVANESCE] tending to fade from sight; vanishing; ephemeral —SYN. see TRANSIENT —**ev'a·nes'cent·ly** *adv.*

e·van·gel (i van'jəl) *n.* [ME. & OFr. *evangile* < L. *evangelium*, good news, in LL.(Ec.), gospel < Gr. *euangelion*, good news in NT., gospel) < *euangelos*, bringing good news < *eu-*, well + *angelos*, messenger] 1. the gospel 2. [E-] any of the four Gospels 3. [Gr. *euangelos*] an evangelist

e·van·gel·i·cal (ē'van jel'i k'l, ev'ən-) *adj.* [< LL.(Ec.) *evangelicus* < Gr. *euangelikos* < *euangelion* (see prec.) + -AL] 1. in, of, or according to the Gospels or the teaching of the New Testament 2. of those Protestant churches, as the Methodist and Baptist, that emphasize salvation by faith in the atonement of Jesus, and reject the efficacy of the sacraments and good works alone 3. of the Low Church party in the Church of England 4. same as EVANGELISTIC Also **e·van·gel'ic** —*n.* a member of an evangelical church —**e'van·gel'i·cal·ly** *adv.*

e·van·gel·i·cal·ism (-iz'm) *n.* 1. evangelical church doctrines 2. acceptance of such doctrines

E·van·ge·line (i van'jə lin, -lǐn) [Fr. *Évangeline* < LL.(Ec.) *evangelium*: see EVANGEL] a feminine name

e·van·gel·ism (-liz'm) *n.* [LGr.(Ec.) *euangelismos*] 1. a preaching of, or zealous effort to spread, the gospel, as in revival meetings 2. any zealous effort in propagandizing for a cause 3. same as EVANGELICALISM —**e·van'gel·is'tic** *adj.* —**e·van'gel·is'ti·cal·ly** *adv.*

e·van·gel·ist (-list) *n.* [ME. & OFr. *evangeliste* < LL.(Ec.) *evangelista* < Gr. *euangelistēs*, bringer of good news (in NT., evangelist): see EVANGEL] 1. [E-] any of the four writers of the Gospels; Matthew, Mark, Luke, or John 2. anyone who evangelizes; esp., a traveling preacher; revivalist

e·van·gel·ize (-līz') *vt.* -ized', -iz'ing [ME. *evangelisen* < OFr. *evangeliser* < LL.(Ec.) *evangelizare* < LGr.(Ec.) *euangelizein* < *euangelion*: see EVANGEL] 1. to preach the gospel to 2. to convert to Christianity —*vi.* to preach the gospel —**e·van'gel·i·za'tion** *n.*

e·van·ish (i van'ish) *vi.* [ME. *evanishen* < OFr. *evaniss-*, extended stem of *esvanir* < VL. *exvanire*, for L. *evanescere*, EVANESCE] [Poet.] same as VANISH

Ev·ans (ev'ənz) 1. Sir Arthur John, 1851–1941; Eng. archaeologist 2. Mary Ann, see George ELIOT 3. Maurice, 1901– ; U.S. actor, born in England

Ev·ans·ton (ev'ən stən) [after Dr. John *Evans*, local philanthropist] city in NE Ill., on Lake Michigan: suburb of Chicago: pop. 80,000

Ev·ans·ville (ev'ənz vil') [after Gen. R. M. *Evans*, who served in the War of 1812] city in SW Ind., on the Ohio River: pop. 139,000

e·vap·o·ra·ble (i vap'ər ə b'l) *adj.* [ML. *evaporabilis*] that can be evaporated —**e·vap'o·ra·bil'i·ty** *n.*

e·vap·o·rate (i vap'ə rāt') *vt.* -rat'ed, -rat'ing [ME. *evaporaten* < L. *evaporatus*, pp. of *evaporare* < *e-*, out, from + *vaporare*, to emit vapor < *vapor*, VAPOR] 1. to change (a liquid or solid) into vapor; drive out or draw off in the form of vapor 2. to remove moisture from (milk, vegetables, fruits, etc.) by heating or drying so as to get a concentrated product 3. *a)* to deposit (a metal, metallic salts, etc.) by sublimation *b)* to drive out (neutrons, electrons, etc.) —*vi.* 1. to become vapor; pass off in the form of vapor 2. to give off vapor 3. to disappear like vapor; vanish —**e·vap'o·ra'tion** *n.* —**e·vap'o·ra'tive** *adj.* —**e·vap'o·ra'tor** *n.*

☆evaporated milk unsweetened milk thickened by evaporation to about half its weight, and then canned and sterilized: cf. CONDENSED MILK

☆e·vap·o·trans·pi·ra·tion (i vap'ō tran'spə rā'shən) *n.* [EVAPO(RATION) + TRANSPIRATION] the total water loss

from the soil, including that by direct evaporation and that by transpiration from the surfaces of plants

e·va·sion (i vā′zhən) *n.* [ME. & OFr. < L. *evasio* < *evasus,* pp. of *evadere:* see EVADE] 1. an evading; specif., an avoiding of a duty, question, etc. by deceit or cleverness 2. a way of doing this; subterfuge

e·va·sive (i vā′siv) *adj.* [< L. *evasus* (see prec.) + -IVE] 1. tending or seeking to evade; not straightforward; tricky; equivocal 2. hard to catch, grasp, etc.; elusive —**e·va′sive·ly** *adv.* —**e·va′sive·ness** *n.*

Eve (ēv) [ME. < LL.(Ec.) *Eva, Heva* < Heb. *ḥawwāh,* lit. ? life, orig. ? serpent] 1. a feminine name: var. *Eva* 2. *Bible* Adam's wife, the first woman: Gen. 3:20

eve (ēv) *n.* [ME., var. of *even* < OE. *æfen,* EVENING] 1. [Poet.] evening 2. [*often* E-] the evening or day before a holiday [Christmas *Eve*] 3. the period immediately before some event [on the *eve* of victory]

e·vec·tion (i vek′shən) *n.* [L. *evectio,* a going up, carrying out < *evectus,* pp. of *evehere* < *e-,* out, from + *vehere,* to carry: see VEHICLE] a periodical variation in the motion of the moon in its orbit, caused by the attraction of the sun —**e·vec′tion·al** *adj.*

Eve·li·na (ev′ə lī′nə) *var. of* EVELINE

Eve·line (ev′ə lin′, -lin) [ONormFr. < *Aveline,* prob. ult. < Gmc.] a feminine name

Eve·lyn (ev′ə lin; *Brit. usually,* ēv′lin) 1. a feminine and masculine name: see EVELINE 2. **John,** 1620-1706; Eng. diarist

e·ven[1] (ē′vən, -v′n) *adj.* [ME. < OE. *efne, efen,* akin to G. *eben,* Goth. *ibus*] 1. flat; level; smooth [*even* country] 2. not irregular; not varying; uniform; constant [an *even* tempo] 3. calm; tranquil; serene; placid [an *even* disposition] 4. in the same plane or line; in line [water *even* with the rim] 5. equally balanced 6. *a)* owing and being owed nothing *b)* with neither a profit nor a loss 7. revenged for a wrong, insult, etc. 8. just; equitable; fair [an *even* exchange] 9. equal or identical in number, quantity, degree, score, etc. 10. exactly divisible by two: said of numbers, and opposed to ODD 11. exact [an *even* mile] —*adv.* 1. [Obs.] in an even manner 2. *used as an intensive or emphatic particle meaning: a)* though it may seem improbable; moreover; indeed; fully [*even* unto death, *even* a fool could understand] *b)* exactly; precisely; just; in no other way but [it happened *even* as I expected] *c)* just as; while [*even* as he spoke, she entered] *d)* still; yet: used in emphasizing a comparison [an *even* worse mistake] *e)* [Archaic] namely; particularly [one there was, *even* John] —*vt., vi.* to make, become, or be even; level (*off*); equalize or be equalized —SYN. see LEVEL, STEADY —☆**break even** [Colloq.] to finish as neither a winner nor a loser —**even if** despite the fact that; though —**e′ven·ly** *adv.* —**e′ven·ness** *n.*

e·ven[2] (ē′vən) *n.* [see EVE] [Poet. or Dial.] evening

e·ven·fall (-fôl′) *n.* [Poet.] twilight; dusk

e·ven·hand·ed (-han′did) *adj.* impartial; fair; just

eve·ning (ēv′niŋ) *n.* [ME. < OE. *æfnung, verbal n.* < *æfnian,* to grow toward evening < *æfen,* evening, akin to G. *abend,* orig. < IE. base **epi-, *opi-,* after, later (whence Gr. *epi,* L. *ob*): basic sense "later part of the day"] 1. the last part of the day; close of the day and early part of night; period between sunset or the last meal of the day and bedtime 2. in some parts of the South, in rural areas, and in parts of England, the period from noon through sunset and twilight 3. the last period, as of life, a career, etc. 4. a part of the night spent in a specified way [a musical *evening*] —*adj.* in, for, or of the evening

evening dress (or **clothes**) formal clothes worn on formal occasions in the evening

evening prayer *same as* EVENSONG

☆**eve·ning-prim·rose** (-prim′rōz′) *adj.* designating a family (Onagraceae) of plants growing chiefly in temperate America, including the fuchsia

☆**evening primrose** any of a genus (*Oenothera*) of plants of the evening-primrose family, with yellow, pink, or white flowers that open in the evening

eve·nings (-niŋz) *adv.* during every evening or most evenings

evening star a bright planet, esp. Venus, that can be seen in the western sky soon after sunset

even money equal stakes in betting, with no odds

e·ven·song (ē′vən sôŋ′) *n.* [ME. < OE. *æfensang:* see EVENING & SONG] 1. R.C.Ch. *same as* VESPERS 2. Anglican Church the worship service assigned to the evening 3. a song sung at evening 4. [Archaic] evening

e·ven-ste·ven, e·ven-ste·phen (ē′v′n stē′v′n) *adj.* [rhyming slang < EVEN[1] + STEVEN] [Colloq.] [*often* S-] *same as* EVEN[1] (senses 4-9): also **even steven, even stephen**

e·vent (i vent′) *n.* [OFr. < L. *eventus,* event, pp. of *evenire,* to happen < *e-,* out + *venire,* COME] 1. a happening or occurrence, esp. when important 2. a result; consequence; outcome 3. a particular contest or item in a program [the pole vault, high jump, and other *events*] —SYN. see OCCURRENCE —**in any event** no matter what happens; anyhow: also **at all events** —**in the event of** if there should happen to be; in case of —**in the event that** if it should happen than

e·ven-tem·pered (ē′vən tem′pərd) *adj.* not quickly angered or excited; placid; calm

e·vent·ful (i vent′fəl) *adj.* 1. full of outstanding events [an *eventful* year] 2. having an important outcome; momentous [an *eventful* conversation ever after] —**e·vent′ful·ly** *adv.* —**e·vent′ful·ness** *n.*

e·ven·tide (ē′vən tid′) *n.* [ME. < OE. *æfentid:* see EVENING & TIDE[1]] [Archaic or Poet.] evening

e·ven·tu·al (i ven′choo wəl) *adj.* [< L. *eventus* (see EVENT) + -AL] 1. [Archaic] contingent or possible 2. happening at the end of, or as a result of, a series of events; ultimate; final [*eventual* success]

e·ven·tu·al·i·ty (i ven′choo wal′ə tē) *n., pl.* -ties a possible event, outcome, or condition; contingency

e·ven·tu·al·ly (i ven′choo wəl ē, -chə lē) *adv.* [EVENTUAL + -LY[2]] finally; ultimately; in the end

☆**e·ven·tu·ate** (-choo wāt′) *vi.* -at′ed, -at′ing [< L. *eventus* (see EVENT) + -ATE[1]] to happen in the end; result (often with *in*)

ev·er (ev′ər) *adv.* [ME. < OE. *æfre,* prob. < WGmc. bases of OE. *a,* always, ever (see AYE[1]) + ? *feorr,* FAR] 1. at all times; always [lived happily *ever* after] 2. at any time [have you *ever* seen an eclipse?] 3. at all; by any chance; in any way [how can I *ever* repay you?] *Ever* is also used colloquially as an intensifier [was she *ever* tired!] —**ever and anon** (or **again**) [Archaic] now and then; occasionally —**ever so** [Colloq.] very; extremely —**for ever and a day** always: also **for ever and ever**

Ev·er·est (ev′ər ist, ev′rist), **Mount** peak of the Himalayas, on the border of Nepal & Tibet: highest known mountain in the world: 29,028 ft.

Ev·er·ett[1] (ev′ər it, ev′rit) [Du. *Evert, Everhart* < OFr. *Everart* < OHG. *Eburhart* < *ebur,* wild boar + *harto,* strong (see HARD): hence, lit., strong (as a) wild boar] 1. a masculine name 2. **Edward,** 1794-1865; U.S. statesman, orator, & scholar

Ev·er·ett[2] (ev′ər it, ev′rit) 1. [after Edward EVERETT] city in E Mass.: suburb of Boston: pop. 43,000 2. [after *Everett Colby,* son of a founder] port in NW Wash., on Puget Sound: pop. 54,000: see SEATTLE

☆**ev·er·glade** (ev′ər glād′) *n.* [< ? *ever*(lasting) *glades:* see GLADE] a tract of marshy land covered in places with tall grass; swampland —**the Everglades** large tract of swampland in S & SE Fla.: c. 100 mi. long, 50-75 mi. wide

THE EVERGLADES

Everglades National Park national park in the S part of the Everglades: wildlife refuge: c. 2,000 sq. mi.

ev·er·green (ev′ər grēn′) *adj.* having green leaves throughout the year: opposed to DECIDUOUS —*n.* 1. an evergreen plant or tree, including most conifers and many broad-leaved plants, as some rhododendrons, hollies, etc. 2. [*pl.*] the branches and twigs of evergreens, used for decoration

ev·er·last·ing (ev′ər las′tiŋ, -läs′-) *adj.* 1. never coming to an end; lasting forever; eternal 2. going on for a long time; lasting indefinitely; durable 3. going on too long or happening too often; seeming never to stop —*n.* 1. eternity 2. *a)* any of various plants, mostly of the composite family, whose blossoms keep their color and shape when dried; esp., an annual (*Xeranthemum annuum*) with pink, lilac, or white flowers *b)* the blossom of such a plant —**the Everlasting** God —**ev·er·last′ing·ly** *adv.* —**ev·er·last′ing·ness** *n.*

ev·er·more (-môr′) *adv.* [ME. *evermor,* earlier *efre ma* < OE. *æfre ma:* see EVER & MORE] 1. forever; constantly 2. [Archaic or Poet.] for all future time —**for evermore** forever; always

e·ver·si·ble (ē vur′sə b′l) *adj.* [< L. *eversus* (see ff.) + -IBLE] that can be everted

e·ver·sion (ē vur′zhən, -shən) *n.* [ME. & OFr. < L. *eversio* < *eversus,* pp. of *evertere*] an everting or being everted

e·vert (ē vurt′) *vt.* [L. *evertere* < *e-,* out + *vertere,* to turn: see VERSE] to turn outward or inside out, as an eyelid

e·ver·tor (-ər) *n.* a muscle that everts or rotates a part, esp. the foot, outward

ev·er·y (ev′rē; *occas.* -ər ē) *adj.* [ME. *everiche* < OE. *æfre ælc,* lit., ever each] 1. each, individually and separately; each, and including all [*every* man among you] 2. the fullest possible; all that there could be [given *every* chance to do the job] 3. each group or interval of (a specified number or

time) *[take a pill every three hours]* —**every now and then** from time to time; occasionally: also [Colloq.] **every so often** —**every other** each alternate, as the first, third, fifth, etc. —**every which way** [Colloq.] in every direction; in complete disorder

ev·er·y·bod·y (-bäd′ē, -bud′ē) *pron.* every person; everyone

ev·er·y·day (-dā′) *adj.* 1. daily *[one's everyday routine]* 2. suitable for ordinary days *[everyday shoes]* 3. usual; common *[an everyday occurrence]*

ev·er·y·one (-wən, -wun′) *pron.* every person; everybody

every one every person or thing of those named *[to remind every one of the students]*

ev·er·y·thing (-thing′) *pron.* 1. every thing; all things; all 2. all things pertinent to a specified matter 3. the most important thing *[money is everything to him]*

ev·er·y·where (-hwer′, -wer′) *adv.* in or to every place

e·vict (i vikt′) *vt.* [ME. *evicten* < L. *evictus*, pp. of *evincere*, EVINCE] 1. formerly, to recover (property) through court judgment or superior claim 2. to remove (a tenant) from leased premises by legal procedure, as for failure to pay rent —*SYN.* see EJECT —**e·vic′tion** *n.*

ev·i·dence (ev′ə dəns) *n.* [ME. < OFr. < L. *evidentia* < *evidens*, clear, evident < *e-*, from + *videns*, prp. of *videre*, to see: see WISE[1]] 1. the condition of being evident 2. something that makes another thing evident; indication; sign 3. something that tends to prove; ground for belief 4. *Law* something legally presented before a court, as a statement of a witness, an object, etc., which bears on or establishes the point in question: distinguished from TESTIMONY and PROOF: see also STATE'S EVIDENCE —*vt.* **-denced, -denc·ing** 1. to make evident; indicate; show 2. to bear witness to; attest —*SYN.* see PROOF —**in evidence** plainly visible or perceptible

ev·i·dent (-dənt, -dent′) *adj.* [ME. < OFr. < L. *evidens* (gen. *evidentis*): see EVIDENCE] easy to see or perceive; clear; obvious; plain; apparent —**ev′i·dent·ly** *adv.*

SYN.—**evident** and **apparent** apply to that which can be readily perceived or easily inferred, but **evident** implies the existence of external signs *[his evident disappointment]* and **apparent** suggests the use of deductive reasoning *[it's apparent he'll win]*; **manifest** applies to that which is immediately, often intuitively, clear to the understanding; **obvious** refers to that which is so noticeable or obtrusive that no one can fail to perceive it; **palpable** applies esp. to that which can be perceived through some sense other than that of sight *[palpable signs of fever]*; **clear** implies that there is no confusion or obscurity to hinder understanding *[clear proof]*; **plain** implies such simplicity or lack of complexity as to be easily perceptible *[the plain facts are these]*

ev·i·den·tial (ev′ə den′shəl) *adj.* 1. of, serving as, or based on evidence 2. providing, or having the nature of, evidence —**ev′i·den′tial·ly** *adv.*

e·vil (ē′v'l) *adj.* [ME. *ivel* < OE. *yfel*, akin to G. *übel* < IE. **upelo-** < base **upo-**, up from under, whence Sans. *upa*, toward, UP[1]] 1. *a)* morally bad or wrong; wicked; depraved *b)* resulting from or based on conduct regarded as immoral *[an evil reputation]* 2. causing pain or trouble; harmful; injurious 3. offensive or disgusting *[an evil odor]* 4. threatening or bringing misfortune; unlucky; disastrous; unfortunate *[an evil hour]* —*adv.* in an evil, wicked, or offensive way: now only in hyphenated compounds *[evil-hearted]* —*n.* 1. anything morally bad or wrong; wickedness; depravity; sin 2. anything that causes harm, pain, misery, disaster, etc. —*SYN.* see BAD[1] —**the Evil One** the Devil; Satan —**e′vil·ly** *adv.* —**e′vil·ness** *n.*

e·vil·do·er (-dʊ̄′ər) *n.* a person who does evil, esp. habitually —**e′vil·do′ing** *n.*

evil eye a look or stare which, in superstitious belief, is able to harm or bewitch the one stared at; also, the supposed power to cast such a look: with *the*

e·vil-mind·ed (-mīn′did) *adj.* having an evil mind or disposition; specif., *a)* malicious or wicked *b)* habitually putting an evil interpretation, esp. a salacious or prurient one, on even innocent things —**e′vil-mind′ed·ly** *adv.* —**e′vil-mind′ed·ness** *n.*

e·vince (i vins′) *vt.* **e·vinced′, e·vinc′ing** [L. *evincere*, to conquer, win one's point < *e-*, intens. + *vincere*, to conquer: see VICTOR] 1. to show plainly; indicate; make manifest; esp., to show that one has (a specified quality, feeling, etc.) 2. [Obs.] to overcome —**e·vin′ci·ble** *adj.*

e·vin·cive (i vin′siv) *adj.* serving to prove

e·vis·cer·ate (i vis′ə rāt′) *vt.* **-at·ed, -at·ing** [< L. *evisceratus*, pp. of *eviscerare* < *e-*, out + *viscera*, VISCERA] 1. to remove the viscera, or entrails, from; disembowel 2. to deprive of an essential part; take away the force, significance, etc. of 3. *Surgery* to remove the contents of (an organ) —*vi.* 1. to protrude through a surgical incision, as the viscera 2. to experience such a protrusion —**e·vis′cer·a′tion** *n.*

e·vi·ta·ble (ev′ə tə b'l) *adj.* [L. *evitabilis* < *evitare*, to shun < *e-*, from + *vitare*, to avoid] avoidable

ev·o·ca·ble (ev′ə kə b'l, i vō′kə b'l) *adj.* [Fr. *évocable*: see EVOKE] that can be evoked

ev·o·ca·tion (ev′ə kā′shən, ē′vō-) *n.* [ME. *evocacion* < L. *evocatio* < pp. of *evocare*] 1. an evoking, or calling forth 2. *same as* INDUCTION (sense 5)

e·voc·a·tive (i väk′ə tiv) *adj.* [L. *evocativus*] tending to evoke —**e·voc′a·tive·ly** *adv.* —**e·voc′a·tive·ness** *n.*

ev·o·ca·tor (ev′ə kāt′ər) *n.* [L.] a person who evokes

e·voke (i vōk′) *vt.* **e·voked′, e·vok′ing** [Fr. *évoquer* < L.

evocare < *e-*, out, from + *vocare*, to call < *vox* (gen. *vocis*), VOICE] 1. to call forth or summon (a spirit, demon, etc.), as by chanting magical words; conjure up 2. to draw forth or elicit (a particular mental image, reaction, etc.) —*SYN.* see EXTRACT

ev·o·lute (ev′ə loot′) *n.* [< L. *evolutus*: see ff.] *Geom.* a curve that is the locus of the center of curvature of another curve (called the *involute*); the envelope of the perpendiculars, or normals, of the involute

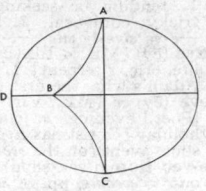

EVOLUTE
(ABC, evolute of ADC)

ev·o·lu·tion (ev′ə lōō′shən) *n.* [L. *evolutio*, an unrolling or opening < *evolutus*, pp. of *evolvere*: see EVOLVE] 1. an unfolding, opening out, or working out; process of development, as from a simple to a complex form, or of gradual, progressive change, as in a social and economic structure 2. a result or product of this; thing evolved 3. *a)* a movement that is part of a series or pattern *b)* a pattern produced, or seemingly produced, by such a series of movements *[the evolutions of a fancy skater]* 4. a setting free or giving off, as of gas in a chemical reaction 5. *Biol.* *a)* the development of a species, organism, or organ from its original or primitive state to its present or specialized state; phylogeny or ontogeny *b)* the theory, now generally accepted, that all species of plants and animals developed from earlier forms by hereditary transmission of slight variations in successive generations: see also DARWINIAN THEORY, LAMARCKISM, MUTATION, NATURAL SELECTION 6. *Math.* the extracting of a root from a given power: opposed to INVOLUTION 7. [Fr. *évolution*] *Mil.* any of various movements or maneuvers by which troops, ships, etc. change formation —**ev′o·lu′tion·al** *adj.* —**ev′o·lu′tion·al·ly** *adv.* —**ev′o·lu′tion·ar′y** *adj.*

ev·o·lu·tion·ist (-ist) *n.* 1. a person who accepts the principles of biological evolution 2. a person who believes in the possibility of political and social progress by gradual, peaceful steps —*adj.* 1. of the theory of evolution 2. of evolutionists —**ev′o·lu′tion·ism** *n.* —**ev′o·lu′tion·is′tic** *adj.* —**ev′o·lu′tion·is′ti·cal·ly** *adv.*

e·volve (i välv′) *vt.* **e·volved′, e·volv′ing** [L. *evolvere*, to roll out or forth < *e-*, out + *volvere*, to roll: see WALK] 1. to develop by gradual changes; unfold 2. to set free or give off (gas, heat, etc.) 3. to produce or change by evolution —*vi.* 1. to develop gradually by a process of growth and change ☆2. to become disclosed; unfold —**e·volve′ment** *n.*

e·vul·sion (i vul′shən) *n.* [ME. *evulsion* < L. *evulsio* < pp. of *evellere*, to pull out < *e-*, out + *vellere*, to pluck < IE. base **wel-**, to tear, injure, whence OE. *wæl*, slaughter] a pulling out by force, or uprooting

Ev·voi·a (ev′ē ə) large Greek island in the Aegean Sea, off the E coast of Greece: 1,492 sq. mi.; pop. 166,000

ev·zone (ev′zōn′) *n.* [< ModGr. *euzōnos* < Gr., well-equipped, lit., well-girdled < *eu-*, well (see EU-) + *zōnē*, a girdle: see ZONE] a member of a special unit of riflemen in the Greek army whose uniform includes a wide skirt

ewe (yōō; *dial.* yō) *n.* [ME. *ewe* < OE. *eowu*, fem. of *eow*, sheep, akin to G. dial *aue*, a ewe < IE. base **owi-s**, sheep, whence L. *ovis*] a female sheep

E·we (ā′wā) *n., pl.* **E′wes, E′we** 1. a member of an agricultural people of Togo and parts of Ghana and Dahomey 2. their Kwa language

Ew·ell (yōō′əl), **Richard Stod·dert** (städ′ərt) 1817–72; Confederate general in the Civil War

ewe-neck (-nek′) *n.* a thin, badly arched neck sometimes occurring in horses and dogs —**ewe′-necked′** (-nekt′) *adj.*

ew·er (yōō′ər) *n.* [ME. < Anglo-Fr. < OFr. *evier* < VL. **aquarium**, water pitcher: see AQUARIUM] a large water pitcher with a wide mouth

ex[1] (eks) *prep.* [L.] 1. without; exclusive of *[ex dividend, ex interest]* 2. out of; free of *[ex warehouse* means "free of charges until removed from the warehouse"]* ☆3. of (the specified college class), but not having graduated with it *[Wm. Jones, Yale ex '61]* —*n., pl.* **ex′es** [Colloq.] one's divorced husband or wife

ex[2] (eks) *n., pl.* **ex′es** the letter X, x

ex-[1] (iks, igz; *also occas.* for *1*, eks, egz; *for 2, always* eks) [ME. < OFr. or L., akin to Gr. *ex-*, *exō* < IE. base **eĝhs**, out] 1. *a prefix meaning:* *a)* forth, from, out *[expel, exert, exempt, excoriate]* *b)* beyond *[excess]* *c)* away from, out of *[expropriate, expatriate]* *d)* thoroughly *[exterminate]* *e)* upward *[exalt]* *f)* without, not having *[examinate]* It is assimilated to *ef-* before *f [efface]*; *e-* before *b, d, g, l, m, n, r*, and *v [educe, egress, elect, emit, etc.]*; often *ec-*, before *c* or *s [eccentric, ecstasy]*; and, in many words of French origin, *es- [escape]* 2. [orig. < L. phrases like *ex consule, ex magistro]* a prefix, used in hyphenated compounds, meaning former, previous, previously *[ex-president, ex-convict, ex-wife]*

ex-[2] (eks) *same as* EXO-: used before a vowel

Ex. Exodus

EWER

ex. 1. examined 2. example 3. except(ed) 4. exchange 5. excursion 6. executed 7. executive 8. export 9. express 10. extra 11. extract

ex·ac·er·bate (ig zas'ər bāt') *vt.* **-bat'ed, -bat'ing** [< L. *exacerbatus,* pp. of *exacerbare,* to exasperate, make angry < *ex-,* intens. + *acerbus,* bitter, harsh, sour: see ACERBITY] 1. to make more intense or sharp; aggravate (disease, pain, annoyance, etc.) 2. to exasperate; annoy; irritate; embitter —**ex·ac'er·ba'tion** *n.*

ex·act (ig zakt') *adj.* [L. *exactus* < pp. of *exigere,* to drive out, measure, determine < *ex-,* out + *agere,* to do: see ACT] 1. characterized by, requiring, or capable of accuracy of detail; very accurate; methodical; correct [an *exact* science] 2. not deviating in form or content; without variation; precise [an *exact* replica] 3. being the very (person or thing specified or understood) [the *exact* spot where I put it] 4. strict; severe; rigorous [an *exact* disciplinarian] —*vt.* [ME. *exacten*] 1. to force payment of; extort (with *from* or *of*) 2. to demand and get by authority or force; insist on (with *from* or *of*) 3. to call for; make necessary; require —*SYN.* see CORRECT, DEMAND, EXPLICIT —**ex·act'a·ble** *adj.* —**ex·act'ness** *n.* —**ex·ac'tor, ex·act'er** *n.*

ex·act·ing (-iŋ) *adj.* 1. making severe or excessive demands; not easily satisfied; strict [an *exacting* teacher] 2. demanding great care, patience, effort, etc.; arduous [an *exacting* job] —*SYN.* see ONEROUS —**ex·act'ing·ly** *adv.* —**ex·act'ing·ness** *n.*

ex·ac·tion (ig zak'shən) *n.* [ME. < OFr. < L. *exactio*] 1. an exacting, as of money, time, etc. 2. an excessive demand; extortion 3. an exacted fee, tax, etc.

ex·ac·ti·tude (ig zak'tə tōōd', -tyōōd') *n.* [Fr.] the quality of being exact; precision; accuracy

ex·act·ly (ig zakt'lē) *adv.* in an exact manner; accurately; correctly; precisely: also used as an affirmative reply, equivalent to "I agree," "quite true"

ex·ag·ger·ate (ig zaj'ə rāt') *vt.* **-at'ed, -at'ing** [< L. *exaggeratus,* pp. of *exaggerare,* to increase, exaggerate < *ex-,* out, up + *aggerare,* to heap up < *agger,* a heap < *aggerere,* to bring toward < *ad-* + *gerere,* to carry: see GESTURE] 1. to think, speak, or write of as greater than is really so; magnify beyond the fact; overstate 2. to increase or enlarge to an extreme or abnormal degree; overemphasize; intensify —*vi.* to give an exaggerated description or account —**ex·ag'ger·a'tion** *n.* —**ex·ag'ger·a'tive** *adj.* —**ex·ag'ger·a'tor** *n.*

ex·alt (ig zôlt') *vt.* [ME. *exalten* < OFr. *exalter* < LL.(chiefly Ec.) *exaltare* < *ex-,* out, up + *altus,* high: see OLD] to raise on high; elevate; lift up; specif., *a*) to raise in status, dignity, power, honor, wealth, etc. *b*) to praise; glorify; extol *c*) to fill with joy, pride, etc.; elate: used in the passive or in participial form *d*) to heighten or intensify the action or effect of —**ex·alt'er** *n.*

ex·al·ta·tion (eg'zôl tā'shən) *n.* [ME. *exaltacioun* < LL.(Ec.) *exaltatio*] 1. an exalting or being exalted 2. a feeling of great or excessive joy, pride, power, etc.; elation; rapture

ex·am (ig zam') *n.* [Colloq.] examination

ex·a·men (ig zā'men) *n.* [L.: see EXAMINE] an examination or detailed study; specif., *Eccles.* a methodical scrutiny of one's conscience

ex·am·i·na·tion (ig zam'ə nā'shən) *n.* [ME. *examinacioun* < OFr. *examination* < L. *examinatio:* see EXAMINE] 1. an examining or being examined; investigation; inspection; scrutiny; inquiry; testing 2. means or method of examining 3. a set of questions asked in testing or interrogating; test —**ex·am'i·na'tion·al** *adj.*

ex·am·i·na·to·ri·al (ig zam'ə nə tôr'ē əl) *adj.* of or having to do with an examiner or examination

ex·am·ine (ig zam'ən) *vt.* **-ined, -in·ing** [ME. *examinen* < OFr. *examiner* < L. *examinare,* to weigh, ponder, examine < *examen,* tongue of a balance, examination < *ex-,* out + base of *agere,* to lead, move: see ACT] 1. to look at or into critically or methodically in order to find out the facts, condition, etc. of; investigate; inspect; scrutinize; inquire into 2. to test by carefully questioning in order to find out the knowledge, skill, qualifications, etc. of (a student, witness, job applicant, etc.) —*SYN.* see SCRUTINIZE —**ex·am'i·na·ble** *adj.*

ex·am·i·nee (ig zam'ə nē') *n.* a person being examined; candidate for examination

ex·am·in·er (ig zam'ə nər) *n.* a person who examines; specif. one whose work is examining records, people, etc.: also **ex·am'i·nant** (-nənt)

ex·am·ple (ig zam'p'l, -zäm'-) *n.* [ME. & OFr. < L. *exemplum,* sample, example < *eximere,* to take out < *ex-,* out + *emere,* to buy < IE. base *em-,* to take, whence Lith. *imù*] 1. something selected to show the nature or character of the rest; single part or unit used as a sample; typical instance 2. a case, punishment, etc. that serves as a warning or caution [to fine a speeder as an *example* to others] 3. a person or thing to be imitated; model; pattern; precedent 4. a problem, as in mathematics, designed to illustrate a principle or method —*vt.* **-pled, -pling** [Obs. except in the passive] to exemplify —*SYN.* see INSTANCE, MODEL —**set an example** to behave so as to be a pattern or

model for others to imitate —**without example** having no precedent

ex·an·i·mate (ig zan'ə mit) *adj.* [L. *exanimatus,* pp. of *exanimare,* to deprive of air, kill < *ex-,* out of + *anima,* air, spirit: see ANIMAL] 1. dead; inanimate 2. without animation; spiritless; inert

ex·an·them (ek san'thəm) *n.* [< LL. *exanthema* < Gr. *exanthēma,* efflorescence, eruption < *exanthein,* to bloom < *ex-,* out + *anthein,* to flower < *anthos:* see ANTHO-] 1. a skin eruption or rash occurring in certain infectious diseases, as measles 2. an infectious disease characterized by such eruptions Also **ex'an·the'ma** (ek'san thē'mə), *pl.* **-mas, -ma·tas** (-them'ə təz, -thē'mə təz)

ex·arch¹ (ek'särk) *n.* [LL. *exarchus,* overseer of monasteries < Gr. *exarchos,* leader, chief (in LGr., prefect, bishop): see EX-¹ & -ARCH] 1. a governor of an outlying province in the ancient Byzantine Empire 2. the supreme head of the independent Orthodox Church of Bulgaria 3. *Orthodox Eastern Ch.* orig., an archbishop, or patriarch; later, a bishop or other clergyman serving as a patriarch's deputy or legate —**ex'arch'al** *adj.*

ex·arch² (ek'särk) *adj.* [< EX-¹ + Gr. *archē,* beginning] *Bot.* having the primary xylem maturing from the outer part, as of a stem, toward the center

ex·arch·ate (ek'sär'kāt, -kit) *n.* [ML. *exarchatus*] the position, rank, or province of an exarch: also **ex'arch'y** (-kē)

ex·as·per·ate¹ (ig zas'pə rāt') *vt.* **-at'ed, -at'ing** [< L. *exasperatus,* pp. of *exasperare* < *ex-,* out, from + *asperare,* to roughen < *asper,* rough: see ASPERITY] 1. to irritate or annoy very much; make angry; vex 2. [Now Rare] to intensify (a feeling, disease, etc.); aggravate —*SYN.* see IRRITATE

ex·as·per·ate² (-rit) *adj.* [< L. *exasperatus:* see prec.] 1. [Archaic] exasperated 2. *Bot.* having rough and prickly skin

ex·as·per·a·tion (ig zas'pə rā'shən) *n.* an exasperating or being exasperated; great irritation or annoyance

Ex·cal·i·bur (cks kal'ə bər) *n.* [ME. < OFr. *Escalibor* < ML. *Caliburnus* < Celt.] *Arthurian Legend* King Arthur's sword: in one version of the legend, he drew it out of a stone; in another, it was given to him by Vivian, the Lady of the Lake

ex ca·the·dra (eks' kə thē'drə, -kath'l drə) [ModL., lit., from the chair < L. *ex,* from + *cathedra,* CHAIR, esp. of a teacher or, in LL.(Ec.), of a bishop] with the authority that comes from one's rank or office: often specif. with reference to papal pronouncements, on matters of faith or morals, that have authoritative finality

ex·ca·vate (eks'kə vāt') *vt.* **-vat'ed, -vat'ing** [< L. *excavatus,* pp. of *excavare* < *ex-,* out + *cavare,* to make hollow < *cavus,* hollow: see CAVE¹] 1. to make a hole or cavity in, as by digging; hollow out 2. to form by hollowing out; dig [to *excavate* a tunnel] 3. to uncover or expose by digging; unearth [to *excavate* ancient ruins] 4. to dig out (earth, soil, etc.)

ex·ca·va·tion (eks'kə vā'shən) *n.* [L. *excavatio*] 1. an excavating or being excavated 2. a hole or hollow made by excavating 3. something unearthed by excavating —*SYN.* see HOLE

ex·ca·va·tor (eks'kə vāt'ər) *n.* a person or thing that excavates; specif., a steam shovel, dredge, etc.

ex·ceed (ik sēd') *vt.* [ME. *exceden* < OFr. *exceder* < L. *excedere* < *ex-,* out, beyond + *cedere,* to go] 1. to go or be beyond (a limit, limiting regulation, measure, etc.) [to *exceed* a speed limit] 2. to be more than or greater than; surpass; outdo [to *exceed* one's expectations] —*vi.* to surpass others, as in a quality or quantity; be outstanding

ex·ceed·ing (-iŋ) *adj.* surpassing; extraordinary; extreme —*adv.* [Archaic] *same as* EXCEEDINGLY

ex·ceed·ing·ly (-iŋ lē) *adv.* extremely; to a great degree; extraordinarily

ex·cel (ik sel') *vi., vt.* **-celled', -cel'ling** [ME. *excellen* < OFr. *exceller* < L. *excellere,* to raise, surpass, excel < *ex-,* out of, from + *-cellere,* to rise, project < IE. base *kel-,* to project, whence HILL, Gr. *kolophōn*] to be better or greater than, or superior to (another or others)

SYN.—**excel** implies superiority in some quality, skill, achievement, etc. over all or over the one (or ones) specified [to *excel* at chess]; **surpass** implies a going beyond (someone or something specified) in degree, amount, or quality [no one *surpasses* him in generosity]; **transcend** suggests a surpassing to an extreme degree [it *transcends* all understanding]; **outdo** implies a going beyond someone else or a previous record in performance [he will not be *outdone* in bravery]

ex·cel·lence (ek's'l əns) *n.* [ME. < OFr. < L. *excellentia* < prp. of *excellere*] 1. the fact or condition of excelling; superiority; surpassing goodness, merit, etc. 2. something in which a person or thing excels; particular virtue 3. [E-] *same as* EXCELLENCY

ex·cel·len·cy (-ən sē) *n., pl.* **-cies** [ME. *excellencie* < L. *excellentia*] 1. [E-] a title of honor applied to various persons of high position, as an ambassador, bishop, governor, etc. (with *His, Her,* or *Your*) 2. *same as* EXCELLENCE

ex·cel·lent (-ənt) *adj.* [ME. < OFr. < L. *excellens*, prp. of *excellere*, EXCEL] **1.** outstandingly good of its kind; of exceptional merit, virtue, etc. **2.** [Obs.] excelling; surpassing —**ex′cel·lent·ly** *adv.*

☆**ex·cel·si·or** (ek sel′sē ôr′; *for n.* ik sel′sē ər) *adj., interj.* [L., compar. of *excelsus*, lofty, high < pp. of *excellere*, EXCEL: *n.* < orig. use as trademark] higher; always upward: used as a motto (as on the New York State seal) —*n.* long, thin wood shavings used for packing breakable things or as stuffing in some furniture

ex·cept (ik sept′) *vt.* [ME. *excepten* < OFr. *excepter* < L. *exceptare*, to take out, except < *exceptus*, pp. of *excipere* < *ex-*, out + *capere*, to take] to leave out or take out; make an exception of; exclude; omit —*vi.* to take exception (with *to* or *against*); object [*to except* to a remark] —*prep.* [ME. < L. *exceptus*] leaving out; other than; but [*to* everyone *except* me] —*conj.* **1.** [Archaic] unless **2.** [Colloq.] were it not that; only [I′d quit *except* I need the money] —**except for** if it were not for

ex·cept·ing (-iŋ) *prep., conj. same as* EXCEPT

ex·cep·tion (ik sep′shən) *n.* [ME. *excepcioun* < OFr. *exception* < L. *exceptio*] **1.** an excepting or being excepted; omission; exclusion **2.** anything that is excepted; specif., *a)* a case to which a rule, general principle, etc. does not apply *b)* a person or thing different from or treated differently from others of the same class **3.** objection or opposition; specif., *Law* a formal objection or reservation to court action or opinion in the course of a trial —**take exception 1.** to object; demur **2.** to resent something; feel offended —**the exception proves the rule** the exception tests the rule: often used to mean "the exception establishes the rule"

ex·cep·tion·a·ble (-ə b′l) *adj.* liable to exception; open to objection —**ex·cep′tion·a·bly** *adv.*

ex·cep·tion·al (-əl) *adj.* **1.** constituting, or occurring as, an exception; not ordinary or average; esp., much above average in quality, ability, etc. [*exceptional* talents] ☆**2.** needing special attention or presenting a special problem, as in education, because mentally gifted or, esp., because mentally, physically, or emotionally handicapped —**ex·cep′tion·al′i·ty** (-al′ə tē) *n., pl.* -**ties** —**ex·cep′tion·al·ly** *adv.*

ex·cep·tion·al·ism (-əl iz′m) *n.* the fact or state of being an exception to some rule or general principle

ex·cep·tive (ik sep′tiv) *adj.* [ML. *exceptivus*] **1.** of, containing, or forming an exception **2.** [Now Rare] inclined to take exception; captious

ex·cerpt (ik surpt′; *also, and for n. always,* ek′surpt′) *vt.* [< L. *excerptus*, pp. of *excerpere*, to pick out, choose < *ex-*, out + *carpere*, to pick, pluck < IE. *kerp-* < base *(s)ker-*, to cut, scrape, whence HARVEST] to select, take out, or quote (passages from a book, etc.); extract —*n.* a passage selected or quoted from a book, article, etc.; extract —**ex·cerp′tion** *n.*

ex·cess (ik ses′; *also, and for adj. usually,* ek′ses′) *n.* [ME. & OFr. *exces* < L. *excessus* < pp. of *excedere:* see EXCEED] **1.** action or conduct that goes beyond the usual, reasonable, or lawful limit **2.** lack of moderation; intemperance; overindulgence **3.** an amount or quantity greater than is necessary, desirable, usable, etc.; too much; superfluity **4.** the amount or degree by which one thing exceeds another; remainder; surplus —*adj.* more than usual; extra; surplus [*excess* profits] —**in excess of** more than —**to excess** to too great an extent or degree; too much

ex·ces·sive (ik ses′iv) *adj.* [ME. & OFr. *excessif* < ML. *excessivus*] characterized by excess; being too much or too great; immoderate; inordinate —**ex·ces′sive·ly** *adv.* —**ex·ces′sive·ness** *n.*

SYN.—**excessive** applies to that which goes beyond what is proper, right, or usual [*excessive* demands]; **exorbitant** is applied to that which is unreasonably excessive and often connotes a greedy desire for more than is just or due [*exorbitant* prices]; **extravagant** and **immoderate** both imply excessiveness resulting from a lack of restraint or of prudence [*extravagant* praise, *immoderate* laughter]; **inordinate** implies a going beyond the orderly limits of convention or the bounds of good taste [*his inordinate* pride]

ex·change (iks chānj′) *vt.* -**changed′**, -**chang′ing** [ME. *eschaungen* < OFr. *eschangier* < VL. *excambiare:* see EX-¹ & CHANGE] **1.** *a)* to give, hand over, or transfer (for another thing in return) *b)* to receive or give another thing for (something returned) **2.** to give and receive (equivalent or similar things); interchange [*to exchange* gifts] **3.** to give up for a substitute or alternative [*to exchange* honor for wealth] —*vi.* **1.** to make an exchange; barter; trade **2.** *Finance* to pass in exchange [*currency* that *exchanges* at par] —*n.* **1.** a giving or taking of one thing for another; trade; barter **2.** a giving to one another of similar things [*an exchange* of greetings] **3.** the substituting of one thing for another [*an exchange* of tears for smiles] **4.** a thing given or received in exchange **5.** a place for exchanging; esp., a place where trade is carried on in securities or commodities by brokers, merchants, etc. [*a stock exchange*] ☆**6.** a central office, or a system operated by it, providing telephone communication in a community or in part of a city: formerly identified by an assigned call name **7.** *Commerce, Finance a)* the payment of debts by negotiable drafts or bills of exchange, without actual transfer of money *b)* a bill of exchange *c)* a fee paid for settling accounts or collecting a draft, bill of exchange, etc. *d)* an exchanging of a sum of money of one country or of a depreciated issue for the equivalent in the money of another country or of a current issue *e)* the rate of exchange; value of one currency in terms of the other; difference in value between currencies *f)* [*pl.*] the checks, drafts, etc. presented for exchange and settlement between banks in a clearinghouse **8.** *Law* a contract by which parties agree to exchange one thing for another —*adj.* **1.** exchanged; interchanged [*an exchange* student] **2.** having to do with an exchange [*an exchange* broker] —**ex·change′a·bil′i·ty** *n.* **ex·change′a·ble** *adj.* —**ex·chang′er** *n.*

exchange rate the ratio of the value of one currency in relation to the value of another

ex·cheq·uer (iks chek′ər, eks′chek ər) *n.* [ME. *escheker*, lit., chessboard, court of revenue, treasury < OFr. *eschequier:* see CHECKER¹] **1.** [E-] *a)* under the Norman kings of England, an administrative and judicial state department in charge of revenue: so called from a table marked into squares, on which accounts of revenue were kept with counters *b)* later, the British Court of Exchequer, which had jurisdiction over all cases relating to government revenue, now merged in the Queen's Bench Division of the High Court of Justice *c)* [*often* E-] the British state department in charge of the national revenue **2.** the funds in the British treasury **3.** a treasury, as of a country or organization **4.** money in one's possession; funds; finances

ex·cide (ik sīd′) *vt.* -**cid′ed**, -**cid′ing** [L. *excidere* < *ex-*, out + *caedere*, to cut: see -CIDE] to cut out

ex·cip·i·ent (ik sip′ē ənt) *n.* [< L. *excipiens*, prp. of *excipere:* see EXCEPT] *Pharmacy* any of various inert substances added to a prescription to give the desired consistency or form

ex·cis·a·ble (ik sī′zə b′l, ek′sī-) *adj.* **1.** subject to an excise tax **2.** that can be excised, or cut out

ex·cise¹ (ek′sīz, -sīs; *for v.* ik sīz′) *n.* [altered (after ff.) < earlier *accise* < MDu. *accijs*, earlier *assijs* < OFr. *assise:* see ASSIZE] **1.** orig., any tax **2.** a tax or duty on the manufacture, sale, or consumption of various commodities within a country, as liquor, tobacco, etc.: also **excise tax 3.** a fee paid for a license to carry on certain occupations, sports, etc. —*vt.* -**cised′**, -**cis′ing** to put an excise on

ex·cise² (ik sīz′) *vt.* -**cised′**, -**cis′ing** [< L. *excisus*, pp. of *excidere:* see EXCISE] to remove, as a tumor, by cutting out or away —**ex·ci′sion** (-sizh′ən) *n.*

ex·cise·man (ik sīz′mən) *n., pl.* -**men** (-mən) in Great Britain, a government official who collects excises and enforces the laws concerning them

ex·cit·a·ble (ik sīt′ə b′l) *adj.* **1.** that is easily excited **2.** *Physiol.* capable of responding to the proper stimulus —**ex·cit′a·bil′i·ty** *n.* —**ex·cit′a·bly** *adv.*

ex·cit·ant (-ənt) *adj.* [L. *excitans*, prp. of *excitare:* see EXCITE] stimulating —*n.* a stimulant

ex·ci·ta·tion (ek′sī tā′shən, -si-) *n.* [ME. *excitacioun* < LL. *excitatio*] an exciting or being excited (esp. in senses 4, 5, 6)

ex·cit·a·tive (ik sīt′ə tiv) *adj.* [ML. *excitativus*] exciting or tending to excite: also **ex·cit′a·to′ry** (-ə tôr′ē)

ex·cite (ik sīt′) *vt.* -**cit′ed**, -**cit′ing** [ME. *exciten* < OFr. *exciter* < L. *excitare*, to call forth, excite, freq. of *exciere*, to call forth < *ex-*, out + pp. of *ciere*, to call, summon: see CITE] **1.** to put into motion or activity; stir up [*tapping* on the hive *excited* the bees] **2.** to call forth; arouse; provoke [the rumors *excited* her curiosity] **3.** to arouse the feelings or passions of [the news *excited* us] **4.** *Elec. a)* to supply electric current to (the field winding of a motor, generator, or other device); also, to produce in this way a magnetic field in *b)* to supply a signal to (any stage of a vacuum-tube or transistor circuit) **5.** *Physics* to raise (a nucleus, atom, etc.) to a higher energy state **6.** *Physiol.* to produce or increase the response of (an organism, organ, tissue, etc.) to a proper stimulus —*SYN.* see PROVOKE

ex·cit·ed (-id) *adj.* **1.** emotionally aroused; agitated **2.** *Physics* in a state of excitation —**ex·cit′ed·ly** *adv.*

ex·cite·ment (-mənt) *n.* [ME. < OFr.] **1.** an exciting or being excited; agitation **2.** something that excites

ex·cit·er (-ər) *n.* **1.** a person or thing that excites **2.** *Elec. a)* a small generator that provides field current for a large generator or motor *b)* an oscillator that provides the carrier frequency voltage driving the various stages, as in a radio transmitter

ex·cit·ing (-iŋ) *adj.* causing excitement or agitation; stirring, thrilling, etc. —**ex·cit′ing·ly** *adv.*

ex·ci·tor (-ər) *n.* [ME. *exciter*] **1.** *same as* EXCITER **2.** *Physiol.* a nerve which, when stimulated, causes increased activity of the part that it supplies

ex·claim (iks klām′) *vi., vt.* [Fr. *exclamer* < L. *exclamare* < *ex-*, out + *clamare*, to cry, shout: see CLAMOR] to cry out; speak or say suddenly and vehemently, as in surprise, anger, etc. —**ex·claim′er** *n.*

ex·cla·ma·tion (eks′klə mā′shən) *n.* [ME. *exclamacioun* < L. *exclamatio*] **1.** the act of exclaiming; sudden, vehement utterance; outcry **2.** something exclaimed; exclamatory word or phrase; interjection

☆**exclamation mark** (or **point**) a mark (!) used after a word or sentence in writing or printing to express surprise, strong emotion, determination, etc.

ex·clam·a·to·ry (iks klam'ə tôr'ē) *adj.* [< L. *exclamatus*, pp. of *exclamare* (see EXCLAIM) + -ORY] of, containing, expressing, or using exclamation

ex·clave (eks'klāv) *n.* [EX-¹ + (EN)CLAVE] a territory (of a nearby specified country) surrounded by foreign territory [East Prussia was an *exclave* of Germany]: distinguished from ENCLAVE

ex·clo·sure (iks klō'zhər) *n.* [EX-¹ + (EN)CLOSURE] an area protected against the entrance of animals, etc.

ex·clude (iks klōōd') *vt.* -clud'ed, -clud'ing [ME. *excluden* < L. *excludere* < *ex-*, out + *claudere*, CLOSE²] 1. to refuse to admit, consider, include, etc.; shut out; keep from entering, happening, or being; reject; bar 2. to put out; force out; expel —**ex·clud'a·ble** *adj.* —**ex·clud'er** *n.*
SYN.—**exclude** implies a keeping out or prohibiting of that which is not yet in [to *exclude* someone from membership]; **debar** connotes the existence of some barrier, as legal authority or force, which excludes someone from a privilege, right, etc. [to *debar* certain groups from voting]; **disbar** refers only to the expulsion of a lawyer from the group of those who are permitted to practice law; **eliminate** implies the removal of that which is already in, usually connoting its undesirability or irrelevancy [to *eliminate* waste products]; **suspend** refers to the removal, usually temporary, of someone from some organization, institution, etc., as for the infraction of some rule [to *suspend* a student from school] —ANT. admit, include

ex·clu·sion (-klōō'zhən) *n.* [ME. *exclusioun* < L. *exclusio* < pp. of *excludere*] 1. an excluding or being excluded 2. a thing excluded —**to the exclusion of** so as to keep out, bar, etc. —**ex·clu'sion·ar·y** *adj.*

ex·clu·sion·ist (-ist) *n.* a person in favor of excluding another or others, as from some privilege —*adj.* of, favoring, or causing exclusion —**ex·clu'sion·ism** *n.*

exclusion principle *same as* PAULI EXCLUSION PRINCIPLE

ex·clu·sive (iks klōō'siv) *adj.* [ML. *exclusivus* < L. *exclusus*, pp. of *excludere*] 1. excluding or tending to exclude all others; shutting out other considerations, happenings, existences, etc. [an *exclusive* interest in sports] 2. excluding all but what is specified ["only" is an *exclusive* particle] 3. given or belonging to no other; not shared or divided; sole [an *exclusive* right to sell something] 4. a) excluding certain people or groups, as for social or economic reasons [an *exclusive* club] b) snobbish; undemocratic 5. dealing only in costly items [an *exclusive* shop] 6. being the only one of its kind [an *exclusive* dress] —*n.* something exclusive; specif., a news item, feature article, etc. which only one newspaper or other periodical is carrying —**exclusive of** not including or allowing for; ignoring [the cost *exclusive* of taxes] —**ex·clu'sive·ly** *adv.* —**ex·clu'sive·ness** *n.*

ex·clu·siv·i·ty (eks'klōō siv'ə tē) *n.* the condition or practice of being exclusive; esp., clannishness or isolationism: also **ex·clu'siv·ism** —**ex·clu'siv·ist** *n., adj.* —**ex·clu'siv·is'tic** *adj.*

ex·cog·i·tate (eks käj'ə tāt') *vt.* -tat'ed, -tat'ing [< L. *excogitatus*, pp. of *excogitare*: see EX-¹ & COGITATE] 1. to think out carefully and fully 2. to contrive, devise, or invent by such thought —**ex·cog'i·ta'tion** *n.* —**ex·cog'i·ta'tive** *adj.*

ex·com·mu·ni·cate (eks'kə myōō'nə kāt'; *for adj. and n., usually* -kit) *vt.* -cat'ed, -cat'ing [ME. *excommunicaten* < LL.(Ec.) *excommunicatus*, pp. of *excommunicare*: see EX-¹ & COMMUNICATE] to exclude, by an act of ecclesiastical authority, from the sacraments, rights, and privileges of a church; censure by cutting off from communion with a church —*adj.* excommunicated —*n.* an excommunicated person —**ex'com·mu'ni·ca'tion** *n.* —**ex'com·mu'ni·ca'tive** (-kāt'iv, -kə tiv) *adj.* —**ex'com·mu'ni·ca'tor** *n.* —**ex'com·mu'ni·ca·to'ry** (-kə tôr'ē) *adj.*

ex·co·ri·ate (ik skôr'ē āt') *vt.* -at'ed, -at'ing [ME. *excoriaten* < L. *excoriatus*, pp. of *excoriare* < *ex-*, out, off + *corium*, the skin: see CORIUM] 1. to strip, scratch, or rub off the skin of; flay, abrade, chafe, etc. 2. to denounce harshly —**ex·co'ri·a'tion** *n.*

ex·cre·ment (eks'krə mənt) *n.* [Fr. *excrément* < L. *excrementum*, that which is sifted out, refuse < *excretus*: see EXCRETE] waste matter from the bowels; feces —**ex'cre·men'tal** (-men't'l), **ex'cre·men·ti'tious** (-men tish'əs) *adj.*

ex·cres·cence (iks kres'ns) *n.* [ME. < OFr. < L. *excrescentia*, excrescences < *excrescere*, to grow out < *ex-*, out + *crescere*, to grow: see CRESCENT] 1. [Now Rare] a normal outgrowth; natural appendage, as a fingernail 2. an abnormal or disfiguring outgrowth or addition, as a bunion

ex·cres·cen·cy (-'n sē) *n.* 1. the condition of being excrescent 2. *pl.* -**cies** *same as* EXCRESCENCE

ex·cres·cent (-'nt) *adj.* [ME. < L. *excrescens*, prp. of *excrescere*] 1. forming an excrescence; growing abnormally; superfluous 2. *Phonet.* designating or of an epenthetic sound or letter in a word, as the unhistorical *b* in *mumble* or the extra syllable in the pronunciation (ath'ə lēt') for *athlete*

ex·cre·ta (eks krēt'ə) *n.pl.* [L., neut. pl. of *excretus*] waste matter excreted from the body, esp. sweat or urine —**ex·cre'tal** *adj.*

ex·crete (iks krēt') *vt., vi.* -cret'ed, -cret'ing [< L. *excretus*, pp. of *excernere*, to sift out < *ex-*, out of + *cernere*, to sift

(see CERTAIN)] 1. to separate (waste matter) from the blood or tissue and eliminate from the body, as through the kidneys or sweat glands 2. *Bot.* to eliminate (waste matter) from the cells

ex·cre·tion (-krē'shən) *n.* [VL. *excretio*] 1. the act or process of excreting 2. waste matter excreted; sweat, urine, etc.

ex·cre·to·ry (eks'krə tôr'ē) *adj.* [VL. *excretorius*] of or for excretion —*n., pl.* -ries an excretory organ

ex·cru·ci·ate (iks krōō'shē āt') *vt.* -at'ed, -at'ing [< L. *excruciatus*, pp. of *excruciare* < *ex-*, intens. + *cruciare*, to torture, crucify < *crux* (gen. *crucis*), CROSS] 1. to cause intense bodily pain to; torture 2. to subject to mental anguish; torment —**ex·cru'ci·a'tion** *n.*

ex·cru·ci·at·ing (-āt'iŋ) *adj.* 1. causing intense physical or mental pain; agonizing 2. intense or extreme [with *excruciating* attention to detail] —**ex·cru'ci·at'ing·ly** *adv.*

ex·cul·pate (eks'kəl pāt', ik skul'pāt) *vt.* -pat'ed, -pat'ing [< L. *ex*, out + *culpatus*, pp. of *culpare*, to blame < *culpa*, fault] to free from blame; declare or prove guiltless —**ex·cul·pa·ble** (ik skul'pə b'l) *adj.* —**ex'cul·pa'tion** *n.* —**ex·cul'pa·to'ry** *adj.*

ex·cur·rent (ek skur'ənt) *adj.* [L. *excurrens*, prp. of *excurrere*, to run out, project < *ex-*, out + *currere*, to run: see CURRENT] 1. running out or forth 2. *Bot.* a) projecting beyond the tip, as the midrib of certain leaves b) having an undivided projecting main stem, as fir trees 3. *Zool.* of ducts, tubes, or passages whose contents flow outward

ex·cur·sion (iks kur'zhən) *n.* [L. *excursio*, a running out or forth < *excursus*, pp. of *excurrere*: see prec.] 1. a short trip taken with the intention of returning to the point of departure; short journey, as for pleasure; jaunt 2. a round trip (on a train, bus, ship, etc.) at reduced rates, usually with limits set on the dates of departure and return 3. a group taking such a trip or journey 4. a deviation or digression 5. [Obs.] a military sortie; raid 6. *Physics* a) a single movement outward from the mean position in an oscillating or alternating motion b) the distance involved in such a movement c) a sudden, very rapid rise in the neutron flux and power of a nuclear reactor 7. *Med.* the extent of movement from a central position, as of the eyes from a midmost location or of the chest during respiration —*adj.* of or for an excursion [*excursion* rates]

ex·cur·sion·ist (-ist) *n.* a person making an excursion

ex·cur·sive (ik skur'siv) *adj.* rambling; desultory; digressive —**ex·cur'sive·ly** *adv.* —**ex·cur'sive·ness** *n.*

ex·cur·sus (-səs) *n., pl.* -**sus·es** or -**sus** [L. *excursus*, a running forth, digression, pp. of *excurrere*: see EXCURRENT] 1. a detailed discussion of some point in a work, added as an appendix 2. a digression, as in a literary work

ex·cus·a·ble (ik skyōō'zə b'l) *adj.* [ME. < OFr. < *excusabilis*] that can be excused; pardonable; justifiable —**ex·cus'a·bly** *adv.*

ex·cus·a·to·ry (-tôr'ē) *adj.* [ML. *excusatorius*] of or containing an excuse or excuses; apologetic

ex·cuse (ik skyōōz'; *for n.* -skyōōs') *vt.* -cused', -cus'ing [ME. *excusen* < OFr. *escuser* & L. *excusare*, to free from a charge < *ex-*, from + *causa*, a charge: see CAUSE] 1. to try to free (a person) of blame; seek to exonerate 2. to try to minimize or pardon (a fault); apologize or give reasons for 3. to consider (an offense or fault) as not important; overlook; pardon [*excuse* my rudeness] 4. to release from an obligation, duty, promise, etc. 5. to permit to leave 6. to serve as an explanation or justification for; justify; exculpate; absolve [a selfish act that nothing will *excuse*] —*n.* 1. a plea in defense of or explanation for some action or behavior; apology 2. a release from obligation, duty, etc. 3. something that excuses; extenuating or justifying factor 4. a pretended reason for conduct; pretext —**a poor** (or **bad**, etc.) **excuse for** a very inferior example of —**excuse oneself** 1. to ask that one's fault be overlooked; apologize 2. to ask for permission to leave —**make one's excuses** to express one's regret over not being able to attend a social gathering, etc.

ex·ec (ig zek') *n.* [Colloq.] an executive officer

exec. 1. executive 2. executor

ex·e·cra·ble (ek'si krə b'l) *adj.* [L. *execrabilis*] 1. deserving to be execrated; abominable; detestable 2. very inferior; of poorest quality —**ex'e·cra·bly** *adv.*

ex·e·crate (-krāt') *vt.* -crat'ed, -crat'ing [< L. *execratus*, pp. of *execrare*, to curse < *ex-*, out + *sacrare*, to consecrate < *sacer*, sacred] 1. orig., to call down evil upon; curse 2. to speak abusively or contemptuously of; denounce scathingly 3. to loathe; detest; abhor —*vi.* to curse —SYN. see CURSE —**ex'e·cra'tive, ex'e·cra·to'ry** (-krə tôr'ē) *adj.* —**ex'e·cra'tor** *n.*

ex·e·cra·tion (ek'si krā'shən) *n.* [L. *execratio*: see prec.] 1. the act of execrating; a cursing, denouncing, etc. 2. a curse 3. a person or thing cursed or detested

ex·ec·u·tant (ig zek'yə tənt) *n.* [Fr. *exécutant*, prp. of *exécuter*: see ff.] a person who gets something done; esp., a performer, as on a musical instrument

ex·e·cute (eks'ə kyōōt') *vt., vi.* -cut'ed, -cut'ing [ME. *executen* < OFr. *executer*, back-formation < *executeur*: see EXECUTOR] 1. to follow out or carry out; do; perform; fulfill

[to execute another's orders] **2.** to carry into effect; administer (laws, etc.) **3.** to put to death in accordance with a legally imposed sentence **4.** to create or produce in accordance with an idea, plan, blueprint, etc. *[to execute* a statue in marble] **5.** to perform (a piece of music, a part in a play, etc.) **6.** *Law* to complete or make valid (a deed, contract, etc.) as by signing, sealing, and delivering —**SYN.** see KILL¹, PERFORM —**ex'e·cut'a·ble** *adj.* —**ex'e·cut'er** *n.*

ex·e·cu·tion (ek'sə kyōō'shən) *n.* [ME. *execucion* < Anglo-Fr. < OFr. *execution* < L. *executio, exsecutio:* see EXECUTOR] **1.** the act of executing; specif., *a)* a carrying out, doing, producing, etc. *b)* a putting to death in accordance with a legally imposed sentence **2.** the manner of doing or producing something, as of performing a piece of music or a role in a play **3.** [Archaic] effective action, esp. of a destructive nature **4.** *Law a)* a writ or order, issued by a court, giving authority to put a judgment into effect *b)* the legal method afforded for the enforcement of a judgment of a court *c)* the act of carrying out the provisions of such a writ or order *d)* the making valid of a legal instrument, as by signing, sealing, and delivering

ex·e·cu·tion·er (-ər) *n.* a person who carries out the death penalty imposed by a court, as a hangman

ex·ec·u·tive (ig zek'yə tiv) *adj.* [ME. < ML. *executivus* < L. *executus:* see EXECUTOR] **1.** of, capable of, or concerned with, carrying out duties, functions, etc. or managing affairs, as in a business organization **2.** empowered and required to administer (laws, government affairs, etc.); administrative: distinguished from LEGISLATIVE, JUDICIAL **3.** of administrative or managerial personnel or functions —*n.* **1.** a person, group of people, or branch of government empowered and required to administer the laws and affairs of a nation **2.** any person whose function is to administer or manage affairs, as of a corporation, school, etc.

☆**Executive Mansion 1.** the White House (in Washington, D.C.), official home of the President of the U.S. **2.** the official home of the governor of a State

executive officer *Mil.* an officer who is chief assistant to the commanding officer

ex·ec·u·tor (ek'sə kyōōt'ər; *for 2* ig zek'yə tər) *n.* [ME. *executour* < OFr. & < ML. *executor,* both < L. < pp. of *exequi, exsequi,* to follow up, pursue < *ex-,* intens. + *sequi,* to follow: see SEQUENT] **1.** a person who gets something done or produced **2.** a person appointed by a testator to carry out the provisions and directions in his will: cf. ADMINISTRATOR —**ex·ec'u·to'ri·al** *adj.* —**ex·ec·u·trix** (ig zek'yə triks) *n.fem., pl.* **-trix·es, -tri'ces** (-trī'sēz)

ex·ec·u·to·ry (ig zek'yə tôr'ē) *adj.* [LL. *exsecutorius* < L. *exsecutus:* see prec.] **1.** executive; administrative **2.** in force; effective, as a law **3.** *Law* designed to be, or capable of being, put into effect at the appropriate time

ex·e·dra (ek'si drə, ik sē'-) *n., pl.* **-drae** (-drē') [L. < Gr. *exedra* < *ex-,* out + *hedra,* a seat: see SIT¹] in ancient Greece, a room, building, or outdoor area with seats, where conversations were held

ex·e·ge·sis (ek'sə jē'sis) *n., pl.* **-ge'ses** (-sēz) [Gr. *exēgēsis,* explanation < *exēgeisthai,* to lead, explain < *ex-,* out + *hēgeisthai,* to lead, guide < IE. base *seg-, *sag-,* to trace, suspect, whence L. *sagire,* to perceive quickly & E. SEEK] explanation, critical analysis, or interpretation of a word, literary passage, etc., esp. of the Bible —**ex'e·get'ic** (-jet'ik), **ex'e·get'i·cal** *adj.* —**ex'e·get'i·cal·ly** *adv.*

ex·e·gete (ek'sə jēt') *n.* an expert in exegesis

ex·e·get·ics (ek'sə jet'iks) *n.pl.* [*with sing. v.*] the science, study, or practice of exegesis

ex·em·plar (ig zem'plär, -plər) *n.* [ME. < OFr. *exemplaire* < LL. *exemplarium* < L. *exemplum,* a pattern, EXAMPLE] **1.** a person or thing regarded as worthy of imitation; model; pattern; archetype **2.** a typical specimen or example **3.** a copy of a book, pamphlet, etc.

ex·em·pla·ry (-plə rē) *adj.* [LL. *exemplaris:* see prec.] **1.** serving as a model or example; worth imitating *[exemplary* behavior] **2.** serving as a warning or deterrent *[exemplary* punishment] **3.** serving as a sample, instance, type, etc.; illustrative *[exemplary* extracts] —**ex·em·pla·ri·ly** (eg'zəm pler'ə lē) *adv.* —**ex·em'pla·ri·ness** *n.*

exemplary damages *Law* damages awarded to the plaintiff beyond the actual loss, imposed as a punishment for the defendant's wrong

ex·em·pli·fi·ca·tion (ig zem'plə fi kā'shən) *n.* [ME. < ML. *exemplificatio:* see ff.] **1.** a showing by example **2.** something that exemplifies; example **3.** *Law* a legally attested or certified copy or transcript

ex·em·pli·fy (ig zem'plə fī') *vt.* **-fied', -fy'ing** [ME. *exemplifien* < OFr. *exemplifier* < ML. *exemplificare* < L. *exemplum,* an example + *facere,* to make (see -FY)] **1.** to show by example; serve as an example of **2.** to make a legally attested or certified copy or transcript of (a document, etc.) under seal

ex·em·plum (-pləm) *n., pl.* **-pla** (-plə) [L., EXAMPLE] **1.** an example; illustration **2.** a moralized tale or anecdote, esp. one included in a medieval sermon

ex·empt (ig zempt') *vt.* [ME. *exempten* < Anglo-Fr. *exempter* < L. *exemptus,* pp. of *eximere,* to take out: see EXAMPLE] to free from a rule or obligation which applies to others; excuse; release —*adj.* [L. *exemptus*] not subject to nor bound by a rule, obligation, etc. applying to others —*n.* an exempted person —**ex·empt'i·ble** *adj.*

ex·emp·tion (ig zemp'shən) *n.* [ME. *exempcioun* < OFr. *exemption* < L. *exemptio*] **1.** an exempting or being exempted; freedom or release from a liability, obligation, etc.; immunity **2.** *a)* the exempting from an individual's taxable income of a specified sum for himself and each of his dependents *b)* the sum specified *c)* any such dependent **SYN.**—**exemption** implies release from some obligation or legal requirement, esp. where others are not so released *[exemption* from the military draft]; **immunity** implies freedom from or protection against something disagreeable or menacing to which all or many are liable *[immunity* from a penalty, disease, taxes]; **impunity** specifically implies escape or freedom from punishment *[to* commit a crime with *impunity]* —**ANT. liability**

ex·en·ter·ate (ek sen'tə rāt') *vt.* **-at'ed, -at'ing** [< L. *exenteratus,* pp. of *exenterare,* Latinized < Gr. *exenterizein* < *ex-,* out + *enteron,* intestine: see ENTERO-] **1.** orig., to disembowel **2.** *Surgery* to take out (an organ) —**ex·en'ter·a'tion** *n.*

ex·e·qua·tur (ek'sə kwāt'ər) *n.* [L., 3d pers. sing., pres. subj., of *exequi, exsequi,* to follow out, perform: see EXECUTOR] an official document given to a consul or commercial agent by the government of the country in which he is stationed, authorizing him to perform his duties there

ex·e·quies (ek'sə kwēz) *n.pl.* [ME. *exequies,* pl. < OFr. *exequies* < L. *exequiae < exequi:* see EXECUTOR] earlier var. of OBSEQUIES

ex·er·cise (ek'sər sīz') *n.* [ME. & OFr. *exercice* < L. *exercitium* < pp. of *exercere,* to drive out (farm animals to work), hence drill, exercise < *ex-,* out + *arcere,* to enclose < IE. base *areq-,* to protect, enclose, whence Gr. *archein*] **1.** active use or operation; employment *[the exercise* of an option] **2.** performance (of duties, functions, etc.) **3.** activity for the purpose of training or developing the body or mind; systematic practice; esp., bodily exertion for the sake of health **4.** a regular series of specific movements designed to strengthen or develop some part of the body or some faculty *[finger exercises* for the piano] **5.** a problem or group of written examples, passages, etc. to be studied and worked out for developing technical skill, as in mathematics, grammar, etc. ☆**6.** *[pl.]* a set program of formal ceremonies, speeches, etc. *[graduation exercises]* —*vt.* **-cised', -cis'ing 1.** to put into action; use; employ *[to exercise* self-control] **2.** to carry out (duties, etc.); perform; fulfill **3.** [Now Rare] to use habitually; practice; train: used reflexively or in the passive *[she was exercised* in virtue] **4.** to put (the body, a muscle, the mind, a skill, etc.) into use so as to develop or train **5.** to drill (troops) **6.** to engage the attention and energy of, esp. so as to worry, perplex, or harass: used esp. in the passive *[greatly exercised* about the decision] **7.** to exert or have (influence, control, authority, etc.) —*vi.* to take exercise; do exercises —**SYN.** see PRACTICE —**ex'er·cis'a·ble** *adj.* —**ex'er·cis'er** *n.*

ex·er·ci·ta·tion (ig zur'sə tā'shən) *n.* [ME. *exercitacioun* < OFr. *exercitation* < L. *exercitatio* < pp. of *exercitare,* intens. of *exercere:* see EXERCISE] [Now Rare] exercise; esp., the exercising or display of special abilities, skills, etc.

ex·ergue (ig zurg', ek'surg) *n.* [Fr. *exergue,* lit., that which is out of the work, exergue < ModL. *exergum* < Gr. *ex,* out, outside of + *ergon,* WORK] **1.** the space on a coin or medal below or around the pictures or designs, often used for the date, place, etc. **2.** the inscription in this space

ex·ert (ig zurt') *vt.* [L. *exsertare,* freq. of *exserere,* to stretch out, put forth < *ex-,* out + *serere,* to join, fasten together: see SERIES] **1.** to put forth or use energetically; put into action or use *[to exert* strength, influence, etc.] **2.** to apply (oneself) with great energy or straining effort —**ex·er'tive** *adj.*

ex·er·tion (ig zur'shən) *n.* **1.** the act, fact, or process of exerting; active use of strength, power, etc.; exercise **2.** energetic activity; effort —**SYN.** see EFFORT

Ex·e·ter (eks'ə tər) city in Devonshire, SW England: pop. 80,000

ex·e·unt (eks'ē ənt, -oont) [L., 3d pers. indic., of *exire:* see EXIT] they (two or more specified characters) leave the stage: a stage direction

exeunt om·nes (äm'nēz) [L.] all (of the characters who are on stage) leave: a stage direction

ex·fo·li·ate (eks fō'lē āt') *vt., vi.* **-at'ed, -at'ing** [< LL. *exfoliatus,* pp. of *exfoliare,* to strip of leaves < L. *ex-,* out + *folium,* a leaf: see FOIL²] **1.** to cast or come off in flakes, scales, or layers, as skin, bark, etc. **2.** to expand or develop by or as by unfolding foliage —**ex·fo'li·a'tion** *n.* —**ex·fo'li·a'tive** *adj.*

ex·hal·ant (eks hā'lənt, ek sā'-) *adj.* [L. *exhalans,* prp. of *exhalare*] of or for exhalation —*n.* an organ or duct used for exhalation

ex·ha·la·tion (eks'hə lā'shən, ek'sə-) *n.* [L. *exhalatio*] **1.** an exhaling or being exhaled; expiration or evaporation **2.** something exhaled, as air, steam, or an odor; emanation; effluvium

ex·hale (eks hāl', ek sāl') *vi.* **-haled', -hal'ing** [Fr. *exhaler* < L. *exhalare < ex-,* out + *halare,* to breathe < IE. base *an-,* whence Gr. *anemos,* L. *animus*] **1.** to breathe forth air; expire **2.** to be given off or rise into the air as vapor; evaporate —*vt.* **1.** to breathe forth (air) **2.** to give off (vapor, fumes, etc.)

ex·haust (ig zôst') *vt.* [< L. *exhaustus,* pp. of *exhaurire,* to draw out, exhaust < *ex-,* out + *haurire,* to draw, drain < IE. base *aus-,* whence ON. *ausa*] **1.** to draw off or let out

completely (air, gas, etc.), as from a container 2. to use up; expend completely [to exhaust one's resources] 3. a) to empty completely; draw off the contents of; drain [to exhaust a well] b) to create a vacuum in 4. to drain of power, resources, etc. [war exhausts nations] 5. to tire out; make very weary; weaken 6. to deal with, study, or develop completely and thoroughly [to exhaust a subject] —vi. to be discharged or let out, as gas or steam from an engine —n. 1. a) the withdrawing of air, gas, etc. from a container or enclosure, as by means of a fan or pump b) an apparatus for doing this, as in getting rid of fumes, dust, stale air, etc. 2. a) the discharge or release of used steam, gas, etc. from the cylinders of an engine at the end of every working stroke of the pistons b) the pipe through which such steam, gas, etc. is released 3. something given off or let out, as fumes from a gasoline engine —ex·haust'i·bil'·i·ty n. —ex·haust'i·ble adj. —ex·haust'less adj.

ex·haus·tion (ig zôs'chən) n. [LL. exhaustio] 1. the act of exhausting 2. the state of being exhausted; esp., a) great fatigue or weariness b) the condition of being used up; complete consumption

ex·haus·tive (ig zôs'tiv) adj. [ML. exhaustivus] 1. exhausting or tending to exhaust 2. leaving nothing out; covering every possible detail [exhaustive research] —ex·haus'tive·ly adv.

ex·hib·it (ig zib'it) vt. [ME. exhibiten < L. exhibitus, pp. of exhibere, to hold forth, present < ex-, out + habere, to hold: see HABIT] 1. to present or expose to view; show; display 2. to present to public view for entertainment, instruction, advertising, judgment in a competition, etc. 3. to give evidence of; reveal [to exhibit impatience] 4. Law to present (evidence, etc.) officially to a court 5. Med. to administer (a drug, etc.) as a remedy —vi. to put pictures, wares, etc. on public display —n. 1. a show; display; presentation 2. a thing exhibited; esp., an object or objects displayed publicly 3. Law a document or object produced as evidence in a court —SYN. see PROOF, SHOW

ex·hib·it·er (-ər) n. same as EXHIBITOR

ex·hi·bi·tion (ek'sə bish'ən) n. [ME. & OFr. exhibicion < LL. exhibitio < pp. of L. exhibere: see EXHIBIT] 1. the act or fact of exhibiting 2. the thing or things exhibited 3. a public show or display, as of art, industrial products, athletic feats, etc. 4. [Brit.] a sum of money awarded by a school or university to help a student continue his studies

ex·hi·bi·tion·er (-ər) n. [Brit.] a student who is awarded an exhibition (sense 4)

ex·hi·bi·tion·ism (-iz'm) n. 1. a tendency to call attention to oneself or show off one's talents, skill, etc. 2. Psychol. a) a tendency to expose parts of the body that are conventionally concealed, esp. in seeking sexual stimulation or gratification b) an instance of such exposure —ex'hi·bi'tion·ist n. —ex'hi·bi'tion·is'tic adj.

ex·hib·i·tive (ig zib'ə tiv) adj. serving or tending to exhibit (usually with of)

ex·hib·i·tor (-tər) n. [LL.] one that exhibits; esp., a) a person, company, etc. that enters an exhibit in a fair, show, competition, etc. ☆b) the owner or manager of a motion-picture theater

ex·hib·i·to·ry (-tôr'ē) adj. [LL. exhibitorius] 1. exhibiting 2. of or for exhibition

ex·hil·a·rant (ig zil'ə rənt) adj. [Fr. < L. exhilarans, prp. of exhilarare] that exhilarates; exhilarating —n. a thing that exhilarates

ex·hil·a·rate (ig zil'ə rāt') vt. -rat'ed, -rat'ing [< L. exhilaratus, pp. of exhilarare, to gladden < ex-, intens. + hilarare, to gladden < hilaris, glad: see HILARIOUS] 1. to make cheerful, merry, or lively 2. to invigorate or stimulate —SYN. see ANIMATE —ex·hil'a·ra'tive adj.

ex·hil·a·ra·tion (ig zil'ə rā'shən) n. [LL. exhilaratio] 1. the act of exhilarating 2. an exhilarated condition or feeling; liveliness; high spirits; stimulation

ex·hort (ig zôrt') vt., vi. [ME. exhorten < L. exhortari, to exhort < ex-, out + hortari, to urge: see HORTATORY] to urge earnestly by advice, warning, etc. (to do what is proper or required); admonish strongly —SYN. see URGE

ex·hor·ta·tion (eg'zôr tā'shən, ek'sər-) n. [ME. exhortacion < OFr. < L. exhortatio] 1. the act of exhorting 2. a plea, sermon, etc. that exhorts

ex·hor·ta·to·ry (ig zôr'tə tôr'ē) adj. [ME. < LL. exhortatorius] of, or having the nature of, exhortation; meant to exhort; admonitory: also ex·hor'ta·tive (-tiv)

ex·hume (ig zyōōm', iks hyōōm') vt. -humed', -hum'ing [ME. exhumen < ML. exhumare < L. ex, out + humus, the ground: see HUMUS] 1. to dig out of the earth; disinter 2. to bring to light; disclose; reveal —ex·hu·ma·tion (eks/hyoo mā'shən) n.

ex·i·gen·cy (ek'sə jən sē, ek sij'ən-) n., pl. -cies [ML. exigentia] 1. the condition or quality of being exigent; urgency 2. a situation calling for immediate action or attention 3. [pl.] pressing needs; demands; requirements Also ex'i·gence (-jəns) —SYN. see EMERGENCY, NEED

ex·i·gent (ek'sə jənt) adj. [L. exigens, prp. of exigere, to drive out: see EXACT] 1. calling for immediate action or attention; urgent; critical 2. requiring more than is reasonable; demanding; exacting —ex'i·gent·ly adv.

ex·i·gi·ble (ek'sə jə b'l) adj. [Fr. < L. exigere (see EXACT)] that can be demanded or exacted

ex·ig·u·ous (eg zig'yoo wəs) adj. [L. exiguus, small < exigere: see EXACT] scanty; little; small; meager —ex·i·gu·i·ty (ek'sə gyōō'ə tē) n.

ex·ile (eg'zīl, ek'sīl) n. [ME. & OFr. exil < L. exilium < exul, an exile, one banished < ex-, out + IE. base *al-, to wander aimlessly, whence Gr. alaomai, I wander, am banished] 1. a prolonged living away from one's country, community, etc., usually enforced; banishment, sometimes self-imposed 2. a person in exile —vt. -iled, -il·ing to force (a person) to leave his own country, community, etc.; banish —SYN. see BANISH —the Exile the period in the 6th cent. B.C. during which the Jews were held captive in Babylonia

ex·il·ic (ig zil'ik, ik sil'ik) adj. of exile, esp. the exile of the Jews in Babylonia

ex·ist (ig zist') vi. [Fr. exister < L. existere, exsistere, to come forth, stand forth < ex-, out + sistere, to cause to stand, set, place, caus. of stare, STAND] 1. to have reality or actual being; be 2. to occur or be present [the qualities that exist in a person] 3. to continue being; live

ex·ist·ence (-əns) n. [ME. < OFr. < ML. existentia < prp. of L. existere] 1. the act of existing; state or fact of being 2. continuance of being; life; living 3. occurrence; specific manifestation 4. a manner of existing, being, or living [a happy existence] 5. a being; entity; thing that exists

ex·ist·ent (-ənt) adj. [L. existens, prp. of existere, EXIST] 1. having existence or being; existing 2. existing now; present; immediate

ex·is·ten·tial (eg'zis ten'shəl, ek'sis-) adj. [ModL. existentialis] 1. of, based on, or expressing existence 2. of, relating to, or as conceived of in, existentialism 3. Logic implicitly or explicitly asserting actuality as opposed to conceptual possibility

ex·is·ten·tial·ism (-shəl iz'm) n. [Fr. existentialisme < existenciel: see prec.] a philosophical and literary movement, variously religious and atheistic, stemming from Kierkegaard and represented by Sartre, Heidegger, etc.: it is based on the doctrine that existence takes precedence over essence and holds that man is totally free and responsible for his acts, and that this responsibility is the source of the dread and anguish that encompass him —ex'is·ten'·tial·ist adj., n.

ex·it (eg'zit, ek'sit) n. [L. exitus, orig. pp. of exire, to go out < ex-, out + ire, to go < IE. base *ei-, whence Sans. émi, Goth. iddja (I went)] 1. an actor's departure from the stage 2. a going out; departure 3. a way out; doorway or passage leading out 4. [L., 3d pers. sing., pres. indic., of exire] he (or she) leaves the stage: a direction in a play script —vi. to leave a place; depart

ex li·bris (eks lē'bris, lī-) [L., lit., from the books (of)] 1. belonging to the library of: an inscription followed by the owner's name, often used on bookplates 2. a bookplate

Ex·moor (eks'moor) hilly region of moors in SW England, mostly in Somersetshire

ex·o- (ek'sō, -sə) [< Gr. exō, without < ex-, EX-¹] a prefix meaning outside, outer, outer part [exogamy]

ex·o·bi·ol·o·gy (ek'sō bī äl'ə jē) n. [EXO- + BIOLOGY] the branch of biology investigating the possibility of the existence of living organisms elsewhere in the universe than on earth —ex'o·bi'o·log'i·cal adj. —ex'o·bi·ol'o·gist n.

ex·o·carp (ek'sō kärp') n. [EXO- + -CARP] the outer layer of a ripened ovary or fruit, as the skin of a plum

ex·o·cen·tric (ek'sə sen'trik) adj. Linguis. designating or of a construction whose syntactic function is different from that of any of its constituents (Ex.: all the way in the sentence "he ran all the way"): cf. ENDOCENTRIC

ex·o·crine (ek'sə krin, -krīn', -krēn') adj. [EXO- + -crine, as in ENDOCRINE] designating or of any gland secreting externally, either directly or through a duct —n. any such gland, as a sweat gland, or its secretion

Exod. Exodus

☆ex·o·don·tics (ek'sə dän'tiks) n.pl. [ModL. < L. ex, out + Gr. odōn (gen. odontos), TOOTH + -ICS] the branch of dentistry having to do with the extraction of teeth: also ex'o·don'tia (-shə) —ex'o·don'tist n.

ex·o·dus (ek'sə dəs) n. [< LL. Exodus (OT. book) < Gr. Exodos, lit., a going out < ex-, out + hodos, way: see -ODE¹] a going out or forth, esp. in a large group —[E-] 1. the departure of the Israelites from Egypt (with the) 2. the second book of the Pentateuch, which describes this

ex of·fi·ci·o (eks' ə fish'ē ō') [L., lit., from office] by virtue of one's office, or position

ex·og·a·my (ek säg'ə mē) n. [EXO- + -GAMY] 1. the custom, often inviolable, of marrying only outside one's own tribe, clan, etc.; outbreeding: opposed to ENDOGAMY 2. cross-pollination among flowers of different plants —ex·og'a·mous, ex·o·gam·ic (ek'sə gam'ik) adj.

ex·o·gen (ek'sə jen) n. [< Fr. exogène: see EXO- & -GEN] former term for DICOTYLEDON

ex·og·e·nous (ek säj'ə nəs) adj. [prec. + -OUS] 1. developing from without; originating externally 2. Biol. of or relating to external factors, as food, light, etc., that have an effect upon an organism —ex·og'e·nous·ly adv.

ex·on·er·ate (ig zän′ə rāt′) *vt.* -at′ed, -at′ing [< L. *exoneratus*, pp. of *exonerare*, to disburden < *ex-*, out + *onerare*, to load < *onus* (gen. *oneris*), a burden: see ONUS] 1. orig., to relieve of (a burden, obligation, etc.); unload 2. to free from a charge or the imputation of guilt; declare or prove blameless; exculpate —*SYN.* see ABSOLVE — **ex·on′er·a′tion** *n.* —**ex·on′er·a′tive** *adj.* —**ex·on′er·a′tor** *n.*

ex·o·pep·ti·dase (ek′sō pep′tə dās′) *n.* any of a number of enzymes that split off the terminal amino acid of a protein

exophthalmic goiter a disease characterized by enlargement of the thyroid gland, overproduction of the thyroid hormone, and abnormal protrusion of the eyeballs

ex·oph·thal·mos (ek′säf thal′məs) *n.* [ModL. < Gr. *exophthalmos*, with prominent eyes < *ex-*, out + *ophthalmos*, an eye: see OPHTHALMIC] abnormal protrusion of the eyeball, caused by disease: also **ex′oph·thal′mus** (-məs), **ex′oph·thal′mi·a** (-mē ə) —**ex′oph·thal′mic** *adj.*

ex·o·ra·ble (ek′sər ə b'l) *adj.* [L. *exorabilis* < *exorare*, to move by entreaty < *ex-*, out + *orare*: see ORATION] that can be persuaded or moved by pleas

ex·or·bi·tance (ig zôr′bə təns) *n.* [ME. *exorbitaunce*: see EXORBITANT] 1. a going beyond what is right or reasonable, as in demands, prices, etc.; extravagance 2. [Archaic] lawlessness Also **ex·or′bi·tan·cy**

ex·or·bi·tant *adj.* [ME. < L. *exorbitans*, prp. of *exorbitare*, to go out of the track < *ex-*, out + *orbita*, a track, ORBIT] going beyond what is reasonable, just, proper, usual, etc.; excessive; extravagant; immoderate: said esp. of charges, prices, etc. —*SYN.* see EXCESSIVE —**ex·or′bi·tant·ly** *adv.*

ex·or·cise, ex·or·cize (ek′sôr sīz′) *vt.* -cised′ or -cized′, -cis′ing or -ciz′ing [ME. *exorcisen* < LL.(Ec.) *exorcizare* < Gr. *exorkizein*, to swear a person (in NT., to banish an evil spirit) < *ex-*, out + *horkizein*, to make one swear < *horkos*, an oath, akin to *horkanē*, enclosure, *herkos*, fence, prob. < IE. base *ser-*, wickerwork, whence L. *sarcire*, to patch] 1. to drive (an evil spirit or spirits) out or away by ritual prayers, incantations, etc. 2. [Rare] to adjure (such a spirit or spirits) 3. to free from such a spirit or spirits

ex·or·cism (-siz′m) *n.* [ME. *exorcisme* < LL.(Ec.) *exorcismus* < Gr. *exorkismos*] 1. the act of exorcising 2. a verbal formula or ritual used in exorcising

ex·or·cist (-sist) *n.* [ME. < LL. *exorcista* < Gr. *exorcistēs*] 1. a person who exorcises 2. R.C.Ch. a member of the second highest of the four minor orders

ex·or·di·um (ig zôr′dē əm) *n.*, *pl.* -di·ums, -di·a (-ə) [L. < *exordiri*, to begin a web, begin < *ex-*, from + *ordiri*, to lay the warp, begin: for IE. base see ORDER] 1. a beginning 2. the opening part of a speech, treatise, etc. —**ex·or′di·al** *adj.*

ex·o·skel·e·ton (ek′sō skel′ə t'n) *n.* any hard, external, secreted supporting structure, as the shell of an oyster, cuticle of a lobster, etc.: distinguished from ENDOSKELETON —**ex′o·skel′e·tal** (-t'l) *adj.*

ex·os·mo·sis (ek′säs mō′sis, -säz-) *n.* [altered (after OSMOSIS) < *exosmose* < Fr., coined by Dutrochet (1826) < Gr. *exo*, out + *ōsmos*, impulse] in osmosis, the slower diffusion of the more dense fluid through the semipermeable membrane to mingle with the less dense: opposed to ENDOSMOSIS —**ex′os·mot′ic** (-mät′ik) *adj.*

☆**ex·o·sphere** (ek′sə sfir′) *n.* [EXO- + SPHERE] the outermost portion of the earth's atmosphere

ex·o·spore (ek′sə spôr′) *n.* [EXO- + SPORE] *Bot.* 1. the outer layer of the covering of a spore 2. *same as* CONIDIUM

ex·os·to·sis (ek′säs tō′sis) *n.*, *pl.* -ses′ (-sēz′) [ModL. < Gr. *exostōsis* < *ex-*, outside + *osteon*, a bone: see OSTEO-] an abnormal bony growth on the surface of a bone or tooth

ex·o·ter·ic (ek′sə ter′ik) *adj.* [LL. *exotericus* < Gr. *exōterikos*, external < compar. of *exō*, outside: see EX-¹] 1. of the outside world; external 2. not limited to a select few or an inner group of disciples; suitable for the uninitiated 3. that can be understood by the public; popular Opposed to ESOTERIC —**ex′o·ter′i·cal·ly** *adv.*

ex·o·ther·mic (ek′sə thur′mik) *adj.* [EXO- + THERMIC] designating or of a chemical change in which there is a liberation of heat, as in combustion: also **ex′o·ther′mal**

ex·ot·ic (ig zät′ik) *adj.* [L. *exoticus* < Gr. *exōtikos* < *exō*, outside (see EX-¹)] 1. foreign; not native 2. strange or different in a way that is striking or fascinating; strangely beautiful, enticing, etc. —*n.* 1. a foreign or imported thing 2. a plant that is not native 3. *same as* EXOTIC DANCER —**ex·ot′i·cal·ly** *adv.* —**ex·ot′i·cism** (-ə siz′m) *n.*

ex·ot·i·ca (-i kə) *n.pl.* [ModL. < L., neut. pl. of *exoticus*, EXOTIC] foreign or unfamiliar things, as curious or rare art objects, strange customs, etc.

☆**exotic dancer** a belly dancer, stripteaser, or the like

ex·o·tox·in (ek′sō täk′sən) *n.* [EXO- + TOXIN] any of a group of toxic substances excreted by certain disease-producing bacteria

ex·o·tro·pi·a (ek′sə trō′pē ə) *n.* [ModL. < EXO- + -tropia, -TROPY] a condition in which only one eye fixes on an object while the other turns outward; walleye

exp. 1. expenses 2. experiment 3. export 4. express

ex·pand (ik spand′) *vt.* [ME. *expanden* < L. *expandere* < *ex-*, out + *pandere*, to spread, extend < IE. base *pet-*, to spread out (esp. the arms), whence FATHOM] 1. to spread out; open out; stretch out; unfold (the eagle *expanded* its wings) 2. to make greater in size, bulk, scope, etc.; en-

large; dilate; extend 3. to enlarge upon (a topic, idea, etc.); develop in detail 4. to work out or show the full form of (a contraction, mathematical equation, etc.) —*vi.* 1. to become expanded; spread out, unfold, enlarge, etc. 2. to become affable, warmly communicative, etc. —**ex·pand′er** *n.*

SYN.—**expand** implies an increasing in size, bulk, or volume and is the broadest term here, being applicable when the enlarging force operates from either the inside or the outside or when the increase comes about by unfolding, puffing out, spreading, or opening; **swell** implies expansion beyond the normal limits or size; **distend** implies a swelling as a result of pressure from within that forces a bulging outward; **inflate** suggests the use of air or gas, or of something insubstantial, to distend or swell a thing; **dilate** suggests a widening or stretching of something circular —ANT. **contract**

ex·pand·ed (-id) *adj.* 1. increased in size, area, scope, etc. 2. *Printing* same as EXTENDED

expanded metal sheet metal that has been cut into parallel, attached strips and stretched into a latticelike form: used to reinforce concrete, as a plaster lath, etc.

ex·panse (ik spans′) *n.* [ME. *expans* < L. *expansum*, neut. pp. of *expandere*: see EXPAND] 1. a large, open area or unbroken surface; wide extent; great breadth 2. expansion

ex·pan·si·ble (ik span′sə b'l) *adj.* that can be expanded: also **ex·pand′a·ble** —**ex·pan′si·bil′i·ty** *n.*

ex·pan·sile (-s'l; *Brit.* -sil) *adj.* 1. tending to expand 2. of or characteristic of expansion

ex·pan·sion (ik span′shən) *n.* [LL. *expansio* < L. *expansus*: see EXPANSE] 1. an expanding or being expanded; enlargement; dilation 2. an expanded thing or part 3. the amount, degree, or extent of expansion 4. a development or full treatment, as of a topic 5. the process or result of working out or giving the full form of a contraction, equation, etc. 6. *Mech.* the expanding in volume of steam in the cylinder of a steam engine after cutoff, or of gas in the cylinder of an internal-combustion engine after explosion

ex·pan·sion·ar·y (-er′ē) *adj.* directed toward expansion

expansion bolt a bolt with an attachment that expands and acts as a wedge as it is screwed inward, used in holes drilled in stone, concrete, etc.

ex·pan·sion·ism (-iz′m) *n.* the policy of expanding a nation's territory or its sphere of influence, often at the expense of other nations —**ex·pan′sion·ist** *adj.*, *n.* —**ex·pan′sion·is′tic** *adj.*

ex·pan·sive (ik span′siv) *adj.* [< L. *expansus* (see EXPANSE) + -IVE] 1. tending or being able to expand 2. of, or working by means of, expansion 3. widely extended; broad; extensive; comprehensive 4. characterized by a free and generous nature; sympathetic; demonstrative; open [an *expansive* person] 5. *Psychiatry* in or of a state characterized by overestimation of oneself, overgenerosity, euphoria, and, at times, delusions of grandeur —**ex·pan′sive·ly** *adv.* —**ex·pan′sive·ness, ex·pan·siv′i·ty** (ek′span siv′ə tē) *n.*

ex par·te (eks pärt′ē) [L., lit., from the side or party: see EX-¹ & PART] on, or in the interest of, one side only; one-sided

ex·pa·ti·ate (ik spā′shē āt′) *vi.* -at′ed, -at′ing [< L. *expatiatus*, pp. of *expatiari*, *exspatiari*, to go out of one's course, wander < *ex-*, out + *spatiari*, to walk, roam < *spatium*, SPACE] 1. orig., to roam or wander freely 2. to speak or write in great detail; elaborate or enlarge (on or upon) —**ex·pa′ti·a′tion** *n.*

ex·pa·tri·ate (eks pā′trē āt′; *for adj.* & *n.*, *usually* -it) *vt.*, *vi.* -at′ed, -at′ing [< pp. of ML. *expatriare*, to leave the homeland < L. *ex*, out of + *patria*, fatherland < *pater*, FATHER] 1. to drive (a person) from his native land; exile 2. to withdraw (oneself) from one's native land or from allegiance to it —*adj.* that has become an expatriate; expatriated —*n.* an expatriated person —*SYN.* see BANISH —**ex·pa′tri·a′tion** *n.*

ex·pect (ik spekt′) *vt.* [L. *expectare*, *exspectare* < *ex-*, out + *spectare*, to look, freq. of *specere*, to see: see SPECTACLE] 1. orig., to await; wait for 2. to look for as likely to occur or appear; look forward to; anticipate [I *expected* you sooner] 3. to look for as due, proper, or necessary [to *expect* a reward] 4. [Colloq.] to suppose; presume; guess —**be expecting** [Colloq.] to be pregnant —**ex·pect′a·ble** *adj.*

SYN.—**expect** implies a considerable degree of confidence that a particular event will happen [to *expect* guests for dinner]; **anticipate** implies a looking forward to something with a foretaste of the pleasure or distress it promises, or a realizing of something in advance, and a taking of steps to meet it [to *anticipate* trouble]; **hope** implies a desire for something, accompanied by some confidence in the belief that it can be realized [to *hope* for the best]; **await** implies a waiting for, or a being ready for, a person or thing [a hearty welcome *awaits* you]

ex·pect·an·cy (ik spek′tən sē) *n.*, *pl.* -cies [ML. *expectantia* < L. *expectans*: see ff.] 1. an expecting or being expected; expectation 2. that which is expected, esp. on a statistical basis [life *expectancy*] Also **ex·pect′ance** (-təns)

ex·pect·ant (-tənt) *adj.* [ME. < OFr. < L. *expectans*, prp. of *expectare*] expecting; specif., *a*) having or showing expectation *b*) waiting, as for a position, the birth of a child, etc. —*n.* a person who expects something —**ex·pect′ant·ly** *adv.*

ex·pec·ta·tion (ek′spek tā′shən) *n.* [L. *expectatio* < pp. of *expectare*: see EXPECT] 1. a looking forward to; anticipa-

tion **2.** a looking for as due, proper, or necessary **3.** a thing looked forward to **4.** [also *pl.*] a reason or warrant for looking forward to something; prospect for the future, as of advancement or prosperity **5.** the degree of probability of the occurrence, duration, etc. of something, esp. as indicated by statistics —**in expectation** in the state of being looked for —**ex·pec·ta·tive** (ik spek′tə tiv) *adj.*

ex·pec·to·rant (ik spek′tər ənt) *adj.* [L. *expectorans*, prp. of *expectorare*] causing or easing the bringing up of phlegm, mucus, etc. from the respiratory tract —*n.* an expectorant medicine

ex·pec·to·rate (-tə rāt′) *vt., vi.* **-rat′ed, -rat′ing** [< L. *expectoratus*, pp. of *expectorare*, to expel from the breast < *ex-*, out + *pectus* (gen. *pectoris*), breast] **1.** to cough up and spit out (phlegm, mucus, etc.) **2.** to spit —**ex·pec′to·ra′-tion** *n.*

ex·pe·di·en·cy (ik spē′dē ən sē) *n., pl.* **-cies 1.** the quality or state of being expedient; suitability for a given purpose; appropriateness to the conditions **2.** the doing or consideration of what is of selfish use or advantage rather than of what is right or just; self-interest **3.** an expedient Also **ex·pe′di·ence**

ex·pe·di·ent (-ənt) *adj.* [ME. < OFr. < L. *expediens*, prp. of *expedire*: see EXPEDITE] **1.** useful for effecting a desired result; suited to the circumstances or the occasion; advantageous; convenient **2.** based on or offering what is of use or advantage rather than what is right or just; guided by self-interest; politic —*n.* **1.** an expedient thing; means to an end **2.** a device used in an emergency; makeshift; resource —*SYN.* see RESOURCE —**ex·pe′di·ent·ly** *adv.*

ex·pe·di·en·tial (ik spē′dē en′shəl) *adj.* based on or guided by expediency

ex·pe·dite (ek′spə dīt′) *vt.* **-dit′ed, -dit′ing** [< L. *expeditus*, pp. of *expedire*, lit., to free one caught by the feet, hence hasten, dispatch < *ex-*, out + *pes* (gen. *pedis*), FOOT] **1.** to speed up or make easy the progress or action of; hasten; facilitate **2.** to do quickly **3.** [Rare] to send off; issue officially; dispatch —*adj.* **1.** [Obs.] not impeded **2.** [Obs.] prompt, ready, or alert

ex·pe·dit·er (-ər) *n.* a person who expedites; esp., one employed by an industry, government agency, etc. to expedite urgent or involved projects

ex·pe·di·tion (ek′spə dish′ən) *n.* [ME. *expedicioun* < OFr. *expedition* < L. *expeditio* < pp. of *expedire*: see EXPEDITE] **1.** *a)* a sending forth or starting out on a journey, voyage, march, etc. for some definite purpose, as exploration or battle *b)* the journey, etc. itself *c)* the people, ships, equipment, etc. on such a journey **2.** efficient speed; dispatch —*SYN.* see HASTE, TRIP —**ex′pe·di′tion·ar′y** *adj.*

ex·pe·di·tious (ek′spə dish′əs) *adj.* done with or characterized by expedition; efficient and speedy; prompt —**ex′pe·di′tious·ly** *adv.*

ex·pel (ik spel′) *vt.* **-pelled′, -pel′ling** [ME. *expellen* < L. *expellere* < *ex-*, out + *pellere*, to thrust: see PULSE] **1.** to drive out by force; force out; eject **2.** to dismiss or send away by authority; deprive of rights, membership, etc. —*SYN.* see EJECT —**ex·pel′la·ble** *adj.* —**ex·pel·lee** (ek′spel ē′) *n.* —**ex·pel′ler** *n.*

ex·pel·lant, ex·pel·lent (-ənt) *adj.* [< L. *expellans*, prp. of *expellere*] expelling or tending to expel —*n.* an expellant medicine

ex·pend (ik spend′) *vt.* [ME. *expenden* < L. *expendere*, to weigh out, pay out < *ex-*, out + *pendere*, to weigh < IE. base *(s)pen(d)-*, to pull, spin, whence SPIN, SPAN¹] **1.** to spend **2.** to consume by using; use up

ex·pend·a·ble (ik spen′də b'l) *adj.* **1.** that can be expended **2.** *Mil. a)* designating supplies or equipment expected to be used up or destroyed in service and therefore not entered on a certificate of expenditure *b)* designating equipment or men considered replaceable and therefore worth sacrificing to gain an objective —*n.* a person or thing considered expendable —**ex·pend′a·bil′i·ty** *n.*

ex·pend·i·ture (-də chər) *n.* [< ML. *expenditus*, irreg. pp. for L. *expendere* + -URE] **1.** the act of expending; a spending or using up of money, time, etc. **2.** the amount of money, time, etc. expended; expense

ex·pense (ik spens′) *n.* [ME. < Anglo-Fr. *expense* < LL. *expensa (pecunia)*, paid out (money) < L. *expensum*, neut. pp. of *expendere*] **1.** formerly, the act of expending; a spending or using up **2.** financial cost; fee; charge **3.** any cost or sacrifice **4.** [*pl.*] *a)* charges or costs met with in running a business, doing one's work, maintaining property, etc. *b)* money to pay for these charges **5.** a cause of spending; drain on one's finances [a car can be a considerable *expense*] —**at the expense of** with the payment, onus, loss, etc. borne by

☆**expense account 1.** an arrangement whereby certain expenses of an employee in connection with his work are paid for by his employer **2.** a record of such expenses

ex·pen·sive (ik spen′siv) *adj.* requiring or involving much expense; high-priced; dear —*SYN.* see COSTLY —**ex·pen′sive·ly** *adv.* —**ex·pen′sive·ness** *n.*

ex·pe·ri·ence (ik spir′ē əns) *n.* [ME. < OFr. < L. *experientia*, trial, proof, experiment < *experiens*, prp. of *experiri*, to try, test < *ex-*, out + base as in *peritus*, experienced < IE. base **per-*, to attempt, venture, whence Gr. *peira*, experience & OE. *fær*, danger (cf. FEAR)] **1.** the act of living through an event or events; personal involvement in or observation of events as they occur **2.** anything observed or lived through [an *experience* he'll never forget] **3.** *a)* all that has happened to one in his life to date [not within his *experience*] *b)* everything done or undergone by a group, people in general, etc. **4.** effect on a person of anything or everything that has happened to him; individual reaction to events, feelings, etc. **5.** *a)* activity that includes training, observation of practice, and personal participation *b)* the period of such activity *c)* knowledge, skill, or practice resulting from this —*vt.* **-enced, -enc·ing** to have experience of; personally encounter or feel; meet with; undergo

ex·pe·ri·enced (-ənst) *adj.* **1.** having had much experience, as in a particular occupation or activity **2.** having learned from experience; made wise, competent, etc. by experience

ex·pe·ri·en·tial (ik spir′ē en′shəl) *adj.* [< L. *experientia* + -AL] of or based on experience; empirical —**ex·pe′ri·en′-tial·ly** *adv.*

ex·per·i·ment (ik sper′ə mənt, -spir′-; *for v., also* -ment′) *n.* [ME. < OFr. < L. *experimentum*, a trial, test < *experiri*: see EXPERIENCE] **1.** a test or trial of something; specif., *a)* any action or process undertaken to discover something not yet known or to demonstrate something known *b)* any action or process designed to find out whether something is effective, workable, valid, etc. **2.** the conducting of such tests or trials; experimentation —*vi.* to make an experiment or experiments —*SYN.* see TRIAL —**ex·per′i·ment′er** *n.*

ex·per·i·men·tal (ik sper′ə men′t'l, -spir′-) *adj.* [ME. < ML. *experimentalis*: see prec.] **1.** of or based on experience rather than on theory or authority **2.** based on, tested by, or having the nature of, experiment **3.** for the sake of experiment; designed to test **4.** tentative **5.** of or used for experiments —**ex·per′i·men′tal·ly** *adv.*

ex·per·i·men·tal·ism (-iz′m) *n.* **1.** the theory or practice of depending on experimentation; empiricism **2.** fondness for experimenting or for new experiences, procedures, etc. —**ex·per′i·men′tal·ist** *n., adj.*

ex·per·i·men·ta·tion (ik sper′ə mən tā′shən, -men-) *n.* [ML. *experimentatio*] the conducting of experiments

ex·pert (ek′spərt; *also, for adj.,* ik spurt′) *adj.* [ME. < OFr. < L. *expertus*, pp. of *experiri*: see EXPERIENCE] **1.** very skillful; having much training and knowledge in some special field **2.** of or from an expert [an *expert* opinion] —*n.* [Fr.] a person who is very skillful or highly trained and informed in some special field —**ex′pert·ly** *adv.* —**ex′pert·ness** *n.*

ex·per·tise (ek′spər tēz′) *n.* [Fr.] the skill, knowledge, judgment, etc. of an expert

ex·pi·a·ble (ek′spē ə b'l) *adj.* [Fr.] that can be expiated

ex·pi·ate (ek′spē āt′) *vt.* **-at′ed, -at′ing** [< L. *expiatus*, pp. of *expiare*, to make satisfaction or atonement < *ex-*, out + *piare*, to appease, akin to *pius*, pious] **1.** to make amends or reparation for (wrongdoing or guilt); atone for **2.** to pay the penalty of; suffer for —**ex′pi·a′tion** *n.* —**ex′pi·a′tor** *n.*

ex·pi·a·to·ry (ek′spē ə tôr′ē) *adj.* [LL. *expiatorius*] that expiates or is meant to expiate

ex·pi·ra·tion (ek′spə rā′shən) *n.* [ME. *expiracioun* < L. *expiratio, exspiratio* < pp. of *exspirare*, EXPIRE] **1.** a breathing out, as of air from the lungs **2.** *a)* something breathed out *b)* a sound, etc. made by breathing out **3.** a breathing one's last; dying **4.** a coming to an end; close

ex·pir·a·to·ry (ik spīr′ə tôr′ē) *adj.* of expiration; relating to breathing out air from the lungs

ex·pire (ik spīr′) *vt.* **-pired′, -pir′ing** [ME. *expiren* < L. *exspirare* < *ex-*, out + *spirare*, to breathe: see SPIRIT] **1.** to breathe out (air from the lungs) **2.** [Obs.] to give off (an odor etc.) —*vi.* **1.** to breathe out air **2.** to breathe one's last breath; die **3.** to come to an end; terminate; cease [the lease *expired*] —*SYN.* see DIE¹

ex·pi·ry (ik spīr′ē, ek′spə rē) *n., pl.* **-ries** [EXPIR(E) + -Y⁴] **1.** a coming to an end; termination **2.** [Archaic] death

ex·plain (ik splān′) *vt.* [ME. *explanen* < L. *explanare*, to flatten < *ex-*, out + *planare*, to make level < *planus*, level (see PLANE²): sp. infl. by PLAIN¹] **1.** to make clear, plain, or understandable **2.** to give the meaning or interpretation of; expound **3.** to account for; state reasons for —*vi.* to give an explanation —**explain away** to state reasons for so as to justify, often by minimizing, or make understandable —**explain oneself 1.** to make clear what one means **2.** to give reasons justifying one's conduct —**ex·plain′a·ble** *adj.*

SYN.—**explain** implies a making clear or intelligible of something that is not known or understood [to *explain* how a machine operates]; **expound** implies a systematic and thorough explanation, often one made by a person having expert knowledge [to *expound* a theory]; **explicate** implies a scholarly analysis or exposition that is developed in detail [the *explication* of a Biblical passage]; **elucidate** implies a shedding light upon by clear and specific explanation, illustration, etc. [to *elucidate* the country's foreign policy]; to **interpret** is to bring out meanings not immediately

apparent, as by translation, searching insight, or special knowledge [how do you *interpret* his silence?]; **construe** suggests a particular interpretation of something whose meaning is ambiguous [his statement is not to be lightly construed]

ex·pla·na·tion (eks'plə nā'shən) *n.* [ME. *explanacioun* < L. *explanatio* < pp. of *explanare*] **1.** the act of explaining **2.** something that explains **3.** the interpretation, meaning, or sense given in explaining **4.** a mutual defining of terms, declaration of motives, etc. to clear up a misunderstanding or settle a dispute

ex·plan·a·to·ry (ik splan'ə tôr'ē) *adj.* [LL. *explanatorius*] explaining or intended to explain: also **ex·plan'a·tive** (-ə tiv) —**ex·plan'a·to'ri·ly** *adv.*

ex·plant (eks plant') *vt.* [EX-¹ + PLANT, *v.*] to transfer (living tissue) for culture in an artificial medium —**ex'plan·ta'tion** (-plan tā'shən) *n.*

ex·ple·tive (eks'plə tiv) *n.* [LL. *expletivus*, serving to fill < L. *expletus*, pp. of *explere*, to fill < *ex-*, out, up + *plere*, to fill: for IE. base see FULL¹] **1.** an oath or exclamation **2.** a word, phrase, etc. not needed for the sense but used merely to fill out a sentence or metrical line, for grammar, rhythm, balance, etc. [there in "there is nothing left" is an *expletive*] **3.** [Rare] anything serving as a filler —*adj.* used to fill out a sentence, line, etc.: also **ex'ple·to'ry** (-tôr'ē)

ex·pli·ca·ble (eks'pli kə b'l, iks plik'ə b'l) *adj.* [L. *explicabilis* + *explicare*: see ff.] that can be explained; explainable

ex·pli·cate (eks'pli kāt') *vt.* -**cat'ed**, -**cat'ing** [< L. *explicatus*, pp. of *explicare*, to unfold < *ex-*, out + *plicare*, to fold: see COMPLICATE] to make clear or explicit (something obscure or implied); explain fully —*SYN.* see EXPLAIN —**ex'pli·ca'tion** *n.* —**ex·pli·ca·tive** (-kāt'iv, ik splik'ə tiv), **ex·pli·ca·to·ry** (eks'pli kə tôr'ē, ik splik'ə-) *adj.* —**ex'pli·ca'tor** *n.*

‡**explication de texte** (ek splē kà syōn' də tekst') [Fr.] an intensive and exhaustive scrutiny and interpretation of a written work, often word by word

ex·plic·it (ik splis'it) *adj.* [OFr. *explicite* < ML. *explicitus* < L., pp. of *explicare*: see EXPLICATE] **1.** clearly stated and leaving nothing implied; distinctly expressed; definite: distinguished from IMPLICIT **2.** saying what is meant, without reservation or disguise; outspoken **3.** plain to see; readily observable —**ex·plic'it·ly** *adv.* —**ex·plic'it·ness** *n.* *SYN.*—**explicit** is applied to that which is so clearly stated or distinctly set forth that there should be no doubt as to the meaning; **express** adds to explicit the ideas of directness and positiveness; **exact** and **precise**, in this connection, both suggest that which is strictly defined, accurately stated, or made unmistakably clear; **definite** implies precise limitations as to the nature, character, meaning, etc. of something; **specific** implies the pointing out of details or the particularizing of references —*ANT.* **vague, ambiguous**

explicit function *Math.* a function whose values may be computed directly

ex·plode (ik splōd') *vt.* -**plod'ed**, -**plod'ing** [orig., to drive off the stage by clapping and hooting < L. *explodere* < *ex-*, off + *plaudere*, to applaud] **1.** to cause to be rejected; expose as false; discredit [to *explode* a theory] **2.** to make burst with a loud noise; blow up; detonate **3.** to cause to change suddenly and violently from a solid or liquid to a quickly expanding gas **4.** to cause rapid nuclear fusion or fission in, with accompanying destructive force —*vi.* **1.** to be exploded; burst noisily and violently **2.** to break forth noisily [to *explode* with anger] **3.** to increase very rapidly [an *exploding* population]—**ex·plod'a·ble** *adj.*—**ex·plod'er** *n.*

exploded view a photograph or drawing showing separately but in proper sequence and relationship the various parts of an assembly, as of a machine

ex·ploit (eks'ploit; *also, and for v. usually,* ik sploit') *n.* [ME. & OFr. *esploit*, an exploit, action < L. *explicitum*, neut. pp. of *explicare*: see EXPLICATE] an act remarkable for brilliance or daring; bold deed —*vt.* **1.** to make use of; turn to account; utilize productively **2.** to make unethical use of for one's own advantage or profit; specif., to make profit from the labor of (others) **3.** *Advertising* to stir up interest in; promote [to *exploit* a product] —**ex·ploit'a·ble** *adj.*—**ex·ploit'er** *n.*

ex·ploi·ta·tion (eks'ploi tā'shən) *n.* an exploiting or being exploited (in various senses)

ex·ploi·ta·tive (ik sploit'ə tiv) *adj.* **1.** exploiting **2.** of exploitation Also **ex·ploi'tive**

ex·plo·ra·tion (eks'plə rā'shən, -plô-) *n.* [L. *exploratio* < pp. of *explorare*: see EXPLORE] an exploring or being explored

ex·plor·a·to·ry (ik splôr'ə tôr'ē) *adj.* [ME. < L. *exploratorius*] of, in, or for exploration: also **ex·plor'a·tive** (-tiv)

ex·plore (ik splôr') *vt.* -**plored'**, -**plor'ing** [L. *explorare*, to search out < *ex-*, out + *plorare*, to cry out, wail] **1.** to look into closely; examine carefully; investigate **2.** to travel in (a region previously unknown or little known) in order to learn about its natural features, inhabitants, etc. **3.** *Med.* to examine (an organ, wound, etc.) by operation, probing, etc., as in order to make a diagnosis —*vi.* to explore new regions, etc.

ex·plor·er (-ər) *n.* a person who explores; esp., one who explores an unknown or little-known region

ex·plo·sion (ik splō'zhən) *n.* [L. *explosio* < pp. of *explodere*: see EXPLODE] **1.** an exploding; esp., a blowing up, or bursting with a loud noise; detonation **2.** the noise made by exploding **3.** a noisy outburst; loud breaking forth [an

explosion of wrath] **4.** a sudden, rapid, and widespread increase [the population *explosion*] **5.** *Phonet.* same as PLOSION

ex·plo·sive (-siv) *adj.* **1.** of, causing, or having the nature of, an explosion **2.** tending to explode; tending to burst forth noisily **3.** *Phonet.* same as PLOSIVE —*n.* **1.** a substance that can explode, as gunpowder **2.** *Phonet.* same as PLOSIVE —**ex·plo'sive·ly** *adv.* —**ex·plo'sive·ness** *n.*

ex·po·nent (ik spō'nənt; *for n. 3, usually* ek'spō'nənt) *adj.* [L. *exponens*, prp. of *exponere*: see EXPOUND] explaining, interpreting, or expounding —*n.* **1.** a person who sets forth, expounds, or promotes (principles, methods, etc.) **2.** a person or thing that is an example or symbol (*of* something); representative **3.** *Algebra* a small figure or symbol placed above and at the right of another figure or symbol to show how many times the latter is to be used as a factor (Ex.: $b^3 = b \times b \times b$)

ex·po·nen·tial (eks'pō nen'shəl) *adj. Math.* **1.** of or relating to an exponent **2.** involving a variable or unknown quantity as an exponent —**ex'po·nen'tial·ly** *adv.*

ex·port (ik spôrt'; *also, and for n. & adj. always,* eks'pôrt) *vt.* [L. *exportare* < *ex-*, out + *portare*, to carry: see PORT³] **1.** to carry or send (goods, etc.) to another country or other countries, esp. for purposes of sale **2.** to carry or send (ideas, culture, etc.) from one place to another **3.** [Now Rare] to carry off; transport —*n.* **1.** something exported **2.** the act or process of exporting —*adj.* of or for exporting or exports —**ex·port'a·ble** *adj.* —**ex·port'er** *n.*

ex·por·ta·tion (eks'pôr tā'shən) *n.* [L. *exportatio*] **1.** the act or process of exporting **2.** anything exported

ex·pos·al (eks pōz'l) *n.* same as EXPOSURE

ex·pose (ik spōz') *vt.* -**posed'**, -**pos'ing** [ME. *exposen* < OFr. *exposer* < L. *expositus*, pp. of *exponere* (see EXPOUND) but infl. in OFr. by *poser* < L. *pausare*: see POSE¹] **1.** *a*) to lay open (*to* danger, attack, ridicule, etc.); leave unprotected *b*) to make accessible or subject (*to* an influence or action) **2.** to put or leave out in an unprotected place; abandon [some ancient peoples *exposed* unwanted infants] **3.** to allow to be seen; disclose; reveal; exhibit; display **4.** *a*) to make (a crime, fraud, etc.) known; unmask *b*) to make known the crimes, etc. of **5.** *Photog.* to subject (a sensitized film or plate) to radiation having a photochemical effect —*SYN.* see SHOW —**ex·pos'er** *n.*

ex·po·sé (eks'pō zā') *n.* [Fr. < pp. of *exposer*: see EXPOSE] a public disclosure of a scandal, crime, etc.

ex·po·si·tion (eks'pə zish'ən) *n.* [ME. *exposicioun* < OFr. *exposition* < L. *expositio* < *expositus*, pp. of *exponere*: see EXPOUND] **1.** a setting forth of facts, ideas, etc.; detailed explanation **2.** writing or speaking that sets forth or explains **3.** [< Fr.] an exhibition; esp., a large public exhibition or show, often international in scope **4.** that part of a play, etc. which reveals what has happened before, who the characters are, etc. **5.** the first section of certain musical forms, which introduces the main theme or themes, as in a sonata, or all the voices, as in a fugue —**ex'po·si'tion·al** *adj.*

ex·pos·i·tor (ik späz'ə tər) *n.* [ME. *expositour* < OFr. *expositeur* < L. *expositor* < *expositus*, pp. of *exponere*: see EXPOUND] a person who expounds or explains

ex·pos·i·to·ry (-ə tôr'ē) *adj.* [ML. *expositorius*] of, like, or containing exposition; explanatory: also **ex·pos'i·tive** (-ə tiv)

ex post fac·to (eks pōst fak'tō) [L., from (the thing) done afterward] done or made afterward, esp. when having retroactive effect [an *ex post facto* law]

ex·pos·tu·late (ik späs'chə lāt') *vi.* -**lat'ed**, -**lat'ing** [< L. *expostulatus*, pp. of *expostulare*, to demand vehemently, require < *ex-*, intens. + *postulare*: see POSTULATE] to reason with a person earnestly, objecting to his actions or intentions; remonstrate (*with*) —*SYN.* see OBJECT —**ex·pos'tu·la'tion** *n.* —**ex·pos'tu·la'tor** *n.* —**ex·pos'tu·la·to·ry** (-lə tôr'ē) *adj.*

ex·po·sure (ik spō'zhər) *n.* [EXPOS(E) + -URE] **1.** an exposing or being exposed **2.** a location, as of a house, in relation to the sun, winds, etc. [an eastern *exposure*] **3.** appearance, esp. frequent appearance, before the public, as in the theater, on radio and TV, etc. **4.** the fact of being exposed in a helpless condition to the elements **5.** *Photog.* *a*) the subjection of a sensitized film or plate to the action of light rays, X-rays, etc. *b*) a sensitized surface or section of a film for making one picture *c*) the time during which such a surface or film is exposed

exposure meter *Photog.* an instrument for measuring the intensity of light on the subject and thus determining the correct exposure

ex·pound (ik spound') *vt.* [ME. *expounden* < OFr. *expondre* < L. *exponere*, to put forth, expound < *ex-*, out + *ponere*, to put: see POSITION] **1.** to set forth point by point; state in detail **2.** to explain or interpret; clarify —*SYN.* see EXPLAIN —**ex·pound'er** *n.*

ex·press (ik spres') *vt.* [ME. *expressen* < ML. *expressare* < L. *expressus*, pp. of *exprimere*, to express, lit., force out < *ex-*, out + *premere*: see PRESS¹] **1.** to press out or squeeze out (juice, etc.) **2.** to get by pressure; elicit by force; extort **3.** to put into words; represent by language; state **4.** to make known; reveal; show [his face *expressed* sorrow] **5.** to picture, represent, or symbolize in music, art, etc. **6.** to show by a sign; symbolize; signify [the sign + *expresses* addition] ☆**7.** to send by express —*adj.* [ME. & OFr. *expres*

< L. *expressus*] **1.** *a)* expressed and not implied; explicit [to give *express* orders] *b)* specific [his *express* reason for going] **2.** exact [she is the *express* image of her aunt] **3.** made for or suited to a specific purpose [*express* regulations] **4.** [orig., for the *express* purpose of running to one station] fast, direct, and making few stops [an *express* train] **5.** characterized by speed or velocity; specif., *a)* for fast driving [an *express* highway] *b)* high-speed [an *express* bullet] *c)* for high-speed projectiles [an *express* rifle] *d)* having to do with railway express, pony express, etc.: see the *n.* —*adv.* by express —*n.* **1.** [Chiefly Brit.] *a)* a special messenger; courier *b)* a message delivered by such a messenger; dispatch sent swiftly **2.** *a)* an express train, bus, elevator, etc. *b)* an express rifle **3.** the pony express ☆**4.** *a)* a method or service for transporting goods or sending money rapidly: express is usually more expensive than freight *b)* the goods transported or money sent by express *c)* a business concern operating such a service **5.** any method or means of swift transmission —*SYN.* see EXPLICIT, UTTER[2] —**express oneself 1.** to state one's thoughts **2.** to give expression to one's feelings, imagination, etc., usually in creative or artistic activity —**ex·press'er** *n.* —**ex·press'i·ble** *adj.*

☆**ex·press·age** (-ij) *n.* **1.** the carrying of packages, etc. by express **2.** the charge for this

ex·pres·sion (ik spresh'ən) *n.* [ME. *expressioun* < L. *expressio* < *expressus*: see EXPRESS] **1.** a pressing out or squeezing out, as of juice **2.** a putting into words or representing in language **3.** a picturing, representing, or symbolizing in art, music, etc. **4.** a manner of expressing; esp., a meaningful and eloquent manner of speaking, singing, etc. [to read with *expression*] **5.** a particular word, phrase, or sentence ["catch cold" is an idiomatic *expression*] **6.** a showing of feeling, character, etc. [laughter as an *expression* of joy] **7.** a look, intonation, sign, etc. that conveys meaning or feeling [a quizzical *expression* on the face] **8.** a symbol or set of symbols expressing some mathematical fact, as a quantity or operation **9.** a showing by a symbol, sign, figures, etc. **10.** *Genetics* the manifestation of a trait caused by a particular gene

ex·pres·sion·ism (-iz'm) *n.* an early 20th-cent. movement in art, literature, and drama, characterized by distortion of reality and the use of symbols, stylization, etc. to give objective expression to inner experience —**ex·pres'sion·ist** *adj., n.* —**ex·pres'sion·is'tic** *adj.* —**ex·pres'sion·is'ti·cal·ly** *adv.*

ex·pres·sion·less (-lis) *adj.* lacking expression; blank and impassive —**ex·pres'sion·less·ly** *adv.*

ex·pres·sive (ik spres'iv) *adj.* [ME. < ML. *expressivus*] **1.** of or characterized by expression **2.** that expresses or shows; indicative (*of*) [a song *expressive* of joy] **3.** full of meaning or feeling [an *expressive* nod] —**ex·pres'sive·ly** *adv.* —**ex·pres'sive·ness** *n.*

ex·pres·siv·i·ty (eks'pres iv'ə tē) *n.* **1.** the quality of being expressive **2.** *Genetics* the relative degree to which a trait caused by a particular gene is manifested in an individual

ex·press·ly (ik spres'lē) *adv.* **1.** in a plain and definite way; explicitly **2.** for the specific purpose; especially; particularly

☆**ex·press·man** (-mən) *n., pl.* **-men** (-mən) a person employed by an express company; esp., a driver of an express truck, who collects and delivers packages

ex·pres·so (ek spres'ō) *n. same as* ESPRESSO

express rifle a hunting rifle using a large charge and a light bullet of large caliber, discharged with a high initial velocity: used to kill large game at short range

☆**ex·press·way** (ik spres'wā) *n.* [EXPRESS + (HIGH)WAY] a divided highway for high-speed, through traffic, with full or partial control of access and with grade separations at all or most intersections

ex·pro·pri·ate (eks prō'prē āt') *vt.* **-at'ed, -at'ing** [< ML. *expropriatus*, pp. of *expropriare*, to deprive of one's own < L. *ex-*, out + *proprius*, one's own] **1.** to take (land, property, etc.) from its owner; esp., to take for public use or in the public interest, as by right of eminent domain; dispossess **2.** to transfer (property) from another to oneself —**ex·pro'pri·a'tion** *n.* —**ex·pro'pri·a'tor** *n.*

ex·pul·sion (ik spul'shən) *n.* [ME. *expulsioun* < OFr. *expulsion* < L. *expulsio* < *expulsus*, pp. of *expellere*] an expelling, or forcing out, or the condition of being expelled —**ex·pul'sive** (-siv) *adj.*

ex·punc·tion (ik spuŋk'shən) *n.* [LL. *expunctio* < L. *expunctus*, pp.] an expunging or being expunged

ex·punge (ik spunj') *vt.* **-punged', -pung'ing** [L. *expungere*, to mark (with points) for omission, erase < *ex-*, out + *pungere*, to prick: see POINT] to erase or remove completely; blot out or strike out; delete; cancel; efface —*SYN.* see ERASE

ex·pur·gate (eks'pər gāt') *vt.* **-gat'ed, -gat'ing** [< L. *expurgatus*, pp. of *expurgare*, to purge, cleanse < *ex-*, out + *purgare*, PURGE] to remove passages considered obscene or otherwise objectionable from (a book, etc.) —**ex'pur·ga'tion** *n.* —**ex'pur·ga'tor** *n.* —**ex·pur·ga·to·ry** (eks pur'gə tôr'ē) *adj.*

ex·qui·site (eks'kwi zit, ik skwiz'it) *adj.* [ME., carefully

sought out < L. *exquisitus*, pp. of *exquirere*, to search out < *ex-*, out + *quaerere*, to ask] **1.** carefully done or elaborately made [an *exquisite* design] **2.** very beautiful or lovely, esp. in a delicate or carefully wrought way [*exquisite* lace] **3.** of highest quality; consummate [*exquisite* technique] **4.** highly sensitive; keenly discriminating; fastidious [an *exquisite* ear for music] **5.** sharply intense; keen [*exquisite* pain] —*n.* a person who makes a great show of being very sensitive, refined, and fastidious in his tastes, etc. —*SYN.* see DELICATE —**ex'qui·site·ly** *adv.* —**ex'qui·site·ness** *n.*

ex·san·guine (eks saŋ'gwin) *adj.* bloodless; anemic

ex·scind (ek sind') *vt.* [L. *exscindere* < *ex-*, out + *scindere*, to cut: see SCISSION] to cut out; excise; extirpate

ex·sect (ek sekt') *vt.* [< L. *exsectus*, pp. of *exsecare* < *ex-*, out + *secare*, to cut] to cut out —**ex·sec'tion** *n.*

ex·sert (ek surt') *vt.* [< L. *exsertus*, pp. of *exserere*, to stretch out: see EXERT] to thrust out; protrude; project —*adj. same as* EXSERTED —**ex·ser'tile** (-sur't'l) *adj.* —**ex·ser'tion** *n.*

ex·sert·ed (-id) *adj.* projecting, as from a sheath or pod

ex·sic·cate (ek'si kāt') *vt., vi.* **-cat'ed, -cat'ing** [ME. *exsiccaten* < L. *exsiccatus*, pp. of *exsiccare*, to make dry < *ex-*, out + *siccare*, to dry < *siccus*, dry: see DESICCATE] to dry up —**ex'sic·ca'tion** *n.*

ex·stip·u·late (eks stip'yoo lit, -lāt') *adj. Bot.* having no stipules

ex·stro·phy (eks'trə fē) *n.* [< EX-[1] + Gr. *strophē*, a turning: see STROPHE] *Med.* the turning inside out of an organ; esp., such a congenital condition of the urinary bladder

ext. 1. extension **2.** exterior **3.** external **4.** extinct **5.** extra **6.** extract

ex·tant (ek'stənt, ik stant') *adj.* [L. *extans, exstans*, prp. of *exstare*, to stand out or forth < *ex-*, out + *stare*, STAND] **1.** still existing; not extinct; not lost or destroyed **2.** [Archaic] standing out; conspicuous

ex·tem·po·ral (ik stem'pər əl) *adj.* [L. *extemporalis*: see EXTEMPORE] *archaic var. of* EXTEMPORANEOUS

ex·tem·po·ra·ne·ous (ik stem'pə rā'nē əs) *adj.* [LL. *extemporaneus*: see EXTEMPORE] **1.** made, done, or spoken without any preparation; unpremeditated; offhand [an *extemporaneous* speech] **2.** spoken with some preparation but not written out or memorized: distinguished from IMPROMPTU **3.** speaking or adept at speaking without preparation **4.** made for the occasion; improvised —*SYN.* see IMPROMPTU —**ex·tem'po·ra'ne·ous·ly** *adv.*

ex·tem·po·rar·y (ik stem'pə rer'ē) *adj. same as* EXTEMPORANEOUS —*SYN.* see IMPROMPTU —**ex·tem'po·rar'i·ly** *adv.* —**ex·tem'po·rar'i·ness** *n.*

ex·tem·po·re (ik stem'pə rē) *adv., adj.* [L., lit., out of the time < *ex*, from, out of + *tempore*, abl. of *tempus*, time: see TEMPER] without preparation; offhand [a speech given *extempore*] —*SYN.* see IMPROMPTU

ex·tem·po·rize (-rīz') *vi., vt.* **-rized', -riz'ing 1.** to speak, perform, or compose extempore; improvise **2.** to furnish or contrive (things) in a makeshift way to meet a pressing need —**ex·tem'po·ri·za'tion** *n.* —**ex·tem'po·riz'er** *n.*

ex·tend (ik stend') *vt.* [ME. *extended* < L. *extendere* < *ex-*, out + *tendere*, to stretch: see TEND[2]] **1.** to stretch out or draw out to a certain point, or for a certain distance or time **2.** to enlarge in area, scope, influence, meaning, effect, etc.; widen; broaden; expand; spread **3.** to stretch or thrust forth; hold out; proffer **4.** to present for acceptance; offer; accord; grant **5.** to stretch or straighten out (a flexed limb of the body) **6.** *a)* to make longer in time or space; prolong *b)* to allow a period of time for the payment of (a loan, mortgage, etc.) beyond that originally set **7.** to make (oneself) work or try very hard **8.** to give added bulk or body to (a substance) by adding another, usually cheaper or inferior, substance **9.** [Obs.] to gain control of by force **10.** *Law a)* in Great Britain, to assess; value *b)* to seize or levy upon, as by a writ of extent —*vi.* **1.** to be extended **2.** to lie or stretch [the fence *extends* to the meadow] *SYN.*—**extend** and **lengthen** both imply a making longer in space or time, but **extend**, in addition, may signify an enlarging in area, scope, influence, meaning, etc.; **elongate** is a synonym for **lengthen** in the spatial sense and is more commonly used in technical applications; **prolong** and **protract** both primarily imply an extending in time, **prolong** suggesting continuation beyond the usual or expected time, and **protract** a being drawn out needlessly or wearyingly

ex·tend·ed (ik sten'did) *adj.* **1.** stretched out; spread out **2.** prolonged; continued **3.** enlarged in influence, meaning, scope, effect, etc.; extensive; widespread **4.** *Printing* designating type with a wider face than is standard for the height

ex·tend·er (-dər) *n.* **1.** a substance or ingredient added to another to give more bulk or body or to adulterate or dilute it **2.** a part added or attached, for lengthening

ex·tend·i·ble (-də b'l) *adj. same as* EXTENSIBLE

ex·ten·si·ble (-sə b'l) *adj.* [Fr. < ML. *extensibilis* < L. *extensus*, pp. of *extendere*] that can be extended: also **ex·ten'sile** (-s'l) —**ex·ten'si·bil'i·ty** *n.*

ex·ten·sion (ik sten'shən) *n.* [ME. *extensioun* < L. *extensio* < pp. of *extendere*] **1.** an extending or being ex-

tended **2.** the amount or degree to which something is or can be extended; range; extent **3.** a part that forms a continuation or addition [an *extension* to a factory] **4.** an extra period of time allowed a debtor for making payment **5.** a branch of a university for students who cannot attend the university proper **6.** an extra telephone connected to the same line as the main telephone **7.** *a)* the straightening of a flexed limb *b)* traction applied to a fractured or dislocated limb so as to bring it into its normal position **8.** *Logic* the total number of objects to which a single term applies; denotation: opposed to INTENSION **9.** *Physics* that property of a body by which it occupies space —☆*adj.* designating a device that can be extended or that extends something else [*extension* ladder, *extension* cord] —**ex·ten′sion·al** *adj.*

ex·ten·si·ty (-sə tē) *n.* **1.** the quality of having extension **2.** *Psychol.* that quality of sensation which permits the perception of space or size

ex·ten·sive (-siv) *adj.* [ME. < L. *extensivus* < *extensus:* see EXTENSIBLE] **1.** having great extent; covering a large area; vast **2.** having a wide scope, effect, influence, etc.; far-reaching; comprehensive **3.** of or characterized by extension **4.** designating or of farming in which large areas of land are used with comparatively little cultivation — **ex·ten′sive·ly** *adv.* —**ex·ten′sive·ness** *n.*

ex·ten·som·e·ter (eks′ten säm′ə tər) *n.* [< L. *extensus* (see EXTENSIBLE) + -METER] an instrument for measuring extremely small degrees of expansion, contraction, or deformation, as in a test piece of metal subjected to tension, compression, etc.

ex·ten·sor (ik sten′sər) *n.* [LL. *extensor,* stretcher < L. *extensus:* see EXTENSIBLE] any of various muscles that extend or straighten some part of the body, esp. a flexed arm or leg

ex·tent (ik stent′) *n.* [ME. *extente* < Anglo-Fr. *extente* < OFr. *estente* < *estendre* < L. *extendere*] **1.** the space, amount, or degree to which a thing extends; size; length; breadth **2.** range or limits of anything; scope; coverage **3.** an extended space; vast area [an *extent* of woodland] **4.** formerly, in Britain, an assessment or valuation, as of land **5.** *Law a)* in Great Britain, a writ (**writ of extent**) by which the person, goods, and property of a debtor could formerly be seized to force payment *b)* seizure by such a writ *c)* in the U.S., a writ giving to a creditor temporary ownership of his debtor's lands

ex·ten·u·ate (ik sten′yōo wāt′) *vt.* -**at′ed, -at′ing** [< L. *extenuatus,* pp. of *extenuare* < *ex-,* out + *tenuare,* to make thin < *tenuis,* THIN] **1.** orig., to make thin or lean **2.** [Now Rare] to diminish or weaken **3.** to lessen or seem to lessen the seriousness of (an offense, guilt, etc.) by giving excuses or serving as an excuse [*extenuating* circumstances] **4.** [Archaic] to underrate; underestimate **5.** [Obs.] to belittle or disparage —**ex·ten′u·a′tor** *n.*

ex·ten·u·a·tion (ik sten′yōo wā′shən) *n.* [ME. *extenuacioun* < L. *extenuatio*] **1.** an extenuating or being extenuated; esp., mitigation, as of the seriousness of a crime, offense, etc. **2.** a thing that extenuates; partial excuse

ex·ten·u·a·to·ry (ik sten′yōo wə tôr′ē) *adj.* extenuating or tending to extenuate: also **ex·ten′u·a′tive** (-wāt′iv)

ex·te·ri·or (ik stir′ē ər) *adj.* [L., compar. of *exter, exterus,* on the outside: see EXTERNAL] **1.** *a)* on the outside; outer; outermost [an *exterior* wall] *b)* to be used on the outside [*exterior* paint] **2.** originating outside; acting or coming from without [*exterior* forces] —*n.* **1.** an outside or outside surface **2.** an outward appearance [a misleading *exterior*] ☆**3.** a picture, view, stage setting, etc. of a scene outdoors —**ex·te′ri·or·ly** *adv.*

exterior angle 1. any of the four angles formed on the outside of two straight lines by a straight line cutting across them **2.** an angle formed by any side of a polygon and the extension of the adjacent side

ex·te·ri·or·i·ty (ik stir′ē ôr′ə tē) *n.* **1.** the state or quality of being exterior or exteriorized **2.** external aspect

ex·te·ri·or·ize (ik stir′ē ə rīz′) *vt.* -**ized′, -iz′ing 1.** to give or attribute an external form or objective character outside the self to (states of mind, attitudes, etc.) **2.** same as EXTERNALIZE —**ex·te′ri·or·i·za′tion** *n.*

EXTERIOR ANGLES
(CEL, LER, ADT, TDF)

ex·ter·mi·nate (ik stur′mə nāt′) *vt.* -**nat′ed, -nat′ing** [< L. *exterminatus,* pp. of *exterminare,* lit., to drive beyond the boundaries, hence drive out, destroy < *ex-,* out + *terminus,* boundary: see TERM] to destroy or get rid of entirely, as by killing; wipe out; annihilate —**ex·ter′mi·na′tion** *n.*

SYN.—exterminate implies the complete, wholesale destruction of living beings or things whose existence is considered undesirable; **extirpate** and **eradicate** both suggest the extinction or abolition of something, **extirpate** implying a deliberate and violent destruction at the very source so that the thing cannot be regenerated, and **eradicate** connoting less violence and, often, the working of natural processes or a methodical plan

ex·ter·mi·na·tor (-nāt′ər) *n.* [LL.(Ec.)] a person or thing that exterminates; specif., ☆*a)* a person whose work or business is exterminating rats, cockroaches, and other vermin ☆*b)* any of various powders, liquids, etc. for exterminating vermin

ex·ter·mi·na·to·ry (-nə tôr′ē) *adj.* exterminating or tending to exterminate: also **ex·ter′mi·na′tive** (-nāt′iv)

ex·tern (ek′stərn) *n.* [Fr. *externe* < L. *externus:* see ff.] a person having some connection with, but not living in, an institution, as a nonresident doctor in a hospital: opposed to INTERN

ex·ter·nal (ik stur′n'l) *adj.* [ME. < L. *externus,* outward, external < *exter, exterus,* on the outside, compar. form < *ex,* out of (see EX-¹) + -AL] **1.** on or having to do with the outside; outer; exterior **2.** on, or for use on, the outside of the body [a medicine for *external* use only] **3.** *a)* outwardly visible *b)* existing apart from the mind; material **4.** originating outside; acting or coming from without [an *external* force] **5.** *a)* for outward appearance or show; superficial [*external* politeness] *b)* not basic or essential [*external* factors] **6.** having to do with foreign countries and international affairs —*n.* **1.** an outside or outward surface or part **2.** [*pl.*] outward appearance or behavior; superficialities —**ex·ter′nal·ly** *adv.*

ex·ter·nal-com·bus·tion engine (-kəm bus′chən) an engine, as a steam engine, that obtains its power from heat produced by burning fuel outside the cylinder or cylinders

external galaxy any of the vast number of galaxies like the one containing the solar system

ex·ter·nal·ism (-iz'm) *n.* **1.** *same as* EXTERNALITY (sense 1) **2.** too great a regard for externals

ex·ter·nal·i·ty (eks′tər nal′ə tē) *n.* **1.** the quality or state of being external **2.** *pl.* -**ties** an external thing

ex·ter·nal·ize (ik stur′n'l īz′) *vt.* -**ized′, -iz′ing 1.** to make external; embody **2.** *same as* EXTERIORIZE — **ex·ter′nal·i·za′tion** *n.*

external respiration exchange of oxygen and carbon dioxide across external or respiratory surfaces, as gills or lungs, in multicellular organisms: cf. INTERNAL RESPIRATION

ex·ter·o·cep·tor (ek′stər ō sep′tər) *n.* [L. *exter* (see EXTERNAL) + -o- + (RE)CEPTOR] a sense organ of the skin

ex·ter·ri·to·ri·al (eks′ter ə tôr′ē əl) *adj.* same as EXTRATERRITORIAL

ex·tinct (ik stiŋkt′) *adj.* [ME. < L. *extinctus, exstinctus,* pp. of *exstinguere:* see EXTINGUISH] **1.** *a)* having died down or burned out; extinguished [an *extinct* fire] *b)* no longer active [an *extinct* volcano] **2.** no longer in existence or use; specif., having no living descendant [an *extinct* species] **3.** that no living person holds or can claim: said of offices, titles, etc. —*SYN.* see DEAD

ex·tinc·tion (ik stiŋk′shən) *n.* [ME. *extinccioun* < L. *exstinctio < exstinctus:* see prec.] **1.** a putting out or being put out, as of a fire **2.** a destroying or being destroyed; annihilation; abolition **3.** the fact or state of being or becoming extinct; dying out, as of a race, species of animal, etc.

ex·tinc·tive (-tiv) *adj.* [ME. *extinctif:* see EXTINCT] serving or tending to extinguish

ex·tin·guish (ik stiŋ′gwish) *vt.* [L. *extinguere, exstinguere,* to quench, destroy < *ex-,* out + *stinguere,* to extinguish (for IE. base see STICK) + -*ish,* as in ABOLISH, BANISH] **1.** to put out (a fire, etc.); quench; smother **2.** to put an end to; destroy or cause to die out **3.** to put in the shade; eclipse; obscure **4.** *Law a)* to make void; nullify *b)* to settle (a debt) by payment, etc. —**ex·tin′guish·a·ble** *adj.* —**ex·tin′guish·ment** *n.*

ex·tin·guish·er (-ər) *n.* a person or thing that extinguishes; esp., *same as* FIRE EXTINGUISHER

ex·tir·pate (ek′stər pāt′, ik stur′pāt) *vt.* -**pat′ed, -pat′ing** [< L. *extirpatus,* pp. of *extirpare, exstirpare,* to root out < *ex-,* out + *stirps,* lower part of a tree, root < IE. base *ster-,* stiff: cf. STARE, STARVE, STARK] **1.** to pull up by the roots; root out **2.** to destroy or remove completely; exterminate; abolish —*SYN.* see EXTERMINATE —**ex′tir·pa′tion** *n.* —**ex′tir·pa′tive** *adj.* —**ex′tir·pa′tor** *n.*

ex·tol, ex·toll (ik stōl′) *vt.* -**tolled′, -tol′ling** [ME. *extollen* < L. *extollere,* to raise up < *ex-,* out, up + *tollere,* to raise: see TOLERATE] to praise highly; laud —*SYN.* see PRAISE —**ex·tol′ler** *n.* —**ex·tol′ment, ex·toll′ment** *n.*

ex·tort (ik stôrt′) *vt.* [< L. *extortus,* pp. of *extorquere,* to twist or turn out < *ex-,* out + *torquere,* to twist: see TORT] to get (money, etc.) from someone by violence, threats, misuse of authority, etc.; exact or wrest (*from*) —*SYN.* see EXTRACT —**ex·tort′er** *n.* —**ex·tor′tive** *adj.*

ex·tor·tion (ik stôr′shən) *n.* [ME. *extorcioun* < OFr. *extorcion* < LL.(Ec.) *extorsio* < L. *extortus*] **1.** *a)* the act of extorting, or getting money, etc. by threats, misuse of authority, etc.: sometimes applied to the exaction of too high a price *b)* the legal offense committed by an official who extorts **2.** something extorted

ex·tor·tion·ate (-it) *adj.* **1.** characterized by, or having the nature of, extortion **2.** excessive; exorbitant [an *extortionate* price]: also **ex·tor′tion·ar′y** (-er′ē)

ex·tor·tion·er (-ər) *n.* a person guilty of extortion: also **ex·tor′tion·ist**

ex·tra (eks′trə) *adj.* [contr. < EXTRAORDINARY; also < L. *extra,* additional, extra < *extra,* adv., more than, outside: see ff.] **1.** more, larger, or better than is normal, expected, usual, necessary, etc.; additional or superior **2.** to be

paid for by an added charge —*n.* an extra person or thing; specif., *a)* an additional charge: *often used in pl.* ☆*b)* a special edition of a newspaper as formerly put out between regular editions to cover news of unusual importance *c)* an extra benefit or additional feature *d)* a spare or leftover copy, duplicate, etc. *e)* an extra worker *f) Cricket* a run not made from a hit, as a bye *g) Motion Pictures* an actor hired by the day to play a minor part, as a member of a mob scene, etc. —*adv.* more than usually; esp., exceptionally *[extra* good quality*]*

ex·tra- (eks′trə) [L. < *exter, exterus:* see EXTERNAL] *an adj.-forming prefix meaning* outside, outside the scope or region of, beyond, besides, as in the following list:

extracellular	extramarital
extracerebral	extraofficial
extracontinental	extraplanetary
extracorporeal	extraprofessional
extrafamilial	extrasocial
extragovernmental	extrasolar
extrahistoric	extraterrestrial

☆**ex·tra-base hit** (-bās′) *Baseball* any hit greater than a single; double, triple, or home run

ex·tra-bold (-bōld′) *n. Printing* a style of type heavier than boldface

ex·tra·ca·non·i·cal (-kə nän′i k'l) *adj.* not included in the canon; not among the authorized books

ex·tract (ik strakt′; *for n.* eks′trakt) *vt.* [ME. *extracten* < L. *extractus,* pp. of *extrahere,* to draw out < *ex-,* out + *trahere,* to DRAW] **1.** to draw out by effort; pull out *[to extract* a tooth, to *extract* a promise from someone*]* **2.** to remove or separate (metal) from ore **3.** to obtain as an extract by pressing, distilling, using a solvent, etc. *[to extract* juice from fruit*]* **4.** to obtain as if by drawing out; deduce (a principle), derive or elicit (information, pleasure, etc.), or the like **5.** to copy out or quote (a passage from a book, etc.); excerpt **6.** *Math.* to compute (the root of a quantity) —*n.* something extracted; specif., *a)* a concentrated form, whether solid, viscid, or liquid, of a food, flavoring, etc. *[beef extract] b)* a passage selected from a book, etc.; excerpt; quotation *c) Pharmacy* the substance obtained by treating a drug with some solvent, as ether or alcohol, and then evaporating the preparation —**ex·tract′a·ble, ex·tract′i·ble** *adj.*

SYN.—**extract** implies a drawing out of something, as if by pulling, sucking, etc. *[to extract* a promise*];* **educe** suggests a drawing out or evolving of something that is latent or undeveloped *[laws were educed* from tribal customs*];* **elicit** connotes difficulty or skill in drawing out something hidden or buried *[his jokes elicited* no smiles*];* **evoke** implies a calling forth or summoning, as of a mental image, by stimulating the emotions *[the odor evoked* a memory of childhood*];* **extort** suggests a forcing or wresting of something, as by violence or threats *[to extort* a ransom*]*

ex·trac·tion (ik strak′shən) *n.* [ME. *extraccioun* < ML. *extractio*] **1.** the act or process of extracting; specif., the extracting of a tooth by an oral surgeon **2.** origin; lineage; descent *[a* man of French *extraction]* **3.** a thing extracted; extract

ex·trac·tive (-tiv) *adj.* [ME. *extractif* < ML. *extractivus*] **1.** extracting or having to do with extraction **2.** capable of being extracted **3.** having the nature of an extract —*n.* **1.** an extractive substance **2.** an extract

ex·trac·tor (-tər) *n.* a person or thing that extracts; specif., the part of a breechloading gun that withdraws the cartridge or shell case from the chamber

☆**ex·tra·cur·ric·u·lar** (eks′trə kə rik′yə lər) *adj.* not part of the required curriculum; outside the regular course of study but under the supervision of the school *[dramatics, athletics, and other extracurricular* activities*]*

ex·tra·dit·a·ble (eks′trə dīt′ə b'l) *adj.* **1.** that can be extradited **2.** making liable to extradition

ex·tra·dite (eks′trə dīt′) *vt.* -**dit′ed, -dit′ing** [backformation < ff.] **1.** to turn over (an alleged criminal, fugitive, etc.) to the jurisdiction of another country, State, etc. **2.** to obtain the extradition of

ex·tra·di·tion (eks′trə dish′ən) *n.* [Fr. < L. *ex,* out + *traditio,* a surrender: see TRADITION] the turning over of an alleged criminal, fugitive, or prisoner by one country, State, etc. to another

ex·tra·dos (eks′trə däs′, -dōs′; ik strā′däs) *n.* [Fr. < L. *extra,* beyond + Fr. *dos* < L. *dorsum,* back] *Archit.* the outside curved surface of an arch

ex·tra·ga·lac·tic (eks′trə gə lak′tik) *adj.* outside or beyond the Galaxy, or Milky Way

ex·tra·ju·di·cial (-jōō dish′əl) *adj.* **1.** outside or beyond the jurisdiction of a court **2.** outside the usual course of justice —**ex′tra·ju·di′cial·ly** *adv.*

ex·tra·le·gal (-lē′g'l) *adj.* outside of legal control or authority; not regulated by law —**ex′tra·le′gal·ly** *adv.*

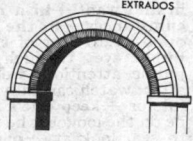

EXTRADOS

ex·tra·mun·dane (-mun′dān) *adj.* [LL. *extramundanus:* see EXTRA- & MUNDANE] outside the physical world; not of this world

ex·tra·mu·ral (-myoor′əl) *adj.* [see EXTRA- & MURAL] outside the walls or limits of a city, school, university, etc. *[extramural* activities*]*

ex·tra·ne·ous (ik strā′nē əs) *adj.* [L. *extraneus,* external, foreign < *extra:* see EXTRA-] **1.** coming from outside; foreign *[an extraneous* substance*]* **2.** not truly or properly belonging; not essential **3.** not pertinent; irrelevant — *SYN.* see EXTRINSIC —**ex·tra′ne·ous·ly** *adv.* —**ex·tra′ne·ous·ness** *n.*

ex·tra·nu·cle·ar (eks′trə nōō′klē ər, -nyōō′-) *adj.* located or occurring outside of the nucleus of a cell

ex·traor·di·nar·y (ik strôr′d'n er′ē; *for 3* eks′trə ôr′-) *adj.* [ME. *extraordinari* < L. *extraordinarius* < *extra ordinem,* out of the usual order < *extra* + acc. of *ordo,* ORDER] **1.** not according to the usual custom or regular plan *[an extraordinary* session of Congress*]* **2.** going far beyond the ordinary degree, measure, limit, etc.; very unusual; exceptional; remarkable **3.** outside of the regular staff; sent on a special errand; having special authority or responsibility *[an* envoy *extraordinary]* —**ex·traor′di·nar′i·ly** *adv.* —**ex·traor′di·nar′i·ness** *n.*

ex·trap·o·late (ik strap′ə lāt′) *vt., vi.* -**lat′ed, -lat′ing** [L. *extra* (see EXTRA-) + (INTER)POLATE] **1.** *Statistics* to estimate or infer (a value, quantity, etc. beyond the known range) on the basis of certain variables within the known range, from which the estimated value is assumed to follow **2.** to arrive at (conclusions or results) by hypothesizing from known facts or observations **3.** to speculate as to consequences on the basis of (known facts or observations) —**ex·trap′o·la′tion** *n.* —**ex·trap′o·la′tive** *adj.* —**ex·trap′o·la′tor** *n.*

ex·tra·sen·so·ry (eks′trə sen′sər ē) *adj.* designating or of perception that seems to occur apart from, or in addition to, the normal function of the usual senses

ex·tra·sys·to·le (-sis′tə lē′) *n.* [EXTRA- + SYSTOLE] a disturbance of heart rhythm resulting in an extra contraction of the heart between regular beats —**ex′tra·sys·tol′ic** (-sis täl′ik) *adj.*

ex·tra·ter·ri·to·ri·al (-ter′ə tôr′ē əl) *adj.* **1.** outside the territorial limits or jurisdiction of the country, State, etc. **2.** of extraterritoriality *[extraterritorial* rights*]* —**ex′tra·ter′ri·to′ri·al·ly** *adv.*

ex·tra·ter·ri·to·ri·al·i·ty (-ter′ə tôr′ē al′ə tē) *n.* **1.** freedom from the jurisdiction of the country in which one is living, as in the case of foreign diplomats **2.** jurisdiction of a country over its citizens in foreign lands

ex·tra·u·ter·ine (-yōōt′ər in) *adj.* outside the uterus

ex·trav·a·gance (ik strav′ə gəns) *n.* [Fr.: see ff.] **1.** a going beyond reasonable or proper limits in conduct or speech; unreasonable excess **2.** a spending of more than is reasonable or necessary; excessive expenditure; wastefulness **3.** an instance of excess in spending, behavior, or speech Also **ex·trav′a·gan·cy,** *pl.* -**cies**

ex·trav·a·gant (-gənt) *adj.* [ME. & Anglo-Fr. *extravagaunt* < ML. *extravagans,* prp. of *extravagari,* to stray < L. *extra,* beyond + *vagari,* to wander: see VAGUE] **1.** orig., straying beyond bounds; wandering **2.** going beyond reasonable limits; excessive or unrestrained *[extravagant* demands*]* **3.** too ornate or showy *[extravagant* designs*]* **4.** costing or spending too much; wasteful —*SYN.* see EXCESSIVE, PROFUSE —**ex·trav′a·gant·ly** *adv.*

ex·trav·a·gan·za (ik strav′ə gan′zə) *n.* [respelled after L. < It. *estravaganza,* extravagance < *estravagante* < ML. *extravagans:* see prec.] **1.** a literary, musical, or dramatic fantasy characterized by a loose structure and farce **2.** a spectacular, elaborate theatrical production, as some musical shows

ex·trav·a·gate (ik strav′ə gāt′) *vi.* -**gat′ed, -gat′ing** [< ML. *extravagatus,* pp.: see EXTRAVAGANT] [Rare] **1.** to stray; wander **2.** to go beyond reasonable limits; be extravagant —**ex·trav′a·ga′tion** *n.*

ex·trav·a·sate (ik strav′ə sāt′) *vt.* -**sat′ed, -sat′ing** [L. *extra* (see EXTRA-) + *vas,* a vessel + -ATE[1]] to allow or force (blood, etc.) to flow from its normal vessels into the surrounding body tissues —*vi.* **1.** to flow out or escape into surrounding tissues: said of blood, lymph, etc. **2.** to flow out in liquid form, as lava from a vent —**ex·trav′a·sa′tion** *n.*

ex·tra·vas·cu·lar (eks′trə vas′kyə lər) *adj.* outside the vascular system, or the blood and lymph vessels

☆**ex·tra·ve·hic·u·lar** (-vē hik′yoo lər) *adj.* designating or of activity by an astronaut outside a vehicle in space

ex·tra·ver·sion (eks′trə vur′zhən) *n. same as* EXTROVERSION (sense 2) —**ex′tra·vert′** (-vurt′) *n., adj.*

ex·treme (ik strēm′) *adj.* [ME. & OFr. < L. *extremus,* last, outermost, superl. of *exterus,* outer: see EXTERNAL] **1.** at the end or outermost point; farthest away; most remote; utmost **2.** *a)* in or to the greatest degree; very great or greatest *[extreme* pain*] b)* to an excessive degree; immoderate **3.** far from what is usual or conventional **4.** deviating to the greatest degree from the center of opinion, as in politics **5.** very severe; drastic *[extreme* measures*]* **6.**

[Archaic] last; final —*n.* **1.** either of two things that are as different or far as possible from each other **2.** an extreme degree **3.** an extreme act, expedient, etc. **4.** an extreme state or condition [an *extreme* of distress] **5.** [Obs.] an extreme point; extremity **6.** *Logic a)* the subject or predicate of a proposition *b)* the major or minor term of a syllogism **7.** *Math.* the first or last term of a proportion —**go to extremes** to be excessive or immoderate in speech or action —**in the extreme** to the utmost degree —**ex·treme′ly** *adv.* —**ex·treme′ness** *n.*

extremely high frequency *Radio* any frequency between 30,000 and 300,000 megahertz

extreme unction *same as* ANOINTING OF THE SICK

ex·trem·ism (ik strēm′iz′m) *n.* the quality or state of going to extremes, esp. the extreme right or extreme left in politics —**ex·trem′ist** *adj., n.*

ex·trem·i·ty (ik strem′ə tē) *n., pl.* **-ties** [ME. & OFr. *extremite* < L. *extremitas* < *extremus*: see EXTREME] **1.** the outermost or utmost point or part; end **2.** the greatest degree **3.** a state of extreme necessity, danger, etc. **4.** the end of life; dying **5.** an extreme measure; severe or strong action: *usually used in pl.* **6.** *a)* a body limb *b)* [pl.] the hands and feet

ex·tre·mum (ik strē′məm) *n., pl.* **-tre·ma** (-mə) [ModL. < L., an end, neut. of *extremus*: see EXTREME] *Math.* the maximum or minimum value of a function

ex·tri·cate (eks′trə kāt′) *vt.* **-cat′ed, -cat′ing** [< L. *extricatus*, pp. of *extricare*, to disentangle < *ex-*, out + *tricae*, hindrances, vexations] to set free; release or disentangle (*from* a net, difficulty, embarrassment, etc.) —**ex′tri·ca·bil′i·ty** *n.* —**ex′tri·ca·ble** (-kə b′l) *adj.* —**ex′tri·ca′tion** *n.*

ex·trin·sic (ek strin′sik) *adj.* [Fr. *extrinsèque* < L. *extrinsecus*, from without, outer < *exter*, without + *secus*, following, otherwise < base of *sequi*, to follow] **1.** not really belonging to the thing with which it is connected; not inherent **2.** being, coming, or acting from the outside; extraneous Opposed to INTRINSIC —**ex·trin′si·cal·ly** *adv.* **SYN.**—*extrinsic* refers to that which coming from outside a thing is not inherent in its real nature [the *extrinsic* advantages of wealth]; **extraneous,** often synonymous with *extrinsic,* may connote the possibility of integration of the external object into the thing to which it is added [*extraneous* grace notes]; **foreign** implies that the external object is organically so different that it cannot become assimilated [a *foreign* substance in the blood]; **alien** emphasizes the incompatibility of the external object with the subject in question ["nothing human is *alien* to me"] —**ANT. intrinsic**

extrinsic factor *same as* VITAMIN B₁₂

ex·tro- (eks′trə) *same as* EXTRA- (when opposed to INTRO-)

ex·trorse (eks trôrs′) *adj.* [Fr. < LL. *extrorsus* < L. *extra*, outside + *versus*, pp. of *vertere*, to turn] *Bot.* turned outward or away from the axis of growth: opposed to INTRORSE —**ex·trorse′ly** *adv.*

ex·tro·ver·sion (eks′trə vur′zhən, -shən) *n.* [altered < G. *extraversion* < L. *extra-* (see EXTRA-) + ML. *versio*, a turning: see VERSION] **1.** *Med. same as* EXSTROPHY **2.** [G.] *Psychol.* an attitude in which a person directs his interest to things outside himself and to other persons rather than to his own experiences and feelings: opposed to INTROVERSION

ex·tro·vert (eks′trə vurt′) *n.* [see prec.] *Psychol.* a person whose interest is more in his environment and in other people than in himself; person who is active and expressive, or other than introspective: opposed to INTROVERT —*adj. same as* EXTROVERTED

ex·tro·vert·ed (-id) *adj.* characterized by extroversion

ex·trude (ik strōōd′) *vt.* **-trud′ed, -trud′ing** [L. *extrudere*, to thrust out or forth < *ex-*, out + *trudere*, THRUST] **1.** to push or force out; expel **2.** to force (metal, plastic, etc.) through a die or very small holes to give it a certain shape —*vi.* to be extruded; esp., to protrude —**ex·trud′er** *n.* —**ex·tru′sion** (-strōō′zhən) *n.*

ex·tru·sive (ik strōōs′iv) *adj.* **1.** extruding or tending to extrude **2.** *Geol.* forced out in a molten state through the earth's crust; volcanic [*extrusive* rock]

ex·tu·bate (eks tōō′bāt, -tyōō′-) *vt.* **-bat·ed, -bat·ing** [EX-¹ + TUB(E) + -ATE¹] to remove a tube from (a part of the body, as an air passage) —**ex′tu·ba′tion** *n.*

ex·u·ber·ance (ig zōō′bər əns, -zyōō′-) *n.* [Fr. *exubérance* < L. *exuberantia* < L. *exuberans*, prp. of *exuberare*, to come forth in abundance < *ex-*, intens. + *uberare*, to bear abundantly < *uber*, UDDER] **1.** the state or quality of being exuberant; great abundance; luxuriance **2.** an instance of this; esp., action or speech showing high spirits Also **ex·u′ber·an·cy** (-ən sē), *pl.* **-cies**

ex·u·ber·ant (-ənt) *adj.* [ME. < L. *exuberans*: see prec.] **1.** growing profusely; luxuriant or prolific [*exuberant* vegetation] **2.** characterized by good health and high spirits; full of life; uninhibited **3.** overly elaborate; flowery **4.** very great; extreme —**ex·u′ber·ant·ly** *adv.*

ex·u·ber·ate (-bə rāt′) *vi.* **-at′ed, -at′ing** [ME. *exuberaten* < L. *exuberatus*, pp. of *exuberare*] [Rare] to be exuberant; abound

ex·u·date (eks′yə dāt′, -ə-; ig zyōō′dāt) *n.* [L. *exudatus*, pp. of *exudare*: see EXUDE] matter exuded

ex·u·da·tion (eks′yə dā′shən, -ə-) *n.* [< prec. + -ION] **1.** the act of exuding **2.** something exuded, as sweat

ex·ude (ig zōōd′, -zyōōd′) *vt., vi.* **-ud′ed, -ud′ing** (L. *exudare, exsudare* < *ex-*, out + *sudare*, to sweat < *sudor*,

SWEAT] **1.** to pass out in drops through pores, an incision, etc.; ooze; discharge **2.** to diffuse or seem to radiate [to *exude* joy]

ex·ult (ig zult′) *vi.* [Fr. *exulter* < L. *exultare, exsultare*, to leap up, leap for joy < *ex-*, intens. + *saltare*, freq. of *salire*: see SALIENT] **1.** to rejoice greatly; be jubilant; glory **2.** [Obs.] to leap up; leap with joy —**ex·ult′ing·ly** *adv.*

ex·ult·ant (-′nt) *adj.* [L. *exsultans*, prp. of *exsultare*] exulting; triumphant; jubilant —**ex·ult′ant·ly** *adv.*

ex·ul·ta·tion (eg′zəl tā′shən, ek′səl-) *n.* [ME. *exultacion* < L. *exultatio, exsultatio* < pp. of *exsultare*] the act of exulting; rejoicing; jubilation; triumph: also **ex·ult′ance** (ig zul′tns), **ex·ult′an·cy** (-t′n sē)

☆**ex·urb** (eks′urb′) *n.* [EX-¹ + (SUB)URB: coined (1955) by A. C. Spectorsky (1910–), U.S. author and editor] a region, generally semirural, beyond the suburbs of a city, inhabited largely by persons in the upper-income group —**ex·ur′ban** *adj.*

☆**ex·ur·ban·ite** (eks ur′bə nīt′) *n.* [coined (1955) by A. C. Spectorsky < EX-¹ + (SUB)URBANITE] a person living in an exurb; esp., one commuting to the city as a business or professional person —*adj.* of or characteristic of exurbia or exurbanites

☆**ex·ur·bi·a** (eks ur′bē ə) *n.* the exurbs collectively: usually used to connote the pseudo-Bohemianism, exclusivity, etc. regarded as characteristic of exurbanites

ex·u·vi·ae (ig zōō′vē ē′, ik sōō′-) *n.pl., sing.* **-vi·a** (-ə) [L., that which is stripped off, spoils < *exuere*, to strip off < *ex-*, away + base < IE. *eu-*, to put on, whence Lith. *aviù*, to wear footwear] *Zool.* castoff coverings of animals, as the skins of snakes, crab shells, etc. —**ex·u′vi·al** *adj.*

ex·u·vi·ate (-vē āt′) *vt., vi.* **-at·ed, -at·ing** [EXUVI(AE) + -ATE¹] to cast off (a skin, shell, etc.); molt —**ex·u′vi·a′tion** *n.*

-ey (ē, i) *same as* -Y²: used esp. after words ending in *y* [*clayey*]

ey·as (ī′əs) *n.* [ME., by faulty division (infl. by *ey*, egg) of *a nyas*, *a niais* < Fr. *niais*, nestling < VL. **nidax* < L. *nidus*, NEST] an unfledged bird; nestling; esp., a young hawk taken from its nest for training in falconry

eye (ī) *n.* [ME. *ey, eie* < OE. *eage*, akin to G. *auge* < IE. base **okw-*, to see, whence Gr. *ōps*, L. *oculus*] **1.** the organ of sight in man and animals **2.** *a)* the eyeball *b)* the iris [brown *eyes*] **3.** the area around the eye, including the eyelids [to get a black *eye*] **4.** [*often pl.*] the power of seeing; sight; vision [weak *eyes*] **5.** a look; glance; gaze [to cast an *eye* on something] **6.** attention; regard; observation **7.** the power of judging, estimating, discriminating, etc. by eyesight [a good *eye* for distances] **8.** [*often pl.*] judgment; opinion; estimation [in the *eyes* of the law] **9.** a thing like an eye in appearance or function; specif., *a)* a bud of a potato *b)* the spot on a peacock's tail feather *c)* the center of a flower; disk *d)* a hole in a tool, as for a handle *e)* the threading hole in a needle *f)* a loop of metal or thread *g)* an organ sensitive to light, as in certain lower forms of life *h) same as* PHOTOELECTRIC CELL ☆**10.** [Slang] a detective: esp. in **private eye** **11.** *Meteorol.* the calm, low-pressure center of a hurricane),

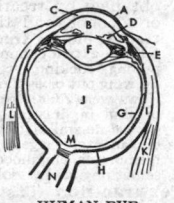

HUMAN EYE (A, conjunctiva; B, anterior chamber; C, cornea; D, iris; E, ciliary body; F, lens; G, retina; H, choroid; I, sclera; J, vitreous body; K, lateral rectus muscle; L, medial rectus muscle; M, optic disc; N, optic nerve)

around which winds of high velocity move —*vt.* **eyed, eye′-ing** or **ey′ing** **1.** to look at; watch carefully; observe **2.** to provide with eyes, or holes —*vi.* [Obs.] to appear (to the eyes) —**all eyes** extremely attentive —**an eye for an eye** punishment or retaliation similar or equivalent to the injury suffered —**catch one's eye** to attract one's attention —☆**easy on the eyes** [Slang] attractive —**eyes right** (or **left**) *Mil.* a command to snap the head to the right (or left) while marching, as a salute when passing in review —**feast one's eyes on** to look at with pleasure or admiration —☆**give (a person) the eye** [Slang] to look at (a person), esp. in an admiring or inviting way —**have an eye for** to have a keen appreciation of —**have an eye to** to watch out for; attend to —**have eyes for** [Colloq.] to be very interested in and want —**in a pig's eye** [Slang] never; under no circumstances —**in the eye of the wind** *Naut.* in a direction opposite to that of the wind; close to the wind —**in the public eye 1.** much seen in public **2.** often brought to public attention; well-known —**keep an eye on** to look after; watch carefully —☆**keep an eye out for** to be watchful for —**keep one's eyes open (or peeled or skinned)** to be on the lookout; be watchful —**lay (or set or clap) eyes on** to see; look at —**make eyes at** to look at amorously or flirtatiously —**my eye!** [Slang] an exclamation of contradiction, astonishment, etc. —**open one's eyes** to make one aware of the facts, real reasons, etc. —**run one's eye over** to glance at hurriedly —**see eye to eye** to agree completely in viewpoint —**see with half an eye** to see or understand (something) easily because it is so evident —**shut one's eyes to** to refuse to see or think about —**with an eye to** paying attention to; considering

eye·ball (-bôl′) *n.* the ball-shaped part of the eye, enclosed by the socket and eyelids —☆*vt., vi.* [Slang] to examine or observe (something) visually

eye·beam (-bēm′) *n.* [Archaic] a beam, or glance, of the eye; quick look

eye·bright (-brīt′) *n.* any of a genus (*Euphrasia*) of plants of the figwort family, esp. a small European plant (*Euphrasia officinalis*) having flowers in leafy clusters, marked with white, yellow, and purple: formerly used in treating eye disorders

eye·brow (-brou′) *n.* [ME. *eiebrou*: see EYE & BROW] **1.** the bony arch over each eye **2.** the arch of hair growing on this —**raise** (or **lift**) **an eyebrow** to appear or feel skeptical, surprised, etc.

☆**eye-catch·er** (-kach′ər) *n.* something that especially attracts one's attention —**eye′-catch′ing** *adj.*

☆**eye·cup** (-kup′) *n.* a small cup whose rim is shaped to fit over the eye, used in applying medicine to the eyes or in washing them

eyed (īd) *adj.* **1.** having eyes (of a specified kind) [blue-*eyed*] **2.** having markings that look like eyes; spotted

☆**eye·drop·per** (ī′dräp′ər) *n.* same as DROPPER (sense 2)

eye·ful (-fool′) *n.* **1.** a quantity of something squirted or blown into the eye **2.** a full look at something; good look **3.** [Slang] a person or thing that looks striking or unusual

eye·glass (-glas′, -gläs′) *n.* **1.** a lens to help or correct faulty vision; monocle **2.** [*pl.*] a pair of such lenses, usually in a frame; glasses **3.** same as EYEPIECE **4.** [Chiefly Brit.] same as EYECUP

eye·hole (-hōl′) *n.* **1.** the socket for the eyeball **2.** a peephole **3.** same as EYELET (sense 1)

eye·lash (-lash′) *n.* **1.** any of the hairs on the edge of the eyelid **2.** a fringe of these hairs

eye·less (-lis) *adj.* without eyes; blind

eye·let (-lit) *n.* [ME. *oylet* < OFr. *oeillet*, dim. of *oeil*, eye < L. *oculus*, EYE] **1.** a small hole for receiving a rope, cord, hook, etc. **2.** a metal ring or short tube for lining such a hole **3.** a small hole edged by stitching in embroidered work **4.** a peephole or loophole **5.** a small eye; ocellus —*vt.* to provide with eyelets

eye·lid (-lid′) *n.* [ME. *eielid, eien lidd*: see EYE & LID] either of the two movable folds of flesh that cover and uncover the front of the eyeball

eye liner a cosmetic preparation applied in a thin line on the eyelid at the base of the eyelashes

ey·en (ī′ən) *n. archaic & dial. pl.* of EYE

☆**eye-o·pen·er** (-ō′p′n ər) *n.* **1.** a surprising piece of news, sudden realization, etc. **2.** [Colloq.] an alcoholic drink, esp. one taken early in the day

eye·piece (-pēs′) *n.* in a telescope, microscope, or other optical instrument, the lens or lenses nearest the viewer's eye: see MICROSCOPE, illus.

eye rhyme a partial rhyme in which the words are similar in spelling but pronounced differently (Ex.: lone, none)

☆**eye shadow** a cosmetic preparation of any of various colors, usually green or blue, applied to the upper eyelids

eye·shot (-shät′) *n.* the distance that a person can see; range of vision

eye·sight (-sīt′) *n.* **1.** the power of seeing; sight; vision **2.** the range of vision

eye·sore (-sôr′) *n.* [ME. *eie sor*] a thing that is unpleasant to look at

eye splice a splice made by turning the end of a rope back and interlacing it with the rope, forming an end loop, or eye: see SPLICE, illus.

eye·spot (-spät′) *n.* **1.** a spot of color that looks like an eye **2.** a small spot of pigment sensitive to light, found in many invertebrates

eye·stalk (-stôk′) *n.* a movable stalk with a compound eye at the tip, as in lobsters, shrimps, snails, and certain other crustaceans and mollusks

eye·strain (-strān′) *n.* a tired or strained condition of the eye muscles, caused as by too much use or an incorrect use of the eyes

eye·tooth (-tōōth′) *n., pl.* **-teeth′** either of the two pointed teeth in the upper jaw between the bicuspids and the incisors; upper canine tooth —**cut one's eyeteeth** to become experienced or sophisticated

eye·wash (-wôsh′, -wäsh′) *n.* **1.** a lotion for the eyes **2.** [Slang] *a)* nonsense *b)* flattery *c)* something done only to impress an observer

eye·wink (-wiŋk′) *n.* **1.** a wink of the eye **2.** an instant

eye·wit·ness (-wit′nis) *n.* **1.** a person who sees or has seen something happen, as an accident, crime, etc. **2.** a person who testifies to what he has seen

eyre (er) *n.* [ME. & Anglo-Fr. *eire* < OFr. *erre* < *errer*, to travel: see ERRANT] *Eng. History* **1.** a tour or circuit: chiefly in the phrase **justices in eyre 2.** a circuit court held by justices in eyre

Eyre (cr) **Lake** shallow salt lake in NE South Australia, varying from occasionally dry to c. 4,000 sq. mi.

Eyre Peninsula peninsula in S South Australia, east of the Great Australian Bight: base, 250 mi. across

ey·rie, ey·ry (er′ē, ir′-) *n., pl.* **-ries** same as AERIE

ey·rir (ā′rir) *n., pl.* **au′rar** (mi′rär) [Ice. < ON., a coin, unit of weight < L. *aureus*, a gold coin, orig. adj., golden: see AUREATE] an Icelandic monetary unit equal to 1/100 krona

E·zek·i·el (i zē′kē əl, -kyəl) [LL.(Ec.) *Ezechiel* < Gr. *Iezekiēl* < Heb. *yeḥezq′ēl*, lit., God strengthens] **1.** a masculine name: dim. *Zeke* **2.** *Bible a)* a Hebrew prophet of the 6th cent. B.C. *b)* the book containing his prophetic writings: abbrev. **Ezek. 3.** *Moses Jacob*, 1844–1917; U.S. sculptor

Ez·ra (ez′rə) [LL.(Ec.) < Heb. *ezrā*, lit., help] **1.** a masculine name **2.** *Bible a)* a Hebrew scribe, prophet, and religious reformer of the 5th cent. B.C. *b)* the book telling of his life and teachings: abbrev. **Ez., Ezr.**

F

F, f (ef) *n., pl.* **F's, f's 1.** the sixth letter of the English alphabet: a modification of the Old Greek digamma (Ϝ), ultimately from the Phoenician **2.** the sound of *F* or *f*, normally a voiceless labiodental fricative **3.** a type or impression for *F* or *f* **4.** *a symbol for* the sixth in a sequence or group **5.** *Genetics* the symbol for filial generation **6.** *Photog.* the symbol for F-NUMBER —*adj.* **1.** of *F* or *f* **2.** sixth in a sequence or group

F (ef) *n.* **1.** an object shaped like *F* **2.** *Chem.* fluorine **3.** *Educ. a)* a grade indicating failing work *b)* sometimes, a grade indicating fair or average work **4.** *Music a)* the fourth tone or note in the ascending scale of C major *b)* a key, string, etc. producing this tone *c)* the scale having this tone as the keynote **5.** *a symbol for a) Math.* function *b) Physics* farad *c) Printing* folio —*adj.* shaped like *F*

F 1. Fahrenheit **2.** farad **3.** fathom

F/, f/, f:, *f*. f-number

F- fighter (plane)

F. 1. Fahrenheit **2.** February **3.** Fellow **4.** France **5.** French **6.** Friday

F., f. 1. farad **2.** farthing **3.** fathom **4.** feminine **5.** fine **6.** fluid **7.** folio(s) **8.** following **9.** *Music* forte **10.** franc(s) **11.** frequency **12.** *Pharmacy a)* [L. *fiat*] let there be made *b)* [L. *fac*] make

fa (fä) *n.* [ME. < ML. < *fa*(*muli*): see GAMUT] *Music* a syllable representing the fourth tone of the diatonic scale: see SOLFEGGIO

FA field artillery

f.a. 1. free alongside **2.** freight agent

FAA Federal Aviation Agency

F.A.A.A.S. 1. Fellow of the American Association for the Advancement of Science **2.** Fellow of the American Academy of Arts and Sciences

fa·ba·ceous (fə bā′shəs) *adj.* [L. *fabaceus* < *faba*, BEAN] of the legume family of plants

Fa·bi·an (fā′bē ən) *adj.* [L. *Fabianus*, of Fabius: see FABIUS] ☆**1.** using a cautious strategy of delay and avoidance of battle **2.** of the Fabian Society —*n.* a member of the Fabian Society —**Fa′bi·an·ism** *n.*

Fabian Society an organization of English socialists, established in 1884, aiming to bring about socialism by gradual reforms rather than revolutionary action

Fa·bi·us (fā′bē əs) (full name *Quintus Fabius Maximus Verrucosus*) ?–203 B.C.; Rom. general & statesman: defeated Hannibal in the second Punic War by a cautious strategy of delay and avoidance of direct encounter: called *Cunctator* (the Delayer)

fa·ble (fā′b′l) *n.* [ME. < OFr. < L. *fabula*, a story < *fari*, to speak: see FAME] **1.** a fictitious story meant to teach a moral lesson: the characters are usually talking animals **2.**

a myth or legend **3.** a story that is not true; falsehood **4.** [Archaic] the plot of a literary work —*vi., vt.* **-bled, -bling** to write or tell (fables, legends, or falsehoods) —**fa′bler** *n.*

fa·bled (fā′b'ld) *adj.* **1.** told of in fables or legends; mythical; legendary **2.** unreal; fictitious

fab·li·au (fab′lē ō′; *Fr.* få blē ō′) *n.*, *pl.* **-aux′** (-ōz′; *Fr.* -ō′) [*Fr.* < OFr., dial. form of *fable,* dim. of *fable,* FABLE] in medieval literature, esp. French and English literature, a short story in verse telling comic incidents of ordinary life, usually with earthy realism

Fa·bre (få′br′), **Jean Hen·ri** (zhän än rē′), 1823–1915; Fr. entomologist

fab·ric (fab′rik) *n.* [MFr. *fabrique* < L. *fabrica,* a workshop, trade, product, fabric < *faber,* a workman < IE. base **dhabh-,* to fit together, whence OE. (*ge*)*dæfte,* fit] **1.** *a)* anything constructed or made of parts put together; structure; building *b)* the framework or basic structure of anything **2.** the style or plan of construction **3.** *a)* a material made from fibers or threads by weaving, knitting, felting, etc., as any cloth, felt, lace, or the like *b)* the texture of such material **4.** [Brit.] the construction and upkeep of a church building

fab·ri·cant (fab′ri kənt) *n.* [Fr. < L. *fabricans,* prp.: see ff.] [Now Rare] a builder or manufacturer

fab·ri·cate (fab′rə kāt′) *vt.* **-cat′ed, -cat′ing** [ME. *fabricaten* < L. *fabricatus,* pp. of *fabricari,* to construct, build < *fabrica:* see FABRIC] **1.** to make, build, construct, etc., esp. by assembling parts; manufacture **2.** to make up (a story, reason, lie, etc.); invent —*SYN.* see LIE², MAKE¹ —**fab′ri·ca′tor** *n.*

fab·ri·ca·tion (fab′rə kā′shən) *n.* [ME. *fabricacioun* < L. *fabricatio*] **1.** a fabricating or being fabricated; construction; manufacture **2.** a fabricated thing; esp., a falsehood, false excuse, etc.

☆**Fab·ri·koid** (fab′rə koid′) [see FABRIC & -OID] *a trademark for* a fabric processed with pyroxylin to resemble leather, used for upholstery, bookbinding, etc.

fab·u·list (fab′yoo list) *n.* [Fr. *fabuliste* < L. *fabula:* see FABLE] **1.** a person who writes or tells fables **2.** a liar

fab·u·lous (fab′yoo ləs) *adj.* [ME. < L. *fabulosus,* fabled < *fabula*] **1.** of or like a fable; imaginary, fictitious, or legendary **2.** hard to believe; incredible; astounding **3.** [Colloq.] very good; wonderful —*SYN.* see FICTITIOUS —**fab′u·lous·ly** *adv.* —**fab′u·lous·ness** *n.*

fa·cade, fa·çade (fə säd′) *n.* [Fr. < It. *facciata* < *faccia* < VL. *facia:* see ff.] **1.** the front of a building; part of a building facing a street, courtyard, etc. **2.** the front part of anything: often used figuratively, with implications of an imposing appearance concealing something inferior

FAÇADE

face (fās) *n.* [ME. < OFr. < VL. *facia* < L. *facies,* the face, appearance < base of *facere,* DO¹] **1.** the front of the head from the top of the forehead to the bottom of the chin, and from ear to ear; visage; countenance **2.** the expression of the countenance **3.** a surface of a thing; esp., *a)* the main surface or side *b)* the front, upper, or outer surface or part *c)* any one of the surfaces of a geometric figure or crystal **4.** the side or surface that is marked, as of a clock, playing card, domino, etc., or that is finished, as of fabric, leather, etc. **5.** the appearance; outward aspect; semblance **6.** [< Chin. idiom] dignity; self-respect; prestige: usually in **to lose** (or **save**) **face 7.** the topography (of an area) **8.** the functional or striking surface (of a tool, golf club, etc.) **9.** [Colloq.] effrontery; audacity **10.** what is shown by the language of a document, without explanation or addition **11.** *Mining* the end of a tunnel, drift, etc., where work is being done **12.** *Typography a)* the type surface on which a letter is cut; printing part of a letter or plate *b)* the design of type —*vt.* **faced, fac′ing** [ME. *facen* < the *n.*] **1.** to turn, or have the face turned, toward; have its front toward [the building *faces* the square] **2.** to meet or confront squarely or face to face **3.** to confront with boldness, courage, etc. **4.** to realize and be ready to meet (a condition, fact, etc.) **5.** to put another material on the surface of **6.** to put a smooth surface on (a stone, tool, etc.) **7.** to turn (a card, etc.) with the face up **8.** *Mil.* to cause (a formation of soldiers) to pivot by giving the appropriate command **9.** *Sewing* to apply a facing to (a collar, edge, etc.) —*vi.* **1.** to turn, or have the face turned, toward a specified thing or person, or in a specified direction **2.** *Mil.* to pivot in a specified direction: usually in the form of a command [*right face!*] —**face down** to disconcert or overcome by a confident, bold manner —**face off** *Hockey* to start or resume play with a face-off —**face to face 1.** confronting one another **2.** very near; in the presence of: followed by *with* —**face up to 1.** to face with courage; confront and resist **2.** to realize and be ready to meet (a fact, condition, etc.) —**fly in the face of** to be rashly defiant of —**in the face of 1.** in the presence of **2.** in spite of —**make a face** to distort the face, esp. in a way expressing contempt, distaste, etc.; grimace —**on the face of it** to all appearances; apparently —**pull** (or **wear**) **a long face** to look sad, glum,

disapproving, etc. —**put a bold face on** to seem bold or confident about —**set one's face against** to be determinedly against; disapprove of; resist —**show one's face** to come and be seen; appear —**to one's face** in one's presence; openly and without fear

SYN.—**face** is the basic, direct word for the front of the head; **countenance** refers to the face as it reflects the emotions or feelings and is, hence, often applied to the facial expression [his happy *countenance*]; **visage** refers to the form, proportions, and expression of the face, especially as indicative of general temperament [a man of stern *visage*]; **physiognomy** refers to the general cast of features, esp. as characteristic of an ethnic group or as supposedly indicative of character [the *physiognomy* of an honest man]

face card any king, queen, or jack in a deck of cards

faced (fāst) *adj.* having a face of a specified kind [round-faced]

face-hard·en (-här′d'n) *vt. same as* CASEHARDEN (sense 1)

face·less (fās′lis) *adj.* **1.** lacking a face **2.** lacking a distinct character; without individuality; anonymous

☆**face lifting 1.** plastic surgery for removing wrinkles, sagging flesh, etc. from the face **2.** an altering, repairing, cleaning, etc., as of the exterior of a building Also **face lift** —**face′-lift′** *vt.*

face-off (-ôf′) *n. Hockey* the act of starting or resuming play when the referee drops the puck between two opposing players

face·plate (-plāt′) *n.* **1.** a disk fastened to the spindle of a lathe that holds in place work to be turned **2.** a protective cover, as over a light switch, journal box, etc.

face powder a cosmetic powder, as of flesh-colored talc, applied to the face

fac·er (fā′sər) *n.* **1.** a person or thing that faces **2.** [Brit. Colloq.] *a)* a sudden blow in the face *b)* any sudden, unexpected difficulty or defeat

face-sav·ing (fās′sā′viŋ) *adj.* preserving or intended to preserve one's dignity or self-respect

fac·et (fas′it) *n.* [Fr. *facette,* dim. of *face:* see FACE] **1.** any of the small, polished plane surfaces of a cut gem **2.** any of a number of sides or aspects, as of a personality **3.** *Anat.* any small, smooth surface on a bone or other hard part **4.** *Archit.* the raised plane between the flutes of a column **5.** *Zool.* any of the many small surfaces of a compound eye, as in typical insects and some crustaceans —*vt.* **-et·ed** or **-et·ted, -et·ing** or **-et·ting** to cut or make facets on —*SYN.* see PHASE

fa·ce·ti·ae (fə sē′shē ē′) *n.pl.* [L., pl. of *facetia,* a jest < *facetus,* elegant, witty, akin to *fax,* torch < IE. base **ĝhwok-,* to gleam, whence Gr. *phaos,* light] **1.** witty sayings **2.** ribald or coarsely witty books

fa·ce·tious (fə sē′shəs) *adj.* [Fr. *facétieux* < L. *facetia:* see prec. & -OUS] joking or trying to be jocular, esp. at an inappropriate time —*SYN.* see WITTY —**fa·ce′tious·ly** *adv.* —**fa·ce′tious·ness** *n.*

face value 1. the value printed or written on a bill, bond, etc. **2.** the seeming value [to take a promise at *face value*]

fa·ci·a (fā′shē ə, -shə) *n.* [Brit., var. of FASCIA] **1.** [Brit.] *a)* an instrument panel or dashboard, as of an automobile *b)* a board over a shop front with the proprietor's name **2.** *same as* FASCIA

fa·cial (fā′shəl) *adj.* [Fr. < ML. *facialis* < VL. *facia:* see FACE] of or for the face —☆*n.* a treatment intended to improve the appearance of the skin of the face, as by massage, the application of creams and astringents, etc. —**fa′cial·ly** *adv.*

facial angle the angle made by the intersection of two lines drawn from the base of the nostrils, one to the base of the skull and the other to the most prominent part of the forehead

facial index the ratio of the length to the width of the face

$$\frac{\text{length} \times 100}{\text{width}}$$

☆**facial tissue** a sheet of soft tissue paper used for cleansing, as a handkerchief, etc.

-fa·cient (fā′shənt) [< L. *faciens* (gen. *facientis*), prp. of *facere,* to make, DO¹] *an adj.-forming suffix meaning* making or causing to become [lique-facient]

FACIAL ANGLE

fa·ci·es (fā′shē ēz′; fā′shēz, -sēz) *n.,* pl. **fa′ci·es′** [L., FACE] **1.** the general appearance, aspect, or nature of anything **2.** *Ecol.* a particular modification of the appearance or composition of a community **3.** *Geol.* the characteristics of a rock body or part of a rock body that differentiate it from others, as in appearance, composition, etc. **4.** *Med. a)* the appearance of the face as indicative of a specific disease or condition *b)* a surface

fac·ile (fas′'l; *chiefly Brit.,* -īl) *adj.* [Fr. < L. *facilis* < *facere,* DO¹] **1.** not hard to do or achieve; easy **2.** acting, working, or done easily, or in a quick, smooth way; fluent; ready [a *facile* wit] **3.** using or showing little effort and not sincere or profound; superficial [a *facile* solution, *facile* emotions] **4.** [Now Rare] easy to influence or persuade; affable —*SYN.* see EASY —**fac′ile·ly** *adv.* —**fac′ile·ness** *n.*

fa·cil·i·tate (fə sil′ə tāt′) *vt.* **-tat′ed, -tat′ing** [< Fr.

faciliter, after It. *facilitare* < L. *facilis* (see FACILE) + -ATE[1]) to make easy or easier

fa·cil·i·ta·tion (fə sil/ə tā/shən) *n.* **1.** the act of facilitating **2.** *Psychol.* increased ease of performance of any action, resulting from the lessening of nerve resistance by the continued successive application of the necessary stimulus —**fa·cil/i·ta/tive** *adj.*

fa·cil·i·ty (fə sil/ə tē) *n., pl.* **-ties** [ME. & OFr. *facilite* < L. *facilitas*, easiness < *facilis*, FACILE] **1.** ease of doing or making; absence of difficulty **2.** a ready ability; skill; dexterity; fluency **3.** [*usually pl.*] the means by which something can be done [poor transportation *facilities*] **4.** a building, special room, etc. that facilitates or makes possible some activity [a new *facility* for outpatient treatment] **5.** [Now Rare] a tendency to be easygoing, yielding, etc.

fac·ing (fās/iŋ) *n.* **1.** a lining, often decorative, sewn on the inside edge of a garment or on a part that is turned back, as a collar **2.** any material used for this **3.** a covering of contrasting material to decorate or protect a building **4.** [*pl.*] the trimmings, collar, and cuffs of certain military coats

fac·sim·i·le (fak sim/ə lē) *n.* [L. *fac*, imperative of *facere*, DO[1] + *simile*, neut. of *similis*, SIMILAR] **1.** (an) exact reproduction or copy **2.** the transmission and reproduction of graphic matter by electrical means, as by radio or wire —*adj.* of, or having the nature of, a facsimile —*vt.* **-led,** **-le·ing** to make a facsimile of —*SYN.* see COPY

fact (fakt) *n.* [L. *factum*, that which is done, deed, fact, neut. pp. of *facere*, to do, act < IE. base *dhē-*, to put, place, whence DO[1], Gr. *tithenai*, to place] **1.** a deed; act: now esp. in the sense of "a criminal deed" in the phrases **after the fact, before the fact** [an accessory *after the fact*] **2.** a thing that has actually happened or that is really true; thing that has been or is **3.** the state of things as they are; reality; actuality; truth [*fact* as distinct from fancy] **4.** something said to have occurred or supposed to be true [to check the accuracy of one's *facts*] **5.** *Law* an actual or alleged incident or condition, as distinguished from its legal consequence —**as a matter of fact** in reality; really; actually; also **in fact, in point of fact** —☆**the facts of life 1.** basic information about life, esp. about sexual reproduction **2.** the harsh, unpleasant facts about a situation in life

fac·tion (fak/shən) *n.* [< Fr. *faction* & L. *factio*, a making, doing, faction < pp. of *facere*: see FACT] **1.** a group of people inside a political party, club, government, etc. working in a common cause against other such groups or against the main body; clique **2.** partisan conflict within an organization or a country; dissension —**fac/tion·al** *adj.* —**fac/tion·al·ly** *adv.*

fac·tion·al·ism (-əl iz'm) *n.* **1.** factional dissension **2.** affiliation with a faction —**fac/tion·al·ist** *n., adj.*

fac·tious (fak/shəs) *adj.* [L. *factiosus* < *factio*] **1.** producing or tending to produce faction; causing dissension **2.** produced or characterized by faction —**fac/tious·ly** *adv.* —**fac/tious·ness** *n.*

fac·ti·tious (fak tish/əs) *adj.* [L. *facticius* < pp. of *facere*: see FACT] not natural, genuine, or spontaneous; forced or artificial [*factitious* needs created by advertising] —**fac·ti/tious·ly** *adv.* —**fac·ti/tious·ness** *n.*

fac·ti·tive (fak/tə tiv) *adj.* [ModL. *factitivus*, irreg. < L. *factus* (see FACT)] designating or of a verb that expresses the idea of making, calling, or thinking something to be of a certain character, using a noun, pronoun, or adjective as a complement to its direct object (Ex.: *make the dress short, elect him mayor*)

fac·tor (fak/tər) *n.* [ME. *factour* < OFr. *facteur* < L. *factor*, doer, maker < pp. of *facere*, DO[1] (see FACT)] **1.** *a)* a person who carries on business transactions for another; commission merchant; agent for the sale of goods entrusted to his possession *b)* an agent, as a banking or finance company, engaged in financing the operations of certain companies, or in financing wholesale and retail sales, through the purchase of accounts receivable *c)* in certain States, a person legally appointed to take care of forfeited or sequestered property *d)* [Scot.] a person who manages an estate for another; steward; bailiff **2.** [< fig. use of 4] any of the circumstances, conditions, etc. that bring about a result; element or constituent that makes a thing what it is **3.** *Biol.* same as GENE **4.** *Math.* any of two or more quantities which form a product when multiplied together —*vt. Math.* to resolve into factors; factorize —*vi.* to act in the capacity of a factor —*SYN.* see AGENT, ELEMENT —**fac/tor·a·ble** *adj.* —**fac/tor·ship** *n.*

fac·tor·age (-ij) *n.* **1.** the business of a factor; buying and selling on commission **2.** a factor's commission

fac·to·ri·al (fak tôr/ē əl) *adj.* **1.** of a factor. **2.** *Math.* of factors or factorials —*n. Math.* the product of a given series of consecutive whole numbers beginning with 1 and ending with the specified number [the *factorial* of 5 is 1 x 2 x 3 x 4 x 5, or 120]

fac·tor·ize (fak/tə rīz') *vt.* **-ized', -iz'ing** *Math.* same as FACTOR —**fac/tor·i·za/tion** *n.*

factor of safety the ratio of the maximum strength of a piece of material or a part to the probable maximum load to be applied to it

fac·to·ry (fak/tə rē, -trē) *n., pl.* **-ries** [Fr. *factorie* < *facteur*: see FACTOR] **1.** a building or buildings in which things are manufactured; manufacturing plant **2.** [after Port. *feitoria*] a trading settlement maintained by factors

fac·to·tum (fak tōt/əm) *n.* [ModL. < L. *fac*, imperative of *facere*, DO[1] + *totum*, neut. of *totus*, all, the whole] a person hired to do all sorts of work; handyman: now a humorously formal usage

fac·tu·al (fak/choo wəl) *adj.* [FACT + (ACT)UAL] **1.** of or containing facts **2.** having the nature of fact; real; actual —**fac/tu·al·ly** *adv.*

fac·tu·al·ism (-iz'm) *n.* adherence or devotion to facts

fac·ture (fak/chər) *n.* [ME. < OFr. < L. *factura* < *facere*, to make, DO[1]] **1.** [Archaic] *a)* the act of making something *b)* the thing made **2.** the manner of making something, esp. a work of art

fac·u·lae (fak/yoo lē') *n.pl., sing.* **-la** (-lə) [L., dim. of *fax* (gen. *facis*), torch: see FACETIAE] bright areas visible on the surface of the sun, esp. near its edge

fac·ul·ta·tive (fak/'l tāt/iv) *adj.* [Fr. *facultatif* < L. *facultas*: see FACULTY] **1.** *a)* granting a faculty, or permission; permissive *b)* optional **2.** that may or may not happen or be; contingent **3.** having to do with a faculty or faculties **4.** *Biol.* capable of living under varying conditions; e.g., able to live in the presence or absence of oxygen, as a parasite or nonparasite, etc.

fac·ul·ty (fak/'l tē) *n., pl.* **-ties** [ME. & OFr. *faculte* < L. *facultas* < *facilis*: see FACILE] **1.** formerly, the power to do; ability to perform an action **2.** any natural or specialized power of a living organism; sense [the *faculty* of hearing, speech, etc.] **3.** power or ability to do some particular thing; skill developed by practice; special aptitude; knack [a *faculty* for making friends] **4.** [ME. < ML. *facultas*, transl. of Aristotle's *dynamis*, branch of learning] [Now Rare] any of the departments of learning in a university ☆**5.** all the teachers of a school, college, or university or of one of its departments or divisions **6.** all the members of any of the learned professions **7.** a power or privilege conferred by authority; specif., *R.C.Ch.* a power granted to a bishop, priest, etc. permitting the performance of certain acts or functions otherwise prohibited to him **8.** [Archaic] what a person is trained to do; trade **9.** *Psychol.* any of the powers formerly thought of as composing the mind, such as will, reason, etc. —*SYN.* see TALENT

fad (fad) *n.* [19th c. < Brit. Midland dial.] a custom, style, etc. that many people are interested in for a short time; passing fashion; craze —*SYN.* see FASHION

fad·dish (-ish) *adj.* **1.** having the nature of a fad **2.** fond of fads; following fads —**fad/dish·ly** *adv.* —**fad/dish·ness** *n.*

fad·dism (-iz'm) *n.* the practice of following fads, or a tendency to do so —**fad/dist** *n.*

fade (fād) *vi.* **fad/ed, fad/ing** [ME. *faden* < OFr. *fader* < *fade*, pale < VL. *fatidus*, prob. < L. *fatuus* (see FATUOUS), infl. by *vapidus*, VAPID] **1.** to become less distinct; lose color, brilliance, etc. **2.** to lose freshness or strength; wither; wane **3.** to disappear slowly; die out **4.** to lose braking power: said of brakes that heat and glaze the lining in repeated hard use **5.** to curve from its direct course, as a golf ball **6.** *Radio & TV* to vary in intensity: said of a signal —*vt.* **1.** to cause to fade ☆**2.** [Slang] to meet the bet of; cover: dice player's term —*n.* the act of fading —*SYN.* see VANISH —☆**fade back** *Football* to move back from the line of scrimmage, as in order to throw a forward pass —**fade in** (or **out**) *Motion Pictures, Radio & TV* to appear (or disappear) gradually; become more (or less) distinct

☆**fade-in** (-in') *n. Motion Pictures, Radio & TV* a fading in; gradual appearance or becoming distinct of a scene or sound

fade·less (-lis) *adj.* that will not fade; unfading

☆**fade-out** (-out') *n. Motion Pictures, Radio & TV* a fading out; gradual disappearance or becoming indistinct of a scene or sound

fa·do (fä/doo) *n.* [Port., lit., fate < L. *fatum*: see FATE] a kind of Portuguese folk song, usually melancholy and nostalgic

fae·ces (fē/sēz) *n.pl.* same as FECES —**fae/cal** *adj.*

‡**fa·e·na** (fä ā/nä) *n.* [Sp., lit., work] in bullfighting, the series of passes at the bull immediately before the kill, for displaying the matador's skill

fa·er·ie, fa·er·y (fer/ē; *also, for 1,* fā/ər ē) *n.* [OFr. *faerie* (see FAIRY): E. use due to Spenser] [Archaic] **1.** fairyland **2.** *pl.* **-ies** a fairy —*adj.* [Archaic] fairy Also written **faërie, faëry**

Faer·oe Islands (fer/ō) group of Danish islands in the N Atlantic, between Iceland & the Shetland Islands: 540 sq. mi.; pop. 35,000: also **Faer·oes**

Faer·o·ese (fer/ə wēz') *n.* **1.** *pl.* **Faer/o·ese'** a native or inhabitant of the Faeroe Islands **2.** the North Germanic language of the Faeroe Islands, akin to Icelandic —*adj.* of the Faeroe Islands, their people, language, etc.

Faf·nir (fäv/nir, fäf/nər) [ON. *Fáfnir*] *Norse Myth.* a giant who, in the form of a dragon, guarded the Nibelung treasure: he was slain by Sigurd

fag[1] (fag) *vi.* **fagged, fag/ging** [< ?: cf. FAG END] **1.** to work hard and become very tired **2.** [Brit. Colloq.] to serve as a

fag or servant —*vt.* **1.** to make tired by hard work **2.** [Brit. Colloq.] to employ (a boy) as a fag or servant —*n.* **1.** [Brit. Colloq.] *a)* hard, tiring work; drudgery *b)* fatigue; weariness *c)* a boy in an English public school who acts as a servant for another boy in a higher form, or class *d)* a menial worker; drudge ☆**2.** [Slang] a male homosexual

fag² (fag) *n.* [< FAG END] [Old Slang] a cigarette

fag end [< ME. *fagge*, broken thread] **1.** *a)* the last part or coarse end of a piece of cloth *b)* the frayed, untwisted end of a rope **2.** the last and worst part of anything; remnant

fag·got¹ (fag'ət) *n., vt. same as* FAGOT

☆**fag·got²** (fag'ət) *n.* [prob. extended < *fag* (homosexual), after prec.] [Slang] a male homosexual —**fag'got·y** *adj.*

fag·ot (fag'ət) *n.* [ME. < OFr., with change of suffix < VL. *facellum* < Gr. *phakelos*, a bundle] **1.** a bundle of sticks, twigs, or branches, esp. for use as fuel **2.** *Metallurgy* a bundle or heap of iron or steel pieces to be worked into bars by hammering or rolling at welding temperature —*vt.* **1.** to make into a fagot; form fagots of **2.** *Sewing* to decorate with fagoting

fag·ot·ing, fag·got·ing (-iŋ) *n.* **1.** a kind of drawnwork or hemstitch with wide spaces **2.** openwork decoration in which the thread is drawn in crisscross or barlike stitches across the open seam

Fah., Fahr. Fahrenheit

Fahr·en·heit (fer'ən hīt', fär'-) *adj.* [after Gabriel Daniel *Fahrenheit* (1686–1736), G. physicist who devised the scale] designating or of a thermometer on which, under laboratory conditions, 32° is the freezing

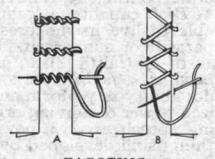

FAGOTING
(A, bar; B, crisscross)

point and 212° is the boiling point of water: abbrev. **F:** the formula for converting a Fahrenheit temperature to Celsius is F° = 9/5C° + 32°—: this thermometer or its scale

fa·ience (fī äns', fā-) *n.* [Fr. < *Faenza*, Italy, original place of its manufacture] glazed earthenware formed as pottery or in blocks or tiles as a wall facing

fail (fāl) *vi.* [ME. *failen* < OFr. *faillir*, to fail, miss < L. *fallere*, to deceive, disappoint < IE. base *ĝhwel-*, to bend, deviate, whence Sans. *hválati*, (he) loses the way, errs, Gr. *phēloein*, to deceive] **1.** to be lacking or insufficient; fall short [the water supply is *failing*] **2.** to lose power or strength; weaken; die away **3.** to stop operating or working [the brakes *failed*] **4.** to be deficient or negligent in an obligation, duty, or expectation; default **5.** to be unsuccessful in obtaining a desired end; be unable to do or become; miss **6.** to become bankrupt **7.** *Educ.* to get a grade of failure; not pass —*vt.* **1.** to be useless or not helpful to; be inadequate for; disappoint **2.** to leave; abandon [his courage *failed* him] **3.** to miss, neglect, or omit: used with an infinitive [he *failed* to go] **4.** *Educ. a)* to give a grade of failure to (a pupil) *b)* to get a grade of failure in (a subject) —*n.* [ME. *faile* < OFr. *faile* < the *v.*] failure: now only in the phrase **without fail,** without failing (to occur, do something, etc.) —**fail of** to fail to achieve; be without

fail·ing (-iŋ) *n.* **1.** a failure **2.** a slight fault or defect; weakness —*prep.* without; lacking [*failing* some rain soon, the crops will wither] —*SYN.* see FAULT

faille (fil, fāl) *n.* [Fr.] a ribbed, soft, plainly woven fabric of silk or rayon, for dresses, coats, etc.

fail-safe (fāl'sāf') *adj.* [FAIL, *v.* + SAFE, *adj.*] designating, of, or involving a procedure designed to prevent malfunctioning or unintentional operation, often specif. of nuclear-armed aircraft, through an intricate system of protective devices

fail·ure (fāl'yər) *n.* [< earlier *failer* < Anglo-Fr. < OFr. *faillir:* see FAIL] **1.** the act, state, or fact of failing; specif., *a)* a falling short *b)* a losing of power or strength *c)* a breakdown in operation or function *d)* neglect or omission *e)* a not succeeding in doing or becoming *f)* a becoming bankrupt **2.** a person or thing that fails **3.** *Educ. a)* a failing to pass ☆*b)* a grade or mark (usually F) indicating a failing to pass

fain (fān) *adj.* [ME. *fain*, joyful, joyfully, < OE. *fægen*, glad, akin to ON. *feginn* < IE. base *pek-*, to be satisfied: cf. FAIR¹] [Archaic] **1.** glad; ready **2.** compelled by circumstances; reluctantly willing **3.** eager —*adv.* [Archaic] with eagerness; gladly: used with *would* [he would *fain* stay]

fai·né·ant (fā'nē ənt; *Fr.* fā nā än') *adj.* [Fr. < OFr. *faignant*, an idler, orig. prp. of *faindre* (see FEIGN); altered by folk etym. as if < Fr. *fait*, (he) does + *néant*, nothing] lazy; idle —*n.* a lazy, idle person

faint (fānt) *adj.* [ME. *feint* < OFr., sluggish, orig. pp. of *feindre:* see FEIGN] **1.** without strength; weak; feeble **2.** without courage or hope; timid **3.** done without strength, vigor, or enthusiasm; halfhearted **4.** feeling weak and dizzy, as if about to swoon **5.** dim; indistinct; unclear **6.** far from certain [a *faint* chance] —*n.* **1.** a condition of temporary loss of consciousness as a result of an inadequate flow of blood to the brain; swoon **2.** [*pl.*] the crude, impure spirits given off in the first and last stages of the distillation of liquor —*vi.* **1.** to fall into a faint; swoon (often with *away*) **2.** [Archaic or Poet.] *a)* to weaken;

languish *b)* to lose courage or hope —**faint'ish** *adj.* —**faint'ly** *adv.* —**faint'ness** *n.*

faint·heart·ed (-här'tid) *adj.* cowardly; timid; shy —**faint'heart'ed·ly** *adv.* —**faint'heart'ed·ness** *n.*

fair¹ (fer) *adj.* [ME. < OE. *fæger*, akin to FAIN, Goth. *fagrs*, apt, fit < IE. base *pek-*, to be content, whence Lith. *púošiu*, to ornament] **1.** attractive; beautiful; lovely **2.** unblemished; clean [a *fair* name] **3.** [< notion that dark coloring was foul] light in color; blond [*fair* hair] **4.** clear and sunny; free from storm or the threat of storm **5.** easy to read; clear [a *fair* hand] **6.** just and honest; impartial; unprejudiced; specif., free from discrimination based on race, religion, sex, etc. [*fair* employment practices, *fair* housing] **7.** according to the rules [a *fair* blow] **8.** likely; promising; advantageous [he is in a *fair* way to make money] **9.** pleasant and courteous **10.** favorable; helpful [a *fair* wind] **11.** of moderately good size [a *fair* fortune] **12.** neither very bad nor very good; average [in *fair* condition] **13.** apparently favorable but really false; specious [*fair* words] **14.** [Archaic] without obstacles; clear and open [a *fair* road] —*n.* **1.** [Obs.] beauty **2.** [Archaic] a woman **3.** [Archaic] something fair, or good —*adv.* **1.** in a fair manner **2.** straight; squarely [struck *fair* in the face] —*vi.* [Dial.] to become clear: said of the weather —*vt.* to give a smooth or streamlined surface to —**fair and square** [Colloq.] with justice and honesty —**fair to middling** [Colloq.] moderately good; passable --**fair'ness** *n.*

SYN.—**fair,** the general word, implies the treating of both or all sides alike, without reference to one's own feelings or interests [a *fair* exchange]; **just** implies adherence to a standard of rightness or lawfulness without reference to one's own inclinations [a *just* decision]; **impartial** and **unbiased** both imply freedom from prejudice for or against any side [an *impartial* chairman, an *unbiased* account]; **dispassionate** implies the absence of passion or strong emotion, hence, connotes cool, disinterested judgment [a *dispassionate* critic]; **objective** implies a viewing of persons or things without reference to oneself, one's feelings, interests, etc. [an *objective* newspaper] See also BEAUTIFUL —**ANT. prejudiced, biased**

fair² (fer) *n.* [ME. *feire* < OFr. < ML. *feria* < LL., holiday (in eccles. use, weekday) < L. *feriae*, pl., festivals < OL. *fesiae*, akin to L. *festus* (cf. FEAST) < IE. base *dhēs-*, used in religious terms, whence Oscan *fíísnu*, temple, Arm. *dik'*, gods] **1.** orig., a gathering of people held at regular intervals for barter and sale of goods **2.** a festival or carnival where there is entertainment and things are sold, often for charity; bazaar ☆**3.** an exhibition, often competitive, of farm, household, and manufactured products, or of international displays, usually with various amusement facilities and educational displays; exposition

☆**fair ball** *Baseball* a batted ball that stops in the infield, or first strikes the ground there, and does not pass the foul line before reaching first or third base, or that first strikes the ground inside the foul line after passing first or third base

Fair·banks (fer'baŋks') [after C. W. *Fairbanks*, prominent political figure] city in EC Alas.: pop. 15,000

☆**fair catch** *Football* a catch of a kicked ball made after giving the proper signal that no attempt will be made to run with the ball: the opposing players are penalized if they interfere with the catcher

fair copy an exact copy of a document after final corrections have been made on it

Fair·field (fer'fēld') **1.** [after an Eng. village of the same name] suburb of Bridgeport, in SW Conn.: pop. 56,000 **2.** [after prec.] city in W Calif., near Vallejo: pop. 44,000

fair game **1.** game that may lawfully be hunted **2.** any legitimate object of attack or pursuit

fair·ground (-ground') *n.* [often *pl.*] an open space where fairs are held

fair-haired (-herd') *adj.* **1.** having blond hair ☆**2.** [Colloq.] favorite [the *fair-haired* boy of the family]

fair·ing (-iŋ) *n.* [see FAIR¹, *vt.*] *Engineering* an additional part or structure added to an aircraft, etc. to smooth the outline and thus reduce drag

fair·ing² (-iŋ) *n.* [Brit.] a gift, esp. one got at a fair

fair·ish (-ish) *adj.* moderately good, well, large, etc.

Fair Lawn borough in NE N.J., near Paterson: pop. 38,000

fair·lead (-lēd') *n.* [< earlier *fair-leader*] *Naut.* a ring, block, or piece of wood with holes in it that acts as a guide for the running rigging or a rope, to prevent its being cut or chafed

fair·ly (-lē) *adv.* [ME.: see FAIR¹ & -LY²] **1.** justly; equitably **2.** moderately; somewhat [*fairly* hot] **3.** clearly; distinctly **4.** completely or really [his voice *fairly* rang] **5.** [Obs.] *a)* softly *b)* courteously

fair-mind·ed (-mīn'did) *adj.* just; impartial; unbiased —**fair'-mind'ed·ly** *adv.* —**fair'-mind'ed·ness** *n.*

fair play the act or fact of abiding by the rules in sports, games, or any other activity; fairness and honor in dealing with competitors, customers, etc.

fair sex women collectively: used with *the*

☆**fair shake** [Colloq.] fair, just, or equitable treatment; square deal

fair-spo·ken (-spō'kən) *adj.* speaking or spoken civilly and pleasantly; polite; courteous; bland; plausible

fair-trade (-trād') *adj.* ☆designating or of an agreement whereby a seller undertakes to charge no less than the

minimum price set by a manufacturer, on a specified trademarked or brand-name commodity —*vt.* -**trad′ed,** -**trad′ing** to sell (a commodity) under a fair-trade agreement

fair·way (-wā′) *n.* **1.** a navigable channel in a river, harbor, etc. **2.** the mowed part of a golf course between a tee and a green

fair-weath·er (-we*th*′ər) *adj.* **1.** suitable only for fair weather **2.** helpful, dependable, etc. only in agreeable, easy circumstances [*fair-weather* friends]

Fair·weath·er (-we*th*′ər), **Mount** [named by James Cook after the state of the weather] mountain on the border between SE Alas. & NW British Columbia: 15,300 ft.

fair·y (fer′ē) *n., pl.* **fair′ies** [ME., fairyland, fairy < OFr. *faerie* < *fée:* see FAY¹] **1.** a tiny, graceful, delicate imaginary being in human form, supposed to have magic powers **2.** [Slang] a male homosexual —*adj.* **1.** of fairies **2.** fairylike; graceful; delicate —**fair′y·like′** *adj.*

fair·y·land (-land′) *n.* **1.** the imaginary land where the fairies live **2.** a lovely, enchanting place

fairy ring a circle of mushrooms often seen on grassy ground, originating from one initial mycelium and often accompanied by a circle of contrasting color in the grass: so called because formerly thought to have been made by the dancing of fairies

fairy shrimp any of an order (Anostraca) of crustaceans formed in temporary freshwater pools in early spring, having delicate colors and a graceful swimming motion

fairy tale 1. a story about fairies, giants, magic deeds, etc. **2.** an unbelievable or untrue story; lie

‡**fait ac·com·pli** (fe tȧ kôn plē′) [Fr., lit., an accomplished fact] a thing already done, so that opposition or argument is useless

Faith (fāth) [see next entry] a feminine name

faith (fāth) *n.* [ME. *feith* < OFr. *feid, fei* (Fr. *foi*) < L. *fides,* confidence, belief (in LL.(Ec.), the Christian religion) < *fidere,* to trust < IE. base *bheidh-,* to urge, be convinced, whence Gr. *peithein,* to persuade, L. *foedus,* a compact & BIDE] **1.** unquestioning belief that does not require proof or evidence **2.** unquestioning belief in God, religious tenets, etc. **3.** a religion or a system of religious beliefs [the Catholic *faith*] **4.** anything believed **5.** complete trust, confidence, or reliance **6.** allegiance to some person or thing; loyalty —*interj.* indeed; in faith —**SYN.** see BELIEF —**bad faith** insincerity; dishonesty; duplicity —**break (or keep) faith 1.** to be disloyal (or loyal) to one's beliefs, principles, etc. **2.** to break (or keep) a promise —**good faith** sincerity; honesty —**in faith** indeed; really ☆**faith cure 1.** a method of trying to cure illness by having religious faith, praying, etc. **2.** a cure allegedly brought about by such methods

faith·ful (-fəl) *adj.* [ME.] **1.** keeping faith; maintaining allegiance to someone or something; constant; loyal [*faithful* friends] **2.** having or showing a strong sense of duty or responsibility; conscientious [*faithful* attendance] **3.** accurate; reliable; exact [a *faithful* copy] **4.** [Obs.] full of faith, esp. religious faith —**the faithful 1.** the true believers (in any specified religion) **2.** the loyal adherents —**faith′ful·ly** *adv.* —**faith′ful·ness** *n.*

SYN.—**faithful** implies continued, steadfast adherence to a person or thing to which one is bound by an oath, duty, obligation, etc. [a *faithful* wife]; **loyal** implies undeviating allegiance to a person, cause, institution, etc. which one feels morally bound to support or defend [a *loyal* friend]; **constant** suggests freedom from fickleness in affections or loyalties [a *constant* lover]; **staunch** (or **stanch**) implies such strong allegiance to one's principles or purpose as not to be turned aside by any cause [a *staunch* defender of the truth]; **resolute** stresses unwavering determination, often in adhering to one's personal ends or aims [she was *resolute* in her decision to stay] —**ANT. faithless**

☆**faith healing** same as FAITH CURE —**faith healer**

faith·less (-lis) *adj.* [ME. *feithles*] **1.** not keeping faith; dishonest; disloyal **2.** unreliable; undependable **3.** [Rare] without faith, esp. religious faith —**faith′less·ly** *adv.* —**faith′less·ness** *n.*

SYN.—**faithless** implies failure to adhere to an oath, duty, obligation, etc. [a *faithless* wife]; **false,** in this connection more or less synonymous with **faithless,** stresses failure in devotion to someone or something that has a moral claim to one's support [a *false* friend]; **disloyal** implies a breach of allegiance to a person, cause, institution, etc. [*disloyal* to one's family]; **traitorous** strictly implies the commission of an act of treason; **treacherous** suggests an inclination to commit treason or a tendency to betray a trust [his *treacherous* colleagues]; **perfidious** adds to the meaning of **treacherous** a connotation of sordidness or depravity [a *perfidious* informer] —**ANT. faithful**

fai·tour (fāt′ər) *n.* [ME. < OFr., lit., a doer, maker < L. *factor:* cf. FACTOR] [Obs.] an impostor; rogue

Fai·yûm (fi yŏom′, fä-) city in N Egypt, just west of the Nile: pop. 102,000: also **Fayum, El Faiyûm**

fake¹ (fāk) *vt., vi.* **faked, fak′ing** [earlier *feague, feake,* ult. < ? Gr. *fegen,* to sweep, in 17th-c. thieves' slang, to clean out a (victim's) purse] **1.** to make (something) seem real, satisfactory, etc. by any sort of deception; practice deception by simulating or tampering with (something); counterfeit ☆**2.** *Jazz* to improvise (a chorus, solo passage,

etc.) —*n.* anything or anyone not genuine; fraud; counterfeit —*adj.* fraudulent; not genuine; sham; false —**SYN.** see FALSE —**fake (someone) out** [Colloq.] to deceive or outmaneuver (someone) by a feint, bluff, deceptive act, etc. —**fak′er** *n.* —**fak′er·y** *n.*

fake² (fāk) *n.* [< ?] *Naut.* a loop of coiled rope, cable, etc. —*vt.* faked, fak′ing to coil (a rope, etc.)

fa·kir (fə kir′) *n.* [Ar. *faqir,* lit., poor, a poor man] **1.** a member of a Moslem holy sect who lives by begging **2.** a Hindu ascetic **3.** any Moslem or Hindu itinerant beggar, often one claiming to perform miracles Also sp. **fa·keer′**

fa la, fal la (fä lä′, fä′ lä) **1.** syllables used as a refrain in some old songs **2.** a type of 16th- and 17th-century part song with this refrain

Fa·lange (fā′lanj; *Sp.* fä län′he) *n.* [Sp., lit., phalanx < L. *phalanx,* PHALANX] a fascist organization that became the only official political party of Spain under Franco following the Spanish civil war (1936–39)

Fa·lang·ist (fə lan′jist) *n.* a member of the Falange

Fa·la·sha (fä lä′shə) *n.* a member of a Hamitic tribe living in Ethiopia and practicing the Jewish religion

fal·cate (fal′kāt) *adj.* [L. *falcatus* < *falx* (gen. *falcis*), a sickle < ? IE. base *dhelg-,* to pierce, needle, whence G. *dolch,* dagger] sickle-shaped; curved; hooked

fal·chion (fôl′chən, -shən) *n.* [ME. & OFr. *fauchon* < VL. *falcio* < L. *falx:* see prec.] **1.** a medieval sword with a short, broad, slightly curved blade **2.** [Poet.] any sword

fal·ci·form (fal′sə fôrm′) *adj.* [< L. *falx,* a sickle (see FALCATE) + -FORM] same as FALCATE

fal·con (fal′kən, fôl′-, fô′-) *n.* [ME. < OFr. *faucon* < LL. *falco* (gen. *falconis*), derived by folk etym. < L. *falx* (see FALCATE) because of its curved beak and talons, but < ? Gmc. *falco* (OHG. *falcho*) < ? IE. base *pel-,* FALLOW²] **1.** any hawk trained to hunt and kill small game: in falconry the female is called a *falcon,* the male a *tercel* **2.** *Zool.* any of several related hawklike birds (family Falconidae), with long, pointed wings and a short, curved, notched beak **3.** a small cannon used from the 15th to the 17th centuries

fal·con·er (-ər) *n.* [ME. < OFr. *fauconnier*] **1.** a person who breeds and trains falcons **2.** a person who hunts with falcons

fal·con·et (-et′) *n.* [dim. of FALCON] **1.** *Zool.* any small falcon, esp. any of various Asiatic kinds **2.** [It. *falconetto* < OIt. *falcone,* FALCON] an obsolete type of light cannon

fal·con-gen·tle (-jen′t'l) *n.* [ME. *faucoun gentil* < Fr.: see FALCON & GENTLE] the female of the peregrine falcon

fal·con·ry (-rē) *n.* [OFr. *fauconnerie*] **1.** the art of training falcons to hunt game **2.** the sport of hunting with falcons

fal·de·ral (fôl′də rôl′, fal′də ral′) *n.* [nonsense syllables] **1.** a showy but worthless trinket **2.** mere nonsense **3.** a refrain in some old songs

fald·stool (fôld′stŏol′) *n.* [ME. *foldstol* < ML. *faldistolium,* prob. via OFr. *faldestoel* < Frank. *faldistol* (see FOLD¹ & STOOL), akin to OHG. *faltstuol,* OE. *fyldestol*] **1.** a portable stool or desk used in praying **2.** *R.C.Ch.* a backless chair used as by a bishop when officiating in a church other than his own, or when not on his throne **3.** *Anglican Ch.* a desk at which the litany is read

Fal·kirk (fôl′kərk, fô′-) city in C Scotland, in Stirlingshire: site of a battle (1298) in which the Scots under Wallace were defeated by the English: pop. 38,000

Falk·land Islands (fôk′lənd) Brit. crown colony consisting of a group of islands in the South Atlantic, east of the tip of S. America: 4,700 sq. mi.; pop. 2,000

fall (fôl) *vi.* **fell, fall′en, fall′ing** [ME. *fallen* < OE. *feallan,* to fall, akin to G. *fallen* < IE. base *phol-,* to fall] **I.** to come down by the force of gravity; drop; descend; specif., **1.** to come down because detached, pushed, dropped, etc.; move down and land forcibly [apples *fall* from the tree] **2.** to come down suddenly from a standing or sitting position; tumble; topple; become prostrate **3.** to be wounded or killed in battle **4.** to come down in ruins; collapse [the building *fell*] **5.** to hang down [hair *falling* about her shoulders] **6.** to strike; hit [the arrow *fell* wide of its mark] **II.** to pass to a position, condition, etc. regarded as lower; specif., **1.** to take a downward direction [land *falling* away to the sea] **2.** to become lower in amount, number, degree, intensity, value, etc.; drop; abate [prices *fell*] **3.** to lose power; be overthrown [the government has *fallen*] **4.** to lose status, reputation, dignity, etc. **5.** to yield to temptation; do wrong; sin; specif. in earlier use (esp. of women), to lose chastity **6.** to be captured or conquered **7.** to take on a look of disappointment or dejection [his face *fell*] **8.** to become lower in pitch or volume [her voice *fell*] **III.** to happen as if by dropping; specif., **1.** to take place; occur [the meeting *fell* on a Friday] **2.** to come by lot, distribution, inheritance, etc. [the estate *falls* to the son] **3.** to pass into a specified condition; become [to *fall* ill] **4.** to come at a specified place [the accent *falls* on the third syllable] **5.** to be directed by chance [his eye *fell* on a misspelled word] **6.** to be spoken in an involuntary way [the news *fell* from his lips] **7.** to be born: said of animals **8.** to be divided (into) [to *fall* into two classes] —*vt.* [Dial.] to fell (a tree, etc.) —*n.* [< the *v.*] **1.** a dropping; descending; coming

down 2. a coming down suddenly from a standing or sitting position **3.** a hanging down, or a part hanging down **4.** a downward direction or slope **5.** a becoming lower or less; reduction in value, price, etc. **6.** a lowering of the voice in pitch or volume **7.** a capture; overthrow; ruin **8.** a loss of status, reputation, etc. **9.** a yielding to temptation; wrongdoing; moral lapse **10.** *a)* a birth: said of animals *b)* the number of animals born at one birth; litter **11.** *a)* something that has fallen [a *fall* of leaves] *b)* a felling of trees, or timber felled at one time **12.** the season when leaves fall; autumn **13.** the amount of what has fallen [a six-inch *fall* of snow] **14.** the distance that something falls **15.** [*usually pl., often with sing. v.*] water falling over a cliff, etc.; cascade **16.** a broad, turned-down ruff or collar worn in the 17th cent. **17.** a piece of cloth hanging from a woman's hat, usually in back; kind of veil **18.** a long tress of hair, often synthetic, used by women to fill out their coiffure **19.** *Mech.* the loose end of a cable or chain of a tackle **20.** *Naut.* either of the lines used to lower or hoist a boat at the davits **21.** *a) Wrestling* the act of throwing an opponent on his back so that both shoulders touch the floor *b)* a bout or division of a wrestling match —*adj.* of, for, or in the autumn —☆**fall (all) over oneself** [Colloq.] to behave in too eager or zealous a manner —**fall among** to come among by chance —**fall away 1.** to take away friendship, support, etc.; desert **2.** to become less in size, strength, etc.; specif., to grow thin and weak —**fall back** to withdraw; give way; retreat —**fall back on** (or **upon**) **1.** to turn, or return, to for security or help **2.** to retreat to —**fall behind 1.** to be outdistanced; drop behind **2.** to fail to pay on time; be in arrears —☆**fall down on** [Slang] to fail or be unsuccessful in (a job, etc.) —**fall flat** to fail to have the desired effect; be completely unsuccessful —☆**fall for** [Colloq.] **1.** to fall in love with; become infatuated with **2.** to be tricked or deceived by —**fall foul** (or **afoul**) of **1.** *Naut.* to collide with **2.** to become entangled with **3.** to have trouble with; get into a quarrel with —**fall in 1.** to collapse inward; cave in **2.** to agree **3.** *Mil.* to line up in proper formation —**fall in with 1.** to meet by chance **2.** to meet and join **3.** to agree with; comply with —**fall off 1.** to become smaller, less, lighter, etc. **2.** to become worse; decline **3.** *Naut.* to swing to leeward or off the wind —**fall on** (or **upon**) **1.** to attack **2.** to be the duty of —**fall out 1.** to have a disagreement; quarrel **2.** to happen; result **3.** *Mil.* to leave one's place in a formation —**fall short 1.** to be lacking **2.** to fail to meet a standard or goal (with *of*) —**fall through** to come to nothing; fail —**fall to 1.** to begin; start; specif., *a)* to start attacking *b)* to start eating —**fall under 1.** to come under (an influence, etc.) **2.** to be listed or classified as —**ride for a fall** to behave in a manner likely to cause one trouble or injury —**the Fall (of Man)** *Christian Theol.* Adam's sin of yielding to temptation in eating the forbidden fruit, and his subsequent loss of grace: see ORIGINAL SIN

Fal·la (fä′lyä), **Ma·nuel de** (mä nwel′ *the*) 1876–1946; Sp. composer

fal·la·cious (fə lā′shəs) *adj.* [L. *fallaciosus*] **1.** containing a fallacy; erroneous [*fallacious* reasoning] **2.** *a)* misleading or deceptive *b)* causing disappointment; delusive —**fal·la′-cious·ly** *adv.* —**fal·la′cious·ness** *n.*

fal·la·cy (fal′ə sē) *n., pl.* **-cies** [ME. *fallace* < OFr. < L. *fallacia*, deception, artifice < *fallax* (gen. *fallacis*), deceitful < *fallere*, to deceive: see FAIL] **1.** orig., deception **2.** aptness to mislead; deceptive or delusive quality [the *fallacy* of the senses] **3.** a false or mistaken idea, opinion, etc.; error **4.** an error in reasoning; flaw or defect in argument; specif., *Logic* an argument based on incorrect demonstration, as a vicious circle

fal·lal (fa lal′) *n.* [? contr. < rare *falbala* < Fr. *falbala*, furbelow] a useless piece of finery or frippery

fall·back (fôl′bak′) *n.* **1.** something in reserve that one can turn to for help **2.** a withdrawing; retreat

fall·en (fôl′ən) *adj.* [ME., pp. of *fallen*, to FALL] **1.** having come down; dropped **2.** on the ground; prostrate **3.** having lost status or moral reputation; degraded **4.** captured; overthrown **5.** ruined; destroyed **6.** dead

fall·er (-ər) *n.* **1.** a device, as in a spinning machine, that works by falling **2.** a person who fells trees

☆**fall·fish** (-fish′) *n., pl.* **-fish′, -fish′es:** see FISH² [prob. so named because often found near falls or rapids] a large chub (*Semotilus corporalis*) found in clear waters of NE U.S.

☆**fall guy** [Slang] a person made the victim, or left to face the consequences, of a scheme that has miscarried

fal·li·ble (fal′ə b'l) *adj.* [ME. < ML. *fallibilis* < L. *fallere*, to deceive: see FAIL] **1.** liable to be mistaken or deceived **2.** liable to be erroneous or inaccurate —**fal′li·bil′i·ty, fal′li·ble·ness** *n.* —**fal′li·bly** *adv.*

fall·ing-out (fôl′iŋ out′) *n.* a disagreement; quarrel

falling sickness former name for EPILEPSY

falling star same as METEOR (sense 1)

☆**fall line 1.** the geographical line indicating the beginning of a plateau, usually marked by many waterfalls and rapids **2.** [F- L-] the line east of the Appalachian Mountains, marking the end of the coastal plains and the beginning of the Piedmont Plateau **3.** *Skiing* the line of direct descent down a hill

☆**fall·off** (-ôf′) *n.* the act of becoming less or worse; decline

Fal·lo·pi·an tube (fa lō′pē ən) [after Gabriel *Fallopius* (L. form of Gabriello *Fallopio*), It. anatomist (1523–62) who first described them] either of two slender tubes that carry ova from the ovaries to the uterus

fall·out (fôl′out′) *n.* ☆**1.** the descent to earth of radioactive particles, as after a nuclear explosion ☆**2.** these particles **3.** whatever comes as an incidental consequence

fal·low¹ (fal′ō) *n.* [ME. *falow* < OE. *fealh*, harrow, felly (of wheel) < IE. base **pelk-*, to turn] **1.** land plowed but not seeded for one or more growing seasons, to kill weeds, make the soil richer, etc. **2.** the plowing of land to be left idle thus —*adj.* **1.** left uncultivated or unplanted **2.** untrained; inactive: said esp. of the mind —*vt.* [ME. *falwen* < OE. *fealgian* < *fealh*, fallow land; infl. by *fealwian*, to fade < *fealo:* see ff.] to leave (land) unplanted after plowing —**lie fallow** to remain uncultivated, unused, unproductive, etc. for a time —**fal′low·ness** *n.*

fal·low² (fal′ō) *adj.* [ME. *falwe* < OE. *fealo*, akin to G. *fahl*, fallow < Gmc. **falwa* < IE. base **pel-*, gray, pale, whence L. *pallidus*] pale-yellow; brownish-yellow

fallow deer a small European deer (*Dama dama*) having a yellowish coat spotted with white in summer

Fall River [transl. of Algonquian name of the Taunton River, which flows into the ocean here] seaport in SE Mass.: pop. 97,000

Fal·mouth (fal′məth) seaport & resort in Cornwall, SW England, on an inlet (**Falmouth Bay**) of the English Channel: pop. 17,000

false (fôls) *adj.* **fals′er, fals′est** [ME. < OFr. < *fals* < L. *falsus*, pp. of *fallere*, to deceive: see FAIL] **1.** not true; in error; incorrect; mistaken [a *false* argument] **2.** untruthful; lying; dishonest [a *false* witness] **3.** disloyal; unfaithful [a *false* friend] **4.** deceiving or meant to deceive; misleading [a *false* scent] **5.** not real; artificial; counterfeit [*false* teeth] **6.** not properly so named; deceptively resembling [*false* jasmine] **7.** based on wrong or mistaken ideas [*false* pride] **8.** *Mech.* temporary, nonessential, or added on for protection, disguise, etc. [a *false* drawer] **9.** *Music* pitched inaccurately —*adv.* in a false manner —**play (a person) false** to deceive, cheat, hoodwink, or betray (a person) —**put in a false position** to cause misunderstanding of the intentions, opinions, etc. of —**false′ly** *adv.* —**false′ness** *n.*

SYN.—false, in this comparison, refers to anything that is not in essence that which it purports to be and may or may not connote deliberate deception [*false* hair]; **sham** refers to an imitation or simulation of something and usually connotes intent to deceive [*sham* piety]; **counterfeit** and the colloquial **bogus** apply to a very careful imitation and always imply intent to deceive or defraud [*counterfeit*, or *bogus*, money]; **fake** is a less formal term for any person or thing that is not genuine [a *fake* doctor, chimney, etc.] See also FAITHLESS —**ANT. genuine, real**

false arrest *Law* any forceful and unlawful restraint of a person by another

false bottom 1. a bottom, as of a box, between which and the real bottom there is a secret compartment **2.** a bottom, as of a whiskey glass, formed to give the illusion that the glass holds more than it does

false·face (-fās′) *n.* a mask, esp. a comical or grotesque one

false fruit *Bot.* a fruitlike structure formed from the separate carpels of one flower or from the uniting of a cluster of flowers, as the accessory fruit of the strawberry or the aggregate fruit of the raspberry

false·heart·ed (-här′tid) *adj.* disloyal; deceitful

false·hood (-hood′) *n.* [ME. *falshod:* see FALSE & -HOOD] **1.** lack of accuracy or truth; falsity; deception **2.** the telling of lies; lying **3.** a false statement; lie **4.** a false belief, theory, idea, etc.

false imprisonment *Law* the unlawful arrest or detention of another person

false keel a narrow keel below the main keel, for protection and increased steadiness

false pretenses *Law* deliberate misrepresentation of fact in speech or action in order to obtain another's property

false relation same as CROSS RELATION

false ribs the five lower ribs on each side of the body: so called because not directly attached to the breastbone

false step 1. a misstep; stumble **2.** a social blunder

false teeth an artificial denture, esp. a complete one

fal·set·to (fôl set′ō) *n., pl.* **-tos** [It., dim. of *falso*, false < L. *falsus*, FALSE] **1.** an artificial way of singing or speaking, in which the voice is placed in a register much higher than that of the natural voice **2.** the voice used in such singing, esp. by tenors, usually having a soft, colorless quality **3.** a person singing or speaking in falsetto: also **fal·set′tist** —*adj.* of or singing in falsetto —*adv.* in falsetto

☆**fals·ies** (fôl′sēz) *n.pl.* [Colloq.] pads worn with a brassiere to make the breasts look fuller

fal·si·fy (fôl′sə fī′) *vt.* **-fied′, -fy′ing** [ME. *falsifien* < OFr. *falsifier* < ML. *falsificare* < L. *falsificus*, that acts falsely < *falsus*, FALSE + *facere*, to make, DO¹] **1.** to make false; specif., *a)* to give an untrue or misleading account of; misrepresent *b)* to alter (a record, etc.) fraudulently *c)* to alter from the accepted rule or form [a poet sometimes *falsifies* accent] **2.** to prove or show to be untrue or unfounded [to *falsify* their hopes] —*vi.* to tell falsehoods; lie —**fal′si·fi·ca′tion** *n.* —**fal′si·fi′er** *n.*

fal·si·ty (-tē) *n., pl.* **-ties** [ME. *falsete* < OFr. < L. *falsitas*] **1.** the condition or quality of being false; specif., *a)* incorrectness *b)* dishonesty *c)* deceitfulness *d)* disloyalty **2.** something false; esp., a lie

Fal·staff, Sir John (fôl′staf, -stäf) in Shakespeare's *Henry IV* and *The Merry Wives of Windsor*, a fat, jovial, witty knight, bold in talk but cowardly —**Fal·staff′i·an** *adj.*

Fal·ster (fäl′stər) one of the islands of Denmark, in the Baltic Sea: 198 sq. mi.

falt·boat (fält′bōt′) *n.* [G. *faltboot* < *falten*, FOLD¹ + *boot*, BOAT] *same as* FOLDBOAT

fal·ter (fôl′tər) *vi.* [ME. *faltren*, prob. < ON., as in *faltra(sk)*, to be encumbered] **1.** to move uncertainly or unsteadily; totter; stumble **2.** to stumble in speech; speak haltingly; stammer **3.** to act hesitantly; show uncertainty; waver; flinch [to *falter* under enemy fire] **4.** to lose strength, certainty, etc.; weaken [the economy *faltered*] —*vt.* to say haltingly, hesitantly, or timidly —*n.* **1.** an act of faltering **2.** a faltering sound —**SYN.** see HESITATE —**fal′ter·er** *n.* —**fal′ter·ing·ly** *adv.*

fam. 1. familiar **2.** family

F.A.M. Free and Accepted Masons

fame (fām) *n.* [ME. < OFr. < L. *fama*, fame, reputation, akin to *fari*, to speak < IE. base *bhā-*, to speak, whence Gr. *phēmē*, utterance, report & BAN¹, BOON¹] **1.** [Rare or Archaic] public report; rumor **2.** reputation, esp. for good **3.** the state of being well known or much talked about; renown; celebrity —*vt.* **famed, fam′ing** [Archaic] to tell about widely; make famous

famed (fāmd) *adj.* [pp. of prec.] much talked about or widely known; famous; renowned (*for* something)

Fa·meuse (fə myōōz′) *n.* [Fr., fem. of *fameux*, FAMOUS] a late fall variety of apple

fa·mil·ial (fə mil′yəl) *adj.* [Fr.: see FAMILY & -AL] of, involving, or common to a family

fa·mil·iar (fə mil′yər) *adj.* [ME. *familier* < OFr. < L. *familiaris*, of a household, domestic < *familia*, FAMILY] **1.** orig., having to do with a family **2.** friendly, informal, or intimate [to be on *familiar* terms] **3.** too friendly; unduly intimate or bold; presumptuous **4.** having an intimate knowledge of; closely acquainted (*with*) [familiar with the Bible] **5.** well-known; often encountered; common; ordinary [a *familiar* sight] **6.** domesticated: said of animals —*n.* **1.** a close friend **2.** in superstitious belief, a spirit, often in animal form, believed to act as a servant, as to a witch **3.** [Obs.] a member of a family **4.** *R.C.Ch. a)* a lay servant in a monastery, bishop's household, etc. *b)* an official of the Inquisition who arrested and imprisoned those accused, as of heresy —**fa·mil′iar·ly** *adv.*

SYN.—**familiar** is applied to that which is known through constant association, and, with reference to persons, suggests informality, or even presumption, such as might prevail among members of a family; **close** is applied to persons or things very near to one in affection, attraction, interests, etc.; **intimate** implies very close association, acquaintance, relationship, etc. or suggests something of a very personal or private nature; **confidential** implies a relationship in which there is mutual trust and a sharing of private thoughts, problems, etc. See also COMMON

fa·mil·i·ar·i·ty (fə mil′yar′ə tē, -mil′ē ar′-) *n.*, *pl.* **-ties** [ME. *familiarite* < OFr. < L. *familiaritas* < *familiaris*: see prec.] **1.** close association; intimacy **2.** free and intimate behavior; absence of formality and ceremony **3.** intimacy that is too bold or unwelcome **4.** a highly intimate act, remark, etc.; often, specif., a caress or other act of sexual intimacy **5.** close acquaintance (*with* something)

fa·mil·iar·ize (fə mil′yə rīz′) *vt.* **-ized′, -iz′ing 1.** to make commonly known [WWII *familiarized* the term "radar"] **2.** to make (another or oneself) accustomed or fully acquainted [*familiarize* yourself with the job] —**fa·mil′iar·i·za′tion** *n.*

fam·i·lism (fam′ə liz′m) *n.* a pattern of social structure in which the family unit and strong family feeling occupy a position of great importance —**fam′i·lis′tic** *adj.*

fam·i·ly (fam′ə lē, fam′lē) *n.*, *pl.* **-lies** [ME. *familie* < L. *familia*, household establishment < *famulus*, servant < ? IE. *dhe-mo-*, house (< *dhē-*: see DO¹), whence Sans. *dhāman*, household] **1.** orig., all the people living in the same house; household **2.** *a)* a social unit consisting of parents and the children that they rear *b)* the children of the same parents *c)* one's husband (or wife) and children **3.** a group of people related by ancestry or marriage; relatives **4.** all those claiming descent from a common ancestor; tribe or clan; lineage **5.** a group of things having a common source or similar features; specif., *a) Biol.* a category in the classification of plants or animals, ranking above a genus and below an order and including one or more similar genera: family names of plants have the suffix *-aceae;* those of animals, *-idae b) Ecol.* a community composed of organisms of the same species *c) Linguis.* a group of related languages assumed to be descended from a common ancestral language *d) Math.* a set of curves, functions, or other entities with some shared property —*adj.* of or for a family —**in a family way** [Colloq.] pregnant; with child

family circle 1. the close members of a family and intimate friends ☆**2.** in some theaters, a section of less expensive seats in the upper balcony

family man 1. a man who has a wife and children **2.** a man devoted to his family and home

family name a surname

family planning the regulation, by birth control methods, of the number of children that a woman will have

☆**family style** a way of serving food, as in boardinghouses and some restaurants, by which each person at the table helps himself from large platters passed around

family tree 1. a chart showing the relationship of all the ancestors and descendants in a given family **2.** all the ancestors and descendants in a given family

fam·ine (fam′ən) *n.* [ME. < OFr. < VL. *famina* < L. *fames*, hunger < IE. base *dhē-*, to wither away, whence DAZE] **1.** an acute and general shortage of food, or a period of this **2.** any acute shortage or dearth **3.** [Archaic] starvation; great hunger

fam·ish (-ish) *vt.*, *vi.* [ME. *famishen*, altered (after verbs ending in *-ish-:* cf. CHERISH) < *famen*, aphetic < OFr. *afamer* < VL. *affamare* < L. *ad*, to + *fames*, hunger: see prec.] **1.** to make or be very hungry; make or become weak from hunger **2.** [Obs.] to starve to death —**fam′ish·ment** *n.*

fa·mous (fā′məs) *adj.* [ME. < L. *famosus* < *fama:* see FAME] **1.** much talked about; having fame, or celebrity; renowned **2.** [Colloq.] excellent; very good; first-rate **3.** [Archaic] notorious —**fa′mous·ly** *adv.*

SYN.—**famous** is applied to persons or things that have received wide public attention and are generally known and talked about; **renowned** suggests a being named publicly again and again for some outstanding quality, achievement, etc.; **celebrated** is applied to persons or things that have received much public honor or praise; **noted** implies a being brought to the wide notice of the public for some particular quality; **notorious**, in current usage, suggests a being widely but unfavorably known or talked about; **distinguished** implies a being noted as superior in its class or of its kind; **eminent** more strongly stresses the conspicuous superiority of persons or things; **illustrious** suggests a reputation based on brilliance of achievement or splendidness of character —ANT. obscure, unknown

fam·u·lus (fam′yoo ləs) *n.*, *pl.* **-li′** (-lī′) [< L., a servant: see FAMILY] an attendant or assistant, esp. of a medieval sorcerer or scholar

fan¹ (fan) *n.* [ME. *fanne* < OE. *fann* < L. *vannus*, basket for winnowing grain < IE. base *wē-*, to blow, flutter, whence WIND², WINNOW] **1.** orig., a device for winnowing grain **2.** any device or machine used to set up a current of air for ventilating or cooling; specif., *a)* any flat surface moved by hand *b)* a folding device made of paper, cloth, etc. which when opened has the shape of a sector of a circle *c)* a device consisting of one or more revolving blades or vanes attached to a rotary hub and operated by a motor **3.** anything in the shape of a fan (*n.* 2 *b*), as the tail of a bird **4.** in a windmill, a small vane that keeps the large vanes, or sails, at right angles to the wind —*vt.* **fanned, fan′ning** [ME. *fannen* < OE. *fannian*] **1.** to move or agitate (air) with or as with a fan **2.** to direct a current of air toward or on with or as with a fan; blow on **3.** to stir up; excite **4.** to blow or drive away with a fan **5.** to spread out into the shape of a fan (*n.* 2 *b*) **6.** to separate (grain) from chaff ☆**7.** [Slang] *a)* to spank *b)* to fire (a pistol) several times quickly in succession by slapping the hammer back as with the alternate hand between shots ☆**8.** *Baseball* to strike (a batter) out —*vi.* ☆*Baseball* to strike out —**fan out** to scatter or spread out like an open fan (*n.* 2 *b*) —**fan the air** to strike at but fail to hit something

☆**fan²** (fan) *n.* [contr. < FANATIC] [Colloq.] a person enthusiastic about a specified sport, pastime, or performer; devotee [a baseball *fan*, movie *fan*]

fa·nat·ic (fə nat′ik) *adj.* [< L. *fanaticus*, of a temple, hence enthusiastic, inspired < *fanum*, a temple: see FANE] unreasonably enthusiastic; overly zealous: also **fa·nat′i·cal** —*n.* a person whose extreme zeal, piety, etc. goes beyond what is reasonable; zealot —**SYN.** see ZEALOT —**fa·nat′i·cal·ly** *adv.*

fa·nat·i·cism (-ə siz′m) *n.* excessive and unreasonable zeal —**fa·nat′i·cize′** (-sīz′) *vt.* **-cized′, -ciz′ing**

fan·cied (fan′sēd) *adj.* imaginary; imagined

fan·ci·er (fan′sē ər) *n.* a person with a special interest in and knowledge of something, particularly of the breeding of plants or animals [a dog *fancier*]

fan·ci·ful (fan′si fəl) *adj.* **1.** full of fancy; indulging in fancies; imaginative in a playful way; whimsical **2.** created in the fancy; imaginary; not real [a *fanciful* tale] **3.** showing fancy in construction or design; quaint; odd [*fanciful* costumes] —**SYN.** see IMAGINARY —**fan′ci·ful·ly** *adv.* —**fan′ci·ful·ness** *n.*

fan·cy (fan′sē) *n.*, *pl.* **-cies** [ME. *fantsy*, contr. < *fantasie:* see FANTASY] **1.** *a)* orig., imagination in general *b)* decorative, light, whimsical, playful, or capricious imagination: the current literary sense See IMAGINATION **2.** illusion or delusion **3.** a mental image **4.** an arbitrary idea; notion; caprice; whim **5.** an inclination, liking, or fondness, often transient [to take a *fancy* to someone] **6.** [Rare] critical taste or judgment in art, dress, etc. —*adj.* **-ci·er, -ci·est 1.** based on fancy; capricious; whimsical; fanciful **2.** higher than real value; extravagant [a *fancy* price] **3.** made or added to please the fancy; ornamental; decorated; not plain; elaborate [a *fancy* necktie] **4.** of superior skill; intricate and difficult [*fancy* diving] **5.** of superior quality,

and therefore more expensive [canned goods graded *fancy*] **6.** bred for some special feature or excellence of type: said of animals —*vt.* -cied, -cy·ing **1.** to form an idea of; imagine **2.** to have a liking for; be fond of [to *fancy* rich desserts] **3.** to believe something without being sure; suppose [they are, I *fancy*, still friends] —*fancy* (that)! can you imagine (that)! —**the fancy** formerly, the enthusiasts of some sport or hobby, esp. boxing —**fan′ci·less** *adj.* —**fan′ci·ly** *adv.* —**fan′ci·ness** *n.*

☆**fancy dan** [FANCY + (prob.) *Dan*, nickname for DANIEL] [Slang] a flashy, ostentatious person, often one who lacks real skill, stamina, etc.

fancy dress a masquerade costume

fan·cy-free (-frē′) *adj.* **1.** free to fall in love; not married, engaged, etc. **2.** free from worry; carefree

fancy man a man supported by a woman; esp., a pimp

fancy woman **1.** a mistress **2.** a prostitute

fan·cy·work (-wurk′) *n.* embroidery, crocheting, and other ornamental needlework

fan·dan·go (fan daŋ′gō) *n., pl.* -gos [Sp.] **1.** a lively Spanish dance in rhythm varying from slow to quick 3/4 time **2.** music for this **3.** a foolish act

fane (fān) *n.* [L. *fanum*, sanctuary, temple < *fasnom* < IE. base *dhēs-*: see FAIR²] [Archaic or Poet.] a temple or church

Fan·euil Hall (fan′əl, -yəl) [after Peter *Faneuil* (1700-43), its builder] old market building & public hall in Boston, Mass.: called the *Cradle of Liberty* from its use by Revolutionary patriots as a meeting place

fan·fare (fan′fer′) *n.* [Fr. < *fanfarer*, to blow trumpets, prob. < *fanfaron*, braggart: see ff.] **1.** a loud flourish of trumpets **2.** noisy or showy display

fan·fa·ron·ade (fan′fər ə nād′) *n.* [Fr. < Sp. *fanfarronada* < Sp. *fanfarrón*, boaster, prob. < Ar. *farfār*, boastful] boasting talk or showy action; bluster

fang (faŋ) *n.* [ME., that which is seized < OE. < base of *fon*, to take, catch, akin to G. *fangen* < IE. base *pak*, to fasten, tie, whence L. *pangere* (see PACT), Sans. *páś-*, noose] **1.** a) one of the long, pointed teeth with which meat-eating animals seize and tear their prey; canine tooth b) one of the long, hollow or grooved teeth through which poisonous snakes inject their venom c) formerly, the root of a tooth **2.** the pointed part of something —*SYN.* see TOOTH —**fanged** (faŋd) *adj.*

FANGS

fan·jet (fan′jet′) *n. same as* TURBOFAN (sense 1)

fan·light (fan′līt′) *n.* a semicircular window, often with sash bars in a fanlike arrangement, over a door or larger window

☆**fan mail** letters, esp. of praise or adulation from strangers, received by a prominent or well-known person

fan·ner (fan′ər) *n.* a person or thing that fans

Fan·nie, Fan·ny (fan′ē) a feminine name: see FRANCES

☆**Fannie Mae** (or **May**) Federal National Mortgage Association

☆**fan·ny** (fan′ē) *n., pl.* -nies [< ? FAN¹, *vt.* 7 a] [Slang] the buttocks

fan·on (fan′ən) *n.* [ME. *fanoun* < OFr. *fanon* < Frank. *fano*, piece of cloth, akin to G. *fahne*, banner < IE. base *pan-*, fabric, whence Gr. *pēnos*, L. *pannus*] **1.** a narrow band worn hanging over the left arm by priests celebrating Mass; maniple **2.** a capelike vestment worn by the Pope when celebrating Mass

fan palm any palm tree with broad, fan-shaped leaves

☆**fan·tab·u·lous** (fan tab′yoo ləs) *adj.* [FANT(ASTIC) + (F)ABULOUS] [Slang] remarkably good

fan·tail (fan′tāl′) *n.* **1.** a part, tail, or end spread out like an opened fan **2.** *Naut.* a) the overhanging portion of the deck on some ships b) the part of the main deck at the stern **3.** *Zool.* a) a variety of domestic pigeon b) an Australian flycatcher (genus *Rhipidura*) with a very broad tail c) a breed of goldfish with a fanlike tail

fan-tan (fan′tan′) *n.* [< Chin. *fan*, number of times + *t'an*, apportion] **1.** a Chinese gambling game in which the players bet on the number of beans, etc. that will be left from a pile after it has been counted off in fours **2.** a card game in which the players seek to discard all their cards in proper sequence Also **fan tan**

fan·ta·si·a (fan tā′zhə, -zē ə; fan′tə zē′ə) *n.* [It. < L. *phantasia*: see FANTASY] **1.** a) a musical composition of no fixed form, with a structure determined by the composer's fancy b) a literary work similarly constructed **2.** a medley of familiar tunes

fan·ta·size (-sīz′) *vt.* -sized′, -siz′ing [FANTAS(Y) + -IZE] to create or imagine in a fantasy; have daydreams about —*vi.* to indulge in fantasies, as by daydreaming —**fan′ta·sist** (-sist) *n.*

fan·tasm (fan′taz'm) *n. same as* PHANTASM

fan·tast (-tast) *n.* an impractical dreamer; visionary

fan·tas·tic (fan tas′tik) *adj.* [ME. *fantastik* < OFr. *fantastique* < ML. *fantasticus* < LL. *phantasticus* < Gr. *phantastikos*, able to present or represent to the mind < *phantazein*, to make visible < *phainein*, to show: see FANTASY] **1.** existing in the imagination; imaginary; unreal [*fantastic* terrors] **2.** having a strange or weird appearance; grotesque; odd; quaint [*fantastic* designs] **3.** thought of by unrestrained fancy; extravagant; capricious; eccentric [a *fantastic* plan] **4.** seemingly impossible; incredible [fan-

tastic progress in science] Also **fan·tas′ti·cal** —*n.* [Archaic] a person who is fantastic in behavior, dress, etc.; eccentric —**fan·tas′ti·cal·ly** *adv.* —**fan·tas′ti·cal·ness** *n.*
SYN.—**fantastic** implies a lack of restraint in imagination, suggesting that which is extravagantly fanciful or unreal in design, conception, construction, etc. [*fantastic* notions]; **bizarre** suggests that which is extraordinarily eccentric or strange because of startling incongruities, extreme contrasts, etc. [music with a *bizarre* atonality]; **grotesque** suggests a ludicrously unnatural distortion of the normal or real, or a fantastic combination of elements [the *grotesque* grimaces of the comedian] See also IMAGINARY

fan·tas·ti·cate (-ti kāt′) *vt.* -cat′ed, -cat′ing to make fantastic —**fan·tas′ti·ca′tion** *n.*

fan·ta·sy (fan′tə sē, -zē) *n., pl.* -sies [ME. *fantasie* < OFr. < L. *phantasia*, idea, notion < Gr. *phantasia*, appearance of a thing < *phainein*, to show < IE. base *bhā-*, to gleam, shine, whence OE. *bonian*, to ornament] **1.** imagination or fancy; esp., wild, visionary fancy **2.** an unnatural or bizarre mental image; illusion; phantasm **3.** an odd notion; whim; caprice **4.** a highly imaginative poem, play, etc. **5.** *Music* a fantasia **6.** *Psychol.* a) a more-or-less connected series of mental images, as in a daydream, usually involving some unfulfilled desire b) the activity of forming such images —*vt.* -sied, -sy·ing to form fantasies about —*vi.* to indulge in fantasies, as by daydreaming

fan·tod (fan′täd) *n.* [prob. < FANT(ASTIC) + -od < ?] a nervous condition: now usually in the humorous phrase **the fantods**, a state of restless anxiety

fan·tom (fan′təm) *n., adj. same as* PHANTOM

fan tracery the decoration on fan vaulting

fan vaulting *Archit.* vaulting in which the ribs are spread out like those of a fan

fan·wise (fan′wīz′) *adv.* opened out like a folding fan

fan·wort (-wurt′) *n. same as* CABOMBA

FAO Food and Agriculture Organization (of the United Nations)

far (fär) *adj.* **far′ther, far′thest:** see also FURTHER, FURTHEST [ME. *farr, fer* (whence dial. form *fur*) < OE. *feorr*, akin to OHG. *ferro* < IE. base *per-*, forward, beyond, whence L. *per*, Gr. *per*] **1.** distant in space or time; not near; remote **2.** extending a long way [a *far* journey] **3.** more distant [the *far* side of the room] **4.** very different in quality or nature [*far* from poor] —*adv.* **1.** very distant in space, time, or degree **2.** to or from a great distance in time or position **3.** very much; considerably [*far* better] **4.** to a certain distance or degree [how *far* did you go?] —*n.* a distant place [to come from *far*] —**as far as** **1.** to the distance, extent, or degree that **2.** [Colloq.] with reference to; as for —**by far** considerably; to a great degree; very much: also **far and away** —**far and near** everywhere —**far and wide** widely; everywhere —**far be it from me** I would not presume or wish —**far gone** in an advanced state of deterioration —**far out** *same as* FAR-OUT (see below) —**few and far between** scarce; rare —**go far 1.** to cover much extent; last long **2.** to have a strong tendency **3.** to accomplish much; achieve much success —**in so far as** to the extent or degree that —**so far** up to this place, time, or degree —**so far as** to the extent or point that —**so far, so good** up to this point everything is all right
SYN.—**far** generally suggests that which is an indefinitely long way off in space, time, relation, etc. [*far* lands]; **distant**, although also suggesting a considerable interval of separation [a *distant* sound], is the term used when the measure of any interval is specified [desks four feet *distant* from one another]; **remote** is applied to that which is far off in space, time, connection, etc. from a place, thing, or person understood as a point of reference [a *remote* village]; **removed**, used predicatively, stresses separateness, distinctness, or lack of connection more strongly than **remote** —*ANT.* near, close

far·ad (far′ad, -əd) *n.* [after M. FARADAY] a unit of capacitance, equal to the amount that permits the storing of one coulomb of charge for each volt of applied potential

far·a·day (far′ə dā′) *n.* [after ff.] a unit of quantity of electricity, used especially in electrolysis, equal to the amount necessary to free one gram atomic weight of a univalent element: its value is equal to approximately 96,494 coulombs

Far·a·day (far′ə dā′), **Michael** 1791-1867; Eng. scientist: noted esp. for his work in electricity & magnetism; discovered electromagnetic induction

fa·rad·ic (fə rad′ik) *adj.* [see FARAD] *Elec.* of or pertaining to an intermittent, asymmetric alternating current produced by the secondary winding of an induction coil

far·a·dize (far′ə dīz′) *vt.* -dized′, -diz′ing [Fr. *faradiser*, after Michael FARADAY: see -IZE] to treat or stimulate with faradic current —**far′a·di·za′tion** *n.*

far·an·dole (far′ən dōl′) *n.* [Fr. < Pr. *farandoulo*] **1.** a lively dance of S France, in 6/8 time, by a winding chain of dancers **2.** the music for this dance

far·a·way (fär′ə wā′) *adj.* **1.** distant in time, place, degree, etc. **2.** dreamy; abstracted [a *faraway* look]

farce (färs) *n.* [Fr., stuffing, hence farce < VL. *farsa* < pp. of L. *farcire*, to stuff: early farces were used to fill interludes between acts] **1.** orig., stuffing, as for a fowl **2.** an exaggerated comedy based on broadly humorous, highly unlikely situations **3.** broad humor of the kind found in such plays **4.** something absurd or ridiculous, as an obvious pretense [his show of grief was a *farce*] —*vt.* **farced, farc′ing** to fill out with or as with stuffing or seasoning [to *farce* a play with old jokes]

‡**far·ceur** (fàr sër′) *n.* [Fr.] **1.** an actor in farces **2.** a writer of farces **3.** a joker; humorist; wag —**far·ceuse′** (-söz′) *n.fem.*

far·ci·cal (fär′si k'l) *adj.* of, or having the nature of, a farce; absurd, ridiculous, ludicrous, etc. —*SYN.* see FUNNY —**far′ci·cal′i·ty** (-kal′ə tē) *n.*, *pl.* -ties —**far′ci·cal·ly** *adv.*

far·cy (fär′sē) *n.* [ME. *farsine* < OFr. *farcin* < ML. *farcina* (for LL. *farciminum*) < L. *farcimen*, a sausage < *farcire*, to stuff] a disease, esp. of horses, affecting the lymphatic glands: a form of glanders

far·del (fär′d'l) *n.* [ME. < OFr., < It. *fardello*, dim. < OIt. *fardo*, a bundle, pack < Ar. *fardah*, a bundle, camel's load] [Archaic] **1.** a pack; bundle **2.** a burden; misfortune

fare (fer) *vi.* **fared, far′ing** [ME. *faren* < OE. *faran*, to go, wander, akin to G. *fahren* < IE. base *per-*, to come over, transport, whence L. *portare*, to carry, Gr. *peran*, to pass over, *peira*, a trial, *poros*, a way] **1.** [Chiefly Poet.] to travel; go **2.** to happen; result *[how did it fare with him?]* **3.** to be in a specified condition or position; get on; go through an experience *[he fared well on his trip]* **4.** to eat or be given food —*n.* **1.** money paid for transportation in a train, taxi, plane, etc. **2.** a passenger who pays a fare **3.** *a)* food *b)* the usual kind of diet **4.** [Archaic] the condition of things —*SYN.* see FOOD

Far East countries of E Asia, including China, Japan, Korea, & Mongolia: the term sometimes includes the countries of Southeast Asia & the Malay Archipelago

fare-thee-well (fer′*thē* wel′) *n.* ☆the highest or ultimate degree: usually in the phrase **to a fare-thee-well:** also **fare-you-well**

fare·well (fer′wel′; *for adj.* -wel′) *interj.* [ME. (imperative) + WELL[2]] goodbye —*n.* **1.** words spoken at parting, usually of good wishes **2.** a leaving or going away —*adj.* parting; last; final *[a farewell gesture]*

Farewell, Cape southernmost tip of Greenland

☆**fare·well-to-spring** (-tə spriŋ′) *n.* a western American plant (*Godetia amoena*) of the evening-primrose family, with showy purple or pink flowers

far·fetched (fär′fecht′) *adj.* **1.** resulting or introduced in a forced, or unnatural, way; strained **2.** [Archaic] brought from a distance

far-flung (-fluŋ′) *adj.* extending over a wide area

Far·go (fär′gō) [after W. G. *Fargo*, of Wells, Fargo & Co., express shippers] city in E N.Dak., on the Red River of the North: pop. 53,000

fa·ri·na (fə rē′nə) *n.* [ME. < L., ground corn, meal < *far*, sort of grain, spelt < IE. base *bhares-*, whence OE. *bere*, BARLEY] **1.** flour or meal made from cereal grains (esp. whole wheat), potatoes, nuts, etc. and eaten as a cooked cereal **2.** potato starch or other starch

far·i·na·ceous (far′ə nā′shəs) *adj.* [LL. *farinaceus* < L. *farina:* see prec.] **1.** containing, consisting of, or made from flour or meal **2.** like meal **3.** containing starch

far·i·nose (far′ə nōs′) *adj.* [LL. *farinosus*] **1.** producing farina **2.** full of meal; mealy **3.** Bot., Zool. covered with a powderlike substance

☆**far·kle·ber·ry** (fär′k'l ber′ē) *n.*, *pl.* -ries [< ?] a shrub or small tree (*Vaccinium arboreum*) of the heath family, with bell-shaped, white flowers and round, black, inedible berries, found in the southern U.S.

farm (färm) *n.* [ME. < OFr. *ferme* < ML. *firma*, fixed payment, farm < *firmare*, to farm, lease, orig., to make a contract < L., to make firm, secure < *firmus*, FIRM[1]] **1.** *a)* orig., a fixed sum payable at regular intervals, as rent, taxes, etc. *b)* the letting out, for a fixed amount, of the collection of taxes, with the privilege of keeping all that is collected *c)* the condition of being let out at a fixed rent **2.** a district of a country leased out by a government for the collection of taxes **3.** a piece of land (with house, barns, etc.) on which crops or animals are raised: orig., such land let out to tenants **4.** any place where certain things are raised *[a tract of water for raising fish is a fish farm]* ☆**5.** Baseball a minor-league team having an agreement with a major-league team to train its young or inexperienced players: in full, **farm club** (or **team**) —*vt.* **1.** to cultivate (land) **2.** to collect the taxes and other fees of (a business) on a commission basis or for a fixed amount **3.** to turn over to another for a fee **4.** formerly, to arrange for the care of (paupers, etc.) —*vi.* to work on or operate a farm; raise crops or animals on a farm —**farm out 1.** to rent (land, a business, etc.) in return for a fixed payment **2.** to send (work) from a shop, office, etc. to workers on the outside **3.** to let out the labor of (a convict, etc.) for a fixed amount **4.** to destroy the fertility of (land), as by failing to rotate crops ☆**5.** Baseball to assign to a farm

farm·er (fär′mər) *n.* [ME. *fermour*, farmer, bailiff < Anglo-Fr. *fermer* < OFr. *fermier* < *ferme:* see FARM] **1.** a person who earns his living by farming; esp., one who manages or operates a farm **2.** a person who pays for a right, as, formerly, to collect and keep taxes **3.** a person who contracts to do something for a fixed price

☆**farm·er·ette** (fär′mə ret′) *n.* [Colloq.] a girl or woman farm worker

farm·hand (färm′hand′) *n.* a hired laborer on a farm

farm·house (-hous′) *n.* a house on a farm; esp., the main dwelling house on a farm

farm·ing (fär′miŋ) *adj.* of or for agriculture —*n.* **1.** the business of operating a farm; agriculture **2.** the letting out to farm of land, revenue, etc.

farm·stead (färm′sted′) *n.* the land and buildings of a farm

farm·yard (-yärd′) *n.* the yard surrounding or enclosed by the farm buildings

far·o (fer′ō) *n.* [Fr. *pharaon:* ? after the representation of an ancient PHARAOH on one of the cards] a gambling game in which the players bet on the cards to be turned up from the top of the dealer's pack

Far·oe Islands (fer′ō) same as FAEROE ISLANDS

Far·o·ese (fer′ō ēz′) same as FAEROESE

far-off (fär′ôf′) *adj.* distant; remote

fa·rouche (fə rōōsh′) *adj.* [Fr. < OFr. *forasche*, ill-tamed < LL. *forasticus*, out-of-doors < L. *foras*, outside of, out-of-doors, akin to *foris*, a DOOR] **1.** wild; savage; fierce **2.** unsociable in a fierce or surly way; lacking social grace

far-out (fär′out′) *adj.* ☆[Colloq.] very advanced, experimental, or nonconformist; esp., avant-garde

far point the farthest point at which vision is distinct when the lens, muscles, etc. of the eye are relaxed

Far·quhar (fär′kwar, -kər), **George** 1678-1707; Brit. playwright, born in Ireland

far·ra·go (fə rā′gō, -rä′-) *n.*, *pl.* -goes [L., mixed fodder for cattle, mixture, medley < *far:* see FARINA] a confused mixture; jumble; medley; hodgepodge —**far·rag′i·nous** (-raj′ə nəs) *adj.*

Far·ra·gut (far′ə gət), **David Glasgow** (born *James Glasgow Farragut*) 1801-70; U.S. admiral; Union naval commander in the Civil War

Far·rar (fə rär′), **Geraldine** 1882-1967; U.S. operatic soprano

far-reach·ing (fär′rēch′iŋ) *adj.* having a wide range, extent, influence, or effect

Far·rell (far′əl), **James T(homas)** 1904- ; U.S. novelist

far·ri·er (far′ē ər) *n.* [ME. *ferrour* < OFr. *ferreor* < ML. *ferrator* < VL. *ferrare*, to shoe horses < L. *ferrum*, iron] [Brit.] a man who shoes horses; blacksmith; also, sometimes, one who treats the diseases of horses

far·ri·er·y (-ē) *n.*, *pl.* -er·ies [Brit.] the work or shop of a farrier

far·row[1] (far′ō) *n.* [altered (after *v.*) < OE. *fearh*, young pig; for IE. base see PORK] **1.** a litter of pigs **2.** [Obs.] a young pig —*vt.*, *vi.* [ME. *farwen*] to give birth to (a litter of pigs)

far·row[2] (far′ō) *adj.* [earlier *ferow*, prob. akin to Early ModDu. *verrekoe*, barren cow, G. *färse*, heifer, OE. *fearr*, bull] [Scot. or Dial.] not bearing a calf in a given season: said of a cow

far·see·ing (fär′sē′iŋ) *adj.* same as FARSIGHTED (senses 1 & 2)

far·sight·ed (-sīt′id) *adj.* **1.** capable of seeing far **2.** having or showing prudent judgment and foresight **3.** having better vision for distant objects than for near ones; hypermetropic —**far′sight′ed·ly** *adv.* —**far′sight′ed·ness** *n.*

fart (färt) *vi.*, *vt.* [ME. *ferten* < OE. **feortan*, akin to OHG. *ferzan* < IE. base **perd-*, whence Sans. *párdatē*, Gr. *perdomai*] to pass, or emit as, gas from the intestines through the anus —*n.* [ME.] **1.** such a passing of gas **2.** [Slang] a person, esp. an old one, regarded as a fool, nuisance, etc. Now a vulgar term

far·ther (fär′*th*ər) *adj. compar.* of FAR [ME. *ferther*, var. of *further*, substituted for regular *ferrer* (compar. of *fer*) < OE. *fyrre*, compar. of *feorr*, FAR] **1.** more distant or remote **2.** additional; further —*adv. compar.* of FAR **1.** at or to a greater distance or more remote point in space or time **2.** to a greater degree or extent; further **3.** in addition; further In sense 2 of the *adj.* and senses 2 and 3 of the *adv.*, FURTHER is more commonly used

far·ther·most (-mōst′) *adj.* most distant; farthest

far·thest (fär′*th*ist) *adj. superl.* of FAR [ME. *ferthest:* see FARTHER] **1.** most distant; most remote **2.** [Rare] most extended; longest —*adv. superl.* of FAR **1.** at or to the greatest distance or most remote point in space or time **2.** to the greatest degree or extent; most

far·thing (fär′*th*in) *n.* [ME. *ferthing* < OE. *feorthing*, lit., a fourthling, fourth part, dim. of *feortha*, FOURTH] **1.** a former small British coin, equal to one fourth of a penny **2.** a thing of little value; the least amount

far·thin·gale (fär′*th*in gāl′) *n.* [OFr. *verdugalle*, farthingale < Sp. *verdugado*, provided with hoops, farthingale < *verdugo*, young shoot of a tree, rod, hoop < *verde* < L. *viridis*, green] **1.** a hoop, openwork frame, or circular pad worn about the hips by women in the 16th and 17th centuries **2.** a skirt or petticoat worn over this

FARTHINGALE

f.a.s. free alongside ship

fas·ces (fas′ēz) *n.pl.* [L., pl. of *fascis*, a bundle, fagot, packet < OE. base *bhasko-*, bundle, whence MIr. *basc*, neckband] a bundle of rods bound about an ax with projecting blade, carried before ancient Roman magistrates as a symbol of authority: later the symbol of Italian fascism

‡**Fa·sching** (fäsh′iŋ) *n.* [G.] the pre-Lenten period of uninhibited revelry celebrated in Austria and parts of Germany

fas·ci·a (fash′ē ə, fash′ə) *n., pl.* **-ci·ae′** (-ē′), **-ci·as** [L., a band, sash] 1. a flat strip; band; fillet 2. *same as* FACIA 3. *Anat.* a thin layer of connective tissue covering, supporting, or connecting the muscles or inner organs of the body 4. *Archit.* a flat, horizontal band, esp. one of two or three making up an architrave 5. *Biol.* a distinct band of color —**fas′ci·al** *adj.*

fas·ci·ate (fash′ē āt′) *adj.* [L. *fasciatus*, pp. of *fasciare*, to swathe, wrap with bands < *fascia*, a band, FASCIA] 1. bound with a band or fillet 2. *Bot. a)* abnormally enlarged and flattened, as some plant stems *b)* growing in a fascicle 3. *Zool.* marked by broad colored bands Also **fas′ci·at·ed**

fas·ci·a·tion (fash′ē ā′shən, fas′-) *n.* [Fr.] 1. the condition of being fasciate 2. a binding up 3. *Bot.* an abnormal broadening and flattening of plant stems

fas·ci·cle (fas′i k'l) *n.* [ME. < OFr. < L. *fasciculus*, dim. of *fascis*: see FASCES] 1. any of the sections of a book or other work being brought out in installments prior to its publication in completed form 2. a small bundle; specif., *Bot.* a small tuft or cluster of fibers, leaves, stems, roots, etc.

fas·ci·cled (-k'ld) *adj. Bot.* growing in a fascicle

fas·cic·u·late (fə sik′yoo lit, -lāt′) *adj.* [< L. *fasciculus*, dim. of *fascis* (see FASCES) + -ATE¹] formed of, or growing in, bundles or clusters: also **fas·cic′u·lat′ed** (-lāt′id), **fas·cic′u·lar** (-lər)

fas·ci·cule (fas′i kyōōl′) *n.* [Fr.] *same as* FASCICULUS

fas·cic·u·lus (fə sik′yoo ləs) *n., pl.* **-u·li′** (-lī′) [L., dim. of *fascis*, a bundle: see FASCES] 1. a small bundle of fibers; specif., a bundle of nerve fibers in the central nervous system 2. *same as* FASCICLE (sense 1)

fas·ci·nate (fas′ə nāt′) *vt.* **-nat′ed, -nat′ing** [< L. *fascinatus*, pp. of *fascinare*, to bewitch, charm < *fascinum*, an enchanting] 1. orig., to put under a spell; bewitch 2. to attract or hold motionless, as by a fixed look or by inspiring terror 3. to hold the attention of by being very interesting or delightful; charm; captivate —*SYN.* see ATTRACT —**fas′ci·nat′ing·ly** *adv.*

fas·ci·na·tion (fas′ə nā′shən) *n.* 1. a fascinating or being fascinated 2. strong attraction; charm; allure

fas·ci·na·tor (fas′ə nāt′ər) *n.* [L., an enchanter] 1. a person who fascinates ☆2. a woman's light scarf, knitted or crocheted, worn around the head or neck: an old-fashioned term

fas·cine (fa sēn′) *n.* [Fr. < OFr. < L. *fascina*, a bundle of sticks, a fagot < *fascis*: see FASCES] a bundle of sticks bound together, formerly used to fill ditches, strengthen the sides of trenches, etc.

fas·cism (fash′iz'm) *n.* [It. *fascismo* < *fascio*, political group < L. *fascis*: see FASCES] 1. [F-] the doctrines, methods, or movement of the Fascisti 2. [*sometimes* F-] a system of government characterized by rigid one-party dictatorship, forcible suppression of opposition, private economic enterprise under centralized governmental control, belligerent nationalism, racism, and militarism, etc.: first instituted in Italy in 1922 3. *a)* a political movement based on such doctrines and policies *b)* fascist behavior See also NAZI

fas·cist (-ist) *n.* [It. *fascista*: see ff.] 1. [F-] *a)* a member of the Fascisti *b)* a member of some similar party; Nazi, Falangist, etc. 2. a person who believes in or practices fascism —*adj.* 1. [F-] of Fascists or Fascism 2. of, believing in, or practicing fascism —**fa·scis′tic** (fa shis′tik) *adj.* —**fa·scis′ti·cal·ly** *adv.*

Fa·scis·ti (fa shis′tē; *It.* fä shē′stē) *n.pl., sing.* **-scis′ta** (-tə; *It.* -stä) [It. < *fascio*: see FASCISM] an Italian political organization which seized power and set up a fascist dictatorship (1922–43) under Mussolini

fash (fash) *vt., vi.* [< OFr. *faschier*, to vex < VL. *fasticare*, altered < *fastidiare*, to disgust, for L. *fastidire*, to feel loathing < L. *fastidium*: see FASTIDIOUS] [Scot.] to trouble; annoy; vex —*n.* vexation

fash·ion (fash′ən) *n.* [ME. *fasoun* < OFr. *faceon* < L. *factio*, a making: see FACTION] 1. the make, form, or shape of a thing 2. [Now Rare] kind; sort 3. the way in which something is made or done; manner 4. the current style or mode of dress, speech, conduct, etc. 5. something, esp. a garment, in the current style 6. fashionable people as a group [a man of *fashion*] —*vt.* 1. to make in a certain way; give a certain form to; shape; mold 2. to fit; accommodate (*to*) [music *fashioned* to our taste] 3. [Archaic] to think up; contrive —**after** (or **in**) **a fashion** in some way or to some extent, but not very well —**fash′ion·er** *n.*

SYN.—**fashion** is the prevailing custom in dress, manners, speech, etc. of a particular place or time, esp. as established by the dominant section of society or the leaders in the fields of art, literature, etc.; **style**, often a close synonym for **fashion**, in discriminating use suggests a distinctive fashion, esp. the way of dressing, living, etc. that distinguishes persons with money and

taste; **mode**, the French word expressing this idea, suggests the height of fashion in dress, behavior, etc. at any particular time; **vogue** stresses the general acceptance or great popularity of a certain fashion; **fad** stresses the impulsive enthusiasm with which a fashion is taken up for a short time; **rage** and **craze** both stress an intense, sometimes irrational enthusiasm for a passing fashion See also MAKE¹, METHOD

fash·ion·a·ble (-ə b'l) *adj.* 1. following the current style; in fashion; stylish 2. of, characteristic of, or used by people who follow the current style of dress, speech, conduct, etc. —*n.* a fashionable person —**fash′ion·a·ble·ness** *n.* —**fash′ion·a·bly** *adv.*

☆**fashion plate** 1. a picture showing a current style in dress 2. a fashionably dressed person

fast¹ (fast, fäst) *adj.* [ME. < OE. *fæst*, akin to G. *fest*, firm, stable < IE. base *pasto-*, fixed, secure, whence Arm. *hast*] 1. not easily moved, freed, or separated; firm, fixed, or stuck [the ship was *fast* on the rocks] 2. firmly fastened or shut [make the shutters *fast*] 3. loyal; devoted [*fast* friends] 4. that will not fade [*fast* colors] 5. rapid in movement or action; swift; quick; speedy 6. permitting or facilitating swift movement [a *fast* highway] 7. taking or lasting a short time [a *fast* lunch] 8. showing or keeping to a time in advance of a standard or scheduled time [his watch is *fast*] 9. *a)* living in a reckless, wild, dissipated way [a *fast* crowd] *b)* promiscuous sexually ☆10. [Colloq.] glib and deceptive [a *fast* talker] 11. [Slang] acting, gotten, done, etc. quickly and often dishonestly [out for a *fast* buck] 12. *Bacteriology* resistant to staining or destruction, as certain bacteria 13. *Photog.* adapted to very short exposure time 14. [Obs. or Dial.] complete; sound [a *fast* sleep] —*adv.* [ME. *faste* < OE. *fæste* < *adj.*] 1. firmly; fixedly 2. thoroughly; soundly [*fast* asleep] 3. rapidly; swiftly; quickly; speedily 4. ahead of time 5. in a reckless, dissipated way; wildly 6. [Obs. or Poet.] close; near [*fast* by the river] —*n.* something that fastens or is used in fastening, as a rope for mooring —**a fast one** [Slang] a tricky or deceptive act [to pull a *fast one* on someone] —**play fast and loose** to behave with reckless duplicity or insincerity

SYN.—**fast** and **rapid** are generally interchangeable in expressing the idea of a relatively high rate of movement or action, but **fast** more often refers to the person or thing that moves or acts, and **rapid** to the action [a *fast* typist, *rapid* transcription]; **swift** implies great rapidity, but in addition often connotes smooth, easy movement; **fleet** suggests a nimbleness or lightness in that which moves swiftly; **quick** implies promptness of action, or occurrence in a brief space of time, rather than velocity [a *quick* reply]; **speedy** intensifies the idea of quickness, but may also connote high velocity [a *speedy* recovery, a *speedy* flight]; **hasty** suggests hurried action and may connote carelessness, rashness, or impatience —*ANT.* slow

fast² (fast, fäst) *vi.* [ME. *fasten* < OE. *fæstan*, akin to G. *fasten*, Goth. *fastan*, all ult. < base of prec.] 1. to abstain from all or certain foods, as in observing a holy day 2. to eat very little or nothing —*n.* 1. the act of fasting 2. a day or period of fasting —**break one's fast** to eat food for the first time after fasting, or for the first time in the day

☆**fast·back** (-bak′) *n.* an automobile body whose roof forms an unbroken curve from windshield to rear bumper

fast day a religious holy day, etc. observed by fasting

fas·ten (fas′'n, fäs′-) *vt.* [ME. *fastnen* < OE. *fæstnian* < base of *fæst* (see FAST¹)] 1. to join (one thing *to* another); attach; connect 2. to make fast or secure, as by locking, shutting, buttoning, etc.; fix firmly in place 3. to hold, fix, or direct (the attention, gaze, etc.) steadily (*on*) 4. to cause to be connected or attributed; impute [to *fasten* a crime on someone] 5. to force (oneself *on* or *upon* another) in an annoying way —*vi.* 1. to become attached or joined 2. to take a firm hold (*on* or *upon*); seize; cling 3. to concentrate (*on* or *upon*) —*SYN.* see TIE

fas·ten·er (-ər) *n.* 1. a person who fastens 2. any of various devices for fastening things together; fastening

fas·ten·ing (-iŋ) *n.* 1. the act or way of making something fast, or secure 2. anything used to fasten; bolt, clasp, hook, lock, button, etc.

fas·tid·i·ous (fas tid′ē əs, fəs-) *adj.* [ME. < L. *fastidiosus* < *fastidium*, a loathing, disgust < *fastus*, disdain, contempt, pride (< ? IE. base *bhars-*, projection, point, BRISTLE) + *taedium*: see TEDIUM] 1. not easy to please; very critical or discriminating 2. refined in a too dainty or oversensitive way, so as to be easily disgusted —*SYN.* see DAINTY —**fas·tid′i·ous·ly** *adv.* —**fas·tid′i·ous·ness** *n.*

fas·tig·i·ate (fas tij′ē it, -āt′) *adj.* [LL. *fastigiatus*, for L. *fastigatus* < *fastigium*, a slope, roof < IE. *bharsti-* < base *bhars-*: see prec.] sloping toward a point; conelike, as the blossom of a plant: also **fas·tig′i·at′ed** (-āt′id)

fas·tig·i·um (-əm) *n.* [ModL. < L., an extremity, orig., the top of a gable < IE. *bhars-*, point, projection < base *bhar-*, point, BRISTLE] 1. the most severe point in the course of an illness 2. the part of the cerebellum that forms an angle in the roof of the fourth ventricle of the brain

fast·ness (fast′nis, fäst′-) *n.* [ME. *fastnesse* < OE. *fæstnes*: see FAST¹ & -NESS] 1. the quality or condition of being fast 2. a secure place; stronghold

☆**fast time** *same as* DAYLIGHT-SAVING TIME

fas·tu·ous (fas′choo wəs) *adj.* [L. *fastuosus* < *fastus*, scornful contempt, pride: see FASTIDIOUS] 1. haughty; lofty 2. ostentatious; pretentious

fat (fat) *adj.* **fat′ter, fat′test** [ME. < OE. *fætt*, pp. of

fǣtan, to fatten, akin to G. *feist*, plump < OHG. *feizzen*, to make fat < IE. **poid-* < base **pi-*, to be fat, distended, whence Gr. *pimelē*, lard, Sans. *pínā-*, fat] **1.** *a)* containing or full of fat; oily; greasy *b)* having much fat in relation to lean: said of meat *c)* containing volatile oil *[fat coal] d)* containing much resin *[fat wood]* **2.** *a)* fleshy; plump *b)* too plump; corpulent; obese **3.** thick; broad *[the fat part of the bat]* **4.** containing something valuable in great quantity; fertile; productive *[fat land]* **5.** profitable; lucrative *[a fat job]* **6.** prosperous **7.** supplied plentifully; ample **8.** stupid; dull **9.** [Slang] desirable because large or important *[a fat role for an actor]* —*n.* **1.** any of various solid or semisolid oily or greasy materials found in animal tissue and in the seeds of plants, composed of glycerides of fatty acids, soluble in organic solvents, and causing translucent markings on paper **2.** any such substance used in cooking **3.** fleshiness; plumpness; corpulence **4.** the richest or finest part of anything **5.** anything unnecessary or superfluous that can be trimmed away **6.** *Chem.* a class of glyceryl esters of fatty acids, insoluble in water —*vt.,* *vi.* **fat′ted, fat′ting** [ME. *fatten* < OE. *fǣttian*] to make or become fat: now usually FATTEN —☆**a fat chance** [Slang] very little or no chance —**a fat lot** [Slang] very little or nothing —**chew the fat** [Slang] to talk together; chat —**the fat is in the fire** the unfortunate thing has happened and cannot be undone —**the fat of the land** [after LL.(Ec.) *medulla terrae*, Gen. 45:18] the best things obtainable; great luxury —**fat′ly** *adv.* —**fat′ness** *n.*

fa·tal (fāt′'l) *adj.* [ME. < OFr. & < L. *fatalis* < *fatum*, FATE] **1.** orig., fated; destined; inevitable **2.** important in its outcome; fateful; decisive *[the fatal day arrived]* **3.** resulting in death **4.** very destructive; most unfortunate; disastrous **5.** concerned with or determining fate —**fa′tal·ness** *n.*
SYN.—**fatal** implies the inevitability or actual occurrence of death or disaster *[a fatal disease, a fatal mistake]*; **deadly** is applied to a thing that can and probably (but not inevitably) will cause death *[a deadly poison]*; **mortal** implies that death has occurred and is applied to the immediate cause of the death *[he has received a mortal blow]*; **lethal** is applied to that which in its nature or purpose is a cause of death *[a lethal weapon]*

fa·tal·ism (-iz'm) *n.* **1.** the belief that all events are determined by fate and are hence inevitable **2.** acceptance of every event as inevitable —**fa′tal·ist** *n.* —**fa′tal·is′tic** *adj.* —**fa′tal·is′ti·cal·ly** *adv.*

fa·tal·i·ty (fə tal′ə tē, fā-) *n., pl.* **-ties** [Fr. *fatalité* < LL. *fatalitas* < L. *fatalis,* FATAL] **1.** fate or necessity; subjection to fate **2.** something caused by fate **3.** an inevitable liability to disaster **4.** a fatal quality; deadly effect; deadliness *[the fatality of any specified disease]* **5.** a death caused by a disaster, as in an accident, war, etc.

fa·tal·ly (fāt′'l ē) *adv.* **1.** as determined by fate; inevitably **2.** so as to cause death or disaster; mortally

fa·ta mor·ga·na (fät′ə môr gän′ə) [It., lit., MORGAN LE FAY] a mirage, esp. one sometimes seen off the coast of Sicily near the Strait of Messina: so called because formerly supposed to be the work of Morgan le Fay

☆**fat·back** (fat′bak′) *n.* **1.** fat from the back of a hog, usually dried and salted in strips **2.** *same as* MENHADEN

☆**fat cat** [Slang] a wealthy, influential person; esp., a heavy contributor to a political party or campaign

fate (fāt) *n.* [ME. < L. *fatum*, prophetic declaration, oracle < neut. pp. of *fari*, to speak: see FAME] **1.** the power or agency supposed to determine the outcome of events before they occur; destiny **2.** *a)* something inevitable, supposedly determined by this power *b)* what happens or has happened to a person or entity; lot; fortune **3.** final outcome **4.** death; destruction; doom —*vt.* **fat′ed, fat′ing** to destine: now usually in the passive —**the Fates** *Gr. & Rom. Myth.* the three goddesses who control human destiny and life: see CLOTHO, LACHESIS, and ATROPOS
SYN.—**fate** refers to the inevitability of a course of events as supposedly predetermined by a god or other agency beyond human control; **destiny** also refers to an inevitable succession of events as determined supernaturally or by necessity, but often implies a favorable outcome *[it was her destiny to become famous]*; **portion** and **lot** refer to what is supposedly distributed in the determining of fate, but **portion** implies an equitable apportionment and **lot** implies a random assignment; **doom** always connotes an unfavorable or disastrous fate

fat·ed (fāt′id) *adj.* **1.** ordained or determined by fate; destined **2.** destined to destruction; doomed

fate·ful (-fəl) *adj.* **1.** revealing what is to come; prophetic **2.** having important consequences; significant; decisive **3.** controlled by or as if by fate **4.** bringing about death or destruction —*SYN.* OMINOUS —**fate′ful·ly** *adv.* —**fate′ful·ness** *n.*

fat·head (fat′hed′) *n.* [Slang] a stupid person; blockhead —**fat′head′ed** *adj.*

fa·ther (fä′thər) *n.* [ME. *fader* < OE. *fæder*, akin to ON. *fathir*, OHG. *fater*, Goth. *fadar* < IE. **pəter*, whence L. *pater*, Gr. *patēr*, Sans. *pitár*: ult. origin prob. echoic of baby talk, as in PAPA, Hind. *bābū*] **1.** a man who has engendered a child; esp., a man as he is related to his child or children **2.** *a)* a stepfather *b)* a father-in-law **3.** the male parent of an animal **4.** a person regarded as a male parent; protector **5.** [F-] God, or God as the first person of the Trinity **6.** a forefather; ancestor: *usually used in the pl.* **7.** an originator, founder, or inventor **8.** any man deserving respect or reverence because of age, position, etc. **9.** a senator of ancient Rome **10.** any of the leaders of a city, assembly, etc.: *usually used in the pl.* **11.** *[often* F-] any of the early Christian religious writers considered reliable authorities on the doctrines and teachings of the Church **12.** a Christian priest: used esp. as a title —*vt.* **1.** to be the father of; beget **2.** to care for as a father does; protect, rear, etc. **3.** to bring into being; found, originate, or invent **4.** to take the responsibility for **5.** to impose improperly as a responsibility; foist *[the mistake was fathered on him]*

father confessor **1.** a priest who hears confessions, as in the Roman Catholic Church **2.** a person to whom one habitually tells private matters

fa·ther·hood (-hood′) *n.* [ME. *faderhod:* see -HOOD] the state of being a father; paternity

father image (or **figure**) a person substituted in one's mind for one's father and often the object of emotions felt toward the father

fa·ther-in-law (-ən lô′) *n., pl.* **fa′thers-in-law′** **1.** the father of one's wife or husband **2.** [Rare] a stepfather

fa·ther·land (-land′) *n.* [often after Du. *vaderland,* G. *vaterland*] a person's native land or, sometimes, the land of his ancestors

fa·ther·less (-lis) *adj.* [ME. *faderles* < OE. *fæderleas*] **1.** not having a father living, or lacking a father's protection **2.** not knowing who one's father is

fa·ther·ly (-lē) *adj.* [ME. *faderly* < OE. *fæderlic*] **1.** belonging to a father *[fatherly duties]* **2.** like or characteristic of a father; kindly; protective —*adv.* [Archaic] in a fatherly manner —**fa′ther·li·ness** *n.*

☆**Father's Day** the third Sunday in June, a day set aside (in the U.S.) in honor of fathers

Father Time time personified as a very old man carrying a scythe and an hourglass

fath·om (fath′əm) *n.* [ME. *fadme* < OE. *fæthm* (akin to OFris. *fethm,* OS. pl. *fathmōs*), the two arms outstretched (to embrace, measure), akin to G. *faden,* thread < IE. base **pet-,* to stretch out, whence L. *patere,* to stretch out] a length of 6 feet, used as a unit of measure for the depth of water or the length of a rope or cable —*vt.* **1.** to measure the depth of; sound **2.** to get to the bottom of; understand thoroughly —**fath′om·a·ble** *adj.*

☆**Fa·thom·e·ter** (fath äm′ə tər) *a trademark for a sonar device used to measure depth of oceans, etc.* —*n.* [f-] such a device

fath·om·less (fath′əm lis) *adj.* **1.** too deep to be measured **2.** incomprehensible —**fath′om·less·ness** *n.*

fa·tid·ic (fə tid′ik, fā-) *adj.* [L. *fatidicus,* prophesying < *fatum,* FATE + *dicere,* to say: see DICTION] of divination or prophecy; prophetic: also **fa·tid′i·cal**

fat·i·ga·ble (fat′i gə b'l) *adj.* that can be fatigued; easily tired —**fat′i·ga·bil′i·ty** *n.*

fa·tigue (fə tēg′) *n.* [Fr. < *fatiguer* < L. *fatigare,* to weary, prob. < base of *fames,* hunger (see FAMINE) + *agere,* to drive, make (see ACT)] **1.** physical or mental exhaustion; weariness **2.** the cause of this; hard work; toil **3.** any manual labor or menial duty, other than drill or instruction, assigned to soldiers: in full, **fatigue duty** **4.** *[pl.]* sturdy work clothing worn by soldiers doing fatigue duty: also **fatigue clothes** or **clothing** **5.** the tendency of a metal or other material to crack and fail under repeated applications of stress **6.** *Physiol.* the decreased ability to function or inability to respond of an organism or one of its parts as because of prolonged exertion or repeated stimulation —*vt., vi.* **-tigued′, -tigu′ing** **1.** to make or become tired or exhausted; weary **2.** to subject to or undergo fatigue

Fat·i·ma (fat′i mə, fät′-; fə tē′mə) 606?-632 A.D.; daughter of Mohammed

Fat·i·mid (fat′i mid) *adj.* **1.** descended from Mohammed's daughter, Fatima **2.** designating or of a dynasty of Moslem rulers, descended from Fatima and Ali, that ruled over Egyptian Islam and parts of N Africa (909–1171) —*n.* any Fatimid ruler or descendant Also **Fat′i·mite′** (-mīt′)

fat·ling (fat′liŋ) *n.* [FAT + -LING[1]] a calf, lamb, kid, or young pig fattened before being slaughtered

fat-sol·u·ble (fat′säl′yə b'l) *adj.* soluble in fats or in solvents for fats

fat·ten (fat′'n) *vt.* **1.** to make fat, or plump, as by feeding **2.** to make (land) fertile **3.** to make richer, fuller, etc. —*vi.* to become fat —**fat′ten·er** *n.*

fat·tish (-ish) *adj.* somewhat fat

fat·ty (-ē) *adj.* **-ti·er, -ti·est** **1.** containing, consisting of, or made of fat **2.** very plump; obese **3.** resembling fat; greasy; oily —*n.* [Colloq.] a fat person —**fat′ti·ness** *n.*

fatty acid **1.** any of a series of saturated, monobasic organic acids having the general formula, $C_nH_{2n+1}COOH$ **2.** any of a number of saturated or unsaturated, monobasic organic acids usually having an even number of carbon atoms in a straight chain and occurring naturally in the form of glycerol esters in fats and oils

fatty degeneration *Pathology* the abnormal occurrence of fat particles in tissue cells

fa·tu·i·ty (fə tōō'ə tē, -tyōō'-; fa-) n., pl. **-ties** [Fr. fatuité < L. fatuitas < fatuus: see ff.] **1.** stupidity, esp. complacent stupidity; smug foolishness **2.** a fatuous remark, act, etc. **3.** [Archaic] idiocy or imbecility —**fa·tu'i·tous** adj.

fat·u·ous (fach'oo wəs) adj. [L. fatuus, foolish < IE. base *bhāt-, to strike] **1.** complacently stupid or inane; silly; foolish **2.** [Archaic] like an ignis fatuus; illusory; unreal —SYN. see SILLY —**fat'u·ous·ly** adv. —**fat'u·ous·ness** n.

fat-wit·ted (fat'wit'id) adj. thick-headed; dull; stupid

‡fau·bourg (fō bōōr'; E. fō'boorg) n. [Fr. for earlier faux bourg, lit., false town, folk-etym. form of OFr. forsbourg, lit., outside town, hence suburb < fors (Fr. hors), outside + bourg, town] **1.** a suburb **2.** a city district that was at one time a suburb

fau·cal (fôk''l) adj. [< ff. + AL] of or produced in the fauces: said of certain vocal sounds

fau·ces (fô'sēz) n.pl. [L., throat, gullet] the passage leading from the back of the mouth into the pharynx —**fau'cial** (-shəl) adj.

fau·cet (fô'sit) n. [ME. < OFr. fausset, prob. < OFr. faulser, to make a breach in, falsify < LL. falsare < L. falsus, FALSE] a device with a hand-operated valve for regulating the flow of a liquid from a pipe, barrel, etc.; cock; tap

faugh (fô: conventionalized pronun.; actually, an expulsion of air, often with vibration of the lips) interj. an exclamation of disgust, scorn, etc.

Faulk·ner (fôk'nər), **William** 1897-1962; U.S. novelist

fault (fôlt) n. [ME. faute < OFr. faulte, a lack < VL. *fallita < *fallitus, for L. falsus < pp. of L. fallere, to deceive (see FAIL)] **1.** orig., failure to have or do what is required; lack; default; neglect **2.** something that mars the appearance, character, structure, etc.; flaw; failing; imperfection; defect **3.** something done wrongly; specif., a) a misdeed; offense b) an error; mistake **4.** responsibility for something wrong; blame [it's her fault that they are late] **5.** Elec. a defect or point of defect in a circuit, which prevents the current from following the intended course **6.** Geol. a fracture or zone of fractures in rock strata together with movement that displaces the sides relative to one another **7.** Hunting a break in the line of the scent **8.** Tennis, Squash, etc. a) an error in service, as failure to serve to the proper court b) a ball improperly served —vt. **1.** to find fault with; blame or criticize **2.** Geol. to cause a fault in —vi. **1.** to commit a fault: archaic except in tennis, etc. **2.** Geol. to develop a fault —**at fault 1.** unable to find the scent, as hunting dogs **2.** not knowing what to do; perplexed **3.** guilty of error; deserving blame —**find fault (with)** to seek and point out faults (of); complain (about); criticize —**in fault** guilty of error; deserving blame —**to a fault** too much; excessively

SYN.—**fault**, in this comparison, refers to a definite, although not strongly condemnatory, imperfection in character [her only fault is stubbornness]; **failing** implies an even less serious shortcoming, usually one of those common to mankind [tardiness was one of his failings]; **weakness** applies to a minor shortcoming that results from a lack of perfect self-control [fattening foods are her weakness]; **foible** refers to a slight weakness that is regarded more as an amusing idiosyncrasy than an actual defect in character [eating desserts first is one of his foibles]; **vice**, although stronger in its implication of moral failure than any of the preceding terms, does not in this connection suggest actual depravity or wickedness [gambling is his only vice] —ANT. virtue

fault·find·er (-fīn'dər) n. a person given to finding fault; chronic, captious complainer

fault·find·ing (-fīn'diŋ) n., adj. finding fault; calling attention to defects —SYN. see CRITICAL

fault·less (-lis) adj. without any fault or defect; perfect —**fault'less·ly** adv. —**fault'less·ness** n.

fault·y (-ē) adj. **fault'i·er**, **fault'i·est** [ME. fauti] having a fault or faults; defective, blemished, imperfect, or erroneous —**fault'i·ly** adv. —**fault'i·ness** n.

faun (fôn) n. [ME. < L. faunus: see FAUNUS] any of a class of minor Roman deities, usually represented as having the body of a man, but the horns, pointed ears, tail, and hind legs of a goat: see also SATYR

fau·na (fô'nə) n., pl. **-nas, -nae** (-nē) [ModL. < LL. Fauna, sister or wife of FAUNUS: adopted by Linnaeus (1746) as term parallel to FLORA] **1.** the animals of a specified region or time [the fauna of N. America] **2.** a descriptive list of such animals —**fau'nal** adj.

Fau·nus (fô'nəs) [L. < ? IE. *dhaunos, wolf, strangler < base *dhau-, to strangle, whence Gr. Daunos; infl. by Roman folk-etym. association with L. favere, to favor] Rom. Myth. a god of nature, the patron of farming and animals: identified with the Greek god Pan

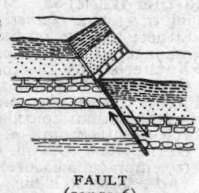

FAULT
(sense 6)

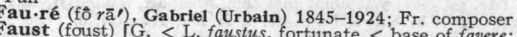

FAUN

Fau·ré (fō rā'), **Gabriel (Urbain)** 1845-1924; Fr. composer

Faust (foust) [G. < L. faustus, fortunate < base of favere:

see FAVOR] the hero of several medieval legends, and later literary and operatic works, an old philosopher who sells his soul to the devil in exchange for knowledge and power: also **Faus'tus** (-təs, fous'-) —**Faust'i·an** adj.

‡faute de mieux (fōt də myё') [Fr.] for want of (something) better

‡fau·teuil (fō tё'y') n. [Fr. < OFr. faldestoel, FALDSTOOL] an upholstered chair; esp., one with open arms

fau·vism (fō'viz'm) n. [Fr. fauvisme < fauve, wild beast, orig. adj., fawn-colored, dun < OFr. < Frank. *falw < Gmc. *falwa, FALLOW[2]] [often F-] a French expressionist movement in painting at the beginning of the 20th cent., involving Matisse, Derain, Vlaminck, etc.: it was characterized by bold distortion of form and the use of strong, pure color —**tauve** (tōv), **fau'vist** n., adj.

‡faux (fō) adj. [Fr.] false; artificial; synthetic

faux pas (fō' pä') pl. **faux pas** (fō' päz') [Fr., lit., false step] a social blunder; error in etiquette; tactless act or remark —SYN. see ERROR

fa·va bean (fä'və) [It. fava, bean (< L. faba < IE. *bhabhā-, BEAN) + BEAN] same as BROAD BEAN

‡fa·vel·a (fä vel'ä) n. [Port.] a slum

fa·ve·o·late (fə vē'ə lāt') adj. [< ModL. faveolus, dim. of L. favus, a honeycomb + -ATE[1]] honeycombed; containing cells; alveolate

fa·vo·ni·an (fə vō'nē ən) adj. [L. Favonianus < Favonius, west wind < favere: see ff.] of or like the west wind; esp., gentle, mild, etc.

fa·vor (fā'vər) n. [ME. favour < OFr. < L. favor < favere, to favor < IE. base *ghow-, to perceive, whence OE. (ofer) gumian, to neglect, Czech hověti, to take precautions (with), spare] **1.** friendly or kind regard; good will; approval; liking **2.** unfair partiality; favoritism **3.** a kind, obliging, friendly, or generous act [to do someone a favor] **4.** [pl.] consent (of a woman) to sexual intimacy **5.** a small gift, souvenir, or token (orig., a token of love) **6.** [Chiefly Brit.] a business letter or note [your favor of the 15th June] **7.** [Archaic] a) appearance or look b) face or countenance **8.** [Obs.] attractiveness; charm —vt. **1.** to regard with favor; approve or like **2.** to be indulgent or too indulgent toward; be partial to; prefer unfairly **3.** to be for; support; advocate; endorse **4.** to make easier; help; assist [rain favored his escape] **5.** to do a kindness for **6.** to look like; resemble in facial features [to favor one's mother] **7.** to use gently; spare [to favor an injured leg] —**by (or under) the favor of 1.** [Rare] with the help of **2.** [Archaic] with the kind indulgence of —**find favor to** be regarded with favor; be pleasing to —**in favor** favored; liked —**in favor of 1.** approving; supporting; endorsing **2.** to the advantage of **3.** payable to, as a check, etc. —**in one's favor** to one's advantage or credit —**out of favor** not favored; not liked —**fa'vor·er** n.

fa·vor·a·ble (-ə b'l) adj. [ME. < OFr. < L. favorabilis] **1.** approving or commending **2.** helpful or advantageous **3.** pleasing or desirable [a favorable impression] —**fa'vor·a·ble·ness** n. —**fa'vor·a·bly** adv.

SYN.—**favorable** applies to that which is distinctly helpful or advantageous in gaining an end [a favorable climate for citrus fruits]; **auspicious** refers to something regarded as a good omen of some undertaking [he made an auspicious debut]; **propitious** is now usually applied to a circumstance or a time that appears favorable for doing or beginning something [a propitious moment] —ANT. adverse, unfavorable

fa·vored (fā'vərd) adj. **1.** regarded or treated with favor; specif., a) provided with advantages; talented b) specially privileged **2.** having (specified) features: often in hyphenated compounds [ill-favored]

fa·vor·ite (fā'vər it, fāv'rit) n. [MFr. < It. favorito, pp. of favorire, to favor < favore < L. favor, FAVOR] **1.** a person or thing regarded with special liking, or more highly than others; specif., a person liked very much and granted special privileges as by a king, high official, etc. **2.** a contestant regarded as most likely to win —adj. held in special regard; best liked; preferred

☆favorite son 1. a famous man honored and praised in his native city, district, etc. because of his achievements **2.** a candidate favored by the political leaders of his own State, city, etc., as for presidential nomination

fa·vor·it·ism (-iz'm) n. **1.** the showing of more kindness and indulgence to some person or persons than to others; act of being unfairly partial **2.** the condition of being a favorite

fa·vour (fā'vər) n., vt. Brit. var of FAVOR

fa·vus (fā'vəs) n. [ModL. < L., a honeycomb] an infectious skin disease of man and certain domestic animals, caused by a fungus (as Trichophyton schoenleini) and characterized by itching and the formation of yellow crusts usually about the hair follicles, esp. on the head

Fawkes (fôks), **Guy** 1570-1606; Eng. conspirator: executed for participating in the Gunpowder Plot, a plot (1605) to blow up the king & both Houses of Parliament

fawn[1] (fôn) vi. [ME. faunen < OE. fagnian < fagen, var. of fægen: see FAIN] **1.** to show friendliness by licking hands, wagging its tail, etc.: said of a dog **2.** to act servilely; cringe and flatter [courtiers fawning on a king] —**fawn'er** n. —**fawn'ing·ly** adv.

fawn[2] (fôn) n. [ME. < OFr. faon, feon < LL. *feto (gen. *fetonis), young animal, child < L. fetus: see FETUS] **1.** a young deer less than one year old **2.** a pale, yellowish

brown —*adj.* of this color —*vi.*, *vt.* to bring forth (young): said of deer

☆**fawn lily** *same as* DOGTOOTH VIOLET (sense 1)

Fay, Faye (fā) [< ? ME. *faie* (see ff.) or ? ME. *fai*, FAY²] a feminine name

fay¹ (fā) *n.* [ME. *faie* < OFr. *feie* < VL. *fata*, one of the Fates < L. *fatum*: see FATE] a fairy

fay² (fā) *n.* [ME. *fei* < OFr. *fei*: see FAITH] [Archaic] faith: used in oaths [by my *fay!*]

fay³ (fā) *vt.*, *vi.* [ME. *feien* < OE. *fegan*, to join, fit < same base as *fæger*: see FAIR¹] *Shipbuilding* to fit closely or exactly; join —☆**fay in** (with) to fit exactly into place

Fay·ette·ville (fā′ət vil′) [after the Marquis de (LA)FAYETTE] city in SC N.C.: pop. 54,000

Fayyum *same as* FAIYŪM

faze (fāz) *vt.* **fazed, faz′ing** [var. of FEEZE] [Colloq.] to disturb; disconcert —*SYN.* see EMBARRASS

fb. *Football* fullback

FBA, F.B.A. Fellow of the British Academy

FBI, F.B.I. Federal Bureau of Investigation

f.c. 1. fire control 2. *Printing* follow copy

FCA, F.C.A. Farm Credit Administration

fcap., fcp. foolscap

FCC, F.C.C. Federal Communications Commission

FCIC, F.C.I.C. Federal Crop Insurance Corporation

F clef *same as* BASS CLEF

F.D. 1. Fire Department 2. free dock

FDA, F.D.A. Food and Drug Administration

FDIC, F.D.I.C. Federal Deposit Insurance Corporation

Fe [L. *ferrum*] *Chem.* iron

fe·al·ty (fē′əl tē) *n., pl.* **-ties** [ME. *feute, fealtye* < OFr. *feauté, fealté* < L. *fidelitas*, FIDELITY] 1. *a)* the duty and loyalty owed by a vassal or tenant to his feudal lord *b)* an oath of such loyalty 2. [Archaic or Poet.] loyalty; fidelity —*SYN.* see ALLEGIANCE

fear (fir) *n.* [ME. *fer* < OE. *fær*, lit., sudden attack, akin to OHG. *fāra*, ambush, snare, G. *(ge)fahr*, danger, peril: basic sense, "trap" < IE. base *per-*: see FARE] 1. a feeling of anxiety and agitation caused by the presence or nearness of danger, evil, pain, etc.; timidity; dread; terror; fright; apprehension 2. respectful dread; awe; reverence 3. a feeling of uneasiness or apprehension; concern [a *fear* that it will rain] 4. a cause for fear; possibility; chance [there was no *fear* of difficulty] —*vt.* 1. to be afraid of; dread 2. to feel reverence or awe for 3. to expect with misgiving; suspect [I *fear* I am late] 4. [Obs.] to fill with fear; frighten —*vi.* 1. to feel fear; be afraid 2. to be uneasy, anxious, or doubtful —**for fear of** in order to avoid or prevent; lest

SYN.—fear is the general term for the anxiety and agitation felt at the presence of danger; **dread** refers to the fear or depression felt in anticipating something dangerous or disagreeable [to live in *dread* of poverty]; **fright** applies to a sudden, shocking, usually momentary fear [the mouse gave her a *fright*]; **alarm** implies the fright felt at the sudden realization of danger [he felt *alarm* at the sight of the pistol]; **terror** applies to an overwhelming, often paralyzing fear [the *terror* of soldiers in combat]; **panic** refers to a frantic, unreasoning fear, often one that spreads quickly and leads to irrational, aimless action [the cry of "fire!" created a *panic*]

Fear, Cape cape on an island (*Smith Island*) off the SE coast of N.C.

fear·ful (-fəl) *adj.* 1. causing fear; terrifying; dreadful 2. feeling fear; afraid 3. showing or resulting from fear [a *fearful* look] 4. [Colloq.] very bad, offensive, great, etc. [a *fearful* liar] —*SYN.* see AFRAID —**fear′ful·ness** *n.*

fear·ful·ly (-fəl ē) *adv.* 1. in a fearful manner 2. to a fearful extent 3. [Colloq.] very much; very [*fearfully* busy]

fear·less (-lis) *adj.* without fear; not afraid; brave; intrepid —**fear′less·ly** *adv.* —**fear′less·ness** *n.*

fear·nought, fear·naught (-nôt′) *n.* 1. a heavy woolen cloth used for coats 2. a coat made of this

fear·some (-səm) *adj.* 1. causing fear; dreadful; frightful; horrible 2. frightened; timid; timorous —**fear′some·ly** *adv.* —**fear′some·ness** *n.*

fea·sance (fē′z'ns) *n.* [Anglo-Fr. *fesance* (Fr. *faisance*) < stem of *faire*, to do: see ff.] *Law* the performance of an act, condition, obligation, etc.

fea·si·ble (fē′zə b'l) *adj.* [ME. *faisible* < OFr. < stem of *faire*, to do < L. *facere*: see FACT] 1. capable of being done or carried out; practicable; possible [a *feasible* scheme] 2. within reason; likely; probable [a *feasible* story] 3. capable of being used or dealt with successfully; suitable [land *feasible* for cultivation] —*SYN.* see POSSIBLE —**fea′si·bil′i·ty** *pl.* **-ties, fea′si·ble·ness** *n.* —**fea′si·bly** *adv.*

feast (fēst) *n.* [ME. *feste* < OFr. < VL. *festa* < pl. of L. *festum*, festival < *festus*, festal, joyful, orig., of days for religious observance: see FAIR²] 1. a celebration or festival; esp., a religious festival honoring a god, saint, event, etc. 2. a rich and elaborate meal; banquet 3. anything that gives pleasure because of its abundance or richness; special treat —*vi.* [ME. *festen* < OFr. *fester* < the *n.*] 1. to eat a rich, elaborate meal 2. to have a special treat —*vt.* 1. to entertain at a feast or banquet 2. to give pleasure to; delight [to *feast* one's eyes on a sight] —**feast′er** *n.*

Feast of Lots *same as* PURIM

---

feat¹ (fēt) *n.* [ME. *fet* < Anglo-Fr. < OFr. *fait* < L. *factum*, a deed < neut. pp. of *facere*: see FACT] an act or accomplishment showing unusual daring, skill, endurance, etc.; remarkable deed; exploit

feat² (fēt) *adj.* [ME. *fet* < OFr. *fait*, pp. of *faire*, to do < L. *facere*: see FACT] [Archaic] 1. fitting; suitable 2. neat or neatly dressed 3. skillful; adroit

feath·er (feth′ər) *n.* [ME. *fether* < OE. *fether*, akin to G. *feder* < IE. base *pet-*, to fall, fly, whence Gr. *piptein*, L. *petere*, to fall, Sans. *pātati*, (he) flies] 1. *Zool.* any of the growths covering the body of a bird and making up a large part of the wing surface: it consists typically of a horny central shaft, partly hollow, from which light, soft, narrow barbs, with interlocking barbules and barbicels, extend to form a thin, flat surface 2. a feather or feather-like part fastened to the shaft of an arrow to help control its flight 3. anything like or suggesting a feather or feathers in appearance, lightness, etc.; specif., *a)* a trifle *b)* a projecting part, as one for fitting into a groove *c)* an irregular flaw in a gem *d)* the wake left by a submarine's periscope *e)* the fringe of hair along the tail and along the back of the legs of some dogs 4. [*pl.*] *a)* plumage *b)* attire; dress 5. class; kind [birds of a *feather*] 6. frame of mind; mood; temper; vein 7. the act of feathering an oar or propeller —*vt.* 1. to provide (an arrow, etc.) with a feather 2. to cover, fit, adorn, or fringe with or as with feathers 3. to give a featheredge to 4. to join by inserting a wedge-shaped part into a groove 5. to turn (the blade of an oar) nearly parallel to the water's surface in recovering after a stroke 6. *a)* to turn (the blade of a propeller) on its shaft so that its leading and trailing edges are nearly parallel with the airplane's line of flight, thus offering minimum resistance or drag when idle *b)* to change the angle of the blades of a helicopter rotor —*vi.* 1. to grow, or become covered with, feathers 2. to move, grow, or extend like feathers 3. to look like feathers 4. to feather an oar or propeller —**feather in one's cap** a distinctive accomplishment; achievement worthy of pride —**feather one's nest** to grow rich by taking advantage of circumstances —**in feather** feathered —**in fine** (or **high** or **good**) **feather** in very good humor, health, or form —**feath′er·less** *adj.*

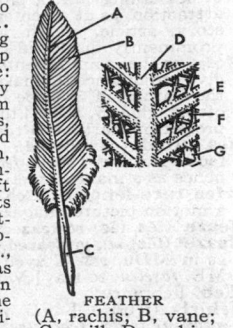

FEATHER
(A, rachis; B, vane; C, quill; D, rachis; E, barb; F, barbule; G, hooks)

feath·er·bed (-bed′) *adj.* ☆of, facilitating, or having to do with featherbedding —☆*vi.*, *vt.* **-bed′ded, -bed′ding** to engage in or subject to featherbedding

feather bed a strong cloth container thickly filled with feathers or down, used as a mattress

☆**feath·er·bed·ding** (-bed′iŋ) *n.* the practice of limiting output or requiring extra workers, as by union contract, in order to provide more jobs and prevent unemployment

☆**feath·er·bone** (-bōn′) *n.* a substitute for whalebone prepared from the quills of domestic fowls

feath·er·brain (-brān′) *n.* a silly, foolish, or frivolous person —**feath′er·brained′** *adj.*

☆**feath·er·cut** (-kut′) *n.* a woman's style of haircut characterized by many curls with feathery tips

feath·ered (feth′ərd) *adj.* 1. having feathers; covered with or decorated with or as with feathers 2. winged; swift

feath·er·edge (-ej′) *n.* a very thin edge, as on a board or tool, that can be easily broken or curled —*vt.* **-edged′, -edg′ing** to give such an edge to

feath·er·head (-hed′) *n. same as* FEATHERBRAIN

feath·er·ing (-iŋ) *n.* 1. an especially delicate and light method of bowing rapid passages on the violin 2. the act of one who feathers 3. feathers collectively

feather palm any palm with featherlike, or pinnate, leaves

feather star any of a number of unattached, free-swimming crinoids related to the sea lilies; comatulid

feath·er·stitch (-stich′) *n.* [so called from resemblance to the arrangement of barbs on a feather] an embroidery stitch forming a zigzag line —*vt.*, *vi.* to embroider with such a stitch

feath·er·weight (-wāt′) *n.* 1. any person or thing of comparatively light weight or small size 2. an unimportant person or thing 3. a boxer who weighs over 118 but not over 126 pounds 4. a wrestler who weighs over 123 but not over 134 pounds 5. the minimum weight that a race horse may carry in a handicap —*adj.* 1. of featherweights 2. light or trivial

feath·er·y (-ē) *adj.* 1. covered with or as with feathers 2. resembling feathers; soft, light, etc. —**feath′er·i·ness** *n.*

FEATHERSTITCH

---

fat, āpe, cär; ten, ēven; is, bīte; gō, hôrn, tōōl, look; oil, out; up, fur; get; joy; yet; chin; she; thin, *then*; zh, leisure; ŋ, ring; ə for a in ago, e in agent, i in sanity, o in comply, u in focus; ' as in able (ā′b'l); Fr. bāl; ë, Fr. coeur; ö, Fr. feu; Fr. mon; ô, Fr. coq; ü, Fr. duc; r, Fr. cri; H, G. ich; kh, G. doch. See inside front cover. ☆ Americanism; ‡foreign; *hypothetical; < derived from

suitably; aptly **2.** neatly **3.** skillfully; adroitly —*adj.* [Archaic] neat; graceful

fea·ture (fē'chər) *n.* [ME. *feture* < OFr. *faiture* < L. *factura*, a making, formation < pp. of *facere*, to make: see FACT] **1.** orig., *a)* the make, shape, form, or appearance of a person or thing *b)* attractive appearance; physical beauty **2.** *a)* [*pl.*] the form or look of the face; facial appearance *b)* any of the parts of the face, as the eyes, nose, mouth, etc. **3.** a distinct or outstanding part, quality, or characteristic of something ☆**4.** a prominently displayed or publicized attraction, as at an entertainment, sale, etc. ☆**5.** a special story, article, etc. in a newspaper or magazine, often prominently displayed ☆**6.** a full-length motion picture, esp. as the main presentation —*vt.* **-tured, tur·ing** ☆**1.** to give prominence to; make a feature of **2.** to sketch or show the features of **3.** to be a feature of ☆**4.** [Slang] to conceive of; imagine **5.** [Dial.] to look like; favor —☆*vi.* to have a prominent part —**fea'ture·less** *adj.*

fea·tured (-chərd) *adj.* **1.** having (a specified kind of) facial features [broad-*featured*] ☆**2.** given special prominence as a main attraction

☆**fea·ture-length** (fē'chər leŋth') *adj.* full-length: said of a motion picture, magazine article, etc.

feaze[1] (fēz, fāz) *vt.* feazed, feaz'ing *same as* FAZE

feaze[2] (fēz) *vt., vi.* feazed, feaz'ing [prob. < LowG. or Du., as in MDu. *vese*, frayed edge, akin to OE. *fæs*, a fringe, ME. *faselen*, to fray] *Naut.* to unravel

Feb. February

feb·ri- (feb'rə) [< L. *febris*, FEVER] *a combining form meaning fever* [*febrifuge*]

fe·brif·ic (fi brif'ik) *adj.* [< Fr. *febrifique*: see FEBRI- & -FIC] [Archaic] having or producing a fever

feb·ri·fuge (feb'rə fyo͞oj') *n.* [Fr. *fébrifuge* (see FEBRI- & -FUGE), after LL. *febrifugia* (see FEVERFEW), the centaury, regarded as an antipyretic] any substance for reducing fever; antipyretic —*adj.* reducing fever

fe·brile (fē'brəl, -bril; feb'rəl) *adj.* [Fr. *fébrile* < L. *febris*, FEVER] **1.** of or characterized by fever; feverish **2.** caused by fever

Feb·ru·ar·y (feb'rə wer'ē, feb'yo͞o wer'ē) *n.* [ME. *Februarie* < L. *Februarius* (*mensis*), orig. month of expiation < *februa*, Rom. festival of purification held Feb. 15, pl. of *februum*, means of purification, prob. < IE. **dhwes-*, to fumigate, smoke: cf. DOZE, DUST] the second month of the year, having 28 days in regular years and 29 days in leap years: abbrev. **Feb., F.**

fec. [L. *fecit*] he (or she) made (it): formerly used with an artist's signature on a painting, etc.

fe·cal (fē'kəl) *adj.* of or consisting of feces

fe·ces (fē'sēz) *n.pl.* [L. *faeces*, pl. of *faex*, dregs, lees] waste matter expelled from the bowels; excrement

Fech·ner (feH'nər), **Gus·tav The·o·dor** (goos'täf tā'ō dôr') 1801–87; Ger. philosopher & psychologist

feck·less (fek'lis) *adj.* [Scot. < *feck* (aphetic for EFFECT) + -LESS] **1.** weak; ineffective **2.** careless; irresponsible — **feck'less·ly** *adv.* —**feck'less·ness** *n.*

fec·u·lence (fek'yo͞o ləns) *n.* [Fr. *féculence* < L. *faeculentia*: see ff.] **1.** the state or quality of being feculent **2.** *a)* dregs; sediment *b)* filth

fec·u·lent (-lənt) *adj.* [ME. < L. *faeculentus* < *faecula*, dim. < *faex*: see FECES] containing, or having the nature of, feces; filthy; foul

fe·cund (fē'kənd, fek'ənd) *adj.* [ME. *fecound* < OFr. *fecond* < L. *fecundus*, fertile: for IE. base see FETUS] fruitful or fertile; productive; prolific —*SYN.* see FERTILE — **fe·cun·di·ty** (fi kun'də tē) *n.*

fe·cun·date (fē'kən dāt', fek'ən-) *vt.* **-dat'ed, -dat'ing** [< L. *fecundatus*, pp. of *fecundare*, to make fruitful < *fecundus*: see prec.] **1.** to make fecund **2.** to fertilize; impregnate; pollinate —**fe·cun·da'tion** *n.*

fed[1] (fed) *pt. & pp.* of FEED —**fed up** [Colloq.] having had enough to become disgusted, bored, or annoyed

fed[2] (fed) *n.* [*often* **F-**] ☆[Slang] a Federal agent or officer —☆**the Fed** the Federal Reserve System

Fed. **1.** Federal **2.** Federation

fed·a·yeen (fed'ä yēn') *n.pl.* [< Ar., lit., those who sacrifice themselves] Arab irregulars or guerrillas in the Middle East

fed·er·al (fed'ər əl, fed'rəl) *adj.* [< L. *foedus* (gen. *foederis*), a league, compact, treaty: see FAITH & -AL] **1.** of or formed by a compact; specif., designating or of a union of states, groups, etc. in which each member agrees to subordinate its governmental power to that of the central authority in certain specified common affairs **2.** designating, of, or having to do with a central authority or government in such a union; specif., ☆[*usually* **F-**] designating, of, or having to do with the central government of the U.S. ☆**3.** [**F-**] of or supporting the Federalist Party or its principle of centralized government ☆**4.** [**F-**] of or supporting the government of the U.S. in the Civil War; Union; pro-Union —*n.* ☆**1.** [**F-**] a Federalist ☆**2.** [**F-**] a supporter or soldier of the U.S. government in the Civil War ☆**3.** [**F-**] a Federal agent or officer —**fed'er·al·ly** *adv.*

☆**Federal Bureau of Investigation** a branch of the U.S. Department of Justice whose duty is to investigate all violations of Federal laws except those, as of currency, tax, and postal laws, dealt with by other Federal agencies

☆**Federal Communications Commission** a Federal agency whose duty is to regulate communication by wire and radio, including the licensing of radio and TV stations

fed·er·al·ism (-iz'm) *n.* **1.** *a)* the federal principle of government or organization *b)* support of this principle ☆**2.** [**F-**] the principles of the Federalist Party

fed·er·al·ist (-ist) *n.* **1.** a person who believes in or supports federalism ☆**2.** [**F-**] a member or supporter of the Federalist Party —*adj.* **1.** of or supporting federalism ☆**2.** [**F-**] of or supporting the Federalist Party or its principles Also **fed'er·al·is'tic** —☆**The Federalist** a set of 85 articles by Alexander Hamilton, James Madison, and John Jay, published in 1787 and 1788, analyzing the Constitution of the U.S. and urging its adoption

☆**Federalist Party** a political party in the U.S. (1789–1816), led by Alexander Hamilton and John Adams, which advocated the adoption of the Constitution and the establishment of a strong, centralized government

fed·er·al·ize (fed'ər ə līz', fed'rə-) *vt.* **-ized', -iz'ing 1.** to unite (states, etc.) in a federal union **2.** to put under the authority of a federal government —**fed'er·al·i·za'tion** *n.*

☆**Federal Land Bank** any of twelve regional banks established in 1916 to provide farmers with long-term loans secured by first mortgages on their farm property

☆**Federal Reserve Bank** any of the twelve district banks of the Federal Reserve System

Federal Reserve note a note issued by the individual Federal Reserve Banks in various denominations of from 1 to 10,000 dollars, now the prevailing form of U.S. paper currency in circulation

☆**Federal Reserve System** a centralized banking system in the U.S. under a Board of Governors (formerly called the **Federal Reserve Board**) with supervisory powers over twelve Federal Reserve Banks, each a central bank for its district, and about 6,000 member banks: it was established in 1913 to develop a currency which would fluctuate with business demands, and to regulate the member banks of each district

☆**Federal Trade Commission** a Federal agency whose duty is to investigate unfair methods of competition in business, fraudulent advertising, etc., and to prosecute those guilty of such practices

fed·er·ate (fed'ər it; *for v.* -ə rāt') *adj.* [L. *foederatus*, pp. of *foederare*, to league together < *foedus*: see FAITH] united by common agreement under a central government or authority —*vt., vi.* **-at'ed, -at'ing** to unite in a federation

fed·er·a·tion (fed'ə rā'shən) *n.* [Fr. *fédération* < ML. *federatio* < L. *foederatus*: see FEDERATE] **1.** the act of uniting or of forming a union of states, groups, etc. by agreement of each member to subordinate its power to that of the central authority in common affairs **2.** an organization formed by such an act; league; specif., a federal union of states, nations, etc.

fed·er·a·tive (fed'ə rāt'iv, -ər ə tiv) *adj.* of, forming, or having the nature of, a federation —**fed'er·a'tive·ly** *adv.*

☆**fe·do·ra** (fə dôr'ə) *n.* [Fr. < *Fédora* (1882), play by Sardou: the hat style was worn by one of the characters] a soft felt hat with the crown creased lengthwise and a somewhat curved brim

fee (fē) *n.* [ME., estate, fief, payment < Anglo-Fr. (< OFr. *feu, fief* < Gmc., as in OHG. *feho, fihu*, akin to OE. *feoh* < IE. base **pek-*, whence L. *pecus*: cf. PECUNIARY) & < OE. *feoh*, cattle, property] **1.** orig., *a)* heritable land held from a feudal lord in return for service; fief; feudal benefice *b)* the right to hold such land *c)* payment, service, or homage due a superior **2.** payment asked or given for professional services, admissions, licenses, tuition, etc.; charge **3.** [Now Rare] a present of money; tip; gratuity **4.** *Law* an inheritance in land: see FEE SIMPLE, FEE TAIL —*vt.* **feed, fee'ing** [Now Rare] to give a fee, or tip, to —*SYN.* see WAGE — **hold in fee** to own; possess

fee·ble (fē'b'l) *adj.* **-bler, -blest** [ME. *feble* < OFr. < L. *flebilis*, to be wept over < *flere*, to weep < IE. base **bhle-*, to howl, whence BLEAT, BLARE] weak; not strong; specif., *a)* infirm [a *feeble* old man] *b)* without force or effectiveness [a *feeble* light, a *feeble* attempt] *c)* easily broken; frail [a *feeble* barrier] —*SYN.* see WEAK —**fee'ble·ness** *n.* — **fee'bly** *adv.*

fee·ble-mind·ed (-mīn'did) *adj.* **1.** mentally retarded; subnormal in intelligence: term no longer used in psychology **2.** [Rare] having a weak will; irresolute —**fee'-ble-mind'ed·ly** *adv.* —**fee'ble-mind'ed·ness** *n.*

feed (fēd) *vt.* **fed, feed'ing** [ME. *feden* < OE. *fedan* < base of *foda*, FOOD] **1.** to give food to; provide food for **2.** *a)* to provide as food [to *feed* oats to horses] *b)* to serve as food for **3.** to provide something necessary for the growth, development, or existence of; nourish; sustain [to *feed* one's anger] **4.** to provide (material to be used up, processed, etc.) [to *feed* coal into a stove] **5.** to provide with material [*feed* the stove] **6.** to provide satisfaction for; gratify [to *feed* one's vanity] **7.** *Sports* to pass (the ball, puck, etc.) to (a teammate intending to make a shot, try for a goal, etc.) **8.** *Theater* to supply (an actor) with (cue lines) —*vi.* **1.** to eat: said chiefly of animals **2.** to flow steadily, as into a machine for use, processing, etc. —*n.* **1.** *a)* food given to animals; fodder *b)* the amount of fodder given at one time **2.** *a)* the material fed into a machine *b)* the part of the machine supplying this material *c)* the supplying of this material **3.** [Colloq.] a meal —**feed·on** (or **upon**) **1.** to take as food; eat **2.** to get satisfaction, support, etc. from —**off one's feed** [Slang] without appetite for food; somewhat sick

feed·back (-bak′) *n.* **1.** *Elec.* the transfer of part of the output of an active circuit or device back to the input, either as an unwanted effect or in an intentional use, as to reduce distortion **2.** a process in which the factors that produce a result are themselves modified, corrected, strengthened, etc. by that result

☆**feed bag** a bag filled with grain, fastened over a horse's muzzle for feeding —**put on the feed bag** [Slang] to eat a meal

feed·er (-ər) *n.* **1.** a person or thing that feeds; specif., *a)* a device that feeds material into a machine *b)* a device that supplies food to animals or birds **2.** an animal, esp. a steer, being fattened for market **3.** anything that supplies or leads into something else; tributary; specif., a branch transportation line (in full, **feeder line**) **4.** *Elec.* a conductor supplying energy to a center from which the energy is distributed into various channels

feel (fēl) *vt.* **felt, feel′ing** [ME. *felen* < OE. *felan*, akin to G. *fühlen* prob. akin to L. *palpare*, to stroke < ? IE. base *pel-*, to push into movement, whence L. *pellere*, to push, impel] **1.** to touch or handle in order to become aware of; examine or test by touching or handling **2.** to perceive or be aware of through physical sensation [to *feel* rain on the face] **3.** *a)* to experience (an emotion or condition) [to *feel* joy, pain, etc.] *b)* to be moved by or very sensitive to [to *feel* a death keenly] **4.** to be aware of through intellectual perception [to *feel* the weight of an argument] **5.** to think or believe, often for unanalyzed or emotional reasons [he *feels* that we should go] —*vi.* **1.** to have physical sensation; be sentient **2.** to appear to be to the senses, esp. to the sense of touch [the water *feels* warm] **3.** to have the indicated emotional effect [it *feels* good to be wanted] **4.** to try to find something by touching; grope (*for*) **5.** to be or be aware of being [to *feel* sad, sick, certain, etc.] **6.** to be moved to sympathy, pity, etc. (*for*) —*n.* **1.** the act of feeling; perception by the senses **2.** the sense of touch **3.** the nature of a thing perceived through touch [the *feel* of wet sawdust] **4.** an emotional sensation or effect **5.** instinctive ability or appreciation [a *feel* for design] —☆**feel (a person) out** to find out the opinions or attitude of (a person) by a cautious and indirect approach —☆**feel like** [Colloq.] to have an inclination or desire for —**feel (like) oneself** to feel normally healthy, fit, etc. —**feel one's way** to move or advance cautiously, by or as if by groping —**feel strongly about** to have decided opinions concerning —**feel up to** [Colloq.] to feel capable of

feel·er (-ər) *n.* **1.** a person or thing that feels **2.** a specialized organ of touch in an animal or insect, as a tentacle or antenna **3.** an action, remark, question, offer, etc. made to feel out another or others

feel·ing (-iŋ) *adj.* [ME. *feling*: see FEEL & -ING] full of or expressing emotion or sensitivity; sympathetic —*n.* **1.** that one of the senses by which sensations of contact, pressure, temperature, and pain are transmitted through the skin; sense of touch **2.** the power or faculty of experiencing physical sensation **3.** an awareness; consciousness; sensation [a *feeling* of pain] **4.** an emotion **5.** [*pl.*] sensitivities; sensibilities [to hurt one's *feelings*] **6.** a kindly, generous attitude; sympathy; pity **7.** *a)* an opinion or sentiment [a *feeling* that he is honest] *b)* a premonition [a *feeling* that we will win] **8.** what is attributed to something as a result of one's own impression or emotion; air; atmosphere [the lonely *feeling* of the city at night] **9.** a natural ability or sensitive appreciation [a *feeling* for music] **10.** the emotional quality in a work of art —**feel′ing·ly** *adv.*

SYN.—**feeling**, when unqualified in the context, refers to any of the subjective reactions, pleasurable or unpleasurable, that one may have to a situation and usually connotes an absence of reasoning [I can't trust my own *feelings*]; **emotion** implies an intense feeling with physical as well as mental manifestations [her breast heaved with *emotion*]; **passion** refers to a strong or overpowering emotion, connoting especially sexual love or intense anger; **sentiment** applies to a feeling, often a tender one, accompanied by some thought or reasoning [what are your *sentiments* in this matter?]

fee simple [Anglo-Fr.: see FEE & SIMPLE] absolute ownership (of land) with unrestricted rights of disposition

☆**fee-split·ting** (fē′split′iŋ) *n.* the unethical practice whereby a medical specialist turns over a part of his fee to the physician who has referred a patient to him

feet (fēt) *n.* *pl. of* FOOT —**feet of clay** a weakness or defect of character (in an otherwise strong person) —**have one's feet on the ground** to be practical, realistic, etc. —**on one's feet** **1.** in a standing position **2.** firmly established **3.** in a healthy condition —**sit at the feet of** to be an admiring disciple or pupil of —**stand on one's own feet** to be independent —**sweep (or carry) off one's feet** **1.** to fill with enthusiasm **2.** to make a deep impression on

fee tail [Anglo-Fr. *fee tailé* < *fee* (see FEE) + *tailé*, pp. of *taillir*, to cut, limit (OFr. *taillier*): see TAILOR] ownership (of land) restricted to a specified class of heirs

feeze (fēz, fāz) *vt.* **feezed, feez′ing** [ME. *fesen*, to drive, put to flight < OE. *fesan*, to drive < *fus*, eager] **1.** [Obs.

or Dial.] *a)* to drive; drive off *b)* to frighten *c)* to beat; chastise **2.** *same as* FAZE —*n.* [< the *v.*] **1.** [Brit. Dial.] a rush, hard impact, or rub **2.** [Colloq.] perturbation; agitation

feh (fā) *n.* [Heb.] a variant of peh, the seventeenth letter of the Hebrew alphabet (פ ף)

feign (fān) *vt.* [ME. *feinen* < OFr. *feindre* (prp. *feignant*) < L. *fingere*, to touch, handle, shape: see FIGURE] **1.** orig., to form; shape **2.** to make up (a story, excuse, etc.); invent; fabricate **3.** to make a false show of; pretend; imitate; simulate **4.** [Archaic] to imagine —*vi.* to pretend; dissemble —*SYN.* see ASSUME —**feign′er** *n.*

feigned (fānd) *adj.* **1.** [Now Rare] fictitious; imagined **2.** pretended; simulated; sham

Fei·ning·er (fī′niŋ ər), **Ly·o·nel (Charles Adrian)** (lī′ə n′l) 1871–1956; U.S. painter

feint (fānt) *n.* [Fr. *feinte* < pp. of *feindre:* see FEIGN] **1.** a false show; sham **2.** a pretended blow or attack intended to take the opponent off his guard, as in boxing, fencing, warfare, etc. —*vi.*, *vt.* to deliver (such a blow or attack)

feis (fesh) *n.* [Ir. < MIr., a feast < IE. base *wes-*, to feast, whence ON. *vist*, OHG. *wist*, food] a cultural festival of the arts held annually in Ireland or by people of Irish ancestry elsewhere

☆**feist** (fīst) *n.* [orig., lit., a fart < ME. *fīst*, akin to OE. *fisting* < IE. base *(s)peis-*, to blow: see SPIRIT] [Dial.] a small, snappish dog

☆**feist·y** (-ē) *adj.* **feist′i·er, feist′i·est** [prec. + -Y²] [Colloq. or Dial.] full of spirit; specif., *a)* lively, energetic, exuberant, etc. *b)* quarrelsome, aggressive, belligerent, etc.

feld·spar (feld′spär′, fel′-) *n.* [altered < G. *feldspath* (now *feldspat*) < *feld*, field + *spath*, spar < IE. base *spe-*, long, flat board, whence SPOON, SPADE¹] any of several crystalline minerals made up of aluminum silicates with sodium, potassium, or calcium, usually glassy and moderately hard, found in igneous rocks —**feld·spath′ic** (-spa′thik), **feld·spath′ose** (-ōs) *adj.*

Fe·li·ci·a (fə lish′ē ə, -lish′ə) a feminine name: see FELIX

fe·li·cif·ic (fē′lə sif′ik) *adj.* [< L. *felix* (gen. *felicis*), happy + -FIC] producing or tending to produce happiness

fe·lic·i·tate (fə lis′ə tāt′) *vt.* **-tat′ed, -tat′ing** [< L. *felicitatus*, pp. of *felicitare*, to make happy < *felix*, happy] **1.** to wish happiness to; congratulate **2.** [Archaic] to make happy —*adj.* [Obs.] made happy —**fe·lic′i·ta′tion** *n.* —**fe·lic′i·ta′tor** *n.*

fe·lic·i·tous (-təs) *adj.* [< ff. + -OUS] **1.** used or expressed in a way suitable to the occasion; aptly chosen; appropriate; apt **2.** having the knack of expressing oneself in an appropriate and pleasing way —**fe·lic′i·tous·ly** *adv.* —**fe·lic′i·tous·ness** *n.*

fe·lic·i·ty (-tē) *n.*, *pl.* **-ties** [ME. *felicite* < OFr. *felicité* < L. *felicitas*, happiness < *felix* (gen. *felicis*), happy, orig., fertile, fruitful: see FETUS] **1.** happiness; bliss **2.** anything producing happiness; good fortune **3.** a quality or knack of appropriate and pleasing expression in writing, speaking, painting, etc. **4.** an apt expression or thought

fe·lid (fē′lid) *n.* [< ModL. *Felidae*, the cat family < L. *felis:* see ff.] any animal of the cat family

fe·line (-līn) *adj.* [L. *felinus* < *feles*, *felis*, a cat] **1.** of a cat or the cat family **2.** catlike; esp., *a)* crafty, sly, stealthy, etc. *b)* graceful in a sleek way —*n.* any animal of the cat family, including the cat, leopard, lion, lynx, panther, puma, tiger, etc. —**fe′line·ly** *adv.* —**fe·lin′i·ty** (fi lin′ə tē) *n.*

Fe·lix (fē′liks) [L., lit., happy: see FELICITY] a masculine name: fem. Felicia

fell¹ (fel) *pt. of* FALL

fell² (fel) *vt.* [ME. *fellen* < OE. *fællan*, *fellan* (< Gmc. *falljan*), caus. of *feallan* (< Gmc. *fallan*), FALL] **1.** to cause to fall; knock down [to *fell* an opponent with a blow] **2.** to cut down (a tree or trees) **3.** *Sewing* to turn over (the rough edge of a seam) and sew down flat on the underside —*n.* **1.** the trees cut down in one season **2.** *Sewing* a felled seam —**fell′a·ble** *adj.* —**fell′er** *n.*

fell³ (fel) *adj.* [ME. *fel* < OFr. < ML. *fello:* see FELON¹] **1.** fierce; terrible; cruel **2.** [Archaic] causing death; deadly [a *fell* plague] —**fell′ness** *n.*

fell⁴ (fel) *n.* [ME. *fel* < OE., akin to G. *fell* < IE. base *pel-*, skin, hide, whence L. *pellis*, skin & FILM] **1.** an animal's hide or skin **2.** a thin membrane under the hide

fell⁵ (fel) *n.* [ME. *fel* < Scand., as in ON. *fjall*, mountain, akin to G. *fels*, rock, cliff < IE. base *pels-*, whence Gr. *pella*] [Brit.] **1.** a rocky or barren hill **2.** a moor; down

fel·lah (fel′ə) *n.*, *pl.* **fel′lahs; Ar. fel·la·heen, fel·la·hin** (fel′ə hēn′) [Ar. *fallāh* (pl. *fellahīn*) < *falāha*, to plow] a peasant or farm laborer in Egypt or some other countries where Arabic is spoken

fel·la·ti·o (fə lāt′ē ō′, -lat′-, -lā′shē ō′) *n.* [ModL. < L. *fellatus*, pp. of *fellare*, to suck < IE. base *dhe-:* cf. FEMALE] a sexual activity involving oral contact with the male genitals

fell·mon·ger (fel′muŋ′gər) *n.* [FELL⁴ + MONGER] formerly, a dealer in sheepskins or other animal skins

fel·loe (fel′ō) *n. same as* FELLY¹

fel·low (fel′ō, -ə) *n.* [ME. *felaghe* < Late OE. *feolaga*,

partner < *feoh* (see FEE) + *laga*, a laying down (see LAW), after cognate ON. *félagi:* basic sense, "one laying down wealth for a joint undertaking"; senses 5, 6, 7 after L. *socius* (cf. ASSOCIATE)] **1.** orig., a person who shares; partner or accomplice **2.** a companion; associate **3.** a person of the same class or rank; equal; peer **4.** either of a pair of corresponding things; mate **5.** a graduate student who holds a fellowship in a university or college **6.** a member of a learned society **7.** at some British and U.S. universities, a member of the governing body **8.** [Obs.] *a)* a person of a lower social class *b)* a coarse, rough man **9.** [Colloq.] *a)* a man or boy: often in familiar address *b)* a person; one [*a fellow* must eat] **10.** [Colloq.] a suitor; beau —*adj.* having the same ideas, position, work, etc.; in the same condition; associated [*fellow* workers]

fellow servant each of two or more persons who perform similar tasks for the same employer: under rule of common law, an employer cannot ordinarily be held liable for injuries suffered by one fellow servant through the negligence of another

fel·low·ship (-ship') *n.* [ME. *felauship*] **1.** companionship; friendly association **2.** a mutual sharing, as of experience, activity, interest, etc. **3.** a group of people with the same interests; company; brotherhood **4.** an endowment, or a sum of money paid from such an endowment, for the support of a graduate student, scholar, etc. doing advanced study in some field **5.** the rank or position of a fellow in a university or college

fellow traveler [transl. of Russ. *poputchik*] a person who espouses the cause of a party, esp. a Communist Party, without being a member; sympathizer

fel·ly[1] (fel'ē) *n., pl.* **-lies** [ME. *felwe* < OE. *felg*, akin to G. *felge* < IE. **pelk-*, to turn: cf. FALLOW[1]] the rim of a spoked wheel, or a segment of the rim

fel·ly[2] (fel'lē) *adv.* in a fell manner; with cruelty

‡**fe·lo-de-se** (fel'ō də sā', fē'lō də sē') *n., pl.* **fe'los-de-se'** (-lōz-), **fe·lo'nes-de-se'** (fi lō'nēz-, fel'ə nēz'-) [Anglo-L., felon of (one)self] *Law* suicide, or one who commits suicide

fel·on[1] (fel'ən) *n.* [ME. < OFr. < ML. *felo*, earlier *fello* < ?] **1.** [Obs.] a villain **2.** *Law* a person guilty of a major crime; criminal —*adj.* [Poet.] wicked; base; criminal

fe·on[2] (fel'ən) *n.* [ME. < ? same base as prec.] a painful, pus-producing infection at the end of a finger or toe, near the nail; whitlow

fe·lo·ni·ous (fə lō'nē əs) *adj.* [altered (after FELONY) < ME. *felonous* < OFr. *feloneus*] **1.** [Poet.] wicked; base **2.** *Law* of, like, or constituting a felony

fel·on·ry (fel'ən rē) *n.* felons collectively

fel·o·ny (fel'ə nē) *n., pl.* **-nies** [ME. *felonie* < OFr. < ML. *felonia*, treason, treachery < *felo*, FELON[1]] a major crime, as murder, arson, rape, etc., for which statute provides a greater punishment than for a misdemeanor: the penalty is usually death or imprisonment in a penitentiary for over one year

fel·site (fel'sīt) *n.* [FELS(PAR) + -ITE[1]] a fine-grained igneous rock consisting mainly of feldspar and quartz

fel·spar (fel'spär') *n.* [altered < FELDSPAR, after G. *fels*, rock] *same as* FELDSPAR

felt[1] (felt) *n.* [ME. < OE., akin to G. *filz*, Du. *filt* (basic sense, "cloth made by pounding or beating") < IE. base **pel-*, to beat, strike, whence L. *pellere*, to beat, drive] **1.** a fabric of wool, often mixed with fur or hair or with cotton, rayon, etc., the fibers being worked together by pressure, heat, chemical action, etc. instead of by weaving or knitting **2.** any fabric or material with a fuzzy, springy surface like that of felt; esp., a heavy insulating material made of asbestos fibers matted together **3.** anything made of felt —*adj.* made of felt —*vt.* **1.** *a)* to make into felt *b)* to cover with felt **2.** to cause (fibers) to mat together —*vi.* to become matted together

felt[2] (felt) *pt. and pp. of* FEEL

felt·ing (fel'tin) *n.* **1.** the making of felt **2.** the material of which felt is made **3.** felted cloth

fe·luc·ca (fə luk'ə, -lōō'kə; fe-) *n.* [It. *feluca*, prob. < Ar.] a small, narrow ship propelled by oars or lateen sails and used esp. in the Mediterranean

fem. feminine

fe·male (fē'māl) *adj.* [ME., altered after MALE < *femelle* < OFr. < L. *femella*, dim. of *femina*, a woman < IE. base **dhē-*, to suck, suckle, whence L. *felare*, to suck, *filius*, son, *fetus*, progeny, Gr. *thēlazein*, to suckle] **1.** designating or of the sex that produces ova and bears offspring: opposed to MALE: biological symbol, ♀ **2.** of, characteristic of, or suitable to members of this sex; feminine **3.** consisting of women or girls **4.** designating or having a hollow part shaped to receive a corresponding inserted part (called *male*): said of pipe fittings, electric sockets, etc. **5.** *Bot. a)* having pistils, archegonia, or oogonia and no stamens or antheridia *b)* designating or of a reproductive structure or part containing large gametes (eggs) that can be fertilized by smaller, motile gametes (sperms) *c)* designating or of any structure or part that produces fruit after it is fertilized —*n.* **1.** a female person; woman or girl **2.** a female animal or plant —**fe'male·ness** *n.*

SYN.—**female** is the basic term applied to members of the sex that is biologically distinguished from the male sex and is used of animals or plants as well as of human beings; **feminine** is now the preferred term for references, other than those basically biological, to qualities characteristic of women or things appropriate to them,

as delicacy, gentleness, etc.; **womanly** suggests the noble qualities one associates with a woman, esp. one who has maturity of character; **womanish**, in contrast, suggests the weaknesses and faults that are regarded as characteristic of women; **effeminate**, used chiefly in reference to a man, implies delicacy, softness, or lack of virility; **ladylike** refers to manners, conduct, etc. such as are expected from a refined or well-bred woman See also WOMAN —*ANT.* **male, masculine, manly, mannish**

feme (fem) *n.* [ME. < OFr. (Fr. *femme*) < L. *femina:* see prec.] **1.** *Law* a wife **2.** [Obs.] a woman

feme covert [OFr., lit., woman covered] *Law* a married woman

feme sole [OFr., lit., woman alone] *Law* an unmarried woman; spinster, divorcée, or widow

fem·i·na·cy (fem'ə nə sē) *n.* [Rare] feminine nature; femininity: also **fem'i·nal'i·ty** (-nal'ə tē), **fem'i·ne'i·ty** (-nē'ə tē)

fem·i·nine (fem'ə nin) *adj.* [ME. < OFr. < L. *femininus* < *femina*, woman] **1.** female; of women or girls **2.** having qualities regarded as characteristic of women and girls, as gentleness, weakness, delicacy, modesty, etc.; womanly **3.** suitable to or characteristic of a woman **4.** effeminate; womanish: said of a man **5.** *Gram.* designating or of the gender of words denoting or referring to females or things orig. regarded as female **6.** *Music* designating or of a cadence ending on an unaccented note or chord **7.** *Prosody* designating or of a rhyme of two, or sometimes three, syllables of which only the first is stressed (Ex.: danger, stranger; haziness, laziness) —*n. Gram.* **1.** the feminine gender **2.** a word or form in this gender —*SYN.* see FEMALE —**fem'i·nine·ly** *adv.*

fem·i·nin·i·ty (fem'ə nin'ə tē) *n., pl.* **-ties** [ME. *femininite* < ML. *foemininitas*] **1.** the quality or state of being feminine; womanliness **2.** a feminine trait **3.** women in general; womankind

fem·i·nism (fem'ə niz'm) *n.* [< L. *femina*, woman + -ISM] **1.** *a)* the principle that women should have political, economic, and social rights equal to those of men *b)* the movement to win such rights for women **2.** [Rare] feminine qualities —**fem'i·nist** *n., adj.* —**fem'i·nis'tic** *adj.*

fem·i·nize (fem'ə nīz') *vt., vi.* **-nized', -niz'ing** [< L. *femina*, woman + -IZE] to make or become feminine or effeminate —**fem'i·ni·za'tion** *n.*

femme (fem; *Fr.* fàm) *n., pl.* **femmes** (femz; *Fr.* fàm) [Fr.] [Slang] a woman or wife

‡**femme de cham·bre** (fàm' də shän'br') [Fr.] **1.** a chambermaid **2.** a lady's maid

‡**femme fa·tale** (fà tàl') *pl.* **femmes fa·tales** (fà tàl') [Fr., lit., deadly woman] an alluring woman, esp. one who leads men to their downfall or ruin

fem·to- (fem'tō-) [< Dan. *femten*, fifteen < ODan. *femtan* < *fem*, five + *-tjan*, -teen] *a combining form meaning* one quadrillionth; the factor 10⁻¹⁵ [*femtosecond*]

fe·mur (fē'mər) *n., pl.* **fe'murs**, **fem'o·ra** (fem'ər ə) [ModL. < L., thigh] **1.** *same as* THIGHBONE **2.** a long leg segment in arthropods; specif., the third segment from the body in the leg of an insect See SKELETON, illus. —**fem·o·ral** (fem'ər əl) *adj.*

fen[1] (fen) *n.* [ME. < OE., akin to G. *fenne*, marsh, Goth. *fani*, mud < IE. base **pen-*, wet, slime, mire, whence G. *feucht*, damp] an area of low, flat, marshy land; swamp; bog

fen[2] (fen) *n.* a monetary unit equal to 1/100 of a Chinese yuan

fe·na·gle (fə nā'g'l) *vi., vt.* **-gled, -gling** *same as* FINAGLE

fence (fens) *n.* [ME. *fens*, aphetic for *defens*, DEFENSE] **1.** orig., a protection; defense **2.** a barrier, as of wooden or metal posts, rails, wire mesh, etc., used as a boundary or means of protection or confinement **3.** the art of self-defense with foil, saber, etc.; fencing **4.** *a)* a person who deals in stolen goods *b)* a place where stolen goods are bought and sold —*vt.* **fenced, fenc'ing 1.** to enclose, restrict, or hamper with or as with a fence (with *in*, *off*, etc.) **2.** to keep (*out*) by or as by a fence **3.** [Archaic] to ward off; protect; defend —*vi.* **1.** to practice the art of fencing **2.** to avoid giving a direct reply; be evasive (*with*); parry **3.** to buy or sell stolen goods —☆**mend** (one's) **fences** to engage in politicking; look after one's political interests —☆**on the fence** uncommitted or undecided in a controversy —**fence'less** *adj.*

fenc·er (fen'sər) *n.* **1.** a person who fences with a foil, saber, etc. **2.** one who makes or repairs fences

fen·ci·ble (fen'sə b'l) *adj.* [ME. *fensable*, aphetic for *defensible*] [Scot.] that can defend or be defended

fenc·ing (fen'sin) *n.* [< FENCE, *v.*] **1.** the art or sport of fighting with a foil or other sword **2.** *a)* material for making fences *b)* a system of fences

fend (fend) *vt.* [ME. *fenden*, aphetic for *defenden*, DEFEND] [Archaic or Poet.] to defend —*vi.* to resist; parry —**fend for oneself** to manage by oneself; get along without help —**fend off** to ward off; parry

fend·er (fen'dər) *n.* anything that fends off or protects something else; specif., ☆*a)* any of the metal frames over the wheels of an automobile or other vehicle to protect against splashing mud, etc. ☆*b)* a device on the front of a streetcar or locomotive to catch or push aside anything on the track *c)* a low screen or frame in front of a fireplace to keep the hot coals in *d)* a pad or cushion of rope, wood, etc. hung over a ship's side to protect it in docking

Fé·ne·lon (fàn lōn'; *E.* fen''l än'), **Fran·çois de Sa·lig·nac**

de la Mothe (frän swä′ də så lē nyàk′ də là môt′) 1651–1715; Fr. clergyman & writer

fen·es·tel·la (fen′ə stel′ə) *n.*, *pl.* **-tel′lae** (-ē) [L., dim. of *fenestra*, window] a small window or opening

fe·nes·tra (fi nes′trə) *n.*, *pl.* **-trae** (-trē) [ModL. < L., window] **1.** a small opening, as in the inner wall of the middle ear **2.** a small, transparent spot, as in the wings of some insects **3.** any small opening in a membrane —**fe·nes′tral** *adj.*

fe·nes·trat·ed (fi nes′trāt′id, fen′ə strāt′id) *adj.* [pp. of rare v. < L. *fenestratus*, pp. of *fenestrare*, to furnish with openings < *fenestra*, window] **1.** having windows, openings, or perforations **2.** *Biol.* having fenestrae Also **fe·nes′trate** (-trit, -trāt)

fen·es·tra·tion (fen′ə strā′shən) *n.* [see prec. & -ION] **1.** the arrangement of windows and doors in a building **2.** the surgical operation of making an opening into the inner ear in certain cases of otosclerosis

Feng·chieh (fuŋ′jye′) city in E Szechwan province, China, on the Yangtze River: pop. 250,000: also sp. **Fengkieh**

Fe·ni·an (fē′nē ən, fēn′yən) *n.* [< pl. of Ir. Gael. *Fiann*, the old militia of Ireland < *Finn*, *Fionn*, hero of Irish tradition: associated with OIr. *fēne*, inhabitant of Ireland] **1.** any of a group of legendary military heroes of ancient Ireland ☆**2.** a member of a secret Irish revolutionary brotherhood formed in New York about 1858 to free Ireland from English rule —*adj.* of the Fenians —**Fe′ni·an·ism** *n.*

fen·nec (fen′ek) *n.* [Ar. *fanak*] a small, fawn-colored desert fox (*Fennecus zerda*) with large ears and eyes, found in N Africa and Arabia

fen·nel (fen′'l) *n.* [ME. *fenel* < OE. *finul* < L. *faeniculum*, dim. of *faenum*, hay] a tall herb (*Foeniculum vulgare*) of the parsley family, with yellow flowers: its aromatic seeds are used as a seasoning and in medicine

fen·nel-flow·er (-flou′ər) *n.* [so named from being confused with prec.] any of a genus (*Nigella*) of plants of the buttercup family, with finely divided foliage and blue, yellow, or white flowers

fen·ny (fen′ē) *adj.* [ME. *fenni* < OE. *fennig*] **1.** full of fens; marshy **2.** of or found in fens

Fen·ris (fen′ris) [ON.] *Norse Myth.* a great wolf, bound by the gods with a magic rope: also **Fen′rir** (-rir)

fen·u·greek (fen′yoo grēk′) *n.* [Fr. *fenugrec* < L. *faenumgraecum*, lit., Greek hay] a plant (*Trigonella foenumgraecum*) of the legume family, native to SE Europe and W Asia, used for forage, as a potherb, and formerly in medicine

feoff (fef, fēf) *vt.* [Early ME. *feoffen* < Anglo-Fr. *feoffer* < OFr. *fieuffer, fieffer* < *fieu*, fief] to give or sell a fief to; enfeoff —*n.* a fief —**feoff′ment** *n.* —**feof′for, feoff′er** *n.*

feoff·ee (fef ē′, fēf ē′) *n.* [ME. *feoffe* < Anglo-Fr. *feoffé*, pp. of *feoffer*] a person granted a fief

FEP Fair Employment Practice(s)

-fer (fər) [< Fr. *-fère* or L. *-fer* < *ferre*, BEAR¹] *a* n. *-forming suffix meaning* bearer, producer [*conifer*]

fe·ra·cious (fə rā′shəs) *adj.* [< L. *ferax* (gen. *feracis*) < *ferre*, BEAR¹ + -OUS] [Rare] producing abundantly; fruitful —**fe·rac′i·ty** (-ras′ə tē) *n.*

†**fe·rae na·tu·rae** (fir′ē nə toor′ē) [L., of a wild nature] *Law* nondomesticated animals and fowls that are not the private property of anyone

fe·ral¹ (fir′əl) *adj.* [ML. *feralis* < L. *fera*, wild animal < *ferus*, FIERCE + -AL] **1.** untamed; wild **2.** savage

fe·ral² (fir′əl) *adj.* [L. *feralis*, of the dead] **1.** [Poet.] gloomy; funereal **2.** [Archaic] deadly; fatal

fer·bam (fur′bam) *n.* [*fer*(*ric dimethyl-dithiocar*)*bam*(*ate*)] a fungicide, FeC₉H₁₈N₃S₆, used to control certain diseases, esp. of fruit trees

Fer·ber (fur′bər), Edna 1887–1968; U.S. novelist

fer-de-lance (fer′də läns′) *n.* [Fr., iron tip of a lance] a large, poisonous pit viper (*Bothrops atrox*), related to the rattlesnake, found in tropical America

Fer·di·nand (fur′d'n and′) [Fr.; prob. < Gmc. *frithu-*, peace (see FREDERICK) + **nanths*, courage, whence Goth. (*ana*)*nanthjan*, to be bold, OE. *nethan*, to dare; hence, lit., ? bold (in) peace] **1.** a masculine name: equiv. It. *Ferdinando, Ferrando*, Sp. *Fernando, Hernando* **2. Ferdinand I** *a*) 1000?–65; king of Castile (1033–65) & of León (1037–65): called *the Great b*) 1503–64; emperor of the Holy Roman Empire (1558–64), born in Spain *c*) (*Maximilian Karl Leopold Maria*) 1861–1948; king of Bulgaria (1908–18): abdicated: father of *Boris III* **3. Ferdinand II** 1578–1637; emperor of the Holy Roman Empire (1619–37) **4. Ferdinand V** 1452–1516; king of Castile (1474–1504); (as **Ferdinand II**) king of Aragon & Sicily (1479–1516); (as **Ferdinand III**) king of Naples (1504–16): husband of Isabella I of Castile: called *the Catholic*

fere (fir) *n.* [ME. *fere* < OE. (Anglian) *fera*, aphetic for *gefera* < *ge-*, together + *-fera* < base of *faran*, to go: see FARE] [Archaic] **1.** a companion; mate **2.** a husband or wife

fer·e·to·ry (fer′ə tôr′ē) *n.*, *pl.* **-ries** [altered < ME. *fertre* < OFr. *fiertre* < L. *feretrum*, a litter, bier < Gr. *pheretron* < *pherein*, BEAR¹: akin to BIER] **1.** a portable reliquary **2.** a place for keeping this

Fer·gus (fur′gəs) [MIr. & MGael.] *Irish Legend* a hero of the army that attacked Cuchulain at Ulster

fe·ri·a (fir′ē ə) *n.*, *pl.* **-ri·as, -ri·ae** (-ē′) [LL.: see FAIR²] **1.** [*pl.*] in ancient Rome, holidays or festivals **2.** *Eccles.* any day except Saturday or Sunday, esp. one not designated a festival or a vigil —**fe′ri·al** *adj.*

fe·rine (fir′in) *adj.* [L. *ferinus < ferus*, FIERCE] *same as* FERAL¹

fer·i·ty (fer′ə tē) *n.* [L. *feritas < ferus*, FIERCE] the state or quality of being wild, savage, or untamed

Fer·man·agh (fər man′ə) county of SW Northern Ireland: 653 sq. mi.; pop. 52,000

fer·ma·ta (fer mät′ə) *n.* [It. < *fermare*, to stop, confirm < L. *firmare*, to make firm < *firmus*, FIRM¹] *Music* **1.** the holding of a tone or rest beyond its written value, at the discretion of the performer **2.** the sign (⌒) or (‿) indicating this

fer·ment (fur′ment; *for v.* fər ment′) *n.* [ME. < OFr. < L. *fermentum*, leaven, yeast < *fervere*, to boil, be agitated: see BARM] **1.** a substance or organism causing fermentation, as yeast, bacteria, enzymes, etc. **2.** *same as* FERMENTATION **3.** a state of excitement or agitation —*vt.* **1.** to cause fermentation in **2.** to excite; agitate —*vi.* **1.** to be in the process of fermentation **2.** to be excited or agitated; seethe —**fer·ment′a·ble** *adj.*

fer·men·ta·tion (fur′mən tā′shən, -men-) *n.* [ME. *fermentacioun < LL. fermentatio*: see prec.] **1.** the breakdown of complex molecules in organic compounds, caused by the influence of a ferment [bacteria cause milk to curdle by *fermentation*] **2.** excitement; agitation

fer·ment·a·tive (fər men′tə tiv) *adj.* of, causing, or resulting from fermentation

fer·mi (fer′mē, fur′-) *n.* [after ff.] *Physics* a unit of length equal to 10⁻¹³ centimeter

Fer·mi (fer′mē), **En·ri·co** (en rē′kō) 1901–54; It. nuclear physicist, in U.S. after 1938

fer·mi·on (fer′mē än′) *n.* [after prec. + -ON] a subatomic particle, as an electron, proton, or neutron, that obeys the Pauli exclusion principle

☆**Fermi surface** an aspect of electronic structure that can be visualized in a three-dimensional graph and is based on the distribution of electrons into different states of momentum as they move in different directions

☆**fer·mi·um** (fer′mē əm) *n.* [after E. FERMI] a radioactive chemical element produced by intense neutron irradiation of plutonium, as in a cyclotron: symbol, Fm; at. wt., 257(?); at. no., 100

fern (furn) *n.* [ME. < OE. *fearn*, akin to Sans. *parṇa*, feather, leaf] any of a widespread class (Filicineae) of nonflowering plants having roots, stems, and fronds, and reproducing by spores instead of by seeds —**fern′y** *adj.*

Fer·nan·do de No·ro·nha (fer nän′doo də nô rō′nya) island in the South Atlantic, northeast of Natal, Brazil: with neighboring islets it constitutes a territory of Brazil: c. 10 sq. mi.; pop. 1,400

Fer·nan·do Pó·o (fer nän′dô pô′ô) island in the Gulf of Guinea, off the coast of Cameroun, forming with another island a province of Equatorial Guinea: 770 sq. mi.; pop. 72,000: Eng. name **Fer·nan·do Po** (fər nan′dō pō′)

FERN

fern·er·y (fur′nər ē) *n.*, *pl.* **-er·ies 1.** a place where ferns are grown **2.** a collection of growing ferns

fern seed the dustlike spores of ferns: formerly believed to make invisible the person who carried them

fe·ro·cious (fə rō′shəs) *adj.* [< L. *ferox* (gen. *ferocis*), wild, untamed < *ferus*, FIERCE + base akin to *oculus*, eye (see OCULO-) + -OUS] **1.** fierce; savage; violently cruel **2.** [Colloq.] very great [a *ferocious* appetite] —**fe·ro′cious·ly** *adv.* —**fe·ro′cious·ness** *n.*

fe·roc·i·ty (fə räs′ə tē) *n.*, *pl.* **-ties** [Fr. *ferocité* < L. *ferocitas*] wild force or cruelty; ferociousness

-ferous (fər əs) [L. *-fer < ferre*, BEAR¹ + -OUS] *a suffix meaning* bearing, producing [*coniferous*]

Fer·ra·ra (fə rär′ə) commune in NC Italy, in the Emilia-Romagna region: pop. 158,000

fer·rate (fer′āt) *n.* [< L. *ferrum*, iron (see FERRO-) + -ATE²] a salt of the hypothetical ferric acid, containing the divalent radical, =FeO₄

fer·re·dox·in (fer′ə däk′sin) *n.* [FER(RO)- + REDOX + -IN¹] a protein containing iron that is found in chloroplasts and is a basic component in the process of photosynthesis

fer·re·ous (fer′ē əs) *adj.* [L. *ferreus < ferrum*, iron + -OUS] of, like, or containing iron

fer·ret¹ (fer′it) *n.* [< It. *fioretti*, floss silk, orig. pl. of *fioretto*, dim. of *fiore*, a flower < L. *flos* (gen. *floris*), FLOWER] a narrow ribbon of cotton, wool, silk, etc.: also **fer′ret·ing**

fer·ret² (fer'it) n. [ME. *feret* < OFr. *furet* < LL. *furetus*, dim. of *furo*, a ferret < L. *fur*, thief < IE. base **bher-*, BEAR¹ (hence, orig., one who carries off), whence Gr. *phōr*, thief] 1. a small, weasellike animal (genus *Mustela*) related to the European polecat, with pink eyes and yellowish fur, easily tamed for hunting rabbits, rats, etc. 2. a rare, black-footed weasel (*Mustela nigripes*) of the W U.S. —vt. 1. to force out of hiding with or as if with a ferret 2. to search for persistently and discover (facts, the truth, etc.); search (*out*) 3. [Archaic] to keep after; harass —vi. 1. to hunt with ferrets 2. to search around —fer'ret·er n. —fer'ret·y (-ē) adj.

FERRET (19 1/2–21 in. long, including tail)

fer·ri- (fer'i, -ī) [< L. *ferrum*, iron] a combining form meaning containing ferric iron: see FERRO-

fer·ri·age (fer'ē ij) n. [< FERRY + -AGE] 1. transportation by ferry 2. the charge for this

fer·ric (fer'ik) adj. [FERR(O)- + -IC] 1. of, containing, or derived from iron 2. *Chem.* designating or of iron with a valence of three, or compounds containing such iron: distinguished from FERROUS

ferric oxide a brown or reddish oxide of iron, Fe_2O_3, occurring naturally as hematite or prepared by the oxidation of iron: used as a pigment, in polishing compounds, in magnetic tapes, etc.

fer·ri·cy·an·ic acid (fer'i sī an'ik, fer'i-) adj. [FERRI- + CYANIC] a brown, crystalline, unstable acid, $H_3Fe(CN)_6$

fer·ri·cy·a·nide (-sī'ə nīd') n. a salt of ferricyanic acid

fer·rif·er·ous (fə rif'ər əs) adj. [FERRI- + -FEROUS] bearing or containing iron

☆**Fer·ris wheel** (fer'is) [after George W. G. *Ferris* (1859–96), U.S. engineer who constructed the first one for the World's Fair in Chicago in 1893] a large, upright wheel revolving on a fixed axle and having seats hanging from the frame: used as an amusement ride

fer·rite (fer'īt) n. [FERR(O)- + -ITE¹] 1. any of various yellowish or reddish-brown crystalline substances occurring in rocks and having the general formula MFe_2O_4, where M is some divalent metal as nickel, zinc, etc. 2. one of the forms of pure metallic iron, having high magnetic permeability and occurring as a constituent of ordinary iron and steel 3. any of various compounds in which ferric oxide may be regarded as combined with a more basic metallic oxide, as calcium ferrite, $Ca(FeO_2)_2$

fer·ro- (fer'ō, -ə) [< L. *ferrum*, iron] a combining form meaning: 1. iron [*ferromagnetic*] 2. iron and [*ferromanganese*] 3. containing ferrous iron [*ferrocyanide*]

fer·ro·al·loy (fer'ō al'oi, -ə loi') n. any of various alloys of iron used in the manufacture of steel: named from the added metal, as ferrochromium, ferromanganese, etc.

fer·ro·chro·mi·um (-krō'mē əm) n. an alloy of iron and chromium: also **fer'ro·chrome'** (-krōm')

fer·ro·con·crete (-kän'krēt, -kän krēt') n. same as REINFORCED CONCRETE

fer·ro·cy·an·ic acid (-sī an'ik) [FERRO- + CYANIC] a colorless crystalline acid, $H_4Fe(CN)_6$

fer·ro·cy·a·nide (-sī'ə nīd', -nid) n. a salt of ferrocyanic acid

fer·ro·e·lec·tric (-i lek'trik) n. any of various crystalline, solid materials that have a natural polarization of the electric fields in the crystal lattice and that exhibit exceptional piezoelectric and elastic properties

Ferrol same as EL FERROL

fer·ro·mag·ne·sian (-mag nē'shən, -nē'zhən) adj. *Mineralogy* containing iron and magnesium

fer·ro·mag·net·ic (-mag net'ik) adj. designating a material, as iron, nickel, or cobalt, having a high magnetic permeability which varies with the magnetizing force — **fer'ro·mag'net·ism** (-mag'nə tiz'm) n.

fer·ro·man·ga·nese (-man'gə nēs', -nēz') n. an alloy of iron and manganese, used for making hard steel

fer·ro·sil·i·con (-sil'i kən) n. a compound of iron and silicon, used in making steel, as a deoxidizing agent, etc.

fer·ro·type (fer'ō tīp') n. [FERRO- + -TYPE] 1. a positive photograph taken directly on a thin plate of iron coated with a sensitized film; tintype 2. the process of making such photographs

fer·rous (fer'əs) adj. [< L. *ferrum*, iron + -OUS] 1. of, containing, or derived from iron 2. *Chem.* designating or of iron with a valence of two, or compounds containing it: distinguished from FERRIC

ferrous oxide the monoxide of iron, FeO, a black powder that is a strong base and absorbs carbon dioxide

ferrous sulfate same as COPPERAS

fer·ru·gi·nous (fə roo'ji nəs) adj. [L. *ferruginus* < *ferrugo*, iron rust, color of iron rust < *ferrum*, iron] 1. of, containing, or having the nature of, iron 2. having the color of iron rust; reddish-brown

fer·rule (fer'əl, -ool) n. [formerly *verrel* < ME. & OFr. *virole*, iron ring on a staff < L. *viriola*, dim. of *viriae*, bracelets, via Celt. < IE. **weir-*, wire, twisted work (whence WIRE) < base **wei-*, to bend, twist, whence L. *viere*, to twist, bind around; sp. altered after L. *ferrum*, iron] 1. a metal ring or cap put around the end of a cane,

tool handle, etc. to prevent splitting or to give added strength 2. *Mech.* a short tube or bushing for tightening a joint —vt. **-ruled, -rul·ing** to furnish with a ferrule

fer·ry (fer'ē) vt. **-ried, -ry·ing** [ME. *ferien* < OE. *ferian*, to carry, convey, esp. by water, caus. of *faran*, to go (see FARE), akin to Goth. *faran*, ON. *ferja*] 1. to take (people, cars, etc.) across a river or narrow body of water in a boat, raft, etc. 2. to cross (a river, etc.) on a ferry 3. to deliver (airplanes) by flying to the destination 4. to transport by airplane —vi. to cross a river, etc. by ferry —n., pl. **-ries** 1. a system for carrying people, cars, or goods across a river, etc. by boat 2. a boat used for this 3. the place where a ferry docks on either shore 4. the legal right to transport by ferry for a fee 5. the delivery of airplanes to their destination by flying them

fer·ry·boat (-bōt') n. same as FERRY (sense 2)

fer·ry·man (-mən) n., pl. **-men** (-mən) a man who owns, manages, or works on a ferry

fer·tile (fur't'l; chiefly Brit., -tīl) adj. [ME. < OFr. < L. *fertilis* < stem of *ferre*, BEAR¹] 1. producing abundantly; rich in resources or invention; fruitful; prolific 2. causing or helping fertility [the sun's *fertile* warmth] 3. able to produce young, seeds, fruit, pollen, spores, etc. 4. capable of development into a new individual; fertilized [*fertile* eggs] —**fer'tile·ly** adv. —**fer'tile·ness** n.

SYN.—**fertile** implies a producing, or power of producing, fruit or offspring, and may be used figuratively of the mind; **fecund** implies the abundant production of offspring or fruit, or, figuratively, of creations of the mind; **fruitful** specifically suggests the bearing of much fruit, but it is also used to imply fertility (of soil), favorable results, profitableness, etc.; **prolific**, a close synonym for **fecund**, more often carries derogatory connotations of overly rapid production or reproduction —ANT. **sterile, barren**

fertile material nonfissionable material which can be converted into a fissionable material by a neutron-induced nuclear reaction, as uranium 238

fer·til·i·ty (fur til'ə tē) n. the quality, state, or degree of being fertile; fecundity

fer·til·ize (fur't'l īz') vt. **-ized', -iz'ing** 1. to make fertile; make fruitful or productive; enrich [nitrates *fertilize* soil] 2. to spread fertilizer on 3. *Biol.* to make (the female reproductive cell or female individual) fruitful by introducing the male germ cell; impregnate or pollinate —**fer'til·iz'a·ble** adj. —**fer'til·i·za'tion** n.

fer·til·iz·er (-ī'zər) n. a person or thing that fertilizes; specif., any material, as manure, chemicals, etc., put on or in the soil to improve the quality or quantity of plant growth

fer·u·la (fer'yoo lə, -oo-) n., pl. **-lae'** (-lē') [L., giant fennel, hence, stick, whip, rod, prob. akin to *festuca*, blade of grass] 1. any of a genus (*Ferula*) of plants of the parsley family, valuable as a source of various gums, as asafetida 2. same as FERULE

fer·ule (fer'əl, -ool) n. [ME. *ferul* < L. *ferula*: see FERULA] a flat stick or ruler used for punishing children —vt. **-uled, -ul·ing** to strike or punish with a ferule

fer·ven·cy (fur'vən sē) n. [ME. < OFr. *fervence* < L. *fervens*: see ff.] great warmth of feeling; ardor

fer·vent (fur'vənt) adj. [ME. < OFr. & < L. *fervens* (gen. *ferventis*), prp. of *fervere*, to glow, boil, rage < IE. **bhreu-*, to boil up < base **bher-*, to boil, whence BREW, BURN¹] 1. hot; burning; glowing 2. having or showing great warmth of feeling; intensely devoted or earnest; ardent —SYN. see PASSIONATE —**fer'vent·ly** adv.

fer·vid (fur'vəd) adj. [L. *fervidus* < *fervere*: see prec.] 1. hot; glowing 2. impassioned; fervent —SYN. see PASSIONATE —**fer'vid·ly** adv. —**fer'vid·ness** n.

fer·vor (fur'vər) n. [ME. < OFr. < L. < *fervere*: see FERVENT] 1. intense heat 2. great warmth of emotion; ardor; zeal Brit. sp. **fer'vour** —SYN. see PASSION

Fès (fes) same as FEZ

Fes·cen·nine (fes'ə nīn', -nin) adj. [L. *Fescenninus* < *Fescennia*, city in Etruria noted for scurrilous verse] [often f-] vulgar; obscene; scurrilous

fes·cue (fes'kyoo) n. [ME. *festu* < OFr. < L. *festuca*, a straw, blade of grass] 1. any of a genus (*Festuca*) of grasses, many of which are used in the temperate zone as lawn and pasture grasses 2. [Rare] a long stick, straw, etc., used as a teacher's pointer

fess, fesse (fes) n. [ME. *fesse* < OFr. < L. *fascia*, a band, FASCIA] *Heraldry* a horizontal band forming the middle third of an escutcheon

☆**-fest** (fest) [< G. *fest*, a celebration < L. *festum*: see FEAST] a combining form used in forming colloquial and slang words, meaning an occasion of much [*funfest*]

fes·ta (fes'tə) n. [It.] a holiday celebration; festival

fes·tal (fes't'l) adj. [< L. *festum*, FEAST + -AL] of or like a joyous celebration; festive —**fes'tal·ly** adv.

fes·ter (fes'tər) n. [ME. *festre* < OFr. < L. *fistula*: see FISTULA] a small sore filled with pus; pustule —vi. [ME. *festren* < the n.] 1. to form pus; ulcerate 2. to grow embittered; rankle 3. to decay —vt. 1. to cause the formation of pus in 2. to make rankle; embitter

fes·ti·nate (fes'tə nāt'; for adj. -nit) vt., vi. **-nat'ed, -nat'ing** [< L. *festinatus*, pp. of *festinare*, to hurry < IE. base **bheres*, quick, whence MIr. *bras*, fast, Russ. *borzój*, swift] [Rare] to hurry; speed —adj. [Rare] hurried

fes·ti·na·tion (fes'tə nā'shən) n. [L. *festinatio*, haste: see prec.] an involuntary inclination to hurry in walking, esp.

seen in certain nervous diseases, as Parkinson's disease

fes·ti·val (fes′tə v'l) *n.* [ME., n. & adj. < OFr. < ML. *festivalis* < L. *festivus*: see ff.] **1.** a time or day of feasting or celebration; esp., a periodic religious celebration **2.** a celebration, entertainment, or series of performances of a certain kind, often held periodically [a Bach *festival*] **3.** merrymaking; festivity —*adj.* of, for, or fit for a festival

fes·tive (fes′tiv) *adj.* [L. *festivus* < *festum* (see FEAST)] of, for, or suited to a feast or festival; merry; joyous —**fes′tive·ly** *adv.* —**fes′tive·ness** *n.*

fes·tiv·i·ty (fes tiv′ə tē) *n., pl.* **-ties** [ME. *festivite* < OFr. < L. *festivus*: see prec.] **1.** merrymaking; gaiety; joyful celebration **2.** *a)* a festival *b)* [*pl.*] festive proceedings; things done in celebration

fes·toon (fes tōōn′) *n.* [Fr. *feston* < It. *festone* < *festa*, FEAST] **1.** a wreath or garland of flowers, leaves, paper, etc. hanging in a loop or curve **2.** any carved or molded decoration resembling this, as on furniture —*vt.* **1.** to adorn or hang with festoons **2.** to form into a festoon or festoons **3.** to join by festoons

fes·toon·er·y (-ər ē) *n.* an arrangement of festoons

Fest·schrift (fest′shrift′) *n., pl.* **-schrift′en** (-shrif′t'n), **-schrifts′** [G. < *fest*, festival, holiday + *schrift*, a writing] [*also* **f-**] a collection of articles by the colleagues, former students, etc. of a noted scholar, published in his honor

fet·a (cheese) (fet′ə) [< ModGr. (*tyri*) *pheta* < *tyri*, cheese (< Gr. *tyros*) + *pheta* < It. *fetta*, a slice, ult. < L. *offa*, a morsel, piece] a white, soft cheese made in Greece from ewe's milk or goat's milk

fe·tal (fēt′'l) *adj.* of, pertaining to, or like a fetus

fe·ta·tion (fē tā′shən) *n.* fetal development; also, pregnancy

fetch¹ (fech) *vt.* [ME. *fecchen* < OE. *feccan*, earlier *fetian* < IE. *pedyo-* (extension of base *ped-*, FOOT), whence G. *fassen*, to grasp] **1.** to go after and come back with; bring; get **2.** to cause to come; produce; elicit **3.** to draw (a breath) or heave (a sigh, groan, etc.) **4.** [Rare] to derive or infer **5.** to come to; reach: said of a ship **6.** to bring as a price; sell for **7.** [Colloq.] to attract; charm; captivate **8.** [Colloq.] to deliver or deal (a blow, stroke, etc.) —*vi.* **1.** to go after things and bring them back; specif., to retrieve game: said of hounds **2.** *Naut. a)* to take or hold a course *b)* to veer —*n.* **1.** the act of fetching **2.** a trick; dodge —*SYN.* see BRING —**fetch and carry** to do minor tasks or chores —**fetch up 1.** [Colloq.] to reach; stop **2.** [Dial.] to bring up or raise (a child, pet, etc.)

fetch² (fech) *n.* [< ?] the apparition of a living person; wraith

fetch·ing (-in) *adj.* attractive; charming —**fetch′ing·ly** *adv.*

fete, fête (fāt) *n.* [Fr. *fête* < OFr. *feste*: see FEAST] an entertainment; esp., a gala entertainment held outdoors —*vt.* **fet′ed** or **fêt′ed**, **fet′ing** or **fêt′ing** to celebrate or honor with a fete; entertain

‡**fête cham·pê·tre** (fet shän pe′tr′) [Fr., rural festival] an outdoor feast or entertainment

☆**fet·e·ri·ta** (fet′ə rēt′ə) *n.* [< Ar. dial. name] a cultivated strain of grain sorghum with large, white seeds, grown for grain and forage in the SW U.S.

fe·ti- (fēt′ə) *a combining form meaning fetus [fetiparous]:* also **fe·to-** (fēt′ə)

fe·tial (fē′shəl) *n.* [L. *fetialis* < *fetiales*, pl., college of priests < OL. *fetis* < IE. *dhē-ti-s*, statute < base *dhē-* (see FACT)] in ancient Rome, any of a group of twenty priests who conducted diplomatic negotiations, declared war, and presided at ceremonies at war's end: also **fe·ti·a·lis** (fē′shē ā′lis), *pl.* **-a′les** (-lēz) —*adj.* of these priests or their functions

fe·ti·cide (fēt′ə sīd′) *n.* [< FETUS + -CIDE] the killing of a fetus; illegal abortion —**fe′ti·ci′dal** (-sī′d'l) *adj.*

fet·id (fet′id, fēt′-) *adj.* [ME. < L. *fetidus*, *foetidus* < *foetere*, to stink < IE. *dhwoitos* < base *dheu-*, to blow about, as dust, odors (whence DOWN³, DUMB)] having a bad smell, as of decay; stinking; putrid —*SYN.* see STINKING —**fet′id·ly** *adv.* —**fet′id·ness** *n.*

fe·tip·a·rous (fē tip′ər əs) *adj.* [FETI- + -PAROUS] designating or of animals whose young are born incompletely developed, as marsupials

fet·ish (fet′ish, fēt′-) *n.* [Fr. *fétiche* < Port. *feitiço*, a charm, sorcery; orig. adj. < L. *facticius*, FACTITIOUS] **1.** any object believed by superstitious people to have magical power **2.** any thing or activity to which one is irrationally devoted [to make a *fetish* of sports] **3.** *Psychiatry* any nonsexual object, such as a foot or a glove, that abnormally excites erotic feelings Also sp. **fet′ich**

fet·ish·ism (-iz'm) *n.* **1.** [Fr. *fétichisme*] worship of or belief in fetishes **2.** *Psychiatry* an abnormal condition in which erotic feelings are excited by a nonsexual object, as a foot, glove, etc. Also sp. **fet′ich·ism** —**fet′ish·ist** *n.* — **fet′ish·is′tic** *adj.*

fet·lock (fet′läk′) *n.* [ME. *fitlok* (understood in ME. as compound of *fet*, FEET + *lok*, LOCK²) < MDu. or MLowG. cognate of MHG. *vizzeloch* < *vissel*, dim. (< base of OHG. *fuoz*, FOOT) + *-och*, -OCK] **1.** a tuft of hair on the back of the leg of a horse, donkey, etc., just above the hoof **2.** the joint or projection bearing this tuft

fe·tor (fēt′ər, fē′tôr) *n.* [L. *fetor*, *foetor* < *foetere*: see FETID] a strong, disagreeable smell; stench

fet·ter (fet′ər) *n.* [ME. *feter* < OE. *feter* < base of *fot*, FOOT, akin to G. *fessel*] **1.** a shackle or chain for the feet **2.** anything that holds in check; restraint —*vt.* [ME. *feterien* < OE. (*ge*)*feterian*] **1.** to bind with fetters; shackle; chain **2.** to hold in check; restrain; confine —*SYN.* see HAMPER¹

☆**fet·ter·bush** (-boosh′) *n.* **1.** any of a genus (*Leucothoë*) of plants of the heath family, found in E U.S., with white, bell-shaped flowers **2.** any of various other plants of the heath family

fet·ter·lock (-läk′) *n. same as* FETLOCK

fet·tle (fet′'l) *vt.* **fet′tled**, **fet′tling** [ME. *fetlen*, to make ready, prob. < OE. *fetel*, belt (akin to fair, FETTER), confused with *fætel*, container < *fæt*, VAT] **1.** [Dial.] to put in order or readiness; arrange **2.** to line or cover (the hearth of a puddling furnace) with ore, silica, or other loose material —*n.* **1.** condition of body and mind [in fine *fettle*] **2.** *same as* FETTLING

fet·tling (fet′lin) *n.* [see prec.] a loose material, as silica, used to fettle a puddling furnace

fet·tuc·ci·ne (fet′ōō chē′nē) *n.pl.* [*often with sing. v.*] [It., lit., little ribbons] broad, flat noodles served with sauce, butter, etc.: also sp. **fet′tu·ci′ne, fet′tu·ci′ni**

fe·tus (fēt′əs) *n., pl.* **-tus·es** [ME. < L. *fetus*, *foetus*, a bringing forth, progeny; as *adj.*, pregnant, fruitful: for IE. base see FEMALE] **1.** the unborn young of an animal while still in the uterus or egg, esp. in its later stages **2.** in man, the offspring in the womb from the end of the third month of pregnancy until birth: distinguished from EMBRYO

feu (fyōō) *n.* [Scot. for FEE] *Scot. History & Law* a renting of land paid for by the holder in grain or money rather than in military service, or the land so held —*vt.* to grant (land) on feu

Feucht·wang·er (foiHt′väŋ ər), **Li·on** (lē′ōn) 1884–1958; Ger. novelist, in exile in U.S. after 1940

feud¹ (fyōōd) *n.* [ME. *fede* < OFr. *faide* < Frank. *faida*, akin to OHG. *fehida*, enmity, revenge < IE. base *peik-*, hostile, whence Lith. *piktas*, angry & FOE] a bitter, long-continued, and deadly quarrel, esp. between clans or families —*vi.* to carry on a feud; quarrel

feud² (fyōōd) *n.* [ME. < ML. *feodum* < OHG. *feho*, cattle, property (see FEE) + *od*, *ot*, wealth, akin to OE. *ead*] land held from a feudal lord in return for service; fief

feu·dal¹ (fyōōd′'l) *adj.* [ML. *feudalis*] **1.** of a feud (land) **2.** of or like feudalism —**feu′dal·ly** *adv.*

feu·dal² (fyōōd′'l) *adj.* of or like a feud (quarrel)

feu·dal·ism (-iz'm) *n.* the economic, political, and social system in medieval Europe, in which land, worked by serfs who were bound to it, was held by vassals in exchange for military and other services given to overlords —**feu′dal·ist** *n.* —**feu′dal·is′tic** *adj.*

feu·dal·i·ty (fyōō dal′ə tē) *n., pl.* **-ties** [Fr. *feodalité*] **1.** the quality or state of being feudal **2.** a feudal holding or estate; fief

feu·dal·ize (fyōōd′'l īz′) *vt.* **-ized′**, **-iz′ing** to make feudal; establish feudalism in —**feu′dal·i·za′tion** *n.*

feudal system *same as* FEUDALISM

feu·da·to·ry (fyōō′də tôr′ē) *n., pl.* **-ries** [ML. *feodatorius* < *feodare*, to enfeoff < *feodum*, *feudum*: see FEUD²] **1.** a person holding land by feudal tenure **2.** the land held; fief —*adj.* **1.** of the feudal relationship between vassal and lord **2.** owing feudal allegiance (*to*)

feud·ist¹ (fyōō′dist) *n.* a participant in a feud (quarrel)

feud·ist² (fyōō′dist) *n.* a specialist in feudal law

Feu·er·bach (foi′ər bäkh′), **Lud·wig An·dre·as** (loot′vikh än drā′äs) 1804–72; Ger. materialist philosopher

‡**feuil·le·ton** (fö yə tōn′) *n.* [Fr. < *feuillet*, a leaf, sheet < dim. of OFr. *fuil*: see FOIL²] **1.** that part of a French newspaper which contains serialized fiction, light reviews, etc. **2.** a piece printed in this section **3.** any light, popular piece of writing

feuil·le·ton·ist (fö′yə tən ist) *n.* a writer of feuilletons

fe·ver (fē′vər) *n.* [ME. < OE. & OFr. *fievre*, both < L. *febris* < IE. base *dhegwh-*, to burn, whence L. *fovere*, to warm, MIr. *daig*, fire] **1.** a state of abnormally increased body temperature, often accompanied by a quickened pulse, delirium, etc. **2.** any of various diseases characterized by a high fever [yellow *fever*] **3.** a condition of nervousness or restless excitement —*vt.* to cause fever in — **fe′vered** *adj.*

fever blister (or **sore**) *same as* COLD SORE

fe·ver·few (-fyōō′) *n.* [ME. *fevyrfue* < OE. *feverfuge* & Anglo-Fr. *fewerfue*, both < LL. *febrifuga* < L. *febris*, FEVER + *fugia* < *fugare*, to drive away: see FUGITIVE] a bushy plant (*Chrysanthemum parthenium*) of the composite family, with finely divided foliage and small white heads of flowers

fe·ver·ish (-ish) *adj.* **1.** having fever, esp. slight fever **2.** of, like, or caused by fever **3.** causing fever **4.** greatly excited or agitated Also **fe′ver·ous** —**fe′ver·ish·ly** *adv.* —**fe′ver·ish·ness** *n.*

fever therapy formerly, treatment of a disease by artificially inducing a rise in bodily temperature to kill or make ineffective the organisms causing the disease

---

fat, āpe, cär; ten, ēven; is, bīte; gō, hôrn, tōōl, look; oil, out; up, fur; get; joy; yet; chin; she; thin, *then*; zh, leisure; ŋ, ring; ə for *a* in *ago*, *e* in *agent*, *i* in *sanity*, *o* in *comply*, *u* in *focus*; ' as in *able* (ā′b'l); Fr. bāl; ë, Fr. coeur; ö, Fr. feu; Fr. mon; ō, Fr. coq; ü, Fr. duc; r, Fr. cri; H, G. ich; kh, G. doch. See inside front cover. ☆ Americanism; ‡foreign; *hypothetical; <derived from

fe·ver·wort (-wʉrt′) *n.* ☆*same as* HORSE GENTIAN: also **fe′ver·root′**

few (fyōō) *adj.* [ME. *fewe* < OE. *feawe, feawa,* pl., akin to OFris. *fē,* Goth. *fawai,* pl. < IE. base *pōu-,* small, little, whence L. *paucus,* Gr. *pauros,* little] not many; a small number of [*few* seats were left, a *few* people came] —*pron., n.* not many; a small number [many left, *few* stayed; a *few* of the men wore hats] —☆**quite a few** [Colloq.] a rather large number —**the few** the minority; esp., a small select group —**few′ness** *n.*

fey (fā) *adj.* [ME. *feie* < OE. *fæge,* fated, akin to. G. *feige,* cowardly (OHG. *feigi,* doomed) < IE. base *peik-,* hostile, whence L. *piger,* averse & FEUD[1], FEY] **1.** [Archaic or Scot.] *a)* orig., fated; doomed to death *b)* in an unusually excited or gay state, formerly believed to portend sudden death **2.** strange or unusual in any of certain ways, as, variously, eccentric, whimsical, puckish, otherworldly, visionary, etc.

Fez (fez) city in NC Morocco: pop. 235,000

fez (fez) *n., pl.* **fez′zes** [Fr. < Turk. *fes* < prec.] a brimless, conical felt hat, usually red, tapering to a flat crown from which a long, black tassel hangs: formerly the Turkish national headdress of men

Fez·zan (fe zän′) region, & former province, of SW Libya, in the Sahara: c. 200,000 sq. mi.

FEZ

ff. 1. folios **2.** following (pages, lines, etc.) **3.** fortissimo

F.F.A. Future Farmers of America

F.F.A., f.f.a. *Naut.* free from alongside

FHA Federal Housing Administration

F.I. Falkland Islands

fi·a·cre (fē ä′kər) *n.* [Fr., after the Hotel St. *Fiacre* in Paris] in France, a small carriage for hire

fi·an·cé (fē′än sā′, fē än′sā) *n.* [Fr., pp. of *fiancer* < OFr. *fiance,* a promise < *fier,* to trust < VL. *fidare,* for L. *fidere:* see FAITH] the man to whom a woman is engaged to be married

fi·an·cée (fē′än sā′, fē än′sā) *n.* [Fr., fem. pp. of *fiancer:* see prec.] the woman to whom a man is engaged to be married

Fi·an·na (fē′ə nə) *n.* the organization of the Fenians

fi·as·co (fē as′kō) *n., pl.* **-coes, -cos** [Fr. < It. (*far*) *fiasco,* to fail < *fiasco,* bottle (< Gmc. *flasko,* FLASK): orig. prob. transl. of Fr. *bouteille,* BOTTLE[1], student slang for "error, blunder"] a complete failure; esp., an ambitious project that ends as a ridiculous failure

fi·at (fī′at, -ət) *n.* [L., 3d pers. sing., pres. subj., of *fieri,* to become, come into existence < IE. base *bheu-,* whence BE] **1.** an order issued by legal authority, usually beginning with *fiat* (let it be done); decree **2.** a sanction; authorization **3.** any arbitrary order

☆**fiat money** paper currency made legal tender by law or fiat, although not backed by gold or silver and not necessarily redeemable in coin

fib (fib) *n.* [16th- & 17th-c. slang: said to be clipped form of obs. *fible-fable,* redupl. form of FABLE] a lie about something unimportant —*vi.* **fibbed, fib′bing** to tell such a lie or lies —*SYN.* see LIE[2] —**fib′ber** *n.*

fi·ber, fi·bre (fī′bər) *n.* [Fr. *fibre* < L. *fibra,* ? akin to *filum,* thread: see FILE[1] **1.** *a)* a slender, threadlike structure that combines with others to form animal or vegetable tissue *b)* the tissue so formed [muscle *fiber*] **2.** a slender, threadlike structure made from a mineral or synthetically [rayon *fibers*] **3.** *a)* any substance that can be separated into threads or threadlike structures for spinning, weaving, etc. [cotton *fiber*] *b)* any such thread or structure [wool *fibers*] **4.** a threadlike root **5.** the texture of something [a fabric of coarse *fiber*] **6.** character or nature; quality [a man of strong moral *fiber*] —**fi′ber·like′** *adj.*

fi·ber·board (-bôrd′) *n.* **1.** a flexible boardlike material made from pressed fibers of wood, etc., used in building **2.** a piece of this material

☆**fi·ber·fill** (-fil′) *n.* a resilient, lightweight, fluffy filling for quilts, etc., made of synthetic fibers

☆**Fi·ber·glas** (-glas′, -gläs′) *a trademark for* finespun filaments of glass made into yarn that is woven into textiles, used in woolly masses as insulation, and pressed and molded as plastic material —*n.* [f-] this substance: usually **fiberglass, fiber glass,** or **fiber-glass**

fiber optics 1. the branch of optics dealing with the transmission of light and images, as around bends and curves, through a flexible bundle of plastic optical fibers **2.** the fibers thus used —**fi′ber-op′tic** *adj.*

fibr- *same as* FIBRO-: used before a vowel

fi·bril (fī′brəl) *n.* [< ModL. *fibrilla,* dim. of L. *fibra,* FIBER] **1.** a small fiber **2.** a root hair —**fi′bril·lar** (-brə lər), **fi′bril·lar′y** (-brə ler′ē) *adj.*

fi·bril·la·tion (fib′rə lā′shən, fī′brə-) *n.* [< FIBRIL + -ATION] a rapid, uncoordinated series of contractions of the heart muscle, causing weak, irregular, and ineffectual heartbeats

fi·bril·lose (fī′brə lōs′) *adj.* of or like fibrils

fi·brin (fī′brən) *n.* [FIBR(E) + -IN[1]] an elastic, threadlike, insoluble protein formed from fibrinogen by the action of thrombin in the clotting of blood, and forming the network of the clot

fi·bri·no- (fī′brə nō′) a combining form meaning fibrin [*fibrinosis*]

fi·brin·o·gen (fī brin′ə jən, -jen′) *n.* [prec. + -GEN] a protein of the blood plasma that is converted to fibrin by the action of the enzyme thrombin in the clotting of blood

fi·brin·o·gen·ic (fī′brə nō jen′ik) *adj.* **1.** of or like fibrinogen **2.** able to form fibrin Also **fi′bri·nog′e·nous** (-näj′ə nəs)

fi·bri·nol·y·sin (fī′brə näl′ə sin) *n.* [FIBRINO- + LYSIN] any of various enzymes, as plasmin, capable of digesting fibrin

fi·bri·nol·y·sis (-sis) *n.* [FIBRINO- + -LYSIS] the digestion or dissolution of fibrin —**fi′bri·no·lyc′ic** (-nō lit′ik) *adj.*

fi·brin·ous (fī′brə nəs) *adj.* of, like, or containing fibrin

fi·bro- (fī′brō) [< L. *fibra,* FIBER] *a combining form meaning* of fibrous matter or structure [*fibrosis*]

fi·bro·blast (fī′brə blast′) *n.* [FIBRO- + -BLAST] a large, flat, oval cell found in connective tissue and responsible for the formation of fibers —**fi′bro·blas′tic** *adj.*

fi·broid (fī′broid) *adj.* [FIBR- + -OID] like, composed of, or forming fibrous tissue —*n.* a fibrous tumor, esp. a benign tumor of the uterus

fi·bro·in (fī′brō in) *n.* [FIBRO- + -IN[1]] a white albuminoid protein forming almost the entire thread of a spider and the core of raw silk

fi·bro·ma (fī brō′mə) *n., pl.* **-mas, -ma·ta** (-mə tə) [ModL. < FIBR- + -OMA] a nonmalignant tumor composed largely of fibrous tissue —**fi·bro′ma·tous** (-mə təs) *adj.*

fi·bro·sis (fī brō′sis) *n.* [ModL. < FIBR- + -OSIS] an abnormal increase in the amount of fibrous connective tissue in an organ, part, or tissue —**fi·brot′ic** (-brät′ik) *adj.*

fi·bro·si·tis (fī′brə sīt′is) *n.* [ModL. < *fibrosus,* FIBROUS + -ITIS] an excessive growth of white fibrous tissue, as of the muscle sheaths, resulting from inflammation

fi·brous (fī′brəs) *adj.* [< ModL. *fibrosus*] **1.** containing or composed of fibers **2.** like fiber

fi·bro·vas·cu·lar (fī′brō vas′kyoo lər) *adj.* [FIBRO- + VASCULAR] *Bot.* having or composed of fibers and ducts for transporting a fluid, as sap

fib·ster (fib′stər) *n.* [Colloq.] a person who tells fibs

fib·u·la (fib′yoo lə) *n., pl.* **-lae′** (-lē′), **-las** [L., a clasp, pin (< base of *figere,* to fasten, FIX): the bone, as it appears in man, is like a clasp] **1.** the long, thin, outer bone of the human leg between the knee and the ankle **2.** a similar bone in the hind leg of other animals **3.** in ancient Greece or Rome, a buckle or clasp for fastening garments —**fib′u·lar** (-lər) *adj.*

-fic (fik) [< Fr. & L.; Fr. *-fique* < L. *-ficus* < unstressed form of *facere,* to make, DO[1]] *an adj.-forming suffix meaning* making, creating [*terrific, scientific*]

FICA Federal Insurance Contributions Act

-fi·ca·tion (fi kā′shən) [< Fr. & L.; Fr. *-fication* < L. *-ficatio* < *-ficare,* unstressed combining form of *facere,* to make, DO[1]] *a n.-forming suffix meaning* a making, creating, causing [*calcification, glorification*]

Fich·te (fiH′tə), **Jo·hann Gott·lieb** (yō′hän gôt′lēp) 1762–1814; Ger. philosopher

fich·u (fish′ōō; *Fr.* fē shü′) *n.* [Fr. < pp. of *ficher,* to thrust in, attach < VL. *figicare,* for L. *figere,* FIX] a three-cornered lace or muslin cape for women, worn with the ends fastened or crossed in front

fick·le (fik′'l) *adj.* [ME. *fikel* < OE. *ficol,* tricky < base of *befician,* to deceive, akin to *gefic,* betrayal, deceit: for IE. base see FEY] changeable or unstable in affection, interest, loyalty, etc.; capricious —*SYN.* see INCONSTANT —**fick′le·ness** *n.*

fi·co (fē′kō) *n., pl.* **-coes** [< It. *fico,* fig, *fica,* derisive gesture, vulva < VL. *fica,* for L. *ficus,* FIG[1]] **1.** [Archaic] a worthless trifle; fig **2.** [Obs.] *same as* FIG[1] (sense 4)

fic·tile (fik′t'l; *chiefly Brit.,* -tīl) *adj.* [L. *fictilis* < pp. of *fingere:* see ff.] **1.** that can be molded; plastic **2.** formed of molded clay **3.** of pottery or ceramics

fic·tion (fik′shən) *n.* [ME. *ficcioun* < OFr. *fiction* < L. *fictio,* a making, counterfeiting < pp. of *fingere,* to form, mold: see FIGURE] **1.** a making up of imaginary happenings; feigning **2.** anything made up or imagined, as a statement, story, etc. **3.** *a)* any literary work portraying imaginary characters and events, as a novel, story, or play *b)* such works collectively **4.** *Law* something accepted as fact for the sake of convenience, although not necessarily true —**fic′tion·al** *adj.* —**fic′tion·al·ly** *adv.*

fic·tion·al·ize (-'l īz′) *vt.* **-ized′, -iz′ing** to deal with (historical events, a person's life, etc.) as fiction: also **fic′tion·ize′** —**fic′tion·al·i·za′tion** *n.*

fic·tion·eer (fik′shə nir′) *n.* a prolific writer of mediocre fiction

fic·tion·ist (fik′shən ist) *n.* a writer of fiction

fic·ti·tious (fik tish′əs) *adj.* [L. *ficticius* < pp. of *fingere,* to form, devise: see FIGURE] **1.** of or like fiction; imaginary **2.** not real; pretended; false [*fictitious joy*] **3.** assumed for disguise or deception [a *fictitious* name] —**fic·ti′tious·ly** *adv.*

SYN.—**fictitious** refers to that which is invented by the imagination and is therefore not real, true, or actually existent [Gulliver is a *fictitious* character]; **fabulous** suggests that which is incredible or astounding, but does not necessarily connote nonexistence [the man's wealth is *fabulous*]; **legendary** refers to something that may have a historical basis in fact but, in popular tradition, has undergone great elaboration and exaggeration [the *legendary*

amours of Don Juan*]*; **mythical** basically applies to the highly imaginary explanation of natural or historical phenomena by a people and, therefore, connotes that what it qualifies is a product of the imagination; **apocryphal** suggests that which is of doubtful authenticity or authorship —*ANT.* **real, true, factual**

fic·tive (fik′tiv) *adj.* [Fr. *fictif* < ML. *fictivus*] **1.** of fiction or the production of fiction **2.** not real; imaginary; feigned —**fic′tive·ly** *adv.*

fid (fid) *n.* [Early ModE. naut. term < ?] **1.** a hard, tapering pin for separating the strands of a rope in splicing **2.** a wooden or metal bar or pin for supporting something; specif., a square bar for supporting a topmast

-fid (fid) [L. *-fidus*, split < base of *findere*, to cleave: for IE. base see BITE] *a combining form meaning* split or separated into (a specified number or kind of) parts [*palmatifid*]

fid·dle (fid′'l) *n.* [ME. *fithele* < OE. *fithele* < VL. **vitula*] **1.** any stringed instrument played with a bow, esp. the violin: now usually a familiar or jocular term ☆**2.** [Slang] a petty swindle **3.** *Naut.* a frame or railing on a ship's table to keep dishes, etc. from sliding off in rough weather —*vt.* **-dled, -dling 1.** [Colloq.] to play (a tune) on a fiddle **2.** [Slang] to swindle in a petty way —*vi.* **1.** [Colloq.] to play on a fiddle **2.** to tamper or tinker (*with*), esp. in a nervous way —**fiddle around** [Colloq.] to pass time aimlessly —**fiddle away** to waste (time) —**fit as a fiddle** in excellent health; physically fit

fid·dle-dee-dee (fid′'l dē dē′) *n., interj.* [prob. < prec., with addition of nonsense syllables] nonsense

fid·dle-fad·dle (fid′'l fad′'l) *n., interj.* [redupl. of FIDDLE or obs. *faddle*, to trifle] nonsense —*vi.* [Colloq.] to be concerned with trifles; fuss

fid·dle·head (-hed′) *n.* **1.** a carved decoration on a ship's bow, curved like the scroll of a violin head **2.** *same as* CROSIER (sense 2)

fid·dler (fid′lər) *n.* **1.** a person who fiddles ☆**2.** *same as* FIDDLER CRAB

☆**fiddler crab** a small, burrowing crab (genus *Uca*), the male of which has one claw much larger than the other

fid·dle·stick (fid′'l stik′) *n.* **1.** the bow for a fiddle **2.** a trifle; mere nothing

fid·dle·sticks (-stiks′) *interj.* nonsense!

fid·dle·wood (-wood′) *n.* **1.** any of several tropical American timber trees (family Verbenaceae) valuable for their hard wood **2.** the wood

fid·dling (fid′liŋ) *adj.* **1.** that plays the fiddle **2.** trifling; useless; petty

fi·de·ism (fē′dā iz′m, fī′dē iz′m) *n.* [ModL. *fideismus* < L. *fides*, FAITH + *-ismus*, -ISM] the belief that faith alone is the basis of knowledge rather than reason —**fi′de·ist** *n.* —**fi′de·is′tic** *adj.*

Fi·del·is·mo (fē′del ēz′mō) *n.* [AmSp. < *Fidel* Castro + *-ismo*, -ISM] [*also* f-] the social revolution in Cuba led by Fidel Castro, or its principles

Fi·del·is·ta (-ēs′tə) *n.* [*also* f-] an adherent of Fidelismo

fi·del·i·ty (fə del′ə tē, fī-) *n., pl.* **-ties** [ME. *fidelite* < OFr. < L. *fidelitas* < *fidelis*, faithful, trusty < *fides*, FAITH] **1.** faithful devotion to duty or to one's obligations or vows; loyalty; faithfulness **2.** accuracy of a description, translation, etc. or of the reproduction of sound, an image, etc. —*SYN.* see ALLEGIANCE

fidg·et (fij′it) *n.* [< obs. *fidge*, to fidget < ME. *fichen* < ? or akin to ON. *fikja*, to fidget] **1.** the state of being restless, nervous, or uneasy **2.** a fidgety person —*vi.* to move about in a restless, nervous, or uneasy way —*vt.* to make restless or uneasy —**the fidgets** restless, uneasy feelings or movements

fidg·et·y (-ē) *adj.* nervous; uneasy —**fidg′et·i·ness** *n.*

fi·du·cial (fi dōō′shəl, -dyōō′-) *adj.* [L. *fiducialis* < *fiducia*, trust: see ff.] **1.** based on firm faith **2.** used as a standard of reference for measurement or calculation [a *fiducial* point] **3.** *same as* FIDUCIARY

fi·du·ci·ar·y (-shē er′ē, -shə rē) *adj.* [L. *fiduciarius* < *fiducia*, trust, thing held in trust < *fidere*, to trust: see FAITH] **1.** designating or of a person who holds something in trust for another; of a trustee or trusteeship [a *fiduciary* guardian for a minor child] **2.** held in trust [*fiduciary* property] **3.** valuable only because of public confidence and support: said of certain paper money —*n., pl.* **-ar′ies** a trustee

fie (fī) *interj.* [ME. *fi* < OFr., of echoic origin, as in L. *fu*, Gr. *phy*] for shame!: now often used in mock reproach

fief (fēf) *n.* [Fr.: see FEE] **1.** under feudalism, heritable land held from a lord in return for service **2.** the right to hold such land

field (fēld) *n.* [ME. *feld* < OE., akin to G. *feld*, Du. *veld* < IE. **pelt-* < base **pele-*, **pla-*, flat and broad, whence L. *planus*, plane, Gr. *palamē*, flat hand] **1.** a wide stretch of open land; plain **2.** a piece of cleared land, set off or enclosed, for raising crops or pasturing livestock **3.** a piece of land used for some particular purpose [a landing *field*] **4.** an area of land producing some natural resource [a gold *field*] **5.** any wide, unbroken expanse [a *field* of ice] **6.** *a)* a battlefield *b)* a battle **7.** *a)* an area of military operations *b)* a military area away from the post or headquarters **8.** *a)* an area where practical work is done, as by a social worker, geologist, etc., away from the central office, laboratory, or the like *b)* a realm of knowledge or of special work or opportunity [the *field* of electronics] **9.** an area of observation, as in a microscope **10.** the background, as on a flag or coin **11.** *a)* an area where games or athletic events are held *b)* the part of such an area, usually inside a closed racing track, where contests in the high jump, long jump, shot put, pole vault, etc. are held ☆*c)* in baseball, the outfield *d)* all the entrants in a contest *e)* all the active players on the field, as in baseball or football *f)* all the entrants in a contest except the one(s) specified *g)* the team not at bat, as in baseball, cricket, etc. **12.** *Heraldry* the surface or part of the surface of a shield **13.** *Math.* a set of numbers or other algebraic elements for which arithmetic operations (except by zero) are defined in a consistent manner to yield another element of the set **14.** *Physics* a space within which magnetic or electrical lines of force are active **15.** *TV a)* the area viewed by the camera *b)* the area that the scanning element covers in one vertical sweep —*adj.* **1.** of, operating in, or held on the field or fields **2.** growing in fields; having a field as its habitat —*vt. Baseball, Cricket,* etc. **1.** to stop or catch or to catch and throw (a ball) in play **2.** to put (a player) into a field position —*vi. Baseball, Cricket,* etc. to play as a fielder —**keep** (or **hold**) **the field** to continue activity, as in games, military operations, etc. —**play the field** to take a broad area of operations; not confine one's activities to one object —**take** (or **leave**) **the field** to begin (or withdraw from) activity in a game, military operation, etc.

Field (fēld) **1. Cyrus West,** 1819–92; U.S. industrialist: promoted the first transatlantic cable **2. Eugene,** 1850–95; U.S. journalist & poet

field army *same as* ARMY (sense 2)

field artillery movable artillery capable of accompanying an army into battle

field battery a number of field artillery pieces, usually four, employed as a unit

☆**field corn** any variety or strain of corn (maize) grown for feeding livestock

field day 1. a day devoted to military exercises and display ☆**2.** a day of athletic events and contests ☆**3.** a day spent in outdoor scientific study **4.** a day of enjoyably exciting events or highly successful activity

field·er (-ər) *n. Baseball, Cricket,* etc. a player in the field

☆**fielder's choice** *Baseball* an attempt by a fielder to retire a runner already on base rather than the batter: the batter is not credited with a base hit if he reaches first base safely

field event any of the contests held on the field in a track meet, as the high jump, shot put, etc.

field·fare (-fer′) *n.* [ME. *feldefare*, altered (after *faren*, FARE) < OE. *feldeware*, lit., "field-dweller" < *feld*, FIELD + *wærian*, to guard, inhabit: ? folk etym.] a European thrush (*Turdus pilaris*) with a grayish head and brown wings

field glass a small, portable, binocular telescope: *usually used in pl.* (**field glasses**)

☆**field goal 1.** *Basketball* a basket toss made from play, scoring two points **2.** *Football* a goal kicked from the field, scoring three points

☆**field hand 1.** orig., a plantation slave who worked in the fields **2.** a hired farm laborer

field hockey *same as* HOCKEY (sense 2)

field hospital a temporary military hospital near the combat zone, for emergency treatment

☆**field house 1.** a building near an athletic field, with lockers, showers, etc. for the athletes' use **2.** a large building for basketball games, indoor track meets, etc.

Field·ing (fēl′diŋ), **Henry** 1707–54; Eng. novelist

field magnet the magnet used to create and maintain the magnetic field in a motor or generator

field marshal in some armies, an officer of the highest rank

field mouse any of several kinds of mice (genus *Microtus*) that live in fields

field music 1. military musicians, as buglers, drummers, etc. **2.** their music

field officer a colonel, lieutenant colonel, or major in the army

field of force *same as* FIELD (*n.* 14)

field of honor 1. a dueling place **2.** a battleground

field pea a strain of the common pea (*Pisum sativum arvense*) of the legume family, with mottled leaves and purplish flowers, grown for forage

field·piece (-pēs′) *n.* a mobile artillery piece

fields·man (fēldz′mən) *n., pl.* **-men** (-mən) a fielder in cricket

field sparrow ☆a rust-colored N. American sparrow (*Spizella pusilla*) with a whitish belly

☆**field-strip** (-strip′) *vt.* **-stripped′, -strip′ping** to disassemble (a firearm) for cleaning and inspection

☆**field-test** (-test′) *vt.* to test (a device, method, etc.) under actual operating conditions

FIDDLER CRAB
(width to 1 2/3 in., length to 1 in.)

field theory the concept that, within the space in the vicinity of a particle, there exists a field containing energy and momentum, and that this field interacts with neighboring particles and their fields

field trial a competition in which the performance of hunting dogs is tested in the field

field trip a trip away from the classroom to permit the gathering of data at first hand

field winding the winding of a field magnet

field·work (fēld'wurk') *n.* **1.** any temporary fortification, as an earthen barrier, made by troops in the field **2.** the work of collecting scientific data in the field, as by a geologist, botanist, etc. —**field'work'er** *n.*

fiend (fēnd) *n.* [ME. *fend, feend* < OE. *feond,* lit., the one hating, orig. prp. < base of *feogan,* to hate, akin to Goth. *fijands* < *fijan,* to hate: for IE. base see FEY] **1.** an evil spirit; devil **2.** an inhumanly wicked or cruel person ☆**3.** [Colloq.] *a)* a person addicted to some activity, habit, etc. [a dope *fiend,* fresh-air *fiend*] *b)* a person who is excellent at some activity [a *fiend* at tennis] —**the Fiend** the Devil; Satan

fiend·ish (-ish) *adj.* **1.** of or like a fiend; devilish; inhumanly wicked or cruel **2.** extremely vexatious or difficult —**fiend'ish·ly** *adv.* —**fiend'ish·ness** *n.*

fierce (firs) *adj.* **fierc'er, fierc'est** [ME. *fers* < OFr. *fers, fier* < L. *ferus,* wild, savage < IE. base **ĝhwer-,* wild animal, whence Gr. *thēr,* animal] **1.** of a violently cruel nature; savage; wild [a *fierce* dog] **2.** violent; uncontrolled [a *fierce* storm] **3.** intensely eager; intense; ardent [a *fierce* effort] ☆**4.** [Colloq.] very distasteful, disagreeable, bad, etc. —**fierce'ly** *adv.* —**fierce'ness** *n.*

fi·er·y (fī'ər ē) *adj.* **-er·i·er, -er·i·est** [ME. *firi*] **1.** containing or consisting of fire **2.** like fire; glaring, hot, etc. **3.** characterized by strong emotion; ardent; spirited [*fiery* words] **4.** easily stirred up; excitable [a *fiery* nature] **5.** easily set on fire; flammable [*fiery* fumes] **6.** inflamed [a *fiery* sore] —**fi'er·i·ly** *adv.* —**fi'er·i·ness** *n.*

fiery cross 1. a wooden cross with charred or bloody ends, used by ancient Scottish clans as a signal calling men to battle ☆**2.** a burning cross, used by the Ku Klux Klan as an emblem or to inspire terror

Fie·so·le (fye'zō le), **Gio·van·ni da** (jō vän'nē dä) *see* Fra ANGELICO

☆**fi·es·ta** (fē es'tə) *n.* [Sp. < VL. *festa:* see FEAST] **1.** a religious festival; esp., a saint's day **2.** any gala celebration; holiday

Fife (fīf) county of E Scotland, on the Firth of Forth: 505 sq. mi.; pop. 321,000: also **Fife'shire** (-shir)

fife (fīf) *n.* [G. *pfeife,* a pipe, fife < MHG. *pfīfe* < OHG. *pfīfa* < VL. **pīpa,* PIPE] a small, shrill-toned musical instrument resembling a flute, used mainly with drums in playing marches —*vt., vi.* **fifed, fif'ing** to play on a fife —**fif'er** *n.*

fife rail a rail around a ship's mast to hold belaying pins for the rigging

fif·teen (fif'tēn') *adj.* [ME. *fiftene* < OE.: see FIVE & -TEEN] five more than ten —*n.* the cardinal number between fourteen and sixteen; 15; XV

fif·teenth (-tēnth') *adj.* [ME. *fiftenthe* < *fifteotha* < *fiftene:* see prec. & -TH²] **1.** preceded by fourteen others in a series; 15th **2.** designating any of the fifteen equal parts of something —*n.* **1.** the one following the fourteenth **2.** any of the fifteen equal parts of something; 1/15

fifth (fifth) *adj.* [ME. *fifte* < OE. *fifta* < *fif,* FIVE] **1.** preceded by four others in a series; 5th **2.** designating any of the five equal parts of something —*n.* **1.** the one following the fourth **2.** any of the five equal parts of something; 1/5 ☆**3.** a fifth of a gallon **4.** *Music a)* the fifth tone of an ascending diatonic scale, or a tone four degrees above or below any given tone in such a scale; dominant *b)* the interval between two such tones, or a combination of them —**fifth'ly** *adv.*

☆**Fifth Amendment** an amendment to the U.S. Constitution mainly guaranteeing certain protections in criminal cases, specif. the clause protecting a person from being compelled to be a witness against himself

fifth column [first used by the Sp. Nationalist General Mola (1936), who, besieging Madrid with four columns from the outside, boasted of having a "fifth column" within] **1.** those people in Madrid who aided the forces of Francisco Franco in his uprising against the Spanish republic (1936–39) **2.** any group of people who give aid and support to the enemy from within their own country —**fifth columnist**

Fifth Republic the republic set up in France in 1958

fifth wheel 1. a horizontal wheellike structure placed over the front axle of a vehicle to support it on turns **2.** an unnecessary or superfluous person or thing

fif·ti·eth (fif'tē ith) *adj.* [ME. *fiftithe* < OE. *fiftigotha* < *fiftig:* see ff. & -TH²] **1.** preceded by forty-nine others in a series; 50th **2.** designating any of the fifty equal parts of something —*n.* **1.** the one following the forty-ninth **2.** any of fifty equal parts of something; 1/50

fif·ty (fif'tē) *adj.* [ME. *fifti* < OE. *fiftig:* see FIVE & -TY²] five times ten —*n., pl.* **-ties** the cardinal number between forty-nine and fifty-one; 50; L —**the fifties** the numbers or years, as of a century, from fifty through fifty-nine

☆**fif·ty-fif·ty** (fif'tē fif'tē) *adj.* [Colloq.] having equal shares; equal; even —*adv.* [Colloq.] equally

fig¹ (fig) *n.* [ME. *fige* < OFr. < VL. **fica,* for L. *ficus,* fig tree, fig] **1.** the hollow, pear-shaped false fruit (syconium) of the fig tree, with sweet, pulpy flesh containing numerous, tiny, seedlike true fruits (achenes) **2.** any of a genus (*Ficus*) of fig-bearing trees of the mulberry family, esp. a cultivated tree (*Ficus carica*) bearing edible figs **3.** a trifling amount; little bit [not worth a *fig*] **4.** a gesture of contempt or disdain made as by placing the thumb between the first two fingers or under the upper teeth

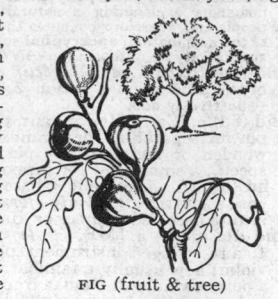
FIG (fruit & tree)

fig² (fig) *vt.* **figged, fig'ging** [altered < obs. *feague,* to whip, polish; confused with the contr. for FIGURE, prob. from the use of this contracted form in reference to plates in books of fashions] to dress showily (with *out* or *up*) —*n.* [Colloq.] **1.** dress; appearance **2.** shape; condition —**in full fig** [Colloq.] completely dressed or outfitted, esp. in a showy manner

fig. 1. figurative **2.** figuratively **3.** figure; figures

fig·eat·er (-ēt'ər) *n.* ☆a large, green, velvety beetle (*Cotinus nitida*), the adults of which feed on ripe fruit: the June bug of the southeastern U.S.

fight (fīt) *vi.* **fought, fight'ing** [ME. *fighten* < OE. *feohtan,* akin to G. *fechten* < IE. base **pek-,* to pluck hair or wool, whence OE. *feoh* (see FEE) & L. *pecten,* a comb] **1.** *a)* to take part in a physical struggle or battle; struggle *b)* to box, esp. professionally **2.** to struggle or work hard in trying to beat or overcome someone or something; contend —*vt.* **1.** *a)* to oppose physically or in battle, as with fists, weapons, etc. *b)* to box with in a contest **2.** to try to overcome; struggle against or contend with, as by argument, legislation, etc. **3.** to engage in or carry on (a war, conflict, case, etc.) **4.** to gain by struggle [to *fight* one's way to the top] **5.** to cause to fight; manage (a boxer, gamecock, etc.) —*n.* [ME. < OE. *feoht*] **1.** a physical struggle; battle; combat **2.** any struggle, contest, or quarrel **3.** power or readiness to fight; pugnacious spirit [full of *fight*] —*SYN.* see CONFLICT —**fight it out** to fight until one side is defeated —**fight off** to fight to keep away; struggle to avoid

fight·er (-ər) *n.* **1.** one that fights or is inclined to fight **2.** a prizefighter; pugilist **3.** a small, fast, highly maneuverable airplane for aerial combat

☆**fighting chance** a chance to win or succeed, but only after a hard struggle

☆**fighting words** a remark that stirs up antagonism

fig leaf 1. a leaf of a fig tree **2.** a representation of such a leaf used, as in sculpture, to conceal the genitals of a nude figure

fig marigold any of a genus (*Mesembryanthemum*) of fleshy plants of the carpetweed family, with showy flowers, grown in warm, dry climates

fig·ment (fig'mənt) *n.* [ME. < L. *figmentum* < *fingere,* to make, devise: see FIGURE] something merely imagined or made up in the mind

fig·u·line (fig'yoo lin, -līn') *adj.* [L. *figulinus* < *figulus,* a potter < *fingere:* see FIGURE] [Rare] of or like clay —*n.* a clay pot, statue, etc.

fig·u·ral (fig'yər əl) *adj.* of or made up of figures, as a painting; representational

fig·u·rant (fig'yə rant'; *Fr.* fē gü rän') *n.* [Fr., masc. prp. of *figurer,* to FIGURE] **1.** a member of a corps de ballet **2.** a supernumerary on the stage —**fig'u·rante'** (-rant'; *Fr.* -ränt') *n.fem.*

fig·u·ra·tion (fig'yə rā'shən) *n.* [ME. *figuracioun* < L. *figuratio* < *figuratus:* see ff.] **1.** a forming; shaping **2.** form; appearance **3.** representation or symbolization **4.** *Music* the use of incidental figures —**fig'u·ra'tion·al** *adj.*

fig·u·ra·tive (fig'yər ə tiv) *adj.* [ME. < OFr. *figuratif* < LL. *figurativus* < L. *figuratus,* pp. of *figurare,* to form, fashion < *figura,* FIGURE] **1.** representing by means of a figure, symbol, or likeness **2.** having to do with figure drawing, painting, etc. **3.** not in its original, usual, literal, or exact sense or reference; representing one concept in terms of another that may be thought of as analogous with it; metaphorical [in "screaming headlines," the word "screaming" is a *figurative* use] **4.** containing or using figures of speech —**fig'u·ra·tive·ly** *adv.*

fig·ure (fig'yər; *chiefly Brit.* fig'ər) *n.* [ME. < OFr. < L. *figura* < *fingere,* to form, shape < IE. base **dheigh-,* to knead (clay, dough), whence DOUGH] **1.** the outline or shape of something; form **2.** the shape of the human body; human form **3.** a person, esp. one seen or thought of in a specified way [a great social *figure*] **4.** a likeness or representation of a person or thing **5.** an illustration; diagram; picture; drawing **6.** an artistic design in fabrics, etc.; pattern **7.** *a)* the symbol for a number [the *figure* 5] *b)* [pl.] calculation with such symbols; arithmetic [very good at *figures*] **8.** a sum of money **9.** *Dancing & Skating* a series or pattern of steps or movements **10.** *Geom.* a

surface or space bounded on all sides by lines or planes **11.** *Logic* the form of a syllogism with reference to the position of the middle term **12.** *Music* a series of consecutive tones or chords forming a distinct group which with other similar groups completes a phrase or theme; motif **13.** *Rhetoric* same as FIGURE OF SPEECH —*vt.* **-ured, -ur·ing** [ME. *figuren* < the *n.*] **1.** to represent in definite form; give a shape to **2.** to represent mentally; imagine **3.** to ornament with a design **4.** to compute with figures **5.** [Colloq.] to believe; consider; decide **6.** to represent by a figure of speech **7.** *Music* to indicate chords for (the bass) by writing the appropriate figures next to the notes —*vi.* **1.** to appear prominently; be conspicuous **2.** to do arithmetic ☆**3.** [Colloq.] to consider; calculate ☆**4.** [Colloq.] to be just as expected or as anticipated —*SYN.* see FORM —**figure in** ☆to add in; include —☆**figure on 1.** to count on; rely on **2.** to consider as part of a scheme or project; plan on —☆**figure out 1.** to solve; compute **2.** to understand; reason out —**fig'ur·er** *n.*

fig·ured (-yərd) *adj.* **1.** shaped; formed **2.** represented or shown by a picture, diagram, etc. **3.** having a design or pattern **4.** *Music* marked with figures (Arabic numerals) representing the appropriate accompanying chords: said of the bass

fig·ure·head (fig'yər hed') *n.* **1.** a carved figure on the bow of a ship **2.** a person put in a position of leadership because of his name, rank, etc., but having no real power, authority, or responsibility

fig·ure-of-eight knot (-əv āt') a kind of knot: see KNOT, illus.

figure of speech an expression, as a metaphor or simile, using words in a nonliteral or unusual sense to add vividness, beauty, etc. to what is said

figure skating ice skating in which the performer traces various elaborate figures on the ice

fig·u·rine (fig'yə rēn') *n.* [Fr. < It. *figurina*, dim. of *figura* < L.: see FIGURE] a small sculptured or molded figure; statuette

fig wasp any of a family (Agaontidae) of small wasps living in certain figs, esp. a wasp (*Blastophaga psenes*) active in the pollination of certain cultivated strains

fig·wort (fig'wurt') *adj.* designating a large family (Scrophulariaceae) of plants including the foxglove, snapdragon, etc. —*n.* any of a genus (*Scrophularia*) of plants of the figwort family, with square stems and small flowers

Fi·ji (fē'jē) country occupying a group of islands (**Fiji Islands**) in the SW Pacific, north of New Zealand: a member of the Brit. Commonwealth: c. 7,000 sq. mi.; pop. 512,000; cap. Suva

Fi·ji·an (fē'jē ən) *adj.* of the Fiji Islands, their people, language, or culture —*n.* **1.** a member of a Melanesian people of the Fiji Islands **2.** their Melanesian language

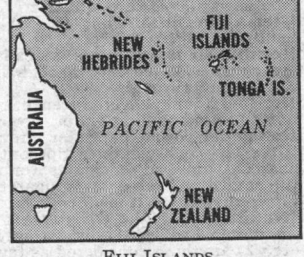

FIJI ISLANDS

fi·la (fī'lə) *n.* *pl.* of FILUM

fil·a·ment (fil'ə mənt) *n.* [Fr. < ML. *filamentum* < VL. *filare*, to spin < L. *filum*: see FILE¹] **1.** a very slender thread or fiber **2.** a threadlike part; specif., *a)* the fine metal wire in a light bulb which becomes incandescent when heated by an electric current *b)* the cathode of a thermionic tube, usually in the form of a wire, which may be electrically heated **3.** *Bot.* the stalk of a stamen bearing the anther —**fil'a·men'ta·ry** (-men'tər ē) *adj.* —**fil'a·men'tous** (-men'təs) *adj.*

fi·lar (fī'lər) *adj.* [< L. *filum*, a thread (see FILE¹) + -AR] **1.** of a thread **2.** having fine threads or hairs stretched across the field of view, as a micrometer

fi·lar·i·a (fi ler'ē ə) *n., pl.* **fi·lar'i·ae** (-ē ē') [ModL. < L. *filum*: see FILE¹] any of several kinds of threadlike parasitic worms (order Filarioidea) that live in the blood and tissues of vertebrate animals: they are carried and transmitted by mosquitoes and other invertebrates —**fi·lar'i·al, fi·lar'i·an** *adj.*

fi·lar·i·a·sis (fil'ə rī'ə sis) *n.* [ModL.: see FILARIA] a disease caused by filarial worms transmitted by mosquitoes: the worms invade lymphatic vessels and lymphoid tissue, causing chronic swelling of the lower extremities and other parts of the body

fil·a·ture (fil'ə chər) *n.* [Fr. < pp. of VL. *filare*, to spin < *filum*, a thread: see FILE¹] **1.** a spinning into threads **2.** *a)* a reeling of raw silk from cocoons *b)* a reel for this *c)* a place where this is done

fil·bert (fil'bərt) *n.* [ME. *filberde, philliberd*, prob. via ONormFr. (*noix de*) *filbert*, (nut of) Philibert < St. *Philibert*, whose feast came in the nutting season] **1.** the edible nut of a cultivated European hazel tree (*Corylus avellana* or *Corylus maxima*) of the birch family **2.** a tree bearing this nut **3.** *same as* HAZELNUT

filch (filch) *vt.* [ME. *filchen*] to steal (usually something small or petty); pilfer —*SYN.* see STEAL

file¹ (fil) *vt.* **filed, fil'ing** [ME. *filen* < OFr. *filer*, to string documents on thread, orig., to spin thread < VL. *filare*, to spin < L. *filum*, thread < IE. base *gwhislo-*, whence Lith. *gýsla*, sinew] **1.** *a)* to arrange (papers, etc.) in order for future reference *b)* to put (a paper, etc.) in its proper place or order ☆**2.** to dispatch (a news story) to a newspaper office **3.** to register (an application, etc.) **4.** to put (a legal document) on public record **5.** to initiate (a divorce suit or other legal action) —*vi.* **1.** to move in a line [to *file* out of a building] ☆**2.** to register oneself as a candidate (*for* a political office) **3.** to make application (*for* divorce proceedings, etc.) —*n.* [senses 1 & 2 < the *v.*; 3 & 4 < Fr. *file* < L. *filum*] **1.** a container, as a folder, cabinet, etc., for keeping papers in order **2.** an orderly arrangement of papers, cards, etc., as for reference **3.** a line of persons or things situated one behind another: cf. RANK **4.** any of the vertical rows of squares on a chessboard —**in file** in line, one behind another —**on file** kept as in a file for reference —**file'a·ble** *adj.* —**fil'er** *n.*

file² (fil) *n.* [ME. < OE. *feol* (Mercian *fil*), akin to G. *feile* < Du. *vijl*, prob. < IE. base *peik-*, to scratch, prick, whence L. *pingere* (see PICTURE), Gr. *pikros*, sharp] **1.** a steel tool with a rough, ridged surface for smoothing, grinding down, or cutting through something **2.** [Brit. Slang] a crafty rascal —*vt.* **filed, fil'ing** to smooth, grind down, or cut through as with a file

file³ (fil) *vt.* **filed, fil'ing** [ME. *filen* < OE. *-fylan* < *ful*, dirty, FOUL] [Archaic] to make foul; defile

☆**fi·lé** (fi lā') *n.* [AmFr. < Fr., pp. of *filer*, to twist, spin < L. *filare* < *filum*, a thread: see FILE¹] powdered sassafras leaves, used in Creole cooking

file clerk a person hired to keep office files in order

file·fish (fil'fish') *n., pl.* **-fish', -fish'es** see FISH² any of various fishes (family Balistidae) with a compressed body and very small, rough scales

fi·let (fi lā', fil'ā) *n.* [ME. < OFr.: see FILLET] **1.** a net or lace with a simple pattern on a square mesh background **2.** *same as* FILLET (*n.* 6) —*vt.* **-leted** (-lād'), **-let'ing** (-lā'iŋ) *same as* FILLET (*vt.* 2)

fi·let mi·gnon (fi lā' min yōn', -yän'; *Fr.* fē le mē nyōn') [Fr., lit., tiny fillet] a thick, round cut of lean beef tenderloin broiled, usually with mushrooms and bacon

fil·i·al (fil'ē əl, fil'yəl) *adj.* [ME. < LL.(Ec.) *filialis*, of a son or daughter < L. *filius*, son, *filia*, daughter < base of *femina*, fetus: see FEMALE] **1.** of, suitable to, or due from a son or daughter [*filial* devotion] **2.** *Genetics* designating or of any generation following the parental: the first filial generation is designated F₁, the second (produced from the first) F₂, etc.

fil·i·a·tion (fil'ē ā'shən) *n.* [ME. *filiacion* < OFr. *filiation* < LL. *filiatio* < L. *filius*, a son, *filia*, a daughter: see prec.] **1.** the state or fact of being a son or daughter; relation of a child to its parent **2.** descent from or as from a parent; derivation **3.** *a)* the forming of a new branch or affiliation of a society, etc. *b)* such a branch **4.** *Law* the determination by a court of the paternity of a child

fil·i·beg (fil'ə beg') *n.* [Gael. *feileadh beag* < *feileadh*, a fold + *beag*, little] a kilt

fil·i·bus·ter (fil'ə bus'tər) *n.* [Sp. *filibustero* < MDu. *vrijbuiter*, freebooter < *vrij*, FREE + *buit*, BOOTY] **1.** an adventurer who engages in unauthorized warfare against a country with which his own country is at peace; specif., any of the 19th-cent. U.S. adventurers who led armed expeditions into Latin-American countries; freebooter ☆**2.** a member of a legislative body, esp. of the Senate, who obstructs the passage of a bill by making long speeches, introducing irrelevant issues, etc.: also **fil'i·bus'ter·er** ☆**3.** the use of such methods to obstruct a bill —*vi.* **1.** to engage in unauthorized warfare as a freebooter ☆**2.** to engage in a filibuster —*vt.* ☆to obstruct the passage of (a bill) by a filibuster

fil·i·cide (fil'ə sīd') *n.* [< L. *filius*, son, *filia*, daughter (see FILIAL) + -CIDE] **1.** the act of murdering one's child **2.** a parent who does this —**fil'i·cid'al** *adj.*

fil·i·form (fil'ə fôrm', fi'lə-) *adj.* [< L. *filum*, a thread (see FILE¹) + -FORM] having the form of a thread or filament

fil·i·gree (fil'ə grē') *n.* [altered from earlier *filigrain* < Fr. *filigrane* < It. *filigrana* < L. *filum*, a thread (see FILE¹) + *granum*, GRAIN] **1.** delicate, lacelike ornamental work of intertwined wire of gold, silver, etc. **2.** any delicate work or design like this —*adj.* like, made of, or made into filigree —*vt.* **-greed', -gree'ing** to ornament with filigree

fil·ing (fil'iŋ) *n.* a small piece, as of metal, scraped off with a file: *usually used in pl.*

FILES
(A, mill; B, knife; C, taper; D, flat bastard)

Fil·i·pine (fil′ə pēn′) *adj. same as* PHILIPPINE

Fil·i·pi·no (fil′ə pē′nō) *n.* [Sp.] **1.** *pl.* **-nos** a native or citizen of the Philippines **2.** *see also* PILIPINO —*adj.* Philippine

fill (fil) *vt.* [ME. *fillen, fullen* < OE. *fyllan* < base of *full,* FULL¹] **1.** *a)* to put as much as possible into; make full *b)* to put a considerable quantity of something into [to *fill* the tub for a bath, to *fill* one's life with joy] **2.** *a)* to take up or occupy all or nearly all the capacity, area, or extent of [the crowd *filled* the room] *b)* to spread or be diffused throughout **3.** *a)* to occupy (an office, position, etc.) *b)* to put a person into (an office, position, etc.) ☆**4.** to fulfill (an engagement to perform, speak, etc.) ☆**5.** *a)* to supply the things needed or called for in (an order, prescription, etc.) *b)* to satisfy (a need, requirement, etc.) **6.** *a)* to close or plug (holes, cracks, etc.) *b)* to insert a filling in (a tooth) **7.** to satisfy the hunger or desire of; feed or satiate ☆**8.** to raise the level of (low land) by adding earth, gravel, etc. **9.** *Naut. a)* to swell (a sail) *b)* to trim (a sail) so as to catch the wind on the after side ☆**10.** *Poker* to draw the card or cards needed to complete (a straight, flush, or full house) —*vi.* to become full —*n.* **1.** all that is needed to make full **2.** all that is needed to satisfy [to eat or drink one's *fill*] ☆**3.** anything that fills or is used to fill; esp., earth, gravel, etc. used for filling a hole or depression ☆**4.** a piece of land artificially raised to a required level, as a railroad embankment —**fill away** *Naut.* to move along with the wind: said of a ship —**fill in 1.** to fill with some substance **2.** to make complete by inserting or supplying something **3.** to insert or supply for completion ☆**4.** to be a substitute —☆**fill one in on** [Colloq.] to provide one with additional facts, details, etc. about —**fill out 1.** to make or become larger, rounder, shapelier, etc. ☆**2.** to make (a document, etc.) complete by inserting or supplying information —**fill up** to make or become completely full

†**fille** (fē′y′) *n.* [Fr. < L. *filia:* see FILIAL] **1.** a daughter **2.** a girl; maid **3.** a spinster

†**fille de joie** (də zhwä′) [Fr., lit., daughter of joy] a prostitute

filled gold brass or other base metal covered with a layer of gold

☆**filled milk** skimmed milk with vegetable oils added to increase the fat content

fill·er (fil′ər) *n.* a person or thing that fills; specif., *a)* matter added to some other to increase bulk, improve consistency, etc. *b)* a preparation used to fill in the cracks, grain, etc. of wood before painting or varnishing *c)* the tobacco rolled in the leaf of a cigar *d)* a short, space-filling item in a newspaper *e)* a pad of paper to be inserted into a loose-leaf notebook, etc. *f)* *Archit.* a small joist resting on a girder

fil·lér (fēl′er) *n., pl.* **-lér, -lérs** [Hung.] a Hungarian monetary unit equal to 1/100 of a forint

fil·let (fil′it; *for n. 6 & vt. 2, usually* fil′ā, fi lā′) *n.* [ME. *filet* < OFr., dim. of *fil:* see FILE¹] **1.** a narrow band worn around the head as to hold the hair in place **2.** a thin strip or band **3.** *same as* FAIRING¹ **4.** *Archit. a)* a flat, square molding separating other moldings *b)* a narrow band between two flutings in a column **5.** *Bookbinding* an ornamental line impressed on a book cover **6.** *Cooking* a boneless, lean piece of meat or fish **7.** *Heraldry* a horizontal band on a shield, just below the chief and one-fourth its width —*vt.* **1.** to bind or decorate with a band, molding, etc. **2.** to bone and slice (meat or fish)

fill-in (fil′in′) *n.* **1.** a person or thing that fills a vacancy or gap, often temporarily ☆**2.** [Colloq.] a brief summary of the pertinent facts —*adj.* of or by a fill-in

fill·ing (fil′iŋ) *n.* **1.** the act of one that fills **2.** a thing used to fill something else or to supply what is lacking; specif., *a)* the metal, plastic, etc. inserted by a dentist into a prepared cavity in a tooth *b)* the foodstuff used between the slices of a sandwich, in a pastry shell, etc. ☆**3.** the horizontal threads crossing the warp in a woven fabric; woof

☆**filling station** *same as* SERVICE STATION (sense 2)

fil·lip (fil′əp) *n.* [echoic extension of FLIP¹ (cf. CHIRRUP, CHIRP)] **1.** the snap made by a finger which is held down toward the palm by the thumb and then suddenly released **2.** a light blow or tap given in this way **3.** anything that stimulates or livens up; piquant element —*vt.* **1.** to strike, impel, or snap with a fillip **2.** to stimulate or liven up —*vi.* to make a fillip

FILLIP

☆**fil·li·peen** (fil′ə pēn′) *n. same as* PHILOPENA

fil·lis·ter (fil′is tər) *n.* [< ?] **1.** a plane for cutting grooves **2.** a groove, as for receiving the glass in a window frame

Fill·more (fil′môr), **Mill·ard** (mil′ərd) 1800–74; 13th president of the U.S. (1850–53)

fil·ly (fil′ē) *n., pl.* **-lies** [ME. *filli* < ON. *fylja,* fem. of *foli,* FOAL] **1.** a young female horse, specif. one under five years of age **2.** [Colloq.] a vivacious young woman or girl

film (film) *n.* [ME. < OE. *filmen,* membrane, foreskin: for IE. base see FELL⁴] **1.** a fine, thin skin, surface, layer, or coating **2.** a sheet or roll of a flexible cellulose material covered with a substance sensitive to light and used in taking photographs or making motion pictures **3.** a thin veil, haze, or blur **4.** an opacity of the cornea **5.** a motion picture **6.** *a)* a fine filament *b)* a gauzy web of filaments —*vt.* **1.** to cover with or as with a film **2.** to take a photograph of **3.** to make a motion picture of (a novel, play, etc.) —*vi.* **1.** to become covered with a film **2.** *a)* to make a motion picture *b)* to be filmed or suitable for filming [this novel won't *film* well] —**film′er** *n.*

film·ic (fil′mik) *adj.* of or having to do with motion pictures or the art of making them

film pack several sheets of photographic film in a frame that fits in the back of a camera

film·strip (-strip′) *n.* a length of film containing still photographs, often of illustrations, diagrams, charts, etc., arranged in sequence for projection separately and used as a teaching aid

film·y (fil′mē) *adj.* **film′i·er, film′i·est 1.** of or like a film; hazy, gauzy, etc. **2.** covered with or as with a film; blurred —**film′i·ly** *adv.* —**film′i·ness** *n.*

fi·lo·po·di·um (fil′ə pō′dē əm, fī′lə-) *n., pl.* **-di·a** (-ə) [ModL. < L. *filum,* thread (see FILE¹) + -PODIUM] a thin, narrow pseudopodium consisting primarily of ectoplasm

fi·lose (fī′lōs) *adj.* [< L. *filum* (see FILE¹) + -OSE²] **1.** threadlike **2.** having a threadlike projection

☆**fils¹** (fēs) *n.* [Fr. < L. *filius:* see FILIAL] a son or a youth: often used like English "Jr." [Dumas *fils*]

fils² (fēls, fils) *n., pl.* **fils** [Ar., earlier *fals* < LGr. *phollis,* a small coin, 1/288 of a solidus] a unit of money in Iraq, Jordan, Bahrain, Southern Yemen, and Kuwait, equal to 1/1000 dinar

fil·ter (fil′tər) *n.* [ME. *filtre* < OFr. < ML. *filtrum, feltrum,* felt, fulled wool (used for straining liquors) < Gmc.: see FELT¹] **1.** a device for separating solid particles, impurities, etc. from a liquid or gas by passing it through a porous substance **2.** any porous substance used or suitable for this, as sand, charcoal, felt, etc. **3.** *Physics a)* a device or substance that passes electric currents of certain frequencies or frequency ranges while preventing the passage of others *b)* a device or substance that partially or completely absorbs certain light rays [a color *filter* for a camera lens] —*vt.* [Fr. *filtrer* < the *n.*] **1.** to pass (a liquid or gas) through a filter **2.** to remove or separate (solid particles, impurities, etc.) from a liquid or gas by means of a filter (often with *out*) **3.** to act as a filter for —*vi.* **1.** to pass through or as if through a filter **2.** to move or pass slowly [the news *filtered* through town]

fil·ter·a·ble (fil′tər ə b′l, -trə b′l) *adj.* that can be filtered —**fil′ter·a·bil′i·ty** *n.*

filterable virus any virus: so called because most viruses are capable of passing through fine filters that bacteria cannot pass through

filter bed a tank, covered trench, etc. with a sand or gravel bottom, used to filter water, sewage, etc.

filter paper porous paper for filtering liquids

☆**filter tip 1.** a cigarette tip containing cellulose, cotton, charcoal, etc. and serving as a mouthpiece through which the smoke is filtered **2.** a cigarette having such a tip —**fil′ter-tip′, fil′ter-tipped′** *adj.*

filth (filth) *n.* [ME. < OE. *fylthe* < base of *ful* (see FOUL) + -*th,* nominal suffix] **1.** disgustingly offensive dirt, garbage, etc. **2.** anything considered as foul as this; esp., anything viewed as grossly indecent or obscene **3.** gross moral corruption

filth·y (fil′thē) *adj.* **filth′i·er, filth′i·est** [ME. *filthi*] **1.** full of filth; disgustingly foul **2.** grossly obscene **3.** morally vicious or corrupt —*SYN.* see DIRTY —**filth′i·ly** *adv.* —**filth′i·ness** *n.*

fil·tra·ble (fil′trə b′l) *adj. same as* FILTERABLE —**fil′tra·bil′i·ty** *n.*

fil·trate (fil′trāt) *vt.* **-trat·ed, -trat·ing** [< ML. *filtratus,* pp. of *filtrare* < *filtrum,* FILTER] to filter —*n.* a filtered liquid —**fil·tra′tion** *n.*

fi·lum (fī′ləm) *n., pl.* **fi′la** (-lə) [L., a thread: see FILE¹] *Anat.* any threadlike part; filament

fim·bri·a (fim′brē ə) *n., pl.* **-bri·ae** (-brē ē) [ModL. < L., fiber, fringe] *Biol.* a fringe or border of hairs, fibers, etc. or a fringelike process, esp. at the opening of an oviduct in mammals

fim·bri·ate (fim′brē āt′) *adj.* [L. *fimbriatus,* fringed: see prec.] having a fringe of hairs, fibers, etc. —**fim′bri·a′tion** *n.*

fin¹ (fin) *n.* [ME. < OE. *finn,* akin to Du. *vin,* G. *finne* < IE. *(s)pina,* point < base *(s)pei-,* pointed stick, whence SPIT¹, SPIKE¹] **1.** any of several winglike, membranous organs on the body of a fish, dolphin, etc., used in swimming, turning, and balancing **2.** anything like a fin in shape or use; specif., *a)* any narrow edge or ridge formed in manufacturing, as on a casting by metal forced through the halves of the mold *b)* any fixed or movable airfoil whose chief function is to give stability in flight *c)* a stabilizing or steering projection on boats or submarines *d)* a stabilizing projection on a racer car *e)* [Slang] a hand or arm —*vt.* **finned, fin′ning** to cut the fins from (a fish) —*vi.* to move the fins, esp. in a violent way

☆**fin²** (fin) *n.* [< Yid. *finnif, finf* < MHG. *vinf* < OHG. *fimf,* FIVE] [Slang] a five-dollar bill

†**fin³** (fan) *n.* [Fr.] the end; finish; conclusion

Fin. 1. Finland **2.** Finnish

fin. 1. finance 2. financial 3. finis 4. finished

fin·a·ble (fī'nə b'l) *adj.* liable to a fine

fi·na·gle (fə nā'g'l) *vt.* **-gled**, **-gling** [< ?] [Colloq.] to get, arrange, or maneuver by cleverness, persuasion, etc., or esp. by craftiness, trickery, etc. —*vi.* to use craftiness, trickery, etc. —**fi·na'gler** *n.*

fi·nal (fī'n'l) *adj.* [ME. < OFr. < L. *finalis* < *finis*, end: see FINISH] 1. of or coming at the end; last; concluding [the *final* chapter] 2. leaving no further chance for action, discussion, or change; deciding; conclusive [a *final* decree] 3. having to do with the basic or ultimate purpose, aim, or end [a *final* cause] —*n.* 1. anything final 2. [*pl.*] the last of a series of athletic contests, trials, etc. 3. a final or concluding examination —*SYN.* see LAST¹

fi·na·le (fə nä'lē, -lä; -nal'ē) *n.* [It., orig. adj. < L. *finalis*, FINAL] 1. the concluding movement or passage of a musical composition 2. the last scene or feature of an entertainment 3. the conclusion or last part; end

fi·nal·ist (fī'n'l ist) *n.* a contestant who participates in the final and deciding contest or contests of a series

fi·nal·i·ty (fī nal'ə tē, fə-) *n.* [LL. *finalitas*] 1. the quality or condition of being final, settled, or complete; conclusiveness 2. *pl.* **-ties** anything final

☆**fi·nal·ize** (fī'n'l īz') *vt.* **-ized'**, **-iz'ing** [FINAL + -IZE] to make final; bring to completion —**fi·nal·i·za'tion** *n.*

fi·nal·ly (-ē) *adv.* 1. at the end; in conclusion 2. decisively; conclusively; irrevocably

fi·nance (fə nans', fī'nans) *n.* [ME. *finaunce*, a fine, forfeit < OFr. *finance*, wealth, revenue < *finer*, to end, settle accounts, pay ransom < *fin*: see FINE²] 1. [*pl.*] the money resources, income, etc. of a nation, organization, or person 2. the managing or science of managing money matters, credit, etc. —*vt.* **-nanced'**, **-nanc'ing** 1. to supply money, credit, or capital to or for 2. to obtain money, credit, or capital for

☆**finance company** a company specializing in the lending of money to consumers, the purchasing of accounts receivable, and the extension of credit to businesses

fi·nan·cial (fə nan'shəl, fī-) *adj.* of finance, finances, or financiers —**fi·nan'cial·ly** *adv.*

SYN.—**financial** implies reference to money matters, esp. where large sums are involved [a *financial* success]; **fiscal** is used with reference to government revenues and expenditures or the administering of the financial affairs of an organization or corporation [a *fiscal* year]; **monetary** refers directly to money itself and is used in connection with coinage, circulation, standards, relative values, etc. [the *monetary* unit of a country]; **pecuniary** is applied to money matters of a practical or personal nature [*pecuniary* motives]

fin·an·cier (fin'ən sir', fī'nan-; *Brit. & Canad., usually* fī nan'syər, fi-) *n.* [Fr.] 1. a person trained or skilled in finance 2. a person who engages in financial operations on a large scale —*vi.* to engage in financial operations, often specif. in a dishonest way

☆**fin·back** (fin'bak') *n.* any of a genus (*Balaenoptera*) of whalebone whales, esp. a large whale (*Balaenoptera physalus*) of the E coast of the U.S., with a prominent dorsal fin

‡**fin·ca** (fēŋ'kä) *n.* [Sp.] an estate or plantation in Spain or Spanish America

finch (finch) *n.* [ME. < OE. *finc*, akin to G. *fink* < IE. echoic base *(s)pingo-, chirping bird, W. *pink*, Gr. *spingos*, finch] any of a large group of small, short-beaked, seed-eating songbirds (family Fringillidae), including the bunting, canary, cardinal, goldfinch, and sparrow

Finch·ley (finch'lē) city in Middlesex, SE England: suburb of London: pop. 69,000

find (find) *vt.* **found**, **find'ing** [ME. *finden* < OE. *findan*, akin to G. *finden*, Goth. *finthan* < IE. base *pent-, to walk, go, whence L. *pons* (gen. *pontis*), a plank causeway, bridge] 1. to happen on; come upon; meet with; discover by chance 2. to get by searching or by making an effort [find the answer] 3. to get sight or knowledge of; perceive; learn [I *find* that I was wrong] 4. to experience or feel [to *find* pleasure in music] 5. *a)* to get or recover (something lost) [to *find* a missing book] *b)* to get or recover the use of [we *found* our sea legs] 6. to realize as being; consider; think [to *find* a book boring] 7. to get to; reach; attain [the blow *found* his chin] 8. to decide and declare [the jury *found* him innocent] 9. to supply; furnish: cf. FOUND³ —*vi.* to reach and announce a decision [the jury *found* for the accused] —*n.* 1. the act of finding 2. something found, esp. something interesting or valuable —**find oneself** 1. to learn what one's real talents and inclinations are, and begin to apply them [to *find oneself* in trouble] —**find out** 1. to discover; learn 2. to learn the true character or identity of (someone or something)

find·er (fīn'dər) *n.* 1. a person or thing that finds 2. a camera device, as a special lens, that helps in adjusting the position of the camera by showing what will appear in the photograph 3. a small, low-powered telescope attached to a larger one, used to locate objects for closer view with the more powerful telescope ☆4. a person who, for a fee (**finder's fee**), initiates a business transaction between principals

‡**fin de siè·cle** (fant sye'kl') [Fr., lit., end of the century] of or characteristic of the last years of the 19th cent.: formerly used to refer to progressive ideas and customs, but now generally used to indicate decadence

find·ing (fīn'diŋ) *n.* [see FIND] 1. the act of one who finds; discovery 2. something found or discovered 3. [*pl.*] miscellaneous small articles or materials used in making garments, shoes, jewelry, etc., as buttons, buckles, clasps, etc. 4. [*often pl.*] the conclusion reached after an examination or consideration of facts or data by a judge, coroner, scholar, etc.

Find·lay (find'lē) [after James *Findlay* (d. 1825), local legislator] city in NW Ohio: pop. 36,000

fine¹ (fīn) *adj.* **fin'er**, **fin'est** [ME. *fin* < OFr. < ML. *finus*, for L. *finis*, an end, limit: see FINISH] 1. orig., finished; perfected 2. superior in quality; better than average; excellent; very good [a *fine* sample] 3. of exceptional character or ability [a *fine* teacher] 4. with no impurities; refined 5. containing a specified proportion of pure metal: said usually of gold or silver 6. clear and bright: said of the weather 7. *a)* not heavy or gross *b)* not coarse; in very small particles [*fine* sand] 8. *a)* very thin or slender [*fine* thread] *b)* very small [*fine* print] 9. sharp; keen [a knife with a *fine* edge] 10. *a)* discriminating; subtle [*fine* distinctions] *b)* involving precise accuracy [a *fine* adjustment] 11. of delicate composition [*fine* lace] 12. [Now Rare] attractive; handsome [a *fine* child] 13. trained and developed physically to the maximum extent: said of athletes, horses, etc. 14. *a)* elegant *b)* too elegant; showy [*fine* writing] —*adv.* 1. *same as* FINELY 2. [Colloq.] very well; all right —*vt.*, *vi.* **fined**, **fin'ing** to make or become fine or finer

fine² (fīn) *n.* [ME. < OFr. *fin* < L. *finis*: see FINISH] 1. orig., a finish; end; conclusion 2. a sum of money paid to settle a matter; esp., a sum required to be paid as punishment or penalty for an offense —*vt.* **fined**, **fin'ing** to require the payment of a fine from —**in fine** 1. in conclusion 2. in brief

fi·ne³ (fē'nā) *n.* [It. < L. *finis*: see FINISH] *Music* the end: a direction marking the close of a repetition

‡**fine⁴** (fēn) [Fr.] ordinary French brandy

fine·a·ble (fī'nə b'l) *adj.* *same as* FINABLE

fine art [orig. considered purely aesthetic, as distinguished from the "useful" arts] 1. any of the art forms that include drawing, painting, sculpture, and ceramics, or, occasionally, architecture, literature, music, dramatic art, or dancing: *usually used in pl.* 2. artistic objects, as paintings, sculpture, etc. collectively [an exhibition of *fine art*] 3. any highly creative or intricate skill

☆**fine-cut** (fīn'kut') *adj.* cut into small, narrow shreds of equal width: said of tobacco and opposed to ROUGH-CUT

fine-draw (-drô') *vt.* **-drew'**, **-drawn'**, **-draw'ing** [FINE¹ + DRAW] to sew together (torn edges of cloth) so carefully that the seam cannot be seen

fine-drawn (-drôn') *adj.* 1. drawn out until very fine, as wire 2. extended to a high degree of subtleness: said of reasoning, arguments, etc.

fine-grained (-grānd') *adj.* having a fine, smooth grain, as some kinds of wood, leather, etc.

fine·ly (-lē) *adv.* [ME. *finliche*] in a fine manner

fine·ness (-nis) *n.* 1. the quality or state of being fine 2. the proportion of pure gold or silver in an alloy

fin·er·y¹ (fīn'ər ē) *n.*, *pl.* **-er·ies** showy, gay, elaborate decoration, esp. clothes, jewelry, etc.

fin·er·y² (fīn'ər ē) *n.*, *pl.* **-er·ies** [Fr. *finerie* < *finer*, to refine < ML. *finire*, to refine < L., FINISH] a refinery where malleable iron or steel is made

fines (fīnz) *n.pl.* fine fragments or tiny particles, as of crushed rock, esp. when separated by screening

fine·spun (fīn'spun') *adj.* 1. spun or drawn out to extreme fineness; delicate; fragile 2. extremely subtle 3. too subtle; not practical

fi·nesse (fi nes') *n.* [Fr. < OFr. *fin*, FINE¹] 1. adroitness and delicacy of performance 2. the ability to handle delicate and difficult situations skillfully and diplomatically 3. cunning; skill; artfulness; craft 4. *Bridge* an attempt to take a trick with a lower card while holding a higher card not in sequence with it, in the hope that an intervening card is held in the hand of an opponent who has already played —*vt.* **-nessed'**, **-ness'ing** 1. to manage by finesse; bring by finesse (*into* a certain condition) 2. *Bridge* to make a finesse with (a card) —*vi.* to use or make a finesse

☆**fine-toothed comb** (fīn'tōōtht') a comb with fine, closely set teeth: also **fine-tooth comb** —**go over with a fine-toothed comb** to examine very carefully and thoroughly

Fin·gal's Cave (fiŋ'g'lz) large cavern on an islet (called *Staffa*) west of Mull in the Hebrides

fin·ger (fiŋ'gər) *n.* [ME. < OE., akin to G. *finger*, Goth. *figgrs* < ? IE. base *penkwe, FIVE] 1. any of the five jointed parts projecting from the palm of the hand; esp., any of these other than the thumb 2. the part of a glove covering one of these parts 3. anything resembling a finger in shape or use 4. a rough unit of measurement based on the breadth of a finger (3/4 inch to 1 inch), as in measuring whiskey in a glass, or the length of the middle finger (about 4 1/2 inches), as in measuring cloth 5. *Mech.* a projecting

fat, āpe, cär; ten, ēven; is, bīte; gō, hôrn, tōōl, look; oil, out; up, fʉr; get; joy; yet; chin; she; thin, then; zh, leisure; ŋ, ring; ə for *a* in ago, *e* in agent, *i* in sanity, *o* in comply, *u* in focus; ' as in able (ā'b'l); Fr. bal; ë, Fr. coeur; ö, Fr. feu; Fr. mon; ô, Fr. coq; ü, Fr. duc; r, Fr. cri; H, G. ich; kh, G. doch. See inside front cover. ☆ Americanism; ‡foreign; *hypothetical; <derived from

part coming into contact with another part and controlling its motion —*vt.* **1.** to touch or handle with the fingers; use the fingers on **2.** [Now Rare] to take; steal ☆**3.** [Slang] to point out; indicate or designate, specif. in senses of PUT THE FINGER ON (see phr. below) **4.** *Music* **a)** to play (an instrument) by using the fingers in a certain way or sequence on strings, keys, etc. **b)** to mark (a score) with directions for the way to use the fingers —*vi.* **1.** to use the fingers in a certain way or sequence on a musical instrument **2.** to be fingered: said of musical instruments **3.** to extend (*out, across,* etc.) like a finger —**burn one's fingers** to cause oneself trouble by being too inquisitive, meddlesome, etc. —**have a finger in the pie 1.** to help do something; participate **2.** to be meddlesome —**have (or keep) one's fingers crossed** to hope for or against something —**lift a finger** to make even the slightest effort —**put one's finger on** to indicate or ascertain exactly —☆**put the finger on** [Slang] **1.** to identify as for the police; inform on **2.** to indicate as the place to be robbed, victim to be killed, etc.

fin·ger·board (-bôrd′) *n.* **1.** a strip of hard wood in the neck of a violin or other stringed instrument, against which the strings are pressed with the fingers to produce the desired tones **2.** a keyboard of a piano, organ, etc.

finger bowl a small bowl to hold water for rinsing the fingers at table after a meal

fin·ger·breadth (-bredth′) *n.* the breadth of a finger, roughly 3/4 inch to 1 inch in measure

fin·gered (fiŋ′gərd) *adj.* **1.** having fingers (of a specified kind or number): used in hyphenated compounds [light-*fingered*] **2.** soiled or marred by touching **3.** *Bot.* **a)** digitate **b)** fingerlike in form **4.** *Music* marked to show the fingering: said of a score

fin·ger·ing (-iŋ) *n.* **1.** a touching or handling with the fingers **2.** *Music* **a)** act or technique of applying the fingers to the strings, keys, etc. of an instrument to produce the tones **b)** directions on a musical score for using the fingers in a certain way or sequence

Finger Lakes group of long, narrow glacial lakes in WC N.Y.

fin·ger·ling (-liŋ) *n.* [ME.: see FINGER & -LING¹] **1.** anything very small or trifling **2.** a small fish about the length of a finger, or a young fish up to the end of the first year

finger mark a mark or smudge left as by an unclean finger —**fin′ger-marked′** (-märkt′) *adj.*

fin·ger·nail (-nāl′) *n.* the horny substance growing on the upper part of the end joint of a finger

FINGER LAKES

☆**finger painting 1.** the art or process of painting by using the fingers, hand, or arm to spread paints made of starch, glycerin, and pigments (**finger paints**) on moistened paper **2.** a painting made in this manner —**fin′ger-paint′** (-pānt′) *vi., vt.*

finger post a post with a sign, often shaped like a pointing finger or hand, indicating a direction

fin·ger·print (-print′) *n.* an impression of the lines and whorls on the inner surface of the end joint of the finger, used in the identification of a person —*vt.* to take the fingerprints of

fin·ger·stall (-stôl′) *n.* [ME. *fingir stall:* see STALL¹] a protective covering of rubber, leather, etc. for an injured finger

finger tip 1. the tip of a finger **2.** a shield to protect the end of a finger, as from the bowstring in archery —**have at one's finger tips 1.** to have available for instant use **2.** to be completely familiar with —**to one's (or the) finger tips** entirely; altogether

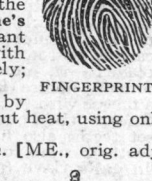

FINGERPRINT

☆**finger wave** a loose wave made by dampening and shaping the hair without heat, using only fingers and comb

fin·i·al (fin′ē əl; *chiefly Brit.,* fī′nē-) *n.* [ME., orig. adj., FINAL] a decorative, terminal part at the tip of a spire, gable, lamp shade support, etc., or projecting upward from the top of a cabinet, breakfront, etc.

fin·i·cal (fin′i k'l) *adj.* [< FINE¹] same as FINICKY —**fin′i·cal′i·ty** (-i kal′ə tē) *n.* —**fin′i·cal·ly** *adv.*

fin·ick·ing (fin′i kiŋ) *adj.* [< FINICAL] same as FINICKY: also **fin′i·kin** (-kin)

fin·ick·y (-kē) *adj.* [< prec.] too particular or exacting; overly dainty or fastidious; fussy —**fin′ick·i·ness** *n.*

fin·ing (fī′niŋ) *n.* [ME. < *finen,* to refine < *fin,* FINE¹] **1.** the refining

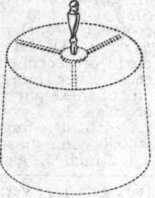

FINIAL

or clarifying of liquids, metals, etc. **2.** [*pl.*] any substance used for clarifying liquors

fi·nis (fin′is, fī′nis; *often taken as Fr.* fē nē′) *n., pl.* **-nis·es** [L.: see ff.] the end; finish; conclusion: used at the end of some books or movies

fin·ish (fin′ish) *vt.* [ME. *finishen* < extended stem of OFr. *finir* < L. *finire,* to end < *finis,* an end, limit, orig., boundary (post), something fixed in the ground < IE. base **dhīgw-,* to stick in, whence DIKE¹, L. *figere,* FIX] **1. a)** to bring to an end; complete [to *finish* the work] **b)** to come to the end of [to *finish* reading a book] **2.** to use up; consume entirely [*finish* your milk] **3.** to give final touches to; embellish or perfect **4.** to give (cloth, leather, wood, etc.) a desired surface effect **5. a)** to cause the defeat, collapse, death, etc. of **b)** to render worthless, useless, helpless, etc. —*vi.* **1.** to come to an end; terminate **2.** to complete something being done —*n.* **1.** the last part; end **2.** anything used to give a desired surface effect, as paint, varnish, polish, wax, etc. **3.** completeness; perfection **4.** the manner or method of completion **5.** the way in which the surface, as of furniture, is painted, varnished, smoothed, polished, etc. **6.** refinement in manners, speech, etc.; polish in social or cultural matters **7.** defeat, collapse, etc. or that which brings it about; downfall **8.** *Carpentry* **a)** joiner work, as doors, stairs, panels, etc., which completes the interior of a building **b)** high-quality lumber used for this —*SYN.* see CLOSE² —**finish off 1.** to end or complete **2.** to kill or destroy —**finish up 1.** to end or complete **2.** to consume all of —**finish with 1.** to end or complete **2.** to end relations with; become indifferent to —**in at the finish** being present or taking part at the conclusion, as of a contest —**fin′ish·er** *n.*

fin·ished (fin′isht) *adj.* **1.** ended; concluded **2.** completed **3.** highly skilled or polished; perfected; accomplished **4.** given a certain kind of finish or surface, as of paint, wax, etc. **5.** defeated, ruined, dying, etc.

finishing school a private school for girls that specializes in imparting social poise and polish

Fin·is·terre (fin′is ter′), **Cape** promontory at the westernmost point of Spain

fi·nite (fī′nīt) *adj.* [ME. *finit* < L. *finitus,* pp. of *finire,* FINISH] **1.** having measurable or definable limits; not infinite **2.** *Gram.* having limits of person, number, and tense: said of a verb that can be used in a predicate **3.** *Math.* **a)** capable of being reached, completed, or surpassed by counting: said of numbers or sets **b)** neither infinite nor infinitesimal: said of a magnitude —*n.* anything that has measurable limits; finite thing —**fi′nite·ly** *adv.* —**fi′nite·ness** *n.*

fin·i·tude (fin′ə tood′, fī′nə-; -tyood′) *n.* the state or quality of being finite

☆**fink** (fiŋk) *n.* [< ?] [Slang] **1.** an informer or strikebreaker; esp., a professional strikebreaker **2.** a person regarded as contemptible, obnoxious, etc.

fin keel a deep, narrow metal keel, shaped somewhat like a dorsal fin, used on some sailboats to give stability and prevent lateral drift

Fin·land (fin′lənd) **1.** country in N Europe, northeast of the Baltic Sea: 130,119 sq. mi.; pop. 4,631,000; cap. Helsinki: Finn. name, SUOMI **2. Gulf of,** arm of the Baltic Sea, between Finland & the U.S.S.R.: c. 250 mi. long

Fin·lay, Fin·ley (fin′lē) [< Celt.] a masculine name

Finn (fin) *n.* **1.** a native or inhabitant of Finland **2.** any person speaking a Finnic language

Finn. Finnish

fin·nan had·die (fin′ən had′ē) [prob. < *Findhorn haddock,* after fishing port and river of *Findhorn,* Scotland; often associated with *Findon,* Scotland] smoked haddock: also **finnan haddock**

finned (find) *adj.* having a fin or fins

Finn·ic (fin′ik) *adj.* **1.** Finnish **2.** designating or of the group of languages to which Finnish belongs: see FINNO-UGRIC

fin·nick·y (fin′i kē) *adj. same as* FINICKY

Finn·ish (fin′ish) *adj.* **1.** of Finland **2.** of the Finns, their language, or culture —*n.* the Finno-Ugric language of the Finns

Fin·no- (fin′ō-) *a combining form meaning* Finn or Finnish [*Finno*-Ugric]

Fin·no-U·gric (fin′ō ōō′grik, -yōō′-) *adj.* designating or of a subfamily of the Uralic group of languages spoken in NE Europe, W Siberia, and Hungary: it includes the Finnic (Finnish, Estonian, Lapp, etc.) and the Ugric (Hungarian, Vogul, Ostyak) languages —*n.* this subfamily of languages Also **Fin′no-U′gri·an** (-grē ən)

fin·ny (fin′ē) *adj.* **1. a)** having fins **b)** like a fin **2. a)** of or being fish **b)** [Poet.] full of fish

fi·noc·chi·o (fi nō′kē ō′) *n.* [It. < VL. *fenuculum* < L. *feniculum,* FENNEL] a variety of fennel (*Foeniculum vulgare dulce*), cooked as a vegetable: its celerylike, anise-flavored, thick stalks are also eaten raw: also called **Florence fennel, sweet fennel**

Fins·bur·y (finz′ber′ē; *Brit.* -bə ri) metropolitan borough of London, north of the Thames: pop. 32,000

Fin·sen (fin′sən), **Niels Ry·berg** (nēls rōō′berg, nils) 1860–1904; Dan. physician: founder of phototherapy

Fin·ster·aar·horn (fin′stər är′hôrn) mountain in SC Switzerland: highest peak in the Bernese Alps: 14,026 ft.

fiord (fyôrd) *n.* [Norw. *fjord* < ON. *fjörthr,* akin to OE. *ford,* FORD] a narrow inlet or arm of the sea bordered by steep cliffs, esp. in Norway

‡**fio·ri·tu·ra** (fyō′rē tōō′rä) *n., pl.* **-tu′re** (-re) [It., lit., blossoming] *Music* a trill, appoggiatura, or other ornamentation added to a melody, as in virtuosic singing

☆**fip·pen·ny bit** (fip′ə nē, fip′ nē) [altered < *five-penny bit*] a Spanish silver coin worth about six cents, circulated in the U.S. before 1857

fip·ple flute (fip′'l) [< ?] any of a class of vertical flutes, as the recorder, in which a plug **(fipple)** near the mouthpiece diverts the breath in producing the tones

fir (fur) *n.* [ME. *firre* < OE. *fyrh,* akin to G. *föhre* < IE. base **perkwus,* name of the tree, oak, whence L. *quercus,* oak] **1.** any of a genus (*Abies*) of cone-bearing evergreen trees of the pine family, having flattened single needles and erect cones whose scales drop at maturity **2.** any of various other coniferous trees, as the Douglas fir **3.** the wood of any of these trees

Fir·dau·si (fir dou′sē) (born *Abul Kasim Mansur*) 940?–1020?; Per. epic poet: also **Fir·dou·si** (-dou′sē), **Fir·du·si** (-dōō′sē)

fire (fīr) *n.* [ME. *fyr* < OE. *fyr,* akin to G. *feuer* < IE. base **pewōr,* whence Gr. *pyra,* PYRE, Czech *pýř,* glowing embers] **1.** the active principle of burning, characterized by the heat and light of combustion **2.** something burning, as fuel in a furnace **3.** a destructive burning [a forest *fire*] **4.** any preparation that will burn and make a brilliant display [red *fire*] **5.** *a)* anything like fire, as in heat or brilliance *b)* firelike brilliance **6.** death, torture, or trial by burning **7.** extreme suffering or distress that tries one's endurance; tribulation or ordeal **8.** a feverish or inflamed condition of the body. **9.** strong feeling; excitement; ardor [a speech full of *fire*] **10.** vivid imagination **11.** *a)* a discharge of firearms or artillery; shooting *b)* anything like this in speed and continuity of action [a *fire* of criticism] —*vt.* **fired, fir′ing** [ME. *firen* < OE. *fyrian*] **1.** to apply fire to; make burn; ignite **2.** to supply with fuel; tend the fire of [to *fire* a furnace] **3.** to bake (bricks, pottery, etc.) in a kiln **4.** to dry by heat **5.** to make bright or illuminate, as if by fire **6.** *a)* to animate or inspire *b)* to excite, stimulate, or inflame **7.** *a)* to shoot or discharge (a gun, bullet, etc.) *b)* to make explode by igniting **8.** to hurl or direct with force and suddenness [*fire* a rock, *fire* questions] ☆**9.** [pun on *discharge*] to dismiss from a position; discharge —*vi.* **1.** to start burning; flame **2.** to tend a fire **3.** to become excited or aroused **4.** to react in a specified way to firing in a kiln [a glaze that *fires* bright blue] **5.** to shoot a firearm **6.** to discharge a projectile [the gun *fired*] **7.** to become yellow prematurely, as corn or grain —**between two fires** between two attacks; shot at, criticized, etc. from both sides —**catch (on) fire** to begin burning; ignite —**fire away** [Colloq.] to begin; start, esp. to talk or ask questions —**fire up 1.** to start a fire in a furnace, stove, etc. **2.** to start or warm up (an engine, etc.) **3.** to become suddenly angry —**go through fire and water** to undergo great difficulties or dangers —**miss fire 1.** to fail to fire, as a gun **2.** to fail in an attempt —**on fire 1.** burning **2.** greatly excited; full of ardor —**open fire 1.** to begin to shoot **2.** to begin; start —**play with fire** to do something risky —**set fire to** to make burn; ignite —**set the world on fire** to become famous through brilliant achievements —**strike fire** to make a spark, as with tinder —**take fire 1.** to begin to burn **2.** to become excited —**under fire 1.** under attack, as by gunfire **2.** subjected to criticism, censure, etc. —**fir′er** *n.*

fire alarm 1. a signal to announce the outbreak of a fire **2.** a bell, siren, whistle, etc. to give this signal

fire ant any of a genus (*Solenopsis*) of ants whose sting causes a burning sensation, esp. a S. American species (*Solenopsis saevissima*) that has become a severe pest in the S U.S.

fire·arm (-ärm′) *n.* any weapon from which a shot is fired by the force of an explosion; esp., such a weapon small enough to be carried, as a rifle or pistol

fire·ball (-bôl′) *n.* **1.** something resembling a ball of fire; specif., *a)* a large, bright meteor *b)* same as BALL LIGHTNING *c)* a high-temperature, luminous ball of gas which forms shortly after a nuclear explosion **2.** formerly, a ball of explosive or combustible material thrown as a weapon in battle ☆**3.** [Colloq.] a vigorous, energetic person

fire·bird (-burd′) *n.* ☆any of various birds with brilliant coloring, as the scarlet tanager and the Baltimore oriole

fire blight ☆a disease of fruit trees, as pear, apple, etc. caused by a bacterium (*Erwinia amylovora*), that kills the branches and blackens the leaves

FIORD

☆**fire·boat** (-bōt′) *n.* a boat equipped with fire-fighting equipment, used along waterfronts

fire·bomb (-bäm′) *n.* a bomb or missile intended to start a fire; incendiary bomb —*vt.* to attack, damage, or destroy with a firebomb

fire·box (-bäks′) *n.* **1.** the place for the fire in a locomotive engine, stove, etc. **2.** [Obs.] a tinderbox

fire·brand (-brand′) *n.* **1.** a piece of burning wood **2.** a person who stirs up others to revolt or strife

☆**fire·break** (-brāk′) *n.* a strip of land cleared or plowed to stop the spread of fire, as in a forest or prairie

fire·brick (-brik′) *n.* a brick made to withstand great heat, used to line fireplaces, furnaces, etc.

fire brigade *chiefly Brit. var. of* FIRE DEPARTMENT

☆**fire·bug** (-bug′) *n.* [Colloq.] a person who deliberately sets fire to buildings, etc.; pyromaniac; incendiary

☆**fire chief** the officer in charge of a fire department

fire·clay (-klā′) *n.* a kind of clay capable of resisting intense heat, used for making firebricks, furnace linings, etc.

fire company 1. a body of men organized to fight fires, esp. one of a number of such groups constituting a fire department **2.** [Brit.] a business firm selling fire insurance

☆**fire·crack·er** (-krak′ər) *n.* a roll of paper that contains an explosive and an attached fuse, and makes a sharp noise when exploded: used at celebrations, etc.

☆**fire-cure** (-kyoor′) *vt.* **-cured′, -cur′ing** to cure (tobacco, etc.) by direct exposure to the smoke of wood fires

fire·damp (-damp′) *n.* a gas, largely methane, formed in coal mines, which is explosive when mixed with a certain proportion of air

☆**fire department** a municipal department, usually consisting of one or more fire companies, whose work is fighting fires and preventing their occurrence

fire·dog (-dôg′) *n.* [sense developed as in Fr. *chenet,* andiron, dim. of *chien,* dog] *same as* ANDIRON

fire door ☆a door of metal or other fire-resistant material designed to keep a fire from spreading

fire·drake (-drāk′) *n.* [see FIRE & DRAKE²] *Germanic Myth.* a fire-breathing dragon

fire drill ☆a drill in which buildings are vacated, fire stations manned, etc. in a quick, orderly way to teach proper procedure in case of fire

fire-eat·er (-ēt′ər) *n.* **1.** a performer at circuses, etc. who pretends to eat fire **2.** a hot-tempered person always ready to quarrel or fight

fire engine 1. a motor truck with a special pumping apparatus for spraying water, chemicals, etc. on fires to put them out **2.** loosely, any motor truck for carrying firemen and equipment to a fire

fire escape 1. a fireproof stairway down an outside wall, to help people escape from a burning building **2.** a ladder, chute, rope, etc. used for the same purpose

fire extinguisher a portable device containing chemicals that can be sprayed on a fire to put it out

fire·fly (-flī′) *n., pl.* **-flies′** any of several winged beetles (family Lampyridae), active at night, whose abdomen glows with a luminescent light: the luminescent larvae and wingless females are called *glowworms*

fire·guard (-gärd′) *n. same as* FIRE SCREEN

☆**fire·house** (-hous′) *n. same as* FIRE STATION

☆**fire hydrant** *same as* FIREPLUG

fire insurance insurance against loss or damage resulting from fire

fire irons the poker, shovel, and tongs used for tending a fireplace

fire·less (-lis) *adj.* without a fire

☆**fireless cooker** an insulated container which when heated stays hot enough to finish cooking the food in it

fire·light (-līt′) *n.* light from a fire, esp. an open fire

fire·lock (-läk′) *n.* **1.** an early type of gunlock in which the priming was ignited by sparks; wheel lock or flintlock **2.** an early type of musket with such a lock

fire·man (-mən) *n., pl.* **-men** (-mən) **1.** a man whose work is fighting fires; member of a fire department **2.** a man who tends a fire in a furnace, locomotive engine, etc. ☆**3.** *U.S. Navy* an enlisted man who is nonrated and whose general duties are concerned with the ship's engines, etc. ☆**4.** [Slang] *Baseball* a relief pitcher

☆**fire marshal** the officer in charge of a fire prevention bureau, as within a fire department

fire-new (-nōō′, -nyōō′) *adj. archaic var. of* BRAND-NEW

Fi·ren·ze (fē ren′dze) *It. name of* FLORENCE, Italy

fire opal a reddish opal usually exhibiting a brilliant play of colors in bright light

fire·place (-plās′) *n.* a place for a fire, esp. an open place built in a wall, at the base of a chimney

fire·plug (-plug′) *n.* a street hydrant to which a hose can be attached for fighting fires

fire·pow·er (-pou′ər) *n. Mil.* **1.** the effectiveness of a weapon in terms of the accuracy and volume of its fire **2.** the capacity of a given unit to deliver fire

fire·proof (-prōōf′) *adj.* that does not burn or is not easily destroyed by fire —*vt.* to make fireproof

fire reel [Canad.] *same as* FIRE ENGINE

☆**fire sale** a sale at lowered prices of goods damaged in a fire

fire screen a screen to be set in front of a fire to protect against heat or sparks

fire ship a ship filled with explosive materials, set afire and floated among an enemy's ships to destroy them

fire·side (-sīd′) n. 1. the part of a room near a fireplace; hearth 2. home or home life

fire station a place where fire engines are kept and where firemen stay when on duty

fire·stone (-stōn′) n. 1. formerly, flint or iron pyrites used for striking fire 2. a stone that can withstand intense heat

fire·storm (-stôrm′) n. an intense fire over a large area, as one initiated by an atomic explosion, that is sustained and spread by the inrushing winds created by the strong draft of rising hot air

☆**fire·thorn** (-thôrn′) n. any of a small genus (*Pyracantha*) of thorny Eurasian plants of the rose family, grown for the masses of brilliant red or orange fruits

fire tower a tower, usually in a forest, where a lookout is posted to watch for fires and give the alarm

fire·trap (-trap′) n. a building unsafe in case of fire because it will burn easily or because it lacks adequate exits or fire escapes

☆**fire wall** a fireproof wall to prevent the spread of fire, as from one room or compartment to the next

☆**fire warden** an official assigned to prevent or fight fires, as in forests, public buildings, etc.

☆**fire·wa·ter** (-wôt′ər, -wät′ər) n. [prob. transl. of AmInd. term, perhaps Algonquin *scoutiouabou*, firewater] alcoholic liquor: now humorous

☆**fire·weed** (-wēd′) n. any of a number of plants that grow readily on cleared or burned-over land; esp., a species (*Epilobium angustifolium*) of willow herb, with purplish-red flowers

fire·wood (-wood′) n. wood used as fuel

fire·works (-wûrks′) n.pl. 1. firecrackers, rockets, etc., exploded or burned, as in celebrations, to produce noises or brilliant lighting effects: *sometimes used in sing.* 2. a display of or as of fireworks

fir·ing (fir′iŋ) n. 1. the application of heat to harden or glaze pottery 2. the stoking of a fire, furnace, etc. 3. the shooting of firearms, etc. 4. fuel for a fire ☆5. the scorching of plants, as from heat, drought, or disease

firing line 1. the line from which gunfire is directed against the enemy 2. the troops stationed along this line 3. the front position in any kind of activity

firing order the order in which explosions occur in the cylinders of an internal-combustion engine

firing pin that part in the bolt or breech of a firearm which strikes the primer and explodes the charge

firing squad (or **party**) 1. a group of soldiers detailed to shoot to death someone so sentenced by a military court 2. a group detailed to fire a volley of shots over the grave at a military funeral as a tribute

fir·kin (fûr′kin) n. [ME., contr. < *firdekyn* < MDu. dim. of *vierdel*, fourth] 1. a small wooden tub for butter, lard, etc. 2. a measure of capacity equal to 1/4 barrel

firm¹ (fûrm) adj. [ME. *ferm* < OFr. < L. *firmus*, prob. < IE. base *dher-*, to hold, support, whence OE. *darian*, to lurk, be hidden, Gr. *thronos*, armchair] 1. not yielding easily under pressure; solid; hard 2. not moved or shaken easily; fixed; stable 3. continued steadily; remaining the same [a *firm* friendship] 4. unchanging; resolute; constant [a *firm* faith] 5. showing determination, strength, etc. [a *firm* command] 6. legally or formally concluded; definite; final [a *firm* contract, a *firm* order] 7. *Commerce* not rising or falling very much; steady: said of prices, etc. —vt., vi. 1. to make or become firm, or solid, steady, stable, definite, etc.: often with *up* —**stand** (or **hold**) **firm** to be or remain steadfast in conviction despite attack, efforts to persuade, etc. —**firm′ly** adv. —**firm′ness** n.

SYN.—**firm**, in referring to material consistency, suggests a compactness that does not yield easily to, or is very resilient under, pressure [*firm* flesh]; **hard** is applied to that which is so firm that it is not easily penetrated, cut, or crushed [hard as rock]; **solid** suggests a dense consistency throughout a mass or substance that is firm or hard and often connotes heaviness or substantialness [*solid* brick]; **stiff** implies resistance to bending or stretching [a *stiff* collar]

firm² (fûrm) n. [It. *firma*, signature, hence title of a business < L. *firmare*, to strengthen < *firmus*: see prec.] 1. a business company or partnership of two or more persons: distinguished from CORPORATION in that a firm is not legally recognized as a person apart from the members forming it 2. popularly, any business company, whether or not unincorporated

fir·ma·ment (fûr′mə mənt) n. [ME. < OFr. < LL.(Ec.) *firmamentum* < L., a strengthening, support < *firmare*, to strengthen < *firmus*: see FIRM¹] the sky, viewed poetically as a solid arch or vault —**fir′ma·men′tal** (-men′t'l) adj.

fir·man (fûr′mən, fər män′) n., pl. **-mans** [Per. *fermān*] a decree or sanction given by an Oriental ruler

firm·er (fûr′mər) adj. [Fr. *fermoir*, altered < *formoir* < *former*, to FORM] designating a carpenter's chisel or gouge with a thin blade fixed in a handle —n. a firmer chisel or gouge

firn (firn) n. [G. < *firn*, of last year, old, akin to OE. *fyrn*, former < IE. base *per-*, beyond, whence FAR, FIRST] the granular snow, not in a completely compacted mass, that accumulates at the top of a glacier

fir·ry (fûr′ē) adj. 1. full of firs 2. of or made of fir

first (fûrst) adj. [< OE. *fyrst*, lit., foremost, superl. of *fore*, before (see FORE), akin to OHG. *furist*, G. *fürst*, prince, lit., foremost < IE. base *per-*, beyond, whence L. *prae*, before, Gr. *para*, beside, beyond] 1. preceding all others in a series; before any others; 1st: used as the ordinal of ONE 2. happening or acting before all others; earliest 3. ranking before all others; foremost in rank, quality, importance, etc.; principal 4. *Music* playing or singing the part highest in pitch or the leading part —adv. 1. *a*) before any other person or thing; at the beginning *b*) before doing anything else 2. as the first point; to begin with 3. for the first time 4. sooner; preferably —n. 1. the one before the second 2. any person, thing, class, place, etc. that is first 3. the first day of a month 4. the beginning; start 5. a first happening or thing of its kind 6. [pl.] the best quality of merchandise 7. the winning place in a race or competition 8. the first or lowest forward gear ratio of a motor vehicle; low gear 9. *Music* the highest or leading voice or instrument in an ensemble —**first thing** as the first thing; before anything else —**in the first place** firstly; to begin with

first aid emergency treatment for injury or sudden illness, before regular medical care is available —**first′-aid′** adj.

☆**first base** *Baseball* the first position on the diamond, which a batter who has hit fairly must reach ahead of the ball —**get to first base** [Slang] to accomplish the first step of an undertaking

first·born (-bôrn′) adj. born first in a family; oldest —n. the firstborn child

first cause 1. a primary cause of anything; source 2. *Theol.* [**F- C-**] God as the unproduced cause of all being

first-class (-klas′, -kläs′) adj. 1. of the highest class, rank, excellence, etc.; of the best quality 2. designating or of the most expensive accommodations [a *first-class* cabin on a ship] ☆3. designating or of a class of mail consisting of sealed matter in writing, as letters, and all other matter sealed against ready inspection: such mail carries the highest regular postage rates —adv. 1. with the most expensive accommodations [to travel *first-class*] 2. as or by first-class mail

first cousin the son or daughter of one's uncle or aunt

First day Sunday: term used by the Society of Friends

first estate *see* ESTATE (sense 2)

first finger the finger next to the thumb; index finger

first floor 1. the ground floor of a building 2. chiefly in Europe and Great Britain, the floor above this

first fruits [orig. transl. of Vulgate *primitiae*: see Ex. 23:16] 1. the earliest produce of the season 2. the first products, results, or profits of any activity

first-gen·er·a·tion (-jen′ə rā′shən) adj. 1. designating a naturalized, foreign-born citizen of a country 2. sometimes, designating a native-born citizen of a country whose parents had immigrated into that country

first·hand (-hand′) adj., adv. from the original producer or source; direct

☆**first lady** [often **F- L-**] the wife of the U.S. president

first lieutenant 1. a U.S. military officer ranking above a second lieutenant and below a captain 2. *U.S. Navy* the officer in charge of maintenance of a ship or station

first·ling (-liŋ) n. 1. the first of a kind 2. the first fruit, produce, etc. 3. the first-born of an animal

first·ly (-lē) adv. in the first place; first: used chiefly in enumerating topics

first mate a merchant ship's officer next in rank below the captain: also **first officer**

first mortgage a mortgage having priority over all other liens or encumbrances on the same property, except those, as real estate taxes, given priority by statute

☆**first name** *same as* GIVEN NAME

first night the opening night of a play, opera, etc.

first-night·er (-nīt′ər) n. a person who regularly attends the opening performances of plays, operas, etc.

first offender a person convicted for the first time of an offense against the law

☆**first papers** *popular name for* the documents by which an alien formerly made a declaration of his intention to become a U.S. citizen

first person 1. that form of a pronoun (as *I*) or verb (as *am*) which refers to the speaker or speakers 2. narration characterized by the general use of such forms

first quarter 1. the time of month between new moon and first half-moon 2. the phase of the moon at the first of the two points when half of its hemisphere is visible

first-rate (-rāt′) adj. [orig. applied to the highest of the rates, or classes, of warships] of the highest class, rank, or quality; very good; excellent —adv. [Colloq.] very well

First Republic the republic established in France in 1792 after the Revolution, and lasting until the establishment of the Empire by Napoleon in 1804

☆**first sergeant** *U.S. Army & Marine Corps* the noncommissioned officer, usually a master sergeant, serving as chief administrative assistant to the commander of a company, battery, etc.

☆**first-string** (-striŋ′) adj. [Colloq.] 1. *Sports* that is the first choice for regular play at the specified position 2. first-class; excellent

first water the best quality and purest luster: said of diamonds, pearls, etc., but also used figuratively

firth (furth) *n.* [ME. < ON. *fjörthr*, akin to OE. *ford*, FORD] a narrow inlet or arm of the sea; estuary

fisc (fisk) *n.* [Fr. < L. *fiscus*: see ff.] [Rare] a royal or state treasury; exchequer

fis·cal (fis'kəl) *adj.* [Fr. < LL. *fiscalis* < L. *fiscus*, basket of rushes, public chest < IE. *bhidh-*, pot (whence ON. *bitha*, milk jug) < base *bheidh-*, to weave, tie] 1. having to do with the public treasury or revenues 2. financial —*n.* in some countries, a public prosecutor or other official — *SYN.* see FINANCIAL —**fis'cal·ly** *adv.*

☆**fiscal year** a twelve-month period between settlements of financial accounts: the U.S. government fiscal year legally ends June 30

Fisch·er (fish'ər) 1. *Emil*, 1852–1919; Ger. organic chemist 2. *Hans*, 1881–1945; Ger. organic chemist

fish[1] (fish) *n.* [Fr. *fiche*, pin, peg < *ficher*, to fix < OFr. *fichier* < VL. *figicare*, intens. for L. *figere*: see FIX] a piece of wood, metal, etc. fastened to another or to a joint to strengthen it —*vt.* to strengthen or join by using such a piece

fish[2] (fish) *n.*, *pl.* **fish**; in referring to different species, **fish'es**: see PLURAL, II, D, 2 [ME. < OE. *fisc*, akin to G. *fisch* < IE. base *pisk-*, whence L. *piscis*] 1. any of a large group of cold-blooded vertebrate animals living in water, and having permanent gills for breathing, fins, and, usually, scales 2. loosely, any animal living in water only, as

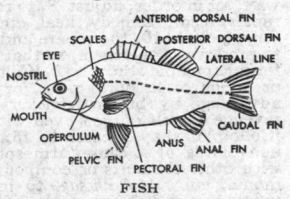
ANTERIOR DORSAL FIN; POSTERIOR DORSAL FIN; SCALES; EYE; LATERAL LINE; NOSTRIL; MOUTH; OPERCULUM; PELVIC FIN; ANUS; CAUDAL FIN; ANAL FIN; PECTORAL FIN
FISH

a dolphin, crab, oyster, etc.: often used in combination [*shellfish*, *jellyfish*] 3. the flesh of a fish used as food 4. [Colloq.] a person thought of as like a fish in being easily lured by bait, lacking intelligence or emotion, etc. 5. *Naut.* a device for raising an anchor —[F-] Pisces, the constellation and twelfth sign of the zodiac —*vi.* [OE. *fiscian*] 1. to catch or try to catch fish, or shrimps, lobsters, etc. 2. to try to get something indirectly or by cunning (often with *for*) —*vt.* 1. to catch or try to catch fish, shrimps, etc. in [to *fish* a stream] 2. to get by fishing 3. to grope for, find, and bring to view: often with *out* or *up* [to *fish* a coin from one's pocket] 4. *Naut.* to raise (an anchor) with a fish (*n.* 5) —*adj.* 1. of fish or fishing 2. selling fish —**drink like a fish** to drink heavily, esp. alcoholic liquor —**fish in troubled waters** to try to gain something by taking advantage of a confused or troubled situation —**fish or cut bait** to proceed energetically with a task or give it up altogether —**fish out** to deplete the stock of fish in (a lake, etc.) —**like a fish out of water** out of one's element; in surroundings not suited to one —**neither fish, flesh, nor fowl (nor good red herring)** not anything definite or recognizable —**other fish to fry** other, more important things to attend to —**fish'a·ble** *adj.* —**fish'like** *adj.*

Fish (fish), *Hamilton* 1808–93; U.S. statesman

fish and chips [Chiefly Brit.] fried, batter-coated fillets of fish served with French fried potatoes

☆**fish ball** (or **cake**) a fried ball (or patty) of minced fish, often mixed with mashed potato

fish·bowl (-bōl') *n.* 1. a glass bowl in which goldfish, snails, etc. are kept; small aquarium 2. any place where one's activities are open to public view

☆**fish crow** a fish-eating crow (*Corvus ossifragus*) of the Atlantic and Gulf coasts of the U.S.

fish·er (-ər) *n.* 1. a person who fishes; fisherman 2. a boat used in fishing 3. *pl.* **fish'ers**, **fish'er**: see PLURAL, II, D, 1 *a)* a flesh-eating animal (*Martes pennanti*) of the marten family, like a weasel but much larger and with very dark fur *b)* this fur

Fish·er (fish'ər), **Dorothy Can·field** (kan'fēld) (born *Dorothy Frances Canfield*) 1879–1958; U.S. writer

fish·er·man (-mən) *n.*, *pl.* -**men** (-mən) 1. a person who fishes for sport or for a living 2. a ship used in fishing

fish·er·man's bend (-mənz) a kind of knot: see KNOT, illus.

fish·er·y (-ē) *n.*, *pl.* -**er·ies** 1. the business of catching, packing, or selling fish, or lobsters, shrimp, etc. 2. a place where fish, etc. are caught; fishing ground 3. the legal right to catch fish in certain waters or at certain times 4. a place where fish are bred

fish·eye lens (fish'ī') a camera lens designed to record a full 180-degree field of vision

fish flake [Canad.] a platform for drying fish

☆**fish flour** fish-protein concentrate in pulverized form

fish hawk *same as* OSPREY

fish·hook (-hook') *n.* a hook, usually barbed, for catching fish

fish·ing (-iŋ) *n.* 1. the catching of fish for sport or for a living 2. a place to fish

fishing banks (or **grounds**) a place where fish are abundant, as off Newfoundland

☆**fishing pole** a simple device for fishing, often one that is improvised, consisting of a pole, line, and hook

fishing rod a slender pole with an attached line, hook, and usually a reel, used in fishing

fishing tackle the equipment, as hooks, lines, rods, reels, etc., used in fishing

fish joint a joint, as of two railroad rails, held together by fishplates along the sides

☆**fish ladder** an ascending series of pools so arranged as to permit fish to leap or swim upward from level to level and thus pass over dams and waterfalls

fish line a line, usually with a hook at one end, used in fishing

fish meal ground, dried fish, used as fertilizer or fodder

fish·mon·ger (-muŋ'gər, -män'-) *n.* a dealer in fish

fish·plate (-plāt') *n.* [prob. < Fr. *fiche*, means of fixing: see FISH[1]] either of a pair of steel plates bolting two rails together lengthwise, as on a railroad

fish·pond (-pänd') *n.* a pond where fish are kept or bred

☆**fish·pound** (-pound') *n.* [Dial.] a submerged net for catching fish; weir

fish-skin disease (-skin') *same as* ICHTHYOSIS

☆**fish stick** a small oblong fillet or cake of fish breaded and fried

☆**fish story** [from the conventional exaggeration by fishermen of the size of the fish that escaped being caught] [Colloq.] an unbelievable story; exaggeration

fish tackle hook and tackle for raising the flukes of an anchor up to the gunwale of a ship

fish·tail (-tāl') *vi.* to retard the speed of a landing airplane by swinging the tail from side to side

fish·wife (-wīf') *n.*, *pl.* -**wives** (-wīvz') 1. a woman who sells fish 2. a coarse, scolding woman

☆**fish·worm** (-wurm') *n.* same as ANGLEWORM

fish·y (fish'ē) *adj.* **fish'i·er**, **fish'i·est** 1. of or full of fish 2. like a fish in odor, taste, etc. 3. like that of a fish; dull or expressionless [a *fishy* stare] 4. [Colloq.] causing doubt or suspicion; questionable —**fish'i·ly** *adv.* —**fish'i·ness** *n.*

Fiske (fisk) 1. *John*, (born *Edmund Fisk Green*) 1842–1901; U.S. historian & philosopher 2. *Minnie Mad·dern* (mad'ərn), (born *Minnie Davey*) 1865–1932; U.S. actress

fis·sile (fis'l; *chiefly Brit.*, -il) *adj.* [L. *fissilis* < *fissus*, pp. of *findere*, to cleave: see ff.] 1. that can be split 2. *same as* FISSIONABLE —**fis·sil·i·ty** (fi sil'ə tē) *n.*

fis·sion (fish'ən) *n.* [L. *fissio* < *fissus*, pp. of *findere*, to cleave, split < IE. base *bheid-*, to split, whence BEETLE[1], BITE, BOAT] 1. a splitting apart; division into parts 2. *same as* NUCLEAR FISSION 3. *Biol.* a form of asexual reproduction, found in various simple plants and animals, in which the parent organism divides into two or more approximately equal parts, each becoming an independent individual —*vi.*, *vt.* to undergo or cause to undergo nuclear fission —**fis'sion·a·ble** *adj.*

fis·sip·a·rous (fi sip'ər əs) *adj.* [< L. *fissus* (see prec.) + -PAROUS] *Biol.* reproducing by fission

fis·si·ped (fis'i ped') *adj.* [< L. *fissipes* (gen. *fissipedis*), cloven-footed < *fissus* (see FISSION) + *pes*, foot] *Zool.* having the toes separated from each other: also **fis·sip·e·dal** (fi sip'ə dəl) —*n.* any of a suborder (Fissipedia) of flesh-eating mammals, including cats, dogs, etc.

fis·si·ros·tral (fis'i räs'trəl) *adj.* [< L. *fissi-*, cloven (< *fissus*: see FISSION) + *rostrum*, beak (see ROSTRUM) + -AL] 1. broad and deeply cleft: said of the beaks of certain birds 2. having such a beak: said of certain birds, as the swifts and nighthawks

fis·sure (fish'ər) *n.* [ME. < OFr. < L. *fissura* < *fissus*: see FISSION] 1. a long, narrow, deep cleft or crack 2. a dividing or breaking into parts 3. *Anat.* a groove between lobes or parts of an organ, as in the brain 4. *Med.* a break or ulceration where skin and mucous membrane join, esp. at the anus —*vt.*, *vi.* -**sured**, -**sur·ing** to break into parts; crack or split apart

fist (fist) *n.* [ME. < OE. *fyst*, akin to G. *faust* (OHG. *füst*) < ? IE. *pnksti* or < ? *penkwe*, FIVE, in sense "clenched five (fingers)"] 1. a hand with the fingers closed tightly into the palm, as for hitting; clenched hand 2. [Colloq.] *a)* a hand *b)* the grasp 3. *Printing* the sign (☞), used to direct special attention to something —*vt.* 1. to hit with the fist 2. *Naut.* to grasp or handle

fist·ful (-fool) *n.* same as HANDFUL

fist·ic (fis'tik) *adj.* having to do with boxing; fought with the fists; pugilistic

fis·ti·cuffs (fis'ti kufs') *n.pl.* [< FIST + CUFF[2]] 1. a fight with the fists 2. the science of boxing

fis·tu·la (fis'choo la) *n.*, *pl.* -**las**, -**lae'** (-lē') [ME. < OFr. < L., a pipe, ulcer] 1. [Rare] a pipe or tube 2. an abnormal passage from an abscess, cavity, or hollow organ to the skin or to another abscess, cavity, or organ

fis·tu·lous (-ləs) *adj.* [ME. < L. *fistulosus* < *fistula*] 1. shaped like a pipe or tube; tubular 2. of or like a fistula Also **fis'tu·lar** (-lər)

fit[1] (fit) *vt.* **fit'ted** or **fit**, **fit'ted**, **fit'ting** [ME. *fitten* < ? or

akin ? to ON. *fitja*, to knit, tie ends of thread, akin to OHG. *fizza*, skein of thread, ult. < IE. **pedyo-*, of the foot < base **ped-*, FOOT] **1.** to be suitable or adapted to; be in accord with [let the punishment *fit* the crime] **2.** to be the proper size, shape, etc. for **3.** *a)* to make or alter so as to fit *b)* to measure (a person) for something that must be fitted [*fit* him for a brace] **4.** to make suitable or qualified [his training *fits* him for the job] **5.** *a)* to insert, as into a receptacle [to *fit* a key in a lock] *b)* to make a place for (with *in* or *into*) [to *fit* another passenger into the crowded car] **6.** to equip; outfit (often with *out*) —*vi.* **1.** to be suitable or proper **2.** to be suitably adapted; be in accord or harmony (often with *in* or *into*) **3.** to have the proper size or shape for a particular figure, space, etc. [his coat *fits* well, this won't *fit* into the box] —*adj.* **fit′ter**, **fit′test** [ME. *fyt*] **1.** adapted, adjusted, qualified, or suited to some purpose, function, situation, etc. [food *fit* to eat] **2.** proper; right; appropriate **3.** in good physical condition; healthy **4.** [Colloq.] disturbed enough; inclined [she was *fit* to scream] —*n.* [prob. < the *v.*] **1.** the condition of fitting or being fitted **2.** the manner or degree of fitting or of fitting together [a good *fit*, a tight *fit*] **3.** anything that fits —☆**fit to be tied** [Colloq.] frustrated and angry
SYN.—**fit**, the broadest term here, means having the qualities or qualifications to meet some condition, circumstance, purpose, or demand [*fit* for a king]; **suitable** is applied to that which accords with the requirements or needs of the occasion or circumstances [shoes *suitable* for hiking]; **proper** implies reference to that which naturally or rightfully belongs to something or suggests a fitness or suitability dictated by good judgment [*proper* respect for one's elders]; that is **appropriate** which is especially or distinctively fit or suitable; **fitting** is applied to that which accords harmoniously with the character, spirit, or tone of something; **apt**, in this connection, is used of that which is exactly suited to the purpose [an *apt* phrase]

fit² (fit) *n.* [ME. < OE. (rare) *fitt*, conflict] **1.** any sudden, uncontrollable attack; paroxysm [a *fit* of coughing] **2.** *a)* a sharp, brief display of feeling [a *fit* of anger] *b)* a transient mood [a *fit* of the blues] **3.** a temporary burst of activity **4.** *Med.* a seizure in which the victim loses consciousness or has convulsions or both —**by fits (and starts)** in an irregular way; in bursts of activity followed by periods of inactivity —**have (or ☆throw) a fit** [Colloq.] to become very angry or upset

fit³ (fit) *n.* [ME. *fitte* < OE. *fitt*, akin to OS. (Latinized) pl. *vitteas*, sections of a poem (the *Heliand*), OHG. *fizza*: see FIT¹] [Archaic] a short section of a poem, ballad, or song

fitch (fich) *n.* [ME. *ficheu* < OFr. *fichau* < MDu. *vitsche*, akin to OHG. *wiessa*, WEASEL] **1.** *same as* POLECAT (sense 1) **2.** its pelt or fur Also **fitch′et** (-it), **fitch′ew** (-ōō)

Fitch (fich) **1.** (**William**) **Clyde**, 1865–1909; U.S. playwright **2. John**, 1743–98; U.S. inventor of a steamboat

Fitch·burg (fich′bərg) [after John *Fitch*, local civic leader] city in N Mass.: pop. 43,000

fit·ful (fit′fəl) *adj.* [FIT² + -FUL] characterized by irregular or intermittent activity, impulses, etc.; spasmodic; restless —**fit′ful·ly** *adv.* —**fit′ful·ness** *n.*

fit·ly (fit′lē) *adv.* **1.** in a fit manner; suitably **2.** at the right time

fit·ment (-mənt) *n.* [Chiefly Brit.] any of various furnishings, fixtures, or detachable parts

fit·ness (-nis) *n.* the condition of being fit; suitability, appropriateness, healthiness, etc.

fit·ted (fit′id) *adj.* designed to conform to the contours of that which it covers [*fitted* bed sheets, a *fitted* coat]

fit·ter (-ər) *n.* a person who fits; specif., *a)* a person who alters or adjusts garments to fit *b)* a person who supplies, installs, or adjusts machinery, pipes, etc.

fit·ting (-iŋ) *adj.* suitable; proper; appropriate —*n.* **1.** an adjustment or trying on of clothes, etc. for fit **2.** a small part used to join, adjust, or adapt other parts, as in a system of pipes **3.** [*pl.*] the fixtures, furnishings, or decorations of a house, office, automobile, etc. —*SYN.* see FIT¹ —**fit′ting·ly** *adv.*

Fitz·Ger·ald (fits jer′əld), **Edward** (born *Edward Purcell*) 1809–83; Eng. poet & translator of *The Rubáiyát*: also written **Fitzgerald**

Fitz·ger·ald (-jer′əld), **F(rancis) Scott (Key)** 1896–1940; U.S. author

Fiu·me (fyōō′me) former (*It.*) name of RIJEKA

five (fiv) *adj.* [ME. < OE. *fif*, with assimilated nasal, akin to G. *fünf* (OHG. < Goth. *fimf*) < IE. base **penkue-*, whence Sans. *páñca*, Gr. *pente*, L. *quinque*] totaling one more than four —*n.* **1.** the cardinal number between four and six; 5; V **2.** any group of five people or things, esp. ☆a basketball team **3.** something numbered five or having five units, as *a)* a playing card, domino, face of a die, etc. ☆*b)* [Colloq.] a five-dollar bill

☆**five-and-ten-cent store** (-'n ten′sent′) a store that sells a wide variety of inexpensive merchandise, orig. with many articles priced at five or ten cents: also **five′-and-ten′, five′-and-dime′** (-'n dīm′) *n.*

Five Civilized Tribes the Cherokee, Chickasaw, Choctaw, Creek, and Seminole tribes of the Indian Territory (now the eastern part of Oklahoma)

five-fin·ger (-fiŋ′gər) *n.* [OE. *fiffingre*] **1.** *same as* CINQUEFOIL (sense 1) ☆**2.** *same as* VIRGINIA CREEPER **3.** any of various plants having leaves with five parts or flowers with five petals

five·fold (-fōld′) *adj.* [see -FOLD] **1.** having five parts **2.** having five times as much or as many —*adv.* five times as much or as many

☆**five hundred** a variety of euchre or rummy in which the object is to score five hundred points

☆**Five Nations** a confederation of Iroquoian Indians, including the Mohawks, Oneidas, Onondagas, Cayugas, and Senecas: see also SIX NATIONS

fiv·er (fī′vər) *n.* [Slang] ☆**1.** a five-dollar bill **2.** [Brit.] a five-pound note

fives (fīvz) *n.* [< ? *five* fingers of the hand] a kind of handball played in England

fix (fiks) *vt.* **fixed**, **fix′ing** [ME. *fixen* < *fix*, fixed < L. *fixus*, pp. of *figere*, to fasten, attach: for IE. base see FINISH] **1.** *a)* to make firm, stable, or secure *b)* to fasten or attach firmly **2.** to set firmly in the mind **3.** *a)* to direct steadily [to *fix* the eyes on a target] *b)* to direct one's eyes steadily at [to *fix* the target] **4.** to make rigid or stiff [to *fix* one's jaw] **5.** to make permanent or lasting [color is *fixed* in dyeing] **6.** to arrange or establish definitely; set [to *fix* the date of a wedding] **7.** to arrange properly or in a certain way; set in order; adjust **8.** to restore to proper condition; repair, mend, remedy, heal, etc. **9.** to bank, refuel, and tend (a fire) **10.** to prepare and cook (food or meals) **11.** to preserve (a specimen) so that its tissue, etc. can be used for microscopic study ☆**12.** [Colloq.] to influence the result or action of (a horse race, jury, election, etc.) to one's advantage by bribery, trickery, etc. ☆**13.** [Colloq.] to revenge oneself on; get even with; punish or chastise **14.** [Colloq.] to spay or castrate **15.** *Chem. a)* to make solid or nonvolatile *b)* to cause (atmospheric nitrogen) to combine with other elements or compounds to form nitrates, ammonia, etc. **16.** *Photog.* to make (a film, print, etc.) permanent and prevent from fading by washing in a chemical solution —*vi.* **1.** to become fixed, firm, or stable **2.** [Colloq. or Dial.] to prepare or intend [I'm *fixing* to go hunting] —*n.* **1.** the position of a ship or aircraft determined from the bearings of two or more known points or from radio signals ☆**2.** [Colloq.] a difficult or awkward situation; predicament ☆**3.** [Slang] *a)* the act of fixing the outcome of a contest, situation, etc. *b)* a contest, situation, etc. that has been fixed **4.** [Slang] an injection of a narcotic, as heroin, by an addict —*SYN.* see PREDICAMENT —**fix on** (or **upon**) to choose; settle on —**fix up** [Colloq.] **1.** to repair, mend, remedy, etc. **2.** to arrange properly; set in order **3.** to make arrangements for —**fix′a·ble** *adj.*

fix·ate (fik′sāt) *vt., vi.* **-at·ed**, **-at·ing** [< ML. *fixatus*, pp. of *fixare*: see FIX] to make or become fixed; specif., **1.** to direct and focus (the eyes) on (a point or object) **2.** *Psychoanalysis* to attach or arrest (the expression of the libidinal or aggressive drive) at an early stage of psychosexual development

fix·a·tion (fik sā′shən) *n.* [ME. *fixacioun* < ML. *fixatio* < *fixatus*: see prec.] **1.** a fixing, or fixating, or a being fixed, or fixated; specif., *a)* the directing and focusing of the eyes *b)* popularly, an exaggerated preoccupation; obsession **2.** *Chem. a)* reduction into a solid or nonvolatile form *b)* the fixing of atmospheric nitrogen: see NITROGEN FIXATION **3.** *Photog.* the treatment of a film, print, etc. to make it permanent **4.** *Psychoanalysis* an arrest of the expression of the libidinal or aggressive drives at an early stage of psychosexual development, or a persistent attachment to some object or person that derives from this

fix·a·tive (fik′sə tiv) *adj.* [FIX + -ATIVE] that is able or tends to make permanent, prevent fading, etc. —*n.* a substance that makes something permanent, prevents fading, etc., as a mordant

fixed (fikst) *adj.* **1.** firmly placed or attached; not movable **2.** established; settled; set [a *fixed* price] **3.** steady; unmoving; resolute [a *fixed* purpose] **4.** remaining in the same position relative to the earth [a *fixed* satellite] **5.** persisting obstinately in the mind and tending to control the thoughts and action; obsessive [a *fixed* idea] **6.** *Chem. a)* nonvolatile: see FIXED OIL *b)* incorporated into a stable compound from its free state, as atmospheric nitrogen ☆**7.** [Colloq.] supplied with something needed, specif. money [comfortably *fixed* for life] ☆**8.** [Slang] with the outcome dishonestly arranged beforehand [a *fixed* race] —**fix·ed·ly** (fik′sid lē) *adv.* —**fix′ed·ness** *n.*

☆**fixed charge** any of certain charges, as taxes, rent, interest, etc., which must be paid, usually at regular intervals, without being changed and without reference to the amount of business done

fixed oil a nonvolatile oil, esp. one found in fatty animal tissue and the seeds of some plants

fixed star a star whose great distance from the earth makes it appear to keep the same position in relation to other stars

fix·er (fik′sər) *n.* **1.** a person or thing that fixes ☆**2.** [Colloq.] a person who pays bribes or uses his influence to manipulate results, as in keeping others from being punished for illegal acts ☆**3.** [Slang] a person who sells narcotics illegally to addicts

fix·ings (-siŋz) *n.pl.* ☆[Colloq.] accessories or trimmings [roast turkey and all the *fixings*]

fix·i·ty (-sə tē) *n.* **1.** the quality or state of being fixed; steadiness or permanence **2.** *pl.* **-ties** anything fixed

fixt (fikst) *poet. pt. and pp. of* FIX

fix·ture (fiks′chər) *n.* [< ME. *fixure* (< LL. *fixura* < L.

fixus: see FIX), altered after MIXTURE] **1.** anything firmly in place **2.** any of the fittings or furniture of a house, store, etc. attached to the building and, ordinarily, considered legally a part of it [bathroom *fixtures*] **3.** any person or thing that has remained in a situation or place so long as to seem fixed there **4.** [Chiefly Brit.] a well-established, regularly occurring sports or social event

fizz (fiz) *n.* [echoic] **1.** a hissing, sputtering sound, as of an effervescent drink **2.** an effervescent drink —*vi.* **fizzed, fiz′zing 1.** to make a hissing or bubbling sound **2.** to give off gas bubbles; bubble up; effervesce

fiz·zle (fiz′'l) *vi.* **-zled, -zling** [ME. *fesilen,* to break wind silently, akin to *fisten,* MDu. *vijsten,* ON. *fisa*] **1.** to make a hissing or sputtering sound **2.** [Colloq.] to fail, esp. after a successful beginning (often with *out*) —*n.* **1.** a hissing or sputtering sound **2.** [Colloq.] an attempt that ends in failure; fiasco

fiz·zy (-ē) *adj.* **-zi·er, -zi·est** fizzing; effervescent

fjeld (fyeld) *n.* [Norw. < ON. *fiall, fjall,* FELL⁵] a barren plateau in Scandinavian countries

fjord (fyôrd) *n.* same as FIORD

Fl. **1.** Flanders **2.** Flemish

fl. **1.** floor **2.** florin(s); also, guilder(s) **3.** [L. *floruit*] (he or she) flourished **4.** fluid

Fla. Florida

flab (flab) *n.* [back-formation < FLABBY] [Colloq.] sagging, flaccid flesh

flab·ber·gast (flab′ər gast) *vt.* [18th-c. slang < ? FLABBY + AGHAST] to make speechless with amazement; astonish —*SYN.* see SURPRISE

flab·by (flab′ē) *adj.* **-bi·er, -bi·est** [var. of *flappy* < FLAP] **1.** lacking firmness; limp and soft; flaccid [flabby muscles] **2.** lacking force; weak —**flab′bi·ly** *adv.* —**flab′bi·ness** *n.*

fla·bel·late (flə bel′āt) *adj.* [< FLABELLUM + -ATE¹] fan-shaped. also **fla·bel′li·form′** (-ə fôrm′)

fla·bel·lum (-əm) *n., pl.* **-bel·la** (-ə) [L., a fan, dim. of *flabrum,* a breeze < *flare,* to blow: for IE. base see BLADDER] **1.** a large fan carried by the Pope's attendants on ceremonial occasions **2.** *Zool.* a fan-shaped organ or structure of the body

flac·cid (flak′sid, flas′id) *adj.* [L. *flaccidus* < *flaccus,* flabby] **1.** hanging in loose folds or wrinkles; soft and limp; flabby [flaccid muscles] **2.** lacking force; weak; feeble —**flac·cid′i·ty** *n.* —**flac′cid·ly** *adv.*

☆**flack** (flak) *n.* [< ?] [Slang] same as PRESS AGENT —*vi.* [Slang] to serve as a press agent —**flack′er·y** *n.*

‡**fla·con** (flà kôn′; E. flak′'n) *n.* [Fr.: see FLAGON] a small flask with a stopper, as for holding perfume

flag¹ (flag) *n.* [LME. *flagge* < ? FLAG⁴, in obs. sense "to flutter"] **1.** a piece of cloth or bunting, often attached to a staff, with distinctive colors, patterns, or symbolic devices, used as a national or state symbol, to signal, etc.; banner; standard; ensign **2.** [pl.] [Now Rare] long feathers or quills, as on a hawk **3.** the tail of a deer **4.** the bushy tail of certain dogs, as setters and some hounds **5.** *Music* any of the lines extending from a stem, indicating whether the note is an eighth, sixteenth, etc. —*vt.* **flagged, flag′ging 1.** to decorate or mark with flags **2.** to signal with or as with a flag; esp., to signal to stop (often with *down*) **3.** to send (a message) by signaling —**dip the flag** to salute by lowering a flag briefly —**strike the** (or **one's**) **flag 1.** to lower the flag **2.** to give up; surrender

flag² (flag) *n.* [ME. *flagge* < ON. *flaga,* slab of stone < IE. base *plāk-,* to spread out, flat, whence L. *placidus,* flat] *same as* FLAGSTONE —*vt.* **flagged, flag′ging** to pave with flagstones

flag³ (flag) *n.* [ME. *flagge,* akin ? to ff.] **1.** *a)* any of various wild irises with flat fans of sword-shaped leaves and white, blue, or yellow flowers *b)* any of various cultivated irises **2.** *same as* SWEET FLAG **3.** *same as* CATTAIL **4.** the flower or leaf of any of these plants

flag⁴ (flag) *vi.* **flagged, flag′ging** [16th c., prob. var. of ME. *flakken* < ? ON. *flakka,* to flutter < IE. base *plāk-,* to strike] **1.** to become limp; droop **2.** to lose strength; grow weak or tired [his enthusiasm *flagged*]

☆**Flag Day** *n.* June 14, anniversary of the day in 1777 when the U.S. flag was adopted **2.** [f- d-] in England, a day when people give to some special fund for charity and get small flags in token of their contribution

flag·el·lant (flaj′ə lənt, flə jel′ənt) *n.* [< L. *flagellans,* prp. of *flagellare:* see FLAGELLATE] a person who whips; esp., one who whips himself or has himself whipped as a religious discipline or for sexual stimulation —*adj.* engaging in flagellation

flag·el·late (flaj′ə lāt′; *for adj., also* flə jel′it) *vt.* **-lat′ed, -lat′ing** [< L. *flagellatus,* pp. of *flagellare,* to whip, scourge < *flagellum,* a whip, dim. of *flagrum* < IE. base *bhlag̑-,* to beat, whence ON. *bluk,* a slap] to whip; flog —*adj.* **1.** having a flagellum or flagella: also **flag′el·lat′ed 2.** shaped like a flagellum —*n.* a flagellate protozoan —**flag′el·la′tor** *n.*

flag·el·la·tion (flaj′ə lā′shən) *n.* [ME. *flagellacioun* < LL.(Ec.) *flagellatio:* see FLAGELLATE] a whipping or flogging, esp. as a religious discipline or for sexual stimulation —**flag′el·la·to·ry** (-lə tôr′ē) *adj.*

fla·gel·li·form (flə jel′ə fôrm′) *adj.* [< ff. + -FORM] shaped

like a whiplash or flagellum; long, slender, round, and tapering

fla·gel·lum (flə jel′əm) *n., pl.* **-la** (-ə), **-lums** [L., a whip. dim. of *flagrum:* see FLAGELLATE] **1.** a whip **2.** *Biol.* a whiplike part or process of some cells, esp. of certain bacteria, protozoans, etc. that is an organ of locomotion or produces a current in the surrounding fluid **3.** *Bot.* a threadlike shoot or runner **4.** *Zool.* the terminal, lashlike portion of the antenna in many insects

flag·eo·let (flaj′ə let′) *n.* [Fr., dim. of OFr. *flageol, flajeol,* a pipe, flute < VL. **flabeolum,* a flute < L. *flare,* to BLOW¹] a small wind instrument of the fipple flute family, similar to a recorder

Flagg (flag), **James Montgomery** 1877–1960; U.S. illustrator

flag·ging¹ (flag′in) *adj.* [prp. of FLAG⁴] weakening or drooping —**flag′ging·ly** *adv.*

flag·ging² (flag′in) *n.* flagstones or a pavement made of flagstones

flag·gy¹ (flag′ē) *adj.* full of flags, or irises

flag·gy² (flag′ē) *adj.* of or like flagstone

fla·gi·tious (flə jish′əs) *adj.* [ME. *flagicious* < L. *flagitiosus* < *flagitium,* shameful act < *flagitare,* to demand, akin to *flagrum:* see FLAGELLATE] shamefully wicked; vile and scandalous —**fla·gi′tious·ly** *adv.* —**fla·gi′tious·ness** *n.*

flag·man (flag′mən) *n., pl.* **-men** (-mən) a person whose work is signaling with a flag or lantern

flag officer ☆*U.S. Navy* any officer above the rank of captain, entitled to display a flag indicating his rank

flag of truce a white flag shown to an enemy to indicate a desire to confer or parley

flag·on (flag′ən) *n.* [ME. < OFr. *flacon* < LL. *flasco* (gen. *flasconis*) < *flascu* < Gmc. **flasko,* FLASK] **1.** a container for liquids, with a handle, a narrow neck, a spout, and, sometimes, a lid **2.** the contents of a flagon

flag·pole (flag′pōl′) *n.* a pole on which a flag is raised and flown; also **flag′staff′** (-staf′, -stäf′)

fla·gran·cy (flā′grən sē) *n.* the quality or state of being flagrant: also **fla′grance**

fla·grant (flā′grənt) *adj.* [L. *flagrans,* prp. of *flagrare,* to flame, blaze < IE. base **bhleg-,* to shine, burn, whence BLACK] **1.** glaringly bad; notorious; outrageous **2.** [Archaic] flaming; blazing —**fla′grant·ly** *adv.*

SYN.—**flagrant** applies to anything that is so obviously bad or wrong as to be notorious [a *flagrant* violation of the law]; **glaring** is used of something bad that is even more conspicuous so that it is immediately perceived [a *glaring* error in arithmetic]; **gross** implies an even greater degree of badness or wrongness, so as to deserve censure [gross negligence]; **rank,** in this connection, is used contemptuously to imply that no exaggeration is intended in the description [it was *rank* folly to send the letter] See also OUTRAGEOUS

‡**fla·gran·te de·lic·to** (flə gran′tē də lik′tō) [L., lit., during the blazing of the crime] in the very act of committing the offense; red-handed: also **in flagrante delicto**

flag·ship (flag′ship′) *n.* **1.** the ship that carries the commander of a fleet or squadron and displays his flag **2.** the finest, largest, or newest ship of a steamship line

Flag·stad (flag′stad; *Norw.* flåg′stä′), **Kir·sten** (kir′sten; *Norw.* kish′t'n) 1895–1962; Norw. soprano

flag station a flag stop on a railroad line

flag·stone (flag′stōn′) *n.* [FLAG² + STONE] **1.** any hard stone that splits into flat pieces and is used in paving walks, terraces, etc. **2.** a piece of such stone

☆**flag stop** a place at which a bus, train, etc. stops only when signaled

flag-wav·ing (flag′wā′vin) *n.* an effort to arouse intense patriotic or nationalistic feelings by a deliberate appeal to the emotions

Fla·her·ty (fla′ər tē), **Robert (Joseph)** 1884–1951; U.S. motion-picture director, esp. of documentaries

flail (flāl) *n.* [ME. *fleil* < OFr. *flaiel* & OE. **flegel* (akin to L. *flagellum,* a whip, scourge)] a farm tool consisting of a free-swinging stick tied to the end of a long handle, used to thresh grain by hand —*vt., vi.* **1.** to thresh with a flail **2.** to strike or beat as with a flail **3.** to move (one's arms) about like flails

flair (fler) *n.* [ME., odor, fragrance < OFr. < *flairer,* to emit an odor < LL. *flagrare,* for L. *fragrare,* to smell, reek < IE. **bhrag-,* prob. < **bher-,* to boil up, whence BARM, BREATH] **1.** orig., sense of smell; hence, keen, natural discernment **2.** a natural talent or ability; aptitude; knack **3.** [Colloq.] a sense of what is stylish and striking; dash

FLAIL

fat, āpe, cär; ten, ēven; is, bīte; gō, hôrn, tōōl, look; oil, out; up, fur; get; yet; chin; she; thin, then; zh, leisure; ŋ, ring; ə for *a* in *ago, e* in *agent, i* in *sanity, o* in *comply, u* in *focus;* ' as in *able* (ā′b'l); Fr. bål; ë, Fr. coeur; ö, Fr. feu; Fr. mon; ô, Fr. coq; ü, Fr. duc; r, Fr. cri; H, G. ich; kh, G. doch. See inside front cover. ☆ Americanism; ‡ foreign; * hypothetical; < derived from

flak (flak) *n.* [G. < *Fl(ieger)a(bwehr)k(anone)*, antiaircraft gun] the fire of antiaircraft guns

flake¹ (flāk) *n.* [ME. < Scand., as in Norw. *flak*, ice floe, ON. *flakna*, to flake off < IE. base **plāg-*, var. of **plāk-*, flat, whence FLAG²] 1. a small, thin mass [a *flake* of snow] 2. a thin piece or layer split off or peeled off from anything; chip —*vt.*, *vi.* **flaked**, **flak'ing** 1. to form into flakes 2. to chip or peel off in flakes 3. to make or become spotted with flakes —**flak'er** *n.*

flake² (flāk) *n.* [ME. *flake*, *fleke* < ON. *flaki*, *fleki*, hurdle, akin to MDu. *vlake*: for IE. base see prec.] a platform or rack for storing or drying food

flake³ (flāk) *n.*, *vt.* **flaked**, **flak'ing** [prob. spec. use of FLAKE¹] *same as* FAKE² —**flake out** [Slang] 1. to go to sleep 2. to faint

flake white a white pigment made of flakes of white lead

flak·y (-ē) *adj.* **flak'i·er**, **flak'i·est** 1. containing or made up of flakes 2. breaking easily into flakes ☆3. [Slang] very eccentric or unconventional —**flak'i·ly** *adv.* —**flak'i·ness** *n.*

flam¹ (flam) *n.* [prob. contr. of obs. *flamfew*, a trifle, gewgaw < OFr. *fanfelue*, tawdry finery, ult. < Gr. *pompholyx*, bubble, boss] 1. a deceptive trick or a lie 2. blarney; humbug —*vt.*, *vi.* **flammed**, **flam'ming** to deceive by lying or flattery

flam² (flam) *n.* [prob. echoic] a drumbeat made by striking the head of a drum with both drumsticks almost but not quite simultaneously

†flam·bé (fläṅ bā′) *adj.* [Fr., lit., flaming] served with a sauce containing brandy, rum, etc. set afire to flame —*n.* a dessert or other dish so served

flam·beau (flam′bō) *n.*, *pl.* **-beaux** (-bōz), **-beaus** [Fr., dim. of OFr. *flambe*: see FLAME] 1. a lighted torch 2. a large, ornamental candlestick

flam·boy·ant (flam boi′ənt) *adj.* [Fr., prp. of OFr. *flamboyer* < *flambe*: see FLAME] 1. designating or of a kind of architecture, as late French Gothic, characterized by flamelike tracery of windows and florid decoration 2. flamelike or brilliant in form or color 3. too showy or ornate; florid, extravagant, etc. [a *flamboyant* costume] —*n.* common name for ROYAL POINCIANA —**flam·boy'ance**, **flam·boy'an·cy** *n.* —**flam·boy'ant·ly** *adv.*

flame (flām) *n.* [ME. < OFr. *flamme* (< L. *flamma*) & *flambe* < L. *flammula*, dim. of *flamma* < base of *flagrare*, to burn: see FLAGRANT] 1. the burning gas or vapor of a fire, seen as a flickering light of various colors; blaze 2. a tongue of light rising from a fire 3. the state of burning with a blaze of light [to burst into *flame*] 4. a) a thing like a flame in heat, brilliance, etc. b) brilliance or bright coloring 5. an intense emotion; strong passion 6. a sweetheart: orig. poetic, now usually humorous —*vi.* **flamed**, **flam'ing** [ME. *flammen* < OFr. *flamer* < L. *flammare*] 1. to burn with a blaze of light; burst into flame 2. to light up with color as if blazing; grow red or hot [a face *flaming* with anger] 3. to show intense emotion; become very excited —*vt.* 1. [Now Rare] to burn or heat with flame 2. to treat with flame 3. [Poet.] to arouse (emotions); inflame — *SYN.* see BLAZE¹ —**flame up** (or **out**) to burst out in or as in flames

flame cell a special, hollow cell found in the excretory tubules of many lower animals, as flatworms, having an internal tuft of cilia that produces movement of the excretory products

fla·men (flā′men) *n.*, *pl.* **fla'mens**, **flam·i·nes** (flam′ə nēz′) [ME. *flamin* < L. *flamen* < IE. **bhlagmen-*, priest, magician, whence Sans. *brahmán-*] in ancient Rome, a priest in the service of one particular god

fla·men·co (flə men′kō) *n.*, *pl.* **-cos** [Sp., Flemish < DuFl. *Flaming*, a Fleming] 1. the Spanish gypsy style of dance (characterized by stamping, clapping, etc.) or music (typically very emotional and mournful) 2. a song or dance in this style

flame·out (flām′out′) *n.* the stopping of combustion in a jet engine, esp. as a result of some abnormal flight condition

flame·proof (-prōōf′) *adj.* 1. not readily damaged by fire 2. not catching fire

flame thrower [transl. of G. *flammenwerfer*] a weapon for shooting a stream of flaming gasoline, oil, napalm, etc. at enemy troops and positions

flame tree 1. an Australian tree (*Brachychiton acerifolium*) of the sterculia family, with maplelike leaves and brilliant scarlet flowers 2. any of various trees with brilliant red flowers

flam·ing (flā′miṅ) *adj.* 1. burning with flames; blazing 2. like a flame in brilliance or heat [*flaming* colors] 3. intensely emotional; ardent; passionate 4. [Now Rare] startling or flagrant —**flam'ing·ly** *adv.*

fla·min·go (flə miṅ′gō) *n.*, *pl.* **-gos**, **-goes** [Port. *flamingo* < Sp. *flamenco*, lit., Flemish (see FLAMENCO): associated with *flama*, FLAME, because of its color] any of a family (Phoenicopteridae) of large, tropical wading birds with long legs, webbed feet, long necks, downward-curving beaks, and bright pink or red feathers

FLAMINGO
(to 4 ft. high,
wingspread 5–6 ft.)

Fla·min·i·an Way (flə min′ē ən) [built (220 B.C.) by the Roman censor Gaius *Flaminius*] ancient Roman paved highway from Rome to Ariminium (Rimini): c. 210 mi.

flam·ma·ble (flam′ə b'l) *adj.* [L. *flammare*, to FLAME + -ABLE] easily set on fire; that will burn readily or quickly: term now preferred to INFLAMMABLE in commerce, industry, etc. —**flam'ma·bil'i·ty** *n.*

Flam·ma·rion (flä ma ryôṅ′), **Camille** 1842–1925; Fr. astronomer

flam·y (flā′mē) *adj.* [Now Rare] of or like flame

flan (flan; *Fr.* flän) *n.* [Fr. < OFr. *flaon* (whence ME. *flawn*, flan) < ML. *flado* (gen. *fladonis*) < OHG. *flado*, flat cake, akin to ME. *flathen*: for IE. base see FLAT¹] 1. a piece of shaped metal ready to be made into a coin by the stamp of a die; blank 2. [Chiefly Brit.] a tart filled with custard, fruit, cheese, etc.

Flan·ders (flan′dərz) region (in medieval times a county) in NW Europe, on the North Sea, including a part of NW France, provinces of East Flanders & West Flanders in Belgium, & a part of SW Netherlands

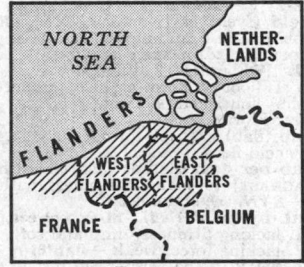
FLANDERS

†flâ·nerie (flä nrē′) *n.* [Fr.: see ff.] idle strolling

†flâ·neur (flä nër′) *n.* [Fr. < *flâner*, to stroll] a person who strolls about idly, as along the boulevards; idler

flange (flanj) *n.* [< ? ME. *flaunch*, a lenticular space on a coat of arms] 1. a projecting rim or collar on a wheel, pipe, rail, etc., to hold it in place, give it strength, guide it, or attach it to something else 2. a tool for making flanges —*vt.* **flanged**, **flang'ing** to put a flange on

FLANGE

flank (flaṅk) *n.* [ME. *flanke* < OFr. *flanc* < Frank. **hlanka*, akin to OHG. *hlanka*, a hip, flank: for IE. base see LANK] 1. the fleshy side of a person or animal between the ribs and the hip 2. a cut of beef from this part 3. loosely, the outer side of the upper part of the human thigh 4. the side of anything 5. *Mil.* the right or left side of a formation or force, or of the projection of a bastion —*adj.* of or having to do with the flank —*vt.* 1. to be at the side of 2. to place at the side, or on either side, of 3. *Mil.* a) to protect the side of (a friendly unit) b) to attack the side of (an enemy unit) c) to pass around the side of (an enemy unit) —*vi.* to be located at the side (with *on* or *upon*)

flank·er (-ər) *n.* 1. *Mil.* a) a fortified position at either flank for protection or attack b) any of several men sent out to protect the flanks of a marching column ☆2. *Football* an offensive back who takes a position closer to the sideline than the rest of the team

flan·nel (flan′'l) *n.* [ME., akin to or < *flanen* < W. *gwlanen* < *gwlan*, wool < IE. base **wel-*, hair, wool, whence L. *lana*, WOOL] 1. a soft, lightweight, loosely woven woolen cloth with a slightly napped surface 2. *same as* COTTON FLANNEL 3. [*pl.*] a) trousers, etc. made of light flannel b) heavy woolen underwear —*vt.* **-neled** or **-nelled**, **-nel·ing** or **-nel·ling** 1. to wrap or clothe in flannel 2. to rub with flannel —**flan'nel·ly** *adj.*

flan·nel·ette, **flan·nel·et** (flan′ə let′) *n.* a soft cotton cloth like cotton flannel but lighter in weight

flan·nel-mouthed (flan′'l mouthd′, -mouthd′) *adj.* 1. speaking thickly, as if one's mouth were full of flannel 2. smooth-talking in an insincere or deceptive way

flap (flap) *n.* [ME. *flappe* < the *v.*] 1. anything flat and broad that is attached at one end and hangs loose or covers an opening [the *flap* of a pocket] 2. the motion or slapping sound of a swinging flap [the *flap* of an awning] 3. a blow with something broad and flat; slap 4. [Slang] a commotion; stir; fuss 5. *Aeron.* a movable airfoil; esp., a section hinged to the trailing edge of a wing between the aileron and the fuselage, usually used to increase lift or drag 6. *Phonet.* a sound produced by slapping the tongue against the roof of the mouth 7. *Surgery* a piece of tissue partly detached from the surrounding tissue, as for grafting —*vt.* **flapped**, **flap'ping** [ME. *flappen*: prob. echoic] 1. to strike with something flat and broad; slap 2. to move back and forth or up and down as in beating the air, usually with some noise [a bird *flapping* its wings] 3. to throw, fling, slam, etc. abruptly or noisily —*vi.* 1. to move back and forth or up and down, as in the wind; flutter 2. to fly or try to fly by flapping the wings 3. to hang down as a flap 4. [Slang] to become excited or confused —**flap'less** *adj.* —**flap'py** *adj.*

flap·doo·dle (flap′dōōd′'l) *n.* [arbitrary formation] [Colloq.] foolish talk; nonsense

flap·drag·on (flap′drag′ən) *n.* [FLAP + DRAGON] earlier name for SNAPDRAGON (sense 2)

flap·jack (flap'jak') *n.* a pancake or griddlecake

flap·per (flap'ər) *n.* 1. a person or thing that flaps; esp., *a*) a flap *b*) a broad fin or flipper *c*) something broad and flat for striking 2. *a*) a young wild duck, partridge, etc. just learning to fly *b*) [Colloq.] in the 1920's, a young woman considered bold and unconventional in actions and dress

flare (fler) *vi.* **flared, flar'ing** [ME. *fleare* < ?] 1. *a*) to blaze up with a sudden, bright light *b*) to burn unsteadily, as a flame whipped about by the wind 2. to burst out suddenly in anger, violence, etc. (often with *up* or *out*) 3. to curve or spread outward, as the bell of a trumpet —*vt.* 1. to make flare 2. to signal with a flare —*n.* 1. a bright, unsteady blaze of light lasting only a little while; outburst of flame 2. *a*) a very bright light used as a distress signal, to light up a landing field, etc. *b*) a substance burned to make such a light 3. a sudden, brief outburst, as of emotion or sound 4. *a*) a curving or spreading outward, as of a skirt *b*) a part that curves or spreads outward 5. *Astron.* a short-lived, spotlike outburst of increased brightness on the sun, esp. near sunspots 6. *Photog.* a foggy spot on film, caused by a reflection of light from the lens —SYN. see BLAZE¹

flare·back (-bak') *n.* a flame shooting out backward or in some other abnormal way from a furnace, cannon, etc.

flare-up (-up') *n.* 1. a sudden outburst of flame 2. a sudden, brief outburst of anger, trouble, etc.

flar·ing (fler'iŋ) *adj.* 1. blazing brightly and unsteadily for a little while 2. gaudy; lurid 3. curving or spreading outward — **flar'ing·ly** *adv.*

flash (flash) *vi.* [ME. *flashen*, to splash, sprinkle; of echoic origin] 1. to send out or reflect a sudden, brief blaze or light, esp. at intervals 2. to sparkle or gleam [eyes *flashing* with anger] 3. to speak abruptly, esp. in anger (usually with *out*) 4. to come, move, or pass swiftly and suddenly; be seen or realized for an instant like a flash of light [an idea *flashed* through his mind] —*vt.* 1. to send out (light, etc.) in sudden, brief spurts 2. to cause to flash 3. to signal with light or reflected light 4. to send (news, messages, etc.) swiftly or suddenly, as by radio 5. to cover (a roof, etc.) with material for weatherproofing 6. [Colloq.] to show briefly or ostentatiously [to *flash* a roll of money] 7. [Archaic] to splash or dash (water) 8. *Glassmaking a*) to put (a colored film of glass) on other glass *b*) to coat with a colored film of glass —*n.* 1. *a*) a sudden, brief light *b*) a sudden burst of flame or heat 2. a brief time; moment 3. a sudden, brief display of thought, understanding, feeling, etc. [a *flash* of wit] ☆4. a brief message or item of news sent by telegraph or radio 5. a gaudy display; showiness 6. *a*) a sudden raising of the water in a channel to help boats over shoals, etc. *b*) a floodgate or other device for doing this 7. a preparation containing burnt sugar, used for coloring liquors 9. anything that flashes; specif., [Colloq.] *a*) a flashlight *b*) a person very quick or adept at something 9. [Archaic] the language of thieves, sharpers, etc. —*adj.* 1. [Colloq.] *a*) flashy; showy; sporty *b*) of thieves, prostitutes, etc. 2. that flashes; happening swiftly or suddenly [a *flash* warning] 3. working with a coordinated flash of light [a *flash* camera] —**flash in the pan** 1. an ineffectual flash of the priming in the pan of a flintlock musket, which fails to explode the charge 2. a sudden, apparently brilliant effort that fails 3. a person who fails after such an effort
SYN.—**flash** implies a sudden, brief, brilliant light; **glance** refers to a darting light, esp. one that is reflected from a surface at an angle; **gleam** suggests a steady, narrow ray of light shining through a background of relative darkness; **sparkle** implies a number of brief, bright, intermittent flashes; **glitter** implies the reflection of such bright, intermittent flashes; **glisten** suggests the reflection of a lustrous light, as from a wet surface; **shimmer** refers to a soft, tremulous reflection of light, as from a slightly disturbed body of water

☆**flash·back** (-bak') *n.* 1. an interruption in the continuity of a story, play, etc. by the narration or portrayal of some earlier episode 2. such an episode

flash·board (-bôrd') *n.* a board or boards placed at the top of a dam to increase the depth or force of the stream

flash·bulb (-bulb') *n.* an electric light bulb giving a brief, dazzling light, for taking photographs

flash burn injury or destruction of body tissue caused by exposure to a flash of intense radiant heat, esp. the heat of a nuclear explosion

☆**flash·card** (-kärd') *n.* any of a set of cards with words, numbers, etc. on them, which are flashed one by one before a class for quick response in a drill

☆**flash·cube** (-kyoob') *n.* a small rotating cube containing a flashbulb in each of four sides, designed for taking pictures rapidly with a flash camera

flash·er (-ər) *n.* a person or thing that flashes; specif., a device for causing lights to go on and off intermittently by closing and opening an electric circuit, or a light that flashes in this way

☆**flash flood** a sudden, violent flood, as after a heavy rain

flash gun a synchronized device that simultaneously sets off a flashbulb and works the camera shutter

flash·ing (-iŋ) *n.* 1. the action of a person or thing that flashes 2. sheets of metal or other material used to weatherproof joints, edges, etc., esp. of a roof

flash·light (-līt') *n.* ☆1. a portable electric light, usually operated by batteries 2. a light that shines in flashes, used for signaling, as in lighthouses, airplane beacons, etc. 3. a brief, dazzling light for taking photographs at night or indoors

flash·o·ver (-ō'vər) *n.* an undesired electrical discharge across an insulator, between a high potential and the ground, etc.

flash point the lowest temperature at which the vapor of a volatile oil will ignite with a flash

FLASHING

flash tube a gaseous discharge tube designed to emit extremely short bursts of very intense light

flash·y (-ē) *adj.* **flash'i·er, flash'i·est** 1. dazzling or bright for a little while; flashing 2. ostentatious and vulgar; gaudy; showy —SYN. see GAUDY¹ —**flash'i·ly** *adv.* —**flash'i·ness** *n.*

flask (flask, fläsk) *n.* [ME. < ML. *flasco* & OE. *flasce*, both < LL. *flasco* < *flasca* < Gmc. *flasko*, bottle, wicker-enclosed jug, prob. < base of OHG. *flechtan*, to weave: for IE. base see FLAX] 1. any small, bottle-shaped container with a narrow neck, used in laboratories, etc. 2. a small, flattened container for liquor, etc., to be carried in the pocket 3. the frame for a mold of sand in a foundry

flask·et (flas'kit, fläs'-) *n.* [ME. < OFr. *flasquet*, dim. of *flasque* < Gmc. *flasko*: see FLASK] 1. a small flask 2. [Archaic] a long, shallow basket

flat¹ (flat) *adj.* **flat'ter, flat'test** [ME. < ON. *flatr*, akin to OHG. *flaz* < IE. *plāt-, plēt-*, wide, flat (whence Gr. *platys*, broad, OE. *flet*, floor: cf. ff.) < IE. base *plā-*, broad] 1. having a smooth, level surface; having little or no depression or elevation 2. *a*) lying extended at full length *b*) spread out smooth and level 3. touching at as many points as possible [with his back *flat* against the wall] 4. *a*) having little depth or thickness; broad, even, and thin *b*) having a flat heel or no heel [*flat* shoes] 5. designating or having an almost straight or level trajectory or flight 6. absolute; positive [a *flat* denial] 7. without variation; not fluctuating [a *flat* rate] 8. without much business activity [a *flat* market] 9. having little or no sparkle or taste; insipid [a *flat* drink] 10. having little or no interest; monotonous; dull 11. not clear or full; blurred [a *flat* sound] ☆12. emptied of air [a *flat* tire] ☆13. [Colloq.] completely without money; penniless 14. without gloss [*flat* paint] 15. *Art a*) lacking relief, depth, or perspective *b*) uniform in tint or shade 16. *Gram. a*) not having the sign *to:* said of an infinitive (Ex.: *go* in *make it go*) *b*) not having an inflectional ending: said esp. of certain adverbs (Ex.: he drove *fast*) 17. *Music a*) below the true or proper pitch *b*) lower in pitch by a half step [D-*flat*] 18. *Phonet.* designating the vowel *a* sounded with the tongue in a relatively level position, as in *can* 19. *Photog.* lacking in contrast —*adv.* 1. in a flat manner; flatly (in various senses) 2. in a prone or supine position 3. *a*) exactly; precisely [to run a race in ten seconds *flat*] *b*) bluntly; abruptly [she left him *flat*] ☆4. *Finance* with no interest 5. *Music* below the true or proper pitch —*n.* 1. a flat surface or part [the *flat* of the hand, of a sword, etc.] 2. an expanse of level land 3. a low-lying marsh 4. a shallow; shoal 5. any of various flat things; specif., *a*) a shallow box or container, as for growing seedlings *b*) a flat-bottomed boat ☆*c*) a flatcar *d*) a piece of theatrical scenery on a flat frame ☆*e*) a deflated tire *f*) [*pl.*] flat-heeled shoes or slippers 6. *Music a*) a note or tone one half step below another *b*) the symbol (♭) indicating such a note —*vt., vi.* **flat'ted, flat'ting** to make or become flat; flatten —SYN. see INSIPID, LEVEL —**fall flat** to fail in the desired effect; arouse no response —**flat'ly** *adv.* —**flat'ness** *n.*

flat² (flat) *n.* [altered < Scot. dial. *flet* (ME. & OE. *flet*), a floor (of a dwelling): see prec.] an apartment or suite of rooms on one floor of a building

flat·bed, flat-bed (-bed') *adj.* ☆1. designating or of a truck, trailer, etc. having a bed or platform without sides or stakes 2. *Printing* designating or of a press having a plane or horizontal printing surface —*n.* ☆1. a flatbed truck, trailer, etc. 2. a flatbed press

flat·boat (-bōt') *n.* a boat with a flat bottom, for carrying freight in shallow waters or on rivers

☆**flat·car** (-kär') *n.* a railroad car without sides or a roof, for carrying certain kinds of freight

flat·fish (-fish') *n.*, *pl.* **-fish', -fish'es:** see FISH² any of an order (Heterosomata) of fishes with a very flat body and both eyes on the uppermost side, as the flounder, halibut, sole, etc.

flat·foot (-foot') *n.* 1. a condition in which the instep arch of the foot has been flattened ☆2. *pl.* **-foots'** [Slang] a policeman: so called from the notion that a policeman's feet are flattened by walking his beat

flat foot a foot having a flattened instep arch

flat-foot·ed (-foot′id) *adj.* **1.** having flatfoot **2.** designating a manner of walking, with the toes pointed outward, as by people with flatfoot ☆**3.** [Colloq.] downright and firm; plain and uncompromising —☆*adv.* [Colloq.] firmly, directly, or abruptly —☆**catch flat-footed** [Colloq.] **1.** to catch unprepared to escape; take by surprise **2.** to catch in the act of committing some offense —**flat′-foot′ed·ly** *adv.* —**flat′-foot′ed·ness** *n.*

☆**Flat·head** (-hed′) *n., pl.* **-heads′, -head′ 1.** *a)* [erroneously so named by confusion with other tribes (such as the Chinooks), which practiced head-flattening] a member of a tribe of Salish Indians living in NW Montana *b)* their Salish dialect **2.** a member of any of several N. American Indian tribes, as the Chinook, Choctaw, Muskogean, etc., that artificially flattened the heads of their children

flat·i·ron (-ī′ərn) *n.* an iron for pressing clothes

flat knot *same as* REEF KNOT

flat·ling (-lin) *adv.* [ME.: see FLAT¹ & -LING²] [Obs. exc. Brit. Dial.] **1.** at full length **2.** with the flat side, as of a sword Also **flat′lings, flat′long** (-lôn) —*adj.* [Obs.] struck with the flat side [a *flatling* blow]

☆**flat silver** silver knives, forks, spoons, etc., as distinguished from silver trays, teapots, bowls, etc.

flat·ten (-'n) *vt.* **1.** to make flat or flatter **2.** to knock down; make prostrate **3.** to level to the ground —*vi.* **1.** to become flat or flatter **2.** to become prostrate —**flatten out 1.** to make or become flat or flatter by spreading out **2.** *Aeron. same as* LEVEL OFF (or OUT) —**flat′ten·er** *n.*

flat·ter¹ (flat′ər) *vt.* [ME. *flateren* < OFr. *flater*, to smooth, caress with flat hand < Frank. *flat*, akin to OHG. *flaz*, FLAT¹] **1.** to praise too much, untruly, or insincerely, as in order to win favor **2.** to try to please, or ingratiate oneself with, by praise and attention **3.** to make seem better or more attractive than is so [his portrait *flatters* him] **4.** to make feel pleased or honored; gratify the vanity of [it's *flattering* to be remembered] **5.** to please or gratify (the eye, ear, senses, etc.) **6.** to encourage, esp. falsely —*vi.* to use flattery —**flatter oneself** to hold the self-satisfying or self-deluding belief (*that*) —**flat′ter·er** *n.* —**flat′ter·ing·ly** *adv.*

flat·ter² (flat′ər) *n.* **1.** a person who flattens something **2.** a drawplate for forming flat strips **3.** a smith's forging tool with a broad, flat face

flat·ter·y (flat′ər ē) *n., pl.* **-ter·ies** [ME. & OFr. *flaterie* (Fr. *flatterie*) < *flater*] **1.** the act of flattering **2.** excessive, untrue, or insincere praise; exaggerated compliment or attention; blandishment

flat·tish (-ish) *adj.* somewhat flat

☆**flat·top** (-täp′) *n.* [Slang] something having a flat or level surface, platform, deck, etc., as an aircraft carrier

flat·u·lent (flach′ə lənt, -yoo-) *adj.* [Fr. < ModL. *flatulentus* < L. *flatus:* see ff.] **1.** of or having gas in the stomach or intestines **2.** producing gas in the stomach or intestines, as certain foods **3.** windy or empty in speech; pompous; pretentious —**flat′u·lence, flat′u·len·cy** *n.* —**flat′u·lent·ly** *adv.*

fla·tus (flāt′əs) *n.* [L. < *flare*, to BLOW¹: for IE. base see BLADDER] gas in the stomach or intestines

flat·ware (flat′wer′) *n.* relatively flat tableware; specif., ☆*a)* knives, forks, spoons, etc. *b)* flat plates, platters, etc. Cf. HOLLOWARE

flat·wise (-wīz′) *adv.* with the flat side foremost, uppermost, or in contact: also **flat′ways′** (-wāz′)

☆**flat·work** (-wurk′) *n.* laundered articles, as sheets, napkins, and other flat pieces, that can be pressed quickly in a mangle

flat·worm (-wurm′) *n. a common name for* PLATYHELMINTH

Flau·bert (flō ber′), **Gus·tave** (güs tàv′) 1821–80; Fr. novelist

flaunt (flônt) *vi.* [15th c. & 16th c., prob. < dial. *flant*, to strut coquettishly, akin to Norw. *flanta* < or akin to ON. *flana*, run back and forth] **1.** to make a gaudy, ostentatious, conspicuous, impudent, or defiant display **2.** to flutter or wave freely —*vt.* to show off proudly, defiantly, or impudently [to *flaunt* one's guilt] —*n.* [Archaic] the act of flaunting —*SYN.* see SHOW —**flaunt′ing·ly** *adv.*

flaunt·y (-ē) *adj.* [Rare] flaunting; showy

flau·tist (flôt′ist, flout′-) *n.* [It. *flautista* < *flauto*, FLUTE] a person who plays the flute; flutist

fla·va·none (flā′və nōn′, flav′ə-) *n.* [FLAV(IN) + -AN(E) + -ONE] a complex, crystalline ketone, $C_{15}H_{12}O_2$, which can be converted into flavones and flavonols **2.** any of the derivatives of this ketone, many of which are found in various plants

fla·vin (flā′vin, flav′in) *n.* [< L. *flavus*, yellow (see FLAVONE) + -IN¹] **1.** a complex heterocyclic ketone, $C_{10}H_8N_4O_2$ **2.** any of a group of yellow pigments occurring in certain plant and animal products or prepared by synthesis; specif., riboflavin **3.** *same as* QUERCETIN

fla·vine (flā′vēn, flav′ēn) *n.* **1.** *same as* FLAVIN **2.** *same as* ACRIFLAVINE

fla·vone (flā′vōn, flav′ōn) *n.* [G. *flavon* < L. *flavus*, yellow (< IE. base *bhlē-wos*, used of light colors, whence BLUE) + G. *-on*, -ONE] **1.** a colorless crystalline compound, $C_{15}H_{10}O_2$, obtained from certain plants or prepared synthetically: it forms a base for some yellow dyes **2.** any derivative of this compound

fla·vo·nol (flā′və nôl′, -nōl′) *n.* [< prec. + -OL¹] **1.** a

yellow crystalline compound, $C_{15}H_{10}O_3$ **2.** any of various derivatives of flavonol, used as yellow pigments and dyes and frequently found in plants

fla·vo·pro·tein (flā′vō prō′tēn, -prōt′ē in) *n.* any of a group of proteins linked chemically with flavins, esp. one that yields riboflavin upon hydrolysis: these proteins play a role in tissue respiration

fla·vo·pur·pu·rin (-pur′par in) *n.* [< L. *flavus*, yellow + PURPURIN] a yellowish, crystalline chemical compound, $C_{14}H_8O_5$, used in making dyes

fla·vor (flā′vər) *n.* [ME. *flavour*, an odor, altered (after *savour*, SAVOR) < OFr. *flaur* < VL. *flator*, odor < L. *flatare*, to blow, freq. of *flare*, BLOW¹, prob. infl. by *foetor*, foul odor] **1.** [Archaic] an odor; smell; aroma **2.** *a)* that quality of a substance that is a mixing of its characteristic taste and smell *b)* taste in general [a soup lacking *flavor*] **3.** any substance added to a food to give it a particular taste; flavoring **4.** the characteristic quality of something; distinctive nature [the *flavor* of the city] —*vt.* to give flavor to —**fla′vor·less** *adj.*

fla·vor·ful (-fəl) *adj.* full of flavor; having a pleasant flavor; also **fla′vor·some** (-səm), **fla′vor·ous** (-əs), **fla′vor·y** (-ē) —**fla′vor·ful·ly** *adv.*

fla·vor·ing (-in) *n.* an essence, extract, etc. added to a food or drink to give it a certain taste

fla·vour (flā′vər) *n., vt. Brit. sp. of* FLAVOR

flaw¹ (flô) *n.* [ME., a flake, scale, splinter, prob. < Scand.: see FLAKE¹] **1.** a break, scratch, crack, etc. that spoils something; blemish [a *flaw* in a diamond] **2.** a defect; fault; error [a *flaw* in a legal document, in one's reasoning, etc.] —*vt., vi.* to make or become faulty —*SYN.* see DEFECT —**flaw′less** *adj.* —**flaw′less·ly** *adv.* —**flaw′less·ness** *n.*

flaw² (flô) *n.* [prob. < ON. *flaga*, sudden onset, or cognate Dan. *flage*, Sw. *flaga*, sudden gust < IE. base *plāk-*, *plāg-*, etc., to strike, beat, whence L. *plangere*, to beat (the breast): cf. PLANGENT] a sudden, brief gust of wind, often with rain or snow; squall

flax (flaks) *n.* [ME. < OE. *flæx*, akin to G. *flachs* < IE. base *plek-*, to plait, interweave, whence L. *plectere*] designating or of a family (Linaceae) of plants, including the flax —*n.* **1.** any of a genus (Linum) of the flax family, esp. a slender, erect, annual plant (Linum usitatissimum) with delicate blue flowers and narrow leaves: the seeds are used to make linseed oil, and the fibers of the stem are spun into linen thread **2.** the threadlike fibers of these plants, ready for spinning **3.** any of a number of flaxlike plants

flax·en (-'n) *adj.* [ME. < OE. *fleaxen*] **1.** of or made of flax **2.** like flax in color; pale-yellow; straw-colored

Flax·man (flaks′mən), **John** 1755–1826; Eng. sculptor

flax·seed (-sēd′) *n.* the seed of the flax; linseed

flax·y (-ē) *adj.* like flax; flaxen

flay (flā) *vt.* [ME. *flan* < OE. *flean*, akin to MDu. *vlaen*, ON. *flá* < IE. base *plēk-*, to tear off, whence FLITCH] **1.** to strip off the skin or hide of, as by whipping **2.** to criticize or scold mercilessly **3.** to rob; pillage; fleece

F layer the highest regular layer of the ionosphere, where high-frequency radio waves are reflected: it is divided into an F_1 layer (c. 125 to 185 miles high), which exists during the day, and an F_2 layer (c. 140 to 250 miles), into the lower part of which the F_1 layer tends to merge in the daytime

fl. dr. fluid dram; fluid drams

flea (flē) *n.* [ME. *fle* < OE. *fleah*, akin to G. *floh* < same Gmc. base as FLEE] **1.** any of an order (Siphonaptera) of small, flattened, wingless insects with large legs adapted for jumping: as adults they are bloodsucking parasites on mammals and birds **2.** *same as* FLEA BEETLE —**flea in one's ear** a stinging rebuke or rebuff or an annoying hint

flea-bag (-bag′) *n.* ☆[Slang] a very cheap hotel

flea·bane (-bān′) *n.* [FLEA + BANE: once thought to drive away fleas] *a common name for* ERIGERON

FLEA
(to 1/8 in. long)

flea beetle any of a number of small jumping beetles (family Chrysomelidae) that feed chiefly on leaves and shoots of plants

flea·bite (-bīt′) *n.* **1.** the bite of a flea **2.** the red spot on the skin caused by the bite of a flea **3.** a minor pain or trifling inconvenience

flea-bit·ten (-bit′'n) *adj.* **1.** bitten by a flea or fleas **2.** infested with fleas **3.** wretched; decrepit; shabby **4.** light-colored with reddish-brown spots: said of horses

☆**flea circus** a number of fleas trained to perform tricks, as for a carnival sideshow

☆**flea-hop·per** (-häp′ər) *n.* any of several small jumping bugs (family Miridae), many of which damage cotton and other cultivated plants

fleam (flēm) *n.* [ME. *fleme* < OFr. *flieme* < VL. *fleutomum* for *phlebotomus:* see PHLEBOTOMY] a sharp lancet formerly used for opening veins

flea market an outdoor bazaar dealing mainly in cheap, secondhand goods

flea·wort (flē′wurt) *n.* **1.** any of several plants that supposedly ward off fleas, as a European aromatic plant (Inula conyza) with rough leaves and yellow flowers **2.** a European plantain (Plantago psyllium) whose seeds,

which more or less resemble fleas, are used as a laxative

flèche (flesh, flāsh) *n.* [Fr., lit., an arrow < OFr. *fleche* < MDu. *vleke*, an arrow, akin to OE. *flacor*, flying (of arrows): for IE. base see FLAW[2]] a slender spire, esp. one over the intersection of the nave and the transept in some Gothic churches

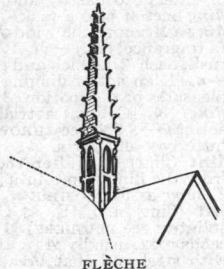

FLÈCHE

fleck (flek) *n.* [ON. *flekkr*, akin to MDu. *vlecke*, G. *fleck*, prob. < IE. base **plek-*, whence FLAY] **1.** a spot or small patch of color, etc.; speck *[flecks* of sunlight] **2.** a small piece; particle; flake —*vt.* [ME. **flekken* (found only in pp. *flekked*), prob. < ON. *flekka* < *flekkr*] to cover or sprinkle with flecks; speckle

flec·tion (flek'shən) *n.* [L. *flexio* < pp. of *flectere*, to bend: see FLEX[1]] **1.** a bending; flexing **2.** a bent part or bend **3.** *Anat.* same as FLEXION **4.** *Gram.* inflection —**flec'tion·al** *adj.*

fled (fled) *pt. & pp. of* FLEE

fledge (flej) *vi.* **fledged, fledg'ing** [< ME. *flegge*, ready to fly < OE. (*un*)*flycge*, (un)fledged, akin to MHG. *vlücke*, MDu. *vlugghe*: for IE. base see FLY[1]] to grow the feathers necessary for flying —*vt.* **1.** to rear (a young bird) until it is able to fly **2.** to supply or adorn with or as if with feathers or down; specif., to fit (an arrow, etc.) with feathers

fledg·ling (flej'liŋ) *n.* **1.** a young bird just fledged **2.** a young, inexperienced person Also, chiefly Brit., **fledge'ling**

flee (flē) *vi.* **fled, flee'ing** [ME. *fleen* < OE. *fleon*, akin to G. *fliehen*, Goth. *thliuhan*] **1.** to run away or escape from danger, pursuit, unpleasantness, etc. **2.** to pass away swiftly; vanish *[night had fled]* **3.** to move rapidly; go swiftly —*vt.* to run away or try to escape from; avoid; shun —**fle·er** (flē'ər) *n.*

fleece (flēs) *n.* [ME. *flees* < OE. *fleos*, akin to G. *vlies* < IE. base **pleus-*, to pluck out, whence L. *pluma*, a feather, down] **1.** the wool covering a sheep or similar animal **2.** the amount of wool cut from a sheep in one shearing **3.** a covering like a sheep's, as of woolly hair **4.** a soft, warm, napped fabric, used for linings, etc. —*vt.* **fleeced, fleec'ing 1.** to shear the fleece from (sheep, etc.) **2.** to steal from by fraud; swindle **3.** to cover or fleck with fleecy masses —**fleec'er** *n.*

fleec·y (-ē) *adj.* **fleec'i·er, fleec'i·est 1.** made of or covered with fleece **2.** like fleece; soft and light *[fleecy* snow] —**fleec'i·ly** *adv.* —**fleec'i·ness** *n.*

fleer (flir) *vi., vt.* [ME. *flerien*, prob. < Scand., as in Dan. dial., Norw. *flire*, to snicker, laugh, prob. < IE. base **plei-*, bald, bare] to laugh derisively (at); sneer or jeer (at) —*n.* a mocking or derisive grimace, laugh, or remark; gibe —**fleer'ing·ly** *adv.*

fleet[1] (flēt) *n.* [ME. *flete* < OE. *fleot* < *fleotan*, to float: see ff.] **1.** *a)* a number of warships under one command, usually in a definite area of operation *b)* the entire naval force of a country; navy **2.** any group of ships, trucks, buses, airplanes, etc. acting together or under one control

fleet[2] (flēt) *vi.* [ME. *fleten* < OE. *fleotan*, akin to G. *fliessen* < IE. **pleud-* < base **pleu-*, to flow, run, whence OFrw. L. *pluere*, to rain] **1.** orig., to float; swim **2.** to move swiftly; flit; fly **3.** [Archaic] to pass away swiftly; disappear **4.** *Naut.* to change position —*vt.* **1.** [Rare] to pass away (time) **2.** *Naut.* to change the position of (a rope, etc.) —*adj.* **1.** swift; rapid **2.** [Poet.] evanescent —*SYN.* see FAST[1] —**fleet'ly** *adv.* —**fleet'ness** *n.*

fleet[3] (flēt) *n.* [ME. *flete* < OE. *fleot*, akin to Du. *vliet:* base as in prec.] [Obs. or Eng. Dial.] a small inlet; creek —**the Fleet 1.** a former small creek in London, now a covered sewer **2.** a debtor's prison which stood near this creek: also **Fleet Prison**

☆**fleet admiral** *U.S. Navy* an admiral of the highest rank, having the insignia of five stars

fleet·ing (flēt'iŋ) *adj.* [OE. *fleotende*, floating: see FLEET[2]] passing swiftly; not lasting —*SYN.* see TRANSIENT —**fleet'ing·ly** *adv.* —**fleet'ing·ness** *n.*

Fleet Street [after *the Fleet* (see FLEET[3]) which crosses beneath it] **1.** old street in C London, where several newspaper & printing offices are located **2.** the London press

Flem·ing (flem'iŋ) *n.* [ME. < OFris. or < MDu. *Vlaming*] **1.** a native of Flanders **2.** a Belgian who speaks Flemish

Fleming, Sir Alexander 1881–1955; Brit. bacteriologist: co-discoverer of penicillin

Flem·ish (-ish) *adj.* of Flanders, the Flemings, or their language —*n.* the West Germanic language of the Flemings, the Dutch dialect of N Belgium —**the Flemish** the people of Flanders

flense (flens) *vt.* **flensed, flens'ing** [< Du. *vlensen* or Dan. *flense*] to cut blubber or skin from (a whale, seal, etc.): also **flench** (flench)

flesh (flesh) *n.* [ME. < OE. *flæsc*, akin to G. *fleisch* < IE. base **plēk-*, to tear off, whence FLAY] **1.** *a)* the soft substance of the body (of a person or animal) between the skin and the bones; esp., the muscular tissue *b)* the surface or skin of the body *[to feel one's flesh* crawl] **2.** the flesh of any animal as food; meat; esp., meat other than fish or fowl **3.** the pulpy or edible part of fruits and vegetables **4.** the human body, as distinguished from the soul *[more than flesh* can bear] **5.** human nature, esp. in its sensual aspect **6.** all living beings, esp. all mankind **7.** kindred or relatives: now mainly in **one's (own) flesh and blood**, one's close relatives or descendants **8.** the typical color of a white person's skin; yellowish pink —*vt.* **1.** to feed (animals) with flesh so as to incite them to hunt or kill **2.** to prepare for or incite to bloodshed, etc. by a foretaste **3.** to harden; inure **4.** to plunge (a weapon) into flesh **5.** to put flesh on; fatten **6.** to fill out as if with flesh; realize or make full, as by the addition of details (usually with *out*) **7.** to remove flesh from (a hide) —*vi.* to grow fleshy or fat (usually with *out* or *up*) —**flesh and blood** the human body, esp. as subject to its natural limitations —**in the flesh 1.** alive **2.** actually present; in person

flesh-col·ored (-kul'ərd) *adj.* having the typical color of a white person's skin; yellowish-pink

flesh-eat·ing (-ēt'iŋ) *adj.* habitually eating flesh; carnivorous

flesh fly any of a family (Sarcophagidae) of viviparous flies that deposit their larvae esp. on flesh

flesh·ings (-inz) *n.pl.* **1.** flesh-colored tights, worn by acrobats, etc. **2.** pieces of flesh scraped from hides

flesh·ly (-lē) *adj.* **-li·er, -li·est** [ME. *fleschlich* < OE. *flæsclic:* see FLESH & -LY[1]] **1.** of the body and its nature; corporeal **2.** fond of bodily pleasures; sensual **3.** fleshy —*SYN.* see CARNAL —**flesh'li·ness** *n.*

flesh·pot (-pät') *n.* **1.** a pot for cooking meat **2.** [after Ex. 16:3] *[pl.] a)* bodily comfort and pleasures; luxuries *b)* a place where such pleasures are provided

flesh wound a wound that does not reach the bones or vital organs

flesh·y (-ē) *adj.* **flesh'i·er, flesh'i·est 1.** having much flesh; fat; plump **2.** of or like flesh **3.** having a firm pulp, as some fruits —**flesh'i·ness** *n.*

fletch (flech) *vt.* [altered (after ff.) < FLEDGE] to fit a feather on (an arrow)

fletch·er (-ər) *n.* [ME. < OFr. *flechier* < *fleche*, an arrow < Gmc. form akin to MDu. *vlieke* < base of *vlegen*, FLY[1]] [Archaic] a person who makes arrows

Fletch·er (flech'ər), **John** 1579–1625; Eng. playwright: collaborated with Francis BEAUMONT

☆**Fletch·er·ism** (-iz'm) *n.* [after Horace *Fletcher* (1849–1919), U.S. dietitian] [*also* f-] the practice of chewing food slowly and thoroughly as an aid to digestion

fleur-de-lis (flur'də lē', -lēz') *n., pl.* **fleurs'-de-lis'** (flur'də lēz') [ME. *flour de lyce* < OFr. *flor de lis*, lit., flower of the lily] **1.** *same as* IRIS (senses 4 & 5) **2.** the coat of arms of the former French royal family **3.** *Heraldry* an emblem resembling a lily or iris Also sp. **fleur-de-lys**

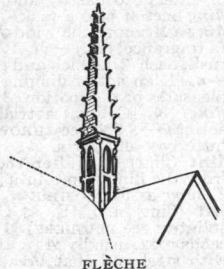

FLEUR-DE-LIS

Fleu·ry (flē rē') **1. An·dré Her·cule de** (än drā' er kül' də), 1653–1743; Fr. cardinal & statesman: prime minister (1726–43) under Louis XV **2. Claude,** 1640–1723; Fr. ecclesiastical historian

flew (flo͞o) *pt. of* FLY[1]

flews (flo͞oz) *n.pl.* [< ?] the loose, hanging parts of the upper lip of a hound or other dog

flex[1] (fleks) *vt., vi.* [< L. *flexus*, pp. of *flectere*, to bend, curve] **1.** to bend (an arm, knee, etc.) **2.** to contract (a muscle)

flex[2] (fleks) *n.* [< FLEXIBLE] [Brit.] flexible, insulated electric cord

flex·i·ble (fleks'ə b'l) *adj.* [ME. < OFr. < L. *flexibilis* < *flexus:* see FLEX[1]] **1.** able to bend without breaking; not stiff or rigid; easily bent; pliant **2.** easily persuaded or influenced; tractable **3.** adjustable to change; capable of modification *[a flexible* voice] —*SYN.* see ELASTIC —**flex'i·bil'i·ty** *n.* —**flex'i·bly** *adv.*

flex·ile (flek'sil) *adj.* [L. *flexilis*] flexible; pliant; mobile

flex·ion (flek'shən) *n.* **1.** *same as* FLECTION **2.** *Anat.* the bending of a joint or limb by means of the flexor muscles —**flex'ion·al** *adj.*

Flex·ner (fleks'nər) **1. Abraham,** 1866–1959; U.S. educator **2. Simon,** 1863–1946; U.S. pathologist: brother of *prec.*

flex·or (flek'sər) *n.* [ModL. < L. *flexus:* see FLEX[1]] a muscle that bends a limb or other part of the body

flex·u·os·i·ty (flek'sho͞o wäs'ə tē) *n.* [LL. *flexuositas*] **1.** the quality or state of being flexuous **2.** *pl.* **-ties** a curve or winding part

flex·u·ous (flek'sho͞o wəs) *adj.* [L. *flexuosus* < *flexus:* see FLEX[1]] **1.** full of bends; winding **2.** wavering —**flex'u·ous·ly** *adv.*

flex·ure (flek'shər) *n.* [L. *flexura*] **1.** a bending, curving, or flexing, as of a heavy object under its own weight **2.** a bend, curve, or fold —**flex'ur·al** *adj.*

flib·ber·ti·gib·bet (flib′ər tē jib′it) *n.* [extended < ME. *flypergebet* < ?] an irresponsible, flighty person

‡flic (flēk) *n.* [Fr. Colloq.] a policeman

flick[1] (flik) *n.* [echoic, but infl. by FLICKER[1]] 1. a light, quick stroke, as with a whip; sudden, jerky movement; snap 2. a light, snapping sound, as of the flick of a whip 3. a fleck; splotch; streak —*vt.* 1. to strike, throw, remove, etc. with a light, quick, snapping stroke, as with the fingernail 2. to make a light, quick, snapping stroke with (a whip, etc.) —*vi.* to move quickly and jerkily; flutter

flick[2] (flik) *n.* [< ff.] [Slang] 1. a movie 2. a movie theater —**the flicks** [Slang] 1. movies collectively 2. a showing of a movie

flick·er[1] (-ər) *vi.* [ME. *flikeren* < OE. *flicorian*, akin to *flacor*, flying, ON. *flokta*, to flutter: for IE. base see FLAW[2]] 1. to flap the wings rapidly, as in hovering; flutter: said of a bird 2. to move with a quick, light, wavering motion 3. to burn or shine unsteadily, as a candle in the wind —*vt.* to cause to flicker or waver —*n.* 1. an act or instance of flickering 2. a dart of flame or light, as in a flickering fire 3. a look or feeling that comes and goes quickly [a *flicker* of fear crossed his face] 4. [Old Slang] a movie: *usually used in pl.* —*SYN.* see BLAZE[1] —**flick′er·y** *adj.*

☆**flick·er**[2] (-ər) *n.* [echoic of its cry] any of several N. American woodpeckers (genus *Colaptes*), esp. a species (*Colaptes auratus*) found east of the Rocky Mountains, with a red, crescent-shaped mark on the back of the head, and wings colored golden on the underside

flick knife [Brit.] *same as* SWITCH-BLADE KNIFE

flied (flīd) *pt. & pp.* of FLY[1] (*vi.* 9)

fli·er (flī′ər) *n.* 1. a thing that flies 2. an aviator ☆3. a bus, train, etc. that has a fast schedule 4. any step in a straight stairway ☆5. a small handbill widely distributed ☆6. [Colloq.] a reckless gamble or speculation, as in the stock market Also, esp. for 2, 3, & 6, **fly′er**

flight[1] (flīt) *n.* [ME. *fliht* < OE. *flyht* (akin to OS. *fluht* Du. *vlucht*) < base of *fleogan*, FLY[1]] 1. the act, manner, or power of flying or moving through space 2. the distance covered or that can be covered at one time by an airplane, bird, projectile, etc. 3. a group of things flying through the air together [a *flight* of birds, arrows, etc.] 4. *a)* a formation of military airplanes in flight *b)* U.S. *Air Force* the smallest tactical unit, a subdivision of a squadron 5. an airplane scheduled to fly a certain route at a certain time 6. a trip by airplane 7. an outburst or soaring above the ordinary [a *flight* of fancy] 8. a set of stairs, as between landings or floors 9. *Archery a)* a contest in distance shooting *b)* a special arrow for such shooting: also **flight arrow** 10. *Sports* a division of contestants grouped according to ability —*vi.* to fly in numbers; migrate: said of birds —*SYN.* see GROUP

flight[2] (flīt) *n.* [ME. *fliht, fluht* < OE. *flyht* < base of *fleon*, FLEE] a fleeing; running away from or as from danger —**put to flight** to force to run away; make flee —**take (to) flight** to run away; flee

flight control 1. the control from the ground, as by radio, of aircraft in flight 2. a station exercising such control

☆**flight deck** the upper deck of an aircraft carrier, that serves as a runway

flight engineer *Aeron.* a crew member who is in charge of mechanical operation during flight

flight feather any of the large feathers of the wings or tail that support a bird in flight

flight formation the orderly arrangement of two or more airplanes flying close together as a unit

flight·less (-lis) *adj.* not able to fly

flight line the portion of an airfield where planes are parked and serviced

☆**flight strip** an emergency runway; airstrip

☆**flight surgeon** a medical officer in the Air Force specializing in aviation medicine

flight-test (-test′) *vt.* to put (an aircraft) through various tests during flight

flight·y (-ē) *adj.* **flight′i·er, flight′i·est** [FLIGHT[1] + -Y[2]] 1. given to sudden whims; not taking things seriously; frivolous or irresponsible 2. slightly demented, foolish, or silly —**flight′i·ly** *adv.* —**flight′i·ness** *n.*

flim·flam (flim′flam′) *n.* [reduplicated < ? FLAM[1]] 1. nonsense; rubbish; humbug 2. a sly trick or deception —*vt.* -**flammed′, -flam′ming** [Colloq.] to trick, swindle, or cheat —**flim′flam′mer·y** *n.*

flim·sy (flim′zē) *adj.* -**si·er, -si·est** [< ?] 1. thin and easily broken or damaged; poorly made and fragile; frail 2. ill-conceived and inadequate; ineffectual [a *flimsy* excuse] —*n.* 1. a sheet of thin paper 2. copy written on such paper, as by newspaper reporters —**flim′si·ly** *adv.* —**flim′si·ness** *n.*

flinch (flinch) *vi.* [earlier also *flench* < OFr. *flenchir*, to bend aside < Frank. **hlankjan*, akin to G. *lenken*, OE. *hlencan*, to twist, bend < IE. base **kleng-*, to bend, whence L. *clingere*] 1. *a)* to draw back, as from a blow *b)* to wince, as from pain 2. to draw back from anything difficult, dangerous, or painful —*n.* an act of flinching —*SYN.* see RECOIL

flin·ders (flin′dərz) *n.pl.* [ME. (northern) *flender* < Scand., as in Norw. *flindra*, splinter < IE. base *(s)plei-*, to split, whence SPLIT, SPLINT, FLINT] splinters or fragments: chiefly in **break** (or **fly**) **into flinders**

fling (flin) *vt.* **flung, fling′ing** [ME. *flingen*, to rush < ON. *flengja*, to whip (Norw. dial., to throw) < IE. base **plāk-*, to strike, whence Gr. *plēssein*, to beat] 1. to throw, esp. with force or violence; hurl; cast 2. to put abruptly or violently [to be *flung* into confusion] 3. to move (one's arms, legs, head, etc.) suddenly or impulsively 4. to move or enter into hastily and with spirit: used reflexively [to *fling* oneself into a task] 5. to throw aside; disregard [to *fling* caution to the winds] 6. [Poet.] to give out or diffuse (a fragrance, etc.) —*vi.* 1. to move suddenly and violently; rush; dash 2. to kick and plunge, as a horse (often with *out*) —*n.* 1. an act of flinging 2. a brief time of unrestrained pleasures or dissipation 3. a spirited dance [the Highland *fling*] 4. [Colloq.] a trial effort; try [to have a *fling* at acting] —*SYN.* see THROW —**fling out** to speak angrily or bitterly —**fling′er** *n.*

Flint (flint) 1. [after the nearby *Flint* River, so called from the flint stones in it] city in SE Mich.: pop. 193,000 2. *same as* FLINTSHIRE

flint (flint) *n.* [ME. < OE., akin to Norw. *flint*, stone splinter: see FLINDERS] 1. a fine-grained, very hard, siliceous rock, usually gray, that produces sparks when struck with steel and that breaks with sharp cutting edges 2. a piece of this stone, used to start a fire, for primitive tools, etc. 3. a small piece of iron-cerium alloy used to strike the spark in a cigarette lighter 4. anything extremely hard or firm like flint

☆**flint corn** a variety of Indian corn with very hard kernels not dented at the tip

flint glass a hard, bright glass containing lead oxide and having a high index of refraction, used for lenses, crystal, etc.

flint·lock (-läk′) *n.* 1. a gunlock in which a flint in the hammer strikes a metal plate to produce a spark that ignites the powder 2. an old-fashioned gun with such a lock

Flint·shire (flint′shir) county of NE Wales, on the Irish Sea & the Dee estuary: 255 sq. mi.; pop. 152,000

flint·y (flin′tē) *adj.* **flint′i·er, flint′i·est** 1. made of or containing flint 2. like flint; extremely hard and firm; inflexible [a *flinty* heart] —**flint′i·ly** *adv.* —**flint′i·ness** *n.*

flip[1] (flip) *vt.* **flipped, flip′ping** [echoic] 1. to toss or move with a quick jerk; flick [*flip* the drawer shut] 2. to snap (a coin) into the air, with the thumb, as in betting on which side will land uppermost 3. to turn or turn over [to *flip* pages in a book] —*vi.* 1. to make a quick, light stroke, as with the finger or a whip; snap 2. to move jerkily 3. to flip a coin, as in letting chance decide something 4. to turn over quickly; specif., to execute a flip 5. to look (*through*) in a quick, random manner ☆6. [Slang] to lose self-control as a result of excitement, anger, madness, etc. —*n.* 1. the act or motion of flipping; snap, tap, jerk, or toss 2. a somersault in the air —☆**flip one's lid** (or **wig**) [Slang] to lose self-control; go berserk

flip[2] (flip) *n.* [prob. < prec.] a sweetened drink, usually hot, of wine, cider, etc. with spices and, sometimes, milk and eggs

flip[3] (flip) *adj.* **flip′per, flip′pest** [contr. < FLIPPANT] [Colloq.] flippant; saucy; impertinent

flip-flop (flip′fläp′) *n.* 1. an acrobatic spring backward from the feet to the hands and back to the feet 2. an abrupt change, as to an opposite opinion 3. a flapping noise 4. *Electronics* a circuit having two stable states and remaining in one until a signal causes it to switch to the other —*vi.* -**flopped′, -flop′ping** to do a flip-flop

flip·pan·cy (flip′ən sē) *n.* 1. the quality or state of being flippant 2. *pl.* -**cies** a flippant act or remark

flip·pant (-ənt) *adj.* [Early ModE., nimble, prob. < FLIP[1]] 1. [Obs.] glib; talkative 2. frivolous and disrespectful; saucy; impertinent —**flip′pant·ly** *adv.*

flip·per (-ər) *n.* [< FLIP[1]] 1. a broad, flat part or limb adapted for swimming, as in seals, whales, etc. 2. a large, flat, paddlelike rubber device worn on each foot by swimmers or skin divers to increase the force of the kick 3. [Slang] the hand

☆**flip side** [Colloq.] the reverse side (of a phonograph record), esp. the less important or less popular side

flirt (flurt) *vt.* [earlier *flert, flurt* < ? OFr. *fleureter*, to touch lightly, lit., move from flower to flower < *fleur*, FLOWER] 1. [Now Rare] to toss or flick quickly 2. to move jerkily back and forth [the bird *flirted* its tail] —*vi.* 1. to move jerkily or unevenly 2. to make love without serious intentions; play at love 3. to trifle or toy [to *flirt* with an idea] —*n.* 1. a quick, jerky movement; flutter 2. a person who plays at love —*SYN.* see TRIFLE

flir·ta·tion (flər tā′shən) *n.* 1. a flirting, or playing at love 2. a frivolous or playful love affair

flir·ta·tious (-shəs) *adj.* 1. inclined to flirt, or play at love 2. of or characteristic of flirtation Also **flirt′y** —**flir·ta′-tious·ly** *adv.*

flit (flit) *vi.* **flit′ted, flit′ting** [ME. *flitten* < ON. *flytja*, akin to OE. *fleotan*, FLEET[2]] 1. to pass lightly and rapidly [memories *flitted* through his mind] 2. to fly lightly and rapidly; flutter 3. [Scot. or Dial.] to move to other quarters, esp. by stealth 4. [Obs.] to change or shift about —*vt.* [Scot. or Dial.] to move to other quarters —*n.* the act of flitting —*SYN.* see FLY[1]

flitch (flich) *n.* [ME. *flicche* < OE. *flicce*, akin to ON. *flikki* < IE. base **pleik-*, to tear (off), whence FLAY] 1. the cured and salted side of a hog; side of bacon 2. a lengthwise strip from the outer part of a tree trunk 3. a beam formed of a steel plate between two beams bolted together: in full, **flitch beam** —*vt.* [< the *n.*] to cut so as to form flitches

flite (flīt) *vi., vt., n.* [ME. *fliten* < OE. *flitan,* akin to OHG. *flizan,* to strive, G. *fleiss,* diligence] [Obs. exc. Dial.] quarrel; dispute

flit·ter[1] (flit′ər) *vi., vt.* [ME. *flitteren,* freq. of *flitten,* FLIT] [Chiefly Dial.] *same as* FLUTTER

flit·ter[2] (flit′ər) *n.* a person or thing that flits

☆**fliv·ver** (fliv′ər) *n.* [< ?] [Old Slang] a small, cheap automobile, esp. an old one

float (flōt) *n.* [ME. *flote,* that which floats, ship, fleet < base of *fleotan* (see FLEET[2])] **1.** anything that stays, or causes something else to stay, on the surface of a liquid or suspended near the surface; specif., *a)* an air-filled bladder, as in a fish *b)* a cork on a fishing line *c)* a floating ball or device that regulates the valve controlling water level, as in a tank, or fuel supply, as in a carburetor *d)* a raftlike platform anchored near a shore, as for use by swimmers ☆*e)* a life preserver *f)* a buoyant device on an aircraft to enable it to land or remain on water **2.** a low, flat, decorated vehicle for carrying exhibits, tableaus, etc. in a parade **3.** a flat tool for smoothing or spreading cement, plaster, etc. **4.** a thread that is brought to the surface of a cloth in weaving, esp. to form a pattern ☆**5.** a cold beverage with ice cream floating in it [root beer *float*] **6.** [Rare] the act of floating ☆**7.** *Banking* the total value of checks or drafts in transit and not yet collected —*vi.* [ME. *flotien* < OE. *flotian*] **1.** to stay on the surface of a liquid or suspended near the surface **2.** to drift or move slowly or easily on water, in air, etc. [leaves *floating* down from the trees] **3.** to move or drift about vaguely and without purpose [idle thoughts *floating* through the mind] —*vt.* **1.** *a)* to cause to stay on the surface of a liquid or suspended near the surface *b)* to bring to the surface and cause to stay there **2.** to flood with a liquid **3.** *a)* to put into circulation; place on the market [to *float* a bond issue] *b)* to establish or start (a business, etc.) **4.** to arrange for (a loan) **5.** to smooth or spread (cement, plaster, etc.)

float·age (-ij) *n. same as* FLOTAGE

float·a·tion (flō tā′shən) *n. same as* FLOTATION

float·er (flōt′ər) *n.* **1.** a person or thing that floats ☆**2.** a person who illegally casts a vote at each of several polling places ☆**3.** a person who changes his place of residence or work at frequent intervals, drifter; esp., a transient laborer **4.** an insurance policy covering movable property irrespective of its location at the time of loss

float·ing (-iŋ) *adj.* **1.** that floats **2.** not fixed; not remaining in one place; moving about **3.** *Finance a)* designating an unfunded, short-time debt resulting from current operations and having no specified date for repayment *b)* not permanently invested; available for current expenses [*floating* capital] **4.** *Mech.* designating or of suspension that reduces vibration **5.** *Med.* displaced from the normal position and moving more freely [a *floating* kidney]

floating (dry) dock a dock that floats and can be lowered in the water for the entrance of a ship, and then raised for use as a dry dock

floating island ☆**1.** a floating mass of earth resembling an island **2.** a dessert of boiled custard topped with a dab or dabs of meringue or whipped cream

floating ribs the eleventh and twelfth pairs of ribs, which are not attached to the breastbone or to other ribs but only to the vertebrae

CONTROL TOWER · SHIP RESTING ON BOTTOM OF DOCK · PUMPS FOR EMPTYING WATER FROM DOCK

FLOATING DOCK

float·plane (-plān′) *n.* a seaplane equipped with pontoons or floats

float valve a valve regulated by a float

floc (fläk) *n.* [contr. < FLOCCULE] **1.** a very fine, fluffy mass formed by the aggregation of fine suspended particles, as in a precipitate **2.** *same as* FLOCK[2]

floc·cose (fläk′ōs) *adj.* [LL. *floccosus* < L. *floccus:* see FLOCCUS] covered with soft wool or woollike tufts

floc·cu·late (fläk′yoo lāt′) *vt., vi.* **-lat′ed, -lat′ing** to collect (soils, clouds, precipitates, etc.) into small, flocculent masses or deposits —*n.* a flocculated mass —**floc′cu·la′tion** *n.* —**floc′cu·la′tor** *n.*

floc·cule (fläk′yool) *n.* [see FLOCCULUS] a small mass of matter resembling a soft tuft of wool, as in a liquid

floc·cu·lent (fläk′yoo lənt) *adj.* [< L. *floccus* (see FLOCCUS) + -ULENT] **1.** like wool or tufts of wool; woolly; fluffy **2.** containing or consisting of small woolly masses **3.** covered with a waxy, woollike substance, as some insects —**floc′cu·lence** *n.* —**floc′cu·lent·ly** *adv.*

floc·cu·lus (-yoo ləs) *n., pl.* **-li′** (-lī′) [ModL., dim. < L. *floccus,* flock of wool: see ff.] **1.** a small, woolly or hairy tuft or mass **2.** *Anat.* a small lobe on the underside of each half of the cerebellum ☆**3.** *Astron.* a former term for PLAGE[2] —**floc′cu·lar** (-lər) *adj.*

floc·cus (fläk′əs) *n., pl.* **floc′ci** (-sī) [L., flock of wool < IE. *bhlok-,* whence OHG. *blaha,* coarse linen cloth] a woolly or hairy tuft or mass

flock[1] (fläk) *n.* [ME. *floc* < OE. *flocc,* a troop, band, akin to ON. *flokkr,* prob. < var. of IE. base *pel-,* to pour, fill, whence L. *plere,* to fill & (prob.) FOLK] **1.** a group of certain animals, as goats or sheep, or of birds, living, feeding or moving together **2.** any group, esp. a large one, of people or things, as the members of a church or the children in a family —*vi.* to assemble or travel in a flock or crowd —*SYN.* see GROUP

flock[2] (fläk) *n.* [ME. *flocke* < OFr. *floc* < L. *floccus:* see FLOCCUS] **1.** a small tuft of wool, cotton, etc. **2.** wool or cotton waste used to stuff upholstered furniture, mattresses, etc. **3.** tiny, fine fibers of wool, rayon, cotton, etc. applied to a fabric, wallpaper, or the like to form a velvetlike surface or pattern **4.** *same as* FLOC —*vt.* to stuff, cover or decorate with flock

flock·ing (-iŋ) *n.* **1.** *same as* FLOCK[2] (*n.* 3) **2.** a material or surface with flock applied to it

flock·y (fläk′ē) *adj.* **flock′i·er, flock′i·est** like or full of flock; flocculent

Flod·den (fläd′n) hilly field in N Northumberland, England: site of a battle (1513) in which the English defeated James IV of Scotland

floe (flō) *n.* [prob. < Norw. *flo,* layer, expanse < ON. < IE. base *plā-,* whence FLAG[2]] *same as* ICE FLOE

flog (fläg, flôg) *vt.* **flogged, flog′ging** [? cant abbrev. of L. *flagellare,* to whip] **1.** to beat, or punish by beating, with a strap, stick, whip, etc. **2.** [Brit. Slang] to sell, esp. dishonestly or illegally —*SYN.* see BEAT —**flog′ger** *n.*

flood (flud) *n.* [ME. *flode* < OE. *flod,* akin to G. *flut:* for IE. base see FLOW] **1.** an overflowing of water on an area normally dry; inundation; deluge **2.** the flowing in of water from the sea, as the tide rises **3.** a great flow or outpouring [a *flood* of words] **4.** [Colloq.] *same as* FLOODLIGHT **5.** [Archaic or Poet.] *a)* water, as opposed to land *b)* a large body of water, as a sea or broad river —*vt.* **1.** to cover or fill with a flood; overflow; inundate **2.** to cover, fill, or overwhelm like a flood [music *flooded* the room] **3.** to put much or too much water, fuel, etc. on or in [to *flood* a carburetor] —*vi.* **1.** to rise in a flood **2.** to come out like a flood; gush out **3.** to become flooded —**the Flood** *Bible* the great flood in Noah's time: Gen. 7

☆**flood control** the protection of land from floods by the construction of dams, reservoirs, river embankments, soil conservation, reforestation, etc.

flood·gate (-gāt′) *n.* **1.** a gate in a stream or canal, to control the height and flow of the water; sluice **2.** any thing like this in controlling a flow or an outburst [the *floodgates* of anger]

flood·light (-līt′) *n.* **1.** an artificial light of high intensity, usually with a reflector that causes it to shine in a broad beam **2.** such a beam of light —*vt.* **-light′ed** or **-lit′, -light′ing** to illuminate by a floodlight or floodlights

flood plain a plain along a river, formed from sediment deposited by floods

flood tide the incoming or rising tide: cf. EBB TIDE

☆**floo·ey, floo·ie** (floo′ē) *adj. same as* BLOOEY

floor (flôr) *n.* [ME. *flor* < OE., akin to G. *flur,* a plain < IE. base *plā-,* broad, flat, whence L. *planus,* PLANE[2]] **1.** the inside bottom surface of a room, hall, etc., on which one stands or walks **2.** the bottom surface of anything [the ocean *floor*] **3.** the platform of a bridge, pier, etc. **4.** a level or story in a building [an office on the sixth *floor*] **5.** *a)* the part of a legislative chamber, stock exchange, etc. occupied by the members and not including the gallery or platform *b)* such members as a group ☆**6.** permission or the right to speak in an assembly [to ask a chairman for the *floor*] **7.** a lower limit set on anything, as by official regulation **8.** *Naut.* the flat part of a ship's bottom —*vt.* **1.** to cover or furnish with a floor **2.** to knock down **3.** [Colloq.] *a)* to be the victor over; defeat *b)* to make unable to act, as by shocking, amazing, confusing, etc. ☆**4.** [Colloq.] to press down to the floor [to *floor* an accelerator]

floor·age (-ij) *n.* the area of a floor: also **floor space**

floor·board (-bôrd′) *n.* **1.** a board in a floor **2.** the floor of an automobile, etc.

floor·ing (-iŋ) *n.* **1.** a floor **2.** floors collectively **3.** material for making a floor

☆**floor leader** a member of a legislature chosen by his political party to direct its actions on the floor

floor plan a scale drawing of the layout of rooms, halls, etc. on one floor of a building

☆**floor show** a show presenting singers, dancers, etc. in a restaurant, nightclub, etc.

☆**floor·walk·er** (-wôk′ər) *n.* formerly, a person employed by a department store to direct customers, supervise sales, etc.: now usually **floor** (or **sales**) **manager**

☆**floo·zy, floo·zie** (floo′zē) *n., pl.* **-zies** [cf. FLOSSY] [Slang] a disreputable woman or girl, esp. one who is promiscuous or a prostitute: also sp. **floo′sy, floo′sie**

flop (fläp) *vt.* **flopped, flop′ping** [echoic var. of FLAP] **1.** to flap, strike, throw, or cause to drop noisily and clumsily **2.** *Photoengraving* to turn (a film negative) face down before exposure to a metal plate, in order to create a desired mirror image —*vi.* **1.** to move or flap around loosely or clumsily, usually with a thud or thuds **2.** to fall or drop in this way [to *flop* into a chair] ☆**3.** to make a sudden change ☆**4.** [Colloq.] to be a failure ☆**5.** [Slang] to sleep —*n.* **1.** the

act or sound of flopping ☆2. [Colloq.] a failure ☆3. [Slang] a place to sleep —*adv.* with a flop —**flop′per** *n.*

☆**flop·house** (-hous′) *n.* [Colloq.] a very cheap hotel frequented chiefly by vagrants

flop·o·ver (-ō′vər) *n. TV* faulty reception in which the picture appears to move repeatedly up or down the screen

flop·py (-ē) *adj.* **-pi·er, -pi·est** [Colloq.] flopping or inclined to flop —**flop′pi·ly** *adv.* —**flop′pi·ness** *n.*

Flo·ra (flôr′ə) [L. < *flos* (gen. *floris*), a flower (see BLOOM[1]): in *n.* 1, used and popularized by Linnaeus (1745)] 1. a feminine name 2. *Rom. Myth.* the goddess of flowers —*n.* [f-] 1. *pl.* **-ras, -rae** (-ē) the plants of a specified region or time [the *flora* of Africa] 2. a descriptive, systematic list of such plants

flo·ral (flôr′əl) *adj.* [L. *floralis*, of Flora: see prec.] of, made of, or like flowers —**flo′ral·ly** *adv.*

floral envelope *same as* PERIANTH

Flor·ence (flôr′əns, flär′-) [Fr. < L. *Florentia*, lit., a blooming < *florens*, prp. of *florere*, to bloom < *flos*: see BLOOM[1]] 1. a feminine name: dim. **Flo, Flossie;** equiv. Ger. *Florenz,* It. *Fiorenza,* Sp. *Florencia* 2. commune in Tuscany, C Italy, on the Arno River: pop. 456,000: It. name, **FIRENZE**

Flor·ence-Gra·ham (-grā′əm) suburb of Los Angeles, in SW Calif.: pop. 43,000

Flor·en·tine (-ən tēn′) *adj.* 1. of Florence, Italy, or its people, culture, or art 2. [*often* f-] designating a metal finish, as for jewelry, with finely incised lines that impart a dull luster —*n.* a native or inhabitant of Florence

Flo·res (flô′res) 1. island of Indonesia, west of Timor & south of Celebes: 5,500 sq. mi. 2. westernmost island of the Azores: 55 sq. mi.

flo·res·cence (flô res′ns, flə-) *n.* [< L. *florescens,* prp. of *florescere,* to begin to bloom, inceptive of *florere,* to bloom < *flos*: see BLOOM[1]] 1. the act, condition, or period of blooming 2. a period of success or achievement —**flo·res′cent** (-'nt) *adj.*

Flores Sea part of the Pacific, between the islands of Celebes & Flores in Indonesia

flo·ret (flôr′it) *n.* [ME. *flourette* < OFr. *florete,* dim. of *flor* (Fr. *fleur*) < L. *flos,* a flower: see BLOOM[1]] 1. a small flower 2. any of the individual flowers making up the head of a plant of the composite family 3. the flowering unit of a grass spikelet, consisting of the flower and its two enveloping bracts

Flo·ri·a·nó·po·lis (flôr′ē ə näp′ə lis) city on an island just off the SE coast of Brazil: capital of Santa Catarina state: pop. 99,000

flo·ri·at·ed (flôr′ē āt′id) *adj.* having floral decorations —**flo′ri·a′tion** *n.*

flo·ri·bun·da (flôr′ə bun′də) *n.* [ModL., fem. of **floribundus,* abounding in blossoms < L. *flos* (gen. *floris*), FLOWER + *-bundus* (as in *moribundus,* MORIBUND), taken to mean "producing": sense infl. by ABUNDANT] any of a class of cultivated roses with clusters of small to medium-sized flowers produced in profusion

flo·ri·cul·ture (flôr′ē kul′chər) *n.* [< L. *flos* (gen. *floris*), a flower + CULTURE] the cultivation of flowers, esp. of decorative flowering plants —**flo′ri·cul′tur·al** *adj.* — —**flo′ri·cul′tur·ist** *n.*

flor·id (flôr′id, flär′-) *adj.* [L. *floridus,* flowery < *flos* (gen. *floris*), a flower: see BLOOM[1]] 1. flushed with red or pink; rosy; ruddy: said of the complexion 2. highly decorated; gaudy; showy; ornate [a *florid* musical passage] 3. [Obs.] decorated with flowers; flowery —*SYN.* see ROSY —**flo·rid′i·ty** (flō rid′ə tē, flə-), **flor′id·ness** *n.* —**flor′id·ly** *adv.*

Flor·i·da (flôr′ə də, flär′-) [Sp. < L., lit., abounding in flowers < *flos* (gen. *floris*): see BLOOM[1]: so named by PONCE DE LEÓN] 1. Southern State of the SE U.S., mostly on a peninsula between the Atlantic & the Gulf of Mexico: admitted 1845; 58,560 sq. mi.; pop. 6,789,000; cap. Tallahassee: abbrev. **Fla., FL** 2. **Straits of,** strait between the S tip of Fla. & Cuba on the south & the Bahamas on the southeast: it connects the Atlantic & the Gulf of Mexico: also called **Florida Strait** —**Flo·rid·i·an** (flô rid′ē ən), **Flor′i·dan** *adj., n.*

Florida Keys chain of small islands extending southwest from the S tip of Fla.: see EVERGLADES, map

flo·rif·er·ous (flô rif′ər əs, flə-) *adj.* [L. *florifer* (< *flos,* a flower + *ferre,* BEAR) + -OUS] bearing flowers; blooming abundantly

☆**flor·i·gen** (flôr′ə jən, flär′-) *n.* [< L. *flos* (gen. *floris*), FLOWER + -GEN: so named at California Institute of Technology] a plant hormone thought to stimulate the flowering of plants

flor·in (flôr′in, flär′-) *n.* [ME. < OFr. < It. *fiorino* < *fiore,* a flower < L. *flos* (gen. *floris*), FLOWER: from the figure of a lily stamped on the original coins] 1. orig., a gold coin of medieval Florence, issued in 1252 2. a British coin equal to two shillings 3. any of various European or South African silver or gold coins

Flo·ri·o (flôr′ē ō′), **John** 1553?-1625; Eng. writer & lexicographer: translator of Montaigne

Flo·ris·sant (flôr′ə sənt) [Fr., flourishing, a prp. of *fleurir,* to bloom, flourish < L. *florere* < *flos* (gen. *floris*), a bloom, flower] city in E Mo.: suburb of St. Louis: pop. 66,000

flo·rist (flôr′ist, flär′-) *n.* [< L. *flos* (gen. *floris*), FLOWER + -IST] a person who cultivates or sells flowers —**flo′ris·try** (-is trē) *n.*

flo·ris·tic (flô ris′tik) *adj.* of or having to do with flowers or floristics —**flo·ris′ti·cal·ly** *adv.*

flo·ris·tics (-tiks) *n.pl.* [*with sing. v.*] [FLORIST + -ICS] the branch of botany dealing with the kinds and number of plant species in particular areas and their distribution

-flo·rous (flôr əs) [< LL. *-florus* < L. *flos* (gen. *floris*), FLOWER] a *suffix meaning* having many or a (specified) number or kind of flowers [*multiflorous, triflorous*]

flos fer·ri (fläs′ fer′ī) [L., flower of iron] an arborescent variety of aragonite, usually found in iron ore

floss (flôs, fläs) *n.* [earlier also *flosh,* prob. < Fr. *floche,* downy, woolly (in *soie floche,* floss silk), ult. < L. *floccus:* see FLOCCUS] 1. the rough silk covering a silkworm's cocoon 2. the short, downy waste fibers of silk 3. a soft, loosely twisted thread or yarn, as of silk (**floss silk**) or linen (**linen floss**), used in embroidery 4. a soft, silky substance resembling floss, as in milkweed pods 5. *same as* DENTAL FLOSS

floss·y (-ē) *adj.* **floss′i·er, floss′i·est** 1. of or like floss; downy; light; fluffy ☆2. [Slang] elegant or stylish in a showy or fancy way —*n.* [Old Slang] a prostitute

flo·tage (flōt′ij) *n.* [< FLOAT, *v.* + -AGE, after OFr. *flotage*] 1. the act, condition, or power of floating 2. anything that floats; esp., floating debris; flotsam

flo·ta·tion (flō tā′shən) *n.* [earlier *floatation,* respelled as if < Fr. *flottaison*] 1. the act or condition of floating; specif., the act of beginning or financing a business, etc., as by selling an entire issue of bonds, securities, etc. 2. *Mining* a method of ore separation in which finely powdered ore is introduced into a bubbling solution to which oils are added: certain minerals float on the surface, and others sink

flo·til·la (flō til′ə) *n.* [Sp., dim. of *flota,* a fleet < OFr. *flote* < OE. *flota:* see FLOAT] 1. a small fleet 2. a fleet of boats or small ships ☆3. *U.S. Navy* a unit consisting of two or more squadrons

Flo·tow (flō′tō), **Baron Frie·drich von** (frē′driH fôn) 1812-83; Ger. operatic composer

flot·sam (flät′səm) *n.* [Anglo-Fr. *floteson* < OFr. *flotaison,* a floating < *floter,* to float < MDu. *vloten* (or cognate OE. *flotian*), to FLOAT] the wreckage of a ship or its cargo found floating on the sea (cf. JETSAM): chiefly in **flotsam and jetsam,** 1. the wreckage of a ship or its cargo found floating on the sea or washed ashore 2. miscellaneous trifles or worthless things 3. transient, unemployed people; vagrants

flounce[1] (flouns) *vi.* **flounced, flounc′ing** [Early ModE., orig., to dive: prob. < Scand., as in Sw. dial. *flunsa,* to dive, dip; ? infl. by BOUNCE] 1. to move with quick, flinging motions of the body, as in anger or impatience 2. to twist or turn abruptly; jerk —*n.* the act of flouncing

flounce[2] (flouns) *n.* [earlier *frounce* < ME. < OFr. *fronce* < *froncir,* to wrinkle < Frank. **hrunkja,* wrinkle, akin to G. *runzel*] a piece of cloth, often gathered or pleated, sewed on by its upper edge to a skirt, sleeve, etc.; wide, ornamental ruffle —*vt.* **flounced, flounc′ing** to trim with a flounce or flounces —**flounc′y** *adj.*

flounc·ing (floun′sin) *n.* 1. material for making flounces 2. a flounce, or flounces collectively

floun·der[1] (floun′dər) *vi.* [16th & 17th c.; also earlier *flunder,* ? var. of FOUNDER[1]] 1. to struggle awkwardly to move, as in deep mud or snow; plunge about in a stumbling manner 2. to speak or act in an awkward, confused manner, with hesitation and frequent mistakes —*n.* the act of floundering

floun·der[2] (floun′dər) *n., pl.* **-ders, -der:** see PLURAL, II, D, 1 [ME. < Scand., as in Sw. *flundra,* akin to G. *flunder* < IE. base **plāt-,* FLAT] any of a large group of flatfishes caught for food, including the halibut and the plaice

flour (flour) *n.* [ME. (see FLOWER): a fig. use as "best, prime" in "flour of wheat," after Fr. *fleur de farine,* lit., flower of meal] 1. a fine, powdery substance, or meal, produced by grinding and sifting grain, esp. wheat, or any of various edible roots, nuts, etc. 2. any finely powdered substance —*vt.* 1. to put flour in or on 2. to grind and sift (grain) into flour

flour·ish (flur′ish) *vi.* [ME. *florishen* < extended stem of OFr. *florir,* to blossom < LL. **florire* < L. *florere* < *flos,* FLOWER] 1. orig., to blossom 2. to grow vigorously; succeed; thrive; prosper 3. to be at the peak of development, activity, influence, production, etc.; be in one's prime 4. to make showy, wavy motions, as of the arms 5. [Now Rare] *a)* to write in an ornamental style *b)* to perform a fanfare, as of trumpets —*vt.* 1. to ornament with something flowery or fanciful 2. [first so used by Wyclif] to wave (a sword, arm, hat, etc.) in the air; brandish —*n.* 1. [Rare] a thriving state; success; prosperity 2. anything done in a showy way, as a sweeping movement of the limbs or body 3. a waving in the air; brandishing 4. a decorative or curved line or lines in writing 5. an ornate musical passage; fanfare 6. [Obs.] a blooming or a bloom —*SYN.* see SUCCEED —**flour′ish·er** *n.* —**flour′ish·ing** *adj.*

flour·y (flour′ē) *adj.* 1. of flour 2. like flour in color or texture; powdery or white 3. covered with flour

flout (flout) *vt.* [prob. special use of ME. *flouten,* to play the flute, hence, whistle (at)] to mock or scoff at; show scorn or contempt for —*vi.* to be scornful; show contempt; jeer; scoff —*n.* a scornful or contemptuous action or speech; mockery; scoffing; insult —*SYN.* see SCOFF[1] —**flout′er** *n.* —**flout′ing·ly** *adv.*

flow (flō) *vi.* [ME. *flouen* < OE. *flowan*, akin to ON. *floa*, to flood, OHG. *flouwen*, to wash < IE. base *pleu-*, to run, flow, whence L. *pluere*, to rain, FLOOD] **1.** to move as a liquid does; move in a stream, like water **2.** to move in a way suggestive of a liquid; stream [crowds *flowing* past] **3.** *a)* to move gently, smoothly, and easily; glide *b)* to have smooth and pleasing continuity [*flowing* lines in a painting] **4.** to stream forth; pour out **5.** to be derived; spring; proceed **6.** to fall in waves; hang loose [hair *flowing* down her back] **7.** to come in; rise, as the tide **8.** to be overflowing or plentiful **9.** *Geol.* to change in shape under pressure without breaking or splitting, as ice in a glacier or rocks deep in the earth —*vt.* **1.** to overflow; flood **2.** [Archaic] to cause to flow —*n.* **1.** the act or manner of flowing **2.** the rate of flow **3.** anything that flows; stream or current **4.** a continuous production [a *flow* of ideas] **5.** the rising of the tide; flood —*SYN.* see RISE —**flow'ing·ly** *adv.*

flow·age (-ij) *n.* **1.** a flowing, overflowing, or flooding **2.** a flooded condition **3.** what flows or overflows **4.** *Geol.* a gradual change in shape of rocks without breaking

☆**flow chart** a diagram showing the progress of work through a sequence of operations, as in manufacturing

flow·er (flou'ər, flour) *n.* [ME. *flowre, flour* < OFr. *flor, flour* (Fr. *fleur*) < L. *flos* (gen. *floris*), for IE. base see BLOOM¹] **1.** *a)* the seed-producing structure of a flowering plant, consisting of a greatly shortened stem bearing four sets of organs, carpels at the tip of the stem and stamens beneath, which are typically surrounded by petals, usually brightly colored, and leaflike sepals *b)* a blossom; bloom *c)* the reproductive structure of any plant **2.** a plant cultivated for its blossoms; flowering plant **3.** the best or finest part or example [the *flower* of a country's youth] **4.** the best period of a person or thing; time of flourishing **5.** something decorative; esp., a figure of speech **6.** [*pl.*] *Chem.* a substance in powder form, made from condensed vapors [*flowers* of sulfur] —*vi.* **1.** to produce blossoms; bloom **2.** to reach the best or most vigorous stage [his genius *flowered* early] —*vt.* to decorate with flowers or floral patterns —**in flower** in a state of flowering —**flow'er·less** *adj.* —**flow'er·like'** *adj.*

FLOWER

flow·er·age (-ij) *n.* **1.** flowers collectively **2.** the act or condition of flowering

☆**flower child** [Slang] *same as* HIPPIE

flow·ered (flou'ərd) *adj.* **1.** bearing or containing flowers **2.** decorated with a design like flowers

flow·er·et (-ər it) *n.* [ME. *flourette*, dim. of *flour*, FLOWER] **1.** *same as* FLORET **2.** [Poet.] a small flower

flower girl 1. a girl or woman who sells flowers in the streets **2.** a little girl who carries flowers and attends the bride at a wedding

flower head *Bot. same as* HEAD (*n.* 17 *a*)

flow·er·ing (-iŋ) *adj.* **1.** having flowers; in bloom **2.** bearing showy or profuse flowers

flowering crab a small tree (*Malus floribunda*) bearing many large, rose-red to light pink flowers

flowering quince *same as* JAPANESE QUINCE

☆**flower-of-an-hour** *n.* a plant (*Hibiscus trionum*) of the mallow family, having yellow flowers with dark centers

flow·er·pot (-pät') *n.* a container, usually made of porous clay, in which to grow plants

flow·er·y (-ē) *adj.* **-er·i·er, -er·i·est 1.** covered or decorated with flowers **2.** of or like flowers **3.** full of figurative or ornate expressions and fine words; said of language, style, etc. —*SYN.* see BOMBASTIC —**flow'er·i·ly** *adv.* —**flow'er·i·ness** *n.*

flown (flōn) *pp. of* FLY¹: sometimes used to form hyphenated adjectives [far-*flown*, high-*flown*]

flown² (flōn) *adj.* [obs. pp. of FLOW] filled too full

flow·stone (flō'stōn') *n.* a calcareous deposit, a kind of travertine, accumulated in caves by the evaporation of seeping water

Floyd (floid) [var. of LLOYD, with *Fl-* for W. *Ll-*] a masculine name

fl. oz. fluid ounce; fluid ounces

flt. flight

flu (flōō) *n.* **1.** *a shortened form for* INFLUENZA **2.** popularly, any of various respiratory or intestinal infections caused by a virus

☆**flub** (flub) *vt., vi.* **flubbed, flub'bing** [? < FL(OP) + (D)UB¹] [Colloq.] to make a botch of (a job, chance, stroke, etc.); bungle —*n.* [Colloq.] a mistake or blunder

fluc·tu·ate (fluk'choo wāt') *vi.* **-at'ed, -at'ing** [< L. *fluctuatus*, pp. of *fluctuare* < *fluctus*, a flowing, wave < pp. stem of *fluere*, to flow < IE. *bhleu-*, to swell up, flow (whence BLUSTER) < base *bhel-*, to swell up (cf. BALL¹)]

1. to move back and forth or up and down; rise and fall; undulate, as waves **2.** to be continually changing or varying in an irregular way [*fluctuating* prices] —*vt.* to cause to fluctuate —*SYN.* see SWING —**fluc'tu·ant** *adj.* —**fluc'tu·a'tion** *n.*

flue¹ (flōō) *n.* [< ? OFr. *fluie*, a flowing, stream] **1.** a tube, pipe, or shaft for the passage of smoke, hot air, gas, etc., as in a chimney **2.** [ME., mouthpiece of a hunting horn] *a)* a flue pipe in an organ *b)* the opening or passage for air in such a flue pipe

flue² (flōō) *n.* [altered < ? FLUKE²] a barbed point; fluke

flue³ (flōō) *n.* [< Fl. *vluwe* < Fr. *velu*, woolly < VL. *villutus*, shaggy < L. *villus*, shaggy hair] a loose, downy mass; fluff

flue⁴ (flōō) *n.* [ME. *flew* < MDu. *vluwe*] any of various kinds of fishing net

☆**flue-cured** (flōō'kyoord') *adj.* cured or dried by hot air passed through flues: said of tobacco

flue·gel·horn, flü·gel·horn (flōō'g'l hôrn', G. flü'-) *n.* [G. < *flügel*, wing + *horn*, horn: because of shape] a brass-wind instrument like the cornet in design and pitch but with a wider bore, larger bell, and mellower tone

flu·en·cy (flōō'ən sē) *n.* [LL. *fluentia* < L. *fluens*: see ff.] the quality or condition of being fluent, esp. in speech or writing

flu·ent (-ənt) *adj.* [L. *fluens* (gen. *fluentis*), prp. of *fluere*, to flow: see FLUCTUATE] **1.** flowing or moving smoothly and easily [*fluent* verse] **2.** able to write or speak easily, smoothly, and expressively —**flu'ent·ly** *adv.*

flue pipe an organ pipe in which the tone is produced by a current of air striking the lip of the mouth, or opening, in the pipe

fluff (fluf) *n.* [? blend of FLUE³ + PUFF] **1.** soft, light down **2.** a loose, soft, downy mass of hair, feathers, cotton, dust, etc. **3.** any light or trivial matter or talk **4.** *Theater, Radio, TV* an error in speaking or reading a line —*vt.* **1.** to shake or pat until loose, feathery, and fluffy **2.** *Theater, Radio, TV* to make an error in speaking or reading (a word, one's lines, etc.) **3.** to make a botch of —*vi.* **1.** to become fluffy **2.** to make a mistake —**bit** (or **piece**) **of fluff** [Slang] a girl or young woman

fluff·y (-ē) *adj.* **fluff·i·er, fluff·i·est 1.** soft and light like fluff; feathery **2.** covered with fluff —**fluff'i·ness** *n.*

flu·id (flōō'id) *adj.* [ME. < L. *fluidus* < *fluere*, to flow: see FLUCTUATE] **1.** that can flow, not solid; able to move and change shape without separating when under pressure **2.** of a fluid or fluids **3.** like a fluid; that can change rapidly or easily; not settled or fixed [*fluid* plans] **4.** marked by or using graceful movements **5.** available for investment [*fluid* capital] **6.** available as cash [*fluid* assets] —*n.* any substance that can flow; liquid or gas —*SYN.* see LIQUID —**flu·id·ic** (flōō wid'ik) *adj.* —**flu·id'i·ty, flu'id·ness** *n.* —**flu'id·ly** *adv.*

fluid dram (or **drachm**) a liquid measure equal to 1/8 fluid ounce

flu·id·ex·tract (-ek'strakt) *n. Pharmacy* a concentrated fluid preparation of a vegetable drug, containing alcohol either as a preservative or a solvent, and of such strength that one cubic centimeter of the solution is equal in activity to one gram of the dry, powdered drug

flu·id·ics (flōō wid'iks) *n.pl.* [*with sing. v.*] [FLUID + -ICS] the science or technology dealing with the control of a flow of air or some other fluid, used like an electronic circuit to perform functions of sensing, control, computing, etc.

flu·id·ize (flōō'ə dīz') *vt.* **-ized', -iz'ing 1.** to make fluid **2.** to give fluid properties to (a solid), as by pulverizing

fluid mechanics the study of the flow properties of liquids and gases

fluid ounce a liquid measure equal to 8 fluid drams, 1/16 pint, or 29.57 ml. (in Great Britain, 1/20 imperial pint, or 28.42 cc.): also **flu'id·ounce'** *n.*

fluid pressure pressure of, or like that of, a fluid: it is constant and uniform in every direction

fluke¹ (flōōk) *n.* [ME. *floke* < OE. *floc*, akin to ON. *floki* < IE. base *plāg-*, broad, flat, whence FLAG², G. *flach*, flat, level] **1.** any of several flatfishes, esp. certain flounders **2.** a parasitic flatworm with a very complex life cycle, found as an adult in the internal organs of vertebrates

fluke² (flōōk) *n.* [prob. < prec., with reference to shape] **1.** the triangular, pointed end of an anchor arm, by which the anchor catches in the ground ☆**2.** a barb or barbed head of an arrow, lance, harpoon, etc. **3.** either of the two lobes of a whale's tail

fluke³ (flōōk) *n.* [19th-c. billiard slang < ?] **1.** [Old Slang] an accidentally good or lucky stroke in billiards, pool, etc. **2.** [Colloq.] a result, esp. a successful one, brought about by accident; stroke of luck —*vt.* **fluked, fluk'ing** [Colloq.] to hit or get by a fluke

fluk·y (flōō'kē) *adj.* **fluk'i·er, fluk'i·est** [< prec.] [Colloq.] **1.** resulting from chance rather than skill or design; lucky **2.** constantly changing; uncertain; fitful [a *fluky* breeze] —**fluk'i·ness** *n.*

flume (flōōm) *n.* [ME. *flum*, river, stream < OFr. < L. *flumen* < *fluere*, to flow: see FLUCTUATE] ☆**1.** an artificial channel, usually an inclined chute or trough, for carrying

water to furnish power, transport logs down a mountainside, etc. ☆2. a narrow gorge or ravine with a stream running through it —☆vt. **flumed, flum′ing** to send (logs, water, etc.) down or through a flume

flum·mer·y (flum′ər ē) n., pl. **-mer·ies** [W. llymru, soured oatmeal < llymus, of a sharp quality] 1. any soft, easily eaten food; esp., a) orig., thick, boiled oatmeal or flour b) a soft custard or blancmange 2. meaningless flattery or silly talk

flum·mox (flum′əks) vt. [< ?] [Old `Slang] to confuse; perplex

flump (flump) vt., vi. [prob. echoic] to drop or move heavily and noisily —n. the act or sound of flumping

flung (flun) pt. & pp. of FLING

☆**flunk** (flunk) vt. [19th-c. college slang < ? FUNK[1] or echoic] [Colloq.] 1. to fail in (schoolwork) [to flunk a science examination] 2. to give a mark of failure to (a student) —vi. [Colloq.] 1. to fail, esp. in schoolwork 2. to give up; retreat —n. [Colloq.] 1. a failure 2. a mark or grade of failure —**flunk out** [Colloq.] to send or be sent away from school or college because of unsatisfactory work

flun·ky (flun′kē) n., pl. **flun′kies** [orig. Scot. < ? Fr. flanquer, to flank, be at the side of, as to render assistance < flanc, FLANK] 1. orig., a liveried manservant, as a footman: term of contempt 2. a) a person who obeys superiors in a servile, cringing way ☆b) a person with very minor or menial tasks Also sp. **flun′key** —**flun′ky·ism** n.

fluo- (flōō′ə) [< FLUOR] a combining form meaning: 1. fluorine 2. fluorescent

flu·or (flōō′ôr, -ōr) n. [ModL. < L., flux < fluere, to flow (see FLUCTUATE): transl. of G. fluss, orig. applied to minerals used as smelting fluxes, but later limited to those containing fluorine] same as FLUORITE

fluor- (flōō′ər, floor) same as FLUORO-: used before a vowel

flu·o·resce (flōō′ə res′; floo res′, flō-) vi. **-resced′, -resc′ing** [back-formation < FLUORESCENCE] to produce, show, or undergo fluorescence; be or become fluorescent

flu·o·res·ce·in (-ē in) n. [< prec. + -IN[1]: from its bright fluorescence in solution] a yellowish-red, crystalline compound, $C_{20}H_{12}O_5$, made synthetically from resorcin and phthalic anhydride: an alkaline solution appears green by reflected light and red by transmitted light: used as a dye and as a liquid coloring material

flu·o·res·cence (-'ns) n. [< FLUOR (SPAR) + -ESCENCE] 1. the property of a substance, such as fluorite, of producing light while it is being acted upon by radiant energy, such as ultraviolet rays or X-rays 2. the production of such light 3. light so produced —**flu′o·res′cent** adj.

fluorescent lamp (or **tube**) a glass tube coated on the inside with a fluorescent substance that gives off light (**fluorescent light**) when mercury vapor in the tube is acted upon by a stream of electrons from the cathode

☆**fluor·i·date** (flôr′ə dāt′, floor′-) vt. **-dat′ed, -dat′ing** to add fluorides to (a supply of drinking water) in order to reduce the incidence of caries in the teeth —**fluor′i·da′tion** n.

flu·o·ride (floor′īd, flôr′-; flōō′ə rīd′) n. a compound of fluorine and one or more elements or radicals

fluor·i·nate (flōr′ə nāt′, floor′-) vt. **-nat′ed, -nat′ing** 1. to introduce fluorine into or cause to combine with fluorine 2. same as FLUORIDATE —**fluor′i·na′tion** n.

flu·o·rine (flōr′ēn, flōr′-; flōō′ə rēn′, -rin) n. [FLUOR + -INE[4]] a corrosive, poisonous, pale greenish-yellow gaseous chemical element, the most reactive nonmetallic element known, forming fluorides with almost all the known elements: symbol, F; at. wt., 18.9984; at. no., 9; density, 1.696 g/l (0°C); melt. pt., −223°C; boil. pt., −188°C

flu·o·rite (floor′īt, flôr′-; flōō′ə rīt′) n. [FLUOR- + -ITE[1]] calcium fluoride, CaF_2, a transparent, crystalline mineral having many colors and perfect cleavage: it is the principal source of fluorine and is used as a flux, in glassmaking, etc.

fluo·ro- (floor′ə-, flôr′-; -ō; flōō′ôr ə, -ə rō′) a combining form meaning: 1. fluorine 2. fluorescence

fluo·ro·car·bon (-kär′bən) n. any of a class of nonreactive organic compounds containing carbon, fluorine, and, in some cases, hydrogen: used as aerosols, lubricants, electrical insulators, etc.

flu·o·rog·ra·phy (floo räg′rə fē, flōō′ə-) n. same as PHOTOFLUOROGRAPHY

☆**flu·o·rom·e·ter** (floo räm′ə tər, flōō′ə-) n. an instrument for measuring the wavelength and intensity of fluorescence —**flu·o·ro·met·ric** (floor′ə met′rik, flōō′ər ə-) adj. —**flu·o·rom′e·try** (-trē) n.

☆**fluor·o·scope** (floor′ə skōp′, flôr′-) n. [FLUORO- + -SCOPE] a machine for examining internal structures by viewing the shadows cast on a fluorescent screen by objects or parts through which X-rays are directed: the shadows vary in intensity according to the density of the object or part —vt. **-scoped′, -scop′ing** to examine with a fluoroscope —**fluor′o·scop′ic** (-skäp′ik) adj. —**fluor′o·scop′i·cal·ly** adv.

☆**flu·o·ros·co·py** (floo räs′kə pē, flōō′ə-) n. examination by means of a fluoroscope —**flu·o·ros′co·pist** n.

flu·o·ro·sis (-rō′sis) n. [ModL.: see FLUORO- & -OSIS] a disorder resulting from the absorption of too much fluorine

fluor spar same as FLUORITE: also **flu′or·spar′** n.

flur·ry (flur′ē) n., pl. **-ries** [< ? ☆1. a sudden, brief rush of wind; gust ☆2. a gust of rain or snow 3. a sudden confusion or commotion 4. a brief fluctuation in stock market prices or increase in trading —vt. **-ried, -ry·ing** to confuse; agitate —vi. to move in a quick, flustered way

flush[1] (flush) vi. [complex of several words, with senses FLASH & ME. flusshen, to fly up suddenly, blended with echoic elements; "flow" senses < ? or akin to OFr. fluir (stem fluiss-), to flow] 1. to flow and spread suddenly and rapidly 2. to become red in the face, as with embarrassment or anger; blush 3. to glow 4. to become cleaned, washed, or emptied out with a sudden flow of water, etc. 5. to start up from cover: said of birds —vt. 1. to make flow 2. to clean, wash, or empty out with a sudden flow of water, etc. 3. to make blush or glow 4. to excite; animate; exhilarate: usually in the passive voice [flushed with victory] 5. to drive (game birds) from cover 6. to make level or even —n. 1. a sudden and rapid flow, as of water in washing out something 2. a sudden, vigorous growth [the first flush of youth] 3. a sudden feeling of excitement or exhilaration 4. a blush; glow 5. a sudden feeling of great heat, as in a fever —adj. 1. well supplied, esp. with money 2. abundant; plentiful 3. [Dial.] lavish; profuse 4. [Rare] full of vigor 5. having a ruddy color; glowing 6. a) making an even or unbroken line or surface; being even or on the same line or plane [a door flush with the walls] b) even with a margin or edge 7. direct; full [a blow flush in the face] —adv. 1. in an even manner; so as to be level or in alignment 2. directly; squarely

flush[2] (flush) n. [Fr. flux: see FLUX] a hand of cards all in the same suit: in poker, a flush ranks just above a straight and below a full house

Flush·ing (flush′in) section of N Queens borough, New York City, on the East River

flus·ter (flus′tər) vt., vi. [ME. flosteren, prob. < Scand., as in Ice. flaustra, to bustle, hurry] to make or become confused, nervous, or befuddled —n. the condition of being flustered

flus·tra·tion (flus trā′shən) n. the condition of being flustered: also **flus′ter·a′tion** (-tər ā′shən)

flute (flōōt) n. [ME. floute < OFr. fleüte, flaute < Pr. flaüt < ?] 1. a) a high-pitched wind instrument consisting of a long, slender tube, played by blowing across a hole near one end: by fingering the holes and keys along its length, the player can produce various tones b) any of various similar instruments, as the fipple flute 2. a) an ornamental groove in cloth, etc. b) Archit. a long, vertical, rounded groove in the shaft of a column 3. a) a flue pipe b) a flue organ stop with a flutelike tone —vt. **flut′ed, flut′ing** 1. to sing, speak, whistle, etc. in a flutelike tone 2. to play on the flute 3. to make long, rounded grooves in (a column, etc.) —vi. 1. to play on the flute 2. to sing, speak, whistle, etc. in a flutelike tone —**flute′like′** adj.

FLUTE

flut·ed (flōōt′id) adj. 1. having a flutelike tone; fluty 2. having long, rounded grooves

flut·er (-ər) n. [ME. floutour < OFr. flauteur] 1. [Rare] a flutist 2. a person or tool that makes flutings

flut·ing (-in) n. 1. a decoration consisting of long, rounded grooves, as in a column 2. such grooves or the act of making them 3. the act of playing the flute or singing, etc. in a flutelike tone

flut·ist (-ist) n. a person who plays the flute; flautist

flut·ter (flut′ər) vi. [ME. floteren < OE. flotorian, freq. of flotian < base of fleotan: see FLEET[2]] 1. to flap the wings rapidly, as in short flight or without flying at all 2. to wave or vibrate rapidly and irregularly [a flag fluttering in the wind] 3. to move with quick vibrations, flaps, etc. 4. to be in a state of tremulous excitement; tremble; quiver 5. to move restlessly; bustle —vt. 1. to cause to move in quick, irregular motions 2. to throw into a state of excitement, alarm, or confusion —n. 1. a fluttering movement; vibration 2. a state of excitement or confusion 3. a condition of the heartbeat in which the contractions are very rapid but generally regular 4. a potentially destructive oscillation of a part of an aircraft, as the wing 5. [Brit.] a small gamble or speculation 6. a) a rapid fluctuation in the amplitude of a reproduced sound b) a flicker in the image on a television screen —SYN. see FLY[1] —**flut′ter·er** n. —**flut′ter·y** adj.

flutter kick a swimming kick in which the legs are moved up and down in short, rapid, steady strokes

flut·y (flōōt′ē) adj. **flut′i·er, flut′i·est** flutelike in tone; soft, clear, and high-pitched

flu·vi·al (flōō′vē əl) adj. [ME. < L. fluvialis < fluvius, a river < fluere, to flow: see FLUCTUATE] of, found in, or produced by a river: also **fluʻvi·a·tile** (-ə til)

flu·vi·o- (flōō′vē ō) [< L. fluvius: see prec.] a combining form meaning by the combined action of a river and [fluvioglacial]

flux (fluks) n. [ME. < OFr. < L. fluxus, a flowing, flow < pp. of fluere, to flow: see FLUCTUATE] 1. a flowing or flow 2. a coming in of the tide 3. a continuous movement or continual change [fashion is always in a state of flux]

4. any excessive or unnatural discharge of fluid body matter, esp. from the bowels   **5.** *a)* a substance, as borax or rosin, used to help metals fuse together by preventing oxidation, as in soldering *b)* a substance used to aid in the extraction of a furnace charge because of its ability to fuse with undesired matter in forming a more liquid slag   **6.** *Physics* the rate of flow of energy, fluids, etc. over a surface —*vt.* **1.** to make fluid **2.** to fuse (metals) by melting —*vi.* [Archaic] to flow or stream out

flux density *Physics* the quantity of a fluid or energy emitted per unit of time through a unit of surface area

flux gate an instrument used to measure the force and direction of the earth's magnetic field

flux·ion (fluk′shən) *n.* [Fr. < VL. *fluxio*, for L. *fluctio*, a flowing < pp. of *fluere*, to flow: see FLUCTUATE] **1.** [Now Rare] continuous change **2.** [Archaic] something that flows; discharge **3.** *Math.* [Archaic] the rate of continuous change in variable quantities; a differential —**flux′ion·al, flux′ion·ar′y** *adj.*

flux·me·ter (fluks′mēt′ər) *n.* an instrument for measuring magnetic flux

fly¹ (flī) *vi.* **flew, flown, fly′ing** [ME. *flien, flegen* < OE. *fleogan*, akin to MDu. *vlegen*, G. *fliegen* < IE. *pleuk-* < *pleu-*, to move forward, extension < *pel-*, to flow, pour, whence FLOW, FLEET²] **1.** to move through the air; specif., *a)* to move through the air by using wings, as a bird *b)* to travel through the air in an aircraft *c)* to be propelled through the air, as a bullet **2.** to operate an aircraft **3.** to wave or float in the air, as a flag or kite **4.** to move swiftly or suddenly [the door *flew* open] **5.** to appear to pass swiftly [time *flies*] **6.** to be used up swiftly: said of money, etc. **7.** to run away from danger or evil; flee **8.** to start with a hawk ☆**9.** **flied, fly′ing** *Baseball* to hit a fly —*vt.* **1.** *a)* to cause to float in the air [*fly* a kite] *b)* to display (a flag) as from a pole **2.** to operate (an aircraft) **3.** to travel over in an aircraft **4.** to carry or transport in an aircraft **5.** to run away from; flee from; avoid **6.** to use (a hawk) to hunt game **7.** *Theater* to suspend (flats, lights, etc.) in the space above the stage —*n., pl.* **flies 1.** [Rare] the act of flying; flight **2.** a flap of cloth that conceals the zipper, buttons, etc. in a garment; esp., such a flap in the front of a pair of trousers **3.** *a)* a flap serving as the door of a tent *b)* a piece of fabric serving as an outer or second top on a tent **4.** *a)* the length of an extended flag measured from the staff outward *b)* the outside edge of a flag **5.** a regulating device, as for a clockwork mechanism, consisting of vanes radiating from a rotating shaft **6.** *same as* **a)** FLYWHEEL **b)** FLYLEAF **7.** [Brit.] a hackney carriage ☆**8.** *Baseball* a ball batted high in the air, esp. within the foul lines **9.** [*pl.*] *Theater* the space behind and above the proscenium arch, containing overhead lights, raised flats, etc. —**fly at** to attack suddenly by or as by flying or springing toward — **fly into** to have a violent outburst of —**fly off** to go away quickly or suddenly; hurry off —☆**fly out** *Baseball* to be put out by hitting a fly that is caught by a fielder —☆**fly right** [Slang] to behave oneself properly —**let fly (at) 1.** to shoot or throw (at) **2.** to direct a verbal attack (at) —**on the fly 1.** while in flight **2.** [Colloq.] while in a hurry
SYN.—**fly** is the general word implying movement through the air on wings [birds, insects, airplanes *fly*]; **flit** suggests a series of quick, brief flights from place to place [sparrows *flitted* about in the trees]; to **hover** is to remain suspended at a point in the air by special movements of the wings [a butterfly *hovered* over the flower]; **soar** implies a flying high into the air in a straight, almost vertical line [the lark *soared* into the sky], or it may also describe a gliding on air currents high in the air [eagles *soaring* near the craggy peaks]; **flutter** suggests a rapid but unsteady flapping of the wings, as in the short flight of a young or injured bird

fly² (flī) *n., pl.* **flies** [ME. *flie* < OE. *fleoge* (akin to G. *fliege*) < base *fleogan*: see prec.] **1.** *a) same as* HOUSEFLY *b)* any of a large group of insects with two transparent wings, including the housefly, gnat, and mosquito *c)* any of several four-winged insects, as the mayfly, caddis fly, etc. **2.** a hook covered with feathers, colored silk, etc. to resemble an insect, used as a lure in fishing: a **wet fly** drifts below the surface of the water, and a **dry fly** floats on it **3.** *Printing a)* formerly, the person whose work was removing sheets from the press as they were printed *b)* a fingered device on the press for removing the printed sheets —**fly in the ointment** anything, esp. a little thing, that reduces or destroys the value or usefulness of something else

fly³ (flī) *adj.* **fli′er, fli′est** [orig., thieves' slang < ? FLY¹] [Slang] alert and knowing; sharp; quick

fly·a·ble (-ə b'l) *adj.* suitable or ready for flying [*flyable* weather, a *flyable* airplane]

fly agaric [orig. used as a fly poison] a poisonous mushroom (*Amanita muscaria*) usually having an orange or russet cap with white flakes and white gills: also **fly amanita**

fly ash airborne bits of unburnable ash, esp. as a factor in air pollution

fly·a·way (-ə wā′) *adj.* **1.** flying in the wind; streaming [*flyaway* hair] **2.** flighty **3.** ready for flight

fly·blow (-blō′) *n.* a blowfly's egg or larva —*vt., vi.* **-blew′, -blown′, -blow′ing 1.** to deposit flyblows in (meat, etc.) **2.** to contaminate; spoil; taint

fly·blown (-blōn′) *adj.* **1.** full of flies' eggs or larvae; maggoty **2.** contaminated; spoiled; tainted **3.** [Colloq.] shabby, dingy, disreputable, etc.

fly·boat (-bōt′) *n.* [Du. *vlieboot*, after the *Vlie*, a channel between the North Sea and the Waddenzee + *boot*, boat] **1.** a fast, flat-bottomed Dutch boat **2.** any of several fast sailing vessels

fly book a booklike case to hold artificial fishing flies

☆**fly·boy** (-boi′) *n.* [Slang] an aviator, esp. in the Air Force

fly·by, fly-by (-bī′) *n., pl.* **-bies′** a flight past a designated point or place by an aircraft or spacecraft

fly-by-night (-bī nīt′) *adj.* not trustworthy; esp., financially irresponsible —*n.* a fly-by-night person; esp., a debtor who runs away from his debts

fly-cast (-kast′, -käst′) *vi.* **-cast′, -cast′ing** to fish by casting artificial flies, using a lightweight, resilient rod (**fly rod**)

fly·catch·er (-kach′ər) *n.* any of various small birds (families Tyrannidae and Muscicapidae), including the kingbird, pewee, and phoebe, that catch insects in flight

fly·er (-ər) *n. same as* FLIER

fly·ing (-iŋ) *adj.* **1.** that flies or can fly **2.** moving as if flying; moving swiftly; fast **3.** like flight through the air **4.** hasty and brief [a *flying* trip] **5.** of or for aircraft or aviators **6.** organized to act quickly, as in an emergency [a *flying* squad] —*n.* the action of a person or thing that flies

flying boat an airplane with a hull that permits it to land on and take off from water

flying bridge *Naut.* a small, often open structure over the main bridge, from which a vessel may be conned

flying buttress a buttress connected with a wall at some distance from it by an arch or part of an arch: it serves to resist outward pressure

flying colors 1. flags flying in the air **2.** notable victory or success

Flying Dutchman 1. a fabled Dutch sailor condemned to sail the seas until Judgment Day **2.** his ghostly ship, considered a bad omen by sailors who think they see it

flying field a field prepared for the landing, taking off, and minor servicing of smaller aircraft

FLYING BUTTRESS

flying fish any of a number of chiefly warm-water sea fishes (family Exocoetidae) with wing-like pectoral fins that enable them to glide through the air

flying fox any of several fruit-eating bats (suborder Megachiroptera) with a foxlike head, living in Africa, Australia, and S Asia

flying frog any of several frogs (genus *Polypedates*) of the East Indies, that have large webbed feet which permit them to make long, gliding leaps

FLYING FISH
(2–18 in. long)

flying gurnard a marine fish (*Dactylopterus volitans*) with winglike pectoral fins, capable of gliding in the air for short distances

flying jib a small, triangular sail in front of the jib, usually on an extension of the jib boom or bowsprit

flying lemur a tree-dwelling mammal (order Dermoptera) of SE Asia, having a broad fold of skin on each side of the body between the forelimbs and the tail, that enables it to make long, gliding leaps

flying machine early term for an airplane or other aircraft

flying mare a throw made in exhibition wrestling by seizing the opponent's wrist, turning, and throwing him over one's back

flying phalanger any of several small Australian marsupials (genera *Acrobates, Petaurus*, and *Schoinobates*) with a thin membrane along the sides of the body, that enable them to make long, sailing leaps

☆**flying saucer** same as UFO

☆**flying squirrel 1.** any of a number of N. American squirrels (genus *Glaucomys*) with winglike folds of skin attached to the legs and body which enable them to make long, gliding leaps **2.** same as FLYING PHALANGER

flying start 1. the start of a race in which the contestants are already moving as they pass the starting line **2.** any rapid beginning

fly·leaf (flī′lēf′) *n., pl.* **-leaves** (-lēvz′) a blank leaf at the beginning or end of a book

fly·o·ver (-ō′vər) *n.* **1.** [Brit.] an overpass or cloverleaf **2.** a flight by one or more aircraft over a particular area or point

fly·pa·per (-pā′pər) *n.* a sticky or poisonous paper set out to catch or kill flies

Fly River river in S New Guinea, flowing through Papua into the Coral Sea: c. 650 mi.

fly sheet [< earlier *flying sheet*] a pamphlet

fly·speck (-spek′) *n.* **1.** a speck of excrement left by a fly **2.** any tiny spot **3.** a petty or insignificant error or flaw —*vt.* to make flyspecks on

flyte (flīt) *vi., vt., n. same as* FLITE

fly·trap (flī'trap') *n.* **1.** any device for catching flies **2.** a plant that catches insects, as the Venus's-flytrap

☆**fly·way** (-wā') *n.* a flying route taken regularly by migratory birds going to and from their breeding grounds

fly·weight (-wāt') *n.* a boxer who weighs 112 pounds or less —*adj.* of flyweights

fly·wheel (-hwēl') *n.* a heavy wheel for regulating the speed and uniformity of motion of the machine to which it is attached

Fm *Chem.* fermium

FM frequency modulation

fm. 1. fathom **2.** from

FMB Federal Maritime Board

FMCS Federal Mediation and Conciliation Service

fn. footnote

f-number *Photog.* the ratio of a lens diameter to its focal length: symbol, F/, f/, f, F, f:, *f.:* the lower the f-number, the shorter the exposure required

fo. folio

F.O. 1. field officer: also **f.o. 2.** Foreign Office

foal (fōl) *n.* [ME. *fole* < OE. *fola,* akin to ON. *foli,* OHG. *folo* (G. *fohlen*) < IE. base **pōu-,* little, small, whence L. *paucus,* little, FEW, FILLY] a young horse, mule, donkey, etc.; colt or filly —*vt., vi.* to give birth to (a foal)

foam (fōm) *n.* [ME. *fom* < OE. *fǣm,* akin to G. *feim,* scum < IE. base **(s)poimno-,* foam, whence Sans. *phēna-,* L. *spuma*] **1.** the whitish mass of bubbles formed on or in liquids by agitation, fermentation, etc. **2.** something like foam, as the heavy sweat of horses, or frothy saliva **3.** [Poet.] the sea **4.** a rigid or spongy cellular mass formed by the dispersal of gas bubbles in liquid rubber, plastic, etc. —*vi.* to form, produce, or gather foam; froth —*vt.* to cause to foam —**foam at the mouth** to be very angry; rage —**foam'less** *adj.*

☆**foam-flow·er** (-flou'ər) *n.* a small plant (*Tiarella cordifolia*) of the saxifrage family, with white flowers that bloom in the spring, found in E N. America

foam rubber rubber that has been treated to form a firm, spongy foam, used in upholstered seats, mattresses, etc.

foam·y (-ē) *adj.* **foam'i·er, foam'i·est** [ME. *fomi* < OE. *famig*] **1.** foaming or covered with foam **2.** consisting of or like foam —**foam'i·ly** *adv.* —**foam'i·ness** *n.*

fob¹ (fäb) *n.* [prob. < dial. G. *fuppe,* a pocket] **1.** a small pocket in the front of a man's trousers, for carrying a watch, etc.; watch pocket ☆**2.** a short ribbon or chain attached to a watch and hanging out of such a pocket ☆**3.** any ornament worn at the end of such a ribbon or chain

fob² (fäb) *vt.* **fobbed, fob'bing** [< ME. *fobben,* to cheat, trick, prob. akin to G. *foppen,* orig. a cant term] [Obs.] to cheat; trick; deceive —**fob off 1.** to trick or put off (a person) with second-rate articles, lies, excuses, etc. **2.** to get rid of (something worthless) by deceit or trickery; palm off

F.O.B., f.o.b. free on board

fo·cal (fō'k'l) *adj.* of or at a focus —**fo'cal·ly** *adv.*

focal infection a localized infection, as in the gall bladder, teeth, or tonsils, from which bacterial toxins may be liberated into the bloodstream so as to cause infection in another part of the body

fo·cal·ize (fō'kə līz') *vt., vi.* **-ized', -iz'ing 1.** to adjust or become adjusted to a focus **2.** *Med.* to limit or be limited to a small area; localize: said of an infection —**fo'cal·i·za'tion** *n.*

focal length the distance from the optical center of a lens to the point where the light rays converge; length of the focus: also **focal distance**

Foch (fôsh), **Fer·di·nand** (fer dē nän') 1851–1929; Fr. marshal; commander in chief of Allied forces (1918)

fo'c's'le (fōk's'l) *n.* forecastle: a phonetic spelling

fo·cus (fō'kəs) *n., pl.* **fo'cus·es, fo'ci** (-sī) [ModL., adopted in math. senses by Kepler (1604) < L., fireplace, hearth < ? IE. base **bhok-,* to flame, burn, whence (?) Arm. *boç,* flame] **1.** the point where rays of light, heat, etc. or waves of sound come together, or from which they spread or seem to spread; specif., the point where rays of light reflected by a mirror or refracted by a lens meet (called *real focus*) or the point where they would meet if prolonged backward through the lens or mirror (called *virtual focus*) **2.** *same as* FOCAL LENGTH **3.** an adjustment of the focal length to make a clear image [to bring a camera into *focus*] **4.** any center of activity, attention, etc. **5.** a part of the body where an infection is localized or most active **6.** the starting point of an earthquake **7.** *Math. a)* either of the two fixed points used in determining an ellipse *b)* any analogous point for a parabola or hyperbola —*vt.* **-cused** or **-cussed, -cus·ing** or **-cus·sing 1.** to bring into focus **2.** to adjust the focal length of (the eye, a lens, etc.) in order to produce a clear image **3.** to fix or settle on one thing; concentrate [to *focus* one's attention on a question] —*vi.* **1.** to meet at a focus **2.** to adjust one's eye or a lens so as to make a clear image —**in focus** clear; distinct; sharply defined —**out of focus** indistinct; blurred; not sharply defined —**fo'cus·er** *n.*

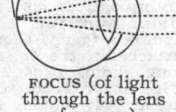

POINT OF FOCUS

FOCUS (of light through the lens of an eye)

fod·der (fäd'ər) *n.* [ME. < OE. *fodor* (akin to G. *futter*) <

base of *foda,* FOOD] coarse food for cattle, horses, sheep, etc., as cornstalks, hay, and straw —*vt.* to feed with fodder

foe (fō) *n.* [ME. *fo, ifo* < OE. *fah,* hostile, (*ge*)*fah,* enemy, akin to OHG. *gefēh,* at feud, hostile: for IE. base see FEUD¹] *same as* ENEMY (in all senses)—*SYN.* see OPPONENT

foehn (fān, fōn) *n.* [G. dial. *fōn* < MHG. *phönne* < OHG. *fonno* < LL. **faunio* < L. *Favonius,* west wind: see FAVONIAN] a warm, dry wind blowing down into the valleys of a mountain, esp. in the Alps

foe·man (fō'mən) *n., pl.* **-men** (-mən) [ME. *foman* < OE. *fahmann,* lit., hostile person] [Archaic or Poet.] a foe; enemy

foe·ti-, foe·to- (fēt'ə) *same as* FETI-

foe·tid (fet'id, fēt'-) *adj. same as* FETID

foe·tus (fēt'əs) *n. same as* FETUS —**foe'tal** *adj.*

fog¹ (fôg, fäg) *n.* [prob. < Scand., as in ON. *fok,* Dan. (*sne*)*fog,* driving snow, Norw. dial. *fjuk,* sea mist < IE. base **pū-,* to puff up, blow, of echoic origin] **1.** a large mass of water vapor condensed to fine particles, at or just above the earth's surface; thick, obscuring mist **2.** a similar mass of smoke, dust, etc. obscuring the atmosphere **3.** a vaporized liquid, as insecticide, dispersed over a large area **4.** a state of mental dimness and confusion; blurred, bewildered state **5.** a blur on a photograph or film —*vi.* **fogged, fog'ging 1.** to become surrounded or covered by fog **2.** to be or become blurred, dimmed, or obscured —*vt.* **1.** to surround or cover with fog **2.** to blur; dim; obscure **3.** to confuse; bewilder **4.** [Slang] to hurl (a baseball, etc.) with great force **5.** *Photog.* to make blurred —*SYN.* see MIST

fog² (fôg, fäg) *n.* [ME. *fogge,* prob. < Scand., as in Norw. dial. *fogg,* long grass in moist place] **1.** a new growth of grass after cutting or grazing **2.** long, rank grass left uncut or ungrazed **3.** [Dial.] moss

fog bank a dense mass of fog

fog·bound (-bound') *adj.* **1.** surrounded or covered by fog **2.** prevented from sailing, flying, etc. because of fog

fog·bow (-bō') *n.* a phenomenon like a white or slightly tinted rainbow, sometimes seen in a fog

fog·dog (-dôg') *n.* a bright spot sometimes seen at the horizon as a fog starts to dissipate

fo·gey (fō'gē) *n., pl.* **-geys** *same as* FOGY

Fog·gia (fôd'jä) commune in Apulia, SE Italy: pop. 128,000

fog·gy (fôg'ē, fäg'-) *adj.* **-gi·er, -gi·est 1.** full of fog; misty; murky **2.** dim; blurred; clouded **3.** confused; perplexed —**fog'gi·ly** *adv.* —**fog'gi·ness** *n.*

fog·horn (-hôrn') *n.* **1.** a horn blown to give warning to ships in a fog **2.** a loud, strident voice

fo·gy (fō'gē) *n., pl.* **-gies** [< ?] a person who is old-fashioned or highly conservative in ideas and actions —**fo'gy·ish** *adj.* —**fo'gy·ism** *n.*

foh (fō) *interj. same as* FAUGH

foi·ble (foi'b'l) *n.* [obs. form of Fr. *faible:* see FEEBLE] **1.** a small weakness; slight frailty in character **2.** the weaker part of a sword blade, from the middle to the point —*SYN.* see FAULT

foil¹ (foil) *vt.* [ME. *foilen* < OFr. *fuler,* to trample on, subdue: see FULL²] **1.** to keep from being successful; thwart; frustrate **2.** *Hunting* to make (a scent, trail, etc.) confused, as by recrossing, in order to balk the pursuers —*n.* **1.** [Archaic] the scent or trail of an animal **2.** [Archaic] a thwarting —*SYN.* see FRUSTRATE

foil² (foil) *n.* [ME. < OFr. *fuil* (Fr. *feuille*), a leaf < VL. *folia* < L. *folium,* leaf: see FOLIATE] **1.** a leaflike, rounded space or design between cusps or in windows, etc., as in Gothic architecture **2.** a very thin sheet or leaf of metal **3.** the metal coating on the back of a mirror **4.** a thin leaf of polished metal placed under an inferior or artificial gem to give it brilliance **5.** a person or thing that sets off or enhances another by contrast **6.** [etym. unc.] *a)* a long, thin fencing sword with a button on the point to prevent injury *b)* [*pl.*] the art or sport of fencing with foils —*vt.* **1.** to cover or back with foil **2.** [Rare] to serve as a contrast to **3.** to decorate (windows, etc.) with foils

foils·man (foilz'mən) *n., pl.* **-men** (-mən) a fencer who uses a foil

foin (foin) *vi., n.* [ME. *foinen* < *foin,* a thrust, stab < OFr. *foisne,* fish spear < L. *fuscina,* a trident] [Archaic] lunge or thrust, as in fencing

foi·son (foi'z'n) *n.* [ME. *foisoun* < OFr. *foison, fuison* < L. *fusio,* a pouring: see FUSION] **1.** [Archaic] a plentiful crop; good harvest; plenty **2.** [Obs. or Dial.] *a)* vitality; strength; ability *b)* [*pl.*] resources

foist (foist) *vt.* [prob. < dial. Du. *vuisten,* to hold in the hand, hence, in dicing, to hide or palm in the hand < *vuist,* a fist, akin to FIST] **1.** to put in slyly or surreptitiously, as a clause into a contract **2.** to pass off (something false) as genuine (with *on* or *upon*); impose by fraud; palm off

Fo·kine (fō kēn'), **Mi·chel** (mē shel') (born *Mikhail Mikhailovich Fokin*) 1880–1942; U.S. choreographer, born in Russia

Fok·ker (fäk'ər), **Anthony Herman Gerard** 1890–1939; U.S. aircraft designer, born in Dutch East Indies: built airplanes for Germany & the Netherlands, 1911–21

fol. 1. folio **2.** following

fo·la·cin (fō'lə sin) *n.* [FOL(IC) AC(ID) + -IN¹] *same as* FOLIC ACID

fold¹ (fōld) *vt.* [ME. *folden* < OE. *faldan* (WS. *fealdan*), akin to G. *falten* < IE. **pel-to* < base **pel-,* to fold, whence

(SIM)PLE, (TRI)PLE] **1.** *a)* to bend or press (something) so that one part is over another; double up on itself [to *fold* a sheet] *b)* to make more compact by so doubling a number of times **2.** to draw together and intertwine [to *fold* the arms] **3.** to draw (wings) close to the body **4.** to clasp in the arms; embrace **5.** to wrap up; envelop —*vi.* **1.** to be or become folded ☆**2.** [Colloq.] to fail; specif.; *a)* to be forced to close, as a business, play, etc. *b)* to succumb, as to exhaustion; collapse —*n.* **1.** a folded part or layer **2.** a mark made by folding **3.** a hollow or crease produced by folded parts or layers **4.** [Brit.] a hollow; small valley **5.** *Geol.* a rock layer folded by pressure —**fold in** *Cooking* to blend (an ingredient) into a mixture, using gentle, cutting strokes

fold² (fōld) *n.* [ME. < OE. *fald*, akin to Du. *vaalt*, enclosed place, Dan. *fold*, sheep pen] **1.** a pen in which to keep sheep **2.** sheep kept together; flock of sheep **3.** a group or organization with common interests, aims, faith, etc., as a church —*vt.* to keep or confine in a pen

-fold (fōld) [ME. *-fold, -fald* < OE. *-feald:* see FOLD¹] *a suffix meaning:* **1.** having (a specified number of) parts [a *tenfold* division] **2.** (a specified number of) times as many, as much, as large [to *fold* tenfold]

☆**fold·a·way** (fōld'ə wā') *adj.* that can be folded together for easy storage [a *foldaway* cot]

fold·boat (fōld'bōt') *n.* a lightweight, collapsible, folding kayak

fold·er (fōl'dər) *n.* **1.** a person or thing that folds **2.** a sheet of cardboard or heavy paper folded for holding loose papers, as in a file ☆**3.** a pamphlet or booklet folded but not stitched

fol·de·rol (fäl'də räl', fōl'də rōl') *n.* same as FALDERAL

folding door a door with hinged leaves or accordion pleats that can be folded back

☆**folding money** [Colloq.] same as PAPER MONEY

fo·li·a (fō'lē ə) *n.* alt. *pl.* of FOLIUM

fo·li·a·ceous (fō'lē ā'shəs) *adj.* [L. *foliaceus < folium*, a leaf: see FOLIATE] **1.** of or like the leaf of a plant **2.** having leaves **3.** consisting of thin layers, as certain rocks

fo·li·age (fō'lē ij) *n.* [ME. *foilage* < OFr. *feuillage < feuille*, a leaf < VL. *folia* < L. *folium:* see FOLIATE] **1.** leaves, as of a plant or tree; mass of leaves; leafage **2.** a decoration consisting of a representation of leaves, branches, flowers, etc.

fo·li·aged (-ijd) *adj.* having foliage: often in hyphenated compounds [dark-*foliaged*]

fo·li·ar (fō'lē ər) *adj.* [ModL. *foliaris < L. folium:* see ff.] of or like a leaf or leaves

fo·li·ate (fō'lē āt'; *for adj., usually* -it) *vt.* **-at'ed, -at'ing** [< L. *foliatus*, leafy *< folium*, a leaf < IE. base **bhel-, **bhlō-*, to swell, blossom, whence BLADE, BLOOM¹] **1.** *a)* to divide into thin layers *b)* to beat into foil **2.** to decorate with leaflike layers or ornamentation **3.** to number the leaves of (a book or manuscript) —*vi.* **1.** to separate into layers **2.** to send out leaves —*adj.* **1.** having or covered with leaves **2.** like a leaf or leaves

fo·li·a·tion (fō'lē ā'shən) *n.* [ML. *foliatio:* see prec.] **1.** a growing of or developing into a leaf or leaves; leaf formation **2.** the state of being in leaf **3.** the way leaves are arranged in the bud; vernation **4.** the act or process of beating metal into layers **5.** *a)* a splitting into leaflike layers: said of certain minerals *b)* the property of splitting into such layers *c)* such layers **6.** the process of backing glass as with metal foil to make a mirror **7.** the consecutive numbering of leaves, rather than pages, of a book **8.** *a)* a decorating with leaflike ornamentation *b)* a leaflike decoration consisting of small arcs or foils

fo·li·a·ture (fō'lē ə chər) *n.* [L. *foliatura:* see FOLIATE] *rare var. of* FOLIAGE

fo·lic acid (fō'lik) [< L. *folium*, a leaf (see FOLIATE) + -IC] a crystalline substance, $C_{19}H_{19}N_7O_6$, found in green leaves and in certain other plant and animal tissues, exhibiting vitamin B activity: used in medicine, esp. for treating certain anemias

‡**fo·lie à deux** (fô lē á dö') [Fr., lit., double insanity] *Psychiatry* a condition in which two closely associated people who are mentally ill share the same delusional beliefs

‡**fo·lie de gran·deur** (də grän dër') [Fr.] delusions of grandeur; megalomania

fo·li·ic·o·lous (fō'lē ik'ə ləs) *adj.* [*folii-* < L. *folium*, leaf: see FOLIATE] + -COLOUS] growing on leaves, as certain lichens, fungi, and algae

fo·lin·ic acid (fa lin'ik) [FOL(IC ACID) + -IN¹ + -IC] a substance, $C_{20}H_{23}N_7O_7$, derived from folic acid: it is important in the utilization of folic acid as a vitamin and appears to be vital to the synthesis of nucleic acids

fo·li·o (fō'lē ō') *n., pl.* **-li·os'** [ME. < L. (*in*) *folio*, (in) a sheet, abl. of *folium*, a leaf (in LL., leaf of paper): see FOLIATE] **1.** a large sheet of paper folded once, so that it forms two leaves, or four pages, of a book, manuscript, etc. **2.** the largest regular size of book, now often 12 by 15 inches, made of sheets folded in this way **3.** a leaf of a manuscript, book, etc. numbered on only one side **4.** the number of a page in a book, etc. **5.** a set number of words (100 in the U.S., 72 or 90 in England) considered as a unit in measuring the length of a legal or official document **6.** *Bookkeeping* a page of a ledger, or facing pages with the same number —*adj.* having sheets folded once; of the size of a folio —*vt.* **-li·oed', -li·o'ing** to number the pages of (a book, etc.) consecutively; page —**in folio** in the form or size of a folio

fo·li·o·late (fō'lē ə lāt') *adj.* [< *foliole*, a leaflet (< Fr. < L. *foliolum*, dim. of L. *folium*, leaf: see FOLIATE) + -ATE¹] having or relating to leaflets

fo·li·ose (fō'lē ōs') *adj.* [L. *foliosus*, leafy *< folium*, a leaf: see FOLIATE] covered with leaves; leafy

-fo·li·ous (fō'lē əs) [< L. *folium*, a leaf + -OUS] an *adj.*-forming combining form meaning leaf

fo·li·um (fō'lē əm) *n., pl.* **-li·ums, -li·a** (-ə) [L.: see FOLIATE] **1.** *Geol.* a thin layer or stratum, as in metamorphic rock **2.** *Geom.* the part of a curve enclosed by the intersection of the two ends at its node; loop

folk (fōk) *n., pl.* **folk, folks** [ME. < OE. *folc*, akin to G. *volk* < IE. base **pel-*, to fill, crowd, whence L. *plebs*, the common people & FULL¹] **1.** *a)* a people, tribe, or nation; ethnic group *b)* the large body of the common people of such a group: with *the* **2.** [*pl.*] people in general; persons [*folks* differ in their tastes] —*adj.* of, originating among, or having to do with the common people, who transmit the general culture of the group through succeeding generations [*folk* art] —**just (plain) folks** [Colloq.] simple and unassuming; not snobbish —**(one's) folks** [Colloq.] (one's) family or relatives, esp. one's parents

folk dance 1. a traditional dance of the common people of a country or region **2.** music for this

‡**Fol·ke·ting, Fol·ke·thing** (fōl'kə tiŋ') *n.* [Dan. < *folke*, people (see FOLK) + *ting*, thing, assembly (see THING²)] **1.** formerly, the lower branch of the Danish legislature **2.** now, the unicameral legislature of Denmark

folk etymology 1. the change that occurs in the form of a word over a period of prolonged usage so as to give it an apparent connection with some other well-known word [''cole slaw'' becomes ''cold slaw'' through *folk etymology*] **2.** unscientific etymology; popular but incorrect notion of the origin and derivation of a word

folk·lore (fōk'lôr') *n.* [FOLK + LORE¹: suggested (1846) by W. J. Thoms to replace earlier *popular antiquities*] **1.** the traditional beliefs, legends, sayings, customs, etc. of a people **2.** the study and scientific investigation of these —**folk'lor'ic** *adj.* —**folk'lor'ist** *n.*

folk medicine the treatment of disease as practiced traditionally among the common people, involving esp. the use of herbs and other natural substances

folk·moot (-mōōt') *n.* [OE. *folcmot, fologemot:* see FOLK & MOOT] [Obs. or Hist.] a general meeting of the people of a town, shire, etc.: also **folk'mote'** (-mōt')

folk music music made and handed down among the common people

☆**folk·nik** (-nik) *n.* [see -NIK] [Slang] a performer or devotee of folk songs

☆**folk-rock** (-räk') *n.* music with a rhythmic rock-and-roll beat combined with words in a folk-song style

folk song [after G. *volkslied*] **1.** a song made and handed down among the common people: folk songs are usually of anonymous authorship and often have many versions **2.** a song composed in imitation of such a song —**folk singer**

☆**folk·sy** (-sē) *adj.* **-si·er, -si·est** [Colloq.] friendly or sociable in a simple, direct manner: sometimes used in a derogatory way of affected or exaggerated familiarity —**folk'si·ly** *adv.* —**folk'si·ness** *n.*

folk tale (or **story**) a story, usually of anonymous authorship and legendary or mythical elements, made and handed down orally among the common people

☆**folk·way** (-wā') *n.* [term first used in 1906 by Wm. Graham SUMNER] any way of thinking, feeling, behaving, etc. common to members of the same social group

fol·li·cle (fäl'i k'l) *n.* [ModL. *folliculus* < L., a small bag, husk, pod, dim. of *follis*, bellows < IE. base **bhel-*, to blow up, swell, whence BALL¹, BULL¹] **1.** *Anat. a)* any small sac, cavity, or gland for excretion or secretion [a hair *follicle*] *b)* [Obs.] a lymph nodule **2.** *Bot.* a dry, one-celled seed capsule or pod, which opens along only one side to release its seeds, as a milkweed pod —**fol·li·cu·lar** (fə lik'yoo lər) *adj.* —**fol'lic'u·late** (-lit, -lāt'), **fol·lic'u·lat'ed** *adj.*

follicle mite any of a number of small, wormlike mites (genus *Demodex*) living as parasites in the hair follicles of mammals, esp. the human follicle mite (*Demodex folliculorum*)

follicle-stimulating hormone a hormone, secreted by the anterior pituitary gland, which stimulates the development of ova in the female and testicular function in the male

fol·lic·u·lin (fə lik'yoo lin) *n.* same as ESTRONE

fol·lies (fäl'ēz) *n.pl.* [pl. of FOLLY] [*with sing. v.*] ☆a revue: formerly used as part of the title

fol·low (fäl'ō) *vt.* [ME. *folwen* < OE. *folgian*, akin to G. *folgen* & (?) W. *olafiad*, follower] **1.** to come or go after **2.** to go after in order to catch; chase; pursue **3.** to go along [*follow* the right road] **4.** to come or occur after in time, in a series, etc. **5.** to provide with something that comes after [to *follow* praise with blame] **6.** to take the place of in rank, position, etc. [Monroe *followed* Madison as president] **7.**

to take up; engage in [to *follow* a trade] **8.** to come or happen as a result of [disease often *follows* malnutrition] **9.** to take as a model; act in accordance with; imitate **10.** to accept the authority of; obey [to *follow* rules] **11.** to support or advocate the ideas, opinions, etc. of **12.** to watch or listen to closely; observe [to *follow* a conversation intently] **13.** to be interested in or attentive to current developments in [to *follow* local politics] **14.** to understand the continuity or logic of [do you *follow* me?] —*vi.* **1.** to come, go, or happen after or next after some thing or person in place, sequence, or time **2.** to occur as a natural or logical consequence; result —*n.* **1.** the act of following **2.** *Billiards* a shot that causes the cue ball to continue rolling after striking the object ball: also **follow shot** —**as follows** as will next be told or explained —**follow out** to carry out fully or completely —**follow through 1.** to continue and complete a stroke or swing after hitting or releasing the ball, puck, etc. **2.** to continue and complete an action —**follow up 1.** to follow closely and persistently **2.** to carry out fully **3.** to add to the effectiveness of by doing something more

SYN.—**follow** is the general word meaning to come or occur after, but it does not necessarily imply a causal relationship with what goes before [sunshine *followed* by rain]; **ensue** implies that what follows comes as a logical consequence of what preceded [clouds appeared and rain *ensued*]; **succeed** implies that what follows takes the place of what preceded [who *succeeded* Polk to the Presidency?]; **result** stresses a definite relationship of cause and effect between what follows and what preceded [superstition *results* from ignorance] —*ANT.* precede

fol·low·er (fäl'ə wər) *n.* [ME. *folwere* < OE. *folgere*] **1.** a person or thing that follows; specif., *a*) a person who follows another's beliefs or teachings; disciple *b*) a servant or attendant **2.** a part (of a machine) that is given motion by another part

SYN.—**follower** is the general term for one who follows or believes in the teachings or theories of someone [a *follower* of Freud]; **supporter** applies to one who upholds or defends opinions or theories that are disputed or under attack [a *supporter* of technocracy]; **adherent** refers to a close, active follower of some theory, cause, etc. [the *adherents* of a political party]; **disciple** implies a personal, devoted relationship to the teacher of some doctrine or leader of some movement [Plato was a *disciple* of Socrates]; **partisan**, in this connection, refers to an unswerving, often blindly devoted, adherent of some person or cause

fol·low·er·ship (-ship') *n.* the ability to follow a leader

fol·low·ing (fäl'ə win) *adj.* **1.** that follows; next after [the *following* year] **2.** to be mentioned immediately; to be dealt with next [the *following* people were chosen] **3.** moving in the same direction that a ship is moving, as the tide or wind —*n.* a group of followers or adherents —*prep.* after [*following* dinner he went home] —**the following 1.** the one or ones to be mentioned immediately **2.** what follows; what comes next

fol·low-through (-ō throō') *n.* **1.** *a*) the act or manner of continuing the swing or stroke of a club, racket, the arm, etc. to its natural end after striking or releasing the ball, puck, etc. *b*) this final part of the stroke **2.** the act of continuing an undertaking to completion

fol·low-up (-up') *adj.* designating or of anything that follows something else as a review, addition, etc. [*follow-up* visits, a *follow-up* letter] —*n.* **1.** a follow-up thing or event **2.** the use of follow-up letters, visits, etc. **3.** a following up

fol·ly (fäl'ē) *n., pl.* **-lies** [ME. *folie* < OFr. < *fol:* see FOOL[1]] **1.** a lack of understanding, sense, or rational conduct; foolishness **2.** any foolish action or belief **3.** any foolish and useless but expensive undertaking **4.** *a*) [Obs.] wickedness or evil; also, lewdness *b*) action that ends or can end in disaster See also FOLLIES

☆**Fol·som man** (fäl'səm, fōl'-) [< *Folsom*, village in NE N.Mex. where a peculiarly fluted type of arrowhead has been found] a member of a people believed to have lived in N. America at the time of the last glacial age

Fo·mal·haut (fō'm'l hôt', -ōt') [Fr. < Ar. *fum al-ḥūt*, lit., mouth of the fish] the brightest star in the constellation Piscis Austrinus

fo·ment (fō ment') *vt.* [ME. *fomenten* < OFr. *fomenter* < LL. *fomentare* < L. *fomentum*, poultice < *fovere*, to keep warm < IE. **dhogwh-* < base **dhegwh-*, to burn, whence MIr. *daig*, fire] **1.** to treat with warm water, medicated lotions, etc. **2.** to stir up (trouble); instigate; incite [to *foment* a riot] —*SYN.* see INCITE

fo·men·ta·tion (fō'mən tā'shən) *n.* [ME. *fomentacioun* < LL. *fomentatio* < L. *fomentum:* see prec.] **1.** treatment of bodily pain or injury by the application of warm, moist substances **2.** any liquid lotion, compress, etc. so applied **3.** a stirring up of trouble; incitement

fond[1] (fänd) *adj.* [ME., contr. of *fonned*, foolish, pp. of *fonnen*, to be foolish: cf. FUN] **1.** [Now Rare] foolish, esp. foolishly naive, credulous, or hopeful **2.** [Dial.] insane, idiotic, or imbecile **3.** tender and affectionate; loving; sometimes, affectionate in a foolish or overly indulgent way; doting **4.** cherished with great or unreasoning affection; doted on [a *fond* hope] —**fond of** having a liking or affection for

fond[2] (fänd; *Fr.* fōn) *n.* [Fr.: see FUND] **1.** foundation; basis; background **2.** [Obs.] supply; fund

fon·dant (fän'dənt) *n.* [Fr. < prp. of *fondre*, to melt: see FOUND[3]] a soft, creamy candy made of sugar, used esp. as a filling for other candies

Fond du Lac (fän' jə lak', də) [Fr., lit., end of the lake] city in E Wis., on Lake Winnebago: pop. 36,000

fon·dle (fän'd'l) *vt.* **-dled, -dling** [freq. of obs. *fond, v.* < FOND[1]] **1.** to stroke or handle in a tender and loving way; caress **2.** [Obs.] to pamper; coddle —*SYN.* see CARESS —**fon'dler** *n.*

fond·ly (fänd'lē) *adv.* [ME.: see FOND[1] & -LY[2]] **1.** with simple trust; naively **2.** lovingly; affectionately **3.** [Archaic] foolishly

fond·ness (-nis) *n.* **1.** tender or doting affection **2.** an inclination; taste **3.** [Archaic] foolishness

fon·due, fon·du (fän dōō', fän'dōō) *n.* [Fr. < pp. of *fondre*, to melt: see FOUND[3]] **1.** a dish made by melting cheese in wine, with a little brandy and seasoning added, used as a dip for cubes of bread **2.** any of various other dishes, as a pot of simmering oil into which cubes of meat are dipped until cooked **3.** cheese soufflé with bread crumbs

Fon·se·ca (fōn sā'kä), **Gulf of** inlet of the Pacific in Central America, on the coasts of El Salvador, Honduras, & Nicaragua

†**fons et o·ri·go** (fänz' et ə rī'gō) [L.] source and origin

font[1] (fänt) *n.* [ME. < OE. < L. *fons* (gen. *fontis*), spring, FOUNTAIN] **1.** a bowl, usually of stone, to hold the water used in baptismal services **2.** a basin for holy water in a church; stoup **3.** [Poet.] a fountain or spring **4.** a source; origin; beginning —**font'al** *adj.*

font[2] (fänt) *n.* [Fr. *fonte* < *fondre*, to cast, FOUND[3]] *Printing* a complete assortment of type in one size and style

Fon·taine·bleau (fōn ten blō'; *E.* fän't'n blō', -blōō') town in N France, near Paris: site of a palace of former kings of France: pop. 21,000

fon·ta·nel, fon·ta·nelle (fän'tə nel') *n.* [ME. *fontinel*, a hollow, pit (of the body) < OFr. *fontanele*, dim. of *fontaine*, FOUNTAIN] **1.** orig., an opening in the body for the discharge of secretions **2.** any of the soft, boneless areas in the skull of a baby or young animal, which are later closed up by the formation of bone

FONTANELS

Foo·chow (fōō'chou'; *Chin.* fōō'jō') city in SE China; capital of Fukien province: pop. 616,000

food (fōōd) *n.* [ME. *fode* < OE. *foda* < IE. *pāt-*, to feed, eat < base **pā-*, to pasture cattle, whence L. *pastor, pabulum*] **1.** any substance taken into and assimilated by a plant or animal to keep it alive and enable it to grow and repair tissue; nourishment; nutriment **2.** solid substances of this sort: distinguished from DRINK **3.** a specified kind of food **4.** anything that nourishes or stimulates; whatever helps something to keep active, grow, etc. [*food* for thought]

SYN.—**food** is the general term for all matter that is taken into the body for nourishment; **fare** refers to the range of foods eaten by a particular organism or available at a particular time and place [the *fare* of horses, a bill of *fare*]; **victuals** is a dialectal or colloquial word for human fare or diet; **provisions**, in this connection, refers to a stock of food assembled in advance [*provisions* for the hike]; **ration** refers to a fixed allowance or allotment of food [the weekly *ration*] and in the plural (**rations**) to food in general [how are the *rations* in this outfit?]

food chain *Ecol.* a sequence (as grass, rabbit, fox) of organisms in a community in which each member of the chain feeds on the member below it

food cycle *Ecol.* all the individual food chains in a community: also **food web**

food poisoning 1. the sickness resulting from eating food contaminated by either bacterial toxins or by certain bacteria, often causing vomiting, diarrhea, and prostration **2.** poisoning resulting from naturally poisonous foods, as certain mushrooms, or from chemical contaminants in food

food·stuff (-stuf') *n.* any material made into or used as food

☆**foo·fa·raw** (fōō'fə rô') *n.* [altered < Fr. *fanfaron*, a swaggering < Sp. *fanfarrón:* see FANFARONADE] [Slang] **1.** unnecessary things added for show; frills **2.** stir or fuss over something trivial

fool[1] (fōōl) *n.* [ME. *fol* < OFr. (Fr. *fou*) < LL. *follis* < L. *follis*, windbag, bellows: see FOLLICLE] **1.** *a*) a person with little or no judgment, common sense, wisdom, etc.; silly or stupid person; simpleton *b*) [Obs.] an idiot or imbecile **2.** a man formerly kept in the household of a nobleman or king to entertain by joking and clowning; professional jester **3.** a victim of a joke or trick; dupe **4.** [Slang] a person especially devoted to or skilled in some activity [a dancing *fool*] —*adj.* [Colloq.] foolish —*vi.* **1.** to act like a fool; be silly **2.** to speak, act, etc. in jest; joke **3.** [Colloq.] to trifle or meddle (*with*) —*vt.* **1.** to make a fool of; trick; deceive; dupe —**be no** (or **nobody's**) **fool** to be shrewd and capable —☆**fool around** [Colloq.] **1.** to spend time in trifling or pointless activity **2.** to trifle or meddle —**fool away** [Colloq.] to fritter away foolishly —**play the fool** to act like a fool; do silly things; clown

fool[2] (fōōl) *n.* [Early ModE. < ? prec.] [Brit.] crushed stewed fruit mixed with cream, esp. whipped cream

fool·er·y (-ər ē) *n., pl.* **-er·ies** foolish behavior or a foolish action

fool·har·dy (-här'dē) *adj.* **-di·er, -di·est** [ME. *folhardi* < OFr. *fol hardi* < *fol*, FOOL + *hardi:* see HARDY[1]] bold or

daring in a foolish way; rash; reckless —**fool′har′di·ly** *adv.* —**fool′har′di·ness** *n.*

☆**fool hen** *same as* SPRUCE GROUSE

fool·ish (-ish) *adj.* [ME. *folish*] **1.** without good sense or wisdom; silly; unwise **2.** *a)* ridiculous; absurd *b)* abashed; embarrassed **3.** [Archaic] humble; worthless —*SYN.* see ABSURD —**fool′ish·ly** *adv.* —**fool′ish·ness** *n.*

☆**fool·proof** (-prōōf′) *adj.* so harmless, simple, or indestructible as not to be mishandled, damaged, misunderstood, etc. even by a fool

fools·cap (fōōlz′kap′) *n.* [so called from the fool's head and cap formerly used as a watermark] any of various sizes of writing paper; esp., in the U.S., a size measuring 13 by 16 inches ☆ also as FOOL'S CAP

fool's cap (fōōlz) a cap, usually with bells, formerly worn by a court fool or jester

fool's errand a foolish, fruitless task or undertaking

☆**fool's gold** iron pyrites (native iron sulfide) or copper pyrites (native copper-iron sulfide), resembling gold in color

fool's paradise a state of deceptive happiness, based on illusions

fool's-pars·ley (-pärs′lē) *n.* a poisonous, foul-smelling European weed (*Aethusa cynapium*) of the parsley family

foot (toot) *n., pl.* **teet**; for sense 8, **foots**: see also sense 6 [ME. < OE., akin to G. *fuss* < IE. base *pĕd-, *pŏd-, foot, to go*, whence Sans. *pad-,* Gr. *pous,* L. *pes* (gen. *pedis*)] **1.** the end part of the leg, on which a person or animal stands or moves **2.** a thing like a foot in some way; specif., *a)* the part that a thing stands on; base *b)* the lowest part; bottom [the *foot* of a page] *c)* the last of a series [go to the *foot* of the line] *d)* the part of a sewing machine that holds the cloth steady *e)* a muscular, ventral disk on a mollusk **3.** the end of a bed, grave, etc. toward which the feet are directed **4.** the end opposite to the end designated the head [at the *foot* of the table] **5.** the part of a stocking, etc. that covers the foot **6.** a measure of length, equal to 12 inches, from an average length of the human foot: symbol, ′ (e.g., 10′): abbrev. **ft.** (sing. & pl.): pl. often **foot** following a number (50 *foot* of lumber) and always in attributive use (a six-*foot* man) **7.** [Brit.] foot soldiers; infantry **8.** the sediment in a liquid: *usually used in pl.* **9.** a group of syllables serving as a unit of meter in verse; esp., such a unit having a specified placement of the stressed syllable or syllables —*vi.* **1.** *a)* to dance *b)* to go on foot: now rare exc. in phr. **foot it**: see below **2.** to move with speed: said of a sailboat —*vt.* **1.** to walk, dance, or run on, over, or through; tread **2.** to make or repair the foot of (a stocking, etc.) **3.** to add (a column of figures) and set down a total (often with *up*) ☆**4.** [Colloq.] to pay (costs, expenses, etc.) [to *foot* the bill] —**foot it** [Colloq.] to dance, walk, or run —**of foot** in walking or running [swift *of foot*] —**on foot 1.** walking or running **2.** going on; in process —**on one's feet 1.** standing **2.** in a sound or recovered condition **3.** alert(ly) —**on the wrong foot** in an inept or unfavorable way at the very beginning —**put one's best foot forward** [Colloq.] **1.** to do the best that one can **2.** to try to appear at one's best —**put one's foot down** [Colloq.] to be firm; act decisively —**put one's foot in it** (or **in one's mouth**) [Colloq.] to make an embarrassing or troublesome blunder —**under foot 1.** on the surface of the ground; on the floor, etc. **2.** in the way

foot·age (foot′ij) *n.* [FOOT + -AGE] ☆the length expressed in feet: said esp. of motion-picture film

foot-and-mouth disease (foot′'n mouth′) an acute, contagious disease of cattle and deer, caused by a virus and characterized by fever and blisters in the mouth and around the hoofs: it can be transmitted to other domestic animals and man

foot·ball (foot′bôl′) *n.* [ME. *foteballe*] **1.** any of several games played with an inflated leather ball by two teams on a field with goals at each end, the object being to get the ball across the opponents' goal: in *association football,* or *soccer,* the form most closely related to the original, the players are not allowed to use their hands or arms in advancing the ball, which is propelled chiefly by kicking; in *Rugby,* a form popular in England, the players may kick, throw, or run with the ball, but are not permitted to be in front of it while it is being carried or kicked by a teammate; in U.S. & Canadian *football,* the elaborated form developed from Rugby, the players may run ahead of the ball variously for interference, forward passes, etc. **2.** *a)* the elliptical, inflated ball used in playing U.S., Canadian, or Rugby football *b)* the spherical, inflated ball used in playing soccer **3.** any issue, problem, etc. that is passed about or shunted from one group to another [a political *football*]

foot·board (-bôrd′) *n.* **1.** a board or small platform for supporting the feet or for standing on **2.** a vertical piece across the foot of a bed

foot·boy (-boi′) *n.* [cf. FOOTMAN] a young manservant or page

foot brake a brake worked by pressure of the foot

foot·bridge (-brij′) *n.* a narrow bridge for pedestrians

foot-can·dle (-kan′d'l) *n.* a unit for measuring illumination: it is equal to the amount of direct light thrown by one candle (*n.* 3 *a*) on a square foot of surface every part of which is one foot away

foot-cloth (-klôth′) *n., pl.* **-cloths** (-klôthz′, -klôths′) **1.** orig., a low-hanging, ornamental cloth over a horse's back **2.** [Now Rare] a carpet or rug

foot·ed (-id) *adj.* **1.** having a foot or feet **2.** having feet of a specified number or kind: used in hyphenated compounds [four-*footed*]

foot·er (foot′ər) *n. same as* FOOTING (*n.* 8)

-foot·er (foot′ər) *a combining form meaning* a person or thing (a specified number of) feet tall, high, long, etc.: used in hyphenated compounds [six-*footer*]

foot·fall (foot′fôl′) *n.* the sound of a footstep

foot fault *Tennis* a rule violation consisting of failure to keep both feet behind the base line, or to keep at least one foot on the ground, when serving

foot·gear (-gir′) *n.* covering for the feet; shoes, boots, etc.

☆**foot·hill** (-hil′) *n.* a low hill at or near the foot of a mountain or mountain range

foot·hold (-hōld′) *n.* **1.** a place to put a foot down securely, as in climbing **2.** a secure position from which it is difficult to be dislodged

foot·ic, foot·y (-ē) *n., pl.* **foot′ies** *same as* FOOTSIE

foot·ing (-in) *n.* [ME. *fotinge*: see FOOT & -ING] **1.** [Now Rare] a moving on the feet; walking, dancing, etc. **2.** a secure placing of the feet [to lose one's *footing*] **3.** *a)* the condition of a surface with regard to its suitability, for walking, running, etc. [poor *footing* following the rain] *b)* a secure place to put the feet; foothold **4.** a secure position or basis [to put a business on a sound *footing*] **5.** a basis for relationship; position in relation to others [to be on a friendly *footing*] **6.** *a)* the making of a foot for a stocking, etc. *b)* the material used for this **7.** *a)* the adding of a column of figures *b)* the sum obtained **8.** *Archit.* the projecting base or enlarged foundation put under a column, wall, etc. to spread its weight and prevent settling

foot·le (foot′'l) *vi.* **-led, -ling** [altered (prob. after FUTILE) < dial. *footer,* to trifle < Fr. *foutre,* orig., to copulate with < L. *futuere*) [Colloq.] to act or talk foolishly —*n.* [Colloq.] foolishness; nonsense; twaddle

foot·less (-lis) *adj.* [ME. *fotles*] **1.** without a foot or feet **2.** not supported; without basis or substance **3.** [Colloq.] not skillful or efficient; clumsy; inept —**foot′less·ly** *adv.* —**foot′less·ness** *n.*

foot·lights (-līts′) *n.pl.* a row of lights along the front of a stage at the actors' foot level, formerly common in stage lighting —**the footlights** the theater, or acting as a profession

foot·ling (foot′lin) *adj.* [prp. of FOOTLE] [Colloq.] silly and unimportant; trivial; trifling

☆**foot·lock·er** (foot′lak′ər) *n.* a small trunk for the belongings of a soldier, usually kept at the foot of his bed

foot·loose (-lōōs′) *adj.* free to go wherever one likes or to do as one likes

foot·man (-mən) *n., pl.* **-men** (-mən) [orig., a man who ran on foot beside his master's horse or carriage] **1.** a male servant who assists the butler in a large household **2.** [Archaic] a foot soldier; infantryman

foot·mark (-märk′) *n. same as* FOOTPRINT

foot·note (-nōt′) *n.* **1.** a note of comment or reference at the bottom of a page **2.** an additional comment, remark, etc. —*vt.* **-not′ed, -not′ing** to add a footnote or footnotes to

foot·pace (-pās′) *n.* **1.** a normal walking pace **2.** a raised platform

foot·pad (-pad′) *n.* [see PAD⁴] a highway robber or holdup man who travels on foot

foot·path (-path′, -päth′) *n.* a narrow path for use by pedestrians only

foot-pound (-pound′) *n.* a unit of energy, equal to the amount of energy required to raise a weight of one pound a distance of one foot

foot-pound·al (-poun′d'l) *n.* a unit of work, equal to the work done when a mass of one pound, accelerating at the rate of one foot per second per second, has moved a distance of one foot

foot-pound-sec·ond (-pound′sek′ənd) *adj.* designating or of the British and American system of measurement in which the foot, pound, and second are used as the units of length, mass, and time, respectively

foot·print (-print′) *n.* an impression or mark made by a foot or shoe, as in sand

foot·race (-rās′) *n.* a race between runners on foot —**foot′rac′ing** *n.*

foot·rest (-rest′) *n.* a support to rest the feet on

foot·rope (-rōp′) *n.* **1.** the part of a boltrope sewn into the lower edge of the sail **2.** a piece of wire rope supported beneath a yard, upon which sailors stand when furling or reefing sail

foot rot ☆**1.** an infection which causes rotting of the stem base and crown of a plant, caused by various microorganisms **2.** a disease of sheep, marked by degeneration of muscle tissue and inflammation of the feet

☆**foot·sie, foot·sy** (-sē) *n., pl.* **-sies** the foot: a child's term —**play footsie (with)** [Colloq.] **1.** to touch feet or rub knees (with) in a caressing way, as under the table **2.** to flirt (with) or have surreptitious, usually underhanded dealings (with)

foot·slog (-släg′) *vi.* **-slogged′, -slog′ging** to march or plod through or as through mud —**foot′slog′ger** *n.*

foot soldier a soldier who moves and fights largely on foot; infantryman

foot·sore (-sôr′) *adj.* having sore or tender feet, as from much walking

foot·stalk (-stôk′) *n.* the stalk of a flower or leaf; peduncle

foot·stall (-stôl′) *n.* the pedestal or base of a column

foot·step (-step′) *n.* **1.** a person's step **2.** the distance covered in a step **3.** the sound of a step; footfall **4.** a footprint **5.** a step in a stairway —**follow in (someone's) footsteps** to follow (someone's) example, vocation, etc.; be or try to be like some predecessor

foot·stock (-stäk′) *n. same as* TAILSTOCK

foot·stone (-stōn′) *n.* a stone put at the foot of a grave

foot·stool (-stōōl′) *n.* a low stool for supporting the feet of a seated person

foot-ton (-tun′) *n.* a unit of energy, equal to the amount of energy required to raise a weight of one long ton a distance of one foot; 2,240 foot-pounds

foot·wall (-wôl′) *n.* the side beneath an inclined fault, vein, lode, or other type of ore body

foot·way (-wā′) *n. same as* FOOTPATH

☆**foot·wear** (-wer′) *n.* shoes, boots, slippers, etc.

foot·work (-wurk′) *n.* the act or manner of moving or using the feet, as in walking, boxing, dancing, etc.

foot·worn (-wôrn′) *adj.* **1.** having tired feet, as from much walking **2.** worn down by feet [footworn stairs]

foot·y (foot′ē) *adj.* [altered (as if < FOOT + -Y²) < Fr. foutu, wretched, orig. pp. of foutre, to copulate: see FOUTER] [Dial.] of little or no importance; paltry; mean

foo·zle (foō′z'l) *vt., vi.* **-zled, -zling** [< ? G. fuseln, to bungle] to make or do (something) awkwardly; esp., to bungle (a stroke in golf) —*n.* the act of foozling; esp., a bad stroke in golf —**foo′zler** *n.*

fop (fäp) *n.* [ME. foppe, a fool, prob. < MDu. or MLowG.: cf. FOB²] **1.** orig., a foolish person **2.** a vain, affected man who pays too much attention to his clothes, appearance, etc.; dandy —**fop′pish** *adj.* —**fop′pish·ly** *adv.* —**fop′pish·ness** *n.*

fop·per·y (-ər ē) *n., pl.* **-per·ies** **1.** the actions, dress, etc. of a fop **2.** something foppish

for (fôr; *unstressed* fər) *prep.* [ME. < OE., akin to G. für < IE. base *per-, whence L. per-, pro-, prae-, Gr. pro, Sans. pári] **1.** in place of; instead of [to use blankets for coats] **2.** as the representative of; in the interest of [to act for another] **3.** in defense of; in favor of [to fight for a cause, to vote for a levy] **4.** in honor of [to give a banquet for someone] **5.** with the aim or purpose of [to carry a gun for protection] **6.** with the purpose of going to [to leave for home] **7.** in order to be, become, get, have, keep, etc. [to walk for exercise, to fight for one's life] **8.** in search of [to look for a lost article] **9.** meant to be received by a specified person or thing, or to be used in a specified way [flowers for a girl, money for paying bills] **10.** suitable to; appropriate to [a room for sleeping] **11.** with regard to; as regards; concerning [a need for improvement, an ear for music] **12.** as being [to know for a fact] **13.** considering the nature of; as concerns [cool for July, clever for a child] **14.** because of; as a result of [to cry for pain] **15.** in spite of; notwithstanding [stupid for all her learning] **16.** in proportion to; corresponding to [two dollars spent for every dollar earned] **17.** to the amount of; equal to [a bill for $50]: when preceded and followed by the same noun, for indicates equality between things compared or contrasted (Ex.: dollar for dollar) **18.** at the price or payment of [to sell a house for $20,000] **19.** to the length, duration, or extent of; throughout; through [to walk for an hour] **20.** at (a specified time) [an appointment for two o'clock] **21.** [Obs.] before —*conj.* because; seeing that; since [comfort him for he is sad]: more formal than because and used to introduce evidence or explanation for an immediately preceding statement —**for (a person or thing)** to that (a person or thing) will, should, ought, must, etc. [to write an order for the grocer to fill] —**O! for** I wish that I had

for- (fôr, fər) [ME. < OE., replacing fer-, fær- (akin to G. ver- < IE. base *per-, as in prec.) & < OFr. for- (as in FORFEIT) < L. foris, beyond, from without] an Old English and Middle English prefix meaning: **1.** away, apart, off [forbid, forget, forgo]: the original senses are now largely obscured **2.** very much, intensely [forlorn, forworn]

for. **1.** foreign **2.** forestry

fo·ra (fôr′ə) *n. alt. pl. of* FORUM

for·age (fôr′ij, fär′-) *n.* [ME. < OFr. fourage < forre, fuerre, fodder < Frank. fodr, food, akin to OE. foda, FOOD] **1.** food for domestic animals; fodder **2.** a search for food or provisions —*vi.* **-aged, -ag·ing** [Fr. fourrager < the n.] **1.** to search for food or provisions **2.** to search for what one needs or wants —*vt.* **1.** a) to get or take food or provisions from b) [Now Rare] to ravage; plunder **2.** to provide with forage; feed **3.** to get by foraging —**for′ag·er** *n.*

forage acre a measure of the vegetation available for grazing on a range or pasture, equal to the total area multiplied by the percentage of surface covered by usable vegetation (Ex.: 10 acres x 30% density = 3 forage acres)

For·a·ker (fôr′ə kər), **Mount** [after J. B. Foraker, 1846-1917, prominent politician] mountain in the Alaska Range, SC Alas.: 17,395 ft.

fo·ra·men (fô rā′mən, fə-) *n., pl.* **-ram′i·na** (-ram′ə nə), **-ra′mens** [L., a hole < forare, BORE¹] a small opening or perforation, esp. in a bone or in a plant ovule —**fo·ram′i·nal** (-ram′ə n'l), **fo·ram′i·nate** (-nit) *adj.*

foramen mag·num (mag′nəm) [ModL., large opening] the opening at the base of the skull through which the spinal cord passes to become the medulla oblongata

for·a·min·i·fer (fôr′ə min′ə fər, fär′-) *n., pl.* **fo·ram·i·nif·er·a** (fə ram′ə nif′ər ə) [< L. foramen (gen. foraminis): see FORAMEN & -FER] any of an order (Foraminifera) of small, one-celled sea animals with calcareous shells full of tiny holes through which slender filaments project: they form the main component of chalk and many deep-sea oozes —**fo·ram′i·nif′er·al, fo·ram′i·nif′er·ous** *adj.*

for·as·much (fôr′əz much′) *conj.* inasmuch (as)

for·ay (fôr′ā) *vt., vi.* [ME. forraien, prob. back-formation < forreier, forager < OFr. forrier < forrer, to forage < forre: see FORAGE] to raid for spoils; plunder; pillage —*n.* [ME. forrai] a sudden attack or raid in order to seize or steal things

☆**forb** (fôrb) *n.* [Gr. phorbē, fodder < pherbein, to feed, graze < ? IE. base *bher-, whence OE. biergan, to taste] a broad-leaved flowering plant, as distinguished from the grasses, sedges, etc.

for·bade, for·bad (fər bad′, fôr-) *pt. of* FORBID

for·bear¹ (fôr ber′, fər-) *vt.* **-bore′** or archaic **-bare′, -borne′, -bear′ing** [ME. forberen < OE. forberan: see FOR- & BEAR¹] **1.** to refrain from; avoid or cease (doing, saying, etc.) **2.** [Archaic or Dial.] to endure; tolerate —*vi.* **1.** to refrain or abstain **2.** to keep oneself in check; control oneself under provocation —*SYN.* see REFRAIN¹ —**for·bear′er** *n.* —**for·bear′ing·ly** *adv.*

for·bear² (fôr′ber′) *n. same as* FOREBEAR

for·bear·ance (fôr ber′əns, fər-) *n.* **1.** the act of forbearing **2.** the quality of being forbearing; self-control; patient restraint **3.** Law the act by which a creditor extends time for payment of a debt or forgoes for a time his right to enforce legal action on the debt —*SYN.* see PATIENCE

Forbes-Rob·ert·son (fôrbz′räb′ərt s'n), **Sir Johnston** 1853-1937; Eng. actor

for·bid (fər bid′, fôr-) *vt.* **-bade′** or **-bad′, -bid′den** or archaic **-bid′, -bid′ding** [ME. forbeden < OE. forbeodan: see FOR- & BID¹] **1.** to rule against; not permit; prohibit **2.** to command to stay away from; exclude or bar from **3.** to make impossible; prevent

SYN.—**forbid** is the basic, direct word meaning to command a person to refrain from some action; **prohibit** implies a forbidding by law or official decree; **interdict** implies legal or ecclesiastical prohibition, usually for a limited time, as an exemplary punishment or to forestall unfavorable developments; **enjoin** implies a legal order from a court prohibiting (or ordering) a given action, under penalty; **ban** implies legal or ecclesiastical prohibition with an added connotation of strong condemnation or censure —*ANT.* permit, allow

for·bid·dance (-'ns) *n.* the act of forbidding; prohibition

for·bid·den (-'n) *adj.* not permitted; prohibited

forbidden fruit **1.** Bible the fruit of the tree of knowledge of good and bad, forbidden to Adam and Eve: Gen. 2:17; 3:3 **2.** any sinful or forbidden pleasure

for·bid·ding (-iŋ) *adj.* looking dangerous, threatening, or disagreeable; repellent —**for·bid′ding·ly** *adv.*

for·bore (fôr bôr′, fər-) *pt. of* FORBEAR¹

for·borne (-bôrn′) *pp. of* FORBEAR¹

for·by, for·bye (fôr bī′) *prep., adv.* [ME. forbi (see FOR- & BY), akin to G. vorbei] [Scot. or Archaic] **1.** close by; near **2.** past **3.** besides

force (fôrs) *n.* [ME. < OFr. < LL. forcia, fortia < L. fortis, strong: see FORT] **1.** strength; energy; vigor; power **2.** the intensity of power; impetus [the force of a blow] **3.** a) physical power or strength exerted against a person or thing [to use force in opening a door] b) the use of physical power to overcome or restrain a person; physical coercion; violence [to resort to force in dispersing a mob] **4.** the power of a person to act effectively and vigorously; moral or intellectual strength [force of character] **5.** a) the power to control, persuade, influence, etc.; effectiveness [the force of circumstances, an argument lacking force] b) a person, thing, or group having a certain influence, power, etc. [a force for good] **6.** the real or precise meaning; basic point [to miss the force of something said] **7.** a) military, naval, or air power b) [pl.] the collective armed strength, as of a nation c) any organized group of soldiers, sailors, etc. **8.** any group of people organized for some activity [a sales force, a police force] **9.** Law binding power; validity **10.** Physics the cause, or agent, that puts an object at rest into motion or alters the motion of a moving object —*vt.* **forced, forc′ing** **1.** to cause to do something by or as if by force; compel **2.** to rape (a woman) **3.** a) to break open, into, or through by force [to force a lock] b) to make (a way, etc.) by force c) to overpower or capture by breaking into, through, etc. [to force the enemy's stronghold] **4.** to get or take by force; wrest; extort [forcing the gun from his hand] **5.** to drive by or as by force; cause to move against resistance; impel [to force an article into a filled box] **6.** to impose by or as by force (with on or upon) [to force one's

attentions on another] **7.** to effect or produce by or as by force; produce by unusual or unnatural effort [to force a smile] **8.** to exert beyond the natural limits or capacity; strain [to force one's voice] **9.** to cause (plants, fruit, etc.) to develop or grow faster by artificial means **10.** [Obs.] a) to give or add force to b) to put in force ☆**11.** Baseball a) to cause (a base runner) to be put out by a force-out: said of a batter b) to cause (a runner) to score or (a run) to be scored by walking the batter with the bases full (often with in) **12.** Card Games to cause (an opponent) to play (a particular card), or to cause (one's partner) to make (a particular bid) —**in force 1.** in full strength; in full number **2.** in effect; operative; valid —**force′a·ble** adj. —**force′less** adj. —**forc′er** n.

SYN.—**force** implies the exertion of power in causing a person or thing to act, move, or comply against his or its resistance and may refer to physical strength or to any impelling motive [circumstances forced him to lie]; **compel** implies a driving irresistibly to some action, condition, etc.; to **coerce** is to compel submission or obedience by the use of superior power, intimidation, threats, etc.; **constrain** implies the operation of a restricting force and therefore suggests a strained, repressed, or unnatural quality in that which results [a constrained laugh] See also STRENGTH

forced (fôrst) adj. **1.** done or brought about by force; not voluntary; compulsory [forced labor] **2.** produced or kept up by unusual effort; not natural or spontaneous; strained or constrained [a forced smile] **3.** due to necessity or emergency [a forced landing] **4.** at a pace faster than usual [a forced march] —**forc·ed·ly** (fôr′sid lē) adv.

‡**force de frappe** (fôrs də fráp′) [Fr.] striking force; specif., the nuclear striking force of France

force-feed (-fēd′) vt. **-fed′, -feed′ing** to feed by force, esp. by means of a tube passing down the throat to the stomach

force feed a method of pressure lubrication used in internal-combustion engines

force·ful (fôrs′fəl) adj. full of force; powerful, vigorous, effective, cogent, etc. —**force′ful·ly** adv. —**force′ful·ness** n.

‡**force ma·jeure** (fôrs má zhër′) [Fr.] overpowering force or coercive power

force·meat (fôrs′mēt′) n. [altered < farce meat < FARCE, v.] meat chopped up and seasoned, usually for stuffing

☆**force-out** (-out′) n. Baseball an out that results when a base runner is forced from a base by a teammate's hit and fails to reach the next base before the ball does

for·ceps (fôr′səps) n., pl. **-ceps** [L., orig., smith's tongs < formus, WARM + capere, to take] small tongs or pincers for grasping, compressing, and pulling, used esp. by surgeons and dentists

force pump a pump with a valveless plunger for forcing a liquid through a pipe, esp. for sending water under pressure to a considerable height

FORCEPS (A, fine bent; B, scissors)

for·ci·ble (fôr′sə b'l) adj. [ME. < OFr.] **1.** done or effected by force; involving the use of force **2.** having force; forceful —**for′ci·ble·ness** n. —**for′ci·bly** adv.

ford (fôrd) n. [ME. < OE., akin to G. furt < IE. prtu, passage < base *per-, to transport, whence L. portus, Goth. faran, FARE] a shallow place in a stream, river, etc., where one can cross by wading or by riding on horseback, in an automobile, etc. —vt. to cross (a stream, etc.) in this way —**ford′a·ble** adj.

Ford (fôrd) **1.** Ford Ma·dox (mad′əks), (born Ford Madox Hueffer) 1873–1939; Eng. writer & editor **2.** Henry, 1863–1947; U.S. automobile manufacturer **3.** John, 1586?–1640?; Eng. dramatist

for·do (fôr dōō′) vt. **-did′, -done′, -do′ing** [ME. fordon < OE.: see FOR- & DO¹] [Archaic] **1.** to destroy, kill, ruin, etc. **2.** to cause to become exhausted: only in the p.

fore (fôr) adv. [ME. < OE. fore, foran, akin to G. vor < IE. base *per-, through, throughout, before, whence L. per-, FOR, FOR-] **1.** at, in, or toward the front part: now only of a ship **2.** [Obs.] previously —adj. **1.** situated in front or in front of some other thing or part **2.** [Obs.] previous; former —n. the thing or part in front —prep. [Obs.] before: used chiefly in oaths —interj. Golf a shout warning those ahead that one is about to hit the ball —**to the fore 1.** to the front; into view; into prominence **2.** at hand; available **3.** still active; alive

'**fore** (fôr) prep. [Poet.] before

fore- (fôr) [ME. < OE.: see FORE] a prefix meaning: **1.** before in time, place, order, or rank [forenoon, foreman] **2.** the front part of [forearm]

fore-and-aft (fôr′n aft′, -äft′) adj. Naut. from the bow to the stern; lengthwise or set lengthwise

fore and aft Naut. **1.** from the bow to the stern; lengthwise or set lengthwise **2.** at, in, or toward both the bow and the stern

fore-and-aft·er (-af′tər, -äf′-) n. a schooner, ketch, or other ship with fore-and-aft rig

fore·arm¹ (fôr′ärm′) n. the part of the arm between the elbow and the wrist

fore·arm² (fôr ärm′) vt. to arm in advance; prepare beforehand for a fight or any difficulty

fore·bear (fôr′ber′) n. [< FORE + BE + -ER] an ancestor

fore·bode (fôr bōd′) vt., vi. **-bod′ed, -bod′ing** [OE. forebodian: see FORE- & BODE¹] **1.** to indicate beforehand; portend; foretell; predict (esp. something bad or harmful) **2.** to have a presentiment of (something bad or harmful) —**SYN.** see FORETELL —**fore·bod′er** n.

fore·bod·ing (-bōd′iŋ) n. [OE. forebodung] a prediction, portent, or presentiment, esp. of something bad or harmful —adj. characterized by foreboding —**SYN.** see OMINOUS —**fore·bod′ing·ly** adv.

fore·brain (fôr′brān′) n. **1.** the front part of the three primary divisions of the brain of a vertebrate embryo **2.** the part of the fully developed brain evolved from this, consisting of the diencephalon and the cerebral hemispheres

fore·cast (fôr′kast′, -käst′; for v., also occas. fôr kast′, -käst′) vt. **-cast′ or -cast′ed, -cast′ing** [ME. forecasten < fore (see FORE) + casten, to contrive: see CAST] **1.** [Now Rare] to plan in advance; foresee **2.** to estimate or calculate in advance; predict or seek to predict (weather, business conditions, etc.) **3.** to serve as a prediction or prophecy of —vi. to make a forecast —n. **1.** [Now Rare] foresight; forethought **2.** a prediction, as of weather conditions —**SYN.** see FORETELL —**fore′cast′er** n.

fore·cas·tle (fōk′s'l; fôr′kas′'l is a sp. pronun.) n. [FORE + CASTLE: from the foremost of the two castlelike structures on the hull of a medieval vessel] **1.** the upper deck of a ship in front of the foremast **2.** the front part of a merchant ship, where the sailors' quarters are located

fore·close (fôr klōz′) vt. **-closed′, -clos′ing** [ME. forclosen < OFr. forclos, pp. of forclore, to exclude < fors (< L. foris), outside + clore (< L. claudere), CLOSE²] **1.** to shut out; exclude; bar **2.** to deprive of the right to redeem a mortgage when regular payments have not been kept up **3.** to take away the right to redeem (a mortgage, etc.) **4.** to hinder the working of **5.** to claim exclusively —vi. to foreclose a mortgage, lien, etc. —**fore·clos′a·ble** adj. —**fore·clo′sure** (-klō′zhər) n.

fore·court (-kôrt′) n. **1.** a court at the front of a building **2.** Tennis, Badminton, etc. the part of the court nearest the net

fore·deck (-dek′) n. the forepart of a ship's deck, esp. of the upper deck

fore·do (fôr dōō′) vt. archaic var. of FORDO

fore·doom (fôr dōōm′; for n. fôr′dōōm′) vt. to doom in advance; condemn beforehand —n. [Archaic] a sentence or judgment in advance; destiny

fore·fa·ther (fôr′fä′thər) n. [ME. forefader: see FORE- & FATHER] an ancestor

☆**Forefathers' Day** December 22, a day celebrated by New Englanders as the anniversary of the Pilgrims' landing at Plymouth, Massachusetts, in 1620

fore·feel (fôr fēl′) vt. **-felt′, -feel′ing** to feel beforehand; have a premonition of

fore·fend (fôr fend′) vt. same as FORFEND

fore·fin·ger (fôr′fiŋ′gər) n. [ME.] the finger nearest the thumb; index finger; first finger

fore·foot (-foot′) n., pl. **-feet′** [ME. forefot] **1.** either of the front feet of an animal with four or more feet **2.** the meeting point of the keel and the stem of a ship

fore·front (-frunt′) n. **1.** the extreme front **2.** the position of most activity, importance, etc.

fore·gath·er (fôr gath′ər) vi. same as FORGATHER

fore·go¹ (-gō′) vt., vi. **-went′, -gone′, -go′ing** [ME. forgon < OE. foregan] to go before in place, time, or degree; precede

fore·go² (-gō′) vt. same as FORGO

fore·go·ing (fôr′gō′iŋ) adj. previously said, written, etc.; preceding —**SYN.** see PREVIOUS —**the foregoing 1.** the one or ones previously mentioned **2.** what has already been said or written

fore·gone (fôr gôn′) adj. **1.** that has gone before; previous; former **2.** previously determined or confidently anticipated; also, inevitable or unavoidable: said of a conclusion

fore·ground (fôr′ground′) n. **1.** the part of a scene, landscape, etc. nearest, or represented in perspective as nearest, to the viewer **2.** the most noticeable or conspicuous position

fore·gut (-gut′) n. the front part of the alimentary canal in vertebrate embryos: the duodenum, stomach, esophagus, and pharynx develop from it

fore·hand (-hand′) n. **1.** [Archaic] the position in front or above; advantage **2.** the part of a horse in front of the rider **3.** a kind of stroke, as in tennis, made with the arm extended and the palm of the hand turned forward —adj. **1.** [Obs.] done or given earlier **2.** foremost; front **3.** done or performed as or with a forehand —adv. with a forehand

fore·hand·ed (fôr han′did) adj. **1.** looking ahead to, or making provision for, the future; thrifty; prudent **2.** well-to-do; well-off; prosperous **3.** same as FOREHAND (adj. 3) —**fore·hand′ed·ly** adv. —**fore·hand′ed·ness** n.

fore·head (fôr′id, fär′-; fôr′hed′, fär′-) n. [ME. forhed < OE. forheafod: see FORE- & HEAD] **1.** the part of the face between the eyebrows and the line where the hair normally begins **2.** the front part of anything

for·eign (fôr'in, fär'-) *adj.* [ME. *forein* < OFr. *forain* < LL. *foranus*, foreign, orig., external < L. *foras*, out-of-doors, orig. acc. pl. of OL. *fora*, DOOR] **1.** situated outside one's own country, province, locality, etc. *[foreign* lands] **2.** of, from, or characteristic of another country or countries *[foreign* languages] **3.** having to do with the relations of one country to another country or countries *[foreign* affairs, *foreign* trade]: often opposed to DOMESTIC **4.** not subject to the laws or jurisdiction of the specified country **5.** *a)* not natural to the person or thing specified; not belonging; not characteristic *[a* trait *foreign* to one's nature] *b)* not pertinent; irrelevant **6.** not organically belonging; introduced from outside: said of substances found in parts of the body or in organisms where they do not naturally occur —*SYN.* see EXTRINSIC —**for'eign·ness** *n.*

foreign bill (of exchange) a bill of exchange drawn in one state or country and payable in another, as one arising from foreign trade operations

for·eign-born (-bôrn') *adj.* born in some other country; not native —**the foreign-born** immigrants of a country

foreign correspondent a journalist who reports events from a foreign country or countries

for·eign·er (-ər) *n.* **1.** a person from another country, thought of as an outsider; alien **2.** any person regarded as an outsider or stranger **3.** something, esp. a ship, from another country —*SYN.* see ALIEN

foreign exchange 1. the transfer of credits to a foreign country to settle debts or accounts between residents of the home country and those of the foreign country **2.** foreign bills or other instruments to settle such accounts

☆**for·eign·ism** (-iz'm) *n.* **1.** a foreign idiom, mannerism, custom, etc. **2.** the quality of being foreign

foreign legion a military force composed mainly of volunteers from foreign countries; esp., **[F- L-]** such a French force, orig. based in North Africa

foreign minister a member of a governmental cabinet in charge of foreign affairs for his country

foreign mission 1. a religious, esp. Christian, mission sent by a church to do missionary work esp. in a non-Christian country **2.** a group sent on diplomatic or other business to a foreign nation

foreign office in some countries, the office of government in charge of foreign affairs

fore·judge[1] (fôr juj') *vt.* **-judged', -judg'ing** to consider or decide before knowing the facts; judge beforehand

fore·judge[2] (-juj') *vt.* **-judged', -judg'ing** [ME. *forjugen* < OFr. *forjugier* < *fors,* outside (< L. *foris:* see FORFEIT) + *jugier:* see JUDGE] *Law* to expel or dispossess by court judgment

fore·know (-nō') *vt.* **-knew', -known', -know'ing** to know beforehand —**fore·know'a·ble** *adj.*

fore·knowl·edge (fôr'näl'ij, fôr näl'ij) *n.* knowledge of something before it happens or exists; prescience

☆**fore·la·dy** (fôr'lā'dē) *n., pl.* **-dies** *same as* FOREWOMAN

fore·land (-lənd) *n.* [ME.] **1.** a headland; promontory **2.** land in relation to the territory behind it

fore·leg (-leg') *n.* either of the front legs of an animal with four or more legs

fore·limb (-lim') *n.* a front limb, as an arm, foreleg, wing, or flipper

fore·lock[1] (-läk') *n.* a lock of hair growing just above the forehead

fore·lock[2] (-läk') *n.* a cotter pin or linchpin —*vt.* to fasten with such a pin or pins

fore·man (-mən) *n., pl.* **-men** (-mən) [orig., foremost man, leader] **1.** the chairman and spokesman of a jury **2.** a man in charge of a department or group of workers in a factory, mill, etc. —**fore'man·ship'** *n.*

fore·mast (fôr'məst', -mäst', -məst) *n.* the mast nearest the bow of a ship

fore·most (-mōst') *adj.* [ME. *foremeste* < OE. *formest* (akin to OFris. *formest,* Goth. *frumists,* etc.), superl. (cf. -EST) of OE. *forma,* itself a superl. of *fore* (see FORE); later understood and spelled as FORE + MOST] **1.** first in place or time **2.** first in rank or importance; leading —*adv.* before all else; first —*SYN.* see CHIEF

fore·name (-nām') *n.* a first name; name before the surname

fore·named (-nāmd') *adj.* named or mentioned before

fore·noon (fôr'nōon', fôr'nōon') *n.* the time from sunrise to noon; morning —*adj.* of, in, or for the forenoon

fo·ren·sic (fə ren'sik) *adj.* [< L. *forensis,* public < *forum* (see FORUM) + adj. suffix *-ensis* + -IC] of, characteristic of, or suitable for a law court, public debate, or formal argumentation —*n.* [*pl.*] debate or formal argumentation —**fo·ren'si·cal·ly** *adv.*

forensic medicine *same as* MEDICAL JURISPRUDENCE

fore·or·dain (fôr'ôr dān') *vt.* to ordain beforehand; predestine —**fore'or·di·na'tion** (-ôr d'n ā'shən) *n.*

fore·part (fôr'pärt') *n.* **1.** the first or early part **2.** the part in front

fore·passed, fore·past (fôr past', -päst') *adj.* [Rare] past; bygone

fore·paw (fôr'pô') *n.* an animal's front paw

fore·peak (-pēk') *n.* the part of a ship's hold in the angle of the bow

fore·play (fôr'plā') *n.* mutual sexual stimulation preceding sexual intercourse

fore·quar·ter (-kwôr'tər) *n.* **1.** the front half of a side of beef or the like **2.** [*pl.*] the front quarters of a horse or other animal, including the forelegs

fore·reach (fôr rēch') *vt.* to overtake and pass, esp. in a sailboat —*vi.* to move forward swiftly and suddenly, as a ship

fore·run (-run') *vt.* **-ran', -run', -run'ning** [Rare or Archaic] **1.** to run before; go before; precede **2.** to be the precursor of; be a prediction or sign of (a thing to follow); foreshadow **3.** to forestall

fore·run·ner (fôr'run'ər, fôr run'ər) *n.* [ME. *forerenner,* after L. *praecursor*] **1.** a person sent before or going before to announce or prepare the way for another or for something to follow; herald **2.** a sign that tells or warns of something to follow; prognostic **3.** *a)* a predecessor *b)* an ancestor

SYN.—**forerunner** and **precursor** both refer to a person or thing that comes before (and presages the appearance of) another, **precursor** more specifically suggesting preparation for the work or achievements of the one that follows; **herald,** originally applied to one who made public proclamations or carried messages of state, now refers to any person or thing that announces something or bears news; **harbinger,** originally applied to one sent in advance to secure lodgings as for a royal party, now often applies to something that arrives as the omen or symbol of something to follow

fore·said (fôr'sed') *adj.* [Now Rare] *same as* AFORESAID

fore·sail (fôr'sāl', -səl) *n.* **1.** the lowest sail on the foremast of a square-rigged ship **2.** the main triangular sail on the foremast of a fore-and-aft-rigged ship, as a schooner

fore·see (fôr sē') *vt.* **-saw', -seen', -see'ing** [ME. *forseyn* < OE. *foreseon*] to see beforehand; know beforehand; foreknow —**fore·see'a·ble** *adj.* —**fore·se'er** *n.*

fore·shad·ow (-shad'ō) *vt.* to be a sign of (something to come); indicate or suggest beforehand; prefigure; presage

fore·shank (fôr'shaŋk') *n.* **1.** the upper part of the front legs of cattle **2.** meat from this part

fore·sheet (-shēt') *n.* **1.** one of the ropes used to trim a foresail **2.** [*pl.*] the space forward in an open boat

fore·shock (-shäk') *n.* a minor earthquake preceding a greater one and originating at or near the same place

fore·shore (-shôr') *n.* **1.** the part of a shore closest to the water **2.** the part of a shore between high-water mark and low-water mark

fore·short·en (fôr shôr't'n) *vt.* **1.** *Drawing, Painting,* etc. to represent some lines of (an object) as shorter than they actually are in order to give the illusion of proper relative size, in accordance with the principles of perspective **2.** to present in condensed form; abridge

FORESHORTENED ARM

fore·show (-shō') *vt.* **-showed', -shown'** or **-showed', -show'ing** [ME. *foreshewen* < OE. *foresceawian*] to show or indicate beforehand; foretell; prefigure

fore·side (fôr'sīd) *n.* [ME.] [Rare or Archaic] the front or upper side

fore·sight (-sīt') *n.* [ME., prob. after L. *providentia*] **1.** *a)* the act of foreseeing *b)* the power to foresee **2.** a looking forward **3.** thoughtful regard or provision for the future; prudent forethought —**fore'sight'ed** *adj.* —**fore'sight'ed·ly** *adv.* —**fore'sight'ed·ness** *n.*

fore·skin (-skin') *n.* the fold of skin that covers the end (*glans*) of the penis and is removed in circumcision; prepuce

fore·speak (fôr spēk') *vt.* **-spoke'** or archaic **-spake', -spok'en** or archaic **-spoke', -speak'ing** [ME. *forspeken:* see FORE- & SPEAK] [Rare] **1.** to foretell; prophesy; predict **2.** to apply for or demand in advance; bespeak

for·est (fôr'ist, fär'-) *n.* [ME. < OFr. (Fr. *forêt*) < ML. (*silva*) *forestis,* as if (wood) unenclosed (< L. *foris,* out-of-doors), but prob. through (wood) under court control (< L. *forum,* court, FORUM)] **1.** a thick growth of trees and underbrush covering an extensive tract of land; large woods: often used figuratively **2.** in Great Britain, any of certain tracts of woodland or wasteland, usually the property of the sovereign, preserved for game —*adj.* of or in a forest; sylvan —*vt.* to plant with trees; change into a forest; afforest

fore·stage (fôr'stāj') *n.* the part of a stage in front of the curtain; apron

fore·stall (fôr stôl') *vt.* [ME. *forestallen* < *forestal,* ambush < OE. *foresteall:* see FORE & STALL[2]] **1.** to prevent or hinder by doing something ahead of time **2.** to act in advance of; get ahead of; anticipate **3.** to interfere with the trading in (a market) by buying up goods in advance, getting sellers to raise prices, etc. **4.** [Obs.] *a)* to intercept *b)* to obstruct by force —*SYN.* see PREVENT —**fore·stall'er** *n.* —**fore·stall'ment** *n.*

☆**for·est·a·tion** (fôr'is tā'shən, fär'-) *n.* the planting or care of forests; afforestation

fore·stay (fôr'stā') *n.* [ME. *forstay:* see FORE- & STAY[1]] a rope or cable reaching from the head of a ship's foremast to the bowsprit, for supporting the foremast

fore·stay·sail (fôr stā'sāl', -s'l) *n.* a triangular sail set from the forestay

for·est·er (fôr'is tər, fär'-) *n.* [ME. < OFr. *forestier* < ML. *forestarius*] **1.** a person trained in forestry **2.** a person in charge of a forest or trees **3.** a person or animal that lives in a forest **4.** any of several metallic-green or velvety-black moths (family Agaristidae)

For·es·ter (fôr′is tər, fär′-), **C(ecil) S(cott)** 1899–1966; Eng. novelist

for·est·ry (fôr′is trē, fär′-) *n.* **1.** [Rare] wooded land; forest land **2.** the science of planting and taking care of forests **3.** systematic forest management for the production of timber, conservation, etc.

fore·taste (fôr′tāst′; *for v.* fôr tāst′) *n.* [ME. *fortaste*] a preliminary or first taste; slight experience of something to be enjoyed, endured, etc. in the future; anticipation —*vt.* **-tast′ed, -tast′ing** [Rare] to taste beforehand; have a foretaste of

fore·tell (fôr tel′) *vt.* **-told′, -tell′ing** [ME. *foretellen*, prob. after L. *praedicere*] to tell, announce, or indicate beforehand; prophesy; predict —**fore·tell′er** *n.*

SYN.—**foretell** is the general term for a telling or indicating beforehand and does not in itself suggest the means used [to *foretell* the future]; **predict**, often interchangeable with **foretell**, more often suggests deduction from facts already known or the use of scientific calculation [the Chaldeans could *predict* eclipses]; **forecast** comes close to **predict**, now commonly implying estimation of the probable course or future condition of things [to *forecast* the weather]; **prophesy**, in discriminating use, implies prediction by divine inspiration or occult knowledge [Jeremiah *prophesied* the Captivity]; to **prognosticate** is to foretell by the study of signs or symptoms [to *prognosticate* a depression]; **presage** and **forebode** are more often used of things than of persons, **presage** referring to either favorable or unfavorable prognostications, and **forebode** to those of an unfavorable nature, based on premonition, presentiment, etc.

fore·thought (fôr′thôt′) *n.* [ME.: see FORE- & THOUGHT[1]] **1.** a thinking or planning beforehand; previous consideration **2.** prudent thought for the future; foresight —*adj.* planned beforehand; premeditated

fore·thought·ful (-f'l) *adj.* showing forethought; prudent —**fore′thought′ful·ly** *adv.*

fore·time (-tīm′) *n.* the past; former time

fore·to·ken (fôr′tō′kən; *for v.* fôr tō′kən) *n.* [ME. *foretokne* < OE. *foretacn*: see FORE- & TOKEN] a prophetic sign; omen; prognostic —*vt.* to be a prophetic sign or omen of; foreshadow

fore·told (fôr tōld′) *pt. & pp.* of FORETELL

fore·tooth (fôr′tōōth′) *n., pl.* **-teeth** [ME. *foretoth* < OE.] a front tooth; incisor

fore·top (fôr′täp′; *also for 1,* təp) *n.* [ME.: see FORE & TOP] **1.** the platform at the top of a ship's foremast **2.** a horse's (or, formerly, a person's) forelock

fore·top·gal·lant (fôr′täp gal′ənt, fôr′tə-) *adj.* designating or of the mast, sail, yard, etc. just above the fore-topmast

fore·top·mast (fôr täp′mast′, -mäst′, -məst) *n.* the section of mast extending above the foremast

fore·top·sail (-sāl′, -s'l) *n.* a sail set on the fore-topmast, above the foresail

for·ev·er (fər ev′ər, fôr-) *adv.* **1.** for eternity; for always; endlessly **2.** at all times; always

for·ev·er·more (fər ev′ər môr′, fôr-) *adv.* for eternity; for always; forever

fore·warn (fôr wôrn′) *vt.* to warn beforehand

fore·went (-went′) *pt.* of FOREGO[1]

fore·wing (fôr′wiŋ′) *n.* either of the front pair of wings attached to the thorax in most insects, sometimes forming a cover for the hind pair

fore·wom·an (-woom′ən) *n., pl.* **-wom′en** a woman serving as a foreman

fore·word (-wurd′, -wərd) *n.* [transl. of G. *vorwort* < *vor,* FORE + *wort,* WORD] an introductory remark, preface, or prefatory note —**SYN.** see INTRODUCTION

fore·worn (fôr wôrn′) *adj.* same as FORWORN

fore·yard (fôr′yärd′) *n.* the lowest yard on a foremast

For·far (fôr′fər) *former name of* ANGUS: also **For′far·shire′** (-shir′)

for·feit (fôr′fit) *n.* [ME. *forfet* < OFr. *forfait,* pp. of *forfaire,* to transgress < ML. *forisfacere,* to do wrong, lit., to do beyond < L. *foris, foras,* out-of-doors, beyond (see FOREIGN) + *facere* (see FACT)] **1.** something that one loses or has to give up because of some crime, fault, or neglect of duty; specif., a fine or penalty **2.** *a)* a thing taken away as a penalty for making some mistake in a game, and redeemable by a specified action *b)* [*pl.*] any game in which such forfeits are taken **3.** the act of forfeiting; forfeiture —*adj.* lost, given up, or taken away as a forfeit —*vt.* to lose, give up, or be deprived of as a forfeit for some crime, fault, etc. —**for′feit·a·ble** *adj.* —**for′feit·er** *n.*

for·fei·ture (fôr′fə choor′) *n.* **1.** the act of forfeiting **2.** anything forfeited; penalty or fine

for·fend (fôr fend′) *vt.* [ME. *forfenden:* see FOR- & FEND] [Archaic] **1.** to forbid **2.** to ward off; prevent

for·fi·cate (fôr′fə kit, -kāt′) *adj.* [< L. *forfex* (gen. *forficis*) pair of shears + -ATE[1]] deeply notched or forked, as some birds' tails

for·gat (fôr gat′) *archaic pt.* of FORGET

for·gath·er (fôr gath′ər) *vi.* [FOR + GATHER, after (?) Du. *vergaderen*] **1.** to come together; meet; assemble **2.** to meet by chance; encounter **3.** to associate or have friendly social relations (*with*)

for·gave (fər gāv′, fôr-) *pt.* of FORGIVE

forge[1] (fôrj) *n.* [ME. < OFr. < L. *fabrica,* workshop, fabric < *faber,* workman < IE. base **dhabh-,* to join, fit, whence DAFT] **1.** a furnace for heating metal to be wrought **2.** a place where metal is heated and hammered or wrought into shape; smithy **3.** a place where wrought iron is made from pig iron or iron ore —*vt.* **forged, forg′ing** [ME. *forgen* < OFr. *forgier* < L. *fabricare,* to make < *fabrica*] **1.** to form or shape (metal) with blows or pressure from a hammer, press, or other machine, usually after heating **2.** to make (something) by or as by this method; form; shape; produce **3.** to make (something false) or imitate (something genuine) for purposes of deception or fraud; esp., to counterfeit (a check, etc.) —*vi.* **1.** to work at a forge **2.** to commit forgery

forge[2] (fôrj) *vt., vi.* **forged, forg′ing** [prob. altered < FORCE] **1.** to move forward steadily, as if against difficulties **2.** to move in a sudden spurt of speed and energy Often with *ahead*

FORGE

forg·er (fôr′jər) *n.* a person who forges; specif., *a)* one who tells false stories *b)* one who forges metal *c)* one who commits forgery

for·ger·y (-jər ē) *n., pl.* **-ger·ies 1.** the act or legal offense of imitating or counterfeiting documents, signatures, works of art, etc. to deceive **2.** anything forged **3.** [Archaic] invention

for·get (fər get′, fôr-) *vt.* **-got′** *or archaic* **-gat′, -got′ten** *or* **-got′, -get′ting** [ME. *forgeten* < OE. *forgitan* (akin to G. *vergessen*): see FOR- & GET] **1.** to lose (facts, knowledge, etc.) from the mind; fail to recall; be unable to remember **2.** to fail to do, bring, etc. as because of carelessness; overlook, omit, or neglect unintentionally [don't *forget* to write] **3.** to overlook, omit, or neglect intentionally [let's *forget* our differences] —*vi.* to forget things; be forgetful —**SYN.** see NEGLECT —**forget it** don't trouble to think about or mention it —**forget oneself 1.** to think only of others; be altruistic or unselfish **2.** to behave in an improper or unseemly manner —**for·get′ta·ble** *adj.* —**for·get′ter** *n.*

for·get·ful (-f'l) *adj.* [ME.] **1.** apt to forget; having a poor memory **2.** heedless or negligent **3.** [Poet.] causing to forget [*forgetful* sleep] —**for·get′ful·ly** *adv.* —**for·get′ful·ness** *n.*

for·get-me-not (-mē nät′) *n.* **1.** any of a genus (*Myosotis*) of marsh plants of the borage family, with clusters of small blue, white, or pink flowers: an emblem of faithfulness and friendship **2.** any of a number of other plants related or similar to this

forg·ing (fôr′jiŋ) *n.* **1.** something forged; esp., a forged piece of metal **2.** the act of one that forges

for·give (fər giv′, fôr-) *vt.* **-gave′, -giv′en, -giv′ing** [ME. *forgeven* < OE. *forgiefan, forgifan* (akin to G. *vergeben*): see FOR- & GIVE] **1.** to give up resentment against or the desire to punish; stop being angry with; pardon **2.** to give up all claim to punish or exact penalty for (an offense); overlook **3.** to cancel or remit (a debt) —*vi.* to show forgiveness; be inclined to forgive —**SYN.** see ABSOLVE —**for·giv′a·ble** *adj.* —**for·giv′er** *n.*

for·give·ness (-nis) *n.* **1.** a forgiving or being forgiven; pardon **2.** inclination to forgive or pardon

for·giv·ing (-iŋ) *adj.* that forgives; inclined to forgive —**for·giv′ing·ly** *adv.* —**for·giv′ing·ness** *n.*

for·go (fôr gō′) *vt.* **-went′, -gone′, -go′ing** [ME. *forgon* < OE. *forgan:* see FOR- & GO[1]] **1.** to do without; abstain from; give up **2.** [Archaic] *a)* to go past *b)* to overlook; neglect —**SYN.** see RELINQUISH —**for·go′er** *n.*

for·got (fər gät′, fôr-) *pt. & alt. pp.* of FORGET

for·got·ten (-'n) *pp.* of FORGET

for·int (fôr′int) *n.* [Hung.] the monetary unit of Hungary: see MONETARY UNITS, table

for·judge (fôr juj′) *vt.* **-judged′, -judg′ing** *same as* FORE-JUDGE[2]

fork (fôrk) *n.* [ME. *forke* < OE. *forca* & < Anglo-Fr. *forque* (Fr. *fourche*), both < L. *furca,* two-pronged fork] **1.** an instrument of greatly varying size with a handle at one end and two or more pointed prongs at the other: forks are variously used as eating utensils and for pitching hay, breaking up soil, etc. **2.** something resembling a fork in shape: cf. TUNING FORK **3.** a division into branches; bifurcation ☆**4.** the point where a river, road, etc. is divided into two or more branches, or where branches join to form a river, road, etc. **5.** any of these branches —*vi.* to divide into branches; be bifurcated [where the road *forks*] —*vt.* **1.** to make into the shape of a fork **2.** to pick up, spear, or pitch with a fork **3.** *Chess* to attack (two chessmen) with a knight, etc. —☆**fork over** (or **out, up**) [Colloq.] to pay out; hand over —**fork′ful′** *n., pl.* **-fuls′**

forked (fôrkt) *adj.* **1.** having a fork or forks; divided into branches; cleft [*forked* lightning] **2.** having prongs: often

in hyphenated compounds [five-*forked*] Also **fork'y, fork'-i·er, fork'i·est**

☆**forked tongue** [prob. transl. of AmInd. expression] lying or deceitful talk

☆**fork·lift** (fôrk'lift') *n.* a device, usually mounted on a truck (**forklift truck**), for lifting, stacking, etc. heavy objects: it consists typically of projecting prongs that are slid under the load and then raised or lowered

For·lì (fôr lē') commune in Emilia-Romagna region, NC Italy: pop. 91,000

for·lorn (far lôrn', fôr-) *adj.* [ME. *forloren* < OE., pp. of *forleosan*, to lose utterly (see FOR- & LOSE)] 1. abandoned or deserted 2. in pitiful condition; wretched; miserable 3. without hope; desperate 4. bereft or deprived (*of*) —**for·lorn'ly** *adv.* —**for·lorn'ness** *n.*

forlorn hope [altered < Du. *verloren hoop*, lit., lost group < *verloren*, pp. of *verliezen*, to lose (akin to prec.) + *hoop*, a band, group (akin to HEAP)] 1. a group of soldiers detached from the main group for a very dangerous mission 2. a desperate undertaking; enterprise with very little chance of success 3. [through confusion with HOPE] a faint hope

form (fôrm) *n.* [ME. *forme* < OFr. < L. *forma*, a shape, figure, image] 1. the shape, outline, or configuration of anything; structure as apart from color, material, etc. 2. *a*) the body or figure of a person or animal *b*) a model of the human figure, esp. one used to display or fit clothes 3. anything used to give shape to something else; mold; specif., a structure of boards or metal into which concrete is poured to set 4. the particular mode of existence a thing has or takes [water in the *form* of vapor] 5. *a*) arrangement; esp., orderly arrangement; way in which parts of a whole are organized; pattern; style: distinguished from CONTENT² *b*) a specific arrangement, esp. a conventional one 6. a way of doing something requiring skill; specif., the style or technique of an athlete, esp. when it is the standard or approved one 7. a customary or conventional way of acting or behaving; ceremony; ritual; formality 8. a fixed order of words; formula [the *form* of a wedding announcement] 9. a printed document with blank spaces to be filled in [an application *form*] 10. a particular kind, type, species, or variety [man is a *form* of animal life] 11. a condition of mind or body in regard to mental or physical performances of skill, speed, etc. [in good *form* for the game] 12. *a*) a chart giving information about horses in a race, as past performances, post positions, odds, etc. *b*) what is or was to be expected, based on past performances [to react according to *form*] 13. the lair or hiding place of a hare, etc. 14. a long, wooden bench without a back, as formerly in a schoolroom 15. a grade or class in some private schools and in British secondary schools 16. [Archaic] beauty 17. *Gram.* any of the different appearances of a word in changes of inflection, spelling, or pronunciation ["am" is a *form* of the verb "be"] 18. *Linguis. same as* LINGUISTIC FORM 19. *Philos.* the ideal nature or essential character of a thing as distinguished from its matter 20. *Printing* the type, engravings, etc. locked in a frame, or chase, for printing or plating —*vt.* 1. to give shape or form to; fashion; make, as in some particular way 2. to mold or shape by training and discipline; train; instruct 3. to develop (habits) 4. to think of; frame in the mind; conceive 5. to come together into; take the formation of; organize into [to *form* a club] 6. to make up; act as; create out of separate elements; constitute [thirteen States *formed* the original Union] 7. *Gram. a*) to build (words) from bases, prefixes, etc. *b*) to construct or make up (a sentence, phrase, etc.) —*vi.* 1. to be formed; assume shape 2. to come into being; take form 3. to take a definite or specific form or shape —**good** (or **bad**) **form** conduct in (or not in) accord with social custom

SYN.—**form** denotes the arrangement of the parts of a thing that gives it its distinctive appearance and is the broadest term here, applying also to abstract concepts; **figure** is applied to physical form as determined by the bounding lines or surfaces; **outline** is used of the lines bounding the limits of an object and, in an extended sense, suggests an undetailed general plan; **shape**, although also stressing outline, is usually applied to something that has mass or bulk and may refer to nonphysical concepts; **configuration** stresses the relative disposition of the inequalities of a surface See also MAKE¹

-form (fôrm) [OFr. *-forme* < L. *-formis* < *forma*, FORM] a *suffix meaning:* 1. having the form of; shaped like [*dentiform*] 2. having (a specified number of) forms [*triform*]

for·mal (fôr'məl) *adj.* [ME. < L. *formalis* < *forma*, FORM] 1. of external form or structure, rather than nature or content 2. of the internal form; relating to the intrinsic or essential character or nature 3. of or according to prescribed or fixed customs, rules, ceremonies, etc. [a *formal* wedding] 4. *a*) having the appearance of being suitable, correct, etc., but not really so *b*) stiff in manner; not warm or relaxed 5. *a*) designed for use or wear at ceremonies, elaborate parties, etc. [*formal* dress] *b*) requiring clothes of this kind [a *formal* dance] 6. done or made in orderly, regular fashion; methodical 7. very regular or orderly in arrangement, pattern, etc.; rigidly symmetrical [a *formal* garden] 8. done or made according to the forms that make explicit, definite, valid, etc. [a *formal* contract] 9. designating education in schools, colleges, etc. 10. designating or of that level of language usage characterized by expanded vocabulary, complete syntactical constructions, complex sentences, etc.: distinguished from COLLOQUIAL or INFORMAL —*n.* 1. a formal dance or ball 2. a woman's evening dress —**go formal** [Colloq.] to go dressed in evening clothes

form·al·de·hyde (fôr mal'də hīd', far-) *n.* [FORM(IC) + ALDEHYDE] a colorless, pungent gas, HCHO, used in solution as a strong disinfectant and preservative, and in the manufacture of synthetic resins, dyes, etc.

For·ma·lin (fôr'mə lin) [FORMAL(DEHYDE) + -IN¹] *a trademark for* a solution of formaldehyde in water, varying from 37% to 50% by volume and usually containing some methanol

for·mal·ism (fôr'məl iz'm) *n.* 1. strict or excessive attention to or insistence on outward forms and customs, as in art or religion 2. an instance of this —**for'mal·ist** *n., adj.* —**for'mal·is'tic** *adj.*

for·mal·i·ty (fôr mal'ə tē) *n., pl.* **-ties** [Fr. *formalité*] 1. the quality or state of being formal; specif., *a*) a following or observing of prescribed customs, rules, ceremonies, etc.; propriety *b*) careful or too careful attention to order, regularity, precision, or conventionality; stiffness 2. a formal or conventional act or requirement; ceremony or form, often without practical meaning —*SYN.* see CEREMONY

for·mal·ize (fôr'mə līz') *vt.* **-ized', -iz'ing** 1. to give definite form to 2. to make formal 3. to make official, valid, etc. by use of an appropriate form [to *formalize* an agreement] —**for'mal·i·za'tion** *n.*

formal logic the branch of logic that studies the validity or correctness of conclusions by investigation of their structural relation to other propositions as evidence

for·mal·ly (-məl ē) *adv.* [ME. *formali, formeliche*] 1. in a formal manner 2. with regard to form

for·mant (fôr'mənt) *n.* [G. < L. *formans*, gen. *formantis*, prp. of *formare*, FORM] *Phonet.* any of the group of sound waves special to a particular vowel sound

for·mat (fôr'mat) *n.* [G. < L. *formatus*, pp. of *formare*: see FORM] 1. the shape, size, binding, type face, paper, and general makeup or arrangement of a book, magazine, etc. 2. general arrangement or plan, as of a television program

for·mate (-māt) *n.* a salt or ester of formic acid

for·ma·tion (fôr mā'shən) *n.* [ME. *formacioun* < OFr. *formation* < L. *formatio* < pp. of *formare*] 1. a forming or being formed 2. a thing formed 3. the way in which something is formed or arranged; structure 4. an arrangement or positioning, as of troops, ships, airplanes in flight, a football team, etc. 5. *Ecol.* the major unit of vegetation usually extending over a large area, as the prairie, deciduous forest, tundra, etc. 6. *Geol.* a rock unit distinguished from adjacent deposits by some common character, as composition, origin, type of fossil, etc.

form·a·tive (fôr'mə tiv) *adj.* [OFr. *formatif* < ML. *formativus* < L. *formatus*, pp. of *formare*] 1. giving or able to give form; helping to shape, develop, or mold [the *formative* influence of a teacher] 2. of formation or development [a child's *formative* years] 3. *Linguis.* serving to form words, as a prefix or suffix —*n. Linguis.* a bound form, as a prefix or suffix

form class *Linguis.* a class made up of words that occur in a distinctive position in constructions and have certain formal features in common, as the form class *noun* in English, made up of all words to which both the plural and possessive suffixes may be added

for·mer¹ (fôr'mər) *adj.* [ME. *formere*, compar. of *forme*, first < OE. *forma*: see FOREMOST] 1. preceding in time; earlier; past [in *former* times] 2. first mentioned of two: opposed to LATTER: often used absolutely (with *the*) [Jack and Bill are twins, but the *former* is taller than the latter] —*SYN.* see PREVIOUS

form·er² (fôr'mər) *n.* a person or thing that forms

for·mer·ly (fôr'mər lē) *adv.* at or in a former or earlier time; in the past

form genus a genus consisting of species superficially resembling each other but probably not closely related in their evolutionary origin

for·mic (fôr'mik) *adj.* [< L. *formica*, an ant < IE. *morm-*, var. of *morwi-*, whence OIr. *moirb*, ON. *maurr*, ant: see PISMIRE] 1. of ants 2. designating or of a colorless acid, HCOOH, that is extremely irritating to the skin: it is found in ants, spiders, etc. as well as in nettles and some other plants, is prepared commercially from oxalic acid and glycerol, and is used as a food preservative, in dyeing, etc.

☆**For·mi·ca** (fôr mīk'ə) [arbitrary coinage] *a trademark for* a laminated, heat-resistant thermosetting plastic used for table and sink tops, etc.

for·mi·car·y (fôr'mə ker'ē) *n., pl.* **-car'ies** [ML. *formicarium* < *formicarius*, of ants < L. *formica*, ant: see FORMIC] an anthill or ants' nest: also **for'mi·car'i·um** (-ē əm) *n., pl.* **-car'i·a** (-ē ə)

for·mi·da·ble (fôr'mə də b'l) *adj.* [ME. < OFr. < L. *formidabilis* < *formidare*, to fear, dread < *formido*, fear < IE. *mormo-*, to feel horror, whence Gr. *mormoros*, fear] 1. causing fear or dread 2. hard to handle or overcome 3. awe-inspiring in size, excellence, etc.; strikingly impressive —**for'mi·da·bil'i·ty, for'mi·da·ble·ness** *n.* —**for'mi·da·bly** *adv.*

form·less (fôrm'lis) *adj.* having no definite or regular form or plan; shapeless —**form'less·ly** *adv.* —**form'less·ness** *n.*

☆**form letter** a letter of standardized form, usually one of a number printed or run off on a duplicating machine, with the date, address, etc. filled in separately

For·mo·sa (fôr mō′sə, -zə) *former (Portuguese) name of* TAIWAN —**For·mo′san** *adj., n.*

Formosa Strait *former name of* TAIWAN STRAIT

for·mu·la (fôr′myə lə) *n., pl.* **-las, -lae′** (-lē′) [L., dim. of *forma*, FORM] 1. a fixed form of words, esp. one that has lost its original meaning or force and is now used only as a conventional or ceremonial expression /"Very truly yours" is a *formula* used in letters/ 2. a rule or method for doing something, esp. when conventional and used or repeated without thought /a *formula* for musical comedies/ 3. an exact statement of religious faith or doctrine 4. *a)* a prescription for preparing a medicine, a baby's food, etc. *b)* something, esp. fortified milk for a baby, prepared according to such a prescription 5. a set of algebraic symbols expressing a mathematical fact, principle, rule, etc. /$A = \pi r^2$ is the *formula* for determining the area of a circle/ 6. *Chem.* an expression of the composition of a compound (or a radical, etc.) by a combination of symbols and figures to show the constituents, usually in their exact proportions: see EMPIRICAL FORMULA, MOLECULAR FORMULA, STRUCTURAL FORMULA

for·mu·lar·ize (-lə rīz′) *vt.* **-ized′, -iz′ing** *same as* FORMULATE (sense 1) —**for′mu·lar′i·za′tion** *n.*

for·mu·lar·y (fôr′myə ler′ē) *n., pl.* **-lar′ies** [Fr. *formulaire* < L. *formula*, FORMULA] 1. a collection of formulas; book of prescribed forms, as prayers, rituals, etc. 2. a formula 3. *Pharmacy* a list of medicines with their formulas and directions for compounding them —*adj.* of, or having the nature of, a formula or formulas

for·mu·late (-lāt′) *vt.* **-lat′ed, -lat′ing** 1. to express in or reduce to a formula 2. to put together and express (a theory, plan, etc.) in a systematic way —**for′mu·la′tion** *n.* —**for′mu·la′tor** *n.*

for·mu·lism (-liz′m) *n.* reliance on or belief in formulas —**for′mu·lis′tic** *adj.*

for·mu·lize (-līz′) *vt.* **-lized′, -liz′ing** *same as* FORMULATE (sense 1) —**for′mu·li·za′tion** *n.*

for·myl (fôr′mil) *n.* [FORM(IC) + -YL] the monovalent radical HCO of formic acid

For·nax (fôr′naks) [L., lit., FURNACE] a S constellation near Eridanus

for·ni·cate[1] (fôr′nə kāt′) *vi.* **-cat′ed, -cat′ing** [< LL.(Ec.) *fornicatus*, pp. of *fornicarī*, to fornicate < L. *fornix* (gen. *fornicis*), a brothel, orig., vault < *fornus*, an oven, akin to *fornax*, FURNACE] to commit fornication —**for′ni·ca′tor** *n.*

for·ni·cate[2] (-kit, -kāt′) *adj.* [L. *fornicatus* < *fornix*, an arch, vault: see prec.] arched or vaulted: also **for′ni·cat′ed** (-kāt′id)

for·ni·ca·tion (fôr′nə kā′shən) *n.* [ME. *fornicacioun* < OFr. *fornication* < LL.(Ec.) *fornicatio* < *fornicatus*: see FORNICATE[1]] 1. voluntary sexual intercourse, generally forbidden by law, between an unmarried woman and a man, esp. an unmarried man: cf. ADULTERY 2. *Bible a)* any unlawful sexual intercourse, including adultery *b)* worship of idols

for·nix (fôr′niks) *n., pl.* **-ni·ces** (-nə sēz′) [ModL. < L., an arch] any of several anatomic arches or folds, such as the vault of the pharynx or the upper part of the vagina

for·rad·er, for·rard·er (fôr′əd ər) *adj.* [Brit. Dial. or Colloq.] further forward or ahead

for·sake (fər sāk′, fôr-) *vt.* **-sook′, -sak′en, -sak′ing** [ME. *forsaken* < OE. *forsacan*, to oppose, forsake < *for-* + *sacan*, to contend, strive < *sacu*: see SAKE[1]] 1. to give up; renounce (a habit, idea, etc.) 2. to leave; abandon —*SYN.* see ABANDON

for·sak·en (-sā′kən) *adj.* abandoned; desolate; forlorn

for·sook (-sook′) *pt.* of FORSAKE

for·sooth (fər sooth′, fôr-) *adv.* [ME. *forsoth* < OE. *for, prep.* + *soth*, truth: see SOOTH] [Archaic] in truth; no doubt; indeed: in later use, mainly ironic

for·spent (fôr spent′) *adj.* [pp. of obs. *forspend* < OE. *forspendan*, to use up: see FOR- & SPEND] [Archaic] exhausted with toil; fatigued

For·ster (fôr′stər), E(dward) M(organ) 1879–1970; Eng. novelist

for·swear (fôr swer′) *vt.* **-swore′** (-swôr′), **-sworn′, -swear′ing** [ME. *forswerien* < OE. *forswerian*: see FOR- & SWEAR] 1. to renounce on oath; promise earnestly to give up 2. to deny earnestly or on oath —*vi.* to swear falsely; commit perjury —**forswear oneself** to swear falsely; perjure oneself

for·sworn (-swôrn′) *pp.* of FORSWEAR —*adj.* perjured

for·syth·i·a (far sith′ē ə, fôr-) *n.* [ModL., after William *Forsyth* (1737–1804), Eng. botanist] any of a genus (*Forsythia*) of shrubs of the olive family, with yellow, bell-shaped flowers, which appear in early spring

fort (fôrt) *n.* [ME. *forte* < OFr. *fort*, orig. adj., strong < L. *fortis* < OL. *forctus* < IE. base **bheregh-*, high, elevated, whence Sans. *bŕmhati*, strengthens, elevates, OHG. *berg*, hill] 1. an enclosed place or fortified building for military defense, equipped as with earthworks, guns, etc. ☆2. a permanent army post, as distinguished from a temporary camp —☆**hold the fort** 1. to make a defensive stand 2.

[Colloq.] to keep things in operation; remain on duty, etc.

fort. 1. fortification 2. fortified

For·ta·le·za (fôr′tə lā′zə) seaport in NE Brazil, on the Atlantic: capital of Ceará state: pop. 515,000

for·ta·lice (fôr′t'l is) *n.* [ME. < ML. *fortalitia* < L. *fortis*, strong: see FORT] [Archaic] 1. a small fort 2. a fortress

Fort Bragg [after Gen. Braxton BRAGG] town in SC N.C., near Fayetteville: pop. 47,000

Fort Collins [after Lt. Col. Wm. O. *Collins*] city in N Colo., north of Denver: pop. 43,000

Fort-de-France (fôr də fräns′) seaport & capital of Martinique, in the Windward Islands: pop. 85,000

forte[1] (fôrt) *n.* [ME. *fort*, strength < OFr.: see FORT] 1. a thing that a person does particularly well; special accomplishment or strong point 2. the strongest part of the blade of a sword, between the middle and the hilt: cf. FOIBLE

for·te[2] (fôr′tā, -tē) *adj., adv.* [It. < L. *fortis*, strong: see FORT] *Music* loud: a direction to the performer: opposed to PIANO[2] —*n.* a forte note or passage

for·te·pia·no (fôr′tā pyä′nō) *adj., adv.* [It.: see FORTE[2] & PIANO[2]] *Music* loud and then soft: a direction to the performer

Forth (fôrth) 1. river in SE Scotland, flowing east into the Firth of Forth: 65 mi. 2. **Firth of**, long estuary of the Forth River, flowing into the North Sea: 51 mi.

forth (fôrth) *adv.* [ME. < OE., akin to FORE] 1. forward in place, time, or degree; onward /from that day *forth*/ 2. out into view, as from hiding 3. [Archaic] abroad —*prep.* [Archaic] out from; out of   See also idiomatic phrases under BACK[1], GIVE, HOLD[1], etc. —**and so forth** and so on; and other such things: equivalent to *etc.*

forth·com·ing (-kum′in) *adj.* 1. about to appear; approaching /the author's *forthcoming* book/ 2. available or ready when needed /the promised help was not *forthcoming*/ —*n.* a coming forth; appearance or approach

forth·right (-rīt′) *adj.* [ME. < OE. *forth riht*: see FORTH & RIGHT] 1. orig., going straight forward 2. straightforward; direct; frank —*adv.* 1. straight forward; directly onward 2. [Archaic] immediately; at once —*n.* [Archaic] a straight path or course —**forth′right′ly** *adv.* —**forth′right′ness** *n.*

forth·with (fôrth′with′, -with′) *adv.* [ME. *forth with* (for OE. *forth mid*): see FORTH & WITH] immediately; at once

for·ti·eth (fôr′tē ith) *adj.* [ME. *fourtithe < feowertigotha*: see FORTY & -TH[2]] 1. preceded by thirty-nine others in a series; 40th 2. designating any of the forty equal parts of something —*n.* 1. the one following the thirty-ninth 2. any of the forty equal parts of something; 1/40

for·ti·fi·ca·tion (fôr′tə fi kā′shən) *n.* [ME. *fortificacioun* < OFr. *fortification* < LL. *fortificatio* < pp. of *fortificare*] 1. the act or science of fortifying 2. something used in fortifying; esp., a fort or defensive earthwork, wall, etc. 3. a fortified place or position

for·ti·fy (fôr′tə fī′) *vt.* **-fied′, -fy′ing** [ME. *fortifien* < OFr. *fortifier* < LL. *fortificare* < L. *fortis*, strong (see FORT) + *facere*, to make: see FACT] 1. to make strong or stronger; strengthen physically, emotionally, etc. 2. to strengthen against attack, as by building or furnishing with forts, walls, etc. 3. to support; corroborate /to *fortify* an argument with statistics/ 4. to strengthen (wine, etc.) by adding alcohol 5. to add vitamins, minerals, etc. to (milk, etc.) so as to increase the food value; enrich —*vi.* to build military defenses —**for′ti·fi′a·ble** *adj.* —**for′ti·fi′er** *n.*

for·tis (fôr′tis) *adj.* [L., strong: see FORT] *Phonet.* articulated with much muscle tension, as most voiceless plosives —*n.* a fortis sound Opposed to LENIS

for·tis·si·mo (fôr tis′ə mō′; *It.* fôr tēs′sē mō′) *adj., adv.* [It., superl. of *forte*, FORTE[2]] *Music* very loud: a direction to the performer: opposed to PIANISSIMO —*n., pl.* **-mos′, -mi′** (-mē′) a passage to be performed fortissimo

for·ti·tude (fôr′tə tōōd′, -tyōōd′) *n.* [ME. < L. *fortitudo* < *fortis*, strong: see FORT] the strength to bear misfortune, pain, etc. calmly and patiently; firm courage —**for′ti·tu′di·nous** (-tōōd′'n əs, -tyōōd′-) *adj.*

SYN.—**fortitude** refers to the courage that permits one to endure patiently misfortune, pain, etc. /to face a calamity with *fortitude*/; **grit** applies to an obstinate sort of courage that refuses to succumb under any circumstances; **backbone** refers to the strength of character and resoluteness that permits one to face opposition unflinchingly; **pluck** and **guts** both refer originally to visceral organs, hence **pluck** implies a strong heart in the face of danger or difficulty and **guts**, a slang word, suggests the sort of stamina that permits one to "stomach" a disagreeable or frightening experience See also PATIENCE —*ANT.* cowardice

Fort Knox [see KNOXVILLE] military reservation in N Ky., near Louisville: site of U.S. gold bullion depository

Fort La·my (fôr lä mē′) capital of Chad, in the SW part, on the Shari River: pop. c. 70,000: also **Fort-Lamy**

Fort Lau·der·dale (lô′dər dāl′) [after a Maj. Wm. *Lauderdale*] city on the SE coast of Fla., near Miami: pop. 140,000 (met. area, incl. Hollywood, 620,000)

Fort Lewis [after Meriwether LEWIS] town in W Wash., near Tacoma: pop. 38,000

Fort Mc·Hen·ry (mək hen′rē) [after James *McHenry*, U.S. Secretary of War, 1796–1800] fort in Baltimore harbor, Md., where the British were repulsed in 1814

fort·night (fôrt′nīt′) n. [ME. fourte(n) niht < OE. feowertyne niht, lit., fourteen nights] [Chiefly Brit.] two weeks

fort·night·ly (-lē) adv., adj. [Chiefly Brit.] (happening or appearing) once in every fortnight, or at two-week intervals —n., pl. **-lies** a periodical issued at two-week intervals

FOR·TRAN (fôr′tran) n. [for(mula) tran(slation)] a digital computer language similar to algebra

for·tress (fôr′trəs) n. [ME. forteresse < OFr. < VL. *fortaricia < L. fortis, strong: see FORT] a fortified place; fort: often used figuratively —vt. to protect by or furnish with a fortress

Fort Smith [after Gen. T. A. Smith, died 1865] city in W Ark., on the Arkansas River: pop. 63,000

Fort Sum·ter (sum′tər) [after Gen. Thomas Sumter, 1734–1832] fort in Charleston harbor, S.C., where Confederate troops fired the first shots of the Civil War (April 12, 1861): now the site of **Fort Sumter National Monument**

for·tu·i·tous (fôr tōō′ə təs, -tyōō′-) adj. [L. fortuitus < fors (gen. fortis), chance, luck < IE. *bhr̥tis < base *bher-, to bring, whence BEAR[1]] 1. happening by chance; accidental 2. bringing, or happening by, good luck; fortunate —SYN. see ACCIDENTAL —for·tu′i·tous·ly adv. —for·tu′i·tous·ness n.

for·tu·i·ty (-tē) n., pl. **-ties** [< L. fortuitus (see prec.) + -ITY] 1. the quality or condition of being fortuitous 2. chance or chance occurrence

For·tu·na (fôr tōō′nə, -tyōō′-) [L. < fortuna] Rom. Myth. the goddess of fortune

for·tu·nate (fôr′chə nit) adj. [ME. fortunat < L. fortunatus, pp. of fortunare, to make fortunate < fortuna, FORTUNE] 1. having good luck; lucky 2. bringing, or coming by, good luck; favorable; auspicious —SYN. see LUCKY —for′tu·nate·ly adv. —for′tu·nate·ness n.

for·tune (fôr′chən) n. [ME. < OFr. < L. fortuna, chance, fate, fortune < fors (gen. fortis), chance: see FORTUITOUS] 1. the supposed power thought of as bringing good or bad to people; luck; chance; fate: often personified 2. what happens or is going to happen to one; one's lot, good or bad, esp. one's future lot 3. good luck; success; prosperity 4. a large quantity of money or possessions; wealth; riches —vt. -tuned, -tun·ing [Archaic] to provide with wealth —vi. [Archaic] to happen; chance —a **small fortune** a very high price or cost —**tell one's fortune** to profess to tell what is going to happen in one's life, as by palmistry, cards, etc. —for′tune·less adj.

☆**fortune cookie** a hollow Chinese cookie with a slip of paper inside bearing a message, often one predicting the future

fortune hunter a person who tries to become rich, esp. by marrying a rich person

for·tune·tell·er (fôr′chən tel′ər) n. a person who professes to foretell events in other people's lives —**for′tune·tell′ing** n., adj.

Fort Wayne [after Anthony WAYNE] city in NE Ind.: pop. 178,000

Fort William [after William McGillivray, a director of the North West Co.] city & port in W Ontario, Canada, on Lake Superior: pop. 48,000

Fort Worth [after Wm. J. Worth (1794–1849)] city in N Tex.: pop. 393,000 (met. area 762,000)

for·ty (fôr′tē) adj. [ME. fourti < OE. feowertig, akin to G. vierzig, Goth. fidwor tigjus: see FOUR & -TY²] four times ten —n., pl. **-ties** the cardinal number between thirty-nine and forty-one; 40; XL —**the forties** the numbers or years, as of a century, from forty through forty-nine

☆**for·ty-nin·er, For·ty-Nin·er** (fôr′tē nī′nər) n. [Colloq.] a person who went to California in the gold rush of 1849

forty winks [Colloq.] a short sleep; nap

fo·rum (fôr′əm) n., pl. **-rums, -ra** (-ə) [L., area out-of-doors, marketplace, prob. < IE. base *dhwor-, door, whence W. dor, DOOR] 1. the public square or marketplace of an ancient Roman city or town, where legal and political business was conducted 2. a law court; tribunal 3. a) an assembly, place, radio program, etc. for the discussion of public matters or current questions b) an opportunity for open discussion —**the Forum** the forum of ancient Rome

for·ward (fôr′wərd) adj. [ME. foreward < OE. foreweard, adj. & adv.: see FORE & -WARD] 1. at, toward, or of the front, or forepart 2. advanced; specif., a) mentally advanced; precocious b) advanced socially, politically, etc.; progressive or radical c) [Now Rare] ahead of time; early 3. moving toward a point in front; onward; advancing 4. ready or eager; prompt 5. too bold or free in manners; pushing; presumptuous 6. of or for the future [forward buying] —adv. 1. toward the front or a point in front or before; ahead 2. toward the future [to look forward] 3. into view or prominence [to bring forward an opinion] —n. Basketball, Hockey, Soccer, etc. any of the players, esp. of the offense, in the front line or in a front position —vt. 1. to help advance; promote 2. to send; dispatch; transmit 3. to send on to one's new address [to forward mail] 4. Bookbinding to round and back (sewed signatures) in preparation for fitting on the cover —SYN. see ADVANCE —for′ward·ness n.

for·ward·er (-wər dər) n. a person or thing that forwards; specif., 1. a person or agency that receives goods and expedites their delivery, as by arranging for warehousing, shipping in carload lots, transshipping, etc. 2. Bookbinding a person who forwards signatures

for·ward-look·ing (-look′iŋ) adj. anticipating or making provision for the future; progressive

for·ward·ly (-lē) adv. 1. boldly; presumptuously ☆2. [Now Rare] at or toward the front, or forepart 3. [Archaic] readily; eagerly

☆**forward pass** Football a pass made from behind the line of scrimmage to a teammate in a position forward of the thrower

for·wards (-wərdz) adv. [ME. forewardes < foreward + adv. gen. -es, akin to G. vorwärts] same as FORWARD

for·went (fôr went′) pt. of FORGO

for·why (fôr hwī′, -wī′) adv. [ME. forwhi < OE. for hwy, wherefore: see FOR & WHY] [Obs. or Dial.] why; wherefore —conj. [Obs.] because

for·worn (-wôrn′) adj. [Early ModE. forworen, pp. of obs. forwear: see FOR- & WEAR¹] [Archaic] worn out

for·zan·do (fôr tsän′dō) adj., adv. [It. < forzare, to force < LL. *fortiare: see FORCE] Music same as SFORZANDO

fos·sa (fäs′ə) n., pl. **-sae** (-ē) [ModL. < L., a ditch, trench, akin to fodere: see FOSSIL] Anat. a cavity, pit, or small hollow —fos′sate (-āt) adj.

fosse, foss (fôs, fäs) n. [ME. < OFr. < L. fossa < fossa (terra), dug (earth) < fossus: see FOSSIL] a ditch or moat, esp. one used in fortifications

fos·sette (fô set′, fä-) n. [Fr., dim. of fosse: see prec.] 1. a small hollow 2. a dimple

fos·sick (fäs′ik) vi. [Eng. dial., prob. ult. < FUSS] [Australian] 1. to prospect or search, as for gold 2. to search about; rummage —vt. to search for; seek out

fos·sil (fäs′'l, fôs′-) n. [Fr. fossile < L. fossilis, dug out, dug up < fossus, pp. of fodere, to dig up < IE. base *bhedh-, to dig in the earth, whence W. bedd, grave, OE. bedd, BED] 1. orig., any rock or mineral dug out of the earth 2. any hardened remains or traces of plant or animal life of some previous geological period, preserved in rock formations in the earth's crust 3. anything fossilized or like a fossil 4. a person who is old-fashioned or has outmoded, fixed ideas —adj. 1. of, having the nature of, or forming a fossil or fossils 2. dug from the earth [coal, petroleum, and natural gas are fossil fuels] 3. belonging to the past; unchanged by progress; antiquated

fos·sil·if·er·ous (fäs′ə lif′ər əs, fôs′-) adj. [< L. fossilis (see prec.) + -FEROUS] containing fossils

fos·sil·ize (fäs′ə līz′, fôs′-) vt. -ized′, -iz′ing 1. to change into a fossil or fossils; petrify 2. to make out of date, rigid, or incapable of change —vi. to become fossilized —fos′sil·i·za′tion n.

fos·so·ri·al (fä sôr′ē əl) adj. [< LL. fossorius < L. fossor, digger < fossus (see FOSSIL) + -AL] digging or adapted for digging; burrowing [fossorial claws]

fos·ter (fôs′tər, fäs′-) vt. [ME. fostren < OE. fostrian, to nourish, bring up < fostor, food, nourishment < base of foda, FOOD] 1. to bring up with care; rear 2. to help to grow or develop; stimulate; promote [to foster discontent] 3. to cling to in one's mind; cherish [foster a hope] —adj. 1. giving, receiving, or sharing the care of one having the standing of a specified member of the family, although not having that standing by birth or adoption [foster parent, foster child, foster brother] 2. designating or relating to such care [foster home] —n. [Obs.] a foster parent —fos′ter·er n.

Fos·ter (fôs′tər, fäs′-) 1. **Stephen Collins,** 1826–64; U.S. composer of songs 2. **William Z**(ebulon), 1881–1961; U.S. Communist Party leader

fos·ter·age (-ij) n. 1. the rearing of a foster child 2. the state of being a foster child 3. a promoting, stimulating, or encouraging

foster home a home in which a child is raised by people other than his natural or adoptive parents

fos·ter·ling (-liŋ) n. [ME. < OE. fostorling: see -LING¹] [Now Rare] a foster child

Fou·cault (fōō kō′), **Jean Ber·nard Lé·on** (zhän ber när′ lä ōn′) 1819–68; Fr. physicist

fou·droy·ant (fōō droi′ənt; Fr. fōō drwä yän′) adj. [Fr., prp. of foudroyer, to strike by lightning < foudre, lightning < LL. fulgere for L. fulgur, akin to flagrare, to burn: see FLAME] 1. dazzling or stunning 2. Med. obs. var. of FULMINANT

‡**fouet·té** (fwe tā′) n. [Fr., pp. of fouetter, to whip < fouet, a whip < MFr., dim. of OFr. fou, beech < L. fagus, BEECH] Ballet any of a series of whipping turns executed rapidly on one leg

fought (fôt) [ME. fauht < OE. feaht, 3d pers. sing., past indic., of feohtan] pt. & pp. of FIGHT

foul (foul) adj. [ME. < OE. ful, akin to G. faul, rotten, lazy < IE. base *pū-, *pu-, to stink (< ? exclamation of disgust), whence L. putere, to rot, Gr. pyos, PUS] 1. so offensive to the senses as to cause disgust; stinking; loathsome [a foul odor] 2. extremely dirty or impure; disgustingly filthy 3. full of or blocked up with dirt or foreign objects [a foul pipe] 4. putrid; rotten: said of food 5. not decent; obscene; profane [foul language] 6. very wicked; abominable [a foul murder] 7. not clear; stormy; unfavorable [foul weather, winds, etc.] 8. tangled or snarled; caught [a foul rope] 9. not according to the rules of a game; unfair, either by accident or intention 10. treacherous; dishonest 11. [Archaic or Brit. Dial.] ugly 12. [Colloq.] unpleasant, disagreeable, etc. ☆13. Baseball not fair: see FOUL BALL, FOUL LINE 14. Printing containing errors or

marked with changes [*foul* copy or proof] —*adv.* in a foul way —*n.* anything foul; specif., *a*) a collision of boats, contestants, etc. *b*) an infraction of the rules, as of a game or sport ☆*c*) *Baseball* same as FOUL BALL —*vt.* 1. to make foul; dirty; soil; defile 2. to dishonor or disgrace 3. to impede or obstruct; specif., *a*) to fill up; encrust; choke [to *foul* a drain with grease] *b*) to cover (the bottom of a ship) with impeding growths *c*) to entangle; catch [a rope *fouled* in the shrouds] *d*) to collide with 4. to make a foul against in a contest or game ☆5. *Baseball* to bat (the ball) so that it falls outside the foul lines —*vi.* 1. to become dirty, filthy, or rotten 2. to be clogged or choked 3. to become tangled 4. to collide 5. to break the rules of a game ☆6. *Baseball* to bat the ball so that it falls outside the foul lines —SYN. see DIRTY —☆**foul out** 1. *Baseball* to be retired as batter by the catch of a foul ball 2. *Basketball* to be disqualified from further play for having committed a specfied number of personal fouls —☆**foul up** [Colloq.] to make a mess of; make disordered or confused; entangle or bungle —**run** (or **fall** or **go**) **foul of** 1. to collide with and become tangled in 2. to get into conflict or trouble with —**foul'ly** *adv.* —**foul'ness** *n.*

fou·lard (fōō lärd′) *n.* [Fr. < ? dial. *foulat*, lit., fulled (cloth) < *fouler*, to full < LL. *fullare*, to FULL¹] 1. a lightweight material of silk, rayon, or sometimes cotton in a plain or twill weave, usually printed with a small design 2. a necktie, scarf, or handkerchief made of this material

☆**foul ball** *Baseball* a batted ball that is not a fair ball: see FAIR BALL

foul·brood (foul′brōōd′) *n.* a deadly bacterial disease of the larvae of honeybees

☆**foul line** 1. *Baseball* either of the lines extending from home plate through the outside corners of first base or third base and onward to the end of the outfield 2. *Basketball* same as FREE-THROW LINE 3. *Tennis, Bowling,* etc. any of various lines bounding the playing area, outside of which the ball must not be hit, the player must not go, etc.

foul-mouthed (-mouthd′, -moutht′) *adj.* using obscene, profane, or scurrilous language

foul play 1. unfair play; action that breaks the rules of the game 2. treacherous action or violence

☆**foul shot** same as FREE THROW

☆**foul tip** *Baseball* a batted ball barely tipped by the bat; it is counted as a strike, but to be counted as a third strike, it must be caught by the catcher

☆**foul-up** (foul′up′) *n.* [Colloq.] a mix-up; botch; mess

found¹ (found) [ME. *funden* < OE. *funden*, pp. of *findan*] *pt. & pp.* of FIND —☆**and found** [Colloq.] with room and board in addition to wages

found² (found) *vt.* [ME. *founden* < OFr. *fonder* < L. *fundare* < *fundus*, bottom < IE. *bhundhos* < base *bhudh-*, whence Sans. *budhnáh*, BOTTOM] 1. to lay the base of; set for support; base [a statement *founded* on facts] 2. to begin to build or organize; bring into being; establish; set up; originate [to *found* a college] —*vi.* [Rare] to be based (on or *upon*)

found³ (found) *vt.* [ME. *founden* < OFr. *fondre* < L. *fundere*, to pour, melt (metal) < IE. base *ĝheu-*, whence OE. *geotan*, Gr. *chein*, pour] 1. to melt and pour (metal or materials for glass) into a mold 2. to make by pouring molten metal into a mold; cast

foun·da·tion (foun dā′shən) *n.* [ME. *foundacioun* < OFr. *fondation* < L. *fundatio* < pp. of *fundare*: see FOUND²] 1. a founding or being founded; establishment 2. *a*) a fund or endowment to maintain a hospital, charity, etc., or to finance projects in research, education, etc. *b*) the organization that administers such a fund *c*) an institution maintained by such a fund 3. the base on which something rests; specif., the supporting part of a wall, house, etc., usually of masonry, concrete, etc., and at least partially underground 4. the fundamental principle on which something is founded; basis 5. a supporting material or part beneath an outer part 6. same as FOUNDATION GARMENT 7. a cosmetic cream, liquid, etc. over which other makeup is applied —SYN. see BASE¹ —**foun·da′tion·al** *adj.*

☆**foundation garment** a woman's corset or girdle, esp. one with an attached brassiere

foun·der¹ (foun′dər) *vi.* [ME. *foundren* < OFr. *fondrer*, to fall in, sink < *fond*, bottom < L. *fundus*, bottom: see FOUND²] 1. to stumble, fall, or go lame 2. to become stuck as in soft ground; bog down 3. to fill with water and sink: said of a ship 4. to become sick from overeating: used esp. of livestock 5. to break down; collapse; fail —*vt.* to cause to founder —*n.* [< the *vi.*, 1] an inflammation of a horse's foot; laminitis

found·er² (-dər) *n.* [ME. *foundour* < OFr. *fondeor* < L. *fundator*] a person who founds, or establishes

found·er³ (-dər) *n.* a person who founds, or casts, metals, glass, etc.

foun·der·ous (-dər əs) *adj.* causing or likely to cause foundering [a *founderous* road]: also **foun′drous** (-drəs)

found·ling (found′liŋ) *n.* [ME. *foundeling* < *founde(n)*, pp. of *finden* (cf. FIND) + *-ling*] an infant of unknown parents that has been found abandoned

found·ry (foun′drē) *n., pl.* **-ries** [see FOUND³ & -ERY] 1. the

act, process, or work of melting and molding metals; casting 2. metal castings 3. a place where metal is cast

foundry proof *Printing* proof from a locked form, submitted for a final reading before plates are cast

fount¹ (fount) *n.* [ME. *font* < OFr. < L. *fons*, FOUNTAIN] 1. [Poet.] a fountain or spring 2. a source

fount² (fount) *n. Brit. var.* of FONT²

foun·tain (foun′t'n) *n.* [ME. < OFr. *fontaine* < LL. *fontana* < fem. of L. *fontanus* < *fons* (gen. *fontis*), spring, prob. < IE. base *dhen-*, to run, flow, whence Sans. *dhanáyati*, (he) runs] 1. a natural spring of water 2. the source or beginning of a stream 3. a source or origin of anything [a *fountain* of knowledge] 4. *a*) an artificial spring, jet, or flow of water *b*) the basin, pipes, etc. where this flows *c*) same as DRINKING FOUNTAIN *d*) same as SODA FOUNTAIN 5. a storage place for liquid; container or reservoir, as for ink, oil, etc.

foun·tain·head (-hed′) *n.* 1. a spring that is the source of a stream 2. the original or main source of anything

Fountain of Youth a legendary spring supposed to restore the health and youth of anyone who drank from it: it was sought in America and the West Indies by Ponce de León and other Spanish explorers

fountain pen a pen in which a nib at the end is fed ink from a supply in a reservoir or cartridge

four (fôr) *adj.* [ME. < OE. *feower*, akin to G. *vier*, Goth. *fidwōr* < IE. base *kwetwer-*, whence L. *quattuor*, W. *pedwar*] totaling one more than three —*n.* 1. the cardinal number between three and five; 4; IV 2. any group of four people or things 3. something numbered four or having four units, as a playing card, face of a die, etc. —**on all fours** 1. on all four feet 2. on hands and knees (or feet) 3. exactly equitable (with)

☆**four-bag·ger** (-bag′ər) *n.* [Slang] same as HOME RUN

four·chette (foor shet′) *n.* [Fr., dim. of *fourche*: see FORK] 1. the side strip of a finger in a glove 2. *Anat.* a small fold of skin connecting the inner lips of the vulva at the posterior end

four-col·or (fôr′kul′ər) *adj.* designating or of a printing process using separate plates in yellow, red, blue, and black, so as to produce any color or colors

four-cy·cle (-sī′k'l) *adj.* having a cycle of four strokes of the piston, as some internal-combustion engines

four-di·men·sion·al (-di men′shən 'l) *adj.* of or in four dimensions, esp. in relativity theory where four coordinates are used to record the space location and time of occurrence of each event

Four·drin·i·er (foor drin′ē ər) *adj.* [after Sealy and Henry *Fourdrinier*, 19th-cent. Eng. papermakers, for whom the machine was developed] designating or of a papermaking machine that produces paper in a continuous strip or roll —*n.* such a machine

☆**four-flush** (fôr′flush′) *vi.* 1. *Stud Poker* to bluff when one holds four cards of the same suit (**four flush**) instead of the five in a true flush 2. [Colloq.] to pretend to be, have, or intend something so as to deceive; bluff —**four′-flush′er** *n.*

four·fold (-fōld′) *adj.* [see -FOLD] 1. having four parts 2. having four times as much or as many —*adv.* four times as much or as many

four-foot·ed (-foot′id) *adj.* [ME. *fourfoted*] having four feet; quadruped

☆**four·gon** (foor gōn′) *n.* [Fr.] a wagon or car for baggage

four-hand·ed (fôr′han′did) *adj.* 1. having four hands 2. for four players, as some games 3. *Music* for two performers, as a piano duet Also **four′-hand′**

☆**Four-H club, 4-H club** (fôr′āch′) [< its aim to improve the *head, hands, heart,* and *health*] a rural youth organization sponsored by the Department of Agriculture, offering instruction in scientific agriculture and home economics

☆**four hundred** [popularized by C. J. Allen, New York *Sun* society reporter, from a remark by Ward McAllister: "There are only 400 people in New York that one really knows"; prob. from limited capacity of Mrs. J. J. Astor's ballroom] [*also* F. H.] the exclusive social set of a particular place (preceded by *the*)

Fou·rier (foo ryā′; E. foor′ē ər) 1. **Fran·çois Ma·rie Charles** (frän swä′ má rē′ shárl), 1772–1837; Fr. socialist & reformer 2. **Baron Jean Bap·tiste Jo·seph** (zhän bá tēst′ zhō zef′), 1768–1830; Fr. mathematician & physicist

☆**Fou·ri·er·ism** (foor′ē ər iz′m) *n.* the doctrines of F. M. C. Fourier, esp. his proposed system for reorganizing society into small, self-sufficient, cooperative communities —**Fou′ri·er·ist** *adj., n.*

Fou·ri·er series (foor′ē ər) [formulated by J. B. J. Fou·rier] *Math.* the expansion of a periodic function into a series of sines and cosines

four-in-hand (fôr′in hand′) *n.* 1. *a*) a team of four horses driven by one man *b*) a coach drawn by such a team 2. *a*) a necktie tied in a slipknot with the ends left hanging —*adj.* designating or of a four-in-hand

four-leaf clover (-lēf′) a clover with four leaves, popularly supposed to bring good luck to the finder

☆**four-letter word** (-let′ər) any of several short words having to do with sex or excrement and generally regarded as offensive or objectionable

---

four-o'clock (-ə kläk′) *adj.* designating a family (Nyctaginaceae) of plants including the four-o'clocks and the bougainvilleas —*n.* any of a genus (*Mirabilis*) of chiefly tropical American plants bearing petalless flowers and, often, brightly colored leaves; esp., a garden plant (*Mirabilis jalapa*) with long-tubed yellow, red, or white blossoms that generally open late in the afternoon

four·pence (fôr′pəns) *n.* **1.** the sum of four British pennies **2.** a former silver coin of this value

four·pen·ny (fôr′pen′ē, fôr′pən ē) *adj.* **1.** costing or valued at fourpence **2.** designating a size of nail: see -PENNY —*n.* fourpence

four-post·er (fôr′pōs′tər) *n.* a bedstead with tall corner posts that sometimes support a canopy or curtains

‡**four·ra·gère** (fōō rȧ zher′) *n.* [Fr. < *fourrager*: see FORAGE, *v.*] a colored and braided cord worn about the shoulder of a uniform; esp., such a cord awarded as a military decoration to an entire unit of troops

four·score (fôr′skôr′) *adj., n.* [ME.] four times twenty; eighty

four·some (-səm) *adj.* [FOUR + -SOME²] [Scot.] of or for four people, as some games —*n.* **1.** a group of four people, as four people playing golf together **2.** *Golf* a game involving four players, often two to a team

four·square (-skwer′) *adj.* **1.** perfectly square **2.** unyielding; unhesitating; firm **3.** frank; honest; forthright —*adv.* **1.** in a square form; squarely **2.** forthrightly —*n.* [Archaic] a square

☆**four-star** (fôr′stär′) *adj.* **1.** designating a general or admiral whose insignia bears four stars **2.** especially important or good, highly recommended, etc.

four·teen (-tēn′) *adj.* [ME. *fourtene* < OE. *feowertyne*: see FOUR & -TEEN] four more than ten —*n.* the cardinal number between thirteen and fifteen; 14; XIV

four·teenth (-tēnth′) *adj.* [ME. *fourtenthe*, altered (after prec.) < OE. *feowerteotha*] **1.** preceded by thirteen others in a series; 14th **2.** designating any of the fourteen equal parts of something —*n.* **1.** the one following the thirteenth **2.** any of the fourteen equal parts of something; 1/14

fourth (fôrth) *adj.* [ME. *feorthe, ferthe* < OE. *feortha*: see FOUR & -TH²] **1.** preceded by three others in a series; 4th **2.** designating any of the four equal parts of something —*n.* **1.** the one following the third **2.** any of the four equal parts of something; 1/4 **3.** the fourth forward gear ratio of an automotive vehicle **4.** *Music* a) the fourth tone of an ascending diatonic scale, or a tone three degrees above or below any given tone in such a scale; subdominant b) the interval between two such tones, or a combination of them —**fourth′ly** *adv.*

fourth-class (-klas′, -kläs′) *adj.* of the class, rank, excellence, etc. next below the third; specif., ☆designating or of a class of mail consisting of merchandise or printed matter not first-class, second-class, or third-class; parcel post —☆*adv.* as or by fourth-class mail; parcel post

fourth dimension a dimension in addition to the ordinary three-space coordinates of length, width, and depth: in the theory of relativity, time is regarded as the fourth dimension: see SPACE-TIME (sense 1) —**fourth′-di·men′sion·al** *adj.*

fourth estate [see ESTATE (sense 2)] [often F- E-] journalism or journalists

☆**Fourth of July** *see* INDEPENDENCE DAY

Fourth Republic the republic established in France in 1945 and lasting until 1958

four-way (fôr′wā′) *adj.* **1.** giving passage in four directions [a *four-way* valve] **2.** involving four participants or elements [a *four-way* debate]

four-wheel (-hwēl′, -wēl′) *adj.* **1.** having or running on four wheels: also **four′-wheeled′** **2.** affecting four wheels [a *four-wheel* drive] —**four′-wheel′er** *n.*

fou·ter, fou·tre (fōōt′ər) *n.* [< OFr. *foutre*, to copulate with < L. *futuere*: for IE. base see BEAT] [Obs.] a fig: euphemism for a strong term of contempt

fo·ve·a (fō′vē ə) *n., pl.* **fo′ve·ae′** (-ē), -ve·as [ModL. < L.] **1.** *Biol.* a small pit, hollow, or depression **2.** *same as* FOVEA CENTRALIS —**fo′ve·al** (-əl), **fo′ve·ate** (-it, -āt′) *adj.* —**fo′ve·i·form′** (-ə fôrm′) *adj.*

fovea cen·tra·lis (sen trā′lis) a rodless depression toward the center of the retina in some vertebrates, the point where the vision is most acute

fo·ve·o·la (fə vē′ə lə) *n., pl.* -**lae** (-lē′), -**las** [ModL., dim. of *fovea*] a small fovea, or pit: also **fo·ve·ole** (fō′vē ōl′) —**fo·ve′o·late** (-lit, -lāt′), **fo·ve·o·lat·ed** (fō′vē ə lāt′id) *adj.*

fowl (foul) *n., pl.* **fowls, fowl:** see PLURAL, II, D, 1 [ME. *foule, foghel* < OE. *fugol*, akin to G. *vogel*, bird] **1.** orig., any bird: now only in combination [wild *fowl*] **2.** any of the larger domestic birds used as food; specif., a) the chicken b) the duck, goose, turkey, etc. c) a full-grown chicken, as distinguished from a springer, etc. **3.** the flesh of any of these birds used for food —*vi.* to catch, trap, hunt, or shoot wild birds for food or sport —**fowl′ing** *n.*

Fow·ler (fou′lər), **H(enry) W(atson)** 1858–1933; Eng. lexicographer and arbiter of linguistic usage

fowling piece a type of shotgun for hunting wild fowl

Fox (fäks) *n.* [transl. of *wagosh*, lit., red fox, tribal name of one of their clans] ☆**1.** any member of a tribe of N. American Indians formerly living in Wisconsin and later merging with the Sauk ☆**2.** the Algonquian language of the Fox, Sauk, and Kickapoo peoples

fox (fäks) *n., pl.* **fox′es, fox:** see PLURAL, II, D, 1 [ME. < OE., akin to G. *fuchs* < Gmc. base *fuh-*; prob. < IE. base *puk-*, thick-haired, bushy, whence Sans. *púccha*, tail] **1.** any of a group of small, wild, flesh-eating mammals (genera *Vulpes, Urocyon*, etc.) of the dog family, with bushy tails and, commonly, reddish-brown or gray fur: the fox is conventionally thought of as sly and crafty: see also RED FOX, SILVER FOX, ARCTIC FOX **2.** the fur of a fox **3.** a sly, crafty, deceitful person **4.** *Naut.* a strand of ropes twisted together **5.** [Obs.] a kind of sword —*vt.* **1.** to make (beer, etc.) sour by fermenting **2.** [from the color of a fox] to stain (book leaves, prints, etc.) with reddish-brown or yellowish discolorations **3.** to trick or deceive by slyness or craftiness **4.** to bewilder or baffle **5.** a) to repair (boots, shoes, etc.) with new upper leather b) to trim (the upper of a shoe) with leather **6.** [Obs.] to intoxicate —*vi.* **1.** to become sour: said of beer, etc. **2.** to become stained: said of book leaves, etc. —**foxed** *adj.*

FOX (average length 42 in., including tail)

Fox (fäks) **1. Charles James,** 1749–1806; Eng. statesman & orator **2. George,** 1624–91; Eng. religious leader: founder of the Society of Friends

Foxe Basin (fäks) arm of the Atlantic Ocean, in NE Canada, west of Baffin Island: c. 3,500 sq. mi.

fox fire the luminescence of decaying wood and plant remains, caused by various fungi

fox·glove (fäks′gluv′) *n.* [ME. *foxes glove* < OE. *foxes glofa*, fox's glove] any of a genus (*Digitalis*) of plants: see DIGITALIS (sense 1)

☆**fox grape** a common wild grape (*Vitis labrusca*) of the grape family, native to E N. America with leaves whose undersides are covered with whitish or reddish woolly hairs: it is the parent of many American vineyard grapes, as the Concord and Catawba

fox·hole (-hōl′) *n.* a hole dug in the ground as a temporary protection for one or two soldiers against enemy gunfire or tanks

fox·hound (-hound′) *n.* any of a breed of hound having great strength and speed and a keen scent: they are bred and trained to hunt foxes and other game

fox hunt a sport in which hunters on horses ride after dogs in pursuit of a fox —**fox′-hunt′** *vi.*

FOXGLOVE

fox·ing (fäk′sin) *n.* [see FOX, *v.*] a piece of leather for repairing or decorating the upper of a shoe

☆**fox snake** a common, harmless snake (*Elaphe vulpina*), with a yellowish background color and a series of dark blotches on the back

☆**fox squirrel** any of several large, variously colored tree squirrels (*Sciurus niger*) of E N. America

fox·tail (fäks′tāl′) *n.* **1.** the tail, or brush, of a fox **2.** any of various grasses (esp. genus *Setaria*) having cylindrical spikes bearing spikelets interspersed with stiff bristles

foxtail lily *a common name for* EREMURUS

☆**foxtail millet** a cultivated annual grass (*Setaria italica*) with dense, lobed, bristly spikes containing small grains, grown in Eurasia for grain and forage and in America mainly for birdseed

fox terrier any of a breed of small, active terriers with a smooth or wire-haired coat, usually white with dark patches: they were formerly trained to drive foxes out of hiding

☆**fox trot 1.** a slow gait in which a horse moves its forelegs in a trot and its hind legs in a long-striding pace **2.** a) a dance for couples in 4/4 time with a variety of steps, both fast and slow b) the music for such a dance —**fox′-trot′** *vi.*, **-trot′ted, -trot′ting**

fox·y (fäk′sē) *adj.* **fox′i·er, fox′i·est 1.** foxlike; crafty; wily; sly **2.** having the reddish-brown color of a fox **3.** covered with brownish or yellowish stains, as an old book ☆**4.** having the characteristic flavor of fox grapes: said of certain wines —*SYN.* see SLY —**fox′i·ly** *adv.* —**fox′i·ness** *n.*

foy (foi) *n.* [MDu. *foy, fooi, voye*, prob. < OFr. *voie* < L. *via*, way, journey: see VIA] [Now Chiefly Scot.] **1.** a feast, present, etc. given by or to a person departing on a journey **2.** a feast at the end of a harvest or fishing season

foy·er (foi′ər, foi′ā, foi yā′) *n.* [orig., greenroom of a theater < Fr., hearth, lobby < ML. *focarius* < L. *focus*, hearth: see FOCUS] an entrance hall or lobby, esp. in a theater, hotel, or apartment house

fp *Music* fortepiano

F.P., f.p. 1. fireplug **2.** *Insurance* a) fire policy b) floating policy **3.** *Music* fortepiano **4.** fully paid

F.P., f.p., fp foot-pound(s)

f.p., fp, fp. freezing point

FPC Federal Power Commission

fpm, f.p.m. feet per minute

FPO *U.S. Navy* Fleet Post Office

fps, f.p.s. 1. feet per second **2.** foot-pound-second **3.** *Photog.* frames per second

Fr *Chem.* francium

Fr. 1. [L. *frater*] Brother 2. Father 3. France 4. *Frau* 5. French 6. Friar 7. Friday

fr. 1. fragment 2. franc(s) 3. frequent 4. from

Fra (frä) *n.* [It., abbrev. of *frate* < L. *frater*, BROTHER] brother: title given to an Italian friar or monk

fra·cas (frā′kəs, frak′əs; *Brit.* frak′ä) *n.* [Fr. < It. *fracasso* < *fracassare*, to smash, prob. blend < *frangere* (< L.: see ff.) + *cassare*, to quash, break < L. *quassare*: see QUASH²] a noisy fight or loud quarrel; brawl

frac·tion (frak′shən) *n.* [ME. < L. *fractio*, a breaking < pp. of *frangere*, BREAK¹] 1. a breaking or dividing: now only of the Eucharistic bread 2. *a)* a small part broken off; fragment; scrap *b)* a small part, amount, degree, etc.; portion 3. *Chem.* a part separated by fractional crystallization, distillation, etc. 4. *Math. a)* an indicated quotient of two whole numbers, as 13/4, 2/5 *b)* any quantity expressed in terms of a numerator and denominator, as $3x/y+2$ —*vt.* to separate into fractions —*SYN.* see PART

frac·tion·al (-əl) *adj.* 1. of or forming a fraction or fractions 2. very small; unimportant; insignificant 3. *Chem.* designating or of any of various processes for separating the constituents of a mixture by taking advantage of differences in their solubility, boiling points, etc. *[fractional distillation]* Also **frac′tion·ar′y** (-er′ē) —**frac′tion·al·ly** *adv.*

☆**fractional currency** small coins or paper money of a denomination less than the standard monetary unit *[dimes and pennies are fractional currency]*

frac·tion·al·ize (-ə līz′) *vt.* -ized′, -iz′ing to divide into fractions, or parts: also **frac′tion·ize′**, -ized′, -iz′ing —**frac′tion·al·i·za′tion**, **frac′tion·i·za′tion** *n.*

frac·tion·ate (-āt′) *vt.* -at′ed, -at′ing 1. to separate into fractions, or parts 2. *Chem.* to separate into fractions by crystallization, distillation, etc. —**frac′tion·a′tion** *n.*

frac·tious (frak′shəs) *adj.* [prob. < FRACTION (in obs. sense "discord") + -OUS] 1. hard to manage; unruly; rebellious; refractory 2. peevish; irritable; cross —**frac′tious·ly** *adv.* —**frac′tious·ness** *n.*

frac·ture (frak′chər) *n.* [ME. < OFr. < L. *fractura*, a breaking, breach, cleft < pp. of *frangere*, BREAK¹] 1. a breaking or being broken 2. a break, crack, or split 3. a break in a bone or, occasionally, a tear in a cartilage: see also COMPOUND FRACTURE 4. the texture of the broken surface of a mineral as distinct from its cleavage —*vt.*, *vi.* -tured, -tur·ing 1. to break, crack, or split 2. to break up; disrupt —*SYN.* see BREAK¹ —**frac′tur·al** *adj.*

frac·tus (frak′təs) *n.* [L., pp. of *frangere*, BREAK¹] a species of cumulus clouds (**cumulus fractus**) or stratus clouds (**stratus fractus**) in which they have a ragged, shredded appearance

frae (frā) *prep.* [Scot.] from

frae·num (frē′nəm) *n.*, *pl.* -nums, -na (-nə) *same as* FRENUM

frag·ile (fraj′′l; *chiefly Brit. & Canad.*, -īl) *adj.* [< OFr. < L. *fragilis* < *frangere*, BREAK¹] easily broken, shattered, damaged, or destroyed; frail; delicate —**fra·gil·i·ty** (frə jil′ə tē) *n.*

SYN.—**fragile** implies such delicacy of structure as to be easily broken *[a fragile china teacup]*; **frangible** adds to this the connotation of liability to being broken because of the use to which the thing is put *[the handle on this axe seems frangible]*; **brittle** implies such inelasticity as to be easily broken or shattered by pressure or a blow *[the bones of the body become brittle with age]*; **crisp** suggests a desirable sort of brittleness, as of fresh celery or soda crackers; **friable** is applied to something that is easily crumbled or crushed into powder *[friable rock]* —*ANT.* tough, sturdy

frag·ment (frag′mənt; *for v.*, *also* frag ment′) *n.* [ME. < L. *fragmentum* < *frangere*, BREAK¹] 1. a part broken away from a whole; broken piece 2. a detached, isolated, or incomplete part *[a fragment of a song]* 3. the part that exists of a literary or other work left unfinished —*vt.*, *vi.* to break into fragments; break up —*SYN.* see PART —**frag′ment·ed** *adj.*

frag·men·tal (frag men′t'l) *adj.* 1. *same as* FRAGMENTARY 2. *Geol.* designating or of rocks formed of the fragments of rocks that had existed previously; clastic —**frag·men′tal·ly** *adv.*

frag·men·tar·y (frag′mən ter′ē) *adj.* consisting of fragments; not complete; disconnected —**frag′men·tar′i·ly** *adv.* —**frag′men·tar′i·ness** *n.*

frag·men·tate (frag′mən tāt′) *vt.*, *vi.* -tat′ed, -tat′ing to break into fragments —**frag′men·ta′tion** *n.*

fragmentation bomb a bomb that scatters in broken, jagged pieces over a wide area when it explodes

frag·ment·ize (frag′mən tīz′) *vt.*, *vi.* -ized′, -iz′ing to break into fragments —**frag′ment·i·za′tion** *n.*

Fra·go·nard (frȧ gō nȧr′), **Jean Ho·no·ré** (zhän ô nô rā′) 1732–1806; Fr. painter

fra·grance (frā′grəns) *n.* [L. *fragrantia*] 1. the quality of being fragrant 2. a sweet smell; pleasant odor Also [Now Rare] **fra′gran·cy**, *pl.* -cies

fra·grant (frā′grənt) *adj.* [ME. < L. *fragrans* (gen. *fragrantis*), prp. of *fragrare*, to emit a (sweet) smell < IE. base *bhrag-*, to smell, whence OHG. *braccho*, bloodhound]

having a pleasant odor; sweet-smelling —**fra′grant·ly** *adv.*

frail¹ (frāl) *adj.* [ME. *frele* < OFr. *frele* < L. *fragilis*, FRAGILE] 1. easily broken, shattered, damaged, or destroyed; fragile; delicate 2. slender and delicate; not robust; weak 3. easily tempted to do wrong; morally weak —☆*n.* [Slang] a woman or girl —*SYN.* see WEAK —**frail′ly** *adv.* —**frail′ness** *n.*

frail² (frāl) *n.* [ME. *fraiel* < OFr. *frael*, rush basket < ML. *fraellum* < L. *flagellum*, young branch, whip: see FLAGELLUM] 1. a basket made of rushes, for packing figs, raisins, etc. 2. the quantity of raisins, etc. packed in such a basket, varying from 50 to 75 pounds

frail·ty (frāl′tē) *n.* [ME. *frelete* < OFr. *frailetē* < L. *fragilitas*, fragility] 1. the quality or condition of being frail; weakness; esp., moral weakness 2. *pl.* -ties any fault or failing arising from such weakness

fraise (frāz) *n.* [Fr., orig., a ruff < *fraiser*, to ruffle] 1. a ruff or high collar of a kind worn esp. in the 16th cent. 2. *Mil.* a barrier consisting of an inclined or horizontal fence of barbed wire, or, formerly, of wooden stakes

‡**fraises des bois** (frez dā bwä′) [Fr.] wild strawberries

frak·tur (fräk toor′) *n.* [G. < L. *fractura* (see FRACTURE): so named from its angular, broken lines] a kind of German black-letter type

fram·be·si·a, **fram·boe·si·a** (fram bē′zhə, -zhē ə) *n.* [ModL. < Fr. *framboise*, raspberry < Frank. *brambasi*, akin to G. *brombeere*: see BRAMBLE & BERRY] *same as* YAWS

‡**fram·boise** (frän bwäz′) *n.* [Fr.: see prec.] raspberry brandy

frame (frām) *vt.* **framed, fram′ing** [ME. *framen* < *frame*, a structure, frame, prob. < ON. *frami*, profit, benefit, akin to *frama*, to further < *fram*, forward (akin to OE. *fram*, FROM); some senses < OE. *framian*, to be helpful: see FURNISH] 1. to shape, fashion, or form, usually according to a pattern; design *[to frame a constitution]* 2. to put together the parts of; construct 3. to put into words; compose; devise; contrive; conceive *[to frame an excuse]* 4. to utter *[his lips framed the words]* 5. to adapt for a particular use; adjust; fit *[a law framed to equalize the tax burden]* 6. to enclose in a border; provide a border for (a mirror, picture, etc.) ☆7. [Colloq.] to falsify evidence, testimony, etc. beforehand in order to make (an innocent person) appear guilty 8. [Obs.] to bring about; cause —*vi.* [Obs.] to proceed or succeed; go —*n.* [ME.: see the *v.*] 1. *a)* formerly, anything made of parts fitted together according to a design *b)* body structure in general; build 2. basic or skeletal structure around which a thing is built and that gives the thing its shape; framework, as of a house 3. *a)* the framework supporting the chassis of an automotive vehicle *b)* same as COLD FRAME *c)* the case or border into which a window, door, etc. is set and which serves as a structural support *d)* a border, often ornamental, surrounding a picture, etc.; also, the picture or other matter inside such a border *e)* [pl.] the framing of a pair of eyeglasses; rims 4. any of various machines built on or in a framework 5. the way that anything is constructed or put together; organization; form 6. a set of circumstances that serve as background to an event 7. mood; humor; temper *[a bad frame of mind]* 8. an established order or system ☆9. [Colloq.] *Baseball* an inning ☆10. [Colloq.] the act of framing (sense 7) 11. *Bowling*, etc. any of the ten divisions of a game, in each of which the pins are set up anew 12. *Linguis.* a syntactic construction with a blank left in it for testing which words will occur there ☆13. *Motion Pictures* each of the small exposures composing a strip of film 14. *Pool a)* the triangular device in which the balls are set up at the beginning of a game *b)* the balls so set up before the break *c)* the period of play required to pocket all the balls 15. *Shipbuilding* any of the transverse structures that form the ribs of a ship's hull and extend from the gunwale to the bilge or to the keel ☆16. *TV* a single scanning of the field of vision by the electron beam —*adj.* ☆having a wooden framework, usually covered with boards *[a frame house]* —**fram′er** *n.*

frame of reference 1. *Math.* the fixed points, lines, or planes from which coordinates are measured 2. the set of ideas, facts, or circumstances within which something exists

☆**frame-up** (-up′) *n.* [Colloq.] 1. a falsifying of evidence, testimony, etc. to make an innocent person seem guilty 2. a surreptitious, underhanded arrangement or scheme made beforehand

frame·work (-wurk′) *n.* 1. a structure, usually rigid, serving to hold the parts of something together or to support something constructed or stretched over or around it; skeletal structure *[the framework of a house]* 2. the basic structure, arrangement, or system 3. *same as* FRAME OF REFERENCE

fram·ing (-iŋ) *n.* 1. the act of a person or thing that frames 2. the way in which something is framed 3. *a)* a frame or framework *b)* a system of frames

Fra·ming·ham (frā′miŋ ham′) [prob. after *Framlingham*, town in England] suburb of Boston, in E Mass.: pop. 64,000

franc (fraŋk) *n.* [Fr. < L. *Francorum rex*, king of the French, device on the coin in 1360] **1.** the monetary unit and a coin of France, Belgium, Switzerland, and Luxembourg: see MONETARY UNITS, table **2.** the monetary unit of various countries formerly ruled by France or Belgium **3.** a unit of money in Morocco, equal to 1/100 dirham

France (frans, fräns) country in W Europe, on the Atlantic & the Mediterranean Sea: 212,821 sq. mi.: pop. 50,620,000; cap. Paris: Fr. name **Ré·pub·lique Fran·çaise** (rä pü blēk⁄ frän sez⁄)

France (frans, fräns), **A·na·tole** (an⁄ə tōl⁄) (pseud. of *Jacques Anatole François Thibault*) 1844–1924; Fr. novelist & literary critic

Fran·ces (fran⁄sis, frän⁄-) [< OFr. fem. form of *Franceis*: see FRANCIS] a feminine name: dim. **Fran, Fannie, Fanny**

Fran·ces·ca (frän ches⁄kä), **Pie·ro del·la** (pye⁄rō del⁄lä) 1420?–92; It. Renaissance painter: also **Piero de·i Fran·ces·chi** (de⁄ē frän ches⁄kē)

Francesca da Ri·mi·ni (dä rē⁄mē nē⁄) 13th-cent. It. woman famous for her adulterous love affair with her brother-in-law, Paolo

Franche-Com·té (fränsh kōn tā⁄) region and former province of E France, on the border of Switzerland

fran·chise (fran⁄chīz) *n.* [ME. < OFr. < *franc,* free: see FRANK¹] **1.** orig., freedom from some restriction, servitude, etc. **2.** *a)* any special right or privilege granted by the government, as to be a corporation, operate a public utility, etc. *b)* the jurisdiction over which this extends **3.** the right to vote; suffrage **4.** the right to market a product or provide a service, often exclusive for a specified area, as granted by a manufacturer or company ☆**5.** the right to own a member team as granted by a league in certain professional sports —*vt.* **-chised, -chis·ing** to grant a franchise to

Fran·cis (fran⁄sis) [OFr. *Franceis* < ML. *Franciscus* < Gmc. *Franco:* see FRANK¹] **1.** a masculine name: dim. *Frank;* equiv. Fr. *François,* Ger. *Franz,* It. *Francesco, Franco,* Sp. *Francisco;* fem. *Frances* **2. Francis I** 1494–1547; king of France (1515–47) **3. Francis II** 1768–1835; last emperor of the Holy Roman Empire (1792–1806) &, as **Francis I,** first emperor of Austria (1804–35)

Fran·cis·can (fran sis⁄kən) *adj.* [< ML. *Franciscus,* Francis] **1.** of Saint Francis of Assisi **2.** designating or of the religious order founded by him in 1209: it is now divided into three independent branches —*n.* any member of this order

Francis Ferdinand 1863–1914; archduke of Austria: his assassination led to the outbreak of World War I: nephew of FRANCIS JOSEPH I

Francis Joseph I 1830–1916; emperor of Austria (1848–1916) and king of Hungary (1867–1916)

Francis of Assisi, Saint (born *Giovanni Bernardone*) 1181?–1226; It. preacher: founder of the Franciscan Order: his day is Oct. 4

Francis of Sales (sālz), **Saint** 1567–1622; Fr. bishop & writer: his day is Jan. 29

Francis Xavier, Saint *see* XAVIER

fran·ci·um (fran⁄sē əm) *n.* [ModL. < FRANCE + -IUM] a radioactive, metallic chemical element of the alkali group, existing in very minute amounts in nature as a decay product of actinium: symbol, Fr; at. wt., 223(?); at. no., 87

Franck (fränk), **Cé·sar** (Auguste) (sā zär⁄) 1822–90; Fr. composer & organist, born in Belgium

Fran·co (fraŋ⁄kō; *Sp.* frän⁄kō), **Fran·cis·co** (fran sis⁄kō; *Sp.* frän thēs⁄kō) 1892– ; Sp. general who led the fascist revolt against the republic; dictator of Spain (1939–)

Fran·co- (fraŋ⁄kō) [ML. < LL. *Francus,* a Frank] *a combining form meaning:* **1.** Frankish **2.** of France or the French [*Francophobe*] **3.** France and; the French and [*Franco-German*]

fran·co·lin (fraŋ⁄kə lin) *n.* [Fr. < It. *francolino*] any of several African and Asiatic partridges (genus *Francolinus*)

Fran·co·ni·a (fraŋ kō⁄nē ə) region of SC Germany, a duchy in the Middle Ages —**Fran·co⁄ni·an** *adj., n.*

Fran·co·phile (fraŋ⁄kə fil⁄) *n.* [FRANCO- + -PHILE] a person who admires or is extremely fond of France, its people, customs, influence, etc. —*adj.* of Francophiles Also **Fran⁄co·phil** (-fil)

Fran·co·phobe (-fōb⁄) *n.* [FRANCO- + -PHOBE] a person who hates or fears France, its people, customs, influence, etc. —*adj.* of Francophobes

Fran·co-Prus·sian War (fraŋ⁄kō prush⁄ən) a war (1870–71) in which Prussia defeated France

‡**franc-ti·reur** (frän tē rër⁄) *n., pl.* **francs-ti·reurs⁄** (frän tē rër⁄) [Fr. < *franc,* free + *tireur,* a gunner < *tirer,* to shoot] any of a group of French irregular soldiers serving as guerrillas, light infantry, etc.

fran·gi·ble (fran⁄jə b'l) *adj.* [ME. < OFr. < ML. *frangibilis* < L. *frangere,* BREAK¹] breakable; fragile —SYN. see FRAGILE —**fran⁄gi·bil⁄i·ty** *n.*

fran·gi·pan·i (fran⁄jə pan⁄-, -pän⁄-) *n., pl.* **-pan⁄i, -pan⁄is** [It. < Marquis *Frangipani* (16th-c. It. nobleman), said to have invented the perfume] **1.** any of several tropical American shrubs and trees (genus *Plumeria*) of the dogbane family, with large, fragrant flowers **2.** a perfume obtained from this flower or like it in scent **3.** a pastry made with ground almonds Also **fran⁄gi·pane⁄** (-pān⁄)

‡**Fran·glais** (frän glā⁄) *n.* [Fr., coined (1964) by René Étiemble, Fr. writer < *Fran(çais),* French + *(An)glais,*

English] English, esp. American, words and phrases adopted into French

Frank (fraŋk) a masculine name: see FRANCIS —*n.* [ME. < OE. *Franca* & < OFr. *Franc* < LL. *Francus:* see ff.] **1.** a member of the Germanic tribes that established the Frankish Empire, which, at its height (beginning of the 9th cent. A.D.), extended over what is now France, Germany, and Italy **2.** any European, esp. western European: term used in the Near East

frank¹ (fraŋk) *adj.* [ME. < OFr. *franc,* free, frank < ML. *francus* < LL. *Francus,* a Frank, hence free man (i.e., member of the ruling race in Gaul) < Gmc. *Frank* (whence OHG. *Franco*) < ? or akin to *franco,* a spear, javelin; whence OE. *franca,* ON. *frakka*] **1.** formerly, free in giving; generous; liberal **2.** open and honest in expressing what one thinks or feels; straightforward; candid **3.** free from reserve, disguise, or guile; clearly evident; plain [*showing frank distaste*] —*vt.* **1.** *a)* to send (mail) free of postage, as by virtue of an official position *b)* to mark (mail) as with one's signature so that it can be sent free **2.** to make easy the passage of (a person); allow to pass freely **3.** to make exempt or immune —*n.* **1.** the privilege of sending mail free **2.** a mark or signature on mail indicating this privilege **3.** any letter, etc. sent free in this way —**frank⁄ness** *n.*

SYN.—frank applies to a person, remark, etc. that is free or blunt in expressing the truth or an opinion, unhampered by conventional reticence [*a frank criticism*]; **candid** implies a basic honesty that makes deceit or evasion impossible, sometimes to the embarrassment of the listener [*a candid opinion*]; **open** implies a lack of concealment and often connotes an ingenuous quality [*her open admiration for him*]; **outspoken** suggests a lack of restraint or reserve in speech, esp. when reticence might be preferable

☆**frank²** (fraŋk) *n.* [Colloq.] a frankfurter

Frank. Frankish

Frank·en·stein (fraŋ⁄kən stīn⁄) the title character in a novel (1818) by Mary Wollstonecraft SHELLEY: he is a young medical student who creates a monster that destroys him —*n.* **1.** any person destroyed by his own creation **2.** *a)* popularly, Frankenstein's monster *b)* anything that becomes dangerous to its creator

Frank·fort (fraŋk⁄fərt) **1.** [orig. *Frank's Ford,* after Stephen *Frank,* a pioneer killed there] capital of Ky., in the NC part: pop. 21,000 **2.** *same as* FRANKFURT

Frank·furt (fraŋk⁄fərt; *G.* fräŋk⁄foort) **1.** city in C West Germany, on the Main River: pop. 688,000: also **Frankfurt am Main 2.** city in E East Germany, on the Oder River: pop. 57,000: also **Frankfurt an der Oder**

Frank·furt·er (fraŋk⁄fər tər), **Felix** 1882–1965; U.S. jurist, born in Austria; associate justice, U.S. Supreme Court (1939–62)

☆**frank·furt·er, frank·fort·er** (fraŋk⁄fər tər) *n.* [G., after FRANKFURT (AM MAIN)] a smoked sausage of beef or beef and pork, etc., usually enclosed in a membranous casing and made in cylindrical links a few inches long; wiener: also **frank⁄furt, frank⁄fort**

frank·in·cense (fraŋ⁄kən sens⁄) *n.* [ME. < OFr. *franc encens:* see FRANK¹ & INCENSE¹] a gum resin obtained from various Arabian and NE African trees (genus *Boswellia*) of a family (Burseraceae), and often burned as incense

Frank·ish (fraŋ⁄kish) *adj.* of the Franks, their language, or culture —*n.* the West Germanic language of the Franks

Frank·lin¹ (fraŋk⁄lin) [see FRANKLIN] **1.** a masculine name **2. Benjamin,** 1706–90; Am. statesman, scientist, inventor, & writer **3. Sir John,** 1786–1847; Eng. arctic explorer

Frank·lin² (fraŋk⁄lin) [see ff.] N district of the Northwest Territories, Canada, including the arctic islands: 549,253 sq. mi.; pop. 6,000

frank·lin (fraŋk⁄lin) *n.* [ME. *frankelein* < Anglo-Fr. *fraunkelain* < ML. *francelengus* < *francus* (see FRANK¹) + Gmc. *-ling* (see -LING¹)] a freeholder; specif., in England in the 14th and 15th cent., a landowner of free but not noble birth, ranking just below the gentry

☆**frank·lin·ite** (fraŋ⁄klə nīt⁄) *n.* [after *Franklin,* borough in N.J., where it is found] an oxide of iron, manganese, and zinc

☆**Franklin stove** a cast-iron heating stove resembling an open fireplace, invented by Benjamin Franklin

frank·ly (fraŋk⁄lē) *adv.* **1.** in a frank manner **2.** to be frank; in truth [*frankly,* he's a bore]

frank·pledge (fraŋk⁄plej⁄) *n.* [ME. *frank-plege* < Anglo-Fr. *fraunc plege* (see FRANK¹ & PLEDGE): prob. orig. a mistransl. of OE. *frith-borh,* lit., peace pledge] **1.** the system in old English law which made each man in a tithing responsible for the actions of other members **2.** a member under this system **3.**

fran·se·ri·a (fran sir⁄ē ə) *n.* [ModL., after Antonio *Franseri,* 18th-c. Sp. botanist] ☆any of a genus (*Franseria*) of W American plants of the composite family

fran·tic (fran⁄tik) *adj.* [ME. *frantik, frenetik:* see PHRENET-IC] **1.** wild with anger, pain, worry, etc.; frenzied **2.** marked by frenzy; resulting from wild emotion **3.** [Archaic] insane —**fran⁄ti·cal·ly** *or* [Rare] **fran⁄tic·ly** *adv.*

FRANKLIN STOVE

Franz Jo·sef I (fränts yō′zef; *E.* fränts jō′zəf) *Ger. name of* FRANCIS JOSEPH I

Franz Josef Land group of islands of the U.S.S.R., in the Arctic Ocean, north of Novaya Zemlya: c. 8,000 sq. mi.

frap (frap) *vt.* **frapped, frap′ping** [ME. *frapen* < OFr. *fraper,* to strike] *Naut.* to pass ropes, cables, etc. around in order to strengthen, support, steady, etc.

☆**frap·pé** (fra pā′) *adj.* [Fr., pp. of *frapper,* to strike] partly frozen; iced; cooled —*n.* **1.** a dessert made of partly frozen beverages, fruit juices, etc. **2.** a drink made of some beverage poured over shaved ice **3.** [Eastern] a milk shake Also, esp. for *n.* 3, **frappe** (frap)

Fra·ser (frā′zər) river in British Columbia, Canada, flowing southward into the Strait of Georgia: 850 mi.

☆**frat** (frat) *n.* [Colloq.] a fraternity, as at a college

fra·ter¹ (frāt′ər) *n.* [ME. *freitour* < Anglo-Fr. *fraitur,* altered < OFr. *refreitor, refeitor* < ML. *refectorium*] [Obs.] the eating room, or refectory, in a monastery

fra·ter² (frāt′ər, frät′ər) *n.* [L., lit., BROTHER] **1.** a comrade, as a fraternity brother **2.** [Obs.] a friar

fra·ter·nal (frə tur′n'l) *adj.* [ME. < ML. *fraternalis* < L. *fraternus,* brotherly < *frater,* BROTHER] **1.** of or characteristic of a brother or brothers; brotherly **2.** of or like a fraternal order or a fraternity **3.** designating twins, of either the same or different sexes, developed from separately fertilized ova and thus having hereditary characteristics not necessarily the same: distinguished from IDENTICAL —**fra·ter′nal·ism** *n.* —**fra·ter′nal·ly** *adv.*

☆**fraternal order** (or **society, association**) a society, often secret, of members banded together for mutual benefit or for work toward a common goal

fra·ter·ni·ty (frə tur′nə tē) *n., pl.* **-ties** [ME. *fraternite* < OFr. *fraternité* < L. *fraternitas* < *fraternus:* see FRATERNAL] **1.** the state or quality of being brothers; fraternal relationship or spirit; brotherliness **2.** a group of men (or, rarely, women) joined together by common interests, for fellowship, etc.; specif., a Greek-letter college organization **3.** a group of people with the same beliefs, interests, work, etc. [the medical *fraternity*]

frat·er·nize (frat′ər nīz′) *vi.* **-nized′, -niz′ing** [Fr. *fraterniser* < L. *fraternus:* see FRATERNAL] **1.** to associate in a brotherly manner; be on friendly terms **2.** to have intimate or friendly relations with any of the enemy: said of soldiers occupying enemy territory —*vt.* [Archaic] to bring into fraternal association —**frat′er·ni·za′tion** *n.* —**frat′er·niz′·er** *n.*

frat·ri·cide (frat′rə sīd′) *n.* [Fr. < LL.(Ec.) *fratricidium* < L. *fratricida,* one who kills a brother < *frater,* BROTHER + *caedere,* to kill (see -CIDE)] **1.** *a)* the act of killing one's own brother or sister *b)* the act of killing relatives or fellow-countrymen, as in a civil war **2.** [ME. < OFr. < L. *fratricida*] a person who kills his brother or sister —**frat′ri·ci′dal** (-sīd′'l) *adj.*

‡**Frau** (frou) *n., pl.* **Frau′en** (-ən) [G. < OHG. *frouwa,* mistress < IE. *prōwo-* < base *per-,* beyond, whence FAR, FIRST, FORE] a married woman; wife: used in Germany as a title corresponding to *Mrs.*

fraud (frôd) *n.* [ME. *fraude* < OFr. < L. *fraus* (gen. *fraudis*) < IE. base *dhwer-,* to trick, whence Sans. *dhvárati,* (he) injures] **1.** *a)* deceit; trickery; cheating *b)* *Law* intentional deception to cause a person to give up property or some lawful right **2.** something said or done to deceive; trick; artifice **3.** a person who deceives or is not what he pretends to be; impostor; cheat —*SYN.* see DECEPTION

fraud·u·lent (frô′jə lənt) *adj.* [ME. < OFr. < L. *fraudulentus* < *fraus,* FRAUD] **1.** acting with fraud; deceitful **2.** based on or characterized by fraud **3.** done or obtained by fraud —**fraud′u·lence, fraud′u·len·cy** *n.* —**fraud′u·lent·ly** *adv.*

fraught (frôt) *adj.* [ME. *fraught,* pp. of *fraughten,* to freight < MDu. *vrachten* < *vracht,* a load, FREIGHT] filled, charged, or loaded (*with*) [a life *fraught* with hardship]

‡**Fräu·lein** (froi′līn; *E.* froi′-, frou′-) *n., pl.* **-lein,** *E.* **-leins** [G. < *frau* (see FRAU) + dim. suffix *-lein*] an unmarried woman: used in Germany as a title corresponding to *Miss*

Fraun·ho·fer lines (froun′hō′fər) [after Joseph von *Fraunhofer* (1787–1826), Bavarian optician. who first mapped them accurately] the dark lines visible in the spectrum of the sun or a star

frax·i·nel·la (frak′sə nel′ə) *n.* [ModL., dim. of L. *fraxinus,* ash tree (the leaves resemble those of the ash): for IE. base see BIRCH] *same as* GAS PLANT

fray¹ (frā) *n.* [ME. *frai,* aphetic < *affrai,* AFFRAY] a noisy quarrel or fight; brawl —*vt.* [ME. *fraien*] [Archaic] to frighten —*vi.* [Archaic] to fight or brawl

fray² (frā) *vt., vi.* [ME. *fraien* < OFr. *freier* < L. *fricare,* to rub: see FRICTION] **1.** to make or become worn, ragged, or raveled by rubbing **2.** to make or become weakened or strained

Fra·zer (frā′zər), Sir **James (George)** 1854–1941; Scot. anthropologist

☆**fra·zil** (ice) (frā′z'l, fraz′'l, frə zil′) [CanadFr. *frasil* < Fr. *fraisil,* charcoal cinders, altered (prob. after *braise,* live coals: see BRAISE) < OFr. *faisil* < VL. *facilis* < L. *fax* (gen. *facis*), a torch < IE. base *bhwok-,* to gleam, glow]

needlelike ice crystals or thin disks of ice, formed in turbulent waters

fraz·zle (fraz′'l) *vt., vi.* **-zled, -zling** [Brit. (*E.* Anglian) dial. & U.S., prob. altered (after FRAY²) < dial. *fazle*] [Colloq.] **1.** to wear or become worn to rags or tatters; fray **2.** to make or become physically or emotionally exhausted —☆*n.* [Colloq.] the state of being frazzled

F.R.C.P. Fellow of the Royal College of Physicians

F.R.C.S. Fellow of the Royal College of Surgeons

freak¹ (frēk) *n.* [Early ModE. < ? OE. *frician,* to dance (whence ME. *freking,* whim, capricious conduct)] **1.** *a)* a sudden fancy; odd notion; whim *b)* an odd or unusual happening **2.** any abnormal animal, person, or plant; monstrosity ☆**3.** [Slang] *a)* a user of a specified narcotic, hallucinogen, etc. [an acid *freak*] *b)* a devotee or buff [a rock *freak*] *c)* *same as* HIPPIE **4.** [Archaic] capriciousness —*adj.* oddly different from what is usual or normal; queer; abnormal —**freak out** [Slang] **1.** to experience, esp. in an extreme way, the mental reactions, hallucinations, etc. induced by a psychedelic drug **2.** to undergo a similar experience without the use of drugs, as at an entertainment in which psychedelic visual and auditory effects are simulated **3.** to become a hippie or act, dress, etc. like one

freak² (frēk) *vt.* [< ?] [Rare] to streak or fleck

freak·ish (frēk′ish) *adj.* **1.** full of or characterized by freaks; whimsical; capricious **2.** having the nature of a freak; odd; queer Also **freak′y** —**freak′ish·ly** *adv.* —**freak′ish·ness** *n.*

freak-out (-out′) *n.* [Slang] the act or an instance of freaking out

☆**freak show** an exhibit of freaks, as in a carnival sideshow

freck·le (frek′'l) *n.* [ME. *frekel,* altered < *frakene* < Scand., as in Norw. dial. *frokle,* freckle & Norw. *frekna,* Dan. *fregne,* Sw. *fräkne,* ON. *freknōttr,* freckled < IE. base *(s)p(h)ereg-,* to strew, sprinkle, whence SPRINKLE, L. *spargere,* to strew] a small, brownish spot on the skin, esp. as a result of exposure to the sun —*vt.* **-led, -ling** to cause freckles to appear on —*vi.* to become spotted with freckles —**freck′led, freck′ly** *adj.*

Fre·da (frē′də) a feminine name: see FRIEDA

Fred·er·i·ca (fred′ə rē′kə, fred′ə rē′kə) [see FREDERICK] a feminine name

Fred·er·ick (fred′rik, ər ik) [Fr. *Frédéric* < G. *Friedrich* < OHG. *Fridurih* < Gmc. **frithu-,* peace (< *fri-,* to love, protect + *-thu-,* substantive particle) + **rik-,* king, ruler (akin to L. *rex,* G. *reich*)] **1.** a masculine name: dim. *Fred;* equiv. Fr. *Frédéric,* Ger. *Friedrich, Fritz,* It. & Sp. *Federico;* fem. *Frederica:* also **Frederic, Fredric, Fredrick 2. Frederick I** *a)* 1123?–90; king of Germany (1152–90) & emperor of the Holy Roman Empire (1155–90): called *Frederick Barbarossa b)* 1657–1713; 1st king of Prussia (1701–13) &, as **Frederick III,** elector of Brandenburg (1688–1701): son of FREDERICK WILLIAM **3. Frederick II** *a)* 1194–1250; emperor of the Holy Roman Empire (1215–50); king of Two Sicilies (1197–1250) *b) same as* FREDERICK THE GREAT **4. Frederick III** 1463–1525; elector of Saxony (1486–1525): protector of Luther after the diet at Worms **5. Frederick IX** 1899– ; king of Denmark (1947–)

Fred·er·icks·burg (fred′riks burg′) [after *Frederick* Louis (1707–51), father of GEORGE III] city in NE Va., on the Rappahannock: scene of a Civil War battle (Dec., 1862) in which Confederate forces were victorious: pop. 14,000

Frederick the Great 1712–86; king of Prussia (1740–86): son of FREDERICK WILLIAM I

Frederick William 1. 1620–88; elector of Brandenburg (1640–88): called *the Great Elector* **2. Frederick William I** 1688–1740; king of Prussia (1713–40) **3. Frederick William II** 1744–97; king of Prussia (1786–97) **4. Frederick William III** 1770–1840; king of Prussia (1797–1840)

Fred·er·ic·ton (fred′ə rik tən) capital of New Brunswick, Canada, on the St. John River: pop. 22,000

Fred·er·iks·berg (fred′ə riks burg′; *Dan.* freth′ə rēks berkh′) borough on Zealand island, Denmark: suburb of Copenhagen: pop. 114,000

free (frē) *adj.* **fre′er, free′est** [ME. *fre* < OE. *freo,* not in bondage, noble, glad, illustrious, akin to G. *frei* < IE. base **prei-,* to be fond of, hold dear, whence Sans. *priyá-,* dear, desired & FRIEND] **1.** *a)* not under the control of some other person or some arbitrary power; able to act or think without compulsion or arbitrary restriction; having liberty; independent *b)* characterized by or resulting from liberty **2.** *a)* having, or existing under, a government that does not impose arbitrary restrictions on the right to speak, assemble, petition, vote, etc.; having civil and political liberty [a *free* people] *b)* not under control of a foreign government **3.** able to move in any direction; not held, as in chains, etc.; not kept from motion; loose **4.** not held or confined by a court, the police, etc.; acquitted **5.** not held or burdened by obligations, debts, discomforts, etc.; unhindered; unhampered [*free* from pain] **6.** at liberty; allowed [*free* to leave at any time] **7.** not confined to the usual rules or patterns; not limited by convention or tradition [*free* verse] **8.** not literal; not exact [a *free* translation] **9.** not held or confined by prejudice or bias **10.** not restricted by anything except its own limitations or nature [*free* will] **11.** not

busy or not in use; available for other work, use, etc.
12. readily done or made; spontaneous [a *free offer*] 13. not constrained or stilted; easy and graceful [a *free gait*] 14. *a*) generous; liberal; lavish [a *free spender*] *b*) profuse; copious 15. frank; straightforward 16. too frank or familiar in speech, action, etc.; forward; indecorous 17. with no charge or cost; gratis [a *free ticket*] 18. not liable to (trade restrictions, etc.); exempt from certain impositions, as taxes or duties 19. clear of obstructions; open and unimpeded [a *free road ahead*] 20. open to all; esp., without restrictions as to trade [a *free market, free port*] 21. not in contact or connection; not fastened [the *free* end of a rope] 22. not united; not combined [*free* oxygen] 23. not opposed; favoring: said of a wind blowing from a direction more than six points from straight ahead 24. *Linguis.* *a*) occurring at the end of a syllable: said of a vowel *b*) designating a minimum form, or morpheme, that occurs as a word (Ex.: *boy* is a *free* form, but *-s* in *boys* is not): opposed to BOUND² —*adv.* 1. without cost or payment 2. in a free manner; without obstruction, burden, obligation, etc. 3. *Naut.* with a favorable wind —*vt.* **freed, free′ing** to make free; specif., *a*) to release from bondage or arbitrary power, authority, obligation, etc. *b*) to clear of obstruction, entanglement, etc.; disengage —**for free** [Colloq.] without cost or payment; gratis —**free and easy** not constrained by formality or conventionality; informal; unceremonious —**free from** (or **of**) 1. lacking; without 2. released or removed from 3. beyond; outside of —**give** (or **have**) **a free hand** to give (or have) liberty to act according to one's judgment —**make free with** 1. to use or treat as if one owned; use freely 2. to take liberties with —**set free** to cause to be free; release; liberate —**with a free hand** with generosity; lavishly —**free′ly** *adv.* —**free′ness** *n.*
SYN.—**free** is the general term meaning to set loose from any sort of restraint, entanglement, burden, etc. [to *free* a convict, one's conscience, etc.]; **release**, more or less interchangeable with **free**, stresses a setting loose from confinement, literally or figuratively [*release* me from my promise]; **liberate** emphasizes the state of liberty into which the freed person or thing is brought [to *liberate* prisoners of war]; **emancipate** refers to a freeing from the bondage of slavery or of social institutions or conventions regarded as equivalent to slavery [*emancipated* from medieval superstition]; **discharge**, in this connection, implies a being permitted to leave that which confines or restrains [*discharged* at last from the army] —**ANT. restrain, bind, confine**

free alongside ship (or **vessel**) delivered by ship to the dock with freight charges paid by the shipper

free association *Psychoanalysis* the technique of having the patient talk spontaneously, expressing without inhibition whatever ideas, memories, etc. come to mind: used to discover and clarify repressed material

☆**free·bie, free·by** (frē′bē) *n., pl.* **-bies** [arbitrary extension of FREE] [Slang] something given or gotten free of charge, as a complimentary theater ticket

free·board (-bôrd′) *n.* the height of a ship's side from the main deck or gunwale to the waterline

free·boot (-boot′) *vi.* [back-formation < ff.] to act as a freebooter

free·boot·er (-boot′ər) *n.* [Du. *vrijbuiter* < *vrijbuiten*, to plunder < *frij*, free + *buit*, plunder] a plunderer; pirate; buccaneer

free·born (-bôrn′) *adj.* 1. born free, not in slavery or serfdom 2. of or fit for a person so born

free city a city that is an autonomous and independent state, as Hamburg and Bremen in the Middle Ages

☆**free coinage** the system by which a government is legally required to coin for a person, either free or at cost, any gold, silver, etc. that he brings to the mint

freed·man (frēd′mən) *n., pl.* **-men** (-mən) a man legally freed from slavery or bondage

free·dom (frē′dəm) *n.* [ME. *fredom* < OE. *freodom*: see FREE & -DOM] 1. the state or quality of being free; esp., *a*) exemption or liberation from the control of some other person or some arbitrary power; liberty; independence *b*) exemption from arbitrary restrictions on a specified civil right; civil or political liberty [*freedom* of speech] *c*) exemption or immunity from a specified obligation, discomfort, etc. [*freedom* from want] *d*) exemption or release from imprisonment *e*) a being able to act, move, use, etc. without hindrance or restraint [to have the *freedom* of the house] *f*) a being able of itself to choose or determine action freely [*freedom* of the will] *g*) ease of movement or performance; facility *h*) a being free from the usual rules, patterns, etc. *i*) frankness or easiness of manner; sometimes, an excessive frankness or familiarity 2. a right or privilege
SYN.—**freedom**, the broadest in scope of these words, implies the absence of hindrance, restraint, confinement, repression, etc. [*freedom* of speech]; **liberty**, often interchangeable with **freedom**, strictly connotes past or potential restriction, repression, etc. [civil *liberties*]; **license** implies freedom that consists in violating the usual rules, laws, or practices, either by consent [poetic *license*] or as an abuse of liberty [*slander* is *license* of the tongue] —**ANT. repression, constraint**

freedom of the city honorary citizenship in a city, now merely nominal as given to distinguished visitors

☆**freedom of the press** freedom to publish any opinions in newspapers, magazines, books, etc. without government interference or censorship: usually modified to exclude libel, sedition, and obscenity

freedom of the seas the principle that all merchant ships may freely travel the open seas at any time

☆**Freedom Rider** [*also* **f- r-**] a demonstrator for civil rights who rides a bus, train, etc. to a Southern State to help desegregate transportation facilities

free enterprise the economic doctrine or practice of permitting private industry to operate under freely competitive conditions with a minimum of governmental control

free fall the unchecked fall of a body through the air; specif., the part of a parachutist's jump before the parachute is opened

free flight the flight of a rocket after the fuel supply has been used up or shut off —**free′-flight′** *adj.*

☆**free-for-all** (frē′fər ôl′) *n.* 1. a contest, race, etc. that anyone may enter 2. a disorganized fight in which many take part; brawl —*adj.* open to anyone

free-form (-fôrm′) *adj.* 1. having an irregular, usually curvilinear form or outline 2. not conforming to the conventional rules of composition, form, etc.; spontaneous, unrestrained, etc.

☆**free gold** gold held by the Federal Reserve Banks in excess of minimum reserve requirements

free·hand (-hand′) *adj.* drawn or done by hand without the use of instruments, measurements, etc.

free·hand·ed (-han′did) *adj.* generous; openhanded

free·heart·ed (-här′tid) *adj.* [ME. *frehertet*] frank, open, generous, impulsive, etc.

free·hold (-hōld′) *n.* [ME. *fre holde*, after Anglo-Fr. *franc tenement*] 1. an estate in land held for life or with the right to pass it on through inheritance: distinguished from LEASEHOLD 2. the holding of an estate, office, etc. in this way —*adj.* of or held by freehold —**free′hold′er** *n.*

free-lance (-lans′, -läns′) *adj.* of or acting as a free lance —*vi.* **-lanced′, -lanc′ing** to work as a free lance

free lance 1. a medieval soldier who sold his services to any state or military leader; mercenary 2. a person who acts according to his own principles and is not influenced by any group; independent 3. a writer, actor, etc. who is not under contract for regular work but sells his writings or services to individual buyers: also **free′-lanc′er** *n.*

☆**free list** 1. a list of goods not subject to tariff duties 2. a list of people admitted free

free-liv·ing (-liv′iŋ) *adj.* 1. indulging freely in eating, drinking, and similar pleasures 2. *Biol.* living independently of any other organism; not parasitic or symbiotic —**free liver**

☆**free-load·er** (-lō′dər) *n.* [Colloq.] a person who habitually imposes on others for free food, lodging, etc.; sponger —**free′load′** *vi.* —**free′load′ing** *adj.*

☆**free love** the principle or practice of sexual relations unrestricted by marriage or other legal obligations

free·man (-mən) *n., pl.* **-men** (-mən) [ME. *fre man* < OE. *freomon*] 1. a person not in slavery or bondage 2. a person who has full civil and political rights in a city or state; citizen

free market any market where buying and selling can be carried on without restrictions as to price, etc.

free·mar·tin (-mär′t'n) *n.* [< ?] an imperfectly developed female calf, usually sterile, born as the twin of a male

Free·ma·son (frē′mās′'n) *n.* [< obs. *freemason*, a skilled itinerant mason, free to move from town to town without restraint by local guilds] a member of an international secret society having as its principles brotherliness, charity, and mutual aid: also **Free and Accepted Mason, Mason**

Free·ma·son·ry (-rē) *n.* 1. the principles, rituals, etc. of Freemasons; Masonry 2. the Freemasons 3. [f-] a natural sympathy and understanding among persons with similar experiences

free on board delivered (by the seller) aboard the train, ship, etc. at the point of shipment, without charge to the buyer

Free·port (frē′pôrt′) [from the fact that trading vessels could formerly slip in through Jones' Inlet without paying duty] village in SE N.Y., on Long Island: pop. 40,000

free port 1. a port open equally to ships of all countries 2. a port or zone where goods may be unloaded, stored, and reshipped without payment of customs or duties, if they are not imported: also **free zone**

fre·er (frē′ər) *adj. compar.* of FREE —*n.* a person or thing that frees

free radical an atom or molecule having at least one unpaired electron: free radicals are usually reactive and unstable

free·si·a (frē′zhē ə, -zhə, -zē ə) *n.* [ModL., after F.H.T. *Freese*, 19th-cent. Ger. physician] any of a genus (*Freesia*) of South African bulbous plants of the iris family, with fragrant, usually white or yellow, funnel-shaped flowers

☆**free silver** the free coinage of silver, esp. at a fixed ratio to the gold coined in the same period

☆**Free-Soil** (-soil′) *adj.* [*also* **f- s-**] opposed to the extension of slavery; specif., designating or of a former (1848–54) political party (**Free-Soil Party**) that opposed the spread of slavery into the Territories —**Free′-Soil′er** *n.*

☆**free soil** territory in which there is no slavery; esp., any territory in the U.S. where slavery was prohibited before the Civil War

free-spo·ken (-spō′k'n) *adj.* free in expressing opinions; frank; outspoken

fre·est (-əst) *adj. superl.* of FREE

free·stand·ing (-stan′din) *adj.* resting on its own support, without attachment or added support

Free State ☆any State of the U.S. in which slavery was forbidden before the Civil War

free·stone (-stōn′) *n.* 1. [ME. *fre ston*, after OFr. *fraunche piere*] a stone, esp. sandstone or limestone, that can be cut easily without splitting 2. [FREE + STONE] *a)* a peach, plum, etc. in which the pit does not cling to the pulp of the ripened fruit *b)* such a pit —*adj.* having such a pit

free·swim·ming (-swim′in) *adj.* capable of swimming about freely, as certain protozoans

free·think·er (-thin′kar) *n.* a person who forms his opinions about religion independently of tradition, authority, or established belief —*SYN.* see ATHEIST —**free′think′ing** *n.*, *adj.* —**free thought**

free throw *Basketball* a free, or unhindered, throw at the basket from a designated line (**free-throw line**), allowed to a player as a penalty imposed on the opponents for some rule infraction: each successful throw counts for one point

Free·town (frē′toun′) seaport & capital of Sierra Leone, on the Atlantic: pop. 128,000

free trade 1. trade carried on without governmental regulations; esp., international trade conducted without quotas on imports or exports, protective tariffs, etc. 2. [Archaic] smuggling —**free′trad′er** *n.*

☆**free university** a loosely organized forum for the study in nontraditional ways of subject matter not generally offered in regular university courses

free verse verse characterized by much rhythmic variation, irregular or unusual stanzaic forms, and either no rhyme or a loose rhyme pattern

☆**free·way** (-wā′) *n.* 1. a multiple-lane divided highway with fully controlled access, as by cloverleafs, for intersecting roads 2. a highway without toll charges

free·wheel (-hwēl′, -wēl′) *n.* 1. in a bicycle, a device in the rear hub that permits the rear wheel to go on turning when the pedals are stopped 2. in some automobiles, a device that permits the drive shaft to go on turning when its speed exceeds that of the engine shaft, thus allowing free coasting with the gears engaged

free·wheel·ing (-in) *n.* 1. a freewheel 2. the use of a freewheel —*adj.* 1. of, having, or using a freewheel 2. [Colloq.] unrestrained in manner, actions, etc.; uninhibited —**free′wheel′er** *n.*

free·will (-wil′) *adj.* 1. freely given or done; voluntary 2. of or holding the doctrine of free will

free will 1. freedom of decision or of choice between alternatives 2. *a)* the freedom of the will to choose a course of action without external coercion but in accordance with the ideals or moral outlook of the individual *b)* the doctrine that people have such freedom: cf. DETERMINISM

freeze (frēz) *vi.* **froze, fro′zen, freez′ing** [ME. *fresen* < OE. *freosan*, akin to OHG. *friosan* (G. *frieren*) < IE. base *preus-*, to freeze, burn like cold, whence L. *pruina*, hoarfrost, *pruna*, glowing coals] 1. to be formed into ice; be hardened or solidified by cold 2. to become covered or clogged with ice 3. to be or become very cold 4. to become attached by freezing [wheels *frozen* to the ground] 5. to die or be damaged by exposure to cold ☆6. to become motionless or fixed 7. to be made momentarily speechless or unable to move or act by a strong, sudden emotion [to *freeze* with terror] 8. to become formal, haughty, or unfriendly 9. *Mech.* to stick or become tight as a result of expansion of parts caused by overheating or inadequate lubrication —*vt.* 1. to cause to form into ice; harden or solidify by cold 2. to cover or clog with ice 3. to make very cold; chill 4. to remove sensation from, as with a local anesthetic 5. to preserve (food) by rapid refrigeration 6. to make fixed or attached by freezing 7. to kill or damage by exposure to cold 8. to make or keep motionless or stiff ☆9. to frighten or discourage by cool behavior, unfriendliness, etc. 10. to make formal, haughty, or unfriendly ☆11. *a)* to fix (prices, employment, an employee, etc.) at a given level or place by authoritative regulation *b)* to stop consumer production or use of (a critical material), as in wartime *c)* to make (funds, assets, etc.) unavailable to the owners —*n.* 1. a freezing or being frozen 2. a period of cold, freezing weather; a frost —☆**freeze (on) to** [Colloq.] to cling to; hold fast to —**freeze out** 1. to die out through freezing, as plants ☆2. [Colloq.] to keep out or force out by a cold manner, competition, etc. —**freeze over** to cover or become covered with ice —**freez′a·ble** *adj.*

☆**freeze-dry** (frēz′drī′) *vt.* **-dried′, -dry′ing** to subject (food, vaccines, etc.) to quick-freezing followed by drying under high vacuum at a low temperature: a freeze-dried product, as food, will keep for long periods at room temperature —**freeze′-dry′er** *n.*

freez·er (-ar) *n.* a person or thing that freezes; specif., ☆*a)* a refrigerator, compartment, or room maintaining temperatures at or below 0°F, for freezing and storing perishable foods *b)* a hand-cranked or electrically operated device for making ice cream and sherbet

freezing point the temperature at which a liquid freezes or becomes solid: the freezing point of water under laboratory conditions is 32°F or 0°C

F region the atmospheric zone within the ionosphere between about 125 and 250 miles above the earth, where the F layers are found

Frei·burg (frī′boork) 1. city in SW West Germany, in Baden-Württemberg: pop. 152,000: also **Freiburg im Breis·gau** (im brīs′gou) 2. *Ger. name of* FRIBOURG

freight (frāt) *n.* [ME. *freit, fraught* < MDu. *vracht* (cf. FRAUGHT)] 1. a method or service for transporting goods, esp. bulky goods, by water, land, or air: freight is usually cheaper but slower than express 2. the cost for such transportation 3. the goods transported; lading; cargo ☆4. *same as* FREIGHT TRAIN 5. any load or burden —*vt.* 1. to load with freight 2. to load; burden 3. to transport as or send by freight

freight·age (-ij) *n.* 1. the charge for transporting goods 2. freight; cargo 3. the transportation of goods

☆**freight car** a railroad car for transporting freight

freight·er (-ar) *n.* 1. a person who loads a ship 2. a person who sends goods by freight 3. a person who receives freighted goods and forwards them to their destination ☆4. a ship or aircraft for carrying freight

☆**freight house** a depot where freight is received and stored

☆**freight train** a railroad train made up of freight cars

Fre·man·tle (frē′man t'l) seaport in Western Australia: suburb of Perth: pop. 22,000

frem·i·tus (frem′it as) *n.* [ModL. < L., a roaring < *fremere*, to roar < IE. base *bherem-*, to murmur, whence W. *brefu*, to bray, G. *brummen*, to grumble] *Med.* a vibration, esp. one felt in palpation of the chest

Fre·mont (frē′mänt) [after ff.] city in W Calif., on San Francisco Bay: suburb of Oakland: pop. 101,000

Fré·mont (frē′mänt), **John Charles** 1813–90; U.S. politician, general, & explorer, esp. in the West

French (french) *adj.* [ME. *Frensh* < *Frenisc* < *Franca*, a FRANK] of France, its people, their language, or culture —*n.* the Romance language spoken by the French —*vt.* [often f-] ☆1. to trim the meat from the end of the bone of (a rib chop) ☆2. to cut (string beans) into long, thin slices before cooking —**the French** the people of France

French (french), **Daniel Chester** 1850–1931; U.S. sculptor

☆**French and Indian War** the American phase (1754-63) of the SEVEN YEARS' WAR

French bulldog any of a breed of bulldog developed in France, having a sturdy frame and ears like a bat's

French Canadian ☆1. a Canadian of French ancestry ☆2. *same as* CANADIAN FRENCH

French chalk a very soft soapstone chalk used for marking lines on cloth or removing grease spots

French Community political union (formed in 1958) comprising France, its overseas departments & territories, and six fully independent member states: Central African Republic, Chad, Congo (Brazzaville), Gabon, Malagasy Republic, & Senegal

French cuff a double cuff, as on the sleeve of a shirt, that is turned back on itself and fastened with a link

French doors two adjoining doors that have glass panes from top to bottom and are hinged at opposite sides of a doorway so that they open in the middle

☆**French dressing** a salad dressing made of vinegar, oil, and various seasonings

☆**French endive** *same as* ENDIVE (sense 2)

French Equatorial Africa former federation of French colonies in C Africa

☆**French fry** [often f- f-] to fry in very hot, deep fat until crisp: French fried potatoes (colloquially, **French fries**) are first cut lengthwise into strips

French Guiana French overseas department in NE S. America, on the Atlantic: 35,135 sq. mi.; pop. 36,000; chief town, Cayenne See GUIANA, map

French Guinea Guinea when it was under French control

French heel a curved high heel on a woman's shoe

French horn a brass-wind instrument with three rotary valves and a long, coiled tube ending in a wide, flaring bell: it has a range of 3 1/2 octaves and a mellow tone

French ice cream very rich ice cream made with eggs and cream of high butterfat content

French·i·fy (-ə fī′) *vt., vi.* **-fied′, -fy′ing** to make or become French or like the French in customs, ideas, manners, etc. —**French′i·fi·ca′tion** *n.*

French India former French territory in India, five small settlements mainly on the E coast

French Indochina Indochina when it was under Fr. control

French knot an embroidery stitch formed by twisting the thread around the needle, which is then inserted at nearly the same point it came through the material

FRENCH HORN

French leave [< 18th-c. custom, prevalent in France, of leaving receptions without taking leave of the host or hostess] an unauthorized, unnoticed, or unceremonious departure; act of leaving secretly or in haste

French·man (-mən) *n.*, *pl.* **-men** (-mən) **1.** a native or inhabitant of France, esp. a man **2.** a French ship

French marigold a small, bushy marigold (*Tagetes patula*) of the composite family, with solitary ray flowers whose yellow petals are blotched with red

French Morocco the former (1912–56) French zone of Morocco, making up most of the country: with Spanish Morocco & Tangier, it became the country of Morocco

French pastry rich pastry, usually filled with preserved fruit, whipped cream, etc.

French polish a preparation, usually shellac dissolved in alcohol, applied to furniture for a glossy finish

French Polynesia French overseas territory in the South Pacific, consisting principally of five archipelagoes: 1,545 sq. mi.; pop. 85,000; cap. Papeete: formerly called **French (Settlements in) Oceania**

French Revolution the revolution of the people against the monarchy in France: it began in 1789, resulted in the establishment of a republic, and ended in 1799 with the Consulate under Napoleon

French Revolutionary Calendar the official calendar of the first French republic, adopted in 1793 and abolished in 1805

French seam a narrow seam sewed on both sides of the material to hide the raw edges of the cloth

French Somaliland French overseas territory in E Africa, on the Gulf of Aden: 8,500 sq. mi.; pop. 81,000; cap. Djibouti: official name (since 1967) *French Territory of the Afars and the Issas*: see SOMALILAND, map

French Sudan former French overseas territory in W Africa: since 1960, the republic of Mali

☆**French telephone** an early kind of handset

☆**French toast** sliced bread dipped in a batter of egg and milk and then fried

French Union former political union (1946–58) of France, its overseas departments & territories, & its protectorates & associated states: succeeded by the FRENCH COMMUNITY

French West Africa former French overseas territory in W Africa, including the present countries of Senegal, Mali, Mauritania, Guinea, Ivory Coast, Upper Volta, Dahomey, & Niger

French West Indies two overseas departments of France in the West Indies, including Martinique & Guadeloupe & the dependencies of Guadeloupe

French windows a pair of casement windows designed like French doors and usually extending to the floor

French·wom·an (-woom′ən) *n.*, *pl.* **-wom′en** (-wim′in) a woman who is a native or inhabitant of France

French·y (-ē) *adj.* **French′i·er, French′i·est** of, characteristic of, or like the French —*n.*, *pl.* **French′ies** [Slang] a Frenchman

Fre·neau (fri nō′), **Philip** (**Morin**) 1752–1832; U.S. poet & journalist

fre·net·ic (frə net′ik) *adj.* [see PHRENETIC] frantic; frenzied: also **fre·net′i·cal** —**fre·net′i·cal·ly** *adv.*

fren·u·lum (fren′yoo ləm) *n.*, *pl.* **-lums, -la** (-lə) [ModL., dim. of *frenum*: see ff.] **1.** a small frenum **2.** *Zool.* a stiff bristle or group of bristles extending forward from the hind wing of some moths and interlocking with a hooklike structure on the front wing, linking the wings together in flight

fre·num (frē′nəm) *n.*, *pl.* **-nums, -na** (-nə) [L., lit., a bridle] a fold of skin or mucous membrane that checks or controls the movement of an organ or part, as the fold under the tongue

fren·zy (fren′zē) *n.*, *pl.* **-zies** [ME. *frenesie* < OFr. < ML. *phrenesia* < L. *phrenesis* < LGr. *phrenēsis* < Gr. *phrenitis*, madness, inflammation of the brain < *phrēn*, mind: see PHRENETIC] wild or frantic outburst of feeling or action; specif., brief delirium that is almost insanity —*vt.* **-zied, -zy·ing** to make frantic; drive mad —*SYN.* see MANIA —**fren′zied** *adj.* —**fren′zied·ly** *adv.*

Fre·on (frē′än) [F(LUORINE) + RE(FRIGERANT) + -*on*, as in NEON] *a trademark for* any of a series of gaseous or low-boiling, inert, nonflammable derivatives of methane or ethane: used as refrigerants and solvents, and as propellants in aerosol products

freq. 1. frequent **2.** frequentative **3.** frequently

fre·quen·cy (frē′kwən sē) *n.*, *pl.* **-cies** [ME. < Fr. < L. *frequentia*: see FREQUENT] **1.** orig., *a)* the condition of being crowded *b)* a crowd **2.** the fact of occurring often or repeatedly; frequent occurrence **3.** the number of times any action or occurrence is repeated in a given period **4.** *Math. & Statistics a)* the number of times an event, value, or characteristic occurs in a given period *b)* the ratio of the number of times a characteristic occurs to the number of trials in which it can potentially occur **5.** *Physics* the number of periodic oscillations, vibrations, or waves per unit of time: usually expressed in cycles per second Also **fre′quence** (-kwəns)

frequency distribution a grouping of the possible values of a variable into broader classifications to indicate the frequency with which the values in a particular interval occur

frequency modulation 1. the variation of the instantane-

ous frequency of a carrier wave in accordance with the signal to be transmitted **2.** the system of radio broadcasting or transmission that uses such modulation Distinguished from AMPLITUDE MODULATION

fre·quent (frē′kwənt; *for v., usually* frē kwent′) *adj.* [ME. < OFr. < L. *frequens* (gen. *frequentis*)] **1.** orig., crowded; filled **2.** occurring often; happening repeatedly at brief intervals **3.** constant; habitual —*vt.* to go to constantly; be at or in habitually [to *frequent* the theater] —**fre·quent′er** *n.*

fre·quen·ta·tion (frē′kwən tā′shən) *n.* [ME. *frequentacioun* < L. *frequentatio* < pp. of *frequentare*] the act or practice of frequenting

fre·quen·ta·tive (frē kwen′tə tiv, frē′kwən-) *adj.* [L. *frequentativus* < *frequentare*, to frequent] *Gram.* expressing frequent and repeated action —*n. Gram.* a frequentative verb: *prickle* is a frequentative of *prick*

fre·quent·ly (frē′kwənt lē) *adv.* at frequent or brief intervals; often

‡**frère** (frer) *n.* [Fr.] **1.** a brother **2.** a friar

fres·co (fres′kō) *n.*, *pl.* **-coes, -cos** [It., fresh < OHG. *frisc*: see ff.] **1.** the art or technique of painting with water colors on wet plaster **2.** a painting or design so made —*vt.* to paint in fresco

fresh[1] (fresh) *adj.* [ME. < OE. *fersc*, but altered after OFr. *fres, fresche* < Gmc. *friska* (whence G. *frisch*) & OE. *fersc*] **1.** recently produced, obtained, or grown; newly made [fresh coffee] **2.** having original strength, vigor, quality, taste, etc.; esp., *a)* not salted, preserved, pickled, etc. [fresh meat] *b)* not spoiled, rotten, or stale *c)* not tired; vigorous; lively [to feel *fresh* after a nap] *d)* not worn, soiled, faded, etc.; vivid; bright; clean *e)* youthful or healthy in appearance [a fresh complexion] **3.** not known before; new; recent [fresh information] **4.** additional; further [a fresh start] **5.** *a)* inexperienced; unaccustomed *b)* having just arrived **6.** original, spontaneous, and stimulating [fresh ideas] **7.** cool and refreshing; invigorating [a fresh spring day] **8.** brisk; strong: said of the wind **9.** not salt: said of water **10.** designating or of a cow that has just begun to give milk, as after having borne a calf —*n.* **1.** the fresh part **2.** a freshet **3.** a pool or stream of fresh water —*adv.* in a fresh manner —*vt., vi.* to make or become fresh —*SYN.* see NEW —**fresh out of** [Slang] having just sold or used up —**fresh′ness** *n.*

☆**fresh**[2] (fresh) *adj.* [< G. *frech*, bold, impudent; confused with prec.] [Slang] bold; saucy; impertinent; impudent —**fresh′ly** *adv.* —**fresh′ness** *n.*

fresh breeze a wind whose speed is 19 to 24 miles per hour: see BEAUFORT SCALE

fresh·en (fresh′ən) *vt.* to make fresh, or vigorous, clean, etc. —*vi.* **1.** to become fresh **2.** to increase in strength: said of the wind **3.** to begin to give milk, as a cow after having a calf —**freshen up** to bathe oneself, change into fresh clothes, etc.

fresh·et (-it) *n.* [see FRESH[1] & -ET] **1.** a stream or rush of fresh water flowing into the sea ☆**2.** a sudden overflowing of a stream because of melting snow or heavy rain

fresh gale a wind whose speed is 39 to 46 miles per hour: see BEAUFORT SCALE

fresh·ly (-lē) *adv.* [ME. *freschli*] **1.** in a fresh manner **2.** just now; recently: followed by a past participle [bread *freshly* baked]

fresh·man (-mən) *n.*, *pl.* **-men** (-mən) [FRESH[1] + MAN] **1.** a beginner; novice **2.** a student in the ninth grade in high school, or one in the first year of college ☆**3.** a person in his first year at any enterprise [a *freshman* in Congress] —*adj.* of or for first-year students [the *freshman* English course]

fresh·wa·ter (-wôt′ər, -wät′ər) *adj.* **1.** of or living in water that is not salty **2.** *a)* accustomed to sailing only on rivers or lakes, not on the sea *b)* inexperienced; unskilled **3.** *a)* in or of the hinterland; inland ☆*b)* somewhat provincial, obscure, etc. [a *freshwater* college]

freshwater eel any of a genus (*Anguilla*) of long, snakelike, bony fishes that live in streams, lakes, etc. and migrate to the sea to spawn

Fres·nel (frā nel′), **Au·gus·tin Jean** (ō güs tan′ zhän) 1788–1827; Fr. physicist

Fresnel mirrors *Optics* two plane mirrors linked together at an angle a little less than 180° so that a beam of light falling on them is reflected by these mirrors in slightly different directions, thus producing interference fringes in the area where this reflected light overlaps

Fres·no (frez′nō) [< Sp. *fresno*, ash tree] city in C Calif.: pop. 166,000

fret[1] (fret) *vt.* **fret′ted, fret′ting** [ME. *freten* < OE. *fretan*, to devour, akin to G. *fressen*, Goth. *fra-itan* < Gmc. prefix **fra-* (OE. *for-*: see FOR-) + **itan*, to eat (OE. *etan*: see EAT)] **1.** to eat away; gnaw **2.** to wear away by gnawing, rubbing, corroding, etc. **3.** to make or form by wearing away **4.** to make rough; disturb [wind *fretting* the water] **5.** to irritate; vex; annoy; worry —*vi.* **1.** to gnaw (*into, on,* or *upon*) **2.** to become eaten, corroded, worn, frayed, etc. **3.** to become rough or disturbed **4.** to be irritated, annoyed, or querulous; worry —*n.* **1.** a wearing away **2.** a worn place **3.** irritation; annoyance; worry —**fret′ter** *n.*

fret[2] (fret) *n.* [ME. *frette*, prob. merging of OFr. *frete* (Fr. *frette*), interlaced work, with OE. *frætwa*, ornament (whence ? OFr. *frete*)] **1.** an ornamental net or network, esp. one formerly worn by women as a headdress **2.** an

ornamental pattern of small, straight bars intersecting or joining one another at right angles to form a regular design, as for a border or in an architectural relief —*vt.* **fret′ted, fret′ting** to ornament with a fret

fret³ (fret) *n.* [OFr. *frette*, a band, ferrule] any of several narrow, lateral ridges fixed across the finger board of a banjo, guitar, mandolin, etc. to regulate the fingering —*vt.* **fret′ted, fret′ting** to furnish with frets

FRETS

fret·ful (fret′fəl) *adj.* tending to fret; irritable and discontented; peevish —**fret′ful·ly** *adv.* —**fret′ful·ness** *n.*

fret saw a saw with a long, narrow, fine-toothed blade, for cutting curved patterns in thin boards or metal plates

fret·work (-wurk′) *n.* work ornamented with frets; decorative carving or openwork, as of interlacing lines

Freud (froid), **Sigmund** 1856–1939; Austrian physician & neurologist: founder of psychoanalysis

Freud·i·an (froi′dē ən) *adj.* of or according to Freud or his theories and practice —*n.* a person who believes in Freud's theories or uses Freud's methods in psychoanalysis See PSYCHOANALYSIS —**Freud′i·an·ism** *n.*

Freudian slip a mistake made in speaking by which, it is thought, the speaker inadvertently reveals his true motives, desires, etc.

Frey (frā) *Norse Myth.* the god of crops, fruitfulness, love, peace, and prosperity: also **Freyr** (frer)

Frey·a, Frey·ja (frā′ə) *Norse Myth.* the goddess of love and beauty, sister of Frey

F.R.G.S. Fellow of the Royal Geographical Society

Fri. Friday

fri·a·ble (frī′ə b'l) *adj.* [Fr. < L. *friabilis* < *friare*, to rub, crumble < IE. base *bhrēi-*, to cut, scrape, whence also in Russ. *briti*, to shave, L. *fricare*, to rub] easily crumbled or crushed into powder —*SYN.* see FRAGILE —**fri′a·bil′i·ty, fri′a·ble·ness** *n.*

fri·ar (frī′ər) *n.* [ME. *frer, frier* < OFr. *frere* < L. *frater*, BROTHER] *R.C.Ch.* a member of any of several mendicant orders; esp., an Augustinian, Carmelite, Dominican, or Franciscan —**fri′ar·ly** *adj.*

fri·ar·bird (-burd′) *n.* any of a genus (*Philemon*) of honey eaters of the SW Pacific and Australia that have a naked, featherless head

Friar Minor *pl.* **Friars Minor** a member of the branch of the Franciscan Order that follows the original rule: see CAPUCHIN, CONVENTUAL

friar's lantern *same as* IGNIS FATUUS

fri·ar·y (-ē) *n.*, *pl.* **-ar·ies** 1. a place where friars live; monastery 2. a brotherhood of friars

frib·ble (frib′'l) *adj.* [altered < ? Fr. *frivole* (cf. FRIVOLOUS)] of little importance; trifling —*n.* 1. a person who wastes time 2. any trifling act or thought —*vi.* **frib′bled, frib′bling** to waste time; trifle —**fribble away** to use wastefully

Fri·bourg (frē boor′) canton of WC Switzerland: 645 sq. mi.; pop. 161,000

fric·an·deau (frik′ən dō′) *n.*, *pl.* **-deaux** (-dōz′) [Fr., irreg. < ? ff.] meat, esp. veal, larded and roasted or braised

fric·as·see (frik′ə sē′, frik′ə sē′) *n.* [Fr. *fricassée*, fem. pp. of *fricasser*, to cut up and fry] a dish consisting of meat cut into pieces, stewed or fried, and served in a sauce of its own gravy —*vt.* **-seed′, -see′ing** to prepare (meat) by this method

fric·a·tive (frik′ə tiv) *adj.* [< L. *fricatus*, pp. of *fricare* (see FRICTION) + -IVE] pronounced by forcing the breath, either voiced or voiceless, through a narrow slit formed at some point in the mouth, as *f, v, z* —*n.* a fricative consonant

Frick (frik), **Henry Clay** 1849–1919; U.S. industrialist & philanthropist

fric·tion (frik′shən) *n.* [Fr. < L. *frictio* < pp. of *fricare*, to rub: see FRIABLE] 1. a rubbing, esp. of one object against another 2. disagreement or conflict because of differences of opinion, temperament, etc. 3. *Mech.* the resistance to motion of two moving objects or surfaces that touch — **fric′tion·less** *adj.*

fric·tion·al (-əl) *adj.* of or caused by friction

fric·tion·al·ly (-əl ē) *adv.* by or with friction

friction clutch a mechanical clutch in which the rotating coaxial shafts are engaged through frictional contact of their surfaces

☆**friction match** a match that lights by friction

friction tape a moisture-resistant adhesive tape, esp. for insulating exposed electrical wires

Fri·day (frī′dē, -dā) *n.* [ME. *fridai* < OE. *frigedæg*, lit., day of the goddess Frig (ON. *Frigg*: see FRIGG), akin to G. *Freitag*, Du. *Vrijdag*, Sw. *Fredag*: transl. LL. *Veneris dies* (Fr. *vendredi*), Venus' day] 1. the sixth day of the week 2. [after the devoted servant of ROBINSON CRUSOE] a faithful follower or efficient helper: usually **man** (or **girl**) **Friday**

Fri·days (-dēz, -dāz) *adv.* on or during every Friday

fridge (frij) *n.* [Chiefly Brit. Colloq.] a refrigerator

fried (frid) [ME. *ifrid*, pp. of *frien*, FRY¹] *pt. & pp.* of FRY¹ —*adj.* ☆[Slang] drunk; intoxicated

Frie·da (frē′də) [G. < OHG. *fridu*, peace: see FREDERICK] a feminine name

☆**fried·cake** (frīd′kāk′) *n.* a small cake fried in deep fat; doughnut or cruller

friend (frend) *n.* [ME. *frend, freond*, friend, lover, akin to G. *freund*, prp. of Gmc. **frijon*, to love (whence OE. *freon*): for IE. base see FREE] 1. a person whom one knows well and is fond of; intimate associate; close acquaintance 2. a person on the same side in a struggle; one who is not an enemy or foe; ally 3. a supporter or sympathizer [*a friend of labor*] 4. something thought of as like a friend in being helpful, reliable, etc. 5. [F-] a member of the Society of Friends; Quaker —*vt.* [Archaic] to act as a friend to; befriend —**make** (or **be**) **friends with** to become (or be) a friend of —**friend′less** *adj.* —**friend′less·ness** *n.*

friend at court a person in an influential position who is friendly toward one and able to help him

friend·ly (-lē) *adj.* **-li·er, -li·est** [ME. *frendli* < OE. *freondlice*] 1. like, characteristic of, or suitable for a friend, friends, or friendship; kindly 2. not hostile; amicable 3. supporting; helping; favorable [*a friendly wind*] 4. showing friendly feelings; ready to be a friend 5. [F-] of the Friends, or Quakers —*adv.* in a friendly manner; as a friend —**friend′li·ly** *adv.* —**friend′li·ness** *n.*

Friendly Islands *same as* TONGA

friend of the court *same as* AMICUS CURIAE

friend·ship (-ship) *n.* [ME. *frendship* < OE. *freondscipe*] 1. the state of being friends 2. attachment between friends 3. friendly feeling or attitude; friendliness

fri·er (frī′ər) *n. same as* FRYER

Frie·sian (frē′zhən) *adj., n. same as* FRISIAN

Fries·land (frēs′lənd, -land′; *Du.* frēs′länt′) province of the N Netherlands, on the North Sea: 1,310 sq. mi.; pop. 496,000; cap. Leeuwarden

Fri·esz (frē′es), **(Achille Émile) O·thon** (ō tōn′) 1879–1949; Fr. painter

frieze¹ (frēz) *n.* [Fr. *frise* < ML. *frisium* (seen also in It. *freggio*) < ? Frank. **frisi*, a curl, border, akin to OE. *fris*, crisped, curled] 1. a decoration or series of decorations forming an ornamental band around a room, mantel, etc. 2. *Archit.* a horizontal band, often decorated with sculpture, between the architrave and cornice of a building

frieze² (frēz) *n.* [ME. *frise* < OFr. < MDu., prob. akin to prec.] a heavy wool cloth with a shaggy, uncut nap on one side

frig·ate (frig′it) *n.* [Fr. *frégate* < It. *fregata*] 1. a fast, medium-sized sailing warship of the 18th and early 19th cent., which carried from 24 to 60 guns 2. a Brit. warship between a corvette and a destroyer ☆3. a U.S. warship larger than a destroyer and smaller than a light cruiser

frigate bird any of several large, tropical sea birds (genus *Fregata*) with extremely long wings and tail and a hooked beak: it commonly robs other birds of their prey

Frigg (frig) [ON., akin to OHG. *Fria* & Sans. *priyā*, beloved: for IE. base see FREE] *Norse Myth.* the wife of Odin and goddess of heaven, presiding over marriage and the home: also **Frig·ga** (frig′ə)

frig·ging (frig′'n) *adj., adv.* [prp. of vulgar *frig*, to copulate, orig. to rub, prob. ult. < L. *fricare*, to rub: see FRICTION] [Slang] darned; damned: a vulgar, generalized intensive

fright (frīt) *n.* [ME. < OE. *fyrhto, fryhto*, fear, akin to G. *furcht*, fear, Goth. *faúrhtei* < IE. base **perg-*, fear, to be afraid] 1. sudden fear or terror; alarm 2. an ugly, ridiculous, startling, or unusual person or thing —*vt.* [ME. *frighten* < OE. *fyrhtan*] [Rare] to frighten; terrify —*SYN.* see FEAR

fright·en (-'n) *vt.* 1. to cause to feel fright; make suddenly afraid; scare; terrify 2. to force (*away, out,* or *off*) or bring (*into* a specified condition) by frightening [*to frighten* someone *into* confessing] —*vi.* to become suddenly afraid —**fright′en·ing·ly** *adv.*

SYN.—**frighten** is the broadest of these terms and implies, usually, a sudden, temporary feeling of fear [*frightened* by a mouse] but sometimes, a state of continued dread [she's *frightened* when she's alone]; **scare**, often equivalent to **frighten**, in stricter use implies a fear that causes one to flee or to stop doing something [I *scared* him from the room]; **alarm** suggests a sudden fear or apprehension at the realization of an approaching danger [*alarmed* by his warning]; to **terrify** is to cause to feel an overwhelming, often paralyzing fear [*terrified* at the thought of war]; **terrorize** implies deliberate intention to terrify by threat or intimidation [the gangsters *terrorized* the city]

fright·ful (-fəl) *adj.* 1. causing fright; terrifying; alarming 2. shocking; terrible 3. [Colloq.] *a)* unpleasant; annoying *b)* great [in a *frightful* hurry] —**fright′ful·ly** *adv.* —**fright′ful·ness** *n.*

frig·id (frij′id) *adj.* [ME. < L. *frigidus* < *frigere*, to be cold < *frigus*, coldness, frost < IE. base **srig-*, coldness whence Gr. *rhigos*, frost] 1. extremely cold; without heat or warmth 2. without warmth of feeling or manner; stiff and formal 3. habitually failing to become sexually aroused, or abnormally repelled by sexual activity: said of a woman —**fri·gid·i·ty** (frə jid′ə tē), **frig′id·ness** *n.* —**frig′id·ly** *adv.*

☆**Frig·id·aire** (frij′ə der′) [arbitrary coinage < FRIGID +

AIR] *a trademark for* an electric refrigerator —*n.* [f-] an electric refrigerator

Frigid Zone either of two zones of the earth (**North Frigid Zone** & **South Frigid Zone**) between the polar circles and the poles: see ZONE, illus.

frig·o·rif·ic (frig′ə rif′ik) *adj.* [Fr. *frigorifique* < L. *frigorificus* < *frigus* (see FRIGID) + *facere*, to make (see FACT)] making cold; freezing or cooling

☆**fri·jol** (frē′hōl) *n., pl.* **fri·jo′les** (frē hō′lēz; *Sp.* frē hō′les) [Sp. *fríjol, fréjol* < L. *faseolus*, earlier *phaselus* < Gr. *phasēlos*, kind of bean] any bean cultivated for food, esp. a variety much used in Mexico and the SW U.S.: also **fri·jo·le** (frē hō′lē; *Sp.* frē hō′le)

frill (fril) *n.* [< ?] **1.** a fold or fringe of hair or feathers around the neck of a bird or animal **2.** any unnecessary ornament; superfluous thing added for show **3.** an edging or trimming of lace, etc., gathered or pleated and attached along one edge but free at the other; ruffle **4.** *Photog.* a wrinkling of the edge of a film —*vt.* **1.** to make a ruffle of; crimp **2.** to decorate with a frill —*vi. Photog.* to become wrinkled, as a film —**frill′y** *adj.* **frill′i·er, frill′i·est**

fringe (frinj) *n.* [ME. *frenge* < OFr. *frenge, fringe* < VL. *frimbia*, metathesis of L. *fimbria*, a fringe, border] **1.** a border or trimming of cords or threads, hanging loose or tied in bunches at the top **2.** *a)* anything like this [a *fringe* of hair] *b)* an outer edge; border; margin [at the *fringes* of the slums] **3.** a part considered to be peripheral, extreme, or minor in relation to the main part [the lunatic *fringe* of a political party] ☆**4.** *same as* FRINGE BENEFIT **5.** *Optics* any of the light or dark bands resulting from the interference or diffraction of light —*vt.* **fringed, fring′ing 1.** to decorate with or as with fringe **2.** to be a fringe for; line [trees *fringed* the lawn] —*adj.* **1.** at the outer edge or border [a *fringe* area of television reception] ☆**2.** additional [*fringe* costs] ☆**3.** less important; minor [*fringe* industries]

☆**fringe benefit** a payment other than wages or salary made to an employee, as in the form of a pension, vacation, insurance, etc.

☆**fringed gentian** any of several plants (genus *Gentiana*) of the gentian family, having blue flowers with fringed petals and native to N U.S. and Canada

☆**fringed polygala** a trailing perennial milkwort (*Polygala paucifolia*) with one to three rosy-lavender flowers having a fringed lower lip, growing in the woods of E N. America

☆**fringe tree** any of a genus (*Chionanthus*) of the olive family; esp., a small tree (*Chionanthus virginica*) native to the SE U.S., having large clusters of drooping white flowers

fringing reef a coral reef growing outward from the shore with no open water between it and the shore: cf. BARRIER REEF

fring·y (frin′jē) *adj.* **fring′i·er, fring′i·est 1.** like a fringe **2.** having a fringe or fringes

frip·per·y (frip′ər ē) *n., pl.* **-per·ies** [orig., castoff clothes < Fr. *friperie* < OFr. *freperie* < *frepe*, a rag < ? ML. *faluppa*, a shaving, straw] **1.** cheap, gaudy clothes; tawdry finery **2.** showy display in dress, manners, speech, etc.; affectation of elegance

Fris. Frisian

☆**Fris·bee** (friz′bē) [altered < *Frisbie:* lids from "Mother Frisbie's" cookie jars were orig. used for the game by Princeton students] *a trademark for* a plastic, saucer-shaped disk tossed back and forth in a game —*n.* [f-] such a disk

Fris·co (fris′kō) [Colloq.] *nickname for* SAN FRANCISCO: not a local usage

fri·sé (fri zā′) *n.* [Fr. < *friser*, to curl, prob. < Frank. *frisi:* see FRIEZE′] a type of upholstery fabric having a thick pile consisting of uncut loops, or, sometimes, of some loops cut to form a design

fri·sette (-zet′) *n.* [Fr., dim. < *friser*, to curl: see prec.] [Rare] a fringe of curls or fluffy bangs, often artificial, worn on the forehead by women

‡**fri·seur** (frē zër′) *n.* [Fr. < *friser:* see FRISÉ] a hairdresser

Fri·sian (frizh′ən, frē′zhən) *adj.* of Friesland, the Frisian Islands, their people, or their language —*n.* **1.** a native or inhabitant of Friesland or the Frisian Islands **2.** a member of an ancient Teutonic tribe of N Holland **3.** the West Germanic language of the Frisians, closely related to Old English

Frisian Islands island chain in the North Sea, extending along the coast of NW Europe: it is divided into three groups, one belonging to the Netherlands (**West Frisian Islands**), one belonging to West Germany (**East Frisian Islands**), & one divided between West Germany & Denmark (**North Frisian Islands**)

frisk (frisk) *adj.* [ME. < OFr. *frisque* < OHG. *frisc*, new, cheerful, lively: see FRESH′] [Obs.] lively;

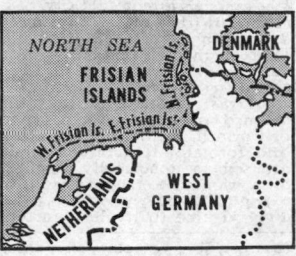

FRISIAN ISLANDS

frisky —*n.* **1.** a lively, playful movement; frolic; gambol **2.** [Slang] the act of frisking a person —*vt.* **1.** to move in a playful, lively manner [the puppy *frisked* its tail] **2.** [Slang] to search quickly; esp., to search (a person) for concealed weapons, stolen articles, etc. by passing the hands quickly over his clothing —*vi.* to dance or move about in a playful, lively manner; frolic

frisk·y (-ē) *adj.* **frisk′i·er, frisk′i·est** inclined to frisk about; lively; playful; frolicsome; merry —**frisk′i·ly** *adv.* —**frisk′i·ness** *n.*

‡**fris·son** (frē sōn′) *n., pl.* **-sons′** (-sōn′) [Fr.] a shudder or shiver, as of excitement, fear, or pleasure

frit (frit) *n.* [Fr. *fritte* < It. *fritta*, fried, pp. of *friggere* < L. *frigere*, FRY′] **1.** the partly fused mixture of sand and fluxes of which glass is made **2.** a partly fused vitreous substance, ground and used as a basis for glazes and enamels —*vt.* **frit′ted, frit′ting** to prepare (materials for glass) by heating; make into frit

frit fly [< ? prec., from the glazed, shining appearance of the fly's body] a tiny, black European fly (*Oscinosoma frit*) whose larvae destroy grain

frith (frith) *n.* [var. of FIRTH] a narrow inlet or arm of the sea; estuary; firth

frit·il·lar·y (frit′′l er′ē) *n., pl.* **-lar·ies** [< ModL. *Fritillaria*, the genus name < L. *fritillus*, dice box: from markings on the petals or wings] **1.** any of a genus (*Fritillaria*) of perennial, bulbous plants of the lily family, related to the tulip but with nodding, bell-shaped flowers **2.** any of a group of medium-sized butterflies (family Nymphalidae), usually having brownish wings with silver spots on the undersides

frit·ter′ (frit′ər) *n.* [< ? OFr. *fraiture* < L. *fractura:* see FRACTURE] [Rare] a small piece; shred —*vt.* [< the *n.*] **1.** [Rare] to break or tear into small pieces **2.** to waste (money, time, etc.) bit by bit on petty things (usually with *away*) —**frit′ter·er** *n.*

frit·ter² (-ər) *n.* [ME. *friture* < OFr. < VL. *frictura* < pp. of *frigere*, FRY′] a small cake of fried batter, usually containing corn, fruit, or other filling

fritz (frits) *n.* [orig., a German (nickname for *Friedrich*): current sense in allusion to cheap German goods exported to U.S. before World War II] ☆[Slang] a broken or non-functioning state: only in the phrase **on the fritz**, not in working order

Fri·u·li-Ve·ne·zia Giu·lia (frē ōō′lē ve ne′tsyä jōō′lyä) autonomous region of NE Italy, on the Adriatic: 3,030 sq. mi.; pop. 1,205,000; cap. Trieste

friv·ol (friv′′l) *vi., vt.* **-oled** or **-olled, -ol·ing** or **-ol·ling** [back-formation < FRIVOLOUS] [Colloq.] to waste (time) on frivolous or trifling things

fri·vol·i·ty (fri väl′ə tē) *n.* [Fr. *frivolité*] **1.** the quality or condition of being frivolous **2.** *pl.* **-ties** a frivolous act or thing

friv·o·lous (friv′ə ləs) *adj.* [ME. < *frivol* (< OFr. *frivole* < L. *frivolus*, fragile, silly, akin to *friare:* see FRIABLE) + *-ous, -OUS*] **1.** of little value or importance; trifling; trivial **2.** not properly serious or sensible; silly and light-minded; giddy —**friv′o·lous·ly** *adv.* —**friv′o·lous·ness** *n.*

fri·zette (fri zet′) *n. same as* FRISETTE

frizz′, **friz** (friz) *vt., vi.* **frizzed, friz′zing** [Fr. *friser*, to curl: see FRIEZE′] to form into small, tight curls —*n.* hair, etc. that is frizzed

frizz² (friz) *vt., vi.* [echoic alteration of FRY′] to fry with a sputtering, hissing noise; sizzle

friz·zle′ (friz′′l) *vt., vi.* **-zled, -zling** [echoic alteration of FRY′, after SIZZLE] **1.** to make or cause to make a sputtering, hissing noise, as in frying; sizzle **2.** to make or become crisp by broiling or frying thoroughly

friz·zle² (friz′′l) *vt., vi.* **-zled, -zling** [freq. of FRIZZ′, prob. akin to Fris. *frislen*, to plait (the hair)] to form into small, tight curls; frizz; crimp —*n.* a small, tight curl

friz·zly (friz′′lē) *adj.* **-zli·er, -zli·est** [< prec. + -Y²] full of or covered with small, tight curls

friz·zy (-ē) *adj.* **-zi·er, -zi·est** *same as* FRIZZLY —**friz′zi·ly** *adv.* —**friz′zi·ness** *n.*

fro (frō) *adv.* [ME. *fra, fro* < ON. *frā*, akin to OE. *fram, FROM*] away; backward; back: now only in *to and fro:* see under TO —*prep.* [Scot. or Dial.] from

Fro·ben (frō′bən), **Jo·hann** (yō′hän) (L. name *Frobenius*) 1460–1527; Ger. printer

Fro·bish·er (frō′bi shər), Sir **Martin** 1535?–94; Eng. navigator & explorer

frock (fräk) *n.* [ME. *frok* < OFr. *froc*, monk's habit (or ML. *froccus*) < OFrank. **hrokk*, cloak, akin to G. *rock*] **1.** a robe worn by friars, monks, etc. **2.** any of various other garments; specif., *a)* a tunic, mantle, or long coat formerly worn by men *b)* a smock or smock frock *c)* a woolen jersey worn by sailors *d)* a girl's or woman's dress *e) same as* FROCK COAT —*vt.* **1.** to clothe in a frock **2.** to ordain as a priest

frock coat a man's double-breasted dress coat with a full skirt reaching to the knees both in front and in back, worn chiefly in the 19th cent.

froe (frō) *n.* [also *frow* (frower): ? contr. of FROWARD, in sense "handle turned away"] a wedge-shaped cleaving tool with a handle set into the blade at right angles to the back

Froe·bel (frō′bəl; *E.* frā′b′l), **Frie·drich (Wilhelm August)** (frē′driH) 1782–1852; Ger. educator: originated the kindergarten system: also sp. **Fröbel**

frog (frôg, fräg) *n.* [ME. *frogge* < OE. *frogga*, akin to G. *frosch*, ON. *froskr* < IE. base **preu-*, to jump, whence Sans. *právaté*, (he) hops] **1.** *a)* any of a large group of tailless, leaping amphibians with long, powerful hind legs, short fore-legs, a smooth skin, and webbed feet: it develops from a tadpole and most species, when grown, are able to live either in water or on land *b)* an animal resembling this, as a tree frog **2.** a triangular horny pad in the posterior half of the sole of a horse's foot **3.** a fastening on a belt for carrying a sword, bayonet, etc. **4.** a corded or braided loop used as a fastener or decoration on clothing ☆**5.** a device on railroad tracks for keeping cars on the proper rails at intersections or switches **6.** a device placed in a bowl, vase, etc. to hold the stems of flowers **7.** the nut of a violin bow —**frog in the throat** a hoarseness due to throat irritation

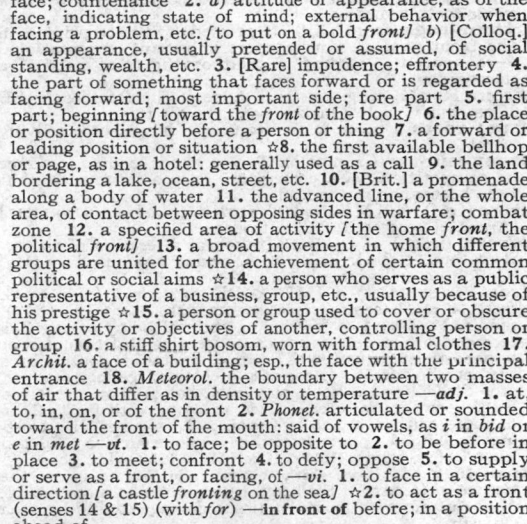

METAMORPHOSIS OF FROG

FROG (sense 4)

frog·fish (-fish′) *n., pl.* -**fish′**, -**fish′es**: see FISH² any of a family (Antennaridae) of bony fishes with compressed, scaleless bodies bearing many warts and flipperlike fins

frog·gy (-ē) *adj.* -**gi·er**, -**gi·est 1.** of or characteristic of a frog **2.** full of frogs

frog·hop·per (-häp′ər) *n.* any of a group of small, leaping insects (family Cercopidae), whose nymphs produce white frothy masses on plants

frog kick a kick used in swimming in which the legs are drawn up and spread outward at the knees and then extended and brought together with a snap

frog·man (-man′) *n., pl.* -**men** (-mən) a person trained and equipped, as with a rubber suit and scuba apparatus, for underwater demolition, exploration, etc.

frog spit (or **spittle**) **1.** *same as* CUCKOO SPIT **2.** mats of filamentous algae floating on the surface of ponds and containing bubbles of oxygen

Froh·man (frō′mən), **Charles** 1860–1915; U.S. theatrical manager & producer

Frois·sart (frwà sàr′; *E.* froi′särt), **Jean** (zhän) 1337?–1410?; Fr. chronicler & poet

frol·ic (fräl′ik) *adj.* [Du. *vroolijk* < MDu. *vrō*, merry, akin to G. *froh*, prob. < IE. base **preu-*, to leap (whence, to hurry, as in Russ. *prýtki*, swift): cf. FROG] [Archaic] full of fun and pranks; merry —*n.* **1.** a playful trick; prank **2.** a lively party or game **3.** merriment; gaiety; fun —*vi.* -**icked, -ick·ing 1.** to make merry; have fun **2.** to play or romp about in a happy, carefree way —*SYN.* see PLAY —**frol′ick·er** *n.*

frol·ic·some (-səm) *adj.* [FROLIC + -SOME¹] full of gaiety or high spirits; playful; merry: also **frol′ick·y**

from (frum, främ; *unstressed* frəm) *prep.* [ME. < OE. *from*, *fram*, akin to Goth. *fram*, forward, away, ON. *frā* < IE. base **pro-*, var. of **per-*, beyond, ahead, whence FOR, FORE, FIRST] a particle used with verbs or other words to indicate **I.** *a point of departure for motion, duration, distance, action, etc.; source or beginning of ideas, action, etc.* **1.** beginning at [to leave *from* the station] **2.** starting with (the first of two named limits) [*from* noon to midnight] **3.** out of; derived or coming out of [to take a comb *from* the pocket] **4.** with (a person or thing) as the maker, sender, speaker, teacher, etc. [a letter *from* Mary, facts learned *from* reading] **II.** *distance, absence, removal, separation, exclusion, prevention, freedom, etc.* **1.** at a place not near to; out of contact with [away *from* danger, far *from* home] **2.** out of the whole of; out of unity or alliance with [take two *from* four] **3.** out of the possibility or use of [kept *from* going] **4.** out of the possession or control of [released *from* jail] **III.** *difference, distinction, etc.* as not being like [to tell one *from* another] **IV.** *reason, cause, motive, etc.* by reason of; caused by; because of [to tremble *from* fear]

frond (fränd) *n.* [L. *frons* (gen. *frondis*), leafy branch, foliage] **1.** a leaf; specif., *a)* the leaf of a fern *b)* the leaf of a palm **2.** the leaflike part, or shoot, of a lichen, seaweed, duckweed, etc. —**frond′ed** *adj.*

‡**Fronde** (frōnd) [Fr., lit., a sling] a French political party organized during the minority of Louis XIV to oppose the court and Cardinal Mazarin; also, the rebellion fomented by it

fron·des·cence (frän des′ns) *n.* [ModL. *frondescentia* < L. *frondescens*, prp. of *frondescere*, to become leafy < *frondere*, to put forth leaves] **1.** the process, state, or period of putting forth leaves **2.** leaves; foliage —**fron·des′cent** *adj.*

frons (fränz) *n.* [L.: see ff.] the upper front portion of the head of an insect

front (frunt) *n.* [ME. < OFr. < L. *frons* (gen. *frontis*), forehead, front < IE. **bhren-*, to project, whence OE. *brant*, steep, high] **1.** formerly, *a)* the forehead *b)* the face; countenance **2.** *a)* attitude or appearance, as of the face, indicating state of mind; external behavior when facing a problem, etc. [to put on a bold *front*] *b)* [Colloq.] an appearance, usually pretended or assumed, of social standing, wealth, etc. **3.** [Rare] impudence; effrontery **4.** the part of something that faces forward or is regarded as facing forward; most important side; fore part **5.** first part; beginning [toward the *front* of the book] **6.** the place or position directly before a person or thing **7.** a forward or leading position or situation ☆**8.** the first available bellhop or page, as in a hotel: generally used as a call **9.** the land bordering a lake, ocean, street, etc. **10.** [Brit.] a promenade along a body of water **11.** the advanced line, or the whole area, of contact between opposing sides in warfare; combat zone **12.** a specified area of activity [the home *front*, the political *front*] **13.** a broad movement in which different groups are united for the achievement of certain common political or social aims ☆**14.** a person who serves as a public representative of a business, group, etc., usually because of his prestige ☆**15.** a person or group used to cover or obscure the activity or objectives of another, controlling person or group **16.** a stiff shirt bosom, worn with formal clothes **17.** *Archit.* a face of a building; esp., the face with the principal entrance **18.** *Meteorol.* the boundary between two masses of air that differ as in density or temperature —*adj.* **1.** at, to, in, on, or of the front **2.** *Phonet.* articulated or sounded toward the front of the mouth: said of vowels, as *i* in *bid* or *e* in *met* —*vt.* **1.** to face; be opposite to **2.** to be before in place **3.** to meet; confront **4.** to defy; oppose **5.** to supply or serve as a front, or facing, of —*vi.* **1.** to face in a certain direction [a castle *fronting* on the sea] ☆**2.** to act as a front (senses 14 & 15) (with *for*) —**in front of** before; in a position ahead of

front. frontispiece

front·age (-ij) *n.* **1.** the front part of a building **2.** the direction toward which this faces; exposure **3.** the land between the front edge of a building and the street **4.** *a)* the front boundary line of a lot facing a street *b)* the length of this line **5.** land bordering a street, river, lake, etc.

fron·tal¹ (-'l) *adj.* [ModL. *frontalis*] **1.** of the front; in, on, at, or against the front **2.** of or for the forehead —*n. same as* FRONTAL BONE —**fron′tal·ly** *adv.*

fron·tal² (-'l) *n.* [ME. *fruuntel* < OFr. *frontel* < ML. *frontellum*, dim. for *frontale* < L. *frontalia*, frontlet < *frons*: see FRONT & -AL] **1.** an ornamental band or piece of armor worn on the forehead **2.** an ornamental drapery for the front of an altar **3.** *a)* a façade *b)* a small pediment over a door, window, etc.

frontal bone the bone comprising the front part of the skull and forming the forehead in man

frontal lobe the largest and foremost subdivision of each cerebral hemisphere

front·bench·er (-ben′chər) *n.* a member of the British House of Commons, who is a leader in his party and occupies a seat near the speaker

Fron·te·nac (frŏnt nak′; *E.* frän′tə nak′), **Comte de (Palluau et de)** (born *Louis de Buade*) 1620–98; Fr. colonial governor in N. America (1672–82; 1689–98)

fron·tier (frun tir′) *n.* [ME. *frontere* < OFr. *frontier* < *front:* see FRONT] **1.** the border between two countries ☆**2.** that part of a settled, civilized country which lies next to an unexplored or undeveloped region **3.** any new field of learning, thought, etc. or any part of a field that is still incompletely investigated: *often used in plural* [the *frontiers* of medicine] —*adj.* of, on, or near a frontier

☆**fron·tiers·man** (-tirz′mən) *n., pl.* -**men** (-mən) a man who lives on the frontier

fron·tis·piece (frun′tis pēs′) *n.* [OFr. < LL. *frontispicium*, front of a church, front view < L. *frons*, FRONT + *specere*, to look: see SPECTACLE] **1.** orig., the first page or title page of a book **2.** an illustration facing the first page or title page of a book or division of a book **3.** *Archit. a)* the main façade *b)* a pediment over a door, window, etc.

front·let (frunt′lit) *n.* [OFr. *frontelet*, dim. of *frontel*: see FRONTAL²] **1.** a frontal or a phylactery worn on the forehead **2.** the forehead of an animal **3.** the forehead of a bird, when distinguishable by the color or texture of the plumage **4.** an ornamental border for an altar frontal

fron·to- (frun′tō) [< L. *frons* (gen. *frontis*): see FRONT] *a combining form meaning:* **1.** of the frontal bone or region and [*fronto-parietal*] **2.** of or connected with a meteorological front [*frontogenesis*]

☆**front office** the management or administration, as of a company

fron·to·gen·e·sis (frun′tō jen′ə sis) *n.* [ModL. < FRONTO- + GENESIS] the coming into contact of two atmospherically different masses or currents of air, thereby forming a meteorological front and usually causing clouds, rain, snow, etc.

fron·tol·y·sis (frun täl′ə sis) *n.* [ModL. < FRONTO- + -LYSIS] the process that tends to destroy a meteorological front, as by mixture of the frontal air

fron·ton (frän′tän; *Sp.* frōn tōn′) *n.* [Sp. *frontón*, orig., wall of a handball court, orig., a pediment < It. *frontone*, aug. derivative < *fronte*, forehead < L. *frons*: see FRONT] **1.** a

building containing a jai alai court or courts **2.** *the Mexican name for* JAI ALAI

☆**front-page** (frunt′pāj′) *adj.* printed or fit to be printed on the front page of a newspaper; important or sensational —*vt.* **-paged′, -pag′ing** to print on the front page of a newspaper

Front Range range on the E edge of the Rockies, in SE Wyo. & NC Colo.: highest peak, 14,274 ft.

front room a room in the front of a house, esp. a living room

front-run·ner (-run′ər) *n.* **1.** one who is leading in a race or competition **2.** a contestant, as in a horse race, that runs best when in the lead

frore (frôr) *adj.* [ME. *frore(n)*, frozen, pp. of *fresen*, FREEZE] [Archaic] very cold; frosty; frozen

☆**frosh** (fräsh) *n., pl.* **frosh** [taken as alteration of FRESH-MAN, but < ? G. dial. *frosch*, young student, lit., frog] [Colloq.] a college freshman

frost (frôst, fräst) *n.* [ME. < OE. *forst, frost* (akin to G. *frost*) < pp. base of *freosan* (see FREEZE) + *-t* (Gmc. *-ta*), nominal suffix] **1.** a freezing or state of being frozen **2.** a temperature low enough to cause freezing **3.** frozen dew or vapor; moisture frozen as a white, crystalline coating on a surface; hoarfrost **4.** coolness of action, feeling, manner, etc. **5.** [Colloq.] a book, play, etc. that is poorly received by the public; failure —*vt.* **1.** to cover with frost **2.** to damage, wither, or kill by freezing **3.** to cover with frost-ing, or icing **4.** to give a frostlike, opaque surface to (glass)

Frost (frôst, fräst), **Robert (Lee)** 1874–1963; U.S. poet

frost·bite (-bīt′) *vt.* **-bit′, -bit′ten, -bit′ing** to injure the tissues (of a part of the body) by exposure to intense cold; nip or numb with frost —*n.* tissue damage caused by such exposure

☆**frost·fish** (-fish′) *n., pl.* **-fish′, -fish′es:** see FISH² **1.** *same as* TOMCOD **2.** any of various fishes that appear in early fall

☆**frost·flow·er** (-flou′ər) *n.* any of various asters

frost·ing (-iŋ) *n.* **1.** a mixture of sugar, butter, flavoring, water or other liquid, whites of eggs, etc. for covering a cake; icing **2.** a dull, frostlike finish on glass, metal, etc. **3.** a mixture of ground glass, varnish, etc., used in orna-mental work

☆**frost line** the limit of penetration of soil by frost

frost·work (-wurk′) *n.* **1.** the tracery formed by frost on glass, etc. **2.** ornamentation like this, as on silver

frost·y (-ē) *adj.* **frost′i·er, frost′i·est 1.** producing frost or cold enough to produce frost; freezing **2.** covered with or as with frost; hoary, glistening, etc. **3.** cold in manner or feeling; austere; unfriendly —**frost′i·ly** *adv.* —**frost′i·ness** *n.*

froth (frôth, fräth) *n.* [ME. *frothe* < ON. *frotha*, akin to OE. *(a)-freothan*, to froth up < IE. **preu-th*, a snorting, slavering < base **per-*, to sprinkle, scatter, whence Gr. *prēmainein*, to blow hard] **1.** a whitish mass of bubbles; foam **2.** foaming saliva caused by disease or great excite-ment **3.** light, trifling, or worthless talk, ideas, etc. —*vt.* [< the *n.*] **1.** to cause to foam **2.** to cover with foam **3.** to spill forth like foam —*vi.* [ME. *frothen*] to produce froth; foam

froth·y (-ē) *adj.* **froth′i·er, froth′i·est 1.** of, like, or covered with froth; foamy **2.** light; trifling; worthless —**froth′i·ly** *adv.* —**froth′i·ness** *n.*

Froude (frood), **James Anthony** 1818–94; Eng. historian

frou·frou (froo′froo′) *n.* [Fr.; echoic] **1.** a rustling or swishing, as of a silk skirt when the wearer moves ☆**2.** [Colloq.] excessive ornateness or affected elegance

frounce (frouns) *vt., vi.* **frounced, frounc′ing** [ME. *frouncen* < OFr. *froncir*, to wrinkle < Frank. **hrunkja*, a wrinkle, akin to ON. *hrukka*] [Obs.] to curl, crease, or wrinkle —*n.* [Archaic] showy display

frow (frō) *n. same as* FROE

fro·ward (frō′ərd, -wərd) *adj.* [ME., turned away, unruly: see FRO & -WARD] **1.** not easily controlled; stubbornly willful; contrary; refractory **2.** [Obs.] adverse; unfavorable —**fro′ward·ly** *adv.* —**fro′ward·ness** *n.*

frown (froun) *vi.* [ME. *frounen* < OFr. *frognier* < *froigne*, sullen face < Gaul. **frogna*, nostrils, akin to OIr. *srón*, nose] **1.** to contract the brows, as in displeasure or con-centrated thought **2.** to show displeasure or disapproval (with *on* or *upon*) —*vt.* **1.** to silence, subdue, etc. with a disapproving look (with *down*) **2.** to express (disapproval, disgust, etc.) by frowning —*n.* **1.** a contracting of the brows in sternness, thought, etc. **2.** any expression of dis-pleasure or disapproval —**frown′er** *n.* —**frown′ing·ly** *adv.* **SYN.**—**frown, scowl,** and **glower** all denote the making of a wry or gloomy face, **frown** implying a contracting of the brows in disapproval, annoyance, or deep thought, **scowl,** a puckering and lowering of the brows in irritation or sullenness, and **glower,** a staring fiercely in great anger or contempt —**ANT.** smile

frowst (froust) *n.* [back-formation < FROWSTY] [Brit.] stale, musty air —*vi.* [Brit.] to lounge about in a hot, stuffy room

frowst·y (-ē) *adj.* [prob. altered < ff.] [Brit.] musty or stuffy

frow·zy (frou′zē) *adj.* **-zi·er, -zi·est** [< ?] **1.** [Rare] bad-smelling; musty **2.** dirty and untidy; slovenly; unkempt Also sp. **frow′sy** —**frow′zi·ly** *adv.* —**frow′zi·ness** *n.*

froze (frōz) *pt. of* FREEZE

fro·zen (-′n) [ME.] *pp. of* FREEZE —*adj.* **1.** turned into or covered with ice; congealed by cold **2.** injured, damaged, or killed by freezing **3.** having heavy frosts and extreme cold

[the *frozen* polar wastes] **4.** preserved by freezing, as food **5.** affected as if turned into ice; made motionless [*frozen* with terror] **6.** without warmth or affection in behavior, manners, etc. **7.** arbitrarily kept at a fixed level or in a fixed position **8.** not readily convertible into cash [*frozen* assets]

☆**frozen custard** a food resembling ice cream, but with a lower butterfat content and a looser consistency

FRS Federal Reserve System

Frs. Frisian

F.R.S. Fellow of the Royal Society

frt. freight

fruc·tif·er·ous (fruk tif′ər əs) *adj.* [< L. *fructifer* (< *fructus*, fruit + *ferre*, to BEAR¹) + -OUS] producing fruit; fruit-bearing

fruc·ti·fy (fruk′tə fī′) *vi.* **-fied′, -fy′ing** [ME. *fructifien* < OFr. *fructifier* < L. *fructificare:* see FRUIT & -FY] to bear fruit; become fruitful —*vt.* to cause to bear fruit; fertilize —**fruc′ti·fi·ca′tion** *n.*

fruc·tose (fruk′tōs, frook′-) *n.* [< L. *fructus*, FRUIT + -OSE¹] a crystalline sugar, C₆H₁₂O₆, found in sweet fruits and in honey; fruit sugar; levulose

fruc·tu·ous (fruk′choo wəs) *adj.* [ME. < OFr. < L. *fructuosus* < *fructus*, FRUIT] fruitful; productive

fru·gal (froo′g′l) *adj.* [L. *frugalis* < *frugi*, fit for food, hence proper, worthy, frugal, orig. dative of *frux* (gen. *frugis*), fruits, produce: for IE. base see FRUIT] **1.** not wasteful; not spending freely or unnecessarily; thrifty; economical **2.** not costly or luxurious; inexpensive or meager [a *frugal* meal] —**SYN.** see THRIFTY —**fru·gal′i·ty** (-gal′ə tē) *n., pl.* **-ties** —**fru′gal·ly** *adv.*

fru·giv·o·rous (froo jiv′ər əs) *adj.* [< L. *frux* (see FRUGAL) + -VOROUS] fruit-eating

fruit (froot) *n.* see PLURAL, II, D, 3 [ME. < OFr. < L. *fructus*, enjoyment, means of enjoyment, fruit, produce, profit < pp. of *frui*, to partake of, enjoy < IE. base **bhrūg-*, fruit, to enjoy, whence BROOK²] **1.** any plant product, as grain, flax, vegetables, etc.: *usually used in pl.* **2.** a sweet and edible plant structure, consisting of a fruit (sense 6) or false fruit of a flowering plant, usually eaten raw or as a dessert: many true fruits which are not sweet, as tomatoes, beans, green peppers, etc., are popularly called *vegetables* **3.** the result, product, or consequence of any action [*fruit* of hard work] **4.** [Slang] a male homosexual **5.** [Archaic] the young of animals or man **6.** *Bot.* the mature ovary of a flowering plant, together with its contents, and any closely connected parts, as the whole peach, pea pod, cucumber, etc. —*vi., vt.* to bear or cause to bear fruit

fruit·age (-ij) *n.* [OFr.: see -AGE] **1.** the bearing of fruit; fruiting **2.** a crop of fruit; fruits collectively **3.** a result; product; consequence

fruit bat any of a suborder (Megachiroptera) of fruit-eating bats, as the flying fox

fruit·cake (-kāk′) *n.* a rich cake containing nuts, preserved fruit, citron, spices, etc.

fruit cup ☆mixed diced fruits served in a sherbet glass, etc. as an appetizer or dessert: also **fruit cocktail**

fruit·er (-ər) *n.* [ME. *fruter* < OFr. *fruitier*] **1.** a tree that bears fruit **2.** a ship for transporting fruit

fruit·er·er (-ər ər) *n.* [ME. *fruterer* (with redundant *-er*) < prec.] [Chiefly Brit.] a person who deals in fruit

fruit fly 1. any of several small flies (family Trypetidae) whose larvae feed on fruits and vegetables **2.** *same as* DROSOPHILA

fruit·ful (-fəl) *adj.* [ME.] **1.** bearing much fruit **2.** produc-ing much; productive; prolific **3.** producing results; profitable [a *fruitful* plan] —**SYN.** see FERTILE —**fruit′-ful·ly** *adv.* —**fruit′ful·ness** *n.*

fruit·ing body (froot′iŋ) the spore-bearing structure of a fungus

fru·i·tion (froo ish′ən) *n.* [ME. *fruicioun* < OFr. *fruition* < LL. *fruitio*, enjoyment < *frui:* see FRUIT] **1.** a pleasure obtained from using or possessing something; enjoyment **2.** [by association with FRUIT] the bearing of fruit **3.** a coming to fulfillment; realization [a book that is the *fruition* of years of research]

☆**fruit jar** a glass jar for canning fruit, vegetables, etc., sealed airtight with a cap

fruit·less (froot′lis) *adj.* [ME. *fruitles*] **1.** without results; unprofitable; unsuccessful; vain **2.** bearing no fruit; sterile; barren —**SYN.** see FUTILE —**fruit′less·ly** *adv.* —**fruit′less·ness** *n.*

fruit sugar *same as* FRUCTOSE

fruit tree a tree that bears edible fruit

fruit·wood (-wood′) *n.* the wood of any of various fruit trees, used in furniture, paneling, etc.

fruit·y (froot′ē) *adj.* **fruit′i·er, fruit′i·est 1.** like fruit in taste or smell; rich in flavor [a *fruity* wine] **2.** rich or mellow in tone, esp. excessively so [a *fruity* voice] **3.** rich in interest; spicy; juicy **4.** [Slang] *a)* eccentric or crazy *b)* of or like a male homosexual —**fruit′i·ly** *adv.* —**fruit′i·ness** *n.*

fru·men·ta·ceous (froo′mən tā′shəs) *adj.* [LL. *frumenta-ceus* < L. *frumentum*, grain < base of *frui:* see FRUIT] of, having the nature of, or like wheat or other grain

fru·men·ty (froo′mən tē) *n.* [ME. *frumente* < OFr. *frumentée* < L. *frumentum:* see prec.] an English dish con-sisting of hulled wheat boiled in milk, sweetened, and flavored with spice

frump (frump) *n.* [prob. shortened n. form < ME. *fromplen*,

to wrinkle < earlier Du. *frompelen, verrompelen* < *rompelen* (see RUMPLE)] a dowdy, unattractive woman —**frump′ish** *adj.* —**frump′y** *adj.*, **frump′i·er, frump′i·est**

Frun·ze (froon′ze) capital of the Kirghiz S.S.R., in SC Asia: pop. 360,000

frus·trate (frus′trāt) *vt.* **-trat·ed, -trat·ing** [ME. *frustraten* < L. *frustratus*, pp. of *frustrare, frustrari*, to disappoint, deceive < *frustra*, in vain: for IE. base see FRAUD] **1.** to cause to have no effect; bring to nothing; counteract; nullify [to *frustrate* plans] **2.** to prevent from achieving an objective; foil; baffle; defeat [to *frustrate* an opponent] **3.** *Psychol.* to prevent from gratifying certain impulses or desires, either conscious or unconscious —*vi.* to become frustrated —*adj.* [Now Rare] frustrated; baffled; defeated **SYN.**—**frustrate** implies a depriving of effect or a rendering worthless of efforts directed to some end; **thwart** implies a frustrating by blocking or acting in opposition to a person or thing moving toward some objective; **foil** implies a throwing something off its course (literally, by confusing the scent or trail) so as to discourage further effort or make it of no avail; to **baffle** is to defeat the efforts of by bewildering or confusing [the crime *baffled* the police]; to **balk** is to frustrate by setting up obstacles or obstructions

frus·tra·tion (frus trā′shən) *n.* [ME. *frustracioun* < L. *frustratio*] **1.** a frustrating or being frustrated **2.** something that frustrates

frus·tule (frus′chool) *n.* [Fr. < L. *frustulum*, dim. of *frustum*, a piece: see ff.] either of the two boxlike halves of the hard, siliceous shell of a diatom cell

frus·tum (frus′təm) *n.*, *pl.* **-tums, -ta** (-tə) [L., a piece, bit < IE. *bhreus-*, to break, crush < base *bher-*, to split, cut, whence BORE[1]] **1.** the solid figure formed when the top of a cone or pyramid is cut off by a plane parallel to the base **2.** the part of a solid figure contained between two planes, esp. two parallel planes

fru·tes·cent (froo tes′′nt) *adj.* [< L. *frutex*, a shrub < IE. base *bhreu-*, to sprout (whence MHG. *briezen*, to bud) + -ESCENT] shrubby or becoming shrubby —**fru·tes′cence** *n.*

fru·ti·cose (froot′ə kōs′) *adj.* [L. *fruticosus* < *frutex*: see prec.] of or like a shrub; shrubby

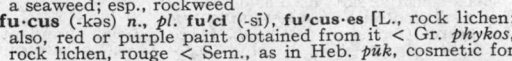
FRUSTUM

fry[1] (frī) *vt., vi.* **fried, fry′ing** [ME. *frien* < OFr. *frire* < L. *frigere*, to fry < IE. base *bher-*, to bake, roast, whence Per. *biriŝtan*, to fry] **1.** to cook or be cooked in a pan or on a griddle over direct heat, usually in hot fat or oil **2.** [Slang] to electrocute or be electrocuted —*n.*, *pl.* **fries 1.** a fried food; esp., [*pl.*] fried potatoes ☆**2.** a social gathering, usually outdoors, at which food is fried and eaten [a fish *fry*]

fry[2] (frī) *n.*, *pl.* **fry** [ME. *frie*, prob. a merging of ON. *frjo*, seed, offspring (akin to Goth. *fraiw*) with Anglo-Fr. *frei* (Fr. *frai*) < OFr. *freier*, to rub, spawn < VL. *frictiare* < L. *fricare*, to rub: see FRIABLE] **1.** young fish **2.** small adult fish, esp. when in large groups **3.** young; offspring; children —**small fry 1.** children **2.** people or things regarded as insignificant

Fry (frī) **1. Christopher,** (born *Christopher Hammond*) 1907– ; Eng. playwright **2. Roger (Eliot),** 1866–1934; Eng. art critic

fry·er (frī′ər) *n.* **1.** a person or thing that fries; specif., a utensil for deep-frying foods **2.** food to be cooked by frying; esp., a chicken young and tender enough to fry

frying pan a shallow pan with a handle, for frying food: also **fry′pan′** *n.* —**out of the frying pan into the fire** from a bad situation into a worse one

FSLIC Federal Savings and Loan Insurance Corporation

f-stop (ef′stäp′) *n.* any of the calibrated settings for the f-number of a camera

ft. 1. foot; feet **2.** fort

FTC Federal Trade Commission

fth., fthm. fathom

ft.-lb. foot-pound

fub·sy (fub′zē) *adj.* **-si·er, -si·est** [< dial. *fub*, plump child] [Brit.] fat and squat; plump

Fuchou same as FOOCHOW

fuch·sia (fyoo′shə) *n.* [ModL., so named by Linnaeus, after Leonhard *Fuchs* (1501–66), G. botanist] **1.** any of a genus (*Fuchsia*) of shrubby plants of the evening-primrose family, with pink, red, or purple flowers hanging from the ends of the branches **2.** purplish red —*adj.* purplish-red

fuch·sin (fook′sin, fyook′-) *n.* [Fr. *fuchsine* < prec. + -*ine*, -IN[1]: from the color] a purplish-red aniline dye, $C_{20}H_{19}N_3HCl$, used as a coloring agent in inks, stains, and dyes: also **fuch′sine** (-sin, -sēn)

fu·coid (fyoo′koid) *adj.* [< ff. + -OID] of or like seaweed, esp. rockweed —*n.* a seaweed; esp., rockweed

fu·cus (-kəs) *n.*, *pl.* **fu′ci** (-sī), **fu′cus·es** [L., rock lichen; also, red or purple paint obtained from it < Gr. *phykos*, rock lichen, rouge < Sem., as in Heb. *pūk*, cosmetic for

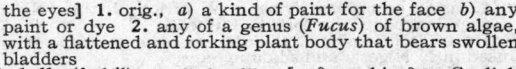
FUCHSIA

the eyes] **1.** orig., *a*) a kind of paint for the face *b*) any paint or dye **2.** any of a genus (*Fucus*) of brown algae, with a flattened and forking plant body that bears swollen bladders

fud·dle (fud′'l) *vt.* **-dled, -dling** [< ? or akin ? to G. dial. *fuddeln*, to swindle] to confuse or stupefy as with alcoholic liquor; befuddle —*vi.* [Rare] to drink heavily; tipple —*n.* a fuddled condition

fud·dy-dud·dy (fud′ē dud′ē) *n.*, *pl.* **-dies** [redupl., prob. based on dial. *fud*, buttocks) [Slang] **1.** a fussy, critical person **2.** an old-fashioned person

fudge (fuj) *n.* [? echoic, as in G. *futsch*, gone, ruined] **1.** empty, foolish talk; nonsense ☆**2.** [< ?] a soft candy made of butter, milk, sugar, and chocolate or other flavoring, etc. **3.** *Printing* a short piece of last-minute news or other matter, inserted directly in the plate of a newspaper page —*vt.* **fudged, fudg′ing** to make or put together dishonestly or carelessly; fake —*vi.* ☆**1.** to refuse to commit oneself or give a direct answer; hedge [to *fudge* on an issue] ☆**2.** to be dishonest; cheat

Fu·e·gi·an (foo ā′jē ən, fwä′jē ən; -gē-) *adj.* of Tierra del Fuego, its Indians, or their culture —*n.* a member of a tribe of South American Indians who live in Tierra del Fuego

fu·el (fyoo′əl, fyool) *n.* [ME. *fewell* < OFr. *fouaille* < ML. *fuale, focale* < *foca*, hearth, for L. *focus*, fireplace: see FOCUS] **1.** any material, as coal, oil, gas, wood, etc., burned to supply heat or power **2.** fissionable material from which atomic energy can be obtained, as in a nuclear reactor **3.** anything that maintains or intensifies strong feeling, etc. —*vt.* **fu′eled** or **fu′elled, fu′el·ing** or **fu′el·ling** to supply with fuel —*vi.* to get fuel —**fu′el·er, fu′el·ler** *n.*

☆**fuel cell** any of various devices that convert chemical energy directly into electrical energy

☆**fuel oil** any oil used for fuel; esp., a petroleum distillate used in diesel engines

fug (fug) *n.* [altered < ? FOG[1]] [Chiefly Brit.] the heavy air in a closed room, regarded as either oppressive and murky or warm and cozy —**fug′gy** *adj.* —**fug′gi·ly** *adv.*

fu·ga·cious (fyoo gā′shəs) *adj.* [< L. *fugax* (gen. *fugacis*) < *fugere* (see FUGITIVE) + -IOUS] **1.** passing quickly away; fleeting, ephemeral **2.** *Bot.* falling soon after blooming, as some flowers —**fu·gac′i·ty** (-gas′ə tē) *n.*

fu·gal (fyoo′g'l) *adj.* of, or having the nature of, a fugue —**fu′gal·ly** *adv.*

-fuge (fyooj) [Fr. < L. *fugere*, to flee: see FUGITIVE] a *n.-forming suffix meaning* something that drives away or out [febrifuge, vermifuge]

Fug·ger (foog′ər) Ger. family of merchants & bankers of the 15th to 19th cent.

fu·gi·tive (fyoo′jə tiv) *adj.* [ME. *fugitif* < OFr. < L. *fugitivus* < pp. of *fugere*, to flee < IE. base *bheug-*, to flee, whence Gr. *phygē*, flight] **1.** fleeing, apt to flee, or having fled, as from danger, justice, etc. **2.** passing quickly away; fleeting; evanescent **3.** having to do with matters of temporary interest [fugitive essays] **4.** roaming; shifting *n.* **1.** a person who flees or has fled from danger, justice, etc. **2.** a fleeting or elusive thing —**fu′gi·tive·ly** *adv.*

fu·gle (fyoo′g'l) *vi.* **-gled, -gling** [back-formation < ff.] [Rare] to act as fugleman; be guide or director

fu·gle·man (-mən) *n.*, *pl.* **-men** (-mən) [altered by dissimilation < G. *flügelmann*, file-leader, lit., wing-man < *flügel*, wing + *mann*, man] **1.** orig., a soldier expert in drilling, detailed to stand at the head of his unit and serve as a model and guide for others **2.** a leader or exemplar

fugue (fyoog) *n.* [Fr. < It. *fuga* < L., a flight < *fugere*: see FUGITIVE] **1.** a musical form or composition designed for a definite number of instruments or voices in which a subject is announced in one voice and then developed contrapuntally in strict order by each of the other voices **2.** *Psychiatry* a state of psychological amnesia during which the subject seems to behave in a conscious and rational way, although upon return to normal consciousness he cannot remember the period of time nor what he did during it; temporary flight from reality —**fugu′ist** *n.*

‡**Füh·rer, Fueh·rer** (fü′rər; E. fyoor′ər) *n.* [G. < *führen*, to lead < Gmc. *forjan*, caus. of *faran*, to go, travel, whence FARE] leader: title assumed by Adolf Hitler as head of Nazi Germany (1934–45)

Fu·ji (foo′jē) extinct volcano on Honshu Island, Japan, southwest of Tokyo: highest peak in Japan: 12,388 ft.: also **Fu·ji·ya·ma** (foo′jē yä′mä), **Fu′ji·san′** (-sän′)

Fu·kien (foo′kyen′) province of SE China, on Taiwan Strait: 47,490 sq. mi.; pop. 14,650,000; cap. Foochow

Fu·ku·o·ka (foo′koo ō′kə) seaport on the N coast of Kyushu island, Japan: pop. 718,000

-ful (fəl, f'l; for 4, *usually* fool) [ME. < OE. < *full*, FULL[1]] a *suffix meaning*: **1.** full of, characterized by, having [joyful, painful] **2.** having the qualities of [masterful] **3.** having the ability or tendency to, apt to [helpful, forgetful] **4.** *pl.* **-fuls** the quantity that fills or would fill [teaspoonful, handful]: the plural is sometimes formed in colloquial usage by adding -s- to the noun stem [cupsful]

Fu·la (foo′lä) *n.*, *pl.* **Fu′las, Fu′la** [< native name] **1.** any member of an Islamic pastoral people of Negroid and

Caucasoid admixture living in W Africa **2.** their Niger-Congo language Also **Fu′lah, Ful** (fōōl)

Fu·la·ni (tōō′lä nē) *n., pl.* **-nis, -ni** *same as* FULA: name used in N Nigeria and adjoining areas

Ful·bright (fool′brīt′) *adj.* [after J. W. *Fulbright* (1905–), U.S. senator from Arkansas] designating, of, or holding a scholarship or grant in a U.S. government program for the exchange of U.S. and foreign scholars, teachers, etc.: the funds are largely derived from the sale of U.S. surplus property abroad —*n.* a Fulbright scholarship, grant, or scholar

ful·crum (fool′krəm, ful′-) *n., pl.* **-crums, -cra** (-krə) [L., bedpost, support, akin to *fulcire*, to support < IE. base *bhel-*, whence Gr. *phalanx*, beam, OE. *balca*, BALK] **1.** *a)* the support or point of support on which a lever turns in raising or moving something *b) Zool.* any structure that supports or acts like a fulcrum **2.** a means of exerting influence, pressure, etc.

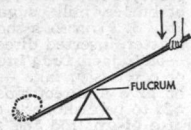

FULCRUM

ful·fill, ful·fil (fool fil′) *vt.* **-filled′, -fill′ing** [ME. *fulfillen* < OE. *fullfyllan:* a pleonasm (see FULL[1] & FILL)] **1.** to carry out (something promised, desired, expected, predicted, etc.); cause to be or happen **2.** to do (something required); obey **3.** to fill the requirements of; satisfy (a condition) or answer (a purpose) **4.** to bring to an end; complete —*SYN.* see PERFORM —**fulfill oneself** to realize completely one's ambitions, potentialities, etc. —**ful·fill′er** *n.* —**ful·fill′ment, ful·fil′ment** *n.*

ful·gent (ful′jənt, fool′-) *adj.* [ME. < L. *fulgens* (gen. *fulgentis*), prp. of *fulgere*, to flash, shine < IE. *bhleg-*, to shine, whence FLAME, BLACK] [Now Rare] very bright; radiant —**ful′gent·ly** *adv.*

ful·gu·rate (ful′gyoo rāt′, fool′-) *vi.* **-rat′ed, -rat′ing** [< L. *fulguratus*, pp. of *fulgurare*, to flash < *fulgur*, lightning, akin to prec.] to give off flashes of or like lightning —*vt.* **1.** to give off in flashes **2.** *Med.* to destroy (tissue) by electrical means —**ful′gu·ra′tion** *n.*

ful·gu·rat·ing (-rāt′in) *adj.* flashing or sudden like lightning [a *fulgurating* pain]: also **ful′gu·rant** (-rənt)

ful·gu·rite (-rīt′) *n.* [L. *fulgur* (see FULGURATE) + -ITE[1]] a glassy substance, usually tube-shaped, formed by fusion when sand, rock, etc. are struck by lightning

ful·gu·rous (-rəs) *adj.* [L. *fulgur* (see FULGURATE) + -OUS] like or full of lightning; flashing

Ful·ham (fool′əm) *n.* metropolitan borough of London, on the N bank of the Thames: pop. 110,000

ful·ham (fool′əm) *n.* [earlier *fullan* < ? *full one*] [Old Slang] one of a pair of loaded dice

fu·lig·i·nous (fyoo lij′ə nəs) *adj.* [LL. *fuliginosus* < L. *fuligo*, soot] **1.** full of smoke or soot **2.** dark; dusky

full[1] (fool) *adj.* [ME. < OE., akin to G. *voll*, Goth. *fulls* < IE. base *pel-*, to fill, whence L. *plenus*, full & *plere*, to fill, Gr. *plēthein*, to be full, W. *llawn*, full, & (?) FOLK] **1.** having in it all there is space for; holding or containing as much as possible; filled [a *full* jar] **2.** *a)* having eaten all that one wants *b)* having had more than one can stand (*of*) **3.** using or occupying all of a given space [a *full* load] **4.** having a great deal or number (*of*); crowded [a room *full* of people] **5.** *a)* well supplied, stocked, or provided; rich or abounding (with *of*) [woods *full* of game] *b)* rich in detail [*full* information] **6.** *a)* filling the required number, capacity, measure, etc.; complete [a *full* dozen] *b)* thorough; absolute [to come to a *full* stop] **7.** *a)* having reached the greatest development, size, extent, intensity, etc. [a *full* moon, *full* speed] ☆*b)* having attained the highest regular rank [a *full* professor] **8.** having the same parents [*full* brothers] **9.** having clearness, volume, and depth [a *full* tone] **10.** plump; round; filled out [a *full* face] **11.** with loose, wide folds; ample; flowing [a *full* skirt] **12.** *a)* greatly affected by emotion, etc. *b)* occupied or engrossed with ideas, thoughts, etc. ☆**13.** *Baseball a)* designating a count of three balls and two strikes on the batter *b)* with a runner at each of the three bases —*n.* the greatest amount, extent, number, size, etc. [to enjoy life to the *full*] —*adv.* **1.** to the greatest degree; completely [a *full*-grown boy] **2.** directly; exactly [to be hit *full* in the face] **3.** very [*full* well] —*vt.* to make (a skirt, etc.) with loose folds; gather —*vi.* to become full: said of the moon —*SYN.* see COMPLETE —**at the full** at the state or time of fullness —**in full 1.** to, for, or with the full amount, value, etc. **2.** with all the words or letters; not abbreviated or condensed —**one's full** as much as one wants —**to the full** fully; completely; thoroughly

full[2] (fool) *vt., vi.* [ME. *fullen* < OFr. *fuler* < LL. *fullare*, to full < L. *fullo*, cloth fuller] to shrink and thicken (cloth, esp. of wool) with moisture, heat, and pressure

full·back (-bak′) *n. Football* a member of the offensive backfield, stationed behind the quarterback: traditionally the back farthest behind the line, used typically for power plays

☆**full blood** [from obs. notion that blood is the medium of heredity] **1.** the relationship between offspring of the same parents **2.** unmixed breed or race

☆**full-blood·ed** (-blud′id) *adj.* **1.** of unmixed breed or race; purebred: also **full′-blood′ 2.** vigorous; lusty **3.** genuine; authentic **4.** rich and full

full-blown (-blōn′) *adj.* **1.** in full bloom; open: said of flowers **2.** fully grown or developed; matured

full-bod·ied (-bäd′ēd) *adj.* **1.** having a rich flavor and much strength [a *full-bodied* wine] **2.** large or broad in body or substance

full-dress (-dres′) *adj.* **1.** of or requiring full dress; formal [a *full-dress* dinner] **2.** complete and thorough [a *full-dress* inquiry]

full dress formal clothes worn on important or ceremonial occasions; esp., formal evening clothes

full·er[1] (fool′ər) *n.* [ME. < OE. *fullere* < L. *fullo*] a person whose work is to full cloth

full·er[2] (-ər) *n.* [< ? obs. *full*, to make full, complete < FULL[1]] **1.** a tool used by blacksmiths to hammer grooves into iron **2.** a groove so made

Ful·ler (fool′ər) **1.** (Sarah) Margaret, (*Marchioness Ossoli*) 1810–50; U.S. writer, critic, & social reformer **2.** Melville Wes·ton (wes′tən), 1833–1910; U.S. jurist; chief justice of the U.S. (1888–1910)

full·er's earth (fool′ərz) a highly absorbent, opaque clay used to remove grease from woolen cloth in fulling, to clarify fats and oils, etc.

Ful·ler·ton (fool′ər tən) [after G. H. *Fullerton*, a founder] city in SW Calif.: suburb of Los Angeles: pop. 86,000

full-faced (fool′fāst′) *adj.* **1.** having a round face **2.** with the face turned directly toward the spectator or in a specified direction —**full′-face′** *adv.*

full-fash·ioned (-fash′′nd) *adj.* knitted to conform to the contours of the body, as hosiery or sweaters

full-fledged (-flejd′) *adj.* **1.** having a complete set of feathers: said of birds **2.** completely developed or trained; of full rank or status

☆**full house** *Poker* a hand containing three of a kind and a pair, as three jacks and two fives: it is higher than a flush but lower than four of a kind

full-length (-leŋkth′, -leŋth′) *adj.* **1.** showing or covering the whole length of an object or all of a person's figure: said of a picture or mirror **2.** of the original, unabridged, or standard length; not shortened [a *full-length* novel, a *full-length* sofa]

full moon 1. the phase of the moon when its entire illuminated hemisphere is seen as a full disk **2.** the time of month when such a moon is seen

full-mouthed (-mouthd′, -moutht′) *adj.* **1.** having a full set of teeth: said of cattle, etc. **2.** uttered loudly

full nelson [see NELSON, *n.*] *Wrestling* a hold in which both arms are placed under the opponent's armpits from behind with the hands pressed against the back of his neck

full·ness (-nis) *n.* [ME. *fulnesse*] the quality or state of being full (in various senses)

fullness of time the appointed or allotted time

full-rigged (-rigd′) *adj.* **1.** having the maximum number of masts and sails: said of a ship **2.** fully equipped

full sail 1. the complete number of sails **2.** with every sail set **3.** with maximum speed and energy

full-scale (-skāl′) *adj.* **1.** of or according to the original or standard scale or measure [a *full-scale* drawing] **2.** to the utmost limit, degree, etc.; complete and thorough; all-out [*full-scale* warfare]

full stop a period (punctuation mark)

full-time (-tīm′) *adj.* designating, of, or engaged in work, study, etc. for specified periods regarded as taking all of one's regular working hours

full time as a full-time employee, student, etc. [to work *full time*]

full·y (-ē) *adv.* [ME. *fulli* < OE. *fullice* < *full*, FULL[1]] **1.** to the full; completely; entirely; thoroughly **2.** abundantly; amply **3.** at least [*fully* two hours later]

ful·mar (fool′mər, -mär) *n.* [ON. < *full*, foul, unpleasant + *mār*, sea gull] a gray sea bird (*Fulmarus glacialis*) of the petrel family, common in arctic regions

ful·mi·nant (ful′mə nənt, fool′-) *adj.* [L. *fulminans*, prp.: see ff.] **1.** fulminating **2.** *Med.* developing suddenly and severely, as a disease

ful·mi·nate (-nāt′) *vi.* **-nat′ed, -nat′ing** [ME. *fulminaten* < L. *fulminatus*, pp. of *fulminare*, to flash or strike with lightning < *fulmen*, lightning, thunderbolt, akin to *fulgere*: see FULGENT] **1.** [Archaic] to thunder and lighten **2.** to explode with sudden violence; detonate **3.** to shout forth denunciations, decrees, etc. —*vt.* **1.** to cause to explode **2.** to shout forth (denunciations, decrees, etc.) —*n.* any of several readily explosive salts of fulminic acid, used in detonators and percussion caps —**ful′mi·na′tion** *n.* —**ful′mi·na′tor** *n.* —**ful′mi·na·to′ry** (-nə tôr′ē) *adj.*

fulminating powder an explosive material used as a detonator, esp. one containing mercuric fulminate

ful·mine (fool′min, fool′-) *vi., vt.* **-mined, -min·ing** [Fr. *fulminer*] *archaic var. of* FULMINATE

ful·min·ic acid (ful min′ik) [< L. *fulmen*, lightning (see FULMINATE) + -IC] an unstable acid, CNOH, an isomer of cyanic acid, known chiefly in the form of highly explosive, shock-sensitive salts used as detonators

ful·ness (fool′nis) *n. same as* FULLNESS

ful·some (fool′səm, ful′-) *adj.* [ME. *fulsom*, abundant, disgustingly excessive < *ful*, FULL[1] + -som, -SOME[1], but infl. by *ful*, FOUL] disgusting or offensive, esp. because excessive or insincere [*fulsome* praise] —**ful′some·ly** *adv.* —**ful′some·ness** *n.*

Ful·ton (fool′t'n), **Robert** 1765–1815; U.S. inventor &

engineer: designer of the 1st commercially successful U.S. steamboat, the *Clermont* (launched 1807)

ful·vous (ful′vəs) *adj.* [L. *fulvus* < IE. base *bhlewos*, whence BLUE] dull reddish-yellow or brownish-yellow; tawny

fu·mar·ic acid (fyoo mar′ik) [< ModL. *fumaria*, fumitory (< L. *fumarium*: see ff.) + -IC] a colorless, crystalline, unsaturated organic acid, $C_2H_2(COOH)_2$, occurring in various plants or produced synthetically from maleic acid: used in making resins and plastics

fu·ma·role (fyoo′mə rōl′) *n.* [It. *fumaruolo* < LL. *fumariolum*, smoke hole, dim. of L. *fumarium*, chimney < *fumus*, smoke: see FUME] a vent in a volcanic area, from which smoke and gases arise —**fu′ma·rol′ic** (-räl′ik) *adj.*

fum·ble (fum′b'l) *vi.*, *vt.* **-bled, -bling** [var. of ME. *famelen*, prob. < ON. *famla*, akin to Du. *fommeln*, G. *fummeln*] 1. to search (*for* a thing) by feeling about awkwardly with the hands; grope clumsily 2. to handle (a thing) clumsily or unskillfully; bungle 3. to lose one's grasp on (a football, etc.) while trying to catch or hold it 4. to make (one's way) clumsily or by groping —*n.* the act or fact of fumbling —**fum′bler** *n.* —**fum′bling·ly** *adv.*

fume (fyoom) *n.* [ME. < OFr. *fum* < L. *fumus* < IE. base *dheu-*, to smoke, be murky, whence DOWN², DUMB] 1. a gas, smoke, or vapor, esp. if offensive or suffocating 2. anything imaginary or without substance 3. [*pl.*] [Rare] anything that weakens clear thinking 4. [Rare] an outburst of anger, annoyance, etc. —*vi.* **fumed, fum′ing** [ME. *fumen* < OFr. *fumer* < L. *fumare* < *fumus*] 1. to give off gas, smoke, or vapor 2. to rise up or pass off in fumes 3. to show, or give way to, anger, annoyance, etc. —*vt.* 1. to expose to fumes; treat or fill with fumes 2. to give off as fumes —**fum′ing·ly** *adv.*

fumed oak oak wood given a darker color and more distinct markings by exposure to ammonia fumes

fu·mi·gant (fyoo′mə gənt) *n.* [< L. *fumigans*, prp. of *fumigare*] any substance used in fumigating

fu·mi·gate (-gāt′) *vt.* **-gat′ed, -gat′ing** [< L. *fumigatus*, pp. of *fumigare*, to smoke < *fumus*, smoke + *agere*, to do: see ACT] 1. to expose to the action of fumes, esp. in order to disinfect or kill the vermin in 2. [Archaic] to perfume —**fu′mi·ga′tion** *n.* —☆**fu′mi·ga′tor** *n.*

fu·mi·to·ry (fyoo′mə tôr′ē) *n.*, *pl.* **-ries** [ME. *fumeter* < OFr. *fumeterre* < ML. *fumus terrae*, lit., smoke of the earth (see FUME & TERRAIN): so called from its smell] any of a genus (*Fumaria*) of plants of the fumitory family, with watery juice and spurred flowers, formerly used in medicine —*adj.* designating a family (Fumariaceae) of plants, including the bleeding heart, Dutchman's breeches, etc.

fum·y (fyoo′mē) *adj.* **fum′i·er, fum′i·est** full of fumes; producing fumes; vaporous

fun (fun) *n.* [< ME. *fonne*, a fool, foolish, or *fonnen*, to be foolish < ?] 1. *a)* lively, gay play or playfulness; amusement, sport, recreation, etc. *b)* enjoyment or pleasure 2. a source or cause of amusement or merriment, as an amusing person or thing —☆*adj.* [Colloq.] intended for, or giving, pleasure or amusement [a *fun* gift] —*vi.* **funned, fun′ning** [< the *n.*] [Colloq.] to make fun; play or joke —**for** (or **in**) **fun** just for amusement; not seriously —**like fun** [Slang] by no means; not at all: used to express emphatic negation or doubt —**make fun of** to mock laughingly; ridicule

fu·nam·bu·list (fyoo nam′byoo list) *n.* [< L. *funambulus* < *funis*, a rope + *ambulare* (see AMBLE) + -IST] a tightrope walker

Fun·chal (foon shäl′) 1. district of Portugal, coextensive with the Madeira Islands: 307 sq. mi.; pop. 269,000 2. capital of this district; seaport on Madeira: pop. 55,000

func·tion (fuŋk′shən) *n.* [OFr. < L. *functio* < pp. of *fungi*, to perform < IE. base *bheug-*, to enjoy, whence Sans. *bhuŋkté*, (he) enjoys] 1. the normal or characteristic action of anything; esp., any of the natural, specialized actions of an organ or part of an animal or plant [the procreative *function*] 2. a special duty or performance required in the course of work or activity [the *function* of an auditor, the *function* of the brakes] 3. occupation or employment 4. a formal ceremony or elaborate social occasion 5. a thing that depends on and varies with something else 6. any of the positions in utterances that a linguistic form can fill 7. *Math.* a quantity whose value depends on that of another quantity or quantities —*vi.* 1. to act in a required or expected manner; do its work 2. to have a function; serve or be used (*as*) —**func′tion·less** *adj.*

SYN.—**function** is the broad, general term for the natural, required, or expected activity of a person or thing [the *function* of the liver, of education, etc.]; **office**, in this connection, refers to the function of a person, as determined by his position, profession, or employment [the *office* of a priest]; **duty** is applied to a task necessary in or appropriate to one's occupation, rank, status, etc. and carries a strong connotation of obligation [the *duties* of a vicar]; **capacity** refers to a specific function or status, not necessarily the usual or customary one [the judge spoke to him in the *capacity* of a friend]

func·tion·al (-əl) *adj.* 1. of or relating to a function or functions 2. *a)* performing or able to perform a function *b)* intended to be useful 3. *Med.* affecting a function of some organ without apparent structural or organic changes [a *functional* disease] —**func′tion·al·ly** *adv.*

☆**functional illiterate** a person whose ability to read is less than that needed for proper functioning in a complex society

func·tion·al·ism (-əl iz'm) *n.* theory or practice emphasizing the necessity of adapting the structure or design of anything to its function —**func′tion·al·ist** *n.*, *adj.* —**func′tion·al·is′tic** *adj.*

functional shift the conversion of a linguistic form from one part of speech to another, as the use of a noun as a verb

func·tion·ar·y (-er′ē) *n.*, *pl.* **-ar′ies** [FUNCTION + -ARY, after Fr. *fonctionnaire*] a person who performs a certain function; esp., an official

function word a word having little or no lexical meaning but used to show syntactical relation or structure, as an article or conjunction

fund (fund) *n.* [L. *fundus*, bottom, land, estate (< IE. *bhundhos* < base *bhudh-*, whence BOTTOM): meaning infl. by Fr. *fond*, stock, provision < same source] 1. a supply that can be drawn upon; stock; store [a *fund* of good humor] 2. *a)* a sum of money set aside for some particular purpose *b)* an organization that administers such a fund *c)* [*pl.*] money available for use, as in a checking account 3. [*pl.*] the British national debt, regarded as stock held by investors (with *the*) —*vt.* 1. to provide money for the payment of interest on (a debt) 2. to put or convert into a long-term debt that bears interest 3. to put in a fund; accumulate 4. to provide for by a fund

fun·da·ment (fun′də mənt) *n.* [ME. *foundement* < OFr. < L. *fundamentum* < *fundare*, to lay the bottom < *fundus*: see prec.] 1. [Obs.] a base or foundation 2. the buttocks 3. the anus

fun·da·men·tal (fun′də men′t'l) *adj.* [LME. < ML. *fundamentalis* < L. *fundamentum*: see prec.] 1. of or forming a foundation or basis; basic; essential [the *fundamental* rules of art] 2. relating to what is basic; radical [a *fundamental* alteration] 3. on which others are based; primary; original [a *fundamental* type] 4. most important; chief [his *fundamental* needs] 5. *Music a)* designating or of the lowest, or root, tone of a chord *b)* designating the prime or main tone of a harmonic series 6. *Physics* designating or of a fundamental —*n.* 1. a principle, theory, law, etc. serving as a basis; essential part 2. *Music a)* the lowest, or root, tone of a chord *b)* the prime or main tone of a harmonic series 3. *Physics* the component having the lowest frequency in a complex vibration; tone produced by a string or column of air vibrating over its entire length —**fun′da·men′tal·ly** *adv.*

fundamental bass *Music* the harmonic part consisting of the root tones of the chords

☆**fun·da·men·tal·ism** (-iz'm) *n.* [*sometimes* F-] 1. religious beliefs based on a literal interpretation of everything in the Bible and regarded as fundamental to Christian faith and morals 2. the 20th-cent. movement among some American Protestants, based on these beliefs —**fun′da·men′tal·ist** *n.*, *adj.*

fundamental particle *same as* ELEMENTARY PARTICLE

fund raising the act or occupation of soliciting money for welfare agencies, political parties, etc. —**fund′-rais′er** *n.* —**fund′-rais′ing** *adj.*

fun·dus (fun′dəs) *n.*, *pl.* **fun′di** (-dī) [ModL. < L., bottom: see FUND] *Anat.* the base of a hollow organ, or the part farthest from the opening, as that part of the uterus farthest from the cervix —**fun′dic** *adj.*

Fun·dy (fun′dē), **Bay of** arm of the Atlantic, between New Brunswick & Nova Scotia, Canada: c. 140 mi. long: noted for its high tides of 60–70 ft.

Fü·nen (fü′nen) *Ger. name of* FYN

fu·ner·al (fyoo′nər əl) *adj.* [ME. < LL. *funeralis* < L. *funus* (gen. *funeris*), a funeral < ? IE. *dheu-*, to fade away, die, whence DEAD, DIE¹] of or having to do with a funeral —*n.* [ME. *funerelles* (pl.) < OFr. *funerailles* < ML. *funeralia* < neut. pl. of *funeralis*] 1. the ceremonies connected with burial or cremation of the dead; obsequies 2. the procession accompanying the body to the place of burial or cremation —**be one's funeral** to be one's problem, worry, etc. and not another's

☆**funeral director** the manager of a funeral home

☆**funeral home** (or **parlor**) a business establishment where the bodies of the dead are prepared for burial or cremation and where funeral services can be held; mortuary

BAY OF FUNDY

fu·ner·ar·y (fyōō'nə rer'ē) *adj.* [LL. *funerarius*] of or having to do with a funeral or burial

fu·ne·re·al (fyoo nir'ē əl) *adj.* [L. *funereus*] of or suitable for a funeral; esp., sad and solemn; gloomy; dismal — **fu·ne're·al·ly** *adv.*

fun·gal (fuŋ'g'l) *adj.* same as FUNGOUS

fun·gi (fun'jī, fuŋ'gī) *n. alt. pl. of* FUNGUS

fun·gi- (fun'jə, fuŋ'gə) *a combining form meaning* fungus or fungi [*fungicide*]

fun·gi·ble (fun'jə b'l) *adj.* [ML. *fungibilis* < L. *fungi*, to perform: see FUNCTION] *Law* designating movable goods, as grain, any unit or part of which can replace another unit, as in discharging a debt —*n.* [ME. (*res*) *fungibilis*] a fungible thing —**fun'gi·bil'i·ty** *n.*

fun·gi·cide (fun'jə sīd', fuŋ'gə-) *n.* [FUNGI- + -CIDE] any substance that kills fungi or checks the growth of spores —**fun'gi·cid'al** *adj.*

fun·gi·form (-fôrm') *adj.* [FUNGI- + -FORM] having the form of a fungus

☆**fun·go** (fuŋ'gō) *n., pl.* **-goes** [< ?] *Baseball* 1. a batted ball, esp. a fly ball, hit, as for fielding practice, by the batter after he has himself tossed the ball into the air 2. the relatively long, thin bat used for this: in full, **fungo bat** (or **stick**)

fun·goid (fuŋ'goid) *adj.* like or characteristic of a fungus —*n.* a fungus

fun·gous (-gəs) *adj.* [ME. < L. *fungosus*, spongy < *fungus*] 1. of, like, or caused by a fungus or fungi 2. growing or arising suddenly, but not lasting or substantial

fun·gus (fuŋ'gəs) *n., pl.* **fun·gi** (fun'jī, fuŋ'gī), **fun'gus·es** [L., a mushroom, fungus, prob. < Gr. *spongos*, SPONGE] 1. any of a large group of thallophytes, including molds, mildews, mushrooms, rusts, and smuts, which are parasites on living organisms or feed upon dead organic material, lack chlorophyll, true roots, stems, and leaves, and reproduce by means of spores 2. something that grows suddenly and rapidly like a fungus —*adj.* of, like, or caused by a fungus; fungous

☆**fun house** an attraction at an amusement park consisting of a series of rooms and passageways with sloping or moving floors, distorting mirrors, and other devices meant to surprise or amuse

fu·ni·cle (fyōō'nə k'l) *n.* [L. *funiculus*, dim. of *funis*, a cord, rope] a little cord or fiber; specif., a funiculus

fu·nic·u·lar (fyoo nik'yoo lər) *adj.* [< L. *funiculus* (see prec.) + -AR] 1. of or like a funiculus or funiculi 2. of, worked by, or hanging from a rope or cable —*n.* a mountain railway on which counterbalanced cars on parallel sets of rails are pulled up and lowered by cables: also **funicular railway**

fu·nic·u·lus (-ləs) *n., pl.* **-li** (-lī') [L., small cord, dim. of *funis*, a cord, rope] 1. *Anat. a*) one of the three major divisions of the white matter of the central nervous system *b*) a small bundle of nerve fibers *c*) [Obs.] the umbilical or spermatic cord 2. *Bot.* the slender stalk of an ovule or seed —**fu·nic'u·late** (-lit, -lāt') *adj.*

funk¹ (fuŋk) *n.* [< ? Fl. *fonck*, dismay] [Colloq.] 1. a cowering or flinching through fear; panic 2. a cowardly or fearful person 3. a low, depressed mood: also **blue funk** —*vi.* [Colloq.] to be in a funk or panic —*vt.* [Colloq.] 1. to be afraid of 2. to avoid because of fear; shrink from; shirk 3. to frighten

funk² (fuŋk) *n.* [cf. FUNKY²] 1. a musty odor, as of moldy tobacco ☆2. funky jazz

fun·ky¹ (fuŋ'kē) *adj.* **-ki·er, -ki·est** in a funk, or panic

fun·ky² (fuŋ'kē) *adj.* **-ki·er, -ki·est** [orig. Negro argot, lit., smelly, hence musty, earthy < obs. *funk*, smell, smoke, prob. < Fr. dial. *funkier*, to smoke < VL. *fumicare*, for L. *fumigare*: see FUMIGATE] ☆*Jazz* having an earthy quality or style derived from early blues

fun·nel (fun'l) *n.* [ME. *fonel* < (prob. via an OFr. form) Pr. *fonilh, enfonilh* < L. *fundibulum, infundibulum*, a funnel < *infundere*, to pour in < *in-*, in + *fundere*, to pour: see FOUND³] 1. an instrument consisting of an inverted cone with a hole at the small end, or a tapering or cylindrical tube with a wide, cone-shaped mouth, for pouring liquids and powders into containers that have small openings 2. a thing shaped like a funnel 3. *a*) a cylindrical smokestack, as of a steamship *b*) a chimney or flue —*vi., vt.* **-neled** or **-nelled, -nel·ing** or **-nel·ling** 1. to move or pour through a funnel 2. to form in the shape of a funnel 3. to move into a central channel or to a central point

fun·nel·form (-fôrm') *adj.* shaped like a funnel

fun·ny (fun'ē) *adj.* **-ni·er, -ni·est** [see FUN & -Y²] 1. causing laughter; laughable; amusing; humorous 2. [Colloq.] *a*) out of the ordinary; strange; queer ☆*b*) deceptive or tricky —☆*n., pl.* **-nies** [Colloq.] same as COMIC STRIP: usually in *pl.* —☆**get funny with** [Colloq.] to be impudent to —**fun'ni·ly** *adv.* —**fun'ni·ness** *n.*

SYN.—**funny** is the simple, general term for anything that excites laughter or mirth; **laughable** applies to that which is fit to be laughed at and may connote contempt or scorn; that is **amusing** which provokes smiles, laughter, or pleasure by its pleasant, entertaining quality; that is **droll** which amuses one because of its quaintness or strangeness, or its wry or waggish humor; **comic** is applied to that which contains the elements of comedy (in a dramatic or literary sense) and amuses one in a thoughtful way; **comical** suggests that which evokes laughter of a more spontaneous, unrestrained kind; **farcical** suggests a broad comical quality based on nonsense, extravagantly boisterous humor, etc. See also ABSURD

funny bone [from its reaction to impact, but prob. suggested also by its relation to the *humerus* (hence, "humorous")] 1. a place on the elbow where the ulnar nerve passes close to the surface: a sharp impact at this place causes a strange, tingling sensation in the arm 2. inclination to laughter; (one's) risibilities

☆**funny paper** the comic-strip section of a newspaper

fur (fur) *n.* [ME. *furre*, prob. contr. < *furrure*, fur lining or blanket < OFr. *fourrure* < *fuerre*, sheath, lining < Frank. *fodr*, akin to G. *futter* < IE. base *po-*, to tend flocks, cover, protect, whence Gr. *poimēn*, Sans. *pālá-*, shepherd] 1. the soft, thick hair covering the body of many mammals 2. a skin bearing such hair, when stripped and processed for making, lining, or trimming garments; dressed pelt 3. any garment, neckpiece, trimming, etc. made of such skins 4. any furlike or fuzzy coating, as diseased matter on the tongue in illness —*adj.* of or having to do with fur —*vt.* **furred, fur'ring** 1. to line, cover, make, or trim with fur 2. to coat with a furry deposit, as of powder 3. to make (a floor, wall, etc.) level by using furring —*vi.* to become coated with a deposit —☆**make the fur fly** 1. to cause dissension or fighting 2. to accomplish much quickly

fu·ran (fyoor'an, fyoo ran') *n.* [contr. < FURFURAN] a colorless, liquid ring compound, C₄H₄O, prepared from wood tar or furfural, and used as a solvent for resins, plastics, etc. or as a tanning agent

fur·be·low (fur'bə lō') *n.* [altered (after FUR) < ModPr. *farbello*, a fringe, flounce, var. of Fr. *falbala*, furbelow] 1. a flounce or ruffle 2. [*usually pl.*] showy, useless trimming or ornamentation —*vt.* to decorate with or as with furbelows

fur·bish (fur'bish) *vt.* [ME. *furbishen* < extended stem of OFr. *forbir* < WGmc. **furbjan*, to clean, whence MHG. *vürben*] 1. to brighten by rubbing or scouring; polish; burnish 2. to make usable or attractive again; renovate (usually with *up*) —**fur'bish·er** *n.*

fur·cate (fur'kāt; *for adj., also* -kit) *adj.* [ML. *furcatus*, cloven < L. *furca*, a fork] forked —*vi.* **-cat·ed, -cat·ing** to branch; fork —**fur'cate·ly** *adv.* —**fur·ca'tion** *n.*

fur·cu·la (fur'kyoo lə) *n., pl.* **-lae** (-lē) [ModL., forked support, dim. of L. *furca*, a fork] *Anat., Zool.* any forked part or organ, as the forked tail in certain springing insects or the wishbone —**fur'cu·lar** (-lər) *adj.*

fur·cu·lum (-ləm) *n., pl.* **-la** (-lə) [ModL., dim. of L. *furca*, a fork] same as FURCULA

fur·fur (fur'fər) *n., pl.* **-fur·es'** (-ēz') [L., bran, redupl. < IE. base **gher-*, to rub, whence Gr. *cheras*, gravel] 1. dandruff; scurf 2. [*pl.*] scaly bits; esp., dandruff scales

fur·fu·ra·ceous (fur'fyə rā'shəs) *adj.* [LL. *furfuraceus*: see prec.] 1. of or like bran 2. covered with dandruff

fur·fu·ral (fur'fə ral', -fyə-) *n.* [L. *furfur* (see FURFUR) + -AL] a colorless, sweet-smelling oily liquid, C₅H₄O₂, produced from corncobs, oat hulls, and other cereal wastes, used as a solvent and to make dyes, lacquers, synthetic resins, etc.

fur·fu·ran (-ran') *n.* [FURFUR(AL) + -AN] same as FURAN

Fu·ries (fyoor'ēz) *n.pl.* [ME. < L. *Furiae*, pl. of *furia*, FURY] *Gr. & Rom. Myth.* the three terrible female spirits with snaky hair (Alecto, Tisiphone, and Megaera) who punished the doers of unavenged crimes

fu·ri·ous (fyoor'ē əs) *adj.* [ME. < OFr. *furieus* < L. *furiosus*] 1. full of fury or wild rage; violently angry 2. moving violently; violently overpowering [a *furious* attack] 3. very great; intense [with *furious* speed] —**fu'ri·ous·ly** *adv.* —**fu'ri·ous·ness** *n.*

furl (furl) *vt.* [< OFr. *ferlier* < *fermlier*, to tie up < *ferm* (< L. *firmus*, FIRM¹) + *lier* (< L. *ligare*, to tie: see LIGATURE)] to roll up tightly and make secure, as a flag to a staff or a sail to a spar —*vi.* to become curled or furled up —*n.* 1. a roll or coil of something furled 2. a furling or being furled

fur·long (fur'lôŋ) *n.* [ME. < OE. *furlang*, a measure, lit., length of a furrow < *furh*, FURROW + *lang*, LONG¹] a measure of distance equal to 1/8 of a mile, or 220 yards

fur·lough (fur'lō) *n.* [earlier *furloff* < Du. *verlof*, after G. *verlaub* < MHG. *verlouben*, to permit < *ver-*, FOR- + *loube*, permission, akin to LEAVE²] a leave of absence; esp., a leave granted to military enlisted personnel for a specified period —*vt.* 1. to grant a furlough to 2. to lay off (employees), esp. temporarily

fur·men·ty (fur'mən tē) *n.* same as FRUMENTY: also **fur'me·ty, fur'mi·ty** (-mə tē)

fur·nace (fur'nəs) *n.* [ME. *furnaise* < OFr. *fornais* < L. *fornax* (gen. *fornacis*), furnace, kiln < *fornus*, oven < IE. **gwhorn-*, heat < base **gwher-*, hot, warm, whence Gr. *thermos*, warm] 1. an enclosed chamber or structure in which heat is produced, as by burning fuel, for warming a building, reducing ores and metals, etc. 2. any extremely hot place 3. a grueling test or trial

Fur·ness (fur'nis), **Horace Howard** 1833-1912; U.S. Shakespearean scholar

fur·nish (fur'nish) *vt.* [ME. *furnishen* < extended stem of OFr. *furnir* < OFrank. **frumjan* (akin to OE. *framian*, G. *frommen*, to benefit), caus. < **fruma* (akin to ON. *frami*, profit): for IE. base see FROM] 1. to supply, provide, or equip with whatever is necessary or useful; esp., to put furniture into (a room, apartment, etc.) 2. to supply;

provide; give [to *furnish* information] —**fur′nish·er** *n.*
SYN.—furnish, as compared here, implies the provision of all the things requisite for a particular service, action, etc. [to *furnish* a house]; to **equip** is to furnish with what is requisite for efficient action [a car *equipped* with overdrive]; to **outfit** is to equip completely with the articles needed for a specific undertaking, occupation, etc. [to *outfit* a hunting expedition]; **appoint**, a formal word now generally used in the past participle, implies the provision of all the requisites and accessories for proper service [a well-*appointed* studio]; **arm** literally implies equipment with weapons, etc. for war but, in extended use, connotes provision with what is necessary to meet any circumstance

fur·nish·ings (-iŋz) *n.pl.* 1. the furniture, carpets, and the like for a room, apartment, etc. 2. articles of dress; things to wear [men's *furnishings*]

fur·ni·ture (fur′ni chər) *n.* [Fr. *fourniture* < *fournir*, FURNISH] 1. orig., the act of furnishing 2. the things, usually movable, in a room, apartment, etc. which equip it for living, as chairs, sofas, tables, beds, etc. 3. the necessary equipment of a machine, ship, trade, etc. 4. [Archaic] full equipment for a man and horse, as armor, harness, etc. 5. *Printing* pieces of wood, metal, etc. used to fill in blank areas in type forms

Fur·ni·vall (fur′ni v'l), **Frederick James** 1825–1910; Eng. philologist & editor

fu·ror (fyoor′ôr) *n.* [ME. *furour* < OFr. *fureur* < L. *furor*, rage, madness: see FURY] 1. fury; rage; frenzy 2. *a)* a great, widespread outburst of admiration or enthusiasm; craze; rage *b)* a state of excitement or confusion; commotion or uproar Also for 2, [Chiefly Brit.] **fu′rore** (-ôr)

furred (furd) *adj.* 1. made, trimmed, or lined with fur 2. having fur: said of an animal 3. wearing fur 4. coated with diseased or waste matter, as the tongue 5. made level with furring strips

fur·ri·er (fur′ē ər) *n.* [ME. *furrere*] 1. a dealer in furs 2. a person who processes furs or makes, repairs, alters, etc. fur garments

fur·ri·er·y (-ē) *n.*, *pl.* **-er·ies** 1. [Obs.] furs collectively 2. the business or work of a furrier

fur·ring (fur′iŋ) *n.* 1. fur used for trimming or lining 2. the act of trimming, lining, etc. with fur 3. a coating of diseased or waste matter, as on the tongue 4. *a)* the leveling of a floor, wall, etc., or the creating of air spaces, with thin strips of wood or metal before adding boards or plaster *b)* the strips (in full, **furring strips**) so used

fur·row (fur′ō) *n.* [ME. *forwe* < OE. *furh*, akin to G. *furche* (OHG. *furuh*) < IE. base *perk-*, to dig up, furrow, whence L. *porca*, furrow, *porcus*, pig (lit., digger)] 1. a narrow groove made in the ground by a plow 2. anything resembling this, as a deep, narrow rut made by a wheel, a deep wrinkle on the face, etc. 3. [Archaic] plowed land —*vt.* [< the *n.*] to make a furrow or furrows in —*vi.* 1. to make furrows 2. to become wrinkled

fur·ry (fur′ē) *adj.* **-ri·er, -ri·est** 1. of or made of fur 2. covered with or wearing fur 3. *a)* like fur, as in texture *b)* having a furlike coating —**fur′ri·ness** *n.*

fur seal any of several seals with soft, thick underfur

Fürth (fürt) city in SE West Germany, in Bavaria, near Nuremberg: pop. 101,000

fur·ther (fur′thər) *adj. alt. compar.* of FAR [ME. < OE. *furthra* (akin to G. *vorder*) < base of *fore*, FORE + compar. suffix < IE. *-tero-* (as in AFTER, OTHER)] 1. additional; more 2. more distant or remote; farther —*adv. alt. compar.* of FAR [ME. < *further*, orig. a neut. acc. of the *adj.*] 1. to a greater degree or extent 2. in addition; moreover 3. at or to a greater distance or more remote point in space or time; farther In sense 2 of the *adj.* and sense 3 of the *adv.*, FARTHER is more commonly used —*vt.* [ME. *furthren* < OE. *fyrthrian* < *furthra*, *furthor*] to give aid to; promote —**SYN.** see ADVANCE —**fur′ther·er** *n.*

fur·ther·ance (-əns) *n.* [ME.] a furthering, or helping forward; advancement; promotion

fur·ther·more (-môr′) *adv.* [ME. *further more*] in addition; besides; moreover: used with conjunctive force

fur·ther·most (-mōst′) *adj.* most distant; furthest

fur·thest (fur′thist) *adj. alt. superl.* of FAR [ME., formed as superl. on analogy of *farther*] most distant; farthest —*adv. alt. superl.* of FAR 1. at or to the greatest distance or most remote point in space or time 2. to the greatest degree or extent; most

fur·tive (fur′tiv) *adj.* [Fr. *furtif* < L. *furtivus*, stolen, hidden < *furtum*, theft < *fur*, a thief] done or acting in a stealthy manner, as if to hinder observation; surreptitious; stealthy; sneaky —**SYN.** see SECRET —**fur′tive·ly** *adv.* —**fur′tive·ness** *n.*

fu·run·cle (fyoor′uŋ k'l) *n.* [L. *furunculus*, petty thief, boil, dim. of *fur*, thief] a small skin abscess, or boil —**fu·run·cu·lar** (fyoo ruŋ′kyoo lər), **fu·run′cu·lous** (-ləs) *adj.*

fu·run·cu·lo·sis (fyoo ruŋ′kyoo lō′sis) *n.* [< prec. + -OSIS] the disorder characterized by the recurrent appearance of furuncles

fu·ry (fyoor′ē) *n.*, *pl.* **-ries** [ME. *furie* < OFr. < L. *furia* < *furere*, to rage, prob. < IE. base *dhus-*, to storm, whence Gr. *thyein*, to storm, L. *fuscus* & DUSK, DUST, DUN] 1. *a)* violent anger; wild rage *b)* a fit of this 2. violence;

vehemence; fierceness [the *fury* of a storm] 3. a violent or vengeful person; esp., such a woman 4. [F-] any of the Furies 5. [Archaic] a frenzy of being inspired —**SYN.** see ANGER —**like fury** [Colloq.] with great violence, speed, etc.

furze (furz) *n.* [ME. *firs* < OE. *fyrs* < IE. base *pūro-*, cereal, whence Czech *pýr*, couch grass] a prickly evergreen shrub (*Ulex europaeus*) of the legume family, with dark-green spines and yellow flowers, native to European wastelands —**furz′y** *adj.*

fu·sain (fyoo zan′) *n.* [Fr., orig., spindle tree < VL. **fusago* (gen. *fusaginis*) < L. *fusus*, a spindle] 1. a type of fine charcoal pencil prepared from the wood of the spindle tree 2. a drawing made with this 3. a constituent of coal resembling charcoal

Fu·san (foo′sän′) former (*Jap.*) name of PUSAN

fus·cous (fus′kəs) *adj.* [L. *fuscus*: see FURY] dark gray or grayish brown in color; dusky

fuse[1] (fyooz) *vt., vi.* **fused, fus′ing** [< L. *fusus*, pp. of *fundere*, to pour out, shed: see FOUND[3]] 1. to melt or to join by melting, as metals 2. to unite as if by melting together; blend —**SYN.** see MIX

fuse[2] (fyooz) *n.* [It. *fuso*, a cord, tube, casing < L. *fusus*, hollow spindle] 1. a narrow tube filled with combustible material, or a wick saturated with such material, for setting off an explosive charge 2. *same as* FUZE[2] (*n.* 2) 3. *Elec.* a wire or strip of easily melted metal, usually set in a plug, placed in a circuit as a safeguard: if the current becomes too strong, the metal melts, thus breaking the circuit —*vt.* **fused, fus′ing** to connect a fuse to —**blow a fuse** 1. to cause an electrical fuse to melt 2. [Colloq.] to become very angry

fused quartz a clear glass obtained when pure silica is fused at high temperature, used in apparatus which is subjected to high or rapidly changing temperatures

fu·see (fyoo zē′) *n.* [Fr. *fusée*, spindleful, rocket, hence fusee < ML. *fusata* < L. *fusus*: see FUSE[2]] 1. formerly, a friction match with a large head, able to burn in a wind ☆2. a colored flare used as a signal by railwaymen, truck drivers, etc. 3. in an old-fashioned clock or watch, a grooved cone upon which the cord from the spring container was unwound to equalize the force of the spring 4. *same as* FUSE[2] (*n.* 1 & 2)

fu·se·lage (fyoo′sə läzh′, -läj′, -lij; -zə-) *n.* [Fr. < *fuselé*, tapering (< OFr. *fus*, spindle < L. *fusus*) + -age, -AGE] the body of an airplane, exclusive of the wings, tail assembly, and engines

fu·sel oil (fyoo′z'l, -s'l) [G. *fusel*, inferior liquor < L. *fusilis*, FUSIL[1]] an oily, acrid, poisonous liquid occurring in imperfectly distilled alcoholic products and consisting generally of a mixture of amyl, butyl, propyl, and isoamyl alcohols: small amounts contribute to the characteristic flavor of a whiskey

Fu·shun (foo′shoon′) city in Liaoning province, NE China: pop. 1,019,000

fu·si·ble (fyoo′zə b'l) *adj.* [ME. < OFr.] that can be fused or easily melted —**fu′si·bil′i·ty** *n.* —**fu′si·bly** *adv.*

fu·si·form (fyoo′zə fôrm′) *adj.* [< L. *fusus*, a spindle + -FORM] shaped like a spindle; rounded, broadest in the middle, and tapering toward each end

fu·sil[1] (fyoo′z'l, -s'l) *adj.* [L. *fusilis* < *fusus*: see FUSE[1]] [Archaic] 1. fusible or fusing 2. *a)* fused; melted *b)* made by melting and molding, or casting; founded Also **fu′sile** (-z'l, -s'l, -sīl)

fu·sil[2] (fyoo′z'l) *n.* [Fr., orig., steel for striking sparks < ML. *focile* < L. *focus*, hearth (in LL., fire): see FOCUS] a light flintlock musket

fu·sil·ier, fu·sil·eer (fyoo′zə lir′) *n.* [Fr. *fusilier* < *fusil*: see prec.] formerly, a soldier armed with a fusil: the term *Fusiliers* is still applied to certain British regiments formerly so armed

fu·sil·lade (fyoo′sə läd′, -läd′; -zə-) *n.* [Fr. < *fusiller*, to shoot < *fusil*: see FUSIL[2]] 1. a simultaneous or rapid and continuous discharge of many firearms 2. something like this [a *fusillade* of questions] —*vt.* **-lad′ed, -lad′ing** to shoot down or attack with a fusillade

fu·sion (fyoo′zhən) *n.* [L. *fusio*] 1. a fusing or melting together 2. *a)* the union of different things by or as if by melting; blending; coalition [a *fusion* of political parties] *b)* the state or fact of being so united 3. anything made by fusing 4. *same as* NUCLEAR FUSION

fusion bomb a nuclear bomb which employs a fusion reaction, rather than fission, to produce the explosion: see HYDROGEN BOMB

fu·sion·ism (-iz'm) *n.* the theory or practice of bringing about a fusion, or coalition, of political parties, factions, etc. —**fu′sion·ist** *n., adj.*

fuss (fus) *n.* [17th-c. slang, prob. echoic] 1. a flurry of nervous, excited, and often unnecessary activity; needless bother; bustle 2. a state of excessive nervousness, agitation, etc. ☆3. [Colloq.] a quarrel or argument 4. [Colloq.] a showy display of delight, approval, etc. —*vi.* 1. to cause or make a fuss 2. to bustle about or worry, esp. over trifles 3. to whine, fret, etc., as a baby —*vt.* [Colloq.] to bother or worry unnecessarily —**fuss around** [Colloq.] to engage in idle, aimless, or annoying activity

☆**fuss·budg·et** (-buj′it) *n.* [FUSS + BUDGET, prob. in sense

"bag, sack"] [Colloq.] a fussy person: also **fuss′pot′** (-pät′)

fuss·y (fus′ē) *adj.* **fuss′i·er, fuss′i·est** **1.** *a)* habitually fussing; bustling about or worrying over trifles *b)* overly exacting and hard to please; finicky *c)* whining, fretting, etc., as a baby **2.** showing or needing careful attention **3.** full of unnecessary or showy details —**fuss′i·ly** *adv.* —**fuss′i·ness** *n.*

fus·tian (fus′chən) *n.* [ME. < OFr. *fustaigne* < ML. *fustaneum* (< L. *fustis*, wooden stick) used as transl. of Gr. *xylinon* < *xylinos*, wooden (in LXX, cotton)] **1.** orig., a coarse cloth of cotton and linen **2.** now, a thick cotton cloth with a short nap, as corduroy, velveteen, etc. **3.** pompous, pretentious talk or writing; bombast; rant —*adj.* **1.** made of fustian **2.** pompous and pretentious but empty

fus·tic (fus′tik) *n.* [ME. *fustik* < OFr. *fustoc* < Ar. *fustuq* < Per. *fistik*, whence Gr. *pistakē*, pistachio] ☆**1.** a tropical American tree (*Chlorophora tinctoria*) of the mulberry family, from whose wood a yellow dye is extracted **2.** the dye **3.** any of several other woods from which dyes are extracted

fus·ti·gate (fus′tə gāt′) *vt.* **-gat′ed, -gat′ing** [< L. *fustigatus*, pp. of *fustigare*, to beat with a stick < *fustis*, a stick + *agere*: see ACT] to beat with a stick; cudgel —**fus′ti·ga′tion** *n.*

fus·ty (fus′tē) *adj.* **fus′ti·er, fus′ti·est** [< *fust*, a musty smell < Early ModE. *fust*, a cask (ME. *foist*) < OFr. *fust*, cask, orig. tree trunk < L. *fustis*, wooden stick] **1.** smelling stale or stuffy; musty; moldy **2.** not up-to-date; old-fashioned; conservative —**fus′ti·ly** *adv.* —**fus′ti·ness** *n.*

fut. future

fu·thark (foo′thärk) *n.* [< the first six letters: *f, u, þ (th), a* (or o), *r, k* (or *c*)] the runic alphabet: also sp. **futharc, futhorc, futhork**

fu·tile (fyoot′′l; *chiefly Brit. & Canad.*, fyoo′tīl) *adj.* [< Fr. or L.: Fr. *futile* < L. *futilis*, lit., that easily pours out, hence untrustworthy, worthless, futile < base of *fundere*: see FOUND³] **1.** *a)* that could not succeed; useless; vain; hopeless *b)* lacking vigor or purpose; inept or ineffective **2.** trifling or unimportant —**fu′tile·ly** *adv.* —**fu′tile·ness** *n.* **SYN.**—*futile* is applied to that which fails completely of the desired end or is incapable of producing any result; *vain* also implies failure but does not have as strong a connotation of intrinsic inefficacy as *futile*; *fruitless* stresses the idea of great and prolonged effort that is profitless or fails to yield results; that is *abortive* which fails to succeed or miscarries at an early stage of its development; that is *useless* which has proved to be ineffectual in practice or is theoretically considered to be of no avail —ANT. *effective, fruitful, effectual*

fu·til·i·tar·i·an (fyoo til′ə ter′ē ən) *adj.* [< ff., after UTILITARIAN] based on or having the belief that everything in life is futile —*n.* a person who has this belief

fu·til·i·ty (fyoo til′ə tē) *n.*, *pl.* **-ties** [Fr. *futilité* < L. *futilitas* < *futilis*, FUTILE] **1.** the quality of being futile **2.** a futile act, thing, etc.

fut·tock (fut′ək) *n.* [< ? pronun. of *foot hook*] any of the upright curved timbers forming the ribs of a wooden ship **futtock plate** an iron plate put horizontally around the top of a ship's lower mast to hold the futtock shrouds **futtock shroud** one of the short iron rods extended from a futtock plate to a band around the lower mast to brace the topmast where it joins the lower mast

Fu·tu·na (fa too′nə) island in the W South Pacific: see WALLIS AND FUTUNA

fu·ture (fyoo′chər) *adj.* [ME. *futur* < OFr. < L. *futurus*, about to be, used as fut. participle of *esse*, to be] **1.** that is to be or come; of days, months, or years ahead **2.** indicating time to come [the *future* tense of a verb] —*n.* **1.** the time that is to come; days, months, or years ahead **2.** what will happen; what is going to be [to seek to foretell the *future*] **3.** the prospective or potential condition of a person or thing; esp., the chance to achieve, succeed, etc. [to have a great *future* in politics] **4.** [*usually pl.*] a contract for a specific commodity bought or sold for delivery at a later date **5.** *Gram. a)* the future tense *b)* a verb form or phrase expressing this tense

fu·ture·less (-lis) *adj.* having no hopes, plans, or prospects for the future

future life *Religion* the state of the soul after death **future perfect** **1.** a tense indicating an action or state as completed in relation to a specified time in the future **2.** a verb form in this tense (Ex.: will have gone)

fu·tur·ism (fyoo′chər iz′m) *n.* [It. *futurismo* < *futuro*, FUTURE] a movement in the arts, originated by Italian painters shortly before World War I: they opposed traditionalism and sought to depict dynamic movement by eliminating conventional form and balance and by stressing the speed, flux, and violence of the machine age —**fu′tur·ist** *n.*, *adj.*

fu·tur·is·tic (fyoo′chər is′tik) *adj.* of or having to do with the future or futurism —**fu′tur·is′ti·cal·ly** *adv.*

fu·tu·ri·ty (fyoo toor′ə tē, -tyoor′-, -choor′-) *n.*, *pl.* **-ties** **1.** *a)* the future *b)* a future condition or event **2.** the quality of being future ☆**3.** *same as* FUTURITY RACE

☆**futurity race** a race, esp. a horse race, in which the contestants are selected long beforehand

fuze¹ (fyooz) *vt.*, *vi.* **fuzed, fuz′ing** *same as* FUSE¹

fuze² (fyooz) *n.* **1.** *same as* FUSE² (*n.* 1) **2.** any of various chemical, electronic, etc. devices for detonating bombs, projectiles, or explosive charges —*vt.* **fuzed, fuz′ing** to connect a fuze to

fu·zee (fyoo zē′) *n.* *same as* FUSEE

fuzz (fuz) *n.* [< ? Du. *voos*, or back-formation < FUZZY] very loose, light particles of down, wool, etc.; fine hairs or fibers [the *fuzz* on a peach] —*vi.*, *vt.* **1.** to cover or become covered with fuzz **2.** to make or become fuzzy —☆**the fuzz** [< ? FUSS, in sense "a fussy (i.e., hard to please) person"] [Slang] a policeman or the police

fuzz·y (-ē) *adj.* **fuzz′i·er, fuzz′i·est** [prob. < LowG. *fussig*, fibrous, spongy, akin to Du. *voos*, spongy < IE. **pus-* < base **pu-*, to rot, whence FOUL] **1.** of, like, or covered with fuzz **2.** not clear, distinct, or precise; blurred [*fuzzy* thinking, a *fuzzy* sound] —**fuzz′i·ly** *adv.* —**fuzz′i·ness** *n.*

f.v. [L. *folio verso*] on the back of the page

fwd. forward

-fy (fī) [ME. *-fyen, -fien* < OFr. *-fier* < L. *-ficare* < *facere*, to make, DO¹: see FACT] *a v.-forming suffix meaning:* **1.** to make; cause to be or become [liquefy] **2.** to cause to have or feel; imbue with [glorify] **3.** to become [putrefy]

☆**fyce** (fīs) *n.* *same as* FEIST

FYI for your information

☆**fyke** (fīk) *n.* [Du. *fuik*, a bow net] a fish net in the form of a long bag reinforced with hoops

fyl·fot (fil′fät) *n.* [< FILL + FOOT: so called because used to fill the foot of a colored window] a swastika

Fyn (fün) a main island of Denmark, between Jutland & Zealand: 1,149 sq. mi.

F.Z.S. Fellow of the Zoological Society

G

G, g (jē) *n.*, *pl.* **G's, g's** **1.** the seventh letter of the English alphabet: from the Greek *gamma*, a borrowing from the Phoenician **2.** a sound of *G* or *g*, either the voiced velar stop (g) of *get* or the voiced alveolar affricate (j) of *siege* **3.** a type or impression for *G* or *g* **4.** *a symbol for* the seventh in a sequence or group **5.** *Physics a)* gravity *b)* acceleration of gravity *c)* a unit of acceleration equal to the acceleration of gravity: used to measure the force on a body undergoing acceleration and expressed as a multiple of the body's weight —*adj.* **1.** of *G* or *g* **2.** seventh in a sequence or group

G (jē) *n.* **1.** [< G(RAND), *n.* 2] [Slang] one thousand dollars **2.** *Educ.* a grade meaning *good* **3.** *Music a)* the fifth tone or note in the ascending scale of C major *b)* a key, string, etc. producing this tone *c)* the scale having this tone as the keynote —*adj.* shaped like *G*

G. **1.** German **2.** specific gravity

G., g. **1.** *Elec.* conductance **2.** gauge **3.** grain **4.** gram(s) **5.** guilder(s) **6.** guinea(s) **7.** gulf

g **1.** *Psychol.* general intelligence **2.** goalkeeper

Ga *Chem.* gallium

Ga. **1.** Gallic **2.** Georgia

G.A. **1.** General Agent **2.** General Assembly

G.A., G/A, g.a. general average

gab (gab) *vi.* **gabbed, gab′bing** [ME. *gabben*, to lie, scoff, talk nonsense < ON. *gabba*, to mock (& < OFr. *gaber* < ON.), akin to OE. *gaffetung*, a scoffing & *gaf-spræc*, foolish speech < IE. base **ĝhebh-* < base **ghē-*, whence GAP, GAPE, GASP] [Colloq.] to talk much or idly; chatter; gabble —*n.* [Colloq.] idle talk; chatter —**gift of (the) gab** [Colloq.] the ability to speak fluently or glibly —**gab′ber** *n.*

gab·ar·dine (gab′ər dēn′, gab′ər dēn′) *n.* [var. of GABERDINE] **1.** a cloth of wool, cotton, rayon, etc. twilled on one side and having a fine, diagonal weave, used for suits, coats, dresses, etc. **2.** a garment made of this cloth **3.** *same as* GABERDINE

gab·ble (gab′l) *vi.* **-bled, -bling** [freq. of GAB] **1.** to talk rapidly and incoherently; jabber; chatter **2.** to utter rapid,

gabbler meaningless sounds, as a goose —*vt.* to utter rapidly and incoherently —*n.* rapid, incoherent talk or meaningless utterance —**gab′bler** *n.*

gab·bro (gab′rō) *n.* [It. < L. *glaber,* bare: see GLABROUS] any of a group of dark, heavy igneous rocks, composed chiefly of pyroxene and feldspar

gab·by (gab′ē) *adj.* **-bi·er, -bi·est** [Colloq.] inclined to chatter; talkative —**gab′bi·ness** *n.*

ga·belle (gə bel′) *n.* [ME. *gabelle* < OFr. < OIt. *gabella* < Ar. *ḳabāla,* tax] a tax levied in certain countries; esp., one on salt levied in France before the Revolution

gab·er·dine (gab′ər dēn′, gab′ər dēn′) *n.* [earlier *gawbardyne* < OFr. *gaverdine,* kind of cloak < ? MHG. *walvart,* pilgrimage < *wallen,* to wander about + *vart,* a trip < *varen,* FARE] **1.** a loose coat or cloak made of coarse cloth, worn in the Middle Ages, esp. by Jews **2.** *chiefly Brit. sp.* of GABARDINE

gab·er·lun·zie (gab′ər lun′zē) *n.* [Scot.; printing form of *gaberlunyie* (with printed *z* for *y* as in pers. name *Menzies* < ?] [Scot.] a wandering beggar

Gabe·rones (gäb rōnz′) capital of Botswana, in the SE part: pop. 12,000

☆**gab·fest** (gab′fest′) *n.* [GAB + -FEST] [Colloq.] **1.** an informal gathering of people to talk with one another **2.** their talk

ga·bi·on (gā′bē ən) *n.* [Fr. < It. *gabbione,* large cage < *gabbia,* cage, coop < L. *cavea;* see CAGE] **1.** a cylinder of wicker filled with earth or stones, formerly used in building fortifications **2.** a similar cylinder of metal, used in building dams, dikes, etc.

ga·ble (gā′b'l) *n.* [ME. < OFr. < Gmc., as in ON. *gafl,* gable, akin to G. *giebel,* gable < IE. base *ghebhel-,* gable, head, whence Gr. *kephalē*] **1.** *a)* the triangular wall enclosed by the sloping ends of a ridged roof *b)* popularly, the whole section, including wall, roof, and space enclosed **2.** the end wall of a building, the upper part of which is a gable **3.** *Archit.* a triangular decorative feature, such as that over a door or window —*vt.* **-bled, -bling** to put a gable or gables on

gable roof a ridged roof forming a gable at each end

gable window 1. a window in a gable (sense 2) **2.** a window with a gable (sense 3) over it

Ga·bo (gä′bō), **Na·um** (nä′ōōm) (born *Naum Pevsner*) 1890– ; U.S. sculptor, born in Russia

Ga·bon (gȧ bōn′) country in WC Africa, on the Gulf of Guinea: a member state of the French Community: 103,089 sq. mi.; pop. 480,000; cap. Libreville —**Gab·on·ese** (gab′ə nēz′) *adj., n. sing. & pl.*

Ga·bo·riau (gȧ bô ryō′), **É·mile** (ā mēl′) 1835–73; Fr. writer of detective stories

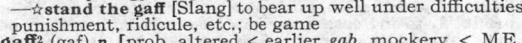
GABLE (sense 1)

Ga·bri·el (gā′brē əl) [Heb. *gabhrī'ēl,* lit., God is (my) strength] a masculine name: dim. *Gabe;* fem. *Gabriella, Gabrielle* **2.** *Bible* one of the seven archangels, the herald of good news: Dan. 8:16; Luke 1:26

Ga·bri·el·la (gab′rē el′ə, gä′brē-) [It. & Sp.] a feminine name: also [Fr.] **Ga′bri·elle′** (-el′): see GABRIEL

ga·by (gā′bē) *n., pl.* **-bies** [< Brit. Midland dial. < ? or akin to ON. *gapi,* reckless person] [Brit. Dial.] a foolish person; simpleton

Gad¹ (gad) [Heb. *gādh,* lit., fortune] *Bible* **1.** the seventh son of Jacob **2.** the tribe of Israel descended from him

Gad² (gad) *interj.* [euphemism for GOD] [*also* g-] a mild oath or expression of surprise, disgust, etc.

gad¹ (gad) *vi.* **gad′ded, gad′ding** [LME. *gadden,* to hurry, perhaps back-formation < *gadeling,* companion in arms < OE. *gædeling:* for IE. base see GATHER] to wander about in an idle or restless way, as in seeking amusement —*n.* an act of gadding: chiefly in the phrase **on** (or **upon**) **the gad,** gadding about —**gad′der** *n.*

gad² (gad) *n.* [ME. *gadd* < ON. *gaddr,* infl. in sense by OE. *gad* (cf. GOAD); akin to Goth. *gazds,* thorn < IE. base *ǵhasto-,* rod, pole, whence YARD¹ & L. *hasta,* rod, shaft] **1.** *same as* GOAD **2.** any of several chisellike or pointed bars used in mining —*vt.* **gad′ded, gad′ding** to break up or loosen (ore) with a gad

gad·a·bout (gad′ə bout′) *n.* [Colloq.] a person who gads about; restless seeker after fun, excitement, etc. —*adj.* fond of gadding

Gad·a·rene (gad′ə rēn′) *adj.* [< the *Gadarene* swine (Luke 8:26–39) that ran into the sea after demons possessed them] moving rapidly and without control; headlong

gad·fly (gad′flī′) *n., pl.* **-flies′** [GAD² + FLY²] **1.** any of several large flies, as the horsefly, that bite livestock **2.** a person who annoys others or rouses them from complacency

gadget (gaj′it) *n.* [< ?] **1.** any small, esp. mechanical contrivance or device **2.** any interesting but relatively useless or unnecessary object —**gadg′et·y** *adj.*

☆**gad·get·eer** (gaj′ə tir′) *n.* [GADGET + -EER] a person who contrives, or takes a special delight in, gadgets

gadg·et·ry (gaj′ət rē) *n.* **1.** gadgets collectively **2.** preoccupation with mere gadgets

Ga·dhel·ic (gə del′ik, -dē′lik) *adj., n. same as* GOIDELIC

ga·did (gā′did) *n.* [< ModL. *Gadidae,* name of the family < *gadus,* cod < Gr. *gados,* kind of fish] a gadoid fish

ga·doid (gā′doid) *adj.* [< ModL. *gadus* (see prec.) + -OID] of or like the cod family of fishes —*n.* any fish of this family

gad·o·lin·ite (gad′'l in it′) *n.* [G. *gadolinit,* after J. *Gadolin* (1760–1852), Finn. chemist who isolated it] a brown or black silicate mineral, containing some metals of the rare-earth group in combination with iron

gad·o·lin·i·um (gad′'l in′ē əm) *n.* [ModL.: so named by J. Marignac, Swiss chemist, who discovered it in GADOLINITE in 1886] a metallic chemical element of the rare-earth group that is very magnetic at low temperatures: symbol, Gd; at. wt., 157.25; at. no., 64; sp. gr., 7.948; melt. pt., 1312°C; boil. pt., 2800°C

ga·droon (gə drōōn′) *n.* [Fr. *godron*] any of various oval-shaped beadings, flutings, or reedings used to decorate molding, silverware, etc. —**ga·droon′ing** *n.*

Gads·den (gadz′dən) [after ff.] city in NE Ala.: pop. 54,000

Gads·den (gadz′dən), **James** 1788–1858; U.S. diplomat: negotiated (1853) a purchase of land (**Gadsden Purchase**) from Mexico, which became part of N.Mex. & Ariz., c. 45,000 sq. mi.

gad·wall (gad′wôl) *n., pl.* **-walls, -wall:** see PLURAL, II, D, 1 [< ?] a grayish-brown wild duck (*Anas strepera*) of the N freshwater regions of America

Gad·zooks (gad zōōks′) *interj.* [< *God's hooks,* nails of the Cross] [Archaic] a mild oath

gae¹ (gā) *vi.* **gaed** (gād), **gaen** (gān), **gae′ing** [Scot.] *same as* GO¹

gae² (gā) [Scot.] *pt.* of GIVE

Gae·a (jē′ə) [Gr. *Gaia* < *gē,* earth] *Gr. Myth.* the earth personified as a goddess, mother of the Titans: identified with the Roman goddess Tellus

Gael (gāl) *n.* [contr. < Gael. *Gaidheal,* akin to Ir. *Gaedheal,* OIr. *Góidel,* W. *gwyddel* (Irishman)] a Celt of Scotland, Ireland, or the Isle of Man; esp., a Celt of the Scottish Highlands

Gael·ic (-ik) *adj.* [< Gael. *Gaidhealach*] **1.** of the Gaels **2.** of the Goidelic subbranch of the Celtic family of languages or its components; of Scottish or Irish Gaelic —*n.* **1.** the Goidelic subbranch of the Celtic family of languages **2.** one of these languages; esp., Scottish or Irish Gaelic Abbrev. **Gael.**

gaff¹ (gaf) *n.* [ME. *gaffe* < OFr. < Pr. *gaf* or Sp. *gafa* < ? or akin to Goth. *gafah,* a catch < *ga-,* intens. + *fahan,* to catch, akin to FANG] **1.** a large, strong hook on a pole, or a barbed spear, used in landing large fish **2.** *a)* a sharp metal spur fastened to the leg of a gamecock *b)* any of the steel points on a linemen's climber **3.** a spar or pole extending from the after side of a mast and supporting a fore-and-aft sail **4.** [Slang] any secret device for cheating **5.** [earlier in sense of "a fair": ? because visitors were *gaffed* there] [Brit. Slang] a cheap theater, dance hall, etc. —*vt.* **1.** to strike or land (a fish) with a gaff **2.** [Chiefly Brit. Slang] to cheat; hoax; trick **3.** [Slang] to rig with a gaff (*n.* 4)

GAFF

☆**stand the gaff** [Slang] to bear up well under difficulties, punishment, ridicule, etc.; be game

gaff² (gaf) *n.* [prob. altered < earlier *gab,* mockery < ME., deceit: cf. GAB] [Brit. Slang] foolish talk; nonsense —**blow the gaff** [Brit. Slang] to reveal a secret

gaffe (gaf) *n.* [Fr.] a blunder; faux pas

gaf·fer (gaf′ər) *n.* [altered < GODFATHER] **1.** an old man, esp. one from the country: now usually contemptuous or humorous: see also GAMMER **2.** a master glass blower ☆**3.** [Slang] head electrician on a movie or TV set **4.** [Brit.] a foreman of a group of workers

gaff sail a fore-and-aft sail supported by a gaff

gaff-top·sail (gaf′täp′s'l, -säl′) *n.* a topsail set above a gaff

gag (gag) *vt.* **gagged, gag′ging** [ME. *gaggen,* of echoic origin] **1.** to cause to retch or choke **2.** to put something over or into the mouth of, so as to keep from talking, crying out, etc. **3.** to keep from speaking or expressing oneself freely, as by intimidation **4.** to prevent or limit speech in (a legislative body) **5.** *Mech.* to choke or stop up (a valve, etc.) —*vi.* **1.** to retch or choke **2.** [Colloq.] to make a gag or gags; joke —*n.* **1.** something put into or over the mouth to prevent talking, crying out, etc. ☆**2.** any restraint of free speech **3.** a dentist's device for holding the jaws open **4.** *a)* a comical remark or act; joke, as one interpolated by an actor on the stage *b)* a practical joke or hoax

ga·ga (gä′gä) *adj.* [Fr., orig., a fool: of echoic orig.] [Slang] **1.** mentally confused; crazy **2.** carried away by love, enthusiasm, etc.

Ga·ga·rin (gä gär′in), **Yu·ri A·lek·se·ye·vich** (yōō′rē ä′lyek sā′yə vich) 1934–68; Soviet cosmonaut; first man to orbit the earth in a space flight

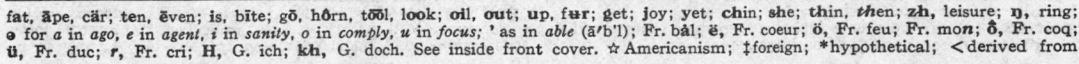

gage[1] (gāj) *n.* [ME. < OFr., a pledge, pawn < (? via ML. *wagium*) Frank. *waddi* or Goth. *wadi*, pledge, akin to G. *wette*, bet: see WED] **1.** something deposited or pledged to insure that an obligation will be fulfilled; security **2.** a pledge to appear and fight, as a glove thrown down by a knight challenging another **3.** a challenge —*vt.* **gaged, gag'ing** [Archaic] **1.** to offer as a pledge; wager **2.** to bind by a pledge

gage[2] (gāj) *n., vt. same as* GAUGE (esp. in technical usage)

gage[3] (gāj) *n. shortened form of* GREENGAGE

Gage (gāj), **Thomas** 1721–87; Brit. general in the American Revolution

gag·ger (gag'ər) *n.* a person or thing that gags; specif., a piece of iron to keep a core in place in a mold

gag·gle (gag'l) *n.* [ME. *gagel* < *gagelen*, to cackle: orig. echoic] **1.** a flock of geese **2.** any group or cluster

☆**gag·man** (-man') *n., pl.* **-men'** a man who devises jokes, bits of comic business, etc., as for entertainers

☆**gag rule** (or **law**) a rule or law limiting or preventing discussion, as in a legislative body

gahn·ite (gän'īt) *n.* [G. *gahnit*, after J. G. *Gahn* (1745–1818), Swed. chemist] a zinc aluminate, ZnAl₂O₄, often containing iron and magnesium, found as almost opaque crystals of green, brown, or black

Gai·a (gā'ə, gī'ə) *same as* GAEA

gai·e·ty (gā'ə tē) *n., pl.* **-ties** [Fr. *gaieté*] **1.** the state or quality of being gay; cheerfulness **2.** merrymaking; festivity **3.** finery; showy brightness

Gail[1] (gāl) [contr. or dim. of *Gaylord*, altered (after LORD) < ME. *Gaylard* < Fr. *Gaillard* < OFr. *gaillard*, brave, prob. ult. < Ir. *gal*, courage < IE. base *gal-*, to be able] a masculine name

Gail[2] (gāl) a feminine name: see ABIGAIL

Gail·lard Cut (gāl'yərd, gā'lärd) [after David DuBose *Gaillard* (1859–1913), U.S. army engineer in charge of its excavation] S section of the Panama Canal cut through the continental divide: c. 8 mi. long

☆**gail·lar·di·a** (gā lär'dē ə) *n.* [ModL., after the 18th-cent. Fr. botanist *Gaillard* de Marentonneau] any of a genus (*Gaillardia*) of American plants of the composite family, having large, showy flower heads with yellow or reddish rays and purple disks

gai·ly (gā'lē) *adv.* [ME.] in a gay manner; specif., *a)* happily; merrily; joyously *b)* brightly; in bright colors

gain[1] (gān) *n.* [ME. < OFr. *gaaigne* < *gaaignier*: see the *v.*] **1.** an increase; addition; specif., *a)* [often *pl.*] an increase in wealth, earnings, etc.; profit; winnings *b)* an increase in advantage; advantage; improvement **2.** the act of getting something; acquisition; accumulation **3.** *Electronics a)* an increase in signal strength when transmitted from one point to another: often expressed in decibels *b)* the ratio of the output current, voltage, or power of an amplifier, receiver, etc. to the respective input —*vt.* [ME. *gainen*, to profit, be of use < OFr. *gaaignier* < Frank. *waidanjan*, to work, earn, akin to OHG. *weidenon*, to pasture < *weide*, pasture < IE. *witi-*, a hunting after < base *wei-*, to go toward, hunt, whence L. *via*, way, *vis*, strength] **1.** to get by labor; earn [to *gain* a livelihood] **2.** *a)* to get by effort or merit, as in competition; win *b)* to cause to be directed toward oneself or itself; attract [to *gain* one's interest] **3.** to get as an increase, addition, profit, or advantage [to *gain* ten pounds] **4.** to make an increase in [to *gain* speed] **5.** to go faster by [my watch *gained* two minutes] **6.** to get to; arrive at; reach —*vi.* **1.** to make progress; improve or advance, as in health, business, etc. **2.** to acquire wealth or profit **3.** to increase in weight; become heavier **4.** to be fast: said of a clock, etc. —*SYN.* see GET, REACH —**gain on 1.** to draw nearer to (an opponent in a race, etc.) **2.** to make more progress than (a competitor) —**gain over** to win over to one's side

☆**gain**[2] (gān) *n.* [< ?] *Carpentry* a joining notch, groove, or mortise

gain·er (gā'nər) *n.* **1.** a person or thing that gains **2.** a fancy dive in which the diver faces forward and does a backward somersault in the air

Gaines·ville (gānz'vil') [after Gen. Edmund P. *Gaines* (1777–1849)] city in NC Fla.: pop. 65,000

gain·ful (gān'f'l) *adj.* producing gain; profitable —**gain'ful·ly** *adv.* —**gain'ful·ness** *n.*

gain·ly (gān'lē) *adj.* **-li·er, -li·est** [ME. *geinli* < *gein*, convenient, ready < ON. *gegn*, straight, fit] shapely and graceful; comely —**gain'li·ness** *n.*

gain·say (gān'sā') *vt.* **-said'** (-sed', -sād'), **-say'ing** [ME. *geinseggen* < *gein-* < OE. *gegn*, against + *seggen* (see SAY)] **1.** to deny **2.** to contradict **3.** to speak or act against; oppose; forbid —*n.* a gainsaying —*SYN.* see DENY —**gain'say'er** *n.*

Gains·bor·ough (gānz'bur'ō, -bər ə), **Thomas** 1727–88; Eng. painter

'gainst, gainst (genst, gānst) *prep. poetic clip of* AGAINST

Gai·ser·ic (gī'zə rik) *same as* GENSERIC

gait (gāt) *n.* [ME. *gate*, a going, gait, orig.; path < ON. *gata*, path between hedges, street, akin to G. *gasse*, lane] **1.** manner of moving on foot; way of walking or running **2.** any of the various foot movements of a horse, as a trot, pace, canter, or gallop —*vt.* to train (a horse) to a particular gait or gaits

gait·ed (-id) *adj.* having a (specified) gait or gaits: used in hyphenated compounds [heavy-*gaited*]

gai·ter (gāt'ər) *n.* [altered (after GAIT) < Fr. *guêtre*, earlier *guietre*, prob. < Frank. *wrist*, instep, akin to WRIST] **1.** a cloth or leather covering for the instep and ankle, and, sometimes, the calf of the leg; spat or legging ☆**2.** a shoe with elastic in the sides and no lacing ☆**3.** a high overshoe with cloth upper

Ga·ius (gā'əs) 110?–180? A.D.; Roman jurist

gal[1] (gal) *n.* [Colloq.] a girl

gal[2] (gal) *n.* [< GAL(ILEO)] a unit of acceleration equal to one centimeter per second per second: used in gravimetry

Gal. Galatians

gal. gallon(s)

GAITERS

ga·la (gā'lə, gal'ə, gä'lə) *n.* [It. *gala* < OFr. *gale*, enjoyment, pleasure, prob. < Gmc. source, as in MDu. *wale*, riches, wealth, akin to WEAL²] **1.** a festive occasion; festival; celebration **2.** [Obs.] festivity —*adj.* festive, or suitable for a festive occasion —**in gala** in festive dress

gal·a·bi·a, gal·a·bi·ya (gal'ə bē'ə) *n.* [Ar. *jallabiyah*] a long, loose cotton gown reaching to the ankles, worn in Arabic countries, esp. by peasants

ga·lac·ta·gogue (gə lak'tə gôg', -gäg') *n.* [GALACT(O)- + -AGOGUE] an agent that stimulates or increases the secretion of milk

ga·lac·tic (gə lak'tik) *adj.* [Gr. *galaktikos*, milky < *gala* (gen. *galaktos*), milk < IE. base *glak-*, whence L. *lac*, milk] **1.** of or obtained from milk; lactic **2.** *Astron.* of or pertaining to the Milky Way or some other galaxy

galactic noise radio waves emanating from sources outside the solar system but within the Milky Way

ga·lac·to- (gə lak'tə, -tō) [Gr. *gala* (gen. *galaktos*): see GALACTIC] *a combining form meaning* milk, milky [*galactometer*]: also, before a vowel, **ga·lact-**

gal·ac·tom·e·ter (gal'ək täm'ə tər) *n. same as* LACTOMETER

ga·lac·tor·rhe·a (gə lak'tə rē'ə) *n.* [GALACTO- + -RRHEA] persistent flow of milk from the breasts

ga·lac·tose (gə lak'tōs) *n.* [GALACT(O)- + -OSE¹] a white, crystalline sugar, C₆H₁₂O₆, prepared by the hydrolysis of lactose

ga·lac·to·se·mi·a (gə lak'tə sē'mē ə) *n.* [GALACTOS(E) + -EMIA] a congenital disease caused by the lack of an enzyme needed to metabolize galactose and producing mental retardation, cataracts, and liver damage

ga·lac·to·side (gə lak'tə sīd') *n.* [GALACTOS(E) + -IDE] **1.** any of a group of fatty substances yielding galactose and a fatty acid on hydrolysis **2.** any of a group of glycosides which contain galactose

ga·lah (gə lä') *n.* [< native name] a pink and gray cockatoo (*Kakatoē roseicapilla*) that is widely distributed in inland Australia and is popular as a cage bird

Gal·a·had (gal'ə had') in late Arthurian legend, a knight who was successful in the quest for the Holy Grail because of his purity and nobility of spirit: he was the son of Lancelot and Elaine —*n.* any man regarded as very pure and noble

ga·lan·gal (gə laŋ'g'l) *n.* [ME. < OFr. *galingal* < ML. *galingala* < Ar. *khalanjān*, ult. < ? Chin.] **1.** either of two plants (genus *Alpinia*) of the ginger family, whose dried rhizomes yield aromatic substances used in medicines **2.** any of various plants (genus *Cyperus*) of the sedge family, some of which have aromatic rootstocks

gal·an·tine (gal'ən tēn') *n.* [ME. *galentine* < OFr. < ML. *galatina*, jelly < L. *gelata*, fem. pp. of *gelare*, to congeal] a mold of boned, seasoned, boiled white meat, as chicken or veal, chilled and served in its own jelly

ga·lan·ty show (gə lan'tē) [earlier also *galanté*, prob. < It. *galante*, gallant: from the stories portrayed] a pantomime made by throwing the shadows of puppet figures on a screen or wall

Ga·lá·pa·gos Islands (gə lä'pə gōs') group of islands in the Pacific on the equator, belonging to Ecuador: 3,028 sq. mi.; pop. 2,400: Sp. name, Archipélago de COLÓN

Ga·la·ta (gal'ə tə) commercial section of Istanbul, Turkey, on the Golden Horn

Gal·a·te·a (gal'ə tē'ə) a statue of a maiden which, in Greek mythology, was given life by Aphrodite after its sculptor, Pygmalion, fell in love with it: name applied in post-classical times

gal·a·te·a (gal'ə tē'ə) *n.* [after a 19th-cent. Eng. warship, H.M.S. *Galatea*: the fabric was used to make sailor suits for little boys] a strong, twill cotton cloth, often striped, used for play clothes, uniforms, etc.

Ga·la·ţi (gä läts') city in E Romania, on the Danube: pop. 113,000

Ga·la·tia (gə lā'shə) ancient kingdom in C Asia Minor, made a Roman province c. 25 B.C. —**Ga·la'tian** *adj., n.*

Ga·la·tians (-shənz) the Epistle to the Galatians, a book of the New Testament which was a message from the Apostle Paul to the Christians of Galatia

gal·a·vant (gal'ə vant') *vi. same as* GALLIVANT

☆**gal·ax** (gā'laks) *n.* [ModL., prob. < Gr. *gala*, milk (see GALACTIC): from its white flower] an evergreen plant (*Galax aphylla*) of the SE U.S., with shiny leaves (often used in wreaths) and small, white flowers

gal·ax·y (gal'ək sē) *n.* [ME. *galaxie* < LL. *galaxias* < Gr. *galaxias*, Milky Way < *gala*, milk (see GALACTIC)] [often G-] *same as* MILKY WAY —*n., pl.* **-ax·ies 1.** any of in-

numerable large groupings of stars, typically containing millions to hundreds of billions of stars **2.** *a)* an assembly of brilliant or famous people *b)* a brilliant array of things

Gal·ba (gal'bə, gôl'-), **(Servius Sulpicius)** 5 B.C.?–69 A.D.; Roman emperor (68–69)

gal·ba·num (gal'bə nəm) *n.* [ME. < L. < Gr. *chalbanē* < Heb. *helbenāh*] a bitter, bad-smelling Asiatic gum resin, obtained from various plants (genus *Ferula*) of the parsley family, formerly used in medicine

gale¹ (gāl) *n.* [< ?] **1.** a strong wind; specif., *Meteorol.* one ranging in speed from 32 to 63 miles per hour: see BEAUFORT SCALE **2.** [Archaic] a breeze ☆**3.** a loud outburst [a *gale* of laughter] —*SYN.* see WIND²

gale² (gāl) *n.* [ME. *gawel* < OE. *gagel*, akin to G. *gagel*] *same as* SWEET GALE

ga·le·a (gā'lē ə) *n.*, *pl.* **ga'le·ae'** (-ē') [ModL. < L., a helmet; prob. < Gr. *galeē*, a weasel, marten (hence, leather, hide, then article made of leather)] *Biol.* a helmet-shaped part, esp. of a corolla or calyx

ga·le·ate (-āt') *adj.* [L. *galeatus*, pp. of *galeare*, to cover with a helmet < *galea*, a helmet] **1.** wearing a helmet **2.** helmet-shaped Also **ga'le·at'ed**

Ga·len (gā'lən) (L. name *Claudius Galenus*) 130?–200? A.D.; Gr. physician & writer on medicine & philosophy —**Ga·len·ic** (gə len'ik), **Ga·len'i·cal** *adj.*

ga·le·na (gə lē'nə) *n.* [L., lead ore, dross of melted lead < ?] native lead sulfide, PbS, a lead-gray mineral with metallic luster: it is the principal ore of lead, often also containing silver

ga·len·i·cal (gə len'i k'l) *n.* [< GALEN] a medicine prepared from plants, according to a fixed recipe, as opposed to drugs of known chemical composition

Ga·len·ism (gā'lən iz'm) *n.* the system of medical practice originated by Galen —**Ga'len·ist** *n.*

ga·len·ite (gə lē'nīt) *n. same as* GALENA

Gales·burg (gālz'bərg) [after Rev. G. W. *Gale* (1789–1861), owner of the site] city in NW Ill.: pop. 36,000

Ga·li·bi (gä lē'bē) *n.*, *pl.* **-bis, -bi** any member of a subdivision of Carib Indians living in Guiana

Ga·li·cia (gə lish'ə) **1.** region of SE Poland & NW Ukrainian S.S.R.: formerly, an Austrian crown land **2.** region & former kingdom in NW Spain

Ga·li·cian (-ən) *adj.* **1.** of Spanish Galicia, its people, or language **2.** of Polish Galicia or its people —*n.* **1.** a native or inhabitant of Spanish Galicia **2.** the Portuguese dialect of the Spanish Galicians **3.** a native or inhabitant of Polish Galicia

Gal·i·le·an¹ (gal'ə lē'ən) *adj.* of Galilee or its people —*n.* **1.** a native or inhabitant of Galilee **2.** [Archaic] a Christian —**the Galilean** Jesus

Gal·i·le·an² (gal'ə lē'ən) *adj.* of Galileo

Gal·i·lee (gal'ə lē') [L. *Galilaea* < Gr. *Galilaia* < Heb. *glil* (*ha-goyim*), lit., district (of the Gentiles)] **1.** region of N Israel **2.** Sea of, lake of NE Israel, on the Syria border: c. 13 mi. long

gal·i·lee (gal'ə lē') *n.* [ME. *galilie* < ML. *galilaea* < L. *Galilaea*, Galilee: ? because, being at the less sacred western end, it was compared with the scriptural "Galilee of the Gentiles"] a porch or chapel at the western entrance of certain medieval churches

Gal·i·le·o (gal'ə lē'ō, -lā'-) (born *Galileo Galilei*) 1564–1642; It. astronomer, mathematician, & physicist: with the telescope, which he improved, he demonstrated the truth of the Copernican theory and was condemned for heresy by the Inquisition

gal·i·ma·ti·as (gal'ə mā'shē əs, -mat'ē əs) *n.* [Fr., prob. < L. *gallus*, lit., a cock, 16th-c. student slang for a candidate engaged in doctoral disputations + Gr. *-mathia*, learning < *mathēma* (see MATHEMATICAL)] meaningless talk; gibberish

gal·in·gale (gal'ən gāl') *n. same as* GALANGAL

gal·i·ot (gal'ē ət) *n. same as* GALLIOT

gal·i·pot (gal'ə pät') *n.* [Fr., earlier *garipot*, prob. altered < MDu. *harpois*, boiled resin] crude turpentine from a pine tree (*Pinus pinaster*) of S Europe

gall¹ (gôl) *n.* [ME. *galle* < OE. (Anglian) *galla* (WS. *gealla*), akin to G. *galle* < IE. base *\\ghel-*, to shine, yellow, whence L. *fel*, gall, Gr. *cholē*, bile, E. YELLOW] **1.** bile, the bitter,

GALILEE

greenish fluid secreted by the liver and stored in the gall bladder **2.** [Archaic] the gall bladder **3.** something that is bitter or distasteful **4.** bitter feeling; rancor ☆**5.** [Colloq.] rude boldness; impudence; audacity —*SYN.* see TEMERITY

gall² (gôl) *n.* [ME. *galle* < OE. *gealla* < L. *galla*: see ff.] **1.** a sore on the skin, esp. of a horse's back, caused by rubbing or chafing **2.** irritation or annoyance, or a cause of this —*vt.* [ME. *gallen* < the *n.* (or < OFr. *galer*, to scratch < *galle* < L. *galla*)] **1.** to injure or make sore by rubbing; chafe **2.** to irritate; annoy; vex —*vi.* [Rare] to become sore from rubbing or chafing

gall³ (gôl) *n.* [ME. *galle* < OFr. < L. *galla*, gallnut, orig., spherical growth < IE. base *\\gel-*, to form into a ball, whence CLAY, CLOT] a tumor on plant tissue caused by stimulation by fungi, insects, or bacteria: galls formed on oak trees have a high tannic acid content and are used commercially

Gal·la (gal'ə) *n.*, *pl.* **-las, -la** [ult. < Ar. *ghaliz*, wild] **1.** any member of various agricultural or pastoral peoples of S Ethiopia and adjoining Somalia **2.** their Cushitic language

gal·lant (gal'ənt; for adj. 4 & n., usually gə lant' or -länt'; for v., always gə lant' or -länt') *adj.* [ME. *galaunt* < OFr. *galant*, gay, brave, prp. of *galer*, to rejoice, make merry < *gale:* see GALA] **1.** showy and gay in dress or appearance **2.** stately; imposing [a *gallant* ship] **3.** brave and noble; high-spirited and daring **4.** *a)* polite and attentive to women in a courtly way *b)* having to do with love; amorous —*n.* [Now Rare] **1.** a high-spirited, stylish man **2.** a man attentive and polite to women **3.** a lover or paramour —*vt.* [Now Rare] **1.** to court (a woman) **2.** to escort or accompany (a woman) **3.** [Now Rare] to court a woman —*SYN.* see CIVIL —**gal'lant·ly** *adv.*

gal·lant·ry (gal'ən trē) *n.*, *pl.* **-ries** [Fr. *galanterie* < *galant:* see prec.] **1.** nobility of behavior or spirit; heroic courage **2.** the courtly manner of a gallant **3.** an act or speech characteristic of a gallant **4.** amorous intrigue **5.** [Archaic] gay or showy appearance

Gal·la·tin (gal'ə tin), **(Abraham Alfonse) Albert** 1761–1849; U.S. statesman & financier, born in Switzerland; secretary of the treasury (1801–13)

gall·blad·der (gôl'blad'ər) *n.* a membranous sac attached to the liver, in which excess gall, or bile, is stored and concentrated

Galle (gäl) seaport in SW Ceylon: pop. 65,000

gal·le·ass (gal'ē as', -əs) *n.* [Fr. *galéasse* < OFr. *galeace* < It. *galeazza* < *galea* < ML. *galea:* see GALLEY] a large, three-masted vessel having sails and oars and carrying heavy guns: used on the Mediterranean in the 16th and 17th cent.

gal·le·in (gal'ē in, gal'ēn) *n.* [GALL(IC ACID) + (PHTHAL)EIN] a violet dye, $C_{20}H_{12}O_7$, formed by treating pyrogallic acid with phthalic anhydride, used as an indicator and as a mordant dye

gal·le·on (gal'ē ən, gal'yən) *n.* [Sp. *galeón* < ML. *galea:* see GALLEY] a large Spanish ship of the 15th and 16th cent., with three or four decks at the stern: used as both a warship and a trader

gal·ler·ied (gal'ər ēd) *adj.* having a gallery or galleries

gal·ler·y (gal'ə rē, gal'rē) *n.*, *pl.* **-ler·ies** [ME. < Fr. *galerie*, gallery < ML. *galeria*, prob. < *galilaea:* see GALILEE] **1.** *a)* a covered walk open at one side or having the roof supported by pillars; colonnade *b)* [Chiefly South] a

GALLEON

veranda or porch **2.** a long, narrow balcony on the outside of a building **3.** a platform or balcony at the quarters or around the stern of an early sailing ship **4.** *a)* a platform or projecting upper floor attached to the back wall or sides of a church, theater, etc.; esp., the highest of a series of such platforms in a theater, with the cheapest seats *b)* the cheapest seats in a theater *c)* the people occupying these seats, sometimes regarded as exemplifying popular tastes *d)* the spectators at a sporting event, legislative meeting, etc. **5.** a long, narrow corridor or room **6.** a place or establishment for exhibiting or dealing in art works **7.** any of the display rooms of a museum **8.** a collection of paintings, statues, etc. ☆**9.** a room or establishment used as a photographer's studio, for practice in shooting at targets, etc. **10.** an underground passage, as one made by an animal, or one used in mining or military engineering —*vt.* **-ler·ied**, **-ler·y·ing** to furnish with a gallery, or balcony —**play to the gallery 1.** *Theater* to act in a manner intended to please those in the gallery **2.** to try to win the approval of the public, esp. in an obvious or showy way

gal·let (gal'it) *n.* [Fr. *galet*, pebble, dim. < dial. *gal*, stone: see ff.] a chip of stone —*vt.* to embed gallets in (joints of fresh masonry)

☆**gal·let·a** (gə yet'ə, gä yät'ə) *n.* [Sp., hardtack < OFr. *galette*, a stone (< Gaul. *\\gallos*) + *-ette:* cf. *-ET*] a coarse, tough forage grass (*Hilaria jamesii*) used for hay and grazing in the SW U.S.

gal·ley (gal′ē) *n., pl.* **-leys** [ME. *galeie* < OFr. *galie* < ML. *galea* < MGr. *galaia*, kind of ship < ? Gr. *galeē*, weasel (in reference to its speed) or < ? Gr. *galeos*, shark] **1.** a long, low, usually single-decked ship propelled by oars and sails, used esp. in ancient and medieval times: the oars were usually manned by chained slaves or convicts **2.** a ship's kitchen **3.** [Brit.] a large rowboat **4.** *Printing a)* a shallow, oblong tray for holding composed type before it is put into a form *b) same as* GALLEY PROOF

GALLEY

galley proof printer's proof taken from type in a galley to permit correction of errors before the type is made up in pages

☆**gal·ley-west** (gal′ē west′) *adv.* [< dial. *colly-west* < ?] [Colloq.] into confusion or inaction: chiefly in the phrase **knock galley-west**

gall·fly (gôl′flī′) *n., pl.* **-flies′** a fly whose eggs or larvae cause galls when deposited in plant stems, or one which lays its eggs in galls produced by other insects

Gal·li·a (gäl′ē ə, gal′-) *Latin genit.* of GAUL

gal·liard (gal′yərd) *adj.* [ME. *gaillard* < OFr.: see GAIL¹] [Obs.] **1.** valiant; sturdy **2.** lively —*n.* **1.** a lively French dance in triple time, for two dancers, popular in the 16th and 17th cent. **2.** music for this

gal·li·ass (gal′ē as′, -əs) *n. same as* GALLEASS

Gal·lic (gal′ik) *adj.* [L. *Gallicus* < *Galli*, the Gauls] **1.** of ancient Gaul or its people **2.** French

gal·lic acid (gal′ik) [Fr. *gallique* < *galle*, GALL³] a nearly colorless, crystalline acid, $(OH)_3C_6H_2COOH$, prepared from nutgalls, tannin, etc. and used in photography and the manufacture of inks, dyes, etc.

Gal·li·can (gal′i kən) *adj.* [ME. < OFr. < L. *Gallicanus*, of the Roman province of *Gallia* < *Gallicus*] **1.** *same as* GALLIC **2.** of the Roman Catholic Church in France, esp. before 1870 **3.** of Gallicanism —*n.* a supporter of Gallicanism

Gal·li·can·ism (-iz'm) *n.* the principles enunciated by the French Roman Catholic Church in 1682, claiming limited autonomy: opposed to ULTRAMONTANISM

Gal·li·cism, gal·li·cism (gal′ə siz′m) *n.* [Fr. *Gallicisme* < L. *Gallicus*, GALLIC] **1.** a French idiom or expression, translated literally into another language **2.** a French custom, way of thought, etc.

Gal·li·cize, gal·li·cize (-sīz′) *vt., vi.* **-cized′, -ciz′ing** [see GALLIC] to make or become French or like the French in thought, language, etc.

Gal·li-Cur·ci (gäl′ə kur′chē; *It.* gäl′lē kŏr′chē), **A·me·li·ta** (ä′mä lē′tä) 1889–1963; U.S. coloratura soprano, born in Italy

gal·li·gas·kins (gal′i gas′kinz) *n.pl.* [altered < Fr. *garguesque* < OFr. *greguesque* < It. *grechesca* < *Grechesca*, Grecian (hence, orig., "Grecian breeches")] **1.** loosely fitting breeches worn in the 16th and 17th cent.: later applied humorously to any loose breeches **2.** [Brit. Dial.] leggings or gaiters

gal·li·mau·fry (gal′ə mô′frē) *n., pl.* **-fries** [Fr. *galimafrée*, prob. < OFr. *galer* (see GALLANT) + dial. (Picardy) *mafrer*, to eat much < MDu. *maffelen*] **1.** orig., a hash made of meat scraps **2.** a hodgepodge; jumble

gal·li·na·cean (gal′ə nā′shən) *adj. same as* GALLINACEOUS —*n.* any gallinaceous bird

gal·li·na·ceous (-shəs) *adj.* [L. *gallinaceus* < *gallina*, hen < *gallus*, a cock] of, or having the nature of, an order (Galliformes) of birds that nest on the ground, including common poultry, pheasants, grouse, etc.

gall·ing (gôl′in) *adj.* [prp. of GALL²] chafing; very annoying; irritating; vexing —**gall′ing·ly** *adv.*

☆**gal·li·nip·per** (gal′ə nip′ər) *n.* [prob. altered (after GAL-LEY) < *gurnipper* < ?] [Colloq.] a large mosquito or other insect that has a painful bite or sting

gal·li·nule (gal′ə nyōōl′, -nōōl′) *n.* [ModL. < L. *gallinula*, pullet, dim. of *gallina*: see GALLINACEOUS] any of various marsh birds (family Rallidae) that both swim and wade, esp. a species (*Gallinula chloropus*) of the E U.S.

gal·li·ot (gal′ē ət) *n.* [ME. < OFr. *galiot*, dim. of *galie* < ML. *galea*, GALLEY] **1.** a small, swift galley with sails and oars, formerly used on the Mediterranean **2.** a light Dutch merchant ship of shallow draft, with a single mast

Gal·lip·o·li (gə lip′ə lē) *same as* GELIBOLU

Gallipoli Peninsula peninsula in S European Turkey, forming the NW shore of the Dardanelles: c. 60 mi. long

gal·li·pot¹ (gal′ə pät′) *n.* [ME. *galy pott*, prob. < *galeie*, GALLEY + *pot*, POT: because shipped in galleys from Italy] a small pot or jar of glazed earthenware, esp. one used by druggists as a container for medicine

gal·li·pot² (gal′ə pät′) *n. same as* GALIPOT

gal·li·um (gal′ē əm) *n.* [ModL. < L. *Gallia*, Gaul; also a pun on L. *gallus*, a cock, transl. of *Lecoq*, in name of the discoverer, Lecoq de Boisbaudran, 19th-cent. Fr. chemist] a soft, bluish-white, metallic chemical element with an unusually low melting point, used as a substitute for mercury in thermometers, dental amalgam, etc.: symbol, Ga; at. wt., 69.72; at. no., 31; sp. gr., 6.095; melt. pt., 30.15°C; boil. pt., 1983°C

gal·li·vant (gal′ə vant′) *vi.* [arbitrary elaboration of GAL-LANT] **1.** orig., to gad about with members of the opposite sex **2.** to go about in search of amusement or excitement —**gal′li·vant′er** *n.*

gal·li·wasp (gal′ə wäsp′, -wôsp′) *n.* [< ?] **1.** any of several large, harmless lizards (genus *Diploglossus*), found in marshes in the West Indies and Central America **2.** a Caribbean lizard fish (*Synodus foetens*)

gall midge (or **gnat**) any of a large number of very small flies (family Cecidomyiidae) that produce galls on plants

gall mite any of various mites (family Eriophyidae) that have only two pairs of legs and produce galls on plants

☆**gall·nut** (gôl′nut′) *n.* a nutlike gall, esp. on oaks

Gal·lo- (gal′ō) [L. < *Gallus*, a Gaul] *a combining form meaning:* **1.** French [*Gallophile*] **2.** French and

gal·lo·glass (gal′ō glas′) *n.* [Ir. *gallóglach*, servant, soldier < *gall*, foreigner + *óglach*, a youth, servant, soldier] an armed follower of any of the old Irish chieftains

gal·lon (gal′ən) *n.* [ME. *galoun* < ONormFr. *galon* < ML. *galo*, gallon, jug] **1.** a liquid measure, equal to 4 quarts (231 cubic inches): the British imperial gallon equals 277.42 cubic inches **2.** a dry measure, equal to 1/8 bushel **3.** any container with a capacity of one gallon Abbrev. **gal.**

gal·lon·age (-ij) *n.* amount or capacity in gallons

gal·loon (gə lōōn′) *n.* [Fr. *galon* < *galonner*, to braid, adorn with lace, ? akin to OFr. *gale*: see GALLANT] a braid or ribbon, as of cotton or silk or of gold or silver thread, used for trimming or ornament

gal·lop (gal′əp) *vi.* [ME. *galopen* < OFr. *galoper* < Frank. *walahlaupan*, to run well < *wala*, akin to WELL² + *hlaupan*, to run, akin to LEAP] **1.** to go at a gallop **2.** to move, progress, or act very fast; hurry —*vt.* to cause to gallop —*n.* [OFr. *galop*] **1.** the fastest gait of a horse or other animal, consisting of a succession of leaping strides with all the feet off the ground at one time **2.** a ride on a galloping animal **3.** any fast pace, speedy action, or rapid progression —**gal′lop·er** *n.*

gal·lo·pade (gal′ə pād′) *n.* [Fr. *galopade* < *galoper*: see prec. & -ADE] *same as* GALOP

gal·lous (gal′əs) *adj.* [GALL(IUM) + -OUS] *Chem.* containing gallium with a valence of two

Gal·lo·way (gal′ə wā′) region in SW Scotland, comprising the counties of Wigtown & Kirkcudbright —*n.* **1.** any of a former Scottish breed of small, hardy horses **2.** any of a Scottish breed of black, hornless beef cattle

gal·low·glass (gal′ō glas′) *n. same as* GALLOGLASS

gal·lows (gal′ōz) *n., pl.* **-lows·es, -lows** [ME. *galwes*, pl. of *galwe* < OE. *galga*, akin to G. *galgen* < IE. base *ĝhalgh-*, pliant tree branch, whence Lith. *žalgà*, long, thin pole: the earliest gallows was a pulled-down branch that carried the victim with it when allowed to spring up] **1.** an upright frame with a crossbeam and a rope, for hanging condemned persons **2.** any structure like this, used for suspending or supporting **3.** the death sentence by hanging

gallows bird [Colloq.] a person who deserves hanging

☆**gallows humor** amused cynicism by one facing disaster; morbid or cynical humor

gallows tree [ME. *galwetre* < OE. *galgtreow*] a gallows

gall·stone (gôl′stōn′) *n.* a small, solid mass sometimes formed in the gallbladder or bile duct; biliary calculus: it is formed of cholesterol, or, occasionally, of calcium salts, and can obstruct the flow of bile, causing pain, jaundice, and other symptoms

gal·lus·es (gal′əs iz) *n.pl.* [< *gallus*, dial. var. of GALLOWS] [Colloq.] suspenders; braces

gall wasp any of various very small insects (family Cynipidae) whose larvae produce galls in plants, esp. oaks and roses

Ga·lois theory (gal wä′) [after Evariste *Galois* (1811–32), Fr. mathematician] a theory for the solution of certain algebraic equations of fifth and higher degrees

ga·loot (gə lōōt′) *n.* [orig., naval slang < ?] [Slang] ☆a person, esp. an awkward, ungainly person

gal·op (gal′əp) *n.* [Fr.: see GALLOP] **1.** a lively round dance in 2/4 time **2.** music for this —*vi.* to dance a galop

ga·lore (gə lôr′) *adv.* [Ir. *go leór*, enough < *go*, to + *leór*, enough] in abundance; plentifully [to attract crowds *galore*] —*n.* [Rare] abundance

ga·losh, ga·loshe (gə läsh′) *n.* [ME. *galoche* < OFr., prob. < LL. *gallicula*, small Gallic shoe, ? infl. by L. *caligula*, dim. of *caliga*, military boot] **1.** orig., *a)* a heavy shoe *b)* any boot or shoe **2.** an overshoe, esp. a high, warmly lined overshoe of rubber and fabric

Gals·wor·thy (gôlz′wur′thē, galz′-), **John** 1867–1933; Eng. novelist & playwright

Gal·ton (gôl′t'n), Sir **Francis** 1822–1911; Eng. scientist & writer: pioneer in eugenics

ga·lumph (gə lumf′) *vi.* [coined by Lewis Carroll < GAL(LOP) + (TRI)UMPH] to march or bound along in a self-satisfied, triumphant manner

Gal·va·ni (gal vä′nē), **Lu·i·gi** (loo wē′jē) 1737–98; It. physiologist and physicist

gal·van·ic (gal van′ik) *adj.* [GALVAN(ISM) + -IC] **1.** of, caused by, or producing an electric current, esp. from a battery **2.** stimulating or stimulated as if by electric shock; startling or convulsive Also **gal·van′i·cal** —**gal·van′i·cal·ly** *adv.*

gal·va·nism (gal′və niz′m) *n.* [Fr. *galvanisme* < It.

galvanismo: so called after L. GALVANI] **1.** electricity produced by chemical action **2.** *Med.* direct electrical current, as from a battery, used to stimulate nerves and muscles

gal·va·nize (gal′və nīz′) *vt.* **-nized′, -niz′ing** [Fr. *galvaniser* < *galvanisme:* see GALVANISM] **1.** to apply an electric current to **2.** to stimulate as if by electric shock; startle; excite **3.** to plate (metal) with zinc, originally by galvanic action —**gal′va·ni·za′tion** *n.*

gal·va·no- (gal′və nō, gal van′ō) *a combining form meaning* galvanic, galvanism [*galvanometer*]

gal·va·no·mag·net·ic (-mag net′ik) *adj.* of or relating to the generation of a transverse electric field in metals and semiconductors in the presence of a magnetic field

gal·va·nom·e·ter (gal′və näm′ə tər) *n.* an instrument for detecting and measuring a small electric current —**gal′va·no·met′ric** (-və nō met′rik) *adj.* —**gal′va·nom′e·try** (-trē) *n.*

Gal·ves·ton (gal′vis tən) [< ff.] seaport in SE Tex., on an island (**Galveston Island**) at the mouth of Galveston Bay: pop. 62,000

Galveston Bay [after Bernardo de *Gálvez* (1746–86), gov. of Louisiana] inlet of the Gulf of Mexico, in SE Tex.: c. 35 mi. long

Gal·way (gôl′wā) **1.** county in Connacht province, W Ireland: 2,293 sq. mi.; pop. 148,000 **2.** its county seat, on an inlet of the Atlantic (**Galway Bay**): pop. 22,000

Gal·we·gian (gal wē′jən) *adj.* of Galloway or its people —*n.* a native or inhabitant of Galloway

gal·yak, gal·yac (gal′yak) *n.* [< word used in Bukhara for a premature lamb < Russ. *golyak,* bare, naked < IE. base *gal-,* whence CALLOW] a flat, glossy fur made from the pelts of lambs or kids

☆**gam**[1] (gam) *n.* [prob. < Scand., as in Norw., Sw. dial. *gams,* loose conversation < ON. *gems,* akin to GAME[1]] **1.** a social visit **2.** an exchange of visits between the crews of whaling ships at sea **3.** a school of whales —*vi.* **gammed, gam′ming 1.** to visit socially, *esp.* at sea **2.** to come together; congregate: said of whales —*vt.* to have a social visit with, esp. at sea

gam[2] (gam) *n.* [var. of GAMB] [Slang] a leg; often, specif., a woman's shapely leg

Gama, Vasco da *see* DA GAMA

☆**ga·ma grass** (gä′mə) [altered < GRAMA grass] any of several tall, perennial, American grasses (genus *Tripsacum*), used for forage

Ga·ma·li·el (gə mā′lē əl, -māl′yəl) [LL. < Gr. *Gamaliēl* < Heb. *gamlī'ēl,* lit., reward of God] **1.** a masculine name **2.** *Bible a*) a teacher of Saul of Tarsus: Acts 22:3 *b*) a ruler of Manasseh: Num. 10:23

gamb, gambe (gamb, gam) *n.* [dial. Fr. *gambe* (Fr. *jambe*) < ML. *gamba,* a leg (in LL., a hoof) < Gr. *kampē,* a turn, joint] an animal's leg or shank, esp. as on a coat of arms

gam·ba·do (gam bā′dō, -bä′dō) *n., pl.* **-dos, -does 1.** [altered < Fr. *gambade* < Pr. *gambado* < It. *gambata,* a kick < *gamba,* a leg: see GAMB] a curvetting leap, as by a horse **2.** a prank or antic **3.** [< It. *gamba,* a leg] a long legging or gaiter, esp. one attached to a saddle to serve as a stirrup

gam·be·son (gam′bi s'n) *n.* [ME. < OFr. < ML. *wambasium* < LGr. *bambax,* cotton: see BOMBAST] a medieval coat, made of leather or quilted cloth, worn as armor

Gam·bet·ta (gam bet′ə; *Fr.* gän be tá′), **Lé·on** (lā ōn′) (**Michel**) 1838–82; Fr. statesman; premier (1881–82)

Gam·bi·a (gam′bē ə) **1.** country on the W coast of Africa, surrounded on three sides by Senegal: formerly a Brit. colony & protectorate, it became independent (1965) & a member of the Brit. Commonwealth: c. 4,000 sq. mi.; pop. 357,000; cap. Bathurst: official name, **The Gambia 2.** river in W Africa, flowing from N Guinea, through Senegal & Gambia, into the Atlantic: c. 700 mi.

gam·bier, gam·bir (gam′bir) *n.* [Malay *gambir*] an astringent substance extracted from the leaves and twigs of a Malayan plant (*Uncaria gambir*) of the madder family, chewed with the betel nut and used in medicine, tanning, and dyeing

gam·bit (gam′bit) *n.* [Fr. < OFr. *gambet* < Sp. *gambito,* a tripping < It. *gamba,* a leg < LL. *gamba:* see GAMB] **1.** *Chess* an opening in which a pawn or other piece is sacrificed to get an advantage in position **2.** a maneuver or action intended to gain an advantage

gam·ble (gam′b'l) *vi.* **-bled, -bling** [prob. dial. var. of ME. *gamen* < OE. *gamenian,* to play, akin to G. dial. *gammeln,* to sport, make merry: form infl. ? by GAMBOL] **1.** to play games of chance for money or some other stake **2.** to take a risk in order to gain some advantage —*vt.* to risk in gambling; bet; wager —*n.* an act or undertaking involving risk of a loss —**gamble away** to squander or lose in gambling —**gam′bler** (-blər) *n.*

gam·boge (gam bōj′, -bōōzh′) *n.* [ModL. *gambogium* < CAMBODIA, where first obtained] **1.** a gum resin obtained from a tropical Asian tree (*Garcinia hanburyi*) of the Saint Johnswort family, used as a yellow pigment and as a cathartic **2.** bright yellow

gam·bol (gam′b'l) *n.* [earlier *gambolde* < Fr. *gambade,* a gambol: see GAMBADO] a jumping and skipping about in

play; frolic —*vi.* **-boled** or **-bolled, -bol·ing** or **-bol·ling** to jump and skip about in play; frolic —*SYN.* see PLAY

gam·brel (-brəl) *n.* [ONormFr. < OFr. *gambe:* see GAMB] **1.** the hock of a horse or similar animal **2.** a frame shaped like a horse's hind leg, used by butchers for hanging carcasses ☆**3.** *same as* GAMBREL ROOF

☆**gambrel roof** a roof with two slopes on each of two sides, the lower steeper than the upper

gam·bu·si·a (gam byōō′zhə, -zhē ə) *n.* [ModL., altered from AmSp. (Cuban) *gambusino*] ☆any of a genus (*Gambusia*) of topminnows, esp. useful in mosquito control: see MOSQUITOFISH

game[1] (gām) *n.* [ME. < OE. *gamen,* akin to OFris. *game,* OHG. *gaman*]

GAMBREL ROOF

1. any form of play or way of playing; amusement; recreation; sport; frolic; play **2.** *a*) any specific amusement or sport involving physical or mental competition under specific rules [football and chess are *games*] *b*) a single contest in such a competition [to win two out of three *games*] *c*) a subdivision of a contest, as in a set in tennis **3.** *a*) the number of points required for winning [the *game* is 25] *b*) the score at any given point in a competition [at the half the *game* was 7 to 6] **4.** that which is gained by winning; victory; win **5.** a set of equipment for a competitive amusement [to sell toys and *games*] **6.** a way or quality of playing in competition [to play a good *game*] **7.** any test of skill, courage, or endurance [the *game* of life] **8.** a project; scheme; plan [to see through another's *game*] **9.** *a*) wild birds or animals hunted for sport or for use as food: see also BIG GAME *b*) the flesh of such creatures used as food **10.** any object of pursuit or attack: usually in **fair game 11.** [Colloq.] a business or vocation, esp. one with an element of risk [the stock-market *game*] —*vi.* **gamed, gam′ing** to play cards, etc. for stakes; gamble —*adj.* **1.** designating or of wild birds or animals hunted for sport or for use as food **2. gam′er, gam′est** *a*) plucky; courageous *b*) having enough spirit or enthusiasm; ready (*for* something) —☆**ahead of the game** [Colloq.] in the position of winning, esp. in gambling —**die game** to die bravely and still fighting —**game away** to squander or lose in gambling —**make game of** to make fun of; make the butt of jokes, teasing, etc.; ridicule —**off one's game** performing poorly —**play the game** [Colloq.] **1.** to act according to the rules of a game **2.** to behave as fairness or custom requires —**The Game** charades —**the game is up** all chances for success (of a risky enterprise) are gone

game[2] (gām) *adj.* [< ?] [Colloq.] lame or injured: said esp. of a leg

game·cock (gām′käk′) *n.* a specially bred rooster trained for cockfighting

game fish any fish regularly caught for sport, esp. any species that fights hard when hooked

game fowl any of a breed of fowl trained for cockfighting

game·keep·er (-kēp′ər) *n.* a person employed to breed and take care of game birds and animals on State farms or private estates

gam·e·lan (gam′ə lan′) *n.* [Jav., a bamboo xylophone] a musical ensemble of Indonesia, consisting of bamboo xylophones, gongs, and other percussion instruments

game laws laws regulating hunting and fishing in order to preserve game

game·ly (gām′lē) *adv.* in a game, or plucky, manner

game·ness (-nis) *n.* a game, or plucky, quality

games·man·ship (gāmz′mən ship′) *n.* [< GAME[1] + (SPORT)SMANSHIP] skill in handling a situation to one's own advantage by the use of ploys

game·some (gām′səm) *adj.* [ME. *gamsum:* see GAME[1] & -SOME] playful; sportive; frolicsome —**game′some·ly** *adv.*

game·ster (-stər) *n.* [GAME[1] + -STER] a gambler

gam·e·tan·gi·um (gam′ə tan′jē əm) *n., pl.* **-gi·a** (-ə) [ModL.: see GAMETO- & ANGIO-] *Bot.* a plant structure in which gametes are produced

gam·ete (gam′ēt; gə mēt′, gə-) *n.* [ModL. *gameta* < Gr. *gametē,* a wife < *gamein,* to marry < GAMO-] a reproductive cell that is haploid and can unite with another gamete to form the cell (*zygote*) that develops into a new individual —**ga·met·ic** (gə met′ik) *adj.*

game theory a method of using mathematical analysis to select the best available strategy in order to minimize one's maximum losses or maximize one's minimum winnings in a game, war, business competition, etc.

ga·me·to- (gə mēt′ō, -ə) *a combining form meaning* gamete [*gametophore*]

ga·me·to·cyte (gə mēt′ə sīt′) *n.* a parent cell, which undergoes meiosis and produces gametes

ga·me·to·gen·e·sis (gə mēt′ə jen′ə sis) *n.* the entire process of consecutive cell divisions and differentiation by which mature eggs or sperm are developed —**ga′me·to·gen′ic** (-jen′ik), **gam′e·tog·e·nous** (gam′ə täj′ə nəs) *adj.* —**gam′e·tog′e·ny** (-nē) *n.*

ga·me·to·phore (gə mēt′ə fôr′) *n.* that part of a plant bearing the organs that produce gametes —**ga·me·to·phor′ic** *adj.*

ga·me·to·phyte (-fīt′) *n.* in plants, the gamete-bearing generation that is haploid and reproduces by eggs and sperms: distinguished from SPOROPHYTE —**ga·me·to·phyt′ic** (-fīt′ik) *adj.*

gam·ic (gam′ik) *adj.* [< Gr. *gamos*, marriage (see GAMO-) + -IC] *Biol.* that can develop only after fertilization

gam·i·ly (gā′mə lē) *adv.* in a gamy manner; esp., pluckily

gam·in (gam′ən) *n.* [Fr.] 1. a neglected child left to roam the streets; street urchin 2. a girl with a roguish, saucy charm: also **ga·mine** (ga mēn′)

gam·i·ness (gā′mē nis) *n.* the quality of being gamy

gam·ing (gā′miŋ) *n.* the act or practice of gambling

gam·ma (gam′ə) *n.* [ME. < Gr. < Sem., as in Heb. *gimel*, akin to *gāmāl*, camel] 1. the third letter of the Greek alphabet (Γ, γ) 2. the third of a group or series 3. a microgram 4. a number indicating the degree of contrast between the darkest and lightest parts of a photographic image 5. a unit of magnetic field intensity equal to 10^{-5} gauss —*adj. Chem. see* ALPHA

gam·ma·di·on (gə mā′dē ən) *n., pl.* **-di·a** (-ə) [MGr., dim. < Gr. *gamma*] a figure made by four capital gammas radiating from a center; esp., such a figure in the form of a swastika

gamma globulin that fraction of blood serum which contains most antibodies, used in the temporary prevention of several infectious diseases, as measles and hepatitis

gamma rays 1. an electromagnetic radiation of great penetrating power, emitted by the nucleus of a radioactive substance: it is somewhat similar to an X-ray, but shorter in wavelength 2. a stream of gamma rays

gam·mer (gam′ər) *n.* [altered < GODMOTHER] an old woman, esp. one from the country: now usually contemptuous or humorous: see also GAFFER

gam·mon[1] (gam′ən) *n.* [ME. *gambon* < ONormFr. < *gambe*; see GAMB] 1. the bottom end of a side of bacon 2. a smoked or cured ham or side of bacon

gam·mon[2] (gam′ən) *n.* [ME. *gammen*, var. of *game*, *gamen*: see GAME[1]] *Backgammon* a victory in which the winner gets rid of all his men before his opponent gets rid of any —*vt.* to defeat by scoring a gammon

gam·mon[3] (gam′ən) *vt.* [< *gammon*, a lashing up < ?] to lash (the bowsprit) to the stem of a vessel

gam·mon[4] (gam′ən) *n., interj.* [prob. orig. thieves' cant < ?] [Brit. Colloq.] nonsense intended to deceive; humbug —*vt., vi.* [Brit. Colloq.] 1. to talk humbug (to) 2. to deceive or mislead

gam·my (gam′i) *adj.* [altered < ? GAME[2]] [Brit. Dial.] *same as* GAME[2]

gam·o- (gam′ə, -ō) [< Gr. *gamos*, marriage < IE. base *ĝem-*, to marry, be related, whence Sans. *jārā-h*, suitor, *jāmā*, daughter-in-law, L. *gener*, son-in-law] *a combining form meaning:* 1. sexually united [*gamogenesis*] 2. joined or united [*gamosepalous*]

gam·o·gen·e·sis (gam′ə jen′ə sis) *n.* reproduction by the uniting of gametes; sexual reproduction —**gam′o·ge·net′ic** (-jə net′ik) *adj.* —**gam′o·ge·net′i·cal·ly** *adv.*

gam·o·pet·al·ous (-pet′′l əs) *adj.* having the petals united so as to form a tubelike corolla

gam·o·phyl·lous (-fil′əs) *adj.* having leaves or leaflike organs joined by their edges

gam·o·sep·al·ous (-sep′′l əs) *adj.* having the sepals united

-ga·mous (gə məs) [< Gr. *gamos* (see GAMO-) + -OUS] *a combining form meaning* marrying, uniting sexually [*heterogamous, polygamous*]

gamp (gamp) *n.* [in allusion to the umbrella of Mrs. *Gamp* in Dickens' *Martin Chuzzlewit*] [Brit.] a large umbrella, esp. one that is bulky or awkwardly wrapped

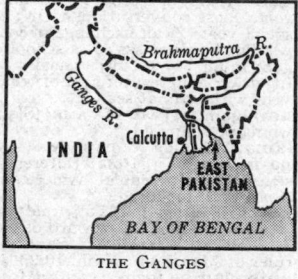

GAMOPETALOUS FLOWER (morning glory)

gam·ut (gam′ət) *n.* [ML. *gamma ut* < *gamma*, the gamut, name used by Guido d'Arezzo for the lowest note of his scale (< Gr. *gamma*, GAMMA) + *ut* < L. *ut*, that, used as a musical note, taken from a medieval song whose phrases began on successive ascending major tones: *Ut queant laxis Resonare fibris, Mira gestorum Famuli tuorum, Solve polluti Labii reatum, Sancte Iohannes*] 1. *Music a)* the lowest note of the medieval scale, corresponding to modern G below middle C *b)* the complete medieval scale *c)* the entire series of recognized notes in modern music *d)* any complete musical scale, esp. the major scale 2. the entire range or extent, as of emotions —*SYN. see* RANGE

gam·y (gā′mē) *adj.* **gam′i·er, gam′i·est** 1. having a strong, tangy flavor like that of cooked game 2. strong in smell or taste; slightly tainted 3. plucky; high-spirited 4. risqué or racy; somewhat salacious

-ga·my (gə mē) [Gr. *-gamia* < *gamos*: see GAMO-] *a combining form meaning* marriage, sexual union [*polygamy*]

gan (gan) *pt. of* GIN[3]

Gand (gän) *Fr. name of* GHENT

Gan·da (gan′də) *n., pl.* **-das, -da** 1. any member of an agricultural people of S Uganda 2. their Bantu language

gan·der (gan′dər) *n.* [ME. < OE. *gan(d)ra*, akin to G. dial., Du., LowG. *gander*, akin to G. *gans*, GOOSE] 1. a male goose 2. a stupid or silly fellow 3. [Slang] a look: chiefly in the phrase **take a gander**

Gan·dhi (gän′dē, gan′-) 1. Mrs. **In·di·ra (Nehru)** (in dir′ə), 1917– ; Indian statesman; prime minister of India (1966–): daughter of Jawaharlal NEHRU 2. **Mo·han·das K(aramchand)** (mō hän′dəs), 1869–1948; Hindu nationalist leader & social reformer: called *Mahatma Gandhi* —**Gan′dhi·an** *adj.*

Gan·dhi·ism (-iz′m) *n.* the political theories of Gandhi, esp. his theories of passive resistance and civil disobedience to achieve reform

☆**gan·dy dancer** (gan′dē) [so named from using tools from the *Gandy* Manufacturing Co. (Chicago)] [Slang] a worker in a railroad section gang

ga·nef, ga·nof (gä′nəf) *n.* [Yid. < Heb. *ganāv*] a thief

gang[1] (gan) *n.* [ME., a band or company, orig., a going, journey < OE. < base of *gangan* (see ff.)] 1. a group of people associated together in some way; specif., *a)* a group of workers directed by a foreman *b)* an organized group of criminals *c)* a squad of convicts at work *d)* a group of youths from one neighborhood banded together for social reasons; often, specif., a band of juvenile delinquents 2. a set of like tools, machines, components, etc., designed or arranged to work together: often used attributively [a *gang* plow] —*vi.* ☆to form, or be associated in, a gang (with *up*) —*vt.* ☆1. [Colloq.] to attack as a gang 2. to arrange in a gang, or coordinated set —☆**gang up on** [Colloq.] to attack or oppose as a group

gang[2] (gan) *vi.* [ME. *gangen* < OE. *gangan*, akin to ON. *ganga*, Goth. *gaggan*, to go < IE. base *ĝhengh-*, whence Sans. *jámhas-*, a step] [Scot.] to go or walk

gang·er (-ər) *n.* [Brit.] a foreman of a gang of workers

Gan·ges (gan′jēz) river in N India & East Pakistan, flowing from the Himalayas into the Bay of Bengal: c. 1,560 mi. —**Gan·get·ic** (gan jet′ik) *adj.*

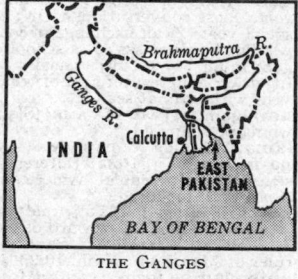

THE GANGES

☆**gang hook** a multiple fishhook consisting of several, usually three, hooks with their shanks joined

☆**gang·land** (-land′) *n.* the sphere of criminal gangs

gan·gli·at·ed (gan′glē āt′id) *adj.* having ganglia: also **gan′gli·ate** (-it, -āt′)

gan·gling (gan′gliŋ) *adj.* [? altered (? after DANGLE) < GANGREL, in obs. sense, "lanky person"] thin, tall, and awkward; of loose, lanky build: also **gan′gly**

gan·gli·o- (gan′glē ə, -ō) *a combining form meaning* ganglion: also, before a vowel, **gan′gli-**

gan·gli·on (gan′glē ən) *n., pl.* **-gli·a** (-ə), **-gli·ons** [special use of LL. *ganglion*, a swelling < Gr. *ganglion*, tumor, prob. redupl. < IE. base *gel-*, to form into a ball, whence CLOT, CLENCH] 1. a mass of nerve cells serving as a center from which nerve impulses are transmitted 2. a center of force, energy, activity, etc. 3. a cystic tumor growing on a tendon sheath —**gan′gli·on′ic** (-än′ik) *adj.*

☆**gang·plank** (gan′plank′) *n.* [< *gang*, a going (see GANG[1]) + PLANK] a narrow, movable platform or ramp forming a bridge by which to board or leave a ship

☆**gang plow** a plow with a number of shares fastened side by side for making several furrows at a time

gan·grel (gan′grəl, -ral) *n.* [ME., a vagabond, tramp, prob. < *gangen* (see GANG[2]) + ending seen also in *wastrel*] [Dial. or Archaic] a roving beggar; vagrant

gan·grene (gan′grēn, gan grēn′) *n.* [Fr. *gangrène* < L. *gangraena* < Gr. *gangraina*, redupl. < *gran*, to gnaw < IE. base *gras-*, whence L. *gramen*, grass, fodder] decay of tissue in a part of the body when the blood supply is obstructed by injury, disease, etc. —*vt., vi.* **-grened, -grening** [Now Rare] to develop gangrene (in) —**gan′gre·nous** (-grə nəs) *adj.*

☆**gang·ster** (gan′stər) *n.* a member of a gang of criminals —**gang′ster·ism** *n.*

Gang·tok (gun′täk′) capital of Sikkim, in the SE part: pop. 12,000

gangue (gan) *n.* [Fr. < G. *gang*, metallic vein, passage, lit., a going, akin to GANG[2]] the commercially worthless mineral matter associated with economically valuable metallic minerals in a deposit

gang·way (gan′wā′) *n.* [OE. *gangweg*, thoroughfare (< GANG[1], in obs. sense "a going" & WAY)] 1. a passageway or opening on a ship; specif., *a)* an opening for loading and unloading freight or for passengers *b) same as* GANGPLANK *c) same as* ACCOMMODATION LADDER 2. a main level in a mine ☆3. an incline for logs, leading up to a saw mill 4. [Brit.] a passageway between rows of seats; aisle; specif., in the House of Commons, the aisle separating front benchers from back benchers —*interj.* make room! clear the way!

gan·is·ter (gan′is tər) *n.* [G. dial. *ganister* < MHG. *ganster*, a spark (cf. GNEISS), akin to OE. *gnast*, spark] a hard, siliceous rock sometimes found underlying coal beds or produced synthetically, used in refractory linings of metallurgical furnaces

gan·ja, gan·jah (gän′jə) *n.* [Hindi *gājā* < Sans. *gañjā*] *same as* MARIJUANA

gan·net (gan′it) *n., pl.* **-nets, -net:** see PLURAL, II, D, 1 [ME. *ganat* < OE. *ganot*, solan goose, lit., a gander, akin to Du. *gent*, OHG. *ganazzo*, gander: for IE. base see GOOSE] any of several large, fish-eating sea birds (family Sulidae); esp., a white, gooselike, web-footed bird (*Morus bassanus*) that breeds on cliffs along the N Atlantic coasts

gan·nis·ter (gan′is tər) *n. var. sp. of* GANISTER

gan·oid (gan′oid) *adj.* [Fr. *ganoïde* < Gr. *ganos*, brightness (prob. < IE. base *gāu-*, to rejoice, whence L. *gaudium*, JOY) + *-eidēs*, -OID] of a group of living and extinct, bony and cartilaginous, primitive fishes covered by rows of hard, glossy, enameled scales or plates, including the sturgeons, gars, bowfins, and paddlefishes —*n.* a ganoid fish

gant·let¹ (gônt′lit, gant′-) *n.* [earlier *gantlope* < Sw. *gatlopp*, a running down a lane < *gata*, lane (akin to G. *gasse*: see GAIT) + *lopp*, a run, akin to LEAP] **1.** *a)* a former military punishment in which the offender had to run between two rows of men who struck him with clubs, etc. as he passed *b)* a series of troubles or difficulties: in these senses, now spelled equally **gaunt′let 2.** a section of railroad track over a narrow passage where two lines of track overlap, one rail of each line being within the rails of the other —*vt.* to overlap (railroad tracks) so as to make a gantlet —**run the gantlet 1.** to be punished by means of the gantlet **2.** to proceed while under attack from both sides, as by criticism, gossip, etc.

gant·let² (gônt′lit, gant′-) *n. same as* GAUNTLET¹

gant·line (gant′lin′) *n.* [altered < ? *girtline* (< GIRT¹ + LINE¹)] *Naut.* a rope passing through an overhead pulley, used for hoisting

gan·try (gan′trē) *n., pl.* **-tries** [ME. *gauntre*, altered (prob. after *tre*, TREE) < OFr. *gantier, chantier* < L. *canterius*, beast of burden, trellis < Gr. *kanthēlios*, a pack ass < *kanthōn*, of same meaning] **1.** a frame on which barrels can be set horizontally **2.** a framework that spans a distance, often moving on wheels at each end, used for carrying a traveling crane **3.** a bridgelike framework over railroad tracks for supporting signals ☆**4.** a wheeled framework with a crane, platforms at different levels, etc., used for positioning and servicing a rocket at its launching site

Gan·y·mede (gan′ə mēd) **1.** *Gr. Myth.* a beautiful youth carried off by Zeus to be the cupbearer to the gods **2.** one of the satellites of the planet Jupiter

gaol (jāl) *n. Brit. sp. of* JAIL —**gaol′er** *n.*

gap (gap) *n.* [ME. < ON. < *gapa*, to yawn, GAPE] **1.** a hole or opening, as in a wall or fence, made by breaking or parting; breach **2.** a mountain pass, cleft, or ravine **3.** an interruption of continuity in space or time; hiatus; lacuna **4.** a lag or disparity between conditions, ideas, natures, etc. **5.** *same as* SPARK GAP —*vt.* **gapped, gap′ping** to make an opening in; breach —*vi.* to come apart; open

gape (gāp; *occas.* gap) *vi.* **gaped, gap′ing** [ME. *gapen* < ON. *gapa* < IE. *ghēp-*, base *ghep-*, to yawn, gape, whence Gr. *chasma*, abyss, L. *hiatus* & GAB] **1.** to open the mouth wide, as in yawning or hunger **2.** to stare with the mouth open, as in wonder or surprise **3.** to open or be opened wide, as a chasm —*n.* **1.** the act of gaping; specif., *a)* an open-mouthed stare *b)* a yawn **2.** a wide gap or opening **3.** *Zool.* the measure of the widest possible opening of a mouth or beak —*SYN.* see LOOK —**the gapes 1.** a disease of poultry and birds, characterized by gaping: see GAPE-WORM **2.** a fit of yawning —**gap′er** *n.* —**gap′ing·ly** *adv.*

gape·worm (-wurm′) *n.* a roundworm (*Syngamus trachea*) parasitic in the respiratory passages of poultry and other birds and causing the gapes

gap-toothed (gap′to͞otht′) *adj.* having a gap between two teeth, as because of a missing tooth

☆**gar** (gär) *n., pl.* **gar, gars:** see PLURAL, II, D, 2 [contr. < GARFISH] **1.** any of a group of freshwater ganoid fishes (genus *Lepisosteus*) characterized by elongated bodies covered with very hard scales, long beaklike snouts, and many sharp teeth **2.** *same as* NEEDLEFISH

G.A.R. Grand Army of the Republic

ga·rage (gə räzh′, -räj′; *Brit.* gar′äzh, -ij) *n.* [Fr. < *garer*, to protect, preserve < Gmc., as in Frank. *waron*, to watch over (or ON. *vara*, to warn, caution): for IE. base see WARD] **1.** a closed shelter for an automotive vehicle or vehicles **2.** a business establishment where automotive vehicles are stored, repaired, serviced, etc. —*vt.* **-raged′, -rag·ing** to put or keep in a garage

Gar·a·mond (gar′ə mänd′) *n.* a style of type orig. designed by Claude Garamond, 16th-cent. Fr. type founder

☆**Gar·and rifle** (gar′ənd, gə rand′) [after John C. *Garand*, U.S. engineer who invented it c. 1930] a semiautomatic, rapid-firing, .30-caliber rifle: formerly, the standard infantry weapon of the U.S. Army

garb (gärb) *n.* [OFr. *garbe*, gracefulness < It. *garbo*, elegance, prob. ult. < Gr. *kalopoios*, making beautiful < *kalos*, beautiful + *poiein*, to make (see POET)] **1.** clothing; manner or style of dress, esp. as characteristic of an occupation, profession, or rank **2.** external form, covering, or appearance **3.** [Obs.] style; manner —*vt.* to clothe; dress; attire

gar·bage (gär′bij) *n.* [ME., entrails of fowls] **1.** spoiled or waste food, as from a market or kitchen, that is thrown away **2.** any worthless, unnecessary, or offensive matter [literary *garbage*]

gar·ban·zo (gär ban′zō; *Sp.* gär vän′thō, -sō) *n., pl.* **-zos** [Sp.] *same as* CHICKPEA

gar·ble (gär′b'l) *vt.* **-bled, -bling** [ME. *garbelen* < It. *garbellare*, to sift < *garbello*, a sieve < Ar. *gharbāl*, earlier *ghirbāl* < LL. *cribellum*, small sieve, dim. of *cribrum*, a sieve, akin to *cernere*: see CRITIC] **1.** [Rare] *a)* to sort by sifting *b)* to select the best parts of **2.** to select, suppress, improperly emphasize, or distort parts of (a story, etc.) in telling, so as to mislead or misrepresent **3.** to confuse or mix up (a quotation, story, etc.) unintentionally —*n.* the act or result of garbling —**gar′bler** *n.*

gar·board (gär′bôrd) *n.* [Du. *gaarbord* < *garen* (contr. of *gaderen*, to GATHER) + *boord*, BOARD] *Shipbuilding* the planks or plates adjoining the keel: also **garboard strake**

Gar·cí·a Lor·ca (gär thē′ä lôr′kä; *E.* gär sē′ə lôr′kə), **Fe·de·ri·co** (fe′de rē′kō) 1899–1936; Sp. poet. & playwright

‡**gar·çon** (gàr sōn′) *n., pl.* **-çons** (-sōn′) [Fr.] **1.** a boy, youth, or young man **2.** a waiter or servant

Gar·da (gär′dä), **Lake** lake in N Italy, on the Lombardy-Veneto border: 143 sq. mi.

gar·dant (gär′dənt) *adj. same as* GUARDANT

gar·den (gär′d'n) *n.* [ME. < ONormFr. *gardin* < Frank. *gardo*, akin to G. *garten*, OE. *geard:* see YARD², GARTH] **1.** a piece of ground for the growing of fruits, flowers, or vegetables, usually close to a house **2.** a well-cultivated region; area of fertile, developed land: also **garden spot 3.** [often *pl.*] a place outdoors for public enjoyment, planted with trees, flowers, etc., and sometimes having special displays of animals or plants —*vi.* to make, work in, or take care of a garden, lawn, etc. —*vt.* to make a garden of —*adj.* **1.** of, for, used in, or grown in a garden **2.** *a)* ordinary; commonplace *b)* hardy —**lead (someone) down the garden path** to mislead or deceive (someone)

Gar·de·na (gär dē′nə) [extended < GARDEN] city in SW Calif.: suburb of Los Angeles: pop. 41,000

☆**garden apartments** a complex of low apartment buildings surrounded by lawns or landscaped areas

garden balsam a fleshy annual garden impatiens (*Impatiens balsamina*), with roselike white, lavender, yellow, pink, or red blossoms borne along the main stem in leaf axils

Garden City city in SE Mich.: suburb of Detroit: pop. 42,000

garden cress an annual plant (*Lepidium sativum*) of the mustard family, sometimes grown as a salad plant

gar·den·er (gärd′nər, gär′d'n ər) *n.* **1.** a person who likes or is skilled at working in a garden **2.** a person whose occupation is making and tending gardens

Garden Grove city in SW Calif.: pop. 123,000: see ANAHEIM

garden heliotrope a tall valerian (*Valeriana officinalis*) with small whitish or pink, very fragrant flowers and a strong-smelling root formerly used in medicine

☆**gar·de·ni·a** (gär dēn′yə, -dē′nē ə) *n.* [ModL., after Alexander *Garden* (1730–91), Am. botanist] any of a genus (*Gardenia*) of chiefly subtropical Old World plants of the madder family, with glossy leaves and highly fragrant, white or yellow, waxy flowers

Gar·di·ner (gärd′nər), **Samuel Raw·son** (rô′s'n) 1829–1902; Eng. historian

gar·dy·loo (gär′di lo͞o′) *interj.* [< Fr. *gare l'eau*, beware (of) the water] formerly, in Edinburgh, a cry warning people below that slops were about to be thrown from a window into the street

Gar·eth (gar′ith) *Arthurian Legend* one of the knights of the Round Table, a nephew of King Arthur

Gar·field (gär′fēld), **James Abram** 1831–81; 20th president of the U.S. (1881): assassinated

Garfield Heights [after prec.] city in NE Ohio: suburb of Cleveland: pop. 41,000

gar·fish (gär′fish′) *n., pl.* **-fish′, -fish′es:** see FISH² [ME. < *gare*, spear (< OE. *gar:* see GORE³) + *fish*, FISH²] *same as* GAR

gar·ga·ney (gär′gə nē) *n.* [prob. < It. dial. *garganello*; prob. echoic of the cry] a small European duck (*Anas querquedula*), living near fresh water and resembling the American blue-winged teal

Gar·gan·tu·a (gär gan′cho͞o wə) a giant king, noted for his size and prodigious feats and appetite, the main character of *Gargantua and Pantagruel*, a satire by Rabelais (1552) —**Gar·gan′tu·an, gar·gan′tu·an** *adj.*

gar·get (gär′gət) *n.* [ME. < OFr. *gargate*, throat < echoic base *garg-:* see ff.] an inflammation of the udders of cows, ewes, etc., usually caused by bacteria

gar·gle (gär′g'l) *vt., vi.* **-gled, -gling** [Fr. *gargouiller* < *gargouille*, throat, waterspout, gargoyle < echoic base *garg-*, as in Gr. *gargarizein*, to gargle, Sans. *gharghara-h*, gurgling] **1.** to rinse or wash (the throat) with a liquid kept in motion by the slow expulsion of air from the lungs **2.** to utter or speak with the sound of gargling —*n.* **1.** a liquid used for gargling **2.** a gargling sound

gar·goyle (gär′goil) *n.* [ME. *gargule*, throat < OFr. *gargouille:* see prec.] 1. a water-spout, usually in the form of a grotesquely carved animal or fantastic creature, projecting from the gutter of a building 2. a projecting ornament (on a building) that looks like this 3. a person with grotesque features —**gar′goyled** *adj.*

gar·i·bal·di (gar′ə bôl′dē) *n.* a woman's loose, high-necked blouse with full sleeves, patterned after the shirt worn by the followers of Garibaldi

GARGOYLE

Gar·i·bal·di (gar′ə bôl′dē; *It.* gä′rē bäl′dē), **Giu·sep·pe** (jōō zep′pe) 1807–82; It. patriot & general: leader in the movement to unify Italy

gar·ish (ger′ish, gar′-) *adj.* [earlier *gaurish*, prob. < ME. *gauren*, to stare] 1. too bright or gaudy; showy; glaring [*garish* colors] 2. gaudily or showily dressed, decorated, written, etc. —*SYN.* see GAUDY[1] —**gar′ish·ly** *adv.* —**gar′ish·ness** *n.*

gar·land (gär′lənd) *n.* [ME. < OFr. *garlande*] 1. a wreath of flowers, leaves, etc., worn on the head or used as decoration, esp. as a symbol of victory, honor, etc. 2. anthology of poems, songs, etc. 3. *Naut.* a band or ring of rope used to hoist spars —*vt.* to form into or decorate with a garland or garlands

Gar·land (gär′lənd) [after A. H. *Garland*, U.S. attorney general (1885–89)] city in NE Tex.: suburb of Dallas: pop. 81,000

Gar·land (gär′lənd), **(Hannibal) Ham·lin** (ham′lin) 1860–1940; U.S. novelist & short-story writer

gar·lic (gär′lik) *n.* [ME. *garlek* < OE. *garleac* < *gar*, a spear (see GARFISH) + *leac*, a LEEK: from the spearlike leaves] 1. a bulbous plant (*Allium sativum*) of the lily family 2. the strong-smelling bulb of this plant, made up of small sections called cloves, used as seasoning in meats, salads, etc. —**gar′lick·y** (-lik ē) *adj.*

gar·ment (gär′mənt) *n.* [ME. < OFr. *garnement* < *garnir:* see GARNISH] 1. *a)* any article of clothing *b)* [*pl.*] clothes; costume 2. a covering —*vt.* to cover with, or as with, a garment; clothe

gar·ner (gär′nər) *n.* [ME. *gerner* < OFr. *grenier* < L. *granarium*, granary < *granum*, GRAIN] 1. a place for storing grain; granary 2. a store of something —*vt.* 1. to gather up and store in or as in a granary 2. to get or earn 3. to collect or gather

gar·net[1] (gär′nit) *n.* [ME. *gernet* < OFr. *grenat* < ML. *granatus* < *granatum*, garnet, lit., pomegranate < L. (see POMEGRANATE): from the resemblance in color] 1. any of a group of hard silicate minerals having the general formula $A_3B_2(SiO_4)_3$, occurring chiefly as well-formed crystals in metamorphic rocks: red varieties are often used as gems, ordinary varieties as abrasives 2. a deep red

gar·net[2] (gär′nit) *n.* [LME. *garnett*, prob. < or akin to Du. *granaat*] *Naut.* a hoisting tackle for loading cargo

Gar·nett (gär′nit), **Constance** (born *Constance Black*) 1862–1946; Eng. translator from Russian

gar·ni (gär nē′) *adj.* [Fr., pp. of *garnir*, to garnish] garnished: said of food

gar·ni·er·ite (gär′nē ə rīt′) *n.* [after Jules *Garnier*, 19th-cent. Fr. geologist, who discovered it] *Mineralogy* an apple-green hydrated silicate of magnesium and nickel, an ore of nickel

gar·nish (gär′nish) *vt.* [ME. *garnischen* < extended stem of OFr. *garnir*, to furnish, protect < Gmc. *warnjan* (whence WARN): for IE. base see WARD] 1. to decorate; adorn; embellish; trim 2. to decorate (food) with something that adds color or flavor [a steak *garnished* with parsley] 3. *Law* to bring garnishment proceedings against; garnishee —*n.* 1. a decoration; ornament 2. something put on or around food to add color or flavor, as parsley or watercress 3. [*Obs.*] a fee, esp. one formerly extorted from new prisoners by inmates of English jails or by the jailer —**gar′nish·er** *n.*

gar·nish·ee (gär′nə shē′) *n.* [prec. + -EE[1]] *Law* a person who has money or other property of a defendant in his possession, and is ordered not to dispose of it pending settlement of the lawsuit —*vt.* **-eed′**, **-ee′ing** *Law a)* to attach (a debtor's property, wages, etc.) by the authority of a court, so that it can be used to pay the debt *b)* to serve (a person) with a garnishment

gar·nish·ment (gär′nish mənt) *n.* 1. a decoration; embellishment 2. *Law* a notice ordering a person not to dispose of a defendant's property or money in his possession pending settlement of the lawsuit

gar·ni·ture (gär′ni chər) *n.* [Fr. < *garnir:* see GARNISH] an ornament; decoration; embellishment; trimming

Ga·ronne (ga rôn′) river in SW France, flowing from the Pyrenees into the Gironde: c. 400 mi.

☆**gar·pike** (gär′pīk′) *n. same as* GAR (sense 1)

gar·ret (gar′it) *n.* [ME. *garite*, a watchtower, loft < OFr. *garir*, to watch < Frank. *warjan*, to protect, akin to OE. *warian:* for IE. base see WARD] the space, room, or rooms just below the roof of a house, esp. under a sloping roof; attic

Gar·rick (gar′ik), **David** 1717–79; Eng. actor & theater manager

gar·ri·son (gar′ə s'n) *n.* [ME. *garison* < OFr. < *garir* (see GARRET, attic); meaning infl. by association with ME. & OFr. *garnison*, a garrison, provisions < *garnir*, to furnish (see GARNISH)] 1. troops stationed in a fort or fortified place 2. a fortified place with troops, guns, etc.; military post or station —*vt.* 1. *a)* to station troops in (a fortified place) for its defense *b)* to occupy and control by sending troops into 2. to place (troops) on duty in a garrison

Gar·ri·son (gar′ə s'n), **William Lloyd** 1805–79; U.S. editor, lecturer, & abolitionist leader

garrison cap *same as a)* OVERSEAS CAP *b)* SERVICE CAP

☆**Gar·ri·son finish** (gar′ə s'n) [after Snapper *Garrison*, 19th-cent. U.S. jockey] a close finish, as in a horse race, in which the winner comes from behind at the last moment

gar·rote (gə rät′, gə rōt′) *n.* [Sp., orig., a stick used to wind a cord, prob. < OFr. *garrot*, crossbow bolt, for earlier *guaroc* < *garokier*, to garrote < Frank. *wrokkan*, to twist] 1. *a)* a method of execution, as formerly in Spain, with an iron collar tightened about the neck by a screw *b)* the iron collar so used 2. *a)* a cord, thong, or length of wire for strangling a robbery victim, enemy sentry, etc. in a surprise attack *b)* a disabling by strangling in this way; strangulation —*vt.* **-rot′ed** or **-rot′ted**, **-rot′ing** or **-rot′ting** 1. to execute or attack with a garrote or by strangling 2. to disable by strangling, as in an attack for robbery Also sp. **ga·rotte′**, **gar·rotte′** —**gar·rot′er** *n.*

gar·ru·lous (gar′ə ləs, gar′yoo-) *adj.* [L. *garrulus* < *garrire*, to chatter: for IE. base see CARE] talking much or too much, esp. about unimportant things; loquacious —*SYN.* see TALKATIVE —**gar·ru·li·ty** (gə rōō′lə tē), **gar·ru·lous·ness** *n.* —**gar′ru·lous·ly** *adv.*

gar·ter (gär′tər) *n.* [ME. < ONormFr. *gartier* < OFr. *garet, jaret*, small of the leg behind the knee < Celt., as in Bret. *gar*, shank of the leg] 1. an elastic band, or a fastener suspended from a band, girdle, etc., for holding a stocking or sock in position 2. an elastic band formerly worn to hold a shirt sleeve up 3. [G-] *a)* the badge of the Order of the Garter *b)* the order itself *c)* membership in it —*vt.* to bind, support, or fasten with or as with a garter

☆**garter belt** a wide belt, usually of elastic fabric, with garters suspended from it, worn by women

☆**garter snake** any of various small, harmless, striped snakes (genus *Thamnophis*) common in N. America

garth (gärth) *n.* [ME. < ON. *garthr*, akin to OE. *geard*, YARD[2]] [Archaic] an enclosed yard or garden

Gar·vey (gär′vē), **Marcus** 1880–1940; West Indian Negro leader in the U.S.

Gar·y (ger′ē, gar′-) [< OE. *Garwig*, lit., spear (of) battle < *gar*, a spear + *wig* < Gmc. *wiga-*, battle < IE. base *wik-*, to be bold, whence L. *vincere*, to conquer] 1. a masculine name 2. [after Elbert H. *Gary* (1846–1927), U.S. industrialist] city in NW Ind., on Lake Michigan: pop. 175,000 (met. area, with Hammond & East Chicago, 633,000)

gas (gas) *n.* [ModL., word invented by the Belgian chemist, Van Helmont (1577–1644), on basis of *chaos*, air (< Gr. *chaos*, chaos), term used by Paracelsus] 1. the fluid form of a substance in which it can expand indefinitely and completely fill its container; form that is neither liquid nor solid; vapor 2. any mixture of flammable gases used for lighting, heating, or cooking 3. any gas, as nitrous oxide, used as an anesthetic 4. any substance, as phosgene, intentionally dispersed through the atmosphere, as in war, to act as a poison, irritant, or asphyxiant 5. a gaseous substance formed in the stomach, bowels, etc. ☆6. [Colloq.] *a)* short for GASOLINE *b)* the accelerator or throttle in an automobile, etc. ☆7. [Slang] *a)* idle or boastful talk *b)* something or someone that is very pleasing, exciting, amusing, etc. 8. *Mining* a mixture of firedamp with air that explodes if ignited —*vt.* **gassed**, **gas′sing** 1. to supply with gas 2. to subject to the action of gas 3. to injure or kill by gas, as in war ☆4. [Slang] to thrill, delight, amuse greatly, etc. —*vi.* 1. to give off gas ☆2. [Slang] to talk in an idle or boastful way —*adj.* of, using, or operated by gas —☆**gas up** [Colloq.] to fill the tank of an automobile, etc. with gasoline —☆**step on the gas** [Slang] 1. to press on the accelerator of an automobile, etc. 2. to hurry; move or act faster

gas bacillus a rod-shaped microorganism (genus *Clostridium*) that infects wounds and causes gas to form in them

gas·bag (-bag′) *n.* 1. a bag to hold gas, as in a balloon ☆2. [Slang] a person who talks too much

gas black *same as* CARBON BLACK

gas burner *same as* GAS JET (sense 2)

gas chamber a room in which people are put to be killed with poison gas

gas coal soft coal from which illuminating gas is distilled

Gas·cogne (gas kōn′y′) Fr. name of GASCONY

Gas·con (gas′kən) *adj.* [Fr. < L. *Vasco* (gen. *Vasconis*), a Basque] 1. of Gascony or its people, reputed to be boastful 2. [g-] boastful; swaggering —*n.* 1. a native of Gascony 2. [g-] a boaster; swaggerer

gas·con·ade (gas′kə nād′) *n.* [Fr. *gasconnade:* see prec. & -ADE] boastful or blustering talk —*vi.* **-ad′ed**, **-ad′ing** to boast or bluster

Gas·co·ny (gas′kə nē) [ME. *Gascoyne* < OFr. *Gascogne* < LL. *Vasconia* < L. *Vascones*, pl., the Basques] region & former province in SW France, on the Bay of Biscay

gas·e·lier (gas′ə lir′) *n.* [GAS + (CHAND)ELIER] an early,

ornamental chandelier with branches ending in gas jets

gas·e·ous (gas'ē əs, gas'yəs, gash'əs; *Brit.* gāz'yəs) *adj.* 1. of, having the nature of, or in the form of, gas 2. [Colloq.] *same as* GASSY (sense 1) **—gas'e·ous·ness** *n.*

gas fitter a person whose work is installing and repairing gas pipes and fixtures

gas fixture a heating or lighting fixture that uses gas

gas furnace 1. a furnace that distills gas from coal, etc. 2. a furnace that burns gas as fuel

gas gangrene a gangrene in which gas bacilli multiply in dirty wounds, producing gas, muscle destruction, and toxemia

gash (gash) *vt.* [earlier *garse* < ME. *garsen* < OFr. *garser* < VL. *charassare < Gr. *charassein*, to point, sharpen, cut: cf. CHARACTER] to make a long, deep cut in; slash —*n.* [ME. *garse* < OFr.] a long, deep cut

☆**gas·house** (gas'hous') *n.* a place where gas for heating and lighting is prepared; gasworks: formerly used figuratively to suggest slum areas, rowdiness, etc.

gas·i·form (gas'ə fôrm') *adj.* in the form of gas; gaseous

gas·i·fy (-fī') *vt., vi.* **-fied'**, **-fy'ing** to change into gas **—gas'i·fi·ca'tion** *n.*

gas jet 1. a flame of illuminating gas 2. a nozzle or burner at the end of a gas fixture

Gas·kell (gas'k'l), Mrs. (**Elizabeth Cleghorn**) (born *Elizabeth Cleghorn Stevenson*) 1810–65; Eng. novelist

gas·ket (gas'kit) *n.* [prob. altered < OFr. *garcette*, small cord] 1. a piece or ring of rubber, metal, paper, etc. placed around a piston or joint to make it leakproof 2. *Naut.* a rope or cord by which a furled sail is tied to the yard **—blow a gasket** [Slang] to become enraged

gas·kin (gas'kin) *n.* [contr. < GALLIGASKINS] 1. [*pl.*] [Obs.] galligaskins 2. the upper part of the hind leg of a horse or other hoofed animal

gas·light (gas'līt') *n.* 1. the light produced by the burning of illuminating gas 2. a gas jet or burner —*adj.* of or characteristic of the period of gaslight illumination [*gaslight* melodrama]

☆**gas log** an imitation log in the form of a hollow, perforated cylinder, used as a gas burner in a fireplace

gas main a large underground pipe that conducts gas into smaller pipes leading into houses, factories, etc.

gas·man (-man') *n., pl.* **-men'** (-men') 1. an employee of a gas company who reads consumers' gas meters for billing purposes 2. *same as* GAS FITTER 3. *Mining* an inspector who checks the ventilation and guards against firedamp

gas mantle a mantle (*n.* 3) to be used over a gas burner

gas mask a device worn over the face to prevent the breathing in of poisonous gases by chemically filtering them out of the air

gas meter an instrument for measuring the quantity of a gas, esp. of illuminating gas consumed as fuel

☆**gas oil** an oily liquid obtained in the fractional distillation of petroleum, boiling between the kerosene and lubricating oil fractions: used esp. as a diesel fuel

gas·o·lier (gas'ə lir') *n. same as* GASELIER

☆**gas·o·line, gas·o·lene** (gas'ə lēn', gas'ə lēn') *n.* [GAS + -OL² + -INE⁴, -ENE] a volatile, highly flammable, colorless liquid mixture of hydrocarbons produced by the fractional distillation of petroleum and used chiefly as a fuel in internal-combustion engines

gas·om·e·ter (gas äm'ə tər) *n.* [Fr. *gazometre*: see GAS & -METER] 1. a container for holding and measuring gas 2. a tank or reservoir for storing gas

gas·om·e·try (-ə trē) *n.* the measurement of gases; esp., the determination of the amount of a gas in a mixture

gasp (gasp) *vi.* [ME. *gaspen* < ON. *geispa*, to yawn: for IE. base see GAPE] to inhale suddenly, as in surprise, or breathe with effort, as in choking —*vt.* to say or tell with gasps —*n.* a gasping; catching of the breath with difficulty **—at the last gasp** 1. just before death 2. just before the end; at the last moment

Gas·pé Peninsula (gas pā') [Fr. < Algonquian (Micmac) *gachepe*, the end] peninsula in S Quebec, Canada, extending into the Gulf of St. Lawrence: c. 150 mi. long

gasp·er (gäs'pər) *n.* [Brit. Slang] a cheap cigarette

gas plant a perennial plant (*Dictamnus albus*) of the rue family, with fragrant white or pink flowers that on hot nights give off a flammable gas

gassed (gast) *adj.* ☆[Slang] drunk; intoxicated

gas·ser (gas'ər) *n.* ☆1. an oil well that produces gas 2. [Slang] *a)* a person who talks a great deal ☆*b)* someone or something that is remarkable, very funny, etc.

Gasset, José Ortega y *see* ORTEGA Y GASSET

☆**gas station** *same as* SERVICE STATION (sense 2)

gas·sy (gas'ē) *adj.* **-si·er**, **-si·est** 1. full of, containing, or producing gas; esp., flatulent 2. like gas 3. [Colloq.] full of talk, esp. boastful talk

gas·ter·o- (gas'tər ə, -ō') *same as* GASTRO-

‡**Gast·haus** (gäst'hous') *n., pl.* **-häus'er** (-hoi'zər) [G., lit., guest house] inn; tavern

Gas·to·ni·a (gas tō'nē ə) [after W. *Gaston* (1778–1844), local jurist] city in S N.C.: pop. 47,000

gastr- *same as* GASTRO-: used before a vowel

gas·trae·a, gas·tre·a (gas trē'ə) *n.* [ModL. < Gr. *gastēr*, belly] the hypothetical ancestral form of flatworms, constructed like the gastrula stage in embryology

gas·trec·to·my (gas trek'tə mē) *n., pl.* **-mies** [GASTR- + -ECTOMY] the surgical removal of all, or esp. part, of the stomach

gas·tric (gas'trik) *adj.* [GASTR- + -IC] of, in, or near the stomach

gastric juice the thin, acid digestive fluid produced by glands in the mucous membrane lining the stomach: it contains enzymes and hydrochloric acid

gastric ulcer an ulcer of the lining of the stomach

gas·trin (gas'trin) *n.* [GASTR- + -IN¹] a hormone that is formed in the stomach and stimulates production of gastric juice: formerly regarded as identical with histamine

gas·tri·tis (gas trīt'is) *n.* [ModL. < GASTR- + -ITIS] inflammation of the stomach, esp. of the stomach lining

gas·tro- (gas'trō, -trə) [< Gr. *gastēr*, stomach] *a combining form meaning:* 1. the stomach [*gastroscope*] 2. the stomach and [*gastrocolic*]

gas·tro·col·ic (gas'trō käl'ik) *adj.* of or attached to the stomach and the transverse colon

gas·tro·derm (gas'trə dʉrm') *n. same as* ENDODERM

gas·tro·en·ter·i·tis (gas'trō en'tə rīt'is) *n.* [ModL. < GASTRO- + ENTER(O)- + -ITIS] an inflammation of the stomach and the intestines

gas·tro·en·ter·ol·o·gy (-en'tə räl'ə jē) *n.* [GASTRO- + ENTER(O)- + -OLOGY] the medical specialty that is concerned with disorders of the digestive system **—gas'tro·en'ter·ol'o·gist** *n.*

gas·tro·in·tes·ti·nal (-in tes'tə n'l) *adj.* of the stomach and the intestines

gas·tro·lith (gas'trə lith) *n.* [GASTRO- + -LITH] a stony concretion formed in the stomach

gas·tro·nome (-nōm') *n.* [Fr. < *gastronomie*: see GASTRONOMY] a person who enjoys and has a discriminating taste for foods: also **gas·tron·o·mer** (gas trän'ə mər), **gas·tron'o·mist** (-mist) **—***SYN.* see EPICURE

gas·tron·o·my (gas trän'ə mē) *n.* [Fr. *gastronomie* < Gr. *Gastronomia*, poem by Archestratus (4th c. B.C.) < *gastēr*, the stomach + *nemein*, to regulate < *nomos*, a rule] the art or science of good eating; epicurism **—gas'tro·nom'ic** (-trə näm'ik), **gas'tro·nom'i·cal** *adj.* **—gas'tro·nom'i·cal·ly** *adv.*

gas·tro·pod (gas'trə päd') *n.* [< ModL. *Gastropoda*, name of the class < GASTRO- + -POD] any of a large class (Gastropoda) of mollusks having one-piece, straight or spiral shells, as snails, limpets, etc., or having no shells or greatly reduced shells, as certain slugs: most gastropods move by means of a broad, muscular, ventral foot **—gas·trop·o·dan** (gas träp'ə dən), **gas·trop'o·dous** (-dəs) *adj.*

gas·tro·scope (gas'trə skōp') *n.* [GASTRO- + -SCOPE] an instrument inserted through the mouth for visually inspecting the inside of the stomach **—gas'tro·scop'ic** (-skäp'ik) *adj.* **—gas·tros·co·pist** (gas träs'kə pist) *n.* **—gas·tros·co·py** (gas träs'kə pē) *n.*

gas·trot·o·my (gas trät'ə mē) *n., pl.* **-mies** [GASTRO- + -TOMY] surgical incision into the stomach

gas·tro·trich (gas'trə trik) *n.* [< ModL. *gastrotricha* < GASTRO- + -*tricha*, ciliated creatures < Gr. neut. pl. of -*trichos*, haired < *thrix* (gen. *trichos*), hair] any of a phylum (Gastrotricha) of minute, freshwater and marine, wormlike animals that swim by means of cilia

gas·tro·vas·cu·lar (gas'trō vas'kyə lər) *adj. Zool.* 1. having both a digestive and a circulatory function 2. of organs with such a dual function

gas·tru·la (gas'troo lə) *n., pl.* **-lae'** (-lē'), **-las** [ModL., dim. < Gr. *gastēr*, the stomach] an embryo in an early stage of development, consisting of a sac with two layers, the ectoderm and endoderm, enclosing a central cavity, the archenteron, that opens to the outside through the blastopore

GASTRULA

gas·tru·la·tion (gas'troo lā'shən) *n.* the process of forming a gastrula

gas turbine a turbine driven by the pressure of hot gases formed by the explosion of a mixture of hot compressed air and fuel in a chamber

gas·works (gas'wʉrks') *n.pl.* [*with sing. v.*] a place where gas for heating and lighting is prepared

gat¹ (gat) *adj. archaic pt.* of GET

gat² (gat) *n.* [< Scand., as in Dan., Sw., ON. *gat*, an opening, passage, akin to OE. *geat*: see GATE¹] a narrow ship channel between cliffs or sandbanks

☆**gat³** (gat) *n.* [< GAT(LING GUN)] [Old Slang] a pistol

gate¹ (gāt) *n.* [ME. < OE. pl. *gatu* of *geat*, a gate, akin to OFris. *jet*, Du. & ON. *gat*, opening < IE. base *ĝhed-, to void, whence Sans. *hadati*, (he) defecates] 1. a movable framework or solid structure, esp. one that swings on hinges, controlling entrance or exit through an opening in a fence or wall 2. an opening providing passageway through a fence or wall, with or without such a structure; gateway 3. any means of entrance, exit, or access, as any

of the numbered exits at a bus terminal **4.** a mountain pass **5.** a movable barrier, as at a railroad crossing or for controlling the start of a horse race **6.** a structure controlling the flow of water, as in a pipe, canal, etc. ☆**7.** a frame in which a saw or saws are set **8.** in slalom racing, an opening between two upright poles through which the skier must pass **9.** *a)* the total amount of money received in admission prices to a performance or exhibition *b)* the total number of spectators who pay to see such an event **10.** *Electronics* a circuit with one output and two or more inputs, whose output is energized only when certain input conditions are satisfied —*vt.* **gat′ed, gat′ing** [Brit.] to confine (a student) to the college grounds —☆**get the gate** [Slang] to be dismissed or rejected —☆**give (someone) the gate** [Slang] to dismiss or reject (someone); get rid of

gate² (gāt) *n.* [altered (after prec.) < OE. *gyte*, a pouring forth, akin to *geotan*, to pour: for IE. base see FOUND³] **1.** a channel through which molten metal is poured into a mold **2.** the waste part of a casting formed at this channel

gate³ (gāt) *n.* [ME. < ON. *gata*, akin to G. *gasse*, Goth. *gatwo*] [Obs. or Dial.] **1.** a road or path **2.** a way of doing something

☆**gate-crash·er** (-krash′ər) *n.* [Colloq.] a person who attends a social affair without an invitation or a performance, etc. without paying admission —**gate′-crash′** *vt.*, *vi.*

☆**gate·fold** (-fōld′) *n.* a page larger than the others in a magazine or book, bound so that it can be folded out

gate·house (-hous′) *n.* a house beside or over a gateway, used as a porter's lodge, etc.

gate·keep·er (-kē′pər) *n.* a person in charge of a gate to control passage through it: also **gate′man**, *pl.* **-men**

gate·leg table (-leg′) a table with drop leaves supported by gatelike legs swung back against the frame to permit the leaves to drop: also **gate′legged′ table**

gate·post (-pōst′) *n.* the post on which a gate is hung or the one to which it is fastened when closed

Gates (gāts), **Horatio** 1728?–1806; Am. general in the Revolutionary War

Gates·head (gāts′hed′) city in Durham, NE England, on the Tyne: pop. 103,000

GATELEG TABLE

gate·way (-wā′) *n.* **1.** an entrance in a wall, fence, etc. fitted with a gate **2.** a means of entrance or access

Gath (gath) [Heb., lit., wine press] *Bible* one of the five great Philistine cities: II Sam. 1:20

gath·er (gath′ər) *vt.* [ME. *gaderen* < OE. *gad(e)rian*, akin to OFris. *gaduria*, Du. *gaderen* < IE. base *ghedh-*, to unite, join, whence (TO)GETHER, GOOD, G. *gatte*, spouse] **1.** to cause to come together in one place or group **2.** to get or collect gradually from various places, sources, etc.; amass; accumulate [*to gather* information] **3.** to bring close [*to gather* a blanket about one's legs] **4.** to pick, pluck, or collect by picking; harvest [*to gather* crops] **5.** to get as an idea or impression; infer; conclude [I *gather* that you disagree] **6.** to prepare or collect (oneself, one's energies) to meet a situation **7.** to gain or acquire gradually [*to gather* speed] **8.** to draw (cloth) into fixed folds or pleats **9.** to wrinkle (one's brow) **10.** to put (the pages or signatures of a book) in proper order for binding —*vi.* **1.** to come together; assemble **2.** to form pus; come to a head, as a boil; fester **3.** to increase **4.** to become wrinkled: said of the brow —*n.* a pleat —**be gathered to one's fathers** to die: cf. Judg. 2:10 —**gather up** **1.** to pick up and assemble **2.** to draw together; make more compact —**gath′er·er** *n.*

SYN.—gather is the general term for a bringing or coming together [*to gather* scattered objects, people *gathered* at the corners]; **collect** usually implies careful choice in gathering from various sources, a bringing into an orderly arrangement, etc. [he *collects* coins]; **assemble** applies especially to the gathering together of persons for some special purpose [*assemble* the students in the auditorium]; **muster** applies to a formal assembling, especially of troops for inspection, roll call, etc. See also INFER

gath·er·ing (-iŋ) *n.* **1.** the act of one that gathers **2.** what is gathered; specif., *a)* a meeting; assemblage; crowd *b)* a series of small pleats in cloth **3.** a boil or abscess

☆**Gat·ling gun** (gat′liŋ) [after R. J. *Gatling* (1818–1903), U.S. inventor] an early kind of machine gun having a cluster of barrels around an axis, designed to be successively discharged when rotated

Ga·tun (gä toon′) town in the N Canal Zone: pop. 700: site of a dam (**Gatun Dam**), 1 1/2 mi. long, which forms a lake (**Gatun Lake**), 163 sq. mi., that is part of the canal route

gauche (gōsh) *adj.* [Fr. < MFr. *gauchir*, to become crooked, warped, ult. < Frank. *wankjan*, to totter (akin to G. *wanken*), confused with *walken*, to beat, full (cloth)] lacking grace, esp. social grace; awkward; tactless —**gauche′ly** *adv.* —**gauche′ness** *n.*

gau·che·rie (gō′shə rē′) *n.* [Fr.: see GAUCHE] **1.** awkwardness; tactlessness **2.** a gauche act or expression

gau·cho (gou′chō) *n.*, *pl.* **-chos** [AmSp., prob. of Araucan origin] a cowboy of mixed Indian and Spanish ancestry, living on the S. American pampas

gaud (gôd) *n.* [ME. *gaude*, a large bead in a rosary, trinket, prob. ult. < L. *gaudium*, JOY] a cheap, tasteless, showy ornament or trinket

‡**gau·de·a·mus** (gou′dā ä′moos, gô′dē ä′məs) *n.* [L., lit., let us be joyful: the opening of a medieval student song] a merrymaking, esp. of college students

gaud·er·y (gôd′ər ē) *n.*, *pl.* **-er·ies** gaudy, or ostentatious, appearance, clothes, etc.; finery

gaud·y¹ (gôd′ē) *adj.* **gaud′i·er, gaud′i·est** [GAUD + -Y²] bright and showy, but lacking in good taste; cheaply brilliant and ornate —**gaud′i·ly** *adv.* —**gaud′i·ness** *n.* **SYN.—gaudy** applies to that which is brightly colored and gay, but inappropriately so or in bad taste [*gaudy* furniture]; **tawdry** is used of something cheap and flimsy that is also gaudy [*tawdry* embroidery]; **garish** implies a glaring brightness of color and excessive ornamentation [*garish* wallpaper]; **flashy** and **showy** imply a conspicuous brightness and display, but **flashy** connotes that it is offensive to subdued tastes [a *flashy* sport coat], while **showy** does not necessarily connote this [*showy* blossoms] —**ANT.** subdued, quiet

gaud·y² (gôd′ē) *n.*, *pl.* **gaud·ies** [< L. *gaudium*, JOY] a feast; esp., an annual dinner or reunion at a British university

gauf·fer (gôf′ər, gäf′-) *vt.*, *n.* same as GOFFER

gauge (gāj) *n.* [ME. < ONormFr.: see the *v.*] **1.** a standard measure or scale of measurement **2.** dimensions, capacity, thickness, etc. **3.** any device for measuring something, as the thickness of wire, the dimensions of a machined part, the amount of liquid in a container, steam pressure, etc. **4.** any means of estimating or judging **5.** the distance between the rails of a railway: cf. STANDARD GAUGE, BROAD GAUGE, NARROW GAUGE **6.** the distance between parallel wheels at opposite ends of an axle **7.** the size of a bore, esp. of a shotgun, expressed in terms of the number per pound of round lead balls of a diameter equal to that of the bore **8.** the thickness of sheet metal, diameter of wire, a screw, etc. **9.** *Building* the part of a slate or shingle remaining exposed when laid **10.** *Carpentry* a tool for scoring a line parallel with the edge of a board **11.** *Knitting* the fineness of a fabric, as of hosiery, expressed in terms of the number of loops per 1 1/2 inches **12.** *Naut.* the position of a ship in relation to another ship and the wind **13.** *Plastering* the amount of plaster of Paris used with common plaster to hasten its setting —*vt.* **gauged, gaug′ing** [ME. *gaugen* < ONormFr. *gaugier*, prob. < VL. *gallicare* < ?] **1.** to measure accurately by means of a gauge **2.** to measure the size, amount, extent, or capacity of **3.** to estimate; judge; appraise **4.** to bring to correct gauge; make conform with a standard **5.** *Masonry* to cut or rub (bricks or stone) to a desired shape **6.** *Plastering* to mix (plaster) in right proportions required for the specified setting time —**SYN.** see STANDARD —**gauge′a·ble** *adj.*

WIRE GAUGE

gaug·er (-ər) *n.* [ME. < Anglo-Fr. *gaugeour* < prec.] **1.** a person or thing that gauges; esp., an official who measures the contents of casks of liquor, etc. to be taxed **2.** a collector of excise taxes

Gau·guin (gō gan′), (**Eugène Henri**) **Paul** (pôl) 1848–1903; Fr. painter, in Tahiti after 1891

Gaul (gôl) **1.** ancient region in E Europe, consisting of what is now mainly France & Belgium: after 5th cent. B.C., also called **Transalpine Gaul 2.** ancient region in N Italy, occupied by the Gauls (5th cent. B.C.): in full, **Cisalpine Gaul 3.** ancient division of the Roman Empire, including Cisalpine Gaul & Transalpine Gaul (1st–5th cent. A.D.) —*n.* **1.** any of the Celtic-speaking people of Gaul **2.** a Frenchman

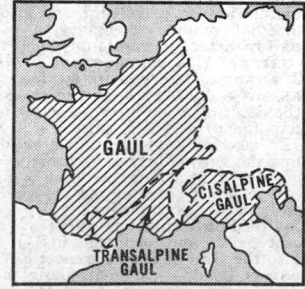

GAUL (in the time of Caesar)

Gaul·ish (-ish) *adj.* of Gaul or the Gauls —*n.* the continental branch of the Celtic languages, spoken in Gaul

Gaull·ism (gôl′iz'm) *n.* the political policies of Charles de Gaulle, characterized by extreme nationalism —**Gaull′ist** *n.*, *adj.*

gaul·the·ri·a (gôl thir′ē ə) *n.* [ModL., name of the genus, after M. *Gaulthier*, 18th-cent. Canad. physician] any of a large genus (*Gaultheria*) of evergreen shrubs of the heath family, including the American wintergreen

gaunt (gônt) *adj.* [ME. *gawnte*, earlier *gant*, slender, thin, gaunt < ?] **1.** thin and bony; hollow-eyed and haggard, as from great hunger or age; emaciated **2.** looking grim, forbidding, or desolate —**SYN.** see LEAN² —**gaunt′ly** *adv.* —**gaunt′ness** *n.*

gaunt·let¹ (gônt′lit, gänt′-) *n.* [ME. < OFr. *gantelet*, dim. of *gant*, a glove < Frank. *want*, a mitten, akin to EFris. *wante*] **1.** a medieval glove, usually of leather covered with metal plates, worn by knights in armor to protect the hand in combat **2.** *a)* a long glove with a flaring cuff covering the lower part of the arm *b)* the flaring cuff —**take up**

the gauntlet 1. to accept a challenge **2.** to undertake the defense of a person, etc. —**throw down the gauntlet** to challenge, as to combat

gaunt·let[2] (gônt′lit, gänt′-) *n. same as* GAUNTLET[1] (esp. *n.* 1)

gaunt·let·ed (-id) *adj.* wearing a gauntlet, or glove

gaun·try (gôn′trē) *n., pl.* **-tries** *same as* GANTRY

gaur (gour) *n., pl.* **gaur, gaurs** [Hind. < Sans. *gaura*, akin to *gáuḥ*, cow: for IE. base see COW[1]] a wild ox of India (*Bibos gaurus*), the largest of the cattle of the world

gauss (gous) *n.* [after Karl F. *Gauss* (1777–1855), Ger. mathematician & astronomer] *Elec.* a cgs unit used in measuring magnetic induction or magnetic flux density, equal to one line of magnetic flux per square centimeter

Gauss·i·an curve (gous′ē ən) [see prec.] *Statistics* a symmetric, bell-shaped probability curve

Gau·ta·ma (gout′ə mə, gôt′-) *n. see* BUDDHA

Gau·tier (gō tyā′) **Thé·o·phile** (tā ō fēl′) 1811–72; Fr. poet, novelist, & critic

gauze (gôz) *n.* [Fr. *gaze*, prob. < Sp. *gasa* < Ar. *ḳazz*, raw silk < Per. *ḳäž*] **1.** any very thin, light, transparent, loosely woven material, as of cotton or silk **2.** any similar but stiff material, as of thin wire **3.** a thin mist

gauz·y (-ē) *adj.* **gauz′i·er, gauz′i·est** thin, light, and transparent, like gauze; diaphanous —**gauz′i·ly** *adv.* —**gauz′i·ness** *n.*

ga·vage (gə väzh′) *n.* [Fr. < *gaver*, to cram, stuff < dial. *gave*, stomach < OFr. < ? Gaul. *gava*] the administration of liquids through a stomach tube, as in forced feeding

gave (gāv) *pt. of* GIVE

☆**gav·el** (gav′'l) *n.* [dial. var. of Scot. *gable*, a fork, tool with forked handle < ME. < OE. *gafol*, akin to G. *gabel*: sense 2 < 1 via Freemasonry] **1.** a mason's hammer for breaking off the rough edges of stones **2.** a small mallet rapped on the table by a presiding officer in calling for attention or silence or by an auctioneer

gav·el·kind (gav′'l kīnd′) *n.* [ME. *gavelkynde* (orig. Kentish) < *gavel*, tribute, tax, rent (< OE. *gafol* < base of *giefan*: see GIVE) + *kynde*, KIND] formerly in Great Britain, a system of land tenure by which: (a) the property of a man dying intestate was divided equally among his sons; (b) the tenant could dispose of his land by feoffment at the age of fifteen; (c) the land did not escheat upon the conviction of the tenant as a felon

ga·vi·al (gā′vē əl) *n.* [Fr. < Hind. *ghaṛiyāl*] **1.** a large crocodile (*Gavialis gangeticus*) of N India, with a very long, slender snout **2.** a closely related, medium-sized crocodile (*Tomistoma schlegeli*) of Borneo and Sumatra

ga·votte (gə vät′) *n.* [Fr. < Pr. *gavoto*, dance of the *Gavots*, a people of Hautes-Alpes, France] **1.** a 17th-cent. dance like the minuet, but faster and livelier **2.** the music for this, in 4/4 time Also sp. **ga·vot′**

G.A.W., GAW guaranteed annual wage

Ga·wain (gä′win, -wān; gə wān′) [Fr. *Gauvain* < ? Gmc. *Gawin*] *Arthurian Legend* a knight of the Round Table, nephew of King Arthur

gawk (gôk) *n.* [prob. dial. var. of GOWK] a clumsy, stupid fellow; simpleton —*vi.* to stare like a gawk, in a stupid way —**gawk′ish** *adj.*

gawk·y (gô′kē) *adj.* **gawk′i·er, gawk′i·est** [prob. < ME. *gouki*, foolish < *gouk*: see GOWK] awkward; clumsy; ungainly —**gawk′i·ly** *adv.* —**gawk′i·ness** *n.*

gawp (gôp) *vi.* [dial., altered < ME. *galpen*, to yawn, gape] [Slang] to stare open-mouthed; gawk or gape

gay (gā) *adj.* [ME. *gai* < OFr. < ? Frank. *gahi*, swift, impetuous, akin to G. *jäh*] **1.** joyous and lively; merry; happy; lighthearted **2.** bright; brilliant [*gay* colors] **3.** given to social life and pleasures [a *gay* life] **4.** wanton; licentious [a *gay* dog] ☆**5.** [Slang] homosexual —*SYN.* see LIVELY —**gay′ness** *n.*

Gay (gā), **John** 1685–1732; Eng. poet & playwright

Ga·ya (gä′yə) city in Bihar, NE India: pop. 151,000

gay·e·ty (gā′ə tē) *n., pl.* **-ties** *same as* GAIETY

Gay-Lus·sac (gā lü säk′), **Jo·seph Louis** (zhō zef′ lwē) 1778–1850; Fr. chemist & physicist

Gay-Lussac's law 1. the statement that the volumes of two or more gases that combine to give a gaseous product are in the proportion of small whole numbers to each other and to the volume of the product **2.** *same as* CHARLES'S LAW

gay·ly (gā′lē) *adv. same as* GAILY

☆**gay·wings** (gā′wiŋz′) *n.* a trailing pink wildflower (*Polygala paucifolia*) of the milkwort family, found in the E U.S. and Canada

gaz. 1. gazette **2.** gazetteer

Ga·za (gä′zə; *for* 2, gā′zə, gaz′ə) **1.** ancient city in Asia Minor, one of the chief cities of the Philistines: Biblical site of Samson's death: Judg. 16:21–30 **2.** city on this site, surrounded by a strip of land (**Gaza Strip**) along the Mediterranean, formerly (until 1967) under United Arab Republic control: 100 sq. mi.

☆**ga·za·bo** (gə zā′bō) *n., pl.* **-bos, -boes** [< Sp. *gazapo*, an artful knave, back-formation < *gazapatón*, foolish talk, ult. < Gr. *kakemphaton*, neut. of *kakemphatos*, ill-sounding, equivocal] [Old Slang] a fellow; guy: often derogatory

gaze (gāz) *vi.* **gazed, gaz′ing** [ME. *gazen* < Scand., as in Norw. & Sw. dial. *gasa*, to stare] to look intently and steadily; stare, as in wonder or expectancy —*n.* a steady look —*SYN.* see LOOK

ga·ze·bo (gə zē′bō, -zā′-) *n., pl.* **-bos, -boes** [said to be jocular formation < prec., after L. *videbo*, I shall see] **1.** a turret, windowed balcony, or summerhouse from which one can gaze at the surrounding scenery ☆**2.** *same as* GAZABO

gaze·hound (gāz′hound′) *n.* [Archaic] a dog that hunts by sight instead of scent, as a greyhound

ga·zelle (gə zel′) *n., pl.* **-zelles′, -zelle′:** see PLURAL, II, D, 1 [Fr. < Ar. *ghazāl*] any of various small, swift, graceful antelopes (genus *Gazella*) of Africa, the near East, and Asia, with spirally twisted, backward-pointing horns and large, lustrous eyes

ga·zette (gə zet′) *n.* [Fr. < It. *gazzetta* < dial. (Venetian) *gazeta*, a small coin, price of the newspaper, orig., prob. dim. of *gaza*, magpie] **1.** a newspaper: now used mainly in some newspaper titles **2.** in England, any of various official publications, as of the government or a university, containing announcements and bulletins —*vt.* **-zet′ted, -zet′ting** [Chiefly Brit.] to publish, announce, or list in a gazette

gaz·et·teer (gaz′ə tir′) *n.* [Fr. *gazettier*] **1.** [Archaic] a person who writes for a gazette **2.** [prob. after L. Echard's use for his geographical dict. (c. 1700)] a dictionary or index of geographical names

Ga·zi·an·tep (gä′zē än tep′) city in S Turkey, near the Syrian border: pop. 124,000

gaz·pa·cho (gäz pä′chō; *Sp.* gäth pä′chō) *n.* [Sp.] a Spanish soup made with tomatoes, chopped cucumbers, peppers, onions, oil, vinegar, etc. and served cold

G.B. Great Britain

GCA *Aeron.* ground control approach

g-cal. gram calorie(s)

G.C.D., g.c.d. greatest common divisor

G.C.F., g.c.f. greatest common factor

G clef *same as* TREBLE CLEF

G.C.M., g.c.m. greatest common measure

gcs gigacycles per second

GCT, G.C.T. Greenwich civil time

Gd *Chem.* gadolinium

gd. guard

G.D. 1. Grand Duchess **2.** Grand Duke

Gdańsk (g′dänsk′) seaport in N Poland, on the Baltic Sea: pop. 319,000: Ger. name, DANZIG

Gdy·nia (g′dēn′yä) seaport in N Poland, on the Baltic Sea: pop. 165,000

Ge[1] (jē, gē) [Gr. *gē*, earth] *same as* GAEA

Ge[2] (zhā) *n.* a family of a number of S. American Indian languages of Brazil, many now extinct

Ge[3] *Chem.* germanium

ge·an·ti·cli·nal (jē an′ti klī′n'l) *n. same as* GEANTICLINE —*adj.* of, or having the nature of, a geanticline

ge·an·ti·cline (jē an′ti klīn′) *n.* [Gr. *gē*, earth + ANTICLINE] *Geol.* a great upward folding of the earth's crust, larger and more complex than an anticline, commonly measured in tens or hundreds of miles

gear (gir) *n.* [ME. *gere*, prob. < ON. *gervi*, preparation, ornament, akin to OE. *gearwe* (see YARE)] **1.** *a)* orig., the clothing and equipment of a soldier, knight, etc. *b)* clothing; apparel **2.** movable property; esp., apparatus or equipment for some particular task, as a workman's tools, the rigging of a ship, a harness, etc. **3.** *a)* a toothed wheel, disk, etc. designed to mesh with another or with the thread of a worm *b)* [often *pl.*] a system of

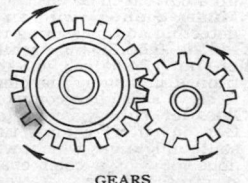

GEARS

two or more gears meshed together so that the motion of one is passed on to the others *c)* a specific adjustment of such a system [high *gear* is for greater speed] *d)* any part of a mechanism performing a specific function [the steering *gear*] —*adj.* [Chiefly Brit. Slang] highly acceptable, attractive, etc. —*vt.* **1.** to furnish with gear; harness **2.** to adapt (one thing) so as to conform with another [to *gear* production to demand] **3.** *Mech. a)* to connect by gears *b)* to furnish with gears *c)* to put into gear —*vi. Mech.* to be in, or come into, proper adjustment or working order —**gear down** (or **up**) to adjust gears in such a way that the driven element goes slower (or faster) than the driving element, with a consequent increase (or decrease) in power —☆**high gear 1.** the arrangement of gears providing the greatest speed but little power **2.** [Colloq.] high speed or efficiency —**in** (or **out of**) **gear 1.** (not) connected to the motor **2.** (not) in proper adjustment or working order —☆**low gear 1.** the arrangement of gears providing little speed but great power **2.** [Colloq.] low speed or efficiency —**reverse gear** the arrangement of gears providing reverse, or backward, motion —☆**shift gears 1.** to change from one gear arrangement to another **2.** to change one's method or approach in handling a problem

gear·box (-bäks′) *n.* **1.** the unit consisting of the transmission gears in a transmission system **2.** a case enclosing gears to protect them from dirt

gear·ing (-in) *n.* **1.** the act or manner of fitting a machine with gears **2.** a system of gears or other parts for transmitting motion

☆**gear·shift** (-shift′) *n.* a device for connecting any of a number of sets of transmission gears to a motor, etc., or for disconnecting them

gear·wheel (-hwēl′, -wēl′) *n.* a toothed wheel in a system of gears; cogwheel

geb. [G. *geboren*] born

geck·o (gek′ō) *n., pl.* **-os, -oes** [Malay *gekok*, echoic of its cry] any of various soft-skinned, insect-eating, tropical and subtropical lizards (family Gekkonidae), with a short, stout body, a large head, and suction pads on the feet

Ged·des (ged′ēz), **Norman Bel** (bel) 1893–1958; U.S. theatrical & industrial design

gee¹ (jē) *interj., n.* [Early ModE. < ?] a word of command to a horse, ox, etc., meaning "turn to the right!" or (usually **gee up**) "go ahead!" —*vt., vi.* **geed, gee′ing** to turn to the right Opposed to HAW²

gee² (jē) *interj.* [euphemistic contr. < JE(SUS)] [Slang] an exclamation of surprise, wonder, etc.

gee³ (jē) *n.* **1.** the letter *g* ☆**2.** [the initial *G* of GRAND] [Slang] one thousand dollars

☆**geek** (gēk) *n.* [< dial. *geck*, fool < Du. *gek*, madman, fool < MLowG. *geck*: orig. echoic of unintelligible cries] [Slang] a performer of grotesque or depraved acts in a carnival, etc., such as biting off the head of a live chicken

Gee·long (jē·lôŋ′) seaport in S Victoria, Australia: pop. (with suburbs) 105,000

Geel·vink Bay (khāl′viŋk) large inlet on the NW coast of New Guinea: c. 200 mi. wide

geese (gēs) *n. pl. of* GOOSE

☆**gee-whiz** (jē′hwiz′, -wiz′) *interj.* [euphemistic alt. of JESUS] a child's exclamation of surprise, objection, etc.

Ge·ez (gē ez′) *n. same as* ETHIOPIC (*n.* 1)

gee·zer (gē′zər) *n.* [< dial. *guiser*, a mummer < GUISE] [Slang] an eccentric old man or, rarely, woman

☆**ge·fil·te fish** (gə fil′tə) [Yid., altered < G. *gefüllter fisch* < *gelfüllt*, pp. of *füllen*, to FILL + *fisch*, FISH²] chopped fish, usually a mixture, as of whitefish, pike, and carp, mixed with chopped onion, egg, seasoning, etc. and boiled, orig. in a casing of the fish skin: it is usually served cold in the form of balls or cakes

ge·gen·schein (gā′gən shīn′) *n.* [G. < *gegen*, against + *schein*, a SHINE, gleam] [also G-] a diffuse, faint light, sometimes visible almost directly opposite the sun in the night sky, and thought to be sunlight reflected from dust

Ge·hen·na (gi hen′ə) [LL.(Ec.) < Gr. *Geenna*, hell < Heb. *gēhinnōm*] **1.** the valley of Hinnom, near Jerusalem, where refuse was burned in Biblical times **2.** *Douay New Testament* hell —*n.* any place of torment

Gei·ger counter (gī′gər) [after Hans *Geiger* (1882–1945), Ger. physicist] an instrument for detecting and counting ionizing particles that pass through it: it consists of a needlelike electrode inside a hollow metallic cylinder filled with gas which, when ionized by the radiation, sets up a current in an electric field: a refined version (**Geiger-Müller counter**) with an amplifying system is used for detecting and measuring radioactivity

Gei·kie (gē′kē), **Sir Archibald** 1835–1924; Scot. geologist

gei·sha (gā′shə) *n., pl.* **-sha, -shas** [Jap.] a Japanese girl trained in singing, dancing, the art of conversation, etc., to serve as a hired companion to men

Geiss·ler tube (gīs′lər) [after H. *Geissler* (1814–79), its Ger. inventor] a glass tube having two electrodes and containing a gas which, when electrified, takes on a luminous glow of a color characteristic of the gas: used in spectroscopy, etc.

gel (jel) *n.* [< GELATIN] a jellylike substance formed by the coagulation of a colloidal solution into a solid phase: cf. SOL³ —*vi.* **gelled, gel′ling** to form a gel; jellify

‡**Ge·län·de·sprung** (gə len′də shproon′) *n.* [G. < *gelände*, open terrain + *sprung*, a leap] *Skiing* a jump, as over an obstacle, made from a crouching position and by propelling oneself with the ski poles

ge·la·ti (gə lät′ē) *n.* [It., pl. of *gelato*, orig., frozen, pp. of *gelare*, to freeze < L.: see ff.] an Italian sherbet made of whole milk, sugar, gelatin, and flavoring: also **ge·la′to** (-ō)

gel·a·tin, gel·a·tine (jel′ət 'n) *n.* [Fr. *gélatine* < It. *gelatina* < *gelata*, a jelly < pp. of L. *gelare*, to freeze < IE. base *gel-*, to freeze, whence COLD] **1.** the tasteless, odorless, brittle substance extracted by boiling bones, hoofs, and animal tissues; also, a similar vegetable substance: gelatin dissolves in hot water, forming a jellylike substance when cool, and is used in the preparation of various foods, medicine capsules, photographic film, etc. **2.** something, as a jelly, made with gelatin **3.** a sheet of translucent material in any of various colors, placed over stage lights for special effects

ge·lat·i·nize (jə lat′'n īz′, jel′ət 'n īz′) *vt.* **-nized′, -niz′ing 1.** to change into gelatin or gelatinous matter **2.** *Photog.* to coat with gelatin —*vi.* to be changed into gelatin or gelatinous matter —**ge·lat′i·ni·za′tion** *n.*

ge·lat·i·noid (-oid′) *adj.* like gelatin —*n.* a gelatinoid substance

ge·lat·i·nous (jə lat′'n əs) *adj.* **1.** of or containing gelatin

2. like gelatin or jelly; having the consistency of gelatin or jelly; viscous —**ge·lat′i·nous·ness** *n.*

ge·la·tion¹ (je lā′shən) *n.* [L. *gelatio* < pp. of *gelare*, to freeze: see GELATIN] solidification by cooling or freezing

ge·la·tion² (je lā′shən) *n.* [GEL + -ATION] the coagulation of a sol to form a gel

geld¹ (geld) *vt.* **geld′ed** or **gelt, geld′ing** [ME. *gelden* < ON. *gelda*, to castrate < *geldr*, barren < IE. base *ghel-*, to cut, whence OW. *gylym*, knife, ON. *gylta*, sow, Goth. *giltha*, scythe] **1.** to castrate (esp. a horse) **2.** to deprive of anything essential; weaken

geld² (geld) *n.* [ML. (Domesday Bk.) *geldum* < OE. *gield*, payment (akin to G. *geld*, money): for IE. base see YIELD] a tax paid to the crown by English landholders under the Anglo-Saxon and Norman kings

Gel·der·land (gel′dər land′; *Du.* khel′dər länt′) province of E Netherlands: 1,941 sq. mi.; pop. 1,410,000; cap. Arnhem

geld·ing (gel′diŋ) *n.* [ME. < ON. *geldingr*: see GELD¹ + -ING] **1.** a gelded animal; esp., a castrated male horse **2.** [Archaic] a eunuch

Ge·li·bo·lu (gel′ē bô lōō′) seaport in S European Turkey, on the Gallipoli Peninsula: pop. 13,000

gel·id (jel′id) *adj.* [L. *gelidus* < *gelu*, frost: see GELATIN] extremely cold; frozen —**ge·lid′i·ty** (jə lid′ə tē) *n.*

gel·ig·nite (jel′ig nīt′) *n.* [GE(LATIN) + L. *lign(um)*, wood + -ITE¹] a blasting explosive that is a mixture of nitroglycerin, nitrocellulose, ammonium nitrate, and some wood pulp

gel·se·mi·um (jel se′mē əm) *n.* [ModL. < It. *gelsomino*, jessamine < Per. *yāsamīn*: see JASMINE] **1.** any of a genus (*Gelsemium*) of twining shrubs of the logania family, bearing fragrant, bright yellow flowers **2.** the root of one variety (*yellow jasmine*), once used as a sedative

Gel·sen·kir·chen (gel′zən kir′Hən) city in North Rhine-Westphalia, West Germany: pop. 371,000

gelt¹ (gelt) *alt. pt. & pp. of* GELD¹

gelt² (gelt) *n.* [G. & Du. *geld* & Yid. *gelt* (< MHG.): see GELD²] [Slang] money

gem (jem) *n.* [ME. *gemme* < OFr. < L. *gemma*, a swelling, bud, precious stone] **1.** a precious or, occasionally, semiprecious stone, cut and polished for use as a jewel **2.** anything prized for its beauty and value, esp. if small and perfect of its kind **3.** a highly valued person ☆**4.** a kind of muffin —*vt.* **gemmed, gem′ming** to adorn or set with or as with gems

CUTS OF GEMS
(A, marquise; B, emerald; C, round; D, pear-shaped)

Ge·ma·ra (gə mä rä′, gə môr′ə) *n.* **1.** [Aram. *gemārā*, completion] the second and supplementary part of the Talmud, providing a commentary on the first part (the MISHNA) **2.** loosely, the Talmud

gem·i·nate (jem′ə nāt′) *adj.* [< L. *geminatus*, pp. of *geminare*, to double < *geminus*, twin] growing or combined in pairs; coupled —*vt.* **-nat′ed, -nat′ing** to arrange in pairs; double —*vi.* to become doubled or paired —**gem′i·na′tion** *n.*

Gem·i·ni (jem′ə nī′, -nē′) [L., twins] **1.** a N constellation between Cancer and Taurus, containing the stars Castor and Pollux, represented as twins sitting together **2.** the third sign of the zodiac (II or □ or ♊), entered by the sun about May 21: see ZODIAC, illus.

gem·ma (jem′ə) *n., pl.* **-mae** (-ē) [L.: cf. GEM] *Biol.* a budlike outgrowth which becomes detached and develops into a new organism, as in certain liverworts —**gem·ma·ceous** (je mā′shəs) *adj.*

gem·mate (jem′āt) *adj.* [L. *gemmatus*, pp. of *gemmare*, to put forth buds < *gemma*, a bud] having, or reproducing by, gemmae —*vi.* **-mat·ed, -mat·ing** to have, or reproduce by, gemmae; bud —**gem·ma′tion** *n.*

gem·mip·a·rous (je mip′ər əs) *adj.* [< L. *gemma*, a bud + -PAROUS] *Biol.* of or reproducing by gemmation; budding

gem·mu·la·tion (jem′yoo lā′shən) *n. Biol.* formation of or reproduction by gemmules

gem·mule (jem′yōōl) *n.* [Fr. < L. *gemmula*, dim. of *gemma*, a bud] *Biol.* a bud of a moss or a reproductive body of an alga or of certain sponges; small gemma

gem·my (jem′ē) *adj.* [ME.] **1.** set with gems **2.** like a gem; glittering

gem·ol·o·gy, gem·mol·o·gy (jem äl′ə jē) *n.* [< L. *gemma* (see GEM) + -O- + -LOGY: sp. infl. by GEM] the science or study of gems and gemstones —**gem′o·log′i·cal, gem′mo·log′i·cal** (-ə läj′i k'l) *adj.* —**gem·ol′o·gist, gem·mol′o·gist** *n.*

ge·mot, ge·mote (gə mōt′) *n.* [OE. < *ge-*, collective prefix (akin to L. *cum*: see COM-) + *mōt*, assembly: see MOOT] an early English public assembly or court, before the Norman Conquest; moot

gems·bok (gemz′bäk′) *n., pl.* **-bok′, -boks′:** see PLURAL, II, D, 2 [Afrik. < G. *gemsbock* < *gemse*, chamois < OHG. *gamuz* < VL. *camox* (see CHAMOIS) + *bock*, BUCK¹] a large antelope (*Oryx gazella*) of S Africa, with long, straight horns and a tufted tail

gem·stone (jem′stōn′) *n.* any mineral or petrified substance that can be used as a gem when cut and polished

‡**ge·müt·lich** (gə müt′liH) *adj.* [G.] agreeable, cheerful, cozy, etc.: indicating a general sense of well-being — **ge·müt′lich·keit′** (-kīt′) *n.*

-gen (jən, jen) [Fr. *-gène* < Gr. *-genēs*, born < base of *gignesthai*, to be born, become: see GENUS] *a n.-forming suffix meaning:* **1.** something that produces [*oxygen*, *hydrogen*] **2.** something produced (in a specified way) [*endogen*]

Gen. **1.** General **2.** Genesis **3.** Geneva

gen. **1.** gender **2.** genera **3.** general **4.** generally **5.** generator **6.** generic **7.** genitive **8.** genus

gen·darme (zhän′därm; *Fr.* zhän därm′) *n., pl.* **-darmes** (-därmz; *Fr.* -därm′) [Fr. < *gens d'armes*, men-at-arms < L. *gens*, a people + *de*, of + *arma*, arms] **1.** formerly, a French cavalryman commanding a squad **2.** in France, Belgium, etc., a soldier serving as an armed policeman **3.** any policeman: a humorous usage

gen·dar·me·rie (zhän där′mə rē; *Fr.* zhän där mə rē′) *n.* [Fr.] gendarmes collectively: also **gen·dar′mer·y**

gen·der[1] (jen′dər) *n.* [ME. < OFr. *gendre*, with unhistoric -*d*- < L. *genus* (gen. *generis*), descent, origin, translating Gr. (Aristotle) *gēnos*: see GENUS] **1.** *Gram. a)* the formal classification by which nouns and pronouns (and often accompanying modifiers) are grouped and inflected, or changed in form, so as to control certain syntactic relationships: although gender is not a formal feature of English, some nouns and the third person singular pronouns are distinguished according to sex or the lack of sex (*man* or *he*, masculine gender; *woman* or *she*, feminine gender; *door* or *it*, neuter gender): in most Indo-European languages, and in others, gender is not necessarily correlated with sex *b)* any one of such groupings, or an inflectional form showing membership in such a group **2.** [Colloq.] sex

gen·der[2] (jen′dər) *vt., vi. archaic var. of* ENGENDER

☆**gene** (jēn) *n.* [< G. *gen* (short for) *pangen* (< *pan*, PAN + -*gen*, -GEN, after *pangenesis*: see PANGENESIS)] *Genetics* any of the units occurring at specific points on the chromosomes, by which hereditary characters are transmitted and determined: each is regarded as a particular state of organization of the chromatin in the chromosome, consisting primarily of DNA and protein: see DOMINANT, RECESSIVE, MENDEL'S LAWS

geneal. genealogy

ge·ne·a·log·i·cal (jē′nē ə läj′i k'l, jen′ē-) *adj.* **1.** of genealogy **2.** tracing a line of descent — **ge′ne·a·log′i·cal·ly** *adv.*

ge·ne·al·o·gy (-äl′ə jē, -al′ə jē), *n., pl.* **-gies** [ME. *genelogi* < OFr. *genealogie* < LL. *genealogia* < Gr. *genealogia* < *genea*, race, stock (cf. GENUS) + *-logia*, -LOGY] **1.** a chart or recorded history of the descent of a person or family from an ancestor or ancestors **2.** the science or study of family descent **3.** descent from an ancestor; pedigree; lineage — **ge′ne·al′o·gist** *n.*

gene pool the total of all the genes of a species

gen·er·a (jen′ər ə) *n. pl. of* GENUS

gen·er·a·ble (jen′ər ə b'l) *adj.* [L. *generabilis*] that can be generated

gen·er·al (jen′ər əl, jen′rəl) *adj.* [ME. < OFr. < L. *generalis* < *genus* (gen. *generis*), kind, class: see GENUS] **1.** of, for, or from the whole or all; not particular nor local [a *general* anesthetic, the *general* welfare] **2.** of, for, or applying to a whole genus, kind, class, order, or race [the *general* classifications of matter] **3.** existing or occurring extensively; common; widespread [a *general* unrest] **4.** most common; usual [the *general* spelling of a word] **5.** concerned with the main or overall features; lacking in details; not specific [the *general* features of a plan] **6.** not precise; vague [to speak in *general* terms] **7.** senior or highest in rank [an attorney *general*] **8.** not connected with or limited to one branch or department of learning, business, etc.; not specialized [a *general* store] —*n.* **1.** the main or overall fact, condition, idea, etc.: opposed to PARTICULAR **2.** the head of a religious order **3.** [Archaic] the public; populace **4.** *a)* any of various military officers ranking above a colonel; specif., *U.S. Army & U.S. Air Force* such an officer, with an insignia of four stars, ranking below a GENERAL OF THE ARMY (or AIR FORCE) and above a LIEUTENANT GENERAL: see also BRIGADIER GENERAL, MAJOR GENERAL *b)* *U.S. Marine Corps* an officer of the highest rank —*SYN.* see COMMON, UNIVERSAL —**in general 1.** in the main; usually **2.** without specific details **3.** with reference to all spoken of

☆**General American** American English as conversationally spoken by most people in the greater part of the U.S., exclusive of much of New England and most of the South: a term no longer much used

general assembly 1. in some States of the U.S., the legislative assembly **2.** [G- A-] the legislative assembly of the United Nations **3.** the highest council or judicatory in certain Protestant, esp. Presbyterian, churches

☆**General Court 1.** orig., a Colonial legislative assembly with limited judicial powers **2.** now, the legislature of New Hampshire or Massachusetts: the official title

general court-martial the highest military court, for judging the gravest offenses: it consists of five or more officers or enlisted men, and can impose the death sentence

gen·er·al·cy (-sē) *n., pl.* **-cies** the rank, commission, tenure of office, or authority of a general

☆**general delivery 1.** delivery of mail at the post office to addressees who call for it **2.** the department of the post office responsible for such delivery

☆**general election 1.** an election to choose from among candidates previously nominated in a primary election, by party convention, etc. **2.** a nationwide or Statewide election

general headquarters *Mil.* the headquarters of a commanding general in the field

gen·er·al·is·si·mo (jen′ər ə lis′ə mō′, jen′rə-) *n., pl.* **-mos′** [It., superl. of *generale*, GENERAL] in certain countries, **1.** the commander in chief of all the armed forces **2.** the commanding officer of several armies in the field

gen·er·al·ist (jen′ər ə list, jen′rə list) *n.* an administrator, teacher, etc. with broad general knowledge and experience in several disciplines or areas, as opposed to a specialist —**gen′er·al·ism** *n.*

gen·er·al·i·ty (jen′ə ral′ə tē) *n., pl.* **-ties** [ME. *generalte* < OFr. *généralité* < LL. *generalitas* < L. *generalis*] **1.** the condition or quality of being general, or applicable to all **2.** a general, nonspecific, or vague statement, expression, idea, principle, etc. **3.** the bulk; main body

gen·er·al·i·za·tion (jen′ər ə li zā′shən, jen′rəl i-) *n.* **1.** the act or process of generalizing **2.** a general idea, statement, etc. resulting from this; inference applied generally

gen·er·al·ize (jen′ər ə līz′, jen′rə-) *vt.* **-ized′, -iz′ing** [ME. *generalisen*] to make general; esp., *a)* to state in terms of a general law or precept *b)* to infer or derive (a general law or precept) from (particular instances) *c)* to emphasize the general character rather than specific details of *d)* to cause to be widely known or used; popularize —*vi.* **1.** to formulate general principles or inferences from particulars **2.** to talk in generalities **3.** to become general or spread throughout a body or area

gen·er·al·ly (-lē; *also, by metathesis*, jen′ər lē) *adv.* **1.** to or by most people; widely; popularly; extensively [a *generally* accepted usage] **2.** in most instances; usually; as a rule **3.** in a general way or sense; without reference to details or individual cases; not specifically

general officer *Mil.* any officer above a colonel in rank

☆**general of the air force** the highest rank in the U.S. Air Force, having the insignia of five stars

☆**General of the Armies** the special rank given John J. Pershing by the Senate on Sept. 3, 1919

☆**general of the army** the highest rank in the U.S. Army, having the insignia of five stars

general order *Mil.* **1.** any of a numbered series of orders under competent authority, including general directives, announcements, etc. **2.** any of the permanent orders giving in general the duties of sentries

general paresis (or **paralysis**) *see* PARESIS

general practitioner a practicing physician who does not specialize in any particular field of medicine

gen·er·al·pur·pose (-pur′pəs) *adj.* having a variety of uses; suitable for general use

☆**general semantics** an educational movement concerned with relations between symbols, esp. language, and reality and with improving the adjustment of people to each other and to the environment

gen·er·al·ship (-ship′) *n.* [see -SHIP] **1.** *a)* the rank, tenure, or authority of a general *b)* the military skill of a general **2.** highly skillful leadership

general staff *Mil.* a group of officers who assist the commander of a high unit in planning, coordinating, and supervising operations

☆**general store** a store where many sorts of merchandise are sold, but not in separate departments

general strike a strike by the workers in an entire industry or throughout an entire community or country

gen·er·ate (jen′ə rāt′) *vt.* **-at′ed, -at′ing** [< L. *generatus*, pp. of *generare*, to beget, produce < *genus* (gen. *generis*), race, kind: see GENUS] **1.** to produce (offspring); beget; procreate **2.** to bring into being; cause to be [to *generate* hope] **3.** to originate or produce by a physical or chemical process [to *generate* electricity] **4.** *Math.* to trace out or form (a line, plane, figure, or solid) by the motion of a point, line, or plane

gen·er·a·tion (jen′ə rā′shən) *n.* [ME. *generacioun* < OFr. *generacion* < L. *generatio* < *generatus*: see GENERATE] **1.** the act or process of producing offspring; procreation **2.** the act or process of bringing into being; origination; production **3.** a single stage or degree in the succession of natural descent [father, son, and grandson are three *generations*] **4.** the average period (about thirty years) between the birth of one generation and that of the next **5.** *a)* all the people born and living at about the same time *b)* a group of such people with some experience, belief, attitude, etc. in common [the beat *generation*] **6.** *Math.* the formation of a line, figure, plane, or solid by the motion of a point, line, or plane —**gen′er·a′tion·al** *adj.*

gen·er·a·tive (jen′ər ə tiv, -ə rāt′iv) *adj.* [ME. *generatif*]

1. of the production of offspring; procreative 2. having the power of producing or originating

☆**generative grammar** a grammatical system consisting of a limited and unchanging set of rules employing a list of symbols and words to generate or describe every possible structure in a language

gen·er·a·tor (jen′ə rāt′ər) n. [L.] 1. a person or thing that generates; specif., a) a machine for producing gas or steam b) a machine for changing mechanical energy into electrical energy; dynamo 2. same as GENERATRIX

gen·er·a·trix (jen′ə rā′triks) n., pl. **-er·a·tri′ces** (-ər ə tri′ sēz, -ə rā′trə sēz′) [L., fem. of generator] Math. a point, line, or plane whose motion generates a line, plane, figure, or solid

ge·ner·ic (jə ner′ik) adj. [ML. genericus: see GENUS + -IC] 1. of, applied to, or referring to a whole kind, class, or group; inclusive or general 2. that is not a trademark 3. Biol. of or characteristic of a genus —SYN. see UNIVERSAL —**ge·ner′i·cal·ly** adv.

gen·er·os·i·ty (jen′ə räs′ə tē) n. [ME. generosite < L. generosus < generosus] 1. the quality of being generous; specif., a) nobility of mind; magnanimity; graciousness b) willingness to give or share; unselfishness 2. pl. **-ties** a generous act

gen·er·ous (jen′ər əs) adj. [L. generosus, of noble birth, excellent, generous < genus: see GENUS] 1. orig., of noble birth 2. having qualities attributed to people of noble birth; noble-minded; gracious; magnanimous 3. willing to give or share; unselfish; liberal 4. large; ample [generous portions] 5. rich in yield; fertile 6. rich, full-flavored, and strong: said of wine —**gen′er·ous·ly** adv. —**gen′er·ous·ness** n.

Gen·e·see (jen′ə sē′) [< Iroquoian (Seneca); ? "beautiful valley"] river flowing from N Pa. across W N.Y. into Lake Ontario: c. 150 mi.

gen·e·sis (jen′ə sis) n., pl. **-ses** (-sēz′) [ME. < OE. & LL. (Ec.) < L. genesis, birth, generation < Gr. genesis (used in LXX for Genesis) < base of gignesthai, to be born: see GENUS] the way in which something comes to be; beginning; origin —[G-] the first book of the Bible, giving an account of the creation of the universe

-gen·e·sis (jen′ə sis) [see prec.] a n.-forming combining form meaning origination, creation, formation, evolution (of something specified) [parthenogenesis]

Ge·nêt (zhə nā′) 1. **Ed·mond Charles E·douard** (ed mōn′ shàrl ā dwàr′), 1763–1834; Fr. diplomat, in the U.S. after 1793: called Citizen Genêt 2. **Jean** (zhän), 1909– ; Fr. playwright & novelist

gen·et¹ (jen′ət, jə net′) n. [ME. < OFr. genette < Sp. gineta < Ar. jarnayt] 1. any of a genus (Genetta) of small, spotted African animals related to the civet 2. the fur of this animal Also **ge·nette** (jə net′)

gen·et² (jen′ət) n. same as JENNET

ge·net·ic (jə net′ik) adj. [< GENESIS] 1. of the genesis, or origin, of something 2. of or having to do with genetics 3. same as GENIC Also **ge·net′i·cal** —**ge·net′i·cal·ly** adv.

genetic code the order in which four chemical constituents are arranged in huge molecules of DNA: these molecules are assumed to transmit genetic information to the cells by synthesizing ribonucleic acid in a corresponding order

ge·net·i·cist (-ə sist) n. a specialist in genetics

ge·net·ics (-iks) n.pl. [with sing. v.] [< GENETIC] 1. the branch of biology that deals with heredity and variation in similar or related animals and plants 2. the genetic features or constitution of an individual, group, or kind

Ge·ne·va (jə nē′və) 1. city in SW Switzerland, on Lake Geneva: pop. 175,000 2. canton of SW Switzerland, largely the city of Geneva & its suburbs: 109 sq. mi.; pop. 291,000 3. **Lake (of)**, lake in SW Switzerland on the border of France: 224 sq. mi.

ge·ne·va (jə nē′və) n. [Du. genever < OFr. genevre, juniper berry < L. juniperus, juniper] same as GIN¹ (sense 1)

Geneva bands [after the clerical garb of GENEVA Calvinists] two white linen strips hanging from the front of the collar, worn by some Protestant clergymen

Geneva Convention an international agreement signed at Geneva in 1864, establishing a code, later revised, for the care and treatment in wartime of the sick, wounded, and dead in battle, and of prisoners of war, including protection of hospitals, ambulances, etc. having the emblem of the Red Cross

Geneva cross same as RED CROSS (sense 1)

Geneva gown [cf. GENEVA BANDS] a long, loose, wide-sleeved black gown, worn by many Protestant clergymen

Ge·ne·van (jə nē′vən) adj. 1. of Geneva or its people 2. same as CALVINISTIC —n. 1. a native or inhabitant of Geneva 2. a Calvinist

Ge·nève (zhə nev′) Fr. name of GENEVA (senses 1 & 2)

Gen·e·vese (jen′ə vēz′) adj., n. sing. & pl. same as GENEVAN

Gen·e·vieve (jen′ə vēv′) [Fr. Geneviève < LL. Genovefa < ? Celt.] a feminine name 2. Saint, 422?–500? A.D.; Fr. nun; patron saint of Paris: her day is Jan. 3

Genf (genf) Ger. name of GENEVA (senses 1 & 2)

Gen·ghis Khan (geŋ′gis kän′, jeŋ′gis) (born Temuchin) 1162?–1227; Mongol conqueror of land from the Black Sea to the Pacific

ge·nial¹ (jēn′yəl, jē′nē əl) adj. [L. genialis, of generation or birth < genius, guardian deity: see GENIUS] 1. orig., of marriage or procreation 2. promoting life and growth;

pleasantly warm, mild, and healthful [a genial climate] 3. cheerful, friendly, and sympathetic; cordial and kindly; amiable 4. [Rare] of or characterized by genius —SYN. see AMIABLE —**ge·ni·al·i·ty** (jē′nē al′ə tē, jēn yal′-) n. —**ge′nial·ly** adv.

ge·ni·al² (ji nī′əl) adj. [< Gr. geneion, a chin (< genys, a jaw: cf. CHIN) + -AL] having to do with the chin

gen·ic (jen′ik) adj. of, having the nature of, or caused by a gene or genes; genetic

-gen·ic (jen′ik) a combining form: 1. used to form adjectives corresponding to nouns ending in -GEN or -GENY [phylogenic] 2. meaning suitable to [photogenic]

ge·nic·u·late (jə nik′yoo lit) adj. [L. geniculatus < geniculum, dim. of genu, KNEE] 1. having a kneelike joint or joints 2. bent sharply like a knee Also **ge·nic′u·lat′ed** (-lāt′id)

ge·nie (jē′nē) n. [Fr. génie (< L. genius: see GENIUS, used to transl. Ar. jinni] same as JINNI

ge·ni·i (jē′nē ī′) n. occas. pl. of GENIUS

gen·i·pap (jen′ə pap′) n. [Port. genipapo < the WInd. (Tupi) name] 1. the brown, edible fruit, about the size of an orange, of a tropical American tree (Genipa americana) of the madder family 2. the tree itself

genit. genitive

gen·i·tal (jen′ə t'l) adj. [ME. < OFr. < L. genitalis < genitus, pp. of genere, gignere, to beget: see GENUS] 1. of reproduction or the sexual organs 2. Psychoanalysis a) designating or of the third stage of infantile psychosexual development in which interest centers around the genital organs b) designating or of the adult or final stage of psychosexual development in which conflicts have been resolved, libidinal drives regulated, and character structure integrated [genital character]: cf. ANAL, ORAL

gen·i·ta·li·a (jen′ə tāl′yə, -tāl′ē ə) n.pl. [L., short for genitalia (membra)] same as GENITALS

gen·i·tals (jen′ə t'lz) n.pl. [< GENITAL] the reproductive organs; esp., the external sex organs

gen·i·ti·val (jen′ə tī′v'l) adj. of or in the genitive case — **gen′i·ti′val·ly** adv.

gen·i·tive (jen′ə tiv) adj. [ME. genitif < OFr. < L. (casus) genitivus, lit., case of origin < genitus (see GENIT.): mistransl. < Gr. genikē, generic (case), (case) of genus < Gr. gēnos, genus] designating, of, or in a relational case, as in Latin, shown by grammatical inflection or by an analytical construction and typically expressing possession, source, or a partitive concept: cf. POSSESSIVE —n. 1. the genitive case 2. a word or construction in the genitive case

gen·i·to- (jen′ə tō) a combining form meaning genital and [genitourinary]

gen·i·to·u·ri·nar·y (jen′ə tō yoor′ə ner′ē) adj. designating or of the genital and urinary organs together

gen·ius (jēn′yəs, jē′nē əs) n., pl. **gen′ius·es** for 3, 4, 5, 6; **ge·ni·i** (jē′nē ī′) for 1 & 2 [L., guardian spirit, natural ability, genius < base of genere, gignere, to produce: see GENUS] 1. a) [often G-] according to ancient Roman belief, a guardian spirit assigned to a person at birth; tutelary deity b) [often G-] the guardian spirit of any person, place, etc. c) either of two spirits, one good and one evil, supposed to influence one's destiny d) a person considered as having strong influence over another 2. same as JINNI 3. the personification of a quality 4. particular character or essential spirit or nature of a nation, place, age, etc. 5. a great natural ability [for a particular activity); strong disposition or inclination 6. a) great mental capacity and inventive ability; esp., great and original creative ability in some art, science, etc. b) a person having such capacity or ability c) popularly, any person with a very high intelligence quotient —SYN. see TALENT

‡**ge·ni·us lo·ci** (jē′nē əs lō′sī) [L., lit., the (guardian) spirit of a place] the general atmosphere of a place

Genk (khenk) city in NE Belgium: pop. 56,000

genl. general

Gen·o·a (jen′ə wə) 1. seaport in NW Italy, at the head of the Gulf of Genoa: pop. 848,000: It. name, GENOVA 2. **Gulf of**, N part of the Ligurian Sea, off NW Italy

☆**gen·o·a** (jen′ə wə) n. [< prec.] [often G-] Naut. a large jib used as on a racing yacht: also **genoa jib**

gen·o·cide (jen′ə sīd′) n. [< Gr. genos, race, kind (see GENUS) + -CIDE: first applied to the attempted extermination of the Jews by Nazi Germany] the systematic killing of, or a program of action intended to destroy, a whole national or ethnic group —**gen′o·ci′dal** (-sī′d'l) adj.

Gen·o·ese (jen′ə wēz′) adj. of Genoa, its people, etc. —n., pl. **-ese′** a native or inhabitant of Genoa

ge·nome (jē′nōm) n. [G. genom < gen, GENE + (chromo-s)om, CHROMOSOME] one complete haploid set of chromosomes of an organism —**ge·nom′ic** (-nō′mik, -nām′ik) adj.

gen·o·type (jen′ə tīp′, jē′nə-) n. [< Gr. genos, race, kind (see GENUS) + -TYPE] 1. the fundamental constitution of an organism in terms of its hereditary factors 2. a group of organisms each having the same combination of hereditary characteristics 3. the type species of a genus —**gen′o·typ′ic** (-tip′ik), **gen′o·typ′i·cal** adj. —**gen′o·typ′i·cal·ly** adv.

-gen·ous (jə nəs) [-GEN + -OUS] a suffix used to form adjectives derived from nouns ending in -GEN, -GENY, meaning: 1. producing, generating [nitrogenous] 2. produced by, generated in [autogenous]

Ge·no·va (je′nō vä′) It. name of GENOA

gen·re (zhän′rə; *Fr.* zhän′r′) *n.* [Fr. < L. *genus* (gen. *generis*): see GENUS, GENDER[1]] **1.** a kind, or type, as of works of literature, art, etc. **2.** *same as* GENRE PAINTING

genre painting painting in which subjects or scenes from everyday life are treated realistically

gen·ro (gen′rō′) *n.pl.* [Jap., lit., first elders] the former elder statesmen of Japan: see ELDER STATESMAN

gens (jenz) *n., pl.* **gen·tes** (jen′tēz) [L., orig., that belonging together by birth < base of *gignere*, to beget: see GENUS] **1.** in ancient Rome, a clan united by descent through the male line from a common ancestor and having both name and religious observances in common **2.** any tribe or clan; esp., an exogamous group that reckons descent only through the male line

Gen·ser·ic (jen′sər ik, gen′-) 400?–477 A.D.; king of the Vandals (427–477): conqueror in N Africa & of Rome

Gent (khent) *Flem. name of* GHENT

gent[1] (jent) *n.* [Colloq.] a gentleman; man: humorous or vulgar term

gent[2] (jent) *adj.* [ME. < OFr. < L. *genitus*, born, pp. of *gignere*, to beget, produce: see GENUS] [Obs.] **1.** of good birth and social standing **2.** pretty; graceful

gen·teel (jen tēl′) *adj.* [< Fr. *gentil* (of same origin as GENTLE & JAUNTY, but reborrowed in 16th c.)] **1.** having or showing the good taste and refinement associated with polite society; elegant, fashionable, etc.: now chiefly an archaic or humorous usage **2.** excessively or affectedly refined, polite, and elegant —**gen·teel′ly** *adv.* —**gen·teel′-ness** *n.*

gen·tian (jen′shən) *adj.* [ME. *genciane* < OFr. *gentiane* < L. *gentiana*] designating a family (Gen-tianaceae) of plants including the fringed gentian and the closed gentian —*n.* **1.** any of a large genus (*Gentiana*) of plants of the gentian family, with blue, white, red, or yellow flowers **2.** the bitter root of the yellow gentian (*Gentiana lutea*), used as a gastrointestinal tonic

gentian violet a violet dye used as an antiseptic and as a stain in microscopy

gen·tile (jen′tīl) *n.* [< Fr. & L.; Fr. *gentil* < L. *gentilis*, of the same gens, clan, or race, also, foreigner (in opposition to Roman), in LL.(Ec.), pagan, heathen (in opposition to Jew and Christian): see GENTLE] [*also* G- *for n. & adj. 1, 2, 3*] **1.** any person not a Jew; often, specif., a Christian **2.** formerly, among Christians, a heathen or pagan ☆**3.** among Mormons, any person not a Mormon —*adj.* **1.** not Jewish **2.** heathen; pagan ☆**3.** not Mormon **4.** of a clan, tribe, or nation **5.** *Gram.* designating a nationality or country [French is a *gentile* adjective] —*SYN.* see PAGAN

gen·ti·lesse (jent′′l es′) *n.* [ME. < OFr. *gentillise* < *gentil*: see GENTLE] [Archaic] good breeding, esp. as shown by refined and courteous behavior

gen·til·i·ty (jen til′ə tē) *n., pl.* **-ties** [ME. *gentilete* < OFr. < L. *gentilitas* < *gentilis*: see GENTLE] **1.** a) the condition of belonging by birth to the upper classes b) members of the upper class, collectively **2.** the quality of being genteel; now, specif., excessive or affected refinement and elegance; genteelness

gen·tis·ic acid (jen tis′ik, -tiz′-) [< *gentisin*, pigment derived from gentian root < ModL. *Gentiana*, genus name + (TRYP)SIN + -IC] a crystalline, water-soluble acid, $C_7H_6O_4$, whose sodium salt has been used in medicine

gen·tle (jent′′l) *adj.* **-tler, -tlest** [ME. *gentil* < OFr., of noble birth < L. *gentilis*, of the same gens (in LL., of a good family) < *gens*: see GENS] **1.** belonging to the upper classes or polite society **2.** like or suitable to polite society; refined, courteous, etc. **3.** [Archaic] noble; chivalrous [a *gentle* knight] **4.** generous; kind [*gentle* reader] **5.** easily handled; tame [a *gentle* dog] **6.** kindly; serene; patient [a *gentle* disposition] **7.** not violent, harsh, or rough [a *gentle* tap, a *gentle* rebuke] **8.** gradual [a *gentle* slope] —*n.* [Archaic] a person of the upper classes —*vt.* **-tled, -tling 1.** [Rare] to make gentle, mild, or pleasant **2.** to tame or train (a horse) **3.** to calm or soothe as by stroking **4.** [Obs.] to raise to the social status of a gentleman —*SYN.* see SOFT —**the gentle craft** (or **art**) **1.** fishing **2.** [Obs.] shoemaking —**gen′tle·ness** *n.*

gentle breeze a wind whose speed is 8 to 12 miles per hour: see BEAUFORT SCALE

gen·tle·folk (-fōk′) *n.pl.* people of high social standing: also **gen′tle·folks′**

gen·tle·man (-mən) *n., pl.* **-men** (-mən) [ME. *gentilman* (after OFr. *gentilz hom*): see GENTLE & MAN] **1.** a) orig., a man born into a family of high social standing b) any man of independent means who does not work for a living **2.** a courteous, gracious man with a strong sense of honor **3.** a man's personal servant; valet: chiefly in the phrase **gentleman's gentleman 4.** any man: polite term, as (chiefly in pl.) of address —☆**the gentleman from** —— in the U.S. House of Representatives, the member from (a specified State)

gen·tle·man-at-arms (-ət ärmz′) *n., pl.* **gen′tle·men-at-arms′** in Great Britain, any of a group of forty men of rank who accompany the sovereign as a military guard on important occasions

gen·tle·man-farm·er (-fär′mər) *n., pl.* **gen′tle·men-farm′ers** a wealthy man who owns and manages a farm as an avocation

gen·tle·man·ly (-lē) *adj.* [ME.] of, characteristic of, or fit for a gentleman; well-mannered: also **gen′tle·man·like′** —**gen′tle·man·li·ness** *n.*

gentleman of fortune *same as* ADVENTURER

☆**gentlemen's** (or **gentleman's**) **agreement 1.** an unwritten agreement secured only by the parties' pledge of honor and not legally binding **2.** such an agreement to discriminate against members of certain minority groups

gen·tle·wom·an (jent′′l woom′ən) *n., pl.* **-wom′en** (-wim/in) [ME. *gentil womman*] **1.** orig., a woman born into a family of high social standing; lady **2.** a courteous, gracious, considerate woman **3.** formerly, a woman in attendance on a lady of rank

gent·ly (jent′lē) *adv.* [ME. *gentilly*] in a gentle manner or to a gentle degree

Gen·too (jen tōō′) *adj., n., pl.* **-toos′** [Port. *gentio*, heathen, gentile < L. *gentilis*: see GENTILE] *archaic var. of* HINDU

gen·try (jen′trē) *n.* [ME. *genterie*, noble or high birth; apparently taken as sing. of *genterise*, gentility of birth < OFr. *gentilise* < *gentil*: see GENTLE] **1.** [Obs.] rank resulting from birth; esp., high rank **2.** people of high social standing; esp., in Great Britain, the class of landowning people ranking just below the nobility **3.** people of a particular class or group [the newspaper *gentry*]

ge·nu (jē′nyōō, jen′-) *n., pl.* **gen·u·a** (jen′yoo wə) [L., KNEE] *Anat.* **1.** the knee **2.** a kneelike part, as in the corpus callosum

gen·u·flect (jen′yə flekt′) *vi.* [ML.(Ec.) *genuflectere* < L. *genu*, KNEE + *flectere*, to bend (see FLEX[1])] **1.** to bend the knee, as in reverence or worship **2.** to act in a submissive or servile way —**gen′u·flec′tion**, chiefly Brit. **gen′u·flex′-ion** (-flek′shən) *n.*

gen·u·ine (jen′yoo wən) *adj.* [L. *genuinus*, orig., inborn, native, hence authentic < base of *gignere*, to be born: see GENUS] **1.** of the original stock; purebred **2.** really being what it is said to be or coming from the alleged source or origin; not counterfeit or artificial; real; true; authentic **3.** sincere and frank; honest and forthright —*SYN.* see AUTHENTIC —**gen′u·ine·ly** *adv.* —**gen′u·ine·ness** *n.*

ge·nus (jē′nəs) *n., pl.* **gen·er·a** (jen′ər ə), sometimes **ge′nus·es** [L., birth, origin, race, species, kind < IE. base **gen-*, to beget, produce, whence L. *gignere*, to beget, Gr. *genos*, race, *gignesthai*, to be born, G. *kind*, child, OE. *(ge)cynd*, kind, *cennan*, to beget; also, with loss of initial *g-*, L. *nascor*, to be born, *natura*, nature] **1.** a class; kind; sort **2.** *Biol.* a classification of plants or animals with common distinguishing characteristics: a genus is the main subdivision of a family and is made up of a small group of closely related species or of a single species; the genus name is capitalized and precedes the species name, which is not capitalized (Ex.: *Homo sapiens*, modern man) **3.** *Logic* a class of things made up of two or more subordinate classes, or species

-ge·ny (jə nē) [Gr. *-geneia*: see -GEN] *a suffix meaning* origin, production, development [*phylogeny*]

ge·o- (jē′ō, -ə) [Gr. *geō-* < *gaia, gē*, the earth] *a combining form meaning* **1.** earth, of the earth [*geocentric, geophyte*] **2.** geographical [*geopolitics*]

ge·o·cen·tric (jē′ō sen′trik) *adj.* [GEO- + CENTRIC] **1.** measured or viewed as from the center of the earth **2.** having or regarding the earth as a center Also **ge′o·cen′-tri·cal** —**ge′o·cen′tri·cal·ly** *adv.*

ge·o·chem·is·try (-kem′is trē) *n.* the branch of chemistry dealing with the chemical composition of the earth's crust and the chemical changes that occur there —**ge′o·chem′i·cal** *adj.* —**ge′o·chem′ist** *n.*

ge·o·chro·nol·o·gy (-krə näl′ə jē) *n.* [GEO- + CHRONOLOGY] the branch of geology dealing with the age of the earth and its materials, the dating of evolutionary stages in plant and animal development, etc. —**ge′o·chron′o·log′i·cal** (-krän′ə läj′i k'l) *adj.*

ge·o·chro·nom·e·try (-krə näm′ə trē) *n.* [GEO- + CHRONOMETRY] the measurement of geologic time, as from the decay of radioactive elements —**ge′o·chro′no·met′ric** (-krän′ə met′rik, -krō′nə-) *adj.*

ge·ode (jē′ōd) *n.* [Fr. *géode* < L. *geodes*, a precious stone < Gr. *geoidēs*, earthlike < *gē*, earth + *eidos*, form] **1.** a globular stone having a cavity lined with inward growing crystals or layers of silica **2.** a) such a cavity b) any formation like this —**ge·od′ic** (-äd′ik) *adj.*

ge·o·des·ic (jē′ə des′ik, -dē′sik) *adj.* **1.** *same as* GEODETIC (sense 1) **2.** a) designating the shortest line between two points on a surface, esp. a curved surface b) of or pertaining to the geometry of such lines —*n.* a geodesic line

ge·od·e·sy (jē äd′ə sē) *n.* [Gr. *geōdaisia* < *gē*, the earth + *daiein*, to divide < IE. base **dā-, dāi-*, to divide, whence TIDE[1]] the branch of applied mathematics concerned with measuring, or determining the shape of, the earth or a

large part of its surface, or with locating exactly points on its surface —**ge·od′e·sist** n.

ge·o·det·ic (jē′ə det′ik) *adj.* **1.** of or determined by geodesy **2.** *same as* GEODESIC (sense 2) Also **ge′o·det′i·cal** —**ge′o·det′i·cal·ly** *adv.*

☆**geo·duck** (gwē′duk′) *n.* [< AmInd. (Chinook) name] a very large, burrowing, edible clam (*Panope generosa*) of intertidal beaches of W N. America

Geof·frey (jef′rē) [ME. *Geffrey* < OFr. *Geoffroi* < Gmc.: first element < *ga-*, district (whence G. *gau*), or *gal-*, spear, or *wala-*, traveler: second element < Gmc. *frithu*, peace (whence G. *friede*)] a masculine name: dim. *Jeff*; var. *Jeffrey*

Geoffrey of Monmouth 1100?–54?; Brit. bishop & chronicler: preserver of the Arthurian legend

geog. 1. geographer **2.** geographical **3.** geography

ge·og·no·sy (jē äg′nə sē) n. [Fr. *géognosie* < Gr. *gē*, earth + *gnōsis*, knowledge < *gignōskein*, to KNOW] the branch of geology dealing with the composition of the earth and the distribution of its various strata and mineral deposits

ge·og·ra·pher (jē äg′rə fər) n. a specialist in geography

ge·o·graph·i·cal (jē′ə graf′i k'l) *adj.* **1.** of or according to geography **2.** with reference to the geography of a particular region Also **ge′o·graph′ic** —**ge′o·graph′i·cal·ly** *adv.*

geographical mile *see* MILE

ge·og·ra·phy (jē äg′rə fē) n., pl. **-phies** [L. *geographia* < Gr. *geōgraphia*, geography < *geō-* (see GEO-) + *graphein*, to write: see GRAPHIC] **1.** the descriptive science dealing with the surface of the earth, its division into continents and countries, and the climate, plants, animals, natural resources, inhabitants, and industries of the various divisions **2.** the physical features, esp. the surface features, of a region, area, or place **3.** a book about geography

ge·oid (jē′oid) n. [G. *geoide* < Gr. *geoeidēs*, earthlike: see GEODE] the earth viewed as a hypothetical ellipsoid with the surface represented as a mean sea level

geol. 1. geologic(al) **2.** geologist **3.** geology

ge·o·log·ic (jē′ə läj′ik) *adj.* of or according to geology: also **ge′o·log′i·cal** —**ge′o·log′i·cal·ly** *adv.*

ge·ol·o·gist (jē äl′ə jist) n. a specialist in geology

ge·ol·o·gize (-jīz′) vi., vt. **-gized′, -giz′ing** [Rare] to study geology or make a geological survey of (an area)

ge·ol·o·gy (-jē) n., pl. **-gies** [ML. *geologia*: see GEO- & -LOGY] **1.** the science dealing with the physical nature and history of the earth, including the structure and development of its crust, the composition of its interior, individual rock types, the forms of life found as fossils, etc. **2.** the structure of the earth's crust in a given region, area, or place **3.** a book about geology

geom. 1. geometric(al) **2.** geometry

ge·o·mag·net·ic (jē′ō mag net′ik) *adj.* of or pertaining to the magnetic properties of the earth —**ge′o·mag′ne·tism** n.

ge·o·man·cy (jē′ə man′sē) n. [ME. *geomancie* < OFr. < ML. *geomantia* < LGr. *geōmanteia*: see GEO- & -MANCY] divination by random figures formed when a handful of earth is thrown on the ground, or as by lines drawn at random —**ge′o·man′cer** n. —**ge′o·man′tic** *adj.*

ge·o·met·ric (jē′ə met′rik) *adj.* [L. *geometricus* < Gr. *geōmetrikos*] **1.** of or according to geometry **2.** characterized by straight lines, triangles, circles, or similar regular forms [a *geometric* pattern] Also **ge′o·met′ri·cal** —**ge′o·met′ri·cal·ly** *adv.*

ge·om·e·tri·cian (jē äm′ə trish′ən, jē′ə mə-) n. a specialist in geometry: also **ge·om·e·ter** (jē äm′ə tər)

geometric mean *Math.* the *n*th root of the product of *n* factors [the *geometric mean* of 2 and 8 (or the mean proportional between 2 and 8) is √2 x 8, or 4]

geometric progression a sequence of terms in which the ratio of each term to the preceding one is the same throughout the sequence (Ex.: 1, 2, 4, 8, 16, 32)

ge·om·e·trid (jē äm′ə trid) n. [< ModL. *Geometridae*, name of the family < L. *geometres*: see GEOMETRY] any of a family (Geometridae) of moths whose larvae move by looping the body

ge·om·e·trize (-trīz′) vi. **-trized′, -triz′ing** [Rare] to use geometric principles —vt. [Rare] to work out geometrically

ge·om·e·try (-trē) n., pl. **-tries** [ME. *geometrie* < OFr. < L. *geometria* < Gr. *geōmetria* < *geōmetrein*, to measure the earth < *gē*, earth + *metria*, measurement < *metrein*, to measure: see METER¹] **1.** the branch of mathematics that deals with points, lines, surfaces, and solids, and examines their properties, measurement, and mutual relations in space: see also PLANE GEOMETRY, SOLID GEOMETRY **2.** a book about geometry **3.** a specific system of geometry

ge·o·mor·phic (jē′ə môr′fik) *adj.* [GEO- + -MORPHIC] of or pertaining to the shape of the earth or its topographic features

ge·o·mor·phol·o·gy (-môr fäl′ə jē) n. [GEO- + MORPHOLOGY] the science dealing with the nature and origin of the earth's topographic features —**ge′o·mor′pho·log′ic** (-môr′fə läj′ik), **ge′o·mor′pho·log′i·cal** *adj.*

ge·oph·a·gy (jē äf′ə jē) n. [GEO- + -PHAGY] the eating of earth, either as a psychotic symptom or to make up for lack of food, as in famine areas

☆**ge·o·phone** (jē′ə fōn′) n. [GEO- + -PHONE] a sensitive electronic receiver designed to pick up vibrations transmitted through rock or other solid material

ge·o·phys·ics (jē′ō fiz′iks) n.pl. [with sing. v.] the science that deals with the physics of the earth, including weather,

winds, tides, earthquakes, volcanoes, magnetism, etc. and their effect on the earth —**ge′o·phys′i·cal** *adj.* —**ge′o·phys′i·cist** n.

ge·o·phyte (jē′ə fīt′) n. [GEO- + -PHYTE] a plant that grows in earth; esp., a perennial whose buds live underground throughout the winter

ge·o·pol·i·tics (jē′ō päl′ə tiks) n.pl. [with sing. v.] [< G. *geopolitik*: see GEO- & POLITICS] **1.** the interrelationship of politics and geography, or the study of this **2.** any program or policy based on this; specif., the Nazi doctrine of aggressive geographical and political expansion leading ultimately to German domination of the world —**ge′o·po·lit′i·cal** (-pə lit′i k'l) *adj.* —**ge′o·po·lit′i·cal·ly** *adv.* —**ge′o·pol′i·ti′cian** n.

ge·o·pon·ic (jē′ə pän′ik) *adj.* [Gr. *geōponikos* < *geōponein*, to till the ground < *geō-* (see GEO-) + *ponein*, to toil < *ponos*, work, toil] [Rare] having to do with agriculture or farming

George (jôrj) [< Fr. & L.; Fr. *Georges* < LL. *Georgius* < Gr. *Geōrgios* < *geōrgos*, husbandman, lit., earthworker < *gaia*, *gē*, earth + base of *ergon*, WORK] **1.** a masculine name: dim. *Georgie*; equiv. Fr. *Georges*, Ger. & Scand. *Georg*, It. *Giorgio*, Sp. *Jorge*; fem. *Georgia*, *Georgiana*, *Georgina* **2.** name of five kings of Great Britain & Ireland: *a)* George I 1660–1727; king (1714–27), born in Germany: great-grandson of JAMES I *b)* George II 1683–1760; king (1727–60), born in Germany: son of prec. *c)* George III 1738–1820; king (1760–1820): grandson of prec. *d)* George IV 1762–1830; king (1820–30); regent (1811–20): son of prec. *e)* George V 1865–1936; king (1910–36): son of EDWARD VII **3.** George VI 1895–1952; king of Great Britain & Northern Ireland (1936–52): son of prec. **4.** Saint, d. 303? A.D.; Christian martyr, possibly from Cappadocia; patron saint of England: his day is April 23 **5.** David Lloyd, *see* LLOYD GEORGE **6.** Henry, 1839–97; U.S. political economist: advocate of the single tax —n. a jeweled figure of St. George slaying a dragon, an insignia of the Order of the Garter —**by George!** an exclamation of mild surprise, determination, etc.

George, Lake lake in NE N.Y.; 33 mi. long

George·town (-toun′) **1.** seaport & capital of Guyana, on the Atlantic: pop. 168,000 **2.** section of Washington, D.C. **3.** former name of PENANG: also **George Town**

geor·gette (jôr jet′) n. [orig. a trademark, after *Georgette de la Plante*, Parisian modiste] a thin, durable, slightly crinkled fabric, originally silk, used for women's dresses, blouses, etc.: also **georgette crepe**

Geor·gia (jôr′jə) **1.** a feminine name: see GEORGE **2.** [after GEORGE II] Southern State of the SE U.S.: one of the 13 original States: 58,876 sq. mi.; pop. 4,590,000; cap. Atlanta: abbrev. **Ga., GA 3.** same as GEORGIAN SOVIET SOCIALIST REPUBLIC **4.** Strait of, arm of the Pacific, between Vancouver Island & British Columbia, Canada: c. 150 mi. long: also **Georgia Strait**

Geor·gian (jôr′jən) *adj.* **1.** *a)* of the reigns of George I, II, III, and IV of England (1714–1830) *b)* designating or of the artistic style of this period **2.** of or characteristic of the period of the reign of George V of England **3.** of the Georgian S.S.R., its people, language, or culture **4.** of the State of Georgia —n. **1.** *a)* a native or inhabitant of the Georgian S.S.R. *b)* the Georgian language: see CAUCASIAN ☆**2.** a native or inhabitant of the State of Georgia

Geor·gi·an·a (jôr′jē an′ə, -jan′ə) a feminine name: see GEORGE

Georgian Bay NE arm of Lake Huron, in Ontario, Canada

Georgian Soviet Socialist Republic republic of the U.S.S.R., in Transcaucasia, on the Black Sea: 26,900 sq. mi.; pop. c. 4,500,000; cap. Tbilisi

geor·gic (jôr′jik) *adj.* [L. *georgicus* < Gr. *geōrgikos*, agricultural < *geōrgos*, husbandman, farmer: see GEORGE] having to do with agriculture or husbandry —n. [L. (Virgil) *georgicum* (*carmen*), georgic (song)] a poem dealing with farming or rural life

ge·o·stat·ic (jē′ō stat′ik, jē′ə-) *adj.* [GEO- + STATIC] **1.** having to do with pressure of earth or a similar substance **2.** capable of supporting such pressure, as a kind of arch

ge·o·stat·ics (-iks) n.pl. [with sing. v.] [< prec.] the branch of physics dealing with the mechanics of the equilibrium of forces in rigid bodies; statics of rigid bodies

ge·o·stroph·ic (-sträf′ik) *adj.* [< GEO- + Gr. *strophē* (see STROPHE) + -IC] designating or of a force producing deflection as a result of the earth's rotation

ge·o·syn·cline (-sin′klīn) n. [GEO- + SYNCLINE] a very large, troughlike depression in the earth's surface containing masses of sedimentary and volcanic rocks

ge·o·tax·is (-tak′sis) n. [ModL.: see GEO- & -TAXIS] any innate movement of a freely moving organism, stimulated by the force of gravity —**ge′o·tac′tic** (-tak′tik) *adj.* —**ge′o·tac′ti·cal·ly** *adv.*

ge·o·tec·ton·ic (-tek tän′ik) *adj.* [GEO- + TECTONIC] having to do with the structure, distribution, shape, etc. of rock bodies and with the structural disturbances and alterations of the earth's crust that produced them

ge·o·ther·mic (-thur′mik) *adj.* [GEO- + THERMIC] having to do with the heat of the earth's interior: also **ge′o·ther′mal**

ge·ot·ro·pism (jē ät′rə piz'm) n. [GEO- + -TROPISM] any movement or growth of a living organism in response to the force of gravity: movement toward the center of the earth,

Geologic Time Chart

MAIN DIVISIONS OF GEOLOGIC TIME			PRINCIPAL PHYSICAL AND BIOLOGICAL FEATURES
ERAS	PERIODS or SYSTEMS	Epochs or Series	
CENOZOIC	QUATERNARY	Recent 12,000*	Glaciers restricted to Antarctica and Greenland; extinction of giant mammals; development and spread of modern human culture.
		Pleistocene 600,000	Great glaciers covered much of N North America & NW Europe; volcanoes along W coast of U.S.; many giant mammals; appearance of modern man late in Pleistocene.
	TERTIARY	Pliocene 10,000,000	W North America uplifted; much modernization of mammals; first possible apelike men appeared in Africa.
		Miocene 25,000,000	Renewed uplift of Rockies & other mountains;** great lava flows in W U.S.; mammals began to acquire modern characters; dogs, modern type horses, manlike apes appeared.
		Oligocene 35,000,000	Many older types of mammals became extinct; mastodons, first monkeys, and apes appeared.
		Eocene 55,000,000	Mountains raised in Rockies, Andes, Alps, & Himalayas; continued expansion of early mammals; primitive horses appeared.
		Paleocene 65,000,000	Great development of primitive mammals.
MESOZOIC	CRETACEOUS 135,000,000		Rocky Mountains began to rise; most plants, invertebrate animals, fishes, and birds of modern types; dinosaurs reached maximum development & then became extinct; mammals small & very primitive.
	JURASSIC 180,000,000		Sierra Nevada Mountains uplifted; conifers & cycads dominant among plants; primitive birds appeared.
	TRIASSIC 230,000,000		Lava flows in E North America; ferns & cycads dominant among plants; modern corals appeared & some insects of modern types; great expansion of reptiles including earliest dinosaurs.
PALEOZOIC	PERMIAN 280,000,000		Final folding of Appalachians & central European ranges; great glaciers in S Hemisphere & reefs in warm northern seas; trees of coal forests declined; ferns abundant; conifers present; first cycads & ammonites appeared; trilobites became extinct; reptiles surpassed amphibians.
	CARBONIFEROUS PENNSYLVANIAN 310,000,000		Mountains grew along E coast of North America & in central Europe; great coal swamp forests flourished in N Hemisphere; seed-bearing ferns abundant; cockroaches & first reptiles appeared.
	CARBONIFEROUS MISSISSIPPIAN 345,000,000		Land plants became diversified, including many ancient kinds of trees; crinoids achieved greatest development; sharks of relatively modern types appeared; land animals little known.
	DEVONIAN 405,000,000		Mountains raised in New England; land plants evolved rapidly, large trees appeared; brachiopods reached maximum development; many kinds of primitive fishes; first sharks, insects, & amphibians appeared.
	SILURIAN 425,000,000		Great mountains formed in NW Europe; first small land plants appeared; corals built reefs in far northern seas; shelled cephalopods abundant; trilobites began decline; first jawed fish appeared.
	ORDOVICIAN 500,000,000		Mountains elevated in New England; volcanoes along Atlantic Coast; much limestone deposited in shallow seas; great expansion among marine invertebrate animals, all major groups present; first primitive jawless fish appeared.
	CAMBRIAN 600,000,000		Shallow seas covered parts of continents; first abundant record of marine life, esp. trilobites & brachiopods; other fossils rare.
PRECAMBRIAN	LATE PRECAMBRIAN‡ (Algonkian) 2,000,000,000		Metamorphosed sedimentary rocks, lava flows, granite; history complex & obscure; first evidence of life, calcareous algae & invertebrates.
	EARLY PRECAMBRIAN‡ (Archean) 4,500,000,000		Crust formed on molten earth; crystalline rocks much disturbed; history unknown.

*Figures indicate approximate number of years since the beginning of each division.
**Mountain uplifts generally began near the end of a division.
‡Regarded as separate eras.

as of the roots of plants growing downward, is *positive geotropism:* movement away from the center of the earth, as of shoots extending upward, is *negative geotropism* — **ge·o·trop·ic** (jē'ə träp'ik) *adj.*

Ger. 1. German **2.** Germany

ger. 1. gerund **2.** gerundive

Ge·ra (gā'rä) city in S East Germany: pop. 108,000

ge·rah (gē'rə) *n.* [Heb. *gērāh*, lit., a bean] an ancient Hebrew coin and weight, equal to 1/20 of a shekel

Ge·raint (jə ränt') [< Celt.] *Arthurian Legend* a knight of the Round Table, husband of Enid

Ger·ald (jer'əld) [< OFr. or OHG.; OFr. *Giraut, Giralt* < OHG. *Gerald, Gerwald* < *ger*, spear (akin to OE. *gar*) + base of *waldan*, to rule] a masculine name: feminine **Ger'·al·dine'** (-əl dēn', -din)

ge·ra·ni·ol (jə rā'nē ôl', -ōl') *n.* [< ModL. *Geranium* (see GERANIUM) + -OL¹: so named because derived from geranium leaves] a terpene alcohol, $C_{10}H_{18}O$, found in many essential oils and having an odor resembling roses: used in perfumery

ge·ra·ni·um (jə rā'nē əm, -rän'yəm) *adj.* [L. < Gr. *geranion*, a plant, crane's-bill, dim. < *geranos*, a crane < IE. base **ger-*, echoic of hoarse cry, whence CRANE] designating a family (Geraniaceae) of plants including the cranesbill and pelargonium —*n.* **1.** any of a large genus (*Geranium*) of plants of the geranium family, having showy pink or purple flowers and leaves with many lobes **2.** *same as* PELARGONIUM **3.** an intense red

Ger·ard (jə rärd') [OFr. *Girart* < OHG. *Gerhart* < *ger*, spear + *hart*, HARD] a masculine name

☆**ger·rar·di·a** (jə rär'dē ə) *n.* [ModL., after John *Gerard* (1545-1612), Eng. botanist] any of a genus (*Gerardia*) of American plants of the figwort family, with showy pink or yellow flowers: it is sometimes parasitic on roots

ger·ber·a (gur'bər ə) *n.* [ModL.: so named after Traugott *Gerber*, 18th-c. Ger. physician and naturalist] an African plant (*Gerbera jamesonii*) of the composite family, with basal rosettes of leaves and single flower heads with numerous long, narrow ray flowers in white, pink, orange, salmon, or violet

ger·bil, ger·bille (jur'b'l) *n.* [Fr. *gerbille* < ModL. *gerbillus* < *gerbo*, JERBOA] any of a subfamily (Gerbillinae) of burrowing rodents related to the mouse, with long hind legs and tail, native to Africa and Asia

ger·ent (jir'ənt) *n.* [< L. *gerens* (gen. *gerentis*), prp. of *gerere*, to bear, conduct] [Rare] a person who manages, directs, governs, or rules

ger·e·nuk (ger'ə nook', gā rən'ək) *n.* [< Somali *garanug*] a small antelope (*Litocranius walleri*) of E Africa, with a very long neck, long legs, and short horns

ger·fal·con (jur'fal'k'n, -fôl'-, -fô'-) *n. same as* GYRFALCON

☆**ger·i·a·tri·cian** (jer'ē ə trish'ən) *n.* a doctor who specializes in geriatrics: also **ger·i·at·rist** (jer'ē at'rist)

☆**ger·i·at·rics** (jer'ē at'riks) *n.pl.* [*with sing. v.*] [< Gr. *gēras*, old age (< IE. base **ger-*, to grow ripe, age, whence Sans. *járant-*, feeble, old, E. CHURL, CORN¹) + -IATRICS] the branch of medicine that deals with the diseases and hygiene of old age —**ger'i·at'ric** *adj.*

germ (jurm) *n.* [ME. *germe*, a bud, sprout < OFr. < L. *germen*, sprig, sprout, bud, germ, embryo < IE. **gen-men*, whence Sans. *janiman-*, birth, origin < base **gen-*: see GENUS] **1.** the rudimentary form from which a new organism is developed; seed, bud, etc. **2.** any microscopic organism, esp. one of the bacteria, that can cause disease **3.** that from which something can develop or grow; origin; basis [the *germ* of an idea]

Ger·man (jur'mən) *adj.* [ME. (only in pl.) < L. *Germanus*, prob. < Celt.] of or like Germany, its people, language, or culture —*n.* **1.** a native or inhabitant of Germany **2.** the Germanic language now spoken chiefly in Germany, Austria, and Switzerland, technically called *New High German:* see also OLD HIGH GERMAN, MIDDLE HIGH GERMAN, HIGH GERMAN, LOW GERMAN **3.** [g-] *a)* a complicated dance for many couples in which partners are changed often; cotillion *b)* a party at which the german is danced

ger·man (jur'mən) *adj.* [ME. *germain, german* < OFr. *germain* < L. *germanus*, akin to *germen*, a sprout, bud: see GERM] closely related; now chiefly in compounds, meaning: *a)* having the same parents [a brother-*german*] *b)* having the same grandparents on either the father's side or the mother's [a cousin-*german* is a first cousin]

German Democratic Republic *see* GERMANY

ger·man·der (jər man'dər) *n.* [ME. *germandre* < OFr. *germandree* < ML. *germandra* < Gr. *chamaidrys* < *chamai*, on the ground (< IE. base **ghm-*, *ghthem-*, whence L. *humus* & OE. *guma*, man) + *drys*, TREE] any of a genus (*Teucrium*) of plants of the mint family, with spikes of flowers that lack an upper lip

ger·mane (jər mān') *adj.* [var. of GERMAN] **1.** truly relevant; pertinent; to the point **2.** akin; german —*SYN.* see RELEVANT

German East Africa former colony of the German Empire, in E Africa: it was the territory now consisting chiefly of Tanganyika, Rwanda, & Burundi

Ger·man·ic (jər man'ik) *adj.* [L. *Germanicus*, of the Germans: orig. applied to a particular tribe, prob. Celtic] **1.** of Germany or the Germans: German **2.** designating or of the original language of the German peoples, or its

speakers; Teutonic **3.** designating or of the languages descended from this language —*n.* **1.** the original language of the Germanic peoples: now called **Proto-Germanic 2.** a principal branch of the Indo-European family of languages, comprising this language and the languages descended from it, including Norwegian, Faroese, Icelandic, Swedish, Danish (all *North Germanic*), New High German, Yiddish, Low German, Dutch, Afrikaans, Flemish, Frisian, and Modern English (all *West Germanic*), the extinct Gothic (*East Germanic*), etc.

Ger·man·i·cus Caesar (jər man'i kəs) 15 B.C.–19 A.D.; Roman general; father of CALIGULA

Ger·man·ism (jur'mən iz'm) *n.* **1.** a German idiom or expression, used in another language **2.** a German custom, way of thought, etc. **3.** fondness for or imitation of German ways

Ger·man·ist (-ist) *n.* a student of or specialist in German life or Germanic linguistics and literature

ger·ma·ni·um (jər mā'nē əm) *n.* [ModL. < L. *Germania*, Germany] a rare, grayish-white, metallic chemical element of the carbon family that can be a semiconductor and is used in making transistors: symbol, Ge; at. wt., 72.59; at. no., 32; sp. gr., 5.35; melt. pt., 947°C; boil. pt., 2700°C

Ger·man·ize (jur'mə niz') *vt.* **-ized', -iz'ing 1.** to make German or like the Germans in thought, language, etc. **2.** to translate into German —*vi.* to adopt German methods, attitudes, etc. —**Ger'man·i·za'tion** *n.*

German measles *same as* RUBELLA

Ger·man·o- (jər man'ə) *a combining form meaning* German, of Germany, or of the Germans [*Germanophobe*]

Ger·man·o·phile (jər man'ə fil') *n.* [GERMANO- + -PHILE] a person who admires or favors Germany, its people, customs, influence, etc.

Ger·man·o·phobe (-fōb') *n.* [GERMANO- + -PHOBE] a person who hates or fears Germany, its people, customs, influence, etc.

German shepherd dog a breed of dog somewhat like a wolf in form and size and noted for its intelligence: it was developed in Germany, mainly for herding sheep, and is now often used in police work and as a guide for the blind: also **(German) police dog**

German silver *same as* NICKEL SILVER

German Southwest Africa *former name of* SOUTH WEST AFRICA

Ger·man·town (jur'mən toun') NW section of Philadelphia, Pa.: formerly a separate town; scene of an American defeat in a Revolutionary War battle (1777)

Ger·ma·ny (jur'mə nē) former country in NC Europe, on the North & Baltic seas: divided (1945) into four zones of occupation, administered respectively by France, Great Britain, the U.S., & the U.S.S.R., and partitioned (1949) into *a)* the **Federal Republic of Germany** country made up of the three W zones (British, French, & U.S.): 95,735 sq. mi.; pop. 59,674,000; cap. Bonn: also called **West Germany** *b)* **German Democratic Republic** country comprising the eastern (U.S.S.R.) zone: c. 41,800 sq. mi.; pop. 17,067,000 (excluding West Berlin); cap. East Berlin: also called **East Germany**

germ cell a cell from which a new organism can develop; egg or sperm cell: opposed to SOMATIC CELL

ger·men (jur'mən) *n., pl.* **-mens, -mi·na** (-mə nə) [L.] [Archaic] a rudimentary form; embryo

ger·mi·cide (jur'mə sid') *n.* [< GERM + -CIDE] any antiseptic, etc. used to destroy germs —**ger'mi·ci'dal** *adj.*

ger·mi·nal (jur'mə n'l) *adj.* [Fr. < ML. *germinalis* < L. *germen* (gen. *germinis*): see GERM] **1.** of, like, or characteristic of germs or germ cells **2.** in an embryonic stage; in the first stage of growth or development —**ger'mi·nal·ly** *adv.*

germinal disc 1. a disclike spot in a fertilized ovum in which the first traces of the embryo are visible **2.** the disclike spot on the yolk of a heavily yolked egg where segmentation begins after fertilization

germinal vesicle the greatly enlarged nucleus of an egg in the prophase of the first meiotic division

ger·mi·nant (jur'mə nənt) *adj.* that germinates; sprouting

ger·mi·nate (-nāt') *vi., vt.* **-nat'ed, -nat'ing** [< L. *germinatus*, pp. of *germinare*, to sprout < *germen*, a sprout, bud: see GERM] **1.** to sprout or cause to sprout, as from a spore, seed, or bud **2.** to start developing or growing —**ger'mi·na'tion** *n.* —**ger'mi·na'tive** *adj.*

Ger·mis·ton (jur'mis tən) city in S Transvaal, South Africa: pop. 214,000

germ layer *Embryology* any of the three primary layers of cells (ectoderm, endoderm, and mesoderm) from which the various organs and parts of the organism develop by further differentiation

germ plasm the reproductive cells of an organism, particularly that portion of the reproductive cells involved in heredity: cf. SOMATOPLASM

germ theory the theory that diseases are transmitted by specific germs, or microorganisms, as has been proved for many infectious diseases

germ warfare the deliberate contamination of enemy territory with disease germs in warfare

Ge·ron·i·mo (jə rän'ə mō') [Sp., Jerome, used as a nickname by the Mexicans] 1829?-1909; Apache Indian chief

ger·on·toc·ra·cy (jer'ən tä'krə sē) *n.* [altered (after -CRACY) < Fr. *gérontocratie* < Gr. *geronto-* < *gerōn*, old man (see GERIATRICS) + -*kratia*, -CRACY] **1.** government by old

men **2.** *pl.* **-cies** a governing group composed of old men —**ge·ron·to·crat·ic** (jə rän′tə krat′ik) *adj.*

ger·on·tol·o·gy (jer′ən täl′ə jē) *n.* [Gr. *geronto-* < *gerōn*, old man + -LOGY] the scientific study of the process of aging and of the problems of aged people: see also GERIATRICS —**ge·ron·to·log·i·cal** (jə rän′tə läj′i k'l) *adj.* — **ger′on·tol′o·gist** *n.*

ge·ron·to·mor·pho·sis (jə rän′tō môr′fə sis) *n.* [*geronto-* (see prec.) + MORPHOSIS] evolutionary development that produces extreme specialization and, ultimately, extinction of a species or race, as with the dinosaurs

-ger·ous (jər əs) [L. *-ger* < *gerere*, to bear + -OUS] *a suffix meaning* producing or bearing [*spinigerous*]

Ger·ry (ger′ē), **El·bridge** (el′brij) 1744–1814; U.S. statesman; vice president of the U.S. (1813–14)

☆**ger·ry·man·der** (jer′i man′dər, ger′-) *vt.* [satirical coinage < prec., governor of Mass. when the method was employed (1812) + SALAMANDER (the shape of the redistricted Essex County)] **1.** to divide (a voting area) so as to give one political party a majority in as many districts as possible **2.** to manipulate unfairly so as to gain advantage —*vi.* to engage in gerrymandering —*n.* a redistricting of voting districts to the advantage of one party

Gersh·win (gursh′win), **George** 1898–1937; U.S. composer

Ger·trude (gur′trood) [< Fr. & G.: Fr. *Gertrude* < G. *Gertrud* < OHG. *Geretrudis* < *ger*, spear + *trut*, dear] a feminine name: dim. *Gert, Gertie, Trudy*

ger·und (jer′ənd) *n.* [LL. *gerundium* < L. *gerundus*, gerundive of *gerere*, to do or carry out] **1.** *Latin Gram.* a verbal noun used in all cases but the nominative (Ex.: *probandi*, in *onus probandi*, the burden of proving) **2.** *English Gram.* a verbal noun ending in -*ing*, that has all the uses of the noun but retains certain characteristics of the verb, such as the ability to take an object or an adverbial modifier (Ex.: *playing* in "Playing golf is his only exercise") —**ge·run·di·al** (jə run′dē əl) *adj.*

ge·run·dive (jə run′div) *adj.* [ME. *gerundif* < LL. *gerundivus* < *gerundium*: see GERUND] **1.** a Latin verbal adjective with a typical gerund stem form, used as a future passive participle expressing duty, necessity, fitness, etc. (Ex.: *delenda* in *delenda est Carthago*, Carthage must be destroyed) **2.** a similar form in any language —**ge·run·di·val** (jer′ən di′val) *adj.*

Ge·ry·on (jir′ē ən, ger′-) [L. < Gr. *Gēryōn* or *Gēryonēs*] *Gr. Myth.* a winged, three-bodied monster killed by Hercules

Ge·sell (gə zel′), **Arnold L**(ucius) 1880–1961; U.S. psychologist: authority on child behavior

ges·ne·ri·a (ges nir′ē ə) *adj.* [after Konrad von *Gesner* (1516–65), Swiss naturalist] designating a tropical family (Gesneriaceae) of somewhat fleshy plants with showy tubular flowers, including the African violets, the gloxinias, and the episcias

ges·so (jes′ō) *n.* [It., gypsum, chalk < L. *gypsum*, GYPSUM] plaster of Paris prepared for use in sculpture or bas-reliefs, or as a surface for painting

gest¹, geste (jest) *n.* [ME. *geste* < OFr. < L. *gesta*, deeds, pl. of pp. of *gerere*, to do, act] **1.** [Archaic] an adventure; deed; exploit **2.** a romantic story of daring adventures, esp. a medieval tale in verse

gest² (jest) *n.* [Fr. *geste* < L. *gestus*, posture, gesture < pp. of *gerere*, to bear, behave] [Archaic] **1.** bearing; deportment; carriage **2.** a gesture

gest. [G. *gestorben*] died

ge·stalt (gə shtält′, -stält′, -stôlt′) *n., pl.* **-stalt′en** (-'n), **-stalts′** [G., lit., shape, form < MHG. pp. of *stellen*, to arrange, fix] [*also* G-] in Gestalt psychology, any of the integrated structures or patterns that make up all experience and have specific properties which can neither be derived from the elements of the whole nor considered simply as the sum of these elements

Gestalt psychology a school of psychology, developed in Germany, which affirms that all experience consists of gestalten, and that the response of an organism to a situation is a complete and unanalyzable whole rather than a sum of the responses to specific elements in the situation

Ge·sta·po (gə stä′pō, -stap′ō; G. -shtä′pō) *n.* [< G. *Ge*(*heime*) *Sta*(*ats*)*po*(*lizei*), secret state police] the secret police force of the German Nazi state, notorious for its terrorism, atrocities, etc.

Ges·ta Ro·ma·no·rum (jes′tə rō′mə nôr′əm) [ML., doings of the Romans] a 14th-cent. European collection of tales in Latin, used as a source of plots by Chaucer, Shakespeare, etc.

ges·tate (jes′tāt) *vt.* **-tat·ed, -tat·ing** [back-formation < ff.] to carry in the uterus during pregnancy

ges·ta·tion (jes tā′shən) *n.* [L. *gestatio* < pp. of *gestare*, freq. of *gerere*, to bear, carry] **1.** the act or period of carrying young in the uterus from conception to birth; pregnancy **2.** a development, as of a plan in the mind

ges·tic (jes′tik) *adj.* [GEST² + -IC] having to do with bodily movement, as dancing: also **ges′ti·cal**

ges·tic·u·late (jes tik′yə lāt′) *vi.* **-lat·ed, -lat·ing** [< L. *gesticulatus*, pp. of *gesticulari*, to make mimic gestures < *gesticulus*, dim. of *gestus*, a gesture, pp. of *gerere*, to bear,

carry, do] to make or use gestures, esp. with the hands or arms, as in adding nuances or force to one's speech, or as a substitute for speech —*vt.* to express by gesticulating —**ges·tic′u·la′tive** *adj.* —**ges·tic′u·la′tor** *n.*

ges·tic·u·la·tion (jes tik′yə lā′shən) *n.* [L. *gesticulatio*] **1.** a gesticulating **2.** a gesture, esp. an energetic one —**ges·tic′u·la·to′ry** (-lə tôr′ē) *adj.*

ges·ture (jes′chər) *n.* [ME. < ML. *gestura*, mode of action < L. *gestus*, pp. of *gerere*, to bear, carry] **1.** a movement, or movements collectively, of the body, or of part of the body, to express or emphasize ideas, emotions, etc. **2.** anything said or done to convey a state of mind, intention, etc.; often, something said or done merely for effect or as a formality [a *gesture* of sympathy] —*vi.* **-tured, -tur·ing** to make or use a gesture or gestures —*vt.* to express with a gesture or gestures —**ges′tur·al** *adj.* —**ges′tur·er** *n.*

‡**Ge·sund·heit** (gə zoont′hit′) *n.* [G.] (your) health: spoken as a toast or as an expression of good wishes to someone who has just sneezed

get (get) *vt.* **got** *or archaic & dial.* **gat, got** *or* **got′ten, get′ting** [ME. *geten* < ON. *geta*, to get, beget, akin to OE. *-gietan* (see BEGET, FORGET), G. *-gessen* in *vergessen*, forget < IE. base **ghend-*, to seize, get hold of, whence L. *prehendere*, to grasp, understand] **1.** to come into the state of having; become the owner or receiver of; receive, win, gain, obtain, acquire, etc. **2.** to reach; arrive at [to *get* home early] **3.** to set up communication with, as by radio or telephone [to *get* Paris] **4.** *a)* to go and bring *b)* to bring [go *get* your books] **5.** *a)* to catch; capture; gain hold of *b)* to become afflicted with (a disease) **6.** to learn; commit to memory **7.** to discover to be as the result of experiment or calculation [add 2 and 2 to *get* 4] **8.** to influence or persuade (a person) to do something [*get* him to leave] **9.** to cause to act in a certain way [*get* the door to shut properly] **10.** *a)* to cause to be [to *get* one's hands dirty] *b)* to cause to arrive at [*get* the copy to the printer] **11.** to take (oneself) away: often used absolutely **12.** to be sentenced to [to *get* ten years for robbery] **13.** to prepare [to *get* lunch] **14.** to give birth to; beget: usually said of animals **15.** [Colloq.] to be obliged to; feel a necessity to (with *have* or *has*) [he's *got* to pass the test] **16.** [Colloq.] to own; possess (with *have* or *has*) [he's *got* red hair] **17.** [Colloq.] to be or become the master of; esp., *a)* to overpower; have complete control of [his illness finally *got* him] *b)* to puzzle; baffle [this problem *gets* me] *c)* to take into custody, wound, or kill ☆*d)* *Baseball*, etc. to put (an opponent) out, as by catching a batted ball **18.** [Colloq.] to strike; hit [the blow *got* him in the eye] ☆**19.** [Colloq.] to catch the meaning or import of; understand ☆**20.** [Slang] to cause an emotional response in; irritate, please, thrill, etc. [her singing *gets* me] ☆**21.** [Slang] to notice or observe [*get* the look on his face] —*vi.* **1.** to come, go, or arrive [to *get* to work on time] **2.** to be or become; come to be (doing something); come to be (in a situation, condition, etc.) [to *get* caught in the rain, *get* in touch with me] **3.** to manage or contrive [to *get* to do something] **4.** [Colloq.] to leave at once *Get* is used as a linking verb in idiomatic phrases, and as an informal auxiliary for emphasis in passive construction [to *get* praised] —*n.* **1.** the young of an animal; offspring; breed **2.** a begetting **3.** *Tennis*, etc. a retrieving of a shot seemingly out of reach —**get about 1.** to move from place to place **2.** to go to many social events, places, etc. **3.** to circulate widely, as news —**get across** [Colloq.] **1.** to clarify or explain convincingly **2.** to be clear; be understood **3.** to succeed, as in making oneself understood or conveying one's personality to an audience —**get after** [Colloq.] **1.** to pursue or attack **2.** to urge or goad persistently —**get along** *see phrase under* ALONG¹ —**get around 1.** to get about (in all senses) ☆**2.** to circumvent or overcome **3.** to influence, outwit, or gain favor with by cajoling, flattering, etc. —**get around to 1.** to find time or occasion for **2.** to get started on, esp. after a delay —**get at 1.** to approach or reach **2.** to apply oneself to (work, etc.) **3.** to find out **4.** to imply or suggest **5.** [Colloq.] to influence by bribery or intimidation —**get away 1.** to go away; leave **2.** to escape **3.** to start, as in a race —☆**get away with** [Slang] to succeed in doing or taking without being discovered or punished —**get back 1.** to return **2.** to recover ☆**3.** [Slang] to retaliate; get revenge (usually with *at*) —**get behind 1.** to move to the rear of **2.** to endorse or support **3.** to fall into arrears, as in making a payment —**get by 1.** to be fairly adequate or acceptable ☆**2.** [Colloq.] to succeed without being discovered or punished **3.** [Colloq.] to survive; manage —**get down 1.** to descend **2.** to dismount —**get down to** to begin to consider or act on —**get in 1.** to enter; join in **2.** to arrive **3.** to put in **4.** to become familiar or closely associated (*with*) —**get it** [Colloq.] ☆**1.** to understand **2.** to be punished —**get nowhere** to make no progress; accomplish nothing —**get off 1.** to come off, down, or out of **2.** to leave; go away **3.** to take off **4.** to escape **5.** *a)* to help escape sentence or punishment *b)* to lessen the sentence or punishment of **6.** to start, as in a race **7.** to utter (a joke, retort, etc.) **8.** to have a holiday; have time off —**get on 1.** to go on or into

2. to put on 3. to proceed; make progress 4. to grow older 5. to succeed, as in making a living 6. to agree; be compatible —**get out** 1. to go out 2. to go away 3. to take out ☆4. to become no longer a secret 5. to publish —**get out of** 1. to go out from 2. *a)* to escape from or avoid *b)* to help escape from or avoid 3. to go beyond (sight, etc.) 4. to find out from —**get over** 1. to recover from 2. to forget or overlook 3. [Colloq.] to get across (in all senses) —**get somewhere** to accomplish something; succeed —**get there** ☆[Colloq.] to succeed —**get through** 1. to finish 2. to manage to survive 3. to secure favorable action upon (a bill, etc.) 4. to establish communication, or make oneself clear (*to*) —**get to** [Colloq.]. 1. to succeed in reaching or communicating with ☆2. to influence, as by bribery or intimidation —**get together** 1. to bring together; accumulate 2. to come together; gather ☆3. [Colloq.] to reach an agreement —**get up** 1. to rise (from a chair, from sleep, etc.) 2. to contrive; organize 3. to dress elaborately 4. to advance; make progress 5. to climb or mount 6. to disgorge (something) ☆7. go forward: used as a command to a horse —**get'ta·ble, get'a·ble** *adj.*

SYN.—**get** is the word of broadest application meaning to come into possession of, with or without effort or volition /to *get* a job, an idea, a headache, etc./; **obtain** implies that there is effort or desire in the getting /he has *obtained* aid/; **procure** suggests active effort or contrivance in getting or bringing to pass /to *procure* a settlement of the dispute/; **secure**, in strict discrimination, implies difficulty in obtaining something and in retaining it /to *secure* a lasting peace/; **acquire** implies a lengthy process in the getting and connotes collection or accretion /he *acquired* a fine education/; **gain** always implies effort in the getting of something advantageous or profitable /to *gain* fame/ —**ANT. lose, forgo**

ge·ta (get'ə, -ä) *n., pl.* **ge'ta, ge'tas** [Jap.] in Japan, a high wooden clog fastened to the foot by a thong between the first and second toes

get·at·a·ble (get at'ə b'l) *adj.* [Colloq.] easy to reach or ascertain; accessible —**get·at'a·bil'i·ty** *n.*

get·a·way (get'ə wā') *n.* 1. the act of starting, as in a race 2. the act of escaping, as from the police

Geth·sem·a·ne (geth sem'ə nē) [Gr. *Gethsēmanē* < Aram. *gath shemānī(m)*, lit., oil press: ? because such a press was located there] *Bible* a garden outside of Jerusalem, scene of the agony, betrayal, and arrest of Jesus: Matt. 26:36 —*n.* [*often* **g-**] any scene or occasion of agony

get-out (get'out') *n.* escape, esp. from an unpleasant situation —☆**all get-out** [Colloq.] the extreme degree, quality, condition, etc. *[big as all get-out]*

get·ter (get'ər) *n.* 1. one that gets 2. a material introduced into certain vacuum tubes and ignited after sealing to remove chemically any residual gases 3. [Canad.] poisoned bait for farm pests

☆**get-to·geth·er** (get'tə geth'ər) *n.* an informal social gathering or meeting

Get·tys·burg (get'iz burg') [after J. *Gettys*, its 18th-cent. founder] town in S Pa.: site of a crucial battle (July, 1863) of the Civil War and of a famous address by Abraham Lincoln at the dedication of the National Cemetery there: pop. 7,000

get-up (get'up') *n.* [Colloq.] 1. general arrangement or composition 2. costume; outfit; dress 3. driving ambition; vigor; energy: also **get'-up'-and-go'**

ge·um (jē'əm) *n.* [ModL. < L.] *same as* AVENS

gew·gaw (gyōo'gô, gōo'-) *n.* [ME. *giuegoue, gugaw*, redupl. formation (?] something showy but useless and of little value; trinket —*adj.* showy but useless

gey (gā) *adj.* [var. of GAY] [Scot.] considerable —*adv.* [Scot.] quite; very

gey·ser (gī'zər, -sər; *Brit.* gā'- for 1, gē'- for 2) *n.* [Ice. *Geysir*, name of a certain hot spring in Iceland, lit., gusher < ON. *gjosa*, to GUSH] 1. a spring from which columns of boiling water and steam gush into the air at intervals 2. [Brit.] a small, gas, hot-water heater of the coil type

gey·ser·ite (-īt') *n.* siliceous material, usually opaline silica, deposited on the edges of geysers and hot springs

Ge·zi·ra (jə zir'ə) region in EC Sudan, between the Blue Nile & the White Nile

g.gr. great gross

GHA Greenwich hour angle

Gha·na (gä'nə) country in W Africa, on the Gulf of Guinea: formed (1957) by a merger of the Gold Coast & the territory of Togoland: it is a member of the Brit. Commonwealth: 91,843 sq. mi.; pop. 8,600,000; cap. Accra —**Gha·na·ian** (gä'nē·ən, -nä-) *adj., n.*

ghar·ry, ghar·ri (gar'ē, gär'-) *n., pl.* **-ries** [Hindi *gāṛī*] in India, a horse-drawn or motorized cab for hire

ghast·ly (gast'lē, gäst'-) *adj.* **-li·er, -li·est** [ME. *gastli* < *gast*, frightened, pp. of *gasten*, to frighten < OE. *gæstan* < *gæst*, var. of *gast* (see GHOST): meaning infl. in ME. by *gostlich*, GHOSTLY; form (*gh-*) infl. by cognate Fl. *gheest*] 1. horrible; frightful 2. ghostlike; pale; haggard 3. [Colloq.] very bad or unpleasant —*adv.* in a ghastly manner —**ghast'li·ness** *n.*

SYN.—**ghastly** suggests the horror aroused by the sight or suggestion of death /a *ghastly* smile on the dead man's face/; **grim** implies hideously repellent aspects /a *grim* joke/; **grisly** suggests an appearance that causes one to shudder with horror /the *grisly* sights of Buchenwald/; **gruesome** suggests the fear and loathing aroused by something horrible and sinister /the *gruesome* details of a murder/; **macabre** implies concern with the gruesome aspects of death /a *macabre* tale/

ghat, ghaut (gôt, gät) *n.* [Hindi *ghāṭ*] 1. in India, a mountain pass 2. a chain of mountains; esp., either of the Ghats ranges 3. in India, a flight of steps leading down to a river landing for ritual bathers

Ghats (gôts, gäts) two mountain ranges forming the east & west edges of the Deccan Plateau, India: highest peak, 8,841 ft.: **Eastern Ghats** (c. 875 mi. long); **Western Ghats** (c. 1,000 mi. long)

gha·zi (gä'zē) *n.* [Ar. *ghāzi*, prp. of *ghazā*, to fight] a Moslem hero, esp. one who wars against infidels

Ghe·ber, Ghe·bre (gā'bər, gē'-) *n.* [Fr. *guèbre* < Per. *gabr*, prob. < Ar. *kāfir*, infidel: see KAFFIR, GIAOUR] *Moslem name for* ZOROASTRIAN

ghee (gē) *n.* [Hind. *ghī*] in India, the liquid butter remaining when butter from cow's milk or buffalo milk is melted, boiled, and strained

Ghent (gent) city in NW Belgium; capital of East Flanders: pop. 158,000

gher·kin (gur'kin) *n.* [< Du. or LowG. *gurken*, cucumber < Pol. *ogórek* < ModGr. *angouri* < LGr. *angourion*, watermelon < Per. *angārah*] 1. a variety of cucumber (*Cucumis anguria*) bearing small, prickly fruit 2. the fruit of this plant, used for pickles 3. the immature fruit of the common cucumber when pickled

ghet·to (get'ō) *n., pl.* **-tos, -toes** [It., lit., foundry (< *gettare*, to pour < VL. **jectare*, for L. *jactare*, to throw, cast), name of a quarter in Venice occupied by Jews, orig. location of a cannon foundry] 1. in certain European cities, a section to which Jews were formerly restricted 2. any section of a city in which many members of some minority group live, or to which they are restricted as by economic pressure or social discrimination

☆**ghet·to·ize** (-īz') *vt.* **-ized', -iz'ing** 1. to restrict to a ghetto 2. to cause to become a ghetto —**ghet'to·i·za'tion** *n.*

Ghib·el·line (gib'ə lin, -lēn') *n.* [It. *Ghibellino*, for G. *Waiblingen*, Hohenstaufen estate in Franconia] any member of a political party in medieval Italy that supported the authority of the German emperors in Italy in opposition to the papal party of the Guelphs —*adj.* of this party

Ghi·ber·ti (gē ber'tē), **Lo·ren·zo** (lō ren'tsō) (born *Lorenzo di Cione di Ser Buonaccorso*) 1378-1455; Florentine sculptor, painter, & worker in metals

ghil·lie (gil'ē) *n.* [var. of GILLIE[1]] 1. a tongueless shoe with loops instead of eyelets, and a lace that is crisscrossed over the instep and may be tied around the ankle: also **ghillie tie** 2. *same as* GILLIE[1]

Ghir·lan·da·io (gir'län dä'yō), **Do·men·i·co** (dō mā'nē kō) (born *Domenico di Tommaso Bigordi*) 1449-94; Florentine painter: also sp. **Ghir'lan·da'jo**

ghost (gōst) *n.* [altered (prob. after Fl. *gheest*) < ME. *goste* < OE. *gast*, soul, spirit, demon, akin to G. *geist* < IE. base **gheizd-*, to be excited, frightened, whence Sans. *hēḍ-*, to be angry] 1. orig., the spirit or soul: now only in **give up the ghost** (to die) and in HOLY GHOST 2. the supposed disembodied spirit of a dead person, conceived of as appearing to the living as a pale, shadowy apparition 3. a haunting memory 4. a faint, shadowy semblance; inkling; slight trace /not a *ghost* of a chance/ ☆5. [Colloq.] *same as* GHOSTWRITER 6. *Optics & TV* an unwanted secondary image or bright spot —*vi.* ☆[Colloq.] to work as a ghostwriter —*vt.* 1. to haunt ☆2. [Colloq.] to be the ghostwriter of —**ghost'-like'** *adj.*

☆**ghost dance** a N. American Indian dance of the 19th cent., in connection with a messianic belief

ghost·ly (-lē) *adj.* **-li·er, -li·est** [ME. *gostlich* < OE. *gastlic*, spiritual, spectral] 1. of, like, or characteristic of a ghost; spectral 2. [Now Rare] having to do with the soul or religion; spiritual —**ghost'li·ness** *n.*

☆**ghost town** the remains of a deserted town, permanently abandoned esp. for economic reasons

ghost word [term invented by W. W. Skeat] a word created through misreading of manuscripts, misunderstanding of grammatical elements, etc. and never really established in a language

☆**ghost·writ·er** (-rīt'ər) *n.* a person who writes speeches, articles, etc. for another who professes to be the author —**ghost'write'** *vt., vi.* **-wrote', -writ'ten, -writ'ing**

ghoul (gōol) *n.* [Ar. *ghūl*, demon of the mountains < *ghāla*, to seize] 1. *Oriental Folklore* an evil spirit that robs graves and feeds on the flesh of the dead 2. a person who robs graves 3. a person who derives pleasure from loathsome acts or things —**ghoul'ish** *adj.* —**ghoul'ish·ly** *adv.* —**ghoul'ish·ness** *n.*

GHQ, G.H.Q. General Headquarters

ghyll (gil) *n. var. of* GILL[4]

gHz, GHz gigahertz

☆**GI** (jē'ī') *adj.* 1. *Mil. a)* orig., galvanized iron /a *GI* can/ *b)* now, government issue: designating clothing, equipment, etc. issued to military personnel 2. [Colloq.] *a)* of or characteristic of the U.S. armed forces or their personnel /a *GI* haircut/ *b)* inclined to a strict observance of military regulations and customs /a captain who is very *GI*/ *c)* of or for veterans of the U.S. armed forces —*n., pl.* **GI's, GIs** [Colloq.] any member of the U.S. armed forces; esp., an enlisted soldier —*vt., vi.* **GI'd, GI'ing** to clean up for official inspection

GI, G.I., g.i. 1. gastrointestinal 2. general issue

gi. gill (unit of measure); gills

Gia·co·met·ti (jä′kô met′tē), **Al·ber·to** (äl ber′tô) 1901-66; Swiss sculptor & painter, mainly in France

gi·ant (jī′ənt) *n.* [ME. *geant* < ONormFr. *geant* (OFr. *jaiant*) < VL. *gagante* < L. *gigas* (pl. *gigantes*), huge fabled beings (in Vulg., giant) < Gr. *gigas* (gen. *gigantos*), in LXX, a man of great size and strength] **1.** *Gr. Myth.* any of a race of huge beings of human form who warred with the gods **2.** any imaginary being of human form but of superhuman size and strength **3.** a person or thing of great size, strength, intellect, etc. —*adj.* like a giant; of great size, strength, etc. —**gi′ant·ess** *n.fem.*

gi·ant·ism (-iz′m) *n.* abnormally great growth of the body, due to an excessive production of growth hormone by the anterior lobe of the pituitary gland

giant panda a large, black-and-white, bearlike mammal (*Ailuropoda melanoleuca*) of China and Tibet that feeds on bamboo shoots

☆**giant powder** an explosive that is like dynamite

Giant's Causeway headland in N Antrim County, Northern Ireland, consisting of thousands of small, vertical basaltic columns: c. 3 mi. long

giaour (jour) *n.* [Turk. *giaur* < Per. *gabr* < Ar. *kāfir*, infidel] in Moslem usage, a non-Moslem; esp., a Christian

GIANT PANDA
(4 ft. high at shoulder)

gib[1] (gib) *n.* [ME. *gibbe*, a swelling < L. *gibba*, a hump < *gibbus*, bent, prob. < IE. base *geibh-*, whence Norw. dial. *keiv*, askew] an adjustable piece of metal, etc. for keeping moving parts of a machine in place or for reducing friction —*vt.* gibbed, gib′bing to fasten or fit with a gib

gib[2] (gib) *n.* [ME. *gibbe*, short for GILBERT, used as a proper name for a cat] a male cat; tomcat; esp., a castrated male cat

Gib. Gibraltar

gib·ber (jib′ər, gib′-) *vi.*, *vt.* [echoic] to speak or utter rapidly and incoherently; chatter unintelligibly —*n.* unintelligible chatter; gibberish

gib·ber·el·lic acid (jib′ə rel′ik) [< ff. + -IC] an acid, $C_{19}H_{22}O_6$, isolated from various fungi and plants, and used to increase the growth of plants and seedlings and to improve the yield of certain fruit-bearing plants

gib·ber·el·lin (-in) *n.* [< ModL. *Gibberella* (dim. of L. *gibber*, hump on the back) + IN[1]] one of a group of organic compounds, secreted by an ascomycetous fungus (*Gibberella fujikuroi*), which behave like plant hormones in stimulating the growth of roots, leaves, and stems, the germination of seeds, etc.

gib·ber·ish (jib′ər ish; *also, & Brit. usually,* gib′-) *n.* [prob. < GIBBER] rapid and incoherent talk; unintelligible chatter; jargon

gib·bet (jib′it) *n.* [ME. *gibet*, gallows, forked stick < OFr. dim. < Frank. *gibb*, forked stick] **1.** a gallows **2.** a structure like a gallows, from which bodies of criminals already executed were hung and exposed to public scorn —*vt.* **1.** to execute by hanging **2.** to hang on a gibbet **3.** to expose to public scorn

gib·bon (gib′ən) *n.* [Fr.] any of several small, slender, long-armed anthropoid apes (genus *Hylobates*) of India, S China, and the East Indies, that live in trees

Gib·bon (gib′ən), **Edward** 1737-94; Eng. historian

Gib·bons (gib′ənz), **Orlando** 1583-1625; Eng. organist & composer

gib·bos·i·ty (gi bäs′ə tē) *n.* [OFr. *gibbosite* < ML. *gibbositas* < L. *gibbosus*] **1.** the state or quality of being gibbous **2.** *pl.* -ties a swelling or protuberance

gib·bous (gib′əs) *adj.* [ME. < L. *gibbosus* < *gibba*: see GIB[1]] **1.** protuberant; rounded and bulging **2.** designating the moon or a planet in that phase in which more than half, but not all, of the disk is illuminated **3.** humpbacked —**gib′bous·ly** *adv.*

GIBBON (18 1/2-25 in. long, head & body)

Gibbs (gibz), **J(osiah) Willard** 1839-1903; U.S. mathematician & physicist

gibe (jīb) *vi.*, *vt.* **gibed**, **gib′ing** [< ? OFr. *giber*, to handle roughly] to jeer, or taunt; scoff (at) —*n.* a jeer; taunt; scoff —*SYN.* see SCOFF[1]

gib·let (jib′lit) *n.* [ME. *gibelet* < OFr., stew made of game] any of various edible parts of a fowl, as the heart, gizzard, or neck, that are usually cooked separately or are used in making gravy

Gi·bral·tar (ji brôl′tər) **1.** small peninsula at the southern tip of Spain, extending into the Mediterranean: 2 1/2 sq. mi.: it consists mostly of a rocky hill (**Rock of Gibraltar**), 1,396 ft. high **2.** Brit. crown colony, including a port & naval base, on this peninsula: pop. 25,000 **3.** Strait of, strait between Spain & Morocco, joining the Mediterranean & the Atlantic: c. 35 mi. long —*n.* any strong fortification; unassailable fortress

☆**Gib·son** (gib′sən) *n.* [after Hugh *Gibson* (1883-1954), U.S.

diplomat] [*also* g-] a dry martini cocktail served with a tiny pickled onion

Gibson Desert C section of the vast desert region of Western Australia

☆**Gibson girl** the American girl of the 1890's as depicted by Charles Dana Gibson (1867-1944), U.S. illustrator

gid (gid) *n.* [< GIDDY] a disease, esp. of sheep, caused by a larval tapeworm (*Multiceps multiceps*) encysted in the brain

gid·dy (gid′ē) *adj.* -di·er, -di·est [ME. *gidie* < OE. *gydig*, insane, prob. < base (*gud) of *god*, GOD + -ig (see -Y[2]): hence, basic meaning "possessed by a god"] **1.** having a whirling, dazed sensation; dizzy; lightheaded **2.** causing or likely to cause such a sensation [a *giddy* height] **3.** turning or circling around very rapidly; whirling **4.** *a)* inconstant; fickle *b)* frivolous; flighty; heedless —*vt.*, *vi.* -died, -dy·ing to make or become giddy —**gid′di·ly** *adv.* —**gid′di·ness** *n.*

☆**gid·dy·ap** (gid′ē ap′) *interj.* [altered < *get up*] start moving! go faster!: a direction to a horse: also **gid′dy·up′** (-up′), **gid·dap** (gi dap′)

Gide (zhēd), **An·dré** (**Paul Guillaume**) (än drā′) 1869-1951; Fr. novelist, critic, etc.

Gid·e·on (gid′ē ən) [Heb. *gidh'ōn*, lit., hewer] **1.** a masculine name **2.** *Bible* a judge of Israel and a leader in the defeat of the Midianites: Judg. 6:11 ff.

☆**Gideons International** a Protestant organization for placing Bibles in hotel rooms, hospitals, etc., founded in 1899 by a group of traveling salesmen

gie (gē) *vt.*, *vi.* **gied** *or* **gae**, **gi·en** (gē′ən), **gie′ing** [Scot. & Brit. Dial.] to give

Gif·ford (gif′ərd) [ME. *Giffard* < ML. *Gifardus*, prob. < Gmc., as in OHG. *Gebahard* < base of *geban*, to GIVE + *hart*, bold, HARD] a masculine name

gift (gift) *n.* [ME. < OE., portion, wedding gift (< *giefan*: see GIVE) & < ON. *gift*, gift (< *gefa*, akin to GIVE), akin to G. *gift*, poison] **1.** something given to show friendship, affection, support, etc.; present **2.** the act, power, or right of giving **3.** a natural ability; talent [a *gift* for languages] —*vt.* **1.** to present a gift to **2.** to present as a gift —*SYN.* see PRESENT, TALENT —**look a gift horse in the mouth** to be critical of a gift or favor: from the practice of judging a horse's age by its teeth

gift·ed (-id) *adj.* **1.** having a natural ability or aptitude; talented **2.** notably superior in intelligence

gift of tongues *same as* GLOSSOLALIA

gift-wrap (-rap′) *vt.* -wrapped′, -wrap′ping to wrap as a gift, with decorative paper, ribbon, etc.

Gi·fu (gē′fōō′) city on C Honshu, Japan, near Nagoya: pop. 358,000

gig[1] (gig) *n.* [ME. *gigge*, whirligig, prob. < Scand., as in Dan. *gig*, whirling object, top, Norw. dial. *giga*, to shake, totter < IE. *gheigh-* < base *ghei-*, to gape (whence GAPE, (?) GIGGLE)] **1.** a light, two-wheeled, open carriage drawn by one horse **2.** a long, light, ship's boat reserved for the commanding officer **3.** [for *gig mill*] a machine for raising nap on cloth —*vi.* **gigged**, **gig′ging** to travel in a gig

gig[2] (gig) *n.* [contr. < earlier *fishgig*, *fizgig* < Sp. *fisga*, kind of harpoon] **1.** a fish spear **2.** a fish line with hooks designed to catch fish by jabbing into their bodies —*vt.*, *vi.* **gigged**, **gig′ging** to spear or jab with or as with a gig

gig[3] (gig) *n.* [< ?] [Slang] **1.** an official record or report of a minor delinquency, as in a military school; demerit **2.** punishment for such a delinquency —*vt.* **gigged**, **gig′ging** [Slang] to give a gig to

☆**gig**[4] (gig) *n.* [< ?] [Slang] **1.** a gathering of musicians for a session of jazz **2.** a job to play or sing jazz, esp. one for a single engagement **3.** any job, performance, or routine; stint

gi·ga- (jig′ə) [< Gr. *gigas*, GIANT] *a combining form meaning* one billion; the factor 10^9 [*gigaton*]

gi·ga·hertz (jig′ə hurts′) *n.* [see prec.] one billion hertz: formerly, **gig′a·cy′cle** (-sī′k'l)

gi·gan·te·an (jī′gan tē′ən, jī gan′tē ən) *adj.* [< L. *giganteus* < *gigas* (see GIANT) + -AN] gigantic; huge

gi·gan·tesque (jī′gan tesk′) *adj.* [Fr. < It. *gagantesco* < *gigante*: see GIANT] like or fit for a giant; gigantic

gi·gan·tic (jī gan′tik) *adj.* [< L. *gigas* (gen. *gigantis*): see GIANT + -IC] **1.** of, like, or fit for a giant **2.** very big; huge; colossal; enormous; immense —*SYN.* see ENORMOUS —**gi·gan′ti·cal·ly** *adv.*

gi·gan·tism (jī gan′tiz′m, jī′gan-) *n.* [see prec. & -ISM] **1.** the quality or state of being gigantic **2.** *same as* GIANTISM

gi·gan·tom·a·chy (jī′gan täm′ə kē) *n.* [LL. *gigantomachia* < Gr. *gigantomachia* < *gigas* (see GIANT) + *machē*, battle] **1.** [G-] *Gr. Myth.* the struggle between the giants and the gods **2.** any war between giants or giant powers

gi·ga·ton (jig′ə tun′) *n.* [GIGA- + TON[1]] the explosive force of a billion tons of TNT: a unit for measuring the power of thermonuclear weapons

gig·gle (gig′'l) *vi.* -gled, -gling [16th c., prob. < Du. *giggelen*: for IE. base see GIG[1]] to laugh with a series of uncontrollable, rapid, high-pitched sounds, suggestive of foolishness, nervousness, etc.; titter —*n.* such a laugh —*SYN.* see LAUGH —**gig′gler** *n.* —**gig′gly** *adj.*, -gli·er, -gli·est

---

fat, āpe, cär; ten, ēven; is, bīte; gō, hôrn, tōōl, look; oil, out; up, fur; get; joy; yet; chin; she; thin, *then*; zh, leisure; ŋ, ring; ə for *a* in *ago*, *e* in *agent*, *i* in *sanity*, *o* in *comply*, *u* in *focus*; ′ as in *able* (ā′b'l); Fr. bal; ë, Fr. coeur; ö, Fr. feu; Fr. mon; ô, Fr. coq; ü, Fr. duc; r, Fr. cri; H, G. ich; kh, G. doch. See inside front cover. ☆ Americanism; ‡foreign; *hypothetical; <derived from

gig·o·lo (jig′ə lō) *n., pl.* **-los** [Fr., masc. back-formation < *gigole*, prostitute, orig., tall, thin woman < OFr. < *gigue*, long-legged, thin girl, thigh, leg, fiddle: see ff.] **1.** a man who is paid to be a dancing partner or escort for women **2.** a man who is the lover of a woman, often a prostitute, and is supported by her

gig·ot (jig′ət, zhē gō′) *n.* [Fr. < OFr., leg of mutton, dim. of *gigue*, a fiddle < MHG. *giga*, a fiddle: for IE. base see JIG] **1.** a leg of mutton, lamb, veal, etc. **2.** a leg-of-mutton sleeve

gigue (zhēg) *n.* [Fr.] a jig, esp. as a movement of a classical suite

☆**GI Joe** [Slang] any man in the U.S. armed forces; esp., an enlisted soldier in World War II

Gi·jón (hē hōn′) seaport in NW Spain: pop. 134,000

Gi·la (hē′lə) [Sp. < Yuman name, lit., salty water] river in S Ariz., flowing southwest into the Colorado: 630 mi. long

☆**Gi·la monster** (hē′lə) [< prec.] a stout, sluggish, poisonous lizard (*Heloderma suspectum*) with a short, stumpy tail and a body covered with beadlike scales arranged in alternating rings of black and orange: found in desert regions of the SW U.S. and in Mexico

GILA MONSTER
(to 24 in. long)

Gil·bert (gil′bərt) [OFr. *Guillebert* < OHG. *Williberht* < *willo*, WILL[1] + *beraht*, BRIGHT] **1.** a masculine name: dim. *Gil* **2. Cass** (kas), 1859–1934; U.S. architect **3. Sir Humphrey**, 1539?–83; Eng. navigator and colonizer in N. America **4. Sir William Schwenck** (shwenk), 1836–1911; Eng. humorous poet & librettist: collaborated with Sir Arthur SULLIVAN in writing comic operas

gil·bert (gil′bərt) *n.* [after William *Gilbert* (1540?–1603), Eng. physician] the cgs unit for magnetomotive force, equal to 0.7958 ampere turn

Gilbert and Ellice Islands Brit. colony in the WC Pacific, consisting principally of four groups of atolls: 369 sq. mi.; pop. 54,000; cap. Tarawa: the colony includes *a)* **Gilbert Islands** group of islands on the equator, east of the Solomon Islands: 100 sq. mi.; pop. 45,000 *b)* **ELLICE ISLANDS** *c)* **LINE ISLANDS**

Gil·ber·ti·an (gil bur′tē ən) *adj.* of or like the characteristic style or humor of Sir William S. Gilbert

gild[1] (gild) *vt.* **gild′ed** or **gilt, gild′ing** [ME. *gilden* < OE. *gyldan* < base (*guld-*) of *gold*, GOLD] **1.** *a)* to overlay with a thin layer of gold *b)* to coat with a gold color **2.** to make appear bright and attractive **3.** to make (something) seem more attractive or more valuable than it is —**gild′er** *n.*

gild[2] (gild) *n. same as* GUILD

gild·ing (gil′diŋ) *n.* **1.** *a)* the art or process of applying gold leaf or a substance like gold to a surface *b)* the substance so applied **2.** an outward appearance covering unpleasant facts, reality, etc.

Gil·e·ad (gil′ē əd) mountainous region of ancient Palestine, east of the Jordan (Gen. 37:25)

Giles (jīlz) [OFr. *Gilles* < L. *Aegidius* < *aegis*: see AEGIS] **1.** a masculine name **2. Saint**, c. 7th cent. A.D.?; semilegendary Athenian hermit in S Gaul: his day is Sept. 1

Gil·ga·mesh (gil′gə mesh′) [< Bab.] a legendary Babylonian king, hero of an epic (*Gilgamesh Epic*) completed about 2000 B.C. and containing an account of a flood like the Biblical Flood: also **Gil′ga·mish′**

gill[1] (gil) *n.* [ME. *gile*, prob. < Anglo-N. form < or akin to ON. *gjolnar*, jaws, gills, older Dan. (*fiske*) *gaeln*, Sw. *gäl* < IE. base *ghelunā-*, jaw, whence Gr. *chelynē*, lip, jaw] **1.** the organ for breathing of most animals that live in water, as fish, lobsters, clams, etc., consisting of a simple saclike or complex feathery evagination of the body surface, usually richly supplied with blood **2.** [*pl.*] *a)* the red flesh hanging below the beak of a fowl; wattle *b)* the flesh under and about the chin and lower jaw of a person **3.** any of the thin, leaflike, radiating plates on the undersurface of a mushroom, on which the basidiospores are produced —**gilled** (gild) *adj.*

gill[2] (jil) *n.* [ME. *gille* < OFr., measure for wine < LL. *gillo*, cooling vessel] a liquid measure, equal to 1/4 pint

gill[3] (jil) [contr. of *Gillian*, proper name < L. *Juliana*, fem. of *Julianus* (see JULIAN)] [Archaic] [*also* G-] a girl or woman; esp., a sweetheart

gill[4] (gil) *n.* [ME. *gille* < ON. *gil*] [Brit.] **1.** a wooded ravine or glen **2.** a narrow stream; brook

gill cleft (or **slit**) *same as* VISCERAL CLEFT

Gil·les·pie (gi les′pē) **Dizzy** (born *John Birks Gillespie*) 1917– ; U.S. jazz musician

Gil·lette (ji let′), **William** (**Hooker**) 1855–1937; U.S. actor

gill fungus (gil) any basidiomycete that has spores borne on the lower side of the cap; agaric

gil·lie¹, gil·ly (gil′ē) *n., pl.* **-lies** [Scot. < Gael. *gille*, lad, page] **1.** in the Scottish Highlands, a sportsman's attendant or guide **2.** a male servant

gil·lie² (gil′ē) *n. same as* GHILLIE

gil·li·flow·er (jil′ē flou′ər) *n.* [altered (after FLOWER) < ME. *gilofre* < OFr. *gilofre*, *girofle*, gilliflower < LL. *caryophyllum* < Gr. *karyophyllon*, clove tree < *karyon*, nut + *phyllon*, leaf] **1.** any of several plants (genus *Dianthus*) with clove-scented flowers, as the clove pink **2.** *same as*

STOCK (sense 6) **3.** *same as* WALLFLOWER (sense 1) Also sp. **gil′ly·flow′er**

☆**gill net** (gil) a net set upright in the water to catch fish by entangling their gills in its meshes

☆**Gil·son·ite** (gil′sə nīt′) [after S. H. *Gilson*, of Salt Lake City, Utah] *a trademark for* UINTAITE

gilt[1] (gilt) *alt. pt. & pp.* of GILD[1] —*adj.* overlaid with gilding —*n. same as* GILDING

gilt[2] (gilt) *n.* [ME. *gilte* < ON. *gyltr*: for IE. base see GELD[1]] a young female pig; immature sow

gilt-edged (-ejd′) *adj.* **1.** having gilded edges, as the pages of a book **2.** of the highest quality, grade, or value [*gilt-edged securities*] Also **gilt′-edge′**

gilt·head (-hed) *n.* any of a number of unrelated sea fishes with gold markings on the head, as the sparoid fish of the Mediterranean or the English cunner

gim·bals (gim′b′lz, jim′-) *n.pl.* [*with sing. v.*] [altered < ME. *gemelles*, twins < L. *gemellus*, dim. of *geminus*, twin] a pair of rings pivoted on axes at right angles to each other so that one is free to swing within the other: a ship's compass, etc. will keep a horizontal position when suspended on gimbals —**gim′baled** (-b′ld) *adj.*

gim·crack (jim′krak′) *adj.* [altered < ME. *gibbecrak*, an ornament, prob. < *gibben*, to be erratic (< OFr. *giber*) + *crak*, a bursting sound] showy but cheap and useless —*n.* a cheap, showy, useless thing; knickknack

gim·crack·er·y (-ər ē) *n.* **1.** gimcracks, collectively **2.** showy but cheap and useless decoration, effects, etc.

gim·el (gim′'l) *n.* [Heb. *gimel*, lit., camel: cf. GAMMA] the third letter of the Hebrew alphabet (ג)

gim·let (gim′lit) *n.* [ME. < OFr. *guimbelet*, altered < *wimbelquin* < MDu. *wimmelkijn*, dim. of *wimpel*, WIMBLE] **1.** a small boring tool with a handle at right angles to a shaft having at the other end a spiral, pointed cutting edge **2.** a cocktail made of lime juice, gin, sugar, and soda —*vt.* to make a hole in with or as with a gimlet

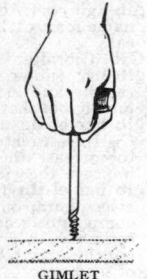

GIMLET

gim·let-eyed (-īd′) *adj.* having a piercing glance

gim·mal (gim′'l, jim′-) *n.* [see GIMBALS] a ring formed of two or more interlocked circlets

☆**gim·mick** (gim′ik) *n.* [< ? GIMCRACK] **1.** [Colloq.] *a)* a secret means of controlling a prize wheel, etc. *b)* anything that tricks or mystifies; deceptive or secret device **2.** [Slang] *a)* an attention-getting device or feature, typically superficial, designed to promote the success of a product, campaign, etc. *b)* any clever little gadget or ruse —*vt.* [Colloq.] to use gimmicks in or add gimmicks to —**gim′mick·y** *adj.*

☆**gim·mick·ry** (-rē) *n.* [Colloq.] **1.** gimmicks collectively **2.** the use of gimmicks Also **gim′mick·er·y**

gimp[1] (gimp) *n.* [< ? Du., akin to G. *gimpf*] a ribbonlike silk, worsted, or cotton braided fabric, sometimes stiffened with wire, used to trim garments, furniture, etc.

☆**gimp[2]** (gimp) *n.* [< ?] [Colloq.] fighting spirit; vigor

☆**gimp[3]** (gimp) *n.* [< ?] [Colloq.] **1.** a lame person **2.** a halting, lame walk; limp —*vi.* to limp —**gimp′y** *adj.*

gin[1] (jin) *n.* [< GENEVA] **1.** a strong, aromatic alcoholic liquor distilled from rye and other grains and flavored with juniper berries **2.** a similar liquor differently flavored, as with coriander **3.** [Slang] alcoholic liquor generally

gin[2] (jin) *n.* [ME., ingenuity, machine < OFr., contr. < *engin*, ENGINE] **1.** a snare, net, or trap, as for game or fish **2.** a machine for hoisting heavy objects ☆**3.** *same as* COTTON GIN —*vt.* **ginned, gin′ning 1.** to catch in a trap **2.** to remove seeds from (cotton) with a gin

gin[3] (gin) *vt., vi.* **gan, gin′ning** [ME. *ginnen*, aphetic form of *beginnen* (see BEGIN) & *onginnen* (OE. *onginnan*, to attempt)] [Archaic & Poet.] to begin

gin[4] (gin) *conj.* [? contr. < GIVEN, infl. ? by Scot. prep. *gin*, by (a certain time)] [Scot.] if; whether

gin[5] (jin) *n.* ☆*same as* GIN RUMMY —*vi.* **ginned, gin′ning** ☆to win in gin rummy with no unmatched cards left in one's hand, thus gaining additional points

gin·gel·li, gin·gel·ly (jin′jə lē) *n. same as* GINGILI

gin·ger (jin′jər) *adj.* [ME. *gingere, gingivere* < OE. *gingifer* & OFr. *ginzivre*, both < ML. *gingiber* < L. *zingiber* < Gr. *zingiberi* < Pali *singivera*] designating a family (Zingiberaceae) of aromatic tropical plants —*n.* **1.** an Asiatic plant (*Zingiber officinale*) of the ginger family, widely cultivated in the tropics for its aromatic rootstalk, used as a spice or perfume and in medicine **2.** the rootstalk, or the spice made from it **3.** a sandy or reddish-brown color ☆**4.** [Colloq.] vigor; spirit —*vt.* **1.** to flavor with ginger **2.** to invigorate; enliven

ginger ale a carbonated, sweet soft drink flavored with ginger

ginger beer a drink like ginger ale but with a stronger flavor

gin·ger·bread (-bred′) *n.* [ME. *ginge bred*, altered (after *bred*, BREAD) < *gingebras*, preserved ginger, ginger pudding < OFr. *gingembraz*: see GINGER] **1.** a cake flavored with ginger and molasses **2.** showy ornamentation, as gaudy or fancy carvings on furniture, gables, etc. —*adj.* cheap and showy; gaudy: also **gin′ger·bread′y**

gingerbread palm, gingerbread tree *same as* DOUM

gin·ger·ly (-lē) *adv.* [altered (after GINGER) < ? OFr. *genzor*, compar. of *gent*, delicate + -LY²] in a very careful or cautious way —*adj.* very careful; cautious —**gin′ger·li·ness** *n.*

gin·ger·snap (-snap′) *n.* a crisp, spicy cookie flavored with ginger and molasses

gin·ger·y (-ē) *adj.* 1. like or flavored with ginger; spicy; pungent 2. sandy or reddish in color 3. lively, vigorous, sharp, etc.

ging·ham (giŋ′əm) *n.* [< Du. *gingang* or Fr. *guingan*, ult. < Malay *ginggang*, striped (cloth)] a yarn-dyed cotton cloth, usually woven in stripes, checks, or plaids

gin·gi·li (jin′jə lē) *n.* [Hindi *jinjali*] 1. *same as* SESAME 2. the oil of sesame seed

gin·gi·va (jin ji′və) *n.* [L. < IE. base *geng-*, lump, ball, whence Gr. *gongros*, CONGER] *same as* GUM² —**gin·gi′val** (-v′l, jin′jə v′l) *adj.*

gin·gi·vi·tis (jin′jə vīt′əs) *n.* [ModL. < prec. + -ITIS] inflammation of the gums

ging·ko (giŋ′kō) *n., pl.* **ging′koes** *same as* GINKGO

gink (giŋk) *n.* [< ? dial. *gink*, a trick (whence Scot. *ginkie*, term of reproach applied to a woman)] [Slang] a man or boy, esp. one regarded as odd

gink·go (giŋ′kō) *n., pl.* **gink′goes** [Jap. *ginkyo* < Chin.] an Asiatic tree (*Ginkgo biloba*) with fan-shaped leaves and fleshy, yellow, foul-smelling seeds enclosing an edible inner kernel

☆**gin mill** (jin) [Slang] a bar or saloon

☆**gin·ner** (jin′ər) *n.* a person who operates a cotton gin

☆**gin rummy** [orig., a play on GIN¹, suggested by *rhum*, early form of RUMMY¹, *n.*] a variety of rummy in which a hand with unmatched cards totaling no more than 10 points may be exposed: the hand exposed wins or loses points, according as the opponent's unmatched cards add up to a higher or lower total: see also GIN⁵

gin·seng (jin′seŋ) *adj.* [Chin. *ien shen*] designating a family (Araliaceae) of plants having flat clusters of small, white or greenish flowers and, often, fragrant leaves, as the ginseng and English ivy —*n.* 1. any of several perennial plants (genus *Panax*) of the ginseng family, with thick, forked, aromatic roots, esp. a Chinese species (*Panax schinseng*) and a N. American species (*Panax quinquefolius*) 2. the root of these plants, used medicinally by the Chinese

Gio·con·da, La (lä′ jō kän′də; *It.* jō kôn′dä) [It., lit., the cheerful one] a portrait by Leonardo da Vinci, more commonly called MONA LISA

‡**gio·co·so** (jō kō′sō) *adj., adv.* [It.: see JOCOSE] *Music* with a gay, playful quality

Gior·gio·ne, Il (ēl jôr jō′ne) (born *Giorgio Barbarelli*) 1478?–1510; Venetian painter

Giot·to (di Bon·do·ne) (jôt′tô dē bôn dô′ne; *E.* jät′ō) 1266?–1337; Florentine painter & architect

gip (jip) *n., vt., vi. same as* GYP¹

gi·pon (ji pän′, jip′än) *n.* [ME. < OFr. *gipon, jupon:* see JUPON] *same as* JUPON

gip·sy (jip′sē) *n., adj., vi. same as* GYPSY

gi·raffe (jə raf′, -räf′) *n., pl.* **-raffes′, -raffe′:** see PLURAL, II, D, 1 [Fr. < It. *giraffa* < Ar. *zarāfa*] either of two species of large cud-chewing animals of Africa (genus *Giraffa*), with a very long neck and legs: the tallest of existing animals, they often reach a height of 18 ft. —[G-] *same as* CAMELO-PARDUS

gir·an·dole (jir′ən dōl′) *n.* [Fr. < It. *girandola* < *girare*, to turn < LL. *gyrare* < *gyrus*, a circle < Gr. *gyros:* see GYRO²] 1. a revolving cluster of fireworks 2. a revolving water jet 3. a branched candleholder 4. a pendant or earring with small stones grouped around a larger one Also **gi·ran·do·la** (ji ran′də la)

Gi·rard (jə rärd′), **Stephen** 1750–1831; Am. financier & philanthropist, born in France

gir·a·sol (jir′ə sōl′, -säl′, -sôl′) *n.* [Fr. < It. *girasole* < *girare* (see GIRANDOLE) + *sole* (< L. *sol*, the sun: see SOL)] 1. *same as* JERUSALEM ARTICHOKE 2. *same as* FIRE OPAL Also **gir′a·sole** (-sōl′)

Gi·rau·doux (zhē rō dōo′), **(Hippolyte) Jean** (zhän) 1882–1944; Fr. playwright & novelist

gird¹ (gurd) *vt.* **gird′ed** or **girt, gird′ing** [ME. *girden* < OE. *gyrdan*, akin to G. *gürten* < IE. base *gherdh-*, to enclose, whence YARD², GIRTH] 1. to encircle or fasten with a belt or band 2. to surround, encircle, or enclose 3. *a)* to equip, furnish, clothe, etc. *b)* to endow with some attribute 4. to prepare (oneself) for action

gird² (gurd) *n., vi., vt.* [ME. *girden*, to strike, assail with words < ? OE. *gyrdan* for *gierdan*, lit., to rod < *gierd, gerd*, a rod (see YARD¹): infl. by prec.] gibe; taunt; scoff; jeer

gird·er (gur′dər) *n.* [GIRD¹ + -ER] a large beam, usually horizontal, of timber or steel, for supporting the joists of a floor, the framework of a building, the superstructure of a bridge, etc.

gir·dle (gur′d'l) *n.* [ME. *girdil* < OE. *gyrdel* < base of *gyrdan* (see GIRD¹): akin to G. *gürtel*] 1. a belt or sash for the waist 2. anything that surrounds or encircles 3. a woman's elasticized undergarment for supporting or mold-

ing the waist and hips 4. the rim of a cut gem ☆5. a ring made by removing bark around the trunk of a tree, so as to kill it 6. *Anat.* a bony arch or zone supporting the limbs [the pelvic *girdle*] —*vt.* **-dled, -dling** 1. to surround or bind, as with a girdle 2. to encircle ☆3. to cut a ring of bark from (a tree)

gir·dler (gur′dlər) *n.* [ME. *girdeler:* see prec. & -ER] 1. a person who makes girdles 2. a person or thing that girdles, or encircles ☆3. any insect that cuts girdles in trees, esp. an American beetle (*Oncideres cingulata*) that lays its eggs in holes bored into twigs

girl (gurl) *n.* [ME. *girle, gurle,* youngster of either sex < ? OE. *gyrele,* ? akin to Brit. southern dial. *girls,* primrose blooms, & LowG. *gore,* young person (of either sex) < ? IE. base *gher-*, small] 1. a female child 2. a young, unmarried woman 3. a female servant or other employee 4. [Colloq.] a woman of any age, married or single 5. [Colloq.] a sweetheart

☆**girl·friend** (gurl′frend′) *n.* [Colloq.] 1. a sweetheart of a boy or man 2. a girl who is one's friend

girl guide a member of a British organization (**Girl Guides**) that is like the Girl Scouts

girl·hood (-hood′) *n.* 1. the state or time of being a girl 2. girls collectively

girl·ie, girl·y (gur′lē) *n., pl.* **girl′ies** [Slang] a girl or woman —☆*adj.* [Slang] designating or of magazines, shows, etc. chiefly devoted to displaying nude or nearly nude young women, esp. in a tasteless or vulgar way

girl·ish (-ish) *adj.* of, like, or suitable to a girl or girlhood —**girl′ish·ly** *adv.* —**girl′ish·ness** *n.*

☆**girl scout** a member of the **Girl Scouts**, an organization founded by Juliette Low in Savannah, Georgia, in 1912 (as *Girl Guides*) to provide healthful, character-building activities for girls

girn (gurn) *n., vi., vt.* [ME. *girnen*, var. of *grennen:* see GRIN] [Brit. Dial.] snarl

Gi·ronde (jə ränd′; *Fr.* zhē rônd′) 1. estuary in SW France, formed by the juncture of the Garonne & Dordogne rivers and flowing into the Bay of Biscay: c. 45 mi. long 2. department in SW France, on the Bay of Biscay: cap. Bordeaux 3. the Girondist party

Gi·ron·dist (jə rän′dist) *n.* [so named because at first led by deputies from Gironde] a member of a French political party (1791–93) that advocated moderate republican principles: it was suppressed by the Jacobins —*adj.* designating or of this party

girt¹ (gurt) *alt. pt. & pp. of* GIRD¹

girt² (gurt) *vt.* [ME. *girten*, var. of *girden:* see GIRD¹] 1. to gird; girdle 2. to fasten with a girth 3. to measure the girth of —*vi.* to measure in girth

girth (gurth) *n.* [ME. *gerth* < ON. *gjörth* < base of *gyrtha*, to encircle, akin to OE. *gyrdan* (see GIRD¹)] 1. a band put around the belly of a horse or other animal for holding a saddle, pack, etc. 2. the circumference, as of a tree trunk or person's waist —*vt.* 1. to gird; encircle 2. to fasten or bind with a girth —*vi.* to measure in girth

gi·sarme (gi zärm′) *n.* [ME. < OFr. < ? ML. *gisarum*] a battle-ax or halberd with a long shaft, formerly carried by foot soldiers

☆**gis·mo** (giz′mō) *n.* [Slang] *same as* GIZMO

Gis·sing (gis′iŋ), **George (Robert)** 1857–1903; Eng. novelist

gist (jist) *n.* [ME. *giste* < OFr., abode, point at issue < 3d pers. sing., pres. indic., of *gesir*, to lie < L. *jacere*, to lie; sense infl. by Anglo-Fr. legal phrase *l'action gist*, lit., the action lies] 1. *Law* the grounds for action in a lawsuit 2. the essence or main point, as of an article or argument

git·tern (git′ərn) *n.* [ME. *giterne* < OFr. *guiterne*, altered < OSp. *guitarra:* see GUITAR] an obsolete, wire-strung musical instrument somewhat like a guitar

give (giv) *vt.* **gave, giv′en, giv′ing** [ME. *given* (with g- < ON. *gefa*, to give), *yeven* < OE. *giefan*, akin to G. *geben* < IE. base *ghabh-*, to grasp, take, whence L. *habere*, to have: the special ONe. sense of this base results from its use as a substitute for IE. *dō-* (as in L. *dare*, to give)] 1. to turn over the possession or control of to someone without cost or exchange; make a gift of 2. to hand or pass over into the trust or keeping of someone [to *give* the porter a bag to carry, to *give* a daughter in marriage] 3. to hand or pass over in exchange for something else; sell (goods, services, etc.) for a price or pay (a price) for goods, services, etc. 4. to relay; pass along [to *give* regards to someone] 5. to produce in a person or thing; cause to have; impart [to *give* pleasure, to *give* someone a cold] 6. to confer or assign (a title, position, name, etc.) 7. to act as host or sponsor of (a party, dance, etc.) ☆8. to put in communication with, as by telephone 9. to be the source, origin, or cause of; produce; supply [cows give milk] 10. *a)* to part with for some cause; sacrifice [to *give* one's life for a cause] *b)* to devote to some occupation, pursuit, etc. [to *give* one's life to art] 11. to concede; yield [to *give* a point in an argument] 12. to offer or yield (oneself) to a man for sexual intercourse 13. to show; exhibit [to *give* every indication of being a fool] 14. to put forward for acceptance or rejection; offer; proffer [to *give* a suggestion] 15. *a)* to perform [to

give a concert/ *b*) to introduce or present (a speaker, the subject of a toast, etc.) **16.** to make (a gesture, movement, etc.) /to *give* a leap/ **17.** to perform (a physical act) /to *give* someone a hug, kiss, etc./ **18.** to administer or dispense (medicine, etc.) **19.** to utter, emit, or produce (words, sounds, etc.); put in words; state /to *give* a reply/ **20.** to inflict or impose (punishment, sentence, etc.) —*vi.* **1.** to make gifts or donations; contribute **2.** to bend, sink, move, break down, yield, etc. from force or pressure **3.** to be springy; be resilient **4.** to provide a view of, or a way of getting to, someplace; open (usually with *on*, *upon*, or *onto*) /the window *gives* on the park/ **5.** [Colloq.] to occur; happen: chiefly in the phrase **what gives?** —*n.* **1.** a bending, moving, sinking, etc. under pressure **2.** a tendency to be springy; resiliency —**give and take** to exchange on an even basis —**give away 1.** to make a gift of; donate; bestow **2.** in a marriage ceremony, to present (the bride) ritually to the bridegroom ✩**3.** [Colloq.] to reveal, expose, or betray —**give back** to return or restore —**give forth** to send forth; emit; issue —**give in 1.** to hand in **2.** to abandon a claim, fight, or argument; surrender; yield —**give it to** [Colloq.] to punish; beat or scold —**give off** to send forth or out; emit —**give or take** plus or minus /a price of $1.00, *give or take* a few cents/ —**give out 1.** to send forth or out; emit **2.** to cause to be known; make public **3.** to distribute **4.** to become worn out or used up; fail to last —**give over 1.** to hand over **2.** to stop; cease **3.** to set apart for some purpose —**give to understand** (or **believe,** etc.) to cause to understand (or believe, etc.) —**give up 1.** to hand over; turn over; relinquish; surrender **2.** to stop; cease **3.** to admit failure and stop trying **4.** to lose hope for; despair of **5.** to sacrifice; devote wholly

SYN.—**give** is the general word meaning to transfer from one's own possession to that of another; **grant** implies that there has been a request or an expressed desire for the thing given /to grant a favor/; **present** implies a certain formality in the giving and often connotes considerable value in the gift /he *presented* the school with a library/; **donate** is used especially of a giving to some philanthropic or religious cause; **bestow** stresses that the thing is given gratuitously and often implies condescension in the giver /to *bestow* charity upon the poor/; **confer** implies that the giver is a superior and that the thing given is an honor, privilege, etc. /to *confer* a title, a college degree, etc./

give-and-take (-'n tāk′) *n.* **1.** a yielding on one or more points, in return for equal concessions by the opposing side **2.** an exchange of remarks or retorts on equal terms; repartee; banter

give·a·way (-ə wā′) *n.* [Colloq.] ✩**1.** an unintentional revelation or betrayal **2.** something given free or sold cheap so as to attract customers, etc. ✩**3.** the appropriation of public lands, resources, etc. for private profit ✩**4.** a radio or television program in which prizes are given to contestants

giv·en (giv′'n) *pp.* of GIVE —*adj.* **1.** bestowed; presented **2.** accustomed, as from habit or inclination; prone /given to lying/ **3.** stated; specified /a given date/ **4.** taken as a premise; assumed; granted **5.** issued or executed (on the specified date by the specified person): used in official documents

given name the first name of a person; name given at birth or baptism, as distinguished from the surname

giv·er (giv′ər) *n.* a person who gives: often in compounds /lawgiver, almsgiver/

give-up (-up′) *n.* a type of fee-splitting in which a stockbroker is instructed by a customer to give up part of the commission to a trade to another firm

Gi·za (gē′zə) city in N Egypt, near Cairo: site of the Sphinx & three pyramids: pop. 250,000: also sp. **Gi′zeh**

✩**giz·mo** (giz′mō) *n.* [< ? Sp. *gisma*, obs. or dial. var. of *chisme*, trifle, jigger, ult. < L. *cimex*, a bug] [Slang] **1.** any gadget or contrivance **2.** a gimmick

giz·zard (giz′ərd) *n.* [ME. *giser* (+ unhistoric -*d*) < OFr. *gisier* < L. *gigeria*, pl., cooked entrails of poultry] **1.** the second stomach of a bird: it has thick muscular walls and a tough lining for grinding food that has been partially digested in the first stomach **2.** [Colloq.] the stomach: humorous usage

Gk. Greek

g/l grams per liter

gla·bel·la (glə bel′ə) *n., pl.* **-lae** (-ē) [ModL. < fem. of L. *glabellus*, without hair < *glaber*: see GLABROUS] the smooth prominence on the forehead between the eyebrows and just above the nose —**gla·bel′lar** *adj.*

gla·brate (glā′brāt, -brit) *adj.* [< L. *glabratus*, pp. of *glabrare*, lit., to make smooth, deprive of hair < *glaber*: see ff.] **1.** glabrous or nearly glabrous **2.** becoming glabrous when old or mature

gla·brous (-brəs) *adj.* [< L. *glaber*, smooth, bald (< IE. *ghladh-ros* < base *ghel-*, to gleam, whence GLAD[1], GLARE[1]) + -OUS] *Biol.* without hair, down, or fuzz; bald —**gla′brous·ness** *n.*

gla·cé (gla sā′) *adj.* [Fr., pp. of *glacer*, to freeze < L. *glaciare* < *glacies*, ice: see ff.] **1.** having a smooth, glossy surface, as certain leathers or silks **2.** candied or glazed, as fruits —*vt.* **-céed′, -cé′ing** to glaze (fruits, etc.)

gla·cial (glā′shəl) *adj.* [L. *glacialis*, icy, frozen < *glacies*, ice, prob. akin to *gelu*, COLD] **1.** of or like ice or glaciers **2.** of or produced by a glacier or a glacial epoch or period **3.** freezing; frigid /glacial weather/ **4.** cold and unfriendly

/a *glacial* stare/ **5.** as slow as the movement of a glacier /*glacial* progress/ **6.** *Chem.* having an icelike, crystalline appearance /*glacial* acetic acid/ —**gla′cial·ly** *adv.*

glacial epoch 1. any period of geological time when large parts of the earth were covered with glaciers **2.** the latest of these periods, the Pleistocene, when a large part of the Northern Hemisphere was intermittently covered with glaciers

gla·cial·ist (-ist) *n.* a student of glaciers and their action

glacial period the period including the glacial epochs; ice age

gla·ci·ate (glā′shē āt′, -sē-) *vt.* **-at′ed, -at′ing** [< L. *glaciatus*, pp. of *glaciare*, to turn into ice, freeze: see GLACIAL & -ATE[1]] **1.** *a*) to cover over with ice or a glacier *b*) to form into ice; freeze **2.** to expose to or change by glacial action —**gla′ci·a′tion** *n.*

gla·cier (glā′shər) *n.* [Fr. (orig., Savoy dial., whence also G. *gletscher*) < VL. *glaciarium* < *glacia* (whence Fr. *glacé*), for L. *glacies*, ice: see GLACIAL] a large mass of ice and snow that forms in areas where the rate of snowfall constantly exceeds the rate at which the snow melts: it moves slowly outward from the center of accumulation or down a mountain slope or valley until it melts or breaks away

Glacier National Park national park in NW Mont., on the Canadian border: it contains over 200 lakes & 60 small glaciers: 1,577 sq. mi.

gla·ci·ol·o·gy (glā′shē äl′ə jē, -sē-) *n.* [*glacio-* (< GLACIER) + -LOGY] **1.** the scientific study of the formation, movements, etc. of glaciers **2.** the glacial formations of a particular region —**gla′ci·o·log′i·cal** (-ə läj′i k'l) *adj.* —**gla′ci·ol′o·gist** *n.*

gla·cis (glā′sis, glas′is) *n., pl.* **-cis** (-sēz), **-cis·es** (-sis əz) [Fr. < OFr. *glacier*, to slip < *glace*, ice: see GLACIER] **1.** a gradual slope **2.** an embankment sloping gradually up to a fortification, so as to expose attackers to defending gunfire

glad[1] (glad) *adj.* **glad′der, glad′dest** [ME. < OE. *glæd*, akin to G. *glatt*, smooth, (the orig. Gmc. sense) < IE. *ghlādh-*, shining, smooth < base *ghel-*, to shine, whence GOLD] **1.** feeling or characterized by pleasure or joy; happy; pleased **2.** causing pleasure or joy; making happy **3.** very willing /I'm glad to help/ **4.** bright or beautiful —*vt., vi.* **glad′ded, glad′ding** [ME. *gladen* < OE. *gladian*] [Archaic] to gladden —*SYN.* see HAPPY —**glad′ly** *adv.* —**glad′ness** *n.*

glad[2] (glad) *n.* [Colloq.] *same as* GLADIOLUS

glad·den (-'n) *vt., vi.* [< GLAD[1] + -EN] to make or become glad

glade (glād) *n.* [ME., prob. < *glad*, GLAD[1]: orig. sense prob. "bright, smooth place," use similar to G. *lichtung*, glade < *licht*, light, Fr. *clairière* < *clair*, clear] **1.** an open space in a wood or forest ✩**2.** an everglade

glad eye [Slang] an inviting or flirtatious glance: usually in **give** (or **get**) **the glad eye**

✩**glad hand** [Slang] a cordial, effusive, or demonstrative welcome —**glad′-hand′** *vt., vi.* —**glad′-hand′er** *n.*

glad·i·ate (glad′ē āt′, glā′dē-; -it) *adj.* [< L. *gladius*, sword (see ff.) + -ATE[1]] *Bot.* sword-shaped

glad·i·a·tor (glad′ē āt′ər) *n.* [L. < *gladius*, sword, via Celt. (as in W. *cleddyf*, sword) < IE. base *kel-*, to strike, whence L. *calamitas*] **1.** in ancient Rome, a man who fought other men or animals with a sword or other weapon in an arena, for the entertainment of spectators: gladiators were slaves, captives, or paid performers **2.** any person involved in a public controversy or fight —**glad·i·a·to·ri·al** (glad′ē ə tôr′ē əl) *adj.*

glad·i·o·la (glad′ē ō′lə; *occas.* glə dī′ə lə) *n.* [mistaken as sing. of ff.] *same as* GLADIOLUS

glad·i·o·lus (glad′ē ō′ləs; *occas.* glə dī′ə ləs) *n., pl.* **-lus·es, -li** (-lī) [ModL. < L., sword lily, small sword, dim. of *gladius*: see GLADIATOR] **1.** any of a genus (*Gladiolus*) of plants of the iris family, with swordlike leaves in flat fans and tall spikes of funnel-shaped flowers in various colors **2.** *Anat.* the central part of the sternum

✩**glad rags** [Slang] fine or dressy clothes

glad·some (glad′səm) *adj.* [see GLAD[1], *adj.* & -SOME[1]] joyful or cheerful —**glad′some·ly** *adv.*

Glad·stone (glad′stōn; *Brit.* -stən) *n.* [after ff.] a traveling bag hinged so that it can open flat into two compartments of equal size: in full, **Gladstone bag**

Glad·stone (glad′stōn; *Brit.* -stən), **William Ew·art** (yōō′ərt) 1809–98; Brit. statesman; prime minister (1868–74; 1880–85; 1886; 1892–94)

Glad·ys (glad′is) [W. *Gwladys*, prob. < L. *Claudia*: see CLAUDIA] a feminine name

glai·kit, glai·ket (glā′kit) *adj.* [ME.] [Chiefly Scot.] foolish; flighty; giddy

glair (gler) *n.* [ME. *glaire* < OFr. < VL. *claria* < L. *clarus*, clear] **1.** raw white of egg, used in sizing or glazing **2.** a size or glaze made from this **3.** any sticky matter resembling raw egg white —*vt.* to cover with glair —**glair′y** *adj.*

glaive (glāv) *n.* [ME. < OFr., a lance < L. *gladius*, sword: see GLADIATOR] [Archaic] **1.** a kind of halberd with a swordlike blade **2.** a sword; esp., a broadsword

Gla·mor·gan·shire (glə môr′gən shir′) county of SE Wales, on the Bristol Channel: 818 sq. mi.; pop. 1,242,000; county seat, Cardiff: also **Gla·mor′gan**

glam·or·ize (glam′ə rīz′) *vt.* **-ized′, -iz′ing** to make glamorous —**glam′or·i·za′tion** *n.*

glam·or·ous, glam·our·ous (glam′ər əs) *adj.* full of glamour; fascinating; alluring —**glam′or·ous·ly** *adv.*

glam·our, glam·or (glam′ər) *n.* [Scot. var. of *grammar* (with sense of GRAMARYE), popularized by Sir Walter Scott; orig. esp. in *cast the glamour*, to cast an enchantment] **1.** orig., a magic spell or charm **2.** seemingly mysterious and elusive fascination or allure, as of some person, object, scene, etc.; bewitching charm: the current sense

glance[1] (glans, gläns) *vi.* **glanced, glanc′ing** [ME. *glansen, glenchen*, prob. a blend < OFr. *glacier*, to slip (see GLACIS) + *guenchir*, to elude < Frank. *wenkjan*, to totter, akin to OE. *wancol*, unstable] **1.** to strike a surface obliquely and go off at an angle (usually with *off*) **2.** to make an indirect or passing reference (with *over, at,* etc.) **3.** to flash or gleam **4.** to look suddenly and briefly; take a quick look —*vt.* to cause to strike (a surface) at an angle and be deflected —*n.* **1.** a glancing off; deflected impact **2.** a flash or gleam **3.** a quick look —*SYN.* see FLASH

glance[2] (glans, gläns) *n.* [G. *glanz*, lit., luster: for IE. base see GLASS] any of various ores with a metallic luster: now applied to only a few metallic ores, such as silver glance (ARGENTITE) and lead glance (GALENA)

gland[1] (gland) *n.* [Fr. *glande* < OFr. *glandre* < L. *glandula,* tonsil, dim. of *glans* (gen. *glandis*), acorn (< IE. base *gwel-*, oak, acorn, whence Gr. *balanos*)] **1.** any organ or specialized group of cells that separates certain elements from the blood and secretes them in a form for the body to use, as epinephrine, or throw off, as urine or sweat: some glands, as the liver and kidneys, have ducts that empty into an organ: the ductless (or endocrine) glands, as the thyroid and adrenals, pass their secretions directly into the bloodstream **2.** loosely, any similar structure that is not a true gland [lymph *glands*] **3.** *Bot.* an organ or layer of cells that produces and secretes some substance

gland[2] (gland) *n.* [< ?] *Mech.* a movable part that compresses the packing on a stuffing box

glan·dered (glan′dərd) *adj.* having glanders

glan·ders (glan′dərz) *n.pl.* [*with sing. v.*] [OFr. *glandres* < L. *glandulae,* swollen glands in the neck, pl. of *glandula:* see GLAND[1]] a contagious disease of horses, mules, etc. characterized by fever, swelling of glands beneath the lower jaw, inflammation of the nasal mucous membranes, etc.: it can be transmitted to certain other animals and man

glan·du·lar (glan′jə lər) *adj.* [Fr. *glandulaire:* see GLANDULE] **1.** of, like, or functioning as a gland **2.** having or consisting of glands **3.** derived from or affected by glands —**glan′du·lar·ly** *adv.*

glandular fever *same as* INFECTIOUS MONONUCLEOSIS

glan·dule (glan′jool) *n.* [Fr. < L. *glandula:* see GLAND[1]] a small gland

glans (glanz) *n., pl.* **glan·des** (glan′dēz) [L., lit., acorn: see GLAND[1]] **1.** the head, or end, of the penis (**glans penis**) **2.** the corresponding part of the clitoris

glare[1] (gler) *vi.* **glared, glar′ing** [ME. *glaren* < or akin to MDu. *glaren,* to gleam, glare & OE. *glær,* amber: for IE. base see GLASS] **1.** to shine with a strong, steady, dazzling light **2.** to be too bright or showy **3.** to stare fiercely or angrily —*vt.* to send forth or express with a glare —*n.* **1.** a strong, steady, dazzling light or brilliant reflection, as from sunlight on ice **2.** a too bright or dazzling display **3.** a fierce or angry stare —*SYN.* see BLAZE[1], LOOK

glare[2] (gler) *n.* [prob. < prec.] a smooth, bright, glassy surface, as of ice —*adj.* smooth, bright, and glassy

glar·ing (-in) *adj.* **1.** shining with a too bright, dazzling light **2.** too bright and showy **3.** staring in a fierce, angry manner **4.** too obvious to be overlooked; flagrant [a *glaring* mistake] —*SYN.* see FLAGRANT —**glar′ing·ly** *adv.*

Glar·us (glär′əs) canton in EC Switzerland: 264 sq. mi.; pop. 41,000: Fr. name **Gla·ris** (glä rēs′)

glar·y (gler′ē) *adj.* **glar′i·er, glar′i·est** shining with, or reflecting, a too bright light —**glar′i·ness** *n.*

Glas·gow (glas′kō, glaz′gō) seaport in SC Scotland, on the Clyde: pop. 980,000

Glas·gow (glas′kō, glaz′gō), **Ellen (Anderson Gholson)** 1874–1945; U.S. novelist

glass (glas, gläs) *n.* [ME. *glas* < OE. *glæs,* akin to G. *glas* < IE. base *ghel-*, to shine, whence GLINT, GLOW] **1.** a hard, brittle substance, usually transparent or translucent, made by fusing silicates with soda or potash, lime, and, sometimes, various metallic oxides: the molten mass is cooled rapidly to prevent crystallization **2.** any substance like glass in composition, transparency, brittleness, etc. **3.** *same as* GLASSWARE **4.** *a)* an article made partly or wholly of glass, as a drinking container, mirror, windowpane, telescope, barometer, etc. *b)* [*pl.*] eyeglasses *c)* [*pl.*] binoculars **5.** the quantity contained in a drinking glass —*vt.* **1.** to put into glass jars for preserving **2.** to mirror; reflect **3.** to equip with glass panes; glaze **4.** to look at through a telescope, etc. **5.** to make glassy —*vi.* to become glassy —*adj.* of, made of or with, or like glass —**glass in** to enclose with glass panes

glass blowing the art or process of shaping molten glass into various forms by blowing air into a mass of it at the end of a tube —**glass blower**

glass cutter 1. a person whose work is cutting sheets of glass to desired sizes or shapes **2.** a person whose work is etching designs on glass surfaces **3.** a tool for cutting, or etching designs on, glass —**glass cutting**

glass·ful (-fool′) *n., pl.* **glass′fuls′** the amount that will fill a glass

glass·house (-hous′) *n. Brit. var. of* GREENHOUSE

☆**glass·ine** (gla sēn′) *n.* [GLASS + -INE[1]] a thin but tough, glazed, nearly transparent paper, used for the windows of envelopes, etc.

glass·mak·er (-māk′ər) *n.* a person who makes glass or glassware —**glass′mak′ing** *n.*

glass·man (-mən, -man′) *n., pl.* **-men** (-mən, -men′) **1.** a person who sells glassware **2.** *same as* GLASSMAKER

☆**glass snake** any of several snakelike, legless lizards (genus *Ophisaurus*), found in the S U.S. and other warm regions: so called because its long tail breaks off easily

glass·ware (-wer′) *n.* articles made of glass

glass wool fine fibers of glass intertwined in a woolly mass, used in filters and as insulation

glass·work (-wurk′) *n.* **1.** [*pl., with sing. or pl. v.*] a factory for making glass **2.** the making or ornamentation of glass and glassware **3.** *same as* GLASSWARE —**glass′work′er** *n.*

glass·worm (-wurm′) *n. same as* ARROWWORM

glass·wort (-wurt′) *n.* [GLASS + WORT[2]] any of several fleshy plants (genera *Salicornia* and *Salsola*) of the goosefoot family, often found in saline coastal or desert areas: the ash is rich in soda and formerly was used in making soap and glass

glass·y (-ē) *adj.* **glass′i·er, glass′i·est** [ME. *glasi*] **1.** like glass, as in smoothness or transparency **2.** expressionless or lifeless [a *glassy* stare] —**glass′i·ly** *adv.* —**glass′i·ness** *n.*

Glas·we·gi·an (glas wē′jən, -jē ən) *adj.* of Glasgow —*n.* a native or inhabitant of Glasgow

Glau·ber's salt (or **salts**) (glou′bərz) [after J. R. *Glauber* (1604–68), Ger. chemist] sodium sulfate, $Na_2SO_4 \cdot 10H_2O$, a crystalline salt used as a cathartic, diuretic, etc.: also **Glauber salt** (or **salts**)

glau·co- (glô′kō, -kə) [< Gr. *glaukos,* orig., gleaming < ? IE. base *gel-*, to shine, whence CLEAN] *a combining form meaning* bluish-green, silvery, or gray [*glauconite*] Also, before a vowel, **glauc-**

glau·co·ma (glô kō′mə, glou-) *n.* [L. < Gr. *glaukōma* < *glaukos:* see prec. & -OMA] a disease of the eye, characterized by increased pressure within, and hardening of, the eyeball: it leads to a gradual impairment of sight that can result in blindness —**glau·co′ma·tous** (-təs) *adj.*

glau·co·nite (glôk′ə nit′) *n.* [G. *glaukonit* < Gr. *glaukon,* neut. of *glaukos* (see GLAUCO-)] a greenish silicate of iron and potassium, found in greensand

glau·cous (glô′kəs) *adj.* [L. *glaucus* < Gr. *glaukos:* see GLAUCO-] **1.** bluish-green or yellowish-green **2.** *Bot.* covered with a whitish bloom that can be rubbed off, as grapes, plums, cabbage leaves, etc.

glaucous gull a large, white and gray, northern gull (*Larus hyperboreus*) common in the Arctic

glaze (glāz) *vt.* **glazed, glaz′ing** [ME. *glasen < glas,* GLASS] **1.** *a)* to provide (a building, etc.) with glass windows *b)* to fit (windows, etc.) with glass **2.** to give a hard, glossy finish or coating to; specif., *a)* to overlay (pottery, etc.) with a substance that gives a glassy finish when fused *b)* to make the surface of (leather, etc.) glossy by polishing, etc. *c)* to cover (foods) with a glassy coating of sugar syrup, gelatin, etc. *d)* to coat (a painted surface) with a semitransparent color **3.** to give (the eyes) a glassy look **4.** to cover with a thin layer of ice —*vi.* **1.** to become glassy or glossy **2.** to form a glaze —*n.* **1.** *a)* a glassy finish, as on pottery *b)* any substance used to produce this **2.** a coat of semitransparent color applied to a painted surface to modify the effect **3.** a substance, as hardened sugar syrup, gelatin, etc, forming a glassy coating on foods **4.** a film or coating, as on the eyes **5.** a thin coating of ice —**glaz′er** *n.*

gla·zier (glā′zhər) *n.* [ME. *glasier:* see GLASS & -IER] a person whose work is cutting glass and setting it in windows, etc. —**gla′zier·y** (-ē) *n.*

glaz·ing (glā′zin) *n.* [ME. *glasinge:* see GLASS & -ING] **1.** the work of a glazier in fitting windows, etc. with glass **2.** glass set or to be set in frames **3.** a glaze or application of a glaze

Gla·zu·nov (glä zōō nôf′), **A·lek·san·dr Kon·stan·ti·no·vich** (ä lyek sän′dr′ kôn′stän tē′nō vich) 1865–1936; Russ. composer

gleam (glēm) *n.* [ME. *glem* < OE. *glæm,* akin to OHG. *gleimo,* glowworm & GLIMMER < IE. *ghlei-* < *ghel-*, to shine, gleam, whence GLASS, GLOW] **1.** a flash or beam of light **2.** a faint light **3.** a reflected brightness, as from a polished surface **4.** a brief, faint manifestation or trace, as of hope, understanding, etc. —*vi.* **1.** to shine or reflect with a gleam or gleams **2.** to be manifested briefly; appear or be revealed suddenly —*SYN.* see FLASH —**gleam′y** *adj.*

glean (glēn) *vt., vi.* [ME. *glenen* < OFr. *glener* < VL. *glennare* < Celt., as in OIr. *digleinn,* he gleans < IE.

---

fat, āpe, cär; ten, ēven; is, bite; gō, hôrn, tōol, look; oil, out; up, fur; get; joy; yet; chin; she; thin, *then*; zh, leisure; ŋ, ring; ə for *a* in *ago, e* in *agent, i* in *sanity, o* in *comply, u* in *focus*; ′ as in *able* (ā′b'l); Fr. bál; ë, Fr. coeur; ö, Fr. feu; Fr. mon; ô, Fr. coq; ü, Fr. duc; r, Fr. cri; H, G. ich; kh, G. doch. See inside front cover. ☆Americanism; ‡foreign; *hypothetical; < derived from

*ǵhlend- < base *ǵhel-, to shine, whence GLEAM] **1.** to collect (grain, etc. left by reapers) **2.** to collect the remaining grain, etc. from (a reaped field) **3.** *a*) to collect or find out (facts, information, etc.) gradually or bit by bit *b*) to examine or go through (books, etc.) so as to collect certain information —**glean′er** *n.*

glean·ings (-iŋz) *n.pl.* that which is gleaned

glebe (glēb) *n.* [ME. < L. *gleba*, clod, lump of earth (in ML.(Ec.), glebe), akin to *globus*: see GLOBE] **1.** a piece of church land often forming part or all of a benefice **2.** [Poet.] soil; earth; esp., a piece of cultivated land

glede (glēd) *n.* [ME. < OE. *glida*, akin to ON. *gletha* & GLIDE] the common European kite (*Milvus milvus*): also **gled** (gled)

glee (glē) *n.* [ME. *gle* < OE. *gleo*, entertainment, merriment, akin to (rare) ON. *glý* < IE. base *ghleu-, to be merry, jest, whence Gr. *chleuē*, jest] **1.** lively joy; gaiety; merriment **2.** a part song for three or more voices, usually unaccompanied —*SYN.* see MIRTH

glee club [see GLEE, sense 2] a group formed to sing part songs or short choral compositions

gleed (glēd) *n.* [ME. *glede* < OE. *gled* < base of *glowan* (see GLOW)] [Dial.] a glowing coal

glee·ful (glē′fəl) *adj.* full of glee; merry: also **glee′some** (-səm) —**glee′ful·ly** *adv.* —**glee′ful·ness** *n.*

glee·man (glē′mən) *n., pl.* **-men** (-mən) [ME. *gleman* < OE. *gleoman*: see GLEE & MAN] a medieval minstrel

gleet (glēt) *n.* [ME. *glete* < OFr. *glete* < LL. *glittus*, sticky, akin to LL. *glus*, GLUE < IE. base *glei-, whence CLAY] **1.** formerly, any abnormal discharge from the body in man or animals **2.** chronic inflammation of the urethra, as in gonorrhea, characterized by a mucous discharge

gleg (gleg) *adj.* [ME. (northern dial. & Scot.) < ON. *gleggr*, clear, clearsighted < IE. *ghlou* < base *ghel-, to GLEAM] [Scot.] alert, sharp, keen, etc.

glen (glen) *n.* [ME. < Late MScot. < ScotGael. *glenn* (now *gleann*), mountain valley, akin to W. *glyn*] a narrow, secluded valley

Glen·dale (glen′dāl) [GLEN + DALE] **1.** city in SW Calif.: suburb of Los Angeles: pop. 133,000 **2.** city in SC Ariz.: suburb of Phoenix: pop. 36,000

Glen·dow·er (glen′dou ər, glen dou′ər), Owen 1359?–1416?; Welsh chieftain: rebelled against Henry IV

Glen·gar·ry (glen gar′ē) *n., pl.* **-ries** [< *Glengarry*, valley in Scotland] [*sometimes* g-] a Scottish cap for men, creased lengthwise across the top and often having short ribbons at the back: also **Glengarry bonnet** (or **cap**)

Glen More (glen môr′) valley across N Scotland, traversed by the Caledonian Canal: 60 1/2 mi. long

Glenn, Glen (glen) [Celt.: see GLEN] a masculine name

gle·noid (glen′oid, glē′noid) *adj.* [Gr. *glēnoeidēs* < *glēnē*, socket of a joint + *eidos*, form] forming a smooth, shallow cavity or socket for a bone; esp., designating the cavity on the head of the scapula which, together with the head of the humerus, forms the shoulder joint

GLENGARRY

glen plaid [after *Glenurquhart*, clan of *Glen Urquhart*, valley in NW Scotland] [*also* G-] a plaid pattern or cloth with thin crossbarred stripes in black and white and four or more muted colors: also **Glen·ur′quhart plaid** (glen ur′kərt)

gley (glā) *n.* [Russ. *glei* < IE. base *glei-, to stick together, whence CLAY] a sticky, compact, clayey soil that sometimes develops in highly humid regions

gli·a (glī′ə, glē′ə) *n.* [ModL.: see NEUROGLIA] *same as* NEUROGLIA —**gli′al** *adj.*

gli·a·din (glī′ə din) *n.* [Fr. *gliadine* < MGr. *glia*, glue (akin to Gr. *gloios*: see GLUE) + -*d*- + Fr. -*ine*, -IN¹] any of a group of proteins found in the seeds of wheat and rye

glib (glib) *adj.* **glib′ber, glib′best** [orig., slippery < or akin to Du. *glibberig*, slippery, *glibber*, jelly] **1.** done in a smooth, offhand fashion **2.** speaking or spoken in a smooth, fluent, easy manner, often in a way that is too smooth and easy to be convincing —**glib′ly** *adv.* —**glib′ness** *n.*

glide (glīd) *vi.* **glid′ed, glid′ing** [ME. *gliden* < OE. *glidan*, akin to G. *gleiten*, prob. < IE. *ghlei-dh* (< *ghel-, to shine, whence GLASS, GLOW)] **1.** to flow or move smoothly and easily, as in skating **2.** to move by or pass gradually and almost unnoticed, as time **3.** *Aeron. a*) to fly in a glider *b*) to descend at a normal angle of attack with little or no engine power **4.** *Music, Phonet.* to make a glide —*vt.* to cause to glide —*n.* **1.** the act of gliding; smooth, easy flow or movement ☆**2.** a small disk or ball, as of nylon, attached to the underside of furniture legs, etc. to allow easy sliding **3.** *Music* loosely, a slur, portamento, or the like **4.** *Phonet.* an intermediate, nonphonemic sound produced when the speech organs change from the position for one sound to that for another —*SYN.* see SLIDE

glid·er (glīd′ər) *n.* **1.** a person or thing that glides **2.** an aircraft like an airplane except that it has no engine and is carried along by air currents ☆**3.** a porch seat suspended in a frame so that it can glide or swing back and forth

glim (glim) *n.* [ME. *glimme*, radiance, prob. < Scand., as in OSw. *glimma*, akin to MHG. *glim*, a spark & GLEAM] [Slang] **1.** a light, as a lamp, candle, etc. **2.** an eye

glim·mer (glim′ər) *vi.* [ME. *glimeren*, to shine, freq. formation < base of OE. *glæm* (see GLEAM), akin to Du. *glimmeren*, G. *glimmern*] **1.** to give a faint, flickering light **2.** to appear or be seen faintly or dimly —*n.* **1.** a faint, flickering light **2.** a faint manifestation or dim perception —**glim·mer·ing** (-ər iŋ) *n.* a glimmer

glimpse (glimps) *vt.* **glimpsed, glimps′ing** [ME. *glimsen* (with unhistoric -*p*-) < base of OE. *glæm* (see GLEAM), akin to MHG. *glimsen*, MDu. *glinsen*] to catch a brief, quick view of, as in passing; perceive momentarily and incompletely —*vi.* to look quickly; glance (*at*) —*n.* **1.** a brief, sudden shining; flash **2.** a faint, fleeting appearance; slight trace **3.** a brief, quick view

Glin·ka (glin′kä; E. glin′kə), **Mi·kha·il I·va·no·vich** (mē khä ēl′ i vä′nô vich) 1804–57; Russ. composer

glint (glint) *vi.* [ME. *glenten*, prob. < Scand., as in Sw. dial. *glänta*, akin to MHG. *glinzen*, to glint, G. *glänzen*, to shine < IE. *ghlendh- < base *ghel-, to shine, whence GLOW, GLASS] **1.** to shine or reflect with intermittent flashes of light; gleam, flash, or glitter **2.** [Archaic] to move quickly, esp. glancingly —*n.* **1.** a gleam, flash, or glitter **2.** [Scot.] a glimpse

gli·o·ma (glī ō′mə, glē-) *n., pl.* **-ma·ta** (-mə tə), **-mas** [ModL. < MGr. *glia* (akin to *gloios*), GLUE + -*ōma* (see -OMA)] a tumor of the brain, spinal cord, etc., composed of tissue that forms the supporting structure of nerves —**gli·o′ma·tous** (-təs) *adj.*

glis·sade (gli säd′, -säd′) *n.* [Fr. < *glisser*, to slide, glide, prob. a blend < Frank. *glitan, to GLIDE + OFr. *glacier* (see GLACIS)] **1.** an intentional slide by a mountain climber down a steep slope covered with snow **2.** *Ballet* a gliding step —*vi.* **-sad′ed, -sad′ing** to make a glissade; slide or glide

glis·san·do (gli sän′dō) *n., pl.* **-di** (-dē), **-dos** [formed as if It. prp. equivalent to Fr. *glissant*, prp. of *glisser*, to slide: see prec.] *Music* **1.** a sliding effect achieved by sounding a series of adjacent tones in rapid succession, as by running a finger over the white keys of a piano or the strings of a harp **2.** a passage having this effect —*adj., adv.* (performed) with such an effect

glis·ten (glis′'n) *vi.* [ME. *glistnen* (with unhistoric -*t*-) < OE. *glisnian* < base of *glisian*, to shine < IE. *ghleis- < base *ghel-, whence GLEAM, GLASS] to shine or sparkle with reflected light, as a wet or polished surface —*n.* a glistening —*SYN.* see FLASH

glis·ter (glis′tər) *vi., n.* [ME. *glisteren*, prob. < LowG. source, as in MDu. *glinsteren*, MLowG. *glistern*, akin to prec.] *archaic var. of* GLISTEN

glitch (glich) *n.* [< G. colloq. *glitsche*, a slip < *glitschen*, to slip, slide, intens. of G. *gleiten*: see GLIDE] [Slang] a mishap, error, malfunctioning, etc.

glit·ter (glit′ər) *vi.* [ME. *gliteren*, prob. < ON. *glitra*, akin to G. *glitzern*: for IE. base see GLISTEN] **1.** to shine with a sparkling light; be bright; glisten; sparkle **2.** to be strikingly brilliant, showy, or attractive —*n.* **1.** a bright, sparkling light **2.** striking or showy brilliance or attractiveness **3.** bits of glittering material used for decoration —*SYN.* see FLASH

glitter ice [Canad.] a glaze of ice formed by a quickly freezing rain

glit·ter·y (-ē) *adj.* having glitter; glittering

Gli·wi·ce (gli vē′tse) city in S Poland: pop. 164,000

gloam·ing (glō′miŋ) *n.* [ME. (Scot.) *glomyng* < OE. *glomung* < *glom*, twilight, akin to *glowan*, to GLOW: adopted in literature < Scot. dial.] evening dusk; twilight

gloat (glōt) *vi.* [prob. via dial. < OE. *glotian* or cognate ON. *glotta*, to grin scornfully, akin to G. *glotzen*, E. dial. *glout*, to stare < IE. *ghlud- < base *ghel-, to shine, whence GLOW] to gaze or think with exultation, avarice, or malicious pleasure (often with *over*) —*n.* the act of gloating

glob (gläb) *n.* [prob. contr. < GLOBULE, after BLOB] a somewhat rounded mass or lump, as of a thick liquid or semisolid

glob·al (glō′b'l) *adj.* **1.** round like a ball; globe-shaped **2.** of, relating to, or including the whole earth; worldwide [*global* warfare] **3.** complete or comprehensive —**glob′al·ly** *adv.*

☆**glob·al·ism** (-iz'm) *n.* a policy, outlook, etc. that is worldwide in scope —**glob′al·ist** *n., adj.*

glo·bate (glō′bāt) *adj.* [L. *globatus*, pp. of *globare*, to make into a ball < *globus*, GLOBE] round like a ball

globe (glōb) *n.* [ME. < L. *globus*, a ball: for IE. base see CLIMB] **1.** any round, ball-shaped thing; sphere; specif., *a*) the earth *b*) a spherical model of the earth showing the continents, seas, etc. *c*) a similar model of the heavens, showing the constellations, etc. **2.** anything shaped somewhat like a globe; specif., *a*) a round glass container, as for goldfish *b*) a rounded glass cover for a lamp *c*) a small, golden ball used as a symbol of authority —*vt., vi.* **globed, glob′ing** to form or gather into a globe

globe·fish (-fish′) *n., pl.* **-fish′, -fish′es**: see FISH² any of several tropical fishes (family Diodontidae) that can puff themselves into a globular form as a defensive measure by swallowing air or water

globe·flow·er (-flou′ər) *n.* **1.** any of a genus (*Trollius*) of plants of the buttercup family, with white, orange, or yellow globe-shaped flowers **2.** *same as* KERRIA

globe·trot·ter (-trät′ər) *n.* a person who travels widely about the world, esp. one who does so for pleasure or sightseeing —**globe′-trot′ting** *n., adj.*

glo·big·er·i·na ooze (glō bij′ə rī′nə) [ModL. *Globigerina*, a genus of foraminifera (< L. *globus*, a ball, GLOBE + *ger(ere)*, to bear + ModL. *-ina*, taxonomic suffix < L., pl. of *-inus*, -INE¹) + OOZE²] a fine, deep-sea sediment covering approximately one-third of the ocean floors at depths usually between 6,000 to 12,000 ft., consisting predominantly of the empty, calcareous shells of a surface-dwelling genus (*Globigerina*) of foraminifera

glo·bin (glō′bin) *n.* [< (HEMO)GLOBIN] the protein component of hemoglobin: cf. HEME

glo·boid (-boid) *adj.* shaped somewhat like a globe or ball —*n.* anything globoid

glo·bose (-bōs) *adj.* [ME. < L. *globosus*] same as GLOBOID: also **glo′bous** (-bəs) —**glo′bose·ly** *adv.* —**glo·bos′i·ty** (-bäs′ə tē) *n.*

glob·u·lar (gläb′yə lər) *adj.* **1.** shaped like a globe or ball; spherical; round **2.** made up of globules —*SYN.* see ROUND¹

glob·ule (-yōōl) *n.* [Fr. < L. *globulus*, dim. of *globus*, GLOBE] a tiny ball or globe, esp. a drop of liquid

glob·u·lin (-yə lin) *n.* [GLOBUL(E) + -IN¹] any of a group of proteins, fully soluble only in salt solutions, found in both animal and vegetable tissue

glo·chid·i·um (glō kid′ē əm) *n., pl.* -i·a (-ə) [ModL. < Gr. *glōchis*, projecting point (cf. GLOSS²) + ModL. *-idium*, dim. suffix < Gr. *-idion*] **1.** *Bot.* a barbed hair or bristle, as on certain cacti or on the spore masses of ferns **2.** *Zool.* the parasitic larval stage of freshwater mussels (family Unionidae) which infests the gills, etc. of many fishes —**glo·chid′i·ate** (-it) *adj.*

glock·en·spiel (gläk′ən spēl′, -shpēl′) *n.* [G. < *glocke*, a bell (see CLOCK¹) + *spiel*, play] a percussion instrument with chromatically tuned, flat metal bars set in a frame, that produce bell-like tones when struck with small hammers

glögg, glogg (glög) *n.* [Sw. *glögg* < *glödga*, to mull, lit., to burn < OSw. < *glöth*, glowing coal, akin to OE. *glæd*; see GLEED] a Swedish drink made by heating wines, brandy, etc. with sugar and spices and adding raisins and almonds as a garnish

☆**glom** (gläm) *vt.* **glommed, glom′ming** [earlier *glaum* < Scot. dial., prob. of ScotGael. orig.] [Slang] **1.** to seize; grab **2.** to steal **3.** to look over; view; see —**glom onto** [Slang] to take and hold; obtain; get

glom·er·ate (gläm′ər it) *adj.* [L. *glomeratus*, pp. of *glomerare*, to wind or make into a ball < *glomus*, a ball, sphere, akin to *globus*, GLOBE] formed into a rounded mass or ball; clustered

glom·er·a·tion (gläm′ə rā′shən) *n.* [L. *glomeratio* < *glomeratus*: see prec.] **1.** the act of forming into a rounded mass; agglomeration or conglomeration **2.** something formed into a rounded mass; cluster

glom·er·u·late (glä mer′yoo lit) *adj.* [< ff. + -ATE¹] grouped in small, dense clusters

glom·er·ule (gläm′ər ōōl′) *n.* [Fr. *glomérule* < ModL. *glomerulus*, dim. < L. *glomus* (gen. *glomeris*), a ball, round knot: see GLOMERATE] **1.** a compact cluster, as of a flower head **2.** same as GLOMERULUS

glo·mer·u·lo·ne·phri·tis (glä mer′yoo lō′nef rīt′is) *n.* [ModL.: see prec. & NEPHRITIS] inflammation of the kidneys, primarily involving the glomeruli

glo·mer·u·lus (glä mer′yoo ləs) *n., pl.* -li (-lī′) [ModL.: see GLOMERULE] any of the small globular structures of the kidney, each containing a loop of blood capillaries, which act as filters, initiating the formation of urine —**glo·mer′u·lar** (-lər) *adj.*

Glom·ma (glô′mə) river in SE Norway, flowing south into the Skagerrak: longest river in Scandinavia: 375 mi.

glon·o·in (glän′ō in) *n.* [GL(YCERIN) + O(XYGEN) + N(ITR)O(GEN) + -IN¹] same as NITROGLYCERIN

gloom (glōōm) *vi.* [< ME. *gloum(b)en*, to look morose, prob. < Scand., as in Norw. dial. *glome*, to stare somberly, akin to EFris. *glumen*, to peer secretly (< IE. *ĝhlu-* base *ĝhel-*, whence GLEAM, GLOW): meaning infl. by OE. *glom*, twilight] **1.** to be or look morose, displeased, or dejected **2.** to be, become, or appear dark, dim, or dismal —*vt.* to make dark, dismal, dejected, etc. —*n.* **1.** darkness; dimness; obscurity **2.** a dark or dim place **3.** deep sadness or hopelessness; dejection

gloom·y (-ē) *adj.* **gloom′i·er, gloom′i·est** **1.** overspread with or enveloped in darkness or dimness **2.** *a)* very sad or dejected; hopeless; melancholy *b)* morose or sullen **3.** causing gloom; dismal; depressing —*SYN.* see DARK —**gloom′i·ly** *adv.* —**gloom′i·ness** *n.*

☆**glop** (gläp) *n.* [< ? GL(UE) + (SL)OP] [Slang] any soft, gluey substance; thick liquid

Glo·ri·a (glôr′ē ə, glō′rē ə) [L., glory] a feminine name —*n.* **1.** short for *a)* GLORIA IN EXCELSIS DEO *b)* GLORIA PATRI **2.** the music for either of these **3.** [g-] a halo or its

representation in art **4.** [g-] a closely woven cloth of silk and wool, silk and cotton, etc. with a glossy surface, used for umbrellas, etc.

Gloria in ex·cel·sis De·o (in ek shel′sis dā′ō,- sel′-) [L.] glory (be) to God on high: first words of the greater doxology

Gloria Pa·tri (pä′trē) [L.] glory (be) to the Father: first words of the lesser doxology

glo·ri·fy (glôr′ə fī′) *vt.* **-fied′, -fy′ing** [ME. *glorifien* < OFr. *glorifier* < LL.(Ec.) *glorificare*, to glorify < L. *gloria*, glory + *facere*, to make: see FACT] **1.** to make glorious; give glory to **2.** to exalt and honor (God) as in worship **3.** to praise extravagantly; honor; extol **4.** to make seem better, larger, finer, etc. than is actually the case —**glo′ri·fi·ca′tion** *n.* —**glo′ri·fi′er** *n.*

glo·ri·ole (glôr′i ōl′) *n.* [Fr. < L. *gloriola*, dim. of *gloria*, glory] a halo

glo·ri·ous (glôr′ē əs) *adj.* [ME. & Anglo-Fr. < OFr. *glorios* < L. *gloriosus*] **1.** full of glory; illustrious **2.** giving or bringing glory **3.** receiving or deserving glory **4.** splendid; magnificent **5.** [Colloq.] very delightful or enjoyable —*SYN.* see SPLENDID —**glo′ri·ous·ly** *adv.* —**glo′ri·ous·ness** *n.*

glo·ry (glôr′ē) *n., pl.* -ries [ME. *glorie* < OFr. < L. *gloria*] **1.** *a)* great honor and admiration won by doing something important or valuable; fame; renown *b)* anything bringing this **2.** worshipful adoration or praise **3.** the condition of highest achievement, splendor, prosperity, etc. [Greece in her *glory*] **4.** radiant beauty or splendor; magnificence **5.** heaven or the bliss of heaven **6.** *a)* a halo or its representation in art *b)* any circle of light —*vi.* **-ried, -ry·ing** to be very proud; rejoice; exult (with *in*) —**gone to glory** dead —**in one's glory** at one's best, happiest, etc.

gloss¹ (glôs, gläs) *n.* [prob. < Scand., as in Norw. dial. *glosa*, to gleam: for IE. base see GLASS] **1.** the brightness or luster of a smooth, polished surface; sheen **2.** *a)* deceptively smooth or pleasant outward appearance, as in manners or speech —*vt.* **1.** to give a polished, shiny surface to; make lustrous **2.** [a blend of prec. sense & GLOSS²] to cover up (an error, inadequacy, fault, etc.) or make appear right by specious argument or by minimizing (often with *over*) —*vi.* to become shiny —**gloss′er** *n.*

gloss² (glôs, gläs) *n.* [ME. *glose* < OFr. or < ML. *glosa*, for L. *glossa*, foreign or strange word needing explanation < Gr. *glōssa*, orig., tongue, language < **glōchia*, pointed object < IE. base **glogh-*, thorn, point, whence OSlav. *gloge*, thorn] **1.** words of explanation or translation inserted between the lines of a text **2.** a note of comment or explanation accompanying a text, as in a footnote or margin **3.** a collection of such notes; glossary **4.** a false or misleading interpretation —*vt.* **1.** to furnish (a text) with glosses **2.** to interpret falsely —*vi.* to write notes of explanation for a text; annotate —**gloss′er** *n.*

gloss. glossary

glos·sa (gläs′ə, glôs′-) *n., pl.* -sae (-ē), -sas [ModL. < Gr. *glōssa*, tongue] the tongue of a vertebrate, or any tongue-like structure, as of a butterfly or moth; esp., either of the middle lobes of the labium of an insect

glos·sal (-'l) *adj.* [prec. + -AL] of the tongue

glos·sa·ry (-ə rē) *n., pl.* -ries [ME. *glosarie* < L. *glossarium* < *glossa*: see GLOSS²] a list of difficult, technical, or foreign terms with definitions or translations, as for some particular author, field of knowledge, etc., often included in alphabetical listing at the end of a textbook —**glos·sar·i·al** (glä ser′ē əl) *adj.* —**glos′sar·ist** *n.*

glos·sa·tor (glä sāt′ər, gläs′āt′ər) *n.* [ME. *glosatour* < ML. *glossator*] a person who writes textual glosses

glos·si·tis (glä sīt′is, glō-) *n.* [GLOSS(O)- + -ITIS] *Med.* inflammation of the tongue —**glos·sit′ic** (-sit′ik) *adj.*

glos·so- (gläs′ō, glôs′-) [< Gr. *glōssa*, the tongue: see GLOSS²] *a combining form meaning:* **1.** the tongue, or the tongue and **2.** of words or language Also, before a vowel, **gloss-**

glos·sog·ra·pher (glä säg′rə fər, glô-) *n.* [Gr. *glōssographos* < *glōssa* (see GLOSS²) + *graphein*, to write] a writer of glosses or glossaries —**glos·sog′ra·phy** *n.*

glos·so·la·li·a (gläs′ə lā′lē ə, glôs′-) *n.* [ModL. < Gr. *glōsso-* (< *glōssa*, tongue: see GLOSS²) + *lalia*, a speaking < *lalein*, to speak, prattle, of echoic orig.] an ecstatic or apparently ecstatic utterance of unintelligible speechlike sounds, viewed by some as a manifestation of deep religious experience

gloss·y (glôs′ē, gläs′-) *adj.* **gloss′i·er, gloss′i·est** [GLOSS¹ + -Y²] **1.** having a smooth, shiny appearance or finish **2.** smooth and plausible; specious —*n., pl.* **gloss′ies** **1.** *Photog.* a print with a glossy finish: opposed to MATTE² **2.** [Colloq.] a magazine printed on glossy paper; slick —**gloss′i·ly** *adv.* —**gloss′i·ness** *n.*

glot·tal (glät′'l) *adj.* of or produced in or at the glottis: also **glot′tic** (-ik)

glottal stop a speech sound (IPA symbol [ʔ]) produced by a momentary complete closure of the glottis: it is sometimes heard as a variant for medial *t* (in *bottle, water,* etc.), in some English dialects

glot·tis (glät′is) *n., pl.* **-tis·es, -ti·des** (-ə dēz′) [ModL.

GLOCKENSPIEL

< Gr. *glōttis* < *glōtta*, Attic var. of *glōssa:* see GLOSS²] the opening between the vocal cords in the larynx

glot·to·chro·nol·o·gy (glät′ō krə näl′ə jē) *n.* [see prec. & CHRONOLOGY] a method for estimating the dates when the branches of a family of languages separated from the parent language and from one another

Glouces·ter (gläs′tər, glôs′-) 1. city in SW England, on the Severn: pop. 71,000 2. *same as* GLOUCESTERSHIRE 3. city in NE Mass.: pop. 28,000

Glouces·ter·shire (-shir) county of SW England, on Severn estuary: 1,258 sq. mi.; pop. 1,024,000; county seat, Gloucester

glove (gluv) *n.* [ME. < OE. *glof* & ON. *glofi* < ? Gmc. **ga-lōfa* < **ga-*, together (OE. *ge-*) + **lōfa* (Goth. *lōfa*), palm of the hand: cf. LUFF] 1. a covering for the hand, made of leather, cloth, etc., with a separate sheath for each finger and the thumb 2. *Sports* a) a similar covering of padded leather worn by baseball players in the field: see also MITT b) a padded mitten worn by boxers: usually **boxing glove** —*vt.* **gloved, glov′ing** 1. to supply with gloves 2. to cover with or as with a glove ☆3. *Baseball* to catch (a ball) —**put on the gloves** [Colloq.] to box

glove box a sealed enclosure containing a window for viewing and ports with attached gloves for handling toxic, radioactive, sterile, etc. materials inside the enclosure

glove compartment a compartment built into the dashboard of an automobile, for miscellaneous articles

glov·er (-ər) *n.* one who makes or sells gloves

glow (glō) *vi.* [ME. *glowen* < OE. *glowan*, akin to G. *glühen* < IE. **ghlō-* < base **ghel-*, to shine, whence Gr. *chlóros*, light green & GLEAM, YELLOW] 1. to give off a bright light as a result of great heat; be incandescent or red-hot 2. to give out a steady, even light without flame or blaze 3. to be or feel hot; give out heat 4. to radiate health or high spirits 5. to be elated or enlivened by emotion [to glow with pride] 6. to show brilliant, conspicuous colors; be bright; specif., a) to be flushed, as from emotion, enthusiasm, etc.; be rosy or ruddy b) to gleam; flash; light up: said of the eyes c) to be bright or luminescent: said of colors —*n.* 1. light given off as a result of great heat; incandescence 2. steady, even light without flame or blaze 3. brilliance, vividness, or luminescence of color 4. brightness of skin color, as from good health, emotion, etc.; flush 5. a sensation of warmth and well-being 6. warmth of emotion; ardor, eagerness, etc. —*SYN.* see BLAZE¹ —**glow′ing** *adj.* —**glow′ing·ly** *adv.*

glow·er (glou′ər) *vi.* [ME. *glouren*, var. of *gloren*, prob. < ON., as in Norw. dial. *glora*, Sw. dial. *glora*, to stare, gape < IE. **ghlöu-* < base **ghel-:* see prec.] to stare with sullen anger; scowl —*n.* a sullen, angry, or ill-humored stare; scowl —*SYN.* see FROWN —**glow′er·ing** *adj.* —**glow′er·ing·ly** *adv.*

glow lamp (glō) a type of discharge tube: see DISCHARGE TUBE

glow·worm (-wʉrm′) *n.* any of a number of wingless insects or insect larvae (family Lampyridae) that give off a luminescent light; esp., the wingless female or the larva of the firefly

glox·in·i·a (gläk sin′ē ə) *n.* [ModL., after B. P. *Gloxin,* 18th-c. Ger. botanist] a cultivated tropical plant (*Sinningia speciosa*) of the gesneria family, with large, downy leaves and bell-shaped flowers of various colors

gloze (glōz) *vt.* **glozed, gloz′ing** [ME. *glosen* < OFr. *gloser* < *glose:* see GLOSS²] 1. orig., to make glosses, or comments, on; explain 2. to explain away; gloss (over) —*vi.* [Obs.] to fawn or flatter —*n.* [Archaic or Rare] 1. a gloss; comment 2. flattery 3. specious talk or insincere action

glu·ca·gon (glōō′kə gän) *n.* [G. *glukagon* < *glukose* (< Fr. *glucose,* GLUCOSE) + Gr. *agōn,* a struggle (see AGON): so named from effect on insulin] a hormone formed in the pancreas of vertebrates that increases the concentration of blood sugar and opposes the action of insulin

glu·ci·num (glōō sī′nəm) *n.* [ModL. < Fr. *glucine* < Gr. *glykys,* sweet (see GLUCOSE): from the sweet taste of some of its salts] *a former name for* BERYLLIUM

Gluck (glōōk) 1. **Al·ma** (al′mə), (born *Reba Fiersohn*) 1884–1938; U.S. operatic soprano, born in Romania 2. **Chris·toph Wil·li·bald** (kris′tôf vil′i bält′), 1714–87; Ger. composer

glu·co·nate (glōō′kə nāt′) *n.* a salt or ester of gluconic acid

glu·co·ne·o·gen·e·sis (glōō′kō nē ō jen′ə sis) *n. same as* GLYCONEOGENESIS

glu·con·ic acid (glōō kän′ik) [GLUC(OSE) + -ON(E) + -IC] a syrupy liquid, C₆H₁₂O₇, prepared by the oxidation of dextrose and used in food products and pharmaceuticals, for cleaning metals, etc.

glu·co·pro·tein (glōō′kō prō′tēn, -tē in) *n. same as* GLYCOPROTEIN

glu·cose (glōō′kōs) *n.* [Fr. < Gr. *gleúkos,* sweet wine, sweetness, akin to *glykys,* sweet: see GLYCERIN] a crystalline sugar, C₆H₁₂O₆, occurring naturally in fruits, honey, etc.: the commercial form, also containing dextrin and maltose, is prepared as a sweet syrup or, upon desiccation, as a light-colored solid, by the hydrolysis of starch in the presence of dilute acids

glu·co·side (glōō′kə sīd′) *n.* [GLUCOS(E) + -IDE] any of a class of compounds, either natural or synthetic, which on hydrolysis yield glucose and one or more other substances —**glu′co·sid′ic** (-sid′ik) *adj.*

glue (glōō) *n.* [ME. *gleu* < OFr. *glu,* birdlime < LL. *glus*

(gen. *glutis*), glue, akin to L. *gluten,* glue, Gr. *gloios,* sticky oil: for IE. base see CLAY] 1. a hard, brittle gelatin made by boiling animal skins, bones, hoofs, etc. to a jelly: when heated in water, it forms a sticky, viscous liquid used to stick things together 2. any of various similar adhesive preparations made from casein, resin, etc. —*vt.* **glued, glu′ing** to make stick with or as with glue —**glu′er** *n.*

glue·pot (-pät′) *n.* a pot like a double boiler for melting glue

glue·y (-ē) *adj.* **glu′i·er, glu′i·est** 1. like glue; sticky 2. covered with or full of glue —**glu′i·ly** *adv.*

glum (glum) *adj.* **glum′mer, glum′mest** [prob. < ME. *glomen,* var. of *gloum(b)en:* see GLOOM] feeling or looking gloomy, sullen, or morose —*SYN.* see SULLEN —**glum′ly** *adv.* —**glum′ness** *n.*

glu·ma·ceous (glōō mā′shəs) *adj.* 1. having glumes 2. like glumes

glume (glōōm) *n.* [ModL. *gluma* < L., husk < base of *glubere,* to peel: for IE. base see CLEAVE¹] either of the two empty sterile bracts at the base of a grass spikelet, or a similar structure on the spikelets of sedges

glut (glut) *vi.* **glut′ted, glut′ting** [ME. *glutten* < OFr. *gloter,* to swallow < L. *gluttire,* prob. ult. < IE. base **gel-*, to devour, whence G. *kehle,* OE. *ceole,* throat] to eat like a glutton; overindulge —*vt.* 1. to feed, fill, supply, etc. to excess; surfeit 2. to flood (the market) with certain goods so that the supply is greater than the demand —*n.* [< the *v.*] 1. a glutting or being glutted 2. a supply of certain goods that is greater than the demand —*SYN.* see SATIATE

glu·ta·mate (glōōt′ə māt′) *n.* a salt or ester of glutamic acid

glu·tam·ic acid (glōō tam′ik) [GLUT(EN) + AM(INO) + -IC] an amino acid, C₅H₉O₄N, prepared by the hydrolysis of proteins, as wheat gluten or beet molasses

glu·ta·mine (glōōt′ə mēn′, -min) *n.* [GLUT(EN) + AMINE] a crystalline amino acid, C₅H₁₀O₃, found in the leaves and roots of certain plants

glu·te·al (glōō tē′əl, glōōt′ē-) *adj.* [GLUTE(US) + -AL] of or near the muscles of the buttocks

glu·ten (glōōt′'n) *n.* [L. *gluten,* GLUE] a gray, sticky, nutritious protein substance containing gliadin, found in wheat and other grain: it gives dough its tough, elastic quality —**glu′ten·ous** *adj.*

gluten bread bread made from flour rich in gluten and low in starch

glu·te·us (glōō tē′əs, glōōt′ē-) *n., pl.* **-te′i** (-ī) [ModL. < Gr. *gloutos,* rump, buttock: for IE. base see CLIMB] any of the three muscles that form each of the buttocks and act to extend, abduct, and rotate the thigh

glu·ti·nous (glōōt′'n əs) *adj.* [ME. < L. *glutinosus* < *gluten,* GLUE] gluey; sticky —**glu′ti·nous·ly** *adv.*

glut·ton (glut′'n) *n.* [ME. < OFr. *glotoun* < L. *gluto, glutto* < *glutire, gluttire,* to devour, akin to *gula,* GULLET] 1. a person who greedily eats too much 2. a person with a great capacity for something [a *glutton* for work] 3. [transl. for G. *vielfrass,* lit., great devourer] a furry, northern animal (*Gulo gulo*) related to the marten and weasel but larger: the American variety is the WOLVERINE —*SYN.* see EPICURE —**glut′ton·ize′** *vt., vi.* **-ized′, -iz′ing**

glut·ton·ous (-əs) *adj.* [ME. *glotonous* < OFr. *glotonos:* see GLUTTON] inclined to eat too much and greedily —**glut′ton·ous·ly** *adv.*

glut·ton·y (-ē) *n., pl.* **-ton·ies** [ME. *glotonie* < OFr. < *gloton,* GLUTTON] the habit or act of eating too much

glyc·er·al·de·hyde (glis′ər al′də hīd′) *n.* an aldehyde, C₃H₆O₃, produced by the oxidation of some sugars

glyc·er·ate (glis′ər āt′) *n.* a salt or ester of glyceric acid

gly·cer·ic acid (gli ser′ik, glis′ər-) a syrupy liquid, C₃H₆O₄, occurring in two optically active forms: it is prepared by the oxidation of glycerin

glyc·er·ide (glis′ər īd′) *n.* a natural or synthetic ester of glycerol —**glyc′er·id′ic** (-id′ik) *adj.*

glyc·er·in (glis′ər in, glis′rin) *n.* [Fr. *glycérine* < Gr. *glykeros,* sweet < **dlykeros* < ? IE. base **dlku-,* sweet, whence Gr. *glykys,* L. *dulcis,* sweet] *popular and commercial term for* GLYCEROL: also sp. **glyc′er·ine**

glyc·er·in·ate (glis′ər ə nāt′) *vt.* **-at′ed, -at′ing** to treat with glycerin, or glycerol —**glyc′er·i·na′tion** *n.*

glyc·er·ol (glis′ər ōl′, -ôl′) *n.* [GLYCER(IN) + -OL¹] an odorless, colorless, syrupy liquid, C₃H₈O₃, prepared by the hydrolysis of fats and oils: it is used as a solvent, skin lotion, food preservative, etc., and in the manufacture of explosives, alkyd resins, etc.: cf. GLYCERIN

glyc·er·yl (-il′) *n.* [GLYCER(IN) + -YL] the trivalent radical of glycerol, C₃H₅

gly·cine (glī′sēn) *n.* [< Gr. *glykys,* sweet (see GLYCERIN) + -INE⁴] a sweet, crystalline substance, C₂H₅O₂N, the simplest amino acid, obtained by hydrolysis of proteins

gly·co- (glī′kō, -kə) [Gr. *glyko-* < *glykys:* see GLYCERIN] a combining form meaning variously: glycerol, sugar, glycogen, glycine: also, before a vowel, **glyc-**

gly·co·gen (glī′kə jən) *n.* [prec. + -GEN] a partially soluble, starchlike substance, (C₆H₁₀O₅)ₓ, produced in animal tissues, esp. in the liver and muscles, and changed into a simple sugar as the body needs it

gly·co·gen·e·sis (glī′kə jen′ə sis) *n.* [ModL. < prec., after -GENESIS] the formation of glycogen

gly·co·gen·ic (-jen′ik) *adj.* of glycogen or glycogenesis

gly·col (glī′kōl, -kôl) *n.* [GLYC(ERIN) + -OL¹] 1. *same as*

ETHYLENE GLYCOL 2. any of a group of alcohols of which ethylene glycol is the type

gly·col·ic acid (gli käl′ik) a crystalline acid, $C_2H_4O_3$, found naturally in unripe grapes or prepared by the oxidation of glycol

gly·col·y·sis (-ə sis) n. [GLYCO- + -LYSIS] the breakdown of sugars, glycogen, or other carbohydrates by enzymes into simpler compounds, such as lactic acid, through the intermediate production of ATP —**gly·co·lyt·ic** (glī′kə lit′ik) adj.

gly·co·ne·o·gen·e·sis (glī′kō nē′ə jen′ə sis) n. [GLYCO- + NEO- + -GENESIS] the production of carbohydrates, esp. glycogen, from substances not glucosidic

gly·co·pro·tein (-prō′-, -tē in) n. any of a class of compounds in which a protein is combined with a carbohydrate group

gly·co·side (glī′kə sīd′) n. [Fr. < glycose (altered after Gr. glykys), for glucose, GLUCOSE + -ide, -IDE] any of a group of sugar derivatives, widely distributed in plants, which on hydrolysis yield a sugar and one or more other substances —**gly′co·sid′ic** (-sid′ik) adj.

gly·co·su·ri·a (glī′kə syoor′ē ə, -soor′-) n. [ModL.: see GLYCO- & -URIA] the presence of sugar in the urine, often associated with diabetes mellitus —**gly′co·su′ric** adj.

glyph (glif) n. [Gr. glyphē, a carving < glyphein, to carve, cut < IE. base *gleubh-, whence CLEAVE[1]] 1. a pictograph or other symbolic character or sign, esp. when cut into a surface or carved in relief 2. Archit. a vertical channel or groove —**glyph′ic** adj.

glyph·og·ra·phy (gli fäg′rə fē) n. [< Gr. glyphē (see GLYPH) + -GRAPHY] a method of producing a printing plate by engraving on a wax-coated copperplate which is then used to make an electrotype

glyp·tic (glip′tik) adj. [Fr. glyptique < Gr. glyptikos < Gr. glyptos, carved < glyphein; see GLYPH] having to do with carving or engraving, esp. on gems

glyp·tics (-tiks) n.pl. [with sing. v.] [< prec.] the art of carving or engraving designs on gems, etc.

glyp·to·dont (glip′tə dänt′) n. [ModL. < Gr. glyptos (see GLYPTIC) + -ODONT: so called from its fluted teeth] an extinct S. American mammal, related to the armadillo but much larger

GLYPTODONT
(to 9 ft. long)

glyp·to·graph (-graf′) n. [< Gr. glyptos (see GLYPTIC) + -GRAPH] 1. a design cut or engraved on a gem, seal, etc. 2. a gem, seal, etc. so engraved —**glyp·tog·ra·phy** (glip täg′rə fē) n.

gm. gram; grams

G.M. 1. General Manager **2.** Grand Master

G-man (jē-man′) n., pl. G-men′ (-men′) [associated with g(overnment) man, but prob. orig. of officers in the G division of the Dublin Police] [Colloq.] ☆an agent of the Federal Bureau of Investigation

Gmc. Germanic

GMT, G.M.T., G.m.t. Greenwich mean time

gnar, gnarr (när) vi. **gnarred, gnar′ring** [echoic] [Now Rare] to snarl or growl

gnarl[1] (närl) n. [back-formation < GNARLED] a knot on the trunk or branch of a tree —vt. to make knotted or twisted; contort —vi. to form gnarls

gnarl[2] (närl) vi. [freq. of echoic gnar] to snarl; growl

gnarled (närld) adj. [var. of KNURLED] **1.** knotty and twisted, as the trunk of an old tree **2.** roughened, hardened, sinewy, etc., as hands that do rough work Also **gnarl′y, gnarl′i·er, gnarl′i·est**

gnash (nash) vt. [Early ModE. for earlier gnast < ME. gnasten, prob. < ON. gnista, to gnash (the teeth), gnastan, gnashing, prob. < IE. base *ghen-, whence GNAW] **1.** to grind or strike (the teeth) together, as in anger or pain **2.** to bite by grinding the teeth —vi. to grind the teeth together —n. the act of gnashing

gnat (nat) n. [ME. < OE. gnæt, akin to G. dial. gnatze, LowG. gnatte < IE. *ghnedh- < base *ghen-, whence GNAW] **1.** any of various unrelated, small, two-winged insects of which can bite or sting **2.** [Brit.] a mosquito —**strain at a gnat** to hesitate or have scruples about trifles: Matt. 23:24 —**gnat′ty** adj.

gnath·ic (nath′ik) adj. [< Gr. gnathos, the jaw (for IE. base see CHIN) + -IC] of the jaw

gnathic index a measurement of the relative amount of protrusion of the jaw, expressed in terms of the ratio of the distance from the nasion to the basion (arbitrarily taken as 100) to the distance from the basion to the middle point of the alveolar process

gna·thite (nā′thīt, nath′īt) n. [< Gr. gnathos, jaw + -ITE[1]] a mouth appendage of an arthropod, modified for chewing

gna·thon·ic (na thän′ik) adj. [< Gnatho, sycophant in Terence's play Eunuchus] [Rare] fawning or flattering

-gnathous [< Gr. gnathos (see GNATHIC)] a combining form meaning having (a specified kind of) jaw [prognathous]

gnaw (nô) vt. **gnawed, gnawed** or, rarely, **gnawn, gnaw′ing** [ME. gnawen < OE. gnagen, akin to G. nagen (OHG. gnagan) < IE. base *ghen- < base *ghen-, to gnaw away, rub away, whence GNASH, GNAT] **1.** to cut, bite, and wear away bit by bit with the teeth **2.** to make by gnawing [to gnaw a hole] **3.** to consume; wear away; corrode **4.** to torment, as by constant pain, fear, etc.; harass —vi. **1.** to bite repeatedly (with on, away, at, etc.) **2.** to produce an effect of continual biting, consuming, corroding, etc. (with on, away, at, etc.); torment

gnaw·ing (-in) n. **1.** a sensation of dull, constant pain or suffering **2.** [pl.] pangs, esp. of hunger

gneiss (nis) n. [G. gneiss < OHG. gneisto, a spark, akin to ON. gneisti, OE. gnast: from the luster of certain of the components] a coarse-grained, metamorphic rock resembling granite, consisting of alternating layers of different minerals, such as feldspar, quartz, mica, and hornblende, and having a banded appearance —**gneiss′ic** adj. —**gneiss′oid** adj.

gnoc·chi (nä′kē, nô′-; It. nyôk′kē) n. [It., pl. of gnocco, dumpling, altered < nocchio, knot (in wood), prob. < Langobardic word akin to MHG. knoche, a knot, gnarl] small, variously shaped dumplings of flour, and sometimes potato, served with a sauce

gnome[1] (nōm) n. [Fr. < ModL. gnomus < Gr. gnōmē (see ff.): so called by Paracelsus, prob. from the belief that gnomes had occult knowledge of the earth] Folklore any of a race of small, misshapen dwarfs, supposed to dwell in the earth and guard its treasures —**gnom′ish** adj.

gnome[2] (nōm) n. [LL. gnome, a sentence, maxim < Gr. gnōmē, thought, judgment, intelligence < gignōskein, to KNOW] a wise, pithy saying; maxim

gno·mic (nō′mik) adj. [Gr. gnōmikos < gnōmē: see prec.] **1.** wise and pithy; full of aphorisms **2.** designating or of a writer of aphorisms

gno·mon (nō′män) n. [L. < Gr. gnōmōn, one who knows or examines, index of a sundial < base of gignōskein, to KNOW] **1.** a column, pin on a sundial, etc. that casts a shadow indicating the time of day: see SUNDIAL, illus. **2.** the part of a parallelogram remaining after a similar, smaller parallelogram has been taken from one of its corners

gno·mon·ic (nō män′ik) adj. **1.** of a gnomon, or sundial **2.** of the measurement of time by sundials

-gnomy [Gr. -gnōmia < gnōmē: see GNOME[2]] a combining form meaning art or science of judging or determining [physiognomy]

gno·sis (nō′sis) n. [LL.(Ec.) < Gr. gnōsis, knowledge < gignōskein, to KNOW] positive, intuitive knowledge in spiritual matters, such as the Gnostics claimed to have

-gnosis [< Gr. gnōsis: see prec.] a combining form meaning knowledge, recognition [diagnosis]

gnos·tic (näs′tik) adj. [Gr. gnōstikos < gnōsis: see GNOSIS] **1.** of or having knowledge **2.** [G-] of the Gnostics or Gnosticism —n. [LL.(Ec.) gnosticus < Gr. gnōstikos] [G-] a believer in Gnosticism

Gnos·ti·cism (näs′tə siz'm) n. a system of belief combining ideas derived from Greek philosophy, Oriental mysticism, and, ultimately, Christianity, and stressing salvation through gnosis

GNP gross national product

gnu (nōō, nyōō) n., pl. **gnus, gnu:** see PLURAL, II, D, 1 [< the native (Bushman) name] either of two large African antelopes (genus Connochaetes) with an oxlike head, horns that curve forward, and a horselike mane and tail; wildebeest

GNU (40–50 in. high at shoulder)

go[1] (gō) vi. **went, gone, go′ing** [ME. gon < OE. gan, akin to Du. gaan, G. gehen < IE. base *ghē-, orig., to leave behind, go away, whence Sans. jihīlē, (he) goes; the pt. WENT is < WEND replacing OE. eode, ME. yede] I. indicating motion without reference to destination or point of departure **1.** to move along; travel; proceed [to go 90 miles an hour] **2.** to be moving [who goes there?] **3.** a) to be in operation, as a mechanism, action, etc. b) to work or operate properly; function [a clock that isn't going] **4.** to behave in a certain way; gesture, act, or make sounds as specified or shown [the balloon went "pop"] **5.** to take or follow a particular course, line of action, etc.; specif., a) to turn out; result [the war went badly] b) to be guided, regulated, or directed by a procedure, method, etc. [to go by what someone says] c) to take its course; proceed [how is the evening going?] Sometimes used merely to emphasize a following verb [did you have to go and do that?] **6.** to pass: said of time **7.** to pass from person to person [a rumor went through the office] **8.** to be known or accepted [to go by the name of Lindsay] **9.** to move about or be in a certain condition or state, usually for some time [to go in rags] **10.** to pass into a certain condition, state, etc.; become; turn [to go mad] **11.** to have a certain form, arrangement, etc.; be expressed,

phrased, voiced, or sung [as the saying *goes*] 12. to be or act in harmony; fit in [a hat that *goes* well with the dress] 13. to put oneself [to go to some trouble] 14. to contribute to a result; tend; help [facts that go to prove a case] ☆15. to have force, validity, acceptance, etc. [that rule still *goes*, anything *goes*] 16. [Colloq.] to perform in an especially inspired or exciting manner [a jazz band that can really *go*] II. *indicating motion from a point of departure* 1. to move off; leave; depart 2. to begin to move off, as in a race: used as a command 3. *a)* orig., to leave a court of justice *b)* to continue (unpunished, unrewarded, unrequited, etc.) 4. to cease to have an effect; come to an end; pass away [the pain has *gone*] 5. to die 6. to be removed or eliminated [the third paragraph had to *go*] 7. to break away; be carried away or broken off [the mast *went* in the storm] 8. to fail; give way [his eyesight is *going*] 9. to be given up or sacrificed [the country house must *go*] 10. to pass into the hands of someone; be allotted, awarded, or given [the prize goes to Jean] 11. to be sold (*for* a specified sum) 12. [Colloq.] to pass bodily waste matter; relieve oneself III. *indicating motion toward a place, point, etc.* 1. to move toward a place or person or in a certain direction [to go to the back of the room] 2. to move out of sight or out of the presence of the speaker: used as a command 3. to make regularly scheduled trips as specified [a bus that *goes* to Chicago] 4. *a)* to extend, lead, reach, run, etc. to a place [a road that *goes* to London] *b)* to be able to extend or reach [the belt won't *go* around his waist] 5. to move toward, enter, or attend and then take part in the activities of, engage in, etc.: *a)* additional meaning is conveyed by the use of a noun governed by *to*, or by a participle [to go to college, to go swimming] *b)* reason for going is indicated by an infinitive, by *and* with a verb, or by a noun governed by *to* [to go to learn, to go to breakfast] 6. to be capable of passing (*through*), fitting (*into*), etc. [it won't go through the door] 7. to be capable of being divided (*into*) [5 goes into 10 twice] 8. to carry one's case, plan, etc. (*to* an authority) 9. to turn to or resort (*to*) [to go to war] 10. to carry one's activity to specified lengths; extend or reach so far in behavior, action, etc. [to go too far in one's protests] 11. to endure; last; hold out 12. to have a particular or regular place or position [the shirts go in the top drawer] —*vt.* 1. to travel or proceed along [he's *going* my way] 2. to bet; wager; ☆3. [Colloq.] to tolerate; put up with [I can't *go* him] 4. [Colloq.] to furnish (bail) for an arrested person 5. [Colloq.] to be willing to pay, bid, etc. (a specified sum) ☆6. [Colloq.] to appreciate or enjoy [could you go a piece of pie?] —*n.*, *pl.* **goes** 1. the act of going 2. something that operates successfully; a success [to make a go of a marriage] 3. [Colloq.] the power of going; animation; energy 4. [Colloq.] a state of affairs ☆5. [Colloq.] an agreement, or bargain [is it a go?] 6. [Colloq.] a try; attempt; endeavor 7. [Brit. Colloq.] a quantity given or taken at one time 8. Cribbage a call made by a player who cannot play a card because any card in his hand will carry the count above 31 —*adj.* [Slang: orig. astronaut's jargon] *a)* functioning properly or ready to go *b)* all right; OK —**as people** (or **things**) **go** in comparison with how other people (or things) are —☆**from the word "go"** from the outset —**go about** 1. to be occupied with; be busy at; do 2. to move from place to place; circulate 3. *Naut.* to tack; change direction —**go after** [Colloq.] to try to catch or get; chase; pursue —**go against** to be or act in opposition to —**go along** 1. to proceed; continue 2. to agree; cooperate 3. to accompany (often with *with*) —**go around** 1. to enclose; surround 2. to be enough to provide a share for each 3. to move from place to place; circulate —**go at** to attack or work at —☆**go back on** [Colloq.] 1. to be faithless or disloyal to; betray 2. to fail (a promise, etc.) —**go beyond** to exceed —**go by** 1. to pass 2. to be guided or led by 3. to be known or referred to by —**go down** 1. to descend; sink; set 2. to suffer defeat; lose 3. to be perpetuated, as in history 4. [Brit.] to leave a university, esp. upon graduation —**go for** 1. to be regarded or taken as 2. to try to get ☆3. to advocate; support ☆4. [Colloq.] to attack 5. [Colloq.] to be attracted by; like very much —**go hard with** to cause trouble or pain to —☆**go in for** [Colloq.] to engage, take part, or indulge in; be given to —**go into** 1. to inquire into 2. to take up as a study or occupation —**go in with** to share expenses or obligations with; join —**go it** [Colloq.] to carry on some activity; proceed; act [to go it alone] —**go off** 1. to go away; leave, esp. suddenly 2. to explode; detonate 3. to happen —**go on** 1. to move ahead; proceed; continue 2. to behave 3. to happen; take place 4. [Colloq.] to chatter or rant 5. *Theater* to make an entrance —**go (a person) one better** [Colloq.] to outdo or surpass (a person) —**go out** 1. to come to an end; specif., *a)* to be extinguished *b)* to become outdated 2. to attend social affairs, the theater, etc. 3. to go on strike 4. to try out (*for* an athletic team, etc.) 5. to play the first nine holes of an 18-hole golf course —**go over** 1. to examine thoroughly 2. to do again 3. to review ☆4. [Colloq.] to be successful —☆**go some** [Colloq.] to do or achieve quite a lot —**go through** 1. to perform thoroughly 2. to endure; suffer; experience ☆3. to look through; search ☆4. to get approval or acceptance 5. to spend —**go through with** to pursue to the end; complete —**go to!** [Archaic] come! indeed!: used to express disapproval, disbelief, etc. —**go together** 1. to match; harmonize ☆2. [Colloq.] to be

sweethearts —**go under** ☆to fail, as in business —**go up** 1. to rise in value, price, etc.; increase 2. [Brit.] to enter a university —**go with** [Colloq.] to be a sweetheart of —**go without** to manage or do without —**have a go at** [Colloq.] to try; attempt —**let go** 1. to set free; let escape 2. to release one's hold or grip 3. to give up; abandon, as one's interest in something 4. to dismiss from a job; fire —**let oneself go** to be unrestrained or uninhibited —**no go** [Colloq.] not possible; without use or value —**on the go** [Colloq.] in constant motion or action —**to go** [Colloq.] ☆1. to be taken out: said of food in a restaurant 2. remaining; still to be completed, etc. [one finished, two to *go*] —☆**what goes?** [Slang] what's happening? See also phrases entered under GOING

SYN.—**go** is the general word indicating motion away from the place where one is; **depart** is a somewhat more formal term and usually suggests a setting out on an expressed or implied journey [he *departed* for France]; **leave** stresses the separation from a person or thing [I can't *leave* while she's ill]; **quit** emphasizes a getting rid of by leaving [he *quit* his job yesterday]; **withdraw** suggests a leaving for a definite, justified, and often unpleasant reason [he *withdrew* from the race because of a strained muscle]; **retire**, often equivalent to the preceding, may imply a permanent withdrawal, a retreat, recession, etc. [he *retired* at 65, she *retired* to a nunnery] —**ANT. come, arrive**

go² (gō) *n.* [Jap.] [*also* G-] a Japanese game played with black and white stones on a board marked with many intersecting lines

GO general order

Go·a (gō′ə) small region on the southwestern coast of India: 1,350 sq. mi.; formerly part of Portuguese India, since 1962 it has formed (with DAMAN & DIU) a territory of India (called **Goa, Daman, and Diu**), 1,426 sq. mi.; pop. 627,000 —**Go′an** *adj., n.*

go·a (gō′ə) *n.* [Tibetan *dgoba*] a small, long-haired, brownish-gray antelope (*Procapra picticaudata*) of Tibet

goad (gōd) *n.* [ME. *gode* < OE. *gad*, akin to Langobardic *gaida*, javelin < IE. base *ĝhei-*, to throw, whence Sans. *hinvati*, (he) hurls] 1. a sharp-pointed stick used in driving oxen 2. any driving impulse; spur —*vt.* to drive with or as with a goad; prod into action; urge on

☆**go·a·head** (gō′ə hed′) *adj.* 1. moving forward 2. enterprising; pushing —*n.* permission or a signal to proceed: usually with *the*

goal (gōl) *n.* [ME. *gol*, boundary < ? or akin ? to OE. *gælan*, to hinder, impede] 1. the line or place at which a race, trip, etc. is ended 2. an object or end that one strives to attain; aim 3. in certain games, *a)* the line, crossbar, or net over or into which the ball or puck must be passed to score *b)* the act of so scoring *c)* the score made —*SYN.* see INTENTION

goal·keep·er (-kēp′ər) *n.* in certain games, a player stationed at a goal to prevent the ball or puck from crossing or entering it: also **goal′ie** (-ē), **goal′tend′er**

goal line a line representing the goal in various games; esp., *Football* either of the two lines, one at each end of the field, across which the ball must be carried or caught for a touchdown

goal post either of a pair of upright posts with a crossbar, used as a goal in football, soccer, etc.: in football the ball must be kicked over the crossbar to score a field goal or an extra point after a touchdown

Goa powder [first used in GOA, c. 1852] same as ARAROBA (sense 1)

goat (gōt) *n.* [ME. *gote* < OE. *gat*, akin to Du. *geit*, G. *geiss* < IE. base *ghaido-*, he-goat, whence L. *haedus*, kid goat] 1. *pl.* **goats, goat**: see PLURAL, II, D, 1 *a)* any of a number of wild or domesticated, cud-chewing mammals (genus *Capra*) with hollow horns, related to the sheep *b)* same as ROCKY MOUNTAIN GOAT 2. a lecherous man ☆3. [Colloq.] a person forced to take the blame or punishment for others; scapegoat —[G-] the constellation Capricorn —☆**get one's goat** [Colloq.] to annoy, anger, or irritate one

goat antelope any of several animals intermediate in their characteristics between goats and antelopes, as the serow and goral of Asia

☆**goat·ee** (gō tē′) *n.* [< GOAT: from the resemblance to a goat's beard] a small, pointed beard on a man's chin

goat·fish (gōt′fish′) *n.*, *pl.* **-fish′, -fish′es**: see FISH² any of several edible tropical fishes (family Mullidae), with large scales, one or more long barbels on the lower jaw, and bright coloration

goat·herd (-hurd′) *n.* one who herds or tends goats

goat·ish (-ish) *adj.* 1. like or characteristic of a goat 2. lustful; lecherous —**goat′ish·ly** *adv.* —**goat′ish·ness** *n.*

goats·beard (gōts′bird′) *n.* 1. a hardy plant (*Aruncus sylvester*) of the rose family, with spikes of white flowers in clusters 2. any of a genus (*Tragopogon*) of plants of the composite family, with flower heads and seed heads that resemble large dandelions, as salsify

goat·skin (gōt′skin′) *n.* 1. the skin of a goat 2. leather made from this 3. a container for wine, water, etc. made of this leather

goat's-rue (gōts′rōō′) *n.* ☆1. a plant (*Tephrosia virginiana*) of the legume family, with yellowish and purple flowers 2. a bushy Old World plant (*Galega officinalis*) with pealike flowers in thick clusters

goat·suck·er (gōt′suk′ər) *n.* [transl. of L. *caprimulgus* < *capri*, goat + *mulgere*, to milk: it was thought to suck

milk from goats] any of various large-mouthed, nocturnal birds (family Caprimulgidae) that feed on insects, including the whippoorwill and nightjar

gob[1] (gäb) *n.* [ME. *gobbe* < OFr. *gobe,* prob. back-formation < *gobet:* see GOBBET] **1.** a lump or mass, as of something soft **2.** [*pl.*] [Colloq.] a large quantity or amount **3.** waste material produced in coal mining, consisting of clay, shale, etc.

☆**gob**[2] (gäb) *n.* [< ?] [Slang] a sailor in the U.S. Navy

gob·bet (gäb′it) *n.* [ME. *gobet,* small piece < OFr. *gobet,* mouthful, prob. < Gaul. *gobbo-,* mouth] [Archaic or Rare] **1.** a fragment or bit, esp. of raw flesh **2.** a lump; chunk; mass **3.** a mouthful

gob·ble[1] (gäb′'l) *n.* [echoic, var. of GABBLE] the characteristic throaty sound made by a male turkey —*vi.* **-bled, -bling** to make this sound

gob·ble[2] (gäb′'l) *vt., vi.* **-bled, -bling** [prob. freq. formation on base of OFr., *gober,* to swallow < *gobe,* mouthful, GOB[1]] **1.** to eat quickly and greedily **2.** to seize eagerly; snatch (*up*)

☆**gob·ble·dy·gook** (gäb′'l dē gook′) *n.* [first used in current sense by Maury Maverick (1895–1954), U.S. Representative: ? echoic of turkey cries] [Slang] talk or writing, esp. of officialdom, that is pompous, wordy, involved, and full of long, Latinized words: also **gob′ble·de·gook′**

gob·bler (gäb′lər) *n.* [GOBBL(E)[1] + -ER] a male turkey

Gob·e·lin (gäb′ə lin, gō′bə-; *Fr.* gô blan′) *adj.* designating, of, or like a kind of tapestry made at the Gobelin works in Paris —*n.* Gobelin tapestry

go-be·tween (gō′bi twēn′) *n.* a person who deals with each of two sides in making arrangements between them; intermediary

Go·bi (gō′bē) desert plateau in E Asia, chiefly in Mongolia: c. 500,000 sq. mi.

go·bi·oid (gō′bē oid′) *adj.* **1.** of or related to the gobies **2.** like a goby —*n.* a gobioid fish

gob·let (gäb′lit) *n.* [ME. *gobelet* < OFr. < *gobel* < ? Bret. *gob, kop*] **1.** orig., a bowl-shaped drinking container without handles **2.** a drinking glass with a base and stem

gob·lin (gäb′lin) *n.* [ME. *gobelin* < OFr. < ML. *gobelinus* < ? VL. *cobalus* < Gr. *kobalos,* sprite] *Folklore* an evil or mischievous sprite, ugly or misshapen in form

☆**go·bo** (gō′bō) *n., pl.* **-bos, -boes** [< ?] **1.** a black screen used to reduce light falling on a camera lens **2.** a screen to shield a microphone from unwanted sounds

go·by (gō′bē) *n., pl.* **-bies, -by:** see PLURAL, II, D, 1 [L. *gobio, gobius,* gudgeon < Gr. *kōbios*] any of a family (Gobiidae) of small, carnivorous, spiny-finned fishes, found throughout tropical and subtropical seas: the ventral fins are sometimes modified into a suction disk

go-by (gō′bī′) *n.* [Colloq.] a passing by; esp., an intentional disregard or slight: chiefly in **give** (or **get**) **the go-by,** to slight (or be slighted)

go-cart (-kärt′) *n.* **1.** a framework mounted on casters, used to support a child learning to walk ☆**2.** a small, low baby carriage **3.** a former type of light carriage **4.** *same as* KART (sense 2)

god (gäd, gôd) *n.* [ME. < OE., akin to G. *gott,* Goth. *guth,* prob. < IE. base *ĝhau-,* to call out to, invoke, whence Sans. *havate,* (he) calls upon] **1.** any of various beings conceived of as supernatural, immortal, and having special powers over the lives and affairs of people and the course of nature; deity, esp. a male deity **2.** an image that is worshiped; idol **3.** a person or thing deified or excessively honored and admired —[G-] in monotheistic religions, the creator and ruler of the universe, regarded as eternal, infinite, all-powerful, and all-knowing; Supreme Being; Almighty Often used in exclamations [good *God! God* almighty! my *God!*] —**God willing** if God is willing

Go·da·va·ri (gō dä′vər ē) river in C India, flowing from the Western Ghats into the Bay of Bengal: c. 900 mi.

god·child (gäd′chīld′) *n., pl.* **-chil′dren** (-chil′drən) [ME.] the person for whom a godparent is sponsor

god-damned (-damd′) *adj.* strongly cursed or damned: used as a curse or strong intensive, often shortened to **god′damn′, god′dam′**

god·daugh·ter (gäd′dôt′ər) *n.* [ME. *goddoughter* < OE. *goddohtor*] a female godchild

god·dess (gäd′is) *n.* [ME. *godesse*] **1.** a female god **2.** a woman greatly admired, as for her beauty

☆**go-dev·il** (gō′dev′'l) *n.* **1.** any of certain kinds of sled used in logging, farming, etc. **2.** a rotary tool for scraping out obstructions from an oil pipeline **3.** a metal weight dropped into an oil well to set off an explosive charge **4.** a railroad handcar

god·fa·ther (gäd′fä′*th*ər) *n.* a male godparent

God-fear·ing (-fir′iŋ) *adj.* [*occas.* g-] **1.** fearing God **2.** devout; pious

God-for·sak·en (-fər sā′kən) *adj.* [*occas.* g-] **1.** depraved; wicked **2.** desolate; forlorn

God·frey (gäd′frē) [OFr. *Godefrei* < OHG. *Godafrid* < *god,* God + *fridu,* peace: hence, lit., peace (of) God] a masculine name: equiv. Ger. *Gottfried*

God-giv·en (gäd′giv′ən) *adj.* [*occas.* g-] **1.** given by God **2.** very welcome; suitable or opportune

god·head (-hed′) *n.* [ME. *godhede:* see -HEAD] **1.** godhood; divinity **2.** [G-] God (usually with *the*)

god·hood (-hood) *n.* [ME. *godhod:* see -HOOD] the state or quality of being a god; divinity

Go·di·va (gə dī′və) an 11th-cent. noblewoman of Coventry who, according to legend, on the dare of her husband, rode naked through the streets on horseback so that he would abolish a heavy tax

god·less (gäd′lis) *adj.* [ME. *godles* < OE. *godleas*] **1.** denying the existence of God or a god; irreligious; atheistic **2.** impious; wicked —**god′less·ness** *n.*

god·like (-līk′) *adj.* [ME.] like or suitable to God or a god; divine

god·ling (-liŋ) *n.* [see -LING[1]] a minor god

god·ly (-lē) *adj.* **-li·er, -li·est** [ME.: see GOD & -LY[1]] **1.** of or from God; divine **2.** devoted to God; pious; devout; religious —**god′li·ness** *n.*

god·moth·er (-mu*th*′ər) *n.* a female godparent

go·down (gō doun′) *n.* [Anglo-Ind. < Malay *gedong* < Telugu *giḍaṅgi*] in the Far East, a warehouse

god·par·ent (gäd′per′ənt, -par′-) *n.* a person who sponsors a child, as at baptism, and assumes responsibility for its faith; godmother or godfather

☆**God's acre** a burial ground, esp. one in a churchyard

god·send (gäd′send′) *n.* [contr. of *God's send:* ME. *sande,* mission, message < OE. *sand* < *sendan,* to send] anything unexpected and needed or desired that comes at the opportune moment, as if sent by God

god·son (-sun′) *n.* a male godchild

God·speed (-spēd′) *n.* [contr. of *God speed you*] success; good fortune: a wish for the welfare of a person starting on a journey or venture

Godt·haab (gôt′hôp) capital of Greenland, on the SW coast: pop. 3,000

Go·du·nov (gō′doo nôf′), **Bo·ris Fë·do·ro·vich** (bô rēs′ fyô′dô rô′vich) 1552?–1605; czar of Russia (1598–1605)

God·win (gäd′win) [OE. *Godewine,* friend (of) God: see EDWIN] **1.** a masculine name **2. Mary Woll·stone·craft** (wool′stən kraft′), 1759–97; Eng. writer: wife of *ff.* & by him mother of Mary Wollstonecraft SHELLEY **3. William,** 1756–1836; Eng. political philosopher & writer

Godwin Austen mountain in the Karakorum range, N Jammu & Kashmir, near the Sinkiang border: second highest mountain in the world: 28,250 ft.

god·wit (gäd′wit) *n.* [orig. prob. echoic of cry] any of a genus (*Limosa*) of brownish wading birds of the snipe family, with a long bill that curves up

Goeb·bels (gö′bəls), **Joseph Paul** 1897–1945; Ger. Nazi propagandist

go·er (gō′ər) *n.* one that goes

Goe·ring (gö′riŋ), **Her·mann (Wilhelm)** (her′män) 1893–1946; Ger. Nazi field marshal: also sp. **Gö′ring**

Goe·thals (gō′thalz), **George Washington** 1858–1928; U.S. army officer & engineer: in charge of building the Panama Canal (1907–14)

Goe·the (gö′tə; *also Anglicized to* gur′tə, gāt′ə), **Jo·hann Wolf·gang von** (yō′hän vôlf′gäŋ fôn) 1749–1832; Ger. poet and dramatist

goe·thite (gur′thīt, gō′-; -tīt) *n.* [G. *göthit,* after prec., in honor of his studies in geology and mineralogy] a hydrous oxide mineral of iron, $Fe_2O_3 \cdot H_2O$

gof·fer (gäf′ər, gôf′-) *vt.* [Fr. *gaufrer,* to crimp < *gaufre,* waffle < Du. *wafel,* waffle, honeycomb] to pleat, crimp, or flute (cloth, paper, etc.) —*n.* **1.** an iron used to goffer cloth, etc. **2.** the act of pleating or fluting; also, a series of pleats, crimps, or flutes: also **gof′fer·ing**

Gog and Ma·gog (gäg′ 'n mā′gäg) [Heb. *gōgh, māgōgh*] *Bible* the nations that, under Satan, are to war against the kingdom of God: Rev. 20:8

☆**go-get·ter** (gō′get′ər) *n.* [Colloq.] an enterprising and aggressive person who usually gets what he wants

gog·gle (gäg′'l) *vi.* **-gled, -gling** [ME. *gogelen,* to look obliquely, freq. formation prob. < Celtic base, as in Ir. *gog,* a nod, W. *gogi,* to shake] **1.** *a)* to stare with bulging or wide-open eyes *b)* to roll the eyes **2.** *a)* to bulge or open wide in a stare *b)* to roll: said of the eyes —*n.* **1.** a staring with bulging eyes **2.** [*pl.*] large spectacles, esp. those fitted with side guards to protect the eyes against dust, wind, sparks, etc. —*adj.* bulging, staring, or rolling: said of the eyes

gog·gle-eye (-ī′) *n.* ☆any of various fishes with large, bulging eyes, as the rock bass

gog·gle-eyed (-īd′) *adj.* having eyes that bulge or roll

gog·gler (-lər) *n.* **1.** one who goggles ☆**2.** *same as* GOGGLE-EYE

Gogh, Vincent van see VAN GOGH

gog·let (gäg′lit) *n.* [Port. *gorgoleta,* dim., ult. < L. *gurgulio,* gullet, akin to *gurges:* see GORGE] a porous earthenware container with a long neck, for keeping water cool by evaporation

go-go (gō′gō′) *adj.* [short for *à gogo* < Fr., in plenty, ad lib., in clover < *à,* to + *gogo,* child's word for throat: semantic development obscure] **1.** of rock-and-roll dancing or dancers or the discothèques, cafés, etc. where such dancing is featured **2.** [Slang] lively, energetic, up-to-date, etc.

Go·gol (gô′gôl; *E.* gō′gəl), **Ni·ko·lai Va·sil·ie·vich** (nē′kô lī′ vä sēl′yə vich) 1809–52; Russ. novelist & dramatist

Goi·â·ni·a (goi ä′nē ə) city in C Brazil; capital of Goiás state: pop. 130,000

Goi·ás (goi äs′) state of C Brazil: 247,800 sq. mi.; pop. 1,955,000; cap. Goiânia

Goi·del·ic (goi del′ik) *adj.* [< OIr. *Goidel:* see GAEL] 1. of the Gaels 2. designating or of their languages —*n.* the subbranch of the Celtic languages that includes Irish Gaelic, Scottish Gaelic, and Manx

go·ing (gō′iŋ) *n.* 1. the act of one who goes: usually used in compounds [opera-*going*] 2. a leaving; departure 3. the condition of the ground or land as it affects traveling, walking, etc. 4. circumstances affecting progress —*adj.* 1. moving; running; working 2. conducting its business successfully [a *going* concern] 3. in existence or available [the best bet *going*] 4. commonly accepted; current [the *going* rate for plumbers] —**be going to** to be intending to; will or shall —☆**get going** [Colloq.] to start; begin —☆**get one going** [Slang] to cause a person to be excited, angry, etc. —**going on** [Colloq.] nearing or nearly (a specified age or time) —☆**have (something) going for one** [Slang] to have (something) working to one's advantage

go·ing-o·ver (-ō′vər) *n.* [Colloq.] ☆1. an inspection or examination, esp. a thorough one ☆2. a severe scolding or beating

go·ings-on (gō′iŋz än′) *n.pl.* [Colloq.] actions or events, esp. when regarded with disapproval

goi·ter, goi·tre (goit′ər) *n.* [Fr. *goitre*, back-formation < OFr. *goitron*, throat < VL. **guttrione*, for L. *guttur*, throat: see GUTTURAL] an enlargement of the thyroid gland, often visible as a swelling in the lower part of the front of the neck

goi·trous (goi′trəs) *adj.* [Fr. *goitreux*] 1. of, having the nature of, or having goiter 2. designating a geographical area where goiter is prevalent

☆**Go Kart** (kärt) *a trademark for* a kind of kart (sense 2)

Gol·con·da (gäl kän′də) ancient city, now ruins, in SC India, near Hyderabad: noted for diamond cutting in the 16th cent. —*n.* a source of great wealth, as a mine

gold (gōld) *n.* [ME. < OE. *gold*, akin to G. *gold*, ON. *goll* < IE. base **ghel-*, to shine, gleam, whence GLOW, YELLOW] 1. a heavy, yellow, inert, metallic chemical element with a high degree of ductility and malleability: it is a precious metal and is used in the manufacture of coins, jewelry, alloys, etc.: symbol, Au; at. wt., 196.967; at. no., 79; sp. gr., 19.4; melt. pt., 1063°C; boil. pt., 2600°C 2. *a)* gold coin *b)* money; riches; wealth 3. the bright yellow color of gold 4. something regarded as having the value, brilliance, etc. of gold [a voice of pure *gold*] —*adj.* 1. of, made of, like, or containing gold 2. having the color of gold 3. secured by or redeemable in gold; based on gold

gold·beat·er (-bēt′ər) *n.* a person who pounds gold into thin leaves for use in gilding —**gold′beat′ing** *n.*

☆**gold beetle** any of a large number of unrelated gold-colored beetles: also **gold′bug′** (-bug′)

☆**gold·brick** (-brik) *n.* 1. [Colloq.] a worthless metal bar gilded and sold as solid gold in a swindle 2. [Colloq.] anything worthless passed off as genuine or valuable 3. [Mil. Slang] a person who tries to avoid work; shirker; loafer: also **gold′brick′er** —*vi.* [Mil. Slang] to shirk a duty or avoid work; loaf

☆**gold certificate** 1. formerly, a type of U.S. paper currency redeemable in gold 2. a U.S. Treasury note issued to and used only among Federal Reserve Banks, as in transferring balances: it represents a claim on their gold reserves held by the Treasury

Gold Coast 1. former Brit. territory in W Africa, on the Gulf of Guinea: see GHANA ☆2. [Colloq.] a district where rich people live, esp. along a shore, as of a lake

☆**gold digger** [Slang] a woman who in her personal relations with men tries to get money and gifts from them

gold dust gold in very small bits or as a powder, the normal state in which it is found in placer mining

gold·en (gōl′d'n) *adj.* [ME. *golden* < *gold* (for earlier *gilden*)] 1. made of, containing, or yielding gold 2. having the color and luster of gold; bright-yellow 3. very valuable or precious; excellent 4. prosperous and joyful; flourishing 5. favorable; auspicious [a *golden* opportunity] 6. gifted in a way that promises future success [a *golden* boy] 7. richly mellow, as a voice —**gold′en·ly** *adv.* —**gold′en·ness** *n.*

Golden Age [after L. (Ovid) *aurea aetas*] 1. *Gr. & Rom. Myth.* an imaginary early age in which mankind was ideally happy, prosperous, and innocent 2. [g- a-] a period of great progress, prosperity, or cultural achievement 3. [also g- a-] of or for golden agers

golden ag·er (ā′jər) [Colloq.] [also G- A-] an elderly person, specif. one who is 65 or older and retired

☆**golden aster** any of a genus (*Chrysopsis*) of N. American plants of the composite family, with golden ray flowers

☆**golden bantam corn** a variety of sweet corn with bright-yellow kernels on small ears

golden calf 1. a calf of gold worshiped by the Israelites while Moses was at Mount Sinai: Ex. 32:4 2. riches regarded as an object of worship and greedy pursuit

golden eagle a large, strong eagle (*Aquila chrysaëtos*) found in mountainous districts of the N Hemisphere, with brown feathers on the back of its head and neck

gold·en·eye (gōl′d'n ī′) *n.,* pl. **-eyes, -eye:** see PLURAL, II, D, 1 a swift, diving wild duck (*Bucephala clangula*) of

N. America and the Old World, with yellow eyes, a dark-green back, and a white breast

Golden Fleece *Gr. Myth.* the fleece of gold that hung in a sacred grove at Colchis guarded by a dragon until taken away by Jason and the Argonauts

Golden Gate strait between San Francisco Bay and the Pacific: 2 mi. wide

☆**golden glow** a tall garden plant (*Rudbeckia laciniata*) of the composite family, with numerous globular, yellow ray flower heads

Golden Horde [from the splendors of their leader's camp] the Mongol armies that invaded Europe in 1237 and, under the Khans, ruled Russia for two centuries

Golden Horn arm of the Bosporus in European Turkey, forming the harbor of Istanbul

golden mean [transl. of L. (Horace) *aurea mediocritas*] the safe, prudent way between extremes; moderation

golden nematode a small, European nematode worm (*Heterodera rostochiensis*) now found in the E U.S. as a destructive potato parasite

golden pheasant a pheasant (*Chrysolophus pictus*) of China and Tibet, with brightly colored feathers and an orange crest

☆**golden retriever** any of a breed of hunting dog with a thick, golden coat, used in retrieving waterfowl, etc.

gold·en·rod (-räd′) *n.* any of a genus (*Solidago*) of chiefly N. American plants of the composite family, typically with long, branching stalks bearing one-sided clusters of small, yellow flower heads through the late summer and fall

golden rule the precept that one should behave toward others as he would want others to behave toward him: see Matt. 7:12; Luke 6:31

☆**gold·en·seal** (-sēl′) *n.* an American plant (*Hydrastis canadensis*) of the buttercup family, with large, round leaves and a thick, yellow rootstock, formerly much used in medicine

☆**golden warbler** any of a number of small, yellow, American songbirds, as the yellow warbler

golden wedding the 50th anniversary of a wedding

gold-filled (gōld′fild′) *adj.* made of a base metal overlaid with gold

gold·finch (-finch′) *n.* [ME. < OE. *goldfinc:* see GOLD & FINCH] 1. a European songbird (*Carduelis carduelis*) with yellow-streaked wings, often kept as a cage bird ☆2. any of several small American finches (genus *Spinus*), esp. a species (*Spinus tristis*), the male of which has a yellow body with a black cap on the head and black markings on the wings

gold·fish (-fish′) *n.,* pl. **-fish′, -fish′es:** see FISH[2] a small, golden-yellow or orange fish (*Carassius auratus*) of the carp family, often kept in ponds or fishbowls

gold foil [ME. *golde foyle*] gold beaten into thin sheets slightly thicker than gold leaf

Gold·i·locks (gōl′dē läks′) a little girl in a folk tale who visits the home of three bears —*n.* [g-] 1. a person with yellow hair 2. a European plant (*Linosyris vulgaris*) of the composite family, with clusters of small, yellow flowers

gold leaf gold beaten into very thin sheets, used for gilding —**gold′-leaf′** *adj.*

Gold·mark (gōld′märk), **Karl** 1830–1915; Hung. composer

gold mine 1. a mine from which gold ore is obtained 2. [Colloq.] a source of something very valuable or profitable

Gol·do·ni (gôl dô′nē), **Car·lo** (kär′lô) 1707–93; It. dramatist

gold plate tableware made of gold

☆**gold reserve** the gold kept in the U.S. Treasury for meeting foreign banking obligations and, formerly, for redeeming gold certificates

☆**gold rush** a rush of people to territory where gold has recently been discovered, as to California in 1849

gold·smith (-smith′) *n.* [ME. < OE.] 1. a skilled worker who makes articles of gold 2. a dealer in such articles

Gold·smith (gōld′smith), **Oliver** 1728–74; Brit. poet, playwright, and novelist, born in Ireland

goldsmith beetle ☆1. a large, bright-yellow American beetle (*Cotalpa lanigera*) that feeds on tree foliage 2. a shiny, golden-yellow European beetle (*Cetonia aurata*)

☆**gold standard** a monetary standard solely in terms of gold, in which the basic currency unit is made equal to and redeemable by a specified quantity of gold

☆**gold star** a small, gold-colored star displayed to represent a member of the U.S. armed forces killed in war

gold·stone (-stōn′) *n. same as* AVENTURINE (sense 1)

gold·thread (-thred′) *n.* ☆any of several N. American plants (genus *Coptis*) of the buttercup family, esp. a small perennial (*Coptis groenlandica*) with white flowers and yellow rhizomes, used in folk medicine

go·lem (gō′ləm) *n.* [Heb., orig., embryo; later, monster (hence Yid. *goylem*, dolt), akin to Ar. *ghulām*, lad] *Jewish Legend* a man artificially created by cabalistic rites; robot; automaton

golf (gôlf, gälf) *n.* [LME. (Scot.) *golf*, *gouff*, usually derived < Du. *kolf*, a club, but all early forms have *g-*, and the *-l-* may be unhistoric, hence < ? Scot. *gowf*, to strike < *gowf*, a blow (with the open hand)] an outdoor game played on a large course with a small, hard ball and a set of clubs, the object being to hit the ball into each of a series of nine or eighteen holes in turn, using the fewest possible strokes —*vi.* to play golf —**golf′er** *n.*

golf club 1. any of the various clubs with a wooden or metal head and a long, slender shaft, used in golf 2. an organization owning a golf course, clubhouse, etc., for the use of its members

golf course (or **links**) a tract of land for playing golf, with tees, greens, fairways, hazards, etc.

Gol·gi apparatus (gôl′jē) [after Camillo *Golgi* (1844–1926), It. neurologist, who first observed it (1909)] a network of fibers, often in the form of rods, granules, etc., found within the cytoplasm of cells and made visible by special stains: also **Golgi body**

GOLF CLUBS (A, putter; B, iron; C, driver)

Gol·go·tha (gäl′gə thə) [LL.(Ec.) < Gr.(Ec.) *golgotha* < Aram. *gulgalta* < Heb. *gulgōleth*, skull, place of a skull] the place where Jesus was crucified; Calvary: Mark 15:22 —*n.* [g-] 1. a burial place 2. a place of agony or sacrifice

gol·iard (gôl′yərd) *n.* [contr. < ME. *goliardeis* < OFr. *goliardois*) & < OFr. *goliart*, ult. < *Golias* (Goliath), a gluttonous giant in OFr. epic poems + *-art*, *-ARD*] any of a class of wandering students of the late Middle Ages who wrote satirical Latin verse and often served as minstrels and jesters —**gol·iar′dic** (-yär′dik) *adj.*

Go·li·ath (gə lī′əth) [LL.(Ec.) < Heb. *golyāth*] *Bible* the Philistine giant killed by David with a stone shot from a sling: I Sam. 17:4, 49

gol·li·wog, gol·li·wogg (gäl′ē wäg′) *n.* [arbitrary formation,? after POLLIWOG] 1. a grotesque black doll used in illustrations by Florence K. Upton (d. 1922) for a series of children's books 2. a grotesque person

gol·ly (gäl′ē) *interj.* an exclamation of surprise, etc.: a euphemism for *God*

go·losh, go·loshe (gə läsh′) *n. Brit. var. of* GALOSH

gom·broon (gäm broon′) *n.* [< *Gombroon* (Bandar Abbas), town on the Persian Gulf] a type of white, semitransparent Persian pottery

Go·mel (gô′mel) city in SE Byelorussian S.S.R.: pop. 226,000

gom·er·al, gom·er·el, gom·er·il (gäm′ər əl) *n.* [< ? obs. *gome*, a man (< OE. *guma*) + -(e)rel, depreciatory suffix < OFr. *-erel*] [Scot.] a simpleton; fool

Go·mor·rah, Go·mor·rha (gə môr′ə) [Gr. *Gomorrha* < Heb.] *see* SODOM

Gom·pers (gäm′pərz), **Samuel** 1850–1924; U.S. labor leader, born in England

gom·pho·sis (gäm fō′sis) *n.* [ModL. < Gr. *gomphōsis*, a nailing together < *gomphos*, a nail, bolt: for IE. base see COMB¹] a form of immovable joint in which a bone or other hard part, as a tooth, fits into a socket

go·mu·ti (gō mōōt′ē) *n.* [Malay *gumuti*] 1. *a*) a Malayan palm (*Arenga pinnata*) with feathery leaves and a sweet sap from which a crude sugar and an alcoholic beverage, arrack, are made *b*) the wiry fibers from the stalks of its leaves, used in making ropes, brushes, etc. 2. a Malayan palm (*Metroxylon sagu*) which yields a kind of sago starch, used for food and for sizing and filling textiles

-gon (gän, gən) [Gr. *-gōnon* < *gōnia*, an angle: for IE. base see KNEE] *a combining form used to form nouns meaning* a figure having (a specified number of) angles [*pentagon*]

go·nad (gō′nad; *occas.* gän′ad) *n.* [< ModL. *gonas* (pl. *gonades*) < Gr. *gonē*, a seed, generation < IE. *gon-* < base *gen-*, to produce, bear, whence L. *gignere*, to bear] an organ in animals that produces reproductive cells; esp., an ovary or testis —**go·nad′al** *adj.*

go·na·do·trop·in (gō nad′ə trō′pin) *n.* a hormone which supports and stimulates the function and growth of the gonads: also **go′na·do·tro′phin** (-fin) —**go′na·do·trop′ic** (-träp′ik), **go′na·do·troph′ic** (-träf′ik) *adj.*

Gon·court (gôN koor′), **Ed·mond Louis An·toine Hu·ot de** (ed mōN′ lwē′ än twän′ ü ō′ də) 1822–96 & his brother **Jules Al·fred Huot de** (zhül′ ål fred′) 1830–70; Fr. collaborating novelists & art critics

Gond (gänd) *n.* [< native (Gondi) name] a member of a Dravidian culture group living in C India

Gon·dar (gän′dər) city in NW Ethiopia: former capital: pop. 29,000

Gon·di (gän′dē) *n.* 1. a group of Dravidian dialects spoken in C India 2. the principal dialect of this group

gon·do·la (gän′də lə, gän dō′lə) *n.* [It. (Venetian) < ?] 1. a long, narrow canalboat with a seat in the middle and a high, pointed prow and stern, used on the canals of Venice: it is propelled by a pole or one oar at the stern ☆2. a flat-bottomed river barge ☆3. a railroad freight car with low sides and no top: also **gondola car** 4. a cabin suspended under a dirigible or balloon, for holding the motors, instruments, passengers, etc. 5. a car suspended from and moved along a cable, for holding passengers

GONDOLA

gon·do·lier (gän′də lir′) *n.* [Fr. < It. *gondoliere* < *gondola*] a man who rows or poles a gondola

Gond·wa·na·land (gänd wän′ə land′) [after the *Gondwana Series*, an extensive tillite deposit in *Gondwana*, region in Central India < GOND] a hypothetical ancient continent that included what are now India, Australia, Africa, S. America and Antarctica, supposed to have separated and moved apart at about the end of the Paleozoic Era

gone (gôn, gän) [ME. *gon* < OE. *gan*] *pp. of* GO¹ —*adj.* 1. moved away; departed 2. ruined 3. lost 4. dead 5. faint; weak 6. used up; consumed 7. ago; past ☆8. [Slang] *a*) excellent; first-rate *b*) enraptured or inspired *c*) pregnant —**far gone** 1. much advanced; deeply involved 2. very tired 3. nearly dead —**gone on** [Colloq.] in love with

gon·ef (gän′if) *n.* [Slang] *same as* GANEF

gon·er (gôn′ər, gän′-) *n.* [< GONE + -ER] [Colloq.] a person or thing that is beyond help or seems certain to die soon, be ruined, etc.

Gon·er·il (gän′ər əl) in Shakespeare's *King Lear*, the elder of Lear's two cruel and disloyal daughters

gon·fa·lon (gän′fə lən, -län′) *n.* [Fr. < OFr. *gonfanon*, banner < Frank. *gundfano*, battle standard (akin to OE. *guthfana*) < *gund* (OE. *guth*), battle + *fano* (OE. *fana*), banner: see FANON] a flag hanging from a crosspiece instead of an upright staff, usually ending in streamers; esp., such a standard of any of the medieval republics of Italy

gon·fa·lon·ier (gän′fə lə nir′) *n.* [< Fr. or It.: Fr. *gonfalonier* < It. *gonfaloniere*] 1. the bearer of a gonfalon 2. in some medieval republics of Italy, a high official

gon·fa·non (gän′fə nən) *n. obs. var. of* GONFALON

gong (gôn, gän) *n.* [Malay *gun:* echoic] 1. a slightly convex metallic disk that gives a loud, resonant tone when struck: used as a signal, percussion instrument, etc. 2. a saucer-shaped bell with such a tone 3. [Brit. Slang] a medal, esp. a military medal

Gon·go·rism (gän′gər iz′m) *n.* [after the style of Luis de *Góngora* y Argote, Sp. poet (1561–1627)] a literary style characterized by affected metaphor and the use of strained conceits

go·nid·i·um (gō nid′ē əm) *n., pl.* **-nid′i·a** (-ə) [ModL., dim. < Gr. *gonos:* see GONAD] 1. a reproductive cell produced asexually in certain algae 2. any of the chlorophyll-bearing algal cells in lichens —**go·nid′i·al** *adj.*

gon·iff, gon·if (gän′if) *n.* [Slang] *same as* GANEF

go·ni·o- (gō′nē ō′) [< Gr. *gōnia*, an angle: see KNEE] *a combining form meaning* angle [*goniometry*]

go·ni·om·e·ter (gō′nē äm′ə tər) *n.* [prec. + -METER] 1. an instrument for measuring angles, esp. of solid bodies 2. *Radio* an electrical device used to determine the direction or angle of signals coming from a transmitting station

go·ni·om·e·try (-ə trē) *n.* [GONIO- + -METRY] the theory or science of measuring angles —**go′ni·o·met′ric** (-ə met′rik) *adj.*

go·ni·on (gō′nē än′) *n., pl.* **-ni·a** (-ə) [ModL. < Gr. *gonia*, an angle: see KNEE] the point at the apex of the angle formed by the horizontal and ascending sides of the lower jaw

-go·ni·um (gō′nē əm) [ModL. < Gr. *gonos:* see ff.] *a combining form used to form nouns meaning* a cell or structure in which reproductive cells are formed [*archegonium, sporogonium*]

gon·o- (gän′ə-, -ō) [< Gr. *gonos, gonē*, procreation, offspring, semen, seed: see GONAD] *a combining form meaning* reproductive, sexual [*gonococcus, gonophore*]

gon·o·coc·cus (gän′ə käk′əs) *n., pl.* **-coc′ci** (-käk′sī) [ModL. < prec. + COCCUS] the microorganism (*Neisseria gonorrhoeae*) that causes gonorrhea —**gon′o·coc′cal** (-käk′əl) *adj.*

gon·of, gon·oph (gän′əf) *n.* [Slang] *same as* GANEF

gon·o·phore (gän′ə fôr′) *n.* [GONO- + -PHORE] 1. an extension of the axis of a flower, lifting the pistil and stamens above the floral envelope 2. a nonfeeding hydranth of a hydroid colony, specialized for the asexual production of offspring —**gon′o·phor′ic** (-fôr′ik), **go·noph·o·rous** (gə näf′ə rəs) *adj.*

gon·o·pore (gän′ə pôr′) *n.* [GONO- + PORE²] an external genital opening through which gametes are released, as in earthworms, insects, etc.

gon·or·rhe·a, gon·or·rhoe·a (gän′ə rē′ə) *n.* [LL. *gonorrhoea* < Gr. *gonorrhoia* < *gonos*, a seed, semen (see GONAD) + *rhoia*, *rhein*, to flow] a venereal disease caused by gonococci, characterized by inflammation of the mucous membrane of the genitourinary tract and a discharge of mucus and pus: it can seriously affect other mucous membranes, esp. those of the eye, as in a baby during childbirth —**gon′or·rhe′al, gon′or·rhoe′al** *adj.*

-go·ny (gə nē) [L. *-gonia* < Gr. *-gonia* < base of *gignesthai*, to be born: see GENESIS] *a combining form used to form nouns meaning* something generated, produced, descended, etc. [*cosmogony, theogony*]

☆**goo** (gōō) *n.* [prob. < baby talk] [Slang] 1. anything sticky, as glue 2. anything sticky and sweet 3. excessive sentimentality

☆**goo·ber** (gōō′bər) *n.* [< Kongo *nguba*] [Chiefly South] a peanut

good (good) *adj.* **bet′ter, best** [ME. *gode* < OE. *god*, akin to G. *gut* < IE. base *ghedh-*, to unite, be associated, suitable, whence GATHER] **I.** *a general term of approval or commendation, meaning* "as it should be" or "better than average" **1.** *a)* suitable to a purpose; effective; efficient [a lamp *good* to read by] *b)* producing favorable results; beneficial; salutary [*good* exercise for the legs] **2.** fertile [*good* soil] **3.** fresh; unspoiled; uncontaminated [*good* eggs] **4.** valid; genuine; real [*good* money, a *good* excuse] **5.** healthy; strong; vigorous [*good* eyesight] **6.** financially safe or sound [a *good* investment] **7.** honorable; worthy; respectable [one's *good* name] **8.** enjoyable, desirable, pleasant, happy, etc. [a *good* life] **9.** dependable; reliable; right [*good* advice] **10.** thorough; complete [a *good* job of cleaning up] **11.** *a)* excellent of its kind [a *good* novel] *b)* best or considered best [her *good* china] **12.** adequate; ample; sufficient; satisfying [a *good* meal] **13.** morally sound or excellent; specif., *a)* virtuous; honest; just *b)* pious; devout *c)* kind, benevolent, generous, sympathetic, etc. *d)* well-behaved; dutiful **14.** proper; becoming; correct [*good* manners] **15.** able; skilled; expert [a *good* swimmer] **16.** loyal or conforming [a *good* Democrat] **17.** *Law* effectual; valid [*good* title] **II.** *a general intensive, meaning* **1.** to a considerable amount, extent, or degree [a *good* many, a *good* beating] **2.** at least; full [we waited a *good* six hours] —*n.* something good; specif., *a)* that which is morally right *b)* worth; virtue; merit [the *good* in a man] *c)* something contributing to health, welfare, happiness, etc.; benefit; advantage [the greatest *good* of the greatest number] *d)* something desirable or desired See also GOODS —*interj.* an exclamation of satisfaction, pleasure, agreement, etc. In some exclamatory phrases expressing surprise, consternation, etc. (Ex.: *good* gracious! *good* grief!), *good* is a euphemism for *God* —*adv.* well, completely, fully, etc.: variously regarded as substandard, dialectal, or colloquial —**as good as** in effect; virtually; nearly —**come to no good** to come to a bad end; end in failure, trouble, etc. —**for good (and all)** for always; finally; permanently —☆**good and** [Colloq.] very or altogether —**good for 1.** able to survive, endure, or be used for (a specified period of time) **2.** worth [a coupon *good for* 10¢] **3.** able to pay, repay, or give **4.** sure to result in [*good for* a laugh] ☆Also used to express approval [*good for* you!] —☆**make good 1.** to give or do something as a substitute for; repay or replace **2.** to fulfill **3.** to succeed in doing; accomplish **4.** to be successful **5.** to prove —**no good** useless or worthless —**the good 1.** those who are good **2.** what is morally good —**to the good** as a profit, benefit, or advantage

good afternoon a salutation of greeting or farewell used in the afternoon

Good Book the Bible (usually with *the*)

good·bye, good-bye (good′bī′) *interj., n., pl.* **-byes′** [contr. of *God be with ye*] farewell: a term used at parting: also sp. **good′by′, good·by′**

good cheer 1. merrymaking; revelry **2.** good food and drink; feasting **3.** cheerful or courageous spirit

☆**Good Conduct Medal** *U.S. Armed Forces* a bronze medal awarded to enlisted men for exemplary behavior, efficiency, and fidelity

good day a salutation of greeting or farewell

good evening a salutation of greeting or farewell used in the evening

good fellow an agreeable, convivial person

good-fel·low·ship (-fel′ō ship′) *n.* [GOOD FELLOW + -SHIP] hearty, convivial companionship

good-for-noth·ing (good′fər nuth′iŋ) *adj.* useless or worthless —*n.* a useless or worthless person

Good Friday the Friday before Easter Sunday, observed in commemoration of the crucifixion of Jesus

good-heart·ed (good′härt′id) *adj.* kind and generous —**good′-heart′ed·ly** *adv.* —**good′-heart′ed·ness** *n.*

Good Hope, Cape of 1. cape at the SW tip of Africa, on the Atlantic **2.** province of South Africa, in the southernmost part: 278,465 sq. mi.; pop. 5,363,000; cap. Cape Town

good humor a cheerful, agreeable, pleasant mood

good-hu·mored (-hyōō′mərd) *adj.* having or showing good humor; cheerful and agreeable —**good′-hu′mored·ly** *adv.*

good·ish (-ish) *adj.* **1.** fairly good **2.** fairly large

good-look·ing (-look′iŋ) *adj.* pleasing in appearance; beautiful or handsome —*SYN.* see BEAUTIFUL

good looks (looks) attractive personal appearance; esp., pleasing facial features

good·ly (-lē) *adj.* **-li·er, -li·est 1.** of attractive appearance; good-looking **2.** of good quality; fine **3.** rather large; ample [a *goodly* sum] —**good′li·ness** *n.*

good·man (-mən) *n., pl.* **-men** (-mən) [ME.: see GOOD & MAN] [Archaic] **1.** a husband or a master of a household **2.** a title equivalent to *Mr.*, applied to a man ranking below a gentleman

good morning a salutation of greeting or farewell used in the morning

good nature a pleasant, agreeable, or kindly disposition; amiability; geniality

good-na·tured (-nā′chərd) *adj.* having or showing good nature; pleasant; agreeable; affable —*SYN.* see AMIABLE —**good′-na′tured·ly** *adv.*

good·ness (-nis) *n.* [ME. *goodnesse* < OE. *godnes*] **1.** the state or quality of being good; specif., *a)* virtue; excellence *b)* kindness; generosity; benevolence **2.** best part,

essence, or valuable element of a thing —*interj.* an exclamation of surprise or wonder: a euphemism for God [for *goodness*' sake!]

good night a salutation of farewell used at night in parting or going to bed

goods (goodz) *n.pl.* **1.** movable personal property **2.** merchandise; wares **3.** fabric; cloth **4.** [Brit.] freight: usually used attributively —☆**deliver the goods** [Colloq.] to do or produce the thing required —☆**get (or have) the goods on** [Slang] to discover (or know) something incriminating about —☆**the goods** [Slang] what is required, genuine, or valid

good Samaritan a person who pities and helps another or others unselfishly: see Luke 10:30–37

Good Shepherd an *epithet* for JESUS: John 10:11

good-sized (good′sīzd′) *adj.* ample; big or fairly big

good speed success; good luck: a farewell expressing good wishes to a person starting on a trip or venture

good-tem·pered (-tem′pərd) *adj.* having a good temper; not easily angered or annoyed; amiable —**good′-tem′-pered·ly** *adv.*

good-time Charlie (or **Charley**) (-tīm′) [Colloq.] a carefree, sociable, pleasure-seeking fellow

good turn a good deed; friendly, helpful act; favor

good·wife (-wīf′) *n., pl.* **-wives′** (-wīvz′) [ME.: see GOOD & WIFE] [Archaic] **1.** a wife or a mistress of a household **2.** a title equivalent to *Mrs.*, applied to a woman ranking below a lady

good will 1. a friendly or kindly attitude; benevolence **2.** cheerful consent; willingness; readiness **3.** the value of a business in patronage, reputation, etc., over and beyond its tangible assets Also **good′will′** (-wil′)

good·y¹ (-ē) *n., pl.* **-ies** [Colloq.] **1.** something considered very good to eat, as a piece of candy ☆**2.** same as GOODY-GOODY —*adj.* [Colloq.] same as GOODY-GOODY —*interj.* a child's exclamation of approval or delight

good·y² (-ē) *n., pl.* **good′ies** [< GOODWIFE] [Archaic] a woman, esp. an old woman or housewife, of lowly social status: used as a title with the surname

Good·year (good′yir′), **Charles** 1800–60; U.S. inventor: originated the process for vulcanizing rubber

good·y-good·y (good′ē good′ē) *adj.* [redupl. of GOODY¹] [Colloq.] moral or pious in an affected or canting way —*n.* [Colloq.] a goody-goody person

☆**goo·ey** (gōō′ē) *adj.* **goo′i·er, goo′i·est** [GOO + -EY] [Slang] **1.** sticky, as glue **2.** sticky and sweet **3.** overly sentimental

goof (gōōf) *n.* [prob. < dial. *goff* < Fr. *goffe*, stupid < It. *goffo*] [Slang] **1.** a stupid, silly, or credulous person **2.** a mistake; blunder —*vi.* [Slang] **1.** to make a mistake; blunder, fail, etc. **2.** to waste time, shirk one's duties, etc. (usually with *off* or *around*)

☆**goof·ball** (-bôl′) *n.* [GOOF + BALL¹] [Slang] a barbiturate, or sometimes a stimulant drug, tranquilizer, etc., esp. when used nonmedically: also **goof ball**

goof-off (-ôf′) *n.* [Slang] a person who wastes time, neglects his duties, or avoids work; shirker

goof·y (-ē) *adj.* **goof′i·er, goof′i·est** [Slang] like or characteristic of a goof; stupid and silly —**goof′i·ly** *adv.* —**goof′i·ness** *n.*

☆**goo·gol** (gōō′gôl) *n.* [arbitrary use by Edward Kasner (1878–1955), U.S. mathematician, of a child's word] **1.** a number 1 followed by 100 zeros; 10^{100} **2.** any very large number

☆**goo·gol·plex** (-pleks′) *n.* [prec. + L. -*plex*, -fold] the number 1 followed by a googol of zeros

☆**goo-goo** (gōō′gōō′) *n.* [< *Goo(d) Go(vernment Association*), a Boston reform society] a person who advocates or works for political reform

goo-goo eyes (-gōō′) [Slang] amorously inviting glances

☆**gook** (gook, gōōk) *n.* [GOO + (GUN)K] [Slang] any sticky, greasy, or slimy substance

☆**goon** (gōōn) *n.* [Slang] **1.** [< ? *goon*, dial. var. of GUN] a ruffian or thug, esp. one hired to help break a strike, etc. **2.** [after a grotesque comicstrip figure created by E. C. Segar (1894–1938), U.S. cartoonist] a person who is awkward, grotesque, stupid, etc.

goo·ney bird (gōō′nē) [< *gooney*, sailors' name for the albatross, orig. simpleton, prob. < or akin to ME. *gonen*, to gape < OE. *ganian*: see YAWN] the black-footed albatross (*Diomedea nigripes*): also **goo′ny bird**

☆**goop** (gōōp) *n.* [GOO + (SOU)P] [Slang] any sticky, semi-liquid substance —**goop′y** *adj.* **goop′i·er, goop′i·est**

goos·an·der (gōō san′dər) *n.* [prob. < GOOSE, after *bergander*, sheldrake] same as MERGANSER

goose (gōōs) *n., pl.* **geese**; for 4 & 5, **goos′es** [ME. *gose* < OE. *gos*, akin to Du. & G. *gans* < IE. *ghans*, whence L. *anser*; *vt.* **1.** prob. from the fact that geese sometimes attack children from the rear] **1.** any of a large group of long-necked, web-footed, wild or domestic birds (subfamily Anserinae) that are like ducks but larger; esp., a female of this group, as distinguished from a gander **2.** the flesh of a goose, used for food **3.** a silly person **4.** a tailor's pressing iron with a long handle curved somewhat like the neck of a goose **5.** [Slang] a sudden, playful prod in the backside —*vt.* **goosed, goos′ing** [Slang] ☆**1.** to prod suddenly and playfully in the backside so as to startle ☆**2.** to feed gasoline to (an engine) in irregular spurts ☆**3.** to prod, or stir, into action —**cook one's goose** [Colloq.] to spoil one's chances, hopes, etc.

goose barnacle [from the fable that geese grew from them] any of a number of barnacles (genera *Lepas* and *Mitella*) that attach themselves by a long, fleshy stalk to rocks, ship bottoms, etc.: also called **gooseneck barnacle**

GOOSE BARNACLES
(1/2–3 1/2 in. long)

goose·ber·ry (gōōs'ber'ē, -bə rē; gōōz'-) n., pl. **-ries** [as if < GOOSE + BERRY, but prob. folk-etym. form for *grose berie*, akin to dial. *grosel*, gooseberry (< Fr. *groseille*), Du. *kruisbezie*, G. *krausbeere*] 1. a small, sour berry used in making preserves, pies, etc.: it resembles a currant but is larger 2. any of various prickly shrubs (genus *Ribes*) of the saxifrage family which produce gooseberries

goose egg [Slang] ☆1. zero or a score of zero 2. a large swelling or lump, esp. one caused by a blow

goose flesh a roughened condition of the skin in which the papillae are erected, caused by cold, fear, etc.: also ☆**goose bumps** (or **pimples** or **skin**)

goose·foot (-foot') adj. designating a family (Chenopodiaceae) of plants including spinach and beets —n., pl. **-foots** any of a genus (*Chenopodium*) of plants of the goosefoot family, with small green flowers and, frequently, scurfy or fleshy foliage

goose·herd (-hurd') n. [ME. *gosherde*: see HERD²] a person who tends geese

goose·neck (-nek') n. any of various mechanical devices shaped like a goose's neck, as an iron joint for pipes, a flexible rod for supporting a desk lamp, etc.

goose step a marching step, as of troops passing in review, in which the legs are raised high and kept stiff and unbent —**goose'-step'** vi. **-stepped', -step'ping**

goos·ey, goos·y (-ē) adj. **goos'i·er, goos'i·est** 1. a) like or characteristic of a goose b) foolish; stupid 2. [Slang] a) easily upset or disturbed by a sudden, playful prod in the backside b) nervous; jumpy

GOP, G.O.P. Grand Old Party (Republican Party)

☆**go·pher** (gō'fər) n. [< ? Fr. *gaufre*, honeycomb (see GOFFER): so called from its habit of burrowing] 1. any of several burrowing rodents (family Geomyidae), about the size of a large rat, with wide cheek pouches: also **pocket gopher** 2. any of a number of striped ground squirrels (genus *Citellus*) related to the chipmunks, found on the prairies of N. America 3. [earlier *magofer*, prob. < AmInd.] a burrowing land tortoise (*Gopherus polyphemus*) found in SE U.S. 4. [G-] a native or inhabitant of Minnesota (called the **Gopher State**)

GOPHER
(7 1/2–25 in. long,
including tail)

☆**gopher snake** 1. same as BULL SNAKE (sense 1) 2. same as INDIGO SNAKE (sense 1)

gopher wood [Heb. *gōpher*] Bible the wood that Noah's ark was made of: Gen. 6:14

Go·rakh·pur (gô'rək poor') city in Uttar Pradesh, NE India: pop. 180,000

go·ral (gô'rəl) n., pl. **-rals, -ral:** see PLURAL, II, D, 1 [< native (Himalayan) name] any of several goat antelopes (genus *Naemorhedus*) similar to the chamois of Europe, found from the S Himalayas into China

gor·cock (gôr'käk') n. [prob. < GORE¹ + COCK¹, because of its color] [Brit. Dial.] the male red grouse

Gor·di·an knot (gôr'dē ən) 1. Gr. Legend a knot tied by King Gordius of Phrygia, which an oracle revealed would be undone only by the future master of Asia: Alexander the Great, failing to untie it, cut the knot with his sword 2. any perplexing problem —**cut the Gordian knot** to find a quick, bold solution for a perplexing problem

gor·di·an worm (gôr'dē ən) any of a phylum (Nematomorpha) of worms parasitic in insects when immature and free-swimming as adults

Gor·don (gôr'd'n) [Scot. < surname *Gordon*] 1. a masculine name 2. **Charles George**, 1833–85; Brit. general in China, Egypt, & Sudan: called **Chinese Gordon**

Gordon setter [after a Scot. dog fancier, the 4th Duke of *Gordon* (1745?–1827?)] a large hunting dog of a breed having a silky, black coat marked with brown

gore¹ (gôr) n. [ME. *gore*, filth < OE. *gor*, dung, filth, akin to ON. *gor*, W. *gor*, MDu. *gore* < IE. base *gwher-*, hot, whence WARM & L. *fornax*, furnace] blood shed from a wound; esp., clotted blood

gore² (gôr) vt. **gored, gor'ing** [ME. *goren* < *gore*, a spear < OE. *gar:* see ff.] to pierce with or as with a horn or tusk

gore³ (gôr) n. [ME. < OE. *gara*, corner < base of *gar*, a spear, akin to MDu. *gheere*, G. *gehre*, gusset < IE. *ghaiso-*, a stake, javelin, whence G. *geissel*, a whip] 1. [Dial.] a triangular piece of land 2. a tapering piece of cloth made or inserted in a skirt, sail, etc. to give it fullness —vt. **gored, gor'ing** to make or insert a gore or gores in

Gor·gas (gôr'gəs), **William Crawford** 1854–1920; U.S. army medical officer: chief sanitary officer in the Canal Zone during construction of the Panama Canal

gorge (gôrj) n. [ME. < OFr., throat, gullet < LL. *gurga*, throat, narrow pass, for L. *gurges*, whirlpool < IE. base *gwer-*, to swallow up, whence L. *vorare*] 1. the throat or gullet 2. the crop or craw of a hawk 3. a) the maw or stomach of a voracious being or animal b) food or a meal to fill or stuff the stomach c) the contents of the stomach 4. a feeling of resentment, disgust, anger, etc. [to make one's *gorge* rise] 5. the entrance from the rear into a bastion or projecting section of a fortification 6. a deep, narrow pass between steep heights ☆7. a mass that blocks up a passage [an ice *gorge*] —vi. **gorged, gorg'ing** to eat gluttonously —vt. 1. to fill the gorge of; glut 2. to swallow greedily

gor·geous (gôr'jəs) adj. [ME. *gorgeouse*, altered < OFr. *gorgias*, beautiful, glorious, also ruff for the neck < *gorge:* see prec.] 1. brilliantly colored; magnificent; resplendent 2. [Slang] wonderful, wonderful, delightful, etc.: a counter word of approval —SYN. see SPLENDID —**gor'geous·ly** adv. —**gor'geous·ness** n.

gor·ger·in (gôr'jər in) n. [Fr. < *gorgère*, ruff for the throat < *gorge:* see GORGE] Archit. the part of a column just below the top molding or between the shaft and the capital

gor·get (gôr'jit) n. [ME. < OFr. *gorgete* < *gorge:* see GORGE] 1. a piece of armor to protect the throat: see ARMOR, illus. 2. a collar 3. an article of clothing covering the neck and breast, formerly worn by women 4. a patch of color on the throat of a bird

Gor·gon (gôr'gən) n. [ME. < L. Gorgo (gen. Gorgonis) < Gr. Gorgō < gorgos, terrible, fierce] 1. Gr. Myth. any of three sisters with snakes for hair, so horrible that the beholder was turned to stone 2. [g-] any ugly, terrifying, or repulsive woman —**Gor·go·ni·an** (gôr gō'nē ən) adj.

gor·go·ni·an (gôr gō'nē ən) n. [ModL. *gorgonia*, name of the genus < L., coral (< *Gorgo*, GORGON) + -AN] any of an order (Gorgonacea) of colonial, attached, marine coelenterates with a horny, axial skeleton that branches, as in the sea whips, or forms an open network, as in the sea fans

gor·gon·ize (gôr'gə nīz') vt. **-ized', -iz'ing** [GORGON + -IZE] to petrify or stupefy, as with a look

Gor·gon·zo·la (gôr'gən zō'lə) n. [It. < Gorgonzola, town in Italy near Milan] a white Italian pressed cheese with veins of blue-green mold and a strong flavor

gor·hen (gôr'hen') n. [prob. < GORE¹ + HEN, with reference to the color] the female red grouse; moor hen

☆**go·ril·la** (gə ril'ə) n. [< Gr. gorillai, a tribe of hairy women, recorded by Hanno, Carthaginian navigator, as the native name in use in W Africa in the 5th cent. B.C. for wild creatures found there] 1. the largest and most powerful of the manlike apes (*Gorilla gorilla*) native to the jungles of equatorial Africa: the adult male weighs up to 500 pounds 2. [Slang] a) a person regarded as like a gorilla in appearance, strength, etc. b) a gangster; thug

GORILLA
(50–70 in. high)

Gor·ki, Gor·kiy, Gor·ky (gôr'kē) city in E European R.S.F.S.R., at the Volga & Oka rivers: pop. 1,100,000

Gor·ki (gôr'kē), **Max·im** (mak'sim) (pseud. of *Aleksei Maximovich Peshkov*) 1868–1936; Russ. novelist & playwright: also sp. **Gor'ky**

Gör·litz (gör'lits) city in SE East Germany, on the Neisse: pop. 96,000

Gor·lov·ka (gär lôf'kä) city in SE Ukrainian S.S.R., in the Donets Basin: pop. 348,000

gor·mand (gôr'mənd) n. same as GOURMAND

gor·mand·ize (gôr'mən dīz') n. [< Fr. gourmandise < gourmand] rare var. of GOURMANDISE —vi., vt. **-ized', -iz'ing** [< the n.] to eat or devour like a glutton —**gor'mand·iz'er** n.

gorm·less (gôrm'lis) adj. [altered < dial. gaumless < gaum, gome, care < ME. gome < ON. gaum, akin to OE. gieme, care, Goth. gaumjan, to heed] [Brit.] slow-witted; stupid

gorse (gôrs) n. [ME. gorst < OE. < IE. base *ghers-*, to stiffen, bristle, whence L. horrere, to stand on end] same as FURZE —**gors'y** adj.

gor·y (gôr'ē) adj. **gor'i·er, gor'i·est** 1. full of, covered with, or like gore; bloody 2. characterized by much bloodshed or slaughter [a gory fight] —**gor'i·ly** adv. —**gor'i·ness** n.

☆**gosh** (gäsh) interj. an exclamation of surprise, wonder, etc.: a euphemism for God

gos·hawk (gäs'hôk') n. [ME. goshauk < OE. goshafoc: see GOOSE & HAWK¹] a large, swift, powerful hawk (*Accipiter gentilis*) with short wings and a long, rounded tail

Go·shen (gō′shən) [Heb. *gōshen*] *Bible* the fertile land assigned to the Israelites in Egypt: Gen. 45:10 —*n.* a land of plenty

gos·ling (gäz′liŋ) *n.* [ME. *goslynge* (see GOOSE & -LING¹), for *geslynge* < ON. *gæslingr*, cognate formation] 1. a young goose 2. a young and foolish person

gos·pel (gäs′p'l) *n.* [ME. *godspell, gospel* (with assimilated *-d-*) < OE. *gōdspel*, orig., good story, good news: intended as transl. of LL.(Ec.) *evangelium* (see EVANGEL), tidings, but later by shortening of *o* it became *gŏdspel* as if < *god*, God + *spel*, story] 1. [*often* G-] *a*) the teachings of Jesus and the Apostles; specif., the Christian doctrine of the redemption of man through Jesus as Christ *b*) the history of the life and teachings of Jesus 2. [G-] *a*) any of the first four books of the New Testament *b*) an excerpt from any of these books read in a religious service 3. anything proclaimed or accepted as the absolute truth: also **gospel truth** 4. any doctrine or rule widely or ardently maintained 5. a style of folk singing originally associated with evangelistic revival meetings —*adj.* [*often* G-] of or having to do with (the) gospel or with evangelism

gos·pel·er, gos·pel·ler (-ər) *n.* [ME. *gospellere* < OE. *godspellere*] 1. a person who reads the Gospel in church services 2. a person who claims for himself and his sect the sole possession of gospel truth: formerly applied derisively to Puritans, Nonconformists, etc.

‡**gos·po·din** (gäs pä dyēn′) *n.*, *pl.* **-da·** (-dä′) [Russ., lit., lord] a Russian title of respect, equivalent to *Mr.*

Gos·port (gäs′pôrt) seaport in Hampshire, S England, on Portsmouth harbor: pop. 70,000

gos·port (tube) (gäs′pôrt) [after prec.] a flexible speaking tube for communicating between different compartments in an airplane

gos·sa·mer (gäs′ə mər) *n.* [ME. *gosesomer*, lit., goose summer: with allusion to the warm period in fall (*St. Martin's summer*) when geese are in season and gossamer is chiefly noticed] 1. a filmy cobweb floating in the air or spread on bushes or grass 2. a very thin, soft, filmy cloth ☆3. formerly, a lightweight waterproof coat 4. anything like gossamer in lightness, flimsiness etc. —*adj.* light, thin, and filmy: also **gos′sa·mer·y** (-mər ē)

gos·san (gäs′'n) *n.* [Corn. *gossen* < *gos*, blood < OCorn. *guit*] *Mining* rusty iron deposits often occurring where the upper part of a vein has been weathered and oxidized

Gosse (gôs, gäs), Sir **Edmund William** 1849–1928; Eng. poet, critic, & biographer

gos·sip (gäs′əp) *n.* [ME. *godsip, gossyp* (with assimilated *-d-*) < Late OE. *godsibbe*, godparent: see GOD & SIB] 1. [Obs. *or* Dial.] *a*) a godparent *b*) a close friend 2. a person who chatters or repeats idle talk and rumors, esp. about the private affairs of others 3. *a*) such talk or rumors *b*) chatter —*vi.* to be a gossip; indulge in idle talk or rumors about others —**gos′sip·y** *adj.*

gos·soon (gä sōōn′) *n.* [altered < Fr. *garçon*, boy, attendant] [Irish] 1. a boy 2. a servant boy

got (gät) *pt. & alt. pp. of* GET

Go·ta·ma (gō′tə mə) *same as* GAUTAMA (*see* BUDDHA)

Gö·te·borg (yö′tə bôr′y′) seaport in SW Sweden, on the Kattegat: pop. 422,000

Goth (gäth, gôth) *n.* [< LL. *Gothi*, pl. (OE. *Gotan*) < Gr. *Gothoi*, pl. < base of Goth. **Gutans*, pl., or *Gut* (*thiuda*) Gothic (people)] 1. any member of a Germanic people that invaded and conquered most of the Roman Empire in the 3d, 4th, and 5th centuries A.D.: see also OSTROGOTH, VISIGOTH 2. an uncouth, uncivilized person; barbarian

Goth., goth. Gothic

Goth·am (gäth′əm, gō′thəm; *for* 1, *Brit.* gät′-) 1. a village near Nottingham, England, whose inhabitants, the "wise men of Gotham," were, according to legend, very foolish 2. *nickname for* NEW YORK CITY —**Goth′am·ite** (-ït′) *n.*

Goth·ic (gäth′ik) *adj.* [LL. *Gothicus:* see GOTH] 1. of the Goths or their language 2. designating of, or related to a style of architecture developed in W Europe between the 12th and 16th cent. and characterized by the use of ribbed vaulting, flying buttresses, pointed arches, steep, high roofs, etc. 3. [*sometimes* g-] *a*) medieval *b*) not classical *c*) barbarous; uncivilized 4. of or in a style of literature using a medieval setting, atmosphere, etc., esp. to suggest horror and mystery —*n.* 1. the East Germanic language of the Goths: it is known chiefly from the Bible translation of Bishop Ulfilas (4th cent. A.D.) 2. Gothic style, esp. in architecture 3. *Printing* ☆*a*) [*often* g-] a plain style of type having straight lines of uniform width, and lacking serifs or other extra strokes *b*) [Brit.] *same as* BLACK LETTER —**Goth′i·cal·ly** *adv.* —**Goth′ic·ness** *n.*

Gothic arch a pointed arch

Goth·i·cism (-ə siz'm) *n.* 1. barbarism; rudeness 2. conformity to or use of Gothic style —**Goth′i·cist** *n.*

Goth·i·cize (-ə sïz′) *vt.* **-cized′, -ciz′ing** to make Gothic

Got·land (gät′lənd; *Sw.* gôt′-) Swed. island in the Baltic, off the SE coast of Sweden: 1,167 sq. mi.

got·ten (gät′'n) *alt. pp. of* GET

‡**Göt·ter·däm·mer·ung** (göt′ər dem′ər ooŋ) *n.* [G., twilight of the gods] 1. Ger. *name for* RAGNAROK 2. an opera by Richard Wagner on the theme of Ragnarok: see RING OF THE NIBELUNG

Göt·ting·en (göt′iŋ ən) city in E West Germany, in Lower Saxony: pop. 111,000

gouache (gwäsh) *n.* [Fr. < It. *guazzo*, water color, spray,

pool < L. *aquatio*, watering, watering place < *aqua*, water] 1. a way of painting with opaque colors ground in water and mixed with a preparation of gum 2. a pigment of this sort 3. a painting made with such pigments

Gou·da (cheese) (gou′də, gōō′-) *n.* [< *Gouda*, Netherlands, city where orig. produced] a mild, semisoft to hard cheese made from curds and usually coated with red wax

Gou·dy (gou′dē), **Frederic William** 1865–1947; U.S. printer & designer of printing types

gouge (gouj) *n.* [ME. < OFr. < VL. *gubia*, for LL. *gulbia* < Celt. (as in OIr. *gulban*, goad, thorn) < IE. base **gelebh-*, to scrape, hollow out, whence Gr. *glaphein*, to carve] 1. a chisel with a curved, hollowed blade, for cutting grooves or holes in wood 2. *a*) the act of gouging *b*) the groove or hole made by gouging ☆3. [Colloq.] unfair exaction of money; extortion or swindle —*vt.* **gouged, goug′ing** 1. to make grooves or holes in with or as with a gouge 2. to scoop out; dig or force out [to *gouge* out dirt] ☆3. in fighting, to push one's thumb into the eye of ☆4. [Colloq.] to cheat out of money, etc.; also, to charge too high a price to —☆**goug′er** *n.*

GOUGE

gou·lash (gōō′läsh, -lash) *n.* [G. *gulasch* < Hung. *gulyás*, lit., cattle herder (< *gulya*, cattle), hence herdsman's food] a stew made of beef or veal and vegetables seasoned with paprika, etc.: also **Hungarian goulash**

Gould (gōōld), **Jay** 1836–92; U.S. financier

Gou·nod (gōō nō′; *E.* gōō′nō), **Charles (François)** (shär′l) 1818–93; Fr. composer

gou·ra·mi (goor′ə mē, goo rä′mē) *n.*, *pl.* **-mis, -mi:** see PLURAL, II, D, 1 [Malay *gurami*] 1. a food fish (*Osphronemus goramy*) of SE Asia, that builds a nest 2. any of a number of related fishes, mostly brightly colored, that are often kept in aquariums, as the **kissing gourami** (*Helostoma temmincki*)

gourd (gôrd, goord) *adj.* [ME. *gourde* < OFr. *gouorde* < L. *cucurbita*] designating a family (Cucurbitaceae) of plants that includes the squash, melon, pumpkin, etc. —*n.* 1. any trailing or climbing plant belonging to the gourd family 2. *a*) *same as* CALABASH (sense 2 *a*) *b*) any of the ornamental, inedible fruits of related plants, esp. of a yellow-flowered variety (*Cucurbita pepo ovifera*) ☆3. the dried, hollowed-out shell of such a fruit, used as a drinking cup, dipper, etc.

gourde (goord) *n.* [Fr., fem. of *gourd*, numb, heavy, dull < L. *gurdus*, dull, heavy, stupid] the monetary unit and a coin of Haiti: see MONETARY UNITS, table

gour·mand (goor′mənd, goor mänd′; *Fr.* gōōr män′) *n.* [ME. *gourmaunt* < OFr. *gourmand*] 1. orig., a glutton 2. a person with a hearty liking for good food and drink and a tendency to indulge in them to excess 3. *same as* GOURMET —*SYN.* see EPICURE

gour·man·dise (goor mən dēz′) *n.* [Fr.] the tastes or connoisseurship of a gourmand

gour·met (goor′mā; *Fr.* gōōr me′) *n.* [Fr. < OFr. *gourmet, groumet*, servant, wine taster, vintner's assistant: meaning infl. by prec.] a person who likes and is an excellent judge of fine foods and drinks; epicure —*SYN.* see EPICURE

Gour·mont (gōōr môn′), **Ré·my de** (rə mē′ də) 1858–1915; Fr. poet, novelist, & literary critic

gout (gout) *n.* [ME. *goute* < OFr. *goute*, gout, lit., a drop < L. *gutta*, a drop: orig. attributed to a discharge of drops of humors] 1. a disease resulting from a disturbance of uric acid metabolism, characterized by an excess of uric acid in the blood and deposits of uric acid salts in various tissues, esp. in the joints of the feet and hands: it causes swelling and severe pain, notably in the big toe 2. a spurt, splash, glob, etc.

gout·y (-ē) *adj.* **gout′i·er, gout′i·est** 1. having, or tending to have, gout 2. of or like gout 3. resulting from or causing gout 4. swollen with gout —**gout′i·ly** *adv.* —**gout′i·ness** *n.*

gov., Gov. 1. government 2. governor

gov·ern (guv′ərn) *vt.* [ME. *governen* < OFr. *gouverner* < L. *gubernare*, to pilot (a ship), direct, guide < Gr. *kybernan*, to steer, govern] 1. to exercise authority over; rule, administer, direct, control, manage, etc. 2. to influence the action or conduct of; guide; sway [to *govern* public opinion] 3. to hold in check; restrain; curb [to *govern* one's temper] 4. to regulate the speed of (an automobile, etc.) by means of a governor 5. to be a rule or law for; determine [the scientific principles *governing* a phenomenon] 6. *Gram. a*) to require (a word) to be in a particular case or mood *b*) to require (a particular case or mood) In English grammar, the term may apply to any interrelationship between forms, as to that between a preposition and a following pronoun —*vi.* to exercise the function of governing; rule —**gov′ern·a·ble** *adj.*

SYN.—**govern** implies the exercise of authority in controlling the actions of the members of a body politic and directing the affairs of state, and generally connotes as its purpose the maintenance of public order and the promotion of the common welfare; **rule** now usually signifies the exercise of arbitrary or autocratic power; **administer** implies the orderly management of governmental affairs by executive officials

gov·ern·ance (-ər nəns) *n.* [ME. < OFr. *gouvernance* < ML. *gubernantia* < prp. of L. *gubernare:* see GOVERN] the act, manner, function, or power of government

gov·ern·ess (-ər nəs) *n.* **1.** a woman employed in a private home to train and teach a child or children **2.** [Obs.] a woman governor

gov·ern·ment (guv'ər mənt, -ərn mənt) *n.* [OFr. *gouvernement:* see GOVERN & -MENT] **1.** *a)* the exercise of authority over a state, district, organization, institution, etc.; direction; control; rule; management *b)* the right, function, or power of governing **2.** *a)* a system of ruling, controlling, etc. *b)* an established system of political administration by which a nation, state, district, etc. is governed *c)* the study of such systems; political science **3.** all the people or agencies that administer or control the affairs of a nation, state, institution, etc.; administration **4.** [*often* G-] the executive or administrative branch of government of a particular nation as constituted by the political party or coalition in power **5.** a governed territory **6.** *Gram.* the influence of one word over the case or mood of another —☆**gov′ern·men′tal** *adj.* —☆**gov′ern·men′tal·ly** *adv.*

gov·er·nor (guv′ə nər, -ər nər) *n.* [ME. *governour* < OFr. *governeor* < L. *gubernator*, a pilot, steersman, governor] **1.** a person who governs; esp., *a)* a person appointed to govern a dependency, province, town, fort, etc. ☆*b)* the elected head of any State of the U.S. *c)* any of the group of persons who direct an organization or institution [the board of *governors* of a hospital] *d)* [Chiefly Brit.] the person in charge of an organization or institution **2.** a mechanical device for automatically controlling the speed of an engine or motor as by regulating the intake of fuel, steam, etc. **3.** [Brit. Colloq.] a person having authority; esp., one's father or employer: often a term of address

governor general *pl.* **governors general, governor generals** a governor who has subordinate or deputy governors under him, as in the British Commonwealth: also, Brit., **gov′er·nor-gen′er·al** *n.*, *pl.* **gov′er·nors-gen′er·al**

gov·er·nor·ship (-ship′) *n.* the position, function, or term of office of a governor

Governors Island [set aside (1698) as the home for Eng. governors] island in Upper New York Bay at the mouth of the East River: a U.S. Coast Guard station now occupies the entire island: 173 acres

govt., Govt. government

gow·an (gou′ən) *n.* [< Obs. *gollan*, yellow flower < ME. *gollan* < or akin to ON. *goll*, GOLD] [Scot.] any yellow or white field flower; esp., the common daisy

Gow·er (gou′ər, gō′ər), **John** 1325?-1408; Eng. poet

gowk (gouk, gōk) *n.* [ME. *goke, gouk* < ON. *gaukr*, akin to OE. *geac*, G. *gauch*, of echoic orig.] [Brit. Dial.] **1.** a cuckoo **2.** a simpleton

gown (goun) *n.* [ME. *goune* < OFr. < LL. *gunna*, loose robe, orig., fur cloak] **1.** a long, loose outer garment; specif., *a)* a woman's dress, esp. one that is elegant or formal *b)* a dressing gown *c)* a nightgown, nightshirt, etc. *d)* a loose, cotton smock worn by a surgeon *e)* a long, flowing robe worn as a symbol of office or status by certain officials, clergymen, scholars, etc. **2.** the members of a college or university as distinct from the other residents of the community [conflicts between town and *gown*] —*vt.* to dress in a gown, as in an academic or ecclesiastic robe

gowns·man (gounz′mən) *n.*, *pl.* **-men** (-mən) a person entitled to wear the gown of his profession or office

‡**goy** (goi) *n.*, *pl.* **goy′im** (-im) [Yid. < Heb. *gōi*, tribe, nation] a non-Jew; gentile

Go·ya (**y Lu·cien·tes**) (gō′yä ē lōō thyen′tās), **Fran·cis·co Jo·sé de** (frän thēs′kō hō se′ *the*) 1746-1828; Sp. painter

G.P., g.p. 1. general paresis **2.** general practitioner

g.p. *Printing* great primer

gpm, g.p.m. gallons per minute

GPO, G.P.O. Government Printing Office

gps, g.p.s. gallons per second

Gr. 1. Grecian **2.** Greece **3.** Greek

gr. 1. grade **2.** grain(s) **3.** gram(s) **4.** grammar **5.** gravity **6.** great **7.** gross **8.** group

Graaf·i·an follicle (or **vesicle**) (gräf′ē ən, graf′-) [after Regnier de *Graaf* (1641-73), Du. anatomist] any of the small, round, fluid-filled sacs in the ovary of higher mammals, each of which contains a maturing ovum

grab¹ (grab) *vt.* **grabbed, grab′bing** [prob. < MDu., MLowG. *grabben*, akin to ON. *grapa*, GRASP < IE. base *ghrebh-*, whence Sans. *grabh-*, to seize] **1.** to seize or snatch suddenly; take roughly and quickly **2.** to get possession of by unscrupulous methods ☆**3.** [Slang] to have a strong emotional impact on —*vi.* to grab or try to grab something (often with *for, at, onto*, etc.) —*n.* **1.** the act of grabbing **2.** something grabbed **3.** any of various mechanical devices for clutching something to be hoisted; specif., [Chiefly Brit.] same as CLAMSHELL (sense 2) —*SYN.* see TAKE —☆**up for grabs** [Slang] for sale, as to the highest bidder, or available to the most aggressive, competitive, etc. —**grab′ber** *n.*

grab² (grab) *n.* [Anglo-Ind. < Ar. *ghurāb*, lit., raven] an Oriental, usually two-masted, ship used in coastal trade

☆**grab bag** a large container holding various wrapped or bagged articles that are sold unseen, the buyer drawing one at random and paying a fixed price

grab·ble (grab′'l) *vi.* **grab′bled, grab′bling** [Du. *grabbelen*, freq. of *grabben*, GRAB¹] **1.** to feel about with the hands; grope **2.** to sprawl —*vt.* to seize

☆**grab·by** (-ē) *adj.* **-bi·er, -bi·est** grasping; avaricious

gra·ben (grä′bən) *n.* [G., a ditch < OHG. *grabo* < *graban*, to dig: see GRAVE²] a relatively long, narrow area of the earth's crust that has subsided between two bordering faults: cf. HORST

Grac·chus (grak′əs), **Ga·ius Sem·pro·ni·us** (gā′əs sem prō′nē əs), 153?-121 B.C., & **Ti·ber·i·as Sempronius** (tī bir′ē əs), 163?-133 B.C., Roman statesmen & social reformers Called **the Grac′chi** (-ī)

Grace (grās) [see ff.] a feminine name

grace (grās) *n.* [ME. < OFr. < L. *gratia*, pleasing quality, favor, thanks < *gratus*, pleasing < IE. base *gwer-*, to lift up the voice, praise, whence Sans. *grnāti*, (he) sings, praises & OIr. *bard*, bard] **1.** beauty or charm of form, composition, movement, or expression **2.** an attractive quality, feature, manner, etc. **3.** *a)* a sense of what is right and proper; decency *b)* thoughtfulness toward others **4.** good will; favor **5.** [Archaic] mercy; clemency **6.** *a)* a period of time granted beyond the date set for the performance of an act or the payment of an obligation; temporary exemption *b)* favor shown by granting such a delay **7.** a short prayer in which blessing is asked, or thanks are given, for a meal **8.** [G-] a title of respect or reverence used in speaking to or of an archbishop, duke, or duchess, preceded by *His, Her*, or *Your* **9.** *Music* [*pl.*] ornamental notes or effects collectively, as appoggiaturas, slides, trills, etc. **10.** *Theol. a)* the unmerited love and favor of God toward man *b)* divine influence acting in man to make him pure and morally strong *c)* the condition of a person thus influenced *d)* a special virtue given to a person by God —*vt.* **graced, grac′ing 1.** to give or add grace or graces to; decorate; adorn **2.** to bring honor to; dignify **3.** *Music* to add a grace note or notes to —**fall from grace** to do wrong; sin —**have the grace** to be so aware of what is proper as (to do something) —**in the good** (or **bad**) **graces of** in favor (or disfavor) with —**with bad grace** sullenly or reluctantly —**with good grace** graciously or willingly

grace cup 1. *a)* a cup passed around for drinking a toast after grace at the end of a meal *b)* the toast **2.** a parting drink or toast

grace·ful (-f'l) *adj.* having grace, or beauty of form, composition, movement, or expression —**grace′ful·ly** *adv.* —**grace′ful·ness** *n.*

grace·less (-lis) *adj.* **1.** lacking any sense of what is right or proper **2.** without grace; clumsy or inelegant —**grace′less·ly** *adv.* —**grace′less·ness** *n.*

grace note *Music* a note not necessary to the melody, added only for ornamentation: it is usually printed as a small note with a slant line through the stem, just before the note that it embellishes, from which its short time value is usually subtracted

Grac·es (grā′siz) [transl. of L. *Gratiae* (see GRACE), transl. of Gr. *Charites*, pl. of *Charis*] *Gr. Myth.* the three sister goddesses who had control over pleasure, charm, and beauty in human life and in nature: Aglaia (Brilliance), Euphrosyne (Joy), and Thalia (Bloom)

‡**gra·ci·as** (grä′thē äs, -sē-) *interj.* [Sp.] thank you

grac·ile (gras′'l) *adj.* [L. *gracilis*, scanty] **1.** slender; slim **2.** [by assoc. with GRACE] gracefully slender —**gra·cil·i·ty** (grə sil′ə tē) *n.*

gra·ci·o·so (grä′shē ō′sō, grä′sē-; *Sp.* grä thyō′sō) *n.* [Sp.] a clown or buffoon in Spanish comedies

gra·cious (grā′shəs) *adj.* [ME. < OFr. < L. *gratiosus*, in favor, popular, kind < *gratia:* see GRACE] **1.** having or showing kindness, courtesy, charm, etc. **2.** merciful; compassionate **3.** indulgent or polite to those held to be inferiors **4.** characterized by the taste, luxury, and social ease associated with prosperity, education, etc. [*gracious* living] **5.** [Archaic] having pleasing qualities; attractive —*interj.* an expression of surprise —**gra′cious·ly** *adv.* —**gra′cious·ness** *n.*

grack·le (grak′'l) *n.* [L. *graculus*, jackdaw < IE. echoic base *ger-*, *grak-*, whence CRANE, CROW¹, CRAKE] ☆any of several American blackbirds (family Icteridae), somewhat smaller than a crow; esp., the purple grackle (*Quiscalus quiscula*)

☆**grad** (grad) *n.* [Colloq.] a graduate

grad. 1. graduate **2.** graduated

gra·date (grā′dāt) *vt., vi.* **-dat·ed, -dat·ing** [back-formation < GRADATION] to pass or cause to pass by imperceptible degrees from one to another; shade into one another, as colors

gra·da·tion (grā dā′shən) *n.* [Fr. < L. *gradatio* < *gradatus*, having steps or grades < *gradus:* see GRADE] **1.** the act or process of forming or arranging in grades, stages, or steps **2.** a gradual change by steps or stages from one condition, quality, etc. to another **3.** a gradual shading of one tint, tone, or color into another **4.** a step, stage, or degree in a graded series; transitional stage [the many *gradations*

between good and bad/ 5. *Geol.* the process of wearing away high areas of land by erosion and building up low areas by deposition 6. *Linguis.* a) same as ABLAUT b) a change in vowel conditioned by a change in stress, as *a* in man and policeman —**gra·da'tion·al** *adj.* —**gra·da'tion·al·ly** *adv.*

grade (grād) *n.* [Fr. < L. *gradus*, a step, degree, rank < *gradi*, to step, walk < IE. base *ghredh-*, to stride, whence Goth. *griths*, step] 1. any of the stages in an orderly, systematic progression; step; degree 2. *a*) a degree or rating in a scale classifying according to quality, rank, worth, intensity, etc. *[grade* A eggs*]* b) any of the official ranks or ratings of officers or enlisted men *[*an army colonel and a navy captain are in *grade* O-6*]* c) an accepted standard or level *[*up to *grade]* d) a group of people of the same rank, merit, worth, etc. ☆3. *a*) the degree of rise or descent of a sloping surface, as of a highway, railroad, etc. b) such a sloping part 4. the ground level around a building ☆5. *a*) any of the divisions in a school curriculum usually equal to one year: most systems in the U.S. include twelve grades after the kindergarten b) a group of pupils forming such a division in a school ☆6. a mark or rating on an examination, in a school course, etc. ☆7. *Animal Husbandry* an animal with one parent of pure breed 8. *Linguis.* any of the various forms in which a vowel may appear in grammatically or etymologically related forms as a result of gradation —*vt.* **grad'ed, grad'ing** 1. to arrange or classify by grades; rate according to quality, rank, worth, etc.; sort ☆2. to give a grade (sense 6) to 3. to gradate ☆4. to make (ground) level or slope (ground) evenly for a roadway, etc. ☆5. *Animal Husbandry* to improve by crossing with a pure breed (often with *up*) —*vi.* 1. to assume an indicated rank or position in a series; be of a certain grade 2. to change gradually; go through a series of stages —☆**at grade** on the same level or degree of rise —☆**make the grade** 1. to get to the top of a steep incline 2. to overcome obstacles and reach a desired goal —☆**the grades** elementary school

-grade (grād) [< L. *gradi*, to walk: see prec.] *a combining form meaning* (a specified manner of) walking or moving *[*plantigrade*]*

☆**grade crossing** the place where a railroad intersects another railroad or a roadway on the same level

☆**grad·er** (grā'dər) *n.* 1. a person or thing that grades 2. a pupil in a specified grade at school *[*a fifth *grader]*

☆**grade school** same as ELEMENTARY SCHOOL

☆**grade separation** a crossing with an overpass or underpass

gra·di·ent (grā'dē ənt, -dyənt) *adj.* [L. *gradiens* (gen. *gradientis*), prp. of *gradi*, to step: see GRADE] ascending or descending with a uniform slope —*n.* 1. *a*) a slope, as of a road or railroad b) the degree of such slope 2. *Biol.* a gradation in rate of growth, metabolism, etc. in an organism, growing part, or developing embryo 3. *Physics a*) the rate of change of temperature, pressure, etc. b) a diagram or curve representing this

gra·din (grād'n) *n.* [Fr. < It. *gradino*, dim. of *grado* < L. *gradus*: see GRADE] 1. one of a series of steps or seats arranged in tiers 2. a shelf behind an altar, for candlesticks, etc. Also **gra·dine** (grə dēn', grā'dēn)

grad·u·al (graj'oo wəl) *adj.* [ML. *gradualis* < L. *gradus*: see GRADE] taking place by almost imperceptible steps or degrees; developing little by little, not sharply or suddenly —*n.* [ML. *graduale*, book of hymns orig. sung on steps of a pulpit < L. *gradus] Eccles.* 1. a verse or chant, esp. from the Psalms, presented after the Epistle at Mass 2. a book containing such verses or chants —**grad'u·al·ly** *adv.* —**grad'u·al·ness** *n.*

☆**grad·u·al·ism** (-iz'm) *n.* the principle of seeking to achieve social or political changes or goals gradually rather than rapidly or immediately —**grad'u·al·ist** *n.,' adj.* —**grad'u·al·is'tic** *adj.*

grad·u·ate (graj'oo wit; *for v., and occas. for n.,* -wāt') *n.* [< ML. *graduatus,* pp. of *graduare,* to graduate < L. *gradus:* see GRADE] 1. a person who has completed a course of study at a school or college and has received a degree or diploma 2. a flask, tube, or other container marked with a progressive series of degrees (lines or numbers or both) for measuring liquids or solids —*vt.* **-at'ed, -at'ing** 1. to give a degree or diploma to in recognition of the completion of a course of study at a school or college 2. to mark (a flask, tube, gauge, etc.) with degrees for measuring 3. to arrange or classify into grades according to amount, size, quality, etc. —*vi.* 1. to become a graduate of a school or college 2. to change, esp. advance, by degrees —*adj.* 1. having been graduated from a school, college, etc. ☆2. designating, of, or for instruction or research in various fields leading to degrees above the bachelor's —**grad'u·a'tor** *n.*

grad·u·a·tion (graj'oo wā'shən) *n.* [ML. *graduatio* < pp. of *graduare:* see GRADUATE] 1. *a*) a graduating or being graduated from a school or college b) the ceremony connected with this; commencement 2. *a*) a marking of a flask, tube, gauge, etc. with a series of degrees for measuring b) one or all of the degrees marked; a degree or scale 3. an arrangement or classification into grades according to amount, size, quality, etc.

gra·dus (grā'dəs) *n.* [< L. *Gradus (ad Parnassum),* lit., step (to Parnassus), title of a book on prosody] 1. a dic-tionary of prosody for help in writing poetry, esp. in Greek or Latin 2. a book of piano studies, études, etc. arranged in a progressive order of difficulty

Grae·ae (grē'ē) [L. < Gr. *Graiai,* pl. of *graia,* old woman < *grais,* old, akin to *gēras,* old age: see GERIATRICS] *Gr. Myth.* the three daughters of Phorcus, a sea god: they acted as guards for the Gorgons and had but one eye and one tooth to share among them

Grae·cism (grē'siz'm) *n.* same as GRECISM

Grae·cize (-sīz') *vt., vi.* -cized', -ciz'ing same as GRECIZE

Grae·co- (grē'kō) same as GRECO-

‡**Graf** (gräf) *n., pl.* **Graf'en** (-'n) [G.] a German, Austrian, or Swedish title of nobility corresponding to *earl* or *count*

graf·fi·to (grə fēt'ō) *n., pl.* **-fi'ti** (-ē) [It., a scribbling < *graffio,* a scratch < L. *graphium:* see ff.] an inscription, slogan, drawing, etc. crudely scratched or scribbled on a wall or other public surface

graft (graft, gräft) *n.* [with unhistoric *-t,* for earlier *graff* < ME. *graffe* < OFr., a pencil < L. *graphium* < Gr. *grapheion,* stylus (see GRAPH): from resemblance of the scion to a pointed pencil] 1. *a*) a shoot or bud of one plant or tree inserted or to be inserted into the stem or trunk of another, where it continues to grow, becoming a permanent part; scion b) the act or process of inserting such a bud or shoot c) the place on a plant or tree where such a bud or shoot has been inserted d) a tree or plant with such an insertion 2. a joining of one thing to another as if by grafting ☆3. *a*) the act of taking advantage of one's position to gain money, property, etc. dishonestly, as in politics b) anything acquired by such illegal methods, as an illicit profit from government business 4. *Surgery a*) a piece of skin, bone, or other living tissue transplanted or to be transplanted from one body, or place on a body, to another, where it grows and becomes a permanent part b) such a transplanting —*vt.* 1. *a*) to insert (a shoot or bud) as a graft b) to insert a graft of (one plant) in another c) to produce (a fruit, flower, etc.) by means of a graft 2. to join or make as one ☆3. to obtain (money, etc.) by graft 4. *Surgery* to transplant (a graft) —*vi.* 1. to be grafted 2. to make a graft on a plant ☆3. to obtain money or property by graft —**graft'er** *n.*

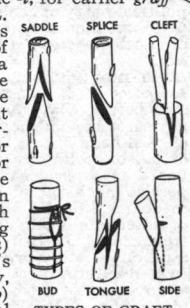

SADDLE SPLICE CLEFT

BUD TONGUE SIDE

TYPES OF GRAFT

graft·age (-ij) *n.* 1. the act or science of grafting 2. the state of being grafted

☆**gra·ham** (grā'əm) *adj.* [< Sylvester *Graham* (1794–1851), U.S. dietary reformer] designating or made of finely ground, whole-wheat flour *[graham* crackers*]*

Gra·ham (grā'əm), **Martha** 1893?– ; U.S. dancer

Grai·ae (grā'ē, grī'ē) same as GRAEAE

Gra·ian Alps (grā'ən) division of the W Alps, along the French-Italian border: highest peak c. 13,320 ft.

Grail (grāl) [ME. *graal* < OFr. < ML. *gradalis,* flat dish, cup < ?] *Medieval Legend* the cup or platter used by Jesus at the Last Supper, and by Joseph of Arimathea to collect drops of Jesus' blood at the Crucifixion: the quest for the Grail, which disappeared, is treated in Malory's *Morte d'Arthur,* Wagner's *Parsifal,* etc.: also called **Holy Grail**

grain (grān) *n.* [ME. *greyne* < OFr. *grein,* a seed, grain (< L. *granum,* a seed, kernel) & *grainne,* seed or grain collectively (< LL. *grana,* fem., orig. pl. of L. *granum*) < IE. base *ĝer-,* to become ripe, whence CORN[1], KERNEL] 1. a small, hard seed or seedlike fruit, esp. that of any cereal plant, as wheat, rice, corn, rye, etc. 2. *a*) cereal seeds in general b) the seeds of a specific cereal c) any plant or plants producing cereal seeds In Great Britain, commonly called *corn* 3. *a*) a tiny, solid particle, as of salt or sand b) a crystal or crystals collectively; also crystallization, esp. of sugar 4. a tiny bit; slightest amount *[*a *grain* of sense*]* 5. [orig. from the weight of a grain of wheat] the smallest unit in the system of weights used in the U.S. and Great Britain, equal to 0.0648 gram: one pound avoirdupois equals 7,000 grains; one pound troy equals 5,760 grains 6. *a*) the arrangement or direction of fibers, layers, or particles of wood, leather, stone, paper, etc. b) the markings or texture due to a particular arrangement c) paint or other surface finish imitating such markings or texture d) a granular surface appearance 7. *a*) that side of a piece of leather from which the hair has been removed b) the markings on that side 8. *a*) disposition; nature b) essential quality 9. [Obs.] *a*) kermes or cochineal b) a red dye made from either c) any fast dye d) [Archaic] color or shade —*vt.* 1. to form into grains; granulate 2. to paint or otherwise finish (a surface) in imitation of the grain of wood, marble, etc. 3. *a*) to remove the hair from (hides) b) to put a finish on the grain surface of (leather) —*vi.* to form grains —**against the** (or **one's**) **grain** contrary to one's feelings, nature, wishes, etc.; irritating or displeasing

grain alcohol ethyl alcohol, esp. when made from grain

☆**grain elevator** a tall building for storing grain

grain·field (-fēld') *n.* a field where grain is grown

Grain·ger (grān′jər), **Percy** (**Aldridge**) 1882–1961; U.S. composer & pianist, born in Australia

grain sorghum any of various strains of sorghum grown primarily for grain

grain·y (-ē) *adj.* **grain′i·er**, **grain′i·est** **1.** having a clearly defined grain: said of textures or surfaces, as of wood **2.** consisting of grains; coarsely textured; granular —**grain′i·ness** *n.*

gral·la·to·ri·al (gral′ə tôr′ē əl) *adj.* [L. *grallator*, stilt-walker < *grallae*, stilts (akin to *gradi*: see GRADE) + -IAL] of or pertaining to the wading birds, including the cranes, herons, etc., characterized by their long legs

gram[1] (gram) *n.* [Fr. *gramme* < LL. *gramma*, weight of two oboli < Gr. *gramma*, small weight, lit., what is written < *graphein*, to write: see GRAPHIC] the basic unit of weight in the metric system, equal to about 1/28 of an ounce (.0022046 pound or 15.4324 grains troy): it was meant to be, and virtually is, the weight of one cubic centimeter of distilled water at 4°C

gram[2] (gram) *n.* [Port. *grão* < L. *granum*: see GRAIN] any of certain plants of the legume family, used as fodder; esp., the chickpea

-gram (gram) [< Gr. *gramma*: see GRAM[1]] *a combining form used to form nouns meaning:* **1.** something written down, drawn, or recorded [*telegram, electrocardiogram*] **2.** *a)* a specified number of grams [*kilogram*] *b)* a specified fraction of a gram [*centigram*]

gram. **1.** grammar **2.** grammarian **3.** grammatical

☆**gra·ma** (grä′mə, gram′ə) *n.* [Sp. < L. *gramen*, GRASS] any of a genus (*Bouteloua*) of native range grasses of the W U.S.: also **grama grass**

gram·a·rye, gram·a·ry (gram′ər ē) *n.* [ME. *gramery*, grammar, magic < OFr. *gramaire*: see GRAMMAR & GLAM-OUR] [Archaic] magic; occult knowledge

gram atom *Chem.* the quantity of an element having a weight in grams numerically equal to the element's atomic weight: a gram atom of copper, the atomic weight of which is 63.54, is a quantity of copper weighing 63.54 grams: also **gram-a·tom·ic weight** (gram′ə täm′ik)

gram calorie *same as* CALORIE (sense 1)

gra·mer·cy (grə mur′sē, gram′ər sē) *interj.* [ME. < OFr. *grant merci* < *grant*, GRAND + *merci*, thanks: see MERCY] [Archaic] **1.** thank you very much; many thanks **2.** an exclamation of surprise

☆**gram·i·ci·din** (gram′ə sīd′'n) *n.* [GRAM(-POSITIVE) + -*i*- + -CID(E) + -IN[1]] any of a group of chemically related antibiotic substances effective in treating various bacterial infections, esp. of the skin and eyes

gra·min·e·ous (grə min′ē əs) *adj.* [L. *gramineus* < *gramen*, GRASS] **1.** of the grass family **2.** of or like grass; grassy

gram·i·niv·o·rous (gram′ə niv′ər əs) *adj.* [< L. *gramen*, GRASS + -VOROUS] feeding on grasses; grass-eating

gram·mar (gram′ər) *n.* [ME. *gramer* < OFr. *gramaire* < L. *grammatica* (*ars*, art) < Gr. *grammatikē* (*technē*, art), grammar, learning < *gramma*, something written (see GRAM[1]): in L. & Gr. a term for the whole apparatus of literary study: in the medieval period, specif., "the study of Latin," hence "all learning as recorded in Latin" (cf. GRAMMAR SCHOOL in Brit. usage), and "the occult sciences as associated with this learning" (cf. GRAMARYE, GLAMOUR)] **1.** that part of the study of language which deals with the forms and structure of words (*morphology*), with their customary arrangement in phrases and sentences (*syntax*), and now often with language sounds (*phonology*): usually distinguished from the study of word meanings (*semantics, semasiology*) **2.** the system of word structures and word arrangements of a given language at a given time **3.** a body of rules for speaking and writing a given language, based on the study of its grammar (sense 2) or on some adaptation of another, esp. Latin, grammar **4.** *same as* GENERATIVE GRAMMAR **5.** a book or treatise on grammar **6.** one's manner of speaking or writing as judged by pre-scriptive grammatical rules [his *grammar* was poor] **7.** *a)* the elementary principles of a field of knowledge *b)* a book or treatise on these

gram·mar·i·an (grə mer′ē ən) *n.* [ME. *gramarian* < MFr. *gramarien*] a specialist or expert in grammar

grammar school ☆**1.** [Now Rare] an elementary school: the term was variously applied to different school levels, esp. to that between the fifth and eighth grades **2.** in England, *a)* orig., a school where Latin was taught *b)* a government-supported secondary school preparing pupils for college

gram·mat·i·cal (grə mat′i k'l) *adj.* [LL. *grammaticalis* < L. *grammatica*: see GRAMMAR] **1.** of or according to grammar **2.** conforming to the prescribed rules of grammar —**gram·mat′i·cal·ly** *adv.* —**gram·mat′i·cal·ness** *n.*

gramme (gram) *n. same as* GRAM[1]

gram molecule *same as* MOLE[4]: also **gram-mo·lec·u·lar weight** (gram′mə lek′yoo lər)

Gram-neg·a·tive (gram′neg′ə tiv) *adj.* [*also* g-] designating bacteria that do not retain the color stain: see GRAM'S METHOD

☆**gram·o·phone** (gram′ə fōn′) *n.* [arbitrary inversion of PHONOGRAM] *chiefly Brit. var. of* PHONOGRAPH

Gram·pi·an Mountains (gram′pē ən) mountain range extending across C & N Scotland, dividing the Highlands from the Lowlands: highest peak, Ben Nevis: also **Grampian Hills, Grampians**

Gram-pos·i·tive (gram′päz′ə tiv) *adj.* [*also* g-] designating bacteria that retain the color stain: see GRAM'S METHOD

gram·pus (gram′pəs) *n., pl.* **-pus·es** [earlier *graundepose*, altered (after GRAND) < ME. *grapays* < OFr. *graspeis* < L. *crassus piscis* < *crassus*, fat (see CRASS) + *piscis*, FISH[2]] any of several small, black, fierce varieties of toothed whales (genus *Grampus*) related to the dolphins

Gram's method (gramz) [after Hans C. J. *Gram* (1853–1938), Dan. physician] a method of staining bacteria for the purpose of classification, involving treatment with gentian violet, an iodine solution, and alcohol: the violet stain is retained (by **Gram-positive** bacteria) or lost (by **Gram-negative** bacteria) when the alcohol is applied

Gra·na·da (grə nä′də; *Sp.* grä nä′thä) **1.** former Moorish kingdom in S Spain **2.** province in this region, on the Mediterranean: 4,838 sq. mi.; pop. 769,000 **3.** capital of this province: site of the Alhambra: pop. 162,000

gran·a·dil·la (gran′ə dil′ə) *n.* [Sp. < dim. of *granada*, pomegranate < L. *granatus*, containing seeds < *granum*, seed: see GRAIN] the edible fruit of certain passionflowers (genus *Passiflora*)

gran·a·ry (gran′ər ē, grā′nər ē) *n., pl.* **-ries** [L. *granarium* < *granum*, GRAIN] **1.** a building for storing threshed grain **2.** a region that produces much grain

Gran Cha·co (grän chä′kō) *same as* CHACO

grand (grand) *adj.* [ME. *graunt* < OFr. *grand, grant* < L. *grandis*, full-grown, great (replacing *magnus* in LL. & Romance languages), prob. < IE. base **gwrendh-*, to swell up, whence Gr. *brenthos*, pride] **1.** higher in rank, status, or dignity than others having the same title [a *grand duke*] **2.** most important; chief; main; principal [the *grand* ballroom] **3.** imposing because of great size, beauty, and extent; magnificent [*grand* scenery] **4.** handsome and luxurious; characterized by splendor and display [a *grand* banquet] **5.** eminent; distinguished; illustrious **6.** self-important; pretentious; haughty **7.** lofty and dignified, as in style **8.** overall; comprehensive [the *grand* total] **9.** [Colloq.] very good; excellent, delightful, admirable, etc.: a general term of approval **10.** *Music* full; complete [a *grand* chorus] —*n.* **1.** *same as* GRAND PIANO ☆**2.** [Slang] a thousand dollars —**grand′ly** *adv.* —**grand′ness** *n.*

SYN.—**grand** is applied to that which makes a strong impression because of its greatness (in size or some favorable quality), dignity, and splendor [the *Grand* Canyon]; **magnificent** suggests a sur-passing beauty, richness, or splendor, or an exalted or glorious quality [a *magnificent* voice]; **imposing** suggests that which strikingly impresses one by its size, dignity, or excellence of char-acter [an *imposing* array of facts]; **stately** suggests that which is imposing in dignified grace and may imply a greatness of size [a *stately* mansion]; **majestic** adds to stately the idea of lofty grandeur [the *majestic* Rockies]; **august** suggests an exalted dig-nity or impressiveness such as inspires awe [an *august* personage]; **grandiose** is often used disparagingly of a grandeur that is affected or exaggerated [a *grandiose* manner]

grand- (grand) [OFr. (see prec.), replacing OE. *ealde-*, ME. *olde-* (see OLD)] *a combining form meaning* of the generation older (or younger) than [*grandfather, grandson*]

gran·dam (gran′dam, -dəm) *n.* [ME. *grandame* < Anglo-Fr. *graund dame*: see prec. & DAME] [Archaic or Rare] **1.** a grandmother **2.** an old woman Also sp. **gran′dame**

☆**Grand Army of the Republic** an association (1866–1949) of Union veterans of the Civil War

grand-aunt (grand′ant′, -änt′) *n. same as* GREAT-AUNT

Grand Banks (or **Bank**) large shoal in the North Atlantic, southeast of Newfoundland: noted fishing grounds: c. 500 mi. long See GULF STREAM, map

Grand Canal **1.** canal in NE China, extending from Tien-tsin to Hangchow: c. 1,000 mi. **2.** main canal in Venice, Italy

Grand Canyon **1.** deep gorge of the Colorado River, in NW Ariz.: over 200 mi. long; 4–18 mi. wide; 1 mi. deep **2.** national park (**Grand Canyon National Park**) including 105 mi. of this gorge: 1,052 sq. mi.

grand·child (gran′chīld′) *n., pl.* **-chil′dren** (-chil′drən) a child of one's son or daughter

Grand Cou·lee (koo′lē) dam on the Columbia River, NE Wash.: 550 ft. high; over 4,000 ft. long

grand·dad, grand-dad (gran′dad′) *n.* [Colloq.] grand-father: an affectionate or children's term

grand·daugh·ter (-dôt′ər) *n.* a daughter of one's son or daughter

grand duchess **1.** the wife or widow of a grand duke **2.** a woman who has the rank of a grand duke and rules a grand duchy **3.** in czarist Russia, a princess of the royal family

grand duchy the territory or a country ruled by a grand duke or a grand duchess

grand duke **1.** the sovereign ruler of a grand duchy, ranking just below a king **2.** in czarist Russia, a prince of the royal family

grande dame (gränd däm) [Fr., great lady] a woman, esp. an older one, of formidable dignity or impressive accomplishments

gran·dee (gran dē′) n. [Sp. & Port. *grande*: see GRAND] 1. a Spanish or Portuguese nobleman of the highest rank 2. a man of high rank; important personage

Grande-Terre (grän′ter′) E island of the two major islands of Guadeloupe, West Indies: also **Grand Terre**

gran·deur (gran′jər, -joor) n. [Fr. < *grand*: see GRAND] the quality of being grand; specif., *a)* splendor; magnificence *b)* moral and intellectual greatness; nobility

Grand Falls waterfall on the upper Hamilton River, W Labrador: over 300 ft. high

grand·fa·ther (gran′fä′*th*ər, grand′-) n. 1. the father of one's father or mother: also a term of respectful familiarity to any elderly man 2. a male ancestor; forefather

☆**grandfather clause** 1. a former law in some Southern States waiving electoral literacy requirements for those whose forebears voted before the Civil War, thus keeping the franchise for illiterate whites 2. a clause in some legislation forbidding a certain activity, which exempts those already engaged in it before the legislation was passed

☆**grandfather** (or **grandfather's**) **clock** a large clock with a pendulum, contained in a tall, upright case

grand·fa·ther·ly (-lē) adj. 1. of a grandfather 2. having the characteristics conventionally attributed to a grandfather; kindly, indulgent, benignant, etc.

Grand Forks [in allusion to the junction of two rivers] city in E N.Dak., on the Red River of the North: pop. 39,000

‡**Grand Gui·gnol** (grän gē nyôl′) [the name of a former theater in Paris noted for such drama] [*occas.* g- g-] any dramatic production designed to shock and horrify its audience with its gruesome or macabre content

gran·dil·o·quent (gran dil′ə kwənt) adj. [< L. *grandiloquus*, grandiloquent < *grandis*, GRAND + *loqui*, to speak, after ELOQUENT] using high-flown, pompous, bombastic words and expressions —SYN. see BOMBASTIC —**gran·dil′o·quence** n. —**gran·dil′o·quent·ly** adv.

gran·di·ose (gran′dē ōs′) adj. [Fr. < It. *grandioso* < L. *grandis*, great, GRAND] 1. having grandeur or magnificence; imposing; impressive 2. seeming or trying to seem very grand or important; pompous and showy —SYN. see GRAND —**gran′di·ose′ly** adv. —**gran′di·os′i·ty** (-äs′ə tē) n.

‡**gran·dio·so** (grän dyō′sō) adj., adv. [It.] *Music* in a grand, noble style: a direction to the performer

grand jury a special jury of a statutory number of citizens, usually more than 12, that investigates accusations against persons charged with crime and indicts them for trial before a petit jury if there is sufficient evidence

Grand Lama same as DALAI LAMA

grand larceny *Law* 1. theft in which the property stolen has a value equaling or exceeding a certain amount fixed by law: the amount varies from State to State but is usually between $25 and $60: distinguished from PETIT LARCENY 2. in some States, the theft of property of any value directly from the person of the victim, but without the use of force

grand·ma (gran′mä, gra′mä) n. [Colloq.] grandmother

grand mal (gran′ mal′; *Fr.* grän mäl′) [Fr., lit., great ailment] a type of epilepsy in which there are generalized convulsions and loss of consciousness: distinguished from PETIT MAL

Grand Ma·nan (mə nan′) island of New Brunswick at the entrance to the Bay of Fundy: 57 sq. mi.; pop. 2,500

‡**grand monde** (grän′ mōnd′) [Fr., lit., great world] fashionable society

grand·moth·er (gran′mu*th*′ər, grand′-, gra′-) n. 1. the mother of one's father or mother: also a term of respectful familiarity to any elderly woman 2. a female ancestor; ancestress

grand·moth·er·ly (-lē) adj. 1. of a grandmother 2. having the characteristics conventionally attributed to a grandmother; kindly, indulgent, etc.

grand·neph·ew (gran′nef′yōō, grand′-; *chiefly Brit.,* -nev′yōō) n. the grandson of one's brother or sister

grand·niece (-nēs′) n. the granddaughter of one's brother or sister

grand opera opera, generally on a serious theme, in which the whole text is set to music

grand·pa (gran′pä, grand′-, gram′-) n. [Colloq.] grandfather

grand·par·ent (-per′ənt) n. a grandfather or grandmother

grand piano a large piano with strings set horizontally in a harp-shaped case

Grand Prairie city in NE Tex.: suburb of Dallas: pop. 51,000

Grand Pré (gran prā′; *Fr.* grän prā′) village in C Nova Scotia, on Minas Basin: site of an early Acadian settlement & the setting of Longfellow's *Evangeline*

‡**grand prix** (grän prē′) [Fr., lit., great prize] first prize; highest award in a competition

Grand Rapids [after the *rapids* on the *Grand* River] city in SW Mich.: pop. 198,000 (met. area 539,000)

grand right and left *Folk Dancing* an interweaving of two concentric circles of dancers, one moving clockwise, one counterclockwise, giving right and left hands alternately to successive partners

grand·sire (gran′sir′, grand′-) n. [Archaic] 1. a grandfather 2. a male ancestor 3. an old man

grand slam ☆1. *Baseball* (designating) a home run hit when there is a runner on each base: also **grand′-slam′mer** 2. *a) Bridge* the winning of all the tricks in a deal ☆*b)* the winning of all of a group of select competitions in a particular sport, as golf

grand·son (gran′sun′, grand′-) n. a son of one's son or daughter

grand·stand (-stand′) n. the main seating structure for spectators at a sporting event, etc. —☆vi. [Colloq.] to try to gain the applause of an audience by or as by making an unnecessarily showy play (**grandstand play**), as in baseball —**grand′stand′er** n.

Grand Te·ton National Park (tē′tän) [Fr., lit., big breast: from the contours of the mountains] national park in NW Wyo., including a section of a range (**Teton Range**) of the Rockies: highest peak, 13,766 ft.; 472 sq. mi.

grand tour 1. a tour of continental Europe formerly taken by young men of the British aristocracy to complete their education 2. any tour like this 3. a conducted inspection tour, as of a building

grand·un·cle (grand′un′k'l) n. same as GREAT-UNCLE

grange (grānj) n. [ME. < Anglo-Fr. *graunge* (OFr. *grange*) < ML. *granica* < L. *granum*, GRAIN] 1. orig., a granary 2. a farm with its dwelling house, barns, etc. ☆3. [G-] *a)* the Patrons of Husbandry, an association of farmers organized in the U.S. in 1867 for mutual welfare and advancement *b)* any of its local lodges

grang·er (-ər) n. ☆1. a farmer ☆2. [G-] a member of the Grange —**grang′er·ism** n.

grang·er·ize (grān′jə rīz′) vt. -ized′, -iz′ing [after James *Granger*, author of a *Biographical History of England* (1769), which included blank pages for such illustrations] [Brit.] 1. to illustrate (a book already printed) with engravings, prints, etc. obtained elsewhere, often by clipping them from other books 2. to damage (a book) by clipping such engravings, etc. —**grang′er·i·za′tion, grang′er·ism** n.

gran·i- (gran′i) [< L. *granum*, GRAIN] a combining form meaning grain [*granivorous*]

Gra·ni·cus (grə ni′kəs) river in ancient Mysia (W Asia Minor): site of a battle (334 B.C.) in which Alexander the Great defeated the Persians

gra·nif·er·ous (grə nif′ər əs) adj. [< L. *granifer*: see GRAIN & -FEROUS] bearing grain

gran·ite (gran′it) n. [It. *granito*, granite, lit., grained, pp. of *granire*, to reduce to grains < *grano* < L. *granum*, a seed, GRAIN] a very hard, crystalline, plutonic rock, gray to pink in color, consisting of feldspar, quartz, and smaller amounts of dark ferromagnesian minerals —**gra·nit·ic** (grə nit′ik, gra-) adj.

Granite City [from the graniteware made there] city in SW Ill., near St. Louis: pop. 40,000

gran·ite·ware (-wer′) n. 1. a variety of ironware for household use, coated with a hard enamel that looks somewhat like granite 2. a variety of fine, hard pottery

gran·it·oid (gran′it oid′) adj. like, or having the structure of, granite

gra·niv·o·rous (grə niv′ər əs) adj. [GRANI- + -VOROUS] feeding on grain and seeds

gran·ny, gran·nie (gran′ē) n., pl. -nies [Colloq.] 1. a grandmother 2. an old woman 3. any fussy, exacting person ☆4. [South] a midwife 5. same as GRANNY KNOT

granny knot a knot like a square knot but with the ends crossed the wrong way, forming an awkward, insecure knot: see KNOT, illus.: also **granny's knot**

gran·o- (gran′ə) [G. *grano-*: see GRANOPHYRE] a combining form meaning of or like granite [*granolith*]

Gran·o·lith (gran′ə lith′) [prec. + -LITH] a trademark for a concrete used for flooring, pavement, etc., containing crushed or chipped granite or other stone —n. [g-] such a concrete —**gran′o·lith′ic** adj.

gran·o·phyre (-fir′) n. [G. *granophyr*, arbitrary blend < *granit*, GRANITE + *porphyr*, PORPHYRY] a rock similar to granite in composition and appearance, but containing larger crystals of quartz and feldspar in a matrix of a finer grain —**gran′o·phyr′ic** (-fir′ik) adj.

grant (grant, gränt) vt. [ME. *granten* < OFr. *graanter, craanter*, to promise, assure < VL. *credentare*, to promise, yield < L. *credens*, prp. of *credere*, to believe: see CREED] 1. to give (what is requested, as permission, etc.); assent to; agree to fulfill 2. *a)* to give or confer formally or according to legal procedure *b)* to transfer (property) by a deed 3. to acknowledge for the sake of argument; admit as true without proof; concede —n. 1. the act of granting 2. something granted, as property, a tract of land, an exclusive right or power, money from a fund, etc. ☆3. a territorial subdivision in Maine, New Hampshire, or Vermont —SYN. see GIVE —**take for granted** to consider as true, already settled, requiring no special attention, etc.; accept as a matter of course —**grant′a·ble** adj. —**grant′er,** *Law* **grant′or** n.

Grant (grant), **Ulysses Simp·son** (simp′sən) (born *Hiram Ulysses Grant*) 1822-85; 18th president of the U.S. (1869-77); commander in chief of the Union forces in the Civil War

grant·ee (grant ē′, gränt-) n. *Law* a person to whom a grant is made

☆**grant-in-aid** (grant′in ād′) *n., pl.* **grants′-in-aid′** a grant of funds, as by the Federal government to a State or by a foundation to a writer, scientist, artist, etc., to support a specific program or project

gran·u·lar (gran′yə lər) *adj.* [< LL. *granulum* (see GRAN-ULE) + -AR] **1.** containing or consisting of grains or granules **2.** like grains or granules; granulated **3.** having a grainy surface —**gran′u·lar′i·ty** (-ler′ə tē) *n.* —**gran′u·lar·ly** *adv.*

granular snow *same as* CORN SNOW

gran·u·late (gran′yə lāt′) *vt., vi.* -**lat′ed, -lat′ing 1.** to form into grains or granules **2.** to make or become rough on the surface by the development of granules or tiny bulges —**gran′u·la′tor, gran′u·lat′er** *n.*

gran·u·la·tion (gran′yə lā′shən) *n.* **1.** formation into granules or grains **2.** *Med. a)* the formation of a small mass of tiny red granules of newly formed capillaries, as on the surface of a wound that is healing *b)* the mass itself

gran·u·la·tive (gran′yə lāt′iv, -lə tiv) *adj.* of or characterized by granulation

gran·ule (gran′yool) *n.* [< LL. *granulum*, dim. of L. *granum*, GRAIN] **1.** a small grain **2.** a small, grainlike particle or spot; specif., any of the small, bright markings on the sun's photosphere that last only a few minutes

gran·u·lite (gran′yə līt′) *n.* [prec. + -ITE¹] a metamorphic rock consisting of uniformly sized, interlocked mineral grains in which coarse and finer bands may alternate — **gran′u·lit′ic** (-lit′ik) *adj.*

gran·u·lo·cyte (-lō sīt′) *n.* [GRANUL(E) + -o- + -CYTE] any of several types of white blood cells with a granular cytoplasm —**gran′u·lo·cyt′ic** (-sit′ik) *adj.*

gran·u·lo·ma (gran′yə lō′mə) *n., pl.* -**mas, -ma·ta** (-mə tə) [GRANUL(E) + -OMA] a nodule of firm tissue formed by the body as a reaction to chronic inflammation, as from foreign bodies, tuberculosis bacteria, etc. —**gran′u·lo′ma·tous** (-təs) *adj.*

gran·u·lose (gran′yə lōs′) *adj. same as* GRANULAR

Gran·ville (gran′vil), **1st Earl** *see* CARTERET

Gran·ville-Bar·ker (gran′vil bär′kər), **Har·ley** (här′lē) 1877-1946; Eng. playwright, critic, & actor

grape (grāp) *n.* [ME. *grap*, replacing earlier *winberie* (cf. WINE & BERRY) < OFr. *grape*, bunch of grapes < *graper*, to gather with a hook < Frank. *krappo* (OHG. *chrapfo*), hook: for IE. base see CRAM] **1.** any of various small, round, smooth-skinned, juicy berries, generally purple, red, or green, growing in clusters on woody vines: grapes are eaten raw, used to make wine, or dried to make raisins **2.** any of various vines (genus *Vitis*) of the grape family that bear grapes; grapevine **3.** a dark purplish red **4.** *same as* GRAPESHOT —*adj.* designating a family (Vitaceae) of tendril-bearing, climbing, woody vines

☆**grape·fruit** (-frōōt′) *n.* [so named because it grows in clusters] **1.** a large, round, edible citrus fruit with a pale-yellow rind, juicy pulp, and a somewhat sour taste **2.** the semitropical evergreen tree (*Citrus paradisi*) of the rue family, that bears grapefruit

grape hyacinth any of a group of small, hardy, bulbous plants (genus *Muscari*) of the lily family, with spikes of small, bell-shaped flowers of blue or white

grape ivy an evergreen climbing vine (*Cissus rhombifolia*) of the grape family, native to N S. America and common as a house plant

grap·er·y (grāp′ər ē) *n., pl.* -**er·ies** a place, esp. an enclosed area or building, where grapes are grown

grape·shot (-shät′) *n.* a cluster of small iron balls formerly fired from a cannon as a dispersing charge

grape sugar *same as* DEXTROSE

grape·vine (-vīn′) *n.* **1.** any of the woody vines that bear grapes ☆**2.** a secret means of spreading or receiving information; also, the spreading of news or gossip from one person to another (with *the*): in full, **grapevine telegraph** ☆**3.** an unfounded report; hearsay; rumor

graph¹ (graf, gräf) *n.* [short for *graphic formula*] **1.** a diagram, as a curve, broken line, series of bars, etc., representing the successive changes in the value of a variable quantity or quantities **2.** *Math. a)* a curve or surface showing the locus of a function on a series of coordinates *b)* a diagram consisting of nodes and links and representing logical relationships or sequences of events —*vt.* to put in the form of, or represent by, a graph

GRAPH

graph² (graf, gräf) *n.* [cf. ff.] a writing-system unit which may be a representation of a phoneme, a syllable, etc.

-**graph** (graf, gräf) [Gr. -*graphos* < *graphein*, to write: see GRAPHIC] *a combining form meaning:* **1.** something that writes or records [*telegraph*] **2.** something written [*monograph*]

graph·eme (graf′ēm) *n.* [*graph*, a spelling, occurrence of an allograph (< -GRAPH) + -*eme* (as in PHONEME)] all the allographs representing a single letter of the alphabet, or all those representing a single phoneme

-**graph·er** (-grə fər) *a combining form used to form nouns of agent corresponding to nouns ending in* -GRAPH *or* -GRAPHY [*telegrapher, stenographer*]

graph·ic (graf′ik) *adj.* [L. *graphicus* < Gr. *graphikos*, capable of painting or drawing, of writing < *graphē*, a drawing, writing < *graphein*, to write, orig., scratch, incise < IE. base *gerebh-*, whence CARVE, CRAB¹] **1.** describing or described in realistic and vivid detail; vivid **2.** of the GRAPHIC ARTS **3.** *a)* of handwriting; used or expressed in handwriting *b)* written, inscribed, or recorded in letters of the alphabet, meaningful symbols, etc. **4.** having markings suggestive of written or printed characters [*graphic* granite] **5.** *a)* of graphs or diagrams *b)* shown by graphs or diagrams Also **graph′i·cal** —**graph′i·cal·ly** *adv.* —**graph′ic·ness** *n.*

SYN.—**graphic**, with reference to speech or writing, imply description that calls forth a mental image as sharply defined as the visual impression made by a picture; **vivid** implies the bringing of strikingly real or lifelike images to the mind; **picturesque** language is full of unusual or quaint imagery and may achieve interesting pictorial effects at the expense of reality

-**graph·ic** (graf′ik) *a combining form used to form adjectives from, or corresponding to, nouns ending in* -GRAPH [*telegraphic, stenographic*]: also -**graph′i·cal**

graphic arts 1. broadly, any form of visual artistic representation, esp. painting, drawing, photography, etc. **2.** specif., those arts in which impressions are printed from various kinds of blocks, plates, screens, etc. as engraving, etching, lithography, serigraphy, dry point, offset, etc.

graph·ics (-iks) *n.pl.* [*with sing. v.*] [< GRAPHIC] **1.** the art of making drawings, as in architecture or engineering, in accordance with mathematical rules **2.** calculation of stresses, etc. from such drawings **3.** *Linguis.* the study of writing systems

graph·ite (graf′īt) *n.* [G. *graphit* < Gr. *graphein*, to write (see GRAPHIC): from its use as writing material] a soft, black, lustrous form of carbon found in nature and used for lead in pencils, for crucibles, lubricants, electrodes, etc. —**gra·phit·ic** (gra fit′ik) *adj.*

graph·i·tize (graf′ə tīz′) *vt.* -**tized′, -tiz′ing 1.** to change into graphite by heating or annealing **2.** to put graphite in or on —**graph′i·ti·za′tion** *n.*

graph·o- (graf′ə) [Fr. < Gr. *graphē*, a writing < *graphein*: see GRAPHIC] *a combining form meaning* writing or drawing [*graphology*]

graph·ol·o·gy (gra fäl′ə jē) *n.* [Fr. *graphologie*: see GRAPHO- & -LOGY] the study of handwriting, esp. as a clue to character, aptitudes, etc. —**graph·ol′o·gist** *n.*

graph·o·mo·tor (graf′ə mōt′ər) *n.* [GRAPHO- + MOTOR] *Physiol.* of or affecting the movements made in writing

☆**Graph·o·phone** (-fōn′) [arbitrary inversion (as if GRAPHO- + -PHONE) < PHONOGRAPH] *a trademark for* an early type of phonograph

graph paper paper with small ruled squares on which to make graphs, diagrams, etc.

-**graph·y** (grə fē) [L. -*graphia* < Gr. -*graphia*, writing < *graphein*, to write: see GRAPHIC] *a combining form meaning:* **1.** a process or method of writing, or graphically representing [*calligraphy, photography*] **2.** a descriptive science or a treatise dealing with such a science [*geography*]

grap·nel (grap′n'l) *n.* [ME. *grapnell*, dim. < OFr. *grapin, grapil* < Pr. *grapa*, a hook < Frank. *krappo*: see GRAPE] **1.** a small anchor with several flukes **2.** an iron bar with claws at one end for grasping and holding things

‡**grap·pa** (grä′pä) *n.* [It.] an Italian brandy distilled from the lees left after pressing grapes to make wine

grap·ple (grap′'l) *n.* [OFr. *grapil*: see GRAPNEL] **1.** *same as* GRAPNEL (sense 2) **2.** a device consisting of two or more hinged, movable iron prongs for grasping and moving heavy objects **3.** a coming to grips; hand-to-hand fight —*vt.* **grap′pled, grap′pling** to grip and hold; seize —*vi.* **1.** to use a grapnel (sense 2) **2.** to struggle in hand-to-hand combat; wrestle **3.** to struggle or try to cope (*with*) [to grapple with a problem]—**grap′pler** *n.*

GRAPNEL

grappling iron (or **hook**) *same as* GRAPNEL (sense 2): also **grap′pling** *n.*

grap·y (grā′pē) *adj.* [ME. *grapi*] of or like grapes; specif., tasting distinctly of grapes: said of some wines

grasp (grasp, gräsp) *vt.* [ME. *graspen*, by metathesis < *grapsen*, prob. < MLowG. (as in LowG., Fris. *grapsen*), akin to Norw. dial. *grapsa*, to scratch, ON. *grapa*, to snatch: for IE. base see GRAB] **1.** to take hold of firmly with or as with the hand or arms; grip **2.** to take hold of eagerly or greedily; seize **3.** to take hold of mentally; understand; comprehend —*vi.* **1.** to reach for and try to seize (with *at*) **2.** to accept eagerly (with *at*) —*n.* **1.** the

act of grasping; grip or clasp of the hand or arms **2.** a firm hold; control; possession **3.** the power to hold or seize; reach **4.** power of understanding; comprehension —*SYN.* see TAKE —**gras′pa·ble** *adj.* —**grasp′er** *n.*

grasp·ing (-iŋ) *adj.* **1.** that grasps **2.** eager for gain; avaricious —*SYN.* see GREEDY —**grasp′ing·ly** *adv.*

grass (gras, gräs) *n.* [ME. *gras* < OE. *gærs, græs, akin to* G. *gras* < IE. base *ghrō-*, to grow, become green, grass, whence L. *gramen,* grass & GROW] **1.** any of a family (Gramineae) of plants with long, narrow leaves, jointed stems, flowers in spikelets, and seedlike fruit, as wheat, rye, barley, oats, sugar cane, bamboo, etc. **2.** any of various green plants with typically long, narrow leaves that grow densely in meadows and are eaten by grazing animals, or that are cultivated for lawns, etc. **3.** ground covered with grass; pasture land or lawn **4.** grasslike lines on a radarscope produced by interference of random noise signals ✰**5.** [Slang] marijuana —*vt.* **1.** to put (an animal or animals) out to pasture or graze **2.** to grow grass over; cover with grass **3.** to lay (textiles, etc.) on the grass for bleaching by the sun —*vi.* **1.** to become covered with grass —go to **grass 1.** to graze **2.** to rest or retire ✰**3.** go to the devil! —**let the grass grow under one's feet** to waste one's time or neglect one's opportunities —**grass′like′** *adj.*

grass cloth a cloth made of plant fibers, as of jute, ramie, hemp, etc.

grass·hop·per (-häp′ər) *n.* [ME. *grashoppere,* modified form, with *-er* suffix (see -ER); of *greshoppe* < OE. *gærshoppe* < *gærs* (see GRASS) + base of *hoppian* (see HOP[1])] **1.** any of a large group of leaping, plant-eating orthopterous insects (families Acrididae and Tettigoniidae) with powerful hind legs adapted for jumping ✰**2.** *Mil. Slang* a small, light airplane for scouting, liaison, and observation

GRASSHOPPER
(1 1–4 in: long)

grass·land (-land′) *n.* **1.** land with grass growing on it, used for grazing; pasture land **2.** land or region where grass predominates; prairie

grass·plot (-plät′) *n.* a piece of ground with grass growing on it; esp., a lawn

grass roots [Colloq.] ✰**1.** the common people, orig. those esp. of rural or non-urban areas, thought of as best representing the basic, direct political interests of the electorate ✰**2.** the basic or fundamental source or support, as of a movement —**grass′-roots′** *adj.*

grass snake ✰**1.** either of two harmless, slender, N. American green snakes (genus *Opheodrys*) living mostly in meadows ✰**2.** *same as* GARTER SNAKE

✰**grass snipe** *same as* PECTORAL SANDPIPER

grass tree any of a genus (*Xanthorrhoea*) of plants of the lily family, native to Australia, with short, thick, woody trunks and grasslike leaves: some produce fragrant resins of commercial value

grass widow [Early ModE., discarded mistress (similar to Du. *grasweduwe,* G. *strohwittwe*): prob. allusion is to bed of grass or straw as opposed to the conjugal bed] a woman divorced or otherwise separated from her husband

grass widower a man divorced or otherwise separated from his wife

grass·y (-ē) *adj.* **grass′i·er, grass′i·est 1.** of or consisting of grass **2.** covered with or containing grass **3.** green like growing grass —**grass′i·ness** *n.*

grate[1] (grāt) *vt.* **grat′ed, grat′ing** [ME. *graten* < OFr. *grater* (Fr. *gratter*) < Frank. *kratton,* akin to OHG. *chrazzōn* (G. *kratzen*), to scratch < IE. base *gred-,* whence Alb. *gërrusë,* scraper] **1.** to grind into shreds or particles by rubbing or scraping **2.** to rub against (an object) with a harsh, scraping sound **3.** to grind (the teeth) together with a rasping sound **4.** to irritate; annoy; fret —*vi.* **1.** to grind or rub with a harsh scraping or rasping sound **2.** to make a harsh or rasping sound **3.** to have an irritating or annoying effect

grate[2] (grāt) *n.* [ME., trellis, lattice < ML. *grata, crata* < L. *cratis,* a hurdle, CRATE] **1.** *same as* GRATING[1] (sense 1) **2.** a frame of metal bars for holding fuel in a fireplace, stove, or furnace **3.** a fireplace **4.** *Mining* a screen for grading crushed ores —*vt.* **grat′ed, grat′ing** to provide with a grate or grates

grate·ful (grāt′fəl) *adj.* [obs. *grate* (< L. *gratus:* see GRACE), pleasing + -FUL] **1.** feeling or expressing gratitude; thankful; appreciative **2.** causing gratitude; welcome; pleasing —**grate′ful·ly** *adv.* —**grate′ful·ness** *n.*

grat·er (grāt′ər) *n.* a utensil with a rough surface on which to grate spices, vegetables, cheese, etc.

Gra·tian (grā′shən) (L. name *Flavius Gratianus*) 359–383 A.D.; Roman emperor (375–383)

grat·i·fi·ca·tion (grat′ə fi kā′shən) *n.* [Fr. < L. *gratificatio*] **1.** a gratifying or being gratified **2.** something that gratifies; cause for satisfaction **3.** [Archaic] reward or recompense for services or benefits

grat·i·fy (grat′ə fī′) *vt.* **-fied′, -fy′ing** [Fr. *gratifier* < L. *gratificare, gratificari,* to oblige, please < *gratus,* pleasing (see GRACE) + *-ficare,* -FY] **1.** to give pleasure or satisfaction to **2.** to give in to; indulge; humor **3.** [Archaic] to reward —**grat′i·fi′er** *n.*

gra·tin (grät′'n, grat′-; *Fr.* grå taṇ′) *n. see* AU GRATIN

grat·ing[1] (grāt′iŋ) *n.* [< GRATE[2] + -ING] **1.** a framework of parallel or latticed bars set in a window, door, etc. **2.** *same as* DIFFRACTION GRATING

grat·ing[2] (grāt′iŋ) *adj.* [prp. of GRATE[1]] **1.** harsh and rasping **2.** irritating or annoying —**grat′ing·ly** *adv.*

gra·tis (grat′is, grāt′-) *adv., adj.* [L. < *gratia,* a favor: see GRACE] without charge or payment; free

grat·i·tude (grat′ə tood′, -tyood′) *n.* [Fr. < ML. *gratitudo* < L. *gratus,* pleasing: see GRACE] a feeling of thankful appreciation for favors or benefits received; warm, appreciative response to kindness; thankfulness

Grat·tan (grat′'n), **Henry** 1746–1820; Ir. statesman & orator

gra·tu·i·tous (grə too′ə təs, -tyoo′-) *adj.* [L. *gratuitus* < *gratus:* see GRACE] **1.** *a)* given or received without charge or payment; free *b)* granted without obligation **2.** without cause or justification; uncalled-for —**gra·tu′i·tous·ly** *adv.* —**gra·tu′i·tous·ness** *n.*

gratuitous contract *Law* a contract for the benefit of the person for whom it is made, without a reciprocal promise of benefit to the maker

gra·tu·i·ty (grə too′ə tē, -tyoo′-) *n., pl.* **-ties** [Fr. *gratuité* < ML. *gratuitas* < L. *gratuitus:* see GRATUITOUS] a gift of money, etc., esp. that given over payment due for a service rendered; tip —*SYN.* see PRESENT

grat·u·late (grach′ə lāt′) *vt.* **-lat′ed, -lat′ing** [< L. *gratulatus,* pp. of *gratulari,* CONGRATULATE] [Archaic] **1.** to express joy or gratification at the sight of **2.** to congratulate —**grat′u·la′tion** *n.* —**grat′u·la·to′ry** (-lə tôr′ē), **grat′u·lant** (-lənt) *adj.*

Grau·bün·den (grou′bün′dən) easternmost canton of Switzerland: 2,745 sq. mi.; pop. 143,000

grau·pel (grou′pəl) *n.* [G. < *graupeln,* to sleet < *graupelein,* dim. of *graupe,* hulled barley, granule of ice < Slav., as in Pol., Serb. *krupa,* kernel of grain, hail] *Meteorol.* brittle, white ice particles having a snowlike structure; soft hail

gra·va·men (grə vā′mən) *n., pl.* **-mens, gra·vam′i·na** (-vam′ə na) [LL., lit., a burden, trouble < L. *gravare,* to weigh down < *gravis:* see ff.] **1.** a grievance **2.** *Law* the essential part of a complaint or accusation

grave[1] (grāv) *adj.* [Fr. < L. *gravis,* heavy, weighty < IE. base *gwer-,* heavy, mill, whence Sans. *gurúh,* grave & QUERN] **1.** requiring serious thought; important; weighty [*grave* doubts] **2.** of a threatening nature; indicating great danger; ominous [a *grave* illness] **3.** dignified and solemn or sedate in manner or mien **4.** somber; dull [*grave* colors] **5.** low or deep in pitch —*n. same as* GRAVE ACCENT —*SYN.* see SERIOUS —**grave′ly** *adv.* —**grave′ness** *n.*

grave[2] (grāv) *n.* [ME. < OE. *græf* (akin to OFris. *gref,* G. *grab*) < base of *grafan,* to dig: see the *vt.*] **1.** *a)* a hole in the ground in which to bury a dead body *b)* any place of burial; tomb **2.** final end or death; extinction —*vt.* **graved, grav′en** or **graved, grav′ing** [ME. *graven* < OE. *grafan;* akin to G. *graben* < IE. base *ghrebh-,* to scratch, scrape] **1.** [Obs.] *a)* to dig *b)* to bury **2.** to shape by carving; carve out; sculpture **3.** [Archaic] to engrave; incise **4.** to impress sharply and clearly; fix permanently —**have one foot in the grave** to be very ill, old, or infirm; be near death —**make one turn (over) in one's grave** to be or do something that would have shocked or distressed one now dead

grave[3] (grāv) *vt.* **graved, grav′ing** [ME. *graven,* prob. < OFr. *grave* (Fr. *grève*), beach, coarse sand (see GRAVEL): ships were orig. beached for cleaning the hulls] to clean (the hull of a wooden ship) by removing the barnacles, etc. and coating with pitch or tar

‡**gra·ve[4]** (grä′ve) *adj., adv.* [It.] *Music* slow and with solemnity: a direction to the performer

grave accent a mark (`) used to indicate: **1.** in French, the quality of an open *e* (è), as in *chère,* or a distinction in meaning, as in *où,* meaning "where" (distinguished from *ou,* meaning "or") **2.** full pronunciation of a syllable normally elided in speech, as in *lovèd* **3.** secondary stress, as in *týpewrìter*

grave·clothes (grāv′klōz′, -klōthz′) *n.pl.* the clothes in which a dead body is buried; cerements

grave·dig·ger (-dig′ər) *n.* a person whose work is digging graves

grav·el (grav′'l) *n.* [ME. < OFr. *gravelle,* dim. of *grave* (Fr. *grève*), coarse sand, seashore < *are* or akin to Gaul. *grava,* stone < IE. base *ghreu-,* to rub hard, pulverize, whence GRIT] **1.** a loose mixture of pebbles and rock fragments coarser than sand, often mixed with clay, etc. **2.** *Med.* a deposit of small concretions that form in the kidneys or gallbladder and that may be retained, passed on to the urinary bladder, or passed from the body —*vt.* **-eled** or **-elled, -el·ing** or **-el·ling 1.** to cover (a walk, driveway, etc.) with gravel **2.** to embarrass or perplex **3.** [Colloq.] to irritate or annoy

grav·el-blind (-blīnd′) *adj.* [intens. synonym for SAND-BLIND] almost completely blind

grav·el·ly (-ē) *adj.* **1.** full of, like, or consisting of gravel **2.** sounding harsh or rasping [a *gravelly* voice]

grav·en (grāv′'n) *alt. pp.* of GRAVE[2]

Gravenhage *see* 'S GRAVENHAGE

graven image an idol made from stone, wood, etc.

Gra·ven·stein (grä′vən stēn′, grā′vən-; -stīn′) *n.* [< *Gravenstein,* village in Denmark] a variety of large, yellow apple with red streaks

grav·er (grā′vər) *n.* [ME.: see GRAVE², *v.* & -ER] **1.** a cutting tool used by engravers and sculptors **2.** an engraver; esp., a carver in stone

Graves (gräv) *n.* a light red or white wine from the region of Graves in SW France

Graves (grāvz), **Robert (Ranke)** 1895– ; Eng. poet, novelist, & critic

Graves' disease (grāvz) [after R. J. *Graves* (1797-1853), Ir. physician] *same as* EXOPHTHALMIC GOITER

☆**grave·side** (grāv′sīd′) *n.* the area alongside a grave —*adj.* being, or taking place, beside a grave

grave·stone (grāv′stōn′) *n.* [ME. *graveston*] an engraved stone marking a grave; tombstone

Gra·vet·ti·an (grə vet′ē ən) *adj.* [< La *Gravette*, France, site of archaeological discoveries + -IAN] designating or of an upper paleolithic culture, characterized by flint points resembling a pointed knife blade with a blunted back

grave·yard (grāv′yärd′) *n.* a burial ground; cemetery

☆**graveyard shift** [Colloq.] a work shift that starts during the night, usually at midnight

grav·id (grav′id) *adj.* [L. *gravidus* < *gravis*, heavy: see GRAVE¹] pregnant —**gra·vid·i·ty** (grə vid′ə tē) *n.*

gra·vim·e·ter (grə vim′ə tər) *n.* [Fr. *gravimètre* < L. *gravis*, heavy + Fr. *-mètre*, -METER] **1.** a device used to determine specific gravity, esp. of liquids **2.** an instrument used to measure the earth's gravitational pull at different places on the earth

grav·i·met·ric (grav′ə met′rik) *adj.* [< L. *gravis* (see GRAVE¹) + METRIC] **1.** of or in terms of measurement by weight **2.** of or pertaining to measurements of the pull of gravity Also **grav′i·met′ri·cal** —**grav′i·met′ri·cal·ly** *adv.*

gra·vim·e·try (grə vim′ə trē) *n.* [< L. *gravis* (see GRAVE¹) + -METRY] the measurement of weight or density

grav·i·tate (grav′ə tāt′) *vi.* -tat′ed, -tat′ing [< ModL. *gravitatus*, pp. of *gravitare* (coined by Newton) < L. *gravitas* (see GRAVITY)] **1.** to move or tend to move in accordance with the force of gravity **2.** [Rare] to sink or fall; tend to settle at a bottom level **3.** to be attracted or tend to move (*toward* something or someone) —*vt.* to cause to gravitate

grav·i·ta·tion (grav′ə tā′shən) *n.* [ModL. *gravitatio*: see prec.] **1.** the act, process, or fact of gravitating **2.** *Physics* *a)* the force by which every mass or particle of matter, including photons, attracts and is attracted by every other mass or particle of matter *b)* the tendency of these masses or particles toward each other —**grav′i·ta′tion·al** *adj.* —**grav′i·ta′tion·al·ly** *adv.*

grav·i·ta·tive (grav′ə tāt′iv) *adj.* **1.** of or caused by gravitation **2.** tending or causing to gravitate

grav·i·ty (grav′ə tē) *n.*, *pl.* -ties [L. *gravitas*, weight, heaviness < *gravis*, heavy: see GRAVE¹] **1.** the state or condition of being grave; esp., *a)* solemnity or sedateness of manner or character; earnestness *b)* danger or threat; ominous quality [the *gravity* of his illness] *c)* seriousness, as of a situation **2.** weight; heaviness: see SPECIFIC GRAVITY, CENTER OF GRAVITY **3.** lowness of musical pitch **4.** gravitation, esp. terrestrial gravitation; force that tends to draw all bodies in the earth's sphere toward the center of the earth: see ACCELERATION OF GRAVITY —*adj.* operated by the force of gravity

gra·vure (grə vyoor′) *n.* [Fr. < *graver*, to carve < Frank. *graban*, akin to GRAVE², *v.*] **1.** *a)* any process that makes or uses intaglio printing plates *b)* a plate or print made by such a process **2.** *clipped form of* PHOTOGRAVURE or ROTOGRAVURE

gra·vy (grā′vē) *n.*, *pl.* -vies [ME. *grave*, ? a misreading of OFr. *grané* < ? *grain*, used as a name for cooking ingredients] **1.** the juice given off by meat in cooking **2.** a sauce made by combining this juice with flour, seasoning, etc. ☆**3.** [Slang] *a)* money easily or illegally obtained *b)* any extra benefit or value beyond that expected

gravy boat a boat-shaped dish for serving gravy

☆**gravy train** [Slang] a sinecure, subsidy, etc. that allows one to live luxuriously without much work

gray (grā) *adj.* [ME. *grai* < OE. *grǣg*, akin to G. *grau* < IE. base *gher-*, to shine, gleam, whence Czech *zŕiti*, to see] **1.** of a color that is a mixture or blend of black and white **2.** *a)* darkish; dull *b)* dreary; dismal **3.** *a)* having hair that is gray *b)* old, or old and respected **4.** wearing gray garments or uniforms **5.** *a)* designating a vague, intermediate area, as between morality and immorality *b)* designating an urban area that is deteriorating into a slum —*n.* **1.** an achromatic color made by mixing or blending black and white: see COLOR **2.** an animal or thing colored gray; esp., a gray horse **3.** gray or unbleached fabric or clothing **4.** [often G-] a person dressed in a gray uniform; specif., ☆a Confederate soldier —*vt.*, *vi.* to make or become gray —**gray′ly** *adv.* —**gray′ness** *n.*

Gray (grā) **1. Asa,** 1810-88; U.S. botanist **2. Thomas,** 1716-71; Eng. poet

gray·back (-bak′) *n.* any of certain birds, fish, whales, etc. with grayish coloring, as the hooded crow, dogfish, alewife, scaup duck, etc.

gray·beard (-bird′) *n.* an old man

gray eminence *same as* ÉMINENCE GRISE

gray·fish (-fish′) *n.*, *pl.* -fish′, -fish′es: see FISH² *same as* DOGFISH (sense 1)

Gray Friar a Franciscan friar

gray-head·ed (-hed′id) *adj.* **1.** having gray hair **2.** old

gray hen the female of the black grouse

gray·hound (-hound′) *n.* *same as* GREYHOUND

gray·ish (-ish) *adj.* somewhat gray

gray·lag (-lag′) *n.* [short for *gray lag* goose: from its color and its late migration] the European wild gray goose (*Anser anser*)

gray·ling (-liŋ) *n.*, *pl.* -ling, -lings: see PLURAL, II, D, 2 [GRAY + -LING¹: from the color] **1.** a freshwater salmonoid game fish (family Thymallidae) with a long dorsal fin, found mainly in cold and arctic waters **2.** any of several varieties of gray or brown butterfly (*Cercyonis alope*)

gray matter 1. grayish nerve tissue of the brain and spinal cord, consisting chiefly of nerve cells, with few nerve fibers: distinguished from WHITE MATTER **2.** [Colloq.] intellectual capacity; brains

Gray's Inn *see* INN OF COURT

Gray·son (grā′sən), **David** *see* Ray Stannard BAKER

☆**gray squirrel** any of several large, gray squirrels (genus *Sciurus*), native to the U.S.

gray·wacke (-wak′) *n.* [partial transl. of G. *grauwacke*: see GRAY & WACKE] *an old term with various meanings:* commonly, *a)* a nonporous, dark-colored sandstone containing angular grains and fragments of other rocks *b)* a fine-grained conglomerate resembling sandstone

☆**gray whale** a whalebone whale (*Eschrichtius glaucus*) of the N Pacific, black with many white spots

☆**gray wolf** a large, gray wolf (*Canis lupus*) that hunts in packs and was formerly common throughout the northern part of the Northern Hemisphere

Graz (gräts) city in SE Austria; capital of Styria province: pop. 237,000

graze¹ (grāz) *vt.* grazed, graz′ing [ME. *grasen* < OE. *grasian* < base of *græs*, *gærs*, GRASS] **1.** to feed on (growing grass, herbage, a pasture, etc.) **2.** to put livestock to graze on (growing grass, herbage, etc.) **3.** to tend (grazing livestock) **4.** to be pasture or grazing for —*vi.* to feed on growing grass, etc. —**graz′er** *n.*

graze² (grāz) *vt.* grazed, graz′ing [prob. < prec. in sense "to come close to the grass"] **1.** to touch or rub lightly in passing **2.** to scrape or scratch in passing [a bullet *grazed* his thigh] —*vi.* to scrape, touch, or rub lightly against something in passing —*n.* **1.** the act of grazing **2.** a slight scratch or scrape caused by grazing

gra·zier (grā′zhər; *Brit.* -zyər) *n.* [Chiefly Brit.] a person who grazes beef cattle for sale

graz·ing (grā′ziŋ) *n.* land to graze on; pasture

†**gra·zio·so** (grä tsyō′sō) *adj.*, *adv.* [It. < L. *gratiosus*: see GRACIOUS] *Music* with grace; in a smooth, elegant manner: a direction to the performer

Gr. Brit., Gr. Br. Great Britain

grease (grēs; *for v.*, *also* grēz) *n.* [ME. *gresse* < OFr. < VL. *crassia* < L. *crassus*, fat, thick: see CRASS] **1.** melted animal fat **2.** any thick, oily substance or lubricant **3.** an inflammation of the skin of a horse's fetlocks, accompanied by an oily discharge **4.** *a)* the oily substance in uncleaned wool *b)* an uncleaned fleece: also **grease wool** —*vt.* **greased, greas′ing 1.** to smear or lubricate with grease; put grease on or in **2.** to influence by giving money to; bribe or tip: chiefly in **grease the palm** (or **hand**) **of** —in (the) **grease 1.** fat and ready to be killed: said of game animals **2.** in an uncleaned condition: said of wool or fur —**greas′er** *n.*

grease cup a small cup over a bearing in machinery, for holding a supply of grease to lubricate the bearing

☆**grease monkey** [Slang] a mechanic, esp. one who works on automobiles or airplanes

grease·paint (-pānt′) *n.* a mixture of grease and coloring matter used by performers in making up for the stage, etc.

☆**grease·wood** (-wood′) *n.* **1.** a thorny plant (*Sarcobatus vermiculatus*) of the goosefoot family, found in the desert regions of the W U.S., having fleshy leaves and dry papery fruits: often grazed by livestock **2.** any of several other similar plants

greas·y (grē′sē, grē′zē) *adj.* **greas′i·er, greas′i·est 1.** smeared or soiled with grease **2.** containing grease, esp. much grease **3.** like grease; oily; unctuous; slippery —**greas′i·ly** *adv.* —**greas′i·ness** *n.*

☆**greasy spoon** [Slang] a small restaurant that serves cheap food under unsanitary conditions

great (grāt) *adj.* [ME. *grete* < OE. *great*, akin to G. *gross* < IE. base *ghreu-*, to rub away, grind down, whence GRIT, W. *gro*, sand: basic sense "coarse, coarsegrained"] **1.** of much more than ordinary size, extent, volume, etc.; esp., *a)* designating a thing or group of things larger than others of the same kind [the *great* cats are tigers, lions, etc.; the *Great* Lakes] *b)* large in number, quantity, etc.; numerous [a *great* company] *c)* long in duration [a *great* while] **2.** much higher in some quality or degree; much above the ordinary or average; esp., *a)* existing in a high degree; intense [a *great* light, *great* pain] *b)* very much of a; acting much as (something specified) [a *great* reader] *c)* eminent; distinguished; illustrious; superior [a *great* playwright] *d)*

very impressive or imposing; remarkable *[great* ceremony*]* e) having or showing nobility of mind, purpose, etc.; grand *[* a *great* man, *great* ideas*]* 3. of most importance; highest in its class; main; chief *[* the *great* seal*]* 4. designating a relationship one generation removed; older or younger by one generation: used in hyphenated compounds *[great*-grandmother*]* 5. [Colloq.] clever; expert; skillful (usually with *at*) *[great* at tennis*]* ☆6. [Colloq.] excellent; splendid; fine: a generalized term of approval 7. [Archaic or Dial.] pregnant: chiefly in **great with child** —*adv.* [Colloq.] very well —*n.* a great or distinguished person: *usually used in pl.* —**SYN.** see LARGE —**great on** [Colloq.] enthusiastic about —**the great** those who are great —**great′ly** *adv.* —**great′-ness** *n.*

great ape any anthropoid ape, as the gorilla, chimpanzee, etc.

great auk a large sea bird (*Pinguinus impennis*) of the N. Atlantic, extinct since 1844, that was incapable of flight

great-aunt (-ant′, -änt′) *n.* a sister of any of one's grandparents; grandaunt

Great Australian Bight wide bay of the Indian Ocean, indenting S Australia: c. 720 mi. wide

Great Barrier Reef coral reef off the NE coast of Queensland, Australia: 1,250 mi. long

Great Basin vast inland region of the W U.S., between the Sierra Nevada & the Wasatch Mountains, covering E Calif., W Utah, most of Nev., & parts of Oreg. & Ida.: the rivers & streams flowing into this region form lakes which have no outlet to the sea: c. 200,000 sq. mi.

Great Bear the constellation Ursa Major: its seven brightest stars form the Big Dipper

Great Bear Lake lake in C Mackenzie District, Northwest Territories, Canada: 12,275 sq. mi.

Great Britain 1. principal island of the United Kingdom, including England, Scotland, & Wales, & administratively including adjacent islands except the Isle of Man & the Channel Islands 2. popularly, the United Kingdom of Great Britain and Northern Ireland

great calorie *see* CALORIE (sense 2)

great circle any circle described on the surface of a sphere by a plane which passes through the center of the sphere; specif., such a circle on the earth's surface: a course (**great-circle course**) plotted along a great circle of the earth is the shortest route between any two points on the earth's surface

great·coat (grāt′kōt′) *n.* a heavy overcoat

Great Dane any of a breed of large, powerful dog with short, smooth hair

☆**Great Divide** 1. a principal mountain watershed; specif., the CONTINENTAL DIVIDE 2. any important dividing line —**cross the Great Divide** to die

Great Dividing Range series of mountain ranges along the eastern coast of Australia: highest peak, Mt. KOSCIUSKO

great·en (grāt′'n) *vt., vi.* to make or become great or greater

Great·er (-ər) *adj.* designating a large city together with its suburbs *[Greater* London*]*

Greater Antilles group of islands in the West Indies, made up of the N & W Antilles, including the islands of Cuba, Jamaica, Hispaniola, & Puerto Rico

Greater Khingan Mountains *see* KHINGAN MOUNTAINS

Greater Wol·lon·gong (wool′ən gän′, -gôn′) city in SE New South Wales, Australia: pop. 151,000

Great Falls city in WC Mont., on the Missouri River: pop. 60,000

Great Glen of Scotland *same as* GLEN MORE

great-grand·child (grāt′gran′child′) *n., pl.* -**chil′dren** a child of any of one's grandchildren —**great′-grand′-daugh′ter** *n.* —**great′-grand′son′** *n.*

great-grand·par·ent (-gran′per′ənt) *n.* a parent of any of one's grandparents —**great′-grand′fa′ther** *n.* —**great′-grand′moth′er** *n.*

great-great- (grāt′grāt′) *a combining form used with nouns of relationship to indicate* two degrees of removal in an ascending (or descending) scale *[great-great-*grandparent, *great-great-*grandson*]*: each additional **great-** indicates one further degree of removal

great gross a unit of quantity equal to twelve gross

great-heart·ed (-härt′id) *adj.* 1. brave; fearless; courageous 2. generous; magnanimous; unselfish

great horned owl a large, pale gray and brownish N. American owl (*Bubo virginianus*) with two prominent tufts of black feathers on its head

Great Karroo *see* KARROO

Great Khingan Mountains *see* KHINGAN MOUNTAINS

Great Lakes chain of freshwater lakes in EC N. America, emptying into the St. Lawrence River; Lakes Superior, Michigan, Huron, Erie, & Ontario

☆**great laurel** a large, E American shrub (*Rhododendron maximum*) of the heath family, with thick, oblong, dark-green leaves and delicate, pink flowers in cone-shaped clusters

Great Mogul 1. the title of the ruler of the Mongol empire in India in the 16th cent. 2. [**g- m-**] a person of importance

great-neph·ew (-nef′yōō; *chiefly Brit.,* -nev′-) *n.* a grandson of one's brother or sister; grandnephew —**great′-niece′** (-nēs′) *n.fem.*

Great Plains sloping region of valleys & plains in WC N. America, extending from Tex. north to S Alberta,

Canada, & stretching east from the base of the Rockies for c. 400 mi.

great primer a large size of type, 18 point

Great Rift Valley depression of SW Asia & E Africa, extending from the Jordan River valley across Ethiopia & Somalia to the lakes region of E Africa

Great Russian the major dialect of Russian, that spoken chiefly in C and NE European Russia

Great Salt Lake shallow saltwater lake in NW Utah, fluctuating greatly in size from c. 1,100 to c. 2,300 sq. mi.

Great Sandy Desert N section of the vast desert region of Western Australia

Great Schism 1. the division or conflict in the Roman Catholic Church from 1378 to 1417, when there were rival popes at Avignon and Rome: also called **Schism of the West** 2. the separation, final in 1472, of the Orthodox Eastern Church from the Roman Catholic Church: also called **Schism of the East**

great seal 1. the chief seal of a nation, state, etc., with which official papers are stamped as proof of their approval 2. [**G- S-**] *a)* the Lord Chancellor of Great Britain, keeper of the great seal *b)* his position

Great Slave Lake lake in S Mackenzie District, Northwest Territories, Canada: 10,980 sq. mi.

Great Smoky Mountains mountain range of the Appalachians, along the Tenn.-N.C. border: highest peak, Clingman's Dome: site of a national park (**Great Smoky Mountains National Park**): 795 sq. mi.

Great St. Bernard Pass mountain pass in the Pennine Alps, on the border between SW Switzerland & Italy: 8,110 ft. high

great-un·cle (-uŋ′k'l) *n.* a brother of any of one's grandparents; granduncle

Great Victoria Desert S section of the vast desert region of Western Australia

Great Vowel Shift the complicated series of sound developments (c. 1400 to c. 1750) which changed the vowel system of Middle English into that of Modern English: Middle English long high vowels (ē and ōō) changed to Modern English diphthongs (ī and ou), and long mid and low vowels (ā, ō, and ä) were raised in their tongue positions to the Modern English sounds (ē, ōō, and ā), but the orthography remained largely the same

Great Wall of China stone & earth wall extending across N China, built as a defense against invaders in the 3d cent. B.C., with later extensions: 15–30 ft. high; 12–20 ft. wide; c. 1,500 mi. long

Great War World War I

Great Week *Orthodox Eastern Ch.* the week preceding Easter; Holy Week

☆**Great White Father** *name given by the American Indians to* the president of the U.S.

☆**Great White Way** the brightly lighted, former theater district in New York City, on Broadway near Times Square

great world [after Fr. *grand monde*] fashionable society and its way of life

Great Yarmouth seaport on the eastern coast of England, in Norfolk: pop. 53,000

great year one full cycle of precession of the equinoxes, equal to c. 25,800 years

greaves¹ (grēvz) *n.pl.* [whaling term < LowG. *greven*, pl., MDu. *grēve*, akin to G. *griebe*: basic sense "coarse elements that will not melt": for IE. base see GREAT] the sediment of skin, etc. formed when animal fat is melted down for tallow; specif., cracklings

greaves² (grēvz) *n.pl.* [ME. *greves* < OFr. pl. of *greve*, shin, shin armor] armor for the legs from the ankle to the knee: see ARMOR, illus.

grebe (grēb) *n., pl.* **grebes, grebe:** see PLURAL, II, D, 1 [< Fr. *grèbe*] any of a worldwide family (Podicipitidae) of diving and swimming birds related to the loons, with partially webbed feet, and legs set far back on the body

Gre·cian (grē′shən) *adj.* [< L. *Graecia*, Greece + -AN] *same as* GREEK (sense 1) —*n.* 1. a Greek 2. [Archaic] a scholar of Greek

Grecian profile a profile in which the nose and forehead form an almost straight line

Gre·cism (grē′siz'm) *n.* [Fr. *grécisme* < ML. *Graecismus* < L. *Graeci*, the Greeks] 1. *a)* an idiom of the Greek language *b)* an imitation of this 2. the spirit of Greek culture 3. imitation of Greek style in the arts

Gre·cize (grē′sīz) *vt.* -**cized**, -**ciz·ing** [Fr. *gréciser* < L. *Graecizare* < *Graeci*, the Greeks] to make Greek; give a Greek form to; Hellenize —*vi.* to imitate the Greeks in language, manner, etc. Also **Gre′cian·ize′**

Gre·co- (grē′kō) [< L. *Graecus*] *a combining form meaning:* 1. Greek or Greeks 2. Greek and or Greece and

Greco, El *see* EL GRECO

Gre·co-Ro·man (grē′kō rō′mən) *adj.* of or influenced by both Greece and Rome *[Greco-Roman* art*]*

gree¹ (grē) *n.* [ME. *gre* < OFr. *gre*, *gred* < L. *gratum*, neut. of *gratus:* see GRACE] [Obs.] good will —**do** (or **make**) **gree** [Archaic] to give satisfaction for an injury

gree² (grē) *n.* [ME. *gre* < OFr. *gré*, a step < L. *gradus*, a step: see GRADE] [Scot.] superiority, pre-eminence, or victory

gree³ (grē) *vt., vi.* **greed, gree′ing** [ME. *green* < OFr. *grēer* < *gré*, pleasure (see AGREE); also aphetic < ME. *agreen*] to agree or make agree

Greece (grēs) country in the S Balkan Peninsula, including many islands in the Aegean, Ionian, & Mediterranean seas: 50,534 sq. mi.; pop. 8,612,000; cap. Athens: in ancient times, the region was comprised of a number of small monarchies and republics

ANCIENT GREECE

greed (grēd) n. [back-formation < GREEDY] excessive desire for getting or having, esp. wealth; desire for more than one needs or deserves; avarice; cupidity

greed·y (-ē) adj. **greed'-i·er, greed'i·est** [ME. gredie < OE. grædig < base of græd- (in grædum, eagerly) + -ig (see -Y²), akin to Goth. grēdags, lit., hungry < IE. base *gher-, to crave, whence Gr. charis, grace, favor] **1.** wanting or taking all that one can get, with no thought of others' needs; desiring more than one needs or deserves; avaricious; covetous **2.** having too strong a desire for food and drink; gluttonous; voracious **3.** intensely eager —**greed'i·ly** adv. —**greed'i·ness** n.

SYN.—**greedy** implies an insatiable desire to possess or acquire something to an amount inordinately beyond what one needs or deserves and is the broadest of the terms compared here; **avaricious** stresses greed for money or riches and often connotes miserliness; **grasping** suggests an unscrupulous eagerness for gain that manifests itself in a seizing upon every opportunity to get what one desires; **acquisitive** stresses the exertion of effort in acquiring or accumulating wealth or material possessions to an excessive amount; **covetous** implies greed for something that another person rightfully possesses ;

Greek (grēk) n. [ME. Greke < OE. Grec < L. Graecus < Gr. Graikos] **1.** a native or inhabitant of ancient or modern Greece **2.** the branch of the Indo-European language family consisting of the dialects of Greece, ancient or modern: see also LATE GREEK, MEDIEVAL GREEK, MODERN GREEK ☆**3.** [Colloq.] a member of a Greek-letter fraternity **4.** [Obs.] a close companion —adj. [ME. Grec < the n. & < Fr. grec < L. Graecus] **1.** of ancient or modern Greece, its people, language, or culture **2.** designating, of, or using the rite (or ritual) of the Orthodox Eastern Church: see also GREEK CATHOLIC & GREEK ORTHODOX CHURCH —**be Greek to one** to be incomprehensible or unintelligible to one

Greek Catholic 1. a member of an Orthodox Eastern Church **2.** a Uniate

Greek cross a cross with four equal arms at right angles

Greek fire [from its first use by Greeks of Byzantium] an incendiary material used in ancient and medieval warfare, described as able to burn in water

☆**Greek-let·ter** (grēk'let'ər) adj. designating or of a student fraternity or sorority whose name is designated by a combination of Greek letters

Greek (Orthodox) Church 1. the established church of Greece, an autonomous part of the Orthodox Eastern Church **2.** popular name for ORTHODOX EASTERN CHURCH

Gree·ley (grē'lē) [after ff.] city in NC Colo., northeast of Denver: pop. 39,000

Gree·ley (grē'lē), **Horace** 1811–72; U.S. journalist & political leader

green (grēn) adj. [ME. grene < OE., akin to G. grün, Du. groen: for IE. base see GRASS] **1.** of the color that is characteristic of growing grass **2.** overspread with or characterized by green plants or foliage [a green field] **3.** keeping the green grass of summer; snowless; mild [a green December] **4.** sickly or bilious, as from illness, fear, etc. **5.** a) flourishing; active [to keep someone's memory green] b) of the time of one's youth [the green years] **6.** not mature; unripe [green bananas] **7.** not trained; inexperienced **8.** easily led or deceived; simple; naive **9.** not dried, seasoned, or cured; unprocessed [green lumber] **10.** fresh; new **11.** [cf. GREEN-EYED] [Colloq.] jealous —n. **1.** the color of growing grass; any color between blue and yellow in the spectrum: green can be produced by blending blue and yellow pigments **2.** any green pigment or dye **3.** anything colored green, as clothing **4.** [pl.] green leaves, branches, sprigs, etc., used for ornamentation **5.** [pl.] green leafy plants or vegetables eaten cooked or raw, as spinach, turnip tops, lettuce, etc. **6.** an area of smooth turf set aside for special purposes [a village green, a bowling green] ☆**7.** [Slang] money, esp. paper money: chiefly in **long green, folding green 8.** Golf a) the plot of carefully tended turf immediately surrounding each of the holes to facilitate putting b) an entire golf course —vt., vi. to make or become green —**green with envy** very envious —**the Green** Ireland's national color —**green'ish** adj. —**green'ly** adv.

Green (grēn) **1. John Richard,** 1837–83: Eng. historian **2. Paul (Eliot),** 1894– ; U.S. playwright **3. William,** 1873–1952; U.S. labor leader

green algae a division (Chlorophyta) of algae in which the chlorophyll is not obscured by other pigments

Green·a·way (grēn'ə wā'), **Kate** 1846–1901; Eng. painter & illustrator, esp. of children's books

☆**green·back** (grēn'bak') n. any piece of U.S. paper money printed in green ink on the back

☆**Greenback Party** a political party organized in the U.S. after the Civil War, which advocated that fiat money issued by the Federal government be the only currency —**Green'back'er** n.

Green Bay [transl. of Fr. Baie Verte] **1.** arm of Lake Michigan, extending into NE Wis.: c. 100 mi. long **2.** city & port in Wis., on this bay: pop. 88,000

☆**green bean** the edible, immature pod of the kidney bean

green·belt (-belt') n. a beltlike area around a city, reserved by official authority for park land, farms, etc.

☆**green·bri·er** (-brī'ər) n. same as CAT BRIER

☆**green corn** young ears of sweet corn, in the milky stage

green dragon ☆an American wildflower (Arisaema dracontium) of the arum family, similar to the jack-in-the-pulpit but with a very long spadix and a greenish spathe

Greene (grēn) **1. Nathanael,** 1742–86; Am. general in the Revolutionary War **2. Robert,** 1558?–92?; Eng. poet, dramatist, & pamphleteer

green·er·y (grēn'ər ē) n., pl. **-er·ies 1.** green vegetation; verdure **2.** greens: see GREEN (n. 4) **3.** a greenhouse

green-eyed (-īd') adj. **1.** having green eyes **2.** [cf. Othello III, iii] very jealous

green·finch (-finch') n. a finch (Chloris chloris) with olive-green and yellow feathers, native to Europe

green·gage (-gāj') n. [after Sir William Gage, who introduced it into England from France, c. 1725] a large plum with golden-green skin and flesh

green-gro·cer (-grō'sər) n. [Brit.] a retail dealer in fresh vegetables and fruit —**green'gro'cer·y** n.

green·heart (-härt') n. **1.** any of various tropical trees whose wood is valued for its hardness and resistance to fungi and insects **2.** the wood

green·horn (-hôrn') n. [orig. with reference to a young animal with immature horns] **1.** a) an inexperienced person; beginner; novice ☆b) [Now Rare] a newly arrived immigrant **2.** a person easily deceived; dupe

green·house (-hous') n. a building made mainly of glass, in which the temperature and humidity can be regulated for the cultivation of delicate or out-of-season plants

greenhouse effect the retention of heat from sunlight at the earth's surface, caused by atmospheric carbon dioxide that admits shortwave radiation but absorbs the long-wave radiation emitted by the earth

green·ing (-in) n. [MDu. groeninc < groen: see GREEN] any of various apples having greenish-yellow skins when ripe

Green·land (grēn'lənd) [orig. so called (ON. Grönland, 986 A.D.) to attract settlers] island of Denmark northeast of N. America: it is the world's largest island: 840,000 sq. mi. (ice-free land 131,930 sq. mi.); pop. 40,000; cap. Godthaab: Dan. name, GRØNLAND

Greenland Sea southern part of the Arctic Ocean, east of Greenland

☆**green·let** (-lit) n. same as VIREO

☆**green light** [after the green phase of a traffic light, the signal to go ahead] [Colloq.] permission or authorization to proceed with some undertaking: usually in **give** (or **get**) **the green light**

green·ling (-lin) n. any of a genus (Hexagrammus) of large, flesh-eating fishes of the North Pacific, with long dorsal fins

green manure 1. a crop of growing plants, as clover, plowed under while still green to fertilize the soil **2.** fresh manure; manure not yet decayed

green mold any of various species of a fungus (esp. genus Penicillium) that produce greenish masses of spores

green monkey a small, long-tailed, African monkey (Cercopithecus sabaeus) with greenish hair

☆**Green Mountain Boys** the Vermont soldiers organized and led by Ethan Allen in the American Revolution

Green Mountains range of the Appalachians, extending the length of Vermont: highest peak 4,393 ft.

green·ness (-nis) n. the quality or state of being green

Green·ock (grē'nək, gren'ək) seaport in SW Scotland, on the Firth of Clyde: pop. 72,000

green·ock·ite (grē'nə kīt') n. [after C. M. Cathcart, Lord Greenock (1783–1859), who found some of the crystals in 1840 + -ITE¹] a rare yellow sulfide of cadmium, CdS, occurring usually as earthy crusts

green onion an immature onion with a long stalk and green leaves, eaten raw as a relish or in salads; scallion

Gree·nough (grē'nō), **Horatio** 1805–52; U.S. sculptor

☆**green pepper** the green, immature fruit of the sweet red pepper, eaten as a vegetable

☆**green revolution** the simultaneous development of new varieties of food plants and improved agricultural techniques, resulting in greatly increased crop yields, esp. in underdeveloped areas

fat, āpe, cär; ten, ēven; is, bīte; gō, hôrn, tōōl, look; oil, out; up, fur; get; joy; yet; chin; she; thin, then; zh, leisure; ŋ, ring; ə for a in ago, e in agent, i in sanity, o in comply, u in focus; ' as in able (ā'b'l); Fr. bal; ë, Fr. coeur; ö, Fr. feu; ô, Fr. mon; ô, Fr. coq; ü, Fr. duc; r, Fr. cri; H, G. ich; kh, G. doch. See inside front cover. ☆ Americanism; ‡foreign; *hypothetical; < derived from

Green River river flowing from W Wyo. south into the Colorado River in SE Utah: 730 mi.

☆**Green River Ordinance** [after such an ordinance passed in 1931 in *Green River*, Wyo.] a local ordinance prohibiting door-to-door selling

green·room (-rōōm', -room') *n.* a waiting room in some theaters, for use by actors when they are offstage

green·sand (-sand') *n.* a green, sandy deposit containing much glauconite

Greens·bor·o (grēnz'bur'ō) [after Nathanael GREENE] city in NC N.C.: pop. 144,000 (met. area, with Winston-Salem & High Point, 604,000)

green·shank (-shaŋk) *n.* a European sandpiper (*Tringa nebularia*) with greenish legs

green·sick·ness (-sik'nis) *n. same as* CHLOROSIS (sense 2)

☆**green snake** any of a genus (*Opheodrys*) of small, harmless, slender, green snakes of N. America

green soap a soft soap made of potash, linseed oil, and alcohol, used in treating skin diseases: so called because originally greenish

green·stick fracture (-stik') a partial bone fracture in which only one side of the bone is broken

green·stone (-stōn') *n.* any of various altered basic igneous rocks having a dark-green color

green·sward (-swôrd') *n.* green, grassy ground or turf

green tea tea prepared from leaves not fermented before drying: distinguished from BLACK TEA

☆**green thumb** an apparent skill or talent for growing plants easily

green turtle a large, edible marine turtle (*Chelonia mydas*) with an olive-colored shell marbled with yellow

Green·ville (grēn'vil) [after Nathanael GREENE] 1. city in NW S.C.: pop. 61,000 2. city in W Miss., on the Mississippi: pop. 40,000

green vitriol *same as* COPPERAS

Green·wich (gren'ich; *chiefly Brit.*, grin'ij; *for 2, also* grēn'wich) 1. metropolitan borough of London, located on the prime meridian: pop. 86,000: formerly the site of an astronomical observatory: see HERSTMONCEUX 2. suburb of Stamford, in SW Conn.: pop. 60,000

Greenwich (mean) time mean solar time of the meridian at Greenwich, England, used as the basis for standard time throughout most of the world

Green·wich Village (gren'ich) section of New York City, on the lower west side of Manhattan: noted as a center for artists, writers, etc.: formerly a village

green·wood (grēn'wood') *n.* a forest in leaf

greet¹ (grēt) *vt.* [ME. *greten* < OE. *gretan, grētan*, akin to Du. *groeten*, G. *grüssen* and to ff.] 1. to speak or write to with expressions of friendliness, respect, pleasure, etc., as in meeting or by letter; hail; welcome 2. to meet, receive, address, or acknowledge (a person, utterance, or event) in a specified way [the speech was *greeted* with cheers, he was *greeted* by a rifle shot] 3. to come or appear to; meet [a roaring sound *greeted* his ears] —**greet'er** *n.*

greet² (grēt) *vi.* [ME. *greten* < OE. *grætan*, akin to Goth. *gretan*] [Archaic or Dial.] to weep; lament

greet·ing (grēt'iŋ) *n.* 1. the act or words of a person who greets; salutation; welcome 2. [*often pl.*] a message of regards from someone absent

greeting card *same as* CARD¹ (*n. 1 g*)

greg·a·rine (greg'ə rin', -ər in) *n.* [< ModL. *Gregarina*, the type genus < L. *gregarius* (see ff.): name suggested by the 19th-cent. Fr. zoologist L. Dufour] any of an order (Gregarinida) of sporozoan protozoans that are parasites in the digestive tract of insects, crustaceans, earthworms, etc. —*adj.* of or pertaining to these protozoans: also **greg·a·rin·i·an** (greg'ə rin'ē ən)

gre·gar·i·ous (grə ger'ē əs) *adj.* [L. *gregarius*, belonging to a flock < *grex* (gen. *gregis*), a flock, herd < IE. base **ger-*, to collect, whence Gr. *ageirein*, to assemble] 1. living in herds or flocks 2. fond of the company of others; sociable 3. having to do with a herd, flock, or crowd 4. *Bot.* growing in clusters —**gre·gar'i·ous·ly** *adv.* —**gre·gar'i·ous·ness** *n.*

gre·go (grē'gō, grā'-) *n.* [< It. *Greco* or Port. *Grego*, both < L. *Graecus*, Greek] a short cloak of coarse cloth with an attached hood, worn in the Levant

Gre·go·ri·an (grə gôr'ē ən) *adj.* of or introduced by Pope Gregory I or Pope Gregory XIII

Gregorian calendar a corrected form of the Julian calendar, introduced by Pope Gregory XIII in 1582 and now used in most countries of the world: it provides for an ordinary year of 365 days and a leap year of 366 days every fourth even year, exclusive of century years, which are leap years only if exactly divisible by 400

Gregorian chant the ritual plainsong introduced under Pope Gregory I and used in the Roman Catholic Church: it is unharmonized and unaccompanied, and is not divided into measures

Greg·o·ry (greg'ər ē) [LL. *Gregorius* < Gr. *Grēgorios*, lit., vigilant, hence, watchman < dial. form of *egeirein*, to awaken] 1. a masculine name: dim. *Greg*; equiv. Fr. *Gregoire*, Ger. & Scand. *Gregor*, It. & Sp. *Gregorio* 2. Gregory I, Saint 540?-604 A.D.; Pope (590-604): his day is Mar. 12: called *the Great* 3. Gregory VII, Saint (born Hildebrand) 1020?-85; Pope (1073-85): his day is May 25 4. Gregory XIII (born *Ugo Buoncompagni*) 1502-85; Pope (1572-85): see GREGORIAN CALENDAR 5. Lady Augusta, (born *Isabella Augusta Persse*) 1852-1932; Ir. playwright

Gregory of Nys·sa (nis'ə), Saint 331?-395? A.D.; Gr. theologian & bishop in Cappadocia: brother of Saint BASIL: his day is Mar. 9

Gregory of Tours, Saint 538?-594? A.D.; Frankish historian & bishop: his day is Nov. 17

greige (grāzh) *n.* [Fr. *grège*, raw (silk) < It. (*seta*) *greggia* < ?] 1. unbleached and undyed cloth or yarn 2. a color blending gray and beige —*adj.* grayish-beige

grei·sen (gri'z'n) *n.* [G., var. of *greiss* < dial. *greissen*, to split] a crystalline, igneous rock consisting mainly of quartz and white mica

gre·mi·al (grē'mē əl) *n.* [LL. *gremialis* < L. *gremium*, bosom, lap < IE. **grem-* < base **ger-*, to collect: cf. GREGARIOUS] a lap cloth placed across the knees of a bishop, as when he sits during the celebration of Mass

grem·lin (grem'lən) *n.* [prob. < Dan. **græmling*, imp, dim. of obs. Dan. *gram*, a devil < ON. *gramr*, angry, akin to OE. *gremian*, to enrage: for IE. base see GRIM] an imaginary small creature humorously blamed for the faulty operation of airplanes or the disruption of any procedure

Gre·na·da (grə nā'də) 1. southernmost island of the Windward group in the West Indies: 120 sq. mi. 2. this island & the S Grenadines, constituting a self-governing colony under Brit. control: 133 sq. mi.; pop. 92,000

gre·nade (grə nād') *n.* [Fr. < OFr., pomegranate < L. (*malum*) *granatum*, (apple) with seeds, pomegranate < *granatus*, seedy < *granum*, seed, GRAIN] 1. a small bomb detonated by a fuse and thrown by hand or fired from a rifle 2. a glass container to be thrown so that it will break and disperse the chemicals inside: used for putting out fires, spreading tear gas, etc.

gren·a·dier (gren'ə dir') *n.* [Fr. < *grenade*] 1. orig., an infantry soldier employed to carry and throw grenades 2. a member of a special regiment or corps, as of the Grenadier Guards of the British Army, attached to the royal household 3. any of a family (Macrouridae) of deep-sea fishes related to the cod, with a long, tapering tail, large head, and soft fins

gren·a·dine¹ (gren'ə dēn', gren'ə dēn') *n.* [Fr. < *grenade*, pomegranate] a syrup made from pomegranate juice, used for flavoring drinks, etc.

gren·a·dine² (gren'ə dēn', gren'ə dēn') *n.* [Fr. < *grenade* (see GRENADE): from being spotted with "grains"] a thin, loosely woven cotton, wool, silk, or rayon cloth, used for blouses, dresses, curtains, etc.

Gren·a·dines (gren'ə dēnz) chain of small islands of the Windward group in the West Indies, dependencies of Grenada & St. Vincent: c. 30 sq. mi.

Gren·del (gren'd'l) the male monster slain by Beowulf: see BEOWULF

Gren·fell (gren'fel'), Sir **Wilfred Thom·a·son** (täm'ə sən) 1865-1940; Eng. physician, writer, & medical missionary to Labrador

Gre·no·ble (grə nō'b'l; *Fr.* grə nô'bl') city in SE France, in the Alps: pop. 157,000

Gren·ville (gren'vil) 1. George, 1712-70; Eng. statesman; prime minister (1763-65) 2. Sir Richard, 1541?-91; Eng. naval commander: also sp. Greynville

Gresh·am's law (gresh'əmz) [after Sir Thomas *Gresham* (1519-79), Eng. financier, formerly thought to have formulated it] the theory that when two or more kinds of money of equal denomination but unequal intrinsic value are in circulation at the same time, the one of greater value will tend to be hoarded or exported; popularly, the principle that bad money will drive good money out of circulation

gres·so·ri·al (gre sôr'ē əl) *adj.* [< L. *gressus*, pp. of *gradi*, to step, go: see GRADE] adapted for walking, as the feet of certain birds: also **gres·so'ri·ous**

Gret·a (gret'ə, gret'ə) [Sw. < or < G. *Grete*] [Sw. < or < G. *Grete*] a feminine name: see MARGARET

Gretch·en (grech'n) [G.] a feminine name: see MARGARET

Gret·na Green (gret'nə) 1. a border village in Scotland, where, formerly, many eloping English couples went to be married 2. any similar village or town

Greuze (grēz), **Jean Bap·tiste** (zhän bá tēst') 1725-1805; Fr. painter

grew (grōō) [ME. *greu* < OE. *greow*] *pt. of* GROW

grew·some (grōō'səm) *adj. same as* GRUESOME

grey (grā) *adj., n., vt., vi. Brit. sp. of* GRAY

Grey (grā) 1. **Charles**, 2d Earl Grey, 1764-1845; Eng. statesman; prime minister (1830-34) 2. Sir **Edward**, Viscount Grey of Fallodon, 1862-1933; Eng. statesman; foreign secretary (1905-16) 3. Lady **Jane**, Lady Jane Dudley, 1537-54; queen of England (July 10-19, 1553): beheaded 4. **Zane** (zān), 1875-1939; U.S. novelist

grey·hound (grā'hound') *n.* [ME. *grehounde* < OE. *grighund* & ON. *greyhundr:* 1st element OE. *grig-* for **grieg-*, ON. *grey*, bitch, coward < IE. **ghrū-*, var. of **gher-*, to shine, as in GRAY) prob. means "gray animal," hence "dog"] any of a breed of tall, slender, swift hound with a narrow, pointed head and a smooth coat

GREYHOUND (28 in. high at shoulder)

grib·ble (grib′'l) *n.* [prob. dim. < base of GRUB] a small marine crustacean (order Isopoda) that bores into wooden objects under water and destroys them

grid (grid) *n.* [short for GRIDIRON] **1.** a framework of parallel bars; gridiron; grating **2.** a network of evenly spaced horizontal and vertical bars or lines, esp. one for locating points when placed over a map, chart, building plan, etc. **3.** *Elec.* a metallic plate in a storage cell for conducting the electric current and supporting the active material **4.** *Electronics* an electrode, usually a wire spiral or mesh, having one or more openings for controlling the passage of electrons or ions in an electronic tube —☆*adj.* [Slang] of football

grid bias the direct-current voltage applied to the control grid of an electron tube to make it negative with respect to the cathode

grid current the flow of electrons between a grid and the cathode of an electron tube

☆**grid·der** (grid′ər) *n.* [< GRID, *adj.* & GRIDIRON] [Slang] a football player

grid·dle (grid′'l) *n.* [ME. *gredil* < Anglo-Fr. *gridil* < OFr. *gredil*, var. of *grail* < L. *craticula*, small gridiron < *cratis*, wickerwork: see CRATE] a heavy, flat, metal plate or pan for cooking pancakes, etc. —*vt.* **-dled, -dling** to cook on a griddle

grid·dle·cake (-kāk′) *n.* a thin, flat batter cake cooked on a griddle; pancake

gride (grid) *vt.*, *vi.* **grid′ed, grid′ing** [metathesis of ME. *girden*, to pierce (see GIRD²), adopted (< Lydgate) & popularized by Spenser] **1.** to scrape or grate with a rasping sound **2.** [Obs.] to pierce or wound —*n.* a harsh, rasping sound made by scraping or grating

grid·i·ron (grid′i′ərn) *n.* [ME. *gredirne*, folk etym. on *irne* (see IRON) < *gredire*, var. of *gredil*: see GRIDDLE] **1.** a framework of metal bars or wires on which to broil meat or fish; grill **2.** any framework or network resembling a gridiron ☆**3.** a football field

grief (grēf) *n.* [ME. *gref* < OFr., sorrow, grief < *grever*: see GRIEVE] **1.** intense emotional suffering caused by loss, disaster, misfortune, etc.; acute sorrow; deep sadness **2.** a cause or the subject of such suffering **3.** [Obs.] *a)* hardship, suffering, or pain *b)* a cause of any of these —*SYN.* see SORROW —**come to grief** to fail or be ruined

grief-strick·en (-strik′'n) *adj.* stricken with grief; keenly distressed; sorrowful

Grieg (grēg; *Norw.* grig), **Ed·vard** (**Hagerup**) (ed′värd; *Norw.* ed′vārt) 1843–1907; Norw. composer

griev·ance (grē′vəns) *n.* [ME. *grevaunce* < OFr. *grevance* < *grever*: see ff.] **1.** a circumstance thought to be unjust or injurious and ground for complaint or resentment **2.** complaint or resentment, or a statement expressing this, against a real or imagined wrong **3.** [Obs.] *a)* the inflicting of injury or hardship *b)* a cause of injury or hardship —*SYN.* see INJUSTICE

grieve (grēv) *vt.* **grieved, griev′ing** [ME. *greven* < OFr. *grever* < L. *gravare*, to burden, grieve < *gravis*, heavy, grievous: see GRAVE¹] **1.** to cause to feel grief; afflict with deep, acute sorrow or distress **2.** [Archaic] to harm; injure —*vi.* to feel deep, acute sorrow or distress; mourn; lament —**griev′er** *n.*

griev·ous (grē′vəs) *adj.* [ME. *grevous* < OFr. < *grever*: see prec.] **1.** causing grief **2.** showing or characterized by grief [a grievous cry] **3.** causing suffering; hard to bear; severe [grievous pain] **4.** deplorable; atrocious; heinous [a grievous crime] —**griev′ous·ly** *adv.* —**griev′ous·ness** *n.*

griffe (grif) *n.* [Fr., lit., a claw < OFr. *grif* < Frank. **grif*, akin to OHG. *grif*: see GRIPE] *Archit.* a clawlike ornament extending from the base of a column

grif·fin (grif′ən) *n.* [ME. *griffon* < OFr. *grifoun* < OHG. or It. *grifo*, both < Gr. *gryps*, griffin < *grypos*, hooked, curved (prob. so called from its hooked beak) < IE. base **ger-*, whence CROOK] a mythical animal with the body and hind legs of a lion and the head and wings of an eagle

Grif·fith (grif′ith) [W. *Gruffydd* < ? L. *Rufus*: see RUFUS] **1.** a masculine name **2. D(avid) (Lew·elyn) W(ark)**, 1875–1948; U.S. motion-picture producer & director

GRIFFIN

grif·fon (grif′ən) *n.* [Fr., lit., a griffin] **1.** *same as* GRIFFIN **2.** any of a Belgian breed of very small dog with a flat face **3.** any of a Dutch breed of medium-sized dog with a wiry coat

☆**grift·er** (grif′tər) *n.* [prob. altered < GRAFTER] [Slang] a petty swindler, as one who operates a dishonest gambling device at a carnival; confidence man —**grift** *n., vt., v.*

grig (grig) *n.* [ME. *grege*, anything diminutive, dwarf, prob. < Scand., as in Norw. *krek*, Sw. dial. *krik*, little animal] **1.** a lively, animated person **2.** [Obs. or Dial.] a small eel **3.** [Obs. or Dial.] a grasshopper or cricket

Gri·gnard reagent (grē nyärd′) [after F. A. V. Grignard (1871–1935), Fr. chemist] any of a class of reagents with the general formula RMgX, in which R is an alkyl or aryl radical and X is a halide: these reagents react with a great variety of compounds and are used in the synthesis of organic compounds

☆**gri·gri** (grē′grē) *n. same as* GRIS-GRIS

grill¹ (gril) *n.* [Fr. *gril* < OFr. *grail*: see GRIDDLE] **1.** a framework of metal bars or wires on which to broil meat or fish; gridiron **2.** a large griddle **3.** grilled food **4.** *short for* GRILLROOM —*vt.* [Fr. *griller* < the *n.*] **1.** to cook on a grill; broil **2.** to torture by applying heat ☆**3.** to question relentlessly; cross-examine searchingly —*vi.* to be subjected to grilling

grill² (gril) *n. same as* GRILLE

gril·lage (-ij) *n.* [Fr., wirework, grating, frame < *grille*: see ff.] a system of beams laid crosswise to form a foundation for a building in soft soil

grille (gril) *n.* [Fr. < OFr. *graille* < L. *craticula*: see GRIDDLE] **1.** an open grating of wrought iron, bronze, wood, etc., forming a screen to a door, window, or other opening, or used as a divider **2.** *Court Tennis* a square opening high on the back wall of the court on the hazard side

grilled (grild) *adj.* **1.** having a grille **2.** cooked on a grill or gridiron; broiled

Grill·par·zer (gril′pär′tsər), **Franz** (fränts) 1791–1872; Austrian dramatist

grill·room (gril′rōōm′) *n.* a restaurant, club, or dining room that makes a specialty of grilled foods

grill·work (-wurk′) *n.* a grille, or something worked into the form of a grille

grilse (grils) *n., pl.* **grilse, grils′es:** see PLURAL, II, D, 2 [ME. *grills* < ? OFr. *grisle*, dim. < *gris*, gray] a young salmon on its first return from the sea to fresh water

grim (grim) *adj.* **grim′mer, grim′mest** [ME. < OE. *grimm*, akin to G. *grimm* < IE. base **ghrem-*, to make a loud sound, roar angrily, whence Russ. *grom*, thunder & GRUMBLE] **1.** fierce; cruel; savage **2.** hard and unyielding; relentless; stern; resolute [grim courage] **3.** appearing stern, forbidding, harsh, etc. [a grim face] **4.** repellent; uninviting [a grim task] **5.** dealing with unpleasant subjects; frightful; ghastly [grim humor] —*SYN.* see GHASTLY —**grim′ly** *adv.* —**grim′ness** *n.*

gri·mace (gri mās′, grim′əs) *n.* [Fr., altered (with pejorative suffix) < OFr. *grimuche*, prob. < Frank. **grima*, a mask, akin to OE. *grima* < IE. base **ghrei-*, to smear, rub over, whence Gr. *chrisma*, ointment & GRISLY] a twisting or distortion of the face, as in expressing pain, contempt, disgust, etc., or a wry look, as in seeking to amuse —*vi.* **-maced′, -mac′ing** to make grimaces —**gri·mac′er** *n.*

Gri·mal·di man (gri mäl′de, -môl′-) [from the remains found near *Grimaldi*, village in Italy] an Aurignacian man, similar to the Cro-Magnon

gri·mal·kin (gri mal′kin, -môl′-) *n.* [earlier *gray malkin*] **1.** a cat; esp., an old female cat **2.** a malicious old woman

grime (grim) *n.* [Early ModE., prob. < Fl. *grijm*: for IE. base see GRIMACE] dirt, esp. sooty dirt, rubbed into or covering a surface, as of the skin —*vt.* **grimed, grim′ing** to make very dirty or griny

☆**Grimes (Golden)** (grimz) [short for *Grimes Golden Pippin*, variety grown (c. 1790) by T. P. *Grimes*, W.Va. fruit grower] a yellow autumn eating apple

Grimm (grim), **Ja·kob (Ludwig Karl)** (yä′kôp), 1785–1863 & **Wil·helm (Karl)** (vil′helm), 1786–1859; Ger. brother philologists & collaborators in the collection of fairy tales

Grimm's law (grimz) [after formulation (1822) by Jakob GRIMM of parallels noticed by R. K. Rask & himself] a systematic statement of a series of prehistoric changes of Indo-European reconstructed consonants to proto-Germanic consonants: these assumed prehistoric sound shifts are reflected by consonant correspondences between Germanic words and their cognates in non-Germanic Indo-European languages: (1) IE. voiceless stops (p, t, k) = Gmc. voiceless fricatives (f, th, h); hence, L. *pater* (cf. PATERNAL) = E. *father*, L. *tenuis* (cf. TENUOUS) = E. *thin*, Gr. *kardia* (cf. CARDIAC) = E. *heart* (2) IE. voiced aspirated stops (bh, dh, gh) = Gmc. voiced fricatives or stops (b, d, g); hence, Sans. *bhrātar* (L. *frater*: cf. FRATERNAL) = E. *brother*, Sans. *madhu*, honey (Gr. *methy*, wine: cf. METHYL) = E. *mead*, L. *hostis* (IE. **ghostis*: cf. HOSTILE) = E. *guest* (3) IE. voiced stops (b, d, g) = Gmc. voiceless stops (p, t, k); hence, L. *bucca* (cf. BUCCAL) = OE. *pohha*, a sack, L. *decem* (cf. DECIMAL) = E. *ten*, L. *genu* (cf. GENUFLECT) = E. *knee* These correspondences show the kinship, stressed in the etymologies of this dictionary, between various native English words and the English words borrowed from the Classical or Romance languages

Grims·by (grimz′bē) seaport in Lincolnshire, NE England, at the mouth of the Humber estuary: pop. 95,000

grim·y (gri′mē) *adj.* **grim′i·er, grim′i·est** covered with or full of grime; very dirty —*SYN.* see DIRTY —**grim′i·ly** *adv.* —**grim′i·ness** *n.*

grin (grin) *vi.* **grinned, grin′ning** [ME. *grennen* < OE. *grennian*, to gnash or bare the teeth, akin to OHG. *grennan*,

to mutter, MHG. *grennen*, to grin] **1.** to smile broadly as in amusement or pleasure, or, sometimes, in foolish embarrassment **2.** to draw back the lips and show the teeth in pain, scorn, etc. —*vt.* to express by grinning —*n.* the act or look of one who grins —**grin and bear it** to accept philosophically something burdensome or painful —*SYN.* see SMILE —**grin′ner** *n.* —**grin′ning·ly** *adv.*

grind (grīnd) *vt.* **ground, grind′ing** [ME. *grinden* < OE. *grindan* < IE. *ghrendh-*, base **ghren-*, to rub away, pulverize: cf. GROUND[1]] **1.** to crush into bits or fine particles between two hard surfaces; pulverize **2.** to afflict with cruelty, hardship, etc.; crush; oppress [a people *ground* by tyranny] **3.** to sharpen, shape, or smooth by friction **4.** to press down or together with a crushing, turning motion; rub harshly or gratingly [to *grind* one's teeth] **5.** to operate by turning the crank of [to *grind* a coffee mill] **6.** to make or produce by grinding —*vi.* **1.** to perform the act of grinding something **2.** to be capable of being ground; undergo grinding **3.** to grate **4.** [Colloq.] to work or study hard and steadily **5.** [Slang] to move the hips in a circular motion, as in striptease dancing —*n.* **1.** the act or operation of grinding **2.** the degree of fineness of something ground into particles **3.** long, difficult, tedious work or study; drudgery ☆**4.** [Colloq.] a student who studies very hard ☆**5.** [Slang] a circular movement of the hips made by or as by a striptease dancer —*SYN.* see WORK —**grind out** to produce by steady or laborious, often uninspired, effort —**grind′ing·ly** *adv.*

☆**grin·de·li·a** (grin dēl′yə, -dē′lē ə) *n.* [ModL., after Hieronymus *Grindel* (1776–1836), professor of botany at Riga] any of a genus (*Grindelia*) of coarse plants of the composite family, with large, yellow flower heads: the dried stems and leaves have been used medicinally

grind·er (grīn′dər) *n.* [ME. & OE. *grindere*] **1.** a person who grinds; esp., one whose work is sharpening tools, etc. **2.** a thing that grinds; specif., *a*) any of various machines for crushing or sharpening *b*) a molar tooth *c*) [*pl.*] [Colloq.] the teeth ☆**3.** *regional var. of* HERO (SANDWICH)

grind·stone (grīnd′stōn′) *n.* **1.** orig., a millstone **2.** a revolving stone disk for sharpening bladed tools or shaping and polishing things —**keep** (or **have** or **put**) **one's nose to the grindstone** to work hard and steadily

☆**grin·go** (grin′gō) *n., pl.* **-gos** [MexSp. < Sp., gibberish, altered < *Griego*, Greek < L. *Graecus*, GREEK] in Latin America, a foreigner, esp. an American or Englishman: hostile and contemptuous term

grip[1] (grip) *n.* [ME. *gripe* < OE., a clutch, *gripa*, handful < base of *gripan* (see GRIPE)] **1.** the act of taking firmly and holding fast with the hand, teeth, an instrument, etc.; secure grasp; firm hold **2.** the manner in which this is done **3.** any special manner of clasping hands by which members of a secret or fraternal society identify one another as such **4.** the power of grasping firmly [to lose one's *grip*] **5.** the power of understanding; mental grasp [to have a good *grip* on a matter] **6.** firm control; mastery [in the *grip* of disease, to get a *grip* on oneself] **7.** a mechanical contrivance for clutching or grasping **8.** the part by which a tool, weapon, etc. is grasped; handle; hilt **9.** [short for GRIPSACK] a small bag or satchel for holding clothes, etc. in traveling ☆**10.** [Slang] *same as* STAGEHAND **11.** *Sports* the manner of holding a bat, club, racket, etc. —*vt.* **gripped** or **gript, grip′ping 1.** to take firmly and hold fast with the hand, teeth, an instrument, etc. **2.** to give a grip (*n.* 3) to **3.** to fasten or join firmly (*to*) **4.** *a*) to get and hold the attention of *b*) to have a strong emotional impact on —*vi.* to get a grip —**come to grips 1.** to engage in hand-to-hand fighting **2.** to struggle or try to cope (*with*) —**grip′per** *n.*

grip[2] (grip) *n. same as* GRIPPE

gripe (grīp) *vt.* **griped, grip′ing** [ME. *gripen* < OE. *gripan*, to seize, akin to G. *greifen* < IE. base **ghreib-*, to grasp, akin to **ghrebh*, whence GRAB[1]] **1.** formerly, *a*) to grasp; clutch *b*) to distress; oppress; afflict **2.** to cause sudden, sharp pain in the bowels of ☆**3.** [Slang] to annoy; irritate —*vi.* **1.** to feel sharp pains in the bowels ☆**2.** [Slang] to complain; grumble —*n.* **1.** the pressure or pain of something distressing or afflicting **2.** a sudden, sharp pain in the bowels: *usually used in pl.* **3.** [Rare] a handle **4.** a device that grips; specif., [*pl.*] Naut. hooks, traps, etc. for holding a ship's boat in place ☆**5.** [Slang] a complaint **6.** [Archaic] *a*) a grasping or clutching *b*) control; mastery —**grip′er** *n.*

grippe (grip) *n.* [Fr., lit., a seizure < *gripper* < Frank. **gripan*, akin to GRIPE] *earlier term for* INFLUENZA —**grip′py** *adj.,* **-pi·er, -pi·est**

grip·ple (grip′'l) *adj.* [ME. *gripel* < base of *gripan:* see GRIPE] [Brit. Dial.] miserly; avaricious

☆**grip·sack** (grip′sak′) *n.* [GRIP[1] + SACK[1]] *earlier term for* GRIP[1] (*n.* 9)

gript (gript) *alt. pt. & pp. of* GRIP[1]

Gris (grēs), **Juan** (hwän) (born *José Victoriano González*) 1887–1927; Sp. painter, in France after 1906

gri·saille (gri zī′, -zāl′; *Fr.* grē zä′y′) *n.* [Fr. < *gris*, gray < Frank. **gris*, akin to Du. *grijs*, gray] a style of painting, esp. on glass, using only gray tints and giving the effect of sculpture in relief

Gri·sel·da (gri zel′də, -sel′-) [Fr. or It. < G. *Griseldis, Grishilda*] **1.** a feminine name **2.** the heroine of various medieval tales, famous for her meek, long-suffering patience

gris·e·ous (gris′ē əs, griz′-) *adj.* [ML. *griseus* < of Gmc. origin: cf. GRISAILLE] gray; esp., pearl-gray

gri·sette (gri zet′) *n.* [Fr., orig., gray woolen cloth used for dresses worn by working girls < *gris*, gray: cf. GRISAILLE] a French working girl

☆**gris-gris** (grē′grē) *n., pl.* **gris-gris** [Louisiana Fr., of Afr. orig.: ult. < ? Ar. *hirz acihr*, amulet of enchantment] an amulet, charm, or spell associated with voodoo

gris·kin (gris′kin) *n.* [dim. of obs. *grice*, pig < ME. *gris* < ON. *griss*, young pig, hog] [Brit.] the lean section of pork loin

gris·ly (griz′lē) *adj.* **-li·er, -li·est** [ME. *grislich* < OE. *grislic* (akin to OFris. *grislyk*) < base of *a-grisan*, to shudder with fear, prob. < IE. base **ghrei-*, to rub hard, smear, whence OE. *grima*, mask] terrifying; horrible; ghastly —*SYN.* see GHASTLY —**gris′li·ness** *n.*

Gri·sons (grē zōn′) *Fr. name of* GRAUBÜNDEN

grist (grist) *n.* [ME. < OE., akin to OHG. *grist-* in *grist-grimmon*, to gnash the teeth: for prob. IE. base see GRISLY] grain that is to be or has been ground; esp., a batch of such grain —**grist to** (or **for**) **one's mill** anything that one can use profitably

gris·tle (gris′'l) *n.* [ME. *gristel* < OE. *gristle* (akin to OFris. *gristel*) < ? IE. base **ghrei:* cf. GRISLY] cartilage, now esp. as found in meat —**grist′li·ness** *n.* —**grist′ly** (gris′lē) *adj.*

grist·mill (grist′mil′) *n.* a mill for grinding grain, esp. for individual customers

grit (grit) *n.* [with Early ModE. vowel shortening < ME. *grete* < OE. *greot*, akin to G. *griess* < IE. base **ghreu-*, to grind down, crush, whence GREAT & Gr. *chrōma*, skin, color] **1.** rough, hard particles of sand, stone, etc. **2.** the texture of stone, with regard to the fineness or coarseness of its grain **3.** any of several sandstones with large, sharp grains, often used for grindstones ☆**4.** stubborn courage; brave perseverance; pluck —*vt.* **grit′ted, grit′ting 1.** to cover with grit **2.** to clench or grind (the teeth) in anger or determination —*vi.* to make a grating sound —*SYN.* see FORTITUDE

grith (grith) *n.* [ME. < OE. < ON., orig., home] [Obs.] **1.** security, protection, or peace, esp. as guaranteed by someone or in some place **2.** a sanctuary

☆**grits** (grits) *n.pl.* [ME. *gryttes* (pl.) < OE. *grytte*, akin to G. *grütze:* for IE. base see GRIT] wheat or corn ground more coarsely than for flour or meal; esp., [South] fine hominy

grit·ty (grit′ē) *adj.* **-ti·er, -ti·est 1.** of, like, or containing grit; sandy **2.** brave; plucky —**grit′ti·ly** *adv.* —**grit′ti·ness** *n.*

griv·et (griv′it) *n.* [Fr.] a long-tailed, olive-green African monkey (*Cercopithecus aethiops*), related to the vervet

griz·zle[1] (griz′'l) *n.* [< ME. *grisel* < OFr. *grisel, adj.* < *gris*, gray: see GRISAILLE] **1.** [Archaic] *a*) gray hair *b*) a gray wig **2.** gray —*vt., vi.* **-zled, -zling** to make or become gray —*adj.* [Archaic] gray

griz·zle[2] (griz′'l) *vt.* **-zled, -zling** [Brit.] **1.** to grumble; complain **2.** to fret or whimper

griz·zled (griz′'ld) *adj.* [< GRIZZLE[1] + -ED] **1.** gray or streaked with gray **2.** having gray hair

griz·zly (-lē) *adj.* **-zli·er, -zli·est** grayish; grizzled —*n., pl.* **-zlies** *short for* GRIZZLY BEAR

grizzly bear [prec. + BEAR[2]: infl. by association with GRISLY] a large, ferocious, brownish, grayish, or yellowish bear (*Ursus horribilis*) of W N. America, having a shoulder hump and long front claws

gro. gross

groan (grōn) *vi.* [ME. *gronien* < OE. *granian*, akin to G. *greinen*, to weep & GRIN] **1.** to utter a deep sound expressing pain, distress, or disapproval **2.** to make a creaking or grating sound, as from great strain [a heavy gate *groaning* on its hinges] **3.** to be weighed down or overburdened to the point of groaning —*vt.* to utter with a groan or groans —*n.* a sound made in groaning —**groan′er** *n.* —**groan′ing·ly** *adv.*

groat (grōt) *n.* [ME. *grote* < MDu. *groot* or MLowG. *grote*, altered < MHG. *grosse* < ML. (*denarius*) *grossus*, lit., thick (denarius): cf. GROSS] **1.** an obsolete English silver coin worth fourpence **2.** a trifling sum

groats (grōts) *n.pl.* [ME. *grotes* < OE. *grotan*, pl.: for IE. base see GRIT] hulled, or hulled and coarsely cracked, grain, esp. wheat, buckwheat, oats, or barley

gro·cer (grō′sər) *n.* [ME. *grosser* < OFr. *grossier* < *gros:* see GROSS] a storekeeper who sells food and various household supplies

gro·cer·y (grō′sər ē) *n., pl.* **-cer·ies** [ME. *grocerye* < OFr. *grosserie*] ☆**1.** a grocer's store **2.** [*pl.*] the food and supplies sold by a grocer

Grod·no (grōd′nō) city in W Byelorussian S.S.R., on the Neman River: pop. 73,000

grog (gräg) *n.* [after Old *Grog*, nickname of Admiral Edward VERNON, who ordered the sailors' rum to be diluted: he was so called because he wore a *grogram* cloak] **1.** an alcoholic liquor, esp. rum, diluted with water **2.** any alcoholic liquor

☆**grog·ger·y** (-ər ē) *n., pl.* **-ger·ies** [Archaic] a saloon

grog·gy (-ē) *adj.* **-gi·er, -gi·est** [< GROG + -Y[2]] **1.** orig., drunk; intoxicated **2.** shaky or dizzy, as from a blow, lack of sleep, etc. —**grog′gi·ly** *adv.* —**grog′gi·ness** *n.*

grog·ram (gräg′rəm) *n.* [earlier *grogran* < OFr. *gros grain* < *gros*, coarse, gross + *grain*, GRAIN] **1.** a coarse fabric in former use, made of silk, or of silk, worsted, and mohair, often stiffened with gum **2.** an article of clothing made of this

grog·shop (gräg′shäp) *n.* [Chiefly Brit.] a saloon

groin (groin) *n.* [Early ModE. phonetic rendering of *grine*, var. of *grinde* < ME. *grynde*, prob. < OE. *grynde*, abyss, in sense "depression" (akin to *grund*, GROUND¹)] **1.** the hollow or fold where the abdomen joins either thigh **2.** *Archit. a)* the sharp, curved edge formed at the junction of two intersecting vaults *b)* the rib of wood, stone, etc. covering this edge —*vt.* to build or provide with groins

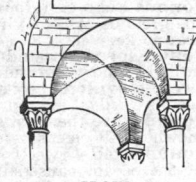

GROIN

☆**grok** (gräk) *vt., vi.* **grokked, grok'king** [coined in a science-fiction novel (1961) by R. A. Heinlein] [Slang] to understand thoroughly because of having empathy (with)

Gro·li·er (grō'lē ər; *Fr.* grō lyā') *adj.* designating a style of bookbinding, with ornamentation in gilt scrolls, bands, or ribbons, designed by Jean Grolier de Servières (1479–1565), *Fr.* bibliophile

grom·met (gräm'it, grum'-) *n.* [< obs. Fr. *gromette* (now *gourmette*), a curb, curb chain < *gourmer*, to curb] **1.** a ring of rope or metal used to fasten the edge of a sail to its stay, hold an oar in place, etc. **2.** an eyelet, as of metal or plastic, protecting an opening in cloth, leather, etc.

grom·well (gräm'wəl, -wel) *n.* [altered < ME. *gromil* < OFr. < ML. *gruinum milium*, kind of millet < *gruinus*, of a crane (< L. *grus*, crane) + L. *milium*, millet] any of a genus (*Lithospermum*) of plants of the borage family, with yellow or orange flowers and hard, stonelike nutlets

Gro·my·ko (grō mē'kō; *E.* grə mē'kō), **An·drei An·dre·e·vich** (än drā' än drā'yi vich) 1909– ; Soviet diplomat

Gro·ning·en (grō'niŋ ən; *Du.* khrō'niŋ ən) **1.** province of the N Netherlands: 898 sq. mi.; pop. 503,000 **2.** its capital: pop. 154,000

Grøn·land (grön'län) *Dan.* name of GREENLAND

groom (grōōm, groom) *n.* [ME. *grom*, boy, groom < ?] **1.** a man or boy whose work is tending, feeding, and currying horses **2.** any of a group of officials in charge of particular departments of the British Royal household **3.** *same as* BRIDEGROOM **[**Archaic**]** *a)* a manservant *b)* any man: a somewhat contemptuous usage —*vt.* **1.** to clean and curry (a horse, dog, etc.) **2.** to make neat and tidy ☆**3.** to train for a particular purpose [to *groom* a man for politics]

grooms·man (grōōmz'mən, groomz'-) *n., pl.* **-men** (-mən) a man who attends a bridegroom at the wedding

groove (grōōv) *n.* [ME. *grofe* < ON. *grof*, a pit & < MDu. *groeve*, both akin to G. *grube*, a pit, hole, ditch: for IE. base see GRAVE²] **1.** a long, narrow furrow or hollow cut in a surface with a tool, as the track cut in a phonograph record for the needle to follow **2.** any channel or rut cut or worn in a surface **3.** a habitual way of doing something; settled routine **4.** *Anat.* any narrow furrow, depression, or slit occurring on the surface of an organ, esp. of bone **5.** *Printing* the indentation on the bottom of a piece of type —*vt.* **grooved, groov'ing** to make a groove or grooves in —*vi.* ☆[Slang] to react in a nonanalytical empathic way to persons, situations, etc. outmoded one

☆**groov·y** (grōō'vē) *adj.* **groov'i·er, groov'i·est** [< old slang *in the groove*, working effortlessly] [Slang] very pleasing or attractive: a generalized term of approval

grope (grōp) *vi.* **groped, grop'ing** [ME. *gropien* < OE. *grapian*, to touch, seize, akin to G. *greifen*, to grasp: for IE. base see GRIPE] to feel or search about blindly, hesitantly, or uncertainly; feel one's way —*vt.* to seek or find (one's way) by groping —*n.* an act or instance of groping —**grop'er** *n.* —**grop'ing·ly** *adv.*

Gro·pi·us (grō'pē əs), **Walter** 1883–1969; Ger. architect, in the U.S. since 1937: founder of the BAUHAUS

Gros (grō), **Baron An·toine Jean** (än twän' zhän) 1771–1835; Fr. painter

gros·beak (grōs'bēk') *n.* [Fr. *grosbec*: see GROSS & BEAK] any of various finchlike birds (family Fringillidae), with a thick, strong, conical bill

gro·schen (grō'shən) *n., pl.* **-schen** [G. < 14th-c. dial. *grosch(e)* < Czech *groš* < ML. (*denarius*) *grossus*: cf. GROAT] **1.** in Austria, a unit of currency and a coin equal to 1/100 schilling **2.** in Germany, formerly, a small silver coin of varying value

gros de Lon·dres (or **lon·dres**) (grō də lôn'drə) [Fr., lit., London gross: cf. GROGRAM] a shiny fabric of lightweight silk having alternate wide and narrow ribs

gros·grain (grō'grān') *n.* [Fr.: see GROGRAM] a closely woven silk or rayon fabric with prominent, crosswise ribbing, used for ribbons, trimming, etc.

gross (grōs) *adj.* [ME. *grose* < OFr. *gros*, big, thick, coarse < LL. *grossus*, thick] **1.** big or fat and coarse-looking; corpulent; burly **2.** glaring; flagrant; very bad [a *gross* miscalculation] **3.** dense; thick **4.** *a)* lacking fineness, as in texture *b)* lacking fine distinctions or specific details **5.** lacking in refinement or perception; insensitive; dull **6.** vulgar; obscene; coarse [*gross* language] **7.** total; entire; with no deductions: opposed to NET² [*gross* income] **8.** [Archaic] evident; obvious —*n.* [ME. *groos* < OFr. *grosse*,

orig. fem. of *gros*] **1.** *pl.* **gross'es** overall total, as of income, before deductions are taken **2.** *pl.* **gross** twelve dozen —*vt., vi.* [Colloq.] to earn (a specified total amount) before expenses are deducted —*SYN.* see COARSE, FLAGRANT —**in the gross 1.** in bulk; as a whole **2.** wholesale: also **by the gross** —**gross'ly** *adv.* —**gross'ness** *n.*

gross national product the total value of a nation's annual output of goods and services

gross ton a unit of weight, equal to 2,240 pounds

gros·su·lar·ite (gräs'yoo lə rīt') *n.* [G. *grossularit* < ModL. *grossularia*, orig. gooseberry genus (in reference to color of some varieties)] a kind of garnet, $Ca_3Al_2(SiO_4)_3$, occurring in various colors

gross weight the total weight of a commodity, including the weight of the packaging or container

Gros Ventre (grō' vänt') [Fr., lit., big belly] **1.** a member of a western tribe of the Arapaho **2.** *same as* HIDATSA

grosz (grôsh) *n., pl.* **grosz'y** (-ē) [Pol., akin to Czech *groš:* see GROSCHEN] a unit of currency and a coin in Poland, equal to 1/100 zloty

Grosz (grōs), **George** 1893–1959; U.S. painter & caricaturist, born in Germany

grot (grät) *n.* [Fr. *grotte* < It. *grotta*] [Poet.] a grotto

Grote (grōt), **George** 1794–1871; Eng. historian

gro·tesque (grō tesk') *adj.* [Fr. < It. *grottesca* (*pittura*), orig., (picture) in a cave < *grotta*, a grotto: from resemblance to designs found in Roman caves] **1.** in or of a style of painting, sculpture, etc. in which forms of persons and animals are intermingled with foliage, flowers, fruits, etc. in a fantastic or bizarre design **2.** characterized by distortions or striking incongruities in appearance, shape, manner, etc.; fantastic; bizarre **3.** ludicrously eccentric or strange; ridiculous; absurd —*n.* **1.** a grotesque painting, sculpture, design, etc. **2.** a grotesque thing or quality —*SYN.* see FANTASTIC —**gro·tesque'ly** *adv.* —**gro·tesque'ness** *n.*

gro·tes·quer·ie, gro·tes·quer·y (-ər ē) *n., pl.* **-quer·ies** [< prec.] **1.** a grotesque thing **2.** the quality or state of being grotesque

Gro·ti·us (grō'shē əs), **Hugo** (born *Huig de Groot*) 1583–1645; Du. scholar, jurist, & statesman

grot·to (grät'ō) *n., pl.* **-toes, -tos** [It. *grotta* < ML. *grupta* < VL. *crupta*, for L. *crypta*, CRYPT] **1.** a cave **2.** a cavelike summerhouse, shrine, etc.

☆**grouch** (grouch) *vi.* [< earlier *grutch* < ME. *grucchen:* see GRUDGE] to grumble or complain in a sulky way —*n.* **1.** a person who grouches continually **2.** a grumbling or sulky mood **3.** a complaint

☆**grouch·y** (-ē) *adj.* **grouch'i·er, grouch'i·est** in a grouch; grumbling; sulky —**grouch'i·ly** *adv.* —**grouch'i·ness** *n.*

ground¹ (ground) *n.* [ME. *grund* < OE., ground, bottom, akin to G. *grund*, ON. *grunnr*, orig. prob. sand < IE. base *ghren-*, to pulverize, rub hard over, whence Gr. *chrainein*, to graze & GRIND] **1.** *a)* orig., the lowest part, base, or bottom of anything *b)* the bottom of a body of water **2.** the surface of the earth, specif. the solid surface **3.** the soil of the earth; earth; land **4.** *a)* any particular piece of land; esp., one set aside for a specified purpose [a hunting *ground*] *b)* [*pl.*] land surrounding or attached to a house or other building; esp., the lawns, gardens, etc. of an estate **5.** any particular area of reference, discussion, work, etc.; topic; subject [arguments covering the same *ground*] **6.** [*often pl.*] basis; foundation **7.** [*often pl.*] the logical basis of a conclusion, action, etc.; valid reason, motive, or cause **8.** the background or surface over which other parts are spread or laid, as the main surface of a painting **9.** [*pl.*] the particles that settle to the bottom of a liquid; dregs; sediment [coffee *grounds*] **10.** *Elec. a)* a conducting body (as the earth, or an object connected with the earth) whose potential is taken as zero and to which an electric circuit can be connected *b)* the connection of an electrical conductor with a ground *c)* a device, as a stake, iron pipe, etc., that makes such a connection —*adj.* **1.** of, on, or near the ground **2.** growing or living in or on the ground —*vt.* **1.** to set on, or cause to touch, the ground **2.** to cause (a ship, etc.) to run aground **3.** to found on a firm basis; establish **4.** to base (a claim, argument, etc.) on something specified **5.** to instruct (a person) in the elements or first principles of **6.** to provide with a background **7.** to keep (an aircraft or pilot) from flying **8.** *Elec.* to connect (an electrical conductor) with the ground, which becomes part of the circuit —*vi.* **1.** to strike the bottom or run ashore: said of a ship ☆**2.** *Baseball a)* to hit a grounder *b)* to be put out on a grounder (usually with *out*) —**break ground 1.** to dig; excavate **2.** to plow **3.** to start building **4.** to start any undertaking —**cover ground 1.** to move or traverse a certain distance **2.** to make a certain amount of progress —**cut the ground from under one** (or **one's feet**) to deprive one of effective defense or argument —☆**from the ground up** from the first or elementary principles, methods, etc. to the last or most advanced; completely; thoroughly —**gain ground 1.** to move forward **2.** to make progress **3.** to gain in strength, extent, popularity, etc. —☆**get off the ground** to get (something) started; begin or cause to begin to

progress —**give ground** to withdraw under attack; retreat; yield —**hold** (or **stand**) **one's ground** to keep one's position against attack or opposition; not withdraw or retreat —**lose ground 1.** to drop back; fall behind **2.** to lose in strength, extent, popularity, etc. —**on delicate ground** in a situation requiring tact —**on firm ground 1.** in a safe situation · **2.** firmly supported by facts or evidence —**on one's own ground 1.** dealing with a situation or subject that one knows well **2.** at home —☆**run into the ground** [Colloq.] to do too long or too often; overdo —**shift one's ground** to shift one's position; change one's argument or defense —**suit (right) down to the ground** [Colloq.] to suit completely

ground² (ground) *pt. & pp. of* GRIND

ground·age (groun′dij) *n.* [GROUND¹ + -AGE] [Brit.] a fee charged for permitting a ship to remain in a port

☆**ground ball** *same as* GROUNDER

ground bass *Music* a short phrase, usually of four to eight measures, played repeatedly in the bass against the melodies and harmonies of the upper parts

ground beetle any of a large family (Carabidae) of nocturnal beetles that live under rocks, rubbish, etc. and prey on other insects

☆**ground-cher·ry** (-cher′ē) *n.* any of a genus (*Physalis*) of plants of the nightshade family, including the Chinese-lantern plant, having small tomatolike fruits completely enclosed by a papery calyx

ground control personnel, electronic equipment, etc. on the ground, serving to guide airplanes and spacecraft in take-off, flight, and landing operations

ground cover any of various low, dense-growing plants, as ivy, myrtle, etc., used for covering the ground, as in places where it is difficult to grow grass

ground crew a group of people in charge of the maintenance and repair of aircraft

ground·er (groun′dər) *n. Baseball, Cricket,* etc. a batted ball that strikes the ground almost immediately and rolls or bounces along

ground fir any of several plants (genus *Lycopodium*) of the club-moss family, having forking stems covered with leaves resembling the needles of some evergreens

ground·fire (ground′fir′) *n.* gunfire directed at aircraft from the ground

ground floor that floor of a building which is approximately level with the ground; first floor —☆**in on the ground floor** [Colloq.] in at the beginning (of a business, etc.) and thus in an especially advantageous position

ground glass 1. glass whose surface has been ground so that it diffuses light and is therefore not transparent **2.** glass ground into fine particles

ground hemlock a low, spreading evergreen plant (*Taxus canadensis*) of the yew family, native to the NE U.S.

☆**ground·hog** (ground′hôg′, -häg′) *n.* [prob. transl. of Du. *aardvark,* AARDVARK] *same as* WOODCHUCK: also **ground hog**

☆**Groundhog Day** February 2, when, according to an old tradition, the groundhog comes out of hibernation: if it is sunny and he sees his shadow, he supposedly returns to his hole for six more weeks of winter weather

ground ice *same as* ANCHOR ICE

☆**ground ivy** a creeping plant (*Glechoma hederacea*) of the mint family, with round, toothed leaves and loose clusters of blue flowers

ground·less (-lis) *adj.* without reason or cause; unjustified —**ground′less·ly** *adv.* —**ground′less·ness** *n.*

ground·ling (-liŋ) **1.** *a)* a fish that lives close to the bottom of the water *b)* an animal that lives on or in the ground *c)* a plant that grows close to the ground **2.** *a)* in an Elizabethan theater, a person who watched the performance from cheap standing room in the pit *b)* a person lacking critical ability or taste

ground loop a sudden, sharp turn sometimes made by a taxiing airplane in taking off or landing

ground·mass (-mas′) *n. Geol.* the small-grained matrix in which larger crystals are embedded

ground meristem the basic primary tissue of the growing tip of a stem or root, excluding the epidermis and vascular bundles, which gives rise to the cortex, rays, and pith

ground·nut (-nut′) *n.* **1.** any of various plants with edible tubers or tuberlike parts, as the peanut **2.** the edible tuber or tuberlike part

ground pine ☆*same as* GROUND FIR

ground plan 1. *same as* FLOOR PLAN **2.** a first or basic plan

ground plate 1. *same as* GROUNDSILL **2.** a metal plate put in the ground to connect an electric circuit with the earth

☆**ground plum** a low, perennial, prairie milk vetch (*Astragalus crassicarpus*), with plump, thick-walled, edible pods

ground rent [Chiefly Brit.] rent paid for land on which the occupant can build, make improvements, etc.

☆**ground rule 1.** *Baseball* any of a set of rules adapted to playing conditions in a specific ballpark **2.** any of a set of rules governing a specific activity

ground·sel (ground′s'l, groun′-) *n.* [ME. *grundeswylie* < OE. *grundeswylige,* altered (after *grund,* GROUND¹) < earlier *gundeswelge,* ? lit., pus swallower < *gund,* pus + *swelgan,* to swallow (from use in poultices)] any of a large genus (*Senecio*) of plants of the composite family, with usually yellow, rayed flower heads

ground·sill (ground′sil) *n.* the bottom horizontal timber in a framework: also **ground′sel** (-s′l)

grounds·keep·er (groundz′kē′pər) *n.* a person who tends the grounds of a playing field, estate, cemetery, etc.: also **ground′keep′er**

ground·speed (ground′spēd) *n.* the speed of an aircraft in flight relative to the ground it passes over

☆**ground squirrel** any of various small, burrowing animals (genus *Citellus*) related to the tree squirrels and chipmunks

ground state the most stable state of an atom or molecule in which all electrons exist at their lowest energy levels

ground·swell (-swel′) *n.* **1.** a violent swelling or rolling of the ocean, caused by a distant storm or earthquake **2.** a rapidly growing wave of popular sentiment, opinion, etc. Also **ground swell**

ground-to-air (-tə er′) *adj. same as* SURFACE-TO-AIR

ground-to-ground (-tə ground′) *adj. same as* SURFACE-TO-SURFACE

ground water water found underground in porous rock strata and soils, as in a spring

ground wave a radio wave that follows the curvature of the earth near the ground

☆**ground wire** a wire acting as a conductor from an electric circuit, antenna, etc. to the ground

ground·work (ground′wurk′) *n.* a foundation; basis —SYN. see BASE¹

☆**ground zero** the surface area directly below or above the point of detonation of a nuclear bomb

group (grōōp) *n.* [Fr. *groupe* < It. *gruppo,* a knot, lump, group < Gmc. **kruppa,* round mass: for IE. base see CROP] **1.** a number of persons or things gathered closely together and forming a recognizable unit; cluster; aggregation; band [a *group* of houses] **2.** a collection of objects or figures forming a design or part of a design, as in a work of art **3.** a number of persons or things classified together because of common characteristics, community of interests, etc. **4.** *Chem. a) same as* RADICAL (*n.* 4) *b)* a number of elements with similar properties, forming one of the vertical columns of the periodic table *c)* a number of elements having similar chemical reactions **5.** *Geol.* a stratigraphic unit consisting of two or more formations **6.** *Math.* a collection of elements with an associative rule for combination of elements in which the product of any two elements is in the set, every element in the set has an inverse, and a unit (or identity) element is contained in the set ☆**7.** *U.S. Air Force* a unit, usually a subdivision of an air wing, under the command of a colonel ☆**8.** *U.S. Mil.* a unit made up of two or more battalions or squadrons —*vt., vi.* to assemble or form into a group or groups —*adj.* of, characteristic of, or involving a group [*group* attitudes]

SYN.—**group** is the basic, general word expressing the simple idea of an assembly of persons, animals, or things without further connotation; **herd** is applied to a group of cattle, sheep, or similar large animals feeding, living, or moving together; **flock,** to goats, sheep, or birds; **drove,** to cattle, hogs, or sheep; **pack,** to hounds or wolves; **pride,** to lions; **swarm,** to insects; **school,** to fish, porpoises, whales, or the like; **bevy,** to quails; **covey,** to partridges or quails; **flight,** to birds flying together In extended applications, **flock** connotes guidance and care, **herd, drove,** and **pack** are used contemptuously of people, **swarm** suggests a thronging, and **bevy** and **covey** are used of girls or women

group·er (grōōp′ər) *n., pl.* **-ers, -er:** see PLURAL, II, D, 1 [Port. *garoupa,* prob. of S.Am. origin] any of several large fishes (esp. genera *Epinephelus* and *Myctoperca*) found in warm seas

☆**group insurance** insurance, esp. life or health insurance, available to employees or members of an organization as a group at special, low rates

☆**group medicine 1.** the practice of medicine by a number of specialists working together in association **2.** medical care provided, esp. by such an association, to the members of a group at a fixed, usually annual, rate

group therapy (or **psychotherapy**) a form of treatment for a group of patients with similar emotional problems or disorders, as by mutual criticism, psychodrama, etc., usually under a therapist's supervision

group work social work in which the worker helps further the social development and growth of individuals by guiding them in cultural and recreational group activities —**group worker**

grouse¹ (grous) *n., pl.* **grouse** [Early ModE. < ?] any of a number of game birds (family Tetraonidae) with a round, plump body, firm, feathered legs, feather-covered nostrils, and mottled feathers, as the ruffed grouse, sage hen, etc.

grouse² (grous) *vi.* **groused, grous′ing** [orig. Brit. army slang < ?] [Colloq.] to complain; grumble —*n.* [Colloq.] a complaint —**grous′er** *n.*

grout (grout) *n.* [ME. *grut* < OE., silt, sand, akin to *greot,* GRIT] **1.** *a)* coarse meal *b)* [*pl.*] *same as* GROATS **2.** [*usually pl.*] [Brit.] sediment; dregs **3.** a thin mortar used to fill chinks or cracks, as between tiles **4.** a fine plaster for finishing surfaces —*vt.* to fill or finish with or as with grout —**grout′er** *n.*

grout·y (-ē) *adj.* **grout′i·er, grout′i·est** [< Dial. *grout,* to grumble + -y²] [Dial.] cross; sulky

grove (grōv) *n.* [ME. *grof* < OE. *graf,* akin to *græfa,* thicket] **1.** a small wood or group of trees without undergrowth **2.** a group of trees planted and cultivated to bear fruit, nuts, etc.; orchard

grov·el (gruv''l, gräv'-) *vi.* **-eled** or **-elled, -el·ing** or **-el·ling** [back-formation (first found in Shakespeare) < *grovelling*, down on one's face (assumed to be prp.) < ME. *grufelinge* < *gruf*, for *o grufe*, on the face (< ON. *ā grūfu*) + *-ling*, -LING²] 1. to lie prone or crawl in a prostrate position, esp. abjectly 2. to behave humbly or abjectly, as before authority; debase oneself in a servile fashion 3. to wallow in what is low, sordid, or contemptible —**grov'el·er, grov'el·ler** *n.*

grow (grō) *vi.* **grew, grown, grow'ing** [ME. *growen* < OE. *growan,* akin to ON. *grōa,* OHG. *gruoen* < IE. base **ghrō-,* to grow, turn green, whence GREEN, GRASS] 1. to come into being or be produced naturally; spring up; sprout 2. to exist as living vegetation; thrive [*cactus grows* in sand] 3. to increase in size and develop toward maturity, as a plant or animal does by assimilating food 4. to increase in size, quantity, or degree, or in some specified manner [to *grow* in wisdom] 5. to come to be; become [to *grow* weary] 6. to become attached or united by growth —*vt.* 1. to cause to grow; raise; cultivate 2. to cover with a growth: used in the passive 3. to allow to grow [to *grow* a beard] 4. to cause to be or to exist; develop —**grow into** 1. to develop so as to become [a boy *grows into* a man] 2. to grow or develop so as to fit or be suited to —**grow on** to have a gradually increasing effect on; come gradually to seem more important, dear, or admirable to —**grow out of** 1. to develop from 2. to outgrow —**grow up** 1. to reach maturity; become adult or attain full growth 2. to come to be; develop; arise —**grow'er** *n.*

growing pains 1. recurrent pains in the joints and muscles, esp. of the legs, of growing children: a loose term with no precise medical meaning 2. difficulties experienced in the early development of an institution or enterprise

growing point the apex of a stem or root, containing actively dividing and elongating cells

growl (groul) *vi.* [ME. *groulen,* to rumble < ? OFr. *grouter,* prob. < MDu. *grollen,* to be noisy, grumble] 1. to make a low, rumbling, menacing sound in the throat, as a dog does 2. to complain in an angry or surly manner 3. to rumble, as thunder, cannon, etc. —*vt.* to express by growling —*n.* 1. the act or sound of growling ☆2. *Jazz* a growling sound produced in playing a trumpet, trombone, etc. —**growl'ing·ly** *adv.*

growl·er (-ər) *n.* 1. a person, animal, or thing that growls ☆2. [Slang] *a)* formerly, a pail or can to carry out beer bought at a saloon, etc. *b)* a keg of beer, equal to 1/8 barrel 3. a small iceberg ☆4. an electromagnetic device used to find short circuits in coils and for magnetizing and demagnetizing

grown (grōn) *pp.* of GROW —*adj.* 1. having completed its growth; fully developed; mature 2. covered with a specified growth 3. cultivated in a specified way or place [home-*grown*]

grown-up (grōn'up'; *for n.* -up') *adj.* 1. that is an adult 2. of, for, or like an adult —*n.* an adult: also **grown'up'**

growth (grōth) *n.* 1. the process of growing or developing; specif., *a)* gradual development toward maturity *b)* formation and development 2. *a)* degree of increase in size, weight, power, etc. *b)* the full extent of such increase 3. something that grows or has grown [a thick *growth* of grass] 4. an outgrowth or offshoot 5. a tumor or other abnormal mass of tissue developed in or on the body

growth factor any element in the nutriment or diet of an organism whose absence prevents normal growth

Groz·ny (grōz'nē) city in the SW R.S.F.S.R., at the northern foot of the Caucasus Mountains: pop. 319,000

grub (grub) *vi.* **grubbed, grub'bing** [ME. *grubben,* to dig, prob. < OE. **grybban* (akin to OHG. *grubilōn,* to bore into): for IE. base see GRAVE²] 1. to dig in the ground 2. to work hard, esp. at something menial or tedious; drudge 3. to search about; rummage 4. [< *n.* 3] [Old Slang] to eat —*vt.* 1. to clear (ground) of roots and stumps by digging them up 2. to dig up by or as by the roots; root out; uproot —*n.* [ME. *grubbe,* prob. < the *v.*] 1. the short, fat, wormlike larva of an insect, esp. of a beetle 2. a person who works hard at some menial or tedious work; drudge 3. [< ? notion "what is grubbed for"] [Slang] food —**grub'ber** *n.*

grub·by (-ē) *adj.* **-bi·er, -bi·est** 1. infested with grubs, esp. with botfly larvae, as cattle or sheep 2. dirty; messy; untidy 3. inferior, contemptible, mean, etc. —**grub'bi·ly** *adv.* —**grub'bi·ness** *n.*

☆**grub·stake** (-stāk') *n.* [GRUB, *n.* 3 + STAKE] [Colloq.] 1. money or supplies advanced to a prospector in return for a share in his findings 2. money advanced for any enterprise —*vt.* [Colloq.] **-staked', -stak'ing** to provide with a grubstake —**grub'stak'er** *n.*

Grub·street (grub'strēt') *n.* [< earlier name of a London street where many literary hacks lived] literary hacks: also **Grub Street** —*adj.* [*also* g-] of or like literary hacks or their work

grudge (gruj) *vt.* **grudged, grudg'ing** [LME. *gruggen,* var. of *grucchen* < OFr. *grouchier*] 1. to envy and resent (someone) because of his possession or enjoyment of (something); begrudge [to *grudge* a person his success] 2. to give with reluctance [the miser *grudged* his dog its food] —*n.* 1. a

strong, continued feeling of hostility or ill will against someone over a real or fancied grievance 2. a reason or cause for this —*SYN.* see MALICE —**grudg'er** *n.* —**grudg'ing·ly** *adv.*

grue (grōō) *n.* [< dial. *grue,* to shudder: see GRUESOME] a shudder of fear

gru·el (grōō'əl, grōōl) *n.* [ME. < OFr., coarse meal < ML. **grutellum,* dim. of *grutum,* meal, mash < Gmc. **grut,* hulled dried grain, akin to GROATS] 1. thin, easily digested broth made by cooking meal in water or milk: it is often fed to invalids 2. [Brit. Colloq.] punishment

gru·el·ing, gru·el·ling (-iŋ) *adj.* [prp. of obs. v. *gruel,* to punish: see prec.] extremely trying; exhausting —*n.* [Brit.] harsh treatment or punishment

grue·some (grōō'səm) *adj.* [< dial. *grue,* to shudder (< ME. *gruwen,* akin to MHG. *gruwen*) + -SOME¹] causing horror or loathing; grisly —*SYN.* see GHASTLY —**grue'some·ly** *adv.* —**grue'some·ness** *n.*

gruff (gruf) *adj.* [< Early ModDu. *grof,* akin to G. *grob,* coarse, surly < OHG. *gerob* < *ge-,* intens. + base akin to OE. *hreof,* rough, scabby < IE. base **kreup-,* scurf] 1. rough or surly in manner or speech; brusquely rude 2. harsh and throaty; hoarse —*SYN.* see BLUNT —**gruff'ly** *adv.* —**gruff'ness** *n.*

gru·gru (grōō'grōō') *n.* [Sp. *grugrú,* prob. < native Carib name] 1. a West Indian palm (*Acrocomia sclerocarpa*) with spiny trunk and leaves and edible nuts 2. the large, wormlike, edible larva of a weevil (*Rhynchophorus palmarum*) infesting this palm

grum (grum) *adj.* **grum'mer, grum'mest** [< ? GR(IM) + (GL)UM] [Now Rare] gloomy or glum

grum·ble (grum'b'l) *vi.* **-bled, -bling** [prob. < Du. *grommelen,* akin to G. *grummeln,* OE. *gremman,* to enrage: for IE. base see GRIM] 1. to make low, unintelligible sounds in the throat; growl 2. to mutter or mumble in discontent; complain in a surly or peevish manner 3. to rumble, as thunder —*vt.* to express by grumbling —*n.* 1. the act of grumbling, esp. in complaint 2. a rumble —**grum'bler** *n.* —**grum'bling·ly** *adv.* —**grum'bly** *adj.*

grume (grōōm) *n.* [< LL. *grumus,* little heap: for IE. base see CRUMB] [Rare] 1. a thick, sticky fluid 2. a clot of blood —**gru·mous** (grōō'məs) *adj.*

grum·met (grum'it) *n. same as* GROMMET

grump (grump) *n.* [prob. echoic of ill-tempered cry] 1. [*often pl.*] a fit of bad humor 2. a grumpy person —*vi.* to complain and grumble

grump·y (grum'pē) *adj.* **grump'i·er, grump'i·est** [prec. + -y²] grouchy; peevish; bad-tempered: also **grump'ish** —**grump'i·ly** *adv.* —**grump'i·ness** *n.*

Grun·dy, Mrs. (grun'dē) [a neighbor repeatedly referred to (but never appearing) in Tom Morton's play *Speed the Plough* (1798) with the question "What will Mrs. Grundy say?"] a personification of conventional social disapproval, hence of prudishness, narrow-mindedness, etc. —**Grun'dy·ism** *n.*

Grü·ne·wald (grü'nə vält'), **Mat·thi·as** (mä tē'äs) (born *Mathis Neithardt-Gothardt*) 1480?-1528?; Ger. painter

☆**grun·ion** (grun'yən) *n., pl.* **-ion, -ions:** see PLURAL, II, D, 2 [prob. < Sp. (colloq.) *gruñón, grunter*] a sardine-shaped fish (*Leuresthes tenuis*) of the California coast: it spawns on sandy beaches during certain spring tides

grunt (grunt) *vi.* [ME. *grunten* < OE. *grunnettan* (akin to G. *grunzen*), freq. of *grunian,* to grunt: origin echoic, as in L. *grunnire*] 1. to make the short, deep, hoarse sound of a hog 2. to make a sound like this, as in annoyance, contempt, effort, etc. —*vt.* to express by grunting [to *grunt* one's disapproval] —*n.* 1. the sound made in grunting 2. any of various related saltwater fishes (family Haemulidae) that grunt when removed from water

grunt·er (-ər) *n.* [ME. *gruntare*] 1. a person or animal that makes a grunting sound; esp., a hog 2. *same as* GRUNT (*n.* 2)

Grus (grus) [L., a crane] a S constellation, the Crane

Gru·yère (cheese) (grōō yer', grē-; *Fr.* grü yer') [< *Gruyère,* district in W Switzerland, where first produced] a light-yellow Swiss cheese, very rich in butterfat, or an American cheese resembling this

gr. wt. gross weight

gryph·on (grif'ən) *n. same as* GRIFFIN

GS German silver

G.S., g.s. 1. general secretary 2. general staff 3. ground speed

GSA, G.S.A. 1. General Services Administration 2. Girl Scouts of America

GSC, G.S.C. General Staff Corps

GSO, G.S.O. General Staff Officer

☆**G-string** (jē'striŋ') *n.* [< ?] 1. a narrow loincloth 2. a similar cloth or band, usually with spangles or tassels, as worn by striptease dancers

☆**G-suit** (-sōōt') *n.* [G for *gravity*] a garment for pilots or astronauts, pressurized to counteract the effects on the body of rapid acceleration or deceleration or of the force of gravity

GT gross ton

gt. 1. gilt 2. great 3. *pl.* **gtt.** *Pharmacy* gutta

Gt. Brit., Gt. Br. Great Britain

G.T.C., g.t.c. good till canceled (or countermanded)

gtd. guaranteed

GU, g.u. genitourinary

☆**gua·ca·mo·le** (gwä′kə mō′lā) *n.* [AmSp. < Nahuatl *ahuacamolli* < *ahuacatl*, AVOCADO + *molli*, a sauce (altered after Sp. *mole*, soft)] a thick sauce or paste of seasoned, puréed avocados, served as a dip, in salads, etc.

gua·cha·ro (gwä′chə rō′) *n., pl.* **-ros′** [Sp. *guácharo*, lit., sickly: prob. so named from its cry] a S. American night bird (*Steatornis caripensis*): the fat of the young birds, when rendered, is used for cooking and lighting

gua·co (gwä′kō) *n.* [AmSp., prob. < native name] any of several S. American plants (genera *Mikania* and *Aristolochia*), believed to be valuable in treating snake bites

Gua·da·la·ja·ra (gwä′d′l ə här′ə; *Sp.* gwä′thä lä hä′rä) city in W Mexico; capital of Jalisco: pop. 1,183,000

Gua·dal·ca·nal (gwä′d′l kə nal′) largest island of the Brit. Solomon Islands Protectorate, in the SW Pacific: c. 2,500 sq. mi.

Gua·dal·quiv·ir (-kwiv′ər; *Sp.* gwä′thäl kē vir′) river in S Spain, flowing into the Atlantic: c. 375 mi.

Gua·de·loupe (gwä′də loop′) overseas department of France consisting of two islands (BASSE-TERRE & GRANDE-TERRE) and five island dependencies in the Leeward Islands: 688 sq. mi.; pop. 316,000; cap. Basse-Terre

Gua·di·a·na (gwä′dē ä′nə) river flowing from SC Spain west & then south into the Atlantic, forming part of the Spanish-Portuguese border: c. 510 mi.

guai·ac (gwī′ak) *n.* [< GUAIACUM] 1. a greenish-brown resin from the wood of two species of guaiacum (*Guaiacum sanctum* and *Guaiacum officinale*) used as a reagent in tests for blood traces, in varnishes, etc. 2. *same as* GUAIACUM (sense 2)

guai·a·col (gwī′ə kôl′, -kōl′) *n.* [< ff. + -OL¹] a white, crystalline solid or colorless, oily liquid, $C_6H_4(OH)OCH_3$, prepared from guaiacum or wood creosote and used in medicine and as a chemical reagent

guai·a·cum (-kəm) *n.* [ModL. < Sp. *guayaco* < native (Taino) name] 1. any of a genus (*Guaiacum*) of trees of a family (Zygophyllaceae) native to tropical America, with blue or purple flowers and fruit growing in capsules 2. the hard, dense wood of any of these trees: see LIGNUM VITAE 3. *same as* GUAIAC (sense 1)

Guam (gwäm) largest of the Mariana Islands, in the W Pacific: a possession of the U.S.: 209 sq. mi.; pop. 87,000; cap. Agaña

guan (gwän) *n.* [AmSp. < the native (Carib) name] any of a large number of chickenlike game birds (family Cracidae) of Central and South America that feed on fruits

Gua·na·ba·ra (gwä′nä bä′rä) state of SE Brazil: 452 sq. mi.; pop. 3,307,000; cap. Rio de Janeiro

gua·na·co (gwə nä′kō) *n., pl.* **-cos, -co:** see PLURAL, II, D, 1 [Sp. < Quechua *huanacu*] a woolly, reddish-brown, wild animal (*Lama guanacoe*) of the Andes, related to the camel and llama

Gua·na·jua·to (gwä′nä hwä′tô) 1. state of C Mexico: rich mining center, esp. for silver: 11,805 sq. mi.; pop. 2,193,000 2. its capital: pop. 23,000

gua·nay (gwə nī′) *n.* [Sp. < the native (Quechua) name] a white-breasted, crested cormorant (*Phalacrocorax bougainvillii*) of Peru and Chile: it is a major source of guano

guan·i·dine (gwä′nə dēn′, -din) *n.* [< GUANINE] a strongly basic, crystalline substance, $NHC(NH_2)_2$, formed by the oxidation of guanine or by heating ammonium thiocyanate

GUANACO
(4 ft. high
at shoulder)

gua·nine (gwä′nēn) *n.* [< GUANO (a commercial source of the base) + -INE⁴] an organic base, $C_5H_5N_5O$, that is a constituent of ribonucleic acid and deoxyribonucleic acid and is found in all plant and animal tissues

gua·no (gwä′nō) *n., pl.* **-nos** [Sp. < Quechua *huanu*, dung] 1. manure of sea birds, found especially on islands off the coast of Peru: it is used as a fertilizer 2. any fertilizer, artificial or natural, resembling this

Guan·tá·na·mo (gwän tä′nə mō′) city in SE Cuba: pop. 125,000

Guantánamo Bay inlet of the Caribbean, on the SE coast of Cuba: site of a U.S. naval station: 12 mi. long

Gua·po·ré (gwä′pô re′) river in C S. America, flowing from C Brazil northwest along the Brazil-Bolivia border into the Mamoré: c. 750 mi.

guar (gwär) *n.* [Hind. *guār*] an annual plant (*Cyamopsis tetragonoloba*) of the legume family, native to India and grown in the SW U.S. for forage

guar. guaranteed

Gua·ra·ní (gwä′rä ne′) *n.* [Guaraní, lit., warrior] 1. *pl.* **-nís′, -ní′** a member of a tribe of S. American Indians who lived in an area between the Paraguay River and the Atlantic 2. the Tupian language of this tribe 3. [g-] *pl.* **-nís′** the monetary unit of Paraguay, equal to 100 centimos: see MONETARY UNITS, table

guar·an·tee (gar′ən tē′, gär′-) *n.* [altered < GUARANTY, after words ending in -EE¹] 1. *same as* GUARANTY (*n.* 1 & 3) 2. a pledge or assurance; specif., *a*) a pledge that some-

thing is as represented and will be replaced if it does not meet specifications *b*) a positive assurance that something will be done in the manner specified 3. a guarantor 4. a person who receives a guaranty 5. something that serves as an assurance of, or promises the happening of, some event [the dark clouds were a *guarantee* of rain] —*vt.* **-teed′, -tee′ing** 1. to give a guarantee or guaranty for [to *guarantee* a product] 2. to state with confidence; promise [to *guarantee* that a thing will be done]

guar·an·tor (gar′ən tôr′, -tər; gär′-) *n.* one who makes or gives a guaranty or guarantee

guar·an·ty (-tē) *n., pl.* **-ties** [OFr. *garantie* < *garantir*, to guarantee < *garant*, *warant*, a warrant, supporter < Frank. *warand*, prp. of *warjan*, to verify, akin to OHG. *werēn* < *wār* (G. *wahr*), true < IE. *weros*, true (whence L. *verus*)] 1. a pledge by which a person commits himself to the payment of another's debt or the fulfillment of another's obligation in the event of default 2. an agreement that secures the existence or maintenance of something 3. something given or held as security 4. a guarantor —*vt.* **-tied, -ty·ing** *same as* GUARANTEE

guard (gärd) *vt.* [LME. *garde* < the *n.*] 1. to keep safe from harm; watch over and protect; defend; shield 2. to watch over; specif., *a*) to keep from escape or trouble *b*) to hold in check; control; restrain *c*) *Sports* to keep (an opponent) from making a gain or scoring; also, to cover (a goal or area) in defensive play *d*) to supervise entrances and exits through (a door, gate, etc.) 3. to cover (a piece of machinery) with a device to protect the operator 4. [Archaic] to escort —*vi.* 1. to keep watch; take precautions (*against*) 2. to act as a guard —*n.* [ME. *garde* < OFr. < *garder*, to protect < Gmc. *wardon* (whence G. *warten*), to wait, OS. *wardon*, to watch over) < IE. base *wer-*, to take heed, whence L. *vereri*, to fear & WARE²] 1. the act or duty of guarding; careful watch; wariness; defense; protection 2. *a*) a posture of alert readiness for defense, as in boxing, fencing, etc. *b*) the arms or weapon in such a posture 3. any device that protects against injury or loss; specif., *a*) the part of the handle of a sword, knife, or fork that protects the hand *b*) a chain or cord attached to a watch, bracelet, etc. to protect against loss *c*) a ring worn to keep a more valuable ring from slipping off the finger *d*) a safety device, as in machinery ☆*e*) an article worn to protect a part of the body, as in a sport [a catcher's shin *guards*] 4. a person or group that guards; specif., *a*) a sentinel or sentry *b*) a railway brakeman or gateman *c*) [Brit.] a railroad conductor *d*) a person who guards prisoners *e*) [*pl.*] a special unit of troops connected with the household of the British sovereign *f*) a military unit with a special ceremonial function [a color *guard*] ☆5. *Basketball* either of the two players whose basic position is at the rear of the court on offense ☆6. *Football* either of two players on offense at the left and the right of the center —*SYN.* see DEFEND —**mount guard** to go on sentry duty —**off (one's) guard** not alert for protection or defense —**on (one's) guard** alert for protection or defense; vigilant —**stand guard** to do sentry duty —**guard′er** *n.*

guard·ant (-′nt) *adj.* [Fr. *gardant*, prp. of *garder*: see prec.] *Heraldry* designating an animal represented with the face fully turned toward the observer

guard cell either of the two bean-shaped cells which surround a stoma, or air pore, in the epidermis of a plant

guard·ed (-id) *adj.* 1. kept safe; watched over and protected; defended 2. kept from escape or trouble; held in check; supervised 3. cautious; noncommittal [a *guarded* reply] —**guard′ed·ly** *adv.* —**guard′ed·ness** *n.*

guard hair any of the coarse protective hairs in the outer fur of certain mammals

guard·house (-hous′) *n. Mil.* 1. a building used by the members of a guard when not walking a post 2. a building where personnel are confined for minor offenses or while awaiting court-martial

guard·i·an (-ē ən) *n.* [ME. *gardein* < OFr. *gardien* < *garder*, to GUARD] 1. a person who guards, protects, or takes care of another person, property, etc.; custodian 2. a person legally placed in charge of the affairs of a minor or of someone incapable of managing his own affairs —*adj.* protecting —**guard′i·an·ship′** *n.*

guard·rail (-rāl′) *n.* 1. a protective railing, as on a staircase ☆2. an extra rail alongside the main rail of a railroad at a crossing, etc., as to keep the cars on the track

guard·room (-room′) *n. Mil.* a room used by the members of a guard when they are not walking a post

guards·man (gärdz′mən) *n., pl.* **-men** (-mən) a member of any military body called a "guard"; specif., ☆a member of a National Guard

Guar·ne·ri (gwär ne′rē) (L. name *Guarnerius*) It. family of violin-makers of Cremona (fl. 17th–18th cent.): also **Gius·ep·pe An·to·nio** (joo zep′pe än tô′nyô), 1687?–1745

Guar·ner·i·us (gwär ner′ē əs) *n.* a violin made by a member of the Guarneri family

Gua·te·ma·la (gwä′tə mä′lə) 1. country in Central America, south & east of Mexico: 42,042 sq. mi.; pop. 5,014,000 2. its capital: pop. 577,000: also **Guatemala City** —**Gua′te·ma′lan** *adj., n.*

gua·va (gwä′və) *n.* [Sp. *guayaba* < native (prob. Arawakan) name in Brazil] 1. any of several tropical American plants (genus *Psidium*) of the myrtle family, esp. a tree (*Psidium*

guajava) bearing a yellowish, pear-shaped, edible fruit
2. the fruit, used for jelly, preserves, etc.
Guay·a·quil (gwī′ä kēl′) seaport in W Ecuador: pop.
506,000
Guay·na·bo (gwī nä′bō, -vō) city in NE Puerto Rico,
near San Juan: pop. 54,000
☆**gua·yu·le** (gwä yōō′lē) *n.* [AmSp. < Nahuatl *quauholli*
< *quauhitl*, plant + *olli*, gum] **1.** a small shrub (*Parthenium
argentatum*) of the composite family, grown in N Mexico,
Texas, etc. for the rubber obtained from it **2.** this rubber:
also **guayule rubber**
gu·ber·na·to·ri·al (gōō′bər nə tôr′ē əl) *adj.* [L. *gubernator*,
helmsman, governor < pp. of *gubernare* (see GOVERN) +
-IAL] of a governor or his office
gu·ber·ni·ya (goo ber′nē yə) *n.* [Russ. < base of L.
gubernare: see GOVERN] orig., a province of czarist Russia;
now, a small administrative unit in the Soviet Union
☆**guck** (guk) *n.* [< ? G(OO) + (M)UCK] [Slang] any thick,
viscous, sticky or slimy substance
gudg·eon[1] (guj′ən) *n.* [ME. *gogeon* < OFr. *goujon* < L.
gobio < Gr. *kōbios*] **1.** a small, European freshwater fish
(*Gobio fluviatilis*), easily caught, and used for bait **2.** a
goby or killifish **3.** a person easily cheated or tricked;
dupe **4.** a bait —*vt.* to cheat; trick; dupe
gudg·eon[2] (guj′ən) *n.* [ME. *gogoun* < OFr. *gojon*, pivot]
1. a metal pin or shaft at the end of an axle, on which a
wheel turns **2.** the socket of a hinge, into which the pin
is fitted **3.** the part of a shaft that revolves in a bearing
Gud·run (good′rŏon) [ON. *Guthrūn* < *guthr*, war, battle
+ *runa*, close friend: see RUNE] *Norse Legend* the daughter
of the Nibelung king: she lured Sigurd away from the
Valkyrie Brynhild and married him
guel·der-rose (gel′dər rōz′) *n.* [after *Guelderland* (or
GELDERLAND)] *same as* SNOWBALL (sense 2)
Guelph[1], **Guelf** (gwelf) *n.* [It. *Guelfo*, for MHG. *Welf*, a
family name < OHG. *welf*, a whelp: the war cry of the
anti-imperialists at the battle of Weinsberg (1140)] any
member of a political party in medieval Italy that supported the authority of the Pope in opposition to the
aristocratic party of the Ghibellines
Guelph[2] (gwelf) city in SE Ontario, Canada: pop. 51,000
gue·non (gə nōn′) *n.* [Fr.] any of a number of long-tailed
African monkeys (esp. genus *Cercopithecus*) including the
green monkey, grivet, and vervet
guer·don (gur′d'n) *n.* [ME. *guerdoun* < OFr. *gueredon*,
altered (after L. *donum*, gift) < Frank. & OHG. *widarlōn*
< OHG. *widar*, back, counter + *lōn*, reward < IE. base
lāu-, to capture, whence L. *lucrum*, riches] [Archaic] a
reward; recompense —*vt.* [Archaic] to reward
Guern·sey (gurn′zē) Brit. island in the English Channel:
25 sq. mi.; pop. 45,000 —*n.*, *pl.* **-seys 1.** any of a breed of
dairy cattle, originally from this island, usually fawn-
colored with white markings **2.** [orig. made on the island]
[g-] a closefitting knitted woolen shirt, worn by seamen
Guer·re·ro (ge re′rō) state of S Mexico: 24,887 sq. mi.;
pop. 1,524,000
guer·ril·la (gə ril′ə) *n.* [Sp., dim. of *guerra*, war < Fr.
guerre or It. *guerra*, both < OHG. *werra*: see WAR[1]] **1.**
formerly, warfare carried on by guerrillas **2.** any member
of a small defensive force of irregular soldiers, usually
volunteers, making surprise raids, esp. behind the lines
of an invading enemy army —*adj.* of or by guerrillas Also
sp. **gue·ril′la**
guess (ges) *vt.*, *vi.* [ME. *gessen*, to judge, estimate, prob.
< MDu. *gessen*, akin to Dan. *gisse*, Sw. *gissa*, ON. *geta*:
for IE. base see GET] **1.** to form a judgment or estimate of
(something) without actual knowledge or enough facts
for certainty; conjecture; surmise **2.** to judge correctly
by doing this **3.** to think or suppose [I *guess* I can do it]
—*n.* **1.** the act of guessing **2.** a judgment or estimate
formed by guessing; conjecture; surmise —**guess′er** *n.*
SYN.—**guess** implies the forming of a judgment or estimate
(often a correct one) haphazardly [he *guessed* the number of
beans in the jar]; to **conjecture** is to infer or predict from incomplete or uncertain evidence [I cannot *conjecture* what his
plans are]; **surmise** implies a conjecturing through mere intuition
or imagination [she *surmised* the truth]
☆**guess·ti·mate** (ges′tə mit; *for vt.* -māt′) *n.* [GUESS +
(ES)TIMATE] [Slang] an estimate based on a guess or conjecture —*vt.* -**mat′ed**, -**mat′ing** [Slang] to form a guess-
timate of Also sp. **guess′ti·mate**
guess·work (-wurk′) *n.* **1.** the act of guessing **2.** a judgment, result, etc. arrived at by guessing
guest (gest) *n.* [ME. *gest* < ON. *gestr*, akin to OE. *gæst*,
G. *gast* < IE. base *ghostis*, stranger, guest, whence L.
hostis] **1.** *a)* a person entertained at the home of another;
visitor *b)* a person entertained by another acting as host
at a restaurant, theater, etc. **2.** any paying customer of
a hotel, restaurant, etc. **3.** a person receiving the hospitality of a club, institution, etc. of which he is not a member
4. a person who appears or performs on a program by
special invitation **5.** *same as* INQUILINE —*adj.* **1.** for
guests **2.** performing by special invitation [a *guest* artist]
—*vt.* to entertain as a guest —*vi.* to be, or perform as,
a guest —*SYN.* see VISITOR

guest rope 1. a rope in addition to the tow rope, used to
steady a vessel being towed **2.** a rope fastened along a
ship's side for attaching boats coming alongside
☆**guff** (guf) *n.* [echoic] [Slang] **1.** foolish talk; nonsense
2. brash or insolent talk
guf·faw (gə fô′) *n.* [echoic] a loud, coarse burst of laughter
—*vi.* to laugh in this way —*SYN.* see LAUGH
Gug·gen·heim (gōōg′ən him′) family of U.S. industrialists and philanthropists, including **Daniel** (1856–1930),
Solomon R. (1861–1949), & **Simon** (1867–1941), who set
up a foundation granting fellowships (**Guggenheims**) to
scholars, writers, & artists
gug·gle (gug′'l) *n.*, *vi.*, *vt.* -**gled**, -**gling** [echoic] *same as*
GURGLE
Gui·a·na (gē an′ə, -ä′nə) **1.** region in N S. America, including Guyana, Suri-
nam (Dutch Guiana),
and French Guiana
2. an area including
this region, SE Vene-
zuela, & part of N
Brazil, bounded by
the Orinoco, Negro, &
Amazon rivers & the
Atlantic Ocean
guid·ance (gīd′ns) *n.*
1. the act of guiding;
direction; leadership
2. something that
guides **3.** advice or
assistance, as that
given to students by
vocational or educa-
tional counselors **4.**
the process of direct-
ing the course of a
spacecraft, missile, etc.

GUIANA

guide (gīd) *vt.* **guid′ed**, **guid′ing** [ME. *giden* < OFr. *guider*,
late var. of *guier* (whence ME. *gien*, to guide & GUY[1])
< Frank. *witan*, to show the way, observe, akin to OE.
witan, to see: for IE. base see WISE[1]] **1.** to point out the
way for; direct on a course; conduct; lead **2.** to direct
the course or motion of (a vehicle, implement, etc.) by
physical action **3.** to give instruction to; train **4.** to direct
(the policies, actions, etc.) of; manage; regulate —*vi.* to
act as a guide —*n.* a person or thing that guides; specif.,
a) a person whose work is conducting strangers or tourists
through a region, building, etc. *b)* a person who directs,
or serves as the model for, another in his conduct, career,
etc. *c)* a part that controls the motion of other parts of a
machine *d)* a guidebook *e)* a book giving instruction in
the elements of some subject; handbook [a *guide* to
mathematics] *f)* *Mil.* a soldier at the right front of a
column, who regulates its pace and alignment and indicates its route —**guid′a·ble** *adj.*
SYN.—**guide** implies the showing of the way by one who is
thoroughly familiar with the course, and connotes his continuous
presence or direction along the way [to *guide* a tourist, a mule,
one's hand]; **lead** implies a going ahead in order to show the way
and, figuratively, suggests a taking of the initiative [he *led* them
to victory]; **steer** suggests a maneuvering of the controls in order
to maintain the correct course [to *steer* a ship]; **pilot** suggests a
guiding over a difficult course, esp. one filled with obstacles or
intricate twists [he *piloted* us through the maze of tunnels] —*ANT.*
follow
guide·book (-book′) *n.* a book containing directions and
information for tourists
guided missile a military missile whose course is controlled
by radio signals, radar devices, etc.
guide dog a dog trained to lead a blind person
guide·line (-līn′) *n.* ☆ a standard or principle by which to
make a judgment or determine a policy or course of action
guide·post (-pōst′) *n.* **1.** a post with a sign and directions
for travelers, placed at a roadside or crossroads **2.** anything
that serves as a guide, standard, example, etc.; guideline
guide word *same as* CATCHWORD (sense 2)
Gui·do d'A·rez·zo (gwē′dō dä ret′tsō) 995?–1050?; It.
monk & musical theorist: also called **Guido Aretino**
gui·don (gīd′'n, gī′dän) *n.* [Fr. < It. *guidone* < *guidare*:
see GUIDE] **1.** formerly, a small flag or pennant carried by
the guide of mounted cavalry **2.** the identification flag of
a military unit or the soldier carrying it
Gui·enne (güē yen′) *same as* GUYENNE
guild (gild) *n.* [ME. *gild*, blend of ON. *gildi*, guild, guild-
feast & OE. *gyld*, association (of paying members), akin to
OHG. *gelt*, OFris. *ield*, all < base seen in OE. *gieldan*, to
pay: see YIELD] **1.** in medieval times, a union of men in the
same craft or trade to uphold standards and protect the
members **2.** any association for mutual aid and the promotion of common interests **3.** *an old term for* a group of
plants in some way dependent upon other plants, as the
epiphytes, saprophytes, parasites, or climbing vines
guil·der (gil′dər) *n.* [ME. *gilder*, altered (with unhistoric
-r-) < MDu. *gulden*, florin: see GULDEN] **1.** the monetary
unit and a coin of the Netherlands: see MONETARY UNITS,

fat, āpe, cär; ten, ēven; is, bīte; gō, hôrn, tōōl, look; oil, out; up, fur; get; joy; yet; chin; she; thin, *then*; zh, leisure; ŋ, ring;
ə for a in ago, e in agent, i in sanity, o in comply, u in focus; ' as in able (ā′b'l); Fr. bâl; ë, Fr. coeur; ö, Fr. feu; ô, Fr. mon; ð, Fr. coq;
ü, Fr. duc; r, Fr. cri; H, G. ich; kh, G. doch. See inside front cover. ☆ Americanism; ‡foreign; *hypothetical; < derived from

table 2. a former gold or silver coin of the Netherlands, Germany, or Austria

guild·hall (gild′hôl′) *n.* [ME. *gildhall* < OE. *gildheall*] 1. a hall where a guild meets 2. a town hall; specif., [G-] the hall of the Corporation of the City of London

guilds·man (gildz′mən) *n., pl.* **-men** (-mən) a member of a guild

guild socialism a form of socialism proposed in England in the early 20th cent., consisting in government ownership of all industries, each to be managed by a guild of workers

guile (gīl) *n.* [ME. *gile* < OFr. *guile*, prob. < Frank. *wigila*, guile, akin to OE. *wigle:* see WILE] slyness and cunning in dealing with others; craftiness

guile·ful (-fəl) *adj.* full of guile; deceitful; tricky —**guile′ful·ly** *adv.* —**guile′ful·ness** *n.*

guile·less (-lis) *adj.* without guile; candid; frank —**guile′less·ly** *adv.* —**guile′less·ness** *n.*

guil·le·mot (gil′ə mät′) *n.* [Fr., dim. of *Guillaume,* William: cf. ROBIN] any of various narrow-billed, northern diving birds (genera *Uria* and *Cepphus*), as the black guillemot (*Cepphus grylle*)

guil·loche (gi lōsh′) *n.* [Fr. *guillochis* < *guillocher,* to ornament with lines < OIt. *ghiocciare,* to drop, drip < LL. *guttiare* < L. *gutta,* a drop] a decorative design in which two or more curved lines or bands are interwoven, forming a series of spaces between them

guil·lo·tine (gil′ə tēn′, gē′ə-; *for v., usually* gil′ə tēn′, gē′ə-) *n.* [Fr., after J. I. *Guillotin* (1738–1814), Fr. physician who advocated its use during the French Revolution in preference to less humane methods] 1. an instrument for beheading by means of a heavy blade dropped between two grooved uprights 2. an instrument, working on a similar principle, for cutting paper, metal, etc. 3. [Brit.] a method of limiting Parliamentary debate on a bill by voting at a previously fixed time —*vt.* **-tined′, -tin′ing** [Fr. *guillotiner* < the *n.*] to behead with a guillotine

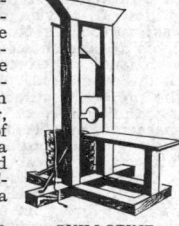

GUILLOTINE

guilt (gilt) *n.* [ME. *gilt* < OE. *gylt,* a sin, offense] 1. *a)* the act or state of having done a wrong or committed an offense; culpability, legal or ethical *b)* a painful feeling of self-reproach resulting from a belief that one has done something wrong or immoral 2. conduct that involves guilt; crime; sin

guilt·less (-lis) *adj.* 1. free from guilt; innocent 2. having no knowledge or experience (with *of*) —**guilt′less·ly** *adv.* —**guilt′less·ness** *n.*

guilt·y (gil′tē) *adj.* **guilt′i·er, guilt′i·est** [ME. *gilti* < OE. *gyltig*] 1. having guilt; deserving blame or punishment; culpable 2. having one's guilt proved; legally judged an offender 3. showing or conscious of guilt [a *guilty* look] 4. of or involving guilt or a sense of guilt [a *guilty* conscience] —**guilt′i·ly** *adv.* —**guilt′i·ness** *n.*

guimpe (gimp, gamp) *n.* [Fr. < OFr. *guimple* < Frank. *wimpil:* see WIMPLE] 1. a blouse worn under a pinafore or jumper 2. a wide piece of cloth used in some nuns' habits to cover the neck and shoulders

Guin·ea (gin′ē) 1. coastal region of W Africa, extending from S Senegal to E Nigeria 2. country in this region: 94,925 sq. mi.; pop. 3,608,000; cap. Conakry: formerly FRENCH GUINEA 3. **Gulf of,** part of the Atlantic, off the W coast of Africa —**Guin′e·an** *adj., n.*

guin·ea (gin′ē) *n.* 1. [the gold of which it was first made came from *Guinea*] a former English gold coin, last minted in 1813, equal to 21 shillings: the word is still used in England to mean a sum of 21 shillings, as in giving prices of luxury items 2. *same as* GUINEA FOWL

guinea fowl [orig. imported from *Guinea*] a domestic fowl (*Numida meleagris*) native to Africa, with a featherless head, rounded body, and dark feathers spotted with white

guinea hen 1. a female guinea fowl 2. any guinea fowl

Guinea pepper 1. any of several African plants (genus *Xylopia*) of the custard-apple family, esp. a tree (*Xylopia aethiopica*) with fruits used in spices and folk medicine 2. the fruit of any of these plants

guinea pig [prob. orig. brought to England by ships plying between England, Guinea, and S. America] 1. a small, fat mammal (genus *Cavia*) of the rat family, with short ears and no external tail; it is domesticated and used in biological experiments ☆2. any person or thing used in an experiment or test

Guinea worm a nematode worm (*Dracunculus medinensis*) of tropical Africa and S Asia, parasitic as an adult in the subcutaneous tissues of man: the female can reach a length of 3 ft.

GUINEA PIG
(to 10 in. long)

Guin·e·vere (gwin′ə vir′) [< Celt.; first element prob. W. *gwen,* white] 1. a feminine name 2. *Arthurian Legend* the wife of King Arthur and mistress of Sir Lancelot Also **Guin′e·ver′** (-vir′, -vər)

gui·pure (gē pyoor′; *Fr.* gē pür′) *n.* [Fr. < *guiper,* to cover with silk < Frank. **wipan,* to wind, akin to WHIP] 1. lace without any ground mesh, having the patterns held together by connecting threads 2. a kind of gimp (fabric)

Guise (gēz) Fr. ducal family of the 16th & 17th cent.; esp., *a)* **Fran·cois de Lor·raine** (frän swä′ də lô ren′), 2d Duc de Guise, 1519–63; general & statesman *b)* **Hen·ri de Lorraine** (än rē′), 3d Duc de Guise, 1550–88; general & statesman: son of *prec.*

guise (gīz) *n.* [ME. *gise* < OFr. *guise* < OHG. *wisa,* way, manner, akin to WISE²] 1. formerly, *a)* manner or way *b)* customary behavior, manner, or carriage 2. manner of dress; garb 3. outward aspect; semblance 4. a false or deceiving appearance; pretense [under the *guise* of friendship] —*vt.* **guised, guis′ing** 1. [Archaic] to dress or arrange (*in* a specified manner) 2. [Brit. Dial.] to disguise —*vi.* [Brit. Dial.] to go in disguise —SYN. see APPEARANCE

gui·tar (gi tär′) *n.* [Fr. *guitare* < Sp. *guitarra* < Ar. *qītāra* < Gr. *kithara,* lyre, lute] a musical instrument related to the lute but having a flat back and usually six strings that are plucked or strummed with the fingers or a plectrum —**gui·tar′ist** *n.*

☆**gui·tar·fish** (-fish′) *n., pl.* **-fish′, -fish′es:** see FISH² any of various skates (genus *Rhinobatos*) with a long, narrow tail and a broad, somewhat guitar-shaped body

Gui·try (gē′trē; *Fr.* gē trē′), **Sa·cha** (sä′shə; *Fr.* sà shä′) (born *Alexandre Pierre Georges Guitry*) 1885–1957; Fr. playwright & actor, born in Russia

Gui·zot (gē zō′), **Fran·cois Pierre Guil·laume** (frän swä′ pyer gē yōm′) 1787–1874; Fr. historian & statesman

Gu·ja·rat (goo′jə rät′) state of W India: 72,245 sq. mi.; pop. 20,633,000; cap. Ahmedabad

Gu·ja·ra·ti (goo′jə rä′tē) *n.* the Indo-European, Indic language spoken in the region of Gujarat

Guj·ran·wa·la (gooj′rən wäl′ə) city in NE West Pakistan: pop. 121,000

gu·lar (gyoo′lər, goo′-) *adj.* [< L. *gula,* throat (see GULLET) + -AR] of or on the throat

☆**gulch** (gulch) *n.* [prob. < dial. *gulch,* to swallow greedily < ME. *gulchen*] a steep-walled valley cut by a swift stream; deep, narrow ravine

gul·den (gool′dən) *n., pl.* **-dens, -den** [MDu., short for *gulden florijn,* golden florin: orig. applied only to coins of gold] *same as* GUILDER

gules (gyoolz) *n.* [ME. *goules* < OFr. *goules,* gules, red-dyed ermine, orig. pl. of *goule,* the mouth < L. *gula,* throat: see GULLET] red, esp. as a color in heraldry: indicated in black-and-white engravings by parallel vertical lines

gulf (gulf) *n.* [ME. *goulf* < OFr. *golfe* < It. *golfo* < LGr. *kolphos,* for Gr. *kolpos,* a fold, bosom, gulf, prob. < IE. **kwolpos* < base **kwel-,* to turn, whence G. *wölben,* to arch] 1. a large area of ocean, larger than a bay, reaching into land 2. a wide, deep chasm or abyss 3. a wide or impassable gap or separation; cleavage 4. an eddy that draws objects down; whirlpool —*vt.* to swallow up; engulf

Gulf·port (gulf′pôrt′) seaport in S Miss., on the Gulf of Mexico: pop. 41,000

Gulf States States on the Gulf of Mexico: Fla., Ala., Miss., La., & Tex.

Gulf Stream warm ocean current flowing from the Gulf of Mexico along the E coast of the U.S., and turning east at the Grand Banks toward Europe: c. 50 mi. wide

gulf·weed (-wēd′) *n.* a greenish-brown seaweed (genus *Sargassum*) with berrylike air sacs, found floating in the Gulf Stream and the Sargasso Sea

gulf·y (gul′fē) *adj.* full of whirlpools

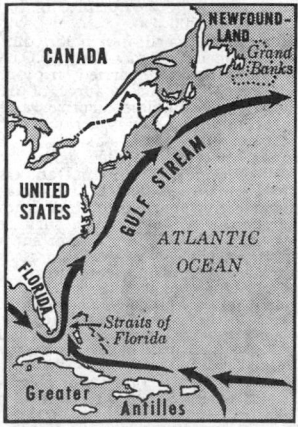

GULF STREAM

gull¹ (gul) *n., pl.* **gulls, gull:** see PLURAL, II, D, 1 [ME. < Celt., as in Corn. *gullan,* W. *gwylan,* Bret. *gwelan*] any of a large, widely distributed group of water birds (family Laridae), with large wings, slender legs, webbed feet, a strong, hooked bill, and feathers of chiefly white and gray

gull² (gul) *n.* [prob. < ME. *golle,* silly fellow, lit., unfledged bird < ?] a person easily cheated or tricked; dupe —*vt.* to cheat or trick; dupe

☆**Gul·lah** (gul′ə) *n.* [< ? *Gola* (*Gula*), tribal group in Liberia, or < ? *Ngola,* tribal group in

GULL (23–32 in. long, including tail and beak)

the Hamba basin in Angola] **1.** any of a group of Negroes living in coastal S.Carolina and Georgia and esp. on the nearby sea islands **2.** the English dialect of the Gullahs

gul·let (gul'ət) *n.* [ME. *golet* < OFr. *goulet*, throat, narrow passage, dim. of *goule* < L. *gula*, throat < IE. base *gel-*, to swallow, whence OE. *ceole*, G. *kehle*, throat] **1.** the tube leading from the mouth to the stomach; esophagus **2.** the throat or neck **3.** any depression or channel like a gullet, as a water gully

gul·li·ble (gul'ə b'l) *adj.* [GULL², *v.* + -IBLE] easily cheated or tricked; credulous: also [Rare] **gul'la·ble** —**gul'li·bil'i·ty** *n.* —**gul'li·bly** *adv.*

Gul·li·ver's Travels (gul'ə vərz) a political and social satire (1726) of 18th-century England by Jonathan Swift, telling of the adventures of the shipwrecked Lemuel Gulliver in four imaginary lands, Lilliput, Brobdingnag, Laputa, and the land of the Houyhnhnms

gul·ly¹ (gul'ē) *n.*, *pl.* -lies [altered < ME. *golet*, water channel, orig., gullet: see GULLET] a channel or hollow worn by running water; small, narrow ravine —*vt.* -lied, -ly·ing to make a gully or gullies in

gul·ly² (gul'ē) *n.*, *pl.* -lies [< ?] [Scot. & Brit. Dial.] a large knife

gu·los·i·ty (gyōō läs'ə tē) *n.* [LL. *gulositas* < *gulosus*, gluttonous < *gula*, GULLET] [Now Rare] greediness

gulp (gulp) *vt.* [ME. *gulpen*, prob. < Du. *gulpen*, to gulp down, akin to OE. *gielpan* (see YELP)] **1.** to swallow hastily, greedily, or in large amounts **2.** to choke back as if swallowing; repress (a sob, etc.) —*vi.* **1.** to catch the breath in or as in swallowing a large amount —*n.* **1.** the act of gulping **2.** the amount swallowed at one time —**gulp'er** *n.* —**gulp'ing·ly** *adv.*

gum¹ (gum) *n.* [ME. *gomme* < OFr. < L. *gumma* (? via Gr. *kommi*) < Egypt. *kemā*, *kemai*] **1.** a sticky, colloidal carbohydrate found in certain trees and plants, which dries into an uncrystallized, brittle mass that dissolves or swells in water **2.** any similar plant secretion, as resin **3.** any plant gum processed for use in industry, art, etc. **4.** *a)* an adhesive, as on the back of a postage stamp *b)* any of various sticky or viscous substances or deposits **5.** *a)* same as GUM TREE *b)* the wood of a gum tree **6.** [Now Rare] *a)* pure rubber *b)* [*pl.*] rubber overshoes **7.** same as CHEWING GUM ☆**8.** [Dial.] a hollowed gum log used as a trough, etc. —*vt.* **gummed, gum'ming** to coat, unite, or stiffen with gum —*vi.* **1.** to secrete or form gum **2.** to become sticky or clogged —**by gum!** [Colloq.] by God!: a euphemism —☆**gum up** [Slang] to put out of working order; cause to go awry

gum² (gum) *n.* [ME. *gome* < OE. *goma*, akin to G. *gaumen*, roof of the mouth < IE. base *ĝhēu-*, *ĝhōu-*, to yawn, gape, whence Gr. *chaos*] [often *pl.*] the firm flesh covering the jaws on the inside of the mouth and surrounding the base of the teeth —☆*vt.* **gummed, gum'ming** to bite or chew with toothless gums —☆**beat one's gums** [Slang] to talk much and idly

gum ammoniac same as AMMONIAC

gum arabic [after L. *gummi Arabicum*] a gum obtained from several African acacias (esp. *Acacia senegal*), used in medicine and candy, for stabilizing emulsions, etc.

☆**gum·bo** (gum'bō) *n.* [< Bantu name for okra] **1.** same as OKRA (senses 1 & 2) **2.** a soup thickened with unripe okra pods **3.** a fine, silty soil of the Western prairies, which becomes sticky and nonporous when wet: also **gumbo soil 4.** [often G-] a French patois spoken by Creoles and Negroes in Louisiana and the French West Indies

gum·boil (gum'boil) *n.* a small abscess on the gum

gum boot [Chiefly Brit.] a high rubber boot

☆**gum·drop** (-dräp') *n.* a small piece of candy of a firm, jellylike consistency, made of sweetened gum arabic or gelatin, usually colored and flavored, and covered with sugar

gum elemi same as ELEMI

gum·ma (gum'ə) *n.*, *pl.* **gum'mas, gum'ma·ta** (-ə tə) [ModL. < L. *gummi*, GUM¹] a soft, rubbery tumor occurring in tertiary syphilis —**gum'ma·tous** *adj.*

gum·mite (gum'īt) *n.* [< L. *gummi*, GUM¹ + -ITE¹: so named (1868) by J. D. DANA] a yellowish or reddish-brown mineral containing uranium and having a gumlike appearance

gum·mo·sis (gə mō'sis) *n.* [ModL. < L. *gummi*, GUM¹ + -OSIS] the giving off of gummy substances as a result of cell degeneration: a characteristic of certain plant diseases, esp. of stone fruits

gum·mous (gum'əs) *adj.* [L. *gummosus*] of or like gum

gum·my (gum'ē) *adj.* -mi·er, -mi·est **1.** having the nature of gum; sticky; viscid **2.** covered with or containing gum **3.** yielding gum —**gum'mi·ness** *n.*

gump·tion (gump'shən) *n.* [< Scot. dial. < ? ME. *gome*, attention < ON. *gaumr*), with jocose Latinate suffix] [Colloq.] **1.** orig., shrewdness in practical matters; common sense **2.** courage and initiative; enterprise and boldness: the current sense

gum resin a mixture of gum and resin, given off by certain trees and plants

☆**gum·shoe** (gum'shōō') *n.* [GUM¹ (rubber) + SHOE] **1.** *a)* a rubber overshoe *b)* [*pl.*] sneakers **2.** [Slang] a detective

—*vi.* **-shoed', -shoe'ing** [Slang] to sneak or go about quietly, as a detective; act with stealth

☆**gum tree** any of various trees that yield gum, as the sour gum, sweet gum, eucalyptus, etc.

gum·wood (gum'wood') *n.* the wood of a gum tree

gun (gun) *n.* [ME. *gunne, gonne*, contr. < *gonnilde*, a cannon < ON. *Gunnhildr*, fem. name (< *gunnr*, war + *hildr*, battle)] **1.** a weapon consisting of a metal tube from which a projectile is discharged by the force of an explosive; specif., *a)* technically, a heavy weapon with a relatively long barrel fixed in a mount, as a cannon or machine gun *b)* a rifle ☆*c)* popularly, a pistol or revolver **2.** any similar device not discharged by an explosive [an air gun] **3.** a discharge of a gun in signaling or saluting **4.** anything like a gun in shape or use ☆**5.** [Slang] same as GUNMAN (sense 1) **6.** [Slang] the throttle of a engine —*vi.* **gun'ning** to shoot or hunt with a gun; go shooting or hunting —*vt.* ☆**1.** [Colloq.] to shoot (a person) **2.** [Slang] to advance the throttle of (an engine) so as to increase the speed —**big gun** [Slang] **1.** an important and influential person **2.** a high-ranking military officer —**give it the gun** [from the resemblance of early airplane accelerators to the trigger of a gun] [Slang] to cause something to start or gain speed —**go great guns** [Slang] to act with speed and efficiency —☆**gun for 1.** to hunt for with a gun **2.** to look for in order to shoot or harm **3.** [Slang] to try to get; seek —**jump the gun** [Slang] **1.** to begin a race before the signal has been given **2.** to begin anything before the proper time —**spike one's guns** to frustrate or defeat one —**stick to one's guns** to hold one's position under attack; not withdraw or retreat; be firm

gun·boat (-bōt') *n.* **1.** a small armed ship of shallow draft, used to patrol rivers, harbors, etc. **2.** [*pl.*] [Slang] shoes; esp., a pair of large shoes

gun·cot·ton (-kät'n) *n.* nitrocellulose in a highly nitrated form, used as an explosive substance

gun dog a dog, as a pointer, setter, or hound, trained to help a hunter by finding or retrieving game

gun·fight (-fīt') *n.* ☆a fight between persons using pistols or revolvers —☆**gun'fight'er** *n.*

gun·fire (-fīr') *n.* **1.** the firing of a gun or guns **2.** the use of firearms or artillery, as distinguished from other military tactics

gun·flint (-flint') *n.* a piece of flint in the hammer of a flintlock, for striking a spark to set off the charge

☆**gung-ho** (guŋ'hō') *adj.* [Chin., lit., work together: slogan of Lt. Col. Evans F. Carlson's Marine Raiders in World War II] enthusiastic, cooperative, enterprising, etc. in an unrestrained, often naive way

☆**Gun·ite** (gun'īt) [< GUN + -ITE¹] *a trademark for* a concrete mixture sprayed under pressure over steel reinforcements, as in making swimming pools —*n.* [g-] this substance

☆**gunk** (guŋk) *n.* [< ? G(OO) + (J)UNK¹] [Slang] any oily, viscous, or thick, messy substance —**gunk'y** *adj.*

☆**gunk hole** [< ?] a sheltered cove or small basin used for anchoring small watercraft

gun·lock (gun'läk') *n.* in some guns, the mechanism by which the charge is set off

gun·man (-mən) *n.*, *pl.* -men (-mən) ☆**1.** a man armed with a gun, esp. an armed gangster or hired killer **2.** a man skilled in the use of a gun

gun·met·al (-met'l) *n.* **1.** a kind of bronze formerly used for making cannon **2.** any metal or alloy treated to resemble tarnished gunmetal **3.** the dark gray color of tarnished gunmetal: also **gunmetal gray** —*adj.* dark gray

☆**gun moll** [Slang] the mistress or female accomplice of a gunman (sense 1)

Gun·nar (goon'är) [ON. *Gunnarr* < *gunnr*, older form of *guthr*, war, battle] *Norse Legend* the brother of Gudrun and husband of Brynhild

gun·nel¹ (gun'l) *n.* [< ?] a small, slimy, blennylike fish (*Pholis gunnellus*), found in the N Atlantic

gun·nel² (gun'l) *n.* same as GUNWALE

gun·ner (gun'ər) *n.* [ME. *gonner* < *gonne*, GUN] **1.** a soldier, sailor, etc. who fires or helps fire an artillery piece **2.** a naval warrant officer who has charge of a ship's guns **3.** a hunter who uses a gun

gun·ner·y (-ē) *n.* **1.** heavy guns **2.** the science of making and using heavy guns and projectiles

☆**gunnery sergeant** *Marine Corps* a noncommissioned officer ranking above a staff sergeant and below a master sergeant or first sergeant

gun·ny (gun'ē) *n.*, *pl.* -nies [Hind. *gōnī*, gunny bag < Sans. *gōnī*, a sack] **1.** a coarse, heavy fabric of jute or hemp, used for sacks **2.** same as GUNNYSACK

gun·ny·sack (-sak') *n.* a sack or bag made of gunny: also **gun'ny·bag'**

☆**gun·play** (gun'plā') *n.* an exchange of gunshots, as between gunmen and police

☆**gun·point** (-point') *n.* the muzzle of a gun: chiefly in **at gunpoint**, under threat of being shot with a gun

gun·pow·der (-pou'dər) *n.* **1.** an explosive powder, esp. a mixture of sulfur, saltpeter, and charcoal, used as a charge in cartridges, shells, etc., for blasting, in fireworks, etc. **2.** same as GUNPOWDER TEA

Gunpowder Plot see Guy FAWKES

gunpowder tea Chinese green tea whose leaves are rolled into pellets

gun room 1. on British warships, the junior officers' quarters; orig., the quarters of the gunner and his mates **2.** a room for displaying a collection of guns

gun·run·ning (-run'iŋ) *n.* the smuggling of guns and ammunition into a country —**gun'run'ner** *n.*

☆**gun·sel** (gun's'l) *n.* [orig., boy (with implication of perversion), prob. altered < Yid. *genzel*, gosling < MHG. *gensel*, dim. of *gans*, GOOSE] [Slang] **1.** a catamite **2.** [infl. by GUN] same as GUNMAN (sense 1)

gun·shot (-shät') *n.* [ME. *gunnes shott*] **1.** *a)* shot fired from a gun *b)* the shooting of a gun **2.** the range of a gun —*adj.* caused by a shot from a gun [a *gunshot* wound]

gun-shy (-shī') *adj.* easily frightened at the firing of a gun [a *gun-shy* dog] —**gun'-shy'ness** *n.*

☆**gun·sling·er** (-sliŋ'ər) *n.* [Slang] same as GUNMAN (sense 1)

gun·smith (-smith') *n.* a person who makes or repairs small guns

gun·stock (-stäk') *n.* the wooden handle or butt to which the barrel of a gun is attached

Gun·ter's chain (gun'tərz) [after Edmund *Gunter* (1581-1626), Eng. mathematician who invented it] a surveyor's chain 66 feet in length: it consists of 100 links, each 7.92 inches long

Gun·ther (goon'tər) [G. < Gmc. *gund-, *gunt-, war (whence ON. *gunnr*, *guthr*: cf. GUN) + *har- (whence OE. *here*), army] in the *Nibelungenlied*, a king of Burgundy and husband of Brunhild

Gun·tur (goon toor') city in Andhra Pradesh, SE India, in the Kistna River delta: pop. 187,000

gun·wale (gun''l) *n.* [LME. *gonne walle* (cf. GUN & WALE[1]): first applied to bulwarks supporting a ship's guns] the upper edge of the side of a ship or boat

gup·py (gup'ē) *n., pl.* -**pies** [after R. J. L. *Guppy*, of Trinidad, who first provided specimens for the British Museum] a tiny freshwater fish (*Lebistes reticulatus*) found in Barbados, Trinidad, and Venezuela: it is often kept in aquariums because of its brilliant coloring

gurge (gurj) *n.* [L. *gurges*: cf. GORGE] [Now Rare] a whirlpool

gur·gi·ta·tion (gur'jə tā'shən) *n.* [< pp. of LL. *gurgitare*, to flood < L. *gurges*, whirlpool: see GORGE] [Now Rare] a whirling or surging, as of liquid

gur·gle (gur'g'l) *vi.* -**gled**, -**gling** [prob. of echoic origin, as in G. *gurgeln*, or ? akin to It. *gorgogliare* < L. *gurgulio*, gullet] **1.** to flow with a bubbling or rippling sound, as water from a narrow-necked bottle **2.** to make a bubbling or rippling sound in the throat, as a contented baby does —*vt.* to utter with a gurgling sound —*n.* the act or sound of gurgling

gur·glet (gur'glət) *n.* [Port. *gorgoleta*] same as GOGLET

Gur·kha (goor'kə, gur'-) *n.* any of a warlike Rajput people living in the mountains of Nepal

gur·nard (gur'nard) *n., pl.* -**nards**, -**nard**: see PLURAL, II, D, 1 [ME. < OFr. *gornart* < *grogner*, to grunt (< L. *grunnire*): from "grunting" when caught: cf. GRUNT, *n.* 2] **1.** same as FLYING GURNARD **2.** same as SEA ROBIN

☆**gur·ry** (gur'ē) *n.* [< ?] fish offal, as from a fish cannery —*vt.* -**ried**, -**ry·ing** to foul with fish offal

gu·ru (goor'oo, goo roo') *n.* [Hind. *guru* < Sans. *guru-ḥ*, venerable, orig. heavy < IE. base *gweru-: cf. GRAVE[1]] **1.** in Hinduism, one's personal spiritual adviser or teacher **2.** any leader highly regarded by a group of followers: sometimes used derisively

gush (gush) *vi.* [ME. *guschen*, prob. akin to ON. *gjosa*, to gush & *gustr*, GUST[1]] **1.** to flow out suddenly and plentifully; pour out; spout **2.** to have a sudden, plentiful flow of blood, tears, etc. (often followed by *with*) **3.** to express oneself with exaggerated enthusiasm or feeling; talk or write effusively —*vt.* to cause to flow out suddenly and plentifully —*n.* **1.** a gushing; sudden, plentiful outflow **2.** gushing talk or writing —**gush'ing** *adj.* —**gush'ing·ly** *adv.*

gush·er (-ər) *n.* **1.** a person who gushes ☆**2.** an oil well from which oil spouts without being pumped

gush·y (-ē) *adj.* **gush'i·er**, **gush'i·est** given to or characterized by gush; effusive —SYN. see SENTIMENTAL —**gush'i·ly** *adv.* —**gush'i·ness** *n.*

gus·set (gus'it) *n.* [ME. *guschet* < OFr. *gousset*] **1.** a piece of chain mail or a metal plate protecting the opening of a joint in a suit of armor **2.** a triangular or diamond-shaped piece inserted in a garment, glove, etc. to make it stronger or roomier **3.** a triangular metal brace for reinforcing a corner or angle —*vt.* to furnish with a gusset

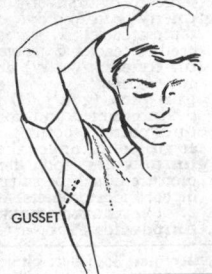

GUSSET

☆**gus·sie, gus·sy** (gus'ē) *vt., vi.* -**sied**, -**sy·ing** [< *Gussie*, nickname for AUGUSTA] [Slang] to dress (*up*) or decorate in a fine or showy way

gust[1] (gust) *n.* [ON. *gustr*, gust, blast < *gjosa*, to gush, break out < IE. *gheus-, < base *gheu-, to pour, whence L. *fundere* & GUT] **1.** a sudden, strong rush of air or wind **2.** a sudden burst of rain, smoke, fire, sound, etc. **3.** an outburst of laughter, rage, etc. —*vi.* to blow in gusts —SYN. see WIND[2]

gust[2] (gust) *n.* [ME. *guste* < L. *gustus*: see GUSTO] [Archaic] **1.** taste; relish; flavor; savor **2.** enjoyment or appreciation —*vt.* [Scot.] to taste or relish —**gust'a·ble** *adj., n.*

Gus·taf V (goos'täf) 1858-1950; king of Sweden (1907-50): also called **Gustav(us) V**

Gustaf VI (Adolf) 1882- ; king of Sweden (1950-): son of Gustaf V: also **Gustav(us) VI**

gus·ta·tion (gəs tā'shən) *n.* [L. *gustatio* < pp. of *gustare*, to taste < *gustus*, a taste: see GUSTO] **1.** the act of tasting **2.** the sense of taste

gus·ta·to·ry (gus'tə tôr'ē) *adj.* [< L. *gustatus*, pp. (see GUSTATION) + -ORY] of or having to do with tasting or the sense of taste: also **gus'ta·tive** (-tiv), **gus'ta·to'ri·al** (-tôr'ē əl)

Gus·ta·vus (gəs tā'vəs, -tä'-) [ModL. < G. *Gustav* or Sw. *Gustaf*, lit., prob. staff of the Goths] **1.** a masculine name: dim. *Gus;* equiv. Fr. *Gustave,* Sw. *Gustaf,* Ger. *Gustav,* It. & Sp. *Gustavo* **2. Gustavus I** (*Gustavus Eriksson Vasa*) 1496-1560; king of Sweden (1523-60) **3. Gustavus II** (*Gustavus Adolphus*) 1594-1632; king of Sweden (1611-32): grandson of *prec.* **4. Gustavus III** 1746-92; king of Sweden (1771-92) **5. Gustavus IV** 1778-1837; king of Sweden (1792-1809); deposed: son of *prec.* See also GUSTAF V & GUSTAF VI (ADOLF)

gus·to (gus'tō) *n.* [It. & Sp. < L. *gustus*, taste < IE. base *ĝeus-, to enjoy, taste, whence CHOOSE] **1.** taste; liking **2.** keen enjoyment; enthusiastic appreciation; zest; relish **3.** great vigor or liveliness **4.** [Archaic] artistic style

gust·y (gus'tē) *adj.* **gust'i·er**, **gust'i·est 1.** characterized by gusts of air or wind **2.** characterized by sudden bursts or outbursts —**gust'i·ly** *adv.* —**gust'i·ness** *n.*

gut (gut) *n.* [ME. < OE. *guttas*, pl. < base of *geotan*, to pour: for IE. base see GUST[1]] **1.** *a)* [*pl.*] the bowels; entrails *b)* the stomach or belly Now generally regarded as an inelicate usage **2.** all or part of the alimentary canal, esp. the intestine **3.** tough cord made from animal intestines, used for violin strings, surgical sutures, etc.; catgut **4.** the little bag of silk removed from a silkworm before it has spun its cocoon: made into strong cord for use in fishing tackle **5.** a narrow passage or gully, as of a stream or path **6.** [*pl.*] [Colloq.] the basic, inner or deeper parts **7.** [*pl.*] [Slang] *a)* daring, courage, perseverance, vigor, etc. *b)* impudence; effrontery *c)* power or force —*vt.* **gut'ted**, **gut'ting 1.** to remove the intestines from; eviscerate **2.** to destroy the interior of, as by fire —*adj.* [Slang] **1.** urgent and basic or fundamental [the *gut* issues of a campaign] **2.** easy; simple [a *gut* course in college] —**hate someone's guts** [Slang] to hate someone intensely

☆**gut·buck·et** (-buk'it) *adj.* [? < *bucket* to catch gin that *gutters* from barrels in a barrelhouse] designating or of a raucous style of jazz resembling barrelhouse

Gu·ten·berg (goot'n burg'), **Jo·hann** (yō'hän) (born *Johannes Gensfleisch*) 1400?-68; Ger. printer: reputedly the first European to print with movable type

Gutenberg Bible a Latin Bible produced at Mainz sometime before 1456, attributed in part to Gutenberg: it is generally considered to be the first book printed from movable type

Guth·rie (guth'rē) [orig. Scot. surname & place name] a masculine name

gut·less (gut'lis) *adj.* [see GUT, *n.* 7] [Slang] lacking courage, daring, perseverance, etc. —**gut'less·ness** *n.*

guts·y (gut'sē) *adj.* **guts'i·er**, **guts'i·est** [Slang] full of guts; daring, courageous, forceful, plucky, etc.

gut·ta (gut'ə) *n., pl.* **gut'tae** (-ē) [ME., drop of gum < L.] **1.** *Pharmacy* a drop **2.** any of a series of small, droplike ornaments on a Doric entablature

gut·ta-per·cha (gut'ə pur'chə) *n.* [< Malay < *gĕtah*, gum + *pĕrchah*, tree from which it is obtained: form influenced by L. *gutta*, a drop] a rubberlike gum produced from the latex of various SE Asian trees (esp. genera *Palaquium* and *Payena*) of the sapodilla family and used in electric insulation, dentistry, golf balls, etc.

gut·tate (gut'āt) *adj.* [L. *guttatus* < *gutta*, a drop] **1.** in the form of drops **2.** spotted, as with drops

gut·ter (gut'ər) *n.* [ME. *gotere* < OFr. *gutiere* < L. *gutta*, a drop] **1.** a trough or channel along or under the eaves of a roof, to carry off rain water **2.** a narrow channel along the side of a road or street, to carry off water, as to a sewer **3.** a place or state of living characterized by filth, poverty, squalor, etc. **4.** a channel or groove like a gutter, as the groove on either side of a bowling alley **5.** the adjoining inner margins of two facing pages in a book, magazine, etc. —*vt.* to furnish with gutters; make gutters in —*vi.* **1.** to flow in a stream **2.** to melt rapidly so that the wax runs down the side in channels: said of a candle

gut·ter·snipe (-snīp') *n.* [orig. (Brit. dial.), the common snipe, which picks food out of gutters] a child of the slums who spends most of his time in the streets: contemptuous term applied to anyone regarded as having the manners, morals, etc. of the gutter

gut·tle (gut''l) *vi., vt.* -**tled**, -**tling** [blend of GUT & GUZZLE] to eat greedily; gormandize —**gut'tler** *n.*

gut·tur·al (gut'ər əl) *adj.* [L. *guttur*, throat < IE. *gut-, *gutr, throat < base *ĝēu-, to curve, whence COD[2]] **1.** of the throat **2.** *a)* loosely, produced in the throat; harsh, rasping, etc.: said of sounds *b)* characterized by such

sounds *[a gutturall language]* **3.** formed by placing the back of the tongue close to or against the soft palate, as the *k* in *keen;* velar —*n.* **1.** a sound produced in this way **2.** a symbol representing such a sound The term is now seldom used by phoneticians —**gut′tur·al·ly** *adv.* —**gut′-tur·al·ness** *n.*

gut·tur·al·ize (-īz′) *vt.* **-ized′, -iz′ing** [prec. + -IZE] **1.** to pronounce gutturally **2.** to give a guttural sound to; velarize —**gut′tur·al·i·za′tion** *n.*

gut·ty (gut′ē) *adj.* **-ti·er, -ti·est** [Slang] *same as* GUTSY

Guy (gī) [Fr. *Gui, Guy,* lit., leader: see ff.] a masculine name: equiv. It. & Sp. *Guido*

guy[1] (gī) *n.* [ME. *gie* < OFr. *guie,* a guide < *guier,* to GUIDE] a rope, chain, or rod attached to something to steady or guide it —*vt.* to guide or steady with a guy

guy[2] (gī) *n.* [after Guy FAWKES] **1.** in England, an effigy of Guy Fawkes displayed and burned on Guy Fawkes Day, Nov. 5 **2.** a person whose appearance or dress is odd ☆**3.** [Slang] *a)* a man or boy; fellow *b)* any person —*vt.* to make fun of; ridicule; josh; tease

Guy·a·na (gī an′ə, -än′ə) country in NE S. America that is a member of the Brit. Commonwealth: formerly (1814–1966) a Brit. colony (called *British Guiana*): 83,000 sq. mi.; pop. 662,000; cap. Georgetown: see GUIANA, map —**Guy·a·nese** (gī′ə nēz′) *adj., n.*

Guy·enne (güē yen′) region, formerly a province, of SW France, on the Atlantic, roughly corresponding to earlier Aquitaine

☆**guy·ot** (gē ō′) *n.* [after A. H. *Guyot* (1807–84), U.S. geologist] a flat-topped, steeply rising seamount; table-mount

guz·zle (guz′'l) *vi., vt.* **-zled, -zling** [< ? OFr. *gosillier* < *gosier,* throat < Gaul. *geusiae,* throat] to drink (or, rarely, eat) greedily or immoderately —**guz′zler** *n.*

g.v. gravimetric volume

Gwa·li·or (gwä′lē ôr′) city in Madhya Pradesh, NC India: pop. (with nearby Lashkar) 301,000

Gwen·do·len, Gwen·do·line, Gwen·do·lyn (gwen′d'l ən) [< Celt.; see GUINEVERE] a feminine name: dim. *Gwen*

Gwin·nett (gwi net′), **But·ton** (but′'n) 1735?–77; Am. patriot, born in England: signer of the Declaration of Independence

Gwyn (gwin), **Nell** (born *Eleanor Gwyn*) 1650–87; Eng. actress; mistress of Charles II: also sp. **Gwynne**

gybe (jīb) *n., vi., vt.* **gybed, gyb′ing** *same as* JIBE[1]

gym (jim) *n.* [Colloq.] **1.** *same as* GYMNASIUM ☆**2.** *same as* PHYSICAL EDUCATION

gym·kha·na (jim kä′nə) *n.* [Anglo-Ind., prob. altered (after GYMNASIUM) < Hind. & Urdu *gend-khāna,* racket court] **1.** a place where athletic contests or games are held **2.** any of various contests involving skill, as in horse-back riding, automobile racing, etc.

gym·na·si·arch (jim nā′zē ärk′) *n.* [L. *gymnasiarchus* < Gr. *gymnasiarchos* < *gymnasion,* gymnasium + *archos,* -ARCH] in ancient Greece, an official who supervised athletic games, contests, and schools

gym·na·si·ast (-ast) *n.* **1.** a student in a European Gymnasium **2.** a gymnast

gym·na·si·um (-əm) *n., pl.* **-si·ums, -si·a** (-ə) [L. < Gr. *gymnasion,* place for exercising < *gymnazein,* to train naked < *gymnos,* naked, stripped < IE. base **nogw-,* whence NAKED, L. *nudus*] **1.** a room or building equipped for physical training and athletic games and sports **2.** [G-] (gim nä′zē oom) in Germany and some other European countries, a secondary school for students preparing to enter a university

gym·nast (jim′nast) *n.* [Gr. *gymnastēs,* trainer of athletes] an expert in gymnastics

gym·nas·tic (jim nas′tik) *adj.* [L. *gymnasticus* < Gr. *gymnastikos* < *gymnazein:* see GYMNASIUM] of or having to do with gymnastics: also **gym·nas′ti·cal** —**gym·nas′-ti·cal·ly** *adv.*

gym·nas·tics (-tiks) *n.pl.* [< prec.] **1.** exercises that develop and train the body and the muscles; esp., exercises that can be done in a gymnasium, as calisthenics, tumbling, etc. **2.** *[with sing. v.]* the art or sport of such exercises

gym·no- (jim′nə, -nō) [< Gr. *gymnos,* naked: see GYM-NASIUM] *a combining form meaning* naked, stripped, bare *[gymnosperm]:* also, before a vowel, **gymn-**

gym·nos·o·phist (jim näs′ə fist) *n.* [ME. *genosophis* < L. *gymnosophistae,* pl. < Gr. *gymnosophistai:* see prec. & SOPHIST] a member of an ancient Hindu sect of ascetics who wore little or no clothing

gym·no·sperm (jim′nə spurm′) *n.* [ModL. *gymnospermus* < Gr. *gymnospermos:* see GYMNO- & -SPERM] any of a large class (Gymnospermae) of seed plants having the ovules borne on open scales, usually in cones, and usually lacking true vessels in the woody tissue: the class includes the pines, spruces, cedars, cycads, ephedras, and the ginkgo —**gym′no·sper′mous** (-məs) *adj.* —**gym′no·sper′-my** (-mē) *n.*

☆**gym shoe** *same as* SNEAKER (sense 2)

gyn- (jin, jīn, gīn) *same as* GYNO-: used before a vowel

gyn·ae·ce·um (jī′nə sē′əm, jin′ə-) *n., pl.* **-ce′a** (-ə) [L. < Gr. *gynaikeion* < *gynaikeios,* of women, feminine <

gynē, woman: see GYNO-] **1.** in ancient Greek and Roman houses, the section of rooms set apart for women **2.** *same as* GYNOECIUM

gyn·ae·co- (jin′ə kō′, gī′nə-) *same as* GYNECO-

gyn·an·dro·morph (ji nan′drə môrf′, gī-) *n.* [< Gr. *gynandros* (see ff.) + -MORPH] an abnormal organism whose physical features are a mixture of male and female characteristics —**gyn·an′dro·mor′phic, gyn·an′dro·mor′-phous** *adj.* —**gyn·an′dro·mor′phism, gyn·an′dro·mor′-phy** *n.*

gyn·an·drous (ji nan′drəs, gī-, jī-) *adj.* [Gr. *gynandros,* of doubtful sex < *gynē,* a woman + *anēr* (gen. *andros*), a man] **1.** *Bot.* having the stamen, or male organ, and pistil, or female organ, united in one column, as in the orchids **2.** characterized by gynandry

gyn·an·dry (-drē) *n.* [GYN- + ANDR- + -Y[3]] [Now Rare] feminine pseudohermaphroditism

gyn·arch·y (jin′är′kē, gī′när′-) *n., pl.* **-arch′ies** [GYN- + -ARCHY] government by a woman or women

gy·ne·ci·um (ji nē′sē əm, jī-, gī-) *n., pl.* **-ci·a** (-ə) *same as* GYNOECIUM

gyn·e·co- (jin′ə kō′, gī′nə-, jī′nə-) [Gr. *gynaiko-* < *gynē,* a woman: see GYNO-] *a combining form meaning* woman, female *[gynecocracy]:* also, before a vowel, **gyn·ec-**

gyn·e·coc·ra·cy (jin′ə käk′rə sē, jī′nə-, gī′nə-) *n., pl.* **-cies** [Gr. *gynaikokratia:* see prec. & -CRACY] government by a woman or women

gyn·e·coid (jin′ə koid′, jī′nə-, gī′nə-) *adj.* [GYNEC- + -OID] of or characteristic of a woman or women; female; feminine

gyn·e·col·o·gy (gī′nə käl′ə jē, jin′ə-, jī′nə-) *n.* [GYNECO- + -LOGY] the branch of medicine dealing with the specific functions, diseases, etc. of women —**gyn′e·co·log′ic** (-kə läj′ik), **gyn′e·co·log′i·cal** *adj.* —**gyn′e·col′o·gist** *n.*

gyn·e·pho·bi·a (jin′ə fō′bē ə, jī′nə-, gī′nə-) *n.* [< prec. + -PHOBIA] an abnormal fear of women

gyn·i·at·rics (jin′ē at′riks, jī′nē-, gī′nē-,) *n.pl.* *[with sing. v.]* [< ff. + -IATRICS] the branch of medicine dealing with the treatment of women's diseases

gyn·o- (jin′ō, jī′nō, gī′nō; -ə, -nə) *a combining form mean-ing:* **1.** woman or female **2.** female reproductive organ, ovary, pistil *[gynophore]*

gy·noe·ci·um (ji nē′sē əm, jī-, gī-) *n., pl.* **-ci·a** (-ə) [ModL., altered (after Gr. *oikos,* house) < L. *gynaeceum*] the female organ or organs of a flower; pistil or pistils; the carpels, collectively

gyn·o·phore (jin′ə fôr′, jī′nə-, gī′nə-) *n.* [GYNO- + -PHORE] a stalk bearing the gynoecium above the petals and stamens —**gy′no·phor′ic** *adj.*

-gyn·ous (ji nəs) [ModL. -*gynus* < Gr. -*gynos* < *gynē:* see GYNO-] *a combining form meaning:* **1.** woman or female *[polygynous]* **2.** having female organs or pistils as specified *[monogynous, androgynous]*

-gyn·y (ji nē) *a n.-forming combining form corresponding to* -GYNOUS

Győr (dyör) city in NW Hungary: pop. 74,000

☆**gyp**[1] (jip) *n.* [prob. < GYPSY] [Colloq.] **1.** an act of cheating; swindle; fraud **2.** a swindler: also **gyp′per, gyp′ster** —*vt., vi.* **gypped, gyp′ping** [Colloq.] to swindle; cheat

gyp[2] (jip) *n.* [< ? GYPSY] [Brit.] a servant at a college

gyp·se·ous (jip′sē əs) *adj.* [ME. *gipseous* < LL. *gypseus* < L. *gypsum*] **1.** like gypsum **2.** containing or consisting of gypsum

gyp·sif·er·ous (jip sif′ər əs) *adj.* [< GYPSUM + -FEROUS] containing or yielding gypsum

gyp·soph·i·la (jip säf′ə lə) *n.* [ModL.: see GYPSUM & -PHIL] any of a genus (*Gypsophila*) of plants of the pink family, bearing clusters of small white or pink flowers with a delicate fragrance, as baby's breath

gyp·sum (jip′səm) *n.* [ME. < L. < Gr. *gypsos,* chalk, gypsum < Sem.] a hydrated sulfate of calcium, $CaSO_4\cdot 2H_2O$, occurring naturally in sedimentary rocks and used for making plaster of Paris, in treating soil, etc.

gypsum board (or **wallboard**) *same as* PLASTERBOARD

Gyp·sy (jip′sē) *n., pl.* **-sies** [earlier *gypcien,* short for *Egipcien,* Egyptian: orig. thought to have come from Egypt] **1.** [*also* **g-**] a member of a wandering Caucasian people with dark skin and black hair, found throughout the world and believed to have originated in India: they are known as musicians, fortunetellers, etc. **2.** *same as* ROMANY (sense 2) **3.** [**g-**] a person whose appearance or habits are like those of a Gypsy —*adj.* of or like a Gypsy or Gypsies —*vi.* [**g-**] **-sied, -sy·ing** [Rare] to wander or live like a Gypsy

gypsy moth a European moth (*Lymantria dispar*), brownish or white, now common in the E U.S.: its larvae feed on leaves, doing much damage to trees and plants

gy·ral (jī′rəl) *adj.* [< GYRE + -AL] **1.** moving in a circular or spiral path; gyratory **2.** of a gyrus

gy·rate (-rāt) *vi.* **-rat·ed, -rat·ing** [< L. *gyratus,* pp. of *gyrare,* to turn, whirl < *gyrus* < Gr. *gyros,* a circle < IE. *guros* < base **geu-, gū-,* to bend, arch, whence COD[2], COP[1]] to move in a circular or spiral path; rotate or revolve on an axis; whirl —*adj.* spiral, coiled, circular, or convolute

---

fat, āpe, cär; ten, ēven; is, bīte; gō, hôrn, tōōl, look; oil, out; up, fur; get; joy; yet; chin; she; thin, *then;* zh, leisure; ŋ, ring; ə for *a* in *ago, e* in *agent, i* in *sanity, o* in *comply; u* in *focus;* ′ as in *able* (ā′b'l); Fr. bål; ë, Fr. coeur; ö, Fr. feu; ö, Fr. mon; ô, Fr. coq; ü, Fr. duc; r, Fr. cri; H, G. ich; kh, G. doch. See inside front cover. ☆ Americanism; ‡foreign; *hypothetical; <derived from

—*SYN.* see TURN —**gy′ra′tor** *n.* —**gy′ra·to′ry** (-rə tôr′ē) *adj.*

gy·ra·tion (jī rā′shən) *n.* **1.** the act of gyrating; circular or spiral motion **2.** something gyrate, as a whorl

gyre (jīr) *n.* [L. *gyrus* < Gr. *gyros*, a circle: see GYRATE] [Chiefly Poet.] **1.** a circular or spiral motion; whirl; revolution **2.** a circular or spiral form; ring or vortex —*vi., vt.* **gyred**, **gyr′ing** [Chiefly Poet.] to whirl

☆**gy·rene** (jī rēn′) *n.* [< ?: cf. *Am. Speech*, Vol. XXXVII, No. 3, Oct., 1962] [Slang] a member of the U.S. Marine Corps

gyr·fal·con (jur′fal′kən, -fôl′-, -fô′-) *n.* [ME. *gerfaucoun* < OFr. *girfaucon* < Frank. *gerfalko* < *ger* (OHG. *gir*, hawk), lit., greedy (one) < IE. base *ghi, *ghe-*, whence GAPE + *falko*, FALCON] a large, fierce, strong falcon (*Falco rusticolus*) of the arctic regions

gy·ro (jī′rō) *n., pl.* **-ros 1.** *short for* GYROSCOPE **2.** *short for* GYROCOMPASS

gy·ro- (jī′rō, -rə) [< Gr. *gyros*, a circle: see GYRATE] *a combining form meaning:* **1.** gyrating [*gyroscope*] **2.** gyroscope [*gyrocompass*] Also, before a vowel, **gyr-**

gy·ro·com·pass (-kum′pəs) *n.* a compass consisting of a motor-operated gyroscope whose rotating axis, kept in a horizontal plane, takes a position parallel to the axis of the earth's rotation and thus points to the geographic north pole instead of to the magnetic pole

gyro horizon *same as* ARTIFICIAL HORIZON (sense 1)

gy·ro·mag·net·ic (jī′rō mag net′ik) *adj.* of or pertaining to the magnetic properties of rotating charged particles

gy·ro·pi·lot (jī′rō pī′lət) *n. same as* AUTOMATIC PILOT

gy·ro·plane (jī′rə plān′) *n.* [GYRO- + PLANE²] any aircraft having wings that rotate about a vertical or nearly vertical axis, as the autogiro or helicopter

gy·ro·scope (-skōp′) *n.* [GYRO- + -SCOPE] a wheel mounted in a ring so that its axis is free to turn in any direction: when the wheel is spun rapidly, it will keep its original plane of rotation no matter which way the ring is turned: gyroscopes are used in gyrocompasses and to keep moving ships, airplanes, etc. level —**gy′ro·scop′ic** (-skäp′ik) *adj.* —**gy′ro·scop′i·cal·ly** *adv.*

GYROSCOPE

gy·rose (jī′rōs) *adj.* [< GYRE + -OSE²] *Bot.* marked with wavy lines or convolutions

gy·ro·sta·bi·liz·er (jī′rō stā′bə lī′zər) *n.* a device consisting of a gyroscope spinning in a vertical plane, used to stabilize the side-to-side rolling of a ship

gy·ro·stat (jī′rə stat′) *n.* [GYRO- + -STAT] a gyroscope consisting of a rotating wheel set in a case, used for demonstrating the dynamics of rotating bodies

gy·ro·stat·ic (jī′rə stat′ik) *adj.* **1.** of a gyrostat **2.** of gyrostatics

gy·ro·stat·ics (-iks) *n.pl.* [*with sing. v.*] [GYRO- + STATICS] the branch of physics dealing with rotating bodies and their tendency to maintain their plane of rotation

gy·rus (jī′rəs) *n., pl.* **-ri** (-rī) [ModL. < L.: see GYRE] *Anat.* a convoluted ridge or fold between fissures, or sulci, esp. of the cortex of the brain

gyve (jīv) *n., vt.* **gyved**, **gyv′ing** [ME. *give* < Anglo-Fr. *gyves*, pl. < ? ME. *withe*, thong, band: cf. WITHY] [Archaic or Poet.] fetter; shackle

H

H, h (āch) *n., pl.* **H's, h's 1.** the eighth letter of the English alphabet: from the Greek *eta*, a borrowing from the Phoenician **2.** the sound of *H* or *h*, phonetically a rough breathing (aspirate): a glottal fricative in which the glottis gradually narrows toward the position for voicing the following vowel while the tongue and lips assume the position for articulating it; in many words originally from French, as *honor*, *honest*, initial *h* is silent **3.** a type or impression for *H* or *h* **4.** a symbol for the eighth in a sequence or group —*adj.* **1.** of *H* or *h* **2.** eighth in a sequence or group

H (āch) *n.* **1.** an object shaped like *H* **2.** *Chem. the symbol for* hydrogen **3.** *Physics the symbol for:* a) henry b) the horizontal component of terrestrial magnetism **4.** [Slang] heroin —*adj.* shaped like *H*

H., h. 1. harbor **2.** hard **3.** hardness **4.** height **5.** high **6.** *Baseball* hits **7.** hour(s) **8.** hundred **9.** husband

ha (hä) *interj.* [echoic] an exclamation variously expressing wonder, surprise, anger, triumph, etc.: repeated (**ha-ha**) it may indicate laughter, derision, etc. —*n.* the sound of this exclamation or of a laugh

ha. hectare(s)

h.a. [L. *hoc anno*] in this year

Haa·kon VII (hô′koon) 1872–1957; king of Norway (1905–57)

Haar·lem (här′ləm) city in NW Netherlands; capital of North Holland province: pop. 172,000

Haar·lem·mer·meer (här′lə mər mer′) city in NW Netherlands, on the site of a former lake: pop. 51,000

Ha·bak·kuk (hab′ə kuk, hə bak′ək) [Heb. *habhaqqūq*, prob. < *hābaq*, to embrace] *Bible* **1.** a Hebrew prophet of about the 7th century B.C. **2.** the book containing his prophecies: abbrev. **Hab.** Also, in the Douay Bible, **Ha′ba·cuc**

Ha·ba·na (ä bä′ nä), (La) *Sp. name of* HAVANA

ha·ba·ne·ra (hä′bə ner′ə; *Sp.* ä′bä nā′rä) *n.* [Sp., lit., of HABANA] **1.** a slow Cuban dance similar to the tango **2.** the music for this

‡**ha·be·as cor·pus** (hā′bē əs kôr′pəs) [ME. < L., (that) you have the body] *Law* any of various writs ordering a person to be brought before a court; specif., a writ or order requiring that a detained person be brought before a court at a stated time and place to decide the legality of his detention or imprisonment: in full, **habeas corpus ad sub·ji·ci·en·dum** (ad′ səb yik′ē en′dəm): the right of *habeas corpus* safeguards one against illegal detention or imprisonment

Ha·ber (hä′bər), **Fritz** 1868–1934; Ger. chemist

hab·er·dash·er (hab′ər dash′ər, hab′ə-) *n.* [ME. *haberdashere*, prob. < Anglo-Fr. *hapertas*, kind of cloth] **1.** a person whose work or business is selling men's furnishings, such as hats, shirts, neckties, gloves, etc. **2.** [Brit.] a dealer in various small articles, such as ribbons, thread, needles, etc.

hab·er·dash·er·y (-ē) *n., pl.* **-er·ies** [ME. *haberdasshrie*] **1.** things sold by a haberdasher **2.** a haberdasher's shop

hab·er·geon (hab′ər jən) *n.* [ME. *habergoun* < OFr. *haubergeon*, dim. of *hauberc:* see HAUBERK] **1.** a short, high-necked jacket of mail, usually sleeveless **2.** *same as* HAUBERK

hab·ile (hab′il) *adj.* [ME. *habil* < OFr. *habile* < L. *habilis* < base of *habere:* see HABIT] [Now Rare] able; skillful; handy; clever

ha·bil·i·ment (hə bil′ə mənt) *n.* [MFr. *habillement* < *habiller*, to clothe, make fit < *habile:* see prec.] **1.** [*usually pl.*] clothing; dress; attire **2.** [*pl.*] furnishings or equipment; trappings

ha·bil·i·tate (-tāt′) *vt.* **-tat′ed, -tat′ing** [< ML. *habilitatus*, pp. of *habilitare*, to make suitable < L. *habilis* (see HABILE)] **1.** to clothe; equip; outfit **2.** to educate or train (the mentally or physically handicapped, the disadvantaged, etc.) to function better in society **3.** *Mining* to provide (a mine) with the capital and equipment needed to work (it) —**ha·bil′i·ta′tion** *n.* —**ha·bil′i·ta′tive** *adj.*

hab·it (hab′it) *n.* [ME. < OFr. < L. *habitus*, condition, appearance, dress < pp. of *habere*, to have, hold < IE. base *ghabh-*, to grasp, take, whence GIVE] **1.** formerly, costume; dress **2.** a particular costume showing rank, status, etc.; specif., a) a distinctive religious costume [a monk's *habit*] b) a costume worn for certain occasions [a riding *habit*] **3.** habitual or characteristic condition of mind or body; disposition **4.** a) a thing done often and hence, usually, done easily; practice; custom b) a pattern of action that is acquired and has become so automatic that it is difficult to break **5.** a tendency to perform a certain action or behave in a certain way; usual way of doing **6.** an addiction, esp. to narcotics **7.** *Biol.* the tendency of a plant or animal to grow in a certain way; characteristic growth [a twining *habit*] —*vt.* **1.** to dress; clothe **2.** [Archaic] to inhabit

SYN.—**habit** refers to an act repeated so often by an individual that it has become automatic with him [his *habit* of tugging at his ear in perplexity]; **practice** also implies the regular repetition of an act but does not suggest that it is automatic [the *practice* of reading in bed]; **custom** applies to any act or procedure carried on by tradition and often enforced by social disapproval of any violation [the *custom* of dressing for dinner]; **usage** refers to custom or practice that has become sanctioned through being long established [*usage* is the only authority in language]; **wont** is a literary or somewhat archaic equivalent for **practice** [it was his *wont* to rise early]

hab·it·a·ble (-ə b'l) *adj.* [ME. < OFr. < L. *habitabilis* < *habitare*, to have possession of, inhabit: see prec. & -ABLE] that can be inhabited; fit to be lived in —**hab'it·a·bil'i·ty** *n.* —**hab'it·a·bly** *adv.*

hab·it·ant (-ənt) *n.* [Fr. < L. *habitans*, prp.: see HABITABLE] 1. an inhabitant; resident 2. (*also Fr.* á bē tän*/*) a farmer in Louisiana or Canada of French descent: also **hab·i·tan** (á bē tän*/*)

hab·i·tat (hab'ə tat*/*) *n.* [L., it inhabits: see HABITABLE] 1. the region where a plant or animal naturally grows or lives; native environment 2. the place where a person or thing is ordinarily found

hab·i·ta·tion (hab'ə tā'shən) *n.* [ME. *habitacioun* < OFr. *habitacion* < L. *habitatio*: see HABITABLE] 1. the act of inhabiting; occupancy 2. a place in which to live; dwelling; home 3. a colony or settlement

hab·it-form·ing (hab'it fôr'miŋ) *adj.* resulting in the formation of a habit or in addiction

ha·bit·u·al (hə bich'ōō wəl) *adj.* [ML. *habitualis*, of habit or dress: see HABIT] 1. formed or acquired by continual use; done by habit or fixed as a habit; customary 2. being or doing a certain thing by habit; steady; inveterate [a *habitual* smoker] 3. much seen, done, or used; usual; frequent —*SYN.* see USUAL —**ha·bit'u·al·ly** *adv.* —**ha·bit'u·al·ness** *n.*

ha·bit·u·ate (-ōō wāt*/*) *vt.* -at'ed, -at'ing [< LL. *habituatus*, pp. of *habituare*, to bring into a condition or habit of the body < L. *habitus*: see HABIT] 1. to make used (*to*); accustom; familiarize: often used reflexively 2. [Archaic] to attend or visit often; frequent —**ha·bit'u·a'tion** *n.*

hab·i·tude (hab'ə tōōd*/*, -tyōōd*/*) *n.* [ME. *abitude* < MFr. *habitude* < L. *habitudo*, condition, habit: see HABIT] 1. habitual or characteristic condition of mind or body; disposition 2. usual way of doing something; custom

ha·bit·u·é (hə bich'ōō wā*/*) *n.* [Fr. < pp. of *habituer*, to accustom < LL. *habituare*: see HABITUATE] a person who frequents a certain place or places [a *habitué* of nightclubs]

hab·i·tus (hab'ə təs) *n., pl.* **hab'i·tus'** (-tōōs*/*) [ModL. < L., HABIT] 1. *same as* HABIT (*n.* 5, 7) 2. general physical appearance and body build, sometimes related to a predisposition to certain diseases

Habs·burg (häps'boorkh) *same as* HAPSBURG

ha·chure (hə shoor*/*; *also, for n.,* hash'oor) *n.* [Fr. < OFr. *hacher*, to chop < *hache*, ax < Frank. *hupju*, sickle < IE. base *(s)kep-*, whence SHAFT & L. *capo*, capon, Gr. *koptein*, to chop] any of a series of short parallel lines used, esp. in map making, to represent a sloping or elevated surface —*vt.* -chured', -chur'ing to show by, or shade with, hachures

☆**ha·ci·en·da** (hä'sē en'də, has'ē-) *n.* [Sp. < OSp. *facienda*, employment, estate < L. *facienda*, things to be done < *facere*: see FACT] in Spanish America, 1. a large estate, ranch, or plantation 2. the main dwelling on any of these

Ha·ci·en·da Heights (hä'sē en'də, has'ē-) suburb of Los Angeles, in SW Calif.: pop. 36,000

hack¹ (hak) *vt.* [ME. *hacken* < OE. *haccian*, akin to G. *hacken* < IE. base *keg-*, peg, hook, whence HOOK, HATCHEL] 1. *a)* to chop or cut crudely, roughly, or irregularly, as with a hatchet *b)* to shape, trim, damage, etc. with or as with rough, sweeping strokes 2. to break up (land) with a hoe, mattock, etc. ☆3. *Basketball* to foul by striking the arm of (an opponent who has the ball) with the hand or arm 4. *Rugby* to foul by kicking (an opponent) on the shins —*vi.* 1. to make rough or irregular cuts 2. to give harsh, dry coughs ☆3. *Basketball* to hack an opponent —*n.* 1. a tool for cutting or hacking; ax, hoe, mattock, etc. 2. a slash, gash, or notch made by a sharp implement 3. a hacking blow 4. a harsh, dry cough —**hack around** [Colloq.] to engage in aimless activity; spend time idly —**hack'er** *n.*

hack² (hak) *n.* [contr. < HACKNEY] 1. *a)* a horse for hire *b)* a horse for all sorts of work *c)* a saddle horse *d)* an old, worn-out horse 2. a person hired to do routine, often dull, writing; literary drudge ☆3. a worker for a political party, usually holding office through patronage, who serves his leaders devotedly and unquestioningly 4. a carriage or coach for hire 5. [Colloq.] *a)* a taxicab *b)* a hackman or cabdriver —*vt.* 1. to employ as a hack 2. to hire out (a horse, etc.) 3. to wear out or make stale by constant use —*vi.* 1. [Brit.] to jog along on a horse ☆2. [Colloq.] to drive a taxicab —*adj.* 1. employed as a hack [a *hack* writer] 2. done by a hack [*hack* work] 3. stale; trite; hackneyed

hack³ (hak) *n.* [orig., board on which a falcon's meat was put, var. of HATCH²] 1. a grating or rack for drying cheese or fish, holding food for cattle, etc. 2. a pile or row of unburned bricks set out to dry —*vt.* to place on a hack for drying

☆**hack·a·more** (hak'ə môr*/*) *n.* [altered < Sp. *jaquima*, halter < Ar. *shakīma*] [Western] a rope or rawhide halter with a headstall, used in breaking horses

hack·ber·ry (hak'ber'ē) *n., pl.* -ries [< Scand., as in Dan. *hæggebær*, Norw. *haggebär*, ON. *heggr*: for IE. base see HEDGE] ☆1. any of a genus (*Celtis*) of American trees of the elm family, with a small fruit resembling a cherry ☆2. its fruit or its wood

hack·but (hak'but*/*) *n.* [Fr. *haquebut* < obs. Du. *hakebus* < *hake*, haak, HOOK + *bus*, a gun, gun barrel, lit., box: so named from method of support during firing] an obsolete type of portable firearm; kind of harquebus

Hack·en·sack (hak'n sak*/*) [< Du. < AmInd. (Delaware) name] city in NE N.J.: pop. 36,000

hack hammer a tool like an adz with a hammerhead, used in dressing stone

☆**hack·ie** (hak'ē) *n.* [Colloq.] a taxicab driver

hack·le¹ (hak'l) *n.* [ME. *hechele* (akin to G. *hechel*) < OE. *hæcel* < IE. base *keg-*, peg, hook, whence HACK¹, HOOK: senses 2, 3, & 4, prob. infl. by dial. *hackle*, bird's plumage, animal's skin < OE. *hacele*] 1. a comblike instrument for separating the fibers of flax, hemp, etc. 2. *a)* any of the long, slender feathers at the neck of a rooster, peacock, pigeon, etc. *b)* such feathers, collectively 3. *Fishing a)* a tuft of feathers from a rooster's neck, used in making artificial flies *b)* a fly made with a hackle 4. [*pl.*] the hairs on a dog's neck and back that bristle, as when the dog is ready to fight —*vt.* -led, -ling 1. to separate the fibers of (flax, hemp, etc.) with a hackle 2. [Rare] to supply (a fishing fly) with a hackle —**get one's hackles up** to become tense with anger; bristle

hack·le² (hak'l) *vt., vi.* -led, -ling [freq. of HACK¹] to cut roughly; hack; mangle

☆**hack·man** (hak'mən) *n., pl.* -men (-mən) the driver of a hack or carriage for hire

☆**hack·ma·tack** (hak'mə tak*/*) *n.* [AmInd. (Algonquian)] 1. *same as* TAMARACK 2. the balsam poplar (*Populus balsamifera*) of the willow family 3. the wood of either of these trees

hack·ney (hak'nē) *n., pl.* -neys [ME. *hakene*, *hakenei* < *Hakeney* (now *Hackney*), an English village] 1. a horse for ordinary driving or riding 2. a carriage for hire 3. [Obs.] a person hired for dull, monotonous work; drudge —*adj.* [Obs.] 1. hired out 2. trite; commonplace —*vt.* [Now Rare] 1. to hire out 2. to make trite by overuse

hack·neyed (-nēd*/*) *adj.* made trite and commonplace by overuse —*SYN.* see TRITE

hack·saw (hak'sô*/*) *n.* a saw for cutting metal, consisting of a narrow, fine-toothed blade held in a frame: also **hack saw**

HACKSAW

had (had; *unstressed* həd, əd) [ME. *hadde*, *had* < OE. *hæfde*] *pt. & pp. of* HAVE: also used to indicate preference or necessity, with adverbs, adjectives, and phrases of comparison, such as *rather*, *better*, *as well* (Ex.: I *had* better leave)

had·dock (had'ək) *n., pl.* -dock, -docks: see PLURAL, II, D, 2 [ME *hadok* < ? OFr. *hadot*, kind of salt fish] a food fish (*Melanogrammus aeglefinus*) related to the cod, found off the coasts of Europe and N. America

hade (hād) *n.* [< dial. *hade*, to slope, incline < ?] *Geol.* the angle between the plane of a fault or vein and the vertical plane —*vi.* had'ed, had'ing *Geol.* to incline from the vertical plane, as a fault, vein, or lode

Ha·des (hā'dēz) [Gr. *Haidēs*] 1. *Gr. Myth. a)* the home of the dead, beneath the earth *b)* the ruler of the underworld 2. *Bible* the state or resting place of the dead: name used in some modern translations of the New Testament —*n.* [*often* h-] [Colloq.] hell: a euphemism

Ha·dhra·maut, Ha·dra·maut (hä'drä môt*/*) 1. region on the S coast of Arabia, in E Southern Yemen: c. 58,500 sq. mi. 2. river valley (**Wadi Hadhramaut**) that crosses this region: c. 350 mi.

hadj (haj) *n. same as* HAJJ

hadj·i (-ē) *n. same as* HAJJI

had·n't (had'nt) had not

Ha·dri·an (hā'drē ən) (L. name *Publius Aelius Hadrianus*) 76–138 A.D.; Roman emperor (117–138)

Hadrian's Wall stone wall across N England, from Solway Firth to the Tyne: built (122–128 A.D.) by Hadrian to protect Roman Britain from N tribes: 73 1/2 mi.

hadst (hadst) *archaic 2d pers. sing., past indic., of* HAVE: *used with* thou

hae (hā, ha) *vt.* [Scot.] to have

Haeck·el (hek'əl), **Ernst Hein·rich** (ernst hīn'riH) 1834–1919; Ger. biologist & philosopher

haem-, haema-, haemat-, haemato-, haemo- *same as* HEM-, HEMA-, HEMAT-, HEMATO-, HEMO-

hae·ma·tox·y·lon (hē'mə täk'sə län*/*, hem'ə-) *n.* [ModL. *haematoxylon* < HAEMATO- + Gr. *xylon*, wood] *same as* LOGWOOD: see also HEMATOXYLIN

-hae·mi·a (hē'mē ə) *same as* -EMIA

hae·res (hē'rēz) *n., pl.* **hae·re·des** (hə rē'dēz) *same as* HERES

Ha·fiz (hä fiz*/*) (born *Shams-ud-Din Mohammed*) 14th cent.; Per. lyric poet

ha·fiz (häf'iz*/*) *n.* [Ar. *ḥāfiz*, a person who remembers] *title for* a Moslem who has memorized the Koran

haf·ni·um (haf'nē əm) *n.* [ModL. < L. *Hafnia*, Roman name of Copenhagen] a metallic chemical element found with zirconium and somewhat resembling it: used in the manufacture of tungsten filaments and in reactor control

rods: symbol, Hf; at. wt., 178.49; at. no., 72; sp. gr., 13.31; melt. pt., 2230°C; boil. pt., 3200°+C

haft (haft, häft) *n.* [ME. < OE. *hæft*, a handle < base of *hebban:* see HEAVE] a handle or hilt of a knife, ax, etc. —*vt.* to fit with, or fix in, a haft

haf·ta·ra (häf'tä rä', -tôr'ə) *n. same as* HAPHTARAH

hag¹ (hag) *n.* [ME. *hagge*, a witch, hag, contr. < OE. *hægtes < haga*, hedge, akin to G. *hexe* (OHG. *hagazissa*): sense comparable to ON. *tūnritha*, lit., hedge rider, hence witch] **1.** orig., a female demon or evil spirit **2.** a witch; enchantress **3.** an ugly, often vicious old woman **4.** *same as* HAGFISH

hag² (hag) *vt.* [Scot. < Anglo-N. form of ON. *höggva*, to cut, hack, akin to OE. *heawan*, HEW] [Scot. & Brit. Dial.] to cut; hack —*n.* [< Anglo-N. form of ON. *högg*, a cutting, chopping < base of the *vt.*] [Scot. & Brit. Dial.] **1.** *a)* a cutting of wood *b)* felled trees **2.** *a)* the edge of a cutting in a peat bog *b)* a marsh or marshy spot *c)* a firm spot in a bog or marsh

Hag. Haggai

Ha·gar (hā'gər) [Heb. *hāghār*, lit., prob. fugitive < ? base akin to Ar. *hajara*, to forsake: cf. HEGIRA] **1.** a feminine name **2.** *Bible* a concubine of Abraham and slave of Abraham's wife Sarah: see ISHMAEL

hag·born (hag'bôrn') *adj.* having a hag, or witch, for a mother

hag·but (hag'but) *n. same as* HACKBUT

Ha·gen¹ (hä'gən) city in W West Germany, in the Ruhr valley, North Rhine-Westphalia: pop. 203,000

Ha·gen² (hä'gən) [G.] in the *Nibelungenlied*, Gunther's uncle, who murders Siegfried at Brunhild's bidding

Ha·gers·town (hā'gərz toun') [after Jonathan *Hager*, early settler] city in N Md.: pop. 36,000

hag·fish (hag'fish') *n., pl.* **-fish'**, **-fish'es:** see FISH² [HAG¹ + FISH²] any of a number of small, jawless, eellike saltwater cyclostomes (order Myxinoidea), with a round, sucking mouth and horny teeth, with which they bore into other fish and devour them

Hag·ga·da, Hag·ga·dah (hä gä dä'; *E.* hə gä'də) *n., pl.* **-ga·dot'** (-dōt') [Heb. *haggādāh < higgid*, to tell, relate] **1.** *a)* [*often* h-] in the *Talmud*, an anecdote or parable that explains or illustrates some point of law *b)* the part of the Talmud devoted to such narratives See also HALAKHA **2.** *a)* a narrative of the Exodus read at the Seder during Passover *b)* a book containing this narrative and the Seder ritual —**hag·gad·ic** (hə gad'ik, -gä'dik) *adj.*

hag·ga·dist (hə gä'dist) *n.* a haggadic writer or scholar —**hag·ga·dis·tic** (hag'ə dis'tik) *adj.*

Hag·ga·i (hag'ē ī', hag'ī) [Heb. *haggai*, lit., festal] *Bible* **1.** a Hebrew prophet who lived c. 500 B.C. **2.** the book attributed to him

hag·gard (hag'ərd) *adj.* [MFr. *hagard*, untamed, untamed hawk] **1.** *Falconry* designating a hawk captured after reaching maturity **2.** untamed; unruly; wild **3.** *a)* wild-eyed *b)* having a wild, wasted, worn look, as from sleeplessness, grief, illness, hunger, etc.; gaunt; drawn —*n. Falconry* a haggard hawk —**hag'gard·ly** *adv.* —**hag'gard·ness** *n.*

Hag·gard (hag'ərd), **Sir H(enry) Rider** 1856–1925; Eng. novelist

hag·gis (hag'is) *n.* [ME. *hagas*, kind of pudding < ? or akin to HAG²] a Scottish dish made of the lungs, heart, etc. of a sheep or calf, mixed with suet, seasoning, and oatmeal and boiled in the animal's stomach

hag·gish (hag'ish) *adj.* of, like, or characteristic of a hag —**hag'gish·ly** *adv.* —**hag'gish·ness** *n.*

hag·gle (hag''l) *vt.* **-gled**, **-gling** [freq. of HAG²] to chop or cut crudely; hack; mangle —*vi.* to argue about terms, price, etc.; bargain; wrangle —*n.* the act of haggling —**hag'gler** *n.*

hag·i·arch·y (hag'ē är'kē, hā'jē-) *n., pl.* **-arch'ies** [< ff. + -ARCHY] *same as* HAGIOCRACY

hag·i·o- (hag'ē ō', hā'jē-) [< Gr. *hagios*, holy] a prefix meaning saintly, sacred, holy [*hagiocracy*]: also, before a vowel, **hag'i-**

hag·i·oc·ra·cy (hag'ē äk'rə sē, hā'jē-) *n., pl.* **-cies** [prec. + -CRACY] rule by priests, saints, or others considered holy; theocracy

Hag·i·og·ra·pha (-äg'rə fə) *n.pl.* [LL.(Ec.) < Gr.(Ec.) *hagiographa* (*biblia*), transl. of Heb. *kethābhē haqqōdhesh*, lit., writings of holiness: see HAGIO- & -GRAPH] the third and final part of the Jewish Scriptures, those books not in the Law or the Prophets

hag·i·og·ra·pher (-äg'rə fər) *n.* **1.** any of the authors of the Hagiographa **2.** any sacred or holy writer **3.** an author of lives of the saints

hag·i·o·graph·ic (hag'ē ə graf'ik, hā'jē-) *adj.* **1.** of hagiography or the Hagiographa **2.** idealizing its subject: said of a biography Also **hag'i·o·graph'i·cal**

hag·i·og·ra·phy (-äg'rə fē) *n., pl.* **-phies** [HAGIO- + -GRAPHY] **1.** the writing or study of lives of the saints **2.** a book or books containing such lives

hag·i·ol·a·try (-äl'ə trē) *n.* [HAGIO- + -LATRY] reverence for or worship of saints —**hag'i·ol'a·ter** *n.*

hag·i·ol·o·gy (-äl'ə jē) *n., pl.* **-gies** [HAGIO- + -LOGY] **1.** literature about saints' lives and legends, sacred writings, etc. **2.** a book or collection of saints' lives and legends **3.** a catalog or list of saints —**hag'i·o·log'ic** (-ə läj'ik), **hag'i·o·log'i·cal** *adj.*

hag·i·o·scope (hag'ē ə skōp', hā'jē-) *n.* [HAGIO- + -SCOPE] a narrow opening in an inside wall of a medieval church to let those in a side aisle, or transept, see the main altar

hag·rid·den (hag'rid''n) *adj.* **1.** orig., ridden by a hag, or witch **2.** obsessed or harassed, as by fears

Hague (hāg), **The** city in W Netherlands; seat of the government (cf. AMSTERDAM): pop. 593,000: Du. name, 'S GRAVENHAGE

Hague Tribunal the Permanent Court of Arbitration founded in 1899: it selects the nominees for election to the International Court of Justice

hah (hä) *interj., n. same as* HA

ha-ha¹ (hä'hä', hä'-) *interj., n. see* HA

ha-ha² (hä'hä') *n.* [Fr. *haha* < ?] a fence, wall, etc. set in a ditch around a garden or park so as not to hide the view from within: also sp. **ha'ha'**

Hahn (hän), **Otto** 1879–1968; Ger. nuclear physicist

Hah·ne·mann (hä'nə mən), (**Christian Friedrich**) **Samuel** 1755–1843; Ger. physician: founder of homeopathy

Hai·da (hī'də) *n.* [< the native name, lit., people] **1.** *pl.* **-das, -da** a member of a tribe of Indians who live in British Columbia and Alaska **2.** their isolated language, the unique member of a family

Hai·fa (hī'fə) seaport in NW Israel, on the Mediterranean: pop. 205,000

Haig (hāg), **Douglas,** 1st Earl Haig, 1861–1928; Brit. commander in chief, World War I

haik (hīk, häk) *n.* [Ar. *ḥāyk < ḥāka*, to weave] a sheetlike piece of woolen or cotton cloth worn by Arabs as an outer garment

hai·ku (hī'kōō) *n.* [Jap.] **1.** a Japanese verse form of three unrhymed lines of 5, 7, and 5 syllables respectively (total 17 syllables), usually on some subject in nature **2.** *pl.* **-ku** a poem in this form

hail¹ (hāl) *vt.* [ME. *hailen*, to salute, greet < ON. *heilla < heill*, whole, sound, akin to OE. *hal* (see HALE¹, WHOLE): used as a salutation] **1.** to welcome, greet, etc. with or as with cheers; acclaim **2.** to name by way of tribute; salute as [they *hailed* him their leader] **3.** to call out to or signal to, as in summoning or greeting [to *hail* a taxi] —*vi. Naut.* to call out or signal to a ship —*n.* **1.** the act of hailing or greeting **2.** the distance that a shout will carry [within *hail*] —*interj.* an exclamation of tribute, greeting, etc. —**hail fellow well met** very sociable or friendly to everyone, esp. in a superficial manner: also **hail fellow, hail-fellow** —**hail from** to be from; come from (one's birthplace or established residence) —**hail'er** *n.*

hail² (hāl) *n.* [ME. *haile* < OE. *hægel*, var. of *hagol*, akin to G. *hagel* < IE. base *kaghlo-*, small pebble, whence Gr. *kachlēx*] **1.** small, rounded pieces of ice that sometimes fall during thunderstorms; frozen raindrops; hailstones **2.** a falling, showering, etc. of hail, or in the manner of hail [a *hail* of bullets] —*vi.* [ME. *hailen* < OE. *hagalian*] to drop or pour down hail: usually in an impersonal construction [it is *hailing*] —*vt.* to shower, hurl, pour, etc. violently in the manner of hail (often with *on* or *upon*) [to *hail* curses on someone]

☆**hail Columbia** [euphemism for HELL] [Old Slang] a severe beating, punishment, scolding, etc.

Hai·le Se·las·sie (hī'lē sə las'ē, -läs'ē) (born *Tafari Makonnen*) 1891– ; emperor of Ethiopia (1930–)

Hail Mary *pl.* **Hail Marys** *same as* AVE MARIA (sense 2)

hail·stone (hāl'stōn') *n.* [ME. *hawelston*] a pellet of hail

hail·storm (-stôrm') *n.* a storm in which hail falls

Hai·nan (hī'nän') island off the S coast of China, in the South China Sea: part of Kwangtung province: c. 13,000 sq. mi.

Hai·naut (e nō') province of SW Belgium: 1,437 sq. mi.; pop. 1,333,000; cap. Mons

Hai·phong (hī'fäŋ') seaport in N North Vietnam, in the delta of the Red River: pop. 369,000

hair (her) *n.* [ME. *here* < OE. *hær* (akin to G. *haar*, OFrank. **harja* < ? OFr. *haire*, hair shirt < OFrank. **harja*, both < IE. base **ker(s)-*, bristle, whence Lith. *šerȳs*] **1.** any of the fine, threadlike outgrowths from the skin of an animal or human being **2.** a growth of these; esp., *a)* the growth covering the human head *b)* the growth covering all or part of the skin of most mammals **3.** material woven from hair **4.** an extremely small space, margin, degree, etc. [to miss by a *hair*] **5.** *Bot.* a threadlike growth on a plant —*adj.* **1.** made of or with hair **2.** for the care of the hair [*hair* tonic] —☆**get in one's hair** [Slang] to annoy one —**hair of the dog (that bit one)** [Colloq.] a drink of alcoholic liquor taken as a supposed cure for a hangover —**have** (or **get**) **by the short hairs** [Slang] to have (or get) completely at one's mercy —**let one's hair down** [Slang] to be very informal, relaxed, and free in behavior —**make one's hair stand on end** to terrify or horrify one —**not turn a hair** to show no fear, surprise, embarrassment, etc.; stay calm and unruffled —**split hairs** to make petty distinctions; quibble —**to a hair** exactly; perfectly; right in every detail —**hair'like'** *adj.*

hair·ball (-bôl') *n.* a rounded mass of hair often found in the stomach of a cow, cat, or other animal that licks its coat

hair·breadth (-bredth') *n.* an extremely small space or amount —*adj.* very narrow; close [a *hairbreadth* escape]

hair·brush (-brush') *n.* a brush for grooming the hair

hair·cloth (-klôth′) *n.* cloth woven from horsehair, camel's hair, etc., used mainly for covering furniture

hair·cut (-kut′) *n.* **1.** a cutting or clipping of the hair of the head **2.** the style in which the hair is cut —**hair′cut′ter** *n.*

☆**hair·do** (-dōō′) *n., pl.* **-dos′** the style in which (a woman's) hair is arranged; coiffure

hair·dress·er (-dres′ər) *n.* a person whose work is dressing (women's) hair —**hair′dress′ing** *n., adj.*

haired (herd) *adj.* having hair of a specified kind [*fair-haired, short-haired*]

hair·less (-lis) *adj.* having little or no hair or having lost the hair; bald

hair·line (-līn′) *n.* **1.** orig., a line, cord, etc. made of hair **2.** a very thin line **3.** *a)* a very thin stripe *b)* cloth patterned with such stripes **4.** a very narrow margin or degree of difference **5.** the outline of the hair on the head, esp. of the hair above the forehead **6.** *Printing* a very thin stroke on a type face or impression

hair·net (-net′) *n.* a net or fine-meshed cap of silk, etc., for keeping a woman's coiffure in order

hair·piece (-pēs′) *n.* **1.** a toupee or wig **2.** a switch of hair, often styled, for a woman's hairdo

hair·pin (-pin′) *n.* a small, usually U-shaped, piece of wire, shell, etc., for keeping the hair or headdress in place —*adj.* formed like a hairpin [*a hairpin turn*]

hair-rais·ing (-rā′ziŋ) *adj.* [Colloq.] causing, or thought of as causing, the hair to stand on end; terrifying or shocking —**hair′-rais′er** *n.*

hairs·breadth, hair's-breadth (herz′bredth′) *n., adj.* *same as* HAIRBREADTH

hair seal any of various earless seals that do not have fine underfur

hair shirt a shirt or girdle of haircloth, worn for self-punishment by religious ascetics and penitents

hair space *Printing* the narrowest metal space used between words, equal to about 1/2 point

hair·split·ting (-split′iŋ) *adj., n.* making overnice or petty distinctions; quibbling —**hair′split′ter** *n.*

hair·spring (-spriŋ′) *n.* a very slender, hairlike coil that controls the regular movement of the balance wheel in a watch or clock

hair·streak (-strēk′) *n.* any of a number of small, usually dark-colored butterflies (family Lycaenidae) with each hind wing commonly having narrow taillike projections

hair stroke a very fine line in writing or printing

hair-trig·ger (-trig′ər) *adj.* [see ff.] set in motion or operation by a very slight impulse

hair trigger a trigger so delicately adjusted that a very slight pressure on it discharges the firearm

hair·worm (-wurm′) *n. same as* GORDIAN WORM

hair·y (-ē) *adj.* **hair′i·er, hair′i·est 1.** covered with hair; hirsute **2.** of or like hair ☆**3.** [Slang] difficult, distressing, harrowing, etc. —**hair′i·ness** *n.*

hairy vetch a common, annual, leguminous plant (*Vicia villosa*) with hairy foliage and numerous small blue flowers, grown for forage

Hai·ti (hāt′ē) **1.** country occupying the W portion of the island of Hispaniola, West Indies: 10,714 sq. mi.; pop. 4,485,000; cap. Port-au-Prince **2.** *former name of* HISPANIOLA

Hai·tian (hā′shən, hāt′ē ən) *adj.* of Haiti, its people, or culture —*n.* **1.** a native or inhabitant of Haiti **2.** the creolized language derived from French and spoken in Haiti: in full, **Haitian Creole**

hajj (haj) *n.* [Ar. *ḥajj* < *ḥajja*, to set out, go on a pilgrimage] the pilgrimage to Mecca that every Moslem is expected to take at least once

haj·i, haj·i (haj′ē) *n.* [Ar. *ḥajji*, form of *ḥajj*, pilgrim: see prec.] a Moslem who has made a pilgrimage to Mecca: a title of honor

hake (hāk) *n., pl.* **hake, hakes:** see PLURAL, II, D, 2 [ME., prob. < ON. *haki*, a hook (from the shape of the jaw), whence Norw. *hakefisk*, trout, salmon, lit., hookfish: for IE. base see HOOK] **1.** any of various marine food fishes (family Merlucciidae) related to the cod, as the **silver hake, European hake,** etc. **2.** any of certain fishes (genus *Urophycis*) of the codfish family, as the **white hake, squirrel hake,** etc.

ha·kim¹ (hä kēm′) *n.* [Ar. *ḥakim*, wise, learned, hence physician] in Moslem regions, a doctor; physician

ha·kim² (hä′kēm, -kim) *n.* [Ar. *ḥākim*, governor < *ḥakama*, to exercise authority] in Moslem regions, a ruler, judge, or governor

Hak·luyt (hak′lōōt) **Richard** 1552?-1616; Eng. geographer & chronicler of explorations & discoveries

Ha·ko·da·te (hä′kō dä′tā) seaport on the SW coast of Hokkaido, Japan: pop. 243,000

hal- (hal) *same as* HALO-: used before a vowel

Ha·la·kha, Ha·la·cha (hä lä khä′, hä lä′khə) *n., pl.* **-la·khot′, -la·chot′** (-khōt′) [Heb. *halākhāh*, rule by which to go < *halākh*, to go] **1.** [*often* h-] *Talmud* any of the laws or ordinances not written down in the Scriptures but based on an oral interpretation of the laws and ordinances See also HAGGADA

ha·la·khist, ha·la·chist (häl′ə khist, hə lä′khist) *n.* any of the contributors to the Halakha

ha·la·tion (hā lā′shən; ha-) *n.* [HAL(O) + -ATION] *Photog.* an undesirable spreading or reflection of light on a negative, appearing like a halo around highlights

hal·berd (hal′bərd) *n.* [LME. *haubert* < OFr. *hallebarde* & MDu. *hellebaerde,* both < MHG. *helmbarte* < *helm,* handle, staff (see HELM²) + *barte,* an ax] a combination spear and battle-ax used in the 15th and 16th cent.: also **hal′bert** (-bərt) —**hal′berd·ier** (-bər dir′) *n.*

hal·cy·on (hal′sē ən) *n.* [ME. *alcioun* < L. *alcyon* < Gr. *alkyōn,* kingfisher, altered by folk etymology after Gr. *hals,* sea] **1.** a legendary bird, identified with the kingfisher, which was supposed to have a peaceful, calming influence on the sea at the time of the winter solstice **2.** *Zool.* any of a genus (*Halcyon*) of kingfishers of SE Asia and Australia —*adj.* **1.** of the halcyon **2.** tranquil, happy, idyllic, etc.: esp. in phr. **halcyon days,** usually with nostalgic reference to earlier times

Hal·dane (hôl′dān) **1. J(ohn) B(urdon) S(anderson),** 1892-1964; Eng. biologist & writer **2. Richard Bur·don** (bur′dən), **1st Viscount Haldane of Cloan,** 1856-1928; Scot. statesman & philosopher: uncle of *prec.*

HALBERD

hale¹ (hāl) *adj.* [northern ME. *hal,* same as Midland *hool* (see WHOLE) < OE. *hal,* sound, healthy] sound in body; vigorous and healthy: now esp. with reference to an older person —*SYN.* see HEALTHY

hale² (hāl) *vt.* **haled, hal′ing** [ME. *halen, halien* < OFr. *haler,* prob. < ODu. *halen:* see HAUL] **1.** [Archaic] to pull forcibly; drag; haul **2.** to force (a person) to go [*haled* him into court]

Hale (hāl) **1. Edward Everett,** 1822-1909; U.S. clergyman & writer **2. Nathan,** 1755-76; Am. soldier in the Revolutionary War: hanged by the British as a spy

Ha·le·a·ka·la National Park (hä′lä ä′kä lä′) national park on the island of Maui, Hawaii, including a dormant volcano (**Haleakala**), 10,023 ft. high, with a crater of 19 sq. mi.

Ha·leb (hä leb′) *Arabic name of* ALEPPO

hal·er (häl′ər) *n., pl.* **-er·u′** (-ə rōō′), **-ers** [Czech < MHG. *haller:* see HELLER²] a unit of currency in Czechoslovakia, equal to 1/100 koruna

Ha·lé·vy (á lā vē′), **Jacques** (zhäk) (born *Jacques François Fromental Élie Lévy*) 1799-1862; Fr. composer

half (haf, häf) *n., pl.* **halves** [ME. < OE. *healf,* part, half, akin to ON. *halfr,* Gr. *halb* < IE. *(s)kelep-,* lit., divided (cf. SCALP) < base *(s)kel-,* to cut, whence SKILL, HELM²] **1.** *a)* either of the two equal parts of something *b)* either of two approximately equal parts [the larger *half* of a divided pie] **2.** *a)* a half hour [*half* past one] ☆*b)* a half dollar ☆*3. a)* *Baseball* either of the two parts of an inning ☆*b)* *Basketball, Football,* etc. either of the two equal periods of the game, between which the players rest *c)* *Football same as* HALFBACK —*adj.* **1.** *a)* being either of the two equal parts *b)* being about a half of the amount, length, etc. [a *half* mask covered his eyes] **2.** incomplete; fragmentary; partial —*adv.* **1.** to an extent approximately or exactly fifty percent of the whole **2.** [Colloq.] to some extent; partly [to be *half* convinced] **3.** [Colloq.] by any means; at all: used with *not* [not *half* bad] —**by half** considerably; very much —**in half** into halves —**not the half of** only a small part of

half-and-half (haf′n haf′, häf′n häf′) *n.* something that is half of one thing and half of another; esp., ☆*a)* a mixture of equal parts of milk and cream *b)* [Chiefly Brit.] a mixture of equal parts of porter and ale, beer and stout, etc. —*adj.* combining two things equally —*adv.* in two equal parts

half·back (-bak′) *n.* **1.** *Football* either of two players whose position is behind the line of scrimmage together with the fullback and the quarterback **2.** any of various players directly behind the forward line, as in soccer

half-baked (-bākt′) *adj.* **1.** only partly baked **2.** not completely planned or thought out [a *half-baked* scheme] **3.** having or showing little intelligence and experience

half·beak (-bēk′) *n.* any of several small, long-bodied tropical sea fishes (family Hemiramphidae) somewhat like the gar, with a greatly extended lower jaw and a short upper jaw

half binding a style of book binding in which leather or other ornamental material is used to surround the spine and cover the corners

half-blood (-blud′) *n.* [based on the obsolete notion that the blood is the medium of heredity] **1.** a person related to another through one parent only ☆*2. same as* HALF-BREED ☆*3.* a half-blooded animal —*adj.* half-blooded

half blood 1. kinship through one parent only [sisters of the *half blood*] **2.** *same as* HALF-BLOODED

half-blood·ed (-blud′id) *adj.* **1.** having kinship through one parent only **2.** born of parents of different races **3.**

Animal Husbandry having a sire or dam of poor pedigree in contrast to that of the other parent

half boot a boot extending halfway up the lower leg

☆**half-breed** (-brēd′) *n.* a person whose parents are of different races; esp., an offspring of an American Indian and a white person —*adj.* half-blooded Sometimes regarded as a hostile or contemptuous term

half brother a brother through one parent only

half-caste (-kast′, -käst′) *n.* a person whose parents are of different races; esp., an offspring of one European parent and one Asiatic parent —*adj.* of, or having the position of, a half-caste

half-cell (-sel′) *n.* a cell consisting of an electrode immersed in a suitable electrolyte, designed to measure single electrode potentials

half cock the halfway position of the hammer of a firearm, when the trigger is locked and cannot be pulled

half-cocked (-käkt′) *adj.* having the hammer at half cock: said of a firearm —**go off half-cocked** 1. to go off too soon: said of a firearm 2. to speak or act thoughtlessly or too hastily: also **go off at half cock**

half crown a British coin equal to two shillings and six-pence (2 1/2 shillings)

☆**half dollar** a coin of the U.S. and Canada, worth 50 cents: the U.S. half dollar is made of silver and copper

☆**half eagle** a gold coin of the U.S., worth $5.00: it is no longer current

half-ev·er·green (-ev′ər grēn′) *adj.* having leaves which tend to remain green in mild winters, as myrtle

half gainer a fancy dive in which the diver springs from the board facing forward and does a back flip in the air so as to enter the water headfirst, facing the board

half·heart·ed (-här′tid) *adj.* with little enthusiasm, determination, interest, etc.; spiritless —**half′heart′ed·ly** *adv.*

half hitch a knot made by passing the end of the rope around the rope and then through the loop thus made: it is the simplest kind of hitch: see KNOT, illus.

half-hour (-our′) *n.* 1. half of an hour; thirty minutes 2. the point thirty minutes after any given hour —*adj.* 1. lasting for thirty minutes 2. occurring every thirty minutes —**half′-hour′ly** *adj., adv.*

half-length (-leŋkth′, -leŋth′) *adj.* 1. of half the full length 2. showing a person from the waist up: said of a portrait —*n.* a half-length portrait

half-life (-līf′) *n.* the period required for the disintegration of half of the atoms in a sample of some specific radioactive substance: also **half life**

half-mast (-mast′, -mäst′) *n.* the position of a flag lowered about halfway down its pole or staff as a sign of mourning or a signal of distress —*vt.* to hang (a flag) at half-mast

half-moon (-mōōn′) *n.* 1. the moon between new moon and full moon, at either the first quarter or last quarter, when only half its disk is clearly seen 2. anything shaped like a half-moon or crescent

half mourning 1. the second period of mourning, during which black clothes are lightened or replaced by gray, white, or purple 2. the clothes worn then

half nelson a wrestling hold in which one arm is placed under the opponent's arm from behind with the hand pressed against the back of his neck

half note *Music* a note (♩) having one half the duration of a whole note: see NOTE, illus.

half-pen·ny (hā′pə nē, hā′pə′nē) *n., pl.* **-pence** (hā′pəns), **-pen·nies** a British coin equal to half a penny —*adj.* 1. worth a halfpenny 2. trifling; insignificant

half pint 1. a liquid or dry measure equal to 1/4 quart ☆2. [Slang] a small person

half sister a sister through one parent only

half size any of a series of sizes in women's garments for short-waisted, mature figures

half slip a woman's slip without a top

half-sole (-sōl′) *vt.* **-soled′, -sol′ing** to repair (shoes or boots) by attaching new half soles

half sole a sole (of a shoe or boot) from the arch to the toe

half sovereign a former British gold coin equal to ten shillings

☆**half-staff** (-staf′, -stäf′) *n.* same as HALF-MAST

half step 1. *Mil.* a short marching step of fifteen inches (in double time, eighteen inches) 2. *Music* same as SEMITONE

half tide the condition or period halfway between flood tide and ebb tide

half-tim·bered (-tim′bərd) *adj. Archit.* made of a wooden framework having the spaces filled with plaster, brick, etc.

☆**half time** the rest period between halves of a football game, basketball game, etc.

half title 1. the title of a book, often abbreviated, appearing on the odd page preceding (or sometimes following) the main title page 2. the title of a subdivision of a book appearing on the odd page immediately preceding that division

half·tone (-tōn′) *n.* 1. *Art* a tone or shading between light and dark 2. *Music* same as SEMITONE 3. *Photoengraving a)* a technique of representing shadings by dots produced by photographing the object from behind a fine screen *b)* a photoengraving so made

☆**half-track** (-trak′) *n.* an army truck, armored vehicle, etc. with tractor treads instead of rear wheels, but with a pair of wheels in front

half-truth (-trōōth′) *n.* a statement or account containing only some of the facts, the rest often being left out with the intention of deceiving

half-vol·ley (-väl′ē) *vt., vi.* to return (a ball) with a half volley

half volley *Tennis, Cricket,* etc. a stroke made by hitting the ball just as it begins to bounce after striking the ground

half·way (-wā′) *adj.* 1. equally distant between two points, states, etc.; midway 2. incomplete; partial *[halfway measures]* —*adv.* 1. half the distance; to the midway point 2. incompletely; partially —**meet halfway** to be willing to compromise with

halfway house 1. a midway inn or stopping place on or as on a journey ☆2. a place where persons are aided in readjusting to society following a period of imprisonment, hospitalization, etc.

half-wit (-wit′) *n.* a stupid, silly, or imbecilic person; fool; dolt —**half′-wit′ted** *adj.*

hal·i·but (hal′ə bət, häl′-) *n., pl.* **-but, -buts:** see PLURAL, II, D, 2 [ME. *halybutte* < *hali,* holy + *butt,* a flounder (so called because eaten on holidays): see HOLY + BUTT[1]] any of a number of large, edible flatfish (subfamily Hippoglossinae) found in northern seas, esp. the **Atlantic halibut** (*Hippoglossus hippoglossus*): they sometimes weigh hundreds of pounds

Hal·i·car·nas·sus (hal′ə kär nas′əs) ancient city in SW Asia Minor, on the Aegean: site of the MAUSOLEUM

hal·ide (hal′īd, hā′līd) *n.* [HAL(OGEN) + -IDE] *Chem.* a compound of a halogen with another element or a radical —*adj.* same as HALOID

hal·i·dom (hal′i dəm) *n.* [ME. < OE. *haligdom:* see HOLY & -DOM] [Archaic] 1. a holy place 2. a thing considered holy; sacred relic Also **hal′i·dome′** (-dōm′)

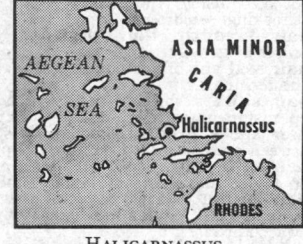

HALICARNASSUS

Hal·i·fax (hal′ə faks′) [after the 2d Earl of *Halifax* (1716–71)] 1. capital of Nova Scotia, Canada; seaport on the Atlantic: pop. 87,000 2. city in Yorkshire, N England: pop. 95,000

hal·ite (hal′īt, hā′līt) *n.* [< Gr. *hals,* SALT + -ITE[1]] native sodium chloride; rock salt

☆**hal·i·to·sis** (hal′ə tō′sis) *n.* [ModL. < L. *halitus,* breath (< *halare,* to breathe) + -OSIS] bad-smelling breath

hall (hôl) *n.* [ME. *halle* < OE. *heall* (akin to G. *halle*), lit., that which is covered < base of *helan,* to cover < IE. base *kel-,* to cover, whence L. *celare,* to conceal & HELL] 1. orig., *a)* the great central room in the dwelling of a king or chieftain, where banquets, games, etc. were held *b)* the dwelling itself 2. the main dwelling on the estate of a baron, squire, etc. 3. [*sometimes* H-] a building containing public offices or the headquarters of an organization, for transacting business, holding meetings, etc. 4. a large public or semipublic room or auditorium for gatherings, entertainments, exhibits, etc. 5. [*sometimes* H-] a college dormitory, classroom building, eating center, etc. 6. a passageway or room between the entrance and the interior of a building; vestibule, foyer, or lobby 7. a passageway, corridor, or area onto which rooms open

Hall (hôl) 1. **Charles Martin,** 1863–1914; U.S. chemist: discovered electrolytic process for reducing aluminum from bauxite 2. **G(ranville) Stanley,** 1844–1924; U.S. psychologist & educator

hal·lah (khä′lə, hä′-) *n.* [Heb. *hallāh*] the traditional loaf of rich white bread, usually braided or twisted, eaten by Jews on the Sabbath and holidays

Hal·lam (hal′əm), **Henry** 1777–1859; Eng. historian

☆**hall bedroom** a small bedroom off a corridor; esp., a small bedroom formed by partitioning off the end of an upstairs corridor

Hal·le (häl′ə; *E.* hal′ē) city in SC East Germany: pop. 276,000

hal·lel (hä lāl′, häl′el) *n.* [Heb. *hallēl,* praise] a part of the Jewish religious services consisting of *Psalms* 113 to 118 inclusive, recited or sung on certain festivals

hal·le·lu·jah, hal·le·lu·iah (hal′ə lōō′yə) *interj.* [LL. (Ec.) *alleluja* < Gr.(Ec.) *hallēlouia* < Heb. < *hallelū,* praise (imperative) + *yāh,* Jehovah] praise (ye) the Lord! —*n.* an exclamation, hymn, or song of praise to God

Hal·ley's comet (hal′ēz) a famous comet, last seen in 1910, whose periodic reappearance (c. 75 years) was predicted by Edmund Halley (1656–1742), Eng. astronomer

hal·liard (hal′yərd) *n. same as* HALYARD

hall·mark (hôl′märk′) *n.* 1. the official mark stamped on gold and silver articles at Goldsmiths' Hall in London or at British government assay offices as a guarantee of genuineness 2. any mark or symbol of genuineness or high quality —*vt.* to put a hallmark on

hal·lo, hal·loa (hə lō′) *interj., n., vi., vt. same as* HALLOO

Hall of Fame a memorial in New York City containing busts and tablets honoring celebrated Americans

hal·loo (hə lōō′) *vi., vt.* **-looed′, -loo′ing** [ME. *halowen* <

halou, interj.: prob. also < OFr. *halloer,* to follow after with much noise] **1.** to shout or call out in order to attract the attention of (a person) **2.** to urge on (hounds) by shouting or calling out "halloo" **3.** to shout or yell, as in greeting or surprise —*interj., n.* a shout or call, esp. one to attract a person's attention or to urge on hounds in hunting

hal·low[1] (hal'ō) *vt.* [ME. *halowen* < OE. *halgian* (used for L. *sanctificare*) < Gmc. base of *halig* (see HOLY): akin to G. *heiligen*] **1.** to make holy or sacred; sanctify; consecrate **2.** to regard as holy; honor as sacred; venerate —*SYN.* see DEVOTE

hal·low[2] (hə lō', hal'ō) *vi., vt., interj., n.* same as HALLOO

hal·lowed (hal'ōd; *in poetry or liturgy, often* hal'ə wid) *adj.* [pp. of HALLOW[1]] **1.** made holy or sacred **2.** honored as holy; venerated —*SYN.* see HOLY

Hal·low·een, Hal·low·e'en (hal'ə wēn', häl'-) *n.* [contr. < *all hallow even; hallow* < OE. *halga,* definite form of *halig* (see HOLY) in sense "holy person, hence saint"] the evening of October 31, which is followed by All Saints' Day, or Allhallows: Halloween is now generally celebrated with fun-making and masquerading: see TRICK OR TREAT

Hal·low·mas (hal'ō məs, -mas') *n.* [< *all hallow mass:* cf. prec.] *former name for* ALL SAINTS' DAY

Hall·statt (hôl'stat', häl'shtät') *adj.* [from archaeological findings at *Hallstatt,* near Salzburg, Austria] designating or of an Iron Age culture (c. 700–400 B.C.) in C Europe, characterized by swords of bronze or iron with winged metal terminals and by the domestication of horses

☆**hall tree** a clothes tree, esp. one in an entrance hall

hal·lu·ci·nate (hə lōō'sə nāt') *vt.* **-nat'ed, -nat'ing** [< L. *hallucinatus,* pp. of *hallucinari,* to wander mentally, rave < Gr. *aluein,* to be confused + ending after L. *vaticinari,* to prophesy, rant] to cause to have hallucinations —*vi.* to have hallucinations

hal·lu·ci·na·tion (hə lōō'sə nā'shən) *n.* [L. *hallucinatio* < *hallucinari:* see prec.] **1.** the apparent perception of sights, sounds, etc. that are not actually present: it may occur in certain mental disorders **2.** the imaginary object apparently seen, heard, etc. —*SYN.* see DELUSION —**hal·lu·ci·na'tive** *adj.*

hal·lu·ci·na·to·ry (hə lōō'sə nə tôr'ē) *adj.* **1.** of or characterized by hallucination **2.** producing hallucination

hal·lu·ci·no·gen (hə lōō'sə nə jen, hal'yōō sin'ə jen) *n.* [< HALLUCIN(ATION) + -o- + -GEN] a drug or other substance that produces hallucinations —**hal·lu'ci·no·gen'ic** *adj.*

hal·lu·ci·no·sis (hə lōō'sə nō'sis) *n.* [ModL. < L. *hallucinatio* + -OSIS] a mental disorder characterized by hallucinations

hal·lux (hal'əks) *n., pl.* **-lu·ces** (-yoo sēz') [ModL., altered < L. *hallex, allex,* great toe] the first toe on either of the hind legs of a terrestrial vertebrate; in man, the great toe

☆**hall·way** (hôl'wā') *n.* **1.** a passageway or room between the entrance and the interior of a building; vestibule **2.** a passageway; corridor; hall

halm (hôm) *n. same as* HAULM

Hal·ma·he·ra (häl'mə her'ə) largest of the Molucca Islands, Indonesia, east of Celebes: 6,870 sq. mi.

ha·lo (hā'lō) *n., pl.* **-los, -loes** [L. *halos* (gen. & acc. *halo*) < Gr. *halōs,* circular threshing floor, round disk of the sun or moon, hence halo around the sun or moon < *halein,* to grind] **1.** a ring of light that seems to encircle the sun, moon, or other luminous body: it results from the refraction of light through ice particles in the atmosphere **2.** a symbolic ring or disk of light shown around the head of a saint, etc., as in pictures; nimbus: often used as a symbol of virtue or innocence **3.** the splendor or glory with which a famed, revered, or idealized person or thing is invested —*vt.* **-loed, -lo·ing** to encircle with a halo

hal·o- (hal'ō, -ə; hā'lō) [< Gr. *hals* (gen. *halos*), SALT, hence sea] *a combining form meaning:* **1.** of the sea [*halobiont*] **2.** having to do with a salt [*halophyte*] **3.** having to do with a halogen [*haloid*]

hal·o·bi·ont (hal'ō bī'änt) *n.* [HALO- + BIONT] an organism living in a saline environment, as in the sea

hal·o·gen (hal'ə jən) *n.* [HALO- + -GEN] any of the five very active, nonmetallic chemical elements, fluorine, chlorine, bromine, astatine, and iodine —**ha·log·e·nous** (hə läj'ə nəs) *adj.*

hal·o·ge·nate (hal'ə jə nāt') *vt.* **-nat'ed, -nat'ing 1.** to treat with a halogen or with a hydrogen halogen **2.** to introduce a halogen, usually chlorine or bromine, into (a compound) —**hal'o·ge·na'tion** *n.*

hal·o·ge·ton (hal'ə jə tän', hə läj'ə tän') *n.* [ModL. < HALO- + Gr. *geitōn,* neighbor] a poisonous Asiatic weed (*Halogeton glomeratus*) of the goosefoot family, with fleshy cylindrical leaves and minute papery flowers, becoming widespread in the W U.S.

hal·oid (hal'oid, hā'loid) *adj.* [HAL(O)- + -OID] of or like a binary compound of a halogen with another element or radical —*n. same as* HALIDE

hal·o·phile (hal'ə fil') *n.* [HALO- + -PHILE] an organism living in a salty environment —**hal'o·phil'ic** (-fil'ik), **ha·loph·i·lous** (hə läf'ə ləs) *adj.*

hal·o·phyte (-fīt') *n.* [HALO- + -PHYTE] a plant that can grow in salty or alkaline soil

hal·o·thane (-thān') *n.* [HALO- + (E)TH(ER) + -ANE] a nonexplosive liquid, $CF_3CHBrCl$, whose vapor is inhaled to produce general anesthesia

Hals (häls), **Frans** (fräns) 1580?–1666; Du. painter

Hal·sey (hôl'zē), **William Frederick** 1882–1959; U.S. admiral in World War II

Häl·sing·borg (hel'siŋ bôr'y') seaport in SW Sweden, on the Öresund, opposite Helsingør, Denmark: pop. 79,000

halt[1] (hôlt) *n.* [orig. in phr. *to make halt,* transl. partly from Fr. *faire halte* and partly from G. *halt machen* < imper. of *halten* (see HOLD[1])] a stop, esp. a temporary one, as in marching; pause or discontinuance —*vi., vt.* **1.** to come or bring to a halt; stop, esp. temporarily —☆**call a halt** to order a stop

halt[2] (hôlt) *vi.* [ME. *halten* < OE. *healtian* < *healt* (see the *adj.*), akin to MHG. *halzen*] **1.** [Archaic] to walk with a crippled gait; limp; hobble **2.** to be uncertain; waver; hesitate [*to halt in one's speech*] **3.** to have defects; esp., *a*) to have a faulty meter: said of verse *b*) to be illogical: said of argument —*adj.* [ME. *halte* < OE. *healt, halt,* akin to MHG. *halz* < IE. base **kel-,* to strike, hew (whence L. *calamitas*): basic sense "lamed by wounding"] limping; crippled; lame —*n.* [Archaic] a halting or limping; lameness —**the halt** those who are lame; cripples

hal·ter[1] (hôl'tər) *n.* [ME. < OE. *hælftre* (akin to G. *halfter*) < base of *helfe* (see HELVE): basic sense "that by which something is held"] **1.** *a*) a rope, cord, strap, etc., usually with a headstall, for tying or leading an animal *b*) a bitless headstall, with or without a lead rope **2.** *a*) a rope for hanging a person; hangman's noose *b*) execution by hanging **3.** a garment for covering the breast, held up by a cord or loop around the neck, and worn by women and girls to bare the shoulders and back —*vt.* **1.** to put a halter on (an animal); tie with a halter **2.** to hang (a person)

HALTER (sense 1*b*)

hal·ter[2] (hôl'tər, hal') *n., pl.* **hal·ter·es** (-tir'ēz) [ModL. < L., lead weights < Gr. *haltēr,* weight held (to give impetus) in leaping < *hallesthai,* to leap < IE. base **sel-,* whence L. *salire*] either of a pair of knobbed, threadlike, modified second wings serving as balancing organs in dipteran insects: also **hal'tere** (-tir)

ha·lutz (khä lōōts', hä) *n., pl.* **ha'lutz·im'** (-lōōt sēm') [Heb. *haluts,* warrior] a Jewish pioneer in the agricultural settlements of modern Israel

hal·vah, hal·va (häl vä') *n.* [Turk. *helwa* < Ar. *halwa*] a Turkish confection consisting of a paste made of ground sesame seeds and nuts mixed with honey, etc.

halve (hav, häv) *vt.* **halved, halv'ing** [ME. *halven* < *half,* HALF] **1.** to divide into two equal parts **2.** to share equally (*with* someone) [*to halve* one's winnings with another] **3.** to reduce by fifty percent; reduce to half **4.** *Carpentry* to fit together (two pieces of wood) by cutting each to half its thickness at its place of joining **5.** *Golf* to play (a hole, match, etc.) in the same number of strokes as one's opponent

halves (havz, hävz) *n. pl. of* HALF —**by halves 1.** halfway; imperfectly **2.** halfheartedly —**go halves** to share expenses, etc. equally

hal·yard (hal'yərd) *n.* [altered (after YARD[1]) < ME. *halier* < *halien* (see HALE[2])] a rope or tackle for raising or lowering a flag, sail, etc.

Ham (ham) *Bible* Noah's second son: Gen. 6:10

ham (ham) *n.* [ME. *hamme* < OE. *hamm,* akin to G. dial. *hamme* < IE. base **konemo-,* shin bone (whence Gr. *knēmē*): sense 5 & 6 influenced by AM(ATEUR)] **1.** the part of the leg behind the knee **2.** *a*) the back of the thigh *b*) the thigh and the buttock together **3.** the hock or hind leg of a four-legged animal **4.** the upper part of a hog's hind leg, or meat from this, salted, dried, smoked, etc. ☆**5.** [Colloq.] an amateur radio operator ☆**6.** [< *hamfatter,* said to be so named from former use of ham fat to remove makeup] [Slang] an incompetent actor or performer, esp. one who overacts —*vi., vt.* **hammed, ham'ming** [Slang] to act with exaggeration; overact: sometimes in the phrase **ham it up**

Ha·ma, Ha·mah (hä'mä) city in W Syria: pop. 156,000: called, in the Bible, **Ha·math** (hā'math)

Ha·ma·dan (ham'ə dan') city in W Iran: pop. 115,000

ham·a·dry·ad (ham'ə drī'əd, -ad) *n.* [L. *Hamadryas* < Gr. *Hamadryas* < *hama,* together with + *dryas,* DRYAD] **1.** [also H-] *Gr. Myth.* a dryad; wood nymph whose life was bound up with that of the tree in which she lived **2.** same as KING COBRA **3.** an Arabian and North African baboon (*Comopithecus hamadryas*) with an ashy-gray fur

ha·mal (hə mäl', -môl') *n.* [Ar. *hammāl* < *hamala,* to carry] in the Middle East, a porter: also **ha·maul'** (-môl')

Ha·ma·ma·tsu (hä'mä mä'tsōō) city on the SC coast of Honshu, Japan: pop. 393,000

Ha·man (hā'mən) *Bible* a Persian official who sought the destruction of the Jews and was hanged when his plot was exposed to Ahasuerus by Esther: Esth. 7

Ham·ble·to·ni·an (ham′b'l tō′nē ən) *n.* [name of a famous American stallion (1849–76)] **1.** any of a breed of American trotting horses **2.** an annual harness race for three-year-old trotters

Ham·burg (ham′bərg; *G.* häm′boorkh) seaport & state in N West Germany, on the Elbe River: 288 sq. mi.; pop. 1,854,000 —*n.* a European variety of small chicken

☆**ham·burg·er** (ham′bûr′gər) *n.* [earlier *Hamburg steak*, after HAMBURG] **1.** beef ground and, usually, seasoned **2.** a fried, broiled, or baked patty of such meat **3.** a sandwich made with such a patty, usually in a round bun Also **ham′burg**

Ham·den (ham′dən) [after J. *Hampden* (1594–1643), Puritan leader] suburb of New Haven, in S Conn.: pop. 49,000

hame[1] (hām) *n.* [ME. < MDu., horse collar: for IE. base see HEM[1]] either of the two rigid pieces along the sides of a horse's collar, to which the traces are attached

hame[2] (hām) *n.* [Scot.] home

Ham·e·lin (ham′ə lin) city in N West Germany: pop. 50,000: cf. PIED PIPER: Ger. name **Ha·meln** (hä′məln)

Ha·mil·car Bar·ca (hə mil′kär bär′kə; ham′l kär′) 270?–228? B.C.; Carthaginian general: father of HANNIBAL

Ham·il·ton (ham′əl t'n) **1.** [after George *Hamilton*, local farmer (c. 1813)] city & port in SE Ontario, Canada, at the W end of Lake Ontario: pop. 298,000 **2.** [after Alexander HAMILTON] city in SW Ohio, near Cincinnati: pop. 68,000 **3.** city in N North Island, New Zealand: pop. 63,000 **4.** city in Lanarkshire, SC Scotland, on the Clyde River: pop. 46,000 **5.** capital of Bermuda, on the main island: pop. 2,800 **6.** river in S Labrador, flowing east to **Hamilton Inlet**, an arm of the Atlantic: 208 mi. (with upper course, 560 mi.)

Ham·il·ton (ham′əl t'n) **1. Alexander,** 1757–1804; Am. statesman; 1st secretary of the U.S. treasury (1789–95) **2. Lady Emma,** (born *Emma Lyon*) 1765?–1815; mistress of Lord Nelson

Ham·il·to·ni·an (ham′əl tō′nē ən) *adj.* of or characteristic of Alexander Hamilton or his federalist principles —*n.* a follower of Alexander Hamilton

Ham·ite (ham′īt) *n.* **1.** a person regarded as descended from Ham **2.** a member of any of several usually dark-skinned, Caucasoid peoples native to N and E Africa, including the Egyptians, Berbers, etc.

Ham·it·ic (ha mit′ik, ha-) *adj.* **1.** of Ham or the Hamites **2.** designating or of a group of African languages, including the Egyptian, Berber, and Cushitic subfamilies of the Afro-Asiatic family of languages

Ham·i·to-Se·mit·ic (ham′ə tō sə mit′ik) *adj.* same as AFRO-ASIATIC

Ham·let (ham′lit) **1.** a famous tragedy by Shakespeare (c. 1602) **2.** the hero of this play, a Danish prince who avenges the murder of his father, the king, by killing his uncle Claudius, the murderer

ham·let (ham′lit) *n.* [ME. *hamelet* < OFr. (Anglo-Fr. *hamelete*), dim. of *hamel* (Fr. *hameau*), itself dim. of LowG *hamm*, enclosed area, akin to OE. *hamm*: for IE. base see HEM[1]] a very small village

Ham·lin (ham′lin), **Hannibal** 1809–91; vice president of the U.S. (1861–65)

Ham·mar·skjöld (häm′är shüld′), **Dag (Hjalmar Agne Carl)** (däg) 1905–61; Swed. statesman; secretary-general of the United Nations (1953–61)

ham·mer (ham′ər) *n.* [ME. *hamer* < OE. *hamor*, akin to G. *hammer*, ON. *hamarr*, crag, cliff < IE. *komor-*, stone hammer < base *ak-m- < ak-*, sharp, sharp stone] **1.** a tool for pounding, usually consisting of a metal head fastened across one end of a handle: one end of the head may be a pronged claw for pulling nails **2.** a thing like this tool in shape or use; specif., *a)* the mechanism that strikes the firing pin or percussion cap in a firearm *b)* a device for striking a bell, gong, metal bar, etc. to make a sound *c)* any of the felt-covered mallets that strike against the strings of a piano *d)* a power tool fitted with a metal block or oscillating chisel, for pounding metal into shape, breaking up paved surfaces, etc. **3.** the malleus, one of the bones of the middle ear: see EAR, illus. **4.** an auctioneer's gavel **5.** a metal ball weighing usually sixteen pounds, hung from a wire handle and thrown for distance in a track and field competition —*vt.* **1.** to strike repeatedly with or as with a hammer **2.** to make or fasten with a hammer **3.** to drive, force, or shape with or as with hammer blows [to *hammer* an idea into someone's head] —*vi.* **1.** to strike repeated blows with or as with a hammer —**hammer and tongs** [with reference to a blacksmith's work] with all one's might; very vigorously —**hammer (away) at 1.** to work continuously or energetically at **2.** to keep emphasizing or talking about —**hammer out 1.** to shape, construct, or produce by hammer-

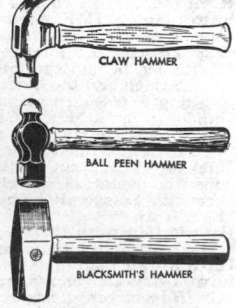

CLAW HAMMER

BALL PEEN HAMMER

BLACKSMITH'S HAMMER

TYPES OF HAMMER

ing **2.** to make flat by hammering **3.** to take out by or as by hammering **4.** to develop or work out by careful thought or repeated effort —**under the hammer** [cf. *n.* 4] for sale at auction —**ham′mer·er** *n.*

hammer and sickle the emblem of Communist parties in some countries, consisting of a sickle (symbolizing peasants) placed across a hammer (symbolizing workers)

ham·mered (ham′ərd) *adj.* shaped or marked by hammer blows: said of metalwork

Ham·mer·fest (häm′ər fest′) seaport on an island in N Norway: northernmost city in Europe: pop. 4,000

ham·mer·head (ham′ər hed′) *n.* **1.** the head of a hammer **2.** any of several medium-sized sharks (genus *Sphyrna*) that have a mallet-shaped head with an eye near the center of each end **3.** a small sea fish (*Catostomus nigricans*) of the sucker family **4.** any of several African bats (genus *Hypsignathus*) that live on fruit **5.** a large, brownish, crested, African bird (*Scopus umbretta*) related to the herons and storks

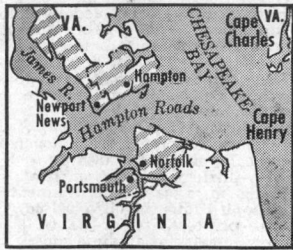

HAMMERHEAD SHARK (to 15 ft. long)

ham·mer·less (-lis) *adj.* having the hammer or other striking device enclosed, as some firearms

ham·mer·lock (-läk′) *n.* a wrestling hold in which one arm of the opponent is twisted upward behind his back

Ham·mer·smith (ham′ər smith′) metropolitan borough of London: pop. 108,000

Ham·mer·stein II (ham′ər stīn′), **Oscar** 1895–1960; U.S. librettist & lyricist of musical comedies

ham·mer·toe (-tō′) *n.* **1.** a condition in which the first joint of a toe is permanently bent downward, resulting in a clawlike deformity **2.** such a toe

ham·mock[1] (ham′ək) *n.* [Sp. *hamaca* of Arawakan origin] a length of netting, canvas, etc. swung from ropes at both ends and used as a bed or couch

ham·mock[2] (ham′ək) *n.* [var. of HUMMOCK] ☆ [Southern] a raised piece of very fertile land with hardwood trees growing on it

Ham·mond (ham′ənd) [after G. H. *Hammond*, local meat-packer] city in NW Ind., near Chicago: pop. 108,000: see GARY

Ham·mu·ra·bi (hä′moo rä′bē, ham′ə-) fl. 18th cent. B.C.; king of Babylon: a famous code of laws is attributed to him

ham·my (ham′ē) *adj.* **-mi·er, -mi·est** ☆[Slang] like or characteristic of a ham (actor); overacting

Hamp·den (hamp′dən, ham′-) **1. John,** 1594–1643; Eng. statesman & Parliamentarian **2. Walter,** (born *Walter Hampden Dougherty*) 1879–1955; U.S. actor

ham·per[1] (ham′pər) *vt.* [northern ME. *hampren*, akin to *hamelian*, to maim, with freq. *-er* & intrusive *-p-* (cf. Brit. dial. *hamble*) < IE. base *kem-*, to press together, whence HEM[1]] to keep from moving or acting freely; hinder; impede; encumber —*n. Naut.* necessary but encumbering articles, as a ship's rigging

SYN.—**hamper** implies an impeding or encumbering so as to keep from moving or acting freely [*hampered* by a heavy load, by a lack of cooperation]; **fetter, shackle,** and **manacle** all imply a checking or restraining so that freedom of movement or progress is curtailed, **fetter,** as if by tying the feet with chains, **shackle,** as if by confining the wrists, ankles, etc. with metal bands, and **manacle,** as if by binding the wrists with handcuffs [a mind *fettered* by superstition, *shackled* to a jealous husband, a *manacled* press]

ham·per[2] (ham′pər) *n.* [var. of HANAPER] a large basket, usually with a cover

Hamp·shire (hamp′shir, ham′-) **1.** county on the S coast of England: 1,503 sq. mi.; pop. 1,406,000; county seat, Winchester: official name, SOUTHAMPTON **2.** formerly, a county of England including Hampshire (sense 1) & the Isle of Wight: name still sometimes so applied

Hamp·stead (-stid, -sted) metropolitan borough of London: pop. 98,000

Hamp·ton (-tən) [after a town in England] seaport in SE Va., on Hampton Roads: pop. 121,000

Hamp·ton (-tən), **Wade** 1818–1902; U.S. politician & Confederate general

Hampton Roads [see HAMPTON & ROAD (sense 4)] channel & harbor in SE Va., linking the James River estuary with Chesapeake Bay

ham·ster (ham′stər) *n.* [G. < OHG. *hamustro*, prob. < OSlav. *chomēstorū* < or akin to Iran. *hamaēstar*, one who knocks down] any of several ratlike, burrowing animals of Europe and Asia, with large cheek pouches in which they carry grain: one variety (*Mesocricetus auratus*) is used, like the guinea pig, in scientific experiments, or is often kept as a pet

HAMPTON ROADS

ham·string (ham′strin′) *n.* **1.** one of the tendons at the

back of the human knee **2.** the great tendon at the back of the hock in a four-legged animal —*vt.* **-strung′, -string′ing 1.** to disable by cutting a hamstring **2.** to lessen or destroy the power or effectiveness of

Ham·sun (häm′sŏŏn; *E.* ham′sən), **Knut** (knŏŏt) 1859–1952; Norw. novelist

ham·u·lus (ham′yŏŏ ləs) *n., pl.* **-u·li′** (-lī′) [ModL. < L., dim. of *hamus*, a hook] a small hook or hook-shaped part, as at the ends of the barbicels of feathers, at the ends of some bones, etc.

Han[1] (hän) river in C China, flowing from Shensi province southeast into the Yangtze at Wuhan: c. 900 mi.

Han[2] (hän) a Chinese dynasty (202 B.C.–220 A.D.), characterized by the introduction of Buddhism, a renewal of the arts, and territorial expansion —*n.* an ethnic group in China constituting the majority of the Chinese and distinguished from the Manchus, Mongols, etc.

han·a·per (han′ə pər) *n.* [ME. *haniper* < OFr. *hanapier* < *hanap*, a cup < Frank. **hnap*, a beaker (akin to G. *napf*)] a small wicker container formerly used to hold official papers

Han Cities *see* WUHAN

Han·cock (han′käk) **1. John,** 1737–93; Am. statesman; president of the Continental Congress (1775–77) & 1st signer of the Declaration of Independence: see also JOHN HANCOCK **2. Win·field Scott** (win′fēld), 1824–86; Union general in the Civil War

hand (hand) *n.* [ME. < OE., akin to Goth. *handu* < ? var. of *hinthan*, to seize (hence, basic sense "grasper")] **I. 1.** the part of the human arm below the wrist, including the palm, fingers, and thumb, used for grasping or gripping **2.** a corresponding part in some animals; specif., *a)* any of the four feet in apes, monkeys, etc., used like human hands for grasping and gripping *b)* the end part of the forelimb in many of the higher vertebrates *c)* the pincer-like claw of a crustacean **3.** a side, direction, or position indicated by one hand or the other [at one's right *hand*] **II.** *denoting some function or activity of the hand* **1.** the hand as an instrument for making or producing **2.** the hand as a symbol of its grasping or gripping function; specif., *a)* possession [the documents now in his *hands*] *b)* control; power; authority [to strengthen one's *hand*] *c)* care; charge; supervision [in the *hands* of one's lawyer] *d)* agency; influence [to see someone's *hand* in a matter] *e)* an active part; share [take a *hand* in the work] **3.** the hand as a symbol of promise; specif., *a)* a clasp or handshake as a pledge of agreement, friendship, etc. *b)* a promise to marry [to ask for a girl's *hand*] **III.** *denoting the manner in which the hand is used* **1.** skill; ability; dexterity [work that shows a master's *hand*] **2.** manner of doing something [to play the piano with a light *hand*] **IV.** *denoting something produced by the hand* **1.** *a)* handwriting *b)* a signature **2.** a clapping of hands; applause [to receive a big *hand* for one's performance] **3.** assistance; aid; help [to lend a *hand*] **V.** *denoting a person as producing or transmitting with the hands* **1.** a person whose chief work is with his hands; esp., one of a staff or crew, as a sailor, farm laborer, etc. **2.** a person regarded as having some special skill or characteristic [quite a *hand* at sewing] **3.** a person (or sometimes thing) from or through which something comes; source [essays by several *hands*]: often used with an ordinal number [to get a story at second *hand*] **VI.** *denoting something like a hand* **1.** a conventional drawing of a hand (☛) used on signposts, etc. **2.** an indicator; pointer [the *hands* of a clock] **3.** the breadth of the human palm, used as a unit of measurement, esp. for the height of horses: now usually taken to be 4 inches **4.** *Commerce* a banana cluster **VII.** *denoting something held in the hand* **1.** *Card Games a)* the cards held by a player at any one time *b)* the conventional number of cards dealt to each player *c)* a player *d)* a round of play ☆**2.** a small tied bundle, esp. of tobacco leaves **3.** the way cloth held in the hand feels —*adj.* **1.** of or for the hand or hands **2.** made by hand **3.** controlled by hand; manual —*vt.* **1.** to pass or give with or as with the hand; transfer; transmit; deliver **2.** to give; provide with [it *handed* them a laugh] **3.** to help, conduct, steady, etc. by means of the hand [to *hand* a lady into her car] **4.** *Naut.* to make (a sail) snug; furl —**(at) first hand** from the original source; directly —**at hand 1.** near; close by **2.** immediately available —**(at) second hand 1.** not from the original source; indirectly **2.** not new; previously used —**at the hand (or hands) of** through the action of —**by hand** not by machines but with the hands —**change hands** to pass from one owner to another —**eat out of one's hand** to be completely dominated by or devoted to one —**force one's hand** [orig., a whist term] to force one to act, or declare his intentions, before he is ready —**from hand to hand** from one person's possession to another's —**from hand to mouth** with just enough for immediate needs and nothing left over for the future —**hand and foot 1.** so that the hands and feet cannot move [bound *hand and foot*] **2.** constantly and diligently [to wait on someone *hand and foot*] —**hand down 1.** to give as an inheritance; bequeath ☆**2.** to announce or deliver (a verdict, etc.)

—**hand in** to give; submit —**hand in** (or **and**) **glove** in intimate association; in close agreement or cooperation —**hand in hand 1.** holding one another's hand **2.** together; in cooperation or correlation —☆**hand it to** [Slang] to give deserved credit to —**hand on** to pass along; transmit —**hand out** to distribute; deal out —**hand over** to give up; deliver —**hand over fist** [Colloq.] easily and in large amounts —**hands down** without effort; easily —**hands off!** don't touch! don't interfere! —**hands up!** ☆raise your hands over your head!: an order given by a person pointing a gun, etc. —**hand to hand** at close quarters: said of fighting —**have one's hands full** to be extremely busy; be doing as much as one can —**hold hands** to hold each other's hand, esp. in affection —**in hand 1.** in order or control **2.** in possession **3.** being worked on; in process —**join hands 1.** to become associates; enter into partnership **2.** to become husband and wife —**keep one's hand in** to keep in practice in order to retain one's skill —**lay hands on 1.** to attack, injure, or punish physically **2.** to get hold of; seize; take **3.** to touch with the hands ceremonially in blessing, ordaining, confirming, etc. —**not lift a hand** to do nothing; not even try —**off one's hands** no longer in one's care; out of one's responsibility —**on every hand** on all sides; in all directions —**on hand 1.** near ☆**2.** available or ready ☆**3.** present —**on one's hands** in one's care; being one's responsibility —**on the one hand** from one point of view —**on the other hand** from the opposed point of view —**out of hand 1.** out of control **2.** immediately; without preliminaries or delay **3.** over and done with —**show** (or **tip**) **one's hand** [orig. with reference to card playing] to disclose one's intentions —**take in hand 1.** to take control of or responsibility for **2.** to take up; handle; treat **3.** to try; attempt —**throw up one's hands** to give up in despair —**to hand 1.** near; accessible **2.** in one's possession —**turn** (or **put**) **one's hand to** to undertake; work at —**wash one's hands of** to refuse to go on with or take responsibility for —**with a heavy hand 1.** in a heavy manner; without delicacy or grace **2.** with severity or sternness —**with a high hand** with arrogance; in an arbitrary or dictatorial manner —**with clean hands** without guilt; as an innocent person

hand- (hand; *also often* han) *an initial combining form meaning* of, with, by, or for a hand or hands [*handclasp, handcuff*]

Hand (hand), (**Billings**) **Lear·ned** (lur′nid) 1872–1961; U.S. jurist

hand ax (or **axe**) a stone tool of the paleolithic period rounded at one end for grasping and flaked to make a point at the other end and sharp edges at the sides

hand·bag (hand′bag′) *n.* **1.** a small container for money, toilet articles, keys, etc., carried by women; purse **2.** a small suitcase or valise

hand·ball (-bôl′) *n.* **1.** a game in which a small ball is batted against a wall or walls with the hand, alternately by opposing teams of one or two players **2.** the small rubber ball used in this game

hand·bar·row (-bar′ō) *n.* a frame carried by two people, each holding a pair of handles attached at either end

hand·bill (-bil′) *n.* a small printed notice, advertisement, etc. to be passed out by hand

hand-blown (-blōn′) *adj.* shaped individually by a glass-blower: said of glassware

hand·book (-book′) *n.* [OE. *handboc*, after L. *manuale* (cf. MANUAL): modern senses after G. *handbuch*] **1.** a compact reference book on some subject; manual of facts or instructions **2.** *same as* GUIDEBOOK ☆**3.** a book in which bets are recorded, as on horse races

hand·breadth (-bredth′, -bretth′) *n.* the breadth of the human palm: see HAND (*n.* VI, 3)

☆**hand·car** (-kär′) *n.* a small, open car, orig. hand-powered, used on railroads to transport workers, etc.

hand·cart (-kärt′) *n.* a small cart, often with only two wheels, pulled or pushed by hand

hand·clasp (-klasp′, -kläsp′) *n.* a clasping of each other's hand in greeting, farewell, etc.

hand·craft (-kraft′, -kräft′) *n. same as* HANDICRAFT —*vt.* to make by hand with craftsmanship —**hand′craft′ed** *adj.*

hand·cuff (-kuf′) *n.* either of a pair of connected metal rings that can be locked about the wrists, as in restraining a prisoner or fastening him to a policeman: *usually used in pl.* —*vt.* **1.** to put handcuffs on; manacle **2.** to check or hinder the activities of

hand·ed (han′did) *adj.* **1.** having, or for use by one having, a specified handedness [*right-handed*] **2.** having or using a specified number of hands [*two-handed*] **3.** involving (a specified number of) players [*three-handed* pinochle]

hand·ed·ness (-nis) *n.* ability in using one hand more skillfully than, and in preference to, the other

Han·del (han′d'l), **George Frederick** (born *Georg Friedrich Händel*) 1685–1759; Eng. composer, born in Germany

hand·fast (hand′fast′, -fäst′) *n.* [< the *v.*] [Obs.] **1.** a firm hold, as with the hands **2.** a contract, esp. of marriage or betrothal, confirmed by a handclasp —*adj.* **1.** [Obs.] betrothed or married **2.** [Rare] tightfisted —*vt.* [ME.

hand·fast·en < OE. *handfæstan*, to make fast, ratify & < ON. *handfesta:* see HAND & FASTEN] [Obs.] to betroth or marry by joining hands

hand·fast·ing (-fas'tiŋ, -fäs'tiŋ) *n.* [OE. *handfæstunge:* see prec.] [Archaic] 1. a betrothal 2. a form of irregular or trial marriage ceremonialized by a joining of hands

hand-feed (-fēd') *vt.* **-fed', -feed'ing** to feed by hand

hand·ful (-fool') *n., pl.* **-fuls'** [ME. < OE. *handfull*] 1. as much or as many as the hand will hold 2. a relatively small number or amount [a mere *handful* of people] 3. [Colloq.] as much as one is able to manage; someone or something hard to manage

hand glass 1. a magnifying glass for reading small print, etc. 2. a small mirror with a handle

hand grenade a small grenade thrown by hand and exploded by a timed fuse or by impact

hand·grip (-grip') *n.* 1. a handclasp or handshake 2. a handle, as on a bicycle handlebar —**come to handgrips** to engage in hand-to-hand fighting

hand·gun (-gun') *n.* any firearm that is held and fired with one hand, as a pistol

hand·hold (-hōld') *n.* 1. a secure grip or hold with the hand or hands 2. a part or thing to take hold of

hand·i·cap (han'dē kap') *n.* [orig. a game in which forfeits were drawn from a cap or hat < *hand in cap*] 1. *a)* a race or other competition in which difficulties are imposed on the superior contestants, or advantages given to the inferior, to make their chances of winning equal *b)* such a difficulty or advantage 2. something that hampers a person; disadvantage; hindrance —*vt.* **-capped', -cap'ping** 1. to give a handicap or handicaps to (contestants) 2. to cause to be at a disadvantage; hinder; impede —**the handicapped** those who are physically disabled or mentally retarded

hand·i·cap·per (-kap'ər) *n.* 1. an official who assigns handicaps to contestants, as in a tournament ☆2. a person, as a sports writer, who tries to predict the winners in horse races on the basis of past records, track conditions, etc.

hand·i·craft (han'dē kraft', -kräft') *n.* [ME. *handiecrafte*, altered (after *handiwerk*, HANDIWORK) < *handcrafte* < OE. *handcræft*] 1. expertness with the hands; manual skill 2. an occupation or art calling for skillful use of the hands, as weaving, pottery, etc. —**hand'i·crafts'man** (-mən) *n., pl.* **-men** (-mən)

hand·i·ly (han'd'l ē) *adv.* 1. in a handy manner; deftly or conveniently 2. with no trouble; easily [to win *handily*]

hand·i·ness (han'dē nis) *n.* the quality of being handy

hand·i·work (-wurk') *n.* [ME. *handiwerk* < OE. *handgeweorc* < *hand* (see HAND) + *geweorc* < *ge-*, collective prefix + *weorc* (see WORK)] 1. *same as* HANDWORK 2. anything made or done by a particular person

hand·ker·chief (haŋ'kər chif, -chēf') *n., pl.* **-chiefs** (-chifs, -chēfs', -chivz', -chēvz') [HAND + KERCHIEF] 1. a small piece of linen, cotton, silk, etc., usually rectangular, for wiping the nose, eyes, or face, or carried or worn for ornament 2. *same as* KERCHIEF

hand-knit (hand'nit') *adj.* knit by hand instead of by machine: also **hand'-knit'ted**

han·dle (han'd'l) *n.* [ME. *handil* < OE. *handle* (akin to Du. *handel*) < *hand*, HAND] 1. that part of a utensil, tool, etc. which is to be held, turned, lifted, pulled, etc. with the hand 2. a thing like a handle in appearance, use, etc. 3. the total amount of money bet over a specified period of time, as at a race track 4. [Colloq.] a person's name, nickname, or title —*vt.* **-dled, -dling** [ME. *handlien* < OE. *handlian*] 1. to touch, lift, etc. with the hand or hands 2. to manage, operate, or use with the hand or hands; manipulate 3. to manage, control, direct, train, etc. 4. to deal with or treat in a particular way [to *handle* a problem tactfully] ☆5. to sell or deal in (a certain commodity) 6. to behave toward; treat —*vi.* to respond or submit to control [the car *handles* well] —☆**fly off the handle** [Colloq.] to become suddenly or violently angry or excited

SYN. —**handle** implies the possession of sufficient (or a specified degree of) skill in managing or operating with or as with the hands [to *handle* a tool, a problem, etc.]; **manipulate** suggests skill, dexterity, or craftiness in handling [to *manipulate* a machine, an account, etc.]; **wield** implies skill and control in handling effectively [to *wield* an ax, influence, etc.]; **ply** suggests great diligence in operating [to *ply* an oar, one's trade, etc.]

han·dle·bar (-bär') *n.* 1. [often *pl.*] a curved or bent metal bar with handles on the ends, for steering a bicycle, motorcycle, etc. ☆2. [Colloq.] a mustache with long, curved ends, resembling a handlebar: in full, **handlebar mustache**

hand·ler (han'dlər) *n.* a person or thing that handles; specif., *a)* a boxer's trainer and second *b)* a person who trains and manages a horse, dog, etc. in a show, contest, or the like

hand·less (han'dlis) *adj.* 1. not having any hands 2. [Dial.] inexpert, clumsy, or awkward

hand·made (hand'mād') *adj.* made by hand, not by machine; made by a process requiring the manual skills of a craftsman

hand·maid·en (-mād''n) *n.* 1. [Archaic] a woman or girl servant or attendant 2. that which accompanies in a useful but subordinate capacity [law is the *handmaiden* of justice] Also **hand'maid'**

hand-me-down (-mē doun') *n.* [Colloq.] something, esp.

an article of clothing, which is used and then passed along to someone else —*adj.* [Colloq.] 1. used; secondhand 2. ready-made and cheap

☆**hand-off** (-ôf') *n. Football* an offensive maneuver in which a back hands the ball directly to another back

☆**hand organ** a barrel organ played by turning a crank by hand

☆**hand-out** (hand'out') *n.* 1. a gift of food, clothing, etc., as to a beggar or tramp 2. a pamphlet or leaflet handed out as for publicity or propaganda 3. a statement or story prepared for release to the news media, as by a government

hand-pick (-pik') *vt.* 1. to pick (fruit or vegetables) by hand 2. to choose with care or for a special purpose, as to gain an advantage —**hand'picked'** *adj.*

hand-rail (-rāl') *n.* a rail serving as a guard or support to be held by the hand, as along a stairway

hand-run·ning (-run'iŋ) *adv.* [Dial. or Colloq.] in succession; without break or interruption: also **hand running**

hand-saw (-sô') *n.* a saw used with one hand

hand's-breadth (handz'bredth', -bretth') *n. same as* HANDBREADTH

hand·sel (han's'l, hant'-) *n.* [ME. *handsel* < OE. (rare) *handselen*, a giving into hand & ON. *handsal*, sealing of a bargain by a handclasp (transl. of L. *mancipatio:* cf. EMANCIPATION), both < *hand* + base of SELL, SALE] 1. a present for good luck, as at the new year or on the launching of a new business 2. [Rare] *a)* a first payment or first installment *b)* the first money taken in by a new business or on any day of business 3. the first use or specimen of anything, regarded as a token of what is to follow —*vt.* **-seled** or **-selled, -sel·ing** or **-sel·ling** [ME. *handsellen* < ON. *handselja*] 1. to give a handsel to 2. to begin or launch with ceremony and gifts 3. to use, do, etc. for the first time

☆**hand·set** (hand'set') *n.* a telephone mouthpiece and receiver in a single unit, for holding in one hand

hand·shake (-shāk') *n.* a gripping and shaking of each other's hand in greeting, farewell, agreement, etc.

hands-off (handz'ôf') *adj.* designating or of a policy, attitude, etc. of not interfering or intervening

hand·some (han'səm) *adj.* [orig., easily handled, convenient < ME. *handsom:* see HAND & -SOME[1]] 1. *a)* [Now Rare] moderately large *b)* large; impressive; considerable [a *handsome* sum] 2. generous; magnanimous; gracious [a *handsome* gesture] 3. good-looking; of pleasing appearance: said esp. of attractiveness that is manly, dignified, or impressive rather than delicate and graceful [a *handsome* lad, a *handsome* chair] —*SYN.* see BEAUTIFUL —**hand'some·ly** *adv.* —**hand'some·ness** *n.*

HANDSET

hand·spike (hand'spīk') *n.* [altered (after SPIKE[1]) < Early ModDu. *handspaeke* (Du. *handspaak*) < *hand*, hand + *spaeke*, rod, pole] a heavy bar used as a lever for shifting heavy objects, esp. on ships

hand·spring (-spriŋ') *n.* a tumbling feat in which the performer turns over in midair with one or both hands touching the ground

hand·stand (-stand') *n.* a gymnastic feat of supporting oneself upright on the hands with the arms outstretched

hand-to-hand (han'tə hand') *adj.* in close contact; at close quarters: said of fighting

hand-to-mouth (-mouth') *adj.* characterized by the necessity of spending or consuming all that is obtained; at or below the level of mere subsistence

hand·work (hand'wurk') *n.* work done or made by hand, not by machine —**hand'worked'** *adj.*

hand-wo·ven (-wō'vən) *adj.* woven on a loom operated manually, not by machine power

hand·writ·ing (-rīt'iŋ) *n.* 1. writing done by hand, with pen, pencil, chalk, etc. 2. a style or way of forming letters and words in writing 3. [Archaic] something written by hand; manuscript —**see the handwriting on the wall** to see the signs of impending disaster, misfortune, etc.: Dan. 5:5–28

hand·writ·ten (-rit''n) *adj.* written by hand, with pen, pencil, etc.

hand·y (han'dē) *adj.* **hand'i·er, hand'i·est** [HAND + -Y[2]] 1. close at hand; easily reached; conveniently located; accessible 2. easily used; saving time or work; convenient [a *handy* device] 3. easily managed or handled; said of a ship, etc. 4. clever with the hands; deft; adroit —*SYN.* see DEXTEROUS

Han·dy (han'dē), **W**(illiam) **C**(hristopher) 1873–1958; U.S. jazz musician & composer

han·dy·man (-man') *n., pl.* **-men'** a man employed at various small tasks; one who does odd jobs

hang (haŋ) *vt.* **hung, hang'ing** for vt. 3 & vi. 5, **hanged** is preferred pt. & pp. [ME. *hangen*, with form < OE. *hangian, vi.* & ON. *hanga, vi.;* senses < these, also < OE. *hon, vt.* & ON. *hengja, caus. v.;* akin to G. *hangen, vi., hängen, vt., henken,* to execute (caus.): all ult. < IE. base **kenk*, to sway, hang (prob. akin to **keg-*, whence HOOK)] 1. to attach to something above with no support from below; suspend 2. to attach so as to permit free motion at

the point of attachment [to *hang* a door on its hinges]
3. to put to death by tying a rope about the neck and suddenly suspending the body so as to snap the neck or cause strangulation **4.** to fasten (pictures, etc.) to a wall by hooks, wires, etc. **5.** to ornament or cover (*with* things suspended) [to *hang* a room with pictures and drapes] **6.** to paste (wallpaper) to walls **7.** to exhibit (pictures) in a museum or gallery **8.** to let (one's head) droop downward **9.** to fasten (an ax head, scythe, etc.) with correct balance **10.** to pin and sew the hem of (a dress) evenly at a desired distance from the floor ☆**11.** to deadlock (a jury), as by withholding one's vote **12.** to cause (something) to be associated with some person or thing —*vi.* **1.** to be attached to something above with no support from below **2.** to hover or float in the air, as though suspended **3.** to swing, as on a hinge **4.** to fall, flow, or drape, as cloth, a coat, etc. **5.** to die by hanging **6.** to incline; lean; droop; bend **7.** to be doubtful or undecided; hesitate **8.** to have one's pictures exhibited in a museum or gallery —*n.* **1.** the way that a thing hangs **2.** a pause in, or suspension of, motion —☆**get** (or **have**) **the hang of 1.** to learn (or have) the knack of **2.** to understand the significance or idea of —☆**hang around** (or **about**) **1.** to cluster around **2.** [Colloq.] to loiter or linger around —**hang back** (or **off**) to be reluctant to advance, as from timidity or shyness —**hang fire 1.** to be slow in firing: said of a gun **2.** to be slow in doing something **3.** to be unsettled or undecided —**hang it!** an exclamation of anger or exasperation —**hang on 1.** to keep hold of **2.** to go on doing; persevere **3.** to depend on; be contingent on **4.** to lean on; be supported by **5.** to be a burden **6.** to listen attentively to —☆**hang one on** [Slang] **1.** to hit with a blow **2.** to go on a drunken spree —**hang out 1.** to lean out **2.** to display, as by suspending **3.** [Slang] *a*) to reside *b*) to spend much of one's time; frequent —**hang over 1.** to project over; overhang **2.** to hover over **3.** to loom over; threaten **4.** to be left from a previous time or state —**hang to** to hold or clutch tenaciously —**hang together 1.** to stick or remain together **2.** to make sense in a coherent way —**hang up 1.** to put on a hanger, hook, etc., esp. in the proper place **2.** to put a telephone receiver or handset back in place in ending a call **3.** to delay or suspend the progress of [cars that are *hung up* in traffic] —**not care** (or **give**) **a hang about** to not care the least bit about

hang·ar (haŋ'ər) *n.* [Fr., a shed, prob. < Frank. *haimgard*, enclosed area: see HOME & YARD²] a repair shed or shelter for aircraft —*vt.* to put or keep in a hangar

☆**hang·bird** (haŋ'bʉrd') *n.* the Baltimore oriole or any other bird that builds a hanging nest

Hang·chow (haŋ'chou', *Chin.* hän'jō') port in E China; capital of Chekiang province: pop. 784,000

hang·dog (-dôg') *n.* **1.** orig., a person considered fit only for hanging dogs, or to be hanged like a dog **2.** a contemptible, sneaking person —*adj.* **1.** contemptible, sneaking, or abject **2.** ashamed and cringing [a *hangdog* expression]

hang·er (haŋ'ər) *n.* **1.** a person who hangs things [a *paperhanger*] **2.** [Rare] a hangman; executioner **3.** a thing that hangs down; esp., a short sword formerly hung from the belt **4.** a thing on which or by means of which objects are, or can be, hung; specif., *a*) a hook, chain, rope, strap, bracket, etc. for this purpose *b*) a small frame on which a garment is hung to keep it in shape

hang·er-on (haŋ'ər än') *n.*, *pl.* **hang'ers-on'** [< HANG ON + -ON] a follower or dependent; specif., *a*) a person who attaches himself to another, to some group, etc. although not wanted *b*) a follower who seeks personal gain; sycophant; parasite —*SYN.* see PARASITE

hang·ing (haŋ'iŋ) *adj.* **1.** attached to something overhead and not supported from below; suspended; pendulous **2.** designed for objects to be hung on **3.** leaning over; inclining; overhanging **4.** located on a steep slope or slant **5.** deserving, causing, or inclined to impose the death penalty **6.** designating or of indention in which the first line of a paragraph touches the left margin, the other lines being indented beneath it **7.** not yet decided; unsettled **8.** [Poet.] of downcast or gloomy appearance —*n.* **1.** a suspending or being suspended **2.** a putting to death by hanging **3.** something hung on a wall, window, etc., as a drapery, tapestry, etc.

hang·man (haŋ'mən) *n.*, *pl.* **-men** (-mən) an executioner who hangs convicted criminals

hang·nail (-nāl') *n.* [altered (by popular association with HANG) < AGNAIL] a bit of torn or cracked skin hanging at the side or base of a fingernail

☆**hang·out** (-out') *n.* [Slang] a place frequented by some person or group

☆**hang·o·ver** (-ō'vər) *n.* **1.** something remaining from a previous time or state; a survival **2.** headache, nausea, etc. occurring as an aftereffect of drinking much alcoholic liquor

☆**hang·tag** (-tag') *n.* a tag attached to an article of merchandise, giving instructions for its use and care

☆**hang-up** (-up') *n.* [Slang] a problem or difficulty, esp. of a personal or emotional nature and apparently not resolvable

hank (haŋk) *n.* [LME., prob. < Scand., as in ON. *hǫnk*, a coil, skein, *hanki*, hasp, clasp < IE. base *keg-, *kenk-, whence HOOK] **1.** a loop or coil of something flexible **2.** a specific length of coiled thread or yarn: a hank of worsted yarn contains 560 yd.; a hank of cotton contains 840 yd. **4.** *Naut.* a ring of wood, metal, or rope on the edge of a staysail, sliding on the controlling stay

hank·er (haŋ'kər) *vi.* [Early ModE., prob. < Du. or LowG. source, as in Fl. *hankeren*, to desire, long for, Du. *hunkeren*, freq. formation & metaphorical extension < base of HANG] to crave, long, or yearn (followed by *after, for*, or an infinitive)

hank·er·ing (-iŋ) *n.* a craving; yearning

han·kie, han·ky (-kē) *n., pl.* **-kies** [Colloq.] a handkerchief

Han·kow (haŋ'kou', *Chin.* hän'kō') former city in EC China: see WUHAN

han·ky-pan·ky (haŋ'kē paŋ'kē) *n.* [altered ? after (SLEIGHT OF) HAND < HOCUS POCUS] [Colloq.] trickery or deception, orig. as used in tricks of illusion or sleight of hand, now esp. in connection with shady dealings or illicit sexual activity

Han·na (han'ə), **Mark** (born *Marcus Alonzo Hanna*) 1837–1904; U.S. financier & politician

Han·nah, Han·na (han'ə) **1.** a feminine name: see ANNA, JOAN **2.** *Bible* the mother of Samuel: I Sam. 1:20

Han·ni·bal (han'ə b'l) 247?–183? B.C.; Carthaginian general: crossed the Alps to invade Italy in the 2d Punic War

Han·o·ver (hä nō'vər, -fər) *Ger.* name of HANOVER

Ha·noi (hä noi', ha-) capital of North Vietnam, on the Red River: pop. 644,000

Han·o·ver (han'ō vər) ruling family of England (1714–1901), founded by George I, orig. Elector of Hanover

Han·o·ver (han'ō vər) **1.** former province (1886–1945) of Prussia, in NW Germany; earlier, an electorate (1692–1815) & a kingdom (1815–86): incorporated into the West German state of Lower Saxony (1945) **2.** city in N West Germany; capital of Lower Saxony: pop. 553,000

Han·o·ve·ri·an (han'ō vir'ē ən) *adj.* **1.** of Hanover, Germany **2.** of the English royal house of Hanover —*n.* **1.** a native or inhabitant of Hanover **2.** a supporter of the house of Hanover

Hans (hans, hanz; *G.* häns) [G. abbrev. of *Johannes*: equivalent to JACK'] a masculine name

han·sa (han'sə) *n.* same as HANSE

Han·sard (han'sərd) *n.* [after Luke Hansard (1752–1828) and descendants, by whom the reports were compiled and printed until 1889] the official record of proceedings in the British Parliament

hanse (hans) *n.* [ME. < MFr. & < ML. *hansa*, both < MHG. & MLowG. *hanse*, association of merchants < OHG. *hansa*, band of men, akin to OE. *hos*, a troop] **1.** a medieval guild of merchants **2.** the fee paid to join this guild, or a toll exacted from nonmembers —**the Hanse** a medieval league of free towns in N Germany and adjoining countries, formed to promote and protect their economic interests: the leading members were Bremen, Lübeck, and Hamburg: also **Hanseatic League**

Han·se·at·ic (han'sē at'ik) *adj.* [ML. *hanseaticus*] of the Hanse or the towns that formed it

han·sel (han's'l) *n.* same as HANDSEL

Han·sen's disease (han's'nz, hän'-) [after A. *Hansen* (1841–1912), Norw. physician who discovered its causative bacterium] same as LEPROSY

han·som (cab) (han'səm) [after J. A. *Hansom* (1803–82), Eng. inventor] a two-wheeled covered carriage for two passengers, pulled by one horse: the driver's seat is above and behind the cab

Han·son (han's'n), **Howard** 1896– ; U.S. composer

hant, ha'nt (hant) *vt., n. dial. var. of* HAUNT

Hants (hants) *short form of* HAMPSHIRE

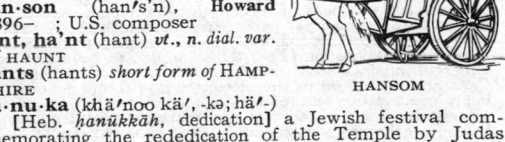

HANSOM

Ha·nu·ka (khä'noo kä', -kə; hä'-) *n.* [Heb. *hanukkāh*, dedication] a Jewish festival commemorating the rededication of the Temple by Judas Maccabaeus in 165 B.C. and celebrated for 8 days beginning the 25th day of Kislev: also **Ha'nuk·kah, Ha'nuk·ka**

han·u·man (hun'oo män', hän'-) *n.* [Hind. *Hanumān* < Sans. *hanumant*, having (big) jaws < *hánu-*, jaw < IE. base *ĝenu-*, whence CHIN] a small, slender-bodied, leaf-eating monkey (*Presbytis entellus*) with a long tail, found in SE Asia —[H-] *Hindu Myth.* a demigod in the form of a monkey

Han·yang (hän'yän') former city in EC China: see WUHAN

†**hao·le** (hou'lā') *n.* [Haw., foreigner] in Hawaii, a non-Polynesian; esp., a white person, or Caucasian

hap¹ (hap) *n.* [ME. < ON. *happ*, akin to OE. (ge)hæp, convenient, suitable < IE. base *kob-*, to be fitted to, suit, whence OIr. *cob*, victory] **1.** chance; luck; lot **2.** [Archaic] an occurrence or happening, esp. an unfortunate

one: *usually used in pl.* —*vi.* **happed, hap′ping** [ME. *happen* < the *n.* or < ? (rare) OE. *hæppan,* to go by chance < same base] to occur by chance; happen

hap² (hap) *vt.* **happed, hap′ping** [ME. *happen* < ?] [Scot. or Dial.] to cover, as with extra bedclothes —*n.* [Scot. or Dial.] any covering

†ha·pax le·go·me·non (hā′paks li gäm′ə nän′, hap′aks) *pl.* **hapax le·go′me·na** (-nə) [Gr., (something) said only once] something unique or occurring only once, as a nonce word or phrase

hap·haz·ard (hap′haz′ərd) —*n.* [HAP¹ + HAZARD] mere chance; accident; fortuity —*adj.* not planned; casual; random —*adv.* by chance; casually —*SYN.* see RANDOM —**hap′haz′ard·ly** *adv.* —**hap′haz′ard·ness** *n.*

haph·ta·ra (häf′tä rä′, -tôr′ə) *n., pl.* **-ta·roth** (-rōth′) [Heb. *haphṭārāh,* conclusion] any of the readings from the Prophets, following the reading from the Pentateuch, in synagogue services on the Sabbath and holidays

hap·less (hap′lis) *adj.* [HAP¹ + -LESS] unfortunate; unlucky; luckless —**hap′less·ly** *adv.* —**hap′less·ness** *n.*

hap·lo- (hap′lō) [< Gr. *haploos,* single < IE. *smplos,* whence L. *simplus,* SIMPLE] a combining form meaning single; simple: also, before a vowel, **hapl-** [*haploid*]

hap·loid (hap′loid) *adj.* [HAPL- + -OID] *Biol.* having the full number of chromosomes normally occurring in the mature germ cell or half the number of the usual animal somatic cell — *n.* a haploid cell or gamete —**hap′loi′dy** (-loi′dē) *n.*

hap·lol·o·gy (hap läl′ə jē) *n.* [HAPLO- + -LOGY] the dropping of one of two similar or identical successive syllables or sounds in a word (Ex.: *interpretive* for *interpretative*)

hap·lont (hap′länt) *n.* [HAPL- + *-ont* < Gr. *ōn* (gen. *ontos*): see ONTO-] an organism in which the nuclei of the somatic cells are haploid

hap·lo·sis (hap lō′sis) *n.* [HAPL- + -OSIS] *Biol.* a halving of the number of chromosomes during meiosis, through the division of a diploid cell into two haploids

hap·ly (hap′lē) *adv.* [ME. *hapliche:* see HAP¹ & -LY²] [Archaic] by chance or accident; perhaps

hap·pen (hap′n) *vi.* [ME. *happenen:* see HAP¹ & -EN] 1. to take place; occur; befall 2. to be or occur by chance or without plan [it *happened* to rain] 3. to have the luck or occasion; chance [I *happened* to see it] 4. to come by chance (*along, by, in,* etc.) —**happen on** (or **upon**) to meet or find by chance —**happen to** to be done to; befall *SYN.*—**happen** is the general word meaning to take place or come to pass and may suggest either direct cause or apparent accident; **chance,** more or less equivalent to **happen,** always implies apparent lack of cause in the event; **occur** is somewhat more formal and usually suggests a specific event at a specific time [what *happened?,* the accident *occurred* at four o'clock]; **transpire** is now frequently used as an equivalent for **happen** or **occur** [what *transpired* at the conference?], apparently by confusion with its sense of to become known, or leak out [reports on the conference never *transpired*]

hap·pen·ing (-iŋ) *n.* 1. something that happens; occurrence; incident; event ☆2. a theatrical performance of unrelated and bizarre or ludicrous actions, often spontaneous and with some participation by the audience

☆**hap·pen·stance** (-stans′) *n.* [HAPPEN + (CIRCUM)STANCE] [Colloq.] chance or accidental happening

hap·py (hap′ē) *adj.* **-pi·er, -pi·est** [ME. *happi* < *hap:* see HAP¹] 1. favored by circumstances; lucky; fortunate 2. having, showing, or causing a feeling of great pleasure, contentment, joy, etc.; joyous; glad; pleased 3. exactly appropriate to the occasion; suitable and clever; apt; felicitous [a *happy* suggestion] 4. [Slang] intoxicated, or irresponsibly quick to action, as if intoxicated: sometimes used in hyphenated compounds: see SLAP-HAPPY, TRIGGER-HAPPY —**hap′pi·ly** *adv.* —**hap′pi·ness** *n.* *SYN.*—**happy** generally suggests a feeling of great pleasure, contentment, etc. [a *happy* marriage]; **glad** implies more strongly an exultant feeling of joy [your letter made her so *glad*], but both **glad** and **happy** are commonly used in merely polite formulas expressing gratification [I'm *glad,* or *happy,* to have met you]; **cheerful** implies a steady display of bright spirits, optimism, etc. [he's always *cheerful* in the morning]; **joyful** and **joyous** both imply great elation and rejoicing, the former generally because of a particular event, and the latter as a matter of usual temperament [the *joyful* throng, a *joyous* family] See also LUCKY—*ANT.* **sad**

hap·py-go-luck·y (-gō luk′ē) *adj.* taking things as they come; easygoing; unworrying; trusting to luck; light-hearted —*adv.* in a haphazard way; by chance

Haps·burg (haps′burg′; *G.* häps′bōōrkh) ruling family of Austria & Austria-Hungary (1278–1918), of Spain (1516–1700), & of the Holy Roman Empire (1438–1806)

hap·ten (hap′ten) *n.* [G. < Gr. *haptein,* to fasten, touch + G. *-en,* -ENE] a compound which, when coupled with a protein or other large molecule, can cause the formation of antibodies: also **hap′tene** (-tēn′) —**hap·ten′ic** (-ten′ik) *adj.*

hap·tic (hap′tik) *adj.* [< Gr. *haptein,* to touch + -IC] of or having to do with the sense of touch; tactile

ha·ra-ki·ri (hä′rə kir′ē, har′ə-; *popularly,* her′ē ker′ē) *n.* [Jap. *hara,* belly + *kiri,* a cutting, cut] ritual suicide by disembowelment: it is called *seppuku* by the Japanese, and was practiced by high-ranking Japanese in lieu of execution or to avoid disgrace

ha·rangue (hə raŋ′) *n.* [ME. (Scot.) *arang* < OFr. *arenge* (Fr. *harangue*) < OIt. *aringa* < *aringo,* site for horse races

and public assemblies < Goth. **hrings,* circle: see RING²] a long, blustering, noisy, or scolding speech; tirade —*vi., vt.* **-rangued′, -rangu′ing** to speak or address in a harangue —**ha·rangu′er** *n.*

Ha·rar (här′ər) city in EC Ethiopia: pop. 40,000

har·ass (hə ras′, har′əs) *vt.* [Fr. *harasser* < OFr. *harer,* to set a dog on < *hare,* cry to incite dogs < Frank.] 1. to trouble, worry, or torment, as with cares, debts, repeated questions, etc. 2. to trouble by repeated raids or attacks, continuous gunfire, etc.; harry —**har·ass′er** *n.* —**har·ass′ment** *n.*

Har·bin (här′bin) city in NE China, on the Sungari River; capital of Heilungkiang province: pop. 1,800,000

har·bin·ger (här′bin jər) *n.* [ME. *herbergeour* (with intrusive *-n-*) < OFr. *herbergeor,* provider of lodging < *herberge,* a shelter < Frank. (or OHG.) *heriberga,* shelter for soldiers < *heri,* army (see HARRY) + *berga,* a shelter < *bergan,* to protect (see BURY)] 1. formerly, an advance representative of an army or royal party, who arranged for lodging, entertainment, etc. 2. a person or thing that comes before to announce or give an indication of what follows; herald —*vt.* to serve as harbinger of; announce; foretell —*SYN.* see FORERUNNER

har·bor (här′bər) *n.* [ME. *herberwe* < OE. *herebeorg* (& ON. *herbergi*), lit., army shelter < *here,* army + *beorg,* a shelter), akin to OHG. *heriberga:* see prec.] 1. a place of refuge, safety, etc.; retreat; shelter 2. a protected inlet, or branch of a sea, lake, etc., used as a shelter and anchorage for ships, esp. one with port facilities —*vt.* 1. to serve as, or provide, a place of protection to; shelter or house; conceal or hide 2. to be the dwelling place or habitat of 3. to hold in the mind; cling to [to *harbor* a grudge] —*vi.* 1. to take shelter, as in a harbor 2. to live or exist —**har′bor·er** *n.* —**har′bor·less** *n.*

har·bor·age (-ij) *n.* 1. a shelter for ships; port; anchorage 2. shelter or lodgings

harbor master the official in charge of enforcing the regulations governing the use of a harbor

☆**harbor seal** an earless seal (*Phoca vitulina*) common in N Atlantic coastal waters of the U.S.

har·bour (här′bər) *n., vt., vi.* Brit. *sp.* of HARBOR

hard (härd) *adj.* [ME. < OE. *heard,* akin to G. *hart* < IE. base **kar-,* hard, whence Gr. *karyon,* nut, *kratos,* strength] 1. not easily dented, pierced, cut, or crushed; resistant to pressure; firm and unyielding to the touch; rigid; solid and compact 2. having firm muscles; in good bodily trim; vigorous and robust 3. showing, or done with, great force or strength; powerful; violent; vigorous [a *hard* blow] 4. demanding great physical or mental effort or labor; fatiguing; difficult; specif., *a)* difficult to do [*hard* work] *b)* difficult to understand, explain, or answer [a *hard* question] *c)* difficult to deal with; not easily managed or controlled [a man *hard* to live with] *d)* firmly fastened or tied [a *hard* knot] 5. *a)* not easily moved; unfeeling; callous [a *hard* heart] *b)* unfriendly; hostile [*hard* feelings] 6. practical and shrewd or calculating [a *hard* customer] 7. *a)* firm, settled, or definite [to follow a *hard* policy] *b)* undeniable, reliable, or actual [*hard* facts] 8. causing pain or discomfort; specif., *a)* difficult to endure; trying; exhausting [a *hard* life] *b)* harsh; severe; stern [a *hard* master, *hard* words] 9. very cold, stormy, etc.; inclement [a *hard* winter] 10. *a)* harsh, stiff, and wiry: said of fibers or cotton *b)* having no nap: said of a finish for fabric 11. *a)* clearly defined or having sharp contrast; distinct [*hard* outlines] *b)* too clear, bright, or penetrating to be pleasant [a *hard* red] 12. having in solution mineral salts that interfere with the lathering and cleansing properties of soap: said of water 13. energetic and persistent; steady and earnest [a *hard* worker] 14. *a)* fermented; alcoholic [*hard* cider] *b)* containing relatively much alcohol; strong: said of alcoholic liquors 15. *a)* of metal, not paper [*hard* money] *b)* that can be exchanged for gold or silver [*hard* currency] 16. designating the letter *c* sounded as in *can* or the letter *g* sounded as in *gun;* also, voiceless, as the *th* in *thin:* a popular term not used by phoneticians 17. *Agric.* high in gluten content [*hard* wheat] 18. *Commerce* high and stable: said of a market, prices, etc. 19. *Mil.* heavily fortified, as an underground installation [*hard* base] 20. *Radiology* of high penetrating power: said of X-rays —*adv.* 1. energetically and persistently; steadily and earnestly [work *hard*] 2. with strength, violence, or severity [hit *hard*] 3. with difficulty: often used in hyphenated compounds [*hard*-earned, *hard*-sought] 4. so as to withstand much wear, use, etc. [*hard*-wearing clothes] 5. deeply; fully; soundly [sleep *hard*] 6. firmly; tightly [hold on *hard*] 7. close; near [we live *hard* by the woods] 8. so as to be or make firm, solid, or rigid [to freeze *hard*] 9. with vigor and to the fullest extent: used esp., in indicating direction [*Hard* alee! turn *hard* right] —**be hard on** 1. to treat severely; be harsh toward 2. to be difficult, unpleasant, or painful for —**hard and fast** 1. invariable; strict: said of rules, etc. 2. not able to be moved: said of a ship run aground —**hard of hearing** partially deaf —**hard put to it** having considerable difficulty or trouble —**hard up** [Colloq.] in great need of something, esp. money; in desperate straits *SYN.*—**hard,** in this comparison, is the simple and general word for whatever demands great physical or mental effort [*hard* work, a *hard* problem]; **difficult** applies especially to that which requires

great skill, intelligence, tact, etc. rather than physical labor [a *difficult* situation]; **arduous** implies the need for diligent, protracted effort [the *arduous* fight ahead of us]; **laborious** suggests long, wearisome toil [the *laborious* task of picking fruit] See also FIRM —*ANT.* **easy, simple**

hard·back (-bak′) *n.* a hard-cover book

☆**hard·ball** (-bôl′) *n. same as* BASEBALL

hard-bit·ten (-bit′n) *adj.* 1. orig., that bites hard; tough in fighting: said of dogs 2. stubborn; tough; enduring; dogged [*hard-bitten* soldiers]

☆**hard·board** (-bôrd′) *n.* a boardlike material made in sheets by subjecting fibers from wood chips to pressure and heat

hard-boiled (-boild′) *adj.* 1. cooked in boiling water until both the white and yolk solidify: said of eggs 2. [Colloq.] not affected by sentiment, pity, etc.; tough; callous

hard-bound (-bound′) *adj. same as* HARD-COVER

hard coal *same as* ANTHRACITE

hard-core (-kôr′) *adj.* 1. constituting or of a hard core 2. absolute; unqualified

hard core the firm, unyielding, or unchanging central part or group

hard-cov·er (-kuv′ər) *adj.* designating any book bound in a relatively stiff cover, as of cloth-covered cardboard: distinguished from PAPERBACK

☆**hard drug** [Colloq.] any drug, such as heroin or cocaine, that is addictive and potentially very damaging to the body or mind

hard·en (här′d'n) *vt., vi.* [ME. *hardnen* < ON. *harthna* & < ME. *hard*, hard] to make or become hard (in various senses)

hard·ened (-d'nd) *adj.* 1. made or become hard or harder (in various senses) 2. confirmed or inveterate in a callous way —*SYN.* see CHRONIC

hard·en·er (-ər) *n.* a person or thing that hardens; specif., *a*) a person who tempers metal tools *b*) a substance used to give a harder film to paint, varnish, etc.

har·den·ing (-in) *n.* 1. a making or becoming hard 2. a substance used to harden something

hard-fea·tured (-fē′chərd) *adj.* having coarse, cruel, stern, or harsh features

hard-fist·ed (-fis′tid) *adj.* stingy; miserly

hard-goods (-goodz′) *n.pl.* durable goods, such as automobiles, furniture, etc.: also **hard goods**

☆**hard·hack** (-hak′) *n.* [HARD + HACK¹] *same as* STEEPLE-BUSH

hard-hand·ed (-han′did) *adj.* 1. having hands made hard by work 2. severe; tyrannical; ruthless: said of a ruler or rule —**hard′hand′ed·ness** *n.*

hard hat ☆1. a protective helmet worn by construction workers, miners, etc. ☆2. [Slang] such a worker

hard·head (-hed′) *n.* 1. a shrewd person, not easily moved 2. *a*) any of various fishes, as the salmon trout, sculpin, etc. ☆*b*) a slender, river minnow (*Mylopharodon conocephalus*) of C and N California

hard·head·ed (-hed′id) *adj.* 1. shrewd and unsentimental; practical; matter-of-fact 2. stubborn; obstinate; dogged —**hard′head′ed·ly** *adv.* —**hard′head′ed·ness** *n.*

hardhead sponge any of several coarse-fibered, commercial sponges from the Caribbean area

hard-heart·ed (-härt′id) *adj.* unfeeling; pitiless; cruel —**hard′heart′ed·ly** *adv.* —**hard′heart′ed·ness** *n.*

har·di·hood (här′dē hood′) *n.* [< HARDY + -HOOD] 1. boldness, daring, fortitude, etc. 2. impudence; insolence

har·di·ly (här′d'l ē) *adv.* in a hardy manner

har·di·ness (-dē nis) *n.* the quality of being hardy; specif., *a*) physical endurance; strength *b*) hardihood; boldness

Har·ding (här′din), **Warren Gamaliel** 1865–1923; 29th president of the U.S. (1921–23)

hard labor compulsory physical labor imposed, together with imprisonment, as a punishment for some crimes

☆**hard landing** a landing, as of a rocket on the moon, made at relatively high speed, with an impact that may destroy all or much of the equipment —**hard′-land′** *vi., vt.*

☆**hard-line** (härd′līn′) *adj.* characterized by an aggressive, unyielding position in politics, foreign policy, etc.

hard·ly (härd′lē) *adv.* [ME. *hardliche* < OE. *heardlice:* see HARD & -LY²] 1. [Now Rare] *a*) with effort or difficulty *b*) severely; harshly 2. only just; barely; scarcely: often used ironically or politely to mean "not quite," or "not at all" [*hardly* the person to ask] 3. probably not; not likely

☆**hard maple** *same as* SUGAR MAPLE

hard·ness (-nis) *n.* 1. the state or quality of being hard (in various senses) 2. the relative capacity of a substance for scratching another or for being scratched or indented by another

☆**hard-nosed** (-nōzd′) *adj.* [Slang] 1. indomitable; tough; stubborn 2. shrewd and practical —**hard′nose′** *n.*

hard palate the bony part of the roof of the mouth, behind the upper teethridge

hard·pan (-pan′) *n.* 1. a layer of hard soil cemented by almost insoluble materials that restrict the downward movement of water and roots 2. solid, unplowed ground ☆3. the hard, underlying part of anything; solid foundation

hard pressed confronted with a difficulty or harassment

hard rubber vulcanized rubber that is firm and comparatively inelastic

hards (härdz) *n.pl.* [ME. *hardes* < OE. *heordan, pl.*, flax hards, akin to MLowG. *herde* < IE. base *kes-* to scrape, comb, whence Gr. *keskeon*, tow] *same as* TOW²

☆**hard sauce** a sweet, creamy mixture of butter, powdered sugar, and flavoring, served with plum pudding, etc.

☆**hard sell** high-pressure salesmanship —**hard′-sell′** *adj.*

hard-set (härd′set′) *adj.* 1. in trouble or difficulty 2. rigid; fixed; firm 3. stubborn

hard-shell (-shel′) *adj.* 1. *a*) having a hard shell *b*) having a shell not recently molted: said of crabs, crayfish, etc. Also **hard′-shelled′** 2. [Colloq.] strict; strait-laced; uncompromising, esp. in religious matters

hard-shelled (or **hard-shell**) **clam** *same as* QUAHOG

☆**hard-shelled** (or **hard-shell**) **crab** a crab, esp. an edible sea crab, before it has shed its hard shell

hard·ship (-ship′) *n.* [ME. *heardschipe:* see HARD & -SHIP] 1. hard circumstances of life 2. a thing hard to bear; specific cause of discomfort or suffering, as poverty, pain, etc. —*SYN.* see DIFFICULTY

hard-spun (-spun′) *adj.* spun with a firm, close twist: said of yarn

☆**hard·stand** (-stand′) *n.* a paved area for parking aircraft or other vehicles

hard·tack (-tak′) *n.* [HARD + TACK, *n.* 5] unleavened bread made in very hard, large wafers: it is traditionally a part of army and navy rations

☆**hard·top** (-täp′) *n.* an automobile resembling a convertible in having no post between the front and rear windows, but with a metal top that cannot be folded back

hard·ware (-wer′) *n.* 1. articles made of metal, as tools, nails, fittings, utensils, etc. ☆2. heavy military equipment or its parts, esp. weapons, vehicles, missiles, etc. ☆3. *a*) apparatus used for controlling spacecraft, etc. *b*) the mechanical, magnetic, and electronic design, structure, and devices of a computer: cf. SOFTWARE

hard·wood (-wood′) *n.* 1. any tough, heavy timber with a compact texture 2. *Forestry* the wood of a broad-leaved tree (*angiosperm*) possessing true vessels, in contrast to the softwood of a needle-bearing conifer (*gymnosperm*) which lacks vessels 3. a tree yielding hardwood

har·dy¹ (här′dē) *adj.* -di·er, -di·est [ME. & OFr. *hardi*, pp. of *hardir*, to make bold < Frank. *hardjan*, to make hard < *hard-*, HARD] 1. bold and resolute; daring; courageous 2. too bold; full of temerity; rash 3. able to withstand fatigue, privation, etc.; robust; vigorous 4. able to survive the winter without special care: said of plants

har·dy² (här′dē) *n.* [prob. HARD + -Y²] a chisel with a square shank, used by blacksmiths: it fits into a square hole (**hardy hole**) in the anvil

Har·dy (här′dē), **Thomas** 1840–1928; Eng. novelist & poet

hare (her) *n., pl.* **hares, hare:** see PLURAL, II, D, 1 [ME. < OE. *hara*, akin to G. *hase* < IE. base *kas-*, gray, whence L. *canus*, hoary] any of a large group of swift mammals (order Lagomorpha) related to the rabbits, with long ears, soft fur, a cleft upper lip, a short tail, and long, powerful hind legs; specif., any member of this group that does not burrow and whose young are furry at birth —**hare off** [Brit. Colloq.] to leave hurriedly; run off

hare and hounds a game in which some players, called "hounds," chase others, called "hares," who have left a trail of paper scraps along their route

hare·bell (-bel′) *n.* [ME. *harebelle:* see HARE & BELL¹] a slender, delicate perennial (*Campanula rotundifolia*), with clusters of blue, bell-shaped flowers

hare·brained (-brānd′) *adj.* having no more intelligence than a hare; reckless, flighty, giddy, rash, etc.

hare·lip (-lip′) *n.* 1. a congenital deformity of one or both lips, usually only the upper one, consisting of a cleft like that of a hare's lip 2. such a lip —**hare′lipped′** *adj.*

ha·rem (her′əm, har′-) *n.* [Ar. *harim*, lit., prohibited (place, thing) < *harama*, to forbid] 1. that part of a Moslem's household in which the women live; seraglio 2. the wives, concubines, women servants, etc. occupying a harem 3. a number of female animals, as of fur seals, who mate and lodge with one male Also **ha·reem** (hä rēm′)

Har·gei·sa (här gā′sa) city in NW Somalia: formerly, capital of British Somaliland: pop. 53,000

Har·greaves (här′grēvz, -grāvz), **James** ?–1778; Eng. inventor of the spinning jenny

Har·ia·na (hər yä′nə) state of NW India: 16,988 sq. mi.; pop. c. 7,000,000; cap. Chandigarh

har·i·cot (har′ə kō′) *n.* [Fr. < *harigoter*, to cut to pieces < ? MDu. *harigod*, sharp tool < *haren*, to sharpen + *god*, a tool] 1. a highly seasoned stew of lamb or mutton and vegetables 2. [altered (after the stew) < ? Nahuatl *ayecotli*, bean] [Chiefly Brit.] *a*) *same as* KIDNEY BEAN *b*) the pod or seed of any of various other edible beans

ha·ri·ka·ri (her′ē ker′ē, hä′rē kä′rē) *n. same as* HARA-KIRI

hark (härk) *vi.* [ME. *herkien* (akin to G. *horchen*) < ? unrecorded OE. *heorcian* or < OE. *heorcnian* (see HEARKEN)] to listen carefully: usually in the imperative, with the effect of an exclamation —*vt.* [Archaic] to listen to; hear —**hark back** 1. to return to an earlier point so as to pick

fat, āpe, cär; ten, ēven; is, bīte; gō, hôrn, tool, look; oil, out; up, fur; get; joy; yet; chin; she; thin, *then*; zh, leisure; ŋ, ring; ə for *a* in *ago*, *e* in *agent*, *i* in *sanity*, *o* in *comply*, *u* in *focus*; ′ as in *able* (ā′b'l); Fr. bäl; ë, Fr. coeur; ö, Fr. feu; ô, Fr. mon; đ, Fr. coq; ü, Fr. duc; r, Fr. cri; H, G. ich; kh, G. doch. See inside front cover. ☆ Americanism; ‡foreign; *hypothetical; < derived from

up the scent or trail again **2.** to go back in thought or speech; revert

hark·en (härʹk'n) *vi., vt. same as* HEARKEN

harl (härl) *n.* [ME. *herle,* prob. < MLowG. *harle*] **1.** a filament, esp. of hemp or flax **2.** *same as* HERL

Har·lan (härʹlən) [< the surname *Harlan*] **1.** a masculine name **2. John Marshall,** 1899– ; U.S. jurist; associate justice, Supreme Court (1955–71)

Har·le·ian (härʹlē ən; *chiefly Brit.,* här lēʹən) *adj.* designating or of the library, esp. the manuscripts now in the British Museum, collected by Robert Harley (1661–1724) and his son Edward (1689–1741)

Har·lem (härʹləm) [var. of HAARLEM] section of New York City, in N Manhattan

Harlem River river separating Manhattan Island from the Bronx &, with Spuyten Duyvil creek, connecting the East River with the Hudson: c. 8 mi.

Har·le·quin (härʹlə kwin, -kin) [Fr. *harlequin, arlequin* < OFr. *hierlekin, hellequin,* demon: Fr. sense & form infl. by It. *arlecchino* < same OFr. source] a traditional comic character in pantomime, who wears a mask and gay, spangled, diamond-patterned tights of many colors, and sometimes carries a wooden wand or sword —*n.* [h-] a clown; buffoon —*adj.* [h-] **1.** comic; ludicrous **2.** of many colors; colorful

har·le·quin·ade (härʹlə kwi nādʹ) *n.* [Fr. *arlequinade*] **1.** that part of a play or pantomime in which the Harlequin and the clown play leading parts **2.** comic pranks; gay, mischievous antics; buffoonery

☆**harlequin bug** a black and red bug (*Murgantia histrionica*) that feeds on cabbages and related plants

☆**harlequin snake** the American coral snake (*Micrurus fulvius*)

har·lot (härʹlət) *n.* [ME. (< OFr., rogue, vagabond), orig. a euphemism for *whore*] *same as* PROSTITUTE

har·lot·ry (-rē) *n.* **1.** prostitution **2.** prostitutes, collectively

harm (härm) *n.* [ME. < OE. *hearm,* akin to G. harm < IE. base *kormo-,* pain, torment, whence MPer. *šarm,* shame] **1.** hurt; injury; damage **2.** moral wrong; evil —*vt.* [ME. *harmen* < OE. *hearmian* < the *n.*] to do harm to; hurt, damage, etc. —*SYN.* see INJURE —**harmʹer** *n.*

har·mat·tan (härʹmə tanʹ) *n.* [Sp. *harmatán* < the native (Twi) name in W Africa] a dry, dusty wind that blows from the interior of Africa toward the Atlantic, esp. from November to March

harm·ful (härmʹfəl) *adj.* causing or able to cause harm; hurtful —**harmʹful·ly** *adv.* —**harmʹful·ness** *n.*

harm·less (-lis) *adj.* **1.** [Rare] not harmed **2.** causing or seeking to cause no harm; not harmful; inoffensive —**harmʹless·ly** *adv.* —**harmʹless·ness** *n.*

Har·mo·ni·a (här mōʹnē ə) [L. < Gr. *Harmonia* (see HARMONY)] *Gr. Myth.* the daughter of Aphrodite and Ares, and wife of Cadmus: she personified harmony and order

har·mon·ic (här mänʹik) *adj.* [L. *harmonicus* < Gr. *harmonikos* < *harmonia,* HARMONY] **1.** harmonious in feeling or effect; agreeing **2.** *Math.* designating or of a series of numbers whose reciprocals are in arithmetical progression **3.** *Music a)* of or pertaining to harmony rather than to melody or rhythm *b)* pertaining to an overtone —*n.* **1.** *same as* OVERTONE (sense 1) **2.** *Elec.* an alternating-current voltage or current or a component of such voltage or current, whose frequency is some integral multiple of a fundamental frequency —**har·monʹi·cal·ly** *adv.*

☆**har·mon·i·ca** (-i kə) *n.* [L., fem. of *harmonicus* (see prec.): earlier *armonica* < It., fem. of *armonico,* of same orig.: so named by B. FRANKLIN, who developed it from an earlier instrument] **1.** a musical instrument consisting of a conveniently arranged series of graduated glasses from which tones are produced by rubbing the edges with a wet finger **2.** a former percussion instrument consisting of metal or glass strips which were struck with small mallets **3.** a small wind instrument played with the mouth; mouth organ: it has a series of graduated metal reeds that vibrate and produce tones when air is blown or sucked across them

harmonic analysis 1. the study of Fourier series **2.** the act of breaking a periodic function into components, each expressed as a sine or cosine function

harmonic mean the reciprocal of the arithmetic mean of the reciprocals of a limited series of numbers

harmonic motion a periodic motion, or vibration, along a straight line in which the restoring force is proportional to the displacement: it may be simple with only one frequency and amplitude, or it may have two or more simple components

☆**har·mon·i·con** (här mänʹi kən) *n., pl.* **-ca** (-kə) [Gr. *harmonikon,* neut. of *harmonikos:* see HARMONIC] **1.** *same as* HARMONICA **2.** *same as* ORCHESTRION

harmonic progression a series of quantities whose reciprocals form an arithmetic progression

har·mon·ics (-iks) *n.pl.* [*with sing. v.*] [< HARMONIC] the physical science dealing with musical sounds

har·mo·ni·ous (här mōʹnē əs) *adj.* [Fr. *harmonieux:* see HARMONY] **1.** having parts combined in a proportionate, orderly, or pleasing arrangement; congruous **2.** having similar or conforming feelings, ideas, interests, etc.; in accord **3.** having musical tones combined to give a pleasing effect; consonant —**har·moʹni·ous·ly** *adv.* —**har·moʹni·ous·ness** *n.*

har·mo·nist (härʹmə nist) *n.* **1.** a musician expert in harmony **2.** a scholar who arranges a harmony (sense 4) —**harʹmo·nisʹtic** *adj.* —**harʹmo·nisʹti·cal·ly** *adv.*

har·mo·ni·um (här mōʹnē əm) *n.* [Fr.: so named by Debain (1809–77), Fr. organ maker < *harmonie,* HARMONY] a small kind of reed organ

har·mo·nize (härʹmə nīzʹ) *vi.* **-nized´, -nizʹing** [Fr. *harmoniser:* see ff. & -IZE] **1.** to be in harmony; accord; agree **2.** to sing in harmony —*vt.* **1.** to make harmonious; bring into agreement **2.** to add chords to (a melody) so as to form a harmony **3.** to arrange into a harmony (sense 4) —*SYN.* see AGREE —**harʹmo·ni·zaʹtion** *n.* —**harʹmo·nizʹer** *n.*

har·mo·ny (härʹmə nē) *n., pl.* **-nies** [ME. *armony* < OFr. *harmonie* < L. *harmonia* < Gr. *harmonia* < *harmos,* a fitting < IE. base *ar-:* cf. ART[1], ARM[1]] **1.** a combination of parts into a pleasing or orderly whole; congruity **2.** agreement in feeling, action, ideas, interests, etc.; peaceable or friendly relations **3.** a state of agreement or proportionate arrangement of color, size, shape, etc. **4.** an arrangement of parallel passages of different authors, esp. of the Scriptures, so as to bring out corresponding ideas, qualities, etc. **5.** agreeable sounds; music **6.** *Music a)* the simultaneous sounding of two or more tones, esp. when satisfying to the ear *b)* structure in terms of the arrangement, modulation, etc. of chords: distinguished from MELODY, RHYTHM *c)* the study of this structure —*SYN.* see SYMMETRY

Harms·worth (härmzʹwurthʹ), **Alfred Charles William** *see* NORTHCLIFFE

har·ness (härʹnis) *n.* [ME. *harneis* < OFr. *harneis,* armor < ON. *hernest,* military supplies < *herr,* army, akin to HARRY] **1.** *orig.,* armor and other military equipment for a man or horse **2.** the leather straps and metal pieces by which a horse, mule, etc. is fastened to a vehicle, plow, or load **3.** any trappings or gear similar to this; specif., *a)* the straps, etc. by which a parachute is fastened to its wearer *b)* a device for raising and lowering the warp threads on a loom —*vt.* **1.** to put harness on (a horse, etc.) **2.** to control so as to use the power of [to harness one's energy] **3.** [Archaic] to put armor on —**in double harness**

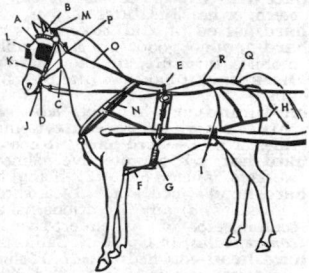

HARNESS
(A, blinker strap; B, brow band; C, throatlatch; D, bit; E, terret; F, martingale; G, bellyband; H, breeching; I, loin strap; J, curb; K, noseband; L, blinker; M, crown piece; N, collar; O, side check; P, runner; Q, crupper; R, back strap)

1. in a harness for two animals pulling the same carriage, plow, etc. **2.** married **3.** working at two jobs —**in harness** in or at one's routine work —**in harness with** in cooperation with

harness hitch a kind of knot: see KNOT, illus.

☆**harness race** a horse race between either trotters or pacers, each pulling a sulky and driver

Har·old (harʹəld) [OE. *Hereweald* & *Harald* < ON. *Haraldr,* both < Gmc. **Hariwald,* lit., leader of the army < **harja-,* army (OE. *here*) + **waldan,* to rule (cf. WIELD)] **1.** a masculine name: dim. *Hal* **2. Harold I** ?–1040; king of England (1035–40): son of CANUTE: called **Harold Harefoot** **3. Harold II** 1022?–66; last Saxon king of England (1066): killed in the Battle of Hastings

harp (härp) *n.* [ME. < OE. *hearpe,* akin to G. *harfe* < IE. base **(s)kerb(h)-,* to bend, curve (whence SHRIMP): from the shape of the instrument] **1.** a musical instrument with strings stretched across an open, triangular frame, held upright and played by plucking with the fingers: the modern harp has usually forty-six strings and a series of foot pedals which permit the playing of halftones **2.** a harp-shaped object or implement—[H-] Lyra, a N constellation —*vi.* **1.** to play a harp **2.** to persist in talking or writing tediously or continuously (*on* or *upon* something) —*vt.* [Rare] to give voice to; express —**harpʹer** *n.*

HARP

Har·pers Ferry (härʹpərz) [the site of a ferry owned (c. 1747) by Robert

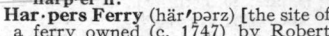

Harper] town in W.Va., at the juncture of the Potomac & Shenandoah rivers: site of the U.S. arsenal captured by John BROWN (1859): pop. 400

harp·ings (härʹpinz) *n.pl.* [prob. < ON. *harpa*, to squeeze, cramp: for IE. base see HARP] **1.** wooden strips or planks on the bow of a ship to give it added strength **2.** wooden pieces used as supports during the construction of a ship Also **harpʹins** (-pinz)

harp·ist (härʹpist) *n.* a person who plays the harp

har·poon (här poōnʹ) *n.* [MDu. *harpoen* < MFr. *harpon* < *harper*, to claw, grip < ON. *harpa*, to squeeze, cramp: for IE. base see HARP] a barbed javelin or spear with a line attached to it, used for spearing whales or other large sea animals —*vt.* to strike, kill, or catch with a harpoon —**har·poonʹer** n.

harp·si·chord (härpʹsi kôrdʹ) *n.* [obs. Fr. *harpechorde* or It. *arpicordo* < *arpa* (LL. *harpa* < Gmc. *harpa:* see HARP) + *corda* (see CORD): -*s*- is intrusive] a stringed musical instrument with a keyboard, predecessor of the piano: the strings are plucked by points of leather or quill when the keys are pressed, producing short, abrupt tones: cf. CLAVICHORD —**harpʹsi·chordʹist** n.

Har·py (härʹpē) *n., pl.* **-pies** [MFr. *harpie* < L. *harpyia* < Gr. *harpyiai*, pl., lit., snatchers < *harpazein*, to snatch] **1.** *Gr. Myth.* any of several hideous, filthy, rapacious winged monsters with the head and trunk of a woman and the tail, legs, and talons of a bird **2.** [h-] a relentless, greedy, or grasping person **3.** [h-] *same as* HARPY EAGLE

harpy eagle a large, black and white, short-winged, tropical American eagle (*Harpia harpyja*), with a double crest and a powerful bill and claws

har·que·bus (härʹkwi bəs) *n.* [Fr. *arquebuse* < It. *archibuso* < MFr. *harquebusche* < Du. *haakbuse:* cf. HACKBUT] an early type of portable gun, supported on a hooked staff or forked rest during firing

har·ri·dan (harʹi d'n) *n.* [prob. altered < Fr. *haridelle*, worn-out horse, jade] a disreputable, shrewish old woman

har·ri·er¹ (harʹē ər) *n.* [< HARE + -IER] **1.** a dog similar to but smaller than the English foxhound, used in packs for hunting hares and rabbits **2.** [*pl.*] a pack of such dogs and the hunters in a hunt **3.** a cross-country runner

har·ri·er² (-ē ər) *n.* **1.** a person who harries **2.** any of several hawks (esp. genus *Circus*) that prey on small mammals, reptiles, etc.; specif., the marsh hawk

Har·ri·et (harʹē it) [fem. dim. of HARRY] a feminine name: var. *Harriot, Harriott;* dim. *Hattie*

Har·ri·man (harʹə mən), **Edward Henry** 1849–1909; U.S. financier & railroad magnate

Har·ris (harʹis) **1. Joel Chan·dler** (chanʹdlər), 1848–1908; U.S. writer: author of the *Uncle Remus* stories **2. Roy (Ellsworth)**, 1898– ; U.S. composer

Har·ris·burg (harʹis bʉrgʹ) [after John *Harris*, Jr., the founder] capital of Pa., in the S part, on the Susquehanna: pop. 68,000

Har·ri·son (harʹə s'n) **1. Benjamin**, *a)* 1726?–91; Am. Revolutionary patriot: signer of the Declaration of Independence: father of *William Henry b)* 1833–1901; 23d president of the U.S. (1889–93): grandson of *ff.* **2. William Henry**, 1773–1841; U.S. general; 9th president of the U.S. (1841): called *Tippecanoe*

Harris tweed [< *Harris*, a district (see LEWIS WITH HARRIS) in the Outer Hebrides where the cloth is made] *a trademark for* a soft, all-wool tweed, hand-woven on the islands of the Outer Hebrides

Har·ro·vi·an (ha rōʹvē ən, hə rōvʹyən) *adj.* of Harrow —*n.* a student or former student of Harrow

Har·row (harʹō) **1.** city in Middlesex, SE England, near London: pop. 210,000: also **Harrow-on-the-Hill 2.** private preparatory school for boys, in this city

har·row¹ (harʹō) *n.* [ME. *harwe*, prob. < or akin to ON. *harfr* < IE. *(s)kerp-:* cf. HARVEST] a heavy frame with spikes or sharp-edged disks, drawn by a horse or tractor and used for breaking up and leveling plowed ground, covering seeds, rooting up weeds, etc. —*vt.* **1.** to draw a harrow over (land) **2.** [Rare] to cut; lacerate **3.** to cause mental distress to; torment; vex —*vi.* to take harrowing [ground that *harrows* well] —**harʹrow·er** n. —**harʹrow·ing** *adj.* —**harʹrow·ing·ly** *adv.*

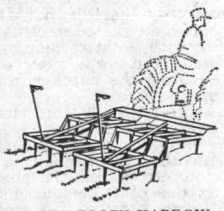

SPIKE-TOOTH HARROW

har·row² (harʹō) *vt.* [ME. *harwen, herien* < OE. *hergian:* see HARRY] [Archaic] to rob, plunder, or pillage —**harrow hell** [Archaic] to enter hell and rescue the righteous: said of Christ

har·rumph (hə rumpfʹ: *conventionalized pronun.*) *vi.* [echoic] **1.** to clear one's throat, esp. in a studied, pompous way **2.** to protest or complain in a pompous or self-righteous way —*n.* the act or sound of harrumphing

Har·ry (harʹē) [ME. *Herry* < HENRY] a masculine name: fem. *Harriet*

har·ry (harʹē) *vt.* **-ried, -ry·ing** [ME. *hergien* < OE. *hergian* < base of *here*, army (G. *heer*) < IE. base *koryos, army, var. of *koros, war, whence Lith. *kāras*, war, MIr. *cuire*, host] **1.** to raid, esp. repeatedly, and ravage or rob; pillage; plunder **2.** to torment or worry; harass **3.** to force or push along

harsh (härsh) *adj.* [ME. *harsk*, akin to G. *harsch*, rough, raw < IE. base *kars, to scratch, comb, whence L. *carduus*, thistle, *carrere*, to card (wool)] **1.** unpleasantly sharp or rough; specif., *a)* grating to the ear; discordant *b)* too bright or vivid to the eye; glaring *c)* too strong to the taste; bitter *d)* not smooth to the touch; coarse **2.** unpleasantly crude, abrupt, or strained so as to be offensive to the mind or feelings [the *harsh* realities of death] **3.** rough, crude, or forbidding in appearance [beneath his *harsh* exterior] **4.** excessively severe; cruel or unfeeling [a *harsh* punishment] —*SYN.* see ROUGH —**harshʹly** *adv.* —**harshʹness** n.

hars·let (härsʹlit) *n. same as* HASLET

hart (härt) *n., pl.* **harts, hart:** see PLURAL, II, D, 1 [ME. *hert* < OE. *heorot*, akin to G. *hirsch* < IE. base **ker-*, head, what is on the head, horn, whence L. *cervus*, hart & HORN, REIN(DEER)] a male of the European red deer, esp. after its fifth year, when the crown antlers are formed; stag

har·tal (här tälʹ) *n.* [Hindi *haṭtāl* < *hāt*, a shop + *tālā*, a lock] in India, a suspension of work and business, esp. as an expression of political protest

Harte (härt), **Bret** (bret) (born *Francis Brett Hart*) 1836–1902; U.S. writer, esp. of short stories

har·te·beest (härʹtə bēstʹ, härtʹbēstʹ) *n., pl.* **-beests', -beest':** see PLURAL, II, D, 1 [obs. Afrik. < *harte*, hart + *beest*, beast] a large, swift South African antelope (*Alcelaphus caama*), now rare, having a reddish-brown coat with a yellow patch on each haunch, and long horns curved backward at the tips

HARTEBEEST
(4–5 ft. high at shoulder)

Hart·ford (härtʹfərd) [after HERTFORD] capital of Conn., in the C part, on the Connecticut River: pop. 158,000 (met. area 664,000)

harts·horn (härtsʹhôrnʹ) *n.* **1.** a hart's horn, or antler **2.** [Now Rare] ammonium carbonate, used in smelling salts; sal volatile: so called because formerly obtained from deer's antlers

hart's-tongue, harts·tongue (-tunʹ) *n.* a fern (*Phyllitis scolopendrium*) with narrow, simple fronds, found in Europe, Asia, and NE N. America

har·um-scar·um (herʹəm skerʹəm) *adj.* [< ? HARE + SCARE + 'EM] acting or done in a reckless or rash way; irresponsible —*adv.* in a harum-scarum manner —*n.* a harum-scarum person or action

Ha·run al-Ra·shid (hä rōōnʹ äl rä shēdʹ) 764?–809 A.D.; caliph of Baghdad (786–809): given popular fame as a hero of the *Arabian Nights*

ha·rus·pex (hə rusʹpeks, harʹəs peks) *n., pl.* **-rus'pi·ces'** (-pə sēzʹ) [L., lit., inspector of entrails < *haru-* (see YARN) + -*spex* (see AUSPEX)] any of a class of lesser priests and soothsayers in ancient Rome, who professed to foretell the future by interpreting the entrails of sacrificial animals —**ha·rus'pi·cal** (-pi k'l) *adj.*

Har·vard (härʹvərd), **John** 1607–38; Eng. clergyman, in America: principal endower of Harvard College

har·vest (härʹvist) *n.* [ME. *hervest* < OE. *hærfest*, akin to G. *herbst* (OHG. *herbist*) < IE. **(s)kerp-* < base **(s)ker-*, to cut, whence SHEAR, SHORT: basic sense "time of cutting"] **1.** the time of the year when matured grain, fruit, vegetables, etc. are reaped and gathered in **2.** a season's yield of grain, fruit, etc. when gathered in or ready to be gathered in; crop **3.** the gathering in of a crop **4.** the outcome or consequence of any effort or series of events [the tyrant's *harvest* of hate] —*vt., vi.* **1.** to gather in (a crop, etc.) **2.** to gather the crop from (a field) **3.** to get (something) as the result of an action or effort —**harʹvest·a·ble** *adj.*

har·vest·er (-ər) *n.* **1.** a person who gathers in a crop of grain, fruit, etc. ☆**2.** any of various farm machines for harvesting crops

☆**harvest fly** *same as* CICADA

harvest home 1. the bringing home of the last harvest load; end of the harvest **2.** an English festival celebrating this **3.** a song sung by harvesters bringing home the last load

har·vest·man (-mən) *n., pl.* **-men** (-mən) **1.** a man who harvests **2.** any of a group of spiderlike animals (order Phalangida) with long, thin legs and a short, broad, segmented abdomen; daddy-longlegs

☆**harvest mite** *same as* CHIGGER (sense 1)

harvest moon the full moon at or about the time of the autumnal equinox, September 22 or 23

harvest mouse 1. a very small European mouse (*Micromys minutus*) that builds its nest among the stalks of wild plants and growing grain **2.** any of several very small New World mice (genus *Reithrodontomys*) with a very long tail
Har·vey (här′vē) [Fr. *Hervé* < OHG. *Herewig*, lit., army battle < Gmc. **harja*, army (cf. HARRY) + **wig-*, fight, akin to OE. *wig* < IE. base **weik-*, whence L. *vincere*, conquer] **1.** a masculine name **2. William**, 1578–1657; Eng. physician: discovered the circulation of the blood
Har·ya·na (hər yä′nə) *same as* HARIANA
Harz (Mountains) (härts) mountain range in C Germany, extending from Lower Saxony to the Elbe River: highest peak, Brocken
has (haz; *unstressed*, həz, əz; *before "to"* has) 3d pers. sing., *pres. indic.*, *of* HAVE
Ha·sa (hä′sə) region in NE Saudi Arabia, on the Persian Gulf: c. 28,000 sq. mi.: also **El Hasa**
has-been (haz′bin′) *n.* [Colloq.] a person or thing that was formerly popular or effective but is no longer so
Has·dru·bal (haz′drŏŏ bəl) **1.** ?–221 B.C.; Carthaginian general; brother-in-law of HANNIBAL **2.** ?–207 B.C.; Carthaginian general: crossed the Alps (207) to aid Hannibal, his brother: son of HAMILCAR BARCA
ha·sen·pfef·fer (häs′n fef′ər, häz′-) *n.* [G. < *hase*, rabbit (see HARE) + *pfeffer*, pepper] a German dish made of rabbit meat marinated in seasoned vinegar, browned, and stewed in the marinade
hash (hash) *vt.* [Fr. *hacher*, to chop, mince: see HACHURE] **1.** to chop (meat or vegetables) into small pieces for cooking **2.** [Colloq.] to make a mess or botch of; bungle —*n.* **1.** a chopped mixture of cooked meat and vegetables, usually baked or browned **2.** a mixture, as of things used before in different forms; rehash **3.** a hodgepodge; muddle; mess —☆**hash out** [Colloq.] to settle or resolve by prolonged discussion —☆**hash over** [Colloq.] to talk over in detail; discuss at length —**make (a) hash of** [Colloq.] **1.** to bungle; botch **2.** to destroy or defeat (an opponent, argument, etc.) —**settle one's hash** [Colloq.] to overcome or subdue one
Hash·em·ite Kingdom of Jordan (hash′ə mīt′) *official name of* JORDAN
☆**hash house** [Slang] a cheap restaurant
hash·ish (hash′ēsh, -ish) *n.* [Ar. *hashish*, dried hemp: cf. ASSASSIN] a drug made from the leaves and stalks of Indian hemp, chewed or smoked for its intoxicating and narcotic effects: also **hash′eesh** (-ēsh)
☆**hash mark** [Mil. Slang] *same as* SERVICE STRIPE
Has·i·dim (has′ə dim; *Heb.* khä sē′dim) *n.pl., sing.* **Has·id** (has′id; *Heb.* khä′sid) [< Heb. *hāsid*, a pious person] the members of a sect of Jewish mystics that originated in Poland in the 18th century and that emphasizes joyful worship of an immanent God —**Ha·sid′ic** (-sid′ik) *adj.* —**Has′i·dism** *n.*
has·let (has′lit, häz′-) *n.* [ME. *hastelet* < OFr. < *haste*, meat cooked on a spit < Gmc. **harst*, a roast: form and sense infl. by L. *hasta*, a spear] the heart, liver, lungs, etc. of a pig or other animal, used for food
has·n't (haz′'nt) has not
hasp (hasp, häsp) *n.* [ME. < OE. *hæsp*, by methathesis < *hæpse*, akin to G. *haspe* < IE. base **kap-*, to grasp, whence L. *capere*, to take, E. HAVE] a hinged metal fastening for a door, window, lid, etc.; esp., a metal piece fitted over a staple and fastened by a bolt or padlock —*vt.* [Rare] to fasten with or as with a hasp
Has·sam (has′əm), **(Frederick) Childe** (child) 1859–1935; U.S. painter & etcher
☆**has·sle** (has′l) *n.* [< ?] [Colloq.] a heated argument; squabble —*vi.* **-sled**, **-sling** to have a heated argument
has·sock (has′ək) *n.* [ME. *hassok* < OE. *hassuc*, (clump of) coarse grass < ?] **1.** [Now Rare] a thick clump or tuft of grass; tussock **2.** a firmly stuffed cushion used as a footstool or seat
hast (hast; *unstressed* həst, əst) *archaic 2d pers. sing.*, *pres. indic.*, *of* HAVE: *used with* thou
‡**has·ta la vis·ta** (äs′tä lä vēs′tä) [Sp., lit., until the meeting] goodbye
‡**hasta lue·go** (lwe′gō) [Sp., lit., until (some time) soon] goodbye
‡**hasta ma·ña·na** (mä nyä′nä) [Sp., lit., until tomorrow] goodbye
has·tate (has′tāt) *adj.* [L. *hastatus* < *hasta*, a spear: see YARD¹] having a triangular shape like a spearhead, as some leaves: see LEAF, illus.
haste (hāst) *n.* [ME. < OFr. (Fr. *hâte*) < Frank. **haist*, violence, akin to OE. *hæst* < IE. base **keibh-*, quick, violent, whence Sans. *śibham*, quick] **1.** the act of hurrying; quickness of motion; rapidity **2.** the act of hurrying carelessly or recklessly [*haste* makes waste] **3.** necessity for hurrying; urgency [the air of *haste* which marks the undertaking] —*vt., vi.* **hast·ed**, **hast′ing** [Rare] *same as* HASTEN —**in haste 1.** in a hurry **2.** in too great a hurry; without enough care or thought —**make haste** to hasten; hurry
SYN.—haste implies quick or precipitate movement or action, as from the pressure of circumstances or intense eagerness; **hurry**, often interchangeable with **haste**, specifically suggests excitement, bustle, or confusion [the *hurry* of city life]; **speed** implies rapidity

of movement, operation, etc., suggesting effectiveness and the absence of excitement or confusion [to increase the *speed* of an assembly line]; **expedition** adds to **speed** the implication of efficiency and stresses the facilitation of an action or procedure; **dispatch** comes close to **expedition** in meaning but more strongly stresses promptness in finishing something —ANT. **slowness**, **delay**

has·ten (hās′n) *vt.* [extended form of prec., *v.*] to cause to be or come faster; speed up; accelerate —*vi.* to move or act swiftly; hurry; be quick
Has·tings (hās′tinz) city in Sussex, SE England, on the English Channel: near the site of the decisive battle (**Battle of Hastings**, 1066) in the Norman Conquest of England: pop. 67,000
Has·tings (hās′tinz), **Warren** 1732–1818; Eng. statesman; 1st governor general of India (1773–84)
hast·y (hās′tē) *adj.* **hast′i·er**, **hast′i·est** [ME. *hasti* < OFr. *hasti*, *hastif*: see HASTE] **1.** done or made with haste; quick; hurried [a *hasty* lunch] **2.** done or made too quickly and with too little thought; rash [a *hasty* decision] **3.** short-tempered or impetuous **4.** showing irritation or impatience [*hasty* words] —SYN. see FAST¹ —**hast′i·ly** *adv.* —**hast′i·ness** *n.*
hasty pudding [so called because quickly prepared] ☆**1.** mush made of cornmeal **2.** [Brit.] mush made of flour or oatmeal
hat (hat) *n.* [ME. < OE. *hætt*, akin to OFris. *hat*, G. *hut* < IE. base **kadh-*, to cover, protect, whence L. *cassis*, helmet & HOOD¹] **1.** a covering for the head, usually with a brim and a crown: sometimes distinguished from BONNET, BERET, CAP, etc. **2.** *R.C.Ch.* *a*) the official red hat of a cardinal *b*) the rank or position of a cardinal —*vt.* **hat′ted**, **hat′ting** to cover or provide with a hat: used chiefly in the pp. —☆**pass the hat** to take up a collection, as at a meeting —**take one's hat off to** to salute or congratulate —☆**talk through one's hat** [Colloq.] to make irresponsible or foolish statements; talk nonsense —**throw one's hat into the ring** to enter a contest, esp. one for political office —☆**under one's hat** [Colloq.] strictly confidential; secret
hat·a·ble (hāt′ə b'l) *adj. same as* HATEABLE
hat·band (hat′band′) *n.* a band of cloth around the crown of a hat, just above the brim
hat·box (-bäks′) *n.* a box or case for carrying or storing a hat or hats
hatch¹ (hach) *vt.* [ME. *hacchen*, akin to G. *hecken*, to breed & OE. *hagan*, the genitals < ? IE. base* *kak-*, to be able, help, whence Sans. *śaknōti*, (he) can] **1.** *a*) to bring forth (young) from an egg or eggs by applying warmth *b*) to bring forth young from (an egg or eggs) **2.** to bring (a plan, idea, etc.) into existence; esp., to plan in a secret or underhanded way; plot —*vi.* **1.** to bring forth young; develop embryos: said of eggs **2.** to come forth from the egg **3.** to brood: said of a bird —*n.* **1.** the process of hatching **2.** the brood hatched **3.** a result or outcome —**hatch′er** *n.*
hatch² (hach) *n.* [ME. *hacche* < OE. *hæcc*, grating, lattice gate, akin to Du., LowG. *hek* < IE. base **kagh-*, to enclose, wickerwork, whence HEDGE] **1.** the lower half of a door, gate, etc. that has two separately movable halves **2.** *same as* HATCHWAY **3.** a covering, orig. a grating, for a ship's hatchway, or a lid or trapdoor for a hatchway in a building **4.** a barrier to regulate the flow of water in a stream; floodgate —**down the hatch!** [Colloq.] drink up!: a toast
hatch³ (hach) *vt.* [OFr. *hacher*, to hack: see HACHURE] to mark or engrave with fine, crossed or parallel lines so as to indicate shading —*n.* any of these lines
hatch·el (hach′əl) *n., vt.* **-eled** or **-elled**, **-el·ing** or **-el·ling** *same as* HACKLE¹
hatch·er·y (hach′ər ē) *n., pl.* **-er·ies** a place for hatching eggs, esp. those of fish or poultry
hatch·et (hach′it) *n.* [ME. *hachet* < OFr. *hachet* < *hache*, an ax: see HACHURE] **1.** a small ax with a short handle, for use with one hand ☆**2.** *same as* TOMAHAWK —☆**bury the hatchet** to stop fighting; make peace
hatchet face a lean, sharp face, suggesting the cutting edge of a hatchet —**hatch′et-faced′** (-fāst′) *adj.*
☆**hatchet job** [Colloq.] a biased, malicious attack on the character or activities of a person, institution, etc.
☆**hatchet man** [Colloq.] **1.** a man hired to commit murder **2.** any person assigned to carry out disagreeable or unscrupulous tasks for his superior, employer, party, etc.
hatch·ing (hach′in) *n.* [HATCH³ + -ING] **1.** the drawing or engraving of fine, parallel or crossed lines to show shading **2.** such lines
hatch·ment (hach′mənt) *n.* [for earlier *atcheament*, altered < ACHIEVEMENT] *Heraldry* a diamond-shaped tablet or panel bearing the coat of arms of a man who has recently died, displayed for a time before his house
hatch·way (-wā′) *n.* **1.** a covered rectangular opening in a ship's deck, through which cargo can be lowered or

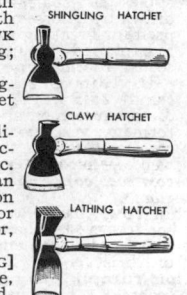

SHINGLING HATCHET

CLAW HATCHET

LATHING HATCHET

TYPES OF HATCHET

HASP

entrance made to a lower deck **2.** a similar opening in the floor or roof of a building

hate (hāt) *vt.* **hat′ed, hat′ing** [ME. *hatien* < OE. *hatian,* akin to G. *hassen* < IE. base **kād-,* bad temper, whence Gr. *kēdein,* to trouble, distress & W. *cas,* hate] **1.** to have strong dislike or ill will for; loathe; despise **2.** to dislike or wish to avoid; shrink from [to *hate* arguments] —*vi.* to feel hatred —*n.* **1.** a strong feeling of dislike or ill will; hatred **2.** a person or thing hated —**hat′er** *n.*
SYN.—**hate** implies a feeling of great dislike or aversion, and, with persons as the object, connotes the bearing of malice; **detest** implies vehement dislike or antipathy; **despise** suggests a looking down with great contempt upon the person or thing one hates; **abhor** implies a feeling of great repugnance or disgust; **loathe** implies utter abhorrence —*ANT.* love, like

hate·a·ble (-ə b'l) *adj.* that deserves to be hated
hate·ful (-fəl) *adj.* **1.** [Now Rare] feeling or showing hate; malicious; malevolent **2.** causing or deserving hate; loathsome; detestable; odious —**hate′ful·ly** *adv.* —**hate′ful·ness** *n.*
SYN.—**hateful** is applied to that which provokes extreme dislike or aversion; **odious** stresses a disagreeable or offensive quality in that which is hateful; **detestable** refers to that which arouses vehement dislike or antipathy; **obnoxious** is applied to that which is very objectionable to one and causes great annoyance or discomfort by its presence; that is **repugnant** which is so distasteful or offensive that one offers strong resistance to it; that is **abhorrent** which is regarded with extreme repugnance or disgust; **abominable** is applied to that which is execrably or degradingly offensive or loathsome
☆**hate·mon·ger** (-muŋ′gər, -män′-) *n.* a propagandist who seeks to provoke hatred and prejudice, esp. against a minority group or groups
hath (hath) *archaic 3d pers. sing., pres. indic.,* of HAVE
Hath·a·way (hath′ə wā′), **Anne** 1557?–1623; *maiden name of the wife of William Shakespeare*
Hath·or (hath′ôr) [Gr. *Hathōr* < Egypt. *Ḥet-Ḥert,* lit., the house above] *Egypt. Myth.* the goddess of love, mirth, and joy, usually represented as having the head or ears of a cow **Ha·thor·ic** (ha thôr′ik) *adj.*
hat·pin (hat′pin′) *n.* a long, ornamental pin for fastening a woman's hat to her hair
hat·rack (-rak′) *n.* a rack, set of pegs or hooks, etc. to hold hats
ha·tred (hā′trid) *n.* [ME. < *hate,* hate + *-red, -reden* < OE. *-ræden,* state, condition] strong dislike or ill will; hate
hat·ter (hat′ər) *n.* a person who makes, sells, or cleans hats, esp. men's hats
Hat·ter·as (hat′ər əs), **Cape** [< name of an Algonquian Indian tribe] cape on an island (**Hatteras Island**) of N.C., between Pamlico Sound & the Atlantic: site of a national recreational area (**Cape Hatteras National Seashore**), 39 sq. mi.

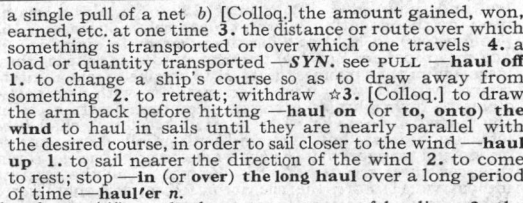

CAPE HATTERAS

Hat·tie (hat′ē) a feminine name: see HARRIET
Hat·ties·burg (hat′ēz burg′) [after *Hattie* Hardy, wife of a railroad builder] city in SE Miss.; pop. 38,000
☆**hat tree** a stand with arms or hooks to hold hats, coats, etc.
hat trick [orig. term in cricket: from the practice of rewarding the feat with a new hat] *Sports* any of various unusual feats; esp., the act by a single player in ice hockey, soccer, etc. of scoring three goals in one game
hau·ber·geon (hô′bər jən) *n. obs. var. of* HABERGEON
hau·berk (hô′bərk) *n.* [ME. *hauberc* < OFr. < Frank. **halsberg* (akin to OE. *healsbeorg),* protection for the neck, gorget < *hals,* the neck + *bergan,* to protect] a medieval coat of armor, usually of chain mail
haugh·ty (hôt′ē) *adj.* **-ti·er, -ti·est** [ME. *haut,* high, haughty < OFr. *haut,* high < L. *altus* (with *h-* after Frank. **hoh,* high) + *-y²*: *gh* prob. inserted by analogy with NAUGHTY] **1.** having or showing great pride in oneself and disdain, contempt, or scorn for others; proud; arrogant; supercilious **2.** [Archaic] lofty; noble —*SYN.* see PROUD —**haugh′ti·ly** *adv.* —**haugh′ti·ness** *n.*
haul (hôl) *vt.* [17th-cent. phonetic sp. of HALE² < ME. *halen* < OFr. *haler,* to draw < ODu. *halen,* akin to G. *holen,* to fetch < IE. base **kel-,* to cry out (whence L. *calare*): basic sense "to call hither"] **1.** to pull with force; move by pulling or drawing; tug; drag **2.** to transport by wagon, truck, etc. [to *haul* coal for a living] **3.** *same as* HALE² **4.** *Naut.* to change the course of (a ship) by setting the sails —*vi.* **1.** to pull; tug **2.** to shift direction: said of the wind **3.** *Naut.* to change the course of a ship by trimming sail, usually so as to travel closer to the wind —*n.* **1.** the act of hauling; pull; tug **2.** *a)* the amount of fish taken in

a single pull of a net *b)* [Colloq.] the amount gained, won, earned, etc. at one time **3.** the distance or route over which something is transported or over which one travels **4.** a load or quantity transported —*SYN.* see PULL —**haul off 1.** to change a ship's course so as to draw away from something **2.** to retreat; withdraw ☆**3.** [Colloq.] to draw the arm back before hitting —**haul on** (or **to, onto**) **the wind** to haul in sails until they are nearly parallel with the desired course, in order to sail closer to the wind —**haul up 1.** to sail nearer the direction of the wind **2.** to come to rest; stop —**in** (or **over**) **the long haul** over a long period of time —**haul′er** *n.*
haul·age (-ij) *n.* **1.** the act or process of hauling **2.** the charge made for hauling, as by a railroad
haulm (hôm) *n.* [ME. *halm* < OE. *healm, halm,* straw, akin to G. *halm* < IE. **kolemos,* reed, cane, whence Gr. *kalamos,* L. *culmus*] **1.** the stalks or stems of cultivated cereal plants, beans, peas, etc., esp. after the crop has been gathered **2.** straw or hay used for thatching, bedding, etc. **3.** a stem of grass or grain
haunch (hônch, hänch) *n.* [ME. *haunche* < OFr. *hanche* < Gmc., as in MDu. *hanke,* haunch, hip] **1.** the part of the body including the hip, buttock, and thickest part of the thigh; hindquarter **2.** an animal's loin and leg together; joint of venison, mutton, etc. **3.** *Archit.* either of the sides of an arch from the point of rising to the vertex
haunch bone the ilium, or hipbone
haunt (hônt, hänt; *for n. 2, usually* hant) *vt.* [ME. *haunten* < OFr. *hanter,* to frequent < Gmc. **haimetan* (akin to OE. *hamettan,* to domicile) < **haim,* HOME] **1.** to visit (a place) often or continually; frequent **2.** to seek the company or companionship of; run after **3.** to appear or recur repeatedly to, often to the point of obsession [memories *haunted* her] **4.** to be associated with; fill the atmosphere of; pervade [memories of former gaiety *haunt* the house] *Haunt* is often used with a ghost, spirit, etc. as its stated or implied subject —*n.* **1.** *a)* a place often visited [to make the library one's *haunt*] *b)* a lair or feeding place of animals **2.** [Dial.] a ghost
haunt·ed (-id) *adj.* supposedly frequented by ghosts
haunt·ing (-iŋ) *adj.* often recurring to the mind; not easily forgotten [a *haunting* tune] —**haunt′ing·ly** *adv.*
Haupt·mann (houpt′män), **Ger·hart** (ger′härt) 1862–1946; Ger. dramatist, novelist, & poet
Hau·sa (hou′sə, -sä) *n., pl.* **-sas, -sa** any member of an Islamic people living principally in N Nigeria and in Niger and adjacent areas **2.** their Chad language, used as a trade language in many parts of W Africa
hau·sen (hô′z'n, hou′-) *n.* [G.] *same as* BELUGA (sense 1)
haus·tel·lum (hô stel′əm) *n., pl.* **-tel′la** (-ə) [ModL. < L. *haustus,* pp. of *haurire,* to drink, draw water] a tubelike sucking organ, or proboscis, as in various insects —**haus·tel′late** (-it, hô′stə lāt′) *adj.*
haus·to·ri·um (hô stôr′ē əm) *n., pl.* **-ri·a** (-ə) [ModL. < L. *haustus:* see prec.] a root or rootlike outgrowth in certain parasitic plants, through which food is absorbed from the host —**haus·to′ri·al** (-əl) *adj.*
haut·boy (hō′boi′, ō′-) *n.* [Fr. *hautbois* < *haut,* high (see HAUGHTY) + *bois,* wood < Frank. **busk,* forest: cf. BUSH¹] earlier name for OBOE
‡**haute cou·ture** (ōt kōō tür′) [Fr., lit., high sewing] the leading designers and creators of new fashions in clothing for women, or their creations; high fashion
‡**haute cui·sine** (ōt kwē zēn′) [Fr., lit., high kitchen] the preparation of fine food by highly skilled chefs, or the food so prepared
hau·teur (hō tur′; *Fr.* ō tër′) *n.* [Fr. < *haut:* see HAUGHTY] disdainful pride; haughtiness; snobbery
Haute-Vol·ta (ōt vôl tà′) *Fr.* name of UPPER VOLTA
‡**haut monde** (ō mōnd′) [Fr.] high society
Ha·van·a (hə van′ə) capital of Cuba; seaport on the Gulf of Mexico; pop. 788,000: Sp. name, HABANA —*n.* **1.** a cigar made in Havana, or in Cuba, or of Cuban tobacco **2.** Cuban tobacco
have (hav; həv, əv; *before* "to" haf) *vt.* **had** (had; *unstressed* həd, əd), **hav′ing;** the unstressed forms usually occur when the verb is used as auxiliary [ME. *haven* (earlier *habben*) < OE. *habban,* akin to OHG. *haben,* ON. *hafa,* Goth. *haban* < IE. base **kap-,* to grasp, whence L. *capere,* to take: primary sense, "to hold, have in hand"] **1.** to hold in the hand or in control; own; possess [to *have* wealth] **2.** to possess or contain as a part, characteristic, attribute, etc. [to *have* blue eyes, the week *has* seven days] **3.** to be affected with or afflicted with [to *have* a cold] **4.** to possess by way of experience; experience; undergo [*have* a good time] **5.** to possess an understanding of; know [to *have* only a little Spanish] **6.** to hold or keep in the mind [to *have* an idea] **7.** to declare or state [so gossip *has* it] **8.** to gain possession, control, or mastery of **9.** *a)* to get, take, receive, or obtain [to *have* news of someone, *have* a look at it] *b)* to consume; eat or drink [*have* some tea] **10.** to bear or beget (offspring) **11.** to perform; carry on; engage in [to *have* an argument] **12.** *a)* to cause to [*have* him walk home] *b)* to cause to be [*have* this done first] **13.** to be in a certain relation to [to *have* brothers and sisters] **14.** to

feel and show [*have* pity on her] 15. to permit; tolerate: used in the negative [I won't *have* this nonsense] 16. [Colloq.] *a*) to hold at a disadvantage or to overcome [I *had* my opponent now] *b*) to deceive; take in; cheat [they were *had* in that business deal] *c*) to engage in sexual intercourse with *Have* is used as an auxiliary with past participles to form phrases expressing completed action, as in the perfect tenses (Ex.: I *have* left, I *had* left, I shall *have* left, I would *have* left, etc.), and with infinitives to express obligation or necessity (Ex.: we *have* to go) *Have got* often replaces *have:* see GET *Have* is conjugated in the present indicative: (I) *have*, (he, she, it) *has*, (we, you, they) *have;* in the past indicative (I, he, she, it, we, you, they) *had* Archaic forms are: (thou) *hast, hadst*, (he, she, it) *hath;* the present subjunctive is *have*, the past subjunctive *had* —*n.* a person or nation with relatively much wealth or rich resources —**have at** to attack; strike —**have done** to stop; get through; finish —**have had it** [Slang] 1. to be exhausted, defeated, disgusted, bored, ready to quit, etc. 2. to be no longer popular, useful, accepted, etc. —**have it good** [Colloq.] to be in comfortable circumstances —**have it out** to settle an issue, disagreement, etc. by fighting or discussion —**have on** to be wearing; be dressed in —**have to be** ☆[Colloq.] to be unquestionably or without doubt [this *has to be* the best movie of the year] —**to have and to hold** to possess permanently: form used in certain marriage ceremonies
SYN.—**have**, the broadest term here, predicates the relation between a subject and an object (physical or nonphysical) that belongs to it in any of the various senses in which *belong* is understood [he had wealth, the poetry has charm, you have odd notions]; **hold** means to have in one's grasp or keeping, or, in extended use, to control as by keeping in a certain place, condition, etc. [to hold a book, one's attention, etc.]; **own** implies the holding or controlling of something as one's personal property [to own lands]; **possess** is in its basic sense equivalent to **own**, and in extended senses means to have as an attribute, quality, faculty, etc. [to *possess* wisdom] —**ANT.** lack, want
Ha·vel (hä′fəl) river in C East Germany, flowing southwest into the Elbe: c. 215 mi.
☆**have·lock** (hav′läk) *n.* [after Sir Henry *Havelock* (1795–1857), Eng. general in India] a light cloth covering for a military cap, falling over the back of the neck for protection against the sun
ha·ven (hā′vən) *n.* [ME. < OE. *hæfen*, akin to G. *hafen*, LowG. *haff* < IE. *kapnos*, haven < base *kap-:* see HAVE] 1. a sheltered anchorage; port; harbor 2. any sheltered, safe place; refuge —*vt.* to provide a haven for
have-not (hav′nät′) *n.* a person or nation with little or no wealth or resources
have·n't (hav′'nt) have not
ha·ver (hā′vər) *vi.* [< ?] [Brit.] to talk foolishly or waste time talking foolishly
Ha·ver·hill (hā′vər əl, -vrəl) [after *Haverhill*, town in England] city in NE Mass., on the Merrimack River, near Lawrence: pop. 46,000
ha·vers (hā′vərz) *interj.* [Brit.] rubbish! nonsense!
hav·er·sack (hav′ər sak′) *n.* [Fr. *havresac* < G. *habersack*, lit., sacks of oats < *haber* (now *hafer* < LowG. cognate), akin to E. dial. *haver*, oats [? orig. "goat food" < IE. base *kapro-*, whence L. *caper*, goat) + G. *sack*, SACK¹] a canvas bag for carrying rations, etc., generally worn over one shoulder, as by soldiers or hikers
Ha·ver·sian (hə vur′shən) *adj.* [after Clopton *Havers*, Eng. physician (1650?–1702)] designating or of the canals through which blood vessels pass in bone
hav·oc (hav′ək) *n.* [earlier esp. in phrase CRY HAVOC (see below) < ME. & Anglo-Fr. *havok* < OFr. *havot*, prob. < *haver*, to hook, take, *hef*, a hook < Frank. *haf-*, to seize (for IE. base see HAVE)] great destruction and devastation, as that resulting from hurricanes, wars, etc. —*vt.* -ocked, -ock·ing [Obs.] to lay waste; devastate —*SYN.* see RUIN —**cry havoc** 1. orig., to give (an army) the signal for pillaging 2. to warn of great, impending danger —**play havoc with** to devastate; destroy; ruin
Havre, Le see LE HAVRE
haw¹ (hô) *n.* [ME. *hawe* < OE. *haga*, haw, hedge, akin to *hecg*, HEDGE] 1. the berry of the hawthorn 2. *same as* HAWTHORN
haw² (hô) *interj., n.* [< ?] a word of command to a horse, ox, etc., esp. one driven without reins, meaning "turn to the left!" —*vt., vi.* to turn to the left Opposed to GEE¹
haw³ (hô) *vi.* [echoic] to hesitate in speaking; grope for words; falter: usually in HEM AND HAW (see HEM²) —*interj., n.* a conventionalized expression of the sound often made by a speaker when hesitating briefly
haw⁴ (hô) *n.* [< ?] 1. *same as* NICTITATING MEMBRANE 2. [often *pl.*] inflammation of the haw
Haw. Hawaiian
Ha·wai·i (hə wä′ē, -yē, -yä) [Haw. < ?] 1. a State of the U.S., consisting of a group of islands (**Hawaiian Islands**) in the North Pacific: admitted 1959; 6,424 sq. mi.; pop. 769,000; cap. Honolulu: abbrev. HI 2. largest & southern-

most of the islands of Hawaii, southeast of Oahu: 4,021 sq. mi.; pop. 63,000
Ha·wai·ian (-yən) *adj.* of Hawaii, its people, language, etc. —*n.* 1. a native or inhabitant of Hawaii; specif., a native of Polynesian descent 2. the Polynesian language of the Hawaiians
☆**Hawaiian Standard Time** a standard time used in Hawaii and corresponding to ALASKA STANDARD TIME
Hawaii Volcanoes National Park national park on the island of Hawaii, including Mauna Loa: 280 sq. mi.
haw·finch (hô′finch′) *n.* [HAW¹ + FINCH] the common grosbeak (*Coccothraustes coccothraustes*) of Europe
haw-haw (hô′hô′) *n., interj. see* HA
hawk¹ (hôk) *n.* [ME. *hauk* < OE. *hafoc*, akin to G. *habicht*, Pol. *kobuz*, falcon] 1. any of a large group of birds of prey (order Falconiformes) characterized by short, rounded wings, a long tail and legs, and a hooked beak and claws; broadly, any such bird active by day except the vultures and eagles: hawks include the falcons, buzzards, harriers, kites, and caracaras; in a more restricted sense, the term is used of birds belonging to the subfamily of falcons typified by the sparrow hawk of Europe and Cooper's hawk of N. America 2. an advocate of all-out war or of measures in international affairs designed to provoke or escalate open hostilities: cf. DOVE¹ 3. a person regarded as having the preying or grasping nature of a hawk; cheater; swindler —*vi.* 1. to hunt birds or other small game with the help of falcons or other hawks 2. to attack by or as by swooping and striking —*vt.* to attack or prey on as a hawk does —**hawk′ish** *adj.* —**hawk′like′** *adj.*
hawk² (hôk) *vt., vi.* [< HAWKER¹] to advertise or peddle (goods) in the streets by shouting
hawk³ (hôk) *vi.* [echoic] to clear the throat audibly —*vt.* to bring up (phlegm) by coughing —*n.* an audible clearing of the throat
hawk⁴ (hôk) *n.* [< ?] a small, square board with a handle underneath, for holding mortar or plaster
hawk·er¹ (hôk′ər) *n.* [altered by folk etym. (after HAWK²) < MLowG. *hoker*, huckster (Du. *heuker*, G. *höker*) < MLowG. *hoken*, to peddle, orig., to crouch (as with a burden) < IE. base *keu-*, to bend, stoop, arch, whence HOBBLE, HIGH] a person who hawks goods in the street; peddler; huckster
hawk·er² (-ər) *n.* [OE. *hafocere*] a person who uses hawks for hunting; falconer
☆**Hawk·eye** (hôk′ī′) *n.* [Colloq.] a native or inhabitant of Iowa, called the **Hawkeye State**
hawk-eyed (-īd′) *adj.* keen-sighted like a hawk
hawk·ing (-iŋ) *n.* falconry; hunting with hawks
Haw·kins (hô′kinz), Sir **John** 1532–95; Eng. naval officer & slave trader
hawk-moth (hôk′môth′) *n.* any of a family (Sphingidae) of moths with a thick, tapering body, slender wings, and a long feeding tube used for sucking the nectar of flowers
hawk's-beard (hôks′bird′) *n.* any of a genus (*Crepis*) of plants of the composite family, with milky juice and small, yellow-flowered heads borne in clusters
hawks·bill (turtle) (-bil′) a medium-sized turtle (*Eretmochelys imbricata*) found in warm seas, having a hawklike beak and a horny shell from which tortoise shell is obtained
hawk·shaw (hôk′shô′) *n.* [after a character in *The Ticket of Leave Man*, a play by Tom Taylor (1817–80), Eng. dramatist] [Colloq.] ☆a detective
hawk·weed (-wēd′) *n.* any of a genus (*Hieracium*) of plants of the composite family, usually with conspicuous basal leaves and stalked clusters of heads with yellow or scarlet ray flowers, including devil's paintbrush
hawse (hôz) *n.* [LME. *halse* < ON. *hals*, the neck, part of the bow of a ship: for IE. base see COLLAR] 1. that part of the bow of a ship containing the hawseholes 2. *same as* HAWSEHOLE 3. the space between the bow of a ship and the anchors 4. the arrangement of a ship's cables when the ship is moored with both a starboard anchor and a port anchor out from forward
hawse·hole (-hōl′) *n.* any of the holes in a ship's bow through which a hawser or cable is passed
hawse·pipe (-pīp′) *n.* an iron or steel pipe in the hawsehole through which the hawser runs
haw·ser (hô′zər) *n.* [ME. *haucer* < Anglo-Fr. *hauceour* < OFr. *haucier* < VL. *altiare* < L. *altus*, high (see ALTITUDE)] a large rope or small cable, often of steel, by which a ship is anchored, moored, or towed
hawser bend a kind of knot for tying one hawser to another: see KNOT, illus.
haw·ser-laid (-lād′) *adj. same as* CABLE-LAID
haw·thorn (hô′thôrn′) *n.* [ME. *hei* < OE. *hagethorn* < OE. *hagathorn* < *haga*, hedge, HAW¹ + *thorn*, akin to G. *hagedorn*] any of a group of thorny shrubs and small trees (genus *Crataegus*) of the rose family, with flowers of white, pink, or red, and red fruits (*haws*) resembling miniature apples
Haw·thorne (hô′thôrn′) [after ff.] city in SW Calif.: suburb of Los Angeles: pop. 53,000
Haw·thorne (hô′thôrn′), **Nathaniel** 1804–64; U.S. novelist & short-story writer
hay¹ (hā) *n.* [ME. *hei* < OE. *hieg* (akin to G. *heu*) < base of OE. *heawan*, to cut (see HEW)] 1. grass, alfalfa, clover, etc. cut and dried for use as fodder 2. [Slang] bed, specif. as a place for sexual intercourse [roll in the *hay*] —*vi.*

HAVELOCK

to mow grass, alfalfa, etc., and spread it out to dry —*vt.* [Rare] **1.** to furnish with hay **2.** to grow grass on (land) for hay —☆**hit the hay** [Slang] to go to bed to sleep —**make hay** to mow grass, alfalfa, etc., and spread it out to dry —**make hay (out) of** to turn (something) to one's advantage —**make hay while the sun shines** to make the most of an opportunity —☆**not hay** [Slang] not a trifling sum; much money

hay² (hā) *n.* [OFr. *haye*] an old country dance with much winding in and out

Hay (hā), **John** (Milton) 1838–1905; U.S. statesman & writer; secretary of state (1898–1905)

hay·cock (hā′käk′) *n.* a small, conical heap of hay drying in a field

Hay·dn (hīd′'n), **Franz Jo·seph** (fränts yō′zef) 1732–1809; Austrian composer

Hayes (hāz) **1. Carl·ton J**(oseph) **H**(untley) (kärl′tən), 1882– ; U.S. historian **2. Ruth·er·ford B**(irchard) (ruth′ər fərd), 1822–93; 19th president of the U.S. (1877–81)

hay fever an acute inflammation of the eyes and upper respiratory tract, accompanied by sneezing: it is an allergic reaction, caused mainly by the pollen of some grasses and trees; pollenosis

hay·field (hā′fēld′) *n.* a field of grass, alfalfa, etc. to be made into hay

hay·fork (-fôrk′) *n.* **1.** *same as* PITCHFORK ☆**2.** a mechanically operated device for lifting or moving hay

hay·loft (-lôft′) *n.* a loft, or upper story, in a barn or stable, for storing hay

hay·mak·er (-mā′kər) *n.* **1.** a person who cuts hay and spreads it out to dry ☆**2.** [Slang] a powerful blow with the fist, intended to cause a knockout

Hay·mar·ket Square (hā′mär′kit) square in Chicago: site of a battle between police & workmen (**Haymarket Riot**) on May 4, 1886, following a demonstration for the eight-hour day

hay·mow (hā′mou′) *n.* **1.** a pile of hay in a barn **2.** *same as* HAYLOFT

Hayns·worth (hānz′wərth), **Clement F**(urman), **Jr.**, 1912– ; associate justice, U. S. Supreme Court (1969–)

hay·rack (hā′rak′) *n.* **1.** a rack or frame from which cattle, horses, etc. eat hay ☆**2.** *a)* a framework extending up from a wagon, to permit carrying larger quantities of hay *b)* a wagon having this

hay·rick (-rik′) *n.* a large heap of hay; haystack

☆**hay·ride** (-rīd′) *n.* a pleasure ride in a wagon partly filled with hay, taken by a group on an outing

Hays (hāz), **Arthur Garfield** 1881–1954; U.S. lawyer & civil libertarian

hay·seed (hā′sēd′) *n.* **1.** grass seed shaken from mown hay **2.** bits of chaff and straw from hay ☆**3.** [Old Slang] an awkward, unsophisticated person regarded as typical of rural areas; rustic

hay·stack (-stak′) *n.* a large heap of hay piled up outdoors

Hay·ward (hā′wərd) [after William *Hayward*, local postmaster] city in W Calif.: suburb of Oakland: pop. 93,000

hay·ward (hā′wôrd, -wərd) *n.* [ME. *heiward* < *hei*, hedge (< OE. *hege*, akin to *haga*, HAW¹ + OFr. *haie* < Frank. *hagja*, cognate with OE. *hege*) + *ward*, a guardian: see WARD] [Now Rare] an official in charge of fences or hedges around public pastures, who impounds stray cattle

☆**hay·wire** (hā′wīr′) *n.* wire for tying up bales of hay, straw, etc. —*adj.* [prob. < *haywire outfit*, loggers' term for a camp with poor equipment that had to be held together with haywire] [Slang] **1.** out of order; disorganized; confused **2.** crazy: usually in **go haywire** to become, or act as if, crazy

ha·zan (hä′z'n; *Heb.* khä zän′) *n.,* *pl.* **ha·zan′im** (-zän′im) [ModHeb. *ḥazzān*] a cantor in a synagogue: also sp. **haz′zan**

haz·ard (haz′ərd) *n.* [ME. < OFr. *hasard*, game of dice, adventure < Ar. *az-zahr*] **1.** an early game of chance played with dice, from which craps is derived **2.** chance, or a chance occurrence **3.** *a)* risk; peril; danger; jeopardy *b)* [Archaic] something risked **4.** an obstacle on a golf course, such as a trap, bunker, or pond **5.** *Court Tennis* any of the three openings on the side (**hazard side**) of the court in which service is received: see WINNING OPENING —*vt.* **1.** to expose to danger; chance; risk **2.** to attempt or venture [to *hazard* a try] —*SYN.* see DANGER

haz·ard·ous (-əs) *adj.* **1.** of or involving chance **2.** risky; dangerous; perilous —**haz′ard·ous·ly** *adv.*

haze¹ (hāz) *n.* [prob. back-formation < HAZY] **1.** a thin vapor of fog, smoke, dust, etc. in the air that reduces visibility **2.** slight confusion or vagueness of mind —*vi., vt.* **hazed, haz′ing** to make or become hazy (often with *over*) —*SYN.* see MIST

haze² (hāz) *vt.* **hazed, haz′ing** [< ? OFr. *haser*, to irritate, annoy] **1.** *Naut.* to oppress, punish, or harass by forcing to do hard and unnecessary work ☆**2.** to initiate or discipline (fellow students) by forcing to do ridiculous, humiliating, or painful things

Ha·zel (hā′z'l) [Heb. *ḥazā'ēl*, lit., God sees] a feminine name

ha·zel (hā′z'l) *n.* [ME. *hasel* < OE. *hæsel*, akin to G. *hasel* < IE. *kos(*e*)*lo*-, hazel, whence L. *corulus*, hazel bush, OIr. *coll*, hazel] **1.** any of a genus (*Corylus*) of shrubs or trees of the birch family, bearing edible nuts **2.** *same as* HAZELNUT **3.** *a)* the wood of this tree or shrub *b)* a stick of this wood **4.** the color of a ripened hazelnut; reddish brown —*adj.* **1.** of the hazel tree or its wood **2.** light reddish-brown or yellowish-brown: hazel eyes are usually flecked with green or gray —**ha′zel·ly** *adj.*

hazel hen (or **grouse**) a European woodland grouse (*Tetrastes bonasia*) related to the ruffed grouse

ha·zel·nut (-nut′) *n.* the small, edible, roundish nut of the hazel; filbert

Haz·litt (haz′lit), **William** 1778–1830; Eng. essayist

ha·zy (hā′zē) *adj.* **-zi·er, -zi·est** [prob. < or akin to OE. *hasu*, gray, dusky (akin to MHG. *heswe*, pale): cf. HARE] **1.** characterized by the presence of haze; somewhat foggy, misty, or smoky **2.** somewhat vague, obscure, confused, or indefinite [*hazy* thinking] —**ha′zi·ly** *adv.* —**ha′zi·ness** *n.*

Hb *the symbol for* hemoglobin

hb. *Football* halfback

H.B.M. His (or Her) Britannic Majesty

☆**H-bomb** (āch′bäm′) *n. same as* HYDROGEN BOMB

H.C. 1. Heralds' College **2.** Holy Communion **3.** House of Commons

h.c. [L. *honoris causa*] for the sake of honor

H.C.F., h.c.f. highest common factor

h.c.l., HCL [Colloq.] high cost of living

HD heavy duty

hd. head

hdbk. handbook

hdqrs. headquarters

he¹ (hē; *unstressed* hi, ē, i) *pron. for pl. see* THEY [ME. & OE. (where it contrasts with *heo*, she, *hie*, they < same base) < IE. base **ko-, kē-*, this one, whence HERE, HITHER, L. *cis*, on this side: orig. a demonstrative] **1.** the man, boy, or male animal (or, sometimes, the object regarded as male) previously mentioned **2.** the person; the one; anyone [*he* who laughs last laughs best] *He* is the nominative case form, *him* the objective, *his* the possessive, and *himself* the intensive and reflexive, of the masculine third personal pronoun —*n., pl.* **hes** a man, boy, or male animal

he² (hā) *n.* [Heb., lit., window] the fifth letter of the Hebrew alphabet (ה)

he- (hē) *a combining form meaning* male: used in hyphenated compounds [*he*-dog]

He *Chem.* helium

H.E. 1. high explosive **2.** His Eminence **3.** His Excellency

head (hed) *n.* [ME. *hede, heved* < OE. *heafod*, akin to G. *haupt* (OHG. *houbit*, Goth. *haubith*) < IE. base *kaput- (orig. prob. cup-shaped), whence L. *caput*: merged in Gmc. with word akin to OHG. *hūba*, a cap, crest (G. *haube*) < IE. *keu-, to bend, curve] **1.** *a)* the top part of the body in man, the apes, etc., or the front part in most other animals: in higher animals it is a bony structure containing the brain, and including the jaws, eyes, ears, nose, and mouth *b)* this part exclusive of the face **2.** *a)* the head as the seat of reason, memory, and imagination; mind; intelligence [to use one's *head*] *b)* aptitude; ability [to have a *head* for mathematics] *c)* [Colloq.] a headache, esp. as part of a hangover **3.** the head as a symbol for the individual; person [dinner at five dollars a *head*] **4.** *pl.* **head** the head as a unit of counting [fifty *head* of cattle] **5.** a representation of a head, as in painting or sculpture **6.** the obverse of a coin, usually with such a representation: often **heads 7.** the highest or uppermost part or thing; top; specif., *a)* the top of a page, column of figures, etc. *b)* a printed title at the top of a page, section of writing, etc. *c)* a chief point of discussion; topic of a section, chapter, etc. in a speech or written work *d)* a headline for a newspaper story *e)* froth floating on newly poured effervescent beverages, esp. on beer *f)* that end of a cask or barrel which is uppermost at any time *g)* the upper edge of a sail **8.** the foremost part of a thing; front; specif., *a)* a part associated with the human head [the *head* of a bed] *b)* the part of a pier farthest from land *c)* the front part of a ship; bow *d)* *Naut.* a toilet, or lavatory *e)* the front position, as of a column of marching men *f)* either end of something; extremity **9.** the projecting part of something; specif., *a)* the part designed for holding, pushing, striking, etc. [the *head* of a pin, the *head* of a golf club] *b)* a jutting mass of rock, land, etc., as of a mountain *c)* a point of land; promontory; headland *d)* a projecting place in a boil or other inflammation where pus is about to break through *e)* the part of a tape recorder that imposes or plays back the magnetic arrangements on the tape **10.** the membrane stretched across the end of a drum, tambourine, etc. **11.** the source of a flowing body of water; beginning of a stream, river, etc. **12.** *a)* a source of water kept at some height to supply a mill, etc. *b)* the height of such a source of water or the vertical distance through which it falls *c)* a rush of water, as in a riptide **13.** the pressure in an enclosed fluid, as steam, from its own weight or applied externally, expressed in

lbs. per sq. in. **14.** a position of leadership, honor, or first importance [the *head* of the class] **15.** the person who is foremost or in charge; leader, ruler, chief, director, etc. **16.** a headmaster **17.** *Bot. a)* a dense, flattened cluster of sessile flowers attached to a common receptacle, as in the dandelion *b)* a large, compact bud [a *head* of cabbage] *c)* the uppermost part of a plant's foliage [the *head* of a tree] **18.** *Linguis.* any word or word group in a greater group that functions grammatically like the entire group **19.** *Mining* same as HEADING (sense 4) **20.** *Music* the rounded part of a note, at the end of the stem **21.** [Slang] a drug addict: often in combination [*acidhead*] —*adj.* **1.** of or having to do with the head **2.** most important; principal; commanding; first **3.** to be found at the top or front **4.** striking against the front [*head* current] —*vt.* **1.** to be the chief of or in charge of; command; direct **2.** *a)* to be at the top or beginning of; lead; precede (often with *up*) [to *head* a list] *b)* to take a lead over, as in a race or competition **3.** to supply (a pin, etc.) with a head **4.** [Rare] to behead; decapitate **5.** to trim the higher part from (a tree or plant); poll ☆**6.** to go round the head of [to *head* a stream] **7.** to turn or cause to go in a specified direction [to *head* a car for home] **8.** *Soccer* to hit (the ball) with one's head —*vi.* **1.** to grow or come to a head **2.** to set out; travel [to *head* eastward] ☆**3.** to originate, as a river —**by a head 1.** by the length of the animal's head, as in horse racing **2.** by a very small margin —**by (or down by) the head** *Naut.* with the bow deeper in the water than the stern —**come to a head 1.** to be about to suppurate, as a boil **2.** to culminate, or reach a crisis —**get it through one's head** to cause one to understand —**give one his head** to let one do as he likes —**go to one's head 1.** to confuse, excite, or intoxicate one **2.** to make one vain or overconfident —**hang (or hide) one's head** to lower one's head or conceal one's face in or as in shame —**head and shoulders above** definitely superior to —**head off** to get ahead of and cause to stop or turn away; intercept —**head over heels 1.** tumbling as if in a somersault **2.** deeply; completely **3.** hurriedly; impetuously; recklessly —**heads up!** [Colloq.] look out! be careful! —**keep one's head** to keep one's poise, self-control, etc.; not become excited or flustered —**keep one's head above water 1.** to remain afloat; not sink **2.** to keep oneself alive, out of debt, etc. —**lose one's head** to lose one's poise, self-control, etc.; become excited or flustered —**make head** to make headway; go forward; advance —**make head or tail of** to understand: usually in the negative —**on (or upon) one's head** as one's burden, responsibility, or misfortune —**one's head off** a great deal: preceded by a verb [to talk *one's head off*] —**out of (or off) one's head** [Colloq.] **1.** crazy **2.** delirious; raving —**over one's head 1.** *a)* too difficult for one to understand *b)* so that one cannot understand **2.** in spite of one's prior claim **3.** without consulting one; to a higher authority —**put (or lay) heads together** to consult or scheme together —**take it into one's head** to conceive the notion, plan, or intention —**turn one's head 1.** to make one dizzy **2.** to make one vain or overconfident

-head (hed) *same as* -HOOD [*godhead*]
head·ache (hed′āk′) *n.* [ME. *hevedeche* < OE. *heafodece*] **1.** a continuous pain in the head ☆**2.** [Colloq.] a cause of worry, annoyance, or trouble
head·band (-band′) *n.* **1.** a band worn around the head ☆**2.** an ornamental printed band at the top of a page or the beginning of a chapter **3.** *Bookbinding* a cloth band fastened to the top and bottom of the back of a book under the spine
head·board (-bôrd′) *n.* a board or frame that forms the head of a bed, etc.
☆**head·cheese** (-chēz′) *n.* a loaf of jellied, seasoned meat made from parts of the head and feet of hogs
head cold a common cold characterized chiefly by congestion of the nasal passages
head doctor [Slang] a psychiatrist
head·dress (-dres′) *n.* **1.** a covering or decoration for the head **2.** a style of arranging the hair; coiffure
head·ed (-id) *adj.* **1.** formed into a head, as cabbage **2.** having a heading
-head·ed (-id) *a combining form meaning:* **1.** having a (specified kind of) head [*clearheaded*] **2.** having a (specified number of) heads [*two-headed*]
head·er (-ər) *n.* **1.** a person or device that puts heads on pins, nails, rivets, etc. ☆**2.** a machine that takes off the heads of grain and sends them up an inclined plane into a wagon **3.** a pipe, tube, etc. that connects other pieces to permit the flow of a fluid through them **4.** [Colloq.] a headlong fall or dive **5.** *Carpentry* a wooden beam, as in flooring, placed between two long beams with the ends of short beams resting against it **6.** *Masonry* a brick or building stone laid across the thickness of a wall so that a short end is exposed in the face of the wall
head·first (-fʉrst′) *adv.* **1.** with the head in front; headlong **2.** in a reckless way; rashly; impetuously Also **head′fore′most′** (-fôr′mōst′)
☆**head·fish** (-fish′) *n. same as* OCEAN SUNFISH
☆**head gate** a gate that controls the flow of water into a canal lock, sluice, etc.
head·gear (-gir′) *n.* **1.** a covering for the head; hat, cap, headdress, etc. **2.** the harness for the head of a horse,

mule, etc. **3.** *Mining* the lifting apparatus at the opening of a shaft
head·hunt·er (-hun′tər) *n.* **1.** a member of any of certain primitive tribes who remove the heads of slain enemies and preserve them as trophies ☆**2.** [Slang] an agent or agency specializing in the recruitment of executive or highly skilled personnel —**head′hunt′ing** *n.*
head·i·ly (-′l ē) *adv.* in a heady manner
head·i·ness (-ē nis) *n.* the quality or condition of being heady
head·ing (-in) *n.* **1.** something forming or used to form the head, top, edge, or front; specif., an inscription at the top of a paragraph, chapter, page, section, etc., giving the title, topic, etc. **2.** a division of a subject; topic or category **3.** the direction in which a ship, plane, etc. is moving: usually expressed as a compass reading **4.** *Mining a)* a gallery; drift *b)* the end of a gallery
☆**head·lamp** (-lamp′) *n. same as* HEADLIGHT
head·land (-lənd; *for* 1, *also* -land′) *n.* [ME. *hedelonde* < OE. *heafod lond*] **1.** the unbroken soil at the edge of a plowed field, esp. at the ends of the furrows **2.** a cape or point of land reaching out into the water; esp., a promontory
head·less (-lis) *adj.* [ME. *hevedles* < OE. *heafodleas*] **1.** without a head; specif., *a)* organically without a head; acephalous *b)* beheaded **2.** without a leader or director **3.** stupid; foolish; brainless
☆**head·light** (-līt′) *n.* a light with a reflector and lens, at the front of a locomotive, automobile, etc.
head·line (-līn′) *n.* **1.** a line at the top of a page in a book, giving the running title, page number, etc. ☆**2.** a line or lines, usually in larger type, at the top of a newspaper article, giving a short statement of its contents **3.** an important item of news —*vt.* **-lined′**, **-lin′ing 1.** to provide (a news article) with a headline **2.** to give (a performer or performance) featured billing or publicity
☆**head·lin·er** (-lī′nər) *n.* an actor or entertainer advertised as a leading attraction
head·lock (-läk′) *n. Wrestling* a hold in which one contestant's head is locked between the arm and the body of the other
head·long (-lôŋ′) *adv.* [LME. *hedlong*, altered (after *-long*, -LONG) < ME. *hedelinge(s)* < *hede*, head + *-linge*, adv. suffix] **1.** with the head first; headfirst **2.** with uncontrolled speed and force **3.** recklessly; rashly; impetuously —*adj.* **1.** [Rare or Poet.] steep; dizzy; precipitous [a *headlong* height] **2.** having the head first **3.** moving with uncontrolled speed and force **4.** reckless; impetuous
head·man (hed′man; *also, for* 1, -man′) *n., pl.* **-men** (-mən; *also, for* 1, -men′) [ME. *hevidman* < OE. *heafodmann*] **1.** a leader, chief, or overseer **2.** [Rare] a headsman; executioner
head·mas·ter (-mas′tər, -mäs′-) *n.* in certain schools, esp. private schools for boys, the man in charge of the school; principal —**head′mas′ter·ship′** *n.*
head·mis·tress (-mis′tris) *n.* in certain schools, esp. private schools for girls, the woman in charge of the school; principal
head money 1. *same as* POLL TAX **2.** a reward paid for killing or capturing an enemy, outlaw, etc.
head·most (-mōst′) *adj.* in the lead; foremost
head·note (-nōt′) *n.* a brief explanatory note prefacing a chapter, poem, story, legal report, etc.
☆**head-on** (-än′) *adj., adv.* **1.** with the head or front foremost [a *head-on* collision] **2.** directly; esp., in direct opposition [to meet a problem *head-on*]
head·phone (-fōn′) *n.* a telephone or radio receiver held to the ear by a band over the head
head·piece (-pēs′) *n.* **1.** a covering for the head, esp. a protective covering; helmet **2.** the head; mind; intellect **3.** *Printing* an ornamental design engraved at the beginning of a book, chapter, etc.
head·pin (-pin′) *n.* the pin at the front of a triangle of bowling pins
head·quar·ters (-kwôr′tərz) *n.pl.* [*often with sing. v.*] **1.** the main office, or center of operations and control, of anyone in command, as in an army, police force, etc. **2.** the main office or center of control in any organization —**head′quar′ter** *vt.*

HEADPHONE

head·race (-rās′) *n.* the channel or race furnishing water as to a mill wheel: opposed to TAILRACE
head register the upper register of the voice, in which the higher range of tones is produced
head·rest (-rest′) *n.* a support for the head, as on a dentist's chair, barber's chair, etc.
head·room (-rōōm′) *n.* space or clearance overhead, as in a doorway, tunnel, etc.; headway
head·sail (-sāl′, -s′l) *n.* any sail forward of the mast or foremast
head·set (-set′) *n.* an earphone or earphones, often with a mouthpiece transmitter attached
head·ship (-ship′) *n.* the position or authority of a chief or leader; leadership; command

head·shrink·er (-shriŋ′kər) *n.* **1.** a headhunter who shrinks the heads of his victims ☆**2.** [Slang] a psychiatrist

heads·man (hedz′mən) *n., pl.* **-men** (-mən) [ME. *heddys-man* < *heddys, hefdes* (gen. of *hede, heved,* HEAD) + MAN] **1.** an executioner who beheads those condemned to die **2.** [Rare] a leader; headman

head·spring (hed′spriŋ′) *n.* [ME. *hedspring:* see HEAD & SPRING] a fountain, origin, or source

head·stall (-stôl′) *n.* [see HEAD & STALL¹] the part of a bridle or halter that fits over a horse's head

head·stand (-stand′) *n.* the act of supporting oneself upright on the head, usually with the help of the hands

head start an early start or other advantage given to or taken by a contestant or competitor

head·stock (-stäk′) *n.* a bearing or support for a revolving or moving part of a machine; specif., the part of a lathe supporting the spindle

head·stone (-stōn′) *n.* **1.** [Rare or Poet.] the main stone in a foundation; cornerstone **2.** a stone marker placed at the head of a grave

head·stream (-strēm′) *n.* a stream forming the source of another and larger stream

head·strong (-strôŋ′) *adj.* [ME. *heedstronge:* see HEAD & STRONG] **1.** determined not to follow orders, advice, etc. but to do as one pleases; self-willed **2.** showing such determination [*headstrong* desire]

head tone any of the tones produced in the head register by a singer

head·wait·er (-wāt′ər) *n.* a supervisor of waiters, often in charge of table reservations

head·wa·ters (-wôt′ərz, -wät′ərz) *n.pl.* the small streams that are the sources of a river

head·way (-wā′) *n.* **1.** forward motion **2.** progress or success in work, etc. **3.** *same as* HEADROOM ☆**4.** the difference in time or miles between two trains, ships, etc. traveling in the same direction over the same course

head wind a wind blowing in the direction directly opposite the course of a ship or aircraft

head·word (-wurd′) *n.* **1.** a word or phrase that is a heading for a paragraph, chapter, etc. **2.** *Linguis.* a word functioning as a head in a structure of modification

head·work (-wurk′) *n.* mental effort; thought

head·y (-ē) *adj.* **head′i·er, head′i·est** [ME. *hevedi:* see HEAD & -Y²] **1.** impetuous; rash; willful **2.** tending to affect the senses; intoxicating [*heady* wine]

heal (hēl) *vt.* [ME. *helen* < OE. *hælan* (akin to G. *heilen*) < base of *hal,* sound, healthy: see HALE¹, WHOLE] **1.** to make sound, well, or healthy; restore to health [*heal* the sick] **2.** *a)* to cure or get rid of (a disease) *b)* to cause (a wound, sore, etc.) to become closed or scarred so as to restore a healthy condition **3.** to free from grief, troubles, evil, etc. **4.** *a)* to remedy or get rid of (grief, troubles, etc.) *b)* to make up (a breach, differences, etc.); reconcile —*vi.* **1.** to become sound, well, or healthy again; be cured; get well **2.** to become closed or scarred: said of a wound —SYN. see CURE

heal-all (hēl′ôl′) *n. same as* SELFHEAL

heal·er (-ər) *n.* [ME. *helere*] a person or thing that heals; specif., one who tries to heal through prayer or faith

health (helth) *n.* [ME. *helthe* < OE. *hælth* < base of *hal,* sound, healthy (see HALE¹, HEAL, WHOLE) + *-th*] **1.** physical and mental well-being; freedom from disease, pain, or defect; normality of physical and mental functions; soundness **2.** condition of body or mind [good or bad *health*] **3.** a wish for a person's health and happiness, as in drinking a toast **4.** soundness or vitality, as of a society or culture

health·ful (-fəl) *adj.* **1.** helping to produce, promote, or maintain health; salutary; wholesome **2.** [Rare] *same as* HEALTHY —**health′ful·ly** *adv.* —**health′ful·ness** *n.*

☆**health physics** a discipline dealing with protection against the potential hazards of harmful radiations in the environment —**health physicist**

health·y (hel′thē) *adj.* **health′i·er, health′i·est** **1.** having good health; well; sound **2.** showing or resulting from good health [a *healthy* color] **3.** *same as* HEALTHFUL **4.** [Colloq.] large, vigorous, etc. [a *healthy* yell] —**health′i·ly** *adv.* —**health′i·ness** *n.*
SYN.—**healthy** implies normal physical and mental vigor and freedom from disease, weakness, disorder, etc.; **sound** implies perfectness of health, suggesting a condition in which there is no sign of disease or defect; **hale,** closely synonymous with **sound,** is used esp. of vigorous elderly people who are free from the infirmities of old age; **robust** implies a vitality and hardiness that is immediately apparent in muscular build, good color, abundance of energy, etc.; **well** simply implies freedom from illness, without further connotation —ANT. ill, diseased, infirm, frail

heap (hēp) *n.* [ME. *hepe,* a troop, heap < OE. *heap,* a troop, band, multitude, akin to Du. *hoop* < IE. *keub-* < base *keu-,* to bend, arch, whence HOP¹, L. *cupa,* vat] **1.** a pile, mass, or mound of things jumbled together **2.** [Colloq.] a large amount; great deal [to earn a *heap* of money] ☆**3.** [Slang] an automobile, esp. an old one —*vt.* **1.** to make a heap of; bring together into a pile **2.** to give or supply in large amounts; load [to *heap* gifts

upon someone] **3.** to fill (a plate, dry measure, etc.) full or to overflowing —*vi.* to accumulate or rise in a heap, or pile

hear (hir) *vt.* **heard** (hurd), **hear′ing** [ME. *heren* < OE. *hieran,* akin to G. *hören* (Goth. *hausjan*) < IE. base *keu-,* to notice, observe, whence L. *cavere,* be on one's guard, Gr. *koein,* to perceive, hear] **1.** to perceive or sense (sounds), esp. through stimulation of auditory nerves in the ear by sound waves **2.** to listen to and consider; specif., *a)* to take notice of; pay attention to [*hear* what I tell you] *b)* to listen to officially; give a formal hearing to [to *hear* a child's lessons] *c)* to conduct an examination or hearing of (a law case, etc.); try *d)* to consent to; grant [*hear* my plea] *e)* to be a member of the audience at (an opera, lecture, etc.) **3.** to be informed of; be told; learn [to *hear* a rumor] —*vi.* **1.** to have a normally functioning ear or ears; be able to hear sounds **2.** to listen **3.** to be told or informed (*of* or *about*) —**hear from 1.** to get a letter, telegram, etc. from **2.** to get a criticism or reprimand from —**hear! hear!** well said!: an expression of approval or agreement —**hear out** to listen to until the end —**hear tell** [Dial.] to be told; learn —**not hear of** to forbid or refuse to consider —**hear′er** *n.*

hear·ing (-iŋ) *n.* [ME. *heringe:* see prec.] **1.** the act or process of perceiving sounds **2.** the sense by which sounds are perceived **3.** opportunity to speak, sing, etc.; chance to be heard; audience **4.** *a)* a court appearance before a judge or court referee, other than an actual formal trial *b)* a formal meeting (as of an investigative body or legislative committee) before which evidence is presented, testimony is given, etc. **5.** the distance that a sound, esp. that of the unaided voice, will carry [to be within *hearing*]

hearing aid a small, battery-powered electronic device worn to compensate for hearing loss

heark·en (här′kən) *vi.* [ME. *herknen* < OE. *heorcnean, hyrcnian* < base of *hieran* (see HEAR)] to give careful attention; listen carefully —*vt.* [Archaic] to pay attention to; hear; heed

Hearn (hurn), **Laf·ca·di·o** (laf kad′ē ō) (born *Patricio Lafcadio Tessima Carlos Hearn*; Jap. name *Yakumo Koizumi*) 1850–1904; U.S. writer, born in Greece; became a citizen of Japan (c. 1890)

hear·say (hir′sā′) *n.* [< phrase *to hear say,* parallel to G. *hörensagen*] something one has heard but does not know to be true; rumor; gossip —*adj.* having the nature of or based on hearsay

hearsay evidence *Law* evidence based on something the witness has heard someone else say rather than on what he has himself seen or experienced: it is usually inadmissible as testimony

hearse (hurs) *n.* [ME. *herce* < OFr., a harrow, grated portcullis < L. *hirpex,* a harrow] **1.** an automobile, carriage, etc. used in a funeral for carrying the corpse **2.** *a)* a framelike structure above a coffin or tomb, on which to place candles, hangings, etc. *b)* a triangular framework for holding candles at Tenebrae services **3.** [Archaic] a bier or coffin —*vt.* **hearsed, hears′ing** [Poet.] to carry or put in a hearse

Hearst (hurst), **William Randolph** 1863–1951; U.S. newspaper & magazine publisher

heart (härt) *n.* [ME. < OE. *heorte,* akin to G. *herz* < IE. base *kerd-, krd-,* heart, whence L. *cor,* (gen. *cordis*) & Gr. *kardia*] **1.** *a)* the hollow, muscular organ in a vertebrate animal that receives blood from the veins and pumps it through the arteries by alternate dilation and contraction *b)* an analogous part in most invertebrate animals **2.** the part of the human body thought of as containing the heart; breast; bosom **3.** any place or part like a heart, in that it is near the center; specif., *a)* the central core of a plant or vegetable [*hearts* of celery] *b)* the center or innermost part of a place or region [the *heart* of a city] **4.** the central, vital, or main part; real meaning; essence; core **5.** the human heart considered as the center or source of emotions, personality attributes, etc.; specif., *a)* inmost thought and feeling; consciousness or conscience [to know in one's *heart*] *b)* the source of emotions: contrasted with HEAD, the source of intellect *c)* one's emotional nature; disposition [to have a kind *heart*] *d)* any of various humane feelings; love, devotion, sympathy, etc. *e)* mood; feeling [to have a heavy *heart*] *f)* spirit, resolution, or courage [to lose *heart*] **6.** a person, usually one loved or admired in some specified way [he is a valiant *heart*] **7.** something like a heart in shape; conventionalized design or representation of a heart, shaped like this: ♥ **8.** *a)* any

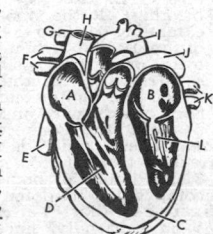

HUMAN HEART
(A, right atrium; B, left atrium; C, myocardium; D, right ventricle; E, inferior vena cava; F, pulmonary veins; G, pulmonary artery; H, superior vena cava; I, aorta; J, pulmonary artery; K, pulmonary veins; L, left ventricle)

of a suit of playing cards marked with such symbols in red *b)* [*pl.*] this suit of cards ☆*c)* [*pl.*] a card game in which the object is to avoid getting any hearts in the tricks taken —*vt.* [Rare] to hearten, or encourage —**after one's own heart** that suits or pleases one perfectly —**at heart** in one's innermost or hidden nature; secretly or fundamentally —**break one's heart** to cause one to be overcome with grief or disappointment —**by heart** by or from memorization —☆**change of heart** a change of mind, affections, loyalties, etc. —**do one's heart good** to make one happy; please one —**eat one's heart out** to brood or feel keenly unhappy over some frustration or in regret —**from (the bottom of) one's heart** very sincerely or deeply —☆**have a heart** to be kind, sympathetic, generous, etc. —**have one's heart in one's mouth** (or **boots**) to be full of fear or nervous anticipation —**have one's heart in the right place** to be well-intentioned or well-meaning —**heart and soul** with all one's effort, enthusiasm, etc. —**in one's heart of hearts** in one's innermost nature or deepest feelings; fundamentally —**lay to heart** to consider seriously and try to profit by —**lose one's heart (to)** to fall in love (with) —**near one's heart** dear or important to one —**set one's heart at rest** to set aside one's doubts, fears, or worries —**set one's heart on** to have a fixed desire for; long for —**steal one's heart** to cause one to feel love or affection —**take heart** to have more courage or confidence; cheer up —**take to heart** 1. to consider seriously 2. to be troubled or grieved by —**to one's heart's content** as much as one desires —**wear one's heart on one's sleeve** to behave so that one's feelings or affections are plainly evident —**with all one's heart** 1. with complete sincerity, devotion, etc. 2. very willingly; with pleasure —**with half a heart** halfheartedly

heart·ache (-āk′) *n.* [OE. *heortece*: see HEART & ACHE] sorrow or grief; mental anguish

heart·beat (-bēt′) *n.* one pulsation, or full contraction and dilation, of the heart; heartthrob

heart block a disorder in which there is defective transmission of impulses regulating the heartbeat, resulting in independent contractions of the atria and ventricles

heart·break (-brāk′) *n.* overwhelming sorrow, grief, or disappointment —**heart′break′ing** *adj.*

heart·bro·ken (-brō′k'n) *adj.* overwhelmed with sorrow, grief, or disappointment

heart·burn (-burn′) *n.* 1. a burning sensation beneath the breastbone resulting from a spastic backflow of acid stomach contents into the esophagus 2. *same as* HEART-BURNING

heart·burn·ing (-bur′niŋ) *n.* jealousy or discontent

heart cherry a heart-shaped variety of sweet cherry

heart·ed (-id) *adj.* [ME.] having a (specified kind of) heart: used in compounds [*stouthearted*]

heart·en (-'n) *vt.* [HEART + -EN] to cheer up; encourage

heart failure the inability of the heart to pump enough blood to maintain an adequate flow to and from the body tissues

heart·felt (-felt′) *adj.* [HEART + pp. of FEEL] with or expressive of deep feeling; sincere —*SYN.* see SINCERE

heart-free (-frē′) *adj.* not in love

hearth (härth) *n.* [ME. *herth* < OE. *heorth*, akin to G. *herd* < IE. base **ker-*, to burn, glow, whence Sans. *kuṣāku-*, burning] 1. the stone or brick floor of a fireplace, often extending out into the room 2. *a)* the fireside as the center of family life *b)* family life; home 3. the part of a brick oven, or of a blacksmith's forge, on which the fire rests 4. *Metallurgy a)* the lowest part of a blast furnace, on which the molten metal and slag are deposited *b)* the floor of a furnace on which the ore or metal rests for exposure to the flame

hearth·side (-sīd′) *n. same as* FIRESIDE

hearth·stone (-stōn′) *n.* 1. the stone forming a hearth 2. the home, or home life 3. a soft stone or powdered composition used for scouring a hearth, steps, etc.

heart·i·ly (härt′'l ē) *adv.* [ME. *hertili*: see HEART & -LY²] 1. in a friendly, sincere, cordial way 2. with zest, enthusiasm, or vigor 3. with a good appetite and in large amounts [to eat *heartily*] 4. completely; fully; very [*heartily* sorry]

heart·i·ness (-ē nis) *n.* a hearty quality or state

heart·land (-land′) *n.* a geographically central area having crucial economic, political, or strategic importance; specif., in Nazi ideology, northern, central Eurasia as having such importance in a struggle for world power

heart·less (-lis) *adj.* [ME. *herteles* < OE. *heortleas*] 1. lacking spirit, courage, or enthusiasm 2. lacking kindness or feeling; hard and pitiless: now the usual sense —**heart′-less·ly** *adv.* —**heart′less·ness** *n.*

heart-rend·ing (-ren′diŋ) *adj.* causing much grief or mental anguish —**heart′-rend′ing·ly** *adv.*

hearts·ease, heart's-ease (härts′ēz′) *n.* [see HEART & EASE] 1. peace of mind; calmness of emotion 2. *same as* WILD PANSY: so called because formerly believed to cure the discomforts of love

heart·sick (härt′sik′) *adj.* sick at heart; extremely unhappy or despondent: also **heart′sore′** (-sôr′)

heart·some (-səm) *adj.* [HEART + -SOME¹] [Scot.] 1. heartening; cheering 2. cheerful; lively

heart-strick·en (-strik′'n) *adj.* deeply grieved or greatly dismayed: also **heart′-struck′** (-struk′)

heart·strings (-striŋz′) *n.pl.* [orig. tendons or nerves formerly believed to brace and sustain the heart] deepest feelings or affections

heart·throb (-thräb′) *n.* 1. the throb of a heart; heartbeat 2. [Slang] *a)* tender or mawkish emotion: *usually used in pl.* *b)* a sweetheart

heart-to-heart (-tə härt′) *adj.* intimate and candid

heart urchin any of an order (Spatangoida) of echinoderms with an elongated, somewhat heart-shaped shell

heart·warm·ing (-wôr′miŋ) *adj.* such as to kindle a warm glow of genial feelings

heart-whole (-hōl′) *adj.* 1. not in love; heart-free 2. sincere; wholehearted 3. undismayed; courageous

heart·wood (-wood′) *n.* the hard, nonliving wood at the core of a tree trunk, usually dark in color and impervious to air and water; duramen: cf. SAPWOOD

heart·worm (-wurm′) *n.* a nematode worm (*Dirofilaria immitis*) transmitted by mosquitoes, that is parasitic in the bloodstream, esp. in the heart, of dogs, cats, etc.

heart·y (-ē) *adj.* **heart′i·er, heart′i·est** [ME. *herti*: see HEART & -Y²] 1. extremely warm and friendly; most genial or cordial [a *hearty* welcome] 2. enthusiastic; wholehearted [*hearty* cooperation] 3. strongly felt or expressed; unrestrained [a *hearty* dislike, *hearty* laughter] 4. strong and healthy [a *hearty* young farmer] 5. *a)* satisfying, nourishing, and plentiful [a *hearty* meal] *b)* needing or liking plenty of food [a *hearty* eater] —*n.*, *pl.* **heart′ies** [Archaic] a friend; comrade; esp., a fellow sailor (usually preceded by *my*) —*SYN.* see SINCERE

heat (hēt) *n.* [ME. *hete* < OE. *hætu* < base of *hat* (see HOT), akin to G. *heiss* < IE. base **kai-*, heat] 1. the quality of being hot; hotness: in physics, heat is considered a form of energy whose effect is produced by the accelerated vibration of molecules and into which mechanical energy may be converted: in classical theory, at −273.16°C molecular vibration would stop and there would be no heat 2. *a)* much hotness; great warmth [stifling *heat*] *b)* same as FEVER 3. degree of hotness or warmth [at low *heat*] 4. the perception of heat by the senses, resulting from contact with or nearness to something hot; sensation of hotness or warmth felt through the skin 5. hot weather or climate 6. the warming of a room, house, etc., as by a stove or furnace [his rent includes *heat*] 7. a burning sensation produced by spices, mustard, etc. 8. color or other appearance as an indication of hotness [blue *heat* in metals] 9. strong feeling or emotion; excitement, ardor, anger, zeal, etc. 10. the period or condition of excitement, intensity, stress, etc.; most violent or intense point or stage [in the *heat* of battle] 11. a single effort, round, bout, or trial; esp., any of the preliminary rounds of a race, etc., the winners of which compete in the final round 12. *a)* sexual excitement *b)* the period of sexual excitement in animals; esp., the estrus of females 13. *Metallurgy a)* a single heating of metal, ore, etc. in a furnace or forge *b)* the amount processed in a single heating ☆14. [Slang] *a)* coercion, as by intimidation *b)* great pressure, as in criminal investigation or law enforcement —*vt., vi.* 1. to make or become warm or hot 2. to make or become excited; inflame or become inflamed

heat barrier *same as* THERMAL BARRIER

heat capacity the amount of heat required to raise the temperature of a substance or system one degree, usually expressed in calories per degree centigrade

heat·ed (hēt′id) *adj.* 1. hot 2. vehement, impassioned, or angry —**heat′ed·ly** *adv.*

heat engine an engine for changing heat into mechanical energy, such as a steam engine or gasoline engine

heat·er (hēt′ər) *n.* 1. an apparatus for heating or warming a room, car, water, etc.; stove, furnace, radiator, etc. 2. a person whose work is to heat something 3. in an electron tube, an element set inside the cathode and heated by an electric current so that it indirectly heats the cathode to the temperature at which it will give off electrons ☆4. [Slang] a pistol

heat exchanger any device, as a radiator, for transferring energy in the form of heat to a cooler medium from a warmer one

heat exhaustion a mild form of heatstroke, characterized by faintness, dizziness, heavy sweating, etc.

heath (hēth) *n.* [ME. *hethe* < OE. *hæth*, akin to G. *heide* < IE. base **kaito-*, forested or uncultivated land, whence W. *coed*, forest] 1. a tract of open wasteland, esp. in the British Isles, covered with heather, low shrubs, etc.; moor 2. any plant of the heath family; esp., any of various shrubs and plants (genera *Erica* and *Calluna*) that grow on heaths, as heather —*adj.* designating a family (Ericaceae) of woody plants, including the blueberry, cranberry, azalea, etc. —**one's native heath** the place of one's birth or childhood

Heath (hēth), Edward Richard George 1916– ; Eng. politician; prime minister (1970–)

☆**heath aster** a N. American wildflower (*Aster ericoides*) of the composite family, with small, stiff leaves and white flowers, growing in dry open places

heath·bird (-burd′) *n.* a bird living on heaths; specif., BLACK GROUSE

heath cock *same as* BLACKCOCK

hea·then (hē′thən) *n., pl.* **-thens, -then** [ME. *hethen* < OE. *hæthen*, akin to G. *heide*: ult. < Goth. *haithnō* <

haithi, heath (hence lit., "heath dwellers"), a mistransl. used by Bishop Ulfilas (4th c. A.D.) for LL.(Ec.) *paganus* (see PAGAN), taken in its L. sense, "a countryman, rustic" < *pagus*, the country] **1.** orig., and in the Old Testament, a member of any nation or people not worshiping the God of Israel **2.** anyone not a Jew, Christian, or Moslem; esp., a member of a tribe, nation, etc. worshiping many gods **3.** a person regarded as irreligious, uncivilized, unenlightened, etc. —*adj.* **1.** of or characteristic of heathens; pagan **2.** irreligious, uncivilized, etc. —*SYN.* see PAGAN —**hea'then·dom, hea'then·ry** *n.* —**hea'then·ish** *adj.* —**hea'then·ism** *n.*

hea·then·ize (-īz') *vt., vi.* **-ized', -iz'ing** to make or become heathen

heath·er (he*th*'ər) *n.* [altered (after HEATH) < ME. (northern & Scot.) *haddyr:* form suggests an OE. **hædre*, parallel with *clofre*, clover, *mædre*, madder] any of various plants of the heath family; esp., a plant (*Calluna vulgaris*) common in the British Isles, with scalelike leaves and stalks of small, bell-shaped, purplish-pink flowers —*adj.* like heather in color or appearance —**heath'er·y** *adj.*

heath hen 1. *same as* GRAY HEN ☆**2.** an extinct New England grouse (*Tympanuchus cupido cupido*)

heath·y (hē'thē) *adj.* of, like, or covered with heath

heating pad a pad consisting of an electric heating element covered with fabric, for applying heat to parts of the body

☆**heat lightning** lightning without thunder, seen near the horizon, esp. on hot evenings, and thought to be reflections of lightning on clouds below the horizon

HEATHER

heat of fusion the amount of heat needed to melt a unit mass of a solid that has just reached the melting temperature

heat of vaporization the amount of heat needed to turn one gram of a liquid into a vapor, without a rise in temperature of the liquid

heat prostration *same as* HEAT EXHAUSTION

heat rash *same as* MILIARIA

heat sink a part of a system designed to be at a lower temperature than its surroundings, used to dissipate heat from that system

heat·stroke (-strōk') *n.* a condition resulting from excessive exposure to intense heat, characterized by high fever, collapse, and sometimes convulsions or coma: cf. HEAT EXHAUSTION, SUNSTROKE

heat-treat (-trēt') *vt.* to heat and cool (a metal) so as to change the physical properties, as its ductility, in a desired way

☆**heat wave 1.** unusually hot weather, resulting from a slowly moving air mass of relatively high temperature **2.** a period of such weather in a particular place

heaume (hōm) *n.* [Fr. < OFr. *helme:* see HELMET] a heavy helmet worn in the Middle Ages, covering the entire head and often reaching to the shoulders

heave (hēv) *vt.* **heaved** or (esp. *Naut.*) **hove, heav'ing** [ME. *heven* < OE. *hebban*, akin to G. *heben* (Goth. *hafjan*) < IE. base **kap-*, to seize, grasp, whence L. *capere* & HAVE] **1.** to raise or lift, esp. with effort **2.** to lift in this way and throw or cast **3.** to make rise or swell, as one's chest **4.** to utter (a sigh, groan, etc.) with great effort or pain **5.** *Geol.* to displace (a stratum or vein), as by the intersection of another stratum or vein **6.** *Naut.* a) to raise, haul, pull, move, etc. by pulling with a rope or cable b) to cause (a ship) to move in a specified manner or direction —*vi.* **1.** to swell up; bulge out **2.** to rise and fall rhythmically [*heaving* waves] **3.** to make strenuous, spasmodic movements of the throat, chest, or stomach; specif., a) to retch; vomit or try to vomit b) to pant; breathe hard; gasp **4.** *Naut.* a) to tug or haul (*on* or *at* a cable, rope, etc.) b) to proceed; move [a ship *heaving* into sight] —*n.* **1.** the act or effort of heaving **2.** *Geol.* the extent of horizontal displacement caused by a fault See also HEAVES —**heave ho!** pull hard!: a cry of sailors hauling in the anchor, etc. —**heave to 1.** *Naut.* to stop forward movement by hauling in or shortening sail and heading into the wind **2.** to stop —**heav'er** *n.*

heave-ho (-hō') *n.* [see the phrase HEAVE HO! in prec.] ☆ [Colloq.] dismissal, as from a position: chiefly in the phrase **give (or get) the (old) heave-ho**

heav·en (hev'n) *n.* [ME. *heven* < OE. *heofon* < IE. base **kem-*, to cover (whence L. *camisia*, shirt); akin to OHG. *himil* and to OS. *hevan*, ON, *himinn* (dat. *hifne*), with *-fn, -v-n* < *-mn* by dissimilation] **1.** [*usually pl.*] the space surrounding or seeming to overarch the earth, in which the sun, moon, and stars appear; visible sky; firmament (in pl., used with *the*) **2.** *Theol.* a) [*often* H-] the dwelling place of God and his angels, variously conceived of as the place where the blessed will live after death b) [H-] God; Providence **3.** a) any place of great beauty and pleasure

b) a state of great happiness Often used in exclamations of surprise, protest, etc. [for *heaven's* sake], good *heavens!*] —**move heaven and earth** to do all that can be done; exert the utmost effort, influence, etc.

heav·en·ly (-lē) *adj.* [ME. *hevenlich* < OE. *heofonlic*] **1.** of or in the heavens [planets and other *heavenly* bodies] **2.** a) causing or marked by great happiness, beauty, peace, etc. b) [Colloq.] very attractive, pleasing, etc. **3.** *Theol.* of or in heaven; holy; divine —**heav'en·li·ness** *n.*

heav·en·ward (-wərd) *adv., adj.* [ME. *heveneward:* see -WARD] toward heaven: also **heav'en·wards** *adv.*

heaves (hēvz) *n.pl.* [*with sing. v.*] ☆a respiratory disease of horses, characterized by forced breathing, coughing, heaving of the flanks, etc.

heav·i·ly (hev'ə lē) *adv.* in a heavy manner; specif., a) with a heavy weight [*heavily* burdened] b) as if with a heavy weight; slowly; clumsily; laboriously [to rise *heavily* from one's seat] c) oppressively; severely [*heavily* taxed] d) abundantly [*heavily* populated]

heav·i·ness (-ē nis) *n.* a heavy quality or state

heav·ing-line bend (hē'vin lin') *same as* CLOVE HITCH

Heav·i·side layer (hev'ē sīd') [after Oliver *Heaviside* (1850–1925), Eng. physicist] *same as* E LAYER

heav·y (hev'ē) *adj.* **heav'i·er, heav'i·est** [ME. *hevi* < OE. *hefig* (akin to OHG. *hebig*) < base of *hebban* (see HEAVE) + *-ig* (see *-y²*): prob. basic sense "containing something, full"] **1.** hard to lift or move because of great weight; weighty **2.** of high specific gravity; of concentrated weight for the size **3.** above the usual or defined weight: said of goods, certain animals, etc. **4.** larger, greater, or more intense than usual or normal; specif., a) falling or striking with great force or impact [a *heavy* blow] b) of greater than usual quantity [a *heavy* vote] c) violent and intense; rough [a *heavy* sea] d) loud, deep, and resounding [*heavy* thunder] e) thick, coarse, or massive [*heavy* features] f) going beyond the average; to a greater than usual extent [a *heavy* drinker] g) prolonged and intense [*heavy* applause] **5.** of great importance; serious; grave; profound [a *heavy* responsibility] **6.** hard to endure; oppressive; burdensome; distressing [*heavy* demands] **7.** hard to do or manage; difficult [*heavy* work] **8.** hard to bear [*heavy* sorrow] **9.** burdened with grief; sorrowful; depressed [a *heavy* heart] **10.** burdened with sleep or fatigue [*heavy* eyelids] **11.** capable of carrying a load of great weight [a *heavy* truck] **12.** characterized by density, hardness, fullness, etc. suggestive of weight; specif., a) hard to digest [a *heavy* meal] b) not leavened properly; doughy [a *heavy* cake] c) remaining in the atmosphere; clinging; penetrating [a *heavy* odor] d) overcast; cloudy; gloomy; lowering [a *heavy* sky] e) hard to work with or travel over because of mud, sand, clay, etc. [a *heavy* soil] **13.** tedious, dull, or strained [*heavy* humor] **14.** clumsy; unwieldy; physically awkward [a *heavy* gait] ☆**15.** steeply inclined [a *heavy* grade] **16.** designating any large industry that uses massive machinery and produces raw or processed materials, as steel, basic to other industries **17.** designating, of, or equipped with massive or relatively heavy weapons, armor, etc. **18.** *Chem.* a) designating an isotope of greater atomic weight than the normal or most abundant isotope b) designating a compound containing such isotopes **19.** *Theater* serious, tragic, or villainous —*adv.* heavily: often in hyphenated compounds [*heavy*-laden] —*n., pl.* **heav'ies 1.** something heavy **2.** *Theater* a) a serious, tragic, or villainous role b) an actor who plays such roles —**hang heavy** to pass tediously; drag: said of time —**heavy with child** pregnant **SYN.**—**heavy** implies relatively great density, quantity, intensity, etc. and figuratively connotes a pressing down on the mind, spirits, or senses [*heavy* water, *heavy*-hearted]; **weighty** suggests heaviness as an absolute rather than a relative quality and figuratively connotes great importance or influence [a *weighty* problem]; **ponderous** applies to something that is very heavy because of size or bulk and figuratively connotes a labored or dull quality [a *ponderous* dissertation]; **massive** stresses largeness and solidness rather than heaviness and connotes an impressiveness due to great magnitude [*massive* structures]; **cumbersome** implies a heaviness and bulkiness that makes for awkward handling and, in extended use, connotes unwieldiness [*cumbersome* formalities]— ANT. light

heav·y-du·ty (-dōōt'ē, -dyōōt'ē) *adj.* made to withstand great strain, bad weather, etc. [*heavy-duty* shoes]

heav·y-foot·ed (-foot'id) *adj.* ponderous or clumsy in or as in walking; plodding

heav·y-hand·ed (-han'did) *adj.* **1.** without a light touch; clumsy or tactless **2.** cruel, oppressive, or tyrannical —**heav'y-hand'ed·ly** *adv.* —**heav'y-hand'ed·ness** *n.*

heav·y-heart·ed (-härt'id) *adj.* sad; depressed; despondent —**heav'y-heart'ed·ly** *adv.* —**heav'y-heart'ed·ness** *n.*

heavy hydrogen *same as* DEUTERIUM

heav·y-lad·en (-lād'n) *adj.* **1.** laden, or loaded, heavily **2.** heavily burdened with care and trouble

heav·y·set (-set') *adj.* having a stout or stocky build

heavy spar *same as* BARITE

heavy water water composed of isotopes of hydrogen of atomic weight greater than one or of oxygen greater than 16, or of both; esp., water composed of ordinary

oxygen and the isotope of hydrogen of atomic weight 2; deuterium oxide, D_2O

heav·y·weight (-wāt′) *n.* **1.** a person or animal weighing much more than average **2.** a boxer or wrestler who weighs over 175 pounds ☆**3.** [Colloq.] a very intelligent, influential, or important person

Heb. 1. Hebrew **2.** Hebrews

Heb·bel (heb′əl), **(Christian) Friedrich** (frē′driH) 1813–63; Ger. playwright & poet

heb·do·mad (heb′də mad′) *n.* [L. *hebdomas* (gen. *hebdomadis*) < Gr. *hebdomas*, the number seven, week < *hebdomos*, seventh < *hepta*, SEVEN] seven days; a week —**heb·dom·a·dal** (heb däm′ə dəl) *adj.*

He·be (hē′bē) [L. < Gr. *Hēbē* < *hēbē*, youth] *Gr. Myth.* the goddess of youth, daughter of Hera and Zeus: she was a cupbearer to the gods

he·be·phre·ni·a (hē′bə frē′nē ə) *n.* [ModL. < Gr. *hēbē*, youth + *phrēn*, the mind] a form of schizophrenia characterized by childish or silly behavior, disorganized thinking, delusions, and hallucinations, usually beginning in adolescence —**he′be·phren′ic** (-fren′ik) *adj.*

Hé·bert (ā ber′), **Jacques Re·né** (zhȧk rə nā′) 1755–94; Fr. Revolutionary leader: guillotined

heb·e·tate (heb′ə tāt′) *vt., vi.* -**tat′ed**, -**tat′ing** [< L. *hebetatus*, pp. of *hebetare*, to make blunt or dull < *hebes*, blunt, dull] to make or become dull or stupid —*adj. Bot.* having a blunt point, as certain leaves —**heb′e·ta′tion** *n.*

he·bet·ic (hi bet′ik) *adj.* [Gr. *hēbētikos*, youthful < *hēbē*, youth] of or happening at puberty

heb·e·tude (heb′ə tood′, -tyood′) *n.* [LL. *hebetudo* < L. *hebes* (gen. *hebetis*), blunt, dull] the quality or condition of being dull or lethargic

He·bra·ic (hi brā′ik) *adj.* [LL. *Hebraicus* < Gr. *Hebraïkos*] of or characteristic of the Hebrews, their language, culture, etc.; Hebrew —**He·bra′i·cal·ly** *adv.*

He·bra·ism (hē′brī iz′m, -brā-) *n.* [ModL. *Hebraismus* < LGr. *Hebraismos* < Gr. *Hebraïzein*: see HEBRAIZE] **1.** a Hebrew phrase, idiom, or custom **2.** the characteristic ethical system, moral attitude, etc. of the Hebrews —**He′bra·ist** *n.* —**He′bra·is′tic** *adj.*

He·bra·ize (-īz′) *vt., vi.* -**ized′**, -**iz′ing** [< Gr. *Hebraizein* < *Hebraios:* see ff.] to make or become Hebrew in language, customs, character, etc.

He·brew (hē′brōō) *n.* [ME. *Hebreu* < OFr. < L. *Hebraeus* < Gr. *Hebraios* < Aram. *'Ebrai* < Heb. *'ibhri*, lit., one from across (the river)] **1.** any member of a group of Semitic peoples tracing descent from Abraham, Isaac, and Jacob; Israelite: in modern, esp. earlier, usage interchangeable with *Jew* **2.** *a)* the ancient Semitic language of the Israelites, in which most of the Old Testament was written *b)* the modern form of this language, the official language of Israel —*adj.* **1.** of Hebrew or the Hebrews **2.** *same as* JEWISH

Hebrew calendar *same as* JEWISH CALENDAR

He·brews (-brōōz) *Bible* the Epistle to the Hebrews, a book of the New Testament

Heb·ri·des (heb′rə dēz′) group of islands off the W coast of Scotland, in the counties of Ross and Cromarty, Inverness, & Argyll: they are divided into the **Inner Hebrides,** nearer the mainland, & the **Outer Hebrides:** c. 2,800 sq. mi.; pop. c. 80,000 —**Heb·ri·de·an** (-dē′ən) *adj., n.*

He·bron (hē′brən) city in W Jordan, south of Jerusalem, dating from Biblical times: pop. 143,000: Arabic name **Al Khalil**

Hec·a·te (hek′ə tē; *formerly & still occas.* hek′it) [L. < Gr. *Hekatē*] *Gr. Myth.* a goddess of the moon, earth, and underground realm of the dead, later regarded as the goddess of sorcery and witchcraft

hec·a·tomb (hek′ə tōm′, -tōōm′) *n.* [L. *hecatombe* < Gr. *hekatombē* < *hekaton*, HUNDRED + *bous*, ox: see COW¹] **1.** in ancient Greece, any great sacrifice to the gods; specif., the slaughter of 100 cattle at one time **2.** any large-scale sacrifice or slaughter

heck (hek) *interj., n.* [var. of Scot. dial. *hech*, exclamation of surprise, sorrow, fatigue: Scot. form of HEIGH] [Colloq.] *a euphemism for* HELL

heck·le (hek′'l) *vt.* -**led**, -**ling** [ME. *hekelin* < *hechele:* see HACKLE¹] **1.** *same as* HACKLE¹ **2.** [orig. Scot.] to annoy or harass (a speaker) by interrupting with questions or taunts —*n. same as* HACKLE² —*SYN.* see BAIT —**heck′ler** (-lər) *n.*

hect- (hekt) *same as* HECTO-: used before a vowel

hec·tare (hek′ter) *n.* [Fr.: see HECTO- & ARE²] a unit of surface measure in the metric system, equal to 10,000 square meters (100 ares or 2.471 acres)

hec·tic (hek′tik) *adj.* [altered (after Fr. or L.) < ME. *etik* < OFr. *étique* (Fr. *hectique*) < LL. *hecticus* < Gr. *hektikos*, habitual, hectic < *hexis*, permanent condition or habit of the body < *echein*, to have: for IE. base see SCHOOL] **1.** designating or of the fever accompanying wasting diseases, esp. tuberculosis **2.** of, affected with, or characteristic of a wasting disease, as tuberculosis; consumptive **3.** red or flushed, as with fever **4.** characterized by confusion, rush, excitement, etc. —**hec′ti·cal·ly** *adv.*

hec·to- (hek′tō, -tə) [Fr., contr. < Gr. *hekaton*, HUNDRED] *a combining form meaning* a hundred: the factor 10^2 [*hectogram*]

hec·to·cot·y·lus (hek′tə kät′'l əs) *n., pl.* -**y·li′** (-ī′) [ModL. < *prec.* + Gr. *kotylē*, a cup, hollow object] one of the arms or tentacles of a male octopus, cuttlefish, or other cephalopod, which becomes modified as a sexual organ for impregnating the female

hec·to·gram (hek′tə gram′) *n.* [Fr. *hectogramme:* see HECTO- & GRAM¹] a metric measure of weight, equal to 100 grams (3.527 ounces avoirdupois): also, Brit., **hec′to·gramme′**

hec·to·graph (-graf′, -gräf′) *n.* [Gr. *hektograph* < *hekto* (< Fr. *hecto-*, HECTO-) + *-graph*, -GRAPH] a duplicating device by which written or typed matter is transferred to a glycerin-coated sheet of gelatin, from which many copies can be taken —*vt.* to duplicate by means of a hectograph —**hec′to·graph′ic** *adj.*

hec·to·kil·o- (-kil′ō) [HECTO- + KILO-] *a combining form meaning* one hundred thousand; the factor 10^5 [*hectokilosecond*]

hec·to·li·ter (-lēt′ər) *n.* [Fr. *hectolitre:* see HECTO- & LITER] a metric measure of capacity, equal to 100 liters (26.418 gallons or 2.8378 bushels): also, Brit., **hec′to·li′tre**

hec·to·me·ter (-mēt′ər) *n.* [Fr. *hectomètre:* see HECTO- & METER] a metric measure of length, equal to 100 meters (109.36 yards): also, Brit., **hec′to·me′tre**

Hec·tor (hek′tər) [L. < Gr. *Hektōr*, lit., holding fast < *echein*, to hold, have: for IE. base see SCHOOL] **1.** a masculine name **2.** in Homer's *Iliad,* a Trojan hero killed by Achilles to avenge the death of Patroclus: he was Priam's oldest son

hec·tor (hek′tər) *n.* [see prec.: in early popular drama, Hector became the type of a braggart and bully] a swaggering fellow; bully —*vt., vi.* to browbeat; bully —*SYN.* see BAIT

Hec·u·ba (hek′yoo bə) [L. < Gr. *Hekabē*] in Homer's *Iliad,* wife of Priam and mother of Hector, Troilus, Paris, and Cassandra

he'd (hēd) **1.** he had **2.** he would

hed·dle (hed′'l) *n.* [prob. (by metathesis) < ME. *helde* < OE. *hefeld*, weaving thread (akin to ON. *hafald*) < base of *hebban*, to raise (see HEAVE) + *-eld*, instrumental suffix] any of a series of parallel wires or cords in the harness of a loom, equipped with eyes and used for separating and guiding the warp threads

†he·der (khä′dər) *n., pl.* **ha·dar·im** (khä dä′rēm) [< Heb. (via Yiddish) *hedher*, chamber] a Jewish religious school for young children

hedge (hej) *n.* [ME. *hegge* < OE. *hecg*, akin to G. *hecke* < IE. base **kagh-*, wickerwork, wickerwork pen, whence L. *caulae*, sheepfold: basic sense "woven fence, enclosure"] **1.** a row of closely planted shrubs, bushes, etc. forming a boundary or fence **2.** anything serving as a fence or barrier; restriction or defense **3.** the act or an instance of hedging —*adj.* **1.** of, in, or near a hedge **2.** low, disreputable, irregular, etc. —*vt.* **hedged, hedg′ing 1.** to place a hedge around or along; border or bound with a hedge **2.** to hinder or guard as by surrounding with a barrier (often with *in*) **3.** to try to avoid or lessen loss in (a bet, risk, etc.) by making counterbalancing bets, investments, etc. —*vi.* **1.** to hide or protect oneself, as if behind a hedge **2.** to hide behind words; refuse to commit oneself or give a direct answer **3.** to try to avoid or lessen loss by making counterbalancing bets, investments, etc. —**hedg′er** *n.*

hedge·hog (hej′hôg′, -häg′) *n.* [HEDGE + HOG: prob. from living in hedgerows and from the hoglike snout] **1.** any of several small, insect-eating mammals (family Erinaceidae) of the Old World, with a shaggy coat and sharp spines on the back, which bristle and form a defense when the animal curls up ☆**2.** the American porcupine **3.** *Mil. a)* any of several defensive obstacles set up to slow the enemy's advance *b)* any of a series of defensive fortifications capable of continued resistance after being encircled

HEDGEHOG (5–10 in. long)

☆**hedge·hop** (-häp′) *vi.* -**hopped′**, -**hop′ping** [Colloq.] to fly an airplane very close to the ground, as for spraying insecticide —**hedge′hop′per** *n.*

hedge hyssop a low-growing annual plant (*Gratiola aurea*), common in wet grounds from Maine to Florida

hedge·row (-rō′) *n.* a row of shrubs, bushes, etc., forming a hedge

hedge sparrow a small European warbler (*Prunella modularis*), reddish-brown with white-tipped wings, often found in hedges

He·din (he dēn′), **Sven An·ders** (sven än′ders) 1865–1952; Swed. explorer, esp. in Asia, & writer

he·don·ic (hē dän′ik) *adj.* [Gr. *hēdonikos* < base of *hedys*, sweet < IE. **swad-*, whence SWEET] **1.** having to do with pleasure **2.** [Rare] of hedonism or hedonists; hedonistic

he·don·ics (-iks) *n.pl.* [*with sing. v.*] [< prec.] the branch of psychology dealing with pleasurable and unpleasurable feelings

he·don·ism (hēd′'n iz'm) *n.* [< Gr. *hēdonē*, delight (see HEDONIC) + -ISM] **1.** *Philos.* the ethical doctrine that pleasure, variously conceived of in terms of happiness of the individual or of society, is the principal good and the proper aim of action **2.** *Psychol.* the theory that a person always acts in such a way as to seek pleasure and avoid

pain **3.** the self-indulgent pursuit of pleasure as a way of life —**he'don·ist** *n.* —**he'do·nis'tic** (-is'tik) *adj.* —**he'do·nis'ti·cal·ly** *adv.*

-he·dral (hē'drəl) *a combining form used in adjectives corresponding to nouns ending in* -HEDRON [hexahedral]

-he·dron (-drən) [Gr. *-edron* < *hedra*, a side, base, seat < IE. base *sed-*, whence L. *sedere*, SIT] *a combining form meaning* a geometric figure or crystal with (a specified number of) surfaces [hexahedron]

☆**hee·bie-jee·bies** (hē'bē jē'bēz) *n.pl.* [coined by W. B. De Beck (1890–1942) in his comic strip *Barney Google*] [Old Slang] a state of nervousness; jitters: with *the*

heed (hēd) *vt.* [ME. *heden* < OE. *hēdan* (< **hodjan*: akin to G. *hüten*) < base of *hod* (see HOOD) in the sense "care, keeping, protection": for IE. base see HAT] to pay close attention to; take careful notice of —*vi.* to pay attention; take notice —*n.* close attention; careful notice —**heed'ful** *adj.* —**heed'ful·ly** *adv.*

heed·less (-lis) *adj.* not taking heed; careless; unmindful —**heed'less·ly** *adv.* —**heed'less·ness** *n.*

hee·haw (hē'hô') *n.* [echoic] **1.** the sound that a donkey makes; bray **2.** a loud, often silly laugh like a bray —*vi.* **1.** to bray **2.** to laugh in a loud, often silly way; guffaw

heel[1] (hēl) *n.* [ME. *hele* < OE. *hēla*, akin to Du. *hiel* < Gmc. **hanhila* < **hanha* < IE. base **kenk-*, leg joint, heel] **1.** the back part of the human foot, under the ankle and behind the instep **2.** the corresponding part of the hind foot of an animal **3.** *a)* that part of a stocking, sock, etc. which covers the heel *b)* the built-up part of a shoe, supporting the heel **4.** crushing oppressive or tyrannical power [under the *heel* of fascism] **5.** anything suggesting the human heel in location, shape, or function, as the end of a loaf of bread, a rind end of cheese, the part of the palm of the hand nearest the wrist, the part of the head of a golf club nearest the shaft, the lower end of a ship's mast, a small quantity of liquor left in a bottle, etc. ☆**6.** [Colloq.] a despicable or unscrupulous person; cad —*vt.* **1.** to furnish with a heel **2.** to follow closely at the rear of **3.** to touch, press, or drive forward with or as with the heel **4.** to equip (a gamecock) with metal spurs ☆**5.** [Colloq.] *a)* to provide (a person) with money: usually in the passive *b)* to equip or arm (oneself) **6.** *Golf* to hit (a ball) with the heel of the club —*vi.* **1.** to follow along at the heels of someone [to teach a dog to *heel*] **2.** to move the heels rhythmically in dancing —**at heel** close to one's heels; just behind —**cool one's heels** [Colloq.] to wait or be kept waiting for a considerable time —**down at the heel(s)** **1.** with the heels of one's shoes in need of repair **2.** shabby; seedy; run-down —**heel in** to cover (plant roots) temporarily with earth in preparation for planting —**kick up one's heels** to be lively or merry; have fun —**lay by the heels 1.** to put in fetters, stocks, or jail **2.** to overcome; frustrate; hinder —**on** (or **upon) the heels of** close behind; immediately following —**out at the heel(s)** **1.** having holes in the heels of one's shoes or socks **2.** shabby; seedy; run-down —**show one's** (or **a clean pair of) heels** to run away —**take to one's heels** to run away —**to heel 1.** close to one's heels; just behind **2.** under discipline or control —**turn on one's heel** to turn around abruptly and face in the opposite direction —**heel'less** *adj.*

heel[2] (hēl) *vi.* [with assimilated -*d* < ME. *helden* < OE. *hieldan* (**healdjan*), to incline, slope < base of *heald*, sloping, bent < IE. base **kel-*, to incline, whence (via **klei-*) L. *-clinare*, INCLINE] to lean or tilt to one side; slant; list: said esp. of a ship —*vt.* to make (a ship) list —*n.* **1.** the act of heeling **2.** the extent of this

heel-and-toe (hēl'ən tō') *adj.* designating or of a walking race or step in which the heel of one foot touches the ground before the toes of the other leave it

heeled (hēld) *adj.* **1.** having a heel or heels ☆**2.** [Colloq.] *a)* having money *b)* armed, esp. with a gun

heel·er (hēl'ər) *n.* **1.** one that heels ☆**2.** [Colloq.] *same as* WARD HEELER

heel·piece (hēl'pēs') *n.* a piece forming, affixed to, or like the heel of a shoe, etc.

heel·plate (-plāt') *n.* a thin metal piece put on the bottom of the heel of a shoe to prevent wear

heel·post (-pōst') *n.* **1.** the outer post supporting the partition of a stall in a stable **2.** the post to which a gate or door is hinged

heel·tap (-tap') *n.* **1.** a layer of leather, etc. serving as a lift in the heel of a shoe **2.** a bit of liquor left in a glass after drinking

Heer·len (her'lən) city in SE Netherlands: pop. 77,000

heft (heft) *n.* [< base of HEAVE] [Colloq.] **1.** weight; heaviness **2.** importance; influence ☆**3.** [Rare] the main part; bulk —*vt.* [Colloq.] **1.** to lift or heave **2.** to try to determine the weight of by lifting —*vi.* [Colloq.] to weigh

heft·y (hef'tē) *adj.* **heft'i·er, heft'i·est** [Colloq.] **1.** weighty; heavy **2.** large and powerful **3.** big or fairly big —**heft'i·ly** *adv.* —**heft'i·ness** *n.*

he·gar·i (hi gar'ē, -ger'-) *n.* [Ar. (in Sudan) *hegiri*, for Ar. *ḥajari*, stony] any of a class of grain sorghums characterized by juicy, leafy stalks and erect heads with grayish grain

He·gel (hā'gəl), **Ge·org Wil·helm Frie·drich** (gā ôrkh' vil'helm frē'driH) 1770–1831; Ger. philosopher

He·ge·li·an (hā gā'lē ən, hi jē'-) *adj.* of Hegel or Hegelianism —*n.* a follower of Hegel or his philosophy

He·ge·li·an·ism (-iz'm) *n.* the philosophy of Hegel, who held that every existent idea or fact belongs to an all-embracing mind in which each idea or situation (thesis) evokes its opposite (antithesis) and these two result in a unified whole (synthesis), which in turn becomes a new thesis

he·gem·o·ny (hi jem'ə nē; hej'ə mō'nē, hē'jə-) *n., pl.* **-nies** [Gr. *hēgemonia*, leadership < *hēgemōn*, leader < *hēgeisthai*, to lead, go on ahead < IE. base **sāg-*, to track down, whence SAKE[1], SEEK] leadership or dominance, esp. that of one state or nation over others —**heg·e·mon·ic** (hej'ə män'ik, hē'jə-) *adj.*

he·gi·ra (hi jī'rə, hej'ər ə) *n.* [ML. < Ar. *hijrah*, lit., separation, flight, era of Mohammed < *hajara*, to leave] **1.** [often H-] the forced journey of Mohammed from Mecca to Medina in 622 A.D.: the Moslem era dates from this event **2.** any journey made for the sake of safety or as an escape; flight

he·gu·men (hi gyōō'men) *n.* [Gr. *hēgoumenos*, prp. of *hēgeisthai*, to lead: see HEGEMONY] *Orthodox Eastern Ch.* the elected head of a monastery corresponding to an abbot in the Roman Catholic Church

heh (hā) *n. same as* HE[2]

Hei·deg·ger (hī'di gər), **Martin** 1889– ; Ger. existentialist philosopher

Hei·del·berg (hīd'l'bʉrg'; *G.* hī'dəl berkh') city in SW West Germany, in Baden-Württemberg: site of a famous university (founded 1386): pop. 125,000

Heidelberg man a type of early man, known from a fossil lower jaw discovered in 1907 near Heidelberg, Germany: he is believed to have lived between the second and third glacial periods

heif·er (hef'ər) *n.* [ME. *haifre* < OE. *heahfore*, lit., full-grown young ox < *heah*, high, hence full-grown (see HIGH) | *fearr*, ox, beast of burden, lit., young animal: for IE. base see FARROW[2]] a young cow that has not borne a calf

Hei·fetz (hī'fits), **Ja·scha** (yä'shə) 1901– ; U.S. violinist, born in Russia

heigh (hī, hā) *interj.* an exclamation to attract notice, show pleasure, express surprise, etc.

heigh-ho (-hō) *interj.* an exclamation of mild surprise, boredom, disappointment, fatigue, greeting, etc.

height (hīt; *earlier, and still occas. colloq.*, hītth) *n.* [< earlier *highth* < ME. *heighthe* < OE. *hiehthu* (akin to Goth. *hauhitha*) < *heah* (see HIGH & -TH[1])] **1.** the topmost point of anything **2.** the highest limit; greatest degree; extreme; climax; culmination [the *height* of absurdity] **3.** the distance from the bottom to the top **4.** *a)* elevation or distance above a given level, as above the surface of the earth or sea; altitude *b)* elevation (of the sun, a star, etc.) above the horizon, measured in degrees **5.** *a)* a relatively great distance from bottom to top *b)* a relatively great distance above a given level **6.** [often *pl.*] a point or place considerably above most others; eminence; elevation; hill **7.** [Obs.] high rank

SYN.—**height** refers to distance from bottom to top [a figurine four inches in *height*] or to distance above a given level [he dropped it from a *height* of ten feet]; **altitude** and **elevation** refer especially to distance above a given level (usually the surface of the earth) and generally connote great distance [the *altitude* of an airplane, the *elevation* of a mountain]; **stature** refers especially to the height of a human being standing erect [he was short in *stature*]

height·en (-'n) *vt., vi.* [< prec.] **1.** to bring or come to a high or higher position; raise or rise **2.** to make or become larger, greater, stronger, brighter, etc.; increase; intensify —*SYN.* see INTENSIFY —**height'en·er** *n.*

☆**height of land** [Canad.] a watershed

height to paper *Printing* the standard height of type from face to feet, equal in the U.S. to .9186 inch

Hei·lung·kiang (hā'loon'jyän') province of NE China: 179,000 sq. mi.; pop. 14,860,000; cap. Harbin

Heim·dall (hām'däl') [ON. *Heimdallr*] *Norse Myth.* the watchman of Asgard, home of the gods

‡**hein** (an) *interj.* [Fr.] *Fr. equiv. of* EH

Hei·ne (hī'nə), **Hein·rich** (hin'riH) 1797–1856; Ger. poet & essayist

hei·nous (hā'nəs) *adj.* [ME. *hainous* < OFr. *hainös* (Fr. *haineux*) < *haine*, hatred < *hair*, to hate < Frank. **hatjan*, akin to G. *hassen*, HATE] outrageously evil or wicked; abominable [a *heinous* crime] —*SYN.* see OUTRAGEOUS —**hei'nous·ly** *adv.* —**hei'nous·ness** *n.*

heir (er) *n.* [ME. < OFr. < L. *heres*: see HEREDITY] **1.** a person who inherits or is legally entitled to inherit, through the natural action of the law, another's property or title upon the other's death **2.** anyone who receives property of a deceased person either by will or by law **3.** a person who appears to get some trait from a predecessor or seems to carry on in his tradition

heir apparent *pl.* **heirs apparent** the heir whose right to a certain property or title cannot be denied if he outlives the ancestor: see HEIR PRESUMPTIVE

heir at law the heir who has the right under the laws of intestate descent and distribution to receive the estate of an ancestor who has died without leaving a will

heir·dom (-dəm) *n.* same as HEIRSHIP

heir·ess (-is) *n.* a woman or girl who is an heir, esp. to great wealth

heir·loom (-lōōm′) *n.* [ME. *heir lome:* see HEIR & LOOM[1]] **1.** a piece of personal property that goes to an heir along with an estate **2.** any treasured possession handed down from generation to generation

heir presumptive *pl.* **heirs presumptive** an heir whose right to a certain property or title will be lost if someone more closely related to the ancestor is born before that ancestor dies: see HEIR APPARENT

heir·ship (-ship′) *n.* [see -SHIP] the position or rights of an heir; right to inheritance

Hei·sen·berg (hī′zən berkh), **Wer·ner** (ver′nər) (**Karl**) 1901– ; Ger. theoretical & nuclear physicist

☆ **heist** (hīst) *n.* [< HOIST] [Slang] a robbery or holdup —*vt.* **1.** [Slang] to rob or steal **2.** *dial. var. of* HOIST —**heist′er** *n.*

He·jaz (he jaz′, hē-; -jäz′) district of NW Saudi Arabia, formerly a kingdom and now administered as a vice-royalty: c. 150,000 sq. mi.; pop. c. 2,000,000; cap. Mecca

he·ji·ra (hi ji′rə, hej′ər ə) *n.* same as HEGIRA

Hek·a·te (hek′ə tē) same as HECATE

hek·to- (hek′tō, -tə) same as HECTO-

Hel (hel) [ON.: see HELL] *Norse Myth.* **1.** Loki's daughter, goddess of death and the underworld **2.** the underworld to which the dead not killed in battle were sent: cf. VALHALLA

‡**hé·las** (ā läs′) *interj.* [Fr.] *Fr. equiv. of* ALAS

held (held) *pt. & pp. of* HOLD

‡**hel·den·ten·or** (hel′dən tā nôr′) *n.* [G., heroic tenor] a robust tenor voice particularly suited to roles in Wagner's operas

Hel·en (hel′ən) [< Fr. or L.: Fr. *Hélène* < L. *Helena* < Gr. *Helenē*, lit., torch] a feminine name: dim. *Nell, Nelly, Lena;* var. *Helena, Ellen, Eleanor;* equiv. Fr. *Hélène, Elaine,* It. & Sp. *Elena*

Hel·e·na (hel′i na; *also, for 1,* hə lē′nə) **1.** a feminine name: see *prec.* **2.** capital of Mont., in the WC part: pop. 23,000

Helen of Troy *Gr. Legend* the beautiful wife of Menelaus, king of Sparta: the Trojan War was started because of her abduction by Paris to Troy

Hel·go·land (hel′gō länd′; *G.* -länt′) island of West Germany, in the North Sea; one of the North Frisian Islands: c. 150 acres

he·li- (hē′lē, hel′ē) same as HELIO-

he·li·a·cal (hi lī′ə kəl) *adj.* [LL. *Heliacus*, relating to the sun < Gr. *hēliakos* < *hēlios*, HELIOS + -AL] of or near the sun; solar; specif., *a)* designating the apparent rising of a star when it is first seen again after having been invisible because of its nearness to the sun *b)* designating the last setting of a star before it becomes invisible again in the sun's rays —**he·li′a·cal·ly** *adv.*

he·li·an·thus (hē′lē an′thəs) *n.* [ModL. < *heli-* + Gr. *anthos,* a flower] same as SUNFLOWER

hel·i·cal (hel′i kəl, hē′lə-) *adj.* [HELIC(O)- + -AL] of, or having the form of, a helix; spiral —**hel′i·cal·ly** *adv.*

hel·i·ces (hel′ə sēz′, hē′lə-) *n. alt. pl. of* HELIX

hel·i·cline (hel′ə klīn′) *n.* [HELI(CO)- + (IN)CLINE] a curving ramp that ascends gradually

hel·i·co- (hel′ə kō′, hē′lə-) [< Gr. *helix* (gen. *helikos*): see HELIX] *a combining form meaning* spiral, spiral-shaped: *also, before a vowel,* **helic-**

hel·i·coid (hel′ə koid′, hē′lə-) *adj.* [Gr. *helikoeidēs* < *helix*, a spiral + *eidos*, form] shaped like, or coiled in the form of, a spiral, as the shell of a snail or certain inflorescences: *also* **hel′i·coi′dal** —*n. Geom.* a surface generated by the rotation of a plane or twisted curve about a fixed line so that each point of the curve traces out a circular helix with the fixed line as axis

Hel·i·con (hel′ə kän′, -kən) mountain group in SC Greece, on the Gulf of Corinth: in Greek mythology, the home of the Muses; highest peak, 5,735 ft. —*n.* [prob. < HELICO- + arbitrary ending: from the shape] [h-] a brass-wind instrument, like a bass tuba, consisting of a long, coiled tube that can be carried over the shoulder

hel·i·co·ni·a (hel′ə kō′nē ə) *n.* [ModL. < L., fem. of *Heliconius*, of HELICON] any of a genus (*Heliconia*) of tropical plants of the banana family, having tall, erect leaves and spikes of flowers enclosed in brilliantly colored bracts

hel·i·cop·ter (hel′ə käp′tər, hē′lə-) *n.* [Fr. *hélicoptère:* see HELICO- & PTERO-] a kind of aircraft lifted vertically and moved horizontally in any direction, or kept hovering, by large, motor-driven rotary blades mounted horizontally —*vi., vt.* to travel or convey by helicopter

HELICON

he·li·o- (hē′lē ō′, -ə) [L. < Gr. *hēlio-* < *hēlios*, the sun: see HELIOS] *a combining form meaning* the sun, bright, radiant [*heliocentric, heliograph*]

he·li·o·cen·tric (hē′lē ō sen′trik) *adj.* [HELIO- + -CENTRIC]

1. calculated from, or viewed as from, the center of the sun **2.** having or regarding the sun as the center

he·li·o·chrome (hē′lē ə krōm′) *n.* [HELIO- + -CHROME] an early type of photograph in natural colors

He·li·o·gab·a·lus (hē′lē ə gab′ə las) same as ELAGABALUS

he·li·o·gram (hē′lē ə gram′) *n.* a message sent by heliograph

he·li·o·graph (-graf′, -gräf′) *n.* [HELIO- + -GRAPH] **1.** a print made by an early photoengraving process **2.** a device for sending messages or signaling by flashing the sun's rays from a mirror —*vt., vi.* to signal or communicate by heliograph —**he′li·og′ra·pher** (-äg′rə fər) *n.* —**he′li·o·graph′ic** *adj.* —**he′li·og′ra·phy** *n.*

he·li·o·gra·vure (hē′lē ō′grə vyōōr′) *n.* [Fr. *héliogravure:* see HELIO- & GRAVURE] *old term for* PHOTOGRAVURE

he·li·o·la·try (hē′lē äl′ə trē) *n.* [HELIO- + -LATRY] sun worship —**he′li·o·la′ter** *n.*

he·li·om·e·ter (-äm′ə tər) *n.* [Fr. *héliomètre:* see HELIO- & -METER: so called because orig. used in measuring the sun's diameter] an instrument formerly used for measuring the angular distance between two stars

He·li·op·o·lis (hē′lē äp′ə lis) [Gr. *Hēlioupolis,* lit., city of the sun < *hēlios* (see ff.) + *polis*, city] **1.** ancient city in the Nile delta, just north of where Cairo now stands: it was the center for the worship of the ancient Egyptian sun god Ra **2.** *see* BAALBEK

He·li·os (hē′lē äs′) [Gr. *hēlios*, the sun < IE. base *sawel-* (with variant *swen-*), sun, whence L. *sol*, ON. *sol*, SUN, SOUTH] *Gr. Myth.* the sun god, son of Hyperion

he·li·o·stat (hē′lē ə stat′) *n.* [ModL. *heliostata:* see HELIO- & -STAT] a device consisting of a mirror slowly revolved by clockwork so as to reflect the sun's rays continuously in a fixed direction

he·li·o·tax·is (hē′lē ə tak′sis) *n.* [ModL.: see HELIO- & TAXIS] the tendency of certain plants and animals to move or turn under the influence of sunlight

he·li·o·ther·a·py (-ther′ə pē) *n.* [HELIO- + THERAPY] the treatment of disease by exposing the body to sunlight

he·li·o·trope (hē′lē ə trōp′, hel′yə-; *Brit.* hel′yə-) *n.* [Fr. *héliotrope* < L. *heliotropium* < Gr. *hēliotropion* < *hēlios,* the sun (see HELIOS) + base of *trepein,* to turn (see TROPE)] **1.** formerly, a sunflower or other plant whose flowers turn to face the sun **2.** any of a genus (*Heliotropium*) of plants of the borage family, with fragrant clusters of small white or reddish-purple flowers **3.** same as VALERIAN **4.** reddish purple **5.** a kind of heliograph (sense 2) used in surveying **6.** same as BLOODSTONE —*adj.* reddish-purple

he·li·ot·ro·pism (hē′lē ät′rə piz'm) *n.* [HELIO- + -TROPISM] the tendency of certain plants or other organisms to turn or bend under the influence of light, esp. sunlight: positive heliotropism causes a turning toward the light; negative heliotropism causes a turning away from the light —**he′li·o·trop′ic** (-ə träp′ik) *adj.* —**he′li·o·trop′i·cal·ly** *adv.*

he·li·o·type (hē′lē ə tīp′) *n.* [HELIO- + -TYPE] same as COLLOTYPE —**he′li·o·typ′y** *n.*

he·li·o·zo·an (hē′lē ə zō′ən) *n.* [< ModL. *Heliozoa* (< HELIO- + -ZOA) + -AN] any of an order (Heliozoa) of chiefly freshwater amoeboid protozoans, with numerous slender pseudopodia arranged as rays —**he′li·o·zo′ic** (-ik) *adj.*

hel·i·port (hel′ə pôrt′) *n.* [HELI(COPTER) + (AIR)PORT] a field, rooftop, etc. where helicopters land and take off

he·li·um (hē′lē əm) *n.* [ModL. < Gr. *hēlios* (see HELIOS)] one of the chemical elements, a very light, inert, colorless gas, having the lowest known boiling and melting points: it is used in low-temperature work, as a diluent for oxygen, for inflating balloons, etc.: symbol, He; at. wt., 4.0026; at. no., 2; density, 0.1785 g/l (0°C); melt. pt., −272.2°C; boil. pt., −268.9°C

he·lix (hē′liks) *n., pl.* **-lix·es, -li·ces′** (hel′ə sēz′, hē′lə-) [L., kind of ivy, spiral < Gr. *helix,* a spiral < *helissein,* to turn round < IE. base *wel-,* to turn, twist, whence L. *volvere* & WALK] **1.** any spiral, either lying in a single plane or, esp., moving around a cone, cylinder, etc. as a screw thread does **2.** *Anat.* the folded rim of cartilage around the outer ear **3.** *Archit.* an ornamental spiral, as a volute on a Corinthian or Ionic capital **4.** *Math.* a line so curved around a right circular cylinder that it would become a straight line if the cylinder were unfolded into a plane **5.** *Zool.* any of a genus (*Helix*) of spiral-shelled land mollusks, including the common, edible European snail (*Helix pomatia*)

hell (hel) *n.* [ME. *helle* < OE. *hel* (akin to G. *hölle* & ON. *Hel,* the underworld goddess: see HEL) < base of *helan,* to cover, hide < IE. base *kel-,* to hide, cover up, whence L. *celare,* to hide] **1.** *Bible* the place where the spirits of the dead are: identified with SHEOL and HADES **2.** [*often* H-] *a) Christianity* the place where devils live and to which variously sinners and unbelievers are doomed to eternal punishment after death *b)* those in hell *c)* the powers of evil or darkness **3.** any place or condition of evil, pain, disorder, cruelty, etc. **4.** [Colloq.] *a)* any extremely disagreeable, unsettling, or punishing treatment or experience, or the cause or source of this *b)* devilish spirits or excitement [*full of hell*] —*vi.* [Slang] to live or act in a reckless or dissolute way: often with *around* As profanity *hell* is widely used, both alone and in various combinations, as an interjection expressing irritation, anger, etc. (Ex.:

hell, no! a *hell* of a success), and in various ways, esp. after *in* or *the*, to express surprise, disbelief, disgust, etc. (Ex.: who in *hell* is he? what the *hell!*) —☆**be hell on** [Slang] 1. to be very difficult or painful for 2. to be very strict or severe with 3. to be very destructive or damaging to —**catch** (or **get**) **hell** [Slang] to receive a severe scolding, punishment, etc. —**for the hell of it** [Slang] for no serious reason —☆**hell of a** [Slang] very much of a: sometimes written **helluva**

he'll (hēl; *unstressed* hil, il) 1. he will 2. he shall

Hel·lad·ic (he lad′ik) *adj.* designating or of the preclassical (c. 3000–c. 1100 B.C.) cultures of the peoples living on or around the Greek peninsula

Hel·las (hel′əs) 1. in ancient times, Greece, including the islands & colonies: orig., a town in Thessaly; later, a district 2. *modern Gr. name of* GREECE

☆**hell·bend·er** (hel′ben′dər) *n.* 1. a large, primitive, edible salamander (*Cryptobranchus alleganiensis*), with lidless eyes, found esp. in the Ohio valley 2. [Slang] a drinking bout; spree

☆**hell·bent** (-bent′) *adj.* [Slang] 1. firmly resolved or recklessly determined 2. moving fast or recklessly

hell·box (-bäks′) *n. Printing* a box for broken or discarded type

hell·broth (-brôth′) *n.* a brew for use in black magic

hell·cat (-kat′) *n.* 1. a witch 2. an evil, spiteful, bad-tempered woman

☆**hell·div·er** (-dī′vər) *n. same as* DABCHICK (sense 2)

Hel·le (hel′ē) [L. < Gr. *Hellē*] *Gr. Legend* a girl who, while fleeing with her brother on a ram with golden fleece, fell off and drowned in the Hellespont

hel·le·bore (hel′ə bôr′) *n.* [altered (after Gr.) < ME. *ellebore* < OFr. < L. *helleborus* < Gr. *helleboros*, orig. prob. "plant eaten by fawns" < *hellos*, var. of *ellos*, fawn < base of *elaphos*, deer + *bora*, food (of beasts): for IE. base see ELK & VORACIOUS] 1. any of a genus (*Helleborus*) of winter-blooming plants of the buttercup family, with flowers shaped like buttercups but of various colors: the poisonous rhizomes of the European black variety (*Helleborus niger*) have been used as a heart stimulant and cathartic 2. any of a genus (*Veratrum*) of plants of the lily family: the white hellebore (*Veratrum album* and *Veratrum viride*) have poisonous rhizomes, that have been used in medicine

Hel·len (hel′ən) [L. < Gr. *Hellēn*] the legendary ancestor of the Hellenes, a son of Deucalion and Pyrrha

Hel·lene (hel′ēn) *n.* [Gr. *Hellēn*] a Greek

Hel·len·ic (hə len′ik, he-) *adj.* [Gr. *Hellēnikos* < *Hellēnes*, the Greeks] 1. of the Hellenes; Greek 2. of the history, language, or culture of the ancient Greeks; specif., from the late 8th century B.C. to the death of Alexander the Great (323 B.C.) —*n.* 1. the language of ancient Greece 2. *a former term for* GREEK (*n.* 2)

Hel·len·ism (hel′ən iz′m) *n.* [Gr. *Hellēnismos*, imitation of the Greeks < *Hellēnizein*, to speak Greek] 1. a Greek phrase, idiom, or custom 2. the character, thought, culture, or ethical system of ancient Greece 3. adoption of the Greek language, customs, etc.

Hel·len·ist (-ist) *n.* [Gr. *Hellēnistēs*, imitator of the Greeks < *Hellēnizein*, to speak Greek] 1. a non-Greek, esp. a Jew of the Diaspora, who adopted the Greek language, customs, etc. 2. a specialist or expert in the Greek language and learning 3. any of the Byzantine Greeks of the 15th century who helped revive classical learning in Europe

Hel·len·is·tic (hel′ə nis′tik) *adj.* 1. of or characteristic of Hellenists or Hellenism 2. of Greek history, language, and culture after the death of Alexander the Great (323 B.C.) —**Hel′len·is′ti·cal·ly** *adv.*

Hel·len·ize (hel′ə nīz′) *vt., vi.* **-ized′, -iz′ing** [Gr. *Hellēnizein* < *Hellēnes*, the Greeks] to make or become Greek or Hellenistic, as in customs, ideals, form, or language —**Hel′len·i·za′tion** *n.* —**Hel′len·iz′er** *n.*

☆**hell·er**[1] (hel′ər) *n.* [Slang] a person who is noisy, wild, reckless, etc.

hel·ler[2] (hel′ər) *n., pl.* **hel′ler** [G. < MHG. *haller*, short for *Haller pfenninc*, penny of Hall: first coined (c. 1208) at Hall, Swabia] 1. formerly, a German copper coin or an Austrian bronze coin 2. *same as* HALER

hel·ler·i (hel′ə rī′) *n.* [ModL. (*Xiphophorus*) *Helleri*, swordtail: after C. *Heller*, 20th-cent. aquarist] *same as* SWORDTAIL

Hel·les (hel′is), **Cape**, S tip of the Gallipoli Peninsula, Turkey, at the entrance to the Dardanelles

Hel·les·pont (hel′əs pänt′) [Gr., lit., "sea of Helle"] *ancient name of the* DARDANELLES

hell·fire (hel′fīr′) *n.* [ME. *helle fir* < OE. *hellefyr*] the fire, hence punishment, of hell

Hell Gate [< Du. *Helle Gat*, hell strait: from the whirlpools formerly there] narrow channel of the East River, N.Y., between Manhattan & Queens

☆**hell·gram·mite, hell·gra·mite** (hel′grə mīt′) *n.* [<?] the carnivorous, dark-brown, aquatic larva of the dobsonfly, often used as fish bait

hell·hole (-hōl′) *n.* [Colloq.] any very unpleasant place

hell·hound (-hound′) *n.* 1. a dog of hell, as Cerberus 2. a fiendish, evil person

hel·lion (hel′yən) *n.* [altered (after HELL) < Scot. dial. *hallion*, a low fellow < ? Fr. *haillon*, rag < MHG. *hadel*, var. of *hader*, rag, quarrel] [Colloq.] a person fond of deviltry; mischievous troublemaker; rascal

hell·ish (hel′ish) *adj.* 1. of, from, or like hell 2. devilish; fiendish 3. [Colloq.] very unpleasant; detestable —**hell′ish·ly** *adv.* —**hell′ish·ness** *n.*

hell·kite (hel′kīt′) *n.* [HELL + KITE (the bird)] a fiendish, cruel, pitiless person

Hell·man (hel′mən), **Lillian** 1905– ; U.S. playwright

hel·lo (he lō′, hə lō′, hel′ō, *etc.*) *interj.* [var. of HOLLO] an exclamation *a)* of greeting or response, as in telephoning *b)* to attract attention *c)* of astonishment or surprise —*n., pl.* **-los** a saying or exclaiming of "hello" —*vi.* **-loed′, -lo′ing** to say or exclaim "hello" —*vt.* to say "hello" to

helm[1] (helm) *n., vt.* [ME. < OE., protection, helmet, akin to G. *helm*, helmet, OE. *helmian*, to protect < IE. base **kel-*, to cover, hide, whence L. *celare*, to hide & HULL[1]] *archaic & poet. var. of* HELMET

helm[2] (helm) *n.* [ME. *helme* < OE. *helma*, akin to G. *helm*, handle < IE. **(s)kelmo-* < basc **(s)kel-*, to cut, whence Gr. *skallein*, to dig & SHIELD] 1. *a)* the wheel or tiller by which a ship is steered *b)* the complete steering gear, including the wheel or tiller, rudder, etc. 2. the control or leadership of an organization, government, etc. —*vt.* to guide; control; steer

hel·met (hel′mət) *n.* [OFr., dim. of *helme*, helmet < Frank. **helm*: for IE. base see HELM[1]] 1. a protective covering for the head; specif., *a)* the headpiece of ancient or medieval armor *b)* the metal head covering worn in modern warfare *c)* the rigid head covering used in football *d)* the mesh-faced mask used in fencing *e)* the headpiece of a diver's suit, equipped with air tubes, glass windows, etc. *f)* a fireman's protective hat *g)* a pith hat with a wide brim, worn as a sunshade in hot countries 2. something suggesting such a headpiece in appearance or function, as the arched upper part of the corolla or calyx in certain flowers —*vt.* to cover or equip with a helmet —**hel′met·ed** *adj.*

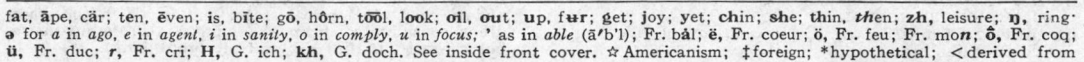

HELMETS

Helm·holtz (helm′hōlts′), **Her·mann Lud·wig Fer·di·nand von** (her′män lōōt′vikh fer′di nänt′ fôn) 1821–94; Ger. physiologist & physicist

hel·minth (hel′minth) *n.* [Gr. *helmins* (gen. *helminthos*), akin to *eilein*, to turn: for IE. base see HELIX] any worm or wormlike animal, esp. a worm parasite of the intestine, as the tapeworm, hookworm, or roundworm

hel·min·thi·a·sis (hel′min thī′ə sis) *n.* [ModL. < Gr. *helminthiān*, to suffer from worms: see prec. & -IASIS] a disease caused or characterized by parasitic worms in the body

hel·min·thic (hel min′thik) *adj.* 1. of, pertaining to, or caused by helminths 2. expelling or destroying helminths —*n.* a helminthic medicine; vermifuge

hel·min·thol·o·gy (hel′min thäl′ə jē) *n.* the scientific study of helminths

helms·man (helmz′mən) *n., pl.* **-men** (-mən) the man at the helm; man who steers a ship

Hel·o·ise (hel′ə wēz′) a feminine name: see ELOISE

Hé·lo·ïse (ā lō ēz′; *E.* hel′ə wēz′) 1101?–64?; mistress &, later, wife of her teacher, Pierre ABÉLARD

Hel·ot (hel′ət, hē′lət) *n.* [L. *Helotes, Hilotae, pl.* < Gr. *Heilōtes, pl.*, taken as < *Helos*, town in Laconia whose inhabitants were enslaved by the Spartans, but < ? base of *haliskesthai*, to be captured < IE. base **wel-*, to tear, injure, whence L. *vellere*, to pluck, tear away] 1. a member of the lowest class of serfs in ancient Sparta 2. [h-] any serf or slave

hel·ot·ism (-iz′m) *n.* 1. the condition of a helot; serfdom or slavery 2. *Biol.* a form of symbiosis, as among some ants, in which one species dominates and uses workers of another species

hel·ot·ry (-rē) *n.* 1. helots as a class; serfs or slaves 2. serfdom or slavery

help (help) *vt.* [ME. *helpen* < OE. *helpan*, akin to G. *helfen* < IE. base **kelb-, *kelp-*, to help, whence OLith. *sélbinos*, to aid] 1. to make things easier or better for (a person); aid; assist; specif., *a)* to give (one in need or trouble) something necessary, as relief, succor, money, etc. [to *help* the poor] *b)* to do part of the work of; ease or share the labor of [to *help* someone lift a load] *c)* to aid in getting (*up, down, in,* etc. or *to, into, out of,* etc.) [*help* her into the house] 2. to make it easier for (something) to exist, happen, develop, improve, etc.; specif., *a)* to make more effective, larger, more intense, etc.; aid the growth of; promote [a tax to *help* the schools] *b)* to cause improvement in; remedy; alleviate; relieve [a medicine that *helps* a cold] 3. *a)* to keep from; avoid [he can't *help* coughing] *b)* to stop, pre-

vent, change, etc. [a misfortune that can't be *helped*] **4.** to serve or wait on (a customer, client, etc.) —*vi.* **1.** to give assistance; be cooperative, useful, or beneficial **2.** to act as a waiter, clerk, servant, etc. —*n.* [ME. < OE. < base of the *v.*; in U.S., sense of "servant," prob. a euphemism to avoid stigma of "serve"] **1.** the act of helping or a thing that helps; aid; assistance **2.** relief; cure; remedy ☆**3.** *a)* a helper; esp., a hired helper, as a domestic servant, farm hand, etc. *b)* hired helpers; employees —**cannot help but** cannot fail to; be compelled or obliged to —**cannot help oneself** to be the victim of circumstances, a habit, etc. —**help oneself to 1.** to serve or provide oneself with (food, etc.) **2.** to take without asking or being given; steal —**help out** to help in getting or doing something; help —**so help me (God)** as God is my witness: used in oaths

SYN.—**help** is the simplest and strongest of these words meaning to supply another with whatever is necessary to accomplish his ends or relieve his wants; **aid** and **assist** are somewhat more formal and weaker, **assist** esp. implying a subordinate role in the helper and less need for help [she *assisted* him in his experiments]; **succor** suggests timely help to one in distress [to *succor* a besieged city] —**ANT. hinder**

help·er (-ər) *n.* a person or thing that helps, esp. an assisting worker who is more or less unskilled
help·ful (-f'l) *adj.* giving help; of service; useful —**help′ful·ly** *adv.* —**help′ful·ness** *n.*
help·ing (-iŋ) *n.* **1.** a giving of aid; assisting **2.** a portion of food served to one person
help·less (-lis) *adj.* **1.** not able to help oneself; weak **2.** lacking help or protection **3.** incompetent, ineffective, or powerless —**help′less·ly** *adv.* —**help′less·ness** *n.*
help·mate (-māt′) *n.* [altered < ff.] a helpful companion; specif., a wife or, sometimes, a husband
help·meet (-mēt′) *n.* [ghost word: mistakenly read as a single word in "an *help meet* for him" (Gen. 2:18)] *same as* HELPMATE
Hel·sing·ør (hel′siŋ ör′) seaport in Denmark, on the Öresund, opposite Hälsingborg, Sweden: pop. 26,000
Hel·sin·ki (hel′siŋ kē) capital of Finland; seaport on the Gulf of Finland: pop. 519,000: Swed. name **Hel·sing·fors** (hel′siŋ fôrs′)
hel·ter-skel·ter (hel′tər skel′tər) *adv.* [arbitrary formation, suggesting confusion] in haste and confusion; in a disorderly, hurried manner —*adj.* hurried and confused; disorderly —*n.* anything helter-skelter
helve (helv) *n.* [ME. *helfe* < OE., akin to MDu. *helf:* for IE. base see HELM², HALF] the handle of a tool, esp. of an ax or hatchet —*vt.* **helved, helv′ing** to put a helve on; equip with a helve
Hel·ve·tia (hel vē′shə) **1.** ancient Celtic country in C Europe, in what is now W Switzerland **2.** *Latin name of* SWITZERLAND
Hel·ve·tian (-shən) *adj.* **1.** of Helvetia or the Helvetii **2.** Swiss —*n.* **1.** a native or inhabitant of Helvetia **2.** a Swiss
Hel·vet·ic (hel vet′ik) *adj. same as* HELVETIAN —*n.* a Swiss Protestant; adherent of Zwingli
Hel·ve·ti·i (hel vē′shē ī′) *n.pl.* [L.] the Celtic people who lived in ancient Helvetia
Hel·vé·tius (el vā syüs′; *E.* hel vē′shē əs), **Claude A·dri·en** (klôd ȧ dre an′) 1715-71; Fr. philosopher
hem¹ (hem) *n.* [ME. < OE., akin to MLowG. *ham,* enclosed piece of land < IE. base **kem-,* to compress, impede, whence HAMPER¹] **1.** the border on a garment or piece of cloth, usually made by folding the edge and sewing it down **2.** any border, edge, or margin —*vt.* **hemmed, hem′ming** to fold back the edge of and sew down; put a hem or hems on —**hem in** (or **around** or **about**) **1.** to encircle; surround **2.** confine or restrain
hem² (hem: *conventionalized pronun.*) *interj., n.* the sound made in clearing the throat —*vi.* **hemmed, hem′ming 1.** to make this sound, as in trying to get attention or in showing doubt **2.** to make this sound, or grope about in speech, while searching for the right words: usually used in the phrase **hem and haw**
hem- (hēm, hem) *same as* HEMO-: used before a vowel
he·ma- (hē′mə, hem′ə) *same as* HEMO-
he·ma·cy·tom·e·ter (hē′mə sī täm′ə ter, hem′ə-) *n.* [HEMA- + CYTO- + -METER] a device used to count the concentration of cells in body fluids, esp. the red and white cells in blood
he·mag·glu·ti·nate (hē′mə glŏŏt′'n āt′, hem′ə-) *vt.* **-nat′ed, -nat′ing** [HEM- + AGGLUTINATE] to cause the clumping of red blood cells in —**he′mag·glu·ti·na′tion** *n.*
he·mag·glu·ti·nin (-glŏŏt′'n in) *n.* a substance, as an antibody, capable of causing hemagglutination
he·mal (hē′məl) *adj.* [HEM- + -AL] **1.** having to do with the blood or blood vessels: also **he′ma·tal 2.** having to do with the side of the body in which the heart and main blood vessels are located
☆**he-man** (hē′man′) *n.* [Colloq.] a strong, virile man
he·ma·te·in (hē′mə tē′in, hem′ə-) *n.* [< HEMAT(OXYLIN) + -IN¹] a reddish-brown, crystalline dye, C₁₆H₁₂O₆, obtained from logwood extracts by oxidation and used as a stain and indicator
he·ma·ther·mal (-thur′m'l) *adj.* [HEMA- + THERMAL] *same as* HOMOIOTHERMAL
he·mat·ic (hi mat′ik) *adj.* [Gr. *haimatikos*] of, filled with, or colored like blood

hem·a·tin (hem′ə tin, hē′mə-) *n.* [HEMAT- + -IN¹] a darkbrown or blackish substance, C₃₄H₃₂N₄O₄·FeOH, obtained by the decomposition of hemoglobin
hem·a·tin·ic (hem′ə tin′ik, hē′mə-) *n.* any substance that increases the amount of hemoglobin in the blood —*adj.* of or relating to hematin
hem·a·tite (hem′ə tīt′, hē′mə-) *n.* [L. *haematites* < Gr. *haimatitēs,* lit., bloodlike, red iron ore < *haima,* blood] native anhydrous ferric oxide, Fe₂O₃, an important iron ore: it is brownish red in the earthy variety or black and crystalline —**hem′a·tit′ic** (-tit′ik) *adj.*
hem·a·to- (hem′ə tō, hē′mə-) [< Gr. *haima* (gen. *haimatos*), blood] *a combining form meaning* blood [*hematology*]: also, before a vowel, **hemat-**
hem·a·to·blast (-blast′) *n.* [prec. + -BLAST] an immature erythrocyte —**hem′a·to·blas′tic** *adj.*
hem·a·to·crit (hi mat′ə krit′) *n.* [< HEMATO- + Gr. *kritēs,* a judge: see CRITIC] **1.** a small centrifuge used to determine the relative volumes of blood cells and fluid in blood **2.** the proportion of blood cells to a volume of blood measured by a hematocrit: also **hematocrit reading**
hem·a·to·gen·e·sis (hem′ə tō jen′ə sis, hē′mə-) *n.* same *as* HEMATOPOIESIS —**hem′a·to·gen′ic** (-jen′ik), **hem′a·to·ge·net′ic** (-jə net′ik) *adj.*
hem·a·tog·e·nous (-täj′ə nəs) *adj.* **1.** forming blood **2.** spread by the bloodstream, as bacteria
he·ma·tol·o·gy (hē′mə täl′ə jē, hem′ə-) *n.* [HEMATO- + -LOGY] the study of the blood and its diseases—**he′ma·to·log′ic** (-tə läj′ik), **he′ma·to·log′i·cal** *adj.* —**he′ma·tol′o·gist** *n.*
he·ma·to·ma (-tō′mə) *n., pl.* **-mas, -ma·ta** (-tə) [ModL.: see HEMAT(O)- & -OMA] a local swelling or tumor filled with effused blood
he·ma·toph·a·gous (-täf′ə gəs) *adj.* [HEMATO- + -PHAGOUS] feeding on blood
hem·a·to·poi·e·sis (hem′ə tō poi ē′sis, hē′mə-) *n.* [< HEMATO- + Gr. *poiēsis,* a making: see POESY] the production of blood cells by the blood-forming organs —**hem′a·to·poi·et′ic** (-et′ik) *adj.*
he·ma·to·ther·mal (-thur′m'l) *adj.* [HEMATO- + THERMAL] *same as* HOMOIOTHERMAL
he·ma·tox·y·lin (hē′mə täk′sə lin, hem′ə-) *n.* [H(A)EMATOXYL(ON) + -IN¹] a colorless, crystalline compound, C₁₆H₁₄O₆·3H₂O, extracted from logwood and used as an indicator and a stain in microscopy: when oxidized it yields hematein dye
hem·a·to·zo·on (hem′ə tə zō′än, hē′mə-) *n., pl.* **-zo′a** (-ə) [ModL.: see HEMATO- & ZOON] any parasitic animal organism in the blood —**hem′a·to·zo′ic** (-ik), **hem′a·to·zo′al** *adj.*
he·ma·tu·ri·a (hē′mə toor′ē ə, -tyoor′-; hem′ə-) *n.* [HEMAT- + -URIA] the presence of red blood cells in the urine
heme (hēm) *n.* [contr. < HEMATIN] the nonprotein, ironcontaining pigment, C₃₄H₃₂N₄O₄Fe, part of the hemoglobin molecule
hem·el·y·tron (he mel′ə trän′) *n., pl.* **-tra** (-trə) [ModL. < HEM(I)- + ELYTRON] either of the forewings of hemipterous insects, having a thickened basal portion and a membranous end: also **hem·el′y·trum** (-trəm), *pl.* **-tra** (-trə)
hem·er·a·lo·pi·a (hem′ər ə lō′pē ə) *n.* [ModL. < Gr. *hēmeralōps,* day blindness (< *hēmera,* day + *alaos,* blind + *ōps,* EYE) + -IA] a defect in the eye in which the vision is reduced in the daylight or in bright light: cf. NYCTALOPIA —**hem′er·a·lop′ic** (-läp′ik) *adj.*
hem·i- (hem′i, -ə, -ē) [Gr. *hēmi-* < IE. **sēmi-,* whence Sans. *sāmí-,* L. *semi-*] *a prefix meaning* half [*hemisphere*]
-he·mi·a (hē′mē ə) [var. of -EMIA] *same as* -EMIA
he·mic (hē′mik, hem′ik) *adj.* [HEM- + -IC] of the blood
hem·i·cel·lu·lose (hem′i sel′yə lōs′) *n.* a substance like cellulose but less complex that is extracted from wood or corn fiber by dilute alkalis and consists of sugars and sugar acids
hem·i·chor·date (-kôr′dāt) *adj.* [HEMI- + CHORDATE] of or pertaining to a phylum (Hemichordata) of wormlike marine animals with visceral clefts and primitive nervous and circulatory systems —*n.* any hemichordate animal
hem·i·cra·ni·a (-krā′nē ə) *n.* [LL. < Gr. *hēmikrania* < *hēmi-,* half + *kranion,* skull] headache in only one side of the head, as in migraine
hem·i·cy·cle (hem′i sī′k'l) *n.* [Fr. *hémicycle* < L. *hemicyclium* < Gr. *hēmikyklion:* see HEMI- & CYCLE] **1.** a half circle **2.** a semicircular room, wall, etc.
hem·i·dem·i·sem·i·qua·ver (hem′ē dem′ē sem′ē kwä′vər) *n.* [HEMI- + DEMISEMIQUAVER] [Chiefly Brit.] *Music* a sixty-fourth note
hem·i·el·y·tron (-el′ə trän′) *n. same as* HEMELYTRON
hem·i·he·dral (hem′i hē′drəl) *adj.* [HEMI- + -HEDRAL] having half the number of planes required for complete symmetry: said of a crystal
hem·i·hy·drate (-hī′drāt) *n.* a hydrate containing half as many molecules of water as of the substance combined with the water
hem·i·me·tab·o·lous (-mə tab′ə ləs) *adj.* designating or of a group of insect orders in which the juvenile stages are aquatic without a pupal stage, and in which the young differ considerably from the adults: also **hem′i·met′a·bol′ic** (-met′ə bäl′ik) —**hem′i·me·tab′o·lism** *n.*

hem·i·mor·phic (-môr′fik) *adj.* [HEMI- + -MORPHIC] designating a crystal with unlike planes at the ends of the same axis

hem·i·mor·phite (-môr′fīt) *n.* [G. *hemimorphit* < *hemimorph*, hemimorphic (< *hemi-*, HEMI- + *-morph*, -MORPH) + *-it*, -ITE¹] a native zinc silicate, $Zn_4Si_2O_7(OH)_2 \cdot H_2O$, that is an important ore of zinc

he·min (hē′min) *n.* [HEM(E) + -IN¹] a brown, crystalline chloride of heme, $C_{34}H_{32}N_4O_4FeCl$, obtained when blood is treated with hydrochloric acid or glacial acetic acid and sodium chloride: its production by this reaction is evidence of the presence of blood in fluids, stains, etc.

Hem·ing·way (hem′iŋ wā′), **Ernest** 1899–1961; U.S. novelist & short-story writer

hem·i·o·la (hem′ē ō′lə) *n.* [< ML. *hemiolia* < Gr. *hēmiolia*, fem. of *hēmiolios*, in the ratio of one and one half to one < *hēmi-* (see HEMI-) + *holos*, whole] *Music* a rhythmical relationship of three beats against two: frequently applied to a passage consisting of two groups of three notes, each against a single group of two: also **hem′i·o′li·a** (-lē ə)

hem·i·par·a·site (hem′i par′ə sit′) *n.* 1. *Zool.* an organism that may be either free living or parasitic; facultative parasite 2. *Bot.* a parasitic plant, as the mistletoe, which carries on some photosynthesis but obtains a portion of its food, water, or minerals from a host plant —**hem′i·par′a·sit′ic** (-sit′ik) *adj.*

hem·i·ple·gi·a (-plē′jē ə, -jə) *n.* [ModL. < MGr. *hēmiplēgia*, paralysis: see HEMI- & -PLEGIA] paralysis of one side of the body —**hem′i·ple′gic** (-jik) *adj., n.*

he·mip·ter·an (hi mip′tər ən) *n.* [< ModL. *Hemiptera*, name of the order (see HEMI- & PTERO-) + -AN] any of a large order (Hemiptera) of insects, including bedbugs, water bugs, lice, aphids, etc., with piercing and sucking mouthparts: they generally have two pairs of wings, the outer pair thickened toward the base —**he·mip′ter·oid** *adj.* —**he·mip′ter·ous** *adj.*

hem·i·sphere (hem′ə sfir′) *n.* [ME. *hemisperie* < L. *hemisphaerium* < Gr. *hēmisphairion*: see HEMI- & SPHERE] 1. half of a sphere or globe; specif., *a)* any of the halves into which the celestial sphere is divided by either the celestial equator or the ecliptic *b)* any of the halves of the earth: the earth is divided by the equator into the Northern and Southern hemispheres and by a meridian into the Eastern Hemisphere (containing Europe, Asia, Africa, and Australia) and the Western Hemisphere (containing the Americas and Oceania) *c)* a model or map of any of these halves 2. the countries and peoples of any of the earth's hemispheres 3. an area of action, knowledge, etc. 4. either lateral half of the cerebrum or cerebellum —**hem′i·spher′i·cal** (-sfer′i kəl), **hem′i·spher′ic** *adj.*

hem·i·sphe·roid (-sfir′oid) *n.* a half of a spheroid

hem·i·stich (hem′i stik′) *n.* [L. *hemistichium* < Gr. *hēmistichion* < *hēmi-*, half + *stichos*, a row, line, verse: see STICH] 1. half a line of verse, esp. either half created by the chief caesura, or rhythmic pause in the middle of a line 2. an incomplete line of poetry or one shorter than the metrical pattern calls for

hem·i·ter·pene (hem′i tur′pēn) *n.* [HEMI- + TERPENE] any of a group of isomeric hydrocarbons with the general formula C_5H_8, as isoprene

hem·i·trope (hem′i trōp′) *adj.* [Fr. *hémitrope*: see HEMI- & -TROPE] designating a crystal formed of two other crystals joined so that corresponding faces are directly opposed: also **hem′i·trop′ic** (-träp′ik) —*n.* such a crystal

hem·line (hem′līn′) *n.* 1. the bottom edge, usually hemmed, of a dress, skirt, coat, etc. 2. the height of this edge above the ground

hem·lock (hem′läk) *n.* [ME. *hemlok* < OE. *hemlic, hymlik,* akin to *hymele,* hop] 1. *a)* a poisonous European plant (*Conium maculatum*) of the parsley family, with compound umbels of small white flowers and finely divided leaves: also **poison hemlock** *b)* a poison made from this plant 2. *same as* WATER HEMLOCK 3. *a)* any of a genus (*Tsuga*) of N. American and Asiatic evergreen trees of the pine family, with drooping branches and short needles: the bark is used in tanning *b)* the wood of such a tree

hem·mer (hem′ər) *n.* 1. a person that hems ☆2. a sewing-machine attachment for making hems

he·mo- (hē′mō, -mə; hem′ō, -ə) [Gr. *haimo-* < *haima,* blood] *a combining form meaning* blood [*hemoglobin*]

he·mo·chro·ma·to·sis (hē′mə krō′mə tō′sis, hem′ə-) *n.* [HEMO- + CHROMAT(O)- + -OSIS] a disorder of iron metabolism, characterized by a bronze-colored skin pigmentation, liver dysfunction, an excess of iron in body organs, and diabetes mellitus

he·mo·cy·a·nin (-sī′ə nin) *n.* [HEMO- + CYAN- + -IN¹] a blue, oxygen-carrying blood pigment containing copper, found in many crustaceans and mollusks

he·mo·cyte (hē′mə sīt′, hem′ə-) *n.* [HEMO- + -CYTE] a blood cell

he·mo·cy·tom·e·ter (hē′mō sī täm′ə tər, hem′ō-) *n.* [HEMO- + CYTO- + -METER] a device for measuring the number of cells in a sample of blood

he·mo·di·al·y·sis (-dī al′ə sis) *n.* the removal of waste substances from the circulating blood by dialysis

he·mo·flag·el·late (-flaj′ə lāt′) *n.* any flagellate protozoan parasite in the bloodstream

he·mo·glo·bin (hē′mə glō′bin, hem′ə-; hē′mə glō′bin, hem′ə-) *n.* [contr. (as if < HEMO-) < earlier *haematoglobulin*: see HEMATO- & GLOBULIN] 1. the red coloring matter of the red blood corpuscles of vertebrates, a protein yielding heme and globin on hydrolysis: it carries oxygen from the lungs to the tissues, and carbon dioxide from the tissues to the lungs 2. any of various respiratory pigments found in the blood or muscle tissue of many invertebrates and in the root nodules of some plants —**he′mo·glo·bin′ic** (-glō bin′ik) *adj.* —**he′mo·glo′bin·ous** (-bin əs) *adj.*

he·mo·glo·bin·u·ri·a (hē′mə glō′bi nyoor′ē ə, hem′ə-) *n.* the presence in the urine of hemoglobin free from the red blood cells —**he′mo·glo′bin·u′ric** *adj.*

he·moid (hē′moid) *adj.* [HEM- + -OID] like blood

he·mo·lymph (hē′mə limf′) *n.* [HEMO- + LYMPH] the circulating fluid in open tissue spaces of invertebrates: it may act as blood, as in arthropods, or be in addition to blood, as in earthworms

he·mo·ly·sin (hē′mə lī′s'n, hem′ə-; hi mäl′ə sin) *n.* [< HEMO- + Gr. *lysis,* a dissolving + -IN¹] a substance formed in the blood, as by bacterial action, that causes the destruction of red corpuscles with liberation of hemoglobin

he·mol·y·sis (hi mäl′ə sis) *n.* [HEMO- + -LYSIS] the destruction of red corpuscles with liberation of hemoglobin into the surrounding fluid —**he·mo·lyt·ic** (hē′mə lit′ik, hem′ə-) *adj.*

he·mo·lyze (hē′mə līz′, hem′ə-) *vi., vt.* **-lyzed′, -lyz′ing** to undergo, or cause to undergo, hemolysis

he·mo·phile (-fīl′) *n.* [HEMO- + -PHILE] a hemophilic bacterium

he·mo·phil·i·a (hē′mə fil′ē ə, hem′ə-; -fil′yə) *n.* [ModL.: see HEMO-, -PHIL, & -IA] a hereditary condition in which one of the normal blood-clotting factors is absent, causing prolonged bleeding from even minor cuts and injuries: it occurs in males and is transmitted by females

he·mo·phil·i·ac (-fil′ē ak, -fil′yak) *n.* a person who has hemophilia

he·mo·phil·ic (-fil′ik) *adj.* 1. of or having hemophilia 2. growing well in a medium containing hemoglobin: said of certain bacteria

he·mop·ty·sis (hi mäp′tə sis) *n.* [ModL. < HEMO- + Gr. *ptysis,* spitting < *ptyein,* to spit out < IE. echoic base (s)*pyū-,* whence L. *spuere,* SPEW] the spitting or coughing up of blood: usually caused by bleeding of the lungs or bronchi

hem·or·rhage (hem′ər ij, hem′rij) *n.* [Fr. *hémorrhagie* < L. *haemorrhagia* < Gr. *haimorrhagia* < *haima,* blood + base of *rhēgnynai,* to break, burst] the escape of large quantities of blood from a blood vessel; heavy bleeding —*vi.* **-rhaged, -rhag·ing** to have a hemorrhage —**hem′or·rhag′ic** (-ə raj′ik) *adj.*

hem·or·rhoid (hem′ə roid′, hem′roid) *n.* [altered (after L. or Gr.) < ME. *emoroid(es)* < L. *haemorrhoidae* < Gr. *haimorrhoïdes (phlebes),* (veins) discharging blood < *haimorrhoos,* flowing with blood < *haima,* blood + *rhein,* to flow, STREAM] a painful swelling of a vein in the region of the anus, often with bleeding: *usually used in pl.* —**hem′or·rhoid′al** *adj.*

hem·or·rhoid·ec·to·my (hem′ə roi dek′tə mē) *n., pl.* **-mies** [see -ECTOMY] the surgical removal of hemorrhoids

he·mo·sta·sis (hi mäs′tə sis) *n.* [ModL. < Gr. *haimostasis:* see HEMO- & STASIS] 1. the stoppage of bleeding 2. the stoppage of the flow of blood in a vein or artery, as with a tourniquet

he·mo·stat (hē′mə stat′, hem′ə-) *n.* [< ff.] anything used to stop bleeding; specif., *a)* a clamplike instrument used in surgery *b)* a medicine that hastens clotting

he·mo·stat·ic (hē′mə stat′ik, hem′ə-) *adj.* [see HEMO- & STATIC] capable of stopping the flow of blood —*n. same as* HEMOSTAT (sense *b*)

he·mo·tox·in (hē′mə täk′sin) *n.* a toxin capable of destroying erythrocytes —**he′mo·tox′ic** *adj.*

hemp (hemp) *n.* [ME. < OE. *hænep* (akin to G. *hanf,* Du. *hennep*) < PGmc. *hanapa-* < *kanab-,* a pre-Germanic borrowing < a (? Scythian) base, whence Gr. *kannabis:* akin ? to Sumerian *kunibu,* hemp] 1. *a)* a tall Asiatic plant (*Cannabis sativa*) of the hemp family, grown for the tough fiber in its stem *b)* the fiber, used to make rope, sailcloth, etc. *c)* a substance, such as marijuana, hashish, etc., made from the leaves and flowers of this plant 2. *a)* any of various plants yielding a hemplike fiber, as the sisal *b)* this fiber —*adj.* designating a family (Cannabinaceae) of plants including hemp and hops

hemp agrimony a European plant (*Eupatorium cannabinum*) of the composite family, with reddish flowers, formerly used in medicine

hemp·en (hem′pən) *adj.* of, made of, or like hemp

hemp nettle any of a genus (*Galeopsis*) of European plants of the mint family; esp., a common prickly weed (*Galeopsis tetrahit*) now found in the U.S.

hemp·seed (-sēd′) *n.* the seed of hemp

Hemp·stead (hemp′sted, hem′-; -stəd) village on W Long Island, N.Y.: pop. 39,000

fat, āpe, cär; ten, ēven; is, bīte; gō, hôrn, tōōl, look; oil, out; up, fur; get; joy; yet; chin; she; thin, *then;* zh, leisure; ŋ, ring; ə for *a* in *ago, e* in *agent, i* in *sanity, o* in *comply, u* in *focus;* ′ as in *able* (ā′b'l); Fr. bal; ë, Fr. coeur; ö, Fr. feu; Fr. mon; ô, Fr. coq; ü, Fr. duc; r, Fr. cri; H, G. ich; kh, G. doch. See inside front cover. ☆ Americanism; ‡foreign; *hypothetical; <derived from

hem·stitch (hem′stich′) n. 1. an ornamental stitch, used esp. at a hem, made by pulling out several parallel threads and tying the cross threads together into small, even bunches 2. decorative needlework done with this stitch — vt. to put a hemstitch or hemstitches on

HEMSTITCH

hen (hen) n. [ME. < OE. henn, fem. of hana, rooster, akin to G. henne (fem. of hahn) < IE. base *kan-, to sing, crow, whence L. canere, to sing, whence carmen (< *canmen), song] 1. the female of the chicken (the domestic fowl): the male is called a rooster, or cock 2. the female of various other birds or of certain other animals, as the lobster 3. [Slang] a woman, esp. an older woman

hen and chickens the common houseleek (Sempervivum tectorum), a flowering plant with a dense rosette of fleshy leaves clustered at the base of the stem from which off-shoots arise

hen·bane (-bān′) n. [ME.: see HEN & BANE] a coarse, hairy, foul-smelling, poisonous plant (Hyoscyamus niger) of the nightshade family: it is used in medicine as a source of hyoscyamine and scopolamine

hen·bit (-bit′) n. [HEN + BIT²] a spreading plant (Lamium amplexicaule) of the mint family, with rounded, opposite leaves and small, pink or lavender flowers

hence (hens) adv. [ME. hennes < henne < OE. heonan(e), from here + -(e)s, adv. gen. suffix (cf. SINCE, THENCE) < IE. base as in HE¹, HERE] 1. from this place; away [go hence] 2. a) from this time; after now [a year hence] b) thereafter; subsequently 3. from this life 4. for this reason; as a result; therefore 5. [Archaic] from this origin or source —interj. [Archaic] depart! go away! —hence with! [Archaic] away with! take away!

hence·forth (-fôrth′) adv. [ME. hennesforth: see HENCE & FORTH] 1. from this time on: also hence′for′ward (-fôr′wərd) 2. thereafter; subsequently

hench·man (hench′mən) n., pl. -men (-mən) [ME. henxtman, hencheman < OE. hengest, stallion (see HENGIST) + -man: orig. sense prob. "horse attendant"] 1. orig., a male attendant; page or squire 2. a trusted helper or follower ☆3. a political underling who seeks mainly to advance his own interests ☆4. any of the followers of a criminal gang leader

hen·coop (hen′kōōp′) n. a coop for poultry

hen·dec·a- (hen′dek ə, hen dek′ə) [< Gr. hendeka, eleven < hen, one (< IE. *sem-, one: see SIMPLE) + deka, TEN] a combining form meaning eleven [hendecasyllable]

hen·dec·a·gon (hen dek′ə gän′) n. [Fr. hendécagone: see prec. & -GON] a plane figure with eleven angles and eleven sides —hen·de·cag·o·nal (hen′də kag′ə nəl) adj.

hen·dec·a·he·dron (hen dek′ə hē′drən) n., pl. -drons, -dra (-drə) [ModL.: see HENDECA- & -HEDRON] a solid figure with eleven plane surfaces —hen·dec′a·he′dral adj.

hen·dec·a·syl·la·ble (-sil′ə b'l) n. [L. hendecasyllabus < Gr. hendekasyllabos: see HENDECA- & SYLLABLE] a line of verse having eleven syllables —hen·dec′a·syl·lab′ic (-sə lab′ik) adj., n.

hen·di·a·dys (hen di′ə dis) n. [ML. < Gr. phrase hen dia dyoin, one (thing) by means of two] a figure of speech in which two nouns joined by and are used instead of a noun and a modifier (Ex.: deceit and words for deceitful words)

Hen·don (hen′dən) city in Middlesex, SE England: suburb of London: pop. 150,000

hen·e·quen (hen′ə kin) n. [Sp. henequén, jeniquén < native (Taino) name in Yucatan] 1. a tropical American agave (Agave fourcroydes) native to Yucatan, cultivated for the hard fiber of the leaves 2. the fiber, similar to the related sisal, used for making rope, binder twine, stuffing for furniture, rugs, etc.

Heng·e·lo (heŋ′ə lō) city in E Netherlands: pop. 67,000

Hen·gist (heŋ′gist) [OE. < hengest, stallion, akin to G. hengst < IE. base *kak-, to leap, spurt forth] ?–488 A.D.; Jute chief; with his brother, Horsa (?–455), he is reputed to have led the first Germanic invasion of England & to have founded the kingdom of Kent

hen·house (hen′hous′) n. a shelter for poultry

Hen·ley (hen′lē) city in SE England, on the Thames: site of an annual rowing regatta; pop. 9,000: also Henley-on-Thames

Hen·ley (hen′lē), William Ernest 1849–1903; Eng. poet, critic, & editor

hen·na (hen′ə) n. [Ar. ḥinnā′] 1. an Old World plant (Lawsonia inermis) of the loosestrife family, with minute white or red flowers having the fragrance of roses 2. a dye extracted from the leaves of this plant, often used to tint the hair auburn 3. reddish brown —adj. reddish-brown —vt. -naed, -na·ing to tint with henna

hen·ner·y (hen′ər ē) n., pl. -ner·ies a place where poultry is kept or raised

hen·o·the·ism (hen′ə thē iz'm) n. [coined (c. 1860) by Max Müller < Gr. hen, one (see HENDECA-) + theos, god] belief in or worship of one god without denying the existence of others —hen′o·the·ist n. —hen′o·the·is′tic adj.

hen party [Colloq.] a party for women only

hen·peck (hen′pek′) vt. to nag and domineer over (one's husband) —hen′pecked′ adj.

Hen·ri·et·ta (hen′rē et′ə) [Fr. Henriette, dim. of Henri: see HENRY] a feminine name: dim. Etta, Hetty, Nettie, Netty

Hen·ry (hen′rē) [Fr. Henri < G. Heinrich < OHG. Haganrih, lit., ruler of an enclosure (< hag-, HAW¹, a hedging in + rihhi, ruler) & also altered < OHG. Heimerich, lit., home ruler (< heim, HOME)] 1. a masculine name: dim. Hal, Hank, Henny; var. Harry; equiv. L. Henricus, Du. Hendrik, Fr. Henri, Ger. Heinrich, It. Enrico, Sp. Enrique; fem. Henrietta 2. 1394–1460; prince of Portugal: called Henry the Navigator 3. Henry I 1068–1135; king of England (1100–35): son of WILLIAM THE CONQUEROR 4. Henry II 1133–89; king of England (1154–89); 1st Plantagenet king 5. Henry III a) 1207–72; king of England (1216–72) b) 1551–89; king of France (1574–89) 6. Henry IV a) 1050–1106; king of Germany (1056–1106) & Holy Roman Emperor (1084–1106) b) 1367–1413; king of England (1399–1413); 1st Lancastrian king: son of JOHN OF GAUNT: called Bolingbroke c) 1553–1610; king of France (1589–1610); 1st Bourbon king: called Henry of Navarre 7. Henry V 1387–1422; king of England (1413–22): defeated the French at AGINCOURT 8. Henry VI 1421–71; king of England (1422–61; 1470–71) 9. Henry VII 1457–1509; king of England (1485–1509); 1st Tudor king 10. Henry VIII 1491–1547; king of England (1509–47): broke with the papacy and established the Church of England 11. O., (pseud. of William Sydney Porter) 1862–1910; U.S. short-story writer 12. Patrick, 1736–99; Am. patriot, statesman, & orator

☆**hen·ry** (hen′rē) n., pl. -rys, -ries [after Joseph Henry (1797–1878), U.S. physicist] Elec. the unit of inductance, equal to the inductance of a circuit in which the variation of current at the rate of one ampere per second induces an electromotive force of one volt

Henry 1. Cape, [after Prince Henry, son of JAMES I] promontory in SE Va., at the entrance of Chesapeake Bay: see HAMPTON ROADS, map 2. Fort, Confederate fort in NW Tenn., on the Tennessee River: captured (1862) by Union forces

Hens·lowe (henz′lō), Philip ?–1616; Eng. theater manager

hent (hent) vt. hent, hent′ing [ME. henten < OE. hentan, akin to huntian, hunt] [Archaic] to grasp; apprehend —n. [Archaic] 1. a grasping 2. something grasped in the mind; conception; purpose

Hen·ty (hen′tē), G(eorge) A(lfred) 1832–1902; Eng. writer of adventure books for boys

☆**hep** (hep) adj. [< ? the drill sergeant's shout (alteration of STEP) marking time for marching troops] [Slang] earlier form of HIP⁴

☆**hep·a·rin** (hep′ər in) n. [Gr. hēpar, the liver (see HEPATIC) + -IN¹] a substance found in various body tissues, esp. in the liver, that prevents the clotting of blood: it is used in surgery and medicine

hep·a·rin·ize (hep′ə rin iz′) vt. -ized′, -iz′ing to treat with heparin

hep·at- (hep′ət, hi pat′) same as HEPATO-: used before a vowel

hep·a·tec·to·my (hep′ə tek′tə mē) n., pl. -mies [prec. + -ECTOMY] the surgical removal of part or all of the liver

he·pat·ic (hi pat′ik) adj. [L. hepaticus < Gr. hēpatikos < hēpar, the liver < IE. base *jekwr̥, whence Sans. yákr̥t, L. jecur] 1. of or affecting the liver 2. like the liver in color or shape 3. of the liverworts —n. same as LIVERWORT

he·pat·i·ca (hi pat′i kə) n. [ModL. (see HEPATIC): in allusion to its liver-shaped, lobed leaves] any of a genus (Hepatica) of small plants of the buttercup family, with three-lobed leaves and white, pink, blue, or purple flowers that bloom in early spring

hep·a·ti·tis (hep′ə tit′is) n. [ModL. < ΗΕΠΑΤ- + -ITIS] inflammation of the liver

hep·a·to- (hep′ə tō′) [Gr. hēpato- < hēpar (gen. hēpatos): see HEPATIC] a combining form meaning the liver

☆**hep·cat** (hep′kat′) n. [HEP + CAT (sense 8)] [Slang] earlier term for a hep, or hip, person

He·phaes·tus (hi fes′təs) [Gr. Hēphaistos] Gr. Myth. the god of fire and the forge, son of Zeus and Hera: identified by the Romans with Vulcan

Hep·ple·white (hep′'l hwit′) adj. [after George Hepplewhite (?–1786), Eng. cabinetmaker] designating or of a style of furniture characterized by the use of graceful curves

hep·ta- (hep′tə) [< Gr. hepta, SEVEN] a combining form meaning: 1. seven [heptagon] 2. Chem. having seven atoms, radicals, etc. of a (specified) substance [heptachlor] Also, before a vowel, hept-

☆**hep·ta·chlor** (hep′tə klôr′) n. an insecticide, $C_{10}H_7Cl_7$, similar to chlordane

hep·tad (hep′tad) n. [Gr. heptas (gen. heptados) < hepta, SEVEN] a series or group of seven

hep·ta·gon (hep′tə gän′) n. [< Gr. heptagōnos, seven-cornered: see HEPTA- & -GON] a plane figure with seven angles and seven sides —hep·tag′o·nal (-tag′ə n'l) adj.

hep·ta·he·dron (hep′tə hē′drən) n., pl. -drons, -dra (-drə) [ModL.: see HEPTA- & -HEDRON] a solid figure with seven plane surfaces —hep′ta·he′dral adj.

hep·tam·er·ous (hep tam′ər əs) adj. [HEPTA- + -MEROUS] having seven parts in each whorl: said of flowers: also written 7-merous

hep·tam·e·ter (hep tam′ə tər) *n.* [HEPTA- + -METER] a line of verse with seven metrical feet

hep·tane (hep′tān) *n.* [HEPT(A)- + -ANE] a paraffin hydrocarbon, C₇H₁₆, existing in several isomeric forms: the normal isomer is used in standard mixtures to test octane ratings

hep·tar·chy (hep′tär kē) *n., pl.* **-chies** [HEPT- + -ARCHY] 1. government by seven rulers 2. a group of seven neighboring or allied kingdoms; specif., [**the H-**] the seven kingdoms supposed to have existed in Anglo-Saxon England before the 9th cent. A.D. (Northumbria, Mercia, Essex, East Anglia, Wessex, Sussex, and Kent)

hep·ta·stich (hep′tə stik′) *n.* [HEPTA- + STICH] a poem or stanza of seven lines

Hep·ta·teuch (-tōōk′, -tyōōk′) *n.* [LL.(Ec.) *Heptateuchos* < Gr.(Ec.) *Heptateuchos* < *hepta*, SEVEN + *teuchos*, a tool, book < *teuchein*, to make < IE. base *dheugh-*, whence DOUGHTY] the first seven books of the Old Testament

hep·ta·va·lent (hep′tə vā′lənt) *adj.* having a valence of seven

hep·tose (hep′tōs) *n.* [HEPT- + -OSE¹] any of several monosaccharides, C₇H₁₄O₇, containing seven carbon atoms in the molecule

her (hur; *unstressed* ər) *pron.* [ME. *hir, her, hire* < OE. *hire*, dat. sing. of *heo*, she, fem. of *he*, HE¹; it replaced the orig. OE. accus., *hie*, in ME.] *objective case of* SHE: also used colloquially as a predicate complement with a linking verb (Ex.: that's *her*) —*possessive pronominal adj.* of, belonging to, made, or done by her

her. heraldry

He·ra (hir′ə) [L. < Gr. *Hēra, Hērē*, lit., protectress: see HERO] *Gr. Myth.* the sister and wife of Zeus, queen of the gods, and goddess of women and marriage: identified by the Romans with Juno

Her·a·cli·tus (her′ə klīt′əs) fl. about 500 B.C.; Gr. philosopher

Her·a·cli·us (her′ə klī′əs, hi rak′lē əs) 575?-641 A.D.; Byzantine emperor (610-641)

Her·a·kles, Her·a·cles (her′ə klēz′) *same as* HERCULES

He·ra·kli·on, He·ra·klei·on (hi rak′lē ən) *Gr. name of* CANDIA

her·ald (her′əld) *n.* [ME. < OFr. *heralt* < *hirauz* < Frank. *hartwald*, army chief: see HAROLD] 1. formerly, any of various officials who made proclamations, carried state messages to other sovereigns, took charge of tournaments, arranged ceremonies, etc. 2. in England, an official in charge of genealogies, heraldic arms, etc. 3. a person who proclaims or announces significant news, etc.: often used as the name of a newspaper 4. a person or thing that comes before to announce, or give an indication of, what follows; forerunner; harbinger —*vt.* 1. to introduce, announce, foretell, etc.; usher in 2. to publicize —SYN. see FORE-RUNNER

he·ral·dic (hə ral′dik) *adj.* of heraldry or heralds

her·ald·ry (her′əl drē) *n., pl.* **-ries** [< HERALD] 1. the art or science having to do with coats of arms, genealogies, etc. 2. the function of a herald (sense 2) 3. *a)* a coat of arms or heraldic device *b)* coats of arms, collectively; armorial bearings 4. heraldic ceremony or pomp

Heralds' College in England, a royal corporation, appointed in 1483, in charge of granting and recording armorial emblems and coats of arms, keeping records of genealogies, etc.: also **College of Arms**

Her·at (he rät′) city in NW Afghanistan: pop. 62,000

herb (urb, hurb) *n.* [ME. *erbe, herbe* < OFr. < L. *herba*, grass, herbage, herb] 1. any seed plant whose stem withers away to the ground after each season's growth, as distinguished from a tree or shrub whose woody stem lives from year to year 2. any plant used as a medicine, seasoning, or flavoring: mint, thyme, basil, and sage are herbs 3. vegetative growth; grass; herbage

her·ba·ceous (hər bā′shəs, ər-) *adj.* [L. *herbaceus*] 1. of, or having the nature of, an herb or herbs 2. like a green leaf in texture, color, shape, etc.

herb·age (ur′bij, hur′-) *n.* [Fr.: see -AGE] 1. herbs collectively, esp. those used as pasturage; grass 2. the green foliage and juicy stems of herbs 3. *Law* the right of pasturing cattle on another's land

herb·al (hur′b'l, ur′-) *adj.* [ML. *herbalis*] of herbs —*n.* formerly, a book about herbs or plants

herb·al·ist (-ist) *n.* 1. orig., a descriptive botanist; author of an herbal 2. a person who grows, collects, or deals in herbs, esp. medicinal herbs

her·bar·i·um (hər ber′ē əm, ər-) *n., pl.* **-i·ums, -i·a** (-ə) [LL. < L. *herba*, herb] 1. a collection of dried plants classified, mounted, and used for botanical study 2. a room, building, case, etc. for keeping such a collection

Her·bart (her′bärt; *E.* hur′bärt), **Jo·hann Frie·drich** (yō′hän frē′driH) 1776-1841; Ger. philosopher & educator —**Her·bart·i·an** (hur bär′tē ən) *adj., n.*

Her·bert (hur′bərt) [OE. *Herebeorht*, lit., bright army < *here* (see HAROLD) + *beorht*, BRIGHT] 1. a masculine name: dim. **Herb, Bert** 2. **George**, 1593-1633; Eng. poet & clergyman 3. **Victor**, 1859-1924; U.S. composer & conductor; born in Ireland

her·bi·cide (hur′bə sīd′, ur′-) *n.* [herbi- (< L. *herba*, HERB) + -CIDE] any chemical substance used to destroy plants, esp. weeds, or to check their growth —**her′bi·ci′dal** *adj.*

her·bi·vore (-vôr′) *n.* [Fr.] a herbivorous animal

her·biv·o·rous (hər biv′ər əs) *adj.* [< L. *herba*, herb + -VOROUS] feeding chiefly on grass or other plants

herb Paris [ML. *herba paris*, lit. prob., herb of a pair (< L. *herba*, HERB + *paris*, gen. of *par*, a pair: see PAR, in allusion to even number of flower parts): associated with PARIS² by folk etym.] a woodland plant (*Paris quadrifolia*) of the lily family, with yellowish-green flowers, similar to the trillium, but having its leaves and flower parts in fours instead of threes

herb Robert [ME. *herbe robert* < ML. *herba Roberti*: so named ? after *Robert*, Duke of Normandy or ? after St. *Robert*, founder of the Carthusians] a plant (*Geranium robertianum*) of the geranium family, with strong-scented compound leaves and purple or white flowers

herb·y (ur′bē, hur′-) *adj.* 1. full of or covered with herbs; grassy 2. of or like an herb or herbs; herbaceous

Her·ce·go·vi·na (hert′sə gō′və nä; *E.* hert′sə gō vē′nə) former independent duchy, later an Austro-Hungarian possession: now, with Bosnia, a republic of Yugoslavia: see BOSNIA AND HERCEGOVINA

Her·cu·la·ne·um (hur′kyə lā′nē əm) ancient city in S Italy, at the foot of Mt. Vesuvius: buried, together with Pompeii, in a volcanic eruption (79 A.D.)

Her·cu·le·an (hur′kyə lē′ən, hər kyōō′lē ən) *adj.* 1. of Hercules 2. [*usually* h-] *a)* having the great size, strength, or courage of Hercules; very powerful or courageous *b)* calling for great strength, size, or courage; very difficult to do [a herculean task]

Her·cu·les (hur′kyə lēz′) [L. < Gr. *Hērakleēs* < *Hēra*, Hera + *kleos*, glory] 1. *Gr. & Rom. Myth.* the son of Zeus and Alcmene, renowned for feats of strength, esp. twelve prodigious labors imposed on him 2. a large N constellation north of Ophiuchus —*n.* [h-] any very large, strong man

☆**Her·cu·les'-club** (-klub′) *n.* [after the club borne by Hercules] 1. a small, very spiny tree (*Aralia spinosa*) of the ginseng family, with clusters of small white flowers, found in the E U.S. 2. a spiny tree or shrub (*Zanthoxylum clava-herculis*) of the rue family, native to the S U.S.

herd¹ (hurd) *n.* [ME. < OE. *heord*, akin to G. *herde* < IE. base *kerdho-*, a row, group, whence Sans. *śardha*, a herd, troop] 1. a number of cattle or other large animals feeding, living, or being driven together 2. *a)* any large group suggestive of this; crowd; company *b)* the common people; masses: contemptuous term —*vt., vi.* to gather together or move as a herd, group, crowd, etc. —SYN. see GROUP

herd² (hurd) *n.* [ME. *herde* < OE. *hierde* (akin to G. *hirt*) < same base as prec.] a herdsman: now chiefly in combination [*cowherd, shepherd*] —*vt., vi.* to tend or drive as a herdsman —☆**ride herd on** 1. to control a moving herd of (cattle) from horseback 2. to keep a close or oppressive watch or control over —**herd′er** *n.*

Her·der (her′dər), **Jo·hann Gott·fried von** (yō′hän gôt′frēt fôn) 1744-1803; Ger. poet & philosopher

☆**her·dic** (hur′dik) *n.* [after the U.S. inventor, Peter *Herdic* (1824-88)] formerly, a low-hung public carriage, with a back entrance and seats along the sides

☆**herd's-grass** (hurdz′gras′, -gräs′) *n.* 1. *same as* REDTOP 2. *same as* TIMOTHY

herds·man (-mən) *n., pl.* **-men** (-mən) a person who keeps or tends a herd —[**H-**] the constellation Boötes

here (hir) *adv.* [ME. < OE. *her*; akin to G. *hier* < IE. base *ko-, *ke-*, this one, whence HE¹, HER, L. *cis*, OIr. *ce*] 1. at or in this place: often used as an intensive [John *here* is a good player]: in dialectal or nonstandard use, often placed between a demonstrative pronoun and the noun it modifies [this *here* man] 2. toward, to, or into this place; hither [come *here*] 3. at this point in action, speech, discussion, etc.; now [*here* the judge interrupted] 4. on earth: in earthly life —*interj.* an exclamation used to call attention, answer a roll call, etc., or, esp. when repeated, to express indignation, remonstrance, etc. —*n.* this place or point —**here and there in**, at, or to various places or points —**here goes!** an exclamation used when the speaker is about to do something new, daring, disagreeable, etc. —**neither here nor there** beside the point; irrelevant

here·a·bout (hir′ə bout′) *adv.* in this general vicinity; about or near here: also **here′a·bouts′**

here·af·ter (hir af′tər, -äf′tər) *adv.* 1. after this; from now on; in the future 2. following this, esp. in a writing, book, etc. 3. in the state or life after death —*n.* 1. the future 2. the state or life after death

here·at (hir at′) *adv.* 1. at this time; when this occurred 2. at this; for this reason

here·by (hir′bī′) *adv.* 1. by or through this; by this means 2. *obs. var. of* HEREABOUT

the·re·des (thə rē′dēz) *n., pl. of* HERES

he·red·i·ta·ble (hə red′i tə b'l) *adj.* [MFr. < LL. *hereditare*, to inherit < L. *hereditas*: see HEREDITY] *same as* HERITABLE

her·ed·it·a·ment (her′ə dit′ə mənt) *n.* [ML. *hereditamentum*] any property that can be inherited

he·red·i·tar·y (hə red′ə ter′ē) *adj.* [L. *hereditarius* < *hereditas*: see HEREDITY] **1.** *a)* of, or passed down by, inheritance from an ancestor to a legal heir; ancestral *b)* having title, etc. by inheritance **2.** of, or passed down by, heredity; designating or of a characteristic transmitted genetically from generation to generation **3.** being such because of attitudes, beliefs, etc. passed down through generations [*hereditary* allies] —*SYN.* see INNATE —**he·red′i·tar′i·ly** *adv.* —**he·red′i·tar′i·ness** *n.*

he·red·i·ty (hə red′ə tē) *n., pl.* **-ties** [Fr. *hérédité* < L. *hereditas*, heirship < *heres*, heir < IE. base *ĝhē-, to be empty, leave behind, whence Gr. *chēres*, bereft & GO¹] **1.** *a)* the transmission of characteristics from parent to offspring by means of genes in the chromosomes *b)* the tendency of offspring to resemble parents or ancestors through such transmission **2.** all the characteristics inherited genetically by an individual

Her·e·ford (her′ə fərd; *for n., usually* hur′fərd) **1.** city in WC England, on the Wye River; county seat of Herefordshire: pop. 42,000 **2.** *same as* HEREFORDSHIRE —*n.* any of a breed of beef cattle originated in Herefordshire, having a white face and a red body with markings

Her·e·ford·shire (-shir′) county in WC England: 842 sq. mi.; pop. 134,000

here·in (hir in′) *adv.* **1.** in here; in or into this place **2.** in this writing **3.** in this matter, detail, etc.

here·in·a·bove (hir′in ə buv′) *adv.* in the preceding part (of this document, speech, etc.): also **here′in·be·fore′** (-bi fôr′)

here·in·af·ter (-af′tər, -äf′tər) *adv.* in the following part (of this document, speech, etc.): also **here′in·be·low′** (-bi lō′)

here·in·to (hir in′tōō) *adv.* **1.** into this place **2.** into this matter, condition, etc.

here·of (hir uv′) *adv.* **1.** of this **2.** concerning this **3.** [Obs.] from this; hence

here·on (-än′) *adv. same as* HEREUPON

‡the·res (hir′ēz) *n., pl.* **he·re·des** (hə rē′dēz) [L.: see HEREDITY] *Law* an heir

here's (hirz) here is

her·e·si·arch (hə rē′zē ärk′, -sē-; -rez′ē-) *n.* [LL.(Ec.) *haeresiarcha* < Gr. *hairesiarchēs*, leader of a school < *hairesis* (see HERESY) + *-archēs*, leader < *archein*, to lead] the founder or head of a heresy or heretical sect

here's to! here's a toast to! I wish success, joy, etc. to!

her·e·sy (her′ə sē) *n., pl.* **-sies** [ME. *heresie* < OFr. < L. *haeresis*, school of thought, sect, in LL.(Ec.), heresy < Gr. *hairesis*, a taking, selection, school, sect, in LGr.(Ec.), heresy < *hairein*, to take] **1.** *a)* a religious belief opposed to the orthodox doctrines of a church; esp., such a belief specifically denounced by the church *b)* the rejection of a belief that is a part of church dogma **2.** any opinion (in philosophy, politics, etc.) opposed to official or established views or doctrines **3.** the holding of any such belief or opinion

her·e·tic (her′ə tik) *n.* [ME. *heretike* < MFr. *hérétique* < LL.(Ec.) *haereticus*, of heresy, heretic < Gr. *hairetikos*, able to choose, in LGr.(Ec.), heretical < *hairein*, to take, choose] a person who professes a heresy; esp., a church member who holds beliefs opposed to church dogma —*adj. same as* HERETICAL

he·ret·i·cal (hə ret′i k'l) *adj.* [ML. *haereticalis*] **1.** of heresy or heretics **2.** containing, characterized by, or having the nature of, heresy —**he·ret′i·cal·ly** *adv.*

here·to (hir tōō′) *adv.* [ME. *her to*] to this (document, matter, etc.) [attached *hereto*]: also **here·un′to** (-un′tōō, -ən tōō′)

here·to·fore (hir′tə fôr′, hir′tə fôr′) *adv.* [ME. *her* (see HERE) + *toforen*, before < OE. *toforan*] up to now; until the present; before this

here·un·der (hir un′dər) *adv.* **1.** under or below this (in a document, etc.) **2.** under the terms stated here

here·up·on (hir′ə pän′, hir′ə pän′) *adv.* **1.** immediately following this; at once **2.** upon this; concerning this subject, etc.

here·with (hir with′, -wiṯẖ′) *adv.* **1.** along with this **2.** by this method or means

her·i·ot (her′ē ət) *n.* [ME. *heriet* < OE. *heregeatwe*, lit., army equipment < *here*, army (see HAROLD) + *geatwe*, earlier *ge-tawe*, equipment, arms < *tawian*, to prepare] in English feudal law, a payment in chattels or money (orig., a restoration of arms, equipment, etc.) made to the lord from the possessions of a tenant who had died

her·it·a·ble (her′it ə b'l) *adj.* [ME. *heretable* < OFr. *héritable*: see ff.] **1.** that can be inherited **2.** that can inherit —**her′it·a·bil′i·ty** *n.*

her·it·age (her′ət ij) *n.* [ME. < OFr. < *heriter* < LL. *hereditare*, to inherit < L. *hereditas*: see HEREDITY] **1.** property that is or can be inherited **2.** *a)* something handed down from one's ancestors or the past, as a characteristic, a culture, tradition, etc. *b)* the rights, burdens, or status resulting from being born in a certain time or place; birthright

SYN.—**heritage**, the most general of these words, applies either to property passed on to an heir, or to a tradition, culture, etc. passed on to a later generation [our *heritage* of freedom]; **inheritance** applies to property, a characteristic, etc. passed on to an heir; **patrimony** strictly refers to an estate inherited from one's father, but it is also used of anything passed on from an ancestor;

birthright, in its stricter sense, applies to the property rights of a first-born son

her·i·tance (-əns) *n.* [ME. *herytaunce* < OFr. *heritance* < *heriter*: see prec.] [Archaic] *same as* INHERITANCE

her·i·tor (-ər) *n.* [ME. *heriter* < OFr. *heritier* < ML. *hereditarius* (for L. *heres*, heir) < L., HEREDITARY] an inheritor, or heir

herl (hurl) *n.* [ME. *herle*: see HARL] **1.** the barb or barbs of a feather, with which an artificial fishing fly is trimmed **2.** a fly trimmed with this

herm (hurm) *n.* [< L. *herma* < Gr. *Hermēs*, Hermes] a square pillar of stone topped by a bust or head, originally of Hermes: such pillars were used as milestones, signposts, etc. in ancient Greece: also **her·ma** (hur′mə), *pl.* **-mae** (-mē), **-mai** (-mī)

Her·man (hur′mən) [G. *Hermann* < OHG. *Hariman* < *heri*, army (see HAROLD) + *man*, man] a masculine name: equiv. Fr. *Armand*, Ger. *Hermann*, It. *Ermanno*

her·maph·ro·dite (hər maf′rə dīt′) *n.* [altered (after L. or Gr.) < ME. *hermofrodite* < L. *hermaphroditus* < Gr. *hermaphroditos* < *Hermaphroditos*, HERMAPHRODITUS] **1.** a person or animal with the sexual organs of both the male and the female **2.** a plant having stamens and pistils in the same flower **3.** *short for* HERMAPHRODITE BRIG —*adj. same as* HERMAPHRODITIC —**her·maph′ro·dit′ism**, **her·maph′ro·dism** (-diz′m) *n.*

hermaphrodite brig a two-masted ship with a square-rigged foremast and a fore-and-aft-rigged mainmast

her·maph·ro·dit·ic (hər maf′rə dit′ik) *adj.* of, or having the nature of, a hermaphrodite: also **her·maph′ro·dit′i·cal** —**her·maph′ro·dit′i·cal·ly** *adv.*

Her·maph·ro·di·tus (-dit′əs) [L. < Gr. *Hermaphroditos*] *Gr. Myth.* the son of Hermes and Aphrodite: when bathing, he became united in a single body with a nymph

her·me·neu·tic (hur′mə nōōt′ik, -nyōōt′-) *adj.* [Gr. *hermēneutikos* < *hermēneuein*, to interpret < *hermēneus*, translator] of hermeneutics; interpretive, esp. of Biblical texts: also **her′me·neu′ti·cal**

her·me·neu·tics (-iks) *n.pl.* [< prec.] [*with sing. v.*] the science of interpretation; esp., the study of the principles of Biblical exegesis

Her·mes (hur′mēz) [L. < Gr. *Hermēs*] *Gr. Myth.* a god who served as herald and messenger of the other gods, identified by the Romans with Mercury and generally pictured with winged shoes and hat, carrying a caduceus: he was also the god of science, commerce, eloquence, and cunning, and guide of departed souls to Hades

Hermes Tris·me·gis·tus (tris′mə jis′təs) [Gr. *Hermēs trismegistos*, lit., Hermes the thrice greatest] the Greek name for the Egyptian god Thoth, mythological founder of alchemy and other occult sciences: identified with Hermes

her·met·ic (hər met′ik) *adj.* [ModL. *hermeticus* < L. *Hermes* < Gr. *Hermēs* (*trismegistos*)] **1.** [*usually* H-] of or derived from Hermes Trismegistus and his lore **2.** [*sometimes* H-] *a)* magical; alchemical *b)* hard to understand; obscure **3.** [from use in alchemy] completely sealed by fusion, soldering, etc. so as to keep air or gas from getting in or out; airtight: also **her·met′i·cal** —**her·met′i·cal·ly** *adv.*

Her·mi·o·ne (hər mī′ə nē) *Gr. Legend* the daughter of Menelaus and Helen of Troy

her·mit (hur′mit) *n.* [ME. *hermite* < OFr. < LL.(Ec.) *eremita* < LGr. *erēmitēs*, a hermit < Gr., of the desert < *erēmos*, desolate < IE. base *er-, loose, distant, to separate, whence Sans. *ārma-* (pl.), fragments, ruins] **1.** a person who lives by himself in a lonely or secluded spot, often from religious motives; recluse **2.** a spiced cookie made with nuts and raisins —**her·mit′ic, her·mit′i·cal** *adj.*

her·mit·age (-ij) *n.* [ME. < OFr.: see -AGE] **1.** the place where a hermit lives **2.** a place where a person can live away from other people; secluded retreat

Her·mit·age (er mē täzh′) *n.* [after *Tain-l′Ermitage*, town in SE France] a full-bodied French wine from vineyards near Valence

hermit crab any of various crabs (esp. family Paguridae) that have asymmetrical, soft-bodied abdomens and live in the empty shells of certain mollusks, as snails

☆**hermit thrush** a N. American thrush (*Hylocichla guttata*) with a brown body, spotted breast, and reddish-brown tail

☆**hermit warbler** a common warbler (*Dendroica occidentalis*) of W N. America, with a yellow and black head, a gray back, and white underparts

Her·mon (hur′mən), **Mount** mountain on the Syria-Lebanon border, in the Anti-Lebanon mountains: 9,232 ft.

Her·mo·sil·lo (er′mō sē′yō) city in NW Mexico; capital of Sonora state: pop. 168,000

hern (hurn) *n. archaic or dial. var. of* HERON

her·ni·a (hur′nē ə) *n., pl.* **-ni·as, -nl·ae′** (-ē′) [L.: for IE. base see YARN] the protrusion of all or part of an organ through a tear in the wall of the surrounding structure; esp., the protrusion of part of the intestine through the abdominal muscles; rupture —**her′ni·al** *adj.*

her·ni·ate (hur′nē āt′) *vi.* -at′ed, -at′ing to protrude so as to form a hernia —**her′ni·a′tion** *n.*

her·ni·o- (hur′nē ō′) *a combining form meaning* hernia

her·ni·or·rha·phy (hur′nē ôr′ə fē) *n., pl.* **-phies** [< HERNIO- + Gr. *-rraphia* < *rhaptein*, to stitch together (cf. RHAPSODY)] the surgical repair of a hernia by suturing

He·ro (hir'ō) [L. < Gr. *Hērō*] **1.** *Gr. Legend* a priestess of Aphrodite at Sestos: her lover, Leander, swam the Hellespont from Abydos every night to be with her; when he drowned one night, Hero threw herself into the sea **2.** *same as* HERON

he·ro (hir'ō, hē'rō) *n., pl.* **-roes** [L. *heros* < Gr. *hērōs* < IE. base *ser-, to watch over, protect, whence Av. *haraiti,* (he) protects, Lith. *sárgas,* watchman] **1.** *Myth. & Legend* a man of great strength and courage, favored by the gods and in part descended from them, often regarded as a half-god and worshiped after his death **2.** any man admired for his courage, nobility, or exploits, esp. in war **3.** any man admired for his qualities or achievements and regarded as an ideal or model **4.** the central male character in a novel, play, poem, etc., with whom the reader or audience is supposed to sympathize; protagonist **5.** the central figure in any important event or period, honored for outstanding qualities ☆**6.** *same as* HERO SANDWICH

Her·od (her'əd) [L. *Herodes* < Gr. *Hērōdēs*] 73?–4 B.C.; Idumaean king of Judea (37–4): called *Herod the Great*

Herod Agrippa either of two kings of Judea; specif., *a)* **Herod Agrippa I** 10? B.C.–44 A.D.; king (37–44): grandson of HEROD (*the Great*) *b)* **Herod Agrippa II** 27?–100? A.D.; king (53–100): son of *prec.*

Herod An·ti·pas (an'ti pas') ?–40? A.D.; tetrarch of Galilee (4? B.C.–39 A.D.): son of HEROD (*the Great*)

He·ro·di·as (hə rō'dē əs) *Bible* the second wife of Herod Antipas & mother of Salome: Mark 6:17–28

He·rod·o·tus (hə räd'ə təs) 485?–425? B.C.; Gr. historian: called the *Father of History*

he·ro·ic (hi rō'ik) *adj.* [L. *heroicus* < Gr. *heroikos,* of a hero < *hērōs,* HERO] **1.** of or characterized by men of godlike strength and courage *[the heroic age of Greece and Rome]* **2.** like or characteristic of a hero or his deeds; strong, brave, noble, powerful, etc. *[heroic conduct, a heroic effort]* **3.** of or about a hero and his deeds; epic *[a heroic poem]* **4.** exalted; eloquent; high-flown *[heroic words]* **5.** daring and risky, but used as a last resort *[heroic measures]* **6.** *Art* larger than life-size but less than colossal *[a heroic statue]* Also **he·ro'i·cal** —*n.* **1.** a) a heroic poem *b)* [*pl.*] *same as* HEROIC VERSE **2.** [*pl.*] pretentious, extravagant, or melodramatic talk or action, meant to seem heroic —**he·ro'i·cal·ly** *adv.*

heroic couplet a pair of rhymed lines in iambic pentameter, first used in English by Chaucer, later developed as a syntactically complete unit, as by Dryden, and brought to perfection by Pope (Ex.: "In every work regard the writer's end Since none can compass more than they intend")

heroic tenor *same as* HELDENTENOR

heroic verse the verse form in which epic poetry is traditionally written, as dactylic hexameter in Greek or Latin, the alexandrine in French, and iambic pentameter in English

her·o·in (her'ə win) *n.* [G., orig. a trademark] a white, crystalline powder, an acetyl derivative of morphine, $C_{21}H_{23}NO_5$: it is a very powerful, habit-forming narcotic whose manufacture and import are prohibited in the U.S.

her·o·ine (her'ə win) *n.* [L. *heroina* < Gr. *hērōinē,* fem. of *hērōs,* HERO] **1.** a girl or woman of outstanding courage, nobility, etc., or of heroic achievements **2.** the central female character in a novel, play, etc., or the one with whom the hero is in love

her·o·ism (-wiz'm) *n.* [Fr. *héroisme*] the qualities and actions of a hero or heroine; bravery, nobility, fearlessness, valor, etc.

Her·on (hir'än) fl. 3d cent. A.D.; Gr. mathematician & inventor: also called **Heron of Alexandria**

her·on (her'ən) *n., pl.* **-ons, -on:** see PLURAL, II, D, 1 [ME. *heroun* < OFr. *hairon* < Frank. *heigro (akin to OHG. *heigir,* ON. *hegri*) < IE. *(*s*)*ker-,* var. of base **ker-,* echoic of hoarse cry: cf. CROW[1], SCREAM] any of a large group of wading birds (family Ardeidae) with a long neck, long legs, and a long, tapered bill, living along marshes and river banks

her·on·ry (-rē) *n., pl.* **-ries** a place where many herons gather to breed

her·ons·bill (her'ənz bil') *n.* any of a genus (*Erodium*) of plants of the geranium family, with fine leaves and white or lavender flowers

☆**hero sandwich** a sandwich made of a large roll sliced lengthwise and filled with various cold meats, cheeses, vegetables, etc.

GREAT BLUE HERON (to 56 in. long, including bill)

hero worship great or excessive reverence or admiration for heroes or other persons —**he'ro-wor'ship** *vt.* —**he'ro-wor'ship·er** *n.*

her·pes (hur'pēz) *n.* [L. < Gr. *herpēs,* lit., a creeping, herpes < *herpein,* to creep: for IE. base see SERPENT] any of several acute, inflammatory virus diseases, characterized by the eruption of small blisters on the skin and mucous membranes —**her·pet'ic** (hər pet'ik) *adj.*

herpes simplex a form of herpes principally involving the mouth, lips, and face

herpes zos·ter (zäs'tər) [L. < *herpes* + *zoster,* shingles < Gr. *zōstēr,* a girdle] a viral infection of certain sensory nerves, causing pain and an eruption of blisters along the course of the affected nerve; shingles

her·pe·tol·o·gy (hur'pə täl'ə jē) *n.* [< Gr. *herpeton,* reptile (see SERPENT) + -LOGY] the branch of zoology having to do with the study of reptiles and amphibians —**her'pe·to·log'ic** (-tə läj'ik), **her'pe·to·log'i·cal** *adj.* —**her'pe·tol'o·gist** *n.*

‡**Herr** (her) *n., pl.* **Her'ren** (-ən) [G.; orig. compar. of *hehr,* noble, venerable, akin to OE. *har,* HOAR] in Germany, a man; gentleman: also used as a title corresponding to *Mr.* or *Sir*

Her·re·ra (e re'rä), **Fran·cis·co de** (frän thes'kō *the*) 1576?–1656; Sp. painter: called *El Viejo* (the Elder)

Her·rick (her'ik), **Robert** 1591–1674; Eng. poet

her·ring (her'iŋ) *n., pl.* **-rings, -ring:** see PLURAL, II, D, 1 [ME. *hering* < OE. *hæring,* akin to G. *häring*] **1.** a small food fish (*Clupea harengus*) of the N Atlantic: the adult fish are eaten cooked, dried, salted, or smoked, and the young are canned as sardines **2.** any of a family (Clupeidae) of bony fishes, including herring, shad, etc. **3.** loosely, any related fish, as the sprat, pilchard, etc.

her·ring·bone (-bōn') *n.* **1.** the spine of a herring, with the ribs extending from opposite sides in rows of parallel, slanting lines **2.** a pattern with such a design or anything having such a pattern, as a kind of cross-stitch, a twill weave, or an arrangement of tiles **3.** a method of climbing a slope on skis with the ski tips turned outward so that the tracks have a herringbone pattern —*adj.* having the pattern of a herringbone —*vi., vt.* **-boned', -bon'ing 1.** to stitch, weave, or arrange in a herringbone pattern **2.** to climb (a slope) on skis, using the herringbone method

Her·riot (er yō'), **É·douard** (ā dwàr') 1872–1957; Fr. statesman & writer; premier (1924–25, 1932)

hers (hurz) *pron.* [LME. *hires, hers* < *hire, her(e),* poss. *adj.* (see HER) + -s after *his*] that or those belonging to her: the absolute form of *her,* used without a following noun, often after *of* [a friend of *hers,* that book is *hers, hers* are better]

Her·schel (hur'shəl) **1.** Sir **John Frederick William,** 1792–1871; Eng. astronomer, chemist, & physicist: son of *ff.* **2.** Sir **William,** (born *Friedrich Wilhelm Herschel*) 1738–1822; Eng. astronomer, born in Germany

her·self (hər self') *pron.* [ME. *hire self* < OE. *hire selfum,* dat. sing. of *hie self:* see HER & SELF] a form of the 3d pers. sing., fem. pronoun, used: *a)* as an intensive *[she went herself] b)* as a reflexive *[she hurt herself] c)* [Irish] as a subject *[herself* will have her tea now] *d)* as a quasi-noun meaning "her real, true, or actual self" *[she is not herself today]:* in this construction *her* may be considered a possessive pronominal adjective and *self* a noun, and they may be separated *[her* own sweet *self]*

Herst·mon·ceux (hurst'mən sōō') village in East Sussex, S England: site of the Royal Greenwich Observatory

Hert·ford·shire (här'fərd shir, härt'-) county in SE England: 632 sq. mi.; pop. 874,000: also called **Hert'ford, Herts** (härts)

Hertogenbosch, 's, *see* 'S HERTOGENBOSCH

hertz (hurts) *n., pl.* **hertz, hertz'es** [see *ff.*] the international unit of frequency, equal to one cycle per second

Hertz (herts; E. hurts), **Hein·rich Ru·dolph** (hīn'riH rōō'dôlf) 1857–94; Ger. physicist

Hertz·i·an waves (hurt'sē ən, hert'-) [after H. R. HERTZ, who discovered them] [*sometimes* h-] radio waves or other electromagnetic radiation resulting from the oscillations of electricity in a conductor

Her·ze·go·vi·na (hert'sə gō vē'nə) *same as* HERCEGOVINA

Herzl (her'ts'l), **The·o·dor** (tā'ō dōr') 1860–1904; Austrian-Jewish writer, born in Hungary: founder of Zionism

he's (hēz) **1.** he is **2.** he has

Hesh·van (khesh vän'; E. hesh'vən) *n.* [Heb.] the second month of the Jewish year: see JEWISH CALENDAR

He·si·od (hē'sē əd, hes'ē-) fl. 8th cent. B.C.; Gr. poet —**He'si·od'ic** (-äd'ik) *adj.*

hes·i·tan·cy (hez'ə tən sē) *n., pl.* **-cies** [L. *haesitantia,* a stammering < *haesitans,* prp. of *haesitare*] hesitation or indecision; doubt: also **hes'i·tance** (-təns)

hes·i·tant (-tənt) *adj.* [L. *haesitans:* see prec.] hesitating or undecided; vacillating; doubtful —*SYN.* see RELUCTANT —**hes'i·tant·ly** *adv.*

hes·i·tate (-tāt') *vi.* **-tat'ed, -tat'ing** [< L. *haesitatus,* pp. of *haesitare,* to stick fast, hesitate, intens. of *haerere,* to stick, cleave < IE. base **ghais-,* to be stuck, neglect, whence prob. Lith. *gaištù,* to neglect] **1.** to stop in indecision; pause or delay in acting, choosing, or deciding because of feeling unsure; waver **2.** to pause; stop momentarily **3.** to be reluctant; not be sure that one should *[hesitating to criticize]* **4.** to pause continually in speaking; stammer —**hes'i·tat'er, hes'i·ta'tor** *n.* —**hes'i·tat'ing·ly** *adv.*

SYN.—**hesitate** implies a pause or delay signifying indecision or reluctance *[I hesitated to ask him];* **waver** suggests esp. a holding

---

fat, āpe, cär; ten, ēven; is, bīte; gō, hôrn, tōōl, look; oil, out; up, fur; get; joy; yet; chin; she; thin, *then;* zh, leisure; ŋ, ring; ə for *a* in *ago, e* in *agent, i* in *sanity, o* in *comply, u* in *focus;* ' as in *able* (ā'b'l); Fr. bâl; ë, Fr. coeur; ö, Fr. feu; Fr. mon; ô, Fr. coq; ü, Fr. duc; r, Fr. cri; H, G. ich; kh, G. doch. See inside front cover. ☆ Americanism; ‡foreign; *hypothetical; < derived from

back or hesitating after a course or decision has been adopted [do not *waver* in your resolution]; **vacillate** implies a shifting back and forth in a decision, opinion, etc., resulting in continued hesitation [she *vacillates* in her affection]; **falter** suggests a pausing or slowing down, as in fear or irresolution [they never *faltered* in the counterattack]

hes·i·ta·tion (hez'ə tā'shən) *n.* [L. *haesitatio*] a hesitating or feeling hesitant; specif., *a)* uncertainty; indecision *b)* reluctance *c)* the act of groping for words; halting speech *d)* a pausing or delaying —**hes'i·ta'tive** *adj.* —**hes'i·ta'tive·ly** *adv.*

Hes·per (hes'pər) [Poet.] *same as* HESPERUS

Hes·pe·ri·a (hes pir'ē ə) [L. < Gr. *Hesperia* < *hesperos:* see ff.] the Western Land: the ancient Greek name for Italy and the Roman name for Spain

Hes·pe·ri·an (-ən) *adj.* [< L. *Hesperius* < Gr. *Hes·perios*, of Hesperus, western, evening < *Hesperos,* the evening star < IE. **wesperos,* evening < base **(a)wes-,* to gleam: cf. VESPER, AURORA] **1.** of Hesperia **2.** western; occidental **3.** [Poet.] of the Hesperides —*n.* [Rare] an inhabitant of Hesperia or any western land

Hes·per·i·des (hes per'ə dēz') *n.pl., sing.* **Hes·per·id** (hes'pər id) *Gr. Myth.* **1.** the nymphs who guarded the golden apples given as a wedding gift by Gaea to Hera **2.** the garden where the apples grew

hes·per·i·din (-din) *n.* [< ModL. *hesperidium,* orange (in allusion to the golden apples of the HESPERIDES) + -IN[1]] a crystalline glucoside, $C_{28}H_{34}O_{15}$, found in unripe citrus fruits, and related to vitamin P

hes·per·i·di·um (hes'pə rid'ē əm) *n., pl.* **-di·a** (-ə) [see prec.] the fruit of a citrus plant, as an orange or lemon

Hes·per·us (hes'pər əs) [L. < Gr. *Hesperos:* see HESPERIAN] the evening star, esp. Venus

Hess (hes), Dame Myra 1890–1965; Eng. pianist

Hesse (hes, hes'i) **1.** state of C West Germany: 8,150 sq. mi.; pop. 5,170,000; cap. Wiesbaden **2.** former region in WC Germany embracing various political units historically Ger. name **Hes·sen** (hes'ən)

Hes·se (hes'ə), **Her·mann** (her'män) 1877–1962; Ger. novelist in Switzerland

Hes·sian (hesh'ən) *adj.* of Hesse or its people —*n.* **1.** a native or inhabitant of Hesse **2.** any of the Hessian mercenaries who fought for the British in the Revolutionary War **3.** [h-] a coarse cloth used for bags

Hessian boots knee-high, tasseled boots, introduced into England by Hessian troops in the 19th cent.

☆**Hessian fly,** a small, two-winged fly (*Phytophaga destructor*) whose larvae destroy wheat crops

hess·ite (hes'īt) *n.* [after G.H. *Hess* (1802–50), Swiss chemist + -ITE[1]] silver telluride, Ag_2Te, a mineral found in gray, sectile masses

hes·so·nite (hes'ə nīt') *n. same as* ESSONITE

hest (hest) *n.* [ME. *hest,* with unhistoric *-t* < OE. *hæs,* command < base of *hatan,* to call, akin to G. *heissen* < IE. base **kēi-,* to set in motion, whence L. *ciere,* Gr. *kinein*] [Archaic] behest; bidding; order

Hes·ter, Hes·ther (hes'tər) a feminine name: see ESTHER

Hes·ti·a (hes'tē ə) [Gr. *Hestia*] *Gr. Myth.* the goddess of the hearth, identified with the Roman Vesta

Hes·ton and I·sle·worth (hes'tən ənd i'z'l wurth') municipal borough in Middlesex, England: suburb of London: pop. 102,000

het, heth (khet) *n.* the eighth letter of the Hebrew alphabet (ח)

he·tae·ra (hi tir'ə) *n., pl.* **-rae** (-ē), **-ras** [Gr. *hetaira,* fem. of *hetairos,* companion] in ancient Greece, a courtesan or concubine, usually an educated slave: also **he·tai'ra** (-tī'rə), *pl.* **-rai** (-rī)

he·tae·rism (-iz'm) *n.* [Gr. *hetairismos* < *hetairizein,* to be a hetaera: see HETAERA] **1.** *same as* CONCUBINAGE **2.** a system of communal marriage supposed to have been practiced among some early peoples Also **he·tai'rism** (-tī'riz'm)

het·er·o- (het'ər ō, -ə) [Gr. *hetero-,* other, different < *heteros,* the other (of two), earlier *hateros* < IE. **sm-tero-* < base **sem-, *sm-,* one, together, whence L. *semper, simplus* (cf. HENDECA-) + **-tero-,* expressing contrast, comparison] *a combining form meaning* other, another, different [*heterosexual*]: opposed to HOMO-: also, before a vowel, **heter-**

het·er·o·cer·cal (-sur'k'l) *adj.* [< prec. + Gr. *kerkos,* a tail + -AL] designating, of, or having a tail fin in which the upper lobe is larger than the lower and contains the upturned end of the spinal column, as in certain fishes, esp. sharks

het·er·o·chro·mat·ic (-krō mat'ik) *adj.* [HETERO- + CHROMATIC] **1.** of, having, or consisting of different or contrasting colors; many-colored **2.** of heterochromatin

het·er·o·chro·ma·tin (-krō'mə tin) *n.* [HETERO- + CHROMATIN] *Biol.* the portion of the chromosome that contains few or no genes and stains very densely: cf. EUCHROMATIN

het·er·o·chro·mo·some (-krō'mə sōm') *n. same as* SEX CHROMOSOME

het·er·o·clite (het'ər ə klīt') *adj.* [Fr. *héteroclite* < LL. *heteroclitus* < Gr. *heteroklitos,* irregularly inflected < *hetero-* (see HETERO-) + *klinein,* to bend, incline: see INCLINE] departing from the standard or norm; abnormal; anomalous: also **het'er·o·clit'ic** (-klit'ik) —*n.* **1.** *Gram.* a

word, esp. a noun, inflected irregularly **2.** [Rare] an anomaly

het·er·o·cot·y·lus (het'ər ō kät'l əs) *n., pl.* **-y·li** (-ī') *same as* HECTOCOTYLUS

het·er·o·cy·clic (-sī'klik, -sik'lik) *adj.* [HETERO- + CYCLIC] designating or of a cyclic molecular arrangement of atoms of carbon and other elements

het·er·o·dox (het'ər ə däks') *adj.* [Gr.(Ec.) *heterodoxos* < Gr. *hetero-,* HETERO- + *doxa,* opinion, akin to *dokein,* to think, seem: for IE. base see DOCTOR] departing from or opposed to the usual beliefs or established doctrines, esp. in religion; inclining toward heresy; unorthodox

het·er·o·dox·y (-däk'sē) *n., pl.* **-dox·ies** [Gr. *heterodoxia*] **1.** the quality or fact of being heterodox **2.** a heterodox belief or doctrine

het·er·o·dyne (-dīn') *adj.* [HETERO- + DYNE] designating or of the combination of two different radio frequencies to produce beats whose frequencies are equal to the sum or difference of the original frequencies —*vi.* **-dyned'**, **-dyn'ing** to combine two different frequencies so as to produce beats

het·er·oe·cious (het'ər ē'shəs) *adj.* [< HETERO- + Gr. *oikia,* a house (see ECONOMY) + -OUS] *Biol.* living as a parasite on first one species of host and then another —**het'er·oe'cism** (-siz'm) *n.*

het·er·o·ga·mete (het'ər ō gam'ēt, -gə mēt') *n.* a gamete differentiated in size, structure, or activity from another with which it unites, typified by the relatively large ovum and the much smaller and more active sperm: opposed to ISOGAMETE —**het'er·o·ga·met'ic** (-gə met'ik) *adj.*

het·er·og·a·mous (het'ər äg'ə məs) *adj.* **1.** characterized by the uniting of heterogametes **2.** characterized by reproduction in which sexual and asexual generations alternate **3.** bearing flowers that are sexually different —**het'er·og'a·my** (-mē) *n.*

het·er·o·ge·ne·ous (het'ər ə jē'nē əs, het'rə-; -jēn'yəs) *adj.* [ML. *heterogeneus* < Gr. *heterogenēs* < *hetero-,* other, HETERO- + *genos,* a race, kind: see GENUS] **1.** differing or opposite in structure, quality, etc.; dissimilar; incongruous; foreign **2.** composed of unrelated or unlike elements or parts; varied; miscellaneous —**het'er·o·ge·ne'i·ty** (-jə nē'ə tē) *n., pl.* **-ties** —**het'er·o·ge·ne·ous·ly** *adv.* —**het'er·o·ge'ne·ous·ness** *n.*

het·er·o·gen·e·sis (-jen'ə sis) *n.* [HETERO- + GENESIS] *same as* ALTERNATION OF GENERATIONS —**het'er·o·ge·net'ic** (-jə net'ik) *adj.*

het·er·og·e·nous (het'ər äj'ə nəs) *adj.* [HETERO- + -GENOUS] of different origin; not from the same source, individual, or species

het·er·og·o·ny (-äg'ə nē) *n.* [HETERO- + -GONY] **1.** *same as* ALTERNATION OF GENERATIONS **2.** *same as* HETEROSTYLY **3.** *same as* ALLOMETRY —**het'er·og'o·nous** (-nəs) *adj.*

het·er·o·graft (het'ər ō graft', -gräft') *n.* a graft of skin, bone, etc. taken from an individual of another species

het·er·og·ra·phy (het'ər äg'rə fē) *n.* [HETERO- + -GRAPHY] **1.** spelling that differs from current standard usage **2.** spelling, as in modern English, in which the same letter does not always represent the same sound —**het'er·o·graph'ic** (-ə graf'ik) *adj.*

het·er·og·y·nous (-äj'ə nəs) *adj.* [HETERO- + -GYNOUS] having two kinds of females, reproductive and nonreproductive, as ants or bees

het·er·o·lec·i·thal (het'ər ō les'ə thəl) *n.* [HETERO- + LECITH(IN) + -AL] having the yolk unevenly distributed, as in bird eggs

het·er·ol·o·gous (het'ər äl'ə gəs) *adj.* [< HETERO- + Gr. *logos,* relation (see LOGIC) + -OUS] **1.** consisting of differing elements; not corresponding, as parts of different organisms or of the same organism that are unlike in structure or origin **2.** *Med. a)* derived from a different species, as a graft *b)* not normal in structure, organization, etc. —**het'er·ol'o·gy** (-jē) *n.*

het·er·ol·y·sis (-äl'ə sis) *n.* [HETERO- + -LYSIS] **1.** the destruction of cells of one species by lysins or enzymes derived from cells of a different species **2.** *Chem.* the breakdown of a compound into two particles with opposite charges —**het'er·o·lyt'ic** (-ə lit'ik) *adj.*

het·er·om·er·ous (-äm'ər əs) *adj.* [HETERO- + -MEROUS] *Bot.* having a whorl or whorls with a different number of parts than that of the other whorls

het·er·o·me·tab·o·lism (het'ər ō mə tab'ə liz'm) *n.* [HETERO- + METABOLISM] insect development in which the young hatch in a form very similar to the adult and then mature without a pupal stage —**het'er·o·met'a·bol'ic** (-met'ə bäl'ik), **het'er·o·me·tab·o·lous** (-mə tab'ə ləs) *adj.*

het·er·o·mor·phic (-môr'fik) [HETERO- + -MORPHIC] **1.** differing from the standard type or form **2.** exhibiting different forms at various stages of development, as insects in the larval and pupal stages Also **het'er·o·mor'phous** —**het'er·o·mor'phism** *n.*

het·er·on·o·mous (het'ər än'ə məs) *adj.* [HETERO- + Gr. *nomos,* custom, law + -OUS] **1.** subject to another's laws or rule **2.** subject to different laws of growth; differentiated or specialized, as parts or organs —**het'er·on'o·my** (-mē) *n.*

het·er·o·nym (het'ər ə nim') *n.* [back-formation < ff. (after SYNONYM)] a word with the same spelling as another but with a different meaning and pronunciation (Ex.: *tear,* a drop of water from the eye, *tear,* to rip)

het·er·on·y·mous (het'ər än'ə məs) *adj.* [Gr. *heterōnymos* < *hetero-*, HETERO- + *onyma*, NAME] **1.** of, or having the nature of, a heteronym **2.** having different names, as a pair of correlatives [*son* and *daughter* are *heteronymous*] **3.** designating or of the two crossed images of something seen when the eyes are focused at a point beyond it —**het'er·on'y·mous·ly** *adv.*

Het·er·o·ou·si·an (het'ər ō ōō'sē ən) *adj.* [Gr. *hetero-ousios* < *hetero-*, HETERO- + *ousia*, essence: see HOMOI-OUSIAN] *Theol.* designating, of, or holding the theory that God the Father and God the Son are different in substance —*n.* an adherent of this theory; Arian

het·er·o·phil (het'ər ə fil') *adj.* [HETERO- + -PHIL] designating or of the agglutination of the red blood cells of one species by the serum of another species

het·er·oph·o·ny (het'ər äf'ə nē) *n.* [HETERO- + -PHONY] the playing of a passage of music with simultaneous variations in melody or rhythm by two or more performers

het·er·o·phyl·lous (het'ər ə fil'əs) *adj.* [HETERO- + -PHYL-LOUS] growing leaves of different forms on the same stem or plant —**het'er·o·phyl'ly** *n.*

het·er·o·phyte (het'ər ə fīt') *n.* [HETERO- + -PHYTE] a plant which obtains its food from other plants or animals, living or dead —**het'er·o·phyt'ic** (-fit'ik) *adj.*

het·er·o·plas·ty (-plas'tē) *n.* [HETERO- + -PLASTY] plastic surgery in which tissue from one individual is grafted onto another —**het'er·o·plas'tic** *adj.*

het·er·o·ploid (-ploid') *adj.* [HETERO- + -PLOID] having a chromosome number that is other than a simple multiple of the haploid number —**het'er·o·ploi'dy** *n.*

het·er·op·ter·ous (het'ər äp'tər əs) *adj.* same as HEMIP-TEROUS

het·er·o·sex·u·al (het'ər ə sek'shoo wəl) *adj.* **1.** of or characterized by sexual desire for those of the opposite sex **2.** *Biol.* of different sexes — *n.* a heterosexual individual —**het'er·o·sex'u·al'i·ty** (-wal'ə tē) *n.*

het·er·o·sis (het'ər ō'sis) *n.* [HETER(O)- + -OSIS] a phenomenon resulting from hybridization, in which offspring display greater vigor, size, resistance, etc. than the parents —**het'er·ot'ic** (-ät'ik) *adj.*

het·er·o·sphere (het'ər ə sfir') *n.* in a division of the earth's atmosphere based on composition, the upper of two regions, beginning at a height of c. 55 mi and characterized by variation in the composition and mean molecular weight of its component gases: cf. HOMOSPHERE —**het'er·o·spher'ic** (-sfer'ik) *adj.*

het·er·os·po·rous (het'ər äs'pər əs, het'ər ə spôr'əs) *adj. Bot.* producing more than one kind of spore; esp., producing microspores and megaspores

het·er·o·sty·ly (het'ər ə stī'lē) *n.* [HETERO- + STYL(E) + -Y³] the condition in which flowers on different plants of the same species have styles of different lengths, thereby encouraging cross-pollination —**het'er·o·sty'lous** *adj.*

het·er·o·tax·is (het'ər ə tak'sis) *n.* [ModL. < HETERO- + Gr. *taxis*, arrangement (see TAXIS)] an abnormal position or arrangement, as of organs of the body, rock strata, etc.: also **het'er·o·tax'i·a** (-sē ə), **het'er·o·tax'y** —**het'er·o·tac'-tic** (-tak'tik), **het'er·o·tac'tous** (-tak'təs), **het'er·o·tax'ic** (-tak'sik) *adj.*

het·er·o·thal·lic (-thal'ik) *adj.* [HETERO- + THALL(US) + -IC] designating or possessing two forms of mycelia that interact as male and female in reproduction —**het'er·o·thal'lism** *n.*

het·er·o·to·pi·a (het'ər ə tō'pē ə) *n.* [ModL. < HETERO- + Gr. *topos*, place (see TOPIC)] the displacement of an organ or part in the body: also **het'er·ot'o·py** (-ät'ə pē) —**het'er·o·top'ic** (-ə täp'ik) *adj.*

het·er·o·troph·ic (-träf'ik) *adj.* [HETERO- + TROPHIC] obtaining food from organic material only; unable to use inorganic matter to form proteins and carbohydrates

het·er·o·typ·ic (-tip'ik) *adj.* [HETERO- + TYPIC(AL)] designating or of the first meiotic division of a germ cell: also **het'er·o·typ'i·cal**

het·er·o·zy·go·sis (het'ər ō zī gō'sis) *n.* [HETERO- + ZYGOSIS] **1.** the condition of being a heterozygote **2.** the production of a heterozygote by the union of unlike gametes

het·er·o·zy·gote (-zī'gōt) *n.* [HETERO- + ZYGOTE] a plant or animal having two different alleles at a single locus on a chromosome, and hence not breeding true to type for the particular character involved; hybrid —**het'er·o·zy'gous** (-zī'gəs) *adj.*

het·man (het'mən) *n., pl.* **-mans** [Pol. < G. *hauptmann*, a captain, lit., head man < *haupt*, HEAD + *mann*, MAN] a Cossack chief or leader; ataman

Het·ty (het'ē) a feminine name: see HENRIETTA

☆**het up** (het) [*het*, dial. pt. & pp. of HEAT] [Slang] excited or angry

heu·land·ite (hyōō'lən dīt') *n.* [named (1822) after Henry *Heuland*, Eng. mineralogist] a hydrous silicate of calcium and aluminum, $CaAl_2Si_6O_{16} \cdot 5H_2O$, a variety of zeolite

heu·ris·tic (hyoo ris'tik) *adj.* [< G. *heuristisch* < Gr. *heuriskein*, to invent, discover: see EUREKA] helping to discover or learn; specif., designating a method of educa-

tion or of computer programming in which the pupil or machine proceeds along empirical lines, using rules of thumb, to find solutions or answers—**heu·ris'ti·cal·ly** *adv.*

heu·ris·tics (-tiks) *n.pl.* **1.** heuristic methods or procedures **2.** [*with sing. v.*] the art or practice of using heuristic methods or procedures

hew (hyōō) *vt.* **hewed, hewed** or **hewn, hew'ing** [ME. *hewen* < OE. *heawan*, akin to G. *hauen* < IE. base *kāu-, *keu-*, to hew, strike, whence L. *caudex, codex, cudere* & HAY¹] **1.** to chop or cut with an ax, knife, etc.; hack; gash **2.** to make or shape by or as by cutting or chopping with an ax, etc. (often with *out*) **3.** to chop (a tree) with an ax so as to cause it to fall (usually with *down*) —*vi.* **1.** to make cutting or chopping blows with an ax, knife, etc. ☆**2.** to conform or adhere (*to* a line, rule, principle, etc.) —**hew'er** *n.*

HEW (Department of) Health, Education, and Welfare

☆**hex** (heks) *n.* [Pa. German *hexe* < G. < OHG. *hagazussa*, akin to OE. *hægtesse*: see HAG¹] **1.** [Dial.] a witch or sorcerer **2.** *a*) a sign, formula, spell, etc. supposed to bring bad luck *b*) same as JINX —*vt.* to cause to have bad luck; jinx

hex·a- (hek'sə) [< Gr. *hex*, SIX] *a combining form meaning* six [*hexagram*]: also, before a vowel, **hex-**

hex·a·chlo·ro·eth·ane (hek'sə klôr'ō eth'ān) *n.* [HEXA- + CHLORO- + ETHANE] a colorless solid, C_2Cl_6, prepared by heating carbon tetrachloride with aluminum amalgam: used in the manufacture of smoke-producing materials and in medicine: also **hex'a·chlor·eth'ane**

hex·a·chlo·ro·phene (-klôr'ə fēn') *n.* [< HEXA- + CHLORO- + PHENOL] a white, odorless powder, $C_{13}Cl_6H_6O_2$, used in deodorants, soaps, cosmetics, etc. to destroy, or prevent the growth of, bacteria

hex·a·chord (hek'sə kôrd') *n.* [< L. *hexachordos*, having six musical strings or stops < Gr.: see HEXA- & CHORD¹] *Medieval Music* a diatonic scale of six tones, with a semitone between the third and the fourth

hex·ad (hek'sad) *n.* [LL. *hexas* (gen. *hexadis*) < Gr. *hexas* (gen. *hexados*), the number six < *hex*, SIX] a series or group of six —**hex·ad'ic** *adj.*

hex·a·em·er·on (hek'sə em'ər än') *n.* [LL.(Ec.) < Gr. (Ec.) *hexaēmeron*, of or in six days < *hex*, SIX + *hēmera*, day] **1.** *Bible a*) the six-day period of the Creation *b*) an account of this, esp. that in Genesis **2.** a treatise dealing with the Creation Also **hex'a·hem'er·on** (-hem'-)

hex·a·gon (hek'sə gän) *n.* [L. *hexagonum* < Gr. *hexa-gōnon*, hexagon, neut. of *hexagōnos*, six-cornered < *hex*, SIX + *gōnia*, a corner, angle: see KNEE] a plane figure with six angles and six sides

hex·ag·o·nal (hek sag'ə n'l) *adj.* [ML. *hexagonalis*] **1.** of, or having the form of, a hexagon **2.** having a six-sided base or section: said of a solid figure **3.** *Crystallography* of or being a crystal system having three axes of equal length intersecting in one plane at 60° and a fourth axis of different length at 90° to the plane of the other three axes —**hex·ag'o·nal·ly** *adv.*

hex·a·gram (hek'sə gram') *n.* [HEXA- + -GRAM] a six-pointed star formed by extending the sides of a regular hexagon, or by placing one equilateral triangle over another so that corresponding sides intersect: see STAR OF DAVID

hex·a·he·dron (hek'sə hē'drən) *n., pl.* **-drons, -dra** (-drə) [ModL. < Gr. *hexaedron*: see HEXA- & -HEDRON] a solid figure with six plane surfaces —**hex'a·he'dral** *adj.*

hex·a·hy·drate (-hī'drāt) *n.* a hydrate containing six gram-molecular weights of water per gram-molecular weight of the substance combined with the water

hex·a·hy·dric (-hī'drik) *adj.* containing six hydroxyl radicals [a *hexahydric* alcohol]

hex·am·er·ous (hek sam'ər əs) *adj.* [HEXA- + -MEROUS] having six parts in each whorl: said of flowers: also written **6-merous**

hex·am·e·ter (hek sam'ə tər) *n.* [L. *hexameter* < Gr. *hexametros*: see HEXA- & METER¹] **1.** a line of verse containing six metrical feet or measures; specif., the six-foot dactylic line of classical verse, the first four feet of which may be either dactyls or spondees, the fifth a dactyl, and the sixth a spondee or trochee **2.** verse consisting of hexameters —*adj.* having six metrical feet or measures —**hex'a·met'ric** (-ə met'rik) *adj.*

hex·a·meth·yl·ene·tet·ra·mine (hek'sə meth'ə lēn tet'-rə mēn') *n.* [HEXA- + METHYLENE + TETRA- + (A)MINE] a crystalline compound, $C_6H_{12}N_4$, used in the vulcanization of rubber and in medicine, explosives, etc.

hex·ane (hek'sān) *n.* [HEX(A)- + -ANE] any of the five colorless, volatile, liquid hydrocarbons, C_6H_{14}, of the paraffin series

hex·an·gu·lar (hek san'gyə lər) *adj.* [HEX(A)- + ANGULAR] having six angles

hex·a·pla (hek'sə plə) *n.pl.* [*with sing. v.*] [Gr. (*ta*) *hexapla*, title of Origen's edition, lit., sixfold, neut. pl. of *hexaploos* < *hex*, SIX + base *-plo-*, < IE. base *pel-, *-plo-*: cf. FOLD¹] an edition having six versions arranged in parallel columns; specif., [H-] Origen's edition of the Old Testament

hex·a·pod (-päd') *n.* [< Gr. *hexapous* (gen. *hexapodos*):

see HEXA- & -POD] *same as* INSECT (sense 1) —*adj.* having six legs, as the true insects: also **hex·ap·o·dous** (hek sap′ə dəs)

hex·a·stich (hek′sə stik′) *n.* [ModL. *hexastichon* < Gr.: see HEXA- & STICH] a poem or stanza of six lines

hex·a·teuch (-tōōk′, -tyōōk′) *n.* [G. < Gr. *hex*, SIX + *teuchos*, book, after PENTATEUCH] the first six books of the Old Testament

hex·a·va·lent (-vā′lənt) *adj.* **1.** having a valence of six **2.** having six valences

hex·en·be·sen (hek′sən bā′z'n) *n.* [G. < *hexe* (see HEX) + *besen* (see BESOM)] *same as* WITCHES'-BROOM

hex·one (hek′sōn) *n.* [HEX(A)- + -ONE] a colorless liquid, $C_6H_{12}O$, used as a solvent for gums and resins, for the extraction of plutonium from irradiated uranium, etc.: also called **methyl isobutyl ketone** —*adj.* designating a group of organic bases containing six carbon atoms in each molecule, formed by the hydrolysis of proteins

hex·o·san (-sə san′) *n.* [< ff. + -AN] any of a group of polysaccharides that form hexoses when hydrolyzed

hex·ose (-sōs) *n.* [HEX(A)- + -OSE¹] any of a group of simple sugars containing six carbon atoms in each molecule, as dextrose or fructose

hex·yl (hek′s'l) *n.* [HEX(A)- + -YL] the univalent hydrocarbon radical C_6H_{13}, derived from hexane

hex·yl·res·or·cin·ol (-rə zôr′sə nôl′, -nōl′) *n.* [prec. + RESORCINOL] a nonpoisonous, pale-yellow, crystalline substance, $C_{12}H_{18}O_2$, used as an antiseptic and germicide, esp. in treating urinary infections

hey (hā) *interj.* [ME. *hei*, echoic formation akin to G. & Du. *hei*] an exclamation used to attract attention, express surprise, etc., or in asking a question

hey·day (hā′dā′) *n.* [prob. ME. *hey*, high + *dei*, day] the time of greatest health, vigor, success, prosperity, etc.; prime —*interj.* [earlier *heyda* prob. < (or akin to) G. & Dan. *heida*, Du. *heidaar*, hey there! (see HEY)] [Archaic] an exclamation of surprise, joy, or wonder

Hey·wood (hā′wood) **1. John,** 1497?–1580?; Eng. writer of interludes, epigrams, poetry, etc. **2. Thomas,** 1574?–1650?; Eng. playwright, poet, & actor

Hez·e·ki·ah (hez′ə kī′ə) [Heb. *hizqiyāh*, lit., God strengthens] **1.** a masculine name **2.** *Bible* any of several persons of the Old Testament; esp., a king of Judah in the time of Isaiah: II Kings 18-20

Hf *Chem.* hafnium

HF, H.F., hf, h.f. high frequency

hf. half

Hg [L. *hydrargyrum*] *Chem.* mercury

HG., H.G. High German

hg. hectogram(s)

hgt. height

H.H. 1. His (or Her) Highness **2.** His Holiness

hhd. hogshead

HHFA Housing and Home Finance Agency

☆**H-hour** (āch′our′) *n.* the hour, usually unspecified, at which a military operation, etc. is to begin

☆**hi** (hī) *interj.* [ME. *hy*, variant of *hei*, HEY] an exclamation of greeting

Hi·a·le·ah (hī′ə lē′ə) [< ? Seminole-Creek *haiyakpo hili*, lit., pretty prairie] city in SE Fla.: suburb of Miami: pop. 102,000

hi·a·tus (hī āt′əs) *n., pl.* **-tus·es, -tus** [L., pp. of *hiare*, to gape < IE. base **g̑hē-, g̑hēi-*, whence GAP, GASP] **1.** a break where a part is missing or lost, as in a manuscript; gap in a sequence; lacuna **2.** any gap or opening **3.** a slight pause in pronunciation between two successive vowels in adjacent words or syllables, as between the successive *e*'s in *he entered* and *reenter*

Hi·a·wa·tha (hī′ə wŏ′thə, hē′-; -wä′-) the Indian hero of *The Song of Hiawatha*, a long narrative poem (1855) by Longfellow: named for an Indian chief thought to have lived in the 16th cent.

hi·ba·chi (hi bä′chē) *n., pl.* **-chis** [Jap. < *hi*, fire + *bachi*, bowl] a charcoal-burning brazier and grill of Japanese design

hi·ber·nac·u·lum (hī′bər nak′yoo ləm) *n., pl.* **-u·la** (-lə) [L., winter residence < *hibernare*: see HIBERNATE] any case or covering for protecting an organism during the winter; specif., *a*) a bud or bulb for protecting a plant *b*) a specially modified bud, as in some freshwater ectoprocts, that can develop into a colony in the spring *c*) a structure in which a dormant animal passes the winter

hi·ber·nal (hī bur′nəl) *adj.* [L. *hibernalis* < *hibernus*: see ff.] of winter; wintry

hi·ber·nate (hī′bər nāt′) *vi.* **-nat·ed, -nat·ing** [< L. *hibernatus*, pp. of *hibernare*, to pass the winter < *hibernus*, wintry < IE. **g̑heimerinos* < base **g̑hei-*, winter, snow, whence L. *hiems*, Gr. *cheima*, Czech *zima*, winter] to spend the winter in a dormant state: opposed to ESTIVATE —**hi′ber·na′tion** *n.* —**hi′ber·na′tor** *n.*

Hi·ber·ni·a (hī bur′nē ə) [L., altered < *Iverna, Juverna* < OCelt. **Iveriu*, whence OIr. *Ériu*: see ERIN] *poet. name for* IRELAND —**Hi·ber′ni·an** *adj., n.*

Hi·ber·ni·cism (hī bur′nə siz′m) *n.* [< HIBERNIA + -IC + -ISM] an Irish characteristic, custom, idiom, etc.

hi·bis·cus (hī bis′kəs, hi-) *n.* [ModL., name of the genus < L. *hibiscus, hibiscum*, prob. < Celt.] any of a genus (*Hibiscus*) of plants, shrubs, and small trees of the mallow family, with large, colorful flowers

hic·cup (hik′əp) *n.* [altered < Early ModE. *hikop, hickock, hicket*, of echoic orig. (as also in WalFr. *hickett*, MDu. *huckup*): sp. infl. by association with COUGH] **1.** a sudden, involuntary contraction of the diaphragm that closes the glottis at the moment of breathing in so that a sharp, quick sound is produced **2.** [*pl.*] a condition characterized by repeated contractions of this kind —*vi.* **-cuped** or **-cupped, -cup·ing** or **-cup·ping** to make a hiccup or hiccups —*vt.* to utter with a hiccup or hiccups Also **hic·cough** (hik′əp)

‡**thic ja·cet** (hik′ jā′sit) [L.] **1.** here lies: inscribed on tombstones **2.** an epitaph

hick (hik) *n.* [altered < RICHARD] [Colloq.] an awkward, unsophisticated person regarded as typical of rural areas; yokel; hayseed: somewhat contemptuous term —*adj.* [Colloq.] of or like a hick or hicks

☆**hick·ey** (hik′ē) *n., pl.* **-eys, -ies** [orig. U.S. dial.] **1.** [Colloq.] any device or gadget; doohickey **2.** a tool used for bending pipe **3.** a coupling for electrical fixtures **4.** [Colloq.] a pimple or pustule

Hick·ok (hik′äk), **James Butler** 1837–76; U.S. frontier scout & marshal: called **Wild Bill Hickok**

☆**hick·o·ry** (hik′ər ē, hik′rē) *n., pl.* **-ries** [contr. < 17th-c. *pohickery* (Virginian term) < AmInd. term recorded by Capt. John SMITH as *pawcohiccora*, product made from crushed kernels of the nut] **1.** any of a genus (*Carya*) of N. American trees of the walnut family, with compound leaves, solid pith, and smooth-shelled nuts **2.** the hard, tough wood of any of these trees **3.** a switch or cane as of this wood **4.** the nut of any of these trees: also **hickory nut**

HICKORY
(leaf & nuts)

Hicks·ville (hiks′vil) [after Valentine *Hicks*, local landowner (c. 1834)] suburb of New York City, on W Long Island: pop. 48,000

hid (hid) [ME. < OE. *hydde*] *pt. & alt. pp. of* HIDE¹

Hi·dal·go (hi dal′gō; *MexSp.* ē däl′gō) state of C Mexico: 8,058 sq. mi.; pop. 1,218,000; cap. Pachuca

hi·dal·go (hi dal′gō; *Sp.* ē thäl′gō) *n., pl.* **-gos** (-gōz; *Sp.* -gōs) [Sp., contr. < *hijo de algo*, son of something < *hijo*, son (< L. *filius*: see FILIAL) + *de*, of + *algo*, something, possessions (< L. *aliquem*)] a Spanish nobleman of secondary rank, below that of a grandee

Hi·dat·sa (hī dä′tsə, -tsä) *n.* [native name] **1.** *pl.* **-sas, -sa** a member of a tribe of Plains Indians who live in N. Dakota **2.** their Siouan language

hid·den (hid′n) [ME., for OE. *gehydd*] *alt. pp. of* HIDE¹ —*adj.* concealed; secret

☆**hid·den·ite** (hid′'n īt′) *n.* [after W. E. Hidden, U.S. mineralogist who discovered it in 1879] a rare, yellowish to emerald-green variety of spodumene, a semiprecious stone

hide¹ (hīd) *vt.* **hid, hid·den** or **hid, hid′ing** [ME. *hiden* < OE. *hydan* < IE. **(s)keudh-* (whence Gr. *keuthein*, to hide) < base **(s)keu-*, to cover, whence HIDE², SKY, L. *cutis*, skin] **1.** to put or keep out of sight; secrete; conceal **2.** to conceal from the knowledge of others; keep secret [*to hide* one's identity] **3.** to keep from being seen by covering up, obscuring, etc. [*fog hid* the road] **4.** to turn away [*to hide* one's head in shame] —*vi.* **1.** to be or lie out of sight or concealed **2.** to keep oneself out of sight; conceal oneself —**hid′er** *n.*

SYN.—**hide**, the general word, refers to the putting of something in a place where it will not easily be seen or found [the view is *hidden* by the billboard]; **conceal**, a somewhat formal equivalent for **hide**, more often connotes intent [*to conceal* one's face, motives, etc.]; **secrete** and **cache** suggest a careful hiding in a secret place [they *secreted*, or *cached*, the loot in the cellar], but **cache** now often refers merely to a storing for safekeeping [let's *cache* our supplies in the cave]; **bury** implies a covering for, or as if for, concealment [*to bury* treasure, they were *buried* in the landslide] —ANT. reveal, expose

hide² (hīd) *n.* [ME. < OE. *hid*, akin to G. *haut* < IE. **(s)keut-* (whence L. *cutis*, skin, Gr. *kytos*, hollow container) < base **(s)keu-* (see prec.)] **1.** an animal skin or pelt, either raw or tanned **2.** [Colloq.] the skin of a person —*vt.* **hid′ed, hid′ing** [Colloq.] to beat severely; flog —SYN. see SKIN —**neither hide nor hair** nothing whatsoever

hide³ (hīd) *n.* [ME. < OE. *higid* < base of *hiwan*, household (akin to OHG. *hiwo*, a husband, master of a household) < IE. **keiwo-* (whence L. *civis*, citizen) < base **kei-*, to lie, camp, whence Gr. *koitos*, bed, sleep & HOME] an old English unit for taxes on land, later a measure of land varying from 80 to 120 acres

hide-and-seek (hīd′'n sēk′) *n.* a children's game in which one player (called "it") tries to find the other players, who have hidden: also **hide′-and-go-seek′**

hide·a·way (hīd′ə wā′) *n.* [Colloq.] a place where one can hide, be secluded, etc.

hide·bound (-bound′) *adj.* **1.** having the hide tight over the bone and muscle structure of the body, as an emaciated cow **2.** obstinately conservative and narrow-minded **3.** having the bark so close that growth is interfered with: said of trees

hid·e·ous (hid′ē əs) *adj.* [ME. *hidous* < Anglo-Fr. < OFr. *hidos* < *hide, hisde,* fright] horrible to see, hear, etc.; very ugly or revolting; dreadful —**hid′e·ous·ly** *adv.* —**hid′e·ous·ness** *n.*

☆**hide-out** (hīd′out′) *n.* [Colloq.] a hiding place, as for gangsters

hid·ey-hole, hid·y-hole (hī′dē hōl′) *n. same as* HIDEAWAY

hid·ing¹ (hīd′iŋ) *n.* [ME. *huydinge*] 1. *a)* the act of one that hides *b)* the condition of being hidden: usually in the phrase **in hiding** 2. a place to hide

hid·ing² (-iŋ) *n.* [< HIDE²] [Colloq.] a severe beating; thrashing; flogging

hi·dro·sis (hi drō′sis, hī-) *n.* [ModL. < Gr. *hidrōsis* < *hidroun,* to perspire < *hidrōs,* SWEAT] 1. perspiration; sweating; esp., excessive sweating 2. any skin condition characterized by excessive sweating

hi·drot·ic (-drät′ik) *adj.* [ML. *hidroticus* < Gr. *hidrōtikos* < *hidrōs,* sweat] 1. having to do with sweat 2. causing sweat; sudorific —*n.* a sudorific drug

hie (hī) *vi., vt.* **hied, hie′ing** or **hy′ing** [ME. *hien* < OE. *higian,* to strive, hasten < IE. **kei-gh,* to leap, IE. base **k̑ēigh-,* fast, whence Russ. *sigát,* to spring] to hurry or hasten: usually used reflexivcly

hi·e·mal (hī′i məl) *adj.* [L. *hiemalis,* of winter < *hiems:* see HIBERNATE] of winter; wintry

hi·er- (hī′ər, hīr) *same as* HIERO-: used before a vowel

hi·er·arch (hī′ə rärk′, hī′rärk) *n.* [ML. *hierarcha* < Gr. *hierarchēs,* presider over sacred rites, chief priest: see HIERO- & -ARCH] the leader or chief of a religious group; high priest

hi·er·ar·chal (hī′ə rär′k'l, hī rär′-) *adj.* of a hierarch or hierarchy

hi·er·ar·chi·cal (-ki k'l) *adj.* of a hierarchy: also **hi′er·ar′chic** —**hi′er·ar′chi·cal·ly** *adv.*

hi·er·ar·chism (hī′ə rär′kiz'm, hī′rär-) *n.* the principles, practices, or authority of a hierarchy —**hi′er·ar′chist** *n.*

hi·er·ar·chy (-kē) *n., pl.* **-chies** [altered (after Gr.) < ME. *ierarchie* < OFr. *jerarchie* < ML.(Ec.) *hierarchia* < LGr. (Ec.) *hierarchia,* power or rule of a hierarch < Gr. *hierarchēs* (see HIERARCH)] 1. a system of church government by priests or other clergy in graded ranks 2. the group of officials, esp. the highest officials, in such a system 3. a group of persons or things arranged in order of rank, grade, class, etc. 4. *Theol. a)* any of the three divisions of angels *b)* all the angels

hi·er·at·ic (hī′ə rat′ik) *adj.* [L. *hieraticus* < Gr. *hieratikos,* of a priest's office, sacerdotal < *hieros,* sacred: see HIERO-] 1. of or used by priests; priestly; sacerdotal 2. designating or of the abridged form of cursive hieroglyphic writing once used by Egyptian priests Also **hi′er·at′i·cal** —**hi′er·at′i·cal·ly** *adv.*

hi·er·o- (hī′ər ə, -ō′; hī′rə, -rō) [< Gr. *hieros,* sacred, holy < IE. base **eis-,* to move violently, excite, whence Sans. **iṣṇáti,* (he) sets in motion, L. *ira,* IRE, ON. *eisa,* to rush on] *a combining form meaning* sacred, holy [*hierocracy*]

hi·er·oc·ra·cy (hī′ə räk′rə sē, hī räk′-) *n., pl.* **-cies** [prec. + -CRACY] government by priests or other clergy; a hierarchy —**hi·er·o·crat·ic** (hī′ər ə krat′ik, hī′rə-), **hi′er·o·crat′i·cal** *adj.*

hi·er·o·dule (hī′ər ə dyo͞ol′, hī′rə-) *n.* [LL. *hierodulus* < Gr. *hierodoulos* < *hieros* (see HIERO-) + *doulos,* slave] in ancient Greece, a temple slave, dedicated to the service of a god

hi·er·o·glyph (-glif′) *n. same as* HIEROGLYPHIC

hi·er·o·glyph·ic (hī′ər ə glif′ik, hī′rə-) *adj.* [Fr. *hiéroglyphique* < LL. *hieroglyphicus* < Gr. *hieroglyphikos* < *hieros,* sacred (see HIERO-) + *glyphein,* to carve, hollow out: see GLYPH] 1. of, or having the nature of, hieroglyphics 2. written in hieroglyphics 3. hard to read or understand Also **hi′er·o·glyph′i·cal** —*n.* 1. a picture or symbol representing a word, syllable, or sound, used by the ancient Egyptians and others instead of alphabetic letters 2. [*usually pl.*] a method of writing using hieroglyphics; picture writing 3. a symbol, sign, etc. hard to understand 4. [*pl.*] writing hard to decipher —**hi′er·o·glyph′i·cal·ly** *adv.*

HIEROGLYPHICS
Translation: "No limit may be set to art, neither is there any craftsman that is fully master of his craft."

hi·er·ol·o·gy (hī′ə räl′ə jē, hī rāl′-) *n., pl.* **-gies** [HIERO- + -LOGY] the religious lore and literature of a people

Hi·er·on·y·mite (hī′ə rän′ə mīt′) *n.* [< L. *Hieronymus,* JEROME + -ITE¹] a member of any of the hermit orders named after Saint Jerome

Hi·er·on·y·mus (hī′ə rän′ə məs) *see* Saint JEROME

hi·er·o·phant (hī′ər ə fant′, hī′rə-) *n.* [LL. *hierophanta* < Gr. *hierophantēs* < *hieros* (see HIERO-) + *phainein,* to show (see FANTASY)] 1. formerly, a priest who presided at sacred mysteries; esp., the high priest of the Eleusinian mysteries 2. an interpreter of sacred mysteries or esoteric principles —**hi′er·o·phan′tic** *adj.*

☆**hi·fa·lu·tin** (hī′fə lo͞ot'n) *adj. same as* HIGHFALUTIN

☆**hi-fi** (hī′fī′) *n.* 1. *same as* HIGH FIDELITY 2. a radio, phonograph, etc. having high fidelity —*adj.* of or having high fidelity of sound reproduction

Hig·gin·son (hig′in sən), **Thomas Went·worth** (went′wurth′) 1823–1911; U.S. writer & social reformer

hig·gle (hig′'l) *vi.* **-gled, -gling** [prob. weakened form of HAGGLE] to argue about terms, price, etc.; haggle —**hig′gler** *n.*

hig·gle·dy-pig·gle·dy (hig′'l dē pig′'l dē) *adv.* [redupl. formation, prob. after PIG] in disorder; in jumbled confusion —*adj.* disorderly; jumbled; confused

high (hī) *adj.* [ME. *heigh, heh, hie* < OE. *heah,* akin to G. *hoch,* Goth. *hauhs* < IE. **keuk-* < base **keu-,* to curve, arch, whence Sans. *kakúd-,* peak, Russ. *kúča,* heap] 1. of more than normal height; lofty; tall: not used of persons 2. extending upward a (specified) distance 3. situated far above the ground or some other level 4. reaching to or done from a height [a *high* jump, a *high* dive] 5. *a)* above other persons or things in rank, position, strength, etc.; most important or powerful *b)* above other persons or things in quality, character, etc.; superior; exalted; excellent 6. grave; very serious [*high* treason] 7. greatly advanced or developed; complex: usually in the comparative degree [*higher* mathematics, the *higher* vertebrates] 8. main; principal; chief [a *high* priest] 9. greater in size, amount, degree, power, intensity, etc. than usual [*high* prices, *high* voltage] 10. advanced to its acme or fullness; fully reached [*high* noon] 11. expensive; costly 12. luxurious and extravagant [*high* living] 13. haughty; overbearing 14. designating or producing tones made by relatively fast vibrations; acute in pitch; sharp; shrill 15. slightly tainted; having a strong smell: said of meat, esp. game 16. extremely formal or rigid in matters of ceremony, doctrine, etc. 17. excited; elated [*high* spirits] 18. far from the equator [a *high* latitude] ☆19. designating or of that gear ratio of a motor vehicle transmission which produces the highest speed 20. [Slang] *a)* drunk; intoxicated *b)* under the influence of a drug 21. *Phonet.* produced with the tongue held in a relatively elevated position: said of a vowel, as (ē) —*adv.* 1. in a high manner 2. in or to a high level, place, degree, rank, etc. —*n.* 1. a high level, place, etc. ☆2. an area of high barometric pressure ☆3. that gear of a motor vehicle, etc. producing the greatest speed 4. [Slang] a condition of euphoria induced as by drugs —**high and dry** 1. out of the reach of the water 2. alone and helpless; stranded —**high and low** everywhere —**high and mighty** [Colloq.] arrogant; haughty —**high on** [Colloq.] enthusiastic about; very interested in or impressed by —☆**high, wide, and handsome** [Colloq.] in a carefree, confident manner —**on high** 1. up in space; high above 2. in heaven

SYN.—**high** refers to something which has greater extension upward than is normal for its kind, or which is placed at a relatively great distance above the given level [a *high* mountain, *high* clouds], but is never used of persons; **tall** is more or less equivalent to **high** but specifically implies relatively small breadth or width [a *tall* woman]; **lofty** and **towering** suggest great, imposing, or conspicuous height [*lofty* peaks, a *towering* castle] —**ANT.** low, short

☆**high·ball** (-bôl′) *n.* [sense 1 < HIGH + *ball,* bartender's slang for "whiskey glass": infl. ? by the *v.*] 1. liquor, usually whiskey or brandy, mixed with water, soda water, ginger ale, etc. and served with ice in a tall glass 2. a railroad signal, originally a ball hung above the tracks, meaning "go ahead": sometimes used figuratively —*vi.* [< *n.* 2] [Slang] to proceed at great speed

☆**high·bind·er** (-bīn′dər) *n.* [< ?: first recorded use in *Highbinders,* name of a New York City gang in early 19th c.] [Colloq.] 1. formerly, *a)* a ruffian; gangster *b)* any of a gang of criminals from the Chinese section of a city who were believed to act as hired assassins 2. an unscrupulous or swindling person; esp., a demagogic politician

high·born (-bôrn′) *adj.* of noble birth

☆**high·boy** (-boi′) *n.* [HIGH + BOY] a high chest of drawers mounted on legs

high·bred (-bred′) *adj.* 1. of superior stock or breed 2. showing good breeding; cultivated; refined

☆**high·brow** (-brou′) *n.* [Colloq.] a person having or affecting highly cultivated, intellectual tastes; intellectual —*adj.* [Colloq.] of or for a highbrow Often a term of contempt or derision

☆**high-bush cranberry** (-boosh) *same as* CRANBERRY BUSH

high·chair (-cher′) *n.* a baby's chair with an attached tray, mounted on long legs

High Church that party of the Anglican Church which emphasizes the importance of the priesthood and of traditional rituals

HIGHBOY

and doctrines: opposed to Low CHURCH, BROAD CHURCH —**High′-Church′** *adj.* —**High′-Church′man** *n.*, *pl.* **-men**

high-class (-klas′, -kläs′) *adj.* of a superior class, rank, quality, etc.

high comedy comedy appealing to, and reflecting the life and problems of, the upper social classes, characterized by a witty, sardonic treatment: cf. LOW COMEDY

high commissioner 1. the chief representative, with ambassadorial status, of the British government to any of the Commonwealth countries, or of one of the Commonwealth countries to the British government 2. the chief administrative officer of a commission appointed to govern a trust territory or mandate 3. the chief officer of an international commission

high day [ME.: cf. HEYDAY, *n.*] a festival day; holiday

high-en·er·gy particle (hī′en′ər jē) an atomic or sub-atomic particle with energy greater than a few hundred kilovolts

high-energy physics the branch of physics employing high-energy particles to study the properties of atomic nuclei and of the elementary particles themselves

higher criticism the study of the authorship, dates of writing, meaning, etc. of the books of the Bible, using the techniques or findings of archaeology, literary criticism, comparative religion, etc.

higher education college or university education

☆**high·er-up** (-up′) *n.* [Colloq.] a person of higher rank or position

high explosive any explosive in which the combustion of the particles is so rapid as to be virtually simultaneous throughout the entire mass, so that it has great shattering effect

☆**high·fa·lu·tin, high·fa·lu·ting** (-fə lo͞ot′'n) *adj.* [altered < *? high-floating*, with insertion of intrusive vowel in ridicule of oratorical speech] [Colloq.] ridiculously pretentious or pompous

high fidelity in radio, sound recording, etc., an approximately exact reproduction of sound achieved by low distortion and a wide range of reproduced frequencies, from approximately 20 to 20,000 hertz

high·fli·er, high·fly·er (-flī′ər) *n.* 1. a person or thing that flies high 2. a person who acts, talks, or thinks in an extravagant or extremist manner —**high′fly′ing** *adj.*

high-flown (-flōn′) *adj.* 1. extravagantly ambitious or aspiring 2. high-sounding but meaningless; bombastic

high frequency any radio frequency between 3 and 30 megahertz

High German [after G. *hochdeutsch* (see DEUTSCHLAND, DUTCH)] 1. the West Germanic dialects spoken in C and S Germany: distinguished from Low GERMAN 2. the official and literary form of the German language, technically called *New High German:* see also OLD HIGH GERMAN, MIDDLE HIGH GERMAN

high-grade (-grād′) *adj.* of fine or superior quality

high·hand·ed (-han′did) *adj.* acting or done in an overbearing or arbitrary manner —**high′hand′ed·ly** *adv.* —**high′hand′ed·ness** *n.*

☆**high-hat** (-hat′) *adj.* [Slang] snobbish and aloof —*n.* [Slang] a snob —*vt.* **-hat′ted, -hat′ting** [Slang] to treat snobbishly; snub

☆**high hat** *same as* TOP HAT

High Holidays the period encompassing Rosh Hashana and Yom Kippur in the Jewish calendar

☆**high·jack** (-jak′) *vt.* [Colloq.] *same as* HIJACK

high jinks *see* JINK (n. 2)

high jump a track-and-field event in which the contestants jump for height over a horizontal bar set between two upright poles: after each successful trial the bar is raised a little

high-keyed (-kēd′) *adj.* emotionally tense; high-strung

high·land (-lənd) *n.* land well above sea level; region higher than adjacent land and containing many hills or mountains —*adj.* of, in, or from such a region —**the Highlands** mountainous region occupying nearly all of the N half of Scotland

high·land·er (-lən dər) *n.* 1. a native or inhabitant of a highland 2. [H-] *a)* a native or inhabitant of the Highlands *b)* a soldier of a Highlands regiment

Highland fling a lively folk dance of the Highlands

Highland Park city in SE Mich., surrounded by Detroit: pop. 35,000

☆**Highland Southern** *an earlier name for* the variety of American speech typically associated with speakers in the southern Appalachian area

high-level (-lev′'l) *adj.* 1. of or by persons of high office or rank 2. in a high office or rank

high life 1. the way of life of fashionable society; luxurious, extravagant way of life 2. a dance with a strong, syncopated beat, originating in W Africa: also **high′life′** *n.*

high·light (-līt′) *n.* 1. *a)* a part on which light is brightest [the *highlights* on the cheeks] *b)* a part of a painting, photograph, etc. on which light is represented as brightest *c)* the representation or effect of such light in a painting, photograph, etc. Also **high light** 2. the most important, interesting, or outstanding part, scene, etc. —*vt.* 1. to give a highlight or highlights to 2. to give prominence to 3. to be the most outstanding in

high liver one who lives in a luxuriant, extravagant way

high·ly (-lē) *adv.* 1. [Rare] in or to a high place 2. in a

high office or rank 3. in or to a high degree; very much; very; extremely 4. with high approval or esteem; favorably 5. at a high level, wage, salary, etc.

High Mass *R.C.Ch.* a sung Mass, usually celebrated with the complete ritual and with incense, at which the celebrant is assisted by a deacon and subdeacon: also **Solemn High Mass, Solemn Mass**

high-mind·ed (-mīn′did) *adj.* 1. [Obs.] haughty; proud; arrogant 2. having or showing high ideals, principles, etc. —**high′-mind′ed·ly** *adv.* —**high′-mind′ed·ness** *n.*

☆**high muck-a-muck** (muk′ə muk′) [< Chinook jargon *hiu muckamuck*, plenty (of) food] [Slang] a person in a position of importance and authority; esp., one who is overbearing: also written **high muckamuck**

high·ness (-nis) *n.* 1. the quality or state of being high; height; loftiness 2. [H-] highest of the nobility: a title used in speaking to or of a member of a royal family, preceded by *His, Her,* or *Your*

☆**high-oc·tane** (-äk′tān) *adj.* having a high octane number: said of gasoline: see OCTANE NUMBER

high-pitched (-picht′) *adj.* 1. high in pitch; shrill 2. lofty; exalted 3. showing intense feeling; agitated 4. steep in slope: said of roofs

high place in early Semitic religions, a place of worship, usually an altar on a hill

High Point [after its location, the highest point on the N.C. Railroad] city in C N.C.: pop. 63,000: see GREENSBORO

high-pow·ered (-pou′ərd) *adj.* very powerful

high-pres·sure (-presh′ər) *adj.* 1. *a)* having, using, or withstanding a high or relatively high pressure *b)* having or indicating a high barometric pressure 2. using or applying forcefully persuasive or insistent methods or arguments —☆*vt.* **-sured, -sur·ing** [Colloq.] to urge or persuade with such methods or arguments

high-priced (-prīst′) *adj.* costly; expensive

high priest [ME. *heyge prest*] a chief priest; specif., the chief priest of the ancient Jewish priesthood

high-proof (-pro͞of′) *adj.* high in alcohol content

high relief 1. relief in which sculptured figures, etc. project from the background by half or more than half their full natural depth 2. sculpture in high relief

☆**high-rise** (-rīz′) *adj.* designating or of a tall apartment house, office building, etc. of many stories —*n.* a high-rise building

high·road (-rōd′) *n.* 1. [Chiefly Brit.] a main road; highway 2. an easy or direct way

high school ☆a secondary school that usually includes grades 10, 11, and 12, and sometimes grade 9, and that offers academic or vocational subjects: see also JUNIOR HIGH SCHOOL, SENIOR HIGH SCHOOL —**high′-school′** *adj.*

high seas open ocean waters outside the territorial limits of any single nation

☆**high sign** a signal, often a prearranged one, given secretly, as in warning

high-sound·ing (-soun′diŋ) *adj.* sounding pretentious or impressive

high-spir·it·ed (-spir′ə tid) *adj.* 1. having or showing a courageous or noble spirit 2. spirited; fiery 3. gay; lively

high-strung (-struŋ′) *adj.* [from the tuning of stringed instruments] highly sensitive or nervous and tense; excitable

hight (hīt) *adj.* [ME. *highte,* merging OE. *hatte,* pass. pt. with *heht,* act. pt. of *hatan,* to command, call: confused in sense with ME. *hoten,* pp. of same *v.:* akin to G. *heissen* < IE. base **kēi-,* to move] [Archaic] named; called [a maiden *hight* Elaine]

☆**high-tail, high·tail** (hī′tāl′) *vi., vt.* [Colloq.] to leave or go in a hurry; scurry off: chiefly in **high-tail it**

high tea [Brit.] a meal somewhat more elaborate and served later than the usual tea

high-ten·sion (hī′ten′shən) *adj.* having, carrying, or operating under a high voltage

high-test (-test′) *adj.* 1. passing severe tests; meeting difficult requirements 2. vaporizing at a relatively low temperature: said of gasoline

high tide 1. the highest level to which the tide rises; high water 2. the time when the tide is at this level 3. any culminating point or time

high time 1. time beyond the proper time but before it is too late; none too soon ☆2. [Slang] a gay, exciting, enjoyable time: also **high old time**

high-toned (-tōnd′) *adj.* 1. [Now Rare] high in tone; high-pitched 2. characterized by dignity, lofty moral or intellectual quality, high principles, etc.: often used ironically or humorously ☆3. [Colloq.] of or imitating the manners, attitudes, etc. of the upper classes

high treason treason against the ruler or government

high·ty-tigh·ty (hīt′ē tīt′ē) *adj., n., interj. same as* HOITY-TOITY

high water 1. *same as* HIGH TIDE 2. the highest level reached by a body of water

high-wa·ter mark (hī′wôt′ər, -wät′ər) 1. the highest level reached by a body of water in tidal flow, flood, etc. 2. the mark left after high water has receded 3. a culminating point; highest point

high·way (-wā′) *n.* [ME. *higewege;* see HIGH & WAY] 1. any road freely open to everyone; public road 2. a main road; thoroughfare 3. a main route by land or water 4. a direct way to some objective

high·way·man (-wā mən) *n., pl.* **-men** (-mən) formerly, a man, esp. one on horseback, who robbed travelers on a highway

☆**high wire** a cable or wire stretched high above the ground, on which aerialists perform; tightrope

H.I.H. His (or Her) Imperial Highness

Hii·u·maa (hē′ōō mä′) island of the Estonian S.S.R., in the Baltic Sea: 373 sq. mi.

☆**hi·jack** (hī′jak′) *vt.* [prob. *hi* (for HIGH) + JACK[1], *v.*] [Colloq.] **1.** to steal (goods in transit, a truck and its contents, etc.) by force **2.** to steal such goods from (a person) by force **3.** to cheat, swindle, etc. by or as by the use of force **4.** to force the pilot of (an aircraft) to fly to a nonscheduled landing point —**hi′jack′er** *n.*

hike (hīk) *vi.* **hiked, hik′ing** [< dial. *heik*, prob. akin to HITCH] **1.** to take a long, vigorous walk; tramp or march, esp. through the country, woods, etc. ☆**2.** to move up out of place —*vt.* [Colloq.] **1.** to pull or jerk up; hoist [to *hike* up one's socks] ☆**2.** to raise (prices, etc.) —☆*n.* **1.** a long, vigorous walk **2.** [Colloq.] a moving upward; rise —**hik′er** *n.*

hi·lar (hī′lər) *adj.* of or relating to a hilum

hi·lar·i·ous (hi ler′ē əs, hī-; -lar′-) *adj.* [< L. *hilaris, hilarus*, cheerful, glad, akin to *hilēnai*, to be gracious (for IE. base see SILLY) + -OUS] **1.** noisily merry; boisterous and gay **2.** provoking laughter; funny —**hi·lar′i·ous·ly** *adv.* —**hi·lar′i·ous·ness** *n.*

hi·lar·i·ty (-ə tē) *n.* [OFr. *hilarité* < L. *hilaritas*] the state or quality of being hilarious; noisy merriment; boisterous gaiety —SYN. see MIRTH

Hil·a·ry (hil′ər ē) [L. *Hilarius*, lit., cheerful: see HILARIOUS] a masculine and feminine name: equiv. Fr. *Hilaire*

Hil·da (hil′də) [G. < Gmc. **hild-*, battle, war (cf. HILT): often contr. of names containing base (e.g., *Hilde*gunde, Brun*hild*e)] a feminine name

Hil·de·garde (hil′də gärd′) [G. < Gmc. **hild-*, battle (cf. HILT) + **gard-*, to protect (see YARD[2]): hence, lit., battle protector] a feminine name: also **Hilda**

hil·ding (hil′diŋ) *n.* [prob. < ME. *heldinge*, bending aside < *helden* (OE. *hieldan*), to incline, bow] [Archaic] a low, contemptible person —*adj.* [Archaic] low and contemptible

hill (hil) *n.* [ME. < OE. *hyll*, akin to MDu. *hille* < IE. base **kel-*, to project, rise high, whence L. *collis*, hill, Gr. *kolophōn*, peak] **1.** a natural raised part of the earth's surface, often rounded and smaller than a mountain **2.** a small pile, heap, or mound [an ant *hill*] **3.** *a)* a small mound of soil heaped over and around plants and tubers [a *hill* of potatoes] *b)* the plant or plants rooted in such a mound —*vt.* **1.** to shape into or like a hill **2.** to cover with a hill (sense 3 *a*) —**over the hill** [Colloq.] **1.** absent without permission; AWOL **2.** in one's decline —**hill′er** *n.*

Hill (hil), **James Jerome** 1838–1916; U.S. railroad magnate & financier, born in Canada

Hil·la·ry (hil′ər ē), **Sir Edmund Percival** 1919– ; New Zealand mountain climber & explorer

☆**hill·bil·ly** (hil′bil′ē) *n., pl.* **-lies** [HILL + *Billy*, dim. of BILL] [Colloq.] a person who lives in or comes from the mountains or backwoods, esp. in the South: sometimes a contemptuous term —*adj.* [Colloq.] of or characteristic of hillbillies [*hillbilly* music]

Hil·lel (hil′el, -əl) 60? B.C.–10? A.D.; Jewish rabbi & scholar in Jerusalem

hill myna an Asiatic bird (*Eulabes religiosa*) resembling the starling: it has the ability to mimic human speech and is often kept as a pet

hil·lo, hil·loa (hil′ō, hi lō′) *interj., n., vi., vt.* archaic var. of HOLLO

hill·ock (hil′ək) *n.* [ME. *hilloc*: see HILL & -OCK] a small hill; mound —**hill′ock·y** *adj.*

☆**hill of beans** [Colloq.] a very small amount or value; trifle: used with a negative [not worth a *hill of beans*]

hill·side (hil′sīd′) *n.* the side or slope of a hill

hill·top (-täp′) *n.* the top of a hill

hill·y (-ē) *adj.* **hill′i·er, hill′i·est 1.** full of hills; rugged, uneven, and rolling **2.** like a hill; steep —**hill′i·ness** *n.*

hilt (hilt) *n.* [ME. *hilt* < OE., akin to ON. *hjalt* < IE. base **kel-*, to strike, whence L. *calamitas*, harm, OE. *hild*, battle] the handle of a sword, dagger, tool, etc. —*vt.* to provide a hilt for —(**up**) **to the hilt** thoroughly; entirely

hi·lum (hī′ləm) *n., pl.* **hi′la** (-lə) [ModL. < L., little thing] **1.** same as HILUS **2.** *Bot. a)* a scar on a seed, marking the place where it was attached to the seed stalk *b)* the nucleus in a starch grain

hi·lus (-ləs) *n., pl.* **hi′li** (-lī) [ModL., var. of HILUM] *Anat.* a small notch, recess, or opening, as where vessels and nerves enter an organ

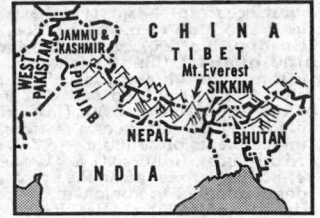
HILUM

Hil·ver·sum (hil′vər səm) city in WC Netherlands, near Amsterdam: pop. 103,000

him (him; *unstressed* im, əm) *pron.* [OE. *him*, dat. of *he*, he, merged in sense with *hine*, acc. of *he*] *objective case of* HE[1]: also used colloquially as a predicate complement with a linking verb (Ex.: that's *him*)

H.I.M. His (or Her) Imperial Majesty

Hi·ma·chal Pra·desh (hi mä′chəl pre desh′) territory of N India: 21,599 sq. mi.; pop. c. 5,000,000; cap. Simla

Hi·ma·la·yan (him′ə lā′ən, hi mäl′yən) *adj.* of the Himalayas —*n.* any of a breed of white rabbit with the tail, feet, nose, and tips of the ears black

Hi·ma·la·yas (-əz, -yəz) mountain system of SC Asia, extending along the India-Tibet border and through West Pakistan, Nepal, & Bhutan: highest peak, Mt. Everest: also **Himalaya Mountains**

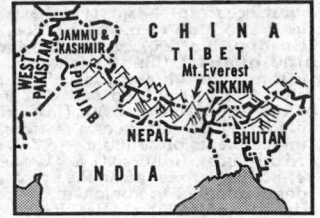
HIMALAYAS

hi·mat·i·on (hi mat′ē än′, -ən) *n., pl.* **-mat′i·a** (-ə) [Gr. *himation*, dim. of *heima*, garment < *hennynai*, to clothe < IE. base **wes-*, whence L. *vestis* & WEAR[1]] an ancient Greek outer garment consisting of a long rectangle of cloth draped over the left shoulder and wound around the body

Him·a·vat (him′ə vat′) [Hind.] *Hindu Myth.* the personification of the Himalayas and father of Devi

Hi·me·ji (hē′me jē′) city on the S coast of Honshu, Japan, near Kobe: pop. 368,000

him·self (him self′) *pron.* [OE. *him selfum*, dat. sing. of *he self*: see HIM & SELF] a form of the 3d pers. sing., masc. pronoun, used: *a)* as an intensive [he went *himself*] *b)* as a reflexive [he hurt *himself*] *c)* [Irish] as a subject [*himself* will have his tea now] *d)* as a quasi-noun meaning "his real, true, or actual self" [he is not *himself* today]

Him·yar·ite (him′yə rīt′) *n.* [< Ar. *Ḥimyar*, a legendary ruler of Yemen + -ITE[1]] **1.** any member of an ancient Arab tribe that lived in southern Arabia **2.** any Arab descended from this tribe —*adj.* of the Himyarites, their language (an Arabic dialect akin to Ethiopic), their culture, etc.: also **Him′yar·it′ic** (-rit′ik)

hin (hin) *n.* [Heb. *hīn*] a unit of liquid measure among the ancient Hebrews, equal to about 1 1/2 gallons

Hi·na·ya·na (hē′nə yä′nə) *n.* [Sans. *hīnayāna*, lit., lesser vehicle] a branch of Buddhism that stresses the original monastic discipline and the attainment of nirvana by the individual through meditation: it developed mainly in Ceylon, Burma, Thailand, and Cambodia

hind[1] (hīnd) *adj.* **hind′er, hind′most** or **hind′er·most′** [ME., prob. back-formation < *hinder*: see HINDER[2]] back; rear; posterior

hind[2] (hīnd) *n., pl.* **hinds, hind:** see PLURAL, II, D, 1 [ME. < OE., akin to G. *hinde* < IE. base **kem-*, not having horns (as applied to horned animal species), whence Gr. *kemas*, young deer] **1.** the female of the red deer, in and after its third year **2.** any of various groupers (genus *Epinephelus*) of the S Atlantic

hind[3] (hīnd) *n.* [< ME. *hine* (with unhistoric -*d*) < OE. *hina*, earlier *higna*, generalized < gen. pl. of *higa*, member of a household: for base see HIDE[3]] **1.** in N England and Scotland, a skilled farm worker or servant **2.** [Archaic] a simple or boorish peasant; rustic

Hind. 1. Hindi **2.** Hindu **3.** Hindustan **4.** Hindustani

hind·brain (-brān′) *n.* the hindmost part of the brain; specif., *a)* the cerebellum, pons, and medulla oblongata; rhombencephalon *b)* the cerebellum and pons only; metencephalon *c)* the cerebellum only

Hin·de·mith (hin′də məth; G. -mit), **Paul** 1895–1963; U.S. composer, born in Germany

Hin·den·burg (hin′dən burg′; G. -boorkh′), **Paul (Ludwig Hans Anton von Beneckendorf und) von** 1847–1934; Ger. field marshal; president of the Weimar Republic (1925–34)

hin·der[1] (hin′dər) *vt.* [ME. *hindren* < OE. *hindrian*, lit., to keep or hold back (akin to G. *hindern*) < base of ff.] **1.** to keep back; restrain; get in the way of; prevent; stop **2.** to make difficult for; thwart; impede; frustrate —*vi.* to delay action; be a hindrance

SYN.—**hinder** implies a holding back of something about to begin and connotes a thwarting of progress [*hindered* by a lack of education]; **obstruct** implies a retarding of passage or progress by placing obstacles in the way [to *obstruct* the passage of a bill by a filibuster]; **block** implies the complete, but not necessarily permanent, obstruction of a passage or progress [the road was *blocked* by a landslide]; **impede** suggests a slowing up of movement or progress by interfering with the normal action [tight garters *impede* the circulation of the blood]; **bar** implies an obstructing as if by means of a barrier [he was *barred* from the club] See also DELAY —ANT. advance, further

hind·er[2] (hīn′dər) *adj.* [ME. *hindre* < OE. *hinder*, adv., back, behind (akin to G. *hinter, prep.*, behind) < ? base of *he* (see HE[1]) + compar. suffix -*der*, akin to Gr. -*tero-*, Sans. -*tara-*: the word is now felt as compar. of HIND[1]] hind; rear; posterior

hind·gut, hind-gut (hīnd′gut′) *n.* **1.** the hindmost part of the embryonic alimentary canal, from which part of

the colon is formed **2.** the posterior part of the digestive tract of arthropods

Hin·di (hin′dē) *adj.* [Hind. *hindī* < *Hind:* see HINDU] of or associated with northern India —*n.* an Indo-Iranian language, the main language of India, now designated the official language

hind·most (hīnd′mōst′) *adj. alt. superl.* of HIND[1] [ME. *henmast:* see HIND[1] + -MOST] farthest back; closest to the rear; last: also **hind′er·most′** (hin′dər-)

Hin·doo (hin′dōō) *adj., n., pl.* **-doos** *same as* HINDU

hind·quar·ter (hīnd′kwôr′tər) *n.* **1.** either of the two hind legs and the adjoining loin of a carcass of veal, beef, lamb, etc. **2.** [*pl.*] the hind part of a four-legged animal

hin·drance (hin′drəns) *n.* [ME. *hinderaunce*] **1.** the act of hindering **2.** any person or thing that hinders; obstacle; impediment; obstruction —*SYN.* see OBSTACLE

☆**hind·sight** (hīnd′sīt′) *n.* **1.** the rear sight of a firearm **2.** ability to see, after the event, what should have been done: opposed to FORESIGHT

Hin·du (hin′dōō) *n.* [Per. *Hindū* < *Hind*, India < OPer. *Hindu*, India, land of the Indus < Sans. *sindhu*, river, the Indus] **1.** any member of those peoples of India that speak an Indic language **2.** a follower of Hinduism **3.** popularly, any native of Hindustan or of India —*adj.* **1.** of the Hindus, their language, etc. **2.** of Hinduism

Hin·du-Ar·a·bic numerals (-ar′ə bik) *same as* ARABIC NUMERALS

Hin·du·ism (hin′dōō wiz′m) *n.* the religion and social system of the Hindus, developed from Brahmanism with elements from Buddhism, Jainism, etc. added

Hindu Kush (kōōsh) mountain range mostly in NE Afghanistan, extending to the Karakoram in NW Kashmir: highest peak, TIRICH MIR

Hin·du·stan (hin′dōō stan′, -stän′) [see ff.] **1.** kingdom in N India in the 15th & 16th cent. **2.** variously, *a*) a region in N India, between the Vindhya Mountains & the Himalayas, where Hindi is spoken *b*) the entire Indian peninsula *c*) the republic of India

Hin·du·sta·ni (hin′dōō stan′ē, -stä′nē) *n.* [Hind. *Hindūstāni*, lit., dweller in northern India, Indian < Per. *Hindūstān*, lit., country of the Hindus < *Hindū* (see HINDU) + *stān*, a place, country] **1.** the most important dialect of Western Hindi, used as a trade language throughout N India: see also HINDI, URDU **2.** a type of speech closely allied to Urdu —*adj.* **1.** of Hindustan or its people **2.** of Hindustani

hinge (hinj) *n.* [ME., earlier *henge* (vowel raised before nasal) < *hengen* (< ON. *hengja*) or < *hangen* (see HANG)] **1.** a joint or device on which a door, gate, lid, etc. swings **2.** a natural joint, as of the bivalve shell of a clam or oyster **3.** a thin, gummed piece of paper, folded for fastening a stamp in an album **4.** anything on which matters turn or depend; cardinal point or principle; pivot —*vt.* **hinged**, **hing′ing** to equip with or attach by a hinge —*vi.* to hang as on a hinge; be contingent; depend [hopes *hinging* on his success]

hinge joint a joint between bones that permits motion in only one plane, as the knee joint

hin·ny (hin′ē) *n., pl.* **-nies** [L. *hinnus* < Gr. *innos*, with *h-* after L. *hinnire*, to whinny] the offspring of a male horse and a female donkey: cf. MULE[1]

TYPES OF HINGE
(A, fast butt; B, loose pin butt; C, T hinge; D, strap; E, spring; F, shutter)

hint (hint) *n.* [prob. var. of HENT] **1.** a slight indication of a fact, wish, etc.; indirect suggestion or piece of advice; intimation; covert allusion [a *hint* that we should leave] **2.** a very small amount or degree; trace [a *hint* of spice] **3.** [Obs.] an occasion; opportunity —*vt.* to give a hint of; suggest indirectly; intimate —*vi.* to make a hint or hints —*SYN.* see SUGGEST —**hint at** to suggest indirectly; intimate —**take a hint** to perceive and act on a hint —**hint′er** *n.*

hin·ter·land (hin′tər land′) *n.* [G. < *hinter* (cf. HINDER[2]), back + *land*, LAND] **1.** the land or district behind that bordering on a coast or river; specif., an inland region claimed by the state that owns the coast **2.** an area far from big cities and towns; back country **3.** the inland trade region served by a port

hip[1] (hip) *n.* [ME. *hipe* < OE. *hype*, akin to G. *hüfte* (OHG. *huf*) < IE. *keub-*, to bend, as at a joint (< base *keu-*, to bend, bend over), whence L. *cubare*, to lie, Gr. *kybos*, hollow above the hips of cattle] **1.** *a*) the part of the human body surrounding and including the joint formed by each thigh bone and the pelvis; esp., the fleshy part between the waist and the upper thigh; haunch *b*) *same as* HIP JOINT **2.** the corresponding part of an animal's body **3.** *Archit.* the angle formed by the meeting of two sloping sides of a roof —*vt.* **hipped**, **hip′ping** to make (a roof) with such an angle or angles —**on** (or **upon**) **the hip** [Rare] at a disadvantage: originally with reference to wrestling —**smite hip and thigh** [Poet.] to attack unsparingly; overwhelm with or as with blows: see Judg. 15:8

hip[2] (hip) *n.* [with Early ModE. shortened vowel < ME. *hepe* < OE. *heope*, akin to OHG. *hiufo*, OS. *hiopo* < IE.

base *keub-*, brier, thorn] the fleshy false fruit of the rose, containing the achenes or true fruits: it is rich in vitamin C

hip[3] (hip) *interj.* an exclamation used in cheers [*hip, hip, hurray!*]

☆**hip[4]** (hip) *adj.* **hip′per, hip′pest** [< *? hep*] [Slang] **1.** *a*) sophisticated; knowing; aware *b*) fashionable; stylish **2.** of or associated with hipsters or hippies —**get** (or **be**) **hip to** [Slang] to become (or be) informed or knowledgeable about —**hip′ness** *n.*

hip·bone (hip′bōn′) *n.* **1.** *same as* INNOMINATE BONE **2.** *same as* ILIUM **3.** the neck of the femur

hip joint the junction between the thigh bone and its socket in the pelvis

hip·parch (hip′ärk) *n.* [Gr. *hipparchos:* see HIPPO- & -ARCH] in ancient Greece, a cavalry commander

Hip·par·chus (hi pär′kəs) 2d cent. B.C.; Gr. astronomer

hipped[1] (hipt) *adj.* **1.** having hips of a specified kind [*broad-hipped*] **2.** having the hip dislocated **3.** *Archit.* having a hip or hips [a *hipped* roof]

hipped[2] (hipt) *adj.* [< HYP(OCHONDRIA)] **1.** [Now Rare] melancholy or depressed ☆**2.** [Colloq.] having a great, often excessive, interest; obsessed (with *on*) [*hipped* on movies]

☆**hip·pie** (hip′ē) *n.* [HIP[4] + -IE] [Slang] any of the young people of the 1960's who, in their alienation from conventional society, have turned variously to mysticism, psychedelic drugs, communal living, avant-garde arts, etc.

Hip·po (hip′ō) *same as* HIPPO REGIUS

hip·po (hip′ō) *n., pl.* **-pos** [Colloq.] *same as* HIPPOPOTAMUS

hip·po- (hip′ō, -ə) [< Gr. *hippos*, a horse < IE. *ekwos*, whence L. *equus*, OE. *eoh*, ON. *iōr*] *a combining form meaning* horse [a *hippophile* is a lover of horses]

hip·po·cam·pus (hip′ə kam′pəs) *n., pl.* **-cam′pi** (-pī) [L., sea horse < Gr. *hippokampos*, hippocampus < *hippos* (see HIPPO-) + *kampos*, sea monster] **1.** *Gr. & Rom. Myth.* a sea monster with the head and forequarters of a horse and the tail of a dolphin or fish **2.** a ridge along each lateral ventricle of the brain —**hip′po·cam′pal** *adj.*

hip·po·cras (hip′ə kras′) *n.* [ME. *ypocras* < OFr. < *Ypocras*, Hippocrates, after ML. *vinum Hippocraticum*, wine of Hippocrates: from being filtered through a strainer called "Hippocrates' sleeve" (L. *manica Hippocratis*)] a former cordial made of wine flavored with spices

Hip·poc·ra·tes (hi päk′rə tēz′) 460?–370? B.C.; Gr. physician: called the *Father of Medicine* —**Hip·po·crat·ic** (hip′ə krat′ik) *adj.*

Hippocratic oath the oath generally taken by students receiving a medical degree: it is attributed to Hippocrates and sets forth an ethical code for the medical profession

Hip·po·crene (hip′ə krēn′, hip′ə krē′nē) [L. < Gr. *Hippokrēnē* < *hippos* (see HIPPO-) + *krēnē*, a spring, fountain] *Gr. Myth.* a fountain on Mt. Helicon, sacred to the Muses: its waters were supposed to inspire poets

hip·po·drome (hip′ə drōm′) *n.* [Fr. < L. *hippodromos* < Gr. *hippodromos:* see HIPPO- & -DROME] **1.** in ancient Greece and Rome, a course for horse races and chariot races, surrounded by tiers of seats in an oval **2.** an arena or building for a circus, games, etc.

hip·po·griff, hip·po·gryph (-grif′) *n.* [Fr. *hippogriffe* < It. *ippogrifo* < Gr. *hippos* (see HIPPO-) + LL. *gryphus*, GRIFFIN] a mythical monster with the hindquarters of a horse and the head and wings of a griffin

Hip·pol·y·ta (hi päl′i tə) *Gr. Myth.* a queen of the Amazons, whose magic girdle was obtained by Hercules as one of his twelve labors: also **Hip·pol′y·te** (-tē)

Hip·pol·y·tus (-təs) *Gr. Myth.* a son of Theseus: when he rejected the love of his stepmother, Phaedra, she turned Theseus against him by false accusations, and at Theseus' request, Poseidon brought about his death

Hip·pom·e·nes (hi päm′ə nēz′) *Gr. Myth.* the youth who won the race against Atalanta: see ATALANTA

hip·po·pot·a·mus (hip′ə pät′ə məs) *n., pl.* **-mus·es, -a·mi** (-mī′), **-a·mus:** see PLURAL, II, D, 1 [L. < Gr. *hippopotamos*, lit., river horse < *hippos* (see HIPPO-) + *potamos*, river < IE. base *pet-*, to fall, fly, whence FEATHER, Gr. *pteryx*, wing] one of several large, plant-eating mammals (family Hippopotamidae, esp. genus *Hippopotamus*), with a heavy, thick-skinned, almost hairless body and short legs: they live chiefly in or near rivers in Africa

Hip·po Re·gi·us (hip′ō rē′jē əs) ancient city in N Africa, near modern Bône, Algeria: capital of ancient Numidia &, later, a Roman colony

-hip·pus (hip′əs) [ModL. < Gr. *hippos:* see HIPPO-] *a combining form meaning* horse [*eohippus*]

☆**hip·py** (hip′ē) *n., pl.* **-pies** [Slang] *same as* HIPPIE

hip roof a roof with sloping ends and sides

hip·shot (hip′shät′) *adj.* **1.** having the hip dislocated **2.** having one hip lower than the other

☆**hip·ster** (-stər) *n.* [Slang] **1.** a hipster, esp. a devotee of modern jazz **2.** *same as* BEATNIK: a term of the 1950's and early 1960's: cf. HIPPIE

Hi·ram (hī′rəm) [Heb. *hīrām*, prob. < ′*ahīrām*, exalted brother] a masculine name: dim. *Hi*

HIP ROOF

hir·cine (hur′sīn, -sin) *adj.* [L. *hircinus* < *hircus*, goat < IE. **gherkwo-* < **ǵher-*, to bristle (cf. HORROR)] of or like a goat; esp., smelling like a goat

hire (hir) *n.* [ME. < OE. *hyr*, wages, akin to Du. *huur*, G. *heuer*] 1. the amount paid to get the services of a person or the use of a thing 2. a hiring or being hired —*vt.* **hired,** **hir′ing** 1. to get the services of (a person) or the use of (a thing) in return for payment; employ or engage 2. to give the use of (a thing) or the services of (oneself or another) in return for payment (often with *out*) 3. to pay for (work to be done) —**for hire** available for work or use in return for payment: also **on hire** —☆**hire out** to work, esp. as a laborer, for payment —**hir′a·ble, hire′a·ble** *adj.* —**hir′er** *n.*

SYN.—to **hire**, in strict usage, means to get, and **let** means to give, the use of something in return for payment, although **hire,** which is also applied to persons or their services, may be used in either sense [to *hire* a hall, a worker, etc., rooms to *let*]; **lease** implies the letting or, in loose usage, the hiring of property (usually real property) by written contract; **rent** implies payment of a specific amount, usually at fixed intervals, for hiring or letting a house, land, or other property; **charter** implies the hiring or leasing of a ship, bus, etc.

hire·ling (-lin) *n.* [see HIRE & -LING¹] a person who is for hire; esp., one who will follow anyone's orders for pay; mercenary —*adj.* of or like a hireling; mercenary

hire purchase [Brit.] *same as* INSTALLMENT PLAN

☆**hiring hall** an employment office, esp. one operated by a union to place its members in jobs in the order of their applications

Hi·ro·hi·to (hir′ō hē′tō) 1901– ; emperor of Japan (1926–)

Hi·ro·shi·ge (hir′ō shē′gä), **An·do** (än′dō) 1797–1858; Jap. painter

Hi·ro·shi·ma (hir′ə shē′mə; *occas.* hi rō′shi mə) seaport in SW Honshu, Japan, on the Inland Sea: largely destroyed (Aug. 6, 1945) by a U.S. atomic bomb, the first ever used in warfare: pop. 504,000

hir·sute (hur′sōōt, hir′-) *adj.* [L. *hirsutus* < *hirtus*, bristly: for IE. base see HIRCINE] hairy; shaggy; bristly —**hir′sute·ness** *n.*

hir·u·din (hir′yə din) *n.* [orig. a trademark: < L. *hirudo*, leech + -IN¹] a substance found in the salivary glands of leeches that prevents the coagulation of blood

hi·ru·di·noid (hi rōōd′'n oid′) *adj.* [< L. *hirudo* (gen. *hirudinis*), a leech + -OID] of or like a leech

hi·run·dine (hi run′din, -dīn) *adj.* [< L. *hirundo* (gen. *hirundinis*), a swallow] of or like the swallow —*n.* any bird of the swallow family

his (hiz; *unstressed* iz) *pron.* [ME. < OE., gen. masc. & neut. of *he*] that or those belonging to him: used without a following noun, often after *of* [a friend of *his*, that book is *his*, *his* are better] —*possessive pronominal adj.* of, belonging to, made, or done by him

His·pa·ni·a (his pā′nē ə, -pä′-) 1. L. name for the IBERIAN PENINSULA 2. *poet. name for* SPAIN

His·pan·ic (his pan′ik) *adj.* [L. *Hispanicus*] Spanish or Spanish and Portuguese —**His·pan′i·cism** (-ə siz′m) *n.* —**His·pan′i·cist** *n.*

His·pan·io·la (his′pan yō′lə) island in the West Indies, between Cuba & Puerto Rico: divided between Haiti & the Dominican Republic: 29,530 sq. mi.

his·pid (his′pid) *adj.* [L. *hispidus*: for base see HIRCINE] covered with rough bristles, stiff hairs, or small spines —**his·pid′i·ty** *n.*

hiss (his) *vi.* [ME. *hissen*, of echoic origin] 1. to make a sound like that of a prolonged *s*, as of a goose or snake when provoked or alarmed, or of escaping steam, air, etc. 2. to show dislike or disapproval by hissing —*vt.* 1. to say or indicate by hissing 2. to show dislike or disapproval of by hissing 3. to force or drive by hissing [to *hiss* (a performer) off the stage] —*n.* the act or sound of hissing —**hiss′er** *n.*

hist (st; hist *is a sp. pronun.*) *interj.* an exclamation to attract attention, call for silence, etc., equivalent to "be quiet! listen!"

hist. 1. historian 2. historical 3. history

his·tam·i·nase (his tam′ə nās′, his′tə mə nās′) *n.* [HISTA-MIN(E) + -ASE] an enzyme found in the animal digestive system, capable of inactivating histamine

his·ta·mine (his′tə mēn′, -mən) *n.* [HIST(IDINE) + AMINE] an amine, C₅H₉N₃, produced by the decarboxylation of histidine and found in all organic matter: it is released by the tissues in allergic reactions, lowers the blood pressure by dilating blood vessels, stimulates gastric secretion, etc. —**his′ta·min′ic** (-min′ik) *adj.*

his·ti·dine (his′tə dēn′, -din) *n.* [< Gr. *histion*, dim. of *histos* (see HISTO-) + -INE⁴] an amino acid, C₆H₉N₃O₂, formed by the hydrolysis of proteins and containing an imidazole group as a major part of the molecule

his·ti·o·cyte (his′tē ə sit′) *n.* [< Gr. *histion*, web, dim. of *histos* (see HISTO-) + -CYTE] a cell found in connective tissue, that participates in the body's reaction to infection and injury —**his′ti·o·cyt′ic** (-sit′ik) *adj.*

his·to- (his′tō, -tə) [< Gr. *histos*, a loom, warp, web, tissue]

a combining form meaning tissue [*histology*]: also, before a vowel, **hist-**

his·to·chem·is·try (his′tō kem′is trē) *n.* the study of the chemical components of cells through the use of chemically specific staining reagents —**his′to·chem′i·cal** (-i k'l) *adj.* —**his′to·chem′i·cal·ly** *adv.*

his·to·gen (his′tə jən) *n.* [HISTO- + -GEN] *Bot.* a group of cells that gives rise to new tissue, such as cambium, phellogen, etc.

his·to·gen·e·sis (his′tə jen′ə sis) *n.* [HISTO- + -GENESIS] the process of tissue development and differentiation —**his′to·ge·net′ic** (-jə net′ik) *adj.* —**his′to·ge·net′i·cal·ly** *adv.*

his·to·gram (his′tə gram′) *n.* [HISTO(RY) + -GRAM] *Math.* a graphic representation of a frequency or relative frequency distribution consisting of vertical rectangles whose widths correspond to a definite range of frequencies and whose heights correspond to the number of frequencies occurring within the range

his·toid (his′toid) *adj.* [HIST- + -OID] *Med.* 1. like normal tissue 2. developed from one kind of tissue only

his·tol·o·gy (his täl′ə jē) *n.* [HISTO- + -LOGY] 1. the branch of biology concerned with the microscopic study of the structure of tissues 2. the tissue structure of an organism or part, as revealed by microscopic study —**his·to·log·ic** (his′tə läj′ik), **his′to·log′i·cal** *adj.* —**his′to·log′i·cal·ly** *adv.* —**his·tol′o·gist** *n.*

his·tol·y·sis (-ə sis) *n.* [HISTO- + -LYSIS] *Biol.* the breaking down and dissolution of organic tissues —**his·to·lyt·ic** (his′tə lit′ik) *adj.*

his·tone (his′tōn) *n.* [< Gr. *histos* (see HISTO-) + -ONE] any of a group of strongly basic, simple proteins that yield amino acids on hydrolysis, as the globin of hemoglobin: they are often poisonous when injected into an animal and prevent the clotting ot blood

his·to·pa·thol·o·gy (his′tō pə thäl′ə jē) *n.* [HISTO- + PATHOLOGY] the study of changes in tissues caused by disease, as revealed by histological examination

his·to·plas·mo·sis (-plaz mō′sis) *n.* [ModL. < *Histoplasma* (*capsulatum*) < HISTO- + PLASMA + -OSIS] a disease caused by a fungus (*Histoplasma capsulatum*) which enters the body via the lungs, and can affect the lungs, spleen, central nervous system, etc.

his·to·ri·an (his tôr′ē ən) *n.* [MFr. *historien*] 1. a writer of history; chronicler 2. an authority on or specialist in history

his·tor·ic (his tôr′ik, -tär′-) *adj.* [L. *historicus* < Gr. *historikos*] historical: esp., famous in history

his·tor·i·cal (-i k'l) *adj.* [< L. *historicus* < Gr. + -AL] 1. of or concerned with history as a science [the *historical* method] 2. providing evidence for a fact of history; serving as a source of history [a *historical* document] 3. based on or suggested by people or events of the past [a *historical* novel] 4. established by history; not legendary or fictional; factual; real 5. showing the development or evolution in proper chronological order [a *historical* account] 6. famous in history: now usually HISTORIC —**his·tor′i·cal·ly** *adv.* —**his·tor′i·cal·ness** *n.*

historical linguistics the branch of linguistics that deals with language changes over a period of time

historical materialism an interpretation of history, esp. in Marxian dialectic, that holds that the chief determinants of society and social institutions are economic factors

historical present the present tense used in telling about past events: also **historic present**

historical school a school of thought, as in economics, legal philosophy, etc., maintaining that the basic facts and principles of a discipline, together with their development, are to be ascertained by the study and interpretation of history

his·tor·i·cism (-i siz′m) *n.* a theory of history that holds that the course of events is determined by unchangeable laws or cyclic patterns —**his·tor′i·cist** *n.*, *adj.*

his·to·ric·i·ty (his′tə ris′ə tē) *n.* the condition of having actually occurred in history; authenticity

his·tor·i·cize (his tôr′ə siz′) *vt.* **-cized′, -ciz′ing** to make, or make seem, historical or historically real

his·to·ried (his′tə rēd) *adj.* having a history or told about in history

his·to·ri·og·ra·pher (his tôr′ē äg′rə fər) *n.* [< OFr. or LL.: OFr. *historiographeur* < LL. *historiographus* < Gr. *historiographos* < *historia* (see HISTORY) + *graphein*, to write (see GRAPHIC)] a historian; esp., one appointed to write the history of some institution, country, etc. —**his·to′ri·o·graph′ic** (-ə graf′ik), **his·to′ri·o·graph′i·cal** *adj.* —**his·to′ri·o·graph′i·cal·ly** *adv.* —**his·to′ri·og′ra·phy** *n.*

his·to·ry (his′tə rē, his′trē) *n.*, *pl.* **-ries** [ME. < L. *historia* < Gr. *historia*, a learning by inquiry, narrative < *histôr*, knowing, learned < base of *eidenai*, to know: for IE. base see WISE¹] 1. an account of what has or might have happened, esp. in the form of a narrative, play, story, or tale 2. a) what has happened in the life or development of a people, country, institution, etc. b) a systematic account of this, usually in chronological order with an analysis and explanation 3. all recorded events of the past 4. the branch

of knowledge that deals systematically with the past; a recording, analyzing, correlating, and explaining of past events *5.* a known or recorded past *[the strange history of his coat]* **6.** something that belongs to the past *[the election is history now]* **7.** something important enough to be recorded **8.** [Rare] a scientific account of a system of natural phenomena —**make history** to be or do something important enough to be recorded

his·tri·on·ic (his'trē än'ik) *adj.* [LL. *histrionicus* < L. *histrio*, actor; ult. of Etruscan orig.] **1.** of, or having the nature of, acting or actors **2.** overacted or overacting; theatrical; artificial; affected —**his'tri·on'i·cal·ly** *adv.*

his·tri·on·ics (-iks) *n.pl.* [*sometimes with sing. v.*] **1.** theatricals; dramatics **2.** an artificial or affected manner, display of emotion, etc.; theatricality

hit (hit) *vt.* **hit, hit'ting** [ME. *hitten* < OE. *hittan* < ON. *hitta*, to hit upon, meet with < IE. base *keid-*, to fall, whence W. *cwydd*, a fall] **1.** to come against, usually with force; strike *[the car hit the tree]* **2.** to give a blow to; strike; knock **3.** to strike so as to deliver (a blow) **4.** to strike by throwing or shooting a missile at *[to hit the target]* **5.** to cause to knock, bump, or strike, as in falling, moving, etc. (often with *on* or *against*) *[to hit one's head on a door]* **6.** to affect strongly or adversely so as to distress or harm *[a town hard hit by floods]* **7.** to come upon by accident or after search; find; light upon *[to hit the right answer]* ☆**8.** to arrive at (a place or point); reach; attain *[stocks hit a new high]* **9.** same as STRIKE, *vt.* 8, 9, 10 (variously) ☆**10.** [Slang] to apply oneself to steadily or frequently *[to hit the books]* **11.** [Slang] to demand or require of (often with *for*) *[to hit someone for a loan]* ☆**12.** *Baseball* to get (a specified base hit) *[to hit a double]* ☆**13.** *Card Games* to deal another card to —*vi.* **1.** to give a blow or blows; strike **2.** to attack suddenly **3.** to knock, bump, or strike (usually with *against*) **4.** to come by accident or after search (with *on* or *upon*) ☆**5.** to ignite the combustible mixture in its cylinders: said of an internal-combustion engine ☆**6.** *Baseball* to get a base hit —*n.* **1.** a blow that strikes its mark **2.** a collision of one thing with another **3.** an effectively witty or sarcastic remark **4.** a stroke of good fortune **5.** a successful and popular song, singer, book, author, etc. **6.** *Backgammon* a game won by a player after one or more of his opponent's men have been removed from the board ☆**7.** *Baseball* same as BASE HIT —*SYN.* see STRIKE —**hit it off** to get along well together; be congenial —**hit off** to mimic or portray briefly and well, usually in a satiric way —**hit or miss** without regard to success or failure; in a haphazard or aimless way —**hit (out) at 1.** to aim a blow at; try to hit **2.** to attack in words; criticize severely —☆**hit the road** [Slang] to leave; go away

☆**hit-and-run** (-'n run') *adj.* **1.** hitting and then escaping: usually of an automobile driver who flees from the scene of an accident in which he is involved **2.** *Baseball* designating a prearranged play in which a runner on base starts running as the pitch is made and the batter must strike at the ball to protect the runner

hitch (hich) *vi.* [ME. *hicchen*, to move jerkily < ?] **1.** to move jerkily; walk haltingly; limp; hobble **2.** to become fastened or caught, as by becoming entangled or hooking on to something **3.** to strike the feet together in moving: said of a horse ☆**4.** [Slang] to hitchhike —*vt.* **1.** to move, pull, or shift with jerks **2.** to fasten with a hook, knot, harness, etc.; unite; tie **3.** [Colloq.] to marry: usually in the passive ☆**4.** [Slang] to hitchhike —*n.* **1.** a short, sudden movement or pull; tug; jerk **2.** a hobble; limp **3.** a hindrance; obstacle; entanglement **4.** a catching or fastening; thing or part used to connect or join together; catch ☆**5.** [Slang] a ride in hitchhiking ☆**6.** [Slang] a period of time served, as of military service, imprisonment, etc. **7.** *Naut.* a kind of knot that can be easily undone —**without a hitch** smoothly, easily, and successfully

☆**hitch·hike** (-hīk') *vi.* -hiked', -hik'ing [prec. + HIKE] to travel by asking for rides from motorists along the way —*vt.* to get (a ride) or make (one's way) by hitchhiking —**hitch'hik'er** *n.*

hith·er (hith'ər) *adv.* [ME. *hider* < OE. (akin to Goth. *hidre*, ON. *hethra*) < base of *he* (see HE¹) + *-der*, suffix as in HINDER²] to or toward this place; here —*adj.* on or toward this side; nearer *[the hither horse]*

hith·er·most (-mōst') *adj.* nearest

hith·er·to (-tōō', hith'ər tōō') *adv.* [see HITHER & TO] **1.** until this time; to now **2.** [Obs.] hither

hith·er·ward (-wərd) *adv.* [OE. *hiderweard*: see -WARD] [Rare] toward this place; hither: also **hith'er·wards**

Hit·ler (hit'lər), **Adolf** 1889–1945; Nazi dictator of Germany (1933–45), born in Austria —**Hit·ler'i·an** (-lir'ē ən) *adj.*

Hit·ler·ism (-iz'm) *n.* the fascist program, ideas, and methods of Hitler and the Nazis —**Hit'ler·ite'** (-īt') *n., adj.*

hit-or-miss (hit'ər mis') *adj.* haphazard; random

☆**hit-skip** (-skip') *adj.* same as HIT-AND-RUN (sense 1)

hit·ter (-ər) *n.* a person who hits

Hit·tite (hit'īt) *n.* [Heb. *ḥitti* (< Hittite *ḥatti*) + -ITE¹] **1.** any of an ancient people of Asia Minor and Syria (fl. 1700–700 B.C.) **2.** the language of the Hittites, considered by most authorities to be associated with Indo-European: it is recorded in divergent cuneiform and hieroglyphic inscriptions —*adj.* of the Hittites, their language, or culture

hive (hīv) *n.* [ME. *hyfe* < OE., akin to ON. < *hūfr*, ship's hull < IE. *keup-* (< base *keu-*, to bend, curve), whence L. *cupa*, a tub: cf. HIP¹, HOP¹] **1.** a box or other shelter for a colony of domestic bees; beehive **2.** a colony of bees living in a hive; swarm **3.** a crowd of busy, very active people **4.** a place where many people are busy or actively engaged —*vt.* **hived, hiv'ing 1.** to put or gather (bees) into a hive **2.** to store up (honey) in a hive **3.** to store up for future use; garner —*vi.* **1.** to enter a hive **2.** to live together in or as in a hive

hives (hīvz) *n.* [orig. Scot. dial.] same as URTICARIA

H.J. [L. *hic jacet*] here lies

hl. hectoliter; hectoliters

H.L. House of Lords

h'm (ham: *conventionalized pronun.*) *interj.* same as HEM² or HUM²

hm. hectometer; hectometers

H.M. 1. Her Majesty **2.** His Majesty

H.M.S. 1. His (or Her) Majesty's Service **2.** His (or Her) Majesty's Ship or Steamer

ho (hō) *interj.* [ME.: a natural emphatic cry] **1.** an exclamation of pleasure, surprise, derision, etc. **2.** an exclamation to attract attention: sometimes used after a destination or direction *[westward ho!]* **3.** [ME. < OFr.] whoa! stop! halt!

Ho *Chem.* holmium

☆**hoa·gy, hoa·gie** (hō'gē) *n., pl.* -gies [< ?] same as HERO SANDWICH

hoar (hôr) *adj.* [ME. *hore* < OE. *har*, akin to G. *herr* (OHG. *hērro*, compar.) < IE. base *kei-*, term used for dark colors, gray, brown, whence ON. *harr*, gray, old, Pol. *szary*, gray & HUE¹] **1.** same as HOARY **2.** [Dial.] moldy; stale —*n.* same as *a*) HOARINESS *b*) HOARFROST

hoard (hôrd) *n.* [ME. *hord* < OE., akin to G. *hort*, Goth. *huzd* < IE. *keus-* < base *(s)keu-*, to cover, conceal, whence HIDE¹, Gr. *skylos*, animal's skin] a supply stored up and hidden or kept in reserve —*vi.* to get and store away money, goods, etc. —*vt.* to accumulate and hide or keep in reserve —**hoard'er** *n.* —**hoard'ing** *n.*

hoard·ing (hôr'diŋ) *n.* [< obs. *hoard*, hoarding < OFr. *hourde* < Frank. *hurda*, a pen, fold: for IE. base see HURDLE] [Brit.] **1.** a temporary wooden fence around a site of building construction or repair **2.** a billboard

hoar·frost (hôr'frôst') *n.* [ME. *horfrost*: see HOAR & FROST] white, frozen dew; white frost; rime

hoar·hound (-hound') *n.* same as HOREHOUND

hoarse (hôrs) *adj.* [ME. *hors, hase* < OE. *has*, akin to ON. *hāss*, OS. *hēs*, OHG. *heisi* < IE. base *kai-*, heat, whence HOT, HEAT] **1.** harsh and grating in sound; sounding rough and husky **2.** having a rough, husky voice —**hoarse'ly** *adv.* —**hoarse'ness** *n.*

hoars·en (hôr's'n) *vt., vi.* to make or become hoarse

hoar·y (hôr'ē) *adj.* **hoar'i·er, hoar'i·est** [HOAR + -Y²] **1.** white, gray, or grayish-white **2.** having white or gray hair because very old **3.** very old; ancient —**hoar'i·ly** *adv.* —**hoar'i·ness** *n.*

hoar·y-head·ed (-hed'id) *adj.* having white or gray hair because very old

☆**hoary marmot** a marmot (*Marmota caligata*) found in the mountains of NW N. America

ho·at·zin (hō at'sin, -wät'-) *n.* [AmSp. < Nahuatl *uatzin*] a crested, olive-colored S. American bird (*Opisthocomus hoazin*): the wings of its young have claws

hoax (hōks) *n.* [altered < ? HOCUS] a trick or fraud, esp. one meant as a practical joke —*vt.* to deceive with a hoax —*SYN.* see CHEAT —**hoax'er** *n.*

hob¹ (häb) *n.* [? var. of HUB] **1.** a projecting ledge at the back or side of a fireplace, used for keeping a kettle, saucepan, etc. warm **2.** a peg used as a target in quoits, etc. **3.** a device for cutting teeth in a gearwheel, etc.

hob² (häb) *n.* [ME., old familiar form for ROBIN, ROBERT] [Eng. Dial.] **1.** a rustic; lout **2.** an elf or goblin —[H-] Robin Goodfellow, or Puck —**play** (or **raise**) **hob with** to make trouble for; interfere with and make disordered

Ho·bart (hō'bərt, -bärt) capital of Tasmania; seaport on the SE coast; pop. (with suburbs) 124,000

Hob·be·ma (häb'ə mä), **Mein·dert** (mīn'dərt) 1638–1709; Du. painter

Hobbes (häbz), **Thomas** 1588–1679; Eng. social philosopher; author of *Leviathan* —**Hobbes'i·an** *adj., n.*

Hob·bism (häb'iz'm) *n.* the philosophy of Thomas Hobbes, who believed that a strong government, esp. an absolute monarchy, is necessary to control conflicting individual interests and desires

hob·bit (häb'it) *n.* [coined in a novel (1938) by J. R. R. TOLKIEN] an imaginary being having a very small human form with some rabbitlike qualities, and characterized by sociability, domesticity, and a peace-loving nature

hob·ble (häb''l) *vi.* -bled, -bling [ME. *hobelen* (akin to Du. *hobbelen*, G. dial. *hobbeln*) < base of *hoppen* (see HOP¹) + freq. suffix] **1.** to go unsteadily, haltingly, etc. **2.** to walk lamely or awkwardly; limp —*vt.* **1.** to cause to go haltingly or lamely **2.** to hamper the movement of (a horse, etc.) by tying two feet together **3.** to hamper; hinder —*n.* **1.** an awkward, halting walk; limp **2.** a rope, strap, etc. used to hobble a horse; fetter **3.** [Rare] an awkward situation; difficulty —**hob'bler** *n.*

☆**hob·ble·bush** (-boosh') *n.* a plant (*Viburnum alnifolium*) of the honeysuckle family, with clusters of small, white flowers and red to purple berries

hob·ble·de·hoy (häb′'l dē hoi′) *n.* [also early vars. *hober-dihoye, hobbedihoy,* prob. based on HOB² with cross associations < HOBBLE, HOBBY¹] a boy or adolescent youth, esp. one who is awkward and gawky

hobble skirt a woman's long skirt so narrow below the knees as to hinder the wearer's movements; esp., such a skirt popular from 1910 to 1914

hob·by¹ (häb′ē) *n., pl.* **-bies** [ME. *hoby* < ? Du. *hobben* (see ff.)] **1.** [Archaic] a medium-sized, vigorous horse **2.** *same as* HOBBYHORSE **3.** [< prec. sense, with notions as in ff. phrase] something that a person likes to do or study in his spare time; favorite pastime or avocation —**ride a hobby** to be excessively devoted to one's favorite pastime or subject —**hob′by·ist** *n.*

hob·by² (häb′ē) *n., pl.* **-bies** [ME. *hobi* < OFr. *hobet,* dim. of *hobe,* a hawk, prob. < Du. *hobben,* to move back and forth (akin to HOP¹)] a small European falcon (*Falco subbuteo*), formerly trained for hawking

hob·by·horse (-hôrs′) *n.* **1.** *a)* a figure of a horse attached to the waist of a person doing a morris dance so that he seems to be riding it *b)* such a dancer **2.** a child's toy consisting of a stick with a horse's head at one end: it is straddled in a pretense of riding **3.** *same as* ROCKING HORSE

hob·gob·lin (häb′gäb′lin) *n.* [HOB², sense 2 + GOBLIN] **1.** an elf; goblin **2.** a frightening apparition; bogy; bugbear —[H-] Robin Goodfellow; Puck

hob·nail (-nāl′) *n.* [HOB¹, sense 2 + NAIL] **1.** a short nail with a broad head, put on the soles of heavy shoes to prevent wear or slipping **2.** one of a series of knoblike decorations, as on the edge of a glass plate —*vt.* to put hobnails on

hob·nob (-näb′) *adv.* [earlier *habnab,* lit., to have and not have < ME. *habben,* to have + *nabben* (< *ne habben*), not to have, esp. with reference to alternation in drinking] at random —*vi.* **-nobbed′, -nob′bing 1.** [Now Rare] to drink together **2.** to be on close terms (*with* someone); associate in a familiar way —*n.* a friendly chat

☆**ho·bo** (hō′bō) *n., pl.* **-bos, -boes** [< ? *ho! beau!,* formerly a greeting between vagrants] **1.** a migratory worker: so used by such workers themselves **2.** a vagrant; tramp —*SYN.* see VAGRANT

Ho·bo·ken (hō′bō k'n) [< Du. *hopoakan,* at the place of the tobacco pipe: infl. by *Hoboken,* town in Belgium] city in NE N.J., across the Hudson from New York City: pop. 45,000

Hob·son's choice (häb′sənz) [after Thomas *Hobson* (1544?-1631), of Cambridge, England, who owned livery stables and let horses in strict order according to their position near the door] a choice of taking what is offered or nothing at all; lack of an alternative

Ho Chi Minh (hō′ chē′ min′) (born *Nguyen Van,* or *That, Thanh*) 1890?-1969; president of North Vietnam (1945-69)

hock¹ (häk) *n.* [S Brit. var. of Scot. *hough* < ME. *hoh, heel* < OE. < Gmc. *hanha* (cf. HEEL¹) with loss of nasal as in SOFT, TOOTH < IE. base *kenk-,* heel, whence Lith. *kinka*] **1.** the joint bending backward in the hind leg of a horse, ox, etc., but corresponding to the human ankle **2.** the corresponding joint in the leg of a fowl —*vt.* to disable by cutting the tendons of the hock

hock² (häk) *n.* [contr. of *hockamore,* altered < G. *Hoch-heimer*] [Chiefly Brit.] any white Rhine wine, orig. that from Hochheim, Germany

☆**hock³** (häk) *vt., n.* [< Du. *hok,* prison, (slang) debt] [Slang] *same as* PAWN¹

hock·ey (häk′ē) *n.* [Early ModE., prob. < OFr. *hoquet,* bent stick, crook, dim. of *hoc,* hook < MDu. *hoec,* HOOK] ☆**1.** a team game played on ice, in which the players, using a curved stick with a flat blade (**hockey stick**) and wearing skates, try to drive a hard rubber disk (*puck*) into their opponents' goal; ice hockey **2.** a similar game played on foot on a field with a small ball instead of a puck; field hockey

☆**hock·shop** (häk′shäp′) *n.* [Slang] *same as* PAWNSHOP

ho·cus (hō′kəs) *vt.* **-cused** or **-cussed, -cus·ing** or **-cus·sing** [contr. < ff.] **1.** to play a trick on; dupe; hoax **2.** to drug **3.** to put drugs in (a drink)

ho·cus-po·cus (-pō′kəs) *n.* [imitation L., prob. altered < *hax pax* (*max Deus adimax*), arbitrary magic formula attributed to medieval traveling scholars] **1.** meaningless words used as a formula by conjurers **2.** a magician's trick or trickery; sleight of hand; legerdemain **3.** any meaningless action or talk meant to draw attention away from some trick or deception **4.** trickery; deception —*vt., vi.* **-cused** or **-cussed, -cus·ing** or **-cus·sing** [Colloq.] to trick; dupe

hod (häd) *n.* [prob. < MDu. *hodde,* akin to G. *hotte*] **1.** a wooden trough with a long handle, used for carrying bricks, mortar, etc. on the shoulder **2.** a coal scuttle

hod carrier a worker who assists a bricklayer, plasterer, or mason by carrying bricks, mortar, etc. on a hod

hod·den (häd′n) *n.* [< ?] [Scot.] a coarse, undyed woolen cloth: a gray variety (**hodden gray**) is made by mixing white and black fleece

Ho·dei·da (hō dā′də) seaport in W Yemen, on the Red Sea: pop. 30,000

hodge·podge (häj′päj′) *n.* [ME. *hogpoch:* see HOTCHPOTCH] **1.** a kind of stew: now usually HOTCHPOTCH **2.** any jumbled mixture; mess; medley

Hodg·kin's disease (häj′kinz) [after Dr. Thomas *Hodgkin* (1798-1866), Eng. physician by whom first described] a neoplastic disease characterized by progressive enlargement of the lymph nodes and inflammation of other lymphoid tissues, esp. of the spleen

hod·man (häd′mən) *n., pl.* **-men** (-mən) [Brit.] *same as* HOD CARRIER

hoe (hō) *n.* [ME. *houe* < OFr. < OHG. *houwa* < *houwan,* to cut, HEW] a tool with a thin, flat blade set across the end of a long handle, used for weeding, loosening soil, etc. —*vt., vi.* **hoed, hoe′ing** to dig, cultivate, weed, etc. with a hoe —**ho′er** *n.*

☆**hoe·cake** (-kāk′) *n.* a thin bread made of cornmeal, orig. baked on a hoe at the fire

☆**hoe·down** (-doun′) *n.* [prob. of U.S. Negro origin; associated with BREAKDOWN, sense 2] **1.** a lively, rollicking dance, often a square dance **2.** music for this **3.** a party at which hoedowns are danced

Ho·fei (hu′fā′) city in E China; capital of Anhwei province: pop. 360,000

Hoff·mann (hôf′män), **Ernst The·o·dor Am·a·de·us** (ernst tā′ō dôr ä′mä dā′oos) 1776-1822; Ger. writer & composer

Hof·mann (häf′mən, hôf′-) **1. Hans,** 1880-1966; U.S. painter, born in Germany **2. Josef,** 1876-1957; U.S. pianist & composer, born in Poland

Hof·manns·thal (hôf′mäns täl′), **Hu·go von** (hoō′gō fôn) 1874-1929; Austrian playwright & poet

Ho·fuf (hoō fōof′) city in E Saudi Arabia, near the Persian Gulf: pop. c. 100,000

hog (hôg, häg) *n., pl.* **hogs, hog:** see PLURAL, II, D, 1 [ME. < OE. *hogg* < ? or akin to ON. *höggva,* to cut (akin to OE. *heawan,* HEW), in basic sense "castrated"] **1.** *a)* a pig; esp., a castrated boar or full-grown pig of more than 120 lbs. raised for its meat *b)* any of several omnivorous animals (family Suidae) including the wild boar **2.** [Scot. & Brit. Dial.] a young sheep not yet shorn **3.** [Colloq.] a selfish, greedy, gluttonous, coarse, or filthy person —*vt.* **hogged, hog′ging 1.** *a)* to arch (the back) like a hog's *b)* to cause (a ship, keel, etc.) to arch in the center like a hog's back **2.** to trim (a horse's mane) in order to make it bristly ☆**3.** [Slang] to grab greedily; take all of or an unfair share of —*vi.* to arch in the center, as the bottom of a ship —**go (the) whole hog** [Slang] to go all the way; do or accept something fully —☆**high on** (or **off**) **the hog** [Colloq.] in a luxurious or costly way —☆**hog wild** [Colloq.] highly excited; without moderation or restraint

☆**ho·gan** (hō′gôn, -gän, -gən) *n.* [Navaho *qoghan,* house] the typical dwelling of the Navaho Indians, built of earth walls supported by timbers

Ho·garth (hō′gärth), **William** 1697-1764; Eng. painter & engraver: known for his satirical pictures of 18th-cent. English life —**Ho·garth′i·an** *adj.*

hog·back (hôg′bak, häg′-) *n.* a ridge with a sharp crest and abruptly sloping sides, often formed by the outcropping edge of steeply dipping rock strata

☆**hog cholera** an infectious virus disease of hogs, characterized by fever, loss of appetite, and frequently by a patchy redness of the skin and congestion and hemorrhages in the lymph glands and kidneys

hog deer *same as* AXIS²

hog-fish (-fish′) *n., pl.* **-fish′, -fish′es:** see FISH² [orig. ? transl. of OFr. *porpeis:* see PORPOISE] **1.** any of several fishes whose head supposedly resembles that of a hog, as the pigfish **2.** a bright-red food fish (*Lachnolaimus maximus*), found off the SE coast of the U.S.

Hogg (hôg, häg), **James** 1770-1835; Scot. poet

hog·gish (hôg′ish, häg′-) *adj.* like a hog; very selfish, greedy, gluttonous, coarse, or filthy —**hog′gish·ly** *adv.* —**hog′gish·ness** *n.*

hog·ma·nay (häg′mə nā′) *n.* [< ?] [Scot.] New Year's Eve, when young people go about singing and seeking gifts

☆**hog-nose snake** (hôg′nōz′, häg′-) any of several small, harmless N. American snakes (genus *Heterodon*), with a flat snout and a thick body: also **hog′nosed′ snake**

☆**hog-nut** (-nut′) *n. same as* PIGNUT

☆**hog peanut** a twining vine (genus *Amphicarpa*) of the legume family, native to E N. America: the flowers borne near the ground develop bladdery pods underground

hogs·head (hôgz′hed′, hägz′-) *n.* [ME. *hoggeshede,* lit.,

Types of hoe illustration

TYPES OF HOE
(A, nursery; B, weeding; C, gardening; D, serrated)

HOBNAILS

hog's head: reason for name unc.] **1.** a large barrel or cask holding from 63 to 140 gallons **2.** any of various liquid measures, esp. one equal to 63 gallons (52 1/2 imperial gallons)

☆**hog·tie** (hôg′tī′, häg′-) *vt.* **-tied′, -ty′ing** or **-tie′ing 1.** to tie the four feet or the hands and feet of **2.** [Colloq.] to make incapable of effective action, as if by tying up

hog·wash (-wôsh′, -wäsh′) *n.* **1.** refuse fed to hogs; swill **2.** useless or insincere talk, writing, etc.

hog·weed (-wēd′) *n.* any of various coarse weeds, as ragweed

Hoh·en·stau·fen (hō′ən shtou′fən) ruling family of Germany (1138–1208; 1215–54) & of Sicily (1194–1268)

Hoh·en·zol·lern (hō′ən tsôl′ərn; *E.* -zäl′ərn) **1.** ruling family of Brandenburg (1415–1918), of Prussia (1701–1918), & of Germany (1871–1918) **2.** region of SW West Germany, formerly a province of Prussia

ho-hum (hō′hum′) *interj.* [conventionalized representation of a yawn] an exclamation expressing boredom, lack of interest, weariness, etc.

hoicks (hoiks) *interj.* [< ?] a hunter's call to the hounds: also **hoick**

hoi·den (hoid′'n) *n., adj., vi.* same as HOYDEN

hoi pol·loi (hoi′ pə loi′) [Gr., the many] the common people; the masses: usually patronizing or contemptuous; popularly and redundantly preceded by *the*

hoise (hoiz) *vt.* **hoised** or **hoist, hois′ing** [Early ModE. phonetic sp. of earlier *hyce* < Du. *hijschen* < or akin to LowG. *hissen:* of nautical origin] *obs. var. of* HOIST

hoist (hoist) *vt.* [< prec. + unhistoric *-t* (< ? the pp.)] to raise aloft; lift or pull up, esp. by means of a cable, pulley, crane, etc. —*n.* **1.** the act of hoisting **2.** an apparatus for raising heavy things; elevator or tackle **3.** *Naut. a)* the perpendicular height of a sail or flag *b)* flags hoisted together as a signal —*SYN.* see LIFT

hoi·ty-toi·ty (hoit′ē toit′ē) *adj.* [redupl. of obs. *hoit,* to indulge in noisy mirth] **1.** [Brit.] giddy or flighty; capricious **2.** haughty; arrogant; condescending **3.** petulant; touchy; huffy —*n.* hoity-toity behavior —*interj.* an exclamation used in rebuking a display of arrogance or huffiness

☆**hoke** (hōk) *vt.* **hoked, hok′ing** [< HOKUM] [Slang] to treat in a mawkishly sentimental, crudely comic, or falsely contrived way: usually with *up* —*n.* [Slang] same as HOKUM —**hok′ey** *adj.*

ho·key·po·key, ho·ky·po·ky (hō′kē pō′kē) *n.* [altered < HOCUS-POCUS] **1.** hocus-pocus; trickery **2.** formerly, a kind of ice cream or flavored ice sold by street vendors

Hok·kai·do (hō kī′dō) one of the four main islands of Japan, north of Honshu: 30,364 sq. mi.; pop. 5,039,000; chief city, Sapporo

hok·ku (hō′kōō) *n.* same as HAIKU

☆**ho·kum** (hō′kəm) *n.* [altered < HOCUS (-POCUS)] [Slang] **1.** crudely comic or mawkishly sentimental elements in a play, story, etc., used to gain an immediate emotional response **2.** nonsense; humbug; claptrap

Ho·ku·sai (hō′koo sī′), **Ka·tsu·shi·ka** (kä′tsoo shē′kä) 1760–1849; Jap. painter & wood engraver

Hol·arc·tic (häl ärk′tik, hōl-) *adj.* [HOL(O)- + ARCTIC] designating or of the biogeographic region consisting of both the Nearctic and Palearctic realms

Hol·bein (hōl′bīn), **Hans** 1. 1460?–1524; Ger. painter: called *the Elder* 2. 1497?–1543; Ger. portrait painter in England: son of *prec.*: called *the Younger*

hold[1] (hōld) *vt.* **held, hold′ing;** archaic pp. **hold′en** [ME. *holden* < Anglian OE. *haldan* (WS. *healdan*), akin to G. *halten,* Goth. *haldan,* to tend sheep < IE. base *kel-,* to drive, incite to action, whence Gr. *kelēs,* swift horse, L. *celer,* swift: prob. sense development: drive (cattle, etc.)— tend (cattle, etc.)—possess (cattle, etc.)] **1.** to take and keep with the hands, arms, or other means; grasp; clutch; seize ☆**2.** to keep from going away; not let escape [to hold a prisoner, hold the train] **3.** to keep in a certain place or position, or in a specified condition [to hold one's head up] **4.** to restrain or control as by keeping in a certain place or by handling; specif., *a)* to keep from falling; bear the weight of; support; sustain [pillars holding the roof] *b)* to keep from acting; keep back [hold your tongue] *c)* to keep from advancing or attacking *d)* to keep from getting an advantage *e)* to get and keep control of; keep from relaxing [to hold someone's attention] *f)* to continue; maintain [to hold a course] ☆*g)* to keep (a letter, etc.) for delivery later *h)* to keep (a room, etc.) for use later *i)* to keep under obligation; bind [hold him to his word] **5.** to have and keep as one's own; have the duties, privileges, etc. of; own; possess; occupy [to hold shares of stock, to hold the office of mayor] **6.** to keep against an enemy; guard; defend [hold the fort] **7.** to have or conduct together; specif., *a)* carry on (a meeting, conversation, etc.) *b)* perform (a function, service, etc.) [to hold classes in the morning] **8.** to call together or preside over [to hold court] **9.** to have or keep within itself; have room or space for; contain [a bottle that holds a quart] **10.** to have or keep in the mind **11.** to have an opinion or belief about; regard; consider [to hold a statement to be untrue] **12.** *Law a)* to decide; adjudge; decree *b)* to bind by contract *c)* to possess by legal title [to hold a mortgage] **13.** *Music* to prolong (a tone or rest) —*vi.* **1.** to retain a hold, firm contact, etc. [hold tight] **2.** to go on being firm,

loyal, etc. [to hold to a resolution] **3.** to remain unbroken or unyielding; not give way [the rope held] **4.** to have right or title (usually with *from* or *of*) **5.** to be in effect or in force; be true or valid [a rule that holds in any case] **6.** to keep up; continue [the wind held from the north] **7.** to go no further; stop oneself; halt: usually in the imperative —*n.* **1.** the act or manner of grasping or seizing; grip; specif., a way of gripping an opponent in wrestling **2.** a thing to hold or hold on by **3.** a thing for holding or containing something else **4.** *a)* a controlling or dominating force; restraining authority [to have a firm hold over someone] *b)* being aware or in control [to lose one's hold on life] **5.** a means of confinement; prison **6.** a temporary halt or delay, as to make repairs, or an order to make such a halt **7.** an order reserving something **8.** [Archaic] a stronghold **9.** [Obs.] the act or fact of guarding, possessing, etc. **10.** *Music* same as FERMATA —*SYN.* see CONTAIN, HAVE —**catch hold of** to take; seize; grasp —**get hold of 1.** to take; seize; grasp **2.** to acquire —**hold back 1.** to restrain **2.** to refrain **3.** to retain —**hold down 1.** to keep down or under control; restrain ☆**2.** [Colloq.] to have and keep (a job) —**hold forth** [cf. Phil. 2:16] **1.** to speak at some length; preach; lecture **2.** to offer; propose —**hold in 1.** to keep in or back **2.** to control oneself or one's impulses —**hold off 1.** to keep away or at a distance **2.** to keep from attacking or doing something —**hold on 1.** to retain one's hold **2.** to continue; persist **3.** [Colloq.] stop! wait! —**hold one's own** to maintain one's place or condition in spite of obstacles or reverses —**hold out 1.** to last; endure; continue **2.** to continue resistance; stand firm; not yield **3.** to offer ☆**4.** [Colloq.] to fail or refuse to give (what is to be given) —**hold out for** [Colloq.] to stand firm in demanding —**hold over 1.** to postpone consideration of or action on **2.** to keep or stay for an additional period or term ☆**3.** to keep as a threat or advantage over —**hold up 1.** to keep from falling; prop up **2.** to show; exhibit **3.** to last; endure; continue **4.** to stop; delay; impede ☆**5.** to stop forcibly and rob ☆**6.** [Colloq.] to overcharge —**hold with 1.** to agree or side with **2.** to approve of —**lay (or take) hold of 1.** to take; seize; grasp **2.** to get control or possession of —**no holds barred** [Colloq.] with no set rules or limits

hold[2] (hōld) *n.* [altered (after prec.) < HOLE or < MDu. < *hol,* a hole, cave, ship's hold] **1.** the interior of a ship below decks, esp. below the lower deck, in which the cargo is carried **2.** the compartment for cargo in an aircraft

hold·all (hōld′ôl′) *n.* [Chiefly Brit.] a large traveling case for carrying clothes, equipment, etc.

hold·back (-bak′) *n.* **1.** a thing that holds back; curb; check; hindrance ☆**2.** a strap or iron attached to the shaft of a wagon, carriage, etc. and to the harness, to enable a horse to stop or back the vehicle

hold·en (-ən) *archaic pp.* of HOLD[1]

hold·er (-ər) *n.* [ME. *holdere*] **1.** a person who holds or possesses; specif., *a)* one who is legally entitled to payment of a bill, note, or check *b)* a tenant *c)* a possessor **2.** a device for holding something

hold·fast (-fast′, -fäst′) *n.* **1.** the act of holding fast **2.** any of various devices that hold something else in place; hook, nail, clamp, etc. **3.** *Bot.* a part, other than a root, by which plants, as certain algae, cling to a support **4.** *Zool.* an organ of a parasitic or sessile organism, specialized for attachment to a host or other object

hold·ing (-iŋ) *n.* [ME. *holdinge:* see HOLD[1]] **1.** land, esp. a farm, rented from another **2.** [usually pl.] property owned, esp. stocks or bonds **3.** in certain sports, the illegal use of the hands and arms to hinder the movements of an opponent

☆**holding company** a corporation organized to hold bonds or stocks of other corporations, which it usually controls

hold·out (-out′) *n.* **1.** the act of holding out ☆**2.** *a)* a player in a professional sport who has not signed a contract at the regular time because he is insisting upon better terms *b)* any person who resists joining in a certain action, coming to an agreement, etc.

hold·o·ver (-ō′vər) *n.* ☆[Colloq.] a person or thing staying on from a previous period; specif., an officeholder who continues in office or an entertainer whose engagement is extended

☆**hold·up** (-up′) *n.* **1.** a stoppage; delay or hindrance **2.** the act of stopping forcibly and robbing **3.** [Colloq.] the act of overcharging **4.** *Chem. a)* the amount of liquid retained or delayed during fractional distillation and certain types of solvent extractions *b)* the free volume between the resin particles in an ion exchange column **5.** *Physics* the amount of fissionable material being processed or in storage for irradiation in a reactor cycle

hole (hōl) *n.* [ME. < OE. *hol,* orig. neut. of *holh, adj.,* hollow, akin to G. *hohl,* hollow < IE. base *kaul-, *kul-,* hollow, hollow stalk, whence L. *caulis,* Gr. *kaulos,* stalk] **1.** a hollow or hollowed-out place; cavity; specif., *a)* an excavation or pit ☆*b)* a small bay or inlet; cove: often in place names *c)* a pool or deep, relatively wide place in a stream [a swimming hole] *d)* an animal's burrow or lair; den **2.** a small, dingy, squalid place; any dirty, badly lighted room, house, etc. **3.** a prison cell **4.** *a)* an opening in or through anything; break; gap [a hole in the wall] *b)* a tear or rent, as in a garment **5.** a flaw; fault; blemish; defect [holes in an argument] ☆**6.** the cards that are dealt

face down in stud poker **7.** [Colloq.] an embarrassing situation or position; predicament **8.** *Golf a)* a small, cylindrical cup sunk into a green, into which the ball is to be hit *b)* any of the distinct sections of a course, including the tee, the fairway, and the green [played the fifth *hole* in par] **9.** *Physics* a nuclear or atomic energy state, as in a semiconductor, nuclear shell structure, etc., in which one particle (nucleon or electron) is missing, whereas adjacent states above and below are frequently occupied —*vt.* **holed, hol'ing 1.** to make a hole or holes in **2.** to put, hit, or drive into a hole **3.** to create by making a hole [to *hole* a tunnel through a mountain] —**burn a hole in one's pocket** to make one eager to spend it: said of money —**hole high** *Golf* at a spot on or near the green that is as far as the hole is from where the ball was hit —**hole in one** *Golf* the act of getting the ball into the hole on the drive from the tee —**hole out** *Golf* to hit the ball into the hole —**hole up** [Colloq.] **1.** to hibernate, usually in a hole **2.** to shut oneself in **3.** to hide out —☆**in the hole** [Colloq.] financially embarrassed or behind [fifty dollars *in the hole*] —**make a hole in** to use up a sizable amount of —**pick holes in** to pick out errors or flaws in

SYN.—**hole** is the general word for an open space in a thing and may suggest a depression in a surface or an opening from surface to surface [a *hole* in the ground, a *hole* in a sock]; **hollow** basically suggests an empty space within a solid body, whether or not it extends to the surface, but it may also be applied to a depressed place in a surface [a wooded *hollow*]; **cavity**, the Latin-derived equivalent of **hollow**, has special application in formal and scientific usage [the thoracic *cavity*]; an **excavation** is a hollow made in or through ground by digging [the *excavations* at Pompeii]

☆**hole in the wall** a small, dingy room, shop, etc., esp. one in a remote or unfrequented place

hol·e·y (-ē) *adj.* [ME.] having a hole or holes

Hol·guin (ôl gēn′) city in E Cuba: pop. 227,000

hol·i·day (häl′ə dā′) *n.* [< ME. *holidei*, with shortened first vowel < OE. *hāligdæg*: see HOLY & DAY] **1.** a religious festival: see HOLY DAY **2.** a day of freedom from labor; day set aside for leisure and recreation **3.** [*often pl.*] [Chiefly Brit.] a period of leisure or recreation; vacation **4.** a day set aside by law or custom for the suspension of business, usually in commemoration of some event —*adj.* of or suited to a holiday; joyous; gay [the *holiday* spirit] —*vi.* [Chiefly Brit.] to take a vacation or vacation trip

hol·i·days (-dāz′) *adv.* on every holiday or most holidays

☆**ho·li·er-than-thou** (hō′lē ər *th*an thou′) *adj.* sanctimonious or self-righteous to an annoying degree

ho·li·ly (hō′lə lē) *adv.* [ME. *holiliche* < OE. *haliglice*] in a holy manner; piously, devoutly, or sacredly

ho·li·ness (-lē nis) *n.* [ME. *holinesse* < OE. *halignesse*] **1.** the quality or state of being holy **2.** [H-] a title of the Pope (with *His* or *Your*)

Ho·lins·hed (häl′inz hed′, -in shed′), **Raphael** ?–1580?; Eng. chronicler: also **Hol·lings·head** (häl′iŋz hed′)

ho·lism (hō′liz′m) *n.* [HOL(O-) + -ISM] the view that an organic or integrated whole has a reality independent of and greater than the sum of its parts —**ho′list** *n.* —**ho·lis′tic** *adj.* —**ho·lis′ti·cal·ly** *adv.*

hol·la (häl′ə, hä lä′) *interj., n., vt., vi.* [< Fr. *holà* < *ho*, ho + *là*, there < L. *illac*, there] *same as* HOLLO

Hol·land (häl′ənd) **1.** former county of the Holy Roman Empire on the North Sea, now divided into two provinces (NORTH HOLLAND & SOUTH HOLLAND) of the Netherlands **2.** *same as* NETHERLANDS —**Hol′land·er** *n.*

hol·land (häl′ənd) *n.* [< prec., where first made] a linen or cotton cloth, sometimes glazed, used for clothing, window shades, etc.

hol·lan·daise sauce (häl′ən dāz′) [Fr. *hollandaise*, fem. of *hollandais*, of Holland] a creamy sauce for fish or vegetables, made of butter, egg yolks, lemon juice, etc.

Hol·lan·di·a (hä lan′dē ə) *former name of* KOTABARU

Hol·lands (häl′əndz) *n.* [Du. *hollandsch* (*genever*)] gin made in the Netherlands: also **Hollands** (or **Holland**) **gin**, orig. **Hollands geneva**

hol·ler[1] (häl′ər) *vi., vt.* [altered < HOLLO, HOLLA] [Colloq.] to shout or yell —*n.* [Colloq.] **1.** a shout or yell ☆**2.** a working song sung by U.S. Negro field workers

hol·ler[2] (häl′ər) *adj., adv., n. dial. var.* of HOLLOW

hol·lo (häl′ō, ha lō′) *interj., n., pl.* **-los** [var. of HOLLA, HALLO] **1.** a shout or call, as to attract a person's attention or to urge on hounds in hunting **2.** a shout of greeting or surprise —*vi., vt.* **-loed, -lo·ing 1.** to shout (at) in order to attract the attention **2.** to urge on (hounds) by calling out "hollo" **3.** to shout or call, as in greeting or surprise Also **hol′loa** Cf. HELLO

hol·low (häl′ō) *adj.* [ME. *holwe* < OE. *holh*: see HOLE] **1.** having an empty space, or only air, within it; having a cavity inside; not solid **2.** depressed below the surrounding surface; shaped like a cup or bowl; concave **3.** deeply set; sunken [*hollow* cheeks] **4.** empty or worthless; not real or meaningful [*hollow* praise] **5.** hungry **6.** deep-toned, dull, and muffled, as though resounding from something hollow —*adv.* in a hollow manner —*n.* **1.** a hollow formation or place; cavity; hole **2.** a valley —*vt., vi.* to make or become hollow —*SYN.* see HOLE, VAIN —**beat all hollow** [Colloq.]

to outdo or surpass by far —**hollow out** to make by hollowing —**hol′low·ly** *adv.* —**hol′low·ness** *n.*

hol·lo·ware (häl′ō wer′) *n.* serving dishes and table accessories, esp. of silver, that are relatively hollow or concave: also **hol′low-ware′**: cf. FLATWARE

hol·low-eyed (häl′ō īd′) *adj.* having deep-set eyes or dark areas under the eyes, as from sickness or fatigue

hol·ly (häl′ē) *n., pl.* **-lies** [ME. *holi, holin* < OE. *holegn* < IE. base **kel-*, to prick, whence W. *celyn*, holly, Sans. *katambá-*, arrow] **1.** any of a genus (*Ilex*) of small trees and shrubs of the holly family, with stiff, glossy, sharp-pointed leaves and clusters of bright-red berries **2.** the leaves and berries, used as Christmas ornaments —*adj.* designating a family (Aquifoliaceae) of trees and shrubs found mostly in Central and South America

hol·ly·hock (häl′ē häk′) *n.* [ME. *holihoc*, lit., holy hock < OE. *halig*, holy + *hoc*, mallow] **1.** a tall, biennial plant (*Althaea rosea*) of the mallow family, with palmately lobed leaves, a hairy stem, and large, showy flowers of various colors in elongated spikes **2.** its flower

Hol·ly·wood (häl′ē wood′) [HOLLY + WOOD[1]] **1.** section of Los Angeles, Calif., once the site of many U.S. motion-picture studios; hence, the U.S. motion-picture industry or its life, world, etc. **2.** city on the SE coast of Fla.: pop. 107,000: see FORT LAUDERDALE

☆**Hollywood bed** a bed consisting typically of a mattress on a box spring that rests on a metal frame or has attached legs: it sometimes has a headboard

holm[1] (hōm) *n.* [ME. < OE., sea: sense infl. by cognate ON. *holmr*, island < IE. base **kel-*, to project, whence HILL] [Brit.] **1.** a small island in a river or lake, near the mainland or a larger island: used chiefly in place names **2.** low, flat land by a river or stream; bottoms

holm[2] (hōm) *n.* [altered < *holn*, form of ME. *holin*: see HOLLY] *same as:* **1.** HOLM OAK **2.** [Dial.] HOLLY

Holman-Hunt *see* William Holman HUNT

Holmes (hōmz, hōlmz) **1. John Haynes** (hānz) 1879–1964; U.S. clergyman & reformer **2. Oliver Wen·dell** (wen′d'l), *a)* 1809–94; U.S. writer & physician *b)* 1841–1935; associate justice, U.S. Supreme Court (1902–32): son of *prec.* **3. Sherlock,** *see* SHERLOCK HOLMES

hol·mi·um (hōl′mē əm) *n.* [ModL. < *Holmia*, Latinized form of *Stockholm*] a trivalent, metallic chemical element of the rare-earth group: symbol, Ho; at. wt., 164.930; at. no., 67; sp. gr., 8.803; melt. pt., 1461°C; boil. pt., 2600°C

holm oak [see HOLM[2]] **1.** a south European evergreen oak (*Quercus ilex*) of the beech family, with hollylike leaves **2.** its wood

hol·o- (häl′ə, -ō; hō′lə, -lō) [Fr. < L. < Gr. *holos*, whole < IE. base **solo-*, well-preserved, whole, whence L. *salus*, sound] *a combining form meaning* whole, entire [*holomorphic*]

hol·o·blas·tic (häl′ə blas′tik, hō′lə-) *adj.* [prec. + -BLAST + -IC] *Embryology* undergoing complete cleavage into daughter cells (*blastomeres*): said of certain ova with little yolk: cf. MEROBLASTIC

Hol·o·caine (häl′ə kān′, hō′lə-) [HOLO- + (CO)CAINE] *trademark for* PHENACAINE

hol·o·caust (häl′ə kôst′, hō′lə-) *n.* [ME. < OFr. *holocauste* < LL.(Ec.) *holocaustum*, a whole burnt offering < Gr. *holokauston* (neut. of *holokaustos*), burnt whole < *holos*, whole + *kaustos*, burnt: see CAUSTIC] **1.** an offering the whole of which is burned; burnt offering **2.** great or total destruction of life, esp. by fire

Hol·o·cene (-sēn′) *adj.* [HOLO- + -CENE] designating or of the Recent Epoch of geological time

ho·lc·crine (-krin, -krīn′, -krēn′) *adj.* [HOLO- + Gr. *krinein*, to separate: see CRISIS] designating or of a gland whose secretion results from the disintegration of the gland's cells

ho·lo·en·zyme (häl′ō en′zīm, hō′lō-) *n.* a complete enzyme, formed from an apoenzyme and a coenzyme

Hol·o·fer·nes (häl′ə fur′nēz) *Bible* the general of Nebuchadnezzar's army, killed by Judith to save her people: see JUDITH

ho·log·a·mous (hə läg′ə məs) *adj.* [HOLO- + -GAMOUS] having gametes essentially the same in size and form as other cells —**ho·log′a·my** (-mē) *n.*

hol·o·gram (häl′ə gram′, hō′lə-) *n.* a photographic plate containing the record of the interference pattern produced by means of holography

hol·o·graph (-graf′, -gräf′) *adj.* [Fr. *holographe* < LL. *holographus* < LGr. *holographos* < Gr. *holos*, whole (see HOLO-) + *graphein*, to write: see GRAPHIC] written entirely in the handwriting of the person under whose name it appears —*n.* a holograph document, letter, etc.

hol·o·graph·ic (häl′ə graf′ik, hō′lə-) *adj.* **1.** *same as* HOLOGRAPH **2.** of or having to do with holography

ho·log·ra·phy (hə läg′rə fē) *n.* [HOLO- + -GRAPHY] a lensless, photographic method that uses laser light to produce three-dimensional images by splitting the laser beam into two beams and recording on a photographic plate the minute interference patterns made by the reference light waves reflected directly from a mirror and the waves modulated when simultaneously reflected from the subject: the virtual image can be reconstructed by shining laser light, white light, etc. through the developed film

hol·o·he·dral (häl′ə hē′drəl, hō′lə-) *adj.* [HOLO- + -HEDRAL] having the full number of planes required for complete symmetry: said of a crystal

hol·o·me·tab·o·lism (-mə tab′ə liz′m) *n.* same as COMPLETE METAMORPHOSIS —**hol′o·me·tab′o·lous** *adj.*

hol·o·mor·phic (-môr′fik) *adj.* [HOLO- + -MORPHIC] having the two ends symmetrical in form: said of a crystal

hol·o·par·a·site (-par′ə sit′) *n.* an obligate parasite —**hol′o·par′a·sit′ic** (-sit′ik) *adj.*

hol·o·phras·tic (-fras′tik) *adj.* [< HOLO- + Gr. *phrastikos,* suited for expressing < *phrazein,* to speak] expressing an entire sentence or phrase in one word

hol·o·phyt·ic (-fit′ik) *adj.* [HOLO- + -PHYT(E) + -IC] obtaining nutrition by photosynthesis, as do green plants and some bacteria

hol·o·plank·ton (-plaŋk′tən) *n.* an organism which spends all stages of its life cycle as a member of the plankton community: cf. MEROPLANKTON

hol·o·thu·ri·an (-thoor′ē ən) *n.* [< L. *holothuria,* pl. < Gr. *holothouria,* pl. of *holothourion,* kind of water polyp] any of a class (Holothuroidea) of echinoderms with an elongated, flexible, wormlike body and a mouth surrounded by tentacles; sea cucumber: see TREPANG

hol·o·type (häl′ə tip′, hō′lə-) *n.* [HOLO- + TYPE] *Taxonomy* the single specimen chosen as the type of a new species or subspecies in the original description —**hol′o·typ′ic** (-tip′ik) *adj.*

hol·o·zo·ic (häl′ə zō′ik, hō′lə-) *adj.* [HOLO- + ZO- + -IC] ingesting and using complex organic material as food, as most animals

holp (hōlp) [ME. *holpe,* S dial. form of ff.] *archaic or dial. pt. & obs. pp.* of HELP

hol·pen (hōl′p′n) [ME.] *archaic or dial. pp.* of HELP

Hol·stein (hōl′stīn; *G.* hôl′shtīn; *for n., usually* hōl′stēn) region of N West Germany, formerly a duchy of Denmark: see SCHLESWIG-HOLSTEIN —*n.* ☆any of a breed of large, black-and-white cattle raised for both milk and beef: also **Hol′stein-Frie′sian** (-frē′zhən)

hol·ster (hōl′stər) *n.* [Du., akin to Goth. *hulistr,* a cover, ON. *hulstr,* a sheath, OE. *heolstor,* darkness, cover < IE. base *kel-,* to conceal (cf. HALL, HULL¹) + Gmc. noun suffix *-stra-*] a pistol case, usually of leather and attached to a belt or a saddle

holt (hōlt) *n.* [ME. < OE., akin to G. *holz,* wood < IE. *kldos* (< base *kel-,* to strike), whence Gr. *klados,* young sprout: cf. HILT] [Archaic] **1.** a small wood or grove **2.** a wooded hill

ho·lus-bo·lus (hō′ləs bō′ləs) *adv.* [mock-Latin < WHOLE + BOLUS] all at once; in one lump

ho·ly (hō′lē) *adj.* **-li·er, -li·est** [ME. *holie* < OE. *halig* (akin to G. *heilig*) < base of OE. *hal,* sound, whole, happy (cf. HALE¹, WHOLE): first used in OE. as transl. of L. *sacer, sanctus* in the Vulgate] [*often* H-] **1.** dedicated to religious use; belonging to or coming from God; consecrated **2.** spiritually perfect or pure; untainted by evil or sin; sinless; saintly **3.** regarded with or deserving deep respect, awe, reverence, or adoration ☆**4.** [Slang] very much of a: a generalized intensive [*a holy terror*] Often used in interjectional compounds to express astonishment, emphasis, etc. [*holy* cow! *holy* smoke!] —*n., pl.* **-lies** a holy thing or place

SYN.—holy suggests that which is held in deepest religious reverence or is basically associated with a religion and, in extended use, connotes spiritual purity [*the Holy Ghost, a holy love*]; **sacred** refers to that which is set apart as holy or is dedicated to some exalted purpose and, therefore, connotes inviolability [*Parnassus was sacred to Apollo, a sacred trust*]; **consecrated** and **hallowed** describe that which has been made sacred or holy, **consecrated,** in addition connoting solemn devotion or dedication [*a life consecrated to art*], and **hallowed,** inherent or intrinsic holiness [*hallowed ground*]; **divine** suggests that which is of the nature of, is associated with, or is derived from God or a god [*the divine right of kings*], and, in extended use, connotes supreme greatness [*the Divine Duse*] or, colloquially, great attractiveness —ANT. **profane, unholy**

Holy Alliance an alliance formed in 1815 by the rulers of Russia, Austria, and Prussia to suppress the democratic revolutionary movement in Europe

Holy Bible *same as* BIBLE

Holy City a city regarded as a sacred traditional center by the believers of a particular religion

Holy Communion any of various Christian rites in which bread and wine are consecrated and received as the body and blood of Jesus or as symbols of them; sacrament of the Eucharist, or the Lord's Supper

Holy Cross, Mount of the peak in WC Colo.: snow-filled crevices on it form a large cross: 13,996 ft.

holy day a day consecrated to religious observances or to a religious festival

holy day of obligation any of certain major religious festivals on which Roman Catholics are obliged to attend Mass and to abstain from nonessential manual labor

Holy Father a title of the Pope

Holy Ghost [ME. *haligast,* transl. of LL.(Ec.) *Spiritus sanctus*] the third person of the Trinity

Holy Grail *see* GRAIL

Holy Innocents' Day December 28, the day commemorating the slaughter of the children by Herod: Matt. 2:16

Holy Land *same as* PALESTINE (sense 1)

Holy Mother Mary, mother of Jesus

Holy Office *R.C.Ch. former name for* a tribunal for the protection of faith and morals, the suppression of heresy, etc.: cf. INQUISITION

holy of holies [transl. of Heb. *qōdesh haqadōshīm*] **1.** the innermost part of the Jewish tabernacle and Temple, where the ark of the covenant was kept **2.** any most sacred place

Hol·yoke (hōl′yōk) [after Rev. Edward *Holyoke* (1689–1769), president of Harvard] city in SW Mass., on the Connecticut River: pop. 50,000: see SPRINGFIELD

holy orders **1.** the sacrament or rite of ordination **2.** the position of being an ordained Christian minister or priest **3.** ranks or grades of the Christian ministry; specif., *a) R.C.Ch. same as* MAJOR ORDERS or, sometimes, MINOR ORDERS *b) Anglican Ch.* bishops, priests, and deacons —**take holy orders** to be ordained as a Christian minister or priest

☆**Holy Roller** a member of a minor religious sect that expresses religious emotion by shouting and moving about during services of worship: generally an offensive term

Holy Roman Empire empire of WC Europe, comprising the German-speaking peoples & N Italy: begun in 800 A.D. with the papal crowning of Charlemagne or, in an alternate view, with the crowning of Otto I in 962, it lasted until Francis II (of Austria) resigned the title in 1806

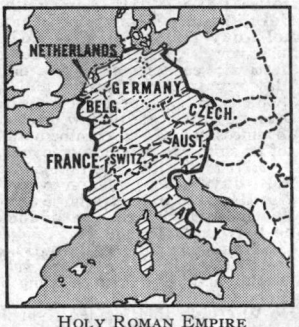

HOLY ROMAN EMPIRE (12th cent.)

Holy Rood [*sometimes* h- r-] **1.** the cross on which Jesus was crucified **2.** any cross or crucifix symbolizing Christianity, as on a rood screen

Holy Saturday the Saturday before Easter

Holy Scripture (or **Scriptures**) the Bible: among Jews, the Pentateuch, the Prophets, and the Hagiographa; among Christians, the Old and New Testaments

Holy See the position, authority, or court of the Pope; Apostolic See

Holy Spirit the spirit of God; specif., the third person of the Trinity

ho·ly·stone (-stōn′) *n.* [< ?] a large, flat piece of sandstone used for scouring a ship's wooden decks —*vt.* **-stoned′, -ston′ing** to scour with a holystone

Holy Synod the administrative council of any branch of the Orthodox Eastern Church

Holy Thursday *same as:* **1.** MAUNDY THURSDAY **2.** ASCENSION DAY

ho·ly·tide (-tīd′) *n.* [HOLY + TIDE¹] [Archaic] a holy season; day or period of religious observance

holy water water blessed by a priest

Holy Week the week before Easter

Holy Writ the Bible

hom- (hōm, häm) *same as* HOMO-: used before a vowel

hom·age (häm′ij, äm′-) *n.* [ME. < OFr. *hommage* < ML. *hominaticum,* vassal's service, homage < L. *homo,* a man < IE. *ĝhom-* < base *ĝhthem-,* earth, ground, whence L. *humus,* Gr. *chthōn,* earth, OE. *guma,* man] **1.** orig., *a)* a public avowal of allegiance by a vassal to his lord *b)* an act done or thing given to show the relationship between lord and vassal **2.** anything given or done to show reverence, honor, or respect: usually with *do* or *pay* [to pay *homage* to a hero] —SYN. see ALLEGIANCE, HONOR

hom·ag·er (-ij ər) *n.* a person who does homage, esp. as a vassal

hom·a·lo·graph·ic (häm′ə lə graf′ik) *adj. same as* HOMOLOGRAPHIC

☆**hom·bre** (äm′brā, -brē) *n.* [Sp. < L. *homo,* man: see HOMAGE] [Slang] a man; fellow

hom·bre² (äm′bər) *n. same as* OMBER

hom·burg (häm′bərg) *n.* [< *Homburg,* Prussia, where first made] a man's felt hat with a crown dented front to back and a brim, slightly curved brim

home (hōm) *n.* [ME. < OE. *ham,* akin to G. *heim* < IE. base *kei-,* to lie, homestead, whence Gr. *keimai,* to lie down, rest, L. *civis,* townsman, HIDE³, ON. *heimr,* home: basic sense "place where one lies; dwelling"] **1.** the place where a person (or family) lives; one's dwelling place; specif., *a)* the house, apartment, etc. where one lives or is

living temporarily; living quarters *b*) the region, city, state, etc. where one lives **2.** the place where one was born or reared; one's own city, state, or country **3.** a place thought of as home; specif., *a*) a place where one likes to be; restful or congenial place *b*) the grave **4.** the members of a family as a unit; a household and its affairs *[homes* broken up by divorce*]* **5.** an institution for the care of orphans, people who are old or helpless, etc. **6.** *a*) the place that is the natural environment of an animal, plant, etc. *b*) the place where something is or has been originated, developed, etc. *[Paris is the home of fashion]* **7.** in many games, the base or goal; esp., the home plate in baseball —*adj.* **1.** of home or a home; specif., *a*) of the family, household, etc.; domestic *b*) of one's country, government, etc.; domestic: opposed to FOREIGN *c*) of or at the center of activity or headquarters *[home* office*]* **2.** reaching its goal; effective; forceful; to the point **3.** played in the city, at the school, etc. where the team originates *[a home* game*]* —*adv.* [orig. the *n.* as acc. of direction] **1.** at, to, or in the direction of home or a home **2.** to the place where it must ultimately go; to the point aimed at *[to* drive a nail *home]* **3.** to the center or heart of a matter; closely; directly; deeply —*vi.* homed, hom'ing **1.** to go or return to one's home **2.** to have a home —*vt.* to send to, put into, or provide with a home —**at home 1.** in one's own house, neighborhood, city, or country **2.** as if in one's own home; comfortable; at ease; familiar **3.** willing to receive visitors —**bring (something) home to 1.** to impress upon or make clear to **2.** to fasten the blame for (something) on (someone) —**come home 1.** to return, as to one's home **2.** *Naut.* to fail to hold, as an anchor —**home free** [Slang] beyond the point of doubt in approaching success or victory —**home in on** to direct, or be directed as by radar, to (a destination or target) —**home'less** *adj.*

☆**home·bod·y** (-bäd'ē) *n., pl.* -**bod'ies** a person mainly concerned with affairs of the home, or one who prefers to stay at home

home·bound (-bound') *adj.* **1.** going home **2.** confined to the home

home·bred (-bred') *adj.* **1.** bred or reared at home; domestic; native **2.** not cultivated, polished, or sophisticated; crude

home·brew (-brōō') *n.* an alcoholic beverage, esp. beer, made at home

home·com·ing (-kum'iŋ) *n.* **1.** a coming or returning to one's home ☆**2.** in many colleges and universities, an annual celebration attended by alumni

☆**home economics** the science and art of homemaking, including nutrition, clothing, budgeting, and child care

home-grown (-grōn') *adj.* grown at home or for local consumption: said of fruits and vegetables

home·land (-land') *n.* the country in which one was born or makes one's home

home·like (-līk') *adj.* having qualities associated with home; comfortable, familiar, cozy, etc.

home·ly (-lē) *adj.* -**li·er**, -**li·est** [ME. *homli*] **1.** orig., *a*) of the home; domestic *b*) same as HOMELIKE **2.** *a*) characteristic of or suitable for home or home life; simple and unpretentious or plain and everyday *[homely* virtues*]* *b*) not elegant or polished; crude **3.** not good-looking or handsome; plain or unattractive —**home'li·ness** *n.*

home·made (-mād') *adj.* **1.** made at home or on the premises **2.** as if made at home; esp., plain, simple, or crude

home·mak·er (-māk'ər) *n.* a person who manages a home; esp., a housewife —**home'mak'ing** *n.*

ho·me·o- (hō'mē ə, häm'-) [Gr. *homoio-* < *homos*, same: for IE. base see SAME] *a combining form meaning* like, the same, similar *[homeomorphism]*

Home Office the department of government in Great Britain corresponding to the Department of the Interior in the U.S.

ho·me·o·mor·phism (hō'mē ə môr'fiz'm, häm'ē ə-) *n.* [HOMEO- + -MORPH + -ISM] similarity in structure and form; esp., a close similarity of crystalline forms between substances of different chemical composition —**ho'me·o·mor'phous** (-fəs) *adj.*

ho·me·o·path (hō'mē ə path', häm'ē ə-) *n.* a person who practices or accepts the principles of homeopathy: also **ho'me·op'a·thist** (-äp'ə thist)

ho·me·op·a·thy (hō'mē äp'ə thē, häm'ē-) *n.* [G. *homöopathie*, lit., likeness of feeling (see HOMEO- & -PATHY): coined c. 1800 by S. Hahnemann (1755–1843), Ger. physician] a system of medical treatment based on the theory that certain diseases can be cured by giving very small doses of drugs which in a healthy person and in large doses would produce symptoms like those of the disease: opposed to ALLOPATHY —**ho'me·o·path'ic** (-ə path'ik) *adj.*

☆**ho·me·o·sta·sis** (hō'mē ō stā'sis, häm'ē-) *n.* [ModL.: see HOMEO- & STASIS] **1.** *Physiol.* the tendency to maintain, or the maintenance of, normal, internal stability in an organism by coordinated responses of the organ systems that automatically compensate for environmental changes **2.**

any analogous maintenance of stability or equilibrium, as within a social group —**ho'me·o·stat'ic** (-stat'ik) *adj.*

ho·me·o·ther·mal (-thur'məl) *adj. same as* HOMOIOTHER-MAL

ho·me·o·typ·ic (-tip'ik) *adj.* [HOMEO- + TYPIC] designating the second division of the nuclei of germ cells in meiosis

home·own·er (hōm'ō'nər) *n.* a person who owns the house he lives in

☆**home plate** *Baseball* the five-sided slab that the batter stands beside, across which the pitcher must throw the ball for a strike: it is the last of the four bases that a runner must touch in succession to score a run

Ho·mer (hō'mər) [L. *Homerus* < Gr. *Homēros* < *homēros*, a pledge, hostage, one led, hence blind] **1.** a masculine name **2.** semilegendary Gr. epic poet of c. 8th cent. B.C.: the *Iliad* & the *Odyssey* are both attributed to him **3.** Winslow, 1836–1910; U.S. painter

ho·mer[1] (hō'mər) *n.* [Heb. *hōmer*, homer, mound < *hāmar*, to surge up, swell up] **1.** an early Hebrew unit of dry measure, equal to about 6 1/4 bushels **2.** an early Hebrew unit of liquid measure equal to about 58 gallons

hom·er[2] (hō'mər) *n.* [Colloq.] ☆**1.** *Baseball same as* HOME RUN **2.** *same as* HOMING PIGEON —☆*vi.* [Colloq.] to hit a home run

home range *Ecol.* the area within which an animal normally ranges in the course of a day or a season

Ho·mer·ic (hō mer'ik) *adj.* of, like, or characteristic of the poet Homer, his poems, or the Greek civilization that they describe (c. 1200–800 B.C.): also **Ho·mer'i·cal**

Homeric laughter loud, unrestrained laughter

☆**home·room** (hōm'rōōm') *n.* **1.** the room where a class in school meets every day to be checked for attendance, receive school bulletins, etc. **2.** the students in a specific homeroom Also **home room**

home rule the administration of the internal affairs of a country, colony, district, city, etc. granted to the citizens who live in it by a superior governing authority or state; local self-government

☆**home run** *Baseball* a safe hit that allows the batter to touch all bases and score a run

home·sick (-sik') *adj.* [back-formation < *homesickness*, 18th-c. rendering of G. *heimweh*] unhappy or depressed at being away from home and family; longing for home **home'sick'ness** *n.*

home·spun (-spun') *n.* **1.** cloth made of yarn spun at home **2.** coarse, loosely woven cloth like this —*adj.* **1.** spun or made at home **2.** made of homespun **3.** plain; unpretentious; homely *[homespun* virtues*]*

home·stead (-sted') *n.* [OE. *hamstede*: see HOME & STEAD] ☆**1.** a place where a family makes its home, including the land, house, and outbuildings **2.** *Law* such a place occupied by the owner and his family and exempted from seizure or forced sale to meet general debts ☆**3.** a tract of public land (160 acres by the **Homestead Act** of 1862) granted by the U.S. government to a settler to be developed as a farm —☆*vi.* to become a settler on a homestead —☆*vt.* to settle on as a homestead

☆**home·stead·er** (-sted'ər) *n.* **1.** a person who has a homestead **2.** a settler who holds a homestead granted by the U.S. government

☆**homestead law 1.** a law exempting a homestead from seizure or forced sale to meet general debts **2.** any law granting to settlers tracts of public land to be developed as farms **3.** in certain States, any of various laws granting specific privileges or tax exemptions to owners of homesteads

☆**home·stretch** (-strech') *n.* **1.** the part of a race track between the last turn and the finish line **2.** the final part of any undertaking

home·ward (-wərd) *adv., adj.* [ME. *hamward* < OE. *hamweard*] toward home: also **home'wards** *adv.*

home·work (-wurk') *n.* **1.** work, esp. piecework, done at home **2.** lessons to be studied or school work to be done outside the classroom

home·y (-ē) *adj.* **hom'i·er, hom'i·est** having qualities usually associated with home; comfortable, familiar, cozy, etc. —**home'y·ness** *n.*

hom·i·ci·dal (häm'ə sīd'l, hō'mə-) *adj.* **1.** of, having the nature of, or characterized by homicide **2.** having a tendency to homicide; murderous —**hom'i·ci'dal·ly** *adv.*

hom·i·cide (häm'ə sid', hō'mə-) *n.* **1.** [ME. < OFr. < LL. *homicidium*, manslaughter, murder < L. *homicida*, murderer < *homo*, a man (see HOMAGE) + *caedere*, to cut, kill < IE. base *(s)k(h)ai-*, to strike, whence MDu. *heien*, to strike, ram] any killing of one human being by another: cf. MURDER, MANSLAUGHTER **2.** [ME. < OFr. < L. *homicida*] a person who kills another

hom·i·let·ic (häm'ə let'ik) *adj.* [LL.(Ec.) *homileticus* < Gr. *homilētikos*, of or for conversation < *homilein*, to be in company, converse < *homilos*: see HOMILY] **1.** having the nature of or characteristic of a homily **2.** of homiletics Also **hom'i·let'i·cal** —**hom'i·let'i·cal·ly** *adv.*

hom·i·let·ics (-iks) *n.pl.* [*with sing. v.*] [< prec.] the branch of theology dealing with the writing and preaching of sermons

---

fat, āpe, cär; ten, ēven; is, bīte; gō, hôrn, tōōl, look; oil, out; up, fur; get; joy; yet; chin; she; thin, *then*; zh, leisure; ŋ, ring; ə for *a* in *ago*, *e* in *agent*, *i* in *sanity*, *o* in *comply*, *u* in *focus*; ' as in *able* (ā'b'l); Fr. bāl; ë, Fr. coeur; ö, Fr. feu; ô, Fr. mon; ō̃, Fr. coq; ü, Fr. duc; r, Fr. cri; H, G. ich; kh, G. doch. See inside front cover. ☆ Americanism; ‡foreign; *hypothetical; < derived from

hom·i·list (häm'ə list) *n.* a person who writes or delivers homilies

hom·i·ly (-lē) *n., pl.* **-lies** [ME. *omelye* < OFr. *omelie* < LL.(Ec.) *homilia*, sermon < Gr. *homilia*, converse, instruction (in LGr.(Ec.), sermon) < *homilos*, assembly, prob. < *homou*, together + *ilē*, a crowd] **1.** a sermon, esp. one about something in the Bible **2.** a solemn, moralizing talk or writing, esp. a long, dull one

hom·ing (hō'miŋ) *adj.* **1.** going home; homeward bound **2.** having to do with guidance homeward or to a goal, target, etc.

homing pigeon a pigeon trained to find its way home from distant places: see CARRIER PIGEON

hom·i·nid (häm'ə nid) *n.* [< ModL. *Hominidae* < L. *homo* (gen. *hominis*: cf. HOMAGE) + *-idae, -IDAE*] any of a family (Hominidae) of two-legged primates including all forms of man, extinct and living —*adj.* designating or of this family

hom·i·noid (-noid) *n.* [< ModL. *Hominoidea*: see HOMO¹ & -OIDEA] any of a superfamily (Hominoidea) of primates that includes the manlike apes and all forms of man —*adj.* of or like man; manlike

☆**hom·i·ny** (häm'ə nē) *n.* [contr. < *rockahominy* < AmInd. (Algonquian), as in Virginian *rokahamen*, meal from parched corn] dry corn (maize) with the hull and germ removed and often coarsely ground (**hominy grits**): it is boiled for food

ho·mo¹ (hō'mō) *n., pl.* **hom·in·es** (häm'ə nēz') [L.: see HOMAGE] any of a genus (*Homo*) of primates comprising modern man (*Homo sapiens*) and several extinct species of man (*Homo habilis, Homo erectus,* etc.)

ho·mo² (hō'mō) *n., pl.* **-mos** [Slang] *short for* HOMOSEXUAL

ho·mo- (hō'mə, häm'ə) [Gr. *homo-* < *homos,* SAME] *a combining form meaning* same, equal, like [*homogenize, homograph*]

ho·mo·cen·tric (hō'mə sen'trik, häm'ə-) *adj.* [ModL. *homocentricus:* see HOMO- & -CENTRIC] having the same center

ho·mo·cer·cal (-sur'k'l) *adj.* [< HOMO- + Gr. *kerkos,* a tail + -AL] designating, of, or having a tail fin in which the upper and lower lobes are symmetrical and in which the spine is shortened and ends at or near the center of the base, as in most bony fishes

ho·mo·chro·mat·ic (-krō mat'ik) *adj.* [HOMO- + CHROMATIC] of, having, or consisting of a single color: also **ho'mo·chro'mous** (-krō'məs)

ho·moe·cious (hō mē'shəs) *adj.* [< HOMO- + Gr. *oikos,* house (see ECONOMY) + -OUS] designating or of parasites that spend their entire life cycle on one species of host

ho·mo·e·o- (hō'mē ə, häm'ē ə) *same as* HOMEO-

ho·mo·erot·i·cism (hō'mō i rät'ə siz'm) *n.* [HOMO- + EROTICISM] *same as* HOMOSEXUALITY —**ho'mo·e·rot'ic** *adj.*

ho·mog·a·my (hō mäg'ə mē) *n.* [G. *homogamie:* see HOMO- & -GAMY] **1.** the condition of having all flowers sexually alike **2.** the condition of having stamens and pistils mature at the same time **3.** interbreeding and inbreeding in an isolated group of individuals of the same species —**ho'mog'a·mous** (-məs) *adj.*

☆**ho·mog·e·nate** (hə mäj'ə nāt') *n.* a substance produced by homogenizing

ho·mo·ge·ne·ous (hō'mə jē'nē əs, häm'ə-; -jēn'yəs) *adj.* [ML. *homogeneus* < Gr. *homogenēs,* of the same race or kind: see HOMO- & GENUS] **1.** the same in structure, quality, etc.; similar or identical **2.** composed of similar or identical elements or parts; uniform **3.** *same as* HOMOGENOUS **4.** *Math. a)* of the same kind *b)* having all terms of the same dimensions —**ho'mo·ge·ne'i·ty** (-jə nē'ə tē) *n.* —**ho'mo·ge'ne·ous·ly** *adv.* —**ho'mo·ge'ne·ous·ness** *n.*

ho·mog·e·nize (hə mäj'ə nīz') *vt.* **-nized', -niz'ing** **1.** to make homogeneous **2.** to make more uniform throughout in texture, mixture, quality, etc. by breaking down and blending the particles; specif., ☆to process (milk) so that the fat particles are so finely divided and emulsified that the cream does not separate on standing —**ho·mog'e·ni·za'tion** *n.*

ho·mog·e·nous (-ə nəs) *adj.* [HOMO- + -GENOUS] having similarity in structure because of common descent —**ho·mog'e·ny** (-nē) *n.*

ho·mog·o·ny (hō mäg'ə nē) *n.* [HOMO- + -GONY] *same as* HOMOSTYLY —**ho·mog'o·nous** (-nəs) *adj.*

ho·mo·graft (hō'mə graft', häm'ə-; -gräft') *n.* a graft of skin, bone, etc. taken from an individual of the same species

hom·o·graph (häm'ə graf', hō'mə-; -gräf') *n.* [HOMO- + -GRAPH] a word with the same spelling as another but with a different meaning and origin (Ex.: *bow,* the front part of a ship, *bow,* to bend) —**hom'o·graph'ic** *adj.*

ho·moi·o- (hō moi'ō) *same as* HOMEO-

ho·moi·o·ther·mal (hō moi'ō thur'məl) *n.* [HOMOIO- + THERMAL] *Zool.* warmblooded: also **ho·moi'o·ther'mic**

Ho·moi·ou·si·an (hō'moi ōō'sē ən, -zē-) *n.* [LGr.(Ec.) *homoiousios,* of like substance < *homoios,* like + *ousia,* essence < *ōn,* being: see ONTO-] *Theol.* designating, of, or holding the theory that God the Father and God the Son are neither identical nor different in substance, but similar —*n.* an adherent of this theory

ho·mo·lec·i·thal (hō'mō les'i thəl) *adj.* [HOMO- + LECITH(IN) + -AL] having the yolk small in amount and more or less evenly distributed, as in mammal eggs

ho·mol·o·gate (hō mäl'ə gāt') *vt.* **-gat'ed, -gat'ing** [< ML. *homologatus,* pp. of *homologare* < Gr. *homologein,* to agree, assent < *homos,* SAME + *legein,* say: see LOGIC] **1.** to approve or countenance **2.** *Civil Law* to confirm officially, as by a court of justice —*vi.* [Rare] to agree —**ho·mol'o·ga'tion** *n.*

ho·mo·log·i·cal (hō'mə läj'i k'l, häm'ə-) *adj. same as* HOMOLOGOUS —**ho'mo·log'i·cal·ly** *adv.*

ho·mol·o·gize (hō mäl'ə jīz', hə-) *vt.* **-gized', -giz'ing** **1.** to make homologous **2.** to demonstrate homology in —*vi.* to be homologous

ho·mol·o·gous (-ə gəs) *adj.* [Gr. *homologos,* agreeing: cf. HOMOLOGATE] **1.** corresponding in structure, position, character, etc.: opposed to HETEROLOGOUS **2.** *Biol.* corresponding in basic type of structure and deriving from a common primitive origin [the wing of a bat and the foreleg of a mouse are *homologous*] **3.** *Chem. a)* designating or of a series of compounds each member of which has a structure differing regularly by some increment (as a CH₂ group) from that of the adjacent members *b)* having this relation with another or other compounds of such a series *c)* designating or of a series of elements in the same group or period of the periodic table, as the halogens, actinides, etc. **4.** *Immunology* having the relationship of a serum and the bacterium from which it is made **5.** *Med. same as* HOMOPLASTIC (sense 2)

hom·o·lo·graph·ic (häm'ə lə graf'ik) *adj.* [altered (after HOMO-) < *homalographic* < Gr. *homalos,* even, level (akin to *homos,* SAME) + -GRAPHIC] keeping the parts in proper relative size and form

homolographic projection an equal-area map projection

hom·o·logue, hom·o·log (häm'ə lôg', hō'mə-; -läg') *n.* [Fr. < Gr. *homologos*] a homologous part, thing, organ, etc.

ho·mol·o·gy (hō mäl'ə jē, hə-) *n., pl.* **-gies** [LL. *homologia* < Gr.: see HOMO- & -LOGY] **1.** the quality or state of being homologous **2.** a homologous correspondence or relationship, as of animal organs, chemical compounds, etc.

ho·mol·o·sine projection (hə mäl'ə sin, hō-; -sīn') [< Gr. *homalos* (akin to *homos,* SAME) + SINE] a map of the earth's surface combining certain features of homolographic and sinusoidal projections so as to allow a minimum of distortion for the continents

HOMOLOSINE PROJECTION

ho·mo·mor·phism (hō'mə môr'fiz'm, häm'ə-) *n.* [HOMO- + -MORPH + -ISM] **1.** similarity in form **2.** *Biol.* resemblance or similarity, without actual relationship, in structure or origin: said of organs or organisms **3.** *Bot.* uniformity in shape or size, as of pistils and stamens **4.** *Zool.* similarity between an insect's larva and its matured form Also **ho'mo·mor'phy** —**ho'mo·mor'phic, ho'mo·mor'phous** *adj.*

hom·o·nym (häm'ə nim, hō'mə-) *n.* [Fr. *homonyme* < L. *homonymus* < Gr. *homōnymos,* having the same name < *homos,* SAME + *onyma,* NAME] **1.** a word with the same pronunciation as another but with a different meaning, origin, and, usually, spelling (Ex.: *bore* and *boar*); homophone **2.** loosely, a homograph **3.** either of two people with the same name; namesake **4.** *Biol.* a name for a genus, species, etc. unsuitable because it has already been used for another taxonomic classification —**hom'o·nym'ic** *adj.*

ho·mon·y·mous (hō män'ə məs) *adj.* **1.** of, or having the nature of, a homonym **2.** having the same name —**ho·mon'y·my** (-mē) *n.*

Ho·mo·ou·si·an (hō'mō ōō'sē ən) *adj.* [LL.(Ec.) *homoousianus* < LGr.(Ec.) *homoousios,* consubstantial < *homos,* SAME + *ousia,* essence (see HOMOIOUSIAN)] *Theol.* designating, of, or holding the theory that God the Father and God the Son are identical in substance —*n.* an adherent of this theory

ho·mo·phile (hō'mō fīl', häm'ə-) *n., adj.* [HOMO- + -PHILE] *same as* HOMOSEXUAL

hom·o·phone (häm'ə fōn') *n.* [< Gr. *homophōnos:* see HOMOPHONIC] **1.** any of two or more letters or groups of letters having the same pronunciation (Ex.: *c* in *civil* and *s* in *song*) **2.** *same as* HOMONYM (sense 1) —**ho·moph·o·nous** (hō mäf'ə nəs) *adj.*

hom·o·phon·ic (häm'ə fän'ik, hō'mə-) *adj.* [< Gr. *homophōnos,* of the same sound (< *homos,* SAME + *phōnē,* sound: see PHONE¹) + -IC] **1.** *Music a)* formerly, having the same pitch; in unison *b)* having a single part, or voice, carrying the melody; monodic; monophonic **2.** *same as* HOMONYMOUS —**ho·moph·o·ny** (hō mäf'ə nē) *n., pl.* **-nies**

ho·mo·plas·tic (hō'mə plas'tik, häm'ə-) *adj.* [HOMO- + -PLASTIC] **1.** of or having to do with homoplasy **2.** derived from a member of the same species, as a graft —**ho'mo·plas'ti·cal·ly** *adv.*

ho·mo·pla·sy (hō'mə plas'ē, -plā'sē; hō mäp'lə sē) *n.* [HOMO- + -PLASY] *same as* ANALOGY (sense 3)

ho·mop·ter·an (hō mäp'tər ən) *adj. same as* HOMOPTEROUS —*n.* a homopterous insect

ho·mop·ter·ous (-əs) *adj.* [HOMO- + -PTEROUS] belonging to an order (Homoptera) of insects with sucking mouth-

parts and two pairs of membranous wings of uniform thickness throughout, as aphids, cicadas, scale insects, etc.

Ho·mo sa·pi·ens (hō′mō sā′pē enz′, sap′ē enz) [ModL.: see HOMO[1] & SAPIENT] modern man; mankind; human being: the scientific name for the only living species of the genus *Homo*

ho·mo·sex·u·al (hō′mə sek′shoo wəl) *adj.* of or characterized by sexual desire for those of the same sex as oneself —*n.* a homosexual individual —**ho′mo·sex′u·al′i·ty** (-wal′ə tē) *n.* —**ho′mo·sex′u·al·ly** *adv.*

ho·mo·sphere (hō′mə sfir′) *n.* the lower of two divisions of the earth's atmosphere, extending to a height of c. 55 mi. and maintaining a relatively constant composition: cf. HETEROSPHERE —**ho′mo·spher′ic** (-sfer′ik) *adj.*

ho·mos·po·rous (hō mäs′pər əs, hō′mə spôr′əs) *adj.* *Bot.* producing only one kind of spore

ho·mo·sty·ly (hō′mō sti′lē) *n.* [HOMO- + STYL(E) + -Y[3]] the condition in which flowers of the same species have styles of equal length —**ho′mo·sty′lous** *adj.*

ho·mo·tax·is (hō′mō tak′sis, häm′ə-) *n.* [ModL. < HOMO- + -TAXIS] *Geol.* a similarity in the arrangement of layers, or in the fossil content, between strata of different regions not necessarily formed at the same time —**ho′mo·tax′i·al** (-tak′sē əl) *adj.*

ho·mo·thal·lic (-thal′ik) *adj.* [HOMO- + THALL(US) + -IC] designating or possessing a mycelium that produces two kinds of cells which function as male and female —**ho′mo·thal′lism** *n.*

ho·mo·ther·mal (-thur′məl) *adj.* same as HOMOIOTHERMAL: also **ho′mo·ther′mic**

ho·mo·trans·plant (-trans′plant) *n.* same as HOMOGRAFT —**ho′mo·trans′plan·ta′tion** *n.*

ho·mo·zy·go·sis (-zī gō′sis) *n.* [ModL. < HOMO- + ZYGOSIS] **1.** the condition of being a homozygote **2.** the production of a homozygote for any one pair or for several pairs of genes —**ho′mo·zy·got′ic** (-gät′ik) *adj.*

ho·mo·zy·gote (-zī′gōt) *n.* [HOMO- + ZYGOTE] a plant or animal having two identical alleles at a single locus on a chromosome, and hence breeding true to type for the particular character involved; purebred —**ho′mo·zy′gous** (-zī′gəs) *adj.*

Homs (hôms) city in W Syria: pop. 164,000

ho·mun·cu·lus (hō mun′kyoo ləs) *n.*, *pl.* **-li** (-lī′) [L., dim. of *homo*, man: see HOMAGE] a little man; dwarf; manikin

hom·y (hō′mē) *adj.* **hom′i·er**, **hom′i·est** same as HOMEY —**hom′i·ness** *n.*

Hon., hon. 1. honorable **2.** honorary

Ho·nan (hō′nän′) province of EC China: 64,479 sq. mi.; pop. 48,670,000; cap. Chengchow

Hond. Honduras

Hon·du·ras (hän door′əs, -dyoor′-) country in Central America, with coast lines on the Pacific & the Caribbean: 43,227 sq. mi.; pop. 2,363,000; cap. Tegucigalpa —**Hon·du′ran** *adj., n.*

hone[1] (hōn) *n.* [ME. < OE. *han*, a stone, akin to ON. *hein*, a hone < IE. base *kōi-*, to sharpen, whet, whence L. *cos*, whetstone, *cotes*, sharp rock, Gr. *kōnos*, cone] a fine-grained, hard stone used to sharpen cutting tools, esp. razors —*vt.* **honed**, **hon′ing 1.** to sharpen with or as with a hone **2.** *Mech.* to enlarge or smooth (a bore) to exact specifications with a rotating stick (**honing stone**) containing abrasive material —**hon′er** *n.*

hone[2] (hōn) *vi.* **honed**, **hon′ing** [ME. *honen* < ONormFr. *honer* < OFr. *hogner*, to mutter, murmur] [Dial.] **1.** to yearn; long **2.** to grumble; moan

Ho·neg·ger (hän′ə gər, hō′neg ər; *Fr.* ô ne ger′), **Arthur** 1892–1955; Swiss composer in France

hon·est (än′əst) *adj.* [ME. < OFr. *honeste* < L. *honestus* < *honor*, honor] **1.** orig., *a*) held in respect; honorable *b*) respectable, creditable, commendable, seemly, etc.: a generalized epithet of commendation **2.** that will not lie, cheat, or steal; truthful; trustworthy **3.** *a*) showing fairness and sincerity; straightforward; free from deceit [an *honest* effort] *b*) gained or earned by fair methods, not by cheating, lying, or stealing [an *honest* living] **4.** being what it seems; genuine; pure [to give *honest* measure] **5.** frank and open [an *honest* face] **6.** [Archaic] virtuous; chaste —*adv.* [Colloq.] honestly; truly: an intensive —*SYN.* see UPRIGHT

hon·est·ly (-lē) *adv.* **1.** in an honest manner **2.** truly; really: used as an intensive [*honestly*, it is so]

hon·es·ty (än′əs tē) *n.* [ME. *honeste* < OFr. *honesté* < L. *honestas* < *honestus*] **1.** the state or quality of being honest; specif., *a*) orig., honor *b*) a refraining from lying, cheating, or stealing; a being truthful, trustworthy, or upright *c*) sincerity; fairness; straightforwardness *d*) [Archaic] chastity **2.** any of a genus (*Lunaria*) of plants of the mustard family, with purple flowers and large, flat, oval pods; esp., a plant (*Lunaria annua*) whose pods are used in winter bouquets

SYN.—**honesty**, the most general of these terms, implies freedom from lying, stealing, cheating, etc. [*honesty* is the best policy/; **honor** implies faithful adherence to the moral or ethical principles that are expected of one in his social class, profession, position, etc. [*honor* among thieves/; **integrity** implies an incorruptible soundness of moral character, esp. as displayed in fulfilling trusts [elect men of *integrity*/; **probity** suggests honesty or rectitude that is tried and proved; **veracity** specifically stresses honesty as displayed in habitual truthfulness [a witness of unquestioned *veracity*] —*ANT.* dishonesty, deceitfulness

hone·wort (hōn′wurt′) *n.* [obs. *hone*, a swelling < WORT[2]: formerly used to treat such swellings] a perennial weed (*Cryptotaenia canadensis*) of the parsley family, with small, white flowers, found in shady places in the E U.S.

hon·ey (hun′ē) *n.*, *pl.* **-eys** [ME. *honi*, *hunig* < OE. *hunig*, akin to G. *honig* (OHG. *honang*) < IE. base **kenekó-*, honey-yellow, whence Sans. *kāñcana-*, golden] **1.** a thick, sweet, syrupy substance that bees make as food from the nectar of flowers and store in honeycombs **2.** *a*) anything like honey in texture, color, etc. *b*) sweet quality; sweetness **3.** sweet one; darling; dear: often a term of affectionate address **4.** [Colloq.] something pleasing or excellent of its kind [a *honey* of an idea] —*adj.* **1.** of or like honey **2.** sweet; dear —*vt.* **-eyed** or **-ied**, **-ey·ing 1.** to make sweet or pleasant as with honey **2.** to speak sweetly or lovingly to **3.** to flatter —*vi.* to speak sweetly or lovingly; be very affectionate, attentive, or coaxing

honey bear *a popular name for: a*) KINKAJOU *b*) SLOTH BEAR

hon·ey·bee (-bē) *n.* a bee that makes honey; esp., the common hive bee (*Apis mellifera*)

☆**hon·ey·bunch** (-bunch′) *n.* [Colloq.] darling; dear: often used in affectionate address: also **hon′ey·bun′**

hon·ey·comb (-kōm′) *n.* [ME. *hunicomb* < OE. *hunigcamb* < *hunig*, HONEY + *camb*, COMB[1]] **1.** the structure of six-sided wax cells made by bees to hold their honey, eggs, etc. **2.** anything like this in structure or appearance —*vt.* **1.** to fill with holes like a honeycomb; riddle **2.** to permeate or undermine [*honeycombed* with intrigue] —*vi.* to become full of holes like a honeycomb —*adj.* of, like, or patterned after a honeycomb: also **hon′ey·combed′**

honey creeper 1. any of several bright-colored, insect-eating, Hawaiian singing birds (family Drepaniidae) **2.** any of a family (Coerebidae) of small, slender-billed birds of tropical America that feed on nectar and fruits

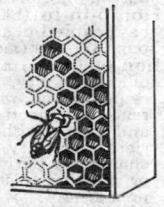

HONEYCOMB

hon·ey·dew (-dōō′, -dyōō′) *n.* **1.** a sweet fluid, as manna, exuded from various plants **2.** a sweet substance secreted by aphids and other juice-sucking plant insects, and sometimes by a fungus ☆**3.** short for HONEYDEW MELON

☆**honeydew melon** a variety of melon with a smooth, whitish rind and very sweet, greenish flesh

honey eater any of a large family (Meliphagidae) of Australasian birds with a long, brushlike tongue that can be protruded to catch insects or draw nectar from flowers

hon·ey·eyed (hun′ēd) *adj.* [ME. *honyede*] **1.** sweetened, covered, or filled with honey **2.** sweet as honey; flattering or affectionate [*honeyed* words]

honey guide any of a family (Indicatoridae) of small, heavily built, drab-colored birds of Africa, Asia, and the East Indies: they are said to lead men and animals to bees' nests in order to eat the grubs when the honeycombs are taken

☆**honey locust** a N. American tree (*Gleditsia triacanthos*) of the legume family, with strong, thorny branches, featherlike foliage, and large, twisted pods containing beanlike seeds and a sweet pulp

hon·ey·moon (hun′ē mōōn′) *n.* [as if < HONEY + MOON (? in reference to the waning of the affection of newlyweds), but ? folk-etym. for ON. *hjūnōttsmānathr*, lit., wedding-night month] **1.** formerly, the first month of marriage **2.** the holiday or vacation spent together by a newly married couple **3.** a brief period of apparent agreement, as between political parties after an election —*vi.* to have or spend a honeymoon —**hon′ey·moon′er** *n.*

honey pot any of a caste of workers in certain species of ants, that serve as living storehouses for a honeylike material later used by the whole colony

hon·ey·suck·er (-suk′ər) *n.* **1.** same as HONEY EATER **2.** a small Australian marsupial (*Tarsipes spenceri*) with a long tongue and snout: it feeds on nectar and small insects

hon·ey·suck·le (-suk′'l) *n.* [ME. *honisocle*, dim. (see -LE) < OE. *hunigsuce* (Brit. dial. *honeysuck*) < *hunig*, HONEY + *sucan*, to SUCK] **1.** any of a genus (*Lonicera*) of plants of the honeysuckle family, with small, fragrant flowers of red, yellow, or white **2.** any of several similar plants with fragrant flowers, esp. columbine and several species of rhododendron —*adj.* designating a family (Caprifoliaceae) of largely woody plants including the coralberry, elder, and honeysuckle

hong (häŋ, hôŋ) *n.* [Chin. *hŏng*, a row, series, factory] formerly in China, a warehouse or factory for foreign trade

Hong Kong (häŋ′ käŋ′, hôŋ′ kôŋ′) **1.** Brit.

HONEYSUCKLE

crown colony in SE China, on the South China Sea: it consists of a principal island (**Hong Kong Island**), nearby islands, Kowloon Peninsula, & an area of adjacent mainland leased from China: 398 sq. mi.; pop. 3,836,000; cap. Victoria 2. *same as* VICTORIA², its capital Also **Hong'kong'**

HONG KONG

hon·ied (hun'ēd) *adj. same as* HONEYED

†**ho·ni soit qui mal y pense** (ô nē swä' kē mäl ē päns') [Fr.] shamed be (anyone) who thinks evil of it: motto of the Order of the Garter

☆**honk** (hôŋk, häŋk) *n.* [echoic] 1. the call of a wild goose 2. any similar sound, as of an automobile horn —*vi.* to make any such sound —*vt.* 1. to express by honking 2. to sound (an automobile horn)

☆**honk·y-tonk** (hôŋ'kē tôŋk', häŋ'kē täŋk') *n.* [< ?] [Slang] a cheap, disreputable, noisy cabaret or nightclub —*adj. same as* RICKY-TICK; specif., designating such music played on a piano adjusted to give a tinkling sound

Hon·o·lu·lu (hän'ə lōō'lōō, hō'nə-) [Haw., lit., sheltered bay] capital of Hawaii; seaport on the SE coast of Oahu: pop. 325,000 (met. area 631,000)

hon·or (än'ər) *n.* [ME. *honour* < OFr. < L. *honor, honos*, official dignity, repute, esteem] 1. high regard or great respect given, received, or enjoyed; esp., *a)* glory; fame; renown *b)* good reputation; credit 2. a keen sense of right and wrong; adherence to action or principles considered right; integrity [to conduct oneself with *honor*] 3. *a)* chastity or purity *b)* reputation for chastity 4. high rank or position; distinction; dignity [the great *honor* of the presidency] 5. [H-] a title of respect given to certain officials, as judges (preceded by *His, Her,* or *Your*) 6. something done or given as a token or act of respect; specif., *a)* formerly, a curtsy; bow *b)* a social courtesy or privilege [may I have the *honor* of this dance?] *c)* a badge, token, decoration, etc. given to a person *d)* [*pl.*] public acts or ceremonies of respect [buried with full military *honors*] *e)* [*pl.*] special distinction or credit given to students, esp. at commencement, for high academic achievement; also, an advanced course of study in place of or in addition to the regular course, for exceptional students 7. a person or thing that brings respect and fame to a school, country, etc. 8. *Bridge a)* any of the five highest cards in a suit *b)* [*pl.*] the four or five highest cards of the trump suit *c)* [*pl.*] in a no-trump hand, the four aces 9. *Golf* the privilege of driving first from the tee —*vt.* 1. to respect greatly; regard highly; esteem 2. to show great respect or high regard for; treat with deference and courtesy 3. to worship (a deity) 4. to do or give something in honor of 5. to accept and pay when due [to *honor* a check] 6. to make a bow to in square dancing —*adj.* of or showing honor [*honor* roll] —**do honor to** 1. to show great respect for 2. to bring or cause honor to —**do the honors** to act as host or hostess, esp. by making introductions, proposing toasts, serving at table, etc. —**honor bright** [Colloq.] honestly! truthfully! —**on** (or **upon**) **one's honor** staking one's good name on one's truthfulness, trustworthiness, or reliability

SYN.—**honor**, as compared here, implies popular acknowledgment of one's right to great respect as well as any expression of such respect [in *honor* of the martyred dead]; **homage** suggests great esteem shown in praise, tributes, or obeisance [to pay *homage* to the genius of Milton]; **reverence** implies deep respect together with love [he held her memory in *reverence*]; **deference** suggests a display of courteous regard for a superior, or for one to whom respect is due, by yielding to his claims or wishes [in *deference* to his age] See also HONESTY

hon·or·a·ble (-ə b'l) *adj.* [ME. *honourable* < OFr. *honorable* < L. *honorabilis* < *honorare*] 1. worthy of being honored; specif., *a)* of, or having a position of, high rank or worth: used as a title of courtesy for certain officials and for the children of certain British peers *b)* noble; illustrious *c)* of good reputation; respectable 2. having or showing a sense of right and wrong; characterized by honesty and integrity; upright 3. bringing honor to the owner or doer 4. doing honor; accompanied with marks of respect [an *honorable* burial] —*SYN.* see UPRIGHT —**hon'or·a·bil'i·ty, hon'or·a·ble·ness** *n.* —**hon'or·a·bly** *adv.*

honorable mention a citation of honor, esp. to one who was not a winner, as in a competition

hon·o·ra·ri·um (än'ə rer'ē əm) *n., pl.* **-ri·ums, -ri·a** (-ə) [L. *honorarium* (*donum*), honorary (gift)] a payment as to a professional person for services on which no fee is set or legally obtainable

hon·or·ar·y (än'ə rer'ē) *adj.* [L. *honorarius*, of or conferring honor] 1. given as an honor only, without the usual requirements or privileges [an *honorary* degree] 2. *a)* designating an office or position held as an honor only, without service or pay *b)* holding such a position or office

3. depending on one's honor; that cannot be legally enforced or collected: said of debts, etc. —**hon'or·ar'i·ly** *adv.*

hon·or·if·ic (än'ə rif'ik) *adj.* [L. *honorificus* < *honor* + *facere*, to make: see FACT] conferring honor; showing respect [an *honorific* title or word]: also **hon'or·if'i·cal** —*n.* in Japanese and some other Oriental languages, any of a grammatical class of forms used in speaking of or to a person or thing that commands respect —**hon'or·if'i·cal·ly** *adv.*

†**hon·or·is cau·sa** (ä nôr'is kô'zə) [L., for the sake of honor] conferred as an honor [a law degree *honoris causa*]

honors of war special privileges granted to a defeated army, as that of continuing to bear arms

☆**honor system** in some schools, prisons, etc., a system whereby individuals are trusted to obey the rules, do their work, take tests, etc. without direct supervision

hon·our (än'ər) *n., vt., adj. Brit. var. of* HONOR

Hon·shu (hän'shōō') largest of the islands forming Japan: 88,946 sq. mi.; pop. 71,354,000; chief city, Tokyo

☆**hooch** (hōōch) *n.* [contr. of Alaskan Ind. *hoochinoo*, crude alcoholic liquor made by the *Hoochinoo* Indians (< *Hutsnuwu*, lit., grizzly bear fort)] [Slang] alcoholic liquor; esp., liquor made or obtained surreptitiously, as during prohibition

Hooch (hōkh), **Pie·ter de** (pē'tər də) 1629?-84?; Du. painter

hood¹ (hood) *n.* [ME. < OE. *hod*, akin to G. *hut*, hat: for IE. base see HAT, HEED] 1. a covering for the head and neck and, sometimes, the face, worn separately or as part of a robe or cloak [a monk's cowl is a *hood*] 2. anything resembling a hood in shape or use; specif., *a)* a fold of cloth over the back of an academic gown, judge's robe, etc., often with distinguishing colors to indicate the wearer's degree, college affiliation, etc. ☆*b)* the metal cover over the engine of an automobile *c)* a protective canopy, as over a door, window, etc. *d)* the cowl of a chimney *e)* a covering for a horse's head *f)* *Falconry* the covering for a falcon's head when it is not chasing game 3. *Zool. a)* a bird's crest *b)* the fold of skin near a cobra's head when expanded in excitement —*vt.* to cover or provide with or as with a hood

☆**hood²** (hood, hōōd) *n.* [Slang] *short for* HOODLUM

-hood (hood) [ME. *-had, -hod* < OE. *had*, order, condition, quality, rank, akin to G. *-heit* < IE. *(s)kāit-*, bright, gleaming: basic sense "appearance by which known"] a *n.-forming suffix meaning:* 1. state, quality, condition [*childhood*] 2. the whole group of (a specified class, profession, etc.) [*priesthood*]

Hood (hood) 1. **John Bell**, 1831-79; Confederate general in the Civil War 2. **Thomas**, 1799-1845; Eng. poet & humorist

Hood, Mount mountain of the Cascade Range, in N Oreg.: a peak of volcanic origin: 11,245 ft.

Hood, Robin *see* ROBIN HOOD

hood·ed (hood'id) *adj.* 1. having or covered with a hood 2. shaped like a hood; cucullate 3. *Zool. a)* having the head different in color from the body *b)* having a crest like a hood *c)* capable of expanding the skin at each side of the neck by movements of the ribs, as the cobra and puff adder

hooded crow a European crow (*Corvus cornix*) with black wings, head, and tail and a gray back and breast

hooded seal a large, dark-gray seal (*Cystophora cristata*) of the North Atlantic: the male has on its head a hoodlike sac that can be inflated

☆**hood·lum** (hood'ləm, hōōd'-) *n.* [prob. < G. dial. (esp. Swiss) *hudilump*, wretch, miserable fellow < MHG. *hudel*, rag, wretch + *lump*, rag, tatter, wretch] a wild, lawless person, often a member of a gang of criminals —**hood'lum·ism** *n.*

hood·man-blind (hood'mən blind') *n.* [Archaic] *same as* BLINDMAN'S BUFF

☆**hoo·doo** (hōō'dōō) *n., pl.* **-doos** [var. of VOODOO] 1. *same as* VOODOO 2. [Colloq.] *a)* a person or thing that causes bad luck *b)* bad luck 3. a natural rock formation of fantastic shape, esp. as found in the W U.S. —*vt.* [Colloq.] to bring bad luck to

hood·wink (hood'wiŋk') *vt.* [HOOD¹ + WINK] 1. orig., to blindfold 2. to mislead or confuse by trickery or deception; dupe

☆**hoo·ey** (hōō'ē) *interj., n.* [echoic] [Slang] nonsense; bunk

hoof (hoof, hōōf) *n., pl.* **hoofs, hooves** (hoovz, hōōvz) [ME. *hoof* < OE. *hof*, akin to G. *huf* < IE. base *kapho-*, whence Sans. *śaphá-*, hoof, claw] 1. the horny covering on the feet of cattle, deer, swine, horses, etc. 2. the entire foot of such an animal 3. [Slang] the human foot —*vt., vi.* 1. to kick or trample with the hoofs 2. [Colloq.] to walk (often with *it*) ☆3. [Slang] to dance —☆**on the hoof** not butchered; alive

hoof-and-mouth disease (-'n mouth') *same as* FOOT-AND-MOUTH DISEASE

hoof·beat (-bēt') *n.* the sound made by the hoof of an animal when it runs, walks, etc.

hoof·bound (-bound') *adj.* having dryness and contraction of the hoof, which causes pain and lameness

hoofed (hooft, hōōft) *adj.* having hoofs; ungulate

☆**hoof·er** (hoof'ər, hōōf'-) *n.* [Slang] a professional dancer, esp. a tap dancer, soft-shoe dancer, etc.

Hoogh (hōkh), **Pieter de** *same as* Pieter de HOOCH

Hoogh·ly (hōōg'lē) river in West Bengal, India, flowing

into the Bay of Bengal; westernmost channel of the Ganges delta: c. 160 mi.

hoo-ha (hōō'hä'; *for interj.* hōō'hä') *n.* [echoic] [Chiefly Brit. Colloq.] a commotion or fuss —*interj.* an exclamation used to express surprise, excitement, etc., often in a mocking way

hook (hook) *n.* [ME. < OE. *hoc,* akin to HAKE, MDu. *hoec,* ON. *hakr* < IE. base **keg-,* peg for hanging] **1.** a curved or bent piece of metal, wood, etc. used to catch, hold, or pull something; specif., *a*) a curved piece of wire or bone with a barbed end, for catching fish *b*) a curved piece of metal, wood, etc. fastened to a wall or chain at one end, used to hang things on, raise things up, etc. [a coat *hook*] *c*) a small metal catch inserted in a loop, or eye, to fasten clothes together *d*) [Naut. Slang] an anchor **2.** a curved metal implement for cutting grain, etc. **3.** something shaped like a hook; specif., *a*) a curving cape or headland: used in place names [Sandy *Hook*] *b*) a bend in a stream **4.** a trap; snare **5.** the stationary part of a hinge, used to hold the pin **6.** *a*) the path of a hit or thrown ball that curves away to the left from a right-handed player or to the right from a left-handed player *b*) a ball that follows such a path **7.** *Boxing* a short blow delivered with the arm bent at the elbow **8.** *Music* same as FLAG[1] (sense 5) —*vt.* **1.** to attach or fasten with or as with a hook or hook and eye **2.** to take hold of with a hook **3.** to catch with or as with a hook **4.** to attack with the horns, as a bull; gore **5.** to make into the shape of a hook ☆**6.** to make (a rug) by drawing strips of cloth or yarn back and forth with a hook through a canvas or burlap backing **7.** t hit or throw (a ball) in a hook (*n.* 6 *a*) **8.** [Colloq.] to steal; snatch **9.** *Boxing* to hit with a hook —*vi.* **1.** to curve as a hook does **2.** to be fastened with a hook or hooks **3.** to be caught by a hook —**by hook or by crook** in any way whatever; by any means, honest or dishonest —☆**get the hook** [Slang] to be discharged or dismissed: from the former practice of pulling incompetent actors off the stage with a long hooked pole —☆**hook, line, and sinker** [Colloq.] completely; altogether: orig., a fisherman's expression —**hook up 1.** to connect or attach with a hook or hooks **2.** to arrange and connect the parts of (a radio, etc.) —**off the hook** [Colloq.] out of trouble, embarrassment, or a state of burdensome responsibility —☆**on one's own hook** [Colloq.] by oneself; without getting help, advice, etc.

hook-ah, hook-a (hook'ə) *n.* [Ar. *huqqah,* pipe for smoking, vase] an Oriental tobacco pipe with a long, flexible tube so arranged that it draws the smoke through water in a vase or bowl and cools it; narghile

HOOKAH

hook and eye a device for fastening clothes, etc., consisting of a small loop and a hook that catches on it

☆**hook and ladder** a fire engine that carries long ladders, hooks for tearing down ceilings, and other equipment

hook-bill (hook'bil') *n.* a parrot or related bird

Hooke (hook), **Robert** 1635–1703; Eng. physicist, mathematician, & inventor

hooked (hookt) *adj.* **1.** curved like a hook **2.** having a hook or hooks ☆**3.** made with a hook [a *hooked* rug] ☆**4.** [Slang] *a*) addicted as to the use of a drug (often with *on*) *b*) preoccupied or obsessed with a person, fad, etc. (often with *on*) **5.** [Slang] married

HOOK & EYE

hook-er[1] (hook'ər) *n.* **1.** one that hooks ☆**2.** [Slang] a large drink of whiskey ☆**3.** [Slang] a prostitute

hook-er[2] (hook'ər) *n.* [Du. *hoeker* < MDu. *hoeck-boot,* lit., hook boat: see HOOK] **1.** a small Dutch fishing ship with two masts **2.** an Irish or English fishing smack with one mast **3.** any clumsy, old ship

Hook-er (hook'ər) **1. Joseph,** 1814–79; Union general in the Civil War **2. Richard,** 1554?–1600; Eng. clergyman & writer **3. Thomas,** 1586?–1647; Eng. Puritan clergyman, in America after 1633

hook-nose (-nōz') *n.* a nose curved downward somewhat like a hook; aquiline nose —**hook'nosed'** *adj.*

☆**hook shot** *Basketball* a one-handed shot in which the extended arm is brought back over the head, tossing the ball toward the basket

☆**hook-up** (-up') *n.* [HOOK + UP[1]] **1.** the arrangement and connection of parts, circuits, etc. in a radio, telephone system, network of radio stations, etc. **2.** [Colloq.] a connection or alliance between two governments, parties, etc.

☆**hook-worm** (-wurm') *n.* any of a number of small, parasitic roundworms (family Ancylostomatidae) with hooks around the mouth, infesting the small intestine of man and other animals, esp. in tropical climates

☆**hookworm disease** a disease caused by hookworms, characterized by anemia, weakness, and abdominal pain: the larvae enter the body through the skin, usually of the bare feet; ancylostomiasis

☆**hook-y** (hook'ē) *n.* see PLAY HOOKY

hoo-li-gan (hōō'li gən) *n.* [< ? *Hooligan* (or *Houlihan*), name of an Irish family in Southwark, London] [Slang] a hoodlum, esp. a young one —**hoo'li-gan-ism** *n.*

hoop (hōōp) *n.* [ME. < OE. *hop,* akin to Du. *hoep,* OFris. *hop,* prob. < IE. **keub-* < base **keu-,* to bend, curve, whence Lith. *kabê,* a hook] **1.** a circular band or ring for holding together the staves of a barrel, cask, etc. **2.** anything like a hoop; specif., *a*) a large, circular band rolled along the ground by children *b*) any of the rings of whalebone, steel, etc. forming the framework of a hoop skirt ☆*c*) *Basketball* the metal rim of the basket *d*) *Croquet* same as WICKET —*vt.* to bind or fasten as with a hoop or hoops; encircle

hoop-er (-ər) *n.* same as COOPER

☆**hoop-la** (hōōp'lä, hoop'-) *n.* [< ?] [Colloq.] **1.** great excitement; bustle **2.** showy publicity; ballyhoo

hoo-poe (hōō'pōō) *n.* [earlier *houpe* < Fr. *huppe* < L. *upupa,* prob. echoic of its cry] any of a number of Old World birds (family Upupidae), esp. the European species (*Upupa epops*) with a long curved bill and erectile crest

☆**hoop skirt** a skirt worn over a framework of hoops, or rings, to make it spread out

☆**hoop snake** any of several American snakes alleged in folklore to take the tail in mouth and roll along like a hoop

hoo-ray (hoo rā', hə-, hōō-) *interj., n., vi., vt.* same as HURRAH

☆**hoose-gow, hoos-gow** (hōōs'gou) *n.* [< Sp. *juzgado,* court of justice < pp. of *juzgar,* to judge < L. *judicare* < *judex,* JUDGE] [Slang] a jail or guardhouse

☆**Hoo-sier** (hōō'zhər) *n.* [prob. < dial. (Cumberland) *hoozer,* something big] [Colloq.] a native or inhabitant of Indiana

HOOP SKIRT

hoot[1] (hōōt) *vi.* [ME. *houten,* of echoic orig., as also in Sw., Norw. *huta*] **1.** to utter its characteristic hollow sound: said of an owl **2.** to utter a sound like this **3.** to shout or cry out, esp. in scorn or disapproval —*vt.* **1.** to express (scorn, disapproval, etc.) by hooting **2.** to express scorn or disapproval of by hooting **3.** to drive or chase away by hooting [to *hoot* an actor off the stage] —*n.* **1.** the sound that an owl makes **2.** any sound like this **3.** a loud shout or cry of scorn or disapproval ☆**4.** the least bit; whit [not worth a *hoot*] —**hoot'er** *n.*

hoot[2] (hōōt) *interj.* [? var. of *prec.*] [Scot. & North Eng.] an exclamation of objection, irritation, or impatience: also **hoots**

☆**hootch** (hōōch) *n.* [Slang] same as HOOCH

☆**hoot-chy-koot-chy** (hōōch'ē kōōch'ē) *n., pl.* **-koot'chies** [< ?] same as COOCH: also sp. **hoot'chie-koot'chie**

☆**hoot-en-an-ny** (hōōt''n an'ē) *n., pl.* **-nies** [orig. in sense of "dingus," "thingamajig"; a fanciful coinage] a meeting of folk singers, as for public entertainment

hoot owl any of various owls that hoot; esp., the great horned owl

Hoo-ver (hōō'vər) **1. Herbert Clark,** 1874–1964; 31st president of the U.S. (1929–33) **2. J(ohn) Edgar,** 1895– ; U.S. government official; director of the FBI (1924–)

Hoover Dam [after Pres. HOOVER] dam on the Colorado River, on the Ariz.-Nev. border: 726 ft. high

hooves (hōōvz, hoovz) *n. rare pl.* of HOOF

hop[1] (häp) *vi.* **hopped, hop'ping** [ME. *hoppen* < OE. *hoppian,* akin to G. *hüpfen* < IE. **keub-* < base **keu-,* to bend, curve, whence HIP[1], L. *cumbere,* to lie: basic sense prob. "to bend forward"] **1.** to make a short leap or leaps on one foot **2.** to move by leaping or springing on both (or all) feet at once, as a bird, frog, etc. **3.** [Colloq.] *a*) to go or move briskly or in bounces *b*) to take a short, quick trip (with *up, down,* or *over*) —*vt.* **1.** to jump over [to *hop* a fence] ☆**2.** to get aboard [to *hop* a train] **3.** [Colloq.] to fly over in an airplane —*n.* **1.** an act or instance of hopping ☆**2.** a bounce, as of a baseball **3.** [Colloq.] a dance, esp. an informal one **4.** [Colloq.] a short flight in an airplane —*SYN.* see SKIP —**hop on** (or **all over**) [Slang] to scold; reprimand

hop[2] (häp) *n.* [LME. *hoppe* < MDu. *hoppe,* akin to G. *hopfen*] **1.** a rough twining vine (*Humulus lupulus*) of the hemp family, having the female flowers borne in small cones covered with bladdery bracts **2.** [*pl.*] the dried ripe cones of the female flowers, used for flavoring beer, ale, etc., and in medicine ☆**3.** [Slang] a narcotic drug; esp., opium —*vt.* **hopped, hop'ping** to flavor or treat with hops —**hop up** [Slang] **1.** to stimulate by or as by a drug **2.** to supercharge (an automobile engine, etc.)

hop clover any of a group of clovers with yellow flowers resembling hops when dry

Hope (hōp) [< ff.] **1.** a feminine name **2.** Anthony, (pseud. of *Sir Anthony Hope Hawkins*) 1863–1933; Eng. novelist

hope (hōp) *n.* [ME. < OE. *hopa*, akin to Du. *hoop*; see the *v.*] **1.** a feeling that what is wanted will happen; desire accompanied by expectation **2.** the thing that one has a hope for **3.** a reason for hope **4.** a person or thing on which one may base some hope **5.** [Archaic] trust; reliance —*vt.* hoped, hop'ing [ME. *hopen* < OE. *hopian*, to expect, look for, akin to G. *hoffen* < ? same IE. base as HOP¹: orig. sense (?) "to leap up in expectation"] **1.** to want and expect **2.** to want very much —*vi.* **1.** to have hope (*for*) **2.** [Archaic] to trust or rely —*SYN.* see EXPECT —**hope against hope** to continue having hope though it seems baseless —**hop'er** *n.*

☆**hope chest** a chest in which a young woman collects linen, clothing, etc. in anticipation of getting married

hope·ful (-fəl) *adj.* [ME.] **1.** feeling or showing hope; expecting to get what one wants **2.** inspiring or giving hope [a *hopeful* sign] —*n.* a person who hopes, or seems likely, to succeed —**hope'ful·ness** *n.*

hope·ful·ly (-ē) *adv.* **1.** in a hopeful manner **2.** it is to be hoped (that) [to leave early, *hopefully* by six]: regarded by some as a loose usage, but widely current

Ho·pei (hō'pā'; *Chin.* hu'bā') province of NE China, on the gulf of Po Hai: 78,263 sq. mi.; pop. 43,730,000; cap. Tientsin

hope·less (-lis) *adj.* **1.** without hope [a *hopeless* prisoner] **2.** allowing no hope; causing despair [a *hopeless* situation] **3.** impossible to solve, deal with, teach, etc. —**hope'less·ly** *adv.* —**hope'less·ness** *n.*

SYN.—**hopeless** means having no expectation of, or showing no sign of, a favorable outcome [a *hopeless* situation]; **despondent** implies a being in very low spirits due to a loss of hope and a sense of futility about continuing one's efforts [her rejection of his suit left him *despondent*]; **despairing** implies utter loss of hope and may suggest the extreme dejection that results [the *despairing* lover spoke of suicide]; **desperate** implies such despair as makes one resort to extreme measures [hunger makes men *desperate*]. —*ANT.* hopeful, optimistic

☆**hop·head** (häp'hed') *n.* [HOP², *n.* 3 + HEAD, *n.* 21] [Slang] a drug addict

hop hornbeam 1. any of a genus (*Ostrya*) of N. American trees of the birch family, with gray bark and hoplike cones **2.** the hard wood of this tree, often used in tool handles

☆**Ho·pi** (hō'pē) *n.* [Hopi *Hópitu*, lit., good, peaceful] **1.** *pl.* **-pis, -pi** a member of a Pueblo tribe of Indians in NE Arizona **2.** their Shoshonean language

Hop·kins (häp'kinz) **1.** Gerard Man·ley (man'lē), 1844–89; Eng. poet & Jesuit priest **2.** Johns, 1795–1873; U.S. financier & philanthropist **3.** Mark, 1802–87; U.S. educator

Hop·kin·son (häp'kin sən), Francis 1737–91; Am. jurist & poet: signer of the Declaration of Independence

hop·lite (häp'līt') *n.* [Gr. *hoplitēs* < *hoplon*, a tool < *hepein*, to prepare, care for < IE. base *sep-, to concern oneself with, whence Sans. *sápati*, (he) woos, cultivates, L. *sepelire*, to bury] a heavily armed foot soldier of ancient Greece

hop-o'-my-thumb (häp'ə mi thum') *n.* [earlier *hop on my thombe* (< HOP¹)] a very small person; midget

hop·per (häp'ər) *n.* [ME. *hoppere*] **1.** a person or thing that hops **2.** any hopping insect **3.** [so called from making material "hop"] a box, tank, or other container, often funnel-shaped, from which the contents can be emptied slowly and evenly [the *hopper* of an automatic coal stoker] ☆**4.** a freight car with an open top and a collapsible bottom through which to unload freight: in full, **hopper car**

hop·ple (häp'l) *n.*, *vt.* **-pled, -pling** *same as* HOBBLE

☆**hop·sack·ing** (häp'sak'iŋ) *n.* [lit., sacking for hops] **1.** a coarse material for bags, made of jute or hemp **2.** a sturdy fabric somewhat simulating this, made from cotton, wool, linen, or synthetic fiber and used for suits, coats, etc. Also **hop'sack'**

hop·scotch (-skäch') *n.* [HOP¹ + SCOTCH¹] a children's game in which a player tosses a small stone into one section after another of a figure drawn on the ground, hopping from section to section to pick up the stone after each toss

hor. 1. horizon **2.** horizontal

ho·ra (hōr'ə, hō'rə) *n.* [ModHeb. *hōrāh* < Romanian *horă* < Turk. *hora*] **1.** a lively Romanian and Israeli folk dance performed in a circle **2.** music for this dance

Hor·ace (hôr'is, här'-) [< L. *Horatius*] **1.** a masculine name: see HORATIO **2.** (L. name *Quintus Horatius Flaccus*) 65–8 B.C.; Roman poet: known for his odes

Hor·ae (hō'rē) *n.pl.* [L. < Gr. *Hōrai*] Gr. Myth. *same as* HOURS

ho·ral (hōr'əl) *adj.* [LL. *horalis* < L. *hora*, HOUR] of an hour or hours

ho·ra·ry (hôr'ə rē) *adj.* [ML. *horarius* < L. *hora*, HOUR] **1.** of or indicating an hour or hours **2.** occurring once every hour; hourly

Ho·ra·tian (hə rā'shən, hō-) *adj.* [L. *Horatianus* < *Horatius*, Horace] of, like, or characteristic of Horace or his poetry

Ho·ra·ti·o (hə rā'shō, -shē ō; hō-) [altered (after L.) < It. *Orazio* < L. *Horatius*, name of a Roman gens] a masculine name: var. *Horace*

Ho·ra·ti·us (-shəs, -shē əs) *Rom. Legend* a hero who defended a bridge over the Tiber against the Etruscans

horde (hôrd) *n.* [Fr. < G. *horde*, earlier *horda* < Pol. *horda* < Turk. *ordū*, a camp < Tat. *urdu*, a camp, lit., something erected < *urmak*, to pitch (a camp): see URDU] **1.** a nomadic tribe or clan of Mongols **2.** any wandering tribe or group **3.** a large, moving crowd or throng; swarm —*vi.* hord'ed, hord'ing to form or gather in a horde —*SYN.* see CROWD¹

Ho·reb (hōr'eb) *Bible* a mountain usually identified with Mt. Sinai: Ex. 3:1

hore·hound (hôr'hound') *n.* [ME. *horehune* < OE. *harhune* < *har*, white, HOAR + *hune*, horehound] **1.** a bitter plant (*Marrubium vulgare*) of the mint family, with white, downy leaves **2.** a bitter juice extracted from its leaves **3.** cough medicine or candy made with this juice **4.** any of various other mints

ho·ri·zon (hə rī'z'n) *n.* [altered (after L.) < ME. *orizont* < OFr. *orizonte* < L. *horizon* < Gr. *horizōn* (*kyklos*), the bounding (circle), horizon < prp. of *horizein*, to bound, limit < *horos*, boundary, limit, prob. < IE. base *weru-, to draw, whence L. *urvus*, city boundary, orig., furrow around city] **1.** the line where the sky seems to meet the earth: called **visible** or **apparent horizon 2.** [*usually pl.*] the limit or extent of one's outlook, experience, interest, knowledge, etc. [travel broadens one's *horizons*] **3.** an archaeological level or an area of culture as indicated by surviving artifacts **4.** *Astron.* the great circle in which a plane perpendicular to the direction of gravity at the place of observation intersects the celestial sphere **5.** *Geol.* a layer or small thickness of soil or rock identified by physical characteristics, particular fossils, etc.

hor·i·zon·tal (hôr'ə zän't'l, här'-) *adj.* [ModL. *horizontalis* < L. *horizon* (gen. *horizontis*): see prec.] **1.** of or near the horizon **2.** *a)* parallel to the plane of the horizon; not vertical *b)* placed, operating, or acting chiefly in a horizontal direction **3.** flat and even; level **4.** at, or made up of elements at, the same level or status [*horizontal* union] —*n.* a horizontal line, plane, etc. —**hor'i·zon'tal·ly** *adv.*

horizontal bar a metal bar fixed in a horizontal position for chinning and other gymnastic exercises

hor·mone (hôr'mōn) *n.* [< Gr. *hormōn*, prp. of *horman*, to stimulate, excite < *hormē*, impulse < IE. base *ser-, to stream, whence Sans. *sará-, fluid, L. *serum*, whey] **1.** a substance formed in some organ of the body, as the adrenal glands, the pituitary, etc., and carried by a body fluid to another organ or tissue, where it has a specific effect: now often prepared synthetically **2.** a similar substance produced in a plant, esp. auxin —**hor·mo'nal** (-mō'n'l), **hor·mon'ic** (-män'ik) *adj.*

Hor·muz (hôr'muz), **Strait of** strait joining the Persian Gulf & the Gulf of Oman, between Arabia & Iran

horn (hôrn) *n.* [ME. < OE., akin to G. *horn* < IE. base *ker-, upper part of the body, head, whence L. *cornu*, Gr. *kēras*: cf. CAIRN, HART] **1.** *a)* a hard, bony or keratinous, permanent projection that grows on the head of cattle, sheep, and some other hoofed animals *b)* either of a pair of branched, bonelike projections that grow on the head of a deer and are shed annually **2.** anything that protrudes naturally from the head of an animal, as one of the tentacles of a snail, a tuft of feathers on certain birds, etc. **3.** [*usually pl.*] the projections imagined as growing on the brow of a cuckold **4.** *a)* the substance that horns are made of *b)* any similar, now often synthetic, substance **5.** *a)* a container made by hollowing out a horn [a powder *horn*] *b)* a drink contained in a horn **6.** *same as* CORNUCOPIA **7.** anything shaped like or suggesting a horn; specif., *a)* a peninsula or cape *b)* either end of a crescent *c)* the beak of an anvil ☆*d)* a projection above the pommel of a cowboy's saddle **8.** *a)* an instrument made of horn and sounded by blowing, as the shofar *b)* any brass-wind instrument; specif., the French horn; also, ☆*Jazz*, any wind instrument *c)* a device sounded to give a warning [a *foghorn*] *d)* a horn-shaped loudspeaker *e)* a horn-shaped antenna **9.** *Bible* an emblem of glory, strength, or honor **10.** *Geol.* a jagged mountain peak resulting from the erosion of several cirques against one headland, as the Matterhorn in the Alps —*vt.* **1.** to strike, butt, or gore with the horns **2.** to furnish with horns **3.** [Archaic] to cuckold —*adj.* made of horn [*horn*-rimmed glasses] —☆**around the horn** *Baseball* (thrown) from third base to second to first in trying for a double play —**blow one's own horn** [Colloq.] to praise oneself; boast —☆**horn in** (on) [Colloq.] to intrude or meddle (in); butt in —**lock horns** ☆to have a disagreement or conflict —**on the horns of a dilemma** having to make a choice between two things, both usually unpleasant —**pull** (or **draw** or **haul**) **in one's horns 1.** to hold oneself back; restrain one's impulses, efforts, etc. **2.** to withdraw; recant —**horn'less** *adj.* —**horn'like'** *adj.*

Horn, Cape southernmost point of S. America; cape on an island (**Horn Island**) in Tierra del Fuego, Chile

horn·beam (-bēm') *n.* [HORN + BEAM] **1.** any of a genus (*Carpinus*) of small, hardy trees of the birch family, with smooth, gray bark and large clusters of light-green nuts **2.** the very hard, white wood of this tree, which takes a hornlike polish

horn·bill (-bil') *n.* any of a family (Bucerotidae) of large, tropical, Old World birds with partly united toes and a huge, curved bill, often with a bony protuberance

horn·blende (-blend') *n.* [G.: see HORN & BLENDE] a black, rock-forming mineral, a type of amphibole, con-

taining iron and silicate of aluminum, magnesium, calcium, etc., common in some granitic rocks

horn·book (-book′) *n.* 1. a sheet of parchment with the alphabet, table of numbers, etc. on it, mounted on a small board with a handle and protected by a thin, transparent plate of horn: it was formerly used as a child's primer 2. an elementary treatise

horned (hôrnd; *poet.* hôr′nid) *adj.* 1. having a horn or horns: often in hyphenated compounds *[two-horned]* 2. having a hornlike projection 3. [Archaic] cuckolded

☆**horned pout** *same as* BULLHEAD; esp., the brown bull-head (*Ameiurus nebulosus*) of the E U.S.: also **horn pout, horn′pout** *n.*

☆**horned toad** any of several small, scaly, insect-eating, New World lizards (genus *Phrynosoma*) with a flattened body, short tail, and hornlike spines

horned viper a poisonous N African snake (*Cerastes cornutus*) with a hornlike spine above each eye; asp

hor·net (hôr′nit) *n.* [ME. *harnette* < OE. *hyrnet*, akin to G. *hornisse* < IE. base **ker-*, cf. (see HORN), whence L. *crabro]* any of several large social wasps (family Vespidae), strikingly colored yellow and black

☆**horn fly** a fly (*Haematobia irritans*) superficially resembling the housefly: it is a pest on cattle and sucks blood, esp. at the base of the horns

hor·ni·to (hôr nēt′ō; *Sp.* ôr nē′tō) *n., pl.* **-tos** (-tōz; *Sp.* -tōs) [Sp., dim. of *horno*, oven < L. *furnus:* see FURNACE] a small, beehive-shaped mound built up from clots of molten lava ejected from an underlying volcanic tube

horn-mad (hôrn′mad′) *adj.* 1. maddened enough to gore: said of horned animals 2. enraged; furious

horn of plenty *same as* CORNUCOPIA

horn·pipe (-pīp′) *n.* [ME.] 1. an obsolete wind instrument with a bell and mouthpiece made of horn 2. a lively dance to the music of the hornpipe, formerly popular with sailors 3. music for this

Horn·sey (hôrn′zē) city in Middlesex, SE England: suburb of London: pop. 98,000

horn silver *same as* CERARGYRITE

horn·stone (hôrn′stōn′) *n.* [transl. of G. *hornstein:* so named from its appearance] [Obs.] flint or chert

☆**horn·swog·gle** (-swäg′'l) *vt.* **-gled, -gling** [fanciful coinage, orig. ? associated with cuckoldry] [Slang] to swindle or hoax; trick

horn·tail (-tāl′) *n.* any of several four-winged insects (family Siricidae), related to the sawfly: the adult female has a horny, taillike extension for depositing eggs in tree trunks, in which the larvae burrow

☆**horn·worm** (-wurm′) *n.* the larval caterpillar of various hawk moths, with a horny growth on the last segment

horn·wort (-wurt′) *n.* [after ModL. *Ceratophyllum:* see CERATO- & -PHYLL] any of a genus (*Ceratophyllum*) of a family (Ceratophyllaceae) of plants growing entirely submerged in lakes and slow-moving streams and having whorls of finely divided leaves

horn·y (hôr′nē) *adj.* **horn′i·er, horn′i·est** [ME.] 1. of, like, or made of horn 2. having horns 3. toughened and calloused *[horny* hands] 4. [Slang] sexually aroused; lustful —**horn′i·ness** *n.*

horol. horology

ho·ro·loge (hôr′ə lōj′, här′-) *n.* [ME. < OFr. < L. *horologium* < Gr. *hōrologion* < *hōra*, HOUR + *legein*, to say: see LOGIC] a timepiece; clock, hourglass, sundial, etc.

hor·o·log·ic (hôr′ə läj′ik, här′-) *adj.* [L. *horologicus*] of horology or horologes: also **hor′o·log′i·cal**

ho·rol·o·gist (hô räl′ə jist) *n.* an expert in horology; maker of or dealer in timepieces: also **ho·rol′o·ger**

Hor·o·lo·gi·um (hôr′ə lō′jē əm, här′-) [L.: see HOROLOGE] a S constellation just below the southern extension of Eridanus

ho·rol·o·gy (hô räl′ə jē) *n.* [< Gr. *hōra*, HOUR + -LOGY] the science or art of measuring time or making timepieces

hor·o·scope (hôr′ə skōp′, här′-) *n.* [Fr. < L. *horoscopus* < Gr. *hōroskopos*, observer of the hour of birth < *hōra*, HOUR + *skopos*, watcher, by metathesis < IE. **spokos* < base **spek-*, to spy, scrutinize, whence L. *specere*, to see, OHG. *spehōn*, to SPY] 1. the position of the planets and stars with relation to one another at a given time, esp. at the time of a person's birth, regarded in astrology as determining his destiny 2. a chart of the zodiacal signs and the positions of the planets, etc., by which astrologers profess to tell a person's future —**hor′o·scop′ic** (-skäp′ik) *adj.*

ho·ros·co·py (hô räs′kə pē) *n.* the practice of drawing up horoscopes

Hor·o·witz (hôr′ə wits, här′-), **Vlad·i·mir** (vlad′ə mir′) 1904– ; Russ. pianist, mainly in the U.S.

hor·ren·dous (hô ren′dəs, hə-) *adj.* [L. *horrendus* < prp. of *horrere*, to bristle] horrible; frightful —**hor·ren′dous·ly** *adv.*

hor·rent (hôr′ənt, här′-) *adj.* [L. *horrens* (gen. *horrentis*), prp. of *horrere:* see HORRID] [Archaic] 1. standing up like bristles; bristling 2. horrified; shuddering

hor·ri·ble (hôr′ə b'l, här′-) *adj.* [ME. < OFr. < L. *horribilis* < *horrere:* see HORRID] 1. causing a feeling of horror;

terrible; dreadful; frightful 2. [Colloq.] very bad, ugly, shocking, unpleasant, etc.

hor·ri·bly (-ə blē) *adv.* 1. in a horrible manner 2. to a horrible degree 3. [Colloq.] very; extremely

hor·rid (hôr′id, här′-) *adj.* [L. *horridus* < *horrere*, to bristle, shake, be afraid < IE. base **ĝhers-*, to bristle, whence GORSE: cf. HIRSUTE] 1. orig., bristling; shaggy; rough 2. causing a feeling of horror; terrible; revolting 3. very bad, ugly, unpleasant, etc.: the current sense —**hor′rid·ly** *adv.* —**hor′rid·ness** *n.*

hor·rif·ic (hô rif′ik, hə-) *adj.* [Fr. *horrifique* < L. *horrificus* < *horrere*, to bristle (see HORRID) + *facere*, to make (see FACT)] horrifying; terrible

hor·ri·fy (hôr′ə fī, här′-) *vt.* **-fied′, -fy′ing** [L. *horrificare* < *horrificus:* see HORRIFIC] 1. to cause to feel horror 2. [Colloq.] to shock or disgust —SYN. see DISMAY —**hor′ri·fi·ca′tion** *n.*

hor·rip·i·late (hô rip′ə lāt′) *vt.* **-lat′ed, -lat′ing** [< L. *horripilatus*, pp. of *horripilare*, to bristle with hairs < *horrere*, to bristle (see HORRID) + *pilus*, hair] to produce horripilation —*vi.* to experience horripilation; bristle or shudder

hor·rip·i·la·tion (hô rip′ə lā′shən) *n.* [LL. *horripilatio:* see prec.] the erection of hair of the head or body, as from fear, disease, or cold; goose flesh

hor·ror (hôr′ər, här′-) *n.* [ME. *horrour* < OFr. < L. *horror* < *horrere*, to bristle (see HORRID)] 1. orig., *a*) a bristling *b*) a shuddering 2. the strong feeling caused by something frightful or shocking; shuddering fear and disgust; terror and repugnance 3. strong dislike or aversion; loathing 4. the quality of causing horror 5. something that causes horror 6. [Colloq.] something very bad, ugly, disagreeable, etc. —*adj.* intended to cause horror *[horror* movies] —**the horrors** [Colloq.] a fit of extreme nervousness, panic, depression, revulsion, etc.

Hor·sa (hôr′sə) [OE.: see HORSE] *see* HENGIST

‡**thors con·cours** (ôr kōn kōōr′) [Fr.] outside or beyond competition

‡**thors de com·bat** (ôr′ də kôn bá′) [Fr., lit., out of combat] put out of action; disabled

hors d'oeu·vre (ôr′ durv′, -duv′; *Fr.* ôr dö′vr′) *pl.* **hors′ d'oeuvres′** (durvz′, duvz′; *Fr.* durv′) [Fr., lit., outside of work < *hors*, outside (< L. *foris*) + *de*, of (see DE-) + *oeuvre*, work (< L. *opera*, works)] an appetizer, as olives, anchovies, canapés, etc., served usually at the beginning of a meal

horse (hôrs) *n., pl.* **hors′es, horse:** see PLURAL, II, D, 1 [ME. *hors* < OE. *hors, hros*, akin to G. *ross* (OHG. *hros*), prob. < IE. base **(s)ker-*, to leap (or < ? **kers-*, to run, whence L. *cursus*)] 1. any of several varieties of large, strong animal (*Equus caballus*) with four legs, solid hoofs, and flowing mane and tail, long ago domesticated for drawing or carrying loads, carrying riders, etc. 2. the full-grown male of the horse; gelding or stallion 3. anything like a horse in that a person sits, rides, or is carried on it 4. a device, esp. a frame with legs, to support something; specif., *a*) a sawing frame *b*) a clotheshorse 5. a man: a joking, friendly, or insolent term 6. [Colloq.] *Chess* a knight ☆7. [Colloq.] *same as* PONY (sense 4) 8. *slang for a*) HORSEPOWER ☆*b*) HEROIN 9. *Gym.* a padded block on legs, used for jumping or vaulting 10. *Mil.* [with *pl. v.*] mounted troops; cavalry 11. *Mining* a mass of earth or rock inside a vein or coal seam 12. *Zool.* any member of a family (Equidae) including the horse, ass, zebra, etc. —*vt.* **horsed, hors′ing** 1. to supply with a horse or horses; put on horseback 2. *a*) to place on a man's back or a wooden horse for flogging *b*) to flog 3. [Colloq.] to shove; push ☆4. [Slang] to subject to horseplay —*vi.* to mount or go on horseback —*adj.* 1. of a horse or horses 2. mounted on horses 3. large, strong, or coarse of its kind *[horse* mackerel] —☆**back the wrong horse** 1. to bet on a horse that loses the race 2. to choose or support the losing side —**beat (or flog) a dead horse** [Colloq.] to argue an issue that is already settled —**from the horse's mouth** [Colloq.] from the original or authoritative source of information —☆**hold one's horses** [Slang] to curb one's impatience —☆**horse around** [Slang] to engage in horseplay —**horse of another (or different) color** an entirely different matter —**on one's high horse** [Colloq.] acting in an arrogant, haughty, or disdainful manner —**to horse!** get or your horse! mount!

HORSE
(sense 9)

horse·back (-bak′) *n.* 1. the back of a horse ☆2. a low sharp ridge; hogback —*adv.* on horseback

☆**horse·car** (-kär′) *n.* 1. a streetcar drawn by horses 2. a car for transporting horses

horse-chest·nut (-ches′nət) *adj.* designating a family (Hippocastanaceae) of trees including the horse chestnuts and buckeyes

horse chestnut [transl. of obs. botanical L. *Castanea*

equina: reason for name unc.] **1.** *a)* a tree (*Aesculus hippocastanium*) of the horse-chestnut family with large palmately compound leaves, clusters of white flowers, and glossy brown seeds growing in burs *b)* its seed **2.** any of various related shrubs or trees, including the buckeyes

horse·feath·ers (-feth′ərz) *n., interj.* [Slang] nonsense; bunk

horse·flesh (-flesh′) *n.* **1.** the flesh of the horse, esp. when used as food **2.** horses collectively

horse·fly (-flī′) *n., pl.* **-flies′** [ME. *hors fleege*] **1.** any of a number of related large flies (family Tabanidae), the female of which sucks the blood of horses, cattle, etc. **2.** any of various other flies troublesome to horses, as the botfly

☆**horse gentian** any of a genus (*Triosteum*) of coarse, weedy plants of the honeysuckle family, with opposite leaves, inconspicuous flowers, and leathery, orange fruit

Horse Guard a body of cavalry; esp., the cavalry brigade forming the household guard of the English sovereign

horse·hair (-her′) *n.* [ME. *horsher*] **1.** hair from the mane or tail of a horse **2.** a stiff fabric made from this hair; haircloth —*adj.* **1.** of horsehair **2.** covered or stuffed with horsehair

horse·hide (-hīd′) *n.* **1.** the hide of a horse **2.** leather made from this

horse latitudes [reason for name unc.] either of two belts over the oceans at c. 30°–35° N. and S. latitude, characterized by calms, light winds, and high barometric pressure

horse·laugh (-laf′, -läf′) *n.* a loud, boisterous, usually derisive laugh; guffaw

horse·leech (-lēch′) *n.* **1.** a large leech (*Haemopis marmoratis*) said to attach itself to the mouth of horses while they are drinking **2.** [Archaic] a veterinarian

horse·less (-lis) *adj.* **1.** without a horse **2.** not requiring a horse; self-propelled *[an automobile was formerly called a* horseless *carriage]*

horse mackerel 1. the largest fish of the mackerel family, the tuna, or tunny **2.** any of various other fishes, as the saurel, cavally, etc.

horse·man (-mən) *n., pl.* **-men** (-mən) [ME. *horsman*] **1.** a man who rides on horseback **2.** a cavalryman **3.** a man skilled in the riding, managing, or care of horses —**horse′man·ship′** *n.*

horse·mint (-mint′) *n.* [ME. *horsminte*] ☆any of a genus (*Monarda*) of N. American plants of the mint family, with heads of showy flowers, usually red or purplish

☆**horse nettle** a weed (*Solanum carolinense*) of the nightshade family, with yellow prickles, white or blue flowers, and yellow berries

☆**horse opera** [Slang] a motion picture or play about cowboys, cattle rustlers, etc., esp. in the W U.S.

horse pistol a large pistol formerly carried by horsemen

horse·play (-plā′) *n.* rough, boisterous fun

horse·pow·er (-pou′ər) *n.* [said to have been first adopted by James WATT] **1.** the power exerted by a horse in pulling **2.** a unit for measuring the power of motors or engines, equal to 746 watts or to a rate of 33,000 foot-pounds per minute (the force required to raise 33,000 pounds at the rate of one foot per minute)

horse·pow·er-hour (-our′) *n.* a unit of work equal to 1,980,000 foot-pounds

horse·pox (-päks′) *n.* an acute infectious disease of horses, a modified form of smallpox

horse·rad·ish (-rad′ish) *n.* **1.** a plant (*Armoracia lapathifolia*) of the mustard family, grown for its pungent, white, fleshy root **2.** a relish made of the grated root of this plant

☆**horse sense** [Colloq.] ordinary common sense

horse·shoe (hôr′shōō′, hôrs′-) *n.* [ME. *horscho*, contr. of *horsis sho*] **1.** a flat, U-shaped metal plate nailed to a horse's hoof for protection **2.** anything shaped like this **3.** [*pl.*] a game in which the players toss horseshoes at two facing stakes driven into the ground 40 feet apart, the object being to encircle the stake or come as close to it as possible —*vt.* **-shoed′, -shoe′ing** to fit with a horseshoe or horseshoes —**horse′sho′er** *n.*

horseshoe arch an arch shaped like a horseshoe: see ARCH[1], illus.

☆**horseshoe crab** any of several horseshoe-shaped sea animals (genus *Xiphosura*) with a long, spinelike tail

☆**horse's neck** an iced drink consisting of ginger ale or ginger ale and soda water, garnished with lemon, and sometimes containing an alcoholic liquor

horse·tail (hôrs′tāl) *n.* **1.** a horse's tail **2.** any of a genus (*Equisetum*) of rushlike plants having hollow, jointed stems, with scalelike leaves at the joints and spores borne in terminal cones

☆**horse trade 1.** an exchange of horses **2.** any bargaining session marked by shrewd calculation by each side — **horse′-trade′** *vi.* **-trad′ed, -trad′ing** —**horse′-trad′er** *n.*

☆**horse·weed** (-wēd′) *n.* **1.** a common weed (*Conyza canadensis*) of the composite family, with a wandlike stem and a panicle of many small, green heads **2.** same as WILD LETTUCE

horse·whip (-hwip′, -wip′) *n.* a whip for driving or managing horses —*vt.* **-whipped′, -whip′ping** to lash with a horsewhip

horse·wom·an (-woom′ən) *n., pl.* **-wom′en** (-wim′in) **1.** a woman who rides on horseback **2.** a woman skilled in the riding or managing of horses

horst (hôrst) *n.* [G., orig., thicket, prob. < IE. base **kert-*, to twist, weave: cf. HURDLE] *Geol.* a raised, usually elongated, rock mass between two faults

hors·y (hôr′sē) *adj.* **hors′i·er, hors′i·est 1.** of, having the nature of, or suggesting a horse or horses **2.** *a)* connected with or fond of horses, fox hunting, or horse racing *b)* having the manners, attitudes, etc. of people who are fond of horses, hunting, etc. Also **hors′ey** —**hors′i·ly** *adv.* —**hors′i·ness** *n.*

hort. 1. horticultural **2.** horticulture

hor·ta·to·ry (hôr′tə tôr′ē) *adj.* [LL.(Ec.) *hortatorius* < pp. of L. *hortari*, to incite, encourage, freq. of *horiri*, to urge, encourage < IE. base **ĝher-*, to desire, whence YEARN, Gr. *charis*] **1.** serving to encourage or urge to good deeds **2.** exhorting; giving advice Also **hor′ta·tive** (-tiv)

Hor·tense (hôr tens′, hôr′tens; *Fr.* ôr täns′) [Fr. < L. *Hortensia*, fem. of *Hortensius*, name of a Roman gens, lit., gardener < *hortensius*, of a garden < *hortus*, a garden] **1.** a feminine name **2.** (born *Hortense de Beauharnais*) 1783–1837; queen of Holland (1806–10): wife of *Louis Bonaparte*

hor·ti·cul·ture (hôr′tə kul′chər) *n.* [< L. *hortus*, a garden (< IE. base **ĝher-*, to enclose, whence Gr. *chortos*, farmyard, W. *garth*, fold) + *cultura:* see CULTURE] the art or science of growing flowers, fruits, vegetables, and shrubs, esp. in gardens or orchards —**hor′ti·cul′tur·al** *adj.* —**hor′ti·cul′tur·ist** *n.*

Ho·rus (hôr′əs) [L. < Gr. *Hōros* < Egypt. *Ḥeru*, hawk] the ancient Egyptian sun god, represented as having the head of a hawk: the son of Osiris and Isis

Hos. Hosea

ho·san·na (hō zan′ə) *n., interj.* [ME. *osanna* < OE. < LL.(Ec.) < Gr.(Ec.) *hōsanna* < Heb. *hōshī′āh nnā*, lit., save, we pray] an exclamation of praise to God

hose (hōz) *n., pl.* **hose** or, for 3, usually **hos′es** [ME. < OE. *hosa*, leg covering, akin to G. *hose* < IE. **(s)keus-* < base **(s)keu-*, to conceal, hide, whence HOUSE, HOARD] **1.** orig., a tight-fitting outer garment worn by men, covering the hips, legs, and feet, or extending only to the knees or ankles, and attached to the doublet by cords or ribbons (called *points*) **2.** [*pl.*] *a)* stockings *b)* socks **3.** [prob. infl. by Du. *hoos*, water pipe, of same origin] *a)* a flexible pipe or tube, used to convey fluids, esp. water from a hydrant *b)* such a pipe equipped with a nozzle and attachments —*vt.* **hosed, hos′ing 1.** to put water on with a hose; sprinkle or drench with a hose (often with *down*) ☆**2.** [Slang] to beat as with a hose

Ho·se·a (hō zē′ə, -zā′ə) [Heb. *hōshēa′*, lit., salvation] **1.** a masculine name **2.** *Bible a)* a Hebrew prophet of the 8th cent. B.C. *b)* the book containing his writings

ho·sen (hō′z′n) *archaic pl.* of HOSE (*n.* 1 & 2)

ho·sier (hō′zhər) *n.* [ME. < *hose*, HOSE] [Chiefly Brit.] a person who makes or sells hosiery

ho·sier·y (hō′zhər ē) *n.* [< prec.] **1.** hose; stockings and socks **2.** [Chiefly Brit.] other similar knitted or woven goods

hosp. hospital

hos·pice (häs′pis) *n.* [Fr. < L. *hospitium*, hospitality, inn, lodging < *hospes*, host, guest < **hostipots*, akin to *hostis*, stranger, enemy < IE. base **ghostis*, stranger, guest, whence OSlav. *gospodi* & GUEST] **1.** a place of shelter for travelers, esp. such a shelter maintained by monks **2.** a home for the sick or poor

hos·pi·ta·ble (häs′pi tə b′l, häs pit′ə b′l) *adj.* [MFr. < ML. *hospitabilis* < L. *hospitare*, to receive as a guest < *hospes:* see prec.] **1.** *a)* friendly, kind, and solicitous toward guests *b)* prompted by or associated with friendliness and solicitude toward guests *[a hospitable act]* **2.** favoring the health, growth, comfort, etc. of new arrivals; not adverse *[a hospitable climate]* **3.** receptive or open, as to new ideas —**hos′pi·ta·bly** *adv.*

hos·pi·tal (häs′pi t′l) *n.* [ME. < OFr. < LL. *hospitale*, a house, inn < L. (*cubiculum*) *hospitale*, guest (room), neut. of *hospitalis*, of a guest < *hospes:* see HOSPICE] **1.** orig., *a)* a place of shelter and rest for travelers, etc. *b)* a charitable institution for providing and caring for the aged, infirm, orphaned, etc.: now only in names **2.** an institution where the ill or injured may receive medical, surgical, or psychiatric treatment, nursing care, food and lodging, etc.

hospital corners neat, secure corners made by tucking in bedclothes at the foot with a double fold

hos·pi·tal·er, hos·pi·tal·ler (-ər) *n.* [ME. < OFr. *hospitalier* < ML. < *hospitalarius* < LL. *hospitale*] **1.** [Rare] a person receiving hospital care **2.** [usually H-] a member of a religious military society organized during the Middle Ages to care for the sick, needy, etc.

Hos·pi·ta·let (ôs′pē tä let′) city in NE Spain: suburb of Barcelona: pop. 175,000

hos·pi·tal·i·ty (häs′pə tal′ə tē) *n., pl.* **-ties** [L. *hospitalitas* < *hospitalis:* see HOSPITAL] the act, practice, or quality of being hospitable; friendly and solicitous entertainment of guests

hos·pi·tal·i·za·tion (häs′pi t′l i zā′shən) *n.* **1.** a hospitalizing or being hospitalized ☆**2.** [Colloq.] same as HOSPITALIZATION INSURANCE

☆**hospitalization insurance** insurance providing hospitalization for the subscriber and, usually, members of his immediate family

hos·pi·tal·ize (häs′pi t'l īz′) *vt.* **-ized′, -iz′ing** to send to, put in, or admit to a hospital

host¹ (hōst) *n.* [ME. *hoste* < OFr. *hoiste* < ML.(Ec.) *hostia*, consecrated host < L., animal sacrificed, prob. < *hostire*, to recompense, requite] a wafer of the Eucharist; esp., [H-] a consecrated wafer

host² (hōst) *n.* [ME. *hoste* < OFr., host, guest < L. *hospes* (gen. *hospitis*): see HOSPICE] **1.** a man who entertains guests either in his own home or, away from home, at his own expense **2.** a man who keeps an inn or hotel; innkeeper **3.** *a)* any organism on or in which another (called a *parasite*) lives for nourishment or protection *b)* an individual, esp. an embryo, into which a graft is inserted —*vi., vt.* to act as host (to) —**reckon without one's host** to make plans or decisions without considering some important factor or factors

host³ (hōst) *n.* [ME. < OFr. < ML. *hostis*, army, hostile force < L.: see HOSPICE] **1.** an army **2.** a multitude; great number —*SYN.* see CROWD¹

hos·tage (häs′tij) *n.* [ME. < OFr. < *hoste:* see HOST²] **1.** a person given as a pledge, or taken prisoner by an enemy, until certain conditions are met **2.** [Obs.] the state of being a hostage —*SYN.* see PLEDGE —**give hostages to fortune** to get and be responsible for a wife and children

hos·tel (häs′t'l) *n.* [ME. < OFr. < LL. *hospitale:* see HOSPITAL] a lodging place; inn; hostelry; specif., *same as* YOUTH HOSTEL

hos·tel·er (-ər) *n.* [ME. < OFr. *hostelier*] **1.** [Archaic] the keeper of a hostel; innkeeper **2.** a traveler who stops at youth hostels

hos·tel·ry (-rē) *n., pl.* **-ries** [ME. *hostellerie* < OFr. < *hostel:* see HOSTEL] a lodging place; inn; hotel

hostel school any of a number of boarding schools operated by the Canadian government for Eskimo and Indian children, esp. in Northwest Territories

host·ess (hōs′tis) *n.* [ME. < OFr. *hostesse*, fem. of *hoste*, HOST²] **1.** a woman who entertains guests in her own home or at her own expense; often, the wife of a host **2.** a woman innkeeper or the wife of an innkeeper **3.** *a)* a woman whose work is seeing that guests or travelers are comfortable, as on an airplane *b)* a woman employed in a restaurant to supervise the waitresses, assign guests to tables, etc. *c)* a woman who serves as a paid partner at a public dance hall

hos·tile (häs′t'l; *chiefly Brit.*, -tīl) *adj.* [L. *hostilis* < *hostis*, enemy: see HOSPICE] **1.** of or characteristic of an enemy; warlike **2.** having or showing ill will; unfriendly; antagonistic **3.** not hospitable or compatible; adverse —*n.* a hostile person —**hos′tile·ly** *adv.*

hos·til·i·ty (häs til′ə tē) *n., pl.* **-ties** [Fr. *hostilité* < LL. *hostilitas* < L. *hostilis*, HOSTILE] **1.** a feeling of enmity, ill will, unfriendliness, etc.; antagonism **2.** *a)* an expression of enmity and ill will; hostile act *b)* [*pl.*] open acts of war; warfare —*SYN.* see ENMITY

hos·tler (häs′lər, äs′-) *n.* [contr. of HOSTELER] **1.** a person who takes care of horses at an inn, stable, etc.; groom ☆**2.** a person who services a truck or a railroad engine at the end of a run **3.** [Obs.] an innkeeper

hot (hät) *adj.* **hot′ter, hot′test** [ME. < OE. *hat*, akin to G. *heiss*, Goth. *heito*, fever < IE. base **kai-*, heat, whence Lith. *kaistù*, to become hot] **1.** *a)* having a high temperature, esp. one that is higher than that of the human body *b)* characterized by a relatively or abnormally high temperature; very warm **2.** producing a burning sensation in the mouth, throat, etc. *[hot pepper]* **3.** full of or characterized by any very strong feeling, or by intense activity, speed, excitement, etc., as *a)* impetuous; fiery; excitable *[a hot temper] b)* violent; raging; angry *[a hot battle, hot words] c)* full of enthusiasm; eagerly intent; ardent *d)* inflamed with sexual desire; lustful *e)* very controversial *f)* [Colloq.] very lucky or effective *[a hot streak in gambling]* **4.** *a)* following or pressing closely *[in hot pursuit] b)* close to what is being sought: said of the seeker ☆**5.** as if heated by friction; specif., *a)* thrown or batted hard or with great speed: said of a ball *b)* electrically charged, esp. with a current of high voltage *[a hot wire] c)* highly radioactive **6.** designating or of color that suggests heat, as intense red, orange, etc. **7.** [Colloq.] that has not had time to lose heat, freshness, currency, etc.; specif., *a)* recently issued or announced *[hot news] b)* just arrived *[hot from the front] c)* clear; intense; strong *[a hot scent]* ☆*d)* recent and from an inside source *[a hot tip] e)* currently very popular *[a hot recording]* ☆**8.** [Slang] *a)* recently stolen *b)* contraband *c)* sought by the police *d)* dangerous or risky for use as a hiding place **9.** [Slang] excellent, good, funny, etc.: a counter word of approval, sometimes used ironically **10.** *Jazz* designating of music or playing characterized by exciting rhythmic and tonal effects, imaginative improvisation, and, often, a fast, driving tempo —*adv.* in a hot manner; hotly —(**all**) **hot and bothered** [Slang] flustered, excited, etc. —**get hot** ☆[Slang] to act, perform, etc. with great spirit or enthusiasm —**hot under the collar** [Slang] extremely angry or provoked —**hot up** [Slang] to heat or

warm up —**make it hot for** [Colloq.] to make things disagreeable, difficult, or uncomfortable for —**hot′ly** *adv.* —**hot′ness** *n.*

hot air ☆[Slang] empty or pretentious talk or writing

hot·bed (-bed′) *n.* **1.** a bed of earth covered with glass and heated by manure, for forcing plants **2.** any place that fosters rapid growth or extensive activity

hot-blood·ed (-blud′id) *adj.* **1.** easily excited; excitable; ardent, passionate, reckless, etc. **2.** of Thoroughbred stock: said of horses

☆**hot·box** (-bäks′) *n.* an overheated bearing on an axle or shaft

☆**hot cake** *same as* GRIDDLECAKE —**sell like hot cakes** [Colloq.] to be sold rapidly and in large quantities

hot cell a protected enclosure, usually made of concrete, containing shielded windows and manipulators operated by remote control, used to handle radioactive materials, as for processing, testing, etc.

hotch·pot (häch′pät′) *n.* [ME. *hochepot* < OFr., stew < *hocher*, to shake < Frank. **hottisōn*, akin to LowG. *hotzen* < IE. base **kwet-*, to shake, whence L. *quatere*) + *pot*, POT] *Eng. Law* a pooling of property of different persons for equal redistribution

hotch·potch (-päch′) *n.* [< prec.] **1.** a thick stew of various meats and vegetables **2.** *same as: a)* HODGEPODGE *b)* HOTCHPOT

hot cock·les (käk′lz) formerly, a game in which a blindfolded player tried to guess who hit him

hot cross bun a bun marked with a cross usually made of frosting, eaten esp. during Lent

☆**hot dog** [orig. (?) so called (c. 1900) by Tad Dorgan, U.S. cartoonist (d. 1929), prob. in allusion to popular notion that the sausage was made of dog meat) [Colloq.] a frankfurter or wiener, esp. one served hot in a long, soft roll, with mustard, relish, etc. —*interj.* [Slang] an exclamation expressing delight

ho·tel (hō tel′) *n.* [Fr. *hôtel* < OFr. *hostel*, HOSTEL] **1.** an establishment providing lodging, and frequently meals and certain other services, for the accommodation of travelers, semipermanent residents, etc. **2.** in France, the mansion of a person of wealth or rank

‡**hôtel de ville** (ō tel′ də vēl′) [Fr.] *same as* TOWN HALL

ho·tel·ier (hō′tel yā′, -tə lir′) *n.* [Fr. *hotelier* < OFr.: see HOTEL & -IER] an owner or manager of a hotel

hot flash the sensation of a wave of heat passing over the body, often experienced by women during the menopause

hot·foot (hät′foot′) *adv.* [ME. *hot fot*] [Colloq.] in great haste —*vi.* [Colloq.] to hurry; hasten: with *it* —☆*n., pl.* **-foots′** the prank of secretly inserting a match between the sole and upper of a victim's shoe and then lighting it

hot·head (-hed′) *n.* a hotheaded person

hot·head·ed (-hed′id) *adj.* **1.** quick-tempered; easily made angry **2.** hasty; impetuous; rash —**hot′head′ed·ly** *adv.* —**hot′head′ed·ness** *n.*

hot·house (-hous′) *n.* a building made mainly of glass, artificially heated for growing plants; greenhouse —*adj.* **1.** grown in a hothouse **2.** needing very careful treatment, as if grown in a hothouse; delicate

☆**hot line** a means of direct, instant communication, as by telephone or telegraph, for use in emergency or crisis; specif., a direct teletype circuit (installed in 1963) between Washington and Moscow

hot pepper 1. any of various pungent peppers, esp. small-fruited varieties of the chili pepper **2.** a plant on which these grow

hot plate a small, portable device for cooking food, usually with only one or two gas or electric burners

hot pot [Chiefly Brit.] meat and potatoes cooked together in a tightly covered pot

hot potato ☆[Colloq.] a troubling or seemingly insoluble problem, issue, etc. that no one wants to handle

hot-press (-pres′) *vt.* to exert heat and pressure on with dies or tools, as in glossing paper or cloth —*n.* a machine for doing this

☆**hot rod** [Slang] **1.** an automobile, usually an old one stripped of extraneous parts, that is adjusted or rebuilt for quick acceleration and great speed **2.** *same as* HOT RODDER

☆**hot rod·der** (räd′ər) [Slang] a person, typically a teenager, who drives hot rods —**hot rod′ding**

☆**hots** (häts) *n.* [Slang] strong sexual desire: with *the*

☆**hot seat** [Slang] **1.** *same as* ELECTRIC CHAIR **2.** any difficult position subjecting a person to harassment, criticism, etc.

☆**hot·shot** (hät′shät′) *n.* [Slang] **1.** a person regarded or regarding himself as an expert in some activity or as very important, aggressive, etc.: often used ironically and attributively **2.** a fast freight train Also **hot shot, hot-shot**

☆**hot spot** [Slang] **1.** an area of actual or potential trouble or violence **2.** a lively nightclub, resort area, etc. **3.** an area of especially intense heat, radiation, etc.

hot spring a spring whose water is above 98°F

Hot Springs city in C Ark., adjoining a national park (**Hot Springs National Park**, 1 1/2 sq. mi.) that has 47 hot mineral springs: pop. 36,000

---

fat, āpe, cär; ten, ēven; is, bīte; gō, hôrn, tōōl, look; oil, out; up, fur; get; joy; yet; chin; she; thin, *then*; zh, leisure; ŋ, ring; ə for *a* in ago, *e* in agent, *i* in sanity, *o* in comply, *u* in focus; ' as in able (ā′b'l); Fr. bâl; ë, Fr. coeur; ö, Fr. feu; Fr. mon; ô, Fr. coq; ü, Fr. duc; r, Fr. cri; H, G. ich; kh, G. doch. See inside front cover. ☆ Americanism; ‡foreign; *hypothetical; < derived from

hot·spur (hät′spur′) *n.* [nickname of Sir Henry PERCY: cf. Shakespeare's *Henry IV*] a rash, hotheaded person

☆**hot·sy-tot·sy** (hät′sē tät′sē) *adj.* [rhyming slang, based on HOT: coined c. 1925 by Billy De Beck, U.S. cartoonist (*d.* 1942)] [Slang] fine, splendid, perfect, etc.

hot-tem·pered (hät′tem′pərd) *adj.* having a fiery temper; easily made angry

Hot·ten·tot (hät′'n tät′) *n.* [Afrik., lit., *hot & tot,* echoic of click consonants characteristic of their language] **1.** a member of a nomadic pastoral people of SW Africa **2.** their Khoisan language —*adj.* of the Hottentots or their language

hot war actual warfare: opposed to COLD WAR

hot water 1. water that is hot, esp. when continuously provided as a utility in an apartment, home, etc. **2.** [Colloq.] trouble; difficulty (preceded by *in, into,* etc.)

hou·dah (hou′də) *n.* *same as* HOWDAH

Hou·dan (hōō′dan) *n.* [Fr. < *Houdan,* town in NC France] one of a French breed of crested, five-toed chickens with white or black-and-white feathers

Hou·din·i (hōō dē′nē), **Harry** (born *Erich Weiss*) 1874–1926; U.S. stage magician

Hou·don (ōō dōn′; E. hōō′dän), **Jean An·toine** (zhän än twän′) 1741–1828; Fr. sculptor

hound[1] (hound) *n.* [ME. < OE. *hund,* a dog (generic term), akin to G. *hund* < IE. base *kwon-, dog, whence Gr. *kyōn,* L. *canis:* sense 1 shows specialization, accompanied by generalization of OE. *dogga* (see DOG)] **1.** any of several breeds of large hunting dogs characterized by long, drooping ears, short hair, and a deep-throated bark **2.** any dog **3.** a contemptible person ☆**4.** [Slang] a devotee or fan [autograph *hound*] —*vt.* **1.** to hunt or chase with or as with hounds; chase or follow continually; nag [to *hound* a debtor] **2.** to urge on; incite as to pursuit —**SYN.** see BAIT —**follow the** (or **ride to**) **hounds** to hunt (a fox, etc.) on horseback with hounds

hound[2] (hound) *n.* [< ME. *houn* < ON. *hūnn,* knob (< IE. base *keu-,* to swell, arch, whence L. *cavus,* hollow), with unhistoric *-d* after HOUND[1]] **1.** *Shipbuilding* a projection at the masthead for supporting the top trestletrees and the upper parts of the lower rigging **2.** a side bar in a vehicle, for increasing the rigidity of the parts connected

hound's-tongue (houndz′tuŋ′) *n.* any of a genus (*Cynoglossum*) of weedy plants of the borage family, with reddish-purple flowers and hairy leaves shaped somewhat like a hound's tongue

hounds·tooth check (-tōōth′) a pattern of irregular broken checks, used in woven material for jackets, shirts, etc.: also **hound's-tooth check**

hour (our) *n.* [ME. < OFr. *hore* < L. *hora* < Gr. *hōra,* hour, time, period, season < IE. base *yē-,* year, summer (< *ei-,* to go), whence YEAR] **1.** *a)* a division of time, one of the twenty-four parts of a day; sixty minutes *b)* one of the twelve points on a clock, watch, etc. marking the beginning or end of such a division [the ninth *hour*] **2.** a point or period of time; specif., *a)* a fixed point or period of time for a particular activity, occasion, etc. [the dinner *hour*] *b)* an indefinite period of time of a specified kind [his finest *hour*] *c)* [pl.] a period fixed for work, receiving patients, etc. [office *hours* from 2 to 5] *d)* [pl.] the usual times for getting up or going to bed [to keep late *hours*] **3.** the time of day as indicated by a timepiece or as reckoned from midnight to midnight, expressed in hours and minutes [arrival at 14:30 *hours*] **4.** a measure of distance set by the normal amount of time passed in traveling it [two *hours* from New York to Philadelphia by rail] **5.** *Astron.* a sidereal hour; angular unit of right ascension equaling 15° measured along the celestial equator **6.** *Eccles. a) same as* CANONICAL HOUR *b)* the prayers said at a canonical hour See BREVIARY ☆**7.** *Educ.* a class session of approximately one hour: each hour of a course per week is a unit of academic credit —**after hours** after the regular hours for business, school, etc. —**hour after hour** every hour —**hour by hour** each hour —**of the hour** most prominent at this time —**one's hour** the time of one's death —**the small** (or **wee**) **hours** the hours just after midnight

hour angle *Astron.* the angle formed at the pole between the hour circle of a heavenly body and the observer's celestial meridian

hour circle *Astron.* any great circle of the celestial sphere which passes through the celestial poles and is therefore perpendicular to the celestial equator

hour·glass (-glas′, -gläs′) *n.* an instrument for measuring time by the trickling of sand, mercury, water, etc., through a small opening from one glass bulb to another below it, in a fixed period of time, esp. one hour

hour hand the short hand of a clock or watch, which indicates the hours and moves around the dial once every twelve hours

hou·ri (hoor′ē, hou′rē) *n., pl.* **-ris** [Fr. < Per. *ḥūrī* < Ar. *ḥūrīyah,* black-eyed woman, ult. < *ḥawira,* to be dark-eyed] **1.** any of the beautiful nymphs of the Moslem Paradise, among the rewards of faithful Moslems **2.** a seductively beautiful woman

hour·ly (our′lē) *adj.* **1.** done, taken, or happening every hour **2.** completed or hap- HOURGLASS

pening in the course of an hour [the *hourly* output] **3.** reckoned by the hour [*hourly* wage] **4.** frequent or continual [to live in *hourly* dread] —*adv.* **1.** at or during every hour **2.** at any hour; soon **3.** with frequency; continually

Hours (ourz) *n.pl.* [see HOUR] *Gr. Myth.* the goddesses of the seasons, justice, order, etc.

house (hous; *for v.* houz) *n., pl.* **hous·es** (hou′ziz) [ME. *hous* < OE. *hus,* akin to G. *haus* (OHG. *hūs*) < IE. *(s)keus-* < base *(s)keu-,* to cover, whence HIDE[1]] **1.** a building for human beings to live in; specif., *a)* the building or part of a building occupied by one family or tenant; dwelling place *b)* a college in a university *c)* an inn; tavern; hotel *d)* a building where a group of people live as a unit [a fraternity *house*] *e)* a monastery, nunnery, or similar religious establishment ☆*f)* [Colloq.] a brothel **2.** the people who live in a house, considered as a unit; social group; esp., a family or household **3.** a family as including kin, ancestors, and descendants, esp. a royal or noble family [the *House* of Tudor] **4.** something regarded as a house; place that provides shelter, living space, etc.; specif., *a)* the habitation of an animal, as the shell of a mollusk *b)* a building or shelter where animals are kept [the monkey *house* in a zoo] *c)* a building where things are kept when not in use [a carriage *house*] *d) same as* DECKHOUSE **5.** any place where something is thought of as living, resting, etc. **6.** *a)* a theater *b)* the audience in a theater **7.** *a)* a place of business *b)* a business firm; commercial establishment ☆**8.** the management of a gambling establishment **9.** a church, temple, or synagogue [*house* of worship] **10.** [*often* H-] *a)* the building or rooms where a legislature or branch of a legislature meets *b)* a legislative assembly or governing body [the *House* of Representatives] **11.** *Astrol. a)* any of the twelve parts into which the heavens are divided by great circles through the north and south points of the horizon *b)* a sign of the zodiac considered as the seat of a planet's greatest influence —*vt.* **housed** (houzd), **hous′ing 1.** to provide, or serve as, a house or lodgings for **2.** to store in a house **3.** to cover, harbor, or shelter by or as if by putting in a house **4.** *Archit., Mech.* to insert into a housing —*vi.* **1.** to take shelter **2.** to reside; live —**bring down the house** [Colloq.] to receive enthusiastic applause from the audience —**clean house 1.** to clean and put a home in order ☆**2.** to get rid of all unwanted things, undesirable conditions, etc. —**keep house** to take care of the affairs of a home; run a house —**like a house on fire** with speed and vigor —☆**on the house** given free, at the expense of the establishment —**play house** to pretend in child's play to be grown-up people with the customary household duties and routine —**set** (or **put**) **one's house in order** to put one's affairs in order

House (hous), **Edward Man·dell** (man′d'l) 1858–1938; U.S. diplomat: called *Colonel House*

house arrest detention of an arrested person in his own home, often under guard

house·boat (-bōt′) *n.* a large, flat-bottomed boat with a superstructure resembling a house, usually moored and used as a residence

house·boy (-boi′) *n. same as* HOUSEMAN

house·break (-brāk′) *vt.* **-broke′, -brok′, -brok′en, -break′ing** [back-formation < HOUSEBROKEN] to make housebroken

house·break·ing (-brāk′iŋ) *n.* **1.** the act of breaking and entering into another's house to commit theft or some other felony: it is itself a felony **2.** [Brit.] the dismantling of houses —**house′break′er** *n.*

house·bro·ken (-brōk′ən) *adj.* **1.** trained to live in a house (i.e., to defecate and urinate outdoors or in a special place): said of a dog, cat, etc. **2.** made docile, conventional, etc.

house·carl (-kärl′) *n.* [Late OE. *huscarl* < ON. *hūskarl,* lit., houseman: see HOUSE & CHURL] a member of the bodyguard or household troops of a Danish or English king or nobleman in late Anglo-Saxon times

☆**house·clean·ing** (-klēn′iŋ) *n.* **1.** the cleaning of the furniture, floors, woodwork, etc. of a house **2.** a getting rid of superfluous things, undesirable conditions, etc. —**house′clean′** *vi., vt.*

☆**house·coat** (-kōt′) *n.* a woman's garment, typically long and loose, for casual wear at home

house·dress (-dres′) *n.* any fairly cheap dress, as of printed cotton, worn at home for housework, etc.

house·fly (-flī′) *n., pl.* **-flies′** a two-winged fly (*Musca domestica*) found worldwide in and around houses: it feeds on garbage, manure, and food, and is a carrier of typhoid and other diseases

house·ful (-fool′) *n.* as much or as many as a house will hold or accommodate [a houseful of guests]

house·hold (-hōld′) *n.* [ME. *household:* see HOUSE & HOLD[1], *n.*] **1.** all the persons who live in one house; family, or family and servants **2.** the home and its affairs —*adj.* **1.** of a household or home; domestic **2.** common; ordinary

☆**household arts** *same as* HOME ECONOMICS

house·hold·er (-hōl′dər) *n.* [ME. *householdere*] **1.** a person who owns or maintains a house as his own **2.** the head of a household or family

household word a common word, saying, thing, etc. that is familiar to nearly everyone

house·keep·er (-kēp′ər) *n.* a woman who manages a home, esp. one who is hired to do so —

house·keep·ing (-kēp′iŋ) *n.* **1.** the work of a housekeeper **2.** internal management of affairs, as of a business

hou·sel (hou′z′l) *n.* [ME. < OE. *husel*, akin to Goth. *hunsl*, a sacrifice < Gmc. **kun-s-lo* < IE. base **kwen-*, to sanctify] [Obs.] *same as* EUCHARIST —*vt.* [Obs.] to administer the Eucharist to

house·leek (hous′lēk′) *n.* [ME. *houslek*: see HOUSE & LEEK] *common name for* SEMPERVIVUM

house·lights (-līts′) *n.pl.* the lights that illuminate the part of a theater where the audience is seated

house·line (-lin′) *n. Naut.* a small line of three strands laid counterclockwise, used for seizing

house·maid (-mād′) *n.* a girl or woman servant who does housework

housemaid's knee an inflammation of the saclike cavity covering the kneecap, caused by much kneeling

house·man (-man′, -mən) *n., pl.* **-men** (-men′, -mən) a man employed to do cleaning or other routine work in a house, hotel, etc.

house·moth·er (-mu*th*′ər) *n.* a woman who has charge of a group of people living together, as in a dormitory or sorority house, and serves as chaperon and, often, housekeeper

☆**House of Burgesses** the lower branch of the colonial legislature of Virginia

house of cards any flimsy structure, plan, etc.

House of Commons the lower branch of the legislature of Great Britain or Canada

house of correction a place of short-term confinement for persons convicted of minor offenses and regarded as capable of being reformed

House of Delegates ☆the lower branch of the legislature of Maryland, Virginia, or West Virginia

House of Keys (kēz) the lower, elective branch of the legislature of the Isle of Man

House of Lords the upper branch of the legislature of Great Britain, made up of the nobility and high-ranking clergy

☆**House of Representatives** the lower branch of the legislature of the U.S., certain other countries, and most of the States of the U.S.

☆**house organ** a periodical published by a business firm for distribution among its employees, affiliates, etc.

house party 1. the entertainment of guests overnight or over a period of a few days in a home, usually a country home, or fraternity house, etc. **2.** the guests

house physician a resident physician of a hospital, hotel, etc.: also **house doctor**

☆**house-rais·ing** (hous′rā′ziŋ) *n.* a gathering of the members of a rural community to help a neighbor build his house or its framework

house·room (-rōōm′, -room′) *n.* room or available space in a house; accommodation

house sparrow *same as* ENGLISH SPARROW

house·top (-täp′) *n.* the top of a house; roof —**from the housetops** publicly and widely

house·wares (-werz′) *n.pl.* articles for household use, esp. in the kitchen, such as dishes, glassware, etc.

house·warm·ing (-wôr′miŋ) *n.* a party given by or for someone moving into a new home

house·wife (-wif′; *for 2, usually* huz′if) *n., pl.* **-wives**′ (-wivz′; *for 2, usually* huz′ivz) [ME. *houswif, huswif*] **1.** a woman, esp. a married woman, whose principal occupation is managing a household and taking care of domestic affairs **2.** a small sewing kit

house·wife·ly (-wif′lē) *adj.* of or characteristic of a good housewife; thrifty, orderly, and managing well —*adv.* in the manner of a good housewife

house·wif·er·y (-wif′ər ē, -wif′rē) *n.* the work or function of a housewife; housekeeping

house·work (-wurk′) *n.* the work involved in housekeeping, such as cleaning, cooking, and laundering

hous·ing¹ (hou′ziŋ) *n.* [ME. *husing*] **1.** the act of providing shelter or lodging **2.** shelter or lodging; accommodation in houses, apartments, etc.: often used attributively [the *housing* problem] **3.** houses collectively **4.** a shelter; covering **5.** *Archit., Carpentry* a space or recess made in a solid part, as to receive the end of a beam **6.** *Mech.* a frame, box, etc. for containing some part, mechanism, etc. **7.** *Naut.* the part of the mast below decks

hous·ing² (hou′ziŋ) *n.* [< ME. *house, houce*, housing < OFr. *houce* < Frank. **hulfti*: for IE. base see HOLSTER] **1.** [*often pl.*] *a*) an ornamental covering draped over a horse or other animal *b*) a decorative saddlecloth **2.** [*pl.*] trappings; ornamentation

Hous·man (hous′mən), **A**(**lfred**) **E**(**dward**) 1859–1936; Eng. poet & classical scholar

Hous·ton (hyōōs′tən) [after ff.] city in SE Tex., a port on a ship canal connected with the Gulf of Mexico: pop. 1,233,000 (met. area 1,985,000)

Hous·ton (hyōōs′tən), **Samuel** 1793–1863; U.S. general & statesman; president of the Republic of Texas (1836–38; 1841–44); U.S. senator (1846–59)

☆**hous·to·ni·a** (hōōs tō′nē ə) *n.* [ModL., after Wm. *Houston* (1695–1733), Eng. botanist] any of a genus (*Houstonia*) of small N. American plants of the madder family, with blue, white, or purple flowers, as the bluet

Hou·yhn·hnm (hōō in′əm, hwin′əm) *n.* [coined by Swift to suggest horse's *whinny*] in Swift's *Gulliver's Travels*, any of a race of horses with reasoning power and human virtues: see also YAHOO

hove (hōv) *alt. pt. & pp. of* HEAVE

hov·el (huv′'l, häv′-) *n.* [ME. < ?] **1.** a low, open shed for sheltering animals, storing supplies or equipment, etc. **2.** any small, miserable dwelling; hut —*vt.* **-eled** or **-elled, -el·ing** or **-el·ling** to shelter in a hovel

hov·er (huv′ər, häv′-) *vi.* [ME. *hoveren*, freq. of *hoven*, to stay (suspended)] **1.** to stay suspended or flutter in the air near one place **2.** to linger or wait close by, esp. in an overprotective, insistent, or anxious way **3.** to be in an uncertain condition; waver (*between*) —*n.* the act of hovering —*SYN.* see FLY¹ —**hov′er·er** *n.*

Hov·er·craft (-kraft′, -kräft′) [HOVER + (AIR)CRAFT] *a trademark for* a vehicle which travels across land or water just above a cushion of air provided by a downward jet, as from its engines, propellers, etc. —*n.* [h-] a vehicle of this kind

how¹ (hou) *adv.* [ME. *hwu, hu* < OE., akin to OHG. *hweo* (G. *wie*), Goth. *hwai-wa* < IE. interrogative base **kwo-, *kwe-*, whence WHY, WHO, L. *quo*, Sans. *kā*] **1.** in what manner or way; by what means **2.** in what state or condition **3.** for what reason or purpose; why [*how* is it that you don't know?] **4.** by what name **5.** with what meaning; to what effect **6.** to what extent, degree, amount, etc. **7.** at what price ☆**8.** [Colloq.] what: usually a request to repeat something said *How* is also used in exclamations, as a conjunction with many of the above meanings, and as an intensive —*n.* the way of doing; manner; method —**how about** what is your thought or feeling concerning? —**how now?** how is that? what is the meaning of this? —**how so?** how is it so? why? —**how then? 1.** what is the meaning of this? **2.** how else?

☆**how²** (hou) *interj.* a greeting attributed to, and still used humorously in imitation of, American Indians

How·ard (hou′ərd) **1.** [< the surname *Howard*] a masculine name **2. Catherine**, 1520?–42; 5th wife of HENRY VIII: beheaded **3. Henry,** *see* SURREY **4. Roy Wilson**, 1883–1964; U.S. editor & newspaper publisher **5. Sidney Coe** (kō), 1891–1939; U.S. playwright

how·be·it (hou bē′it) *adv.* [HOW¹ + BE + IT] **1.** [Archaic] however it may be; nevertheless **2.** [Obs.] although

how·dah (hou′də) *n.* [Anglo-Ind. < Hind. *hauda* < Ar. *haudaj*] a canopied seat for riding on the back of an elephant or camel

how-do-you-do, how-d'-ye-do (hou′də yə dōō′, hou′ dyə-) *n.* [Colloq.] an annoying or awkward situation: usually preceded by *fine, pretty, nice*, etc. Also **how′-de-do′** (-dē dōō′)

How do you do? How is your health?: a conventionalized expression used in greeting a person or upon being introduced

how·dy (hou′dē) *interj.* [< prec.] [Dial. or Colloq.] an expression of greeting

Howe (hou) **1. Elias**, 1819–67; U.S. inventor of a sewing machine **2. Julia Ward**, 1819–1910; U.S. social reformer & poet **3. Sir William**, 5th Viscount Howe, 1729–1814; commander in chief of Brit. forces in American Revolution (1775–78)

How·ells (hou′əlz), **William Dean** 1837–1920; U.S. novelist, critic, & editor

how·ev·er (hou ev′ər) *adv.* [ME. *hou-ever*] **1.** no matter how; in whatever manner **2.** to whatever degree or extent **3.** by what means: intensive of HOW¹ [*However* did he escape?] **4.** nevertheless; yet; in spite of that; all the same: often used as a conjunctive adverb —*conj.* [Archaic] although Also [Poet.] **how·e′er′** (-er′)

how·itz·er (hou′it sər) *n.* [Du. *houvietser* < Early ModG. *haufenis* < Czech *haufnice*, howitzer, orig., a sling] a short cannon with a low muzzle velocity, firing shells in a relatively high trajectory

howl (houl) *vi.* [ME. *hulen*, akin to G. *heulen* < IE. echoic base **kāu-*, whence Sans. *kāuti*, (it) cries, OHG. *hūwila*, owl] **1.** to utter the long, loud, wailing cry of wolves, dogs, etc. **2.** to utter a similar cry of pain, anger, grief, etc. **3.** to make a sound like this [a *howling* wind] **4.** to shout or laugh in scorn, mirth, etc. —*vt.* **1.** to utter with a howl or howls **2.** to drive or effect by howling —*n.* **1.** a long, loud, wailing cry of a wolf, dog, etc. **2.** any similar sound **3.** [Colloq.] something hilarious; joke —**howl down** to drown out with shouts of scorn, anger, etc. —**one's night to howl** one's time for unrestrained pleasure

howl·er (-ər) *n.* **1.** a person or thing that howls **2.** *same as* HOWLING MONKEY **3.** [Colloq.] a ludicrous blunder

howl·et (hou′lit) *n.* [ME. *howlat*, akin ? to Fr. *hulotte* < OFr. *huler*, to howl] [Archaic] an owl

howl·ing (houl′iŋ) *adj.* **1.** that howls **2.** mournful; dreary **3.** [Slang] great [a *howling* success]

howling monkey any of a group of long-tailed monkeys (family Cebidae) with a loud, howling cry, found in Central and South America

---

How·rah (hou′rə) city in S West Bengal, India, on the Hooghly River, opposite Calcutta: pop. 513,000

how·so·ev·er (hou′sō ev′ər) *adv.* [ME. *hou so evere*] **1.** to whatever degree or extent **2.** by whatever means; in whatever manner

☆**how-to** (hou′tōō′) *adj.* [< phrase *how to make* (or *do*) *something*] [Colloq.] giving elementary instruction in some handicraft, hobby, etc. [*a how-to book*]

hoy[1] (hoi) *n.* [ME. *hoye* < MDu. *hoei*] **1.** a former type of small fore-and-aft-rigged vessel resembling a sloop **2.** a heavy barge

hoy[2] (hoi) *interj.*, *n.* [ME.] an exclamation to attract attention, drive hogs, etc.

hoy·den (hoid′'n) *n.* [Early ModE., a rude fellow < ? Du. *heiden*, HEATHEN] a bold, boisterous girl; tomboy —*adj.* bold and boisterous; tomboyish —*vi.* to behave like a hoyden —**hoy′den·ish** *adj.*

Hoyle (hoil) *n.* a book of rules and instructions for indoor games, esp. card games, orig. compiled by Edmond Hoyle (1672–1769), English authority on card games and chess —**according to Hoyle** according to the rules and regulations; in the prescribed, fair, or correct way

HP, H.P., hp, h.p. 1. high-powered **2.** high pressure **3.** [Brit.] hire purchase **4.** horsepower

HQ, H.Q., hq, h.q. headquarters

hr. *pl.* **hrs.** hour; hours

H.R. 1. Home Rule **2.** House of Representatives

h.r., hr, HR home run

Hra·dec Krá·lo·vé (hrä′dets krä′lô ve) city in Bohemia, NW Czechoslovakia: in a battle at nearby Sadová (1866) the Prussians defeated the Austrians: pop. 62,000

Hr·dlič·ka (hur′dlich kə), **A·leš** (ä′lesh) 1869–1943; U.S. anthropologist, born in Bohemia

H.R.H. 1. Her Royal Highness **2.** His Royal Highness

Hrolf (rälf, rôlf) *see* ROLLO

H.S., h.s. high school

Hsia·men (shyä′mun′) *same as* AMOY

H.S.M. 1. Her Serene Majesty **2.** His Serene Majesty

HT high tension

ht. 1. heat **2.** *pl.* **hts.** height

HUAC (hōō′ak′, hyōō′-) House Un-American Activities Committee

☆**hua·ra·ches** (hə rä′chēz; *Sp.* wä rä′ches) *n.pl.* [pl. of MexSp. *huarache*] flat sandals whose uppers are made of straps or woven leather strips

Huás·car (wäs′kär) 1495?–1533; Inca king of Peru, deposed by his half brother Atahualpa

Huas·ca·rán (wäs′kä rän′) mountain of the Andes, in WC Peru: 22,205 ft.

Huas·tec (wäs′tek) *n.* [< native name] **1.** a member of a tribe of Mexican Indians living in N Veracruz and adjacent states **2.** their Mayan language

hub (hub) *n.* [prob. ult. < IE. base *keu-*, to bend, mound, boss; ? akin to HOB[1]: cf. HIGH, HOBBLE] **1.** the center part of a wheel, etc., the part fastened to the axle, or turning on it **2.** a center of interest, importance, or activity —☆**the Hub** Boston: a nickname

☆**Hub·bard squash** (hub′ərd) a hard winter squash with a green or yellow rind and firm, yellow flesh

hub·ble-bub·ble (hub′'l bub′'l) *n.* [echoic] **1.** a tobacco pipe in which the smoke is drawn through water, causing a bubbling sound; simple type of hookah **2.** a bubbling sound **3.** hubbub; uproar

☆**hub·bly** (hub′lē) *adj.* [Colloq.] rough or bumpy; uneven

hub·bub (hub′ub′) *n.* [prob. < Celt., as in Gael. *ubub*, exclamation of aversion] a confused sound of many voices; uproar; tumult —*SYN.* see NOISE

hub·by (hub′ē) *n.*, *pl.* **-bies** [Colloq.] a husband

hub·cap (hub′kap′) *n.* a tightfitting metal cap for the hub of a wheel, esp. of an automobile

Hu·bert (hyōō′bərt) [Fr. < OHG. *Huguberht*, lit., bright (in) spirit < *hugu*, mind, spirit + *beraht*, BRIGHT] a masculine name: equiv. It. *Uberto*

Hub·li (hōōb′lē) city in Mysore state, SW India: pop. 171,000

hu·bris (hyōō′bris) *n.* [Gr. *hybris* < IE. *ud-*, up (cf. OUT) + *gwerī-*, heavy: basic sense prob. "to rush at impetuously"] wanton insolence or arrogance resulting from excessive pride or from passion —**hu·bris′tic** *adj.*

huck·a·back (huk′ə bak′) *n.* [< ?] a coarse linen or cotton cloth with a rough surface, used for toweling: also **huck**

huck·le (huk′'l) *n.* [dim. (see -LE) of obs. *huck* in same sense: ? akin to ON. *hūka*, to crouch < same IE. base as HIP[1]] [Archaic] the hip or haunch

☆**huck·le·ber·ry** (huk′'l ber′ē) *n.*, *pl.* **-ries** [prob. altered < HURTLEBERRY] **1.** any of a genus (*Gaylussacia*) of plants of the heath family, having dark-blue berries resembling blueberries, but with ten large seeds **2.** the fruit of any of these shrubs **3.** loosely, a blueberry

huck·le·bone (-bōn′) *n.* [see HUCKLE] [Archaic] **1.** the hipbone **2.** the anklebone; talus

huck·ster (huk′stər) *n.* [ME. *hokestere* < MDu. *hoekster* < *hoeken*, to peddle, akin to G. *hökern*: see HAWKER[1]] **1.** a peddler or hawker of wares, esp. of fruits, vegetables, etc. **2.** an aggressive or haggling merchant, esp. one who uses questionable methods ☆**3.** [Colloq.] a person engaged in advertising, esp. for radio and television —*vt.* **1.** to peddle or sell **2.** to sell or advertise in an aggressive, questionable way —**huck′ster·ism** *n.*

HUD (Department of) Housing and Urban Development

Hud·ders·field (hud′ərz fēld′) city in SW Yorkshire, NC England: pop. 132,000

hud·dle (hud′'l) *vi.* **-dled, -dling** [orig. (16th c.), to put out of sight, prob. var. of ME. *hoderen* in same sense (akin to HIDE[1])] **1.** to crowd, push, or nestle close together, as cows do in a storm **2.** to draw or hunch oneself up, as from cold [to *huddle* under a blanket] ☆**3.** to hold a private, informal conference ☆**4.** *Football* to gather in a huddle —*vt.* **1.** to crowd close together **2.** to hunch or draw (oneself) up **3.** to do, put, or make hastily and carelessly **4.** to push or thrust in a hurried or disordered manner —*n.* **1.** a confused crowd or heap of persons or things **2.** confusion; muddle; jumble ☆**3.** [Slang] a private, informal conference ☆**4.** *Football* a grouping of a team behind the line of scrimmage to receive signals before a play

Hu·di·bras·tic (hyōō′də bras′tik) *adj.* like, or in the style of, Samuel Butler's *Hudibras*, a mock-heroic satirical poem (1663–78) in tetrameter couplets, ridiculing the Puritans

Hud·son (hud′s'n) [after Henry HUDSON] river in E N.Y. flowing southward into Upper New York Bay: c. 315 mi.

Hudson 1. Henry, ?–1611; Eng. explorer, esp. of the waters about NE N. America **2. W(illiam) H(enry),** 1841–1922; Eng. naturalist & writer

Hudson Bay [after Henry HUDSON] inland sea in NE Canada; arm of the Atlantic: c. 475,000 sq. mi.

☆**Hudson seal** muskrat fur processed to resemble seal

Hudson Strait strait in NE Canada, connecting Hudson Bay with the Atlantic: c. 430 mi. long; 37–120 mi. wide

Hue (hwā, wä) city in N South Vietnam, on the South China Sea: pop. 104,000

hue[1] (hyōō) *n.* [ME. *hewe* < OE. *heow*, akin to Goth. *hiwi*, appearance, form < IE. *ki-wo* < base *kei-*, (dark-)colored, whence OE. *hæwen*, blue, *har*, HOAR] **1.** orig., general appearance; aspect **2.** color; esp., the distinctive characteristics of a given color that enable it to be assigned a position in the spectrum **3.** a particular shade or tint of a given color —*SYN.* see COLOR

hue[2] (hyōō) *n.* [ME. *hu* < OFr., a warning interjection] a shouting; outcry: now only in ff. phrase —**hue and cry** [Anglo-Norm. *hu e cri*] **1.** orig., *a*) a loud shout or cry by those pursuing a felon: all who heard were obliged to join in the pursuit *b*) the pursuit itself **2.** any loud outcry or clamor

hued (hyōōd) *adj.* [ME. *hewed*, pp. of *heowien*, to color < OE. *heowian* < *heow*: see HUE[1]] having some (specified) shade or intensity of color or (a specified number of) colors [rosy-*hued*, many-*hued*]

huff (huf) *vt.* [prob. echoic] **1.** orig., to blow, swell, or puff up **2.** to treat insolently; bully; hector **3.** to make angry; offend —*vi.* **1.** to blow; puff **2.** to become angry; take offense **3.** [Obs.] to swell with pride or arrogance —*n.* a condition of smoldering anger or resentment

huff·ish (-ish) *adj.* [HUFF + -ISH] **1.** peevish; petulant; sulky **2.** [Obs.] inclined to be arrogant —**huff′ish·ly** *adv.* —**huff′ish·ness** *n.*

huff·y (-ē) *adj.* **huff′i·er, huff′i·est 1.** easily offended; touchy **2.** angered or offended **3.** [Obs.] arrogant —**huff′i·ly** *adv.* —**huff′i·ness** *n.*

Hu·fuf (hōō fōōf′) *same as* HOFUF

hug (hug) *vt.* **hugged, hug′ging** [prob. via dial. < ON. *hugga*, to comfort, console] **1.** to put the arms around and hold closely; esp., to embrace tightly and affectionately **2.** to squeeze tightly between the forelegs, as a bear does **3.** to cling to or cherish (a belief, opinion, etc.) **4.** to keep close to [to *hug* the shoreline in sailing] —*vi.* to clasp or embrace one another closely —*n.* **1.** a close, affectionate embrace **2.** a tight clasp or hold with the arms, as in wrestling **3.** a bear's squeeze

huge (hyōōj, yōōj) *adj.* [ME. < OFr. *ahuge, ahoge*] very large; gigantic; immense —*SYN.* see ENORMOUS —**huge′ly** *adv.* —**huge′ness** *n.*

hug·ger-mug·ger (hug′ər mug′ər) *n.* [earlier also *hoker-moker*, apparently rhyming compound based on ME. *mokeren*, to hoard, conceal, whence the basic sense "secrecy"] **1.** a confusion; muddle; jumble **2.** [Archaic] secrecy —*adj.* **1.** confused; muddled; jumbled **2.** [Archaic] secret —*adv.* **1.** in a confused or jumbled manner **2.** [Archaic] secretly —*vt.* to keep secret —*vi.* to behave in a secretive or confused way

Hugh (hyōō) [OFr. *Hue* < OHG. *Hugo*, prob. < *hugu*, heart, mind] a masculine name: var. *Hugo*

Hugh Capet *see* Hugh CAPET

Hughes (hyōōz) **1. Charles Evans,** 1862–1948; U.S. statesman & jurist; chief justice (1930–41) **2. (James) Lang·ston** (laŋ′stən), 1902–67; U.S. poet & writer **3. Thomas,** 1822–96; Eng. writer & social reformer

Hu·go (hyōō′gō; for 2, also Fr. ü gō′) **1.** a masculine name: see HUGH **2. Vic·tor Ma·rie** (vēk tôr′ mä rē′), 1802–85; Fr. poet, novelist, & playwright

Hu·gue·not (hyōō′gə nät′) *n.* [MFr., orig., supporter of group in Geneva opposing annexation to Savoy: altered (after *Hugues* Besançon, leader of the group) < earlier *eidgnot* < G. *eidgenosse*, a confederate, ally: name later applied to Protestants in reference to the Calvinist Reformation in Geneva] any French Protestant of the 16th or 17th century

huh (hu, hun) *interj.* an exclamation used to express contempt, surprise, etc., or to ask a question

Hu·he·hot (hōō′hä′hōt′) city in N China; capital of Inner Mongolian Autonomous Region: pop. 860,000

☆**hui·sa·che** (wē′sä chē) n. [AmSp. < Nahuatl *huixachi* < *huitztli*, a spine + *izachi*, plentiful] a spiny plant (*Acacia farnesiana*), native to Texas and Mexico, with fragrant yellow flowers used in perfumery

Hui·zing·a (hī′ziŋ ə), **Jo·han** (yō′ hän′) 1872–1945; Du. historian

☆**hu·la** (hōō′lə) n. [Haw.] a native Hawaiian dance marked by flowing, pantomimic gestures: also **hu′la-hu′la**

☆**Hu·la-Hoop** (-hōōp′) [< prec. + HOOP] *a trademark for* a light hoop twirled around the body in play or exercise by rotating the hips —**hula hoop** such a hoop

hulk (hulk) n. [ME. < OE. *hulc* < ML. *hulcus* < Gr. *holkas*, towed vessel < IE. *solkos*, a pull, something dragged < base *selk-*, to pull, whence Gr. *hēlkein*, to pull, OE. *sulh*, a plow] **1.** a) orig., any ship b) a big, unwieldy ship **2.** a) the body of a ship, esp. if old and dismantled b) [*usually pl.*] a ship, esp. an old, dismantled ship, used as a prison or the like and not intended to be seagoing c) a deserted wreck or ruins **3.** a big, clumsy person or thing —*vi.* **1.** to rise bulkily (usually with *up*) **2.** [Dial.] to slouch or lounge about in a heavy, clumsy manner

hulk·ing (hul′kiŋ) adj. large, heavy, and often unwieldy or clumsy: also **hulk′y** (-kē)

Hull (hul) **1.** seaport in SE Yorkshire, England, on the Humber estuary: pop. 298,000: officially *Kingston upon Hull* **2.** city in SW Quebec, Canada, on the Ottawa River, opposite Ottawa: pop. 60,000

hull¹ (hul) n. [ME. *hule* < OE. *hulu*, akin to G. *hülle*, covering: for IE. base see HALL] **1.** the outer covering of a seed or fruit, as the husk of grain, pod of peas, shell of nuts, etc. **2.** the calyx of some fruits, as the raspberry, strawberry, etc. **3.** any outer covering —*vt.* to take the hull or hulls off —**hull′er** n.

hull² (hul) n. [special use of prec., prob. infl. by Du. *hol*, ship's hold] **1.** the frame or body of a ship, excluding the spars, sails, and rigging **2.** a) the main body of an airship b) the frame or main body of a flying boat, amphibian, hydrofoil, etc., on which it floats when in the water —*vt.* to pierce the hull of (a ship) with a shell, torpedo, etc. —**hull down** far enough away so that the hull is below the horizon

Hull (hul), **Cor·dell** (kôr′del) 1871–1955; U.S. statesman; secretary of state (1933–44)

hul·la·ba·loo (hul′ə bə lōō′) n. [echoic duplication based on HULLO] loud noise and confusion; hubbub

Hull-House (hul′hous′) a social settlement house founded in Chicago in 1889 by Jane Addams

hul·lo (hə lō′) interj., n., vt., vi. same as **1.** HOLLO **2.** HELLO

hum¹ (hum) vi. hummed, hum′ming [ME. *hummen*, of echoic origin, as in G. *hummel*, bumblebee, MDu. *hommeln*, hum] **1.** to make a low, continuous, murmuring sound like that of a bee or a motor **2.** to sing with the lips closed, not producing words **3.** to give forth a confused, droning sound [a room *humming* with voices] **4.** [Colloq.] to be busy or full of activity —*vt.* **1.** to sing (a tune, etc.) with the lips closed **2.** to produce an effect on by humming [to *hum* a child to sleep] —*n.* **1.** the act of humming **2.** a continuous, murmuring sound —**hum′mer** n.

hum² (həm: *conventionalized pronun.*) interj., n. **1.** same as HEM² **2.** same as HUMPH —*vi.* hummed, hum′ming same as HEM²

hu·man (hyōō′mən, yōō′-) adj. [ME. *humayne* < OFr. *humaine* < L. *humanus*, akin to *homo*, a man: see HOMAGE] **1.** of, belonging to, or typical of mankind [the *human* race] **2.** consisting of or produced by men [*human* society] **3.** having or showing qualities, as rationality or fallibility, viewed as distinctive of such individuals [a *human* act, a *human* failing] —*n.* a person: the phrase **human being** is still preferred by some —**hu′man·ness** n.

hu·mane (hyōō mān′, hyoo-, yōō-) adj. [earlier var. of HUMAN, now usually associated directly with L. *humanus*] **1.** having what are considered the best qualities of mankind; kind, tender, merciful, sympathetic, etc. **2.** civilizing; humanizing [*humane* learning] —**hu·mane′ly** adv. —**hu·mane′ness** n.

hu·man·ism (hyōō′mə niz′m, yōō′-) n. **1.** the quality of being human; human nature **2.** any system of thought or action based on the nature, dignity, interests, and ideals of man; specif., a modern, nontheistic, rationalist movement that holds that man is capable of self-fulfillment, ethical conduct, etc. without recourse to supernaturalism **3.** the study of the humanities **4.** [H-] the intellectual and cultural secular movement that stemmed from the study of classical literature and culture during the Middle Ages and was one of the factors giving rise to the Renaissance

hu·man·ist (-nist) n. **1.** a student of human nature and human affairs **2.** a student of the humanities **3.** an adherent of any system of humanism **4.** [H-] a follower of Humanism —adj. of humanism or the humanities —**hu′man·is′tic** adj. —**hu′man·is′ti·cal·ly** adv.

hu·man·i·tar·i·an (hyōō man′ə ter′ē ən, hyoo-, yōō-) n. **1.** a person devoted to promoting the welfare of humanity, esp. through the elimination of pain and suffering; philanthropist **2.** an adherent of humanitarianism (senses 2 & 3)

—adj. **1.** helping humanity **2.** of humanitarianism —*SYN.* see PHILANTHROPIC

hu·man·i·tar·i·an·ism (-iz′m) n. **1.** the beliefs or actions of a humanitarian (sense 1) **2.** *Ethics* a) the doctrine that man's obligations are limited to the welfare of mankind b) the doctrine that man may perfect his own nature without divine aid **3.** *Theol.* the doctrine that Jesus was of a human, not a divine, nature

hu·man·i·ty (hyōō man′ə tē, hyoo-, yōō-) n., pl. **-ties** [ME. *humanite* < OFr. < L. *humanitas*] **1.** the fact or quality of being human; human nature **2.** [pl.] human qualities or characteristics, esp. those considered desirable **3.** the human race; mankind; people **4.** the fact or quality of being humane; kindness, mercy, sympathy, etc. —the **humanities 1.** languages and literature, esp. the classical Greek and Latin **2.** the branches of learning concerned with human thought and relations, as distinguished from the sciences; esp., literature, philosophy, the fine arts, history, etc.

hu·man·ize (hyōō′mə nīz′, yōō′-) vt. **-ized′, -iz′ing 1.** to make human; give a human nature or character to **2.** to make humane; make kind, merciful, considerate, etc.; civilize; refine —*vi.* to become human or humane —**hu′man·i·za′tion** n. —**hu′man·iz′er** n.

hu·man·kind (hyōō′mən kīnd′, yōō′-) n. the human race; mankind; people

hu·man·ly (-lē) adv. **1.** in a human manner **2.** within human ability or knowledge; by human means **3.** from a human viewpoint

human nature the common qualities of all human beings; esp., *Sociology* the pattern of responses inculcated by the tradition of the social group

hu·man·oid (-oid′) adj. [HUMAN + -OID] nearly human, as in appearance or behavior —n. a nearly human creature; specif., a) any of the earliest ancestors of modern man b) in science fiction, a living, reasoning creature inhabiting another planet

hu·mate (hyōō′māt) n. a salt or ester of humic acid

Hum·ber (hum′bər) estuary in NE England, formed by the Ouse & Trent rivers: c. 40 mi. long

Hum·bert I (hum′bərt) (It. name *Umberto I*) 1844–1900; king of Italy (1878–1900)

hum·ble (hum′b'l, um′-) adj. **-bler, -blest** [ME. < OFr. < L. *humilis*, low, small, slight, akin to *humus*, soil, earth (see HUMUS)] **1.** having or showing a consciousness of one's defects or shortcomings; not proud; not self-assertive; modest **2.** low in condition, rank, or position; lowly; unpretentious [a *humble* home] —*vt.* **-bled, -bling 1.** to lower in condition, rank, or position; abase **2.** to lower in pride; make modest or humble in mind —**hum′ble·ness** n. —**hum′bler** n. —**hum′bly** adv.

SYN.—**humble**, in a favorable sense, suggests an unassuming character in which there is an absence of pride and assertiveness [a *humble* genius] and, unfavorably, connotes an almost abject lack of self-respect; **lowly** is an older equivalent for **humble** but never carries the unfavorable connotation of abjectness [he answered in *lowly* terms]; **meek** stresses a mildness and patience of disposition which is not easily stirred to anger or resentment and, in an unfavorable sense, connotes spineless submissiveness; **modest** implies the absence of pretensions, boastfulness, conceit, etc. [to be *modest* about one's achievements] See also DEGRADE —*ANT.* **proud, conceited**

hum·ble·bee (-bē′) n. [ME. *humbylbee* < *humblen*, to hum, akin to *hummen* (see HUM¹) + *bee*] same as BUMBLEBEE

humble pie [earlier *umble pie* < *umbles*, entrails of a deer < ME. *nombles* < OFr. < L. *lumbulus*, dim. of *lumbus*, loin: see LUMBAR] formerly, a pie made of the inner parts of a deer, served to the servants after a hunt —**eat humble pie** to undergo humiliation, esp. that of admitting one's error and apologizing

Hum·boldt (hoom′bōlt; E. hum′bōlt) **1.** Baron (**Friedrich Heinrich**) **A·le·xan·der von** (ä′lek sän′dər fôn), 1769–1859; Ger. scientist, explorer, & writer **2.** Baron **Karl Wil·helm von** (vil′helm fôn), 1767–1835; Ger. statesman & philologist: brother of prec.

Humboldt current [after A. von HUMBOLDT] the cold ocean current flowing north along the coasts of Chile & Peru

hum·bug (hum′bug′) n. [18th-c. slang: orig. reference unc.] **1.** a) something made or done to cheat or deceive; fraud; sham; hoax b) misleading, dishonest, or empty talk; nonsense **2.** a person who is not what he claims to be; impostor **3.** a spirit of trickery, deception, etc. **4.** [Brit.] a striped hard candy —*vt.* **-bugged′, -bug′ging** to dupe; deceive —interj. nonsense! —**hum′bug′ger** n. —**hum′bug′ger·y** n.

☆**hum·ding·er** (hum′diŋ′ər) n. [fanciful coinage] [Slang] a person or thing considered excellent of its kind

hum·drum (hum′drum′) adj. [echoic extension (after DRUM¹) of HUM¹] lacking variety; dull; monotonous; boring —n. humdrum talk, routine, etc.; monotony

Hume (hyōōm), **David** 1711–76; Scot. philosopher & historian

hu·mec·tant (hyōō mek′tənt) n. [< L. *humectans*, var. of *umectans*, prp. of *humectare*, to moisten < *umectus*, moist < *umere*, to be moist: see HUMOR] a substance, as glycerol, added or applied to another to help it retain moisture

hu·mer·al (hyōō′mər əl) *adj.* [ModL. *humeralis* < L. *humerus*] **1.** of or near the humerus **2.** of or near the shoulder or shoulders

humeral veil *Eccles.* a long, broad, scarflike cloth worn over the shoulders as by a priest during certain liturgical functions

hu·mer·us (hyōō′mər əs) *n., pl.* **-mer·i′** (-ī′) [L. *humerus, umerus,* the shoulder, upper arm < IE. *om(e)sos,* the shoulder, whence Sans. *áṃsa-,* Gr. *ōmos*] the bone of the upper arm or forelimb, extending from the shoulder to the elbow

hu·mic (hyōō′mik) *adj.* of or derived from humus

humic acid a brown powder consisting of organic acids, derived from humus

hu·mid (hyōō′mid, yōō′-) *adj.* [Fr. *humide* < L. *humidus* < *humere,* altered (after *humus*) < *umere,* to be moist: see HUMOR] full of water vapor; damp; moist —*SYN.* see WET —**hu′mid·ly** *adv.*

hu·mid·i·fy (hyōō mid′ə fī′, yōō-) *vt.* **-fied′, -fy′ing** to make humid; moisten; dampen —**hu·mid′i·fi·ca′tion** *n.* —**hu·mid′i·fi′er** *n.*

☆**hu·mid·i·stat** (-stat′) *n.* [HUMIDI(TY) + -STAT] an automatic device for controlling the extent to which a humidifier or dehumidifier modifies the relative humidity

hu·mid·i·ty (-tē) *n., pl.* **-ties** [ME. *humydite* < OFr. *humidite* < LL. *humiditas* < L. *humidus:* see HUMID] **1.** moistness; dampness **2.** the amount or degree of moisture in the air **—relative humidity** the amount of moisture in the air as compared with the maximum amount that the air could contain at the same temperature, expressed as a percentage

☆**hu·mi·dor** (hyōō′mə dôr′, yōō′-) *n.* [HUMID + -OR] **1.** a device, as a tube containing a moistened sponge, for keeping the air moist in a tobacco jar, cigar case, etc. **2.** a case, jar, etc. equipped with such a device

hu·mil·i·ate (hyōō mil′ē āt′, hyoo-, yōō-) *vt.* **-at′ed, -at′ing** [< LL. *humiliatus,* pp. of *humiliare,* to humiliate < L. *humilis,* HUMBLE] to hurt the pride or dignity of by causing to be or seem foolish or contemptible; mortify —*SYN.* see DEGRADE —**hu·mil′i·a′tion** *n.*

hu·mil·i·ty (hyōō mil′ə tē) *n.* [ME. *humilite* < OFr. < L. *humilitas*] the state or quality of being humble; absence of pride or self-assertion

hum·mer (hum′ər) *n.* **1.** a person or thing that hums ☆**2.** same as HUMMINGBIRD

hum·ming (-iŋ) *adj.* **1.** that buzzes, drones, or hums **2.** [Colloq.] full of activity; lively; brisk

☆**hum·ming·bird** (-bʉrd′) *n.* any of a large family (Trochilidae) of very small, brightly colored, New World birds with a long, slender bill for feeding on nectar, and narrow wings that vibrate rapidly, often with a humming sound

HUMMINGBIRD
(4 1/4–4 3/4 in. long)

hum·mock (hum′ək) *n.* [orig. naut. < ?] **1.** a low, rounded hill; knoll; hillock **2.** a ridge or rise in an ice field ☆**3.** a tract of fertile, heavily wooded land, higher than a surrounding marshy area —☆**hum′mock·y** *adj.*

hu·mor (hyōō′mər, yōō′-) *n.* [ME. < OFr. < L. *humor, umor,* moisture, fluid, akin to *umere,* to be moist < IE. base *ʷegw-, ʷugw-,* moist, moisten, whence Gr. *hygros,* moist, fluid, Du. *wak,* wet, WAKE²] **1.** orig., any fluid or juice of an animal or plant; esp., any of the four fluids (**cardinal humors**) formerly considered responsible for one's health and disposition; blood, phlegm, choler (yellow bile), or melancholy (black bile) **2.** *a*) a person's disposition or temperament *b*) a mood; state of mind **3.** whim; fancy; caprice **4.** the quality that makes something seem funny, amusing, or ludicrous; comicality **5.** *a*) the ability to perceive, appreciate, or express what is funny, amusing, or ludicrous *b*) the expression of this in speech, writing, or action **6.** any fluid or fluidlike substance of the body; blood, lymph, bile, etc. [the aqueous *humor*] —*vt.* **1.** to comply with the mood or whim of (another); indulge **2.** to act in agreement with the nature of; adapt oneself to —*SYN.* see INDULGE, MOOD¹, WIT¹ **—out of humor** not in a good mood; cross; disagreeable

hu·mor·al (-əl) *adj.* [ModL. (Paracelsus) *humoralis* < L. *humor*] of or relating to the humors of the body

hu·mor·esque (hyōō′mə resk′) *n.* [G. *humoreske* < *humor* (see HUMOR, *n.* 3) + *-eske,* -ESQUE] a light, fanciful or playful musical composition; capriccio

hu·mor·ist (hyōō′mər ist, yōō′-) *n.* [HUMOR + -IST] **1.** a person with a good sense of humor **2.** a person skilled in the expression of humor; esp., a professional writer or teller of amusing stories, jokes, etc. —**hu′mor·is′tic** *adj.*

hu·mor·ous (-əs) *adj.* [HUMOR + -OUS; sense 2 < Fr. *humoreux* (< L.), sense 3 < L. *humorosus*] **1.** having or expressing humor; funny; amusing; comical **2.** [Archaic] whimsical; capricious **3.** [Obs.] *a*) moist *b*) humoral —*SYN.* see WITTY —**hu′mor·ous·ly** *adv.*

hu·mour (hyōō′mər, yōō′-) *n., vt.* Brit. *sp.* of HUMOR

hump (hump) *n.* [< or akin to LowG. *humpe,* thick piece <

IE. **kumb-* (< base **keu-,* to bend, curve), whence Sans. *kumba-,* thick end (of a bone), Gr. *kymbē,* a bowl: cf. HIP¹, HIVE] **1.** a rounded, protruding lump, as the fleshy mass on the back of a camel: in man, a hump is caused by a deformity of the spine **2.** a hummock; mound **3.** [Brit. Colloq.] a fit of melancholy —*vt.* **1.** to hunch; arch [the cat *humped* its back] **2.** [Australian Colloq.] to carry on the back **3.** [Slang] to have sexual intercourse with —*vi.* ☆[Slang] **1.** to exert (oneself) **2.** to hurry —☆**over the hump** [Colloq.] over the worst or most difficult part

hump·back (-bak′) *n.* **1.** a humped, deformed back **2.** a person having a humped back; hunchback ☆**3.** a large whale (*Megaptera novaeangliae*) with long flippers and a dorsal fin resembling a humpback ☆**4.** a male pink salmon (*Oncorhynchus gorbuscha*) at the time it travels up rivers to spawn —**hump′backed′** *adj.*

humped (humpt) *adj.* having a hump; humpbacked

Hum·per·dinck (hoom′pər diŋk′; E. hum′pər diŋk′), **Eng·el·bert** (eŋ′gəl bert′) 1854–1921; Ger. composer

humph (humf: *conventionalized pronun.: usually uttered as a voiced snort with the mouth closed*) *interj., n.* a snorting or grunting sound expressing doubt, surprise, disdain, disgust, etc.

Hum·phrey (hum′frē) [OE. *Hunfrith* < Gmc. **hun,* strength + OE. *frith,* peace] **1.** a masculine name: equiv. Ger. *Humfried,* It. *Onfredo:* also sp. **Hum′phry 2. Hubert** **H**(*oratio*)**,** (**Jr.**)**,** 1911– ; vice president of the U.S. (1965–69)

Hump·ty Dump·ty (hump′tē dump′tē) a short, squat character in an old nursery rhyme, a personification of an egg, who fell from a wall and broke into pieces

hump·y (hum′pē) *adj.* **hump′i·er, hump′i·est 1.** having humps **2.** like a hump

hu·mus (hyōō′məs, yōō′-) *n.* [L., earth, ground, soil < IE. **ĝhom-:* see HOMAGE] a brown or black substance resulting from the partial decay of plant and animal matter; organic part of the soil

Hun (hun) *n.* [OE. *Hune* < LL. *Hunni* (pl.) < native name, whence Chin. *Hiong-nu, Han*] **1.** a member of a warlike Asiatic people who, led by Attila, invaded eastern and central Europe in the 4th and 5th centuries A.D. **2.** [*often* h-] any savage or destructive person; vandal: term of contempt applied to German soldiers esp. in World War I

Hu·nan (hōō′nän′) province of SE China: 81,274 sq. mi.; pop. 36,220,000; cap. Changsha

hunch (hunch) *vt.* [< ?] to draw (one's body, etc.) up so as to form a hump; arch into a hump —*vi.* **1.** to move forward jerkily; push; shove **2.** to sit or stand with the back arched —*n.* **1.** a hump **2.** a chunk; lump; hunk **3.** [Colloq.] a feeling about something not based on known facts; premonition or suspicion: from the superstition that it brings good luck to touch a hunchback

hunch·back (-bak′) *n.* same as HUMPBACK (senses 1 & 2) —**hunch′backed′** *adj.*

hun·dred (hun′drid, -dərd) *n.* [ME. < OE., akin to OS. *hunderod,* ON. *hundrath* < PGmc. base **hund-,* 100 (< IE. base **kmto-,* whence L. *centum:* see CENT) + **rath-,* to count (whence Goth. *-rathjan*) < IE. base **rē-:* see REASON] **1.** the cardinal number next above ninety-nine; ten times ten; 100; C **2.** a division of an English county: orig., probably, 100 hides of land **3.** a corresponding division in the early U.S., still surviving in Delaware —*adj.* ten times ten

Hundred Days the days from March 20 to June 28, 1815, the period from Napoleon's recapture of power, after his escape from Elba, to his final defeat

hun·dred·fold (-fōld′) *adj.* having a hundred times as much or as many —*adv.* a hundred times as much or as many: with *a* (or, British, *an*) —*n.* a number or an amount a hundred times as great

hun·dredth (hun′dridth) *adj.* [HUNDRED + -TH²] **1.** preceded by ninety-nine others in a series; 100th **2.** designating any of the hundred equal parts of something —*n.* **1.** the one following the ninety-ninth **2.** any of the hundred equal parts of something; 1/100

hun·dred·weight (hun′drid wāt′, -dərd-) *n.* a unit of weight equal to 100 pounds in the U.S. and 112 pounds in England: abbrev. **cwt.**

Hundred Years' War a series of English-French wars (1337 to 1453), in which England lost all her possessions in France except Calais (lost to France in 1558)

hung (huŋ) *pt. & pp.* of HANG —**hung over** [Slang] suffering from a hangover —☆**hung up (on)** [Slang] **1.** emotionally disturbed (by); neurotic, repressed, etc. **2.** baffled, frustrated, stymied, etc. (by) **3.** addicted or committed (to), or obsessed (by)

Hung. 1. Hungarian **2.** Hungary

Hun·gar·i·an (huŋ ger′ē ən) *adj.* of Hungary, its people, their language, or culture —*n.* **1.** a native or inhabitant of Hungary **2.** the Finno-Ugric language of the Hungarians; Magyar

Hun·ga·ry (huŋ′gər ē) country in SC Europe: 35,919 sq. mi.; pop. 10,198,000; cap. Budapest: Hung. name, MAGYARORSZÁG

hun·ger (huŋ′gər) *n.* [ME. < OE. *hungor,* akin to G. *hunger* < IE. base **kenk-,* to burn, dry up, whence Lith. *kankà,* pain] **1.** *a*) the discomfort, pain, or weakness caused by a need for food *b*) famine; starvation **2.** a

desire, need, or appetite for food **3.** any strong desire; craving —*vi.* **1.** to feel hunger; be hungry; need food **2.** to have a strong desire; crave (with *for* or *after*) —*vt.* [Rare] to subject to hunger; starve

hunger strike a refusal of a prisoner, protester, etc. to eat until certain demands are granted

Hung·nam (hŏōŋ′näm′) seaport in E North Korea, on the Sea of Japan: pop. 150,000

hun·gry (huŋ′grē) *adj.* **-gri·er, -gri·est** [ME. < OE. *hungrig*] **1.** feeling, having, or showing hunger; specif., *a)* wanting or needing food *b)* craving; eager [*hungry* for praise] **2.** [Rare] producing hunger **3.** not fertile; barren: said of soil —**hun′gri·ly** (-grə lē) *adv.* —**hun′gri·ness** (-grē nis) *n.*

SYN.—hungry is the general word expressing any degree of wanting or needing food; **ravenous** suggests extreme, often frenzied hunger, but may imply mere greediness; **famished** suggests hunger to the point of actual weakness or suffering; **starved** implies a continued lack or inadequacy of food resulting in emaciation or death. Both **famished** and **starved** are often used colloquially as hyperbolic equivalents of **hungry** —ANT. sated, satiated

hunk (huŋk) *n.* [Fl. *hunke*, hunk] [Colloq.] a large piece, lump, or slice of bread, meat, etc.; chunk

hun·ker (huŋ′kər) *vi.* [orig. dial., prob. < or akin to Faroese *hokna*, to crouch < ON. *hokra*, to creep] to settle down on one's haunches; squat or crouch: often with *down* —*n.* [*pl.*] **1.** haunches **2.** buttocks; rump

hunks (huŋks) *n., pl.* **hunks** [< ?] [Now Rare] a stingy, disagreeable, surly person

☆**hun·ky-do·ry** (huŋ′kē dôr′ē) *adj.* [*hunky* (< U.S. local *hunk*, goal, home, as in the game of tag, hence safe place, all right < Du. *honk*, a post, station, goal) + *-dory* < ?] [Slang] all right; satisfactory; fine: also, esp. formerly, **hun′ky**

Hun·nish (hun′ish) *adj.* **1.** of or like the Huns **2.** barbarous; savage and destructive

hunt (hunt) *vt.* [ME. *hunten* < OE. *huntian*, prob. < base of *hentan*, to seize: see HENT] **1.** to go out to kill or catch (game) for food or sport **2.** to search eagerly or carefully for; try to find **3.** *a)* to pursue; chase; drive **4.** to hound; harry; persecute **4.** *a)* to go through (a woods, fields, etc.) in pursuit of game *b)* to search (a place) carefully **5.** to use (dogs or horses) in chasing game —*vi.* **1.** to go out after game; take part in the chase **2.** to search; seek **3.** *Bell Ringing* to change the order of bells in a hunt: cf. *n.* 5 —*n.* **1.** the act of hunting; the chase **2.** a group of people who hunt together **3.** a district covered in hunting **4.** a search **5.** *Bell Ringing* a series of regularly varying sequences in ringing a group of from five to twelve bells —**hunt down 1.** to pursue until successful in catching or killing **2.** to search for until successful in finding —**hunt up 1.** to hunt for; search for **2.** to find by searching

Hunt (hunt) **1.** (**James Henry**) **Leigh,** 1784–1859; Eng. poet, critic, & essayist **2.** (**William**) **Hol·man** (hōl′mən), 1827–1910; Eng. painter

hunt·er (hunt′ər) *n.* [ME. *huntere*] **1.** a person who hunts **2.** a horse or dog trained for hunting **3.** a watch with a hunting case: also **hunting watch**

Hun·ter (hunt′ər), **John** 1728–93; Brit. physiologist & surgeon, born in Scotland

hunter green a dark, slightly yellowish, green

hunter's moon the full moon after the harvest moon

hunt·ing (hunt′iŋ) *n.* [ME. < OE. *huntung*] **1.** the act of a person or animal that hunts **2.** a periodic oscillation of the rotor of a synchronous electrical machine about its average position **3.** a periodic oscillation in the controlled function of any feedback control system, as a thermostat, caused by fluctuation in the control system **4.** any similar fluctuation, as of a control surface, compass, indicator, etc. —*adj.* of or for hunting

hunting case a watchcase with a hinged cover to protect the crystal: so called from use by foxhunters

Hun·ting·don·shire (hun′tiŋ dən shir′) county in EC England: 366 sq. mi.; pop. 88,000: also **Hunt′ing·don**

hunting horn a signaling horn used during a hunt

☆**hunting knife** a large, sharp knife used by hunters to skin and cut up game

Hun·ting·ton (hun′tiŋ tən) [after Collis P. *Huntington* (1821–1900), its founder] city in W W.Va., on the Ohio River: pop. 74,000

Hun·ting·ton (hun′tiŋ tən), **Samuel** 1731–96; Am. statesman: signer of the Declaration of Independence

Huntington Beach [after Henry E. *Huntington*, U.S. railroad executive] city in SW Calif.: suburb of Los Angeles: pop. 116,000

☆**Hun·ting·ton's chorea** (-tənz) [after G. *Huntington* (1851–1916), U.S. physician] a progressive hereditary chorea, accompanied by increasing mental deterioration

hunt·ress (hun′tris) *n.* **1.** a woman or girl who hunts **2.** a mare used for hunting

Hunts short for HUNTINGDONSHIRE

hunts·man (hunts′mən) *n., pl.* **-men** (-mən) **1.** a hunter **2.** the manager of a hunt, in charge of the hounds

hunts·man's-cup (hunts′mənz kup′) *n.* same as PITCHER PLANT

hunt's-up (hunts′up′) *n.* [contr. < *the hunt is up* (i.e., the hunt is starting)] a rousing tune played on a hunting horn to get the hunters out

Hunts·ville (hunts′vil) [after John *Hunt*, its first settler (1805)] city in N Ala.: pop. 138,000

Hu·nya·di (hoo′nyä dē), **Já·nos** (jä′nōsh) 1387?–1456; Hung. general & national hero: also sp. **Hu′nya·dy**

Hu·on pine (hyoo′än) [after the *Huon*, river in Tasmania] a large Tasmanian tree (*Dacrydium franklinii*) of the yew family, with scalelike leaves and close-grained wood

Hu·pa (hoo′pə) *n.* **1.** any member of a tribe of N. American Indians of NW California **2.** their Athapascan language

Hu·peh, Hu·pei (hoo′bä′) province in EC China: 72,394 sq. mi.; pop. 30,790,000; cap. Wuhan

hur·dle (hur′d'l) *n.* [ME. *hirdel* < OE. *hyrdel* < base **hurd-*, wickerwork, hurdle, akin to *hyrd*, door, Frank. *hurda*, a pen, fold < IE. base **kert-*, to plait, twist together, whence L. *cratis* (cf. CRATE), Gr. *kyrtos*, bird cage] **1.** [Chiefly Brit.] a portable frame made of interlaced twigs, etc., used as a temporary fence or enclosure **2.** a kind of frame or sled on which prisoners in England were drawn through the streets to execution **3.** any of a series of framelike barriers over which horses or runners must leap in a special race (the **hurdles**) **4.** a difficulty to be overcome; obstacle —*vt.* **-dled, -dling 1.** to enclose or fence off with hurdles **2.** to jump over (a barrier), as in a race **3.** to overcome (an obstacle) —**hur′dler** *n.*

HURDLES

hurds (hurdz) *n.pl.* [var. of HARDS] same as HARDS

hur·dy-gur·dy (hur′dē gur′dē) *n., pl.* **-gur′dies** [prob. echoic] **1.** an early lutelike instrument played by turning a crank attached to a rosined wheel that scrapes the strings and produces sound **2.** same as BARREL ORGAN

hurl (hurl) *vt.* [ME. *hurlen*, prob. < ON. echoic origin, as in Dan. *hurle*, to whirl, Norw. *hurla*, to buzz] **1.** to throw or fling with force or violence **2.** to cast down; overthrow **3.** to utter vehemently [to *hurl* insults] ☆**4.** [Colloq.] *Baseball* to pitch —*vi.* **1.** to throw or fling something **2.** to move with force or violence; rush ☆**3.** [Colloq.] *Baseball* to pitch —*n.* a hurling —SYN. see THROW —**hurl′er** *n.*

hurl·ing (-iŋ) *n.* [< prec.] an Irish game resembling field hockey

hurl·y (-ē) *n.* [< HURL] [Archaic] uproar; turmoil

hurl·y-burl·y (hur′lē bur′lē) *n., pl.* **-burl′ies** [prob. extended < prec.] a turmoil; uproar; hubbub; confusion —*adj.* disorderly and confused

Hu·ron (hyoor′ən, -än) *n.* [Fr., coarse fellow, ruffian < *hure*, unkempt head] **1.** *pl.* **-rons, -ron** a member of a confederation of Indian tribes that lived between Georgian Bay and Lake Ontario, Canada, and now live in Oklahoma and Quebec **2.** their Iroquoian language

Huron, Lake second largest of the Great Lakes, between Mich. & Ontario, Canada: 24,328 sq. mi.; 247 mi. long

hur·rah (hə rô′, -rä′) *interj.* [ult. of echoic orig.] a shout of joy, triumph, approval, etc. —*n.* **1.** a shouting of "hurrah" **2.** excitement, tumult, commotion, etc. —*vi.* to shout "hurrah"; cheer Also **hur·ray′** (-rā′)

hur·ri·cane (hur′ə kān′, -kən) *n.* [Sp. *huracán* < WInd. (Taino) *huracan*] **1.** a violent tropical cyclone with winds moving at 73 or more miles per hour, often accompanied by torrential rains, and originating usually in the West Indian region: winds of hurricane force sometimes occur in the absence of a hurricane system: see BEAUFORT SCALE **2.** anything like a hurricane in force and speed

☆**hurricane deck** the upper deck of a passenger ship, esp. of a river steamer

hurricane lamp 1. an oil lamp or candlestick with a tall glass chimney to keep the flame from being blown out **2.** an electric lamp in imitation of this

hur·ried (hur′ēd) *adj.* in a hurry; rushed or rushing; hasty —**hur′ried·ly** *adv.* —**hur′ried·ness** *n.*

hur·ry (hur′ē) *vt.* **-ried, -ry·ing** [prob. < echoic base seen in HURL or ? in ON. *hurra*, to whir, whirl around] **1.** to cause to move or act more rapidly or too rapidly; drive, move, send, force, or carry with haste **2.** to cause to occur or be done more rapidly or too rapidly; accelerate the preparation or completion of; urge on **3.** to urge or cause to act soon or too soon —*vi.* to move or act with haste; move faster than is comfortable or natural —*n.* **1.** a hurrying or being hurried; rush; urgency **2.** eagerness to do, act, go, etc. quickly —SYN. see HASTE —**hur′ri·er** *n.*

hur·ry-scur·ry, hur·ry-skur·ry (-skur′ē) *n.* [redupl. of prec.] an agitated, confused rushing about; disorderly confusion —*vi.* **-ried, -ry·ing** to hurry and scurry about; act hurriedly and confusedly —*adj.* hurried and confused —*adv.* in a hurried, confusing manner

hurst (hurst) *n.* [ME. < OE. *hyrst*, hillock, wooded mound, prob. < IE. base **kert-*, to plait, entwine, whence

HURDLE] **1.** a hillock, knoll, or mound **2.** a grove or wooded hillock Now usually in place names, as *Sandhurst*

hurt (hurt) *vt.* **hurt, hurt'ing** [ME. *hurten,* to knock, hurt < OFr. *hurter,* to push, thrust, hit, prob. < Frank. **hurt,* a thrust, blow (as by a ram); akin to ON. *hrutr,* a ram] **1.** to cause physical pain or injury to; wound **2.** to harm or damage in some way; be bad for **3.** to cause mental distress or pain to; wound the feelings of; offend —*vi.* **1.** to cause injury, damage, or pain **2.** to give or have the sensation of pain; be sore *[a leg that hurts]* —*n.* **1.** the act or an instance of hurting; pain, injury, or wound **2.** harm, wrong, or damage **3.** something that wounds the feelings —*adj.* injured; damaged *[a sale of hurt books]* —*SYN.* see INJURE

hurt·ful (-fəl) *adj.* causing hurt; harmful —**hurt'ful·ly** *adv.* —**hurt'ful·ness** *n.*

hur·tle (hurt'l) *vi.* **-tled, -tling** [ME. *hurtlen,* freq. of ME. *hurten:* see HURT] **1.** orig., to dash (*against* or *together*) with great force or crushing impact; collide **2.** to move swiftly and with great force —*vt.* to throw, shoot, or fling with great force; hurl —*n.* [Poet.] the act of hurtling; collision; clash

hur·tle·ber·ry (hurt'l ber'ē) *n., pl.* **-ries** [ME. *hurtilberye* < OE. *horte,* a whortleberry (+ *-il* suffix) + ME. *berie:* see BERRY] **1.** *same as* WHORTLEBERRY ☆**2.** *same as* HUCKLEBERRY

hurt·less (hurt'lis) *adj.* **1.** causing no hurt; harmless **2.** [Archaic] unhurt

Hus (hoos), **Jan** (yän) *Czech name of* John HUSS

hus·band (huz'bənd) *n.* [ME. *husbonde,* householder, husband < Late OE. *husbonda* < ON. *hūsbōndi,* lit., householder < *hūs,* house + *bondi,* freeholder, yeoman < earlier *būandi,* prp. of *būa,* to dwell: see BONDAGE] **1.** *a)* a man with reference to the woman to whom he is married *b)* any married man **2.** [Archaic] a manager, as of a household —*vt.* **1.** to manage economically; conserve **2.** [Archaic] to provide with a husband or become the husband of; marry **3.** [Archaic] to cultivate (soil or plants)

hus·band·man (-mən) *n., pl.* **-men** (-mən) [ME.: see prec.] [Archaic or Poet.] a farmer

hus·band·ry (huz'bən drē) *n.* [ME. *husbonderie:* see HUSBAND] **1.** orig., management of domestic affairs, resources, etc. **2.** careful, thrifty management; thrift; frugality **3.** farming

hush (hush) *vt.* [ME. *huschen* < *huscht,* quiet (mistaken as pp.): of echoic origin] **1.** to stop from making noise; make quiet or silent **2.** to soothe; calm; lull —*vi.* to stop making noise; be or become quiet or silent —*adj.* [Archaic] silent; hushed —*n.* absence of noise; quiet; silence —*interj.* an exclamation calling for silence —**hush up 1.** to keep quiet **2.** to keep from being told; suppress the report or discussion of

hush·a·by (-ə bī') *interj.* [see HUSH & LULLABY] an exclamation once used to hush infants

hush-hush (hush'hush') *adj.* [Colloq.] very secret; most confidential

Hu Shih (hoo' shē', shē') 1891–1962; Chin. diplomat, philosopher, & writer

hush money money paid to a person to keep him from telling something

☆**hush puppy** [< ?] in the southern U.S., a small, fried ball of cornmeal dough

husk (husk) *n.* [ME. *huske,* prob. < MDu. *huuskijn,* dim. of *huus,* HOUSE] **1.** the dry outer covering of various fruits or seeds, as of an ear of corn **2.** the dry, rough, or useless outside covering of anything —*vt.* to remove the husk or husks from —**husk'er** *n.*

☆**husk·ing** (bee) (hus'kiŋ) *same as* CORNHUSKING

☆**husk-to·ma·to** (husk'tə māt'ō) *n., pl.* **-toes** *same as* GROUND-CHERRY

☆**hus·ky[1]** (hus'kē) *n., pl.* **-kies** [altered < ? ESKIMO] [*sometimes* H-] a hardy dog used for pulling sleds in the Arctic

husk·y[2] (hus'kē) *adj.* **husk'i·er, husk'i·est 1.** *a)* full of, containing, or consisting of husks *b)* like a husk **2.** dry in the throat; hoarse ☆**3.** [with reference to the toughness of a HUSK] big and strong; robust; burly —☆*n., pl.* **husk'ies** a husky person —**husk'i·ly** *adv.* —**husk'i·ness** *n.*

Huss (hus), **John** 1369?–1415; Bohemian religious reformer and martyr, burned as a heretic

hus·sar (hoo zär', hə-) *n.* [Hung. *huszár,* orig., highwayman < Serb. *husar, gusar* < VL. **cursarius,* running swiftly: see CORSAIR] **1.** orig., a member of the light cavalry of Hungary or Croatia **2.** a member of any European regiment of light-armed cavalry, usually with brilliant dress uniforms

Hus·sein I (hoo sān') 1935– ; king of Jordan (1952–)

Huss·ite (hus'īt) *n.* a follower of John Huss —*adj.* of John Huss or his religious beliefs

hus·sy (huz'ē, hus'-) *n., pl.* **-sies** [contr. < ME. *huswife,* housewife] **1.** a woman, esp. one of low morals: contemptuous or playful term **2.** a bold, saucy girl; minx **3.** [Dial.] a small sewing kit

hus·tings (hus'tiŋz) *n.pl.* [*usually with sing. v.*] [ME. *husting* < ON. *hūsthing,* lit., house council < *hūs,* a house + *thing,* assembly: orig., a lord's household assembly as distinct from a general assembly] **1.** orig., *a)* a deliberative assembly *b)* a court held in various English cities and still occasionally in London *c)* the platform in London Guildhall where such a court was formerly held *d)* the temporary platform where candidates for Parliament formerly stood for nomination and spoke **2.** the proceedings at an election **3.** the route followed by a campaigner for political office

hus·tle (hus'l) *vt.* **-tled, -tling** [Du. *hutseln, husselen,* to shake up (coins, lots), freq. of MDu. *hutsen,* to shake] **1.** to push or knock about; shove or jostle in a rude, rough manner **2.** to force in a rough, hurried manner *[to hustle a rowdy customer out of a bar]* ☆**3.** [Colloq.] to cause to be done, prepared, sent, etc. quickly or too quickly; hurry ☆**4.** [Slang] to get, sell, victimize, etc. by aggressive, intense effort —*vi.* **1.** to push one's way; move hurriedly **2.** [Colloq.] to work or act rapidly or energetically ☆**3.** [Slang] *a)* to obtain money by aggressive or dishonest means *b)* to work as a prostitute —*n.* **1.** the act of hustling; esp., rough jostling, pushing, or shoving ☆**2.** [Colloq.] energetic action or effort; drive; push —**hus'tler** *n.*

hut (hut) *n.* [Fr. *hutte* (in 17th-c. military usage) < MHG. *hütte* < OHG. *hutta:* for IE. base see HIDE[1]] a little house or cabin of the plainest or crudest kind —*vt., vi.* **hut'ted, hut'ting** to shelter or be sheltered in or as in a hut or huts

hutch (huch) *n.* [ME. *hucche* < OFr. *huche,* bin, kneading trough < ML. *hutica,* a chest] **1.** a bin, chest, or box for storage ☆**2.** a china cabinet with open shelves on top of drawers and cupboards **3.** a pen or coop for small animals **4.** a hut **5.** a mining trough for washing ore **6.** a car or truck for carrying ore out of a mine —*vt.* to store or put in or as in a hutch

Hutch·ins (huch'inz), **Robert May·nard** (mā'nərd) 1899– ; U.S. educator

Hutch·in·son (huch'in sən) [after C. C. *Hutchinson,* its founder (c. 1871)] city in C Kans., on the Arkansas River: pop. 37,000

Hutch·in·son (huch'in sən) **1. Anne,** (born *Anne Marbury*) 1591?–1643; Am. religious leader, born in England: a founder of Rhode Island **2. Thomas,** 1711–80; colonial governor of Mass. (1771–74)

hut·ment (hut'mənt) *n.* [< HUT + -MENT] a hut or group of huts, as in an army camp

Hutt (hut) city in S North Island, New Zealand, near Wellington: pop. 115,000

☆**Hut·ter·ite** (hut'ər it') *n.* [< Jacob *Hutter,* 16th-c. Austrian religious reformer + -ITE[1]] any member of a group of Anabaptists, originally from Moravia, who live communally in settlements in the Dakotas, Montana, and Alberta, Canada, and hold beliefs similar to those of the Mennonites

☆**hutz·pah** (hoots'pə, khoots'-; -pä) *n. same as* CHUTZPAH

Hux·ley (huks'lē) **1. Al·dous (Leonard)** (ôl'dəs), 1894–1963; Eng. novelist & essayist, in the U.S. after c. 1935 **2. Sir Julian (Sorrell),** 1887– ; Eng. biologist & writer: brother of prec. **3. Thomas Henry,** 1825–95; Eng. biologist & writer: grandfather of *Aldous & Julian*

Huy·gens, Huy·ghens (hī'gənz; Du. hoi'gəns), **Christian** 1629–95; Du. physicist, mathematician, & astronomer

huz·zah, huz·za (hə zä') *interj., n., vi., vt.* [echoic] *former var. of* HURRAH

H.V., HV, h.v., hv high voltage

Hwang Hai (hwän' hī') *Chin. name of the* YELLOW SEA

Hwang Ho (hwän' hō') river in N China, flowing from Tibet into the gulf of Po Hai: c. 2,900 mi.

H.W.M., h.w.m. high-water mark

hwy. highway

hy·a·cinth (hī'ə sinth') *n.* [L. *hyacinthus* < Gr. *hyakinthos,* wild hyacinth, bluebell, blue larkspur, hence a blue gem] **1.** *a)* among the ancients, a blue gem, probably the sapphire *b)* any of the reddish-orange or brownish varieties of zircon or certain other minerals, used as a semiprecious stone. **2.** *a)* any of a genus (*Hyacinthus*) of plants of the lily family, with narrow channeled leaves and spikes of fragrant, bell-shaped flowers in white, yellow, red, blue, or purple *b)* the bulb of any of these plants *c)* the flower **3.** a bluish purple —**hy'a·cin'thine** (-sin'thin, -thin) *adj.*

HYACINTH

Hy·a·cin·thus (hī'ə sin'thəs) [L. < Gr. *Hyakinthos,* lit., HYACINTH] *Gr. Myth.* a youth loved and accidentally slain by Apollo, who caused to grow from his blood a flower bearing the letters AI AI (a Greek cry of sorrow)

Hy·a·des (hī'ə dēz') *n.pl.* [L. *Hyades* < Gr. *Hyades*] **1.** *Gr. Myth.* the daughters of Atlas, placed in the sky by Zeus **2.** an open cluster of more than 200 stars in the constellation Taurus, whose five brightest members form a V

hy·ae·na (hī ē'nə) *n. same as* HYENA

hy·a·lin (hī'ə lin) *n.* [HYAL(O)- + -IN[1]] any of various glassy translucent substances, esp. such a substance occurring normally in vertebrate cartilage

hy·a·line (-lin, -līn') *adj.* [LL. *hyalinus* < Gr. *hyalinos,* glassy < *hyalos,* glass] **1.** transparent as glass; glassy **2.** of or relating to hyalin —*n.* anything transparent or glassy, as a smooth sea or clear sky

hyaline membrane disease a disease of newborn infants,

a respiratory disorder caused by an abnormal membrane of protein lining the alveoli of the lungs

hy·a·lite (hī′ə līt′) *n.* [HYAL(O)- + -ITE¹] a colorless variety of opal, transparent or whitish and translucent

hy·a·lo- (hī′ə lō′, hī al′ə) [< Gr. *hyalos*, glass] *a combining form meaning* glass, glassy, transparent [*hyaloplasm*]: also, before a vowel, **hyal-**

hy·al·o·gen (hī al′ə jən) *n.* [prec. + -GEN] any of the various insoluble, mucoidlike substances found in animal tissue and producing hyalins upon hydrolysis

hy·a·loid (hī′ə loid′) *adj.* [Gr. *hyaloeidēs < hyalos*, glass + *eidos*, appearance] *same as* HYALINE

hyaloid membrane a delicate membrane containing the vitreous humor of the eye

hy·a·lo·plasm (hī′ə lō plaz′m, hī al′ə-) *n.* [HYALO- + -PLASM] the basic substance of the protoplasm of a cell: it is clear and fluid, as distinguished from the granular and reticulate parts

hy·al·u·ron·ic acid (hī′əl yoo rän′ik) [< HYAL(O)- + Gr. *ouron*, urine + -IC] a polymer occurring naturally in such body fluids as the vitreous humor of the eye and the synovial fluid of the joints, and responsible for their jelly-like consistency

hy·al·u·ron·i·dase (-rän′ə dās′) *n.* [< prec. + -ID(E) + -ASE] an enzyme that inactivates hyaluronic acid by breaking down its polymeric structure, thus promoting the diffusion of substances through tissues: found in sperm cells, certain venoms and bacteria, etc.

hy·brid (hī′brid) *n.* [L. *hybrida*, offspring of mixed parentage] **1.** the offspring produced by crossing two individuals of unlike genetic constitution; specif., the offspring of two animals or plants of different races, varieties, species, etc. **2.** anything of mixed origin, unlike parts, etc. **3.** *Linguis.* a word made up of elements from different languages, as *companionway* —*adj.* of, or having the nature of, a hybrid —**hy′brid·ism, hy·brid′i·ty** *n.*

hy·brid·ize (hī′brə dīz′) *vt., vi.* -**ized′,** -**iz′ing** to produce or cause to produce hybrids; crossbreed —**hy′brid·i·za′tion** *n.* —**hy′brid·iz′er** *n.*

hybrid vigor *same as* HETEROSIS

hyd. 1. hydraulics **2.** hydrostatics

hy·da·thode (hī′də thōd′) *n.* [G. < Gr. *hydōr* (gen. *hydatos*), WATER + *hodos*, way] a specialized microscopic pore or stoma on the leaves of many plants, through which water may be excreted

hy·da·tid (-tid) *n.* [Gr. *hydatis* (gen. *hydatidos*), watery vesicle < base of *hydōr*, WATER] a cyst containing watery fluid and the larvae of certain tapeworms, esp. a tapeworm (genus *Echinococcus*) found in the body of many animals, esp. canines —*adj.* of or like such a cyst

Hyde (hīd) **1. Douglas,** 1860–1949; Ir. statesman & writer; president of Eire (1938–45) **2. Edward,** see CLARENDON, 1st Earl of **3.** see Dr. JEKYLL

Hyde Park 1. public park in London, noted for the public meetings on popular issues that take place there **2.** village in SE N.Y., on the Hudson: site of the estate & burial place of Franklin D. Roosevelt

Hy·der·a·bad (hī′dər ə bad′, -bäd′; hī′drə-) **1.** city in SC India; capital of Andhra Pradesh state: pop. 1,119,000 **2.** city in S West Pakistan, on the Indus River: pop. 242,000 **3.** former state of SC India

hydr- *same as* HYDRO-: used before vowels

Hy·dra (hī′drə) [ME. *ydre* (< OFr. < L.), *ydra* < L. *Hydra* < Gr., water serpent, akin to *hydōr*, WATER] **1.** *Gr. Myth.* the nine-headed serpent slain by Hercules: when any one of its heads was cut off, it was replaced by two others **2.** a long, irregular, S constellation, south of Cancer, Leo, and Virgo —*n., pl.* -**dras,** -**drae** (-drē) [h-] **1.** any persistent or ever-increasing evil with many sources and causes **2.** any of a group (as genus *Hydra*) of small, soft-bodied, freshwater polyps with a tubelike body and a mouth surrounded by tentacles

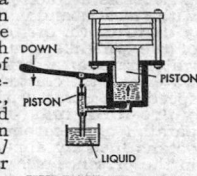

HYDRA
(1/4–1/2
inch in
length

hy·drac·id (hī dras′id) *n.* an acid that does not contain oxygen, as HCl, H₂S, HCN, etc.

hy·dran·ge·a (hī drān′jə, -dran′-; -jē ə) *n.* [ModL. < HYDR- + Gr. *angeion*, vessel] any of a genus (*Hydrangea*) of shrubby plants of the saxifrage family, with opposite leaves and large, showy clusters of white, blue, or pink flowers, often sterile

☆**hy·drant** (hī′drənt) *n.* [< Gr. *hydōr*, WATER] **1.** a large discharge pipe with a valve for drawing water from a water main; fireplug **2.** [Dial.] a faucet

hy·dranth (hī′dranth) *n.* [< HYDR- + Gr. *anthos*, a flower: see ANTHO-] *Zool.* any of the feeding individuals (*zooids*) of a hydroid colony

hy·drar·gy·rum (hī drär′jə rəm) *n.* [ModL. < L. *hydrargyrus < Gr. hydrargyros < hydōr*, WATER + *argyros*, silver] mercury: symbol, Hg

hy·dras·tine (hī dras′tēn, -tin) *n.* [ModL. *Hydrastis*, name of the genus of herbs (< Gr. *hydōr*, WATER) + -INE⁴] a bitter, crystalline alkaloid, C₂₁H₂₁O₆N, extracted from the rootstalk of the goldenseal

hy·dras·tis (-tis) *n.* [see prec.] the rhizome and roots of the goldenseal, containing hydrastine: formerly much used in medicine

hy·drate (hī′drāt) *n.* [HYDR- + -ATE²] a compound formed by the chemical combination of water and some other substance in a definite molecular ratio [plaster of Paris, 2CaSO₄·H₂O, is a hydrate] —*vt., vi.* -**drat·ed,** -**drat·ing 1.** to become or cause to become a hydrate **2.** to combine with water —**hy·dra′tion** *n.* —**hy′dra·tor** *n.*

hy·drau·lic (hī drô′lik, -drä′-) *adj.* [Fr. *hydraulique* < L. *hydraulicus* < Gr. *hydraulikos*, of a water organ < *hydraulis*, water organ < *hydōr*, WATER + *aulos*, tube, pipe < IE. base **aulos*, whence (with metathesis) L. *alvus*, the belly] **1.** of hydraulics **2.** operated by the movement and force of liquid; specif., operated by the pressure created when a liquid is forced through an aperture, tube, etc. [hydraulic brakes] **3.** setting or hardening under water [hydraulic mortar] —**hy·drau′li·cal·ly** *adv.*

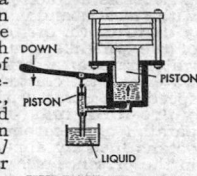

DOWN   PISTON
PISTON   LIQUID
HYDRAULIC PRESS

hydraulic ram a device for delivering a small portion of a flowing liquid to a higher elevation by using the momentum of the flowing liquid as the energy source

hy·drau·lics (-liks) *n.pl.* [with sing. v.] the branch of physics having to do with the mechanical properties of water and other liquids in motion and with the application of these properties in engineering

hy·dra·zide (hī′drə zīd′) *n.* [HYDRAZ(INE) + -IDE] any of several derivatives of hydrazine in which at least one of the hydrogens has been replaced by an acyl group, RCO-

hy·dra·zine (hī′drə zēn′, -zin) *n.* [HYDR- + AZINE] a colorless, corrosive, liquid base, NH₂NH₂, used as a jet and rocket fuel, a reducing agent, antioxidant, etc.

hy·dra·zo·ate (hī′drə zō′āt) *n.* any salt of hydrazoic acid

hy·dra·zo·ic acid (-ik) [HYDR- + AZO- + -IC] a colorless, volatile, poisonous acid, HN₃, from which the hydrazoates are derived: used in the manufacture of explosives

hy·dric (hī′drik) *adj.* [HYDR- + -IC] of or containing hydrogen

-hy·dric (hī′drik) [see prec.] *a combining form meaning* having (a specified number of) hydroxyl radicals or replaceable hydrogen atoms in the molecule [monohydric]

hy·dride (hī′drīd) *n.* [HYDR- + -IDE] a compound of hydrogen with another element or a radical

hy·dri·od·ic acid (hī′drē äd′ik) [HYDR- + IODIC] a strong acid, HI, that is a solution of the gas hydrogen iodide in water

hy·dro¹ (hī′drō) *n., pl.* -**dros** [Brit. Colloq.] a place, such as a spa, where people go to get hydropathic treatments

hy·dro² (hī′drō) *n.* [Canad.] **1.** hydroelectric power **2.** *pl.* -**dros** a hydroelectric power plant —*adj.* [Canad.] hydroelectric

hy·dro- (hī′drō, -drə) [< Gr. *hydōr*, WATER] *a combining form meaning:* **1.** water [hydrostatic, hydrometer] **2.** containing hydrogen [hydrocyanic]

hy·dro·bro·mic acid (hī′drə brō′mik) [HYDRO- + BROMIC] a strong acid, HBr, that is a solution of the gas hydrogen bromide in water

hy·dro·car·bon (hī′drə kär′bən) *n.* any compound containing only hydrogen and carbon: benzene and methane are hydrocarbons

hy·dro·cele (hī′drə sēl′) *n.* [L. < Gr. *hydrokēlē < hydōr*, WATER + *kēlē*, tumor: see -CELE] a collection of watery fluid in a cavity of the body, esp. in the scrotum or along the spermatic cord

hy·dro·ceph·a·lus (hī′drə sef′ə ləs) *n.* [ModL. < Gr. *hydrokephalon < hydōr*, WATER + *kephalē*, head: see CEPHALIC] a condition characterized by an abnormal increase in the amount of fluid in the cranium, esp. in young children, causing enlargement of the head and destruction of the brain: also **hy′dro·ceph′a·ly** (-lē) —**hy′dro·ce·phal′ic** (-sə fal′ik) *adj., n.* —**hy′dro·ceph′a·lous** (-ləs) *adj.*

hy·dro·chlo·ric acid (hī′drə klôr′ik) [HYDRO- + CHLORIC] a strong, highly corrosive acid, HCl, that is a solution of the gas hydrogen chloride in water: it is widely used in ore processing, for cleaning metals, as a reagent, etc.

hy·dro·chlo·ride (-klôr′īd) *n.* a compound of hydrochloric acid and an organic base

hy·dro·col·loid (-käl′oid) *n.* [HYDRO- + COLLOID] any of several substances that form gels with water

☆**hy·dro·cor·ti·sone** (-kôrt′ə sōn′, -zōn′) *n.* [HYDRO- + CORTISONE] *same as* CORTISOL

hy·dro·cy·an·ic acid (-sī an′ik) [HYDRO- + CYANIC] a weak, highly poisonous acid, HCN, produced by treating a cyanide with an acid or by reacting ammonia with hydrocarbons, and existing as a colorless liquid with the odor of bitter almonds: it is used as a fumigant, poison gas, in metallurgy, etc.

hy·dro·dy·nam·ic (-dī nam′ik) *adj.* **1.** having to do with hydrodynamics **2.** of, derived from, or operated by, the action of water, etc. in motion —**hy′dro·dy·nam′i·cal·ly** *adv.*

hy·dro·dy·nam·ics (-dī nam′iks) *n.pl.* [*with sing. v.*] the branch of physics having to do with the motion and action of water and other liquids; dynamics of liquids

hy·dro·e·lec·tric (-i lek′trik) *adj.* producing, or having to do with the production of, electricity by water power or by the friction of water or steam —**hy′dro·e·lec′tric′i·ty** *n.*

hy·dro·fluor·ic acid (hī′drə flôr′ik, -floor′-) [HYDRO- + FLUOR(INE) + -IC] an acid, H_4F_6, H_3F_4, H_2F_2, or HF (depending on the temperature), produced by the reaction of concentrated sulfuric acid with solid fluorides, and existing as a colorless, fuming, corrosive liquid: it reacts with silicates and is therefore used in etching glass

hy·dro·foil (hī′drə foil′) *n.* [HYDRO- + (AIR)FOIL] 1. any of the winglike structures attached to the hull of some watercraft: at a certain speed the hull is lifted above the water and the craft skims along on the hydrofoils at great speeds 2. a craft with hydrofoils

hy·dro·form·ing (-fôr′miŋ) *n.* a process for converting paraffin hydrocarbons of low octane numbers into high-octane fuels by applying high temperatures and pressures in the presence of hydrogen and a catalyst

hy·dro·gen (hī′drə jən) *n.* [Fr. *hydrogène* (see HYDRO- & -GEN): coined in 1787 by the Fr. chemist G. de Morveau, in reference to the generation of water from the combustion of hydrogen] a flammable, colorless, odorless, gaseous chemical element, the lightest of all known substances: symbol, H; at. wt., 1.00797; at. no., 1; density 0.0899 g/l (0°C); melt. pt., −259.14°C; boil. pt., −252.8°C —**hy·drog·e·nous** (hī drä j′ə nəs) *adj.*

hy·dro·gen·ate (hī′drə jə nāt′, hī dräj′ə-) *vt.* -at′ed, -at′ing to combine with, treat with, or expose to the action of, hydrogen [oil is *hydrogenated* to produce a solid fat] —**hy′dro·gen·a′tion** *n.*

☆**hydrogen bomb** an extremely destructive kind of atom bomb operating on the principle of nuclear fusion, in which the atoms of heavy isotopes of hydrogen (deuterium and tritium) are fused with each other under the extraordinarily intense heat and pressure created by explosion of a nuclear-fission unit in the bomb: cf. NUCLEAR FUSION

hydrogen bond a bond formed through a hydrogen atom between an electronegative atom or group and a similar atom or group attached to a different molecule

hydrogen ion the positively charged ion in all acids: symbol, H⁺

hy·dro·gen·ize (hī′drə jə nīz′, hī dräj′ə-) *vt.* -ized′, -iz′ing *same as* HYDROGENATE

hydrogen peroxide an unstable compound, H_2O_2, a colorless, syrupy liquid, often used in dilute solution as a bleaching or disinfecting agent, and in more concentrated form as a rocket fuel, in the production of foam rubber, etc.

hydrogen sulfide a flammable, poisonous gas, H_2S, with the characteristic odor of rotten eggs, widely used as a reagent in analytical chemistry

hy·drog·ra·phy (hī dräg′rə fē) *n.* [Fr. *hydrographie*: see HYDRO- & -GRAPHY] 1. the study, description, and mapping of oceans, lakes, and rivers, esp. with reference to their navigational and commercial uses 2. the oceans, lakes, rivers, etc. of a region, esp. as dealt with on a map or in a survey, treatise, etc. —**hy·drog′ra·pher** *n.* —**hy·dro·graph·ic** (hī′drə graf′ik), **hy′dro·graph′i·cal** *adj.*

hy·droid (hī′droid) *adj.* [HYDR(A) + -OID] 1. like a hydra or polyp 2. of or related to the group of hydrozoans of which the hydra is a member —*n.* any member of a large group of colonial hydrozoans, mostly marine, typically consisting of two kinds of polyps, individuals specialized for feeding the colony and asexual individuals specialized for reproduction

hy·dro·ki·net·ic (hī′drō ki net′ik) *adj.* [HYDRO- + KINETIC] of the motions of fluids or the forces producing or influencing such motions —**hy′dro·ki·net′i·cal·ly** *adv.*

hy·dro·ki·net·ics (-iks) *n.pl.* [*with sing. v.*] [HYDRO- + KINETICS] the branch of physics having to do with fluids in motion

hy·drol·o·gy (hī dräl′ə jē) *n.* [ModL. *hydrologia*: see HYDRO- & -LOGY] the science dealing with the waters of the earth, their distribution on the surface and underground, and the cycle involving evaporation, precipitation, flow to the seas, etc. —**hy·dro·log·ic** (hī′drə läj′ik), **hy′dro·log′i·cal** *adj.* —**hy·drol′o·gist** *n.*

hy·drol·y·sate (hī dräl′ə sāt′, -zāt′) *n.* a product resulting from hydrolysis: also **hy·drol′y·zate′** (-zāt′)

hy·drol·y·sis (hī dräl′ə sis) *n., pl.* -ses′ (-sēz′) [HYDRO- + -LYSIS] a chemical reaction in which a compound reacts with the ions of water (H⁺ and OH⁻) to produce a weak acid, a weak base, or both —**hy·dro·lyt·ic** (hī′drə lit′ik) *adj.*

hy·dro·lyte (hī′drə līt′) *n.* any substance undergoing hydrolysis

hy·dro·lyze (-līz′) *vt., vi.* -lyzed′, -lyz′ing to undergo or cause to undergo hydrolysis —**hy′dro·lyz′a·ble** *adj.*

hy·dro·mag·net·ics (hī′drō mag net′iks) *n.pl.* [*with sing. v.*] *same as* MAGNETOHYDRODYNAMICS —**hy′dro·mag·net′ic** *adj.*

hy·dro·man·cy (hī′drə man′sē) *n.* [ME. *idromancie* < OFr. *ydromancie* < L. *hydromantia* < Gr. *hydromanteia*: see HYDRO- & -MANCY] divination by the observation of water —**hy′dro·man′cer** (-sər) *n.*

hy·dro·me·chan·ics (hī′drō mə kan′iks) *n.pl.* [*with sing. v.*] [HYDRO- + MECHANICS] the branch of physics having to do with the laws governing the motion and equilibrium of fluids —**hy′dro·me·chan′i·cal** *adj.*

hy·dro·me·du·sa (-mə dōō′sə, -dyōō′-; -zə) *n., pl.* -sae (-sē) [ModL.: see HYDRA & MEDUSA] a jellyfish (*medusa*) formed from a bud produced asexually on a hydroid

hy·dro·mel (hī′drə mel′) *n.* [ME. *ydromel* (prob. via OFr. *ydromelle*) < L. *hydromeli* < Gr. *hydromeli* < *hydōr*, WATER + *meli*, honey: for IE. base see MELLIFLUOUS] a mixture of honey and water that becomes mead when fermented

hy·dro·met·al·lur·gy (hī′drə met′′l ʉr′jē) *n.* [HYDRO- + METALLURGY] the recovery of metals from ores by a liquid process, as by leaching the ore with an acid

hy·dro·me·te·or (-mēt′ē ər) *n.* any product formed of atmospheric water vapor, as rain, snow, fog, dew, etc.

hy·drom·e·ter (hī dräm′ə tər) *n.* [HYDRO- + -METER] an instrument for measuring the specific gravity of liquids: it is a graduated, weighted tube that sinks in a liquid up to the point determined by the density of the liquid —**hy·dro·met·ric** (hī′drə met′rik), **hy′dro·met′ri·cal** *adj.* —**hy·drom′e·try** *n.*

hy·dro·mor·phic (hī′drə môr′fik) *adj.* [HYDRO- + -MORPHIC] *Bot.* having properties of structure adapted to growth wholly or partially in water

☆**hy·dro·naut** (hī′drə nôt′) *n.* [HYDRO- + (ASTRO)NAUT] *U.S. Navy* a person trained to operate deep submergence vehicles

hy·drop·a·thy (hī dräp′ə thē) *n.* [HYDRO- + -PATHY] a method of treatment that attempts to cure all diseases by the external or internal use of water —**hy·dro·path·ic** (hī′drə path′ik) *adj.* —**hy·drop′a·thist** *n.*

hy·dro·phane (hī′drə fān′) *n.* [HYDRO- + -PHANE] an opaque variety of opal that becomes translucent or transparent when wet —**hy·droph·a·nous** (hī dräf′ə nəs) *adj.*

hy·dro·phil·ic (hī′drə fil′ik) *adj.* [HYDRO- + -PHIL(IA) + -IC] capable of uniting with or taking up water: also **hy′dro·phile′** (-fīl′)

hy·droph·i·lous (hī dräf′ə ləs) *adj.* [HYDRO- + -PHILOUS] 1. *same as* HYDROPHYTIC 2. requiring the presence of water for fertilization

hy·dro·pho·bi·a (hī′drə fō′bē ə) *n.* [LL. < Gr. *hydrophobia*: see HYDRO- & -PHOBIA] 1. an abnormal fear of water 2. [from the symptomatic inability to swallow liquids] *same as* RABIES

hy·dro·pho·bic (-fō′bik, -fäb′ik) *adj.* 1. of or having hydrophobia 2. not capable of uniting with or absorbing water: also **hy′dro·phobe′** (-fōb′) —**hy′dro·pho·bic′i·ty** (-fō bis′ə tē) *n.*

hy·dro·phone (hī′drə fōn′) *n.* [HYDRO- + -PHONE] an instrument for detecting, and registering the distance and direction of, sound transmitted through water

hy·dro·phyte (-fīt′) *n.* [HYDRO- + -PHYTE] any plant growing only in water or very wet earth —**hy′dro·phyt′ic** (-fit′ik) *adj.*

hy·dro·plane (-plān′) *n.* [HYDRO- + PLANE⁴] 1. a small, light motorboat with hydrofoils or with a flat bottom rising in steps to the stern so that it can skim along the water's surface at high speeds 2. *same as* SEAPLANE 3. an attachment for an airplane that enables it to glide along on the water 4. a horizontal rudder used to submerge or raise a submarine —*vi.* -planed′, -plan′ing 1. to drive or ride in a hydroplane 2. to skim along like a hydroplane

☆**hy·dro·pon·ics** (hī′drə pän′iks) *n.pl.* [*with sing. v.*] [HYDRO- + (GEO)PON(IC) + -ICS] the science of growing plants in solutions or moist inert material containing the necessary minerals, instead of in soil —**hy·dro·pon′ic** *adj.* —**hy·dro·pon′i·cal·ly** *adv.* —**hy′dro·pon′i·cist** (-ə sist), **hy·drop·o·nist** (hī dräp′ə nist) *n.*

hy·dro·pow·er (hī′drə pou′ər) *n.* hydroelectric power

hy·drops (hī′dräps′) *n.* [< Gr. *hydrōps*: see DROPSY] accumulation of fluid within an organ or tissue —**hy·drop′ic** *adj.*

hy·dro·qui·none (hī′drō kwi nōn′, -kwin′ōn) *n.* [HYDRO- + QUINONE] a white, crystalline substance, $C_6H_4(OH)_2$, used in medicine and photography, as an antioxidant, etc.: also **hy′dro·quin′ol** (-kwin′ōl, -ōl)

hy·dro·scope (hī′drə skōp′) *n.* [HYDRO- + -SCOPE] a device like a periscope, for viewing things at some distance below the surface of water

hy·dro·ski (hī′drō skē′) *n.* an elongated planing surface, similar to a snow ski, allowing an aircraft to take off or land on water, snow, etc.

hy·dro·sol (hī′drə säl′, -sôl′) *n.* [HYDRO- + SOL(UTION)] a colloidal dispersion in which water is the dispersing medium

hy·dro·space (-spās′) *n.* the ocean waters and ocean depths of the earth, esp. as a realm to be explored and investigated scientifically

hy·dro·sphere (-sfir′) *n.* [HYDRO- + -SPHERE] 1. all the water on the surface of the earth, including oceans, lakes, rivers, etc. 2. the moisture in the atmosphere surrounding the earth

hy·dro·stat·ics (hī′drə stat′iks) *n.pl.* [*with sing. v.*] [< Fr. *hydrostatique* < ModL. *hydrostaticus*: see HYDRO- & -STATIC] the branch of physics having to do with the pressure and equilibrium of water and other liquids; statics of liquids —**hy′dro·stat′ic**, **hy′dro·stat′i·cal** *adj.* —**hy′dro·stat′i·cal·ly** *adv.*

hy·dro·sul·fide (-sul′fīd) *n.* a compound containing the

HS radical and some other radical or element, produced by the partial replacement of the hydrogen in hydrogen sulfide

hy·dro·sul·fite (-sul′fīt) *n.* **1.** *same as* HYPOSULFITE (sense 1) **2.** sodium hydrosulfite, $Na_2S_2O_4$, a bleaching and reducing agent

hy·dro·sul·fu·rous acid (-sul fyoor′əs, -sul′fər əs) *same as* HYPOSULFUROUS ACID

hy·dro·tax·is (hī′drō tak′sis) *n.* [HYDRO- + TAXIS] the response of an organism to the stimulus of moisture —**hy′dro·tac′tic** (-tak′tik) *adj.*

hy·dro·ther·a·peu·tics (-ther′ə pyoot′iks) *n.pl.* [*with sing. v.*] *same as* HYDROTHERAPY —**hy′dro·ther′a·peu′tic** *adj.*

hy·dro·ther·a·py (-ther′ə pē) *n.* [HYDRO- + THERAPY] the treatment of disease, esp. in physical therapy, by the use of baths, compresses, etc.

hy·dro·ther·mal (-thur′məl) *adj.* [HYDRO- + THERMAL] having to do with hot water; esp., having to do with the action of hot water in producing minerals and springs or in dissolving, shifting, and otherwise changing the distribution of minerals in the earth's crust

hy·dro·tho·rax (-thôr′aks) *n.* [ModL.: see HYDRO- & THORAX] a condition marked by the accumulation of watery fluid in the pleural cavity

hy·drot·ro·pism (hī drät′rə piz′m) *n.* [HYDRO- + -TROPISM] movement or growth, as of a plant root, in response to the stimulus of moisture —**hy·dro·trop·ic** (hī′drə träp′ik) *adj.*

hy·drous (hī′drəs) *adj.* [HYDR- + -OUS] containing water, esp. water of crystallization of hydration, as certain minerals and chemical compounds

hy·drox·ide (hī dräk′sīd) *n.* [HYDR- + OXIDE] a compound consisting of an element or radical combined with the hydroxyl radical (OH)

hy·drox·y (hī dräk′sē) *adj.* containing or related to hydroxyl

hy·drox·y- (hī dräk′sē) *a combining form meaning* hydroxyl (in organic chemistry): also, before a vowel, **hy′drox**

hydroxy acid an organic acid, as lactic acid, in which both the hydroxyl and carboxyl radicals occur

hy·drox·y·bu·tyr·ic acid (hī dräk′sē byoo tir′ik) any of three isomeric acids, C_3H_7OCOOH: the beta isomer is found in the urine of diabetics

hy·drox·y·ke·tone (-kē′tōn) *n.* a ketone containing the hydroxyl radical

hy·drox·yl (hī dräk′sil) *n.* [HYDR- + OX(YGEN) + -YL] the monovalent radical OH, present in all hydroxides —**hy·drox·yl·ic** (hī′dräk sil′ik) *adj.*

hy·drox·yl·a·mine (hī dräk′sil ə mēn′, -am′in) *n.* [HYDROXYL + AMINE] a colorless, odorless base, NH_2OH, used as a reducing agent

hy·drox·yl·ate (hī dräk′sə lāt′) *vt.* -at′ed, -at′ing to introduce the hydroxyl group into (a compound) —**hy·drox′yl·a′tion** *n.*

hy·dro·zo·an (hī′drə zō′ən) *adj.* [< HYDRA + ZO- + -AN] of a class (Hydrozoa) of coelenterate animals having a saclike body consisting of two layers of cells, and a mouth that opens directly into the body cavity —*n.* any animal of this class, as a hydra, hydroid, etc.

Hy·drus (hī′drəs) [L. < Gr. *hydros*, water snake, akin to *hydōr*, water] S constellation near the south celestial pole

hy·e·na (hī ē′nə) *n.* [L. *hyaena* < Gr. *hyaina*, hyena, lit., sow (so called from its hog-like mane) < *hys*, a hog (+ *-aina*, fem. suffix) < IE. base *sus*, hog: cf. SWINE, SOW[1]] any of a group of wolflike animals (family Hyaenidae) of Africa and Asia, with powerful jaws, a bristly mane, short hind legs, and a characteristic shrill cry: hyenas feed on carrion and are thought of as cowardly

hy·e·to- (hī′ə tō′, -tə) [< Gr. *hyetos*, rain < *hyein*, to rain < IE. base *seu-*, juice, moisture, rain, whence L. *sugere*, SUCK] *a combining form meaning* rain, rainfall [*hyetograph*]: also, before a vowel, **hyet-**

hy·e·to·graph (hī′ə tə graf′, -gräf′) *n.* [prec. + -GRAPH] a chart showing the distribution of rainfall over a particular period of time or a particular area

hy·e·tog·ra·phy (hī′ə täg′rə fē) *n.* [HYETO- + -GRAPHY] the branch of meteorology having to do with the geographical distribution and annual variation of rainfall —**hy·e·to·graph·ic** (hī′ə tə graf′ik), **hy′e·to·graph′i·cal** *adj.*

Hy·ge·ia (hī jē′ə) [L. *Hygea* < Gr. *Hygeia*, *Hygieia* < *hygiēs*: see ff.] *Gr. Myth.* the goddess of health

hy·giene (hī′jēn) *n.* [Fr. *hygiène* < Gr. *hygieinē* (*technē*), (art) of health < *hygiēs*, healthy, sound < IE. *su-gwiyēs*, living well < base *su-*, well (whence Sans. *su-*, well) + base *gwei-*, to live, whence Gr. *bios*, life, L. *vivus*, living] **1.** the science of health and its maintenance; system of principles for the preservation of health and prevention of disease **2.** sanitary practices; cleanliness [*personal hygiene*]

hy·gi·en·ic (hī′jē en′ik, -jē′nik, -jen′ik) *adj.* **1.** of hygiene or health **2.** promoting health; healthful; sanitary —**hy′gi·en′i·cal·ly** *adv.*

hy·gi·en·ics (-iks) *n.pl.* [*with sing. v.*] the science of health; hygiene

hy·gi·en·ist (hī′jē ə nist, -jē′nist; hī jē′nist) *n.* an expert in hygiene

hy·gro- (hī′grə) [< Gr. *hygros*, wet, moist: for IE. base see HUMOR] *a combining form meaning* wet, moisture [*hygrometer*]: also, before a vowel, **hygr-**

hy·gro·graph (hī′grə graf′, -gräf′) *n.* a hygrometer for continuously recording atmospheric humidity

hy·grom·e·ter (hī gräm′ə tər) *n.* [Fr. *hygromètre*: see HYGRO- & -METER] any of various instruments for measuring the absolute or relative amount of moisture in the air —**hy·gro·met·ric** (hī′grə met′rik) *adj.* —**hy·grom′e·try** (-trē) *n.*

hy·gro·phyte (hī′grə fīt′) *n.* [HYGRO- + -PHYTE] *same as* HYDROPHYTE

hy·gro·scope (-skōp′) *n.* [HYGRO- + -SCOPE] an instrument that indicates, without actually measuring, changes in atmospheric humidity

hy·gro·scop·ic (hī′grə skäp′ik) *adj.* **1.** *a)* attracting or absorbing moisture from the air *b)* changed or altered by the absorption of moisture **2.** of or according to a hygroscope —**hy′gro·scop′i·cal·ly** *adv.* —**hy′gro·sco·pic′i·ty** (-skō pis′ə tē) *n.*

hy·gro·ther·mo·graph (-thur′mə graf′, -gräf′) *n.* [HYGRO- + THERMOGRAPH] an instrument that measures and records atmospheric humidity and temperature on the same graph

hy·ing (hī′in) *alt. prp. of* HIE

Hyk·sos (hik′sōs, -säs) [Gr. *Hyksōs* < Egypt. *Hiq shasu*, chief of the nomadic tribes] foreign (prob. Semitic) kings of Egypt (1700?–1550? B.C.), traditionally considered to have formed the XVth & XVIth dynasties

hy·la (hī′lə) *n.* [ModL. < Gr. *hylē*, wood] any of a large genus (*Hyla*) of tree frogs, as the spring peeper

hy·lo- (hī′lō, -lə) [< Gr. *hylē*, wood, matter] *a combining form meaning:* **1.** wood [*hylophagous*] **2.** matter, substance [*hylozoism*] Also, before a vowel, **hyl-**

hy·loph·a·gous (hī läf′ə gəs) *adj.* [HYLO- + -PHAGOUS] feeding on wood, as some insects

hy·lo·zo·ism (hī′lə zō′iz'm) *n.* [< HYLO- + Gr. *zōē*, life + -ISM] the doctrine that all matter has life, or that life is inseparable from matter —**hy′lo·zo′ic** *adj.* —**hy′lo·zo′ist** *n.* —**hy′lo·zo·is′tic** *adj.*

Hy·men (hī′mən) [L. < Gr. *Hymēn*: see ff.] *Gr. Myth.* the god of marriage —*n.* [h-] [Poet.] *a)* marriage *b)* a wedding song or poem

hy·men (hī′mən) *n.* [Gr. *hymēn*, membrane < IE. **syumen-*, ligature: for base see SEAM] the thin mucous membrane that usually closes part of the opening of the vagina in a virgin; maidenhead —**hy′men·al** *adj.*

hy·me·ne·al (hī′mə nē′əl) *adj.* [< L. *hymenaeus* < Gr. *hymenaios* (see HYMEN) + -AL] of marriage —*n.* [Poet.] **1.** a wedding song **2.** [*pl.*] a marriage

hy·me·ni·um (hī mē′nē əm) *n.*, *pl.* **-ni·a** (-ə), **-ni·ums** [ModL.: see HYMEN & -IUM] a superficial layer of spore-producing cells in fungi —**hy·me′ni·al** *adj.*

hy·me·nop·ter·an (hī′mə näp′tər ən) *n.* [< Gr. *hymenopteros*, membrane-winged < *hymēn*, membrane (see HYMEN) + *pteron*, a wing (see PTERO-) + -AN] any of a large, highly specialized order (Hymenoptera) of insects having complete metamorphosis and often living in social colonies: it includes wasps, bees, ants, etc., which have a biting or sucking mouth and, when winged, four membranous wings —*adj.* of or belonging to the hymenopterans: also **hy′me·nop′ter·ous**

Hy·met·tus (hī met′əs) mountain range in EC Greece, near Athens: highest peak, 3,367 ft.

hymn (him) *n.* [ME. *ymen* < OE. *ymen* & OFr. *ymne*, both < LL.(Ec.) *hymnus* < Gr. *hymnos*, a hymn, festive song, ode] **1.** a song in praise or honor of God, a god, or gods **2.** any song of praise or glorification —*vt.* to express or praise in a hymn —*vi.* to sing a hymn

hym·nal (him′nəl) *n.* [ME. *hymnale* < ML. < L. *hymnus*] a collection of religious hymns: also **hymn′book′**, **hym′na·ry** (-nə rē), *pl.* **-ries** —*adj.* of hymns

hym·nist (-nist) *n.* a composer of hymns

hym·no·dy (-nə dē) *n.* [ML. *hymnodia* < Gr. *hymnoidia*: see HYMN & ODE] **1.** the singing of hymns **2.** hymns collectively **3.** *same as* HYMNOLOGY —**hym′no·dist** *n.*

hym·nol·o·gy (him näl′ə jē) *n.* [ML. *hymnologia*, praise in song < Gr. *hymnologia*: see HYMN & -LOGY] **1.** the study of hymns, their history, use, etc. **2.** the writing or composition of hymns **3.** *same as* HYMNODY (sense 2) —**hym·nol′o·gist** *n.*

hy·oid (hī′oid) *adj.* [Fr. *hyoïde* < ModL. *hyoides* < Gr. *hyoeidēs*, shaped like the letter *v* (upsilon) < *hy*, upsilon + *eidos*, form] designating or of a bone or bones at the base of and supporting the tongue, U-shaped in man —*n.* the hyoid bone or bones

hy·o·scine (hī′ə sēn′, -sin) *n.* [HYOSC(YAMUS) + -INE[4]] *same as* SCOPOLAMINE

hy·os·cy·a·mine (hī′ə sī′ə mēn′, -min) *n.* [< L. *hyoscyamus*, henbane < Gr. *hyoskyamos* < *hys*, pig (see HYENA) + *kyamos*, bean) + -INE[4]] a colorless, crystalline, very poisonous alkaloid, $C_{17}H_{23}NO_3$, obtained from henbane and

HYENA
(2 1/2–3 ft. high at shoulder)

other plants of the nightshade family: it is used in medicine as a sedative, antispasmodic, etc.

hy·os·cy·a·mus (-məs) *n.* [L.: see prec.] same as HENBANE

hyp (hip) *n.* [Obs. Colloq.] [*often pl.*] a fit of melancholy; hypochondria (usually with *the*)

hyp- (hip, hip) same as HYPO-: used before a vowel

hyp. 1. hypotenuse **2.** hypothesis **3.** hypothetical

hyp·a·byss·al (hip'ə bis'l) *adj.* [HYP- + ABYSSAL] *Geol.* designating or of igneous rocks solidified at moderate depths, generally as sills or dikes

hy·pae·thral (hi pē'thrəl, hi-) *adj.* [< L. *hypaethrus*, uncovered, in the open air (< Gr. *hypaithros* < *hypo-*, HYPO- + *aithēr*, ether, clear sky: see ETHER) + -AL] open to the sky; roofless: said of buildings and courts in classical architecture

hy·pan·thi·um (hi pan'thē əm, hi-) *n.*, *pl.* **-thi·a** (-ə) [ModL.: see HYPO- & ANTHO- & -IUM] an enlarged cup or rim of tissue in flowers, as of the rose family, which supports the sepals, petals, and stamens —**hy·pan'thi·al** *adj.*

☆**hype** (hip) *vt.* **hyped, hyp'ing** [< HYPODERMIC] [Slang] to stimulate, excite, enliven, etc. artificially by or as by the injection of a narcotic drug: usually with *up* [*hyped*-up glamour]

hy·per- (hi'pər) [Gr. < *hyper*, over, above, concerning: for IE. base see SUPER] *a prefix meaning:* **1.** over, above, more than the normal, excessive [*hypercritical, hyperopia*] **2.** existing in a space of four or more dimensions [*hyperplane*] **3.** *Chem.* formerly, same as PER- [*hyperoxide*]

hy·per·ac·id·i·ty (hi'pər ə sid'ə tē) *n.* excessive acidity, as of the gastric juice —**hy'per·ac'id** (-as'id) *adj.*

hy·per·ac·tive (-ak'tiv) *adj.* extremely, esp. abnormally, active —**hy'per·ac·tiv'i·ty** (-ak tiv'ə tē) *n.*

hy·per·bar·ic (-bar'ik) *adj.* [HYPER- + BARIC] **1.** of or having a pressure or specific gravity greater than that within the body tissues or fluids **2.** designating or of a pressurized, usually oxygenated, chamber, used in the experimental treatment of various diseases and conditions —**hy'per·bar'ism** *n.*

hy·per·bo·la (hi pur'bə lə) *n.*, *pl.* **-las,** occas. **-lae'** (-lē') [ModL. < Gr. *hyperbolē*, a throwing beyond, excess < *hyperballein*, to throw beyond < *hyper-* (see HYPER-) + *ballein*, to throw (see BALL[1])] the locus of a point whose difference in distances from two fixed points, or foci, is constant; curve formed by the section of a cone cut by a plane more steeply inclined to the base than to the side of the cone

HYPERBOLA

hy·per·bo·le (-bə lē) *n.* [L. < Gr.: see prec.] exaggeration for effect, not meant to be taken literally (Ex.: He's as strong as an ox)

hy·per·bol·ic (hi'pər bäl'ik) *adj.* [LL. *hyperbolicus* < Gr. *hyperbolikos* < *hyperbolē*] **1.** of, having the nature of, or using hyperbole; exaggerated or exaggerating **2.** of, or having the form of, a hyperbola **3.** designating or of any of a set of six functions (**hyperbolic sine, hyperbolic cosine,** etc.) related to the hyperbola in a manner similar to that by which the trigonometric functions are related to the circle Also **hy'per·bol'i·cal** —**hy'per·bol'i·cal·ly** *adv.*

hy·per·bo·lism (hi pur'bə liz'm) *n.* **1.** the use of hyperbole **2.** a hyperbolic statement

hy·per·bo·lize (-liz') *vt.*, *vi.* **-lized', -liz'ing** to express with or use hyperbole

hy·per·bo·loid (-loid) *n.* a quadric surface distinguished by the fact that its plane sections are hyperbolas for some orientations and ellipses for others

hy·per·bo·re·an (hi'pər bôr'ē ən, -bə rē'ən) *adj.* [LL. *Hyperboreanus* < L. *Hyperboreus* < Gr. *hyperboreos*, beyond the north wind < *hyper-* (see HYPER-) + *boreas*, north wind: see BOREAS] **1.** of the far north **2.** very cold; frigid **3.** [H-] of the Hyperboreans —*n.* **1.** [H-] *Gr. Myth.* an inhabitant of a northern region of sunshine and everlasting spring, beyond the mountains of the north wind **2.** a person of a far northern region

hy·per·cat·a·lec·tic (-kat'l ek'tik) *adj.* [LL. *hypercatalecticus* < Gr. *hyperkatalēktikos*: see HYPER- & CATALECTIC] having one or more extra syllables following the last regular measure: said of a line of verse

hy·per·crit·ic (-krit'ik) *n.* a hypercritical person

hy·per·crit·i·cal (-krit'i k'l) *adj.* too critical; too severe in judgment; hard to please —SYN. see CRITICAL —**hy'per·crit'i·cal·ly** *adv.* —**hy'per·crit'i·cism** *n.*

hy·per·du·li·a (hi'pər doo li'ə, -dyoo-) *n.* [HYPER- + DULIA] *R.C.Ch.* the special homage paid to the Virgin Mary as holier than any other created being

hy·per·e·mi·a (-ē'mē ə) *n.* [ModL.: see HYPER- & -EMIA] an increased blood flow or congestion of blood anywhere in the body —**hy'per·e'mic** (-ē'mik) *adj.*

hy·per·es·the·sia (-es thē'zhə) *n.* [ModL.: see HYPER- & ESTHESIA] an abnormal sensitivity of the skin or some sense organ —**hy'per·es·thet'ic** (-es thet'ik) *adj.*

hy·per·eu·tec·tic (-yoo tek'tik) *adj.* containing more of the lesser component than is present in a eutectic solution or alloy —**hy'per·eu·tec'toid** *adj.*

hy·per·fo·cal distance (-fō'k'l) the distance from a photographic lens to a point beyond which all objects are substantially in focus

hy·per·gly·ce·mi·a (-gli sē'mē ə) *n.* [ModL. < HYPER- + Gr. *glykys* (see GLYCERIN) + -EMIA] an abnormally high concentration of sugar in the blood —**hy'per·gly·ce'mic** (-mik) *adj.*

hy·per·gol·ic (hi'pər gäl'ik, -gôl'-) *adj.* [< G. *hypergol*, a hypergolic liquid fuel (< *hyp-*, for HYPER- + Gr. *ergon*, work + L. *oleum*, OIL) + -IC] igniting spontaneously when mixed together, as rocket fuel and oxidizer combinations

hy·per·in·su·lin·ism (-in'sə lin iz'm) *n.* excessive secretion of insulin from the pancreas, resulting in hypoglycemia

Hy·pe·ri·on (hi pir'ē ən) [L. < Gr. *Hyperiōn*] *Gr. Myth.* **1.** a Titan, son of Uranus and Gaea, and father of the sun god Helios **2.** Helios himself

hy·per·ker·a·to·sis (-ker'ə tō'sis) *n.*, *pl.* **-to'ses** (-sēz) [HYPER- + KERATOSIS] **1.** an increase in the thickness of the horny layer of the skin **2.** an increase of the cells of the cornea of the eye —**hy'per·ker'a·tot'ic** (-tät'ik) *adj.*

hy·per·ki·ne·sis (-ki nē'sis) *n.* [ModL. < HYPER- + Gr. *kinēsis*, motion] a condition of abnormally increased muscular movement: also **hy'per·ki·ne'sia** (-zhə) —**hy'per·ki·net'ic** (-net'ik) *adj.*

hy·per·me·tric (-met'rik) *adj.* [< Gr. *hypermetros*, beyond measure: see HYPER- & METRIC] *Prosody* having an extra syllable or syllables: also **hy'per·met'ri·cal**

hy·per·me·tro·pi·a (-mi trō'pē ə) *n.* [ModL. < Gr. *hypermetros*, excessive (see HYPER- & METRIC) + -ōpia, -OPIA] the condition of being farsighted; abnormal vision in which the rays of light are focused behind the retina so that distant objects are seen more clearly than near ones —**hy'per·me·trop'ic** (-träp'ik) *adj.*

hy·perm·ne·sia (hi'pərm nē'zhə) *n.* [ModL.: see HYPER- & AMNESIA] abnormally sharp memory or vivid recall of details, seen in certain mental illnesses —**hy'perm·ne'sic** (-zik) *adj.*

Hy·perm·nes·tra (hi'pərm nes'trə) [L. < Gr. *Hypermnēstrē*] *Gr. Myth.* the only one of the Danaides who did not kill her husband

hy·per·on (hi'pər än') *n.* [HYPER- + (BARY)ON] any of a class of baryons which are heavier than the nucleons

hy·per·o·pi·a (hi'pər ō'pē ə) *n.* [ModL. < HYPER- + -OPIA] same as HYPERMETROPIA —**hy'per·op'ic** (-äp'ik) *adj.*

hy·per·os·to·sis (-äs tō'sis) *n.*, *pl.* **-ses** (-sēz) [ModL. < HYPER- + OSTOSIS] an abnormal increase or thickening of bone tissue —**hy'per·os·tot'ic** (-tät'ik) *adj.*

hy·per·ox·i·a (-äk'sē ə) *n.* [ModL.: see HYPER- & OXY-[1] & -IA] an excess of oxygen in the body

hy·per·phys·i·cal (-fiz'i k'l) *adj.* **1.** beyond the physical; esp., supernatural **2.** separate from the physical —**hy'per·phys'i·cal·ly** *adv.*

hy·per·pi·tu·i·ta·rism (-pi tōō'ə tər iz'm, -tyōō'-) *n.* **1.** excessive activity of the pituitary gland, esp. of its anterior lobe **2.** a condition resulting from this, as giantism —**hy'per·pi·tu'i·tar'y** (-ter'ē) *adj.*

hy·per·plane (-plān') *n. Math.* a plane in a space of four or more dimensions

hy·per·pla·si·a (-plā'zhə, -zhē ə) *n.* [ModL. < HYPER- + -PLASIA] an abnormal increase in the number of cells composing a tissue or organ —**hy'per·plas'tic** (-plas'tik) *adj.*

hy·per·pne·a (hi'pər nē'ə, -pərp-) *n.* [ModL. < HYPER- + Gr. *pnoē*, breathing < *pnein*, to breathe: see PNEUMA] abnormally rapid breathing; panting: also sp. **hy'per·pnoe'a** —**hy'per·pne'ic** *adj.*

hy·per·py·rex·i·a (-pi rek'sē ə) *n.* [ModL. < HYPER- + PYREXIA] an abnormally high fever —**hy'per·py·ret'ic** (-ret'ik) *adj.*

hy·per·sen·si·tive (-sen'sə tiv) *adj.* abnormally or excessively sensitive —**hy'per·sen'si·tiv'i·ty** *n.*

hy·per·son·ic (-sän'ik) *adj.* designating, of, or traveling at a speed equal to about five times the speed of sound or greater: see SONIC

hy·per·sthene (hi'pər sthēn') *n.* [altered (after Gr.) < Fr. *hyperstène*: coined by Haüy (1803) < Gr. *hyper-*, HYPER- + *sthenos*, strength] a lustrous, greenish-black or dark-brown mineral of the pyroxene group, a silicate of iron and magnesium —**hy'per·sthen'ic** (-sthen'ik) *adj.*

hy·per·ten·sion (hi'pər ten'shən) *n.* **1.** any abnormally high tension **2.** abnormally high blood pressure, or a disease of which this is the chief sign —**hy'per·ten'sive** *adj.*, *n.*

hy·per·thy·roid (-thi'roid) *adj.* of, characterized by, or having hyperthyroidism —*n.* a hyperthyroid person

hy·per·thy·roid·ism (-thi'roid iz'm) *n.* **1.** excessive activity of the thyroid gland **2.** the disorder resulting from this or from taking too much thyroid extract, characterized by loss of weight, nervousness, a rapid pulse, etc.

hy·per·ton·ic (-tän'ik) *adj.* **1.** having abnormally high tension or tone, esp. of the muscles **2.** having an osmotic pressure higher than that of an isotonic solution —**hy'per·to·nic'i·ty** (-tə nis'ə tē) *n.*

hy·per·tro·phy (hi pur'trə fē) *n.* [ModL.: see HYPER- & -TROPHY] a considerable increase in the size of an organ or tissue, caused by enlargement of its cellular components —*vi.*, *vt.* **-phied, -phy·ing** to undergo or cause to undergo hypertrophy —**hy'per·troph·ic** (hi'pər träf'ik) *adj.*

hy·per·ven·ti·la·tion (hi'pər ven't'l ā'shən) *n.* [HYPER- + VENTILATION] extremely rapid or deep breathing that overoxygenates the blood, causing dizziness, fainting, etc. —**hy'per·ven'ti·late'** (-āt') *vi.*, *vt.* **-lat·ed, -lat'ing**

hy·per·vi·ta·min·o·sis (-vit'ə mi nō'sis) *n.* a disorder resulting from excessive dosage with one or more vitamins

hyp·es·the·si·a (hip es thē'zhə, -zhē ə, -zē ə) *n.* [ModL.: see HYP- & ESTHESIA] impaired power of sensation; esp.,

diminished sensitivity to touch —**hyp′es·the′sic** (-thē′sik), **hyp′es·thet′ic** (-thet′ik) *adj.*

hy·pe·thral (hi pē′thrəl, hī-) *adj.* same as HYPAETHRAL

hy·pha (hī′fə) *n., pl.* **-phae** (-fē) [ModL. < Gr. *hyphē*, a web < IE. base *webh-*, whence WEAVE, WEB] any of the threadlike parts making up the mycelium of a fungus —**hy′phal** *adj.*

hy·phen (hī′f'n) *n.* [LL. < Gr. *hyphen* (for *hyph' hen*), a hyphen, lit., under one, together, in one < *hypo-*, under + *hen*, neut. acc. of *heis*, one: for IE. base see SAME] a mark (-) used between the parts of a compound word or the syllables of a divided word, as at the end of a line —*vt.* same as HYPHENATE

hy·phen·ate (-āt′) *vt.* **-at′ed**, **-at′ing** 1. to connect or separate by a hyphen 2. to write or print with a hyphen —*adj.* hyphenated —**hy′phen·a′tion** *n.*

hy·phen·ize (-īz′) *vt.* **-ized′**, **-iz′ing** same as HYPHENATE —**hy′phen·i·za′tion** *n.*

hyp·na·gog·ic (hip′nə gäj′ik) *adj.* [HYPN(O)- + -AGOG(UE) + -IC] 1. causing sleep; soporific 2. designating or of the state intermediate between wakefulness and sleep [*hypnagogic* fantasies]

hyp·no- (hip′nō, -nə) [< Gr. *hypnos*, sleep < IE. *supnos* < base *swep-*, to sleep, whence L. *sopire*, to lull to sleep, OE. *swefan*, to sleep] *a combining form meaning:* 1. sleep [*hypnology*] 2. hypnotism [*hypnotherapy*] Also, before a vowel, **hypn-**

hyp·no·a·nal·y·sis (hip′nō ə nal′ə sis) *n.* the use of hypnosis or hypnotic drugs in combination with psycho-analytic techniques

hyp·no·gen·e·sis (-jen′ə sis) *n.* [ModL. < HYPNO- + -GENESIS] the inducing of sleep or hypnosis —**hyp′no·gen′ic** (-jen′ik), **hyp′no·ge·net′ic** (-jə net′ik) *adj.*

hyp·noid (hip′noid) *adj.* resembling sleep or hypnosis: also **hyp·noid′al**

hyp·nol·o·gy (hip näl′ə jē) *n.* [HYPNO- + -LOGY] the science dealing with sleep and hypnotism

hyp·no·pom·pic (hip′nō päm′pik) *adj.* [HYPNO- + Gr. *pompē*, procession (see POMP) + -IC] designating or of the state intermediate between sleep and complete awakening [*hypnopompic* visions]

Hyp·nos (hip′näs) [Gr. *Hypnos* < *hypnos*: see HYPNO-] *Gr. Myth.* the god of sleep, identified by the Romans with Somnus

hyp·no·sis (hip nō′sis) *n., pl.* **-ses** (-sēz) [ModL.: see HYPNO- & -OSIS] 1. a sleeplike condition psychically induced, usually by another person, in which the subject is in a state of altered consciousness and responds, with certain limitations, to the suggestions of the hypnotist 2. same as HYPNOTISM

hyp·no·ther·a·py (hip′nō ther′ə pē) *n.* [HYPNO- + THERAPY] the treatment of disease by hypnotism

hyp·not·ic (hip nät′ik) *adj.* [Fr. or LL. *hypnotique* < LL. *hypnoticus* < Gr. *hypnōtikos*, tending to sleep < *hypnos*: see HYPNO-] 1. causing sleep; soporific 2. of, characterized by, having the nature of, or inducing hypnosis 3. easily hypnotized —*n.* 1. any agent causing sleep; soporific 2. a hypnotized person or one easily hypnotized —**hyp·not′i·cal·ly** *adv.*

hyp·no·tism (hip′nə tiz′m) *n.* 1. the act or practice of inducing hypnosis 2. the science of hypnosis

hyp·no·tist (-tist) *n.* a person who induces hypnosis

hyp·no·tize (-tīz′) *vt.* **-tized′**, **-tiz′ing** 1. to put into a state of hypnosis 2. to affect or influence by or as if by hypnotism; spellbind —**hyp′no·tiz′a·ble** *adj.*

Hyp·nus (hip′nəs) same as HYPNOS

hy·po[1] (hī′pō) *n., pl.* **-pos** (-pōz) *short for* ☆a) HYPODERMIC b) HYPOCHONDRIAC —☆*vt.* **-poed**, **-po·ing** [Slang] to boost, stimulate, etc. by or as if by a hypodermic injection

hy·po[2] (hī′pō) *n.* [contr. < HYPOSULFITE] same as SODIUM THIOSULFATE

hy·po- (hī′pō, -pə; *occas.* hip′ō, -ə) [Gr. *hypo-* < *hypo*, under, less than: for IE. base see UP[1]] *a prefix meaning:* 1. under, beneath, below [*hypodermic*] 2. less than, subordinated to [*hypotaxis*] 3. *Chem.* having a lower state of oxidation [*hypophosphorous*]

hy·po·blast (hī′pə blast′) *n.* [HYPO- + -BLAST] same as ENDODERM —**hy′po·blas′tic** *adj.*

hy·po·caust (hī′pə kôst′) *n.* [L. *hypocaustum* < Gr. *hypokauston* < *hypokaiein*, to heat by applying fire below < *hypo-* (see HYPO-) + *kaiein*, to burn] a space below the floor in some ancient Roman buildings, into which hot air was piped to warm the rooms

hy·po·cen·ter (hī′pə sen′tər) *n.* the point on the ground lying directly below the center of a nuclear bomb blast

hy·po·chlo·rite (hī′pə klôr′īt) *n.* any salt of hypochlorous acid

hy·po·chlo·rous acid (-klôr′əs) [HYPO- + CHLOROUS] an unstable acid, HClO, known only in solution and used as a bleaching and oxidizing agent

hy·po·chon·dri·a (hī′pə kän′drē ə) *n.* [ModL. < LL., pl., abdomen < pl. of Gr. *hypochondrion*, soft part of the body below the cartilage of the breastbone < *hypo-* (see HYPO-) + *chondros*, cartilage, by dissimilation < IE. *ghren-* < base *gher-*, to pulverize, rub hard, whence

GRIND, GROUND[1]] abnormal anxiety over one's health, often with imaginary illnesses and severe melancholy

hy·po·chon·dri·ac (-ak′) *adj.* [Fr. *hypocondriaque* < Gr. *hypochondriacus*] 1. designating or of the region of the hypochondrium 2. of or having hypochondria —*n.* a person who has hypochondria —**hy′po·chon·dri′a·cal** (-kən drī′ə k'l) *adj.* —**hy′po·chon·dri′a·cal·ly** *adv.*

hy·po·chon·dri·a·sis (-kən drī′ə sis) *n.* same as HYPOCHONDRIA: term preferred in medicine

hy·po·chon·dri·um (-kän′drē əm) *n., pl.* **-dri·a** (-ə) [ModL.: see HYPOCHONDRIA] either side of the abdomen just below the lowest rib

hy·po·co·ris·tic (hī′pə kə ris′tik, hip′ə-) *adj.* [< Gr. *hypokoristikos* < *hypokorizesthai*, to call by endearing names < *hypo-* (see HYPO-) + *korizesthai*, to pet < *korē*, girl] of or being a pet name or a diminutive or term of endearment —**hy·poc·o·rism** (hī päk′ə riz′m) *n.* —**hy′po·co·ris′ti·cal·ly** *adv.*

hy·po·cot·yl (-kät′'l) *n.* [HYPO- + COTYL(EDON)] the part of the axis, or stem, below the cotyledons in the embryo of a plant

hy·poc·ri·sy (hi päk′rə sē) *n., pl.* **-sies** [ME. *ipocrisie* < OFr. < L. *hypocrisis*, mimicry (in LL.(Ec.), pretended sanctity) < Gr. *hypokrisis*, acting a part (in LXX and NT., hypocrisy) < *hypokrinesthai*, to play a part < *hypo-*, HYPO- + *krinesthai*, to dispute < *krinein*, to separate, choose: for IE. base see CRISIS] a pretending to be what one is not, or to feel what one does not feel; esp., a pretense of virtue, piety, etc.

hyp·o·crite (hip′ə krit) *n.* [ME. *ipocrite* < OFr. < L. *hypocrita*, stage actor (in LL.(Ec.), hypocrite) < Gr. *hypokritēs*, an actor (in LXX & NT., a pretender, hypocrite) < *hypokrinesthai*: see prec.] a person who pretends to be what he is not; one who pretends to be better than he really is, or to be pious, virtuous, etc., without really being so —**hyp′o·crit′i·cal** (-krit′i k'l) *adj.* —**hyp′o·crit′i·cal·ly** *adv.*

hy·po·cy·cloid (hī′pə si′kloid) *n.* [HYPO- + CYCLOID] *Geom.* the curve traced by a point on the circumference of a circle that rolls around the inner circumference of another circle

hy·po·derm (hī′pə durm′) *n.* [ModL.: see HYPO- & DERMA] same as HYPODERMIS: also **hy′po·der′ma** (-dur′mə)

hy·po·der·mal (hī′pə dur′məl) *adj.* 1. of the hypoderm or hypodermis 2. lying under the epidermis

hy·po·der·mic (-dur′mik) *adj.* [HYPODERM + -IC] 1. of the parts under the skin 2. injected under the skin 3. of the hypodermis 4. stimulating or exciting, as though resulting from a hypodermic injection —*n.* same as 1. HYPODERMIC INJECTION 2. HYPODERMIC SYRINGE —**hy′po·der′mi·cal·ly** *adv.*

hypodermic injection the injection of a medicine or drug under the skin

hypodermic syringe a piston syringe as of glass, attached to a hollow metal needle (**hypodermic needle**), used for giving hypodermic injections

hy·po·der·mis (hī′pə dur′mis) *n.* [ModL.: see HYPO- & DERMIS] 1. *Bot.* a specialized layer of cells, as for support or water storage, lying immediately beneath the epidermis of a plant organ 2. *Zool.* a layer of cells that lies beneath, and secretes, the cuticle of annelids, arthropods, etc.

hy·po·eu·tec·tic (hī′pō yoo tek′tik) *adj.* containing less of the secondary component than is present in the eutectic mixture of the same components —**hy′po·eu·tec′toid** *adj.*

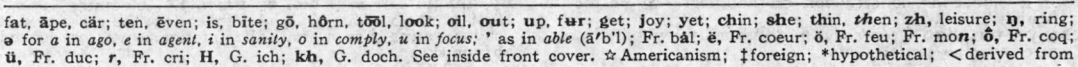

HYPODERMIC SYRINGE

hy·po·gas·tri·um (hī′pə gas′trē əm) *n., pl.* **-tri·a** (-ə) [ModL. < Gr. *hypogastrion*, lower belly, neut. of *hypogastrios*, abdominal < *hypo-*, HYPO- + *gastēr*, the belly] the lower, middle part of the abdomen —**hy′po·gas′tric** *adj.*

hy·po·ge·al (-jē′əl) *adj.* [< LL. *hypogeus*, underground (< Gr. *hypogaios* < *hypo-*, under + *gē*, earth) + -AL] 1. of, or occurring in, the region below the surface of the earth 2. *Bot.* growing or maturing underground, as peanuts, truffles, etc.: said esp. of cotyledons 3. *Zool.* burrowing, living, or developing beneath the ground, as certain insect larvae, animals, etc. Also **hy′po·ge′an**

hy·po·gene (hī′pə jēn′, hip′ə-) *adj.* [HYPO- + Gr. -*genēs* (see -GEN)] *Geol.* 1. produced or formed within the earth, as plutonic and metamorphic rocks 2. designating minerals or ore deposits formed by waters ascending from great depths

hy·pog·e·nous (hī päj′ə nəs, hi-) *adj.* [HYPO- + -GENOUS] growing on the lower surface of something, as spores on the underside of some fern leaves

hy·po·ge·ous (hī′pə jē′əs) *adj.* same as HYPOGEAL

hy·po·ge·um (-jē′əm) *n., pl.* **-ge′a** (-ə) [L. < Gr. *hypogaios*: see HYPOGEAL] an underground cellar, vault, tomb, etc.

hy·po·glos·sal (-gläs′'l, -glôs′-) *adj.* [HYPO- + GLOSSAL] under the tongue; esp., designating or of the motor nerves of the tongue —*n.* a hypoglossal nerve

hy·po·gly·ce·mi·a (-glī sē′mē ə) *n.* [ModL. < HYPO- +

Gr. *glykys* (see GLYCERIN) + -EMIA] an abnormally low concentration of sugar in the blood —**hy′po·gly·ce′mic** (-mik) *adj.*

hy·pog·na·thous (hī päg′nə thəs) *adj.* [HYPO- + -GNA-THOUS] having a protruding lower jaw

hy·pog·y·nous (hī päj′ə nəs) *adj.* [HYPO- + -GYNOUS] 1. growing attached to the receptacle, below and free from the pistil: said of the parts of some flowers 2. having the parts so arranged *[hypogynous* flowers] —**hy·pog′y·ny** (-nē) *n.*

hy·poid gear (hī′poid) [contr. < *hyperboloidal* < HYPER-BOL(A) + -OID + -AL] a bevel gear in a system in which the driven gear is not in the same plane as the driving gear

hy·po·ki·ne·sis (hī′pō ki nē′sis) *n.* [ModL. < HYPO- + Gr. *kinēsis,* motion] a condition of abnormally diminished muscular movement: also **hy′po·ki·ne′sia** (-zhə) —**hy′po·ki·net′ic** (-net′ik) *adj.*

hy·po·lim·ni·on (-lim′nē än′) *n.* [ModL. < HYPO- + Gr. *limnion,* dim. of *limnē,* a pool of standing water] the lowermost, noncirculating layer of cold water in a thermally stratified lake, usually deficient in oxygen

hy·po·ma·ni·a (hī′pə mā′nē ə, -mān′yə) *n.* [HYPO- + -MANIA] a mild form of mania, specif. of the manic phase of manic-depressive psychosis —**hy′po·man′ic** (-man′ik) *adj.*

hy·po·nas·ty (hī′pə nas′tē) *n.* [< HYPO- + -NASTY] *Bot.* the condition in which an organ, as a leaf, turns upward because of the more rapid growth of the cells of the undersurface: opposed to EPINASTY —**hy′po·nas′tic** *adj.*

hy·po·ni·trite (hī′pə nī′trīt) *n.* a salt or ester of hyponitrous acid

hy·po·ni·trous acid (-nī′trəs) [HYPO- + NITROUS] a nitrogenous dibasic acid, $H_2N_2O_2$, an active reducing and oxidizing agent

hy·po·phos·phate (-fäs′fāt) *n.* a salt or ester of hypophosphoric acid

hy·po·phos·phite (-fäs′fīt) *n.* a salt or ester of hypophosphorous acid

hy·po·phos·phor·ic acid (-fäs fôr′ik) an acid, $H_4P_2O_6$, or H_2PO_3, obtained when phosphorus is slowly oxidized in moist air

hy·po·phos·pho·rous acid (-fäs′fər əs, -fäs fôr′əs) a monobasic acid of phosphorus, H_3PO_2: it is a strong reducing agent

hy·poph·y·sis (hī päf′ə sis) *n., pl.* **-ses′** (-sēz′) [ModL. < Gr. *hypophysis,* undergrowth, process < *hypophyein* < *hypo-,* under + *phyein,* to cause to grow: for IE. base see BE] the pituitary gland or body

hy·po·pi·tu·i·ta·rism (hī′pō pi tōō′ə tər iz′m, -tyōō′-) *n.* 1. deficient activity of the pituitary gland, esp. of its anterior lobe 2. the condition resulting from this, characterized by decreased growth in children or decreased activity of the gonads, thyroid gland, or adrenal glands —**hy′po·pi·tu′i·tar′y** (-ter′ē) *adj.*

hy·po·pla·si·a (hī′pə plā′zhə, -zhē ə) *n.* [ModL. < HYPO- + -PLASIA] a condition of decreased or arrested growth of an organ or tissue of the body —**hy′po·plas′tic** (-plas′tik) *adj.*

hy·po·py·on (hī pō′pē än′) *n.* [ModL. < Gr. *hypopyon,* kind of ulcer, neut. sing. of *hypopyos,* tending to suppurate < *hypo-,* under (see HYPO-) + *pyon,* PUS] an accumulation of pus in the cavity between the cornea and the lens of the eye

hy·po·sen·si·tize (hī′pō sen′sə tīz′) *vt.* **-tized′, -tiz′ing** [HYPO- + SENSITIZE] to treat with frequent, small injections of an antigen so as to decrease the symptoms of an allergy to that antigen —**hy′po·sen′si·ti·za′tion** *n.*

hy·po·sta·sis (hī päs′tə sis) *n., pl.* **-ses′** (-sēz′) [Gr. *hypostasis,* a supporting, foundation < *hyphistanai,* to set under, pass, stand under < *hypo-,* under (see HYPO-) + *histanai,* to STAND, cause to stand] 1. the masking or suppression of a gene by one or more genes that are not its allelomorphs 2. *Med. a)* a deposit, or sediment *b)* a settling of blood in the lower parts of the body as a result of a slowing down of the blood flow 3. *Philos.* the underlying principle or nature; essence; substance 4. *Theol. a)* orig., the unique essence or nature of the Godhead and, therefore, of the three persons of the Trinity *b)* any of the three persons of the Trinity *c)* the personality of Christ as distinguished from his two natures, human and divine —**hy·po·stat·ic** (hī′pə stat′ik) *adj.*

hy·pos·ta·tize (hī päs′tə tīz′) *vt.* **-tized′, -tiz′ing** [< Gr. *hypostatos* (< *hyphistanai:* see prec.) + -IZE] to make into, or consider as, a distinct substance or a reality; attribute substantial or personal existence to —**hy′pos′ta·ti·za′tion** *n.*

hy·po·style (hī′pə stīl′, hip′ə-) *adj.* [Gr. *hypostylos,* resting on pillars < *hypo-,* under + *stylos,* a pillar: see HYPO- & STEER[1]] having a roof supported by rows of pillars or columns —*n.* a hypostyle structure

hy·po·sul·fite (-sul′fīt) *n.* 1. any salt of hyposulfurous acid. 2. same as HYDROSULFITE (sense 2) 3. *a popular but erroneous var.* of SODIUM THIOSULFATE

hy·po·sul·fu·rous acid (-səl fyoor′əs) an unstable acid, $H_2S_2O_4$, which has very strong reducing properties and forms stable salts

hy·po·tax·is (-tak′sis) *n.* [ModL. < Gr. *hypotaxis,* submission: see HYPO- & -TAXIS] *Gram.* the dependent relation of a clause or construction on another —**hy′po·tac′tic** (-tak′tik) *adj.*

hy·po·ten·sion (-ten′shən) *n.* abnormally low blood pressure —**hy′po·ten′sive** *adj.*

hy·pot·e·nuse (hī pät′'n ōōs′, -yōōs′) *n.* [L. *hypotenusa* < Gr. *hypoteinousa,* lit., subtending, properly fem. of prp. of *hypoteinein,* to subtend, stretch under < *hypo-,* under + *teinein,* to stretch: see HYPO- & THIN] the side of a right-angled triangle opposite the right angle: also **hy·poth′e·nuse** (hī päth′-)

hypoth. 1. hypothesis 2. hypothetical

hy·po·thal·a·mus (hī′pə thal′ə məs) *n., pl.* **-mi′** (-mī′) [ModL.: see HYPO- & THALAMUS] the part of the brain that forms the floor of the third ventricle and regulates many basic body functions, as temperature —**hy′po·tha·lam′ic** (-thə lam′ik) *adj.*

hy·poth·ec (hī päth′ik, hi-) *n.* [Fr. *hypothèque* < LL. *hypotheca,* a pledge, security < Gr. *hypothēkē,* something put under (obligation), pledge < *hypotithenai,* to put under, pledge: see HYPOTHESIS] *Law* security or right given to a creditor over a debtor's property without transfer of possession or title

hy·poth·e·car·y (-ə ker′ē) *adj.* [LL. *hypothecarius*] of or secured by a hypothec

hy·poth·e·cate (-ə kāt′) *vt.* **-cat′ed, -cat′ing** [< ML. *hypothecatus,* pp. of *hypothecare,* to hypothecate < LL. *hypotheca:* see HYPOTHEC] 1. to pledge (property) to another as security without transferring possession or title; mortgage 2. *same as* HYPOTHESIZE —**hy·poth′e·ca′tion** *n.* —**hy·poth′e·ca′tor** *n.*

hy·po·ther·mal (hī′pə thur′məl) *adj.* 1. tepid, or lukewarm 2. of or characterized by hypothermia 3. produced at a temperature of 300°C or more: said of certain mineral deposits

hy·po·ther·mi·a (-thur′mē ə) *n.* [ModL. < HYPO- + Gr. *thermē,* heat: see WARM] a subnormal body temperature

hy·poth·e·sis (hī päth′ə sis, hi-) *n., pl.* **-ses′** (-sēz′) [Gr. *hypothesis,* groundwork, foundation, supposition < *hypotithenai,* to place under < *hypo-,* under + *tithenai,* to place: see HYPO- & DO[1]] an unproved theory, proposition, supposition, etc. tentatively accepted to explain certain facts or **(working hypothesis)** to provide a basis for further investigation, argument, etc. —*SYN.* see THEORY

hy·poth·e·size (-sīz′) *vi.* **-sized′, -siz′ing** to make a hypothesis —*vt.* to assume; suppose

hy·po·thet·i·cal (hī′pə thet′i k'l) *adj.* [< Gr. *hypothetikos* (< *hypothesis*) + -AL] 1. based on, involving, or having the nature of, a hypothesis; assumed; supposed 2. given to the use of hypotheses [a *hypothetical* mind] 3. *Logic* conditional [a *hypothetical* proposition] Also **hy′po·thet′ic** —**hy′po·thet′i·cal·ly** *adv.*

hy·po·thy·roid (hī′pō thī′roid) *adj.* of, characterized by, or having hypothyroidism —*n.* a hypothyroid person

hy·po·thy·roid·ism (-thī′roid iz′m) *n.* 1. deficient activity of the thyroid gland 2. the disorder resulting from this, characterized by a retarded rate of metabolism and resulting sluggishness, puffiness, etc.

hy·po·ton·ic (-tän′ik) *adj.* 1. having abnormally low tension or tone, esp. of the muscles 2. having an osmotic pressure lower than that of an isotonic solution —**hy′po·to·nic′i·ty** (-tə nis′ə tē) *n.*

hy·po·xan·thine (-zan′thēn, -thin) *n.* a nitrogenous compound, $C_5H_4N_4O$, found with xanthine in the muscles, spleen, etc.

hy·pox·i·a (hī päk′sē ə, hi-) *n.* [ModL.: see HYPO- & OXY-[1] & -IA] an abnormal condition resulting from a decrease in the oxygen supplied to or utilized by body tissue

hyp·so- (hip′sō, -sə) [< Gr. *hypsos,* height < IE. *ups-,* high < base *upo-:* cf. UP[1]] *a combining form meaning* height, high [*hypsometer*]: also, before a vowel, **hyps-**

hyp·sog·ra·phy (hip säg′rə fē) *n.* [HYPSO- + -GRAPHY] 1. the science of measuring the configuration of land or underwater surfaces with respect to a datum plane, as sea level 2. the configuration of such surfaces; topographic relief 3. the representation or description of relief features on a map or chart, as by tints, hachures, etc. 4. *same as* HYPSOMETRY —**hyp′so·graph′ic** (-sə graf′ik) *adj.*

hyp·som·e·ter (-säm′ə tər) *n.* [HYPSO- + -METER] 1. a device for determining height above sea level by measuring atmospheric pressure as indicated by the boiling point of water 2. an instrument for measuring heights of trees by triangulation

hyp·som·e·try (-säm′ə trē) *n.* [HYPSO- + -METRY] the measurement of surface elevations above a datum plane, esp. sea level —**hyp′so·met′ric** (hip′sə met′rik) *adj.*

hy·ra·coid (hī′rə koid′) *n.* [< ModL. *Hyracoidea,* name of the genus: see HYRAX & -OID] *same as* HYRAX —*adj.* designating or of the hyraxes

hy·rax (hī′raks) *n., pl.* **-rax·es, -ra·ces′** (-rə sēz′) [ModL. < Gr. *hyrax,* shrew mouse < IE. base **swer-,* to hum, buzz, whence SWARM[1]] any of an order (Hyracoidea) of small, hoofed mammals of Africa and SW Asia that feed on plants and live in rocky areas (genus *Procavia*) or in trees (genus *Dendrohyrax*): the former is the coney of the Bible

Hyr·ca·ni·a (hər kā′nē ə) province of the ancient Persian & Macedonian empires, on the S & SE coast of the Caspian Sea —**Hyr·ca′ni·an** *adj., n.*

hy·son (hī′s'n) *n.* [Chin. *hsi-tchun,* lit., blooming spring, first crop] a variety of Chinese green tea: the early crop is called **young hyson,** and the inferior leaves are called **hyson skin**

hys·sop (his′əp) *n*. [ME. *isope* < OE. *ysope* & OFr. *ysope*, both < L. *hyssopus* < Gr. *hyssōpos, hyssōpon* < Heb. *ēzōbh*] **1.** *a*) a fragrant, blue-flowered plant (*Hyssopus officinalis*) of the mint family, used in folk medicine as a tonic, stimulant, etc. *b*) its flower ☆**2.** any of several American plants of the mint and figwort families **3.** *Bible* a plant whose twigs were used for sprinkling in certain ancient Jewish rites

hys·ter·ec·to·my (his′tə rek′tə mē) *n., pl.* **-mies** [HYSTER- (O)- + -ECTOMY] surgical removal of all or part of the uterus

hys·ter·e·sis (his′tə rē′sis) *n*. [ModL. < Gr. *hysterēsis*, a deficiency < *hysterein*, to be behind, come short < *hysteros*, later, behind < IE. **udteros*, compar. of base **ud-*, up, whence OUT] *Physics* a lag of effect when the forces acting on a body are changed, as a lag in magnetization (**magnetic hysteresis**) of a ferromagnetic substance when the magnetizing force is changed —**hys′ter·et′ic** (-et′ik) *adj.*

hys·te·ri·a (his tir′ē ə, -ter′-) *n*. [ModL. < ff. + -IA] **1.** a psychiatric condition variously characterized by emotional excitability, excessive anxiety, sensory and motor disturbances, or the unconscious simulation of organic disorders, such as blindness, deafness, etc. **2.** any outbreak of wild, uncontrolled excitement or feeling, such as fits of laughing and crying

hys·ter·ic (his ter′ik) *adj*. [L. *hystericus* < Gr. *hysterikos*, suffering in the womb, hysterical < *hystera*, uterus: from the ancient notion that women were hysterical more often than men] hysterical —*n*. **1.** [*usually pl., occas. with sing.*

v.] a hysterical fit; hysteria (sense 2) **2.** a person subject to hysteria

hys·ter·i·cal (-i k′l) *adj*. [prec. + -AL] **1.** of or characteristic of hysteria **2.** *a*) like or suggestive of hysteria; emotionally uncontrolled and wild *b*) extremely comical **3.** having or subject to hysteria

hys·ter·o- (his′tər ō, -ə) [< Gr. *hystera*, uterus, womb: cf. HYSTERIC] *a combining form meaning:* **1.** uterus, womb [*hysterotomy*] **2.** hysteria, hysteria and [*hysterocatalepsy*] Also, before a vowel, **hyster-**

hys·ter·o·gen·ic (-jen′ik) *adj*. [HYSTERO- + -GENIC] causing hysteria

hys·ter·oid (his′tər oid′) *adj.* [HYSTER(O)- + -OID] resembling hysteria

hys·ter·on pro·te·ron (his′tər än′ prät′ər än′) [LL. < Gr. *hysteron*, neut. of *hysteros*, latter + *proteron*, neut. of *proteros*, earlier] **1.** a figure of speech in which the logical order of ideas is reversed (Ex.: "I die, I faint, I fail") **2.** *Logic* the fallacy of assuming as true, and using as an argument, what is to be proved; begging the question

hys·ter·ot·o·my (his′tə rät′ə mē) *n., pl.* **-mies** [HYSTERO- + -TOMY] incision of the uterus, as in a Caesarean section

hys·tri·co·mor·phic (his′tri kə môr′fik) *adj.* [< ModL. *Hystricomorpha*, name of the division < L. *hystrix*, porcupine (< Gr. *hystrix*) + Gr. *morphē*, form + -IC] designating or of a suborder (Hystricomorpha) of rodents including the porcupines, chinchillas, etc.

Hz, hz hertz

I

I, i (ī) *n., pl.* **I's, i's** (īz) **1.** the ninth letter of the English alphabet: via Latin from the Greek *iota*, a modification of the Phoenician (Semitic *yodh*, a hand): this letter, first dotted in the 11th cent., was not distinguished from *j* until the 17th cent. **2.** a sound of *I* or *i*: in most European languages the letter primarily represents a high, front, tense, unrounded vowel, IPA [i]; in English it represents a high, front, unrounded vowel that is either lowered or tense, IPA [ɪ, i], a diphthong, IPA [aɪ], or a neutral sound, IPA [ə] **3.** a type or impression for *I* or *i* **4.** *a symbol for* the ninth in a sequence or group —*adj.* **1.** of *I* or *i* **2.** ninth in a sequence or group

I¹ (ī) *n*. **1.** an object shaped like *I* **2.** a Roman numeral for 1: placed after another numeral, it adds one unit (e.g., VI =6), and placed before another numeral, it subtracts one unit (e.g., IV = 4) **3.** *Chem.* iodine **4.** *Dentistry* the symbol for incisor **5.** *Logic* a particular affirmative proposition **6.** *Physics* the symbol for *a*) electric current *b*) moment of inertia —*adj.* shaped like *I*

I² (ī) *pron.* [for *pl.* see WE] [ME. *i, ich, ih* < OE. *ic*, akin to G. *ich*, Goth. *ik* < IE. base **ĕgom*, orig. prob. neut. n. meaning "(my) presence here," whence L. *ego*, Gr. *egō*, Sans. *ahám*] the person speaking or writing: *I* is the nominative case form, *me* the objective, *my* and *mine* the possessive, and *myself* the intensive and reflexive, of the first personal singular pronoun —*n., pl.* **I's** the ego; the self

i (ī) *n*. **1.** a Roman numeral for 1 [*page iii*] **2.** *Astron.* the inclination of a planet's orbit to some reference plane, as the ecliptic **3.** *Math. the symbol for* √−1, the square root of minus one

i- (ī) [Archaic] *same as* Y-

I. 1. Independent **2.** Island

I., i. 1. imperator **2.** island; islands **3.** isle; isles

i. 1. interest **2.** intransitive

-i·a (ē ə, yə) [for 1, 2, 7, (& sometimes 4), L. *-ia* & Gr. *-ia* < *-i-*, thematic vowel + *-a*, noun suffix of 1st declension; for 3, 5, 6, (& sometimes 4), L. *-ia* & Gr. *-ia*, neut. pl. ending of L. nouns in *-ium* & Gr. nouns in *-i-*, thematic vowel + *-a*, suffix] *a n.-forming suffix used in:* **1.** the names of countries [*India*] **2.** the names of diseases [*pneumonia*] **3.** the names of classic festivals [*Lupercalia*] **4.** Greek and Latin words carried over into English [*militia*] **5.** English plurals of Greek and Latin words [*paraphernalia*] **6.** *Bot.* the generic names of some plants [*zinnia*] **7.** *Zool.* the names of some classes, orders, etc. [*Reptilia*]

Ia. Iowa

IAEA International Atomic Energy Agency

I·a·go (ē ä′gō) the villain in Shakespeare's *Othello*: see OTHELLO

-i·al (ē əl, yəl, əl) [L. *-ialis, -iale*] *same as* -AL [*magisterial, jovial, artificial*]

i·amb (ī′amb, -am) *n*. [Fr. *iambe* < L. *iambus* < Gr. *iambos*] a metrical foot of two syllables, the first unaccented and the other accented, as in English verse, or the first short and the other long, as in Greek and Latin verse (Ex.: "Tŏ strĭve, | tŏ sĕek, | tŏ fĭnd, | ănd nŏt | tŏ yĭeld")

i·am·bic (ī am′bik) *adj*. [< Fr. or L.: Fr. *iambique* < L. *iambicus* < Gr. *iambikos*] of or made up of iambs —*n*. **1.** an iamb **2.** an iambic verse **3.** a piece of satirical verse written in iambs

i·am·bus (-bəs) *n., pl.* **-bus·es, -bi** (-bī) [L.] *same as* IAMB

-i·an (ē ən, yən, ən) [Fr. or L.: Fr. *-ien* < L. *-ianus* < *-i-* stem ending + *-anus*: see -AN] *same as* -AN [*Indian, reptilian, Grecian*]

-i·an·a (ē an′ə) *same as* -ANA

IAS indicated airspeed

Ia·şi (yäsh, yä′shē) city in NE Romania: pop. 126,000

-i·a·sis (ī′ə sis) [ModL. < Gr. *-iasis*] *a combining form meaning:* **1.** process or condition **2.** pathological or morbid condition [*hypochondriasis*]

i·at·ric (ī at′rik) *adj*. [Gr. *iatrikos* < *iatros*, physician < *iasthai*, to cure, heal] of medicine or medical doctors; medical or medicinal: also **i·at′ri·cal**

-i·at·rics (-riks) [see IATRIC] *a combining form meaning* treatment of disease [*pediatrics*]

i·at·ro- (ī at′rō, -rə) [Gr. *iatro-* < *iatros*: see IATRIC] *a combining form meaning* medicine, medical, medicinal [*iatrogenic*]

i·at·ro·gen·ic (ī at′rə jen′ik) *adj*. [IATRO- + -GENIC] caused by medical treatment: said esp. of imagined symptoms, ailments, or disorders induced by a physician's words or actions

-i·a·try (ī′ə trē) [ModL. *-iatria* < Gr. *iatreia*, healing] *a combining form meaning* medical treatment [*podiatry, psychiatry*]

ib. *same as* IBID.

I·ba·dan (ē bä′dän) city in SW Nigeria: pop. 600,000

Ibáñez see BLASCO IBÁÑEZ

I-beam (ī′bēm′) *n*. a steel beam shaped like an I in cross section

I·be·ri·a (ī bir′ē ə) [L.] **1.** ancient region in the S Caucasus, in what is now the Georgian S.S.R. **2.** *same as* IBERIAN PENINSULA

I·be·ri·an (-ē ən) *adj*. of Iberia (either region), its people, etc. —*n*. **1.** *a*) any member of an ancient people in the S Caucasus, believed to be the ancestors of the Georgians *b*) any member of an ancient people of the Iberian Peninsula **2.** a native or inhabitant of the Iberian Peninsula **3.** any of the languages spoken by the ancient Iberians

Iberian Peninsula peninsula in SW Europe, comprising Spain & Portugal

Iberville see D'IBERVILLE

i·bex (ī′beks) *n., pl.* **i′bex·es, i·bi·ces** (ib′ə sēz′, ī′bə-),
i′bex: see PLURAL, II, D, 1 [L.,
prob. < IE. word in an Alpine
language, signifying "climber,"
akin to IVY] any of several varieties of wild goat (genus *Capra*)
of Europe, Asia, or Africa, as the
Alpine ibex (*Capra ibex*) formerly
abundant in the Alps: the male
has large, backward-curved horns
Ib·i·bi·o (ib′ə bē′ō) *n., pl.* **-bi′os,
-bi′o** 1. any of a people of SE Nigeria 2. their Niger-Congo language
ibid. [L. *ibidem*] in the same place:
used in referring again to the
book, page, etc. cited just before
-i·bil·i·ty (ə bil′ə tē) *pl.* **-ties** [L.
-ibilitas < -*i*-, thematic vowel +
-bilitas: see -ABILITY] *a n.-forming suffix corresponding to*
-IBLE [*sensibility*]
i·bis (ī′bis) *n., pl.* **i′bis·es, i′bis:** see PLURAL, II, D, 1 [L. <
Gr. *ibis* < Egypt. *hib*] any of several large wading birds
(family Threskiornithidae) related to the herons, with long
legs and a long, slender, curved bill, found chiefly in
tropical regions, as the sacred ibis of the Nile (*Threskiornis
aethiopica*)
-i·ble (i b′l, ə b′l) [L. *-ibilis*] *same as* -ABLE: used in forming
adjectives derived directly from Latin verbs ending in
-ire or *-ere* [*divisible, legible*]
ib·n- (ib′'n) [Ar.] *a combining form meaning* son of: used
in many hyphenated Arabic names
ibn-Rushd (ib′'n roosht′) *Ar.* name of AVERROËS
☆**I·bo** (ē′bō) *n.* [< the native name] 1. *pl.* **I′bos, I′bo** any
member of an African people of SE Nigeria 2. their Kwa
language
Ib·sen (ib′s'n), **Hen·rik** (hen′rik) 1828–1906; Norw. playwright & poet —**Ib′sen·ism** *n.*
-ic (ik) 1. [< Fr. or L. or Gr.; Fr. *-ique* < L. *-icus* < Gr.
-ikos: akin to G. *-isch*, OE. *-ig* (see -Y²)] *an adj.-forming
suffix meaning:* a) of, having to do with [*volcanic*] b) like,
having the nature of, characteristic of [*angelic*] c) produced
by, caused by [*anaerobic*] d) producing, causing [*psychedelic*] e) consisting of, containing, forming [*dactylic*] f)
having, showing, affected by [*lethargic*] g) *Chem.* of or
derived from [*benzoic, citric*]; also, having a higher valence
than is indicated by the suffix *-ous* [*nitric, phosphoric*] 2.
[< ME. or L. or Gr.: ME. *-ike* < L. *-icus* < Gr. *-ikos:* from
substantive use of respective adjectives] *a n.-forming suffix
meaning* a person or thing: a) having, showing, affected by
[*hysteric, paraplegic*] b) supporting, adhering to [*Gnostic*]
c) belonging to, characteristic of [*cynic, Philippic*] d)
derived from [*patronymic*] e) producing, causing [*hypnotic*]
f) affecting [*stomachic*] Adverbs corresponding to adjectives in *-ic* are formed by adding *-ally* or, less often, *-ly*
IC integrated circuit
I·çá (ē sä′) *Brazilian name of the* PUTUMAYO River
-i·cal (i k′l, ə k′l) [LL. *-icalis* < -*icus, -ic* + *-alis, -AL*] *same
as* -IC: adjectives formed with -*ical* sometimes have special
or differentiated meanings (e.g., *historical, economical*)
beyond those of the corresponding -*ic* forms
ICAO International Civil Aviation Organization
I·car·i·a (i ker′ē ə, i-) Gr. island in the Aegean Sea, southwest of Samos: 99 sq. mi.
I·car·i·an (-ən) *adj.* [L. *Icarius* < Gr. *Ikarios*, of Icarus] of,
like, or characteristic of Icarus; esp., too daring; foolhardy;
rash
Icarian Sea ancient name for the S part of the Aegean Sea,
between the Cyclades & Asia Minor
Ic·a·rus (ik′ə rəs) [L. < Gr. *Ikaros*] *Gr. Myth.* the son of
Daedalus: escaping from Crete by flying with wings made
by Daedalus, Icarus flew so high that the sun's heat melted
the wax by which his wings were fastened, and he fell to
his death in the sea
ICBM intercontinental ballistic missile
ICC, I.C.C. Interstate Commerce Commission
ice (īs) *n.* [ME. *is* < OE., akin to G. *eis* (OHG. ĭs), ON. *iss*
< IE. base *eis, ein-*, whence Av. *isu-*, icy, OBulg. *inej,*
snow flurry] 1. the glassy, brittle, crystalline form of water
made solid by cold; frozen water 2. a piece, layer, or sheet
of this 3. anything like frozen water in appearance,
structure, etc. 4. coldness in manner or attitude 5. a) a
frozen dessert, usually made of water, fruit juice, egg
white, and sugar b) [Brit.] ice cream 6. icing; frosting
☆7. [Slang] a diamond or diamonds ☆8. [Slang] a) the
illegal profit made in ticket scalping, as through extra
payment by ticket brokers to theater management b) any
money paid in bribes or graft —*vt.* **iced, ic′ing** 1. to change
into ice; freeze 2. to cover with ice; apply ice to 3. to cool
by putting ice on, in, or around 4. to cover (cake, etc.)
with icing 5. *Ice Hockey* to shoot (the puck) from defensive
to offensive territory —*vi.* to freeze (often with *up* or *over*)
—**break the ice** 1. to make a start by getting over initial
difficulties 2. to make a start toward getting better
acquainted —☆**cut no ice** [Colloq.] to have no influence or
effect —☆**on ice** [Slang] 1. in readiness, reserve, or safekeeping 2. in abeyance 3. with success or victory assured
—**on thin ice** [Colloq.] in a risky, dangerous situation
-ice (is, əs) [ME. *-ice, -ise, -is* < OFr. *-ice* < L. *-itius*, masc.,

-itia, fem., *-itium*, neut.] *a suffix meaning* condition, state,
or quality of [*justice, malice*]
Ice. 1. Iceland 2. Icelandic
ice age *same as* GLACIAL EPOCH
ice bag a bag, as of rubber, for holding ice, applied to the
body to reduce a swelling, ease pain, etc.
ice·berg (īs′bʉrg) *n.* [prob. via Du. *ijsberg*, lit., ice mountain < Scand., as in Dan. *isberg* < *is*, ICE + *berg*, mountain]
a great mass of ice broken off from a glacier and floating in
the sea
☆**iceberg lettuce** a variety of lettuce with crisp, medium-
green leaves tightly folded into a round, compact head
ice·blink (-bliŋk′) [ICE + BLINK, after Du. *ijsblink* or Dan.
isblink] a brightness in the sky caused by the reflection of
light from an expanse of ice
ice·boat (-bōt′) *n.* 1. a light, boatlike frame, often triangular, designed to skim over frozen lakes, rivers, etc. on
runners and driven along by a sail or by a propeller or jet
engine 2. *same as* ICEBREAKER (sense 1)
ice·bound (-bound′) *adj.* 1. held fast by ice, as a boat 2.
made inaccessible by ice, as a port
☆**ice·box** (-bäks′) *n.* a cabinet with ice in it for keeping
foods, etc. cold; also, any refrigerator
☆**ice·break·er** (-brā′kər) *n.* 1. a sturdy boat for breaking a
channel through ice 2. a wedgelike structure for protecting
a pier, etc. from floating ice 3. anything serving to lessen
formality or break down reserve
ice·cap (-kap′) *n.* a mass of glacial ice that spreads slowly
out in all directions from a center
ice-cold (īs′kōld′) *adj.* very cold
☆**ice cream** [orig., *iced cream*] a rich, sweet, creamy, frozen
food made from variously flavored cream and milk
products churned or stirred to a smooth consistency during
the freezing process and often containing gelatin, eggs,
fruits, or nuts, etc. —**ice′-cream′** *adj.*
ice·fall (-fôl′) *n.* ☆1. a jumbled mass of pulverized ice
broken from the terminus of a glacier at the edge of a
mountain shelf 2. that part of a valley glacier descending
an unusually steep slope where the ice is broken by
crevasses
ice field 1. an extensive mass of thick ice, generally in a
highland area, which may feed valley glaciers about its
borders; icecap 2. an extensive area of floating sea ice,
specif. an area five or more miles across
ice floe 1. *same as* ICE FIELD (sense 2) 2. a single piece,
large or small, of floating sea ice
ice foot [ICE + FOOT, after Dan. *isfod*] a fringe of sea ice
frozen to the shore in polar regions
ice hockey hockey played on ice: see HOCKEY (sense 1)
ice·house (-hous′) *n.* 1. a building where ice is stored 2. a
place where artificial ice is made
Ice·land (īs′lənd) 1. island in the North Atlantic, southeast of Greenland 2. country including this island & a few
small nearby islands: 39,768 sq. mi.; pop. 192,000; cap.
Reykjavik —**Ice′land·er** *n.*
Ice·lan·dic (īs lan′dik) *adj.* of Iceland, its people, their
language, or culture —*n.* the N. Germanic language of the
Icelanders, considered the most conservative of Germanic
languages
Iceland moss an arctic lichen (*Cetraria islandica*) sometimes used as a food and in folk medicine
Iceland poppy an arctic poppy (*Papaver nudicaule*) with
fragrant, nodding flowers, cultivated in gardens
Iceland spar a transparent, colorless calcite, found esp. in
Iceland: it is used by opticians for making double-
refracting prisms
ice·man (īs′man′, -mən) *n., pl.* **-men′** (-men′, -mən) ☆a
person who sells or delivers ice
☆**ice milk** a frozen dessert like ice cream, but with a lower
butterfat content
ice needle *Meteorol.* a thin piece of ice, so light that it
floats in the air in clear, cold weather
I·ce·ni (i sē′nī) *n.pl.* [L.] an ancient British people who, led
by their queen Boadicea, rebelled against the Romans in
61 A.D. —**I·ce′ni·an** (-sē ən) *adj.*
ice pack 1. a large, floating expanse of broken ice masses
frozen together 2. an ice bag, folded cloth, etc. filled with
crushed ice and applied to the body, as to reduce a swelling
or ease pain
☆**ice pick** a sharply pointed metal tool used to chop ice
into small pieces
ice plant a succulent Old World plant (*Cryophytum crystal-
linum*) of the carpetweed family, having thick leaves
covered with thin, glistening cells that look like ice crystals
ice sheet a thick layer of ice covering an extensive area for
a long period, as in the ice age
ice shelf a thick mass of glacial ice extending along a polar
shore, often resting on the bottom near the shore with the
seaward edge afloat: it may protrude hundreds of miles
out to sea
ice skate a skate for skating on ice: see SKATE¹ (sense 1)
—**ice′-skate′** *vi.* **-skat′ed, -skat′ing** —**ice skater**
☆**ice storm** a storm in which freezing rain falls and forms a
glaze on surfaces
ice water 1. melted ice 2. water chilled as with ice
IC4A, I.C.4-A Intercollegiate Association of Amateur
Athletes of America
ICFTU International Confederation of Free Trade Unions
Ich·a·bod (ik′ə bäd′) [Heb. *ī-khābhōdh*, lit., according to

pop. etym., inglorious: orig. meaning unc.] a masculine
name

ich·neu·mon (ik nyōō′mən, -nōō′-) *n.* [L. < Gr. *ichneu-
mōn*, ichneumon, lit., tracker < *ichneuein*, to track out,
hunt after < *ichnos*, a track, footstep (from its supposed
practice of locating and destroying crocodile eggs)] 1. the
Egyptian species (*Herpestes ichneumon*) of mongoose 2.
same as ICHNEUMON FLY

ichneumon fly any of a large family (Ichneumonidae) of
hymenopteran insects whose larvae live as parasites in or
on other insect larvae: also **ichneumon wasp**

ich·nite (ik′nīt′) *n.* [ICHN(O)- + -ITE[1]] a fossil footprint:
also **ich′no·lite′** (-nə līt′)

ich·no- (ik′nō) [< Gr. *ichnos*, footprint] *a combining form
meaning* track, footprint, trace *[ichnology]*: also, before a
vowel, **ichn-**

ich·nog·ra·phy (ik näg′rə fē) *n.* [< Fr. or L.; Fr. *ichnog-
raphie* < L. *ichnographia* < Gr. *ichnographia*, a tracing out,
ground plan: see ICHNO- & -GRAPHY] 1. a scale drawing of
the ground plan of a building; floor plan 2. the art of
drawing such plans

ich·nol·o·gy (ik näl′ə jē) *n.* [ICHNO- + -LOGY] the scientific
study of fossil footprints —**ich′no·log′i·cal** *adj.*

i·chor (ī′kôr, -kər) *n.* 1. [Gr. *ichōr*] *Gr. Myth.* the ethereal
fluid flowing instead of blood in the veins of the gods 2.
[ModL. < Gr.] a thin, acrid, watery discharge from a
wound or sore —**i′chor·ous** (-kər əs) *adj.*

ich·thy·ic (ik′thē ik) *adj.* [ICHTHY(O)- + -IC] of or characteristic of a fish or fishes

ich·thy·o- (ik′thē ō, -ə) [Gr. *ichthyo-* < *ichthys*, a fish, akin
to Lith. *žuvìs*, Arm. *jukn*, fish] *a combining form meaning*
fish, like a fish *[ichthyology]*: also, before a vowel, **ichthy-**

ich·thy·oid (ik′thē oid′) *adj.* [Gr. *ichthyoeidēs*: see
ICHTHY0- & -OID] like a fish — *n.* a fishlike vertebrate

ich·thy·o·lite (-ə līt′) *n.* [ModL.: see ICHTHYO- & -LITE] a
fossil of a fish or of part of a fish

ich·thy·ol·o·gy (ik′thē äl′ə jē) *n.* [ModL. *ichthyologia:*
see ICHTHYO- & -LOGY] the branch of zoology dealing with
fishes, their structure, classification, and life history —
ich′thy·o·log′i·cal (-ə läj′i k′l), **ich′thy·o·log′ic** *adj.* —
ich′thy·ol′o·gist *n.*

ich·thy·oph·a·gous (-äf′ə gəs) *adj.* [Gr. *ichthyophagos:*
see ICHTHYO- & -PHAGOUS] living on fish; fish-eating —
ich′thy·oph′a·gy (-jē) *n.*

ich·thy·or·nis (-ôr′nis) *n.* [ModL. < ICHTHYO- + Gr.
ornis, bird] any of a genus (*Ichthyornis*) of prehistoric birds,
now extinct, which had well-developed teeth set in sockets

ich·thy·o·saur (ik′thē ə sôr′) *n.* [< ModL. < ICHTHYO- +
Gr. *sauros*, lizard] any of an order (Ichthyosauria) of prehistoric marine reptiles, now extinct, which had a fishlike
body, four paddle-shaped flippers, and a dolphinlike head
—**ich′thy·o·sau′ri·an** (-sôr′ē ən) *adj.*

ich·thy·o·sis (ik′thē ō′sis) *n.* [ModL.: see ICHTHY- &
-OSIS] a congenital, hereditary skin disease characterized
by roughening and thickening of the horny layer of the
skin, producing dryness and scaling —**ich′thy·ot′ic**
(-ät′ik) *adj.*

-i·cian (ish′ən) [Fr. *-icien:* see -IC & -IAN] *n.-forming
suffix meaning* a person engaged in, practicing, or specializing in (a specified field) *[beautician]*

i·ci·cle (ī′si k′l) *n.* [ME. *isikel* < OE. *isgicel* (akin to ON.
isjökull) < *is*, ice + *gicel*, piece of ice, icicle (Brit. dial.
ickle), akin to ON. *jökull*, icicle, glacier, *jaki*, lump of ice <
IE. base *yeg-*, ice, whence MIr. *aig*, W. *iā*, ice, MCorn.
yeyn, cold] a tapering, pointed, hanging piece of ice,
formed by the freezing of dripping or falling water —
i′ci·cled *adj.*

i·ci·ly (ī′sə lē) *adv.* in an icy manner; very coldly

i·ci·ness (ī′sē nis) *n.* the quality or state of being icy

ic·ing (ī′siŋ) *n.* a mixture of sugar, butter, flavoring, and,
sometimes, egg whites, etc. for covering a cake or pastries;
frosting

ICJ International Court of Justice

☆**ick·y** (ik′ē) *adj.* **ick′i·er, ick′i·est** [baby talk, short for
STICKY] [Slang] 1. unpleasantly sticky or gluey 2. cloyingly sweet or sentimental 3. very distasteful; disgusting
—**ick′i·ly** *adv.* —**ick′i·ness** *n.*

i·con (ī′kän) *n.* [L. < Gr. *eikōn*, an image, figure (in LGr.,
sacred image) < IE. base *weik-*, to resemble, whence
Lith. *į-vỹkti*, to happen, become true] 1. an image; figure;
representation 2. *Orthodox Eastern Ch.* an image or picture
of Jesus, Mary, a saint, etc., venerated as sacred

i·con·ic (ī kän′ik) *adj.* [L. *iconicus* < Gr. *eikonikos* < *eikōn*,
an image: see prec.] 1. of, or having the nature of, an icon
2. done in a fixed or conventional style: said of certain
statues and busts

I·co·ni·um (ī kō′nē əm) *ancient Roman name of* KONYA

i·con·o- (ī kän′ō, -ə) [< Gr. *eikōn*, a figure, image: see ICON]
a combining form meaning image, likeness, figure *[iconol-
atry]*: also, before a vowel, **icon-**

i·con·o·clasm (ī kän′ə klaz′m) *n.* [< ICONO- < Gr. *klasma*,
broken thing] the actions or beliefs of an iconoclast

i·con·o·clast (-klast′) *n.* [ML. *iconoclastes* < MGr.
eikonoklastēs < LGr. *eikōn* (see ICON) + *klaein*, to break:
for IE. base see CALAMITY] 1. anyone opposed to the reli-

gious use of images or advocating the destruction of such
images; specif., a member of a group in the Orthodox
Eastern Church in the 8th and 9th cent. who denounced
the use of icons 2. a person who attacks or ridicules
traditional or venerated institutions or ideas regarded by
him as erroneous or based on superstition —**i·con′o·clas′-
tic** *adj.* —**i·con′o·clas′ti·cal·ly** *adv.*

i·co·nog·ra·phy (ī′kə näg′rə fē) *n.* [ML. *iconographia* <
Gr. *eikonographia*, a sketch, description: see ICONO- &
-GRAPHY] 1. the art of representing or illustrating by
pictures, figures, images, etc. 2. the study or description of
pictures, images, etc.; esp., the study of the portraits of a
specific person 3. *same as* ICONOLOGY —**i′co·nog′ra·pher**
n. —**i·con·o·graph·ic** (ī kän′ə graf′ik), **i·con′o·graph′i-
cal** *adj.*

i·co·nol·a·try (ī′kə näl′ə trē) *n.* [ICONO- + -LATRY] the
worship of images —**i′co·nol′a·ter** *n.*

i·co·nol·o·gy (-ə jē) *n.* [ICONO- + -LOGY] 1. the study of
icons, images, etc. 2. icons collectively 3. symbolic representation; symbolism —**i·con·o·log·i·cal** (ī kän′ə läj′i k′l)
adj. —**i′co·nol′o·gist** *n.*

☆**i·con·o·scope** (ī kän′ə skōp′) *n.* [ICONO- + -SCOPE] a
television camera electron tube, consisting of a vacuum
tube enclosing a photosensitive plate on which the image is
projected and an electron gun that scans the image with a
narrow focused beam

i·co·nos·ta·sis (ī′kə näs′tə sis) *n., pl.* **-ses′** (-sēz′)
[ModGr.(Ec.) *eikonostasis* < Gr. *eikōn*, an image + *stasis*,
a standing < *histasthai*, to stand] *Orthodox Eastern Ch.* a
partition or screen, decorated with icons, separating the
sanctuary from the rest of the church: also **i·con·o·stas**
(ī kän′ə stas′)

i·co·sa·he·dron (ī′kō sə hē′drən) *n., pl.* **-he′dra** (-drə),
-drons [Gr. *eikosaedron:* see ff. & -HEDRON] a solid figure
with twenty plane surfaces —**i′co·sa·he′dral** *adj.*

i·co·si- (ī′kō sē, -sə) [Gr. *eikosi-* < *eikosi*, twenty <
IE. *wikṃti*, twenty < *wi-*, two + *dkṃt-*, ten: cf. VIGINTI-]
a combining form meaning twenty: also **i′co·sa-** (-sə) or,
before a vowel, **icos-**

-ics (iks) [-IC + -s (pl.)]: used as transl. of Gr. *-ika* (L. *-ica*),
neut. pl. of *-ikos* (L. *-icus*)] *a n.-forming pl. suffix meaning:*
1. *[usually with sing. v.]* art, science, study *[linguistics]*
2. *[usually with sing. v.]* arrangement, system *[architecton-
ics]* 3. *[usually with pl. v.]* activities, practices *[histrionics]*
4. *[usually with pl. v.]* qualities, properties *[atmospherics]*

ic·ter·ic (ik ter′ik) *adj.* [L. *ictericus* < Gr. *ikterikos* <
ikteros, jaundice] relating to or having jaundice

ic·ter·us (ik′tər əs) *n.* [ModL. < Gr. *ikteros*, jaundice]
same as JAUNDICE

Ic·ti·nus (ik tī′nəs) 5th cent. B.C.; Gr. architect who
designed the Parthenon

ic·tus (ik′təs) *n., pl.* **-tus·es, -tus** [L., a blow, stroke,
metrical stress < pp. of *icere*, to strike, hit, beat < IE. base
aik-, ik-, spear, to strike with a sharp weapon, whence Gr.
aichmē, a spear] 1. rhythmical or metrical stress, or accent
2. *Med.* a convulsion, stroke, or sudden attack

i·cy (ī′sē) *adj.* **i′ci·er, i′ci·est** [ME. *isy* < OE. *isig*] 1.
having much ice; full of or covered with ice 2. of ice 3.
like ice; specif., *a)* slippery *b)* very cold; frigid 4. cold in
manner or attitude; unfriendly

id (id) *n.* [ModL. < L., it, neut. sing. of *is*, he: used as
transl. of G. *es*, it] *Psychoanalysis* that part of the psyche
which is regarded as the reservoir of the instinctual drives
and the source of psychic energy: it is dominated by the
pleasure principle and irrational wishing, and its impulses
are controlled through the development of the ego and
superego

-id (id, əd) *a n.-forming suffix meaning:* 1. [< L. *-is*, pl.
-ides < Gr. *-is*, pl. *-idēs*, patronymic suffix] a thing belonging to or connected with; specif., *a)* a meteor that seems to
radiate from a (specified) constellation *[Leonid]* *b)* [< Fr.
or ModL.: Fr. *-ide* < ModL. *-idae* (see -IDAE)] an animal
belonging to a (specified) group *[ephemerid]* 2. *Chem. same
as* -IDE 3. *Med.* an allergic reaction of the skin to (specified)
bacteria, fungi, etc. in the body

ID, I.D. 1. identification 2. inside diameter 3. Intelligence
Department —*n.* (ī′dē′), *pl.* **ID′s, I.D.′s** ☆a card (**ID card**)
or document, as a birth certificate, that serves to identify
a person, prove his age, etc.

id. [L. *idem*] the same

I'd (īd) 1. I had 2. I would 3. I should

I·da (ī′də) [ML. < OHG.: akin ? to ON. *Ithunn*, goddess of
youth] a feminine name

Ida. Idaho

I·da (ī′də), **Mount** 1. highest mountain in Crete, in the C
part: 8,058 ft. 2. mountain in NW Asia Minor, in ancient
Phrygia & Mysia near the site of Troy: c. 5,800 ft.: Turk.
name *Kazdaği*

-i·dae (i dē′) [ModL., pl. of L. *-ides* < Gr. *-idēs*, patronymic
suffix] *a suffix used to form the name of* a zoological family
[Canidae (the dog family)]

I·da·ho (ī′də hō′) [< tribal (Shoshonean) name < ?]
Mountain State of the NW U.S.: admitted 1890; 83,557
sq. mi.; pop. 713,000; cap. Boise: abbrev. **Ida., ID** —**I′da-
ho′an** (*or* ī′də hō′ən) *adj., n.*

fat, āpe, cär; ten, ēven; is, bīte; gō, hôrn, tōōl, look; oil, out; up, fur; get; joy; yet; chin; she; thin, *then*; zh, leisure; ŋ, ring;
ə for *a* in *ago*, *e* in *agent*, *i* in *sanity*, *o* in *comply*, *u* in *focus*; ' as in *able* (ā'b'l); Fr. bál; ë, Fr. coeur; ö, Fr. feu; Fr. mon; ɔ, Fr. coq;
ü, Fr. duc; r, Fr. cri; H, G. ich; kh, G. doch. See inside front cover. ☆Americanism; ‡foreign; *hypothetical; <derived from

Idaho Falls city in SE Ida., on the Snake River: pop. 36,000

-ide (īd; *occas.* id) [< (OX)IDE] *a suffix added to part of the name of* the nonmetallic or electronegative element or radical in a binary compound [sodium *chloride*, potassium *hydroxide*] *or used in forming the name of* a class of related compounds [glucoside]

i·de·a (ī dē′ə) *n.* [L. < Gr. *idea*, form or appearance of a thing as opposed to its reality < IE. *widswo- < base *weid-*, to see, know, whence L. *videre*, to see, Gr. *idein*, to see, OE. *witan*, to know (cf. WIT)] 1. something one thinks, knows, or imagines; a thought; mental conception or image; notion 2. an opinion or belief 3. a plan; scheme; project; intention; aim 4. a hazy perception; vague impression; fanciful notion; inkling 5. meaning or significance 6. *Music* a theme or figure 7. *Philos.* according to Plato, a model or archetype of which all real things are but imperfect imitations and from which their existence derives: in modern philosophy, used variously to mean the immediate object of thought, an ultimate principle apprehended by reason, absolute truth, etc.
SYN.—**idea**, the most general of these terms, may be applied to anything existing in the mind as an object of knowledge or thought; **concept** refers to a generalized idea of a class of objects, based on knowledge of particular instances of the class [his *concept* of a republic]; **conception**, often equivalent to **concept**, specifically refers to something conceived in the mind, or imagined [my *conception* of how the role should be played]; **thought** is used of any idea, whether or not expressed, that occurs to the mind in reasoning or contemplation [she rarely speaks her *thoughts*]; **notion** implies vagueness or incomplete intention [I have a *notion* to go]; **impression** also implies vagueness of an idea provoked by some external stimulus [I have the *impression* that she's unhappy]

i·de·al (ī dē′əl; *also, esp. for adj.* 2 & 4, *n.* 1 & 2, ī dēl′) *adj.* [Fr. *idéal* < LL. *idealis*, existing in idea, ideal < L. *idea*: see prec.] 1. existing as an idea, model, or archetype; consisting of ideas (sense 7) 2. thought of as perfect or as a perfect model; exactly as one would wish; of a perfect kind 3. of, or having the nature of, an idea or conception; identifying or illustrating an idea or conception; conceptual 4. existing only in the mind as an image, fancy, or concept; visionary; imaginary 5. *Philos.* of idealism; idealistic —*n.* 1. a conception of something in its most excellent or perfect form 2. a person or thing regarded as fulfilling this conception; perfect model 3. something that exists only in the mind 4. a goal or principle, esp. one of a noble character

i·de·al·ism (ī dē′əl iz′m) *n.* [< Fr. *idéalisme* or G. *ideal ismus*] 1. behavior or thought based on a conception of things as they should be or as one would wish them to be; idealization 2. a striving to achieve one's ideals 3. imaginative treatment in art or literature that seeks to show the artist's or author's conception of perfection; representation of imagined types, or ideals: cf. REALISM 4. *Philos.* any of various theories which hold that the objects of perception are actually: *a*) ideas which the mind knows directly and are not the objects themselves: cf. REALISM *b*) manifestations of an independent realm of essences or forms that are unique and changeless: cf. MATERIALISM

i·de·al·ist (-ist) *n.* 1. *a*) a person whose behavior or thought is based on ideals *b*) one who follows his ideals to the point of impracticality; visionary or dreamer 2. an adherent or practitioner of idealism in art, literature, or philosophy —*adj. same as* IDEALISTIC

i·de·al·is·tic (ī′dē ə lis′tik, ī dē′ə-) *adj.* 1. of or characteristic of an idealist 2. of, characterized by, or based on idealism —**i′de·al·is′ti·cal·ly** *adv.*

i·de·al·i·ty (ī′dē al′ə tē) *n.* 1. the state or quality of being ideal or of existing only in the mind 2. *pl.* **-ties** something that is only ideal and has no reality 3. creative ability or imaginative faculty: orig. a term in theory

i·de·al·ize (ī dē′ə līz′) *vt.* **-ized′, -iz′ing** to make ideal; think of or represent as ideal; regard or show as perfect or more nearly perfect than is true —*vi.* 1. to form an ideal or ideals 2. to represent things in the manner of an idealist —**i·de′al·i·za′tion** *n.* —**i·de′al·iz′er** *n.*

i·de·al·ly (ī dē′əl ē) *adv.* 1. in accordance with an ideal or ideals; in an ideal manner; perfectly 2. in theory

ideal point the point on a line or curve which lies at infinity

i·de·ate (ī′dē āt′, ī dē′āt) *vt., vi.* **-at′ed, -at′ing** to form an idea (of); imagine or conceive

i·de·a·tion (ī′dē ā′shən) *n.* [ML. *ideatio*] the formation or conception of ideas by the mind —**i′de·a′tion·al** *adj.* —**i′de·a′tion·al·ly** *adv.*

‡i·dée fixe (ē dā fēks′) [Fr.] a fixed idea; obsession

‡i·dée re·çue (rə sü′) [Fr., lit., received idea] a generally accepted idea; convention; commonplace

‡i·dem (ī′dem, ē′-) *pron.* [L.] the same as that previously mentioned

i·den·tic (ī den′tik, i-) *adj.* [ML. *identicus* < LL. *identitas*: see IDENTITY] identical; esp., having exactly the same wording, form, etc.: said of diplomatic messages or action by two or more governments

i·den·ti·cal (-ti k'l) *adj.* [prec. + -AL] 1. the very same 2. exactly alike or equal 3. designating twins, always of the same sex, developed from a single fertilized ovum and very much alike in physical appearance: cf. FRATERNAL —*SYN.* see SAME —**i·den′ti·cal·ly** *adv.*

identical proposition *Logic* a proposition whose subject and predicate are identical in content and extent (Ex.: that which is mortal is not immortal)

i·den·ti·fi·ca·tion (ī den′tə fi kā′shən, i-) *n.* [Fr.] 1. an identifying or being identified 2. anything by which a person or thing can be identified [the use of fingerprints for *identification*] 3. *Psychoanalysis* a mainly unconscious process by which a person formulates a mental image of another person important to him, and then thinks, feels, and acts in a way which resembles this image

i·den·ti·fy (ī den′tə fī′, i-) *vt.* **-fied′, -fy′ing** [LL. *identificare*: see ff. & -FY] 1. to make identical; consider or treat as the same [to *identify* one's interests with another's] 2. to recognize as being or show to be the very person or thing known, described, or claimed; fix the identity of [to *identify* a biological specimen] 3. to connect, associate, or involve closely [to *identify* a person with a school of thought] 4. *Psychoanalysis* to make an identification of (oneself) with someone else: often used absolutely —*vi.* to put oneself in another's place, so as to understand and share the other's thoughts, feelings, problems, etc.; sympathize (*with*) —**i·den′ti·fi′a·ble** *adj.* —**i·den′ti·fi′er** *n.*

I·den·ti·kit (ī den′tə kit′) [IDENTI(FICATION) + KIT[1]] *a trademark for* a set of transparencies carrying drawings of types of eyes, noses, mouths, etc. that can be variously overlaid to form a composite picture corresponding to descriptions given, as of a person sought by the police —*adj.* [often **i-**] designating or of a picture made from such a set

i·den·ti·ty (ī den′tə tē, i-) *n., pl.* **-ties** [Fr. *identité* < LL. *identitas*, coined (prob. after LL. *essentitas*, essence) < L. *idem*, the same, akin to Sans. *idám*, the same < IE. base *e-, ei-*, he, that, whence Sans. *ayám*, OIr. *ē*, Goth. *is*, he] 1. the condition or fact of being the same or exactly alike; sameness; oneness [groups united by *identity* of interests] 2. *a*) the condition or fact of being a specific person or thing; individuality *b*) the condition of being the same as a person or thing described or claimed 3. *Math.* an equation which is true for all permissible sets of values of the variables which appear in it: Ex. $x^2 - y^2 = (x + y)(x - y)$

id·e·o- (id′ē ə, ī′dē ə) [< Fr. or Gr.: Fr. *idéo-* < Gr. *idea*] *a combining form meaning* idea [ideology]

id·e·o·gram (id′ē ə gram′, ī′dē-) *n.* [prec. + -GRAM] 1. a graphic symbol representing an object or idea without expressing, as in a phonetic system, the sounds that form its name 2. a symbol representing an idea rather than a word (Ex.: 5, +, ÷) Also **id′e·o·graph′**

id·e·o·graph·ic (id′ē ə graf′ik) *adj.* of, or having the nature of, an ideogram or ideography: also **id′e·o·graph′i·cal** —**id′e·o·graph′i·cal·ly** *adv.*

id·e·og·ra·phy (id′ē äg′rə fē) *n.* the use of ideograms; representation of objects or ideas by graphic symbols

i·de·o·log·i·cal (ī′dē ə läj′i k'l, id′ē ə-) *adj.* of or concerned with ideology: also **i·de·o·log′ic** —**i′de·o·log′i·cal·ly** *adv.*

i·de·ol·o·gist (-äl′ə jist) *n.* 1. a student of or expert in ideology 2. a person occupied mainly with ideas; esp., an idle theorist or visionary 3. an exponent of a specified ideology; theorist

i·de·ol·o·gize (-jīz′) *vt.* **-gized′, -giz′ing** 1. to analyze ideologically 2. to convert to a certain ideology

i·de·o·logue (ī′dē ə lôg′, id′ē-; id′ē-) *n.* [Fr. *idéologue*, back-formation < *idéologie*: see ff.] *same as* IDEOLOGIST

i·de·ol·o·gy (ī′dē äl′ə jē, id′ē-) *n., pl.* **-gies** [Fr. *idéologie*: see IDEO- & -LOGY] 1. the study of ideas, their nature and source 2. thinking or theorizing of an idealistic, abstract, or impractical nature; fanciful speculation 3. the doctrines, opinions, or way of thinking of an individual, class, etc.; specif., the body of ideas on which a particular political, economic, or social system is based

i·de·o·mo·tor (ī′dē ə mōt′ər, id′ē-) *adj.* [IDEO- + MOTOR] *Psychol.* designating or of an unconscious body movement made in response to an idea

i·de·o·phone (-fōn′) *n.* [IDEO- + PHONE[1]] *Linguis.* the expression of an idea, as in many African languages, by means of a sound, often reduplicated, that creates an image of an action, object, etc.

ides (īdz) *n.pl.* [often with sing. v.] [Fr. < L. *idus*] in the ancient Roman calendar, the 15th day of March, May, July, or October, or the 13th of the other months

‡id est (id est) [L.] that is (to say)

id·i·o- (id′ē ō, -ə) [Gr. *idio- < idios*, one's own < IE. *swedyos < base *swe-*, possessive, whence L. *suus*, his, her, one's, Goth. *swēs*, own, OE. *swæs*, beloved, own] *a combining form meaning* one's own, personal, distinct [idiomorphic]

id·i·o·blast (id′ē ə blast′) *n.* [IDIO- + -BLAST] a specialized plant cell, usually thick-walled and without chlorophyll, occurring isolated among other cells of different type —**id′i·o·blas′tic** *adj.*

id·i·o·cy (id′ē ə sē) *n., pl.* **-cies** [IDIO(T) + -CY] 1. the state of being an idiot 2. behavior like that of an idiot; great foolishness or stupidity 3. an idiotic act or remark

id·i·o·lect (id′ē ə lekt′) *n.* [IDIO- + (DIA)LECT] *Linguis.* the dialect of an individual

id·i·om (id′ē əm) *n.* [< Fr. & LL.: Fr. *idiome* < LL. *idioma* < Gr. *idiōma*, peculiarity, idiom < *idios*: see IDIO-] 1. the language or dialect of a people, region, class, etc. 2. the usual way in which the words of a particular language are joined together to express thought 3. an accepted phrase, construction, or expression contrary to the usual patterns of the language or having a meaning different from the literal (Ex.: not a word did he say; to catch one's eye) 4.

the style of expression characteristic of an individual [the *idiom* of Carlyle] 5. a characteristic style, as in art or music

id·i·o·mat·ic (id′ē ə mat′ik) *adj.* [Gr. *idiōmatikos*, peculiar, characteristic] 1. in accordance with the individual nature of a language; characteristic of a particular language 2. using or having many idioms 3. of, or having the nature of, an idiom or idioms —**id′i·o·mat′i·cal·ly** *adv.*

id·i·o·mor·phic (-môr′fik) *adj.* [IDIO- + -MORPHIC] having its own proper form; specif., *Mineralogy* having the normal faces characteristic of a particular mineral: said of crystals in rock that have developed without interference

id·i·o·path·ic (-path′ik) *adj.* [< Gr. *idiopatheia*, feeling for oneself alone (see IDIO- & -PATHY) + -IC] designating or of a disease whose cause is unknown or uncertain —**id′i·op′a·thy** (-äp′ə thē) *n.*, *pl.* -**thies**

id·i·o·phone (id′ē ə fōn′) *n.* [IDIO- + -PHONE] *Music* any of a class of nonmembranous percussion instruments consisting of some elastic material, as wood or metal, capable of vibrating with a distinctive sound, as the triangle

id·i·o·plasm (-plaz′m) *n.* [IDIO- + -PLASM] the chromatin in a cell regarded as the part of the cell transmitting hereditary qualities: cf. TROPHOPLASM

id·i·o·syn·cra·sy (id′ē ə siŋ′krə sē, -sin′-) *n.*, *pl.* -**sies** [Gr. *idiosynkrasia* < *idio-*, one's own, peculiar (see IDIO-) + *synkrasis*, a mixing together, tempering < *synkerannynai*, to mix together < *syn-*, together + *kerannynai*, to mix < IE. *kere-, to mix, whence G. *rühren*, to stir] 1. the temperament or mental constitution peculiar to a person or group 2. any personal peculiarity, mannerism, etc. 3. an individual reaction to a drug, food, etc. that is different from the reaction of most people —**id′i·o·syn·crat′ic** (-sin krat′ik) *adj.* —**id′i·o·syn·crat′i·cal·ly** *adv.*
SYN.—**idiosyncrasy** refers to any personal mannerism or peculiarity and connotes strong individuality [the *idiosyncrasies* of a writer's style]; **eccentricity** implies considerable deviation from what is normal or customary and connotes whimsicality or even mental aberration [his *eccentricity* of wearing overshoes in the summer]

id·i·ot (id′ē ət) *n.* [ME. *idiote* < OFr. < L. *idiota*, ignorant and common person < Gr. *idiōtēs*, layman, ignorant person < *idios*, one's own, peculiar (see IDIO-)] 1. a mentally retarded person with an intelligence quotient of less than 25; adult person mentally equal or inferior to a child two years old: an obsolescent term: see MENTAL RETARDATION 2. a very foolish or stupid person

☆**idiot board** (or **card**) [Slang] a board, placard, etc. bearing the lines to be spoken by a television performer, used in prompting him

id·i·ot·ic (id′ē ät′ik) *adj.* [L. *idioticus*, uneducated, ignorant < Gr. *idiōtikos*, private, peculiar, rude] of, having the nature of, or characteristic of an idiot; very foolish or stupid —**id′i·ot′i·cal·ly** *adv.*

id·i·ot·ism (id′ē ə tiz′m) *n.* [Fr. *idiotisme* < IDIOT & -ISM] 1. idiotic action or behavior 2. [Archaic] idiocy 3. [Obs.] *same as* IDIOM

i·dle (ī′d'l) *adj.* **i′dler, i′dlest** [ME. *idel* < OE., empty, akin to G. *eitel*, vain, empty < ? IE. base *ai-dh, to burn, shine: basic sense, either "only apparent, seeming" or "burned out"] 1. *a)* having no value, use, or significance; worthless; useless [*idle* talk] *b)* vain; futile; pointless [an *idle* wish] 2. baseless; unfounded [*idle* rumors] 3. *a)* unemployed; not busy *b)* inactive; not in use [*idle* machines] *c)* not filled with activity [*idle* hours] 4. not inclined to work; lazy —*vi.* **i′dled, i′dling** [< the *adj.*: parallel with OE. *idlian*, to come to nothing, be useless] 1. to move slowly or aimlessly; loaf 2. to spend time unprofitably; be unemployed or inactive 3. to operate without transmitting power; esp., to operate with gears disengaged [an *idling* motor] —*vt.* 1. to waste; squander (usually with *away*) [to *idle* away one's youth] 2. to cause (a motor, etc.) to idle 3. to cause to be inactive or unemployed —*SYN.* see INACTIVE, LOITER, VAIN —**i′dle·ness** *n.* —**i′dly** *adv.*

i·dler (īd′lər) *n.* 1. a person who wastes time and does no work; lazy person 2. *a)* a gearwheel placed between two others to transfer motion from one to the other without changing their direction or speed: also **idler gear** (or **wheel**), **idle wheel** *b)* a pulley riding loosely on a shaft, pressing against a belt to guide it or take up the slack: also **idler pulley**

IDLE WHEEL

i·dlesse (īd′lis) *n.* [< IDLE + -ESS: a pseudo-archaic coinage] [Poet.] idleness; indolence

I·do (ē′dō) [an Esperanto affix used as a complete word, meaning "offspring"] an artificial, international auxiliary language, a modified form of Esperanto

i·do·crase (ī′dō krās′, id′ō-) *n.* [Fr. < Gr. *eidos*, form + *krasis*, mixture] *same as* VESUVIANITE

i·dol (ī′d'l) *n.* [ME. *idole* < OFr. < L. *idolum*, an image, form, specter, apparition (in LL.(Ec.), idol) < Gr. *eidōlon*, an image, phantom (in LGr.(Ec.), idol) < *eidos*, form, shape;

1. an image of a god, used as an object or instrument of worship 2. in monotheistic belief, any heathen deity 3. any object of ardent or excessive devotion or admiration 4. [Archaic] anything that has no substance but can be seen, as an image in a mirror 5. [Obs.] *a)* any image or effigy *b)* an imposter 6. *Logic* a material fallacy resulting from some common prejudice

i·dol·a·ter (ī däl′ə tər) *n.* [ME. *idolatre* < OFr. < LL.(Ec.) *idolatres* < LGr.(Ec.) *eidōlolatrēs* < *eidōlon* (see IDOL) + *latris*, hired servant] 1. a person who worships an idol or idols 2. a devoted admirer; adorer —**i·dol′a·tress** (-tris) *n.fem.*

i·dol·a·trize (-trīz′) *vt.*, *vi.* -**trized′, -triz′ing** to worship as an idolater

i·dol·a·trous (-trəs) *adj.* 1. of, or having the nature of, idolatry 2. worshiping an idol or idols 3. having or showing excessive admiration or devotion —**i·dol′a·trous·ly** *adv.* —**i·dol′a·trous·ness** *n.*

i·dol·a·try (-trē) *n.*, *pl.* -**tries** [ME. *idolatrie* < OFr. < LL.(Ec.) *idolatria* < Gr. (NT.) *eidōlolatreia*: see IDOLATER] 1. worship of idols 2. excessive devotion to or reverence for some person or thing

i·dol·ism (ī′d'l iz'm) *n.* 1. *same as* IDOLATRY 2. [Archaic] a fallacious notion; false reasoning

i·dol·ize (-īz′) *vt.* -**ized′, -iz′ing** 1. to make an idol of 2. to love or admire excessively; adore —*vi.* to worship idols —**i′dol·i·za′tion** *n.*

I·dom·e·neus (ī däm′ə nyōōs′, -nōōs′) *Gr. Legend* a king of Crete who led his subjects against Troy in the Trojan War

Id·u·mae·a, Id·u·me·a (id′yoo mē′ə, īd′-) *Gr. name of* EDOM —**Id′u·mae′an, Id′u·me′an** *adj.*, *n.*

I·dun (ē′dōōn) *Norse Myth.* the goddess of youth and spring, wife of Bragi: also **I′dun·a** (-ə)

i·dyll, i·dyl (ī′d'l; *Brit.* often id′'l) *n.* [L. *idyllium* < Gr. *eidyllion*, dim. of *eidos*, a form, figure, image: see -OID] 1. a short poem or prose work describing a simple, pleasant, peaceful scene of rural, pastoral, or domestic life 2. a scene or incident suitable for such a work 3. an extended narrative poem ["The *Idylls* of the King"] 4. *Music* a simple, pastoral composition

i·dyl·lic (ī dil′ik) *adj.* 1. of, or having the nature of, an idyll 2. pleasing and simple; pastoral or picturesque —**i·dyl′li·cal·ly** *adv.*

i·dyll·ist (ī′d'l ist) *n.* a writer or composer of idylls

-ie (ē) [earlier form of -Y¹: revitalized in back-formation (MOV)IE] *a suffix meaning: a)* small, little [*lassie, doggie*]: often used to express affection *b)* one that is as specified [a *softie*]

IE., I.E. Indo-European

i.e. [L. *id est*] that is (to say)

Ie·per (ē′pər) *Flem. name of* YPRES

-i·er (ir, ər, ē′ər, yər) [< various sources: *1.* ME. < OFr. < L. *-arius; 2.* Fr. < OFr. as in *l*, with the primary stress in Eng. on the suffix; *3.* ME. var. of -ER; *4.* ME. < *-i-* ending of prec. stem + -*er*] *a n.-forming suffix meaning* a person concerned with (a specified action or thing) [*furrier, bombardier, glazier*]

if (if) *conj.* [ME. < OE. *gif*, akin to G. *ob* (OHG. *oba, ibu*, Goth. *ibai*): ult. source unc.] 1. on condition that; in case that; supposing that [*if* I come, I'll see him; *if* I were you, I wouldn't do that] 2. allowing that; granting that [*if* he was there, I didn't see him] 3. whether: used to introduce an indirect question [ask him *if* he knows her] *If* is also used to introduce an exclamation expressing: *a)* a wish [*if* I had only known!] *b)* surprise, annoyance, etc. [well, *if* that isn't the limit!] —*n.* 1. a supposition or speculation 2. a condition or qualification [a clause filled with *ifs*] —**as if** as the situation would be if; as though

IF, I.F., i.f., i-f intermediate frequency

IFC International Finance Corporation

I·fe (ē′fe) city in SW Nigeria, near Ibadan: pop. 111,000

IFF Identification, Friend or Foe: an electronic system for recognition of friendly aircraft, ships, etc.

if·fy (if′ē) *adj.* [see IF & -Y²] [Colloq.] not definite; containing doubtful elements; dependent upon varying conditions [an *iffy* situation]

If·ni (ēf′nē) former Sp. province in NW Africa, ceded to Morocco in 1969: 580 sq. mi.; pop. 52,000

IFR Instrument Flight Rules

IG, I.G. 1. Indo-Germanic 2. Inspector General

Ig·bo (ēg′bō) *n. same as* IBO

Ig·dra·sil (ig′drə sil′) *same as* YGDRASIL

ig·loo (ig′lōō) *n.*, *pl.* -**loos** [Esk. *igdlu*, snow house] an Eskimo house or hut, usually dome-shaped and built of blocks of packed snow

ign. 1. ignition 2. [L. *ignotus*] unknown

Ig·na·tius (ig nā′shəs) [L. < Gr. *Ignatios*] 1. a masculine name 2. Saint, 50?-110? A.D.; Christian martyr & bishop of Antioch: his day is Feb. 1

IGLOO

Ignatius (of) Loyola, Saint (born *Iñigo López de Recalde*) 1491–1556; Sp. priest: founder of the Society of Jesus (Jesuit order): his day is July 31

ig·ne·ous (ig′nē əs) *adj.* [L. *igneus* < *ignis,* a fire < IE. base **egnis,* whence Sans. *agníḥ,* fire, Lith. *ugnìs*] **1.** of, containing, or having the nature of, fire; fiery **2.** produced by the action of fire; specif., formed by volcanic action or intense heat, as rocks solidified from molten magma at or below the surface of the earth

ig·nes·cent (ig nes′'nt) *adj.* [L. *ignescens,* prp. of *ignescere,* to take fire, burn < *ignis:* see prec.] **1.** bursting into flame **2.** giving off sparks when struck with steel —*n.* an ignescent substance

‡**ig·nis fat·u·us** (ig′nis fach′oo wəs) *pl.* **ig·nes fat·u·i** (ig′nēz fach′oo wī′) [ML. < L. *ignis,* a fire + *fatuus,* foolish] **1.** a light seen at night moving over swamps or marshy places, believed to be caused by the combustion of gases arising from decaying organic matter: popularly called *will-o'-the-wisp* or *jack-o'-lantern* **2.** a deceptive hope, goal, or influence; delusion

ig·nite (ig nīt′) *vt.* **-nit′ed, -nit′ing** [< L. *ignitus,* pp. of *ignire,* to set on fire < *ignis:* see IGNEOUS] **1.** to set fire to; cause to burn **2.** to heat to a great degree; make glow with heat **3.** to arouse the feelings of; excite —*vi.* to catch on fire; start burning —**ig·nit′a·ble, ig·nit′i·ble** *adj.* —**ig·nit′er, ig·ni′tor** *n.*

ig·ni·tion (ig nish′ən) *n.* [ModL. (Paracelsus) *ignitio* < L. *ignitus:* see IGNITE] **1.** a setting on fire or catching on fire **2.** the means by which a thing is ignited **3.** in an internal-combustion engine, *a)* the igniting of the explosive mixture in the cylinder *b)* the device or system for doing this **4.** *Chem.* the heating of a compound or mixture to the point of complete combustion, complete chemical change, or complete removal of volatile material

ig·ni·tron (ig nī′trän, ig′nə trän′) *n.* [IGNI(TE) + (ELEC)-TRON] a type of mercury-arc rectifier tube having a mercury-pool cathode and a single graphite anode: when a current is passed through an igniter rod into the pool, the mercury vapor is ionized and an arc starts between the cathode and anode: used in resistance welders, the control equipment for much high-energy research apparatus, etc.

ig·no·ble (ig nō′b'l) *adj.* [MFr. < L. *ignobilis,* unknown, obscure < *in-,* not + *nobilis* (OL. *gnobilis*), known: see NOBLE] **1.** formerly, not noble in birth or position; of the common people **2.** not noble in character or quality; dishonorable; base; mean —*SYN.* see BASE² —**ig·no′ble·ness** *n.* —**ig·no′bly** *adv.*

ig·no·min·i·ous (ig′nə min′ē əs) *adj.* [Fr. *ignominieux* < L. *ignominiosus*] **1.** characterized by or bringing on ignominy; shameful; dishonorable; disgraceful **2.** contemptible; despicable **3.** degrading; humiliating —**ig′no·min′i·ous·ly** *adv.* —**ig′no·min′i·ous·ness** *n.*

ig·no·min·y (ig′nə min′ē) *n., pl.* **-min′ies** [Fr. *ignominie* < L. *ignominia* < *in-,* without, not + *nomen,* NAME] **1.** loss of one's reputation; shame and dishonor; infamy **2.** disgraceful, shameful, or contemptible quality, behavior, or act —*SYN.* see DISGRACE

ig·no·ra·mus (ig′nə rā′məs, -ram′əs) *n., pl.* **-mus·es** [< the name of a lawyer in Geo. Ruggle's play *Ignoramus* (1615); L., lit., we take no notice (a legal term formerly written on a bill of indictment by a grand jury that finds it to be not a true bill)] an ignorant and stupid person

ig·no·rance (ig′nər əns) *n.* [ME. < OFr. < L. *ignorantia*] **1.** the condition or quality of being ignorant; lack of knowledge, education, etc. **2.** unawareness (*of*)

ig·no·rant (-ənt) *adj.* [ME. < OFr. < L. *ignorans,* prp. of *ignorare:* see IGNORE] **1.** *a)* having little knowledge, education, or experience; uneducated; inexperienced *b)* lacking knowledge (*in a particular area or matter*) **2.** caused by or showing lack of knowledge or education **3.** unaware (*of*) —**ig′no·rant·ly** *adv.*

SYN.—**ignorant** implies a lack of knowledge, either generally [an *ignorant* man] or on some particular subject [*ignorant* of the reason for their quarrel]; **illiterate** implies a failure to conform to some standard of knowledge, esp. an inability to read or write; **unlettered,** sometimes a milder term for **illiterate,** often implies unfamiliarity with fine literature [although a graduate engineer, he is relatively *unlettered*]; **uneducated** and **untutored** imply a lack of formal or systematic education, as of that acquired in schools [his brilliant, though *uneducated,* mind]; **unlearned** suggests a lack of learning, either generally or in some specific subject [*unlearned* in science] —*ANT.* educated, erudite, learned

‡**ig·no·ra·ti·o e·len·chi** (ig′nə rät′ē ō′ i len′kī; -kē) [L., lit., ignorance of the refutation] *Logic* the fallacy of irrelevant conclusion or missing the point where a proposition other than the one at issue is established by appeal to emotion

ig·nore (ig nôr′) *vt.* **-nored′, -nor′ing** [Fr. *ignorer* < L. *ignorare,* to have no knowledge of, ignore < *in-,* not + base of *gnarus,* knowing < IE. base **ĝnā-, *ĝnē-,* to know, whence Gr. *gnōrizein,* to make known, G. *kennen,* KNOW] **1.** to disregard deliberately; pay no attention to; refuse to consider **2.** *Law* to reject (a bill of indictment) for lack of evidence —*SYN.* see NEGLECT —**ig·nor′er** *n.*

I·go·rot (ig′ə rōt′, ē′gə-) *n., pl.* **-rots′, -rot′** [Sp. *Igorrote,* prob. < *Igolot,* name used in certain older records: of Tagalog origin] **1.** a member of a Malayan people, some formerly headhunters, living in Luzon, in the Philippines **2.** their Indonesian language

I·graine (i grān′) [akin ? to OFr. *Iguerne* < ? Celt.] *Arthurian Legend* the mother of King Arthur

I·gua·çú (ē′gwä soo′) river in S Brazil, flowing into the Paraná River: 380 mi.: also sp. **I′gua·zú′, I′guas·sú′**

i·gua·na (i gwä′nə) *n.* [Sp. < native S.Am. (Arawak) *iuana*] any of a large family (Iguanidae) of lizards, chameleons, etc.: esp., any of several harmless, large, tropical American lizards (genus *Iguana*) with a row of spines from neck to tail and feeding on insects or vegetation

i·guan·o·don (i gwän′ə dän′) *n.* [ModL. < prec. + -ODON(T)] any of a genus (*Iguanodon*) of very large, vegetarian, two-footed dinosaurs: also **i·guan′o·dont′** (-dänt′)

IGY International Geophysical Year

IH, I.H. Indo-Hittite

IHP, I.H.P., ihp., i.h.p. indicated horsepower

LAND IGUANA (to 5 ft. long)

ih·ram (i räm′) *n.* [Ar. *iḥrām,* a prohibiting < *ḥarama,* to forbid] **1.** a costume worn by Moslem pilgrims to Mecca, consisting of one piece of white cotton around the waist and hips and another over the shoulder **2.** the restrictions and rules that must be observed by a pilgrim so dressed

IHS [< L. miscopying of IHΣ, for which the proper L. form would be IES] a contraction derived from the Greek word IHΣOYΣ, Jesus, used as a symbol or monogram: later misunderstood as a Latin abbreviation **I.H.S.** and expanded variously as *Iesus Hominum Salvator,* Jesus, Saviour of Men; *In Hoc Signo* (*Vinces*), in this sign (thou shalt conquer); *In Hoc* (*Cruce*) *Salus,* in this (cross) salvation

IJs·sel (ī′səl) river in the E Netherlands, flowing from the Rhine north into the IJsselmeer: 70 mi.: also sp. **Ijs·sel, Ij′sel**

IJs·sel·meer (-mer′) shallow freshwater lake in N & C Netherlands: formerly part of the Zuider Zee, until cut off by a dam (1932): also sp. **Ijs′sel·meer′, Ij′sel·meer′**

‡**i·ke·ba·na** (ē′ke bä′nä) *n.* [Jap.] the Japanese art of arranging cut flowers in rhythmic, decorative designs

Ikh·na·ton (ik nät′'n) ?–1358? B.C.; king of Egypt (as *Amenhotep IV,* 1375?–58?) & religious reformer

i·kon (ī′kän) *n. var. of* ICON

il- (il) *see* IN-¹, IN-²

-il (il) *see* -ILE

ILA International Longshoremen's Association

i·lang-i·lang (ē′läŋ ē′läŋ) *n. same as* YLANG-YLANG

-ile (il, əl, 'l; *also, chiefly Brit.* īl) [< Fr. or L.: Fr. *-il, ile* < L. *-ilis*] a *suffix meaning* of, having to do with, that can be, like, suitable for [*docile, missile*]: sometimes **-il** [*civil, fossil*]

il·e·ac (il′ē ak′) *adj.* of or having to do with the ileum: also **il′e·al** (-əl)

Île-de-France (ēl də fräns′) region & former province of NC France, surrounding Paris

Île du Dia·ble (ēl dü dyȧ′bl′) *Fr. name of* DEVIL'S ISLAND

il·e·i·tis (il′ē ī′tis) *n.* inflammation of the ileum

il·e·o- (il′ē ō, -ə) a *combining form meaning:* **1.** of the ileum [*ileostomy*] **2.** ileum and [*ileocolic*] Also, before a vowel, **ile-**

il·e·os·to·my (il′ē äs′tə mē) *n.* the surgical operation of making an opening in the ileum

il·e·um (il′ē əm) *n., pl.* **il′e·a** (-ə) [ModL. < L., flank, groin (var. of *ilium, ile*): form prob. after *ileus* (see ff.) < ?] the lowest part of the small intestine, opening into the large intestine

il·e·us (-əs) *n.* [ModL. < L. *ileus, ileos* < Gr. *eileos,* colic, altered (after *eilein,* to twist) < *eilyos* < *eilyein,* to envelop, creep along < IE. **wel-,* to turn, roll, whence WALK] an abnormal condition caused by paralysis or obstruction of the intestines and resulting in the failure of intestinal contents to pass through properly

i·lex (ī′leks) *n.* [L., holm oak] **1.** *same as* HOLLY **2.** *same as* HOLM OAK

Il·ford (il′fərd) city in Essex, England, near London: pop. 177,000

il·i·ac (il′ē ak′) *adj.* [LL. *iliacus,* relating to colic < L. *ileus* (see ILEUS), but with meaning as if < L. *ileum*] of or near the ilium

Il·i·ad (il′ē əd) [L. *Ilias* (gen. *Iliadis*) < Gr. *Ilias* (*poiēsis*) < *Ilios, Ilion,* Ilium, Troy < *Ilos,* Ilus, legendary founder of Troy] a long Greek epic poem, ascribed to Homer, about events growing from the wrath of Achilles: it is set in the tenth year of the Trojan War —*n.* a series of disasters

Il·i·am·na (il′ē am′nə) lake in SW Alas., at the base of the Alaska Peninsula: 1,000 sq. mi.

il·i·o- (il′ē ō, -ə) a *combining form meaning:* **1.** of the ilium **2.** iliac and

-il·i·ty (il′ə tē) *pl.* **-ties** a *n.-forming suffix corresponding to* -ILE, -IL [*imbecility, civility*]

Il·i·um (il′ē əm) [see ILIAD] L. *name for* TROY

il·i·um (il′ē əm) *n., pl.* **il′i·a** (-ə) [ModL.: see ILEUM] the flat, uppermost portion of the three sections of the innominate bone

ilk¹ (ilk) *adj.* [Scot. dial. < ME. *ilke* < OE. *ilca,* same; prob. < **ī-līca* < *ī-,* lit., the + *-līca,* like (see LIKE¹)] [Obs.] same; like —*n.* kind; sort; class: only in **of** that; **of his, her,** etc.) **ilk,** of the same sort or class: from a misunderstanding of the phrase *of that ilk* as used in Scotland to mean "of the

same name (as the place he owns or from which he comes)" [MacDonald *of that ilk* (i.e., MacDonald of MacDonald)]

ilk² (ilk) *adj.* [ME., Northern & Midlands var. of *ilch*, *ælch* < OE. *ælc*: see EACH] [Chiefly Scot.] each; every: also **il·ka** (il′kə)

ill (il) *adj.* **worse, worst** [ME. < ON. *illr* (replacing OE. *yfel*, evil, in many senses): prob. < Gmc. **ilhila* < IE. base **elk-*, hungry, bad, whence OIr. *elc*, bad] **1.** characterized by, causing, or tending to cause harm or evil; specif., *a)* morally bad or wrong; evil [*ill repute*] *b)* causing pain, hardship, etc.; adverse [*ill fortune*] *c)* not kind or friendly; harsh; cruel [*ill will*] *d)* promising trouble; unfavorable; unfortunate; unpropitious [an *ill omen*] **2.** not healthy, normal, or well; having a disease; sick; indisposed **3.** not according to rule, custom, desirability, etc.; faulty; imperfect [*ill breeding*] —*n.* anything causing harm, trouble, wrong, pain, unhappiness, etc.; specif., *a)* an evil or misfortune *b)* a disease —*adv.* **worse, worst 1.** in an ill manner; specif., *a)* badly; wrongly; improperly; imperfectly *b)* harshly; cruelly; unkindly [*ill-spoken*] **2.** with difficulty; scarcely [he can *ill* afford to refuse] —*SYN.* see BAD¹, SICK —**go ill with** to be unfortunate for or unfavorable to —**ill at ease** uneasy; uncomfortable —**take ill** to be annoyed or offended at

I'll (il) **1.** I shall **2.** I will

Ill. Illinois

ill. 1. illustrated **2.** illustration

ill-ad·vised (il′əd vīzd′) *adj.* showing or resulting from a lack of sound advice or proper consideration; unwise — **ill′-ad·vis′ed·ly** (-vī′zid lē) *adv.*

Il·lam·pu (ē yäm′pōō) mountain of the Andes, in WC Bolivia: highest peak c. 21,500 ft.

il·la·tion (i lā′shən) *n.* [LL. *illatio* < L. *illatio* < *illatus* (used as pp. of *inferre*, to bring in) < *in-*, in + *latus* (used as pp. of *ferre*, to bring) < earlier **tlatus* < IE. **tḷtós* < base **tel-*, to lift, bear, whence L. *tolerare* (see TOLERATE), Gr. *tlēnai*, to bear] **1.** the act of drawing a conclusion or making an inference from premises **2.** the conclusion drawn; inference

il·la·tive (il′ə tiv, i lāt′iv) *adj.* [L. *illativus*: see prec.] **1.** expressing or introducing an inference: said of such words as *therefore* **2.** of, or having the nature of, an illation; inferential —*n.* **1.** an illative word or phrase **2.** an illation or inference —**il′la·tive·ly** *adv.*

ill-be·ing (il′bē′iŋ) *n.* an unhealthy, unhappy, or unprosperous condition

ill-bod·ing (-bōd′iŋ) *adj.* boding evil; ominous

ill-bred (-bred′) *adj.* badly brought up; lacking good manners; rude; impolite

ill-con·sid·ered (-kən sid′ərd) *adj.* not properly considered; not suitable or wise

ill-de·fined (-di fīnd′) *adj.* poorly defined; not clear or definite

ill-dis·posed (-dis pōzd′) *adj.* **1.** having a bad disposition; malicious or malevolent **2.** unfriendly or unfavorable (*toward*)

il·le·gal (i lē′gəl) *adj.* [< Fr. *illégal* or ML. *illegalis*: see IN-² & LEGAL] prohibited by law; against the law; unlawful; illicit; also, not authorized or sanctioned, as by rules — **il·le·gal·i·ty** (il′ē gal′ə tē) *n., pl.* **-ties** —**il·le′gal·ly** *adv.*

il·leg·i·ble (i lej′ə b'l) *adj.* [< IN-² + LEGIBLE] very difficult or impossible to read because badly written or printed, faded, obscured by age, etc. —**il·leg′i·bil′i·ty** *n.* — **il·leg′i·bly** *adv.*

il·le·git·i·ma·cy (il′ə jit′ə mə sē) *n., pl.* **-cies** [< ff. + -CY] the fact, condition, or quality of being illegitimate; specif., bastardy

il·le·git·i·mate (-ə mit) *adj.* [< ML. *illegitimatus*, pp. of *illegitimare*, to make illegitimate < L. *illegitimus*, not lawful: see IN-² & LEGITIMATE] **1.** born of parents not married to each other; bastard **2.** incorrectly deduced or concluded; not logical **3.** contrary to law or rules; illegal; unlawful **4.** not in keeping with accepted usage: said of words or phrases —**il′le·git′i·mate·ly** *adv.*

ill fame bad reputation —**house of ill fame** a house of prostitution; brothel

ill-fat·ed (il′fāt′id) *adj.* **1.** having or certain to have an evil fate or unlucky end **2.** causing misfortune; unlucky

ill-fa·vored (-fā′vərd) *adj.* **1.** of unpleasant or evil appearance; ugly **2.** unpleasant; offensive

ill-found·ed (-foun′did) *adj.* not supported by facts or sound reasons

ill-got·ten (-gät′'n) *adj.* obtained by evil, unlawful, or dishonest means [*ill-gotten* gains]

ill humor a disagreeable, cross, or sullen mood or state of mind —**ill′-hu′mored** *adj.* —**ill′-hu′mored·ly** *adv.*

il·lib·er·al (i lib′ər əl) *adj.* [Fr. *illibéral* < L. *illiberalis*: see IN-² & LIBERAL] **1.** [Archaic] lacking a liberal education; without culture; unrefined **2.** intolerant; bigoted; narrow-minded **3.** not generous; stingy —**il·lib′er·al′i·ty** (-ə ral′ə tē) *n.* —**il·lib′er·al·ly** *adv.*

il·lic·it (i lis′it) *adj.* [Fr. *illicite* < L. *illicitus*, not allowed: see IN-² & LICIT] not allowed by law, custom, rule, etc.; unlawful; improper; prohibited; unauthorized —**il·lic′it·ly** *adv.* —**il·lic′it·ness** *n.*

Il·li·ma·ni (ē′yē mä′nē) mountain of the Andes, in WC Bolivia: c. 21,200 ft.

il·lim·it·a·ble (i lim′it ə b'l) *adj.* [< IN-² + LIMITABLE] without limit or bounds; immeasurable —**il·lim′it·a·bil′i·ty, il·lim′it·a·ble·ness** *n.* —**il·lim′it·a·bly** *adv.*

☆**il·lin·i·um** (i lin′ē əm) *n.* [ModL. after the University of *Illinois*, where research on it was done] *former name for* PROMETHIUM

Il·li·nois (il′ə noi′; *occas.* -noiz′) *n.* [Fr. < Illinois *ileniwe*, man] **1.** *pl.* **Il′li·nois′** a member of a tribe or confederacy of Indians who lived in N Illinois, S Wisconsin, and parts of Iowa and Missouri **2.** their dialect of the Algonquian language —**1.** Middle Western State of the U.S.: admitted 1818; 56,400 sq. mi.; pop. 11,114,000; cap. Springfield: abbrev. **Ill., IL 2.** river in Ill., flowing from southwest of Chicago into the Mississippi, near St. Louis: c. 273 mi. —**Il′li·nois′an** (-noi′ən, -noiz′ən) *adj., n.*

il·liq·uid (i lik′wid) *adj.* [< IN-² + LIQUID] **1.** not readily convertible into cash **2.** characterized by an insufficiency of cash —**il′li·quid′i·ty** (-li kwid′ə tē) *n.*

☆**il·lite** (il′īt) *n.* [< ILL(INOIS) + -ITE¹] any of a group of clay minerals usually consisting of interlayered mica and montmorillonite

il·lit·er·a·cy (i lit′ər ə sē) *n.* **1.** the state or quality of being illiterate; lack of education or culture; esp., an inability to read or write **2.** *pl.* **-cies** a mistake (in writing or speaking) suggesting poor or inadequate education

il·lit·er·ate (-it) *adj.* [L. *illiteratus*, unlettered: see IN-² & LITERATE] **1.** ignorant; uneducated; esp., not knowing how to read or write **2.** having or showing limited knowledge, experience, or culture, esp. in some particular field [musically *illiterate*] **3.** violating accepted usage in language [an *illiterate* sentence] —*n.* an illiterate person; esp., one not knowing how to read or write —*SYN.* see IGNORANT —**il·lit′er·ate·ly** *adv.*

ill-look·ing (il′look′iŋ) *adj.* **1.** unattractive; ugly **2.** of evil or sinister appearance

ill-man·nered (-man′ərd) *adj.* having or showing bad manners; rude; impolite —*SYN.* see RUDE

ill nature an unpleasant, disagreeable, or mean disposition —**ill′-na′tured** *adj.* —**ill′-na′tured·ly** *adv.*

ill·ness (-nis) *n.* **1.** the condition of being ill, or in poor health; sickness; disease **2.** [Obs.] wickedness

il·log·ic (i läj′ik) *n.* the quality of being illogical

il·log·i·cal (-i k'l) *adj.* [< IN-² + LOGICAL] not logical or reasonable; using, based on, or caused by faulty reasoning —**il·log′i·cal′i·ty** (-i kal′ə tē), **il·log′i·cal·ness** *n.* —**il·log′i·cal·ly** *adv.*

ill-o·mened (il′ō′mənd) *adj.* having bad omens; ill-fated; inauspicious

ill-sort·ed (-sôrt′id) *adj.* badly arranged or matched [an *ill-sorted* pair]

ill-spent (-spent′) *adj.* misspent; spent wastefully

ill-starred (-stärd′) *adj.* [< astrological notion of being born or conceived under an evil star] unlucky or doomed to disaster

ill-suit·ed (-sōōt′id) *adj.* not suited or appropriate

ill-tem·pered (-tem′pərd) *adj.* having or showing a bad temper; quarrelsome; sullen; irritable

ill-timed (-tīmd′) *adj.* coming or done at the wrong time; inopportune [an *ill-timed* remark]

ill-treat (-trēt′) *vt.* to treat unkindly, cruelly, or unfairly; harm; abuse; maltreat —**ill′-treat′ment** *n.*

il·lume (i lōōm′) *vt.* **-lumed′, -lum′ing** [Poet.] to illuminate

il·lu·mi·nance (i lōō′mə nəns) *n. same as* ILLUMINATION (sense 2)

il·lu·mi·nant (-nənt) *adj.* [L. *illuminans*, prp. of *illuminare*] giving light; illuminating —*n.* something that illuminates, or gives light

il·lu·mi·nate (-nāt′) *vt.* **-nat′ed, -nat′ing** [< L. *illuminatus*, pp. of *illuminare*, to light up < *in-*, in + *luminare*, to light < *lumen* (gen. *luminis*), a light < IE. **leuksmen* < base **leuk-*: see ILLUSTRATE] **1.** *a)* to give light to; light up *b)* to brighten; animate **2.** *a)* to make clear; explain; elucidate *b)* to inform; instruct; enlighten **3.** to make illustrious, glorious, or famous **4.** to decorate with lights **5.** *a)* to decorate (an initial letter or word) with designs, tracings, etc. of gold, silver, or bright colors *b)* to decorate (a manuscript, page border, etc.) with such initial letters, miniature pictures, etc. —*adj.* [Archaic] **1.** made bright with light **2.** enlightened in mind or spirit —*n.* [Archaic] a person who has or claims to have special knowledge —**il·lu′mi·na·ble** *adj.*

il·lu·mi·na·ti (i lōō′mə nät′ē) *n.pl. sing.* **-to** (-ō) [It. (or ModL.) < L., pl. of *illuminatus*: see ILLUMINATE] **1.** people who have or profess to have special intellectual or spiritual enlightenment **2.** [I-] any of various societies, usually secret, composed of such people

il·lu·mi·na·tion (-nā′shən) *n.* [ME. *illumynacyon* < OFr. *illumination* < LL. *illuminatio*] **1.** an illuminating or being illuminated; specif., *a)* a lighting up; supplying of light *b)* clarification; explanation *c)* enlightenment; instruction *d)* decoration with lights *e)* decoration of initial letters, manuscripts, etc. with designs, colors, etc. **2.** the intensity of light per unit of area **3.** the designs, tracings, etc. used

in decorating manuscripts **4.** the lights used in decorating a city, etc.

il·lu·mi·na·tive (i lōō'mə nāt'iv) *adj.* [ML. *illuminativus*] illuminating or tending to illuminate

il·lu·mi·na·tor (-ər) *n.* [LL.(Ec.), an enlightener] a person or thing that illuminates; specif., *a)* any apparatus or device for giving, concentrating, or reflecting light *b)* one who decorates manuscripts, etc.

il·lu·mine (i lōō'min) *vt.* **-mined, -min·ing** [ME. *illuminen* < OFr. *illuminer* < L. *illuminare*] to illuminate; light up

il·lu·min·ism (-min iz'm) *n.* the doctrines or claims of any of the Illuminati —**il·lu'min·ist** *n.*

illus. 1. illustrated **2.** illustration

ill-us·age (il'yōō'sij, -zij) *n.* unfair, unkind, or cruel treatment; abuse: also **ill usage**

ill-use (-yōōz'; *for n.* -yōōs') *vt.* **-used', -us'ing** to treat unfairly, unkindly, or cruelly; use badly; abuse —*n. same as* ILL-USAGE

il·lu·sion (i lōō'zhən) *n.* [ME. *illusioun* < OFr. *illusion* < L. *illusio*, a mocking (in LL.(Ec.), deceit, illusion) < *illusus*, pp. of *illudere*, to mock, play with < *in-*, on + *ludere*, to play, akin to Gr. *loidorein*, to revile] **1.** a false idea or conception; belief or opinion not in accord with the facts **2.** an unreal, deceptive, or misleading appearance or image [a large mirror giving the *illusion* of space in a small room] **3.** *a)* a false perception, conception, or interpretation of what one sees *b)* the misleading image resulting in such a false impression **4.** *same as* HALLUCINATION **5.** a delicate, gauzy silk tulle used for veils, etc. —*SYN.* see DELUSION —**il·lu'sion·al, il·lu'sion·ar'y** *adj.*

il·lu·sion·ism (-iz'm) *n.* **1.** the theory or doctrine that the material world exists only in illusive sense impressions **2.** the use of illusions in art —**il·lu'sion·is'tic** *adj.*

il·lu·sion·ist (-ist) *n.* **1.** a person subject to illusions, or false impressions; visionary **2.** a believer in illusionism **3.** an entertainer who performs sleight-of-hand tricks **4.** an artist who employs illusionism

il·lu·sive (i lōō'siv) *adj.* illusory; unreal —**il·lu'sive·ly** *adv.* —**il·lu'sive·ness** *n.*

il·lu·so·ry (-sər ē) *adj.* producing, based on, or having the nature of, illusion; deceptive; unreal; illusive —**il·lu'so·ri·ly** *adv.* —**il·lu'so·ri·ness** *n.*

illust. 1. illustrated **2.** illustration

il·lus·trate (il'ə strāt', i lus'trāt) *vt.* **-trat'ed, -trat'ing** [< L. *illustratus*, pp. of *illustrare*, to light up, illuminate < *in-*, in + *lustrare*, to illuminate < *lustrum* < IE. **leukstrom*, illumination < base **leuk-*, to light, whence Gr. *leukos*, gleaming, L. *lux*, LIGHT[1]] **1.** *a)* to make clear; explain *b)* to make clear or easily understood by examples, comparisons, etc.; exemplify **2.** *a)* to furnish (books, etc.) with explanatory or decorative drawings, designs, or pictures *b)* to explain or decorate: said of pictures, etc. **3.** [Obs.] *a)* to make luminous; illuminate *b)* to enlighten *c)* to make bright; adorn *d)* to make illustrious —*vi.* to offer an example for clarification

il·lus·tra·tion (il'ə strā'shən) *n.* [ME. *illustracione* < OFr. *illustration* < L. *illustratio*] **1.** an illustrating or being illustrated **2.** an example, story, analogy, etc. used to help explain or make something clear **3.** a picture, design, diagram, etc. used to decorate or explain something —*SYN.* see INSTANCE —**il'lus·tra'tion·al** *adj.*

il·lus·tra·tive (i lus'trə tiv, il'ə strāt'iv) *adj.* [ML.(Ec.) *illustrativus*] serving as an illustration or example —**il·lus'tra·tive·ly** *adv.*

il·lus·tra·tor (il'ə strāt'ər, i lus'trāt ər) *n.* [LL.(Ec.), an enlightener] a person or thing that illustrates; esp., an artist who makes illustrations for books, magazines, etc.

il·lus·tri·ous (i lus'trē əs) *adj.* [< L. *illustris*, clear, conspicuous, distinguished (back-formation < *illustrare*: see ILLUSTRATE) + -OUS] **1.** orig., *a)* lustrous; shining; bright *b)* very clear; evident **2.** very distinguished; famous; eminent; outstanding —*SYN.* see FAMOUS —**il·lus'tri·ous·ly** *adv.* —**il·lus'tri·ous·ness** *n.*

il·lu·vi·al (i lōō'vē əl) *adj.* of or relating to illuvium or illuviation

il·lu·vi·ate (-āt') *vi.* **-at'ed, -at'ing** to be subjected to illuviation

il·lu·vi·a·tion (i lōō'vē ā'shən) *n.* [see ff. & -ATION] the accumulation in an underlying soil layer of materials, as colloids, soluble salts, etc., that have been leached out of an upper layer

il·lu·vi·um (i lōō'vē əm) *n., pl.* **-vi·ums, -vi·a** (-ə) [ModL. < IL- + (AL)LUVIUM] soil materials which have been leached from an upper layer of soil and deposited in a lower layer

ill will unfriendly feeling; hostility; hate; dislike —*SYN.* see MALICE

ill-wish·er (il'wish'ər) *n.* a person who wishes evil or misfortune to another

il·ly (il'lē) *adv.* [Now Dial.] badly; ill

Il·lyr·i·a (i lir'ē ə) ancient region along the E coast of the Adriatic: see GREECE, map

Il·lyr·i·an (-ən) *adj.* of Illyria, its people, or culture —*n.* **1.** a native or inhabitant of Illyria **2.** the extinct language of the Illyrians, generally regarded as a distinct branch of the Indo-European family

Il·lyr·i·cum (-i kəm) Roman province including Illyria; later, Roman prefecture including much of the Balkan Peninsula & some of the area north of the Adriatic

il·men·ite (il'mə nīt') *n.* [G. *ilmenit* < the *Ilmen* Mts. in the southern Urals + *-it*, -ITE[1]] a lustrous black mineral, FeTiO₃, an oxide of iron and titanium

ILO, I.L.O. International Labor Organization

I·lo·ca·no (ē'lō kä'nō) *n.* **1.** *pl.* **-nos, -no** any member of a people of N Luzon **2.** their Indonesian language

I·lo·i·lo (ē'lō ē'lō) seaport on S Panay, in the Philippines: pop. 151,000

ILS instrument landing system

I'm (im) I am

im- (im) *see* IN-[1], IN-[2]

I.M. Isle of Man

im·age (im'ij) *n.* [ME. < OFr. < *imagene* < L. *imaginem*, acc. of *imago*, imitation, copy, image < base of *imitari*, to imitate] **1.** *a)* an imitation or representation of a person or thing, drawn, painted, photographed, etc.; esp., a statue *b)* a sculptured figure used as an idol **2.** the visual impression of something produced by reflection from a mirror, refraction through a lens, etc. **3.** a person or thing very much like another; copy; counterpart; likeness **4.** *a)* a mental picture of something; conception; idea; impression ☆*b)* the concept of a person, product, institution, etc. held by the general public, often one deliberately created or modified by publicity, advertising, propaganda, etc. **5.** a type; typical example; symbol; embodiment [the very *image* of laziness] **6.** a vivid representation; graphic description [a drama that is the *image* of life] **7.** a figure of speech, esp. a metaphor or simile **8.** *Psychoanalysis* a picture or likeness of a person, as of a parent, usually idealized, constructed in the unconscious and remaining there; imago —*vt.* **-aged, -ag·ing** [< the *n.*; also < Fr. *imager* < the *n.*] **1.** to make a representation or imitation of; portray; delineate **2.** to reflect; mirror **3.** to picture in the mind; imagine **4.** to be a symbol or type of **5.** to describe graphically, vividly, or with figures of speech

image converter *Electronics* a device in which a primary optical image is converted to an electron image which is focused in turn by an electron lens on a secondary screen or plate

☆**image dissector** *Electronics* a television pickup tube of low sensitivity but long life in which the primary electron image is scanned past a small photocathode

☆**image orthicon** *Electronics* a television camera tube of high sensitivity that combines an image converter, an orthicon, and an electron-multiplier amplifier

im·age·ry (im'ij rē, -ər ē) *n., pl.* **-ries** [ME. *imagerie* < OFr.] **1.** [Now Rare] images generally; esp., statues **2.** mental images, as produced by memory or imagination **3.** descriptions and figures of speech

i·mag·i·na·ble (i maj'ə nə b'l) *adj.* [ME. *ymaginable* < LL. *imaginabilis*] that can be imagined —**i·mag'i·na·bly** *adv.*

i·mag·i·nal[1] (i maj'ə n'l) *adj.* of or having to do with the imagination or mental images

i·mag·i·nal[2] (i maj'ə n'l, -mā'gə-) *adj. Zool.* of an imago

i·mag·i·nar·y (i maj'ə ner'ē) *adj.* [L. *imaginarius*] **1.** existing only in the imagination; fanciful; unreal **2.** *Math.* designating or of the square root of a negative quantity —**i·mag'i·nar'i·ly** *adv.* —**i·mag'i·nar'i·ness** *n.*

SYN.—**imaginary** applies to that which exists in the imagination only and is, therefore, unreal [*imaginary* enemies]; **fanciful** refers to that which has been conceived in the fancy and usually connotes quaintness or whimsicality [*fanciful* tales]; **visionary** refers to something unreal conceived of in, or as in, a vision and usually connotes impracticality [the airplane was once a *visionary* dream]; **fantastic** applies to something which seems to be so highly fanciful or odd as to be beyond belief [a *fantastic* scheme for storing energy] —*ANT.* **real, actual**

imaginary number a complex number in the form *a* + *bi* where *b* is not zero: when *a* is zero, it is a **pure imaginary number**

imaginary part the part of a complex number which is a real number multiplied by the square root of minus one, e.g., 5 in (3 + 5*i*)

imaginary unit the square root of minus one; $\sqrt{-1}$: symbol *i*

i·mag·i·na·tion (i maj'ə nā'shən) *n.* [ME. *ymaginacioun* < OFr. *imagination* < L. *imaginatio* < pp. of *imaginari*: see IMAGINE] **1.** *a)* the act or power of forming mental images of what is not actually present *b)* the act or power of creating mental images of what has never been actually experienced, or of creating new images or ideas by combining previous experiences; creative power **2.** anything imagined; mental image; creation of the mind; fancy **3.** a foolish notion; empty fancy **4.** the ability to understand and appreciate imaginative creations of others, esp. works of art and literature **5.** resourcefulness in dealing with new or unusual experiences **6.** [Obs.] an evil plan or scheme

i·mag·i·na·tive (i maj'ə nə tiv, -nāt'iv) *adj.* [ME. *imaginatif* < OFr. < ML. *imaginativus*] **1.** having, using, or showing imagination; having great creative powers **2.** given to imagining **3.** of or resulting from imagination [*imaginative* literature] —**i·mag'i·na·tive·ly** *adv.* —**i·mag'i·na·tive·ness** *n.*

i·mag·ine (i maj'in) *vt.* **-ined, -in·ing** [ME. *imaginen* < OFr. *imaginer* < L. *imaginari* < *imago*, a likeness, IMAGE] **1.** to make a mental image of; form an idea or notion of; conceive in the mind; create by the imagination **2.** to suppose; guess; think —*vi.* **1.** to use the imagination **2.** to

suppose; guess; think —*interj.* an exclamation of surprise, expostulation, etc.

im·ag·ism (im′ə jiz′m) *n.* [< *Des imagistes*, title of the first anthology of imagist poetry (1914)] a movement in modern poetry (c. 1909–1917), characterized by the use of precise, concrete images, free verse, and suggestion rather than complete statement —**im′ag·ist** *n., adj.* —**im′ag·is′tic** *adj.*

i·ma·go (i mā′gō) *n., pl.* **-goes, -gos, i·mag·i·nes** (i maj′ə nēz′) [ModL., special use (by Linnaeus) of L., an IMAGE, likeness] **1.** an insect in its final, adult, reproductive stage, generally having wings **2.** *Psychoanalysis* same as IMAGE

i·mam (i mäm′) *n.* [Ar. *imām,* a guide, leader < *amma,* to walk before, precede] **1.** the leader of prayer in a Moslem mosque **2.** [*often* I-] a title for any of various Moslem leaders and rulers

i·mam·ate (-āt) *n.* [see -ATE²] **1.** the territory ruled by an imam **2.** the office or function of an imam

i·ma·ret (i mä′ret) *n.* [Turk. *'imārat* < Ar. *'imārah,* building] in Turkey, an inn or hospice

im·bal·ance (im bal′əns) *n.* lack of balance, as in proportion, force, functioning, etc.

im·be·cile (im′bə s'l) *n.* [Fr. *imbécile* < L. *imbecilis, imbecillus,* feeble, weak, prob. < *in-,* without + *baculus,* staff (see BACILLUS): hence, "without support"] **1.** a mentally retarded person with an intelligence quotient ranging from 25 to 50; adult person mentally equal to a child between three and eight years old: an obsolescent term: see MENTAL RETARDATION **2.** a very foolish or stupid person —*adj.* showing feeble intellect; foolish or stupid: also **im′be·cil′ic** (-sil′ik)

im·be·cil·i·ty (im′bə sil′ə tē) *n., pl.* **-ties** [Fr. *imbécilité* < L. *imbecillitas*] **1.** the state of being an imbecile **2.** behavior like that of an imbecile; great foolishness or stupidity **3.** an imbecile act or remark

im·bed (im bed′) *vt. same as* EMBED

im·bibe (im bīb′) *vt.* **-bibed′, -bib′ing** [ME. *enbiben* < L. *imbibere* < *in-,* in + *bibere,* to drink < **pibere* < IE. *pi-, pōi-,* to drink, whence Sans. *pāti,* (he) drinks, L. *potare*] **1.** *a)* to drink (esp. alcoholic liquor) *b)* to take in with the senses; drink in **2.** *a)* to absorb (moisture) *b)* to inhale **3.** to take into the mind and keep, as ideas, principles, etc. —*vi.* to drink, esp. alcoholic liquor —**im·bib′er** *n.*

im·bi·bi·tion (im′bi bish′ən) *n.* [LME.: see IMBIBE & -ITION] the absorption or adsorption of water by certain colloids, as in seeds, wood, etc., with resultant swelling of the tissues

im·bit·ter (im bit′ər) *vt. same as* EMBITTER

im·bod·y (im bäd′ē) *vt. same as* EMBODY

im·bos·om (im booz′əm, -bōō′zəm) *vt. same as* EMBOSOM

im·bow·er (im bou′ər) *vt., vi. same as* EMBOWER

im·bri·cate (im′brə kit; *also, and for v. always,* -kāt′) *adj.* [LL. *imbricatus,* pp. of *imbricare,* to cover with gutter tiles < L. *imbrex,* gutter tile < *imber,* rain < IE. base **mbh-,* var. of **nebh-,* moist, water, whence Gr. *nephos,* cloud, G. *nebel,* fog] **1.** overlapping evenly, as tiles or fish scales **2.** ornamented with overlapping scales or a pattern like this —*vt.* **-cat′ed, -cat′ing** to place (tiles, shingles, etc.) in overlapping order —*vi.* to overlap —**im′bri·cate·ly** *adv.*

im·bri·ca·tion (im′brə kā′shən) *n.* [see prec.] **1.** an overlapping, as of tiles or scales **2.** an ornamental pattern like this

im·brown (im broun′) *vt. same as* EMBROWN

im·brue (im brōō′) *vt.* **-brued′, -bru′ing** [ME. *enbrewen* < OFr. *embreuver,* to moisten < VL. **imbiberare,* for L. *imbibere:* see IMBIBE] to wet, soak, or stain, esp. with blood —**im·brue′ment** *n.*

im·brute (im brōōt′) *vt., vi.* **-brut′ed, -brut′ing** [IM- + BRUTE] to make or become brutal

im·bue (im byōō′) *vt.* **-bued′, -bu′ing** [L. *imbuere,* to wet, soak] **1.** [Rare] to fill with moisture; saturate **2.** to fill with color; dye; tinge **3.** to permeate or inspire (*with* principles, ideas, emotions, etc.)

im·id·az·ole (im′id az′ōl, -ə zōl′) *n.* [IMID(E) + AZOLE] a colorless, heterocyclic, crystalline base, $C_3H_4N_2$

im·ide (im′id, -id) *n.* [arbitrary alteration of AMIDE] an organic compound having the divalent radical NH combined with two acid radicals

im·i·do (im′ə dō′, i mē′dō) *adj.* of an imide or imides

i·mid·o- (i mid′ə, -mē′də) [< IMIDE] a combining form meaning of or containing the divalent radical NH combined with two acid radicals: also, before a vowel, **imid-**

im·ine (im′ēn, -in; i mēn′) *n.* [arbitrary alteration of AMINE] a compound containing the divalent radical NH united to alkyl or other nonacid radicals

im·i·no (im′ə nō′, i mē′nō) *adj.* of an imine or imines

i·min·o- (i min′ə, -mē′nə) [< IMINE] a combining form meaning of or containing the divalent radical NH united to alkyl or other nonacid radicals

imit. **1.** imitation **2.** imitative

im·i·tate (im′ə tāt′) *vt.* **-tat′ed, -tat′ing** [< L. *imitatus,* pp. of *imitari,* to imitate] **1.** to seek to follow the example of; take as one's model or pattern **2.** to act the same as; impersonate; mimic **3.** to reproduce in form, color, etc.; make a duplicate or copy of **4.** to be or become like in appearance; resemble [glass made to *imitate* diamonds] —**im′i·ta·ble** (-tə b'l) *adj.* —**im′i·ta′tor** *n.*

SYN.—**imitate** implies the following of something as an example or model but does not necessarily connote exact correspondence with the original [the child *imitates* the father's mannerisms]; **copy** implies as nearly exact imitation or reproduction as is possible [to *copy* a painting]; **mimic** suggests close imitation, often in fun or ridicule [to *mimic* the speech peculiarities of another]; **mock** implies imitation with the intent to deride or affront ["I can't," she echoed *mockingly*]; **ape** implies close imitation either in mimicry or in servile emulation [she *aped* the fashions of the court ladies]

im·i·ta·tion (im′ə tā′shən) *n.* [L. *imitatio*] **1.** the act of imitating **2.** *a)* the result or product of imitating; artificial likeness; copy *b)* a counterfeit **3.** *Biol.* same as MIMICRY **4.** *Music* the repetition of a theme in different parts of a composition, with or without slight changes in rhythm, intervals, etc. **5.** *Philos.* *a)* in Platonism, the process wherein sensible objects participate in archetypal forms, essences, or ideas *b)* in Aristotelianism, artistic portrayal not as copying but as gathering the meaning of what might or could happen —*adj.* made to resemble something specified, usually something superior or genuine; not real; sham; bogus [*imitation* leather]

im·i·ta·tive (im′ə tāt′iv) *adj.* [L. *imitativus*] **1.** formed from a model; reproducing the qualities of an original or another **2.** given to imitating; inclined to imitate others **3.** not genuine or real; imitation **4.** approximating in sound the thing or action signified; echoic: said of such words as *hiss, ripple, clang* —**im′i·ta′tive·ly** *adv.* —**im′i·ta′tive·ness** *n.*

im·mac·u·late (i mak′yə lit) *adj.* [ME. < L. *immaculatus* < *in-,* not + *maculatus,* pp. of *maculare,* to spot, soil < *macula,* a spot] **1.** perfectly clean; without a spot or stain; unsoiled **2.** perfectly correct; without a flaw, fault, or error **3.** pure; innocent; without sin **4.** *Biol.* of a solid color, without marks or spots —**im·mac′u·late·ly** *adv.* —**im·mac′u·late·ness, im·mac′u·la·cy** (-lə sē) *n.*

Immaculate Conception *R.C.Ch.* the doctrine that the Virgin Mary, though conceived naturally, was from the moment of conception free from any stain of original sin: sometimes confused with VIRGIN BIRTH

im·mane (i mān′) *adj.* [L. *immanis* < *in-,* not + *manus,* good] [Archaic] **1.** huge; immense **2.** cruel or brutal

im·ma·nent (im′ə nənt) *adj.* [LL. *immanens,* prp. of *immanere,* to remain in or near < *in-,* in + *manere,* to remain: see MANOR] **1.** living, remaining, or operating within; inherent **2.** *Theol.* present throughout the universe: said of God —**im′ma·nence, im′ma·nen·cy** *n.* —**im′ma·nent·ly** *adv.*

im·ma·nent·ism (-iz′m) *n.* **1.** *Philos.* the theory that objects of knowledge are within the mind **2.** *Theol.* the theory that God pervades the universe

Im·man·u·el (i man′yoo wəl) [Heb. *'immānūēl* < *'im,* with + *ānū,* us + *ēl,* God, hence, lit., God with us] **1.** a masculine name: var. *Emmanuel, Manuel* **2.** a name given by Isaiah to the Messiah of his prophecy (Isa. 7:14), often applied to Jesus (Matt. 1:23)

im·ma·te·ri·al (im′ə tir′ē əl) *adj.* [ME. *immateriel* < LL. *immaterialis:* see IN-² & MATERIAL] **1.** not consisting of matter; incorporeal; spiritual **2.** that does not matter; not pertinent; unimportant —**im′ma·te′ri·al′i·ty** (-al′ə tē) *n., pl.* **-ties** —**im′ma·te′ri·al·ly** *adv.*

im·ma·te·ri·al·ism (-iz′m) *n.* the theory or doctrine that material things exist only as mental perceptions or ideas —**im′ma·te′ri·al·ist** *n.*

im·ma·te·ri·al·ize (im′ə tir′ē ə līz′) *vt.* **-ized′, -iz′ing** to make immaterial

im·ma·ture (im′ə toor′, -tyoor′, -choor′) *adj.* [L. *immaturus*] **1.** not mature or ripe; not completely grown or developed **2.** not finished or perfected; incomplete **3.** *Geol.* worn down only slightly by erosion, as a land surface having steeply entrenched stream valleys that lack well-developed flood plains —**im′ma·ture′ly** *adv.* —**im′ma·tu′ri·ty, im′ma·ture′ness** *n.*

im·meas·ur·a·ble (i mezh′ər ə b'l) *adj.* that cannot be measured; boundless; vast —**im·meas′ur·a·bil′i·ty, im·meas′ur·a·ble·ness** *n.* —**im·meas′ur·a·bly** *adv.*

im·me·di·a·cy (i mē′dē ə sē) *n.* the quality or condition of being immediate; esp., direct pertinence or relevance to the present time, place, purpose, etc.

im·me·di·ate (i mē′dē it) *adj.* [LL. *immediatus:* see IN-² & MEDIATE] having nothing coming between; with no intermediary; specif., *a)* not separated in space; in direct contact; closest; nearest; also, close by; near *b)* not separated in time; acting or happening at once; without delay; instant *c)* of the present time *d)* next in order, succession, etc.; next in line; also, directly or closely related [one's *immediate* family] *e)* directly affecting; direct; first-hand [an *immediate* cause] *f)* understood or perceived directly or intuitively [an *immediate* inference]

immediate constituent any of the meaningful structural layers, usually two, into which a complex linguistic structure may be divided and which may in turn be subdivided

im·me·di·ate·ly (-lē) *adv.* in an immediate manner; specif., *a)* without intervening agency or cause; directly *b)* without delay; at once; instantly —*conj.* [Chiefly Brit.] at the very moment that; as soon as *(return immediately you are done)*

im·med·i·ca·ble (i med′i kə b'l) *adj.* [L. *immedicabilis*: see IN-² & MEDICABLE] that cannot be healed; incurable

Im·mel·mann (turn) (im′əl män′, -mən) [after Max *Immelmann*, Ger. ace (1890–1916)] a maneuver in which an airplane is half looped to an upside-down position and then half rolled back to normal, upright flight: used to gain altitude while reversing direction

im·me·mo·ri·al (im′ə môr′ē əl) *adj.* [ML. *immemorialis*: see IN-² & MEMORIAL] extending back beyond memory or record; ancient —**im′me·mo′ri·al·ly** *adv.*

im·mense (i mens′) *adj.* [Fr. < L. *immensus* < *in-*, not + *mensus*, pp. of *metiri*, to measure: see METER] **1.** orig., unmeasured; limitless; infinite **2.** very large; vast; huge **3.** [Slang] very good; excellent —*SYN.* see ENORMOUS —**im·mense′ly** *adv.* —**im·mense′ness** *n.*

im·men·si·ty (i men′sə tē) *n., pl.* **-ties** [Fr. *immensité* < L. *immensitas*] the state or quality of being immense; specif., *a)* vastness; great size or limitless extent *b)* infinite space or being; infinity

im·men·su·ra·ble (i men′shoor ə b'l, -soor-) *adj.* [< Fr. or LL.: Fr. *immensurable* < LL. *immensurabilis*: see IN-² & MENSURABLE] *same as* IMMEASURABLE

im·merge (i murj′) *vt.* -merged′, -merg′ing [L. *immergere*: see ff.] *archaic var. of* IMMERSE —*vi.* to plunge or disappear, as in a liquid —**im·mer′gence** *n.*

im·merse (i murs′) *vt.* -mersed′, -mers′ing [< L. *immersus*, pp. of *immergere*, to dip, plunge into: see IN-¹ & MERGE] **1.** to plunge, drop, or dip into or as if into a liquid, esp. so as to cover completely **2.** to baptize by dipping under water **3.** to plunge into a specified state; absorb deeply; engross *(immersed in study)*

im·mersed (i murst′) *adj.* **1.** plunged into or as if into a liquid **2.** baptized by immersion **3.** *Biol.* embedded in another organ or part **4.** *Bot.* growing completely under water

im·mers·i·ble (i murs′ə b'l) *adj.* ☆that can be immersed in water without harm, as some electric appliances

im·mer·sion (i mur′shən, -zhən) *n.* [LL.(Ec.) *immersio*] **1.** an immersing or being immersed **2.** baptism in which the whole body is dipped under water **3.** *Astron.* [Now Rare] occultation or eclipse

immersion heater an electric coil or rod that heats water while directly immersed in it

im·mesh (i mesh′) *vt. archaic var. of* ENMESH

im·me·thod·i·cal (im′ə thäd′ə k'l) *adj.* not methodical —**im′me·thod′i·cal·ly** *adv.*

☆**im·mie** (im′ē) *n.* [short for *imitation agate*] [Colloq.] an agate (sense 3)

☆**im·mi·grant** (im′ə grənt) *n.* [< L. *immigrans*, prp.] **1.** a person who immigrates **2.** a plant or animal that has recently appeared for the first time in a locality —*adj.* immigrating —*SYN.* see ALIEN

im·mi·grate (-grāt′) *vi.* -grat′ed, -grat′ing [< L. *immigratus*, pp. of *immigrare*, to go or remove into: see IN-¹ & MIGRATE] to come into a new country, region, or environment, esp. in order to settle there: opposed to EMIGRATE —*vt.* to bring in as an immigrant or immigrants —*SYN.* see MIGRATE

im·mi·gra·tion (im′ə grā′shən) *n.* **1.** an act or instance of immigrating **2.** the number of immigrants entering a country or region during a specified period

im·mi·nence (im′ə nəns) *n.* [L. *imminentia*] **1.** the quality or fact of being imminent: also **im′mi·nen·cy 2.** something imminent; impending evil, danger, etc.

im·mi·nent (-nənt) *adj.* [L. *imminens*, prp. of *imminere*, to project over, threaten < *in-*, on + *minere*, to project: see MENACE] likely to happen without delay; impending; threatening: said of danger, evil, misfortune, etc. —**im′mi·nent·ly** *adv.*

im·min·gle (i miŋ′g'l) *vt., vi.* -gled, -gling *same as* INTERMINGLE

im·mis·ci·ble (i mis′ə b'l) *adj.* [< IN-² + MISCIBLE] that cannot be mixed or blended, as oil and water —**im·mis′·ci·bil′i·ty** *n.* —**im·mis′ci·bly** *adv.*

im·mit·i·ga·ble (i mit′i gə b'l) *adj.* [LL. *immitigabilis*: see IN-² & MITIGATE] that cannot be mitigated —**im·mit′i·ga·bly** *adv.*

im·mix (i miks′) *vt., vi.* [back-formation < obs. *immixt*, mixed in with (< L. *immixtus*, pp. of *immiscere* < *in-*, in + *miscere*, to MIX), taken as Eng. pp.] to mix thoroughly —**im·mix′ture** (-chər) *n.*

im·mo·bile (i mō′b'l, -bēl, -bīl) *adj.* [ME. *inmobill* < OFr. *immobile* < L. *immobilis*: see IN-² & MOBILE] **1.** not movable; firmly set or placed; stable **2.** not moving or changing; motionless —**im′mo·bil′i·ty** *n.*

im·mo·bi·lize (i mō′bə līz′) *vt.* -lized′, -liz′ing [Fr. *immobiliser*] **1.** to make immobile; prevent the movement of; keep in place **2.** to prevent the movement of (a limb or joint) with splints or a cast —**im·mo′bi·li·za′tion** *n.*

im·mod·er·ate (i mäd′ər it) *adj.* [ME. < L. *immoderatus*] **1.** not moderate; without restraint; unreasonable; excessive **2.** [Obs.] boundless —*SYN.* see EXCESSIVE —**im·mod′er·ate·ly** *adv.* —**im·mod′er·a′tion, im·mod′er·ate·ness, im·mod′er·a·cy** (-ə sē) *n.*

im·mod·est (i mäd′ist) *adj.* [L. *immodestus*, excessive, immoderate: see IN-² & MODEST] not modest; specif., *a)* not decorous; indecent *b)* not shy or humble; bold; forward —**im·mod′est·ly** *adv.* —**im·mod′es·ty** *n.*

im·mo·late (im′ə lāt′) *vt.* -lat′ed, -lat′ing [< L. *immolatus*, pp. of *immolare*, to sprinkle a victim with sacrificial meal < *in-*, on + *mola*, MEAL] to sacrifice; esp., to offer or kill as a sacrifice —**im′mo·la′tion** *n.* —**im′mo·la′tor** *n.*

im·mo·ral (i môr′əl, -mär′-) *adj.* [< IN-² + MORAL] not in conformity with accepted principles of right and wrong behavior; contrary to the moral code of the community; wicked; sometimes, specif., not in conformity with the accepted standards of proper sexual behavior; unchaste; lewd —**im·mor′al·ly** *adv.*

im·mor·al·ist (-ist) *n.* an immoral person; specif., one who advocates immorality

im·mo·ral·i·ty (im′ə ral′ə tē, im′ô-) *n.* **1.** the state or quality of being immoral **2.** immoral behavior **3.** *pl.* **-ties** an immoral act or practice; vice

im·mor·tal (i môr′t'l) *adj.* [ME. < L. *immortalis*: see IN-² & MORTAL] **1.** not mortal; deathless; living or lasting forever **2.** of immortal beings or immortality **3.** lasting a long time; enduring **4.** having lasting fame; long-remembered *(an immortal poet)* —*n.* an immortal being; specif., *a)* [*pl.*] the ancient Greek or Roman gods *b)* a person having lasting fame —**im′mor·tal′i·ty** (-tal′ə tē) *n.* —**im·mor′tal·ly** *adv.*

im·mor·tal·ize (i môr′tə līz′) *vt.* -ized′, -iz′ing to make immortal; esp., to give lasting fame to —**im·mor′tal·i·za′tion** *n.* —**im·mor′tal·iz′er** *n.*

im·mor·telle (im′ôr tel′) *n.* [Fr. fem. of *immortel*, IMMORTAL] *same as* EVERLASTING (*n.* 2)

im·mo·tile (i mōt′'l) *adj.* not motile; unable to move

im·mov·a·ble (i moōv′ə b'l) *adj.* [ME. *immouable*] **1.** that cannot be moved; firmly fixed; not capable of movement **2.** not moving; immobile; motionless; stationary **3.** that cannot be changed; unyielding; steadfast **4.** unemotional; impassive **5.** *Law* of or pertaining to immovables —*n.* [*pl.*] *Law* objects or property, as land, trees, buildings, etc., which, by their own nature, cannot be removed —**im·mov′·a·bil′i·ty, im·mov′a·ble·ness** *n.* —**im·mov′a·bly** *adv.*

im·mune (i myoōn′) *adj.* [ME. *immun* < L. *immunis*, free from public service, exempt < *in-*, without + *munia*, duties, functions: for IE. base see COMMON] having immunity; specif., *a)* exempt from or protected against something disagreeable or harmful *b)* not susceptible to some specified disease because of the presence of the specific antibodies —*n.* an immune person

immune body *same as* ANTIBODY

im·mu·ni·ty (i myoōn′ə tē) *n., pl.* **-ties** [ME. *ynmunite* < OFr. *immunité* < L. *immunitas*, freedom from public service < *immunis*: see IMMUNE] **1.** exemption or freedom from something burdensome or otherwise unpleasant, as a legal obligation **2.** resistance to or protection against a specified disease; power to resist infection, esp. as a result of antibody formation —*SYN.* see EXEMPTION

im·mu·nize (im′yə nīz′) *vt.* -nized′, -niz′ing to give immunity to, as by inoculation —**im′mu·ni·za′tion** *n.*

im·mu·no- (im′yoo nō′, i myoō′nō) *a combining form meaning* immune, immunity *[immunology]*

im·mu·no·chem·is·try (-kem′is trē) *n.* the study of the chemical reactions and phenomena of immunity —**im′·mu·no·chem′i·cal** (-i k'l) *adj.*

im·mu·no·flu·o·res·cence (-floō′ə res′əns, -floō res′-, -flô′-) *n.* the use of the fluorescent microscope and antibodies labeled with fluorescent dyes to locate specific antigens in tissues —**im′·mu′no·flu′o·res′cent** *adj.*

im·mu·no·ge·net·ics (-jə net′iks) *n.pl.* [with sing. v.] the branch of immunology dealing with the relationship between immunity to certain diseases and genetics —**im′·mu·no·ge·net′ic** *adj.*

im·mu·no·gen·ic (-jen′ik) *adj.* producing immunity —**im′mu·no·gen′i·cal·ly** *adv.*

im·mu·no·glob·u·lin (-gläb′yə lin) *n.* a globulin protein that participates in the immune reaction as the antibody for a specific antigen

☆**im·mu·nol·o·gy** (im′yoo näl′ə jē) *n.* [IMMUNO- + -LOGY] the branch of medicine dealing with *a)* antigens and antibodies, esp. immunity to disease *b)* hypersensitive biological reactions, as allergies, the rejection of foreign tissues, etc. —**im′mu·no·log′i·cal** (-nə läj′i k'l), **im′mu·no·log′ic** *adj.* —**im′mu·no·log′i·cal·ly** *adv.* —**im′mu·nol′o·gist** *n.*

im·mu·no·re·ac·tion (im′yoo nō′rē ak′shən) *n.* the reaction between an antigen and its antibody

im·mu·no·sup·pres·sion (-sə presh′ən) *n.* the inactivation of a specific antibody by various agents, thus permitting the acceptance of a foreign substance, as a transplant, by an organism

im·mure (i myoor′) *vt.* -mured′, -mur′ing [< OFr. or ML.: OFr. *emmurer* < ML. *immurare* < L. *in-*, in + *murus*, wall: for IE. base see MERE²] **1.** to shut up within or as within walls; imprison, confine, or seclude **2.** to entomb in a wall —**im·mure′ment** *n.*

im·mu·ta·ble (i myoōt′ə b'l) *adj.* [ME. < L. *immutabilis*: see IN-² & MUTABLE] never changing or varying; unchangeable —**im·mu′ta·bil′i·ty, im·mu′ta·ble·ness** *n.* —**im·mu′ta·bly** *adv.*

Im·o·gen (im′ə jən) [first recorded in Shakespeare's *Cymbeline* (First Folio): ? misprint for Holinshed's *Innogen*] a feminine name: also **Im′o·gene**′ (-jēn′)

imp (imp) *n.* [ME. *impe* < OE. *impa* < *impian*, to graft in, akin to OHG. *impfôn* < VL. **imputare* (< *im-*, in + *putare*, to prune), transl. of Gr. *emphyteyein*, to engraft < *emphyta*, scion < *em-*, in + *phyton*, growth, plant: for IE. base see BONDAGE] **1.** orig., *a*) a shoot or graft *b*) a child; offspring **2.** a devil's offspring; young demon **3.** a mischievous child —*vt.* [ME. *impen* < OE. *impian*] [Archaic] **1.** to implant, esp. by grafting **2.** to repair (the wing or tail of a falcon) by grafting on (feathers) **3.** to furnish with wings **4.** to help out by adding to, increasing, etc.

Imp. Imperator

imp. **1.** imperative **2.** imperfect **3.** imperial **4.** impersonal **5.** import **6.** imported **7.** importer **8.** imprimatur

im·pact (im pakt′; *for n.* im′pakt) *vt.* [< L. *impactus*, pp. of *impingere*, to press firmly together: see IMPINGE] to force tightly together; pack; wedge —*vi.* to hit with force —*n.* **1.** a striking together; violent contact; collision **2.** the force of a collision; shock **3.** the power of an event, idea, etc. to produce changes, move the feelings, etc. —**im·pac′tion** *n.*

im·pact·ed (im pak′tid) *adj.* **1.** pressed tightly together; driven firmly in; wedged in; esp., firmly lodged in the jaw: said of a tooth unable to erupt because of its abnormal position ☆**2.** densely populated; overcrowded [an *impacted* area]

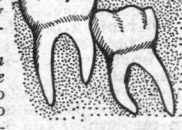

IMPACTED TOOTH

im·pair (im per′) *vt.* [ME. *empeiren* < OFr. *empeirer* < VL. **impejorare* < L. *in-*, intens. + LL. *pejorare*, to make worse < L. *pejor*, worse] to make worse, less, weaker, etc.; damage; reduce —*SYN.* see INJURE —**im·pair′ment** *n.*

im·pa·la (im pä′lə, -pal′ə) *n., pl.* **-la, -las:** see PLURAL, II, D, 2 [Zulu] a medium-sized, reddish antelope (*Aepyceros melampus*) of C and S Africa

im·pale (im pāl′) *vt.* **-paled**′, **-pal′ing** [Fr. *empaler* < ML. *impalare* < L. *in-*, on + *palus*, a stake, POLE¹] **1.** [Rare] to surround with or as with a palisade **2.** *a*) to pierce through with, or fix on, something pointed; transfix *b*) to punish or torture by fixing on a stake **3.** to make helpless, as if fixed on a stake [*impaled* by her glance] **4.** *Heraldry* to join (two coats of arms) side by side on one shield —**im·pale′ment** *n.*

im·pal·pa·ble (im pal′pə b'l) *adj.* [Fr. < ML. *impalpabilis:* see IN-² & PALPABLE] **1.** not perceptible to the touch; that cannot be felt **2.** too slight or subtle to be grasped easily by the mind —**im·pal′pa·bil′i·ty** *n.* —**im·pal′pa·bly** *adv.*

im·pa·na·tion (im′pə nā′shən) *n.* [ML. *impanatio* < pp. of *impanare*, to embody in bread < L. *in-*, in + *panis*, bread < IE. base **pa-*, to feed, whence FOOD] *Theol.* the doctrine that the body and blood of Christ are present in the bread and wine of the Eucharist after consecration by the priest, with no actual change in their substance: cf. TRANSUBSTANTIATION

im·pan·el (im pan′'l) *vt.* **-eled** or **-elled, -el·ing** or **-el·ling** **1.** to enter the name or names of on a jury list **2.** to choose (a jury) from such a list —**im·pan′el·ment** *n.*

im·par·a·dise (im par′ə dīs′) *vt.* **-dised**′, **-dis′ing** **1.** to make as happy as though in paradise; transport; enrapture **2.** to make into a paradise

im·par·i·ty (im par′ə tē) *n., pl.* **-ties** [LL. *imparitas* < L. *impar*, unequal: see IN-² & PAR] [Rare] disparity; lack of equality

im·park (im pärk′) *vt.* [LME. *imparken* < Anglo-Fr. *enparker*, for OFr. *enparquer*] [Archaic] **1.** to shut up (animals) in a park **2.** to enclose (land) for a park

im·part (im pärt′) *vt.* [ME. *imparten* < OFr. *empartir* < L. *impartire:* see IN-¹ & PART] **1.** to give a share or portion of; give **2.** to make known; tell; reveal —**im·part′a·ble** *adj.* —**im′par·ta′tion** *n.* —**im·part′er** *n.*

im·par·tial (im pär′shəl) *adj.* [< IN-² + PARTIAL] favoring no one side or party more than another; without prejudice or bias; fair; just —*SYN.* see FAIR¹ —**im·par′ti·al′i·ty** (-shē al′ə tē) *n.* —**im·par′tial·ly** *adv.*

im·part·i·ble (im pär′tə b'l) *adj.* [LL. *impartibilis:* see IN-² & PARTIBLE] that cannot be partitioned or divided; indivisible: said of an estate —**im·part′i·bly** *adv.* —**im·part′i·bil′i·ty** *n.*

im·pass·a·ble (im pas′ə b'l) *adj.* that cannot be passed, crossed, or traveled over [an *impassable* highway] —**im·pass′a·bil′i·ty** *n.* —**im·pass′a·bly** *adv.*

im·passe (im′pas, im pas′) *n.* [Fr.: see IN-² & PASS²] **1.** a passage open only at one end; blind alley **2.** a situation offering no escape; difficulty without solution or an argument where no agreement is possible; deadlock

im·pas·si·ble (im pas′ə b'l) *adj.* [ME. < OFr. < LL.(Ec.) *impassibilis:* see IN-² & PASSIBLE] **1.** that cannot feel pain; incapable of suffering **2.** that cannot be injured; invulnerable **3.** that cannot be moved emotionally; unfeeling —**im·pas′si·bil′i·ty** *n.* —**im·pas′si·bly** *adv.*

im·pas·sion (im pash′ən) *vt.* [It. *impassionare*] to fill with passion; arouse emotionally

im·pas·sioned (-ənd) *adj.* filled with passion; having or showing strong feeling; passionate; fiery; ardent —*SYN.* see PASSIONATE —**im·pas′sioned·ly** *adv.*

im·pas·sive (im pas′iv) *adj.* [< IN-² + PASSIVE] **1.** not feeling pain; not liable to suffering; insensible **2.** not feeling or showing emotion; placid; calm; serene —**im·pas′sive·ly** *adv.* —**im·pas·siv·i·ty** (im′pə siv′ə tē) *n.* *SYN.*—**impassive** means not having or showing any feeling or emotion, although it does not necessarily connote an incapability of being affected [his *impassive* face did not betray his anguish]; **apathetic** stresses an indifference or listlessness from which one cannot easily be stirred to feeling [an *apathetic* electorate]; **stoic** implies an austere indifference to pleasure or pain and specifically suggests the ability to endure suffering without flinching [he received the bad news with *stoic* calm]; **stolid** suggests dullness, obtuseness, or stupidity in one who is not easily moved or excited; **phlegmatic** is applied to one who by temperament is not easily disconcerted or aroused

im·paste (im pāst′) *vt.* **-past′ed, -past′ing** [It. *impastare* < *in-* (see IN-¹) + *pasta*, PASTE] **1.** to enclose or crust over with or as with paste **2.** to make a paste or crust of **3.** to apply a thick coat as of paint to

im·pas·to (im päs′tō) *n.* [It. < *impastare:* see prec.] **1.** painting in which the paint is laid thickly on the canvas **2.** paint so laid on

im·pa·tience (im pā′shəns) *n.* [ME. *impacience* < L. *impatientia*] lack of patience; specif., *a*) annoyance because of delay, opposition, etc. *b*) restless eagerness to do something, go somewhere, etc.

im·pa·ti·ens (im pā′shē enz′, -shənz) *n.* [ModL. < L.: see ff.] any of a genus (*Impatiens*) of plants of the balsam family, with spurred flowers and pods that burst and scatter their seeds when ripe

im·pa·tient (im pā′shənt) *adj.* [ME. *impacient* < OFr. < L. *impatiens:* see IN-² & PATIENT] feeling or showing a lack of patience; specif., *a*) feeling or showing annoyance because of delay, opposition, etc. *b*) feeling or showing restless eagerness to do something, go somewhere, etc. —**impatient of** not willing to bear or tolerate —**im·pa′tient·ly** *adv.*

im·pav·id (im pav′id) *adj.* [L. *impavidus:* see IN-² & PAVID] [Archaic] not afraid; fearless —**im·pav′id·ly** *adv.*

im·pawn (im pôn′) *vt.* [Now Rare] *same as* PAWN¹

im·peach (im pēch′) *vt.* [ME. *empechen* < OFr. *empechier*, to hinder < LL. *impedicare*, to fetter, entangle < L. *in-*, in + *pedica*, a fetter < *pes*, FOOT] **1.** to challenge or discredit (a person's honor, reputation, etc.) **2.** to challenge the practices or honesty of; accuse; esp., to bring a (public official) before the proper tribunal on a charge of wrongdoing —*n.* [Obs.] impeachment —*SYN.* see ACCUSE —**im·peach′ment** *n.*

im·peach·a·ble (im pēch′ə b'l) *adj.* **1.** liable to be impeached **2.** making one liable to be impeached [an *impeachable* act] —**im·peach′a·bil′i·ty** *n.*

im·pearl (im purl′) *vt., vi.* [Fr. *emperler:* see IM-² & PEARL¹] [Now Rare] **1.** to form into pearls or pearllike drops **2.** to decorate with or as with pearls

im·pec·ca·ble (im pek′ə b'l) *adj.* [L. *impeccabilis* < *in-*, not + *peccare*, to sin] **1.** not liable to sin or wrongdoing **2.** without defect or error; faultless; flawless —**im·pec′ca·bil′i·ty** *n.* —**im·pec′ca·bly** *adv.*

im·pec·cant (im pek′ənt) *adj.* [< L. *in-*, not + *peccans'* prp. of *peccare*, to sin] free from sin or wrong; blameless —**im·pec′can·cy** (-ən sē) *n.*

im·pe·cu·ni·ous (im′pi kyōō′nē əs) *adj.* [< IN-² + obs. *pecunious*, rich < ME. < OFr. *pécunieux* < L. *pecuniosus*, wealthy < *pecunia*, money: see PECUNIARY] having no money; poor; penniless —*SYN.* see POOR —**im′pe·cu′ni·os′i·ty** (-äs′ə tē) *n.,* **im′pe·cu′ni·ous·ness** *n.* —**im′pe·cu′ni·ous·ly** *adv.*

im·ped·ance (im pēd′'ns) *n.* [IMPED(E) + -ANCE] **1.** the total opposition offered by an electric circuit to the flow of an alternating current of a single frequency: it is a combination of resistance and reactance and is measured in ohms **2.** the ratio of the force per unit area to the volume displacement of a given surface across which sound is being transmitted

im·pede (im pēd′) *vt.* **-ped′ed, -ped′ing** [L. *impedire*, to entangle, ensnare, lit., to hold the feet < *in-*, in + *pes* (gen. *pedis*), FOOT] to bar or hinder the progress of; obstruct or delay —*SYN.* see DELAY, HINDER —**im·ped′er** *n.*

im·ped·i·ment (im ped′ə mənt) *n.* [ME. < L. *impedimentum*, hindrance] **1.** [Now Rare] an impeding or being impeded; obstruction **2.** anything that impedes; specif., *a*) a speech defect; stutter, lisp, stammer, etc. *b*) anything preventing the making of a legal contract, esp. of a marriage contract —*SYN.* see OBSTACLE

im·ped·i·men·ta (im ped′ə men′tə) *n.pl.* [L., pl. of *impedimentum:* see prec.] things hindering progress, as on a trip; encumbrances; esp., baggage, supplies, or equipment, as those carried along with an army

im·pel (im pel′) *vt.* **-pelled**′, **-pel′ling** [ME. *impellen* < L. *impellere* < *in-*, in + *pellere*, to drive < IE. base **pel-*, to

push into motion, drive, whence FELT¹] **1.** to push, drive, or move forward; propel **2.** to force, compel, or urge; incite; constrain —**im·pel′lent** *adj.* *n.* —**im·pel′ler** *n.*

im·pend (im pend′) *vi.* [L. *impendere*, to overhang, threaten < *in-*, in + *pendere*, to hang, prob. < IE. base *(s) pend-*, to pull, stretch, whence SPIN] **1.** [Now Rare] to hang or be suspended (*over*) **2.** to be about to happen; be imminent; threaten [an *impending* disaster]

im·pend·ent (-ənt) *adj.* [L. *impendens*, prp. of *impendere*] impending; about to happen —**im·pend′ence, im·pend′-en·cy** *n.*

im·pen·e·tra·ble (im pen′i trə b'l) *adj.* [ME. *inpenetrable* < Fr. *impénétrable* < L. *impenetrabilis*] **1.** that cannot be penetrated or passed through [an *impenetrable* jungle] **2.** that cannot be solved or understood; unfathomable; inscrutable **3.** unreceptive to ideas, impressions, influences, etc. **4.** *Physics* having that property of matter by which two bodies are prevented from occupying the same space at the same time —**im·pen′e·tra·bil′i·ty** *n.* —**im·pen′e·tra·bly** *adv.*

im·pen·i·tent (im pen′ə tənt) *adj.* [LL.(Ec.) *impaenitens*] without regret, shame, or remorse; unrepentant —*n.* an impenitent person —**im·pen′i·tence, im·pen′i·ten·cy** *n.* —**im·pen′i·tent·ly** *adv.*

imper. imperative

im·per·a·tive (im per′ə tiv) *adj.* [LL. *imperativus*, commanding < pp. of L. *imperare*, to command: see EMPEROR] **1.** having the nature of, or indicating, power or authority; commanding [an *imperative* gesture] **2.** absolutely necessary; urgent; compelling [it is *imperative* that I go] **3.** *Gram.* designating or of the mood of a verb that expresses a command, strong request, or exhortation —*n.* **1.** a binding or compelling rule, duty, requirement, etc. **2.** a command; order **3.** *Gram.* a) the imperative mood b) a verb in this mood —**im·per′a·tive·ly** *adv.* —**im·per′a·tive·ness** *n.*

im·pe·ra·tor (im′pə rāt′ər, -rät′-; -ôr) *n.* [L., commander in chief: see EMPEROR] in ancient Rome, a title of honor given originally to generals and later to emperors —**im·per·a·to·ri·al** (im pir′ə tôr′ē əl) *adj.*

im·per·cep·ti·ble (im′pər sep′tə b'l) *adj.* [Fr. < ML. *imperceptibilis*: see IN-² & PERCEPTIBLE] not plain or distinct to the senses or the mind; esp., so slight, gradual, subtle, etc. as not to be easily perceived —**im′per·cep′ti·bil′i·ty** *n.* —**im′per·cep′ti·bly** *adv.*

im·per·cep·tive (-tiv) *adj.* not perceiving; lacking perception: also **im′per·cip′i·ent** (-sip′ē ənt) —**im′per·cep′tive·ness** *n.*

imperf. **1.** imperfect **2.** imperforate

im·per·fect (im per′fikt) *adj.* [ME. *inperfit* < OFr. *imparfit* < L. *imperfectus*: see IN-² & PERFECT] **1.** not finished or complete; lacking in something **2.** not perfect; having a defect, fault, or error **3.** in the grammar of certain inflected languages, designating or of the tense of a verb that indicates a past action or state as incomplete, continuous, customary, or going on at the same time as another: "was writing" and "used to write" are forms corresponding to the imperfect tense in such languages **4.** *Music* diminished —*n.* *Grammar* **1.** the imperfect tense **2.** a verb in this tense —**im·per′fect·ly** *adv.* —**im·per′fect·ness** *n.*

imperfect flower a diclinous flower

imperfect fungi any of a large group of fungi for which no sexual stage of reproduction is known

im·per·fec·tion (im′pər fek′shən) *n.* [ME. *imperfeccioun* < OFr. *imperfection* < LL. *imperfectio*] **1.** the quality or condition of being imperfect **2.** a shortcoming; defect; fault; blemish —*SYN.* see DEFECT

im·per·fec·tive (-tiv) *adj.* *Gram.* designating or of an aspect of verbs, as in Russian and other Slavic languages, expressing incompletion, or continued repetition, of the action —*n.* **1.** the imperfective aspect **2.** a verb in this aspect

im·per·fo·rate (im pur′fər it, -fə rāt′) *adj.* [< IN-² & PERFORATE] **1.** having no holes or openings; unpierced **2.** having a straight edge without perforations: said of a postage stamp, etc. **3.** *Anat.* lacking the normal opening Also **im·per′fo·rat′ed** —*n.* an imperforate stamp —**im·per′fo·ra′tion** *n.*

im·pe·ri·al (im pir′ē əl) *adj.* [ME. < OFr. < L. *imperialis* < *imperium*, EMPIRE] **1.** of an empire **2.** of a country having control or sovereignty over other countries or colonies **3.** of, or having the rank of, an emperor or empress **4.** having supreme authority; sovereign **5.** majestic; august; imperious **6.** of great size or superior quality **7.** *a*) of or pertaining to the British Commonwealth *b*) according to the standard of weights and measures fixed by British law: discontinued in favor of the metric system, 1971 —*n.* **1.** [I-] a supporter or a soldier of any of the Holy Roman emperors **2.** a gold coin of the former Russian Empire **3.** the roof or top of a coach, or a case carried on it **4.** an article of great size or superior quality **5.** a size of writing paper measuring 23 by 31 inches (in England, 22 by 30 or 32 inches) ☆**6.** [after the emperor LOUIS NAPOLEON, who set this fashion] a pointed tuft of beard on the lower lip and chin —**im·pe′ri·al·ly** *adv.*

imperial gallon the standard British gallon, equal to 277.42 cubic inches or about 1 1/5 U.S. gallons

im·pe·ri·al·ism (-iz'm) *n.* **1.** imperial state, authority, or system of government **2.** the policy and practice of form-

ing and maintaining an empire in seeking to control raw materials and world markets by the conquest of other countries, the establishment of colonies, etc. **3.** the policy and practice of seeking to dominate the economic or political affairs of underdeveloped areas or weaker countries —**im·pe′ri·al·ist** *n.*, *adj.* —**im·pe′ri·al·is′tic** *adj.* —**im·pe′ri·al·is′ti·cal·ly** *adv.*

☆**imperial moth** a large American moth (*Basilona imperialis*) having yellow wings with purple markings

Imperial Valley [after *Imperial* Land Co., developer of the region] a rich agricultural region in S Calif. & N Baja California, Mexico, reclaimed from the Colorado Desert

im·per·il (im per′əl) *vt.* -**iled** or -**illed**, -**il·ing** or -**il·ling** to put in peril; endanger —**im·per′il·ment** *n.*

im·pe·ri·ous (im pir′ē əs) *adj.* [L. *imperiosus* < *imperium*, EMPIRE] **1.** overbearing, arrogant, domineering, etc. **2.** urgent; imperative —*SYN.* see MASTERFUL —**im·pe′ri·ous·ly** *adv.* —**im·pe′ri·ous·ness** *n.*

im·per·ish·a·ble (im per′ish ə b'l) *adj.* not perishable; that will not die or decay; indestructible; immortal —**im·per′ish·a·bil′i·ty** *n.* —**im·per′ish·a·bly** *adv.*

im·pe·ri·um (im pir′ē əm) *n.*, *pl.* -**ri·a** (-ə) [L.: see EMPIRE] **1.** supreme power; absolute authority or rule; imperial sovereignty; empire **2.** *Law* the right of a state to use force in maintaining the law

im·per·ma·nent (im pur′mə nənt) *adj.* not permanent; not lasting; fleeting; temporary —**im·per′ma·nence, im·per′ma·nen·cy** *n.* —**im·per′ma·nent·ly** *adv.*

im·per·me·a·ble (im pur′mē ə b'l) *adj.* [LL. *impermeabilis*] not permeable; not permitting fluids to pass through it; impenetrable —**im·per′me·a·bil′i·ty** *n.* —**im·per′me·a·bly** *adv.*

im·per·mis·si·ble (im′pər mis′ə b'l) *adj.* not permissible —**im′per·mis′si·bil′i·ty** *n.*

im·per·son·al (im pur′s'n əl) *adj.* [LL. *impersonalis*] **1.** not personal; specif., *a*) without connection or reference to any particular person [an *impersonal* comment] *b*) not existing as a person [an *impersonal* force] **2.** *Gram.* *a*) designating or of a verb occurring only in the third person singular, in English generally with *it* as the indefinite subject (Ex.: "it is snowing") *b*) indefinite: said of a pronoun —*n.* an impersonal verb or pronoun —**im·per′son·al′i·ty** (-al′ə tē) *n.* —**im·per′son·al·ly** *adv.*

im·per·son·al·ize (-ə līz′) *vt.* -**ized′**, -**iz′ing** to make impersonal

im·per·son·ate (im pur′sə nāt′) *vt.* -**at·ed**, -**at·ing** **1.** [Now Rare] to represent in the form of a person; personify; embody **2.** to act the part of; specif., *a*) to mimic the appearance, manner, etc. of (a person) for purposes of entertainment *b*) to pretend to be for purposes of fraud [to *impersonate* an officer] —**im·per′son·a′tion** *n.* —**im·per′son·a′tor** *n.*

im·per·ti·nence (im pur′t'n əns) *n.* [Fr.] **1.** the quality or fact of being impertinent; specif., *a*) lack of pertinence; irrelevance *b*) insolence; impudence **2.** an impertinent act, remark, etc. Also **im·per′ti·nen·cy**, *pl.* -**cies**

im·per·ti·nent (-ənt) *adj.* [ME. < OFr. < L. *impertinens*] **1.** not pertinent; having no connection with a given matter; irrelevant **2.** not showing proper respect or manners; saucy; insolent; impudent **3.** [Rare] not suitable to the circumstances; inappropriate —**im·per′ti·nent·ly** *adv.* *SYN.*—**impertinent** implies a forwardness of speech or action that is disrespectful and oversteps the bounds of propriety or courtesy; **impudent** implies a shameless or brazen impertinence; **insolent** implies defiant disrespect as displayed in openly insulting and contemptuous speech or behavior; **saucy** implies a flippancy and provocative levity toward one to whom respect should be shown

im·per·turb·a·ble (im′pər tur′bə b'l) *adj.* [LL. *imperturbabilis*: see IN-², PERTURB, -ABLE] that cannot be disconcerted, disturbed, or excited; impassive —**im′per·turb′a·bil′i·ty** *n.* —**im′per·turb′a·bly** *adv.*

im·per·tur·ba·tion (im′pər tər bā′shən) *n.* [LL.(Ec.) *imperturbatio* (see IN-² & PERTURBATION)] freedom from excitement; serenity; calmness

im·per·vi·ous (im pur′vē əs) *adj.* [L. *impervius*: see IN-² & PERVIOUS] **1.** incapable of being passed through or penetrated [a fabric *impervious* to moisture] **2.** not affected by (with *to*) [*impervious* to pity] —**im·per′vi·ous·ly** *adv.* —**im·per′vi·ous·ness** *n.*

im·pe·ti·go (im′pə tī′gō) *n.* [L. < *impetere*, to attack: see IMPETUS] any of certain skin diseases characterized by the eruption of pustules; esp., a contagious disease of this kind, caused by staphylococci —**im′pe·tig′i·nous** (-tij′ə nəs) *adj.*

im·pe·trate (im′pə trāt′) *vt.* -**trat′ed**, -**trat′ing** [< L. *impetratus*, pp. of *impetrare*, to accomplish < *in-*, intens. + *patrare*, to accomplish] **1.** to get by request or entreaty **2.** [Rare] to implore —**im′pe·tra′tion** *n.*

im·pet·u·os·i·ty (im pech′oo wäs′ə tē, im′pech-) *n.* [MFr. *impétuosité* < LL. *impetuositas* < L. *impetuosus*] **1.** the quality of being impetuous **2.** *pl.* -**ties** an impetuous action or feeling

im·pet·u·ous (im pech′oo wəs) *adj.* [ME. *impetuouse* < OFr. *impetueuse* < LL. *impetuosus* < L. *impetus*: see ff.] **1.** moving with great force or violence; having great impetus; rushing; furious [*impetuous* winds] **2.** acting or done suddenly with little thought; rash; impulsive —*SYN.* see SUDDEN —**im·pet′u·ous·ly** *adv.* —**im·pet′u·ous·ness** *n.*

im·pe·tus (im′pə təs) *n.*, *pl.* -**tus·es** [L. < *impetere*, to rush upon < *in-*, in + *petere*, to rush at < IE. base *pet-*, to rush

at, fly, fall, whence FEATHER] **1.** the force with which a body moves against resistance, resulting from its mass and the velocity at which it is set in motion **2.** anything that stimulates activity; driving force or motive; incentive; impulse

impf. imperfect

imp. gal. imperial gallon

Imp·hal (imp′hul) city in NE India; capital of Manipur territory: pop. 68,000

im·pi·e·ty (im pī′ə tē) *n.* [ME. *impietie* < OFr. or L.: OFr. *impiété* < L. *impietas*] **1.** a lack of piety; specif., *a)* lack of reverence for God *b)* lack of respect or dutifulness, as toward a parent **2.** *pl.* **-ties** an impious act or remark

im·pinge (im pinj′) *vi.* **-pinged′, -ping′ing** [L. *impingere* < *in-*, in + *pangere*, to strike: for IE. base see FANG] **1.** *a)* to strike, hit, or dash (*on, upon,* or *against* something) *b)* to touch (*on* or *upon*); have an effect [an idea that *impinges* on one's mind] **2.** to make inroads or encroach (*on* or *upon* the property or rights of another) —**im·pinge′ment** *n.* —**im·ping′er** *n.*

im·pi·ous (im′pē əs) *adj.* [L. *impius*] not pious; specif., *a)* lacking reverence for God *b)* lacking respect or dutifulness, as toward a parent —**im′pi·ous·ly** *adv.* —**im′pi·ous·ness** *n.*

imp·ish (im′pish) *adj.* of or like an imp; mischievous — **imp′ish·ly** *adv.* —**imp′ish·ness** *n.*

im·plac·a·ble (im plak′ə b'l, -plā′kə-) *adj.* [Fr. < L. *implacabilis*] **1.** not placable; that cannot be appeased or pacified; relentless; inexorable **2.** [Rare] that cannot be eased, lessened, or allayed —*SYN.* see INFLEXIBLE — **im·plac·a·bil′i·ty** *n.* —**im·plac′a·bly** *adv.*

im·pla·cen·tal (im′plə sen′t'l) *adj.* [< IN-¹ + PLACENTAL] *same as* APLACENTAL: also **im′pla·cen′tate** (-tāt)

im·plant (im plant′, -plänt′; *for n.* im′plant′, -plänt′) *vt.* [Fr. *implanter*: see IN-¹ & PLANT] **1.** to plant firmly or deeply; embed **2.** to fix firmly in the mind; instill; inculcate **3.** *Med.* to insert (a substance, organ, or piece of living tissue) within the body, as in grafting —*n. Med.* an implanted substance, organ, or piece of tissue —*SYN.* see INSTILL —**im′plan·ta′tion** (-plan tā′shən) *n.*

im·plau·si·ble (im plô′zə b'l) *adj.* not plausible —**im·plau′si·bil′i·ty** *n., pl.* **-ties** —**im·plau′si·bly** *adv.*

im·plead (im plēd′) *vt., vi.* [ME. *enpleden* < Anglo-Fr. *enpleder* < OFr. *emplaidier*: see IN-¹ & PLEAD] **1.** to prosecute or sue in a law court **2.** [Archaic] to plead (a cause, etc.)

im·ple·ment (im′plə mənt; *for v.* -ment′) *n.* [ME. < LL. *implementum*, a filling up < L. *implere*, to fill up < *in-*, in + *plere*, to fill: see FULL¹] **1.** any article or device used or needed in a given activity; tool, instrument, utensil, etc. **2.** any thing or person used as a means to some end —*vt.* **1.** to carry into effect; fulfill; accomplish **2.** to provide the means for the carrying out of; give practical effect to **3.** to provide with implements —**im′ple·men′tal** *adj.* —**im′ple·men·ta′tion** (-mən tā′shən) *n.*

SYN.—**implement** applies to any device used to carry on some work or effect some purpose [agricultural *implements*]; **tool** is commonly applied to manual implements such as are used in carpentry, plumbing, etc.; **instrument** specifically implies use for delicate work or for scientific or artistic purposes [surgical *instruments*] and may also be applied, as are **tool** and **implement**, to a thing or person serving as a means to an end; **appliance** specifically suggests a mechanical or power-driven device, esp. one for household use; **utensil** is used of any implement or container for domestic use, esp. a pot, pan, etc.

im·ple·tion (im plē′shən) *n.* [LL.(Ec.) *impletio* < pp. of L. *implere*; to implement] [Rare] a filling or being filled

im·pli·cate (im′plə kāt′) *vt.* **-cat′ed, -cat′ing** [< L. *implicatus*, pp. of *implicare*, to enfold, involve: see IMPLY] **1.** *a)* to show to have a connection with a crime, fault, etc.; involve *b)* to have a resulting effect on **2.** to imply **3.** [Archaic] to twist or fold together; intertwine; entangle —**im′pli·ca′tive** *adj.* —**im′pli·ca′tive·ly** *adv.*

im·pli·ca·tion (im′plə kā′shən) *n.* [ME. < L. *implicacioun* < L. *implicatio*] **1.** an implicating or being implicated **2.** an implying or being implied **3.** something implied, from which an inference may be drawn; specif., *Logic* a formal relationship between two propositions such that if the first is true then the second is necessarily or logically true

im·plic·it (im plis′it) *adj.* [L. *implicitus*, pp. of *implicare*: see IMPLY] **1.** suggested or to be understood though not plainly expressed; implied; distinguished from EXPLICIT **2.** necessarily or naturally involved though not plainly apparent or expressed; essentially a part or condition; inherent **3.** without reservation or doubt; unquestioning; absolute **4.** [Obs.] implicated; entangled —**im·plic′it·ly** *adv.* —**im·plic′it·ness** *n.*

implicit function the mathematical rule or function which permits computation of one variable directly from another when an equation relating both variables is given

im·plied (im plīd′) *adj.* involved, suggested, or understood without being openly or directly expressed

im·plode (im plōd′) *vt., vi.* **-plod′ed, -plod′ing** [< IN-¹ + (EX)PLODE] **1.** to burst inward **2.** to pronounce by implosion

im·plore (im plôr′) *vt.* **-plored′, -plor′ing** [L. *implorare*, to beseech, entreat < *in-*, intens. + *plorare*, to cry out, weep] **1.** to ask or beg earnestly for; beseech **2.** to ask or beg (a person) to do something; entreat —*SYN.* see BEG — **im·plor′ing·ly** *adv.*

im·plo·sion (im plō′zhən) *n.* [< IN-¹ + (EX)PLOSION] an imploding; specif., *a)* a bursting inward *b)* *Phonetics* the rush of air into the pharynx following the release of a stop

im·plo·sive (-siv) *adj.* formed by implosion —*n.* an implosive sound or consonant —**im·plo′sive·ly** *adv.*

im·ply (im plī′) *vt.* **-plied′, -ply′ing** [ME. *implien* < OFr. *emplier* < L. *implicare*, to involve, entangle < *in-*, in + *plicare*, to fold < IE. base *plek-*, to plait, wrap together, whence Gr. *plekein*, to braid: cf. FLAX] **1.** to have as a necessary part, condition, or effect; contain, include, or involve naturally or necessarily [drama *implies* conflict] **2.** to indicate indirectly or by allusion; hint; suggest; intimate [an attitude *implying* boredom] **3.** [Obs.] to enfold; entangle —*SYN.* see SUGGEST

im·pol·i·cy (im päl′ə sē) *n., pl.* **-cies** [< IN-² + POLICY¹, after IMPOLITIC] an unwise policy or act

im·po·lite (im′pə līt′) *adj.* [L. *impolitus*, unpolished] not polite; ill-mannered; discourteous —*SYN.* see RUDE — **im′po·lite′ly** *adv.* —**im′po·lite′ness** *n.*

im·pol·i·tic (im päl′ə tik) *adj.* not politic; unwise; unjudicious; inexpedient —**im·pol′i·tic·ly** *adv.*

im·pon·der·a·ble (im pän′dər ə b'l) *adj.* not ponderable; specif., *a)* that cannot be weighed or measured *b)* that cannot be conclusively determined or explained —*n.* anything imponderable —**im·pon′der·a·bil′i·ty** *n.* —**im·pon′der·a·bly** *adv.*

im·pone (im pōn′) *vt.* **-poned′, -pon′ing** [L. *imponere*, to set upon: see IMPOSE] [Obs.] to wager; stake

im·port (im pôrt′; *also, and for n. always,* im′pôrt) *vt.* [ME. *importen* < L. *importare*, to bring in, introduce < *in-*, in + *portare*, to carry; *vt.* 2, 3, & *vi.* < ML. *importare*, to imply, mean, be of importance < L.] **1.** *a)* to bring in from the outside; introduce *b)* to bring (goods) from another country or countries, esp. for purposes of sale **2.** to mean; signify [an action that *imports* trouble] **3.** [Archaic] to be of importance to; concern —*vi.* to be of importance; matter —*n.* **1.** the act or business of importing (goods) **2.** something imported **3.** meaning; signification **4.** importance —*adj.* of or for importing or imports —*SYN.* see MEANING —**im·port′a·ble** *adj.* —**im·port′er** *n.*

im·por·tance (im pôr′t'ns) *n.* [MFr. < OIt. *importanza*] **1.** the state or quality of being important; significance; consequence **2.** [Obs.] *a)* a matter or consequence *b)* import, or meaning *c)* importunity

SYN.—**importance,** the broadest of these terms, implies greatness of worth, meaning, influence, etc. [news of *importance*]; **consequence,** often interchangeable with the preceding, more specifically suggests importance with regard to outcome or result [a disagreement of no *consequence*]; **moment** expresses this same idea of importance in effect with somewhat stronger force [affairs of great *moment*]; **weight** implies an estimation of the relative importance of something [his word carries great *weight* with us]; **significance** implies an importance or momentousness because of a special meaning that may or may not be immediately apparent [an event of *significance*]

im·por·tant (-t'nt) *adj.* [Fr. < OIt. *importante* < ML. *importans,* prp. of *importare*: see IMPORT] **1.** meaning a great deal; having much significance, consequence, or value **2.** having, or acting as if having, power, authority, influence, high position, etc. **3.** [Obs.] *same as* IMPORTUNATE —**im·por′tant·ly** *adv.*

im·por·ta·tion (im′pôr tā′shən) *n.* **1.** an importing or being imported **2.** something imported

im·por·tu·nate (im pôr′chə nit) *adj.* [< L. *importunus* (see ff.) + -ATE¹] **1.** urgent or persistent in asking or demanding; insistent; refusing to be denied; annoyingly urgent or persistent **2.** [Obs.] troublesome; annoying — **im·por′tu·nate·ly** *adv.* —**im·por′tu·nate·ness** *n.*

im·por·tune (im′pôr tōōn′, -tyōōn′; im pôr′chən) *vt.* **-tuned′, -tun′ing** [Fr. *importuner* < the *adj.*] **1.** to trouble with requests or demands; urge or entreat persistently or repeatedly **2.** [Archaic] to ask for urgently; demand **3.** [Obs.] *a)* to trouble; annoy *b)* to impel —*vi.* to be importunate —*adj.* [ME. < OFr. *importun* < L. *importunus,* unsuitable, troublesome < *in-*, not + (*op*)-*portunus*: see OPPORTUNE] *rare var. of* IMPORTUNATE — *SYN.* see BEG, URGE —**im′por·tune′ly** *adv.* —**im′por·tun′er** *n.*

im·por·tu·ni·ty (-tōōn′ə tē, -tyōōn′-) *n., pl.* **-ties** [Fr. *importunité* < L. *importunitas*] an importuning or being importunate; persistence in requesting or demanding

im·pose (im pōz′) *vt.* **-posed′, -pos′ing** [Fr., altered after *poser* (see POSE¹) < L. *imponere*, to place upon < *in-*, on + *ponere*: see POSITION] **1.** to place or set (a burden, tax, fine, etc. *on* or *upon*) as by authority **2.** to force (oneself, one's presence or will, etc.) on another or others without right or invitation; obtrude **3.** to pass off; palm off; foist, esp. by deception [to *impose* false cures on unsuspecting patients] **4.** to arrange (pages of type or plates) in a frame in the proper order of printing **5.** [Archaic] to place; put; deposit **6.** [Obs.] to lay (the hands) on a person being ordained or

confirmed —**impose on** (or **upon**) **1.** [Rare] to make a strong impression on **2.** to take advantage of; put to some trouble or use unfairly for one's own benefit **3.** to cheat or defraud —**im·pos′er** n.

im·pos·ing (-pō′ziŋ) adj. making a strong impression because of great size, strength, dignity, etc.; impressive —SYN. see GRAND —**im·pos′ing·ly** adv.

im·po·si·tion (im′pə zish′ən) n. [ME. < OFr. < L. im-positio, a laying upon, application] **1.** an imposing or imposing on; specif., a) the forcing of oneself, one's presence or will, etc. on another or others without right or invitation; obtrusion b) a taking advantage of friendship, etc. c) the laying on of hands, as in ordination or confirmation **2.** something imposed; specif., a) a tax, fine, etc. b) an unjust burden or requirement; specif., a deception; fraud **3.** the arrangement of type pages or plates in the proper order of printing

im·pos·si·bil·i·ty (im päs′ə bil′ə tē) n. [OFr. impossibilite < LL. impossibilitas] **1.** the fact or quality of being impossible **2.** pl. **-ties** something impossible

im·pos·si·ble (im päs′ə b'l) adj. [ME. < OFr. < L. im-possibilis: see IN-² & POSSIBLE] **1.** not capable of being, being done, or happening **2.** not capable of being done easily or conveniently **3.** not capable of being endured, used, agreed to, etc. because disagreeable or unsuitable [an impossible novel, an impossible request] —**im·pos′si·ble·ness** n. —**im·pos′si·bly** adv.

im·post¹ (im′pōst) n. [OFr. < ML. impostus < L. im-positus, pp. of imponere: see IMPOSE] **1.** a tax; esp., a duty on imported goods **2.** Racing the weight assigned to a horse in a handicap race —vt. to classify (imported goods) in order to assess the proper taxes

im·post² (im′pōst) n. [Fr. imposte < It. imposta < L. impositus: see prec.] the top part of a pillar, pier, or wall supporting an arch

im·pos·tor (im päs′tər) n. [Fr. imposteur < LL. impostor < pp. of L. imponere: see IMPOSE] a person who deceives or cheats others, esp. by pretending to be someone or something that he is not —SYN. see QUACK²

im·pos·tume (-chōōm, -tyōōm) n. [Late ME. < MFr. < L. apostema < Gr. apostēma, lit., separation < apostenai, to stand off from: see APOSTATE] [Archaic] an abscess: also **im·pos′thume** (-thōōm, -thyōōm)

im·pos·ture (-chər) n. [Fr. < LL. impostura] the act or practice of an impostor; fraud; deception

im·po·tence (im′pə təns) n. [ME. < OFr. < L. impotentia] the quality or condition of being impotent: also **im′po·ten·cy**, pl. **-cies**

im·po·tent (-tənt) adj. [ME. < OFr. < L. impotens: see IN-² & POTENT] **1.** lacking physical strength; weak **2.** ineffective, powerless, or helpless [impotent rage] **3.** unable to engage in sexual intercourse, esp. because of an inability to have an erection **4.** [Obs.] having no self-control —SYN. see STERILE —**im′po·tent·ly** adv.

im·pound (im pound′) vt. **1.** to shut up (an animal) in a pound **2.** to take and hold (a document, evidence, etc.) in legal custody **3.** to gather and enclose (water) for irrigation, etc. —**im·pound′ment** n.

im·pov·er·ish (im päv′ər ish, -päv′rish) vt. [ME. empov-erishen < extended stem of OFr. empovrir < em- (< L. in-, in) + povre < L. pauper, POOR] **1.** to make poor; reduce to poverty **2.** to deprive of strength, resources, etc. —**im·pov′er·ish·ment** n.

im·pow·er (im pou′ər) vt. obs. var. of EMPOWER

im·prac·ti·ca·ble (im prak′ti kə b'l) adj. [< IN-² + PRACTI-CABLE] **1.** not capable of being carried out in practice [an impracticable plan] **2.** not capable of being used [an im-practicable road] **3.** [Now Rare] not capable of being managed or dealt with; intractable [an impracticable person] —**im·prac′ti·ca·bil′i·ty, im·prac′ti·ca·ble·ness** n. —**im·prac′ti·ca·bly** adv.

im·prac·ti·cal (im prak′tə k'l) adj. not practical; specif., a) not workable or useful; impracticable b) not handling practical matters well c) given to theorizing; idealistic —**im·prac′ti·cal′i·ty, im·prac′ti·cal·ness** n.

im·pre·cate (im′prə kāt′) vt. **-cat′ed, -cat′ing** [< L. im-precatus, pp. of imprecari, to invoke, pray to < in-, in, on + precari, to PRAY] **1.** to pray for or invoke (evil, a curse, etc.) **2.** [Rare] to invoke evil upon; curse —SYN. see CURSE —**im′pre·ca′tor** n.

im·pre·ca·tion (im′prə kā′shən) n. [L. imprecatio] **1.** the act of imprecating evil, etc. on someone **2.** a curse —**im′pre·ca·to′ry** (-kə tôr′ē) adj.

im·pre·cise (im′pri sīs′) adj. not precise, exact, or definite; vague —**im′pre·cise′ly** adv. —**im′pre·ci′sion** (-sizh′ən) n.

im·preg·na·ble¹ (im preg′nə b'l) adj. [ME. imprenable < OFr.: see IN-² & PREGNABLE] **1.** not capable of being captured or entered by force **2.** unshakable; unyielding; firm [an impregnable belief] —**im·preg′na·bil′i·ty** n. —**im·preg′na·bly** adv.

im·preg·na·ble² (im preg′nə b'l) adj. [IMPREGN(ATE) + -ABLE] that can be impregnated

im·preg·nate (im preg′nāt; for adj. -nit) vt. **-nat·ed, -nat·ing** [< LL. impraegnatus, pp. of impraegnare, to make pregnant < L. in-, in + praegnans, PREGNANT] **1.** to fertilize (an ovum) **2.** to make pregnant **3.** to fertilize (land); make fruitful **4.** to fill or saturate; cause to be permeated [clothing impregnated with smoke] **5.** to indoctrinate or imbue (with ideas, feelings, principles, etc.) —

adj. impregnated; pregnant —SYN. see SOAK —**im′preg·na′tion** n. —**im·preg′na·tor** n.

im·pre·sa (im prā′zə) n. [It.: see ff.] [Obs.] a device or emblem, usually with a motto

im·pre·sa·ri·o (im′prə sär′ē ō, -ser′-) n., pl. **-ri·os** [It. < impresa, enterprise < imprendere, to undertake < VL. *imprehendere: see EMPRISE] the organizer, manager, or director of an opera or ballet company, concert series, etc.

im·pre·scrip·ti·ble (im′pri skrip′tə b'l) adj. [Fr.: see IN-² & PRESCRIPTIBLE] that cannot rightfully be taken away, lost, or revoked; inviolable —**im′pre·scrip′ti·bly** adv.

im·press¹ (im pres′; for n. im′pres) vt. [< IN-¹ + PRESS²] **1.** to draft or force (men) into public service, esp. into a navy **2.** to levy, seize, or requisition (money, property, etc.) for public use —n. same as IMPRESSMENT

im·press² (im pres′; for n. im′pres) vt. [ME. impressen < L. impressus, pp. of imprimere: see IN-¹ & PRESS¹] **1.** to use pressure on so as to leave a mark [to impress clay with a die] **2.** to mark by using pressure; stamp; imprint **3.** to apply with pressure [to impress a die into clay] **4.** a) to have a marked effect on the mind or emotions of b) to arouse the interest or approval of **5.** to implant firmly on the mind or fix in the memory **6.** Elec. to apply (a voltage or current) to a circuit or device, as from a generator —n. **1.** the act of impressing **2.** any mark, imprint, etc. made by pressure; stamp; impression **3.** a distinctive quality or effect produced by some strong influence —SYN. see AFFECT¹

im·press·i·ble (-ə b'l) adj. [ML. impressibilis] that can be impressed; impressionable —**im·press′i·bil′i·ty** n. —**im·press′i·bly** adv.

im·pres·sion (im presh′ən) n. [ME. impressioun < OFr. impression < L. impressio] **1.** the act of impressing **2.** a result or effect of impressing; specif., a) a mark, imprint, etc. made by physical pressure b) an effect produced, as on the mind or senses, by some force or influence c) the effect produced by any effort or activity [hard cleaning made little impression on the stain] **3.** a notion, feeling, or recollection, esp. a vague one **4.** a first or single coat of paint or color **5.** an imitation or mimicking intended as a caricature or amusing impersonation **6.** Dentistry the imprint of the teeth and surrounding tissues in wax, plaster, etc., used as a mold in making dentures **7.** Printing a) the pressing or pressure of type or plates on paper, etc.; printing b) a printed copy c) all the copies printed in a single operation from a set of unaltered type or plates —SYN. see IDEA —**im·pres′sion·al** adj.

im·pres·sion·a·ble (im presh′ən ə b'l) adj. [Fr.] easily affected by impressions; esp., capable of being influenced intellectually, emotionally, or morally; sensitive —**im·pres′sion·a·bil′i·ty** n. —**im·pres′sion·a·bly** adv.

im·pres·sion·ism (-iz'm) n. [< Fr. impressionisme, coined in 1874 after a Monet painting entitled "Impression, sunrise"] a theory and school of painting exemplified chiefly by Monet, Pissarro, and Sisley, but also by Manet, Renoir, etc., whose chief aim is to capture a momentary glimpse of a subject, esp. to reproduce the changing effects of light by applying paint to canvas in short strokes of pure color: the term has been extended to literature, as in the novels of the Goncourt brothers and in symbolist poetry, and to music, as by Debussy and Ravel, which seeks to produce moods and impressions by various characteristic devices

im·pres·sion·ist (-ist) n. **1.** a painter, writer, or composer who practices impressionism **2.** an entertainer who does impressions, or impersonations —adj. of impressionism or impressionists

im·pres·sion·is·tic (im presh′ə nis′tik) adj. **1.** same as IMPRESSIONIST **2.** conveying a quick or overall impression —**im·pres′sion·is′ti·cal·ly** adv.

im·pres·sive (im pres′iv) adj. having or tending to have a strong effect on the mind or emotions; eliciting wonder or admiration —**im·pres′sive·ly** adv.

im·press·ment (-mənt) n. [IMPRESS¹ + -MENT] the practice or act of impressing men or property for the use or service of the public

im·pres·sure (im presh′ər) n. [IMPRESS² + -URE] [Archaic] same as IMPRESSION

im·prest (im′prest) n. [It. impresto, a loan < (dare) in prestito, (to give) in loan < in, in + prestito, a loan < presture, to lend < L. praestare, to become surety for, lit., to stand before; prae-, before + stare, to STAND] a loan or advance of money, as from government funds —adj. Accounting designating a fund, as of petty cash, that is replenished in exactly the amount expended from it

im·pri·ma·tur (im′pri mä′tər, -māt′-) n. [ModL., lit., let it be printed, 3d pers. sing., pres. subj. pass., of L. impri-mere: see IMPRINT] **1.** license or permission to publish or print a book, article, etc.; specif., R.C.Ch. such permission granted by an ecclesiastical censor **2.** any sanction or approval

im·pri·mis (im prī′mis) adv. [ME. inprimis < L. in primis, lit., among the first < in, among + primis, abl. pl. of primus, first: see PRIME] in the first place

im·print (im print′; for n. im′print) vt. [ME. emprenten < OFr. empreinter < empreinte, an imprint < pp. of em-preindre < L. imprimere < in-, on + premere, to PRESS¹] **1.** to mark by or as by pressing or stamping; impress [to imprint a paper with a seal] **2.** to make as a mark or impression **3.** to press or apply [to imprint a kiss on the fore-

head/ **4.** to implant firmly on the mind or fix in the memory —*n.* **1.** a mark made by imprinting **2.** a lasting effect or characteristic result [the *imprint* of starvation] **3.** a publisher's or printer's note on the title page or its reverse or at the end of a book, giving his name, the time and place of publication, etc.

im·print·ing (im print′iŋ) *n. Psychol.* a learning mechanism operating very early in the life of an animal, in which a particular stimulus immediately establishes an irreversible behavior pattern with reference to the same stimulus in the future

im·pris·on (im priz′'n) *vt.* **1.** to put or keep in prison; jail **2.** to restrict, limit, or confine in any way —**im·pris′on·ment** *n.*

im·prob·a·ble (im präb′ə b'l) *adj.* [L. *improbabilis*] not probable; not likely to happen or be true; unlikely—**im′prob·a·bil′i·ty** *n., pl.* **-ties** —**im·prob′a·bly** *adv.*

im·pro·bi·ty (im prō′bə tē) *n., pl.* **-ties** [ME. *improbite* < L. *improbitas*] lack of probity; dishonesty

im·promp·tu (im prämp′tōō, -tyōō) *adj., adv.* [Fr. < L. *in promptu*, in readiness < *in*, in + *promptu*, abl. of *promptus*, readiness < *promptus*, brought out, ready, PROMPT] without preparation or advance thought; offhand —*n.* an impromptu speech, performance, etc.

SYN.—**impromptu** is applied to that which is spoken, made, or done on the spur of the moment to suit the occasion and stresses spontaneity; **extemporaneous, extempore** (more commonly used as an adverb), and **extemporary** may express the same idea but are now more often used of a speech that has received some preparation, but has not been written out or memorized; **improvised** applies to something composed or devised without any preparation and, with reference to things other than music, suggests the ingenious use of whatever is at hand to fill an unforeseen and immediate need

im·prop·er (im präp′ər) *adj.* [OFr. *impropre* < L. *improprius*: see IN-² & PROPER] **1.** not suitable for or consistent with the purpose or circumstances; ill-adapted; unfit **2.** not in accordance with the truth, fact, or rule; wrong; incorrect **3.** contrary to good taste or decency; indecorous **4.** not normal or regular —**im·prop′er·ly** *adv.* —**im·prop′er·ness** *n.*

SYN.—**improper**, the word of broadest application in this list, refers to anything that is not proper or suitable, esp. to that which does not conform to conventional standards; **unseemly** applies to that which is improper or inappropriate to the particular situation [her *unseemly* laughter at the funeral]; **unbecoming** applies to that which is inappropriate to a certain kind of person, his character, etc. [his rigid views are most *unbecoming* in a teacher]; **indecorous** refers to that which violates propriety or good taste in behavior, speech, etc. [his *indecorous* interruption of their chat]; **indelicate** implies a lack of propriety or tact and connotes immodesty or coarseness [an *indelicate* anecdote]; **indecent** is used of that which is regarded as highly offensive to morals or modesty [*indecent* exposure] —*ANT.* **proper, decorous**

improper fraction a fraction in which the denominator is less than the numerator (Ex.: 5/3)

im·pro·pri·ate (im prō′prē āt′; *for adj., usually* -it) *vt.* **-at′ed, -at′ing** [< ML.(Ec.) *impropriatus*, pp. of *impropriare*, to take as one's own < L. *in*, in + *proprius*, one's own] **1.** to transfer (church income or property) to private individuals or corporations **2.** [Obs.] to appropriate —*adj.* having been impropriated —**im·pro′pri·a′tion** *n.* —**im·pro′pri·a′tor** *n.*

im·pro·pri·e·ty (im′prə prī′ə tē) *n., pl.* **-ties** [< MFr. *impropriété* (or) < L. *improprietas*: see IN-² & PROPRIETY] **1.** the quality of being improper **2.** improper action or behavior **3.** an improper use of a word or phrase (Ex.: "borrow" for "lend"): see also BARBARISM, SOLECISM

im·prove (im prōōv′) *vt.* **-proved′, -prov′ing** [earlier *improw* < Anglo-Fr. *emprower* < *en-*, in + *prou*, gain, advantage < LL. *prode*, advantage (back-formation < L. *prodesse*, to be of advantage): see PRO-² + IS] **1.** to use profitably or to good advantage [to *improve* one's leisure by studying] **2.** to raise to a better quality or condition; make better ☆**3.** to make (land or structures) more valuable by cultivation, construction, etc. —*vi.* to become better in quality or condition —**improve on** (or **upon**) to do or make better than, as by additions or changes —**im·prov′a·bil′i·ty** *n.* —**im·prov′a·ble** *adj.* —**im·prov′er** *n.*

SYN.—**improve** and **better** both imply a correcting or advancing of something that is not in itself necessarily bad, the former by supplying a lack or want [to *improve* a method] and the latter by seeking something more satisfying [he's left his job to *better* himself]; **ameliorate** implies a bad, oppressive, or intolerable condition to begin with [to *ameliorate* the lot of the poor] —*ANT.* **worsen, impair**

im·prove·ment (-mənt) *n.* [Anglo-Fr. *emprowement*] **1.** an improving or being improved; esp., *a)* betterment *b)* an increase in value or in excellence of quality or condition *c)* profitable use **2.** *a)* an addition or change that improves something *b)* a person or thing representing a higher degree of excellence **3.** a change or addition to land or real property, as a sewer, fence, etc., to make it more valuable

im·prov·i·dent (im präv′ə dənt) *adj.* [< L. *improvidus* < *in-*, not + *providus*, foreseeing, cautious < *providere*: see PROVIDE] failing to provide for the future; lacking foresight or thrift—**im·prov′i·dence** *n.*—**im·prov′i·dent·ly** *adv.*

im·prov·i·sa·tion (im präv′ə zā′shən, im′prə vi-) *n.* **1.** the act of improvising **2.** something improvised —**im·prov′i·sa′tion·al** *adj.*

im·prov·i·sa·to·ri·al (im präv′i zə tôr′ē əl) *adj.* of, or having the nature of, an improviser or improvisation: also **im·pro·vi·sa·to·ry** (im′prə vī′zə tôr′ē)

im·pro·vise (im′prə vīz′) *vt., vi.* **-vised′, -vis′ing** [Fr. *improviser* < It. *improvvisare* < *improvviso*, unprepared < L. *improvisus*, unforeseen < *in-*, not + *provisus*, pp. of *providere*, to foresee, anticipate: see PROVIDE] **1.** to compose, or simultaneously compose and perform, on the spur of the moment and without any preparation; extemporize **2.** to make, provide, or do with the tools and materials at hand, usually to fill an unforeseen and immediate need [to *improvise* a bed out of leaves] —**im′pro·vis′er, im′pro·vi′sor, im·prov′i·sa·tor** (-präv′ə zāt′ər) *n.*

im·pru·dent (im prōōd′'nt) *adj.* [ME. < L. *imprudens*: see IN-² & PRUDENT] not prudent; without thought of the consequences; lacking in judgment or caution; rash; indiscreet —**im·pru′dence** *n.* —**im·pru′dent·ly** *adv.*

im·pu·dence (im′pyōō dəns) *n.* [ME. < OFr. < L. *impudentia*] **1.** the quality of being impudent **2.** impudent speech or behavior: also **im′pu·den·cy** *n., pl.* **-cies**

im·pu·dent (-dənt) *adj.* [ME. < L. *impudens* < *in-*, not + *pudens*, modest, orig. prp. of *pudere*, to feel shame] **1.** orig., immodest; shameless **2.** shamelessly bold or disrespectful; saucy; insolent —*SYN.* see IMPERTINENT —**im′pu·dent·ly** *adv.*

im·pu·dic·i·ty (im′pyoo dis′ə tē) *n.* [Fr. *impudicité* < LL. *impudicitas*, for L. *impudicitia* < *impudicus* < *in-*, not + *pudicus*, modest] immodesty; shamelessness

im·pugn (im pyōōn′) *vt.* [ME. *impugnen* < OFr. *impugner* < L. *impugnare* < *in-*, on, against + *pugnare*, to fight: for IE. base see POINT] **1.** orig., to attack physically **2.** to attack by argument or criticism; oppose or challenge as false or questionable —*SYN.* see DENY —**im·pugn′a·ble** *adj.* —**im·pug·na·tion** (im′pəg nā′shən) *n.* —**im·pugn′er** *n.*

im·pu·is·sance (im pyōō′ə s'ns, -pwis′'ns) *n.* [Fr.: see IN-² & PUISSANCE] lack of power; weakness —**im·pu′is·sant** *adj.*

im·pulse (im′puls) *n.* [L. *impulsus* < pp. of *impellere*: see IMPEL] **1.** *a)* an impelling, or driving forward with sudden force *b)* an impelling force; sudden, driving force; push; thrust; impetus *c)* the motion or effect caused by such a force **2.** *a)* incitement to action arising from a state of mind or some external stimulus *b)* a sudden inclination to act, without conscious thought *c)* a motive or tendency coming from within [prompted by an *impulse* of curiosity] **3.** *Elec.* a momentary surge in one direction of voltage or current **4.** *Mech.* the change in momentum effected by a force, measured by multiplying the average value of the force by the time during which it acts **5.** *Physiol.* a stimulus transmitted in a muscle or nerve fiber, which causes or inhibits activity in the body

impulse turbine a kind of turbine having rotor blades so shaped that the force of jets of fluid striking against the blades moves the wheel, without pressure drop occurring across the blades

im·pul·sion (im pul′shən) *n.* [L. *impulsio* < *impulsus*: see prec.] **1.** an impelling or being impelled **2.** an impelling force **3.** movement or tendency to move resulting from this force; impetus **4.** *same as* IMPULSE (sense 2)

im·pul·sive (-siv) *adj.* [< MFr. or ML.: MFr. *impulsif* < ML. *impulsivus* < L. *impulsus*, IMPULSE] **1.** impelling; driving forward **2.** *a)* acting or likely to act on impulse [an *impulsive* person] *b)* produced by or resulting from a sudden impulse [an *impulsive* remark] **3.** *Mech.* acting briefly and as a result of impulse —*SYN.* see SPONTANEOUS —**im·pul′sive·ly** *adv.* —**im·pul′sive·ness** *n.*

im·pu·ni·ty (im pyōō′nə tē) *n.* [Fr. *impunité* < L. *impunitas* < *impunis*, free from punishment < *in-*, without + *poena*, punishment: see PAIN] exemption from punishment, penalty, or harm —*SYN.* see EXEMPTION

im·pure (im pyoor′) *adj.* [L. *impurus*] not pure; specif., *a)* unclean; dirty *b)* unclean according to religious ritual; defiled *c)* immoral; obscene; unchaste *d)* mixed with foreign matter; adulterated *e)* mixed so as to lack purity in color, tone, style, etc. *f)* characterized by solecisms, barbarisms, foreign words or idioms, etc.: said of language or speech —**im·pure′ly** *adv.* —**im·pure′ness** *n.*

im·pu·ri·ty (-pyoor′ə tē) *n.* [OFr. *impurité* < L. *impuritas*] **1.** the state or quality of being impure **2.** *pl.* **-ties** an impure thing or element

im·put·a·ble (im pyōōt′ə b'l) *adj.* [ML. *imputabilis*] that can be imputed; ascribable —**im·put′a·bil′i·ty** *n.* —**im·put′a·bly** *adv.*

im·pute (im pyōōt′) *vt.* **-put′ed, -put′ing** [ME. *imputen* < OFr. *imputer* < L. *imputare* < *in-*, in, to + *putare*, to estimate, think, orig., to cut, clean: for IE. base see PURE] **1.** to attribute (esp. a fault or misconduct) to another; charge with; ascribe **2.** *Theol.* to ascribe (goodness or guilt) to a person as coming from another —*SYN.* see ASCRIBE —**im′pu·ta′tion** (-pyoo tā′shən) *n.* —**im·put′a·tive** (-pyōōt′ə tiv) *adj.*

impv. imperative

in (in, ən, 'n) *prep.* [ME. < OE., akin to G. *in* < IE. base *en-*, whence Gr. *en*, L. *in* (OL. *en*), OIr. *in*, OSlav. *on-*, Sans. *an-*] **1.** contained or enclosed by; inside; within [*in* the room, *in* the envelope] **2.** wearing; clothed by [to dress *in* furs] **3.** during the course of [done *in* a day] **4.** at, before, or after the end of [return *in* an hour] **5.** perceptible to (one of the senses) [to be *in* sight] **6.** limited by the scope of [*in* my opinion] **7.** being a member of or worker at [to be *in* business] **8.** out of a group or set of [one *in* ten will fail] **9.** amidst; surrounded by [*in* a storm] **10.** affected by; having [to be *in* trouble] **11.** engaged or occupied by [*in* a search for truth] **12.** with regard to; as concerns [weak *in* faith, to vary *in* size] **13.** so as to form [arranged *in* curls] **14.** with; by; using [to paint *in* oil, written *in* English] **15.** made of [done *in* wood] **16.** because of; for [to cry *in* pain] **17.** by way of [do this *in* my defense] **18.** as a part of the capacity or function of; belonging to [he didn't have it *in* him to cheat] **19.** into [come *in* the house]: *into* is generally preferred in this sense *In* expresses inclusion with relation to space, place, time, state, circumstances, manner, quality, substance, a class, a whole, etc. —*adv.* **1.** from a point outside to one inside [to invite visitors *in*] **2.** to or toward a certain place or direction [he flies *in* today, they live ten miles *in*] **3.** at or inside one's home, office, etc. [forced to stay *in* for a day] **4.** *a)* so as to be contained by a certain space or condition *b)* so as to be in office or power **5.** so as to be agreeing or involved [he fell *in* with our plans] **6.** so as to form a part [mix *in* the cream] —*adj.* **1.** that is successful or in power [the *in* group] **2.** inner; inside **3.** coming or going inside or inward [the *in* door, the *in* boat] **4.** completed, gathered, counted, etc. [the votes are *in*] **5.** [Colloq.] profiting to the extent of [to be *in* $100] **6.** [Colloq.] currently smart, popular, fashionable, etc. [an *in* joke] —*n.* **1.** a person, group, etc. that is in power, in office, or in a favored position: *usually used in pl.* ☆**2.** [Colloq.] special influence or favor; pull —*vt.* **inned, in'ning** [Chiefly Brit. Dial.] **1.** to collect; gather in [*in* the hay before it rains] **2.** to enclose —**have it in for** [Colloq.] to hold a grudge against —**in for** certain to have or get (usually an unpleasant experience) —**in on** having a share or part of —**ins and outs 1.** all the complex physical details of a place **2.** all the details and intricacies —**in that** because; since —**in with** associated with as a partner, friend, etc.

in-¹ (in) [< the prep. IN; also ME. < OE. & < MFr. *in-* or OFr. *en-* < L. *in-* < *in*: see prec.] *a prefix meaning* in, into, within, on, toward [*inbreed, infer, induct*]: also used as an intensive in some words of Latin origin [*instigate*] and assimilated to *il-* before *l* [*illuminate*], *ir-* before *r* [*irrigate*], and *im-* before *m, p,* and *b* [*immigrate, impeach, imbibe*]

in-² (in) [ME. < OFr. & ML. < L. < IE. *ṇ-,* initial negative particle, var. of *ne, nei,* whence L. *ne-:* cf. NO] *a prefix meaning* no, not, without, non- [*insignificant*]: assimilated to *il-* before *l* [*illiterate*], *ir-* before *r* [*irresponsible*], and *im-* before *m, p,* and *b* [*immaterial, impossible, imbecile*]

-in¹ (in) [see -INE⁴] *a n.-forming suffix meaning:* **1.** *a)* a neutral carbohydrate [*inulin*] *b)* a glucoside [*amygdalin*] *c)* a protein [*albumin*] *d)* a glyceride [*palmitin*] *e)* an enzyme [*rennin*] *f)* an antibiotic [*streptomycin*] **2.** *same as* -INE⁴ (sense 2 *b*) [*codein*]: an infrequent variant **3.** a pharmaceutical preparation [*riboflavin*] **4.** a commercial product, material, or mixture [*Weirzin*] **5.** an antigen [*tuberculin*]

-in² (in) a combining form used in compounding terms formed by analogy with SIT-IN to describe various similar actions in mass demonstrations [*teach-in, be-in*]

In *Chem.* indium

in. inch; inches

-i·na (ē′nə) [L., fem. of *-inus*] *a suffix used to form* feminine names, titles, occupational designations, etc. [*Christina, czarina, ballerina*]

in·a·bil·i·ty (in′ə bil′ə tē) *n.* [ME. *inabilite:* see IN-² & ABILITY] the quality or state of being unable; lack of ability, capacity, means, or power

in ab·sen·ti·a (in ab sen′shə, ab sen′shē ə) [L., lit., in absence] although not present [to receive a college degree *in absentia*]

in·ac·ces·si·ble (in′ək ses′ə b'l) *adj.* [Fr. < LL. *inaccessibilis*] not accessible; specif., *a)* impossible to reach or enter *b)* that cannot be seen, talked to, influenced, etc.; inapproachable *c)* not obtainable —**in′ac·ces′si·bil′i·ty** *n.* —**in′ac·ces′si·bly** *adv.*

in·ac·cu·ra·cy (in ak′yər ə sē) *n.* **1.** the quality of being inaccurate; lack of accuracy **2.** *pl.* **-cies** something inaccurate; error; mistake

in·ac·cu·rate (-yər it) *adj.* not accurate; not correct; not exact; in error —**in·ac′cu·rate·ly** *adv.*

in·ac·tion (in ak′shən) *n.* absence of action or motion; inertness or idleness

in·ac·ti·vate (in ak′tə vāt′) *vt.* **-vat′ed, -vat′ing** to make inactive; specif., *a)* to cause (a military unit, governmental bureau, etc.) to go out of existence; dissolve *b) Biochem.* to destroy the activity of (a substance) by heat —**in·ac′ti·va′tion** *n.*

in·ac·tive (in ak′tiv) *adj.* **1.** not active or moving; inert **2.** not inclined to act; idle; dull; sluggish **3.** not in use or force; not functioning **4.** not in active service in the armed forces **5.** not affecting the plane of polarized light: said of

some isomers of certain optically active crystalline substances —**in·ac′tive·ly** *adv.* —**in′ac·tiv′i·ty** *n.*

SYN.—**inactive** is a general word applied to any person or thing that is not active, operating, working, in force, etc. [an *inactive* machine, ballplayer, contract, etc.]; **idle** is used especially of persons who are not at the moment occupied, either voluntarily, as through indolence, or of necessity [the shutdown left 2000 workers *idle*]; **inert** is applied to anything which has no inherent power of motion or action [*inert* matter] or to any person who seems inherently indisposed to action [the *inert* electorate]; **passive** refers to something that is acted upon but does not act in return and, hence, often connotes submissiveness or failure to resist [*passive* compliance] —ANT. active, lively, dynamic

in·ad·e·qua·cy (in ad′ə kwə sē) *n., pl.* **-cies** quality, state, or instance of being inadequate

in·ad·e·quate (-kwət) *adj.* not adequate; not sufficient; not equal to what is required —**in·ad′e·quate·ly** *adv.* —**in·ad′e·quate·ness** *n.*

in·ad·mis·si·ble (in′əd mis′ə b'l) *adj.* not admissible; not to be allowed, accepted, granted, or conceded —**in′ad·mis′si·bil′i·ty** *n.* —**in′ad·mis′si·bly** *adv.*

in·ad·vert·ence (in′əd vur′təns) *n.* [ML. *inadvertentia:* see IN-² & ADVERTENCE] **1.** the quality of being inadvertent **2.** an instance of this; oversight; mistake Also **in′ad·vert′en·cy** *pl.* **-cies**

in·ad·vert·ent (-tənt) *adj.* [prob. back-formation < prec.] **1.** not attentive or observant; heedless **2.** due to oversight; unintentional —**in′ad·vert′ent·ly** *adv.*

in·ad·vis·a·ble (in′əd vī′zə b'l) *adj.* not advisable; not wise or prudent —**in′ad·vis·a·bil′i·ty** *n.*

-i·nae (ī′nē) [ModL., fem. pl. of adjectives in *-inus* (in agreement with understood *bestiae,* animals) < L.] *a suffix used to form* the name of a zoological subfamily [*Felinae* (a cat subfamily)]

†in ae·ter·num (in ē ter′nəm) [L., to eternity] forever

in·al·ien·a·ble (in āl′yən ə b'l) *adj.* [Fr. *inaliénable:* see IN-² & ALIENABLE] that may not be taken away or transferred [*inalienable* rights] —**in·al′ien·a·bil′i·ty** *n.* —**in·al′ien·a·bly** *adv.*

in·al·ter·a·ble (in ôl′tər ə b'l) *adj.* [ML. *inalterabilis*] that cannot be altered; unchangeable —**in·al′ter·a·bil′i·ty** *n.* —**in·al′ter·a·bly** *adv.*

in·am·o·ra·ta (in am′ə rät′ə, in′am-) *n.* [It., fem. of *innamorato,* lover, orig. pp. of *innamorare,* to fall in love < *in-* (see IN-¹) + *amore* < L. *amor,* love] a woman in relation to the man who is her lover; sweetheart or mistress

in-and-in (in′ənd in′) *adj., adv.* repeatedly with individuals of the same or closely related stocks [*in-and-in* breeding]

in·ane (in ān′) *adj.* [L. *inanis*] **1.** empty; vacant **2.** lacking sense or meaning; foolish; silly —*n.* that which is inane; esp., the void of infinite space —**in·ane′ly** *adv.*

in·an·i·mate (in an′ə mit) *adj.* [LL. *inanimatus*] **1.** not animate; not endowed with (animal) life **2.** not animated; dull; spiritless —SYN. see DEAD —**in·an′i·mate·ly** *adv.* —**in·an′i·mate·ness** *n.*

in·a·ni·tion (in′ə nish′ən) *n.* [ME. *in-anisioun* < OFr. *inanition* < LL. *inanitio* < L. *inanitus,* pp. of *inanire,* to empty < *inanis,* inane] emptiness; specif., *a)* exhaustion from lack of food or an inability to assimilate it *b)* lack of strength or spirit

in·an·i·ty (in an′ə tē) *n.* [Fr. *inanité* < L. *inanitas,* emptiness] **1.** the quality or condition of being inane; specif., *a)* emptiness *b)* lack of sense or meaning; silliness **2.** *pl.* **-ties** something inane; senseless or silly act, remark, etc.

in·ap·par·ent (in′ə par′ənt) *adj.* not apparent

in·ap·peas·a·ble (in′ə pē′zə b'l) *adj.* not to be appeased

in·ap·pe·tence (in ap′ə təns) *n.* [IN-² + APPETENCE] lack of appetite or desire: also **in·ap′pe·ten·cy** —**in·ap′pe·tent** *adj.*

in·ap·pli·ca·ble (in ap′li kə b'l) *adj.* not applicable; not suitable; inappropriate —**in′ap·pli·ca·bil′i·ty** *n.* —**in·ap′pli·ca·bly** *adv.*

in·ap·po·site (in ap′ə zit) *adj.* not apposite; irrelevant —**in·ap′po·site·ly** *adv.* —**in·ap′po·site·ness** *n.*

in·ap·pre·ci·a·ble (in′ə prē′shə b'l, -shē ə-) *adj.* [IN-² + APPRECIABLE] too small to be observed or have any value; negligible —**in′ap·pre′ci·a·bly** *adv.*

in·ap·pre·ci·a·tive (-shə tiv, -shē ə-, -shē āt′iv) *adj.* not feeling or showing appreciation —**in′ap·pre′ci·a·tive·ly** *adv.* —**in′ap·pre′ci·a·tive·ness** *n.*

in·ap·pre·hen·si·ble (in′ap ri hen′sə b'l) *adj.* that cannot be apprehended, or understood

in·ap·pre·hen·sion (-shən) *n.* lack of apprehension

in·ap·pre·hen·sive (-siv) *adj.* **1.** lacking the ability to apprehend, or understand **2.** not perceiving danger, trouble, etc. —**in′ap·pre·hen′sive·ly** *adv.*

in·ap·proach·a·ble (in′ə prō′chə b'l) *adj.* that cannot be approached —**in′ap·proach·a·bil′i·ty** *n.*

in·ap·pro·pri·ate (in′ə prō′prē it) *adj.* not appropriate; not suitable, fitting, or proper —**in′ap·pro′pri·ate·ly** *adv.* —**in′ap·pro′pri·ate·ness** *n.*

in·apt (in apt′) *adj.* **1.** not apt; not suitable; inappropriate **2.** lacking skill or aptitude; inept —**in·apt′i·tude′** (-ap′tə tōōd′, -tyōōd′) *n.* —**in·apt′ly** *adv.* —**in·apt′ness** *n.*

in·arch (in ärch′) *vt.* [IN-¹ + ARCH¹, *v.*] to graft (a plant) by uniting a shoot to another plant while both are growing on their own roots

in·ar·tic·u·late (in′är tik′yə lit) *adj.* [LL. *inarticulatus*: see IN-[2] & ARTICULATE] **1.** produced without the normal articulation of understandable speech: said of vocal sounds *[an inarticulate cry]* **2.** *a)* not able to speak, as because of strong emotion; mute *b)* not able to speak understandably, effectively, or coherently **3.** not expressed or able to be expressed *[inarticulate passion]* **4.** *Zool.* without joints, segments, hinges, or valves —**in′ar·tic′u·late·ly** *adv.* —**in′ar·tic′u·late·ness** *n.*

in·ar·ti·fi·cial (in′är tə fish′′l) *adj.* [Now Rare] **1.** not artificial; natural **2.** inartistic; unskillful **3.** unaffected; simple

in·ar·tis·tic (in′är tis′tik) *adj.* not artistic; specif., *a)* not conforming to the standards or principles of art *b)* lacking artistic taste —**in′ar·tis′ti·cal·ly** *adv.*

in·as·much as (in′əz much′ əz) **1.** seeing that; since; because **2.** to the extent that

in·at·ten·tion (in′ə ten′shən) *n.* failure to pay attention; heedlessness; negligence

in·at·ten·tive (-tiv) *adj.* not attentive; heedless; negligent —*SYN.* see ABSENT-MINDED —**in′at·ten′tive·ly** *adv.* —**in′at·ten′tive·ness** *n.*

in·au·di·ble (in ô′də b′l) *adj.* [LL. *inaudibilis*] not audible; that cannot be heard —**in′au·di·bil′i·ty** *n.* —**in·aud′i·bly** *adv.*

in·au·gu·ral (in ô′gyə rəl, -gə rəl) *adj.* [Fr.] **1.** of an inauguration **2.** that begins a series; first —*n.* ☆**1.** a speech made at an inauguration ☆**2.** an inauguration

in·au·gu·rate (-rāt′) *vt.* -rat′ed, -rat′ing [< L. *inauguratus*, pp. of *inaugurare*, to practice augury: see IN-[1] & AUGUR] **1.** to induct (an official) into office with a formal ceremony **2.** to make a formal beginning of; start *[to inaugurate a new policy]* **3.** to celebrate formally the first public use of; dedicate *[to inaugurate a new library]* —*SYN.* see BEGIN —**in·au′gu·ra′tion** *n.* —**in·au′gu·ra′tor** *n.*

☆**Inauguration Day** the day on which a president of the U.S. is inaugurated: January 20 (before 1934, March 4) of the year following his election

in·aus·pi·cious (in′ô spish′əs) *adj.* not auspicious; unfavorable; unlucky; ill-omened —**in′aus·pi′cious·ly** *adv.* —**in′aus·pi′cious·ness** *n.*

in·be·ing (in′bē′iŋ) *n.* **1.** inherent existence **2.** basic nature; essence

in·board (in′bôrd′) *adv., adj.* [< in board: see BOARD[2]] **1.** inside the hull or bulwarks of a ship or boat **2.** close or closer to the fuselage or hull of an aircraft **3.** *Mech.* toward the inside —*n.* **1.** a marine motor mounted inboard and connected by a drive shaft to a propeller below the boat **2.** a boat with such a motor

☆**in·board-out·board** (-out′bôrd′) *adj.* designating or of a power unit for small watercraft that has an inboard engine connected by a drive shaft with a universal joint to a propeller at the stern of the boat —*n.* a boat with such a power unit

in·born (in′bôrn′) *adj.* [OE. *inboren*] present in the organism at birth; innate; natural; not acquired —*SYN.* see INNATE

in·bound (-bound′) *adj.* traveling or going inward

in·breathe (in′brēth′) *vt.* -breathed′, -breath′ing [ME. *inbrethen* (see IN-[1] & BREATHE), after L. *inspirare*] [Rare] **1.** to inhale **2.** to inspire

in·bred (in′bred′) *adj.* [pp. of ff.] **1.** innate or deeply instilled **2.** bred from closely related parents; resulting from inbreeding —*SYN.* see INNATE

in·breed (in′brēd′) *vt.* -bred′, -breed′ing **1.** [Rare] to form or develop within **2.** to breed by continual mating of individuals of the same or closely related stocks —*vi.* **1.** to engage in such breeding **2.** to become too refined, effete, etc. as the result of arbitrarily narrow social or cultural association

inc. 1. inclosure **2.** included **3.** including **4.** inclusive **5.** income **6.** incorporated **7.** increase

In·ca (in′kə) *n.* [Sp. < Quechua, prince of the royal family] **1.** any member of a group of Quechuan or related Indian tribes that dominated ancient Peru until the Spanish conquest: the Incas had a highly developed civilization **2.** a ruler or member of the ruling family of these tribes; specif., the emperor —**In′can** *adj.*

in·cal·cu·la·ble (in kal′kyə lə b′l) *adj.* **1.** that cannot be calculated; too great or too many to be counted **2.** too uncertain to be counted on; unpredictable —**in·cal′cu·la·bil′i·ty** *n.* —**in·cal′cu·la·bly** *adv.*

in·ca·les·cent (in′kə les′′nt) *adj.* [L. *incalescens*: see IN-[1] & CALESCENT] [Rare] becoming hotter —**in′ca·les′cence** *n.*

in cam·er·a (in kam′ər ə) [L., in chamber] **1.** in a judge's private office rather than in open court **2.** in closed session, as a committee meeting or hearing not open to the public; secretly

in·can·desce (in′kən des′) *vi., vt.* -desced′, -desc′ing [L. *incandescere*] to become or make incandescent

in·can·des·cent (-des′′nt) *adj.* [L. *incandescens*, prp. of *incandescere*: see IN-[1] & CANDESCENT] **1.** glowing with intense heat; red-hot or, esp., white-hot **2.** very bright; shining brilliantly; gleaming —**in′can·des′cence** *n.* —**in′can·des′cent·ly** *adv.*

incandescent lamp a lamp in which the light is produced by a filament of conducting material contained in a vacuum and heated to incandescence by an electric current

in·can·ta·tion (in′kan tā′shən) *n.* [ME. *incantacion* < Fr. *incantation* < LL. *incantatio* < pp. of L. *incantare*, ENCHANT] **1.** the chanting of magical words or formulas that are supposed to cast a spell or perform other magic **2.** words or a formula so chanted **3.** any magic or sorcery —**in′can·ta′tion·al** *adj.* —**in·can′ta·to′ry** (-kan′tə tôr′ē) *adj.*

in·ca·pa·ble (in kā′pə b′l) *adj.* [LL. *incapabilis*] not capable; specif., *a)* lacking the necessary ability, competence, strength, etc. *b)* not legally qualified or eligible — **incapable of 1.** not allowing or admitting; not able to accept or experience *[incapable of change]* **2.** lacking the ability or fitness for *[incapable of sustained thought]* **3.** not legally qualified for —**in·ca·pa·bil′i·ty**, **in·ca′pa·ble·ness** *n.* —**in·ca′pa·bly** *adv.*

in·ca·pa·cious (in′kə pā′shəs) *adj.* [< LL. *incapax*, incapable + -IOUS] **1.** not capacious or able to hold much **2.** [Archaic] mentally deficient

in·ca·pac·i·tate (in′kə pas′ə tāt′) *vt.* -tat′ed, -tat′ing [INCAPACIT(Y) + -ATE] **1.** to make unable or unfit; esp., to make incapable of normal activity; disable **2.** *Law* to make ineligible; disqualify —**in′ca·pac′i·ta′tion** *n.*

in·ca·pac·i·ty (in′kə pas′ə tē) *n., pl.* -ties [Fr. *incapacité* < ML. *incapacitas*] **1.** lack of capacity, power, or fitness; disability **2.** legal ineligibility or disqualification

In·cap·a·ri·na (in kap′ə rē′nə) *n.* [*INCAP* (acronym for Institute of Nutrition in Central America and Panama) + (F)ARINA] a low-cost protein food made of cottonseed, corn, and sorghum flours, yeast, etc. and used, esp. in Latin America, in preventing protein deficiency diseases

in·cap·su·late (in kap′sə lāt′) *vt.* -lat′ed, -lat′ing *same as* ENCAPSULATE

in·car·cer·ate (in kär′sə rāt′) *vt.* -at′ed, -at′ing [< ML. *incarceratus*, pp. of *incarcerare*, to imprison < L. *in-*, in + *carcer*, prison] **1.** to imprison; jail **2.** to shut up; confine —**in·car′cer·a′tion** *n.* —**in·car′cer·a′tor** *n.*

in·car·di·nate (in kär′də nāt′) *vt.* -nat′ed, -nat′ing [< pp. of ML. *incardinare*: see IN-[1] & CARDINAL] *R.C.Ch.* **1.** to attach (a cleric) to a particular diocese **2.** to elevate to the rank of cardinal —**in·car′di·na′tion** *n.*

in·car·na·dine (in kär′nə din′, -din, -dēn′) *adj.* [Fr. *incarnadin* < It. *incarnatino* < *incarnato* < LL.(Ec.) *incarnatus*: see ff.] **1.** flesh-colored; pink **2.** red; esp., blood-red —*n.* the color of either flesh or blood —*vt.* **-dined′**, **-din′ing** to make incarnadine

in·car·nate (in kär′nit; *also, and for v. always*, -nāt) *adj.* [ME. < LL.(Ec.) *incarnatus*, pp. of *incarnari*, to be made flesh < L. *in-*, in + *caro* (gen. *carnis*), flesh] **1.** endowed with a human body; in human form; personified *[evil incarnate]* **2.** *a)* flesh-colored; pink *b)* red; rosy —*vt.* **-nat·ed**, **-nat·ing 1.** to provide with flesh or a body; embody **2.** to give actual form to; make real **3.** to be the type or embodiment of *[to incarnate the frontier spirit]*

in·car·na·tion (in′kär nā′shən) *n.* [ME. *incarnacion* < OFr. *incarnatiun* < LL.(Ec.) *incarnatio* < pp. of *incarnari*: see prec.] **1.** *a)* endowment with a human body; appearance in human form *b)* *Theol.* [I-] the taking on of human form and nature by Jesus conceived of as the Son of God **2.** any person or animal serving as the embodiment of a god or spirit **3.** any person or thing serving as the type or embodiment of a quality or concept *[the incarnation of courage]*

in·case (in kās′) *vt.* -cased′, -cas′ing *same as* ENCASE

in·cau·tion (in kô′shən) *n.* lack of caution

in·cau·tious (-shəs) *adj.* not cautious; not careful or prudent; reckless; rash —**in·cau′tious·ly** *adv.* —**in·cau′tious·ness** *n.*

in·cen·di·ar·y (in sen′dē er′ē) *adj.* [L. *incendiarius*, setting on fire, an incendiary < *incendium*, a fire < *incendere*: see ff.] **1.** having to do with the willful destruction of property by fire **2.** causing or designed to cause fires, as certain substances, bombs, etc. **3.** willfully stirring up strife, riot, rebellion, etc. —*n., pl.* -ar′ies **1.** a person who willfully destroys property by fire **2.** a person who willfully stirs up strife, riot, rebellion, etc. **3.** an incendiary bomb, substance, etc. —**in·cen′di·a·rism** (-ə riz′m) *n.*

in·cense[1] (in′sens) *n.* [ME. *encens* < OFr. *encens* < LL. *incensum*, incense < neut. of L. *incensus*, pp. of *incendere*, to kindle, inflame < *in-*, in, on + *candere*, to burn, shine: see CANDESCENT] **1.** any of various substances, as gums or resins, producing a pleasant odor when burned: used in some religious ceremonies **2.** the smoke or fragrance from such a substance **3.** any pleasant odor **4.** pleasing attention, praise, or admiration —*vt.* -censed, -cens·ing **1.** to make fragrant with or as with incense; perfume **2.** to burn or offer incense to —*vi.* to burn incense

in·cense[2] (in sens′) *vt.* -censed′, -cens·ing [ME. *encensen* <

OFr. *incenser* < L. *incensus*: see prec.] to make very angry; fill with wrath; enrage —**in·cense'ment** *n.*

☆**incense cedar** a large, W N. American tree (*Libocedrus decurrens*) of the cypress family with reddish bark and flattened, scalelike leaves

in·cen·tive (in sen'tiv) *adj.* [ME. < LL. *incentivum* < neut. pp. of L. *incinere*, to sing < *in-*, in, on + *canere*, to sing: see CHANT] stimulating one to take action, work harder, etc.; encouraging; motivating —*n.* something that stimulates one to take action, work harder, etc.; stimulus; encouragement —*SYN.* see MOTIVE

in·cept (in sept') *vt.* [L. *inceptare*, to begin, freq. of *incipere*: see INCIPIENT] **1.** [Obs.] to begin or undertake **2.** to take in; receive; specif., to ingest [amoebas *incept* food particles] —*vi.* [Brit.] to receive a master's or doctor's degree at Cambridge University

incept. inceptive

in·cep·tion (in sep'shən) *n.* [L. *inceptio* < *inceptus*, pp. of *incipere*: see INCIPIENT] the act of beginning; start; commencement —*SYN.* see ORIGIN

in·cep·tive (-tiv) *adj.* [OFr. *inceptif* < LL. *inceptivus* < L. *inceptus*: see prec.] **1.** beginning; introductory; initial **2.** *Gram.* expressing the beginning of an action —*n.* an inceptive verb or form, as in Latin —**in·cep'tive·ly** *adv.*

in·cer·ti·tude (in sur'tə tood', -tyood') *n.* [Fr. < ML. *incertitudo*: see IN-² + CERTITUDE] **1.** an uncertain state of mind; doubt **2.** an uncertain state of affairs; insecurity

in·ces·sant (in ses'ənt) *adj.* [Early ModE. < LL. *incessans* < L. *in-*, not + *cessans*, prp. of *cessare*, to CEASE] never ceasing; continuing or being repeated without stopping or in a way that seems endless; constant —*SYN.* see CONTINUAL —**in·ces'san·cy, in·ces'sant·ness** *n.* —**in·ces'sant·ly** *adv.*

in·cest (in'sest) *n.* [ME. < L. *incestum*, unchastity, incest < neut. of *incestus*, unchaste < *in-*, not + *castus*, chaste] sexual intercourse between persons too closely related to marry legally

in·ces·tu·ous (in ses'choo wəs) *adj.* [L. *incestuosus*] **1.** guilty of incest **2.** of, or having the nature of, incest —**in·ces'tu·ous·ly** *adv.* —**in·ces'tu·ous·ness** *n.*

inch¹ (inch) *n.* [ME. *inche* < OE. *ynce* < L. *uncia*, twelfth part, inch, OUNCE] **1.** a measure of length equal to 1/12 foot (2.54 centimeters): symbol, " (e.g., 10"): abbrev. **in.** (*sing. & pl.*) **2.** a fall (of rain, snow, etc.) equal to the amount that would cover a surface to the depth of one inch **3.** a unit of pressure as measured by a barometer or manometer, equal to the pressure balanced by the weight of a one-inch column of liquid, usually mercury, in the instrument **4.** a very small amount, degree, or distance; trifle; bit —*vt., vi.* to move by inches or degrees; move very slowly —**every inch** in all respects; thoroughly —**inch by inch** gradually; slowly; by degrees: also **by inches** —**within an inch of** very close to; almost to —**within an inch of one's life** almost to one's death

inch² (inch) *n.* [ME. < Gael. *innis*, island] in Scotland and Ireland, an isolated piece of land, as a small island or hill

inch·meal (inch'mēl') *adv.* [INCH¹ + -MEAL] gradually; inch by inch: also **by inchmeal**

in·cho·ate (in kō'it) *adj.* [L. *inchoatus, incohatus*, pp. of *inchoare, incohare*, to begin, orig. rural term, "hitch up, harness" < *in-*, in + *cohum*, the strap from plow beam to yoke < IE. base *kagh-*, to hold, enclose, whence HEDGE] **1.** just begun; in the early stages; incipient; rudimentary **2.** not yet clearly or completely formed or organized; disordered **3.** *Law* not yet completed or made effective; pending —**in·cho'ate·ly** *adv.* —**in·cho'ate·ness** *n.*

in·cho·a·tion (in'kō ā'shən) *n.* [L. *incohatio*: see prec.] a beginning; early stage

in·cho·a·tive (in kō'ə tiv) *adj.* [LL. *incohativus*] **1.** [Rare] same as INCHOATE (sense 1) **2.** *Gram.* expressing the beginning of an action; inceptive, as, in English, through the use of the auxiliary *get* (Ex.: we got going early) —*n.* an inchoative verb or phrase

In·chon (in'chän') seaport in NW South Korea, on the Yellow Sea: pop. 465,000

☆**inch·worm** (inch'wurm') *n. same as* MEASURING WORM

in·ci·dence (in'si dəns) *n.* [ME. (North) < OFr. < LL. *incidentia*] **1.** the act, fact, or manner of falling upon or influencing **2.** the degree or range of occurrence or effect; extent of influence **3.** *Geom.* partial coincidence between two figures, as of a line and a point contained in it **4.** *Physics a)* the falling of a line, or a ray of light, projectile, etc. moving in a line, on a surface *b)* the direction of such falling See also ANGLE OF INCIDENCE

in·ci·dent (-dənt) *adj.* [ME. < OFr. < ML. < prp. of L. *incidere*, to fall upon < *in-*, on + *cadere*, to fall: see CASE¹] **1.** likely to happen as a result or concomitant; incidental (*to*) [the cares *incident* to parenthood] **2.** falling upon, striking, or affecting [*incident* rays] **3.** *Law* dependent upon or involved in something else —*n.* [ME. *incydente*] **1.** something that happens; happening; occurrence **2.** something that happens as a result of or in connection with something more important; minor event or episode, esp. one in a novel, play, etc. **3.** an apparently minor conflict, disturbance, etc., as between persons, states, etc., that may have serious results **4.** *Law* something incident to something else —*SYN.* see OCCURRENCE

in·ci·den·tal (in'si den't'l) *adj.* [ML. *incidentalis*] **1.** *a)* happening as a result of or in connection with something more important; casual [*incidental* benefits] *b)* likely to happen as a result or concomitant (with *to*) [troubles *incidental* to divorce] **2.** secondary or minor, but usually associated [*incidental* expenses] —*n.* **1.** something incidental **2.** [*pl.*] miscellaneous or minor items or expenses —*SYN.* see ACCIDENTAL

in·ci·den·tal·ly (-dent'l'ē, -den't'l ē) *adv.* **1.** in an incidental manner; as something less important but associated **2.** by the way: an expression used in introducing a new but related topic

incidental music music played in connection with the presentation of a play, motion picture, poem, etc. in order to heighten the mood or effect on the audience

in·cin·er·ate (in sin'ə rāt') *vt., vi.* -at'ed, -at'ing [< ML. *incineratus*, pp. of *incinerare*, to burn to ashes < L. *in*, in, to + *cinis* (gen. *cineris*), ashes < IE. *kenis* < base *ken-*, to scratch, rub, whence Gr. *konis*, dust, ashes] to burn to ashes; burn up; cremate —**in·cin'er·a'tion** *n.*

in·cin·er·a·tor (-rāt'ər) *n.* a person or thing that incinerates; esp., a furnace or other device for incinerating trash

in·cip·i·ent (in sip'ē ənt) *adj.* [L. *incipiens*, prp. of *incipere*, to begin, lit., take up < *in-*, in, on + *capere*, to take] in the first stage of existence; just beginning to exist or to come to notice [an *incipient* illness] —**in·cip'i·ence, in·cip'i·en·cy** *n.* —**in·cip'i·ent·ly** *adv.*

‡**in·ci·pit** (in'si pit) [L.] (here) begins: a word sometimes placed at the beginning of medieval manuscripts

in·cise (in sīz') *vt.* -cised', -cis'ing [Fr. *inciser* < L. *incisus*, pp. of *incidere*, to cut into < *in-*, into + *caedere*, to cut: see -CIDE] to cut into with a sharp tool; specif., to cut (designs, inscriptions, etc.) into (a surface); engrave; carve

in·cised (-sīzd') *adj.* **1.** *a)* cut into *b)* engraved or carved *c)* made by cutting into with a sharp tool **2.** having the edges deeply notched, as a leaf

in·ci·sion (-sizh'ən) *n.* [ME. < OFr. < L. *incisio*] **1.** the act or result of incising; cut; gash **2.** incisive quality **3.** a deep notch, as in the edge of a leaf **4.** *Surgery* a cut made into a tissue or organ

in·ci·sive (in sī'siv) *adj.* [ML. *incisivus* < L. *incisus*: see INCISE] **1.** cutting into **2.** sharp; keen; penetrating; acute [an *incisive* mind] **3.** of the incisors —**in·ci'sive·ly** *adv.* —**in·ci'sive·ness** *n.*

SYN.—**incisive** is applied to speech or writing that seems to penetrate directly to the heart of the matter, resulting in a clear and unambiguous statement [an *incisive* criticism]; **trenchant** implies clean-cut expression that results in sharply defined categories, differences, etc. [a *trenchant* analysis]; **cutting** implies incisive qualities but also connotes such harshness or sarcasm as to hurt the feelings [his *cutting* allusion to her inefficiency]; **biting** implies a caustic or stinging quality that makes a deep impression on the mind [his *biting* satire]

in·ci·sor (in sī'zər) *n.* [ModL. < L. *incisus* (see INCISE) + -OR] a cutting tooth; any of the front teeth between the canines in either jaw: in man there are eight incisors

in·cite (in sīt') *vt.* -cit'ed, -cit'ing [ME. *inciten* < OFr. *inciter* < L. *incitare* < *in-*, in, on + *citare*, to set in motion, urge: see CITE] to urge to action; stir up; rouse —**in·cite'ment, in·ci·ta·tion** (in'sī tā'shən, -si-) *n.* —**in·cit'er** *n.*

SYN.—**incite** implies an urging or stimulating to action, either in a favorable or unfavorable sense [*incited* to achievement by rivalry]; **instigate** always implies responsibility for initiating the action and usually connotes a bad or evil purpose [who *instigated* the assassination?]; **arouse**, in this connection, means little more than a bringing into being or action [it *aroused* my suspicions]; **foment** suggests continued incitement over an extended period of time [the unjust taxes *fomented* rebellion] —*ANT.* restrain, inhibit

in·ci·vil·i·ty (in'sə vil'ə tē) *n., pl.* -ties [Fr. *incivilité* < LL. *incivilitas* < L. *incivilis*, impolite: see IN-² & CIVIL] **1.** a lack of courtesy or politeness; rudeness **2.** a rude or discourteous act

incl. **1.** inclosure **2.** including **3.** inclusive

in·clem·ent (in klem'ənt) *adj.* [L. *inclemens*: see IN-² & CLEMENT] **1.** rough; severe; stormy [*inclement* weather] **2.** lacking mercy or leniency; harsh —**in·clem'en·cy** *n., pl.* -cies —**in·clem'ent·ly** *adv.*

in·clin·a·ble (in klīn'ə b'l) *adj.* **1.** *a)* having an inclination or tendency *b)* favorably disposed **2.** that can be inclined

in·cli·na·tion (in'klə nā'shən) *n.* [ME. < OFr. < L. *inclinatio* < pp. of *inclinare*, INCLINE] **1.** the act of bending, leaning, or sloping; esp., a bowing or nodding **2.** an inclined surface or plane; slope; incline; slant **3.** the extent or degree of incline from a horizontal or vertical position, course, etc. **4.** the difference in direction of two lines, planes, or surfaces as measured by the angle between them; specif., a property of a line in a plane, being the angle measured from the positive portion of the x-axis to the line in question **5.** *a)* a particular disposition or bent of mind; bias; tendency *b)* a liking or preference **6.** any action, practice, or thing, toward which one is inclined —**in'cli·na'tion·al** *adj.*

SYN.—**inclination** refers to a more or less vague mental disposition toward some action, practice, or thing [he had an *inclination* to refuse]; **leaning** suggests a general inclination toward something but implies only the direction of attraction and not the final choice [Dr. Green had always had a *leaning* toward the study of law]; **bent** and **propensity** imply a natural or inherent inclination, the latter also connoting an almost uncontrollable attraction [she has a *bent* for art, he has a *propensity* for getting into trouble]; **proclivity** usually suggests strong inclination as a result of habitual indulgence, usually toward something bad or wrong [a *proclivity* to falsehood]

in·cline (in klīn′; *for n., usually* in′klīn) *vi.* **-clined′, -clin′ing** [ME. *enclinen* < OFr. *encliner* < L. *inclinare* < *in-*, on, to + *clinare*, to lean < IE. base **klei-*, to bend, lean, whence Gr. *klinein*, OE. *hleonian*: cf. LEAN[1], LADDER] **1.** to deviate from a horizontal or vertical position, course, etc.; lean; slope; slant **2.** to bend or bow the body or head **3.** *a)* to have a particular disposition or bent of mind, will, etc. *b)* to have a tendency **4.** to have a preference or liking —*vt.* **1.** to cause to lean, slope, slant, etc.; bend **2.** to bend or bow (the body or head) **3.** to give a tendency to; make willing; dispose; influence —*n.* an inclined plane or surface; slope; grade; slant —**incline one's ear** to pay heed; listen willingly —**in·clin′er** *n.*

in·clined (in klīnd′) *adj.* **1.** having an inclination; specif., *a)* at or on a slant; sloping; leaning *b)* disposed; willing; tending **2.** forming an angle with another line, plane, or body

inclined plane a plane surface set at any angle other than a right angle against a horizontal surface

in·cli·nom·e·ter (in′klə näm′ə tər) *n.* [< INCLINE + -METER] **1.** *same as* DIP NEEDLE **2.** *same as* CLINOMETER **3.** an instrument that measures the inclination of an axis of an airplane or ship in relation to the horizontal

INCLINED PLANE

in·close (in klōz′) *vt.* **-closed′, -clos′ing** *same as* ENCLOSE
in·clo·sure (in klō′zhər) *n. same as* ENCLOSURE
in·clude (in klōōd′) *vt.* **-clud′ed, -clud′ing** [ME. *includen* < L. *includere* < *in-*, in + *claudere*, to shut, CLOSE[1]] **1.** to shut up or in; enclose **2.** to have as part of a whole; contain; comprise [the cost *includes* taxes] **3.** to consider as part of a whole; take into account; put in a total, category, etc. [to be *included* as a candidate] —**in·clud′a·ble, in·clud′i·ble** *adj.*
SYN.—include implies a containing as part of a whole; **comprise,** in discriminating use, means to consist of and takes as its object the various parts that make up the whole [his library *comprises* 2000 volumes and *includes* many first editions]; **comprehend** suggests that the object is contained within the total scope or range of the subject, sometimes by implication [the word "beauty" *comprehends* various concepts]; **embrace** stresses the variety of objects comprehended [he had *embraced* a number of hobbies]; **involve** implies inclusion of an object because of its connection with the subject as a consequence or antecedent [acceptance of the office *involves* responsibilities] —**ANT.** exclude
in·clud·ed (-id) *adj.* **1.** enclosed, contained, or involved **2.** with stamens and pistils wholly contained within the petals, sheath, etc.
in·clu·sion (in klōō′zhən) *n.* [L. *inclusio* < *inclusus,* pp. of *includere*] **1.** an including or being included **2.** something included; specif., *a)* a solid, liquid, or gaseous foreign substance encased in mineral or rock *b)* *Biol.* a separate body, as a grain of starch, within the protoplasm of a cell
inclusion body any of various small particles of foreign material occurring in body cells infected with a filterable virus
in·clu·sive (in klōō′siv) *adj.* [LL. *inclusivus* < L. *inclusus,* pp. of *includere*] **1.** including or tending to include; esp., taking everything into account; reckoning everything **2.** including the terms, limits, or extremes mentioned [ten days, from the third to the twelfth *inclusive*] —**inclusive of** including; taking into account —**in·clu′sive·ly** *adv.* —**in·clu′sive·ness** *n.*
in·co·er·ci·ble (in′kō ur′sə b'l) *adj.* that cannot be coerced
incog. incognito
in·cog·i·ta·ble (in käj′ə tə b'l) *adj.* [L. *incogitabilis*: see IN-[2] & COGITABLE] [Rare] unthinkable; inconceivable
in·cog·i·tant (-tənt) *adj.* [L. *incogitans* < *in-*, not + *cogitans,* prp. of *cogitare,* to COGITATE] unthinking; thoughtless
in·cog·ni·to (in′käg nēt′ō, in käg′ni tō′) *adv., adj.* [It. < L. *incognitus,* unknown < *in-*, not + *cognitus:* see COGNITION] with true identity unrevealed or disguised; under an assumed name, rank, etc. —*n., pl.* **-tos 1.** a person who is incognito **2.** *a)* the state of being incognito *b)* the disguise assumed —*SYN.* see PSEUDONYM —**in·cog·ni·ta** (-ə, -tə) *adj., n.fem., pl.* **-tas**
in·cog·ni·zant (in käg′ni zənt; *occas.* -kän′ə-) *adj.* not cognizant (*of*); unaware (*of*) —**in·cog′ni·zance** *n.*
in·co·her·ence (in′kō hir′əns) *n.* **1.** lack of coherence; the quality or state of being incoherent **2.** incoherent speech, thought, etc. Also **in′co·her′en·cy,** *pl.* **-cies**
in·co·her·ent (-ənt) *adj.* not coherent; specif., *a)* lacking cohesion; not sticking together *b)* not logically connected; disjointed; rambling *c)* characterized by incoherent speech, thought, etc. —**in′co·her′ent·ly** *adv.*
in·com·bus·ti·ble (in′kəm bus′tə b'l) *adj.* [ME. < ML. *incombustibilis*] not combustible; that cannot be burned; fireproof —*n.* an incombustible substance —**in′com·bus′ti·bil′i·ty** *n.*
in·come (in′kum) *n.* [ME.: see IN & COME] **1.** [Archaic] the act or an instance of coming in **2.** the money or other gain received, esp. in a given period, by an individual, corporation, etc. for labor or services or from property, investments, operations, etc.

income statement a statement that summarizes the various transactions of a business during a specified period, showing the net profit or loss: also **income account**
income tax a tax on net income or on that part of income which exceeds a certain amount
in·com·ing (in′kum′iŋ) *adj.* [ME. < *incomen,* to come in < OE. *incuman*] coming in or about to come in [the *incoming* tide, the *incoming* mayor] —*n.* **1.** an act or instance of coming in **2.** [*usually pl.*] income
in·com·men·su·ra·ble (in′kə men′shər ə b'l, -sər-) *adj.* [LL. *incommensurabilis:* see IN-[2] & COMMENSURABLE] **1.** that cannot be measured or compared by the same standard or measure; without a common standard of comparison **2.** not worthy of comparison [a statement *incommensurable* with truth] **3.** having no common divisor: said of two or more numbers or quantities —*n.* an incommensurable thing, quantity, etc. —**in′com·men′su·ra·bil′i·ty** *n.* —**in′com·men′su·ra·bly** *adv.*
in·com·men·su·rate (-it) *adj.* not commensurate; specif., *a)* not proportionate; not adequate [a supply *incommensurate* to the demand] *b)* *same as* INCOMMENSURABLE (sense 1) —**in′com·men′su·rate·ly** *adv.*
in·com·mode (in′kə mōd′) *vt.* **-mod′ed, -mod′ing** [Fr. *incommoder* < L. *incommodare* < *incommodus,* inconvenient < *in-*, not + *commodus,* convenient: see COMMODE] to inconvenience; put to some trouble; bother
in·com·mo·di·ous (-mō′dē əs) *adj.* [IN-[2] + COMMODIOUS] **1.** causing inconvenience; uncomfortable; troublesome **2.** inconveniently small, narrow, etc. —**in′com·mo′di·ous·ly** *adv.* —**in′com·mo′di·ous·ness** *n.*
in·com·mod·i·ty (in′kə mäd′ə tē) *n., pl.* **-ties** [ME. *incommodite* < OFr. *incommodité* < L. *incommoditas:* see INCOMMODE] inconvenience; discomfort
in·com·mu·ni·ca·ble (in′kə myōō′ni kə b'l) *adj.* [LL. *incommunicabilis*] that cannot be communicated or told —**in′com·mu′ni·ca·bil′i·ty** *n.* —**in′com·mu′ni·ca·bly** *adv.*
☆**in·com·mu·ni·ca·do** (in′kə myōō′nə kä′dō) *adj* [Sp. *incomunicado* < pp. of *incomunicar,* to isolate, cut off from communication < *in-* (< L. *in-,* IN-[2]) + *comunicar* < L. *communicare,* to COMMUNICATE] unable or not allowed to communicate with others [prisoners held *incommunicado*]
in·com·mu·ni·ca·tive (in′kə myōō′nə kāt′iv, -ni kə tiv) *adj.* not communicative; reserved; taciturn
in·com·mut·a·ble (in′kə myōōt′ə b'l) *adj.* [ME. < L. *incommutabilis:* see IN-[2] & COMMUTABLE] that cannot be changed or exchanged —**in′com·mut′a·bil′i·ty** *n.* —**in′com·mut′a·bly** *adv.*
in·com·pact (in′kəm pakt′) *adj.* not compact; loosely assembled; not solid
in·com·pa·ra·ble (in käm′pər ə b'l; *occas.* in′kəm par′ə b'l) *adj.* [ME. < OFr. < L. *incomparabilis*] that cannot be compared; specif., *a)* having no common basis of comparison; incommensurable *b)* beyond comparison; unequaled; matchless [*incomparable* skill] —**in·com′pa·ra·bil′i·ty** *n.* —**in·com′pa·ra·bly** *adv.*
in·com·pat·i·ble (in′kəm pat′ə b'l) *adj.* [ML. *incompatibilis*] **1.** not compatible; not able to exist in harmony or agreement; not going, or getting along, well together; incongruous, conflicting, discordant, etc. (often followed by *with*) **2.** that cannot be held at one time by the same person: said of positions, ranks, etc. **3.** *Logic a)* both not true at the same time: said of propositions *b)* not predicable of the same subject without contradiction: said of terms **4.** *Math.* logically contradictory: said of equations or other statements **5.** *Med., Pharmacy* not suitable for being mixed or used together: said of substances having an undesirable action on each other or, when mixed, on the body —*n.* an incompatible person or thing: *usually used in pl.* —**in′com·pat′i·bil′i·ty** *n., pl.* **-ties** —**in′com·pat′i·bly** *adv.*
in·com·pe·tent (in käm′pə tənt) *adj.* [Fr. *incompétent* < LL. *incompetens:* see IN-[2] & COMPETENT] **1.** without adequate ability, knowledge, fitness, etc.; failing to meet requirements; incapable; unskillful **2.** not legally qualified **3.** lacking strength and sufficient flexibility to transmit pressure, thus breaking or flowing under stress: said of rock structures —*n.* an incompetent person; esp., one who is mentally retarded —**in·com′pe·tence, in·com′pe·ten·cy** *n.* —**in·com′pe·tent·ly** *adv.*
in·com·plete (in′kəm plēt′) *adj.* [ME. *incompleet* < LL. *incompletus:* see IN-[2] & COMPLETE] **1.** lacking a part or parts; not whole; not full **2.** unfinished; not concluded **3.** not perfect; not thorough —**in′com·plete′ly** *adv.* —**in′com·plete′ness, in′com·ple′tion** *n.*
in·com·pli·ant (in′kəm plī′ənt) *adj.* not compliant; not yielding; not pliant —**in′com·pli′ance, in·com·pli′an·cy** *n.* —**in′com·pli′ant·ly** *adv.*
in·com·pre·hen·si·ble (in′käm pri hen′sə b'l, in käm′-) *adj.* [ME. < OFr. or L.: OFr. *incompréhensible* < L. *incomprehensibilis*] **1.** not comprehensible; that cannot be understood; obscure or unintelligible **2.** [Archaic] illimitable —**in′com·pre·hen′si·bil′i·ty** *n.* **in′com·pre·hen′si·bly** *adv.*

in·com·pre·hen·sion (-shən) *n.* lack of comprehension; inability to understand

in·com·pre·hen·sive (-siv) *adj.* **1.** not inclusive; including little **2.** not able to comprehend well; understanding little —**in'com·pre·hen'sive·ly** *adv.*

in·com·press·i·ble (in'kəm pres'ə b'l) *adj.* that cannot be compressed —**in'com·press'i·bil'i·ty** *n.*

in·com·put·a·ble (in'kəm pyōōt'ə b'l) *adj.* that cannot be computed —**in'com·put'a·bly** *adv.*

in·con·ceiv·a·ble (in'kən sē'və b'l) *adj.* that cannot be conceived; that cannot be thought of, understood, imagined, or believed —**in'con·ceiv'a·bil'i·ty, in'con·ceiv'a·ble·ness** *n.* —**in'con·ceiv'a·bly** *adv.*

in·con·clu·sive (in'kən klōō'siv) *adj.* not conclusive or final; not leading to a definite result —**in'con·clu'sive·ly** *adv.* —**in'con·clu'sive·ness** *n.*

in·con·den·sa·ble, in·con·den·si·ble (in'kən den'sə b'l) *adj.* that cannot be condensed —**in'con·den'sa·bil'i·ty, in'con·den'si·bil'i·ty** *n.*

in·con·dite (in kän'dit, -dīt) *adj.* [L. *inconditus < in-,* not + *conditus,* pp. of *condere,* to put together: see CONDITION] **1.** poorly constructed: said of literary works **2.** lacking finish or refinement; crude

in·con·form·i·ty (in'kən fôr'mə tē) *n.* [ML. *inconformitas*] lack of conformity; nonconformity

in·con·gru·ent (in kän'grōō wənt, in'kən grōō'ənt) *adj.* [L. *incongruens*] not congruent —**in·con'gru·ence** *n.* —**in·con'gru·ent·ly** *adv.*

in·con·gru·i·ty (in'kən grōō'ə tē) *n.* [ML. *incongruitas <* L. *incongruus*] **1.** the condition, quality, or fact of being incongruous; specif., *a)* lack of harmony or agreement *b)* lack of fitness or appropriateness **2.** *pl.* **-ties** something incongruous

in·con·gru·ous (in kän'grōō wəs) *adj.* [L. *incongruus*] not congruous; specif., *a)* lacking harmony or agreement; incompatible *b)* having inconsistent or inharmonious parts, elements, etc. *c)* not corresponding to what is right, proper, or reasonable; unsuitable; inappropriate —**in·con'gru·ous·ly** *adv.*

in·con·nu (in'kə nōō') *n., pl.* **-nus', -nu':** see PLURAL, II, D, 1 [Fr., an unknown, stranger] a large, oily, freshwater fish (*Stenodus mackenzii*) of NW N. America and NE Asia

in·con·sec·u·tive (in'kən sek'yə tiv) *adj.* not consecutive

in·con·se·quent (in kän'sə kwent', -kwənt) *adj.* [L. *inconsequens*] not consequent; specif., *a)* not following as a result *b)* not following as a logical inference or conclusion; irrelevant *c)* not proceeding in logical sequence; characterized by lack of logic —**in·con'se·quence'** *n.* —**in·con'se·quent·ly** *adv.*

in·con·se·quen·tial (in kän'sə kwen'shəl) *adj.* **1.** inconsequent; illogical **2.** of no consequence; unimportant; trivial —*n.* something inconsequential —**in·con'se·quen'ti·al'i·ty** (-shē al'ə tē) *n.* —**in·con'se·quen'tial·ly** *adv.*

in·con·sid·er·a·ble (in'kən sid'ər ə b'l) *adj.* not worth consideration; unimportant; trivial; small —**in'con·sid'er·a·ble·ness** *n.* —**in'con·sid'er·a·bly** *adv.*

in·con·sid·er·ate (-it) *adj.* [L. *inconsideratus*] **1.** [Now Rare] insufficiently considered; ill-advised **2.** without thought or consideration for others; thoughtless; heedless —**in'con·sid'er·ate·ly** *adv.* —**in'con·sid'er·ate·ness, in'con·sid'er·a'tion** (-ə rā'shən) *n.*

in·con·sis·ten·cy (in'kən sis'tən sē) *n.* **1.** the quality or state of being inconsistent **2.** *pl.* **-cies** an inconsistent act, remark, etc. Also **in'con·sis'tence**

in·con·sis·tent (-tənt) *adj.* not consistent; specif., *a)* not in agreement, harmony, or accord; incompatible [*acts inconsistent* with belief] *b)* not uniform; self-contradictory [*inconsistent* testimony] *c)* not always holding to the same principles or practice; changeable —**in'con·sis'tent·ly** *adv.*

inconsistent equations two or more equations impossible to satisfy by any one set of values for the variables (Ex.: *x + y* = 1 and *x + y* = 2)

in·con·sol·a·ble (in'kən sōl'ə b'l) *adj.* [L. *inconsolabilis*] that cannot be consoled; disconsolate; brokenhearted —**in'con·sol'a·bil'i·ty, in'con·sol'a·ble·ness** *n.* —**in'con·sol'a·bly** *adv.*

in·con·so·nant (in kän'sə nənt) *adj.* [L. *inconsonans*] not consonant; not in harmony or agreement; discordant —**in·con'so·nance** *n.* —**in·con'so·nant·ly** *adv.*

in·con·spic·u·ous (in'kən spik'yōō wəs) *adj.* [L. *inconspicuus*] not conspicuous; hard to see or perceive; attracting little attention; not striking —**in'con·spic'u·ous·ly** *adv.* —**in'con·spic'u·ous·ness** *n.*

in·con·stant (in kän'stənt) *adj.* [ME. < OFr. < L. *inconstans*] not constant; changeable; specif., *a)* not remaining firm in mind or purpose *b)* unsteady in affections or loyalties; fickle *c)* not uniform in nature, value, etc.; irregular; variable —**in·con'stan·cy** *n.* —**in·con'stant·ly** *adv.*

SYN.—**inconstant** implies an inherent tendency to change or a lack of steadfastness [an *inconstant* lover]; **fickle** suggests an even greater instability or readiness to change, especially in affection [spurned by a *fickle* public]; **capricious** implies an instability or irregularity that seems to be the product of whim or erratic impulse [a *capricious* climate]; **unstable,** in this connection, applies to one who is emotionally unsettled or variable [an *unstable* person laughs and cries easily] —**ANT. constant, reliable**

in·con·sum·a·ble (in'kən sōō'mə b'l, -syōō'-) *adj.* that cannot be consumed —**in'con·sum'a·bly** *adv.*

in·con·test·a·ble (in'kən tes'tə b'l) *adj.* [Fr. < *in-,* IN-² + *contestable < contester,* CONTEST] not to be contested; indisputable; unquestionable —**in'con·test'a·bil'i·ty** *n.* —**in'con·test'a·bly** *adv.*

in·con·ti·nent¹ (in känt''n ənt) *adj.* [ME. < OFr. < L. *incontinens:* see IN-² & CONTINENT] **1.** *a)* without self-restraint, esp. in regard to sexual activity *b)* unrestrained **2.** incapable of containing, holding, keeping, etc. [*incontinent* of ire] **3.** unable to restrain a natural discharge, as of urine, from the body —**in·con'ti·nence** *n.* —**in·con'ti·nent·ly** *adv.*

in·con·ti·nent² (in känt''n ənt) *adv.* [ME. < OFr. < L. *in continenti (tempore),* in continuous (time): see CONTINENT] [Archaic] immediately; without delay

in·con·trol·la·ble (in'kən trōl'ə b'l) *adj.* that cannot be controlled; uncontrollable

in·con·tro·vert·i·ble (in kän trə vur'tə b'l, in kän'-) *adj.* that cannot be controverted; not disputable or debatable; undeniable —**in'con·tro·vert'i·bil'i·ty** *n.* —**in'con·tro·vert'i·bly** *adv.*

in·con·ven·ience (in'kən vēn'yəns) *n.* [ME. < OFr. < LL. *inconvenientia*] **1.** the quality or state of being inconvenient; lack of comfort, ease, etc.; bother; trouble **2.** anything inconvenient Also **in'con·ven'ien·cy** (-yən sē), *pl.* **-cies** —*vt.* **-ienced, -ienc·ing** to cause inconvenience to; cause trouble or bother to; incommode

in·con·ven·ient (-yənt) *adj.* [ME. < OFr. < L. *inconveniens*] not convenient; specif., *a)* not favorable to one's comfort; difficult to do, use, or get to; causing trouble or bother; unhandy *b)* [Obs.] not appropriate —**in'con·ven'ient·ly** *adv.*

in·con·vert·i·ble (in'kən vur'tə b'l) *adj.* [LL.(Ec.) *inconvertibilis*] that cannot be converted; that cannot be changed or exchanged [paper money that is *inconvertible* into silver] —**in'con·vert'i·bil'i·ty** *n.* —**in'con·vert'i·bly** *adv.*

in·con·vin·ci·ble (in'kən vin'sə b'l) *adj.* [LL.(Ec.) *inconvincibilis*] that cannot be convinced

in·co·or·di·nate (in'kō ôr'd'n it) *adj.* not coordinate

in·co·or·di·na·tion (-ôr'd'n ā'shən) *n.* lack of coordination; esp., inability to adjust the harmonious action of muscles in producing complex movements

incorp., incor. incorporated

in·cor·po·ra·ble (in kôr'pər ə b'l) *adj.* that can be incorporated

in·cor·po·rate¹ (in kôr'pər it; *for v.* -pə rāt') *adj.* [ME. *incorporat <* LL. *incorporatus,* pp. of *incorporare:* see IN-¹ & CORPORATE] *same as* INCORPORATED —*vt.* **-rat'ed, -rat'ing** [ME. *incorporaten*] **1.** to combine or join with something already formed; make part of another thing; include; embody **2.** to bring together into a single whole; merge **3.** to admit into a corporation or association as a member **4.** to form (individuals or units) into a legally organized group that acts as one individual; form into a corporation **5.** to give substantial, material, or physical form to —*vi.* **1.** to unite or combine into a single whole; be combined or merged **2.** to form a corporation —**in·cor'po·ra'tion** *n.* —**in·cor'po·ra'tive** *adj.*

in·cor·po·rate² (in kôr'pər it) *adj.* [L. *incorporatus:* see IN-² & CORPORATE] [Archaic] *same as* INCORPOREAL

in·cor·po·rat·ed (in kôr'pə rāt'id) *adj.* **1.** combined into one body or unit; united **2.** organized as a legal corporation [an *incorporated* town]

in·cor·po·ra·tor (-ər) *n.* **1.** a person who incorporates **2.** any of the original members of a corporation, whose names appear in its charter

in·cor·po·re·al (in'kôr pôr'ē əl) *adj.* [L. *incorporeus* (see ff.) + -AL] **1.** not consisting of matter; without material body or substance **2.** of spirits or angels **3.** *Law* without physical existence in itself but belonging as a right to a material thing or property, as a patent, copyright, etc. —**in'cor·po're·al·ly** *adv.*

in·cor·po·re·i·ty (in'kôr pə rē'ə tē) *n.* [ML. *incorporeitas <* L. *incorporeus < in-,* IN-² + *corporeus,* CORPOREAL] **1.** the quality or state of being incorporeal **2.** *pl.* **-ties** an incorporeal entity or attribute

in·cor·rect (in'kə rekt') *adj.* [ME. < L. *incorrectus*] not correct; specif., *a)* improper *b)* untrue; inaccurate; wrong; faulty —**in'cor·rect'ly** *adv.* —**in'cor·rect'ness** *n.*

in·cor·ri·gi·ble (in kôr'i jə b'l, -kär'-) *adj.* [ME. *incorygibile <* OFr. < LL. *incorrigibilis*] not corrigible; that cannot be corrected, improved, or reformed, esp. because firmly established, as a habit, or because set in bad habits, as a child —*n.* an incorrigible person —**in·cor'ri·gi·bil'i·ty, in·cor'ri·gi·ble·ness** *n.* —**in·cor'ri·gi·bly** *adv.*

in·cor·rupt (in'kə rupt') *adj.* [ME. *incorrupte <* L. *incorruptus*] not corrupt; specif., *a)* [Obs.] uncontaminated; not rotten *b)* morally sound; not depraved, evil, impure, or perverted *c)* not taking bribes; upright; honest *d)* containing no errors, alterations, or foreign admixtures: said of texts, languages, etc.

in·cor·rupt·i·ble (-rup'tə b'l) *adj.* [ME. *incorruptyble <* LL.(Ec.) *incorruptibilis*] that cannot be corrupted, esp. morally —**in'cor·rupt'i·bil'i·ty** *n.* —**in'cor·rupt'i·bly** *adv.*

in·cor·rup·tion (in'kə rup'shən) *n.* [LL.(Ec.) *incorruptio*] [Archaic] the quality or state of being incorrupt or incorruptible

incr. 1. increase **2.** increased **3.** increasing

in·cras·sate (in kras'āt) *vt., vi.* **-sat·ed, -sat·ing** [< L. *incrassatus,* pp. of *incrassare,* to make thick < *in-,* in +

crassare, to thicken < *crassus*, thick: see CRASS] [Now Rare] to make or become thick or thicker, esp. in consistency —*adj. Biol.* thickened; swollen —**in·cras'sa·tion** *n.*

in·crease (in krēs'; *also, and for n. always,* in'krēs) *vi.* -**creased'**, -**creas'ing** [ME. *encresen* < OFr. *encreistre* < L. *increscere* < *in-*, in, on + *crescere*, to grow: see CRESCENT] 1. to become greater in size, amount, degree, etc.; grow 2. to become greater in numbers by producing offspring; multiply; propagate —*vt.* to cause to become greater in size, amount, degree, etc.; add to; augment —*n.* [ME. *encrese*] 1. an increasing or becoming increased; specif., *a)* growth, enlargement, etc. *b)* [Archaic] multiplication, as of offspring 2. the result or amount of an increasing [a population *increase* of 10%] —**on the increase** increasing —**in·creas'a·ble** *adj.* —**in·creas'er** *n.*
SYN.—**increase**, the general word in this list, means to make or become greater in size, amount, degree, etc. [to *increase* one's weight, one's power, debts, etc.]; **enlarge** specifically implies a making or becoming greater in size, volume, extent, etc. [to *enlarge* a house, a business, etc.]; **augment**, a more formal word, generally implies increase by addition, often of something that is already of a considerable size, amount, etc. [to *augment* one's income]; **multiply** suggests increase in number, specif. by procreation [rabbits *multiply* rapidly] —ANT. decrease, diminish, lessen

in·creas·ing·ly (in krēs'iŋ lē) *adv.* more and more; to an ever-increasing degree

in·cre·ate (in'krē āt', in'krē āt') *adj.* [ME. < LL. *increatus*] not created: said of divine beings or attributes

in·cred·i·ble (in kred'ə b'l) *adj.* [L. *incredibilis*] 1. not credible; unbelievable 2. seeming too unusual or improbable to be possible —**in·cred'i·bil'i·ty** *n.* —**in·cred'i·bly** *adv.*

in·cre·du·li·ty (in'krə dōō'lə tē, -dyōō'-) *n.* [ME. *incredulite* < OFr. *incrédulité* < L. *incredulitas*: see IN-² & CREDULITY] unwillingness or inability to believe; doubt; skepticism —SYN. see UNBELIEF

in·cred·u·lous (in krej'oo ləs) *adj.* [L. *incredulus*: see IN-² & CREDULOUS] 1. unwilling or unable to believe; doubting; skeptical 2. showing doubt or disbelief [an *incredulous* look] —**in·cred'u·lous·ly** *adv.*

in·cre·ment (in'krə mənt, iŋ'-) *n.* [ME. < L. *incrementum* < base of *increscere*, to INCREASE] 1. the fact of becoming greater or larger; increase; gain; growth 2. amount of increase [an annual *increment* of $300 in salary] 3. *Math.* the quantity, usually small, by which a variable increases or is increased: a negative increment results in a decrease —**in'cre·men'tal** (-men't'l) *adj.*

in·cres·cent (in kres'nt) *adj.* [L. *increscens*, prp. of *increscere*, to INCREASE] increasing; growing; waxing: said esp. of the moon

in·cre·tion (in krē'shən) *n.* [IN-¹ + (SE)CRETION] *same as* INTERNAL SECRETION

in·crim·i·nate (in krim'ə nāt') *vt.* -**nat'ed**, -**nat'ing** [< ML. *incriminatus*, pp. of *incriminare*: see IN-¹ & CRIMINATE] 1. to charge with a crime; accuse 2. to involve in, or make appear guilty of, a crime or fault —**in·crim'i·na'tion** *n.* —**in·crim'i·na·to·ry** (-nə tôr'ē) *adj.*

in·cross (in'krôs') *n.* an organism formed by close inbreeding within a stock —*vt. same as* INBREED (sense 2)

in·crust (in krust') *vt.* [OFr. *encrouster* < L. *incrustare*: see IN-¹ & CRUST] 1. to cover with or as with a crust, or hard coating 2. to decorate elaborately, esp. with gems —*vi.* to form a crust

in·crus·ta·tion (in'krus tā'shən, in krus'-) *n.* [LL. *incrustatio*] 1. an incrusting or being incrusted 2. a crust; hard layer or coating 3. an elaborate decorative coating, inlay, etc. 4. *Med.* a crust, scale, scab, etc.

in·cu·bate (in'kyə bāt', in'-) *vt.* -**bat'ed**, -**bat'ing** [< L. *incubatus*, pp. of *incubare*, to lie in or upon < *in-*, IN-¹ + *cubare*, to lie: see CUBE¹] 1. to sit on and hatch (eggs) 2. to keep (eggs, embryos, bacteria, etc.) in a favorable environment for hatching or developing 3. to cause to develop or take form, as by thought or planning —*vi.* 1. to go through the process of incubation 2. to develop or take form, esp. gradually

in·cu·ba·tion (in'kyə bā'shən, in'-) *n.* [L. *incubatio*] 1. an incubating or being incubated 2. the phase in the development of a disease between the infection and the first appearance of symptoms —**in'cu·ba'tion·al** *adj.* —**in'cu·ba'tive** *adj.*

in·cu·ba·tor (in'kyə bāt'ər, in'-) *n.* a person or thing that incubates; specif., *a)* an artificially heated container for hatching eggs *b)* a similar apparatus in which premature babies are kept for a period *c)* an apparatus for developing bacterial cultures

in·cu·bus (in'kyə bəs, in'-) *n., pl.* -**bus'es**, -**bi'** (-bī') [ME. < LL., nightmare (in ML., demon supposed to cause nightmares) < L. *incubare*: see INCUBATE] 1. a spirit or demon thought in medieval times to lie on sleeping persons, esp. on women for the purpose of sexual intercourse: see also SUCCUBUS 2. a nightmare 3. anything oppressive; burden

in·cu·des (in kyōō'dēz) *n. pl. of* INCUS

in·cul·cate (in kul'kāt, in'kul kāt') *vt.* -**cat'ed**, -**cat'ing** [< L. *inculcatus*, pp. of *inculcare*, to tread in, tread down <

in-, in, on + *calcare*, to trample underfoot < *calx*, heel] to impress upon the mind by frequent repetition or persistent urging —SYN. see INSTILL —**in'cul·ca'tion** *n.* —**in·cul'-ca·tor** *n.*

in·culpable (in kul'pə b'l) *adj.* [LL. *inculpabilis*] not culpable; free from blame or guilt

in·cul·pate (in kul'pāt, in'kul pāt') *vt.* -**pat·ed**, -**pat·ing** [< ML. *inculpatus*, pp. of *inculpare*, to blame < L. *in*, in, on + *culpa*, fault, blame] *same as* INCRIMINATE —**in'cul·pa'tion** *n.* —**in·cul'pa·to·ry** (-pə tôr'ē) *adj.*

in·cult (in kult') *adj.* [L. *incultus*: see IN-² & CULT] [Rare] 1. uncultivated: said of land 2. unrefined

in·cum·ben·cy (in kum'bən sē) *n., pl.* -**cies** 1. the quality or condition of being incumbent 2. something incumbent, as a duty or obligation 3. *a)* the holding and administering of a position; esp., the holding of a church benefice *b)* tenure of office

in·cum·bent (-bənt) *adj.* [L. *incumbens*, prp. of *incumbere*, to recline or rest on < *in-*, on + *cubare*, to lie down: see CUBE¹] 1. lying, resting, or pressing with its weight on something else 2. currently in office —*n.* the holder of an office or benefice —**incumbent on** (or **upon**) resting upon as a duty or obligation

in·cum·ber (in kum'bər) *vt. same as* ENCUMBER

in·cum·brance (-brəns) *n.* 1. *Law* a lien, charge, or claim attached to the real or personal property of another, as a mortgage 2. *same as* ENCUMBRANCE

in·cu·nab·u·la (in'kyoo nab'yə lə) *n.pl.sing.* -**u·lum** (-ləm) [L., neut. pl., swaddling clothes, cradle, origin < *in-*, in + *cunabula*, neut. pl., a cradle, dim. of *cunae*, fem. pl., a cradle: for IE. base see CITY] 1. the very first stages of anything; infancy; beginnings 2. early printed books; esp., books printed before 1500 —**in'cu·nab'u·lar** *adj.*

in·cur (in kur') *vt.* -**curred'**, -**cur'ring** [ME. *incurren* < L. *incurrere*, to run into or toward, attack < *in-*, in, toward + *currere*, to run: see CURRENT] 1. to come into or acquire (something undesirable) [to *incur* a debt] 2. to become subject to through one's own action; bring upon oneself [to *incur* someone's wrath]

in·cur·a·ble (in kyoor'ə b'l) *adj.* [ME. < OFr. < LL. *incurabilis*] not curable; that cannot be remedied or corrected —*n.* a person having an incurable disease or disorder —**in·cur'a·bil'i·ty** *n.* —**in·cur'a·bly** *adv.*

in·cu·ri·ous (in kyoor'ē əs) *adj.* [L. *incuriosus*] not curious; not eager to find out; uninterested; indifferent —SYN. see INDIFFERENT —**in·cu·ri·os·i·ty** (in'kyoor ē äs'ə tē), **in·cu'ri·ous·ness** *n.* —**in·cu'ri·ous·ly** *adv.*

in·cur·rence (in kur'əns) *n.* the act of incurring

in·cur·rent (-ənt) *adj.* [L. *incurrens*, prp. of *incurrere*: see INCUR] flowing in; esp., characterized by the flowing in of water [the *incurrent* canals of sponges]

in·cur·sion (in kur'zhən; *chiefly Brit.*, -shən) *n.* [ME. < L. *incursio* < *incurrere*: see INCUR] 1. a running in or coming in, esp. when undesired; inroad 2. a sudden, brief invasion or raid —**in·cur'sive** (-siv) *adj.*

in·cur·vate (in kur'vit; *also, and for v. always*, -vāt) *adj.* [L. *incurvatus*, pp. of *incurvare*: see INCURVE] bent or curving inward —*vt., vi.* -**vat·ed**, -**vat·ing** to bend or curve inward —**in·cur'va·tion**, **in·cur'va·ture** (-və chər) *n.*

in·curve (in kurv'; *for n.* in'kurv') *vt., vi.* -**curved'**, -**curv'-ing** [L. *incurvare* < *in-*, IN-¹ + *curvare*, to CURVE] to curve inward —*n.* 1. an act or instance of incurving ☆2. [IN-¹ + CURVE, *n.*] *Baseball same as* SCREWBALL

in·cus (iŋ'kəs) *n., pl.* **in·cu·des** (in kyoo'dēz) [ModL. < L., anvil < *incusus*: see ff.] the central one of the three small bones in the middle ear: it is shaped somewhat like an anvil

in·cuse (in kyooz', -kyoos') *adj.* [L. *incusus*, pp. of *in·cudere*, to forge with a hammer < *in-*, in, on + *cudere*, to strike, hit < IE. base *kāu-*, whence HEW] hammered or stamped in: said of the design on a coin, etc. —*n.* such a design

Ind (ind) [ME. & OFr. *Inde* < L. *India*] 1. [Poet.] India 2. [Obs.] the Indies

Ind. 1. India 2. Indian 3. Indiana 4. Indies

ind. 1. independent 2. index 3. indicative 4. indigo 5. indirect 6. industrial

in·da·ba (in dä'bä) *n.* [Zulu *in-daba*, subject, matter] a council or conference, esp. between or with South African natives

in·da·mine (in'də mēn', -min) *n.* [IND(IGO) + AMINE] any of a group of blue or blue-green organic dyes containing the NH group; esp., phenylene blue, NH:C₆H₄:N·C₆H₄·NH₂

in·debt·ed (in det'id) *adj.* [ME. *endetted*, after OFr. *endeté*, pp. of *endetter* < *en-* (L. *in-*) + *dette*: see DEBT] 1. in debt or under legal obligation to repay something received 2. owing gratitude, as for a favor received

in·debt·ed·ness (-nis) *n.* 1. the state of being indebted 2. the amount owed; all one's debts

in·de·cen·cy (in dē's'n sē) *n.* [L. *indecentia*] 1. the state or quality of being indecent; lack of modesty, taste, or propriety 2. *pl.* -**cies** an indecent act, statement, etc.

in·de·cent (-s'nt) *adj.* [< Fr. or L.: Fr. *indécent* < L. *indecens*] not decent; specif., *a)* not proper and fitting; unseemly; improper *b)* morally offensive; obscene —SYN. see IMPROPER —**in·de'cent·ly** *adv.*

in·de·cid·u·ous (in′di sij′ŏo wəs) *adj.* not deciduous

in·de·ci·pher·a·ble (in′di sī′fər ə b'l) *adj.* that cannot be deciphered; illegible —**in′de·ci′pher·a·bil′i·ty** *n.*

in·de·ci·sion (in′di sizh′ən) *n.* [Fr. *indécision* < *indécis*, undecided < ML. *indecisus*] lack of decision; inability to decide or a tendency to change the mind frequently; hesitation or vacillation

in·de·ci·sive (-sī′siv) *adj.* 1. not decisive; not conclusive or final 2. characterized by indecision; hesitating or vacillating —**in′de·ci′sive·ly** *adv.* —**in′de·ci′sive·ness** *n.*

in·de·clin·a·ble (in′di klīn′ə b'l) *adj.* not declinable; having no case inflections

in·de·com·pos·a·ble (in′dē kəm pō′zə b'l) *adj.* that cannot be decomposed

in·dec·o·rous (in dek′ər əs; *occas.* in′di kôr′əs) *adj.* [L. *indecorus*] not decorous; lacking decorum, propriety, good taste, etc.; unseemly —*SYN.* see IMPROPER —**in·dec′o·rous·ly** *adv.* —**in·dec′o·rous·ness** *n.*

in·de·co·rum (in′di kôr′əm) *n.* [L., neut. of *indecorus*] 1. lack of decorum; lack of propriety, good taste, etc. 2. indecorous conduct, speech, etc.

in·deed (in dēd′) *adv.* [ME. *indede*: see IN, *prep.* & DEED] certainly; truly; admittedly: often used for emphasis or confirmation [it is *indeed* warm] or, in questions, to seek confirmation [did he *indeed* tell you that?] —*interj.* an exclamation of surprise, doubt, sarcasm, etc.

indef. indefinite

in·de·fat·i·ga·ble (in′di fat′i gə b'l) *adj.* [MFr. *indéfatigable* < L. *indefatigabilis* < *in-*, not + *defatigare*, to tire out, weary: see DE- & FATIGUE] that cannot be tired out; not yielding to fatigue; untiring —**in′de·fat′i·ga·bil′i·ty** *n.* —**in′de·fat′i·ga·bly** *adv.*

in·de·fea·si·ble (in′di fē′zə b'l) *adj.* not defeasible; that cannot be undone or made void —**in′de·fea′si·bil′i·ty** *n.* —**in′de·fea′si·bly** *adv.*

in·de·fect·i·ble (in′di fek′tə b'l) *adj.* [IN-² + DEFECT + -IBLE] 1. not likely to fail, decay, become imperfect, etc. 2. without a fault or blemish; perfect —**in′de·fect′i·bil′i·ty** *n.* —**in′de·fect′i·bly** *adv.*

in·de·fen·si·ble (in′di fen′sə b'l) *adj.* 1. that cannot be defended or protected 2. that cannot be justified or excused; inexcusable —**in′de·fen′si·bil′i·ty** *n.* —**in′de·fen′si·bly** *adv.*

in·de·fin·a·ble (in′di fīn′ə b'l) *adj.* [ML. *indeffinabilis*] that cannot be defined —**in′de·fin′a·bil′i·ty** *n.* —**in′de·fin′a·bly** *adv.*

in·def·i·nite (in def′ə nit) *adj.* [L. *indefinitus*] not definite; specif., *a)* having no exact limits *b)* not precise or clear in meaning; vague *c)* not sharp or clear in outline; blurred; indistinct *d)* not sure or positive; uncertain *e)* Bot. of no fixed number, or too many to count: said of the stamens, etc. of certain flowers *f)* Gram. not limiting or specifying [*a* and *an* are *indefinite* articles, *any* is an *indefinite* pronoun] —**in·def′i·nite·ly** *adv.* —**in·def′i·nite·ness** *n.*

indefinite integral *Math.* any function which when differentiated yields a specified function

in·de·his·cent (in′di his′'nt) *adj.* not dehiscent; not opening at maturity to discharge its seeds [*indehiscent* fruits] —**in′de·his′cence** *n.*

in·del·i·ble (in del′ə b'l) *adj.* [L. *indelibilis* < *in-*, not + *delibilis*, perishable < *delere*, to destroy: see DELETE] 1. that cannot be erased, blotted out, eliminated, etc.; permanent; lasting 2. leaving an indelible mark [*indelible* ink] —**in·del′i·bil′i·ty** *n.* —**in·del′i·bly** *adv.*

in·del·i·ca·cy (in del′i kə sē) *n.* 1. the quality of being indelicate 2. *pl.* -**cies** something indelicate

in·del·i·cate (-kit) *adj.* not delicate; coarse; crude; rough; esp., lacking, or offensive to, propriety or modesty; gross —*SYN.* see COARSE, IMPROPER —**in·del′i·cate·ly** *adv.* —**in·del′i·cate·ness** *n.*

in·dem·ni·fi·ca·tion (in dem′nə fi kā′shən) *n.* 1. an indemnifying or being indemnified 2. something that indemnifies; recompense —*SYN.* see REPARATION

in·dem·ni·fy (in dem′nə fī′) *vt.* -**fied**′, -**fy**′**ing** [< L. *indemnis*, unhurt < *in-*, not + *damnum*, hurt, harm, damage (see DAMN) + -FY] 1. to protect against or keep free from loss, damage, etc.; insure 2. *a)* to repay for what has been lost or damaged; compensate for a loss, etc.; reimburse *b)* to redeem or make good (a loss) —*SYN.* see PAY —**in·dem′ni·fi′er** *n.*

in·dem·ni·ty (-tē) *n., pl.* -**ties** [Fr. *indemnité* < LL. *indemnitas* < L. *indemnis*: see prec.] 1. protection or insurance against loss, damage, etc. 2. legal exemption from penalties or liabilities incurred by one's actions 3. repayment or reimbursement for loss, damage, etc.; compensation

in·de·mon·stra·ble (in′di män′strə b'l; *chiefly Brit.*, in dem′ən-) *adj.* [LL. *indemonstrabilis*] not demonstrable; that cannot be proved

in·dene (in′dēn) *n.* [IND(OLE) + -ENE] a colorless, oily hydrocarbon, C₉H₈, obtained from coal tar and used in the manufacture of synthetic resins

in·dent¹ (in dent′; *for n., usually* in′dent) *vt.* [ME. *indenten* < OFr. *endenter* or ML. *indentare*, both < L. *in*, in + *dens*, TOOTH] 1. *a)* to cut toothlike points into (an edge or border); notch; also, to join by mating notches *b)* to make jagged or zigzag in outline 2. to sever (a written contract, etc.) along an irregular line, so that the parts may be identified 3. to write out (a contract, etc.) in duplicate 4. to bind (a servant or apprentice) by indenture 5. to space

(the first line of a paragraph, an entire paragraph, a column of figures, etc.) in from the regular margin 6. to order by an indent —*vi.* 1. to form or be marked by notches, points, or a jagged border 2. to space in from the margin; make an indentation 3. to draw up an order or requisition in duplicate or triplicate —*n.* 1. a notch or cut in an edge 2. an indenture, or written contract 3. *a)* a space in from the margin; indention *b)* an indented line, paragraph, etc. 4. *Business* an order form used in foreign trade and usually drawn up in duplicate or triplicate; specif., *a)* any order for foreign merchandise *b)* an export order to buy certain goods at stated terms

in·dent² (in dent′; *for n., usually* in′dent) *vt.* [IN-¹ + DENT¹] 1. to make a dent, or slight hollow, in 2. to apply (a mark, etc.) with pressure; impress; stamp in —*n.* a dent

in·den·ta·tion (in′den tā′shən) *n.* [INDENT¹ or INDENT² + -ATION] 1. an indenting or being indented 2. a result of indenting; specif., *a)* a notch, cut, or inlet on a coastline, etc. *b)* a dent, or slight hollow *c)* an indention; space in from a margin

in·den·tion (in den′shən) *n.* [INDENT¹ or INDENT² + -ION] 1. a spacing in from the margin 2. an empty or blank space left by this 3. *a)* a dent, or slight hollow *b)* the making of a dent

in·den·ture (in den′chər) *n.* [ME. *endenture* < OFr. & < ML. *indentura*: see INDENT¹: now used also as if < INDENT²] 1. [Now Rare] *same as* INDENTATION 2. a written contract or agreement: originally, it was in duplicate, the two copies having correspondingly notched edges for identification 3. [*often pl.*] a contract binding a person to work for another for a given length of time, as an apprentice to a master, or an immigrant to service in a colony 4. an official, authenticated list, inventory, etc. —*vt.* -**tured**, -**tur·ing** 1. to bind by indenture 2. [Archaic] *same as* INDENT²

In·de·pend·ence (in′di pen′dəns) [in honor of Andrew Jackson, in allusion to his *independence* of character] city in W Mo.: suburb of Kansas City: pop. 112,000

in·de·pend·ence (in′di pen′dəns) *n.* [ML. *independentia*] 1. the state or quality of being independent; freedom from the influence, control, or determination of another or others 2. [Now Rare] an income sufficient for a livelihood

☆**Independence Day** the Fourth of July, the anniversary of the adoption of the Declaration of Independence on July 4, 1776: a legal holiday in the U.S.

in·de·pend·en·cy (-dən sē) *n., pl.* -**cies** 1. *same as* INDEPENDENCE 2. [I-] the church polity of the Independents 3. an independent nation, province, etc.

in·de·pend·ent (-dənt) *adj.* [ML. *independens*: see IN-² & DEPENDENT] 1. free from the influence, control, or determination of another or others; specif., *a)* free from the rule of another; controlling or governing oneself; self-governing *b)* free from influence, persuasion, or bias; objective [an *independent* observer] *c)* relying only on oneself or one's own abilities, judgment, etc.; self-confident; self-reliant [*independent* in his thinking] *d)* not adhering to any political party or organization [an *independent* voter] *e)* not connected or related to another, to each other, or to a group; separate [an *independent* grocer] 2. *a)* not depending on another or others, esp. for financial support *b)* large enough to enable one to live without working: said of an income, a fortune, etc. *c)* having an independent income; not needing to work for a living 3. [I-] of or having to do with Independents —*n.* 1. a person who is independent in thinking, action, etc.; ☆specif. [*often* I-] a voter who is not an adherent of or committed to any political party 2. [I-] *a)* a person who believes that a local organized Christian church is or should be self-sufficient and not dependent on external ecclesiastical authority *b)* in England, a Congregationalist —**independent of** apart from; regardless of —**in′de·pend′ent·ly** *adv.*

independent clause *Gram. same as* MAIN CLAUSE

independent variable *Math.* a quantity whose value may be determined freely without reference to other variables

in-depth (in′depth′) *adj.* carefully worked out, detailed, profound, thorough, etc. [an in-depth study]

in·de·scrib·a·ble (in′di skrī′bə b'l) *adj.* that cannot be described; beyond the power of description —**in′de·scrib′a·bil′i·ty** *n.* —**in′de·scrib′a·bly** *adv.*

in·de·struct·i·ble (in′di struk′tə b'l) *adj.* not destructible; that cannot be destroyed —**in′de·struct′i·bil′i·ty** *n.* —**in′de·struct′i·bly** *adv.*

in·de·ter·mi·na·ble (in′di tʉr′mi nə b'l) *adj.* [LL. *indeterminabilis*] not determinable; specif., *a)* that cannot be decided or settled *b)* that cannot be definitely learned or ascertained —**in′de·ter′mi·na·ble·ness** *n.* —**in′de·ter′mi·na·bly** *adv.*

in·de·ter·mi·na·cy (-sē) *n.* the state or quality of being indeterminate

indeterminacy principle *same as* UNCERTAINTY PRINCIPLE

in·de·ter·mi·nate (-nit) *adj.* [LL. *indeterminatus*] 1. not determinate; specif., *a)* inexact in its limits, nature, etc.; indefinite; uncertain; vague [an *indeterminate* amount] *b)* not yet settled, concluded, or known; doubtful or inconclusive 2. *Bot. a) same as* RACEMOSE *b)* having the floral leaves separate and not overlapping in the bud —**in′de·ter′mi·nate·ly** *adv.* —**in′de·ter′mi·nate·ness** *n.*

indeterminate cleavage *Zool.* the division of an egg into cells, each of which has the potential of developing into a complete organism: cf. TWINNING

in·de·ter·mi·na·tion (in′di tʉr′mə nā′shən) n. [LL. *indeterminatio*] 1. lack of determination 2. the state or quality of being indeterminate

in·de·ter·min·ism (in′di tʉr′mə niz′m) n. [IN-² + DETERMINISM] 1. the doctrine that the will is free or to some degree free, or that one's actions and choices are not altogether determined by a sequence of causes independent of one's will 2. the quality or condition of being indeterminate —**in′de·ter′min·ist** n., adj. —**in′de·ter′min·is′tic** adj.

in·dex (in′deks) n., pl. **-dex·es, -di·ces′** (-də sēz′) [L., informer, that which points out < *indicare*, INDICATE] 1. short for INDEX FINGER 2. a pointer or indicator, as the needle on a dial 3. a thing that points out; indication; sign; representation [performance is an *index* of ability] 4. a) an alphabetical list of names, subjects, etc. together with the page numbers where they appear in the text, usually placed at the end of a book or other publication b) short for THUMB INDEX c) a list describing the items of a collection and where they may be found; catalog [a library *index*] 5. a) the relation or ratio of one amount or dimension to another, or the formula expressing this relation [cranial *index*] b) a number used to measure change in prices, wages, employment, production, etc.: it shows percentage variation from an arbitrary standard, usually 100, representing the status at some earlier time: in full **index number** 6. [I-] same as a) INDEX LIBRORUM PROHIBITORUM b) INDEX EXPURGATORIUS 7. [Obs.] a table of contents, preface, prologue, or statement of subject 8. Math. a) an exponent (sense 3) b) a subscript c) an integer or symbol placed above and to the left of a radical (Ex.: $\sqrt[3]{8}$, $\sqrt[n]{x}$) 9. *Printing* a sign (☞) calling special attention to certain information; fist —vt. 1. a) to make an index of or for b) to include in an index c) to supply with a thumb index 2. to be an index, or sign, of; indicate —**in′dex·er** n. —**in·dex′i·cal** adj.

‡Index Ex·pur·ga·to·ri·us (eks pʉr′gə tôr′ē əs) [ModL., expurgatory index] formerly, a list of books that the Roman Catholic Church forbade its members to read unless certain passages condemned as dangerous to faith, morality, etc. were deleted or changed

index finger the finger next to the thumb; forefinger

index fossil any fossil of wide geographic distribution and a short range in time, used to determine the age of strata in which it is found and of associated fossils

‡Index Lib·ro·rum Pro·hib·i·to·rum (li brôr′əm prō hib′ə tôr′əm) [ModL., index of prohibited books] formerly, a list of books that the Roman Catholic Church forbade its members to read (except by special permission) as dangerous to faith, morality, etc.

index of refraction the ratio of the sine of the angle of incidence to the sine of the angle of refraction for a ray of light crossing from one medium into another

In·di·a (in′dē ə) [L. < Gr. *India* < *Indos*, the Indus < OPer. *Hindu*, India: see HINDU] 1. region in S Asia, south of the Himalayas, including a large peninsula between the Arabian Sea & the Bay of Bengal: it contains India (sense 2), Pakistan, Nepal, & Bhutan 2. republic in C & S India: member of the Brit. Commonwealth: 1,177,000 sq. mi.; pop. 536,984,000 (see also JAMMU AND KASHMIR): cap. New Delhi 3. same as INDIAN EMPIRE

INDIA

India ink 1. a black pigment of lampblack mixed with a gelatinous substance and dried into cakes or sticks 2. a liquid ink made from this, used in writing, drawing, etc.

In·di·a·man (in′dē ə mən) n., pl. **-men** [see MAN, n. 10] formerly, a merchant ship sailing regularly between England and India; esp., a large ship of this sort belonging to the English East India Company

In·di·an (in′dē ən) adj. [LL. *Indianus* < L. *India*] 1. of India or the East Indies, their people, or culture 2. of any of the aboriginal peoples (**American Indians**) of N. America, S. America, or the West Indies, or of their cultures 3. of a type used or made by Indians 4. made of maize, or Indian corn —n. 1. a native of India or the East Indies 2. a member of any of the aboriginal peoples of N. America, S. America, or the West Indies: originally so named from the belief, held by early explorers, that these regions were part of Asia 3. popularly, any of the languages spoken by the American Indians

In·di·an·a (in′dē an′ə) [ModL., "land of the Indians"] Middle Western State of the U.S.: admitted 1816; 36,291 sq. mi.; pop. 5,194,000; cap. Indianapolis: abbrev. **Ind.**, **IN** —**In′di·an′i·an** adj., n.

☆Indian agent a U.S. or Canadian official representing the government in dealings with American Indians, as on reservations

In·di·an·ap·o·lis (in′dē ə nap′ə lis) [INDIANA + Gr. *polis*, city] capital of Indiana, in the C part of the State: pop. 745,000 (met. area 1,110,000)

☆Indian bread 1. bread made from cornmeal 2. same as TUCKAHOE

☆Indian club a club of wood, metal, etc. shaped like a tenpin and swung in the hand for exercise

☆Indian corn same as CORN¹ (sense 3)

Indian Desert same as THAR DESERT

Indian Empire formerly, territories in & near India, under Brit. control: dissolved in 1947

☆Indian file same as SINGLE FILE: it was the American Indians' way of walking a trail

☆Indian giver [Colloq.] a person who gives something and then asks for it back: from the belief that American Indians expected an equivalent in return when giving something

☆Indian hemp 1. a perennial American plant (*Apocynum cannabinum*) of the dogbane family, with a tough bark formerly used in ropemaking by the Indians and a medicinal root 2. same as HEMP (sense 1)

Indian licorice same as JEQUIRITY (sense 2)

Indian mallow a tall weed (*Abutilon theophrasti*) of the mallow family, with small, yellow flowers and large, heart-shaped, velvety leaves

☆Indian meal meal made from corn (maize); cornmeal

Indian Mutiny an uprising of native troops in India against British colonial policy (1857–58)

Indian Ocean ocean south of Asia, between Africa & Australia: 28,356,000 sq. mi.

☆Indian paintbrush any of a large genus (*Castilleja*) of plants of the figwort family, with brilliantly colored orange or red flowers and red or yellow upper leaves

☆Indian pipe a leafless, fleshy, white, saprophytic plant (*Monotropa uniflora*) of the heath family, native to the forests of the N Hemisphere: its unbranched, erect stalks each bear a single, nodding, white flower

☆Indian pudding a cornmeal pudding made with milk, molasses, etc.

Indian red 1. a yellowish-red ocher, orig. from an island in the Persian Gulf, used in early times as a pigment ☆2. an impure native iron oxide used by N. American Indians as a reddish war paint, and by early American painters

☆Indian sign a hex or jinx: chiefly in the phr. **to have** (or **put**) **the Indian sign on**

Indian States and Agencies formerly, a number of semidependent native states & agencies in India

☆Indian summer [INDIAN, adj., 2 + SUMMER²; reason for name obscure] 1. a period of mild, warm, hazy weather following the first frosts of late autumn 2. the final period, as of a person's life, regarded as being serene, tranquil, reminiscent, etc.

Indian Territory former territory (1834–90) of the U.S., reserved for the settlement of Indians: now a part of Oklahoma

☆Indian tobacco a poisonous annual plant (*Lobelia inflata*) of the bellflower family, common over the E U.S., with light blue flowers in slender spikes, and inflated pods

☆Indian turnip the jack-in-the-pulpit or its root

☆Indian wrestling 1. a contest in which two persons grasp each other's hand, with their elbows resting on a flat surface: the one who forces the other's arm down to the surface wins 2. a contest in which two persons, each placing a foot alongside the other's corresponding foot and grasping a hand of the other, try to force each other off balance

India paper [< INDIA in generalized sense "Far East"] 1. a thin, absorbent paper made in China and Japan from vegetable fiber, used in taking proofs from engraved plates 2. a thin, strong, opaque printing paper, used for some Bibles, dictionaries, etc.

India (or **india**) **rubber** crude, natural rubber obtained from latex; caoutchouc —**In′di·a-rub′ber** adj.

In·dic (in′dik) adj. [L. *Indicus* < Gr. *Indikos*] 1. of India 2. designating or of a subgroup of the Indo-Iranian branch of the Indo-European language family, including many of the languages spoken, or formerly spoken, in India, Pakistan, Ceylon, etc.

indic. 1. indicating 2. indicative 3. indicator

in·di·can (in′də kan) n. [< L. *indicum*, INDIGO + -AN] 1. a glucoside, $C_{14}H_{17}NO_6$, found in a natural state in the indigo plant: it is converted by water and oxygen into indigo 2. an indigo-forming substance, $C_8H_6NOSO_2OH$, the potassium salt of which is present in animal urine

in·di·cant (in′di kənt) adj. [L. *indicans*] indicating; pointing out —n. something that indicates or points out

in·di·cate (in′də kāt′) vt. **-cat′ed, -cat′ing** [< L. *indicatus*, pp. of *indicare*, to indicate, show < *in-*, in, to + *dicare*, to point out, declare: see DICTION] 1. to direct attention to; point to or point out; show 2. to be or give a sign, token, or indication of; signify; betoken [fever *indicates* illness] 3. to show the need for; call for; make necessary [a fabric

for which dry cleaning is *indicated*] **4.** to show or point out as a cause, nature, treatment, or outcome: said of a disease, etc. **5.** to express briefly or generally [to *indicate* guidelines for action]

in·di·ca·tion (in′də kā′shən) *n.* [L. *indicatio*] **1.** the act of indicating **2.** something that indicates, points out, or signifies; sign **3.** something that is indicated as necessary **4.** the amount or degree registered by an indicator

in·dic·a·tive (in dik′ə tiv) *adj.* [Fr. *indicatif* < L. *indicativus*] **1.** giving an indication, suggestion, or intimation; showing; signifying [a look *indicative* of joy]: also **in·dic·a·to·ry** (in dik′ə tôr′ē, in′dik-) **2.** designating or of that mood of a verb used to express an act, state, or occurrence as actual, or to ask a question of fact: it is the usual form of the verb: cf. SUBJUNCTIVE, IMPERATIVE —*n.* **1.** the indicative mood **2.** a verb in this mood —**in·dic′a·tive·ly** *adv.*

in·di·ca·tor (in′də kāt′ər) *n.* [LL.] **1.** a person or thing that indicates; specif., *a)* any device, as a gauge, dial, register, or pointer, that measures or records and visibly indicates *b)* an apparatus that diagrams the varying fluid pressure of an engine in operation **2.** any of various substances used to indicate the acidity or alkalinity of a solution, the beginning or end of a chemical reaction, the presence of certain substances, etc., by changes in color **3.** *Ecol.* a species of plant or animal, or a community, whose occurrence serves as evidence that certain environmental conditions exist

in·di·ces (in′də sēz′) *n. alt. pl. of* INDEX

in·di·ci·a (in dish′ē ə, -dish′ə) *n.pl. sing.* **in·di′ci·um** (-əm) [L., pl. of *indicium*, a notice, information < *index* (gen. *indicis*): see INDEX] characteristic marks or tokens; ☆esp., printed markings substituted on mail or on mailing labels for stamps or cancellations

in·dict (in dīt′) *vt.* [altered (after L.) < ME. *enditen*, to write down, accuse < Anglo-L. *indictare* < LL. *indictare* < L. *in*, against + *dictare*: see DICTATE] to charge with the commission of a crime; esp., to make formal accusation against on the basis of positive legal evidence: usually said of the action of a grand jury —*SYN.* see ACCUSE —**in·dict′er, in·dict′or** *n.*

in·dict·a·ble (-ə b'l) *adj.* [ME. *enditable*] **1.** that should be indicted **2.** making indictment possible, as an offense

in·dic·tion (in dik′shən) *n.* [ME. *indictioun* < L. *indictio* < pp. of *indicere*, to declare, announce < in-, in + *dicere*, to say, tell: see DICTION] **1.** the edict of a Roman emperor, orig. of Constantine, fixing the tax valuation of property for each fifteen-year period **2.** the tax so levied **3.** *a)* a cycle of fifteen years *b)* a particular year in such a cycle

in·dict·ment (in dīt′mənt) *n.* [ME. & Anglo-Fr. *enditement*] **1.** an indicting or being indicted **2.** a charge; accusation; specif., a formal written accusation charging one or more persons with the commission of a crime, presented by a grand jury to the court when the jury has found, after examining the evidence presented, that there is a valid case

In·dies (in′dēz) **1.** *same as a)* EAST INDIES *b)* WEST INDIES **2.** formerly, SE Asia & the Malay Archipelago

in·dif·fer·ence (in dif′ər əns, -dif′rəns) *n.* [Fr. < L. *indifferentia*] the quality, state, or fact of being indifferent; specif., *a)* lack of concern, interest, or feeling; apathy *b)* lack of importance, meaning, or worth Also [Archaic] **in·dif′fer·en·cy**

in·dif·fer·ent (-ənt, -rənt) *adj.* [ME. < OFr. < L. *indifferens*: see IN-² & DIFFERENT] **1.** having or showing no partiality, bias, or preference; neutral **2.** having or showing no interest, concern, or feeling; uninterested, apathetic, or unmoved **3.** of no consequence or importance; immaterial **4.** not particularly good or bad, large or small, right or wrong, etc.; fair, average, etc. **5.** not really good; rather poor or bad **6.** neutral in quality, as a chemical, magnet, etc.; inactive: chiefly in scientific use **7.** capable of developing in various ways, as the cells of an embryo that are not yet specialized; undifferentiated —**in·dif′fer·ent·ly** *adv.*

SYN.—**indifferent** implies either apathy or neutrality, esp. with reference to choice [to remain *indifferent* in a dispute]; **unconcerned** implies a lack of concern, solicitude, or anxiety, as because of callousness, ingenuousness, etc. [to remain *unconcerned* in a time of danger]; **incurious** suggests a lack of interest or curiosity [*incurious* about the details]; **detached** implies an impartiality or aloofness resulting from a lack of emotional involvement in a situation [he viewed the struggle with *detached* interest]; **disinterested** strictly implies a commendable impartiality resulting from a lack of selfish motive or desire for personal gain [a *disinterested* journalist], but it is now often used colloquially to mean not interested, or indifferent

in·dif·fer·ent·ism (-iz′m) *n.* the state of being indifferent; esp., *a)* systematic indifference to religion *b)* the belief that all religions have equal validity —**in·dif′fer·ent·ist** *n.*

in·di·gence (in′di jəns) *n.* [ME. < OFr. < L. *indigentia*] the condition of being indigent: also **in′di·gen·cy** —*SYN.* see POVERTY

in·di·gene (-jēn′) *n.* [Fr. *indigène* < L. *indigena* < OL. *indu* (L. *in*), in + *gignere*, to be born: see GENUS] a native animal or plant: also **in′di·gen** (-jən)

in·dig·e·nous (in dij′ə nəs) *adj.* [LL. *indigenus* < L. *indigena*: see prec.] **1.** existing, growing, or produced naturally in a region or country; belonging (*to*) as a nature **2.** innate; inherent; inborn —*SYN.* see NATIVE —**in·dig′e·nous·ly** *adv.* —**in·dig′e·nous·ness** *n.*

in·di·gent (in′di jənt) *adj.* [ME. *indygent* < OFr. < L. *indigens*, prp. of *indigere*, to be in need < OL. *indu* (L. *in*), in + *egere*, to need < IE. base *eg-*, lack, whence ON. *ekla*] **1.** in poverty; poor; needy; destitute **2.** [Archaic] lacking; destitute (*of*) —*n.* an indigent person —*SYN.* see POOR —**in′di·gent·ly** *adv.*

in·di·gest·ed (in′di jes′tid, -dī-) *adj.* [IN-² + DIGESTED] **1.** not well considered or thought out **2.** confused; chaotic **3.** not digested; undigested

in·di·gest·i·ble (-jes′tə b'l) *adj.* [L. *indigestibilis*] that cannot be digested; not easily digested —**in′di·gest′i·bil′i·ty** *n.*

in·di·ges·tion (-jes′chən, -jesh′-) *n.* [Fr. < LL. *indigestio*] **1.** inability to digest, or difficulty in digesting, food; dyspepsia **2.** the discomfort caused by this

in·di·ges·tive (-jes′tiv) *adj.* having or characterized by indigestion

in·dign (in dīn′) *adj.* [Fr. *indigne* < L. *indignus* < in-, not + *dignus*, worthy: see DIGNITY] [Obs. or Poet.] **1.** undeserving; unworthy **2.** disgraceful

in·dig·nant (in dig′nənt) *adj.* [L. *indignans*, prp. of *indignari*, to consider as unworthy or improper, be displeased at < in-, not + *dignari*, to deem worthy < *dignus*, worthy: see DIGNITY] feeling or expressing anger or scorn, esp. at unjust, mean, or ungrateful action or treatment —**in·dig′nant·ly** *adv.*

in·dig·na·tion (in′dig nā′shən) *n.* [ME. *indignacion* < OFr. < L. *indignatio* < pp. of *indignari*: see prec.] anger or scorn resulting from injustice, ingratitude, or meanness; righteous anger —*SYN.* see ANGER

in·dig·ni·ty (in dig′nə tē) *n., pl.* -ties [L. *indignitas*, unworthiness, vileness: see IN-² & DIGNITY] **1.** something that humiliates, insults, or injures the dignity or self-respect; affront **2.** [Obs.] *a)* unworthiness or disgrace *b)* indignation

in·di·go (in′di gō′) *n., pl.* -gos′, -goes′ [Sp. < L. *indicum* < Gr. *indikon* (*pharmakon*), lit., Indian (dye) < *Indikos*, Indian < *India*, INDIA] **1.** a blue dye obtained from certain plants, esp. a plant (*Indigofera tinctoria*) native to India, or made synthetically, usually from aniline **2.** any of a genus (*Indigofera*) of plants of the legume family that yield indigo **3.** a deep violet-blue, designated by Newton as one of the seven prismatic or primary colors —*adj.* of this color

indigo blue 1. *same as* INDIGOTIN **2.** *same as* INDIGO (sense 3) —**in′di·go-blue′** *adj.*

☆**indigo bunting** a small finch (*Passerina cyanea*) native to the E U.S.: the male is indigo-blue, the female brown: also **indigo bird**

in·di·goid (in′də goid′) *adj.* [INDIG(O) + -OID] of a class of dyes that produce a color resembling indigo and contain the chromophoric group -C:O·C:C-C:O- —*n.* a dye of this class

☆**indigo snake 1.** a large, harmless, dark-blue snake (*Drymarchon corais couperi*), occurring in lowlands from S. Carolina to Texas **2.** *same as* BULL SNAKE (sense 1)

in·dig·o·tin (in dig′ə tin, in′di gō′tin) *n.* [INDIGO- + -*t* + -IN¹] a dark-blue powder, $C_{16}H_{10}N_2O_2$, with a coppery luster, the coloring matter and chief ingredient in indigo (the dye)

in·di·rect (in′di rekt′, -dī-) *adj.* [ME. < ML. *indirectus*] not direct; specif., *a)* not straight; deviating; roundabout *b)* not straight to the point, or to the person or thing aimed at [an *indirect* reply] *c)* not straightforward; not fair and open; dishonest [*indirect* dealing] *d)* not immediate; secondary [an *indirect* result] —**in′di·rect′ly** *adv.* —**in′di·rect′ness** *n.*

indirect discourse statement of what a person said, without quoting his exact words (Ex.: she said that she could not go)

in·di·rec·tion (-rek′shən) *n.* [< INDIRECT, after DIRECTION] **1.** roundabout act, procedure, or means **2.** deceit; dishonesty **3.** lack of direction or purpose

indirect lighting lighting reflected, as from a ceiling, or diffused so as to provide an even illumination without glare or shadows

indirect object the word or words denoting the person or thing indirectly affected by the action of the verb: it generally names the person or thing to which something is given or for which something is done (Ex.: *him* in "give *him* the ball," "do *him* a favor")

indirect tax a tax on certain manufactured goods, imports, etc. that is paid indirectly by the consumer because it is included in the price

in·dis·cern·i·ble (in′di sur′nə b'l, -zur′-) *adj.* [LL. *indiscernibilis*] that cannot be discerned; imperceptible —**in′dis·cern′i·bly** *adv.*

in·dis·ci·pline (in dis′ə plin) *n.* lack of discipline

in·dis·creet (in′dis krēt′) *adj.* [ME. *indiscrete* < L. *indiscretus*, unseparated (in LL. & ML., careless, indiscreet): see IN-² & DISCREET] not discreet; lacking prudence, as in speech or action; unwise —**in′dis·creet′ly** *adv.* —**in′dis·creet′ness** *n.*

in·dis·crete (in′dis krēt′) *adj.* [L. *indiscretus*: see prec.] not discrete; not separated in distinct parts —**in′dis·crete′ly** *adv.* —**in′dis·crete′ness** *n.*

in·dis·cre·tion (in′dis kresh′ən) *n.* [ME. *indiscrecyone* < OFr. *indiscrétion* < LL. *indiscretio*] **1.** lack of discretion, or good judgment; imprudence **2.** an indiscreet act or remark

in·dis·crim·i·nate (in'dis krim'ə nit) *adj.* 1. not based on careful selection or a discerning taste; confused, random, or promiscuous 2. not discriminating; not making careful choices or distinctions —**in'dis·crim'i·nate·ly** *adv.*

in·dis·crim·i·na·tion (-krim'ə nā'shən) *n.* the condition of being indiscriminate; lack of discrimination —**in'dis·crim'i·na'tive** *adj.*

in·dis·pen·sa·ble (in'dis pen'sə b'l) *adj.* 1. that cannot be dispensed with or neglected 2. absolutely necessary or required —*n.* an indispensable person or thing —*SYN.* see ESSENTIAL —**in'dis·pen'sa·bil'i·ty** *n.* —**in'dis·pen'sa·bly** *adv.*

in·dis·pose (in'dis pōz') *vt.* -posed', -pos'ing [prob. back-formation < ff.] 1. to make unfit or unable; disqualify 2. to make unwilling or disinclined 3. to make slightly ill

in·dis·posed (-pōzd') *adj.* [ME. *indisposid* < *in-*, IN-[2] + pp. of *disposen*, DISPOSE] 1. slightly ill 2. unwilling; disinclined —*SYN.* see SICK[1]

in·dis·po·si·tion (in'dis pə zish'ən) *n.* the condition of being indisposed; specif., *a)* a slight illness *b)* unwillingness; disinclination

in·dis·pu·ta·ble (in'dis pyōōt'ə b'l, in dis'pyōō tə b'l) *adj.* [LL. *indisputabilis*] that cannot be disputed or doubted; unquestionable —**in'dis·pu'ta·bil'i·ty** *n.* —**in'dis·pu'ta·bly** *adv.*

in·dis·sol·u·ble (in'di säl'yoo b'l) *adj.* [L. *indissolubilis*] that cannot be dissolved, decomposed, broken, or destroyed; firm, stable, lasting, permanent, etc. —**in'dis·sol'u·bil'i·ty** *n.* —**in'dis·sol'u·bly** *adv.*

in·dis·tinct (in'dis tiŋkt') *adj.* [L. *indistinctus*] not distinct; specif., *a)* not seen, heard, or perceived clearly; faint; dim; obscure *b)* not separate or separable; not clearly marked off; not plainly defined —**in'dis·tinct'ly** *adv.* —**in'dis·tinct'ness** *n.*

in·dis·tinc·tive (-tiŋk'tiv) *adj.* 1. not distinctive; lacking distinction 2. making no distinction; incapable of distinguishing —**in'dis·tinc'tive·ly** *adv.*

in·dis·tin·guish·a·ble (-tiŋ'gwish ə b'l) *adj.* 1. that cannot be distinguished as being different or separate 2. that cannot be discerned or recognized; imperceptible —**in'dis·tin'guish·a·bly** *adv.*

in·dite (in dīt') *vt.* **dit'ed, dit'ing** [ME. *enditen* < OFr. *enditer* < LL. **indictare:* see INDICT] 1. [Archaic] to express or describe in prose or verse 2. to put in writing; compose and write 3. [Obs.] to dictate —**in·dite'ment** *n.* —**in·dit'er** *n.*

in·di·um (in'dē əm) *n.* [ModL. < L. *indicum*, INDIGO + -IUM: from the two indigo lines in its spectrum] a rare metallic chemical element, soft, ductile, and silver-white, occurring in some zinc ores: symbol, In; at. wt., 114.82; at. no., 49; sp. gr., 7.30; melt. pt., 156.6°C; boil. pt., 2000°C

in·di·vert·i·ble (in'di vurt'ə b'l) *adj.* that cannot be diverted or turned aside —**in'di·vert'i·bly** *adv.*

in·di·vid·u·al (in'di vij'oo wəl, -vij'ol) *adj.* [ML. *individualis* < L. *individuus* (< *in-*, IN-[2] + *dividuus*, divisible < *dividere*, to DIVIDE) + -AL] 1. orig., not divisible; not separable 2. existing as a single, separate thing or being; single; separate; particular 3. of, for, or by a single person or thing 4. relating to or characteristic of a single person or thing 5. distinguished from others by special characteristics; of a unique or striking character [an *individual* style] —*n.* 1. a single thing, being, or organism, esp. when regarded as a member of a class, species, group, etc. 2. a person —*SYN.* see CHARACTERISTIC, SINGLE

in·di·vid·u·al·ism (-iz'm) *n.* [Fr. *individualisme*] 1. individual character; individuality 2. an individual peculiarity 3. the doctrine that individual freedom in economic enterprise should not be restricted by governmental or social regulation; laissez-faire 4. the doctrine that the state exists for the individual and not the individual for the state 5. the doctrine that self-interest is the proper goal of all human actions; egoism 6. *a)* action based on any of these doctrines *b)* the leading of one's life in one's own way without conforming to prevailing patterns —**in'di·vid'u·al·ist** *n., adj.* —**in'di·vid'u·al·is'tic** *adj.*

in·di·vid·u·al·i·ty (in'di vij'oo wal'ə tē) *n., pl.* -ties [ML. *individualitas*] 1. *a)* the sum of the characteristics or qualities that set one person or thing apart from others; individual character *b)* personal identity; personality 2. the condition of existing as an individual; separate existence; oneness 3. a single person or thing; individual 4. [Obs.] indivisibility

in·di·vid·u·al·ize (-vij'oo wə līz', -vij'oo līz') *vt.* -ized', -iz'ing 1. to make individual; mark as different from other persons or things 2. to suit to the use, taste, requirements, etc. of a particular individual 3. to consider individually; specify; particularize —**in'di·vid'u·al·i·za'tion** *n.*

in·di·vid·u·al·ly (-vij'oo wəl ē, -vij'əl ē) *adv.* 1. as an individual or individuals rather than as a group; one at a time; separately; singly 2. as an individual with special characteristics; personally 3. in a way showing individual characteristics; distinctively

in·di·vid·u·ate (-vij'oo wāt') *vt.* -at'ed, -at'ing [< ML. *individuatus*, pp. of *individuare*: see INDIVIDUAL] 1. to make individual or distinct; specif., to

differentiate from others of the same species or kind 2. to form into an individual; develop as a separate organic unit —**in'di·vid'u·a'tion** *n.*

in·di·vis·i·ble (in'di viz'ə b'l) *adj.* [ME. *indyvysible* < LL. *indivisibilis:* see IN-[2] & DIVISIBLE] 1. that cannot be divided 2. *Math.* that cannot be divided without leaving a remainder —*n.* anything indivisible —**in'di·vis'i·bil'i·ty** *n.* —**in'di·vis'i·bly** *adv.*

In·do- (in'dō) [Gr. < *Indos:* see INDIA] *a combining form meaning:* 1. of India, of Indian (Hindu) stock 2. of India and

In·do-Ar·y·an (in'dō ar'ē ən, -er'-; -yən) *adj.* [prec. + ARYAN] 1. of the Indo-Aryans 2. *same as* INDIC (sense 2) —*n.* a native of India who speaks an Indic language The term is now seldom used

In·do·chi·na (in'dō chī'nə) 1. large peninsula south of China, including Burma, Thailand, Indochina (sense 2), & Malaya 2. E part of this peninsula, formerly under Fr. control, consisting of Laos, Cambodia, & Vietnam Also sp. **Indo-China, Indo China**

In·do·chi·nese, In·do-Chi·nese (-chī nēz') *adj.* 1. of Indochina, its Mongoloid people, their language, or their culture 2. *same as* SINO-TIBETAN: term now seldom used —*n., pl.* -nese' a native or inhabitant of Indochina

INDOCHINA

in·doc·ile (in däs'') *adj.* [Fr. < L. *indocilis*] not docile; not easy to teach or discipline —**in·do·cil·i·ty** (in'dä sil'ə tē, -dō-) *n.*

in·doc·tri·nate (in däk'trə nāt') *vt.* -nat'ed, -nat'ing [prob. (after ML. *doctrinatus*, pp. of *doctrinare*, to instruct < L. *doctrina*) < ME. *endoctrinen* < OFr. *endoctriner:* see IN-[1] & DOCTRINE] 1. to instruct in, or imbue with, doctrines, theories, or beliefs, as of a sect 2. to instruct; teach —**in·doc'tri·na'tion** *n.* —**in·doc'tri·na'tor** *n.*

In·do-Eu·ro·pe·an (in'dō yoor'ə pē'ən) *adj.* designating or of a family of languages that includes most of those spoken in Europe and many of those spoken in southwestern Asia and India —*n.* 1. the Indo-European family of languages: its principal branches are Indo-Iranian, Armenian, Tocharian, Greek, Albanian, Italic, Celtic, Germanic, and Balto-Slavic 2. the hypothetical language, reconstructed by modern linguists, from which these languages are thought to have descended Abbrev. IE., I.E.

In·do-Ger·man·ic (-jər man'ik) *adj., n.* [transl. of G. *Indogermanisch*] *same as* INDO-EUROPEAN: term now chiefly used by German-trained scholars

In·do-Hit·tite (-hit'īt) *n.* 1. according to a recent theory, the language family comprising the Indo-European and Anatolian languages 2. the hypothetical parent language from which the Indo-European and Hittite languages descended: most scholars now believe Hittite to be a branch of Indo-European

In·do-I·ra·ni·an (-i rā'nē ən) *adj.* designating or of a subfamily of the Indo-European language family that includes the Indic and Iranian branches —*n.* the hypothetical parent language from which all Indic and Iranian languages have descended

in·dole (in'dōl) *n.* [< INDIGO + PHENOL] a white, crystalline compound, C_8H_7N, obtained from indigo and other sources and formed as a product of the intestinal putrefaction of proteins: it is used in perfumery, as a reagent, etc.

in·dole·a·ce·tic acid (in'dōl ə sēt'ik) a plant hormone, $C_{10}H_9NO_2$, that promotes the growth of plants and roots

in·dole·bu·tyr·ic acid (-byoo tir'ik) a plant hormone, $C_{12}H_{13}NO_2$, that promotes the growth of roots

in·do·lent (in'də lənt) *adj.* [< LL. *indolens* < L. *in-*, not + *dolens*, prp. of *dolere*, to feel pain: see DOLEFUL] 1. disliking or avoiding work; idle; lazy 2. *Med.* *a)* causing little or no pain [an *indolent* cyst] *b)* slow to heal [an *indolent* ulcer] —**in'do·lence** *n.* —**in'do·lent·ly** *adv.*

in·dom·i·ta·ble (in däm'it ə b'l) *adj.* [LL. *indomitabilis* < L. *indomitus*, untamed, ungoverned < *in-*, not + *domitus*, pp. of *domitare*, to tame, intens. < *domare*, to TAME] not easily discouraged, defeated, or subdued; unyielding; unconquerable —**in·dom'i·ta·bil'i·ty, in·dom'i·ta·ble·ness** *n.* —**in·dom'i·ta·bly** *adv.*

In·do·ne·sia (in'də nē'zhə, -shə) republic in the Malay Archipelago, consisting of Java, Sumatra, most of Borneo, West Irian, Celebes, & many smaller nearby islands: formerly, until 1945, the Netherlands Indies: 736,510 sq. mi.; pop. 113,721,000; cap. Jakarta

In·do·ne·sian (-zhən, -shən) *adj.* 1. of Indonesia, its people, etc. 2. designating or of a group of some two hun-

dred Malayo-Polynesian languages spoken in Indonesia, the Philippines, Java, etc., including Malay, Tagalog, Javanese, etc. —*n.* **1.** a member of a light-brown people of Indonesia, the Philippines, Java, etc., apparently of mixed Polynesian and Mongoloid stock **2.** an inhabitant of Indonesia **3.** the Indonesian languages **4.** the official Malay language of Indonesia: in full, **Bahasa Indonesia**

in·door (in′dôr′) *adj.* [for earlier *within-door*] **1.** of the inside of a house or building **2.** living, belonging, or carried on within a house or building

☆**indoor baseball** the game of softball, adapted for playing indoors

in·doors (in′dôrz′) *adv.* [< *within doors*] in or into a house or other building

in·do·phe·nol (in′dō fē′nōl, -nôl) *n.* [IND(IG)O + PHENOL] any of a series of synthetic blue dyes derived from the oxidation of mixtures of phenols and diamines, used for dyeing wool and cotton

In·dore (in dôr′) **1.** city in Madhya Pradesh, C India: pop. 395,000 **2.** former state of C India

in·dorse (in dôrs′) *vt.* **-dorsed′, -dors′ing** [var. of ENDORSE, after ML. *indorsare*] *same as* ENDORSE

in·dox·yl (in däk′s'l) *n.* [IND(IGO) + (HYDR)OXYL] a compound, C_8H_7NO, produced by the hydrolysis of indican and synthesized by several methods: it is important in the synthesis of indigo

In·dra (in′drə) [Sans.] the chief god of the early Hindu religion, associated with rain and thunderbolts

in·draft (in′draft′, -dräft′) *n.* **1.** a drawing in; inward pull or attraction **2.** an inward flow, stream, or current Also, Brit. sp., **in′draught′**

in·drawn (in′drôn′) *adj.* **1.** drawn in **2.** introspective

in·dri (in′drē) *n.* [Fr. < Malagasy *indry*, behold!: erroneously taken for the name of the animal] any of a genus (*Indri*) of black and white, tailless lemurs of Madagascar

in·du·bi·ta·ble (in dōō′bi tə b'l, -dyōō′-) *adj.* [L. *indubitabilis*: see IN-² & DUBITABLE] that cannot be doubted; unquestionable —**in·du′bi·ta·bly** *adv.*

induc. induction

in·duce (in dōōs′, -dyōōs′) *vt.* **-duced′, -duc′ing** [ME. *enducen* < L. *inducere* < *in-*, in + *ducere*, to lead: see DUCT] **1.** to lead on to some action, condition, belief, etc.; prevail on; persuade **2.** to bring on; bring about; cause; effect [to *induce* vomiting with an emetic] **3.** to draw (a general rule or conclusion) from particular facts; infer by induction **4.** *Physics* to bring about (an electric or magnetic effect) in a body by exposing it to the influence or variation of a field of force —*SYN.* see PERSUADE —**in·duc′er** *n.* —**in·duc′i·ble** *adj.*

in·duce·ment (-mənt) *n.* **1.** an inducing or being induced **2.** anything that induces; motive; incentive **3.** *Law a)* an explanatory introduction in a pleading *b)* the benefit which a party is to receive for entering into a contract —*SYN.* see MOTIVE

in·duct (in dukt′) *vt.* [ME. *inducten* < L. *inductus*, pp. of *inducere*: see INDUCE] **1.** formerly, to bring or lead in **2.** to place in a benefice or official position with formality or ceremony; install **3.** *a)* to bring formally into a society or organization; initiate *b)* to provide with knowledge or experience of something, esp. something not open to all [*inducting* him into the secrets of the trade] ☆*c)* to enroll (esp. a draftee) in the armed forces

in·duct·ance (-duk′təns) *n.* [prec. + -ANCE] **1.** the property of an electric circuit by which a varying current in it produces a varying magnetic field that induces voltages in the same circuit or in a nearby circuit: it is measured in henrys **2.** the capacity of an electric circuit for producing a counter electromotive force when the current changes

☆**in·duct·ee** (in duk′tē′) *n.* a person inducted or being inducted, esp. into the armed forces

in·duc·tile (in dukt′t'l) *adj.* not ductile; not malleable, pliant, etc. —**in′duc·til′i·ty** (-til′ə tē) *n.*

in·duc·tion (in duk′shən) *n.* [ME. < OFr. *induction* < L. *inductio*] **1.** an inducting or being inducted; installation, initiation, etc. **2.** [Archaic] an introduction; preface or prelude **3.** an inducing, or bringing about **4.** a bringing forward of separate facts or instances, esp. so as to prove a general statement **5.** *Embryology* the influence of one tissue upon the development of adjacent tissue, as by the diffusion of a chemical substance to nearby tissue **6.** *Logic* reasoning from particular facts or individual cases to a general conclusion; also, a conclusion reached by such reasoning: opposed to DEDUCTION **7.** *Math.* a method of proving a theorem which holds true for all whole numbers and zero by demonstrating that it holds true for the first number and by showing that, if it holds true for all the numbers preceding a given number, then it must hold for the next following number: in full, **mathematical induction 8.** *Physics a)* the act or process by which an electric or magnetic effect is produced in an electrical conductor or magnetizable body when it is exposed to the influence or variation of a field of force *b)* the transference of the explosive mixture of air and fuel from the carburetor to the cylinder of an internal-combustion engine

induction coil an apparatus made up of two magnetically coupled coils in a circuit in which interruptions of the direct-current supply to one coil produce an alternating current of high potential in the other

induction heating the heating of a conducting material by

means of electric current induced by an externally applied alternating magnetic field

in·duc·tive (in duk′tiv) *adj.* [LL. *inductivus*] **1.** [Rare] inducing; leading on **2.** of, or proceeding by methods of, logical induction [*inductive* reasoning] **3.** produced by induction **4.** of inductance or electrical or magnetic induction **5.** [Rare] introductory **6.** *Physiol.* producing a change or response in an organism —**in·duc′tive·ly** *adv.*

in·duc·tor (-tər) *n.* [L., one who stirs up, lit., one who leads or brings in] **1.** a person who inducts **2.** *Chem.* a substance that speeds up a slow chemical reaction **3.** *Elec.* a device designed primarily to introduce inductance into an electric circuit

in·due (in dōō′, -dyōō′) *vt.* **-dued′, -du′ing** [L. *induere*, to put on, dress oneself < OL. *indu* (L. *in*), in, on + base < IE. **eu-*, to put on, whence Arm. *aganim*, I put (something) on: cf. EXUVIAE] *same as* ENDUE

in·dulge (in dulj′) *vt.* **-dulged′, -dulg′ing** [L. *indulgere*, to be kind to, yield to] **1.** to yield to or satisfy (a desire); give oneself up to [to *indulge* a craving for sweets] **2.** to gratify the wishes of; be very lenient with; humor **3.** to grant an ecclesiastical indulgence or dispensation to **4.** [Archaic] to grant a kindness, favor, or privilege —*vi.* to give way to one's own desires; indulge oneself (*in* something) —**in·dulg′er** *n.*

SYN.—**indulge** implies a yielding to the wishes or desires of oneself or another, as because of a weak will or an amiable nature; **humor** suggests compliance with the mood or whim of another [they *humored* the dying man]; **pamper** implies overindulgence or excessive gratification; **spoil** emphasizes the harm done to the personality or character by overindulgence or excessive attention [grandparents often *spoil* children]; **baby** suggests the sort of pampering and devoted care lavished on infants and connotes a potential loss of self-reliance [because he was sickly, his mother continued to *baby* him] —*ANT.* discipline, restrain

in·dul·gence (in dul′jəns) *n.* [ME. < OFr. < L. *indulgentia*] **1.** an indulging or being indulgent **2.** a thing indulged in **3.** the act of indulging oneself, or giving way to one's own desires **4.** a favor or privilege **5.** *Business* an extension of time to make payment on a bill or note, granted as a favor **6.** [sometimes I-] *Eng. History* the grant of certain religious liberties to Dissenters and Roman Catholics by Charles II and James II **7.** *R.C.Ch.* a remission of temporal or purgatorial punishment still due for a sin after the guilt has been forgiven in the sacrament of penance —*vt.* **-genced, -genc·ing** *R.C.Ch.* to apply an indulgence to

in·dul·gent (-jənt) *adj.* [L. *indulgens*] indulging or inclined to indulge; kind or lenient, often to excess —**in·dul′gent·ly** *adv.*

in·du·line (in′dyoo lēn′, -lin) *n.* [IND(IGO) + -UL(E) + -INE⁴] any of a series of blue or black azine dyes

in·dult (in dult′) *n.* [< ML.(Ec.) *indultum* < LL., indulgence, favor < neut. of L. *indultus*, pp. of *indulgere*: see INDULGE] *R.C.Ch.* a privilege or special permission granted by the Pope to bishops and others to do something otherwise prohibited by the general law of the Church

in·du·pli·cate (in dōō′plə kit, -dyōō′-) *adj.* [IN-¹ + DUPLICATE] having the edges folded or rolled in, but not overlapping: said of the arrangement of leaves in a leaf bud or of the calyx or corolla in a flower bud

in·du·rate (in′doo rāt′, -dyoo-) *vt.* **-rat′ed, -rat′ing** [< L. *induratus*, pp. of *indurare*, to make hard < *in-*, in + *durare*, to harden < *durus*, hard: see DURABLE] **1.** to make hard; harden **2.** to make callous, unfeeling, or stubborn **3.** to cause to be firmly established —*vi.* to become indurated —*adj.* **1.** hardened **2.** made callous, unfeeling, or stubborn —**in′du·ra′tion** *n.* —**in′du·ra′tive** *adj.*

In·dus¹ (in′dəs) river in S Asia, flowing from SW Tibet through Kashmir & West Pakistan into the Arabian Sea: c. 1,900 mi.

In·dus² (in′dəs) [L., the Indian] a S constellation

in·du·si·um (in dōō′zē əm, -dyōō′-; -zhē-) *n., pl.* **-si·a** (-ə) [ModL. < L., undergarment, tunic; associated with *induere*, to put on (see INDUE), but prob. < Gr. *endysis*, dress, clothing < *endyein*, to go into, put on] **1.** *Anat. & Zool. a)* any covering membrane, as the amnion *b)* a case enclosing an insect larva or pupa **2.** *Bot. a)* a membranous outgrowth of the leaf epidermis in certain ferns, covering the sporangia *b)* the annulus of certain fungi —**in·du′si·al** (-əl) *adj.*

in·dus·tri·al (in dus′trē əl) *adj.* [< Fr. & ML.: Fr. *industriel* < ML. *industrialis*] **1.** having the nature of or characterized by industries **2.** of, connected with, or resulting from industries **3.** working in industries **4.** of or concerned with people working in industries **5.** for use by industries: said of products —*n.* **1.** a stock, bond, etc. of an industrial corporation or enterprise **2.** [Rare] a person working in industry —**in·dus′tri·al·ly** *adv.*

industrial arts the mechanical and technical skills used in industry, ☆esp. as taught in industrial schools

industrial disease *same as* OCCUPATIONAL DISEASE

in·dus·tri·al·ism (-iz'm) *n.* social and economic organization characterized by large industries, machine production, concentration of workers in cities, etc.

in·dus·tri·al·ist (-ist) *n.* a person who owns, controls, or has an important position in the management of an industrial enterprise

in·dus·tri·al·ize (in dus′trē ə līz′) *vt.* **-ized′, -iz′ing 1.** to make industrial; establish or develop industrialism in **2.** to

organize as an industry —*vi.* to become industrial —**in·dus'tri·al·i·za'tion** *n.*

☆**industrial park** an area that is zoned for industrial and business use, usually located on the outskirts of a city and characterized by coordinated plant design

industrial relations relations between industrial employers and their employees

Industrial Revolution [*often* **i- r-**] the change in social and economic organization resulting from the replacement of hand tools by machine and power tools and the development of large-scale industrial production: applied to this development in England from about 1760 and to later changes in other countries

industrial school 1. a secondary school offering instruction in technical and industrial skills **2.** such a school to which neglected or delinquent youths are sent for habilitation

industrial union a labor union to which all workers in a given industry may belong, regardless of occupation or trade: distinguished from CRAFT UNION

in·dus·tri·ous (in dus'trē əs) *adj.* [< Fr. or L.: Fr. *industrieux* < L. *industriosus* < *industria*: see ff.] **1.** orig., skillful or clever **2.** characterized by earnest, steady effort; hard-working; diligent —*SYN.* see BUSY —**in·dus'tri·ous·ly** *adv.* —**in·dus'tri·ous·ness** *n.*

in·dus·try (in'dəs trē) *n., pl.* **-tries** [LME. < MFr. *industrie* < L. *industria* < *industrius*, active, industrious] **1.** orig., *a)* skill or cleverness *b)* the application of this **2.** earnest, steady effort; constant diligence in or application to work **3.** systematic work; habitual employment **4.** *a)* any particular branch of productive, esp. manufacturing, enterprise [the paper *industry*] *b)* any large-scale business activity [the motion-picture *industry*] **5.** *a)* manufacturing productive enterprises collectively, esp. as distinguished from agriculture *b)* the owners and managers of industry —*SYN.* see BUSINESS

in·dwell (in dwel') *vi., vt.* **-dwelt'**, **-dwell'ing** [ME. *indwellen*: used by Wycliffe to translate L. *inhabitare*] to dwell (in); reside (within): said of an animating spirit or essential element —**in'dwell'er** *n.*

Indy, Vincent d' *see* D'INDY

-ine[1] (*variously* in, in, ēn, ən) *a suffix meaning* of, having the nature of, like: **1.** [Fr. *-in*, *-ine* < L. *-inus*, masc., *-ina*, fem., *-inum*, neut.] added to bases of Latin origin to form adjectives, and nouns derived from them [*aquiline, divine, marine*] **2.** [L. *-inus* < Gr. *-inos*] used to form adjectives [*adamantine, crystalline*]

-ine[2] (*variously* in, ən, in, ēn) *a suffix of various sources*, used to form feminine nouns: **1.** [< L. *-ina* < Gr. *-inē*] [*heroine*] **2.** [< L. *-ina*] [*Clementine*] **3.** [< G. *-in*, after Fr. *-ine*] [*landgravine*]

-ine[3] (in, ən) [Fr. < L. *-ina*, suffix of fem. abstract nouns] *a suffix used to form certain abstract nouns* [*medicine, doctrine*]

-ine[4] (*variously* ēn, in, in, ən) [arbitrary use of L. *-inus*, masc., *-ina*, fem., n. & adj. ending] **1.** *a suffix used to form the commercial names of certain products* [*Vaseline*] **2.** *a suffix used to form the chemical names of a)* halogens [*iodine*] *b)* alkaloids or nitrogen bases [*morphine*] *c)* certain types of hydrides [*stibine*] The names of neutral substances, as carbohydrates, glucosides, proteins, etc., are formed with *-in* (Ex.: *inulin, amygdalin, albumin*)

in·earth (in urth') *vt.* [Archaic] to put into the earth; bury; inter

in·e·bri·ant (in ē'brē ənt) *adj., n.* [L. *inebrians*, prp. of *inebriare*] *same as* INTOXICANT

in·e·bri·ate (-āt'; *for adj. & n., usually* -it) *vt.* **-at'ed**, **-at'ing** [< L. *inebriatus*, pp. of *inebriare*, to intoxicate < *in-*, intens. + *ebriare*, to make drunk < *ebrius*, drunk] **1.** to make drunk; intoxicate **2.** to excite; exhilarate —*adj.* drunk; intoxicated —*n.* a drunken person, esp. a drunkard —**in·e'bri·a'tion** *n.*

in·e·bri·at·ed (-āt'id) *adj.* drunk; intoxicated —*SYN.* see DRUNK

in·e·bri·e·ty (in'ē brī'ə tē) *n.* [< INEBRIATE, after earlier *ebriety*] drunkenness; intoxication

in·ed·i·ble (in ed'ə b'l) *adj.* not edible; not fit to be eaten —**in·ed·i·bil'i·ty** *n.*

in·ed·it·ed (in ed'it id) *adj.* **1.** unpublished **2.** not edited

in·ed·u·ca·ble (in ej'ə kə b'l) *adj.* thought to be incapable of being educated

in·ef·fa·ble (in ef'ə b'l) *adj.* [ME. < MFr. < L. *ineffabilis* < *in-*, not + *effabilis*, utterable < *effari*, to speak out < *ex-*, out + *fari*, to speak: see FAME] **1.** too overwhelming to be expressed or described in words; inexpressible [*ineffable* beauty] **2.** too awesome or sacred to be spoken [God's *ineffable* name] —**in'ef·fa·bil'i·ty, in·ef'fa·ble·ness** *n.* —**in·ef'fa·bly** *adv.*

in·ef·face·a·ble (in'i fās'ə b'l) *adj.* that cannot be effaced; impossible to wipe out or erase; indelible —**in'ef·face'a·bil'i·ty** *n.* —**in'ef·face'a·bly** *adv.*

in·ef·fec·tive (in'i fek'tiv) *adj.* **1.** not effective; not producing the desired effect; ineffectual [an *ineffective* plan] **2.** not capable of performing satisfactorily; incompetent; inefficient [an *ineffective* mayor] —**in'ef·fec'tive·ly** *adv.* —**in'ef·fec'tive·ness** *n.*

in·ef·fec·tu·al (-choo wəl) *adj.* not effectual; not producing

or not able to produce the desired effect —**in'ef·fec'tu·al'i·ty** (-wal'ə tē), **in'ef·fec'tu·al·ness** *n.* —**in'ef·fec'tu·al·ly** *adv.*

in·ef·fi·ca·cious (in'ef ə kā'shəs) *adj.* not efficacious; unable to produce the desired effect [an *inefficacious* medicine] —**in'ef·fi·ca'cious·ly** *adv.* —**in'ef·fi·ca'cious·ness** *n.*

in·ef·fi·ca·cy (in ef'i kə sē) *n.* [LL. *inefficacia*] lack of efficacy; inability to produce the desired effect

in·ef·fi·cient (in'ə fish'ənt) *adj.* not efficient; specif., *a)* not producing the desired effect with a minimum use of energy, time, etc.; ineffective *b)* lacking the necessary ability; unskilled; incapable —**in'ef·fi'cien·cy** *n.* —**in'ef·fi'cient·ly** *adv.*

in·e·las·tic (in'i las'tik) *adj.* not elastic; inflexible, rigid, unyielding, unadaptable etc. —*SYN.* see STIFF —**in'e·las·tic'i·ty** (-las tis'ə tē) *n.*

inelastic collision *Physics* a collision process whereby part of the total kinetic energy of the system is converted into a different form of energy, such as radiant energy

in·el·e·gance (in el'ə gəns) *n.* **1.** lack of elegance **2.** something inelegant Also **in·el'e·gan·cy**, *pl.* **-cies**

in·el·e·gant (-gənt) *adj.* [Fr. *inélégant* < L. *inelegans*] not elegant; lacking refinement, good taste, grace, etc.; coarse; crude —**in·el'e·gant·ly** *adv.*

in·el·i·gi·ble (in el'i jə b'l) *adj.* [ML. *ineligibilis*] not eligible; not legally or morally qualified; not fit to be chosen; not suitable —*n.* an ineligible person —**in·el'i·gi·bil'i·ty** *n.* —**in·el'i·gi·bly** *adv.*

in·el·o·quent (in el'ə kwənt) *adj.* not eloquent; not fluent, forceful, and persuasive —**in·el'o·quence** *n.* —**in·el'o·quent·ly** *adv.*

in·e·luc·ta·ble (in'i luk'tə b'l) *adj.* [L. *ineluctabilis* < *in-*, not + *eluctabilis*, that can be resisted by struggling < *eluctari*, to struggle < *ex-*, out + *luctari*, to struggle < IE. base **leug-*, to bend, whence LOCK[1], Gr. *lygos*, supple twig] not to be avoided or escaped; certain; inevitable [*ineluctable* fate] —**in'e·luc'ta·bil'i·ty** *n.* —**in'e·luc'ta·bly** *adv.*

in·e·lud·i·ble (in'i lōōd'ə b'l) *adj.* that cannot be eluded

in·ept (in ept') *adj.* [Fr. *inepte* < L. *ineptus* < *in-*, not + *aptus*, suitable, APT] **1.** not suitable to the purpose; unfit **2.** wrong in a foolish and awkward way [*inept* praise] **3.** clumsy or bungling; inefficient —*SYN.* see AWKWARD —**in·ept'ly** *adv.* —**in·ept'ness** *n.*

in·ept·i·tude (in ep'tə tōōd', -tyōōd') *n.* [L. *ineptitudo*] **1.** the quality or condition of being inept **2.** an inept act, remark, etc.

in·e·qual·i·ty (in'i kwäl'ə tē, -kwôl'-) *n., pl.* **-ties** [ME. *inequalitie* < MFr. *inequalité* < L. *inaequalitas*] **1.** the quality of being unequal; lack of equality **2.** an instance of lack of equality; specif., *a)* difference or variation in size, amount, rank, quality, social position, etc. *b)* unevenness in surface; lack of levelness *c)* lack of proper proportion; unequal distribution **3.** *Math.* the relation between two unequal quantities, or an expression of this relationship: Ex.: a ≠ b (a is not equal to b), 3a > 2b (3a is greater than 2b)

in·eq·ui·ta·ble (in ek'wit ə b'l) *adj.* not equitable; unfair; unjust —**in·eq'ui·ta·bly** *adv.*

in·eq·ui·ty (in ek'wət ē) *n.* [IN-[2] + EQUITY] **1.** lack of justice; unfairness **2.** *pl.* **-ties** an instance of this

in·e·qui·valve (in ē'kwə valv') *adj.* having the two valves of the shell unequal, as an oyster

in·e·rad·i·ca·ble (in'i rad'ə kə b'l) *adj.* that cannot be eradicated —**in'e·rad'i·ca·bly** *adv.*

in·e·ras·a·ble (in'i rās'ə b'l) *adj.* that cannot be erased

in·er·ra·ble (in er'ə b'l, -ur'-) *adj.* [L. *inerrabilis*] not erring; infallible —**in·er'ra·bil'i·ty** *n.*

in·er·rant (-ənt) *adj.* [L. *inerrans*, not wandering, fixed: see IN-[2] & ERRANT] not erring; making no mistakes; infallible —**in·er'ran·cy** *n.*

in·ert (in urt') *adj.* [L. *iners*, without skill or art, idle < *in-*, not + *ars* (gen. *artis*), skill, ART[1]] **1.** having inertia; without power to move, act, or resist **2.** tending to be physically or mentally inactive; dull; slow **3.** having few or no active properties [*inert* matter in a fertilizer, an *inert* gas] —*SYN.* see INACTIVE —**in·ert'ly** *adv.* —**in·ert'ness** *n.*

in·er·tia (in ur'shə) *n.* [L., lack of art or skill, ignorance < *iners*: see prec.] **1.** *Physics* the tendency of matter to remain at rest if at rest, or, if moving, to keep moving in the same direction, unless affected by some outside force **2.** a tendency to remain in a fixed condition without change; disinclination to move or act —**in·er'tial** *adj.*

inertial guidance (or **navigation**) the guidance (or navigation) of a ship, aircraft, etc. along a preassigned course by means of self-contained, automatic instruments that utilize the laws of accelerated motion and gravitation

in·es·cap·a·ble (in'ə skāp'ə b'l) *adj.* that cannot be escaped or avoided; inevitable —**in'es·cap'a·bly** *adv.*

‡**in es·se** (in es'ē) [L.] in being; in existence

in·es·sen·tial (in'ə sen'shəl) *adj.* **1.** [Rare] without essence or existence; immaterial **2.** not essential; not really necessary or important; unessential —*n.* something inessential

in·es·ti·ma·ble (in es'tə mə b'l) *adj.* [ME. < OFr. < L. *inaestimabilis*] that cannot be estimated or reckoned; esp.,

too great or valuable to be properly measured or appreciated; invaluable —**in·es′ti·ma·bly** *adv.*

in·ev·i·ta·ble (in ev′ə tə b'l) *adj.* [ME. < L. *inevitabilis:* see IN-² & EVITABLE] that cannot be avoided or evaded; certain to happen —**in·ev′i·ta·bil′i·ty** *n.* —**in·ev′i·ta·bly** *adv.*

in·ex·act (in′ig zakt′) *adj.* not exact; not accurate or precise —**in′ex·act′i·tude** (-zak′tə tōōd′, -tyōōd′), **in′ex·act′ness** *n.* —**in′ex·act′ly** *adv.*

in·ex·cus·a·ble (in′ik skyōō′zə b'l) *adj.* that cannot or should not be excused; unpardonable; unjustifiable —**in′-ex·cus′a·bil′i·ty** *n.* —**in′ex·cus′a·bly** *adv.*

in·ex·er·tion (in′ig zur′shən) *n.* lack of exertion; failure to exert oneself

in·ex·haust·i·ble (in′ig zôs′tə b'l) *adj.* that cannot be exhausted; specif., *a)* that cannot be used up or emptied *b)* that cannot be tired out; tireless —**in′ex·haust′i·bil′i·ty** *n.* —**in′ex·haust′i·bly** *adv.*

in·ex·ist·ent (in′ig zis′tənt) *adj.* [LL. *inexistens*] not existent; not having being —**in′ex·ist′ence** *n.*

in·ex·o·ra·ble (in ek′sər ə b'l) *adj.* [L. *inexorabilis:* see IN-² & EXORABLE] 1. that cannot be moved or influenced by persuasion or entreaty; unrelenting 2. that cannot be altered, checked, etc. [his *inexorable* fate] —**in·ex′o·ra·bil′i·ty** *n.* —**in·ex′o·ra·bly** *adv.*

in·ex·pe·di·ent (in′ik spē′dē ənt) *adj.* not expedient; not suitable or practicable for a given situation; inadvisable; unwise —**in′ex·pe′di·en·cy, in′ex·pe′di·ence** *n.* —**in′ex·pe′di·ent·ly** *adv.*

in·ex·pen·sive (in′ik spen′siv) *adj.* not expensive; costing relatively little; low-priced; cheap —*SYN.* see CHEAP —**in′ex·pen′sive·ly** *adv.* —**in′ex·pen′sive·ness** *n.*

in·ex·pe·ri·ence (in′ik spir′ē əns) *n.* [Fr. *inexpérience* < LL. *inexperientia*] lack of experience or of the knowledge or skill resulting from experience —**in′ex·pe′ri·enced** *adj.*

in·ex·pert (in ek′spərt, in′ik spurt′) *adj.* [ME. < MFr. < L. *inexpertus*] not expert; unskillful; amateurish —**in·ex′pert·ly** *adv.* —**in·ex′pert·ness** *n.*

in·ex·pi·a·ble (in ek′spē ə b'l) *adj.* [L. *inexpiabilis*] 1. that cannot be expiated or atoned for [an *inexpiable* sin] 2. [Archaic] that cannot be appeased; implacable —**in·ex′pi·a·bly** *adv.*

in·ex·plain·a·ble (in′ik splān′ə b'l) *adj.* that cannot be explained; inexplicable

in·ex·pli·ca·ble (in eks′pli kə b'l, in′iks plik′ə b'l) *adj.* [Fr. < L. *inexplicabilis*] not explicable; that cannot be explained, understood, or accounted for —**in·ex′pli·ca·bil′i·ty** *n.* —**in·ex′pli·ca·bly** *adv.*

in·ex·plic·it (in′ik splis′it) *adj.* [L. *inexplicitus*] not explicit; vague; indefinite; general —**in′ex·plic′it·ly** *adv.* —**in′ex·plic′it·ness** *n.*

in·ex·press·i·ble (in′ik spres′ə b'l) *adj.* that cannot be expressed; indescribable or unutterable —**in′ex·press′i·bil′i·ty, in′ex·press′i·ble·ness** *n.* —**in′ex·press′i·bly** *adv.*

in·ex·pres·sive (in′ik spres′iv) *adj.* 1. [Archaic] *same as* INEXPRESSIBLE 2. not expressive; lacking meaning or expression —**in′ex·pres′sive·ly** *adv.* —**in′ex·pres′sive·ness** *n.*

in·ex·pug·na·ble (in′ik spug′nə b'l) *adj.* [ME. < MFr. < L. *inexpugnabilis* < in-, not + *expugnabilis*, that can be taken by storm < *expugnare*, to take by storm < *ex-*, intens. + *pugnare*, to fight: see PUGNACIOUS] that cannot be defeated by force; unconquerable; unyielding —**in′ex·pug′na·ble·ness** *n.* —**in′ex·pug′na·bly** *adv.*

in·ex·ten·si·ble (in′ik sten′sə b'l) *adj.* not extensible

‡**in ex·ten·so** (in ik sten′sō) [L.] at full length; without abridgment

in·ex·tin·guish·a·ble (in′ik stiŋ′gwish ə b'l) *adj.* not extinguishable; that cannot be quenched, put out, or stopped —**in′ex·tin′guish·a·bly** *adv.*

in·ex·tir·pa·ble (in′ik stur′pə b'l) *adj.* [L. *inextirpabilis*] that cannot be extirpated, or rooted out

‡**in ex·tre·mis** (in′ ik strē′mis) [L., in extremity] at the point of death

in·ex·tri·ca·ble (in eks′tri kə b'l, in′ik strik′ə b'l) *adj.* [L. *inextricabilis* < in-, IN-² + *extricabilis*] 1. that one cannot extricate himself from 2. that cannot be disentangled or untied 3. so complicated or involved as to be insolvable —**in·ex′tri·ca·bil′i·ty** *n.* —**in·ex′tri·ca·bly** *adv.*

I·nez (ī′niz, ī′nez′, ī nez′) [Sp. *Iñez*] a feminine name: see AGNES

Inf., inf. infantry

inf. 1. [L. *infra*] below 2. infinitive 3. information

in·fal·li·ble (in fal′ə b'l) *adj.* [ML. *infallibilis:* see IN-² & FALLIBLE] 1. incapable of error; never wrong 2. not liable to fail, go wrong, make a mistake, etc.; dependable; reliable; sure 3. *R.C.Ch.* incapable of error in setting forth doctrine on faith and morals: said esp. of the Pope speaking *ex cathedra* (i.e., in his official capacity) —*n.* an infallible person or thing —**in·fal′li·bil′i·ty** *n.* —**in·fal′li·bly** *adv.*

in·fa·mous (in′fə məs) *adj.* [ME. < OFr. *infameux* < ML. *infamosus* < L. *infamis:* see IN-² & FAMOUS] 1. having a very bad reputation; notorious; in disgrace or dishonor 2. causing or deserving a bad reputation; scandalous; outrageous 3. *Law a)* punishable by imprisonment in a penitentiary: said of certain crimes, usually felonies *b)* guilty of such a crime —*SYN.* see VICIOUS —**in′fa·mous·ly** *adv.*

in·fa·my (-mē) *n., pl.* -**mies** [ME. *infamye* < OFr. *infamie* < L. *infamia* < *infamis:* see INFAMOUS] 1. very bad reputation; notoriety; disgrace; dishonor 2. the quality of being infamous; great wickedness 3. an infamous act 4. *Law* loss of character and of certain civil rights sustained by a person convicted of an infamous crime —*SYN.* see DISGRACE

in·fan·cy (in′fən sē) *n., pl.* -**cies** [LME. < L. *infantia*] 1. the state or period of being an infant; babyhood; very early childhood 2. the beginning or earliest stage of anything 3. *Law* the state or period of being a minor; period before the age of legal majority, usually twenty-one; minority

in·fant (in′fənt) *n.* [ME. *infaunt* < OFr. *enfant* < L. *infans* (gen. *infantis*), child < *adj.*, not yet speaking < *in-*, not + *fans*, prp. of *fari*, to speak: see FAME] 1. a very young child; baby 2. a person in the state of legal infancy; minor —*adj.* 1. of or for infants or infancy 2. in a very early stage

in·fan·ta (in fan′tə, -fän′-) *n.* [Sp. & Port., fem. of *infante:* see ff.] 1. any daughter of a king of Spain or Portugal 2. the wife of an infante

in·fan·te (-tā) *n.* [Sp. & Port. < L. *infans:* see INFANT] any son of a king of Spain or Portugal, except the heir to the throne

in·fan·ti·cide (in fan′tə sīd′) *n.* [Fr. < LL. *infanticidium* < *infanticida*, one who kills an infant: see INFANT & -CIDE] 1. the murder of a baby 2. [Fr. < LL. *infanticida*] a person guilty of this

in·fan·tile (in′fən tīl′, -til) *adj.* [L. *infantilis*] 1. of or having to do with infants or infancy 2. like, suitable for, or characteristic of an infant; babyish; childish or childlike; immature 3. in the earliest stage of development

infantile paralysis *same as* POLIOMYELITIS

in·fan·ti·lism (in′fən t'l iz'm; *esp. in psychol.*, in fan′-) *n.* immature or childish behavior; specif., *Psychol.* an abnormal state in which such behavior persists into adult life: it is marked by retarded mental and physical growth and by failure to mature sexually

in·fan·tine (in′fən tīn′, -tin) *adj.* [Fr. *infantin, enfantin*] infantile; babyish; childish or childlike

in·fan·try (in′fən trē) *n., pl.* -**tries** [Fr. *infanterie* < It. *infanteria*, very young person, knight's page, foot soldier < L. *infans:* see INFANT] 1. foot soldiers collectively; esp., that branch of an army consisting of soldiers trained and equipped to fight chiefly on foot 2. [I-] a (designated) infantry regiment [the 274th *Infantry*]

in·fan·try·man (-mən) *n., pl.* -**men** (-mən) a soldier in the infantry

in·farct (in färkt′) *n.* [ML. *infarctus*, for L. *infartus*, pp. of *infarcire* < *in-*, in + *farcire*, to stuff: see FARCE] an area of dying or dead tissue resulting from obstruction of the blood vessels normally supplying the part

in·farc·tion (in färk′shən) *n.* 1. the development of an infarct 2. *same as* INFARCT

in·fare (in′far′, -fer′) *n.* [ME. *infer*, entrance < OE. *infær* < *in-*, IN + *fær*, a going < *faran:* see FARE] [Dial.] a reception or dinner party after a wedding, usually on the day after

in·fat·u·ate (in fach′ōō wāt′) *vt.* -**at′ed**, -**at′ing** [< L. *infatuatus*, pp. of *infatuare*, to make a fool of < *in-*, intens. + *fatuus*, foolish: see FATUOUS] 1. to make foolish; cause to lose sound judgment 2. to inspire with foolish or shallow love or affection —*adj.* infatuated —*n.* a person who is infatuated

in·fat·u·at·ed (-id) *adj.* 1. lacking sound judgment; foolish 2. completely carried away by foolish or shallow love or affection —**in·fat′u·at′ed·ly** *adv.*

in·fat·u·a·tion (in fach′ōō wā′shən) *n.* [LL. *infatuatio*] an infatuating or being infatuated —*SYN.* see LOVE

in·fea·si·ble (in fē′zə b'l) *adj.* not feasible; not easily done; impracticable —**in·fea′si·bil′i·ty** *n.*

in·fect (in fekt′) *vt.* [ME. *infecten* < MFr. *infecter* < L. *infectus*, pp. of *inficere*, to put or dip into, tinge, stain < *in-*, in + *facere*, to DO¹] 1. to contaminate with a disease-producing organism or matter 2. to cause to become diseased by bringing into contact with such an organism or matter 3. to invade an individual, organ, tissue, etc.: said of a pathogenic organism 4. to affect or imbue with one's feelings or beliefs, esp. in a harmful or undesirable way —**in·fec′tor** *n.*

in·fec·tion (in fek′shən) *n.* [ME. *infeccioun* < OFr. *infection* < LL. *infectio*] 1. an infecting; specif., *a)* the act of causing to become diseased *b)* the act of affecting with one's feelings or beliefs 2. the fact or state of being infected, esp. by the presence in the body of bacteria, protozoans, viruses, or other parasites 3. something that results from infecting or being infected; specif., *a)* a disease resulting from infection (sense 2) *b)* a feeling, belief, influence, etc. transmitted from one person to another 4. anything that infects

in·fec·tious (-shəs) *adj.* 1. likely to cause infection; containing disease-producing organisms or matter 2. designating a disease that can be communicated by infection (sense 2) 3. tending to spread or to affect others; catching [an *infectious* laugh] 4. [Obs.] infected with disease —**in·fec′tious·ly** *adv.* —**in·fec′tious·ness** *n.*

infectious hepatitis a viral disease causing inflammation of the liver and characterized by jaundice, fever, etc.

infectious mononucleosis an acute disease, esp. of young people, characterized by fever, swollen lymph nodes, sore throat, and abnormalities of the lymphocytes: it is presumed to be caused by a virus

in·fec·tive (in fek′tiv) *adj.* [ME. *infectif* < OFr. < L. *infectivus*] likely to cause infection; infectious

in·fe·cund (in fē′kənd, -fek′ənd) *adj.* [ME. *infecunde* < L. *infecundus*] not fecund; not fertile; barren —**in·fe·cun·di·ty** (in′fi kun′də tē) *n.*

in·fe·lic·i·tous (in′fə lis′ə təs) *adj.* not felicitous; unfortunate or unsuitable —**in′fe·lic′i·tous·ly** *adv.*

in·fe·lic·i·ty (-tē) *n.* [L. *infelicitas* < *infelix*, unfortunate: see IN-² & FELICITY] 1. the quality or condition of being infelicitous 2. *pl.* **-ties** something infelicitous; unsuitable or inapt remark, action, etc.

in·fer (in fur′) *vt.* **-ferred′, -fer′ring** [L. *inferre*, to bring or carry in, infer < *in-*, in + *ferre*, to carry, BEAR¹] 1. orig., to bring on or about; cause; induce 2. to conclude or decide from something known or assumed; derive by reasoning; draw as a conclusion 3. *a)* to lead to as a conclusion; indicate *b)* to indicate indirectly; imply: in this sense, still sometimes regarded as a loose usage —*vi.* to draw inferences —**in·fer′a·ble** *adj.* —**in·fer′a·bly** *adv.* —**in·fer′rer** *n.* **SYN.—infer** suggests the arriving at a decision or opinion by reasoning from known facts or evidence [from your smile, I *infer* that you're pleased]; **deduce**, in strict discrimination, implies inference from a general principle by logical reasoning [the method was *deduced* from earlier experiments]; **conclude** strictly implies an inference that is the final logical result in a process of reasoning [I must, therefore, *conclude* that you are wrong]; **judge** stresses the careful checking and weighing of premises, etc. in arriving at a conclusion; **gather** is an informal substitute for **infer** or **conclude** [I *gather* that you don't care]

in·fer·ence (in′fər əns) *n.* [ML. *inferentia*] 1. the act or process of inferring; specif., the deriving of a conclusion in logic by either induction or deduction 2. something inferred; specif., a conclusion arrived at in logic

in·fer·en·tial (in′fə ren′shəl) *adj.* [< ML. *inferentia* + -AL] based on or having to do with inference —**in′fer·en′tial·ly** *adv.*

in·fe·ri·or (in fir′ē ər) *adj.* [ME. < L., compar. of *inferus*, low, below < IE. *ndheros*, whence UNDER] 1. lower in space; placed lower down 2. low or lower in order, status, rank, etc.; subordinate 3. lower in quality or value than (with *to*) 4. poor in quality; below average 5. *Anat.* located below or directed downward 6. *Astron.* between the earth and the sun [Mercury and Venus are *inferior* planets] 7. *Bot.* having the sepals, petals, and stamens attached at the apex: said of the ovary of an epigynous flower 8. *Printing* placed below the type line, as 2 in NO₂ —*n.* an inferior person or thing —**in·fe′ri·or′i·ty** (ôr′ə tē, -är′-) *n.*

inferiority complex 1. *Psychol.* a neurotic condition resulting from various feelings of inferiority, such as derive from real or imagined physical or social inadequacy and often manifested through overcompensation in excessive aggressiveness, a domineering attitude, etc. 2. popularly, any feeling of inferiority, inadequacy, etc.: cf. SUPERIORITY COMPLEX

in·fer·nal (in fur′n'l) *adj.* [ME. < OFr. < LL. *infernalis* < L. *infernus*, underground, lower, infernal < *inferus*: see INFERIOR] 1. *a)* of the ancient mythological world of the dead *b)* of hell 2. hellish; diabolical; fiendish; inhuman 3. [Colloq.] hateful; outrageous —**in·fer′nal·ly** *adv.*

infernal machine *earlier name for* a booby trap or time bomb

in·fer·no (in fur′nō) *n., pl.* **-nos** [It. < LL. *infernus*: see INFERNAL] hell or any place suggesting hell, usually characterized by great heat or flames —**[I-]** that section of Dante's *Divine Comedy* which describes hell and the sufferings of the damned

in·fe·ro- (in′fə rō′) [< L. *inferus*: see INFERIOR] *a combining form meaning* below and [*inferoanterior*]

in·fe·ro·an·te·ri·or (in′fə rō′an tir′ē ər) *adj.* [prec. + ANTERIOR] lying below and in front

in·fer·tile (in fur′t'l; *chiefly Brit.*, -tīl) *adj.* [MFr. < L. *infertilis*] 1. not fertile; not productive; barren 2. not fertilized, as an egg —**SYN.** see STERILE —**in·fer·til·i·ty** (in′fur til′ə tē) *n.*

in·fest (in fest′) *vt.* [Fr. *infester* < L. *infestare*, to attack, trouble < *infestus*, hostile < *in-*, in + IE. base *dhers-*, to be bold, attack, whence DARE] 1. to overrun or inhabit in large numbers, usually so as to be harmful or bothersome; swarm in or over 2. to be parasitic in or on —**in′fes·ta′tion** *n.* —**in·fest′er** *n.*

in·feu·da·tion (in′fyoo dā′shən) *n.* [ML. *infeudatio* < pp. of *infeudare*, to enfeoff < *in-*, in + *feudum*: for IE. base see FEE] in feudal law, the granting of an estate in fee; enfeoffment

in·fi·del (in′fə d'l) *n.* [ME. < MFr. *infidèle* < L. *infidelis*, unfaithful (in LL.(Ec.), unbelieving) < *in-*, IN-² + *fidelis*: see FIDELITY] 1. a person who does not believe in a particular religion, esp. the prevailing religion; specif., *a)* among Christians, a non-Christian *b)* among Moslems, a non-Moslem 2. a person who holds no religious belief 3. a person who does not accept some particular theory, belief, etc. —*adj.* 1. that is an infidel; unbelieving 2. of infidels —**SYN.** see ATHEIST

in·fi·del·i·ty (in′fə del′ə tē) *n., pl.* **-ties** [L. *infidelitas* < *infidelis*: see prec.] 1. the fact or state of being an infidel

2. unfaithfulness or disloyalty to another; esp., sexual unfaithfulness of a husband or wife; adultery 3. an unfaithful or disloyal act

in·field (in′fēld′) *n.* [IN, *adv.* + FIELD] 1. the land of a farm nearest the farmhouse ☆2. *a)* the area enclosed by the four base lines on a baseball field *b)* the infielders collectively, or the area covered by them Distinguished from OUTFIELD ☆3. the area inside a race track or running track: field events of a track meet are often held on it

☆**in·field·er** (-ər) *n. Baseball* a player whose position is in the infield; shortstop, first baseman, second baseman, or third baseman: the pitcher and the catcher are considered infielders when fielding the ball

in·fight·ing (in′fīt′iŋ) *n.* 1. fighting, esp. boxing at close range 2. intense competition or conflict, often bitterly personal, as between political opponents or within an organization or group —**in′fight′er** *n.*

in·fil·trate (in fil′trāt, in′fil trāt′) *vi., vt.* **-trat·ed, -trat·ing** [IN-¹ + FILTRATE] 1. to pass, or cause (a fluid) to pass, through small gaps or openings; filter 2. to pass through, as in filtering 3. to pass, or cause (individual troops) to pass, through weak places in the enemy's lines in order to attack the enemy's flanks or rear 4. to penetrate, or cause to penetrate, (a region or group) gradually or stealthily, so as to attack or to seize control from within —*n.* something that infiltrates —**in′fil·tra′tion** *n.* —**in′fil·tra′tive** *adj.* —**in′fil·tra′tor** *n.*

infin. infinitive

in·fi·nite (in′fə nit) *adj.* [ME. < L. *infinitus*: see IN-² & FINITE] 1. lacking limits or bounds; extending beyond measure or comprehension; without beginning or end; endless 2. very great; vast; immense 3. *a) Math.* indefinitely large; greater than any finite number however large *b)* capable of being put into one-to-one correspondence with a part of itself [*infinite* set] —*n.* something infinite, as space or time —**the Infinite (Being)** God —**in′fi·nite·ly** *adv.* —**in′fi·nite·ness** *n.*

in·fin·i·tes·i·mal (in′fin ə tes′ə məl, in fin′-) *adj.* [ModL. *infinitesimus* < L. *infinitus* (see INFINITE), after *centesimus*, hundredth < *centum*, one hundred] 1. too small to be measured; infinitely small 2. *Math.* of or pertaining to an infinitesimal —*n.* 1. an infinitesimal quantity 2. *Math.* a variable nonzero number which is understood to be smaller in absolute value than any preassigned nonzero number —**in′fin·i·tes′i·mal·ly** *adv.*

infinitesimal calculus the methods of mathematical analysis of differential and integral calculus

in·fin·i·tive (in fin′ə tiv) *adj.* [LL. *infinitivus* < L. *infinitivus (modus)*, lit., unlimited (mood) < *infinitus* (see INFINITE): so named because it is not limited to any person, number, or tense] *Gram.* of or connected with an infinitive —*n. Gram.* the form of the verb which expresses existence or action without reference to person, number, or tense and can also function as a noun: in English, it is usually the form of the first person singular present preceded by the marker *to* [*to go, to think*] or by another verb form [*can he go, make him try*] —**in·fin′i·ti′val** (-tī′vəl) *adj.*

in·fin·i·tude (-tōōd′, -tyōōd′) *n.* [< L. *infinitus*, INFINITE, prob. after MAGNITUDE] 1. the quality of being infinite 2. an infinite quantity, number, or extent

in·fin·i·ty (-tē) *n., pl.* **-ties** [ME. < OFr. *infinité* < L. *infinitas*] 1. the quality of being infinite 2. anything infinite; endless or unlimited space, time, distance, quantity, etc. 3. an indefinitely large number or amount 4. *Geom.* a location infinitely distant from the origin or base point of the space being considered 5. *Math.* the numerical value of an infinite quantity: symbol, ∞ 6. *Photog. a)* a distance so far from a camera that rays of light reflected from a subject there may be regarded as parallel *b)* a setting for such a distance on a camera's focusing scale —**to infinity** without limit or end

in·firm (in furm′) *adj.* [ME. < L. *infirmus*] 1. not firm or strong physically; weak; feeble, as from old age 2. not firm in mind or purpose; not resolute; vacillating 3. not stable, firm, or sound; frail; shaky, as a structure 4. not secure or valid [an *infirm* title to property] —**SYN.** see WEAK —**in·firm′ly** *adv.* —**in·firm′ness** *n.*

in·fir·ma·ry (in fur′mə rē) *n., pl.* **-ries** [ML. *infirmaria, infirmarium* < L. *infirmus*] a place for the care of the sick, injured, or infirm; esp., a building or room, as in a school, that serves as a hospital or dispensary

in·fir·mi·ty (-mə tē) *n.* [ME. *infirmite* < L. *infirmitas*] 1. the quality or state of being infirm; feebleness; weakness 2. *pl.* **-ties** an instance of this; specif., *a)* a physical weakness or defect; frailty or ailment, as from old age *b)* a moral weakness; defect

in·fix (in fiks′; *also, and for n. always,* in′fiks′) *vt.* [< L. *infixus,* pp. of *infigere,* to fix or drive in: see IN-¹ & FIX] 1. to fasten or set firmly in or on, esp. by inserting or piercing 2. to fix firmly in the mind; instill; implant 3. to place (an infix) within the body of a word —*n. Linguis.* a bound morpheme that is added within a word that has no affixes or within that part of a word to which affixes are added (Ex.: Arabic *-ta-* in *iq-ta-riba,* to cause oneself to come near < *qariba,* to come near)

‡in fla·gran·te de·lic·to (in flə gran'tē di lik'tō) [L.] in the very act of committing the offense; red-handed

in·flame (in flām') vt. -flamed', -flam'ing [ME. enflamen < OFr. enflammer < L. inflammare: see IN-¹ & FLAME] 1. to set on fire 2. to arouse passion, desire, or violence in; excite intensely, as with anger 3. to increase the intensity of (passion, desire, violence, etc.) 4. to cause inflammation in (some organ or tissue) —vi. 1. to become roused, excited, stimulated, etc. 2. to catch fire 3. to become hot, feverish, swollen, red, sore, etc. —in·flam'er n.

in·flam·ma·ble (in flam'ə b'l) adj. [Fr. < ML. inflammabilis < L. inflammare: see INFLAME] 1. same as FLAMMABLE 2. easily roused, provoked, or excited —n. anything flammable —in·flam'ma·bil'i·ty, in·flam'ma·ble·ness n. —in·flam'ma·bly adv.

in·flam·ma·tion (in'flə mā'shən) n. [Fr. < L. inflammatio] 1. the act of inflaming 2. the state of being inflamed; specif., a condition of some part of the body that is a reaction to injury, infection, irritation, etc. and is characterized by redness, pain, heat, swelling, and loss of function

in·flam·ma·to·ry (in flam'ə tôr'ē) adj. [< L. inflammatus, pp. of inflammare (see INFLAME) + -ORY] 1. rousing or likely to rouse excitement, anger, violence, rioting, etc. [an inflammatory speech] 2. Med. of, caused by, or characterized by inflammation

in·flate (in flāt') vt. [-flat'ed, -flat'ing [< L. inflatus, pp. of inflare, to blow into, inflate < in-, in + flare, to BLOW¹] 1. to blow full or swell out as with air or gas; distend; expand; dilate 2. to raise in spirits; make proud or elated 3. to increase or raise beyond what is normal or valid; specif., to cause inflation of (money, credit, etc.) —vi. to become inflated; swell Opposed to DEFLATE —SYN. see EXPAND —in·flat'a·ble adj. —in·flat'er, in·fla'tor n.

in·flat·ed (-id) adj. 1. puffed out; swollen 2. pompous; bombastic; high-flown 3. increased or raised beyond what is normal or valid 4. characterized or caused by inflation

in·fla·tion (in flā'shən) n. [ME. inflacioun < L. inflatio] 1. an inflating or being inflated ☆2. an increase in the amount of money in circulation, resulting in a relatively sharp and sudden fall in its value and rise in prices Opposed to DEFLATION

in·fla·tion·ar·y (-er'ē) adj. of, causing, or characterized by inflation

☆inflationary spiral a continuous and accelerating rise in the prices of goods and services, primarily due to the interaction of increases in wages and costs

in·fla·tion·ism (-iz'm) n. the advocacy or promotion of monetary inflation —in·fla'tion·ist adj., n.

in·flect (in flekt') vt. [ME. inflecten < L. inflectere < in-, in + flectere, to bend] 1. to turn, bend, or curve, usually inward 2. to vary or change the tone or pitch of (the voice); modulate 3. Gram. to change the form of (a word) by inflection, as in conjugating or declining —vi. to be changed by inflection —in·flec'tive adj.

in·flec·tion (in flek'shən) n. [L. inflexio < inflexus, pp. of inflectere: see prec.] 1. a turning, bending, or curving 2. a turn, bend, or curve 3. any change in tone or pitch of the voice; modulation [to signal a question by a rising inflection] 4. a change of a curve or arc from convex to concave or the reverse 5. Gram. a) the change of form by which some words indicate certain grammatical relationships, as number, case, gender, tense, etc. b) an inflected form c) an inflectional element, as those bound forms used in English to form the plural and possessive case of nouns (ships, ship's) and the past tense and third person singular, present indicative, of verbs [he shipped, he ships]

in·flec·tion·al (-'l) adj. of, having, or showing grammatical inflection, as a language in which the subject-object relation is indicated by inflection: Greek and Latin are inflectional languages, whereas English is syntactically analytical —in·flec'tion·al·ly adv.

in·flexed (in flekst', in'flekst) adj. [< L. inflexus (see INFLECT) + -ED] Biol. bent sharply downward or inward; turned toward the axis

in·flex·i·ble (in flek'sə b'l) adj. [ME. < L. inflexibilis: see IN-² & FLEXIBLE] 1. that cannot be bent or curved; stiff; rigid 2. firm in mind or purpose; stubborn; unyielding; unshakable 3. that cannot be changed; fixed; unalterable [an inflexible rule] —in·flex'i·bil'i·ty, in·flex'i·ble·ness n. —in·flex'i·bly adv.

SYN.—inflexible implies an unyielding or unshakable firmness in mind or purpose, sometimes connoting stubbornness [his inflexible attitude]; adamant implies a firm or unbreakable resolve that remains unaffected by temptation or pleading [adamant to her entreaties]; implacable suggests the impossibility of pacifying or appeasing [implacable in his hatred]; obdurate implies a hardheartedness that is not easily moved to pity, sympathy, or forgiveness [her obdurate refusal to help] See also STIFF —ANT. flexible, yielding, compliant

in·flex·ion (-shən) n. Brit. var. of INFLECTION

in·flict (in flikt') vt. [< L. inflictus, pp. of infligere, to strike or beat against < in-, on, against + fligere, to strike < IE. base *bhlīĝ-, to strike, whence W. blif, catapult] 1. to give or cause (pain, wounds, blows, etc.) by or as by striking; cause to be borne 2. to impose (a punishment, disagreeable task, etc. on or upon) —in·flict'er, in·flic'tor n. — in·flic'tive adj.

in·flic·tion (in flik'shən) [LL. inflictio] 1. the act of inflicting 2. something inflicted, as punishment

in·flight (in'flīt') adj. done, occurring, shown, etc. while an aircraft is in flight [in-flight movies]

in·flo·res·cence (in'flô res'ns, -flə-) n. [ModL. inflorescentia < LL. inflorescens, prp. of inflorescere, to begin to blossom: see IN-¹ & FLORESCENCE] Bot. 1. the producing of blossoms; flowering 2. the arrangement of flowers on a stem or axis 3. a flower cluster on a common axis 4. flowers collectively 5. a solitary flower, regarded as a reduced cluster — in'flo·res'cent adj.

in·flow (in'flō') n. 1. a flowing in or into 2. anything that flows in

in·flu·ence (in'floo wəns) n. [ME. < OFr. < ML. influentia, a flowing in < L. influens, prp. of influere, to flow in < in-, in + fluere, to flow: see FLUCTUATE] 1. orig., the supposed flowing of an ethereal fluid or power from the stars, thought by astrologers to affect the characters and actions of people 2. a) the power of persons or things to affect others, seen only in its effects b) the action or effect of such power 3. the ability of a person or group to produce effects indirectly by means of power based on wealth, high position, etc. 4. a person or thing that has influence 5. Elec. the effect of an external field —vt. -enced, -enc·ing to exert or have influence on; have an effect on the nature, behavior, development, action, or thought of

SYN.—influence implies the power of persons or things (whether or not exerted consciously or overtly) to affect others [he owed his position to influence]; authority implies the power to command acceptance, belief, obedience, etc., based on strength of character, expertness of knowledge, etc. [a statement made on good authority]; prestige implies the power to command esteem or admiration, based on brilliance of achievement or outstanding superiority; weight implies influence that is more or less preponderant in its effect [he threw his weight to the opposition] See also EFFECT

in·flu·ent (in'floo ənt) adj. [L. influens: see prec.] flowing in —n. 1. anything flowing in, as a tributary 2. an organism that has important interactions within an ecological community, but is not a dominant

in·flu·en·tial (in'floo wen'shəl) adj. [ML. influentialis] having or exerting influence, esp. great influence; powerful; effective —in'flu·en'tial·ly adv.

in·flu·en·za (in'floo wen'zə) n. [It., lit., an influence (because attributed by astrologers to the influence of the stars) < ML. influentia: see INFLUENCE] 1. an acute, contagious, infectious disease, caused by any of a specific group of viruses and characterized by inflammation of the respiratory tract, fever, and muscular pain 2. any of various virus diseases of domestic animals, characterized by inflammation of the respiratory tract —in'flu·en'zal adj.

in·flux (in'fluks') n. [Fr. < LL. influxus < pp. of influere: see INFLUENCE] 1. a) a flowing in; inpouring; inflow, as of a liquid, gas, etc. b) a continual coming in of persons or things [an influx of customers] 2. the point where a river joins another body of water

in·fold (in fōld') vt. same as ENFOLD

in·form¹ (in fôrm') vt. [ME. informen < OFr. enformer < L. informare: see IN-¹ & FORM] 1. a) [Obs.] to give form to b) to give character to; be the formative principle of c) to give, imbue, or inspire with some specific quality or character; animate 2. [Rare] to form or shape (the mind); teach; instruct 3. to give knowledge of something to; tell; acquaint with a fact, etc. —vi. 1. to give information 2. to give information laying blame or accusation upon another —SYN. see NOTIFY

in·form² (in fôrm') adj. [Fr. informe < L. informis] [Archaic] without form; formless

in·for·mal (in fôr'məl) adj. not formal; specif., a) not according to prescribed or fixed customs, rules, ceremonies, etc. b) casual, easy, unceremonious, or relaxed c) designed for use or wear on everyday occasions d) not requiring formal dress e) same as COLLOQUIAL —in·for'mal·ly adv.

in·for·mal·i·ty (in'fôr mal'ə tē) n. 1. the quality or state of being informal 2. pl. -ties an informal act

in·for·mant (in fôr'mənt) n. [< L. informans, prp. of informare, to inform] a person who gives, or serves as a source of, information; specif., a native speaker of a language whose pronunciations, usages, etc. are studied and recorded by linguistic investigators

‡in for·ma pau·pe·ris (in fôr'mə pô'pər is) [L., in the

TYPES OF INFLORESCENCE
(A, spike; B, catkin; C, raceme; D, spadix; E, head with disk flowers and ray flowers; F, umbel; G, compound umbel)

manner of a pauper] as a poor person; i.e., without paying court costs [to initiate litigation *in forma pauperis*]

in·for·ma·tion (in'fər mā'shən) *n.* [ME. *informacioun* < OFr. *information* < L. *informatio*, a representation, outline, sketch] **1.** an informing or being informed; esp., a telling or being told of something **2.** something told; news; intelligence; word **3.** knowledge acquired in any manner; facts; data; learning; lore **4.** a person or agency answering questions as a service to others **5.** in information theory and computer science, a precise measure of the information content of a message, measured in bits and ranging from zero when the entire message is known in advance to some maximum when nothing is known of its content **6.** any data that can be stored in and retrieved from a computer **7.** *Law* an accusation, under oath, of a criminal offense, not by indictment of a grand jury, but by a public officer, such as a prosecutor —**in·for·ma'tion·al** *adj.*

SYN.—**information** applies to facts that are gathered in any way, as by reading, observation, hearsay, etc. and does not necessarily connote validity [*inaccurate information*]; **knowledge** applies to any body of facts gathered by study, observation, etc. and to the ideas inferred from these facts, and connotes an understanding of what is known [*man's knowledge of the universe*]; **learning** is knowledge acquired by study, especially in languages, literature, philosophy, etc.; **erudition** implies profound or abstruse learning beyond the comprehension of most people; **wisdom** implies superior judgment and understanding based on broad knowledge —**ANT.** ignorance

information theory the study of processes of communication and the transmission of messages; specif., the study dealing with the information content of messages and with the probability of signal recognition in the presence of interference, noise, distortion, etc.

in·form·a·tive (in fôr'mə tiv) *adj.* [ML. *informativus* < L. *informatus*, pp. of *informare* (see INFORM[1])] giving information; educational; instructive: also **in·form'a·to'ry** — **in·form'a·tive·ly** *adv.*

in·formed (in fôrmd') *adj.* having much information, knowledge, or education

in·form·er (in fôr'mər) *n.* a person who informs; esp., a person who secretly accuses, or gives evidence against, another, often for a reward

in·fra- (in'frə) [< L. *infra*, *adv. & prep.*, below: for IE. base see INFERIOR] *a prefix meaning* below, beneath [*infrared*]

in·fract (in frakt') *vt.* [< L. *infractus*, pp. of *infringere*: see INFRINGE] [Rare] to break or violate (a law, pledge, etc.) —**in·frac'tor** *n.*

in·frac·tion (in frak'shən) *n.* [L. *infractio*: see prec.] a breaking of a law, pact, etc.; violation; infringement

in·fra dig (in'frə dig') [< L. *infra dig(nitatem)*] [Colloq.] beneath one's dignity

in·fra·hu·man (in'frə hyoō'mən) *adj.* below man on the evolutionary scale; esp., anthropoid

in·fra·lap·sar·i·an (in'frə lap ser'ē ən, -sar'-) *n.* [< INFRA- + L. *lapsus*, a fall + -ARIAN] any of a group of Calvinists who held that God's plan of salvation for some people followed and was a consequence of the fall of man from grace: opposed to SUPRALAPSARIAN —*adj.* of this doctrine —**in'fra·lap·sar'i·an·ism** *n.*

in·fran·gi·ble (in fran'jə b'l) *adj.* [MFr.: see IN-[2] & FRANGIBLE] **1.** that cannot be broken or separated **2.** that cannot be violated or infringed —**in·fran'gi·bil'i·ty**, **in·fran'gi·ble·ness** *n.* —**in·fran'gi·bly** *adv.*

in·fra·red (in'frə red') *adj.* designating or of those invisible rays just beyond the red end of the visible spectrum: their waves are longer than those of the spectrum colors but shorter than radio waves, and have a penetrating heating effect: used in cooking, photography, etc.

in·fra·son·ic (-sän'ik) *adj.* [INFRA- + SONIC] designating or of a frequency of sound below the range audible to the human ear

in·fra·spe·cif·ic (-spə sif'ik) *adj.* of or pertaining to any taxon or category within a species, as a subspecies

in·fra·struc·ture (in'frə struk'chər) *n.* [INFRA- + STRUCTURE] a substructure or underlying foundation; esp., the basic installations and facilities on which the continuance and growth of a community, state, etc. depend, as roads, schools, power plants, transportation and communication systems, etc. —**in'fra·struc'tur·al** *adj.*

in·fre·quent (in frē'kwənt) *adj.* [L. *infrequens*] not frequent; happening seldom or at long intervals; rare; uncommon —**SYN.** see RARE[1] —**in·fre'quen·cy**, **in·fre'quence** *n.* —**in·fre'quent·ly** *adv.*

in·fringe (in frinj') *vt.* -**fringed'**, -**fring'ing** [L. *infringere*, to break off, break, impair, violate < *in-*, in + *frangere*, to BREAK[1]] to break (a law or agreement); fail to observe the terms of; violate —**infringe on** (or **upon**) to break in on; encroach or trespass on (the rights, patents, etc. of others) —**in·fringe'ment** *n.*

in·fun·dib·u·lar (in'fən dib'yoo lər) *adj.* **1.** shaped like a funnel **2.** of or having an infundibulum Also **in'fun·dib'u·late** (-lit, -lāt')

in·fun·dib·u·li·form (-lə fôrm') *adj.* shaped like a funnel

in·fun·dib·u·lum (-ləm) *n., pl.* -**la** (-lə) [ModL. < L., a

funnel < *infundere*: see INFUSE] *Anat.* any of various funnel-shaped organs or passages, as *a*) the extension of the third ventricle of the brain to the pituitary body *b*) the calyx of a kidney *c*) the ovarian end of a Fallopian tube

in·fu·ri·ate (in fyoor'ē āt'; *for adj.* -it) *vt.* -**at'ed**, -**at'ing** [< ML. *infuriatus*, pp. of *infuriare*, to enrage < L. *in-*, in + *furiare*, to enrage < *furia*, rage, FURY] to cause to become very angry; enrage —*adj.* [Archaic] furious; very angry; enraged —**in·fu'ri·at'ing·ly** *adv.* —**in·fu'ri·a'tion** *n.*

in·fus·cate (in fus'kit, -kāt) *adj.* [L. *infuscatus*, pp. of *infuscare*, to make dark, obscure < *in-*, in + *fuscare*, to darken < *fuscus*, dark: for IE. base see FURY] darkened or tinged with brown, as the wings of an insect: also **in·fus'cat·ed** (-kāt id)

in·fuse (in fyōoz') *vt.* -**fused'**, -**fus'ing** [ME. *infusen* < L. *infusus*, pp. of *infundere*, to pour in < *in-*, in + *fundere*, to pour: see FOUND[3]] **1.** formerly, to pour (a liquid) in, into, or upon **2.** to put (a quality, idea, etc.) into, as if by pouring; instill; impart **3.** to fill (*with* a quality, feeling, etc.); imbue; inspire **4.** to steep or soak (tea leaves, etc.) so as to extract flavor or other qualities —**SYN.** see INSTILL — **in·fus'er** *n.*

in·fu·si·ble (in fyōo'zə b'l) *adj.* [IN-[2] + FUSIBLE] that cannot be fused or melted —**in·fu'si·bil'i·ty** *n.*

in·fu·sion (in fyōo'zhən) *n.* [< Fr. or L.: Fr. *infusion* < L. *infusio*] **1.** the act or process of infusing **2.** something infused; tincture; admixture **3.** the liquid extract that results from steeping a substance in water **4.** *Med.* the slow introduction of a solution into the body, specif. into a vein

in·fu·sion·ism (-iz'm) *n. Theol.* the doctrine that the pre-existing human soul enters the body by divine infusion at conception or birth —**in·fu'sion·ist** *n.*

in·fu·sive (in fyōo'siv) *adj.* tending or able to infuse

in·fu·so·ri·al (in'fyoo sôr'ē əl, -zôr'-) *adj.* of, consisting of, containing, or having the nature of, infusorians

in·fu·so·ri·an (-ən) *n.* [< MpdL. (*animalcula*) *infusoria*, neut. pl. of *infusorius*, pertaining to infusions (< L. *infusus*: see INFUSE) + -AN] **1.** any of a former large group (Infusoria) of microscopic organisms consisting of those found in infusions of decayed organic matter and in stagnant water **2.** any of a former class (Infusoria) of protozoans found in most water, characterized by cilia which permit free movement, as paramecia, stentors, etc. —*adj.* of this group or class

-ing (in; *in context often* 'ŋ, in, ən, 'n) **1.** [ME. -ing, -yng, orig. -end, -and, -ind < OE. -ende, suffix of prp. of verbs] *a suffix used to form the present participle* [*hearing, noticing*] **2.** [ME. -ing, -yng < OE. -ung] *a suffix added to verbs or, sometimes, nouns, to form verbal nouns meaning: a*) the act or an instance of (a specified verb) [*talking, digging*] *b*) something produced by the action of (a specified verb) [*a painting*] *c*) something that does the action of (a specified verb) [*a covering for her head*] *d*) material used for (a specified thing) [*blanketing, carpeting*] **3.** [ME. < OE.] *a n.-forming suffix, sometimes with diminutive force, meaning* a person or thing of a specified kind or origin [*atheling, farthing*]

in·gath·er (in gath'ər) *vt., vi.* [Archaic] **1.** to gather in or draw together **2.** to harvest

Inge (iŋ), **William Ralph** 1860-1954; Eng. theologian: dean of St. Paul's Cathedral, London (1911-34)

in·gem·i·nate (in jem'ə nāt') *vt.* -**nat'ed**, -**nat'ing** [< L. *ingeminatus*, pp. of *ingeminare*, to redouble, repeat: see IN-[1] & GEMINATE] [Now Rare] to stress or make more forceful by repeating —**in·gem'i·na'tion** *n.*

in·gen·er·ate[1] (in jen'ər it; *for v.* -ə rāt') *adj.* [L. *ingeneratus*, pp. of *ingenerare*: see ENGENDER] [Archaic] innate; inborn —*vt.* -**at'ed**, -**at'ing** [Archaic] to produce or create within; engender

in·gen·er·ate[2] (-ər it) *adj.* [LL. *ingeneratus*: see IN-[2] & GENERATE] [Rare] not generated or produced, but originating and existing in itself

in·gen·ious (in jēn'yəs) *adj.* [LME. < MFr. *ingenieux* < L. *ingeniosus*, of good capacity, gifted with genius, ingenious < *ingenium*, innate quality, ability < *in-*, in + *gignere*: see GENUS] **1.** orig., having genius; having great mental ability **2.** clever, resourceful, original, and inventive **3.** made or done in a clever or original way —**SYN.** see CLEVER —**in·gen'ious·ly** *adv.* —**in·gen'ious·ness** *n.*

in·gé·nue (an'zhə noō', -jə-; *Fr.* an zhā nü') *n., pl.* -**nues'** (-noōz'; *Fr.* -nü') [Fr., fem. of *ingénu* < L. *ingenuus*, INGENUOUS] **1.** an innocent, inexperienced, unworldly young woman **2.** *Theater a*) the role of such a character *b*) an actress playing such a role or roles

in·ge·nu·i·ty (in'jə noō'ə tē, -nyoō'-) *n.* [L. *ingenuitas* < *ingenuus* (see ff.): sense 1 affected by association with INGENIOUS] **1.** the quality of being ingenious; cleverness, originality, skill, etc. **2.** *pl.* -**ties** an ingenious device **3.** [Archaic] the quality of being ingenuous

in·gen·u·ous (in jen'yoo wəs) *adj.* [L. *ingenuus*, native, inborn, freeborn, noble, frank < *ingignere*, to ingenerate < *in-*, in + *gignere*, to produce: see GENUS] **1.** orig., of noble birth or nature **2.** frank; open; candid **3.** simple; artless; naive; without guile —**SYN.** see NAIVE —**in·gen'u·ous·ly** *adv.* —**in·gen'u·ous·ness** *n.*

In·ger·soll (in′gər sôl′, -səl), **Robert Green** 1833–99; U.S. lawyer & lecturer: exponent of agnosticism

in·gest (in jest′) *vt.* [< L. *ingestus*, pp. of *ingerere*, to carry, put into < *in-*, into + *gerere*, to carry] to take (food, drugs, etc.) into the body, as by swallowing or absorbing —**in·ges′tion** *n.* —**in·ges′tive** *adj.*

in·ges·ta (in jes′tə) *n.pl.* [L., neut. pl. of *ingestus*: see prec.] things ingested: sometimes used figuratively

in·gle (in′g′l) *n.* [Scot. < Gael. *aingeal*, fire] [Brit. Dial.] 1. a fire or blaze, esp. on a hearth 2. a fireplace

in·gle·nook (-nook′) *n.* [Chiefly Brit.] a corner by a fireplace; chimney corner: also **ingle nook**

In·gle·wood (in′g′l wood′) [after the home town in Canada of the owner of the site] city in SW Calif.: suburb of Los Angeles: pop. 90,000

in·glo·ri·ous (in glôr′ē əs) *adj.* [L. *ingloriosus*: see IN-² & GLORIOUS] 1. not giving, receiving, or deserving glory; shameful; disgraceful; dishonorable 2. [Now Rare] without glory; not famous; little-known —**in·glo′ri·ous·ly** *adv.* —**in·glo′ri·ous·ness** *n.*

in·go·ing (in′gō′in) *adj.* going in; entering

in·got (in′gət) *n.* [ME. < MFr. *lingot* (with faulty separation of *l-*, as if *l′*, for *le*, the) < OPr., prob. < *lingo*, var. of *lengo*, tongue (< L. *lingua*: see LANGUAGE): from the elongated form] 1. orig., a mold for casting metal into a bar 2. a mass of metal cast into a bar or other convenient shape

ingot iron a ductile, rust resistant, highly purified steel with the impurity level below 0.15%

in·graft (in graft′, -gräft′) *vt.* same as ENGRAFT

in·grain (in grān′; *for adj. & n.* in′grān) *vt.* [see ENGRAIN] 1. to dye in the fiber before manufacture 2. to work into the fiber; infuse deeply: chiefly in a figurative sense, and in the past participle —*adj.* 1. dyed in the fiber, before manufacture; thoroughly dyed 2. made of fiber or yarn dyed before weaving: said of rugs, carpeting, etc. 3. deeply infused —*n.* yarn, fiber, carpeting, etc. dyed before manufacture

in·grained (in grānd′, in′grānd) *adj.* 1. worked into the fiber; firmly fixed or established [*ingrained* principles] 2. inveterate; thoroughgoing [an *ingrained* liar]

in·grate (in′grāt) *adj.* [ME. *ingrat* < OFr. < L. *ingratus*, unpleasant, ungrateful < *in-*, not + *gratus*, grateful: see GRACE] [Obs.] ungrateful —*n.* an ungrateful person

in·gra·ti·ate (in grā′shē āt′) *vt.* -at′ed, -at′ing [prob. via It. *ingratiare* (now *ingraziare*) < L. phr. *in gratiam*, for the favor of < *in*, in + *gratia*, favor, GRACE] to make acceptable; esp., to bring (oneself) into another's favor or good graces by conscious effort —**in·gra′ti·at′ing** *adj.* —**in·gra′ti·at′ing·ly** *adv.* —**in·gra′ti·a′tion** *n.* —**in·gra′ti·a·to·ry** (-ə tôr′ē) *adj.*

in·grat·i·tude (in grat′ə tood′, -tyood′) *n.* [ME. < OFr. < LL. *ingratitudo*: see INGRATE] lack of gratitude; ungratefulness

in·gra·ves·cent (in′grə ves′′nt) *adj.* [L. *ingravescens*, prp. of *ingravescere*, to become heavier, grow worse < *in-*, IN-¹ + *gravis*, heavy, severe, GRAVE¹] [Now Rare] becoming more and more severe, as a disease

in·gre·di·ent (in grē′dē ənt) *n.* [ME. < L. *ingrediens*, prp. of *ingredi*: see INGRESS] 1. any of the things that a mixture is made of 2. a component part, or constituent, of anything —SYN. see ELEMENT

In·gres (an′gr′), **Jean Au·guste Do·mi·nique** (zhän ō güst′ dô mē nēk′) 1780–1867; Fr. painter

in·gress (in′gres) *n.* [ME. < L. *ingressus*, pp. of *ingredi*, to step into, enter < *in-*, into + *gradi*, to go: see GRADE] 1. the act of entering: also **in·gres·sion** (in gresh′ən) 2. the right or permission to enter 3. a place or means of entering; entrance

in·gres·sive (in gres′iv) *adj.* [ML. *ingressivus*] 1. having to do with ingress 2. *Gram.* same as INCEPTIVE

Ing·rid (in′grid) [< Scand.; ult. < ON. *Ingvi*, name of a Gmc. god + *rida*, ride] a feminine name

in·group (in′groop′) *n.* any group of people with common interests that give them a sense of solidarity and exclusivity as regards all nonmembers

in·grow·ing (in′grō′in) *adj.* growing within, inward, or into; esp., growing into the flesh [an *ingrowing* hair]

in·grown (-grōn′) *adj.* 1. grown within, inward, or into; esp., grown into the flesh, as a toenail that curves under at the sides 2. inborn; native; innate

in·growth (-grōth′) *n.* 1. a growing inward 2. something ingrowing or ingrown

in·gui·nal (in′gwə n′l) *adj.* [L. *inguinalis* < *inguen* (gen. *inguinis*), the groin] of or near the groin

in·gui·no- (in′gwə nō′, -nə) *a combining form meaning* inguinal and: also, before a vowel, **inguin-**

in·gulf (in gulf′) *vt.* same as ENGULF

in·gur·gi·tate (in gur′jə tāt′) *vt.*, *vi.* -tat′ed, -tat′ing [< L. *ingurgitatus*, pp. of *ingurgitare*, to pour in like a flood, guzzle: see IN-¹ & GURGITATION] to swallow up greedily or in large amounts; gulp; gorge; guzzle —**in·gur′gi·ta′tion** *n.*

in·hab·it (in hab′it) *vt.* [ME. *enhabiten* < OFr. *enhabiter* < L. *inhabitare* < *in-*, in + *habitare*, to dwell < *habitus*: see HABIT] to dwell or live in (a region, house, etc.); occupy —*vi.* [Archaic] to dwell; live —**in·hab′it·er** *n.*

in·hab·it·a·ble¹ (-ə b′l) *adj.* that can be inhabited; fit to live in; habitable —**in·hab′it·a·bil′i·ty** *n.*

in·hab·it·a·ble² (-ə b′l) *adj.* [Rare] not habitable — **in·hab′it·a·bil′i·ty** *n.*

in·hab·it·an·cy (in hab′i tən sē) *n.*, *pl.* -cies 1. an inhabiting or being inhabited 2. place of residence; home; dwelling Also [Obs.] **in·hab′it·ance**

in·hab·it·ant (-tənt) *n.* [ME. *inhabitaunt* < OFr. *inhabitant* < L. *inhabitans*, prp. of *inhabitare*] a person or animal that inhabits some specified region, dwelling, etc.; permanent resident

in·hab·i·ta·tion (in hab′ə tā′shən) *n.* [ME. *inhabitacioun* < LL. *inhabitatio*] an inhabiting or being inhabited

in·hab·it·ed (in hab′it id) *adj.* having inhabitants; lived in; occupied

in·hal·ant (in hāl′ənt) *adj.* [< L. *inhalans*, prp. of *inhalare*] used in inhalation; inhaling —*n.* a medicine or other substance to be inhaled as a vapor

in·ha·la·tion (in′hə lā′shən) *n.* [< pp. of L. *inhalare*] 1. the act of inhaling 2. same as INHALANT

☆**in·ha·la·tor** (in′hə lāt′ər) *n.* 1. an apparatus for administering medicinal vapors in inhalation 2. same as RESPIRATOR (sense 2)

in·hale (in hāl′) *vt.* -haled′, -hal′ing [L. *inhalare* < *in-*, in + *halare*, to breathe: see EXHALE] to draw (air, vapor, etc.) into the lungs; breathe in —*vi.* 1. to draw air, vapor, etc. into the lungs 2. to draw tobacco smoke into the lungs when smoking

in·hal·er (-ər) *n.* 1. a person who inhales 2. same as RESPIRATOR (sense 1) 3. same as INHALATOR (sense 1)

in·har·mon·ic (in′här män′ik) *adj.* not harmonic; out of harmony; discordant

in·har·mo·ni·ous (-mō′nē əs) *adj.* not harmonious; discordant, in conflict, etc. —**in′har·mo′ni·ous·ly** *adv.* — **in′har·mo′ni·ous·ness** *n.*

in·har·mo·ny (in här′mə nē) *n.* lack of harmony; discord; conflict

in·haul (in′hôl′) *n.* a rope used to haul in a sail: also **in′haul′er**

in·here (in hir′) *vi.* -hered′, -her′ing [L. *inhaerere*, to stick in, adhere to < *in-*, in + *haerere*, to stick] to be inherent; exist as a quality, characteristic, or right (*in*); be innate

in·her·ence (in hir′əns, -her′-) *n.* [ME. *inhaerentia*] the fact or state of inhering or being inherent; specif., *Philos.* the relation of an attribute to its subject

in·her·en·cy (-ən sē) *n.*, *pl.* -cies 1. same as INHERENCE 2. something inherent

in·her·ent (-ənt) *adj.* [L. *inhaerens*, prp. of *inhaerere*: see INHERE] existing in someone or something as a natural and inseparable quality, characteristic, or right; innate; basic; inborn —**in·her′ent·ly** *adv.*

in·her·it (in her′it) *vt.* [ME. *enheriten* < OFr. *enheriter* < LL. *inhereditare*, to appoint as heir, inherit < L. *in-*, in + *heres*, HEIR] 1. orig., to transfer property to (an heir) 2. *a*) to receive (property, a title, etc.) by the laws of inheritance from an ancestor at his death *b*) to receive (property) by bequest 3. to receive as if by inheritance from a predecessor 4. to have (certain characteristics) by heredity —*vi.* to receive an inheritance; become an heir —**in·her′i·tor** *n.* —**in·her′i·tress** (-i tris), **in·her′i·trix** (-i triks) *n.fem.*

in·her·it·a·ble (-ə b′l) *adj.* [ME. *enheritable* < Anglo-Fr. < OFr.] 1. capable of inheriting; having the rights of an heir 2. capable of being inherited —**in·her′it·a·bil′i·ty**, **in·her′it·a·ble·ness** *n.*

in·her·it·ance (-əns) *n.* [ME. *inheritauns* < Anglo-Fr. & OFr. *enheritance*] 1. the action of inheriting 2. something inherited or to be inherited; legacy; bequest 3. ownership by virtue of birthright; right to inherit 4. anything received as if by inheritance from a predecessor 5. any characteristic passed on by heredity —SYN. see HERITAGE

inheritance tax a tax levied by the state upon the right of beneficiaries to receive property of a deceased person

in·he·sion (in hē′zhən) *n.* [< L. *inhaesio* < pp. of L. *inhaerere*: see INHERE] [Rare] same as INHERENCE

in·hib·it (in hib′it) *vt.* [< L. *inhibitus*, pp. of *inhibere*, to hold back, restrain, curb < *in-*, in, on + *habere*, to have, hold: see HABIT] 1. to hold back or keep from some action, feeling, etc.; check or repress 2. [Rare] to prohibit; forbid —SYN. see RESTRAIN —**in·hib′i·tive**, **in·hib′i·to·ry** (-i tôr′ē) *adj.*

in·hi·bi·tion (in′hi bish′ən, -ə bish′ən) *n.* [ME. *inhibicion* < OFr. < L. *inhibitio*] 1. an inhibiting or being inhibited 2. anything that inhibits; esp., a mental or psychological process that restrains or suppresses an action, emotion, or thought

in·hib·i·tor (in hib′it ər) *n.* a person or thing that inhibits; esp., any substance that slows or prevents a chemical or organic reaction: also **in·hib′it·er**

in·ho·mo·ge·ne·ous (in′hō mə jē′nē əs, -häm ə-) *adj.* not homogeneous

in·hos·pi·ta·ble (in häs′pi tə b′l, in′häs pit′ə b′l) *adj.* [ML. *inhospitabilis*] 1. not hospitable; not offering hospitality 2. not offering protection, shelter, etc.; barren; forbidding [an *inhospitable* climate] —**in·hos′pi·ta·ble·ness** *n.* —**in·hos′pi·ta·bly** *adv.*

in·hos·pi·tal·i·ty (in′häs pi tal′ə tē, in häs′-) *n.* lack of hospitality; inhospitable treatment

in·house (in′hous′) *adj.* originating within an organization, company, etc., rather than brought in from outside

in·hu·man (in hyoo′mən, -yoo′-) *adj.* [LME. *inhumayn*

< MFr. *inhumain* < L. *inhumanus*] not human; esp., not having the qualities considered normal to or for human beings; unfeeling, heartless, cruel, barbarous, etc. —*SYN.* see CRUEL —**in·hu′man·ly** *adv.*

in·hu·mane (in′hyo͞o mān′, -yoo-) *adj.* [IN-[2] + HUMANE] not humane; unmoved by the suffering of others; cruel, brutal, unkind, etc. —**in′hu·mane′ly** *adv.*

in·hu·man·i·ty (-man′ə tē) *n.* [LME. *inhumanite* < MFr. < L. *inhumanitas*] 1. the quality or condition of being inhuman or inhumane 2. *pl.* **-ties** an inhuman or inhumane act or remark

in·hume (in hyo͞om′) *vt.* **-humed′, -hum′ing** [Fr. *inhumer* < L. *inhumare* < *in-*, in + *humus*, earth: see HUMUS] to bury (a dead body); inter —**in′hu·ma′tion** *n.*

in·im·i·cal (in im′i k′l) *adj.* [LL. *inimicalis* < L. *inimicus*, hostile, ENEMY] 1. like an enemy; hostile; unfriendly 2. in opposition; adverse; unfavorable *[laws inimical* to freedom] —**in·im′i·cal·ly** *adv.*

in·im·i·ta·ble (in im′ə tə b′l) *adj.* [L. *inimitabilis:* see IN-[2] & IMITABLE] that cannot be imitated or matched; too good to be equaled or copied —**in·im′i·ta·bil′i·ty, in·im′i·ta·ble·ness** *n.* —**in·im′i·ta·bly** *adv.*

in·i·on (in′ē ən) *n.* [ModL. < Gr. *inion*, the back of the head < *is* (gen. *inos*), sinew, muscle, lit., strength] the bulging part at the rear of the human skull

in·iq·ui·tous (in ik′wə təs) *adj.* showing iniquity; wicked; unjust —*SYN.* see VICIOUS —**in·iq′ui·tous·ly** *adv.* —**in·iq′ui·tous·ness** *n.*

in·iq·ui·ty (-wə tē) *n.* [ME. *iniquite* < OFr. *iniquité* < L. *iniquitas* < *iniquus*, unequal < *in-*, not + *aequus*, EQUAL] 1. lack of righteousness or justice; wickedness 2. *pl.* **-ties** a wicked, unjust, or unrighteous act

init. initial

in·i·tial (i nish′əl) *adj.* [< Fr. or L.: Fr. *initial* < L. *initialis* < *initium*, a beginning < *inire*, to go into, enter upon, begin < *in-*, into, in + *ire*, to go < IE. base *ei-*, whence Goth. *iddja*] having to do with, indicating, or occurring at the beginning *[the initial* stage of a disease, the *initial* letter of a word] —*n.* 1. a capital, or upper-case, letter; specif., *a*) an extra-large capital letter at the start of a printed paragraph, chapter, etc. *b*) the first letter of a name 2. *Biol.* a primordial cell that determines the basic pattern of derived tissues; specif., a meristematic cell —*vt.* **-tialed** or **-tialled, -tial·ing** or **-tial·ling** to mark or sign with an initial or initials

in·i·tial·ly (-ē) *adv.* at the beginning; at first

Initial Teaching Alphabet an alphabet of 44 characters, with a single sound for each character, devised by Sir James Pitman (1901–) of England for teaching beginners to read English: orig. called *Augmented Roman*

in·i·ti·ate (i nish′ē āt′; *for adj. & n., usually* -it) *vt.* **-at′ed, -at′ing** [< L. *initiatus*, pp. of *initiare*, to enter upon, initiate < *initium:* see INITIAL] 1. to bring into practice or use; introduce by first doing or using; start *[to initiate* a new course of studies] 2. to teach the fundamentals of some subject to; help to begin doing something *[to initiate* someone into the game of chess] 3. to admit as a member into a fraternity, club, etc., esp. with a special or secret ceremony —*adj.* 1. initiated 2. [Archaic] just begun —*n.* a person who has recently been, or is about to be, initiated —*SYN.* see BEGIN —**in·i′ti·a′tor** *n.*

in·i·ti·a·tion (i nish′ē ā′shən) *n.* [L. *initiatio*] 1. an initiating or being initiated 2. the ceremony by which a person is initiated into a fraternity, etc.

in·i·ti·a·tive (i nish′ē ə tiv, -nish′ə-) *adj.* [ML. *initiativus*] of, or having the nature of, initiation; introductory; initial —*n.* 1. the action of taking the first step or move; responsibility for beginning or originating 2. the characteristic of originating new ideas or methods; ability to think and act without being urged; enterprise 3. *a*) the right of a legislature to introduce new legislation on some specified matter *b*) the right of a group of citizens to introduce a matter for legislation either to the legislature or directly to the voters *c*) the procedure by which such matters are introduced, usually a petition signed by a specified percentage of the voters

in·i·ti·a·to·ry (-tôr′ē) *adj.* 1. beginning; introductory; initial 2. of or used in an initiation

in·ject (in jekt′) *vt.* [< L. *injectus*, pp. of *injicere*, to throw, cast, or put in < *in-*, in + *jacere*, to throw] 1. to force or drive (a fluid) into some passage, cavity, or chamber; esp., to introduce or force (a liquid) into some part of the body by means of a syringe, hypodermic needle, etc. 2. to fill by, or subject to, injection 3. to introduce (a missing feature, quality, etc.) *[to inject* a note of humor into a story] 4. to interject (a remark, opinion, etc.) as into a discussion —**in·ject′a·ble** *adj.*

in·jec·tion (in jek′shən) *n.* [L. *injectio*] 1. an act or instance of injecting 2. something injected; esp., *a*) a liquid injected into the body *b*) a fuel under pressure forced into a combustion chamber

injection molding a method of shaping certain materials, as thermoplastic substances, by forcing the heated, syrupy resin into water-chilled molds for cooling and setting —**in·jec′tion-mold′ed** *adj.*

in·jec·tor (-tər) *n.* a person or thing that injects, as a device for injecting fuel into a combustion chamber or for injecting water into a steam boiler

in·ju·di·cious (in′jo͞o dish′əs) *adj.* [IN-[2] + JUDICIOUS] showing poor judgment; not discreet or wise —**in′ju·di′cious·ly** *adv.* —**in′ju·di′cious·ness** *n.*

in·junc·tion (in junk′shən) *n.* [LL. *injunctio* < pp. of *injungere*, to ENJOIN] 1. an enjoining; bidding; command 2. something enjoined; command; order 3. a writ or order from a court prohibiting a person or group from carrying out a given action, or ordering a given action to be done —**in·junc′tive** *adj.*

in·jure (in′jər) *vt.* **-jured, -jur·ing** [altered < earlier *injury*, to harm < LME. *injurien* < MFr. *injurier* < L. *injuriari* < *injuria:* see INJURY] 1. to do physical harm or damage to; hurt 2. to offend (one's feelings, pride, etc.); wound 3. to weaken or otherwise cause a loss in value to (a business, reputation, etc.) 4. to be unjust to; wrong —**in′jur·er** *n.* *SYN.*—**injure** implies the marring of the appearance, health, soundness, etc. of a person or thing *[injured* goods]; **harm** more strongly suggests the pain or distress caused *[he wouldn't harm* a fly]; **damage** stresses the loss, as in value, usefulness, etc., resulting from an injury *[damaged* goods]; **hurt** implies a wounding physically or emotionally or a causing of any kind of harm or damage *[the rumors hurt* his business]; to **impair** something is to cause it to deteriorate in quality or to lessen in value, strength, etc. *[impaired* hearing]; **spoil** implies such serious impairment of a thing as to destroy its value, usefulness, etc. *[the canned food was spoiled]*

in·ju·ri·ous (in joor′ē əs) *adj.* [LME. *iniuryous* < MFr. *injurieux* < L. *injuriosus*] 1. injuring or likely to cause injury; harmful; damaging 2. offensive or abusive; slanderous or libelous —**in·ju′ri·ous·ly** *adv.* —**in·ju′ri·ous·ness** *n.*

in·ju·ry (in′jər ē) *n., pl.* **-ries** [ME. *iniurie* < L. *injuria* < *injurius*, wrongful, unjust < *in-*, not + *jus* (gen. *juris*), right, justice: see JUST[1]] 1. physical harm or damage to a person, property, etc. 2. an injurious act; specif., *a*) an offense against a person's feelings, dignity, etc. *b*) loss in value inflicted on a business, reputation, etc. *c*) a violation of rights; injustice; wrong 3. [Obs.] an insult —*SYN.* see INJUSTICE

in·jus·tice (in jus′tis) *n.* [ME. < OFr. < L. *injustitia*] 1. the quality of being unjust or unfair; lack of justice; wrong 2. an unjust act; injury; wrong *SYN.*—**injustice** implies unjust treatment of another or a violation of his rights; **injury** and **wrong** have special application to injustices for the redress or punishment of which legal action can be taken, both applying to a violation of the private rights of an individual, and **wrong** alone, to crimes and misdemeanors which affect the whole community; a **grievance** is a circumstance considered by the person affected to be unjust and ground for complaint or resentment —*ANT.* justice

ink (iŋk) *n.* [ME. *enke* < OFr. *enque* < LL. *encaustum* < Gr. *enkauston*, purple or red ink < *enkaustos*, burned in < *enkaiein*, to burn in < *en-*, in + *kaiein*, to burn] 1. a colored liquid used for writing, drawing, etc. 2. a sticky, colored paste used in printing; printer's ink 3. a dark, liquid secretion squirted out by cuttlefish, octopuses, etc. to cloud the water for protection —*vt.* 1. to cover with ink; spread ink on 2. to draw, mark, or color with ink (often with *in*) ☆3. [Slang] to sign one's name to

☆**ink·ber·ry** (-ber′ē) *n., pl.* **-ries** 1. an evergreen holly (*Ilex glabra*) with shiny, leathery leaves, native to E N. America 2. the dark-purple fruit of this plant 3. *same as* POKEWEED

ink·blot (-blät′) *n.* any of a group of irregular patterns made by blots of ink and used in psychological testing: see RORSCHACH TEST

ink·er (iŋ′kər) *n.* a person or thing that inks; specif., *Printing* a roller for spreading ink on type

ink·horn (-hôrn′) *n.* a small container made of horn or other material, formerly used to hold ink

in·kle (iŋ′k′l) *n.* [< ? obs. Du. *inckel* (Du. *enkel*), single (with reference to the narrow width)] [Now Rare] 1. a kind of braided linen tape 2. the thread or yarn from which this is made

ink·ling (iŋk′liŋ) *n.* [ME. *ingkiling* < *inclen*, to give an inkling of] 1. an indirect suggestion; slight indication; hint 2. a vague idea or notion; suspicion

ink·stand (iŋk′stand′) *n.* 1. a small stand holding an inkwell, pens, etc. 2. *same as* INKWELL

Ink·ster (iŋk′stər) [after Robert *Inkster*, local citizen] city in SE Mich.: suburb of Detroit: pop. 39,000

ink·well (iŋk′wel′) *n.* a container for holding ink, usually set in the top of a desk, inkstand, etc.

☆**ink·wood** (-wood′) *n.* a tropical tree (*Exothea paniculata*) of a family (Sapindaceae) found in Florida and the West Indies, having dark, hard wood used for pilings, fence posts, etc.

ink·y (iŋ′kē) *adj.* **ink′i·er, ink′i·est** 1. like ink in color; dark; black 2. colored, marked, stained, or covered with ink —**ink′i·ness** *n.*

inky cap any of several mushrooms (genus *Coprinus*) whose cap liquefies and forms an inky material

in·lace (in lās′) *vt.* **-laced′, -lac′ing** *same as* ENLACE

in·laid (in′lād′, in lād′) *adj.* **1.** set in pieces into a surface of another material so as to form a smooth surface *[a* pine table with an *inlaid* walnut design*]* **2.** decorated with a surface made in this way *[an inlaid* floor*]*

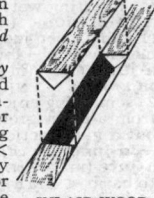

INLAID WOOD

in·land (in′lənd; *for n. & adv., usually* -land′) *adj.* [IN-¹ + LAND] **1.** of, located in, or confined to the interior of a country or region; away from the coast or border **2.** [Brit.] carried on or operating within a country; domestic —*n.* [ME. < OE. *in-lande]* the interior of a country or region; inland areas —*adv.* into or toward the interior; away from the coast or border

in·land·er (in′lən dər) *n.* a person living inland

☆**Inland Passage** *same as* INSIDE PASSAGE

Inland Sea arm of the Pacific surrounded by the Japanese islands of Honshu, Shikoku, & Kyushu

in·law (in′lô′) *n.* [< (MOTHER-)IN-LAW, etc.] [Colloq.] a relative by marriage

in·lay (in′lā′; *for v., also* in lā′) *vt.* **-laid′**, **-lay′ing** [IN-¹ & LAY¹] **1.** *a)* to set (pieces of wood, metal, etc.) into a surface to make a design that is usually level with the surface *b)* to decorate with such pieces **2.** to fit or insert (an illustration) into a mat **3.** to add extra silver to (silver-plated objects) —*n., pl.* **-lays′** **1.** inlaid decoration or material **2.** a filling for a tooth made from a mold of the cavity and then cemented in —**in′lay′er** *n.*

in·let (in′let; *for n.* in′let, -lit) *vt.* **-let′**, **-let′ting** [ME. *inletan:* see IN-¹ & LET¹] to inlay or insert —*n.* [ME. *inlate* < the *v.*] **1.** *a)* a narrow strip of water extending into a body of land from a river, lake, ocean, etc.; small bay or creek *b)* a narrow strip of water between islands **2.** the act of letting something in **3.** an entrance, opening, or passage, as to a culvert **4.** something inlaid or inserted

in·li·er (in′lī′ər) *n.* [< IN-¹ + LIE¹ + -ER] an outcrop area of older rocks entirely surrounded by younger rocks

‡**in loc. cit.** [L. *in loco citato]* in the place cited

‡**in lo·co pa·ren·tis** (in lō′kō pə ren′tis) [L.] in the place of a parent, or of a parent's authority

in·ly (in′lē) *adv.* [ME. *inliche* < OE. *inlice:* see IN-¹ & -LY²] [Poet.] **1.** inwardly **2.** intimately

in·mate (in′māt′) *n.* [IN-¹ + MATE¹] a person living with others in the same building, now esp. one confined with others in a prison or institution

‡**in me·di·as res** (in mā′dē äs rās′) [L., lit., into the midst of things] in the middle of the action rather than at the beginning, as in commencing an epic

in me·mo·ri·am (in mə môr′ē əm) [L.] in memory (of): put on tombstones, in obituary notices, etc.

in·mesh (in mesh′) *vt. same as* ENMESH

in·mi·grant (in′mi′grənt) *adj.* coming in from another region of the same country *[in-migrant* workers] —*n.* an in-migrant person or animal —**in′-mi′grate** (-grāt) *vi.* **-grat·ed**, **-grat·ing** —**in′-mi·gra′tion** *n.*

in·most (in′mōst′) *adj.* [ME. *innemest* < OE.: see IN-¹ & -MOST] **1.** located farthest within **2.** most intimate or secret; innermost *[inmost* thoughts]

Inn (in) river flowing from E Switzerland, across W Austria & SE Bavaria, into the Danube: c. 320 mi.

inn (in) *n.* [ME. *yn* < OE. *inn* (akin to ON. *inni*) < *inne, adv.,* within: cf. IN] **1.** orig., any dwelling or lodging **2.** *a)* an establishment or building providing food, drink, bedrooms, etc. for travelers; hotel, esp. one in the country or along a highway *b)* a restaurant or tavern Now usually only in the names of such places **3.** [Brit.] formerly, any of various houses in London providing lodging for students: see INN OF COURT —*vt., vi.* [Archaic] to lodge at an inn

in·nards (in′ərdz) *n.pl.* [altered < INWARDS] [Dial. or Colloq.] **1.** the internal organs of the body; viscera; entrails **2.** the inner parts of anything

in·nate (i nāt′, in′āt) *adj.* [L. *innatus,* pp. of *innasci,* to be born in, originate in < *in-,* in + *nasci,* to be born: see NATIVE] **1.** *a)* existing naturally rather than acquired; that seems to have been in one from birth *[innate* talent] *b)* existing as an inherent attribute *[the innate* humor of a situation] **2.** *Bot.* borne at the apex of the support, as an anther —**in·nate′ly** *adv.* —**in·nate′ness** *n.*

SYN.—**innate** and **inborn** are often interchangeable, but **innate** has more extensive connotations, describing that which belongs to something as part of its nature or constitution, and **inborn,** the simpler term, more specifically suggesting qualities so much a part of one's nature as to seem to have been born in or with one *[inborn* modesty]; **inbred** refers to qualities that are deeply ingrained by breeding *[an inbred* love of learning]; **congenital** implies existence at or from one's birth, specifically as a result of prenatal environment *[congenital* blindness]; **hereditary** implies acquirement of characteristics by transmission genetically from parents or ancestors *[hereditary* blondness]

in·ner (in′ər) *adj.* [ME. < OE. *innerra,* compar. of *inne,* within, IN] **1.** located farther within; interior; internal *[inner* organs] **2.** of the mind or spirit *[inner* peace] **3.** more intimate, central, or secret *[inner* emotions]

inner circle a small, exclusive group of people who control or influence customs, thought, etc.

☆**inner city** the sections of a large city in or near its center, esp. when crowded or blighted

☆**in·ner-di·rect·ed** (-di rek′tid) *adj.* guided by or concerned with goals or ideals determined by oneself rather than by others; nonconformist

Inner Hebrides *see* HEBRIDES

Inner Light in Quaker doctrine, a guiding influence resulting from the presence of God in the soul

inner man 1. one's spiritual being; mind or soul **2.** humorously, one's stomach or palate

Inner Mongolia region in NE China, south & southeast of the Mongolian People's Republic, comprising mainly the **Inner Mongolian Autonomous Region,** 454,633 sq. mi.; pop. 9,200,000; cap. Huhehot

in·ner·most (in′ər mōst′) *adj.* [< INMOST, after INNER] **1.** located farthest within **2.** most intimate or secret

in·ner·sole (-sōl′) *n. same as* INSOLE

☆**inner space** any space deep within, as contrasted with outer space; specif., *a)* the spiritual world within a person *b)* the sea or depths of the sea

in·ner·spring mattress (in′ər spriŋ′) a mattress with built-in coil springs

Inner Temple *see* INN OF COURT

inner tube a rubber tube used in a pneumatic tire: see TUBE (sense 2)

in·ner·vate (i nur′vāt, in′ər vāt′) *vt.* **-vat·ed**, **-vat·ing** [< IN-¹ + NERVE + -ATE¹] *Med.* **1.** to supply (a part of the body) with nerves **2.** to stimulate (a nerve, muscle, etc.) to movement or action —**in′ner·va′tion** *n.*

in·nerve (i nurv′) *vt.* **-nerved′**, **-nerv′ing** **1.** *same as* INNERVATE **2.** to give strength or courage to

In·ness (in′is), **George** 1825–94; U.S. painter

in·ning (in′iŋ) *n.* [ME. *inninge* < OE. *innung,* gerund of *innian,* to get in, put in] **1.** [Now Rare] *a)* an enclosing or reclaiming, as of wasteland *b)* [pl.] lands reclaimed, as from the sea **2.** *Baseball & (pl.) Cricket a)* the period of play in which a team has a turn at bat, completed in baseball by three outs *b)* a numbered round of play in which both teams have a turn at bat: a baseball game normally consists of nine innings **3.** [often *pl.*] the period of or opportunity for action, expression, exercise of authority, etc. *[the* election gave him his *innings]*

inn·keep·er (in′kē′pər) *n.* the proprietor or manager of an inn

in·no·cence (in′ə səns) *n.* [ME. < OFr. < L. *innocentia]* **1.** the quality or state of being innocent; specif., *a)* freedom from sin or moral wrong *b)* freedom from legal guilt *c)* freedom from guile or cunning; simplicity *d)* lack of sophistication; naïveté *e)* harmlessness *f)* ignorance **2.** an innocent person ☆**3.** *same as* BLUET

in·no·cen·cy (-sən sē) *n.* [Archaic] **1.** *same as* INNOCENCE (senses 1 & 2) **2.** *pl.* **-cies** an instance of this

In·no·cent (in′ə sənt) any of 13 popes, including **1. Innocent I,** Saint ?–417 A.D.; Pope (401–417): his day is July 28 **2. Innocent II** (born *Gregorio Papareschi*) ?–1143; Pope (1130–43) **3. Innocent III** (born *Lotario de' Conti de' Segni)* 1161?–1216; Pope (1198–1216) **4. Innocent IV** (born *Sinibaldo de' Fieschi)* ?–1254; Pope (1243–54) **5. Innocent XI** (born *Benedetto Odescalchi*) 1611–89; Pope (1676–89)

in·no·cent (-sənt) *adj.* [ME. < OFr. < L. *innocens < in-,* not + *nocens,* prp. of *nocere,* to do wrong to: for IE. base see NECRO-] **1.** free from sin, evil, or guilt; specif., *a)* doing or thinking nothing morally wrong; pure *b)* not guilty of a specific crime or offense; guiltless *c)* free from harmful effect or cause; that does not harm, injure, or corrupt *d)* not malignant; benign *[an innocent* tumor] **2.** *a)* knowing no evil *b)* without guile or cunning; artless; simple *c)* naïve *d)* ignorant **3.** totally lacking (with *of)* *[innocent* of adornment] —*n.* **1.** a person knowing no evil or sin, such as a child **2.** a very naïve or simple-minded person —**in′no·cent·ly** *adv.*

in·noc·u·ous (i näk′yoo wəs) *adj.* [L. *innocuus < in-,* not + *nocuus,* harmful < *nocere,* to harm, injure: see NECRO-] **1.** that does not injure or harm; harmless *[an innocuous* insect] **2.** not controversial, offensive, or stimulating; dull and uninspiring *[an innocuous* speech] —**in·noc′u·ous·ly** *adv.* —**in·noc′u·ous·ness** *n.*

Inn of Court [cf. INN, 3] **1.** one of the four London legal societies having the exclusive right to admit persons to practice at the bar **2.** one of the four groups of buildings *(Inner Temple, Middle Temple, Lincoln's Inn,* and *Gray's Inn)* belonging to these societies

in·nom·i·nate (i näm′ə nit) *adj.* [LL. *innominatus:* see IN-² & NOMINATE] **1.** not named; anonymous **2.** having no specific name

innominate bone either of the two large, irregular bones that, together with the sacrum and coccyx, make up the pelvis: it is formed of three bones, the ilium, ischium, and pubis, which become fused in the adult

in·no·vate (in′ə vāt′) *vi.* **-vat′ed**, **-vat′ing** [< L. *innovatus,* pp. of *innovare,* to renew < *in-,* in + *novare,* to renew, alter < *novus,* NEW] to introduce new methods, devices, etc. —*vt.* to bring in as an innovation —**in′no·va′tive** *adj.* —**in′no·va′tor** *n.*

in·no·va·tion (in′ə vā′shən) *n.* [LL. *innovatio]* **1.** the act or process of innovating **2.** something newly introduced; new method, custom, device, etc.; change in the way of doing things —**in′no·va′tion·al** *adj.*

in·nox·ious (i näk′shəs) *adj.* [L. *innoxius]* not noxious; harmless; innocuous

Inns·bruck (inz′brook′; *G.* ins′brook) capital of the Tirol, W Austria, on the Inn River: pop. 101,000

in·nu·en·do (in′yoo wen′dō) [L., by nodding to, abl. of gerund of *innuere*, to nod to, hint < *in-*, in + *-nuere* (in comp.), to nod < IE. base *neu-*, to jerk, beckon, nod, whence Sans. *návatē*, (he) turns, L. *numen*, a nod] that is to say; meaning: Latin formula for introducing explanatory material in legal documents; hence —*n.*, *pl.* **-does, -dos 1.** *Law* explanatory material so introduced; esp., that part of a complaint in an action for libel or slander which explains the expressions alleged to be libelous or slanderous **2.** an indirect remark, gesture, or reference, usually implying something derogatory; insinuation

in·nu·mer·a·ble (i nōō′mər ə b′l, -nyōō′-) *adj.* [ME. < L. *innumerabilis*: see IN-² & NUMERABLE] too numerous to be counted; very many; countless: also [Poet.] **in·nu′mer·ous** —*SYN.* see MANY —**in·nu′mer·a·bil′i·ty, in·nu′mer·a·ble·ness** *n.* —**in·nu′mer·a·bly** *adv.*

in·nu·tri·tion (in′nōō trish′ən, -nyōō-) *n.* lack of nutrition —**in′nu·tri′tious** (-shəs) *adj.*

in·ob·serv·ance (in′əb zur′vəns) *n.* **1.** lack of attention; disregard **2.** failure to observe a custom, rule, etc. — **in′ob·serv′ant** *adj.*

in·oc·u·la·ble (i näk′yoo lə b′l) *adj.* [INOCUL(ATE) + -ABLE] **1.** that can be communicated by inoculation **2.** that can be infected with a disease by inoculation **3.** that may be used in inoculation —**in·oc′u·la·bil′i·ty** *n.*

in·oc·u·late (-lāt′) *vt.* **-lat′ed, -lat′ing** [ME. *enoculaten* < L. *inoculatus*, pp. of *inoculare*, to engraft a bud in another plant < *in-*, in + *oculus*, a bud, EYE] **1.** *a)* to inject a serum, vaccine, etc. into (a living organism) esp. in order to create immunity *b)* to communicate (a disease) in this way **2.** to put or implant microorganisms into (soil, a culture medium, etc.) to develop a culture, stimulate growth, fix nitrogen, etc. **3.** to introduce ideas, etc. into the mind of; imbue; infect —**in·oc′u·la′tive** *adj.* —**in·oc′u·la′tor** *n.*

in·oc·u·la·tion (i näk′yoo lā′shən) *n.* [L. *inoculatio*] the act or process of inoculating; esp., *a)* the injection of a disease agent into an animal or plant, usually to cause a mild form of the disease and build up immunity to it *b)* the putting of bacteria, serum, etc. into soil, a culture medium, etc.

in·oc·u·lum (i näk′yoo ləm) *n.* [ModL.] material used in an inoculation, as bacteria, viruses, spores, etc.: also **in·oc′u·lant**

in·o·dor·ous (in ō′dər əs) *adj.* [L. *inodorus*] not odorous; having no odor; odorless

in·of·fen·sive (in′ə fen′siv) *adj.* not offensive; not objectionable; causing no harm, discomfort, or annoyance —**in′of·fen′sive·ly** *adv.* —**in′of·fen′sive·ness** *n.*

in·of·fi·cious (in′ə fish′əs) *adj.* [L. *inofficiosus*, undutiful: see IN-² & OFFICIOUS] *Law* showing neglect of moral duty: said esp. of a will that unreasonably deprives an heir of his just inheritance

I·nö·nü (ē nö nü′), **Is·met** (is met′) 1884– ; Turk. statesman; president of Turkey (1938–50); prime minister (1923–24; 1925–37; 1961–65)

in·op·er·a·ble (in äp′ər ə b′l) *adj.* not operable; specif., *a)* not practicable *b)* that will not practically allow of surgical operation [*an inoperable cancer*]

in·op·er·a·tive (-ər ə tiv, -ə rāt′iv) *adj.* not operative; not working; not functioning; without effect

in·op·er·cu·late (in′ō pur′kyoo lit) *adj.* [IN-² + OPERCULATE] lacking a definite, separable lid, as some spore cases

in·op·por·tune (in äp′ər tōōn′, -tyōōn′) *adj.* [L. *inopportunus*] not opportune; coming or happening at a poor time; not appropriate —**in·op′por·tune′ly** *adv.* —**in·op′por·tune′ness** *n.*

in·or·di·nate (in ôr′d′n it) *adj.* [ME. *inordinat* < L. *inordinatus*: see IN-² & ORDINATE] **1.** disordered; not regulated **2.** lacking restraint or moderation; too great or too many; immoderate —*SYN.* see EXCESSIVE —**in·or′di·na·cy** (-ə sē) *n.* —**in·or′di·nate·ly** *adv.* —**in·or′di·nate·ness** *n.*

inorg. inorganic

in·or·gan·ic (in′ôr gan′ik) *adj.* not organic; specif., *a)* designating or composed of matter that is not animal or vegetable; not having the organized structure of living things *b)* not like an organism in structure; without design, relation, and coordination of parts *c)* designating or of any chemical compound not classified as organic: most inorganic compounds do not contain carbon and are derived from mineral sources *d)* designating or of the branch of chemistry dealing with these compounds — **in′or·gan′i·cal·ly** *adv.*

in·os·cu·late (in äs′kyoo lāt′) *vt.*, *vi.* **-lat′ed, -lat′ing** [IN-¹ + OSCULATE] **1.** *a)* to join together by openings at the ends: said of arteries, ducts, etc. *b)* to intertwine: said of vines, etc. **2.** to join, blend, or unite intimately —**in·os′cu·la′tion** *n.*

in·o·si·tol (i nō′sə tōl′, -tôl′) *n.* [< Gr. *is* (gen. *inos*), muscle, fiber, strength < IE. base *wei-*, whence L. *vis*, strength + -IT(E)¹ + -OL¹] a sweet crystalline alcohol, $C_6H_6(OH)_6$, existing in nine isomeric forms and found in

both plant and animal tissues, esp. the form found in the vitamin B complex that apparently promotes growth: also **in·o·site** (in′ə sīt′)

in·pa·tient (in′pā′shənt) *n.* a patient who is lodged and fed in a hospital, clinic, etc. while receiving treatment

‡**in per·pe·tu·um** (in′ pər pech′oo wəm) [L.] forever

in per·so·nam (in′ pər sō′nam) [L., against the person] *Law* designating an action or judgment against a person, as distinguished from one against a thing, as property (*in rem*)

‡**in pet·to** (ēn pet′tō) [It., lit., in the breast] secretly; not revealed: said of cardinals appointed by the Pope but not named in consistory

in·phase (in′fāz′) *adj.* *Elec.* being of the same phase

‡**in pos·se** (in pō′sā) [L.] in possibility; only potentially

‡**in pro·pri·a per·so·na** (in prō′prē ə pər sō′nə) [L.] in one's own person or right

in·put (in′poot′) *n.* **1.** the act of putting in **2.** what is put in; specif., *a)* the amount of money, material, effort, etc. put into a project or process; investment *b)* electric current, voltage, or power put into a circuit, machine, etc. *c)* information fed into a computer, etc. **3.** a terminal connection for receiving electric power or signals

in·quest (in′kwest) *n.* [ME. *enqueste* < OFr. < VL. *inquaesita*, fem. pp. of *inquaerere*: see INQUIRE] **1.** a judicial inquiry, as a coroner's investigation of a death **2.** the jury or group holding such an inquiry **3.** the verdict of such an inquiry —*SYN.* see INVESTIGATION

in·qui·e·tude (in kwī′ə tōōd′, -tyōōd′) *n.* [ME. < MFr. *inquiétude* < LL. *inquietudo* < L. *inquietus*, restless: see IN-² & QUIET] restlessness; uneasiness

in·qui·line (in′kwə lin′, -lin) *n.* [L. *inquilinus*, inhabitant < *in-*, in + *colere*, to dwell: for IE. base see CULT] an animal, usually an insect, that lives in the nest or abode of another, with or without harm to the host: cf. COMMENSAL —**in′qui·lin·ism** (-lin iz′m) *n.*

in·quire (in kwīr′) *vi.* **-quired′, -quir′ing** [ME. *enqueren* < OFr. *enquerre* < VL. *inquaerere*, for L. *inquirere* < *in-*, into + *quaerere*, to seek] **1.** to seek information; ask a question or questions **2.** to carry out an examination or investigation (usually with *into*) —*vt.* to seek information about [*to inquire the way*] —*SYN.* see ASK —**inquire after** to pay respects by asking about the health of —**inquire for 1.** to ask to see (someone) **2.** to try to get by asking — **in·quir′er** *n.* —**in·quir′ing·ly** *adv.*

in·quir·y (in′kwə rē, -kwi′-; in kwīr′ē) *n.*, *pl.* **-quir·ies** [earlier *enquery* < ME. *enquere*] **1.** the act of inquiring **2.** an investigation or examination **3.** a question; query

in·qui·si·tion (in′kwə zish′ən) *n.* [ME. *inquicisioun* < OFr. *inquisition* < L. *inquisitio* < *inquisitus*, pp. of *inquirere*] **1.** the act of inquiring; investigation **2.** [I-] *R.C.Ch.* *a)* formerly, the general tribunal established in the 13th cent. for the discovery and suppression of heresy and the punishment of heretics *b)* the activities of this tribunal **3.** *a)* any harsh or arbitrary suppression or punishment of dissidents or nonconformists *b)* any severe or intensive questioning **4.** *Law* *a)* an inquest or any judicial inquiry *b)* the written finding of such an inquiry —*SYN.* see INVESTIGATION —**in′qui·si′tion·al** *adj.*

in·qui·si·tion·ist (-ist) *n.* same as INQUISITOR

in·quis·i·tive (in kwiz′ə tiv) *adj.* [ME. *enquesitif* < OFr. *inquisitif* < LL. *inquisitivus* < L. *inquisitus*, pp. of *inquirere*: see INQUIRE] **1.** inclined to ask many questions or seek information; eager to learn **2.** asking more questions than is necessary or proper; unnecessarily curious; prying —*SYN.* see CURIOUS —**in·quis′i·tive·ly** *adv.* —**in·quis′i·tive·ness** *n.*

in·quis·i·tor (-tər) *n.* [OFr. *inquisitor* < L. *inquisitor* < *inquisitus*, pp.: see INQUIRE] **1.** an official whose work is examining, or making an inquisition **2.** any harsh or prying questioner **3.** [I-] an official of the Inquisition

in·quis·i·to·ri·al (in kwiz′ə tôr′ē əl) *adj.* [< ML. *inquisitorius*] **1.** of, or having the nature of, an inquisitor or an inquisition **2.** inquisitive; unnecessarily or unpleasantly curious —**in·quis′i·to′ri·al·ly** *adv.*

in re (in rē, rā) [L.] in the matter (of); concerning

in rem (in rem) [L., against the thing] *Law* designating an action or judgment against a thing, as property, as distinguished from one against a person (*in personam*)

I.N.R.I. [L., *Iesus Nazarenus, Rex Iudaeorum*] Jesus of Nazareth, King of the Jews

in·road (in′rōd′) *n.* [IN-¹ + ROAD (in obs. sense of "riding")] **1.** a sudden invasion or raid **2.** [*usually pl.*] any injurious or wasting encroachment [*inroads* on one's health]

in·rush (-rush′) *n.* a rushing in; inflow; influx

ins. **1.** inches **2.** insulated **3.** insurance

‡**in sae·cu·la sae·cu·lo·rum** (in sek′yoo lə sek′yoo lôr′əm) [L., into ages of ages] for ever and ever; for eternity

in·sal·i·vate (in sal′ə vāt′) *vt.* **-vat′ed, -vat′ing** [IN-¹ + SALIVATE] to mix (food) with saliva in chewing —**in·sal′i·va′tion** *n.*

in·sa·lu·bri·ous (in′sə lōō′brē əs) *adj.* [< L. *insalubris* < -OUS] not salubrious; not healthful; unwholesome —**in′sa·lu′bri·ty** (-brə tē) *n.*

in·sane (in sān′) *adj.* [L. *insanus*] **1.** not sane; mentally ill

or deranged; demented; mad: not a scientific term: see INSANITY ☆2. of or for insane people /an *insane* asylum/ 3. very foolish, impractical, extravagant, etc.; senseless —in·sane′ly *adv.*

in·san·i·tar·y (in san′ə ter′ē) *adj.* not sanitary; unhealthful; likely to cause disease

in·san·i·ty (in san′ə tē) *n., pl.* -ties [L. *insanitas < insanus*] 1. the state of being insane; mental illness or derangement, usually excluding amentia: not a scientific term; specif., *Law* any form or degree of mental derangement or unsoundness of mind, permanent or temporary, that makes a person incapable of what is regarded legally as normal, rational conduct or judgment: it usually implies a need for hospitalization 2. great folly; extreme senselessness

SYN.—**insanity**, current in popular and legal language but not used technically in medicine (see definition above), implies mental derangement in one who formerly had mental health; **lunacy** specifically suggests periodic spells of insanity, but is now most commonly used in its extended sense of extreme folly; **dementia** is the general term for an acquired mental disorder, now generally one of organic origin, as distinguished from *amentia* (congenital mental deficiency); **psychosis** is the psychiatric term for any of various specialized mental disorders, functional or organic, in which the personality is seriously disorganized —ANT. sanity

in·sa·ti·a·ble (in sā′shə b'l, -shē ə-) *adj.* [see IN-² & SATIATE] constantly wanting more; that cannot be satisfied or appeased; very greedy —in·sa′ti·a·bil′i·ty *n.* —in·sa′ti·a·bly *adv.*

in·sa·ti·ate (-shē it) *adj.* [L. *insatiatus*] never satisfied; insatiable —in·sa′ti·ate·ly *adv.* —in·sa′ti·ate·ness *n.*

in·scribe (in skrīb′) *vt.* -scribed′, -scrib′ing [L. *inscribere*: see IN-¹ & SCRIBE] 1. *a)* to write, mark, or engrave (words, symbols, etc.) on some surface *b)* to write on, mark, or engrave (a surface) 2. to add the name of (someone) to a list; enroll 3. *a)* to dedicate (a book, song, etc.) briefly and informally *b)* to write a short, signed message in (a book, etc. one is presenting as a gift) 4. to fix or impress deeply or lastingly in the mind, memory, etc. 5. *Geom.* to draw (a figure) inside another figure so that their boundaries touch at as many points as possible —in·scrib′er *n.*

in·scrip·tion (in skrip′shən) *n.* [ME. *inscripcioun < L. inscriptio < inscriptus*, pp. of *inscribere*] 1. the act of inscribing 2. something inscribed or engraved, as on a coin or monument 3. *a)* a brief or informal dedication in a book, etc. *b)* a short, signed message written in a book, etc. one is presenting as a gift —in·scrip′tive, in·scrip′tion·al *adj.*

in·scroll (in skrōl′) *vt.* to record on a scroll

in·scru·ta·ble (in skrōōt′ə b'l) *adj.* [ME. < LL.(Ec.) *inscrutabilis < L. in-*, not + *scrutari*, to search carefully, examine: see SCRUTINY] that cannot be easily understood; completely obscure or mysterious; unfathomable; enigmatic —SYN. see MYSTERIOUS —in·scru′ta·bil′i·ty *n.* —in·scru′ta·bly *adv.*

in·seam (in′sēm′) *n.* an inner seam; specif., the seam from the crotch to the bottom of a trouser leg

in·sect (in′sekt) *n.* [< L. *insectum (animale)*, lit., notched (animal), neut. of pp. of *insecare*, to cut into < *in-*, in + *secare*, to cut (see SAW¹): from the segmented bodies: cf. ENTOMO-] 1. any of a large class (Insecta) of small arthropod animals characterized, in the adult state, by division of the body into head, thorax, and abdomen, three pairs of legs on the thorax, and, usually, two pairs of membranous wings: beetles, bees, flies, wasps, mosquitoes, etc. are insects 2. popularly, any of a group of small animals, usually wingless, including spiders, centipedes, wood lice, ticks, mites, etc. 3. an unimportant or contemptible person

INSECT (locust)
(A, spiracles; B, tympanum; C, ovipositor; D, abdomen; E, hind leg; F, middle leg; G, foreleg; H, tarsus; I, tibia; J, femur; K, antennae; L, compound eye; M, head; N, forewing; O, hind wing; P, cercus; Q, thorax; R, anus)

in·sec·tar·i·um (in′sek ter′ē əm) *n., pl.* -i·a (-ə) [ModL.] a place where insects are raised, esp. for study: also in·sec·tar·y (in′sek ter′ē, -tər ē), *pl.* -tar′ies

in·sec·ti·cide (in sek′tə sīd′) *n.* [< INSECT + -CIDE] any substance used to kill insects —in·sec′ti·cid′al *adj.*

☆in·sec·ti·fuge (-fyōōj′) *n.* any substance used to repel or drive away insects

in·sec·tile (in sek′t'l) *adj.* 1. of or like an insect: also in·sec·ti·val (in′sek tī′v'l) 2. consisting of insects

in·sec·ti·vore (in sek′tə vôr′) *n.* [Fr. < ModL. *insectivorus*: see IF.] 1. any of an order (Insectivora) of generally small, primitive mammals that are active mainly at night and that feed principally on insects, as moles, shrews, hedgehogs, etc. 2. any animal or plant that feeds on insects

in·sec·tiv·o·rous (in′sek tiv′ər əs) *adj.* [ModL. *insectivorus*: see INSECT & -VOROUS] feeding chiefly on insects

in·se·cure (in′si kyoor′) *adj.* [ML. *insecurus*] not secure; specif., *a)* not safe from danger *b)* not confident; filled with anxieties; apprehensive *c)* not firm or dependable; unreliable —in′se·cure′ly *adv.* —in′se·cu′ri·ty *n., pl.* -ties

in·sem·i·nate (in sem′ə nāt′) *vt.* -nat′ed, -nat′ing [< L. *inseminatus*, pp. of *inseminare*, to sow in < *in-*, in + *seminare*, to sow < *semen*, seed: see SEMEN] 1. to sow seeds in; esp., to impregnate by sexual intercourse or by artificially injecting semen 2. to implant (ideas, etc.) in (the mind, etc.) —SYN. see INSTILL —in·sem′i·na′tion *n.*

in·sen·sate (in sen′sāt, -sit) *adj.* [LL.(Ec.) *insensatus*, irrational < L. *in-*, IN-² + *sensatus*, gifted with sense < *sensus*, SENSE] 1. lacking sensation; not feeling, or not capable of feeling, sensation; inanimate 2. without sense or reason; foolish; stupid 3. lacking sensibility; without regard or feeling for others; cold; insensitive —in·sen′sate·ly *adv.* —in·sen′sate·ness *n.*

in·sen·si·ble (in sen′sə b'l) *adj.* [ME. < OFr. < L. *insensibilis*: see IN-² & SENSIBLE] 1. lacking sensation; not having the power to perceive with the senses 2. having 'ost sensation; unconscious 3. not recognizing or realizing; unaware; indifferent 4. not responsive emotionally; without feeling 5. so small, slight, or gradual as to be virtually imperceptible 6. not intelligible; without meaning: now chiefly in legal use 7. [Obs.] senseless; stupid —in·sen′si·bil′i·ty *n.* —in·sen′si·bly *adv.*

in·sen·si·tive (-tiv) *adj.* not sensitive; esp., incapable of being impressed, influenced, or affected; having little or no reaction (to) —in·sen′si·tive·ly *adv.* —in·sen′si·tiv′i·ty, in·sen′si·tive·ness *n.*

in·sen·ti·ent (in sen′shē ənt, -shənt) *adj.* not sentient; without life, consciousness, or perception —in·sen′ti·ence *n.*

in·sep·a·ra·ble (in sep′ər ə b'l) *adj.* not separable; that cannot be separated or parted /inseparable friends/ —n. [*pl.*] inseparable persons or things —in·sep′a·ra·bil′i·ty, in·sep′a·ra·ble·ness *n.* —in·sep′a·ra·bly *adv.*

in·sert (in surt′; *for n.* in′sərt) *vt.* [< L. *insertus*, pp. of *inserere < in-*, in + *serere*, to join] to put or fit (something) into something else; put in; introduce —*n.* anything inserted or for insertion; esp., an extra leaf or section inserted in a newspaper, etc. —SYN. see INTRODUCE

in·sert·ed (in sur′tid) *adj. Biol.* joined by natural growth

in·ser·tion (in sur′shən) *n.* [L. *insertio*] 1. an inserting or being inserted 2. something inserted; specif., *a)* a piece of lace or embroidery that can be set into a piece of cloth for ornamentation *b)* a single placement of an advertisement, as in a newspaper 3. *Anat.* the point of attachment of a muscle to the part that it moves

☆in·ser·vice (in′sur′vis) *adj.* designating or of training, as in special courses, workshops, etc., given to employees in connection with their work to help them develop skills, etc.

in·ses·so·ri·al (in′se sôr′ē əl) *adj.* [< ModL. *Insessores, pl.*, perching birds < L. *insessor*, occupant, lit., one who sits in or on < *insidere* (see INSIDIOUS) + -IAL] adapted for perching: said of certain birds

in·set (in set′; *also, and for n. always,* in′set) *vt.* -set′, -set′ting [ME. *insetten < OE. insettan*, to set in, appoint < *in-*, in + *settan*, to SET] to set into something; insert —*n.* something set in; insert; specif., *a)* a smaller picture or map set within the border of a larger one *b)* a piece of material set into a garment

in·sheathe (in shēth′) *vt.* -sheathed′, -sheath′ing *same as* ENSHEATHE

in·shore (in′shôr′, in shôr′) *adv., adj.* 1. in toward the shore 2. near the shore —inshore of nearer than (something else) to the shore

in·side (in′sīd′, -sīd′; *for prep. & adv., usually* in′sīd′) *n.* 1. the part lying within; inner side, surface, or part; interior 2. the part closest to something specified or implied, as the part of a sidewalk closest to the buildings 3. [*pl.*] [Colloq.] the internal organs of the body, as the stomach and intestines —*adj.* 1. on or in the inside; internal 2. of or suited for the inside 3. working or used indoors; indoor ☆4. known only to insiders; secret or private /the *inside* story/ ☆5. *Baseball* passing between home plate and the batter —*adv.* 1. on or to the inside; within 2. indoors —*prep.* inside of; in; within —☆inside of in less than (a specified time or distance); within the space of —inside out 1. with the inside where the outside should be; reversed 2. [Colloq.] thoroughly; completely —on the inside ☆1. in a position allowing access to secret information, special advantage or favor, etc. 2. in one's inner thoughts or feelings

inside job [Colloq.] a crime committed by, or with the aid of, a person employed or trusted by the victim

☆Inside Passage sea route along the W coast of N. America, from Seattle, Wash., to the N part of the Alaska panhandle

in·sid·er (in sī′dər) *n.* 1. a person inside a given place or group 2. a person having or likely to have secret or confidential information

☆inside track 1. the inner, shorter way around a race track 2. a favorable position or advantage

in·sid·i·ous (in sid′ē əs) *adj.* [L. *insidiosus < insidiae*, an ambush, plot < *insidere*, to sit in or on, lie in wait for < *in-*, in + *sedere*, to SIT¹] 1. characterized by treachery or slyness; crafty; wily 2. operating in a slow or not easily

apparent manner; more dangerous than seems evident [an *insidious* disease] —**in·sid′i·ous·ly** *adv.* —**in·sid′-i·ous·ness** *n.*

in·sight (in′sīt′) *n.* [ME. *insiht:* see IN-¹ & SIGHT] 1. the ability to see and understand clearly the inner nature of things, esp. by intuition 2. a clear understanding of the inner nature of some specific thing 3. *a) Psychol.* awareness of one's own mental attitudes and behavior *b) Psychiatry* recognition of one's own mental disorder

in·sight·ful (-fəl) *adj.* having or showing insight

in·sig·ni·a (in sig′nē ə) *n.pl.* (*in sense* 1), *n.sing.* (*in sense* 2) [L., pl. of *insigne*, neut. of *insignis*, distinguished by a mark < *in-*, in + *signum*, a mark, SIGN] 1. *sing.* **in·sig′ne** (-nē) badges, emblems, or other distinguishing marks, as of rank, membership, etc. 2. *pl.* **in·sig′ni·as** such a badge, emblem, etc.

in·sig·nif·i·cant (in′sig nif′ə kənt) *adj.* [IN-² + SIGNIFI-CANT] 1. having little or no meaning 2. having little or no importance; trivial 3. small; unimposing 4. low in position, character, etc.; mean —**in·sig·nif′i·cance, in′-sig·nif′i·can·cy** *n.* —**in′sig·nif′i·cant·ly** *adv.*

in·sin·cere (in′sin sir′) *adj.* [L. *insincerus*] not sincere; deceptive or hypocritical; not to be trusted —**in′sin·cere′-ly** *adv.*

in·sin·cer·i·ty (-ser′ə tē) *n.* 1. the quality of being insincere 2. *pl.* **-ties** an insincere act, remark, etc.

in·sin·u·ate (in sin′yoo wāt′) *vt.* **-at′ed, -at′ing** [< L. *insinuatus*, pp. of *insinuare*, to introduce by windings and turnings, insinuate < *in-*, in + *sinus*, curved surface] 1. to introduce or work into gradually, indirectly, and artfully [to *insinuate* oneself into another's favor] 2. to hint or suggest indirectly; imply —*vi.* to make insinuations —*SYN.* see INTRODUCE, SUGGEST —**in·sin′u·at′ing·ly** *adv.* —**in·sin′u·a′tive** *adj.* —**in·sin′u·a′tor** *n.*

in·sin·u·a·tion (in sin′yoo wā′shən) *n.* [L. *insinuatio*] 1. the act of insinuating 2. something insinuated; specif., *a)* a sly hint or suggestion, esp. against someone *b)* action or a remark intended to win favor; ingratiation

in·sip·id (in sip′id) *adj.* [< Fr. & LL.: Fr. *insipide* < LL. *insipidus* < L. *in-*, not + *sapidus*, savory < *sapere*, to taste: see SAPIENT] 1. without flavor; tasteless 2. not exciting or interesting; dull; lifeless —**in′si·pid′i·ty** *n.*, *pl.* **-ties** —**in·sip′id·ly** *adv.*

SYN.—**insipid** implies a lack of taste or flavor and is, hence, figuratively applied to anything that is lifeless, dull, etc. [*insipid* table talk]; **vapid** and **flat** apply to that which once had, but has since lost, freshness, sharpness, tang, zest, etc. [the *vapid*, or *flat*, epigrams that had once so delighted him]; **banal** is used of that which is so trite or hackneyed as to seem highly vapid or flat [her *banal* compliments] —*ANT.* zestful, spicy, pungent

in·sip·i·ence (in sip′ē əns) *n.* [ME. < OFr. < L. *insipientia* < *insipiens*, unwise, foolish < *in-* + *sapiens*, wise: see IN-² & SAPIENT] [Archaic] lack of wisdom or intelligence; stupidity —**in·sip′i·ent** *adj.*

in·sist (in sist′) *vi.* [MFr. *insister* < L. *insistere*, to stand on, pursue diligently, persist < *in-*, in, on + *sistere*, to stand, akin to *stare*, STAND] to take and maintain a stand or make a firm demand (often with *on* or *upon*) —*vt.* 1. to demand strongly 2. to declare firmly or persistently —**in·sist′er** *n.* —**in·sist′ing·ly** *adv.*

in·sist·ence (in sis′təns) *n.* 1. the quality of being insistent 2. the act or an instance of insisting Also **in·sist′-en·cy**, *pl.* **-cies**

in·sist·ent (-tənt) *adj.* [L. *insistens*] 1. insisting or demanding; persistent in demands or assertions 2. compelling the attention [an *insistent* rhythm] —**in·sist′ent·ly** *adv.*

‡**in si·tu** (in sī′too) [L.] in position; in its original place

in·snare (in sner′) *vt.* **-snared′, -snar′ing** *same as* ENSNARE

in·so·bri·e·ty (in′sə brī′ə tē, -sō-) *n.* lack of sobriety; intemperance, esp. in drinking

in·so·far (in′sə fär′, -sō-) *adv.* to such a degree or extent (usually with *as*) [*insofar* as one can tell]

in·so·late (in′sō lāt′) *vt.* **-lat′ed, -lat′ing** [< L. *insolatus*, pp. of *insolare*, to expose to the sun < *in-*, in + *sol*, the sun: see SOL¹] to expose to the rays of the sun so as to dry, bleach, etc.

in·so·la·tion (in′sō lā′shən) *n.* [L. *insolatio*] 1. the act or an instance of insulating 2. the treatment of disease by exposure to the sun's rays 3. *same as* SUNSTROKE 4. *Meteorol. a)* the radiation from the sun received by a surface, esp. the earth's surface *b)* the rate of such radiation per unit of surface

in·sole (in′sōl′) *n.* 1. the inside sole of a shoe 2. an extra, removable inside sole put in for comfort

INSOLE

in·so·lent (in′sə lənt) *adj.* [ME. < L. *insolens < in-*, IN-² + *solens*, prp. of *solere*, to be accustomed to] 1. boldly disrespectful in speech or behavior; impertinent; impudent 2. [Now Rare] arrogantly contemptuous; overbearing —*SYN.* see IMPERTINENT, PROUD —**in′so·lence** *n.* —**in′so·lent·ly** *adv.*

in·sol·u·ble (in säl′yoo b'l) *adj.* [ME. < L. *insolubilis*] 1. that cannot be solved; unsolvable 2. that

cannot be dissolved; not soluble —**in·sol′u·bil′i·ty, in·sol′u·ble·ness** *n.* —**in·sol′u·bly** *adv.*

in·solv·a·ble (in säl′və b'l) *adj.* that cannot be solved

in·sol·ven·cy (in säl′vən sē) *n.*, *pl.* **-cies** the fact or condition of being insolvent; bankruptcy

in·sol·vent (-vənt) *adj.* 1. not solvent; unable to pay debts as they become due; bankrupt 2. not enough to pay all debts [an *insolvent* inheritance] 3. of insolvents or insolvency —*n.* an insolvent person

in·som·ni·a (in säm′nē ə) *n.* [L. < *insomnis*, sleepless < *in-*, IN-² + *somnus*, sleep: see SOMNOLENT] abnormally prolonged inability to sleep, esp. when chronic —**in·som′-ni·ac′** (-ak′) *n.*, *adj.*

in·so·much (in′sō much′, -sə-) *adv.* 1. to such a degree or extent; so (with *that*) 2. inasmuch (*as*)

in·sou·ci·ant (in soo′sē ənt) *adj.* [Fr. < *in-*, not + *souciant*, prp. of *soucier*, to regard, care < L. *sollicitare*: see SOLICIT] calm and unbothered; carefree; indifferent —**in·sou′ci-ance** (-əns) *n.* —**in·sou′ci·ant·ly** *adv.*

in·soul (in sōl′) *vt. same as* ENSOUL

insp. inspector

in·span (in span′) *vt., vi.* **-spanned′, -span′ning** [Afrik. < Du. *inspannen:* see IN-¹ & SPAN¹] in South Africa, to harness or yoke (animals) to a wagon, etc.

in·spect (in spekt′) *vt.* [L. *inspectare*, freq. < *inspectus*, pp. of *inspicere*, to look into, examine < *in-*, in, at + *specere*, to look at: see SPY] 1. to look at carefully; examine critically, esp. in order to detect flaws, errors, etc. 2. to examine or review (troops, etc.) officially —*SYN.* see SCRUTINIZE —**in·spec′tive** *n.*

in·spec·tion (in spek′shən) *n.* [ME. < OFr. < L. *inspectio* < *inspectus:* see prec.] 1. critical examination 2. official examination or review, as of troops

in·spec·tor (in spek′tər) *n.* [L.] 1. a person who inspects; official examiner; overseer 2. an officer on a police force, ranking next below a superintendent or police chief —**in·spec′to·ral, in′spec·to′ri·al** (-tôr′ē əl) *adj.* —**in·spec′-tor·ship** *n.*

in·spec·to·rate (-it, -āt′) *n.* 1. the position or duties of an inspector 2. inspectors collectively 3. the district supervised by an inspector

in·sphere (in sfir′) *vt.* **-sphered′, -spher′ing** *same as* ENSPHERE

in·spi·ra·tion (in′spə rā′shən) *n.* [ME. *inspiracioun* < OFr. *inspiration* < LL. *inspiratio*] 1. a breathing in, as of air into the lungs; inhaling 2. an inspiring or being inspired mentally or emotionally 3. *a)* an inspiring influence; any stimulus to creative thought or action *b)* an inspired idea, action, etc. 4. a prompting of something written or said 5. *Theol.* a divine influence upon human beings, as that resulting in the writing of the Scriptures

in·spi·ra·tion·al (-'l) *adj.* 1. of or giving inspiration; inspiring 2. produced, influenced, or stimulated by inspiration; inspired —**in·spi·ra′tion·al·ly** *adv.*

in·spir·a·to·ry (in spir′ə tôr′ē) *adj.* [< L. *inspiratus*, pp. of *inspirare* (see ff.) + -ORY] of, for, or characterized by inspiration, or inhalation

in·spire (in spīr′) *vt.* **-spired′, -spir′ing** [ME. *inspiren* < OFr. *inspirer* < L. *inspirare* < *in-*, in, on + *spirare*, to breathe] 1. orig., *a)* to breathe or blow upon or into *b)* to infuse (life, etc. *into*) by breathing 2. to draw (air) into the lungs; inhale 3. to have an animating effect upon; influence or impel; esp., to stimulate or impel to some creative or effective effort 4. to cause, guide, communicate, or motivate as by divine or supernatural influence 5. to arouse or produce (a thought or feeling) [kindness *inspires* love] 6. to affect with a specified feeling or thought [to *inspire* someone with fear] 7. to occasion, cause, or produce 8. to prompt, or cause to be written or said, by influence [to *inspire* a rumor] —*vi.* 1. to inhale 2. to give inspiration —**in·spir′a·ble** *adj.* —**in·spir′er** *n.*

in·spir·it (in spir′it) *vt.* to put spirit into; give life or courage to; cheer; exhilarate

in·spis·sate (in spis′āt, in′spə sāt′) *vt., vi.* **-sat·ed, -sat·ing** [< LL. *inspissatus*, thick < *in-*, in + *spissare*, to thicken < *spissus*, thick < IE. base *spei-*, to flourish, grow fat, whence G. *speck*, bacon, OE. *sped*, SPEED] to thicken, as by evaporation; condense —**in′-spis·sa′tion** *n.* —**in′spis·sa′tor** *n.*

Inst. 1. Institute 2. Institution

inst. 1. instant (*adj.* 2) 2. instrumental

in·sta·bil·i·ty (in′stə bil′ə tē) *n.* lack of stability; unstableness; specif., *a)* lack of firmness or steadiness *b)* lack of determination; irresolution

in·sta·ble (in stā′b'l) *adj.* [L. *instabilis*] *same as* UNSTABLE

in·stall, in·stal (in stôl′) *vt.* **-stalled′, -stall′ing** [ML.(Ec.) *installare < in-*, in + *stallum* < OHG. *stal*, a place, seat, STALL¹] 1. to place in an office, rank, etc., with formality or ceremony 2. to establish in a place or condition; settle [to *install* oneself in a deck chair] 3. to fix in position for use [to *install* new fixtures] —**in·stall′er** *n.*

in·stal·la·tion (in′stə lā′shən) *n.* [ML.(Ec.) *installatio*] 1. an installing or being installed 2. a complete mechanical apparatus fixed in position for use [a heating *installation*] 3. any military post, camp, base, etc.

in·stall·ment, in·stal·ment¹ (in stôl′mənt) *n.* [earlier *estallment* < *estall*, to arrange payments for < OFr. *estaler*, to stop, fix < *estal*, a halt, place < OHG. *stal*: see STALL¹] 1. any of the parts of a debt or other sum of money to be paid at regular times over a specified period 2. any of several parts, as of a serial story, appearing at intervals

in·stall·ment, in·stal·ment² (-mənt) *n.* [INSTALL + -MENT] an installing or being installed; installation

☆**installment plan** a credit system by which debts, as for purchased articles, are paid in installments

in·stance (in′stəns) *n.* [ME. *instaunce* < OFr. *instance* < L. *instantia*, a standing upon or near, being present < *instans*: see INSTANT] 1. orig., an urgent plea; persistent solicitation 2. an example; case; illustration 3. a step in proceeding; occasion or case [in the first *instance*] 4. [Obs.] a motive; cause 5. [Obs.] a token or sign 6. [Obs.] a detail or circumstance 7. *Law* a process or proceeding in a court; suit —*vt.* **-stanced, -stanc·ing** 1. to show by means of an instance; exemplify 2. to use as an example; cite —**at the instance of** at the suggestion or instigation of —**for instance** as an example; by way of illustration
SYN.—**instance** refers to a person, thing, or event that is adduced to prove or support a general statement [here is an *instance* of his sincerity]; **case** is applied to any happening or condition that demonstrates the general existence or occurrence of something [a *case* of mistaken identity]; **example** is applied to something that is cited as typical of the members of its group [his novel is an *example* of romantic literature]; **illustration** is used of an instance or example that helps to explain or clarify something [this sentence is an *illustration* of the use of a word]

in·stan·cy (in′stən sē) *n.* [L. *instantia*] the quality or condition of being instant; specif., *a)* urgency; pressure; insistence *b)* [Rare] imminence; immediateness *c)* [Rare] instantaneousness

in·stant (in′stənt) *adj.* [LME. < MFr. < L. *instans*, prp. of *instare*, to stand upon or near, press < *in-*, in, upon + *stare*, to STAND] 1. urgent; pressing 2. of the current month: an old-fashioned usage [yours of the 13th (day) *instant* received] 3. soon to happen; imminent 4. without delay; immediate [to demand *instant* obedience] 5. designating a food or beverage in readily soluble, concentrated, or precooked form, that can be prepared quickly, as by adding water 6. [Archaic] present; current —*adv.* [Poet.] at once; instantly —*n.* 1. a point or very short space of time; moment 2. a particular moment —**on the instant** without delay; immediately —**the instant** as soon as

in·stan·ta·ne·ous (in′stən tā′nē əs, -tān′yəs) *adj.* [ML. *instantaneus*] 1. done, made, or happening in an instant 2. done or made without delay; immediate [an *instantaneous* reply] 3. existing at a particular instant —**in′·stan·ta′ne·ous·ly** *adv.* —**in′·stan·ta′ne·ous·ness** *n.*

in·stan·ter (in stan′tər) *adv.* [L., earnestly, pressingly < *instans*: see INSTANT] without delay; immediately

in·stant·ly (in′stənt lē) *adv.* 1. in an instant; without delay; immediately 2. [Archaic] urgently; pressingly —*conj.* as soon as; the instant that [I came *instantly* I saw the need]

in·star¹ (in′stär) *n.* [ModL. < L., a shape, form < *instare*: see INSTANT] any of the various stages of an insect or other arthropod between molts

in·star² (in stär′) *vt.* **-starred′, -star′ring** 1. to stud or adorn as with stars 2. [Archaic] to place as a star

in·state (in stāt′) *vt.* **-stat′ed, -stat′ing** [IN-¹ + STATE] 1. to put in a particular status, position, or rank; install 2. [Obs.] to endow; invest (with)

‡**in sta·tu quo** (in stā′tōō kwō, stach′ōō) [L., in the state in which] in the existing, or same, condition

in·stau·ra·tion (in′stô rā′shən) *n.* [L. *instauratio* < *instauratus*, pp. of *instaurare*, to renew, repeat: see STORE] 1. the act of restoring; repair; renewal 2. [Obs.] the act of instituting or founding

in·stead (in sted′) *adv.* [IN + STEAD] in place of the person or thing mentioned; as an alternative or substitute [to feel like crying and laugh *instead*] —**instead of** in place of; rather than

in·step (in′step′) *n.* [prob. IN-¹ + STEP] 1. the upper part of the arch of the foot, between the ankle and the toes 2. the part of a shoe or stocking that covers this 3. the front part of the hind leg of a horse, between the hock and the pastern joint

in·sti·gate (in′stə gāt′) *vt.* **-gat′ed, -gat′ing** [< L. *instigatus*, pp. of *instigare*, to stimulate, incite < *in-*, IN-¹ + *-stigare* (in comp.), to prick: for IE. base see STICK] 1. to urge on, spur on, or incite to some action, esp. to some evil [to *instigate* others to strife] 2. to cause by inciting; foment [to *instigate* a rebellion] —**SYN.** see INCITE —**in′·sti·ga′tion** *n.* —**in′·sti·ga′tive** *adj.* —**in′·sti·ga′tor** *n.*

in·still, in·stil (in stil′) *vt.* **-stilled′, -still′ing** [MFr. *instiller* < L. *instillare* < *in-*, in + *stillare*, to drop < *stilla*, a drop] 1. to put in drop by drop 2. to put (an idea, principle, feeling, etc.) *in* or *into* little by little; impart gradually —**in′·stil·la′tion** *n.* —**in·still′er** *n.* —**in·still′-ment, in·stil′ment** *n.*
SYN.—**instill**, in this figurative connection, implies a gradual imparting of knowledge over an extended period of time [he had *instilled* honesty in his children]; **implant** suggests the imparting of knowledge as if by planting it in the mind, with the implication that it will develop there; **inculcate** implies frequent or insistent repetition so as to impress upon the mind [prejudice is *inculcated*

in one during childhood]; **infuse** suggests the imparting of qualities as if by pouring [he *infused* life into the play]; **inseminate** implies the spreading of ideas throughout a group, nation, etc. as if by sowing seeds

in·stinct (in′stiŋkt; *for adj.* in stiŋkt′) *n.* [< L. *instinctus*, pp. of *instinguere*, to impel, instigate < *in-*, in + **stinguere*, to prick: for IE. base see STICK] 1. (an) inborn tendency to behave in a way characteristic of a species; natural, unacquired mode of response to stimuli [suckling is an *instinct* in mammals] 2. a natural or acquired tendency, aptitude, or talent; bent; knack; gift [an *instinct* for doing the right thing] 3. *Psychoanalysis* a primal biological urge, as hunger, impelling a response, as eating, which brings relief of tension: the human instincts are conceived of as including the self-preservative, the sexual, and, sometimes, the aggressive —*adj.* filled or charged (*with*) [a look *instinct* with pity] —**in·stinc·tu·al** (in stiŋk′chōō wəl) *adj.*

in·stinc·tive (in stiŋk′tiv) *adj.* 1. of, or having the nature of, instinct 2. prompted or done by instinct —**SYN.** see SPONTANEOUS —**in·stinc′tive·ly** *adv.*

in·sti·tute (in′stə tōōt′, -tyōōt′) *vt.* **-tut′ed, -tut′ing** [< L. *institutus*, pp. of *instituere*, to set up, erect, construct < *in-*, in, on + *statuere*, to cause to stand, set up, place: see STATUTE] 1. to set up; establish; found; introduce 2. to start; initiate [to *institute* a search] 3. to install in office, esp. as a minister in a church or parish —*n.* [L. *institutum*, arrangement, plan < the *v.*] something instituted; specif., *a)* an established principle, law, custom, or usage *b)* [*pl.*] a summary or digest of established principles, esp. in law *c)* an organization for the promotion of art, science, education, etc. *d)* a school specializing in art, music, etc. ☆*e)* a college or university specializing in technical subjects *f)* an institution for advanced study, research, and instruction in a restricted field ☆*g)* a short teaching program established for a group concerned with some special field of work *h)* same as INSTITUTION (sense 3) —**in′sti·tut′er, in′sti·tu′tor** *n.*

in·sti·tu·tion (in′stə tōō′shən, -tyōō′-) *n.* [ME. *institucion* < OFr. < L. *institutio*] 1. an instituting or being instituted; establishment 2. an established law, custom, practice, system, etc. 3. *a)* an organization having a social, educational, or religious purpose, as a school, church, hospital, reformatory, etc. *b)* the building housing such an organization 4. [Colloq.] a person or thing long established in a place 5. *Eccles.* *a)* the establishment of a sacrament by Jesus *b)* the ritual of installing a clergyman as minister of a church or parish

in·sti·tu·tion·al (-′l) *adj.* 1. of, characteristic of, or having the nature of, an institution 2. of or to institutions, rather than individuals [*institutional* sales] 3. designating advertising that is intended primarily to gain prestige and good will rather than immediate sales —**in·sti·tu′tion·al·ly** *adv.*

in·sti·tu·tion·al·ism (-iz′m) *n.* 1. a belief in the usefulness or sanctity of established institutions 2. the care of the poor, homeless, or others needing assistance by or in public institutions 3. the nature of such care, regarded as impersonal, standardized, etc.

in·sti·tu·tion·al·ize (-īz′) *vt.* **-ized′, -iz′ing** 1. to make into or consider as an institution 2. to make institutional 3. to place in an institution, as for treatment or detention —**in′sti·tu′tion·al·i·za′tion** *n.*

in·sti·tu·tion·ar·y (in′stə tōō′shə ner′ē, -tyōō′-) *adj.* 1. of legal institutes 2. of institutions; institutional

in·sti·tu·tive (in′stə tōōt′iv, -tyōōt′-) *adj.* instituting or tending to institute; of institution

instr. 1. instructor 2. instrument 3. instrumental

in·struct (in strukt′) *vt.* [ME. *instructen* < L. *instructus*, pp. of *instruere*, to pile upon, put in order, erect < *in-*, in, upon + *struere*, to pile up, arrange, build: see STREW] 1. to communicate knowledge to; teach; educate 2. to give facts or information to on a particular matter; inform or guide [the judge *instructs* the jury] 3. to order or direct [to *instruct* a sentry to shoot] —**SYN.** see COMMAND, TEACH

in·struc·tion (in struk′shən) *n.* [ME. *instruccioun* < OFr. *instruccion* < L. *instructio*] 1. the act of instructing; education 2. *a)* knowledge, information, etc. given or taught *b)* any teaching, lesson, rule, or precept 3. *a)* a command or order *b)* [*pl.*] details on procedure; directions —**in·struc′tion·al** *adj.*

in·struc·tive (-tiv) *adj.* [ML. *instructivus*] serving to instruct; giving knowledge or information —**in·struc′tive·ly** *adv.* —**in·struc′tive·ness** *n.*

in·struc·tor (-tər) *n.* [ME. *instructour* < Anglo-Fr. < L. *instructor*, a preparer (in ML., teacher)] 1. a person who instructs; teacher ☆2. a college teacher ranking below an assistant professor —**in·struc′tor·ship′** *n.* —[Now Rare] —**in·struc′tress** (-tris) *n.fem.*

in·stru·ment (in′strə mənt) *n.* [ME. < OFr. < L. *instrumentum*, a tool or tools, stock, furniture, dress < *instruere*: see INSTRUCT] 1. *a)* a thing by means of which something is done; means *b)* a person used by another to bring something about 2. a tool or implement, esp. one used for delicate work or for scientific or artistic purposes 3. any of various devices for indicating or measuring conditions, performance, position, direction, etc. or, sometimes, for controlling operations, esp. in aircraft or rocket flight 4. any of various devices producing musical sound, as a piano, violin, oboe, etc. 5. *Law* a formal document, as a deed, contract, etc. —*vt.* 1. to provide with instruments 2.

Music to arrange (a composition) for instruments; orchestrate —*SYN.* see IMPLEMENT

in·stru·men·tal (in′strə men′t'l) *adj.* [ME. < MFr. < ML. *instrumentalis*] **1.** serving as a means; helpful (*in* bringing something about) **2.** of or performed with an instrument or tool **3.** of, performed on, or written for a musical instrument or instruments **4.** of instrumentalism **5.** *Gram.* designating or of a case showing means or agency: the instrumental case is found in Old English, Sanskrit, Slavonic, etc. —*n.* a composition for a musical instrument or instruments —**in′stru·men′tal·ly** *adv.*

in·stru·men·tal·ism (-iz′m) *n. Philos.* the pragmatic doctrine that ideas are plans for action serving as instruments for adjustment to the environment and that their validity is tested by their effectiveness

in·stru·men·tal·ist (-ist) *n.* **1.** a person who performs on a musical instrument **2.** a person who believes in instrumentalism —*adj.* of instrumentalism

in·stru·men·tal·i·ty (in′strə men tal′ə tē) *n., pl.* -**ties 1.** the condition, quality, or fact of being instrumental, or serving as a means **2.** a means or agency

in·stru·men·ta·tion (-tā′shən) *n.* [Fr.] **1.** the composition or arrangement of music for instruments; orchestration **2.** the act of developing, using, or equipping with, instruments, esp. scientific instruments **3.** the instruments used, as in a mechanical apparatus or in a particular musical score, band, etc. **4.** *same as* INSTRUMENTALITY

instrument flying the flying of an aircraft by the use of instruments only: distinguished from CONTACT FLYING

instrument landing a landing made by using only the instruments of the aircraft and electronic or radio signals from the ground

instrument panel (or **board**) a panel or board with instruments, gauges, etc. mounted on it, as in an automobile or airplane

in·sub·or·di·nate (in′sə bôr′d'n it) *adj.* [IN-² + SUBORDINATE] not submitting to authority; disobedient —*n.* an insubordinate person —**in′sub·or′di·nate·ly** *adv.* —**in′sub·or′di·na′tion** *n.*

in·sub·stan·tial (in′səb stan′shəl) *adj.* [ML. *insubstantialis*] not substantial; specif., *a)* not real; imaginary *b)* not solid or firm; weak or flimsy —**in′sub·stan′ti·al′i·ty** (-shē al′ə tē) *n.*

in·suf·fer·a·ble (in suf′ər ə b'l) *adj.* not sufferable; intolerable; unbearable —**in·suf′fer·a·bly** *adv.*

in·suf·fi·cien·cy (in′sə fish′ən sē) *n., pl.* -**cies** [LL. *insufficientia*] **1.** lack of sufficiency; deficiency; inadequacy: also [Rare] **in′suf·fi′cience 2.** inability or failure of an organ or tissue to perform its normal function: said esp. of a heart valve or heart muscle

in·suf·fi·cient (-ənt) *adj.* [LL. *insufficiens*] not sufficient; not enough; inadequate —**in′suf·fi′cient·ly** *adv.*

in·suf·flate (in suf′lāt, in′sə flāt′) *vt.* -**flat·ed**, -**flat·ing** [< L. *insufflatus*, pp. of *insufflare*, to blow or breathe into < *in-*, in + *sufflare*, to blow from below < *sub-*, under + *flare*, to BLOW¹] **1.** to blow or breathe into or on **2.** *Eccles.* to breathe on (baptismal waters or a person being baptized) as a rite of exorcism **3.** *Med.* to blow (a powder, vapor, air, etc.) into a cavity of the body —**in′suf·fla′tion** *n.* —**in′suf·fla′tor** *n.*

in·su·lar (in′sə lər, -syoo-) *adj.* [L. *insularis* < *insula*, island: see ISLE] **1.** of, or having the form of, an island **2.** living or situated on an island **3.** like an island; detached; isolated **4.** of, like, or characteristic of islanders, esp. when regarded as narrow-minded, illiberal, or provincial **5.** *Med. a)* characterized by isolated spots *b)* of the islets of Langerhans or other islands of tissue —**in′su·lar′i·ty** (-lar′ə tē), **in′su·lar·ism** *n.* —**in′su·lar·ly** *adv.*

in·su·late (-lāt′) *vt.* -**lat·ed**, -**lat·ing** [< L. *insulatus*, made like an island < *insula*, ISLE] **1.** to set apart; detach from the rest; isolate **2.** to separate or cover with a nonconducting material in order to prevent the passage or leakage of electricity, heat, sound, radioactive particles, etc.

in·su·la·tion (in′sə lā′shən, -syoo-) *n.* **1.** an insulating or being insulated **2.** any material used to insulate

in·su·la·tor (in′sə lāt′ər, -syoo-) *n.* anything that insulates; esp., a nonconductor, usually a device of glass or porcelain for insulating and supporting electric wires

in·su·lin (in′sə lin, -syoo-) *n.* [< L. *insula*, island (see ISLE) + -IN¹: after the islets of Langerhans] **1.** a protein hormone secreted by the islets of Langerhans, in the pancreas, which helps the body use sugar and other carbohydrates **2.** a preparation extracted from the pancreas of sheep, oxen, etc. and used hypodermically in the treatment of diabetes mellitus

insulin shock the abnormal condition caused by an overdose or excess secretion of insulin, resulting in a sudden reduction in the sugar content of the blood: it is characterized by tremors, cold sweat, convulsions, and coma

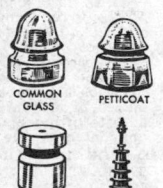

COMMON GLASS   PETTICOAT

PORCELAIN

HIGH TENSION

INSULATORS

in·sult (in sult′; *for n.* in′sult) *vt.* [MFr. *insulter* < L. *insultare*, to leap upon, scoff at, insult < *in-*, in, on + *saltare*, freq. of *salire*: see SALIENT] **1.** to treat or speak to with scorn, insolence, or great disrespect; subject to treatment, a remark, etc. that hurts or is meant to hurt the feelings or pride **2.** [Obs.] to attack; assail —*vi.* [Archaic] to behave arrogantly —*n.* **1.** an insulting act, remark, etc.; affront; indignity **2.** [Archaic] an attack; assault **3.** *Med. a)* damage or injury to tissues or organs of the body *b)* anything that causes this —*SYN.* see OFFEND —**in·sult′er** *n.* —**in·sult′ing** *adj.* — **in·sult′ing·ly** *adv.*

in·su·per·a·ble (in soo′pər ə b′l, -syoo′-) *adj.* [ME. < L. *insuperabilis*] not superable; that cannot be overcome or passed over; insurmountable —**in·su′per·a·bil′i·ty** *n.* —**in·su′per·a·bly** *adv.*

in·sup·port·a·ble (in′sə pôrt′ə b′l) *adj.* [LL.(Ec.) *insupportabilis*] not supportable; specif., *a)* intolerable; unbearable; unendurable *b)* incapable of being upheld, proved, etc. —**in′sup·port′a·bly** *adv.*

in·sup·press·i·ble (in′sə pres′ə b′l) *adj.* not suppressible; that cannot be suppressed —**in′sup·press′i·bly** *adv.*

in·sur·ance (in shoor′əns) *n.* [earlier *ensurance* < OFr. *enseurance*: see ENSURE] **1.** an insuring or being insured against loss; a system of protection against loss in which a number of individuals agree to pay certain sums (*premiums*) periodically for a guarantee that they will be compensated under stipulated conditions for any specified loss by fire, accident, death, etc. **2.** *a)* a contract guaranteeing such protection: usually called **insurance policy:** see POLICY² (sense 1) *b)* the premium specified for such a contract **3.** the amount for which life, property, etc. is insured **4.** the business of insuring against loss

in·sure (in shoor′) *vt.* -**sured′**, -**sur′ing** [ME. *ensuren*: see ENSURE] **1.** to contract to be paid or to pay money in the case of loss of (life, property, etc.); take out or issue insurance on (something or someone) **2.** *same as* ENSURE —*vi.* to give or take out insurance —**in·sur′a·bil′i·ty** *n.* —**in·sur′a·ble** *adj.*

in·sured (in shoord′) *n.* a person whose life, property, etc. is insured against loss

in·sur·er (in shoor′ər) *n.* a person or company that insures others against loss or damage; underwriter

in·sur·gence (in sur′jəns) *n.* a rising in revolt; uprising; insurrection

in·sur·gen·cy (-jən sē) *n.* **1.** the quality, state, or fact of being insurgent **2.** *same as* INSURGENCE

in·sur·gent (-jənt) *adj.* [L. *insurgens*, prp. of *insurgere*, to rise up (against) < *in-*, in, upon + *surgere*, to rise: see SURGE] rising up against established authority; rebellious; specif., *a)* designating or of a revolt or rebellion not well enough organized to be recognized in international law as belligerence *b)* designating or of a faction in revolt against the leadership of a political party —*n.* a person engaged in insurgent activity —**in·sur′gent·ly** *adv.*

in·sur·mount·a·ble (in′sər moun′tə b′l) *adj.* not surmountable; that cannot be passed over or overcome; insuperable —**in′sur·mount′a·bil′i·ty** *n.* —**in′sur·mount′a·bly** *adv.*

in·sur·rec·tion (in′sə rek′shən) *n.* [LME. < MFr. < LL. *insurrectio* < pp. of L. *insurgere*: see INSURGENT] a rising up against established authority; rebellion; revolt —*SYN.* see REBELLION —**in′sur·rec′tion·al** *adj.* —**in′sur·rec′tion·ar′y** *adj., n., pl.* -**ar′ies** —**in′sur·rec′tion·ist** *n.*

in·sus·cep·ti·ble (in′sə sep′tə b′l) *adj.* not susceptible (*to* or *of*); not easily affected or influenced —**in′sus·cep′ti·bil′i·ty** *n.* —**in′sus·cep′ti·bly** *adv.*

int. 1. interest **2.** interim **3.** interior **4.** interjection **5.** internal **6.** international **7.** intransitive

in·tact (in takt′) *adj.* [ME. *intacte* < L. *intactus* < *in-*, not + *tactus*, pp. of *tangere*, to touch: see TACT] with nothing missing or injured; kept or left whole; sound; entire; unimpaired —*SYN.* see COMPLETE —**in·tact′ness** *n.*

in·tag·lio (in tal′yō, -täl′-) *n., pl.* -**ios** [It. < *intagliare*, to cut in, engrave < *in-*, in + *tagliare*, to cut < LL. *taliare*: see TAILOR] **1.** a design or figure carved, incised, or engraved into a hard material so that it is below the surface **2.** something, as a gem or stone, ornamented with such a design or figure: opposed to CAMEO **3.** the art or process of making such designs or figures **4.** a method of printing from a plate on which incised lines, which carry the ink, leave a raised impression **5.** a die cut to produce a design in relief —*vt.* -**ioed**, -**io·ing** to engrave, carve, etc. in intaglio

in·take (in′tāk′) *n.* **1.** the act of taking in **2.** the amount or thing taken in **3.** the place at which a fluid is taken into a pipe, channel, etc. [a sewer *intake*] **4.** a narrowing; an abrupt lessening in breadth **5.** *Mech.* the amount of energy taken in **6.** *Mining* an air shaft

in·tan·gi·ble (in tan′jə b′l) *adj.* [ML. *intangibilis:* see IN-² & TANGIBLE] **1.** that cannot be touched; incorporeal; impalpable **2.** that represents value but has either no intrinsic value or no material being [stocks and bonds are *intangible* property, good will is an *intangible* asset] **3.** that cannot be easily defined, formulated, or grasped;

vague —*n.* something intangible —**in·tan′gi·bil′i·ty** *n.*, *pl.* **-ties** —**in·tan′gi·bly** *adv.*

in·tar·si·a (in tär′sē ə) *n.* [It. *intarsio* < *intarsiare*, to inlay, incrust < *in-*, in + Ar. *tarṣi*, inlay work < *raṣṣa′a*, to inlay] a style of decorative or pictorial inlay, esp. of the Italian Renaissance, involving a mosaic of wood pieces or, sometimes, ivory, metal, etc.

in·te·ger (in′tə jər) *n.* [L., untouched, whole, entire < *in-*, not + base of *tangere*, to touch: see TACT] **1.** anything complete in itself; entity; whole **2.** any positive (e.g., 5, 10) or negative (e.g., −5, −10) whole number or zero: distinguished from FRACTION

†**in·te·ger vi·tae** (in′tə jər vī′tē) [L., lit., unblemished in life] blameless; upright: from Horace, *Odes*, I

in·te·gra·ble (in′tə grə b'l) *adj.* that can be integrated

in·te·gral (in′tə grəl; *also, exc. for adj. 4 & n. 2*, in teg′rəl) *adj.* [LL. *integralis* < L. *integer*: see INTEGER] **1.** necessary for completeness; essential [an *integral* part] **2.** whole or complete **3.** made up of parts forming a whole **4.** *Math.* *a)* of or having to do with an integer or integers; not fractional *b)* of or having to do with integrals or integration —*n.* **1.** a whole **2.** *Math.* *a)* the result of integrating a function: cf. DEFINITE INTEGRAL, INDEFINITE INTEGRAL *b)* a solution of a differential equation —**in′te·gral′i·ty** (-gral′ə tē) *n.* —**in′te·gral·ly** *adv.*

integral calculus the branch of higher mathematics that deals with integration and its use in finding volumes, areas, equations of curves, solutions of differential equations, etc.

in·te·grand (in′tə grand′) *n.* [< L. *integrandus*, gerundive of *integrare*] *Math.* the function or expression to be integrated

in·te·grant (-grənt) *adj.* [L. *integrans*, prp. of *integrare*: see INTEGRATE] integral —*n.* an integral part; constituent

in·te·grate (-grāt′) *vt.* **-grat′ed, -grat′ing** [< L. *integratus*, pp. of *integrare*, to make whole, renew < *integer*: see INTEGER] **1.** to make whole or complete by adding or bringing together parts **2.** to put or bring (parts) together into a whole; unify **3.** to give or indicate the whole, sum, or total of ☆**4.** *a)* to remove the legal and social barriers imposing segregation upon (racial groups) so as to permit free and equal association *b)* to abolish segregation in; desegregate (a school, neighborhood, etc.) **5.** *Math. a)* to calculate the integral or integrals of (a function, equation, etc.) *b)* to perform the process of integration upon **6.** *Psychol.* to cause to undergo integration —*vi.* to become integrated —**in′te·gra′tive** *adj.*

integrated circuit an electronic circuit containing many interconnected amplifying devices and circuit elements formed on a single body, or chip, of semiconductor material

in·te·gra·tion (in′tə grā′shən) *n.* [L. *integratio*] **1.** an integrating or being integrated; specif., ☆the bringing of different racial or ethnic groups into free and equal association **2.** *Math.* the process of finding the quantity or function of which a given quantity or function is the derivative or differential: opposed to DIFFERENTIATION **3.** *Psychol.* the organization of various traits, feelings, attitudes, etc. into one harmonious personality —**in′te·gra′tion·al** *adj.*

☆**in·te·gra·tion·ist** (-ist) *n.* a person who advocates integration, esp. of racial groups —*adj.* believing in or advocating integration

in·te·gra·tor (in′tə grāt′ər) *n.* [L.] **1.** a person or thing that integrates **2.** a mechanical device for calculating integrals

in·teg·ri·ty (in teg′rə tē) *n.* [LME. *integrite* < L. *integritas* < *integer*: see INTEGER] **1.** the quality or state of being complete; unbroken condition; wholeness; entirety **2.** the quality or state of being unimpaired; perfect condition; soundness **3.** the quality or state of being of sound moral principle; uprightness, honesty, and sincerity — *SYN.* see HONESTY

in·teg·u·ment (in teg′yoo mənt) *n.* [L. *integumentum*, a covering < *integere*, to cover < *in-*, in, upon + *tegere*, to cover: see THATCH] an outer covering, as of the body or of a plant; skin, shell, hide, husk, rind, etc. —**in·teg′u·men′ta·ry** (-men′tə rē) *adj.*

in·tel·lect (in′t'l ekt′) *n.* [ME. < L. *intellectus*, a perceiving, understanding < pp. of *intellegere, intelligere*, to perceive, understand < *inter-*, between, among + *legere*, to gather, pick, choose: see LOGIC] **1.** the ability to reason or understand or to perceive relationships, differences, etc.; power of thought; mind **2.** great mental ability; high intelligence **3.** *a)* a mind or intelligence, esp. a superior one *b)* a person of high intelligence *c)* minds or intelligent persons, collectively —**in′tel·lec′tive** *adj.*

in·tel·lec·tion (in′t'l ek′shən) *n.* [ME. *intelleccioun* < ML. *intellectio*] **1.** the process of using the intellect; thinking; cognition **2.** an act of the intellect; a thought or perception

in·tel·lec·tu·al (in′t'l ek′choo wəl) *adj.* [ME. < LL. *intellectualis*] **1.** of or pertaining to the intellect **2.** appealing to the intellect **3.** *a)* requiring or involving the intellect *b)* inclined toward activities that involve the intellect **4.** guided by the intellect rather than by feelings **5.** having or showing a high degree of intellect; having superior reasoning powers —*n.* **1.** a person with intellectual interests or tastes **2.** a person engaged in intellectual work **3.** a member of the intelligentsia —*SYN.* see INTELLIGENT —**in′tel·lec′tu·al′i·ty** (-choo wal′ə tē) *n.* —**in′tel·lec′tu·al·ly** *adv.*

in·tel·lec·tu·al·ism (-iz'm) *n.* **1.** the quality of being intellectual; devotion to intellectual pursuits **2.** *Philos.* the doctrine that knowledge comes wholly from pure reason, without aid from the senses; rationalism —**in′tel·lec′tu·al·ist** *n.* —**in′tel·lec′tu·al·is′tic** *adj.*

in·tel·lec·tu·al·ize (-īz′) *vt.* **-ized′, -iz′ing 1.** to make intellectual; give an intellectual quality to **2.** to examine or interpret rationally, often without proper regard for emotional considerations —*vi.* to reason; think —**in′tel·lec′tu·al·i·za′tion** *n.*

in·tel·li·gence (in tel′ə jəns) *n.* [ME. < OFr. < L. *intelligentia*, perception, discernment < *intelligens*, prp. of *intelligere*: see INTELLECT] **1.** *a)* the ability to learn or understand from experience; ability to acquire and retain knowledge; mental ability *b)* the ability to respond quickly and successfully to a new situation; use of the faculty of reason in solving problems, directing conduct, etc. effectively *c)* *Psychol.* measured success in using these abilities to perform certain tasks *d)* generally, any degree of keenness of mind, cleverness, shrewdness, etc. **2.** news or information **3.** *a)* the gathering of secret information, as for military or police purposes *b)* the persons or agency employed at this **4.** intelligence personified; an intelligent spirit or being —**in·tel′li·gen′tial** (-jen′shəl) *adj.*

intelligence quotient a number indicating a person's level of intelligence: it is the mental age (as shown by intelligence tests) multiplied by 100 and divided by the chronological age

in·tel·li·genc·er (in tel′ə jən sər) *n.* [Now Rare] a person who supplies news or information; esp., a spy or secret agent

intelligence test a standardized series of problems progressively graded in difficulty, intended to test the relative intelligence of an individual

in·tel·li·gent (-jənt) *adj.* [L. *intelligens*, prp. of *intelligere*: see INTELLECT] **1.** having or using intelligence; rational **2.** having or showing an alert mind or high intelligence; bright, perceptive, informed, clever, wise, etc. **3.** [Archaic] having knowledge, understanding, or awareness (*of* something) —**in·tel′li·gent·ly** *adv.*
SYN.—**intelligent** implies the ability to learn or understand from experience or to respond successfully to a new experience; **clever** implies quickness in learning or understanding, but sometimes connotes a lack of thoroughness or depth; **alert** emphasizes quickness in sizing up a situation; **bright** and **smart** are somewhat informal, less precise equivalents for any of the preceding; **brilliant** implies an unusually high degree of intelligence; **intellectual** suggests keen intelligence coupled with interest and ability in the more advanced fields of knowledge —*ANT.* **stupid, dull**

in·tel·li·gent·si·a (in tel′ə jent′sē ə, -gent′-) *n.pl.* [*also with sing. v.*] [Russ. *intelligentsiya* < L. *intelligentia*: see INTELLIGENCE] the people regarded as, or regarding themselves as, the educated and enlightened class; intellectuals collectively

in·tel·li·gi·ble (in tel′i jə b'l) *adj.* [ME. < L. *intelligibilis* < *intelligere*: see INTELLECT] **1.** that can be understood; clear; comprehensible **2.** *Philos.* understandable by the intellect only; conceptual —**in·tel′li·gi·bil′i·ty** *n.* —**in·tel′li·gi·bly** *adv.*

In·tel·sat (in′tel sat′) [*In*(ternational) *Tel*(ecommunications) *Sat*(ellite Consortium)] an international organization for developing and launching communications satellites

in·tem·per·ance (in tem′pər əns) *n.* **1.** a lack of temperance or restraint; immoderation **2.** excessive drinking of alcoholic liquor

in·tem·per·ate (-it) *adj.* [L. *intemperatus*] **1.** not temperate; specif., *a)* not moderate; lacking restraint; excessive; going to extremes *b)* severe or violent; inclement [an *intemperate* wind] **2.** drinking too much alcoholic liquor —**in·tem′per·ate·ly** *adv.*

in·tend (in tend′) *vt.* [ME. *entenden* < OFr. *entendre* < L. *intendere*, to stretch out for, aim at < *in-*, in, at + *tendere*, to stretch: see THIN] **1.** to have in mind as a purpose; plan; purpose **2.** to mean (something) to be or be used (*for*); design; destine [a cake *intended* for the party] **3.** to mean or signify **4.** [Archaic] to direct or turn (the mind, eyes, thoughts, etc.) **5.** *Law* to construe or interpret legally —*vi.* to have a purpose or intention —**in·tend′er** *n.*
SYN.—**intend** implies a having in mind of something to be done, said, etc. [I *intended* to write you]; **mean**, a more general word, does not connote so clearly a specific, deliberate purpose [he always *means* well]; **design** suggests careful planning in order to bring about a particular result [their delay was *designed* to forestall suspicion]; **propose** implies a clear declaration, openly or to oneself. of one's intention [I *propose* to speak for an hour]; **purpose** adds to **propose** a connotation of strong determination to effect one's intention [he *purposes* to become a doctor]

in·tend·ance (in ten′dəns) *n.* [Fr. < *intendant*: see INTENDANT] **1.** superintendence; supervision **2.** same as INTENDANCY **3.** any of various administrative offices, as in France

in·tend·an·cy (-dən sē) *n., pl.* **-cies 1.** the position or duties of an intendant **2.** intendants collectively **3.** the district supervised by an intendant: also **in·tend′en·cy**

in·tend·ant (-dənt) *n.* [Fr. *intendant* or Sp. *intendente*, both < L. *intendens*, prp. of *intendere*: see INTEND] a director, manager of a public business, superintendent, etc.: term applied to certain foreign officials, as to the supervisors of any of certain districts in Spanish America

in·tend·ed (-did) *adj.* **1.** meant; planned; purposed **2.**

prospective; future [one's *intended* wife] —*n.* [Colloq.] the person whom one has agreed to marry; fiancé(e)

in·tend·ing (-diŋ) *adj.* [Chiefly Brit.] prospective; future

in·tend·ment (-mənt) *n.* [ME. *entendement* < OFr.: see INTEND] 1. [Archaic] intention, purpose, or design 2. the true and correct meaning or intention, as of a law

in·ten·er·ate (in ten'ə rāt') *vt.* -**at·ed**, -**at'ing** [IN-1 + L. *tener*, TENDER1 + -ATE1] [Rare] to make tender or soft — **in·ten·er·a'tion** *n.*

intens. 1. intensified 2. intensifier 3. intensive

in·tense (in tens') *adj.* [ME. < MFr. < L. *intensus*, pp. of *intendere*: see INTEND] 1. occurring or existing in a high degree; very strong; violent, extreme, sharp, vivid, etc. [an *intense* light] 2. strained to the utmost; strenuous; earnest; fervent; zealous [*intense* thought] 3. having or showing strong emotion, firm purpose, great seriousness, etc. [an *intense* person] 4. characterized by much action, emotion, etc. —**in·tense'ly** *adv.* —**in·tense'ness** *n.*

in·ten·si·fi·er (in ten'sə fī'ər) *n.* 1. something that intensifies 2. *Gram.* an intensive word, prefix, etc. 3. *Photog.* any of several solutions used to increase the printing density of a negative

in·ten·si·fy (-fī') *vt.* -**fied'**, -**fy'ing** 1. to make intense or more intense; increase; strengthen 2. *Photog.* to make (a film, etc.) more dense or opaque by treating with an intensifier —*vi.* to become intense or increase in intensity —**in·ten'si·fi·ca'tion** *n.*

SYN.—**intensify** implies an increasing in the degree of force, vehemence, vividness, etc. [his absence only *intensified* her longing]; **aggravate** implies a making more serious, unbearable, etc. and connotes something that is unpleasant or troublesome in itself [your insolence only *aggravates* the offense]; to **heighten** is to make greater, stronger, more vivid, etc. so as to raise above the ordinary or commonplace [music served to *heighten* the effect]; **enhance** implies the addition of something so as to make more attractive or desirable [she used cosmetics to *enhance* her beauty] —ANT. diminish, mitigate

in·ten·sion (in ten'shən) *n.* [L. *intensio* < *intensus*, pp. of *intendere*: see INTEND] 1. intentness; determination 2. intensification 3. the quality of being intense; intensity or degree of intensity 4. *Logic* the total number of characteristics which a thing must possess so that a particular term can be applied to it; connotation: opposed to EXTENSION —**in·ten'sion·al** *adj.*

in·ten·si·ty (in ten'sə tē) *n.*, *pl.* -**ties** [ML. *intensitas*] 1. the quality of being intense; specif., *a)* extreme degree of anything *b)* great energy or vehemence of emotion, thought, or activity 2. degree or extent; relative strength, magnitude, vigor, etc. 3. *same as* SATURATION (sense 2) 4. *Physics* the amount of force or energy of heat, light, sound, electric current, etc. per unit area, volume, charge, etc.

in·ten·sive (-siv) *adj.* [ML. *intensivus* < L. *intensus*: see INTENSE & -IVE] 1. increasing or causing to increase in degree or amount 2. of or characterized by intensity; thorough, profound, and intense; concentrated or exhaustive 3. of or characterized by logical intension 4. designating care of an especially attentive nature given to hospital patients immediately following surgery, a heart attack, etc. 5. *Agric.* designating a system of farming which aims at the increase of crop yield per unit area 6. *Gram.* giving force or emphasis; emphasizing ["very" in "the very same man" is an *intensive* adverb] —*n.* 1. anything that intensifies 2. an intensive word, prefix, etc. —**in·ten'sive·ly** *adv.* —**in·ten'sive·ness** *n.*

in·tent (in tent') *adj.* [L. *intentus*, pp. of *intendere*: see INTEND] 1. firmly directed or fixed; earnest; intense [an *intent* look] 2. *a)* having the mind or attention firmly directed or fixed; engrossed [*intent* on his studies] *b)* strongly resolved [*intent* on going] —*n.* [ME. *entente*, *intente* < OFr. *entente* & ML. *intentus*, both < L. *intentus*, a stretching out < *intendere*: see INTEND] 1. an act or instance of intending 2. something intended; specif., *a)* a purpose; object; aim *b)* meaning or import 3. *Law* one's mental attitude, including purpose, will, determination, etc., at the time of doing an act —SYN. see INTENTION —to all intents and purposes in almost every respect; practically; virtually —**in·tent'ly** *adv.* —**in·tent'ness** *n.*

in·ten·tion (in ten'shən) *n.* [ME. *entencioun* < OFr. *entencion* < L. *intentio* < pp. of *intendere*] 1. the act or fact of intending; determination to do a specified thing or act in a specified manner 2. *a)* anything intended or planned; aim, end, or purpose *b)* [*pl.*] purpose in regard to marriage 3. [Rare] meaning or import 4. *Logic* an instrument, such as a concept, for knowing and referring to a thing as it exists in the mind 5. *Surgery* the manner or process by which a wound heals: the three degrees (*first*, *second*, and *third intention*) are distinguished by the relative amounts and types of granulation that occur SYN.—**intention** is the general word implying a having something in mind as a plan or design, or referring to the plan had in mind; **intent**, a somewhat formal term now largely in legal usage, connotes more deliberation [assault with *intent* to kill]; **purpose** connotes greater resolution or determination in the plan [I have a *purpose* in writing you]; **aim** refers to a specific intention and connotes a directing of all efforts toward this [his *aim* is to become a

doctor]; **goal** suggests laborious effort in striving to attain something [the presidency was the *goal* of his ambition]; **end** emphasizes the final result one hopes to achieve as distinct from the process of achieving it [is this *end* justified by the means used?]; **object** is used of an end that is the direct result of a need or desire [the *object* of the discussion was to arouse controversy]; **objective** refers to a specific end that is capable of being reached [her immediate *objective* is to pass the course]

in·ten·tion·al (-shən 'l) *adj.* [ML. *intentionalis*] 1. having to do with intention or purpose 2. done purposely; intended —SYN. see VOLUNTARY —**in·ten'tion·al·ly** *adv.*

in·ten·tioned (-shənd) *adj.* having (specified) intentions: often in hyphenated compounds [well-*intentioned*]

in·ter (in tur') *vt.* -**terred'**, -**ter'ring** [ME. *enteren* < OFr. *enterrer* < VL. *interrare, to put in the earth < L. *in*, in + *terra*, earth: see THIRST] to put (a dead body) into a grave or tomb; bury

in·ter- (in'tər) [L. < *inter*, between, among < IE. *enter, *nter (compar. of *en, in), whence Sans. *antár*, within, OE. *under*, G. *unter*, among] *a combining form meaning:* 1. between or among: the second element is singular in form [*interstate*] 2. with or on each other (or one another), together, mutual, reciprocal, mutually, or reciprocally [*interact*]

in·ter·act (in'tər akt') *vi.* to act on one another; act reciprocally —**in'ter·ac'tive** *adj.*

in·ter·act·ant (-ak'tənt) *n.* any of the elements involved in an interaction; specif., any of the substances involved in a chemical reaction

in·ter·ac·tion (-ak'shən) *n.* action on each other; reciprocal action or effect —**in'ter·ac'tion·al** *adj.*

‡**in·ter a·li·a** (in'tər ā'lē ə, ä'-) [L.] among other things

‡**in·ter a·li·os** (-ōs') [L.] among other persons

in·ter-A·mer·i·can (in'tər ə mer'ə kən) *adj.* between or among nations of the Americas

in·ter·brain (in'tər brān') *n.* same as DIENCEPHALON

in·ter·breed (in'tər brēd') *vt.*, *vi.* -**bred'**, -**breed'ing** same as HYBRIDIZE

in·ter·ca·lar·y (in tur'kə ler'ē) *adj.* [L. *intercalarius*, *inter-calaris* < *intercalare*: see ff.] 1. added to the calendar: said of a day, month, etc. inserted in a leap year to make the calendar correspond to the solar year 2. having such a day, month, etc. added: said of a year 3. interpolated or inserted

in·ter·ca·late (-lāt') *vt.* -**lat'ed**, -**lat'ing** [< L. *intercalatus*, pp. of *intercalare*, to insert < *inter-*, between + *calare*, to call, proclaim: for IE. base see CLAMOR] 1. to insert (a day, month, etc.) in the calendar 2. to interpolate or insert —**in·ter'ca·la'tion** *n.*

in·ter·cede (in'tər sēd') *vi.* -**ced'ed**, -**ced'ing** [L. *intercedere* < *inter-*, between + *cedere*, to go] 1. to plead or make a request in behalf of another or others [to *intercede* with the authorities for the prisoner] 2. to intervene for the purpose of producing agreement; mediate —SYN. see INTERPOSE

in·ter·cel·lu·lar (-sel'yoo lər) *adj.* located between or among cells

in·ter·cept (in'tər sept'; *for n.* in'tər sept') *vt.* [< L. *interceptus*, pp. of *intercipere*, to take between, interrupt < *inter-*, between + *capere*, to take] 1. to seize or stop on the way, before arrival at the intended place; stop or interrupt the course of; cut off [to *intercept* a forward pass] 2. [Now Rare] *a)* to stop, hinder, or prevent *b)* to cut off communication with, sight of, etc. 3. *Math.* to cut off, mark off, or bound between two points, lines, or planes —*n.* 1. *Math.* the part of a line, plane, etc. intercepted 2. *Mil.* the act of intercepting an enemy force, esp. enemy aircraft —**in'ter·cep'tion** *n.* —**in'ter·cep'tive** *adj.*

in·ter·cep·tor (-sep'tər) *n.* a person or thing that intercepts; esp., a fast-climbing military airplane used in fighting off enemy attacks: also **in'ter·cept'er**

in·ter·ces·sion (in'tər sesh'ən) *n.* [L. *intercessio* < *intercessus*, pp. of *intercedere*] the act of interceding; mediation, pleading, or prayer in behalf of another or others —**in'ter·ces'sion·al** *adj.*

in·ter·ces·sor (in'tər ses'ər, in'tər ses'ər) *n.* [ME. *intercessour* < L. *intercessor*] a person who intercedes —**in'ter·ces'so·ry** *adj.*

in·ter·change (in'tər chānj'; *for n.* in'tər chānj') *vt.* -**changed'**, -**chang'ing** [ME. *entrechangen* < OFr. *entre-changier*: see INTER- & CHANGE] 1. to give and take mutually; exchange [to *interchange* ideas] 2. to put (each of two things) in the other's place 3. to alternate; cause to follow in succession [to *interchange* work with play] —*vi.* to change places with each other —*n.* 1. the act or an instance of interchanging 2. any of the places on a freeway where traffic can enter or depart, usually by means of a cloverleaf

in·ter·change·a·ble (in'tər chān'jə b'l) *adj.* [OFr. *entre-changeable*] that can be interchanged; esp., that can be put or used in place of each other —**in'ter·change'a·bil'-i·ty** *n.* —**in'ter·change'a·bly** *adv.*

in·ter·clav·i·cle (-klav'ə k'l) *n.* a bone lying between the tips of the clavicles and on the sternum in certain vertebrates —**in'ter·cla·vic'u·lar** (-klə vik'yə lər) *adj.*

in·ter·col·le·gi·ate (-kə lēʹjət, -jē ət) *adj.* between or among colleges and universities

in·ter·co·lum·ni·a·tion (-kə lumʹnē āʹshən) *n. Archit.* 1. the space between two columns, measured from their axes 2. the system of spacing a series of columns

in·ter·com (inʹtər käm′) *n.* a radio or telephone inter-communication system, as between compartments of an airplane or ship, rooms of a building, etc.

in·ter·com·mu·ni·cate (inʹtər kə myōōʹnə kāt′) *vt., vi.* **-cat′ed, -cat′ing** to communicate with or to each other or one another —**in′ter·com·mun′i·ca′tion** *n.*

in·ter·com·mun·ion (-kə myōōnʹyən) *n.* mutual communion, as among religious groups

in·ter·con·nect (-kə nekt′) *vt., vi.* to connect or be connected with one another —**in′ter·con·nec′tion** *n.*

in·ter·con·ti·nen·tal (-känʹtə nenʹt'l) *adj.* 1. between or among continents 2. able to travel from one continent to another, as a plane, rocket-launched missile, etc.

in·ter·cos·tal (-käsʹt'l) *adj.* [ModL. *intercostalis:* see INTER- & COSTAL] between the ribs —*n.* an intercostal muscle, etc. —**in′ter·cos′tal·ly** *adv.*

in·ter·course (inʹtər kôrs) *n.* [ME. *entercours* < OFr. *entrecours* < L. *intercursus:* see INTER- & COURSE] 1. communication or dealings between or among people, countries, etc.; interchange of products, services, ideas, feelings, etc. 2. the sexual joining of two individuals; coitus; copulation: in full, **sexual intercourse**

in·ter·crop (inʹtər kräp′; *for n.* inʹtər kräp′) *vt., vi.* **-cropped′, -crop′ping** to grow a crop with (another crop) in the same field, as in alternate rows —*n.* any such crop

in·ter·cross (inʹtər krôs′; *for n.* inʹtər krôs′) *vt., vi.* same as HYBRIDIZE —*n.* same as HYBRID (sense 1)

in·ter·cul·tur·al (-kulʹchər əl) *adj.* between or among people of different cultures

in·ter·cur·rent (-kurʹənt) *adj.* [L. *intercurrens,* prp. of *intercurrere:* see INTER- & COURSE] 1. running between; intervening 2. occurring during another disease and modifying it —**in′ter·cur′rent·ly** *adv.*

in·ter·de·nom·i·na·tion·al (-di nämʹə nāʹshən 'l) *adj.* between, among, shared by, or involving different religious denominations

in·ter·den·tal (-denʹt'l) *adj.* 1. situated between the teeth 2. *Phonet.* pronounced with the tip of the tongue between the upper and lower teeth, as *th* in *think*

in·ter·de·part·men·tal (-di pärtʹmenʹt'l) *adj.* between or among departments —**in′ter·de·part′men′tal·ly** *adv.*

in·ter·de·pend·ence (-di penʹdəns) *n.* dependence on each other or one another; mutual dependence: also **in′ter·de·pend′en·cy** —**in′ter·de·pend′ent** *adj.* —**in′ter·de·pend′ent·ly** *adv.*

in·ter·dict (inʹtər dikt′; *for n.* inʹtər dikt′) *vt.* [altered (after L.) < ME. *entrediten* < *entredit, n.:* see *n.* below] 1. to prohibit (an action) or the use of (a thing); forbid with authority 2. to restrain from doing or using something 3. to impede or hinder (the enemy) or isolate (an area, route, etc.) by firepower or bombing 4. *R.C.Ch.* to exclude (a person, parish, etc.) from certain acts, sacraments, or privileges —*n.* [altered (after L.) < ML. *entredit* < OFr. < L. *interdictum* < pp. of *interdicere,* to forbid, prohibit, lit., to speak between < *inter-* (see INTER-) + *dicere,* to speak (see DICTION) an official prohibition or restraint; specif., *a) Scottish Law* an injunction *b) R.C.Ch.* an interdicting of a person, parish, etc. —*SYN.* see FORBID —**in′ter·dic′tion** *n.* —**in′ter·dic′tor** *n.* —**in′ter·dic′to·ry, in′ter·dic′tive** *adj.*

in·ter·dig·i·tate (-dijʹə tāt′) *vi.* **-tat′ed, -tat′ing** to interlock like the fingers of folded hands

in·ter·dis·ci·pli·nar·y (-disʹə pli ner′ē) *adj.* involving, or joining, two or more disciplines, or branches of learning [an *interdisciplinary* approach to cultural history]

in·ter·est (inʹtrist, inʹtər ist; *for v., also* -tə rest′) *n.* [ME. *interesse* < ML. *interesse,* usury, compensation (in L., to be between, be different, interest < *inter-,* between + *esse,* to be: see IS): altered after OFr. *interest* < L., it interests, concerns, 3d pers. sing., pres. indic., of *interesse*] 1. a right or claim to something 2. *a)* a share or participation in something *b)* a business, etc. in which one participates or has a share 3. [*often pl.*] advantage; welfare; benefit 4. [*usually pl.*] a group of people having a common concern or dominant power in some industry, occupation, cause, etc. [the steel *interests*] 5. personal influence 6. *a)* a feeling of intentness, concern, or curiosity about something [an *interest* in politics] *b)* the power of causing this feeling [books of *interest* to children] *c)* something causing this feeling [the academic *interests* of a scholar] 7. importance; consequence [a matter of little *interest*] 8. *a)* money paid for the use of money *b)* the rate of such payment, expressed as a percentage per unit of time 9. an increase or addition over what is owed [to repay kindness with *interest*] —*vt.* [prob. < ME. *interessed < interesse + -ed*] 1. to involve the interest, or concern, of; have an effect upon 2. to cause to have an interest or take part in [can I *interest* you in a game of golf?] 3. to excite the attention or curiosity of —**in the interest**(or **interests**)**of** for the sake of; in order to promote

in·ter·est·ed (-id) *adj.* 1. having an interest or share; concerned 2. influenced by personal interest; biased or prejudiced 3. feeling or showing interest, or curiosity —**in′ter·est·ed·ly** *adv.* —**in′ter·est·ed·ness** *n.*

in·ter·est·ing (-iŋ) *adj.* exciting curiosity or attention; of interest —**in′ter·est·ing·ly** *adv.*

in·ter·face (inʹtər fās′) *n.* a surface that forms the common boundary between two parts of matter or space —*vt.* **-faced′, -fac′ing** to sew material (**interfacing**) between the outer fabric and the facing of (a collar, lapel, etc.) so as to give body or prevent stretching

in·ter·fa·cial (inʹtər fāʹshəl) *adj.* 1. of or having to do with an interface 2. designating the angle between any two faces of a crystal or a crystal form

in·ter·faith (inʹtər fāth′) *adj.* between or involving persons adhering to different religions

in·ter·fere (inʹtər fir′) *vi.* **-fered′, -fer′ing** [OFr. (s′)*entreferir,* to strike (each other) < *entre-,* INTER- + *férir* < L. *ferire,* to strike: for IE. base see BORE[1]] 1. to knock one foot or leg against the other: said of a horse 2. to come into collision or opposition; clash; conflict 3. *a)* to come in or between for some purpose; intervene *b)* to meddle —*Sports* to be guilty of interference 5. *Patent Law* to claim priority for an invention, as when two or more applications for its patent are pending 6. *Physics* to affect each other by interference: said of two waves or streams of vibration 7. *Radio & TV* to create interference in reception —*SYN.* see INTERPOSE —**interfere with** to hinder; prevent —**in′ter·fer′er** *n.*

in·ter·fer·ence (-firʹəns) *n.* 1. an act or instance of interfering 2. something that interferes ☆3. *a) Football* the legal blocking of opposing players in order to clear the way for the ball carrier; also, the player or players who do such blocking *b) Sports* the illegal hindering of an opposing player in any of various ways, as when receiving a pass in football 4. *Physics* the mutual action of two waves or streams of vibration, as of sound, light, etc., in reinforcing or neutralizing each other according to their relative phases on meeting 5. *Radio & TV a)* static, unwanted signals, etc., producing a distortion of sounds or images and preventing good reception *b)* such distorted reception —☆**run interference for** *Football* to accompany (the ball carrier) in order to block opposing players —**in′ter·fe·ren′tial** (-fə renʹshəl) *adj.*

in·ter·fer·om·e·ter (inʹtər fi rämʹə tər) *n.* [< INTERFERE + -METER] an instrument for measuring wavelengths of light and very small distances and thicknesses, for determining indices of refraction, and for analyzing small parts of a spectrum by means of the interference phenomena of light —**in′ter·fer′o·met′ric** (-fir′ə metʹrik) *adj.* —**in′ter·fer·om′e·try** *n.*

in·ter·fer·on (-fir′än) *n.* [INTERFER(E) + -on, arbitrary suffix] a cellular protein produced in response to infection by a virus and acting to inhibit viral growth

in·ter·fer·tile (-furʹt'l) *adj.* able to interbreed, or hybridize —**in′ter·fer·til′i·ty** (-fər tilʹə tē) *n.*

in·ter·fold (-fōld′) *vt., vi.* to fold together or inside one another

in·ter·fuse (-fyōōz′) *vt.* **-fused′, -fus′ing** [< L. *interfusus,* pp. of *interfundere,* to pour between: see INTER- & FOUND[3]] 1. to combine by mixing, blending, or fusing together 2. to cause to pass into or through a substance; infuse 3. to spread itself through; pervade —*vi.* to fuse; blend —**in′ter·fu′sion** *n.*

in·ter·ga·lac·tic (-gə lakʹtik) *adj.* existing or occurring between or among galaxies

in·ter·gla·cial (-glāʹshəl) *adj.* formed or occurring between two glacial epochs

in·ter·grade (inʹtər grād′; *for n.* inʹtər grād′) *vi.* **-grad′ed, -grad′ing** to pass into another form or kind by a series of intermediate grades —*n.* an intermediate grade; transitional form —**in′ter·gra·da′tion** (-grā dāʹshən) *n.*

in·ter·group (inʹtər grōōp′) *adj.* between, among, or involving different groups, esp. different ethnic or racial groups in a society

in·ter·im (inʹtər im) *n.* [L., meanwhile < *inter:* see INTER-] the period of time between; meantime —*adj.* for or during an interim; temporary; provisional [an *interim* council]

in·te·ri·or (in tirʹē ər) *adj.* [ME. < MFr. < L., compar. of *inter,* between: see INTER-] 1. situated within; on the inside; inner 2. away from the coast, border, or frontier; inland 3. of the internal, or domestic, affairs of a country 4. of the inner nature of a person or thing; private, secret, etc. —*n.* 1. the interior part of anything; specif., *a)* the inside of a room or building *b)* the inland part of a country or region *c)* the inner nature of a person or thing 2. a picture, view, etc. of the inside of a room or building 3. the internal, or domestic, affairs of a country [the U.S. Department of the *Interior*] —**in·te′ri·or′i·ty** (-ôr′ə tē) *n.* —**in·te′ri·or·ly** *adv.*

interior angle 1. any of the four angles formed on the inside of two straight lines by a straight line cutting across them 2. the angle formed inside a polygon by two adjacent sides Cf. EXTERIOR ANGLE

interior decoration 1. the decorating and furnishing of the interior of a room, house, etc. 2. the art or business of decorating and furnishing such interiors —**interior decorator**

in·te·ri·or·ize (-īz′) *vt.* **-ized′, -iz′ing** to make (a concept, value, etc.) part of one's inner nature —**in·te′ri·or·i·za′tion** *n.*

interj. interjection

in·ter·ject (inʹtər jekt′) *vt.* [< L. *interjectus,* pp. of *inter-*

jicere, to throw between < *inter-*, between + *jacere*, to throw: see JET[1]] to throw in between; interrupt with; insert; interpose [to *interject* a question] —*SYN*. see INTRODUCE —**in′ter·jec′tor** *n*.

in·ter·jec·tion (-jek′shən) *n*. [ME. *interjeccioun* < MFr. *interjection* < L. *interjectio*] **1.** the act of interjecting **2.** something interjected, as a word or phrase **3.** *Gram.* an exclamation thrown in without grammatical connection (Ex.: ah! ouch! well!)

in·ter·jec·tion·al (-jek′shə n′l) *adj*. **1.** of, or having the nature of, an interjection **2.** interjected **3.** containing an interjection Also **in′ter·jec′to·ry**

in·ter·knit (-nit′) *vt., vi.* **-knit′ted** or **-knit′, -knit′ting** to knit together; intertwine

in·ter·lace (-lās′) *vt., vi.* **-laced′, -lac′ing** [ME. *entrelacen* < OFr. *entrelacier*: see INTER- & LACE] **1.** to unite by passing over and under each other; weave together **2.** to connect intricately —**in′ter·lace′ment** *n*.

In·ter·lak·en (in′tər lä′kən) resort town in the Bernese Alps, C Switzerland, on the Aar River: pop. 4,700

in·ter·lam·i·nate (in′tər lam′ə nāt′) *vt.* **-nat′ed, -nat′ing 1.** to put between laminae **2.** to place in alternate laminae —**in′ter·lam′i·na′tion** *n*.

in·ter·lard (-lärd′) *vt.* [MFr. *entrelarder*: see INTER- & LARD] **1.** orig., to insert strips or pieces of fat, bacon, etc. in (meat to be cooked) **2.** to intersperse; diversify [to *interlard* a lecture with quotations] **3.** *a*) to mix together *b*) to be intermixed in: said of things

in·ter·lay (in′tər lā′) *vt.* **-laid′** (-lād′), **-lay′ing** to lay or put between or among —**in′ter·lay′er** *n*.

in·ter·leaf (in′tər lēf′) *n., pl.* **-leaves′** (-lēvz′) a leaf, usually blank, bound between the other leaves of a book, for notes, etc.

in·ter·leave (in′tər lēv′) *vt.* **-leaved′, -leav′ing** to put an interleaf or interleaves in

in·ter·line[1] (in′tər lin′) *vt.* **-lined′, -lin′ing** [ME. *enterlynen* < ML. *interlineare*: see INTER- & LINE[1]] **1.** to write or print between the lines of (a text, document, etc.) **2.** to insert between the lines [to *interline* notes on pages] Also **in′ter·lin′e·ate′** (-lin′ē āt′) — **in′ter·lin′e·a′tion** *n*.

in·ter·line[2] (in′tər lin′) *vt.* **-lined′, -lin′ing** [INTER- + LINE[2]] to put an inner lining between the outer material and the ordinary lining of (a garment)

in·ter·lin·e·ar (in′tər lin′ē ər) *adj.* [ME. *interlineare* < ML. *interlinearis*] **1.** written or printed between the lines [*interlinear* notes] ☆**2.** having the same text in different languages printed in alternate lines [an *interlinear* Bible] Also **in′ter·lin′e·al**

In·ter·lin·gua (-liŋ′gwə) *n.* [It., coined (c. 1908) by Giuseppe Peano, It. mathematician < L. *inter-*, INTER- + *lingua*, LANGUAGE] an artificial language based largely on languages derived from Latin, for international use esp. in science

in·ter·lin·ing (in′tər li′niŋ) *n.* **1.** an inner lining put between the outer material and the ordinary lining of a garment **2.** any fabric used as an interlining

in·ter·link (in′tər liŋk′) *vt.* to link together

in·ter·lock (-läk′) *vt., vi.* **1.** to lock together; join with one another **2.** to connect or be connected so that neither part can be operated independently —*n.* **1.** the condition of being interlocked **2.** a device or arrangement by means of which the functioning of one part is controlled by the functioning of another, as for safety

interlocking directorates boards of directors having some members in common, so that the corporations concerned are more or less under the same control

in·ter·lo·cu·tion (-lō kyoo′shən) *n.* [L. *interlocutio* < pp. of *interloqui*, to speak between < *inter-*, INTER- + *loqui*, to speak] talk between two or more people; interchange of speech; conversation; dialogue

in·ter·loc·u·tor (-läk′yə tər; *for 2, often* -läk′ə tər) *n.* [< pp. of L. *interloqui*: see prec.] **1.** a person taking part in a conversation or dialogue ☆**2.** an entertainer in a minstrel show who serves as master of ceremonies and as a foil for the end men

in·ter·loc·u·to·ry (-läk′yə tôr′ē) *adj.* [ML.(Ec.) *interlocutorius*: see INTERLOCUTION] **1.** of, having the nature of, or occurring in dialogue; conversational **2.** interjected [*interlocutory* wit] **3.** *Law* pronounced during the course of a suit, pending final decision; not final [an *interlocutory* divorce decree]

in·ter·lope (in′tər lōp′) *vi.* **-loped′, -lop′ing** [prob. < INTER- + LOPE: basic sense prob. "to run about, interfere"] **1.** orig., to intrude on another's trading rights or privileges **2.** to intrude or meddle in others' affairs —*SYN*. see INTRUDE

in·ter·lop·er (in′tər lō′pər) *n.* [prob. < prec.] **1.** *a*) orig., an unauthorized trading vessel in areas assigned to monopolies or chartered companies *b*) any unauthorized trader **2.** a person who meddles in others' affairs

in·ter·lude (in′tər lood′) *n.* [ME. *enterlude* < OFr. *entrelude* < ML. *interludium* < L. *inter-*, between + *ludus*, play: see LUDICROUS] **1.** a short, humorous play formerly presented between the parts of a miracle play or morality play **2.** a short play of a sort popular in the Tudor period, either

farcical or moralistic in tone and with a plot typically derived from French farce or the morality play **3.** any performance between the acts of a play **4.** instrumental music played between the parts of a song, church liturgy, play, etc. **5.** anything that fills time between two events; intervening time or, rarely, space

in·ter·lu·nar (in′tər loo′nər) *adj.* [prob. < MFr. *interlunaire*: see INTER- & LUNAR] of the period of about four days between old and new moon, when the moon cannot be seen because it is too close to the sun

in·ter·mar·riage (-mar′ij) *n.* **1.** marriage between persons of different clans, tribes, races, religions, castes, etc. **2.** marriage between closely related persons

in·ter·mar·ry (-mar′ē) *vi.* **-ried, -ry·ing 1.** to become connected by or unite in marriage: said of persons of different clans, tribes, races, religions, castes, etc. **2.** to marry: said of closely related persons

in·ter·med·dle (-med′'l) *vi.* **-dled, -dling** [ME. *entremedlen* < Anglo-Fr. *entremedler*: see INTER- & MEDDLE] to meddle in the affairs of others —**in′ter·med′dler** *n*.

in·ter·me·di·ar·y (-mē′dē er′ē) *adj.* [Fr. *intermédiaire* < L. *intermedius*: see ff. + -ARY] **1.** acting between two persons; acting as mediator **2.** being or happening between; intermediate —*n., pl.* **-ar′ies 1.** a go-between; mediator **2.** any medium, means, or agency **3.** an intermediate form, phase, etc.

in·ter·me·di·ate (-mē′dē it; *for v.* -āt′) *adj.* [ML. *intermediatus* < L. *intermedius* < *inter-*, between + *medius*, middle: see MID[1]] being or happening between two things, places, stages, etc.; in the middle —*n.* **1.** anything intermediate **2.** *same as* INTERMEDIARY **3.** *Chem.* a substance obtained as a necessary intermediate stage between the original material and the final product —*vi.* **-at′ed, -at′ing** to act as an intermediary; mediate —**in′ter·me′di·ate·ly** *adv.* —**in′ter·me′di·ate·ness, in′ter·me′di·a·cy** (-ə sē) *n.* —**in′ter·me′di·a′tion** *n.* —**in′ter·me′di·a′tor** *n*.

intermediate frequency *Radio* in superheterodyne reception, a frequency resulting from combining the incoming signal with a locally produced signal for amplification prior to detection

intermediate host the organism on or in which a parasite lives during an immature stage

in·ter·me·din (-mē′d′n) *n.* [< L. (*pars*) *intermedia*, intermediate (lobe) + -IN[1]] a hormone produced by the intermediate lobe of the pituitary gland in certain vertebrates that influences the activity of pigment cells

in·ter·ment (in tur′mənt) *n.* the act of interring; burial

in·ter·mez·zo (in′tər met′sō, -med′zō) *n., pl.* **-zos, -zi** (-sē, -zē) [It. < L. *intermedius*: see INTERMEDIATE] **1.** a short, light dramatic, musical, or ballet entertainment between the acts of a play or opera **2.** *Music a*) a short movement connecting the main parts of a composition *b*) any of certain short instrumental pieces similar to this

in·ter·mi·na·ble (in tur′mi nə b′l) *adj.* [ME. < OFr. < LL. *interminabilis*: see IN-[2] & TERMINABLE] without, or apparently without, end; lasting, or seeming to last, forever; endless —**in·ter′mi·na·bly** *adv*.

in·ter·min·gle (in′tər miŋ′g′l) *vt., vi.* **-gled, -gling** to mix together; mingle; blend

in·ter·mis·sion (-mish′ən) *n.* [L. *intermissio* < *intermissus*, pp. of *intermittere*] **1.** an intermitting or being intermitted; interruption **2.** an interval of time between periods of activity; pause, as between acts of a play —**in′ter·mis′sive** (-mis′iv) *adj*.

in·ter·mit (-mit′) *vt., vi.* **-mit′ted, -mit′ting** [L. *intermittere* < *inter-* + *mittere*: see INTER- & MISSION] to stop for a time; cease at intervals; make or be intermittent; discontinue —**in′ter·mit′ter** *n*.

in·ter·mit·tent (-mit′'nt) *adj.* [L. *intermittens*, prp. of *intermittere*: see INTERMIT] stopping and starting again at intervals; pausing from time to time; periodic —**in′ter·mit′tence** *n.* —**in′ter·mit′tent·ly** *adv*.

SYN.—**intermittent** and **recurrent** both apply to something that stops and starts, or disappears and reappears, from time to time, but the former usually stresses the breaks or pauses, and the latter, the repetition or return [an *intermittent* fever, *recurrent* attacks of the hives]; **periodic** refers to something that recurs at more or less regular intervals [*periodic* economic crises]; **alternate** is usually used of two recurrent things that follow each other in regular order [a life of *alternate* sorrow and joy] —*ANT*. continued, continuous

intermittent current an electric current interrupted at intervals but always flowing in the same direction

intermittent fever a fever characterized by periodic intervals when the body temperature returns to normal

in·ter·mix (-miks′) *vt., vi.* to mix together; blend

in·ter·mix·ture (-miks′chər) *n.* **1.** an intermixing or being intermixed **2.** a mixture **3.** an added ingredient; admixture

in·ter·mo·lec·u·lar (-mə lek′yoo lər) *adj.* between or among molecules

☆**in·ter·mon·tane** (-män′tān) *adj.* [< INTER + L. *montanus*, of a mountain < *mons* (gen. *montis*), MOUNTAIN] between or among mountains

☆**in·tern** (in′tərn; *for vt., usually* in turn′) *n.* [Fr. *interne*, resident within < L. *internus*, inward: see ff.] **1.** a doctor

serving an apprenticeship as an assistant resident in a hospital generally just after graduation from medical school: cf. EXTERN ☆2. an apprentice teacher, journalist, etc. —*vi.* to serve as an intern —*vt.* 1. to detain and confine within a country or a definite area [to *intern* aliens in time of war] 2. to detain (ships) in port

in·ter·nal (in tur'n'l) *adj.* [ML. *internalis* < L. *internus*, inward, internal, akin to *inter*: see INTER-] 1. of or having to do with the inside; inner; interior 2. to be taken or applied inside the body [*internal* remedies] 3. having to do with or belonging to the inner nature of a thing; intrinsic [*internal* evidence] 4. having to do with or belonging to the inner nature of man; subjective 5. having to do with the domestic affairs of a country [*internal* revenue] 6. *a) Anat.* situated toward the inside of the body or closer to its center *b)* existing or occurring inside the body or a body part —*n.* 1. [*pl.*] the internal organs of the body; entrails 2. inner, intrinsic, or essential quality or attribute —**in'·ter·nal'i·ty** (-nal'ə tē) *n.* —**in·ter'nal·ly** *adv.*

in·ter·nal-com·bus·tion engine (-kəm bus'chən) an engine, as in an airplane, automobile, etc., that obtains its power from heat produced by the explosion of a fuel-and-air mixture within the cylinder or cylinders

internal ear that part of the ear in the temporal bone consisting of the labyrinth and semicircular canals

in·ter·nal·ize (in tur'n'l īz') *vt.* -**ized'**, -**iz'ing** to make internal; interiorize; specif., to make (others', esp. the prevailing, attitudes, ideas, norms, etc.) a part of one's own patterns of thinking —**in·ter'nal·i·za'tion** *n.*

internal medicine the branch of medicine that deals with the diagnosis and nonsurgical treatment of diseases

internal respiration 1. the exchange of oxygen and carbon dioxide between the blood or lymph and the body cells 2. the metabolic consumption of oxygen and the production of carbon dioxide in the protoplasm of cells

☆**internal revenue** governmental income from taxes on income, profits, amusements, luxuries, etc.

internal rhyme a rhyming of words within the same line of verse or within two separate lines

internal secretion a substance secreted directly into the blood, as by an endocrine gland; hormone

internat. international

in·ter·na·tion·al (in'tər nash'ən 'l) *adj.* 1. between or among nations [an *international* treaty] 2. concerned with the relations between nations [an *international* court] 3. for the use of all nations [*international* waters] 4. of, for, or by people in various nations —*n.* 1. a person having connections with two different countries, as a resident alien, etc. 2. an international group; esp., [I-] any of several international socialist organizations in existence variously from 1864 on —**in'ter·na'tion·al'i·ty** *n.* —**in'ter·na'tion·al·ly** *adv.*

international candle *see* CANDLE (*n. 3b*)

International Court of Justice a court established at the Hague in 1945 as an advisory or arbitrational judicial organ of the United Nations

international date line *same as* DATE LINE

In·ter·na·tio·nale (in'tər nash'ən 'l; *Fr.* an'ter nà syð nál') [Fr.] a revolutionary socialist hymn written in 1871 by Eugène Pottier, with music by Adolphe Degeyter

International Geophysical Year a period (July, 1957–December, 1958) that was set aside for intensive geophysical and astronomical observations by scientists from many cooperating nations

in·ter·na·tion·al·ism (in'tər nash'ən 'l iz'm) *n.* 1. the principle or policy of international cooperation for the common good 2. international character, quality, etc.

in·ter·na·tion·al·ist (-ist) *n.* 1. a person who believes in internationalism 2. a specialist in international law and relations

in·ter·na·tion·al·ize (-īz') *vt.* -**ized'**, -**iz'ing** to make international; bring under international control —**in'ter·na'tion·al·i·za'tion** *n.*

international law the rules generally observed and regarded as binding in the relations between nations

International Phonetic Alphabet a set of phonetic symbols for international use, orig. sponsored in the late 19th cent. by the International Phonetic Association: each symbol represents a single sound or kind of articulation, whether the sound or articulation occurs in only one language or in more than one

international pitch (since 1939) *same as* CONCERT PITCH (sense 2)

☆**in·terne** (in'turn') *n. same as* INTERN

in·ter·ne·cine (in'tər nē'sin, -sīn; -nes'n) *adj.* [L. *internecinus* < *internecare*, to kill, destroy < *inter*-, between + *necare*, to kill: see NECRO-] 1. orig., full of slaughter or destruction 2. deadly or harmful to both sides of a group involved in a conflict, as in a civil war; mutually destructive or harmful

in·tern·ee (in'tər nē') *n.* [INTERN + -EE¹] a person interned as a prisoner of war or enemy alien

in·ter·neu·ron (in'tər noor'än, -nyoor'-) *n. same as* INTERNUNCIAL NEURON

☆**in·ter·nist** (in'tər nist, in tur'nist) *n.* a doctor who specializes in internal medicine

in·tern·ment (in turn'mənt) *n.* an interning or being interned

in·ter·node (in'tər nōd') *n.* [L. *internodium*] 1. *Anat. &*

Zool. the part between two nodes, as a segment of a nerve fiber 2. *Bot.* the section of a plant between two successive nodes or joints —**in'ter·nod'al** *adj.*

‡**in·ter nos** (in'tər nōs') [L.] between (or among) ourselves

☆**in·tern·ship** (in'turn ship') *n.* 1. the position of an intern 2. the period of service as an intern

internuncial neuron any of various nerve cells connecting sensory and motor neurons in the brain and spinal cord

in·ter·nun·ci·o (in'tər nun'sē ō', -noon'-; -shē ō') *n., pl.* -**ci·os'** [It. *internunzio* < L. *internuntius*: see INTER- & NUNCIO] 1. a messenger between two parties; envoy 2. a papal representative ranking below a nuncio —**in'ter·nun'ci·al** *adj.* —**in'ter·nun'ci·al·ly** *adv.*

in·ter·o·ce·an·ic (-ō'shē an'ik) *adj.* between oceans

in·ter·o·cep·tor (in'tər ō sep'tər) *n.* [ModL.: see INTERNAL & RECEPTOR] a specialized cell or end organ that responds to and transmits stimuli from the internal organs, muscles, blood vessels, and the ear labyrinth —**in'ter·o·cep'tive** *adj.*

in·ter·of·fice (in'tər ôf'is, -äf'-) *adj.* between or among the offices within an organization

in·ter·os·cu·late (-äs'kyə lāt') *vi.* -**lat'ed**, -**lat'ing** [INTER- & OSCULATE] 1. to have mutual communication; interpenetrate 2. *Biol.* to have some common characteristics: said of separate species or groups —**in'ter·os'cu·lant** *adj.* —**in'ter·os'cu·la'tion** *n.*

in·ter·pel·late (in'tər pel'āt, in tur'pə lāt') *vt.* -**lat·ed**, -**lat·ing** [< L. *interpellatus*, pp. of *interpellare*, to interrupt in speaking < *inter*-, between + *-pellare* < *pellere*, to drive, urge: see FELT] to ask (a person) formally for an explanation of his action or policy: a form of political challenge to members of the administration in legislative bodies of certain countries —**in'ter·pel'lant** *adj., n.* —**in'ter·pel'la'tor** *n.*

in·ter·pel·la·tion (in'tər pə lā'shən, in tur'-) *n.* [L. *interpellatio*] the act of interpellating; formal calling to account of a cabinet minister, etc. by a legislative body

in·ter·pen·e·trate (in'tər pen'ə trāt') *vt.* -**trat'ed**, -**trat'ing** 1. to penetrate thoroughly; pervade; permeate 2. to penetrate (each other) reciprocally or mutually —*vi.* 1. to penetrate each other 2. to penetrate between parts, etc. —**in'ter·pen'e·tra'tion** *n.* —**in'ter·pen'e·tra'tive** *adj.*

in·ter·per·son·al (-pur'sə n'l) *adj.* 1. between persons [*interpersonal* relationships] 2. of or involving relations between persons —**in'ter·per'son·al·ly** *adv.*

in·ter·phase (in'tər fāz') *n.* the stage of a cell between mitotic divisions

☆**in·ter·phone** (-fōn') *n.* an intercommunication telephone system, as between departments of an office

in·ter·plan·e·tar·y (in'tər plan'ə ter'ē) *adj.* 1. between planets 2. within the solar system but outside the atmosphere of any planet or the sun

in·ter·play (in'tər plā'; *for v.* in'tər plā') *n.* action, effect, or influence on each other or one another; interaction —*vi.* to exert influence reciprocally

in·ter·plead (in'tər plēd') *vi.* -**plead'ed** or -**plead'** (-plēd') or -**pled'**, -**plead'ing** [Anglo-Fr. *entrepleder*: see INTER- & PLEAD] *Law* to initiate an interpleader

in·ter·plead·er (-ər) *n.* [< Anglo-Fr. *entrepleder*, to interplead; substantive use of inf.] a legal proceeding by which a person sued by two or more persons having the same claim against him may compel them to go to trial with each other to arrive at a settlement

In·ter·pol (in'tər pōl') *n.* [*inter*(*national*) *pol*(*ice*)] an international police organization with headquarters in Paris: it coordinates the police activities of participating nations against international criminals: full name, *International Criminal Police Organization*

in·ter·po·late (in tur'pə lāt') *vt.* -**lat'ed**, -**lat'ing** [< L. *interpolatus*, pp. of *interpolare*, to polish, dress up, corrupt < *interpolis*, altered by furbishing, repaired < *inter*-, between + *polire*, to polish] 1. to alter, enlarge, or corrupt (a book, manuscript, etc.) by putting in new words, subject matter, etc. 2. to insert between or among others 3. *Math.* to estimate a missing functional value by taking a weighted average of known functional values at neighboring points —*vi.* to make interpolations —*SYN.* see INTRODUCE —**in·ter'po·lat'er, in·ter'po·la'tor** *n.* —**in·ter'po·la'tion** *n.* —**in·ter'po·la'tive** *adj.*

in·ter·pose (in'tər pōz') *vt.* -**posed'**, -**pos'ing** [Fr. *interposer*, altered (after *poser*: see POSE) < L. *interpositus*, pp. of *interponere*, to set between < *inter*-, between + *ponere*, to put, place: see POSITION] 1. to place or put between; insert 2. to introduce by way of intervention; put forward as interference 3. to introduce (a remark, opinion, etc.) into a conversation, debate, etc.; put in as an interruption —*vi.* 1. to be or come between 2. to intervene or mediate 3. to interrupt —**in'ter·pos'al** *n.* —**in'ter·pos'er** *n.*

SYN.—**interpose**, in this comparison, is the general word, meaning no more than to introduce action, a remark, etc. in some conversation or affair, with no further implication of motive or effect; **intervene** implies an interposing in order to modify action, adjust differences, etc. [to *intervene* in the internal affairs of another country]; **interfere** implies an interposing actively in order to hinder action or effect certain results [don't *interfere* in their decision to move]; **intercede** suggests an intervening in order to plead or argue on behalf of another [he *interceded* for the accused]; **mediate** implies intervention in order to reconcile, or effect a compromise between, opposing parties [to *mediate* a labor dispute] See also INTRODUCE

in·ter·po·si·tion (in'tər pə zish'ən) *n.* [ME. *interposicioun* < OFr. *interposicion* < L. *interpositio* < pp. of *interponere*: see prec.] **1.** an interposing or being interposed **2.** a thing interposed ☆**3.** the disputed doctrine that a State may reject a Federal mandate that it considers to be encroaching on its rights

in·ter·pret (in tur'prit) *vt.* [ME. *interpreten* < MFr. *interpréter* < L. *interpretari* < *interpres*, agent between two parties, broker, interpreter] **1.** to explain the meaning of; make understandable [to *interpret* a poem] **2.** to translate (esp. oral remarks) **3.** to have or show one's own understanding of the meaning of; construe [to *interpret* a silence as contempt] **4.** to bring out the meaning of; esp., to give one's own conception of (a work of art), as in performance or criticism —*vi.* to act as an interpreter; explain or translate —*SYN.* see EXPLAIN —**in·ter'pret·a·ble** *adj.*

in·ter·pre·ta·tion (in tur'prə tā'shən) *n.* [ME. *interpretacioun* < OFr. *entrepretation* < L. *interpretatio*] **1.** the act or result of interpreting; explanation, meaning, translation, exposition, etc. **2.** the expression of a person's conception of a work of art, subject, etc. through acting, playing, writing, criticizing, etc. [the pianist's *interpretation* of the sonata] —**in·ter'pre·ta'tion·al** *adj.*

in·ter·pre·ta·tive (in tur'prə tāt'iv) *adj.* [ML. *interpretativus*] *same as* INTERPRETIVE

in·ter·pret·er (-prə tər) *n.* [ME. *interpretour* < Anglo-Fr. < OFr. *interpreteur* < LL.(Ec.) *interpretator*] a person who interprets; specif., a person whose work is translating a foreign language orally, as in a conversation between people speaking different languages

in·ter·pre·tive (-prə tiv) *adj.* that interprets; explanatory or elucidative

in·ter·ra·cial (in'tər rā'shəl) *adj.* between, among, or involving different races or members of different races: also **in'ter·race'**

in·ter·ra·di·al (-rā'dē əl) *adj.* situated between rays or radii —**in'ter·ra'di·al·ly** *adv.*

in·ter·reg·num (-reg'nəm) *n., pl.* **-reg'nums, -reg'na** (-nə) [L. < *inter-*, between + *regnum*, REIGN] **1.** an interval between two successive reigns, when the country has no sovereign **2.** a suspension of governmental or administrative functions; period without the usual ruler, governor, etc. **3.** any break in a series or in a continuity; pause or interval

in·ter·re·late (-ri lāt') *vt., vi.* **-lat'ed, -lat'ing** to make, be, or become mutually related —**in'ter·re·lat'ed** *adj.* —**in'ter·re·lat'ed·ness** *n.*

in·ter·re·la·tion (-ri lā'shən) *n.* mutual relationship; interconnection —**in'ter·re·la'tion·ship** *n.*

in·ter·rex (in'tər reks') *n., pl.* **in'ter·re'ges** (-rē'jēz) [L. < *inter-*, between + *rex* (gen. *regis*), king: see REGAL] a person acting as ruler during an interregnum

interrog. 1. interrogation **2.** interrogative

in·ter·ro·gate (in ter'ə gāt') *vt.* **-gat'ed, -gat'ing** [< L. *interrogatus,* pp. of *interrogare*, to ask < *inter-*, between + *rogare*, to ask, akin to *regere*, to rule: see REGAL] to ask questions of formally in examining [to *interrogate* a witness] —*vi.* to ask questions —*SYN.* see ASK

in·ter·ro·ga·tion (in ter'ə gā'shən) *n.* [ME. *interrogacion* < MFr. *interrogation* < L. *interrogatio*] **1.** an interrogating or being interrogated; examination **2.** a question **3.** *short for* INTERROGATION MARK

interrogation mark (or point) *same as* QUESTION MARK

in·ter·rog·a·tive (in'tə räg'ə tiv) *adj.* [LL. *interrogativus* see INTERROGATE] **1.** asking, or having the form of, a question **2.** used in asking a question —*n.* an interrogative word, construction, or element (Ex.: what? where?) —**in'ter·rog'a·tive·ly** *adv.*

in·ter·ro·ga·tor (in ter'ə gāt'ər) *n.* **1.** a person who interrogates; questioner **2.** a radio or radar transmitter whose signals actuate a transponder or beacon

in·ter·rog·a·to·ry (in'tə räg'ə tôr'ē) *adj.* [LL. *interrogatorius*] expressing or implying a question —*n., pl.* **-ries** a formal question or set of questions —**in'ter·rog'a·to'ri·ly** *adv.*

in·ter·rupt (in'tə rupt') *vt.* [ME. *interrupten* < L. *interruptus*, pp. of *interrumpere*, to break apart, break off < *inter-*, between + *rumpere*, to break: see RUPTURE] **1.** *a)* to break into or in upon (a discussion, train of thought, etc.) *b)* to break in upon (a person) while he is speaking, working, etc.; stop or hinder **2.** to make a break in the continuity of; cut off; obstruct —*vi.* to make an interruption, esp. in another's speech, action, etc. —**in'ter·rup'tive** *adj.*

in·ter·rupt·ed (-id) *adj.* **1.** broken by interruptions; not continuous **2.** *Bot.* asymmetrical; irregular: said of parts not equally spaced on a stem

interrupted screw a screw having the thread interrupted by a slot or slots to enable it to be locked or released by a partial turn

in·ter·rupt·er (-ər) *n.* **1.** a person or thing that interrupts **2.** *Elec.* a mechanism used to interrupt, or intermittently open and close, a circuit

in·ter·rup·tion (in'tə rup'shən) *n.* [ME. *interrupcion* < OFr. < L. *interruptio*] **1.** an interrupting or being interrupted **2.** anything that interrupts **3.** the interval during which something is interrupted; intermission

in·ter·scho·las·tic (in'tər skə las'tik) *adj.* between or among schools [an *interscholastic* debate]

‡**in·ter se** (in'tər sē', sā') [L.] between (or among) themselves

in·ter·sect (in'tər sekt') *vt.* [< L. *intersectus*, pp. of *intersecare*, to cut between, cut off < *inter-*, between + *secare*, to cut: see SAW[1]] to divide into two parts by passing through or across; cut across [a river *intersects* the plain] —*vi.* to cross each other [lines *intersecting* to form right angles]

in·ter·sec·tion (-sek'shən) *n.* [L. *intersectio*] **1.** the act of intersecting **2.** a place of intersecting; specif., *a)* the point or line where two lines or surfaces meet or cross *b)* the place where two streets cross **3.** *Math.* the set containing all the points common to two or more given sets

in·ter·sec·tion·al (-'l) *adj.* **1.** of or forming an intersection **2.** between sections or regions [*intersectional* football games]

in·ter·sex (in'tər seks') *n. Biol.* an abnormal individual having characteristics intermediate between those of male and female

in·ter·sex·u·al (in'tər sek'shoo wəl) *adj.* **1.** between the sexes [*intersexual* rivalry] **2.** of, or having the characteristics of, an intersex

in·ter·space (in'tər spās'; *for v.* in'tər spās') *n.* a space between —*vt.* **-spaced', -spac'ing 1.** to make spaces between **2.** to fill spaces between

in·ter·spe·cif·ic (in'tər spi sif'ik) *adj.* between different species

in·ter·sperse (in'tər spurs') *vt.* **-spersed', -spers'ing** [< L. *interspersus*, pp. of *interspergere* < *inter-*, among + *spargere*, to scatter: see SPARK[1]] **1.** to scatter among other things; put here and there or at intervals **2.** to decorate or diversify with things scattered here and there —**in'ter·sper'sion** (-spur'zhən, -shən) *n.*

☆**in·ter·state** (in'tər stāt') *adj.* between or among states of a federal government [*interstate* commerce]

Interstate Commerce Commission a U.S. Federal commission created in 1887 to regulate commerce between the States: it has eleven members, appointed by the President

in·ter·stel·lar (in'tər stel'ər) *adj.* [INTER- + STELLAR] between or among the stars [*interstellar* space]

in·ter·stice (in tur'stis) *n., pl.* **-stic·es** (-stis iz. -stə sēz') [Fr. < LL. *interstitium* < *inter-*, between + *sistere*, to set < *stare*, to STAND] a small or narrow space between things or parts; crevice; chink; crack

in·ter·sti·tial (in'tər stish'əl) *adj.* **1.** of, forming, or occurring in interstices **2.** *Anat.* situated between the cellular components of an organ or structure —**in'ter·sti'tial·ly** *adv.*

interstitial cell-stimulating hormone *see* LUTEINIZING HORMONE

in·ter·tex·ture (in'tər teks'chər) *n.* [< L. *intertextus*, pp. of *intertexere*, to interweave (see INTER- & TEXTURE) + -URE] **1.** the act or process of interweaving **2.** something formed by interweaving

in·ter·tid·al (-tīd'l) *adj.* of or pertaining to a shore zone bounded by the levels of low and high tide

in·ter·trib·al (-trī'b'l) *adj.* between or among tribes

in·ter·trop·i·cal (-träp'i k'l) *adj.* within or between the tropics (of Cancer and Capricorn)

in·ter·twine (-twīn') *vt., vi.* **-twined', -twin'ing** to twine together; intertwist

in·ter·twist (-twist') *vt., vi.* to twist together

☆**in·ter·ur·ban** (-ur'bən) *adj.* [INTER- + URBAN] between cities or towns [an *interurban* railway] —*n.* an interurban railway, trolley route, train, car, etc.

in·ter·val (in'tər v'l) *n.* [ME. *enterval, intervalle* < OFr. < L. *intervallum*, lit., space between two palisades or walls < *inter-*, between + *vallum*, palisade, WALL] **1.** a space between two things; gap; distance **2.** a period of time between two points of time, events, etc.; intervening period **3.** the extent of difference between two qualities, conditions, etc. ☆*same as* INTERVALE **5.** *Math.* the set containing all numbers between two given numbers and including one, both, or neither end point **6.** *Music* the difference in pitch between two tones —**at intervals 1.** once in a while **2.** here and there —**in'ter·val'lic** (-val'ik) *adj.*

☆**in·ter·vale** (-vāl') *n.* [a blending of prec. + VALE] [Chiefly New England] low, flat land between hills or along a river or stream; bottom land: also **intervale** (or **interval) land**

in·ter·vene (in'tər vēn') *vi.* **-vened', -ven'ing** [L. *intervenire* < *inter-*, between + *venire*, to COME] **1.** to come, be, or lie between **2.** to take place between two points of time, events, etc. **3.** to come or be in between as something unnecessary or irrelevant **4.** to come between as an influencing force, as in order to modify, settle, or hinder some action, argument, etc. **5.** *Law* to come in as a third party to a suit, for the protection of one's own interests —*SYN.* see INTERPOSE —**in'ter·ven'er, *Law* in'·ter·ve'nor** *n.*

in·ter·ven·ient (in'tər vēn'yənt) *adj.* [L. *interveniens*, prp.] intervening —*n.* an intervening person or thing

in·ter·ven·tion (in'tər ven'shən) n. [LL. *interventio* < L. *intervenire*] 1. the act of intervening 2. any interference in the affairs of others, esp. of one state in the affairs of another

in·ter·ven·tion·ist (-ist) n. a person who favors or practices intervention, esp. in international affairs —adj. 1. of intervention or interventionists 2. favoring or practicing intervention —in'ter·ven'tion·ism n.

in·ter·ver·te·bral (-vur'tə brəl) adj. between the vertebrae —in'ter·ver'te·bral·ly adv.

intervertebral disk a disk of fibrous cartilage between adjacent vertebral surfaces

in·ter·view (in'tər vyoo') n. [Fr. *entrevue*: see INTER- & VIEW] 1. a meeting of people face to face, as for evaluating or questioning a job applicant ☆2. a) a meeting in which a person is asked about his views, activities, etc., as by a reporter or as on a radio program b) a published account of such a meeting —☆vt. to have an interview with —in'ter·view·ee', n. —in'ter·view'er n.

†in·ter vi·vos (in'tər vē'vōs, vī'-) [L., lit., among the living] between living persons; from one living person to another or others [*inter vivos* gifts, trusts, etc.]

in·ter·vo·cal·ic (in'tər vō kal'ik) adj. Phonet. coming between two vowels: said of a consonant

in·ter·volve (in'tər välv') vt., vi. -volved', -volv'ing [< INTER- + L. *volvere*, to roll: see WALK] 1. to wind or roll up together; coil up 2. to involve or be involved with one another

in·ter·weave (-wēv') vt., vi. -wove', -wov'en, -weav'ing 1. to weave together; interlace 2. to connect closely or intricately; intermingle; blend

in·tes·ta·cy (in tes'tə sē) n. the fact or state of dying intestate

in·tes·tate (in tes'tāt, -tit) adj. [ME. < L. *intestatus* < *in-*, not + *testatus*, pp. of *testari*, to make a will: see TESTAMENT] 1. having made no will 2. not disposed of by a will —n. a person who has died intestate

in·tes·tin·al (in tes'ti n'l) adj. of, in, or affecting the intestines —in·tes'tin·al·ly adv.

☆**intestinal fortitude** courage and perseverance; grit; pluck: a euphemism for GUTS (in the same sense)

in·tes·tine (in tes'tin) adj. [L. *intestinus*, inward, internal < *intus*, within, akin to Gr. *entos* < IE. *entos* < base *en-*, in] internal, with regard to a country or community; domestic; civil —n. [L. *intestinum*, neut. sing. of *intestinus*] [usually pl.] the lower part of the alimentary canal, extending from the stomach to the anus and consisting of a convoluted upper part (**small intestine**) and a lower part of greater diameter (**large intestine**); bowel(s): food passes from the stomach into the intestines for further digestion

in·thrall, in·thral (in thrôl') vt. -thralled', -thrall'ing same as ENTHRALL

in·ti·ma (in'tə mə) n., pl. -mae (-mē'), -mas [ModL. < fem. of L. *intimus*: see INTIMATE] the innermost layer or living membrane of an organ or other part, as of an artery, vein, or lymphatic, or of an insect's trachea

in·ti·ma·cy (in'tə mə sē) n., pl. -cies 1. the state or fact of being intimate; intimate association; familiarity 2. an intimate act; esp., [usually pl.] illicit sexual intercourse: a euphemism

in·ti·mate (in'tə mit; for v. -māt') adj. [altered (after the v.) < earlier *intime* < Fr. < L. *intimus*, superl. of *intus*, within: see INTESTINE] 1. pertaining to the inmost character of a thing; fundamental; essential [the *intimate* structure of the atom] 2. most private or personal [one's *intimate* feelings] 3. closely acquainted or associated; very familiar [an *intimate* friend] 4. promoting a feeling of privacy, coziness, romance, etc. [an *intimate* nightclub] 5. a) resulting from careful study or investigation; thorough [an *intimate* knowledge of French] b) very close [an *intimate* acquaintance with the facts] 6. having illicit sexual relations: a euphemism —n. an intimate friend or companion —vt. -mat'ed, -mat'ing [< L. *intimatus*, pp. of *intimare*, to announce < *intimus*] 1. orig., to make known formally; announce 2. to make known indirectly; hint or imply —SYN. see FAMILIAR, SUGGEST —in'ti·mate·ly adv. —in'ti·mate·ness n.

in·ti·ma·tion (in'tə mā'shən) n. [ME. < OFr. *intimacion* < LL. *intimatio*] 1. the act of intimating 2. a formal announcement or declaration: now chiefly in law 3. a hint; indirect suggestion

†in·time (an tēm') adj. [Fr.] same as INTIMATE (esp. sense 4)

in·tim·i·date (in tim'ə dāt') vt. -dat'ed, -dat'ing [< ML. *intimidatus*, pp. of *intimidare*, to make afraid < L. *in-*, in + *timidus*, afraid, TIMID] 1. to make timid; make afraid; overawe 2. to force or deter with threats or violence; cow —in·tim'i·da'tion n. —in·tim'i·da'tor n.

in·ti·mist (in'tə mist) adj. [Fr. *intimiste*] dealing largely with intimate, personal thoughts and feelings in literature and art —n. an intimist writer or painter

in·tinc·tion (in tiŋk'shən) n. [LL.(Ec.) *intinctio*, a dipping in, baptizing < L. *intinctus*, pp. of *intingere*, to dip in < *in-*, in + *tingere*, to dye, TINGE] the act of dipping the Eucharistic bread into the consecrated wine, so that the communicant receives both together

in·tine (in'tēn, -tin) n. [G. < L. *intus*, within + G. *-ine*, -INE⁴] same as ENDOSPORE (sense 2)

in·ti·tle (in tīt'l) vt. -tled, -tling same as ENTITLE

in·tit·ule (in tit'yōōl) vt. -uled, -ul·ing [ME. *intitulen* < OFr. *intituler* < LL. *intitulare*, to ENTITLE] [Chiefly Brit.] to entitle (a legislative act, etc.)

intl. international

in·to (in'tōō, -too, -tə; occas. in poetry, etc., in too') prep. [ME. < OE.: see IN & TO] 1. from the outside to the inside of; toward and within [into a house] 2. advancing or continuing to the midst of (a period of time) [dancing far *into* the night] 3. to the form, substance, or condition of [turned *into* a swan, divided *into* parts] 4. so as to strike [to bump *into* a door] 5. to the work, activity, etc. of [to go *into* teaching] 6. in the direction of [to head *into* a storm] 7. Math. used to indicate division [3 into 21 is 7]

in·tol·er·a·ble (in täl'ər ə b'l) adj. [ME. *intollerable* < L. *intolerabilis*] not tolerable; unbearable; too severe, painful, cruel, etc. to be endured —in·tol'er·a·bil'i·ty, in·tol'er·a·ble·ness n. —in·tol'er·a·bly adv.

in·tol·er·ance (in täl'ər əns) n. [L. *intolerantia*] 1. lack of tolerance, esp. of others' opinions, beliefs, etc.; bigotry 2. an allergy or sensitivity to some food, medicine, etc.

in·tol·er·ant (-ənt) adj. [L. *intolerans*] not tolerant; unwilling to tolerate others' opinions, beliefs, etc. or persons of other races, background, etc.; bigoted; illiberal — **intolerant of** not able or willing to tolerate —in·tol'er·ant·ly adv. —in·tol'er·ant·ness n.

in·to·nate (in'tə nāt') vt. -nat'ed, -nat'ing [< ML. *intonatus*, pp. of *intonare*: see INTONE] same as INTONE

in·to·na·tion (in'tə nā'shən) n. [ML. *intonatio*] 1. the act of intoning 2. the manner of singing or playing tones with regard to accuracy of pitch 3. a) the opening phrase of a Gregorian chant b) the chanting of this 4. Linguis. a) significant levels and variations in pitch sequences within an utterance b) the manner of applying final pitch to a spoken sentence or phrase [to ask a question with a rising *intonation*] —in'to·na'tion·al adj.

intonation pattern Linguis. the set of pitch phonemes occurring between silence and a terminal juncture or between two terminal junctures

in·tone (in tōn') vt. -toned', -ton'ing [ME. *entonen* < OFr. *entoner* < ML. *intonare*: see IN-¹ & TONE] 1. to utter or recite in a singing tone or in prolonged monotones; chant 2. to give a particular intonation to 3. to sing or recite the opening phrase of (a chant, canticle, etc.) —vi. to speak or recite in a singing tone or in prolonged monotones; chant —in·ton'er n.

in·tor·sion (in tôr'shən) n. [Fr. < L. *intortio* < *intortus*] a spiral twisting, bending, or curling, as in plant stems

in·tort (in tôrt') vt. [< L. *intortus*, pp. of *intorquere*, to twist < *in-*, in + *torquere*, to twist: see TORT] [Rare] to twist inward: usually used in the past participle

in·to·to (in tō'tō) [L.] in the whole; as a whole

in·tox·i·cant (in täk'sə kənt) n. [< ML. *intoxicans*, prp. of *intoxicare*] something that intoxicates; esp., alcoholic liquor —adj. that intoxicates; intoxicating

in·tox·i·cate (-kāt'; for adj. -kit) vt. -cat'ed, -cat'ing [< ML. *intoxicatus*, pp. of *intoxicare*, to poison, drug < L. *in-*, in + *toxicare*, to smear with poison < *toxicum*, poison: see TOXIC] 1. to make drunk; inebriate 2. to excite to a point beyond self-control; make wild with excitement or happiness 3. Med. to poison or have a poisonous effect on —adj. [Archaic] intoxicated

in·tox·i·ca·tion (in täk'sə kā'shən) n. 1. an intoxicating or becoming intoxicated; specif., a) a making or becoming drunk b) Med. a poisoning or becoming poisoned, as by a drug, serum, etc. 2. a feeling of wild excitement; rapture; frenzy

intr. intransitive

in·tra- (in'trə) [L. < *intra*, within, inside < *intera*, akin to *interior*, *inter*: see INTER-] a combining form meaning within, inside of [intramural, intravenous]

in·tra·cel·lu·lar (in'trə sel'yoo lər) adj. of or occurring within individual cells

In·tra·coast·al Waterway (in'trə kōs't'l) waterway for small craft extending in two sections from Boston, Mass., to Brownsville, Tex.: it consists of natural and artificial channels within the U.S. coastline except for a stretch of open water along the W Fla. coast: 2,500 to 3,000 mi. long

in·trac·ta·ble (in trak'tə b'l) adj. [L. *intractabilis*] not tractable; specif., a) hard to manage; unruly or stubborn b) hard to work, manipulate, cure, treat, etc. —SYN. see UNRULY —in·trac'ta·bil'i·ty, in·trac'ta·ble·ness n. —in·trac'ta·bly adv.

in·tra·cu·ta·ne·ous test (in'trə kyoo tā'nē əs) the injection of an antigen into the skin in order to determine whether or not the subject is allergic to it

in·tra·der·mal (-dur'm'l) adj. within the skin or between the layers of the skin

in·tra·dos (in'trə däs', -dōs'; in trā'dōs) n. [Fr. < L. *intra*, within + Fr. *dos* < L. *dorsum*, the back] Archit. the inside curve or surface of an arch or vault

INTESTINE
(A, stomach; B, pancreas; C, descending colon; D, rectum; E, appendix; F, ileum; G, jejunum; H, ascending colon; I, transverse colon; J, duodenum; K, liver)

in·tra·mo·lec·u·lar (in′trə mə lek′yə lər) *adj.* acting, existing, or taking place within a molecule or molecules —**in′tra·mo·lec′u·lar·ly** *adv.*

in·tra·mu·ral (-myoor′əl) *adj.* [INTRA- + MURAL] **1.** within the walls or limits of a city, college, etc. **2.** between or among members of the same school, college, etc. [*intramural* athletics] **3.** *Anat.* within the substance of the walls of an organ —**in′tra·mu′ral·ly** *adv.*

in·tra·mus·cu·lar (-mus′kyə lər) *adj.* located or injected within the substance of a muscle —**in′tra·mus′cu·lar·ly** *adv.*

intrans. intransitive

in trans. [L. *in transitu*] on the way; during passage

in·tran·si·gent (in tran′sə jənt) *adj.* [Fr. *intransigeant* < Sp. *intransigente* < L. *in-*, IN-² + *transigens*, prp. of *transigere*, to come to a settlement, TRANSACT] refusing to compromise, come to an agreement, or be reconciled; uncompromising —*n.* a person who is intransigent, esp. in politics —**in·tran′si·gence, in·tran′si·gen·cy** *n.* —**in·tran′si·gent·ly** *adv.*

in·tran·si·tive (in tran′sə tiv) *adj.* [LL. *intransitivus*] not transitive; designating a verb that does not require a direct object to complete its meaning —*n.* an intransitive verb —**in·tran′si·tive·ly** *adv.*

in·tra·psy·chic (in′trə sī′kik) *adj.* existing or occurring within the mind or psyche: also **in′tra·psy′chi·cal** —**in′tra·psy′chi·cal·ly** *adv.*

in·tra·spe·cif·ic (-spi sif′ik) *adj.* within a single species

☆**in·tra·state** (-stāt′) *adj.* within a state; esp., within a State of the U.S.

in·tra·tel·lu·ric (-te loor′ik, -tel yoor′ik) *adj.* [INTRA- + TELLURIC², after G. *intratellurisch*] **1.** formed, located, or occurring deep inside the earth: used esp. to refer to the minerals of igneous rocks before eruption or to phenocrysts formed before the ground mass solidified **2.** designating or of the period of crystallization of a magma before extrusion as a lava

in·tra·u·ter·ine (-yōot′ər in) *adj.* within the uterus

☆**intrauterine (contraceptive) device** any of various devices, as a coil or loop of plastic, inserted in the uterus as a contraceptive

in·trav·a·sa·tion (in trav′ə sā′shən) *n.* [INTRA- + (EXTRA)-VASATION] the entry of a foreign substance into a blood or lymph vessel

in·tra·ve·nous (in′trə vē′nəs) *adj.* [INTRA- + VENOUS] in, or directly into, a vein or veins [an *intravenous* injection] —**in′tra·ve′nous·ly** *adv.*

in·tra·zon·al (-zō′n'l) *adj.* designating or of a soil whose characteristics indicate the dominance of local conditions, such as topography or parent material, over the ordinary effects of climate and vegetation

in·treat (in trēt′) *vt., vi. archaic var. of* ENTREAT

in·trench (in trench′) *vt., vi. same as* ENTRENCH

in·trep·id (in trep′id) *adj.* [L. *intrepidus* < *in-*, not + *trepidus*, alarmed, anxious: see TREPIDATION] not afraid; bold; fearless; dauntless; very brave —*SYN.* see BRAVE —**in′tre·pid′i·ty** (-trə pid′ə tē), **in·trep′id·ness** *n.* —**in·trep′id·ly** *adv.*

Int. Rev. internal revenue

in·tri·ca·cy (in′tri kə sē) *n.* **1.** the quality or state of being intricate; complexity **2.** *pl.* **-cies** something intricate; involved matter, proceeding, etc.

in·tri·cate (in′tri kit) *adj.* [L. *intricatus*, pp. of *intricare*, to entangle, perplex, embarrass < *in-*, in + *tricae*, vexations, perplexities] **1.** hard to follow or understand because full of puzzling parts, details, or relationships [an *intricate* problem] **2.** full of elaborate detail [an *intricate* filigree] —*SYN.* see COMPLEX —**in′tri·cate·ly** *adv.* —**in′tri·cate·ness** *n.*

in·tri·gant (in′tri gənt; *Fr.* an trē gän′) *n., pl.* **-gants** (-gənts; *Fr.* -gän′) [Fr. < It. *intrigante* < *intrigare*, to INTRIGUE] a person given to or involved in intrigue —**in′tri·gante′** (-gant′; *Fr.* -gänt′) *n.fem., pl.* **-gantes** (-gants′; *Fr.* -gänt′)

in·trigue (in trēg′; *for n., also* in′trēg) *vt.* **-trigued′, -trigu′ing** [Fr. *intriguer* < It. *intrigare* < L. *intricare*: see INTRICATE] **1.** to carry on a secret love affair **2.** to plot or scheme secretly or underhandedly —*vt.* **1.** to bring on or get by secret or underhanded plotting **2.** to excite the interest or curiosity of; fascinate [the puzzle *intrigued* her] **3.** [Archaic] to trick or perplex **4.** [Obs.] to entangle —*n.* **1.** an intriguing; secret or underhanded plotting **2.** a secret or underhanded plot or scheme; machination **3.** a secret love affair —*SYN.* see PLOT —**in·trigu′er** *n.*

in·trigu·ing (-trēg′iŋ) *adj.* exciting interest or curiosity; fascinating —**in·trigu′ing·ly** *adv.*

in·trin·sic (in trin′sik, -zik) *adj.* [LME. *intrinsique* < MFr. *intrinsèque* < LL. *intrinsecus*, inward < L., inwardly < *intra-*, within (see INTRA-) + *secus*, close, following, akin to *sequi*: see SEQUENT] **1.** belonging to the real nature of a thing; not dependent on external circumstances; essential; inherent **2.** *Anat.* located within, or exclusively of, a part Also **in·trin′si·cal** Opposed to EXTRINSIC —**in·trin′si·cal·ly** *adv.* —**in·trin′si·cal·ness** *n.*

intrinsic factor a substance secreted by the stomach

which permits the absorption of vitamin B̄₁₂ in the intestines

in·tro- (in′trō, -trə) [L. < *intro*, inwardly, on the inside < **intero*, akin to *inter*: see INTER-] *a combining form meaning* into, within, inward [*introvert*]

introd., intro. **1.** introduction **2.** introductory

in·tro·duce (in′trə dōos′, -dyōos′) *vt.* **-duced′, -duc′ing** [L. *introducere* < *intro-* (see INTRO-) + *ducere*, to lead: see DUKE] **1.** to lead or bring into a given place or position; conduct in **2.** to put in or within; insert [to *introduce* an electric wire into a conduit] **3.** to bring or add as a new feature into some action, composition, etc. [to *introduce* a humorous note in a speech] **4.** to bring into use, knowledge, or fashion; make popular or common; institute [space science has *introduced* many new words] ☆**5.** to offer (a new product) for sale **6.** *a)* to make acquainted; present (*to* another or others or to one another) [please *introduce* me to your friend] *b)* to present (a person) to society, a court, the general public, etc. *c)* to give knowledge or experience of [to *introduce* a freshman to campus life] **7.** to bring forward; bring to notice formally [to *introduce* a bill into Congress] **8.** to start; open; begin [to *introduce* a talk with an anecdote] —**in′tro·duc′er** *n.*

SYN.—**introduce** implies the bringing or putting of someone or something into a place, position, notice, etc., sometimes stressing this as an innovation [to *introduce* a new song to the public]; **insert** suggests the putting of something into a hole or gap or between two things [*insert* the candle into the holder]; **insinuate** implies the slow, indirect, but skillful introduction of something [he *insinuated* himself into her trust]; **interpolate** refers to the introduction of new words or passages, esp. of spurious copy, into a writing [certain phrases in his book were *interpolated* by the editor]; **interpose**, in this connection, and **interject** imply the introduction of a comment or opinion that serves to interrupt [if I may *interpose*, or *interject*, a few remarks at this point] —*ANT.* **withdraw, remove**

in·tro·duc·tion (-duk′shən) *n.* [ME. *introduccion* < MFr. *introduction* < L. *introductio*] **1.** an introducing or being introduced **2.** anything introduced, or brought into use, knowledge, or fashion **3.** anything that introduces, or prepares the way for; specif., *a)* the preliminary section of a book, usually explaining or defining the subject matter and often written by someone other than the author *b)* the preliminary part of a speech, treatise, etc. *c)* an opening section of a musical composition *d)* a preliminary guide or text **4.** the formal presentation of one person to another, to an audience, to society, etc.

SYN.—**introduction**, in strict usage, refers to the preliminary section of a book, etc. that explains and leads into the subject proper; **preface** strictly refers to a statement preliminary to, and distinct from, a book, etc. written by the author or someone else and explaining the purpose, plan, or preparation of the work; **foreword** is usually used for a very brief or simple preface; **preamble** refers to a formal, but usually brief, introduction to a constitution, treaty, etc.; **prologue** applies to the preliminary section of a play, poem, etc., serving as an introduction and, in the play, frequently spoken by one of the characters —*ANT.* **conclusion, epilogue**

in·tro·duc·to·ry (-duk′tər ē) *adj.* [L. *introductorius*] used as an introduction; preliminary: also **in′tro·duc′tive** —**in′tro·duc′to·ri·ly** *adv.*

in·tro·gres·sion (-gresh′ən) *n.* [INTRO- + (DI)GRESSION] the infiltration of genes from the gene pool of one species into that of another —**in′tro·gres′sive** (-gres′iv) *adj.*

in·tro·it (in trō′it; in′trō it, -troit) *n.* [ME. *introite* < MFr. < L. *introitus*, a going in, entrance (in LL.(Ec.), introit of the mass) < *introire* < *intro-*, INTRO- + *ire*, to go: cf. EXIT] **1.** a psalm or hymn sung or played at the opening of a Christian worship service **2.** [I-] *R.C.Ch.* the first variable part of the Mass, consisting typically of a few psalm verses followed by the *Gloria Patri* and then repeated

in·tro·ject (in′trə jekt′) *vt.* [INTRO- + (PRO)JECT(ION)] *Psychoanalysis* to incorporate unconsciously into the psyche (a mental image of an object, person, etc.) and focus aggressive energy upon this image rather than the object itself —**in′tro·jec′tion** *n.*

in·tro·mit (-mit′) *vt.* **-mit′ted, -mit′ting** [L. *intromittere* < *intro-*, INTRO- + *mittere*, to send: see MISSION] **1.** to cause to enter; put in; insert **2.** to allow to enter; let in; admit —**in′tro·mis′sion** (-mish′ən) *n.* —**in′tro·mit′tent** *adj.*

in·trorse (in trôrs′) *adj.* [L. *introrsus*, contr. of *introversus*: see INTRO- & VERSE] *Bot.* facing inward, or toward the center —**in·trorse′ly** *adv.*

in·tro·spect (in′trə spekt′) *vt., vi.* [L. *introspectare*, freq. < *introspectus*, pp. of *introspicere*, to look within < *intro-*, INTRO- + *specere*, to look: see SPECTACLE] [Rare] to look into (one's own mind, feelings, etc.)

in·tro·spec·tion (-spek′shən) *n.* [prec. + -ION] a looking into one's own mind, feelings, etc.; observation and analysis of oneself —**in′tro·spec′tive** *adj.* —**in′tro·spec′tive·ly** *adv.* —**in′tro·spec′tive·ness** *n.*

in·tro·ver·sion (-vur′zhən, -shən) *n.* [ModL. *introversio* < INTRO- + *-versio*, as in L. *conversio*, CONVERSION] **1.** an introverting or being introverted **2.** *Psychol.* an attitude

in which a person directs his interest to his own experiences and feelings rather than upon external objects or other persons: opposed to EXTROVERSION —**in′tro·ver′sive** *adj.* —**in′tro·ver′sive·ly** *adv.*

in·tro·vert (in′trə vurt′; *for v., also* in′trə vurt′) *vt.* [INTRO- + (CON)VERT] 1. to direct (one's interest, mind, or attention) upon oneself; introspect 2. to bend (something) inward 3. *Zool.* to draw (a tubular organ or part) inward upon itself, commonly by invagination —*vi.* to practice introversion; become introverted —*n.* 1. a thing, esp. a tubular organ or part, that can be introverted 2. *Psychol.* a person whose interest is more in himself than in his environment or in other people; introspective person: opposed to EXTROVERT —*adj. same as* INTROVERTED

in·tro·vert·ed (-id) *adj.* characterized by introversion

in·trude (in trood′) *vt.* -trud′ed, -trud′ing [L. *intrudere* < *in*-, in + *trudere*, to thrust, push: see THREAT] 1. to push or force (something *in* or *upon*) 2. to force (oneself or one's thoughts) upon others without being asked or welcomed 3. *Geol.* to force (liquid magma, etc.) into or between solid rocks —*vi.* to intrude oneself —**in·trud′er** *n.* SYN.—**intrude** implies the forcing of oneself or something upon another without invitation, permission, or welcome [to *intrude* upon another's privacy]; **obtrude** connotes even more strongly the distractive nature or the undesirability of the invasion [side issues keep *obtruding*]; **interlope** implies an intrusion upon the rights or privileges of another to the disadvantage or harm of the latter [the *interloping* merchants have ruined our trade]; **butt in** (or **into**) is a slang term implying intrusion in a meddling or officious way [stop *butting into* my business] See also TRESPASS

in·tru·sion (in troo′zhən) *n.* [ME. < OFr. < ML. *intrusio* < L. *intrusus*: see ff.] 1. the act of intruding; specif., *Law* the illegal entering upon another's land without right to possession 2. *Geol.* a) the invasion, as of liquid magma, into or between solid rock b) the body of rock resulting from such invasion

in·tru·sive (-siv) *adj.* [< L. *intrusus*, pp. of *intrudere* (see INTRUDE) + -IVE] 1. intruding or tending to intrude 2. *Geol.* a) forced into or between other rocks while in a molten state b) formed of such rock 3. *Linguis.* added without etymological justification, as the *d* in *spindle*: cf. EXCRESCENT —**in·tru′sive·ly** *adv.* —**in·tru′sive·ness** *n.*

in·trust (in trust′) *vt. same as* ENTRUST

in·tu·bate (in′too bāt′, -tyoo-) *vt.* -bat′ed, -bat′ing [IN-¹ + TUB(E) + -ATE¹] to insert a tube into (an orifice or hollow organ, as the larynx) for the administration of gases or to admit air —**in′tu·ba′tion** *n.*

in·tu·it (in too′it, -tyoo′-; in′too wit) *vt., vi.* [< L. *intuitus*] to know or learn by intuition —**in·tu′it·a·ble** *adj.*

in·tu·i·tion (in′too wish′ən, -tyoo-) *n.* [LL. < L. *intuitus*, pp. of *intueri*, to look at, regard < *in*- + *tueri*, to look at, view] 1. the direct knowing or learning of something without the conscious use of reasoning; immediate apprehension or understanding 2. something known or learned in this way 3. the ability to perceive or know things without conscious reasoning —**in′tu·i′tion·al** *adj.* —**in′tu·i′tion·al·ly** *adv.*

in·tu·i·tion·ism (-iz′m) *n.* 1. the doctrine that all things are apprehended in their real nature through intuition 2. *Ethics* the doctrine that the rightness of acts or fundamental moral principles are apprehended by intuition —**in′tu·i′tion·ist** *adj., n.*

in·tu·i·tive (in too′i tiv, -tyoo′-) *adj.* [ML. *intuitivus* < L. *intuitus*] 1. having to do with intuition 2. having, or perceiving by, intuition 3. that is or can be perceived by intuition [an *intuitive* truth] —**in·tu′i·tive·ly** *adv.* —**in·tu′i·tive·ness** *n.*

in·tu·mesce (in′too mes′, -tyoo-) *vi.* -mesced′, -mesc′ing [L. *intumescere*: see IN-¹ & TUMESCENT] to swell, enlarge, expand, or bubble up, as with heat

in·tu·mes·cence (-mes′ns) *n.* [Fr.] 1. an intumescing or being intumesced 2. a swollen or enlarged organ or mass, as a tumor; swelling —**in′tu·mes′cent** *adj.*

in·tus·sus·cept (in′tə sə sept′) *vt.* [< L. *intus*, within + *susceptus*, pp. of *suscipere*: see ff.] to receive within itself or into another part; specif., to telescope (one section of the intestines) into another; invaginate

in·tus·sus·cep·tion (-sə sep′shən) *n.* [< L. *intus*, within (see INTESTINE) + *susceptio*, a taking up < pp. of *suscipere*, to take up: see SUSCEPTIBLE] 1. an intussuscepting or being intussuscepted 2. the process of taking in food or other foreign matter and interposing the tiny particles among those already present in the cell walls —**in′tus·sus·cep′tive** *adj.*

in·twine (in twin′) *vt., vi.* -twined′, -twin′ing *same as* ENTWINE

in·u·lase (in′yoo lās′) *n.* [< ff. + -ASE] an enzyme that converts inulin into fructose

in·u·lin (-lin) *n.* [< ModL. *Inula*, genus of plants (< L. *inula*, ELECAMPANE) + -IN¹] a white, starchlike polysaccharide which yields fructose when hydrolyzed: found in the roots and tubers of many composite plants

in·unc·tion (in uŋk′shən) *n.* [L. *inunctio*: see IN-¹ & UNCTION] 1. the act of rubbing ointment, etc. into the skin 2. an ointment, liniment, etc.

in·un·dant (in un′dənt) *adj.* [L. *inundans*, prp. of *inundare*: see ff.] overflowing or inundating

in·un·date (in′ən dāt′) *vt.* -dat′ed, -dat′ing [< L. *inundatus*, pp. of *inundare*, to overflow < *in*-, in, on + *undare*,

to move in waves, flood < *unda*, a wave: see WATER] to cover with or as with a flood; deluge; flood —**in′un·da′tion** *n.* —**in·un′da·tor** *n.* —**in·un·da·to·ry** (in un′də tôr′ē) *adj.*

in·ur·bane (in′ur bān′) *adj.* [L. *inurbanus*] not urbane; crude; unpolished —**in′ur·ban′i·ty** (-ban′ə tē) *n.*

in·ure (in yoor′) *vt.* -ured′, -ur′ing [ME. (in pp. *enured*) < *in ure*, in practice < *in*, in + *ure*, practice, work < OFr. *eure, ovre* < L. *opera*, work: see OPERA¹] to make accustomed to something difficult, painful, etc.; habituate —*vi.* to come into use or take effect [sick pay *inures* from the first day of illness] —**in·ure′ment** *n.*

in·urn (in urn′) *vt.* 1. to put (ashes of the dead) into an urn 2. to bury; entomb

in u·ter·o (in yoot′ər ō) [L.] in the uterus; unborn

in·u·tile (in yoot′'l) *adj.* [ME. < MFr. < L. *inutilis* < *in*-, IN-² + *utilis*, useful: see UTILITY] useless; unprofitable —**in·u·til·i·ty** (in′yoo til′ə tē) *n.*

inv. 1. [L. *invenit*] he (or she) designed it 2. invented 3. inventor 4. invoice

†in va·cu·o (in vak′yoo ō′) [L.] in a vacuum

in·vade (in vād′) *vt.* -vad′ed, -vad′ing [ME. *invaden* < L. *invadere* < *in*-, in + *vadere*, to come, go] 1. to enter forcibly or hostilely; come into as an enemy 2. to crowd into; throng [tourists *invading* the beaches] 3. to intrude upon; infringe; violate [to *invade* someone's privacy] 4. to enter and spread through with harmful effects [a body *invaded* by disease] —*vi.* to make an invasion —*SYN.* see TRESPASS —**in·vad′er** *n.*

in·vag·i·nate (in vaj′ə nāt′) *vt.* -nat′ed, -nat′ing [< ML. *invaginatus*, pp. of *invaginare* < L. *in*-, in + *vagina*, a sheath] 1. to place or receive into a sheath 2. *same as* INTUSSUSCEPT —*vi.* to become invaginated —**in·vag′i·na′tion** *n.*

in·va·lid¹ (in′və lid; *for v., Brit & occas. Canad.* in·və lēd′) *adj.* [Fr. *invalide* < L. *invalidus*, feeble: see IN-² & VALID] 1. not well; weak and sickly; infirm 2. of or for invalids [an *invalid* home] —*n.* a weak, sickly person; esp., one who is chronically ill or disabled —*vt.* 1. to make invalid; disable or weaken 2. [Chiefly Brit.] to remove (a soldier, sailor, etc.) from active duty or from a combat zone because of injury or illness —*vi.* [Rare] 1. to become an invalid 2. to retire, as from the army or navy, because of ill health

in·val·id² (in val′id) *adj.* [L. *invalidus*] not valid; having no force; null or void —**in·va·lid·i·ty** (in′və lid′ə tē) *n.* —**in·val′id·ly** *adv.*

in·val·i·date (in val′ə dāt′) *vt.* -dat′ed, -dat′ing [prec. + -ATE¹] to make invalid; deprive of legal force —*SYN.* see NULLIFY —**in·val′i·da′tion** *n.*

in·va·lid·ism (in′və lid iz′m) *n.* the state of being an invalid; chronic ill health or disability

in·val·u·a·ble (in val′yoo wə b'l, -yə b'l) *adj.* extremely valuable; having value too great to measure; priceless —*SYN.* see COSTLY —**in·val′u·a·ble·ness** *n.* —**in·val′u·a·bly** *adv.*

In·var (in vär′) [contr. < INVARIABLE] *a trademark for* a steel alloy containing approximately 36% nickel, used for making precision instruments and thermostatic elements because of its low coefficient of thermal expansion —*n.* [i-] this substance

in·var·i·a·ble (in ver′ē ə b'l) *adj.* [ML. *invariabilis*] not variable; not changing; constant; uniform —*n.* an invariable quantity; constant —**in·var′i·a·bil′i·ty, in·var′-i·a·ble·ness** *n.* —**in·var′i·a·bly** *adv.*

in·var·i·ant (-ənt) *adj.* not varying; constant; specif., having the nature of an invariant —*n. Math.* an entity that is unchanged by a given transformation —**in·var′i·ance** *n.*

in·va·sion (in vā′zhən) *n.* [MFr. < LL. *invasio* < L. *invasus*, pp. of *invadere*] an invading or being invaded; specif., a) an entering or being entered by an attacking military force b) an intrusion or infringement c) the onset or appearance of something harmful or troublesome, as a disease —**in·va′sive** *adj.*

invasion of privacy a wrongful intrusion into one's private activities such as to cause humiliation or mental suffering to a person of average sensibilities

in·vec·tive (in vek′tiv) *adj.* [ME. *invectif* < MFr. *invectif* < LL. *invectivus* < L. *invectus*, pp. of *invehere*: see ff.] inveighing; using, inclined to use, or characterized by strong verbal abuse —*n.* 1. a violent verbal attack; strong criticism, insults, curses, etc.; vituperation 2. an abusive term; insult, curse, etc. —**in·vec′tive·ly** *adv.* —**in·vec′tive·ness** *n.*

in·veigh (in vā′) *vi.* [ME. *invehen* < L. *invehi*, to assail, attack with words, passive of *invehere*, to bring in < *in*-, in, to + *vehere*, to carry: see VEHEMENT] to make a violent verbal attack; talk or write bitterly (*against*); rail —**in·veigh′er** *n.*

in·vei·gle (in vē′g'l, -vā′-) *vt.* -gled, -gling [LME. *invegelen*, altered (after IN-¹) < MFr. *aveugler*, to blind, delude < *aveugle*, blind < L. **aboculus*, blind < L. *ab*, from + *oculus*, an EYE] to lead on with deception; entice or trick into doing or giving something, going somewhere, etc. —*SYN.* see LURE —**in·vei′gle·ment** *n.* —**in·vei′gler** *n.*

in·vent (in vent′) *vt.* [ME. *inventen* < L. *inventus*, pp. of *invenire*, to come upon, meet with, discover < *in*-, in, on + *venire*, to COME] 1. to think up; devise or fabricate in

the mind [to *invent* excuses] **2.** to think out or produce (a new device, process, etc.); originate, as by experiment; devise for the first time **3.** [Archaic] to find; come upon; discover

in·ven·tion (in ven′shən) *n.* [ME. *inuencioun* < OFr. *invencion* < L. *inventio*] **1.** an inventing or being invented **2.** the power of inventing; ingenuity or creativity **3.** something invented; specif., *a)* something thought up or mentally fabricated; esp., a falsehood *b)* something originated by experiment, etc.; new device or contrivance **4.** *Music* a short composition, usually for a keyboard instrument, developing a single short motive in two-voice or three-voice counterpoint; esp., any of a group of these by J. S. Bach

in·ven·tive (-tiv) *adj.* [ME. *inventif* < ML. *inventivus*] **1.** of invention **2.** skilled in inventing **3.** indicating an ability to invent [*inventive* powers] —**in·ven′tive·ly** *adv.* —**in·ven′tive·ness** *n.*

in·ven·tor (-tər) *n.* [L.] a person who invents; esp., one who devises a new contrivance, method, etc.

in·ven·to·ry (in′vən tôr′ē) *n., pl.* **-ries** [ML. *inventorium* < LL. *inventarium* < L. *inventus*: see INVENT] **1.** an itemized list or catalog of goods, property, etc.; esp., such a list of the stock of a business, taken annually **2.** the store of goods, etc. that are or may be so listed; stock **3.** any detailed list **4.** the act of making such a list —*vt.* **-ried**, **-ry·ing 1.** to make an inventory of **2.** to place on an inventory —*SYN.* see LIST —**take inventory 1.** to make an inventory of stock on hand **2.** to make an appraisal, as of one's skills, personal characteristics, etc. —**in′·ven·to′ri·al** *adj.* —**in′ven·to′ri·al·ly** *adv.*

in·ve·rac·i·ty (in′və ras′ə tē) *n.* **1.** lack of veracity; untruthfulness **2.** *pl.* **-ties** a falsehood; lie

In·ver·ness (in′vər nes′) **1.** county of N Scotland: 4,211 sq. mi.; pop. 83,000: also **In′ver·ness′-shire** (-shir) **2.** its county seat, at the head of Moray Firth: pop. 30,000 —*n.* [*often* i-] *a)* an overcoat with a long, removable, sleeveless cape *b)* the cape: also **Inverness cape**

in·verse (in vurs′; *also, for adj. & n.*, in′vurs′) *adj.* [L. *inversus*, pp. of *invertere*] **1.** inverted; reversed in order or relation; directly opposite **2.** *Math.* designating or of an operation which, when applied after a specific operation, cancels it [subtraction is the *inverse* operation of addition] —*n.* **1.** any inverse thing; direct opposite **2.** *Math.* the result of an inversion —*vt.* **-versed′**, **-vers′ing** [Rare] to invert; reverse —**in·verse′ly** *adv.*

inverse function the function obtained by expressing the independent variable of another function in terms of the dependent variable which is then regarded as an independent variable

in·ver·sion (in vur′zhən, -shən) *n.* [L. *inversio < inversus*, pp. of *invertere*] **1.** an inverting or being inverted **2.** something inverted; reversal **3.** *Chem. a)* a chemical change in which an optically active substance is converted into another substance having no effect, or the opposite rotatory effects, on the plane of polarization *b)* the conversion of an isomeric compound to its opposite **4.** *Gram. & Rhetoric* a reversal of the normal order of words in a sentence (Ex.: "said he" for "he said") **5.** *Math. a)* the process of using an opposite rule or method *b)* an interchange of the terms of a ratio **6.** *Meteorol.* an increase with altitude in the temperature of the air, preventing the normal rising of surface air **7.** *Music a)* the reversal of the position of the tones in an interval or chord, as by raising the lower tone by an octave, etc. *b)* the recurrence of a theme, fugue subject, motive, or figure in identical intervals and note values, but consistently in the opposite direction **8.** *Phonet.* a position of the tongue in which the tip is turned upward and backward **9.** *Psychiatry same as* HOMOSEXUALITY —**in·ver′sive** *adj.*

in·vert (in vurt′; *for adj. & n.*, in′vurt′) *vt.* [L. *invertere* < *in-*, in, to, toward + *vertere*, to turn: see VERSE] **1.** to turn upside down **2.** to change to the direct opposite; reverse the order, position, direction, etc. of **3.** to subject to inversion (in various senses) —*adj. Chem.* inverted [*invert* sugar] —*n.* **1.** an inverted person or thing **2.** *Psychiatry same as* HOMOSEXUAL —*SYN.* see REVERSE —**in·vert′i·ble** *adj.*

in·vert·ase (in vur′tās) *n.* [INVERT + -ASE] an enzyme, present in certain plants and in animal intestines, which changes sucrose into dextrose and fructose

in·ver·te·brate (in vur′tə brit, -brāt′) *adj.* [ModL. *invertebratus*] **1.** not vertebrate; having no backbone, or spinal column **2.** of invertebrates **3.** having no moral backbone; lacking courage, resolution, etc. —*n.* any animal without a backbone, or spinal column; any animal other than a fish, amphibian, reptile, bird, or mammal

inverted comma [Brit.] *same as* QUOTATION MARK

inverted mordent *see* MORDENT

in·vert·er (in vur′tər) *n. Elec.* a device for transforming direct current into alternating current

invert sugar a mixture of dextrose and levulose in approximately equal proportions, found in fruits and produced artificially by the hydrolysis of sucrose

in·vest (in vest′) *vt.* [L. *investire* < *in-*, in + *vestire*, to

clothe < *vestis*, clothing: see VEST] **1.** to clothe; array; adorn **2.** *a)* to cover, surround, or envelop like, or as if with, a garment [fog *invests* the city] *b)* to endue with qualities, attributes, etc. **3.** to install in office with ceremony **4.** to furnish with power, privilege, or authority **5.** [Rare] to vest or settle (a power or right) in a person, legislative body, etc. **6.** to put (money) into business, real estate, stocks, bonds, etc. for the purpose of obtaining an income or profit **7.** to spend (time, effort, etc.) with the expectation of some satisfaction **8.** *Mil.* to hem in or besiege (a town, port, enemy salient, etc.) —*vi.* to invest money; make an investment —**in·ves′tor** *n.*

in·ves·ti·gate (in ves′tə gāt′) *vt.* **-gat′ed**, **-gat′ing** [< L. *investigatus*, pp. of *investigare*, to trace out < *in-*, in + *vestigare*, to track < *vestigium*, a track] to search into so as to learn the facts; inquire into systematically —*vi.* to make an investigation —**in·ves′ti·ga·ble** (-gə b'l) *adj.* —**in·ves′ti·ga′tor** *n.*

in·ves·ti·ga·tion (in ves′tə gā′shən) *n.* [ME. *investigacioun* < MFr. < L. *investigatio*] **1.** an investigating or being investigated **2.** a careful search or examination; systematic inquiry —**in·ves′ti·ga′tion·al** *adj.*

SYN.—**investigation** refers to a detailed examination or search, often formal or official, to uncover facts and determine the truth [the *investigation* of a crime]; **probe** applies to an extensive, searching investigation, as by an appointed committee, of alleged corrupt practices, etc.; **inquest** now refers to a judicial inquiry, especially one conducted by a coroner to determine the cause of a suspicious death; **inquisition** strictly refers to any penetrating investigation, but because of its application to the ecclesiastical inquiries for the suppression of heresy, it now usually connotes ruthless, hounding persecution; **research** implies careful, patient study and investigation from original sources of information, as by scientists or scholars

in·ves·ti·ga·tive (in ves′tə gāt′iv) *adj.* [ML. *investigativus*] **1.** of or characterized by investigation **2.** inclined to investigate Also **in·ves′ti·ga·to′ry** (-gə tôr′ē)

in·ves·ti·tive (in ves′tə tiv) *adj.* [< L. *investitus, see* INVEST) + -IVE] **1.** that invests or can invest authority, etc. **2.** of such investing

in·ves·ti·ture (-chər) *n.* [ME. < ML. *investitura* < L. *investire*] **1.** a formal investing with an office, power, authority, etc., often with appropriate symbols, robes, etc. **2.** anything that clothes or covers; vesture **3.** *Feudal Law* ceremonial transfer of land to a tenant

in·vest·ment (in vest′mənt) *n.* **1.** an investing or being invested **2.** an outer covering **3.** *same as* INVESTITURE (sense 1) **4.** *a)* the investing of money *b)* the amount of money invested *c)* anything in which money is or may be invested

investment fund a trust or corporation that invests in securities the funds obtained from the sale of its own shares and distributes a return to its shareholders from the income on the securities

in·vet·er·ate (in vet′ər it) *adj.* [L. *inveteratus*, pp. of *inveterare*, to make or become old < *in-*, in + *vetus*, old: see WETHER] **1.** firmly established over a long period; of long standing; deep-rooted **2.** settled in a habit, practice, prejudice, etc.; habitual —*SYN.* see CHRONIC —**in·vet′er·a·cy** *n.* —**in·vet′er·ate·ly** *adv.*

in·vi·a·ble (in vī′ə b'l) *adj.* not viable; unable to live and develop normally —**in·vi′a·bil′i·ty** *n.*

in·vid·i·ous (in vid′ē əs) *adj.* [L. *invidiosus < invidia:* see ENVY] **1.** *a)* such as to excite ill will, odium, or envy; giving offense *b)* giving offense by discriminating unfairly [*invidious* comparisons] **2.** [Obs.] envious —**in·vid′i·ous·ly** *adv.* —**in·vid′i·ous·ness** *n.*

in·vig·i·late (in vij′ə lāt′) *vi.* **-lat′ed**, **-lat′ing** [< L. *invigilatus*, pp. of *invigilare* < *in-*, in, on + *vigilare*, to watch] [Brit.] to monitor students during a written examination —**in·vig′i·la′tion** *n.*

in·vig·or·ate (in vig′ə rāt′) *vt.* **-at′ed**, **-at′ing** [IN-[1] + VIGOR + -ATE[1]] to give vigor to; fill with energy; enliven —*SYN.* see ANIMATE —**in·vig′or·a′tion** *n.* —**in·vig′or·a′tive** *adj.* —**in·vig′or·a′tor** *n.*

in·vin·ci·ble (in vin′sə b'l) *adj.* [ME. *invyncyble* < MFr. *invincible* < L. *invincibilis:* see IN-[2] & VINCIBLE] that cannot be overcome; unconquerable —**in·vin′ci·bil′i·ty**, **in·vin′ci·ble·ness** *n.* —**in·vin′ci·bly** *adv.*

‡**in vi·no ve·ri·tas** (in vē′nō ver′i tas′) [L.] in wine there is truth: a quotation from Pliny the Elder

in·vi·o·la·ble (in vī′ə lə b'l) *adj.* [MFr. < L. *inviolabilis*] **1.** not to be violated; not to be profaned or injured; sacred [an *inviolable* promise] **2.** that cannot be violated; indestructible [the *inviolable* heavens] —**in·vi′o·la·bil′i·ty** *n.* —**in·vi′o·la·bly** *adv.*

in·vi·o·late (in vī′ə lit, -lāt′) *adj.* [ME. < L. *inviolatus:* see IN-[2] & VIOLATE] not violated; kept sacred or unbroken —**in·vi′o·la·cy** (-lə sē), **in·vi′o·late·ness** *n.* —**in·vi′o·late·ly** *adv.*

in·vis·i·ble (in viz′ə b'l) *adj.* [ME. < OFr. < L. *invisibilis*] **1.** not visible; that cannot be seen **2.** out of sight; not apparent **3.** too small or too faint to be seen; imperceptible; indistinct **4.** not publicized; kept hidden [*invisible* assets] —*n.* an invisible thing or being —**the Invisible 1.**

God 2. the unseen world —**in·vis′i·bil′i·ty, in·vis′i·ble-ness** *n.* —**in·vis′i·bly** *adv.*

invisible ink a colorless ink that cannot be seen on paper until it is treated with heat, vapor, or a chemical

in·vi·ta·tion (in′və tā′shən) *n.* [L. *invitatio* < pp. of *invitare*] 1. an inviting to come somewhere or do something 2. the message or note used in inviting 3. enticement or allurement

in·vi·ta·tion·al (-′l) *adj.* participated in only by those invited [an *invitational* art exhibit]

in·vi·ta·to·ry (in vit′ə tôr′ē) *adj.* [LL. *invitatorius*] containing an invitation —*n., pl.* -**ries** a form of invitation used in worship as a call to prayer or praise; esp., Ps. 95 (94 in the Douay)

in·vite (in vīt′; *for n.* in′vīt) *vt.* -**vit′ed**, -**vit′ing** [Fr. *inviter* < L. *invitare* < *in-*, IN-[1] + ? IE. base **wei-*, to go directly toward, chase after, whence L. *via* & OE. *wædan*, to hunt] 1. to ask courteously to come somewhere or do something; request the presence or participation of 2. to make a request for [to *invite* questions] 3. to tend to bring on; give occasion for [action that *invites* scandal] 4. to tempt; allure; entice —*n.* [Colloq.] an invitation —*SYN.* see CALL

in·vit·ing (-vīt′iŋ) *adj.* tempting; alluring; enticing

in vi·tro (in vē′trō) [L., lit., in glass] isolated from the living organism and artificially maintained, as in a test tube

in vi·vo (in vē′vō) [L., lit., in one that is living] occurring within the living organism

in·vo·cate (in′və kāt′) *vt., vi.* -**cat′ed**, -**cat′ing** [< L. *invocatus*, pp. of *invocare*: see INVOKE] [Rare] to speak or ask in invocation

in·vo·ca·tion (in′və kā′shən) *n.* [ME. < OFr. < L. *invocatio* < pp. of *invocare*: see INVOKE] 1. the act of calling on God, a god, a saint, the Muses, etc. for blessing, help, inspiration, support, or the like 2. *a)* a formal prayer used in invoking, as at the beginning of a church service *b)* a formal plea for aid from a Muse, god, etc., at the beginning of an epic or similar poem 3. *a)* a conjuring of evil spirits *b)* an incantation used in conjuring 4. *Law* a formal request from the bench for the papers or evidence pertaining to a case other than that under trial —**in′vo·ca′tion·al** *adj.* —**in·voc′a·to·ry** (-väk′ə tôr′ē) *adj.*

in·voice (in′vois) *n.* [prob. orig. pl. of ME. *envoie*, a message: see ENVOY[1]] 1. an itemized list of goods shipped to a buyer, or of services rendered, stating quantities, prices, fees, shipping charges, etc., often with a request for payment 2. a shipment of invoiced goods —*vt.* -**voiced**, -**voic·ing** to present an invoice for or to

in·voke (in vōk′) *vt.* -**voked′**, -**vok′ing** [ME. *invoken* < MFr. *invoquer* < L. *invocare* < *in-*, in, on + *vocare*, to call: see VOCATIVE] 1. to call on (God, a god, a saint, the Muses, etc.) for blessing, help, inspiration, support, etc. 2. to resort to or put into use (a law, ruling, penalty, etc.) as pertinent [to *invoke* an article of the U.N. Charter] 3. to call forth; cause 4. to summon (evil spirits) by incantation; conjure 5. to ask solemnly for; beg for; implore; entreat [to *invoke* aid] —**in·vok′er** *n.*

in·vol·u·cel (in väl′yoo sel′) *n.* [ModL. *involucellum*, dim. < L. *involucrum*] a secondary involucre; ring of small leaves, or bracts, at the base of each segment of a cluster —**in·vol′u·cel′late** (-it) *adj.*

in·vo·lu·crate (in′və loo′krit, -krāt) *adj.* having an involucre

in·vo·lu·cre (-kər) *n.* [Fr. < L. *involucrum*, wrapper, case, envelope < *involvere*: see INVOLVE] 1. *Anat.* a membranous covering or envelope 2. *Bot.* a ring of small leaves, or bracts, at the base of a flower, flower cluster, or fruit: involucres are found in all plants of the composite family Also **in′vo·lu′crum** (-krəm), *pl.* -**cra** (-krə) —**in′vo·lu′cral** (-krəl) *adj.*

in·vol·un·tar·y (in väl′ən ter′ē) *adj.* [LL. *involuntarius*] not voluntary; specif., *a)* not done of one's own free will; not done by choice *b)* unintentional; accidental *c)* not consciously controlled; automatic [sneezing is *involuntary*] —*SYN.* see SPONTANEOUS —**in·vol′un·tar′i·ly** *adv.* —**in·vol′un·tar′i·ness** *n.*

in·vo·lute (in′və loot′) *adj.* [L. *involutus*, pp. of *involvere*, INVOLVE] 1. intricate; involved 2. rolled up or curled in a spiral; having the whorls wound closely around the axis [*involute* shells] 3. *Bot.* rolled inward at the edges [*involute* leaves] —*n. Math. a)* the curve traced by any point of a taut string when it is wound upon or unwound from a fixed curve on the same plane with it *b)* the locus of any fixed point on a moving tangent which rolls, but does not slide on a curve: correlative to EVOLUTE —*vi.* -**lut′ed**, -**lut′ing** to become involute or undergo involution

in·vo·lu·tion (in′və loo′shən) *n.* [L. *involutio* < *involutus*, pp. of *involvere*] 1. an involving or being involved; entanglement 2. anything that is involved; complication; intricacy 3. *Anat.* a part formed by rolling or curling inward, as in the formation of a gastrula 4. *Biol.* a retrograde or degenerative change 5.

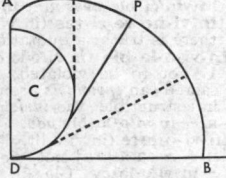

INVOLUTE
(AB, involute made by point P of string unrolled from curve C)

Gram. an involved construction, esp. one created by a clause separating a subject from its predicate 6. *Math.* the raising of a quantity to any given power 7. *Med. a)* the return of an organ to its normal size after distention, as of the womb after childbirth *b)* a decline in the normal functions of the human body, or of an organ, that occurs with age, as the changes taking place at the menopause —**in′vo·lu′tion·al** *adj.* —**in′vo·lu′tion·ar′y** *adj.*

in·volve (in välv′) *vt.* -**volved′**, -**volv′ing** [ME. *involven* < L. *involvere* < *in-*, in + *volvere*, to roll: see WALK] 1. orig., to enfold or envelop as in a wrapping [fog *involved* the shore-line] 2. to make intricate, tangled, or complicated 3. to entangle in trouble, difficulty, danger, etc.; implicate 4. to draw or hold within itself; include [a riot that soon *involved* thousands] 5. to include by necessity; entail; require [a project *involving* years of work] 6. to relate to or affect [his honor is *involved*] 7. to make busy; employ; occupy [*involved* in research] 8. [Obs.] to wind spirally; coil up —*SYN.* see INCLUDE —**in·volve′ment** *n.*

in·volved (-välvd′) *adj.* 1. not easily understood; intricate; complicated 2. implicated, affected, or committed —*SYN.* see COMPLEX

invt. inventory

in·vul·ner·a·ble (in vul′nər ə b'l) *adj.* [L. *invulnerabilis*] not vulnerable; specif., *a)* that cannot be wounded or injured *b)* proof against attack; unassailable —**in·vul′ner·a·bil′i·ty** *n.* —**in·vul′ner·a·bly** *adv.*

in·ward (in′wərd) *adj.* [ME. *inneward* < OE. *inweard*, *inneweard*: see IN-[1] & -WARD] 1. situated within; being on the inside; internal 2. of or belonging to the inner nature of a person; mental or spiritual 3. directed toward the inside; ingoing [the *inward* pull of a centrifuge] 4. [Obs.] *a)* inherent; intrinsic *b)* domestic *c)* intimate; familiar *d)* private; secret —*n.* 1. the inside; inward part 2. [*pl.*] the entrails —*adv.* 1. toward the inside, interior, or center 2. into the mind, thoughts, or soul

in·ward·ly (-lē) *adv.* [ME. *inwardlich* < OE. *inweardlic*: see prec. & -LY[2]] 1. in or on the inside; internally 2. in the mind or spirit [*inwardly* resentful] 3. toward the inside or center

in·ward·ness (-nis) *n.* [ME. *inwardnesse*] 1. the inner nature, essence, or meaning 2. the quality or state of being inward; esp., spirituality 3. depth of thought or feeling; sincerity 4. [Obs.] intimacy; familiarity

in·wards (in′wərdz) *adv.* same as INWARD

in·weave (in wēv′) *vt.* -**wove′**, -**wo′ven** or -**wove′**, -**weav′ing** to weave in; interweave

in·wrap (in rap′) *vt.* -**wrapped′**, -**wrap′ping** same as ENWRAP

in·wrought (in rôt′) *adj.* [IN-[1] + WROUGHT] 1. *a)* worked or woven into a fabric: said of a pattern, etc. *b)* [Archaic] having a decoration worked in 2. closely blended with other things

I·o (ī′ō) [L. < Gr. *Iō*] 1. *Gr. Myth.* a maiden loved by Zeus and changed into a heifer by jealous Hera or, in some tales, by Zeus to protect her: she was watched by Argus and was driven to Egypt, where she regained human form 2. the second satellite of Jupiter

Io *Chem.* ionium

Io·an·ni·na (yô ä′nē nä′) city in Epirus, NW Greece: pop. 35,000

i·o·date (ī′ə dāt′) *vt.* -**dat′ed**, -**dat′ing** [IOD(O)- + -ATE[2]] to treat with iodine —*n.* any salt of iodic acid —**i′o·da′-tion** *n.*

i·od·ic (ī äd′ik) *adj.* designating, of, or containing iodine, esp. iodine with a valence of five

iodic acid a colorless or white crystalline powder, HIO_3, that is a relatively strong acid: used as an analytical reagent and oxidizing agent

i·o·dide (ī′ə dīd′) *n.* [IOD(O)- + -IDE] a compound of iodine with another element, as in sodium iodide, NaI, or with a radical, as in methyl iodide, CH_3I

i·o·di·nate (ī′ə di nāt′) *vt.* -**nat′ed**, -**nat′ing** to treat or cause to combine with iodine —**i′o·di·na′tion** *n.*

i·o·dine (ī′ə dīn′, -din; *also*, *Brit. & among chemists*, -dēn′) *n.* [Fr. *iode*, iodine (< Gr. *iōdēs*, violetlike < *ion*, a violet + *eidos*, form) + -INE[4]] 1. a nonmetallic chemical element belonging to the halogen family and consisting of grayish-black crystals that volatilize into a violet-colored vapor: used as an antiseptic, in the manufacture of dyes, in photography, etc.: symbol, I; at. wt., 126.9044; at. no., 53; sp. gr., 4.93; melt. pt., 113.7°C; boil. pt., 184.35°C: a radioactive isotope of iodine (**iodine 131**) is used esp. in the diagnosis and treatment of thyroid function, in internal radiation therapy, and as a tracer 2. tincture of iodine, used as an antiseptic

i·o·dism (ī′ə diz'm) *n.* [IOD(O)- + -ISM] a disease caused by the excessive use of iodine

i·o·dize (-dīz′) *vt.* -**dized′**, -**diz′ing** [IOD(O)- + -IZE] to treat (a wound, photographic plate, etc.) with iodine or an iodide

iodized salt common table salt to which a small amount of sodium iodide or potassium iodide has been added

i·o·do- (ī ō′də; ī′ə dō′, -ə də) [< Fr. *iode*, IODINE] a combining form meaning iodine or a compound of iodine [*iodoform*]: also, before a vowel, **iod-**

i·o·do·form (ī ō′də fôrm′) *n.* [< prec. + FORM(YL)] a yellowish, crystalline compound of iodine, CHI_3, used as an antiseptic in surgical dressings

I·o·dol (ī′ə dôl′, -däl′) [IOD(O)- + (PYRR)OL(E)] *a trademark*

for a brownish, crystalline compound of iodine, C₄HI₄N, *used as an antiseptic* —*n.* [i-] this substance

i·o·dom·e·try (ī'ə däm'ə trē) *n.* [IODO- + -METRY] quantitative determination of iodine, or of substances that will react with it or liberate it, by volumetric analytical methods —**i'o·do·met'ric** (-dō met'rik) *adj.*

i·o·do·pro·tein (ī'ə dō prō'tēn, -prōt'ē in) *n.* a protein that contains iodine

i·o·dop·sin (ī'ə däp'sin) *n.* [< IOD(O)- + Gr. *opsis*, sight + -IN[1]] a photosensitive, violet-colored pigment-protein thought to be responsible for the translation of light stimuli to nerve impulses by the cones of the retina

i·o·dous (ī ō'dəs, ī'ə dəs) *adj.* [IOD(O)- + -OUS] 1. of or containing iodine 2. designating or of a chemical compound in which iodine has a valence of three

i·o·lite (ī'ə līt') *n.* [altered (after -LITE) < G. *iolith* < Gr. *ion*, violet + *lithos*, stone] *same as* CORDIERITE

☆**I·o moth** (ī'ō) a large, yellowish, N. American moth (*Automeris io*) with an eyelike spot on each hind wing: its caterpillar has poisonous, stinging hairs

i·on (ī'ən, -än) *n.* [arbitrary use (by Faraday) of Gr. *ion*, neut. of *iōn*, prp. of *ienai*, to go] an electrically charged atom or group of atoms, the electrical charge of which results when a neutral atom or group of atoms loses or gains one or more electrons during chemical reactions, by the action of certain forms of radiant energy, etc.: the loss of electrons results in a positively charged ion (*cation*), the gain of electrons in a negatively charged ion (*anion*)

-ion [< Fr. or L.: Fr. *-ion* < L. *-io*, nom., (gen. *-ionis*)] *a n.-forming suffix meaning:* 1. the act or condition of [*translation, condemnation*] 2. the result of [*fusion, conscription, correction*]

☆**ion engine** a reaction engine, as for space vehicles, that uses for propulsion a stream of ionized heavy atoms or molecules, accelerated by an electrostatic field

Io·nes·co (yə nes'kō, ē'ə-), **Eugene** 1912– ; Fr. playwright, born in Romania

ion exchange a chemical process whereby ions are reversibly transferred between an insoluble solid, such as a resin, and a fluid mixture, usually an aqueous solution: widely used in water softening, recovery of metals from waste solutions, etc.

I·o·ni·a (ī ō'nē ə) ancient region in W Asia Minor, including a coastal strip & the islands of Samos & Khíos: colonized by the Greeks in the 11th cent. B.C.

I·o·ni·an (-nē ən) *adj.* 1. of Ionia, its people, or their culture 2. of an ancient Greek people who settled in eastern Greece and Ionia 3. *Music a)* designating or of one of the ancient Greek modes *b)* designating or of a medieval church mode corresponding to the modern major diatonic scale —*n.* an Ionian Greek

Ionian Islands group of islands along the W coast of Greece, forming an administrative division of Greece: 873 sq. mi.; pop. 213,000

Ionian Sea section of the Mediterranean, between Greece, Sicily, & the S part of the Italian peninsula

I·on·ic (ī än'ik) *adj.* [L. *Ionicus* < Gr. *Iōnikos*] 1. of Ionia or its people; Ionian 2. designating or of a branch of the ancient Greek language, including the dialect of Attica 3. designating or of that one of the three orders of Greek architecture characterized by ornamental scrolls (spiral volutes) on the capitals: cf. CORINTHIAN, DORIC 4. of the Ionic of Greek and Latin prosody —*n.* 1. *Gr. & Latin Prosody a)* either of two feet consisting of four syllables, the first two long and the second two short (- - ˘ ˘) (*greater Ionic*) or the first two short and the second two long (˘ ˘ - -) (*smaller* or *lesser Ionic*) *b)* verse or meter of such feet 2. the Ionic dialect

IONIC CAPITAL

i·on·ic (ī än'ik) *adj.* of, or being in the form of, an ion or ions

i·o·ni·um (ī ō'nē əm) *n.* [ION + -IUM] a radioactive isotope of thorium having a mass number of 230 and a half life of 8 x 10⁴ years

ionization chamber any of various devices, as a closed vessel containing a suitable gas, for determining the intensity of X-rays or the disintegration rate of a radioactive material, by measuring the current flow between oppositely charged electrodes in the gas

i·on·ize (ī'ə nīz') *vt., vi.* **-ized', -iz'ing** to change or be changed into ions; dissociate into ions, as a salt dissolved in water, or become electrically charged, as a gas under the influence of radiation or electric discharge —**i'on·i·za'tion** *n.* —**i'on·iz'er** *n.*

i·on·o·gen (ī än'ə jən) *n.* [< ION + -o- + -GEN] a substance that can be ionized or that produces ions —**i·on'o·gen'ic** (-jen'ik) *adj.*

I·o·none (ī'ə nōn') [Gr. *ion*, violet + -ONE] *a trademark for* a colorless liquid, C₁₃H₂₀O, made from citral and acetone and used in perfume manufacture for its violetlike odor —*n.* [i-] this liquid

i·on·o·sonde (ī än'ə sänd') *n.* [< ION + -o- + (RADIO)-SONDE] a pulse radar device operated at a frequency that can be varied from 1 MHz to 25 MHz: used to measure the height, thickness, etc. of ionospheric layers

i·on·o·sphere (ī än'ə sfir') *n.* [< ION + -o- + SPHERE] the outer part of the earth's atmosphere, beginning at an altitude of about 25 miles and extending to the highest parts of the atmosphere: it contains several regions that consist of a series of constantly changing layers characterized by an appreciable electron and ion content: see D LAYER, E LAYER, and F LAYER —**i·on'o·spher'ic** *adj.*

I.O.O.F. Independent Order of Odd Fellows

i·o·ta (ī ōt'ə, ē-) *n.* [Gr. *iōta* < Sem., as in Heb. *yōdh*] 1. the ninth letter of the Greek alphabet (I, ι) 2. a very small quantity; jot

i·o·ta·cism (-siz'm) *n.* [LL. *iotacismus* < Gr. *iōtakismos*] 1. excessive use of *i* (Gr. *iota*) 2. a tendency, esp. in Greek, to give the sound (ē) of this letter to other vowels

IOU, I.O.U. (ī'ō'yōō') 1. I owe you 2. a paper bearing these letters, acknowledging a specified debt and signed by the debtor

-ious (ē əs, yəs, əs) [< -i-, thematic vowel or stem ending + -OUS, for Fr. *-ieux* & L. *-ius*] *an adj.-forming suffix corresponding to* -ION [*rebellious, religious*] *or meaning* having, characterized by [*furious, anxious*]

I·o·wa (ī'ə wə; *occas. for the State,* -wā') *n.* [prob. < AmInd. (Dakota) *Ayuba*, lit., sleepy ones: a scornful appellation] 1. *pl.* **-wa, -was** any member of a tribe of Indians who earlier lived in Iowa and Missouri and now live in Nebraska, Kansas, and Oklahoma 2. their Siouan dialect 3. Middle Western State of NC U.S.: admitted 1846; 56,290 sq. mi.; pop. 2,825,000; cap. Des Moines: abbrev. **Ia., IA** 4. river flowing from N Iowa southeast into the Mississippi: c. 300 mi. —**I'o·wan** (-wən) *adj., n.*

Iowa City city in E Iowa: pop. 47,000

IPA 1. International Phonetic Alphabet 2. International Phonetic Association

☆**ip·e·cac** (ip'ə kak') *n.* [contr. < Port. *ipecacuanha* < Tupi *ipe-kaa-guéne*, small emetic plant] 1. a tropical S. American plant (*Cephaëlis ipecacuanha*) of the madder family, with small, drooping flowers 2. the dried roots of this plant that yield emetine 3. a preparation from the dried roots used to induce vomiting 4. any of several plant roots used in a similar way Also **ip·e·cac·u·an·ha** (ip'ə kak'yoo wan'ə)

Iph·i·ge·ni·a (if'ə jə nī'ə) [L. < Gr. *Iphigeneia*] *Gr. Myth.* a daughter of Agamemnon, offered by him as a sacrifice to Artemis and, in some versions, saved by the goddess, who made her a priestess

I·poh (ē'pō) city in Perak, NW Malaya: pop. 126,000

ip·o·moe·a (ip'ə mē'ə, ī'pə mē'ə) *n.* [ModL. < Gr. *ips* (gen. *ipos*), a worm + *homoios*, like: see SAME] any of a genus (*Ipomoea*) of twining or creeping plants of the morning-glory family, with funnel-shaped flowers and heart-shaped or lobed leaves, including the morning-glory and the sweet potato

Ip·po·li·tov-I·va·nov (ē'pō lü'tōf ē vä'nōf), **Mi·kha·il Mikhai·lo·vich** (mi khä ēl' mi khī'lō vich) 1859–1935; Russ. composer

ips, i.p.s. inches per second

‡**ip·se dix·it** (ip'sē dik'sit) [L., he himself has said (it)] an arbitrary or dogmatic statement

ip·si·lat·er·al (ip'sə lat'ər əl) *adj.* [< L. *ipse*, self + LATERAL] on or affecting the same side of the body —**ip'si·lat'er·al·ly** *adv.*

‡**ip·sis·si·ma ver·ba** (ip sis'i mə vur'bə) [L.] the very words (of a person being quoted)

ip·so fac·to (ip'sō fak'tō) [L., by the fact (or act) itself] by that very fact

‡**ip·so ju·re** (joor'ē) [L.] by the law itself

Ips·wich (ip'swich) 1. river port in Suffolk, E England: pop. 121,000 2. city in SE Queensland, Australia: pop. 50,000

IQ, I.Q. intelligence quotient

i.q. [L. *idem quod*] the same as

I·qui·que (ē kē'ke) seaport in N Chile: pop. 48,000

I·qui·tos (ē kē'tōs) river port in NE Peru, on the Amazon: pop. 63,000

ir- (ir) *see* IN-[1] & IN-[2]

Ir *Chem.* iridium

IR, ir, i-r infrared

Ir. 1. Ireland 2. Irish

I·ra (ī'rə) [Heb. 'īrā, lit., watchful] a masculine name

I.R.A., IRA Irish Republican Army

i·ra·cund (ī'rə kund') *adj.* [L. *iracundus* < *ira*, IRE] [Rare] easily angered; irascible —**i'ra·cun'di·ty** *n.*

i·ra·de (i rä'dē) *n.* [Turk. < Ar. *irādah*, will, desire] formerly, a written decree of a Moslem ruler

I·rak (i räk', -rak'; ē-) *same as* IRAQ

I·rak·li·on (ē räk'lē ōn') *Gr. name of* CANDIA

I·ran (i ran', ī-; ē rän') 1. country in SW Asia, between the Caspian Sea & the Persian Gulf: formerly called *Persia*: 636,000 sq. mi.; pop. 28,237,000; cap. Tehrán 2. **Plateau of,** plateau extending from the Tigris River to the Indus River, mostly in Iran & Afghanistan

Iran. Iranian

I·ra·ni (ē rä'nē) *adj. same as* IRANIAN

I·ra·ni·an (i rā′nē ən, ī-) *adj.* of Iran, its people, their language, or culture —*n.* **1.** one of the people of Iran; Persian **2.** a subbranch of the Indo-Iranian branch of the Indo-European family of languages that includes languages now spoken in the Plateau of Iran and a small area of the Caucasus: among the extant languages of the group are Persian, Kurdish, and Pashto

I·raq (i räk′, -rak′; ē-) country in SW Asia, at the head of the Persian Gulf, coinciding more or less with ancient Mesopotamia: 171,599 sq. mi.; pop. 9,431,000; cap. Baghdad

I·ra·qi (i rä′kē, -rak′ē) *n.* **1.** *pl.* **-qis** a native or inhabitant of Iraq **2.** the dialect of Arabic spoken in Iraq —*adj.* of Iraq, its people, their language, or culture

i·ras·ci·ble (i ras′ə b'l, ī-) *adj.* [ME. *irascibel* < MFr. < LL. *irascibilis* < L. *irasci*: see IRATE] easily angered; quick-tempered —*SYN.* see IRRITABLE —**i·ras′ci·bil′i·ty, i·ras′-ci·ble·ness** *n.* —**i·ras′ci·bly** *adv.*

i·rate (ī rāt′, ī′rāt) *adj.* [L. *iratus* < *irasci*, to be angry < *ira*, IRE] angry; wrathful; incensed —**i·rate′ly** *adv.* —**i·rate′ness** *n.*

IRBM intermediate range ballistic missile

ire (īr) *n.* [ME. < OFr. < L. *ira* < IE. base *eis-, to move quickly, violently, whence Gr. *oima*, stormy attack, ON. *eisa*, to rush on] anger; wrath —*SYN.* see ANGER —**ire′ful** *adj.* —**ire′ful·ly** *adv.* —**ire′ful·ness** *n.*

Ire. Ireland

Ire·land (īr′lənd) **1.** island of the British Isles, west of Great Britain: 32,595 sq. mi. **2.** republic comprising the S provinces of this island & three counties of Ulster province: established as a republic in 1922, it was a member of the Brit. Commonwealth until 1949: 27,136 sq. mi.; pop. 2,921,000; cap. Dublin Cf. NORTHERN IRELAND

I·rene (ī rēn′; *for 2* ī rē′nē) [< Fr. < L: Fr. *Irène* < L. *Irène* < Gr. *Eirēnē*, lit., peace] **1.** a feminine name **2.** *Gr. Myth.* the goddess of peace, daughter of Zeus and Themis: identified with the Roman goddess Pax

i·ren·ic (ī ren′ik, ī rē′nik) *adj.* [Gr. *eirēnikos* < *eirēnē*, peace] promoting peace; peaceful; pacific: also **i·ren′i·cal** —**i·ren′i·cal·ly** *adv.*

i·ren·ics (ī ren′iks, ī rē′niks) *n.pl.* [*with sing. v.*] [see IRENIC & -ICS] the doctrine or practice of promoting peace among Christian churches in relation to theological differences; irenic theology

Ir·i·an (ir′ē än′) *Indonesian name of* NEW GUINEA: see WEST IRIAN

i·rid (ī′rid) *n.* [see IRIS] a plant of the iris family

ir·i·dec·to·my (ir′ə dek′tə mē, ī′rə-) *n., pl.* **-mies** [IRID(O)- + -ECTOMY] the surgical removal of part of the iris of the eye

ir·i·des (ir′ə dēz′, ī′rə-) *alt. pl.* of IRIS

ir·i·des·cent (ir′ə des′'nt) *adj.* [< L. *iris* (gen. *iridis*), rainbow < Gr. *iris*, rainbow (see IRIS) + -ESCENT] having or showing shifting changes in color or an interplay of rainbowlike colors, as when seen from different angles —**ir′i·des′cence** *n.* —**ir′i·des′cent·ly** *adv.*

i·rid·ic (i rid′ik, ī-) *adj.* **1.** of or containing iridium **2.** designating or of a chemical compound in which iridium has a valence of four **3.** of the iris of the eye

i·rid·i·um (-ē əm) *n.* [< L. *iris* (gen. *iridis*), rainbow (see IRIS): from the changing color of some of its salts] a white, heavy, brittle, chemically resistant, metallic chemical element found in platinum ores: alloys of iridium are used for pen points and bearings of watches and scientific instruments: symbol, Ir; at. wt., 192.2; at. no., 77; sp. gr., 22.42; melt. pt., 2454°C; boil. pt., > 4800°C

ir·i·do- (ir′ə dō′, ī′rə-) [< ModL. *iris* (gen. *iridis*): see IRIS] *a combining form meaning* the iris (of the eye) [*iridoparalysis*]: also, before a vowel, **irid-**

ir·i·dos·mine (ir′i däz′min, ī′rə-; -däs′-; -mēn) *n.* [< IRIDIUM + OSMIUM] a native alloy of iridium and osmium containing small amounts of other metals of the platinum group: it crystallizes in the hexagonal system: also **ir′i·dos′mi·um** (-mē əm)

I·ris (ī′ris) [L. < Gr. *Iris*: see ff.] **1.** a feminine name **2.** *Gr. Myth.* the goddess of the rainbow: in the *Iliad*, she is the messenger of the gods

i·ris (ī′ris) *n., pl.* **i′ris·es, ir·i·des** (ir′ə dēz′, ī′rə-) [LME. < L. < Gr. *iris* (gen. *iridos*) < IE. *wir- (whence WIRE) < base *wei-, to turn, bend] **1.** a rainbow **2.** a rainbowlike show or play of colors **3.** the round, pigmented membrane surrounding the pupil of the eye, having muscles that adjust the size of the pupil to regulate the amount of light entering the eye: see EYE, illus. **4.** any of a large genus (*Iris*) of perennial plants of the iris family, with sword-shaped leaves and conspicuous flowers composed of three petals and three drooping sepals of widely varying color **5.** the flower of these plants —*adj.* designating a family (Iridaceae) of plants including irises, crocuses, and gladioluses

iris diaphragm a device consisting of thin, overlapping metal plates that can be adjusted to form an aperture of varying size for camera lenses, etc.

IRIS

I·rish (ī′rish) *adj.* [ME. < base of OE. *Iras*, the Irish < OIr. *Eriu*, Ireland: cf. EIRE] of Ireland, its people, their language, or culture —*n.* **1.** *same as* IRISH GAELIC **2.** the English dialect of Ireland **3.** [Colloq.] temper: chiefly in **get one's Irish up**, to arouse one's temper —**the Irish** the people of Ireland

Irish bull *same as* BULL³

Irish coffee brewed coffee containing Irish whiskey, topped with cream or whipped cream

Irish Free State *former name* (1922-37) of IRELAND (sense 2)

Irish Gaelic the Celtic language of Ireland: see GAELIC

I·rish·ism (-iz'm) *n.* an Irish idiom, custom, etc.

I·rish·man (-mən) *n., pl.* **-men** (-mən) **1.** a native or inhabitant of Ireland, esp. a man **2.** a person of Irish ancestry, esp. a man —**I′rish·wom′an** *n.fem.*, *pl.* -wom′en

Irish moss *same as* CARRAGEEN

Irish potato the common white potato: so called because extensively cultivated in Ireland

Irish Republican Army a secret organization founded to work for Irish independence from England: it continued to exist after the establishment of the Irish Free State, which declared it illegal in 1936

Irish Sea arm of the Atlantic between Ireland & Great Britain

Irish setter any of a breed of setter with a coat of long, silky, reddish-brown hair

Irish stew a stew of meat, orig. mutton, with potatoes, onions, and other vegetables

Irish terrier any of a breed of small, lean, active dog with a wiry, bright-red or golden-red coat

Irish wolfhound any of a breed of very large, heavy, powerful dog with a hard, rough coat

i·ri·tis (ī rīt′is) *n.* [ModL.: see IRIS & -ITIS] inflammation of the iris of the eye —**i·rit′ic** (-rit′ik) *adj.*

irk (ʉrk) *vt.* [ME. *irken*, to loathe, be weary of, akin to northern & north Midland adj. *irk, yrk*, weary, troubled, bored] to annoy, disgust, irritate, tire out, etc. —*SYN.* see ANNOY

irk·some (ʉrk′səm) *adj.* [ME. *irksum*: see IRK & -SOME¹] that tends to irk; tiresome or annoying —**irk′some·ly** *adv.* —**irk′some·ness** *n.*

Ir·kutsk (ir kōōtsk′) city in S Asiatic R.S.F.S.R., near Lake Baikal: pop. 409,000

Ir·ma (ʉr′mə) [G., orig. contr. of *Irmenberta, Irmintrud, Irmgard*, etc. < OHG. *Irmin*, cognomen of the Gmc. war god Tiu] a feminine name

IRO International Refugee Organization

i·ron (ī′ərn) *n.* see PLURAL, II, D, 3 [ME. *iren* < OE. *iren* (chiefly poetic & prob. dissimilated), beside *isern, isen* (akin to Goth. *eisarn*) < Gmc. *isarna*, akin to early Celt. *isarno*, prob. via Illyrian *eisarno- < IE. base *eis-, to move vigorously; strong, holy (cf. IRE): orig. sense prob. "the strong metal," in contrast to the softer bronze] **1.** a white, malleable, ductile, metallic chemical element that can be readily magnetized, rusts rapidly in moist or salty air, and is vital to plant and animal life: it is the most common and important of all metals, and its alloys, as steel, are extensively used: symbol, Fe; at. wt., 55.847; at. no., 26; sp. gr., 7.86; melt. pt., 1535°C; boil. pt., 3000°C **2.** any tool, implement, device, apparatus, etc. made of iron, as *a)* a device with a handle and flat, smooth undersurface, used, when heated, for pressing clothes or cloth; flatiron *b)* a rodlike device with a brand at one end, heated for branding cattle: in full, **branding iron** **3.** [*pl.*] iron shackles or chains **4.** firm strength; power **5.** [Slang] a pistol **6.** *Golf* any of a set of numbered clubs with metal heads having various lofts **7.** *Med.* a tonic or other preparation containing iron —*adj.* **1.** of or consisting of iron **2.** like iron, as *a)* firm; unyielding [an iron will] *b)* capable of great endurance; strong [an iron constitution] **3.** cruel; merciless —*vt.* **1.** to furnish or cover with iron **2.** to put (a prisoner) in irons **3.** to press (clothes or cloth) smooth or flat with a hot iron —*vi.* to iron clothes or cloth —**have many** (or **several**, etc.) **irons in the fire** to have or be engaged in many (or several, etc.) activities, enterprises, or the like —**in irons 1.** shackled with irons; imprisoned **2.** *Naut.* failing to come about or fill away: said of a sailing vessel —☆**iron out** to smooth out; eliminate —**strike while the iron is hot** to act at the opportune time

Iron Age 1. a phase of human culture (in Europe, c. 1000 B.C.-100 A.D.) characterized by the introduction and development of iron tools and weapons: it followed the Bronze Age **2.** *Gr. & Rom. Myth.* the last and worst age of the world, characterized by wickedness, selfishness, and degeneracy

i·ron·bark (-bärk′) *n.* **1.** any of several Australian eucalyptus trees (genus *Eucalyptus*) with hard wood and hard, gray bark **2.** the wood of any of these trees

i·ron·bound (-bound′) *adj.* **1.** bound with iron **2.** hard; rigid; unyielding; inflexible **3.** edged with rocks or cliffs, as a coast

i·ron·clad (-klad′) *adj.* **1.** covered or protected with iron **2.** difficult to change or break [an ironclad lease] —*n.* formerly, a warship armored with thick iron plates

iron curtain [prob. calque of G. *eiserner vorhang*, as used by Nazi propaganda minister J. Goebbels: popularized by Winston Churchill in a speech (1946)] a barrier of secrecy and censorship regarded as isolating the Soviet Union and other countries in its sphere, or a similar barrier to information in other regions

i·ron·er (ī'ər nər) *n.* one that irons; esp., a mangle

iron gray a gray like that of freshly broken cast iron — **i'ron-gray'** *adj.*

iron hand firm, rigorous, severe control —**i'ron·hand'ed** *adj.*

i·ron·heart·ed (ī'ərn här'tid) *adj.* unfeeling; cruel

☆**iron horse** [Old Colloq.] a locomotive

i·ron·i·cal (ī rän'i k'l) *adj.* [< L. *ironicus* < Gr. *eirōnikos* < *eirōneia* (see IRONY¹) + -AL] **1.** meaning the contrary of what is expressed **2.** using, or given to the use of, irony **3.** having the quality of irony; directly opposite to what is or might be expected Also **i·ron'ic** —*SYN.* see SARCASTIC —**i·ron'i·cal·ly** *adv.*

ironing board (or **table**) a cloth-covered board or stand on which clothes are ironed

i·ron·ist (ī'rə nist) *n.* a writer or speaker noted for his frequent use of irony

☆**iron lung** a large metal respirator that encloses all of the body but the head, used for maintaining artificial respiration in a person who has difficulty in breathing as a result of poliomyelitis, gas poisoning, etc.

Iron Maiden a former instrument of torture consisting of a case in the form of a woman, with sharp spikes inside

i·ron·mas·ter (ī'ərn mas'tər) *n.* a manufacturer of iron

i·ron·mon·ger (-muŋ'gər, -mäŋ'-) *n.* [ME. *irenmonger*: see IRON & MONGER] [Brit.] a dealer in hardware —**i'ron·mon'ger·y** *n.*

iron pyrites *same as* PYRITE

I·ron·sides (-sīdz') **1.** nickname of Oliver CROMWELL **2.** *a)* the regiment that Cromwell led in the English Civil War *b)* his whole army —*n.pl.* [i-] [*with sing. v.*] same as IRONCLAD

i·ron·smith (-smith') *n.* an ironworker or blacksmith

i·ron·stone (-stōn') *n.* **1.** any rock rich in iron; specif., siderite occurring as nodules or beds in coal, shale, etc. **2.** a hard variety of white ceramic ware

i·ron·ware (-wer') *n.* things made of iron; hardware

i·ron·weed (-wēd') *n.* [so named from its hard stem] any of a genus (*Vernonia*) of perennial plants of the composite family, with clusters of small, tubular, purple flowers

i·ron·wood (-wood') *n.* **1.** any of various trees, esp. hornbeam and hop hornbeam, with extremely hard, heavy wood **2.** the wood of an ironwood

i·ron·work (-wurk') *n.* articles or parts made of iron

i·ron·work·er (-wur'kər) *n.* **1.** a person who makes iron or articles of iron **2.** a worker who builds the framework of steel bridges, etc.

i·ron·works (-wurks') *n.pl.* [*often with sing. v.*] a place where iron is smelted or heavy iron goods are made

i·ro·ny¹ (ī'rən ē, ī'ər nē) *n., pl.* -**nies** [Fr. *ironie* < L. *ironia* < Gr. *eirōneia* < *eirōn*, dissembler in speech < *eirein*, to speak < IE. basc **wer-*, to speak, whence WORD] **1.** a method of humorous or subtly sarcastic expression in which the intended meaning of the words used is the direct opposite of their usual sense [*the irony of calling a stupid plan "clever"*] **2.** an instance of this **3.** a combination of circumstances or a result that is the opposite of what is or might be expected or considered appropriate [*an irony that the firehouse burned*] **4.** the feigning of ignorance in argument: often **Socratic irony** (after Socrates' use in Plato's *Dialogues*) —*SYN.* see WIT¹

i·ron·y² (ī'ər nē) *adj.* of, like, or containing iron

☆**Ir·o·quoi·an** (ir'ə kwoi'ən) *adj.* [< ff. + -AN] of an important linguistic family of N. American Indians, including speakers of the Seneca, Cayuga, and Onondaga dialects of a single language, and the languages of the Huron (Wyandot), Mohawk, Tuscarora, Oneida, and Cherokee —*n.* **1.** a member of an Iroquoian tribe **2.** the Iroquoian languages collectively

Ir·o·quois (ir'ə kwoi') *n., pl.* -**quois** (-kwoi', -kwoiz') [Fr. < Algonquian *Irinakoiw*, lit., real adders] **1.** a member of a confederation of Iroquoian Indian tribes that lived in W and N New York and in adjacent Quebec and Ontario: their descendants also live in Oklahoma: see FIVE NATIONS **2.** the Iroquoian language family —*adj.* of the Iroquois or their tribes

ir·ra·di·ance (i rā'dē əns) *n.* **1.** an irradiating; radiance **2.** the amount of light or other radiant energy striking a given area of a surface Also **ir·ra'di·an·cy** —**ir·ra'di·ant** *adj.*

ir·ra·di·ate (-āt'; *for adj., usually* -it) *vt.* -**at'ed**, -**at'ing** [< L. *irradiatus*, pp. of *irradiare*, to beam upon, illumine: see IN-¹ & RADIATE] **1.** to shine or throw light upon; light up; make bright **2.** to make clear; illuminate intellectually; enlighten **3.** to radiate; diffuse; spread; give out **4.** to expose to or treat by exposing to X-rays, ultraviolet rays, radium, or some other form of radiant energy **5.** to heat with radiant energy —*vi.* **1.** to emit rays; shine **2.** to become radiant —*adj.* lighted up; irradiated — **ir·ra'di·a'tive** *adj.* —**ir·ra'di·a'tor** *n.*

ir·ra·di·a·tion (i rā'dē ā'shən) *n.* [Fr. < ML. *irradiatio*] **1.** an irradiating or being irradiated; esp., *a)* exposure to radiation *b)* emission of radiant energy *c)* intellectual enlightenment **2.** *same as* IRRADIANCE (sense 2) **3.** *Optics*

the apparent enlargement of a brightly lighted object seen against a dark background

ir·ra·tion·al (i rash'ən 'l) *adj.* [ME. < L. *irrationalis*: see IN-² & RATIONAL] **1.** lacking the power to reason **2.** contrary to reason; senseless; unreasonable; absurd **3.** *Gr. & Latin Prosody* designating *a)* a syllable that does not fit the meter, esp. one that is long when it should be short *b)* a foot with such a syllable **4.** *Math.* not capable of being expressed as an integer or as a quotient of two integers —**ir·ra'tion·al'i·ty** (-ə nal'ə tē) *n., pl.* -**ties** —**ir·ra'tion·al·ly** *adv.*

SYN.—**irrational** implies mental unsoundness or may be used to stress the utterly illogical nature of that which is directly contrary to reason [*an irrational belief that everybody was his enemy*]; **unreasonable** implies bad judgment, willfulness, prejudice, etc. as responsible for that which is not justified by reason [*unreasonable demands*]; —*ANT.* rational, reasonable

ir·ra·tion·al·ism (-iz'm) *n.* irrational thought, belief, or action —**ir·ra'tion·al·ist** *n.*

Ir·ra·wad·dy (ir'ə wä'dē, -wô'-) river flowing from N Burma south into the Andaman Sea: c. 1,000 mi.

ir·re·claim·a·ble (ir'i klā'mə b'l) *adj.* that cannot be reclaimed —**ir're·claim'a·bil'i·ty** *n.* —**ir're·claim'a·bly** *adv.*

ir·rec·on·cil·a·ble (i rek'ən sīl'ə b'l, i rek'ən sīl'-) *adj.* that cannot be reconciled; that cannot be brought into agreement; incompatible, conflicting, or inconsistent —*n.* **1.** a person who is irreconcilable and refuses to make any compromise **2.** [*pl.*] ideas, beliefs, etc. that cannot be brought into agreement with each other —**ir·rec'on·cil'a·bil'i·ty** *n.* —**ir·rec'on·cil'a·bly** *adv.*

ir·re·cov·er·a·ble (ir'i kuv'ər ə b'l) *adj.* that cannot be recovered, rectified, or remedied; irretrievable —**ir'-re·cov'er·a·bly** *adv.*

ir·re·cu·sa·ble (ir'i kyoo'zə b'l) *adj.* [< Fr. or LL.: Fr. *irrécusable* < LL. *irrecusabilis* < *in-*, IN² + *recusabilis*, that should be rejected < *recusare*, to refuse: see RECUSANT] that cannot be refused or rejected —**ir're·cu'sa·bly** *adv.*

ir·re·deem·a·ble (ir'i dēm'ə b'l) *adj.* [see IN-² & REDEEMABLE] **1.** that cannot be bought back ☆**2.** that cannot be converted into coin, as certain kinds of paper money **3.** that cannot be changed; hopeless **4.** that cannot be reformed —**ir're·deem'a·bly** *adv.*

ir·re·den·tist (ir'i den'tist) *n.* [It. *irredentista* < (*Italia*) *irredenta*, unredeemed (Italy) < L. *in-*, not + *redemptus*: see REDEMPTION] **1.** [*usually* I-] any member of an Italian political party, organized in 1878, seeking to recover for Italy adjacent regions inhabited largely by Italians but under foreign control **2.** any person who advocates a similar policy about territory formerly a part of his country —**ir're·den'tism** *n.*

ir·re·duc·i·ble (ir'i dōōs'ə b'l, -dyōōs'-) *adj.* that cannot be reduced —**ir're·duc'i·bil'i·ty** *n.* —**ir're·duc'i·bly** *adv.*

ir·re·fra·ga·ble (i ref'rə gə b'l) *adj.* [LL. *irrefragabilis* < L. *in-*, IN-² + L. *refragari*, to oppose < *re-*, against + (*suf*)*fragari*: see SUFFRAGAN] that cannot be refuted; indisputable —**ir·ref'ra·ga·bil'i·ty** *n.* —**ir·ref'ra·ga·bly** *adv.*

ir·re·fran·gi·ble (ir'i fran'jə b'l) *adj.* [IR- + REFRANGIBLE] **1.** that cannot be broken or violated **2.** that cannot be refracted —**ir're·fran'gi·bly** *adv.*

ir·ref·u·ta·ble (i ref'yoo tə b'l, ir'i fyoot'ə b'l) *adj.* [LL. *irrefutabilis*] that cannot be refuted or disproved —**ir·ref'-u·ta·bil'i·ty** *n.* —**ir·ref'u·ta·bly** *adv.*

irreg. **1.** irregular **2.** irregularly

☆**ir·re·gard·less** (ir'i gärd'lis) *adj., adv.* a substandard or humorous redundancy for REGARDLESS

ir·reg·u·lar (i reg'yə lər) *adj.* [ME. *irregular* < OFr. *irregulier* < ML. *irregularis*: see IN-² & REGULAR] **1.** not conforming to established rule, method, usage, standard, etc.; out of the ordinary; anomalous **2.** not conforming to legal or moral requirements; lawless; disorderly **3.** not straight or even; not symmetrical; not uniform in shape, design, or proportion **4.** uneven in occurrence or succession; variable or erratic ☆**5.** having minor flaws or imperfections: said of merchandise **6.** *Bot.* not uniform in shape, size, etc., as the petals of flowers **7.** *Gram.* not inflected in the usual way [*go* is an *irregular* verb] **8.** *Mil.* not belonging to the regularly established army —*n.* **1.** a person or thing that is irregular **2.** a soldier who belongs to an irregular military force ☆**3.** [*usually in pl.*] irregular merchandise —**ir·reg'u·lar'i·ty** *n., pl.* -**ties** —**ir·reg'u·lar·ly** *adv.*

SYN.—**irregular** implies deviation from the customary or established rule, procedure, etc. [*an irregular marriage*]; **abnormal** and **anomalous** imply deviation from the normal condition or from the ordinary type, **abnormal** stressing atypical form or character [*a man of abnormal height*], and **anomalous**, an exceptional condition or circumstance [*in the anomalous position of a leader without followers*]; **unnatural** applies to that which is contrary to the order of nature or to natural laws [*an unnatural appetite for chalk*] —*ANT.* regular, normal, natural

ir·rel·a·tive (i rel'ə tiv) *adj.* unrelated or irrelevant —**ir·rel'a·tive·ly** *adv.*

ir·rel·e·vant (i rel'ə vənt) *adj.* not relevant; not pertinent; not to the point; not relating to the subject —**ir·rel'e·vance**, **ir·rel'e·van·cy** (*pl.* -**cies**) *n.* —**ir·rel'e·vant·ly** *adv.*

ir·re·liev·a·ble (ir'i lēv'ə b'l) *adj.* that cannot be relieved

ir·re·li·gious (ir'i lij'əs) *adj.* [L. *irreligiosus*] 1. not religious; adhering to no particular religious belief 2. indifferent or hostile to religion 3. not in accord with religious principles; profane; impious —**ir're·li'gion** (-ən) *n.* —**ir're·li'gion·ist** *n.* —**ir're·li'gious·ly** *adv.*

ir·rem·e·a·ble (i rem'ē ə b'l, -rē'mē-) *adj.* [L. *irremeabilis* < *in-*, not + *remeabilis*, returning < *remeare*, to go back < *re-*, back + *meare*, to go < IE. base *mei-*, to go, wander] [Archaic] from which there is no return

ir·re·me·di·a·ble (ir'i mē'dē ə b'l) *adj.* [L. *irremediabilis*] that cannot be remedied or corrected; incurable or irreparable —**ir're·me'di·a·ble·ness** *n.* —**ir're·me'di·a·bly** *adv.*

ir·re·mis·si·ble (-mis'ə b'l) *adj.* [ME. < OFr. *irrémissible* < L. *irremissibilis*] not remissible; specif., *a*) that cannot be excused or pardoned *b*) that cannot be shirked —**ir're·mis'si·bly** *adv.*

ir·re·mov·a·ble (-mōō'və b'l) *adj.* not removable —**ir're·mov'a·bil'i·ty** *n.* —**ir're·mov'a·bly** *adv.*

ir·rep·a·ra·ble (i rep'ər ə b'l) *adj.* [ME. *irreperable* < OFr. *irréparable* < L. *irreparabilis*] not reparable; that cannot be repaired, mended, remedied, etc. —**ir·rep'a·ra·bil'i·ty** *n.* —**ir·rep'a·ra·bly** *adv.*

ir·re·peal·a·ble (ir'i pēl'ə b'l) *adj.* not repealable

ir·re·place·a·ble (-plās'ə b'l) *adj.* not replaceable

ir·re·plev·i·a·ble (-plev'ē ə b'l) *adj.* [ML. *irrepleviabilis*] that cannot be replevied

ir·re·press·i·ble (-pres'ə b'l) *adj.* that cannot be repressed or restrained —**ir're·press'i·bil'i·ty** *n.* —**ir're·press'i·bly** *adv.*

ir·re·proach·a·ble (-prō'chə b'l) *adj.* [Fr. *irréprochable*] not reproachable; beyond reproach; blameless; faultless —**ir're·proach'a·bil'i·ty** *n.* —**ir're·proach'a·bly** *adv.*

ir·re·sist·i·ble (-zis'tə b'l) *adj.* [LL. *irresistibilis*] that cannot be resisted; too strong, fascinating, compelling, etc. to be withstood —**ir're·sist'i·bil'i·ty, ir're·sist'i·ble·ness** *n.* —**ir're·sist'i·bly** *adv.*

ir·res·o·lu·ble (i rez'ə loo b'l, -əl yoo-; ir'i zäl'yoo b'l) *adj.* [L. *irresolubilis*] that cannot be resolved or solved; insoluble

ir·res·o·lute (i rez'ə loot') *adj.* [L. *irresolutus*] not resolute; wavering in decision, purpose, or opinion; indecisive; vacillating —**ir·res'o·lute'ly** *adv.* —**ir·res'o·lute'ness** *n.* —**ir·res'o·lu'tion** (-loo'shən) *n.*

ir·re·solv·a·ble (ir'i zäl'və b'l) *adj.* 1. that cannot be resolved into elements or parts 2. that cannot be solved

ir·re·spec·tive (-spek'tiv) *adj.* [IR- + RESPECTIVE] showing disregard for persons or consequences —**irrespective of** regardless of; independent of —**ir're·spec'tive·ly** *adv.*

ir·re·spir·a·ble (ir'i spir'ə b'l, i res'pər ə b'l) *adj.* [Fr. < LL. *irrespirabilis:* see IN-² & RESPIRE] not suitable to be breathed

ir·re·spon·si·ble (ir'i spän'sə b'l) *adj.* not responsible; specif., *a*) not liable to be called to account for actions *b*) lacking a sense of responsibility; unreliable, shiftless, etc. *c*) said or done as by an irresponsible person —*n.* an irresponsible person —**ir're·spon'si·bil'i·ty, ir're·spon'si·ble·ness** *n.* —**ir're·spon'si·bly** *adv.*

ir·re·spon·sive (-siv) *adj.* not responsive —**ir're·spon'sive·ness** *n.*

ir·re·ten·tive (ir'i ten'tiv) *adj.* not retentive

ir·re·triev·a·ble (-trēv'ə b'l) *adj.* that cannot be retrieved, recovered, restored, or recalled —**ir're·triev'a·bil'i·ty** *n.* —**ir're·triev'a·bly** *adv.*

ir·rev·er·ence (i rev'ər əns) *n.* [ME. < L. *irreverentia*] 1. lack of reverence; disrespect 2. an act or statement showing this 3. the condition of not being treated with reverence —**ir·rev'er·ent** *adj.* —**ir·rev'er·ent·ly** *adv.*

ir·re·vers·i·ble (ir'i vʉr'sə b'l) *adj.* not reversible; specif., *a*) that cannot be repealed or annulled *b*) that cannot be turned inside out, run backward, etc. —**ir're·vers'i·bil'i·ty** *n.* —**ir're·vers'i·bly** *adv.*

ir·rev·o·ca·ble (i rev'ə kə b'l) *adj.* [ME. < MFr. *irrévocable* < L. *irrevocabilis*] that cannot be revoked, recalled, or undone; unalterable —**ir·rev'o·ca·bil'i·ty, ir·rev'o·ca·ble·ness** *n.* —**ir·rev'o·ca·bly** *adv.*

ir·ri·ga·ble (ir'i gə b'l) *adj.* that can be irrigated

ir·ri·gate (ir'ə gāt') *vt.* **-gat'ed, -gat'ing** [< L. *irrigatus*, pp. of *irrigare*, to bring water to or upon < *in-*, in, to, upon + *rigare*, to water, moisten: see RAIN] 1. to refresh by or as by watering 2. to supply (land) with water by means of artificial ditches or channels or by sprinklers 3. *Med.* to wash out or flush (a cavity, wound, etc.) with water or other fluid —**ir'ri·ga'tion** *n.* —**ir'ri·ga'tive** *adj.* —**ir'ri·ga'tor** *n.*

ir·rig·u·ous (i rig'yoo wəs) *adj.* [L. *irriguus* < *in-*, in + *riguus*, watered < *rigare:* see RAIN] [Now Rare] 1. moist; well-watered 2. that irrigates

ir·ri·ta·ble (ir'i tə b'l) *adj.* [L. *irritabilis* < *irritare*, to IRRITATE] 1. easily annoyed or provoked; impatient; fretful 2. *Med.* excessively or pathologically sensitive to a stimulus 3. *Physiol.* able to respond to a stimulus —**ir'ri·ta·bil'i·ty, ir'ri·ta·ble·ness** *n.* —**ir'ri·ta·bly** *adv.*
SYN.—**irritable** implies quick excitability to annoyance or anger, usually resulting from emotional tension, restlessness, physical indisposition, etc.; **irascible** and **choleric** are applied to persons who are hot-tempered and can be roused to a fit of anger at the slightest irritation; **splenetic** suggests a peevish moroseness in one quick to vent his malice or spite; **touchy** applies to one who is acutely irritable or sensitive and is too

easily offended; **cranky** and **cross** suggest moods in which one cannot be easily pleased or satisfied, **cranky** because of stubborn notions or whims, and **cross** because of ill humor

ir·ri·tant (-tənt) *adj.* [L. *irritans*, prp. of *irritare*] causing irritation or inflammation —*n.* something that causes irritation —**ir'ri·tan·cy** *n.*

ir·ri·tate (-tāt') *vt.* **-tat'ed, -tat'ing** [< L. *irritatus*, pp. of *irritare*, to excite, stimulate, irritate, prob. < IE. base *erei-*, to excite, agitate, whence ROAM] 1. to excite to impatience or anger; provoke; annoy; exasperate 2. to cause (an organ or part of the body) to be inflamed or sore 3. *Physiol.* to excite (an organ, muscle, etc.) to a characteristic action or function by a stimulus
SYN.—**irritate**, the broadest in scope of these terms, may suggest temporary superficial impatience, constant annoyance, or an outburst of anger in the person stirred to feeling [their smugness *irritated* him]; to **provoke** is to arouse strong annoyance or resentment, or, sometimes, vindictive anger [*provoked* by an insult]; **nettle** implies irritation that stings or piques rather than infuriates [sly, *nettling* remarks]; **exasperate** implies intense irritation such as exhausts one's patience or makes one lose one's self-control [*exasperating* impudence]; **peeve**, an informal word, means to cause to be annoyed, cross, or fretful [he seems *peeved* about something]

ir·ri·ta·tion (ir'ə tā'shən) *n.* [L. *irritatio*] 1. the act or process of irritating 2. the fact or condition of being irritated 3. something that irritates 4. *Med.* an excessive response to stimulation in an organ or part; specif., a condition of soreness or inflammation in some organ or part

ir·ri·ta·tive (ir'ə tāt'iv) *adj.* 1. causing irritation 2. accompanied or caused by irritation

ir·rupt (i rupt') *vi.* [< L. *irruptus*, pp. of *irrumpere*, to break in: see IN-¹ & RUPTURE] 1. to burst suddenly or violently (*into*) 2. *Ecol.* to increase abruptly in size of population —**ir·rup'tion** *n.* —**ir·rup'tive** *adj.*

IRS, I.R.S. Internal Revenue Service

Ir·tysh (ir tish') river in C Asia, flowing from N Sinkiang, China, northwestward into the Ob River: c. 1,850 mi.: also sp. **Irtish**

Ir·ving¹ (ʉr'vin) [north Brit. surname, prob. orig. a place name] 1. a masculine name 2. Sir Henry, (born *John Henry Brodribb*) 1838–1905; Eng. actor 3. Washington, 1783–1859; U.S. writer

Ir·ving² (ʉr'vin) [prob. an arbitrary selection] city in NE Tex.: suburb of Dallas: pop. 97,000

Ir·ving·ton (ʉr'vin tən) [after Washington IRVING] town in NE N.J.: suburb of Newark: pop. 60,000

Ir·win (ʉr'win) a masculine name: see ERWIN

is (iz) [ME. < OE., akin to G. *ist* < IE. *esti* (whence Sans. *ásti*, Gr. *esti*, L. *est*) < base *es-*, to be + *-ti*, prob. orig. an enclitic pron.] *3d pers. sing., pres. indic., of* BE

is- (is) *same as* ISO-: used before vowels

is. 1. island(s) 2. isle(s)

Isa., Is. Isaiah

I·saac (ī'zək) [LL.(Ec.) *Isaacus* < Gr.(Ec.) *Isaak* < Heb. *yitshāq*, lit., laughter: cf. Gen. 17:17] 1. a masculine name: dim. *Ike* 2. *Bible* one of the patriarchs, son of Abraham and Sarah, and father of Jacob and Esau: Gen. 21:3

Is·a·bel (iz'ə bel') [Sp., prob. an alteration of *Elizabeth*] a feminine name: dim. *Bel;* var. *Isabelle, Isabella*

Is·a·bel·la (iz'ə bel'ə) [It.] 1. a feminine name: dim. *Bella:* see ISABEL 2. Isabella I 1451–1504; wife of Ferdinand V & queen of Castile (1474–1504): gave help to Columbus in his expedition: called **Isabella of Castile** 3. Isabella II 1830–1904; queen of Spain (1833–68): deposed

Is·a·belle (iz'ə bel') [Fr.] a feminine name: dim. *Belle:* see ISABEL

is·a·cous·tic (ī'sə koōs'tik) *adj.* [IS- + ACOUSTIC] of or having to do with equal intensity of sound

Is·a·dor, Is·a·dore (iz'ə dôr') a masculine name: fem. *Isadora:* see ISIDORE

Is·a·do·ra (iz'ə dôr'ə) [var. of Gr. *Isidōra:* see ISIDORE] a feminine name

i·sa·go·ge (ī'sə gō'jē) *n.* [L. < Gr. *eisagōgē* < *eisagein*, to lead in, introduce < *eis-*, into + *agein*, to lead] an introduction, as to a branch of study —**i'sa·gog'ic** (-gäj'ik) *adj.*

i·sa·gog·ics (ī'sə gäj'iks) *n.pl.* [see prec. & -ICS] introductory study; esp., the study of the literary history of the Bible, considered as introductory to the study of Bible interpretation

I·sa·iah (ī zā'ə; chiefly Brit., -zī'-) [LL.(Ec.) *Isaias* < Gr.(Ec.) *Ēsaias* < Heb. *yĕsha 'yah*, lit., God is salvation] 1. a masculine name 2. *Bible a*) a Hebrew prophet of the 8th cent. B.C. *b*) the book containing his teachings Also, in the Douay Bible, **I·sa·ias** (-əs)

i·sal·lo·bar (ī sal'ə bär') *n.* [< IS- + ALLO- + (ISO)BAR] a line on a weather map connecting places having an equal change of barometric pressure over a given period

i·sa·tin (ī'sə tən) *n.* [< L. *isatis*, variety of herb (< Gr. *isatis*, woad) + -IN¹] a reddish-orange, crystalline compound, $C_8H_5NO_2$, produced by the oxidation of indigo and used in making dyes

Is·car·i·ot (is ker'ē ət) [LL.(Ec.) *Iscariota* < Gr.(Ec.) *Iskariōtēs* < Heb. *īsh-qĕrīyōth*, man of Kerioth (town in Palestine)] *see* JUDAS (sense 1)

is·che·mi·a (is kē'mē ə) *n.* [ModL. < Gr. *ischaimos*, stanching blood (< *ischein*, to hold + *haima*, blood: see SCHEME & HEMO-) + -IA] a lack of blood supply in an organ or tissue —**is·che'mic** *adj.*

is·chi·um (is'kē əm) n., pl. **-chi·a** (-ə) [L. < Gr. *ischion*, hip, hip joint] the lowermost of the three sections of the hipbone; bone on which the body rests when sitting — **is'chi·al, is'chi·ad'ic, is'chi·at'ic** adj.

-ise (īz) *chiefly Brit. var. of* -IZE

I·seult (i sōōlt') [Fr.] *same as* ISOLDE

Is·fa·han (is'fä hän') *same as* ESFAHÁN

-ish (ish) **1.** [ME. < OE. *-isc*, akin to G. *-isch*, L. *-iscus*, Gr. *-iskos*] *a suffix meaning: a)* of or belonging to (a specified nation or people) [*Spanish, Irish*] *b)* like or characteristic of [*devilish, boyish*] *c)* tending to, verging on [*bookish, knavish*] *d)* somewhat, rather [*tallish, bluish*] *e)* [Colloq.] approximately, about [*thirtyish*] **2.** [ME. *-ishen, -ischen, -issen* < OFr. *-iss-, -is-*, stem element in pres. tense < L. *-isc-*, stem element in inceptive verbs] *a suffix found in verbs of French origin* [*finish, punish*]

Ish·er·wood (ish'ər wood), **Christopher (William Bradshaw-)** 1904– ; U.S. writer, born in England

Ish·ma·el (ish'mē əl, -mā-) [LL.(Ec.) *Ismaël* < Heb. *yishmā'ē'l*, lit., God hears] *Bible* the son of Abraham and Hagar: he and his mother were made outcasts: Gen. 21:9–21 —n. an outcast

Ish·ma·el·ite (-ə līt') n. **1.** a descendant of Ishmael, the traditional progenitor of Arab peoples **2.** an outcast —**Ish'ma·el·it'ish** adj.

Ish·tar (ish'tär) [Assyr.-Bab.] the Babylonian and Assyrian goddess of love and fertility

Is·i·dore, Is·i·dor (iz'ə dôr') [< G. *Isidor* or Fr. *Isidore*, both < L. *Isidorus* < Gr. *Isidōros* < *Isis* + *dōron*, gift; hence, lit., gift of Isis] a masculine name: dim. *Izzy*; var. *Isador, Isadore*

Isidore of Seville, Saint (L. *Isidorus Hispalensis*) 560?–636 A.D.; Sp. bishop & scholar: his day is April 4

i·sin·glass (ī'z'n glas', -zin-; -gläs') n. [prob. altered < MDu. *huizenblas*, lit., sturgeon bladder < *huizen*, sturgeon + *blas*, bladder] **1.** a form of gelatin prepared from the internal membranes of fish bladders: it is used as a clarifying agent and adhesive **2.** mica, esp. in thin sheets

I·sis¹ (ī'sis) [L. < Gr. *Isis*] the Egyptian goddess of fertility, sister and wife of Osiris, usually represented with a cow's horns surrounding a solar (or lunar) disk

I·sis² (ī'sis) *Eng. name of* the THAMES RIVER, esp. at, & west of, Oxford

Is·ken·de·run (is ken'də rōōn') seaport in S Turkey, on the Mediterranean: pop. 62,000

isl. *pl.* **isls.** **1.** island **2.** isle

Is·lam (is'läm, iz'-; -ləm, -lam; is läm') n. [Ar. *islām*, lit., submission (to God's will) < *salama*, to be resigned] **1.** the Moslem religion, a monotheistic religion in which the supreme deity is Allah and the chief prophet and founder is Mohammed **2.** Moslems collectively **3.** all the lands in which the Moslem religion predominates —**Is·lam'ic** (-lam'-, -läm'-), **Is·lam·it'ic** (-lə mit'ik) adj. —**Is'lam·ism** n. —**Is'lam·ite'** (-lə mīt') n.

Is·lam·a·bad (is läm'ə bäd') designated future capital of Pakistan, under construction in NE West Pakistan

Is·lam·ize (is'lə mīz', iz'-) vt., vi. **-ized', -iz'ing** to subject or adapt to Islam —**Is'lam·i·za'tion** n.

is·land (ī'lənd) n. [< ME. *iland* (respelled after unrelated ISLE) < OE. *igland, iegland*, lit., island land & *ealand*, lit., water land < *ig, ieg*, isle (akin to G. *aue*, ON. *ey* < PGmc. **aujo*, akin to **ahwo*, water) & *ea*, water < PGmc. **ahwo* < IE. **akwa*, whence L. *aqua*: see LAND] **1.** a land mass not as large as a continent, surrounded by water **2.** anything like an island in position or isolation; specif., ☆*a)* a structure above the flight deck of an aircraft carrier *b)* short for TRAFFIC ISLAND **3.** *Anat.* a tissue or cluster of cells differing from surrounding tissue in formation, etc. —vt. **1.** to make into or like an island; isolate **2.** to intersperse with or as with islands [a prairie *islanded* with wooded tracts]

is·land·er (-ər) n. a native or inhabitant of an island

Islands of the Blessed *Gr. & Rom. Myth.* the islands of bliss in the Western Ocean, where dead heroes went

island universe *a former name for* EXTERNAL GALAXY

isle (īl) n. [ME. *ile* < OFr. *ile*, earlier *isle* < ML. *isla*, contr. < L. *insula* < ? (*terra*) *in salo*, (land) in the sea < *salum*, sea: the form *isle* became general in the Renaissance after L. *insula*] an island, esp. a small island —vt. **isled, isl'ing** *same as* ISLAND —vi. to live on an isle

Isle of France *same as* ÎLE-DE-FRANCE

Isle Roy·ale (roi'əl) [Fr., royal island] island in N Lake Superior: it is part of the State of Michigan and, with adjacent islets, constitutes a U.S. national park (**Isle Royale National Park**), 842 sq. mi.

is·let (ī'lit) n. [OFr., dim. of *isle*, ISLE] a very small island

islets (or **islands**) **of Lang·er·hans** (län'ər häns') [after Paul *Langerhans* (1847–88), G. histologist] irregular groups of endocrine cells in the pancreas that produce the hormone insulin: their degeneration is believed to be a cause of diabetes mellitus

Is·ling·ton (iz'liŋ tən) metropolitan borough of London: pop. 227,000

ism (iz'm) n. [< ff.] a doctrine, theory, system, etc., esp. one whose name ends in *-ism*

-ism (iz'm; iz əm) [ME. *-isme* < OFr. & < L. *-isma* (< Gr. *-isma*) & *-ismus* (< Gr. *-ismos*): orig. suffix of action or of state, forming nouns from verbs in L. *-izare*, Gr. *-izein*] *a n.-forming suffix meaning:* **1.** the act, practice, or result of [*terrorism*] **2.** the condition of being [*pauperism*] **3.** action, conduct, or qualities characteristic of [*patriotism*] **4.** the doctrine, school, theory, or principle of [*cubism, socialism*] **5.** devotion to [*nationalism*] **6.** an instance, example, or peculiarity of [*Gallicism, witticism*] **7.** an abnormal condition caused by [*alcoholism*]

Is·ma·il·i·a (is'mä ē lē'ä) city in NE Egypt: pop. 111,000

Is·ma·il·i·an (is'mä il'ē ən) n. any member of a Shiite sect of Moslems holding that the office of imam should have gone to the descendant of Jafar's elder son Ismail (died 760 A.D.) when Jafar, the sixth imam, died in 765 A.D.: also **Is'ma·e'li·an** (-ē'lē-)

is·n't (iz'nt) is not

i·so- (ī'sə, -sō) [< Gr. *isos*, equal] *a combining form meaning: a)* equal, similar, alike, identical [*isomorph*] *b)* isomeric [*isoalloxazine*]

i·so·ag·glu·ti·na·tion (ī'sō ə glōōt'n ā'shən) n. the clumping of the red blood cells of an individual by the blood serum of another member of the same species

i·so·ag·glu·ti·nin (-ə glōōt'n in) n. [ISO- + AGGLUTININ] a substance in the blood that causes isoagglutination

i·so·al·lox·a·zine (-ə läk'sə zēn') n. [ISO- + *alloxazine* < G. *alloxan* (< *all(antoin)* + *ox(alsäure)* + *-an, -ANE*) + AZINE] *same as* FLAVIN (sense 1)

i·so·an·ti·bod·y (-an'ti bäd'ē) n., pl. **-bod'ies** an antibody in one individual for cells or proteins of some other members of the same species

i·so·an·ti·gen (-an'tə jən) n. an antigen derived from one member of a species that can cause the production of antibodies in some other members of the same species

i·so·bar (ī'sə bär') n. [< ISO- + Gr. *baros*, weight] **1.** a line on a map connecting points on the earth's surface having equal barometric pressure over a given period or at a given time **2.** any of two or more forms of an atom having the same atomic weight (or mass number) but different atomic numbers and representing different chemical elements —**i'so·bar'ic** (-bar'ik) adj.

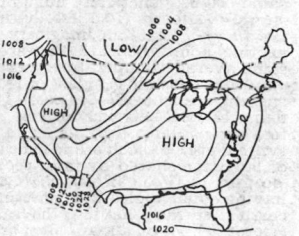

ISOBARS
(figures in millibars)

i·so·bath (-bath') n. [< ISO- + Gr. *bathos*, depth] a contour line on a map connecting points of equal depth in a body of water or below the earth's surface —**i'so·bath'ic** adj.

i·so·bu·tyl·ene (ī'sə byōōt'l ēn') n. a colorless, volatile liquid, $(CH_3)_2C{:}CH_2$ obtained from gases in petroleum cracking: it polymerizes readily and is used in making synthetic rubber and resins: also **i'so·bu'tene** (-tēn)

i·so·cheim (ī'sə kim') n. [< ISO- + Gr. *cheima*, winter (for IE. base see HIBERNATE)] a line on a map connecting points on the earth's surface that have the same mean winter temperature —**i'so·chei'mal** adj.

i·so·chor, i·so·chore (ī'sə kôr') n. [< ISO- + Gr. *chōra*, a place < IE. base **ghēi-*, to be empty, whence OE. *gad*, lack] *Physics* a line on a graph representing the parallel changes in pressure and temperature of something whose volume remains constant —**i'so·chor'ic** adj.

i·so·chro·mat·ic (ī'sə krō mat'ik) adj. [ISO- + CHROMATIC] **1.** *Optics* having the same color: said of lines or curves in figures formed by interfering light waves from biaxial crystals **2.** *same as* ORTHOCHROMATIC

i·soch·ro·nal (ī säk'rə n'l) adj. [< ModL. *isochronus* < Gr. *isochronos* < *isos*, equal + *chronos*, time + -AL] **1.** equal in length of time **2.** occurring at equal intervals of time Also **i·soch'ro·nous** —**i·soch'ro·nal·ly** adv. —**i·soch'ro·nism** n.

i·soch·ro·nize (-nīz') vt. **-nized', -niz'ing** to make isochronal

i·soch·ro·ous (ī säk'rō əs) adj. [ISO- + -CHROOUS] having the same color in every part

i·so·cli·nal (ī'sə klī'n'l) adj. [< ISO- + Gr. *klinein*, to slope (see INCLINE) + -AL] **1.** of similar or equal inclination or dip **2.** connecting or showing points on the earth's surface having equal magnetic inclination or dip [*isoclinal* lines on a map] **3.** *Geol.* dipping in the same direction: said of strata Also **i'so·clin'ic** (-klin'ik) —n. an isoclinal line —**i'so·cli'nal·ly** adv.

i·so·cline (ī'sə klīn') n. [see prec.] **1.** an anticline or syncline so compressed that the strata on both sides of the axis dip with equal inclination in the same direction **2.** an isoclinal line

i·soc·ra·cy (ī säk'rə sē) n., pl. **-cies** [Gr. *isokratia*: see ISO- & -CRACY] a system of government in which all persons have equal political power

---

fat, āpe, cär; ten, ēven; is, bīte; gō, hôrn, tōōl, look; oil, out; up, fur; get; joy; yet; chin; she; thin, then; zh, leisure; ŋ, ring; ə for a in ago, e in agent, i in sanity, o in comply, u in focus; ' as in able (ā'b'l); Fr. bal; ë, Fr. coeur; ö, Fr. feu; Fr. mon; ô, Fr. coq; ü, Fr. duc; r, Fr. cri; H, G. ich; kh, G. doch. See inside front cover. ☆Americanism; ‡foreign; *hypothetical; < derived from

I·soc·ra·tes (ī säk′rə tēz′) 436–338 B.C.; Athenian orator & rhetorician

i·so·cy·a·nate (ī′sō sī′ə nāt′) *n.* [see ff. & -ATE²] any of various compounds containing the group –N:C:O, used in making resins and adhesives

i·so·cy·a·nine (-nēn′, -nin) *n.* [ISO- + CYANINE] any of a group of quinoline dyes used in sensitizing photographic plates and films

i·so·cy·clic (-sī′klik, -sik′lik) *adj.* [ISO- + CYCLIC] consisting of or being a ring of atoms of the same element; specif., *same as* CARBOCYCLIC

i·so·di·a·met·ric (-dī′ə met′rik) *adj.* having equal diameters or axes

i·so·di·mor·phism (-dī môr′fiz′m) *n.* a similarity of crystalline structure between the two forms of two dimorphous substances —**i′so·di·mor′phous** (-fəs) *adj.*

i·so·dose (ī′sə dōs′) *adj.* [ISO- + DOSE] designating or of points representing equal doses of radiation

i·so·dy·nam·ic (ī′sō dī nam′ik) *adj.* [ISO- + DYNAMIC] 1. of or having equal force 2. connecting or showing points on the earth's surface having equal magnetic intensity [*isodynamic* lines on a map]

i·so·e·lec·tric point (-i lek′trik) the point, or pH value, at which a substance is neutral or has zero electric potential

i·so·e·lec·tron·ic (-i lek′trän′ik) *adj.* designating or of any of two or more atoms which have the same number of electrons around the nucleus and similar spectral and physical properties —**i′so·e·lec′tron′i·cal·ly** *adv.*

i·so·ga·mete (-gam′ēt, -gə met′) *n.* a gamete not differentiated in size, structure, or function from another with which it unites: found in some protozoans, fungi, etc.: opposed to HETEROGAMETE —**i′so·ga·met′ic** (-met′ik) *adj.*

i·sog·a·my (ī säg′ə mē) *n.* [ISO- + -GAMY] reproduction by the uniting of isogametes —**i·sog′a·mous** (-məs) *adj.*

i·sog·e·nous (ī säj′ə nəs) *adj.* [ISO- + -GENOUS] *Biol.* of the same origin; genetically uniform —**i·sog′e·ny** (-nē) *n.*

i·so·ge·o·therm (ī′sō jē′ə thurm′) *n.* [< ISO- + GEO- + Gr. *thermē*, heat] an imaginary line or curved plane connecting points beneath the earth's surface that have the same average temperature —**i′so·ge′o·ther′mal** *adj.*

i·so·gloss (ī′sə glôs′, -gläs′) *n.* [< Gr. *glōssa*, tongue, speech: see GLOSS²] *Linguis.* 1. *a)* an imaginary line of demarcation between regions differing in a particular feature of language, as on a point of pronunciation, syntax, etc. *b)* such a line indicated on a map 2. a feature of language shared by most people in a given area

i·so·gon·ic (ī′sə gän′ik) *adj.* [ISO- + -GON + -IC] 1. of or having equal angles 2. connecting or showing points on the earth's surface having the same magnetic declination [*isogonic* lines on a map] 3. of or having to do with isogony Also **i·sog′o·nal** (ī säg′ə n′l) —*n.* an isogonic line

i·sog·o·ny (ī säg′ə nē) *n.* [ISO- + -GONY] equivalent growth of parts of an organism so that size remains proportionate to the whole

i·so·gram (ī′sə gram′) *n.* [ISO- + -GRAM] a line on a particular surface, as on a map, that represents a constant or equal value of a given quantity

i·so·hel (ī′sə hel′) *n.* [< ISO- + Gr. *helios*, the sun] a line on a map connecting points having equal hours of sunshine in a standard period of time

i·so·hy·et (ī′sō hī′ət) *n.* [< ISO- + Gr. *hyetos*, rain] a line on a map connecting points having equal amounts of rainfall —**i′so·hy′et·al** *adj.*

i·so·late (ī′sə lāt′, is′ə-; *for n., usually* -lit) *vt.* **-lat′ed, -lat′-ing** [back-formation < *isolated* < It. *isolato*, pp. of *isolare*, to isolate < *isola* < L. *insula*, island: see ISLE] 1. to set apart from others; place alone 2. *Bacteriology* to grow a pure culture of (a specific bacterium) 3. *Chem.* to separate (an element or compound) in pure form from substances with which it is combined or mixed 4. *Med.* to place (a patient with a contagious disease) apart from others to prevent the spread of infection —*n.* a person or group that is set apart —**i′so·la·ble** (-lə b′l) *adj.* —**i′so·la′tor** *n.*

isolated point *Math.* a point on a curve that is isolated from all other points on the curve

i·so·la·tion (ī′sə lā′shən, is′ə-) *n.* [Fr.] an isolating or being isolated —*SYN.* see SOLITUDE

☆**i·so·la·tion·ist** (-ist) *n.* a person who believes in or advocates isolation; specif., one who opposes the involvement of his country in international alliances, agreements, etc. —*adj.* of isolationists or their policy —**i′so·la′tion·ism** *n.*

I·sol·de (i sōl′də, i sōld′; *G.* ē zōl′də) [G. < OFr. *Isolt, Iseut* < OHG. *Isold*, prob. < *is*, ice + *waltan*, to rule] *Medieval Legend* 1. the Irish princess married to King Mark of Cornwall and beloved by Tristram 2. the daughter of the king of Brittany, married to Tristram Also **I·solt** (i sōlt′) See TRISTRAM

☆**I·so·lette** (ī′sə let′) [arbitrary blend < ISOL(ATE) + (BASSIN)ET] *a trademark for* a kind of incubator for premature babies —*n.* [l-] such an incubator

i·so·leu·cine (ī′sə loō′sēn, -sin) *n.* [ISO- + LEUCINE] an essential amino acid, $C_6H_{13}NO_2$, an isomer of leucine, found in small amounts in most proteins

i·so·line (ī′sə līn′) *n. same as* ISOGRAM

i·sol·o·gous (ī säl′ə gəs) *adj.* [ISO- + (HOMO)LOGOUS] 1. designating or of any of two or more chemical compounds of similar structure but consisting of different atoms of the same valence and usually of the same periodic group 2. designating or of a series formed by such compounds —**i′so·logue′** (ī′sə log′ -sə lôg′, -läg′) *n.*

i·so·mag·net·ic (ī′sō mag net′ik) *adj.* 1. of equal magnetic force 2. connecting or showing points on the earth's surface having the same magnetic intensity [*isomagnetic* lines on a map] —*n.* an isomagnetic line

i·so·mer (ī′sə mər) *n.* [< Gr. *isomerēs*, equally divided < *isos*, equal + *meros*, a part, share < IE. base *(s)mer-*, to allot to, provide for, whence L. *merere*, to deserve, merit, Gr. *moira*, fate] 1. *Chem.* any of two or more chemical compounds having the same constituent elements in the same proportion by weight but differing in physical or chemical properties because of differences in the structure of their molecules 2. *Physics* any of two or more nuclei possessing the same number of neutrons and protons, but existing in different energy states, and thus having different radioactive properties —**i′so·mer′ic** (-mer′ik) *adj.* —**i′so·mer′i·cal·ly** *adv.*

i·som·er·ism (ī säm′ər iz′m) *n.* the state or relation of isomers

i·som·er·ous (-əs) *adj.* [ISO- + -MEROUS] 1. having the same number of parts, markings, etc. 2. *Bot.* having the same number of parts in each whorl 3. *same as* ISOMERIC

i·so·met·ric (ī′sə met′rik) *adj.* [< Gr. *isometros* < *isos*, equal + *metron*, measure (see METER¹) + -IC] 1. of, indicating, or having equality of measure 2. *same as* CUBIC (sense 3) 3. of or having to do with isometrics —*n.* 1. a line, as on a chart, indicating changes of pressure or temperature at constant volume 2. [*pl.*] a method of physical exercise in which one set of muscles is tensed, for a period of seconds, in opposition to another set of muscles or to an immovable object Also **i′so·met′ri·cal** —**i′so·met′ri·cal·ly** *adv.*

isometric projection a method of drawing figures and maps so that three dimensions are shown not in perspective but foreshortened equally

i·so·me·tro·pi·a (ī′sō mə trō′pē ə) *n.* [ModL. < ISO- + Gr. *metron*, measure (see METER¹) + -OPIA] the condition of being equal in refraction: said of the two eyes

i·som·e·try (ī säm′ə trē) *n.* [ISO- + -METRY] 1. equality of measure 2. *Geog.* equality of height above sea level

i·so·morph (ī′sə môrf′) *n.* [ISO- + -MORPH] an organism, substance, or structure that exhibits isomorphism

i·so·mor·phic (ī′sə môr′fik) *adj.* 1. having similar or identical structure or form 2. *Biol., Chem.* showing isomorphism Also **i′so·mor′phous** (-fəs)

i·so·mor·phism (-fiz′m) *n.* [< prec. + -ISM] 1. *Biol.* a similarity in appearance or structure of organisms belonging to different species or races 2. *Chem.* an identity or close similarity in the crystalline form of substances usually containing different elements but having similar composition 3. *Math.* a one-to-one correspondence between the elements of two groups

☆**i·so·ni·a·zid** (ī′sə nī′ə zid) *n.* [ISO- + NI(COTINIC) + (HYDR)AZ(INE) + -ID] an antibacterial drug, $C_6H_7N_3O$, used in treating and preventing tuberculosis

i·son·o·my (ī săn′ə mē) *n.* [Gr. *isonomia*: see ISO- & -NOMY] equality of laws, rights, or privileges

i·so·oc·tane (ī′sə äk′tān) *n.* [ISO- + OCTANE] a liquid hydrocarbon, $(CH_3)_2CHCH_2C(CH_3)_3$, used with normal heptane to prepare antiknock rating standards and arbitrarily assigned an octane rating of 100

i·so·pi·es·tic (ī′sō pī es′tik) *adj.* [< ISO- + Gr. *piestos*, compressible < *piezein*, to press + -IC] indicating equal pressure —*n. same as* ISOBAR

i·so·pleth (ī′sə pleth′) *n.* [< Gr. *isoplēthēs*, equal in number or quantity < *isos*, equal + *plēthos*, number, quantity] the line connecting points on a graph or map that have equal or corresponding values with regard to certain variables

i·so·pod (-päd′) *n.* [ISO- + -POD] any of an order (Isopoda) of mostly aquatic crustaceans with a flat, oval body and seven pairs of walking legs of similar size and form, each pair attached to a segment of the thorax —*adj.* of an isopod or the isopods Also **i·sop·o·dan** (ī säp′ə dən)

i·so·prene (-prēn′) *n.* [coined (1860) by C. G. Williams, Brit. chemist < ISO- + PR(OPYL) + -ENE] a colorless, volatile liquid, C_5H_8, prepared by the dry distillation of raw rubber or synthetically: when heated with sodium or other substances it polymerizes to form a substance closely resembling natural rubber

i·so·pro·pyl (ī′sə prō′pil) *n.* the univalent radical $(CH_3)_2$-CH, an isomer of the univalent propyl radical, C_3H_7

i·sos·ce·les (ī säs′ə lēz′) *adj.* [LL. < Gr. *isoskelēs* < *isos*, equal + *skelos*, a leg < IE. base *(s)kel-*, to bend, whence L. *calx*, heel, *coluber*, serpent] designating a triangle with two equal sides

i·so·seis·mal (ī′sə sīz′m′l, -sis′-) *adj.* [< ISO- + Gr. *seismos*, earthquake + -AL] 1. of equal intensity of earthquake shock 2. connecting or showing points of such equal intensity on the earth's surface [*isoseismal* lines on a map] —*n.* an isoseismal line Also **i′so·seis′mic**

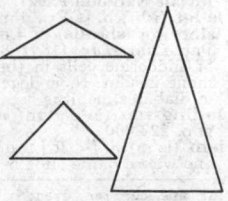

ISOSCELES TRIANGLES

is·os·mot·ic (ī′säs mät′ik) *adj.* [IS- + OSMOTIC] *same as* ISOTONIC (sense 2)

i·so·spon·dy·lous (ī′sə spän′d′l əs) *adj.* [< ISO- + Gr. *spondylos*, vertebra] of or having to do with an order (Isospondyli) of bony fishes that includes the herring and trout

i·so·spo·rous (ī′sə spôr′əs) *adj. same as* HOMOSPOROUS

i·sos·ta·sy (ī säs′tə sē) *n.* [< ISO- + Gr. *stasis*, a standing still (see STASIS)] 1. a condition in which there is equal pressure on every side 2. *Geol.* approximate equilibrium in large, equal areas of the earth's crust, preserved by the action of gravity upon the different substances in the crust in proportion to their densities —**i·so·stat·ic** (ī′sə stat′ik) *adj.*

i·so·there (ī′sə thir′) *n.* [Fr. *isothère* < *iso-* (see ISO-) + Gr. *theros*, summer (see WARM)] a line on a map connecting points on the earth's surface that have the same mean summer temperature —**i·soth·er·al** (ī säth′ər əl) *adj.*

i·so·therm (-thʉrm) *n.* [Fr. *isotherme* < *iso-*, ISO- + Gr. *thermē*, heat < *thermos*, hot: see WARM] 1. a line on a map connecting points on the earth's surface having the same mean temperature or the same temperature at a given time 2. a line representing changes of volume or pressure at constant temperature

i·so·ther·mal (ī′sə thʉr′m′l) *adj.* [Fr. *isotherme* (see prec.) + -AL] 1. of or indicating equality or constancy of temperature 2. of or indicating changes of volume or pressure at constant temperature [an *isothermal* line] 3. of an isotherm or isotherms —*n. same as* ISOTHERM

i·so·tone (ī′sə tōn′) *n.* [ISO- + TONE] any of a number of nuclides having the same excess of neutrons over protons

i·so·ton·ic (ī′sə tän′ik) *adj.* [< Gr. *isotonos* (< *isos*, equal + *tonos*, a stretching) + -IC] 1. having equal tension 2. having the same osmotic pressure; esp., designating or of a salt solution having the same osmotic pressure as blood —**i′so·ton′i·cal·ly** *adv.* —**i′so·to·nic′i·ty** (-tō nis′ə tē) *n.*

i·so·tope (ī′sə tōp′) *n.* [< ISO- + Gr. *topos*, place (see TOPIC)] any of two or more forms of an element having the same or very closely related chemical properties and the same atomic number but different atomic weights (or mass numbers) [U 235, U 238, and U 239 are three *isotopes* of uranium] —**i′so·top′ic** (-täp′ik, -tō′pik) *adj.* —**i′so·top′i·cal·ly** *adv.* —**i·sot·o·py** (ī sät′ə pē, is′ə tō′pē) *n.*

i·so·trop·ic (ī′sə träp′ik, -trō′pik) *adj.* [ISO- + -TROPIC] having physical properties, as conductivity, elasticity, etc., that are the same regardless of the direction of measurement: also **i·sot·ro·pous** (ī sät′rə pəs) —**i·sot′ro·py** (-pē) *n.*

Is·ra·el (iz′rē əl, -rā-) [ME. < OFr. < LL.(Ec.) < Gr. *Israēl* < Heb. *yisrā′ēl*, lit., contender with God < *sārāh*, to wrestle + *ēl*, God] 1. a masculine name: dim. *Izzy* 2. *Bible* Jacob: so named after wrestling with the angel: Gen. 32:28 3. ancient land of the Hebrews, at the SE end of the Mediterranean 4. kingdom in the N part of this region, formed (10th cent. B.C.) by the ten tribes of Israel that broke with Judah & Benjamin 5. country between the Mediterranean Sea & the country of Jordan: established (1948) by the U.N. as a Jewish state: 7,992 sq. mi.; pop. 2,678,000; cap. Jerusalem 6. the Jewish people, as descendants of Jacob 7. any group of Christians regarding themselves as chosen by God

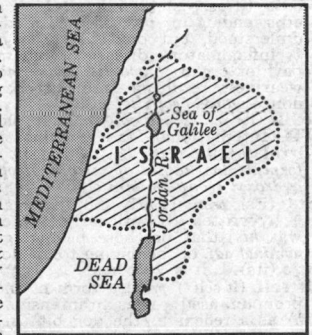
ISRAEL (8th cent. B.C.)

Is·rae·li (iz rā′lē) *adj.* [ModHeb. *yisrĕ′ēli* < Heb.: see prec.] of modern Israel or its people —*n., pl.* **-lis, -li** a native or inhabitant of modern Israel

Is·ra·el·ite (iz′rē ə līt′, -rā-) *n.* [ME. < LL.(Ec.) *Israelita* < Gr. *Israēlitēs*] any of the people of ancient Israel or their descendants; Jew; Hebrew —*adj.* of ancient Israel or the Israelites; Jewish: also **Is′ra·el·it′ish** (-līt′ish), **Is′ra·el·it′ic** (-lit′ik)

Is·sa·char (is′ə kär′) *Bible* 1. ninth son of Jacob: Gen. 30:18 2. the tribe of Israel descended from him

☆**is·sei** (ē′sā′) *n., pl.* **-sei, -seis** [Jap., lit., first generation] [also **I-**] a Japanese who emigrated to the U.S. after the Oriental exclusion proclamation of 1907 and was thus ineligible by law, until 1952, to become a U.S. citizen: cf. NISEI, KIBEI

is·su·a·ble (ish′oo wə b′l) *adj.* 1. that can issue or be issued 2. that can be disputed, debated, or raised as an issue at law —**is′su·a·bly** *adv.*

☆**is·su·ance** (ish′oo wəns) *n.* an issuing; issue

is·su·ant (-wənt) *adj.* 1. [Rare] issuing 2. *Heraldry* with only the upper part visible [a lion *issuant*]

is·sue (ish′oo; *chiefly Brit.,* is′yoo) *n.* [ME. < OFr. *issue*, pp. of *issir*, to go out < L. *exire* < *ex-*, out + *ire*, to go: see YEAR] 1. an outgoing; outflow; passing out; exit 2. a place or means of going out; exit; outlet 3. a result; consequence; upshot 4. offspring; a child or children 5. profits from lands, estates, or fines; produce; proceeds 6. a point, matter, or question to be disputed or decided 7. a sending or giving out; putting forth 8. the thing or set of things issued; all that is put forth and circulated at one time [the July *issue* of a magazine, an *issue* of bonds] 9. *Med. a)* a discharge of blood, pus, etc. *b)* an incision or artificial ulcer for the discharge of pus —*vi.* **-sued, -su·ing** 1. to go, come, pass, or flow out; emerge 2. to be descended; be born 3. to be derived or result (*from* a cause) 4. to end or result (*in* an effect or consequence) 5. to come as revenue; accrue 6. to be published; be put forth and circulated —*vt.* 1. to let out; discharge 2. to give or deal out; distribute [to *issue* supplies] 3. to publish; put forth and circulate [to *issue* bonds] —*SYN.* see EFFECT, RISE —**at issue** 1. in dispute; still to be decided: also **in issue** 2. at variance; in disagreement —**join issue** 1. to enter into conflict, argument, etc. with another or each other 2. to join in submitting an issue for decision at law —**take issue** to disagree; differ —**is′su·er** *n.*

Is·sus (is′əs) ancient town in Cilicia, in SE Asia Minor: site of a battle (333 B.C.) in which Alexander the Great defeated Darius III of Persia

Is·syk Kul (is′ik kool′) mountain lake in SC Asia, in the Kirghiz S.S.R.: c. 2,400 sq. mi.: also **Issyk-Kul**

-ist (ist, əst) [ME. *-iste* < OFr. < L. *-ista* < Gr. *-istēs* < verbs ending in *-izein*] a *n.-forming suffix corresponding to verbs ending in* -IZE *or nouns ending in* -ISM, *meaning:* 1. a person who does, makes, or practices [*moralist, satirist*] 2. a person skilled in or occupied with; an expert in [*druggist, violinist*] 3. an adherent of, believer in [*anarchist*]

Is·tan·bul (is′tan bool′, -tän-; -bool′; *Turk.* is täm′bool′) [altered < ModGr. *'s ten poli* < Gr. *eis tēn polin*, lit., into the city] seaport in NW Turkey, on both sides of the Bosporus: pop. 1,467,000: former name, CONSTANTINOPLE; ancient name, BYZANTIUM

Isth., isth. isthmus

isth·mi·an (is′mē ən) *adj.* [< L. *isthmius* (Gr. *isthmios* < *isthmos:* see ISTHMUS) + -AN] 1. of an isthmus 2. [I-] *a)* of the Isthmus of Panama *b)* of the Isthmus of Corinth or the games held there in ancient times —*n.* a native or inhabitant of an isthmus

isth·mus (is′məs) *n., pl.* **-mus·es, -mi** (-mī) [L. < Gr. *isthmos*, a neck, narrow passage, isthmus] 1. a narrow strip of land having water at each side and connecting two larger bodies of land 2. *Anat. a)* a narrow strip of tissue connecting two larger parts of an organ [the *isthmus* of the thyroid] *b)* a narrow passage between two larger cavities [the *isthmus* of the Fallopian tubes]

-is·tic (is′tik) [MFr. *-istique* < L. *-isticus* < Gr. *-istikos:* also formed in E. < -IST + -IC] an *adj.-forming suffix corresponding to nouns ending in* -ISM *and* -IST [*realistic, artistic*]: also **-is′ti·cal**

is·tle (ist′lē) *n.* [< AmSp. *ixtle* < Nahuatl *ichtli*] a fiber obtained from certain tropical American plants, as various agaves: used for cordage, nets, baskets, etc.

Is·tri·a (is′trē ə) peninsula in NW Yugoslavia, projecting into the N Adriatic, formerly including part of the area around Trieste: also **Istrian Peninsula** —**Is′tri·an** *adj., n.*

it (it) *pron.* [for *pl.* see THEY] [ME. *hit, it* < OE. *hit,* akin to Du. *het,* Goth. *hita,* this: IE. base as in HE[1]: basic sense "this one"] the animal or thing previously mentioned or under discussion *It* is used as: *a)* the subject of an impersonal verb without reference to agent [*it* is snowing] *b)* the grammatical subject of a clause of which the actual subject is another clause or phrase following [*it* is clear that he wants to go] *c)* an object of indefinite sense in certain idiomatic expressions [to lord *it* over someone]; often, specif., an unpleasant consequence [to be in for *it*, let him have *it*] *d)* the antecedent to a relative pronoun from which it is separated by a predicate [*it* is your car that we want] *e)* a term of reference to something indefinite but understood, as the state of affairs [*it*'s all right, I didn't hurt myself] ☆*f)* [Colloq.] an emphatic predicate pronoun referring to the person, thing, situation, etc. which is considered ultimate, final, or perfect [zero hour is here; this is *it*] *g)* [Slang] an emphatic pronoun referring to an attractive personal quality, as vigor, charm, or sex appeal —*n.* the player, as in the game of tag, who must try to touch, catch, or find another —☆**with it** [Slang] alert, informed, or hip

It., Ital. 1. Italian 2. Italic 3. Italy

i/t/a, I.T.A. Initial Teaching Alphabet

it·a·col·u·mite (it′ə käl′yoo mīt′) *n.* [< *Itacolumi,* mountain in Brazil, where found] a type of fine-grained sandstone deposited in flexible layers

---

fat, āpe, cär; ten, ēven; is, bīte; gō, hôrn, tool, look; oil, out; up, fʉr; get; joy; yet; chin; she; thin, *th*en; zh, leisure; ŋ, ring; ə for *a* in *ago, e* in *agent, i* in *sanity, o* in *comply, u* in *focus;* ′ as in *able* (ā′b′l); Fr. bál; ë, Fr. coeur; ö, Fr. feu; Fr. mon; ô, Fr. coq; ü, Fr. duc; r, Fr. cri; H, G. ich; kh, G. doch. See inside front cover. ☆ Americanism; ‡foreign; *hypothetical; <derived from

it·a·con·ic acid (it'ə kän'ik) [arbitrary transposition of *aconitic* (< ACONITE + -IC)] a white crystalline material, C₅H₆O₄, prepared by the fermentation of sugar with a special mold: it is used in making resins and plasticizers

ital. italic (type)

†**I·tal·ia** (ē täl'yä) *It.* name of ITALY

I·tal·ian (i tal'yən) *adj.* [ME. < L. *Italianus* < *Italia*, Italy] of Italy, its people, their language, or culture —*n.* 1. a native or inhabitant of Italy 2. the Romance language of the Italians

I·tal·ian·ate (-it; *also, & for v. always,* -āt') *adj.* [It. *Italianato*] of Italian form, appearance, or character —*vt.* -**at'ed, -at'ing** [It. *italianare*] *same as* ITALIANIZE

Italian East Africa former It. colony in E Africa, consisting of Ethiopia, Eritrea, & Italian Somaliland

I·tal·ian·ism (-iz'm) *n.* 1. an Italian expression, idiom, or custom 2. Italian spirit, quality, etc. 3. fondness for Italian customs, ideas, etc.

I·tal·ian·ize (-īz') *vt., vi.* -**ized', -iz'ing** [Fr. *italianiser*] to make or become Italian in character, form, etc. —**I·tal'-ian·i·za'tion** *n.*

Italian Somaliland former It. colony on the E coast of Africa: merged with British Somaliland to form Somalia

Italian sonnet *same as* PETRARCHAN SONNET

I·tal·ic (i tal'ik) *adj.* [L. *Italicus*] 1. of ancient Italy, its people, etc. 2. designating or of the subfamily of the Indo-European languages that includes Latin, Oscan, Umbrian, other languages of ancient Italy, and the Romance languages —*n.* the Italic languages collectively

i·tal·ic (i tal'ik, i-) *adj.* [see prec.: so called because first used in an Italian edition of Virgil (1501)] designating or of a type in which the characters slant upward to the right, used variously, as to emphasize words, indicate foreign words, set off book titles, etc. [*this is italic type*] —*n.* 1. an italic letter or other character 2. [*usually pl., sometimes with sing. v.*] italic type or print

I·tal·i·cism (i tal'ə siz'm) *n. same as* ITALIANISM (sense 1)

i·tal·i·cize (-sīz') *vt.* -**cized', -ciz'ing** 1. to print in italics 2. to underscore (handwritten or typed matter) with a single line to indicate that it is to be printed in italics — **i·tal'i·ci·za'tion** *n.*

I·tal·o- (i tal'ō) *a combining form meaning:* 1. Italian 2. Italian and [*Italo-American*]

It·a·ly (it'l ē) [L. *Italia*, earlier *Vitalia*] country in S Europe mostly on a peninsula extending into the Mediterranean & including the islands of Sicily & Sardinia: 116,304 sq. mi.; pop. 54,388,000; cap. Rome: It. name, ITALIA

I·tas·ca (i tas'kə), **Lake** [coined by H. R. SCHOOLCRAFT] lake in NW Minn., a source of the Mississippi: c. 2 sq. mi.

itch (ich) *vi.* [ME. *yicchen, icchen* < OE. *giccan*, akin to G. *jucken*] 1. to feel an irritating sensation on the skin, with the desire to scratch the affected part 2. to have a restless desire or hankering —*vt.* 1. to make itch 2. to irritate or annoy —*n.* 1. an irritating sensation on the skin that makes one want to scratch the affected part 2. a restless desire; hankering [*an itch to travel*] —**the itch** any of various skin disorders accompanied by severe irritation of the skin; specif., *same as* SCABIES

itch·y (-ē) *adj.* **itch'i·er, itch'i·est** like, feeling, or causing an itch —**itch'i·ly** *adv.* —**itch'i·ness** *n.*

-ite[1] (it) [ME. < OFr. or L. or Gr.: OFr. *-ite* < L. *-ita, -ites* < Gr. *-itēs*, fem. *-itis*] *a n.-forming suffix meaning:* 1. a native, inhabitant, or citizen of [*Brooklynite*] 2. a descendant from or offspring of [*Israelite*] 3. an adherent of, believer in, or member of [*laborite*] 4. a product, esp. a commercially manufactured one [*lucite, dynamite, vulcanite*] 5. a fossil [*ammonite*] 6. a part of a body or bodily organ [*somite*] 7. [Fr., arbitrary alteration of *-ate, -*ATE[2]] a salt or ester of an acid whose name ends in *-ous* [*nitrite, sulfite*] 8. a (specified) mineral or rock [*anthracite, dolomite*]

-ite[2] (īt; *in some words,* it) [L. *-itus*, ending of some past participles] a suffix used variously to form adjectives, nouns, and verbs [*finite, favorite, unite*]

i·tem (īt'əm) *adv.* [ME. < L. < *ita*, so, thus] also: used before each article in a series being enumerated —*n.* 1. orig., an admonition; hint 2. an article; unit; separate thing; particular; entry in an account 3. a bit of news or information —*vt.* [Archaic] *same as* ITEMIZE

SYN.—**item** applies to each separate article or thing entered or included in a list, inventory, record, etc.; **detail** applies to any single thing or small section that is part of a whole structure, design, etc. [*an architectural detail, the details of a plot*]; **particular** stresses the distinctness of a thing as an individual unit in a whole [*to go into particulars*]

☆**i·tem·ize** (-īz') *vt.* -**ized', -iz'ing** to specify the items of; set down by items [*to itemize a bill of purchases*] —**i'tem·i·za'tion** *n.*

☆**item veto** executive power, as of some State governors, to veto a section of an appropriation bill without vetoing the whole bill

I·té·nez (ē tā'nes) *Bolivian name of* GUAPORÉ River

it·er·ate (it'ə rāt') *vt.* -**at'ed, -at'ing** [< L. *iteratus*, pp. of *iterare*, to repeat < *iterum*, again < **iterus*, compar. of **i-*, pron. stem, whence *is, ea, id*, he, she, it, *ita*, thus] to utter or do again or repeatedly —**SYN.** see REPEAT —**it'er·ant** (-ər ənt) *adj.*

it·er·a·tion (it'ə rā'shən) *n.* [ME. < L. *iteratio*] 1. an iterating or being iterated; repetition 2. something iterated Also **it'er·ance** (-ər əns)

it·er·a·tive (it'ə rāt'iv, -ər ət iv) *adj.* [ME. < MFr. *itératif* < L. *iteratus*] 1. repetitious; repeating or repeated 2. *Gram. same as* FREQUENTATIVE

Ith·a·ca (ith'ə kə) 1. one of the Ionian Islands, off the W coast of Greece: legendary home of Odysseus: 37 sq. mi.: Gr. name **I·tha·ki** (ē thä'kē) 2. city in WC N.Y., on Cayuga Lake: pop. 26,000 —**Ith'a·can** *adj., n.*

I·thunn, I·thun (ē'thoon) *same as* IDUN

ith·y·phal·lic (ith'i fal'ik) *adj.* [L. *ithyphallicus* < Gr. *ithyphallikos* < *ithyphallos*, erect phallus < *ithys*, straight (< IE. base **sidh-*, to go directly toward, whence Sans. *sādhú-*, straight) + *phallos*, PHALLUS] 1. of the phallus carried in the rites of Bacchus 2. lewd; obscene; lascivious 3. in the meter of the Bacchic hymns —*n.* an ithyphallic poem

i·tin·er·an·cy (ī tin'ər ən sē, i-) *n.* 1. *a)* an itinerating, or traveling from place to place *b)* the state of being itinerant 2. a group of itinerant preachers or judges 3. official work requiring constant travel from place to place or frequent change of residence, as preaching or presiding over courts in a circuit Also **i·tin'er·a·cy** (-ə sē)

i·tin·er·ant (-ənt) *adj.* [LL. *itinerans*, prp. of *itinerari*, to travel < L. *iter* (gen. *itineris*), a walk, journey < base of *ire*, to go: see YEAR] traveling from place to place or on a circuit —*n.* a person who travels from place to place — **i·tin'er·ant·ly** *adv.*

SYN.—**itinerant** applies to persons whose work or profession requires them to travel from place to place [*itinerant* laborers, an *itinerant* preacher]; **ambulatory** specifically implies ability to walk about [*an ambulatory* patient]; **peripatetic** implies a walking or moving about in carrying on some activity and is applied humorously to persons who are always on the go; **nomadic** is applied to tribes or groups of people who have no permanent home, but move about constantly in search of food for themselves, pasture for the animals they herd, etc.; **vagrant** is applied to individuals, specif. hobos or tramps, who wander about without a fixed home, and implies shiftlessness, disorderliness, etc.

i·tin·er·ar·y (ī tin'ə rer'ē, i-) *adj.* [LL. *itinerarius* < *itinerans*: see prec.] 1. of traveling, journeys, routes, or roads —*n., pl.* -**ar'ies** [LL. *itinerarium*, neut. of *itinerarius*] 1. a route 2. a record of a journey 3. a guidebook for travelers 4. a detailed plan or outline for a proposed journey

i·tin·er·ate (-rāt') *vi.* -**at'ed, -at'ing** [< LL. *itineratus*, pp. of *itinerari*: see ITINERANT] to travel from place to place or on a circuit —**i·tin'er·a'tion** *n.*

-i·tion (ish'ən) [< Fr. or L.: Fr. *-iton* < L. *-itio* (gen. *-itionis*) < *-i-*, thematic vowel + *-tio* (gen. *-tionis*)] *a n.-forming suffix:* see -ATION [*nutrition*]

-i·tious (ish'əs) [L. *-icius, -itius*] *an adj.-forming suffix corresponding to* -ITION, *meaning of*, having the nature of, characterized by [*nutritious, seditious*]

-i·tis (īt'əs, -is) [ModL. < L. < Gr. *-itis*, orig. fem. of adjs. ending in *-itēs*, used to modify *nosos*, disease (later understood, but omitted)] *a n.-forming suffix meaning:* 1. inflammatory disease or inflammation of (a specified part or organ) [*neuritis, bronchitis*] 2. addiction to, or weariness resulting from preoccupation with: used in nonce words [*golfitis*]

it'll (it''l) 1. it will 2. it shall

ITO International Trade Organization

-i·tol (i tōl', -tôl', -täl') [< -ITE[1] + -OL[1]] *a suffix used in forming the names of certain alcohols with more than one hydroxyl group* [*mannitol*]

its (its) *pron.* [Early ModE. analogical formation < *it* + *'s*; written *it's* until early 19th c.: the ME. & OE. form was *his*] that or those belonging to it —*possessive pronominal adj.* of, belonging to, or done by it

it's (its) 1. it is 2. it has

it·self (it self') *pron.* a form of the 3d pers. sing., neuter pronoun, used: *a)* as an intensive [*the work itself* is easy] *b)* as a reflexive [*the dog bit itself*] *c)* as a quasi-noun meaning "its real, true, or actual self" [*the bird is not itself* today]: in this construction *it* may be considered a possessive pronominal adjective and *self* a noun, and they may be separated [*its* own sweet *self*]

it·ty-bit·ty (it'ē bit'ē) *adj.* [baby talk alteration < *little bit*] [Colloq.] very small; tiny: a facetious imitation of child's talk Also **it·sy-bit·sy** (it'sē bit'sē)

-i·ty (ə tē, i-) [ME. *-ite* < OFr. or L.: OFr. *-ité* < L. *-itas* < *-i-*, ending of stem, or thematic vowel + *-tas*, -TY[1]] *a suffix meaning* state, character, condition, or an instance of any of these [*chastity, possibility*]

IU, I.U. international unit(s)

IUD intrauterine (contraceptive) device: also **IUCD**

-i·um (ē əm, yəm) [ModL. < L., ending of certain neuter nouns] *a suffix used: a)* in forming Modern Latin names for chemical elements [*sodium*] *b)* in designating certain positive ions [*ammonium, carbonium*]

i.v. 1. initial velocity 2. intravenous(ly)

I·van (ī'vən; *Russ.* i vän') [Russ. < Gr. *Iōannēs*: see JOHN] 1. a masculine name 2. Ivan III 1440–1505; grand duke of Muscovy (1462–1505): called *the Great* 3. Ivan IV 1530–84; grand duke of Muscovy (1533–84) & 1st czar of Russia (1547–84): called *the Terrible*

I·va·no·vo (ē vä'nô vô) city in C European R.S.F.S.R.: pop. 398,000

I've (īv) I have

-ive (iv) [ME. < OFr. *-if*, fem. *-ive* < L. *-ivus*] *a suffix*

meaning: **1.** of, relating to, belonging to, having the nature or quality of [native, substantive] **2.** tending to, given to [creative, destructive]

Ives (īvz) **1. Charles Edward,** 1874–1954; U.S. composer **2. James M.,** see CURRIER AND IVES

i·vied (ī′vēd) *adj.* covered or overgrown with ivy

i·vo·ry (ī′vər ē, īv′rē) *n., pl.* **-ries** [ME. < OFr. *yvoire* < L. *eboreus* (adj.) < *ebur* (gen. *eboris*), ivory < Egypt. *āb, ābu,* elephant, ivory] **1.** the hard, white substance, a form of dentine, that makes up the tusks of elephants, walruses, etc. **2.** *a)* dentine in any form *b)* any substance like ivory in appearance, use, etc. **3.** the color of ivory; creamy white **4.** a tusk of an elephant, walrus, etc. **5.** [*pl.*] things made of, resembling, or suggesting ivory; specif., [Slang] *a)* piano keys *b)* teeth *c)* dice *d)* billiard balls —*adj.* **1.** of, made of, or like ivory **2.** creamy-white

☆**i·vo·ry-billed woodpecker** (-bild′) a large blue-black woodpecker (*Campephilus principalis*) with a white bill: formerly of SE U.S., now virtually extinct

ivory black a fine black pigment made from burnt ivory

Ivory Coast 1. country in WC Africa, on the Gulf of Guinea, west of Ghana: a member of the Conseil de l'Entente: 124,500 sq. mi.; pop. 3,750,000; cap. Abidjan **2.** formerly, the African coast in this region

ivory nut *same as* VEGETABLE IVORY (sense 1)

ivory palm the palm tree that yields ivory nuts

☆**ivory tower** figuratively, a place of mental withdrawal from reality and action: used as a symbol of escapism

I·vy (ī′vē) [< ff.] a feminine name

i·vy (ī′vē) *n., pl.* **i·vies** [ME. *ivi* < OE. *ifig, ifegn,* akin to G. *efeu* (OHG. *ebawi, ebah*): orig. sense prob. "climber"] **1.** a climbing vine (*Hedera helix*) of the ginseng family, with a woody stem and evergreen leaves, grown as ornamentation on buildings, walls, etc. **2.** any of various similar climbing plants, as Boston ivy, ground ivy, poison ivy, etc. —*adj.* [*usually* I-] ☆of or characteristic of the Ivy League

☆**Ivy League** [many of the buildings are traditionally ivy-covered] a group of colleges in the NE U.S. forming a league for intercollegiate sports: often used to describe the fashions, standards, attitudes, etc. associated with their students —**Ivy Leaguer**

i·wis (i wis′) *adv.* [ME. < OE. *gewiss* (akin to G. *gewiss*), certain(ly) < *ge-* + *wiss,* certain: for IE. base see WISE¹] [Archaic] certainly; assuredly

I·wo (ē′wō) city in SW Nigeria: pop. 100,000

I·wo Ji·ma (ē′wō jē′mə, ē′wə) small island of the Volcano Islands in the W Pacific: captured from the Japanese by U.S. forces in World War II: c. 8 sq. mi.

I.W.W., IWW Industrial Workers of the World

ix·i·a (ik′sē ə) *n.* [ModL. < Gr. *ixos,* birdlime: from the viscid nature of some of the species] any of a genus (*Ixia*) of South African plants of the iris family, with grasslike leaves and funnel-shaped flowers

Ix·i·on (ik sī′ən) [L. < Gr. *Ixiōn*] *Gr. Myth.* a Thessalian king who was bound to a revolving wheel in Tartarus because he sought the love of Hera

Ix·ta·ci·huatl (ēs′tä sē′wät′l) volcanic mountain in C Mexico, southeast of Mexico City: 17,343 ft.: also sp. **Ix′tac·ci′huatl, Iz′tac·ci′huatl**

ix·tle (iks′tlē, is′-) *n. same as* ISTLE

I·yar (ē yär′, ē′yär) *n.* [Heb.] the eighth month of the Jewish year: see JEWISH CALENDAR

-i·za·tion (ə zā′shən, ī-) *a n.-forming compound suffix corresponding to* -IZE [realization]

-ize (īz) [ME. *-isen* < OFr. *-iser* < LL. *-izare* < Gr. *-izein*] *a v.-forming suffix meaning:* **1.** to cause to be or become; make conform with or resemble; make [democratize, Americanize] **2.** to become, become like, or change into [crystallize] **3.** to subject to, treat with, or combine with [oxidize, galvanize] **4.** to engage in; act in a specified way [soliloquize, theorize]

I·zhevsk (i zhefsk′) city in W European R.S.F.S.R.: pop. 360,000

Iz·mir (iz mir′) seaport in W Turkey, on the Aegean Sea: pop. 361,000; former name, SMYRNA

iz·zard (iz′ərd) *n.* [earlier *ezed, ezod,* var. of ZED] [Archaic or Dial.] the letter Z

J

J, j (jā) *n., pl.* **J's, j's 1.** the tenth letter of the English alphabet: formerly a variant of I, i, in the 17th cent. it became established as a consonant only, as in *Iulius,* originally spelled *Iulius* **2.** the usual sound of this letter in English, phonetically a voiced affricate (j) **3.** a type or impression for J or j **4.** a symbol *for* the tenth in a sequence or group —*adj.* **1.** of J or j **2.** tenth in a sequence or group

J (jā) *n.* **1.** an object shaped like J **2.** a unit vector in the direction of the y-axis **3.** *Physics* a symbol for joule —*adj.* shaped like J

j *Physics* the imaginary number √–1

J. 1. Journal **2.** Judge **3.** Justice

‡**ja** (yä) *adv.* [G.] yes

Ja. January

J.A. 1. Joint Account **2.** Judge Advocate

jab (jab) *vt., vi.* **jabbed, jab′bing** [var. of JOB²] **1.** to poke or thrust, as with a sharp instrument **2.** to punch with short, straight blows —*n.* a quick thrust, blow, or punch

Ja·bal·pur (jub′əl poor′) city in C India, in Madhya Pradesh: pop. 295,000

jab·ber (jab′ər) *vi., vt.* [LME. *jaberen:* prob. echoic] to speak or say quickly, incoherently, or nonsensically; chatter; gibber —*n.* fast, incoherent, nonsensical talk; gibberish —**jab′ber·er** *n.*

jab·ber·wock·y (-wäk′ē) *n.* [< *Jabberwocky,* nonsense poem by Lewis Carroll] meaningless syllables that seem to make sense; gibberish

jab·i·ru (jab′ə rōō′) *n.* [Port. < Tupi *jabirú*] **1.** *same as* WOOD IBIS **2.** either of two large, wading storks; specif., a genus (*Jabiru mycteria*) of tropical America or one (*Ephippiorhynchus senegalensis*) of Africa

jab·o·ran·di (jab′ə ran′dē) *n.* [Port. < Tupi] the dried leaflets of various S. American plants (genus *Pilocarpus*) of the rue family, that yield the alkaloid pilocarpine

ja·bot (zha bō′, ja-) *n.* [Fr., bird's crop, hence, jabot] a trimming or frill, as of lace, attached to the neck or front of a blouse, bodice, or shirt

☆**ja·cal** (hä käl′) *n., pl.* **-cal′es** (-kä′lās), **-cals′** [AmSp. < Nahuatl *xacalli,* contr. < *xamitl calli,* adobe house] a hut in Mexico and the Southwest, with walls of close-set wooden stakes plastered with mud and roofed with straw, rushes, etc.

jac·a·mar (jak′ə mär′) *n.* [Fr. < native (Tupi) name] any of several tropical forest birds (family Galbulidae) of South and Central America that feed on insects

ja·ca·na, ja·ca·na (zhä′sə nä′) *n.* [Port. < Tupi] any of several tropical and subtropical birds (family Jacanidae), with long toes that enable them to walk on the floating leaves of water plants, as the **Mexican jaçana** (*Jacana spinosa*)

jac·a·ran·da (jak′ə ran′də) *n.* [ModL. < Port. < native (Tupi) name in Brazil] any of a genus (*Jacaranda*) of tropical American trees of the bignonia family, with finely divided foliage and large clusters of lavender flowers, often grown in the S U.S.

j'ac·cuse (zhá küz′) [Fr., I accuse: phrase made famous by ZOLA in a public letter attacking irregularities in the trial of Dreyfus] any strong accusation or denunciation

ja·cinth (jā′sinth, jas′inth) *n.* [ME. *jacinte* < L. *hyacinthus:* see HYACINTH] **1.** *same as* HYACINTH (sense 1 *b*) **2.** a reddish-orange color

jack¹ (jak) [ME. *Jacke, Jake* < OFr. *Jaque, Jaques* < LL. (Ec.) *Jacobus, JACOB* [J-] a nickname for John, and, sometimes, for James or Jacob —*n., pl.* for **6, 7, 8, 9 jacks, jack:** see PLURAL, II, D, **1** [< nickname] **1.** [*often* J-] *a)* orig., a common fellow or boy assistant *b)* a man or boy; fellow *c)* a sailor; jack-tar ☆*d)* a lumberjack *e)* a jack-of-all-trades **2.** *same as a)* BOOTJACK *b)* SMOKE-JACK **3.** a fruit-flavored alcoholic liquor, as applejack **4.** any of various machines used to lift, hoist, or move something heavy a short distance [hydraulic *jack,* automobile *jack*] **5.** a wooden bar attached to each key of a harpsichord, etc. that raises the

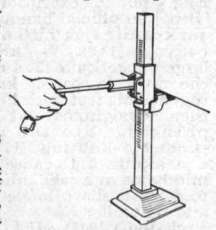

JACK (sense 4)

plectrum when the key is depressed **6.** a male donkey; jackass ☆**7.** *short for* JACK RABBIT **8.** any of various birds, as a jackdaw **9.** *a)* any of various fishes, as the crevalle, pickerel, pike, etc. *b)* a young or small pike ☆**10.** [Slang] money **11.** *Elec.* a plug-in receptacle used to make electric contact **12.** *Games* *a)* a playing card with a page boy's picture on it; knave *b)* a small ball used as the center mark in lawn bowling *c)* one of the small, six-pronged metal pieces or stones used in playing jacks: see JACKS ☆**13.** *Hunting* a torch or light used to attract fish or game at night **14.** *Naut. a)* a small flag flown on a ship's bow as a signal or to show nationality; union jack *b)* a horizontal metal bar at the top of the topgallant mast to help support the royal mast —*vt.* **1.** to raise by means of a jack ☆**2.** to hunt or fish for with a light —*adj.* male: of some animals —**every man jack** every man; everyone —**jack up** **1.** to raise by means of a jack ☆**2.** [Colloq.] to raise (prices, salaries, etc.) ☆**3.** [Colloq.] *a)* to reproach for misbehavior or neglect *b)* to encourage to perform one's duty

jack² (jak) *n.* [ME. *jakke* < OFr. *jaque* < Sp. *jaco* < Ar. *shakk*] **1.** a sleeveless coat, usually of leather, worn by a medieval foot soldier **2.** formerly, a drinking mug of leather; blackjack

jack- (jak) [see JACK¹] *a combining form meaning:* **1.** male [*jackass*] **2.** large or strong [*jackboot*] **3.** boy; fellow: used in hyphenated compounds [*jack-in-the-box*]

jack·al (jak'əl, -ôl) *n., pl.* **-als, -al:** see PLURAL, II, D, 1 [Turk. *chaqāl* < Per. *shagāl* < Sans. *śṛgālá*] **1.** any of several wild dogs (genus *Canis*) of Asia and N Africa, mostly yellowish-gray and smaller than the wolf: they often hunt prey in packs, generally at night, and also eat carrion and certain plants **2.** a person who does dishonest or humiliating tasks for another: from the notion that the jackal hunts game for the lion and eats the leavings **3.** a cheat or swindler

jack·a·napes (jak'ə nāps') *n.* [ME. *Jac Napes*, nickname of William de la Pole, Duke of Suffolk (1396–1450), whose badge was a clog and a chain like a tame ape's] **1.** formerly, a monkey **2.** a conceited, insolent, presumptuous fellow **3.** a pert, mischievous child

jack·ass (jak'as') *n.* [JACK- + ASS¹] **1.** a male donkey **2.** a stupid or foolish person; nitwit

☆**jack bean** a tropical leguminous plant (*Canavalia ensiformis*) often grown in S U.S. for forage and for its edible seeds

jack·boot (-boot') *n.* [JACK- + BOOT¹] a heavy, sturdy military boot that reaches above the knee

jack·daw (-dô') *n.* [JACK- + DAW¹] **1.** a European black bird (*Corvus monedula*) closely related to the crow, but smaller **2.** same as GRACKLE

jack·et (jak'it) *n.* [ME. *jaket* < OFr. *jaquette*, dim. of *jaque*: see JACK²] **1.** a short coat, usually with sleeves **2.** an outer coating or covering; specif., *a)* same as DUST JACKET ☆*b)* a cardboard holder for a phonograph record *c)* the metal covering of a bullet *d)* the insulating casing on a pipe or boiler *e)* the skin of a potato, etc. ☆*f)* a folder or envelope for holding letters or documents —*vt.* **1.** to put a jacket, or coat, on **2.** to cover with a casing, wrapper, etc.

jack·fish (jak'fish') *n., pl.* **-fish', -fish'es:** see FISH² [JACK- + FISH²] *a local name for* any of various fishes; esp., the northern pike

Jack Frost frost or cold weather personified

jack·fruit (-froot') *n.* [JACK- + FRUIT] **1.** an East Indian tree (*Artocarpus integrifolia*) of the mulberry family, like the breadfruit **2.** its large, heavy fruit, containing edible seeds **3.** its yellow, fine-grained wood

☆**jack·ham·mer** (-ham'ər) *n.* [JACK- + HAMMER] a portable type of pneumatic hammer, used for drilling rock, brick, etc.

jack-in-the-box (jak'in thə bäks') *n., pl.* **-box'es** a toy consisting of a box from which a grotesque little figure on a spring jumps up when the lid is lifted: also **jack'-in-a-box'**

☆**jack-in-the-pul·pit** (-pool'pit) *n., pl.* **-pits** an American plant (*Arisaema triphyllum*) of the arum family, with a flower spike partly arched over by a hoodlike covering

Jack Ketch (kech) [after a famous Eng. public executioner, ?–1686] [Brit.] an official hangman

☆**jack·knife** (jak'nīf') *n., pl.* **-knives'** (-nīvz') [JACK- + KNIFE] **1.** a large pocketknife **2.** a dive in which the diver keeps his knees unbent, touches his feet with his hands, and then straightens out just before plunging into the water —*vt.* **-knifed', -knif'ing** **1.** to cut with a jackknife **2.** to cause to jackknife —*vi.* **1.** to bend at the middle as in a jackknife dive **2.** to turn on the hitch so as to form a sharp angle with each other: said of a vehicle and its trailer

JACK-IN-THE-PULPIT

☆**jack·leg** (-leg') *adj.* [JACK¹ (*n.* 1 *e*) + (BLACK)LEG] **1.** *a)* not properly trained or qualified; incompetent *b)* same as MAKESHIFT **2.** unprofessional, unscrupulous, or dishonest —*n.* a jackleg person or thing

☆**jack·light** (-līt') *n.* [JACK- + LIGHT¹] same as JACK¹ (sense 13) —*vt.* same as JACK¹ (sense 13)

jack-of-all-trades (jak'əv ôl'trādz') *n., pl.* **jacks'-** [see

JACK-, 3] [*often* J-] a person who can do many kinds of work acceptably; handyman

jack-o'-lan·tern (jak'ə lan'tərn) *n., pl.* **-terns** **1.** a shifting, elusive light seen over marshes at night; will-o'-the-wisp **2.** a hollow pumpkin, real or artificial, cut to look like a face and used as a lantern

☆**jack pine** a pine (*Pinus banksiana*) of Canada and N U.S., having short needles in pairs and many woody cones

☆**jack·pot** (jak'pät') *n.* [JACK¹, *n.* 12 *a* + POT] **1.** cumulative stakes in a poker game, which can be played for only when some player has a pair of jacks or better with which to open **2.** any cumulative stakes, as in a bingo game, lottery, or slot machine **3.** [Colloq.] the highest stakes that can be won in any enterprise —**hit the jackpot** [Slang] **1.** to win the jackpot **2.** to attain the highest success

☆**jack rabbit** [JACK(ASS) + RABBIT: so named because of its long ears] any of several large hares (genus *Lepus*) of W N. America, with long ears and strong hind legs

jacks (jaks) *n.pl.* [< JACKSTONE] [*with sing. v.*] a children's game in which pebbles or small, six-pronged metal pieces are tossed and picked up in various ways, esp. while bouncing a small ball

jack·screw (jak'skroo') *n.* [JACK- + SCREW] a machine for raising heavy things a short distance, operated by turning a screw

☆**jack·smelt** (jak'smelt') *n.* [JACK¹ + SMELT¹] a common smeltlike silversides (*Atherinopsis californiensis*) of Pacific waters, differing from true smelt by having two dorsal fins

jack·snipe (-snīp') *n., pl.* **-snipes', -snipe':** see PLURAL, II, D, 1 [JACK- + SNIPE] **1.** a small snipe (*Limnocryptes minimus*) of the Old World **2.** any of several American sandpipers, as the pectoral sandpiper

Jack·son (jak's'n) [after Andrew JACKSON] **1.** capital of Miss., in the SW part, on the Pearl River: pop. 154,000 **2.** city in S Mich.: pop. 45,000 **3.** city in W Tenn.: pop. 40,000

Jack·son (jak's'n) **1.** Andrew, (nickname *Old Hickory*) 1767–1845; U.S. general; 7th president of the U.S. (1829–37) **2.** Robert H(oughwout), 1892–1954; U.S. jurist; associate justice, Supreme Court (1941–54) **3.** Thomas Jonathan, (nickname *Stonewall Jackson*) 1824–63; Confederate general in the Civil War

Jack·so·ni·an (jak sō'nē ən) *adj.* of or relating to Andrew Jackson or his policies —*n.* a follower of Jackson

Jack·son·ville (jak'sən vil') [after Andrew JACKSON] port in NE Fla., on the St. Johns River: pop. 529,000

jack·stay (jak'stā') *n.* [JACK- + STAY¹] **1.** a rope or staff along a ship's yard, to which the sail is fastened **2.** a rope or rod that runs up and down a ship's mast, on which the yard moves

jack·stone (-stōn') *n.* [for dial. *checkstone, chackstone* < *check, chuck,* pebble] **1.** same as JACK (*n.* 12 *c*) **2.** [*pl.*, with *sing. v.*] same as JACKS

jack·straw (-strô') **1.** [JACK¹ + STRAW] same as STRAW MAN **2.** [JACK- + STRAW] a narrow strip of wood, plastic, etc. used in a game (**jackstraws**) played by tossing a number of such strips into a jumbled heap and trying to remove them one at a time without moving any of the others

jack-tar (-tär') *n.* [JACK¹ + TAR²] [*often* J-] a sailor

jack towel same as ROLLER TOWEL

Ja·cob (jā'kəb) [LL.(Ec.) *Jacobus* < Gr. *Iakōbos* < Heb. *ja'aqob*, Jacob, lit., seizing by the heel (cf. Gen. 25:26)] **1.** a masculine name: dim. *Jake, Jack;* var. *James;* equiv. Fr. *Jacques,* It. *Giacomo* **2.** *Bible* a son of Isaac and father of the founders of the twelve tribes of Israel: also called *Israel:* Gen. 25–50

Jac·o·be·an (jak'ə bē'ən) *adj.* [< ModL. *Jacobaeus* < *Jacobus,* Latinized form of the name of James I (see JACK¹) + -AN] **1.** of James I of England **2.** of the period in England when he was king (1603–1625) —*n.* a poet, diplomat, etc. of this period

Ja·co·bi·an (jə kō'bē ən, yä-) *n.* [after Karl G. J. *Jakobi* (1804–51), G. mathematician] a determinant whose elements are the first, partial derivatives of a finite number of functions of the same number of variables, with the elements in each row being the derivatives of the same function with respect to each of the variables

Jac·o·bin (jak'ə bin) *n.* [ME. < MFr. *Jacobin* < ML. *Jacobinus* < LL.(Ec.) *Jacobus:* see JACK¹] **1.** a French Dominican friar: the Dominicans were established in a convent at the Church of St. Jacques in Paris **2.** any member of a society of radical democrats in France during the Revolution of 1789: their meetings were held in the Jacobin friars' convent **3.** an extreme political radical —*adj.* of the Jacobins or their policies: also **Jac'o·bin'ic, Jac'o·bin'i·cal** —**Jac'o·bin·ism** *n.*

Jac·o·bite (jak'ə bīt') *n.* [< LL.(Ec.) *Jacobus:* see JACK¹] a supporter of James II of England after his abdication, or of the claims of his son or his son's descendants to the throne —**Jac'o·bit'ic** (-bit'ik), **Jac'o·bit'i·cal** *adj.*

Jacob's ladder **1.** *Bible* the ladder from earth to heaven that Jacob saw in a dream: Gen. 28:12 **2.** a ladder made of rope, wire, etc., used on ships **3.** any of several plants (genus *Polemonium*) of the phlox family, with pinnately compound leaves and small, blue, bell-shaped flowers **4.** same as CARRION FLOWER (sense 1)

Ja·co·bus (jə kō'bəs) *n.* [see JACOBEAN] same as UNITE²

jac·o·net (jak'ə net') *n.* [Urdu *jagannāthī* < *Jagannāth* (now Puri), town in India, where it was manufactured]

1. a soft, white, lightweight cotton textile **2.** cotton cloth glazed on one side and dyed

Jac·quard (jə kärd′) *n.* [after the Fr. inventor, J. M. *Jacquard* (1752–1834)] **1.** *a)* a loom with an endless belt of cards punched with holes arranged to produce a figured weave: also **Jacquard loom** *b)* the distinctive mechanism of this loom **2.** *a)* the weave made: also **Jacquard weave** *b)* a fabric with such a weave

Jac·que·line (jak′wə lin, jak′ə-) [Fr., fem. of *Jacques:* see JACK¹] a feminine name: dim. *Jacky*

‡Jac·que·rie (zhȧk′rē′) [Fr. < *Jacques* *Bonhomme*, nobles' epithet for "peasant"] the French peasants' revolt of 1358 —*n.* [often **j-**] any peasants' revolt

Jacques-Car·tier (zhȧk kȧr tyā′; *E.* zhak′kär tyā′) city is S Quebec, on the St. Lawrence River, opposite Montreal: pop. 53,000

jac·ta·tion (jak tā′shən) *n.* [L. *jactatio*, a throwing, boasting < *jactare:* see JET¹] **1.** the act of bragging **2.** *Med.* same as JACTITATION

jac·ti·ta·tion (jak′ti tā′shən) *n.* [ML. *jactitatio* < L. *jactitare*, to utter, tell in public < *jactare*, to throw: see JET¹] **1.** the act of bragging **2.** *Law* a false boast or false statement that causes harm to another person, esp. to another's title to real estate **3.** *Med.* restless tossing or jerking of the body in severe illness

jade¹ (jād) *n.* [Fr. < Sp. < *piedra de ijada*, stone of the side: from the notion that it cured pains in the side] **1.** a hard stone, either jadeite or nephrite, usually green or white, used in jewelry and artistic carvings **2.** a green color of generally medium hue —*adj.* **1.** made of jade **2.** green like jade

jade² (jād) *n.* [ME. < ON. *jalda*, a mare < Finn.] **1.** a horse, esp. a worn-out, worthless one **2.** a loose or disreputable woman **3.** [Now Rare] a saucy, pert young woman —*vt., vi.* **jad′ed, jad′ing** to make or become tired, weary, or worn-out —**jad′ish** *adj.*

jad·ed (jā′did) *adj.* [pp. of prec., *v.*] **1.** tired; worn-out; wearied **2.** dulled or satiated, as from overindulgence — **jad′ed·ly** *adv.* —**jad′ed·ness** *n.*

jade·ite (jā′dīt) *n.* [JAD(E)¹ + -ITE¹] a hard, translucent, complex silicate of the pyroxene group: a variety of jade

jade plant a thick-leaved plant (*Crassula arborescens*) of the orpine family, native to S Africa and Asia

Ja·dot·ville (zhȧ dō vēl′) city in SE Congo (sense 2): pop. 78,000

jae·ger (yā′gər) *n.* **1.** same as JÄGER **2.** any of several sea birds (genus *Stercorarius*) which force other, weaker birds to leave or give up their prey

Ja·el (jā′əl) [Heb. *yā'el*, lit., mountain goat] *Bible* the woman who killed Sisera by hammering a tent peg through his head while he slept: Judg. 4:17–22

Jaf·fa (yäf′ə, jaf′ə) seaport in C Israel: since 1950, incorporated with Tel-Aviv: see TEL-AVIV-JAFFA

Jaff·na (jaf′nə) seaport in N Ceylon: pop. 94,000

jag¹ (jag) *n.* [ME. *jagge*, projecting point < ? dial. var. < OE. *sceacga:* cf. SHAG¹] **1.** a sharp, toothlike projection or similar indentation **2.** [Archaic] a notch or pointed tear, as in cloth —*vt.* **jagged, jag′ging** [ME. *jaggen, joggen* < the *n.*] **1.** to cut jags in; notch or pink (cloth, etc.) **2.** to cut unevenly; tear raggedly

jag² (jag) *n.* [< ?] **1.** [Dial.] a small load or amount, as of wood, hay, etc. **2.** [Slang] *a)* an intoxicated condition due to liquor or drugs *b)* a drunken celebration; spree *c)* a period of uncontrolled activity [crying *jag*]

JAG, J.A.G. Judge Advocate General

Jag·an·nath (jug′ə nät′, -nôt′) *n.* same as JUGGERNAUT (sense 1)

jä·ger (yā′gər) *n.* [G., huntsman < *jagen*, to hunt] **1.** a hunter **2.** [often **J-**] a rifleman in the old Austrian and German armies **3.** same as JAEGER

jag·ged (jag′id) *adj.* having sharp projecting points; notched or ragged —SYN. see ROUGH —**jag′ged·ly** *adv.* —**jag′ged·ness** *n.*

jag·ger·y (jag′ər ē) *n.* [Anglo-Ind. < Hind. *jāgri* < Sans. *śarkarā*, SUGAR] a dark, crude sugar from the sap of certain species (genera *Phoenix, Borassus*, etc.) of palm trees

jag·gy (jag′ē) *adj.* **-gi·er, -gi·est** jagged; notched

jag·uar (jag′wär, -yoo wär′) *n., pl.* **-uars, -uar:** see PLURAL, II, D, 1 [Port. < Tupi *jaguara*] a large cat (*Panthera onca*), yellowish with black spots, found from SW U.S. to Argentina: it is similar to the leopard, but larger

jag·ua·run·di (jag′wə run′di) *n.* [AmSp. & Port. < Tupi] a small wildcat (*Felis yagouaroundi*) of tropical and subtropical America, with a slender body, and a long tail: also sp. **jag′ua·ron′di**

Jah·veh, Jah·ve, Jah·weh, Jah·we (yä′ve) [see YAHWEH] same as JEHOVAH

jai a·lai (hī′ lī′, -ə lī′) [Sp. < Basque *jai*, celebration + *alai*, merry] a game like handball, popular in Latin America: it is played with a curved basket (*cesta*) fastened to the arm, for catching the ball and hurling it against the wall

jail (jāl) *n.* [ME. *jaile, gaile* < OFr. *jaole, gaole*, a cage, prison < LL. *caveola*, dim. of L. *cavea*, CAGE] **1.** a building for the confinement of people who are awaiting trial or

who have been convicted of minor offenses **2.** imprisonment —*vt.* to put or keep in or as in jail

jail·bird (-burd′) *n.* [Colloq.] **1.** a prisoner or former prisoner in a jail **2.** a person often put in jail; habitual lawbreaker

☆**jail·break** (-brāk′) *n.* the act of breaking out of jail by force

jail delivery ☆**1.** a liberation of prisoners from jail by force **2.** the act of clearing a jail by bringing the prisoners to trial

jail·er, jail·or (-ər) *n.* a person in charge of a jail or of prisoners

Jain (jīn) *n.* [Hindi *Jaina* < Sans. *jina*, saint < base *ji*, to conquer] a believer in Jainism —*adj.* of the Jains or their religion Also **Jai·na** (jī′nə), **Jain′ist**

Jain·ism (-iz′m) *n.* a Hindu religion resembling Buddhism, founded in the 6th cent. B.C.: it emphasizes asceticism and reverence for all living things

Jai·pur (jī′poor′) **1.** city in NW India; capital of Rajasthan state: pop. 403,000 **2.** former state of NW India: since 1950, included in Rajasthan state

Ja·kar·ta (jə kär′tə) capital of Indonesia, on the NW coast of Java: pop. c. 3,500,000

☆**jake** (jāk) *adj.* [prob. < *Jake*, abbrev. of JACOB: sense development unknown] [Slang] just right; satisfactory

jakes (jāks) *n.* [< *Jacques:* cf. JOHN] [Archaic or Dial.] an outdoor toilet; privy

jal·ap (jal′əp) *n.* [Fr. < Sp. *jalapa* < JALAPA, whence it is imported] **1.** the dried root of a Mexican vine (*Ipomoea purga*) of the morning-glory family, formerly used as a purgative **2.** a resin obtained from this root **3.** the plant bearing this root **4.** any of several other plants with similar roots

Ja·la·pa (hä lä′pä) city in E Mexico; capital of Veracruz state: pop. 66,000: official name **Jalapa En·ri·quez** (en rē′kes)

jal·a·pin (jal′ə pin) *n.* a glucoside, $C_{34}H_{62}O_{18}$, contained in jalap

Ja·lis·co (hä lēs′kô) state of W Mexico, on the Pacific: 31,258 sq. mi.; pop. 2,443,000; cap. Guadalajara

☆**ja·lop·y** (jə läp′ē) *n., pl.* **-lop′ies** [earlier *jaloupy* < ?] [Slang] an old, ramshackle automobile

jal·ou·sie (jal′ə sē′; *chiefly Brit.* zhal′oo zē′) *n.* [Fr. < OFr. *gelosie*, JEALOUSY] a window, shade, or door formed of adjustable, horizontal slats of wood, metal, or glass, for regulating the air or light coming through

jam¹ (jam) *vt.* **jammed, jam′ming** [< ?] **1.** to squeeze or wedge into or through a confined space **2.** *a)* to bruise or crush *b)* to force (a thumb, toe, etc.) back against its joint so as to cause impaction **3.** to push, shove, or crowd **4.** to pack full or tight **5.** to fill or block (a passageway, river, etc.) by crowding or squeezing in **6.** *a)* to wedge or make stick so that it cannot move or work *b)* to put out of order by such jamming [to *jam* a rifle] **7.** to make (radio broadcasts, radar signals, etc.) unintelligible, as by sending out others on the same wavelength —*vi.* **1.** *a)* to become wedged or stuck fast *b)* to become unworkable through such jamming of parts **2.** to push against one another in a confined space ☆**3.** [Slang] *Jazz* to improvise freely —*n.* **1.** a jamming or being jammed **2.** a group of persons or things so close together as to jam a passageway, etc. [a traffic *jam*] ☆**3.** [Colloq.] a difficult situation; predicament

JALOUSIES

jam² (jam) *n.* [< ? prec.] a food made by boiling fruit with sugar to a thick mixture: cf. PRESERVE, JELLY

Jam. Jamaica

Ja·mai·ca (jə mā′kə) country on an island in the West Indies, south of Cuba: a member of the Brit. Commonwealth: 4,411 sq. mi.; pop. 1,972,000; cap. Kingston — **Ja·mai′can** *adj., n.*

Jamaica rum a dark, full-bodied rum with a heavy aroma

jamb (jam) *n.* [ME. *jambe* < OFr., a leg, shank, pier, side post of a door < LL. *gamba*, a leg, hoof: see GAMB] **1.** a side post or piece of a framed opening, as for a door, window, or fireplace **2.** a pillar or core **3.** same as JAMBEAU: also **jambe**

☆**jam·ba·lay·a** (jum′bə lī′ə) *n.* [AmFr. (Louisiana) < ModPr. *jambalaia*] **1.** a Creole stew made of rice and shrimp, oysters, crabs, ham, chicken, etc., with spices and, often, vegetables **2.** any jumbled mixture

jam·beau (jam′bō) *n., pl.* **-beaux** (-bōz) [ME. < OFr. *jambe:* see prec.] a piece of medieval armor for the leg

☆**jam·bo·ree** (jam′bə rē′) *n.* [< ?] **1.** [Colloq.] *a)* a boisterous party or noisy revel *b)* a gathering or celebration, with planned entertainment **2.** a national or international assembly of boy scouts

James¹ (jāmz) [ME. < OFr. < LL.(Ec.) *Jacomus*, later form of *Jacobus:* see JACK¹] **1.** a masculine name: dim. *Jamie, Jim, Jimmy:* see JACOB **2.** *Bible a)* a Christian

apostle, Zebedee's son: also called **Saint James** (**the Greater**): his day is July 25 *b*) a Christian apostle, Alphaeus' son: also called **Saint James** (**the Less**): his day is May 1 *c*) a brother of Jesus; also, a book of the New Testament sometimes attributed to him **3. James I** 1566–1625; king of England (1603–25) & (as **James VI**) king of Scotland (1567–1625): son of MARY, QUEEN OF SCOTS **4. James II** 1633–1701; king of England & (as **James VII**) king of Scotland (1685–88): deposed: son of CHARLES I **5. Henry,** *a*) 1811–82; U.S. writer on religion & philosophy *b*) 1843–1916; U.S. novelist, in England: son of *prec.* **6. Jesse (Woodson),** 1847–82; U.S. outlaw **7. William,** 1842–1910; U.S. psychologist & philosopher: exponent of pragmatism: son of *Henry* (sense 5 *a*)

James² (jāmz) **1.** river in Va., flowing from the W part southeast into Chesapeake Bay: 340 mi. **2.** river in E N. Dak. & E S.Dak., flowing south into the Missouri: 710 mi.

James Bay arm of Hudson Bay, extending south into NE Ontario & NW Quebec: c. 275 mi. long

James Edward *see* James Francis Edward STUART

James·i·an (-ē ən) *adj.* of or characteristic of Henry James or of his brother William

James·town (jāmz′toun′) [after JAMES I] **1.** former village near the mouth of the James River, Va.: the 1st permanent Eng. colonial settlement in America (1607) **2.** city in SW N.Y.: pop. 40,000

Jam·mu (jum′ōō) **1.** city in SW Jammu and Kashmir, India: winter capital of the state: pop. 103,000 **2.** former kingdom in N India: merged with Kashmir, 1846

Jammu and Kashmir state of N India: its control is disputed by Pakistan, which occupies c. 31,000 sq. mi. in the NW part: 86,024 sq. mi.; pop. over 4,500,000 (3,601,000 in part controlled by India); caps. Srinagar & Jammu

☆**jam·packed** (jam′pakt′) *adj.* tightly packed; crammed

☆**jam session** an informal gathering of jazz musicians to play improvisations: now usually clipped to **session**

JAMMU & KASHMIR

Jam·shed·pur (jum′shed poor′) city in NE India, in Bihar state: pop. 292,000

Jam·shid, Jam·shyd (jam shēd′) [Per.] *Persian Myth.* the king of the peris: because he boasted that he was immortal, he had to live as a human being on earth

Jan. January

Ja·ná·ček (yä′nə chek′), **Le·oš** (le′ōsh) 1854–1928; Czech composer

Jane (jān) [Fr. *Jeanne* < ML. *Joanna:* see JOANNA] a feminine name: dim. *Janet, Jenny* —*n.* [j-] [Slang] ☆a girl or woman

Jane Doe *see* DOE

Janes·ville (jānz′vil) [after Henry F. *Janes,* early settler] city in S Wis.: pop. 46,000

Jan·et (jan′it) a feminine name: see JANE

Ja·net (zhà ne′), **Pierre (Marie Félix)** (pyer) 1859–1947; Fr. psychologist

jan·gle (jaŋ′g'l) *vi.* **-gled, -gling** [ME. *janglen* < OFr. *jangler,* to jangle, prattle, prob. < Frank. **jangelon,* to jeer] **1.** to make a harsh, inharmonious sound, as of a bell out of tune **2.** to quarrel or argue noisily —*vt.* **1.** to utter in a harsh, inharmonious manner **2.** to cause to make a harsh sound **3.** to irritate very much *[to jangle one's nerves]* —*n.* **1.** noisy or annoying talk **2.** noisy quarrel or arguing **3.** a harsh sound; discordant ringing —**jan′gler** *n.*

Jan·ice (jan′is) [< JANE, JANET] a feminine name

Ja·ni·na (yä′nē nä′) *Serbian name of* IOANNINA

jan·i·tor (jan′i tər) *n.* [L., doorkeeper < *janua,* door < *janus,* arched passageway: see JANUS] **1.** [Now Rare] a doorman or doorkeeper **2.** the custodian of a building, who maintains the heating system, does routine repairs, etc. —**jan′i·to′ri·al** (-ə tôr′ē əl) *adj.* —[Rare] **jan′i·tress** *n.fem.*

jan·i·zar·y (jan′ə zer′ē) *n., pl.* **-zar′ies** [Fr. *janissaire* < It. *giannizzero* < Turk. *yenicheri,* lit., new troops < *yeni,* new + *cheri,* soldiery] *[often* J-] **1.** a soldier (orig. a slave) in the Turkish sultan's guard, established in the 14th cent. and abolished in 1826 **2.** any Turkish soldier **3.** any very loyal or submissive follower or supporter Also **jan′is·sar′y** (-ser′ē)

Jan May·en (yän mī′ən) Norw. island in the Arctic Ocean, between Greenland & N Norway: site of a meteorological station: 145 sq. mi.

Jan·sen (jan′sən; *E.* jan′s'n), **Cor·ne·lis** (kôr nā′lis) (L. name *Jansenius*) 1585–1638; Du. R.C. theologian

Jan·sen·ism (jan′s'n iz'm) *n.* the rigorous doctrines of Cornelis Jansen, who believed in predestination, denied free will, and held that man, though depraved in nature, is unable to resist God's grace —**Jan′sen·ist** *n., adj.* —**Jan′sen·is′tic** *adj.*

Jan·u·ar·y (jan′yoo wer′ē) *n., pl.* **-ar′ies** [ME. *Januere* <

L. *Januarius* (*mensis*), (the month) of Janus, to whom it was sacred] the first month of the year, having 31 days: abbrev. **Jan., Ja.**

Ja·nus (jā′nəs) [L., lit., gate, arched passageway < IE. base *yă-,* var. of *ei-,* to go, whence YEAR] *Rom. Myth.* the god who was guardian of portals and patron of beginnings and endings: he is shown as having two faces, one in front, the other at the back of his head

Ja·nus-faced (-fāst′) *adj.* two-faced; deceiving

Jap. 1. Japan **2.** Japanese

Ja·pan (jə pan′) **1.** island country in the Pacific, off the E coast of Asia, including Hokkaido, Honshu, Kyushu, Shikoku, & many smaller islands: 142,726 sq. mi.; pop. 102,833,000; cap. Tokyo **2. Sea of,** arm of the Pacific, between Japan & E Asia: c. 405,000 sq. mi.

ja·pan (jə pan′) *n.* [orig. from Japan] **1.** a lacquer or varnish giving a hard, glossy finish **2.** a liquid mixture used as a paint drier **3.** objects decorated and lacquered in the Japanese style —*vt.* **-panned′, -pan′ning** to varnish or lacquer with or as with japan

☆**Japan clover** an annual plant (*Lespedeza striata*) of the legume family, grown for hay and forage in the SW U.S.

Japan Current warm ocean current flowing from the Philippine Sea east of Taiwan & northeast past Japan

Jap·a·nese (jap′ə nēz′) *adj.* of Japan, its people, language, culture, etc. —*n. 1. pl.* **-nese′** a native of Japan **2.** the language of Japan

Japanese an·drom·e·da (an dräm′ə də) [cf. ANDROMEDA] an evergreen plant (*Pieris japonica*) of the heath family, with drooping racemes of bell-shaped, white flowers

☆**Japanese beetle** a shiny, green-and-brown beetle (*Popillia japonica*), orig. from Japan, which eats leaves, fruits, and grasses, and is damaging to crops

Japanese iris any of several tall, beardless irises with showy flowers, esp. a species (*Iris kaempferi*) commonly cultivated in gardens

Japanese ivy *same as* BOSTON IVY

Japanese lantern *same as* CHINESE LANTERN

☆**Japanese oyster** a large, edible oyster (*Ostrea gigas*), native to Japan but introduced in the Puget Sound region

☆**Japanese persimmon 1.** an Asiatic persimmon (*Diospyros kaki*), bearing large, soft, edible, red or orange-colored fruit **2.** its fruit

☆**Japanese plum** a cultivated plum tree (*Prunus salicina*) with yellow or reddish fruits, native to China

Japanese quince 1. a spiny plant (*Chaenomeles lagenaria*) of the rose family, with pink or red flowers and hard, fragrant, greenish-yellow fruit **2.** the fruit

Japanese spurge a trailing evergreen plant (*Pachysandra terminalis*) of the box family, used as a ground cover

Jap·a·nesque (jap′ə nesk′) *adj.* of Japanese style

Japan wax a white, waxy fat obtained from the fruit of several Asiatic sumacs (esp. *Toxicodendron vernicifluum* and *Toxicodendron succedanea*) of the cashew family, used in lubricants, polishes, etc.

jape (jāp) *vi.* **japed, jap′ing** [ME. *japen*] **1.** to joke; jest **2.** to play tricks —*vt.* [Now Rare] **1.** to make fun of; mock **2.** to play tricks on; fool —*n.* **1.** a joke or jest **2.** a trick —**jap′er** *n.* —**jap′er·y** *n., pl.* **-er·ies**

Ja·pheth (jā′fith) [LL.(Ec.) < Gr.(Ec.) < Heb. *yepheth,* lit., enlargement: cf. Gen. 9:27] *Bible* the youngest of Noah's three sons: Gen. 5:32

Ja·phet·ic (jə fet′ik) *adj.* **1.** of or from Japheth **2.** *a former name for* INDO-EUROPEAN

ja·pon·i·ca (jə pän′i ka) *n.* [ModL., fem. of *Japonicus,* of Japan < *Japonia,* Japan < Fr. *Japon*] *a popular name for* JAPANESE QUINCE, CAMELLIA, etc.

Ja·pu·rá (zhä′poo rä′) river in S Colombia & NW Brazil, flowing southeast into the Amazon: c. 1,500 mi.

Ja·ques (jā′kwēz) [OFr.: see JACK¹] a cynically philosophical nobleman in Shakespeare's *As You Like It*

Jaques-Dal·croze (zhȧk dȧl krōz′), **É·mile** (ā mēl′) 1865–1951; Swiss composer: originated eurythmics

jar¹ (jär) *vi.* **jarred, jar′ring** [ult. echoic] **1.** to make a harsh sound or a discord; grate **2.** to have a harsh, irritating effect (*on one*) **3.** to shake or vibrate from a sudden impact **4.** to clash, disagree, or quarrel sharply —*vt.* **1.** to make vibrate or shake by sudden impact **2.** to cause to give a harsh or discordant sound **3.** to jolt or shock —*n.* **1.** a harsh, grating sound; discord **2.** a vibration due to a sudden impact **3.** a jolt or shock **4.** a sharp clash, disagreement, or quarrel

jar² (jär) *n.* [Fr. *jarre* < OPr. or Sp. *jarra* < Ar. *jarrah,* earthen water container] **1.** a container made of glass, stone, or earthenware, usually cylindrical, with a large opening and no spout: some jars have handles **2.** as much as a jar will hold: also **jar′ful** (-fool′)

jar³ (jär) *n.* [see AJAR¹] [Archaic] a turn: now only in the phrase **on the jar,** ajar; partly open

jar·di·niere (jär′d'n ir′; *Fr.* zhàr dē nyer′) *n.* [Fr. *jardinière,* a flower stand, orig. fem. of *jardinier,* gardener < *jardin,* GARDEN] **1.** an ornamental bowl, pot, or stand for flowers or plants **2.** a garnish for meats, of different kinds of vegetables cooked separately

Jar·ed (jar′id) [LL.(Ec.) < Gr.(Ec.) < Heb. *yeredh,* lit., descent: cf. Gen. 5:15] a masculine name

jar·gon¹ (jär′gən) *n.* [ME. < MFr., a chattering (of birds): ult. of echoic orig.] **1.** incoherent speech; gibberish **2.** a language or dialect unknown to one so that it seems

incomprehensible or outlandish **3.** a mixed or hybrid language or dialect; esp., pidgin **4.** the specialized vocabulary and idioms of those in the same work, profession, etc., as of sports writers or social workers: a somewhat derogatory term, often implying unintelligibility: see SLANG[1] **5.** speech or writing full of long, unfamiliar, or roundabout words or phrases —*vi. same as* JARGONIZE —*SYN.* see DIALECT —**jar′gon·is′tic** *adj.*

jar·gon² (jär′gän) *n.* [Fr. < It. *giargone* < Ar. *zarqūn* < Per. *zargūn*: see ZIRCON] a colorless or smoky variety of zircon: also **jar·goon′** (-gōōn′)

jar·gon·ize (jär′gə niz′) *vi.* -**ized′**, -**iz′ing** to talk or write in jargon —*vt.* to express in jargon

jarl (yärl) *n.* [ON., akin to OE. *eorl*: see EARL] a Scandinavian chieftain or nobleman in earlier times

jar·o·vize (yär′ə vīz′) *vt.* -**vized′**, -**viz′ing** [< Russ. *yar*′, spring grain + -IZE] *same as* VERNALIZE

Jar·vis (jär′vis) [older *Gervais* < Norm. var. of Fr. *Gervais* < LL. *Gervasius*, name of an early Christian saint and martyr] a masculine name

Jas. James

ja·sey (jā′zē) *n.* [altered < JERSEY] [Brit.] formerly, a wig, esp. one made of worsted

jas·mine, jas·min (jaz′min; *chiefly Brit.*, jas′-) *n.* [Fr. *jasmin* < Ar. *yās*(*a*)*mīn* < Per. *yāsamīn*] **1.** any of various tropical and subtropical plants (genus *Jasminum*) of the olive family, with fragrant flowers of yellow, red, or white, used in perfumes or for scenting tea **2.** any of several other similar plants with fragrant flowers, as YELLOW JASMINE **3.** pale yellow

Ja·son (jā′s′n) [L. *Iāson* < Gr. *Iāson*, lit., healer] **1.** a masculine name **2.** *Gr. Myth.* a prince who led the Argonauts, and, with Medea's help, got the Golden Fleece

Jas·per (jas′pər) [OFr. *Jaspar* < ?] a masculine name: equiv. Fr. *Gaspard*, G. *Kaspar*, Sp. *Gaspar*

jas·per (jas′pər) *n.* [ME. *jaspre* < MFr. < L. *iaspis* < Gr. *iaspis*, a green precious stone, prob. akin to Heb. *yāšpeh*] **1.** an opaque variety of colored, cryptocrystalline quartz, usually reddish, yellow, or brown **2.** *Bible* a precious stone, probably an opaque green quartz **3.** a kind of porcelain developed by Wedgwood, having a dull surface in green, blue, etc., with raised designs, usually in white

Jasper National Park Canadian national park in SW Alberta, in the E Rockies: 4,200 sq. mi.

Jas·pers (yäs′pərz), **Karl** 1883–1969; Ger. philosopher

jas·pil·ite (jas′pə līt′) *n.* [< Gr. *jaspis*, JASPER + -LITE] a rock consisting primarily of alternate bands of red jasper and black iron ore

jas·sid (jas′id) *n.* [< ModL. *Jassidae* < *Jassus*, name of the type genus < L. *Iassus*, ancient town on the coast of Caria + ModL. -*idae*, -IDAE] any of a large family (Jassidae) of leafhoppers that feed on plants

Jas·sy (yä′sē) *same as* IAŞI

Jat (jät, jŏt) *n.* [Hind.] a member of an Indian people of the Vale of Kashmir, the Punjab, and Rajputana

ja·to, JA·TO (jā′tō) *n.* [*j*(*et*)-*a*(*ssisted*) *t*(*ake*)*o*(*ff*)] an airplane takeoff assisted by a jet-producing unit or units, usually small, solid-propellant rockets

jaun·dice (jôn′dis, jän′-) *n.* [ME. *jaundis* < OFr. *jaunisse* < *jaune*, yellow < L. *galbinus*, greenish yellow < *galbus*, yellow, prob. via Celt. *galbos* < IE. base *ghel*-, YELLOW] **1.** *a*) a condition in which the eyeballs, the skin, and the urine become abnormally yellow as a result of bile pigments in the blood *b*) popularly, a disease causing this condition, as hepatitis **2.** a bitter or prejudiced state of mind, caused by jealousy, envy, etc. —*vt.* -**diced**, -**dic·ing** **1.** to cause to have jaundice **2.** to make bitter or prejudiced through jealousy, envy, etc.

jaunt (jônt, jänt) *vi.* [< ?] to take a short trip for pleasure —*n.* such a trip; excursion —*SYN.* see TRIP

jaunting car a light, topless, two-wheeled cart used in Ireland, with seats on both sides

jaun·ty (-ē) *adj.* -**ti·er**, -**ti·est** [earlier *janty*, *genty* < Fr. *gentil*, genteel] **1.** in fashion; stylish; chic **2.** having an easy confidence; gay and carefree; sprightly; perky —**jaun′ti·ly** *adv.* —**jaun′ti·ness** *n.*

Jau·rès (zhō res′), **Jean Lé·on** (zhän lā ōn′) 1859–1914; Fr. Socialist leader & journalist: assassinated

Jav. Javanese

Ja·va (jä′və, jav′ə) large island of Indonesia, southeast of Sumatra: 48,842 sq. mi.; pop. (with Madura) 63,000,000 —*n.* ☆**1.** any of a breed of chickens with black or mottled black plumage ☆**2.** a kind of coffee grown on Java and nearby islands ☆**3.** [*often* j-] [Slang] any coffee

Java man a type of primitive man (*Homo erectus erectus*) known from fossil remains found in Java

Jav·a·nese (jav′ə nēz′, -nēs′) *adj.* of Java, its people, their language, or culture —*n.* **1.** *pl.* -**nese**′ a native or inhabitant of Java; esp., a member of a group of tribes occupying the main part of Java **2.** the Indonesian language of these tribes

Java Sea part of the Pacific, between Java & Borneo: c. 600 mi. long

Java sparrow a white, pink, and gray finch (*Padda oryzivora*) of SE Asia, widely kept as a cage bird

jav·e·lin (jav′lin, jav′ə lin) *n.* [MFr. *javeline*, fem. dim. < *javelot*, a spear, prob. < Gaul. *gabalaccos* < IE. base *ghabh*(*o*)*lo*-, forked branch, fork, whence OE. *gafol*, G. *gabel*] **1.** a light spear for throwing **2.** *a*) a pointed wooden or metal shaft, about 8 1/2 ft. long, thrown for distance as a test of strength and skill *b*) the throwing of the javelin as a field event in track and field meets: in full, **javelin throw**

☆**jav·e·li·na** (hä′və lē′nə) *n.* [Sp. *jabalina*, wild sow, fem. of *jabalí*, boar < Ar. (*hinzir*) *g'abali*, lit., mountain (pig) < *g'abal*, mountain] *same as* PECCARY

Ja·velle (or **Ja·vel**) **water** (zhə vel′) [after *Javel*, former Fr. village (now part of Paris), where it was made] a solution of sodium hypochlorite, NaOCl, in water, used as a bleaching agent or disinfectant

jaw (jô) *n.* [ME. *jowe* < ? OFr. *joue*, cheek] **1.** either of the two bones or bony parts that hold the teeth and frame the mouth in most vertebrates: the **lower jaw** (mandible) is usually hinged and movable, the **upper jaw** (maxilla) is usually not; often, specif., the lower jaw **2.** any of various analogous biting structures of invertebrates **3.** [*pl.*] the mouth **4.** either of two mechanical parts that open and close to grip or crush something, as in a monkey wrench or vise **5.** [*pl.*] the narrow entrance of (a canyon, valley, strait, etc.) **6.** [*pl.*] something grasping or imminent [the *jaws* of death] **7.** [Slang] talk; esp., abusive or boring talk —*vi.* [Slang] to talk, esp. in a boring or abusive way —*vt.* [Slang] to scold or reprove, esp. repeatedly

jaw·bone (-bōn′) *n.* a bone of a jaw, esp. of the lower jaw —☆*vt.*, *vi.* -**boned′**, -**bon′ing** to attempt to persuade by using one's high office or position to apply pressure, as the President might in proposing price and wage controls to business and labor

jaw·break·er (-brā′kər) *n.* **1.** a machine with jaws for crushing rocks, ore, etc. ☆**2.** a hard, usually round candy **3.** [Slang] a word that is hard to pronounce

Jax·ar·tes (jak sär′tēz) *ancient name of* SYR DARYA

jay (jā) *n.* [ME. < OFr. *gai* < LL. *gaius*, a jay, prob. echoic, but sp. infl. by the L. proper name *Gaius*] **1.** any of several birds of the crow family, usually strikingly colored, as the **European jay** (*Garrulus glandarius*) **2.** *same as* BLUE JAY **3.** [Colloq.] a foolish or talkative person

Jay (jā), **John** 1745–1829; Am. statesman & jurist: 1st chief justice of the U.S. (1789–95)

jay·bird (jā′burd′) *n. dial. var. of* JAY

☆**Jay·cee** (jā′sē′) *n.* [< *j*(*unior*) *c*(*hamber*)] any member of a junior chamber of commerce

☆**jay·hawk·er** (jā′hô′kər) *n.* [< ?] **1.** [Slang] an abolitionist guerrilla of Missouri and Kansas in Civil War days **2.** a robber, raider, or plunderer **3.** [J-] [Colloq.] *a nickname for* a Kansan: also **Jay′hawk′**

☆**jay·walk** (jā′wôk′) *vi.* [JAY, 3 + WALK] [Colloq.] to walk in or across a street carelessly without obeying traffic rules and signals, esp. at other than proper crossing places —**jay′walk′er** *n.* —**jay′walk′ing** *n.*

☆**jazz** (jaz) *n.* [etym. unc.: < ? Creole patois *jass*, sexual term applied to the Congo dances (New Orleans)] **1.** a kind of music, originally improvised but now also arranged, characterized by syncopation, rubato, usually heavily accented rhythms, dissonances, individualized melodic variations, and unusual tonal effects on the saxophone, clarinet, trumpet, trombone, etc.: it originated among New Orleans, esp. Negro, musicians: see also SWING, BOP² **2.** loosely, any popular dance music **3.** [Slang] a quality reminiscent of jazz music; lively spirit **4.** [Slang] remarks, acts, concepts, etc. regarded as hypocritical, tiresome, trite, pretentious, etc. —*adj.* of, in, like, or having to do with jazz —*vt.* **1.** to play or arrange as jazz **2.** to speed up **3.** [Slang] to fill with jazz qualities; make exciting or elaborate; enliven or embellish (usually with *up*) —*vi.* [Slang] to move or behave in a lively or carefree way

☆**jazz·man** (jaz′man′) *n.*, *pl.* -**men**′ a jazz musician

☆**jazz·y** (-ē) *adj.* **jazz′i·er**, **jazz′i·est** **1.** characterized by the qualities of jazz music **2.** [Slang] lively, gay, showy, etc. —**jazz′i·ly** *adv.* —**jazz′i·ness** *n.*

J.C. **1.** Jesus Christ **2.** Julius Caesar **3.** jurisconsult

J.C.D. **1.** [L. *Juris Canonici Doctor*] Doctor of Canon Law **2.** [L. *Juris Civilis Doctor*] Doctor of Civil Law

jct. junction

JD juvenile delinquency (or delinquent)

J.D. [L. *Jurum Doctor*] Doctor of Laws

Je. June

jeal·ous (jel′əs) *adj.* [ME. *jelous* < OFr. *gelos* < ML. *zelosus*: see ZEAL] **1.** very watchful or careful in guarding or keeping [*jealous* of one's rights] **2.** *a*) resentfully suspicious of a rival or a rival's influence [a husband *jealous* of other men] *b*) resentfully envious *c*) resulting from such feelings [a *jealous* rage] **3.** [Now Rare] requiring exclusive loyalty [the Lord is a *jealous* God] —**jeal′ous·ly** *adv.* —**jeal′ous·ness** *n.*

jeal·ous·y (-ē) *n.*, *pl.* -**ous·ies** [ME. *jalousie* < OFr. *gelosie* < *gelos*: see prec.] **1.** the quality or condition of being jealous **2.** an instance of this; jealous feeling

Jean (jēn) **1.** a masculine name: see JOHN **2.** a feminine name: see JOANNA

jean (jēn) *n.* [< ME. *Gene* (*fustian*), (fustian) of Genoa < OFr. *Janne* < ML. *Janua* < L. *Genua*, Genoa] **1.** a durable cotton cloth in a twill weave, used for work clothes and casual wear **2.** [*pl.*] trousers of this material, often blue, or of denim, flannel, etc.

Jeanne (jēn) a feminine name: dim. *Jeannette:* see JOANNA

Jeanne d'Arc (zhän därk) *see* JOAN OF ARC

Jean·nette (jə net′) a feminine name: dim. *Nettie, Netty:* see JEANNE

Jeans (jēnz), Sir **James** (**Hopwood**) 1877–1946; Eng. mathematician, physicist, astronomer, & writer

je·bel (jeb′'l) *n.* [Ar. *jebel*] a hill or mountain: often used in Arabic place names

Jebel Druze (drōōz′) region in S Syria, inhabited by the Druzes: 2,584 sq. mi.: also **Jebel ed Druz** (ed)

Jebel Mu·sa (mōō′sə) mountain in N Morocco, opposite Gibraltar: c. 2,700 ft.: cf. PILLARS OF HERCULES

jee (jē) *interj., n., vt., vi. same as* GEE[1]

☆**jeep** (jēp) *n.* [orig. military slang, after a creature (Eugene the Jeep) with extraordinary powers, in comic strip by E. C. Segar (1894–1938): later associated with *G.P.*, abbrev. for General Purpose Car] a small, rugged automotive vehicle with a 1/4-ton capacity and a four-wheel drive, used by U.S. armed forces in World War II —[J-] *a trademark for* a similar vehicle for civilian use

☆**jee·pers** (jē′pərz) *interj.* [euphemistic alteration of *Jesus*] a mild exclamation of surprise, emphasis, etc.

jeer (jir) *vi., vt.* [? altered < CHEER] to make fun of (a person or thing) in a rude, sarcastic manner; mock; taunt; scoff (at) —*n.* a jeering cry or remark; sarcastic or derisive comment; gibe —SYN. see SCOFF —**jeer′er** *n.* —**jeer′ing·ly** *adv.*

jeers (jirz) *n.pl.* [? altered < *gears:* see GEAR] *Naut.* the tackle by which the lower yards are hoisted or lowered

Jef·fers (jef′ərz), (**John**) **Robinson** 1887–1962; U.S. poet

Jef·fer·son (jef′ər s'n) **1.** Joseph, 1829–1905; U.S. actor **2.** Thomas, 1743–1826; Am. statesman; 3d president of the U.S. (1801–09): drew up the Declaration of Independence

Jefferson City [after T. JEFFERSON] capital of Mo., on the Missouri River: pop. 32,000

☆**Jef·fer·so·ni·an** (jef′ər sō′nē ən) *adj.* **1.** of or characteristic of Thomas Jefferson **2.** of or like his ideas and principles; democratic —*n.* a follower of Thomas Jefferson —**Jef′fer·so′ni·an·ism** (-iz′m) *n.*

Jeff·rey (jef′rē) a masculine name: dim. *Jeff:* see GEOFFREY

☆**Jeffrey pine** [after John *Jeffrey*, Scot. botanist (19th c.) who identified it] a pine (*Pinus jeffreyi*) native to Oregon and California, resembling the ponderosa pine and having similar wood

je·had (ji häd′) *n. same as* JIHAD

Je·hol (jə hōl′, ru hō′) former province of NE China: divided (1955) between Hopei & Liaoning provinces & Inner Mongolia

Je·hosh·a·phat (ji häs′ə fat′, -häsh′-) [Heb. *yehōshāphāt*, lit., God has judged] *Bible* a king of Judah in the 9th cent. B.C.: II Chr. 17 ff.

Je·ho·vah (ji hō′və) [modern transliteration of the Tetragrammaton YHWH; the vowels appear through arbitrary transference of the vowel points of *adōnāi*, my Lord: see YAHWEH] God; (the) Lord

Jehovah's Witnesses [name adopted after Isa. 43:10, "Ye are my witnesses"] a proselytizing Christian sect founded by Charles T. Russell (1852–1916)

Je·ho·vist (ji hō′vist) *n. same as* YAHWIST

Je·hu (jē′hōō, -hyōō) [Heb.] *Bible* a king of Israel in the 9th cent. B.C., described as a furious charioteer: II Kings 9 —*n.* [j-] [Colloq.] **1.** a driver of a cab or coach **2.** a fast, reckless driver

je·june (ji jōōn′) *adj.* [L. *jejunus*, empty, dry, barren] **1.** not nourishing; barren **2.** not interesting or satisfying; dull or empty **3.** [? by confusion with JUVENILE] not mature; childish —**je·june′ly** *adv.* —**je·june′ness** *n.*

je·ju·nec·to·my (ji′jōō nek′tə mē) *n., pl.* **-mies** [JEJUN(UM) + -ECTOMY] the surgical removal of all or part of the jejunum

je·ju·nos·to·my (-näs′tə mē) *n., pl.* **-mies** [JEJUN(UM) + -O- + -STOMY] the surgical operation of making an artificial opening into the jejunum

je·ju·num (ji jōō′nəm) *n., pl.* **-na** (-nə) [ML. < neut. of L. *jejunus*, empty: it was formerly thought to be empty after death] the middle part of the small intestine, between the duodenum and the ileum —**je·ju′nal** *adj.*

Je·kyll (jē′k'l, jek′'l), Dr. a kind, good doctor in R. L. Stevenson's story *The Strange Case of Dr. Jekyll and Mr. Hyde*, who discovers drugs that enable him to transform himself into a vicious, brutal creature named Mr. Hyde and back again

☆**jell** (jel) *vi., vt.* [back-formation < JELLY] **1.** to become or cause to become jelly **2.** [Colloq.] to take or cause to take definite form; crystallize [plans that haven't *jelled* yet] —*n.* [Dial.] *same as* JELLY

jel·la·ba (je lä′bä) *n. same as* DJELLABA

Jel·li·coe (jel′i kō′), **John Rush·worth** (rush′wurth′), 1st Earl Jellicoe, 1859–1935; Eng. admiral

jel·li·fy (jel′ə fī′) *vt., vi.* **-fied′, -fy′ing** to change into jelly —**jel′li·fi·ca′tion** *n.*

☆**Jell-O** (jel′ō) *a trademark for* a flavored gelatin eaten as a

dessert or used in molded salads —**jell′o** *n.* such a gelatin

jel·ly (jel′ē) *n., pl.* **-lies** [ME. *gely* < OFr. *gelee*, a frost, jelly < fem. pp. of *geler* < L. *gelare*, to freeze: see GELATIN] **1.** a soft, resilient, partially transparent, semisolid, gelatinous food resulting from the cooling of fruit juice boiled with sugar, or of meat juice cooked down **2.** any substance like this; gelatinous substance —*vt.* **-lied, -ly·ing 1.** to make into jelly **2.** to coat, fill, or serve with jelly —*vi.* to become jelly —**jel′ly·like′** *adj.*

☆**jel·ly·bean** (-bēn′) *n.* a small, bean-shaped, gelatinous candy with a colored sugar coating

jel·ly·fish (-fish′) *n., pl.* **-fish′, -fish′es:** see FISH[2] **1.** any of a number of related free-swimming, mostly marine coelenterates, with a body made up largely of jellylike substance and shaped like an umbrella: it has long, hanging tentacles with stinging cells on them **2.** [Colloq.] a weak-willed person

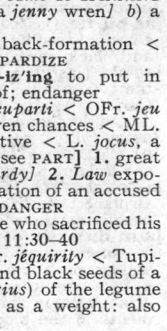

JELLYFISH
(16 in. long)

jel·ly·roll (-rōl′) *n.* a thin sheet of sponge cake spread with jelly and rolled so as to form layers

Je·mi·ma (jə mī′mə) [Heb. *yemīmāh*, lit., a dove] a feminine name

jem·my (jem′ē) *n., pl.* **-mies** [< dim. of JAMES] [Brit.] **1.** *same as* JIMMY **2.** a sheep's head used as food

Je·na (yā′nä) city in SW East Germany: site of a battle (1806) in which the Prussian forces were routed by Napoleon: pop. 81,000

‡**je ne sais quoi** (zhə nə sā kwä′) [Fr., lit., I know not what] something elusive, or hard to describe or express

Jen·ghiz Khan (jen′gis) *same as* GENGHIS KHAN

Jen·ner (jen′ər) **1.** Edward, 1749–1823; Eng. physician: introduced vaccination **2.** Sir William, 1815–98; Eng. physician

jen·net (jen′it) *n.* [ME. *genett* < MFr. *genette* < Sp. *jinete*, horseman, mounted soldier < Ar. *Zenāta*, a tribe of Barbary] **1.** any of a breed of small Spanish horses **2.** a female donkey

Jen·ni·fer (jen′i fər) [altered < GUINEVERE] a feminine name

Jen·ny (jen′ē) a feminine name: see JANE

jen·ny (jen′ē) *n., pl.* **-nies** [< prec.] **1.** *same as* SPINNING JENNY **2.** a) the female of some birds [a *jenny* wren] b) a female donkey

jeop·ard (jep′ərd) *vt.* [ME. *jeoparden*, back-formation < *jeoparti*, JEOPARDY] *now rare var. of* JEOPARDIZE

jeop·ard·ize (jep′ər dīz′) *vt.* **-ized′, -iz′ing** to put in jeopardy; risk loss, damage, or failure of; endanger

jeop·ard·y (-dē) *n., pl.* **-ard·ies** [ME. *jeuparti*, lit., a divided game, game with even chances < ML. *jocus partitus*, an even chance, alternative < L. *jocus*, a game, JOKE + pp. of *partire*, to divide: see PART] **1.** great danger; peril [to have one's life in *jeopardy*] **2.** *Law* exposure to conviction and punishment; situation of an accused person on trial for a crime —SYN. see DANGER

Jeph·thah (jef′thə) [Heb.] *Bible* a judge who sacrificed his daughter in fulfillment of a vow: Judg. 11:30–40

je·quir·i·ty (ji kwir′ə tē) *n., pl.* **-ties** [Fr. *jéquirity* < Tupi-Guarani] **1.** any of the poisonous, red and black seeds of a tropical, climbing plant (*Abrus precatorius*) of the legume family, used for beads and, formerly, as a weight: also **jequirity bean** **2.** the plant it grows on

Jer. Jeremiah

jer·bo·a (jər bō′ə) *n.* [Ar. *yarbū'*] any of various small, nocturnal, leaping rodents (family Dipodidae) of N Africa and Asia, with very long hind legs

JERBOA
(4 1/2–16 in. long, including tail)

jer·e·mi·ad (jer′ə mī′ad, -ad) *n.* [Fr. *jérémiade* < *Jérémie*, Jeremiah: see ff.] a lamentation or tale of woe: in allusion to the *Lamentations of Jeremiah*

Jer·e·mi·ah (-ə) [LL.(Ec.) *Jeremias* < Gr.(Ec.) *Hieremias* < Heb. *yirmeyāh*, lit., the Lord loosens (i.e., from the womb)] a masculine name: dim. *Jerry;* var. *Jeremy* **2.** *Bible* a) a Hebrew prophet of the 7th and 6th cent. B.C. b) the book containing his prophecies —*n.* a person pessimistic about the future

Jer·e·mi·as (-əs) *Douay Bible name for* JEREMIAH

Jer·e·my (jer′ə mē) a masculine name: see JEREMIAH

Je·rez de la Fron·te·ra (he reth′ the lä fron te′rä) city in SW Spain, near Cádiz: noted for the sherry made there: pop. 140,000: also **Jerez**

Jer·i·cho (jer′ə kō′) city in W Jordan, just north of the Dead Sea: pop. 42,000: site of an ancient Canaanite city whose walls, according to the Bible, were miraculously destroyed when trumpets were sounded: Josh. 6

jerk[1] (jurk) *vt.* [var. of archaic *yerk* < ?] **1.** to pull, twist, push, thrust, or throw with a sudden, sharp movement ☆**2.** [Colloq.] to make and serve (ice cream sodas) —*vi.* **1.** to move with a jerk or in jerks **2.** to twitch —*n.* **1.** a sharp, abrupt movement; quick pull, twist, push, etc. **2.** a sudden

muscular contraction caused by a reflex action ☆**3.** [Slang] a person regarded as stupid, dull, foolish, etc. —**jerk out** to utter sharply and abruptly

jerk² (jurk) *vt.* [altered (after prec.) < JERKY²] to preserve (meat) by slicing it into strips and drying these in the sun —*n.* same as JERKY²

jer·kin (jur′kin) *n.* [< ?] a short, closefitting jacket, often sleeveless, or a vest, of a kind worn in the 16th and 17th cent.

☆**jerk·wa·ter** (jurk′wôt′ər, -wät′-) *n.* [JERK¹ + WATER] a train on an early branch railroad —*adj.* [Colloq.] small, unimportant, etc. [a *jerkwater* town]

jerk·y¹ (-ē) *adj.* **jerk′i·er, jerk′i·est 1.** characterized or moving by jerks; making sudden starts and stops or spasmodic movements ☆**2.** [Slang] stupid, dull, foolish, etc. —**jerk′i·ly** *adv.* —**jerk′i·ness** *n.*

☆**jer·ky²** (jur′kē) *n.* [< Sp. *charqui* < Quechua] meat, esp. beef, that has been preserved by being sliced into strips and dried in the sun

Jer·o·bo·am (jer′ə bō′əm) [Heb. *yārobh'ām*, lit., prob., the people increases] *Bible* first king of Israel (sense 4): I Kings 11:26–14:20 —*n.* [*often* j-] a large wine bottle, esp. for champagne, usually one holding about .8 gal.

Je·rome (jə rōm′; *chiefly Brit.*, jer′əm) [Fr. *Jérôme* < L. *Hieronymus* < Gr. *Hierōnymos* < *hieros,* holy + *onyma,* NAME] **1.** a masculine name: dim. *Jerry* **2.** Saint, (born *Eusebius Hieronymus Sophronius*) 340?–420 A.D.; monk & church scholar, born in Pannonia: author of the Vulgate: his day is Sept. 30

jer·ry-built (jer′ē bilt′) *adj.* [originated in England, c. 1860, prob. < name *Jerry,* reinforced by JURY²] built poorly, of cheap materials

jer·ry·can (jer′ē kan′) *n.* [< *jerry,* short for JEROBOAM + CAN³] a large, flat can for holding liquids, esp. gasoline: also sp. **jerry can, jerrican**

Jer·sey (jur′zē) Brit. island in the English Channel; largest of the Channel Islands: 45 sq. mi.; pop. 57,000 —*n., pl.* **-seys** any of a breed of small, reddish-brown dairy cattle, originally from Jersey: its milk has a high butterfat content

jer·sey (jur′zē) *n., pl.* **-seys** [< prec.: orig. used of worsted garments made in Jersey of locally produced wool] **1.** a soft, elastic, knitted cloth of wool, cotton, rayon, etc. **2.** a closefitting pullover sweater or shirt worn by athletes, sailors, etc. **3.** any closefitting, knitted upper garment

Jersey City city in NE N.J., across the Hudson from New York City: pop. 261,000 (met. area 609,000)

Je·ru·sa·lem (jə rōō′sə ləm) capital of Israel (sense 5) in the C part: divided (1948–67) between Israel & Jordan: pop. c. 250,000

Jerusalem artichoke [altered, after prec., by folk etym. < GIRASOL] **1.** a tall N. American sunflower (*Helianthus tuberosus*) of the composite family, with potatolike tubers used as a vegetable **2.** such a tuber

☆**Jerusalem cherry** either of two bushy plants (*Solanum pseudo-capsicum* or *Solanum capsicastrum*) of the nightshade family, with small, star-shaped, white flowers and orange to red berries, grown widely as ornamentals

☆**Jerusalem cricket** any of several burrowing, wingless, long-horned grasshoppers (family Stenopelmatidae) common in dry regions of W U.S.

Jerusalem oak an aromatic Eurasian goosefoot (*Chenopodium botrys*) occurring as a weed in N U.S. and Canada

Jerusalem thorn 1. a tropical American tree (*Parkinsonia aculeata*) of the legume family, with compound leaves and yellow, fragrant flowers: used for hedges **2.** same as CHRIST'S-THORN

Jer·vis (jur′vis; *Brit.* jär′-) a masculine name: see JARVIS

Jervis Bay (jär′vis) inlet of the Pacific, on the SE coast of New South Wales, Australia: peninsula on its S shore is a detached part of Australian Capital Territory

Jes·per·sen (yes′pər sən) (Jens) Otto (Harry) 1860–1943; Dan. linguist, notably of English

jess (jes) *n.* [ME. *ges* < OFr. *gies, gets,* pl. (see JET¹): from its use in letting a hawk fly] a strap for fastening around a falcon's leg, with a ring at one end for attaching a leash: also sp. **jesse** —*vt.* to fasten jesses on

Jes·sa·mine (jes′ə min) [< MFr. *jessemin,* JASMINE] a feminine name —*n.* [j-] **1.** same as JASMINE **2.** same as YELLOW JASMINE

Jes·se (jes′ē) [Heb. *yīshai*] **1.** a masculine name: dim. *Jess* **2.** *Bible* the father of David: I Sam. 16

Jes·sel·ton (jes′l tən) seaport in N Borneo; capital of Sabah, Malaysia: pop. 21,000

Jes·si·ca (jes′i kə) a feminine name

Jes·sie (jes′ē) a feminine name: var. of *prec.*

jest (jest) *n.* [ME. *geste* < OFr., an exploit, tale of exploits < L. *gesta,* neut. pl. pp. of *gerere,* to perform, carry out] **1.** a mocking or bantering remark; jibe; taunt **2.** a joke; witticism **3.** a gay, lighthearted action or mood; fun; joking **4.** something to be laughed at or joked about **5.** [Obs.] a notable deed —*vi.* **1.** to jeer; mock **2.** to be playful in speech and actions; joke —SYN. see JOKE

jest·er (-ər) *n.* a person who jests; esp., a professional fool employed by a medieval ruler to amuse him

Je·su (jē′zōō, -sōō; jā′-, yā′-) *archaic var. of* JESUS

Jes·u·it (jezh′ōō wit, jez′-; -yoo-) *n.* [ModL. *Jesuita* < LL.(Ec.) *Iesus,* Jesus + -*ita,* -ITE¹] **1.** a member of the Society of Jesus, a Roman Catholic religious order for men founded by Ignatius Loyola in 1534 **2.** [j-] a crafty schemer; cunning dissembler; casuist: hostile and offensive term, as used by anti-Jesuits —**Jes′u·it′ic, Jes′u·it′i·cal** *adj.* —**Jes′u·it′i·cal·ly** *adv.*

Jes·u·it·ism (-iz′m) *n.* **1.** the teachings or practice of the Jesuits **2.** [j-] craftiness; duplicity; intrigue: hostile and offensive term, as used by anti-Jesuits Also **Jes′u·it·ry** (-rē)

Jes·u·it·ize (-īz′) *vt.* **-ized′, -iz′ing** to make Jesuitic

Je·sus (jē′zəs, -zaz) [LL.(Ec.) *Iesus* < Gr.(Ec.) *Iēsous* < Heb. *yēshū'a,* contr. of *yehōshū'a* (JOSHUA), help of Jehovah < *yāh,* Jehovah + *hōshīa,* to help] **1.** a masculine name **2.** c. 8–4 B.C.–29? A.D. (see CHRISTIAN ERA); founder of the Christian religion: also called **Jesus Christ, Jesus of Nazareth:** see also CHRIST **3.** the author of *Ecclesiasticus,* a book of the Apocrypha

jet¹ (jet) *vt., vi.* **jet′ted, jet′ting** [< MFr. *jeter,* to throw < OFr. *jeter* < VL. *jectare,* for L. *jactare,* freq. of *jacere,* to throw < IE. base *yē-,* to throw, do, whence Gr. *hienai,* to set in motion, throw, send] **1.** to spout, gush, or shoot out in a stream, as liquid or gas **2.** to travel or convey by jet airplane —*n.* [ME. < OFr. *get, giet,* a throw, spurt < L. *jactus,* a throw, cast] **1.** a stream of liquid or gas emitted or forced out, as from a spout **2.** a spout or nozzle for emitting a stream of water or gas **3.** a jet-propelled airplane: in full, **jet (air)plane** —*adj.* **1.** jet-propelled **2.** of or having to do with jet propulsion or jet-propelled aircraft [the *jet* age]

jet² (jet) *n.* [ME. *get* < OFr. *jaiet* < L. *gagates* < Gr. *gagatēs,* lit. < *Gagas,* town and river of Lycia in Asia Minor] **1.** a hard, black variety of lignite, which takes a high polish: sometimes used in jewelry **2.** a deep, lustrous black —*adj.* **1.** made of jet **2.** black like jet

jet-bead (-bēd′) *n.* a cultivated Japanese shrub (*Rhodotypos tetrapetala*) of the rose family, having white, four-petaled flowers and four shiny, black, beadlike fruits

jet-black (-blak′) *adj.* glossy black, like jet

je·té (zhə tā′) *n.* [Fr., pp. of *jeter,* to throw] *Ballet* a leap from one foot to the other, made with a kicking movement of the leg

jet engine an engine for aircraft, ships, etc., operating on the principle of jet propulsion

jet lag a disruption of circadian rhythms, associated with high-speed travel by jet airplane

jet·lin·er (-lī′nər) *n.* [JET¹ + LINER¹] a commercial jet aircraft for carrying passengers

‡**je·ton** (zhə tōn′; E. jet′'n) *n.* [Fr. < MFr. < *jeter,* to calculate, lit., to throw: see JET¹] a metal disk or counter, as for operating a pay telephone, etc.

jet·port (jet′pôrt′) *n.* [JET¹ + (AIR)PORT] an airport with long runways, for use by jet airplanes

jet-pro·pelled (-prə peld′) *adj.* driven by jet propulsion

jet propulsion a method of propelling airplanes, boats, etc. by the reaction caused when gases are emitted under pressure through a rear vent or vents

jet·sam (jet′səm) *n.* [var. of JETTISON] **1.** that part of the cargo thrown overboard to lighten a ship in danger: cf. FLOTSAM **2.** such discarded cargo washed ashore **3.** discarded things

☆**jet set** a social set of rich, fashionable people who travel widely, as by jet airplane, in pursuit of pleasure

jet stream 1. any of several bands of high-velocity winds moving from west to east around the earth at altitudes of from 8 to 10 mi. **2.** the stream of exhaust from a rocket

jet·ti·son (jet′ə s'n, -z'n) *n.* [ME. *jetteson* < Anglo-Fr. *getteson* < OFr. *getaison,* a throwing, jetsam < L. *jactatio,* a throwing < *jactare,* to throw: see JET¹] **1.** a throwing overboard of goods to lighten a ship, airplane, etc. in an emergency **2.** same as JETSAM —*vt.* **1.** to throw (goods) overboard **2.** to throw (something) away as useless or a burden

jet·ty¹ (jet′ē) *n., pl.* **-ties** [ME. *gete* < OFr. *jetée,* jetty, jutty, orig. pp. of *jeter:* see JET¹] **1.** a kind of wall built out into the water to restrain currents, protect a harbor or pier, etc. **2.** a landing pier **3.** a projecting or overhanging part of a building —*vi.* **-tied, -ty·ing** to project, or jut out

jet·ty² (jet′ē) *adj.* **-ti·er, -ti·est** very black, like jet

‡**jeu** (zhö) *n., pl.* **jeux** (zhö) [Fr.] a game; diversion

‡**jeu de mots** (də mō′) [Fr.] a play on words; pun

‡**jeu d'es·prit** (des prē′) *pl.* **jeux d'es·prit′** (zhö) [Fr., lit., play of intellect] a clever, witty turn of phrase, piece of writing, etc.

‡**jeune fille** (zhën fē′y') [Fr.] a young girl

‡**jeu·nesse** (zhë nes′) [Fr.] youth; young people

Jev·ons (jev′ənz), **William Stanley** 1835–82; Eng. economist & logician

Jew (jōō) *n.* [ME. < OFr. *Giu, Juiu* < L. *Judaeus* < Gr. *Ioudaios* < Heb. *yehūdī,* member of the tribe or kingdom of Judah: see JUDAH] **1.** a person descended, or regarded as descended, from the ancient Hebrews of Biblical times **2.** a person whose religion is Judaism See also HEBREW

jew·el (jōō′əl) *n.* [ME. < OFr. *joel < jeu,* a game, trifle

< L. *jocus*, a trifle, JOKE] **1.** a valuable ring, pin, necklace, etc., esp. one set with a gem or gems **2.** a precious stone; gem **3.** any person or thing that is very precious or valuable **4.** a small gem or hard, gemlike bit, used as one of the bearings in a watch —*vt.* **-eled** or **-elled, -el·ing** or **-el·ling** to decorate or set with jewels

jew·el·er, jew·el·ler (-ər) *n.* [ME. *jueler* < OFr. *joieleor* < *joel*: see prec.] a person who makes, deals in, or repairs jewelry, watches, etc.

jew·el·lery (jōō′əl rē) *n.* Brit. *sp.* of JEWELRY

jew·el·ry (-rē) *n.* jewels collectively

☆**jew·el·weed** (-wēd′) *n.* any of a number of plants (genus *Impatiens*) of the balsam family, bearing yellow or orange-yellow flowers with short spurs, and seed pods that split at the touch when ripe

Jew·ess (jōō′is) *n.* a Jewish woman or girl: term avoided by those who regard the *-ess* suffix as patronizing or discriminatory

Jew·ett (jōō′it), **Sarah Orne** (ôrn) 1849–1909; U.S. writer

jew·fish (-fish′) *n., pl.* **-fish′, -fish′es:** see FISH² [? < JEW + FISH²] any of several large fish found in warm seas, as the **giant sea bass** (*Stereolepis gigas*) found off California or a large grouper (*Epinephelus itajara*) found off Florida

Jew·ish (-ish) *adj.* of or having to do with Jews or Judaism —*n.* [Colloq.] *same as* YIDDISH —**Jew′ish·ness** *n.*

Jewish calendar a calendar used by the Jews in calculating Jewish history, holidays, etc. based on the lunar month and reckoned from 3761 B.C., the traditional date of the Creation

Months of the Jewish Calendar

1. **Tishri** (30 days)	7. **Nisan** (30 days)	
2. **Heshvan** (29 or 30 days)	8. **Iyar** (29 days)	
3. **Kislev** (29 or 30 days)	9. **Sivan** (30 days)	
4. **Tebet** (29 days)	10. **Tammuz** (29 days)	
5. **Shebat** (30 days)	11. **Ab** (30 days)	
6. **Adar** (29 or 30 days)	12. **Elul** (29 days)	

N.B. About once every three years (seven times in each nineteen years) an extra month, **Veadar** or **Adar Sheni** (29 days), falls between *Adar* and *Nisan*, as the Jewish year has only 354 days. *Tishri* begins in late September or early October. The Jewish day is from sunset to sunset.

Jew·ry (jōō′rē) *n., pl.* **-ries** [ME. *jewerie* < OFr. *juerie* < *Giu*: see JEW] **1.** formerly, a district inhabited only or mainly by Jews; ghetto **2.** Jewish people collectively [American *Jewry*] **3.** *obs.* name for JUDEA

jew's-harp, jews'-harp (jōōz′härp′) *n.* [earlier *Jew's trump*, altered (after JEW) < Du. *jeugd-tromp*, child's trumpet < *jeugd*, YOUTH + *tromp*, trumpet < Fr. *trompe*: see TRUMP²] a small musical instrument consisting of a lyre-shaped metal frame held between the teeth and played by plucking a projecting bent piece with the finger: it produces twanging tones

Jez·e·bel (jez′ə bel′, -b'l) [Heb. *Izebhel*] *Bible* the wicked woman who married Ahab, king of Israel: I Kings 21:5–23; II Kings 9:7–10, 30–37 —*n.* [also **j-**] any woman regarded as shameless, wicked, etc.

Jez·re·el (jez rē′əl, -rēl′) **1.** ancient town in Israel, on the plain of Esdraelon **2. Plain of,** *same as* ESDRAELON

JEW'S-HARP

jg, j.g. junior grade: designation of the lower rank of lieutenant in the U.S. Navy

Jhe·lum (jā′ləm) river in India, flowing from the Himalayas in Kashmir through West Pakistan into the Chenab: c. 480 mi.

JHS Jesus: see IHS

JHVH, JHWH *see* TETRAGRAMMATON

jib¹ (jib) *n.* [prob. < GIBBET] **1.** the projecting arm of a crane **2.** the boom of a derrick

jib² (jib) *vi., vt.* **jibbed, jib′bing** [< Dan. *gibbe*, to shift from one side to the other, jibe, akin to Du. *gijpen* < IE. *gheib-* < base *ghe-*, to yawn (cf. GAPE)] *Naut.* to jibe; shift —*n.* [Dan. *gib:* so named because it jibs: see the *v.*] a triangular sail projecting ahead of the foremast —**cut of one's jib** [Colloq.] one's appearance or way of dressing

jib³ (jib) *vi.* **jibbed, jib′bing** [prob. < prec.] **1.** to stop and refuse to go forward; balk **2.** to start or shy (*at* something) —*n.* [prob. < *v.*] an animal that jibs, as a horse —**jib′ber** *n.*

jib boom a spar fixed to and extending beyond the bowsprit of a ship: the jib is attached to it

jibe¹ (jib) *vi.* **jibed, jib′ing** [< Du. *gijpen*, to shift over (of sails), orig., to gasp for air: see JIB²] **1.** to shift from one side of a ship to the other: said of a fore-and-aft sail or its boom when the course is changed in a following or quartering wind **2.** to change the course of a ship so that the sails shift thus; change tack without going about **3.** [Colloq.] to be in harmony, agreement, or accord [accounts that don't *jibe*] —*vt. Naut.* to cause to jibe —*n.* a shift of sail or boom from one side of a ship to another

jibe² (jib) *vi., vt., n. same as* GIBE —**jib′er** *n.*

jib-head·ed (jib′hed′id) *adj.* cut like a jib; triangular: said of fore-and-aft sails

Ji·bu·ti (ji bōōt′ē) *same as* DJIBOUTI

Jid·da, Jid·dah (jid′ə) seaport in Hejaz, Saudi Arabia, on the Red Sea: pop. 150,000

jif·fy (jif′ē) *n., pl.* **-fies** [18th-c. slang < ?] [Colloq.] a very short time; instant [done in a *jiffy*]: also **jiff**

jig (jig) *n.* [prob. < MFr. *giguer*, to gambol, dance < *gigue*, a fiddle < MHG. *giga* (akin to ON. *gigja*) < OHG. **gigan* (G. dial. *geigen*), to move back and forth] **1.** *a)* a fast, gay, springy sort of dance, usually in triple time *b)* the music for such a dance **2.** any of various fishing lures that are jiggled up and down in the water **3.** any of several mechanical devices operated in a jerky manner, as a sieve for separating ores, a pounding machine, or a drill **4.** a device, often with metal surfaces, used as a guide for a tool or as a template —*vi., vt.* **jigged, jig′ging** [< ? *giguer:* see the *n.*] **1.** to dance or perform (a jig) or to dance in jig style **2.** to move jerkily and quickly up and down or to and fro **3.** to use a jig (on) in working **4.** to fish or catch (a fish) with a jig —☆**in jig time** [Colloq.] very quickly—☆ **the jig is up** [Slang] that ends it; all chances for success are gone: said of a risky or improper activity

jig·ger¹ (jig′ər) *n.* [prob. < Afr. origin] ☆*same as* CHIGGER

jig·ger² (jig′ər) *n.* **1.** a person who jigs ☆**2.** *a)* a small cup or glass used to measure liquor, containing usually 1 1/2 fluid ounces *b)* the quantity of liquor in a jigger **3.** any device or contraption whose name does not occur to one; gadget **4.** *same as* JIG (*n.* 3) **5.** *Mech.* any of several devices that operate with a jerky, up-and-down motion **6.** *Naut. a)* a small tackle *b)* a small sail *c)* a small boat with such a sail *d) same as* JIGGER MAST

jigger mast 1. a small mast in the stern of a ship **2.** the mast nearest the stern in a ship with four masts

jig·ger·y-pok·er·y (jig′ər ē pō′kər ē) *n.* [altered < Scot. *joukery-paukery*, rhyming slang < *jouk*, a trick) [Chiefly Brit. Colloq.] trickery or deception; underhanded activity; hanky-panky

jig·gle (jig′'l) *vt., vi.* **-gled, -gling** [dim. or freq. of *jig, v.*] to move in a succession of quick, slight jerks; rock lightly —*n.* a jiggling movement

jig·gly (jig′lē) *adj.* moving or tending to move with a jiggle; unsteady

☆**jig·saw** (jig′sô′) *n.* [JIG, *v.* + SAW¹] a saw with a narrow blade set in a frame, that moves with an up-and-down motion for cutting along wavy or irregular lines, as in scroll work: also **jig saw** —*vt.* to cut or form with a jigsaw

☆**jigsaw puzzle** a puzzle made by cutting up a picture into pieces of irregular shape, which must be put together again to re-form the picture

JIGSAW

ji·had (ji häd′) *n.* [Ar., a contest, war] **1.** a war by Moslems against unbelievers or enemies of Islam, carried out as a religious duty **2.** a fanatic campaign for or against an idea, etc.; crusade

Jill (jil) [var. of GILL³] a feminine name —*n.* [*often* **j-**] [Now Rare] a girl or woman; esp., a sweetheart

jilt (jilt) *n.* [< *jillet*, dim. of prec.] a woman who rejects a lover or suitor after accepting or encouraging him —*vt.* to reject or cast off (a previously accepted lover or sweetheart)

Jim (jim) *a nickname for* JAMES

☆**Jim Crow** [name of an early Negro minstrel song] [also **j- c-**] [Colloq.] discrimination against or segregation of Negroes —**Jim′-Crow′** *vt., adj.* —**Jim Crow′ism**

☆**jim-dan·dy** (jim′dan′dē) *n.* [JIM (used as an intensive) + DANDY] [Colloq.] an excellent or very pleasing person or thing —*adj.* [Colloq.] excellent; very pleasing

Ji·mé·nez (hē me′neth), **Juan Ra·món** (hwän rä mōn′) 1881–1958; Sp. poet, in the Americas after 1937

jim-jams (jim′jamz′) *n.pl.* [arbitrary echoic formation] [Slang] **1.** delirium tremens **2.** a nervous feeling; jitters (usually with *the*)

jim·my (jim′ē) *n., pl.* **-mies** [< dim. of JAMES] a short crowbar, used by burglars to pry open windows, etc. — ☆*vt.* **-mied, -my·ing** to use a jimmy on; pry open with a jimmy or similar tool

☆**jim·son weed** (jim′s'n) [altered < *Jamestown weed* < JAMESTOWN, Va.] a poisonous annual weed (*Datura stramonium*) of the nightshade family, with foul-smelling leaves, prickly fruit, and white or purplish, trumpet-shaped flowers: also **jimp′son weed** (jimp′-)

jin·gle (jiŋ′g'l) *vi.* **-gled, -gling** [ME. *gingelen*, prob. echoic] **1.** to make a succession of light, ringing sounds, as small bells or bits of metal striking together; tinkle **2.** to have obvious, easy rhythm, simple repetitions of sound, etc., as some poetry and music —*vt.* to cause to jingle —*n.* **1.** a jingling sound **2.** a verse that jingles; jingling arrangement of words or syllables [advertising *jingles*] —**jin′gly** (-glē) *adj.*

jin·go (jiŋ′gō) *n., pl.* **-goes** [< phr. *by jingo* in the refrain of a patriotic Brit. music-hall song (1878)] a person who boasts of his patriotism and favors an aggressive, threatening, warlike foreign policy; chauvinist —*adj.* of jingoes; jingoistic —**by jingo!** [prob. euphemism for *by Jesus*] [Colloq.] an exclamation used to indicate strong assertion, surprise, etc. —**jin′go·ism** *n.* —**jin′go·ist** *n.* —**jin′go·is′tic** *adj.* —**jin′go·is′ti·cal·ly** *adv.*

jink (jiŋk) *vi.* [< ?] [Chiefly Brit.] to move swiftly or with sudden turns, as in dodging a pursuer —*n.* **1.** [Chiefly

Brit.] an eluding, as by a quick, sudden turn **2.** [*pl.*] lively pranks; boisterous fun; horseplay: in full, usually, **high jinks**

jinn (jin) *n. pl.* of JINNI: popularly regarded as a singular, with the *pl.* **jinns**

jin·ni (ji nē′, jin′ē) *n., pl.* **jinn** [Ar. *jinnī*, pl. *jinn*] *Moslem Legend* a supernatural being that can take human or animal form and influence human affairs

jin·rik·i·sha (jin rik′shô, -shä) *n.* [Jap. < *jin*, a man + *riki*, power + *sha*, carriage] a small, two-wheeled carriage with a hood, pulled by one or two men, esp. formerly in the Orient: also sp. **jin·rick′sha, jin·rik′sha**

☆**jinx** (jiŋks) *n.* [earlier *jynx* < L. *iynx* < Gr. *iynx*, the wryneck (bird used in black magic)] [Colloq.] **1.** a person or thing supposed to bring bad luck **2.** a spell of bad luck —*vt.* [Colloq.] to bring bad luck to

ji·pi·ja·pa (hē′pē hä′pə) *n.* [Sp. < *Jipijapa*, place in Ecuador] **1.** a Central and South American plant (*Carludovica palmata*) whose leaves yield a flexible, durable straw used for hats **2.** this straw **3.** *same as* PANAMA HAT

☆**jit·ney** (jit′nē) *n., pl.* **-neys** [c. 1903 < ? Fr. JETON] **1.** [Old Slang] a five-cent coin; nickel **2.** a small bus or car, esp. one traveling a regular route, that carries passengers for a low fare, originally five cents

☆**jit·ter** (jit′ər) *vi.* [? echoic] [Colloq.] to be nervous; have the jitters; fidget —**the jitters** [Colloq.] a very uneasy, nervous feeling; the fidgets

☆**jit·ter·bug** (-bug′) *n.* [prec. + BUG¹] **1.** a dance for couples, esp. in the early 1940's, involving fast, acrobatic movements to swing music **2.** a dancer of the jitterbug —*vi.* **-bugged′, -bug′ging** to dance the jitterbug

☆**jit·ter·y** (-ē) *adj.* [Colloq.] having the jitters —**jit′ter·i·ness** *n.*

jiu·jit·su, jiu·jut·su (jōō jit′sōō) *n. var.* of JUJITSU

Jí·va·ro (hē′vä rō′) *n.* [Sp. *Jíbaro* < native name] **1.** *pl.* **-ros′, -ro′** a member of a tribe of Indians who live in S Ecuador and N Peru **2.** their language

☆**jive** (jīv) *vt.* [altered < JIBE²: sense development, to taunt-banter-improvise-swing (music)] [Slang] to use jive, or nonsense talk, to, esp. in an effort to mislead —*vi.* to play, or dance to, jive music —*n.* **1.** [Slang] foolish, exaggerated, or insincere talk; nonsense **2.** *former term* (c. 1930–45) *for* JAZZ *or* SWING

Jl. July

Jno. John

jo (jō) *n., pl.* **joes** [var. of JOY] [Scot.] a sweetheart

Jo·ab (jō′ab) [LL.(Ec.) < Gr.(Ec.) *Iōab* < Heb. *yō′ābh*, lit., Yahweh is (his) father] **1.** a masculine name **2.** *Bible* the commander of David's army

Jo·a·chim (yō′ə kim, yō ä′kim), Joseph 1831–1907; Hung. violinist & composer

Joan (jōn, jō′ən) a feminine name: see JOANNA

Jo·an·na (jō an′ə) [ML., fem. of *Joannes*: see JOHN] a feminine name: var. *Joan, Jane, Jean, Jeanne, Joanne, Johanna*; equiv. L. & Ger. *Johanna*, Fr. *Jeanne*, It. *Giovanna*, Sp. *Juana*

Jo·anne (jō an′) a feminine name: see JOANNA

Joan of Arc (ärk), Saint (Fr. name *Jeanne d'Arc*) 1412–31; Fr. heroine: defeated the English at Orléans (1429): burned at the stake for witchcraft: called the *Maid of Orleans*

Joã·o Pes·so·a (zhoo ounˈ pe sō′ə) city in NE Brazil; capital of Paraíba state: pop. 155,000

Job (jōb) [LL.(Ec.) < Gr.(Ec.) *Iōb* < Heb. *iyyōbh*] **1.** a masculine name **2.** *Bible a)* a man who endured much suffering but did not lose his faith in God *b)* the book telling of him

job¹ (jäb) *n.* [< ?] **1.** a specific piece of work, as in one's trade, or done by agreement for pay **2.** anything one has to do; task; chore; duty **3.** the thing or material being worked on **4.** *a)* the action of doing a task, duty, or piece of work *b)* a result or product of such action ☆**5.** a position of employment; situation; work **6.** [Colloq.] a criminal act or deed, as a theft, etc. **7.** [Colloq.] any happening, affair, matter, object, etc. **8.** [Chiefly Brit.] a thing done supposedly in the public interest but actually for private gain —*adj.* hired or done by the job: see also JOB LOT —*vi.* **jobbed, job′bing 1.** to do odd jobs **2.** to act as a jobber or broker **3.** [Chiefly Brit.] to do public or official business dishonestly for private gain —*vt.* **1.** to buy and sell (goods) as wholesaler; handle as middleman **2.** to let or sublet (work, contracts, etc.) **3.** to hire or let for hire, as a horse or carriage **4.** [Slang] to deceive; trick; cheat **5.** [Chiefly Brit.] to transact (public business) dishonestly for private gain —*SYN.* see POSITION, TASK —**odd jobs** miscellaneous pieces of work —**on the job** [Colloq.] while working at one's job **2.** [Slang] attentive to one's task or duty

job² (jäb) *n., vt., vi.* **jobbed, job′bing** [ME. *jobben*, to peck] *dial. var.* of JAB

☆**job analysis** a study of a specific job, or of all jobs, in an enterprise with respect to operations involved, working conditions, qualifications required, etc.

job·ber (jäb′ər) *n.* **1.** a person who jobs; esp., one who buys goods in quantity from manufacturers or importers and sells them to dealers; wholesaler; middleman **2.** a

person who works by the job; also, one who does piece-work **3.** [Brit.] a person who deals in stock-exchange securities: distinguished from BROKER

job·ber·y (-ər ē, -rē) *n.* [see JOB¹ (*vi.* 3)] [Chiefly Brit.] the carrying on of public or official business dishonestly for private gain

Job Corps a U.S. government program for training underprivileged youth for employment

☆**job·hold·er** (-hōl′dər) *n.* a person who has a steady job; specif., a government employee

job·less (-lis) *adj.* **1.** without a job; unemployed **2.** having to do with the unemployed —**the jobless** those who are unemployed —**job′less·ness** *n.*

job lot 1. an assortment of goods for sale as one quantity **2.** any random assortment, esp. when of inferior quality

job printing commercial printing of such items as letterheads, circulars, invitations, etc. —**job printer**

Job's comforter (jōbz) a person who aggravates one's misery while attempting or pretending to comfort: see Job 16:1-5

Job's-tears (jōbz′tirz′) *n.pl.* [see JOB] **1.** [*with sing. v.*] a coarse, annual tropical grass (*Coix lacryma-jobi*) which bears hard, beadlike structures (modified leaves) that contain edible grains **2.** the beads, often used for rosary or ornamental beads

Jo·cas·ta (jō kas′tə) [L. < Gr. *Iokastē*] *Gr. Myth.* the queen who unwittingly married her own son, Oedipus, and killed herself when she found out

Joc·e·lin, Joc·e·line, Joc·e·lyn (jäs′ə lin, jäs′lin) [OFr. *Joscelin* < Gmc.] a feminine name

jock (jäk) *n. clipped form of:* **1.** JOCKEY **2.** JOCKSTRAP

jock·ey (jäk′ē) *n., pl.* **-eys** [< *Jocky, Jockie*, northern Eng. and Scot. form of *Jacky*, dim. of JACK¹] **1.** a person whose work is riding horses in races ☆**2.** [Slang] one who operates a specified vehicle, machine, etc. —*vt., vi.* **-eyed, -ey·ing 1.** to ride (a horse) in a race **2.** to cheat; trick; swindle **3.** *a)* to maneuver for position or advantage *b)* to bring about by such maneuvering ☆**4.** [Slang] to be the operator, pilot, etc. (of)

jock·o (jäk′ō) *n.* [Fr., earlier *engeco* < *ncheko*, the native name in W Africa] a chimpanzee or a monkey

jock·strap (jäk′strap′) *n.* [slang *jock*, penis + STRAP] **1.** an elastic belt with a groin pouch for supporting the genitals, worn by men while engaging in athletics ·**2.** [Slang] an athlete: often a derogatory term

jo·cose (jō kōs′, jə-) *adj.* [L. *jocosus* < *jocus*, a jest, JOKE] joking or playful; humorous —*SYN.* see WITTY —**jo·cose′ly** *adv.* —**jo·cose′ness** *n.*

jo·cos·i·ty (-käs′ə tē) *n.* [ML. *iocositas*] **1.** the quality or state of being jocose **2.** *pl.* **-ties** a jocose action or remark

joc·u·lar (jäk′yə lər) *adj.* [L. *jocularis* < *joculus*, dim. of *jocus*, JOKE] **1.** joking; humorous; full of fun **2.** said as a joke —*SYN.* see WITTY —**joc′u·lar′i·ty** (-lar′ə tē) *n., pl.* **-ties** —**joc′u·lar·ly** *adv.*

joc·und (jäk′ənd, jō′kənd) *adj.* [ME. < OFr. *jocond* < LL. *jocundus* (altered after L. *jocus*, JOKE) < L. *jucundus*, pleasant, agreeable, helpful < *juvare*, to help] cheerful; genial; gay —**jo·cun·di·ty** (jō kun′də tē) *n., pl.* **-ties** —**joc′und·ly** *adv.*

Jodh·pur (jōd′poor, jäd′-) **1.** city in Rajasthan, NW India: pop. 225,000 **2.** former state of NW India, now merged with Rajasthan

jodh·pur (jäd′pər) *n.* [after prec., where the breeches first became popular] **1.** [*pl.*] riding breeches made loose and full above the knees and tight from the knees to the ankles **2.** a boot high enough to cover the ankle, with an adjustable buckle and strap, or an elastic insert, at the side

Joe (jō) *a nickname for* JOSEPH —☆*n.* [Slang] **1.** [*often* **j-**] fellow; guy ☆**2.** [**j-**] coffee

joe (jō) *n.* [Scot.] *same as* JO

☆**Joe College** [Colloq.] *a personification of* the typical male college student in the United States

Jo·el (jō′əl) [LL.(Ec.) < Gr.(Ec.) *Iōēl* < Heb. *yō′ēl*, lit., the Lord is God] **1.** a masculine name **2.** *Bible a)* Hebrew prophet, probably of the 5th cent. B.C. *b)* the book of his preachings

☆**joe-pye weed** (jō′pī′) [< ? the name of an Indian doctor said to have used the plant as medicine] any of a number of perennial American plants (genus *Eupatorium*) of the composite family, with whorled leaves and clusters of rayless, pinkish or purple flower heads

jo·ey (jō′ē) *n.* [Australian native name *joè*] [Australian] **1.** a young kangaroo **2.** any young animal

Jof·fre (zhô′fr′), **Jo·seph Jacques Cé·saire** (zhô zef′ zhàk sā zer′) 1852–1931; Fr. general; commander in chief of Fr. forces in World War I

jog¹ (jäg) *vt.* **jogged, jog′ging** [ME. *joggen*, to spur (a horse): ? akin to JAG²] **1.** *a)* to give a little shake, shove, or jerk to *b)* to nudge **2.** to shake up or revive (a person's memory) **3.** to cause to jog —*vi.* **1.** to move along at a slow, steady, jolting pace or trot **2.** to go (*on* or *along*) in a steady, slow, heavy manner —*n.* **1.** a little shake, shove, or nudge **2.** a slow, steady, jolting motion or trot —**jog′ger** *n.*

jog² (jäg) *n.* [var. of JAG¹] **1.** a projecting or notched part, esp. one at right angles, in a surface or line **2.** a sharp,

temporary change of direction, as in a road or one's course —*vi.* **jogged, jog′ging** to form or make a jog [*turn left where the road jogs*]

jog·gle¹ (-'l) *vt., vi.* **-gled, -gling** [freq. of JOG¹] to shake or jolt slightly —*n.* a slight jolt

jog·gle² (-'l) *n.* [< JOG²] **1.** *a*) a joint made between two surfaces of wood, stone, etc. by cutting a notch in one and making a projection in the other to fit into it *b*) a notch or projection for such a joint **2.** *same as* DOWEL —*vt.* **-gled, -gling** to fasten or join by joggles

joggle post **1.** a post made of pieces joined by joggles **2.** a post with shoulders to receive the feet of struts

Jog·ja·kar·ta (jäg′yə kär′tə) city in C Java, Indonesia: pop. 313,000

jog trot **1.** a slow, steady trot **2.** a routine, monotonous, or leisurely way of doing something

Jo·han·na (jō han′ə) a feminine name: see JOANNA

jo·han·nes (jō han′ēz) *n., pl.* **-nes** [< ML. *Johannes* for *John* V, king of Portugal (1706–50), who first issued them] a Portuguese gold coin of the 18th and 19th cent.

Jo·han·nes·burg (jō han′is burg′, yō hän′is-) city in the Transvaal, NE South Africa: pop. 1,153,000

Jo·han·nine (jō han′ən, -in) *adj.* [< ML. *Johannes* (see ff.) + -INE¹] of or characteristic of the Apostle John, author of the fourth Gospel

John (jän) [ME. *Jon* < OFr. *Johan, Jehan, Jan* < ML. *Johannes* < LL.(Ec.) *Joannes* < Gr.(Ec.) *Ioannes* < Heb. *yōḥānān,* contr. < *yehōḥānān,* lit., Yahweh is gracious] **1.** a masculine name: dim. *Jack, Johnnie, Johnny;* equiv. Fr. *Jean,* Ger. *Johann, Johannes, Hans,* It. *Giovanni,* Pol. *Jan,* Russ. *Ivan,* Sp. *Juan;* fem. *Jane, Jean, Jeanne, Joan, Joanna, Johanna* **2.** (called *John Lackland*) 1167?–1216; king of England (1199–1216): forced by his barons to sign the Magna Charta (1215): son of HENRY II **3.** *Bible a*) a Christian apostle, credited with having written the fourth Gospel, the three Epistles of John, and the Book of Revelation: called *the Evangelist* and *the Divine:* also called *Saint John:* his day is Dec. 27 *b*) the fourth book of the New Testament *c*) any of the three Epistles of John *d*) *same as* JOHN THE BAPTIST **4. John III** (born *John Sobieski*) 1624–96; king of Poland (1674–96) **5. John XXIII** (born *Angelo Giuseppe Roncalli*) 1881–1963; Pope (1958–63) **6. Augustus (Edwin),** 1879–1961; Eng. painter & etcher

john (jän) *n.* [Slang] **1.** a toilet ☆**2.** [*also* J-] *a*) any man, esp. one who is an easy mark *b*) a customer of a prostitute

John Barleycorn [see BARLEYCORN] *a personification of* corn liquor, malt liquor, etc.

☆**john·boat** (jän′bōt′) *n.* a skiff with a flat bottom

John Bull [title character in John Arbuthnot's *History of John Bull* (1712)] *a personification of* England or an Englishman

John Doe *see* DOE

John Do·ry (dôr′ē) *pl.* **John Do′rys** [JOHN + DORY²] **1.** an edible, saltwater, European fish (*Zeus faber*), with long dorsal spines and a yellow-ringed black spot on each side of its flat body **2.** a similar American fish (*Zenopsis ocellata*) of a silvery color

John Hancock ☆[Colloq.] one's signature: so called because John Hancock's signature on the Declaration of Independence is bold and legible

John Henry ☆**1.** legendary, usually Negro, hero of an American ballad, who died while pitting his strength with a sledge hammer against that of a steam drill ☆**2.** [Colloq.] one's signature

John·ny, John·nie (jän′ē) *a nickname for* JOHN —*n., pl.* **-nies** [cf. JACK¹] [Chiefly Brit. Colloq.] any man or boy

☆**john·ny·cake** (jän′ē kāk′) *n.* [altered (after prec. & CAKE) < north Eng. dial. *jannock, johnnick,* a bread made of oatmeal or coarse wheat flour] a kind of corn bread baked on a griddle

☆**John·ny-come-late·ly** (-kum′lāt′lē) *n.* [Colloq.] one who has only recently arrived at a certain place or position or taken a certain stand

☆**John·ny-jump-up** (-jump′up′) *n.* **1.** *same as* WILD PANSY **2.** *a popular name for* DAFFODIL **3.** any of various American violets

☆**Johnny on the spot** [Colloq.] a person who is ready and at hand whenever needed Also **John′ny-on-the-spot′** *n.*

Johnny Reb (reb) [JOHNNY + REB(EL)] *a personification of* a Confederate soldier

John of Gaunt (gônt) Duke of Lancaster, 1340–99; founder of the house of Lancaster: son of EDWARD III

John·son (jän′s'n) **1. Andrew,** 1808–75; 17th president of the U.S. (1865–69) **2. James Wel·don** (wel′dən), 1871–1938; U.S. writer & diplomat **3. Lyn·don Baines** (lin′dən bānz), 1908– ; 36th president of the U.S. (1963–69) **4. Samuel,** 1709–84; Eng. lexicographer, writer, & critic: known as *Dr. Johnson*

John·son·ese (jän′sə nēz′) *n.* the literary style of, or like that of Samuel Johnson, variously characterized by erudition, Latinisms, heaviness, pomposity, etc.

☆**Johnson grass** a forage and pasture grass (*Sorghum halepense*), widespread in the S U.S., often as a weed

John·so·ni·an (jän sō′nē ən) *adj.* of, like, or characteristic of Samuel Johnson or his style —*n.* an imitator, admirer, or student of Johnson and his work

☆**Johnson noise** [after J. B. *Johnson,* 20th-c. U.S. physicist] thermal background noise in a radio receiver

Johns·ton (jän′stən) **1. Albert Sidney,** 1803–62; Confederate general **2. Joseph Eggleston,** 1807–91; Confederate general

Johns·town (jänz′toun′) [after Joseph *Johns,* local landowner] city in SW Pa.: site of a disastrous flood (1889): pop. 42,000

John the Baptist *Bible* the forerunner and baptizer of Jesus: he was killed by Herod: Matt. 3

Jo·hore (jə hôr′) state of Malaya, at the tip of the Malay Peninsula: 7,330 sq. mi.; pop. 1,217,000

‡**joie de vi·vre** (zhwȧd vē′vr') [Fr.] joy of living; zestful enjoyment of life

join (join) *vt.* [ME. *joinen* < OFr. *joindre* < L. *jungere,* to bind together, YOKE] **1.** to put or bring together; connect; fasten **2.** to make into one; unite [*join* forces, *join* people in marriage] **3.** to become a part or member of; enter into association with [*to join* a club] **4.** to go to and combine with [*the path joins the highway*] **5.** *a*) to enter into the company of; accompany [*join* us later] *b*) to participate or take part with [they *join* me in congratulating you] **6.** [Colloq.] to adjoin **7.** *Geom.* to connect with a straight line or curve —*vi.* **1.** to come together; meet **2.** *a*) to enter into association *b*) to become a member of a group or organization Often with *up* **3.** to participate (*in* a conversation, singing, etc.) —*n.* a place of joining [a seam in a coat is a *join*] —**join battle** to start fighting or competing **SYN.—join** is the general term implying a bringing or coming together of two or more things and may suggest direct contact, affiliation, etc.; **combine** implies a mingling together of things, often with a loss of distinction of elements that completely merge with one another [*to combine* milk and water]; **unite** implies a joining or combining of things to form a single whole [*the United States*]; **connect** implies attachment by some fastening or relationship [*roads connected* by a bridge, the duties *connected* with a job]; **link** stresses firmness of a connection [*linked* together in a common cause]; **associate** implies a joining with another or others as a companion, partner, etc. and, in extended use, suggests a connection made in the mind [*to associate* Freud's name with psychoanalysis]; **consolidate** implies a merger of distinct and separate units into a single whole for resulting compactness, strength, efficiency, etc. [*to consolidate* one's debts] —*ANT.* separate, part

join·der (-dər) *n.* [Fr. *joindre,* a use of inf. as *n.:* see prec.] **1.** a joining; act of meeting or coming together **2.** *Law a*) a joining of causes *b*) a joining of parties as coplaintiffs or codefendants *c*) a uniting on facts or procedure *d*) an accepting of an issue offered

join·er (-ər) *n.* [ME. *joinour* < OFr. *joignour* < *joindre:* see JOIN] **1.** a person or thing that joins **2.** a workman who constructs and finishes interior woodwork, as doors, molding, stairs, etc. ☆**3.** [Colloq.] a person given to joining various organizations

join·er·y (-ər ē) *n.* **1.** the work or skill of a joiner **2.** any of various joints made in woodworking

joint (joint) *n.* [ME. < OFr. < L. *junctus,* pp. of *jungere,* to join, YOKE] **1.** a place or part where two things or parts are joined **2.** the way in which two things are joined at such a part **3.** one of the parts or sections of a jointed whole **4.** a large cut of meat with the bone still in it, as for a roast ☆**5.** [Slang] *a*) a cheap bar, restaurant, nightclub, etc. *b*) any house, building, etc. ☆**6.** [Slang] a marijuana cigarette **7.** *Anat. a*) a place or part where two bones or corresponding structures are joined, usually so that they can move *b*) the way in which they are joined **8.** *Bot.* a point where a branch or leaf grows out of the stem **9.** *Geol.* a fracture in a rock mass, along which displacement has not occurred —*adj.* [OFr. *joint, jointe,* pp. of *joindre:* see JOIN] **1.** joined as to time; concurrent **2.** common to two or more persons, governments, etc. as to ownership or action [a *joint* declaration, *joint* property] **3.** sharing with someone else [a *joint* owner] —*vt.* **1.** to fasten together by a joint or joints **2.** to give a joint or joints to **3.** to prepare (a board or stave) for joining to another **4.** to cut (meat) into joints; separate at the joints —**out of joint** **1.** not in place at the joint; dislocated **2.** disordered or disorganized

joint account a bank account in the name of two or more persons, each of whom may withdraw funds

☆**Joint Chiefs of Staff** a group within the Department of Defense, consisting of the Chief of Staff of the Army, the Chief of Naval Operations, the Chief of Staff of the Air Force, and a chairman

☆**joint committee** a committee with members from both houses of a legislative body, or from two or more organizations

joint·ed (-id) *adj.* having joints

joint·er (-ər) *n.* **1.** a person or machine that joints **2.** a long plane used in dressing boards **3.** a triangular device with an edge, fastened to a plow beam **4.** a tool for pointing joints, as of brickwork

joint·ly (-lē) *adv.* in a joint manner; together

☆**joint resolution** a resolution passed by both houses of a bicameral legislature: it has the force of a law if signed by the chief executive or passed over his veto

joint·ress (join′tris) *n.* [Rare] a woman with a jointure

joint return a single income tax return filed by a married couple, combining their individual incomes

joint stock stock or capital held in a common fund

joint-stock company (joint′stäk′) a business firm with a joint stock, owned by the stockholders in shares which each may sell or transfer independently

join·ture (join′chər) *n.* [ME. < OFr. < L. *junctura,* a joining < *jungere:* see YOKE] **1.** [Now Rare] an act or instance of joining **2.** *Law a)* an arrangement by which a husband grants real property to his wife for her use after his death *b)* the property thus settled; widow's portion *c)* [Obs.] the holding of property jointly

☆**joint·weed** (joint′wēd′) *n.* a plant (*Polygonella articulata*) of the buckwheat family, with threadlike leaves, jointed stems, and clusters of small, white flowers

joint·worm (-wurm′) *n.* ☆the larva of either of two species of small wasp (genus *Harmolita*) which attack grain stems by producing gall-like swellings in the joints

Join·ville (zhwan vēl′), **Jean de** (zhän də) 1224?–1317; Fr. chronicler

joist (joist) *n.* [ME. *giste* < OFr., a bed, couch, beam < *gesir,* to lie < L. *jacere,* to lie] any of the parallel beams that hold up the planks of a floor or the laths of a ceiling —*vt.* to provide with joists

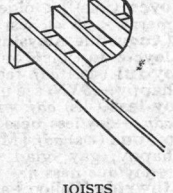

JOISTS

Jó·kai (yō′koi), **Mau·rus** (mou′roos) 1825–1904; Hung. novelist: also called **Mór** (mōr) **Jókai**

joke (jōk) *n.* [L. *jocus,* a joke, game < IE. base *jek-,* to speak, whence OHG. *jehan*] **1.** anything said or done to arouse laughter; specif., *a)* a funny anecdote with a punch line *b)* an amusing trick played on someone **2.** the humorous element in a situation **3.** a thing done or said merely in fun **4.** a person or thing to be laughed at, not to be taken seriously, because absurd, ridiculous, etc. —*vi.* **joked,** **jok′ing** [< the *n.* or L. *jocari,* to joke] **1.** to tell or play jokes **2.** to say or do something as a joke; jest —*vt.* **1.** [Now Rare] to make fun of; make (a person) the object of jokes or teasing **2.** to bring to a specified condition by joking —**no joke** a serious matter —**jok′ing·ly** *adv.* **SYN.**—**joke** is the simple, basic word for anything said or done in fun or to excite laughter and may apply to remarks, anecdotes, pranks, etc.; **jest,** the more formal equivalent, usually is applied to joking language and suggests banter or light, good-natured ridicule; **quip** and **sally** suggest a smart, neatly turned jest; a **witticism** is a witty or amusingly clever saying or remark; **wisecrack,** a slang term, applies to a witty remark that is flippant or facetious

jok·er (jō′kər) *n.* **1.** a person who jokes ☆**2.** a hidden or cunningly worded provision put into a law, legal document, etc. to make it different from what it seems to be ☆**3.** any hidden, unsuspected difficulty ☆**4.** an extra playing card, used in some games to represent the highest trump or any card the holder desires **5.** [Slang] a man; fellow: usually used disparagingly

Jok·ja·kar·ta (jäk′ya kär′ta) *same as* JOGJAKARTA

Jo·li·et (jō′lē et′, -et′) [after et.] [after et.] city in NE Ill.: pop. 80,000

Jo·li·et, Jol·li·et (jō′lē et′, jō′lē et′; *Fr.* zhô lye′), **Louis** 1645–1700; Fr.-Canad. explorer of the Mississippi

Jo·liot-Cu·rie (zhō lyô kü rē′) **1. (Jean) Fré·dé·ric** (frā dā rēk′), (born *Jean Frédéric Joliot*) 1900–58; Fr. nuclear physicist **2. I·rène** (ē ren′), (born *Irène Curie*) 1897–1956; Fr. nuclear physicist: wife of *prec.* & daughter of Pierre & Marie CURIE

jol·li·fy (jäl′ə fī′) *vt., vi.* **-fied′, -fy′ing** [Colloq.] to make or be jolly or merry —**jol′li·fi·ca′tion** *n.*

jol·li·ty (-ə tē) *n.* [ME. *jolite* < OFr. < *joli:* see JOLLY] **1.** the quality or state of being jolly; fun; gaiety **2.** *pl.* **-ties** [Brit.] a jolly occasion; festive gathering —*SYN.* MIRTH

jol·ly (jäl′ē) *adj.* **-li·er, -li·est** [ME. *joli* < OFr., prob. < ON. *jol,* YULE] **1.** full of high spirits and good humor; merry; gay; convivial **2.** [Colloq.] enjoyable; pleasant —*adv.* [Brit. Colloq.] very; altogether —*vt., vi.* **-lied, -ly·ing** [Colloq.] ☆**1.** to try to make (a person) feel good or agreeable by coaxing, flattering, joking, etc. (often with *along*) **2.** to make fun of (someone) —*n., pl.* **-lies** [Brit. Colloq.] a British marine —**get one's jollies** [Slang] to have fun or pleasure —**jol′li·ly** *adv.* —**jol′li·ness** *n.*

jolly (boat) [< MDu. *jolle,* yawl + BOAT] a ship's small boat

Jolly Roger [JOLLY + *Roger,* pirate flag < ROGER] a black flag of pirates, with white skull and crossbones

Jo·lo (hō lō′) island in the Philippines, southwest of Mindanao; largest island in Sulu Archipelago: 345 sq. mi.

jolt (jōlt) *vt.* [earlier *jot,* to jog, bump, of echoic origin: prob. infl. by obs. *jowl,* to strike] **1.** to shake up or jar, as with a bumpy ride or sharp blow **2.** to shock or surprise —*vi.* to move along in a bumpy, jerky manner —*n.* **1.** a sudden jerk, bump, or shake, as from a blow **2.** a shock or surprise ☆**3.** a drink of liquor neat —**jolt′er** *n.* —**jolt′ing·ly** *adv.* —**jolt′y** *adj.*

Jo·nah (jō′na) [LL.(Ec.) *Jonas* < Gr.(Ec.) *Ionas* < Heb. *yōnāh,* lit., a dove] **1.** a masculine name: var. *Jonas* **2.** *Bible a)* a Hebrew prophet: thrown overboard in a storm sent because he had disobeyed God, he was swallowed by a big fish, but three days later was cast up on the shore unharmed *b)* the book telling Jonah's story —*n.* any person said to bring bad luck by being present

☆**Jonah crab** a large, reddish, edible crab (*Cancer borealis*) of the NE coast of N. America

Jo·nas (jō′nas) *Douay Bible name for* JONAH

Jon·a·than (jän′ə thən) [Heb. *yōnāthān,* contr. < *yehōnāthān,* lit., Yahweh has given] **1.** a masculine name: dim. *Jon* **2.** *Bible* Saul's oldest son, a close friend of David: I Sam. 18–20 —*n.* ☆**1.** a late fall variety of apple ☆**2.** *same as* BROTHER JONATHAN

Jones (jōnz) **1. Daniel,** 1881– ; Eng. phonetician **2. Ernest,** 1879–1958; Brit. psychoanalyst **3. Howard Mumford** (mum′fard), 1892– ; U.S. educator & critic **4. In·i·go** (in′i gō′), 1573–1652; Eng. architect and stage designer **5. John Paul,** (born *John Paul*) 1747–92; Am. naval officer in the Revolutionary War, born in Scotland

jon·gleur (jŏŋ′glər; *Fr.* zhôŋ glėr′) *n.* [Fr. < OFr. *jogleor:* see JUGGLER] a wandering minstrel in medieval France and England, who entertained by reciting or singing

jon·quil (jäŋ′kwəl, jän′-) *n.* [Fr. *jonquille* < Sp. *junquillo,* dim. of *junco,* a reed < L. *juncus,* a rush < IE. base *yoini-,* rush, whence MIr. *ain,* rush, ON. *einir,* juniper] **1.** *a)* a species of narcissus (*Narcissus jonquilla*) having relatively small yellow flowers with a very short crown, and long, slender leaves *b)* its bulb or flower **2.** loosely, any narcissus

Jon·son (jän′s'n), **Ben** 1572?–1637; Eng. dramatist & poet —**Jon·so·ni·an** (jän sō′nē ən) *adj.*

Jop·lin (jäp′lin) [after Rev. H. G. *Joplin,* first settler] city in SW Mo.: pop. 39,000

Jop·pa (jäp′a) *ancient name of* JAFFA

Jor·daens (yōr′däns), **Ja·cob** (yä′kôp) 1593–1678; Flem. painter

Jor·dan (jôr′d'n) **1.** river in the Near East, flowing from the Anti-Lebanon mountains south through the Sea of Galilee, through Jordan, into the Dead Sea: 200 mi. **2.** country in the Near East, east of Israel: 37,300 sq. mi.; pop. 2,133,000; cap. Amman: official name the **Hashemite Kingdom of Jordan** —**Jor·da·ni·an** (jôr dā′nē ən) *adj., n.*

jor·dan (jôr′d'n) *n.* [ME. *jurdan* < ?] [Obs. or Dial.] *same as* CHAMBER POT

Jor·dan (jôr′d'n), **David Starr** (stär) 1851–1931; U.S. educator & naturalist

Jordan almond [altered (after the proper name *Jordan*) < ME. *jardyne almaunde* < OFr. *jardin,* garden + ME. *almande,* ALMOND: i.e., a cultivated almond] **1.** a variety of large Spanish almond **2.** a confection consisting of such an almond with a colored coating of sugar

jo·rum (jôr′əm) *n.* [prob. < *Joram* (II Sam. 8:10), bringer of silver vessels] **1.** a large drinking bowl **2.** the amount of liquor that it holds

Jos. 1. Joseph **2.** Josiah

Jo·seph (jō′zəf, -səf) [LL.(Ec.) < Gr.(Ec.) *Iōsēph* < Heb. *yōsēph,* lit., may he add: cf. Gen. 30:24] **1.** a masculine name: dim. *Joe, Jo;* equiv. L. *Josephus,* It. *Giuseppe,* Sp. *José;* fem. *Josepha, Josephine* **2.** *Bible a)* Jacob's eleventh son, who was sold into slavery in Egypt by his jealous brothers but became a high official there: Gen. 37, 39–41 *b)* the husband of Mary, mother of Jesus: Matt. 1:18–25: also called *Saint Joseph:* his day is March 19 —*n.* [in allusion to *Joseph's* coat: Gen. 37:3] a woman's long riding coat, with a cape, worn in the 18th cent.

Jo·se·phine (jō′zə fēn, -sə-) [Fr. *Joséphine* < *Joseph:* see JOSEPH] **1.** a feminine name: dim. *Jo, Josie;* var. *Josepha* **2.** 1763–1814; wife of Napoleon (1796–1809) & empress of France (1804–09): wife (1779–94) of vicomte *Alexandre de Beauharnais,* 1760–94, Fr. army officer

Joseph of Arimathea *Bible* a wealthy disciple who provided a tomb for Jesus' body: Matt. 27:57–60

☆**Joseph's coat** an ornamental species of pigweed (*Amaranthus tricolor*) grown for its colorful red, yellow, and green upper leaves

Jo·se·phus (jō sē′fəs) **1.** a masculine name: see JOSEPH **2. (Flavius),** 37–95? A.D.; Jewish historian

☆**josh** (jäsh) *vt., vi.* [< ?] [Colloq.] to ridicule in a good-humored way; tease jokingly; banter —*n.* good-humored joking —**josh′er** *n.* —**josh′ing·ly** *adv.*

Josh·u·a (jäsh′oo wə) [Heb. *yehōshū'a,* lit., help of Jehovah (see JESUS)] **1.** a masculine name: dim. *Josh* **2.** *Bible a)* Moses' successor, and leader of the Israelites into the Promised Land *b)* the book telling about him Abbrev. **Josh.**

☆**Joshua tree** [? Mormon coinage on the fancied resemblance of the angular branches to the arms of JOSHUA leading the Israelites] a tree (*Yucca brevifolia*) of the agave family, found in the SW U.S. and characterized by branches that are extended grotesquely like upraised arms and by dagger-shaped, spine-tipped leaves

Jo·si·ah (jō sī′ə) [Heb. *yōshīyāh,* lit., the Lord supports] **1.** a masculine name **2.** *Bible* a king of Judah in the 7th cent. B.C.: II Kings 22, 23

Jo·si·as (-əs) *Douay Bible name for* JOSIAH

joss (jäs) *n.* [PidE. < Port. *deos* < L. *deus,* a god: see DEITY] a figure of a Chinese god; Chinese idol

joss house a Chinese temple

joss stick a thin stick of dried paste made of fragrant wood dust, burned by the Chinese as incense

jos·tle (jäs′'l) *vt.*, *vi.* **-tled**, **-tling** [earlier *justle*, freq. < ME. *justen*: see JOUST] **1.** to bump or push, as in a crowd; elbow or shove roughly **2.** to push (one's way) by shoving or bumping **3.** to come or bring into close contact **4.** to contend (*with* someone *for* something) —*n.* the act of jostling; rough bump or shove —**jos′tler** *n.*

Jos·u·e (jäs′yoo wē′) *Douay Bible name for* JOSHUA

jot (jät) *n.* [L. *iota* < Gr. *iōta*, the letter *i*, the smallest letter (hence, very small thing) < Sem., as in Heb. *yōdh*] a trifling amount; the smallest bit —*vt.* **jot′ted**, **jot′ting** [prob. < the *n.*] to make a brief, quick note of (usually with *down*) —**jot′ter** *n.*

jo·ta (hō′tä) *n.* [Sp. < OSp. *sota* < *sotar*, to dance < L. *saltare*, to leap: see SALTANT] a Spanish dance in 3/4 time performed by a man and woman to the rhythm of castanets

jot·ting (jät′iŋ) *n.* a short note jotted down

Jo·tunn, Jo·tun (yō′toon, yō′-) *n.* [ON. *jötunn*, akin to OE. *eoten*, a giant < IE. base *ed-, to eat: hence, orig., glutton or ? man-eater] *Norse Myth.* any of the giants

Jo·tunn·heim, Jo·tun·heim (-hām′) [ON. *jötunheimar*, pl. < *jötunn* (see prec.) + *heimr*, HOME] *Norse Myth.* the home of the giants

Jou·bert (zhoo ber′), **Jo·seph** (zhō zef′) 1754–1824; Fr. essayist

joule (jool, joul) *n.* [after ff.] *Physics* the unit of work or energy in the mks system, being the amount of work done by one newton acting through a distance of one meter and equal to 10,000,000 ergs

Joule (jool), **James Prescott** 1818–89; Eng. physicist

jounce (jouns) *vt.*, *vi.* **jounced**, **jounc′ing** [ME. *jounsen* < ?] to shake, jolt, or bounce, as in riding —*n.* a bounce or jolt —**jounc′y** *adj.*

jour. 1. journal **2.** journeyman

jour·nal (jur′n'l) *n.* [ME., book containing forms of worship for the day hours (Little Hours) < OFr., lit., daily < L. *diurnalis* < *dies*, day (see DEITY): sense 4 prob. via It. *giornale*, of same orig.] **1.** a daily record of happenings, as a diary **2.** a record of the transactions of a legislature, club, etc. **3.** a ship's logbook **4.** a daily newspaper **5.** any newspaper, magazine, or other periodical **6.** *Bookkeeping a)* same as DAYBOOK *b)* a book of original entry, used, in the double-entry system, for recording all transactions with an indication of the special accounts to which they belong **7.** [orig. Scot.] *Mech.* the part of a rotatory axle or shaft that turns in a bearing

journal box *Mech.* a casing or housing for a journal

jour·nal·ese (jur′n'l ēz′) *n.* a style of writing and diction characteristic of many newspapers, magazines, etc.; facile or sensational style, with many clichés

jour·nal·ism (jur′n'l iz'm) *n.* [Fr. *journalisme* < *journal*: see JOURNAL] **1.** the work of gathering, writing, editing, and publishing or disseminating news, as through news-papers and magazines or by radio and television **2.** journalistic writing **3.** newspapers and magazines collec-tively

jour·nal·ist (-ist) *n.* **1.** a person whose occupation is journalism; reporter, news editor, etc. **2.** a person who keeps a journal or diary

jour·nal·is·tic (jur′n'l is′tik) *adj.* of or characteristic of journalists or journalism —**jour′nal·is′ti·cal·ly** *adv.*

jour·nal·ize (jur′n'l īz′) *vt.*, *vi.* **-ized′**, **-iz′ing** to record (transactions, daily events, etc.) in a journal

jour·ney (jur′nē) *n.*, *pl.* **-neys** [ME. *journee* < OFr. < VL. *diurnata*, day's journey, day's work < LL. *diurnum*, a daily portion < L. *diurnus*, daily < *dies*, day: see DEITY] **1.** the act or an instance of traveling from one place to another; trip **2.** any course or passage from one stage or experience to another —*vi.* **-neyed**, **-ney·ing** to go on a trip; travel —SYN. see TRIP —**jour′ney·er** *n.*

jour·ney·man (-mən) *n.*, *pl.* **-men** (-mən) [ME. < *journee* (see JOURNEY), in sense "day's work" + *man*] **1.** *a)* orig., a worker for a daily wage *b)* formerly, a worker who had served his apprenticeship and thus qualified himself to work at his trade *c)* now, a worker who has learned his trade **2.** any sound, experienced, but not brilliant crafts-man or performer

jour·ney·work (-wurk′) *n.* work of a journeyman

joust (joust, just, joost) *n.* [ME. *jouste* < OFr. *jouste* < *jouster*: see the *v.*] **1.** a combat with lances between two knights on horseback; esp., such a formal combat as part of a tournament **2.** [*pl.*] a tournament —*vi.* [ME. *justen* < OFr. *juster* < VL. *juxtare*, to approach, tilt < L. *juxta*: see JUXTA-] to engage in a joust

Jove (jōv) [< L. *Jovis* (gen. of *Juppiter*, JUPITER) < IE. *diwes*, gen. of *dyēus*, whence Gr. *Zeus* < base *dei-, to gleam, shine: cf. DEITY] *same as* JUPITER —**by Jove!** an exclamation of astonishment, emphasis, etc.

jo·vi·al (jō′vē əl, -vyəl) *adj.* [Fr. < LL. *Jovialis*, of Jupiter < L. *Jovis*: see prec.] **1.** [J-] *same as* JOVIAN **2.** full of hearty, playful good humor; genial and gay; jolly: from the astrological notion that people born under the sign of Jupiter are joyful —**jo′vi·al′i·ty** (-al′ə tē) *n.* —**jo′vi·al·ly** *adv.*

Jo·vi·an (jō′vē ən) *adj.* **1.** of or like Jove (the god Jupiter); majestic **2.** of the planet Jupiter

Jow·ett (jou′it), **Benjamin** 1817–93; Eng. classical scholar & translator of Plato and others

jowl¹ (joul, jōl) *n.* [ME. *chavel* < OE. *ceafl*, jaw, cheek, akin to ON. *kjoptr*, MHG. *kivel* < IE. base *ĝebh-, jaw, mouth,

whence OIr. *gop*, mouth, Czech *žábra*, gills (of fish)] **1.** a jawbone or jaw; esp., the lower jaw with the chin and cheeks **2.** the cheek **3.** the meat of a hog's cheek

jowl² (joul, jōl) *n.* [ME. *cholle* < OE. *ceole*, throat, akin to G. *kehle* < IE. base *gel-, to swallow, whence OIr. *gaile*, stomach] **1.** [often *pl.*] the fleshy, hanging part under the lower jaw **2.** *a)* the dewlap of cattle *b)* the wattle of fowl **3.** the head and adjacent parts of a fish —**jowl′y** *adj.* **jowl′i·er, jowl′i·est**

joy (joi) *n.* [ME. *joie* < OFr. < LL. *gaudia*, orig. pl. of L. *gaudium*, joy < IE. base *gāu-, to rejoice, whence Gr. *gēthein*, to rejoice, MIr. *gūaire*, noble] **1.** a very glad feel-ing; happiness; great pleasure; delight **2.** anything causing such feeling **3.** the expression or showing of such feeling —*vi.* to be full of joy; rejoice —*vt.* [Archaic] **1.** to make joyful **2.** to enjoy —SYN. see PLEASURE

joy·ance (-əns) *n.* [Archaic] joy; rejoicing

Joyce (jois) [< older *Jocosa* < L. *jocosa*, fem. of *jocosus*, merry < *jocus*, jest, trifle] **1.** a feminine name **2.** James (**Augustine Aloysius**), 1882–1941; Ir. novelist & poet —**Joyc·e·an** (jois′ē ən) *adj.*

joy·ful (-fəl) *adj.* feeling, expressing, or causing joy; glad; happy —SYN. see HAPPY —**joy′ful·ly** *adv.* —**joy′ful·ness** *n.*

joy·less (-lis) *adj.* without joy; unhappy; sad —**joy′less·ly** *adv.* —**joy′less·ness** *n.*

joy·ous (-əs) *adj.* [ME. < OFr. *joios* < *joie*, JOY] full of joy; happy; gay; glad —SYN. see HAPPY —**joy′ous·ly** *adv.* —**joy′ous·ness** *n.*

☆**joy ride** [Colloq.] an automobile ride merely for pleasure, often with reckless speed and sometimes, specif., in a stolen car —**joy rider** —**joy riding**

joy stick [Slang] the control stick of an airplane

JP jet propulsion

J.P. justice of the peace

Jr., jr. junior

J.S.D. Doctor of Juristic (or Juridical) Science

Ju. June

Ju·an de Fu·ca Strait (hwän də fyoo′kə) strait between Vancouver Island and NW Washington: c. 100 mi. long: also called **Strait of Juan de Fuca**

Juan Fer·nán·dez Islands (hwän fer nän′des; *E.* joo′ən fər nan′dez) group of three islands in the South Pacific, c. 400 mi. west of, & belonging to, Chile: c. 70 sq. mi.; pop. c. 900

Juárez see CIUDAD JUÁREZ

Juá·rez (hwä′res), **Be·ni·to Pa·blo** (be nē′tō pä′blō) 1806–72; Mex. statesman; president of Mexico (1858–72; in exile 1863–67)

Ju·ba (joo′bä) river in Africa, flowing from S Ethiopia south through Somalia into the Indian Ocean: c. 550 mi.

☆**ju·ba** (joo′bə) *n.* [< Zulu, lit., to kick about] a Southern Negro dance, characterized by a lively rhythm marked by clapping the hands

Ju·bal (joo′b'l) [Heb. *yūbhāl*] *Bible* one of Cain's descend-ants, a musician or inventor of musical instruments: Gen. 4:19–21

jub·bah (joob′ə) *n.* [Ar.] a long outer garment worn by both men and women in some Moslem countries

Jub·bul·pore (jub′'l pōr′) *same as* JABALPUR

ju·be (joo′bē) *n.* [imperative of L. *jubere*, to bid, command: from a prayer that begins *Jube*, said from this gallery] a loft or gallery over the rood screen in a church

ju·bi·lant (joo′b'l ənt) *adj.* [L. *jubilans*, prp. of *jubilare*: see JUBILATE²] joyful and triumphant; elated; rejoicing —**ju′bi·lance** n. —**ju′bi·lant·ly** *adv.*

Ju·bi·la·te (yoo′bə lä′tā, joo′-; -tē) *n.* [L., pl. imperative of *jubilare*: see ff.] **1.** *Bible* the 100th Psalm (99th in the Vulgate and Douay versions) **2.** the third Sunday after Easter: so called because the Introit for the day begins *Jubilate*

ju·bi·late (joo′bə lāt′) *vi.* **-lat′ed**, **-lat′ing** [< L. *jubilatus*, pp. of *jubilare*, to shout for joy < *jubilum*, wild shout < IE. base *yu-, an outcry, especially of rejoicing, whence YOWL] to rejoice, as in triumph; exult

ju·bi·la·tion (joo′bə lā′shən) *n.* **1.** a jubilating or a being jubilant **2.** a happy celebration, as of victory

ju·bi·lee (joo′bə lē′, joo bə lē′) *n.* [ME. < OFr. *jubile* < LL.(Ec.) *jubilaeus* < Gr.(Ec.) *iōbēlaios* < Heb. *yōbēl*, a ram, ram's horn used as a trumpet to announce the sabbatical year: infl. by L. *jubilum*: see JUBILATE²] **1.** *Jewish History* a year-long celebration held every fifty years in which all bondmen were freed, mortgaged lands were restored to the original owners, and land was left fallow: Lev. 25:8–17 **2.** *a)* an anniversary, esp. a 50th or 25th anniversary *b)* a celebration of this **3.** a time or occasion of rejoicing **4.** jubilation; rejoicing **5.** *R.C.Ch.* a year of plenary indulgence or remission of punishment for sin, on certain conditions: an **ordinary jubilee** occurs every twenty-five years

Jud. 1. Judges **2.** Judith

Ju·dae·a (joo dē′ə) *same as* JUDEA —**Ju·dae′an** *adj.*, *n.*

Ju·dae·o- (joo dē′ō) *same as* JUDEO-

Ju·dah (joo′də) [Heb. *yehūdhāh* < ?] **1.** a masculine name: dim. *Jude*; fem. *Judith* **2.** *Bible a)* the fourth son of Jacob *b)* the tribe descended from him, strongest of the twelve tribes of Israel **3.** the kingdom in the S part of ancient Palestine formed by the tribes of Judah and Benjamin after they broke with the other ten tribes: I Kings 11:31; 12:17–21

Ju·da·ic (jōō dā'ik) *adj.* [L. *Judaicus* < Gr. *Ioudaikos* < *Ioudaios:* see JEW] 1. of Judah 2. of the Jews or Judaism; Jewish —**Ju·da'i·cal·ly** *adv.*

Ju·da·i·ca (-i kə) *n.* [ModL. < L. *Judaicus*, JUDAIC] a collection of books, papers, objects, data, etc. having to do with Jews or Judaism

Ju·da·ism (jōō'də iz'm, -dē-) *n.* [ME. *Judaisme* < LL.(Ec.) *Judaismus* < Gr.(Ec.) *Ioudaismos* < *Ioudaios:* see JEW] 1. the Jewish religion, a monotheistic religion based on the laws and teachings of the Holy Scripture and the Talmud 2. the Jewish way of life; observance of Jewish morality, traditions, ceremonies, etc. 3. Jews collectively; Jewry —**Ju'da·ist** *n.* —**Ju'da·is'tic** *adj.*

Ju·da·ize (-īz') *vi.* **-ized', -iz'ing** [LL.(Ec.) *Judaizare* < Gr.(Ec.) *Ioudaizein* < *Ioudaios:* see JEW] to conform to Jewish morality, traditions, etc. —*vt.* to bring into conformity with Judaism —**Ju'da·i·za'tion** *n.*

Ju·das (jōō'dəs) [ME. < LL.(Ec.) < Gr.(Ec.) *Ioudas* < Heb. *yehūdhāh*, JUDAH] 1. Judas Iscariot, the disciple who betrayed Jesus: Matt. 26:14, 48 2. Jude, the apostle 3. a brother of Jesus and James: Mark 6:3; Matt. 13:55 —*n.* 1. a traitor or betrayer 2. [*usually* j-] a peephole or small window, as in the door of a prison cell: in full, **judas window** (or **hole**)

Ju·das (jōō'dəs), Saint *see* JUDE

Judas Maccabaeus *see* MACCABAEUS

Judas tree [from the legend that Judas Iscariot hanged himself on one] *a popular name for* CERCIS

jud·der (jud'ər) *vi.* [altered < ? SHUDDER] [Brit.] to shake, wobble, or vibrate

Jude (jōōd) 1. a masculine name: see JUDAH 2. *Bible a)* a Christian apostle: John 14:22; Luke 6:13–16: also called *Judas, Saint Jude:* his day is Oct. 28 *b)* a book of the New Testament, the Epistle of Jude *c)* its author, perhaps the Judas called Jesus' brother See JUDAS

Ju·de·a (jōō dē'ə) ancient region of S Palestine under Persian, Greek, & Roman rule: it corresponded roughly to the Biblical Judah —**Ju·de'an** *adj., n.*

Ju·de·o- (jōō dē'ō, -dā'-) *a combining form meaning:* 1. Judaic; Jewish 2. Jewish and [*Judeo-*Christian]

Judg. Judges

judge (juj) *n.* [ME. *juge* < OFr. < L. *judex*, a judge < *jus*, law + *dicere*, to say, declare (see JURY[1] & DICTION)] 1. an elected or appointed public official with authority to hear and decide cases in a court of law 2. a person designated to

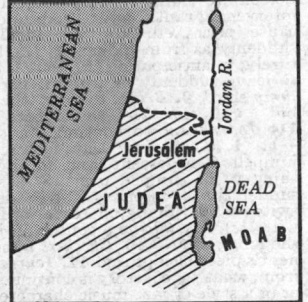

JUDEA (1st cent. AD.).

determine the winner in a contest, settle a controversy, etc. 3. a person qualified to give an opinion or decide on the relative worth of anything [a good *judge* of music] 4. *Jewish History* any of the governing leaders of the Israelites after Joshua and before the time of the kings —*vt., vi.* **judged, judg'ing** [ME. *juggen* < OFr. *juger* < L. *judicare*, to judge, declare the law < *judex:* see the *n.*] 1. to hear and pass judgment on (persons or cases) in a court of law 2. to determine the winner of (a contest) or settle (a controversy) 3. to decree 4. to form an idea, opinion, or estimate about (any matter) 5. to criticize or censure 6. to think or suppose 7. *Jewish History* to govern —**judg'er** *n.*

SYN.—**judge** is applied to one who, by the authority vested in him or by expertness of knowledge, is qualified to settle a controversy or decide on the relative merit of things [a *judge* of a beauty contest]; **arbiter** emphasizes the authoritativeness of decision of one whose judgment in a particular matter is considered indisputable [an *arbiter* of the social graces]; **referee** and **umpire** both apply to a person to whom anything is referred for decision or settlement [a *referee* in bankruptcy] and, in sports, to officials charged with the regulation of a contest, ruling on the plays in a game, etc. [a *referee* in boxing, basketball, etc., an *umpire* in baseball, cricket, etc.] See also INFER

judge advocate *pl.* **judge advocates** a military legal officer; esp., an officer designated to act as prosecutor at a court-martial

judge advocate general, *pl.* **judge advocates general** ☆the head officer of the legal section in the U.S. Army, Navy, or Air Force

judge-made (-mād') *adj.* made by judges or by their decisions taken as precedent

Judg·es (juj'iz) a book of the Bible telling the history of the Jews from the death of Joshua to the birth of Samuel

judge·ship (juj'ship') *n.* the position, functions, or term of office of a judge

judg·mat·ic (jəj mat'ik) *adj.* [< JUDG(E) + (DOG)MATIC] [Colloq.] discerning; judicious: also **judg·mat'i·cal**

judg·ment (juj'mənt) *n.* [ME. *jugement* < OFr. < ML. *judicamentum* < L. *judicare:* see JUDGE, *v.*] 1. the act of judging; deciding 2. a legal decision; order, decree, or sentence given by a judge or law court 3. *a)* a debt or other obligation resulting from a court order *b)* a document recording this obligation 4. a misfortune looked on as a punishment from God 5. an opinion or estimate 6. criticism or censure 7. the ability to come to opinions about things; power of comparing and deciding; understanding; good sense 8. *Bible* justice; right 9. *Logic* the assertion of a belief or proposition 10. [J-] *short for* LAST JUDGMENT Also sp. **judge'ment** —**judg·men'tal** (-men't'l) *adj.*

Judgment Day *Theol.* the time of God's final judgment of all people; end of the world; doomsday

ju·di·ca·ble (jōō'di kə b'l) *adj.* [LL. *judicabilis* < L. *judicatus*, pp. of *judicare:* see JUDGE, *v.*] 1. that can be judged 2. liable to be judged

ju·di·ca·tive (-kāt'iv, -kə tiv) *adj.* [< L. *judicatus*, pp. of *judicare* (see JUDGE, *v.*) + -IVE] judging; judicial

ju·di·ca·to·ry (-kə tôr'ē) *adj.* [LL.(Ec.) *judicatorius* < L. *judicatus:* see prec.] having to do with administering justice; judging —*n., pl.* **-ries** [LL. *judicatorium*] 1. a court of law; tribunal 2. the system of administration of justice 3. law courts collectively

ju·di·ca·ture (-kə chər) *n.* [MFr. < ML. *judicatura* < L. *judicare:* see JUDGE, *v.*] 1. the administering of justice 2. the position, functions, or legal power of a judge 3. the extent of legal power of a judge or court of law; jurisdiction 4. a court of law 5. judges or courts of law collectively

ju·di·cial (jōō dish'əl) *adj.* [ME. < OFr. < L. *judicialis* < *judex:* see JUDGE] 1. of judges, law courts, or their functions 2. allowed, enforced, or set by order of a judge or law court 3. administering justice 4. like or befitting a judge 5. carefully considering the facts, arguments, etc., and reasoning to a decision; fair; unbiased —**ju·di'cial·ly** *adv.*

ju·di·ci·ar·y (jōō dish'ē er'ē, -dish'ər ē) *adj.* [L. *judiciarius* < *judicium*, judgment, court of justice < *judex:* see JUDGE] of judges, law courts, or their functions —*n., pl.* **-ar·ies** 1. the part of government whose work is the administration of justice 2. a system of law courts 3. judges collectively

ju·di·cious (-dish'əs) *adj.* [Fr. *judicieux* < L. *judicium*, judgment < *judex:* see JUDGE] having, applying, or showing sound judgment; wise and careful —SYN. see WISE[1] —**ju·di'cious·ly** *adv.* —**ju·di'cious·ness** *n.*

Ju·dith (jōō'dith) [LL.(Ec.) < Gr.(Ec.) *Ioudith* < Heb. *yehūdhīth*, fem. of *yehūdhāh*, JUDAH] 1. a feminine name: dim. *Judy* 2. *a)* a book of the Apocrypha and the Douay Bible *b)* the Jewish woman told about in this book, who saved her people by killing Holofernes

ju·do (jōō'dō) *n.* [Jap. < *jū*, soft + *dō*, art] a form of jujitsu developed as a sport and as a means of self-defense without the use of weapons

ju·do·ka (jōō'dō kä) *n.* [Jap. < *jūdō*, JUDO + -*ka*, n. suffix] one who performs, or is expert in, judo

Ju·dy (jōō'dē) 1. a feminine name: see JUDITH 2. Punch's wife in a puppet show: see PUNCH-AND-JUDY SHOW

jug[1] (jug) *n.* [echoic] a sound meant to imitate a nightingale's note —*vi.* **jugged, jug'ging** to make a nightingale's sound or a sound imitating this

jug[2] (jug) *n.* [apparently a pet form of JUDITH or JOAN] 1. *a)* a container for liquids, usually large and deep with a small opening at the top and a handle *b)* the contents of such a container 2. [Slang] a jail 3. [Slang] a bottle of whiskey —*vt.* **jugged, jug'ging** 1. to put into a jug 2. to stew (esp. hare) in a covered earthenware container 3. [Slang] to jail —**jug'ful** (-fool) *n.*

ju·gal (jōō'gəl) *adj.* [L. *jugalis* < *jugum*, a YOKE: cf. ZYGOMA] designating or of a bone of the upper cheek

ju·gate (jōō'gāt, -git) *adj.* [L. *jugatus*, pp. of *jugare*, to yoke, connect < *jugum*, YOKE] *Biol.* paired or connected

☆**jug band** a small folk-music or jazz band using harmonicas, kazoos, etc., and for percussive effects, jugs, washboards, washtubs, etc.

Jug·ger·naut (jug'ər nôt') *n.* [altered < Hind. *Jagannāth* < Sans. *Jagannātha*, lord of the world < *jagat*, world + *nātha*, lord] 1. an incarnation of the Hindu god Vishnu, whose idol, it is said, so excited his worshipers when it was hauled along on a large car during religious rites that they threw themselves under the wheels and were crushed 2. [*usually* j-] anything that exacts blind devotion or terrible sacrifice 3. [*usually* j-] any terrible, irresistible force

jug·gle (jug''l) *vt.* **-gled, -gling** [ME. *jogelen* < OFr. *jogler*, to juggle, play false < L. *joculari*, to joke < *joculus*, dim. of *jocus*, JOKE] 1. to perform skillful tricks of sleight of hand with (balls, knives, etc.), as by keeping a number of them in the air continuously 2. to make several awkward attempts to catch or hold (a ball, etc.) 3. to manipulate or practice trickery on so as to deceive or cheat [to *juggle* figures so as to show a profit] —*vi.* to toss up a number of balls, knives, etc. and keep them continuously in the air —*n.* 1. an act of juggling 2. a clever trick or deception —**jug'gler** *n.*

jug·gler·y (-lər ē) *n., pl.* **-gler·ies** [ME. *jugelri* < OFr.

jogelerie] **1.** the art or act of juggling; sleight of hand **2.** trickery; deception

☆**jug·head** (-hed´) *n.* [Slang] a foolish or stupid person

Ju·go·sla·vi·a (yōō´gō slä´vē ə) *same as* YUGOSLAVIA —**Ju´go·slav´** *adj., n.* —**Ju´go·sla´vi·an** *adj., n.* —**Ju´go·slav´ic** *adj.*

jug·u·lar (jug´yōō lər, jōōg´-) *adj.* [LL. *jugularis* < L. *jugulum*, collarbone, neck, throat, dim. of *jugum*, a YOKE] **1.** of the neck or throat **2.** of a jugular vein **3.** *Zool.* of or having ventral fins in front of the pectoral, under the throat —*n. same as* JUGULAR VEIN

jugular vein either of two large veins in the neck carrying blood back from the head to the heart

ju·gu·late (jōō´gyə lāt´) *vt.* **-lat´ed, -lat´ing** [L. *jugulatus*, pp. of *jugulare* < *jugulum*: see JUGULAR] [Now Rare] **1.** to kill by cutting the throat **2.** *Med.* to use extreme measures in arresting (a disease)

ju·gum (jōō´gəm) *n., pl.* **-ga** (-gə), **-gums** [ModL. < L., YOKE] a special process on the forewings of some insects by means of which the forewings and hind wings are hooked together during flight

Ju·gur·tha (jōō gur´thə) ?-104 B.C.; king of Numidia (112?-104 B.C.)

juice (jōōs) *n.* [ME. *juis* < OFr. *jus* < L., broth, juice < IE. **yūs-* < base **yeu-*, to mix, whence Sans. *yuti-*, mixture] **1.** the liquid part of a plant, fruit, or vegetable **2.** a liquid in or from animal tissue [gastric *juice*, meat *juices*] **3.** the essence of anything **4.** [Colloq.] energy; vitality ☆**5.** [Slang] *a)* electricity *b)* gasoline, oil, or any liquid fuel ☆**6.** [Slang] alcoholic liquor (often with *the*) ☆**7.** [Slang] exorbitant interest charged on a loan —*vt.* **juiced, juic´ing** to extract juice from —☆**juice up** to add power, vigor, energy, etc. or interest, excitement, etc. to —**juice´less** *adj.*

☆**juic·er** (jōō´sər) *n.* a device or appliance for extracting juice from fruit

juic·y (jōō´sē) *adj.* **juic´i·er, juic´i·est 1.** full of juice; containing much juice; succulent **2.** [Colloq.] full of interest, as a racy story or bit of gossip; piquant; spicy **3.** [Colloq.] highly profitable [a *juicy* contract] —**juic´i·ly** *adv.* —**juic´i·ness** *n.*

ju·jit·su (jōō jit´sōō) *n.* [Jap. *jū-jutsu*, lit., soft art < *jū*, soft, pliant + *jutsu*, art] a Japanese system of wrestling in which knowledge of anatomy and the principle of leverage are applied so that the strength and weight of an opponent are used against him

ju·ju (jōō´jōō) *n.* [Hausa, an evil spirit, fetish] **1.** a magic charm or fetish used by some West African tribes **2.** its magic **3.** a taboo connected with its use

ju·jube (jōō´jōōb; *for 4, often* jōō´jōō bē´) *n.* [Fr. < ML. *jujuba* < L. *zizyphum* < Gr. *zizyphon*] **1.** the edible, datelike fruit of any of several trees and shrubs (genus *Zizyphus*) of the buckthorn family, growing in warm climates **2.** a tree or shrub bearing this fruit **3.** a jelly made from this fruit **4.** a lozenge of gelatinous fruit-flavored candy

ju·jut·su (jōō jit´sōō, -jut´-) *n. same as* JUJITSU

☆**juke·box** (jōōk´bäks´) *n.* [Gullah *juke*, wicked, disorderly (as in *juke-house*, house of prostitution); of WAfr. orig.] a coin-operated electric phonograph used in restaurants, bars, etc.: a record is chosen by pushing a button: also **juke box**

Jul. July

ju·lep (jōō´ləp) *n.* [ME. < MFr. < Ar. *julāb* < Per. *gulāb* < *gul*, rose + *āb*, water] ☆**1.** *same as* MINT JULEP **2.** a mixture of water with syrup or sugar, as for drinking along with, or after taking, medicine

Jules (jōōlz) *a masculine name:* see JULIUS

Jul·ia (jōōl´yə) [L., fem. of *Julius*: see JULIUS] a feminine name: dim. *Juliet*; equiv. Fr. & Ger. *Julie*, It. *Giulia*

Jul·ian (jōōl´yən) [L. *Julianus* < *Julius*: see JULIUS] **1.** a masculine name: dim. *Jule*; equiv. Fr. *Julien*, It. *Giuliano*; fem. *Juliana* **2.** (L. name *Flavius Claudius Julianus*) 331-363 A.D.; Rom. general; emperor of Rome (361-363 A.D.): called *Julian the Apostate* —*adj.* of Julius Caesar

Ju·li·an·a (jōō´lē an´ə; *for 2, Du.* yü´lē ä´nə) [L., fem. of *Julian*] **1.** a feminine name: equiv. Fr. *Julienne*, It. *Giuliana* **2.** (born *Juliana Louise Emma Marie Wilhelmina*) 1909- ; queen of the Netherlands (1948-): daughter of WILHELMINA

Julian Alps SE range of the Alps, mostly in NW Yugoslavia: highest peak, 9,395 ft.

Julian calendar the calendar introduced by Julius Caesar in 46 B.C., in which the ordinary year had 365 days and every fourth year (leap year) had 366 days: the months were the same as in the Gregorian or New Style calendar now used

ju·li·enne (jōō´lē en´; *Fr.* zhü lyen´) *n.* [Fr., prob. < *Julienne, Juliana*; reason for name unknown] a clear soup containing vegetables cut into strips or bits —*adj. Cooking* cut into strips: said of vegetables

Ju·li·et (jōōl´yət, jōōl´ē ət, jōō´lē et´) [Fr. *Juliette*, dim. < L. *Julia*] **1.** a feminine name: see JULIA **2.** the heroine of Shakespeare's tragedy *Romeo and Juliet*: see ROMEO

Juliet cap a woman's small, brimless cap, worn usually on the back of the head: often a part of bridal attire

Jul·ius (jōōl´yəs) [L., name of a Roman gens] **1.** a masculine name: dim. *Jule, Julie*; equiv. Fr. *Jules*, It. *Giulio*,

Sp. *Julio;* fem. *Julia* **2.** *Julius II* (born *Giuliano della Rovere*) 1443-1513; Pope (1503-13)

Julius Caesar *see* Julius CAESAR

Jul·lun·dur (jul´ən dər) city in N India, in Punjab state: pop. 223,000

Ju·ly (joo lī´, jōō-, jə-) *n., pl.* **-lies´** [ME. *Julie* < Anglo-Fr. < L. *Julius* < *mensis Julius*, the month of Julius (CAESAR)] the seventh month of the year, having 31 days: abbrev. **Jul., Jl., Jy.**

jum·ble[1] (jum´b'l) *n.* [< ? OFr. *jumel, gemel* (Fr. *jumeau*), twin: see GIMBALS] a kind of cookie shaped like a ring: also sp. **jum´bal**

jum·ble[2] (jum´b'l) *vt.* **-bled, -bling** [? blend of JUMP + TUMBLE] **1.** to mix in a confused, disorderly heap **2.** to confuse mentally —*vi.* to be jumbled —*n.* **1.** a confused mixture or heap **2.** a muddle **3.** [Brit.] *same as* RUMMAGE SALE: in full **jumble sale**

☆**jum·bo** (jum´bō) *n., pl.* **-bos** [< Gullah *jamba*, elephant; of Afr. origin: reinforced by P. T. BARNUM's use of it for his famous elephant, *Jumbo*] a very large person, animal, or thing —*adj.* very large; larger than usual of its kind

Jum·na (jum´nə) river in N India, flowing from the Himalayas southwest into the Ganges at Allahabad: 860 mi.

jump (jump) *vi.* [< ?] **1.** to move oneself suddenly from the ground, etc. by using the leg muscles; leap; spring **2.** to be moved with a jerk; bob; bounce **3.** to leap from an aircraft using a parachute **4.** to move, act, or react energetically or eagerly (often with *at*) **5.** to pass suddenly from one thing or topic to another **6.** to rise suddenly [prices have *jumped*] **7.** to break in continuity of action, as a motion-picture image, because of faulty alignment of the film **8.** [Slang] to be lively and animated [the party was *jumping*] **9.** *Bridge* to make a jump bid ☆**10.** *Checkers* to move a piece over an opponent's piece, thus capturing it —*vt.* **1.** *a)* to leap over *b)* to pass over; skip **2.** to cause to leap [to *jump* a horse over a fence] ☆**3.** to advance (a person) to a higher rank or position, esp. by bypassing intervening ranks ☆**4.** to leap upon; spring aboard **5.** to cause (prices, etc.) to rise suddenly **6.** [Colloq.] to attack suddenly as from hiding **7.** [Colloq.] to react to prematurely, in anticipation [to *jump* a traffic light] ☆**8.** [Slang] to leave suddenly or without permission [to *jump* town, *jump* ship] **9.** *Bridge* to raise (the bid) by making a jump bid ☆**10.** *Checkers* to capture (an opponent's piece) **11.** *Journalism* to continue (a story) on another page —*n.* **1.** a jumping; leap; bound; spring **2.** a distance jumped **3.** a descent from an aircraft by parachute **4.** a thing to be jumped over **5.** a sudden transition **6.** a sudden rise, as in prices **7.** a sudden, nervous start or jerk; twitch **8.** [pl.] [Slang] chorea; also, delirium tremens (usually with *the*) **9.** *Athletics* a contest in jumping [the high *jump*, the long *jump*] **10.** *Checkers* a move by which an opponent's piece is captured **11.** *Journalism* a line telling on, or from, what page a story is continued —*adj.* **1.** designating or of a style of jazz music characterized by recurrent short riffs and a strong, fast beat **2.** of or for parachuting or paratroops —**get** (*or* **have**) **the jump on** [Slang] to get (or have) an earlier start than and thus have an advantage over —☆**jump a claim** to seize mining rights or land claimed by someone else —**jump at** to accept hastily and eagerly —☆**jump bail** to forfeit one's bail by running away —**jump in with both feet** to enter into an activity or venture wholeheartedly —**jump off** [Mil. Slang] to start an attack —**jump on** (*or* **all over**) [Slang] to scold; censure severely —☆**jump the track** to go suddenly off the rails —**on the jump** [Colloq.] busily moving about

☆**jump ball** *Basketball* a ball tossed by the referee between two opposing players, as in beginning or resuming play

jump bid *Bridge* a bid that is higher than is necessary to increase the previous bid

jump·er[1] (-ər) *n.* **1.** a person, animal, or thing that jumps ☆**2.** a kind of sled **3.** a short wire to close a break in, or cut out part of, a circuit, or to make a temporary electrical connection **4.** *Mining* a boring tool that is operated with an up-and-down jumping motion

jump·er[2] (jum´pər) *n.* [< earlier dial. *jump*, short coat, prob. altered (after JUMP) < Fr. *jupe* (? via Sp. *aljuba*, Moorish garment) < Ar. *al jubbah* < *al*, the + *jubbah*, cotton undergarment] **1.** a loose jacket or blouse; specif., *a)* one worn by workmen to protect clothing *b)* one with a wide collar hanging down in back, worn by sailors **2.** a sleeveless dress for wearing over a blouse or sweater ☆**3.** [pl.] *same as* ROMPERS

☆**jumping bean** the seed of any of several Mexican plants (genera *Sebastiania* and *Sapium*) of the spurge family, containing the larva of a small moth (*Carpocapsa saltitans*), which by its movements makes the seed jump or roll about

jumping jack a child's toy consisting of a little jointed figure made to jump or dance about by pulling a string or pushing an attached stick

☆**jumping mouse** any of various small N. American and Asiatic rodents (family Zapodidae) with large hind legs and a long tail

☆**jump·ing-off place** (jum´piŋ ôf´) **1.** any isolated or

JUMPER

remote place regarded as the outmost limit of human habitation 2. starting point for a trip, venture, etc.

☆**jump seat** a small folding seat, as one behind the front seat of a limousine, taxi, etc.

☆**jump shot** *Basketball* a shot made by a player while in the air during a jump

☆**jump suit** 1. a coverall worn by paratroops, garage mechanics, etc. 2. a woman's lounging outfit somewhat like this, usually tightfitting

jump·y (jum′pē) *adj.* **jump′i·er, jump′i·est** 1. moving in jumps, jerks, or abrupt variations 2. easily startled; apprehensive —**jump′i·ly** *adv.* —**jump′i·ness** *n.*

Jun., jun. junior

Junc., junc. junction

jun·co (juŋ′kō) *n., pl.* **-cos** [ModL., name of the genus < Sp. *junco*, a rush < L. *juncus*, a rush: see JONQUIL] ☆any of a genus (*Junco*) of sparrowlike birds of North and Central America with a gray or black head and white outer tail feathers, including the snowbird

junc·tion (juŋk′shən) *n.* [L. *junctio* < *jungere*, to JOIN] 1. a joining or being joined 2. a place or point of joining or crossing, as of highways or railroads 3. a region within a single-crystal semiconductor body separating two types of material differing in impurity characteristics: when connections are made to a body containing such a junction, a semiconductor diode or transistor (**junction transistor**) is produced —**junc′tion·al** *adj.*

junc·ture (juŋk′chər) *n.* [L. *junctura* < *jungere*, to JOIN] 1. a joining or being joined 2. a point or line of joining or connection; joint, as of two bones, or seam 3. a point of time 4. a particular or critical moment in the development of events; crisis 5. a state of affairs 6. *Linguis.* the transition from one speech sound to the next, occurring typically within a word (**close juncture**), as between *t* and *r* in *nitrate*, or marking the boundaries between words (**open juncture**), as between *t* and *r* in *night rate*

June (jōon) a feminine name: see JUNIUS —*n.* [ME. < OFr. < L. *Junius* < *mensis Junius*, the month of *Juno*] the sixth month of the year, having 30 days: abbrev. **Je., Ju., Jun.**

Ju·neau (jōo′nō) [after J. *Juneau*, a prospector] capital of Alas.; seaport on the SE coast: pop. 6,000

☆**June·ber·ry** (jōon′ber′ē, -bər i) *n., pl.* **-ries** 1. any of a genus (*Amelanchier*) of trees and shrubs of the rose family, with white flowers, small, purple-black fruits, and simple leaves 2. the fruit

June bug ☆1. any of several large, scarabaeid beetles (genus *Phyllophaga*) appearing in May or June in the N U.S.: also **June beetle** ☆2. same as FIGEATER

Jung (yoon), **Carl Gus·tav** (goos′täf) 1875–1961; Swiss psychologist & psychiatrist —**Jung′i·an** *adj., n.*

Jung·frau (yoon′frou′) mountain of the Bernese Alps, S Switzerland: 13,642 ft.

jun·gle (juŋ′g'l) *n.* [Hindi *jangal*, desert, forest, jungle < Sans. *jangala*, wasteland, desert] 1. land covered with dense growth of trees, tall vegetation, vines, etc., typically in tropical regions, and inhabited by predatory animals 2. any confused, tangled growth, collection, etc. ☆3. [Slang] a hobos' camp ☆4. [Slang] a place or situation in which people engage in ruthless competition or in a struggle for survival —**jun′gly** *adj.*

jungle fever any of several diseases of tropical regions; esp., a severe malarial fever of the East Indies

jungle fowl any of several game birds (genus *Gallus*) native to Malaysia and India, having combs and throat wattles: the red Indian species (*Gallus gallus*) is regarded as the ancestor of the present-day domestic fowl

☆**Jungle Gym** *a trademark for* an apparatus for playgrounds, consisting of bars, ladders, etc. for children to climb on —*n.* [**j- g-**] such an apparatus

jun·ior (jōon′yər) *adj.* [L., contr. of *juvenior*, compar. of *juvenis*, YOUNG] 1. the younger: written *Jr.* after the name of a son who bears the same name as his father: opposed to SENIOR 2. of more recent position or lower status [a junior partner, a junior lien] 3. of later date 4. made up of younger members ☆5. relating to a junior or juniors in a high school or college —*n.* 1. a younger person 2. a person of lower standing or rank ☆3. a student in the next-to-last year of a high school or college ☆4. a size of clothing for slight women and girls with high waistlines —**one's junior** a person younger than oneself

☆**junior college** a school offering courses two years beyond the high school level, either the first two years of the standard college course or terminal study programs in various fields, and awarding a certificate at the completion of the course

☆**junior high school** a school intermediate between elementary school and senior high school: it usually includes the seventh, eighth, and ninth grades

jun·ior·i·ty (jōon yôr′ə tē, -yär′-) *n.* the quality or state of being junior, as in age or rank

☆**Junior League** any of the local branches of the Association of the Junior Leagues of America, Inc., the members of which are young women of leisure and the upper social class, organized to engage in volunteer welfare work —**Junior Leaguer**

☆**junior miss** 1. a girl in her early teens 2. *same as* JUNIOR (*n.* 4)

☆**junior varsity** a team, usually of lowerclassmen, that represents a university, college, or school in a secondary level of competition, esp. in an athletic sport

ju·ni·per (jōo′nə pər) *n.* [ME. *junipur* < L. *juniperus* < IE. base *yoini-*, reed (cf. JONQUIL) + unexplained second element] 1. any of a genus (*Juniperus*) of small evergreen shrubs or trees of the cypress family, with needlelike or scalelike foliage, aromatic wood, and berrylike cones that yield an oil used for flavoring gin and formerly in medicine ☆2. any of several similar trees often grown for ornament

Jun·ius (jōon′yəs) [L., name of a Roman gens] 1. a masculine name: fem. *June* 2. pseudonym of the unknown writer of a series of public letters (1768–1772) criticizing the policies of the British ministry

junk[1] (juŋk) *n.* [< ? Port. *junco*, a reed, rush < L. *juncus*, a rush: see JONQUIL] 1. orig., old cable or rope used for making oakum, mats, etc. 2. old metal, glass, paper, rags, etc. 3. [Colloq.] useless or worthless stuff; trash; rubbish ☆4. [Slang] a narcotic drug; esp., heroin 5. *Naut.* hard salted meat —*vt.* ☆[Colloq.] to throw away as worthless or get rid of by selling as junk; discard; scrap —**junk′y** *adj.* **junk′i·er, junk′i·est**

junk[2] (juŋk) *n.* [Sp. & Port. *junco* < Jav. *joŋ*] a Chinese flat-bottomed ship with battened sails and a high poop

Jun·ker (yoon′kər) *n.* [G. < MHG. *junc herre*, young nobleman < OHG. *jung*, YOUNG + *herro*, lord: cf. HOAR] 1. a member of the privileged, militaristic land-owning class in Germany; Prussian aristocrat 2. a German military officer, esp. one who is autocratic, illiberal, etc.

☆**junk·er** (juŋ′kər) *n.* [< JUNK[1], *vt.*] [Slang] an old, dilapidated car or truck

jun·ket (juŋ′kit) *n.* [ME. *joncate* < ML. **juncata*, a sweetmeat, cream cheese < L. *juncus*, a rush (see JONQUIL): because orig. brought to market in rush baskets] 1. formerly, curds with cream 2. milk sweetened, flavored, and thickened into curd with rennet 3. a feast or picnic 4. an excursion for pleasure ☆5. an excursion, as by a public official, paid for out of public funds —*vi.* to go on a junket or excursion, esp. one paid for out of public funds —*vt.* to entertain at a feast —☆**jun′ket·eer′** (-kə tir′), ☆**jun′ket·er** *n.*

☆**junk·ie, junk·y** (juŋ′kē) *n., pl.* **junk′ies** [< JUNK[1], *n.* 4] [Slang] a narcotics addict, esp. one addicted to heroin

☆**junk jewelry** [Colloq.] inexpensive costume jewelry

☆**junk mail** advertisements, solicitations, etc. mailed indiscriminately in large quantities

☆**junk·man** (juŋk′man′) *n., pl.* **-men′** (-men′) a dealer in old metal, glass, paper, rags, etc.: also **junk dealer**

☆**junk·yard** (-yärd′) *n.* a place where old metal, paper, etc. is kept, sorted, and sold or old cars are junked

Ju·no (jōo′nō) [L.] *Rom. Myth.* the sister and wife of Jupiter; queen of the gods and goddess of marriage: identified with the Greek Hera

Ju·no·esque (jōo′nō esk′) *adj.* stately and regal like Juno

jun·ta (hoon′tə, jun′-) *n.* [Sp. < L. *juncta*, fem. of *junctus*, pp. of *jungere*, to JOIN] 1. an assembly or council; esp., a Spanish or Latin-American legislative or administrative body 2. a group of political intriguers; esp., such a group of military men in power after a coup d'état: also **jun·to** (jun′tō), *pl.* **-tos**

Ju·pi·ter (jōo′pə tər) [L. *Juppiter*, orig. a vocative < bases of *Jovis*, JOVE & *pater*, FATHER] 1. *Rom. Myth.* the god ruling over all other gods and all people: identified with the Greek Zeus 2. the largest planet of the solar system and the fifth in distance from the sun: diameter, c.88,000 mi.; period of revolution, 11.86 yrs.; period of rotation, 9.9 hrs.; symbol, ♃

Jupiter Plu·vi·us (plōo′vē əs) [L., lit., Jupiter who brings rain; *pluvius*, rainy < *pluere*, to rain] Jupiter regarded as the giver of rain

ju·pon (jōo′pän, jōo pän′; *Fr.* zhü pōn′) *n.* [ME. *jopon* < OFr. *jupon* < *jupe*: see JUMPER[2]] a jacket or tunic formerly worn over or under armor

Ju·ra (joor′ə) *n.* the Jurassic period or its rocks

ju·ra (joor′ə, yōo′rə) *n.* [L.] *pl. of* JUS

ju·ral (joor′əl) *adj.* [< L. *jus* (gen. *juris*), right, law (see JURY[1]) + -AL] 1. of law; legal 2. relating to natural rights and duties —**ju′ral·ly** *adv.*

Ju·ra Mountains (joor′ə) mountain range along the border of France & Switzerland: highest peak, 5,652 ft.

ju·rant (joor′ənt) *adj.* [L. *jurans*, prp. of *jurare*, to swear < *jus*: see JURY[1]] *Law* taking an oath; swearing

Ju·ras·sic (joo ras′ik) *adj.* [Fr. *jurassique* < *Jura* (Mountains)] designating or of the second period of the Mesozoic Era, immediately following the Triassic and preceding the Cretaceous, characterized by the dominance of

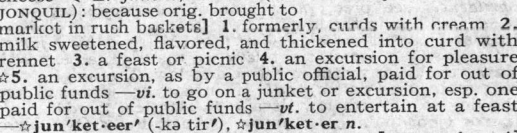

JUNK

dinosaurs and the appearance of flying reptiles and birds —**the Jurassic** the Jurassic Period or its rocks: see GEOLOGY, chart

ju·rat (joor′ət) *n.* [Fr. < ML. *juratus,* lit., one sworn < L. *juratus,* pp. of *jurare:* see JURY[1]] **1.** a municipal officer or magistrate in certain French towns and the Channel Islands **2.** [< L. *juratum,* neut. pp. of *jurare*] *Law* a statement or certification added to an affidavit, telling when, before whom, and, sometimes, where the affidavit was made

ju·ra·to·ry (joor′ə tôr′ē) *adj.* [LL. *juratorius* < L. *jurator,* sworn witness < *jurare:* see JURY[1]] *Law* of or expressed in an oath

ju·rel (hoo rel′) *n.* [Sp., ult. < Gr. *sauros,* horse mackerel: see SAURY] any of a number of related edible fishes (esp. genus *Caranx*) of warm seas, having typically narrow bodies and widely forked tails

ju·rid·i·cal (joo rid′i k'l) *adj.* [L. *juridicus* < *jus* (gen. *juris*), right, law (see JURY[1]) + *dicere,* to point out, declare (see DICTION) + -AL] of judicial proceedings, jurisprudence, or law: also **ju·rid′ic** —**ju·rid′i·cal·ly** *adv.*

juridical days the days on which courts are in session

ju·ris·con·sult (joor′is kən sult′, -kän′səlt) *n.* [L. *jurisconsultus,* lawyer < *jus* (gen. *juris*), law + *consultus:* see CONSULT] *same as* JURIST

ju·ris·dic·tion (-dik′shən) *n.* [ME. *jurisdiccioun,* altered (after L.) < OFr. *juridiction* < L. *jurisdictio,* administration of the law < *jus* (gen. *juris*), right, law + *dictio:* see DICTION] **1.** the administering of justice; authority or legal power to hear and decide cases **2.** authority or power in general **3.** the range or sphere of authority **4.** the territorial range of authority **5.** a law court or system of law courts —SYN. see POWER —**ju′ris·dic′tion·al** *adj.* —**ju′ris·dic′tion·al·ly** *adv.*

jurisp. jurisprudence

ju·ris·pru·dence (joor′is proo′d'ns) *n.* [L. *jurisprudentia* < *jus* (gen. *juris*), right, law + *prudentia,* a foreseeing, knowledge, skill: see PRUDENT] **1.** the science or philosophy of law **2.** a part or division of law *[medical jurisprudence]* —**ju′ris·pru·den′tial** (-proo den′shəl) *adj.* —**ju′ris·pru·den′tial·ly** *adv.*

ju·ris·pru·dent (-d'nt) *n.* [Fr., back-formation < *jurisprudence:* see prec.] a student of jurisprudence; jurist —*adj.* skilled in the law

ju·rist (joor′ist) *n.* [ME. *juriste* < MFr. < ML. *jurista* < L. *jus* (gen. *juris*), right, law: see JURY[1]] **1.** an expert in law; scholar or writer in the field of law **2.** a judge

ju·ris·tic (joo ris′tik) *adj.* of jurists or jurisprudence; having to do with law; legal —**ju·ris′ti·cal·ly** *adv.*

ju·ror (joor′ər) *n.* [ME. *jurour* < Anglo-Fr. < OFr. *jureor* < L. *jurator,* taker of an oath < *jurare,* to swear: see JURY[1]] **1.** a member of a jury or jury panel **2.** a person taking an oath, as of allegiance

Ju·ruá (zhoor wä′) river flowing from the Andes in Peru northeast across NW Brazil into the Amazon: c. 1,200 mi.

ju·ry[1] (joor′ē) *n., pl.* **-ries** [ME. *jure* < Anglo-Fr. *juree* < OFr., oath, judicial inquest < ML. *jurata,* a jury, properly fem. pp. of L. *jurare,* to take an oath, swear < *jus* (gen. *juris*), law < IE. **yewos,* fixed rule, whence OIr. *huisse,* just] **1.** a group of people sworn to hear the evidence and inquire into the facts in a law case, and to give a decision in accordance with their findings **2.** a group of people, often experts, selected to decide the winners and award the prizes in a competition or contest

ju·ry[2] (joor′ē) *adj.* [< ?] *Naut.* for temporary or emergency use; makeshift *[a jury mast, jury rig]*

ju·ry·man (joor′ē mən) *n., pl.* **-men** (-mən) *same as* JUROR (sense 1)

ju·ry-rigged (-rigd′) *adj.* [see JURY[2]] *Naut.* rigged for temporary use

jus (jus, yoos) *n., pl.* **ju·ra** (joor′ə, yoo′rə) [L.: see JURY[1]] **1.** *a*) law; the whole body of law *b*) a particular system of law **2.** a legal principle, right, or power

jus., just. justice

‡**jus ca·no·ni·cum** (kə nän′i kəm) [L.] *same as* CANON LAW

‡**jus ci·vi·le** (sə vī′lē) [L.] *same as* CIVIL LAW

‡**jus di·vi·num** (di vī′nəm) [L.] divine law

‡**jus gen·ti·um** (jen′shē əm) [L., law of nations] **1.** ancient Roman law for aliens **2.** *same as* INTERNATIONAL LAW

jus na·tu·rae (nə tyoor′ē) [L.] law of nature; natural law: also **jus na·tu·ra·le** (nach′oo rā′lē)

jus san·gui·nis (saŋ′gwi nis) [L., right of blood] a right which entitles one to citizenship of a nation of which his natural parents are citizens

jus·sive (jus′iv) *adj.* [< L. *jussus,* a command (< *jubere,* to command < IE. **yeu-dh-,* to be in violent movement, fight, whence Sans. *yúdh-,* fighter) + -IVE] *Gram.* expressing a command —*n. Gram.* a jussive word, form, or mood

jus so·li (sō′lī) [L., right of land] a right which entitles one to citizenship of a nation in which he was born

just[1] (just) *adj.* [ME. < OFr. *juste* < L. *justus,* lawful, rightful, proper < *jus,* right, law: see JURY[1]] **1.** right or fair; equitable; impartial *[a just decision]* **2.** righteous; upright *[a just man]* **3.** deserved; merited *[just praise]* **4.** legally right; lawful; rightful **5.** proper, fitting, etc. *[a just balance of colors]* **6.** well-founded; reasonable *[a just suspicion]* **7.** correct or true *[a just report]* **8.** accurate; exact *[a just measure]* —*adv.* **1.** neither more nor

less than; precisely; exactly *[just one o'clock]* **2.** almost at the point of; nearly *[he is just leaving]* **3.** no more than; only *[just a taste, just teasing you]* **4.** by a very small amount; barely *[to just miss a train]* **5.** a very short time ago *[she has just left]* **6.** immediately *[just east of the church]* **7.** [Colloq.] quite; really *[to feel just fine]* —SYN. see FAIR[1], UPRIGHT —**just now** a moment ago —☆**just the same** [Colloq.] nevertheless —**just′ness** *n.*

just[2] (just) *n., vi. same as* JOUST

jus·tice (jus′tis) *n.* [ME. < OFr. < L. *justitia* < *justus:* see JUST[1]] **1.** the quality of being righteous; rectitude **2.** impartiality; fairness **3.** the quality of being right or correct **4.** sound reason; rightfulness; validity **5.** reward or penalty as deserved; just deserts **6.** *a*) the use of authority and power to uphold what is right, just, or lawful *b*) [J-] the personification of this, usually a blindfolded goddess holding scales and a sword **7.** the administration of law; procedure of a law court **8.** *same as: a*) JUDGE *b*) JUSTICE OF THE PEACE —**bring to justice** to cause (a wrongdoer) to be tried in court and duly punished —**do justice to 1.** to treat fitly or fairly **2.** to treat with due appreciation; enjoy properly —**do oneself justice 1.** to do something in a manner worthy of one's abilities **2.** to be fair to oneself

justice of the peace in some States, a magistrate with jurisdiction over a small district or part of a county, authorized to decide minor cases, commit persons to trial in a higher court, perform marriages, etc.

jus·tice·ship (-ship′) *n.* the position, functions, or term of office of a justice

jus·ti·ci·a·ble (jus tish′ē ə b'l) *adj.* [Anglo-Fr. < OFr. < *justice:* see JUSTICE] **1.** liable for trial in court **2.** subject to court jurisdiction

jus·ti·ci·ar (-ər) *n. same as* JUSTICIARY (*n.* 1 & 2)

jus·ti·ci·ar·y (-er′ē) *n., pl.* **-ar′ies** [ME. < ML. *justitiarius* < L. *justitia:* see JUSTICE] **1.** the chief political and judicial officer under the Norman and early Plantagenet kings **2.** an officer of justice; esp., a judge of a superior court **3.** the jurisdiction of a justiciary —*adj.* relating to the administration of justice or the office of a judge

jus·ti·fi·a·ble (jus′tə fī′ə b'l, jus′tə fī′ə b'l) *adj.* [Fr. < *justifier:* see JUSTIFY] that can be justified or defended as correct —**jus′ti·fi′a·bil′i·ty** *n.* —**jus′ti·fi′a·bly** *adv.*

jus·ti·fi·ca·tion (jus′tə fi kā′shən) *n.* [ME. *justificacioun* < OFr. *justification* < LL. *justificatio* < *justificare:* see JUSTIFY] **1.** a justifying or being justified **2.** a fact that justifies or vindicates **3.** *Printing* the adjustment of type by proper spacing

justification by faith *Theol.* the act by which a sinner is freed through faith from the penalty of his sin and is accepted by God as righteous

jus·ti·fi·ca·to·ry (jəs tif′ə kə tôr′ē) *adj.* [< L. *justificatus,* justified, pp. of *justificare* (see JUSTIFY) + -ORY] justifying; serving to uphold or vindicate: also **jus·ti·fi·ca·tive** (jus′tə fi kāt′iv)

jus·ti·fy (jus′tə fī′) *vt.* **-fied′, -fy′ing** [ME. *justifien* < OFr. *justifier* < LL. (chiefly Ec.) *justificare,* to act justly toward, justify < L. *justus,* just + -ficare < *facere,* to DO[1]] **1.** to show to be just, right, or in accord with reason; vindicate **2.** [Rare exc. Theol.] to free from blame; declare guiltless; absolve **3.** to supply good or lawful grounds for; warrant **4.** *Printing* to adjust (type) by spacing so that the lines will be of the correct length —*vi.* **1.** *Law a*) to show an adequate reason for something done *b*) to prove qualified as surety **2.** *Printing* to fit; be in line or flush, as type —**jus′ti·fi′er** *n.*

Jus·tin (jus′tin) [L. *Justinus* < *justus:* see JUST[1]] **1.** a masculine name: var. *Justus;* fem. *Justina* **2.** Saint, 100?-165? A.D.; Christian apologist & martyr, born in Samaria: called *Justin Martyr:* his day is April 14

Jus·ti·na (jəs tē′nə, -tī′-) [L., fem. of *Justinus:* see JUSTIN] a feminine name: var. *Justine*

Jus·tin·i·an I (jəs tin′ē ən) (L. name *Flavius Ancius Justinianus*) 483-565 A.D.; Byzantine emperor (527-565): known for the codification of Roman law (**Justinian code**) published during his reign: called *the Great*

jus·tle (jus′'l) *n., vi., n. same as* JOSTLE

just·ly (just′lē) *adv.* **1.** in a just manner **2.** rightly **3.** deservedly

Jus·tus (jus′təs) a masculine name: see JUSTIN

jut (jut) *vi., vt.* **jut′ted, jut′ting** [prob. var. of JET[1]] to stick out; project —*n.* a part that juts

Jute (joot) *n.* [< ME. *Jutes,* pl. < ML. *Jutae* or OE. *Iotas* < ON. *Iōtar*] a member of any of several ancient Germanic tribes that lived in Jutland: Jutes invaded SE England in the 5th cent. A.D., settling in what became Kent —**Jut′ish** *adj.*

jute (joot) *n.* [Hind. *jhuto* < Sans. *jūta,* matted hair, *jaṭa,* braid of hair, fibrous roots] **1.** a strong, glossy fiber used for making burlap, sacks, mats, rope, etc. **2.** either of two Indian plants (*Corchorus capsularis* and *Corchorus olitorius*) of the linden family, which yield this fiber

Jut·land (jut′lənd) peninsula of N Europe, forming the mainland of Denmark & the N part of the West German state of Schleswig-Holstein: see SCHLESWIG, map

jut·ty (jut′ē) *n., pl.* **-ties** *same as* JETTY[1] —*vi., vt.* **-tied, -ty·ing** [Obs.] to project or overhang

Ju·ve·nal (joo′və n'l) (L. name *Decimus Junius Juvenalis*) 60?-140? A.D.; Rom. satirical poet

ju·ve·nes·cent (jōō′və nes′'nt) *adj.* [L. *juvenescens*, prp. of *juvenescere*, to become young < *juvenis*, YOUNG] becoming young; growing youthful —**ju′ve·nes′cence** *n.*

ju·ven·ile (jōō′və n'l, -nil′) *adj.* [L. *juvenilis* < *juvenis*, YOUNG] **1.** *a)* young or youthful *b)* immature or childish **2.** of, characteristic of, or suitable for children or young persons **3.** *Geol.* emanating from the interior of the earth for the first time: said of gas, water, etc. —*n.* **1.** a young person; child or youth **2.** an actor who plays youthful roles ☆**3.** a book for children **4.** a two-year-old race horse **5.** *Biol.* a young plant or animal differing variously in form, features, etc. from the adult —*SYN.* see YOUNG

☆**juvenile court** a law court for cases involving children under a specified age, usually 18 years

juvenile delinquency behavior by minors of not more than a specified age, usually 18 years, that is antisocial or in violation of the law —**juvenile delinquent**

juvenile hormone a hormone secreted by insects that regulates growth and metamorphosis and which must be absent for the emergence of an adult: used to inhibit insect growth, as for preventing insect reproduction

ju·ve·nil·i·a (jōō′və nil′ē ə, -nil′yə) *n.pl.* [L., neut. pl. of *juvenilis*, JUVENILE] **1.** writings, paintings, etc. done in childhood or youth **2.** books for children

ju·ve·nil·i·ty (-ə tē) *n.*, *pl.* **-ties** [L. *juvenilitas*] **1.** the quality or state of being juvenile **2.** a childish action, manner, etc.

jux·ta- (juk′stə) [Fr. < L. *juxta*, near, beside < IE. *yugistos*, superl. of base *yug-*, closely connected, var. of *yeug-*, whence YOKE] *a combining form meaning* near, beside, close by [*juxtaposition*]

jux·ta·pose (juk′stə pōz′) *vt.* **-posed′**, **-pos′ing** [Fr. *juxtaposer:* see prec. & POSE¹] to put side by side or close together —**jux′ta·po·si′tion** *n.*

JWB Jewish Welfare Board

J.W.V., JWV Jewish War Veterans

Jy. July

Jyl·land (yül′län) *Dan. name of* JUTLAND

K

K, k (kā) *n.*, *pl.* **K's, k's 1.** the eleventh letter of the English alphabet: from the Greek *kappa*, a borrowing from the Phoenician **2.** the sound of *K* or *k*, normally a voiceless velar stop: when used as the first letter of a word and followed by *n*, it is usually not pronounced (Ex.: *knee, knife*) **3.** a type or impression for *K* or *k* **4.** *a symbol for* the eleventh in a sequence or group (or the tenth if J is omitted) —*adj.* **1.** of *K* or *k* **2.** eleventh (or tenth if J is omitted) in a sequence or group

K¹ (kā) *n.* **1.** an object shaped like *K* **2.** *a symbol for. a)* carat *b)* [ModL. *kalium*] *Chem.* potassium *c) Math.* constant *d) Meteorol.* smoke —*adj.* shaped like *K*

K² l. knit **2.** Chess king

K., k. 1. *Elec.* capacity **2.** karat (carat) **3.** *Physics* Kelvin **4.** kilo **5.** king **6.** knight **7.** kopeck, kopecks

K2 (kā′tōō′) *same as* GODWIN AUSTEN

ka (kä) *n.* [Egypt.] in ancient Egyptian religion, the soul, regarded as dwelling in a person's body or in an image and continuing after death

ka. kathode (cathode)

Kaa·ba (kä′bə, kä′ə bə) [Ar. *ka'bah*, lit., square building < *ka'b*, a cube] the sacred Moslem shrine at Mecca, toward which believers turn when praying: it contains a black stone supposedly given to Abraham by the angel Gabriel

kab (kab) *n. same as* CAB²

kab·a·la, kab·ba·la (kab′ə lə, kə bä′lə) *n. same as* CABALA

ka·bob (kə bäb′) *n. same as* KEBAB

Ka·bu·ki (kä bōō′kē, kə-) *n.* [Jap. < *kabu*, music and dancing + *ki*, spirit] [*also* k-] a form of Japanese drama dating from the 17th cent.: it is based on popular themes, with male and female roles performed exclusively by men, chiefly in formalized pantomime, dance, and song

Ka·bul (kä′bool) capital of Afghanistan, in NE part: pop. 450,000

Ka·byle (kə bīl′) *n.* [Fr. < Ar. *qabā'il*, pl. of *qabīlah*, tribe] **1.** a member of the Algerian or Tunisian Berber tribes **2.** the Berber language of the Kabyles

☆**ka·chi·na** (kə chē′nə) *n.*, *pl.* **-nas, -na** [Hopi *katsina*, prob. of Keres origin] **1.** *Pueblo Folklore* a beneficent spirit, either a minor deity or the spirit of an ancestor **2.** *a)* a male dancer impersonating such a spirit *b)* the mask worn by the dancer **3.** a small wooden doll representing the spirit

kad·dish (käd′ish) *n.* [Aram. *qaddīsh*, holy] *Judaism* a hymn in praise of God, recited as part of the daily service or, in one form, as a mourner's prayer

Ka·desh (kā′desh) city in ancient W Syria

ka·di (kä′dē, kā′-) *n. same as* CADI

Ka·di·yev·ka, Ka·di·ev·ka (kä dē′yef kä) city in SE Ukrainian S.S.R., in the Donets Basin: pop. 192,000

kaf (käf, kôf) *n.* [Heb.] the eleventh letter of the Hebrew alphabet (כ, ך), corresponding to English *K, k*

☆**kaf·fee·klatsch** (kä′fē kläch′, kô′fē klach′) *n.* [G. < *kaffee*, COFFEE + *klatsch*, gossip, of echoic orig.] [*also* K-] an informal gathering, as of housewives during the day, to drink coffee and chat: also **kaffee klatsch**

Kaf·fir (kaf′ər) *n.* [Ar. *kāfir*, infidel < prp. of *kafara*, to be skeptical] **1.** *a)* a member of any of several Bantu-speaking tribes of SE Africa *b) same as* XHOSA In these senses often regarded as contemptuous **2.** [k-] *same as* KAFIR

kaf·fi·yeh (kä fē′yə) *n.* [Ar. *kaffīyah*, var. of *kuffīyeh*, prob. < LL. *cufea*, COIF] a headdress worn by Arabs as a protection against dust and heat: it is a large square of cotton cloth, draped and folded, and held in place by a cord wound about the head

kaf·ir (kaf′ər) *n.* [Ar. *kāfir:* see KAFFIR] **1.** a nonsaccharine grain sorghum with juicy stalks and slender, cylindrical seed heads, grown in dry regions for grain and fodder: also **kafir corn 2.** [K-] *same as* KAFFIR

Ka·fi·ri·stan (kä′fi ri stän′) *former name of* NURISTAN

Kaf·ka (käf′kə), **Franz** (fränts) 1883–1924; Austrian-Czech writer

kaf·tan (kaf′tən, käf tän′) *n. same as* CAFTAN

Ka·ga·wa (kä′gä wä′), **To·yo·hi·ko** (tô′yō hē′kô) 1888–1960; Jap. social reformer & writer

ka·go (kä′gō) *n.* [Jap.] a Japanese palanquin, carried on a pole over the shoulders of two bearers

Ka·go·shi·ma (kä′gō shē′mä) seaport on the S coast of Kyushu, Japan: pop. 328,000

Kahn test (kän) [after R. L. *Kahn* (1887–), U.S. immunologist, who developed it] a modified form of the Wassermann test for the diagnosis of syphilis

Ka·hoo·la·we (kä′hōō lä′wē) [Haw. < ?] island of Hawaii, southwest of Maui: 45 sq. mi.

kai·ak (kī′ak) *n. same as* KAYAK

Kai·e·teur Falls (kī′ə toor′) waterfall in WC Guyana: 741 ft. high

Kai·feng (kī′fuŋ′) city in EC China, near the Yellow River: former capital of Honan province: pop. 318,000

kail (kāl) *n. same as* KALE

kail·yard (kāl′yärd′) *n.* [Scot.] a kaleyard: applied to the fiction of J. M. Barrie and others (the **kailyard school**) dealing with Scottish life and using much Scottish dialect

kai·nite (kī′nīt′, kā′-) *n.* [G. *kainit* < Gr. *kainos*, new < IE. base *ken-*, to sprout forth, whence L. *-cens:* cf. RECENT] a mineral, $MgSO_4 \cdot KCl \cdot 3H_2O$, much used in fertilizers as a source of potassium

Kair·ouan (ker wän′) city in NE Tunisia: holy city of the Moslems: pop. 82,000

kai·ser (kī′zər) *n.* [ME. *caiser* < or akin to OFris. *keiser*, ON. *keisari*, OHG. *kaisar*, Gmc. borrowing < L. *Caesar*, family name of first Roman emperors; reinforced, esp. in senses *b & c*, by G. *kaiser*] emperor: the title [K-] of: *a)* the rulers of the Holy Roman Empire, 962–1806 *b)* the rulers of Austria, 1804–1918 *c)* the rulers of Germany, 1871–1918

Kai·ser (kī′zər), **Henry J(ohn)** 1882–1967; U.S. industrialist

ka·ka (kä′kə) *n.* [Maori: echoic of the bird's cry] a New Zealand parrot (*Nestor meridionalis*) having an olive-brown body with markings of various other colors

ka·ka·po (kä′kə pō′) *n.*, *pl.* **-pos′** [Maori < *kaka*, parrot + *po*, night] a nocturnal burrowing parrot (*Strigops habroptilus*) of New Zealand having a green body with brown and yellow markings

ka·ke·mo·no (kä′kə mō′nō) *n.*, *pl.* **-nos** [Jap. < *kake*, to hang + *mono*, thing] a Japanese hanging or scroll made of silk or paper with an inscription or picture on it and a roller at the bottom

ka·ki (kä′kē) *n., pl.* **-kis** [Jap.] *same as* JAPANESE PERSIMMON

kal. kalends (calends)

ka·la a·zar (kä′lä ä zär′) *n.* [Hind. *kālā-āzār*, lit., black disease] an infectious disease of S Asia and Mediterranean countries caused by a protozoan parasite (*Leishmania donovani*) transmitted by sandflies (genus *Phlebotomus*), and characterized by an enlarged spleen and liver, irregular fever, anemia, etc.: also called **visceral leishmaniasis**

Ka·la·ha·ri (kä′lä hä′rē) desert plateau in S Africa, mostly in Botswana: c. 350,000 sq. mi.

Kal·a·ma·zoo (kal′ə mə zōō′) [< Fr. < Ojibwa < ?] city in SW Mich.: pop. 86,000

Ka·lat (kə lät′) region of West Pakistan, former state of W British India: 99,000 sq. mi.

Kalb *see* DE KALB

kale (kāl) *n.* [Scot. *kale, kail,* var. of COLE] **1.** a hardy cabbage (*Brassica oleracea acephala*) with loose, spreading, curled leaves that do not form a head **2.** [Scot.] *a)* any cabbage or greens *b)* a broth made of cabbage or other greens ☆**3.** [Slang] money; esp., paper money

ka·lei·do·scope (kə lī′də skōp′) *n.* [< Gr. *kalos,* beautiful + *eidos,* form + -SCOPE] **1.** a tubelike instrument containing loose bits of colored glass, plastic, etc. reflected by mirrors so that various symmetrical patterns appear when the tube is held to the eye and rotated **2.** anything that constantly changes, as in color and pattern —**ka·lei′-do·scop′ic** (-skäp′ik) *adj.* —**ka·lei′do·scop′i·cal·ly** *adv.*

kal·ends (kal′əndz) *n.pl. same as* CALENDS

Ka·le·va·la (kä′lə vä′lä) [Finn. < *kaleva,* heroic + -*la,* abode, hence, lit., land of heroes] a Finnish epic poem in unrhymed trochaic verse, compiled by Elias Lönnrot from the oral transmission of folklore and mythology and first published in 1835

kale·yard (kāl′yärd′) *n.* [Scot.] a vegetable garden; esp., a cabbage garden

Kal·gan (käl′gän′) *former name of* CHANGKIAKOW

Ka·li (kä′lē) a Hindu goddess viewed both as destroying life and as giving it

Ka·li·da·sa (kä′lē dä′sä) 5th cent.? A.D.; Hindu poet & dramatist

ka·lif, ka·liph (kā′lif, kal′if) *n. same as* CALIPH

Ka·li·man·tan (kä′lē män′tän) S part of the island of Borneo, constituting four provinces of Indonesia: 208,286 sq. mi.; pop. c. 4,000,000; chief city, Banjermasin

Ka·li·nin (kä lē′nin) city in W European R.S.F.S.R., on the Volga: pop. 311,000

Ka·li·nin·grad (-grät′) seaport in W European R.S.F.S.R., on the Baltic: pop. 261,000

Ka·lisz (kä′lish) city in C Poland: pop. 73,000

Kal·mar (käl′mär) seaport in SE Sweden, on the Baltic: pop. 37,000

☆**kal·mi·a** (kal′mē ə) *n.* [ModL., after Peter Kalm (1715–1779), Swed. botanist] any of a genus (*Kalmia*) of N. American evergreen shrubs of the heath family, as the mountain laurel, with flowers of white or rose

Kal·muck, Kal·muk (kal′muk) *n.* [Turk. *kalmuk,* lit., that part (of the tribe) remaining (at home), orig. pp. of *kalmak,* to remain] **1.** a member of a group of Mongol peoples living chiefly in the NE Caucasus and N Sinkiang **2.** the Altaic, western Mongolic language of the Kalmucks Also **Kal′myk** (-mik)

ka·long (kä′läŋ) *n.* [Jav. *kaloṅ*] a large, long-muzzled, fruit-eating bat (genus *Pteropus*) of the Old World tropics

kal·pak (kal′pak) *n. same as* CALPAC

kal·so·mine (kal′sə mīn′, -min) *n., vt.* **-mined′, -min′ing** *same as* CALCIMINE

Ka·ma[1] (kä′mə) river in European R.S.F.S.R., flowing from the Urals southwest into the Volga: 1,262 mi.

Ka·ma[2] (kä′mə) [Sans. *kāma,* desire, love, god of love] *Hindu Myth.* the god of love

ka·ma·la (kä mä′lə, kam′ə lə) *n.*[Sans.] **1.** an East Indian tree (*Mallotus philippinensis*) of the spurge family **2.** a powder obtained from the coating of the seed pods of this tree, used as the base of an orange-red dye for silk and wool and, formerly, as a vermifuge

Ka·ma·su·tra (kä′mə sōō′trə) [Sans. < *kāma,* love (see KAMA[2]) + *sūtra,* thread guide line, manual] a Hindu love manual written in the 8th cent.: also **Kama Sutra**

Kam·chat·ka (käm chät′kä; *E.* kam chat′kə) peninsula in NE Siberia, between the Sea of Okhotsk & the Bering Sea: c. 750 mi. long; 104,200 sq. mi.

kame (kām) *n.* [north Brit. dial. var. of COOMB] a hill or short, steep ridge of stratified sand or gravel deposited in contact with glacial ice

Ka·me·ha·me·ha I (kä mā′hä mä′hä) 1758?–1819; 1st king of the Hawaiian Islands (1810–19): called *the Great*

ka·mi (kä′mē) *n., pl.* **-mi** [Jap.] *Shintoism* a divine power or aura, often associated or identified with one or more deities or ancestors

ka·mi·ka·ze (kä′mi kä′zē) *n.* [Jap., lit., divine wind < KAMI + *kaze,* the wind] **1.** a suicide attack by a Japanese airplane pilot in World War II **2.** the airplane or pilot in such an attack

Kam·pa·la (käm pä′lä) capital of Uganda, in the S part near Lake Victoria: pop. 77,000

kam·pong (käm′pôn′) *n.* [Malay] a small Malay village or cluster of native huts

kam·seen (kam sēn′) *n. same as* KHAMSIN: also **kam·sin** (kam′sin)

Ka·nak·a (kə nak′ə, kan′ə kə) *n.* [Haw., man] **1.** a Hawaiian **2.** a native of the South Sea Islands

Ka·na·ra (kun′ər ə, kə när′ə) region in SW India, in Mysore state

Ka·na·rese (kä′nə rēz′) *adj.* of Kanara, its people, or their language —*n.* **1.** *pl.* **-rese** any of a group of Kannada-speaking people living chiefly in Kanara **2.** *same as* KANNADA

Ka·na·za·wa (kä′nə zä′wə) city in WC Honshu, Japan, on the Sea of Japan: pop. 336,000

Kan·chen·jun·ga (kän′chən jooŋ′gə) mountain in the E Himalayas, on the Nepal-Sikkim border: 3d highest in the world: 28,146 ft.

Kan·da·har (kən də här′) city in S Afghanistan: pop. 115,000

Kan·din·sky (kan din′skē), **Was·si·ly** (or **Vas·i·li**) (vas′ə lē) 1866–1944; Russ. painter in Germany & France: also sp. **Kandinski**

Kan·dy (kan′dē, kän′-) city in C Ceylon: pop. 68,000

kan·ga·roo (kaŋ′gə rōō′) *n., pl.* **-roos′, -roo′:** see PLURAL, II, D, 1 [said (by James COOK) to be native Australian name in Queensland] any of a group of leaping, plant-eating mammals (family Macropodidae) native to Australia and neighboring islands, with short forelegs, strong, large hind legs, and a long, thick tail: the female has a pouch, or marsupium, in front, for her young

☆**kangaroo court** [said to be so named because its justice progresses by leaps and bounds] [Colloq.] an unauthorized, irregular court, usually disregarding normal legal procedure, as an irregular court in a frontier region or a mock court set up by prison inmates

kangaroo rat ☆**1.** any of various small, long-legged, jumping, mouselike rodents (genus *Dipodomys*) living in desert regions of the SW U.S. and Mexico **2.** *same as* RAT KANGAROO

Kan·na·da (kä′nə də) *n.* a major Dravidian language of Mysore and adjacent districts of S India

Kan·na·po·lis (kə nap′ə lis) [< *Cannon* Mills (textiles) + Gr. *polis,* city] town in C N.C.: pop. 36,000

Ka·no (kä′nō) city in N Nigeria: pop. 130,000

Kan·pur (kän′poor) city in N India, on the Ganges, in Uttar Pradesh: pop. 895,000

Kan·sas (kan′zəs) [Fr. < Siouan tribal and river name: cf. ARKANSAS] **1.** Middle Western State of the NC U.S.: admitted 1861; 82,264 sq. mi.; pop. 2,249,000; cap. Topeka: abbrev. **Kans., KS 2.** river in NE Kans., flowing east into the Missouri at Kansas City: c. 170 mi. —**Kan′san** *adj., n.*

Kansas City 1. city in W Mo., on the Missouri River: pop. 507,000 **2.** city in NE Kans., on the Missouri & Kansas rivers, opposite Kansas City, Mo.: pop. 168,000 (Both cities are in a single met. area, pop. 1,257,000)

Kan·su (gän′sōō′) province of NW China: c. 141,500 sq. mi.; pop. 12,800,000; cap. Lanchow

Kant (kant; *G.* känt), **Immanuel** 1724–1804; Ger. philosopher

kan·tar (kän tär′) *n.* [Ar. *qinṭar* < L. *centenarius:* see CENTENARY] a unit of weight in Moslem countries, varying from c. 100 to c. 700 pounds

Kant·i·an (kan′tē ən) *adj.* of Kant or Kantianism —*n.* a follower of Kant or Kantianism

Kant·i·an·ism (-iz′m) *n.* the philosophy of Kant, who held that the content of knowledge comes a posteriori from sense perception, but that its form is determined by a priori categories of the mind: he also declared that God, freedom, and immortality cannot be proved or denied by empirical knowledge though they are implied by rational morality

Ka·nu·ri (kä noor′ē) *n.* **1.** *pl.* **-ris, -ri** any of a Moslem people of N Nigeria and adjacent regions **2.** their Nilo-Saharan language

Kaoh·siung (gou′shyooŋ′) seaport on the SW coast of Taiwan: pop. 276,000

ka·o·lin (kā′ə lin) *n.* [Fr. < Chin. *kao-ling* (lit., high hill), name of the hill where it was found] a fine white clay used in making porcelain, as a filler in textiles, paper, rubber, etc., and in medicine in the treatment of diarrhea

ka·o·lin·ite (-lə nīt′) *n.* a hydrous aluminum silicate, $Al_2O_3 \cdot 2SiO_2 \cdot 2H_2O$, the main constituent of kaolin

ka·on (kä′än) *n.* [*Ka* (the letter K) + (MES)ON] any of four mesons that are positive, negative, or neutral and have a mass approximately 970 times that of an electron

‡**Ka·pell·meis·ter** (kä pel′mīs′tər) *n., pl.* **-ter** [G., lit., chapel master < *kapelle,* choir < It. *cappella,* a company of musicians (orig. CHAPEL), hence the choir or orchestra in a court chapel) + G. *meister,* a master] the conductor of a choir or orchestra

kaph (käf, kôf) *n. same as* KAF

Ka·pi·tza (kä′pi tsä′), **Pë·tr L(eonidovich)** (pyô′tər) 1894– ; Soviet nuclear physicist

ka·pok (kā′päk) *n.* [Malay *kapoq*] the silky fibers around the seeds of any of several tropical trees of the bombax family, esp. a ceiba (*Ceiba pentandra*): used for stuffing mattresses, life preservers, sleeping bags, etc.

kap·pa (kap′ə) *n.* [Gr. < Sem., as in Heb. *kaph*] the tenth letter of the Greek alphabet (K, κ), corresponding to the English K, k: it often appears as *c* in English words derived from Greek, as in *center, cosmetic*

ka·put (kə pŏŏt′, -pōōt′) *adj.* [G. *kaputt,* lost, ruined,

broken < Fr. *capot*, having lost all tricks (as in piquet)] [Slang] ruined, destroyed, defeated, etc.

Ka·ra·chi (kə rä′chē) seaport in S West Pakistan, on the Arabian Sea: former capital: pop. 1,913,000

Ka·ra·de·niz Bo·ğa·zi (kä′rä deŋ ēz′ bō′gä zē′) *Turk. name of the* BOSPORUS

Ka·ra·fu·to (kä′rä fōō′tō) *Jap. name of* SAKHALIN

Ka·ra·gan·da (kä′rə gän′də) city in EC Kazakh S.S.R.: pop. 489,000

Kar·a·ite (ker′ə it′) *n.* [< Heb. *q'raim*, scripturalists (< *qārā*, to read + *-īm*, pl. suffix) + -ITE¹] any of a Jewish sect, established in the Middle East in the 8th cent., rejecting the rabbinical teachings and interpretations of the Talmud and acknowledging only the Bible as a source of authority in religion —**Kar′a·ism** *n.*

Ka·ra·Kal·pak (kä rä′käl päk′) *n.* **1.** a member of a Turkic people living in the Uzbek S.S.R. **2.** the language of this people

Ka·ra·ko·ram (kä′rä kôr′əm, kar′ə-) mountain range in N India, near the Chinese border; NW extension of the Himalayas: highest peak, GODWIN AUSTEN

kar·a·kul (kar′ə kəl) *n.* [< *Kara Kul* (lit., black lake), lake in E Tadzhik S.S.R.] **1.** a broad-tailed sheep of C Asia **2.** the loosely curled, lustrous, usually black fur made from the fleece of its newborn lambs: in this sense commonly sp. CARACUL

Ka·ra Kum (kä rä′ kōōm′; *E.* kar′ə) desert in the Turkmen S.S.R., east of the Caspian Sea: c. 135,000 sq. mi.; also **Kara-Kum**

Ka·ra Sea (kä′rə) arm of the Arctic Ocean, between Novaya Zemlya & NW Siberia

kar·at (kar′ət) *n.* [var. of CARAT] one 24th part (of pure gold) [14-*karat* gold is 14 parts pure gold and 10 parts alloy]

ka·ra·te (kə rät′ē) *n.* [Jap., lit., open hand < *kara*, empty + *te*, hand] a Japanese system of self-defense characterized chiefly by chopping blows delivered with the side of the open hand

Ka·re·li·a (kə rēl′yə; *Russ.* kä rē′lē ä) an administrative division (**Karelian A.S.S.R.**) of the R.S.F.S.R., in the NW part, east of Finland: 66,500 sq. mi.; pop. 700,000

Ka·re·li·an (kə rēl′ē ən, -rēl′yən) *adj.* of Karelia, its people, etc. —*n.* **1.** a member of a branch of the Finnish people living in Karelia and E Finland **2.** the Finnish dialect of the Karelians

Karelian Isthmus isthmus in Karelia, NW U.S.S.R., between the Gulf of Finland & Lake Ladoga: 90 mi. long

Kar·en¹ (kar′ən) a feminine name: see CATHERINE

Ka·ren² (kə ren′) *n.* **1.** *pl.* **-rens′, -ren′** any member of a group of peoples of S and SE Burma **2.** their Sino-Tibetan language

Ka·ri·ba Dam (kə rē′bə) dam on the Zambezi River, on the Malawi-Rhodesia border: 420 ft. high: it has created a lake (**Kariba Lake**): 2,000 sq. mi.

Karl-Marx-Stadt (kärl′märks′shtät′) city in S East Germany: pop. 295,000: also **Karl Marx Stadt**

Kar·lo·vy Var·y (kär′lō vē vä′rē) city in W Czechoslovakia, famous for its hot springs: pop. 45,000

Karls·bad (kärls′bät; *E.* kärlz′bad) *Ger. name of* KARLOVY VARY

Karls·ruh·e (-rōō ə; *E.* -rōō ə) city in SW West Germany, in Baden-Württemberg, on the Rhine: pop. 253,000

kar·ma (kär′mə, kur′-) *n.* [Sans., a deed, act, fate] **1.** *Buddhism & Hinduism* the totality of a person's actions in any one of the successive states of his existence, thought of as determining his fate in the next **2.** loosely, fate; destiny —**kar′mic** *adj.*

Kar·nak (kär′nak) village in S Egypt, on the Nile: site of ancient Thebes

Kärn·ten (kern′tən) *Ger. name of* CARINTHIA

Ká·ro·lyi (kä′rō yē), Count **Mi·hál·y** (mē′hä y′) 1875-1955; Hung. politician: 1st president of Hungary (1919)

ka·ross (kə räs′) *n.* [Afrik. *karos*] in South Africa, a cape, blanket, or rug made of animal skins

kar·roo, ka·roo (kə rōō′, ka-) *n., pl.* **-roos′** [Hottentot *karo*] in South Africa, a dry tableland —**the Great Karroo** karroo in SC Cape of Good Hope province: c. 350 mi. long & 2,000 to 3,000 ft. high

karst (kärst) *n.* [G. < *Karst*, name of the hinterland of Trieste, altered < Slovenian *Kras*] a region made up of porous limestone containing deep fissures and sinkholes and characterized by underground caves and streams

kart (kärt) *n.* [arbitrary alteration of CART] ☆**1.** any of various small, wheeled, motorized or unmotorized vehicles: so used chiefly as part of certain trademarked names ☆**2.** a small, flat, 4-wheeled, motorized vehicle seating one person and used in special racing events (**karting**)

kar·y·o- (kar′ē ō′, -ə) [ModL. < Gr. *karyon*, a nut, kernel, prob. < IE. base *kar-*, HARD] *a combining form meaning:* **1.** nut, kernel **2.** *Biol.* the nucleus of a cell [*karyoplasm*]

kar·y·o·ki·ne·sis (kar′ē ō ki nē′sis) *n.* [prec. + Gr. *kinēsis*, motion] *same as* MITOSIS —**kar′y·o·ki·net′ic** (-net′ik) *adj.*

kar·y·o·lymph (kar′ē ə limf′) *n.* [KARYO- + LYMPH] a colorless, watery liquid found inside the nucleus of a cell

kar·y·o·plasm (-plaz′m) *n.* [KARYO- + PLASM] *same as* NUCLEOPLASM —**kar′y·o·plas′mic** (-plaz′mik) *adj.*

kar·y·o·some (-sōm′) *n.* [KARYO- + -SOME³] *Biol.* **1.** an aggregation of chromatin in a resting nucleus **2.** the nucleus of a cell

kar·y·o·tin (kar′ē ō′tin) *n.* [KARYO- + (CHROMA)TIN] *same as* CHROMATIN

kar·y·o·type (kar′ē ə tīp′) *n.* the general appearance, including size, number, and shape, of the set of somatic chromosomes —**kar′y·o·typ′ic** (-tip′ik), **kar′y·o·typ′i·cal** *adj.*

Ka·sai (kä sī′) river in SC Africa, flowing from Angola northwest into the Congo River: c. 1,100 mi.

kas·bah (käz′bä) *n. same as* CASBAH

ka·sha (kä′shə) *n.* [Russ., partly via Yid.] cracked buckwheat, wheat, etc. cooked into a mushlike consistency and served with meat, in soup, etc.

ka·sher (kä′shər) *adj., n., vt. same as* KOSHER

Kash·gar (käsh′gär′) city in westernmost Sinkiang province, China: pop. 91,000

Kash·mir (kash′mir, kash mir′) **1.** region in SE Asia, between Afghanistan & Tibet: since 1846, part of Jammu & Kashmir **2.** *same as* JAMMU AND KASHMIR **3.** Vale of, valley of the Jhelum River, in W Kashmir —**Kash·mir′i·an** *adj., n.*

Kash·mir·i (kash mir′ē) *n.* **1.** the Indic language of the Kashmirians **2.** *pl.* **-mir′is, -mir′i** a Kashmirian

kash·rut, kash·ruth (käsh rōōt′, käsh′rōōt) *n.* the dietary regulations of Judaism: see KOSHER

Ka·shu·bi·an (ka shōō′bē ən) *n.* a West Slavic dialect closely related to Polish, spoken in N Poland

Käs·sa·la (kas′ə lə) city in NE Sudan: pop. 49,000

Kas·sel (käs′əl) city in C West Germany, in Hesse state: pop. 215,000

kat (kät) *n. same as* KHAT

kat·a- (kat′ə) *same as* CATA-: also, before a vowel, **kat-**

Ka·tab·a·sis (kə tab′ə sis) *n.* [Gr. *katabainein*, to go down < *kata-*, down + *bainein*, to go: see COME] the retreat to the sea made by the Greek mercenaries who followed Cyrus against Artaxerxes, as described by Xenophon in the *Anabasis* —*n.* [k-] *pl.* **-ses′** (-sēz′) any similar retreat

Kate (kāt) a feminine name: see CATHERINE

‡**ka·tha·rev·ou·sa** (kä′thä rev′ōō sä) *n.* [ModGr., lit., being pure] the form of Modern Greek that conforms to classical Greek usage

Kath·ar·ine, Kath·er·ine (kath′ər in, kath′rin) a feminine name: dim. *Kate, Kay, Kit, Kitty:* also **Kath′ryn** (kath′rin): see CATHERINE

ka·thar·sis (kə thär′sis) *n. same as* CATHARSIS

Kath·leen (kath′lēn, kath lēn′) [Ir.] a feminine name: see CATHERINE

kath·ode (kath′ōd) *n. same as* CATHODE

kat·i·on (kat′ī′ən) *n. same as* CATION

Kat·mai (kat′mī) [Russ. < ?] volcano in SW Alas.: c. 7,000 ft.: included in a volcanic region (**Katmai National Monument**) of the S Alaska Range, 4,215 sq. mi.

Kat·man·du (kät′män dōō′) capital of Nepal, in the C part: pop. 195,000: also **Kath′man·du′**

Ka·to·wi·ce (kä′tô vē′tse) city in S Poland: pop. 286,000

Kat·rine (kat′rin; *Scot.* kät′rin), **Loch** lake in C Scotland: scene of Scott's *Lady of the Lake:* 8 mi. long

Kat·te·gat (kat′i gat′) strait between SW Sweden & E Jutland, Denmark: c. 150 mi. long

☆**ka·ty·did** (kāt′ē did′) *n.* [echoic of the sound made by the males] any of several large, green tree insects (family Tettigoniidae) resembling and related to the grasshopper but with longer antennae: the male has highly developed stridulating organs on the forewings, that produce a shrill sound

☆**katz·en·jam·mer** (kat′s'n jam′ər) *n.* [G. < *katze*, CAT + *jammer*, woe < OHG. *jamar*, orig. adj., sad, akin to OE. *geomor*, miserable: sense 1 infl. by U.S. cartoon strip (*The Katzenjammer Kids*), originated (1897) by Rudolph Dirks] **1.** a farcical quality; travesty **2.** a bewildering hodgepodge or distressing confusion **3.** a severe headache, esp. as part of a hangover

Ka·u·a·i (kä′ōō ä′ē, kou′ī′) an island of Hawaii, northwest of Oahu: 551 sq. mi.; pop. 30,000

Kau·nas (kou′näs) city in SC Lithuanian S.S.R., on the Neman River: pop. 276,000

kau·ri (kou′rē) *n.* [Maori] **1.** a tall evergreen tree (*Agathis australis*) of the pine family, growing in New Zealand **2.** its wood **3.** a resin (**kauri resin, kauri gum**) from this tree, often found as a fossil, used in varnishes, adhesives, and linoleum

ka·va (kä′vä) *n.* [Maori *kawa*, lit., bitter] **1.** a plant (*Piper methysticum*) of the pepper family, with an aromatic odor: its rootstocks have narcotic properties **2.** an intoxicating drink made from the roots Also **ka′va·ka′va**

Ka·vál·la (kä vä′lä) seaport in Macedonia, NE Greece, on the Aegean: pop. 45,000: also sp. **Kavála**

Kavir Desert *same as* DASHT-I-KAVIR

Ka·wa·sa·ki (kä′wä sä′kē) city in C Honshu, Japan, on Tokyo Bay: pop. 855,000

Kay (kā), Sir *Arthurian legend* one of the knights of the Round Table, the boastful, rude, malicious seneschal and foster brother of King Arthur

kay·ak (kī′ak) *n.* [Esk.] **1.** an Eskimo canoe made of skins, esp. sealskins, stretched over a frame of wood to cover it completely except for an opening in the middle for the paddler **2.** any similarly designed canoe for one or two paddlers, made of canvas, plastic, etc.

KAYAK

☆**kay·o** (kā′ō′) *vt.* **-oed′, -o′ing** [< KO] [Slang] *Boxing* to knock out — *n.* [Slang] *Boxing* a knockout

Kay·se·ri (kī′se rē′) city in C Turkey: pop. 103,000

ka·za·chok (kä zä chôk′) *n., pl.* **-zach·ki′** (-zäch kē′) *same as* KAZATSKY

Ka·zakh, Ka·zak (kä zäk′) *n.* a member of a Kirghiz people living chiefly in the Kazakh S.S.R.

Kazakh Soviet Socialist Republic republic of the U.S.S.R., in W Asia: 1,048,000 sq. mi.; pop. 12,100,000; cap. Alma-Ata: also **Ka·zakh·stan** (kä′zäk stän′)

Ka·zan (kä zän′; *Russ.* kǎ zän′y′) city in W R.S.F.S.R., on the Volga: pop. 804,000

Ka·zan·tza·kis (kä′zän tsä′kēs) **Ni·kos** (nē′kôs) 1885–1957; Gr. novelist

ka·zat·sky, ka·zat·ski (kə zät′skē) *n., pl.* **-skies** [Russ.] a vigorous Russian folk dance performed by a man and characterized by a step in which, from a squatting position, each leg is alternately kicked out: also **ka·zat′ska** (-skä)

Kaz·bek (käz bek′) volcanic mountain in the C Caucasus, N Georgian S.S.R.: 16,558 ft.

☆**ka·zoo** (kə zōō′) *n.* [echoic] a toy musical instrument consisting of a small, open tube with a top hole covered by a membrane, as of paper, that vibrates to give a buzzing quality to tones hummed through the tube

KB *Chess* king's bishop

K.B. **1.** King's Bench **2.** Knight Bachelor

k·bar (kā′bär′) *n. clipped form of* KILOBAR

K.B.E. Knight Commander of the British Empire

kc, kc. kilocycle; kilocycles

K.C. **1.** King's Counsel **2.** Knight Commander **3.** Knight (or Knights) of Columbus

kcal. kilocalorie; kilocalories

K.C.B. Knight Commander of the Bath

Kčs koruna; korunas

K.C.V.O. Knight Commander of the Royal Victorian Order

K.D., k.d. *Commerce* knocked down (not assembled)

Ke·a (kā′ä) island of the NW Cyclades, Greece, in the Aegean Sea: 60 sq. mi.

ke·a (kā′ə, kē′ə) *n.* [Maori] a large, green, mountain parrot (*Nestor notabilis*) of New Zealand, which at times kills sheep by tearing at their backs to eat the kidney fat

Kean (kēn) **Edmund** 1787–1833; Eng. actor

Kear·ny (kär′nē) [after U.S. Gen. Philip *Kearny*, 1814–62] town in NE N.J., on the Passaic River: pop. 38,000

Keats (kēts) **John** 1795–1821; Eng. poet

ke·bab (kə bäb′) *n.* [Ar. *kabāb*] **1.** [*often pl.*] a dish consisting of small pieces of marinated meat stuck on a skewer, often alternated with pieces of onion, tomato, etc., and broiled or roasted **2.** a piece of such meat

keb·buck, keb·bock (keb′ək) *n.* [ME. *cabok* < Gael. *ceapag*, a cheese, wheel] [Scot. Dial.] a cheese

Ke·ble (kē′b'l) **John** 1792–1866; Eng. Anglican clergyman & poet: a founder of the Oxford movement

Kech·ua (kech′wä) *n. same as* QUECHUA —**Kech′uan** *adj., n.*

Ke·chu·ma·ran (kech′ōō mə rän′) *n. same as* QUECHUMARAN

keck (kek) *vi.* [echoic] **1.** to retch or heave, as if about to vomit **2.** to feel or show great disgust

Kecs·ke·mét (kech′ke māt′) city in C Hungary: pop. 69,000

Ke·dah (kā′dä) state of NW Malaya, on the Strait of Malacca: 3,660 sq. mi.; pop. 874,000

ked·dah (ked′ə) *n.* [Hindi *khedā*] an elephant trap

kedge (kej) *vt.* **kedged, kedg′ing** [ME. *caggen*, to fasten < ?] to move (a ship) along by hauling on a rope fastened to an anchor dropped at some distance —*vi.* **1.** to move a ship by kedging it **2.** to move by being kedged —*n.* a light anchor, used esp. in kedging a ship: also **kedge anchor**

Ke·dron (kē′drən) *same as* KIDRON

ke·ef (kē ef′) *n. same as* KEF

keek (kēk) *vi.* [ME. *kiken*, prob. < MDu. or MLowG. *kīken*] [Scot. & North Eng. Dial.] to peep; spy

keel[1] (kēl) *n.* [ME. *kele* < ON. *kjølr* < Gmc. *kelu-* < IE. base *gel-*, to swallow, whence L. *gula*, throat] **1.** the chief timber or steel piece extending along the entire length of the bottom of a boat or ship and supporting the frame: it sometimes protrudes beneath the hull **2.** [Poet.] a ship **3.** anything resembling a ship's keel **4.** the assembly of beams, girders, etc. at the bottom of a rigid or semirigid airship to prevent sagging or buckling ☆**5.** *short for* KEELBOAT **6.** *Biol.* a ridgelike part —*vt.* **1.** to furnish with a keel **2.** to turn (a ship) over on its side so as to turn up the keel —*vi.* to turn up the keel —☆**keel over** [Colloq.] **1.** to turn over or upside down; upset; capsize **2.** to fall over suddenly, as in a faint —**on an even keel 1.** in or keeping an upright, level position **2.** steady, stable, well-balanced, etc.

keel[2] (kēl) *n.* [ME. *kele* < MDu. *kiel*, boat < Gmc. *keula* < IE. *geul-*, rounded vessel, whence Sans. *gōlā*, ball, round

jug] **1.** a flat-bottomed ship; esp., a low, flat-bottomed coal barge or lighter, used on the Tyne **2.** *a)* a barge load of coal *b)* a Brit. unit of weight for coal, equal to 21.1 long tons

keel[3] (kēl) *vt.* [ME. *kelen* < OE. *celan* (akin to G. *kühlen*) < base of *col*, COOL] [Obs. or Dial.] to cool (a hot liquid) by stirring, skimming, etc.

keel[4] (kēl) *n.* [prob. < Ir. or Gael. *cīl*, ruddle] a red stain used for marking lumber, etc.; ruddle

☆**keel·boat** (-bōt′) *n.* a large, shallow freight boat with a keel, formerly used on the Mississippi, Missouri, etc.

keel·haul (-hôl′) *vt.* [Du. *kielhalen* < *kiel* (see KEEL[2]) + *halen*, to HAUL] **1.** to haul (a person) through the water under the keel of a ship from one side to the other: a former method of punishment or torture **2.** to scold or rebuke harshly

Kee·ling Islands (kē′liŋ) *same as* COCOS ISLANDS

keel·son (kel′s'n, kēl′-) *n.* [prob. via Du. *kolsem* < Dan. *kjølsvin*, altered (after *svin*, swine) < *kjølsvill* < *kjøl*, KEEL[1] + *sville*, SILL] a longitudinal beam or set of timbers or metal plates fastened inside the hull of a ship along the keel to add structural strength

Kee·lung (kē′loon′) *same as* CHILUNG

keen[1] (kēn) *adj.* [ME. *kene* < OE. *cene*, wise, learned, akin to G. *kühn*, bold < IE. base *ĝen-*, to know, understand, whence KNOW: the material senses spring from the basic notion "capable"] **1.** having a sharp edge or point; that can cut well [a *keen* knife, a *keen* edge] **2.** sharp or cutting in force; piercing [a *keen* appetite, a *keen* wind] **3.** sharp and quick in seeing, hearing, thinking, etc.; acute [*keen* eyes, a *keen* intelligence] **4.** sharp-witted; mentally acute; shrewd **5.** eager; enthusiastic; much interested **6.** strongly felt or perceived; intense; strong [*keen* desire, a *keen* scent] ☆**7.** [Slang] good, fine, excellent, etc.: a generalized term of approval —*SYN.* see EAGER, SHARP —**keen′ly** *adv.* —**keen′ness** *n.*

keen[2] (kēn) *n.* [Ir. *caoine* < *caoinim*, I wail] [Irish] a wailing for the dead; dirge —*vt., vi.* [Irish] to lament or wail for (the dead) —*SYN.* see CRY

keep (kēp) *vt.* **kept, keep′ing** [ME. *kepen* < OE. *cepan*, to behold, watch out for, lay hold of, akin ? to MLowG. *kapen*, to stare at < ? IE. base *gab-*, to look at or for] **1.** to observe or pay regard to; specif., *a)* to observe with due or prescribed acts, ceremonies, etc.; celebrate or solemnize [to *keep* the Sabbath] *b)* to fulfill (a promise, etc.) *c)* to follow or adhere to (a routine, diet, etc.) *d)* to go on maintaining [to *keep* pace] *e)* [Archaic] to attend (church, etc.) regularly **2.** to take care of, or have and take care or charge of; specif., *a)* to protect; guard; defend *b)* to look after; watch over; tend *c)* to raise (livestock) *d)* to maintain in good order or condition; preserve *e)* to supply with food, shelter, etc.; provide for; support *f)* to supply with food or lodging for pay [to *keep* boarders] *g)* to have or maintain in one's service or for one's use [to *keep* servants] *h)* to set down regularly in writing; maintain (a continuous written record) [to *keep* an account of sales] *i)* to make regular entries in; maintain a continuous record of transactions, accounts, or happenings in [to *keep* books of account, to *keep* a diary] *j)* to carry on; conduct; manage **3.** to maintain, or cause to stay or continue, in a specified condition, position, etc. [to *keep* an engine running] **4.** to have or hold; specif., *a)* to have or hold for future use or for a long time *b)* to have regularly in stock for sale **5.** to have or hold and not let go; specif., *a)* to hold in custody; prevent from escaping *b)* to prevent from leaving; detain *c)* to hold back; restrain [to *keep* someone from talking] *d)* to withhold *e)* to conceal; not tell (a secret, etc.) *f)* to continue to have or hold; not lose or give up *g)* to stay in or at; not leave (a path, course, or place) —*vi.* **1.** to stay or continue in a specified condition, position, etc. **2.** to continue; go on; persevere or persist (often with *on*) [to *keep* on talking] **3.** to hold oneself back; refrain [to *keep* from telling someone] **4.** to stay in good condition; not become spoiled, sour, stale, etc.; last **5.** to require no immediate attention [a task that will *keep* until tomorrow] ☆**6.** [Colloq.] to continue in session [will school *keep* all day?] **7.** [Now Rare] to reside; live; stay —*n.* **1.** orig., care, charge, or custody **2.** *a)* the strongest, innermost part or central tower of a medieval castle; donjon *b)* a stronghold; fort; castle **3.** [Rare] a keeping or being kept **4.** what is needed to maintain a person or animal; food and shelter; support; livelihood —☆**for keeps** [Colloq.] **1.** with the agreement that the winner will keep what he wins **2.** forever; permanently —**keep at** to continue doing, practicing, etc.; persist in (an activity) —**keep in with** [Colloq.] to remain on good terms with —**keep to 1.** to persevere in **2.** to avoid swerving from; adhere to **3.** to remain in —**keep to oneself 1.** to avoid the company of others **2.** to treat (information, etc.) as confidential; not tell —**keep up 1.** to maintain in good order or condition **2.** to continue; not stop or end **3.** to maintain the pace; not lag behind **4.** to remain informed about (with *on* or *with*) —**keep up with the Joneses** to strive to get all the material things one's neighbors or associates have

SYN.—**keep,** a general word of broad application, in its simplest sense implies merely a continuing to have or hold; **retain,** a more formal equivalent, often stresses the possibility of loss or seizure [he has managed to *retain* most of his fortune]; **withhold** implies a keeping or holding back and connotes refusal to release [to

withhold information*/*; **reserve** implies a keeping or holding back for some time or for some future use *[*is this table *reserved* for us?*]*
See also CELEBRATE —ANT. relinquish, release

keep·er (-ər) *n.* a person or thing that keeps; specif., *a)* a guard, as of prisoners, animals, etc. *b)* a guardian or protector *c)* a custodian; caretaker *d)* [Brit.] a game-keeper *e)* any of several devices for keeping something in place, as a clasp *f)* something that keeps or lasts (well or poorly)

keep·ing (-iŋ) *n.* **1.** observance (of a rule, holiday, promise, etc.) **2.** care; custody; charge **3.** maintenance or means of maintenance; keep **4.** the condition in which something is kept **5.** retention **6.** reservation for future use; preservation —**in keeping with** in conformity or accord with

keep·sake (-sāk´) *n.* something kept, or to be kept, for the sake of, or in memory of, the giver; memento

☆**keet** (kēt) *n.* [echoic] a young guinea fowl

Kee·wa·tin (kē wä´tin) [< Algonquian (Cree), the north wind] district of Northwest Territories, Canada, on Hudson Bay: 228,160 sq. mi.; pop. 2,300 —*adj. Geol.* designating or of a series of rocks of the Precambrian system in the Lake Superior region

kef (kāf) *n.* [Ar., colloq. form of *kaif*, well-being] **1.** a drowsy, dreamy condition produced by smoking narcotics **2.** Indian hemp or other narcotic smoked to produce such a condition

Ke·fal·li·ni·a (kā´fä lē nē´ä) *Gr.* name of CEPHALONIA

keg (keg) *n.* [ME. *cagge* < or akin to ON. *kaggi*, keg < IE. base *gegh-*, a branch, stake, whence E. dial. *cag*, stump] **1.** a small barrel, usually one holding less than ten gallons **2.** a unit of weight for nails, equal to 100 pounds

☆**keg·ler** (keg´lər) *n.* [G. < *kegel*, (nine)pin, (ten)pin < OHG. *kegil*, a post, stake, dim. of base akin to prec.] [Colloq.] a person who bowls; bowler

keir (kir) *n. same as* KIER

☆**keis·ter, kees·ter** (kēs´tər) *n.* [prob. via Yid. < MHG. *kiste*, a chest < OHG. *kista* < L. *cista*, CHEST] [Slang] **1.** a satchel, suitcase, etc. **2.** the buttocks; rump

Keith (kēth) [Scot. < Gael. base meaning "the wind"] **1.** a masculine name **2.** Sir **Arthur**, 1866–1955; Brit. anthropologist & writer, born in Scotland

keit·lo·a (kīt´lō ə, kāt´-) *n.* [Schuana *kgetlwa*] the large, black, two-horned rhinoceros of S Africa

Ke·lan·tan (kə län´tän´) state of N Malaya: 5,750 sq. mi.; pop. 637,000

☆**kel·ep** (kel´əp) *n.* [native name in Guatemala] a Central American stinging ant (*Ectatomma tuberculatum*) that feeds on insects

Kel·ler (kel´ər), **Helen Adams** 1880–1968; U.S. writer & lecturer: blind & deaf from infancy, she was taught to speak & read

Kel·ly (green) (kel´ē) [*also* k-] a bright, yellowish green

ke·loid (kē´loid) *n.* [Fr. *kéloïde, chéloïde* < Gr. *chēlē*, crab's claw (see CHELA) + *-oeidēs*, -OID] an excessive growth of scar tissue on the skin —**ke·loi´dal** *adj.*

kelp (kelp) *n.* [ME. *culp*] **1.** any of various large, coarse, brown seaweeds belonging to the brown algae **2.** ashes of seaweed, from which iodine is obtained

kel·pie, kel·py (kel´pē) *n., pl.* **-pies** [Scot. < ? Gael. *calpa, colt*] *Gaelic Folklore* a water spirit, supposed to take the form of a horse and drown people

kel·son (kel´s'n) *n. same as* KEELSON

Kelt (kelt) *n. same as* CELT —**Kelt´ic** *adj.*, *n.*

kelt (kelt) *n.* [ME.] [Scot.] a salmon that has spawned

kel·ter (kel´tər) *n.* [Colloq.] *same as* KILTER

Kel·vin (kel´s'n) [< Eng. surname] **1.** a masculine name **2.** 1st **Baron**, (*William Thomson*) 1824–1907; Brit. physicist & mathematician —*adj.* designating, of, or according to the Kelvin scale

Kelvin scale [after Baron KELVIN] *Physics* a scale of temperature measured in degrees Celsius from absolute zero (−273.15°C)

Ke·mal A·ta·turk (ke mäl´ ät ä turk´) 1881–1938; Turk. general; 1st president of Turkey (1923–38): also called **Mustafa Kemal** & **Kemal Pasha**

Kem·ble (kem´b'l) **1. Fanny**, (born *Frances Anne Kemble*) 1809–93; Eng. actress **2. John Philip**, 1757–1823; Eng. tragedian: uncle of *prec.*

Ke·me·ro·vo (kem´e rô vô) city in SC R.S.F.S.R., in the Kuznetsk Basin: pop. 358,000

Kem·pis (kem´pis), **Thomas à** (born *Thomas Hamerken* or *Hammerlein*) 1380?–1471; Ger. monk & scholar

kempt (kempt) *adj.* [ME., combed: in mod. use, back-formation < UNKEMPT] neat; tidy; well-groomed

ken (ken) *vt.* **kenned, ken´ning** [ME. *kennen* < OE. *cennan*, lit., to cause to know < *kannjan* < base of CAN¹, akin to G. *kennen*, ON. *kenna*, to know] **1.** [Scot.] to know **2.** [Archaic] to see; look at; descry **3.** [Archaic or Dial.] to recognize —*vi.* [Scot.] to know (*of* or *about*) —*n.* [contr. < KENNING] **1.** [Rare] range of vision or sight **2.** mental perception or recognition; range of knowledge; understanding

ke·naf (kə naf´) *n.* [Per., akin to *kanab*, HEMP] **1.** a tropical Asiatic plant (*Hibiscus cannabinus*) of the mallow family, grown for its fiber, which is similar to jute **2.** this fiber

kench (kench) *n.* [? var. of Brit. dial. *canch*] a box or bin in which fish or skins are salted

Ken·dal (green) (ken´d'l) [orig. woven and dyed at *Kendal*, city in Westmorland, England] **1.** a coarse, green woolen cloth **2.** its color

Ken·dall (ken´d'l) [earlier *Kendal*; ? after the Eng. city (see prec.)] suburb of Miami, in SE Fla.: pop. 35,000

ken·do (ken´dō) *n.* [Jap.] stylized swordplay in which bamboo swords are used: a Japanese sport

Ken·il·worth (ken´'l wurth´) urban district in Warwick-shire, England, near Coventry: pop. 16,000

Ken·nan (ken´ən), **George F(rost)** 1904– ; U.S. diplomat & historian

Ken·ne·bec (ken´ə bek´) [< Abnaki, lit., long-water place] river in W Me., flowing into the Atlantic: c. 150 mi.

Ken·ne·dy (ken´ə dē), **Cape** [after ff.] cape on the E coast of Fla.: U.S. proving ground for missiles & spacecraft

Kennedy, John Fitzgerald 1917–63; 35th president of the U.S. (1961–63): assassinated

Kennedy Round [*often* K- r-] [after a 1962 act sponsored by President *Kennedy*] trade negotiations to reduce tariffs on imports into the U.S. in return for corresponding reductions on U.S. exports

ken·nel¹ (ken´'l) *n.* [ME. *kenel*, prob. via ONormFr. < OFr. *chenil* < VL. *canile* < L. *canis*, a dog: see CANINE] **1.** a doghouse **2.** [*often pl.*] a place where dogs are bred or kept **3.** a pack of dogs —*vt.* **-neled** *or* **-nelled, -nel·ing** *or* **-nel·ling** to place or keep in a kennel —*vi.* to live or take shelter in a kennel

ken·nel² (ken´'l) *n.* [ME. *canel* < OFr. *canel, chanel,* CHANNEL¹] an open drain or sewer; gutter

Ken·nel·ly-Heav·i·side layer (ken´'l ē hev´ē sīd´) [after A. E. *Kennelly* (1861–1939), U.S. electrical engineer & Oliver *Heaviside* (1850–1925), Eng. physicist] *same as* E LAYER

Ken·ne·saw Mountain (ken´ə sô´) [< Muskhogean (Cherokee) < ?] mountain in NW Ga.: scene of a Civil War battle (1864): 1,800 ft.

Ken·neth (ken´ith) [Scot. < Gael. *Caioneach,* lit., hand-some] a masculine name: dim. *Ken*

ken·ning (ken´iŋ) *n.* [ME.: see KEN] **1.** [Scot.] *a)* knowl-edge or recognition *b)* a tiny quantity; trace **2.** [ON., symbol < *kenna*: see KEN] in early Germanic, as Old English, poetry, a metaphorical name, usually a compound, for something (Ex.: "whale-path" for *sea*)

Ken·ny method (or **treatment**) (ken´ē) [after Elizabeth *Kenny* (1886–1952), Australian nurse who developed it] an earlier method of treating poliomyelitis by the use of hot packs and exercises

☆**ke·no** (kē´nō) *n.* [< Fr. *quine*, five winning numbers < L. *quini*, five each < *quinque*, FIVE] a gambling game resembling lotto

Ke·no·sha (ki nō´shə) [< Fr. *Keinouche* < Algonquian *kinōzhan*, lit., pickerel] city in SE Wis., on Lake Michigan: pop. 79,000

ke·no·sis (ki nō´sis) *n.* [Gr. *kenōsis*, an emptying < *kenos*, empty] *Theol.* Jesus' humbling himself by taking on the form of man —**ke·not´ic** (-nät´ik) *adj.*

Ken·sing·ton (ken´ziŋ tən) borough of W London: pop. 172,000

Kent (kent) county of SE England, on the English Channel: formerly, an Anglo-Saxon kingdom (6th–9th cent. A.D.): 1,525 sq. mi.; pop. 1,748,000; county seat, Maidstone

Kent (kent) **1. James**, 1763–1847; U.S. jurist **2. Rock·well** (räk´wel), 1882–1971; U.S. artist

Kent·ish (-ish) *adj.* of Kent or its people —*n.* the dialect of Kent, esp. in its Old English and Middle English stages

kent·ledge (kent´lij) *n.* [Fr. *quintelage < quintal* (see QUINTAL) + *-age* (see -AGE)] pig iron used as permanent ballast in a ship

Ken·tuck·y (kən tuk´ē, ken-) [< Iroquoian (Wyandot), level land, plain] **1.** EC State of the U.S.: admitted 1792; 40,395 sq. mi.; pop. 3,219,000; cap. Frankfort: abbrev. **Ky., KY 2.** river in E Ky., flowing northwest into the Ohio: 259 mi. —**Ken·tuck´i·an** *adj., n.*

☆**Kentucky coffee tree** a large tree (*Gymnocladus dioica*) of the legume family, with brown, curved pods containing seeds sometimes used as a substitute for coffee: it is native to the E U.S.

☆**Kentucky colonel** a person who has had the unofficial honorary title "Colonel" conferred on him in Kentucky

☆**Kentucky Derby** an annual horse race run at Churchill Downs in Louisville, Kentucky

Kentucky Lake reservoir in SW Ky. & W Tenn., on the Tennessee River: 247 sq. mi.; 184 mi. long

Ken·ya (ken´yə, kēn´-) **1.** a country in EC Africa, on the Indian Ocean, in the Brit. Commonwealth: 224,960 sq. mi.; pop. 10,890,000; cap. Nairobi **2. Mount**, mountain in C Kenya: 17,040 ft. —**Ken´yan** *adj., n.*

Ken·yat·ta (ken yät´ə), **Jo·mo** (jō´mō) 1893?– ; African political leader; president of Kenya (1964–)

Ken·yon (ken´yən), **John Samuel** 1874–1959; U.S. phonetician & educator

Ke·os (kā´ōs) *same as* KEA

kep·i (kep′ē, kā′pē) *n., pl.* **kep′is** [Fr. *képi* < G. dial. *käppi*, dim. of *kappe*, a cap < OHG. *kappa* < VL. *cappa:* see CAP] a cap with a flat, round top and stiff visor, worn by French soldiers

Kep·ler (kep′lər), **Jo·hann** (yō′hän) or **Jo·han·nes** (yō hän′əs) 1571–1630; Ger. astronomer & mathematician

kept (kept) *pt. & pp.* of KEEP —*adj.* maintained as a mistress [*a kept woman*]

☆**ker-** (kər) [echoic] *a humorous intensifier used in nonce formations suggesting* a thump, thud, explosion, etc. [*kerplunk, kerflooey*]

Ker·a·la (ker′ə lə) state of SW India, on the Malabar Coast: 15,002 sq. mi.; pop. 16,904,000; cap. Trivandrum

ke·ram·ic (kə ram′ik) *adj. same as* CERAMIC

ker·a·tec·to·my (ker′ə tek′tə mē) *n., pl.* **-mies** [KERAT(O)- + -ECTOMY] the surgical removal of part or all of the cornea

ker·a·tin (ker′ət ′n) *n.* [KERAT(O)- + -IN[1]] a tough, fibrous, insoluble protein forming the principal matter of hair, nails, horn, etc. —**ke·rat·i·nous** (kə rat′′n əs), **ke·rat′i·noid′** (-oid′) *adj.*

ker·a·ti·tis (ker′ə tīt′is) *n.* [KERAT(O)- + -ITIS] inflammation of the cornea

ker·a·to- (ker′ə tō′, -tə) [< Gr. *keras* (gen. *keratos*), HORN] *a combining form meaning:* **1.** horn, hornlike, horny tissue [*keratogenous*] **2.** the cornea [*keratotomy*] Also, before a vowel, **kerat-**

ker·a·tog·e·nous (ker′ə täj′ə nəs) *adj.* [KERATO- + -GENOUS] causing the growth of horny tissue

ker·a·toid (ker′ə toid′) *adj.* [Gr. *keratoeidēs:* see KERATO- & -OID] hornlike; horny

ker·a·to·plas·ty (ker′ə tō plas′tē) *n., pl.* **-ties** [KERATO- + -PLASTY] the surgical operation of grafting new corneal tissue onto an eye

ker·a·tose (ker′ə tōs′) *adj.* [KERAT(O)- + -OSE[1]] **1.** horny **2.** having horny material in the skeleton, as certain sponges and some other invertebrates

ker·a·to·sis (ker′ə tō′sis) *n., pl.* **-ses** (-sēz) [ModL. < KERAT(O)- + -OSIS] **1.** a horny growth of the skin, as a wart **2.** any disease characterized by horny growths

ker·a·tot·o·my (ker′ə tät′ə mē) *n., pl.* **-mies** [KERATO- + -TOMY] surgical incision of the cornea

kerb (kurb) *n. Brit. sp.* of CURB (*n.* 5)

Kerch (kerch) seaport in W Crimea, U.S.S.R., on a strait (**Kerch Strait**) connecting the Black Sea & the Sea of Azov: pop. 115,000

ker·chief (kur′chif) *n.* [ME. *kerchef, coverchef* < OFr. *covrechef* < *covrir,* to COVER + *chef,* the head: see CHIEF] **1.** a piece of cloth, usually square, worn over the head or around the neck **2.** a handkerchief —**ker′chiefed** (-chift) *adj.*

Ke·ren·sky (kə ren′skē; *Russ.* kye′ryen skē), **A·lek·san·dr Fe·o·do·ro·vich** (ä′lyek sän′dər fyō′dô rô′vich) 1881–1970; Russ. revolutionary leader; prime minister of Russia (July-Nov., 1917), overthrown by the Bolshevik Revolution: in the U.S. after 1940

Ke·res (ke′rəs) *n.* **1.** *pl.* **Ke′res** a member of any of seven Indian pueblos in New Mexico, mostly on the Rio Grande **2.** their language, the unique member of its language family: also **Ker·e·san** (ker′ə sən)

kerf (kurf) *n.* [ME. < OE. *cyrf* (akin to ON. *kurfr,* a cutting, chip) < pp. base of *ceorfan,* to CARVE] the cut or channel made by a saw — *vt.* to make a kerf in

Ker·gue·len Islands (kur′gə lən) group of Fr. islands in the S Indian Ocean, consisting of one large island & over 300 small ones: 2,700 sq. mi.

Kerk·ra·de (kerk′rä də) city in SE Netherlands, on the West German border: pop. 51,000

Kér·ky·ra (ker′kē rä) Gr. name of CORFU

Ker·man (ker män′) city in SE Iran: pop. 75,000

Ker·man·shah (ker′män shä′) city in W Iran: pop. 167,000

ker·mes (kur′mēz) *n.* [Fr. *kermès* < Ar. & Per. *qirmiz:* see CRIMSON] **1.** the dried bodies of the females of certain scale insects (genus *Kermes*), used for making a purple-red dye **2.** this dye **3.** a small, evergreen Mediterranean oak (*Quercus coccifera*) on which the kermes insects are found: also **kermes oak**

ker·mis, ker·mess (kur′mis) *n.* [Du. *kermis,* orig. *kerkmis* < *kerk,* a CHURCH + *mis,* MASS: orig. the feast day of the local patron saint, hence, a fair or carnival held on that day] **1.** in the Netherlands, Belgium, etc., an outdoor fair or carnival ☆**2.** any somewhat similar fair or entertainment, held usually for charity

kern[1] (kurn) *n.* [Fr. *carne,* projecting angle, hinge < dial. form of OFr. *charne,* a hinge, corner, edge < L. *cardo* (gen. *cardinis*), a hinge: see CARDINAL] that part of the face of a letter of type which projects beyond the body — *vt.* to put a kern on (type)

kern[2], kerne (kurn) *n.* [ME. < OIr. *ceitern,* band of soldiers, soldier] **1.** [Archaic] a medieval Irish or Scottish foot soldier armed with light weapons **2.** an Irish peasant

Kern (kurn), **Jerome (David)** 1885–1945; U.S. composer

ker·nel (kur′n'l) *n.* [ME. < OE. *cyrnel* < base of *corn,* seed (see CORN[1]) + *-el,* dim. suffix] **1.** a grain or seed, as of corn, wheat, etc. **2.** the inner, softer part of a nut, fruit pit, etc. **3.** the central, most important part of something; core; essence — *vt.* **-neled** or **-nelled, -nel·ing** or **-nel·ling** to enclose as a kernel

☆**kernel sentence** in generative grammar, a simple declarative sentence in the active voice from which both simpler and more complicated English sentences may be derived by transformation

☆**kern·ite** (kur′nīt′) *n.* [< Kern County, California, where it is mined + -ITE[1]] a monoclinic mineral, $Na_2B_4O_7 \cdot 4H_2O$, an important ore of boron

ker·o·gen (ker′ə jən) *n.* [< Gr. *kēros,* wax (cf. CERE) + -GEN] solid bituminous material in some shales, which yields petroleum when heated

☆**ker·o·sene** (ker′ə sēn′, ker′ə sēn′) *n.* [Gr. *kēros,* wax + -ENE] a thin oil distilled from petroleum or shale oil, used as a fuel, solvent, illuminant, etc.; coal oil: also, esp. in scientific and industrial usage, sp. **kerosine**

ker·ri·a (ker′ē ə) *n.* [ModL., after Wm. *Kerr,* Brit. botanist (d. 1814)] any of a genus (*Kerria*) of Chinese plants of the rose family, esp. an ornamental variety (*Kerria japonica*) with slender, green twigs and bright yellow, often double flowers

Ker·ry (ker′ē) county in Munster province, SW Ireland: 1,815 sq. mi.; pop. 113,000 — *n., pl.* **-ries** any of a breed of small, black dairy cattle, originally from this county

ker·sey (kur′zē) *n., pl.* **-seys** [ME. < *Kersey,* village in Suffolk, England] a coarse, lightweight woolen cloth, usually ribbed and with a cotton warp

ker·sey·mere (-mir′) *n.* [altered (after prec.) < CASSIMERE] *same as* CASSIMERE

ke·ryg·ma (kə rig′mə) *n.* [Gr.(Ec.) *kērygma,* preaching < Gr., a proclamation < *kēryssein,* to proclaim < *kēryx,* a herald < IE. base **kar-,* to praise loudly, whence OE. *hrothor, joy*] *Theol.* **1.** preaching of the Gospel **2.** emphasis on the essence of the Gospel, as in preaching, catechesis, etc. —**ker·yg·mat·ic** (ker′ig mat′ik) *adj.*

kes·trel (kes′trəl) *n.* [ME. *castrel* < OFr. *cresserelle, quercerelle:* origin echoic] a small, brown and gray European falcon (*Falco tinnunculus*) that can hover in the air against the wind

ketch (kech) *n.* [ME. *cache* < *cacchen,* to CATCH: orig. used of fishing vessels] a fore-and-aft rigged sailing vessel with a mainmast toward the bow and a relatively tall mizzenmast, forward of the rudderpost, toward the stern: distinguished from YAWL[1]

Ketch·i·kan (kech′i kan′) [prob. < Tlingit eponymous stream name *Kitschk-hin,* Kitschk's stream] seaport in SE Alas.: pop. 7,000

KETCH

ketch·up (kech′əp) *n.* [Malay *kēchap,* a fish sauce < Chin. *ke-tsiap*] a sauce for meat, fish, etc.; esp., a thick sauce (tomato ketchup) made of tomatoes flavored with onion, salt, sugar, and spice

ke·tene (kē′tēn) *n.* [KET(O)- + -ENE] **1.** a colorless toxic gas, $H_2C:CO$, with a penetrating odor, made by passing acetone or acetic acid through hot metal tubes: used esp. as an acetylating agent **2.** any of a series of related organic compounds containing the >C:CO group

ke·to- (kēt′ō, -ə) *a combining form meaning* ketone, of ketones [*ketogenesis*]: also, before a vowel, **ket-**

ke·to·gen·e·sis (kēt′ō jen′ə sis) *n.* [prec. + -GENESIS] the formation of ketones, such as acetone, in the body as a result of the incomplete oxidation of organic compounds such as fatty acids or carbohydrates —**ke′to·gen′ic** *adj.*

ke·tol (kē′tôl, -tōl) *n.* [KET(ONE) + -OL[1]] any of a group of organic compounds containing a ketone group and an alcohol group in the molecule

ke·tone (-tōn) *n.* [G. *keton,* arbitrary var. of Fr. *acétone:* see ACETONE] an organic chemical compound containing the divalent carbonyl group, CO, in combination with two hydrocarbon radicals

ketone body any of three related substances, including acetone, important in human fat metabolism

ke·to·ne·mi·a (kēt′ə nē′mē ə) *n.* [KETON(E) + -EMIA] an excess of ketone bodies in the blood

ke·to·nu·ri·a (-nyoor′ē ə) *n.* [KETON(E) + -URIA] an excess of ketone bodies in the urine

ke·tose (kē′tōs) *n.* [KET(O)- + -OSE[1]] a sugar that contains a ketone group in the molecule

ke·to·sis (kē tō′sis) *n.* [ModL. < KET(O)- + -OSIS] a condition in which there is excessive formation of ketones in the body

ke·to·ster·oid (kēt′ō stir′oid) *n.* a steroid containing a ketone group in the molecule

Ket·ter·ing (ket′ər in) city in SW Ohio: suburb of Dayton: pop. 70,000

Kettering, Charles Franklin 1876–1958; U.S. electrical engineer & inventor

ket·tle (ket′'l) *n.* [ME. *ketel* < ON. *ketill,* akin to OE *cetel,* G. *kessel,* Goth. *katils,* early Gmc. loanword < L. *catillus,* dim. of *catinus,* container for food] **1.** a metal container for boiling or cooking things; pot **2.** a teakettle **3.** a kettledrum **4.** *Geol. a)* a depression in glacial drift remaining after the melting of an isolated mass of buried ice *b)* a kettle-shaped hole in rock, gravel, etc.: also **kettle hole**

ket·tle·drum (-drum′) *n.* a percussion instrument consisting of a hollow hemisphere of copper or brass and a parchment top that can be tightened or loosened to change the pitch; timpano

kettle of fish 1. a difficult or embarrassing situation **2.** a matter to be dealt with

kev, Kev (kev) *n., pl.* **kev, Kev** [K(ILO)- E(LECTRON)-V(OLTS)] a unit of energy equal to one thousand (10³) electron-volts

kev·el (kev′'l) *n.* [ME. *keuil* < ONormFr. *keville* (Fr. *cheville*) < L. *clavicula*, small key (in LL., a bar, bolt for a door), dim. of *clavis*, key: see CLOSE²] a cleat or peg for fastening the heavy lines of a ship

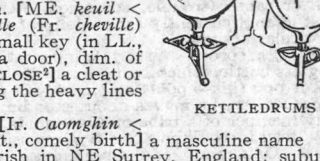

KETTLEDRUMS

Kev·in (kev′in) [Ir. *Caomghin* < OIr. *Coemgen*, lit., comely birth] a masculine name

Kew (kyōō) parish in NE Surrey, England: suburb of London: site of the Royal Botanic Gardens (**Kew Gardens**)

☆**Kew·pie doll** (kyōō′pē) [altered < CUPID] *a trademark for* a chubby, rosy-faced doll with a topknot, patterned after a winged baby fairy originally drawn by Rose O'Neill (?-1944) —*n.* [k-] such a doll

key¹ (kē) *n., pl.* **keys** [ME. *keye* < OE. *cæge*, akin to OFris. *kei, kēia*, to secure, guard] **1.** an instrument, usually of metal, for moving the bolt of a lock and thus locking or unlocking something **2.** any of several instruments or mechanical devices resembling or suggesting this in form or use; specif., *a*) a device to turn a bolt, etc. [a skate key, a watch key] *b*) a pin, bolt, wedge, cotter, or similar device put into a hole or space to lock or hold parts together *c*) something that completes or holds together the parts of another thing, as the keystone of an arch or a roughened surface forming a secure base for plaster *d*) any of a set of levers, or the disks, buttons, etc. connected to them, pressed down in operating a piano, accordion, clarinet, typewriter, linotype, etc. *e*) a device for opening or closing an electric circuit *f*) a small metal piece for fastening a wheel, pulley, etc. to a shaft *g*) a key-shaped emblem presented as an honor [the key to the city] **3.** something regarded as like a key in opening or closing a way, revealing or concealing, etc.; specif., *a*) so located as to give access to or control of a region [Vicksburg was the *key* to the lower Mississippi] *b*) a thing that explains or solves something else, as a book of answers, the explanations on a map, the code to a system of pronunciation, etc. *c*) a controlling or essential person or thing **4.** tone of voice; pitch **5.** *a*) tone or style of thought or expression [in a cheerful *key*] *b*) relative intensity of feeling **6.** the tone of a picture with regard to lightness or darkness or intensity of color **7.** *Biol.* a logical device, usually an ordered, contrastive listing of significant characters of a group of organisms, used to identify unknown individuals for taxonomic classification **8.** *Bot. same as* KEY FRUIT **9.** *Mus. a*) [Obs.] the keynote of a scale *b*) a system of related notes or tones based on and named after a certain note (keynote, tonic) and forming a given scale; tonality *c*) the main tonality of a composition —*adj.* controlling; essential; important [a key position] —*vt.* **keyed, key′ing 1.** to fasten or lock with a key or wedge **2.** to furnish with a key; specif., *a*) to put the keystone in (an arch) *b*) to provide with an explanatory key **3.** to regulate the tone or pitch of **4.** to bring into harmony or accord —**key up 1.** to raise the key of **2.** to bring into a state of nervous tension, as in anticipation

key² (kē) *n., pl.* **keys** [Sp. *cayo*: sp. infl. by prec. & earlier *key* (quay)] a reef or low island

Key (kē), **Francis Scott** 1779–1843; U.S. lawyer: wrote "The Star-Spangled Banner"

key·board (kē′bôrd′) *n.* the row or rows of keys of a piano, typewriter, linotype, etc. —☆*vt., vi.* to set (type) using a keyboard typesetting machine

☆**key club** a private nightclub, restaurant, or café, to which each member has his own key

keyed (kēd) *adj.* **1.** having keys, as some musical instruments **2.** fastened or reinforced with a key or keystone **3.** pitched in a specified key **4.** adjusted so as to conform

key fruit a dry, winged fruit, as of the maple, ash, or elm, containing the seed or seeds; samara

key·hole (kē′hōl′) *n.* **1.** an opening (in a lock) into which a key is inserted ☆**2.** *Basketball* the keyhole-shaped free-throw lane

Key Lar·go (lär′gō) [Sp. *Cayo Largo*, large key] largest island of the Florida Keys, off the SE tip of Fla.: c. 40 sq. mi.

Keynes (kānz), **John Maynard,** 1st Baron Keynes, 1883–1946; Eng. economist & writer

Keynes·i·an (kān′zē ən) *adj.* designating, of, or in accord with the economic theories of Keynes and his followers, which hold that full employment and a stable economy depend on the continued governmental stimulation of spending and investment through adjustment of interest rates and tax rates, deficit financing, etc. —*n.* an adherent of these theories —**Keynes′i·an·ism** *n.*

key·note (-nōt′) *n.* **1.** the lowest, basic note or tone of a musical scale, or key; tonic **2.** the basic idea or ruling principle, as of a speech, policy, etc. —☆*vt.* **-not′ed, -not′-ing 1.** to give the keynote of **2.** to deliver the keynote address at —☆**key′not′er** *n.*

☆**keynote speech** (or **address**) a speech, as at a political convention, that sets forth the main line of policy

key punch a machine, operated from a keyboard, that records data by punching holes in cards that can then be fed into machines for sorting, accounting, etc.

key ring a metal ring for holding keys

key signature *Music* one or more sharps or flats placed after the clef on the staff to indicate the key

key·stone (kē′stōn′) *n.* **1.** the central, topmost stone of an arch, popularly thought of as especially holding the others in place **2.** that one of a number of associated parts or things that supports or holds together the others; main part or principle

☆**Key·stone** (kē′stōn′) *adj.* [< *Keystone* Comedy Co., the film producers] designating, of, or like the slapstick comedy of a series of silent films featuring a bungling, inept squad of policemen (**Keystone Kops,** or **Cops**) in wild chases, etc.

KEYSTONE

Keystone State *nickname of* PENNSYLVANIA: from its central geographical position among the 13 original colonies

key·way (-wā′) *n.* **1.** a groove or slot cut in a shaft, hub, etc. to hold the key **2.** the keyhole in a lock worked by a flat key

Key West [Sp. *Cayo Hueso*, rocky key] **1.** westernmost island of the Florida Keys: c. 4 mi. long **2.** seaport on this island: pop. 28,000

kg, kg. 1. keg(s) **2.** kilogram(s)

K.G. Knight of (the Order of) the Garter

Kha·ba·rovsk (khä bä′rôfsk) **1.** territory in E.R.S.F.S.R., in E Siberia: pop. 1,143,000 **2.** capital of this territory, on the Amur River: pop. 377,000

Kha·cha·tu·ri·an (kach′ə toor′ē ən; *Russ.* khä′chä too ryän′), **A·ram** (ar′əm; *Russ.* ä räm′) 1903?– ; Soviet composer

kha·di (kä′dē) *n.* [Hind. *khādī*] homespun cotton cloth made in India: also **khad·dar** (kä′dər)

khaf (khäf, khôf) *n.* [Heb.] a variant of the eleventh letter (*kaf*) of the Hebrew alphabet (כ, ך)

Khaibar Pass *same as* KHYBER PASS

kha·ki (kak′ē, kä′kē) *adj.* [Hind. *khākī*, dusty, dust-colored < Per. *khāk*, dust, earth] **1.** dull yellowish-brown **2.** made of khaki (cloth) —*n., pl.* **-kis 1.** a dull yellowish brown **2.** strong, twilled wool or, esp., cotton cloth of this color, used esp. for military uniforms **3.** [*often pl.*] a khaki uniform or trousers

kha·lif (kä′lif, kal′if) *n. same as* CALIPH

Khal·kha (kal′kə) *n.* **1.** any member of a Mongolian people of Mongolia **2.** *same as* MONGOL (*n.* 4)

Khal·ki·di·ki (khäl′ki thē′kē) *Gr. name of* CHALCIDICE

Khal·kis (khäl kēs′) *Gr. name of* CHALCIS

kham·sin (kam′sin, kam sēn′) *n.* [Ar. *khamsīn* < *khamsūn*, fifty] a hot south wind from the Sahara that blows in the Near East, esp. Egypt, from late March until early May (about 50 days)

khan¹ (kän, kan) *n.* [ME. *chaan* < Turki *khān*, lord, prince: of Tatar origin] **1.** a title given to Genghis Khan and his successors, who ruled over Turkish, Tatar, and Mongol tribes and dominated most of Asia during the Middle Ages **2.** a title given to various officials and dignitaries in Iran, Afghanistan, etc. —**khan′ate** (-āt) *n.*

khan² (kän, kan) *n.* [Ar. *khān*] in Turkey and other Eastern countries, a public inn; caravansary

Kha·ni·a (khä nyä′) *Gr. name of* CANEA

khaph (khäf, khôf) *n. same as* KHAF

kha·pra beetle (käp′rə) [Hindi *khaprā*, lit., destroyer, akin to Sans. *kṣayati*, (he) destroys < IE. base *gwhthei(e)-*, to pass away, dwindle, destroy, whence Gr. *phthíein*, to waste away: cf. PHTHISIS] an insect (*Trogoderma granarium*) native to S and SE Asia, now a destructive grain pest in much of the world

Khar·kov (kär′kôf; *Russ.* khär′kôf) city in NE Ukrainian S.S.R.: pop. 1,092,000

Khar·toum (kär tōōm′) capital of Sudan, on the Nile: pop., with adjoining cities of OMDURMAN & **Khartoum North,** 312,000

khat (kät) *n.* [Ar. *qat*] a plant (*Catha edulis*) of the staff-tree family, found in Africa and Arabia: the fresh leaf is chewed for its stimulating effects or used in tea

Khayyám, Omar *see* OMAR KHAYYÁM

khed·ah (ked′ə) *n. same as* KEDDAH

khe·dive (kə dēv′) *n.* [Fr. *khédive* < Turk. *khidīv* < Per. *khidīw*, prince, ruler] the title of the Turkish viceroys of Egypt, from 1867 to 1914

Kher·son (kher sôn′) port in S Ukrainian S.S.R., on the Dnepr near its mouth: pop. 222,000

khet, kheth *n. same as* HET

Khin·gan Mountains (shin′gän′) mountain range in NE China, with two divisions: *a)* **Great** (or **Greater**) **Khingan Mountains** W range along the E border of the Mongolian People's Republic: highest peak, 5,670 ft. *b)* **Lesser** (or **Little**) **Khingan Mountains** N range running parallel to the Amur River: highest peak, 4,665 ft.

Khí·os (khē′ŏs) Gr. island in the Aegean, off the W coast of Turkey: with nearby islands it forms a province (335 sq. mi.; pop. 62,000)

Khi·va (khē′və; *E.* kē′və) former khanate in C Asia, now in the U.S.S.R.

Khmer (k′mer) *n.* [< the Khmer name] 1. one of a native people of Cambodia, who had a highly developed civilization in the Middle Ages 2. their Mon-Khmer language

Khoi·san (koi′sän) *n.* a group of S African languages including Hottentot, Bushman, etc.

Khond (känd) *n.* [< Dravidian name] a member of a group of Dravidian tribes of EC India

Kho·war (kō′wär) *n.* an Indo-Iranian language of NW Pakistan

Khrush·chev (kroos′chev, -chôf′; *Russ.* khrōōsh′chyôf′), **Ni·ki·ta Ser·gey·e·vich** (ni kē′tä syer gā′ye vich) 1894–1971; premier of the U.S.S.R. (1958–64)

Khu·fu (kōō′fōō) fl. c. 2650 B.C.; king of Egypt, of the IVth dynasty; builder of the Great Pyramid near Gîza

Khu·zis·tan (khōō′zis tän′) region in W Iran: pop. 2,400,000; cap. Ahvaz

Khy·ber Pass (kī′bər) mountain pass in a range of the Hindu Kush, between Afghanistan & West Pakistan: c. 33 mi. long

kHz kilohertz

Ki. Kings

ki·ang (kē aŋ′) *n.* [< Tibet. *rkyaṅ*] a wild ass (*Equus kiang*) found in Tibet and Mongolia

Kiang·si (kyaŋ′sē′; *Chin.* jyäŋ′sē′) province of SE China: 63,629 sq. mi.; pop. 18,610,000; cap. Nanchang

Kiang·su (-sōō′) province of E China, on the Yellow Sea: 39,459 sq. mi.; pop. 45,230,-000; cap. Nanking

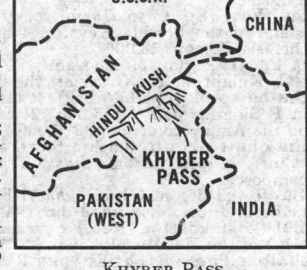

KHYBER PASS

kib·ble (kib′'l) *vt.* **-bled, -bling** [< ?] to grind or form into coarse particles or bits —*n.* meal, prepared dog food, etc. in this form

kib·butz (ki bōōts′, -boots′) *n., pl.* **-but·zim** (kē′bōō tsēm′) [ModHeb.] an Israeli collective settlement, esp. a collective farm

kib·butz·nik (-nik) *n.* [cf. -NIK] a member of a kibbutz

kibe (kīb) *n.* [ME., prob. < W. *cibi*] [Archaic] a chapped or ulcerated chilblain, esp. on the heel

☆**ki·bei** (kē′bā′) *n., pl.* **-bei′, -beis′** [Jap.] [*also* K-] a native U.S. citizen born of immigrant Japanese parents but educated largely in Japan: cf. ISSEI, NISEI

☆**kib·itz** (kib′its) *vi.* [Colloq.] to act as a kibitzer

☆**kib·itz·er** (-ər) *n.* [Yid. < colloq. G. *kiebitzen*, to look on (at cards) < *kiebitz*, meddlesome onlooker, orig., plover, of echoic origin] [Colloq.] 1. an onlooker at a card game, etc., esp. one who volunteers advice 2. a giver of unwanted advice; meddler

kib·lah (kib′lä) *n.* [Ar. *qiblah*, something placed opposite < *qabala*, to be opposite] the point toward which Moslems turn when praying, the location of the black stone at Mecca: see KAABA

ki·bosh (kī′bäsh, ki bäsh′) *n.* [earlier also *kyebosh* < ? Yid.: infl. in Eng. by association with BOSH¹] [Slang] orig., nonsense: now usually in **put the kibosh on,** to put an end to; squelch; veto

kick¹ (kik) *vi.* [ME. *kiken* < ?] 1. to strike out with the foot or feet, as in anger, or in swimming, dancing, etc. 2. to spring back suddenly, as a gun when fired; recoil 3. [Colloq.] to object strongly; complain; grumble 4. *Football* to kick the ball —*vt.* 1. to strike or shove suddenly with the foot or feet 2. to drive or move (a ball, etc.) by striking with the foot 3. to make or force (one's way, etc.) by kicking 4. to score (a goal or point in football) by kicking ☆5. [Slang] *a)* to stop taking (a narcotic drug) *b)* to get rid of (a habit) —*n.* 1. a blow with or thrust of the foot 2. a method of kicking 3. a sudden, sharp thrust or jolt, as the recoil of a gun when fired 4. a sudden burst of speed by a runner toward the end of a race 5. [Colloq.] an objection; complaint ☆6. [Colloq.] a stimulating or intoxicating effect, as of alcoholic liquor ☆7. [Colloq.] [*often pl.*] pleasure; esp., pleasurable excitement 8. [Slang] pocket 9. *Football a)* the act of kicking the ball *b)* the kicked ball *c)* the distance that it travels *d)* one's turn at kicking —☆**kick around** (or **about**) [Colloq.] 1. to treat roughly 2. to move from place to place 3. to lie

about unnoticed or forgotten 4. to think about or discuss informally —**kick back** 1. [Colloq.] to recoil suddenly and in an unexpected way ☆2. [Slang] to give back (a portion of money received as pay, commission, etc.), often as a result of coercion or a previous understanding —**kick down** to shift to a lower gear —☆**kick in** [Slang] to pay (one's share) —**kick off** 1. to put a football into play with a kickoff ☆2. to start (a campaign, etc.) ☆3. [Slang] to die 4. [Slang] to depart; leave —**kick on** [Colloq.] 1. to turn on (a switch, etc.) 2. to begin operating —☆**kick oneself** to blame oneself severely —**kick out** 1. [Colloq.] to get rid of; expel; dismiss 2. *Football* to make a kick out of bounds —**kick up** 1. to raise by kicking 2. [Colloq.] to make or cause (trouble, confusion, etc.) —☆**on** (or **off**) **a kick** [Slang] currently (or no longer) enthusiastic about a particular activity

kick² (kik) *n.* [prob. < prec.] an indentation at the bottom of a glass bottle, which reduces its capacity

☆**Kick·a·poo** (kik′ə pōō′) *n., pl.* **-poos′, -poo′** [< Kickapoo *kiwigapaw*, lit., he moves about standing here and there] 1. any member of a tribe of Algonquian Indians who formerly lived in N Illinois and S Wisconsin and now live in Kansas, Oklahoma, and Chihuahua, Mexico 2. their Algonquian language

☆**kick·back** (kik′bak′) *n.* 1. [Colloq.] a sharp, violent reaction 2. [Slang] *a)* a giving back of part of money received as payment, commission, etc., often as a result of coercion or a previous understanding *b)* the money so returned

kick·ball (-bôl′) *n.* ☆a children's game with the general rules of baseball, but using a large ball that is kicked rather than batted

kick·er (-ər) *n.* 1. one that kicks 2. [Slang] an outboard motor 3. [Slang] *a)* a surprise ending, ironic twist, etc. *b)* a hidden, unsuspected point or difficulty

kick·off (-ôf′) *n.* ☆1. *Football* a place kick from the forty-yard line of the kicking team, that puts the ball into play at the beginning of each half or after a touchdown or field goal ☆2. a beginning or commencement, as of a campaign or drive

kick·shaw (kik′shô′) *n.* [properly *kickshaws*, altered (by folk etym.) < Fr. *quelque chose*, something] 1. a fancy food or dish; delicacy; tidbit 2. a trinket; trifle; gewgaw Also **kick′shaws′** (-shôz′)

☆**kick·stand** (kik′stand′) *n.* a short metal bar attached by a pivot to a bicycle or motorcycle: it holds the stationary cycle upright when kicked down into a vertical position

kick·up (kik′up′) *n.* [Colloq.] a fuss; row

kid (kid) *n.* [ME. *kide*, prob. < Anglo-N., akin to ON. *kith*, Dan. & Sw. *kid*, G. *kitze*] 1. a young goat or, occasionally, antelope 2. its flesh, used as a food 3. leather made from the skin of young goats, used for gloves, shoes, etc. 4. [*pl.*] gloves or shoes made of this leather 5. [Colloq.] a child or young person —*adj.* 1. made of kidskin ☆2. [Colloq.] younger [*my kid sister*] —*vt., vi.* **kid′ded, kid′ding** 1. to give birth to (a kid or kids): said of goats or antelopes 2. [Colloq.] *a)* to deceive or fool in a playful way *b)* to tease or ridicule playfully —☆**no kidding!** [Colloq.] I can hardly believe it!: an exclamation of doubt or surprise —**kid′der** *n.* —**kid′like′, kid′dish** *adj.*

Kidd (kid), **Captain** (**William**) 1645?–1701; Brit. privateer & pirate, born in Scotland: hanged

Kid·der·min·ster (kid′ər min′stər) *n.* a kind of ingrain or reversible carpet, orig. made at Kidderminster, a town in W England

kid·dush (ki dōōsh′, kid′oosh) *n.* [Heb. *qiddūsh*, sanctification] *Judaism* a benediction recited over wine or bread on the eve of the Sabbath or a festival

kid·dy, kid·die (kid′ē) *n., pl.* **-dies** [dim. of KID, *n.* 5] [Colloq.] a child

kid gloves soft, smooth gloves made of kidskin —☆**handle with kid gloves** [Colloq.] to handle or treat with care, tact, etc.

kid·nap (-nap′) *vt.* **-napped′** or **-naped′, -nap′ping** or **-nap′ing** [KID, *n.* 5 + dial. *nap*: see NAB] 1. to steal (a child) 2. to seize and hold or carry off (a person) against his will, by force or fraud, often for ransom —**kid′nap′per, kid′nap′er** *n.*

kid·ney (kid′nē) *n., pl.* **-neys** [ME. *kidenei* < ?] 1. either of a pair of glandular organs in the upper abdominal cavity of vertebrates, which separate water and waste products of metabolism from the blood and excrete them as urine through the bladder 2. the kidney of an animal, used as food 3. *a)* disposition; temperament *b)* class; kind; sort

kidney bean the kidney-shaped seed of the common garden bean (*Phaseolus vulgaris*) of the legume family

kidney stone a hard, mineral deposit (*renal calculus*) formed in the kidney from phosphates, urates, etc.

Ki·dron (kē′drən) 1. valley in Jordan, east of Jerusalem 2.

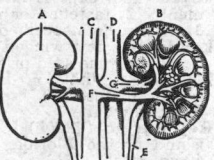

KIDNEYS
(A, right kidney; B, left kidney; C, vena cava; D, aorta; E, ureter; F, renal vein; G, renal artery; left kidney shown in cross section)

brook in this valley, flowing to the Dead Sea: II Sam. 15:23

kid·skin (kid′skin′) *n.* leather from the skin of young goats, used for gloves, shoes, etc.

Kiel (kēl) seaport in N West Germany, on the Kiel Canal: capital of Schleswig-Holstein: pop. 270,000

kiel·ba·sa (kēl bä′sə) *n., pl.* **-si** (-sē), **-sas** [Pol.] a type of smoked Polish sausage, flavored with garlic, etc.

Kiel Canal canal in N West Germany, connecting the North Sea & the Baltic Sea: 61 mi.

kier (kir) *n.* [prob. < ON. *ker*, tub, akin to MLowG. *kar*, Goth. *kas*, tub, keg] a large vat to hold cloth for bleaching, boiling, etc.

KIEL CANAL

Kier·ke·gaard (kir′kə gärd′; *Dan.* kir′kə gôr′), **Sø·ren** (Aabye) (sö′rən) 1813–55; Dan. philosopher & theologian

kie·sel·guhr, kie·sel·gur (kē′z'l goor′) *n.* [G. < *kiesel*, flint + *guhr, gur*, earthy sediment < *gären*, to ferment] *same as* DIATOMITE

kie·ser·ite (kē′zə rīt′) *n.* [G. *kieserit*, after D. G. *Kieser* (1779–1862), G. scientist] hydrous magnesium sulfate, MgSO₄·H₂O

Ki·ev (kē′ef; *E.* kē′ev′, kē′ev) capital of the Ukrainian S.S.R., on the Dnepr: pop. 1,371,000

kif, kief (kif, kēf) *n. same as* KEF

Ki·ga·li (ki gä′lē) capital of Rwanda: pop. 7,000

Ki·kon·go (kē käŋ′gō) *n. same as* KONGO

Ki·ku·yu (kē koo′yoo) *n.* **1.** *pl.* **-yus, -yu** any member of an agricultural people of Kenya **2.** their Bantu language

kil. kilometer; kilometers

Ki·lau·e·a (kē′lou ā′ə) active volcanic crater on the slope of Mauna Loa, Hawaii: c. 8 mi. in circumference

Kil·dare (kil der′) county in Leinster province, E Ireland: 654 sq. mi.; pop. 66,000

kil·der·kin (kil′dər kin) *n.* [ME. *kylderkin*, altered < MDu. *kinderkin*, quarter tun, dim. < *kintal* < ML. *quintale* (see QUINTAL)] **1.** a cask; small barrel **2.** an old English liquid measure of about 18 imperial gallons

Kil·i·man·ja·ro (kil′ə män jä′rō) mountain in NE Tanganyika: highest mountain in Africa: 19,340 ft.

Kil·ken·ny (kil ken′ē) county in Leinster province, E Ireland: 796 sq. mi.; pop. 60,000

kill¹ (kil) *vt.* [ME. *kullen, killen* < ? OE. **cyllan*, special late phonetic development of *cwellan*, to kill (see QUELL)] **1.** to cause the death of; make die **2.** *a)* to destroy the vital or active qualities of *b)* to destroy; put an end to; ruin **3.** to prevent the passage of (legislation); defeat or veto **4.** to spend (time) on matters of little or no importance ☆**5.** *a)* to cause (an engine, etc.) to stop; turn off *b)* to turn off (a light, esp. a theater spotlight) *c)* to muffle (sound) ☆**6.** to prevent publication of [to *kill* a newspaper story] **7.** to spoil the effect of; destroy by contrast: said of colors, etc. **8.** [Colloq.] to overcome with laughter, chagrin, pleasure, surprise, etc. **9.** [Colloq.] to cause to feel great pain or discomfort **10.** [Colloq.] to tire out; exhaust **11.** [Slang] to drink the last, or all, of (a bottle of liquor, etc.); finish off ☆**12.** *Printing* to mark as not to be used; score out; cancel **13.** *Tennis*, etc. to return (the ball) with such force that it cannot be played back; smash —*vi.* **1.** to destroy life **2.** to be killed [plants that *kill* easily] —*n.* **1.** an act or instance of killing **2.** an animal or animals killed **3.** an enemy plane, ship, etc. destroyed —**in at the kill 1.** present when the hunted animal is killed **2.** present at the end of some action

SYN.—**kill** is the general word in this list, meaning to cause the death of in any way and may be applied to persons, animals, or plants; **slay**, now largely a literary word, implies deliberate and violent killing; **murder** applies to an unlawful and malicious or premeditated killing; **assassinate** implies specifically the sudden killing of a politically important person by someone hired or delegated to do this; **execute** denotes a killing in accordance with a legally imposed sentence; **dispatch** suggests a killing by direct action, such as stabbing or shooting, and emphasizes speed or promptness

☆**kill**² (kil) *n.* [Du. *kil* < MDu. *kille*, ? akin to ON. *kīll*, inlet] a stream; channel; creek: used esp. in place names

Kil·lar·ney (ki lär′nē) **1.** town in C Kerry county, SW Ireland: pop. 7,000 **2. Lakes of,** three lakes near this town

☆**kill·deer** (kil′dir′) *n., pl.* **-deers, -deer'**: see PLURAL, II, D, 1 [echoic of its cry] a small, N. American bird (*Oxyechus vociferus*) of the plover family, with a high, piercing cry: also **kill′dee'** (-dē′)

Kil·leen (ki lēn′) [after F. P. *Killeen*, official of the Santa Fe Railroad] city in C Tex.: pop. 36,000

kill·er (kil′ər) *n.* **1.** a person, animal, or thing that kills, esp. one that kills habitually or wantonly **2.** *same as* KILLER WHALE

killer whale any of several fierce, grayish to black, small whales (genera *Grampus* and *Orcinus*) that hunt in large packs and prey on large fish, seals, and whales

kil·lick (kil′ik) *n.* [New England dial.] a small anchor; often, an anchor weighted with a stone, or a stone used as an anchor: also **kil′lock** (-ək)

Kil·lie·cran·kie (kil′ē kraŋ′kē) mountain pass in the Grampians, NE Perthshire, Scotland

☆**kil·li·fish** (kil′ē fish′) *n., pl.* **-fish', -fish'es:** see FISH² [*killie*, killifish (< KILL² + -IE) + FISH²] any of several small, minnowlike freshwater fishes (family Cyprinodontidae) used in mosquito control and as bait: also **kil′lie** (-ē), *pl.* **-lies**

kill·ing (kil′iŋ) *adj.* **1.** causing, or able to cause, death; destructive; deadly **2.** exhausting; fatiguing **3.** [Colloq.] very funny or comical —*n.* **1.** slaughter; murder ☆**2.** [Colloq.] a sudden, great profit or success —**kill′ing·ly** *adv.*

kill-joy (-joi′) *n.* a person who destroys or lessens other people's enjoyment: also **kill′joy'**

Kil·mar·nock (kil mär′nək) city in Ayrshire, SW Scotland: pop. 48,000

Kil·mer (kil′mər), (Alfred) **Joyce** 1886–1918; U.S. poet

kiln (kil, kiln) *n.* [ME. *kylne* < OE. *cylne* < L. *culina*, cookstove, kitchen (cf. CULINARY)] a furnace or oven for drying, burning, or baking something, as bricks, grain, or pottery —*vt.* to dry, burn, or bake in a kiln

kiln-dry (-drī′) *vt.* **-dried', -dry'ing** to dry in a kiln

kil·o (kē′lō, kil′ō) *n., pl.* **-los** [Fr.: abbreviated form] *short for a)* KILOGRAM *b)* KILOMETER

kil·o- (kil′ə, -ō) [Fr. < Gr. *chilioi*, thousand < IE. **ghéslo-*, thousand] *a combining form meaning* a thousand; the factor 10³ [*kilogram*]

kilo. **1.** kilogram **2.** kilometer

kil·o·bar (kil′ə bär′) *n.* [see KILO- & BAR²] a metric unit of pressure equal to one thousand bars

kil·o·cal·o·rie (kil′ə kal′ər ē) *n.* [see KILO- & CALORIE] the amount of heat needed to raise the temperature of one kilogram of water one degree centigrade; 1,000 calories; great calorie

kil·o·cy·cle (-sī′k'l) *n. former name for* KILOHERTZ

kil·o·gram (-gram′) *n.* [Fr. *kilogramme*; see KILO- & GRAM] a unit of weight and mass, equal to 1,000 grams (2.2046 lb.): also, chiefly Brit., **kil′o·gramme':** abbrev. **kg** (sing. & pl.), **k., kilo., kilog.**

kil·o·gram-me·ter (-gram′mēt′ər) *n.* a unit of energy or work, being the amount needed to raise one kilogram one meter: it is equal to 7.2334 foot-pounds: also, chiefly Brit., **kil′o·gram'-me'tre**

kil·o·hertz (-hurts′) *n., pl.* **-hertz'** [see KILO- & HERTZ] one thousand hertz: abbrev. **kHz** (sing. & pl.)

kil·o·li·ter (-lēt′ər) *n.* [Fr. *kilolitre*; see KILO- & LITER] a unit of capacity, equal to 1,000 liters, or one cubic meter (264.18 gal., or 1.308 cu. yd.): also, chiefly Brit., **kil′o·li'tre:** abbrev. **kl.** (sing. & pl.), **kilol.**

ki·lo·me·ter (ki läm′ə tər, kil′ō mēt′ər) *n.* [Fr. *kilomètre:* see KILO- & METER¹] a unit of length or distance, equal to 1,000 meters (3,280.8 ft., or about 5/8 mi.): also, chiefly Brit., **ki·lo′me·tre:** abbrev. **km., kil., kilo., kilom.** —**kil·o·met·ric** (kil′ə met′rik) *adj.*

kil·o·par·sec (kil′ə pär′sek′) *n.* one thousand parsecs; 3,260 light-years

kil·o·ton (-tun′) *n.* [see KILO- & TON¹] the explosive force of 1,000 tons of TNT: a unit for measuring the power of thermonuclear weapons: abbrev. **kt.**

kil·o·volt (-vōlt′) *n.* one thousand volts: abbrev. **kv**

kil·o·volt-am·pere (-am′pir) *n.* one thousand volt-amperes: abbrev. **kva**

kil·o·watt (-wät′) *n.* a unit of electrical power, equal to 1,000 watts: abbrev. **kw.**

kil·o·watt-hour (-our′) *n.* a unit of electrical energy or work, equal to that done by one kilowatt acting for one hour: abbrev. **kwhr, kwh**

kilt (kilt) *vt.* [ME. (northern) *kilten*, prob. < Scand., as in ON. *kilting*, a skirt, *kjalta*, lap: for IE. base see CHILD] **1.** [Scot.] to tuck up (a skirt, etc.) **2.** to pleat **3.** to provide a kilt for —*n.* a pleated skirt reaching to the knees; esp., the tartan skirt worn sometimes by men of the Scottish Highlands

kil·ter (kil′tər) *n.* [< ?] [Colloq.] good condition; proper order: now chiefly in **out of kilter**

Ki·lung (kē′loon′) *same as* CHILUNG

Kim·ber·ley (kim′bər lē) city in N Cape of Good Hope province, South Africa: diamond-mining center: pop. 79,000

kim·ber·lite (kim′bər līt′) *n.* [KIMBER(LEY) + -LITE] a kind of peridotite which sometimes contains diamonds

kim·chi (kim′chē) *n.* [Kor.] a spicy Korean dish consisting of pickled cabbage, peppers, garlic, etc.

ki·mo·no (kə mō′nə, -nō) *n., pl.* **-nos** [Jap.] **1.** a loose outer garment with short, wide sleeves and a sash, part of the traditional costume of Japanese men and women **2.** a woman's loose dressing gown like this

KILT

kin (kin) *n.* [ME. *kyn* < OE. *cynn*, akin to Du. *kunne*, Goth. *kuni*, ON. *kyn* < IE. base *ĝen-*, to produce: see GENUS, GENESIS] **1.** relatives; family; kinfolk; kindred **2.** [Now Rare] family relationship; kinship —*adj.* related, as by blood; kindred —(**near**) **of kin** (closely) related

-kin (kin) [ME. < MDu. *-ken, -kijn,* dim. suffix, akin to G. *-chen*] *a suffix meaning* little [*lambkin*]

Kin·a·ba·lu (kin′ə bə lōō′) mountain in NW Sabah: highest peak on Borneo; 13,455 ft.

kin·aes·the·si·a (kin′is thē′zhə) *n. same as* KINESTHESIA: also **kin′aes·the′sis** (-sis) —**kin′aes·thet′ic** (-thet′ik) *adj.*

ki·nase (kī′nās, kin′ās) *n.* [KIN(ETIC) + -ASE] a substance capable of activating a zymogen into an enzyme

Kin·car·dine (kin kär′din) county of E Scotland: 382 sq. mi.; pop. 25,000: also **Kin·car′dine·shire** (-shir)

kind (kīnd) *n.* [ME. *kynd* < OE. *cynd,* akin to G. *kind,* child, ON. *kundr,* son < IE. *ĝṇti-* (whence L. *natio:* see NATION) < base *ĝen-:* see KIN] **1.** [Archaic] *a)* origin *b)* nature *c)* manner; way **2.** a natural group or division [the rodent *kind*]: sometimes used in compounds [*humankind*] **3.** essential character **4.** sort; variety; class —*adj.* [ME. *kynde* < OE. *gecynde*] **1.** sympathetic, friendly, gentle, tenderhearted, generous, etc. **2.** cordial [*kind* regards] **3.** [Archaic] loving; affectionate **4.** [Obs.] natural; native —**after one's** (or **its**) **kind** [Archaic] in agreement with one's (or its) nature —**in kind 1.** in goods or produce instead of money **2.** with something like that received; in the same way —**kind of** [Colloq.] somewhat; rather; almost —**of a kind 1.** of the same kind; alike **2.** of poor quality; mediocre [*entertainment of a kind*] *SYN.*—**kind** implies the possession of sympathetic or generous qualities, either habitually or specifically, or is applied to actions manifesting these [he is *kind* only to his mother, your *kind* remarks]; **kindly** usually implies a characteristic nature or general disposition marked by such qualities [his *kindly* old uncle]; **benign** suggests a mild or kindly nature and is applied especially to a gracious superior [a *benign* employer]; **benevolent** implies a charitable or altruistic inclination to do good [his *benevolent* interest in orphans] See also TYPE —*ANT.* unkind, unfeeling, cruel

‡**kin·der, kir·che, kü·che** (kin′dər, kir′Hə, kü′Hə) [G.] children, church, and kitchen: a German slogan limiting the sphere of women's activities

kin·der·gar·ten (kin′dər gär′t'n) *n.* [G., lit., garden of children < *kinder,* gen. pl. of *kind,* child (see KIND) + *garten,* GARDEN] a school or class of young children, usually four to six years old, that prepares them for first grade and that develops basic skills and social behavior by games, exercises, music, simple handicraft, etc. —**kin′der·gart′-ner, kin′der·gar′ten·er** (-gärt′nər) *n.*

kind·heart·ed (kīnd′här′tid) *adj.* having or resulting from a kind heart; sympathetic; kindly —**kind′heart′-ed·ly** *adv.* —**kind′heart′ed·ness** *n.*

kin·dle[1] (kin′d'l) *vt.* -**dled, -dling** [ME. *kindlen,* freq. < ON. *kynda,* to set on fire, akin to MHG. *künten*] **1.** to set on fire; ignite **2.** to light (a fire) **3.** to arouse or excite (interest, feelings, etc.) **4.** to cause to light up; make bright —*vi.* **1.** to catch fire; start burning **2.** to become aroused or excited **3.** to light up; become bright [eyes *kindling* with joy] —**kin′dler** *n.*

kin·dle[2] (kin′d'l) *vt., vi.* -**dled, -dling** [ME. *kindlen:* see KIND, *n.*] [Dial.] to give birth to (young)

kind·less (kīnd′lis) *adj.* **1.** [Rare] lacking kindness **2.** [Obs.] lacking natural feeling; unnatural

kin·dling (kin′dlin) *n.* [ME.: see KINDLE[1]] **1.** bits of dry wood or other easily lighted material for starting a fire **2.** the act of one who kindles

kind·ly (kīnd′lē) *adj.* -**li·er, -li·est** [ME. *cyndelich* < OE. (ge)*cyndelic,* natural < *cynde:* see KIND] **1.** kind; gracious; benign **2.** agreeable; pleasant [a *kindly* climate] **3.** [Archaic] natural; native; innate —*adv.* **1.** in a kind, gracious manner **2.** agreeably; favorably **3.** please [*kindly* shut the door] **4.** [Obs.] naturally: now only in **take kindly to** *a)* to be naturally attracted to *b)* to accept willingly —*SYN.* see KIND —**thank kindly** to thank heartily —**kind′li·ness** *n.*

kind·ness (-nis) *n.* [ME. *kyndeness*] **1.** the state, quality, or habit of being kind **2.** kind act or treatment **3.** [Archaic] kind feeling; affection; good will

kin·dred (kin′drid) *n.* [with intrusive *-d-* < ME. *kinreden* < OE. *cynn,* KIN + *ræden,* state, condition, akin to *rædan,* READ] **1.** formerly, relationship by birth or, sometimes, by marriage; kinship **2.** relatives or family; kin; kinfolk **3.** [Archaic] resemblance in qualities; likeness —*adj.* **1.** formerly, related by birth or common origin **2.** of like nature or qualities; similar [*kindred* spirits] —*SYN.* see RELATED

kine (kīn) *n.pl.* [ME. *kin,* double pl. of *cou* (< OE. *cy,* pl. of *cu,* COW[1]) + -(*e*)*n*] [Archaic] cows; cattle

kin·e·mat·ics (kin′ə mat′iks) *n.pl.* [with sing. *v.*] [Fr. *cinématique* < Gr. *kinēma* (gen. *kinēmatos*), motion < *kinein,* to move + -ICS] the branch of mechanics that deals with motion in the abstract, without reference to the force or mass —**kin′e·mat′ic, kin′e·mat′i·cal** *adj.*

☆**kin·e·scope** (kin′ə skōp′) *n.* [KINE(TO)- + -SCOPE] **1.** a cathode-ray tube used in television receivers, monitors, etc. for picture display **2.** a motion-picture record of a television program from a kinescope

ki·ne·sics (ki nē′siks, kī-) *n.pl.* [with sing. *v.*] [< Gr. *kinēsis* (see ff.) + -ICS] the study of bodily movements,

facial expressions, etc. as ways of communication or as accompaniments to speech —**ki·ne′sic** *adj.*

ki·ne·si·ol·o·gy (ki nē′sē āl′ə jē, kī-) *n.* [< Gr. *kinēsis,* motion < *kinein,* to move + -LOGY] the science or study of human muscular movements, esp. as applied in physical education

kin·es·the·si·a (kin′is thē′zhə, -zhē ə) *n.* [ModL. < Gr. *kinein,* to move + *aisthēsis,* perception: for IE. base see AESTHETIC] the sensation of position, movement, tension, etc. of parts of the body, perceived through nerve end organs in muscles, tendons, and joints: also **kin′es·the′sis** (-sis) —**kin′es·thet′ic** (-thet′ik) *adj.*

ki·net·ic (ki net′ik) *adj.* [Gr. *kinētikos* < *kinētos,* movable < *kinein,* to move] **1.** of or resulting from motion **2.** energetic or dynamic

kinetic art an art style, esp. in sculpture or assemblage, involving the use of moving, often motorized, parts, shifting lights, sounds, etc.

kinetic energy that energy of a body which results from its motion: it is equal to half the product of its mass and the square of its velocity

ki·net·ics (-iks) *n.pl.* [with sing. *v.*] [< KINETIC] same as DYNAMICS (sense 1)

kinetic theory the theory that the minute particles of all matter are in constant motion and that the temperature of a substance is dependent on the velocity of this motion, increased motion being accompanied by increased temperature: according to the kinetic theory of gases, the elasticity, diffusion, pressure, and other physical properties of a gas are due to the rapid motion in straight lines of its molecules, to their impacts against each other and the walls of the container, to weak cohesive forces between molecules, etc.

ki·net·o- (ki net′ō, -nēt′-; -ə) [< Gr. *kinētos:* see KINETIC] a combining form meaning moving, motion [*kinetoplast*]

ki·net·o·plast (ki net′ə plast′, -nēt′-) *n.* [KINETO- + -PLAST] a cytoplasmic structure lying at the base of the flagellum in many flagellated protists

kin·folk (kin′fōk′) *n.pl.* family; relatives; kin; kindred: also **kin′folks′**

king (kin) *n.* [ME. < OE. *cyning,* akin to ON. *konungr,* OHG. *kuning* < Gmc. *kuningaz* < *kunja-,* KIN: prob. basic sense, either "head of a kin" or "son of noble kin"] **1.** a male ruler of a nation or state usually called a kingdom; male sovereign, limited or absolute; monarch **2.** *a)* a man who is supreme or highly successful in some field [an oil *king*] *b)* something supreme in its class **3.** a playing card with a conventionalized picture of a king on it **4.** *Checkers* a piece that has moved across the board to the opponent's base and been crowned, so that it can move both forward and backward **5.** *Chess* the chief piece, which can move one square in any direction: the game is won by checkmating the opponent's king —*adj.* chief (in size, importance, etc.): often in combination

King (kin) **1. Martin Luther, Jr.,** 1929-68; U.S. clergyman & leader in the Negro civil rights movement: assassinated **2. (William Lyon) Mackenzie,** 1874-1950; Canad. statesman; prime minister (1921-26; 1926-30; 1935-48)

king·bird (-bʉrd′) *n.* ☆ any of several American flycatchers (genus *Tyrannus*), often called tyrant flycatchers; esp., the **Eastern kingbird** (*Tyrannus tyrannus*), known as the bee martin because it supposedly eats bees

king·bolt (-bōlt′) *n.* a vertical bolt connecting the front axle of a wagon, etc., or the truck of a railroad car, with the body: it acts as a pivot when the vehicle turns

King Charles spaniel an English toy spaniel with white, black, and tan hair: so called because made fashionable by Charles II

king cobra a large, very poisonous snake (*Naja hannah*) native to India; hamadryad

☆**king crab** any of various very large crabs; specif., same as HORSESHOE CRAB

king·craft (-kraft′, -kräft′) *n.* the art of ruling as a monarch; royal statecraft

king·cup (-kup′) *n. same as* BUTTERCUP

king·dom (-dəm) *n.* [ME. < OE. *cyningdom:* see KING & -DOM] **1.** a government or country headed by a king or queen; monarchy **2.** a realm; domain; sphere [the *kingdom* of poetry] **3.** any of the three great divisions into which all natural objects have been classified (the animal, vegetable, and mineral kingdoms) **4.** the spiritual realm of God **5.** [Obs.] the position, rank, or power of a king —**kingdom come** [< "thy kingdom come," in the Lord's Prayer] the hereafter; heaven

king·fish (-fish′) *n., pl.* -**fish′,** -**fish′es:** see FISH[2] any of various large and unrelated food fishes found along the Atlantic or Pacific coast, as the cero or any of several croakers, whitings, etc. ☆**2.** [Colloq.] a person holding absolute power in some group, legislature, etc.

king·fish·er (-fish′ər) *n.* [ME. *kyngys fyschare,* lit., king's fisher] any of a large number of coraciiform birds (family Alcedinidae), usually bright-colored and having a large, crested head, a large, strong beak, and a short tail

King Horn (hôrn) the hero of an English metrical romance (c. 1225)

King James Version same as AUTHORIZED VERSION

King Lear (lir) **1.** a famous tragedy by Shakespeare (1606?) **2.** the main character of this play, a legendary British king

king·let (kiŋ′lit) *n.* [see -LET] **1.** a petty, unimportant king **2.** any of several small songbirds (genus *Regulus*) with a bright-colored crown, as the **golden-crowned kinglet** (*Regulus satrapa*) and the **ruby-crowned kinglet** (*Regulus calendula*)

king·ly (-lē) *adj.* **-li·er**, **-li·est** [ME.] of, like, or fit for a king or kings; royal; regal; noble —*adv.* [Archaic] in the manner of a king —**king′li·ness** *n.*

king·mak·er (-mā′kər) *n.* a politically powerful person who is instrumental in getting candidates into office

king-of-arms (-əv ärmz′) *n.* in Great Britain, any of the chief officers who decide questions of heraldry

king of beasts *an epithet for* a lion

king·pin (-pin′) *n.* **1.** *same as* KINGBOLT **2.** the headpin or the center pin in bowling, tenpins, etc. ☆**3.** [Colloq.] the main or essential person or thing

king post *Carpentry* a vertical supporting post between the apex of a triangular truss and the base, or tie beam, as at the ridge of a roof: cf. QUEEN POST

KING POST

Kings (kiŋz) **1.** either of two books of the Bible (I Kings, II Kings) which give the history of the reigns of the Jewish kings after David **2.** any of four books of the Roman Catholic Bible (Douay Version), including I & II Samuel and I & II Kings (of the Protestant version)

☆**king salmon** *same as* CHINOOK SALMON

King's (or **Queen's**) **Bench** [so called because the sovereign used to sit there on a raised bench] *Brit. Law* formerly, the supreme court of common law; now, one of the three divisions of the High Court of Justice

king's blue *same as* COBALT BLUE

Kings Canyon National Park national park in EC Calif., in the Sierra Nevada mountains: 709 sq. mi.

King's (or **Queen's**) **Counsel** a barrister appointed to be counsel of the British Crown

king's (or **queen's**) **English, the** standard or accepted (esp. British) English usage in speech or writing: so called from the notion of royal sanction

king's (or **queen's**) **evidence** *Brit. Law* *same as* STATE'S EVIDENCE

king's evil [transl. of ML. *regius morbus*: from the old notion that a king's touch could cure it] *obs. name for* SCROFULA

king·ship (kiŋ′ship′) *n.* **1.** the position, rank, dignity, or dominion of a king **2.** the rule of a king; monarchical government **3.** majesty: a title sometimes used (with *his*) in referring to a king

☆**king-size** (-sīz′) *adj.* [Colloq.] of greater than normal size [a *king-size* cigarette]: also **king′-sized′**

Kings·ley (kiŋz′lē), **Charles** 1819–75; Eng. clergyman & novelist

☆**king snake** any of several large, harmless snakes (genus *Lampropeltis*) found in C and S N. America: they eat mice, rats, lizards, and other snakes

Kings·ton (kiŋz′tən, kiŋs′-) **1.** seaport & capital of Jamaica, on the SE coast: pop. c. 120,000 (met. area 379,000) **2.** port in SE Ontario, Canada, at the outlet of Lake Ontario into the St. Lawrence: pop. 59,000

Kingston upon Hull *same as* HULL (sense 1)

king's yellow *same as* ORPIMENT

king·wood (kiŋ′wood′) *n.* **1.** a hard, fine-grained, violet-tinted wood from a Brazilian tree (*Dalbergia cearensis*) of the legume family **2.** the tree

ki·nin (kī′nin) *n.* [< KIN(ETIC) + -IN¹] a short-lived, relatively simple peptide produced in blood and other fluids to fulfill immediate hormonal needs

kink (kiŋk) *n.* [< Scand., as in Sw. & Dan. *kink*, akin to MLowG. *kinke*, Du. *kink*] **1.** a short twist, curl, or bend in a thread, rope, hair, wire, etc. **2.** a painful muscle spasm or cramp in the neck, back, etc.; crick ☆**3.** *a)* a mental twist; queer notion; whim; eccentricity *b)* a quirk; peculiarity **4.** a difficulty or defect in a plan or process —*vi., vt.* to form a kink or kinks

kin·ka·jou (kiŋ′kə joo′) *n.* [Fr., earlier *quincajou*, a misapplication (by BUFFON) of AmInd. (Algonquian) name, whence CARCAJOU] a mammal (*Potos flavus*) of Central and South America, somewhat like a raccoon, with soft, yellowish-brown fur, large eyes, and a long prehensile tail: it lives in trees and moves about at night

kink·y (kiŋ′kē) *adj.* **kink′i·er**, **kink′i·est** ☆**1.** full of kinks; tightly curled [*kinky* hair] **2.** [Chiefly Brit. Slang] weird, bizarre, eccentric, etc.; specif., sexually abnormal or perverse —**kink′i·ness** *n.*

KINKAJOU (32–45 in. long, including tail)

Kin·men (jin′mun′) *same as* QUEMOY

☆**kin·ni·ki·nick, kin·ni·ki·nic** (kin′ē kə nik′) *n.* [AmInd. (Algonquian), lit., that which is mixed] **1.** a mixture, as of tobacco and dried sumac leaves, bark, etc., formerly smoked by certain American Indians and pioneers **2.** any of the plants used for such a mixture

ki·no (kē′nō) *n.* [< WAfr. (Mandingo) native name] a dark-red or reddish-brown gum obtained from certain tropical plants (esp. *Pterocarpus marsupium*) of the legume family: used in tanning, varnishes, and as an astringent in medicine: also **kino gum**

Kin·ross (kin rôs′) county of EC Scotland: 82 sq. mi.; pop. 6,000: also **Kin·ross′shire** (-shir)

Kin·sey (kin′zē), **Alfred Charles** 1894–1956; U.S. zoologist: studied human sexual behavior in the U.S.

kins·folk (kinz′fōk′) *n.pl.* [< KIN + FOLK, after KINSMAN] *earlier form of* KINFOLK

Kin·sha·sa (kēn shä′sä) capital of the Congo (sense 2), in the W part: pop. 503,000

kin·ship (kin′ship′) *n.* [see KIN & -SHIP] **1.** family relationship **2.** relationship; close connection

kins·man (kinz′mən) *n., pl.* **-men** [ME. *kynnesman* < *kynnes*, gen. sing. of *kynne* (see KIN) + *man*] a relative; esp., a male relative —**kins′wom′an** (-woom′ən) *n. fem., pl.* **-wom′en** (-wim′ən)

ki·osk (kē′äsk, kē äsk′) *n.* [Fr. *kiosque* < Turk. *köşk* < Per. *kūshk*, palace] **1.** in Turkey and Persia, a summerhouse or pavilion of open construction **2.** a somewhat similar small structure open at one or more sides, used as a newsstand, bandstand, entrance to a subway, etc.

Kio·to (kyō′tō) *same as* KYOTO

Ki·o·wa (kī′ō wä, -ə wə) *n.* **1.** *pl.* **-was, -wa** any member of a tribe of Plains Indians who formerly lived in Montana and other Western states and now live in Oklahoma **2.** their Tanoan language

kip¹ (kip) *n.* [earlier *kyppe*, prob. < Du. *kip, kijp* (in sense 2)] **1.** the untanned hide of a calf, lamb, or other young or small animal **2.** a set of such hides

kip² (kip) *n.* [< or akin to Dan. *kippe*, low alehouse] [Slang] **1.** a rooming house **2.** a bed **3.** sleep —*vi.* **kipped, kip′ping** [Slang] to sleep

kip³ (kip) *n., pl.* **kips, kip** [Thai] the monetary unit of Laos: see MONETARY UNITS, table

kip⁴ (kip) *n.* [KI(LO) + P(OUND)¹] a unit of weight equal to 1,000 pounds

Kip·ling (kip′liŋ), **(Joseph) Rud·yard** (rud′yərd) 1865–1936; Eng. writer, born in India

kip·per (kip′ər) *vt.* [< ? the *n.*] to cure (herring, salmon, etc.) by cleaning, salting, and drying or smoking —*n.* [ME. *kypre* < OE. *cypera*] **1.** a male salmon or sea trout during or shortly after the spawning season **2.** a kippered herring, salmon, etc.

Kirch·hoff (kirH′hôf), **Gus·tav Ro·bert** (goos′täf rō′bert) 1824–87; Ger. physicist

Kir·ghiz (kir gēz′) *n.* [native name: said to be after a legendary chief] **1.** *pl.* **-ghiz′, -ghiz′es** a member of a Mongolian people in SC Asia **2.** their Turkic language Also sp. **Kir·giz′**

Kirghiz (or **Kirgiz**) **Soviet Socialist Republic** republic of the U.S.S.R., in SC Asia: 76,460 sq. mi.; pop. 2,700,000; cap. Frunze: also **Kir·ghi·zia** (kir gē′zhə, -zhē ə) —**Kir·ghi′zian** *adj., n.*

Ki·rin (kē′rin′) **1.** province of NE China: 72,201 sq. mi.; pop. 12,550,000; cap. Changchun **2.** city in this province, on the Sungari River: pop. 583,000

kirk (kurk) *n.* [Scot. *kirk*] *n.* [Scot. < ME. *kirke* < OE. *cirice* (infl. by the cognate ON. *kirkja*): see CHURCH] [Scot. & North Eng.] a church

Kirk·cal·dy (kər kô′dē, -kôl′dē) seaport in S Fifeshire, Scotland, on the Firth of Forth: pop. 52,000

Kirk·cud·bright (kər koo′brē) county of SW Scotland, on Solway Firth: 900 sq. mi.; pop. 29,000: also **Kir·cud′bright·shire′** (-shir)

kir·mess (kur′mis) *n. var. of* KERMIS

kirn (kurn) *n.* [Scot. *kirn*] *n.* [< ?] in Scotland **1.** a feast to celebrate the end of the harvest; harvest home **2.** the last sheaf of the harvest

Ki·rov (kē′rôf) city in NC European R.S.F.S.R.: pop. 302,000

Ki·rov·a·bad (kē′rô vä bät′) city in NC Azerbaijan S.S.R., in Transcaucasia: pop. 170,000

Ki·rov·o·grad (-grät′) city in SC Ukrainian S.S.R.: pop. 161,000

kirsch·was·ser (kirsh′väs′ər) *n.* [G. < *kirsche*, cherry, akin to OE. *cirse* < Gmc. **kirissa* < L. *cerasus*, CHERRY + *wasser*, WATER] a colorless alcoholic drink distilled from the fermented juice of black cherries: often clipped to **kirsch**

kir·tle (kur′t'l) *n.* [ME. *kirtel* < OE. *cyrtel* (akin to ON. *kyrtill*) < Gmc. **kurt-*, short (< L. *curtus*: see CURT) + *-el*, dim. suffix] [Archaic] **1.** a man's tunic or coat **2.** a woman's dress or skirt

Ki·san·ga·ni (kē′sän gä′nē) city in the NE Congo (sense 2), on the Congo River: pop. 100,000

Kish (kish) ancient Sumerian city on the Euphrates in what is now C Iraq: fl. c. 4,000 B.C.

Ki·shi·nev (ki shi nyôf′; *E.* kish′i nef′) capital of the Moldavian S.S.R., in the C part: pop. 289,000

kish·ke (kish′kə) *n.* [Yid. < Russ. *kishka*, intestine] same as DERMA²: also sp. **kish′ka**

Kis·lev (kis′lef) *n.* [Heb.] the third month of the Jewish year: see JEWISH CALENDAR

kis·met (kiz′met, kis′-) *n.* [Turk. *qismet* < Ar. *qismah*, a portion, lot, fate < *qasama*, to divide] fate; destiny

kiss (kis) *vt.* [ME. *kissen* < OE. *cyssan*, akin to G. *küssen* < IE. base *kus-*, prob. echoic] 1. to give a kiss to (a person or thing); touch or caress with the lips 2. to touch lightly or gently —*vi.* 1. to give a kiss to one another on the lips 2. to touch one another lightly, as billiard balls —*n.* [ME. *kisse* < the *v.*, replacing *cosse* < OE. *coss*] 1. a touch or caress with the lips, often with some pressure and suction, as an act of affection, desire, greeting, etc. 2. a light, gentle touch or slight contact 3. *a)* any of various candies *b)* a baked confection of egg white and sugar —**kiss goodbye** 1. to kiss in taking leave ☆2. [Colloq.] to give up all hope of getting, recovering, realizing, etc. —**kiss′a·ble** *adj.*

kiss·er (-ər) *n.* 1. a person who kisses 2. [Slang] *a)* the mouth or lips *b)* the face

☆**kissing bug** same as CONENOSE

☆**kiss of death** an action or quality, often seemingly helpful, which is actually harmful or ruinous

☆**kiss-off** (-ôf′) *n.* [Slang] dismissal, esp. when rude or abrupt

kist¹ (kist) *n.* [ME. *kiste* < ON. *kista*, akin to G. *kiste* < L. *cista*: see CHEST] [Chiefly Scot. & North Eng. Dial.] a chest, box, or locker

kist² (kist) *n.* same as CIST

Kist·na (kist′nə) river in S India, flowing from the Western Ghats eastward into the Bay of Bengal: c. 800 mi.

Kit (kit) 1. a masculine name: see CHRISTOPHER 2. a feminine name: see CATHERINE

kit¹ (kit) *n.* [ME. *kyt* < MDu. *kitte*, container made of hooped staves] 1. [Brit. Dial.] a small wooden tub or bucket for holding fish, butter, etc. 2. *a)* personal equipment, esp. as packed for travel *b)* a set of tools or implements *c)* equipment for some particular activity, sport, etc. [a first-aid *kit*, a salesman's *kit*] *d)* a set containing a number of parts to be assembled [a model airplane *kit*] 3. a box, bag, or other container for carrying such parts, equipment, or tools 4. [Colloq.] lot; collection: now chiefly in ☆**the whole kit and caboodle**, everybody or everything

kit² (kit) *n.* same as KITTEN

kit³ (kit) *n.* [Early ModE.: abbrev. < ? *cithara*] [Rare] a small violin

Ki·ta·kyu·shu (kē′ta kyōō′shōō) seaport on the N coast of Kyushu, Japan: pop. 1,042,000

kitch·en (kich′ən) *n.* [ME. *kychene* < OE. *cycene* < VL. *cucina* < LL. *coquina* < L. *coquere*, to COOK] 1. a room, place, or equipment for the preparation and cooking of food 2. a staff that cooks and serves food

kitchen cabinet 1. a cabinet or cupboard in a kitchen ☆2. [often K- C-] *a)* the group of unofficial advisers on whom President Jackson relied *b)* any similar group on whom a governmental head relies

kitch·en·er (-ər) *n.* 1. a person who works in a kitchen, esp. in a monastery 2. [Brit.] a stove for cooking

Kitch·e·ner (kich′ə nər) [after H. H. KITCHENER] city in SE Ontario, Canada: pop, 93,000

Kitch·e·ner (kich′ə nər), **Horatio Herbert**, 1st Earl, Kitchener of Khartoum, 1850–1916; Brit. military officer & statesman, born in Ireland

☆**kitch·en·ette, kitch·en·et** (kich′ə net′) *n.* a small, compact kitchen or part of a room arranged as a kitchen, as in some apartments

kitchen garden a garden in which vegetables and, sometimes, fruit are grown, usually for home use

kitch·en·maid (kich′ən mād′) *n.* a domestic worker who helps the cook

kitchen midden [transl. of Dan. *kökkenmödding*] a mound of shells, animal bones, and other refuse such as often marks the location of a prehistoric settlement

☆**kitchen police** 1. soldiers detailed to assist the cooks in an army kitchen 2. this duty

kitch·en·ware (-wer′) *n.* utensils used in the kitchen; pots, pans, etc.

kite (kīt) *n.* [ME. < OE. *cyta*, akin to MLowG. *kuten*, to gossip < IE. echoic base *gou-*, to scream, whence Gr. *goun*, to moan] 1. any of various birds of the hawk family, with long, pointed wings and, usually, a forked tail: they prey esp. on insects, reptiles, and small mammals 2. [Chiefly Brit.] a greedy, grasping person 3. a light frame, usually of wood, covered with paper or cloth, to be flown in the wind at the end of a string 4. [pl.] the highest sails of a ship, used in a light breeze 5. a bad check or similar fictitious or worthless commercial paper used to raise money or maintain credit temporarily —*vi.* **kit′ed, kit′ing** 1. [Colloq.] *a)* to fly like a kite; soar *b)* to move lightly and rapidly 2. to get money or credit by using bad checks, etc. —*vt.* to issue (a bad check, etc.) as a kite

kith (kith) *n.* [ME. < OE. *cyth*, earlier *cyththu* < base of *cuth*, known: see UNCOUTH] friends, acquaintances, or neighbors: now only in **kith and kin**, friends, acquaintances, and relatives; also, often, relatives, or kin

kithe (kith) *vt., vi.* **kithed, kith′ing** [ME. *kithen* < OE.

cythan, akin to *cunnan*, to know: see CAN¹] [Scot. & North Eng. Dial.] to make or become known

kitsch (kich) *n.* [G., gaudy trash < dial. *kitschen*, to smear] art, writing, etc. of a pretentious, but shallow kind, calculated to have popular appeal —**kitsch′y** *adj.*

kit·ten (kit′n) *n.* [ME. *kitoun* < OFr. *chitoun*, var. of *chaton*, dim. of *chat*, CAT] a young cat: occasionally applied to the young of some other small animals —*vi., vt.* to give birth to (kittens)

kit·ten·ish (-ish) *adj.* like a kitten; playful; frisky; often, playfully coy —**kit′ten·ish·ly** *adv.* —**kit′ten·ish·ness** *n.*

kit·ti·wake (kit′i wāk′) *n., pl.* **-wakes, -wake**: see PLURAL, II, D, 1 [echoic of its cry] any of several sea gulls (genus *Rissa*) of the Arctic and North Atlantic, having a short or rudimentary hind toe

kit·tle (kit′l) *vt.* **-tled, -tling** [LME. < *kytylle* < ON. *kitla*, akin to G. *kitzeln*, prob. echoic in origin] [Scot.] 1. to tickle 2. to puzzle —*adj.* [Scot.] ticklish; hard to deal with; skittish

Kit·tredge (kit′rij), **George Ly·man** (lī′mən) 1860–1941; U.S. Shakespearean scholar & educator

Kit·ty (kit′ē) a feminine name: see CATHERINE

kit·ty¹ (kit′ē) *n., pl.* **-ties** 1. a kitten 2. *a pet name for* a cat of any age

kit·ty² (kit′ē) *n., pl.* **-ties** [prob. < KIT¹] 1. in poker, *a)* the stakes or pot *b)* a pool formed from part of the winnings, to pay for refreshments, etc. 2. money pooled for some particular purpose 3. in certain card games, an extra hand, or part of a hand, dealt to the table, etc.

kit·ty-cor·nered (kit′ē kôr′nərd) *adj., adv.* same as CATER-CORNERED: also **kit′ty-cor′ner**

Kitty Hawk [< AmInd. < ?] village on the Outer Banks of N.C., near where the first controlled & sustained airplane flight was made by Orville & Wilbur Wright in 1903: see Cape HATTERAS, map

Ki·tu·ba (kē tōō′bə) *n.* a trade language, spoken chiefly along the lower Congo River and its tributaries: its elements come from Kongo, Lingala, and French

☆**ki·va** (kē′və) *n.* [Hopi] in a Pueblo Indian dwelling, a large room used for religious and other purposes

Ki·vu (kē′vōō), **Lake** lake in EC Africa, on the border of E Congo (sense 2) & Rwanda: c. 1,100 sq. mi.

☆**Ki·wa·nis** (kə wä′nis) *n.* [said to be < AmInd. *keewanis*, to make (oneself) known] an international service club of business and professional men —**Ki·wa′ni·an** (-nē ən) *adj., n.*

ki·wi (kē′wē) *n., pl.* **-wis** [Maori: echoic of its cry] 1. any of a genus (*Apteryx*) of tailless New Zealand birds, with undeveloped wings, hairlike feathers, and a long, slender bill: it feeds chiefly on insects and worms 2. [also K-] the brown, hairy, egg-sized fruit of a subtropical vine (*Actinidia chinensis*), with a sweet, green pulp having a strawberrylike flavor 3. [K-] [Colloq.] a New Zealander

Ki·zil (ki zil′) river in NC Turkey, flowing into the Black Sea: c. 700 mi.: also **Kizil Ir·mak** (ir mäk′), **Ki·zil′ir′mak′**

KJV, K.J.V. King James Version (of the Bible)

K.K.K., KKK Ku Klux Klan

KKt *Chess* king's knight

kl, kl. kiloliter; kiloliters

Kla·gen·furt (klä′gən foort′) city in S Austria: pop. 69,000

Klai·pe·da (klī′pi də) seaport in W Lithuanian S.S.R., on the Baltic: pop. 125,000

Kla·math (klam′əth) [< the name of the tribe] river flowing from S Oreg. southwest across NW Calif., into the Pacific: c. 250 mi. —*n.* 1. *pl.* **-aths, -ath** any member of a N. American Indian tribe living in S Oregon 2. their Penutian language

Klan (klan) *n.* 1. *short for* KU KLUX KLAN 2. any chapter of the Ku Klux Klan —**Klans′man** *n., pl.* **-men**

klatch, klatsch (kläch, klach) *n.* [G. *klatsch*, gossip] [Colloq.] an informal gathering, as for conversation or gossip

☆**Klax·on** (klak′s'n) [arbitrary coinage] *a trademark for* a kind of electric horn with a loud, shrill sound —*n.* [k-] such a horn

Klee (klā), **Paul** 1879–1940; Swiss abstract painter

☆**Klee·nex** (klē′neks) [arbitrary alteration < CLEAN + -*ex*, arbitrary suffix] *a trademark for* soft tissue paper used as a handkerchief, etc. —*n.* [occas. k-] a piece of such paper

klepht (kleft) *n.* [ModGr. *klephtēs*, robber < Gr. *kleptēs*, thief: see *kl.*] 1. a member of the Greek patriot bands who held out in the mountains after the Turkish conquest of Greece 2. a brigand

klep·to·ma·ni·a (klep′tə mā′nē ə) *n.* [ModL. < Gr. *kleptēs*, thief (< IE. base *klep-*, to hide, steal, whence L. *clepere*, Goth. *hlifan*, to steal) + -MANIA] an abnormal, persistent impulse or tendency to steal, not prompted by need —**klep′to·ma′ni·ac′** *n.*

☆**klieg light** (klēg) [after the inventors, Anton *Kliegl* (1872–1927) and his brother John (1869–1959), U.S. lighting engineers] a very bright, hot arc light used to light motion-picture sets: also sp. **kleig**

Kline test (klīn) [after its developer, Benjamin S. *Kline* (1886–1968), U.S. pathologist] a modified form of the Kahn test for the diagnosis of syphilis

klip·spring·er (klip′spriŋ′ər) *n., pl.* **-ers, -er**: see PLURAL, II, D, 1 [Afrik. < *klip*, a rock, cliff + *springer*, springer] a small, agile mountain antelope (*Oreotragus oreotragus*) of S and E Africa

Klon·dike (klän′dīk) [Athapascan < ?] **1.** river in W Yukon Territory, Canada, flowing west into the Yukon River: c. 100 mi. **2.** gold-mining region surrounding this river: site of a gold rush, 1898

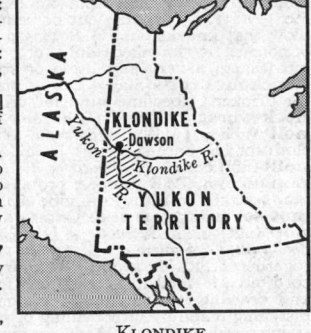

KLONDIKE

klong (klôŋ) *n.* [Thai] any of the canals of Thailand

‡**kloof** (klo͞of) *n.* [Afrik. < Du. *klooven*, to cleave, akin to CLEAVE¹] in South Africa, a deep, narrow valley; gorge

Kluck·hohn (kluk′hōn), **Clyde** (**Kay Mahen**) 1905–60; U.S. anthropologist

klys·tron (klis′trən, klīs′-; -trän) *n.* [< Gr. *klys-* (see CLYSTER) + (ELEC)TRON] an electron tube, used as an oscillator, amplifier, frequency multiplier, etc. in ultrahigh frequency circuits, that employs electric fields and resonant cavities to bunch electrons from a uniform stream and thus vary their velocities, and to transfer energy

km, km. kilometer; kilometers

knack (nak) *n.* [ME. *knak*, sharp blow: see KNOCK] **1.** *a)* a trick; device *b)* a clever expedient or way of doing something **2.** ability to do something easily; particular skill; dexterity **3.** [Archaic] a knickknack; trinket; trifle —*SYN.* see TALENT

knack·er (nak′ər) *n.* [Early ModE., harness maker < ? prec.] [Brit.] **1.** a person who buys and slaughters worn-out horses and sells their flesh as dog's meat, etc. **2.** a person who buys and wrecks old houses, etc. and sells their materials

knack·wurst (näk′wurst′, G. knäk′voorsht′) *n.* [G. < *knacken*, to crack, split (prob. ult. akin to IE. base *gneu̯g-*, whence KNOCK) + *wurst*, sausage] a thick, highly seasoned sausage

knag·gy (nag′ē) *adj.* -**gi·er**, -**gi·est** [< ME. *knag*, a knot, akin to Sw. *knagg*, a knot] knotty; rough

knap¹ (nap) *vt., vi.* **knapped, knap′ping** [LME. *knappen*, akin to Du. *knappen*, to snap, eat < IE. *gnebh-*: for base see KNEAD] [Brit. Dial.] **1.** to knock, rap, or snap **2.** to break or shape (stones or flints) by a quick, hard blow **3.** to bite sharply; snap —*n.* [Brit. Dial.] a sudden blow; rap

knap² (nap) *n.* [ME. < OE. *cnæp*, top, knob, button, akin to ON. *knappr* < IE. *gnebh-*: see prec.] [Chiefly Dial.] **1.** the top of a hill; summit **2.** a hillock

knap·sack (nap′sak′) *n.* [Du. *knapzak* < *knappen* (see KNAP¹) + *zak*, a SACK¹] a leather or canvas bag or case worn on the back, as by soldiers or hikers, for carrying equipment or supplies

knap·weed (nap′wēd′) *n.* [earlier *knopweed*: see KNOP & WEED²] any of several weedy plants (genus *Centaurea*) of the composite family; esp., a hardy perennial (*Centaurea nigra*) with heads of rose-purple flowers

knar (när) *n.* [ME. *knarre* < or akin to LowG. *knarre*, Du. *knar*, a stump, knob, knot < IE. *gner-*: for base see KNEAD] a knot in wood; esp., a bark-covered protuberance on a tree trunk or root —**knarred** *adj.*

knave (nāv) *n.* [ME. *knaue* < OE. *cnafa*, boy, male child, akin to G. *knabe*] **1.** [Archaic] *a)* a serving boy or male servant *b)* a man of humble birth or status **2.** a dishonest, deceitful person; tricky rascal; rogue **3.** a playing card with a page's picture on it; jack

knav·er·y (nāv′ər ē) *n., pl.* -**er·ies 1.** behavior or an act characteristic of a knave; rascality; dishonesty **2.** [Obs.] roguishness; mischievous quality

knav·ish (-ish) *adj.* like or characteristic of a knave; esp., dishonest; tricky —**knav′ish·ly** *adv.* —**knav′ish·ness** *n.*

knead (nēd) *vt.* [ME. *kneden* < OE. *cnedan*, akin to G. *kneten* < IE. *gnet-*, to press together < base *gen-*, to form into a ball, pinch, compress, whence KNOT¹, KNOB] **1.** to mix and work (dough, clay, etc.) into a pliable mass by folding over, pressing, and squeezing, usually with the hands **2.** to press, rub, or squeeze with the hands; massage **3.** to make or form by or as if by kneading —**knead′er** *n.*

knee (nē) *n.* [ME. *kne* < OE. *cneow*, akin to G. *knie* < IE. base *ĝeneu-*, whence Sans. *jâ̄nu*, Gr. *gony*, L. *genu*, a knee] **1.** *a)* the joint between the thigh and the lower part of the human leg *b)* the front part of the leg at this joint **2.** a joint regarded as corresponding or similar to the human knee, as in the hind limb of a vertebrate, in the forelimb of a hoofed, four-footed animal (*carpal joint*), or the tarsal joint of a bird **3.** anything resembling or suggesting a knee, esp. a bent knee; specif., *a)* a bent piece of wood used as a brace *b)* a protuberant, woody growth on certain trees **4.** the part of a stocking, trouser leg, etc. covering the knee

—*vt.* **kneed, knee′ing 1.** to hit or touch with the knee **2.** *Carpentry* to fasten with a knee or knees (sense 3 *a*) — **bring to one's knees** to force to submit or give in

knee breeches *same as* BREECHES (sense 1)

knee·cap (-kap′) *n.* **1.** a movable bone at the front of the human knee; patella: also **knee′pan′** (-pan′) **2.** *same as* KNEEPAD

knee-deep (-dēp′) *adj.* **1.** sunk to the knees [standing *knee-deep* in water] **2.** so deep as to reach to the knees, as water **3.** very much involved or concerned

knee-high (-hī′) *adj.* so high or tall as to reach to the knees

knee-hole (-hōl′) *n.* a space for the knees, as below a desk

knee jerk *same as* PATELLAR REFLEX

kneel (nēl) *vi.* **knelt** or **kneeled, kneel′ing** [ME. *knelen* < OE. *cneowlian* < *cneow*: see KNEE] to bend or rest on a knee or the knees —**kneel′er** *n.*

knee·pad (nē′pad′) *n.* a pad worn to protect the knee, as by a basketball player

knee-piece (-pēs′) *n.* a piece of armor to protect the knee: see ARMOR, illus.

☆**knee-sprung** (-spruŋ′) *adj.* having the knees bent forward as a result of a shortening of the flexor tendons: said of a horse

knell (nel) *vi.* [ME. *knyllen* & (with echoic vowel change) *knellen* < OE. *cnyllan*, akin to MHG. (*er*)*knellen*: prob. echoic] **1.** to ring in a slow, solemn way; toll **2.** to sound ominously or mournfully —*vt.* to call or announce by or as by a knell —*n.* **1.** the sound of a bell, esp. of a bell rung slowly, as at a funeral **2.** an omen of death, failure, etc. **3.** a mournful sound

knelt (nelt) *alt. pt. and pp.* of KNEEL

Knes·set (knes′et) *n.* [Heb., assembly] the unicameral legislature of Israel

knew (no͞o, nyo͞o) *pt.* of KNOW

☆**Knick·er·bock·er** (nik′ər bäk′ər) *n.* [< Diedrich *Knickerbocker*, fictitious Du. author of Washington Irving's *History of New York* (1809)] ☆**1.** a descendant of the early Dutch settlers of New York ☆**2.** any New Yorker **3.** [k-] [*pl.*] short, loose trousers gathered in at or just below the knees, as those worn by Dutch settlers of New York; knickers

knick·ers (nik′ərz) *n.pl.* [contr. < prec.] **1.** *same as* KNICKERBOCKERS **2.** [Chiefly Brit.] a bloomerlike undergarment worn by women or girls

knick·knack (nik′nak′) *n.* [redupl. of KNACK] a small ornamental article or contrivance; gimcrack; trinket

knife (nīf) *n., pl.* **knives** [ME. *knif* < OE. *cnif*, akin to G. *kneif*, ON. *knifr* < IE. *gneibh-* (whence Lith. *gnaibis*, a pinching): for base see KNEAD] **1.** a cutting or stabbing instrument with a sharp blade, single-edged or double-edged, set in a handle **2.** a cutting blade, as in a machine —*vt.* **knifed, knif′ing 1.** to cut or stab with a knife ☆**2.** [Colloq.] to use underhanded methods in order to hurt, defeat, or betray —☆*vi.* to pass into or through something quickly, like a sharp knife —☆**under the knife** [Colloq.] undergoing surgery —**knife′like′** *adj.*

knife-edge (-ej′) *n.* **1.** the edge of a knife **2.** any very sharp edge **3.** a metal wedge whose fine edge serves as the fulcrum for a scale beam, pendulum, etc.

knife switch an electrical switch in which the hinged, knifelike contact blade is pressed down between the contact clips

knight (nīt) *n.* [ME. *kniht* < OE. *cniht*, boy, retainer, akin to G. *knecht*, lad, servant < IE. base *gnegh-*: for base see KNEAD] **1.** in the Middle Ages, *a)* a military servant of the king or other feudal superior; tenant holding land on condition that he serve his superior as a mounted man-at-arms *b)* later, a man, usually one of high birth, who after serving as page and squire was formally raised to honorable military rank and pledged to chivalrous conduct **2.** in Great Britain, a man who for some achievement is given honorary nonhereditary rank next below a baronet, entitling him to use *Sir* before his given name **3.** an ancient Roman, Athenian, etc. whose status is regarded as equivalent to that of a knight **4.** [*usually* K-] a member of any order or society that officially calls its members *knights* **5.** [Poet.] *a)* a lady's devoted champion or attendant *b)* a devoted follower of some cause, person, etc. **6.** *Chess* a piece shaped like a horse's head: it is moved one square, whether occupied or unoccupied, in any vertical or horizontal direction, and then one square diagonally —*vt.* to make (a man) a knight

knight bachelor *pl.* **knights bachelors, knights bachelor** a member of the oldest and lowest class of British knights

knight-er·rant (-er′ənt) *n., pl.* **knights′-er′rant 1.** a medieval knight wandering in search of adventures, esp. ones which allow him to redress wrongs or show his prowess **2.** a chivalrous or quixotic person

knight-er·rant·ry (-er′ən trē) *n., pl.* -**ries 1.** the behavior or action of a knight-errant **2.** quixotic behavior

knight·hood (-hood′) *n.* **1.** the rank or status of a knight **2.** the profession or vocation of a knight **3.** knightly conduct **4.** knights collectively

knight·ly (-lē) *adj.* **1.** of, characteristic of, like, or befitting a knight; chivalrous, brave, etc. **2.** consisting of knights

—*adv.* [Archaic] in a knightly manner —**knight′li·ness** *n.*

☆**Knights of Columbus** an international fraternal, benevolent, and proselyting society of Roman Catholic men, founded in 1882

☆**Knights of Pythias** a fraternal and benevolent society founded in 1864

Knight Templar *pl.* **Knights Templars** for 1, **Knights Templar** for 2 **1.** a member of a military and religious order established among the Crusaders early in the 12th century **2.** a member of a certain order of Masons

knish (kə nish′) *n.* [Yid. < Russ., a kind of cake, akin to Pol. *knysz*] a piece of thin rolled dough folded over a filling, as of mashed potatoes, chopped meat, etc., and baked

knit (nit) *vt.* **knit′ted** or **knit, knit′ting** [ME. *knitten* < OE. *cnyttan* (akin to G. *knütten*, to tie (fishing) nets) < base of *cnotta* (see KNOT)] **1.** to make (cloth or a piece of clothing) by looping yarn or thread together with special needles **2.** to form into cloth in this way instead of by weaving **3.** to join together closely and firmly; unite **4.** to draw (the brows) together; contract in wrinkles **5.** [Archaic or Dial.] to tie or fasten in or with a knot —*vi.* **1.** to make cloth or a piece of clothing by looping together yarn or thread **2.** to be joined together closely and firmly; grow together, as a broken bone **3.** to become drawn together in wrinkles, as the brow —*n.* cloth or a garment made by knitting —**knit′ter** *n.*

knit·ting (-iŋ) *n.* **1.** the action of a person or thing that knits **2.** knitted work

knitting needle an eyeless, usually long, needle of metal, bone, plastic, etc., with a blunt point at one or both ends, used in pairs, etc. in knitting by hand

knit·wear (-wer′) *n.* clothing made by knitting

knives (nīvz) *n. pl. of* KNIFE

knob (näb) *n.* [ME. *knobbe* < or akin to MLowG. *knobbe*, a knot, knob, bud < IE. *gn-eu-bh* < base *gen-:* see KNEAD] **1.** a rounded lump or protuberance **2.** a handle, usually round, of a door, drawer, etc. **3.** a rounded hill or mountain; knoll —**knobbed** *adj.*

knob·by (näb′ē) *adj.* **-bi·er, -bi·est 1.** covered with knobs **2.** like a knob —**knob′bi·ness** *n.*

knob·ker·rie (-ker′ē) *n.* [Afrik. *knopkirie* < Du. *knobbe*, knob + Hottentot *kirri*, a club] a short club with a knobbed end, used by some South African tribes as a throwing and striking weapon: also called **knob′stick′**

knock (näk) *vi.* [ME. *knokken* < OE. *cnocian*, akin to ON. *knoka,* MHG. *knochen,* to press < echoic base whence KNACK] **1.** to strike a blow or blows with the fist or some hard object; esp., to rap on a door **2.** to bump; collide; clash **3.** to make a thumping, pounding, or rattling noise: said of an engine, etc. ☆**4.** [Colloq.] to find fault; criticize adversely ☆**5.** *Gin Rummy* to end a deal by exposing one's hand and showing a surplus of not more than ten points in unmatched cards —*vt.* **1.** to hit; strike **2.** to make by hitting or striking [to *knock* a hole in a wall] ☆**3.** [Colloq.] to find fault with; criticize adversely —*n.* **1.** the act of knocking **2.** a hit; sharp or resounding blow; rap, as on a door **3.** a thumping or rattling noise in an engine, etc., as because of faulty combustion ☆**4.** [Colloq.] an adverse criticism **5.** [Colloq.] a misfortune or trouble [the school of hard *knocks*] —*SYN.* see STRIKE —**knock about** (or **around**) [Colloq.] **1.** to wander about; roam **2.** to treat roughly —**knock down 1.** to hit so as to cause to fall ☆**2.** to take apart for convenience in shipping **3.** to indicate the sale of (an article) at an auction, as by a blow of the auctioneer's hammer **4.** [Slang] to earn as pay —☆**knock for a loop** [Slang] **1.** to punch very hard **2.** to make a deep impression on —☆**knock it off!** [Slang] stop doing that! specif., stop talking! —**knock off 1.** to hit so as to cause to fall **2.** [Colloq.] *a)* to stop working *b)* to leave off (work) **3.** [Colloq.] to deduct **4.** [Colloq.] to do; accomplish ☆**5.** [Slang] to kill, overcome, etc. —☆**knock (oneself) out** to make great efforts; exhaust oneself —**knock out 1.** *Boxing* to defeat (an opponent) by knocking him to the ground so that he cannot rise within a specified time **2.** *a)* to make unconscious *b)* to make exhausted; tire out **3.** to defeat, destroy, etc. **4.** [Colloq.] to do; make; specif., to compose, write, etc., esp. casually or with careless haste —☆**knock out of the box** *Baseball* to make so many hits against (an opposing pitcher) as to cause his removal —**knock over** [Slang] ☆to rob —**knock together 1.** to cause to collide **2.** to make or compose hastily or crudely —**knock up 1.** [Brit. Colloq.] *a)* to tire out; exhaust *b)* to wake (someone), as by knocking at the door ☆**2.** [Slang] to make pregnant

knock·a·bout (-ə bout′) *n.* ☆**1.** a small, one-masted yacht with a mainsail, a jib, and a centerboard or keel, but no bowsprit **2.** something suitable for knockabout use —*adj.* **1.** rough; noisy; boisterous **2.** made or suitable for knocking about or rough use

knock·down (-doun′) *adj.* **1.** so severe as to knock down; overwhelming ☆**2.** made so as to be easily taken apart [a *knockdown* table] —*n.* **1.** a knocking down; felling **2.** a blow, stroke, etc. that knocks one down ☆**3.** [Old Slang] an introduction (to a person)

knocked down ☆not assembled: said of furniture, etc.

knock·er (-ər) *n.* a person or thing that knocks; specif., *a)* a small metal ring, hammer, etc. attached by a hinge to a door, for use in knocking for admittance ☆*b)* [Colloq.] a faultfinder

knock-knee (-nē′) *n.* **1.** a condition in which the legs bend inward so that the knees knock together or touch each other in walking **2.** [*pl.*] such knees —**knock′-kneed′** *adj.*

knock·out (-out′) *adj.* that knocks out: said of a blow, etc. —*n.* **1.** a knocking out or being knocked out **2.** *a)* a blow that knocks out *b) Boxing* a victory won when the opponent is knocked out: cf. TECHNICAL KNOCKOUT ☆**3.** [Slang] a very attractive or striking person or thing

☆**knockout drops** [Slang] a drug put into a drink to cause the drinker to become stupefied or unconscious

knock·wurst (näk′wurst′) *n.* same as KNACKWURST

knoll¹ (nōl) *n.* [ME. < OE. *cnoll,* akin to G. *knollen,* lump, clod: for IE. base see KNOT¹] a hillock; mound

knoll² (nōl) *vi., vt. n., archaic* or *dial. var.* of KNELL

knop (näp) *n.* [ME. *knoppe;* prob. < ON. *knappr* or MDu. *cnoppe;* akin to KNOB] a knob; esp., a knoblike ornament

Knos·sos (näs′əs) same as CNOSSUS

knot¹ (nät) *n.* [ME. *knotte* < OE. *cnotta,* akin to Du. *knot,* Sw. *knut,* G. *knoten* < IE. *gn-eu-t* < base *gen-,* to press together: cf. KNOB, KNEAD] **1.** a lump or knob in a thread, cord, etc., formed by passing one free end through a loop and drawing it tight, or by a tangle drawn tight **2.** a fastening made by intertwining or tying together pieces of string, cord, rope, etc. **3.** an ornamental bow of ribbon or twist of braid; cockade; epaulet **4.** a small group or cluster **5.** something that ties or fastens closely or intricately; bond of union; esp., the bond of marriage **6.** a problem; difficulty; entanglement **7.** a knotlike part; node or lump [a *knot* in a tense muscle]; specif., *a)* a hard lump on a tree where a branch grows out *b)* a cross section of such a lump, appearing as cross-grained in a board or log *c)* a joint on a plant stem where leaves grow out *d)* any of several fungous diseases of trees, in which abnormal protuberances appear **8.** *Naut. a)* orig., a division of the log line, by which a ship's rate of speed is measured *b)* a unit of speed of one nautical mile (6,076.10 feet) an hour [to average a speed of 10 *knots*] *c)* loosely, *same as* NAUTICAL MILE —*vt.* **knot′ted, knot′ting 1.** to tie, fasten, or intertwine in or with a knot or knots; make a knot or knots in **2.** to tie or unite closely or intricately; entangle **3.** to make (fringe) by tying knots —*vi.* **1.** to form a knot or knots; become entangled **2.** to make knots for fringe — **tie the knot** [Colloq.] to get married

KNOTS

(1. figure-of-eight knot; 2. overhand knot; 3. thief knot; 4. half hitch; 5. stevedore's knot; 6. loop knot; 7. harness hitch; 8. square knot; 9. granny knot; 10. bowline knot; 11. bowline on a bight; 12. bowline with a bight; 13. prolonge knot; 14. clove hitch; 15. round turn and two half hitches; 16. running bowline; 17. slide knot; 18. slipknot; 19. fisherman's bend; 20. cat's-paw; 21. single Blackwall hitch; 22. double Blackwall hitch; 23. studding-sail tack bend; 24. magnus hitch; 25. sheepshank; 26. half hitch over pin; 27. rolling hitch; 28. studding-sail halyard bend; 29. timber hitch; 30. timber hitch and a half hitch; 31. surgeon's knot; 32. anchor knot; 33. long splice; 34. surgeon's knot; 35. sheet bend; 36. trefoil knot; 37. throat seizing; 38. outside clinch; 39. inside clinch; 40. double sheet bend; 41. Englishman's tie; 42. single carrick bend; 43. double carrick bend; 44. single bowknot; 45. double bowknot)

knot² (nät) *n.* [rare ME. *knotte* < ?] a small sandpiper (*Calidris canutus*) that breeds in arctic regions and then migrates

knot·grass (nät′gras′, -gräs′) *n.* **1.** any of several weedy plants (genus *Polygonum*) of the buckwheat family; esp., a common weed (*Polygonum aviculare*) with slender stems, narrow leaves, and small axillary flowers ☆**2.** a creeping grass (*Papsalum distichum*) growing in wet places in the S U.S. Also **knot′weed′** (-wēd′)

knot·hole (-hōl′) *n.* a hole in a board, etc. where a knot has fallen out

knot·ted (-id) *adj.* **1.** tied or fastened in or with a knot or knots **2.** having or full of knots **3.** tangled; intricate **4.** puzzling; knotty

knot·ter (-ər) *n.* **1.** a person or thing that ties knots **2.** a remover of knots

knot·ting (-iŋ) *n.* fringe made of knotted threads

knot·ty (-ē) *adj.* **-ti·er, -ti·est** [ME.] **1.** having or full of knots [a *knotty* board] **2.** hard to solve or explain; puzzling [a *knotty* problem] —**knot′ti·ness** *n.*

☆**knotty pine** pine wood having a large number of ornamental knots, used for interior finishing and some furniture

knout (nout) *n.* [Russ. *knut* < Sw. *knut*, a KNOT¹] a leather whip formerly used in Russia to flog criminals —*vt.* to flog with a knout

know (nō) *vt.* **knew, known, know′ing** [ME. *knowen* < OE. *cnawan*, akin to OHG. *-cnāhan* < IE. base **ĝen-, *ĝnō-*, to know, apprehend, whence L. *gnoscere*, to know, Gr. *gignōskein:* cf. CAN¹, KEN, GNOMON, GNOSTIC] **1.** to have a clear perception or understanding of; be sure of or well informed about [to *know* the facts] **2.** to be aware or cognizant of; have perceived or learned [to *know* that one is loved] **3.** to have a firm mental grasp of; have securely in the memory [to *know* the multiplication tables] **4.** to be acquainted or familiar with **5.** to have understanding of or skill in as a result of study or experience [to *know* music] **6.** to recognize [I'd *know* that face anywhere] **7.** to recognize as distinct; distinguish [to *know* right from wrong] **8.** [Archaic] to have sexual intercourse with —*vi.* **1.** to have knowledge **2.** to be sure, informed, or aware — **in the know** [Colloq.] having confidential information — **know better** to be aware that one could or should act better or think more correctly —**know best** to be the best guide, authority, etc. —**know′a·ble** *adj.* —**know′er** *n.*

☆**know-how** (-hou′) *n.* [Colloq.] knowledge of how to do something well; technical skill

know·ing (-iŋ) *adj.* **1.** having knowledge or information **2.** shrewd; clever **3.** implying shrewd understanding or possession of secret or inside information [a *knowing* look] **4.** deliberate; intentional —*n.* awareness or familiarity —**know′ing·ly** *adv.* —**know′ing·ness** *n.*

know-it-all (-it ôl′) *adj.* [Colloq.] pretending or claiming to know much about almost everything —*n.* [Colloq.] a know-it-all person: also **know′-all′**

knowl·edge (näl′ij) *n.* [ME. *knoweleche*, acknowledgment, confession < Late OE. *cnawlæc < cnawan* (see KNOW) + element of unc. orig.] **1.** the act, fact, or state of knowing; specif., *a)* acquaintance or familiarity (with a fact, place, etc.) *b)* awareness *c)* understanding **2.** acquaintance with facts; range of information, awareness, or understanding **3.** all that has been perceived or grasped by the mind; learning; enlightenment **4.** the body of facts, principles, etc. accumulated by mankind **5.** [Archaic] sexual intercourse —*SYN.* see INFORMATION —**to (the best of) one's knowledge** as far as one knows; within the range of one's information

knowl·edge·a·ble (-ə b'l) *adj.* having or showing knowledge or intelligence —**knowl′edge·a·bil′i·ty, knowl′edge·a·ble·ness** *n.* —**knowl′edge·a·bly** *adv.*

known (nōn) *pp. of* KNOW

know-noth·ing (nō′nuth′iŋ) *n.* **1.** an ignorant person; ignoramus **2.** [Rare] an agnostic **3.** [K- N-] a member of a secret political party in the U.S. in the 1850's with a program of keeping out of public office anyone not a native-born American: so called because members professed ignorance of the party's activities

known quantity an algebraic quantity whose value is given: usually represented by an earlier letter of the alphabet, as *a, b,* and *c*

Knox (näks) **1.** John, 1505?-72; Scot. Protestant clergyman & religious reformer **2.** Ronald (Arbuthnott), 1888-1957; Eng. R.C. priest & Bible translator

Knox·ville (näks′vil) [after Gen. Henry *Knox* (1750-1806), 1st secretary of war] city in E Tenn., on the Tennessee River: pop. 175,000

knt. knight

knuck·le (nuk′'l) *n.* [ME. *knokyl* < or akin to MDu. & MLowG. *knokel*, dim. of *knoke*, bone < IE. **gneuĝ-* < base **gen-*, to press together: cf. KNOB, KNOT¹] **1.** *a)* a joint of the finger; esp., the joint connecting a finger to the rest of the hand *b)* the rounded knob formed by the bones at such a joint **2.** the knee or hock joint and nearby parts of a pig or other animal, used as food **3.** something resembling a knuckle, as the joint of a hinge, where the pin goes **4.** [*pl.*] *same as* BRASS KNUCKLES **5.** *Archit.* the central

joint in a gambrel or curb roof **6.** *Shipbuilding* an angular fitting of timbers —*vt.* **-led, -ling** to strike, press, or touch with the knuckles —☆**knuckle down 1.** to rest the knuckles on the ground in shooting a marble **2.** to work energetically; apply oneself seriously —**knuckle under** to yield; give in

☆**knuckle ball** *Baseball* a slow pitch without spin thrown with the first knuckles, or the nails, of the middle two or three fingers pressed against the ball: also **knuck·ler** (nuk′lər)

knuck·le·bone (-bōn′) *n.* **1.** any bone of a human knuckle **2.** *a)* an animal's limb bone with a rounded knob at the joint end *b)* the knob **3.** [*pl.*] an old game played with the knucklebones of sheep

☆**knuck·le·dust·er** (-dus′tər) *n. same as* BRASS KNUCKLES

☆**knuck·le·head** (-hed′) *n.* [Colloq.] a stupid person; fool

knuckle joint 1. any articulation, or point of movement, between two bones forming a knuckle **2.** a hinged joint formed by a projection between two others, with a pin running through aligned holes in the projections

Knud·sen effect (nood′sən) [after Martin *Knudsen* (1871-1949), Dan. chemist] the difference in pressure exerted by two gases confined in containers connected by a capillary tube and maintained at different temperatures

knur (nur) *n.* [ME. *knorre* < or akin to MDu. & MLowG. *knorre* < IE. **gner-:* for base see KNOT¹] a knot, as on the trunk or branch of a tree

knurl (nurl) *n.* [prob. blend of prec. + GNARL¹] **1.** a knot, knob, nodule, etc. **2.** any of a series of small beads or ridges, as along the edge of a coin or on a dial **3.** [Scot.] a short, thickset person —*vt.* to make knurls on; mill —**knurled** *adj.*

knurl·y (-ē) *adj.* **knurl′i·er, knurl′i·est** full of knurls, as wood; gnarled

Knut (k'nōōt) *same as* CANUTE

☆**KO** (kā′ō′) *vt.* **KO'd, KO'ing** [Slang] *Boxing* to knock out —*n., pl.* **KO's** [Slang] *Boxing* a knockout Also **K.O., k.o.**

ko·a (kō′ə) *n.* [Haw.] a Hawaiian acacia tree (*Acacia koa*) of the legume family, valued for its wood, used in building and cabinetmaking, and its bark, used in tanning

ko·a·la (kō ä′lə) *n.* [< the native name in Australia] an Australian, tree-dwelling, marsupial animal (*Phascolarctos cinereus*) with thick, gray fur, sharp claws, and large, tufted ears: it is about two to three feet long, tailless, looks somewhat like a small bear, and feeds exclusively on eucalyptus leaves and buds

ko·an (kō′än) *n.* [Jap., lit., public plan < *kō*, public + *an*, a proposal, plan] in Zen, a nonsense question asked of a student to force him, through contemplation of it, to a greater awareness of reality

kob (käb) *n.* [< native name in Niger-Congo area, as in Wolof *koba*] an orange-red antelope (*Kobus kob*) of SE Africa

Ko·ba·rid (kô′bä red) *see* CAPORETTO

Ko·be (kō′bä′; E. kō′bē) seaport on the S coast of Honshū, Japan, on the Inland Sea: pop. 1,217,000

Kø·ben·havn (kø′b'n houn′) *Dan. name of* COPENHAGEN

Ko·blenz (kō′blents) city in W West Germany, in the Rhineland-Palatinate, on the Rhine: pop. 102,000

ko·bold (kō′bōld, -bäld) *n.* [G.] *Ger. Folklore* **1.** a helpful or mischievous sprite in households; brownie **2.** a gnome in mines and other underground places

Koch (kôk; *G.* kôkh), **Robert** 1843-1910; Ger. bacteriologist & physician

Ko·dá·ly (kō′dä y′), **Zol·tán** (zōl′tän) 1882-1967; Hung. composer

ko·di·ak bear (kō′dē ak′) a very large, brown bear (*Ursus middendorffi*) found on Kodiak Island and in adjacent areas: it can attain a weight of 1,500 pounds

Ko·di·ak Island (kō′dē ak′) [< Russ. < ? native name meaning "island"] large island off the SW coast of Alas.: with nearby islands & a small section of the Alaska Peninsula it constitutes a district of Alas., 8,216 sq. mi., pop. 9,000

ko·el (kō′əl) *n.* [Hindi < Sans. *kokila:* origin echoic] any of various cuckoos (genus *Eudynamis*) of India, the East Indies, and Australia

K. of C. Knight (or Knights) of Columbus

Koff·ka (kôf′kə), **Kurt** (kurt) 1886-1941; U.S. psychologist, born in Germany

K. of P. Knight (or Knights) of Pythias

Ko·hel·eth (kō hel′eth) [Heb. *qōheleth:* see ECCLESIASTES] *same as* ECCLESIASTES; also, its author, traditionally identified with Solomon

Koh·i·noor, Koh-i-noor (kō′ə noor′) [Per. *koh-i-nūr*, lit., mountain of light] a famous large Indian diamond, now one of the British crown jewels

kohl (kōl) *n.* [Ar. *kuhl:* cf. ALCOHOL] a cosmetic preparation, as powdered antimony sulfide, used, esp. in certain Eastern countries, for eye makeup

Köh·ler (kō′lər), **Wolf·gang** (vôlf′gäŋ′) 1887- ; Ger. psychologist in the U.S., born in Estonia

KOALA
(27-35 in. long)

kohl·ra·bi (kōl'rä'bē, kōl'rä'bē) n., pl. **-bies** [G. < It. *cavoli rape*, pl. of *cavolo rapa*, cole rape: cf. COLE & RAPE[2]] a garden vegetable (*Brassica oleracea caulorapa*) related to the cabbage: the edible part is a bulbous portion of the stem just above the ground

koi·ne (koi nā'; koi'nā, -nē) n. [Gr. (*hē*) *koinē* (*dialektos*), (the) common (dialect) < *koinos*: see COENO-] [*also* K-] **1.** the language used throughout the Greek world, from Syria to Gaul, during the Hellenistic and Roman periods: its spoken form consisted of colloquial Attic, supplemented by numerous Ionic words and some borrowings from other dialects: the New Testament is written in the koine **2.** a regional dialect or language that has become the common language of a larger area

KOHLRABI

Ko·kand (kō känt') city in E Uzbek S.S.R.: pop. 128,000

ko·kan·ee (kō kan'ē) n., pl. **-ees, -ee:** see PLURAL, II, D, 1 [prob. after *Kokanee Creek*, a stream in British Columbia] a small, landlocked variety (*Oncorhynchus nerka kennerlyi*) of the sockeye salmon, found in W N. America

Ko·ko·mo (kō'kə mō') [< Algonquian (Miami) name of a village, lit., ? young grandmother] city in C Ind.: pop. 44,000

Ko·ko Nor (kō'kō nôr') **1.** *same as* TSINGHAI (lake) **2.** *former name of* TSINGHAI (province)

Ko·kosch·ka (kō kôsh'kə), **Oskar** 1886– ; Brit. painter, born in Austria

kok·sa·ghyz, kok·sa·gyz (kōk'sə gēz') n. [Russ. < Turk. *kök*, a root + East Turk. *sagiz*, rubber, gum] a dandelion (*Taraxacum kok-saghyz*) grown in parts of the Soviet Union for the rubber obtained from its roots

ko·la (kō'lə) n. *same as* COLA[1]

kola nut the seed of the cola

Ko·la Peninsula (kō'lä) peninsula in NW U.S.S.R., between the White & Barents seas: c. 50,000 sq. mi.

Kol·ha·pur (kōl'hä pōōr') city in W India, in Maharashtra state: pop. 187,000

ko·lin·sky (kə lin'skē, kō-) n., pl. **-skies** [Russ. *kolinski* < *Kola*, district in N Russia] **1.** any of several weasels of Asia, esp. a Russian species (*Mustela siberica*) **2.** the golden-brown fur of such a weasel

kol·khoz (käl khôz') n. [Russ. < *kol*(*lektivnoe*), collective + *khoz*(*aïstvo*), household, farm] a collective farm in the Soviet Union

Koll·witz (kōl'vits), **Kä·the** (ke'tə) (born *Käthe Schmidt*) 1867–1945; Ger. painter, etcher, & lithographer

Köln (köln) *Ger. name of* COLOGNE

Kol Nid·re (kōl nē'drä, nid'rə; *Heb.* kōl'nē drä') [Aram. *kōl nidhrē*, lit., all our vows (opening words of the prayer)] **1.** the prayer of atonement recited in synagogues at the opening of the Yom Kippur eve services **2.** the traditional music to which this is sung

ko·lo (kō'lō) n., pl. **-los** [Serb. < OSlav., wheel < IE. base *kwel-, to turn, whence WHEEL] a Serbian folk dance performed by a group in a circle

Ko·ly·ma (kä lē mä') river in E R.S.F.S.R., flowing north into the East Siberian Sea: c. 1,300 mi.: also sp. **Ko·li·ma'**

Ko·mo·do dragon (kə mō'dō) [< *Komodo* Island, Indonesia] a giant, flesh-eating lizard (*Varanus komodoensis*) of SE Asian jungles: it is the largest living lizard, reaching a length of 9 ft.

Kom·so·mol (käm'sə môl') [Russ. *Kom*(*munisticheskü*) *So*(*yuz*) *Mol*(*odezhi*), Communist League of Youth] the Communist organization for youth in the Soviet Union

Kom·so·molsk-on-A·mur (käm'sə môlsk' än ä moor') city in E R.S.F.S.R., in Khabarovsk territory, on the Amur River: pop. 207,000: also **Kom'so·molsk'**

Kon·go (käŋ'gō) n. **1.** pl. **-gos, -go** any member of a Bantu people of N Angola and the SW Congo (sense 2) **2.** their Bantu language

Kö·nig·grätz (kö'niH grets') *former* (*Ger.*) *name of* HRADEC KRÁLOVÉ

Kö·nigs·berg (-niHs berk') *former* (*Ger.*) *name of* KALININGRAD

Kon·stanz (kôn'stäns) *Ger. name of* CONSTANCE

Kon·ya (kôn'yä) city in S Turkey: pop. 120,000

koo·doo (kōō'dōō) n., pl. **-doos, -doo:** see PLURAL, II, D, 1 *same as* KUDU

☆**kook** (kōōk) n. [prob. contr. < CUCKOO] [Slang] a person regarded as silly, eccentric, crazy, etc.

kook·a·bur·ra (kōō'kə bur'ə, -bûr'ə) n. [< native name in Australia] an Australian kingfisher (*Dacelo gigas*) with an abrupt, harsh cry suggestive of loud laughter

☆**kook·y, kook·ie** (kōō'kē) adj. **kook'i·er, kook'i·est** [Slang] of or characteristic of a kook; silly, eccentric, crazy, etc. —**kook'i·ness** n.

Kooning, Willem de *see* DE KOONING

Koord (kûrd, koord) n. *same as* KURD

Koo·te·nay (kōōt'n ā') [< a native name < ?] **1.** river flowing from SE British Columbia, through Mont. & Ida. into Kootenay Lake, thence into the Columbia River: 407 mi. **2.** elongated lake in the valley of this river, SE British Columbia: 168 sq. mi. —n. *same as* KUTENAI Also, in the U.S., sp. **Kootenai** for sense 1 & for n.

‡**kop** (käp) n. [Afrik. < Du. *kop*, head: see COP[1]] in South Africa, a hill or mountain

ko·peck, ko·pek (kō'pek) n. [Russ. *kopeika* < *kopye*, a lance] **1.** a monetary unit equal to 1/100 of a Russian ruble: abbrev. **k., kop. 2.** a coin of this unit

Ko·peysk, Ko·peisk (kō päsk') city in SW R.S.F.S.R., in the S Urals: pop. 167,000

koph (kōf) n. [Heb. *qōph*] the nineteenth letter of the Hebrew alphabet (ק)

‡**kop·je** (käp'ē) n. [Afrik., dim. of *kop:* see KOP] in South Africa, a small hill; hillock

kor (kôr) n. [Heb. *kōr*] *same as* HOMER[1]

Ko·ran (kō rän', -rän'; kô-, kə-) n. [Ar. *qur'ān*, lit., book, reading, recitation < *qara'a*, to read] the sacred book of the Moslems, written in Arabic: its contents are reported revelations made to Mohammed by Allah —**Ko·ran'ic** adj.

Kor·do·fan (kôr'dō fän') province of C Sudan: 146,930 sq. mi.: pop. 2,052,000; cap. El Obeid

Kor·do·fan·i·an (kôr'də fan'ē ən) n. [< prec.] a subfamily of the Congo-Kordofanian family of African languages, having five branches

Ko·re·a (kō rē'ə, kô-, kə-) peninsula & country in E Asia, extending south from NE China: divided (1948) into *a*) **Korean People's Democratic Republic (North Korea)** occupying the N half of the peninsula: 47,255 sq. mi.; pop. 11,568,000; cap. Pyongyang, and *b*) **Republic of Korea (South Korea)** occupying the S half of the peninsula: 38,030 sq. mi.; pop. 29,608,000; cap. Seoul: war (1950–53) between the two countries ended in a cease-fire & reaffirmation of the division

Ko·re·an (-ən) adj. of Korea, its people, their language, etc. —n. **1.** a native of Korea **2.** the language of the Koreans

Korea Strait strait between Korea & Japan, connecting the Sea of Japan & the East China Sea: c. 110 mi. wide

Ko·rin·thos (kô'rēn thôs') *Gr. name of modern* CORINTH

Kor·sa·koff's psychosis (or **syndrome**) (kôr'sə kôfs') [after S. S. *Korsakoff* (1854?–1900), Russ. neurologist] a severe mental disorder caused by damage to the nervous system from alcohol, vitamin deficiencies, etc., characterized by multiple neuritis, memory loss, disorientation, etc.

ko·ru·na (kō rōō'nä) n., pl. **Ko·ru'nas, ko·run'** [Czech, lit., crown < L. *corona:* see CROWN] **1.** the monetary unit of Czechoslovakia: see MONETARY UNITS, table **2.** a coin of this unit

Kor·zyb·ski (kôr zip'skē), **Alfred (Habdank)** 1879–1950; U.S. semanticist, born in Poland

kos (kōs) n., pl. **kos** [Hind. < Sans. *krósa*, lit., a shout (hence, lit., shouting distance)] in India, a measure of distance whose value varies in different localities from 1.5 to 3 miles

Kos (käs, kôs) Gr. island in the Dodecanese, off the SW coast of Turkey: 111 sq. mi.

Kos·ci·us·ko (käs'ē us'kō; *Pol.* kôsh chōōsh'kō), **Thaddeus** (born *Tadeusz Andrzej Bonawentura Kościuszko*) 1746–1817; Pol. patriot & general: served in the Am. army in the American Revolution

Kosciusko, Mount mountain of the Australian Alps, in SE New South Wales: highest peak in Australia: 7,316 ft.

ko·sher (kō'shər; *for v., usually* käsh'ər) adj. [Heb. *kāshēr*, fit, right, proper] **1.** *Judaism a*) clean or fit to eat according to the dietary laws: Lev. 11 *b*) serving or dealing in such food [a kosher kitchen] **2.** loosely, prepared according to traditional Jewish recipes [kosher pickles] ☆**3.** [Slang] all right, proper, correct, etc. —n. kosher food —vt. to make kosher

Ko·ši·ce (kō'shē tse) city in E Slovakia, Czechoslovakia: pop. 106,000

Kos·suth (käs'ōōth, kä sōōth'; *Hung.* kô'shoot), **Louis** (Hung. name *Lajos Kossuth*) 1802–94; Hung. patriot & statesman

Ko·stro·ma (kō strô mä') city in NW R.S.F.S.R., on the Volga: pop. 205,000

Ko·sy·gin (kō sē'gyin; *E.* kə sē'gin), **A·lek·sei Ni·ko·la·e·vich** (ä lyik sā' nē'kō lä'yi vich) 1904– ; premier of the U.S.S.R. (1964–)

Ko·ta·ba·ru (kōt'ə bär'ōō) capital of West Irian, Indonesia; seaport on the NE coast: pop. 16,000

ko·to (kōt'ō) n. [Jap.] a Japanese musical instrument similar to a zither, consisting of an oblong box with thirteen silk strings stretched over it

Kot·ze·bue (kôt'sə boo'), **Au·gust Fried·rich Fer·di·nand von** (ou'goost frē'driH fer'di nän fôn) 1761–1819; Ger. playwright

Kous·se·vitz·ky (kōō'sə vit'skē) **Serge** (sûrj, serzh) (born *Sergei Alexandrovich Koussevitzky*) 1874–1951; Russ. orchestral conductor in the U.S.

Kov·no (kôv'nô) *Russ. name of* KAUNAS

Kow·loon (kou'lōōn') **1.** peninsula in SE China, opposite Hong Kong island & part of Hong Kong colony: 3 sq. mi. **2.** city on this peninsula: pop. 1,350,000

kow·tow (kou'tou', kou'-) n. [Chin. *k'o-t'ou*, lit., knock head] the act of kneeling and touching the ground with the forehead to show great deference, submissive respect, homage, etc., as formerly in China —vi. **1.** to make a kowtow **2.** to show submissive respect (*to*)

Ko·zhi·kode (kō'zhi kōd') seaport in SW India, on the Arabian Sea, in Kerala state: pop. 193,000

KP, K.P. kitchen police

KR *Chess* king's rook

Kr *Chem.* krypton

kr. 1. kreutzer **2.** krone

Kra (krä), **Isthmus of** narrow strip of land connecting the Malay Peninsula with the Indochinese peninsula

kraal (kräl, krôl) *n.* [Afrik., village, pen, enclosure < Port. *curral*, pen for cattle: see CORRAL] **1.** a village of South African natives, usually surrounded by a stockade **2.** a fenced enclosure for cattle or sheep in South Africa; pen —*vt.* to shut up in a kraal

Krae·pe·lin (krä′pə lin), **Emil** 1856–1926; Ger. psychiatrist

Krafft-E·bing (kraft′ā′biɲ, kräft′-), Baron **Richard von** 1840–1902; Ger. neurologist

kraft (kraft, kräft) *n.* [G., strength: see CRAFT] strong wrapping paper, usually brown, made from wood pulp prepared with a sodium sulfate solution: also **kraft paper**

krait (krīt) *n.* [Hind. *karait*] any of several very poisonous snakes (genus *Bungarus*), generally black or dark brown with tan or yellow bands, found in SC and SE Asia

Kra·ka·tau (krä′kä tou′) small volcanic island of Indonesia, between Java & Sumatra: 2,667 ft.: also **Kra′ka·to′a** (-tō′ə)

kra·ken (krä′k'n) *n.* [Norw.] a legendary sea monster of northern seas

Kra·ków (krä′kou′, krä′-; -kō; *Pol.* krä′koof) city in S Poland, on the Vistula: pop. 517,000

Kras·no·dar (kräs′nō där′) **1.** territory in SW R.S.F.S.R., in the N Caucasus: pop. 3,766,000 **2.** capital of this territory, on the Kuban River: pop. 395,000

Kras·no·yarsk (kräs′nō yärsk′) **1.** territory in C R.S.F.S.R., in Asia: pop. 2,614,000 **2.** capital of this territory, on the Yenisei River: pop. 557,000

kra·ter (krät′ər, krat′-) *n.* [Gr. *kratēr*: see CRATER] an ancient Greek jar or mixing bowl with a broad body, a wide neck, and two handles

Krebs cycle (krebs) [after H. A. *Krebs* (1900–), Brit. biochemist] a series of biochemical reactions which produce carbon dioxide and water from foodstuffs and release energy for the synthesis of ATP molecules

Kre·feld (krā′felt) city in W West Germany, on the Rhine, in North Rhine-Westphalia: pop. 222,000

Kreis·ler (krīs′lər), **Fritz** (frits) 1875–1962; U.S. violinist & composer, born in Austria

krem·lin (krem′lin) *n.* [Fr. < Russ. *kreml′*] in Russia, the citadel of a city —**the Kremlin 1.** the citadel of Moscow, formerly housing government offices of the Soviet Union **2.** the government of the Soviet Union

Krem·lin·ol·o·gy (krem′lin äl′ə jē) *n.* [prec. + -OLOGY] [Colloq.] the study of the government, foreign policy, etc. of the Soviet Union —**Krem′lin·ol′o·gist** *n.*

☆**krep·lach** (krep′läkh, -lakh) *n.pl.* [Yid. *kreplech*, pl. of *krepel* < MHG. dial *kreppel*, var. of MHG. *krepfel*, dim. of *krapfe*, fritter < OHG. *krapfo*, lit., a hook: for IE. base see CRAMP[1]] small casings of dough filled with ground meat, etc., boiled, and served usually in soup

Kre·te, Kri·ti (krē′tē) *Gr.* name of CRETE

kreut·zer, kreu·zer (kroit′sər) *n.* [G. *kreuzer* < *kreuz*, a cross: so called because the coin had the figure of a cross on it] a former small, copper coin of Germany and Austria

krieg·spiel (krēg′spēl′, -shpēl′) *n.* [G. *kriegsspiel* < *kriegs* (gen. of *krieg*, war) + *spiel*, game] a game for teaching or practicing military tactics by the use of small figures representing troops, tanks, etc. moved about on a large map or representation of the terrain

Kriem·hild (krēm′hild; *G.* krēm′hilt) [G. < MHG. *Kriemhilt* < Gmc. **grim-*, a mask, face, visor (cf. GRIMACE) + **hild-*, battle] in the *Nibelungenlied*, the wife of Siegfried and sister of Gunther

krill (kril) *n., pl.* **krill** [Norw. *kril*, young fry (of fish)] a small, shrimplike crustacean (esp. genus *Euphausia*), the main food of baleen whales

krim·mer (krim′ər) *n.* [G. < *Krim*, Crimea] a grayish, tightly curled fur similar to astrakhan, made from the pelts of Crimean lambs

kris (krēs) *n.* [Malay *kerīs*] a dagger with a wavy blade, used by Malays; creese

Krish·na (krish′nə) [Sans. *Kṛṣṇa*] **1.** an important Hindu god, an incarnation of Vishnu, second god of the Hindu trinity **2.** same as KISTNA —**Krish′na·ism** *n.*

☆**Kriss Krin·gle** (kris′ kriɲ′g'l) [G. *Christkindl* < *Christ*, Christ + *kindl*, dim. of *kind*, child] same as SANTA CLAUS

Kri·voi Rog (kri voi′ rōk′) city in SC Ukrainian S.S.R.: pop. 498,000

Kroe·ber (krō′bər), **A(lfred) L(ouis)** 1876–1960; U.S. anthropologist

kro·na (krō′nə; *Sw.* krōō′nə), *n., pl.* **kro′nor** (-nôr) [Sw. < L. *corona*: see CROWN] the monetary unit and a coin of Sweden: see MONETARY UNITS, table

kró·na (krō′nə) *n., pl.* **kró′nur** (-nər) [Ice. < ML. *corona*, CROWN] the standard monetary unit and a coin of Iceland: see MONETARY UNITS, table

kro·ne[1] (krō′nə) *n., pl.* **kro′nen** (-nən) [G. < L. *corona*: see CROWN] **1.** a former German gold coin **2.** the former monetary unit or a silver coin of Austria

kro·ne[2] (krō′nə) *n., pl.* **kro′ner** (-nər) [Dan. < L. *corona*: see CROWN] the monetary unit and a coin of Denmark or Norway: see MONETARY UNITS, table

Kron·shtadt (krōn′shtät′) city & naval fortress on an island in NW R.S.F.S.R., at the head of the Gulf of Finland: pop. 59,000: also, Ger. sp., **Kron′stadt′**

Kro·pot·kin (krō pōt′kin; *E.* krə pät′kin), **Prince Pëtr A·lek·se·ye·vich** (pyōt′r′ ä′lyik sā′yi vich) 1842–1921; Russ. anarchist & writer

Kru·ger (krōō′gər), **Paul** (born *Stephanus Johannes Paulus Kruger*) 1825–1904; South African statesman; president of the South African Republic (1883–1900)

Kru·gers·dorp (krōō′gərz dôrp′) city in the SW Transvaal, South Africa: pop. 90,000

☆**krul·ler** (krul′ər) *n. same as* CRULLER

krumm·horn, krum·horn (kroom′hôrn′, krum′-) *n.* [G. < *krumm*, crooked + *horn*, HORN] an ancient double-reed musical instrument with a curve at the end of the tube

Krung Thep (kroon′ tāp′) *Thai* name of BANGKOK

Krupp (krup; *G.* kroop) family of Ger. steel & munitions manufacturers in the 19th & 20th cent.

Krutch (krōōch), **Joseph Wood** 1893–1970; U.S. critic, essayist, & naturalist

kryp·ton (krip′tän) *n.* [ModL. < Gr. *krypton*, neut. of *kryptos*, hidden: see CRYPT] a rare, gaseous chemical element present in very small quantities in air and inert to all reagents except fluorine: symbol, Kr; at. wt., 83.80; at. no., 36; density, 3.736 g/l(0°C); melt. pt., −156.6°C; boil. pt., −152.9°C

Kshat·ri·ya (kshat′rē ə) *n.* [Sans. *kṣatriya* < *kṣatra*, rule] among the Hindus, a member of the military caste, next below the Brahmans

Kt *Chess* knight

kt. 1. karat **2.** kiloton; kilotons

K.T. 1. Knight of (the Order of) the Thistle **2.** Knight (or Knights) Templar

Kua·la Lum·pur (kwä′lə loom poor′) city in W Malaya; capital of the Federation of Malaya & the Federation of Malaysia: pop. c. 400,000

Ku·ban (kōō ban′; *Russ.* kōō bän′y′) river in the N Caucasus, flowing northwest partly into the Sea of Azov & partly into the Black Sea: c. 550 mi.

Ku·blai Khan (kōō′blī kän′, -blə) 1216?–94; Mongol emperor of China (1260?–94): founder of the Mongol dynasty: grandson of GENGHIS KHAN: also **Ku·bla Khan** (kōō′blə)

☆**ku·chen** (kōō′kən, -khən) *n.* [G., cake: see CAKE] a German coffeecake, made of yeast dough covered with sugar and spices, and often containing raisins, nuts, etc.

Ku·ching (kōō′chin) capital of Sarawak, Malaysia; seaport in the W part: pop. 51,000

ku·dos (kōō′däs, -dōs; kyōō′-) *n.* [Gr. *kydos*, glory, fame < IE. **kud-* < base **keu-*, to pay attention to, hear, feel, whence HEAR] [Colloq.] credit or praise for an achievement; glory; fame: sometimes wrongly taken as a plural (*pron.* -dōz) of an assumed "*kudo*"

ku·du (kōō′dōō) *n., pl.* **-dus, -du:** see PLURAL, II, D, 1 [Hottentot] either of two large, grayish-brown African antelopes (genus *Tragelaphus*), with narrow, white stripes across the back and long, twisted horns

☆**kud·zu** (kood′zōō) *n.* [Jap. *kuzu*] a hairy perennial vine (*Pueraria thunbergiana*) of the legume family, with large, three-part leaves: sometimes planted in the South for soil stabilization or forage

Ku·fic (kōō′fik, kyōō′-) *adj.* [< *Kufa* (Ar. *al-Kūfah*), town on the Euphrates, south of Babylon + -IC] designating or of an early Arabic alphabet with angular letters, used esp. in a region south of Babylon

Kui·by·shev (kwē′bi shef′) **1.** region in SW R.S.F.S.R., in the Volga River basin: pop. 2,257,000 **2.** capital of this region, on the Volga: pop. 969,000

☆**Ku Klux** (kōō′ kluks′, kyōō′) [< Gr. *kyklos*, a circle (cf. CYCLE): prob. suggested by *Kuklos Adelphōn*, a S college fraternity (1812–66)] **1.** *short for* KU KLUX KLAN **2.** a member of the Ku Klux Klan: also **Ku Klux′er**

☆**Ku Klux Klan** (klan) [prec. + *klan*, arbitrary sp. for CLAN] **1.** a secret society of white men founded in the S States after the Civil War to reestablish and maintain white supremacy **2.** a secret society organized in Atlanta, Georgia, in 1915 as "the Invisible Empire, Knights of the Ku Klux Klan": it is anti-Negro, anti-Semitic, anti-Catholic, etc., and uses terrorist methods

ku·lak (kōō läk′) *n.* [Russ., lit., fist, hence, tightwad < Estonian] a well-to-do farmer in Russia who profited from the labor of poorer peasants and who opposed the Soviet collectivization of the land

‡**Kul·tur** (kool tōōr′) *n.* [G., lit., culture] civilization; social organization; specif., the highly systematized social organization of Hohenzollern or Nazi Germany: now usually ironic in application, with reference to chauvinism, militarism, terrorism, etc.

‡**Kul·tur·kampf** (-kämpf′) *n.* [G. < prec. + *kampf*, a battle] the struggle between the Roman Catholic Church and the German government from 1872 to 1887, mainly over the government's efforts to control education, civil marriage, church appointments, etc.

Ku·ma·mo·to (kōō′mä mō′tō) city in W Kyushu, Japan: pop. 407,000

Ku·mas·i (koo mä′sē) city in SC Ghana; capital of Ashanti region: pop. 190,000

ku·miss (kōō′mis) *n.* [G. < Russ. *kumis* < Tatar *kumiz*] **1.** mare's or camel's milk fermented and used as a drink by Tatar nomads of Asia **2.** a similar drink made from cow's milk, used in certain special diets

küm·mel (kim′'l; *G.* küm′əl) *n.* [G., caraway < OHG. *kumil, kumin* < L. *cuminum:* see CUMIN] a colorless liqueur flavored with caraway seeds, anise, cumin, etc.

kum·mer·bund (kum′ər bund′) *n. same as* CUMMERBUND

kum·quat (kum′kwät, -kwôt) *n.* [< dial. pronun. of Chin. *chin-chü,* lit., golden orange] **1.** an orange-colored, oval citrus fruit about the size of a small plum, with a sour pulp and a sweet rind, used in preserves and confections **2.** a tree (genus *Fortunella*) of the rue family that bears this fruit

Kun (koon), **Bé·la** (bā′lä) 1886–1937?; Hung. Communist leader

K'ung Fu-tse (koon′ foo′dzu′) *Chin.* name of CONFUCIUS

Kun·lun Mountains (koon′loon′) mountain system in W China, between Tibet & Sinkiang province: highest peak, c. 25,300 ft.

Kun·ming (koon′miŋ′) city in S China; capital of Yunnan province: pop. 730,000

☆**kunz·ite** (koonts′it) *n.* [after George F. *Kunz* (1856–1932), U.S. gem expert + -ITE¹] a transparent variety of spodumene, occurring in lilac crystals, used as a gem

Kuo·min·tang (kwō′min taŋ′; *Chin.* gwō′min′däŋ′) [Chin. *kuo,* nation(alist) + *min,* people('s) + *tang,* party] nationalist political party of China, organized chiefly by Sun Yat-sen in 1911 and afterward controlled and led by Chiang Kai-shek: see CHINA

Ku·ra (koo rä′) river flowing from NE Turkey west across Transcaucasia, into the Caspian Sea: c. 940 mi.

kur·bash (koor′bash) *n.* [Turk. *qirbāch*] a leather whip formerly used in Turkey, Egypt, etc. for punishing offenders —*vt.* to flog with a kurbash

Kurd (kurd, koord) *n.* [Turk. & Ar.] any of a nomadic Moslem people living chiefly in Kurdistan and the S Caucasus

Kurd·ish (-ish) *adj.* of the Kurds, their language, culture, etc. —*n.* the Iranian language of the Kurds

Kur·dis·tan (kur′di stan′, koor′-; -stän′) region in SW Asia inhabited chiefly by Kurds, occupying SE Turkey, N Iraq, & NW Iran —*n.* any of various rugs made by Kurds, esp. in Iran

Ku·re (koo′rä′) seaport in SW Honshu, Japan, on the Inland Sea: pop. 225,000

Kur·gan (koor gän′) city in SW Siberian R.S.F.S.R.: pop. 205,000

Ku·ril (or **Ku·rile**) **Islands** (kōō′ril, koo rēl′) chain of islands belonging to the U.S.S.R., between N Hokkaido, Japan, and Kamchatka Peninsula: formerly Japanese (1875–1945): c. 6,000 sq. mi.

Kur·land (koor′lənd) *same as* COURLAND

Kur·o·shi·o (koo rō′shē ō′) *same as* JAPAN CURRENT

kur·ra·jong (kur′ə jôŋ′, -jäŋ′) *n.* [< native name in Australia] any of several Australian trees and shrubs; esp., a bottle tree (*Brachychiton populneum*) yielding fibers used by the natives for weaving nets, mats, etc.

Kursk (koorsk) city in SW R.S.F.S.R., near the Ukrainian border: pop. 249,000

kur·to·sis (kər tō′sis) *n.* [< Gr. *kyrtōsis,* a bulging, convexity < *kyrtos,* curved: for IE. base see CURVE] the degree of peakedness of the graph of a statistical distribution

ku·ru (kōō′rōō) *n.* [< native name in New Guinea] a degenerative disease of the central nervous system, found among certain aborigines of the eastern highlands of New Guinea

ku·rus (koo rōōsh′) *n., pl.* -rus′ [Turk.] in Turkey, a monetary unit equivalent to a piaster

Kush (kush) *same as* CUSH

Kus·ko·kwim (kus′kə kwim) river in SW Alas., flowing southwest into the Bering Sea: 550 mi.

Kutch (kuch) **1.** former state of W India, on the Arabian Sea, now part of the state of Gujarat **2. Rann of** (run əv), large salt marsh in W India & S West Pakistan: c. 9,000 sq. mi.

Ku·te·nai, Ku·te·nay (koot′'n ā′) *same as* KOOTENAY —*n.* **1.** a member of a tribe of Indians who live in Montana, Idaho, and British Columbia **2.** their isolated language, the unique member of a family

Ku·tu·zov (koo tōō′zôf), **Mi·kha·il I·la·ri·o·no·vich** (mē′khä ēl′ ē′lä rē ō nô′vich) 1745–1813; Russ. field marshal: defeated Napoleon at Smolensk (1812)

Ku·wait (koo wāt′, -wit′) **1.** independent Arab state in E Arabia, between Iraq & Saudi Arabia: 6,000 sq. mi.; pop. 555,000 **2.** its capital, a seaport on the Persian Gulf: pop. 100,000

Kuyp (koip), **Aelbert** *same as* CUYP

Kuz·netsk Basin (kōōz nyetsk′) industrial & coal-mining region in SC R.S.F.S.R.: c. 10,000 sq. mi.

kv, kv. kilovolt; kilovolts

kvass, kvas (kväs) *n.* [Russ. *kvas*] a Russian fermented drink made from rye, barley, rye bread, etc.

kw. kilowatt; kilowatts

Kwa (kwä) *n.* a branch of the Niger-Congo subfamily of languages, spoken in West and NW Africa and including Akan, Ashanti, etc.

kwa·cha (kwä′chä) *n., pl.* **kwa′cha** [native term, lit., dawn] the monetary unit of Malawi and Zambia: see MONETARY UNITS, table

Kwa·ja·lein (kwä′jə lān′) atoll in the W Pacific, in the Marshall Islands: 6 1/2 sq. mi.

Kwa·ki·u·tl (kwä′kē ōōt′'l) *n.* [native name, lit., beach at the north end of the river] **1.** a member of a tribe of Indians of British Columbia, noted for their potlatches **2.** their Algonquian language

Kwang·chow (kwäŋ′chō′; *Chin.* gwäŋ′jō′) port in SE China, on the Chu Kiang River; capital of Kwangtung province: pop. 2,200,000: also sp. **Kwang′chou′**

Kwang·ju (gwäŋ′jōō′) city in SW South Korea: pop. 240,000

Kwang·si-Chu·ang (gwäŋ′sē′jwäŋ′) autonomous region in S China: 85,097 sq. mi.; pop. 19,390,000; cap. Nanning: formerly **Kwang′si′** province

Kwang·tung (kwäŋ′tooŋ′; *Chin.* gwäŋ′dooŋ′) province of SE China, on the South China Sea: 89,344 sq. mi.; pop. 37,960,000; cap. Kwangchow

Kwan·tung Peninsula (kwan′tooŋ′; *Chin.* gwän′dooŋ′) tip of Liaotung Peninsula in Liaoning province, NE China: leased (1905–45) by Japan

kwa·shi·or·kor (kwä′shē ôr′kôr) *n.* [< native name in Ghana] a severe disease of young children, caused by chronic deficiency of protein and calories in the diet and characterized by stunted growth, edema, and a protuberant belly

Kwei·chow (kwä′chou′; *Chin.* gwä′jō′) province of S China: 67,181 sq. mi.; pop. 16,890,000; cap. Kweiyang

Kwei·lin (kwä′lin′; *Chin.* gwä′lin′) city in Kwangsi province, S China: pop. 145,000

Kwei·yang (kwä′yäŋ′; *Chin.* gwä′yäŋ′) city in S China; capital of Kweichow province: pop. 530,000

kwh, K.W.H., kw.-hr., kw-hr kilowatt-hour

Ky. Kentucky

☆**ky·ack** (kī′ak) *n.* [< ?] [Western] a kind of packsack consisting of two sacklike containers swung on either side of a packsaddle

ky·ak (kī′ak) *n. same as* KAYAK

ky·a·nite (kī′ə nīt′) *n. same as* CYANITE

ky·an·ize (-nīz′) *vt.* -ized′, -iz′ing [after J. H. *Kyan* (1774–1850), Ir. inventor of the process] to make (wood) resistant to decay by treatment with a solution of corrosive sublimate

kyat (kyät) *n.* [< Burmese] the monetary unit of Burma: see MONETARY UNITS, table

Kyd (kid), **Thomas** 1558–94; Eng. dramatist

ky·lix (kī′liks, kil′iks) *n., pl.* **ky·li·kes** (kī′lə kēz′, kil′ə-) [Gr. *kylix*] an ancient Greek two-handled drinking cup with a stem and a wide, shallow bowl

ky·mo·gram (kī′mə gram′) *n.* the chart produced by a kymograph

ky·mo·graph (-graf′, -gräf′) *n.* [< Gr. *kyma,* a wave (see CYME) + -GRAPH] an apparatus consisting of a rotating drum for recording wavelike motions, variations, or modulations, such as muscular contractions, the pulse, etc. —**ky′mo·graph′ic** *adj.* —**ky·mog·ra·phy** (kī mäg′rə fē) *n.*

Kym·ric (kim′rik) *adj., n. same as* CYMRIC

Kym·ry, Kym·ri (-rē) *n., pl.* -ry or -ri, -ries *same as* CYMRY

Kyong·song (kyôŋ′sôŋ′) *same as* SEOUL

Kyo·to (kyō′tō′; *E.* kē ōt′ō) city in S Honshu, Japan: pop. 1,365,000

ky·pho·sis (kī fō′sis) *n.* [ModL. < Gr. *kyphōsis* < *kyphos,* a hump, hunch < IE. **keubh-* < base **keu-,* to bend, arch, whence HIP¹, HUMP] abnormal curvature of the spine resulting in a hump —**ky·phot′ic** (-fät′ik) *adj.*

Kyr·i·e e·le·i·son (kir′ē ā′ e lā′ē sōn′) [Gr.(Ec.) *Kyrie eleēson,* Lord, have mercy (upon us): cf. Ps. 123:3, Matt. 15:22] **1.** an invocation or response used in various Christian churches; specif., a part of the Roman Catholic service after the Introit in the Mass **2.** a musical setting for this

Ky·the·ra (kē′thi rä′) *Gr.* name of CYTHERA

Kyu·shu (kyōō′shōō′) one of the four main islands of Japan, south of Honshu: 16,223 sq. mi.; pop. 12,937,000; chief city, Nagasaki

Kyz·yl Kum (kiz′'l koom′) desert in the Kazakh S.S.R. & the Uzbek S.S.R.: c. 75,000 sq. mi.

L

L, l (el) *n., pl.* **L's, l's** **1.** the twelfth letter of the English alphabet: from the Greek *lambda*, a borrowing from the Phoenician **2.** the sound of *L* or *l*: in English, it is normally a voiced alveolar continuant; in most varieties of American speech, final and preconsonantal *l* (e.g., *feel, field*) has the cavity friction, and hence the sonority, usually associated with vowels: in many words, *l* preceding *f, k, m,* and *v* is silent (c.g., *half, balk, calm,* and *salve*) **3.** a type or impression for *L* or *l* **4.** *a symbol for* the twelfth (or the eleventh if J is omitted) in a sequence or group —*adj.* **1.** of *L* or *l* **2.** twelfth (or eleventh if J is omitted) in a sequence or group

L (el) *n., pl.* **L's** **1.** an object shaped like L; ☆esp., an extension of a house or building that gives the whole a shape resembling L; ell **2.** a Roman numeral for 50: with a superior bar (L̄), 50,000 ☆**3.** [for *el*, short for ELEVATED] an elevated railroad **4.** *Elec.* the symbol for inductance **5.** *Geodesy* the symbol for longitude **6.** *Physics* the symbol for latent heat —*adj.* shaped like L

L- *a prefix meaning* having a spatial arrangement of atoms around an asymmetric carbon atom similar to that of levorotatory glyceraldehyde, the arbitrary standard of comparison *[L-glucose]*

l- *a prefix meaning* levorotatory *[l-limonene]*

L. **1.** Latin **2.** Licentiate **3.** Lodge

L., l. **1.** lake **2.** land **3.** latitude **4.** law **5.** leaf **6.** league **7.** left **8.** length **9.** *pl.* LL., **ll.** line **10.** link **11.** lira; lire **12.** liter **13.** low **14.** [L. *libra*, pl. *librae*] pound(s)

la¹ (lä, lȯ) *interj.* [cf. LO] [Dial. or Archaic] oh! look!: an exclamation of surprise or emphasis

la² (lä) *n.* [ME. < ML. < *labii*, word of a Latin hymn: see GAMUT] *Music* a syllable representing the sixth tone of the diatonic scale: see SOLFEGGIO

La *Chem.* lanthanum

La. Louisiana

L.A. [Colloq.] Los Angeles

laa·ger (lä′gər) *n.* [Afrik. < Du. *leger*, a camp: see LAIR] in South Africa, a temporary camp within an encircling barricade of wagons, etc. —*vt.* to form into a laager —*vi.* to camp in a laager

Laa·land (lô′län) *same as* LOLLAND

lab (lab) *n.* [Colloq.] a laboratory

Lab. Labrador

lab. **1.** labial **2.** labiate **3.** laboratory

La·ban (lā′bən) [Heb. *lābhān*, lit., white] *Bible* the father of Rachel and Leah: Gen. 29:16

lab·a·rum (lab′ə rəm) *n., pl.* **-a·ra** (-rə) [LL. (whence LGr. *labaron*) < ?] the royal cavalry standard carried before the Roman emperors in war, esp. that first carried by Constantine, the first emperor to adopt Christianity: it usually bore the first two letters (XP) of the Greek *Christos* (Christ)

lab·da·num (lab′də nəm) *n.* [ML., altered < L. *ladanum* < Gr. *ladanon* < *lēdon*, mastic < Ar. *lādan* < Per. *lādan*] a dark resin obtained from various rockroses (genus *Cistus*), used in perfumery

La·be (lä′be) *Czech name of the* ELBE

lab·e·fac·tion (lab′ə fak′shən) *n.* [< L. *labefactus*, pp. of *labefacere*, to cause to totter < *labare*, to totter (see LAP¹) + *facere*, to make: see FACT] [Rare] a weakening, ruining, etc.; downfall; deterioration

la·bel (lā′b'l) *n.* [ME. < OFr., a rag, strip < Frank. *labba*, akin to OHG. *lappa*, a rag, shred: for IE. base see LAP¹] **1.** formerly, *a)* a narrow band of cloth, etc.; fillet *b)* a narrow strip of ribbon attached to a document to hold the seal **2.** a card, strip of paper, etc. marked and attached to an object to indicate its nature, contents, ownership, destination, etc. **3.** a descriptive word or phrase applied to a person, group, theory, etc. as a convenient generalized classification ☆**4.** an identifying brand of a company, as of a phonograph recording company **5.** *Archit.* a projecting molding over a door, window, etc.; dripstone **6.** *Heraldry* a horizontal bar with several dependent points on the coat of arms of an eldest son —*vt.* **-beled** or **-belled, -bel·ing** or **-bel·ling** **1.** to attach a label to; mark with a label **2.** to classify as; call; describe **3.** *a)* to differentiate (an element, atom, etc.) by introducing a radioactive isotope or an isotope of unusual mass that may be readily traced through a complex process *b)* to incorporate a labeled element into (a molecule, compound, material, etc.) —**la′bel·er, la′bel·ler** *n.*

la·bel·lum (lə bel′əm) *n., pl.* **-bel′la** (-ə) [ModL. < L., dim. of *labrum*, a lip] the lip, or lowest of the three petals forming the corolla, of an orchid, usually larger than the other two petals, and often spurred

la·bi·a (lā′bē ə) *n. pl. of* LABIUM

la·bi·al (-əl) *adj.* [ML. *labialis* < L. *labium*, a LIP] **1.** of the labia, or lips **2.** *Phonet.* formed mainly with the lips: said esp. of *b, m,* and *p* —*n.* **1.** an organ pipe whose tone is produced by the action of an air current against a liplike edge **2.** a labial sound —**la′bi·al·ly** *adv.*

la·bi·al·ism (-əl iz'm) *n.* **1.** the quality of being labial **2.** the tendency to labialize sounds; esp., a speech defect in which (w) is used for (r) or (l)

la·bi·al·ize (-iz′) *vt.* **-ized′, -iz′ing** [LABIAL + -IZE] *Phonet.* **1.** to pronounce by using the lips, sometimes excessively, as in sounding initial *w* **2.** to round (a vowel) —**la′bi·al·i·za′tion** *n.*

labia ma·jo·ra (mə jôr′ə) [ModL., lit., greater lips] the outer folds of skin of the vulva, one on either side

labia mi·no·ra (mi nôr′ə) [ModL., lit., lesser lips] the two folds of mucous membrane within the labia majora

la·bi·ate (lā′bē āt′, -it) *adj.* [ModL. *labiatus* < L. *labium*, a lip: see LIP] **1.** formed or functioning like a lip **2.** having a lip or lips; lipped **3.** *Bot. a)* having the calyx or corolla so divided that one part overlaps the other like a lip *b)* of or pertaining to the mint family —*n.* a plant of the mint family

la·bile (lā′b'l, -bil) *adj.* [L. *labilis* < *labi*, to slip, fall: see LAP¹] liable to change; unstable *[labile* chemical compounds] —**la·bil·i·ty** (lā bil′ə tē) *n.*

la·bi·o- (lā′bē ō, -ə) [< L. *labium*, LIP] *a combining form meaning* the lips, the lips and *[labiodental]*

la·bi·o·den·tal (lā′bē ō den′t'l) *adj.* [prec. + DENTAL] *Phonet.* formed by placing the lower lip against the upper teeth and forcing the breath through them, as the sounds of *f* and *v* —*n.* a labiodental sound

la·bi·o·na·sal (-nā′z'l) *adj.* [LABIO- + NASAL] *Phonet.* formed with the lips but having nasal resonance, as the sound of *m* —*n.* a labionasal sound

la·bi·o·ve·lar (-vē′lər) *adj.* [LABIO- + VELAR] *Phonet.* formed by rounding and half closing the lips and placing the back of the tongue against or near the velum, or soft palate, as the sound of *w* —*n.* a labiovelar sound

la·bi·um (lā′bē əm) *n., pl.* **-bi·a** (-ə) [L., LIP] a lip or liplike organ; esp., *a) [pl.] same as* LABIA MAJORA or LABIA MINORA *b)* the lower, liplike part of the corolla of certain flowers *c)* the lower lip of an insect, formed by the fusion of the second maxillae

la·bor (lā′bər) *n.* [ME. < OFr. < L., labor, orig., hardship, pain, prob. < base of *labi*, to slip, totter: see LAP¹] **1.** physical or mental exertion; work; toil **2.** a specific task; piece of work **3.** *a)* all wage-earning workers as a group: distinguished from CAPITAL or MANAGEMENT *b)* all manual workers whose work is characterized largely by physical exertion **4.** labor unions collectively **5.** [L-] *same as* LABOR PARTY **6.** the work accomplished by or the role in production of all workers, esp. workers for wages **7.** *Med.* the process or period of childbirth; parturition; esp., the muscular contractions of giving birth —*vi.* [ME. *laboren* < OFr. *laborer* < L. *laborare* < the *n.*] **1.** to work; toil **2.** to work hard; exert oneself to get or do something; strive **3.** *a)* to move slowly and with difficulty *[the car labored* up the hill*] b)* to pitch and roll heavily *[the ship labored* in the rough sea*]* **4.** to be afflicted or burdened with a liability or limitation (with *under) [to labor* under a delusion*]* **5.** to undergo, and suffer the pains of, childbirth —*vt.* [earlier *elabour* < Fr. *élaborer:* see ELABORATE] **1.** to spend too much time and effort on; develop in too great detail *[to labor* a point*]* **2.** to burden; trouble —*SYN.* see WORK

lab·o·ra·to·ry (lab′rə tôr′ē, -ər ə tôr′ē; *Brit.* lə bär′ə tər ē, -e trē) *n., pl.* **-ries** [ML. *laboratorium* < L. *laborare:* see LABOR, *vi.*] **1.** a room or building for scientific experimentation or research **2.** a place for preparing chemicals, drugs, etc. ☆**3.** a place where theories, techniques, and methods, as in education or social studies, are tested, analyzed, demonstrated, etc. —*adj.* of or performed in, or as in, a laboratory

☆**Labor Day** in the U.S. & Canada, the first Monday in September, a legal holiday in honor of labor

---

la·bored (lā′bərd) *adj.* made or done with great effort; not effortless and natural; strained

la·bor·er (lā′bər ər) *n.* [ME. < OFr. *laboreor* < *laborer:* see LABOR] 1. a person who labors; esp., a wage-earning worker whose work is characterized largely by physical exertion 2. an unskilled workman who brings materials to, and does preparatory work for, skilled workers in a trade /mason's *laborer*/

la·bo·ri·ous (lə bô′rē əs) *adj.* [ME. < OFr. *laborios* < L. *laboriosus* < *labor*, LABOR] 1. involving or calling for much hard work; difficult 2. industrious; hard-working —*SYN.* see HARD —**la·bo′ri·ous·ly** *adv.* —**la·bo′ri·ous·ness** *n.*

☆**la·bor·ite** (lā′bə rīt′) *n.* 1. a member or supporter of a labor party 2. [L-] a member or supporter of the British Labor Party: Brit. sp. **La′bour·ite′**

labor of love [see I Thess. 1:3] work done for personal satisfaction or altruistic reasons rather than for material gain

labor party 1. a political party organized to protect and further the rights of workers, or one dominated by organized labor 2. [L- P-] such a party in Great Britain: Brit. sp. **Labour Party**

la·bor-sav·ing (-sā′viŋ) *adj.* eliminating or lessening physical labor [*labor-saving* appliances]

☆**labor union** an association of workers to promote and protect the welfare, interests, and rights of its members, primarily by collective bargaining

la·bour (lā′bər) *n.*, *vt.*, *vi.* Brit. sp. of LABOR

la·bra (lā′brə, lab′rə) *n. pl. of* LABRUM

Lab·ra·dor (lab′rə dôr′) 1. region along the Atlantic coast of NE Canada, constituting the mainland part of the province of Newfoundland: 112,826 sq. mi. 2. large peninsula between the Atlantic & Hudson Bay, containing Quebec & Labrador (sense 1)

Labrador Current icy arctic current flowing south from Baffin Bay past Labrador & Newfoundland into the Gulf Stream

lab·ra·dor·ite (lab′rə dôr īt′) *n.* [after LABRADOR, where specimens have been found] a variety of plagioclase feldspar often showing a play of colors

Labrador retriever any of a breed of medium-sized hunting dog used in retrieving game, having a black, brown, or yellow coat of short, thick hair

la·bret (lā′bret) *n.* [dim. of L. *labrum*, LIP] an ornament of wood, bone, etc. worn, as by some S. American Indians, in a hole pierced through the lip

lab·roid (lab′roid, lā′broid) *adj.* [< ModL. *Labroidea*, name of the family < *Labrus*, type genus < L. *labrus*, kind of fish] belonging to a suborder (*Pharyngognathi*) of sea fishes, including the wrasses and parrot fishes, with well-developed pharyngeal teeth —*n.* a labroid fish

la·brum (lā′brəm, lab′rəm) *n.*, *pl.* **la′bra** (-brə, -rə) [ModL. < L., LIP] a lip or liplike edge; esp., the upper or front lip of insects and other arthropods

La Bru·yère (lá brü yer′), **Jean de** (zhän də) 1645-96; Fr. essayist & moralist

La·bu·an (lä′boo än′) island of Sabah, Malaysia, off the NW coast of Borneo: 35 sq. mi.

la·bur·num (lə bur′nəm) *n.* [ModL. < L.] any of a genus (*Laburnum*) of small, poisonous trees and shrubs of the legume family, with three-part leaves and drooping racemes of yellow flowers

lab·y·rinth (lab′ə rinth′) *n.* [ME. *laborintus* (altered by folk etym. after L. *labor*, LABOR + *intus*, into) < L. *labyrinthus* < Gr. *labyrinthos*] 1. a structure containing an intricate network of winding passages hard to follow without losing one's way; maze; specif., [L-] *Gr. Myth.* such a structure built by Daedalus for King Minos of Crete, to house the Minotaur 2. a complicated, perplexing arrangement, course of affairs, etc. 3. *Anat.* the inner ear: see EAR[1]

LABYRINTH

lab·y·rin·thine (lab′ə rin′thin, -thēn) *adj.* 1. of or constituting a labyrinth 2. like a labyrinth; intricate; complicated; puzzling Also **lab′·y·rin′thi·an** (-thē ən), **lab′y·rin′thic**

lac (lak) *n.* [Hindi *lākh* < Sans. *lākṣā*, var. of *rākṣā*, prob. < IE. base *reg-*, to color (whence Gr. *regma*, colored material); in part via Fr. *laque* < OPr. *laca* < Ar. *lakk* < Per. *lak*, of same orig.] 1. a resinous substance secreted on certain trees in S Asia by various scale insects, esp. a species (*Laccifer laca*) of India: when melted, strained, and rehardened, it forms shellac 2. *same as* LAKH

Lac·ca·dive, Min·i·coy, and A·min·di·vi Islands (lak′ə div′ min′i koi′ ənd äm′ən dē′vē) territory of India, made up of a number of islands in the Arabian Sea, off the Malabar Coast: 11 sq. mi.; pop. 24,000

lac·co·lith (lak′ə lith) *n.* [< Gr. *lakkos*, a cistern + -LITH] an irregular body of igneous rock intruded between the layers of sedimentary rock so as to cause them to bulge upward

lace (lās) *n.* [ME. *las* < OFr. < L. *laqueus*, a noose, snare, trap < IE. base *lēk-*, whence OE. *læla*, a whip] 1. a string, ribbon, etc. used to draw together and fasten the parts of a shoe, corset, etc. by being drawn through eyelets or over hooks 2. an ornamental braid of gold or silver, for trimming uniforms, hats, etc. 3. a fine netting or openwork fabric of linen, cotton, silk, etc., woven in ornamental designs —*vt.* **laced, lac′ing** 1. to draw the ends of (a garment, shoe, etc.) together and fasten with a lace 2. to compress the waist of by lacing a corset, etc. (often with *up*) 3. to pass (a cord, etc.) in and out *through* eyelets, fabric, etc. 4. to weave together; intertwine 5. to ornament with or as with lace 6. *a*) to streak, as with color *b*) to diversify, as with a contrasting element 7. to thrash; whip 8. to add a dash of alcoholic liquor to (a beverage) —*vi.* 1. to be fastened with a lace [these shoes *lace*] 2. [Colloq.] to attack physically or verbally (with *into*)

Lac·e·dae·mon (las′ə dē′mən) *same as* SPARTA —**Lac′·e·dae·mo′ni·an** (-di mō′nē ən) *adj.*, *n.*

lac·er·ate (las′ə rāt′; *also, for adj.*, -ər it) *vt.* **-at′ed, -at′ing** [< L. *laceratus*, pp. of *lacerare*, to tear < *lacer*, lacerated < IE. base *lēk-*, to tear, whence Gr. *lakis*, a tatter] 1. to tear jaggedly; mangle (something soft, as flesh) 2. to wound or hurt (one's feelings, etc.) deeply; distress —*adj.* 1. torn; mangled 2. *Bot.* having jagged edges —**lac′er·a·ble** (-ər ə b′l) *adj.*

lac·er·a·tion (las′ə rā′shən) *n.* [L. *laceratio*] 1. the act of lacerating 2. the result of lacerating; jagged tear or wound

La·cer·ta (lə sur′tə) [L.: see LIZARD] a N constellation in the Milky Way, between Cygnus and Andromeda

la·cer·til·i·an (las′ər til′ē ən) *adj.*, *n.* [< ModL. *Lacertilia*, name of the division < L. *lacertus, lacerta* (see LIZARD) + -IAN] *same as* SAURIAN

lace·wing (lās′wiŋ′) *n.* any of a large group of insects (esp. order Neuroptera) with four delicate, gauzy wings: the larvae feed on aphids and other insect pests

lace·work (-wurk′) *n.* lace, or any openwork decoration like lace

La·chaise (lá shez′), **Gas·ton** (gás tōn′) 1882-1935; U.S. sculptor, born in France

lach·es (lach′iz) *n.* [ME. *lachesse* < OFr. *laschesse* < *lasche*, lax, negligent < VL. *lascus*, metathetic for L. *laxus*, LAX] *Law* failure to do the required thing at the proper time (e.g., inexcusable delay in enforcing a claim)

Lach·e·sis (lak′ə sis) [L. < Gr. *lachesis*, lit., lot < *lanchanein*, to obtain by lot or fate, happen] *Gr. & Rom. Myth.* that one of the three Fates who determines the length of the thread of life

La·chine (lə shēn′) city in S Quebec, Canada, on Montreal Island: pop. 43,000

lach·ry·mal (lak′rə məl) *adj.* [ML. *lacrimalis* < L. *lacrima*, TEAR[2]] 1. of, characterized by, or producing tears 2. *same as* LACRIMAL (sense 1) —*n. same as* LACHRYMATORY

lach·ry·ma·tor (lak′rə māt′ər) *n.* [< L. *lacrima*, TEAR[2] + -ATOR] a substance that irritates the eyes and produces tears, as tear gas

lach·ry·ma·to·ry (-mə tôr′ē) *n.*, *pl.* **-ries** [ML. *lacrimatorium*, neut. of *lacrimatorius*, of tears < L. *lacrima*, TEAR[2]] any of various small vases found in ancient Roman sepulchers, formerly supposed to have been used to catch the tears of mourners —*adj.* of, causing, or producing tears

lach·ry·mose (-mōs′) *adj.* [L. *lacrimosus* < *lacrima*, TEAR[2]] 1. inclined to shed many tears; tearful 2. causing tears; sad —**lach′ry·mose′ly** *adv.*

lac·i·ly (lās′ə lē) *adv.* in a lacy manner or pattern

lac·i·ness (-ē nis) *n.* a lacy quality or state

lac·ing (-iŋ) *n.* 1. the act of a person who laces 2. a thrashing; beating 3. a cord or lace, as a shoelace 4. gold or silver braid used to trim a uniform, etc.

la·cin·i·ate (lə sin′ē āt′, -it) *adj.* [< L. *lacinia*, a flap (akin to *lacer*: see LACERATE) + -ATE[1]] 1. having a fringe; fringed 2. *Bot.* cut deeply into narrow, jagged segments Also **la·cin′i·at′ed** —**la·cin′i·a′tion** *n.*

lack (lak) *n.* [early ME. *lac* < or akin to MLowG., MDu. *lak*, lack: for IE. base see LEAK] 1. the fact or condition of not having enough; shortage; deficiency 2. the fact or condition of not having any; complete absence 3. the thing that is lacking or needed —*vi.* [ME. *lacen* < MDu. *laken*, to be wanting] 1. to be wanting or missing; show a deficiency 2. *a*) to be short (with *in, for,* or, now rarely, *of*) *b*) to be in need —*vt.* 1. to be deficient in or entirely without 2. to fall short by [*lacking* one ounce of being a pound] 3. [Obs.] to need; require

SYN.—**lack** implies an absence or insufficiency of something essential or desired [she *lacks* experience]; **want** (in this sense, chiefly British) and **need** stress the urgency of supplying what is lacking [this matter *needs*, or *wants*, immediate attention]; **require** emphasizes even more strongly imperative need, connoting that what is needed is indispensable [his work *requires* great powers of concentration] —*ANT.* have, possess

lack- (lak) *a combining form meaning* lacking [lackluster]

lack·a·dai·si·cal (lak′ə dā′zi k′l) *adj.* [< *lackadaisy*, altered (after DAISY) < ff.] showing lack of interest or spirit; listless; languid —**lack′a·dai′si·cal·ly** *adv.*

lack·a·day (lak′ə dā′) *interj.* [contr. < ALACKADAY] [Archaic] an exclamation of regret, sorrow, pity, etc.

lack·ey (lak′ē) *n.*, *pl.* **-eys** [Fr. *laquais*, a lackey, soldier < Sp. *lacayo*, lackey, footman < ? Ar. *al-kaid*, the captain] 1. a male servant of low rank, usually in some sort of livery or uniform 2. a follower who carries out another's orders like a servant; toady —*vt.*, *vi.* **-eyed, -ey·ing** [Now Rare] to serve as a lackey

lack·lus·ter (lak′lus′tər) *adj.* lacking brightness; dull *[lackluster eyes]* —*n.* [Rare] absence of brightness; dullness Also, chiefly Brit. sp., **lack′lus′tre**

La·co·ni·a (lə kō′nē ə) province on the S coast of the Peloponnesus, Greece: 1,388 sq. mi.; pop. 119,000: in ancient times, a region dominated by the city of Sparta See GREECE, map —**La·co′ni·an** *adj., n.*

la·con·ic (lə kän′ik) *adj.* [L. *Laconicus* < Gr. *Lakōnikos*, Laconian < *Lakōn*, a Laconian, Spartan] brief or terse in speech or expression; using few words —*SYN.* see CONCISE —**la·con′i·cal·ly** *adv.*

lac·o·nism (lak′ə niz′m) *n.* [Gr. *Lakōnismos* < *Lakō nizein*, to imitate the Laconians] **1.** brevity of speech or expression **2.** a laconic speech or expression Also **la·con·i·cism** (lə kän′ə siz′m)

La Co·ru·ña (lä′ kô rōō′nyä) seaport in NW Spain, on the Atlantic: pop. 182,000

lac·quer (lak′ər) *n.* [Fr. *laquer*, earlier *lacre* < Port. < *laca*, gum lac < Hind. *lākh:* see LAC] **1.** a coating substance consisting of resinous materials, as cellulose esters or ethers, shellac, or gum or alkyd resins, dissolved in ethyl alcohol or other solvent that evaporates rapidly on application leaving a tough, adherent film: pigments are often added to form **lacquer enamels 2.** a resinous varnish obtained from certain trees in China and Japan (esp. *Toxicodendron verniciflua*) of the cashew family, used to give a hard, smooth, highly polished finish to wood **3.** a decorative article or articles made of wood and coated with this lacquer: in full **lac′quer·ware′, lac′quer·work′** —*vt.* to coat with or as with lacquer —**lac′quer·er** *n.*

lac·quey (lak′ē) *n., vt., vi. obs. var. of* LACKEY

lac·ri·mal (lak′rə məl) *adj.* **1.** *Anat.* designating, of, or near the glands that secrete tears **2.** *same as* LACHRYMAL (sense 1)

lac·ri·ma·tion (lak′rə mā′shən) *n.* [L. *lacrimatio*, a weeping < pp. of *lacrimare*, to weep < *lacrima*, a tear (cf. LACHRYMAL] normal or excessive secretion or shedding of tears

lac·ri·ma·tor (lak′rə māt′ər) *n. same as* LACHRYMATOR

lac·ri·ma·to·ry (mə tôr′ē) *adj., n., pl.* **-ries** *same as* LACHRYMATORY

☆**la·crosse** (lə krôs′, -kräs′) *n.* [CanadFr. < Fr. *la*, the + *crosse*, a crutch, hockey stick, CROSS] a ball game in which two teams of ten men each, using long-handled, pouched rackets, try to advance a small rubber ball across the field into the opponents' goal: the game was first played by N. American Indians

La Crosse (lə krôs′, kräs′) [< prec.] city in W Wis., on the Mississippi: pop. 51,000

lact- *same as* LACTO-: used before a vowel

lac·tam (lak′tam) *n.* [LACT(ONE) + AM(INO)] any of a group of organic cyclic compounds containing the –NHCO– group in the ring, formed by the elimination of water from the amino and carboxyl groups; inner anhydride of an amino acid

LACROSSE

lac·ta·ry (lak′tə rē) *adj.* [L. *lactarius* < *lac* (gen. *lactis*), milk: see LACTO-] [Rare] of or pertaining to milk

lac·tase (lak′tās) *n.* [LACT- + (DIAST)ASE] an enzyme, present in certain yeasts and in the intestines of animals, which splits lactose into glucose and galactose

lac·tate (-tāt) *vi.* **-tat·ed, -tat·ing** [< L. *lactatus*, pp. of *lactare*, secrete milk, suckle < *lac* (see LACTO-)] to secrete milk —*n.* any salt or ester of lactic acid

lac·ta·tion (lak tā′shən) *n.* [LL. *lactatio*: see prec.] **1.** the secretion of milk by a mammary gland **2.** the period during which milk is secreted **3.** the suckling of young —**lac·ta′tion·al** *adj.*

lac·te·al (lak′tē əl) *adj.* [< L. *lacteus*, milky < *lac* (gen. LACTO-) + -AL] **1.** of or like milk; milky **2.** containing or carrying chyle, the milky fluid that is a product of digestion —*n.* any of the lymphatic vessels that take up this fluid from the small intestine and carry it to the thoracic duct

lac·tes·cent (lak tes′'nt) *adj.* [L. *lactescens*, prp. of *lactescere*, to turn into milk < *lactare:* see LACTATE] **1.** becoming milky **2.** of a milky appearance **3.** *a)* secreting milk *b)* forming or exuding a milky fluid: said of certain plants —**lac·tes′cence** *n.*

lac·tic (lak′tik) *adj.* [Fr. *lactique:* see LACTO- + -IC] of or obtained from milk

lactic acid a yellowish or clear, syrupy organic acid, C₃H₆O₃, produced by the fermentation of lactose when milk sours or from sucrose and some other carbohydrates by the action of certain microorganisms, and used in tanning leather, as a preservative, in the formation of plasticizers, etc.

lac·tif·er·ous (lak tif′ər əs) *adj.* [LL. *lactifer* < L. *lac* (see ff.) + *ferre*, to BEAR¹ + -OUS] **1.** yielding or conveying milk **2.** forming a milky fluid

lac·to- (lak′tō, -tə) [< L. *lac* (gen. *lactis*), milk < IE. base *glak-:* cf. GALACTIC] *a combining form meaning:* **1.** milk *[lactometer]* **2.** *Chem.* lactic acid or lactate *[lactobacillus, lactone]*

lac·to·ba·cil·lus (lak′tō bə sil′əs) *n., pl.* **-cil′li** (-ī) [ModL. < prec. + BACILLUS] any of a genus (*Lactobacillus*) of bacteria that ferment milk, carbohydrates, etc., producing lactic acid and carbon dioxide

lac·to·fla·vin (-flā′vin) *n.* [LACTO- + FLAVIN] *same as* RIBOFLAVIN

lac·to·gen·ic (-jen′ik) *adj.* [LACTO- + -GENIC] capable of inducing milk secretion *[lactogenic hormone]*

lac·tom·e·ter (lak täm′ə tər) *n.* [LACTO- + -METER] a hydrometer for determining the specific gravity, and hence the richness, of milk

lac·tone (lak′tōn) *n.* [LACT- + -ONE] any of a group of organic cyclic esters formed by the elimination of a molecule of water from the –OH and –COOH groups of a molecule of a hydroxy acid

lac·to·pro·te·in (lak′tō prō′tēn, -prōt′ē in) *n.* [LACTO- + PROTEIN] any of the proteins found in milk

lac·tose (lak′tōs) *n.* [LACT- + -OSE¹] a white, crystalline sugar, C₁₂H₂₂O₁₁, found in milk and prepared by evaporation of the whey and the subsequent crystallization of the sugar: used in infant foods, medicine, etc.

la·cu·na (lə kyoo′nə) *n., pl.* **-nas, -nae** (-nē) [L., a ditch, hole, pool < *lacus:* see LAKE¹] **1.** a space where something has been omitted or has come out; gap; hiatus; esp., a missing portion in a manuscript, text, etc. **2.** *Anat., Biol.* a space, cavity, or depression; specif., any of the very small cavities in bone that are filled with bone cells —**la·cu′nar** (-nər) *adj.* of or having a lacuna or lacunae: also **la·cu′nal** —*n., pl.* **la·cu′nars, lac·u·nar·i·a** (lak′yoo ner′ē ə) [L. < *lacuna:* see LACUNA] *Archit.* **1.** a ceiling made up of sunken panels **2.** a sunken panel in such a ceiling

la·cu·nose (-nōs) *adj.* [L. *lacunosus*] full of lacunae

la·cus·trine (lə kus′trin) *adj.* [< Fr. *lacustre* < L. *lacus*, LAKE¹] **1.** of or having to do with a lake or lakes **2.** found or formed in lakes

lac·y (lā′sē) *adj.* **lac′i·er, lac′i·est 1.** of lace **2.** like lace; having a delicate open pattern

lad (lad) *n.* [ME. *ladde* < ?] **1.** a boy or youth **2.** [Colloq.] any man; fellow: familiar or endearing term

lad·a·num (lad′ə nəm) *n.* [L.] *same as* LABDANUM

lad·der (lad′ər) *n.* [ME. < OE. *hlæder*, akin to G. *leiter* < IE. base *klei-*, to incline, lean, whence LEAN¹, L. *-clinare* (cf. INCLINE)] **1.** a framework consisting of two parallel sidepieces connected by a series of rungs or crosspieces on which a person steps in climbing up or down **2.** anything by means of which a person climbs or rises *[the ladder of success]* **3.** a rising series of steps, stages, or levels **4.** [Chiefly Brit.] a run as in a stocking —*vt., vi.* [Chiefly Brit.] to have or cause to have a ladder, or run

lad·der-back chair (lad′ər bak′) a chair with a back of two upright posts connected by horizontal slats

ladder stitch an embroidery stitch with parallel crossbars in a ladderlike design

lad·die (lad′ē) *n.* [Scot., dim. of LAD] [Chiefly Scot.] a young lad

la·dle (lād′'l) *vt., vi.* **la′dled, la′dled** or **lad′en, lad′ing** [ME. *laden* < OE. *hladan*, akin to G. *laden* < IE. base *klā-*, to set down, lay, place, whence OSlav. *klasti*, to load & LADLE] **1.** to load **2.** to dip or draw out (water, etc.) with a ladle; bail; ladle

lad·en¹ (lād′'n) *alt. pp. of* LADE —*adj.* **1.** loaded **2.** burdened; afflicted *[laden with sorrow]*

lad·en² (-'n) *vi.* [Rare] *same as* LADE

la·di·da (lä′dē dä′) *adj.* [imitation of affected speech] [Colloq.] affected in speech, manners, etc.; pretentiously refined —*n.* [Colloq.] **1.** a la-di-da person **2.** affected speech or behavior —*interj.* an exclamation of derision at affectation, foppishness, etc. Also sp. **la′-de-da′**

☆**Ladies' Day** a special day on which women may attend a certain event, as a baseball game, free or at reduced cost

la·dies'-tress·es (lā′dēz tres′iz) *n.* any of a genus (*Spiranthes*) of wild orchids with small, white flowers arranged spirally on spikes

La·din (lə dēn′) *n.* [Rhaeto-Romanic < L. *Latinus*, Latin] **1.** the dialect of Rhaeto-Romanic spoken in the S Tirol **2.** a native speaker of this dialect

lad·ing (lā′diŋ) *n.* [LME.: see LADE] **1.** the act of one that lades **2.** a load; cargo; freight

La·di·no (lə dē′nō) *n.* [Sp., wise, cunning, learned, lit., Latin < L. *Latinus*] **1.** a Spanish dialect with some elements of Hebrew spoken by Sephardic Jews in Turkey and some other Mediterranean countries **2.** *pl.* **-nos** in Spanish America, a person of mixed ancestry

la·di·no (lə dē′nō, -dī′-) *n.* [prob. < It. *Ladino*, of the Ladin-speaking area of the Tirol and Grisons < L. *Latinus*, LATIN] a large, vigorous strain of the white clover, often grown as a forage crop

la·dle (lā′d'l) *n.* [ME. *ladel* < OE. *hlædel*, a ladle: see LADE] **1.** a long-handled, cuplike spoon for dipping out liquids **2.** any similar device, as a large container for carrying and pouring molten metal —*vt.* **-dled, -dling**

---

fat, āpe, cär; ten, ēven; is, bīte; gō, hôrn, tōōl, look; oil, out; up, fur; get; joy; yet; chin; she; thin, *th*en; zh, leisure; ŋ, ring; ə for *a* in *ago*, *e* in *agent*, *i* in *sanity*, *o* in *comply*, *u* in *focus*; ′ as in *able* (ā′b'l); Fr. bāl; ë, Fr. coeur; ö, Fr. feu; Fr. mon; ð, Fr. coq; ü, Fr. duc; r, Fr. cri; H, G. ich; kh, G. doch. See inside front cover. ☆ Americanism; ‡foreign; *hypothetical; < derived from

1. to dip out with or as with a ladle **2.** to lift out and carry in a ladle —**la′dle·ful′** *n.*, *pl.* **-fuls′**

La·do·ga (lä′dô gä), Lake lake in NW R.S.F.S.R., near the border of Finland: c. 7,000 sq. mi.

la·drone (lə drōn′) *n.* [Sp. *ladrón* < L. *latro*, hired servant, mercenary, freebooter: see LARCENY] a robber or bandit in Spanish-speaking regions

la·dy (lā′dē) *n.*, *pl.* **-dies** [ME. *lavedi* < OE. *hlæfdige*, lady, mistress < *hlaf*, LOAF[1] + *-dige* < base of *dæge*, (bread) kneader: see DOUGH] **1.** the mistress of a household: now obsolete except in the phrase **the lady of the house 2.** a woman who has the rights, rule, or authority of a lord **3.** *a)* a woman of high social position *b)* a woman who is polite, refined, and well-mannered **4.** any woman: a polite or formal term, now generally avoided except in addressing a group of women **5.** [Old-fashioned] a woman with reference to the man who is her devoted attendant, lover, etc. **6.** [L-] the Virgin Mary (usually with *Our*) **7.** [L-] in Great Britain, the title of respect given to a marchioness, countess, viscountess, or baroness, to the daughter of a duke, marquis, or earl, or to the wife of a baronet, knight, or holder of a courtesy title of *Lord* —*adj.* female *[a lady barber]* —*SYN.* see WOMAN

la·dy·bird (**beetle**) (-bʉrd′) [short for *Our Lady's bird*: see LADY, *n.* 6] *same as* LADYBUG: also **lady beetle**

Lady Bountiful [after a character in Farquhar's comedy *The Beaux' Stratagem* (1707)] a charitable woman, esp. one who gives ostentatiously

la·dy·bug (-bug′) *n.* any of certain small, roundish beetles (family Coccinellidae) with spotted backs, usually brightly colored: both larvae and adults feed chiefly on insect pests and their eggs

Lady chapel a chapel, as in a cathedral or parish church, dedicated to the Virgin Mary: it is usually built east of the high altar

Lady Day *Brit.* name for ANNUNCIATION (sense 3 *b*)

la·dy·fin·ger (-fiŋ′gər) *n.* a small spongecake shaped somewhat like a finger

la·dy·fish (-fish′) *n.*, *pl.* **-fish′**, **-fish′es**: see FISH[2] any of several unrelated fishes; esp., a kind of tarpon (*Elops saurus*) occurring in tropical seas

la·dy-in-wait·ing (-in wāt′iŋ) *n.*, *pl.* **la′dies-in-wait′ing** a woman attending, or waiting upon, a queen or princess

la·dy-kill·er (-kil′ər) *n.* [Old Slang] a man to whom women are supposed to be irresistibly attracted

la·dy·kin (-kin) *n.* [LADY + -KIN] a little lady

la·dy·like (-līk′) *adj.* like, characteristic of, or suitable for a lady; refined; well-bred —*SYN.* see FEMALE

la·dy·love (-luv′) *n.* a sweetheart

Lady of the Lake *Arthurian Legend* Vivian, mistress of Merlin: she lived in a castle surrounded by a lake

la·dy·ship (lā′dē ship′) *n.* the rank or position of a lady: used in speaking to or of a woman having the title of *Lady*, always preceded by *your* or *her*

la·dy-slip·per (-slip′ər) *n.* **1.** *same as* CYPRIPEDIUM **2.** any of various cultivated orchids whose flowers somewhat resemble a slipper Also **la′dy's-slip′per**

lady's (or ladies') man a man very fond of the company of women and very attentive to them

la·dy's-smock (lā′dēz smäk′) *n. same as* CUCKOOFLOWER (sense 1)

la·dy's-thumb (-thum′) *n.* an annual plant (*Polygonum persicaria*) of the buckwheat family, with dense spikes of pinkish or purplish flowers

la·dy's-tress·es (-tres′iz) *n. same as* LADIES′-TRESSES

LADY-SLIPPER

lae·o·trop·ic (lē′ə träp′ik) *adj.* [< Gr. *laios*, left (see LEVO-) + -TROPIC] turning from right to left, as the whorls in some gastropod shells

La·er·tes (lā ʉr′tēz) [L. < Gr. *Laertēs*] **1.** *Gr. Myth.* the father of Odysseus **2.** in Shakespeare's *Hamlet*, the brother of Ophelia

lae·vo- (lē′vō, -və) *same as* LEVO-

La Farge (lə färzh′, färj′), **John** 1835-1910; U.S. artist & writer

La·fa·yette (laf′i yet′, lä′fi-; *for 2, also* lə fā′it) [after ff.] **1.** city in W Ind.: pop. 45,000 **2.** city in SC La.: pop. 69,000

La·fa·yette (lä′fi yet′, laf′i ā′), marquis **de** (born *Marie Joseph Paul Yves Roch Gilbert du Motier*) 1757-1834; Fr. general & statesman: served as a volunteer (1777-81) in the Continental army in the American Revolution

La·fitte (là fēt′), **Jean** (zhän) 1780?-1826?; Fr. pirate in the Gulf of Mexico: also sp. **Laf·fite′**

La Fol·lette (lə fäl′it), **Robert Marion** 1855-1925; U.S. legislator, reformer, & Progressive Party leader

La Fon·taine (lä fōn ten′, *E.* lə fän tān′), **Jean de** (zhän də) 1621-95; Fr. poet & writer of fables

lag[1] (lag) *vi.* **lagged, lag′ging** [? akin to MDan. *lakke*, to go slowly] **1.** *a)* to fall, move, or stay behind; loiter; linger *b)* to move or develop more slowly than expected, desired, etc.; be retarded in motion, development, etc. **2.** to become gradually less intense, strong, etc.; wane; flag **3.** to toss one's shooting marble, or taw, toward a line marked on the ground (**lag line**) for deciding the order of play **4.** *Billiards* to strike the cue ball so that it rebounds from the far rail to

stop as close as possible to the near rail or the string line: done to decide the order of play —*n.* **1.** a falling behind or being retarded in motion, development, etc. **2.** the amount of such falling behind; interval between two related events, processes, etc. *[the lag of peak current behind peak voltage]* **3.** a lagging, as in billiards and marbles **4.** [Now Rare] one that lags, or is last

lag[2] (lag) *n.* [prob. < Scand., as in Sw. *lagg*, barrel stave < IE. base *leu-*, to cut off, whence L. *luere*, to cleanse, purge] **1.** a barrel stave **2.** any of the narrow strips of insulating material used for covering boilers, cylinders, etc. —*vt.* **lagged, lag′ging** to cover with lags

lag[3] (lag) *vt.* **lagged, lag′ging** [< ?] [Chiefly Brit. Colloq.] **1.** to put in jail or transport as a criminal **2.** to arrest. —*n.* [Chiefly Brit. Colloq.] **1.** a person transported or sentenced to penal servitude; convict **2.** a term of transportation or penal servitude

lag·an (lag′ən) *n.* [< OFr., goods washed up by the sea < ? base of ON. *leggja*, to lie] *Maritime Law* goods cast overboard, as in a storm, but with a buoy attached to identify the owner

lag bolt *same as* LAG SCREW

Lag b'O·mer (läg′ bô′mər) [Heb. *lag b'ōmer*, 33d (day) of the omer (the count of 49 days from the second day of Passover to the first day of Shabuoth)] a Jewish holiday observed on the 18th day of Iyar

☆**la·ger** (**beer**) (lä′gər) [G. *lagerbier*, lit., store beer < *lager*, storehouse (cf. LAIR) + *bier*, BEER] a beer which is stored for several months for aging and clarification after it has been brewed

La·ger·kvist (lä′gər kvist′), **Pär** (**Fabian**) (par) 1891- ; Swed. poet, novelist, & playwright

La·ger·löf (lä′gər löf′), **Selma** (**Ottiliana Lovisa**) (sel′mä) 1858-1940; Swed. novelist

lag·gard (lag′ərd) *n.* [< LAG[1] + -ARD] a slow person, esp. one who is always falling behind; loiterer —*adj.* slow or late in doing things; falling behind —**lag′gard·ly** *adv.*, *adj.* —**lag′gard·ness** *n.*

lag·ger (lag′ər) *n.* a person or thing that lags

lag·ging (lag′iŋ) *n.* [< LAG[2] + -ING] **1.** strips of wood or other nonconducting material for covering a boiler, cylinder, wall, etc. **2.** the act of covering with lags **3.** an open frame woodwork to support an arch while it is being built **4.** *Mining* planks or timber used to prevent rocks from falling in a shaft or drift

☆**la·gniappe, la·gnappe** (lan yap′, lan′yap) *n.* [Creole < Fr. *la*, the + Sp. *ñapa*, lagniappe < Peruv. (Quechuan) *yapa*] **1.** [Chiefly South] a small present given to a customer with a purchase **2.** a gratuity or the like

lag·o·morph (lag′ə môrf′) *n.* [< Gr. *lagos*, hare + -MORPH] any of an order (Lagomorpha) of plant-eating mammals characterized by a short tail and two pairs of upper incisors, one behind the other, as the rabbits, hares, and pikas —**lag′o·mor′phic** *adj.*

la·goon (lə gōōn′) *n.* [< Fr. *lagune* & It. *laguna* < L. *lacuna*: see LACUNA] **1.** a shallow lake or pond, esp. one connected with a larger body of water **2.** the area of water enclosed by a circular coral reef, or atoll **3.** an area of shallow salt water separated from the sea by sand dunes

La·gos (lä′gäs, -gəs) capital of Nigeria; seaport on the Bight of Benin: pop. 450,000

La·grange (lä gränzh′), comte **Jo·seph Louis** (zhô zef′ lwē′) 1736-1814; Fr. mathematician & astronomer

lag screw a wood screw with a boltlike head

La Guar·di·a (lə gwär′dē ə), **Fi·o·rel·lo H**(enry) (fē′ə rel′ō) 1882-1947; U.S. lawyer & political leader

La Ha·bra (lä hä′brə, lə) [Sp., lit., the pass, or defile] city in SW Calif.: suburb of Los Angeles: pop. 41,000

lah-di-dah, lah-de-dah (lä′dē dä′) *adj.*, *n.*, *interj.* same *as* LA-DI-DA

La·hore (lə hôr′, lä-) capital of West Pakistan, in the NE part: pop. 1,296,000

Lah·ti (lä′tē) city in S Finland: pop. 83,000

lai·bach (lī′bäkh) *Ger.* name of LJUBLJANA

la·ic (lā′ik) *adj.* [LL.(Ec.) *laicus*, not priestly < Gr. *laikos* < *laos*, the people] of the laity; secular; lay: also **la′i·cal** —*n.* a layman

la·i·cism (lā′ə siz'm) *n.* policy and principles opposing clericalism and restricting political influence and power to the laity

la·i·cize (-sīz′) *vt.* **-cized′, -ciz′ing** [LAIC + -IZE] to remove clerical influence from; restrict to laymen; secularize —**la′i·ci·za′tion** *n.*

laid (lād) *pt.* & *pp.* of LAY[1]

laid paper paper having evenly spaced parallel lines watermarked in it

laigh (lākh) *adj.*, *adv.* [Scot.] low

lain (lān) *pp.* of LIE[1]

lair (ler) *n.* [ME. *leir* < OE. *leger*, lit., lying place, hence bed, couch < Gmc. base (*leg-*) of *licgan*, to LIE[1]] a bed or resting place of a wild animal; den —*vi.* to go to, rest in, or have a lair

laird (lerd; *Scot.* lārd) *n.* [Scot. form of LORD] in Scotland, a landowner, esp. a wealthy one —**laird′ly** *adj.*

lais·sez faire (les′ā fer′, lez′-) [Fr., let (people) do (as they please)] the policy or practice of letting people act without interference or direction; noninterference; specif., the policy of letting the owners of industry and business fix the rules of competition, the conditions of labor, etc.

as they please, without governmental regulation or control: also sp. **lais′ser faire′** —**lais′sez-faire′** *adj.*

‡**lais·sez-pas·ser** (le sā pä sā′) *n.* [Fr., lit., let (someone) pass] a pass authorizing access to a place, travel in a country, etc.

la·i·ty (lā′ət ē) *n., pl.* **-ties** [< LAY³] 1. all the people not included among the clergy; laymen collectively 2. all the people not belonging to any given profession

La·ius (lā′yəs) [L. < Gr. *Laios*] *Gr. Myth.* a king of Thebes and the father of Oedipus: see OEDIPUS

lake¹ (lāk) *n.* [ME. < OE. *lacu* & OFr. *lac*, both < L. *lacus*, a basin, lake < IE. base *laku-*, accumulation of water, pond, lake, whence LOCH & OE. *lagu*, water, sea] 1. an inland body of usually fresh water, larger than a pool or pond, generally formed by some obstruction in the course of flowing water 2. a pool of oil or other liquid

lake² (lāk) *n.* [Fr. *laque*: see LAC] 1. *a)* a dark-red pigment prepared from cochineal *b)* its color 2. an insoluble coloring compound precipitated from a solution of a dye by adding a metallic salt, which acts as a mordant: used in the application of certain dyes to cloth, in printing inks, paints, etc.

Lake Charles [after *Charles* Sallier, an early settler] city in SW La.: pop. 78,000

Lake District (or **Country**) lake & mountain region in NW England, in the counties of Cumberland, Westmorland, & Lancashire

lake dwelling a dwelling built on wooden piles rising above the surface of a lake; esp., such a structure built in prehistoric times — **lake dweller**

☆**lake herring** a variety of cisco (*Coregonus artedii*) of the Great Lakes

Lake·land (lāk′land) city in C Fla.: pop. 42,000

Lake of the Woods lake in N Minn. & in Ontario & Manitoba, Canada: 1,485 sq. mi.

LAKE DISTRICT

Lake poets the English poets Wordsworth, Coleridge, and Southey, who lived in the Lake District

☆**lak·er** (lā′kər) *n.* 1. a fish, esp. a trout, found in lakes 2. a ship operating on lakes, esp. the Great Lakes

lake trout any of several varieties of trout and salmon found in lakes; ☆specif., a large, gray game fish (*Salvelinus namaycush*) of deep lakes of the N U.S. and Canada

Lake·wood (lāk′wood) 1. city in NC Colo.: suburb of Denver: pop. 93,000 2. city in SW Calif.: suburb of Los Angeles: pop. 83,000 3. city in NE Ohio, on Lake Erie: suburb of Cleveland: pop. 70,000

lakh (lak) *n.* [Hind. *lākh* (see LAC): prob. in reference to abundance of the insects] in India and Pakistan 1. the sum of 100,000: said specifically of rupees 2. any indefinitely large number

lak·y (lā′kē) *adj.* of the color of the pigment lake

☆**la·la·pa·loo·za, la·la·pa·loo·za** (läl′ə pə lo͞o′zə) *n.* [Slang] *same as* LOLLAPALOOZA

Lal·lan (lal′ən) *adj.* [Scot.] of the Lowlands of Scotland —*n.* the Scottish dialect spoken in the Lowlands: also **Lal′lans**

lal·la·tion (la lā′shən) *n.* [< pp. of L. *lallare*, to sing a lullaby] a pronunciation of *l* so that it sounds like *r* or *w*, or of *r* so that it sounds like *l*

☆**lal·ly·gag** (läl′ē gag′) *vi.* **-gagged′, -gag′ging** [Colloq.] *same as* LOLLYGAG

La·lo (lä lō′), É·douard (Victor Antoine) (e dwär′) 1823-92; Fr. composer

lam¹ (lam) *vt., vi.* **lammed, lam′ming** [< Scand., as in ON. *lemja*, to thrash, beat, flog, lit., to lame: see LAME¹] [Slang] to beat; thrash; flog

☆**lam²** (lam) *n.* [< ? prec.: cf. slang BEAT IT] [Slang] headlong flight, usually to escape punishment for a crime —*vi.* **lammed, lam′ming** [Slang] to flee; escape —**on the lam** [Slang] in flight, as from the police —**take it on the lam** [Slang] to make a getaway; escape

Lam. Lamentations

la·ma (lä′mə) *n.* [Tibetan *blama*, a chief, high priest] a priest or monk in Lamaism: cf. DALAI LAMA

La·ma·ism (lä′mə iz′m) *n.* a form of Buddhism practiced in Tibet and Mongolia, characterized by elaborate ritual and a strong hierarchal organization —**La′ma·ist** *adj., n.* —**La′ma·is′tic** *adj.*

La Man·cha (lä män′chä) flat region in SC Spain

La·marck (lä märk′; E. lə märk′), chevalier **de** (born *Jean Baptiste Pierre Antoine de Monet*) 1744-1829; Fr. naturalist: see LAMARCKISM

La·marck·i·an (lə mär′kē ən) *adj.* of Lamarck or Lamarckism —*n.* an adherent of Lamarckism

La·marck·ism (-kiz′m) *n.* the theory of organic evolution advanced by Lamarck; theory that acquired characters can be inherited: see ACQUIRED CHARACTER

La·mar·tine (lá mär tēn′), **Al·phonse Ma·rie Louis de** (Prat de) (ȧl fōns′ mȧ rē′ lwē dᵊ) 1790-1869; Fr. poet

la·ma·ser·y (lä′mə ser′ē) *n., pl.* **-ser′ies** [Fr. *lamaserie* < *lama*, LAMA] a monastery of lamas

lamb (lam) *n.* [ME. < OE., akin to G. *lamm* (OHG. *lamb*) < IE. *lonbhos* (< base *el-*: see ELK), whence Goth. *lamb*] 1. a young sheep 2. the flesh of a young sheep, used as food 3. lambskin 4. a gentle or innocent person, particularly a child 5. a loved person; dear 6. a person easily tricked or outwitted, as an inexperienced speculator —*vi.* to give birth: said of a ewe —**the Lamb** Jesus: see LAMB OF GOD

Lamb (lam) 1. **Charles,** (pen name *Elia*) 1775-1834; Eng. essayist & critic 2. **Mary** (Ann), 1764-1847; Eng. writer: sister of *prec.* & coauthor with him of *Tales from Shakespeare*

lam·baste (lam bāst′, -bast′) *vt.* **-bast′ed, -bast′ing** [LAM¹ + BASTE³] [Colloq.] 1. to beat soundly; thrash 2. to scold or denounce severely Also sp. **lam·bast′**

lamb·da (lam′də) *n.* [Gr. < Sem., as in Heb. *lāmedh*, LAMED] the eleventh letter of the Greek alphabet (Λ, λ)

lamb·da·cism (lam′də siz′m) *n.* [LL. *lambdacismus* < Gr. *lambdakismos* < *lambdakizein*, to pronounce *l* imperfectly < *lambda*, LAMBDA] *same as* LALLATION

lamb·doid (-doid) *adj.* [Gr. *lambdoeidēs*: see LAMBDA & -OID] shaped like the Greek lambda (Λ); specif., designating the suture that connects the occipital and the parietal bones of the skull

lam·bent (lam′bənt) *adj.* [L. *lambens*, prp. of *lambere*, to lick, lap < IE. echoic base *lab-*, whence LAP²] 1. playing lightly over a surface; flickering: said of a flame, etc. 2. giving off a soft glow [a *lambent* sky] 3. playing lightly and gracefully over a subject: said of wit, humor, etc. —**lam′ben·cy** *n.* —**lam′bent·ly** *adv.*

lam·bert (lam′bərt) *n.* [after J. H. *Lambert* (1728-77), G. mathematician, physicist, & philosopher] the cgs unit of brightness, equal to the brightness of a perfectly diffusing surface that radiates or reflects light at the rate of one lumen per square centimeter

Lam·bert (conformal conic) projection (lam′bərt) [see prec.] a map projection in which all meridians are represented by straight lines radiating from a common point outside the mapped area and the parallels are represented by arcs or circles whose center is this same common point: this projection may have one or two standard parallels that maintain exact scale, while the scale varies along the meridians and, since the meridians and parallels intersect at right angles, angles between locations on the surface of the earth are correctly shown

Lam·beth (lam′bəth) metropolitan borough of London: site of the official residence (**Lambeth Palace**) of the archbishops of Canterbury since 1197: pop. 223,000

lamb·kill (lam′kil′) *n.* ☆*same as* SHEEP LAUREL

lamb·kin (lam′kin) *n.* a little lamb: sometimes applied to a child or young person as a term of affection

lamb·like (-līk′) *adj.* like, or having qualities attributed to, a lamb; gentle, meek, innocent, etc.

Lamb of God Jesus: so called by analogy with the paschal lamb: John 1:29, 36

lam·bre·quin (lam′bər kin, -brə-) *n.* [Fr. < Du. *lamperkin* < *lamper*, a veil + *-kin*, -kin] 1. a fabric covering for a knight's helmet ☆2. a drapery hanging from a shelf or covering the upper part of a window or doorway

lamb·skin (lam′skin′) *n.* 1. the skin of a lamb, esp. with the fleece left on it 2. leather or parchment made from the skin of a lamb

lamb's-quar·ters (lamz′kwôr′tərz) *n.* an annual weed (*Chenopodium album*) of the goosefoot family, with whitened or mealy leaves and dense clusters of small green flowers, sometimes used for greens

lame¹ (lām) *adj.* [ME. < OE. *lama*, akin to G. *lahm*, ON. *lami* < IE. base *lem-*, to break, whence Russ. *lom*, a break] 1. crippled; disabled; esp., having an injured leg or foot that makes one limp 2. stiff and very painful [a *lame* back] 3. poor, weak, unconvincing, ineffectual, etc. [a *lame* excuse] —*vt.* **lamed, lam′ing** to make lame —**lame′ly** *adv.* —**lame′ness** *n.*

lame² (lām; *Fr.* läm) *n.* [Fr. < L. *lamina*: see LAMINA] 1. a thin metal plate 2. [*pl.*] the thin, overlapping metal plates in a piece of armor

la·mé (la mā′) *n.* [Fr., laminated < *lame*: see prec.] a fabric of silk, wool, or cotton interwoven with metal threads, as of gold or silver

☆**lame-brain** (lām′brān′) *n.* [Colloq.] a slow-witted or stupid person; dolt; numskull —**lame′brained′** *adj.*

la·med (lä′mid) *n.* [Heb. *lāmedh*, lit., a whip or club] the twelfth letter of the Hebrew alphabet (ל)

lame duck 1. a disabled, ineffectual, or helpless person or thing ☆2. an elected official whose term extends beyond the time of the election at which he was not reelected

---

fat, āpe, cär; ten, ēven; is, bīte; gō, hôrn, to͞ol, look; oil, out; up, fᵘr; get; joy; yet; chin; she; thin, then; zh, leisure; ŋ, ring; ə for *a* in *ago*, *e* in *agent*, *i* in *sanity*, *o* in *comply*, *u* in *focus*; ′ as in *able* (ā′b'l); Fr. bäl; ë, Fr. coeur; ö, Fr. feu; Fr. moɴ; ō, Fr. coq; ü, Fr. duc; r, Fr. cri; H, G. ich; kh, G. doch. See inside front cover. ☆ Americanism; ‡foreign; *hypothetical; <derived from

la·mel·la (lə mel′ə) n., pl. **-lae** (-ē), **-las** [L., dim. of *lamina:* see LAMINA] a thin, platelike part, layer, organ, or structure; specif., *a)* one of the layers of bone around a Haversian canal *b)* one of the two plates forming a gill in clams and oysters *c)* any of the vertical platelike parts (*gills*) on the underside of the cap of a mushroom or agaric *d)* the cementing layer (*middle lamella*) between two adjacent plant cells —**la·mel′lar** adj. —**la·mel′lar·ly** adv.

lam·el·late (lam′ə lāt′, lə mel′āt) adj. [ModL. *lamellatus*] 1. having, consisting of, arranged in, or resembling a lamella or lamellae 2. same as LAMELLIFORM Also **lam′el·lat′ed** —**lam′el·la′tion** n.

la·mel·li- (lə mel′i) a *combining form meaning* of, like, or consisting of a lamella or lamellae [*lamelliform*]

la·mel·li·branch (lə mel′i brank′) n. [< ModL. *Lamellibranchia*, the class name: see LAMELLI- & BRANCHIAE] any of a class (Pelecypoda) of mollusks, including the clams, oysters, etc., with platelike gills and compressed bodies enclosed in bivalve shells —adj. designating or of these mollusks: also **la·mel′li·bran′chi·ate′** (-bran′kē āt′, -it)

la·mel·li·corn (-kôrn′) adj. [< ModL. *lamellicornis* < LAMELLI- + L. *cornu*, HORN] 1. ending in flattened plates: said of the antennae of some beetles 2. having such antennae: said of a large group of beetles (superfamily Lamellicornia), including the cockchafers and scarabs —n. a lamellicorn beetle

la·mel·li·form (-fôrm′) adj. having the form of a lamella; platelike or scalelike

la·mel·li·ros·tral (lə mel′i räs′trəl) adj. [< ModL. *lamellirostris:* see LAMELLI- & ROSTRAL] of a group of water birds, as ducks, geese, and swans, with fringes of lamellae on the inner edge of the bill: also **la·mel′li·ros′trate** (-trāt)

la·mel·lose (lə mel′ōs, lam′ə lōs′) adj. same as LAMELLATE —**lam′el·los′i·ty** (-läs′ə tē) n.

la·ment (lə ment′) vi. [Fr. *lamenter* < L. *lamentari* < *lamentum*, a mourning, wailing < IE. echoic base *lā-*, whence Arm. *lam*, I weep] to feel deep sorrow or express it as by weeping or wailing; mourn; grieve —vt. 1. to feel or express deep sorrow for; mourn or grieve for 2. to regret deeply —n. 1. an outward expression of sorrow; lamentation; wail 2. a literary or musical composition, as an elegy or dirge, mourning some loss or death

lam·en·ta·ble (lam′ən tə b′l, lə men′tə b′l) adj. [ME. < MFr. < L. *lamentabilis*] 1. to be lamented; grievous; deplorable; distressing 2. [Now Rare] expressing sorrow; mournful —**lam′en·ta·bly** adv.

lam·en·ta·tion (lam′ən tā′shən) n. the act of lamenting; outward expression of grief; esp., a weeping or wailing

Lam·en·ta·tions (-shənz) [LL.(Ec.) *Lamentationes*, transl. in Vulg. for Gr. *thrēnoi*, in LXX] a book of the Bible attributed to Jeremiah

la·ment·ed (-men′tid) adj. mourned for: usually said of someone dead —**la·ment′ed·ly** adv.

La Me·sa (lä mā′sə, lə) [Sp., lit., the MESA] city in SW Calif.: suburb of San Diego: pop. 39,000

la·mi·a (lā′mē ə) n. [ME. *lamya* < L. *lamia* < Gr. *lamia;* akin to *lamos*, abyss < IE. base *lem-*, with gaping mouth, whence L. *lemures*, ghosts (see LEMUR), W. *llef*, voice] 1. in classical folklore, any of a class of monsters, half woman and half serpent, supposed to lure people in order to suck their blood 2. a vampire; female demon; sorceress

lam·i·na (lam′ə nə) n., pl. **-nae′** (-nē′), **-nas** [L., thin piece of metal or wood < ? IE. *(s)tlamen*, a spreading out < base *stel-*, to spread] 1. a thin flake, scale, or layer, as of metal, animal tissue, etc. 2. the flat, expanded part of a leaf; blade, as distinguished from the petiole

lam·i·na·ble (lam′ə nə b′l) adj. that can be laminated

lam·i·nar (lam′ə nər) adj. composed of, arranged in, or like laminae: also **lam′i·nal**

laminar flow the regular, continuous, nonturbulent movement, in a specific direction, of the individual particles of a fluid

lam·i·nar·i·a (lam′ə ner′ē ə) n. [ModL. < L. *lamina:* see LAMINA] any of a genus (*Laminaria*) of marine brown algae having fluted, ribbonlike blades attached at one end to a stalk and holdfast

lam·i·nate (lam′ə nāt′; *for adj. & n., usually* -nit) vt. **-nat′ed**, **-nat′ing** [< ModL. *laminatus* < L. *lamina:* see LAMINA] 1. to form or press into a thin sheet or layer 2. to separate into laminae 3. to cover with or bond to one or more thin layers, as of clear plastic 4. to make by building up in layers —vi. to split into laminae —adj. same as LAMINATED —n. something made by laminating —**lam′i·na′tor** n.

lam·i·nat·ed (-nāt′id) adj. composed of or built in thin sheets or layers, as of fabric, wood, plastic, etc., that have been bonded or pressed together, sometimes under heat

lam·i·na·tion (lam′ə nā′shən) n. 1. a laminating or being laminated 2. a laminated structure; something built up in layers 3. a lamina; thin layer

lam·i·nec·to·my (lam′ə nek′tə mē) n., pl. **-mies** [LAMIN(A) + -ECTOMY] the surgical removal of all or part of the bony arch of a spinal vertebra

lam·i·ni·tis (-nīt′is) n. [ModL.: see -ITIS] an inflammation of laminae in a horse's hoof

Lam·mas (lam′əs) n. [ME. *lammasse* < OE. *hlammæsse*, for *hlafmæsse*, lit., loaf mass, bread feast < *hlaf*, LOAF[1] + *mæsse*, festival, MASS] 1. a harvest festival formerly held in England on August 1, when bread baked from the first crop of wheat was consecrated at Mass 2. this day (**Lammas Day**) or this time (**Lam′mas·tide′**) of the year

lam·mer·gei·er, lam·mer·gey·er (lam′ər gī′ər) n. [G. *lämmergeier* < *lämmer*, pl. of *lamm*, LAMB + *geier*, vulture, akin to *gier*, greed < IE. base *ghī-*, var. of *ghē-*, whence GAPE] a large European and Asiatic bird of prey (*Gypaëtus barbatus*) of the vulture family, with grayish-black plumage streaked with white and a tuft of bristles over the nostrils and under the bill

lamp (lamp) n. [ME. *lampe* < OFr. < VL. *lampade* < L. *lampas* (gen. *lampadis*) < Gr. *lampas* < *lampein*, to shine < IE. base *lāp-*, whence Lett. *lāpa*, torch] 1. a container with a wick for burning oil, alcohol, etc. to produce light or heat: the wick is often enclosed in a glass tube, or chimney, to protect the flame 2. any device for producing light or therapeutic rays, as a gas jet with a mantle, an electric light bulb or tube, or an ultraviolet bulb 3. a holder, stand, or base for such a device 4. a source of knowledge, wisdom, or spiritual strength 5. [Poet.] the sun, moon, a star, etc. 6. [pl.] [Slang] the eyes —vt. ☆[Slang] to look at

lam·pas[1] (lam′pəs) n. [Fr. < OFr. *lampas*, throat: ? akin to *lamper*, to guzzle (nasalized form of *laper*, to lap)] an inflammatory disease of horses, in which the roof of the mouth becomes swollen: also **lam′pers** (-pərz)

lam·pas[2] (lam′pəs) n. [Fr.] an ornamentally designed cloth; esp., a silk cloth like damask

lamp·black (lamp′blak′) n. fine soot produced by the incomplete combustion of oils and other forms of carbon: used as a pigment in paint, ink, etc.

Lam·pe·du·sa (läm′pe dōō′zä) It. island in the Mediterranean, between Malta & Tunisia: 8 sq. mi.

lam·per eel (lam′pər) [dial. *lamper*, var. of LAMPREY] same as LAMPREY

lam·pi·on (lam′pē ən) n. [Fr. < It. *lampione* < *lampa*, lamp < Fr. *lampe*, LAMP] a small oil lamp, usually with a colored glass chimney, formerly used as for a carriage light

lamp·light (lamp′līt′) n. light given off by a lamp

lamp·light·er (-līt′ər) n. 1. a person whose work is lighting and extinguishing gas street lamps ☆2. a roll of paper, a wood splinter, etc. used to light lamps

lam·poon (lam pōōn′) n. [Fr. *lampon* < *lampons*, let us drink (refrain in a drinking song) < *lamper*, to drink: cf. LAMPAS[1]] a piece of strongly satirical writing, usually attacking or ridiculing someone —vt. to attack or ridicule by means of a lampoon —SYN. see CARICATURE —**lam·poon′er, lam·poon′ist** n. —**lam·poon′er·y** n.

lamp·post (lamp′pōst′, lamp′-) n. a post supporting a street lamp

lam·prey (lam′prē) n., pl. **-preys** [ME. *lampreie* < OFr. < ML. *lampreda*] any of a group of eellike cyclostomes (order Petromyzontia) with a funnel-shaped, jawless, sucking mouth surrounded by rasping teeth with which it bores into the flesh of other fishes to suck their blood

lamp shell [from its resemblance to an ancient Roman oil lamp] any of various brachiopods

La·na·i (lä nä′ē) [Haw., var. of *nanai*, a swelling, in allusion to its form] an island of Hawaii, west of Maui: 141 sq. mi.; pop. 2,200

☆**la·nai** (lä nī′, la-) n. [Haw.] a veranda or open-sided living room of a kind found in Hawaii

Lan·ark (lan′ərk) county of SC Scotland: 879 sq. mi.; pop. 1,577,000: also **Lan′ark·shire′** (-shir′)

la·nate (lā′nāt) adj. [L. *lanatus*, woolly < *lana*, WOOL] *Bot., Zool.* having a woolly or hairy covering or appearance

Lan·ca·shire (laŋ′kə shir′) county on the NW coast of England: 1,878 sq. mi.; pop. 5,176,000; county seat, Lancaster

Lan·cas·ter[1] (laŋ′kəs tər) ruling family of England (1399–1461), descended from John of Gaunt

Lan·cas·ter[2] (laŋ′kə stər; *for 3 & 4, usually* laŋ′kas′tər) 1. city in N Lancashire: pop. 48,000 2. same as LANCASHIRE 3. city in SE Pa.: pop. 58,000

Lan·cas·tri·an (laŋ kas′trē ən) adj. 1. of the English royal house of Lancaster 2. from Lancaster or Lancashire —n. 1. a member or follower of the house of Lancaster, esp. in the Wars of the Roses 2. a native or inhabitant of Lancaster or Lancashire

lance (lans, läns) n. [ME. < OFr. < L. *lancea*, light spear, lance, orig., Spanish lance < Celt.] 1. a thrusting weapon consisting of a long wooden shaft with a sharp metal spearhead 2. same as LANCER 3. any sharp instrument resembling a lance, as a fish spear 4. a surgical lancet —vt. **lanced**, **lanc′ing** 1. to attack or pierce with a lance 2. to cut open with a lancet

lance corporal [after obs. *lance-pesade* < MFr. *lance-pessade* < It. *lancia spezzata*, lit., broken lance] 1. *Brit. Army* a private acting temporarily as a corporal ☆2. *U.S. Marine Corps* an enlisted man ranking below a corporal, and above a private first class

lance·let (lans′lit, läns′-) n. [LANCE + -LET] any of a group of small, invertebrate, fishlike sea animals (subphylum Cephalochordata) closely related to the vertebrates; amphioxus

Lan·ce·lot (lan′sə lät′, län′-; -lət) [Fr., double dim. < *Lance* < OHG. *Lanzo* < *lant*, land] *Arthurian Legend* the bravest and most celebrated of the Knights of the Round Table: he was Guinevere's lover

lan·ce·o·late (lan′sē ə lāt′, -lit) *adj.* [LL. *lanceolatus* < *lanceola*, dim.: see LANCE] narrow and tapering like the head of a lance, as certain leaves

lanc·er (lan′sər, län′-) *n.* [Fr. *lancier* < LL. *lancearius*] a cavalry soldier armed with a lance or a member of a cavalry regiment originally armed with lances

lanc·ers (-sərz) *n.pl.* [*with sing. v.*] [< prec.] 1. a 19th-cent. quadrille 2. music for this

lance sergeant [see LANCE CORPORAL] *Brit. Army* a corporal acting temporarily as a sergeant

lan·cet (lan′sit, län′-) *n.* [ME. *lancettis*, pl. < OFr. *lancette* dim. of *lance*, LANCE] 1. a small, pointed surgical knife, usually two-edged, used for making small incisions, skin punctures, etc. 2. *same as:* a) LANCET ARCH b) LANCET WINDOW

lancet arch a narrow, sharply pointed arch

lan·cet·ed (-id) *adj.* having lancet arches or windows

lancet window a narrow, sharply pointed window without tracery, set in a lancet arch

lance·wood (lans′wood′, läns′-) *n.* 1. a tough, elastic wood used for shafts, fishing rods, billiard cues, etc. 2. any of various tropical trees (as *Oxandra lanceolata*) yielding such wood

Lan·chow (lan′chou′, *Chin.* län′jō′) city in NW China, on the Yellow River; capital of Kansu province: pop. 699,000: also sp. **Lanchou**

lan·ci·form (lan′sə fôrm′) *adj.* [< LANCE + -FORM] narrow and pointed, like the head of a lance

lan·ci·nate (-nāt′) *vt.* -nat′ed, -nat′ing [< L. *lancinatus*, pp. of *lancinare*, to tear, to *lacer:* see LACERATE] to stab, pierce, or tear: now rare except in medical use [a *lancinating* pain] — **lan′ci·na′tion** *n.*

land (land) *n.* [ME. < OE., akin to G. *land* < IE. base **lendh*, unoccupied land, heath, steppe, whence Bret. *lann*, heath (whence Fr. *lande*, moor), W. *llan*, enclosure, yard] 1. the solid part of the earth's surface not covered by water 2. a specific part of the earth's surface 3. *a)* a country, region, etc. [a distant *land*, one's native *land*] *b)* the inhabitants of such an area; nation's people 4. ground or soil in terms of its quality, location, etc. [rich *land*, high *land*] 5. *a)* ground considered as property; estate [to invest in *land*] *b)* [*pl.*] specific holdings in land 6. rural or farming regions as distinguished from urban regions [to return to the *land*] 7. that part of a grooved surface which is not indented, as any of the ridges between the grooves in the bore of a rifle ☆8. the Lord: a euphemism [for *land's* sake!] 9. *Econ.* natural resources —*vt.* [ME. *landen* < the *n.*, replacing OE. *lendan* < **land-jan*] 1. to put, or cause to go, on shore from a ship 2. to bring into; cause to enter or end up in a particular place or condition [a fight *landed* him in jail] 3. to set (an aircraft) down on land or water 4. to draw successfully onto land or into a boat; catch [to *land* a fish] 5. [Colloq.] to get, win, or secure [to *land* a job] 6. [Colloq.] to deliver (a blow) —*vi.* 1. to leave a ship and go on shore; disembark 2. to come to a port or to shore: said of a ship 3. to arrive at a specified place; end up 4. to alight or come to rest, as after a flight, jump, or fall —**land on** [Colloq.] ☆to scold or criticize severely

-land (land, lənd) *a combining form meaning:* 1. a kind or quality of land [grassland, highland] 2. a particular place or realm [dreamland]

lan·dau (lan′dou, -dô) *n.* [< *Landau*, town in SW Germany where orig. made] 1. a four-wheeled covered carriage with the top in two sections, either of which can be lowered independently 2. a former style of automobile with a top whose back could be folded down

Lan·dau (län′dou), **Lev** (**Davidovich**) (lyef) 1908–68; Soviet theoretical physicist

lan·dau·let, lan·dau·lette (lan′də let′) *n.* a small landau (sense 1)

land bank ☆a bank that finances transactions in real estate

land breeze a breeze blowing seaward from the land

land contract a contract in which a purchaser of real estate, upon making an initial payment, agrees to pay the seller stipulated amounts at specified intervals until the total purchase price is paid, at which time the seller transfers his interest in the property

land·ed (lan′did) *adj.* 1. owning land [landed gentry] 2. consisting of, or having the nature of, land or real estate [a landed estate]

land·fall (land′fôl′) *n.* 1. a sighting of land from a ship at sea 2. the land sighted 3. a landing by ship or airplane

land·fill (-fil′) *n.* the disposal of garbage or rubbish by burying it under a shallow layer of earth

land·form (-fôrm′) *n.* any topographic feature on the earth's surface, as a plain, valley, hill, etc., caused by erosion, sedimentation, or movement

☆**land-grab·ber** (-grab′ər) *n.* a person who gets possession of land unfairly or fraudulently

☆**land-grant** (-grant′, -gränt′) *adj.* designating any of a number of colleges and universities originally given federal aid, esp. by land grants, on condition that they offer instruction in agriculture and the mechanical arts: they are now supported by the individual States with supplementary Federal funds

☆**land grant** an appropriation of public land by the government for a railroad, State college, etc.

land·grave (-grāv′) *n.* [G. *landgraf* < *land*, LAND + *graf*, a count] 1. in medieval Germany, a count having jurisdiction over a specified territory 2. later, the title of any of certain German princes —**land·gra′vi·ate** (-grā′vē it) *n.* —**land′gra·vine** (-grə vēn′) *n.fem.*

land·hold·er (-hōl′dər) *n.* an owner or occupant of land —**land′hold′ing** *adj., n.*

land·ing (lan′din) *n.* 1. the act of coming to shore or of going or putting ashore 2. the place where a ship is unloaded or loaded 3. a platform at the end of a flight of stairs 4. the act of alighting, or coming to the ground, as after a flight, jump, or fall

landing craft any of various naval craft designed to bring troops and equipment close to shore

landing field a field provided with a smooth surface to enable airplanes to land and take off easily

landing gear the undercarriage of an aircraft, including wheels, pontoons, etc., for support on land or water

landing net a small, baglike net attached to a long handle, for taking a hooked fish from the water

landing strip *same as* AIRSTRIP

Lan·dis (lan′dis), **Kenesaw Mountain** 1866–1944; U.S. jurist; commissioner of professional baseball (1920–44)

land·la·dy (land′lā′dē) *n., pl.* -dies [after LANDLORD] 1. a woman who rents or leases land, houses, etc. to others 2. a woman who keeps a rooming house, inn, etc.

länd·ler (lent′lər) *n.* [G. *ländler* < dial. *Landl*, upper Austria, dim. < *land*, LAND] 1. an Austrian country dance in slow rhythm and triple time 2. music for this

land·less (land′lis) *adj.* not owning land

land·locked (-läkt′) *adj.* 1. entirely or almost entirely surrounded by land, as a bay or a country 2. cut off from the sea and confined to fresh water by a geographical barrier [landlocked salmon]

land·lord (-lôrd′) *n.* [ME. *londelorde* < OE. *landhlaford:* see LAND & LORD] 1. a person, esp. a man, who rents or leases land, houses, etc. to others 2. a man who keeps a rooming house, inn, etc.

land·lord·ism (-lôrd′iz'm) *n.* the economic system under which land is privately owned and rented to tenants

land·lub·ber (-lub′ər) *n.* [LAND + LUBBER] a person who has had little experience at sea, and is therefore awkward aboard a ship: a sailor's term of contempt

land·mark (-märk′) *n.* 1. any fixed object used to mark the boundary of a piece of land 2. any prominent feature of the landscape, as a tree or building, serving to identify a particular locality 3. an event, discovery, etc. considered as a high point or turning point in the history or development of something

land·mass (-mas′) *n.* a very large area of land; esp., a continent

land measure 1. a system of square measure for finding the area of a piece of land 2. any unit of measurement in such a system, as an acre, hectare, etc.

land mine an explosive charge hidden under the surface of the ground and detonated by pressure upon it

☆**land office** a government office that handles and records the sales and transfers of public lands

☆**land-of·fice business** (land′ôf′is) [with reference to Western U.S. land offices in the 19th c.] [Colloq.] a booming business

Land of Nod (näd) 1. *Bible* the country to which Cain journeyed after slaying Abel: Gen. 4:16 2. [l-] the imaginary realm of sleep and dreams

Land of Promise *same as* PROMISED LAND

Land of the Midnight Sun Norway

Land of the Rising Sun Japan

Lan·dor (lan′dər, -dôr′), **Walter Savage** 1775–1864; Eng. writer & poet

land·own·er (land′ō′nər) *n.* a person who owns land —**land′own′er·ship′** *n.* —**land′own′ing** *adj., n.*

Lan·dow·ska (län dôf′skä), **Wan·da** (vän′dä) 1879–1959; Pol. harpsichordist, in the U.S. after 1941

☆**land patent** a legal document granting ownership of a piece of public land

☆**land plaster** finely ground gypsum, used as a fertilizer

☆**land-poor** (-poor′) *adj.* owning land, often much land, but poor, or lacking ready money, because of high taxes on the land, its low yield, etc.

land power 1. military strength on land 2. a nation having great military strength on land

land rail *same as* CORNCRAKE

land reform the redistribution of agricultural land by breaking up large landholdings and apportioning shares to small farmers, peasants, etc.

---

fat, āpe, cär; ten, ēven; is, bīte; gō, hôrn, tōol, look; oil, out; up, fur; get; joy; yet; chin; she; thin, *then*; zh, leisure; ŋ, ring; ə for *a* in *ago*, *e* in *agent*, *i* in *sanity*, *o* in *comply*, *u* in *focus*; ′ as in *able* (ā′b'l); Fr. bâl; ë, Fr. coeur; ö, Fr. feu; Fr. mon; ô, Fr. coq; ü, Fr. duc; r, Fr. cri; H, G. ich; kh, G. doch. See inside front cover. ☆ Americanism; ‡foreign; *hypothetical; <derived from

land·scape (-skāp') n. [17th-c. art borrowing (cf. EASEL, LAY FIGURE) < Du. landschap < land, land + -schap, -SHIP: earlier also landskip, akin to OE. landscipe, G. landschaft] **1.** a picture representing a section of natural, inland scenery, as of prairie, woodland, mountains, etc. **2.** the branch of painting, photography, etc. dealing with such pictures **3.** an expanse of natural scenery seen by the eye in one view —vt. -scaped', -scap'ing to change the natural features of (a plot of ground) so as to make it more attractive, as by adding lawns, trees, bushes, etc. —vi. to work as a landscape architect or gardener —land'scap'er n.

☆**landscape architecture** the art or profession of planning or changing the natural scenery of a place for a desired purpose or effect —**landscape architect**

landscape gardening the art or work of placing or arranging lawns, trees, bushes, etc. on a plot of ground to make it more attractive —**landscape gardener**

land·scap·ist (-skāp'ist) n. a painter of landscapes

Land·seer (land'sir), Sir **Edwin Henry** 1802–73; Eng. painter, esp. of animal pictures

Land's End cape in Cornwall at the southwesternmost point of England: also **Lands End**

land·side (land'sīd') n. the flat side of a plow which is turned toward the land yet unbroken

land·skip (-skip) n. obs. var. of LANDSCAPE

☆**land·slide** (-slīd') n. **1.** the sliding of a mass of loosened rocks or earth down a hillside or slope **2.** the mass of loosened material sliding down **3.** an overwhelming majority of votes for one candidate or party in an election **4.** any overwhelming victory

land·slip (-slip') n. [Chiefly Brit.] same as LANDSLIDE (senses 1 & 2)

lands·man (landz'mən) n., pl. **-men** (-mən) **1.** a person who lives on land: distinguished from SEAMAN **2.** [partly via Yid. lantsman, for earlier lantman < OHG. < lant, LAND + man, MAN] a fellow countryman; compatriot

Land·stei·ner (land'stī'nər; G. länt'shtī'nər), **Karl** 1868–1943; U.S. pathologist & immunologist in Austria

‡**Land·sturm** (länt'shtoorm') n. [G., lit., land storm] **1.** in Germany and, later, other countries, the drafting in time of war of all men under sixty not already in the armed services or in the reserve, as for home defense **2.** the force so drafted

land·ward (land'wərd) adv. toward the land: also **land'wards** —adj. situated or facing toward the land

Land·wehr (länt'ver') n. [G. < land, land + wehr, defense < wehren, to defend: see WEIR] in Germany and, later, other countries, the trained military reserves

land wind a wind blowing seaward from the land

lane[1] (lān) n. [ME. < OE. lanu, akin to Du. laan < ? IE. base *elə-, to be in motion, go] **1.** a narrow way between hedges, walls, buildings, etc.; narrow country road or city street **2.** any narrow way, as an opening in a crowd of people **3.** a) a path or route designated, as for reasons of safety, for ships or aircraft ☆b) a marked strip of road wide enough for a single line of cars, trucks, etc. **4.** any of the parallel courses marked off for contestants in a race **5.** Bowling a) a long, narrow strip of highly polished wood, along which the balls are rolled; alley b) [usually pl.] a bowling establishment

lane[2] (lān) adj. Scot. var. of LONE

Lang (laŋ), **Andrew** 1844–1912; Scot. writer

lang. language

lang·bein·ite (laŋ'bī nīt') n. [G. langbeinit, after A. Langbein, 19th-c. G. chemist who identified it + -it, -ITE[1]] a mineral, $K_2Mg_2(SO_4)_3$, a natural sulfate of potassium and magnesium, used as a source of potash

Lang·er (laŋ'ər), **Susanne K**(**atherina**) (born Susanne Katherina Knauth) 1895– ; U.S. philosopher

Langerhans islets (or **islands**) same as ISLETS OF LANGERHANS

Lang·land (laŋ'lənd), **William** 1332?–1400?; Eng. poet: also **Lang·ley** (laŋ'lē)

‡**lang·lauf** (läŋ'louf') n. [G. < lang, long + lauf, a course < laufen, to run] Skiing a cross-country run —**lang'läuf'er** (-loi'fər) n.

lang·ley (laŋ'lē) n., pl. **-leys** [after ff.] a unit for measuring solar radiation, equal to one small calorie per square centimeter

Lang·ley (laŋ'lē), **Samuel Pier·pont** (pir'pänt) 1834–1906; U.S. astronomer, physicist, & pioneer in airplane construction

Lang·muir (laŋ'myoor), **Irving** 1881–1957; U.S. chemist

Lan·go·bard (laŋ'gō bärd') n. same as LOMBARD (n. 2)

Lan·go·bar·dic (laŋ'gō bär'dik) adj. of the Lombards, their language, or culture —n. the language of the Lombards, a dialect of High German

‡**lan·gouste** (län goost') n. [Fr.] same as SPINY LOBSTER

lan·grage, lan·gridge (laŋ'grij) n. [< ?] a type of irregularly shaped shot formerly used in naval battles to damage rigging and sails: also **lan'grel** (-grəl)

lang·syne (laŋ'sīn', -zīn') adv. [Scot. < lang, LONG[1] + syne, since] [Scot.] long since; long ago —n. [Scot.] the long ago; bygone days Also **lang syne**

Lang·try (laŋ'trē), **Lily** (born Emily Charlotte Le Breton) 1852–1929; Eng. actress

lan·guage (laŋ'gwij) n. [ME. < OFr. langage < langue, tongue < L. lingua, tongue, language, altered (by associa-

tion with lingere, to lick) < OL. dingua < IE. *dņĝhwa, whence OE. tunge, TONGUE] **1.** a) the expression or communication of thoughts and feelings by means of vocal sounds, and combinations of such sounds, to which meaning is attributed; human speech b) the ability to express or communicate by this means c) the vocal sounds so used, or the written symbols for them **2.** a) any means of expressing or communicating, as gestures, signs, animal sounds, etc. b) a special set of symbols, letters, numerals, rules, etc. used for the transmission of information, as in a computer **3.** all the vocal sounds, words, and the ways of combining them common to a particular nation, tribe, or other speech community [the French language] **4.** the particular form or manner of selecting and combining words characteristic of a person, group, or profession; form or style of expression in words [the language of teen-agers] **5.** the study of language in general or of some particular language or languages; linguistics —**speak one's** (or **the same**) **language** to have the same beliefs, attitudes, etc. as another

Langue·doc (läng dôk') region of S France, between the E Pyrenees & the lower Rhone: chief city, Toulouse

‡**langue d'oc** (läng dôk') [Fr., lit., language of oc (Pr. oc, yes < L. hoc, this thing): from characteristic use of oc for affirmation (in contrast to ff.)] a group of French dialects spoken in S France in the Middle Ages and surviving in Provençal

‡**langue d'o·ïl** (dô ēl') [Fr., lit., language of oïl (OFr. oïl, yes < LL. hoc illi < L. hoc, this + ille, that): from characteristic use of oïl (Fr. oui) for affirmation: cf. prec.] a group of French dialects spoken in most of C and N France in the Middle Ages: it is the Old French from which modern French is derived

lan·guet, lan·guette (laŋ'gwit) n. [ME. < MFr., dim. of langue: see LANGUAGE] a thing or part resembling the tongue in shape or use

lan·guid (laŋ'gwid) adj. [Fr. languide < L. languidus < languere, to be faint or listless, akin to laxus: see LAX] **1.** without vigor or vitality; drooping; weak **2.** without interest or spirit; listless; indifferent **3.** sluggish; dull; slow —**lan'guid·ly** adv. —**lan'guid·ness** n.

lan·guish (-gwish) vi. [ME. languishen < extended stem of OFr. languir < L. languescere < languere, to be weary: see prec.] **1.** to lose vigor or vitality; fail in health; become weak; droop **2.** to live under distressing conditions; continue in a state of suffering [to languish in poverty] **3.** to become slack or dull; lose intensity **4.** to suffer with longing; pine **5.** to put on an air of sentimental tenderness or wistful melancholy —**lan'guish·er** n. —**lan'guish·ment** n.

lan·guish·ing (-gwish iŋ) adj. that languishes; specif., a) becoming weak; drooping b) lingering c) slow; not intense d) pining; longing e) tender; sentimental; wistfully amorous —**lan'guish·ing·ly** adv.

lan·guor (laŋ'gər) n. [ME. langour < OFr. langueur < L. languor < languere, to be weary: see LAX] **1.** a lack of vigor or vitality; weakness **2.** a lack of interest or spirit; feeling of listlessness; indifference **3.** tenderness of mood or feeling **4.** the condition of being still, sluggish, or dull —SYN. see LETHARGY —**lan'guor·ous** adj. —**lan'guor·ous·ly** adv. —**lan'guor·ous·ness** n.

lan·gur (luŋ'goor') n. [Hind. langūr < Sans. lāngūlin, lit., having a tail] any of a number of lanky, long-tailed monkeys (genus Presbytis) of SE Asia, with bushy eyebrows and a chin tuft

lan·iard (lan'yərd) n. same as LANYARD

la·ni·ar·y (lā'nē er'ē, lan'ē-) adj. [L. laniarius, of a butcher < lanius, a butcher, of Etruscan origin] adapted for tearing; canine: said of teeth

La·nier (lə nir'), **Sidney** 1842–81; U.S. poet

la·nif·er·ous (lə nif'ər əs) adj. [< L. lanifer + -OUS] bearing wool or fine hairs resembling wool; fleecy: also **la·nig'er·ous** (-nij'-)

lank (laŋk) adj. [ME. < OE. hlanc, slim, flexible < IE. base *kleng-, to bend, wind, whence G. lenken, to bend, ON. hlekkr, a ring] **1.** long and slender; lean **2.** straight and limp; not curly: said of hair —**lank'ly** adv. —**lank'ness** n.

lank·y (laŋ'kē) adj. **lank'i·er** (prec. + -Y[2]) **lank'i·est** awkwardly tall and lean or long and slender —SYN. see LEAN[2] —**lank'i·ly** adv. —**lank'i·ness** n.

lan·ner (lan'ər) n. [ME. lanere < MFr. lanier < VL. *lanarius, for L. laniarius, type of falcon < laniare, to tear, lacerate: see LANIARY] a falcon (Falco biarmicus) of the Mediterranean region; specif., in falconry, the female of this bird

lan·ner·et (lan'ə rēt') n. [ME. lanerette < MFr. laneret, dim.] the male of the lanner: it is smaller than the female

lan·o·lin (lan'l in) n. [< L. lana, WOOL + oleum, oil + -IN[1]] a fatty substance obtained from sheep wool and used as a base for ointments, cosmetics, etc.: also **lan'o·line** (-in, -ēn)

la·nose (lā'nōs) adj. [L. lanosus < lana, WOOL] same as LANATE

Lan·sing (lan'siŋ) [ult. after John Lansing (1751–1829), U.S. jurist] capital of Mich., in the SC part: pop. 132,000

lans·que·net (lans'kə net') n. [Fr. < G. landsknecht, foot soldier < land, country + knecht, servant (see KNIGHT), with Fr. intrusive vowel] **1.** a German mercenary foot soldier of the 15th to the 17th cent. **2.** a card game of German origin

lan·ta·na (lan tā'nə, -tä'-) n. [ModL. < It. dial., viburnum < Gaul. < IE. base *lento-, lithe, flexible, whence L. lentus

& LINDEN] any of a genus (*Lantana*) of shrubby plants of the verbena family, growing in tropical and subtropical America and often cultivated as pot plants

lan·tern (lan′tərn) *n.* [ME. < OFr. *lanterne* < L. *lanterna* < Gr. *lamptēr* < *lampein*, to shine: see LAMP] **1.** a transparent case for holding a light and protecting it from wind and weather: it usually has a handle on its framework so that it can be carried **2.** the room containing the lamp at the top of a lighthouse **3.** an open or windowed structure on the roof of a building or in the upper part of a tower or the like, to admit light or air **4.** *short for* MAGIC LANTERN

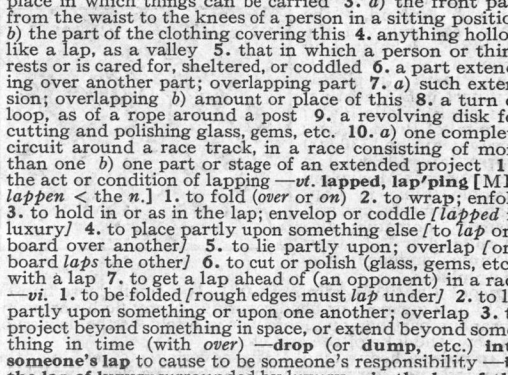

LANTERNS
(A, gasoline; B, garden; C, Chinese; D, electric)

lantern fish any of numerous deep-sea fishes (family Myctophidae), with a large mouth, large eyes, and luminescent organs along each side of the body

lantern fly any of a group of large, brightly colored S. American insects (family Fulgoridae) having a long head with a hollow part formerly thought to emit light

lantern jaw [from resemblance to the early lantern with long sides of thin, concave horn] **1.** a projecting lower jaw **2.** [*pl.*] long, thin jaws, with sunken cheeks, that give the face a lean, gaunt appearance —**lan′tern-jawed′** *adj.*

lantern pinion (or **wheel**) an old type of gearwheel consisting of two circular disks connected by projecting bars around their edges

lantern slide a photographic slide for projection, as, originally, by a magic lantern

lantern tree a Chilean tree (*Crinodendron hookerianum*) having leathery, elliptic leaves and hanging, red flowers with incurving petals, sometimes grown in the far S U.S. as an ornamental

lan·tha·nide series (lan′thə nīd′, -nid) [< ff., first in the series] the rare-earth group of chemical elements from element 57 (lanthanum) through element 71 (lutetium): see PERIODIC TABLE, chart

lan·tha·num (-nəm) *n.* [ModL. < Gr. *lanthanein*, to be concealed < IE. *lādh-* < base *lā-*, hidden, whence L. *latere*, to lurk, be hidden] a silvery, lustrous metallic chemical element of the rare-earth group: symbol, La; at. wt., 138.91; at. no., 57; sp. gr., 6.194; melt. pt., 920°C; boil. pt., 3470°C

lant·horn (lan′tərn) *n.* [altered by folk etym. < LANTERN, after HORN, material once used for the sides] *archaic var.* of LANTERN

Lan·tsang (län′tsäŋ′) *Chin. name of* MEKONG

la·nu·go (lə nōō′gō, -nyōō′) *n.* [L., down < *lana*, WOOL] *a)* the soft, downy hair covering the human fetus *b)* the fine hair covering most of the human body —**la·nu′gi·nous** (-ji nəs), **la·nu′gi·nose′** (-ji nōs′) *adj.*

La·nús (lä nōōs′) city in E Argentina: suburb of Buenos Aires: pop. 244,000

lan·yard (lan′yərd) *n.* [ME. *lanyer* < MFr. *laniere* < OFr. *lasniere* < *lasne*, noose: altered after YARD¹] **1.** a short rope or cord used on board ship for holding or fastening something **2.** a cord worn around the neck, as by sailors, from which to hang something, as a knife, whistle, etc. **3.** a cord with attached hook, for firing certain types of cannon

Lao (lou, lä′ō) *adj., n., pl.* **Lao, Laos** *same as* LAOTIAN

La·oc·o·ön (lä äk′ə wän′) [L. < Gr. *Laokoōn*] *Gr. Legend* a priest of Troy who, with his two sons, was destroyed by two huge sea serpents after he had warned the Trojans against the wooden horse

La·od·i·ce·a (lä äd′ə sē′ə, lā′ə də-) **1.** ancient city in Phrygia, SW Asia Minor **2.** *ancient name of* LATAKIA

La·od·i·ce·an (-ən) *adj.* **1.** of Laodicea **2.** indifferent or lukewarm in religion, as the early Christians of Laodicea (sense 1): Rev. 3:14–16 **3.** indifferent or lukewarm concerning any subject —*n.* **1.** a native or inhabitant of Laodicea **2.** a person who is indifferent or lukewarm, esp. in religion

La·om·e·don (lä äm′ə dän′) [L. < Gr. *Laomedōn*] *Gr. Legend* father of Priam and founder of Troy

La·os (lä′ōs, lous, lä′äs) kingdom in the NW part of the Indochinese peninsula: 91,429 sq. mi.; pop. 2,635,000; caps. Vientiane & Luang Prabang See INDOCHINA, map

La·o·tian (lä ō′shən) *adj.* of Laos, its people, culture, etc. —*n.* **1.** a native or inhabitant of Laos; specif., a member of a Buddhist Thai people **2.** their Thai language

Lao-tse (lou′dzu′) 604? B.C.–?; Chin. philosopher: reputed founder of Taoism: also **Lao-tzu, Lao-tsze**

lap¹ (lap) *n.* [ME. *lappe* < OE. *læppa*, fold or hanging part of a garment, skin; akin to G. *lappen* < IE. base *leb-, lāb-*, to hang down, whence L. *labi*, to fall, sink, *lapsus*, a fall] **1.** [Now Rare] the loose lower part of a garment, which may be doubled or folded over; skirt of a coat or gown **2.**

the front part of the skirt when held up to form a hollow place in which things can be carried **3.** *a)* the front part from the waist to the knees of a person in a sitting position *b)* the part of the clothing covering this **4.** anything hollow like a lap, as a valley **5.** that in which a person or thing rests or is cared for, sheltered, or coddled **6.** a part extending over another part; overlapping part **7.** *a)* such extension; overlapping *b)* amount or place of this **8.** a turn or loop, as of a rope around a post **9.** a revolving disk for cutting and polishing glass, gems, etc. **10.** *a)* one complete circuit around a race track, in a race consisting of more than one *b)* one part or stage of an extended project **11.** the act or condition of lapping —*vt.* **lapped, lap′ping** [ME. *lappen* < the *n.*] **1.** to fold (*over* or *on*) **2.** to wrap; enfold **3.** to hold in or as in the lap; envelop or coddle [*lapped* in luxury] **4.** to place partly upon something else [to *lap* one board over another] **5.** to lie partly upon; overlap [one board *laps* the other] **6.** to cut or polish (glass, gems, etc.) with a lap **7.** to get a lap ahead of (an opponent) in a race —*vi.* **1.** to be folded [rough edges must *lap* under] **2.** to lie partly upon something or upon one another; overlap **3.** to project beyond something in space, or extend beyond something in time (with *over*) —**drop** (or **dump**, etc.) **into someone's lap** to cause to be someone's responsibility —**in the lap of luxury** surrounded by luxury —**in the lap of the gods** beyond human control or power

lap² (lap) *vi., vt.* **lapped, lap′ping** [ME. *lapen* < OE. *lapian*, akin to MDu. *lapen*, OHG. *laffan*, to lick < IE. echoic base *lab-*, to lick loudly, whence L. *lambere*] **1.** to drink (a liquid) by dipping it up with the tongue in the manner of a dog **2.** to move or strike gently with a light, splashing sound such as a dog makes in lapping: said of waves, etc. —*n.* **1.** the act of lapping **2.** the sound of lapping **3.** something that is, or is intended to be, lapped up —**lap up 1.** to take up (liquid or liquid food) by lapping **2.** [Colloq.] to eat or drink greedily **3.** [Colloq.] *a)* to accept with enthusiasm *b)* to believe too readily —**lap′per** *n.*

lap·a·ro· (lap′ə rə) [< Gr. *lapara*, the flank] *a combining form meaning* the flank, the abdominal wall [*laparotomy*]: also, before a vowel, **lapar-**

lap·a·rot·o·my (lap′ə rät′ə mē) *n., pl.* **-mies** [prec. + -TOMY] a surgical incision into the abdomen at the flanks or, less precisely, at any point

La Paz (lä päs′; *E.* lə päz′) **1.** city in W Bolivia: actual seat of government (cf. SUCRE): pop. 461,000 **2.** seaport in N W Mexico, on the Gulf of California; capital of Baja California Sur: pop. 24,000

lap·board (lap′bôrd′) *n.* a flat board placed on or over the lap and used as a table or desk

lap dissolve *Motion Pictures & TV* a dissolving view in which a new scene is blended in with a scene being faded out, as by lapping two exposures on one film or two images on a television screen

lap dog any pet dog small enough to be held in the lap

la·pel (lə pel′) *n.* [dim. of LAP¹] either of the front parts of a coat, jacket, etc. folded back on the chest and forming a continuation of the collar

lap·ful (lap′fool′) *n., pl.* **-fuls′** as much as a lap can hold

lap·i·dar·i·an (lap′ə der′ē ən) *adj. same as* LAPIDARY

lap·i·dar·y (lap′ə der′ē) *n., pl.* **-ies** [ME. *lapidarie* < LL. *lapidarius* < L., of stones < *lapis* (gen. *lapidis*), a stone] **1.** a workman who cuts, polishes, and engraves precious stones **2.** the art of such a workman **3.** an expert in precious stones; collector of or dealer in gems: also **lap′i·dar′ist** —*adj.* [L. *lapidarius*] **1.** of or connected with the art of cutting and engraving precious stones **2.** engraved on stone **3.** like an inscription on a monument; short, precise, and elegant

lap·i·date (lap′ə dāt′) *vt.* **-dat′ed, -dat′ing** [< L. *lapidatus*, pp. of *lapidare*, to stone < *lapis* (see prec.)] **1.** to throw stones at **2.** to stone to death —**lap′i·da′tion** *n.*

la·pid·i·fy (lə pid′ə fī′) *vt., vi.* **-fied′, -fy′ing** [Fr. *lapidifier* < ML. *lapidificare* < L. *lapis* (gen. *lapidis*), a stone + *facere*, to make: see FACT] [Rare] to turn into stone —**la·pid′i·fi·ca′tion** *n.*

la·pil·lus (lə pil′əs) *n., pl.* **-pil′li** (-ī) [L., dim. of *lapis*, stone] a small fragment of igneous rock, up to the size of a walnut, ejected from a volcano

lap·in (lap′in) *n.* [Fr., rabbit] rabbit fur, generally dyed in imitation of more valuable skins

‡**lap·is** (lap′is, läp′-) *n., pl.* **lap·id·es** (lap′ə dēz′) *Latin word for* stone: used esp. in chemistry

lap·is laz·u·li (lap′is laz′yoo lī′, lazh′-; -lē′) [ModL. < L. *lapis*, a stone + ML. *lazuli*, gen. of *lazulus*, azure < Ar. *lāzaward*: see AZURE] **1.** an azure-blue, opaque, semiprecious stone, a mixture of various minerals **2.** its color

lap joint a joint made by lapping one piece or part over another and fastening them together: also **lapped joint** —**lap′-joint′** *vt.*

LAP JOINT

La·place (lä pläs′), marquis **Pierre Si·mon de** (pyer sē mōn′ də) 1749–1827; Fr. mathematician & astronomer

Lap·land (lap′land′) region of N Europe, including the N parts of Norway, Sweden, & Finland, & the NW extremity of the U.S.S.R., inhabited by the Lapps

LAPLAND

La Pla·ta (lä plä′tä) seaport in E Argentina, on the Río de la Plata; capital of Buenos Aires province: pop. 330,000

Lapp (lap) *n.* [Sw.] **1.** a member of a Mongoloid people living in Lapland, formerly, and still partly, nomadic: also **Lap′land′er 2.** their Finnic language: also **Lap′pish**

lap·pet (lap′it) *n.* [dim. of LAP¹] **1.** a small, loose flap or fold of a garment or head covering **2.** any fleshy or membranous part hanging loosely or in a fold, as the dewlap of a cow, the lobe of the ear, etc.

☆**lap robe** a heavy blanket, fur covering, etc. laid over the lap and knees for warmth when riding in a sleigh, watching outdoor sports, etc.

Lap·sang (lap′san) *adj.* designating a fine variety of souchong tea with a smoky flavor

lapse (laps) *n.* [L. *lapsus*, a fall < pp. of *labi*, to slip, fall: see LAP¹] **1.** a slip of the tongue, pen, or memory; small error; fault **2.** *a)* a falling away from a moral standard; moral slip *b)* a falling or slipping into a lower or worse condition, esp. for a short time **3.** a falling away from one's belief or faith **4.** a gliding or passing away, as of time or of anything continuously flowing **5.** [Rare] a falling into ruin **6.** *Law a)* the termination or forfeiture of a right or privilege through disuse, through failure of some contingency, or through failure to meet stated obligations within a stated time *b)* the failure of a bequest or devise to take effect because of the death of the person who was to receive it —*vi.* **lapsed, laps′ing** [L. *lapsare* < *labi*, to slip or fall; esp., to slip into a specified state [to *lapse* into unconsciousness] **2.** to slip or deviate from a higher standard or fall into former erroneous ways; backslide **3.** to pass away; elapse: said of time **4.** to come to an end; stop; end [a subscription that has *lapsed*] **5.** to become forfeit or void because of the holder's failure to pay his premium at the stipulated time: said of an insurance policy **6.** *Law* to pass to another proprietor by reason of negligence or death —*vt.* to make forfeit or void by not meeting standards —**laps′a·ble, laps′i·ble** *adj.* —**laps′er** *n.*

lapse rate the rate of decrease of an atmospheric variable, usually temperature, with increase of altitude

lap·strake (lap′strāk′) *adj.* [LAP¹ + STRAKE] *Shipbuilding* **1.** having a hull built of overlapping planks riveted together; clinker-built **2.** molded, as of fiberglass, to suggest such a hull —*n.* a boat so built or molded Also **lap′streak′** (-strēk′)

‡**lap·sus** (lap′səs) *n.* [L.] a slip; error; lapse

‡**lapsus lin·guae** (lin′gwē) [L.] a slip of the tongue

‡**lapsus me·mo·ri·ae** (me mō′ri ē) [L.] a slip of the memory

Lap·tev Sea (läp′tef) arm of the Arctic Ocean, north of Siberia, between the New Siberian Islands & the Taimyr Peninsula

La·pu·ta (lə pyōōt′ə) in Swift's *Gulliver's Travels*, a flying island inhabited by impractical, visionary philosophers, who engage in various absurd activities —**La·pu′tan** *adj., n.*

lap·wing (lap′win′) *n.* [ME. *lapwinge*, altered (by folk etym. after *lappe*, LAP¹ & *wing*, WING) < OE. *hleapewince* < *hleapan*, to leap + *wince* < *wincian* (see WINK): prob. so called from its irregular flight] an old-world crested plover (*Vanellus vanellus*) noted for its irregular, wavering flight

lar (lär) *n. sing. of* LARES

Lar·a·mie (lar′ə mē) [after Jacques *Laramie* (?–1821), trapper & explorer] city in SE Wyo.: pop. 23,000

lar·board (lär′bərd, -bôrd′) *n.* [ME. *laddeborde*, orig. ? lading side < OE. *hladan*, to lade + *bord*, side: sp. infl. by STARBOARD] the left-hand side of a ship when facing the front end, or bow; port —*adj.* on or of this side Now largely replaced by PORT⁴

lar·ce·ny (lär′sə nē) *n., pl.* **-nies** [ME. < Anglo-Fr. *larcin* < OFr. *larrecin* < L. *latrocinium* < *latrocinari*, to rob, plunder < *latro*, mercenary soldier, robber < Gr. *latrōn* < *latron*, wages, pay < IE. base *lēi-*, to possess, acquire, whence OE. *læs*, landed property] *Law* the unlawful taking away of another's property without his consent and with the intention of depriving him of it; theft: see also GRAND LARCENY, PETIT LARCENY —*SYN.* see THEFT —**lar′ce·nist, lar′ce·ner** *n.* —**lar·ce·nous** *adj.* —**lar′ce·nous·ly** *adv.*

larch (lärch) *n.* [G. *lärche* < L. *larix*] **1.** any of a genus (*Larix*) of trees of the pine family, found throughout the N Hemisphere, bearing cones and needlelike leaves that are shed annually **2.** the tough wood of this tree

lard (lärd) *n.* [ME. < OFr. < L. *lardum*, bacon fat, lard < IE. base *lai-*, fat, whence Gr. *larinos*, fattened, fat, L. *largus*, large] the fat of hogs, melted down and clarified to become a white, soft solid; esp., the inner abdominal fat —*vt.* [ME. *larden* < OFr. *larder*] **1.** to cover or smear with

lard or other fat; grease **2.** to put strips of fat pork, bacon, etc. over, or into slits in (meat or poultry) before cooking; interlard **3.** to add to; embellish; garnish [a talk *larded* with jokes] —**lard′y** *adj.* **lard′i·er, lard′i·est**

lard·er (lär′dər) *n.* [ME. < OFr. *lardier*, orig., storehouse for bacon < ML. *lardarium* < L. *lardum*, LARD] **1.** a place where the food supplies of a household are kept; pantry **2.** a supply of food; provisions

larder beetle a small, mostly black beetle (*Dermestes lardarius*), whose larvae feed on dead animal matter, cheese, etc.

Lard·ner (lärd′nər), **Ring(gold Wilmer)** 1885–1933; U.S. sports reporter & humorist

lar·don (lär′dən) *n.* [ME. < MFr. < *lard*, LARD] a strip of bacon or pork used to lard meat: also **lar·doon′** (-dōōn′)

La·re·do (lə rā′dō) [after *Laredo*, town in Spain] city in S Tex., on the Rio Grande: pop. 69,000

la·res (ler′ēz, lā′rēz) *n.pl., sing.* **lar** [L., pl. of *lar* < ? IE. base *las*-, greedy, wanton, whence LUST] in ancient Rome, guardian spirits; esp., the deified spirits of ancestors, who watched over and protected the households of their descendants

lares and penates 1. the household gods of the ancient Romans: see LARES, PENATES **2.** the treasured belongings of a family or household

lar·gan·do (lär gän′dō) *adj., adv.* [It.] same as ALLARGANDO

large (lärj) *adj.* **larg′er, larg′est** [ME. < OFr. < L. *largus*: see LARD] **1.** [Archaic] liberal; generous **2.** big; great; specif., *a)* taking up much space; bulky *b)* enclosing much space; spacious [a *large* office] *c)* of great extent or amount [a *large* sum] **3.** big as compared with others of its kind; of more than usual or average size, extent, or amount **4.** comprehensive; far-reaching [to have *large* views on a subject] **5.** pompous or exaggerated [*large* talk] **6.** operating on a big scale [a *large* manufacturer] **7.** *Naut.* fair or favorable: said of a wind —*adv.* **1.** in a large way; so as to be large [to write *large*] **2.** *Naut.* with a favoring wind —*n.* liberty: now only in the phrase, **at large 1.** free; not confined; not in jail **2.** fully; in complete detail **3.** in general; taken altogether ☆**4.** representing an entire State or other district rather than only one of its subdivisions [a congressman *at large*] —**large′ness** *n.*

SYN.—**large, big,** and **great** are often interchangeable in meaning of more than usual size, extent, etc. [a *large*, *big*, or *great* oak], but in strict discrimination, **large** is used with reference to dimensions or quantity [a *large* studio, amount, etc.], **big,** to bulk, weight, or extent [a *big* baby, *big* business], and **great,** to size or extent that is impressive, imposing, surprising, etc. [a *great* river, success, etc.] —*ANT.* **small, little**

large·heart·ed (-här′tid) *adj.* generous; kindly

large intestine the relatively large part of the intestines of vertebrates, between the small intestine and the anus, including the cecum, colon, and rectum

large·ly (-lē) *adv.* **1.** much; in great amounts **2.** for the most part; mainly

large-mind·ed (-mīn′did) *adj.* liberal in one's views; tolerant; broad-minded

☆**large-mouth (bass)** (lärj′mouth′) a black bass (*Micropterus salmoides*) found in warm, sluggish waters

large-scale (-skāl′) *adj.* **1.** drawn to a large scale: said of a map, etc. **2.** of wide scope; over a large area; extensive [*large-scale* business operations]

lar·gess, lar·gesse (lär jes′, lär′jis) *n.* [ME. *largesse* < OFr. < *large*, LARGE] **1.** generous giving, as from a patron **2.** a gift or gifts given in a generous, or sometimes showy, way **3.** nobility of spirit

lar·ghet·to (lär get′ō) *adj., adv.* [It. < *largo*: see LARGO] *Music* relatively slow, but faster than largo: a direction to the performer —*n., pl.* **-tos** a larghetto movement or passage

larg·ish (lär′jish) *adj.* rather large

lar·go (lär′gō) *adj., adv.* [It., large, slow < L. *largus*, large: see LARD] *Music* slow and stately: a direction to the performer —*n., pl.* **-gos** a largo movement or passage

☆**lar·i·at** (lar′ē it) *n.* [Sp. *la reata* < *la*, the + *reata*, a rope] **1.** a rope used for tethering grazing horses, etc. **2.** same as LASSO —*vt.* to tie or catch with a lariat

lar·ine (lar′in, -in) *adj.* [< ModL. *Larinae*, name of the subfamily < LL.(Ec.) *larus*, a ravenous seabird < Gr. *laros* < IE. echoic base *lā-*: see LAMENT **1.** designating or of a suborder (Lari) of sea birds comprising the gulls **2.** of or like a gull

La·ri·sa (lä′rē sä, E. lə ris′ə) city in E Thessaly, Greece: pop. 55,000: also sp. **La·ris′sa**

lark¹ (lärk) *n.* [ME. *larke, laverke* < OE. *laferce*, older *læwerce*, akin to G. *lerche* (OHG. *lērahha*), ON. *lævirki* (Dan. *lerke*)] **1.** any of a large family (Alaudidae) of chiefly old-world songbirds; esp., the skylark **2.** any of a number of similar birds, as the pipit and meadowlark

lark² (lärk) *vi.* [? alteration (after prec.) of northern dial. *lake* < ME. *laike*, to play < ON. *leika* & cognate OE. *lacan*, akin to Goth. *laikan*, to hop, leap < IE. base *leig-*, *loig-*, to hop, whence Sans. *rejatē*, (he) hops, quivers] **1.** to play or frolic; have a merry time **2.** to cause one's horse to jump fences, etc. unnecessarily —*n.* a frolic or spree; merry prank —**lark′er** *n.* —**lark′ish, lark′y** *adj.*

lark·spur (lärk′spur′) *n.* a common name for DELPHINIUM

La Roche·fou·cauld (lä′rōsh fōō kō′), **duc Fran·çois de** (frän swä′ də) 1613–80; Fr. moralist & writer of maxims

La Ro·chelle (lä rō shel′) seaport in W France, on the Bay of Biscay: pop. 66,000

La·rousse (lä rōōs′), **Pierre A·tha·nase** (pyer å tå nåz′) 1817–75; Fr. lexicographer & grammarian

lar·ri·gan (ler′i gən) *n.* [prob. of Canad. origin] a high moccasin made of oiled leather, worn by woodsmen

lar·ri·kin (lar′ə k'n) *n.* [ult. < ? LARK²] [Chiefly Australian Slang] a hoodlum or rowdy, esp. a young one

lar·rup (lar′əp) *vt.* [East Anglian dial., prob., with intrusive vowel, for *lerp*, *larp*, akin to or < Du. *larpen*, to thrash] [Colloq.] to whip; flog; beat

Lar·ry (lar′ē) a masculine name: see LAURENCE

lar·va (lär′və) *n., pl.* **-vae** (-vē), **-vas** [L., ghost, specter, akin to *lar*, household spirit: see LARES] the early, free-living, immature form of any animal that changes structurally when it becomes an adult, usually by a complex metamorphosis [the caterpillar is the *larva* of the butterfly, the tadpole is the *larva* of the frog] —**lar′val** *adj.*

lar·vi·cide (-və sīd′) *n.* [< LARVA + -CIDE] a substance used to kill harmful larvae —**lar′vi·cid′al** *adj.*

la·ryn·gal (lə riŋ′gəl) *adj. same as* LARYNGEAL (*adj.* 3 & *n.*)

la·ryn·ge·al (lə rin′jē əl, -jəl) *adj.* 1. of, in, or near the larynx 2. used for treating the larynx 3. produced in the larynx: said of a sound —*n.* a laryngeal sound —**la·ryn′ge·al·ly** *adv.*

lar·yn·gi·tis (lar′ən jīt′əs) *n.* [ModL. < ff. + -ITIS] an inflammation of the larynx, often characterized by a temporary loss of voice —**lar′yn·git′ic** (-jit′ik) *adj.*

la·ryn·go- (lə riŋ′gō, -gə) [< Gr. *larynx* (gen. *laryngos*), larynx] a combining form meaning: 1. the larynx [*laryngoscope*] 2. laryngeal and [*laryngopharyngeal*] Also, before a vowel, **la·ryng′-**

lar·yn·gol·o·gy (lar′in gäl′ə jē) *n.* the branch of medicine having to do with diseases of the larynx and adjacent parts —**la·ryn·go·log·i·cal** (lə rin′gə läj′i k'l) *adj.* —**lar′yn·gol′o·gist** *n.*

la·ryn·go·pha·ryn·ge·al (lə riŋ′gō fə rin′jē əl, -jəl) *adj.* of both the larynx and the pharynx

la·ryn·go·scope (lə riŋ′gə skōp′) *n.* [LARYNGO- + -SCOPE] an instrument for examining the interior of the larynx

lar·yn·gos·co·py (lar′in gäs′kə pē) *n.* examination of the larynx by means of a laryngoscope —**la·ryn·go·scop·ic** (lə riŋ′gə skäp′ik), **la·ryn′go·scop′i·cal** *adj.* —**la·ryn′go·scop′i·cal·ly** *adv.*

lar·yn·got·o·my (-gät′ə mē) *n., pl.* **-mies** [LARYNGO- + -TOMY] the surgical incision of the larynx

lar·ynx (lar′iŋks) *n., pl.* **lar′ynx·es**, **la·ryn·ges** (lə rin′jēz) [ModL. < Gr. *larynx*] 1. the structure of muscle and cartilage at the upper end of the human trachea, containing the vocal cords and serving as the organ of voice 2. a similar structure in many other animals

la·sa·gna (lə zän′yə) *n.* [It. (pl. *lasagne*), the noodle < L. *lasanum*, a pot < Gr. *lasanon*, pot with feet] a dish of wide, flat noodles baked in layers with cheese, tomato sauce, and ground meat: also **la·sa′gne** (-yə)

La·Salle (lə sal′; *Fr.* lå sål′) city in S Quebec, Canada, on Montreal island: pop. 48,000

La Salle (lä säl′; *E.* lə sal′), sieur **Ro·bert Cave·lier de** (rō ber′ kåv lyā′ də) 1643–87; Fr. explorer in N. America

las·car (las′kər) *n.* [Hind. *lashkar*, army, camp < Per. *lashkar*, army < Ar. *al-'askar*, army] an Oriental sailor, esp. one who is a native of India

Las Ca·sas (läs kä′säs), **Bar·to·lo·mé de** (bär tō lō mā′ də) 1474–1566; Sp. missionary & historian in the Americas

Las·caux (lä skō′) cave in the Dordogne region, SW France, containing paleolithic drawings

las·civ·i·ous (lə siv′ē əs) *adj.* [ME. *lascyuyous* < ML. *lasciviosus* < L. *lascivia*, wantonness < *lascivus*, wanton: see LUST] 1. characterized by or expressing lust or lewdness; wanton 2. tending to excite lustful desires —**las·civ′i·ous·ly** *adv.* —**las·civ′i·ous·ness** *n.*

Las Cru·ces (läs krōō′sis) [Sp., lit., the crosses: prob. from crosses marking an early burial spot] city in S N.Mex., on the Rio Grande: pop. 38,000

lase (lāz) *vi.* **lased**, **las′ing** [back-formation < ff.] to emit laser light

☆**la·ser** (lā′zər) *n.* [l(ight) a(mplification by) s(timulated) e(mission of) r(adiation)] a device, containing a crystal, gas, or other suitable substance, in which atoms, when stimulated by focused light waves, amplify and concentrate these waves, then emit them in a narrow, very intense beam; optical maser

lash¹ (lash) *n.* [ME. *lassche* < ?] 1. a whip; esp. the flexible striking part as distinguished from the handle 2. a stroke with or as with a whip; switch 3. a sharp, censuring or rebuking remark 4. an eyelash —*vt.* [ME. *laschen* < ? the *n.*] 1. to strike or drive with or as with a lash; flog 2. to swing or move quickly or angrily; switch [the cat *lashed* her tail] 3. to strike with great force; dash against [waves *lashed* the cliffs] 4. to attack violently in words; censure or rebuke 5. to incite by appealing to the emotions [to *lash* a crowd into a frenzy of anger] —*vi.* 1. to move quickly or violently; switch 2. to make strokes with or as with a whip —**lash out** 1. to strike out violently 2. to speak angrily or in bitter criticism —**lash′er** *n.*

lash² (lash) *vt.* [ME. *lashen* < OFr. *lachier*, var. of *lacier*: see LACE] to fasten or tie with a rope, etc.

lash·ing¹ (-iŋ) *n.* 1. the act of a person or thing that lashes; specif., *a)* a whipping *b)* a strong rebuke 2. [*pl.*] [Chiefly Brit. Colloq.] a large amount; lots

lash·ing² (-iŋ) *n.* 1. the act of fastening or tying with a rope, etc. 2. a rope, etc. so used

Lash·io (läsh′yō) town in EC Burma: see BURMA ROAD

Lash·kar (lush′kər) city in NC India: see GWALIOR

lash-up (lash′up′) *n.* [< *lash up*, to fasten < LASH² + UP¹] [Colloq.] 1. a temporary or improvised contrivance; expedient 2. any arrangement or setup

Las·ki (las′kē), **Harold (Joseph)** 1893–1950; Eng. political scientist & socialist leader

Las Pal·mas (läs päl′məs) seaport in the Canary Islands: pop. 215,000

La Spe·zia (lä spät′syä) seaport in NW Italy, on the Ligurian Sea: pop. 129,000

lass (las) *n.* [north ME. *lasce*, *lasse*: prob. < Anglo-N. *lasqa* (< ON. *løskr*, weak, idle): see LATE] 1. a young woman; girl 2. a sweetheart 3. [Scot.] a girl servant; maid

Las·salle (lə sal′; *G.* lä säl′), **Ferdinand** 1825–64; Ger. socialist & writer

Las·sen Volcanic National Park (las′n) [after Peter Lassen (fl. 1845), Dan. pioneer] national park in N Calif., with an active volcano (Lassen Peak, 10,457 ft.): 166 sq. mi.

las·sie (las′ē) *n.* [dim. of LASS] [Scot.] 1. a young girl 2. a sweetheart

las·si·tude (las′ə tōōd′, -tyōōd′) *n.* [Fr. < L. *lassitudo* < *lassus*, faint, weary: see LATE] a state or feeling of being tired and listless; weariness; languor —*SYN.* see LETHARGY

☆**las·so** (las′ō, -ōō; la sōō′) *n., pl.* **-sos**, **-soes** [Sp. *lazo* < L. *laqueus*, noose, snare: see LACE] a long rope or leather thong with a sliding noose at one end, used to catch cattle or wild horses —*vt.* to catch with a lasso —**las′so·er** *n.*

last¹ (last, läst) *adj. alt. superl. of* LATE [ME. *laste*, earlier *latest*, *latst* < OE. *latost*, superl. of *læt*, *adj.*, *late*, *adv.*: see LATE] 1. being or coming after all others in place; farthest from the first; hindmost 2. *a)* coming after all others in time; furthest from the beginning; latest; final *b)* only remaining 3. most recent; directly before the present [*last* month] 4. furthest from what is expected; least likely [the *last* person to suspect] 5. utmost; greatest 6. coming after all others in importance; lowest in rank: said esp. of a prize 7. newest [the *last* thing in hats] 8. conclusive; authoritative [the *last* word in scientific research] 9. individual: a redundant intensive [to spend every *last* cent] —*adv. alt. superl. of* LATE 1. after all others; at the end. 2. most recently 3. finally; in conclusion —*n.* 1. someone or something which comes last [the *last* of the kings] 2. the final or concluding part; end [friends to the *last*] —at (long) **last** after a long time; finally —**see the last of** to see for the last time

SYN.—**last** implies a coming after all others in a series or sequence and connotes that nothing else follows [he was the *last* one to enter]; **final** implies a coming at the end so as to terminate or conclude and connotes decisiveness [that's my *final* offer]; **terminal** applies to that which marks an end, limit, or extremity [the *terminal* outpost of a settlement]; **ultimate** applies to a concluding point or result beyond which it is impossible to go [his *ultimate* fate is death] —*ANT.* **first**

last² (last, läst) *vi.* [ME. *lasten* < OE. *læstan*, akin to G. *leisten*, *vt.*, to perform, carry out, Goth. *laistjan*, lit., to follow in the track of < IE. base *leis-*, a track, spoor, whence L. *lira*, furrow (cf. DELIRIUM): sense development: to follow—to go on, continue] 1. to remain in existence or operation; continue; go on; endure 2. to remain in good condition; wear well 3. to continue unconsumed, unspent, etc.; be enough (for) [food to *last* (for) a month] —*vt.* to continue or endure throughout: often with *out* [doubtful whether he can *last* (out) the year] —*SYN.* see CONTINUE —**last′er** *n.*

last³ (last, läst) *n.* [ME. *laste* < OE. *læst*, a boot, *læste*, shoemaker's last < base of *last*, footstep, track, furrow < same base as prec.] 1. a block or form shaped like a person's foot, on which shoes are made or repaired 2. a particular form or shape of shoe —*vt.* to form with a last —**stick to one's last** 1. to keep to one's own work 2. to mind one's own business —**last′er** *n.*

last⁴ (last, läst) *n.* [ME. *laste* < OE. *hlæst* (akin to G. *last*, OHG. *hlast*) < base of *hladan* (see LADE)] a measure or weight that varies for different things and in different places, often one equal to 4,000 pounds

last-ditch (-dich′) *adj.* made, done, used, etc. in a final, often desperate act of resistance or opposition

Las·tex (las′teks) [coined word < (E)LAS(TIC) + TEX(TILE)] a trademark for a fine, round rubber thread wound with cotton, rayon, silk, etc. and woven or knitted into fabric

last·ing (las′tiŋ, läs′-) *adj.* that lasts a long time; enduring; durable; permanent [a *lasting* peace] —*n.* 1. a strong, twilled cloth 2. [Archaic] endurance; permanence —**last′ing·ly** *adv.* —**last′ing·ness** *n.*

Last Judgment *Theol.* 1. the final judgment of mankind at the end of the world 2. the time of this

last·ly (last′lē, läst′-) *adv.* in conclusion; finally

last quarter 1. the time of month between second half-moon and new moon **2.** the phase of the moon at the second of the two points when half of its hemisphere is visible

last rites 1. final rites and prayers for a dead person **2.** sacraments administered to a dying person

last straw [from the last straw that broke the back of the overburdened camel in the fable] the last of a sequence of annoyances or troubles that results in a breakdown, defeat, loss of patience, etc.

Last Supper the last supper eaten by Jesus with his disciples before the Crucifixion: cf. LORD'S SUPPER

last word 1. *a)* the final word or speech, regarded as settling the argument *b)* final authority **2.** something regarded as perfect **3.** [Colloq.] the very latest style

Las Ve·gas (läs vā'gəs) [Sp., the plains or meadows] city in SE Nev.: pop. 126,000

Lat. Latin

lat. latitude

La·ta·ki·a (lä'tä kē'ä; *also, esp. for n.,* lat'ə kē'ə) **1.** seaport in W Syria, on the Mediterranean: pop. 68,000 **2.** the Mediterranean coastal district of Syria: 2,433 sq. mi. —*n.* a fine grade of Turkish smoking tobacco, produced near the port of Latakia

latch (lach) *n.* [ME. *lacche* < *lacchen*, to seize, catch hold of < OE. *læccan* < IE. base *(s)lagw-*, to grasp, seize] **1.** a fastening for a door or gate, esp. one capable of being worked from either side by means of a lever and consisting of a bar that falls into a notch in a piece attached to the doorjamb or gatepost: often said of a spring lock on a door **2.** a fastening for a window, etc. —*vt., vi.* to fasten or close with a latch —☆**latch onto** [Colloq.] to get or obtain —**on the latch** fastened by the latch but not bolted

latch·et (lach'it) *n.* [ME. *lachet* < OFr. *lachet,* dial. var. of *lacet,* dim. of *laz:* see LACE] [Archaic] a strap or lace for fastening a sandal or shoe to the foot

latch·key (lach'kē') *n.* a key for drawing back or unfastening the latch of a door, esp. of an outer door, from the outside

latch·string (-striŋ') *n.* a cord fastened to the bar of a latch and passed through a hole in the door so that the latch can be raised from the outside

late (lāt) *adj.* **lat'er** or **lat'ter, lat'est** or **last** [ME. < OE. *læt,* slow, sluggish, tardy, akin to Du. *laat,* G. *lass,* slow, lazy < IE. **lēid-* < base **lēi-,* to neglect, let go, whence LET[1], L. *lassus,* weak] **1.** happening, coming, etc. after the usual, proper, or expected time; tardy; behindhand **2.** *a)* happening, being, continuing, etc. far on in the day, night, year, etc. [the *late* afternoon, a *late* party] *b)* happening, being, continuing, etc. toward the end; far advanced in a period, development, etc. [the *late* Middle Ages] **3.** happening, appearing, etc. just previous to the present time; recent [a *late* news bulletin] **4.** having been so recently but not now [the *late* allies] **5.** having recently died —*adv.* **lat'er, lat'est** or **last** [ME. < OE. < base of the *adj.*] **1.** after the usual, proper, or expected time; tardily **2.** at or until an advanced time of the day, night, year, etc. **3.** toward the end of a given period, development, etc. **4.** recently; lately [*late* as yesterday] —*SYN.* see DEAD, TARDY —**of late** lately —**late'ness** *n.*

lat·ed (lāt'id) *adj.* [Poet.] belated

la·teen (la tēn', lə-) *adj.* [Fr. *latine* < (*voile*) *latine,* Latin (sail) < fem. of L. *Latinus,* LATIN] **1.** designating or of a triangular sail attached to a long yard suspended obliquely from a short mast: now used chiefly on Mediterranean vessels **2.** having such a sail —*n.* a vessel with such a sail: also **la·teen'er**

la·teen-rigged (-rigd') *adj.* having a lateen sail

Late Greek the Greek language of the period after classical Greek: term applied chiefly to the written language seen in patristic writings and texts from c. 200–c. 600 A.D.

LATEEN SAIL

Late Latin the Latin language of the period after classical Latin, seen chiefly in late Western Roman Empire and patristic writings from c. 200–c. 600 A.D.

late·ly (lāt'lē) *adv.* recently; during a recent period; a short while ago

La Tène (lä ten') [name of the site of such a find on Lake of Neuchâtel] designating or of an Iron Age culture (c. 400 B.C.–c. 100 A.D.) of central Europe, characterized by decorations in bronze, gold, and enamel on weapons, utensils, ornaments, etc.

la·tent (lāt''nt) *adj.* [L. *latens,* prp. of *latere,* to lie hidden, lurk < IE. **lāidh-* < base **lā-,* to be hidden, whence ON. *lōmr,* betrayal, deception] **1.** present but invisible or inactive; lying hidden and undeveloped within a person or thing, as a quality or power **2.** *Biol.* dormant but capable of normal development under the best conditions: said of buds, spores, cocoons, etc. **3.** *Psychol.* unconsciously but. not actively so [a *latent* homosexual] —**la'ten·cy** *n.* —**la'tent·ly** *adv.*

SYN.—**latent** applies to that which exists but is as yet concealed or unrevealed [his *latent* ability]; **potential** applies to that

which exists in an undeveloped state but which can be brought to development in the normal course of events [a *potential* concert pianist]; **dormant** suggests a lack of visible activity, as of something asleep [a *dormant* volcano]; **quiescent** implies a stopping of activity, usually only temporarily [the raging sea had become *quiescent*] —ANT. active, actual, operative

latent ambiguity *Law* uncertainty existing where language employed in an instrument is clear and appears to have but one meaning, yet outside evidence makes it capable of more than one meaning: see PATENT AMBIGUITY

latent heat additional heat required to change the state of a substance from solid to liquid at its melting point, or from liquid to gas at its boiling point, after the temperature of the substance has reached either of these points

latent period 1. the interval in the course of a disease between the time of the infection and the first appearance of the symptoms; incubation period **2.** the interval between a stimulus and its response

lat·er (lāt'ər) *alt. compar.* of LATE (*adj.*) —*adv. compar.* of LATE at a later time; after some time; subsequently —**later on** subsequently

lat·er·ad (lat'ə rad') *adv.* [< L. *later(alis)* < gen. of *latus,* side (see ff.) + -AD[2]] *Anat.* toward the side

lat·er·al (lat'ər əl) *adj.* [L. *lateralis* < *latus* (gen. *lateris*), a side, akin to *latus,* broad < IE. base **stel-,* to spread out, whence Arm. *lain,* broad] **1.** of, at, from, or toward the side; sideways [*lateral* movement] **2.** *Phonet.* formed by an occlusion with the tongue in such a way that breath escapes along the sides —*n.* **1.** anything located, done, etc. to the side; lateral part, growth, branch, etc. ☆**2.** *Football short for* LATERAL PASS **3.** *Mining* a drift off to the side of and parallel to a main drift **4.** *Phonet.* a lateral sound —**lat'er·al·ly** *adv.*

lateral line a row of sensory organs along each side of the head and body in fishes and a few amphibians, probably for detecting vibrations, currents, and pressure

☆**lateral pass** *Football* a short pass parallel to the goal line or in a slightly backward direction

Lat·er·an (lat'ər ən) [< L. *Lateranus,* pl. *Laterani,* name of the Roman family (the *Plautii Laterani*) whose palace once occupied the same site] **1.** the church of St. John Lateran, the cathedral of the Pope as bishop of Rome **2.** the palace, now a museum, adjoining this church

lat·er·ite (lat'ə rīt') *n.* [L. *later,* brick, tile (prob. akin to *latus,* broad: see LATERAL) + -ITE[1]] *Geol.* a red, residual soil containing large amounts of aluminum and ferric hydroxides, formed by the decomposition of many kinds of rocks, and found esp. in well-drained tropical rain forests —**lat'er·it'ic** *adj.*

lat·er·i·za·tion (lat'ər i zā'shən) *n.* the process by which rock is converted into laterite —**lat'er·ize'** (-ə rīz') *vt.* **-ized', -iz'ing**

lat·est (lāt'ist) *adj., adv. alt. superl.* of LATE **1.** most recent; newest **2.** [Archaic] last —**at the latest** no later than (the time specified) —**the latest** the most recent thing, development, etc.

la·tex (lā'teks) *n., pl.* **lat·i·ces** (lat'ə sēz'), **la'tex·es** [L. *latex* (gen. *laticis*), a fluid, liquid < Gr. *latax,* a drop, wine lees < IE. base **lat-,* wet, whence MIr. *laith,* beer] **1.** a milky liquid containing resins, proteins, etc., present in certain plants and trees, as the rubber tree, milkweed, and poppy: used esp. as the basis of rubber **2.** a suspension in water of particles of natural or synthetic rubber or plastic: used in rubber goods, adhesives, paints, etc.

lath (lath, läth) *n., pl.* **laths** (lath*z,* laths, läth*z,* läths) [ME. *lathe* (< OE. **læthth,* akin to OHG. *latta*) & *latte* (< OE. *lætt,* akin to ON. *latto*)] **1.** any of the thin, narrow strips of wood used in building lattices or nailed to two-by-fours, rafters, etc. as a groundwork for plastering, tiling, etc. **2.** any framework for plaster, as wire screening or expanded metal **3.** laths collectively —*vt.* to cover with laths

lathe (lāth) *n.* [ME. *lath,* turning lathe, supporting stand, prob. < MDu. *lade* in the same senses (whence also Dan. *dreielad,* turning lathe): for IE. base see LADE] a machine for shaping an article of wood, metal, etc. by holding and turning it rapidly against the edge of a cutting or abrading tool —*vt.* **lathed, lath'ing** to shape on a lathe

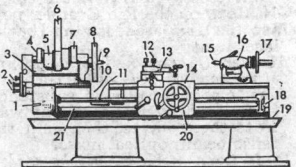

ENGINEER'S LATHE (1. change-speed box; 2. studs carrying change gears; 3. headstock; 4. guards; 5. pulley; 6. driving belt; 7. guard; 8. faceplate; 9. center; 10. gap; 11. lead screw; 12. clamps for securing turning tool; 13. cross slide; 14. saddle; 15. center; 16. loose headstock; 17. wheel for adjusting center; 18. bed; 19. tray for catching turnings; 20. apron holding control levers; 21. shaft giving automatic feeds)

lath·er (la*th*'ər) *n.* [ME. < OE. *leathor,* washing soda or soap, akin to ON. *lauthr,* washing soda, foam < IE. **loutro-* < base **lou-,* wash, whence L. *lavare, lavere,* to wash, bathe & LYE] **1.** the foam or froth formed by soap or other detergent in water **2.** foamy sweat, as that on a race

horse ☆**3.** [Slang] an excited or agitated state —*vt.* **1.** to cover with lather **2.** [Colloq.] to flog soundly —*vi.* to form, or become covered with, lather

lath·er·y (-ər ē) *adj.* made of, covered with, or capable of forming lather

la·thi (lä′tē) *n.* [Hind.] in India, a heavy stick of bamboo and iron, used as a club by police, soldiers, etc.: also sp. **la′thee**

lath·ing (lath′iŋ, läth′-) *n.* **1.** laths collectively, esp. when serving as a base for plastering, etc. **2.** the putting up of laths on walls, ceilings, etc. Also **lath′work′** (-wurk′)

lath·y (-ē) *adj.* **lath′i·er, lath′i·est** like a lath; tall and thin

lat·i·cif·er·ous (lat′ə sif′ər əs) *adj.* [see LATEX & -FEROUS] producing, containing, or secreting latex

lat·i·fun·di·um (lat′ə fun′dē əm) *n., pl.* **-di·a** (-ə) [L. < *latus,* broad (see LATERAL) + *fundus,* estate, orig., bottom: see FOUND²] a large landed estate, typically owned by an absentee landlord and worked by serfs, as in some Latin American countries

Lat·i·mer (lat′ə mər), **Hugh** 1485?-1555; Eng. Protestant bishop & religious reformer: burned at the stake

lat·i·mer·i·a (lat′ə mir′ē ə) *n.* [ModL., after M. E. D. Courtenay-*Latimer* (1907-), director of South African museum: cf. -IA] a deep-sea coelacanth fish (*Latimeria chalumnae*) with large, circular scales and six of its seven fins paddlelike: believed to be extinct until the recent discovery of specimens off the E coast of South Africa, esp. in the Mozambique Channel

Lat·in (lat′'n) *adj.* [L. *Latinus* < *Latium,* Latium (in which Rome was included), orig. ? "flat land" < IE. **tletiom* < base **(s)tel-,* to spread out, whence L. *latus,* broad] **1.** of ancient Latium or its people **2.** of ancient Rome or its people **3.** of or in the language of ancient Latium and ancient Rome **4.** designating or of the languages derived from Latin, the peoples who speak them, their countries, cultures, etc. **5.** of the Roman Catholic Church, esp. as distinguished from the Orthodox Eastern Church —*n.* **1.** a native or inhabitant of ancient Latium or ancient Rome **2.** the Italic language of ancient Latium and ancient Rome: see also OLD LATIN, LATE LATIN, LOW LATIN, MEDIEVAL LATIN, MODERN LATIN **3.** a person whose language is derived from Latin, as a Spaniard, Italian, or Latin American **4.** a Roman Catholic: so called esp. by Eastern Christians

Latin America that part of the Western Hemisphere south of the U.S., in Mexico, Central America, the West Indies, & South America, where Spanish, Portuguese, & French are the official languages —**Latin American**

Lat·in·ate (-āt′) *adj.* of, derived from, or similar to Latin: also **La·tin·ic** (la tin′ik)

Latin Church *same as* ROMAN CATHOLIC CHURCH

Latin cross a plain, right-angle cross whose lowest arm is the longest: see CROSS, illus.

Lat·in·ism (lat′'n iz'm) *n.* **1.** a Latin idiom or expression, used in another language **2.** a Latin quality

Lat·in·ist (-ist) *n.* a scholar in Latin

La·tin·i·ty (la tin′ə tē) *n.* [L. *latinitas*] the use or knowledge of Latin

Lat·in·ize (lat′'n īz′) *vt.* **-ized′, -iz′ing** [LL. *latinizare,* to translate into Latin < L. *Latinus,* LATIN] **1.** to translate into Latin **2.** to give Latin form or characteristics to **3.** to transliterate into the Latin alphabet; Romanize **4.** to make conform to the rites, practices, etc. of the Roman Catholic Church —*vi.* to use Latin expressions, forms, etc. —**Lat′in·i·za′tion** *n.* —**Lat′in·iz′er** *n.*

La·ti·no (la tē′nō, lə-) *n., pl.* **-nos** [AmSp. < Sp., lit., Latin < L. *Latinus,* LATIN] a Latin American

Latin Quarter [transl. of Fr. *Quartier Latin*] a section of Paris, south of the Seine, where many artists and students live

Latin Rite the Latin liturgy used in the Roman Catholic Church

Latin square a square array of numbers, symbols, etc. repeated in columns and rows in such an order that each element occurs only once in any column or row: used in statistical analysis

lat·ish (lat′ish) *adj., adv.* somewhat late

lat·i·tude (lat′ə tōōd′, -tyōōd′) *n.* [ME. < OFr. < L. *latitudo* < *latus,* wide: see LATERAL] **1.** [Rare] breadth; width **2.** extent; scope; range of applicability **3.** freedom from narrow restrictions; freedom of opinion, conduct, or action **4.** *see* ASTRONOMICAL LATITUDE, CELESTIAL LATITUDE **5.** *Geog.* a) angular distance, measured in degrees, north or south from the equator [a ship at forty degrees north *latitude*] b) a region or place as determined by such measurement Cf. LONGITUDE —**lat′i·tu′di·nal** *adj.* —**lat′i·tu′di·nal·ly** *adv.*

lat·i·tu·di·nar·i·an (lat′ə tōōd′'n er′ē ən, -tyōōd′-) *adj.* [< L. *latitudo* (gen. *latitudinis*): see LATITUDE & -ARIAN] liberal in one's views; permitting free thought, esp. in religious matters; very tolerant of differing opinions —*n.* a person who is very liberal in his views and, in religion, cares little about particular creeds and forms —**lat′i·tu′di·nar′i·an·ism** *n.*

La·ti·um (lā′shē əm) [L.: see LATIN] **1.** region of C Italy, on the Tyrrhenian Sea: 6,642 sq. mi.; pop. 3,923,000; chief city, Rome **2.** ancient country in the part of this region southeast of Rome

LATIUM (4th cent. B.C.)

lat·ke (lät′kə) *n., pl.* **-kes** [< Yid. < Russ. *latka,* a patch] a pancake, often, specif., one made of grated raw potatoes

la·tri·a (lə tri′ə) *n.* [LL. (Ec.) < Gr.(Ec.) *latreia* < Gr., hired service < *latreuein,* to serve, worship < *latris,* hired servant: for IE. base see LARCENY] *R.C.Ch.* that worship which is due to God alone: distinguished from DULIA, HYPERDULIA

la·trine (lə trēn′) *n.* [Fr. < L. *latrina,* contr. of *lavatrina,* bath < *lavare,* to wash: see LATHER] a toilet, privy, etc. for the use of a large number of people, as in an army camp

La·trobe (lə trōb′), **Benjamin Henry** 1764-1820; U.S. architect, born in England

-la·try (lə trē) [Gr. -*latreia* < *latreia:* see LATRIA] a combining form meaning worship of or excessive devotion to [*idolatry*]

lat·ten (lat′'n) *n.* [ME. *laton* < OFr. < Ar. *lātūn,* copper] **1.** brass or a brasslike alloy hammered into thin sheets, formerly used for making church vessels **2.** any metal, esp. tin, in thin sheets

lat·ter (lat′ər) *adj. alt. compar. of* LATE [ME. *lattre* < OE. *lættra,* compar. of *læt:* it represents the orig. compar. form; LATER is a new formation] **1.** a) later; more recent b) nearer the end or close [the *latter* part of May] **2.** last mentioned of two: opposed to FORMER¹: often used absolutely (with *the*) [Jack and Bill are twins, but the *latter* is shorter than the former]

lat·ter-day (-dā′) *adj.* of recent or present time; modern

☆**Lat·ter-day Saint** *see* MORMON

lat·ter·ly (lat′ər lē) *adv.* lately; of late; recently

lat·ter·most (-mōst′) *adj.* last in order

lat·tice (lat′is) *n.* [ME. *latis* < OFr. *lattis* < *latte* < MHG. *latte,* a lath: cf. LATH] **1.** an openwork structure of crossed strips or bars of wood, metal, etc. used as a screen, support, etc. **2.** something resembling or suggesting such a structure **3.** a door, gate, shutter, trellis, etc. formed of such a structure **4.** *Physics* a) a three-dimensional pattern of points in space, as of atoms or groups of atoms in a solid or crystal b) *same as* SPACE LATTICE c) the arrangement in a geometrical pattern of fissionable and nonfissionable material in a nuclear reactor —*vt.* **-ticed, -tic·ing** **1.** to arrange like a lattice; make a lattice of **2.** to furnish or cover with a lattice or latticework —**lat′tice·like′** *adj.*

lat·tice·work (-wurk′) *n.* **1.** a lattice **2.** lattices collectively; trelliswork Also **lat′tic·ing**

lat·ti·ci·nio (lat′ə chēn′yō) *n.* [It., lit., food prepared with milk < LL. *lacticinium* < L. *lac,* milk: see GALACTIC] opaque white glass, often used in threads for a decorative pattern on glassware

Lat·vi·a (lat′vē ə) a republic (**Latvian Soviet Socialist Republic**) of the U.S.S.R. in NE Europe, on the Baltic Sea: 24,594 sq. mi.; pop. 2,300,000; cap. Riga

Lat·vi·an (-ən) *adj.* **1.** of Latvia or its people; Lettish **2.** of the group of Baltic dialects spoken in Latvia —*n.* **1.** a native or inhabitant of Latvia **2.** the Baltic language of the Latvians

laud (lôd) *n.* [ME. *laude* < OFr. < ML.(Ec.) *laudes,* pl. < L. *laus* (gen. *laudis*), glory, praise < IE. echoic base **leu-,* whence OE. *leoth,* G. *lied,* song] **1.** praise **2.** any song or hymn of praise **3.** [*pl.*] *Eccles.* [often **L**-] the service of dawn which constitutes the second (or, when said together with matins, the first) of the canonical hours and includes the singing of psalms of praise to God —*vt.* [ME. *lauden* < L. *laudare* < the *n.*] to praise; extol —*SYN.* see PRAISE

Laud (lôd), **William** 1573-1645; Eng. prelate; archbishop of Canterbury (1633-45): executed

laud·a·ble (lôd′ə b'l) *adj.* [L. *laudabilis*] worthy of being lauded; praiseworthy; commendable —**laud′a·bil′i·ty, laud′a·ble·ness** *n.* —**laud′a·bly** *adv.*

laud·a·num (lôd′'n əm, lôd′nəm) *n.* [ModL., altered use (by Paracelsus) of ML. var. of L. *ladanum:* see LABDANUM] **1.** formerly, any of various preparations containing opium **2.** a solution of opium in alcohol

lau·da·tion (lô dā′shən) *n.* [L. *laudatio*] a lauding or being lauded; praise; commendation

laud·a·to·ry (lôd′ə tôr′ē) *adj.* [LL. *laudatorius* < L. *laudare:* see LAUD] expressing praise; eulogistic; commendatory: also **laud′a·tive**

Lau·der (lô′dər), Sir **Harry** (born *Harry MacLennan*) 1870–1950; Scot. comic singer & song writer

laugh (laf, läf) *vi.* [ME. *laughen* < OE. *hleahhan,* akin to G. *lachen* (OHG. *hlahhan*) < IE. base *klēg-,* to cry out, sound, whence Gr. *klangē,* L. *clangor*] **1.** to make the explosive sounds of the voice, and the characteristic movements of the features and body, that express mirth, amusement, ridicule, etc. **2.** to be amused **3.** to feel or suggest joyousness; appear bright and gay *[laughing eyes]* —*vt.* **1.** to express or say with laughter **2.** to bring about, effect, or cause to be by means of laughter *[to laugh one-self hoarse]* —*n.* **1.** the act or sound of laughing **2.** anything that provokes or is fit to provoke laughter **3.** *[pl.]* [Colloq.] mere diversion or pleasure —**have the last laugh** to win after apparent defeat and discomfiture —**laugh at 1.** to be amused by **2.** to make fun of; ridicule; deride **3.** to be indifferent to or contemptuous of; disregard —**laugh away** to get rid of (something unpleasant or embarrassing) by laughter —**laugh down** to silence or suppress by laughing —**laugh in (or up) one's sleeve** to laugh secretly or inwardly —**laugh off** to scorn, avoid, or reject by laughter or ridicule —**laugh out of (or on) the other (or wrong) side of the mouth** to change from joy to sorrow, from amusement to annoyance, etc. —**no laughing matter** a serious matter —**laugh′er** *n.*

SYN.—**laugh** is the general word for the sounds or exhalation made in expressing mirth, amusement, etc.; **chuckle** implies soft laughter in low tones, expressive of mild amusement or inward satisfaction; **giggle** and **titter** both refer to a half-suppressed laugh consisting of a series of rapid, high-pitched sounds, suggesting embarrassment, silliness, etc., but **titter** is also used of a laugh of mild amusement suppressed in affected politeness; **snicker** is used of a sly, half-suppressed laugh, as at another's discomfiture or a bawdy story; **guffaw** refers to loud, coarse laughter

laugh·a·ble (-ə b'l) *adj.* of such a nature as to cause laughter; amusing or ridiculous —*SYN.* see FUNNY— **laugh′a·ble·ness** *n.* —**laugh′a·bly** *adv.*

laugh·ing (-iŋ) *adj.* **1.** that laughs or appears to laugh *[a laughing brook]* **2.** uttered with laughter *[a laughing remark]* —*n.* laughter —**laugh′ing·ly** *adv.*

laughing gas nitrous oxide used as an anesthetic: so called from the reaction of laughter and exhilaration that inhaling it may produce

laughing jackass *same as* KOOKABURRA

laugh·ing·stock (laf′iŋ stäk′, läf′-) *n.* a person or thing made the object of ridicule; butt

laugh·ter (laf′tər, läf′-) *n.* [ME. < OE. *hleahtor* (akin to G. *gelächter*) < base of *hleahhan,* to LAUGH] **1.** the action of laughing or the sound resulting **2.** an indication of amusement *[with laughter in her eyes]* **3.** [Archaic] a matter for or cause of laughter

launce (lôns, lans, läns) *n.* [prob. < LANCE, from its shape] *same as* SAND EEL

launch[1] (lônch, länch) *vt.* [ME. *launchen* < OFr. *lanchier* < LL.(Ec.) *lanceare,* to wield a lance < L. *lancea,* LANCE] **1.** to hurl, discharge, or send off (a weapon, blow, etc.) **2.** to send forth with some force *[to launch* a plane by catapult]* **3.** to cause (a newly built vessel) to slide from the land into the water; set afloat **4.** to set in operation; start *[to launch* an attack] **5.** to start (a person) on some course or career —*vi.* **1.** to put to sea (often with *out* or *forth*) **2.** to start on some new course or enterprise (often with *out* or *forth*) **3.** to throw oneself (*into*) with vigor; rush; plunge *[to launch* into a tirade] —*n.* the act or process of launching a ship, spacecraft, plane, etc. —*adj.* designating or of vehicles, facilities, sites, etc. used in the launching of spacecraft or missiles

launch[2] (lônch, länch) *n.* [Sp. or Port. *lancha* < ?] **1.** formerly, the largest boat carried by a warship **2.** an open, or partly enclosed, motorboat

launch·er (-ər) *n.* **1.** a catapult **2.** a device for launching a grenade from a rifle **3.** a device or structure used to launch and give initial guidance to a missile, spacecraft, etc.

launch pad the platform from which a rocket, guided missile, etc. is launched: also **launching pad**

launch window the period of time during which conditions are favorable for launching a spacecraft on a particular mission

laun·der (lôn′dər, län′-) *n.* [ME., contr. < *lavender,* washerwoman < OFr. *lavandier* < ML. *lavandarius* < LL. *lavandaria,* things to be washed < L. *lavandus,* gerundive of L. *lavare,* to wash: see LATHER] a water trough, esp. one used in mining for washing dirt from the ore —*vt.* to wash, or wash and iron, (clothes, etc.) —*vi.* **1.** to withstand washing *[a fabric that launders well]* **2.** to do laundry —**laun′der·er** *n.* —**laun′der·ing** *n.*

☆**Laun·der·ette** (lôn′də ret′, län′-) *a service mark for a* self-service laundry —*n.* [l-] such a laundry

laun·dress (lôn′dris, län′-) *n.* a woman whose work is washing clothes, ironing, etc.; washerwoman

☆**Laun·dro·mat** (lôn′drə mat′, län′-) [< a trademark for an automatic washing machine] *a service mark for a* self-service laundry —*n.* [l-] such a laundry

laun·dry (lôn′drē, län′-) *n., pl.* **-dries** [ME. *lavenderie* < OFr. < *lavandier:* see LAUNDER] **1.** the act or process of laundering **2.** *a)* a room with facilities for laundering *b)* a commercial establishment for this **3.** a batch of clothes, linens, etc. that has been, or is about to be, laundered

laun·dry·man (-mən) *n., pl.* **-men** (-mən) a man who works in or for a laundry, esp. one who collects and delivers clothes, etc. for laundering service

laun·dry·wom·an (-woom′ən) *n., pl.* **-wom′en** (-wim′in) *same as* LAUNDRESS

Lau·ra (lôr′ə) [It. < ? L. *laurus,* laurel] a feminine name: var. **Lorinda;** dim. **Lolly, Loretta**

Lau·ra·sia (lô rā′zhə, -shə) [LAUR(ENTIAN) + (EUR)ASIA] a hypothetical ancient continent that included what are now N. America and Eurasia, supposed to have separated and moved apart at about the end of the Paleozoic Era

lau·re·ate (lôr′ē it; *for v.* -āt′) *adj.* [ME. < L. *laureatus* < *laurea* (*corona*), laurel (wreath), fem. of *laureus,* of laurel < *laurus,* laurel] **1.** formerly, woven of sprigs of laurel: said of a crown or wreath **2.** crowned with a laurel wreath as a mark of honor or distinction **3.** worthy of honor; distinguished; pre-eminent, esp. among poets —*n.* **1.** a person on whom honor or distinction is conferred **2.** *same as* POET LAUREATE —*vt.* **-at′ed, -at′ing** [Archaic] **1.** to honor or confer distinction upon **2.** to appoint to the position of poet laureate —**lau′re·ate·ship′** *n.*

lau·rel (lôr′əl, lär′-) *n.* [ME. *laurer, lorel* < OFr. *lorier* < L. *laurus*] **1.** any of a genus (*Laurus*) of evergreen trees or shrubs of the laurel family, native to S Europe and widely cultivated in the U.S., with large, glossy, aromatic leaves, greenish-yellow flowers, and black berries; specif., the **poet's laurel** (*Laurus nobilis*) **2.** the foliage of this tree, esp. as woven into wreaths such as those used by the ancient Greeks to crown the victors in various contests **3.** *[pl.] a)* fame; honor *b)* victory ☆**4.** any of various trees and shrubs resembling the true laurel, as the mountain laurel, cherry laurel, California laurel, etc. —*adj.* designating a family (Lauraceae) of shrubs or trees including the bay, sassafras, cinnamon, camphor, etc. —*vt.* **-reled** (or **-relled**), **-rel·ing** (or **-rel·ling**) **1.** to crown with laurel **2.** to honor —**look to one's laurels** to beware of having one's achievements surpassed —**rest on one's laurels** to be satisfied with what one has already achieved

Lau·rence (lôr′əns, lär′-) [L. *Laurentius,* prob. < *laurus,* laurel (or < ? *Laurentius,* town in Latium)] a masculine name: dim. **Larry;** var. **Lorenzo;** equiv. Fr. **Laurent,** Ger. **Lorenz,** It. & Sp. **Lorenzo;** fem. **Laura**

Lau·ren·tian (lô ren′shən) *adj.* [< L. *Laurentius,* Lawrence + -AN] **1.** of or relating to the St. Lawrence River **2.** designating or of a series of rocks of the Precambrian system in E Canada

Laurentian Mountains mountain range in S Quebec, Canada, extending along the St. Lawrence River valley: highest peak, 3,905 ft.: also **Laurentian Highlands**

Laurentian Plateau *same as* CANADIAN SHIELD

lau·res·ti·nus, lau·rus·ti·nus (lô′rə stī′nəs, -stē′-) *n.* [ModL. *laurustinus* < L. *laurus,* laurel + *tinus,* laurestinus] a tall evergreen shrub (*Viburnum tinus*) grown in the Mediterranean regions of Europe for its fragrant, white or pinkish flowers: also **lau′rus·tine** (-stin, -stēn′)

lau·ric acid (lôr′ik, lär′-) [< ModL. *Laurus,* a genus of trees or shrubs < L. *laurus,* LAUREL + -IC] a fatty acid, $C_{12}H_{24}O_2$, occurring in many vegetable fats, used in detergents, soaps, wetting agents, etc.

Lau·ri·er (lô′rē ā′; *Fr.* lô ryā′), Sir **Wilfrid** 1841–1919; Canad. statesman; prime minister (1896–1911)

lau·ryl alcohol (lôr′əl, lär′-) [< ModL. *Laurus* (see LAURIC ACID) + -YL] a white solid, $C_{12}H_{26}O$, which has a low melting point and yields a pleasant-smelling liquid: used in the manufacture of detergents, perfumes, etc.

Lau·sanne (lō zan′) city in W Switzerland, on Lake Geneva: pop. 134,000

la·va (lä′və, lav′ə) *n.* [It. < dial. (Neapolitan) *lave* < L. *labes,* a fall, subsidence < *labi,* to slide < IE. base *lāb-,* to hang loosely: cf. LAP[1], LIP] **1.** melted rock issuing from a volcano **2.** such rock when solidified by cooling

la·va·bo (lə vä′bō, -vā′-) *n., pl.* **-boes** [L., I shall wash: see LATHER] **1.** [*usually* L-] *R.C.Ch. a)* the ritual of washing the celebrant's hands after the offertory, accompanied by the repetition of Psalm 25:6–12 (Vulgate), beginning with *lavabo:* a similar ritual is used in some Episcopal churches *b)* these verses *c)* the basin used: in full **lavabo dish** (or **basin**) **2.** *a)* a basin and a tank for water above it, hung on the wall *b)* a wall planter resembling this

lav·age (lə väzh′, lav′ij) *n.* [Fr. < *laver* < L. *lavare,* to wash: see LATHER] *Med.* the washing out of an organ, as the stomach, intestinal tract, or sinuses

La·val (lə val′) city in SW Quebec, on an island just north of Montreal: pop. 196,000: also **Ville de La·val** (vēl də là vàl′)

La·val (là vàl′; *E.* lə val′), **Pierre** (pyer) 1883–1945; Fr. politician; premier of France (1931–32; 1935–36): executed for treason

la·va·la·va (lä′və lä′və) *n.* [Samoan] a calico loincloth or skirt worn by men and women on the South Sea islands

lav·a·liere, lav·a·lier (lav′ə lir′, lä′və-) *n.* [Fr. *lavallière,* kind of tie < *Duchesse de La Vallière* (1644–1710), mistress of Louis XIV] an ornament hanging from a chain, worn around the neck: also **la·val·lière** (*also Fr.* là và lyer′)

la·va·tion (lə vā′shən) *n.* [L. *lavatio* < *lavare,* to wash: see LATHER] the act of washing; specif., *same as* LAVAGE

lav·a·to·ry (lav′ə tôr′ē) *n., pl.* **-ries** [LL. *lavatorium* < L. *lavare,* to wash: see LATHER] **1.** a bowl or basin, esp. one with faucets and drainage, for washing the face and hands;

washbowl **2.** *a)* a room equipped with a washbowl, flush toilet, etc.; toilet *b)* [Chiefly Brit.] a flush toilet

lave[1] (lāv) *vt.* **laved, lav′ing** [ME. *laven* < OE. & OFr.: OE. *lafian* (akin to MDu. *laven*, OHG. *labon*) < L. *lavare*; OFr. *laver* < L. *lavare*: see LATHER] [Poet.] **1.** to wash or bathe **2.** to flow along or against **3.** to dip or pour with or as with a ladle —*vi.* to wash or bathe

lave[2] (lāv) *n.* [OE. *laf*: see LEAVE[1]] [Scot.] what is left over

lav·en·der (lav′ən dər) *n.* [ME. < Anglo-Fr. *lavendre* < ML. *lavandria*, akin to *lavendula* (whence G. *lavendel*) < L. *lavare*, to wash (see LATHER): from use as bath perfume] **1.** any of a genus (*Lavandula*) of fragrant European plants of the mint family, having spikes of pale-purplish flowers and yielding an aromatic oil (**oil of lavender**) **2.** the dried flowers, leaves, and stalks of this plant, used to fill sachets and to perfume clothes, linens, etc. **3.** a pale purple —*adj.* pale-purple —*vt.* to perfume with lavender

lavender water a perfume or toilet water made from flowers of the lavender plant

la·ver[1] (lā′vər) *n.* [ME. *lavour* < OFr. *laveoir* < L. *lavatorium* < *lavare*, to wash: see LATHER] [Archaic] **1.** a large basin to wash in; esp., the brass basin of the ancient Jewish Temple used by the priests for ceremonial washing **2.** anything that cleanses spiritually; esp., the water of baptism or the font containing this

la·ver[2] (lā′vər) *n.* [L., water plant] any of various large, edible, ribbonlike seaweeds

lav·er·ock (lav′ər ək, lav′rək) *n.* [LME. *laveroc*, var. of *laverke*: see LARK[1]] [Archaic] *same as* LARK[1]

La·vin·i·a (lə vin′ē ə, -vin′yə) [L.] a feminine name

lav·ish (lav′ish) *adj.* [< ME. *lavas*, abundance < MFr. < OFr. *lavasse*, torrent of rain, prob. < *laver*, to wash < L. *lavare*: see LATHER] **1.** very generous or liberal in giving or spending, often extravagantly so; prodigal **2.** more than enough; very abundant; unstinted [*lavish* entertainment] —*vt.* to give or spend generously or liberally [to *lavish* time and money on pets] —*SYN.* see PROFUSE —**lav′ish·ly** *adv.* —**lav′ish·ness** *n.*

La·voi·sier (lá vwá zyā′; *E.* lə vwä′zē ā′), **An·toine Lau·rent** (än twän′ lō rän′) 1743–94; Fr. pioneer in modern chemistry; guillotined

law (lô) *n.* [ME. *lawe* < OE. *lagu* < Anglo-N. *lagu*, akin to ON. *lög*, pl. of *lag*, something laid down or settled < IE. base *legh*-, to lie down (whence LIE[1])] **1.** *a)* all the rules of conduct established and enforced by the authority, legislation, or custom of a given community, state, or other group *b)* any one of such rules **2.** the condition existing when obedience to such rules is general [to establish *law* and order] **3.** the branch of knowledge dealing with such rules; jurisprudence **4.** the system of courts in which such rules are referred to in defending one's rights, securing justice, etc. [to resort to *law* to settle a matter] **5.** all such rules having to do with a particular sphere of human activity [business *law*] **6.** common law, as distinguished from equity **7.** the profession of lawyers, judges, etc. (often with *the*) **8.** *a)* a sequence of events in nature or in human activities that has been observed to occur with unvarying uniformity under the same conditions: often **law of nature** *b)* the formulation in words of such a sequence [the *law* of gravitation, the *law* of diminishing returns] **9.** any rule or principle expected to be observed [the *laws* of health, a *law* of grammar] **10.** inherent tendency; instinct [the *law* of self-preservation] **11.** *Eccles. a)* a divine commandment *b)* all divine commandments collectively **12.** *Math., Logic,* etc. a general principle to which all applicable cases must conform [the *laws* of exponents] **13.** [Brit.] *Sports* an allowance in distance or time, as in a race; handicap —*vi., vt.* [Colloq. or Dial.] to take legal action (against) —**go to law** to take a problem or dispute to a law court for settlement —**lay down the law 1.** to give explicit orders in an authoritative manner **2.** to give a scolding (*to*) —**read law** to study to become a lawyer —**the Law 1.** the Mosaic law, or the part of the Hebrew Scriptures containing it; specif., the Pentateuch ☆**2.** [I-] [Colloq.] a policeman or the police *SYN.*—**law**, in its specific application, implies prescription and enforcement by a ruling authority [the *law* of the land]; a **rule** may not be authoritatively enforced, but it is generally observed in the interests of order, uniformity, etc. [the *rules* of golf]; **regulation** refers to a rule of a group or organization, enforced by authority [military *regulations*]; a **statute** is a law enacted by a legislative body; an **ordinance** is a local, generally municipal, law; a **canon** is, strictly, a law of a church, but the term is also used of any rule or principle regarded as true or in conformity with good usage [the *canons* of taste] See also THEORY

Law (lô) **1. (Andrew) Bon·ar** (bän′ər), 1858–1923; Brit. statesman, born in Canada; prime minister (1922–23) **2. John,** 1671–1729; Scot. financier

law·a·bid·ing (lô′ə bīd′in) *adj.* obeying the law

law·book (-book′) *n.* a book containing or discussing laws, esp. one used as a textbook by law students

law·break·er (-brā′kər) *n.* a person who violates the law —**law′break′ing** *adj., n.*

law court a court for administering justice under the law

law French *same as* NORMAN FRENCH (sense 2)

law·ful (-fəl) *adj.* **1.** in conformity with the principles of the law; permitted by law [a *lawful* act]: see also LEGAL (sense 2) **2.** recognized by or established by law; just or valid [*lawful* debts] **3.** obeying the law; law-abiding — *SYN.* see LEGAL —**law′ful·ly** *adv.* —**law′ful·ness** *n.*

law·giv·er (-giv′ər) *n.* a person who draws up, introduces, or enacts a code of laws for a nation or people; lawmaker; legislator —**law′giv′ing** *n., adj.*

law·less (-lis) *adj.* **1.** without law; not regulated by the authority of law [a *lawless* city] **2.** not in conformity with law; illegal [*lawless* practices] **3.** not obeying the law; unruly; disorderly —**law′less·ly** *adv.* —**law′less·ness** *n.*

law·mak·er (-mā′kər) *n.* a person who makes or helps to make laws; esp., a member of a legislature; legislator —**law′mak′ing** *adj., n.*

law·man (-man′) *n., pl.* **-men** (-men′) a law officer; esp., a marshal, sheriff, constable, etc.

Law·man (lô′mən) *same as* LAYAMON

law merchant all the rules and usages originating in the customs of merchants and now applied to dealings in trade and commerce, where not changed by statute; mercantile or commercial law

lawn[1] (lôn) *n.* [ME. *launde* < OFr., heath < Bret. *lann*, territory, country, akin to W. *llan*, open space: see LAND] **1.** land covered with grass kept closely mowed, esp. in front of or around a house **2.** [Archaic] an open space in a forest; glade —**lawn′y** *adj.*

lawn[2] (lôn) *n.* [ME. *lawne*, for *laune lynen*, Laon linen < *Laon*, city in France, where made] a fine, sheer cloth of linen or cotton, used for blouses, curtains, etc. —**lawn′y** *adj.*

lawn bowling *same as* BOWLS (sense 1)

lawn mower a hand-propelled or power-driven machine for cutting the grass of a lawn

lawn tennis *see* TENNIS

law of mass action the law that the rate of a chemical reaction is directly proportional to the concentrations of the reactants

Law of Moses *same as* MOSAIC LAW

law of nations *same as* INTERNATIONAL LAW

Law·rence[1] (lôr′əns, lär′-) **1.** a masculine name: see LAURENCE **2. D(avid) H(erbert),** 1885–1930; Eng. novelist & poet **3. Ernest O(rlando),** 1901–58; U.S. physicist **4. Sir Thomas,** 1769–1830; Eng. portrait painter **5. T(homas) E(dward),** (changed name, 1927, to *Thomas Edward Shaw*) 1888–1935; Brit. adventurer & writer: called **Lawrence of Arabia**

Lawrence[2] [after A. A. *Lawrence* (1814–86) of Boston] **1.** city in NE Mass.: pop. 67,000 **2.** city in NE Kans., on the Kansas River: pop. 46,000

☆**law·ren·ci·um** (lô ren′sē əm, lä-) *n.* [after E. O. LAWRENCE] a radioactive chemical element produced by bombarding californium with boron nuclei: symbol, Lr; at. wt., 256 (?); at. no., 103

law·suit (lô′sōōt′) *n.* a suit between private parties at law or in equity; case before a civil court

Law·ton (lôt′'n) [< Maj. Gen. Henry W. *Lawton* (1843–99)] city in SW Okla.: pop. 74,000

law·yer (lô′yər) *n.* [ME. *lawyere*: see LAW & -IER] a person who has been trained in the law, esp. one whose profession is advising others in matters of law or representing them in lawsuits
SYN.—**lawyer** is the general term for a person trained in the law and authorized to advise or represent others in legal matters; **counselor** and its British equivalent, **barrister**, refer to a lawyer who conducts cases in court; **attorney**, usually, and its British equivalent, **solicitor**, always, refer to a lawyer legally empowered to act for a client, as in drawing up a contract or will, settling property, etc.; **counsel**, often equivalent to **counselor**, is frequently used collectively for a group of counselors

lax (laks) *adj.* [ME. < L. *laxus* < IE. base *(s)leg*-, to be loose, lax, whence SLACK[1]] **1.** *a)* loose; emptying easily: said of the bowels *b)* having lax bowels **2.** slack; of a loose texture; not rigid or tight **3.** not strict or exact; careless [*lax* morals] **4.** *Bot.* loose; open: said of a flower cluster **5.** *Phonet.* pronounced with the jaw and tongue relatively relaxed: said of certain vowels, as *e* in *met*, *i* in *hill*: opposed to TENSE[1] —*n.* a lax vowel —*SYN.* REMISS —**lax′ly** *adv.* —**lax′ness** *n.*

lax·a·tion (lak sā′shən) *n.* [ME. *laxacion* < L. *laxatio*] the act or process of making or being made lax

lax·a·tive (lak′sə tiv) *adj.* [ME. *laxatif* < OFr. < ML. *laxativus* < LL., mitigating < pp. of L. *laxare*, to relax, slacken < *laxus*: see LAX] tending to make lax; specif., making the bowels loose and relieving constipation —*n.* any laxative medicine; mild cathartic —*SYN.* see PHYSIC

lax·i·ty (-sə tē) *n.* [Fr. *laxité* < L. *laxitas*] the quality or condition of being lax; looseness

Lax·ness (läks′nes), **Hall·dór (Kiljan)** (häl′dōr) (born *Halldór Gudjonsson*) 1902– ; Icelandic novelist

lay[1] (lā) *vt.* **laid, lay′ing** [ME. *leyen*, new formation < 3d pers. sing. of earlier *leggen* < OE. *lecgan*, lit., to make lie (akin to Goth. *lagjan*, G. *legen*) < pt. base of OE. *licgan*, to LIE[1]] **1.** to cause to come down or fall with force; knock down, as from an erect position [a blow *laid* him low] **2.** to cause to lie; place or put so as to be in a resting

or recumbent position; deposit (often with *on* or *in*) *[lay the pen on the desk]* **3.** *a)* to put down or place (bricks, carpeting, etc.) in the correct position or way for a specific purpose *b)* to cause to be situated in a particular place or condition *[the scene is laid in France]* *c)* to establish or prepare as a basis or for use *[to lay the groundwork]* **4.** to place; put; set: esp. of something abstract *[to lay emphasis on accuracy]* **5.** to produce and deposit (an egg or eggs) **6.** *a)* to cause to subside or settle *[lay the dust]* *b)* to allay, suppress, overcome, or appease *[to lay a ghost, lay one's fears]* **7.** to press or smooth down *[to lay the nap of cloth]* **8.** to bet (a specified sum, etc.). **9.** to impose or place (a tax, penalty, etc. *on* or *upon*) **10.** to work out; devise *[to lay plans]* **11.** to prepare (a table) for a meal; set with silverware, plates, etc. **12.** to advance, present, or assert *[to lay claim to property, to lay a matter before the voters]* **13.** to attribute; ascribe; charge; impute *[to lay the blame on someone]* **14.** *a)* to form (the strands of a rope) by twisting yarn *b)* to form (a rope) by arranging and twisting the strands ☆**15.** [Slang] to have sexual intercourse with **16.** *Mil.* to aim (a cannon) at the required elevation —*vi.* **1.** to lay an egg or eggs **2.** to bet; wager **3.** to lie; recline: a dialectal or substandant usage **4.** [Dial.] to get ready; plan *[laying to rob a store]* **5.** *Naut.* to station oneself in a required or specified position *[they lay aft]* —*n.* **1.** the way or position in which something is situated or arranged *[the lay of the land]* ☆**2.** a share in the profits of some enterprise, esp. of a whaling expedition **3.** the direction or amount of twist of the strands of a rope, cable, etc. ☆**4.** [Colloq.] terms of employment, a sale, etc. ☆**5.** [Slang] *a)* an instance of sexual intercourse *b)* a woman regarded as a sexual partner **6.** [Chiefly Brit. Slang] one's occupation, esp. as a criminal —**lay about (one)** **1.** to deliver blows on all sides; strike out in every direction **2.** to act energetically —**lay a course 1.** *Naut.* to proceed in a certain direction without the need for tacking **2.** to make plans to do something —**lay aside 1.** to put to one side; lay out of the way **2.** to save; lay away —**lay away 1.** to set aside for future use; save ☆**2.** to set (merchandise) aside for future delivery ☆**3.** to bury (usually in the passive) —**lay by 1.** to save; lay away **2.** [Dial.] ☆*a)* to cultivate (a crop) for the last time *b)* to harvest (a crop or crops) —**lay down 1.** to sacrifice or give up (one's life) **2.** to assert or declare emphatically **3.** to bet; wager **4.** to store away, as wine in a cellar —**lay for** [Colloq.] to be waiting to attack —**lay in** to get and store away —**lay into** [Slang] **1.** to attack and hit repeatedly; beat **2.** to attack with words; scold —**lay it on (thick)** to exaggerate, esp. in praising or blaming —**lay off 1.** to put (a garment, etc.) aside ☆**2.** to put (an employee) out of work, esp. temporarily **3.** to mark off the boundaries of ☆**4.** [Slang] *a)* to cease *b)* to stop criticizing, teasing, etc. *c)* to stop for a rest **5.** [Slang] to transfer part of (a bet) to another bookmaker so as to minimize risk: said of a bookmaker —**lay on 1.** to spread on **2.** to attack with force; strike repeatedly —**lay oneself open** to expose oneself to attack, blame, etc. —**lay open 1.** to open up; cut open **2.** to expose; uncover —**lay out 1.** to spend **2.** to arrange according to a plan **3.** to spread out (clothes, equipment, etc.) ready for wear, inspection, etc. **4.** to make (a dead body) ready for burial **5.** [Slang] to knock down or make unconscious **6.** [Slang] to scold or censure (someone) —**lay over 1.** to stop a while in a place before going on —**lay to 1.** to attribute to; credit to or blame on **2.** to apply oneself with vigor **3.** *Naut.* *a)* to check the motion of a ship and cause it to become stationary *b)* to lie more or less stationary with the bow to the wind —**lay to rest** to bury; inter —**lay up 1.** to store for future use; hoard **2.** to disable; confine to bed or the sickroom **3.** to put (a ship) in dock, as for repairs

lay[2] (lā) *pt. of* LIE[1]

lay[3] (lā) *adj.* [ME. *lai* < OFr. < LL.(Ec.) *laicus*, lay, not priestly < Gr. *laikos* < *laos*, the people] **1.** of or consisting of the laity, or ordinary people, as distinguished from the clergy **2.** not belonging to or connected with a given profession; nonprofessional *[a legal handbook for lay readers]*

lay[4] (lā) *n.* [ME. & OFr. *lai* < Bret. **laid*, song, akin to Ir. *laod*] **1.** a short poem, esp. a narrative poem, for singing, orig. as by a medieval minstrel **2.** [Archaic or Poet.] a song or melody

lay·a·bout (lā'ə bout') *n.* [Chiefly Brit. Colloq.] a lazy idler or loafer; bum

Lay·a·mon (lā'ə mən, lī'-) fl. c. 1200; Eng. poet and chronicler

lay analyst a psychoanalyst who is not a medical doctor

lay·a·way plan (lā'ə wā') a method of buying by making a deposit on something which is delivered only after it is paid for in full, as by monthly payments

lay brother a member of a monastery who has taken certain simple vows and wears a distinctive habit but is not in holy orders: lay brothers are generally employed in manual labor

lay-by (-bī') *n.* **1.** a widened section of a stream, canal, etc. for vessels to lay over or pass **2.** a railroad siding **3.** [Brit.] a widened section or turnout along a highway, for emergency parking

lay day [short for *delay day*] **1.** *Commerce* any of the days allowed for loading or unloading a ship without payment

of extra charge **2.** *Naut.* any of the days that a ship is delayed in port

lay·er (lā'ər) *n.* **1.** a person or thing that lays **2.** a single thickness, coat, fold, or stratum **3.** a shoot or twig (of a living plant) bent down and partly covered with earth so that it may take root —*vt., vi.* to grow (a plant) by means of a layer (sense 3)

lay·er·age (lā'ər ij) *n.* the growing of plants by layering

☆**layer cake** a cake made in two or more layers, with icing, preserves, etc. between them

lay·ette (lā et') *n.* [Fr., dim. of *laie*, packing box, drawer < Fl. *laeye* < MDu. *lade*, a chest, trunk < Gmc. **hlatho-*, container < base of LADE] a complete outfit for a newborn baby, including clothes, bedding, and accessories

lay figure [earlier *layman* < Du. *leeman* < MDu. *led*, limb, joint, akin to OE. *lith*, limb + *man*, man] **1.** an artist's jointed model of the human form, on which drapery is arranged to get the proper effect **2.** a person who is a mere puppet or a nonentity

lay·man (lā'mən) *n., pl.* -men (-mən) [LAY[3] + MAN] **1.** a member of the laity; person not a clergyman **2.** a person not belonging to or skilled in a given profession *[a medical textbook not for the layman]*

☆**lay-off** (lā'ôf') *n.* [< phr. LAY OFF] the act of laying off; esp., temporary unemployment, or the period of this

lay of the land 1. the way the land is situated; arrangement of the terrain **2.** the existing state or disposition of affairs Also **lie of the land**

☆**lay-out** (lā'out') *n.* **1.** the act of laying something out **2.** the manner in which anything is laid out; arrangement; specif., the plan or makeup of a newspaper, book, page, advertisement, etc. **3.** the thing laid out **4.** the art or process of arranging type, illustrations, etc. in an advertisement, newspaper, etc. **5.** an outfit or set, as of tools **6.** [Colloq.] a residence, factory, etc., esp. when large and complex

☆**lay·o·ver** (-ō'vər) *n.* [< phr. LAY OVER] a stopping for a while in some place during a journey

lay reader a layman authorized to conduct some religious services, as in the Episcopal Church, or to read portions of the service, as in the Roman Catholic Church

lay·up (-up') *n.* ☆*Basketball* a leaping, one-handed shot made from a position very close to the basket, usually off the backboard

la·zar (laz'ər, lā'zər) *n.* [ME. < ML. *lazarus*, leper < LL. (Ec.) *Lazarus* < Gr.(Ec.) *Lazaros*, LAZARUS] [Rare] an impoverished, diseased beggar, esp. a leper

laz·a·ret·to (laz'ə ret'ō) *n., pl.* -tos [It. < Venetian *lazareto, nazareto* < Venetian church of Santa Madonna di *Nazaret*, used as a plague hospital during the 15th c.; initial *l-* after *lazzaro*, leper: see LAZAR] **1.** formerly, a public hospital for poor people having contagious diseases, esp. for lepers **2.** a building or ship used as a quarantine station **3.** in certain ships, a storage space between decks Also, and for 3 usually, **laz'a·ret', laz'a·rette'** (-ret')

Laz·a·rus (laz'ə rəs) [LL.(Ec.) < Gr.(Ec.) *Lazaros* < Heb. *el'āzār*, lit., God has helped] **1.** a masculine name **2.** *Bible* *a)* the brother of Mary and Martha, raised from the dead by Jesus: John 11 *b)* the diseased beggar in Jesus' parable of the rich man and the beggar: Luke 16:19–31 —*n.* [often l-] any horribly diseased beggar, esp. a leper

Laz·a·rus (laz'ə rəs), **Emma** 1849–87; U.S. poet

laze (lāz) *vi.* **lazed, laz'ing** [back-formation < LAZY] to be lazy or idle; loaf —*vt.* to spend (time, etc.) in idleness (often with *away*) —*n.* an act or instance of lazing

laz·u·lite (laz'yoo līt') *n.* [G. *lazulith*, altered (after ML. *lazulum*, azure + Gr. *lithos*, stone) < earlier *lazurstein* < ML. *lazur* (see AZURE) + *stein*, STONE] a glassy, azure-blue mineral, (Mg,Fe)Al₂(PO₄)₂(OH), that is a monoclinic hydrous aluminum phosphate

la·zy (lā'zē) *adj.* **-zi·er, -zi·est** [Early ModE., prob. < MLowG. or MDu., as in MLowG. *lasich*, slack, loose < IE. *les-*, slack, tired, akin to base **lēi-* (see LATE)] **1.** not eager or willing to work or exert oneself; indolent; slothful **2.** slow and heavy; sluggish *[a lazy river]* **3.** tending to cause laziness *[a lazy day]* ☆**4.** designating or of a letter or figure placed on its side in a livestock brand —*vi., vt.* **-zied, -zy·ing** *same as* LAZE —**la'zi·ly** *adv.* —**la'zi·ness** *n.*

la·zy·bones (-bōnz') *n.* [Colloq.] a lazy person

☆**Lazy Susan** a revolving tray placed at the center of a dining table, from which one can help oneself to food

lazy tongs a device consisting of a series of jointed bars crossing each other: it can be extended to pick up or deposit small objects at a distance

laz·za·ro·ne (laz'ə rō'nē; *It.* läd'zä rō'ne) *n., pl.* -ro'ni (-nē) [It. < *lazzaro*, leper: see LAZAR] any of a class of homeless beggars formerly common on the streets of Naples

lb. [L. *libra*, pl. *librae*] pound; pounds

L.B. **1.** [L. *Lit(t)erarum Baccalaureus*] Bachelor of Letters **2.** Local Board

L bar (or **beam**) a steel bar or beam having an L-shaped cross section

lbs. pounds

LC- *U.S. Navy* landing craft (following letter indicates type, as **LCV**, Landing Craft-Vehicle)

L/C, l/c letter of credit

L. C. Library of Congress

LAZY TONGS

l.c. 1. [L. *loco citato*] in the place cited **2.** left center (of the stage) **3.** *Printing* lower case

L.C.D., l.c.d. least (or lowest) common denominator

‡l'cha·im, l'chay·im (lə khä′yim) *interj.* [Heb.] to life: a drinking toast

L.C.L., l.c.l. *Commerce* less than carload lot

L.C.M., l.c.m. least (or lowest) common multiple

LCT, L.C.T. local civil time

LD, L.D. Low Dutch

Ld. Lord

L.D.S. 1. Latter-day Saints **2.** Licentiate in Dental Surgery

-le (′l) *a suffix of various origins and meanings:* **1.** [ME. n. suffix *-el, -le* < OE. *-ol, -ul, -el*] *a)* small [*icicle*] *b)* a person who does (something specified) [*beadle*] *c)* a thing used for doing (something specified) [*girdle, handle*] **2.** [ME. adj. suffix *-el* < OE. *-ol*] having a tendency toward [*brittle, fickle*] **3.** [ME. v. suffix *-len* < OE. *-lian*] used with a *frequentative force* [*babble, prattle*]

le., le *Football* left end

lea¹ (lē) *n.* [ME. *leye* < OE. *leah*, orig., open ground in a wood, akin to Du. *-loo* (in *Waterloo*), G. *-loh*, grove < IE. base *leuk-*, to light, whence LIGHT & L. *lucus*, grove, orig., clearing, glade] [*Chiefly Poet.*] a meadow, grassy field, or pasture; grassland

lea² (lē) *n.* [ME. *lee*, prob. taken as sing. of *leese* < OFr. *lesse*: see LEASH] a measure of yarn varying from 80 to 300 yards, according to the kind of yarn (usually 80 yards for wool, 120 yards for silk and cotton, 300 yards for linen)

lea. **1.** league **2.** leather

leach (lēch) *vt.* [prob. < OE. *leccan*, to water, irrigate, orig. a caus. form of base akin to ON. *leka:* see LEAK] **1.** to cause (a liquid) to filter down through some material **2.** to subject to the washing action of a filtering liquid [*wood ashes are leached* to extract lye] **3.** to extract (a soluble substance) from some material by causing water to filter down through the material [*lye is leached* from wood ashes] *—vi.* **1.** to lose soluble matter as a result of the filtering through of water [*soil that has leached* badly] **2.** to dissolve and be washed away *—n.* **1.** the action of leaching **2.** a sievelike container used in leaching **3.** the solution obtained by leaching *—***leach′a·ble** *adj.* *—***leach′er** *n.*

☆**leach·y** (-ē) *adj.* [prec. + -Y²] porous, as soil

Lea·cock (lē′käk), **Stephen (Butler)** 1869-1944; Canad. humorist & political economist, born in England

lead¹ (lēd) *vt.* **led, lead′ing** [ME. *leden* < OE. *lædan*, caus. of *lithan*, to travel, go, akin to G. *leiten:* see LOAD] **1.** *a)* to show the way to, or direct the course of, by going before or along with; conduct; guide *b)* to show (the way) in this manner *c)* to mark the way for [*lights to lead* you there] **2.** to guide, or cause to follow one, by physical contact, holding the hand, pulling a rope, etc. [*to lead* a horse by the bridle] **3.** to conduct (water, steam, rope, etc.) in a certain direction, channel, or the like **4.** *a)* to guide or direct, as by persuasion or influence, to a course of action or thought [*to lead* pupils to think clearly] *b)* to cause; prompt [*troubles that led* him to drink] **5.** to be the head of; specif., *a)* to proceed at the front of (a parade, etc.) *b)* to act as chief officer of; command the operations of (a military unit) *c)* to direct the operations of (an expedition, etc.) *d)* to direct, conduct, or serve as the leader or conductor of (an orchestra, ballet, etc.) **6.** *a)* to be the first or foremost among; be at the head of [*to lead* one's class in grades] *b)* to be ahead of by a specified margin **7.** *a)* to live; spend; pass [*to lead* a hard life] *b)* to cause to live or spend [*to lead* someone a dog's life] **8.** to aim a rifle, throw a ball, etc. just ahead of (a moving target or receiver) **9.** *Card Games* to begin the play with (a card or suit); lay down as the first card or suit of a hand or round *—vi.* **1.** to show the way by going before or along; act as guide **2.** to be led; submit to being led: said esp. of a horse **3.** to be or form a way (*to, from, under,* etc.); tend in a certain direction; go **4.** to come, or bring one, as a result (with *to*) [one thing led to another, a cold can lead to pneumonia] **5.** to be or go first; act as leader ☆**6.** *Boxing* to aim a first blow or one designed to test an opponent's defense [*to lead* with a right jab] **7.** *Card Games* to play, or have the right to play, the first card of a hand or round *—n.* **1.** the part of director or leader; leadership [*to take the lead* in a project] **2.** example [follow his *lead*] **3.** *a)* first or front place; precedence [the horse in the *lead*] *b)* the amount or distance that one is ahead [*to hold a safe lead*] **4.** same as LEASH (sense 1) **5.** anything that leads or serves as a clue **6.** a long, narrow, navigable passage in an ice pack or ice field ☆**7.** *Baseball* a position taken by a base runner some distance away from his base in the direction of the next **8.** *Boxing* the act of leading, or the blow used **9.** *Card Games* the act or right of playing first, as in a hand, or the card or suit played **10.** *Elec.* a wire carrying current from one point to another in a circuit, or to or from a piece of apparatus **11.** *Journalism* the opening paragraph of a news story, containing all the essential facts of the story ☆**12.** *Mining* a stratum of ore; lode, ledge, or vein **13.** *Music* the leading part or main melody in a harmonic composition **14.** *Naut.* the course of a rope **15.** *Theater a)* the principal role, or a main role, in a play or other production *b)* the actor or

actress who plays such a role *—adj.* acting as leader [the *lead* horse] *—SYN.* see GUIDE *—***lead off 1.** to begin; start ☆**2.** *Baseball* to be the first batter in the lineup or of an inning *—***lead on 1.** to conduct further **2.** to lure or tempt *—***lead one a merry chase** (or **dance**) to cause a person trouble by luring him into a vain pursuit *—***lead up to 1.** to prepare the way for **2.** to approach (a subject, etc.) in a subtle or indirect way *—***lead with one's chin** [Colloq.] to act so imprudently as to invite disaster

lead² (led) *n.* [ME. *lede* < OE. *lead*, akin to Du. *lood*, G. *lot*, plummet, prob. < Celt. (as in MIr. *luiade*, lead)] **1.** a heavy, soft, malleable, bluish-gray metallic chemical element used for piping and in numerous alloys and compounds: symbol, Pb; at. wt., 207.19; at. no., 82; sp. gr., 11.344; melt. pt., 327.43°C; boil. pt., 1515°C **2.** anything made of this metal; specif., *a)* a weight for sounding depths at sea, etc.: it is attached to a line and tossed over the side of the ship *b)* any of the strips of lead used to hold the individual panes in ornamental windows: *usually used in pl. c)* [*pl.*] [Brit.] sheets of lead used for covering a roof *d) Printing* a thin strip of type metal inserted to increase the space between lines of type **3.** bullets **4.** a thin stick of graphite, used in pencils *—adj.* made of or containing lead *—vt.* **1.** to cover, line, weight, or fasten with lead or leads **2.** *Ceramics* to glaze (pottery) with a glaze made primarily of lead **3.** *Printing* to increase the space between (lines of type) by inserting thin strips of type metal

lead acetate a poisonous, colorless, crystalline compound, Pb(C₂H₃O₂)₂·3H₂O, used as a mordant in dyeing, and in making varnishes and paints

lead arsenate a very poisonous, colorless, crystalline compound, Pb₃(AsO₄)₂, used as an insecticide and, sometimes, as a herbicide

lead colic a form of lead poisoning characterized by intense abdominal pain

lead·en (led′'n) *adj.* **1.** made of lead **2.** having the inert heaviness of lead; hard to move or lift **3.** sluggish; dull; heavy in action, feeling, etc. **4.** depressed; dispirited; gloomy **5.** of a dull gray *—***lead′en·ly** *adv.* *—***lead′en·ness** *n.*

lead·er (lē′dər) *n.* **1.** a person or thing that leads; directing, commanding, or guiding head, as of a group or activity **2.** a horse harnessed before all others in the same hitch or as one of the two horses in the foremost span **3.** a pipe for carrying fluid; specif., ☆*a)* a downspout for rain water *b)* a hot-air duct in a heating system **4.** a tendon **5.** a section of blank film or recording tape at the beginning of a reel, for use in threading, etc. ☆**6.** a featured article of trade, esp. one offered at an attractively low price: cf. LOSS LEADER **7.** *Bot.* the central or dominant stem of a plant, esp. of a tree ☆**8.** *Fishing* a short piece of catgut, etc., often used to attach the hook, lure, etc. to the fish line **9.** *Journalism* same as LEADING ARTICLE **10.** *Music a)* a conductor, esp. of a dance band *b)* the main performer in an instrumental or vocal section, generally given the solo passages **11.** *Naut.* a wooden block or metal piece with holes in it for leading lines to their proper places **12.** [*pl.*] *Printing* dots, dashes, etc. in a line, used to direct the eye across the page, as in a table of contents *—***lead′er·less** *adj.*

lead·er·ship (-ship′) *n.* **1.** the position or guidance of a leader **2.** the ability to lead **3.** the leaders of a group

lead glass glass that contains lead oxide

lead-in (lēd′in′) *n.* **1.** the wire leading from an aerial or antenna to a receiver or transmitter **2.** an introduction *—adj.* that is a lead-in

lead·ing¹ (led′in) *n.* **1.** a covering or being covered with lead **2.** strips or sheets of lead, collectively

lead·ing² (lē′diŋ) *n.* the action of one that leads; guidance; direction; leadership *—adj.* **1.** that leads; guiding **2.** principal; chief **3.** playing the lead in a play, motion picture, etc. *—SYN.* see CHIEF

lead·ing article (lē′diŋ) the principal article or, esp. in England, editorial in a newspaper

lead·ing edge (lē′diŋ) *Aeron.* the front edge of a propeller blade or airfoil

lead·ing light (lē′diŋ) an important or influential member of a club, community, etc.

lead·ing question (lē′diŋ) a question put in such a way as to suggest the answer sought

lead·ing strings (lē′diŋ) **1.** strings or straps formerly used to guide and support a young child learning to walk **2.** a condition of childlike dependence or restricting guidance: usually in phr. **in leading strings** (to)

leading tone (lē′diŋ) *Music* the seventh tone of a scale, a half tone below the tonic

lead line (led) *Naut.* a line with a lead weight at one end, used for measuring the depth of water

lead-off (lēd′ôf′) *n.* the first in a series of actions, moves, etc. *—adj.* ☆*Baseball* designating the first batter in a lineup or of an inning

lead pencil (led) a pencil consisting of a slender stick of graphite encased in wood, etc.

☆**lead-pipe cinch** (led′pīp′) [extended (prob. in allusion to the pliability of *lead pipe*) < PIPE, sense 12] [Slang] **1.** a thing very easy to do **2.** a sure thing; certainty

☆**lead·plant** (led′plant′) *n.* a small American plant

(*Amorpha canescens*) thought by early miners to indicate lead deposits

lead poisoning (led) an acute or chronic poisoning caused by the absorption of lead or any of its salts into the body: it may result in anemia, constipation, colic, paralysis, or muscular cramps

leads·man (ledz′mən) *n.*, *pl.* **-men** (-mən) *Naut.* a man who uses a lead line to take soundings

lead tetraethyl *same as* TETRAETHYL LEAD

lead time (lēd) *Manufacturing* the period of time required from the decision to make a product to the beginning of actual production

lead·wort (led′wurt′) *n.* [LEAD² + WORT²] any of several shrubby plants (genus *Plumbago*) grown for their ornamental white, blue, or red flowers, esp. in warm climates

lead·y (led′ē) *adj.* resembling lead; leaden

leaf (lēf) *n.*, *pl.* **leaves** [ME. *lefe* < OE. *leaf*, akin to Du. *loof*, G. *laub* < IE. base *leubh-*, to peel off, pull off, whence Lith. *lupù*, to skin, pare off] 1. any of the flat, thin, expanded organs, usually green, growing laterally from the stem or twig of a plant: it usually consists of a broad blade, a petiole, or stalk, and stipules and is involved in the processes of photosynthesis and transpiration 2. in popular usage *a)* the blade of a leaf *b)* a petal 3. leaves collectively [choice tobacco *leaf*] 4. a design resembling a leaf, used as an ornament in architecture 5. a sheet of paper, esp. as part of a book, with a page on each side 6. *a)* a very thin sheet of metal; lamina *b)* such sheets collectively [covered with gold *leaf*] 7. *a)* a hinged section of a table top, forming an extension when raised into place *b)* a board inserted into a table top to increase its surface 8. a flat, hinged or movable part of a folding door, shutter, etc. ☆9. one of a number of metal strips laid one upon another to make a leaf spring —*vi.* 1. to put forth or bear leaves (often with *out*) 2. to turn the pages of a book, etc., esp. so as to glance quickly (*through*) —*vt.* to turn the pages of —**in leaf** having leaves grown; with foliage —**take a leaf from someone's book** to follow someone's example —**turn over a new leaf** to make a new start —**leaf′less** *adj.* —**leaf′like** *adj.*

leaf·age (-ij) *n.* leaves collectively; foliage

leaf bud a bud from which only stems and leaves develop, in contrast to flower buds, or mixed buds which produce both leaves and flowers

leaf fat fat built up in layers around the kidneys of a hog, used in making lard

☆**leaf hopper** any of a family (Cicadellidae) of homopterous insects that leap from one plant to another, sucking the juices and often transmitting plant diseases

leaf insect any of a number of sluggish, winged insects (order Phasmida) having a striking resemblance to leaves

leaf lard the highest grade of lard, made from leaf fat

leaf·let (-lit) *n.* 1. one of the divisions of a compound leaf 2. a small or young leaf 3. a separate sheet of printed matter, often folded but not stitched

leaf miner any of a large number of unrelated small moths and flies whose larval stages burrow into and eat the soft tissues of leaves and green stems

leaf mold 1. a rich soil consisting largely of decayed leaves 2. a mold that forms on leaves

leaf spot any of various plant diseases characterized by lesions in the form of spots on the leaves

☆**leaf spring** a spring built up of curved strips of metal: see SPRING, illus.

leaf·stalk (-stôk′) *n.* the slender, usually cylindrical portion of a leaf, which supports the blade and is attached to the stem; petiole

leaf·y (lēf′ē) *adj.* **leaf′i·er**, **leaf′i·est** 1. of, covered with, consisting of, or like a leaf or leaves 2. having many leaves 3. having broad leaves or consisting mainly of such leaves [spinach is a *leafy* vegetable] —**leaf′i·ness** *n.*

league¹ (lēg) *n.* [ME. *ligg* < OFr. *ligue* < It. *liga* < *legare* < L. *ligare*, to bind: see LIGATURE] 1. a compact or covenant made by nations, groups, or individuals for promoting common interests, assuring mutual protection, etc. 2. an association or alliance of individuals, groups, or nations formed by such a covenant 3. *Sports* a group of teams organized to compete against one another ☆4. [Colloq.] a division according to grade or quality; class —*vt.*, *vi.* **leagued**, **leagu′ing** to form into a league —*SYN.* see ALLIANCE —**in league** associated for a common purpose; allied

league² (lēg) *n.* [ME. *lege* < OFr. *legue* < LL. *leuga*, *leuca*, Gallic mile, of Celt. origin] 1. a measure of distance varying in different times and countries: in English-speaking countries it is usually about 3 statute miles or 3 nautical miles ☆2. an old measure of land in parts of the U.S. that were formerly Mexican, equal to about 4,400 acres

League of Nations an association of nations (1920–46), established to promote international cooperation and peace: it was succeeded by the United Nations

lea·guer¹ (lē′gər) *n.* [Du. *leger*, a camp, bed: see LAIR] [Archaic] 1. a siege 2. *a)* a besieging army *b)* its camp —*vt.* [Archaic] to besiege

leagu·er² (lē′gər) *n.* a member of a league

Le·ah (lē′ə) [? Heb. *lē′āh*, gazelle, or ? *lā′āh*, to tire, weary] 1. a feminine name 2. *Bible* the elder of the sisters who were wives of Jacob: Gen. 29:13–30

leak (lēk) *vi.* [ME. *leken* < ON. *leka*, to drip < IE. base *leg-*, to drip, trickle, whence OIr. *legaim*, (I) dissolve, W. *llaith*, damp & LACK] 1. to let a fluid substance out or in accidentally [the boat *leaks*] 2. to enter or escape accidentally from an object or container (often with *in* or *out*) 3. to become known little by little, by accident, carelessness, or treachery [the truth *leaked* out] —*vt.* 1. to permit (water, air, light, radiation, etc.) to pass accidentally in or out; allow to leak 2. to allow (ostensibly secret or private information) to become known —*n.* 1. an accidental hole or crack that lets something out or in 2. any means of escape for something that ought not to be let out, lost, etc. 3. the fact of leaking; leakage ☆4. a disclosure, as by a government official, ostensibly accidental but actually intended to produce an effect: in full, **news leak** 5. *a)* a loss of electrical charge through faulty insulation *b)* the point where this occurs 6. [Slang] the act of urinating

leak·age (-ij) *n.* 1. an act or instance of leaking; leak 2. something that leaks in or out 3. the amount that leaks in or out 4. *Commerce* an allowance for a partial loss by leaking, as of liquids in shipment

Lea·key (lē′kē), **L(ewis) S(eymour) B(azett)** 1903– ; Brit. anthropologist, born in Kenya

leak·y (lē′kē) *adj.* **leak′i·er**, **leak′i·est** allowing the accidental entrance or escape of a fluid substance; having a leak or leaks —**leak′i·ness** *n.*

leal (lēl) *adj.* [north Brit. dial. & Scot. < ME. *lele* < OFr. < L. *legalis*: cf. LEGAL, LOYAL] [Archaic or Scot.] loyal; true —**leal′ly** *adv.*

lean¹ (lēn) *vi.* **leaned** or **leant**, **lean′ing** [ME. *lenen* < OE. *hlinian*, to lean, *hlænan*, to cause to lean, akin to G. *lehnen* < IE. base *klei-*, to incline, lean, whence Gr. *klinein* (cf. CLINIC), L. *clinare* (cf. INCLINE)] 1. to bend or deviate from an upright position; stand at a slant; incline 2. to bend or incline the body so as to rest part of one's weight upon or against something [he *leaned* on the desk] 3. to depend for encouragement, aid, etc.; rely (*on* or *upon*) 4. to have a particular mental inclination; tend (*toward* or *to* a certain opinion, attitude, etc.) —*vt.* to cause to lean [to lean one's head back, lean the ladder against the house] —*n.* the act or condition of leaning; inclination; slant —**lean′er** *n.*

lean² (lēn) *adj.* [ME. *lene* < OE. *hlæne*, prob. akin to prec. in sense "leaning, drooping," hence "thin, slender"] 1. with little flesh or fat; thin; spare 2. containing little or no fat: said of meat 3. *a)* lacking in richness, profit, productiveness, etc.; meager *b)* deficient in some quality or substance [a *lean* mixture in the carburetor] *c)* characterized by brevity, incisiveness, directness, etc. [a *lean* style] —*n.* meat containing little or no fat —**lean′ly** *adv.* —**lean′ness** *n.*

SYN.—**lean** implies a healthy, natural absence of fat or fleshiness; **spare** suggests a sinewy frame without any superfluous flesh; **lanky** implies an awkward tallness and leanness, and, often, loose-jointedness; **skinny** and **scrawny** imply extreme thinness that is unattractive and indicative of a lack of vigor; **gaunt** implies a bony thinness such as that caused by a wasting away of the flesh from hunger or suffering See also THIN —*ANT.* fleshy, fat, stout

Le·an·der (lē an′dər) [L. < Gr. *Leiandros* < ? *leōn*, lion + *anēr* (gen. *andros*), a man] 1. a masculine name 2. *Gr. Legend* the lover of Hero: see HERO

lean·ing (lē′niŋ) *n.* 1. the act of a person or thing that leans 2. tendency; inclination; penchant; predilection —*SYN.* see INCLINATION

Leaning Tower of Pisa bell tower in Pisa, Italy, which leans more than 17 ft. from the perpendicular

leant (lent) *alt. pt. & pp. of* LEAN¹

lean-to (lēn′tōō′) *n.*, *pl.* **lean′-tos′** 1. a roof with a single slope, its upper edge abutting a wall or building 2. a shed with a one-slope roof, the upper end of the rafters resting against an external support, such as trees or the wall of a building 3. a structure, as the wing of a building, whose roof is a lean-to —*adj.* having or characterized by such construction

leap (lēp) *vi.* **leaped** or **leapt** (lept, lēpt), **leap′ing** [ME. *lepen* < OE. *hleapan*, akin to MDu. *lopen* (cf. LOPE), G. *laufen*] 1. to move oneself suddenly from the ground, etc. by using one's leg muscles; jump; spring 2. to move suddenly or swiftly, as if by jumping; bound 3. to accept eagerly something offered (with *at*) [to *leap* at a chance] —*vt.* 1. to pass over by a jump 2. to cause or force to leap [to *leap* a horse over a wall] —*n.* 1. the act of leaping; jump; spring 2. the distance covered in a jump 3. a place that is, or is to be, leaped over or from 4. a sudden transition —**by leaps and bounds** very rapidly —**leap in the dark** an act that is risky because its consequences cannot be foreseen —**leap′er** *n.*

leap·frog (-frôg′, -fräg′) *n.* a game in which each player in turn jumps, with legs spread wide, over the bent back of each of the other players —*vi.* **-frogged′**, **-frog′ging** 1. to jump in or as if in leapfrog; skip (*over*) 2. to move or progress in jumps or stages —*vt.* to jump or skip over, as in leapfrog

leap year a year of 366 days, occurring every fourth year: the additional day, February 29, makes up for the time lost annually when the approximate 365 1/4-day cycle is computed as 365 days: a leap year is a year whose number

LEAF FORMS

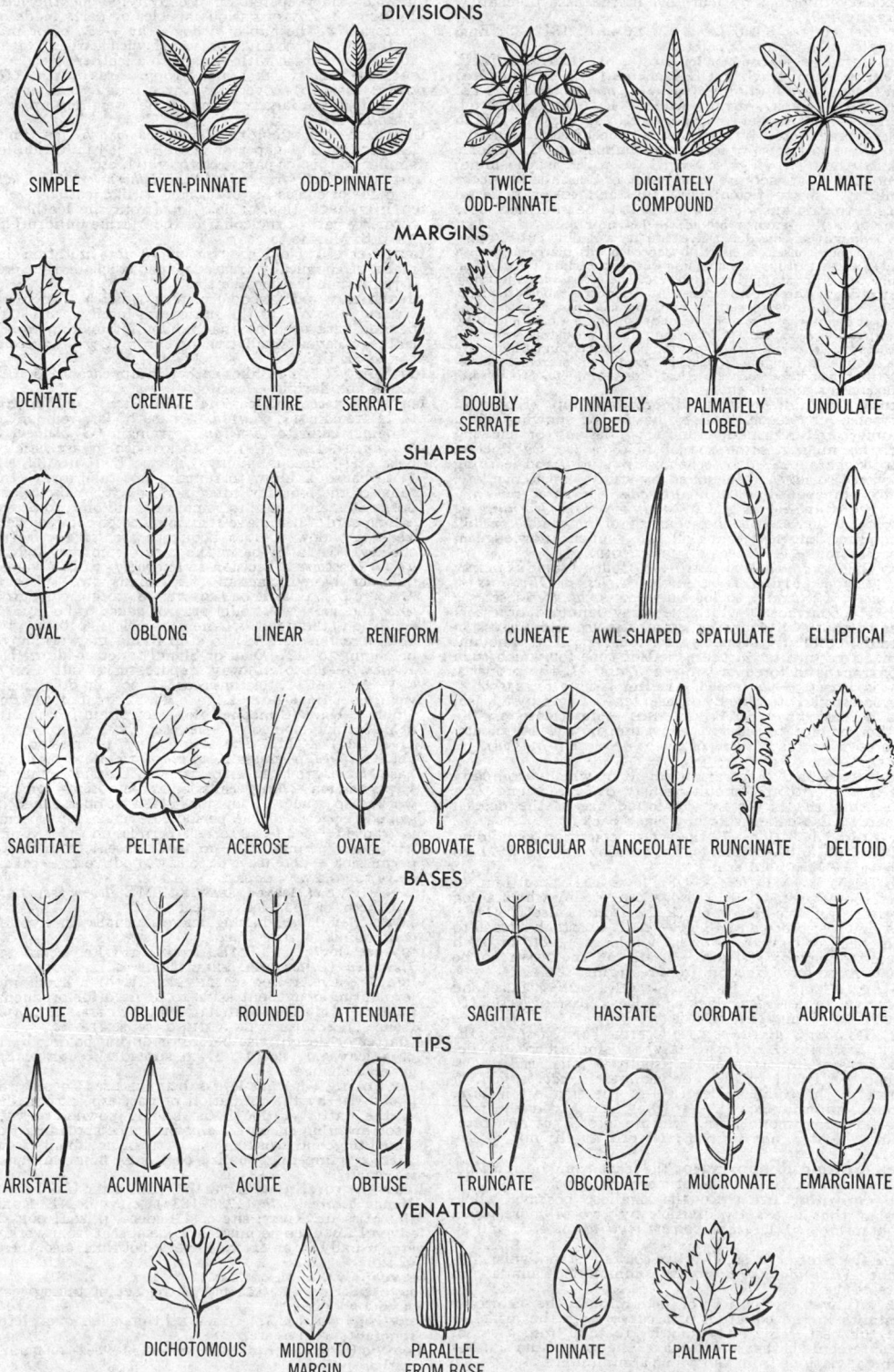

DIVISIONS

SIMPLE   EVEN-PINNATE   ODD-PINNATE   TWICE ODD-PINNATE   DIGITATELY COMPOUND   PALMATE

MARGINS

DENTATE   CRENATE   ENTIRE   SERRATE   DOUBLY SERRATE   PINNATELY LOBED   PALMATELY LOBED   UNDULATE

SHAPES

OVAL   OBLONG   LINEAR   RENIFORM   CUNEATE   AWL-SHAPED   SPATULATE   ELLIPTICAL

SAGITTATE   PELTATE   ACEROSE   OVATE   OBOVATE   ORBICULAR   LANCEOLATE   RUNCINATE   DELTOID

BASES

ACUTE   OBLIQUE   ROUNDED   ATTENUATE   SAGITTATE   HASTATE   CORDATE   AURICULATE

TIPS

ARISTATE   ACUMINATE   ACUTE   OBTUSE   TRUNCATE   OBCORDATE   MUCRONATE   EMARGINATE

VENATION

DICHOTOMOUS   MIDRIB TO MARGIN   PARALLEL FROM BASE TO TIP   PINNATE   PALMATE

is exactly divisible by four, or, in the case of century years, by 400

Lear (lir) **1.** *see* KING LEAR **2. Edward,** 1812–88; Eng. humorist, illustrator, & painter

learn (lʉrn) *vt.* **learned** or **learnt** (lʉrnt), **learn′ing** [ME. *lernen,* to learn, teach < OE. *leornian* (akin to G. *lernen*) < WGmc. *liznŏn (akin to Goth. *laisjan,* to teach) < IE. base **leis-,* track, furrow, whence L. *lira,* furrow (cf. DELIRIOUS)] **1.** to get knowledge of (a subject) or skill in (an art, trade, etc.) by study, experience, instruction, etc. **2.** to come to know [to *learn* what happened] **3.** to come to know how [to *learn* to swim] **4.** to fix in the mind; memorize **5.** to acquire as a habit or attitude [to *learn* humility] **6.** to teach: now substandard or dialectal —*vi.* **1.** to gain knowledge or skill **2.** to be informed; hear (of or *about*) —**learn′a·ble** *adj.* —**learn′er** *n.*
SYN.—**learn,** as considered here, implies a finding out of something without conscious effort [I *learned* of his marriage from a friend]; **ascertain** implies a finding out with certainty by careful inquiry, experimentation, research, etc. [he *ascertained* the firm's credit rating]; **determine** stresses intention to establish the facts exactly, often so as to settle something in doubt [to *determine* the exact denotation of a word]; **discover** implies a finding out, by chance, exploration, etc., of something already existing or known to others [to *discover* a plot, a star, etc.]; **unearth,** in its figurative sense, implies a bringing to light, as by diligent search, of something that has been concealed, lost, forgotten, etc. [to *unearth* old documents, a secret, etc.]

learn·ed (lʉr′nid; *for 3,* lʉrnd) *adj.* [orig. pp. of prec. in obs. sense of "teach"] **1.** *a)* having or showing much learning; well-informed; erudite *b)* having or showing much learning in some special field [a *learned* doctor] **2.** of or characterized by scholarship, study, and learning [a *learned* society] **3.** acquired by study, experience, etc. [a *learned* response] —**learn′ed·ly** *adv.* —**learn′ed·ness** *n.*

learn·ing (lʉr′niŋ) *n.* [ME. *lerning* < OE. *leornung* < *leornian,* to LEARN] **1.** the acquiring of knowledge or skill **2.** acquired knowledge or skill; esp., much knowledge in a special field —*SYN.* see INFORMATION

lear·y (lir′ē) *adj.* lear′i·er, lear′i·est [Colloq.] *same as* LEERY

lease (lēs) *n.* [ME. *leas* < Anglo-Fr. *les* < OFr. *lais* < *laissier* < L. *laxare,* to loosen, relax < *laxus,* loose: see LAX] **1.** a contract by which one party (landlord, or lessor) gives to another (tenant, or lessee) the use and possession of lands, buildings, property, etc. for a specified time and for fixed payments **2.** the period of time for which such a contract is in force [a two-year *lease*] **3.** the property that is leased —*vt.* **leased, leas′ing** [Anglo-Fr. *lesser* < OFr. *laissier*] **1.** to give by a lease; let **2.** to get by a lease; take a lease on —*SYN.* see HIRE —**new lease on life** another chance to lead a happy life, be successful, etc. because of a new turn of events —**leas′a·ble** *adj.* —**leas′er** *n.*

lease-back (-bak′) *n.* an arrangement by which a company sells a property and simultaneously obtains a long-term lease from the buyer for continued use of the deeded property: also called **sale and lease-back**

lease·hold (-hōld′) *n.* **1.** the act or condition of holding by lease **2.** lands, buildings, etc. held by lease —*adj.* held by lease —**lease′hold′er** *n.*

leash (lēsh) *n.* [ME. *lese* < OFr. *lesse* < L. *laxa,* fem. of *laxus,* loose: see LAX] **1.** a cord, strap, etc. by which a dog or other animal is held in check **2.** *Hunting* a set of three, as of hounds; brace and a half —*vt.* **1.** to attach a leash to **2.** to check or control by or as by a leash —**hold in leash** to control; curb; restrain —**strain at the leash** to be impatient to have freedom from restraint

leas·ing (lē′ziŋ) *n.* [ME. *lesinge* < OE. *leasung,* falsehood < *leasian,* to lie < *leas,* lacking, false < base of *leosan,* to LOSE] [Obs.] lying, lies, or a lie

least (lēst) *adj. alt. superl. of* LITTLE [ME. *lest* < OE. *læsest, læst,* superl. of *læssa,* LESS] **1.** smallest in size, degree, extent, importance, etc.; slightest [the *least* movement] **2.** [Dial.] smallest or youngest —*adv. superl. of* LITTLE in the smallest degree —*n.* the smallest in size, amount, importance, etc. —**at (the) least 1.** at the very lowest figure, amount, etc.; with no less **2.** at any rate; in any event —**not in the least** not at all; not in the smallest degree

least common denominator the least common multiple of the denominators of two or more fractions

least common multiple the smallest positive whole number that is exactly divisible by two or more given whole numbers [the *least common multiple* of 4, 5, and 10 is 20]

☆**least flycatcher** a small, olive-colored or brownish flycatcher (*Empidonax minimus*) common in Canada and parts of the U.S.

least squares a method of determining the arbitrary constants in the equation of a curve from the principle that the best value of a quantity to take from a set of measurements is that which makes the sum of the squares of the deviations from this value a minimum

least·ways (-wāz′) *adv.* [< *phr. at the least ways,* at least] [Chiefly Dial.] leastwise; anyway

least·wise (-wīz′) *adv.* [Colloq.] at least; anyway

leath·er (leth′ər) *n.* [ME. *lether* < OE. *lether-,* akin to G. *leder,* ON. *lethr* < Gmc. *lethra < ? or akin ? to Celt. base as in OIr. *lethar,* W. *lledr*] **1.** a material consisting of animal skin prepared for use by removing the hair and tanning **2.** any of various articles or parts made of this material **3.** the flap of a dog's ear —*adj.* of or made of leather —*vt.* **1.** to cover or furnish with leather **2.** [Colloq.] to whip or thrash with or as with a leather strap

leath·er·back (-bak′) *n.* a tropical sea turtle (*Dermochelys coriacea*) covered with a tough, leathery upper shell: it is the largest living turtle, weighing up to 1,200 pounds

Leath·er·ette (leth′ə ret′) *a trademark for* imitation leather made of paper or cloth —*n.* [l-] imitation leather similar to this, of paper, cloth, vinyl, etc.

leath·ern (leth′ərn) *adj.* [ME. *letherne* < OE. *letheren*] **1.** made or consisting of leather **2.** like leather

leath·er·neck (leth′ər nek′) *n.* [from the leather lining, formerly part of the collar of the Marine uniform] [Slang] ☆a U.S. Marine

Leath·er·oid (-oid′) *a trademark for* imitation leather made of chemically treated paper stock or the like —*n.* [l-] imitation leather like this

☆**leath·er·wood** (-wood′) *n.* **1.** a small N. American tree (*Dirca palustris*) of the mezereum family, with a tough, flexible bark used by the Indians for making rope **2.** a leathery-leaved small tree or shrub (*Cyrilla racemiflora*) of the SE U.S.

leath·er·y (-ē) *adj.* like leather in appearance or texture; tough and flexible —**leath′er·i·ness** *n.*

leave[1] (lēv) *vt.* **left, leav′ing** [ME. *leven* < OE. *læfan,* lit., to let remain (< *lafjan < base of *laf,* remnant, what remains), akin to (be)*lifan,* to remain (G. *bleiben,* OHG. *belīban*) < IE. **leip-,* to smear with grease, stick to < base **lei-,* viscous, sticky, whence L. *limus* (cf. LIME[1])] **1.** to cause or allow to remain; not take away [to *leave* some of the food for latecomers] **2.** to make, place, deposit, etc., and cause to remain behind one [to *leave* one's calling card] **3.** to have remaining after one [the deceased *leaves* a widow] **4.** to bequeath [to *leave* a fortune to charity] **5.** to let be in the care of; entrust (with *to* or *up to*) [to *leave* a decision to another] **6.** to give as a remainder by subtraction [ten minus two *leaves* eight] **7.** to reject [take it or leave it] **8.** to go away from [to *leave* the house] **9.** to let stay or cause to be in a certain condition [the flood *left* them homeless] **10.** to give up; abandon; forsake **11.** to stop living in, working for, or belonging to **12.** [Dial. or Slang] to let or allow [leave us go now] —*vi.* to go away, depart, or set out —*SYN.* see GO[1] —**leave off 1.** to stop; cease **2.** to stop doing, using, or wearing —**leave out 1.** to omit **2.** to fail to consider; ignore —**leave (someone) alone** to refrain from bothering or disturbing (someone) —**leav′er** *n.*

leave[2] (lēv) *n.* [ME. *leve* < OE. *leaf,* permission, akin to obs. G. *laube,* permission, *erlauben,* to allow, permit < IE. base **leubh-,* to like, desire, whence L. *libido* & LIEF, LOVE] **1.** permission **2.** *a)* permission to be absent from duty or work, esp. such permission given to personnel in the armed services *b)* the period for which such permission is granted —**beg leave** to ask permission —**by your leave** with your permission —**on leave** absent from duty with permission —**take leave of** to say goodbye to —**take one's leave** to go away; depart

leave[3] (lēv) *vi.* **leaved, leav′ing** [ME. *leven:* see LEAF] to put forth, or bear, leaves; leaf

leaved (lēvd) *adj.* having leaves: usually in hyphenated compounds [narrow-*leaved*]

leav·en (lev′'n) *n.* [ME. *levein* < OFr. *levain* < VL. *levamen (L. *levamen,* alleviation) < L. *levare,* to make light, relieve, raise: see LEVER] **1.** *a)* a small piece of fermenting dough put aside to be used for producing fermentation in a fresh batch of dough *b) same as* LEAVENING (sense 1) **2.** *same as* LEAVENING (sense 2) —*vt.* **1.** to make (batter or dough) rise before or during baking by means of a leavening agent **2.** to spread through, causing a gradual change

leav·en·ing (-iŋ) *n.* **1.** a substance used to make baked goods rise by the formation of gas, esp. carbon dioxide, in the batter or dough, as baking powder, yeast, etc.: also **leavening agent 2.** any influence spreading through something and working on it to bring about a gradual change; tempering quality or thing **3.** a causing to be leavened

Leav·en·worth (lev′'n wʉrth′) [ult. after U.S. Army Col. Henry *Leavenworth* (1783–1834)] city in NE Kans., on the Missouri River: site of a Federal prison: pop. 25,000

leave of absence permission to be absent from work, duty, etc., usually for an extended period of time; also, the period of time

leaves (lēvz) *n. pl. of* LEAF

leave-tak·ing (lēv′tāk′iŋ) *n.* the act of taking leave, or saying goodbye

leav·ings (-iŋz) *n.pl.* [< LEAVE[1]] things left over; leftovers, remnants, refuse, etc.

Lea·vis (lē′vis), F(rank) R(aymond) 1895– ; Eng. literary critic

leav·y (lē′vē) *adj. archaic form of* LEAFY

Leb·a·non (leb′ə nən) **1.** country in SW Asia, at E end of the Mediterranean: c. 4,000 sq. mi.; pop. 2,367,000; cap. Beirut **2.** mountain range extending nearly the entire length of Lebanon: highest peak, 10,131 ft. —**Leb′a·nese′** (-nēz′) *adj., n., pl.* **-nese′**

Le·bens·raum (lā'bəns rowm') n. [G., living space] territory for political and economic expansion: term of German imperialism

‡**Leb·ku·chen** (lāp'koo'khən) n. [G. < MHG. lebekuoche < lebe, loaf, akin to leip (< OHG. leib, hlaib) + OE. hlaf, LOAF[1] + MHG. kuoche, cake < OHG. kuocho, CAKE] a chewy cookie containing candied fruits, often made with honey

Le·brun (lə brön') 1. Al·bert (ȧl ber'), 1871–1950; Fr. statesman; president of France (1932–40) 2. Charles (shȧrl), 1619–90; Fr. historical painter: also Le Brun

lech (lech) vi. [Slang] to behave like a lecher; lust (for, after, etc.) —n. [Slang] 1. a lecherous desire 2. a lecherous person

lech·er (lech'ər) n. [ME. lechoure < OFr. lecheur < lechier, to live a debauched life, lit., lick < Frank. *lekkon, akin to G. lecken, to LICK] a man who indulges in lechery; lewd, grossly sensual man

lech·er·ous (-əs) adj. [ME. < OFr. lecheros] given to, characterized by, or stimulating to lechery; lustful —lech'er·ous·ly adv. —lech'er·ous·ness n.

lech·er·y (-ē) n., pl. -er·ies [ME. lecherie < OFr. < lecheor, LECHER] unrestrained, excessive indulgence of sexual desires; gross sensuality; lewdness

lec·i·thin (les'ə thin) n. [< Gr. lekithos, yolk of an egg + -IN[1]] any of several phosphatides found in nerve tissue, blood, milk, egg yolk, soybeans, corn, etc.: used in medicine, foods, cosmetics, etc. as a wetting, emulsifying, and penetrating agent

lec·i·thin·ase (-thi nās') n. [prec. + -ASE] any of a group of enzymes that hydrolyze lecithin

Leck·y (lek'ē), William Edward Hart·pole (härt'pōl') 1838–1903; Brit. historian, born in Ireland

Le·conte de Lis·le (lə kônt də lēl'), Charles Ma·rie (René) (shȧrl mȧ rē') 1818–94; Fr. poet

Le Cor·bu·sier (lə kôr bü zyā') (pseud. of Charles-Édouard Jeanneret-Gris) 1887–1965; Swiss architect in France

lect. 1. lecture 2. lecturer

lec·tern (lek'tərn) n. [ME. lectorne, altered (after L. forms) < earlier lettrun < OFr. < ML. lectrum < L. lectus, pp. of legere, to read: see LOGIC] 1. a reading desk in a church; esp., such a desk from which a part of the Scriptures is read in a church service 2. a stand for holding the notes, written speech, etc., as of a lecturer

lec·tion (lek'shən) n. [L. lectio < lectus: see prec.] 1. the version in a particular text of a certain passage 2. a part of the Scriptures read in church service

lec·tion·ar·y (-er'ē) n., pl. -ar'ies [ML. (Ec.) lectionarium: see prec. & -ARY] a sequence or list of lections to be read in church services during the year

LECTERN

lec·tor (lek'tər) n. [LME. < L., reader (in ML.(Ec.), church officer) < lectus: see LECTERN] 1. a person who reads the Scripture lessons in a church service 2. R.C.Ch. a member of the second of the four minor orders 3. a college or university lecturer, esp. in certain European countries

lec·ture (lek'chər) n. [ME., act of reading < ML. lectura < pp. of L. legere, to read: see LOGIC] 1. a) an informative talk given before an audience, class, etc., and usually prepared beforehand b) the text of such a talk 2. a lengthy rebuke or scolding —vi. -tured, -tur·ing to give a lecture or lectures —vt. 1. to give a lecture to 2. to rebuke or scold at length —SYN. see SPEECH

lec·tur·er (-ər) n. a person who gives lectures, esp. by profession or in connection with teaching duties, as at a college or university: sometimes used as an academic title for one who teaches at a college or university but does not have the rank or tenure of a regular faculty member —lec'ture·ship' n.

led (led) pt. & pp. of LEAD[1]

Le·da (lē'də) [L. < Gr. Lēda] Gr. Myth. a Spartan queen, wife of Tyndareus: she was the mother (variously by Tyndareus and by Zeus, who visited her in the form of a swan) of Clytemnestra, Helen of Troy, and Castor and Pollux

le·der·ho·sen (lā'dər hō'zən) n. [G. < MHG. lederhose < leder, LEATHER + hose, pants: see HOSE] short leather pants of a kind worn with suspenders by men and boys in the Alps

ledge (lej) n. [ME. legge, prob. < base of leggen, to LAY[1]] 1. a shelf or shelflike projection 2. a) a projecting ridge of rocks b) such a ridge under the surface of the water near the shore 3. Mining a layer of ore-bearing rock; vein —ledg'y adj.

ledg·er (lej'ər) n. [ME. legger, prob. < ME. leggen or liggen after MDu. ligger: see LAY[1], LIE[1]] 1. a large flat stone placed over a tomb 2. a large horizontal timber in a scaffold 3. [< ME. sense "large volume kept in one place in church"] Bookkeeping the book of final entry, in which a record of debits, credits, and all money transactions is kept

ledger board 1. a board attached to studding to carry floor joists; ribbon strip 2. a board forming the topmost rail as of a fence

ledger line same as LEGER LINE

Lee (lē) 1. [var. of LEIGH; also short for LEROY] a masculine or feminine name 2. Ann, 1736–84; Eng. mystic: founder of the Shakers in America (1776) 3. Charles, 1731–82; Am. general in the Revolutionary War, born in England 4. Henry, 1756–1818; Am. general in the Revolutionary War & statesman: called Light-Horse Harry Lee 5. Richard Henry, 1732–94; Am. Revolutionary statesman: signer of the Declaration of Independence: cousin of prec. 6. Robert E(dward), 1807–70; commander in chief of the Confederate army in the Civil War: son of Henry

lee (lē) n. [ME. le < OE. hleo, shelter, akin to ON. hle, Du. lij, G. lee (in sense 3) < IE. *kleu-< base *kel-, warm, whence L. calere, to be warm] 1. shelter; protection 2. a sheltered place, esp. one on that side of anything away from the wind 3. Naut. the side or part sheltered or away from the wind —adj. 1. of or on the side sheltered or away from the wind ☆2. facing or located in the direction toward which a glacier moves: opposed to STOSS

lee·board (-bôrd') n. a large flat board or piece of metal let down into the water on the lee side of a sailboat to lessen its drift to that side

leech[1] (lēch) n. [ME. leche < OE. læce, akin to OHG. lāhhi, Goth. lēkeis, magician, healer, OE. lacnian, to heal, prob. < IE. base *leĝ-, to collect, gather together, whence L. lex (see LEGAL); sense 2 is supposedly same word (from use in medicine), but OE. lyce, ME. liche, MDu. lieke suggest different word assimilated by folk etym.] 1. formerly, a physician 2. any of a number of mostly flattened, annelid worms (class Hirudinea) living in water or wet earth and having a well-developed sucker at each end: most are bloodsuckers, and one species (Hirudo medicinalis) has been used in medicine, esp. in former times, to bleed patients 3. a person who clings to another to get what he can from him; parasite —vt. 1. formerly, to heal 2. to apply leeches to; bleed with leeches 3. to cling to (another) as a parasite; drain dry —vi. to act as a parasite (often with onto) —SYN. see PARASITE

LEECH
(3 in. long)

leech[2] (lēch) n. [LME. lyche, akin to ON. lik < Du. lijk, boltrope < IE. base *leiĝ-, to bind, fasten, whence L. ligare, to tie] 1. the free or outside edge of a fore-and-aft sail 2. either of the vertical edges of a square sail

Leeds (lēdz) city in N England, in West Riding, Yorkshire: pop. 508,000

leek (lēk) n. [ME. lek < OE. leac, akin to G. lauch < ? IE. base *leug-, to bend, whence L. luxus, excess: so named ? from its outward bent leaves] a biennial, onionlike garden vegetable (Allium porrum) of the amaryllis family, having a small bulb with a cylindrical stem, and broad, flat, folded leaves: used in soups, sauces, etc.

leer (lir) n. [< ME. lere, cheek < OE. hleor: in sense "look over one's cheek, look askance"] a sly, sidelong look showing salaciousness, malicious triumph, etc. —vi. to look with a leer —leer'ing·ly adv.

leer·y (lir'ē) adj. leer'i·er, leer'i·est [prob. < ME. lere (var. of lore, LORE[1]) + -Y[2]: current sense infl. by prec.] formerly, knowing; hence, on one's guard; wary; suspicious

lees (lēz) n.pl. [pl. of lee (obs. in sing.) < ME. lie < OFr. < ML. lia < Gaul. *liga, akin to OIr. lige, a bed, layer < IE. base *legh-, whence LIE[1]] dregs or sediment, as of wine

lee shore the shore on the lee side of a ship; shore toward which the wind is blowing and driving a ship

leet (lēt) n. [ME. & Anglo-Fr. lete, akin ? to OE. læth, land division, esp. in southeast England] in England, formerly, a manorial court or its jurisdiction

lee tide a leeward tide

Leeu·war·den (lā'vär'dən) city in N Netherlands; capital of Friesland province: pop. 86,000

Leeu·wen·hoek (lā'vən hook'), An·ton van (än'tôn vän) 1632–1723; Du. naturalist & pioneer in microscopy

lee·ward (lē'wərd; naut. loo'ərd) adj. in the direction toward which the wind blows; of the lee part or side: opposed to WINDWARD —n. the lee part or side —adv. toward the lee —lee'ward·ly adv.

Lee·ward Islands (lē'wərd) 1. N group of islands in the Lesser Antilles of the West Indies, extending from Puerto Rico southeast to the Windward Islands 2. former Brit. colony in this group, constituted in 1960 as four separate colonies

lee·way (lē'wā') n. 1. the leeward drift of a ship or aircraft from the true course 2. [Colloq.] a) margin of time, money, etc. b) room for freedom of action

left[1] (left) adj. [ME. (Kentish) var. of lift < OE. lyft, weak, akin to EFris. luf, weak] 1. a) designating or of that side of one's body which is toward the west when one faces north, the side of the less-used hand in most people b) designating or of the corresponding side of anything c)

closer to the left side of a person directly before and facing the thing mentioned or understood /the top *left* drawer of a desk/ 2. of the side or bank of a river on the left of a person facing downstream 3. of the political left; radical or liberal —*n.* 1. *a)* all or part of the left side *b)* what is on the left side *c)* a direction or location on the left side (often with *the)* *d)* a turn toward the left side /take a *left* at the fork/ 2. *Boxing a)* the left hand *b)* a blow delivered with the left hand 3. *[often* L-] *Politics* a radical or liberal position, esp. one varying from moderate socialism to communism, or a party or group advocating this (often with *the*): from the position of the seats occupied in some European legislatures —*adv.* on or toward the left hand or side —*SYN.* see LIBERAL —**have two left feet** to be very clumsy

left² (left) *pt. & pp.* of LEAVE¹ —☆**get left** [Slang] 1. to be left behind 2. to be outdone or frustrated

Left Bank a district in Paris on the left bank of the Seine, associated with artists, Bohemians, etc.

☆**left field** *Baseball* the left-hand part of the outfield (as viewed from home plate) —**out in left field** [Slang] not reasonable, sensible, or probable

left-hand (left′hand′) *adj.* 1. being on or directed toward the left 2. of, for, or with the left hand

left-hand·ed (-han′did) *adj.* 1. using the left hand more skillfully than, and in preference to, the right 2. done with the left hand 3. clumsy; awkward 4. designating an insincere or ambiguous compliment, esp. one that is indirectly unflattering or derogatory 5. *same as* MORGANATIC: from the custom of having the groom give his left hand to the bride at such a wedding 6. made for use with the left hand 7. turning from right to left; worked by counterclockwise motion —*adv.* with the left hand /to write *left-handed*/ —**left′-hand′ed·ly** *adv.* —**left′-hand′ed·ness** *n.* —**left′-hand′er** *n.*

left heart the half of the heart containing the left ventricle and left atrium which supply blood to all parts of the body except the lungs

left·ist (-ist) *n.* a person whose political position is radical or liberal; member of the left —*adj.* radical or liberal —**left′ism** *n.*

☆**left·o·ver** (-ō′vər) *n.* something left over, as from a meal —*adj.* remaining unused, uneaten, etc.

left·ward (-wərd) *adv., adj.* on or toward the left: also **left′wards** *adv.*

left wing [see LEFT¹, *n.* 3] the more radical or liberal section of a political party, group, etc. —**left′-wing′** *adj.* —**left′-wing′er** *n.*

☆**left·y** (lef′tē) *n., pl.* **left′ies** [Slang] a left-handed person: often used as a nickname

leg (leg) *n.* [ME. < ON. *leggr*, a leg, limb < IE. base **lek-*, limb, whence L. *lacertus*, muscle, *lacerta*, lizard] 1. one of the parts of the body by means of which animals stand and walk: in human beings, one of the lower limbs, often, specif., the part from the knee to the foot 2. a cut of meat consisting of the leg or its lower part 3. the part of a garment covering the leg 4. anything that resembles a leg in shape or use; specif., *a)* a bar or pole used as a support or prop *b)* any of the supports of a piece of furniture *c)* any of the branches of a forked or jointed object 5. the run made by a sailing vessel on one tack 6. any of the stages of a journey or other course 7. *Bridge* the first game of a rubber, for either side 8. *Cricket* that part of the field which lies to the left and back of the batsman 9. *Math.* either of the sides of a triangle other than its base or, in a right-angled triangle, its hypotenuse —*vi.* **legged, leg′ging** [Colloq.] to walk or run: used chiefly in the phr. **leg it,** to go fast —**get up on one's hind legs** [Colloq.] to become assertive, aggressive, belligerent, etc. —**give a leg up** [Colloq.] 1. to help to mount 2. to help to advance —**not have a leg to stand on** [Colloq.] to have absolutely no defense, excuse, or justification —**on one's (or its) last legs** [Colloq.] not far from exhaustion, death, breakdown, etc. —**pull someone's leg** [Colloq.] to make fun of or fool someone by playing on his credulity —**shake a leg** [Slang] 1. to hurry 2. to dance —**stretch one's legs** to walk, esp. after sitting a long time —**take to one's legs** to run away —**leg′less** *adj.*

leg. 1. legal 2. legato 3. legislative 4. legislature

leg·a·cy (leg′ə sē) *n., pl.* **-cies** [ME. *legacie* < OFr. < ML. *legatia* < L. *legatus:* see LEGATE] 1. money or property left to someone by a will; bequest 2. anything handed down from, or as from, an ancestor

le·gal (lē′gəl) *adj.* [MFr. *légal* < L. *legalis* < *lex* (gen. *legis*), law, prob. < IE. base **leg-*, to collect, whence L. *legere*, Gr. *legein*, to read: cf. LOGIC] 1. of, created by, based upon, or authorized by law 2. in conformity with the positive rules of law; permitted by law /a *legal* act/ 3. that can be enforced in a court of law /*legal* rights/ 4. of or applicable to lawyers /*legal* ethics/ 5. in terms of the law /a *legal* offense/ 6. *Theol. a)* of the Mosaic law *b)* of the doctrine of salvation by good works rather than free grace —*n.pl. same as* LEGAL LIST —**le′gal·ly** *adv.*
SYN.—legal implies literal connection or conformity with statute or common law or its administration /*legal* rights/; **lawful,** a more general word, may suggest conformity to the principle rather than to the letter of the law or may broadly refer to that which is not contrary to the law /a *lawful* but shady enterprise/; **legitimate** implies legality of a claim to a title or right /a *legitimate*

heir/ or accordance with what is sanctioned or accepted as lawful, reasonable, etc. /a *legitimate* argument/; **licit** implies strict conformity to the law, especially in trade, commerce, or personal relations /*licit* marriage/ —*ANT.* **illegal, unlawful, illicit**

☆**legal cap** writing paper for use by lawyers, 8 1/2 by 13 or 14 inches, with a ruled margin

le·gal·ese (lē′gə lēz′) *n.* the conventional language of legal forms, documents, etc., involving special vocabulary and formulations, often thought of as abstruse and incomprehensible to the layman

☆**legal holiday** a holiday set by statute, during which government and, usually, business affairs are suspended, schools and courts are closed, etc.

le·gal·ism (lē′gəl iz′m) *n.* 1. strict, often too strict and literal, adherence to law or to a code 2. *Theol.* the doctrine of salvation by good works —**le′gal·ist** *n.* —**le′gal·is′ti·cal·ly** *adv.*

le·gal·i·ty (li gal′ə tē) *n., pl.* **-ties** [ML. *legalitas*] 1. quality, condition, or instance of being legal or lawful; conformity with the law 2. *[pl.]* legal aspects

le·gal·ize (lē′gə līz′) *vt.* **-ized′, -iz′ing** to make legal or lawful —**le′gal·i·za′tion** *n.*

legal list investments that savings banks and certain other fiduciaries are legally authorized to make

☆**legal reserve** the funds that a bank, insurance company, etc. are required by law to maintain as reserves

☆**legal separation** an agreement by which a man and wife live apart but are not divorced

legal tender money that may be legally offered in payment of an obligation and that a creditor must accept

leg·ate (leg′it) *n.* [ME. < OFr. *legat* < L. *legatus*, pp. of *legare*, to send as ambassador < *lex*, law: see LEGAL] 1. an envoy or ambassador, esp. one officially representing the Pope 2. *Rom. History a)* an assistant or deputy of the governor of a province *b)* after 31 B.C., the governor of a province —**leg′ate·ship′** *n.* —**leg′a·tine** (-tin, -tīn′) *adj.*

leg·a·tee (leg′ə tē′) *n.* [< L. *legatus*, pp. of *legare*, to bequeath, appoint (see LEGATE) + -EE¹] one to whom a legacy is bequeathed

le·ga·tion (li gā′shən) *n.* [ME. *legacion* < OFr. < L. *legatio*] 1. *a)* the act of sending a legate on a mission *b)* the mission on which he is sent 2. a diplomatic minister and his staff collectively, representing their government in a foreign country and ranking just below an embassy 3. the residence or offices of such a legation 4. the position or authority of such a legation

le·ga·to (li gät′ō) *adj., adv.* [It., pp. of *legare* < L. *ligare*, to tie, bind: see LEECH²] *Music* in a smooth, even style, with no noticeable interruption between the notes: a direction to the performer: cf. STACCATO

le·ga·tor (li gāt′ər) *n.* one who bequeaths legacies; testator

leg bye *Cricket* a run scored for a ball that touches the batsman on any part of the body except his hand

leg·end (lej′ənd) *n.* [ME. *legende* < OFr. < ML. *legenda*, things read, neut. pl. of L. *legendus*, gerundive of *legere*, to read: see LOGIC] 1. *a)* a story handed down for generations among a people and popularly believed to have a historical basis, although not verifiable: cf. MYTH *b)* all such stories belonging to a particular group of people /famous in Irish *legend*/ 2. *a)* a notable person whose deeds or exploits are much talked about in his own time *b)* the stories told about the exploits of such a person 3. an inscription on a coin, coat of arms, etc. 4. a title, brief description, or key accompanying an illustration or map 5. *[Obs.] a)* a story of the life of a saint *b)* a collection of such stories

leg·end·ar·y (lej′ən der′ē) *adj.* of, based on, or presented in legends; traditional —*SYN.* see FICTITIOUS

Le·gen·dre (lə zhän′d'r′), **A·dri·en Ma·rie** (à drē aN′ mà rē′) 1752–1833; Fr. mathematician

leg·end·ry (lej′ən drē) *n.* legends collectively

Lé·ger (lā zhā′), **Fer·nand** (fer näN′) 1881–1955; Fr. painter

leg·er·de·main (lej′ər di mān′) *n.* [ME. < MFr. *leger de main*, lit., light of hand < *leger* (< LL. *levarius < L. *levis*, light) + *de* (< L. *de*, of, from) + *main* < L. *manus*, hand] 1. sleight of hand; tricks of a stage magician 2. trickery of any sort; deceit

leg·er line (lej′ər) [altered < *ledger line*] *Music* a short line written above or below the staff, for notes beyond the range of the staff

‡**le·ges** (lē′jēz, lā′gās) *n. pl.* of LEX

leg·ged (leg′id, legd) *adj.* having a (specified number or kind of) legs: used in hyphenated compounds /long-*legged*, four-*legged*/

leg·ging (leg′iŋ, -ən) *n.* a covering of canvas, leather, etc. for the leg below the knee

leg·gy (leg′ē) *adj.* **-gi·er, -gi·est** 1. having long and awkward legs /a *leggy* colt/ 2. [Colloq.] having long, well-shaped legs /a *leggy* chorus girl/ —**leg′gi·ness** *n.*

Leg·horn (leg′hôrn, leg′ərn) [altered by folk etym. < It. *Livorno*] seaport in Tuscany, W Italy, on the Ligurian Sea: pop. 170,000: It. name, LIVORNO —*n.* 1. *[sometimes* l-] any of a breed of small chicken originally developed in the Mediterranean region 2. [l-] *a)* a plaiting made of an Italian wheat straw, cut green and bleached when dry *b)* a hat, typically broad-brimmed, made of this straw

leg·i·ble (lej′ə b'l) *adj.* [ME. (northern) *legeable* < LL. *legibilis* < L. *legere*, to read: see LOGIC] 1. that can be

read or deciphered **2.** that can be read or deciphered easily —**leg′i·bil′i·ty** n. —**leg′i·bly** adv.

le·gion (lē′jən) n. [ME. < OFr. < L. *legio* < *legere*, to choose, select: see LOGIC] **1.** *Rom. History* a military division varying at times from 3,000 to 6,000 foot soldiers, with additional cavalrymen **2.** a large group of soldiers; army **3.** a large number; multitude [his honors are *legion*] **4.** [L-] *clipped form of* AMERICAN LEGION, FOREIGN LEGION, etc.

le·gion·ar·y (-er′ē) adj. [L. *legionarius*] of or constituting a legion or legions —n., pl. -**ar′ies** a member of a legion

legionary ant same as ARMY ANT

le·gion·naire (lē′jə ner′) n. [Fr. *légionnaire* < L. *legionarius*] **1.** a member of a legion **2.** [often L-] a member of the American Legion, Foreign Legion, etc.

Legion of Honor a French honorary society founded in 1802 by Napoleon for recognition of distinguished military or civil service

☆**Legion of Merit** a U.S. decoration given to members of the armed forces of the U.S. or of foreign nations for exceptionally meritorious conduct in the performance of outstanding services

legis. 1. legislation **2.** legislative **3.** legislature

leg·is·late (lej′is lāt′) vi. -**lat′ed**, -**lat′ing** [back-formation < LEGISLATOR] to make or pass a law or laws —vt. to cause to be, become, go, etc. by making laws

leg·is·la·tion (lej′is lā′shən) n. [LL. *legislatio* < L. *lex* (gen. *legis*), law (see LEGAL) + *latio*, a bringing, proposing < *latus*, pp. of *ferre*, to bring, BEAR¹] **1.** the act or process of making a law or laws **2.** the law or laws made

leg·is·la·tive (lej′is lāt′iv) adj. **1.** of legislation [*legislative* powers] ☆**2.** of a legislature or its members [*legislative* party whip] **3.** having the power to make laws [a *legislative* assembly] **4.** brought about or enforced by legislation —n. the lawmaking branch of a government; legislature —**leg′is·la′tive·ly** adv.

leg·is·la·tor (-lāt′ər) n. [L. *legis lator*, lit., a proposer of a law: for bases see LEGISLATION] a member of a legislative assembly; lawmaker

leg·is·la·ture (-lā′chər) n. [see prec. + -URE] a body of persons given the responsibility and power to make laws for a country or state; specif., the lawmaking body of a State, corresponding to the U.S. Congress

le·gist (lē′jist) n. [LME. < MFr. *legiste* < ML. *legista* < L. *lex*, law: see LEGAL] a person who has special knowledge of the law, or of some branch of it

le·git (lə jit′) n. [Slang] the legitimate theater, drama, stage, etc. —adj. [Slang] legitimate

le·git·i·ma·cy (lə jit′ə mə sē) n. the quality or state of being legitimate

le·git·i·mate (-mit; *for v.* -māt′) adj. [ML. *legitimatus*, pp. of *legitimare*, to make lawful < L. *legitimus*, lawful < *lex*: see LEGAL] **1.** conceived or born of parents legally married to each other **2.** a) sanctioned by law or custom; lawful [a *legitimate* claim] b) conforming to or abiding by the law **3.** ruling by the rights of heredity [a *legitimate* king] **4.** a) reasonable; logically correct [a *legitimate* inference] b) justifiable or justified **5.** conforming to or in accordance with established rules, standards, or principles **6.** *Theater* designating or of professionally produced stage plays, as distinguished from motion pictures, burlesque, vaudeville, etc. —vt. -**mat′ed**, -**mat′ing** same as LEGITIMIZE (esp. sense 1 c) —SYN. see LEGAL —**le·git′i·mate·ly** adv. —**le·git′i·ma′tion** n.

le·git·i·ma·tize (lə jit′ə mə tīz′) vt. -**tized′**, -**tiz′ing** same as LEGITIMIZE

le·git·i·mist (-mist) n. [Fr. *légitimiste*] a supporter of legitimate authority or, esp., of claims to monarchy based on the rights of heredity —**le·git′i·mism** n.

le·git·i·mize (-mīz′) vt. -**mized′**, -**miz′ing 1.** to make or declare legitimate; specif., a) to make lawful; give legal force or status to b) to give official or formal sanction to; authorize c) to give the status of a legitimate child to (one born out of wedlock) **2.** to make seem just, right, or reasonable; justify —**le·git′i·mi·za′tion** n.

☆**leg·man** (leg′man′) n., pl. -**men′** (-men′) **1.** a newspaperman who gathers information at the scene of events or at various sources, usually transmitting it to the editorial office for rewriting **2.** a person who runs errands or gathers information to assist someone in an office

Leg·ni·ca (leg nēt′tsä) city in SW Poland: pop. 69,000

leg-of-mut·ton (leg′ə mut′'n, -əv-) adj. shaped somewhat like a leg of mutton; specif., designating a sleeve that puffs out toward the shoulder, or a triangular sail

le·gong (lā′gôŋ) n. [Balinese] a traditional Balinese dance, performed by two young girls

Legree, Simon see SIMON LEGREE

leg-room (leg′rōōm′) n. adequate space for the legs while seated, as in a car, theater seat, etc.

leg·ume (leg′yōōm, lə gyōōm′) n. [Fr. *légume* < L. *legumen*, lit., anything that can be gathered < *legere*, to gather: see LOGIC] **1.** any of a large family (Leguminosae) of herbs, shrubs, and trees, including the peas, beans, vetches, clovers, etc., with usually compound leaves, flowers having a single carpel, and fruit that is a dry pod splitting along

two sutures: many legumes are nitrogen-fixing and often are used as green manure and for forage **2.** the pod or seed of some members of this family, used for food

le·gu·min (li gyōō′min) n. a globulin present in legumes

le·gu·mi·nous (-əs) adj. **1.** of, having the nature of, or bearing a legume or legumes **2.** of the family of plants bearing legumes, or pods, to which peas and beans belong

☆**leg·work** (leg′wurk′) n. [Colloq.] travel away from the center of work as a necessary, but routine, part of a job, as of a newspaper reporter

Le·hár (lā′här), **Franz** 1870–1948; Hung. composer of operettas

Le Ha·vre (lə hä′vrə, hä′vər; Fr. lə à′vr′) seaport in NW France, on the English Channel: pop. 184,000

Le·high (lē′hī) river in E Pa., flowing into the Delaware: c. 120 mi.

Leh·mann (lā′mən; G. -män) **1. Lil·li** (lil′ē), 1848–1929; Ger. operatic soprano **2. Lot·te** (lät′ē; G. lôt′ə), 1888– ; U.S. operatic soprano, born in Germany

le·hu·a (lā hōō′ä) n. [Haw.] **1.** a tropical tree (*Metrosideros collina*) of the myrtle family, with clusters of bright-red flowers and hard, durable wood: it grows in Hawaii and other Pacific islands **2.** its wood **3.** its flower

lei¹ (lā, lā′ē) n., pl. **leis** [Haw.] in Hawaii, a wreath of flowers and leaves, generally worn about the neck

lei² (lā) n. pl. of LEU

Leib·niz (līp′nits), Baron **Gott·fried Wil·helm von** (gôt′frēt vil′helm fôn)1646–1716; Ger. philosopher & mathematician: also sp. **Leibnitz**

Leices·ter (les′tər) **1.** city in C England; county seat of Leicestershire: pop. 284,000 **2.** same as LEICESTERSHIRE —n. any of a breed of long-wooled sheep originally developed in Leicestershire

Leicester, Earl of, (*Robert Dudley*) 1532–88; Eng. courtier & general: favorite of Elizabeth I

Leices·ter·shire (-shir′) county of C England: 832 sq. mi.; pop. 697,000

Lei·den (līd′'n) city in W Netherlands: pop. 100,000

Leif (lēf, lāf) [ON. *Leifr*, akin to *ljufr*, beloved: cf. LIEF] a masculine name

Leif Ericsson see ERICSSON

Leigh (lē) [< surname *Leigh* < ME. *leye*: see LEA¹] a masculine or feminine name: var. *Lee*

Lein·ster (len′stər) province of E Ireland: 7,580 sq. mi.; pop. 1,412,000

Leip·zig (līp′sig, -sik; G. līp′tsiH) city in SC East Germany: pop. 596,000

leish·man·i·a·sis (lēsh′mə nī′ə sis) n. [ModL. < *Leishmania*, name of the parasitic genus, after Sir William Boog *Leishman* (1865–1926), Scot. bacteriologist] any of several diseases caused by protozoan parasites (genus *Leishmania*); esp., kala azar

leis·ter (lēs′tər) n. [< Scand., as in ON. *ljoster* < *ljosta*, to strike < IE. base *leu-*, to cut off, whence Gr. *lyein*, to loosen, dissolve] a kind of fish spear, usually with three prongs —vt. to spear (fish) with a leister

lei·sure (lē′zhər, lezh′ər) n. [ME. *leiser* < OFr. *leisir*, subst. use of inf., to be permitted < L. *licere* < IE. base *leik-*, to offer for sale, bargain] free, unoccupied time during which a person may indulge in rest, recreation, etc. —adj. **1.** free and unoccupied; spare [*leisure* time] **2.** having much leisure; not working for a living [the *leisure* class] —at leisure **1.** having free or spare time **2.** with no hurry **3.** not occupied or engaged —at one's leisure when one has the time or opportunity —**lei′sured** adj.

lei·sure·ly (-lē) adj. characterized by or having leisure; without haste; deliberate; slow [to make a *leisurely* inspection of a place] —adv. in an unhurried manner —**lei′sure·li·ness** n.

Leith (lēth) former burgh in Scotland: now a port section of Edinburgh

leit·mo·tif, leit·mo·tiv (līt′mō tēf′) n. [G. *leitmotiv* < *leiten*, to LEAD¹ + *motiv*, MOTIVE] **1.** a short musical phrase representing and recurring with a given character, situation, or emotion in an opera: first developed by Richard Wagner **2.** a dominant theme or underlying pattern

lek (lek) n. the monetary unit of Albania: see MONETARY UNITS, table

Le·ly (lē′lē, lā′-), Sir **Peter** (born *Pieter van der Faes*) 1618–80; Du. portrait painter in England

lem·an (lem′ən, lē′mən) n. [ME. *lemman*, *lefman* < *lef*, dear (see LIEF) + *man*] [Archaic] a sweetheart or lover (man or woman); esp., a mistress

Le·man (lē′mən), **Lake** same as Lake GENEVA: Fr. name **Lac Lé·man** (läk lä män′)

Le Mans (lə män′) city in W France: pop. 132,000

Le·may (lə mā′) [after François *Le Mais*, local ferryman] suburb of St. Louis, in E Mo., on the Mississippi: pop. 40,000

Lem·berg (lem′berk; E. -bərg) Ger. name of LVOV

lem·ma¹ (lem′ə) n., pl. -**mas**, -**ma·ta** (-ə tə) [L. < Gr. *lēmma*, something taken or received, something taken for granted < *lambanein*, to take, assume < IE. base *(s)lagw-*, to grasp, whence LATCH] **1.** a proposition proved, or sometimes assumed, to be true and used in proving a theorem

2. the subject of a gloss, annotation, etc. that is used also as a heading

lem·ma² (lem′ə) *n.* [Gr. *lemma*, a husk < base of *lepein*, to peel (cf. LEPER)] the outer or lower of the two bracts or scales surrounding the flower of a grass

lem·ming (lem′iŋ) *n., pl.* **-mings, -ming:** see PLURAL, II, D, 1 [Dan. < ON. *læmingi*, lemming, orig., prob. "barker" < IE. echoic base *lā-*, whence L. *latrare*, to bark: cf. LAMENT] any of various small arctic rodents (genera *Lemmus* and *Dicrostonyx*) resembling mice but having short tails and fur-covered feet: some species undertake spectacular mass migrations at peaks of population growth, ultimately crowding into the sea to destruction

lem·nis·cus (lem nis′kəs) *n., pl.* **-nis·ci** (-nis′ī) [ModL. < L., hanging ribbon < Gr. *lēmniskos*, ribbon] a band of sensory nerve fibers in the central nervous system, usually terminating in the thalamus

Lem·nos (lem′näs, -nōs) Gr. island in the N Aegean: 186 sq. mi.

lem·on (lem′ən) *n.* [ME. *lymon* < MFr. *limon* < Ar. *laimūn* < Per. *limūn*] **1.** a small, egg-shaped, edible citrus fruit with a pale-yellow rind and a juicy, sour pulp, rich in vitamin C **2.** the small, spiny, semitropical evergreen tree (*Citrus limon*) of the rue family, bearing this fruit **3.** pale yellow ☆**4.** [Slang] *a)* something, esp. a manufactured article, that is defective or imperfect *b)* an inadequate person —*adj.* **1.** pale-yellow **2.** made with or from lemons **3.** having a flavor more or less like that of lemons —**lem′on·y** *adj.*

lem·on·ade (lem′ə nād′) *n.* [Fr. *limonade*] a drink made of lemon juice and water, usually sweetened

lemon balm a perennial mint (*Melissa officinalis*) with white or yellowish flowers and aromatic leaves: used in flavoring food, liqueurs, and medicines

☆**lemon butter** **1.** a spread made of butter flavored with lemon **2.** a sauce of melted butter, lemon juice, and seasoning, used on fish, vegetables, etc.: also **lemon butter sauce**

☆**lemon drop** a small, hard, lemon-flavored candy

lemon verbena a Chilean shrub (*Aloysia triphylla*) of the verbena family, with white flowers and whorls of narrow, lemon-scented leaves

lem·pi·ra (lem pir′ə) *n., pl.* **-ras** [AmSp., after *Lempira*, native chief who resisted the Spaniards] the monetary unit of Honduras: see MONETARY UNITS, table

Lem·u·el (lem′yoo wəl) [Heb. *lemū′ēl*, lit., belonging to God] a masculine name: *dim.* **Lem**

le·mur (lē′mər) *n.* [< L. *lemures*, ghosts, specters (akin to Gr. *lamia:* see LAMIA): so called from its nocturnal habits] any of a group of small, chiefly tree-dwelling primates (suborder Lemuroidea) related to the monkeys, with large eyes, a long, nonprehensile tail, a pointed muzzle, and soft, woolly fur: found mainly in the old-world tropics and active mostly at night —**lem·u·rine** (lem′yoo rīn′, -rin) *adj.* —**lem′u·roid′** (-roid′) *adj., n.*

LEMUR
(27–37 in. long, including tail)

lem·u·res (lem′yoo rēz′) *n.pl.* [L.: see prec.] *Rom. Myth.* the night-walking spirits of the dead

Le·na (lē′nə; *also, for 2, Russ.* lye′nä) **1.** a feminine name: see HELEN, MAGDALENE **2.** river in EC Siberian R.S.F.S.R., flowing northeast into the Laptev Sea: c. 2,680 mi.

Len·a·pe (len′ə pē′) *n., pl.* **-pe** or **-pes** [< Lenape *Leni-lenape*, lit., real man < *leni*, real + *lenape*, man] same as DELAWARE (*n.* 1 & 2)

lend (lend) *vt.* **lent, lend′ing** [< ME. *lenen* (with unhistoric -d < pt.) < OE. *lænan* < *læn*, a LOAN] **1.** to let another use or have (a thing) temporarily and on condition that it, or the equivalent, be returned: opposed to BORROW **2.** to let out (money) at interest **3.** to give; impart [a fire *lends* cheer to a room] —*vi.* to make a loan or loans —**lend itself** (or **oneself**) **to** to be adapted to, useful for, or open to —**lend′a·ble** *adj.* —**lend′er** *n.*

lending library a library from which books may be borrowed, usually for a daily fee

☆**lend-lease** (-lēs′) *n.* in World War II, material aid in the form of munitions, tools, food, etc. granted under specified conditions to foreign countries whose defense was deemed vital to the defense of the U.S. —**lend′-lease′** *vt.* **-leased′, -leas′ing**

L'En·fant (län fän′), **Pierre Charles** (pyer shärl′) 1754–1825; Fr. engineer & architect who served in the Am. Revolutionary army & drew up plans for Washington, D.C.

length (leŋkth, leŋth) *n.* [ME. < OE. *lengthu* < base of *lang*, LONG¹ + -TH¹] **1.** the measure of how long a thing is; measurement of anything from end to end; the greatest of the two or three dimensions of anything **2.** extent in space; distance anything extends **3.** extent in time; duration **4.** a long stretch or extent **5.** the quality, state, or fact of being long **6.** a piece of a certain or standardized length [a *length* of stove pipe] **7.** a unit of measure consisting of the length of an object or animal competing in a race [to win a boat race by two *lengths*] **8.** *Phonet. a)* the duration of the pronunciation of a vowel [the *i* in

bride has greater *length* than the *i* in *bright*] *b)* popularly, the quality of a vowel **9.** *Prosody* syllabic quantity —**at full length** stretched out; completely extended —**at length** **1.** after a long time; finally **2.** in or to the whole extent; in full —**go to any length** (or **great lengths**) to do whatever is necessary; scruple at nothing

-length (leŋkth, leŋth) *a combining form meaning* of a specified length, of such length as to reach a specified point or part [floor-*length*]

length·en (-'n) *vt., vi.* to make or become longer —*SYN.* see EXTEND —**length′en·er** *n.*

length·wise (-wīz′) *adv., adj.* in the direction of the length: also **length′ways′** (-wāz′)

☆**length·y** (-ē) *adj.* **length′i·er, length′i·est** having length; long; esp., too long, or so long as to be tiresome [a *lengthy* voyage, a *lengthy* sermon] —**length′i·ly** *adv.* —**length′i·ness** *n.*

le·ni·ent (lē′nē ənt, lēn′yənt) *adj.* [L. *leniens*, prp. of *lenire*, to soften, alleviate < *lenis*, smooth, soft, mild < IE. base *lei-*: see LATE] **1.** not harsh or severe in disciplining, punishing, judging, etc.; mild; merciful; clement **2.** [Archaic] softening; soothing; relaxing —**le′ni·en·cy,** *pl.* **-cies, le′ni·ence** *n.* —**le′ni·ent·ly** *adv.*

Len·in (len′in; *Russ.* lye′nyin), **V(ladimir) I(lyich)** (orig. surname *Ulyanov;* also called *Nikolai Lenin*) 1870–1924; Russ. leader of the Communist revolution of 1917; premier of the U.S.S.R. (1917–24)

Len·in·grad (len′in grad′; *Russ.* lye′nin grät′) seaport in NW R.S.F.S.R., on the Gulf of Finland: former capital (as *St. Petersburg & Petrograd*) of the Russian Empire (1713–1917): pop. 3,665,000

Len·in·ism (len′in iz′m) *n.* the communist theories, doctrines, policies, and methods of Lenin, including esp. his theory of the dictatorship of the proletariat and analysis of imperialism: a development of Marxism —**Len′in·ist** *n., adj.*

Lenin Peak mountain in S U.S.S.R., on the border between Kirghiz S.S.R. & Tadzhik S.S.R.: c. 23,400 ft.

le·nis (lē′nis, lā′-) *adj.* [L., gentle, smooth, soft, mild: see LENIENT] *Phonet.* articulated with little muscle tension, as voiced continuants —*n.* a lenis sound Opposed to FORTIS

len·i·tive (len′ə tiv) *adj.* [< ML. *lenitivus* < L. *lenitus*, pp. of *lenire*, to soften: see LENIENT] soothing or assuaging; lessening pain or distress —*n.* anything that soothes; esp., a lenitive medicine

len·i·ty (-tē) *n.* [OFr. *lenité* < L. *lenitas* < *lenis*, mild: see LENIENT] **1.** the quality or condition of being lenient; mildness; gentleness; mercifulness **2.** *pl.* **-ties** a lenient act —*SYN.* see MERCY

le·no (lē′nō) *n.* [Fr. *linon* < *lin*, flax: cf. LINEN] **1.** a type of weave in which the warp yarns are paired and twisted **2.** a soft, meshed fabric of this weave

Le·nore (lə nôr′) a feminine name: var. of LEONORA

lens (lenz) *n.* [L., lentil: from the resemblance to the shape of a lentil] **1.** *a)* a piece of glass, or other transparent substance, with two curved surfaces, or one plane and one curved, regularly bringing together or spreading rays of light passing through it: a lens or combination of lenses is used in optical instruments to form an image *b)* a combination of two or more such pieces **2.** any of various devices used to focus microwaves, electrons, or sound waves **3.** *Anat.* a transparent, biconvex body situated between the iris and the vitreous humor of the eye: it focuses upon the retina light rays entering the pupil: see EYE, illus.

LENS
(A, plano-convex; B, double-convex; C, divergent meniscus; D, double-concave; E, plano-concave)

☆**lens·man** (-mən) *n., pl.* **-men** [prec. + -MAN] [Colloq.] a photographer

Lent (lent) *n.* [ME. *lenten* < OE. *lengten*, the spring < Gmc. *langat-tin* < base of LONG¹ + *tina-*, day < IE. base *dei-*, to shine, whence L. *dies*, day: from the lengthening of the days in the spring; akin to G. *lenz*, spring] **1.** the period of forty weekdays from Ash Wednesday to Easter, observed variously in Christian churches by fasting and penitence to commemorate Jesus' fasting in the wilderness **2.** in the Middle Ages, the period from Martinmas (November 11) to Christmas: in full, **St. Martin's Lent**

lent (lent) *pt. & pp.* of LEND

-lent (lənt) [L. *-lentus, -ful*] an *adj.-forming suffix meaning* full of, characterized by [virulent, fraudulent]

len·ta·men·te (len′tə men′tā) *adv.* [It. < *lento*, LENTO] *Music* slowly: a direction to the performer

len·tan·do (len tän′dō) *adv., adj.* [It. < *lentare*, to make slow < *lento*, LENTO] *Music* slowing down by degrees: a direction to the performer

Lent·en (lent′'n) *adj.* [ME. *lenten* < OE. *lengten*, full form of LENT: now felt as LENT + -EN] [*also l-*] **1.** of, connected with, or suitable for Lent **2.** meager; cheerless [*Lenten* fare]

len·tic (lent′ik) *adj.* [< L. *lentus*, slow (see LITHE) + -IC] *Ecol.* designating, of, or living in still water, as lakes, ponds, marshes, etc.: cf. LOTIC

len·ti·cel (len′ti səl) *n.* [ModL. *lenticella*, dim. < L. *lens* (gen. *lentis*), lentil] a spongy area in the bark of a woody plant, serving as a pore to permit the exchange of gases between the stem and the atmosphere —**len′ti·cel′late** (-sel′it) *adj.*

len·tic·u·lar (len tik′yoo lər) *adj.* [L. *lenticularis* < *lenticula*, dim. of *lens:* see LENS] **1.** shaped like a lentil or biconvex lens **2.** of a lens **3.** of the lens of the eye

len·tic·u·late (-lāt′) *vt.* **-lat′ed, -lat′ing** to emboss lenticules on the base side of (a film) in order to produce, with a special color filter, pictures in natural color — **len·tic′u·la′tion** *n.*

len·ti·cule (len′tə kyōōl′) *n.* [< L. *lenticula* (see LENTICULAR)] any of the microscopic lenses lenticulated on a film

len·tig·i·nous (len tij′ə nəs) *adj.* [L. *lentiginosus* < *lentigo*, freckly eruption < *lens*, lentil] **1.** of lentigo **2.** freckled Also **len·tig′i·nose′** (-nōs′)

len·ti·go (-tī′gō) *n., pl.* **len·tig·i·nes** (-tij′ə nēz′) [L. < *lens*, lentil] **1.** a frecklelike mark of the skin which is not influenced by sunlight **2.** *same as* FRECKLE

len·til (lent′'l) *n.* [ME. < OFr. *lentille* < L. *lenticula*, dim. of *lens*, lentil] **1.** an Old World leguminous plant (*Lens culinaris*) with small, edible seeds shaped like biconvex lenses **2.** the seed of this plant

len·tis·si·mo (len tis′ə mō′) *adv., adj.* [It., superl. of *lento:* see ff.] *Music* very slow: a direction to the performer

len·to (len′tō) *adv., adj.* [It. < L. *lentus*, slow: see LITHE] *Music* slow: a direction to the performer

len·toid (len′toid) *adj.* [< L. *lens* (gen. *lentis*): see LENS & -OID] lens-shaped

Le·o (lē′ō) [L.: see LION] **1.** a masculine name: var. *Leon;* fem. *Leona* **2.** a N constellation between Cancer and Virgo, containing the star Regulus **3.** the fifth sign of the zodiac (♌), entered by the sun about July 22: see ZODIAC, illus. (♌) **4.** name of thirteen popes: **Leo I,** Saint 400?–461 A.D.; Pope (440–461): his day is April 11: called *the Great* **5. Leo III,** Saint ?–816 A.D.; Pope (795–816); his day is June 12 **6. Leo XIII** (born *Gioacchino Pecci*) 1810–1903; Pope (1878–1903)

Leo Minor [L., the Lesser Lion] a small N constellation just north of Leo

Le·on (lē′än) a masculine name: see LEO

Le·ón (le ōn′) **1.** region in NW Spain: formerly a kingdom **2.** city in this region: pop. 84,000 **3.** city in C Mexico, in Guanajuato state: pop. 307,000 **4.** city in W Nicaragua: pop. 62,000

Le·o·na (lē ō′nə) a feminine name: see LEO

Leon·ard (len′ərd) [Fr. *Léonard* < OFr. *Leonard* < OHG. *Lewenhart*, lit., strong as a lion < *lewo*, lion (< L. *leo:* see LION) + *hart*, strong, HARD] a masculine name: dim. *Len, Lenny*

Le·o·nar·desque (lē′ə när desk′) *adj.* resembling Leonardo da Vinci or his style of painting

Leonardo da Vinci *see* DA VINCI

Le·on·ca·val·lo (le ōn′kä väl′lō), **Rug·gie·ro** (rōōd je′rō) 1858–1919; It. operatic composer

le·one (lē ōn′) *n.* the monetary unit of Sierra Leone: see MONETARY UNITS, table

Le·on·i·das (lē än′ə dəs) ?–480 B.C.; king of Sparta (491?–480): defeated & killed by the Persians at Thermopylae

Le·o·nids (lē′ə nidz) *n.pl.* [Fr. < L. *Leo* (gen. *Leonis*): see LEO & -ID] a shower of meteors visible yearly about November 15, appearing to radiate from the constellation Leo: also **Le·on·i·des** (lē ōn′ə dēz′)

le·o·nine (lē′ə nīn′) *adj.* [ME. < OFr. *leonin* < L. *leoninus* < *leo*, lion] of, characteristic of, or like a lion

Le·o·no·ra (lē′ə nôr′ə) a feminine name: dim. *Nora;* var. *Lenore, Leonore:* see ELEANOR

Le·o·nore (lē′ə nôr′) a feminine name: var. of LEONORA

leop·ard (lep′ərd) *n., pl.* **-ards, -ard:** see PLURAL, II, D, 1 [ME. *leoparde* < OFr. *leupart* < LL. *leopardus* < Gr. *leopardos* < *leōn*, lion + *pardos*, pard, panther] **1.** a large, ferocious animal (*Panthera pardus*) of the cat family, usually having a tawny coat spotted with black, found in Africa and S Asia **2.** *same as* JAGUAR **3.** *Heraldry* a lion represented in side view, with one foreleg raised and the head facing the viewer —**leop′ard·ess** *n.fem.*

Le·o·par·di (le′ō pär′dē), **Conte Gia·co·mo** (jä′kō mō′) 1798–1837; It. poet

Le·o·pold (lē′ə pōld′) [G. < OHG. *Liutbalt* < *liut*, people (orig., prob., free man, akin to OE. *leod*, man, king) + *balt*, strong, BOLD] **1.** a masculine name **2. Leopold I** *a)* 1640–1705; emperor of the Holy Roman Empire (1658–1705) *b)* 1790–1865; king of Belgium (1831–65) **3. Leopold II** *a)* 1747–92; emperor of the Holy Roman Empire (1790–92): son of MARIA THERESA *b)* 1835–1909; king of Belgium (1865–1909): son of *Leopold I* **4. Leopold III** 1901–   ; king of Belgium (1934–51): abdicated: son of ALBERT I

Lé·o·pold·ville (lē′ə pōld vil′, lā′-) former name of KINSHASA

le·o·tard (lē′ə tärd′) *n.* [after J. *Léotard*, 19th-c. Fr. aerial performer] a one-piece, tight-fitting, sleeved or sleeveless garment that covers the torso: it is worn by acrobats, dancers, etc.

Le·pan·to (li pan′tō, -pän′-) **1. Gulf of,** former name of Gulf of CORINTH **2. Battle of,** naval battle (1571) in the Gulf of Corinth, in which the European powers defeated Turkey

lep·er (lep′ər) *n.* [ME. *lepre*, leprosy < OFr. < LL. *lepra* (L. *leprae*, pl.) < Gr. *lepra* < *lepros*, rough, scaly < *lepein*, to peel < IE. base *lep-*, to peel off, scale, whence OE. *læfer*, rush, reed] **1.** a person having leprosy **2.** a person to be shunned or ostracized, as because of the danger of moral contamination

lep·i·do- (lep′ə dō′) [< Gr. *lepis* (gen. *lepidos*), a scale < *lepein:* see LEPER] *a combining form meaning* scaly *[lepidolite]:* also, before a vowel, **lep′id-**

le·pid·o·lite (li pid′ə lit′, lep′i də lit′) *n.* [prec. + -LITE] mica that contains lithium, commonly occurring in scaly masses of rose, lilac, or gray color

lep·i·dop·ter·an (lep′ə däp′tər ən) *n.* [< ModL. *Lepidoptera*, name of the order (see LEPIDO- & -PTEROUS) + -AN] any of a large order (Lepidoptera) of insects, including the butterflies and moths, characterized by two pairs of broad, membranous wings covered with very fine scales, often brightly colored: the larvae are caterpillars —**lep′i·dop′ter·ous** *adj.*

lep·i·dop·ter·ist (-ist) *n.* a specialist in the study of lepidoptera

lep·i·do·si·ren (lep′ə dō si′rən) *n.* [LEPIDO- + SIREN] any of a genus (*Lepidosiren*) of lungfishes with an eellike form, found in swamps and stagnant waters of the S. American tropics

lep·i·dote (lep′ə dōt′) *adj.* [Gr. *lepidōtos* < *lepis* (gen. *lepidos*), a scale: see LEPIDO-] *Biol.* covered with small flakes, scales, or scalelike hairs; scurfy

Lep·i·dus (lep′ə dəs), **(Marcus Aemilius)** ?–13 B.C.; Rom. triumvir (43–36 B.C.), with Antony & Octavian

Le·pon·tine Alps (li pän′tin) division of the W Alps between Switzerland & Italy: highest peak, 11,684 ft.

lep·o·rid (lep′ə rid) *n., pl.* **le·por·i·dae** (li pôr′ə dē′) [< ModL. *Leporidae*, name of the family < L. *lepus* (gen. *leporis*), a hare] any of a family (Leporidae) of mammals of the order of lagomorphs, consisting of the hares and rabbits —*adj.* of this family

lep·o·rine (lep′ə rīn′, -rin) *adj.* [L. *leporinus* < *lepus* (gen. *leporis*), a hare] of or like a hare or hares

lep·re·chaun (lep′rə kôn′, -kän′) *n.* [Ir. *lupracān* < OIr. *luchorpan* < *lu*, little + *corpan*, dim. of *corp*, body < L. *corpus*, body] *Irish Folklore* a fairy in the form of a little old man who can reveal a buried crock of gold to anyone who catches him

lep·ro·sa·ri·um (lep′rə ser′ē əm) *n., pl.* **-ri·ums, -ri·a** (-ə) [LEPROS(Y) + (SANIT)ARIUM] a hospital or colony for lepers

lep·rose (lep′rōs) *adj.* [LL. *leprosus:* see LEPROUS] *Biol.* scaly; scurfy

lep·ro·sy (lep′rə sē) *n.* [OFr. *leprosie*, prob. < LL. *leprosus*, LEPROUS] a chronic infectious disease caused by a bacterium (*Mycobacterium leprae*) that attacks the skin, flesh, nerves, etc.; it is characterized by nodules, ulcers, white scaly scabs, deformities, and wasting of body parts, and is apparently communicated only after long and close contact

lep·rous (-rəs) *adj.* [ME. *lepros* < OFr. < LL. *leprosus* < L. *lepra* < Gr. *lepra*, leprosy: see LEPER] **1.** of or like leprosy **2.** having leprosy **3.** *same as* LEPROSE

-lep·sy (lep′sē) [ModL. *-lepsia* < Gr. *-lēpsia* < *lēpsis*, an attack < base of *lambanein*, to seize: see LEMMA[1]] *a combining form meaning* a fit, attack, seizure *[catalepsy];* also **-lep′si·a**

lep·to- (lep′tō, -tə) [Gr. *lepto-* < *leptos*, thin: see LEPTON[1]] *a combining form meaning* thin, fine, slender *[leptodactylous]:* also, before a vowel, **lept-**

lep·to·ceph·a·lus (lep′tə sef′ə ləs) *n., pl.* **-li′** (-lī′) [ModL.: see LEPTO- & -CEPHALOUS] the marine larval stage of a genus (*Anguilla*) of freshwater eels, a flattened, transparent animal with a very slender head

lep·to·dac·ty·lous (-dokt′'l əs) *adj.* [LEPTO- + DACTYL- + -OUS] having slender toes, as some birds

lep·ton[1] (lep′tän) *n., pl.* **lep′ta** (-tə) [Gr. < *leptos*, thin, small < *lepein*, to peel: see LEPER] **1.** a small coin of ancient Greece **2.** the 1/100 part of a modern Greek drachma

lep·ton[2] (lep′tän) *n., pl.* **-ta** [LEPT- + -ON] any of a group of primary particles that do not interact strongly with other particles or nuclei, including the electrons, neutrinos, photons, etc.

lep·to·spi·ro·sis (lep′tō spī rō′sis) *n.* [ModL. < *Leptospira* (< LEPTO- + L. *spira:* see SPIRE[1]) + -OSIS] any of several systemic infections of man and domestic animals caused by a genus (*Leptospira*) of spirochetes found in sewage and natural waters, and involving variously the eyes, liver, kidneys, etc. —**lep′to·spi′ral** (-spī′rəl) *adj.*

Le·pus (lē′pəs) [L., the Hare] a S constellation between Eridanus and Canis Major

Ler·mon·tov (lyer′män tôf′), **Mi·kha·il Yur·ie·vich** (mē khä ēl′ yōōr′yə vich) 1814–41; Russ. poet & novelist

Le·roy (lə roi′, lē′roi) [< Fr. *le roi*, the king] a masculine name

Le·sage (lə säzh′), **A·lain Re·né** (à lan′ rə nā′) 1668–1747; Fr. novelist & dramatist: also **Le Sage**

Les·bi·an (lez′bē ən) *adj.* [L. *Lesbius* < Gr. *Lesbios*] 1. of Lesbos, its people, etc. 2. [*usually* l-] [from the eroticism or homosexuality attributed to Sappho and her followers in Lesbos] *a*) of homosexuality between women *b*) [Rare] erotic —*n.* 1. a native or inhabitant of Lesbos 2. [*usually* l-] a homosexual woman —**les′bi·an·ism** *n.*

Les·bos (lez′bäs, -bəs) Gr. island in the Aegean, off the coast of Asia Minor: c. 630 sq. mi.

Les Cayes (lā kā′) seaport on the SW coast of Haiti: pop. 14,000

Le·sche·tiz·ky (le′shə tit′skē), **Theodor** 1830–1915; Pol. pianist, teacher, & composer

lese maj·es·ty (lēz′ maj′is tē) [Fr. *lèse-majesté* < L. *laesa majestas* < *laesa*, fem. of *laesus*, pp. of *laedere*, to hurt, injure + *majestas*, majesty] 1. a crime against the sovereign; offense against a ruler's dignity as head of the state; treason 2. any insolent or slighting behavior toward a person to whom deference is due

le·sion (lē′zhən) *n.* [ME. < MFr. < L. *laesio* < *laesus*, pp. of *laedere*, to harm, injure] 1. an injury; hurt; damage 2. an injury or other change in an organ or tissue of the body tending to result in impairment or loss of function

Les·lie (les′lē, lez′-) [< surname, orig. place name said to be < *less lee* (*lea*), i.e., smaller meadow, dell] a masculine or feminine name

Le·so·tho (le sut′hō, le sō′thō) country in SE Africa, surrounded by South Africa: formerly the Brit. protectorate of Basutoland, it became an independent member of the Brit. Commonwealth in 1966: 11,716 sq. mi.; pop. 975,000; cap. Maseru

☆**les·pe·de·za** (les′pə dē′zə) *n.* [ModL. *Lespedeza*, erroneously for **Zespedesa*, after V. M. de *Zespedes*, 18th-c. Sp. governor of E Florida] any of a genus (*Lespedeza*) of annual or perennial plants of the legume family, cultivated for forage, hay, soil improvement, etc.

less (les) *adj. alt. compar.* of LITTLE [ME. *les* < OE. *læs*, adv. *læssa*, adj., used as compar. of *lytel* (cf. LITTLE), akin to OFris. *lēs* < IE. **leis-* < base **lei-*, to diminish, meager, whence LITTLE] not so much, so many, so great, etc.; smaller; fewer —*adv. compar.* of LITTLE not so much; to a smaller extent —*n.* a smaller amount —*prep.* with the deduction of; minus [\$5,000 *less* taxes] —**less and less** to a decreasing degree; decreasingly —**no less a person than** a person of no lower importance, rank, etc. than

-less (lis, ləs) [ME. *-les, -leas* < OE. *-leas* < *leas*, free, loose: see LOOSE, LOSE] *an adj.-forming suffix meaning:* 1. without, lacking [*pitiless, valueless*] 2. that does not [*relentless, tireless*] 3. that cannot be [*dauntless*]

les·see (les ē′) *n.* [ME. < Anglo-Fr. < OFr. *lessé*, pp. of *lesser*: see LEASE & -EE¹] a person to whom property is leased; tenant

less·en (les′'n) *vt.* 1. to make less; decrease 2. [Archaic] to belittle; minimize; disparage —*vi.* to become less —SYN. see DECREASE

Les·seps (les′əps; *Fr.* le seps′), vicomte **Fer·di·nand Ma·rie de** (fer dē nän′ mà rē′ də) 1805–94; Fr. engineer & diplomat: promoter & planner of the Suez Canal

less·er (les′ər) *adj. alt. compar.* of LITTLE [LESS + -ER] smaller, less, or less important —*adv.* less

Lesser Antilles group of islands in the West Indies, southeast of Puerto Rico, including the Leeward Islands, the Windward Islands, & the islands off the N coast of Venezuela

Lesser Khingan Mountains see KHINGAN MOUNTAINS

lesser panda a reddish, raccoonlike mammal (*Ailurus fulgens*) of the Himalayan region, with a long ringed tail

Les·sing (les′in), **Gott·hold E·phra·im** (gōt′hōlt ā′frä im) 1729–81; Ger. dramatist & critic

les·son (les′'n) *n.* [ME. *lessoun* < OFr. *leçon* < L. *lectio*, a reading, hence text, lesson < pp. of *legere*, to read: see LOGIC] 1. something to be learned; specif., *a*) an exercise or assignment that a student is to prepare or learn within a given time; unit of instruction *b*) the instruction given during one class or instruction period *c*) something that needs to be learned (or the event through which it is learned) for the sake of one's safety, well-being, etc. *d*) [*pl.*] course of instruction [music *lessons*] 2. a selection from the Bible, read as part of a church service 3. a rebuke; reproof —*vt.* [Now Rare] 1. to give a lesson to 2. to rebuke; reprove

les·sor (les′ôr, les ôr′) *n.* [Anglo-Fr. < *lesser*: see LEASE] a person who gives a lease; landlord

lest (lest) *conj.* [ME. *leste* < OE. *the læste* < *thy læs the*, lit., by the less that < *thy*, instrumental of *thæt*, pronoun + *læs* (see LESS) + *the*, particle] 1. for fear that; in case; so that . . . not [*speak low lest* you be overheard] 2. that: used only after an expression denoting fear [afraid *lest* he should fall]

Les·ter (les′tər) [orig. surname < LEICESTER] a masculine name: nickname, **Les**

let¹ (let) *vt.* **let** or obs. **let′ted, let′ting** [ME. *leten* < OE. *lætan*, to leave behind, akin to G. *lassen* < IE. **lēd-* < base **lēi-*, to neglect, leave behind, whence L. *lenis*, gentle, *letum*, death, Gr. *lēdein*, to be tired & LATE] 1. to leave; forsake; abandon: now only in phrases **let alone** (or **let be**), to refrain from bothering, disturbing, touching, etc. 2. *a*) to give the use of (a house, room, etc.) to a tenant in return for rent; rent; hire out *b*) to give out (work), assign (a contract), etc. 3. to allow or cause to escape; cause to flow or come out, as by shedding, emitting, etc. [to *let* blood] 4. to allow to pass, come, or go [*let* me in] 5. to allow; permit: followed by an infinitive, normally without *to* [*let* me help], or by an adverb, etc. with the verb itself unexpressed [*let* me up] 6. to cause to; make: usually with *know* or *hear* [*let* me hear from you] 7. to suppose; assume; regard as When used in commands, suggestions, or dares with a noun or pronoun as object, *let* serves as an auxiliary [*let* us give generously, just *let* him make one false move] —*vi.* to be rented or leased [house to *let*] —**let down** 1. to lower 2. to slow up; relax; slacken 3. *a*) to disappoint or fail *b*) to deject or dishearten —**let off** 1. to give forth (steam, etc.) 2. to excuse from work for a short time 3. to deal leniently with; release with light punishment or none —**let on** [Colloq.] 1. to indicate one's awareness of a fact 2. to pretend —**let out** 1. to allow to flow, run, etc. away; release 2. to give forth; emit 3. to lease or rent out 4. to reveal (a secret, etc.) 5. to make a garment larger by reducing (the seams, hem, etc.) 6. to cut (fur pelts) into strips that are then sewn together to achieve suppleness, attractive shading, etc. ☆7. to dismiss or be dismissed, as school —**let up** 1. to slacken; relax 2. to cease —☆**let up on** [Colloq.] to stop dealing harshly or severely with
SYN.—**let** may imply positive consent but more often stresses the offering of no opposition or resistance, sometimes connoting negligence, lack of power, etc. [don't *let* this happen again]; **allow** and **permit** imply power or authority to give or deny consent, **allow** connoting a refraining from the enforcement of usual requirements [honor students were *allowed* to miss the examinations], and **permit** more positively suggesting formal consent or authorization [he was *permitted* to talk to the prisoner]; **suffer**, now somewhat rare in this sense, is closely synonymous with **allow** and may connote passive consent or reluctant tolerance See also HIRE

let² (let) *vt.* **let′ted** or **let, let′ting** [ME. *letten* < OE. *lettan*, to hinder, lit., to make late (akin to Goth. *latjan*, to delay) < base of *læt*, LATE: cf. prec.] [Archaic] to hinder; obstruct; prevent —*n.* 1. an obstacle or impediment: used in the legal phrase **without let or hindrance** 2. in tennis and other racket games, an interference with the course of the ball in some way specified in the rules, making it necessary to play the point over again

-let (lit, lət) [ME. < MFr. *-el* (< L. *-ellus*) + *-et*, both dim. suffixes] *a n.-forming suffix meaning: a*) small [*ringlet, booklet*] *b*) a small object worn as a band on (a specified part of the body) [*anklet*]

‡**l'é·tat, c'est moi** (lā tà′ se mwà′) [Fr., the state, it is I] I am the state: a saying attributed to Louis XIV of France

letch (lech) *vi., n. same as* LECH

let·down (let′doun′) *n.* 1. a slowing up, relaxing, or feeling of dejection, as after great excitement, effort, etc. 2. the gliding descent of an airplane as it prepares to land 3. a disappointment or disillusionment

le·thal (lē′thəl) *adj.* [L. *letalis, lethalis* < *letum*, death: see LET¹] 1. causing or capable of causing death; fatal or deadly 2. of or suggestive of death —SYN. see FATAL —**le·thal′i·ty** (-thal′ə tē) *n.* —**le′thal·ly** *adv.*

lethal chamber a room where persons are executed by exposure to a deadly gas

lethal gene a gene present in the homozygous state, that causes death during some immature stage in the development of an organism: also **lethal factor**

le·thar·gic (li thär′jik) *adj.* [ME. *litargik* < L. *lethargicus* < Gr. *lēthargikos*] 1. of or producing lethargy 2. having lethargy; abnormally drowsy or dull, sluggish, etc. —**le·thar′gi·cal·ly** *adv.*

leth·ar·gize (leth′ər jīz′) *vt.* **-gized′, -giz′ing** to make lethargic

leth·ar·gy (leth′ər jē) *n., pl.* **-gies** [ME. *litarge* < OFr. < LL. *lethargia* < Gr. *lēthargia* < *lēthargos*, forgetful < *lēthē* (see LETHE) + *argos*, idle < *a-*, not + *ergon*, WORK] 1. a condition of abnormal drowsiness or torpor 2. a great lack of energy; sluggishness, dullness, apathy, etc.
SYN.—**lethargy** implies a dull, sluggish state brought on by illness, great fatigue, overeating, etc.; **languor** now generally suggests an inertia or limpness that results from indolence, enervating weather, a dreamy, tender mood, etc.; **lassitude** suggests a listlessness or spiritlessness resulting from overwork, dejection, etc.; **stupor** suggests a state in which the faculties and senses are deadened, as by emotional shock, alcohol, or narcotics; **torpor** implies a temporary loss of all or part of the power of sensation or motion

Leth·bridge (leth′brij′) city in S Alberta, Canada: pop. 37,000

Le·the (lē′thē) [L. < Gr. *lēthē*, forgetfulness, oblivion < IE. **lāidh-* < base **lā-*, hidden, whence L. *latere*, to be hidden] *Gr. & Rom. Myth.* the river of forgetfulness, flowing through Hades, whose water produced loss of memory in those who drank of it —*n.* oblivion; forgetfulness —**Le·the·an** (lē thē′ən) *adj.*

Le·ti·tia (li tish′ə) [< L. *laetitia*, gladness < *laetus*, gay, glad] a feminine name: dim. *Letty*

let's (lets) let us

Lett (let) *n.* [G. *Lette* < Lett. *Latvi*] 1. a member of a people living in Latvia and adjacent Baltic regions 2. *same as* LETTISH

Lett. Lettish

let·ted (let′id) 1. *obs. pt. & pp.* of LET¹ 2. *alt. pt. & pp.* of LET²

let·ter[1] (let′ər) *n.* [ME. *lettre* < OFr. < L. *littera*, letter of the alphabet, (in pl.) a letter, epistle] **1.** a symbol or character employed, theoretically, to represent a speech sound or sounds: in English, many words contain letters that are no longer pronounced **2.** a written or printed message to a person or group, usually sent by mail in an envelope **3.** an official document giving certain authorities or privileges: *usually used in pl.* **4.** [*pl.*] *a)* literature generally *b)* learning; knowledge, esp. of literature *c)* the profession of a writer **5.** strict interpretation of the literal meaning, or the literal meaning itself; exact wording ✰**6.** the first letter of the name of a school or college, awarded and worn for superior performance in sports, etc. **7.** *Printing a)* a type or impression of a character of the alphabet *b)* a particular style of type —*vt.* **1.** to make hand-printed letters on; mark with letters [*to letter* a poster] **2.** to set down in hand-printed letters [*to letter* one's name] —*vi.* **1.** to make hand-printed letters ✰**2.** [Colloq.] to earn a school letter as in a sport —**to the letter** just as written or directed; precisely —**let′ter·er** *n.*

let·ter[2] (let′ər) *n.* a person who lets, or rents out, property

letter box *same as* MAILBOX

letter carrier a postman; mail carrier

let·tered (let′ərd) *adj.* **1.** able to read and write; literate **2.** very well educated; learned **3.** inscribed or marked with letters

let·ter·head (-hed′) *n.* **1.** the name, address, etc. of a person or firm printed as a heading on a sheet of letter paper **2.** a sheet of letter paper with such a heading printed on it

let·ter·ing (-iŋ) *n.* the process of putting letters on something by inscribing, printing, painting, engraving, etc., or the letters so made

✰**let·ter·man** (-man′) *n., pl.* -men′ (-men′) a student who has won a school letter, as for proficiency in a sport

letter of advice a letter notifying the receiver that a bill of exchange has been drawn on him or that goods have been shipped to him, etc.

letter of credit a letter from a bank asking that the holder of the letter be allowed to draw specified sums of money from other banks or agencies, to be charged to the account of the writer of the letter

let·ter-per·fect (-pur′fikt) *adj.* **1.** correct in all its letters, or in every respect **2.** knowing one's lesson, theatrical role, etc. perfectly

let·ter·press (-pres′) *n.* **1.** *a)* the method of printing from raised surfaces, as set type: cf. OFFSET *b)* matter printed by this method **2.** [Chiefly Brit.] reading matter, as distinguished from illustrations

letters of administration *Law* a document by which an administrator is authorized by the probate court to administer the goods or property of a dead person

letters (or letter) of credence a formal document which a country's diplomatic representative carries as his credentials to a foreign government: also **letters credential**

letters (or letter) of marque formerly, a government document authorizing an individual to make reprisals on the subjects of an enemy nation, specif. to arm a ship and capture enemy merchant ships and cargo: also **letters (or letter) of marque and reprisal**

letters patent a document granting a patent: see PATENT

letters testamentary *Law* a document granted after probate of a will by the probate court or some officer who has authority, directing the person named as executor in the will to act in that capacity

Let·tic (let′ik) *adj. same as* LETTISH

Let·tish (let′ish) *adj.* of the Letts or their language —*n. same as* LATVIAN (n. 2)

†**let·tre de ca·chet** (let r′ də kȧ shā′), *pl.* **let·tres de ca·chet′** (let r′) [Fr.] a sealed letter; esp., in France before the Revolution, a letter containing a royal warrant for the imprisonment without trial of a specified person

let·tuce (let′is) *n.* [ME. *letuse* < OFr. *laituës*, pl. of *laitue* < L. *lactuca* < *lac* (gen. *lactis*), milk (see GALACTIC): from its milky juice] **1.** any of a genus (*Lactuca*) of hardy, annual composite plants; specif., a plant (*Lactuca sativa*) grown for its crisp, succulent, green leaves **2.** the leaves of such a plant, much used for salads **3.** [Slang] paper money

✰**let·up** (let′up′) *n.* [< phr. *let up*] [Colloq.] **1.** a slackening or lessening, as of effort **2.** a stop or pause

le·u (le′oo) *n., pl.* **lei** [Romanian, lit., lion < L. *leo*, LION] **1.** the monetary unit of Romania: see MONETARY UNITS, table **2.** a coin of this value

Leu·cas (loo′kas) *L. name of* LEVKÁS

leu·cine (loo′sēn, -sin) *n.* [< Gr. *leukos*, white (see LIGHT[1]) + -INE[4]] an amino acid, $C_6H_{13}NO_2$, produced by the hydrolysis of proteins by pancreatic enzymes during digestion and by the putrefaction of nitrogenous organic matter

leu·cite (-sīt) *n.* [G. *leucit* (now *leuzit*) < Gr. *leukos*, white (see LIGHT[1]) + -*it*, -ITE[1]] a white or gray mineral, $KAl(SiO_3)_2$, found in potassium-rich igneous rocks

leu·co- (loo′kō, -kə) [< Gr. *leukos*, white: see LIGHT[1]] *a combining form meaning* white, weakly colored, or colorless [*leucoplast*]: also, before a vowel, **leuc-**: many words beginning with *leuc-* or *leuco-* are now usually spelled **leuk-** or **leuko-** in medical and biological usage

leu·co·plast (loo′kə plast′) *n.* [LEUCO- + -PLAST] any of the colorless granules found in the protoplasm of vegetable cells in which starch forms in the absence of light

leu·ke·mi·a (loo kē′mē ə) *n.* [ModL.: see LEUCO- & -EMIA] any of a group of neoplastic diseases of the blood-forming organs, resulting in an abnormal increase in the production of leukocytes, often accompanied by anemia and enlargement of the lymph nodes, spleen, and liver: also sp. **leu·kae′mi·a** —**leu·ke′mic** (-mik) *adj.* —**leu·ke′moid** (-moid) *adj.*

leu·ko·cyte (loo′kə sīt′) *n.* [see LEUCO- & -CYTE] any of the small, colorless cells in the blood, lymph, and tissues, which are important in the body's defenses against infection; white blood corpuscle —**leu′ko·cyt′ic** (-sit′ik) *adj.* —**leu′ko·cyt′oid** (-sit′oid) *adj.*

leu·ko·cy·to·blast (loo′kə sīt′ə blast′) *n.* [see LEUCO- & CYTO- & BLAST] the precursor cell to a mature leukocyte —**leu′ko·cy′to·blas′tic** (-blas′tik) *adj.*

leu·ko·cy·to·sis (-sī tō′sis) *n.* [ModL. < LEUKOCYTE + -OSIS] an increase in the number of leukocytes in the blood: it is a normal response to pregnancy and is found in certain intoxications and in many infections and cases of inflammation **leu′ko·cy·tot′ic** (-tät′ik) *adj.*

leu·ko·der·ma (-dur′mə) *n.* [ModL.: see LEUCO- & -DERM] a lack of pigmentation, often congenital, in areas of the skin, resulting in white patches

leu·ko·ma (loo kō′mə) *n.* [ModL. < Gr. *leukōma* < *leukos*, white: see LIGHT[1]] a dense, white opacity of the cornea, caused by injury or inflammation

leu·ko·pe·ni·a (loo′kə pē′nē ə) *n.* [ModL. < LEUCO- + Gr. *penia*, poverty] a decrease below normal in the number of leukocytes in the blood —**leu′ko·pe′nic** *adj.*

leu·ko·poi·e·sis (-poi ē′sis) *n.* [ModL. < Gr. *leukos*, white + *poiēsis*, a making: see LEUCO- & POESY] the process of forming leucokytes —**leu′ko·poi·et′ic** (-et′ik) *adj.*

leu·kor·rhe·a (loo′kə rē′ə) *n.* [ModL.: see LEUCO- + -RRHEA] an abnormal, whitish discharge from the vagina —**leu′kor·rhe′al** *adj.*

Leu·ven (lö′vən) *Fl. name of* LOUVAIN

lev (lef) *n., pl.* **le·va** (le′va) [Bulg., lit., lion < OSlav. *livu*, ult. < Gr. *leōn*, lion] the monetary unit of Bulgaria: see MONETARY UNITS, table

Lev. Leviticus

Le·val·loi·si·an (lev′ə loi′zē ən) *adj.* [after fl., where such tools were found] designating or of a middle paleolithic culture, characterized by the production of flake tools

Le·val·lois-Per·ret (lə vȧl lwä′pe re′) city in NC France, on the Seine: suburb of Paris: pop. 62,000

Le·vant (lə vant′) [Fr. *levant* < It. *levante* (< L. *levans*, rising, raising), prp. of *levare*, to raise: see LEVER] applied to the East, from the "rising" of the E sun] region on the E Mediterranean, including all countries bordering the sea between Greece & Egypt —*n.* [l-] **1.** *same as* LEVANT MOROCCO **2.** *rare var. of* LEVANTER

le·vant (lə vant′) *vi.* [prob. < Sp. *levantar*, to start suddenly (as game), lit., to rise, ult. < L. *levare*, to raise: see LEVER] [Chiefly Brit.] to disappear unexpectedly, leaving unpaid debts —**le·vant′er** *n.*

LEVANT

le·vant·er (lə van′tər) *n.* [LEVANT + -ER] **1.** a strong wind that blows over the Mediterranean area from the east **2.** [L-] *same as* LEVANTINE

Lev·an·tine (lev′ən tīn′, -tēn′; lə van′tin) *adj.* [Fr. *levantin*] of the Levant —*n.* **1.** a native or inhabitant of the Levant **2.** [l-] a strong, twilled silk cloth

Levant morocco a fine morocco leather with a large, irregular grain, used esp. in bookbinding

le·va·tor (lə vāt′ər) *n., pl.* **le·va·to·res** (lev′ə tôr′ēz), **le·va′tors** [ModL. < pp. of L. *levare*, to raise: see LEVER] **1.** a muscle that raises a limb or other part of the body **2.** a surgical instrument for lifting depressed fragments of bone in a skull fracture

✰**lev·ee**[1] (lev′ē) *n.* [Fr. *levée*, fem. pp. of *lever*, to raise < L. *levare*: see LEVER] **1.** an embankment built alongside a river to prevent high water from flooding bordering land **2.** a landing place along the bank of a river; quay **3.** a low ridge of earth around a field to be irrigated —*vt.* **lev′eed**, **lev′ee·ing** to build a levee along

lev·ee[2] (lev′ē; lə vē′, -vā′) *n.* [Fr. *levé*, for *lever*, substantival use of inf., to raise, *se lever*, to rise: see prec.] **1.** formerly, a morning reception held by a sovereign or person of high rank upon arising **2.** a reception held by the President or other high official **3.** [Brit.] a reception held in the afternoon by the king or his representative, attended only by men

lev·el (lev′'l) *n.* [ME. < OFr. *livel* < VL. **libellus* < L. *libella,* dim. of *libra,* a balance, level, weight] **1.** an instrument for determining, or adjusting a surface to, an even horizontal plane: it has a glass tube partly filled with liquid so as to leave an air bubble that moves to the exact center of the tube when the instrument is on an even horizontal plane **2.**

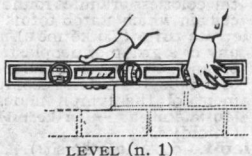

LEVEL (n. 1)

a measuring of differences in altitude with such an instrument **3.** *a)* a horizontal plane or line; esp., such a plane taken as a basis for the measurement of elevation *[sea level] b)* the height, or altitude, of such a plane **4.** a relatively flat and even area of land or other surface; horizontal area **5.** the same horizontal plane *[to keep the tops of pictures on a level]* **6.** usual or normal position with reference to a certain height *[water seeks its level]* **7.** position, elevation, or rank considered as one of the planes in a scale of values *[levels of income]* **8.** a horizontal drift or gallery in a mine **9.** the degree of concentration of a substance in a fluid **10.** *Physics* the ratio of a quantity's magnitude to an arbitrarily selected magnitude —*adj.* **1.** having no part higher than any other; perfectly flat and even; conforming to the surface of still water **2.** conforming to the plane of the horizon; not sloping **3.** being of the same height or being in the same plane; even (*with*) **4.** even with the top of the container; not heaping *[a level teaspoonful]* **5.** *a)* equal in importance, rank, degree, etc. *b)* conforming to a specified level or rank *[high-level talks] c)* equally advanced in development *d)* even or uniform in tone, color, pitch, volume, rate, etc. **6.** *a)* not having or showing sudden differences or inequalities; well-balanced; equable *b)* not excited or disturbed; calm or steady **7.** paid or to be paid in equal amounts over a period of time ☆**8.** [Slang] honest; straight —*adv.* [Now Rare] on a level line —*vt.* **-eled** or **-elled, -el·ing** or **-el·ling** **1.** to make level; specif., *a)* to make perfectly horizontal by means of a level *b)* to make even; give a flat, horizontal surface to *c)* to equalize in height, rank, quality, etc. (often with *down* or *up*) *d)* to make even in tone, color, pitch, etc. **2.** to knock to the ground; demolish; lay low *[the storm leveled the tree]* **3.** to raise (a gun, etc.) to a level position for firing **4.** to aim or direct **5.** *Surveying* to determine the differences in altitude in (a plot of ground) —*vi.* **1.** to aim a gun, etc. (*at*) **2.** to bring people or things to an equal rank, condition, etc. (usually with *down* or *up*) ☆**3.** [Slang] to be frank and honest (*with* someone) —**find one's** (or **its**) **level** to reach one's proper or natural place according to one's qualities, capacity, etc. —**level off** **1.** to give a flat, horizontal surface to; make even with the surfaces immediately surrounding **2.** to become horizontal; specif., *Aeron.* to come or bring to a horizontal line of flight: also **level out** **3.** to become stable or constant —**one's level best** [Colloq.] the best one can do —☆**on the level** [Slang] honest(ly) and fair(ly) —**lev′el·ly** *adv.* —**lev′el·ness** *n.*

SYN.—**level** is applied to a surface that is parallel to, or conforms with, the horizon; **flat** implies the absence to any marked degree of depressions or elevations in a surface, in whatever direction it lies; **plane** describes a real or imaginary surface that is absolutely flat and wholly contains every straight line joining any two points lying in it; **even** is applied to a surface that is uniformly level or flat, or to a surface that is in the same plane with, or a parallel plane to, another; a **smooth** surface has no roughness or projections, often as a result of wear, planing, polishing, etc.

level crossing [Brit.] *same as* GRADE CROSSING

lev·el·er (lev′'l ər) *n.* **1.** one that levels **2.** a person who wishes to abolish political and social inequalities **3.** [L-] a member of an English party that arose in the army of the Long Parliament (c. 1647) and advocated the leveling of all ranks and the establishment of a more democratic government Also sp. **lev′el·ler**

☆**lev·el·head·ed** (lev′'l hed′id) *adj.* having or showing an even temper and sound judgment; sensible —**lev′el·head′ed·ly** *adv.* —**lev′el·head′ed·ness** *n.*

leveling rod (or **staff**) *Surveying* a graduated rod used in determining the difference in elevation between two points

lev·er (lev′ər, lē′vər) *n.* [ME. < OFr. *leveour* < *lever,* to raise < L. *levare* < *levis,* light: see LIGHT²] **1.** a bar used as a pry **2.** a means to an end **3.** *Mech.* a device consisting of a bar turning about a fixed point, the fulcrum, using power or force applied at a second point to lift or sustain a weight at a third point; hence, any handle or other projection used to operate something —*vt.* **1.** to move, lift, etc. with or as with a lever **2.** to use as a lever —*vi.* to use a lever

lev·er·age (-ij) *n.* **1.** the action of a lever **2.** the mechanical power resulting from this **3.** increased means of accomplishing some purpose

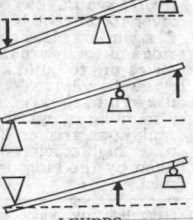

LEVERS

lev·er·et (lev′ər it) *n.* [LME. < MFr. *levrette,* dim. of *levre,* hare < L. *lepus* (gen. *leporis*)] a hare during its first year

Le·vi (lē′vī) [Heb., *lēwī,* lit., joining] **1.** a masculine name: dim. *Lev* **2.** *Bible* the third son of Jacob and Leah: see also LEVITE

lev·i·a·ble (lev′ē ə b'l) *adj.* **1.** that can be levied upon; taxable; assessable **2.** that can be levied

le·vi·a·than (lə vī′ə thən) *n.* [ME. *leuyethan* < LL.(Ec.) < Heb. *liwyāthān* < base akin to Akkad *lawū,* to surround, Ar. *liyatu,* snake] **1.** *Bible* a sea monster, variously thought of as a reptile or a whale **2.** anything huge or very powerful —[L-] a political treatise by Thomas Hobbes (1651) dealing with the organization of the state

lev·i·er (lev′ē ər) *n.* a person who levies taxes, fines, tributes, etc.

lev·i·gate (lev′ə gāt′) *vt.* **-gat·ed, -gat·ing** [< L. *levigatus,* pp. of *levigare,* to make smooth, polish < *levis,* smooth (< IE. base **lei-,* slippery: cf. LIME¹) + *agere,* to make (see ACT)] **1.** to grind to a fine, smooth powder **2.** to separate fine particles from coarse particles of (a substance) by grinding in water so as to suspend the fine particles, which settle to the bottom last

lev·in (lev′in) *n.* [ME. *levene,* prob. ult. < IE. base **leuk-,* to shine, whence LIGHT¹] [Archaic] lightning

lev·i·rate (lev′ər it, lē′vər-; -āt′) *n.* [L. *levir,* husband's brother, brother-in-law (< **daiwer* < IE. **dāiwēr,* whence Sans. *dēvár,* Gr. *daēr,* OE. *tacor*) + -ATE²] a custom of the Jews in Biblical times by which a dead man's brother was obligated to marry the widow if there were no sons: Deut. 25:5–10 —**lev′i·rat′ic** (-ə rat′ik), **lev′i·rat′i·cal** *adj.*

☆**Le·vi's** (lē′vīz) [after *Levi* Strauss, who first made them in San Francisco (c. 1850)] *a trademark for* closefitting trousers of heavy denim, reinforced at the seams, etc. with small copper rivets —*n.pl.* such trousers: usually written **le′vis**

lev·i·tate (lev′ə tāt′) *vt.* **-tat·ed, -tat·ing** [< L. *levis,* LIGHT² by analogy with GRAVITATE] to cause to rise and float in the air —*vi.* to rise and float in the air because of, or as if because of, lightness and buoyancy —**lev′i·ta′tor** *n.*

lev·i·ta·tion (lev′ə tā′shən) *n.* **1.** a levitating or being levitated **2.** the illusion of raising and keeping a heavy body in the air with little or no physical support

Le·vite (lē′vīt) *n.* [LL.(Ec.) *Levites* < Gr.(Ec.) *Leuitēs* < Heb. *lēwī:* see LEVI] *Bible* any member of the tribe of Levi, chosen to assist the priests in the Temple

Le·vit·i·cal (lə vit′i k'l) *adj.* [< LL.(Ec.) *Leviticus* + -AL] **1.** of the Levites **2.** of Leviticus or its laws

Le·vit·i·cus (-kəs) [LL.(Ec.) *Leviticus* (*liber*) < Gr.(Ec.) *Leuitikon* (*biblion*), lit., the Levitical book] the third book of the Pentateuch in the Bible, containing the laws relating to priests and Levites

Lev·it·town (lev′it toun′) [< *Levitt* & Sons, Inc., builders of planned towns] suburb of New York City, on W Long Island: pop. 65,000

lev·i·ty (lev′ə tē) *n., pl.* **-ties** [OFr. *levité* < L. *levitas* < *levis,* LIGHT²] **1.** [Rare] lightness of weight; buoyancy **2.** lightness or gaiety of disposition, conduct, or speech; esp., improper or unbecoming gaiety or flippancy; lack of seriousness; frivolity **3.** fickleness; instability

Lev·kás (lef käs′) one of the Ionian Islands, in the Ionian Sea, off the W coast of Greece: 114 sq. mi.

le·vo- (lē′və, -vō) [< L. *laevus,* left < earlier **laiwos* < IE. **laiwos* (whence Gr. *laios*) < base **lei-, elei,* to bend, curve, whence EL(BOW)] *a combining form meaning:* **1.** toward or on the left-hand side **2.** *Chem.* levorotatory

le·vo·gy·rate (lē′və jī′rāt) *adj.* [LEVO- + GYRATE, *adj.*] *same as* LEVOROTATORY: also **le′vo·gy′rous** (-rəs) *adj.*

le·vo·ro·ta·tion (-rō tā′shən) *n.* [LEVO- + ROTATION] rotation to the left; counterclockwise rotation: usually said of the plane of polarization of light

le·vo·ro·ta·to·ry (-rōt′ə tôr′ē) *adj.* [LEVO- + ROTATORY] **1.** turning or circling to the left, in a counterclockwise direction **2.** that turns the plane of polarized light counterclockwise: said of certain crystals, etc.

lev·u·lin (lev′yoo lin) *n.* [LEVUL(OSE) + -IN¹] a colorless, starchlike carbohydrate ($C_6H_{10}O_5$), which hydrolyzes to form levulose

lev·u·lose (-lōs′) *n.* [LEV(O)- + -UL(E) + -OSE¹: so called because levorotatory] *same as* FRUCTOSE

lev·y (lev′ē) *n., pl.* **lev′ies** [ME. *levee* < MFr., fem. pp. of *lever,* to raise: see LEVER] **1.** an imposing and collecting of a tax or other payment **2.** an amount levied; tax, etc. **3.** *a)* the enlistment, usually compulsory, of personnel, as for military service *b)* a group so enlisted —*vt.* **lev′ied, lev′y·ing** **1.** to impose or collect (a tax, tribute, fine, etc.) **2.** to enlist (troops) for military service, usually by force **3.** to wage (war) —*vi.* **1.** to make a levy **2.** *Law* to seize property in order to satisfy a judgment (often with *on*)

levy en masse [after Fr. *levée en masse*] an armed rising by civilians in a territory in order to resist an approaching invader: also **levy in mass**

lewd (lood) *adj.* [ME. *lewed* < OE. *læwede,* lay, unlearned < ?] **1.** showing, or intended to excite, lust or sexual desire, esp. in an offensive way; lascivious **2.** [Obs.] *a)* unlearned; ignorant *b)* unprincipled; vicious —**lewd′ly** *adv.* —**lewd′ness** *n.*

Lew·es (loo′is), **George Henry** 1817–78; Eng. critic & writer on philosophy

lew·is (lōō′is) *n.* [prob. < the name *Lewis*] an attachment for lifting heavy stones: it consists of a dovetailed iron piece made in sections that fit into a dovetailed opening in the stone: also **lew′is·son** (-i s′n)

Lew·is (lōō′is) **1.** a masculine name: dim. *Lew, Lewie:* see LOUIS **2.** C(ecil) Day, *see* DAY LEWIS **3.** C(live) S(taples), 1898–1963; Brit. writer, born in Ireland **4.** John L(lewellyn), 1880–1969; U.S. labor leader **5.** Mer·i·weth·er (mer′ē weth′ər), 1774–1809; Am. explorer; co-leader of the Lewis & Clark expedition (1804–06) to the Northwest **6.** Sinclair, 1885–1951; U.S. novelist **7.** (Percy) Wynd·ham (win′dəm), 1884–1957; Brit. author & painter, born in the U.S.

Lew·i·sham (lōō′ə shəm, -səm) metropolitan borough of London: pop. 223,000

☆**lew·is·ite** (lōō′ə sit′) *n.* [after W. L. Lewis (1878–1943), U.S. chemist who developed it] a pale yellow, odorless, irritating arsenical compound, ClCH=CHAsCl₂, used as a blistering poison gas

Lewis (machine) gun [after its U.S. inventor, Col. I. N. Lewis (1858–1931)] a former type of air-cooled, automatic firearm having a circular cartridge drum

Lew·is·ton (lōō′is tən) [prob. < a personal name] city in SW Me.: pop. 42,000

Lewis with Harris northernmost island of the Outer Hebrides, Scotland: larger N part (Lewis) is in Ross and Cromarty county & the S part (Harris) is in Inverness county: 770 sq. mi.: also called **Lewis**

‡**lex** (leks) *n., pl.* **le·ges** (lē′jēz, lā′gās) [L.] law

lex. lexicon

☆**Lex·an** (lek′san) *a trademark for* a polycarbonate resin, used in molded products, as a substitute for glass, etc.

lex·eme (lek′sēm) *n.* [LEX(ICON) + -eme, as in PHONEME] *Linguis.* a word or stem that is a meaningful unit in a language as opposed to such a form as part of a grammatical structure —**lex·em′ic** (-sē′mik) *adj.*

lex·i·cal (lek′si k′l) *adj.* [ModL. *lexicalis* < Gr. *lexikon*, lexicon] **1.** of a vocabulary, or stock of words, as of a language: specif., of words as isolated items of vocabulary rather than elements in a grammatical structure **2.** of, or having the nature of, a lexicon or lexicography

lexicog. **1.** lexicographer **2.** lexicography

lex·i·cog·ra·pher (lek′sə käg′rə fər) *n.* [LGr. *lexikographos* < Gr. *lexikon*, LEXICON + *graphein*, to write: see GRAPHIC] a person who writes or compiles a dictionary

lex·i·cog·ra·phy (lek′sə käg′rə fē) *n.* [< Gr. *lexikon*, LEXICON + -GRAPHY] the act, process, art, or work of writing or compiling a dictionary or dictionaries —**lex·i·co·graph·ic** (lek′si kə graf′ik), **lex′i·co·graph′i·cal** *adj.* —**lex′i·co·graph′i·cal·ly** *adv.*

lex·i·col·o·gy (-käl′ə jē) *n.* [< Gr. *lexikon*, LEXICON + -LOGY] the study of the meanings and origins of words —**lex′i·co·log′i·cal** (-kə läj′i k′l) *adj.* —**lex′i·col′o·gist** *n.*

lex·i·con (lek′si kən, -kän′) *n.* [Gr. *lexikon*, neut. of *lexikos*, of words < *lexis*, a saying, phrase, word < *legein:* see LOGIC] **1.** a dictionary, esp. of an ancient language **2.** the special vocabulary of a particular author, field of study, etc. **3.** *Linguis.* the total stock of morphemes in a language

Lex·ing·ton (lek′siŋ tən) **1.** [after ¶] city in NC Ky.: pop. 108,000 **2.** [after Robt. Sutton (1661–1723), 2d Baron of *Lexington*] suburb of Boston, in E Mass.: pop. 32,000: see CONCORD (sense 3)

‡**lex lo·ci** (leks lō′sī) [L.] the law of the place

‡**lex non scrip·ta** (nän skrip′tə) [L., lit., unwritten law] *same as* COMMON LAW

‡**lex scrip·ta** (skrip′tə) [L., lit., written law] *same as* STATUTE LAW

‡**lex ta·li·o·nis** (tal′ē ō′nis) [L.] the law of retaliation

Ley·den (lid′n) *same as* LEIDEN

Leyden, Lucas van *see* LUCAS VAN LEYDEN

Leyden jar (or **vial**) [< LEIDEN, where invented] a condenser for static electricity, consisting of a glass jar with a coat of tin foil outside and inside and a metallic rod connecting with the inner lining and passing through the lid

Ley·te (lāt′ē; *Sp.* lā′tā) island of EC Philippines, between Luzon & Mindanao: 2,785 sq. mi.; pop. (with small nearby islands) 1,177,000

Ley·ton (lāt′n) city in Essex, England, near London: pop. 93,000

leze majesty (lēz) *same as* LESE MAJESTY

LF, L.F., lf, l.f. low frequency

lf. **1.** *Baseball* left field; left fielder **2.** *Printing* lightface

LG., L.G. Low German

lg. **1.** large **2.** *Football* left guard

LGr., L.Gr. Late Greek

lgth. length

lg.tn. long ton

LH luteinizing hormone

l.h., L.H., LH left hand

Lha·sa (lä′sə) capital of Tibet, in the SE part: it is a Buddhist holy city: pop. c. 50,000

L.H.D. [L. *Litterarum Humaniorum Doctor*] Doctor of the Humanities: an honorary degree

LHeb. Late Hebrew

li (lē) *n., pl.* **li** [Chin.] a Chinese measure of distance, equal to about one third of a mile

Li *Chem.* lithium

li, li. link, links (in chain measure)

L.I. Long Island

li·a·bil·i·ty (lī′ə bil′ə tē) *n., pl.* **-ties** **1.** the state of being liable **2.** anything for which a person is liable **3.** [*pl.*] *Accounting* all the entries on a balance sheet showing the debts of a person or business, as accounts and notes payable, incurred but not paid obligations, and long-term debentures **4.** something that works to one's disadvantage

li·a·ble (lī′ə b′l; *also, esp. for 3,* lī′b′l) *adj.* [prob. via Anglo-Fr. < OFr. *lier,* to bind < L. *ligare,* to bind (see LIGATURE) + -ABLE] **1.** legally bound or obligated, as to make good any loss or damage that occurs in a transaction; responsible **2.** likely to have, suffer from, etc.; exposed to or subject to [liable to heart attacks] **3.** subject to the possibility of; likely (to do, have, get, etc. something unpleasant or unwanted) [liable to cause hard feelings] —*SYN.* see LIKELY

li·aise (lē āz′) *vi.* **-aised′, -ais′ing** [back-formation < ff.] [Chiefly Brit. Colloq.] to establish liaison (usually with *with*)

li·ai·son (lē′ə zän′, -zōn′; lē ā′zän; *occas.* lā′ə zän′; *for 3,* lē′ə zōn′; Fr. lye zōn′) *n.* [Fr. < OFr. < L. *ligatio* < *ligare,* to bind: see LIGATURE] **1.** a linking up or connecting of the parts of a whole, as of military units, in order to bring about proper coordination of activities **2.** an illicit love affair **3.** in spoken French, the linking of words, under certain conditions, by pronouncing the final consonant, ordinarily silent, of one word as though it were the initial consonant of the following word, as in the phrase *chez elle* (pronounced shā zel′) **4.** *Cooking* a thickening, as of flour and butter, for sauces, soups, etc.

li·a·na (lē än′ə, -an′ə) *n.* [NormFr. *liane* < Fr. *lierne, liorne,* altered (after *lier,* to bind) < *viorne* < L. *viburnum,* wayfaring tree: cf. VIBURNUM] any luxuriantly growing, woody, tropical vine that roots in the ground and climbs, as around tree trunks: also **li·ane′** (-än′, -an′)

Liao (lyou) river in NE China, flowing from Inner Mongolia west & south into the Yellow Sea: c. 900 mi.

Liao·ning (lyou′niŋ′) province of NE China: 58,301 sq. mi.; pop. 24,090,000; cap. Shenyang

Liao·tung (-dooŋ′) peninsula in Liaoning province, NE China, extending into the Yellow Sea

Liao·yang (-yäŋ′) city in C Liaoning province, NE China: pop. 135,000

li·ar (lī′ər) *n.* [ME. *lier* < OE. *leogere* < base of *leogan,* to tell lies, akin to OHG. *liugari:* see LIE²] a person who tells lies

Li·ard (lē′ärd, lē är′) river in W Canada, flowing from S Yukon southward into the Mackenzie River: 755 mi.

liar's dice a dice game in which the throw of the dice is concealed from the opponents and betting on the throw can involve bluffing: also **liar dice**

Li·as (lī′əs) *n.* [ME. *lyas* < OFr. *liois* (Fr. *liais*), kind of limestone] a series of rocks, the oldest or lowest part of the Jurassic System, noted for its fossils

lib (lib) *n. clipped form of* LIBERATION

Lib. **1.** Liberal **2.** Liberia

lib. **1.** [L. *liber*] book **2.** librarian **3.** library

li·ba·tion (lī bā′shən) *n.* [ME. *libacioun* < L. *libatio* < *libare,* to taste, pour out < IE. base *lei-,* to pour, whence Gr. *leibein*] **1.** the ritual of pouring out wine or oil upon the ground as a sacrifice to a god **2.** the liquid so poured out **3.** an alcoholic drink or the act of drinking: used humorously —**li·ba′tion·al** *adj.*

Lib·by (lib′ē), W(illard) F(rank) 1908—   ; U.S. chemist

li·bel (lī′b′l) *n.* [ME., little book < OFr. < L. *libellus,* little book, writing, lampoon, dim. of *liber,* a book: see LIBRARY] **1.** any false and malicious written or printed statement, or any sign, picture, or effigy, tending to expose a person to public ridicule, hatred, or contempt or to injure his reputation in any way **2.** the act of publishing such a thing **3.** anything that gives an unflattering or damaging picture of the subject with which it is dealing **4.** *Admiralty & Eccles. Law* the plaintiff's written statement of the wrongs he has suffered; initial pleading —*vt.* **-beled** or **-belled, -bel·ing** or **-bel·ling** **1.** to publish or make a libel against **2.** to give an unflattering or damaging picture of **3.** *Admiralty & Eccles. Law* to bring suit against by presenting a written statement of grievances

li·bel·ant, li·bel·lant (lī′b′l ənt) *n.* a person who sues by filing a libel (sense 4)

li·bel·ee, li·bel·lee (lī′b′l ē′) *n.* the defendant in a suit by libel (sense 4)

li·bel·er, li·bel·ler (lī′b′l ər) *n.* a person who commits libel

li·bel·ous, li·bel·lous (-əs) *adj.* **1.** of the nature of, or involving, a libel **2.** given to writing and publishing libels; defamatory —**li′bel·ous·ly, li′bel·lous·ly** *adv.*

‡**li·ber** (lī′bər, lē′ber) *n., pl.* **li·bri** (lī′brī, lē′brē) [L.: see LIBRARY] a book; esp., a book of public records, as of mortgages or deeds

lib·er·al (lib′ər əl, lib′rəl) *adj.* [ME. < OFr. < L. *liberalis* < *liber,* free < IE. **leudhero-,* belonging to the people,

free < base *leudh-*, to grow up, rise, whence G. *leute*, people, OE. *leodan*, to grow] **1.** orig., suitable for a freeman; not restricted: now only in LIBERAL ARTS, LIBERAL EDUCATION, etc. **2.** giving freely; generous **3.** large or plentiful; ample; abundant [a *liberal* reward] ☆**4.** not restricted to the literal meaning; not strict [a *liberal* interpretation of the Bible] **5.** tolerant of views differing from one's own; broad-minded; specif., not orthodox or conventional **6.** of democratic or republican forms of government, as distinguished from monarchies, aristocracies, etc. **7.** favoring reform or progress, as in religion, education, etc.; specif., favoring political reforms tending toward democracy and personal freedom for the individual; progressive **8.** [L-] designating or of a political party upholding liberal principles, esp. such a party in England or Canada **9.** [Obs.] excessively free or indecorous in behavior; licentious —*n.* **1.** a person favoring liberalism **2.** [L-] a member of a liberal political party, esp. that of England or Canada —**lib′er·al·ly** *adv.* —**lib′er·al·ness** *n.* SYN.—**liberal** implies tolerance of others' views as well as openmindedness to ideas that challenge tradition, established institutions, etc.; **progressive**, a relative term as opposed to *reactionary* or *conservative*, is applied to persons favoring progress and reform in politics, education, etc. and connotes an inclination to more direct action than **liberal**; **advanced** specifically implies a being ahead of the times, as in science, the arts, philosophy, etc.; **radical** implies a favoring of fundamental or extreme change, specifically of the social structure; **left**, originally referring to the position in legislatures of the seats occupied by parties holding such views, implies political liberalism or radicalism

liberal arts [transl. of L. *artes liberales*, lit., arts befitting a freeman: so named in contrast to *artes serviles*, lower (lit., servile) arts, and because open to study only by freemen (L. *liberi*); in later use understood as "arts becoming a gentleman"] the subjects of an academic college course, including literature, philosophy, languages, history, and, usually, survey courses of the sciences, as distinguished from professional or technical subjects: sometimes referred to as *arts*, as in BACHELOR OF ARTS

liberal education an education mainly in the liberal arts, providing the student with a broad cultural background rather than any specific professional training

lib·er·al·ism (-iz′m) *n.* the quality or state of being liberal; specif., *a)* a political philosophy advocating personal freedom for the individual, democratic forms of government, gradual reform in political and social institutions, etc. *b)* a movement in Protestantism advocating a broad interpretation of the Bible, freedom from rigid doctrine and authoritarianism, etc.

lib·er·al·i·ty (lib′ə ral′ə tē) *n., pl.* -ties [ME. *liberalite* < OFr. < L. *liberalitas*] **1.** the quality or state of being liberal; specif., *a)* willingness to give or share freely; generosity *b)* absence of narrowness or prejudice in thinking; broad-mindedness **2.** [Now Rare] a gift, etc. indicating generosity

lib·er·al·ize (lib′ər ə līz′, lib′rə-) *vt., vi.* -ized′, -iz′ing to make or become liberal —**lib′er·al·i·za′tion** *n.* —**lib′er·al·iz′er** *n.*

lib·er·ate (lib′ə rāt′) *vt.* -at′ed, -at′ing [< L. *liberatus*, pp. of *liberare*, to set free, release < *liber*, free: see LIBERAL] **1.** to release from slavery, enemy occupation, etc. **2.** [Slang] to steal or loot, esp. from a defeated enemy in wartime **3.** *Chem.* to free from combination in a compound —SYN. see FREE —**lib′er·a′tion** *n.*

lib·er·a·tor (-ər) *n.* [L.] a person who liberates; esp., one who frees his country from an enemy or tyranny

Li·be·rec (lē′bə rets′) city in Bohemia, NW Czechoslovakia: pop. 71,000

Li·ber·i·a (lī bir′ē ə) country on the W coast of Africa: founded by freed U.S. slaves: 43,000 sq. mi.; pop. 1,090,000; cap. Monrovia —**Li·ber′i·an** *adj., n.*

lib·er·tar·i·an (lib′ər ter′ē ən) *n.* [LIBERT(Y) + -ARIAN] **1.** a person who believes in the doctrine of the freedom of the will **2.** a person who advocates full civil liberties —*adj.* of or upholding either of these principles —**lib′er·tar′i·an·ism** *n.*

‡**li·ber·té, é·ga·li·té, fra·ter·ni·té** (lē ber tā′ ā gȧ lē tā′ frȧ ter nē tā′) [Fr.] liberty, equality, fraternity: the motto of the French Revolution of 1789

li·ber·ti·cide (li bur′tə sīd′) *n.* [Fr. *liberticide, adj.*] **1.** a destroyer of liberty **2.** [Rare] the destruction of liberty —*adj.* destroying liberty

lib·er·tine (lib′ər tēn′, -tin) *n.* [ME. *libertyn* < L. *libertinus* < *libertus*, freedman < *liber*, free: see LIBERAL] **1.** in ancient Rome, a person who had been freed from slavery **2.** [prob. via Fr. *libertin*] a man who leads an unrestrained, sexually immoral life; rake **3.** [Archaic] a freethinker —*adj.* morally unrestrained; licentious —**lib′er·tin·ism, lib′er·tin·age** *n.*

lib·er·ty (lib′ər tē) *n., pl.* -ties [ME. & OFr. *liberte* < L. *libertas* < *liber*, free: see LIBERAL] **1.** freedom or release from slavery, imprisonment, captivity, or any other form of arbitrary control **2.** the sum of rights and exemptions possessed in common by the people of a community, state, etc.; see also CIVIL LIBERTIES, POLITICAL LIBERTY **3.** a particular right, franchise, or exemption from compulsion **4.** a too free, too familiar, or impertinent action or attitude **5.** the limits within which a certain amount of freedom may be exercised [to have the *liberty* of the third floor]

6. *a)* permission given to a sailor to go ashore; specif., *U.S. Navy* permission given to an enlisted person to be absent from duty for a period of 72 hours or less *b)* the period of time given **7.** *Philos.* freedom to choose; absence of the control of necessity —SYN. see FREEDOM —**at liberty 1.** not confined; free **2.** permitted (to do or say something); allowed **3.** not busy or in use —**take liberties 1.** to be too familiar or impertinent in action or speech **2.** to deal (*with* facts, data, etc.) in an inaccurate or distorting way

☆**Liberty Bell** the bell of Independence Hall in Philadelphia, rung on July 4, 1776, to proclaim the independence of the U.S.: it cracked in 1835

liberty cap a soft, closefitting, visorless cap, adopted by the French Revolutionists as a symbol of liberty

Liberty Island island in SE N.Y., in New York Bay: site of the Statue of Liberty: c. 10 acres

☆**Liberty Ship** a U.S. merchant ship carrying about 10,000 gross tons, built in large numbers during World War II

li·bid·i·nal (li bid′'n əl) *adj.* of the libido —**li·bid′i·nal·ly** *adv.*

li·bid·i·nous (-əs) *adj.* [ME. *lybidynous* < L. *libidinosus* < *libido*: see ff.] full of or characterized by lust; lewd; lascivious —**li·bid′i·nous·ly** *adv.* —**li·bid′i·nous·ness** *n.*

li·bi·do (li bē′dō, -bī′-) *n.* [ModL. < L., pleasure, wantonness < *libet, lubet*, it pleases: see LOVE] **1.** the sexual urge or instinct **2.** *Psychoanalysis* psychic energy generally; specif., a basic form of psychic energy, comprising the positive, loving instincts and manifested variously at different stages of personality development

Li·bra (lī′brə, lē′-) [L., a balance] **1.** a S constellation between Virgo and Scorpius **2.** the seventh sign of the zodiac (♎), entered by the sun at the autumnal equinox, about September 23: see ZODIAC, illus.

li·bra (lī′brə; *also, and for 3 always,* lē′-) *n., pl.* -brae (-brē) [ME. < L.] **1.** pound: abbrev. lb., L., l.: the British symbol for the monetary unit (£) is derived from the first letter of this word **2.** an ancient Roman unit of weight, equal to about 12 ounces **3.** [Sp.: cf. POUND¹] *a)* a former gold coin of Peru *b)* a unit of weight in Spain, Mexico, and various Central and South American countries, equal to about one pound

li·brar·i·an (lī brer′ē ən) *n.* [< L. *librarius* + -AN] **1.** a person in charge of a library **2.** a library worker trained in library science —**li·brar′i·an·ship′** *n.*

li·brar·y (lī′brer′ē, -brə rē) *n., pl.* -brar′ies [ME. *librarie* < OFr. < *libraire*, copyist < L. *librarius, n.*, transcriber of books, *adj.*, of books < *liber*, a book, orig. inner bark or rind of a tree (which was written on) < IE. base *leubh-*, to peel off, whence Gr. *lepein*, to strip off rind & LEAF] **1.** a room or building where a collection of books, periodicals, musical scores, etc. is kept for reading or reference **2.** a public or private institution in charge of the care and circulation of such a collection **3.** a collection of books etc., esp. a large, systematically arranged collection for reading or reference **4.** a set or series of books issued in a single format by a publishing house

Library of Congress the public national library in Washington, D.C., established in 1800 by the U.S. Congress and housing one of the largest collections of printed material in the world

☆**library science** the study of library organization and management

li·brate (lī′brāt) *vi.* -brat·ed, -brat·ing [< L. *libratus*, pp. of *librare*, to weigh, balance < *libra*, a balance] **1.** to move back and forth slowly like the beam of a balance in coming to rest; oscillate **2.** to remain balanced; hover —**lī′bra·to′ry** (-brə tôr′ē) *adj.*

li·bra·tion (lī brā′shən) *n.* [L. *libratio*] **1.** the act of librating **2.** *Astron.* an apparent or real oscillation of the moon's face which makes it possible to see about nine per cent more of its surface other than the hemisphere which is toward the earth

li·bret·tist (li bret′ist) *n.* a writer of librettos

li·bret·to (li bret′ō) *n., pl.* -tos, -ti (-ē) [It., dim. of *libro* (< L. *liber*), a book: see LIBRARY] **1.** the words, or text, of an opera, oratorio, or other long choral work **2.** a book containing these words

Li·bre·ville (lē br′ vēl′) capital of Gabon; seaport on the Gulf of Guinea: pop. 31,000

‡**li·bri** (lī′brī, lē′brē) *n. pl. of* LIBER

li·bri·form (lī′brə fôrm′) *adj.* [L. *liber* (gen. *libri*), inner bark of a tree (see LIBRARY) + -FORM] *Bot.* designating or of wood fibers which are elongated and have simple pits

☆**Lib·ri·um** (lib′rē əm) [arbitrary coinage < Fr. *libre*, free (< L. *liber*: see LIBERTY) + -IUM] *a trademark for* a tranquilizing drug

Lib·y·a (lib′ē ə) **1.** ancient Greek & Roman name of North Africa, west of Egypt **2.** country in N Africa, on the Mediterranean: 679,359 sq. mi.; pop. 1,682,000; caps. Benghazi & Tripoli

Lib·y·an (-ən) *adj.* of Libya or its people —*n.* **1.** a native or inhabitant of Libya **2.** the earliest form of the Berber language as found in inscriptions in ancient Libya

Libyan Desert E part of the Sahara, in Libya, Sudan, & Egypt west of the Nile

lice (līs) *n. pl. of* LOUSE

li·ce·i·ty (lī sē′ə tē) *n.* [< L. *licere*, to be permitted (see LICENSE) + -ITY] lawfulness

li·cense (līs′'ns) *n.* [ME. < OFr. < L. *licentia* < *licens*, prp. of *licere*, to be permitted: see LEISURE] **1.** a formal permission to do something; esp., authorization by law to do some specified thing *[license* to marry, practice medicine, hunt, etc.*]* **2.** a document, printed tag, permit, etc. indicating that such permission has been granted **3.** *a)* freedom to deviate from strict conduct, rule, or practice, generally permitted by common consent *[poetic license]* *b)* an instance of such deviation **4.** excessive, undisciplined freedom, constituting an abuse of liberty Also, Brit. sp., **licence** —*vt.* **-censed, -cens·ing** to give license or a license to or for; permit formally —*SYN.* see AUTHORIZE, FREEDOM —**li′cens·a·ble** *adj.*

li·cen·see (līs′'n sē′) *n.* a person to whom a license is granted

li·cens·er (līs′'n sər) *n.* a person with authority to grant licenses: also sp., *Law*, **li′cen·sor**

li·cen·sure (-shər, -shoor′) *n.* the act or practice of granting licenses, as to practice a profession

li·cen·ti·ate (lī sen′shē it, -āt′) *n.* [ME. *licenciat* < ML. *licentiatus*, pp. of *licentiare*, to license < L. *licentia*: see LICENSE] **1.** a person licensed to practice a specified profession **2.** in certain European & Canadian universities, an academic degree between that of bachelor and that of doctor —**li·cen′ti·ate·ship′** *n.*

li·cen·tious (lī sen′shəs) *adj.* [L. *licentiosus* < *licentia*: see LICENSE] **1.** [Rare] disregarding accepted rules and standards **2.** morally unrestrained, esp. in sexual activity; lascivious; libertine —**li·cen′tious·ly** *adv.* —**li·cen′tious·ness** *n.*

‡**li·cet** (lī′set) [L.] it is allowed; it is legal

lich (lich) *n.* [ME. < OE. *lic*, akin to G. *leiche*, corpse < IE. base **lig-*, figure, shape, similar, like, whence LIKE²] [Scot. & Eng. Dial.] a dead body; corpse

li·chee (lē′chē′) *n. same as* LITCHI

li·chen (lī′kən) *n.* [L. < Gr. *leichēn*, prob. < *leichein*, to lick] **1.** any of a large group (Lichenes) of small plants composed of a particular fungus and a particular alga growing in an intimate symbiotic association and forming a dual plant, commonly adhering in colored patches or spongelike branches to rock, wood, soil, etc. **2.** any of various skin diseases characterized by papules and enlarged skin markings —*vt.* to cover with lichens —**li′chen·ous, li′chen·ose′** (-ōs′) *adj.*

li·chen·in (-in) *n.* [prec. + -IN¹] a carbohydrate having the same empirical formula as starch, (C₆H₁₀O₅)ₙ, obtained from Iceland moss and other lichens

li·chen·ol·o·gy (lī′kə näl′ə jē) *n.* the study of lichens

Lich·field (lich′fēld′) city in Staffordshire, WC England: birthplace of Samuel Johnson: pop. 16,000

lich gate [see LICH] [Brit.] a roofed gate at the entrance to a churchyard, where a coffin can be set down to await the arrival of the clergyman

licht (liĸht) *adj., adv., n., vi., vt. Scot. var. of* LIGHT

lic·it (lis′it) *adj.* [ME. *lycite* < L. *licitus*, pp. of *licere*, to be permitted: see LEISURE] permitted; lawful —*SYN.* see LEGAL —**lic′it·ly** *adv.* —**lic′it·ness** *n.*

lick (lik) *vt.* [ME. *licken* < OE. *liccian*, akin to G. *lecken* < IE. base **leiǵh-*, to lick, whence Gr. *leichein*, L. *ligurrire*, to lick, *lingere*, to lick up] **1.** to pass the tongue over *[to lick* one's lips*]* **2.** to bring into a certain condition by passing the tongue over *[to lick* one's fingers clean*]* **3.** to pass lightly over like a tongue *[flames licking* the logs*]* **4.** [Colloq.] *a)* to whip; thrash *b)* to overcome, vanquish, or control —*vi.* to move lightly and quickly, as a flame *[waves licking* about her feet*]* —*n.* **1.** the act of licking with the tongue **2.** a small quantity ☆**3.** *short for* SALT LICK **4.** [Colloq.] *a)* a sharp blow *b)* a short, rapid burst of activity, often careless, as in cleaning up, etc.: also **lick and a promise** *c)* a fast pace; spurt of speed; clip ☆**5.** [Slang] a phrase of jazz music, esp. an interpolated improvisation **6.** [often *pl.*] [Slang] chance; turn *[to get one's licks in]* —**lick into shape** [Colloq.] to bring into proper condition by careful, persistent work —**lick one's chops** to anticipate eagerly —**lick up** to consume as by licking or lapping

lick·er·ish (lik′ər ish) *adj.* [altered < *lickerous* < ME. *lykerous* < Anglo-Fr. form of OFr. *lecheros*] **1.** [Archaic] *a)* lecherous; lustful; lewd *b)* greedy or eager, esp. to eat or taste **2.** [Obs.] tempting the appetite

☆**lick·e·ty-split** (lik′ə tē split′) *adv.* [fanciful formation based on LICK, n. 4 *c*] [Colloq.] at great speed

lick·ing (lik′in) *n.* **1.** the act of a person or thing that licks **2.** [Colloq.] *a)* a whipping *b)* a defeat

lick·spit·tle (-spit′'l) *n.* a servile flatterer; toady: also **lick′spit′**

lic·o·rice (lik′ər ish, -is; lik′rish) *n.* [ME. *licorys* < OFr. *licorece* < LL. *liquiritia*, altered (after *liquor*: see LIQUOR) < L. *glycyrrhiza* < Gr. *glycyrrhiza* < *glykys*, sweet (see GLYCERIN) + *rhiza*, ROOT¹] **1.** a European perennial plant (*Glycyrrhiza glabra*) of the legume family, with spikes of blue flowers and short, flat pods **2.** the dried root of this plant or the black extract made from it, used in medicine, esp. as a vehicle and a diluting agent, or as flavoring for candy, tobacco, etc. **3.** candy flavored with this extract or in imitation of it

lic·tor (lik′tər) *n.* [ME. (Wycliffe) *littour* < L. *lictor* < base of *ligare*, to bind (see LIGAMENT), in allusion to the bundles of bound rods which he bore] in ancient Rome, any of a group of minor officials who carried the fasces and cleared the way for the chief magistrates

lid (lid) *n.* [ME. < OE. *hlid* (akin to G. *-lid* in *augenlid*, eyelid) < base seen in OE. *hlidan*, to cover < IE. base **klei-*, to lean, slope, incline, whence LEAN¹] **1.** a movable cover, hinged or unattached, as for a box, trunk, pot, etc.; top **2.** *short for* EYELID ☆**3.** [Colloq.] a curb or restraint *[to put a lid* on gambling*]* **4.** [Slang] a cap, hat, etc. **5.** *Bot.* loosely, an operculum

lid·ded (-id) *adj.* **1.** covered with or as with a lid **2.** having (a specified kind of) eyelids *[heavy-lidded]*

Li·di·ce (lē′di tse; *E.* lid′ə sē′) village in NW Bohemia, Czechoslovakia, near Prague: ruthlessly destroyed by the Nazis in 1942; rebuilt after 1947

lid·less (lid′lis) *adj.* **1.** without a lid **2.** without eyelids **3.** [Poet.] not closed; watchful: said of the eyes

Li·do (lē′dō) island resort in NE Italy, near Venice

li·do (lē′dō) *n.* [< prec.] **1.** a resort at a beach **2.** a swimming pool, esp. one on an ocean liner

lie¹ (lī) *vi.* **lay, lain, ly′ing** [ME. *lien* < 2d & 3d pers. sing. of earlier *liggen* < OE. *licgan*, to lie, akin to G. *liegen* < IE. base **legh-*, to lie, lay oneself down, whence L. *lectus* & Gr. *lēkhos*, bed, *lōchos*, lair] **1.** to be or put oneself in a reclining position along a relatively horizontal surface (often with *down*) **2.** to be in a more or less horizontal position on some supporting surface: said of inanimate things **3.** to be or remain in a specified condition *[motives that lie* hidden*]* **4.** to be situated *[Canada lies* to the north*]* **5.** to extend; stretch *[the road that lies* before us*]* **6.** to be; exist; be found *[the love that lies* in her eyes*]* **7.** to be buried or entombed **8.** [Archaic] to stay overnight or for a short while; lodge **9.** [Archaic] to have sexual intercourse (*with*) **10.** *Law* to be maintainable or admissible *[an action that will not lie]* —*n.* **1.** the way in which something is situated or arranged; lay *[the lie* of the land*]* **2.** an animal's lair or resting place **3.** [Brit.] a period of resting **4.** *Golf* the relative situation of a ball with reference to the advantage it offers the player *[a good lie]* —☆**lie down on the job** [Colloq.] to put forth less than one's best efforts —**lie in** to be in confinement for childbirth —**lie off** *Naut.* to stay at a distance from shore or another ship —☆**lie over** to stay and wait until some future time —**lie to** *Naut.* to lie stationary with the head to the wind: said of a ship —**take lying down** to submit to (punishment, a wrong, etc.) without protest or opposition

lie² (lī) *vi.* **lied, ly′ing** [ME. *lien* < OE. *leogan*, akin to G. *lügen* (Goth. *liugan*) < IE. base **leugh-*, to tell lies, whence Lith. *lūgoti*, to ask] **1.** *a)* to make a statement that one knows is false, esp. with intent to deceive *b)* to make such statements habitually **2.** to give a false impression; deceive one *[statistics can lie]* —*vt.* to bring, put, accomplish, etc. by lying *[to lie* oneself into office*]* —*n.* **1.** a false statement or action, esp. one made with intent to deceive **2.** anything that gives or is meant to give a false impression **3.** the charge of lying —**give the lie to 1.** to charge with telling a lie **2.** to prove to be false; belie —**lie in one's throat** (or **teeth**) to tell a foul or outrageous lie

SYN.—**lie** is the simple direct word meaning to make a deliberately false statement; **prevaricate** strictly means to quibble or confuse the issue in order to evade the truth, but it is loosely used as a formal or affected substitute for **lie**; **equivocate** implies the deliberate use of ambiguity in order to deceive or mislead; **fabricate** suggests the invention of a false story, excuse, etc. intended to deceive and is, hence, sometimes used as a somewhat softer equivalent for **lie**; **fib** implies the telling of a falsehood about something unimportant and is sometimes used as a euphemism for **lie**

Lie (lē) **1. Jonas,** 1880–1940; U.S. painter, born in Norway **2. Jonas** (**Lauritz Edemil**), 1833–1908; Norw. novelist: uncle of *prec.* **3. Tryg·ve** (**Halvdan**) (trig′və), 1896–1968; Norw. statesman; 1st secretary-general of the United Nations (1946–53)

Lieb·frau·milch (lēb′frou milk′; *G.* lēp′frou milkh′) *n.* [G., contr. < *Liebfrauenmilch*, orig. jocular formation (after *Liebfrauenstift*, monastery of our dear lady, i.e., the Virgin Mary) < *lieb*, dear + *frauen*, obs. gen. of *frau*, lady + *milch*, MILK: the wine was first produced at the monastery in Worms] a variety of white Rhine wine

Lie·big (lē′biH), **Baron Jus·tus von** (yōōs′toos fôn) 1803–73; Ger. chemist

Lieb·knecht (lēp′kneHt′), **Karl** (kärl) 1871–1919; Ger. socialist leader

Liech·ten·stein (liĸH′tən shtīn′) country in WC Europe, on the Rhine, between Switzerland & Austria: 61 sq. mi.; pop. 19,000; cap. Vaduz

lied (lēd; *G.* lēt) *n., pl.* **lied·er** (lē′dər; *G.* -dər) [G.: see LAUD] a German song, esp. a song whose words and music are of a lyrical, often popular, character

☆**Lie·der·kranz** (lē′dər krants′) *n.* [G., lit., garland of songs: see prec.] **1.** a group of songs **2.** a men's singing society —*a trademark for* a soft cheese having a strong odor and flavor

☆**lie detector** a polygraph used on persons suspected of lying: it records certain bodily changes assumed to occur when the subject lies in answering questions

lief (lēf) *adj.* [ME. *lef* < OE. *leof*, beloved, dear, akin to G. *lieb* < IE. base *leubh-*, to be fond of, desire, whence LOVE] [Archaic or Obs.] **1.** valued; dear; beloved **2.** willing —*adv.* willingly; gladly: only in **would** (or **had**) **as lief,** etc.

Li·ège (lē äzh′; *Fr.* lyezh) **1.** province of E Belgium: 1,526 sq. mi.; pop. 1,017,000 **2.** its capital, on the Meuse River: pop. 155,000

liege (lēj) *adj.* [ME. < OFr., prob. < Frank. base akin to OHG. *ledig*, free, but infl. by L. *ligare*, to bind] *Feudal Law* a) entitled to the service and allegiance of his vassals [a *liege* lord] b) bound to give service and allegiance to the lord [*liege* subjects] **2.** loyal; faithful —*n. Feudal Law* **1.** a lord or sovereign **2.** a subject or vassal

liege·man (-mən) *n., pl.* **-men** (-mən) **1.** a vassal **2.** a loyal follower Also **liege man**

li·en (lēn, lē′ən) *n.* [Fr. < L. *ligamen*, a band < *ligare*, to bind, tie: see LIGATURE] *Law* a claim on the property of another as security for the payment of a just debt

li·er (lī′ər) *n.* one who lies (reclines)

li·erne (lē urn′) *n.* [Fr.: see LIANA] *Archit.* a short rib used in Gothic vaulting to connect the bosses and intersections of the main ribs

lieu (lōō) *n.* [ME. *liue* < OFr. *lieu* < L. *locus*, place: see LOCUS] place: now chiefly in **lieu of**, in place of; instead of

Lieut. Lieutenant

lieu·ten·ant (lōō ten′ənt; *Brit.* & *Canad. army* lef ten′-) *n.* [ME. *lutenand, luftenand* < MFr. < *lieu* (see LIEU) + *tenant*, holding, prp. of *tenir*, to hold < L. *tenere*, to hold: see THIN] **1.** a person who acts for a superior, as during the latter's absence; aide; deputy **2.** an officer ranking below a captain as in a police or fire department **3.** *U.S. Mil.* a military officer ranking below a captain: see also FIRST LIEUTENANT, SECOND LIEUTENANT **4.** *U.S. Navy* an officer ranking below a lieutenant commander and above a lieutenant junior grade Abbrev. **Lieut., Lt.** —**lieu·ten′-an·cy** (-ən sē) *n., pl.* **-cies**

lieutenant colonel *U.S. Mil.* an officer ranking below a colonel and above a major

lieutenant commander *U.S. Navy* an officer ranking below a commander and above a lieutenant

lieutenant general *U.S. Mil.* an officer ranking below a general and above a major general

lieutenant governor **1.** an elected official of a State who ranks below and substitutes for the governor in case of the latter's absence or death **2.** the official head of the government of a Canadian province, appointed by the governor general: also **lieu·ten′ant-gov′er·nor** *n.*

lieutenant junior grade *U.S. Navy* an officer ranking below a lieutenant and above an ensign

life (līf) *n., pl.* **lives** [ME. < OE. *lif*, akin to ON. *lif*, life, G. *leib*, body < IE. base *leibh-*, to live, whence L. (*cae*)*lebs*, unmarried, orig., living alone (cf. CELIBATE)] **1.** that property of plants and animals which makes it possible for them to take in food, get energy from it, grow, adapt themselves to their surroundings, and reproduce their kind: it is the quality that distinguishes a living animal or plant from inorganic matter or a dead organism **2.** the state of possessing this property [brought back to *life*] **3.** a living being, esp. a human being [the *lives* lost in wars] **4.** living things collectively, often of a specified kind [plant *life*] **5.** the time a person or thing is alive or exists, or a specific portion of such time [his early *life*] **6.** a sentence of imprisonment for the rest of one's life **7.** one's manner of living [a *life* of ease] **8.** the activities of a given time or in a given setting, and the people who take part in them [military *life*] **9.** lives considered together as belonging to a certain class or type [low *life*] **10.** a) an individual's animate existence b) an account of this; biography **11.** the existence of the soul [eternal *life*] **12.** something essential to the continued existence of something else [freedom of speech is the *life* of democracy] **13.** the source of vigor or liveliness [the *life* of the party] **14.** vigor; liveliness; animation; vivacity **15.** the period of flourishing, usefulness, etc.; period during which anything lasts [fads have a short *life*] **16.** [Colloq.] another chance: often in the phrase *get a life* **17.** *Fine Arts* a) a lifelike quality or appearance b) representation from living models [a class in *life*] —*adj.* **1.** for a lifetime [a *life* sentence] **2.** of or relating to the property of life [*life* processes] **3.** using live models [a *life* class in art] —**a matter of life and death 1.** something whose outcome determines whether a person lives or dies **2.** any extremely important matter —**as large** (or **big**) **as life 1.** *same as* LIFE-SIZE **2.** in actual fact; truly —**bring to life 1.** to bring back to consciousness **2.** to make lively; animate —**come to life 1.** to recover consciousness **2.** to become lively or animated —**for dear life** to, or as if to, save one's life; with a desperate intensity —**for life 1.** for the duration of one's life **2.** in order to save one's life —**for the life of me** [Colloq.] even though my life were at stake on it; by any means: used in negative expressions —**from life** from a living model —☆**not on your life** [Colloq.] by no means; certainly not —**see life** to have a wide variety of social experiences —**take life** to kill —**take one's** (**own**) **life** to commit suicide —☆**the life of Riley** [Colloq.] a very

pleasant or luxurious way of living —**to the life** like the living original; exactly —**true to life** corresponding to what happens or exists in real life; true to reality

life belt a life preserver in the form of a belt

life·blood (-blud′) *n.* **1.** the blood necessary to life **2.** a vital element or animating influence

life·boat (-bōt′) *n.* **1.** a strong, seaworthy boat kept in readiness on the shore for use in rescuing people in danger of drowning **2.** one of the small boats carried by a ship for use if the ship must be abandoned

life buoy *same as* LIFE PRESERVER (sense 1)

life cycle 1. the series of changes in form undergone by an organism in development from its earliest stage to the recurrence of the same stage in the next generation **2.** any series of changes like this

life expectancy the number of years that an individual of a given age may expect on the average to live, as projected in statistical tables

life force *same as* ÉLAN VITAL

life-giv·ing (-giv′iŋ) *adj.* **1.** that gives or can give life **2.** strengthening; refreshing; inspiring

life·guard (-gärd′) *n.* ☆an expert swimmer employed at bathing beaches, pools, etc. to prevent drownings

Life Guards [earlier also *liefguard*, prob. after obs. Du. *lijfgarde*, bodyguard < *lijf*, body (cf. LIFE) + *garde* (see GUARD)] two regiments of British cavalry which serve as a bodyguard for the sovereign

life history 1. the history of the changes undergone by an organism in development from the egg, spore, etc. to its death in maturity **2.** one series of such changes **3.** the story of a person's life

life insurance insurance in which a stipulated sum is paid to the beneficiary or beneficiaries at the death of the insured, or, if specified, to the insured when he reaches a specified age

life interest interest (in property) that is payable to a person during his lifetime but cannot be passed on by him to another or others at his death

life jacket (or **vest**) a life preserver in the form of a sleeveless jacket or vest

life·less (-lis) *adj.* **1.** without life; specif., a) that never had life; inanimate b) that no longer has life; dead c) having no living beings [a *lifeless* planet] **2.** dull; listless —SYN. see DEAD —**life′less·ly** *adv.* —**life′less·ness** *n.*

life·like (-līk′) *adj.* **1.** resembling actual life [lifelike dialogue in the movie] **2.** closely resembling a real person or thing [a *lifelike* portrait]

life·line (-līn′) *n.* **1.** a rope or line for saving life, as one thrown to a person in the water, or shot to a ship to establish connection for a breeches buoy, etc. **2.** any rope fastened where it may be clutched by persons in danger of being swept away and drowned **3.** the rope by means of which a diver is raised and lowered, used by him for signaling **4.** a line in the palm of the hand, curving about the base of the thumb, supposed (in palmistry) to reveal facts about the person's life **5.** a commercial, esp. maritime, route of great importance **6.** a route that is the only one over which supplies can be transported to a certain place

life·long (-lôŋ′) *adj.* lasting or not changing during one's whole life [a *lifelong* love]

☆**life net** a strong net used by firemen, etc. as to catch people jumping from a burning building

life preserver 1. a buoyant device for saving a person from drowning by keeping his body afloat, as a ring or sleeveless jacket of canvas-covered cork or kapok **2.** [Chiefly Brit.] *same as* BLACKJACK (sense 3)

lif·er (līf′ər) *n.* [Slang] a person sentenced to imprisonment for life

life raft a small, inflatable raft or boat used as an emergency craft at sea

☆**life·sav·er** (-sā′vər) *n.* **1.** a person or thing that saves people from drowning, as a lifeguard **2.** [Colloq.] a person or thing that gives aid in time of need

☆**life·sav·ing** (-sā′viŋ) *adj.* designed for or connected with the saving of human life —*n.* the saving of human life, esp. through the prevention of drowning

life-size (-sīz′) *adj.* of the same size as the person or thing represented: said of a picture, sculpture, etc.: also **life′-sized′**

life span 1. *same as* LIFETIME **2.** the longest period of time that a typical individual can be expected to live

☆**life style** the consistent, integrated way of life of an individual as typified by his manner, attitudes, possessions, etc.

LIFE
PRESERVERS

life table *same as* MORTALITY TABLE

life·time (-tīm′) *n.* the length of time that someone lives, or that something lasts, functions, or is in effect —*adj.* lasting for such a period [a *lifetime* job]

life·work (-wurk′) *n.* the work to which a person devotes his life; most important work of one's life

life zone any of a series of biogeographic zones into which a continent, region, etc. is divided both by latitude and altitude on the basis of the characteristic animal and plant life in a zone

lift (lift) *vt.* [ME. *liften* < ON. *lypta* < *lopt*, air, akin to OE. *lyft*, G. *luft*, Du. *lucht*] **1.** to bring up to a higher position; raise **2.** to pick up and move or set *[lift* the box down from the shelf*]* **3.** to hold up; support high in the air **4.** to raise in rank, condition, dignity, spirits, etc.; bring to a higher level; elevate; exalt **5.** to pay off (a mortgage, debt, etc.) **6.** to end (a blockade, siege, etc.) by withdrawing forces **7.** to revoke or rescind (a ban or order) **8.** to loosen and remove (bulbs, seedlings, or root crops) from the soil **9.** [Colloq.] to remove from its proper place; esp., to plagiarize *[to lift* a passage from another writer*]* **10.** [Slang] to steal **11.** to change (a person's face) by means of surgery intended, usually, to remove wrinkles **12.** to transport, esp. by aircraft **13.** *Golf* to pick (a ball) up, as from an unplayable position **14.** *Mil.* to change the direction of or cease (fire) —*vi.* **1.** to exert strength in raising or trying to raise something **2.** to rise and vanish; be dispelled *[the fog lifted]* **3.** to become raised or elevated; go up **4.** to stop for a time —*n.* **1.** a lifting, raising, or rising; upward movement **2.** the amount lifted at one time **3.** *a)* the distance through which something is lifted *b)* the extent of rise or elevation **4.** lifting power or influence **5.** elevation of spirits or mood **6.** elevated position or carriage, as of the neck, head, etc. **7.** a ride in the direction in which one is going **8.** help of any kind **9.** a swell or rise in the ground **10.** the means by which a person or thing is lifted; specif., *a)* any layer of leather in the heel of a shoe *b)* [Brit.] *same as* ELEVATOR *c)* any of various devices used to transport people up or down a slope *d)* a device for lifting an automobile for repairs **11.** *Aeron.* the component of total air force acting on a body, as an airfoil or wing, which is perpendicular to the direction of flight and is exerted, normally, in an upward direction **12.** *Mining* a set of pumps in a mine —**lift up one's voice** (or **a shout** or **cry**) to cry or speak out loudly —**lift′er** *n.*

SYN.—**lift**, in its general literal sense, implies the use of some effort in bringing something up to a higher position *[help me lift* the table*]*; **raise**, often interchangeable with **lift**, specifically implies a bringing into an upright position by lifting one end *[to raise* a flagpole*]*; **elevate** is now a less frequent synonym for **lift** or **raise** *[the balloon had been elevated* 500 feet*]*; **rear** is a literary equivalent of **raise** *[the giant trees reared* their branches to the sky*]*; **hoist** implies the lifting of something heavy, usually by some mechanical means, as a block and tackle, crane, etc. *[to hoist* bales of cotton into a ship*]*; **boost** is a colloquial term implying a lifting by or as by a push from behind or below *[boost* me into the tree*]* All these terms are used figuratively to imply a bringing into a higher or better state *[to lift, or hoist,* one's spirits, to *raise* one's hopes, to *elevate* one's mind, to *rear* children, to *boost* sales*]* See also STEAL—**ANT.** lower

lift-drag ratio (lift′drag′) *Aeron.* the ratio of the lift of a body to its drag

☆**lifting body** a vehicle combining features of aircraft and spacecraft, designed for re-entry into the atmosphere, flight and maneuvers at high altitudes, and the ability to land itself

☆**lift-off** (-ôf′) *n.* **1.** the vertical thrust and rise of a spacecraft, missile, helicopter, etc. as it is launched or takes off **2.** the moment at which this occurs

lift pump a suction pump that raises a column of liquid to the level of a spout out of which the liquid runs of its own accord: cf. FORCE PUMP

lig·a·ment (lig′ə mənt) *n.* [L. *ligamentum* < *ligare*, to tie, bind: see LIGATURE] **1.** a bond or tie connecting one thing with another **2.** *Anat.* a band of tough tissue connecting bones or holding organs in place

li·gan (lī′gən) *n. same as* LAGAN

lig·and (lig′ənd, lī′gənd) *n.* [< L. *ligandum*, gerund of *ligare*, to bind: see LIGATURE] an atom, group, ion, radical, or molecule which forms a coordination complex with a central atom or ion

li·gate (lī′gāt) *vt.* **-gat·ed, -gat·ing** [< L. *ligatus*, pp. of *ligare*, to bind, tie: see LIGATURE] to tie or bind with a ligature, as a bleeding artery —**li·ga′tion** *n.*

lig·a·ture (lig′ə chər) *n.* [ME. < MFr. < LL. *ligature* < pp. of L. *ligare*, to bind < IE. base **leig̑-*, to bind, whence MLowG. *lik*, a tie, MHG. *geleich*, joint, Alb. *lidhe*, a bond] **1.** a tying or binding together **2.** a thing used in tying or binding together; tie, bond, etc. **3.** *a)* a written or printed character containing two or more letters united, as *æ, fl, th b)* a curved line connecting such letters in writing **4.** *Music a)* a curved line indicating that the notes which it connects are to be sung or played as one phrase; slur *b)* the notes so connected **5.** *Surgery* a thread or wire used to tie up an artery, etc. —*vt.* **-tured, -tur·ing** to tie or bind together with a ligature; ligate

li·ger (lī′gər) *n.* [LI(ON) + (TI)GER] the offspring of a male lion and a female tiger

light¹ (līt) *n.* [ME. *liht* < OE. *leoht*, akin to G. *licht* < IE. base **leuk-*, to shine, bright, whence Gr. *leukos*, white, L. *lux* & *lumen*, light, *lucere*, to shine, *luna*, moon, W. *llug*, gleam] **1.** *a)* the form of electromagnetic radiation that acts upon the retina of the eye, optic nerve, etc., making sight possible: this energy is transmitted at a velocity of about 186,000 miles per second *b)* a form of radiant energy

similar to this, but not acting on the normal retina, as ultraviolet and infrared radiation **2.** the rate of flow of light radiation with respect to the sense of sight: it is measured in *lumens* **3.** the sensation that light stimulates in the organs of sight **4.** brightness; illumination: usually with reference to a particular case **5.** a source of light, as the sun, a lamp, a light bulb, etc. **6.** *same as* TRAFFIC LIGHT **7.** the light from the sun; daylight or dawn **8.** a thing by means of which something can be started burning *[a light* for a cigar*]* **9.** the means by which light is let in; window or windowpane **10.** mental illumination; knowledge or information; enlightenment *[to shed light* on the past*]* **11.** spiritual inspiration **12.** public knowledge or view *[to bring* new facts *to light]* **13.** the way in which something is seen; aspect *[presented in a favorable light]* **14.** facial expression showing a mental or emotional state*[a light* of recognition in his eyes*]* **15.** a person whose brilliant record makes him an example for others; outstanding figure *[one of the shining lights* of the school*]* **16.** *a)* the quality suggesting light created in a painting, drawing, etc., esp. in certain areas *b)* such an area —*adj.* [ME. *liht* < OE. *leoht*] **1.** having light; not dark; bright **2.** pale in color; whitish; fair —*adv.* not brightly; in a pale way *[light* blue*]* —*vt.* **light′ed** or **lit**, **light′ing** [ME. *lighten* < OE. *lihtan*] **1.** to set on fire; ignite *[to light* a bonfire*]* **2.** to cause to give off light *[to light* a lamp*]* **3.** to give light to; furnish with light; illuminate *[lamps light* the streets*]* **4.** to brighten; animate **5.** to show the way to by giving light *[a beacon lights* the ships to harbor*]* —*vi.* **1.** to catch fire *[the fuse lighted* at once*]* **2.** to be lighted; brighten (usually with *up*) —**according to one's lights** as one's opinions, information, or standards may direct —**in the light of** with knowledge of; considering —**light up 1.** to make or become light **2.** to make or become bright, cheerful, etc. **3.** [Colloq.] to begin smoking (a cigar, etc.) —**see the light (of day) 1.** to come into existence **2.** to come to public view ☆**3.** to understand —**stand in one's own light** to harm oneself or one's reputation by acting foolishly, thoughtlessly, or unwisely —**strike a light** to make a flame, as with a match

light² (līt) *adj.* [ME. < OE. *leoht*, akin to G. *leicht*, Du. *licht* < IE. **lengwhto-* < base **legwh-*, light in movement and weight, whence L. *levis*, Gr. *elaphros*] **1.** having little weight; not heavy **2.** having little weight for its size; of low specific gravity **3.** below the usual or defined weight *[a light* coin*]* **4.** less than usual or normal in amount, extent, intensity, force, etc.; specif., *a)* striking or making contact with little force or impact *[a light* blow*]* *b)* of less than the usual quantity or density *[a light* vote, a *light* rain*]* *c)* not thick, coarse, or massive; delicate and graceful in structure *[light* tracery*]* *d)* not violent or intense; mild *[a light* wind*]* *e)* soft, muted, or muffled *[a light* sound*]* *f)* not prolonged or intense *[light* applause*]* **5.** of little importance; not serious or profound *[light* conversation*]* **6.** easy to bear; not burdensome *[a light* tax*]* **7.** easy to do; not difficult *[light* housekeeping*]* **8.** not burdened with grief or sorrow; gay; happy; buoyant *[light* spirits*]* **9.** of a flighty nature; frivolous; capricious **10.** loose in morals; wanton **11.** dizzy; giddy **12.** of an amusing or nonserious nature *[light* reading*]* **13.** containing little alcohol *[light* wine*]* **14.** characterized by qualities suggestive of little weight; not dense, hard, full, etc.; specif., *a)* not as full as usual; moderate *[a light* meal*]* *b)* easy to digest *c)* well leavened; soft and spongy *[a light* cake*]* *d)* loose in consistency; easily crumbled; porous *[light* sand*]* **15.** moving with ease and nimbleness *[light* on one's feet*]* **16.** carrying little weight or cargo *[a light* vehicle*]* **17.** unstressed or slightly stressed: said of a syllable in phonetics, prosody, etc. **18.** designating or of an industry equipped with relatively light machinery and producing relatively small products **19.** designating, of, or equipped with weapons, armor, ships, etc. of a relatively small size or light weight **20.** [Colloq.] *a)* lacking personnel; short-handed *b)* owing (a specified sum) to the pot in poker *[light* fifty cents*]* —*adv. same as* LIGHTLY —*vi.* **light′ed** or **lit**, **light′ing** [ME. *lihten* < OE. *lihtan*: also aphetic for ALIGHT¹] **1.** [Now Dial.] to get down from a horse or vehicle; dismount; alight **2.** to come to rest after traveling through the air *[ducks lighting* on the pond*]* **3.** to come or happen (*on* or *upon*) by chance **4.** to fall or strike suddenly, as a blow —**light in the head 1.** dizzy; giddy **2.** simple; foolish —☆**light into** [Colloq.] **1.** to attack **2.** to scold; berate —☆**light out** [Colloq.] to depart suddenly —**make light of** to treat as trifling or unimportant; pay little or no attention to —**light′ish** *adj.*

light adaptation the adaptation of the retina of the eye to vision under a wide variety of light intensity

light air a wind whose speed is 1 to 3 miles per hour: see BEAUFORT SCALE

☆**light bread** [South] bread made of wheat flour with yeast as a leavening agent

light breeze a wind whose speed is 4 to 7 miles per hour: see BEAUFORT SCALE

light·en¹ (-'n) *vt.* [ME. *lightnen*] **1.** to make light or bright; illuminate **2.** to make light or bright **3.** to cause to flash

in or as in lightning (with *out* or *forth*)   4. [Archaic] to give knowledge to; enlighten —*vi.* 1. to become light; grow brighter 2. to shine brightly; flash 3. to give off flashes of lightning —**light′en·er** *n.*

light·en² (-′n) *vt.* [ME. *lihtnen*] 1. *a*) to make lighter in weight *b*) to make less heavy; reduce the load of 2. to make less severe, harsh, troublesome, etc. 3. to make more cheerful; gladden —*vi.* 1. to become lighter in weight 2. to become more cheerful —*SYN.* see RELIEVE — **light′en·er** *n.*

light·er¹ (-ər) *n.* a person or thing that lights something or starts it burning *[a cigar lighter]*

light·er² (-ər) *n.* [LME. < MDu. *lichter* < *lichten*, to make light, unload < *licht*, LIGHT²] a large, open barge used chiefly in loading or unloading larger ships wherever shallow water prevents these from coming in to the shore —*vt., vi.* to transport (goods) in a lighter

light·er·age (-ər ij) *n.* 1. the loading or unloading of a ship, or transportation of goods, by means of a lighter, or barge 2. the charge for this

light·er-than-air (-ər thən er′) *adj.* designating or of an aircraft that is a balloon filled with a gas lighter than air

light·face (līt′fās′) *n. Printing* type having thin, light lines —*adj.* having thin, light lines: also **light′faced′**

light·fast (-fast′) *adj.* that will not fade because of exposure to light —**light′fast′ness** *n.*

light-fin·gered (-fiŋ′gərd) *adj.* 1. having a light, delicate touch 2. skillful at stealing, esp. by picking pockets; thievish —**light′-fin′gered·ness** *n.*

light-foot·ed (-foot′id) *adj.* stepping lightly and gracefully; nimble of foot: also [Poet.] **light′-foot′** —**light′-foot′ed·ly** *adv.* —**light′-foot′ed·ness** *n.*

light-hand·ed (-han′did) *adj.* 1. having a light, delicate touch 2. having little to carry

light-head·ed (-hed′id) *adj.* 1. mentally confused or feeling giddy; dizzy 2. not sensible; flighty; frivolous —**light′head′ed·ly** *adv.* —**light′head′ed·ness** *n.*

light-heart·ed (-härt′id) *adj.* free from care; gay; cheerful —**light′heart′ed·ly** *adv.* —**light′heart′ed·ness** *n.*

☆**light heavyweight** a boxer or wrestler between a middle-weight and heavyweight (in boxing, 161–175 pounds)

light horse light-armed cavalry —**light′-horse′man** (-hôrs′mən) *n., pl.* **-men** (-mən)

light·house (-hous′) *n.* a tower located at some place important or dangerous to navigation: it has a very bright light at the top, and often foghorns, sirens, etc., by which ships are guided and warned

lighthouse tube *Radio* any of several electron tubes, shaped somewhat like a lighthouse, used for generating or amplifying very high or ultrahigh frequency signals

light·ing (-iŋ) *n.* 1. a giving light or being lighted; illumination; ignition 2. the distribution of light and shade, as in a painting 3. *Theater, TV a*) the art, practice, or manner of using and arranging lights on a stage *b*) the stage lights collectively

light·ly (-lē) *adv.* 1. with little weight, pressure, or motion; gently 2. to a small degree or amount *[to spend lightly]* 3. nimbly; deftly 4. cheerfully; merrily 5. *a*) with indifference or neglect *b*) so as to slight 6. with little or no reason 7. with little or no punishment *[to let someone off lightly]* 8. [Now Rare] easily; readily

light meter *same as* EXPOSURE METER

light-mind·ed (-mīn′did) *adj.* not serious; frivolous —**light′-mind′ed·ly** *adv.* —**light′-mind′ed·ness** *n.*

light·ness¹ (-nis) *n.* 1. the state, quality, or intensity of lighting; brightness 2. *a*) the state of being nearer to white than to black; paleness *b*) the relative amount of light reflected by an object ranging from black to white or colorless

light·ness² (-nis) *n.* 1. the state of being light, not heavy 2. mildness, nimbleness, delicacy, cheerfulness, lack of seriousness, etc.

light·ning (-niŋ) *n.* [ME. *lightninge* < *lightnen*, to LIGHTEN¹] 1. a flash of light in the sky caused by the discharge of atmospheric electricity from one cloud to another or between a cloud and the earth 2. such a discharge of electricity —*vi.* to give off such a discharge —*adj.* like lightning

☆**lightning arrester** a device that protects radio or electrical equipment from lightning by causing the discharge to be grounded

☆**lightning bug** (or **beetle**) *same as* FIREFLY

☆**lightning rod** a pointed metal rod placed high on a building, etc. and grounded at the lower end to act as a conductor and divert lightning from the structure

light-o'-love (-ə luv′) *n.* a person, usually a woman, who is wanton or inconstant in love

light opera a short, amusing musical play; operetta

☆**light pen** a penlike electronic device employing a phototransistor to detect information displayed on a computer-controlled cathode-ray tube and permitting response to or manipulation of such retrieved data by simply pointing to it

light·proof (-proof′) *adj.* that does not admit light

light quantum *same as* PHOTON

lights (līts) *n.pl.* [ME. *lihtes* < *liht* (see LIGHT²): so called from being lighter in weight than the rest of the body: cf. LUNG] [Dial.] the lungs of animals, as sheep, hogs, cattle, etc., used as food

light·ship (līt′ship′) *n.* a ship moored in a place dangerous to navigation and bearing a light or lights and foghorns, sirens, etc. to warn or guide pilots

light·some¹ (-səm) *adj.* [ME. *lihtsum*: see LIGHT² & -SOME¹] 1. nimble, buoyant, graceful, or lively 2. lighthearted; gay 3. not serious; frivolous

light·some² (-səm) *adj.* [ME. *lyghtesum*: see LIGHT¹ & -SOME¹] 1. giving light; luminous 2. well-lighted; bright

lights out 1. a signal, as in a military camp, etc., to extinguish lights at bedtime 2. bedtime

light-struck (līt′struk′) *adj. Photog.* injured or fogged by being exposed to light accidentally

light verse verse, usually rhymed, in which the subject is treated humorously, as parodies, limericks, etc.

light·weight (-wāt′) *n.* 1. one below normal weight 2. a boxer or wrestler between a bantamweight and a welter-weight (in boxing, 127-135 pounds) ☆3. [Colloq.] a person of limited influence, intelligence, competence, etc. —*adj.* 1. light in weight 2. of lightweights 3. not important or serious

light·wood (-wood′) *n.* [Dial.] very dry wood, ☆esp. southern pine, which burns readily with a bright light

light-year (-yir′) *n. Astron.* a unit of distance equal to the distance that light travels in a vacuum in one year, approximately 6,000,000,000,000 miles: cf. PARSEC

lign·al·oes (lī nal′ōz, lig-) *n.* [ME. *ligne Aloes* < OFr. < L. *lignum aloës*, wood of aloe (see ff. & ALOE)] the resinous wood of the aloes tree (*Aquilaria agallocha*), burned for its pleasant aroma

lig·ne·ous (lig′nē əs) *adj.* [L. *ligneus* < *lignum*, wood < *legnom*, collected wood < base of *legere*, to collect: see LOGIC] of, or having the nature of, wood; woody

lig·ni- (lig′nə) [< L. *lignum*: see prec.] *a combining form meaning* wood *[lignify]*: also **lig′no-** (-nō) or, before a vowel, **lign-**

lig·ni·fy (lig′nə fī′) *vt.* **-fied′**, **-fy′ing** [LIGNI- + -FY] to make into wood —*vi.* to become wood or like wood as a result of the depositing of lignin in the cell walls —**lig′ni·fi·ca′tion** *n.*

lig·nin (lig′nin) *n.* [LIGN- + -IN¹] an amorphous, cellulose-like, organic substance which acts as a binder for the cellulose fibers in wood and certain plants and adds strength and stiffness to the cell walls

lig·nite (lig′nīt) *n.* [Fr.: see LIGNEOUS & -ITE¹] a soft, brownish-black coal in which the texture of the original wood can often still be seen: it is denser and contains more carbon than peat —**lig·nit′ic** (-nit′ik) *adj.*

lig·no·cel·lu·lose (lig′nō sel′yoo lōs′) *n.* [LIGNO- + CELLULOSE] any of several combinations of lignin and hemicellulose, forming the essential part of woody tissue —**lig′no·cel′lu·los′ic** (-lō′sik) *adj.*

lig·num vi·tae (lig′nəm vīt′ē) [ModL. < L. *lignum*, wood (see LIGNEOUS) + *vitae*, gen. of *vita*, life: see QUICK] 1. *same as* GUAIACUM (sense 1) 2. *common commercial name for* the very hard wood of the guaiacum, used in marine and machine bearings, casters, pulleys, etc.

lig·ro·in (lig′rō in) *n.* [arbitrary coinage, prob. < Gr. *liguros*, clear + -IN¹] *chemists' term for* BENZINE

lig·u·la (lig′yoo lə) *n., pl.* **-lae** (-lē′), **-las** [see LIGULE] *Zool.* a structure containing typically the terminal lobes of the labium of an insect

lig·u·late (-lit, -lāt′) *adj.* 1. of or having ligules 2. shaped like a strap

lig·ule (lig′yōōl) *n.* [L. *ligula*, a spoon, tongue of a shoe, shoe strap < IE. base *leiĝh-*, to lick, whence MIr. *liag*, LICK: infl. by association with L. *lingua*, tongue, *ligare*, to bind] 1. a strap-shaped corolla in the flowers of certain composite plants 2. a thin membrane attached to a leaf of grass at the point where the blade meets the leaf sheath 3. any of various similar appendages on the leaves of other plants

lig·ure (lig′yoor) *n.* [LL.(Ec.) *ligurius* < Gr.(Ec.) *ligyrion*] *Bible* one of the twelve precious stones in the breastplate of the Jewish high priest, thought to be yellow jacinth: Ex. 28:19

Li·gu·ri·a (li gyoor′ē ə) region of NW Italy, on the Ligurian Sea: 2,091 sq. mi.; pop. 1,718,000; chief city, Genoa — **Li·gu′ri·an** *adj., n.*

Ligurian Sea part of the Mediterranean, between Corsica & NW Italy

Li Hung-chang (lē′ hoong′jäŋ′) 1823–1901; Chin. statesman & general; prime minister (1895–98)

lik·a·ble (līk′ə b'l) *adj.* having qualities that inspire liking; easy to like because attractive, pleasant, genial, etc. —**lik′a·ble·ness**, **lik·a·bil′i·ty** *n.*

like¹ (līk) *adj.* [ME. *lik*, aphetic for *ilik* < OE. *gelic*, similar, equal, lit., of the same form or shape, akin to G. *gleich* < PGmc. *galīka-* <

LIGURIA

*ga-, prefix of unc. meaning + *līka-, body, (whence ON. lik, Goth. leik, OE. lic): for IE. base see LICH] 1. having almost or exactly the same qualities, characteristics, etc.; similar; equal [a cup of sugar and a like amount of flour] 2. [Rare] alike 3. [Dial.] likely —adv. [Colloq.] likely [like as not, he is already there] —prep. 1. similar to; somewhat resembling [she is like a bird] 2. in a manner characteristic of; similarly to [she sings like a bird] 3. in accord with the nature of; characteristic of [not like her to cry] 4. in the mood for; desirous of [to feel like sleeping] 5. indicative or prophetic of [it looks like a clear day tomorrow] 6. as for example [fruit, like pears and peaches, for dessert] Like was originally an adjective in senses 1, 3, 4, 5, and an adverb in sense 2, and is still considered so by conservative grammarians —conj. [Colloq.] 1. in the way that; as [it was just like you said] 2. as if [it looks like he is late] —n. a person or thing regarded as the equal or counterpart of another or of the person or thing being discussed [did you ever see the like of it?] —vt. liked, lik′ing [Obs.] to compare; liken —vi. [Dial.] to be on the verge; be about (to have done something) [he like to broke the door down] Like is also used without meaning or syntactical function, as in hip talk, before or after a word, phrase, or clause [it's like hot] —and the like and others of the same kind —like anything [Colloq.] very much; exceedingly —like blazes (or crazy, the devil, mad, etc.) [Colloq.] with furious energy, speed, etc. —nothing like not at all like; completely different from —something like almost like; about —the like (or likes) of [Colloq.] any person or thing like

like² (līk) vi. liked, lik′ing [ME. liken < OE. lician (akin to Goth. leikan) < base of lic, body, form (see prec.): sense development: to be pleasing to 1. [Obs.] to please; be agreeable to: with the dative [it likes me not] 2. to be so inclined; choose [leave whenever you like] —vt. 1. to have a taste or fondness for; be pleased with; have a preference for; enjoy 2. to want or wish [I would like to see him] —n. [pl.] preferences, tastes, or affections —lik′er n.

-like (līk) [< LIKE¹] 1. an adj.-forming suffix meaning like, characteristic of, suitable for [doglike, manlike, homelike] 2. an adv.-forming suffix meaning in the manner of Words formed with -like are sometimes hyphenated, always if three l's fall together [ball-like]

like·a·ble (līk′ə b'l) adj. same as LIKABLE

like·li·hood (līk′lē hood′) n. [ME. liklihode: see ff. & -HOOD] the fact of being likely to happen or something that is likely to happen; probability

like·ly (līk′lē) adj. -li·er, -li·est [ME. likly, prob. aphetic < OE. geliclic (or < ? cognate ON. likligr): see LIKE¹ & -LY¹] 1. apparently true to the facts; credible; probable [a likely cause] 2. seeming as if it would happen or make happen; reasonably to be expected; apparently destined [it is likely to rain] 3. such as will probably be satisfactory or rewarding; suitable [a likely man for the job] 4. having good prospects; promising [a likely lad] 5. [Dial.] attractive; agreeable —adv. probably [he will very likely go] SYN.—likely suggests probability or an eventuality that can reasonably be expected [he's not likely to win; liable and apt are loosely or informally used as equivalents of likely, but in strict discrimination, liable implies exposure or susceptibility to something undesirable [he's liable to be killed if he plays with firearms] and apt suggests a natural or habitual inclination or tendency [such people are always apt to be fearful]; prone also suggests a propensity or predisposition to something that seems almost inevitable [he's prone to have accidents] See also PROBABLE —ANT. unlikely, indisposed

like·mind·ed (līk′mīn′did) adj. having the same ideas, plans, tastes, etc.; agreeing mentally —like′-mind′ed·ly adv. —like′-mind′ed·ness n.

lik·en (-'n) vt. to represent or describe as being like, or similar; compare

like·ness (-nis) n. 1. the state or quality of being like; similarity 2. (the same) form or shape; semblance [Jupiter appeared in the likeness of a swan] 3. something that is like; copy, facsimile, portrait, etc. SYN.—likeness implies close correspondence in appearance, qualities, nature, etc. [his remarkable likeness to his brother]; similarity suggests only partial correspondence [your problem bears a certain similarity to mine]; resemblance usually implies correspondence in appearance or in superficial aspects [the resemblance between a diamond and zircon]; analogy refers to a correspondence between attributes or circumstances of things that are basically unlike [the analogy between a calculating machine and the human brain] —ANT. unlikeness, difference

like·wise (-wīz′) adv. [short for in like wise] 1. in the same manner 2. also; too; moreover

lik·ing (līk′kin) n. [ME. < OE. licung < lician: see LIKE²] 1. fondness; affection 2. preference; taste; pleasure; predilection [not to my liking]

li·ku·ta (lē koo′tä) n., pl. ma·ku′ta (mä-) a monetary unit of the Congo (Kinshasa), equal to 1/100 of a zaire

li·lac (lī′lak, -läk, -lak) n. [Fr. (now lilas) < Ar. līlak < Per. lilak, nilak, bluish < nil, indigo < Sans. nila, dark blue, indigo] 1. any of a genus (Syringa) of hardy shrubs or trees of the olive family, with large clusters of tiny,

fragrant flowers ranging in color from white, through many shades of lavender, to deep crimson 2. the flower or flower cluster of this plant 3. the pale-purple color often characteristic of this flower —adj. of a pale-purple color

Lil·i·an (lil′ē ən) [earlier Lilion, prob. < L. lilium, lily] a feminine name: dim. Lil, Lily, Lilly

lil·ied (lil′ēd) adj. 1. having many lilies; decorated or covered with lilies 2. [Archaic] like a lily; fair

Lil·ien·thal (lil′yən thôl′), David E(li) 1899– ; U.S. lawyer & administrator

Lil·ith (lil′ith) [Heb. līlīth < Assyr.-Bab. lilītu, lit., of the night] 1. in ancient Semitic folklore, a female demon or vampire that lived in desolate places 2. in medieval Jewish folklore, a) the first wife of Adam, before the creation of Eve b) a night witch who menaced infants

Li·li·u·o·ka·la·ni (li lē′oo ō′kä lä′nē), Lydia Ka·me·ke·ha (kä′mä kā′hä) 1838–1917; queen of the Hawaiian Islands (1891–93)

Lille (lēl) city in N France, near the Belgian border; pop. 193,000

Lil·li·an (lil′ē ən) var. of LILIAN

lil·li·bul·le·ro (lil′ē bə lir′ō) n. [< lilli burlero: arbitrary formation] 1. part of the refrain of a song popular in England during the revolution of 1688, ridiculing the Irish Catholics 2. this song

Lil·li·put (lil′ə put′, -pət) in Swift's Gulliver's Travels, a land inhabited by tiny people about six inches tall

Lil·li·pu·tian (lil′ə pyoo′shən) adj. 1. of Lilliput or its people 2. very small; tiny 3. narrow-minded; petty —n. 1. an inhabitant of Lilliput 2. a very small person 3. a narrow-minded person

Lil·ly (lil′ē) a feminine name: see LILIAN

lilt (lilt) vt., vi. [ME. lilten, lulten, prob. of echoic orig.] to sing, speak, play, or move with a light, graceful rhythm or swing —n. 1. a gay song or tune with a light, swingy, and graceful rhythm 2. a light, swingy, and graceful rhythm or movement —lilt′ing adj. —lilt′ing·ly adv.

Lil·y (lil′ē) [dim. of Lilian or < ff.] a feminine name

lil·y (lil′ē) n., pl. lil′ies [ME. lilie < OE. < L. lilium] 1. any of a large genus (Lilium) of perennial plants of the lily family, grown from a bulb and having typically trumpet-shaped flowers, white or colored 2. the flower or the bulb of any of these plants 3. any of several plants similar to the true lily, as the water lily 4. the flower of any of these plants 5. the heraldic fleur-de-lis, as in the royal arms of France —adj. 1. designating a family (Liliaceae) of plants including the lilies, tulips, hyacinths, onions, asparagus, etc. 2. like a lily, as in whiteness, delicacy, purity, etc. —gild the lily to attempt vain improvements on something that is already excellent or perfect

lily iron a harpoon with a detachable barbed head

lil·y-liv·ered (lil′ē liv′ərd) adj. [after Shakespeare, Macbeth, V, iii] cowardly; timid

lily of the valley pl. lilies of the valley [after LL.(Ec.) lilium convallium in Song of Solomon 2:1 (Vulg.)] a perennial plant (Convallaria majalis) of the lily family, that grows in the shade and has a single pair of basal, oblong leaves and a single leafless raceme of very fragrant, small, white, bell-shaped flowers

☆lily pad one of the large, flat, floating leaves of the water lily

lily-white (-hwīt′, -wīt′) adj. 1. white as a lily 2. innocent and pure; unsullied: often used sarcastically ☆3. practicing discrimination against, or segregation of, non-whites, esp. Negroes

Li·ma (lē′mə; for 2, lī′-) 1. capital of Peru, in the WC part: pop. 1,716,000 2. [after prec.] city in W Ohio: pop. 54,000

LILY OF THE VALLEY

li·ma bean (lī′mə) [after Lima, Peru: from being native to tropical America] [also L- b-] 1. a common variety of bean (Phaseolus limensis), with creamy flowers and broad pods 2. the broad, flat, nutritious seed of this plant

lim·a·cine (lim′ə sīn′, -sin) adj. [ModL. limacinus < L. limax (gen. limacis), a slug < IE. *leimāk, snail (whence Gr. leimax) < base *(s)lei-, slimy: cf. SLIME] of or like slugs or shell-less snails: also li·mac·i·form (lī mas′ə fôrm′)

limb¹ (lim) n. [with unhistoric -b < ME. lim < OE., akin to ON. limr, limb < IE. base *lei-, *elei-, to bend, whence EL(BOW)] 1. an arm, leg, or wing 2. a large branch of a tree 3. any projecting part like an arm or leg or forming an outgrowth or extension from a larger body 4. a person or thing regarded as a branch, part, agent, or representative [a policeman is a limb of the law] 5. [Chiefly Brit. Colloq.] a naughty child —vt. [Rare] to dismember; disjoint —☆out on a limb [Colloq.] in a precarious or vulnerable position or situation —limb′less adj.

limb² (lim) n. [Fr. limbe, orig., limbo < ML.(Ec.) limbi < L. limbus: see LIMBO¹] a border, margin, or edge; specif., a) the graduated edge of a quadrant b) Astron. the apparent outer edge of a heavenly body c) Bot. the spreading outer portion of the corolla of certain flowers as distinguished from the lower, tubelike part

fat, āpe, cär; ten, ēven; is, bīte; gō, hôrn, tōōl, look; oil, out; up, fur; get; joy; yet; chin; she; thin, then; zh, leisure; ŋ, ring; ə for a in ago, e in agent, i in sanity, o in comply, u in focus; ' as in able (ā′b'l); Fr. bâl; ë, Fr. coeur; ö, Fr. feu; Fr. mon; ô, Fr. coq; ü, Fr. duc; r, Fr. cri; H, G. ich; kh, G. doch. See inside front cover. ☆ Americanism; ‡foreign; *hypothetical; <derived from

lim·bate (lim′bāt) *adj.* [LL. *limbatus* < *limbus*: see LIMBO[1]] having a distinct border or edging, as of a color different from the main part

limbed (limd) *adj.* having (a specified number or kind of) limbs [*straight-limbed, four-limbed*]

lim·ber[1] (lim′bər) *adj.* [< ? LIMB[1]] 1. easily bent; flexible; pliant 2. able to bend the body easily; supple; lithe —*vt.* to make limber [*to limber the fingers*] —*vi.* to make oneself limber, as by exercises (usually with *up*) —**lim′ber·ness** *n.*

lim·ber[2] (lim′bər) *n.* [ME. *lymour* < ?] the two-wheeled, detachable front part of a gun carriage, usually supporting an ammunition chest —*vt., vi.* to attach the limber to (a gun carriage), as in preparing to move off (often with *up*)

lim·bers (lim′bərz) *n.pl.* [prob. < Fr. *lumière*, a hole, aperture, lit., light < VL. *luminaria*, orig. pl. of L. *luminare*, a light, window: see LUMINARY] *Naut.* channels or gutters near a ship's keel or keelson to drain bilge water into the pump well

lim·bo[1] (lim′bō) *n., pl.* **-bos** [ME. < L., abl. of *limbus*, edge, border (in *in limbo*, in or on the border) < IE. base *lemb-, to hang loosely, whence Sans. *lambatē*, hangs down, falls & LIMP[2]] 1. [*often* L-] in some Christian theologies, a region bordering on hell, the abode after death of unbaptized children and righteous people who lived before Jesus 2. [Archaic] a prison 3. a place or condition of oblivion or neglect 4. an indeterminate state midway between two others

lim·bo[2] (lim′bō) *n., pl.* **-bos** [prob. altered < LIMBER[1]] a dance, originated in the West Indies, in which the dancers bend from the knees as far back as possible to pass beneath a bar that is put lower and lower

Lim·burg (lim′bərg) 1. province of NE Belgium: 930 sq. mi.; pop. 624,000: also **Lim′bourg** (*Fr.* laṅ bōōr′) 2. province of SE Netherlands: 859 sq. mi.; pop. 969,000; cap. Maastricht 3. former duchy occupying the general area of these two provinces

Lim·bur·ger (cheese) (lim′bər gər) a semisoft cheese of whole milk, with a strong odor, made originally in Limburg, Belgium: also **Lim′burg (cheese)**

lim·bus (lim′bəs) *n., pl.* **-bi** (-bī) [L.: see LIMBO[1]] a distinct border or edging, often of a contrasting color

lime[1] (līm) *n.* [ME. < OE. *lim*, akin to G. *leim* < IE. base *(s)lei-, slimy, wet and sticky, to smooth over, whence Gr. *leios*, smooth, L. *limus*, slime, *linere*, to smear, OE. *lam*, clay, LOAM] 1. *short for* BIRDLIME 2. a white substance, calcium oxide, CaO, obtained by the action of heat on limestone, shells, and other material containing calcium carbonate, and used in making mortar and cement, and, when hydrated, in neutralizing acid soil —*vt.* **limed, lim′ing** 1. to cement 2. to smear with birdlime 3. to catch with or as with birdlime 4. to apply lime to; treat with lime

lime[2] (līm) *n.* [Fr. < Pr. *limo* < Ar. *līma*: cf. LEMON] 1. a small, lemon-shaped, greenish-yellow citrus fruit with a juicy, sour pulp, rich in vitamin C 2. the small, thorny, semitropical tree (*Citrus aurantifolia*) of the rue family that it grows on, originally native to S Asia but now widely cultivated —*adj.* 1. made with or of limes 2. having a flavor like that of limes

lime[3] (līm) *n.* [< earlier *line* < ME. *lind*: see LINDEN] same as LINDEN

☆**lime·ade** (līm′ād′) *n.* [LIME[2] + -ADE] a drink made of lime juice and water, usually sweetened

lime burner a person who burns limestone, shells, etc. to make lime

Lime·house (līm′hous′) dock district in the London borough of Stepney, on the Thames: former Chinese quarter

lime·kiln (līm′kil′, -kiln′) *n.* a furnace in which limestone, shells, etc. are reduced to lime by burning

lime·light (-līt′) *n.* 1. a brilliant light created by the incandescence of lime, formerly used in theaters to throw an intense beam of light upon a particular part of the stage, a certain actor, etc. 2. the part of a stage where a limelight or spotlight is cast 3. a prominent or conspicuous position before the public

li·men (lī′mən) *n., pl.* **li′mens, lim·i·na** (lim′i nə) [L. *limen* (gen. *liminis*), threshold, akin to *limus* (see LIMES)] used as transl. of G. *schwelle*] *Psychol. & Physiol.* same as THRESHOLD

Lim·er·ick (lim′ər ik, lim′rik) 1. county in SW Ireland, in Munster province: 1,037 sq. mi.; pop. 137,000 2. its county seat: pop. 56,000 —*n.* [l-] [prob. < Ir. refrain containing the name] a nonsense poem of five anapestic lines, now often bawdy, usually with the rhyme scheme aabba, the first, second, and fifth lines having three stresses, the third and fourth, two: the form was popularized by Edward Lear Example: There was a young lady named Harris, / Whom nothing could ever embarrass / Till the bath salts one day / In the tub where she lay / Turned out to be plaster of Paris

li·mes (lī′mēz) *n.* [L., border, boundary, limit, akin to *limus*, aslant, oblique < IE. base *(e)lei-, to bend, whence LIMB[1]] a boundary line or border; orig., a Roman frontier fortification

lime·stone (līm′stōn′) *n.* rock consisting mainly of calcium carbonate, often composed of the organic remains of sea animals, as mollusks, corals, etc., and used as building stone, a source of lime, etc.: when crystallized by heat and pressure it becomes marble

lime sulfur a mixture made by boiling together sulfur, water, and lime: used as an insecticide and fungicide, esp. in the form of a spray

lime twig 1. a twig smeared with birdlime to snare birds 2. any kind of snare

lime·wa·ter (-wôt′ər, -wät′ər) *n.* a solution of calcium hydroxide in water, used to neutralize acids and to absorb carbon dioxide from the air

☆**lim·ey** (lī′mē) *n.* [from the LIME[2] juice formerly served to the crew on British ships to prevent scurvy] [Slang] 1. an English sailor or, sometimes, soldier 2. any Englishman —*adj.* [Slang] British

Lim Fjord (lēm′ fyōrd′) strait across N Jutland, Denmark: c. 110 mi. long

li·mic·o·line (lī mik′ə lin′, -lin) *adj.* [< LL. *limicola*, mud dweller < L. *limus*, mud (see LIME[1]) + *colere*, to dwell (see CULT) + -INE[1]] inhabiting the shore; specif., designating or of a group of wading birds that live along the shore, as the plovers, curlews, killdeers, snipes, sandpipers, etc.

li·mic·o·lous (-ləs) *adj.* [< L. *limicola* (see prec.) + -OUS] living in mud

lim·i·nal (lim′i n′l, līm′i-) *adj.* of or at the limen

lim·it (lim′it) *n.* [ME. < OFr. *limite* < L. *limes* (gen. *limitis*): see LIMES] 1. the point, line, or edge where something ends or must end; boundary or border beyond which something ceases to be or to be possible 2. [*pl.*] bounds; boundary lines 3. the greatest number or amount allowed [to catch the *limit* for a day of trout fishing] 4. the maximum amount by which a bet may be raised at one time, as in poker 5. *Math.* a fixed quantity or value which a varying quantity or value is regarded as approaching indefinitely —*vt.* [ME. *limiten* < OFr. *limiter* < L. *limitare*] to confine within bounds; set a limit to; restrict; curb —**the limit** ☆[Colloq.] any person or thing regarded as unbearable, remarkable, etc. to an extreme degree —**lim′it·a·ble** *adj.* —**lim′it·er** *n.*

SYN.—**limit** implies the prescribing of a point in space, time, extent, etc. beyond which it is impossible or forbidden to go [*limit* your slogan to 25 words]; **bound** implies an enclosing in boundaries or borders [a meadow *bounded* by hills]; **restrict** implies a boundary that completely encloses and connotes a restraining within these bounds [the soldier was *restricted* to the camp area]; **circumscribe** emphasizes more strongly the cutting off or isolation of that which is within the bounds [he leads the *circumscribed* life of a monk]; **confine** stresses the restraint or hampering of enclosing limits [*confined* in jail] —**ANT.** widen, expand

lim·i·tar·y (lim′ə ter′ē) *adj.* [L. *limitaris*] 1. serving as a limit or boundary; restrictive 2. [Now Rare] limited; restricted

lim·i·ta·tion (lim′ə tā′shən) *n.* [ME. *limitacioun* < OFr. *limitacion* < L. *limitatio*] 1. a limiting or being limited 2. something that limits, as some factor in a person's makeup which restricts the scope of his activity or accomplishment; qualification 3. *Law* a period of time, fixed by statute, during which legal action can be brought, as for settling a claim

lim·i·ta·tive (lim′ə tāt′iv) *adj.* [Fr. *limitatif* < ML. *limitativus*] limiting; restrictive

lim·it·ed (lim′it id) *adj.* 1. *a)* confined within bounds; restricted *b)* circumscribed or narrow in scope or extent ☆2. accommodating a restricted number of passengers, making fewer stops than on the regular runs, and often charging extra fare: said of a train, bus, etc. 3. exercising governmental powers under constitutional restrictions; not having absolute power [a *limited* monarch] 4. [Chiefly Brit.] restricting the liability of each partner or shareholder to the amount of his actual investment in the business [a *limited* company] —☆*n.* a limited train, bus, etc. —**lim′it·ed·ly** *adv.* —**lim′it·ed·ness** *n.*

limited edition a special, finely bound edition of a book, of which only a predetermined number of copies are printed

lim·it·ing (-iŋ) *adj.* that limits; specif., *Gram.* designating or of any of a class of adjectives that limit or restrict the words modified (Ex.: *several, four,* etc.)

limiting factor an environmental factor that limits the growth or activities of an organism or that restricts the size of a population or its geographical range

lim·it·less (-lis) *adj.* without limits; unbounded; vast; infinite —**lim′it·less·ly** *adv.* —**lim′it·less·ness** *n.*

li·miv·o·rous (lī miv′ər əs) *adj.* [< L. *limus*, mud, slime (see LIME[1]) + -VOROUS] eating mud or earth for the organic matter in it, as earthworms do

limn (lim) *vt.* **limned, limn·ing** (lim′iŋ, -niŋ) [ME. *limnen*, contr. < *luminen*, for *enluminen* < OFr. *enluminer* < L. *illuminare*, to make light: see ILLUMINE] 1. to paint or draw 2. to portray in words; describe 3. [Obs.] to illuminate (manuscripts) —**limn·er** (lim′ər, -nər) *n.*

lim·net·ic (lim net′ik) *adj.* [< Gr. *limnē,* marsh (cf. ff.) + E. -etic < L. or Gr.: L. -eticus < Gr. -etikos, adj. suffix] designating, of, or living in the open waters of lakes, away from shore vegetation

lim·nol·o·gy (lim näl′ə jē) *n.* [< Gr. *limnē*, marsh, akin to *leimōn* (see LIMONITE) + -LOGY] the science that deals with the physical, chemical, and biological properties and features of fresh waters, esp. lakes and ponds —**lim′no·log′i·cal** (-nə läj′i k′l) *adj.* —**lim·nol′o·gist** *n.*

Li·moges (lē mōzh′; *Fr.* lē mōzh′) city in WC France: pop. 118,000 —*n.* fine porcelain made there: also **Limoges ware**

lim·o·nene (lim′ə nēn′) *n.* [< ModL. *Limonum* (< Fr. *limon*, LEMON) + -ENE] any of three isomeric terpenes, $C_{10}H_{16}$, present in many plant products such as lemon peel, orange oil, pine needles, peppermint, etc.

li·mo·nite (lī′mə nīt′) *n.* [< Gr. *leimōn*, meadow, orig., low ground (for IE. base see LIMB[1]) + -ITE[1]] a brownish, hydrous ferric oxide consisting of several minerals: an important ore of iron —**li′mo·nit′ic** (-nit′ik) *adj.*

Li·mou·sin (lē mōō zan′) region & former province of WC France: chief city, Limoges

lim·ou·sine (lim′ə zēn′, lim′ə zēn′) *n.* [Fr., lit., a hood: from the costume worn in LIMOUSIN] 1. a former kind of automobile with a closed compartment seating three or more passengers and the top extended forward over the driver's seat 2. any large, luxurious sedan, esp. one driven by a chauffeur ☆3. a buslike sedan used to carry passengers to or from an airport, train station, etc.

limp[1] (limp) *vi.* [ME. *lympen* < OE. *limpan*, to befall, occur (in a specialized sense, to walk lamely), akin to MHG. *limpfen*, to walk with a limp, OHG. *limfan*, to befall, happen < IE. *lemb-* < base *leb-*, to hang down, be limp, whence L. *labor*, *limbus*] 1. to walk with or as with a lame or partially disabled leg 2. to move or proceed unevenly, jerkily, or laboriously, as because of being impaired, defective, damaged, etc. —*n.* a halt or lameness in walking —**limp′er** *n.* —**limp′ing·ly** *adv.*

limp[2] (limp) *adj.* [< base of prec., akin to MHG. *lampen*, to hang limply] 1. lacking or having lost stiffness or body; flaccid, drooping, wilted, etc. 2. lacking firmness, energy, or vigor 3. flexible, as the binding of some books —**limp′ly** *adv.* —**limp′ness** *n.*

lim·pet (lim′pit) *n.* [ME. *lempet* < OE. *lempedu* < ML. *lempreda*, limpet, lamprey: cf. LAMPREY] any of several varieties of mostly marine, gastropod mollusks, with a single, low, cone-shaped shell and a thick fleshy foot, by means of which it clings tenaciously to rocks, timbers, water plants, etc.

lim·pid (lim′pid) *adj.* [Fr. *limpide* < L. *limpidus* < OL. *limpa*, *lumpa*, water: see LYMPH] 1. perfectly clear; transparent; not cloudy or turbid [*limpid waters*] 2. clear and simple [*limpid prose*] —**lim·pid′i·ty**, **lim′pid·ness** *n.* —**lim′pid·ly** *adv.*

☆**limp·kin** (limp′kin) *n.* [LIMP[1] + -KIN: from its walk] a raillike wading bird (*Aramus vociferus*), found in Florida, Central America, and the West Indies

Lim·po·po River (lim pō′pō) river in SE Africa, flowing from South Africa across Mozambique into the Indian Ocean: c. 1,000 mi.

limp·sy, limp·sey (limp′sē) *adj.* **-si·er, -si·est** [Dial.] limp, as from exhaustion or weakness

lim·u·lus (lim′yoo ləs) *n., pl.* **-li** (-lī′) [ModL., name of the genus < L. *limulus*, somewhat askance, dim. of *limus*, sidelong (see LIMES) + -OID] same as HORSESHOE CRAB

lim·y (lī′mē) *adj.* **lim′i·er, lim′i·est** 1. covered with, consisting of, or like birdlime; sticky 2. of, like, or containing lime —**lim′i·ness** *n.*

lin. 1. lineal 2. linear

lin·ac (lī′nak) *n. shortened form of* LINEAR ACCELERATOR

lin·age (lī′nij) *n.* 1. the number of written or printed lines on a page or in an article, advertisement, etc. 2. payment based on the number of lines produced by a writer

lin·al·o·ol (li nal′ə ōl′, -ōl′; lin′ə lōōl′) *n.* [< MexSp. *linaloa*, an aromatic Mexican wood (< Sp. *lináloe* < L. *lignum aloës*: cf. LIGNALOES) + -OL[1]] a terpene alcohol, $C_{10}H_{17}OH$, present in several essential oils and used in perfumery

linch·pin (linch′pin′) *n.* [ME. *lynspin* < *lyns* (< OE. *lynis*, linchpin, akin to G. *lünse* < IE. base *elei-*, to bend, whence ELL, Sans. *āṇih*, linchpin) + *pin*, PIN] a pin that goes through the end of an axle outside the wheel to keep the wheel from coming off

Lin·coln (liŋ′kən) 1. [after Pres. LINCOLN] capital of Nebr., in the SE part: pop. 150,000 2. *same as* LINCOLNSHIRE 3. city in Lincolnshire, NE England: pop. 77,000 —*n.* a breed of sheep having long wool: orig. from Lincoln, England

Lin·coln (liŋ′kən), **Abraham** 1809-65; 16th president of the U.S. (1861-65): assassinated —☆**Lin·coln·esque** (liŋ′kə nesk′) *adj.* —☆**Lin·coln·i·an** (liŋ kō′nē ən) *adj.*

Lincoln green a bright-green cloth orig. made in Lincoln, England: associated esp. with Sherwood Forest

Lincoln Park city in SW Mich.: suburb of Detroit: pop. 53,000

Lin·coln·shire (liŋ′kən shir) county in NE England, on the North Sea: 2,663 sq. mi.; pop. 743,000

Lincoln's Inn *see* INN OF COURT

Lind (lind), **Jenny** (born *Johanna Maria Lind*; *Mme. Otto Goldschmidt*) 1820-87; Swed. soprano: called the *Swedish Nightingale*

Lin·da (lin′də) a feminine name: see BELINDA

lin·dane (lin′dān′) *n.* [after T. van der *Linden*, Du. chemist (20th c.) who first isolated the isomer + -ANE] an isomeric form of benzene hexachloride, widely used as an insecticide

Lind·bergh (lind′bərg, lin′-), **Charles Augustus** 1902- ; U.S. aviator: made first nonstop solo flight from New York to Paris (1927)

Lind·en (lin′dən) [from its *linden* trees, brought from Germany] city in NE N.J.: pop. 41,000

lin·den (lin′dən) *n.* [ME., *adj.* < OE. < *lind*, linden, akin to G. *linde*: popularized as *n.* via G. *linden*, pl. of *linde*: prob. < IE. base *lento-*, flexible, yielding, whence LITHE] any of a genus (*Tilia*) of trees of the linden family, with dense, heart-shaped leaves, widely cultivated throughout the North Temperate Zone: the American variety is also called BASSWOOD —*adj.* designating a family (Tiliaceae) of chiefly tropical shrubs and trees including the lindens and jutes

Lind·say (lin′zē, lind′-), (**Nicholas**) **Va·chel** (vā′chəl) 1879-1931; U.S. poet

☆**Lin·dy (Hop)** (lin′dē) [after C. A. LINDBERGH's ("Lindy's") transatlantic "hop"] [*also* l- h-] a lively dance for couples, popular in the early 1930's

line[1] (lin) *n.* [ME. *line*, merging OE. *line*, a cord, with OFr. *ligne* (both < L. *linea*, lit., linen thread, n. use of fem. of *lineus*, of flax < *linum*, flax)] 1. *a)* a cord, rope, wire, string, or the like *b)* a long, fine, strong cord with a hook, sinker, leader, etc. used in fishing *c)* a clothesline *d)* a cord, steel tape, etc. used in measuring or leveling *e)* a rope, hawser, or cable used on a ship *f)* a rein: *usually used in pl.* ☆2. *a)* a wire or wires connecting stations in a telephone or telegraph system *b)* the whole system of such wires *c)* effective contact between stations [*hold the line, please*] 3. any wire, pipe, system of pipes or wires, etc. for conducting water, gas, electricity, etc. 4. a very thin, threadlike mark; specif., *a)* a long, thin mark made by a pencil, pen, chalk, etc. *b)* a similar mark cut in a hard surface, as by engraving *c)* a thin crease in the palm or on the face 5. a mark made on the ground in certain sports; specif., *a)* any of the straight, narrow marks dividing or bounding a football field, tennis court, etc.: often used in combination [*sideline*] *b)* a mark indicating a starting point, a limit not to be crossed, or a point which must be reached or passed ☆6. a border or boundary [the State line] 7. a division between conditions, qualities, classes, etc.; limit; demarcation 8. outline; contour; lineament 9. [Archaic] [*pl.*] lot in life; one's fate 10. [*usually pl.*] a plan of construction; plan of making or doing 11. a row or series of persons or things of a particular kind; specif., *a)* a row of written or printed characters extending across or part way across a page ☆*b)* a row of persons waiting in turn to buy something, enter a theater, etc.; queue *c)* an assembly line or a similar arrangement for the packing, shipping, etc. of merchandise 12. a connected series of persons or things following each other in time or place; succession [a *line* of Democratic presidents] 13. *same as* LINEAGE[1] 14. the descendants of a common ancestor or of a particular breed 15. ☆*a)* a transportation system or service consisting of regular trips by buses, ships, etc. between two or more points ☆*b)* a company operating such a system *c)* one branch or division of such a system [the main *line* of a railroad] *d)* a single track of a railroad 16. the course or direction anything moving takes; path [the *line* of fire] 17. *a)* a course of conduct, action, explanation, etc. [the *line* of an argument] *b)* a course of movement 18. a person's trade or occupation, or the things he deals in [what's his *line*?] ☆19. a stock of goods of a particular type considered with reference to quality, quantity, variety, etc. 20. *a)* the field of one's special knowledge, interest, or ability *b)* a source or piece of information [a *line* on a bargain] 21. a short letter, note, or card [drop me a *line*] 22. a single metrical unit consisting of a specified number of feet; verse of poetry 23. [*pl.*] all the speeches in a play; esp., the speeches of any single character 24. [Colloq.] persuasive or flattering talk that is insincere 25. [*pl.*] [Chiefly Brit.] a marriage certificate: in full, **marriage lines** 26. *Bridge* the horizontal line dividing trick scores from honor scores ☆27. *Football a) short for* LINE OF SCRIMMAGE *b)* the players arranged in a row on either side of the line of scrimmage at the start of each play 28. *Geog.* an imaginary circle of the earth or of the celestial sphere, as the equator or the equinoctial circle 29. *Math. a)* the path of a moving point, thought of as having length but not breadth, whether straight or curved *b)* such a path when considered perfectly straight 30. *Mil. a)* a formation of ships, troops, etc. in which elements are abreast of each other *b)* the area or position in lines closest contact with the enemy during combat *c)* the troops in this area *d)* the officers in immediate command of fighting ships or combat troops ☆*e)* the combatant branches of the army as distinguished from the supporting branches and the staff 31. *Music* any of the long parallel marks forming the staff 32. *TV* a scanning line —*vt.* **lined, lin′ing** 1. to mark with lines 2. to draw or trace with or as with lines 3. to bring or cause to come into a straight row or into conformity; bring into alignment (often with *up*) 4. to form a line along [elms *line* the streets] 5. to place objects along the edge of [*line* the walk with flowers] ☆6. *Baseball* to hit (a pitched ball) in a line drive —*vi.*

1. to form a line (usually with *up*) ☆**2.** *Baseball* to hit a line drive —**all along the line 1.** everywhere **2.** at every turn of events —**bring** (or **come, get**) **into line** to bring (or come or cause to come) into a straight row or into conformity; bring or come into alignment —**down the line** completely; entirely —**draw the** (or **a**) **line** to set a limit —☆**get a line on** [Colloq.] to find out about —**hard lines** [Brit. Slang] misfortune; bad luck —☆**hit the line 1.** *Football* to try to carry the ball through the opposing line **2.** to try boldly or firmly to do something —**hold the line** to stand firm; not permit a breakthrough or retreat: often used figuratively —**in line 1.** in a straight row; in alignment **2.** in agreement or conformity **3.** behaving properly or as required —**in line for** being considered for —**in line of duty** in the performance of authorized or prescribed military duty —**lay** (or **put**) **it on the line 1.** to put up or pay money; pay up **2.** to speak frankly and in detail **3.** to stake (one's reputation, etc.) on something: usually with the object of the verb explicitly stated —**line out** ☆*Baseball* to be put out by hitting a line drive that is caught by a fielder —**line up 1.** to form a line **2.** to bring into a line **3.** to organize effectively, secure a pledge of support from, etc. **4.** to take a position (*against* a competitor or rival) —**on a line** in the same plane; level —**out of line 1.** not in a straight line; not in alignment **2.** not in agreement or conformity **3.** impertinent, insubordinate, etc. —**read between the lines** to discover a hidden meaning or purpose in something written, said, or done —**lin′a·ble, line′a·ble** *adj.*
line² (līn) *vt.* **lined, lin′ing** [ME. *lynen* < *lin,* long-fiber flax, linen cloth < OE. *lin,* ult. < or akin to L. *linum,* flax: from use of linen to line clothes] **1.** to put a layer or lining of a different material on the inside of **2.** to be used as a lining in [cloth *lined* the trunk] **3.** to fill; stuff; now chiefly in **line one's pockets,** to make money, esp. greedily or unethically
lin·e·age¹ (lin′ē ij) *n.* [ME. *linage* < OFr. *lignage* < *ligne:* see LINE¹] **1.** direct descent from an ancestor **2.** ancestry; family; stock **3.** *same as* LINAGE (*n.* 14)
line·age² (lī′nij) *n. same as* LINAGE
lin·e·al (lin′ē əl) *adj.* [ME. < OFr. *linéal* < LL. *linealis* < L. *linea:* see LINE¹] **1.** in the direct line of descent from an ancestor **2.** hereditary **3.** of or composed of lines; linear —**lin′e·al′i·ty** (-al′ə tē) *n.* —**lin′e·al·ly** *adv.*
lin·e·a·ment (lin′ē ə mənt) *n.* [ME. *liniamente* < L. *lineamentum* < *lineare,* to fashion to a straight line < *linea,* LINE¹] **1.** any of the features of the body, usually of the face, esp. with regard to its outline **2.** a distinctive feature or characteristic *Usually used in pl.* —**lin′e·a·men′tal** *adj.*
lin·e·ar (lin′ē ər) *adj.* [L. *linearis*] **1.** of or relating to a line or lines **2.** made of or using lines [*linear* design] **3.** in relation to length only; extended in a line **4.** designating or of a style of art in which forms are sharply delineated and line is emphasized over color, light and shadow, etc. **5.** having an effect or giving a response directly proportional to stimulus, force, or input: used esp. of electronic devices **6.** *Bot.* narrow and uniform in width, as the leaves of grasses **7.** *Math.* of or involving terms of the first degree [a *linear* function] —**lin′e·ar·ly** *adv.*
linear accelerator a high-energy accelerator in which charged particles are given electrostatic acceleration in a straight line at periodic intervals as they pass between metal tubes along the flight path
linear algebra the algebra of vectors and matrices, as distinct from the ordinary algebra of real numbers and the abstract algebra of unspecified entities
Linear B a Minoan pictographic script inscribed on clay tablets discovered on Crete, found to be an archaic form of Greek: **Linear A,** also used in Minoan inscriptions, remains undeciphered
linear equation an algebraic equation whose variable quantity or quantities are in the first power only and whose graph is a straight line (Ex.: a + b − 5 = 0)
lin·e·ar·i·ty (lin′ē ar′ə tē) *n., pl.* **-ties 1.** the quality or state of being linear **2.** *Electronics a)* the extent to which any signal modification process, as detection, is accomplished without amplitude distortion *b)* the fidelity with which a televised image is reproduced as determined by the extent to which there is a uniform distribution of the picture elements on the screen **3.** *Physics* the extent to which any effect is exactly proportional to its cause
lin·e·ar·ize (lin′ē ə rīz′) *vt.* **-ized′, -iz′ing** to give a linear form to —**lin′e·ar·i·za′tion** *n.*
linear measure 1. measurement of length, as distinguished from volume, weight, etc. **2.** a system of measuring length, esp. the system in which 12 inches = 1 foot or that in which 100 centimeters = 1 meter: see TABLE OF WEIGHTS AND MEASURES in Supplement
linear perspective *see* PERSPECTIVE
linear programming *Math.* a procedure for minimizing or maximizing a linear function of many variables, subject to a finite number of linear restrictions on these variables
lin·e·ate (lin′ē it, -āt′) *adj.* [L. *lineatus,* pp. of *lineare,* to fashion to a straight line < *linea,* LINE¹] having or marked with lines; streaked
lin·e·a·tion (lin′ē ā′shən) *n.* [ME. *lyneacion* < L. *lineatio*] **1.** *a)* a marking with lines *b)* a system or series of lines

2. a division into lines **3.** parallelism in rock structures
☆**line·back·er** (līn′bak′ər) *n. Football* any of the players on defense stationed directly behind the line
☆**line breeding** the producing of desired characteristics in animals by inbreeding through several successive generations —**line′-breed′** *vt.* **-bred′, -breed′ing**
line drawing a drawing done entirely in lines, from which a cut (**line cut**) can be photoengraved for printing
☆**line drive** *Baseball* a hard-hit ball that travels close to, and nearly parallel with, the ground
line engraving 1. a kind of engraving in which the effect is produced by lines of varying thickness and nearness to each other **2.** a plate engraved in this way **3.** a print from such a plate
Line Islands group of coral atolls in the C Pacific, divided between the U.S. and Great Britain
line·man (līn′mən) *n., pl.* **-men** (-mən) **1.** a man who carries a surveying line, tape, or chain **2.** a man whose work is setting up and repairing telephone, telegraph, or electric power lines ☆**3.** *Football* one of the players in the line
☆**linemen's climber** a device with sharp spikes or gaffs, fastened to the shoe or strapped to the leg to aid in climbing telephone poles, etc.
lin·en (lin′ən) *n.* see PLURAL, II, D, 3 [ME. < OE. (akin to G. *leinen*) < *lin,* flax: see LINE²] **1.** yarn, thread, or cloth made of flax **2.** [*often pl.*] things made of linen, or of cotton, etc., as tablecloths, sheets, shirts, etc.: cf. BED LINEN, TABLE LINEN **3.** fine stationery orig. made from linen rags —*adj.* **1.** spun from flax [*linen* thread] **2.** made of linen
linen closet a closet with shelves for sheets, towels, table linen, etc.
line of battle troops or ships drawn up to fight
line of credit the maximum amount of credit to be extended, as to a borrower by a bank
line officer 1. *Mil.* a commissioned officer in charge of combat troops **2.** *U.S. Navy* a commissioned officer eligible to command a ship at sea
line of fire 1. the course of a bullet, shell, etc. that has been, or is to be, fired **2.** a position open to attack of any kind
line of force a line in a field of electrical or magnetic force that indicates the direction taken by the force at any point
☆**line of scrimmage** *Football* an imaginary line, parallel to the goal lines, on which the ball rests at the start of each play and on either side of which the teams line up
line of sight 1. an imaginary straight line joining the center of the eye of the observer with the object viewed: also **line of vision 2.** *Radio & TV* the straight path from a transmitting antenna to the horizon, representing the normal range of high-frequency wave propagation —**line′-of-sight′** *adj.*
lin·e·o·late (lin′ē ə lāt′) *adj.* [ModL. *lineolatus* < L. *lineola,* dim. of *linea* (see LINE¹)] *Biol.* marked with fine, usually parallel, lines
lin·er¹ (lī′nər) *n.* **1.** a person or thing that traces lines or stripes ☆**2.** a steamship, passenger airplane, etc. in regular service for a specific line ☆**3.** *same as* LINE DRIVE **4.** a cosmetic applied in a fine line, as along the eyelid or, in the theater, to accentuate a natural line in the face
lin·er² (lī′nər) *n.* **1.** a person who makes or attaches linings **2.** a lining or something that suggests a lining by fitting inside something else [a helmet *liner*] ☆**3.** the cover or jacket of a long-playing record, usually containing information (**liner notes**) on the back about the music, the performers, etc.
lines·man (līnz′mən) *n., pl.* **-men** (-mən) **1.** *same as* LINEMAN **2.** *Football* an official who measures and marks the gains or losses in ground and determines where the ball goes out of bounds **3.** *Tennis* an official who reports whether the ball is inside or outside the lines he is assigned to watch
line squall the line of thunderstorms or windstorms that marks the progress of a cold front
☆**line storm** *same as* EQUINOCTIAL (*n.* 2)
☆**line-up** (līn′up′) *n.* an arrangement of persons or things in or as in a line; specif., *a)* a group of suspected criminals lined up by the police for identification *b)* *Football, Baseball,* etc. the list of a team's players arranged according to the positions they play, their order at bat, etc.
lin·e·y (lī′nē) *adj.* **lin′i·er, lin′i·est** *same as* LINY
ling¹ (liŋ) *n., pl.* **ling,** *see* PLURAL, II, D, 2 [ME. *lenge,* akin to MDu. *lange,* ON. *langa* < base of LONG¹: so named from its shape] **1.** any of several edible fishes of the cod family found in the North Atlantic from Greenland to Norway **2.** *same as* BURBOT
ling² (liŋ) *n.* [ME. < ON. *lyng* < IE. base *lenk*-, to bend: cf. -LING²] *same as* HEATHER
-ling¹ (liŋ) [ME. < OE., combining the bases of -LE + -ING] *a suffix added to nouns, meaning:* **1.** small [*duckling*] **2.** having a connection, esp. of an unimportant or contemptible kind, with the specified thing [*hireling*]
-ling² (liŋ) [ME. *-linge* < OE. *-ling, -lang* < IE. base *lenk*-, to bend, whence Lett. *lùnkans,* flexible] [Archaic or Dial.] *an adv.-forming suffix meaning* direction, extent, or condition [*darkling*]
ling. linguistics

Lin·ga·la (liŋ gä′lə) *n.* a Bantu language used as a lingua franca in the western part of the Congo (sense 2)

lin·gam (liŋ′gəm) *n.* [Sans. *lingam*, lit., token, symbol] the phallic symbol used in the worship of the Hindu god Siva: also **lin′ga:** cf. YONI

ling·cod (liŋ′käd) *n.*, *pl.* **-cod′, -cods′:** see PLURAL, II, D, 2 [LING¹ + COD¹] ☆a large game fish (*Ophiodon elongatus*) of the North Pacific, related to the greenling

lin·ger (liŋ′gər) *vi.* [North ME. *lengeren*, freq. of *lengen*, to delay, stay < OE. *lengan*, to lengthen, delay < base of *lang*, LONG¹] **1.** to continue to stay, esp. through reluctance to leave [*lingering* at the door] **2.** to continue to live or exist although very close to death or the end **3.** to be unnecessarily slow in doing something; delay; loiter —*vt.* to spend (time) idly, slowly, etc. —SYN. see STAY³ —**lin′ger·er** *n.* —**lin′ger·ing** *adj.* —**lin′ger·ing·ly** *adv.*

lin·ge·rie (län′zhə rā′, -rē′; lan′-; -jə-) *n.* [Fr. < *linge*, linen < L. *lineus*, linen < *linum*, flax, linen] **1.** formerly, articles made of linen **2.** women's underwear and night clothes of silk, nylon, lace, etc.

lin·go (liŋ′gō) *n. pl.* **-goes** [Pr. *lingo*, *lengo* < L. *lingua*, tongue: see LANGUAGE] language; esp., a dialect, jargon, or special vocabulary that one is not familiar with [the *lingo* of medical men]: a humorous or disparaging term —SYN. see DIALECT

☆**ling·on·ber·ry** (liŋ′ən ber′ē) *n.*, *pl.* **-ries** [< Sw. *lingon*, lingonberry (akin to ON. *lyng*, heather: cf. LING²) + BERRY] same as COWBERRY

lin·gua (liŋ′gwə) *n.*, *pl.* **-guae** (-gwē) [L.: see LANGUAGE] a tongue or an organ resembling a tongue, as the proboscis of a butterfly or moth

lin·gua fran·ca (liŋ′gwə fraŋ′kə) *pl.* **lin′gua fran′cas, lin′guae fran′cae** (liŋ′gwē fran′sē) [It., lit., Frankish language] **1.** a hybrid language of Italian, Spanish, French, Greek, Arabic, and Turkish elements, spoken in certain Mediterranean ports **2.** any hybrid language used for communication between different peoples, as pidgin English

lin·gual (liŋ′gwəl) *adj.* [ME. < ML. *lingualis* < L. *lingua*, the tongue: see LANGUAGE] **1.** of the tongue **2.** of language or languages **3.** articulated by using the tongue —*n.* *Phonet.* a lingual sound, as *l* or *t* —**lin′gual·ly** *adv.*

lin·gui·form (liŋ′gwə fôrm′) *adj.* [< L. *lingua*, the tongue (see LANGUAGE) + -FORM] shaped like a tongue

lin·gui·ne (liŋ gwē′nē) *n.* [altered < It. *linguini*, pl. of *linguina*, dim. of *lingua*, tongue (< L.: see LANGUAGE)] a kind of pasta like spaghetti but flat, often served with seafood sauces

lin·guist (liŋ′gwist) *n.* [< L. *lingua*, the tongue (see LANGUAGE) + -IST] **1.** a specialist in linguistics: cf. PHILOLOGIST **2.** same as POLYGLOT (sense 1)

lin·guis·tic (liŋ gwis′tik) *adj.* **1.** of language **2.** of linguistics —**lin·guis′ti·cal·ly** *adv.*

linguistic atlas a bound collection of maps charting the geographical distribution of linguistic forms and usages

linguistic form a meaningful unit of speech, as a morpheme, word, phrase, sentence, etc.

linguistic geography the branch of linguistics studying the geographical distribution of linguistic forms and usages —**linguistic geographer**

lin·guis·tics (liŋ gwis′tiks) *n.pl.* [*with sing. v.*] [< LINGUISTIC] **1.** the science of language, including phonology, morphology, syntax, and semantics: often **general linguistics:** usually subdivided into *descriptive, historical, comparative,* and *geographical linguistics* **2.** the study of the structure, development, etc. of a particular language and of its relationship to other languages [English *linguistics*]

linguistic stock 1. a parent language and all the languages and dialects derived from it **2.** all the native speakers of any of these languages or dialects

lin·gu·late (liŋ′gyə lit, -lāt′) *adj.* [L. *lingulatus* < *lingula*, dim. of *lingua*, the tongue: see LANGUAGE] shaped like a tongue; linguiform

lin·i·ment (lin′ə mənt) *n.* [ME. *lynyment* < LL. *linimentum* < L. *linere*, to smear: see LIME¹] a medicated liquid to be rubbed on the skin for soothing sore, sprained, or inflamed areas

li·nin (lī′nin) *n.* [< L. *linum*, flax + -IN¹] the achromatic substance constituting the netlike structure that connects the granules of chromatin in the nucleus of a cell

lin·ing (lī′niŋ) *n.* [see LINE² & -ING] **1.** the act or process of covering the inner surface of something **2.** the material used or suitable for this purpose

link¹ (liŋk) *n.* [ME. *linke* < Scand., as in ON. *hlekkr*, Dan. *lænke*, Sw. *länk*, in same senses, akin to OE. *hlence*, link of a chain, coat of mail < base of *hlencan*, to twist < IE. base *kleng-*, to bend, wind: cf. FLANK] **1.** any of the series of rings or loops making up a chain **2.** *a)* a section of something resembling a chain [a *link* of sausage] *b)* a point or stage in a series of circumstances [a weak *link* in the evidence] **3.** same as CUFF LINK **4.** anything serving to connect or tie [a *link* with the past] **5.** *a)* one division (1/100) of a surveyor's, or Gunter's, chain, equal to 7.92 in. *b)* 1/100 of an engineer's chain, equal to 1 ft. **6.** *Chem.* same as BOND

7. *Elec.* the part of a fuse that melts when the current becomes too strong **8.** *Mech.* a short connecting rod for transmitting power or motion **9.** *Radio & TV* a radio unit for transmitting sound or picture between specific stations —*vt., vi.* to join together with or as with a link or links —SYN. see JOIN —**link′er** *n.*

link² (liŋk) *n.* [prob. < ML. *linchinus*, var. of *lichinus*, a lamp < L. *lychnus*, a light < Gr. *lychnos*, a lamp < IE. **luksnos* < base **leuk-*, to shine, LIGHT¹] a torch made of tow and pitch

link·age (liŋk′kij) *n.* **1.** a linking or being linked **2.** a series or system of links; esp., a series of connecting rods for transmitting power or motion **3.** *Biol.* the tendency of some genes to remain together and act as a unit (**linkage group**) in inheritance, generally in the same chromosome, without segregation throughout maturation **4.** *Chem. a) same as* BOND¹ *b)* the type of bonding between various atoms or groups in a molecule **5.** *Elec.* the product of the number of lines of magnetic flux times the number of turns in the coil surrounding it

link·boy (-boi′) *n.* a boy or man formerly hired to carry a link, or torch, to light one's way at night: also **link′man** (-mən), *pl.* **-men** (-mən)

linking verb a verb that functions chiefly as a connection between a subject and a predicate complement (Ex.: *be, appear, seem, become,* etc.); copula

link motion a valve gear that reverses the motion in steam engines: it operates by a slotted bar linked with the eccentric rods

Lin·kö·ping (lin′chö′piŋ) city in SE Sweden: pop. 72,000

links (liŋks) *n.pl.* [OE. *hlinc*, a slope, akin to *hlence:* see LINK¹] **1.** [Scot.] a stretch of rolling, sandy land, esp. along a seashore **2.** same as GOLF COURSE

link·up (liŋk′up′) *n.* a joining together of two objects, factions, interests, etc.

link·work (liŋk′wurk′) *n.* **1.** anything made in links, as a chain **2.** a gear system operating by links

Lin·lith·gow (lin lith′gō) *former name of* WEST LOTHIAN

linn (lin) *n.* [< OE. *hlynn*, torrent, confused with Gael. *linne*, a pond) [Scot.] **1.** a waterfall or a pool of water at its base **2.** a steep ravine

Lin·nae·an, Lin·ne·an (li nē′ən) *adj.* of Linnaeus; esp., designating or of his system of classifying plants and animals by using a double name, the first word naming the genus, and the second the species

Lin·nae·us (li nē′əs), **Car·o·lus** (kar′ə ləs) (Latinized form of *Karl von Linné*) 1707–78; Swed. botanist

lin·net (lin′it) *n.* [ME. *linet* < OFr. *linette* < *lin*, flax (< L. *linum:* cf. LINEN): so called because it feeds on flaxseed] a small, variously colored songbird (*Acanthis cannabina*) of the finch family, found in Europe, Asia, and Africa

li·no·cut (lī′nə kut′) *n.* [LINO(LEUM) + CUT] **1.** a design cut into the surface of a block of linoleum **2.** a print made from this

li·no·le·ate (li nō′lē āt′) *n.* [< ff. + -ATE²] a salt or ester of linoleic acid

lin·o·le·ic acid (lin′ə lē′ik, li nō′lē ik) [< L. *linum*, flax + OLEIC] an unsaturated fatty acid, $C_{18}H_{32}O_2$, found as a glyceryl ester in linseed oil and other fats and oils: used as a drying agent and in soaps, foods, etc. and considered essential in animal diets

lin·o·le·nate (lin′ə lē′nāt) *n.* [< ff. + -ATE²] a salt or ester of linolenic acid

lin·o·le·nic acid (lin′ə lē′nik) [< LINOL(EIC) + -EN(E) + -IC] an unsaturated fatty acid, $C_{18}H_{30}O_2$, found as a glyceryl ester in fats and oils: used in drying oils, varnishes, resins, paints, etc. and considered essential in animal diets

li·no·le·um (li nō′lē əm) *n.* [coined 1863 by F. Walton, Eng. manufacturer < L. *linum*, flax + *oleum*, OIL] a hard, smooth, washable floor covering made of a mixture of ground cork, ground wood, gums, color pigments, and oxidized linseed oil laid on a burlap or canvas backing

☆**Lin·o·type** (līn′ə tip′) [*line of type*] *a trademark for* a typesetting machine that casts an entire line of type in one bar, or slug: it is operated from a keyboard —*n.* [*often* l-] **1.** a machine of this kind **2.** matter set in this way —*vt., vi.* [l-] **-typed′, -typ′ing** to set (matter) with this machine —**lin′o·typ′ist, lin′o·typ′er** *n.*

lin·sang (lin′saŋ) *n.* [Jav. *linsaŋ, wlinsaŋ*] any of several long-tailed, catlike animals (family Viverridae) about the size of a weasel, found in Australia and the Old World tropics

lin·seed (lin′sēd) *n.* [ME. *linsed* < OE. *linsæd* < *lin*, flax (see LINE²) + *sæd*, SEED] the seed of flax

linseed oil a yellowish oil extracted from flaxseed, and used, because of its drying qualities, in making oil paints, printer's ink, linoleum, etc.

lin·sey-wool·sey (lin′zē wŏōl′zē) *n.*, *pl.* **-wool′seys** [ME. *linsy wolsye* < *lin*, linen (see LINE²) + *wolle*, WOOL + jingling suffix] **1.** a coarse cloth made of linen and wool or cotton and wool: also **lin′sey 2.** [Obs.] an incongruous mixture; jumble

lin·stock (lin′stäk′) *n.* [altered < Du. *lontstok* < *lont*, a match, lunt + *stok*, a stick] a long stick formerly used to hold a lighted match for firing a cannon

lint (lint) *n.* [ME. *linnet*, prob. < *lin*, linen: see LINE[2]] **1.** scraped and softened linen formerly used as a dressing for wounds **2.** cotton fiber used to make yarn **3.** the waste cotton remaining after ginning **4.** bits of thread, ravelings, or fluff from cloth or yarn —*vi.* to give off lint or fluff —**lint′less** *adj.* —**lint′y** *adj.* **lint′i·er, lint′i·est**

lin·tel (lin′t'l) *n.* [ME. < OFr. < VL. *limitellus*, for *limitaris*, altered (after L. *limes*, gen. *limitis:* see LIMES) < L. *liminaris*, of a threshold or lintel < *limen:* see LIMEN] the horizontal crosspiece over a door, window, etc., carrying the weight of the structure above it

☆**lint·er** (lin′tər) *n.* **1.** a machine for removing the short, fuzzy fibers which remain stuck to cotton seeds after ginning **2.** [*pl.*] these fibers, used in making cotton batting, gun cotton, etc.

lint·white (lint′hwit′, -wit′) *n.* [ME. *lynkwhitte*, altered < OE. *lynetuige*, lit., flax-plucker < *lin* (see LINE[2]) + *-twige* < or akin to *twiccian:* see TWITCH] *same as* LINNET

lin·y (li′nē) *adj.* **lin′i·er, lin′i·est 1.** like a line; thin **2.** marked with, or full of, lines or streaks

Linz (lints) city in N Austria, on the Danube: pop. 196,000

li·on (li′ən) *n., pl.* **li′ons, li′on:** see PLURAL, II, D, 1 [ME. < OFr. < L. *leo* (gen. *leonis*) < Gr. *leōn* (gen. *leontos*)] **1.** a large, powerful mammal (*Panthera leo*) of the cat family, found in Africa and SW Asia, with a tawny coat, a tufted tail, and, in the adult male, a shaggy mane: in folklore and fable the lion is considered king of the beasts **2.** a person of great courage or strength **3.** a prominent person who is in demand socially; celebrity —[L-] **1.** [*pl.*] an international service club of business and professional men **2.** Leo, the constellation and fifth sign of the zodiac —**beard the lion in his den** to visit and defy or oppose a person in his own home, etc. —**li′on·ess** *n.fem.*

Li·o·nel (li′ə n'l, -nel′) [Fr., dim. of *lion*, LION: cf. LEO] a masculine name

li·on·heart·ed (li′ən här′tid) *adj.* very brave

li·on·ize (li′ə niz′) *vt.* **-ized′, -iz′ing** [LION + -IZE] **1.** to treat as a celebrity **2.** [Brit.] to visit or explore the interesting sights of (a place) —**li′on·i·za′tion** *n.* —**li′on·iz′er** *n.*

Lions, Gulf of (the) part of the Mediterranean, on the S coast of France, between Toulon & Spain: Fr. name **Golfe du Lion** (gôlf dü lyôn′)

lion's share [from Aesop's fable in which the lion took all the spoils of a joint hunt] the whole thing or, now popularly, the biggest and best portion

lip (lip) *n.* [ME. *lippe* < OE. *lippa*, akin to MDu. *lippe* < IE. base *leb-*, to hang loosely, lip, whence L. *labes*, a falling, *labium*, lip] **1.** either of the two fleshy folds, normally pink or reddish in color, forming the edges of the mouth and important in speech **2.** anything like a lip, as in structure or in being an edge, rim, or margin; specif., *a*) the edge of a wound *b*) the projecting rim of a pitcher, cup, etc. *c*) the mouthpiece of a wind instrument *d*) the cutting edge of any of certain tools *e*) *Anat.* same as LABIUM *f*) *Bot.* same as LABELLUM **3.** the position and use of the lips in playing a wind instrument; embouchure **4.** [Slang] impertinent or insolent talk —*vt.* **lipped, lip′ping 1.** to touch with the lips; specif., *a*) to place the lips in the proper position for playing (a wind instrument) *b*) [Archaic] to kiss **2.** to utter, esp. softly **3.** *Golf* to come just to or across the edge of (the cup): said of the ball —*adj.* **1.** formed with a lip or the lips; labial [*a lip* consonant] **2.** of or for the lips **3.** from the lips only; spoken, but insincere —**bite one's lips** to keep back one's anger, annoyance, etc. —**hang on the lips of** to listen to with close attention —☆**keep a stiff upper lip** [Colloq.] to fail to become frightened or discouraged under difficulties —**smack one's lips** to express great satisfaction in anticipating or remembering something pleasant —**lip′less** *adj.*

Li·pa·ri Islands (lip′ə rē; *It.* lē′pä rē′) group of volcanic islands in the Tyrrhenian Sea, northeast of Sicily: part of Sicily autonomous region: c. 45 sq. mi.

li·pase (li′pās, lip′ās) *n.* [LIP(O)- + -ASE] any of a group of enzymes that aid in digestion by hydrolyzing fats into fatty acids and glycerol

Lip·chitz (lip′shits), **Jacques** (zhäk) (born *Chaim Jacob Lipchitz*) 1891-   ; U.S. sculptor, born in Lithuania

Li·petsk (lē′pyetsk) city in SW European R.S.F.S.R.: pop. 237,000

lip·id (lip′id, li′pid) *n.* [LIP(O)- + -ID] any of a group of organic compounds consisting of the fats and other substances of similar properties: they are insoluble in water, soluble in fat solvents and alcohol, greasy to the touch, and are important constituents of living cells: also **lip′ide** (lip′id, -id; li′pid, -pid)

Li Po (lē′ bō′) 700?-762 A.D.; Chin. poet

lip·o- (lip′ə, -ō) [< Gr. *lipos*, fat < IE. *leip-:* see LEAVE[1]] a combining form meaning of or like fat, fatty [*lipolysis*]: also, before a vowel, **lip-**

li·poid (lip′oid, li′poid) *adj.* [LIP(O)- + -OID] *Biochem., Chem.* resembling fat: also **li·poi′dal** —*n.* a fat or fatlike substance; lipid

li·pol·y·sis (li päl′ə sis) *n.* [ModL.: see LIPO- & -LYSIS] the decomposition of fat, as during digestion —**lip·o·lyt·ic** (lip′ə lit′ik) *adj.*

li·po·ma (li pō′mə, li-) *n., pl.* **-po′ma·ta** (-tə), **-po′mas** [ModL.: see LIPO- & -OMA] a tumor made up of fat tissue —**li·pom′a·tous** (-päm′ə təs) *adj.*

lip·o·phil·ic (lip′ə fil′ik) *adj.* [LIPO- + -PHIL(E) + -IC] having a strong attraction for fats

lip·o·pro·tein (-prō′tēn, -prō′tē in) *n.* any of a group of proteins combined with a lipid, found in blood plasma, egg yolk, brain tissue, etc.

lip·o·trop·ic (-träp′ik) *adj.* [LIPO- + -TROPIC] regulating or reducing the accumulation of fat in the body or its organs —**li·pot·ro·pism** (li pät′rə piz'm) *n.*

Lip·pe (lip′ə) region in the state of North Rhine-Westphalia, West Germany: formerly, a state of Germany

lipped (lipt) *adj.* **1.** having a lip or lips: often in compounds [*tight-lipped*] **2.** having a spoutlike projection in the rim: said of a pitcher, cup, etc. **3.** *Bot.* same as LABIATE

lip·pen (lip′'n) *vt., vi.* [ME. *lipnen* < ?] [Chiefly Scot.] to trust

lip·per (lip′ər) *n.* [N.Eng. & Scot., prob. < base of LAP[2]] *Naut.* **1.** a gentle ruffling movement of the surface of the sea **2.** light spray caused by this

Lip·pi (lēp′pē; *E.* lip′ē) **1.** **Fi·lip·pi·no** (fē′lēp pē′nō), 1457?-1504; Florentine painter **2.** **Fra Fi·lip·po** (fi läp′pō), 1406?-69; Florentine painter; father of *prec.:* also called **Fra Lippo Lippi**

Lipp·mann (lip′mən), **Walter** 1889-   ; U.S. journalist

lip·py (lip′ē) *adj.* **-pi·er, -pi·est** [Slang] impudent, brash, or insolent —**lip′pi·ness** *n.*

lip-read (lip′rēd′) *vt., vi.* **-read′** (-red′), **-read′ing** to recognize (a speaker's words) by lip reading —**lip reader**

lip reading the act or skill of recognizing a speaker's words by watching the movement of his lips: it is taught esp. to the deaf

lip service insincere expression of respect, loyalty, support, etc.

☆**lip·stick** (-stik′) *n.* a small stick of cosmetic paste, set in a case, for coloring the lips

lip-sync (lip′sink′) *vt., vi.* [< *lip sync*(*hronization*)] to synchronize lip movements with (recorded speaking or singing) —*n.* the act or process of lip-syncing

liq. 1. liquid **2.** liquor

li·quate (li′kwāt) *vt.* **-quat·ed, -quat·ing** [< L. *liquatus*, pp. of *liquare*, to melt, akin to *liquere:* see LIQUID] *Metallurgy* to heat (a metal, etc.) in order to separate a fusible substance from one less fusible —**li·qua′tion** *n.*

liq·ue·fa·cient (lik′wə fā′shənt) *adj.* [< L. *liquefaciens*, prp. of *liquefacere*, LIQUEFY] that liquefies, or causes to become liquid —*n.* something that causes liquefaction

liq·ue·fac·tion (-fak′shən) *n.* a liquefying or being liquefied

liquefied petroleum gas a compressed or liquefied gas, generally a mixture of propane and butane, obtained as a byproduct from petroleum refining: used as a domestic or industrial fuel and in certain organic syntheses

liq·ue·fy (lik′wə fi′) *vt., vi.* **-fied′, -fy′ing** [Fr. *liquefier* < L. *liquefacere* < *liquere*, to be liquid (see LIQUID) + *facere*, to make: see FACT] to change into a liquid —*SYN.* see MELT —**liq′ue·fi′a·ble** *adj.* —**liq′ue·fi′er** *n.*

li·ques·cent (li kwes′'nt) *adj.* [L. *liquescens*, prp. of *liquescere*, to become liquid < *liquere:* see LIQUID] becoming liquid; melting —**li·ques′cence** *n.*

li·queur (li kur′) *n.* [Fr.] any of certain strong, sweet, syrupy alcoholic liquors, variously flavored

liq·uid (lik′wid) *adj.* [ME. < OFr. *liquide* < L. *liquidus* < *liquere*, to be liquid, prob. < IE. base *wlikw-*, wet, whence W. *gwlyb*, moist] **1.** readily flowing; fluid; specif., having its molecules moving freely with respect to each other so as to flow readily, unlike a solid, but because of cohesive forces not expanding indefinitely like a gas **2.** clear; limpid [*liquid* eyes] **3.** flowing smoothly and musically, gracefully, etc. [*liquid* verse] **4.** readily convertible into cash [*liquid* assets] **5.** without friction and like a vowel: a nontechnical term used to describe certain consonants, esp. *l* and *r* —*n.* **1.** a liquid substance **2.** a liquid consonant —**liq·uid′i·ty, liq′uid·ness** *n.* —**liq′uid·ly** *adv.*

SYN.—**liquid** refers to a substance that flows readily and assumes the form of its container but retains its independent volume [water that is neither ice nor steam is a *liquid*]; **fluid** applies to any substance that flows [all liquids, gases, and viscous substances are *fluids*] —*ANT.* **solid**

liquid air air brought to a liquid state by being subjected to great pressure and then cooled by its own expansion to a temperature below the boiling point of its main constituents, nitrogen and oxygen: it is used as a refrigerant

liq·uid·am·bar (lik′wid am′bər) *n.* [ModL. *Liquidambar*, name of the genus: see LIQUID & AMBER] **1.** any of a genus (*Liquidambar*) of trees of the witch hazel family, found in Asia and N. America; specif., *same as* SWEET GUM **2.** the balsam from such a tree

liq·ui·date (lik′wə dāt′) *vt.* **-dat·ed, -dat·ing** [< ML. *liquidatus*, pp. of *liquidare*, to make liquid or clear < L. *liquidus*, LIQUID] **1.** to settle by agreement or legal process the amount of (indebtedness, damages, etc.) **2.** to settle the accounts of (a bankrupt business firm that is closing, etc.) by apportioning assets and debts **3.** to pay or settle (a debt) **4.** to convert (holdings or assets) into cash **5.** to dispose of or get rid of, as by killing —*vi.* to liquidate debts, accounts, etc.

liq·ui·da·tion (lik′wə dā′shən) *n.* a liquidating or being liquidated —**go into liquidation** to close one's business by collecting assets and settling all debts

liq·ui·da·tor (lik′wə dāt′ər) *n.* a person who liquidates, esp. one legally appointed to liquidate a company, etc.

liquid crystal a liquid that has certain characteristics of crystals, as interference colors and double refraction

liquid diet a diet restricted to liquids and, sometimes, certain semisolid foods, as custards, gelatin, etc.

liq·uid·ize (lik′wə dīz′) *vt.* **-ized′, -iz′ing** to cause to have a liquid quality

liquid measure 1. the measurement of liquids **2.** a system of measuring liquids; esp., the system in which 4 gills = 1 pint, 2 pints = 1 quart, 4 quarts = 1 gallon: see TABLE OF WEIGHTS AND MEASURES in Supplement

liquid oxygen a light-bluish liquid boiling at −183°C, produced by fractionation of liquid air: used as an oxidizer in liquid-fueled rockets

liq·uor (lik′ər) *n.* [altered (after L.) < ME. *licour* < OFr. *licor* < L. *liquor,* akin to *liquere:* see LIQUID] **1.** any liquid or juice *[meat liquor]* **2.** an alcoholic drink, esp. one made by distillation, as whiskey or rum **3.** *Pharmacy* a solution of some substance in water —*vt., vi.* [Colloq.] to drink or cause to drink alcoholic liquor, esp. to the point of intoxication

liq·uo·rice (lik′ər ish, -is; lik′rish) *n. chiefly Brit. sp.* of LICORICE

li·ra (lir′ə) *n., pl.* **li′re** (-ā), *also, and for 2 always,* **li′ras** [It. < L. *libra,* a balance, pound] the monetary unit of **1.** Italy **2.** Turkey See MONETARY UNITS, table

lir·i·pipe (lir′ə pip′) *n.* [ML. *liripipium* < ?] in early academic and clerical costume, a long tail to a hood

Lis·bon (liz′bən) capital of Portugal: seaport on the Tagus estuary: pop. 802,000 (met. area 1,335,000): Port. name **Lis·bo·a** (lēzh bô′ə)

Lisle *see* LECONTE DE LISLE & ROUGET DE LISLE

lisle (līl) *n.* [< *Lisle,* earlier sp. of LILLE, where orig. made] **1.** a fine, hard, extra-strong cotton thread: in full, **lisle thread 2.** a fabric, or stockings, gloves, etc., knit or woven of lisle —*adj.* made of lisle

lisp (lisp) *vt.* [ME. *lyspen,* earlier *wlispen* < OE. *-wlyspian* < *wlisp, wlips,* a lisping, akin to G. *lispeln,* MLowG. *wlispen, wilspen,* of echoic orig.] **1.** to substitute the sounds (th) and (*th*) for the sounds of *s* and *z,* as in pronouncing *sing* as though it were *thing* **2.** to speak imperfectly or like a child —*vt.* to utter with a lisp or in an imperfect or child-like way —*n.* **1.** the act or speech defect of lisping **2.** the sound of lisping —**lisp′er** *n.* —**lisp′ing·ly** *adv.*

lis pen·dens (lis pen′denz) [L.] *Law* a pending suit: *a lis pendens* involves the legal doctrine that a court acquires jurisdiction over property involved in a suit

lis·some, lis·som (lis′əm) *adj.* [altered < LITHESOME] bending or moving gracefully or with ease and lightness; lithe, supple, limber, agile, etc. —**lis′some·ly, lis′som·ly** *adv.* —**lis′some·ness, lis′som·ness** *n.*

list¹ (list) *n.* [ME. *liste,* merging OE. *liste,* a hem, border & Anglo-Fr. *liste* < OFr. *liste* < Gmc., akin to OE. base *leizd-,* edge, border, whence Alb. *leth,* the raised border of a plot of ground, wall] **1.** formerly, a narrow strip or border; specif., *a)* a strip of cloth *b)* a stripe of color *c)* a boundary **2.** *a)* a narrow strip of wood, esp. sapwood, trimmed from the edge of a board *b) same as* LISTEL **3.** the selvage of cloth **4.** [from the idea of a narrow slip of paper] a series of names, words, numbers, etc. set forth in order; catalog, roll, etc. ☆**5.** a ridge of earth between two furrows **6.** *same as* LIST PRICE **7.** *Finance* the stocks listed for trading on a stock exchange See also LISTS —*vt.* **1.** formerly, to edge with, or arrange in, stripes or bands **2.** *a)* to set forth (a series of names, items, etc.) in order *b)* to enter (a name, item, etc.) in a list, directory, catalog, etc. ☆**3.** to plow (ground) or plant (corn) with a lister **4.** to trim a strip of wood, esp. sapwood, from the edge of (a board) —*vi.* ☆**1.** to plow with a lister **2.** to be listed for sale, as in a catalog (at the price specified) **3.** [Archaic] to enlist in the armed forces

SYN.—list, the broadest in scope of these terms, applies to a series of items of any kind, no matter what the arrangement or purpose; **catalog** implies methodical arrangement, usually alphabetical, and is used of lists of articles for sale or on exhibit, library card files, etc.; an **inventory** is an itemized list of goods, property, etc., especially one made annually in business; a **register** is a book, etc. in which names, events, or other items are formally or officially recorded *[a register of voters];* a **roll** is an official list of the members of an organization, especially as used for checking attendance

list² (list) *vt.* [ME. *listen* < OE. *lystan* < base of *lust,* desire, appetite: see LUST] [Archaic] to be pleasing to; suit —*vi.* [Archaic] to wish; like; choose —*n.* [Archaic] a craving, desire, or inclination

list³ (list) *vt., vi.* [prob. specialized use of prec.] to tilt to one side, as a ship —*n.* a tilting or inclining to one side

list⁴ (list) *vt., vi.* [ME. < OE. *hlystan* < base of *hlyst,* hearing, akin to G. *lauschen,* dial. *laustern* < IE. base *kleu-,* to hear, whence L. *cluere,* to be called] [Archaic] to listen (to)

lis·tel (list′′l) *n.* [Fr. < It. *listello,* dim. of *lista,* a border, strip < Gmc. *lista:* see LIST¹] *Archit.* a narrow molding or band; fillet

lis·ten (lis′′n) *vi.* [ME. *listnen,* felt as freq. of *listen* (see LIST⁴) < OE. *hlysnan* (akin to MHG. *lüsenen*): for base see LIST¹] **1.** to make a conscious effort to hear; attend closely, so as to hear **2.** to give heed; take advice —*vt.* [Archaic] to pay attention to by listening; hear —*n.* the act of listening —☆**listen in 1.** to listen to the conversation of others; esp., to eavesdrop **2.** to listen to a broadcast —**lis′ten·er** *n.*

lis·ten·ing post (-iŋ) **1.** *Mil.* an advanced, concealed position near the enemy's lines, for detecting the enemy's movements by listening **2.** a strategic position or center for securing information or intelligence about an opponent, enemy, rival power, etc.

list·er¹ (lis′tər) *n.* [LIST¹, *vt.* 3 + -ER] ☆a plow with a double moldboard, which heaps the earth on both sides of the furrow: it is sometimes combined with a drill that plants seed in the same operation

list·er² (lis′tər) *n.* a person who compiles a list or lists

Lis·ter (lis′tər), **Joseph** 1st Baron Lister of Lyme Regis, 1827–1912; Eng. surgeon: introduced antiseptic surgery

list·ing (lis′tiŋ) *n.* **1.** the act of making a list **2.** an entry in a list, as in a directory, a real-estate broker's record of property for sale, etc. **3.** a list

list·less (list′lis) *adj.* [LIST² + -LESS] **1.** having no interest in what is going on about one, as a result of illness, weariness, dejection, etc.; spiritless; languid **2.** characterized by such a feeling —**list′less·ly** *adv.* —**list′less·ness** *n.*

list price retail price as given in a list or catalog, variously discounted in sales to dealers

lists (lists) *n.pl.* [ME. *listes,* specialized use of *liste,* border, hedging, boundary (see LIST¹), prob. infl. by OFr. *lisse* (Fr. *lice*) in same sense < Frank. **listia < *lista,* LIST¹] **1.** *a)* in the Middle Ages, a high fence of stakes enclosing the area in which a tournament was held *b)* this area itself or the tournament held there **2.** any place or realm of combat, conflict, etc. —**enter the lists** to enter a contest or struggle

Liszt (list), **Franz** (fränts) 1811–86; Hung. composer & pianist

lit (lit) *alt. pt. & pp.* of LIGHT

lit. 1. liter; liters **2.** literal **3.** literally **4.** literary **5.** literature

Li Tai Po (lē′ tī′ bō′) *same as* LI PO

lit·a·ny (lit′′n ē) *n., pl.* **-nies** [ME. *letanie* < OFr. < LL. (Ec.) *litania* < Gr.(Ec.) *litaneia* < Gr. *litanos,* pleading < *litē,* a request, prob. < IE. **leit-* < base **lei-,* to stroke, smooth over: cf. LIME¹] **1.** a form of prayer in which the clergy and the congregation take part alternately, with recitation of supplications and fixed responses **2.** any dreary or repetitive recital or account

Lit.B., Lit.D. *see* LITT.B., LITT.D.

li·tchi (lē′chē′) *n.* [Chin. *li-chih*] **1.** a Chinese evergreen tree (*Litchi chinensis*) of the soapberry family, cultivated in warm climates for its fruit **2.** the fruit of this tree (**litchi nut**), usually eaten dried or preserved: it consists of a single seed surrounded by a sweet, edible, raisinlike pulp, enclosed in a rough, brown, papery shell

-lite (līt) [Fr., for *-lithe:* see -LITH] *a combining form meaning* stone: used in the names of minerals, rocks, and fossils *[chrysolite, cryolite]*

li·ter (lēt′ər) *n.* [Fr. *litre < litron,* obs. unit of measure < ML. *litra* < Gr. *litra,* a pound] the basic unit of capacity in the metric system, equal to 1 cubic decimeter or 61.025 cubic inches (1.0567 liquid quarts or .908 dry quart): it is the volume of a kilogram of distilled water at 4°C

lit·er·a·cy (lit′ər ə sē) *n.* the state or quality of being literate; ability to read and write

lit·er·al (lit′ər əl) *adj.* [ME. *litterall* < MFr. *litteral* < LL. *litteralis* < L. *littera,* LETTER¹] **1.** of, involving, or expressed by a letter or letters of the alphabet *[literal notation]* **2.** following or representing the exact words of the original; word-for-word *[a literal translation]* **3.** *a)* based on the actual words in their ordinary meaning; not figurative or symbolical *[the literal meaning of a passage]* *b)* giving the actual denotation of the word: said of the senses of words *c)* giving the original or earlier meaning of a word; etymological *[the literal meaning of ponder is "to weigh"]* **4.** habitually interpreting statements or words according to their actual denotation; prosaic; matter-of-fact *[a literal mind]* **5.** real; not going beyond the actual facts; accurate; unvarnished *[the literal truth]:* often used as an intensive with the meaning "virtual": see LITERALLY —**lit′er·al·ness** *n.*

lit·er·al·ism (-iz′m) *n.* **1.** the tendency or disposition to take words, statements, etc. in their literal sense **2.** thoroughgoing realism in art —**lit′er·al·ist** *n.* —**lit′er·al·is′tic** *adj.*

lit·er·al·i·ty (lit′ə ral′ə tē) *n., pl.* **-ties 1.** the state or quality of being literal **2.** a literal meaning or interpretation

lit·er·al·ize (lit′ər ə līz′) *vt.* **-ized′, -iz′ing 1.** to make literal, as a translation **2.** to interpret according to the literal sense —**lit′er·al·i·za′tion** *n.*

lit·er·al·ly (lit′ər əl ē) *adv.* in a literal manner or sense;

specif., *a*) word for word; not imaginatively, figuratively, or freely [to translate a passage *literally*] *b*) actually; in fact [the house *literally* burned to the ground]: used as an intensive, in a sense opposite to that above [he *literally* flew into the room]: this latter usage is generally regarded as loose or erroneous

lit·er·ar·y (lit'ə rer'ē) *adj.* [L. *litterarius* < *littera*, LETTER[1]] **1.** *a*) of, having the nature of, or dealing with literature *b*) of or having to do with books [*literary agents*] **2.** characterized by the more formal, balanced, and polished language of literature rather than the informal language of speech; not colloquial **3.** *a*) familiar with or versed in literature *b*) making literature a profession —**lit'er·ar'i·ness** *n.*

lit·er·ate (lit'ər it) *adj.* [ME. *litterate* < L. *litteratus* < *littera*, LETTER[1]] **1.** able to read and write **2.** well-educated; having or showing extensive knowledge, learning, or culture **3.** [Now Rare] versed in literature —*n.* a literate person —**lit'er·ate·ly** *adv.*

lit·e·ra·ti (lit'ə rät'ē, -rä'tī) *n.pl.* [It. < L. *litterati*, learned, pl. of *litteratus*: see prec.] men of letters; scholarly or learned people

‡**lit·e·ra·tim** (-rät'im, -rät'-) *adv.* [ML. < L. *littera*, LETTER[1]] letter for letter; literally

lit·er·a·ture (lit'ər ə chər, lit'rə choor') *n.* [ME. *litterature* < OFr. < L. *litteratura* < *littera*, LETTER[1]] **1.** the profession of an author; production of writings, esp. of imaginative prose, verse, etc. **2.** *a*) all writings in prose or verse, esp. those of an imaginative or critical character, without regard to their excellence: often distinguished from scientific writing, news reporting, etc. *b*) all of such writings considered as having permanent value, excellence of form, great emotional effect, etc. *c*) all the writings of a particular time, country, region, etc. [*American literature*] *d*) all the writings dealing with a particular subject [the medical *literature*] **3.** all the compositions for a specific musical instrument, voice, or ensemble **4.** [Colloq.] printed matter of any kind, as advertising, campaign leaflets, etc. **5.** [Archaic] acquaintance with books; literary knowledge

-lith (lith) [Fr. *-lithe* < Gr. *lithos*, stone] *a combining form meaning* stone [*eolith, monolith*]

Lith. **1.** Lithuania **2.** Lithuanian

lith. **1.** lithograph **2.** lithography

lith·arge (lith'ärj, li thärj') *n.* [ME. < OFr. *litarge* < L. *lithargyrus* < Gr. *lithargyros*, spume or foam of silver < *lithos*, a stone + *argyros*, silver] an oxide of lead, PbO, used in storage batteries, ceramic cements, paints, etc.

lithe (lith) *adj.* [ME. < OE. *lithe*, soft, mild, akin to OHG. *lindi* < IE. base *lento-*, flexible, bendable, whence L. *lentus*, pliant, flexible & LINDEN] bending easily; flexible; supple; limber; lissome: also **lithe'some** (-səm) —**lithe'ly** *adv.* —**lithe'ness** *n.*

lith·i·a (lith'ē ə) *n.* [ModL. < Gr. *lithos*, stone] lithium oxide, Li₂O, a white, crystalline compound

lith·i·a·sis (li thī'ə sis) *n.* [ModL. < Gr. *lithiasis* < *lithos*, stone] the formation of calculi, or mineral concretions, within the body

lithia water a mineral water containing lithium salts

lith·ic (-ik) *adj.* [Gr. *lithikos* < *lithos*, a stone] **1.** of stone **2.** *Chem.* of lithium **3.** *Med.* of calculi

-lith·ic (lith'ik) *a combining form meaning* of a (specified) stage in the use of stone [*neolithic*]

lith·i·um (lith'ē əm) *n.* [ModL. < LITHIA] a soft, silver-white, metallic chemical element, the lightest known metal: used in thermonuclear explosives, in metallurgy, etc.: symbol, Li; at. wt., 6.939; at. no., 3; sp. gr., 0.534; melt. pt., 179°C; boil. pt., 1317°C

lith·o (lith'ō) *n., pl.* **-os;** *vt., vi.* **-oed, -o·ing** *a clipped form of* LITHOGRAPH

lith·o- (lith'ə) [< Gr. *lithos*, a stone] *a combining form meaning* stone, rock, calculus [*lithosphere, lithograph*]: also, before a vowel, **lith-**

litho., lithog. **1.** lithograph **2.** lithography

lith·o·graph (lith'ə graf', -gräf') *n.* a print made by lithography —*vi., vt.* to make (prints or copies) by this process —**li·thog·ra·pher** (li thäg'rə fər) *n.*

li·thog·ra·phy (li thäg'rə fē) *n.* [LITHO- + -GRAPHY] the art or process of printing from a flat stone or metal plate by a method based on the repulsion between grease and water: the design is put on the surface with a greasy material, and then water and printing ink are successively applied; the greasy parts, which repel water, absorb the ink, but the wet parts do not —**lith·o·graph·ic** (lith'ə graf'ik) *adj.* —**lith·o·graph'i·cal·ly** *adv.*

lith·oid (lith'oid) *adj.* [Gr. *lithoeidēs:* see LITH(O)- & -OID] having the nature of a stone; stonelike: also **li·thoi·dal** (li thoi'd'l)

li·thol·o·gy (li thäl'ə jē) *n.* [LITHO- + -LOGY] **1.** the scientific study of rocks, usually with the unaided eye or with little magnification **2.** loosely, the structure and composition of a rock formation —**lith·o·log·ic** (lith'ə läj'ik), **lith'o·log'i·cal** *adj.* —**lith'o·log'i·cal·ly** *adv.*

lith·o·marge (lith'ə märj') *n.* [< LITHO- + L. *marga*, marl] a smooth, closely packed variety of kaolin

lith·o·me·te·or (lith'ə mēt'ē ər) *n.* [LITHO- + METEOR] solid material, except ice, suspended in the atmosphere, as dust, smoke, pollen, etc.

lith·o·phyte (lith'ə fīt') *n.* [LITHO- + -PHYTE] a plant that grows on rock surfaces —**lith'o·phyt'ic** (-fit'ik) *adj.*

lith·o·pone (-pōn') *n.* [< LITHO- + Gr. *ponos*, a work] a white pigment made by mixing barium sulfate with zinc sulfide, used in paints, linoleum, etc.

lith·o·sphere (-sfir') *n.* [LITHO- + SPHERE] the solid, rocky part of the earth; earth's crust

li·thot·o·my (li thät'ə mē) *n., pl.* **-mies** [LL. *lithotomia* < Gr. *lithotomia:* see LITHO- & -TOMY] *Surgery* the surgical removal of a calculus, or mineral concretion, by cutting into the bladder —**lith·o·tom·ic** (lith'ə täm'ik) *adj.*

li·thot·ri·ty (li thät'rə tē) *n., pl.* **-ties** [< LITHO- + L. *tritus*, pp. of *terere*, to grind, crush] the process of crushing a calculus in the bladder into very small pieces so that it can be eliminated in the urine

Lith·u·a·ni·a (lith'oo wā'nē ə) republic (**Lithuanian Soviet Socialist Republic**) of the U.S.S.R., in NE Europe, on the Baltic Sea: 25,170 sq. mi.; pop. 2,900,000; cap. Vilnius

Lith·u·a·ni·an (-ən) *adj.* of Lithuania, its people, or their language —*n.* **1.** a native or inhabitant of Lithuania **2.** the Baltic language of the Lithuanians

lit·i·ga·ble (lit'i gə b'l) *adj.* that gives cause for litigation, or a lawsuit; actionable

lit·i·gant (lit'ə gənt) *adj.* [Fr. < L. *litigans*] [Rare] engaged in litigation —*n.* a party to a lawsuit

lit·i·gate (-gāt') *vt.* **-gat'ed, -gat'ing** [< L. *litigatus*, pp. of *litigare*, to dispute, carry on a suit < *lis* (gen. *litis*), dispute + *agere*, to do: see ACT] to contest in a lawsuit —*vi.* to carry on a lawsuit —**lit'i·ga'tor** *n.*

lit·i·ga·tion (lit'ə gā'shən) *n.* [LL. *litigatio*] **1.** the act or process of carrying on a lawsuit **2.** a lawsuit

li·ti·gious (li tij'əs) *adj.* [ME. < MFr. *litigieux* < L. *litigiosus* < *litigium*, strife < *litigare:* see LITIGATE] **1.** *a*) given to carrying on lawsuits *b*) quarrelsome **2.** disputable at law **3.** of lawsuits —**li·ti'gious·ly** *adv.* —**li·ti'gious·ness** *n.*

lit·mus (lit'məs) *n.* [ON. *litmose*, lichen used in dyeing < *litr*, color (akin to Goth. *wlits*, face < IE. *wļtu-*, appearance < base *wel-*, to see, whence L. *voltus*, expression, W. *gweled*, to see) + *mosi*, MOSS] a purple coloring matter obtained from various lichens and used as an acid-base indicator in chemical analysis: it turns blue in bases and red in acids

litmus paper absorbent paper treated with litmus and used as an acid-base indicator

li·to·tes (lit'ə tēz) *n.* [Gr. *litotēs* < *litos*, smooth, simple, plain, akin to *leios:* see LIME[1]] understatement for effect, in which something is expressed by a negation of the contrary (Ex.: not a few regrets)

li·tre (lēt'ər) *n. chiefly Brit. sp. of* LITER

Litt.B. [L. *Lit(t)erarum Baccalaureus*] Bachelor of Letters; Bachelor of Literature

Litt.D. [L. *Lit(t)erarum Doctor*] Doctor of Letters; Doctor of Literature

lit·ten (lit'’n) *adj.* [extended < LIT] [Archaic] lighted

lit·ter (lit'ər) *n.* [ME. *litere* < OFr. *litiere* < ML. *literia*, *lectaria* < L. *lectus*, a couch] **1.** a framework having long horizontal shafts near the bottom and enclosing a couch on which a person can be carried **2.** a stretcher for carrying the sick or wounded **3.** straw, hay, leaves, etc. used as bedding for animals, as a protective covering for plants, etc. **4.** the young borne at one time by a dog, cat, or other animal which normally bears several young at a delivery **5.** things lying about in disorder; esp., bits or scraps of rubbish scattered about **6.** untidiness; disorder **7.** *Forestry* the surface layer of the forest floor, in which the leaves are slightly decomposed —*vt.* **1.** to supply with a bed, covering, etc. of straw, hay, or the like **2.** to bring forth (a number of young) at one time: said of certain animals **3.** to make messy or untidy with things scattered about **4.** to scatter about in a careless manner —*vi.* to bear a litter of young

lit·té·ra·teur (lit'ər ə tur'; *Fr.* lē tā rȧ tër') *n.* [Fr.] a literary man; man of letters: also written **litterateur**

☆**lit·ter·bug** (lit'ər bug') *n.* a person who litters highways or other public places with waste paper, garbage, etc.

lit·ter·mate (-māt') *n.* an offspring in a litter in its relation to the others in the litter

lit·ter·y (lit'ər ē) *adj.* covered with litter; untidy

lit·tle (lit''l) *adj.* **lit'tler** *or* **less** *or* **less'er, lit'tlest** *or* **least** [ME. *littel* < OE. *lytel* (akin to G. dial. *lützel*) < base of *lyt*, small (< IE. base *leud-*, to stoop, whence W. *lludded*, fatigue), infl. by ON. *litill*, small (akin to Goth. *leitils*) < IE. base *lei-*, to decline, be lean, whence LESS] **1.** small in size; not big, large, or great **2.** small in amount, number, or degree; not much **3.** short in duration or distance; brief; not long **4.** small in importance or power [the rights of the *little* man] **5.** small in force, intensity, etc.; weak **6.** trivial; trifling **7.** lacking in breadth of vision; narrow-minded; illiberal [a *little* mind] **8.** young: said of children or animals Sometimes used with implications of pleasing or endearing qualities [bless your *little* heart] —*adv.* **less, least 1.** in a small degree; to a slight extent; only slightly; not much **2.** not in the least [he *little* suspects the plot] —*n.* **1.** *a*) a small amount, degree, etc. [a *little* goes a long way] *b*) not much [*little* will be done about it] **2.** a short time or distance —*SYN.* see SMALL —**in little** on a small scale; in miniature **little by little** by slow degrees or small amounts; gradually —**make little of** to consider or treat as not very important; pay little attention to; depreciate —**not a little** very much; very —**lit'tle·ness** *n.*

Little America five operational bases established by the Admiral Byrd expeditions, on the Ross Ice Shelf, Antarctica

Little Bear *same as* URSA MINOR

Little Bighorn river in N Wyo., flowing north into the Bighorn in S Mont.: c. 90 mi.: in a battle near here (**Battle of the Little Bighorn**, 1876) General Custer's troops attacked the Sioux Indians and were annihilated

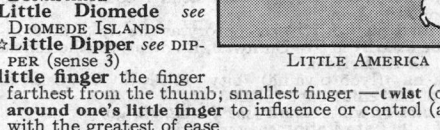

LITTLE AMERICA

Little Corporal *nickname of* NAPOLEON BONAPARTE

Little Diomede *see* DIOMEDE ISLANDS

☆**Little Dipper** *see* DIPPER (sense 3)

little finger the finger farthest from the thumb; smallest finger —**twist** (or **wrap**) **around one's little finger** to influence or control (another) with the greatest of ease

Little Fox *same as* VULPECULA

Little Hours *R.C.Ch.* the hours of prime, terce, sext, and none

Little John *Eng. Legend* a member of Robin Hood's band

Little Khingan Mountains *see* KHINGAN MOUNTAINS

little leaf a disease of stone fruits, apples, grapes, etc., caused by a deficiency of zinc and characterized by crinkled, small leaves and yellowing of the tips of new growth

☆**Little League** a league of baseball teams for boys —**Little Leaguer**

little magazine a noncommercial magazine of limited circulation publishing experimental poetry, fiction, etc.

Little Missouri river in the NW U.S., flowing from Wyo. into the Missouri in N.Dak.: 560 mi.

☆**lit·tle·neck** (lit′'l nek′) *n.* [< *Little Neck*, Long Island] the young of the quahog, a round, thick-shelled clam, usually eaten raw: also **littleneck clam**

Little Office *R.C.Ch.* an office similar to but shorter than the breviary, esp. one in honor of the Virgin Mary

little people the fairies

Little Rock [after a rocky promontory in the river] capital of Ark., on the Arkansas River: pop. 132,000

Little Russian earlier term for UKRAINIAN

little slam *Bridge* the winning of all but one trick

Little St. Bernard Pass mountain pass in the Graian Alps, between France & Italy: 7,178 ft. high

☆**little theater** 1. a small theater, as of a college, art group, etc., usually noncommercial and amateur, that produces experimental drama, often directed at a limited audience 2. drama produced by such theaters

lit·tlish (lit′'l ish) *adj.* rather little

lit·to·ral (lit′ər əl) *adj.* [L. *litoralis* < *litus* (gen. *litoris*), seashore, coast] of, on, or along the shore —*n.* the region along the shore

li·tur·gi·cal (li tur′jə k′l) *adj.* [< Gr. *leitourgikos* + -AL] 1. of or constituting a liturgy 2. used in or using a liturgy —**li·tur′gi·cal·ly** *adv.*

li·tur·gics (-jiks) *n.pl.* [with sing. v.] the study of liturgies, or the forms of public worship

lit·ur·gist (lit′ər jist) *n.* 1. a person who uses, or advocates the use of, a liturgy 2. an authority on liturgies

lit·ur·gy (-jē) *n., pl.* -**gies** [Fr. *liturgie* < ML.(Ec.) *liturgia* < Gr. *leitourgia*, public service to the gods (in LXX & NT., ministry of priests), ult. < *leōs, laos*, people + *ergon*, work] 1. prescribed forms or ritual for public worship in any of various religions or churches 2. the Eucharistic service, esp. (**Divine Liturgy**) in the Orthodox Eastern Church

Lit·vi·nov (lit vē′nôf), **Max·im** (**Maximovich**) (mäk sēm′) 1876-1951; Soviet statesman

liv·a·ble (liv′ə b′l) *adj.* 1. fit or pleasant to live in; habitable: said of a house, room, etc. 2. that can be lived through; endurable: said of life or of a specified sort of existence 3. agreeable to live with (often followed by -*with*): said of a person —**liv′a·bil′i·ty, liv′a·ble·ness** *n.*

live[1] (liv) *vi.* **lived, liv′ing** [ME. *liven* < OE. *libban* (akin to ON. *lifa*, Goth. *liban*, G. *leben*) < base of *lif*, LIFE] 1. to be alive; have life 2. *a)* to remain alive *b)* to last; endure 3. *a)* to pass one's life in a specified manner [to *live* happily] *b)* to regulate or conduct one's life [to *live* by a strict moral code] 4. to enjoy a full and varied life [to really know how to *live*] 5. *a)* to maintain life; support oneself [to *live* on a pension] *b)* to be dependent for a living (with *off*) 6. to feed; subsist; have as one's usual food [to *live* on fruits and nuts] 7. to make one's dwelling; reside 8. to remain in the memory of man [men's good deeds *live* after them] —*vt.* 1. to practice or carry out in one's life [to *live* one's faith] 2. to spend; pass [to *live* a useful life] 3. to act (a role in a play) very convincingly or feelingly —**live and let live** to

as one wishes and let other people do the same; be tolerant —**live down** to live in such a way as to wipe out the memory or shame of (some fault, misdeed, etc.) —**live high** to live in luxury —**live in** to sleep at the place where one is in domestic service —**live it up** [Slang] 1. to have a gay, hilarious time 2. to indulge in pleasures, extravagances, etc. that one usually forgoes —**live out** 1. to live until the end of; last through ☆2. to sleep away from the place where one is in domestic service —**live up to** 1. to live or act in accordance with (one's ideals, reputation, etc.) 2. to fulfill (something expected) —**live well** 1. to live in luxury 2. to lead a virtuous life —**live with** 1. to dwell with; be a lodger at the home of 2. to cohabit with 3. to tolerate; bear; endure —**where one lives** [Slang] in a sensitive or vulnerable area

live[2] (liv) *adj.* [aphetic for ALIVE] 1. having life; not dead 2. of the living state or living beings 3. having positive qualities, as of warmth, vigor, vitality, brightness, brilliance, etc. [a *live* organization, a *live* color] ☆4. of immediate or present interest [a *live* issue] 5. *a)* still burning or glowing [a *live* spark] *b)* not extinct [a *live* volcano] 6. not burned; unstruck [a *live* match] 7. charged for explosion; unexploded [a *live* shell] 8. unused; unexpended [*live* steam] 9. carrying electrical current [a *live* wire] 10. in the native state; not quarried or mined [*live* rocks] 11. having resiliency or elasticity [a *live* rubber ball] 12. fresh; pure: said of the air 13. *a)* involving an appearance or performance in person, rather than a filmed or recorded one; transmitted during the actual performance [a *live* broadcast] *b)* recorded at a public performance 14. *Mech.* imparting motion or power 15. *Printing* set up ready to be printed 16. *Sports* in play [a *live* ball]

live·a·ble (liv′ə b′l) *adj. same as* LIVABLE

live center the center in the revolving spindle of a lathe or other machine on which work is turned

-**lived** (līvd; *occas., by mistaken etym.*, livd) [< ME. *lyved*: see LIFE & -ED] *a combining form meaning* having (a specified kind or duration of) life [short-*lived*]

live-for·ev·er (liv′fər ev′ər) *n. popular name for* SEDUM

live·li·hood (liv′lē hood′) *n.* [ME. *livelode* < OE. *līflad* (**līfgelad*), course of life < *līf*, LIFE + -*lad*, course, akin to OHG. *lībleita*: modern form altered after LIVELY & -HOOD] means of living or of supporting life; subsistence

live load any load not constant in its application, as moving traffic, which a bridge or other structure carries in addition to its own weight

live·long (liv′lôṇ′) *adj.* [ME. *lefe longe*, lit., lief long (cf. LIEF), phr. in which the first word is merely intens., as in G. *die liebe lange nacht*, lit., the lief long night: altered after LIVE[1]] long or tediously long in passing; whole; entire [the *livelong* day]

live·ly (liv′lē) *adj.* -**li·er**, -**li·est** [ME. *liflich* < OE. *liflic*: see LIFE & -LY[1]] 1. full of life; active; vigorous 2. full of spirit; exciting; animated [a *lively* debate] 3. showing or inspiring liveliness; gay; cheerful 4. moving quickly and lightly, as a dance 5. brisk [a *lively* breeze] 6. vivid; keen; intense [*lively* colors] ☆7. bounding back with, or having, great resilience [a *lively* ball] —*adv.* in a lively manner —**live′li·ness** *n.*

SYN.—**lively** implies a being full of life and energy and suggests an active or vigorous quality in something [a *lively* dance, talk, etc.]; **animated** is applied to that which is made alive or bright and suggests a spirited quality [an *animated* face, discussion, etc.]; **vivacious** and, more emphatically, **sprightly** suggest buoyancy of spirit or sparkling brightness [a *vivacious* manner, a *sprightly* tune]; **gay** suggests lightheartedness and unrestrained good spirits [a *gay* life] —**ANT.** dull

liv·en (liv′vən) *vt., vi.* [< LIVE[2] + -EN] to make or become lively or gay; cheer (often with *up*) —**liv′en·er** *n.*

☆**live oak** 1. any of several American oaks; esp., *a)* a widespreading, evergreen oak (*Quercus virginiana*) native to the SE U.S. *b) same as* ENCINA 2. the hard wood of these trees, used in shipbuilding and other construction

liv·er[1] (liv′ər) *n.* [ME. *livere* < OE. *lifer*, akin to G. *leber* < ? IE. base **leip-*, to smear with fat, whence Gr. *liparos*, fat] 1. the largest glandular organ in vertebrate animals, located in the upper or anterior part of the abdomen: it secretes bile, has an important function in the metabolism of carbohydrates, fats, and proteins, and contains a substance essential to the normal production of red blood cells 2. loosely, a similar organ or tissue in invertebrate animals 3. the liver of cattle, fowl, etc. used as food 4. the reddish-brown color of liver 5. [Archaic] the liver thought of as the seat of emotion or desire

liv·er[2] (liv′ər) *n.* a person who lives (in a specified way or place) [a clean *liver*]

liver extract an extract consisting of the water-soluble, nonprotein constituents of fresh mammalian liver, used in treating pernicious anemia

liver fluke any of various trematodes (as

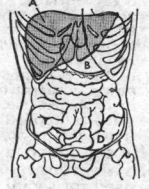

LIVER
(A, liver; B, stomach; C, small intestine; D, large intestine)

Clonorchis sinensis) that in the adult stage live as parasites in the liver of various vertebrates, including man

liv·er·ied (liv′ər ēd, liv′rēd) *adj.* wearing a livery

liv·er·ish (liv′ər ish) *adj.* [Colloq.] **1.** having a disordered liver; bilious **2.** having or displaying a sour disposition; peevish; cross —**liv′er·ish·ness** *n.*

☆**liv·er·leaf** (-lēf′) *n.* same as HEPATICA

Liv·er·more (liv′ər môr′) [after Robt. *Livermore*, a pioneer] city in W Calif., near Oakland: pop. 38,000

Liv·er·pool (liv′ər pōōl′) seaport in NW England, in Lancashire, on the Mersey estuary: pop. 740,000

Liv·er·pud·li·an (liv′ər pud′lē ən) *adj.* [< *Liverpuddle*, jocular alteration of LIVERPOOL + -IAN] of Liverpool or its inhabitants —*n.* a native or inhabitant of Liverpool

liver spot a yellowish-brown, red, or black spot or patch on the skin, formerly attributed to faulty functioning of the liver

liv·er·wort (liv′ər wurt′) *n.* [ME.: see LIVER[1] & WORT[2]: so called from having liver-shaped parts] any of a class (Hepaticae) of bryophytes, often forming dense, green mosslike mats on logs, rocks, or soil in moist places

☆**liv·er·wurst** (-wurst′) *n.* [partial transl. of G. *leberwurst* < *leber*, LIVER[1] + *wurst*, sausage] a sausage containing ground liver: also called **liver sausage**

liv·er·y (liv′ər ē, liv′rē) *n., pl.* -er·ies [ME., allowance of food, gift of clothes to a servant, thing delivered < OFr. *livree*, pp. of *livrer*, to deliver < L. *liberare*, to LIBERATE] **1.** an identifying uniform such as was formerly worn by feudal retainers or is now worn by servants or those in some particular group, trade, etc. **2.** the people wearing such uniforms **3.** characteristic dress or appearance **4.** *a)* the keeping and feeding of horses for a fixed charge *b)* the keeping of horses, vehicles, or both, for hire ☆*c)* same as LIVERY STABLE ☆**5.** a place where boats can be had for hire **6.** *Law* the legal delivery of property, esp. landed property, into the hands of the new owner

livery company any of the London city companies that grew out of earlier trade guilds, characterized by distinctive ceremonial dress

liv·er·y·man (-mən) *n., pl.* -men (-mən) **1.** formerly, a liveried retainer or servant **2.** a member of a livery company **3.** a person who owns or works in a livery stable

livery stable a stable where horses and carriages can be had for hire, or where horses are kept for a fixed charge

lives (līvz) *n. pl.* of LIFE

☆**live steam** steam that comes directly from the boiler before its expansion in work, as distinguished from exhaust steam

live·stock (līv′stäk′) *n.* domestic animals kept for use on a farm or raised for sale and profit

live wire 1. a wire carrying an electric current ☆**2.** [Colloq.] a person who is energetic and enterprising

liv·id (liv′id) *adj.* [< Fr. or L.: Fr. *livide* < L. *lividus*, akin to *livere*, to be black and blue < IE. *(s)līwos-* < base *(s)li-*, bluish, whence SLOE, OSlav. *sliva*, plum] **1.** discolored by a bruise; black-and-blue **2.** grayish-blue; lead-colored *[livid* with rage]: sometimes taken to mean pale, white, or red —*SYN.* see PALE[1] —**li·vid·i·ty** (li vid′ə tē), **liv′id·ness** *n.*

liv·ing (liv′iŋ) *adj.* **1.** alive; having life; not dead **2.** full of vigor; in active operation or use *[a living* institution] **3.** of persons alive *[within living* memory] **4.** in its natural state or place, or having its natural force, motion, etc. *[hewn from the living* rock, a *living* stream] **5.** still spoken and undergoing changes *[a living* language] **6.** true to reality; lifelike *[the living* image of his brother] **7.** of life or the sustaining of life *[living* conditions] **8.** suited for social and recreational activities in a house *[the living* area] **9.** presented in person before a live audience *[living* theater] **10.** very *[the living* daylights] —*n.* **1.** the state of being alive **2.** the means of sustaining life; livelihood *[to work for a living]* **3.** manner of existence *[the standard of living]* **4.** in England, a church benefice —**the living** those that are still alive

SYN.—**living** and **alive**, the latter usually a predicate adjective, are the simple, basic terms for organisms having life or existence; **living** figuratively connoting continued existence or activity *[a living* faith] and **alive**, full force or vigor *[prejudices kept alive* by ignorance]; **animate**, opposed to **inanimate**, is applied to living organisms as distinguished from lifeless ones or inorganic objects; **animated** is applied to inanimate things to which life or, in extended use, motion has been imparted *[animated* cartoons]; **vital** is applied to that which is essential to organic life *[vital* functions] or to the energy, force, etc. manifested by living things

living death a life of unrelieved misery

living room ☆a room in a home, with sofas, chairs, etc., used for social activities, entertaining guests, etc.

Liv·ing·ston (liv′iŋ stən), **Robert R.** 1746–1813; Am. statesman: helped draft the Declaration of Independence

Liv·ing·stone (liv′iŋ stən), **David** 1813–73; Scot. missionary & explorer in Africa

living wage a wage sufficient to enable a person to maintain himself and his family in reasonable comfort

Li·vo·ni·a (li vō′nē ə) former province (1783–1918) of Russia, on the Gulf of Riga: divided (1918) between Latvia & Estonia **2.** [after prec.] city in SE Mich.: suburb of Detroit: pop. 67,000 —**Li·vo′ni·an** *adj., n.*

Li·vor·no (lē vôr′nô) *It.* name of LEGHORN

li·vre (lē′vər; *Fr.* lē′vr′) *n.* [Fr. < L. *libra*, a pound] a former French monetary unit and coin, orig. equivalent in value to a pound of silver

Liv·y (liv′ē) (L. name *Titus Livius*) 59 B.C.–17 A.D.; Rom. historian

lix·iv·i·ate (lik siv′ē āt′) *vt.* -at′ed, -at′ing [see LIXIVIUM & -ATE[1]] same as LEACH —**lix·iv′i·a′tion** *n.*

lix·iv·i·um (lik siv′ē əm) *n., pl.* -i·ums, -i·a (-ə) [LL. < L. *lixivius*, made into lye < *lix*, ashes, lye, akin to *liquere*: see LIQUID] a solution obtained by leaching, as lye

liz·ard (liz′ərd) *n.* [ME. *lesard* < OFr. < L. *lacerta*, lizard: see LEG] **1.** any of a suborder (Sauria) of reptiles characterized by a long slender body and tail, a scaly skin, and four legs, sometimes merely vestigial: most species live in hot, dry regions, as the gecko, horned toad, chameleon, and iguana **2.** loosely, any of various similar reptiles or other animals, as alligators or salamanders

lizard fish any of a family (Synodontidae) of small, brightly colored sea fishes, with a slender body, lizardlike head, and large mouth

Lizard Head (or **Point**) promontory at the tip of a peninsula (**The Lizard**) in SW Cornwall, England: southernmost point of Great Britain

Lju·blja·na (lyōō′blyä nä) city in NW Yugoslavia; capital of Slovenia: pop. 157,000

'll contraction of will or shall *[she'll* sing, *I'll* go]

LL., L.L. 1. Late Latin **2.** Low Latin

ll., ll lines

lla·ma (lä′mə) *n., pl.* -mas, -ma: see PLURAL, II, D, 1 [Sp. < Quechua] **1.** any of a species (*Lama peruana*) of domesticated S. American animals related to the camel but smaller and without humps: some are used as beasts of burden and as sources of wool, meat, and milk **2.** cloth made from the woolly hair of this animal **3.** general term for llama, alpaca, guanaco, and vicuña

Llan·el·ly (lä nel′ē; *W.* hlä ne′ hlē) seaport in Carmarthenshire, SW Wales: pop. 30,000

lla·no (lä′nō; *Sp.* lyä′nō) *n., pl.* -nos (-nōz; *Sp.* -nōs) [Sp. < L. *planus*, plain, PLANE[1]] any of the level, grassy plains covering large areas in Spanish America

LLAMA
(about 4 ft. high at shoulder)

Llano Es·ta·ca·do (lä′nō es′tə kä′dō) [Sp., staked plain] extensive high plain in W Tex. & SE N.Mex.; S extension of the Great Plains: c. 40,000 sq. mi.

LL.B. [L. *Legum Baccalaureus*] Bachelor of Laws

LL.D. [L. *Legum Doctor*] Doctor of Laws

Llew·el·lyn (loo wel′ən) [W. *Llewelyn*, lit., prob., lionlike] a masculine name

LL.M. [L. *Legum Magister*] Master of Laws

Lloyd (loid) [W. *Llwyd*, lit., gray] a masculine name

Lloyd George, David, 1st Earl Lloyd-George of Dwyfor, 1863–1945; Brit. statesman; prime minister (1916–22)

Lloyd's (loidz) *n.* [< *Lloyd's* coffeehouse, meeting place of the original association] an association of insurance underwriters in London formed in the early 18th cent. to subscribe marine insurance policies and to publish shipping news: it now handles many kinds of insurance and publishes an annual descriptive list (**Lloyd's Register**) of the seagoing vessels of all countries

L.M. 1. Licentiate in Medicine **2.** Licentiate in Midwifery **3.** Lord Mayor

lo (lō) *interj.* [ME. < OE. *la*] look! see!: now mainly in **lo and behold!**

loach (lōch) *n.* [ME. *loche* < OFr.] any of various small, old-world freshwater fishes (family Cobitidae), with barbels around the mouth

load (lōd) *n.* [ME. *lode* < OE. *lad*, a course, way, journey < Gmc. base *laido*, way < IE. base *leit(h)-*, to go, leave, whence LEAD[1], ON. *litha*, Goth. *galeithan*, to go: sense infl. by ME. *laden*, LADE] **1.** something carried or to be carried at one time or in one trip; burden; cargo **2.** the amount that can be or usually is carried: a measure of weight or quantity varying with the type of conveyance, often used in combination *[a carload* of coal] **3.** something carried with difficulty; specif., *a)* a heavy burden or weight *b)* a great mental or spiritual burden *[a load* off one's mind] **4.** the weight that a structure bears or the stresses that are put upon it **5.** a single charge, as of powder and bullets, for a firearm ☆**6.** the amount of work carried by or assigned to a person, group, etc. *[the class load* of a teacher, the *case-load* of a social worker] **7.** *[often in pl.]* [Colloq.] a great amount or number *[loads* of friends] **8.** *Elec. a)* the amount of power delivered by a generator, motor, etc. or carried by a circuit *b)* a device to which this power is delivered **9.** *Mech.* the amount of work performed by an engine, etc.; specif., the external resistance offered to an engine by the machine that it is operating —*vt.* **1.** to put something to be carried into or upon; esp., to fill or cover with as much as can be carried *[to load* a wagon with wheat] **2.** to put into or upon a carrier *[to load* coal into a truck] **3.** to weigh down with or as with a heavy load; burden; oppress **4.** to supply in large quantities; give much of something to

[to load a person with honors, a novel loaded with suspense] **5.** to put a charge of ammunition into (a firearm, etc.) **6.** to put (a roll of film or a plate) into (a camera) **7.** to add weight to, esp. so as to make one end or one side heavier *[dice fraudulently loaded]* to fall with a certain face up *f* **8.** to add extra or excessive costs, profits, etc. to *[to load an expense account]* **9.** to add (an adulterant, filler, etc.) to **10.** to phrase (a question, etc.) so as to elicit a desired answer or reaction ☆**11.** *Baseball* to have or cause to have runners on (first, second, and third bases) —*vi.* **1.** to put a charge of ammunition into a firearm **2.** to receive a charge of ammunition *[mortars that load at the muzzle]* **3.** to receive or take on passengers, goods, fuel, etc. *[the bus is loading]* —☆**get a load of** [Slang] **1.** to listen to or hear **2.** to look at or see —**have a load on** [Slang] to be intoxicated —**load′er** *n.* —**load′ing** *n.*

load displacement the displacement of a completely loaded ship

load·ed (-id) *adj.* **1.** carrying a load **2.** filled, charged, weighted, etc. (as indicated by various senses of *load, v.*) **3.** [Slang] under the influence of liquor or drugs ☆**4.** [Slang] well supplied with money

load factor *Elec.* the ratio of average load to greatest load

load·ing (-in) *n.* **1.** the act of one that loads **2.** the thing with which something is loaded **3.** the part of the cost of insurance premiums, stock shares, of mutual funds, etc. added to cover selling and administering expenses, etc. **4.** *same as* WING LOADING

loading coil a coil placed in an electric circuit, as of a telephone cable, to increase its inductance

load line any of the lines along the sides of a ship marking the level to which the ship sinks when loaded under various conditions

load·star (lōd′stär′) *n. same as* LODESTAR

load·stone (lōd′stōn′) *n. same as* LODESTONE

loaf[1] (lōf) *n., pl.* **loaves** (lōvz) [ME. *lof* < OE. *hlaf*, akin to G. *laib*, ON. *hleifr*] **1.** a portion of bread baked in one piece, commonly of oblong shape and in a size convenient for table use **2.** any mass of food shaped somewhat like a loaf of bread and baked *[a salmon loaf]* **3.** a mass of sugar shaped like a cone **4.** [Brit. Slang] head or brain

☆**loaf**[2] (lōf) *vi.* [prob. back-formation < ff.] to spend time idly; loiter or lounge about; idle, dawdle, etc. —*vt.* to spend (time) idly (often with *away*)

☆**loaf·er** (-ər) *n.* [prob. contr. < *land-loafer* < G. *landläufer*, a vagabond (akin to Du. *landlooper*, obs. E. *landloper*) < *land*, LAND + *laufen*, to run (see LEAP)] a person who loafs; lounger; idler —[L-] *a trademark for* a moccasinlike sport shoe for informal wear; also, [l-] a shoe like this

loam (lōm) *n.* [ME. *lome* < OE. *lam:* for IE. base see LIME[1]] **1.** a rich soil composed of clay, sand, and some organic matter **2.** a mixture of clay, sand, and straw used in making foundry molds, plastering, etc. **3.** popularly, any rich, dark soil —*vt.* to fill or cover with loam —**loam′y** *adj.* **loam′i·er, loam′i·est**

loan (lōn) *n.* [ME. *lone* < ON. *lān* (akin to OE. *læn*, lending, loan, *lænan*, to lend) < IE. base *leikw-*, to leave behind, whence L. *linquere*, Gr. *leipein*, Sans. *riṇákti*, (he) leaves] **1.** the act of lending, esp. to use for a short time *[the loan of a pen]* **2.** something lent; esp., a sum of money lent, often for a specified period and repayable with interest —*vt., vi.* to lend —**on loan** lent for temporary use or service to another by the owner, regular employer, etc.

loan collection a collection of pictures, curios, etc. lent for temporary public exhibition

loan·er (-ər) *n.* **1.** a person who loans something **2.** an automobile, radio, typewriter, etc. on loan to a customer while his own is being repaired

☆**loan shark** [Colloq.] a person who lends money at exorbitant or illegal rates of interest

loan·shift (-shift′) *n.* a word borrowed from another language in which native morphemes have replaced some of the original ones in the borrowed word (Ex.: SMEARCASE < G. *schmierkäse*)

loan translation *same as* CALQUE (sense 1)

loan·word (-wurd′) *n.* [after G. *lehnwort*] a word of one language taken into another and naturalized (Ex.: KINDERGARTEN < G., CHAUFFEUR < Fr.)

loath (lōth) *adj.* [ME. *loth* < OE. *lath*, hostile, hateful, akin to G. *leid*, sorrow (orig. *adj.*) < IE. base *leit-*, to detest, abhor, whence Gr. *aleitēs*, sinner] unwilling; reluctant (usually followed by an infinitive) *[to be loath to depart]* —SYN. see RELUCTANT —**nothing loath** not reluctant(ly); willing(ly) —**loath′ness** *n.*

loathe (lōth) *vt.* **loathed, loath′ing** [ME. *lothen* < OE. *lathian*, to be hateful < base of *lath:* see prec.] to feel intense dislike, disgust, or hatred for; abhor; detest —SYN. see HATE —**loath′er** *n.*

loath·ful (lōth′fəl) *adj. rare var. of* LOATHSOME

loath·ing (-in) *n.* [ME. *lothynge*] intense dislike, disgust, or hatred; abhorrence —SYN. see AVERSION

loath·ly[1] (lōth′lē) *adv.* [ME. *lothlie* < OE. *lathlice:* see LOATH & -LY[2]] [Rare] unwillingly; reluctantly

loath·ly[2] (lōth′lē) *adj.* [ME. *lothely* < OE. *lathlice:* see LOATHE & -LY[1]] *rare var. of* LOATHSOME

loath·some (lōth′səm, lōth′-) *adj.* [ME. *lothsum*] causing loathing; disgusting; abhorrent; detestable —**loath′some·ly** *adv.* —**loath′some·ness** *n.*

loaves (lōvz) *n. pl. of* LOAF[1]

lob (läb) *n.* [ME. *lobbe-* (in *lobbe-keling*, large codfish), heavy, thick, akin to EFris., MLowG. *lobbe*, hanging lump of flesh] **1.** [Brit. Dial.] a big, slow, clumsy person **2.** *Cricket* a slow underhand throw **3.** *Tennis* a stroke in which the ball is sent high into the air, usually so as to drop into the back of the opponent's court —*vt.* **lobbed, lob′bing** to throw, toss, etc. slowly and in a high curve; send (a ball) in a lob —*vi.* **1.** to move heavily and clumsily (often with *along*) **2.** to lob a ball —**lob′ber** *n.*

Lo·ba·chev·ski (lō′bä chyef′skē), **Ni·ko·lai I·va·no·vich** (nē kō lī′ ē vä′nō vich) 1793–1856; Russ. mathematician

lo·bar (lō′bər, -bär) *adj.* [ModL. *lobaris*] of a lobe or lobes *[lobar* pneumonia]

lo·bate (-bāt) *adj.* [ModL. *lobatus*] having or formed into a lobe or lobes —**lo′bate·ly** *adv.*

lo·ba·tion (lō bā′shən) *n.* **1.** the condition of having lobes **2.** the process of forming lobes **3.** a lobe

lob·by (läb′ē) *n., pl.* **-bies** [LL. *lobia:* see LODGE] **1.** a hall or large anteroom, as a waiting room or vestibule of an apartment house, hotel, theater, etc. **2.** a large hall adjacent to the assembly hall of a legislature and open to the public ☆**3.** a group of lobbyists representing the same special interest *[the oil lobby]* —☆*vi.* **-bied, -by·ing** to act as a lobbyist —☆*vt.* to get or try to get legislators to vote for or against (a measure) by acting as a lobbyist (often with *through*)

☆**lob·by·ist** (-ist) *n.* a person, acting for a special interest group, who tries to influence the introduction of or voting on legislation or the decisions of government administrators —**lob′by·ism** *n.*

lobe (lōb) *n.* [Fr. < LL. *lobus* < Gr. *lobos* < IE. base *lob-*, var. of *leb-*, to hang loosely: cf. LABOR, LAP[1], SLEEP] a rounded projecting part; specif., *a)* the fleshy lower end of the human ear *b)* any of the main divisions of an organ separated by fissures, etc. *[a lobe of the brain, lung, or liver]* *c)* any of the rounded divisions of the leaves of certain trees *d)* any of the loops in the radiation pattern of a television antenna

lo·bec·to·my (lō bek′tə mē) *n., pl.* **-mies** [prec. + -ECTOMY] the surgical removal of a lobe, as of the brain

lobed (lōbd) *adj.* **1.** *same as* LOBATE **2.** *Bot.* having major divisions which extend almost to the base or center, as the leaves of oaks or maples

lo·be·li·a (lō bē′lyə, -bē′lē ə) *n.* [ModL., after *Lobelius*, Latinized name of Matthias de *L'Obel* (1538–1616), Fl. botanist] any of a genus (*Lobelia*) of annual or perennial plants of the bellflower family, having white, blue, or red flowers of very irregular shape

lo·be·line (lō′bə lēn′, -lin) *n.* [< ModL. *Lobelia* (see prec.) + -INE[4]] a yellow, crystalline, poisonous alkaloid, $C_{22}H_{27}NO_2$, related to nicotine, used in medicine

lob·lol·ly (läb′läl′ē) *n., pl.* **-lies** [16th-c., prob. < dial. *lob*, to bubble, boil + dial. *lolly*, broth, soup] **1.** [Dial.] a thick gruel ☆**2.** [Dial.] a mudhole; muddy puddle ☆**3.** *a)* a common pine (*Pinus taeda*) of the SE U.S., having long needles borne in pairs or threes *b)* the wood of this tree: also **loblolly pine**

☆**loblolly bay** an evergreen tree (*Gordonia lasianthus*) of the tea family, found in the SE U.S. and having large, white, fragrant flowers

☆**lo·bo** (lō′bō) *n.* [Sp. < L. *lupus:* see WOLF] *same as* GRAY WOLF

lo·bot·o·my (lō bät′ə mē) *n., pl.* **-mies** [< LOBE + -TOMY] a surgical operation in which a lobe of the brain, esp. the frontal lobe of the cerebrum, is cut into or across, as in the treatment of certain psychoses

lob·scouse (läb′skous′) *n.* [*lob* (as in LOBLOLLY) + *scouse* < ?] a sailor's stew of meat, vegetables, and hardtack

lob·ster (läb′stər) *n., pl.* **-sters, -ster:** see PLURAL, II, D, 1 [ME. < OE. *loppestre, lopustre* < *loppe*, spider (from the external resemblance) + *-estre:* see -STER] **1.** any of a group of large, edible sea crustaceans (genus *Homarus*), with compound eyes, long antennae, and five pairs of legs, the first pair of which are modified into large, powerful pincers: lobsters are greenish or dark gray in color when alive, but turn bright red when boiled **2.** any of several similar crustaceans, as the spiny lobster **3.** the flesh of these animals used as food

LOBSTER
(to 24 in. long)

lobster pot a basketlike trap for catching lobsters

☆**lobster shift** (or **trick**) [< ?] [Colloq.] the night shift of a newspaper staff, or now of any working force

lobster tail 1. a tail of any of various crustaceans, as the Cape crayfish **2.** the flesh of such a tail prepared as food, often by broiling in the shell

lobster ther·mi·dor (thur′mə dôr′) [cf. THERMIDOR] a dish consisting of lobster flesh, mushrooms, etc. in a sauce, served in half of a lobster shell

lob·ule (läb′yōōl) n. [ModL. *lobulus*, dim.] 1. a small lobe 2. a subdivision of a lobe —**lob′u·lar** (-yoo lər) adj. —**lob′u·late′** (-lāt′) adj.

lob·worm (läb′wurm′) n. same as LUGWORM

lo·cal (lō′k'l) adj. [ME. *locall* < OFr. *local* < LL. *localis* < L. *locus*, a place < IE. *stlokos* < base *stel*-, to set up, stand, location, whence STALK¹, STALL¹, STILL¹, Gr. *stellein*, to put] 1. relating to place 2. of, characteristic of, or confined to a particular place or district [items of *local* interest] 3. not broad; restricted; narrow [*local* outlook] 4. of or for a particular part or specific area of the body; not general ☆5. making all stops along its run [a *local* bus] —n. ☆1. a local train, bus, etc. ☆2. a newspaper item of local interest only ☆3. a chapter or branch of a larger organization, esp. of a labor union 4. [Brit. Colloq.] a neighborhood pub

local color ways of behaving or talking and other features characteristic of a certain region or time, introduced into a novel, play, etc. to supply realism

lo·cale (lō kal′) n. [Fr. *locale*] a place or locality, esp. with reference to events or circumstances connected with it, often as a setting for a story, play, etc.

local government 1. government of the affairs of a town, district, etc. by the people living there 2. the people chosen to administer this government

lo·cal·ism (lō′k'l iz'm) n. 1. a way of acting or speaking peculiar to one locality; local custom or locution 2. a word, meaning, expression, pronunciation, etc. peculiar to one locality 3. fondness for a particular locality 4. narrow outlook; provincialism

lo·cal·i·ty (lō kal′ə tē) n., pl. -ties [Fr. *localité* < LL. *localitas*: see LOCAL] 1. position with regard to surrounding objects, landmarks, etc. [a sense of *locality*] 2. a place; district; neighborhood

lo·cal·ize (lō′kə līz′) vt. -ized′, -iz′ing 1. to make local; limit or confine to a particular place, area, or locality 2. to determine the specific local origin of, as a tradition 3. to concentrate in one area, esp. of the body —**lo′cal·iz′a·ble** adj. —**lo′cal·i·za′tion** n.

lo·cal·iz·er (-ər) n. a directional radio beam designed to assist an airplane in landing to align itself with the runway

lo·cal·ly (lō′k'l ē) adv. 1. in a local way; with respect to place 2. within a given area or areas [the damage done by a tornado *locally*]

local option the right of determining by a vote of the residents whether something, esp. the sale of intoxicating liquors, shall be permitted in their locality

Lo·car·no (lō kär′nō) town in S Switzerland, on Lake Maggiore: site of peace conference (1925): pop. 11,000

lo·cate (lō′kāt, lō kāt′) vt. -cat·ed, -cat·ing [< L. *locatus*, pp. of *locare*, to place < *locus*: see LOCAL] 1. to mark off or designate the site of (a mining claim, etc.) 2. to establish in a certain place [offices *located* downtown] 3. to discover the position of after a search [to *locate* a lost object] 4. to show the position of [to *locate* Guam on a map] 5. to assign to a particular place, function, occupation, etc. —vi. ☆[Colloq.] to make one's home or headquarters; settle [to *locate* in Boston] —**lo′cat·er, lo′ca·tor** n.

lo·ca·tion (lō kā′shən) n. [L. *locatio*] 1. a locating or being located 2. position in space; place where a factory, house, etc. is or is to be; situation 3. an area marked off or designated for a specific purpose ☆4. *Motion Pictures* an outdoor set or setting, away from the studio, where scenes are photographed: chiefly in **on location** —**lo·ca′tion·al** adj.

loc·a·tive (läk′ə tiv) adj. [< L. *locatus* (see LOCATE) + -IVE, after VOCATIVE] *Linguis.* designating or of a case expressing place at which or in which, as in Latin, Greek, Sanskrit, etc. —n. 1. the locative case 2. a word in the locative case

loc. cit. [L. *loco citato*] in the place cited

loch (läk, läkh) n. [ME. *louch* < Gael. & OIr.: for IE. base see LAKE¹] [Scot.] 1. a lake 2. an arm of the sea, esp. when narrow and nearly surrounded by land

lo·chi·a (lō′kē ə, läk′ē ə) n. [ModL. < Gr. *lochia*, neut. pl. of *lochios*, of childbirth < *lochos*, childbirth < IE. *loghos*, bed < base *legh*-, to lie down, whence LIE¹] the uterine discharge from the vagina after childbirth

Loch·in·var (läk′in vär′) the hero of a ballad in Scott's *Marmion*, who boldly rides off with his sweetheart just as she is about to be married to another

lo·ci (lō′sī) n. pl. of LOCUS

lock¹ (läk) n. [ME. < OE. *loc*, a bolt, bar, enclosure, prison, akin to G. *loch*, a hole, ON. *lok*, a lid, prob. IE. base *leug*-, to bend, whence Gr. *lygos*, supple twig, L. *luctāri*, to struggle] 1. a mechanical device furnished with a bolt and, usually, a spring, for fastening a door, strongbox, etc. by means of a key or combination 2. anything that fastens something else and prevents it from opening, turning, etc. 3. a locking together; jam 4. an enclosed part of a canal, waterway, etc. equipped with gates so that the level of the water can be changed to raise or lower boats from one level to another 5. the mechanism of a firearm used to explode the ammunition charge 6. same as AIR LOCK (sense 1) 7. *Wrestling* a hold in which a part of the opponent's body is firmly gripped [armlock]

—vt. 1. to fasten (a door, trunk, etc.) by means of a lock 2. to keep from going in or out; shut (up, in, or out); confine [*locked* in jail] 3. to fit closely; link; intertwine [to *lock* arms] 4. to embrace tightly 5. to jam or force together so as to make immovable [*locked* gears, *locked* brakes] 6. to put in a fixed position [a throttle *locked* in the idle position] ☆7. to equip (a canal, etc.) with a lock or locks 8. to move or pass (a ship) through a lock 9. *Printing* to fasten (type elements) in a chase or on the bed of a press by means of quoins (often with *up*) —vi. 1. to become locked 2. to be capable of being locked 3. to intertwine or interlock; link together 4. to close tightly and firmly [his jaws *locked*] 5. to jam, as gears 6. to pass through the locks of a canal —**lock away** to store or safeguard in a locked box, container, etc. —**lock on** *Aeron.* to track and automatically follow a target, as by radar —**lock out** 1. to shut out by or as by locking the door against 2. to keep (workers) from a place of employment in seeking to force terms upon them —**lock, stock, and barrel** [Colloq.] completely; entirely —**lock up** 1. to fasten the doors of (a house, etc.) by means of locks 2. to enclose or store in a locked container 3. to put in jail 4. to make certain to have the result one wants [to have an election *locked up*] —**under lock and key** locked up; safely put away

lock² (läk) n. [ME. *lokke* < OE. *loc* (akin to G. *locke*): basic sense "a bend, twist": IE. base as in *lock¹*] 1. a curl, tress, or ringlet of hair 2. [pl.] [Poet.] the hair of the head 3. a tuft of wool, cotton, etc.

lock·age (läk′ij) n. 1. the act of moving a ship from one water level to another by means of a lock 2. the charge for such service 3. the construction or operation of locks in a canal, etc. 4. the amount of rise and fall effected by locks in a canal

Locke (läk) 1. **David Ross**, see Petroleum V. NASBY 2. **John**, 1632–1704; Eng. empirical philosopher

lock·er (-ər) n. 1. a person or thing that locks 2. a) a chest, closet, compartment, drawer, etc., usually of metal, which can be fastened with a lock, esp. such a container for individual or specified use ☆b) same as FOOTLOCKER ☆3. a large compartment, as one rented in a cold-storage plant, for freezing and storing foods at or below 0°F

☆**locker room** a room equipped with lockers, as at a gymnasium, swimming pool, factory, etc., for storing one's clothes and equipment

lock·et (läk′it) n. [OFr. *loquet*, dim. of *loc*, a latch, lock < Frank. *lok*, akin to OE. *loc*, LOCK¹] a small, hinged, ornamental case of gold, silver, etc. for holding a picture, lock of hair, etc.; it is usually worn suspended from a necklace or chain

lock·jaw (läk′jô′) n. [short for earlier *locked jaw*] same as TETANUS (sense 1)

lock·mas·ter (-mas′tər) n. one in charge of a canal lock

lock·nut (-nut′) n. 1. a thin nut screwed down hard on an ordinary nut to prevent the latter from working loose 2. a specially designed nut that locks itself when screwed down tight: also **lock nut**

lock·out (-out′) n. the refusal by an employer to allow his employees to come in to work until they agree to his terms

lock·smith (-smith′) n. a person whose work is making or repairing locks and keys

lock step a way of marching in such close file that the corresponding legs of the marchers must keep step precisely

lock stitch the typical sewing-machine stitch formed by the interlocking of two threads

lock·up (-up′) n. 1. the act of locking up 2. a being locked up, as in jail 3. a jail

☆**lo·co** (lō′kō) n. [MexSp. < Sp., mad < L. *ulucus*, owl, akin to *ulula*: see OWL] [Western] 1. same as LOCOWEED 2. same as LOCO DISEASE —vt. -coed, -co·ing 1. to poison with locoweed 2. [Slang] to craze —adj. [Slang] crazy; demented

lo·co- (lō′kə, -kō) [< L. *locus*, a place: see LOCAL] a combining form meaning from place to place [*locomotive*]

‡**lo·co ci·ta·to** (lō′kō si tät′ō) [L.] in the place cited or quoted: referring to a previously cited passage

☆**loco disease** a nervous disease of horses, sheep, and cattle caused by locoweed poisoning: also **lo·co·ism** (lō′kō iz'm) n.

☆**lo·co·fo·co** (lō′kō fō′kō) n., pl. -cos [coined (c. 1834) after LOCO(MOTIVE), interpreted as "self-(moving)" + It. *fuoco*, fire < L. *focus*: see FOCUS: sense 2 from the use of such matches in Tammany Hall, Oct. 22, 1835, by one faction to restore lights extinguished by another] 1. orig., a cigar or match ignited by friction 2. a) [L-] a faction of the Democratic Party in New York (c. 1835), called the Equal Rights party b) a member of this faction 3. formerly, any Democrat

lo·co·mo·bile (lō′kə mō′b'l) adj. [*loco*- (cf. *prec.*) + MOBILE] [Rare] moving by its own power; self-propelling

lo·co·mo·tion (-mō′shən) n. [LOCO- + MOTION] motion, or the power of moving, from one place to another

lo·co·mo·tive (-mō′tiv) adj. [< LOCO- + LL. *motivus*, moving] 1. of locomotion 2. moving or capable of moving from one place to another; not stationary 3. designating or of engines that move under their own power [*locomotive* design] —n. an engine that can move about by its own

power, esp., an electric, steam, or diesel engine on wheels, designed to push or pull a railroad train

lo·co·mo·tor (lō′kə mōt′ər) *n.* [LOCO- + L. *motor*, mover] a person or thing with power of locomotion —*adj.* of or relating to locomotion

locomotor ataxia *same as* TABES DORSALIS

☆**lo·co·weed** (lō′kō wēd′) *n.* any of several perennial plants (genera *Astragalus* and *Oxytropis*) of the legume family, which are common in W N. America and cause the loco disease of cattle, sheep, and, esp., horses

Lo·cris (lō′kris) region of ancient Greece, north of the Gulf of Corinth

loc·u·lar (läk′yə lər) *adj. Biol.* of, having the nature of, or consisting of loculi, or cavities

loc·u·late (-lit, -lāt′) *adj. same as* LOCULAR

loc·u·li·ci·dal (läk′yə li sī′d′l) *adj.* [< ff. + -*i-* + -CIDAL] *Bot.* splitting open along the midribs of the carpels of which it is formed: said of a capsule

loc·u·lus (läk′yə ləs) *n., pl.* -**li** (-lī′) [ModL. < L., dim. of *locus*, place: see LOCAL] any small cavity or chamber in plant or animal tissue: also **loc′ule** (-yool)

lo·cum te·nens (lō′kəm tē′nənz) [ML., holding the place < L. *locum*, acc. of *locus*, a place + *tenens*, prp. of *tenere*, to hold: cf. LIEUTENANT] [Chiefly Brit.] a person taking another's place for the time being; temporary substitute, as for a doctor or clergyman

lo·cus (lō′kəs) *n., pl.* **lo·ci** (-sī) [L.: see LOCAL] **1.** a place **2.** *Genetics* the position on a chromosome occupied by a particular gene **3.** *Math. a)* any system of points, lines, etc. which satisfies one or more given conditions *b)* a line, plane, etc. every point of which satisfies a given condition and which contains no point that does not satisfy this condition

‡**lo·cus clas·si·cus** (lō′kəs klas′i kəs) *pl.* **lo′ci clas′si·ci** (lō′sī klas′i sī′) [L.] a passage often cited as authoritative or illustrative of its subject

‡**locus in quo** (in kwō′) [L.] the place in which

lo·cust (lō′kəst) *n.* [ME. < L. *locusta*, prob. akin to *lacerta*, LIZARD] **1.** any of various large grasshoppers; specif., a migratory grasshopper often traveling in great swarms and destroying nearly all vegetation in areas visited **2.** *same as* SEVENTEEN-YEAR LOCUST ☆**3.** *a)* a spiny tree (*Robinia pseudoacacia*) of the legume family, native to the SW U.S. and having long pendulous racemes of fragrant white flowers: also called **black locust, yellow locust** *b)* the yellowish, hard, durable wood of this tree ☆**4.** *same as* HONEY LOCUST **5.** *same as* CAROB (sense 1)

LOCUST
(to 2 in. long)

lo·cu·tion (lō kyōō′shən) *n.* [ME. < L. *locucion* < L. *locutio*, a speaking < pp. of *loqui*, to speak] **1.** a word, phrase, or expression **2.** a particular style of speech; phraseology

Lod (lōd) city in C Israel: pop. 21,000

lode (lōd) *n.* [sp. var. of LOAD (ME. *lode* < OE. *lad*) retaining etym. senses "course, way"] *Mining* **1.** a vein containing important quantities of metallic ore and filling a well-defined fissure in the rock **2.** any flat deposit of valuable ore separated from the adjoining rock by definite boundaries **3.** any abundant or rich source

lo·den (lō′d′n) *adj.* [G. < MHG. *lode* < OHG. *lodo*, coarse cloth, akin to OE. *lotha*, cloak] **1.** designating or of a fulled, waterproof wool cloth with a short pile, used for coats **2.** of a dark, olive green often used for this cloth

lode·star (lōd′stär′) *n.* [ME. *lodesterre*: see LODE & STAR] **1.** a star by which one directs his course; esp., the North Star **2.** a guiding principle or ideal

lode·stone (-stōn′) *n.* [LODE + STONE] **1.** a strongly magnetic variety of the mineral magnetite **2.** something that attracts as with magnetic force

lodge (läj) *n.* [ME. *loge*, hut, masons' workshop (whence sense 2) < OFr. *loge*, summerhouse, arbor (cf. LOGE) < LL. *lobia* < Gmc. source whence OHG. *louba*, upper roof, porch, leafy cover: for IE. base see LEAF] **1.** *a)* a small house, esp. one for a servant, or one for use during a special season [a caretaker's *lodge*, hunting *lodge*] *b)* a resort hotel or motel **2.** *a)* the meeting place of a local chapter, as of a fraternal organization *b)* such a local chapter **3.** the den or typical lair of certain wild animals, esp. beavers ☆**4.** *a)* the hut or tent of an American Indian *b)* those who live in it —*vt.* **lodged, lodg′ing** [ME. *loggen* < OFr. *logier*] **1.** to provide with a place of temporary residence; house **2.** to rent rooms to; take as a paying guest **3.** to serve as a temporary dwelling for **4.** to serve as a container for **5.** to place or deposit for safekeeping **6.** to put or send into a place or position by shooting, thrusting, etc.; place; land (with *in*) [to *lodge* an arrow in a target] **7.** to bring (an accusation, complaint, etc.) before legal authorities **8.** to confer (powers) upon (with *in*) **9.** to beat down (growing crops), as rain —*vi.* **1.** to live in a certain place for a time; to live (with another or *in* his home) as a paying guest **2.** to come to rest or be placed and remain firmly fixed (with *in*) [a bone *lodged* in her throat]

Lodge (läj) **1. Henry Cabot,** 1850–1924; U.S. senator (1893–1924) **2. Sir Oliver Joseph,** 1851–1940; Eng. physicist & writer

lodg·er (läj′ər) *n.* a person or thing that lodges; esp., one who lives in a rented room in another's home

lodg·ing (-in) *n.* [ME. *loggyng*: see LODGE, *v.*] **1.** the act of one that lodges **2.** a place to live in, esp. temporarily; quarters **3.** [*pl.*] a room or rooms rented in a private home

lodging house *same as* ROOMING HOUSE

lodg·ment (-mənt) *n.* [Fr. *logement*] **1.** a lodging or being lodged **2.** a lodging place **3.** an accumulation of deposited material, often in the nature of an obstruction **4.** *Mil.* a foothold gained in territory held by the enemy Also sp. **lodge′ment**

Lo·di (lō′dē) city in Lombardy, NW Italy: scene of Napoleon's defeat of the Austrians (1796): pop. 37,000

lod·i·cule (läd′i kyōōl′) *n.* [L. *lodicula*, a small coverlet, dim. of *lodix*, a coverlet] one of usually two minute, flat or fleshy outgrowths at the base of the flower of a grass, that swell up at flowering, assisting the escape of anthers and stigmas

Łódź (looj) city in C Poland: pop. 743,000

Loeb (lōb), **Jacques** (zhäk) 1859–1924; U.S. physiologist & biologist, born in Germany

lo·ess (les, lō′es) *n.* [G. *löss*, arbitrary use of dial. *lösch*, loose < base of *lösen*, to loosen: for IE. base see LOSE] a fine-grained, yellowish-brown, extremely fertile loam deposited mainly by the wind and found widely in N. America, Asia, and Europe —**lo·ess′i·al** *adj.*

Loe·wy (lō′ē), **Raymond (Fernand)** 1893– ; U.S. industrial designer, born in France

Lo·fo·ten Islands (lō′fōot ′n) group of Norw. islands off the NW coast of Norway: c. 550 sq. mi.

loft (lôft, läft) *n.* [ME. *lofte* < Late OE. *loft* < ON. *lopt*, upper room, air, sky (akin to OE. *lyft*, air, sky) < IE. base **leup-, *leubh-*, to peel off (whence LEAF)] **1.** *a)* an attic or atticlike space, usually not partitioned off into rooms, immediately below the roof of a house, barn, etc. *b)* any of the upper stories of a warehouse or factory **2.** a gallery [the choir *loft* in a church] **3.** *a)* the slope given to the face of a golf club to aid in knocking the ball in a high curve *b)* the height attained by hitting or throwing a ball in a high curve —*vt.* **1.** to store in a loft **2.** *a)* to hit or throw (a golf ball, baseball, etc.) into the air in a high curve *b)* to throw (a bowling ball) so that it strikes the alley sharply some distance past the foul line —*vi.* to loft a ball —loft′er *n.*

Lof·ting (lôf′tin), **Hugh (John)** 1886–1947; U.S. writer & illustrator, esp. of children's books, born in England

loft·y (lôf′tē) *adj.* **loft′i·er, loft′i·est** **1.** very high [a *lofty* peak in the Alps] **2.** elevated; noble; sublime; grand **3.** haughty; overproud; arrogant —SYN. see HIGH —loft′i·ly *adv.* —loft′i·ness *n.*

log¹ (lôg, läg) *n.* [ME. *logge*, prob. < or akin to ON. *lāg* (Dan. *laag*), felled tree < base of *liggia*, to lie, akin to OE. *licgan*, to LIE¹] **1.** a section of the trunk or of a large branch of a felled tree, either in its natural state or cut up for use in building, as firewood, etc. **2.** [because orig. a quadrant of wood] a device for measuring the speed of a ship: see also LOG CHIP, LOG LINE, LOG REEL **3.** a daily record of a ship's speed and progress; logbook: in it are usually entered the ship's position and any notable events of the trip **4.** *a)* a similar record of an aircraft's flight *b)* a record of a pilot's flying time, experience, etc. **5.** any record of progress or occurrences, as on a journey, in an experiment, etc. —*adj.* made of a log or logs —*vt.* **logged, log′ging** **1.** to saw (trees) into logs ☆**2.** to cut down the trees of (a region) **3.** to enter or record in a log **4.** to sail or fly (a specified distance) **5.** to be credited with a record of (certain accomplishments) —☆*vi.* to cut down trees and transport the logs to a sawmill

log² (lôg, läg) *n. clipped form of* LOGARITHM

-log *same as* -LOGUE

log. logic

Lo·gan (lō′gən), **Mount** mountain in the St. Elias range, SW Yukon, Canada: highest mountain in Canada: 19,850 ft.

☆**lo·gan·ber·ry** (lō′gən ber′ē) *n., pl.* -**ries** [after Judge J. H. *Logan* (1841–1928), of California, who developed it in 1881] **1.** a hybrid bramble (*Rubus loganobaccus*) of the rose family, developed from the blackberry and the red raspberry and extensively grown for its fruit **2.** the highly acid, purplish-red fruit of this shrub

lo·ga·ni·a (lō gā′nē ə) *adj.* [ModL. < James *Logan* (1674–1751), Ir. botanist + -IA] designating a family (Loganiaceae) of chiefly tropical and subtropical, often poisonous plants, including buddleia, nux vomica, and gelsemium

log·a·oe·dic (lôg′ə ē′dic, läg′-) *adj.* [LL. *logaoedicus* < LGr. *logaoidikos* < Gr. *logos*, discourse, prose (see LOGIC) + *aoidē*, song (see ODE)] having a meter of combined dactyls and trochees or anapests and iambs —*n.* a logaoedic verse

log·a·rithm (lôg′ə rith′m, läg′-) *n.* [ModL. *logarithmus* < Gr. *logos*, a word, proportion, ratio (see LOGIC) < *arithmos*, number (see ARITHMETIC)] *Math.* the exponent expressing the power to which a fixed number (the *base*) must be raised in order to produce a given number (the *antilogarithm*): logarithms are normally computed to the base of

10 and are used for shortening mathematical calculations —**log′a·rith′mic** *adj.* —**log′a·rith′mi·cal·ly** *adv.*

log·book (lôg′book′, läg′-) *n. same as* LOG¹ (senses 3, 4, & 5)

log chip a flat piece of wood, usually shaped like a quarter section of a circle, attached to a line and reel and thrown into the water to measure a ship's rate of speed

loge (lōzh) *n.* [Fr.: see LODGE] **1.** a box in a theater **2.** the forward section of a mezzanine or balcony in a theater, set off by an aisle or railing

☆**log·ger** (lôg′ər, läg′-) *n.* a person whose work is logging; lumberjack

log·ger·head (lôg′ər hed′, läg′-) *n.* [dial. *logger,* heavy block of wood (< LOG¹) + HEAD] **1.** a long-handled tool with a ball, or bulb, at the end, used when heated to melt tar, heat liquids, etc. **2.** any of a genus (*Caretta*) of Atlantic sea turtles, with a hard shell and a large head: also **loggerhead turtle 3.** a post on a whaling ship around which a harpoon line is turned to keep it from running out too fast **4.** [Dial.] a stupid fellow; blockhead —**at loggerheads** in disagreement; quarreling

☆**loggerhead shrike** a common N. American shrike (*Lanius ludovicianis*), white below with black markings on the upper parts

log·gi·a (läj′ē ə, lä′jə; lô′-; *It.* lôd′jä) *n., pl.* **-gi·as;** *It.* **log′gie** (-je) [It. < Fr. *loge:* see LODGE] an arcaded or roofed gallery built into or projecting from the side of a building, particularly one over-looking an open court

☆**log·ging** (lôg′iŋ, läg′-) *n.* the occupation of cutting down trees, cutting them into logs, and transporting them to the sawmill

log·i·a (läg′ē ə, lō′gē ə) *n.pl. sing.* **log′i·on** (-än′) [Gr., pl., sayings < *logos,* a word: see ff.] maxims attributed to a religious leader; esp., [L-] sayings attributed to Jesus, esp. those thought to come from hypothetical sources of the Gospels

LOGGIA

log·ic (läj′ik) *n.* [ME. *logike* < OFr. *logique* < L. *logica* < Gr. *logikē* (*technē*), logical (art) < *logikos,* of speaking or reasoning < *logos,* a word, reckoning, thought < *legein,* to speak, calculate, collect < IE. base *leĝ-,* to gather, whence L. *legere,* to collect, OE. *læce,* LEECH¹] **1.** the science of correct reasoning; science which describes relationships among propositions in terms of implication, contradiction, contrariety, conversion, etc.: see also SYMBOLIC LOGIC **2.** a book dealing with this science **3.** correct reasoning; valid induction or deduction [the lack of *logic* in his scheme] **4.** way of reasoning, whether correct or incorrect [to use faulty *logic*] **5.** the system of principles underlying any art or science **6.** necessary connection or outcome, as through the working of cause and effect [the *logic* of events] **7.** the systematized interconnection of digital switching functions, circuits, or devices, as in electronic digital computers

log·i·cal (läj′i k'l) *adj.* [ML. *logicalis*] **1.** of or used in the science of logic **2.** according to the principles of logic, or correct reasoning **3.** necessary or to be expected because of what has gone before; that follows as reasonable **4.** using or accustomed to use correct reasoning —**log′i·cal′i·ty** (-kal′ə tē), **log′i·cal·ness** *n.* —**log′i·cal·ly** *adv.*

-log·i·cal (läj′i k'l) [< Gr. *-logikos* (< LOGIC) + -AL] *an adj.-forming suffix corresponding to* -LOGY [*biological*]: also **-log·ic**

logical positivism a movement in philosophy which tests all statements by reference to experience or the structure of language and is concerned with the unification of the sciences through a common logical language: also called **logical empiricism**

lo·gi·cian (lō jish′ən) *n.* an expert in logic

lo·gis·tic¹ (lō jis′tik) *adj.* of logistics: also **lo·gis′ti·cal** —**lo·gis′ti·cal·ly** *adv.*

lo·gis·tic² (lō jis′tik) *adj.* [ML. *logisticus* < Gr. *logistikos,* skilled in calculation < *logizesthai,* to calculate < *logos,* a word, reckoning: see LOGIC] of calculation —*n.* [Rare] the art of calculation; common arithmetic —**lo·gis′ti·cal·ly** *adv.*

lo·gis·tics (-tiks) *n.pl.* [*with sing. v.*] [Fr. *logistique* < *logis,* lodgings (< *loger,* to quarter: see LODGE): form as if < ML. *logisticus:* see prec.] the branch of military science having to do with procuring, maintaining, and transporting materiel, personnel, and facilities

☆**log·jam** (lôg′jam′, läg′-) *n.* **1.** an obstacle formed by logs jamming together in a stream **2.** an obstacle formed by the accumulation of many items to deal with

log line a graduated line attached to a log chip

log·o (lôg′ō, läg′ō) *n. clipped form of* LOGOTYPE

log·o- (lôg′ō, läg′ō) [Gr. < *logos:* see LOGIC] *a combining form meaning* word, speech, discourse [*logogram*]

log·o·gram (lôg′ə gram′, läg′-) *n.* [prec. + -GRAM] a letter, character, or symbol used to represent an entire word (Ex.: $ for *dollar*): also **log′o·graph′** (-graf′, -gräf′) —**log′o·gram·mat′ic** (-grə mat′ik) *adj.*

lo·gog·ra·phy (lō gäg′rə fē) *n.* [Gr. *logographia,* writing of speeches, office of official recorder in a law court: see LOGO- & GRAPHY] the use of logotypes in printing

log·o·griph (lôg′ə grif′, läg′-) *n.* [LOG- + Gr. *griphos,* fishing basket, riddle, prob. < IE. *grebh-,* whence CRIB] a word puzzle, as an anagram

lo·gom·a·chy (lō gäm′ə kē) *n., pl.* **-chies** [Gr. *logomachia* < *logos,* a word (see LOGIC) + *machē,* a fight, battle] **1.** strife or contention in words only, or an argument about words **2.** a game similar to anagrams

log·or·rhe·a (lôg′ə rē′ə, läg′-) *n.* [ModL.: see LOGO- & -RRHEA] excessive talkativeness, esp. when incoherent and uncontrollable —**log′or·rhe′ic** (-ik) *adj.*

Log·os (läg′äs; lō′gäs, lô′-) *n.* [L. *logos* < Gr. *logos,* a word: see LOGIC] **1.** [*sometimes* l-] *Gr. Philos.* reason, thought of as constituting the controlling principle of the universe and as being manifested by speech **2.** *Christian Theol.* the Word, or ultimate reality; esp., the creative and sustaining spirit of God as revealed in Jesus: John 1

log·o·type (lôg′ə tīp′, läg′-) *n.* [LOGO- + -TYPE] **1.** a single type body or matrix containing a short, often-used set of letters, or word, as *an, qu:* cf. LIGATURE **2.** a distinctive company signature, trademark, colophon, newspaper nameplate, etc.

log reel a reel for winding and unwinding a log line

☆**log·roll** (lôg′rōl′, läg′-) *vi.* [back-formation < LOGROLLING] to take part in logrolling —*vt.* to get passage of (a bill) by logrolling —**log′roll′er** *n.*

☆**log·roll·ing** (-rōl′iŋ) *n.* **1.** the act of rolling logs, as when a group of neighbors help to clear off land by rolling logs into some spot for burning, etc. **2.** *a*) a giving of help, praise, etc. in return for help, praise, etc. *b*) *Politics* mutual aid among politicians, as by reciprocal voting for each other's bills **3.** *same as* BIRLING

-logue (lôg, läg) [Fr. < L. *-logus* < Gr. *-logos* < *logos:* see LOGIC] *a combining form meaning:* **1.** a (specified kind of) speaking or writing [*monologue*] **2.** a student or scholar [*Sinologue*]

log·wood (lôg′wood′, läg′-) *n.* [so called from being imported in logs] **1.** the hard, brownish-red wood of a tropical tree (*Haematoxylon campechianum*) of the legume family, native to Central America and the West Indies: it yields a dye much used in biological stains and formerly for dyeing fabrics **2.** this tree, having thorny branches and small, yellow flowers **3.** the dye

lo·gy (lō′gē) *adj.* **-gi·er, -gi·est** [< ? Du. *log,* heavy, dull] [Colloq.] dull or sluggish, as from overeating —**lo′gi·ness** *n.*

-lo·gy (lə jē) [ME. *-logie* < OFr. < L. *-logia* < Gr. *-logia* < *logos,* word: see LOGIC] *a combining form meaning:* **1.** a (specified kind of) speaking [*eulogy*] **2.** science, doctrine, or theory of [*biology, theology*]

Lo·hen·grin (lō′ən grin′) *Ger. Legend* a knight of the Holy Grail, son of Parsifal

loin (loin) *n.* [ME. *loine* < OFr. *loigne* < VL. *lumbea* < L. *lumbus:* see LUMBAR] **1.** [*usually pl.*] the lower part of the back on either side of the backbone between the hip-bones and the ribs **2.** the front part of the hindquarters of beef, lamb, mutton, veal, etc. with the flank removed: see BEEF, illus. **3.** [*pl.*] the hips and the lower abdomen regarded as a part of the body to be clothed or as the region of strength and procreative power —**gird (up) one's loins** to get ready to do something difficult or strenuous

loin·cloth (-klôth′, -kläth′) *n.* a cloth worn about the loins, as by some tribes in warm climates

Loire (lwär) river flowing from S France north & west into the Bay of Biscay: 625 mi.

Lo·is (lō′is) [LL.(Ec.) < Gr.(Ec.) *Lōis:* cf. II Tim. 1:5] a feminine name

loi·ter (loit′ər) *vi.* [ME. *loitren* < MDu. *loteren* (Du. *leuteren,* to dawdle), akin to OE. *loddere,* beggar < IE. base *(s)leu-,* to hang loosely, whence SLEET, SLUR] **1.** to spend time idly (often with *about*); linger in an aimless way **2.** to walk or move slowly and indolently, with frequent stops and pauses —*vt.* to spend (time) idly —**loi′ter·er** *n.*

SYN.—loiter implies aimlessness or slowness of movement and may suggest a wasting of time in lingering or lagging [to *loiter* around street corners]; **dawdle** implies a wasting of time over trifles or a frittering away of time that makes for slow progress [to *dawdle* over a cup of tea]; **dally** suggests a spending of time in trifling or frivolous pursuits; **idle** suggests habitual avoidance of work, or inactivity, indolence, etc. [to *idle* away the hours]

Lo·ki (lō′kē) [ON.] *Norse Myth.* the god who constantly created discord and mischief

loll (läl) *vi.* [ME. *lollen* < MDu., of echoic orig.] **1.** to lean or lounge about in a relaxed or lazy manner **2.** to hang in a relaxed manner; droop [the dog's tongue *lolled* out] —*vt.* to let droop or hang loosely —*n.* [Archaic] the act of lolling —**loll′er** *n.*

Lol·land (lôl′än) island of Denmark, in the Baltic Sea, south of Zealand: 479 sq. mi.

☆**lol·la·pa·loo·za, lol·la·pa·loo·sa** (läl′ə pə lōō′zə) *n.* [< ?] [Slang] something or someone very striking or exceptional: also **lollypalooza,** etc.

Lol·lard (läl′ərd) *n.* [ME. < MDu. *lollaerd,* lit., mutterer (of prayers, psalms) < *lollen,* to mumble, doze, LOLL] any of the followers of John Wycliffe in 14th- and 15th-cent. England

lol·li·pop, lol·ly·pop (läl′ē päp′) *n.* [child's word: prob. after dial. *lolly,* the tongue + *pop*] a piece of hard candy fixed to the end of a small stick; sucker

lol·lop (läl′əp) *vi.* [extended < LOLL, prob. after GALLOP] [Chiefly Brit.] **1.** to lounge about; loll **2.** to move in a clumsy or relaxed way, bobbing up and down or from side to side

lol·ly (läl′ē) *n., pl.* **-lies** [contr. < LOLLYPOP] [Brit. Slang]
1. money 2. a piece of hard candy
☆**lol·ly·gag** (läl′ē gag′) *vi.* **-gagged′, -gag′ging** [var. of
lallygag < ?] [Colloq.] to waste time in trifling or aimless
activity; fool around
Lo·max (lō′maks), **Alan**, 1915–   , son of **John** (**Avery**),
1867–1948; U.S. collectors of Am. folksongs
Lom·bard (läm′bärd) [after J. L. *Lombard*, local land own-
er] village in NE Ill.: suburb of Chicago: pop. 36,000
Lom·bard (läm′bərd, lum′-; -bärd) *n.* [ME. *Lumbarde*
< ML. *Lombardus* < L. *Langobardus* < Gmc. **lango-*,
LONG¹ + *-barda-*, BEARD] 1. a native or inhabitant of
Lombardy 2. a member of an ancient Germanic tribe
that settled in the Po Valley 3. [from the activity of the
medieval Lombards as pawnbrokers] banker or moneylender —*adj.* of Lombardy or the Lombards —**Lom·bar′-
dic** *adj.*
Lombard Street [after the *Lombard* merchants & bankers
who settled there in the 12th cent.] street in London where
many banks & financial houses are located
Lom·bar·dy (läm′bər dē, lum′-) [the region was invaded
and settled by Lombards in the 6th cent. A.D.] region of
N Italy, on the border of Switzerland: 9,191 sq. mi.; pop.
7,390,000; chief city, Milan: It. name **Lom·bar·dia**
(lōm bär′dyä)
Lombardy poplar a tall, slender variety of the black
poplar (*Populus nigra*), with upward-curving branches
Lom·bok (läm bäk′) island of Indonesia, between Bali &
Sumbawa: 1,825 sq. mi.
Lom·bro·si·an (läm brō′zē ən) *adj.* designating or of the
theories and methods of Lombroso, who regarded the
criminal as a distinct and atavistic type of person
Lom·bro·so (lōm brō′sō), **Ce·sa·re** (che′zä re)1836–1909;
It. physician & criminologist
Lo·mé (lō mā′) capital of Togo; seaport on the Bight of
Benin: pop. 80,000
lo·ment (lō′ment) *n.* [ModL. < L. *lomentum*, bean meal
< pp. of *lavare*, to wash (see LATHER): Roman women
used it in a cosmetic wash] a legume fruit that separates
at its constrictions into one-seeded segments when ripe:
also **lo·men′tum** (-men′təm)   **lo′men·ta′ceous** (-mən
tā′shəs) *adj.*
Lu·mond (lō′mənd), **Loch** lake in WC Scotland, between
Dunbarton & Stirling counties: c. 27 sq. mi.
Lon·don (lun′dən) 1. administrative county in SE England, consisting of the City of London and 28 metropolitan boroughs; capital of England, the United Kingdom,
& the Brit. Commonwealth: 117 sq. mi.; pop. 3,179,000
2. this county with its suburbs: 722 sq. mi.; pop. 8,183,000:
called *Greater London* 3. city in SE Ontario, Canada: pop.
194,000 4. **City of,** historic center of the county of London,
with its ancient boundaries: 677 acres; pop. 4,600 —
Lon′don·er *n.*
Lon·don (lun′dən), **Jack** (born *John Griffith London*)
1876–1916; U.S. novelist & short-story writer
Lon·don·der·ry (-der′ē) 1. county of NW Northern
Ireland: 814 sq. mi.; pop. 174,000 2. seaport in this
county: pop. 56,000
lone (lōn) *adj.* [ME., aphetic < *alone*] 1. by oneself;
alone; solitary 2. lonesome 3. unmarried or widowed
4. *a*) standing apart from others of its kind; isolated
b) unfrequented —*SYN.* see ALONE —**lone′ness** *n.*
lone hand 1. *Card Games* a hand played without help
from a partner 2. a person who manages any activity
without help 3. a position different from that taken by
one's friends, associates, etc.
lone·ly (-lē) *adj.* **-li·er, -li·est** 1. alone; solitary 2. *a*)
standing apart from others of its kind; isolated *b*) unfrequented or uninhabited 3. unhappy at being alone;
longing for friends, company, etc. 4. causing such a
feeling —*SYN.* see ALONE —**lone′li·ly** *adv.* —**lone′li·ness** *n.*
☆**lon·er** (lō′nər) *n.* [Colloq.] one who prefers to be independent of others, as by living or working alone
lone·some (lōn′səm) *adj.* 1. having or causing a lonely
feeling 2. unfrequented; desolate —*n.* [Colloq.] self [all
by my *lonesome*] —*SYN.* see ALONE —**lone′some·ly** *adv.*
—**lone′some·ness** *n.*
Lone Star State *nickname of* TEXAS
☆**lone wolf** *same as* LONER
long¹ (lôŋ) *adj.* [ME. < OE., akin to G. *lang* < IE.
*(d)longho-s < base **del-*, long, whence L. *longus*, Gr.
dolichos, long] 1. measuring much from end to end in space
or from beginning to end in time; not short or brief
2. measured from end to end rather than from side to side
[the *long* dimension] 3. of a specified extent in length
[a foot *long*] 4. of greater than usual or standard length,
height, quantity, etc. [a *long* window, a *long* ton]
5. containing many items or members: said of a
series, list, etc. 6. overextended in length 7. taking too
much time; tedious; slow 8. extending to what is distant
in space or time; far-reaching [a *long* view of the matter]
9. large; big [the *long* odds of 100 to 1, to take a *long*
chance] 10. having an abundance of (with *of* or *on*) [long
on excuses] ☆11. *Finance* holding a supply of a commodity
or security in anticipation of a rise in price 12. *Phonet.*

a) held for a relatively long time: said of a speech sound
b) popularly, having the quality determined by its relative
back position as compared with other vowel variants
13. *a*) requiring a relatively long time to pronounce: said
of syllables in quantitative verse *b*) stressed: said of
syllables in accentual verse —*adv.* 1. for a long time
2. for the duration of; from the beginning to the end [all
day *long*] 3. at a much earlier or a much later time than
the time indicated; remotely [to stay *long* after midnight]
—*n.* 1. a variation of clothing size longer than the average
for that size 2. [*pl.*] long pants 3. a signal, syllable, etc.
of long duration 4. a long time [it won't take long to
finish the work] —**as** (or **so**) **long as** 1. of the same length
as 2. during the time that 3. seeing that; since 4. provided that —**before long** soon —**the long and** (**the**) **short
of** the whole story of in a few words; gist or point of
long² (lôŋ) *vi.* [ME. *longen* < OE. *langian* (akin to G.
langen, to reach, extend) < base of *lang* (see prec.)] to feel
a strong yearning; wish earnestly [to *long* to go home]
long³ (lôŋ) *vi.* [ME. *longen* < OE. *langian*, to belong]
[Archaic & Poet.] to be fitting or appropriate
long. longitude
long·an (läŋ′gən) *n.* [altered < Chin. *lung yen*, lit.,
dragon's eye] 1. an Asiatic tree (*Euphoria longana*) of the
soapberry family, bearing an edible fruit resembling a
small litchi 2. this fruit
lon·ga·nim·i·ty (lôŋ′gə nim′ə tē) *n.* [LL. *longanimitas* <
L. *longus*, LONG¹ + *animus*, mind: see ANIMAL] patient
endurance of injuries; forbearance
Long Beach seaport in SW Calif., on the Pacific: part of
the Los Angeles metropolitan area: pop. 359,000
long·boat (lôŋ′bōt′) *n.* the largest boat carried on a
merchant sailing ship
long·bow (-bō′) *n.* a large bow drawn by hand and shooting a long, feathered arrow: cf. CROSSBOW —**draw** (or
pull) **the longbow** to exaggerate in telling something
long·cloth (-klôth′, -kläth′) *n.* [so called because made in
long pieces] a soft cotton fabric of fine quality
long-day (-dā′) *adj. Bot.* maturing and blooming under
long periods of light and short periods of darkness
☆**long-dis·tance** (-dis′təns) *adj.* 1. to or from a distant
place or places [long-distance telephone calls] 2. that
covers a long distance [a long-distance runner] —*adv.* by
long-distance telephone
☆**long distance** a telephone exchange or operator that
puts through long-distance calls
long division the process of dividing a number by another
number containing, ordinarily, two or more figures, and
of putting the steps down in full
long dozen thirteen
long-drawn (-drôn′) *adj.* continuing for a long or very
long time; prolonged: also **long′-drawn′-out′**
longe (lunj) *n.* [Fr., back-formation < *allonge*, extension
< *allonger* < LL. *elongare*: see ELONGATE] 1. a long rope
fastened to a horse's head and held by the trainer, who
causes the horse to move around in a circle 2. the use of
the longe in training horses —*vt.* **longed**, **longe′ing** or
long′ing to put (a horse) through his paces, using a longe
lon·ge·ron (län′jər ən) *n.* [Fr.] a main structural member
along the length of an airplane fuselage, nacelle, etc.
lon·gev·i·ty (län jev′ə tē, lôn-) *n.* [L. *longaevitas* < *longaevus:* see ff.] 1. *a*) long life; great span of life *b*) length
of life 2. length of time spent in service, employment, etc.
lon·ge·vous (-jē′vəs) *adj.* [L. *longaevus* < *longus*, LONG¹ +
aevum, age: see ETERNAL] [Rare] long-lived
long face a glum, sad, or disconsolate facial expression
—**long′-faced′** (-fāst′) *adj.*
Long·fel·low (lôŋ′fel′ō), **Henry Wads·worth** (wädz′-
wərth′) 1807–82; U.S. poet
☆**long green** [Slang] *same as* PAPER MONEY
☆**long·hair** (-her′) *adj.* [Colloq.] designating or of intellectuals or their tastes; specif., playing or preferring classical
music rather than jazz or popular tunes: also **long′haired′**
—*n.* [Colloq.] 1. an intellectual; specif., a longhair musician 2. *same as* HIPPIE
long·hand (-hand′) *n.* ordinary handwriting, in which the
words are written out in full, as distinguished from shorthand or from typing
long·head (-hed′) *n.* a dolichocephalic person
long·head·ed (-hed′id) *adj.* 1. *same as* DOLICHOCEPHALIC
2. having much foresight, good sense, or shrewdness; sagacious Also **long′head′ed** —**long′-head′ed·ness** *n.*
long·horn (-hôrn′) *n.* ☆any of a breed of long-horned
cattle formerly raised in great numbers in the Southwest
☆**long-horned beetle** (-hôrnd′) any of various slender
beetles (family Cerambycidae) having very long antennae
☆**long-horned grasshopper** any of a family (Tettigoniidae) of greenish grasshoppers with long antennae,
including the katydids
long house ☆a communal home or council hall among the
Iroquois and other Indian tribes
long hundredweight the British hundredweight, equal
to 112 pounds avoirdupois: see HUNDREDWEIGHT
lon·gi- (län′ji) [L. < *longus*, LONG¹] *a combining form
meaning* long [longicorn]

fat, āpe, cär; ten, ēven; is, bīte; gō, hôrn, tōol, look; oil, out; up, fʉr; get; joy; yet; chin; she; thin, then; zh, leisure; ŋ, ring;
ə for *a* in *ago, e* in *agent, i* in *sanity, o* in *comply, u* in *focus*; ′ as in *able* (ā′b'l); Fr. bäl; ë, Fr. coeur; ö, Fr. feu; Fr. mon; ô, Fr. coq;
ü, Fr. duc; r, Fr. cri; H, G. ich; kh, G. doch. See inside front cover. ☆ Americanism; ‡foreign; *hypothetical; < derived from

lon·gi·corn (län′ji kôrn′) *adj.* [< prec. + L. *cornu*, HORN] having long feelers, or antennae, as some beetles

☆**long·ies** (lôŋ′ēz) *n.pl.* [Colloq.] *same as* LONG JOHNS

long·ing (-iŋ) *n.* [see LONG²] strong desire; yearning —*adj.* feeling or showing a yearning —**long′ing·ly** *adv.*

Lon·gi·nus (län jī′nəs), **Dionysius Cassius** 213?–273 A.D.; Gr. Platonic philosopher & rhetorician

long·ish (lôŋ′ish) *adj.* somewhat long

Long Island island in SE N.Y., between Long Island Sound & the Atlantic: 1,411 sq. mi.; pop. 7,115,000

Long Island Sound arm of the Atlantic, between N Long Island & S Conn.: c. 100 mi. long

lon·gi·tude (län′jə tōōd′, -tyōōd′) *n.* [ME. < L. *longitudo* < *longus*, LONG¹] 1. length 2. distance east or west on the earth's surface, measured as an arc of the equator (in degrees up to 180° or by the difference in time) between the meridian passing through a particular place and a standard or prime meridian, usually the one passing through Greenwich, England 3. *Astron. see* CELESTIAL LONGITUDE

lon·gi·tu·di·nal (län′jə tōōd′'n əl, -tyōōd′-) *adj.* [ML. *longitudinalis*] 1. of or in length 2. running or placed lengthwise: opposed to TRANSVERSE 3. of longitude — **lon′gi·tu′di·nal·ly** *adv.*

☆**long johns** [Colloq.] long underwear, usually covering the legs to the ankles

long jump a track and field event that is a jump for distance rather than height, made either from a stationary position or with a running start

☆**long·leaf pine** (lôŋ′lēf′) a pine (*Pinus palustris*) native to the S U.S., having very long needles and valued for its hard, heavy wood

long·lived (-līvd′, -livd′) *adj.* [LONG¹ + -LIVED] having or tending to have a long life span or existence

long measure *same as* LINEAR MEASURE

☆**long moss** *same as* SPANISH MOSS

Lon·go·bard (läŋ′gō bärd′) *n., pl.* **-bards′, Lon′go·bar′di** (-bär′dē) [LL. *Longobardus* < L. *Langobardus:* see LOMBARD] *same as* LOMBARD (*n.* 2) —**Lon′go·bar′dic** *adj.*

Long Parliament the English Parliament that met in 1640, was expelled by Cromwell in 1653, reconvened briefly in 1659, and was dissolved in 1660

long pig human flesh or a human body as food for cannibals: from the Maori and Polynesian term

long play a long-playing record

long·play·ing (lôŋ′plā′iŋ) *adj.* designating or of a phonograph record marked with microgrooves, for playing at 33 1/3 revolutions per minute

long prim·er (prim′ər) a size of type, 10 point

long-range (lôŋ′rānj′) *adj.* 1. designating or of a gun, aircraft, missile, etc. that has a range of great distance 2. taking the future into consideration *[long-range plans]*

long-run (-run′) *adj.* extending over a long time

long·shore (-shôr′) *adj.* [aphetic for ALONGSHORE] existing, occurring, employed, or working along the shore or waterfront —*adv.* along the shore

long·shore·man (-shôr′mən) *n., pl.* **-men** (-mən) [prec. + MAN] a person who works on a waterfront loading and unloading ships

long shot 1. [Colloq.] *a)* in betting, a choice that has only a slight chance of winning and, hence, carries great odds *b)* any venture with only a slight chance of success, but offering great rewards if successful 2. *Motion Pictures, TV* a scene shot with the camera at some distance from the action —☆**not by a long shot** [Colloq.] absolutely not; not at all

long·sight·ed (lôŋ′sīt′id) *adj. same as* FARSIGHTED — **long′sight′ed·ly** *adv.* —**long′sight′ed·ness** *n.*

long·some (-səm) *adj.* [ME. *langsum* < OE. < *lang*, LONG¹ + *-sum*, -SOME¹] [Dial.] lengthy; overly long; tedious

Longs Peak (lôŋz) [after S. H. *Long* (1784–1864), U.S. engineer] peak in Rocky Mountain National Park, NC Colo.: 14,255 ft.

☆**long·spur** (lôŋ′spur′) *n.* [LONG¹ + SPUR] any of a genus (*Calcarius*) of northern birds related to the sparrows and finches and distinguished by their long hind claws

long·stand·ing (-stan′diŋ) *adj.* having continued for a long time

Long·street (lôŋ′strēt′), **James** 1821–1904; Confederate general in the Civil War

long-suf·fer·ing (-suf′ər iŋ) *adj.* bearing injuries, insults, trouble, etc. patiently for a long time —*n.* long and patient endurance of injuries, insults, trouble, etc.: also [Archaic] **long′-suf′fer·ance** —**long′-suf′fer·ing·ly** *adv.*

long suit 1. *Card Games* the suit in which a player holds the most cards 2. something at which one excels

long-term (-turm′) *adj.* 1. for or extending over a long time 2. designating or of a capital gain, loan, etc. that involves a relatively long period

long·time (-tīm′) *adj.* over a long period of time

long ton the British ton, equal to 2,240 pounds avoirdupois: see TON

‡**lon·gueur** (lôn gër′; E. lôŋ gur′) *n.* [Fr.] a long, boring section, as in a novel, musical work, etc.

Long·view (lôŋ′vyōō′) [from the "view" afforded by its altitude] city in NE Tex.: pop. 46,000

long-waist·ed (-wās′tid) *adj.* unusually long between shoulders and waistline; with a low waistline

long wave an electromagnetic wave that is longer than those used in commercial broadcasting, usually a radio wave longer than 1000 meters and below 300 kilohertz in frequency —**long′-wave′** *adj.*

long·ways (-wāz′) *adv. same as* LENGTHWISE

long-wind·ed (-win′did) *adj.* 1. capable of considerable exertion without getting out of breath 2. *a)* speaking or writing at great, often tiresome length *b)* tiresomely long: said of a speech, writing, etc. —**long′-wind′ed·ly** *adv.* —**long′-wind′ed·ness** *n.*

long·wise (-wīz′) *adv. same as* LENGTHWISE

loo¹ (lōō) *n.* [contr. < *lanterloo* < Fr. *lanturelu,* name of the game, orig. fanciful word in refrain of a 17th-cent. song] 1. a card game played for a pool made up of stakes and forfeits 2. a stake or forfeit in the game —*vt.* to cause to pay a forfeit at loo

loo² (lōō) *n.* [< Fr. *lieux, short for les lieux d'aisances,* toilets, lit., places of conveniences] [Brit. Slang] a toilet

loo·by (lōō′bē) *n., pl.* **-bies** [ME. *loby,* prob. akin to LOB, LUBBER] [Now Rare or Dial.] a big, clumsy fellow; lout

loo·fah (lōō′fə) *n.* [Ar. *lūfah*] *same as* LUFFA

loo·ie, loo·ey (lōō′ē) *n.* [Mil. Slang] a lieutenant

look (look) *vi.* [ME. *loken* < OE. *locian,* akin to OS. *lōkōn,* OHG. *luogēn* (G. dial. *lugen*), to spy after, look for] 1. to make use of the sense of sight; see 2. *a)* to direct one's eyes in order to see *b)* to direct one's attention mentally upon something 3. to try to see or find something; search 4. to appear to be; seem *[to look sick]* 5. to be facing or turned in a specified direction 6. to expect (followed by an infinitive) —*vt.* 1. to direct one's eyes on *[to look someone in the face]* 2. to express by one's looks, or appearance *[to look one's disgust]* 3. [Rare] to bring to a certain condition by looking 4. to appear as having attained (some age) *[to look one's years]* —*n.* 1. the act of looking; glance 2. outward impression; appearance; aspect *[the look of a beggar]* 3. [Colloq.] *a)* [*usually pl.*] appearance; the way something seems to be *[from the looks of things]* *b)* [*pl.*] personal appearance, esp. of a pleasing nature *[to have looks and youth]* —*interj.* 1. see! 2. pay attention! —**it looks like** 1. it seems that there will be 2. [Colloq.] it seems as if — **look after** to take care of; watch over —**look alive (or sharp)** [Colloq.] to be alert; act or move quickly: usually in the imperative —**look back** to recall the past; recollect —**look down on (or upon)** 1. to regard as an inferior 2. to regard with contempt; despise —**look for** 1. to search or hunt for 2. to expect; anticipate —**look forward to** to anticipate, esp. eagerly —**look in (on)** to pay a brief visit (to) —**look into** to examine carefully; investigate —**look on** 1. to be an observer or spectator 2. to consider; regard —**look (like) oneself** to appear to be in normal health, spirits, etc. — **look out** to be on the watch; be careful —**look out for** 1. to be wary about 2. to take care of —**look over** to examine; inspect —**look to** 1. to take care of; give attention to 2. to rely upon; resort to 3. to look forward to; expect —**look up** 1. to search for in a book of reference, etc. 2. [Colloq.] to pay a visit to; call on 3. [Colloq.] to get better; improve —**look up and down** 1. to search everywhere 2. to examine with an appraising eye; scrutinize —**look up to** to regard with great respect

SYN.—**look** is the general term meaning to direct the eyes in order to see *[don't look now]*; **gaze** implies a looking intently and steadily, as in wonder, delight, or interest *[to gaze at the stars]*; to **stare** is to look fixedly with wide-open eyes, as in surprise, curiosity, abstraction, etc. *[it is rude to stare at people]*; to **gape** is to stare with the mouth open in ignorant or naive wonder or curiosity *[the child stood gaping at the elephant]*; to **glare** is to stare fiercely or angrily *[he glared at her for talking]*; to **peek** is to take a quick, furtive look, as through a hole or from behind a barrier, at something not supposed to be seen; to **peer** is to look searchingly with the eyes narrowed *[she peered down the well]* See also APPEARANCE

look·er (-ər) *n.* 1. a person who looks ☆2. [Slang] a handsome person; esp., a pretty woman

look·er-on (look′ər än′) *n., pl.* **look′ers-on′** an observer or spectator; onlooker

look-in (look′in′) *n.* 1. a quick glance 2. a brief visit

looking glass a (glass) mirror

look·out (-out′) *n.* 1. an alert, careful watching for someone or something 2. a place for keeping watch, esp. a high place affording an extensive view 3. a person detailed to watch; sentry; observer 4. [Chiefly Brit.] outlook, esp. for the future; prospect 5. [Colloq.] concern; worry *[that's your lookout]*

Lookout Mountain mountain ridge in Tenn., Ga., & Ala.: the section near Chattanooga was the site of a Civil War battle (1863) in which Union forces defeated the Confederates: highest point, 2,125 ft.

look-see (-sē′) *n.* [Slang] a quick look or inspection

loom¹ (lōōm) *n.* [ME. *lome* < OE. *(ge)loma,* tool, utensil] 1. a machine for weaving thread or yarn into cloth 2. the art of weaving (usually with *the*) 3. [ON. *hlumr*] the part of an oar between the handle and the blade —*vt.* to weave on a loom

loom² (lōōm) *vi.* [earlier *lome, loam* < ?] to appear, take shape, or come in sight indistinctly as through a mist, esp. in a large, portentous, or threatening form (often with *up*) *[the peak loomed up before us]*: also used figuratively *[the specter of war loomed ahead]* —*n.* a looming appearance, as of a ship in the fog

loom³ (lōōm) *n.* [Brit. Dial.] *same as* LOON¹

L.O.O.M. Loyal Order of Moose

loon[1] (lōōn) *n.* [altered (after ff.) < earlier *loom* < ON. *lomr* < IE. echoic base *lā-, whence L. *latrare*, to bark] any of a genus (*Gavia*) of fish-eating, diving birds, with a sharp bill and webbed feet, found mainly in subarctic regions: noted for its weird cry

LOON
(to 34 in. long, including bill)

loon[2] (lōōn) *n.* [Scot. *lown, loun* < ?] 1. a clumsy, stupid person 2. a crazy person 3. [Scot.] *a)* a boy *b)* a harlot 4. [Archaic] *a)* a person of low rank *b)* a rogue
loon·y (lōō'nē) *adj.* **loon'i·er,** **loon'i·est** [< LUNATIC] [Slang] crazy; demented —*n., pl.* **loon'ies** [Slang] a loony person Also **loon'ey**
loony bin [Slang] an institution for the mentally ill
loop[1] (lōōp) *n.* [ME. *loup* < Anglo-N. forms corresponding to ON. *hlaup*, a leap, *hlaupa*, to run (akin to LEAP), whence Dan. *løbe(knude)*, lit., running (knot)] 1. *a)* the more or less circular figure formed by a line, thread, wire, etc. that curves back to cross itself *b)* a noose 2. anything having or forming this figure [the *loop* of a written *l*] 3. a sharp bend, as in a mountain road, which almost comes back upon itself 4. a ring-shaped fastening or ornament [*loops* for a belt] 5. a plastic intrauterine contraceptive device (usually *with the*) 6. *Aeron.* a maneuver in which an airplane describes a closed curve or circle in the vertical plane 7. *Elec.* a complete circuit 8. *Physics* the part of a vibrating string, air column, etc. between the nodes; antinode —*vt.* 1. to make a loop or loops in or of 2. to wrap around one or more times [*loop* the wire around the post] 3. to fasten with a loop or loops [to *loop* curtains back] 4. *Elec.* to join (conductors) so as to complete a circuit —*vi.* 1. to form into a loop or loops 2. to progress as a measuring worm does by alternately straightening the body and drawing it up into a loop 3. *Aeron.* to perform a loop or loops —☆**knock** (or **throw**) **for a loop** [Slang] to throw into a state of confusion or shock —**loop the loop** to make a vertical loop in the air, as in an airplane —☆**the Loop** the main business and shopping district in downtown Chicago
loop[2] (lōōp) *n.* [ME. *loupe*, prob. < MDu. *lupen*, to peer] [Archaic] a narrow opening or loophole
loop antenna *Radio* a coil of large diameter, used as an antenna, esp. in direction-finding equipment and in radio receivers
☆**looped** (lōōpt) *adj.* [Slang] intoxicated; drunk
loop·er (lōōp'ər) *n.* 1. a person or thing that makes loops 2. *Zool.* same as MEASURING WORM
loop·hole (-hōl') *n.* [LOOP[2] + HOLE] 1. a hole or narrow slit in the wall of a fort, etc. for looking or shooting through 2. a means of escape; esp., a means of evading or escaping an obligation, enforcement of a law or contract, etc.
loop knot a knot tied in a doubled rope so that a loop extends beyond it: see KNOT, illus.
loop stitch any sewing stitch formed of connected loops
loop·y (lōōp'ē) *adj.* **loop'i·er, loop'i·est** [Slang] crazy; foolish
loose (lōōs) *adj.* [ME. *lous* < ON. *lauss*, akin to OE. *leas* (see -LESS)] 1. not confined or restrained; free; unbound 2. not put up in a special package, box, binding, etc. [*loose* salt] 3. readily available; not put away under lock and key [*loose* cash] 4. not firmly fastened down, on, or in [a *loose* tooth, a *loose* wheel] 5. not taut; slack 6. not tight; giving enough room [*loose* clothing] 7. not compact or compactly constructed [a *loose* frame, *loose* soil] 8. not restrained; irresponsible [*loose* talk] 9. not precise or close; inexact [a *loose* translation] 10. sexually immoral; lewd 11. *a)* not strained or hard [a *loose* cough] *b)* moving freely or excessively [*loose* bowels] 12. [Colloq.] relaxed; easy; unconstrained —*adv.* loosely; in a loose manner —*vt.* **loosed, loos'ing** 1. to make loose; specif., *a)* to set free; unbind *b)* to make less tight *c)* to make less compact *d)* to free from restraint; make less rigid; relax *e)* to free from an obligation or responsibility; absolve 2. to let fly; release [to *loose* an arrow into the air] —*vi.* to loose something or become loose —**break loose** 1. to free oneself by force 2. to shake off restraint —**cast loose** to untie or unfasten; become or set free —**let loose (with)** to set free or give out; release —**on the loose** 1. not confined or bound; free 2. [Colloq.] having fun in a free, unrestrained manner —**set (or turn) loose** to make free; release —**loose'ly** *adv.* —**loose'ness** *n.*
loose ends [from the ends of a spliced rope] final, relatively minor matters still to be taken care of —**at loose ends** [orig. naut., with reference to rope] 1. in an unsettled, disorganized, or confused condition 2. without anything definite to do 3. unemployed
loose-joint·ed (lōōs'join'tid) *adj.* 1. having loose joints 2. moving freely and flexibly; limber —**loose'-joint'ed·ly** *adv.* —**loose'-joint'ed·ness** *n.*
loose-leaf (lōōs'lēf') *adj.* having or designed to have leaves that can easily be removed or replaced [a *loose-leaf* notebook]

loose-limbed (-limd') *adj.* having flexible and limber arms and legs [a *loose-limbed* dancer]
loos·en (lōōs''n) *vt., vi.* to make or become loose or looser; specif., *a)* to free from confinement or restraint; unbind, unfasten, etc. *b)* to make less taut, less tight, less compact, etc. —☆**loosen up** [Colloq.] 1. to talk freely 2. to give money generously 3. to relax —**loos'en·er** *n.*
loose sentence a sentence in which a period could be placed before the end, as any compound sentence
loose smut any of various diseases of cereal grasses caused by smut fungi (esp. genus *Ustilago*) that reduce the kernels to black, dustlike masses of spores
loose-strife (-strīf') *n.* [LOOSE, *v.* + STRIFE: used as transl. of L. *lysimachia* < Gr. *lysimachion* < *lysimachos*, ending strife < *lyein*, to loosen, solve (see LYSIS) + *machē*, battle: from its assumed soothing properties] 1. any of a genus (*Lysimachia*) of plants of the primrose family, with leafy stems and loose spikes of white, rose, or yellow flowers 2. any of a genus (*Lythrum*) of plants of the loosestrife family, esp. **purple loosestrife** (*Lythrum salicaria*) with spikes of purple flowers —*adj.* designating a family (Lythraceae) of chiefly tropical plants, including henna and purple loosestrife
loose-tongued (-tuŋd') *adj.* talking too much; careless or irresponsible in speech
loot (lōōt) *n.* [Hindi *lūt* < Sans. *luṇṭ*, to rob] 1. goods stolen or taken by force, as from a captured enemy city in wartime or by a corrupt official or by rioters; plunder; spoils 2. the act of looting 3. [Slang] *a)* money *b)* items of value; esp., received gifts —*vt.* 1. to plunder; strip of everything valuable; despoil 2. to take or carry off as plunder; steal —*vi.* to engage in plundering —SYN. see SPOIL —**loot'er** *n.*
lop[1] (läp) *vt.* **lopped, lop'ping** [ME. *loppen* < OE. *loppian*, prob. < Scand. (as in Norw. *loppa*) < IE. base *leub-*, to peel off, break off] 1. to trim (a tree, etc.) by cutting off branches, twigs, or stems 2. to remove by or as by cutting off (usually with *off*) —*n.* something lopped off —**lop'per** *n.*
lop[2] (läp) *vi.* **lopped, lop'ping** [prob. akin to LOB] 1. to hang down loosely 2. to move in a halting way —*adj.* hanging down loosely
lope (lōp) *vi.* **loped, lop'ing** [ME. *lopen* < ON. *hlaupa*, to leap, run (or cognate MDu. *lopen*): see LEAP] to move along easily, with a long, swinging stride or in an easy canter —*vt.* to cause to lope —*n.* a long, easy, swinging stride —**lop'er** *n.*
lop-eared (läp'ird') *adj.* having ears that droop or hang down
Lope de Vega see VEGA
lo·pho·branch (lō'fə braŋk', läf'ə-) *adj.* [< ModL. *Lophobranchii*, name of the suborder < Gr. *lophos*, crest, tuft + *branchion*, gill] of a suborder (Lophobranchii) of fishes including the pipefishes and sea horses, having gills arranged in tufts along the branchial arches —*n.* a fish of this suborder
lo·pho·phore (-fôr') *n.* [< Gr. *lophos*, crest, tuft + -PHORE] a usually horseshoe-shaped ring of ciliated tentacles around the mouth of certain aquatic animals, as in brachiopods
lop·py (läp'e) *adj.* **-pi·er, -pi·est** hanging down loosely; drooping
lop·sid·ed (-sīd'id) *adj.* 1. noticeably heavier, bigger, or lower on one side; not symmetrical 2. not balanced; uneven —**lop'sid'ed·ly** *adv.* —**lop'sid'ed·ness** *n.*
loq. *L. loquitur* [he (or she) speaks
lo·qua·cious (lō kwā'shəs) *adj.* [< L. *loquax* (gen. *loquacis*) < *loqui*, to speak + -OUS] very talkative; fond of talking —SYN. see TALKATIVE —**lo·qua'cious·ly** *adv.* —**lo·qua'cious·ness** *n.*
lo·quac·i·ty (-kwas'ə tē) *n.* [L. *loquacitas* < *loquax*: see prec.] talkativeness, esp. when excessive
lo·quat (lō'kwät, -kwat) *n.* [< Chin. (Canton dial.) *lō kwat*, lit., rush orange] 1. a small evergreen tree (*Eriobotrya japonica*) of the rose family, native to China and Japan 2. the small, yellow, edible, plumlike fruit of this tree
Lo·rain (lō rān') [ult. after LORRAINE (France)] city in N Ohio, on Lake Erie: pop. 78,000
lor·al (lôr'əl) *adj.* of or having to do with a lore of a bird or snake
Lor·an (lôr'an) *n.* [< *Lo*(ng) *Ra*(nge) *N*(avigation)] [also l-] a system by which a ship or aircraft can determine its position by the difference in time between radio signals sent from two or more known stations
Lor·ca (lôr'kä) city in SE Spain: pop. 71,000
Lorca, Federico García see GARCÍA LORCA
lord (lôrd) *n.* [ME. < OE. *hlaford* < earlier *hlafweard* < *hlaf* (cf. LOAF[1]) + *weard* (cf. WARD, WARDEN): basic sense— "loaf keeper" (i.e., one who feeds dependents): some senses infl. by use as transl. of L. *dominus*] 1. a person having great power and authority; ruler; master 2. the owner and head of a feudal estate 3. one's husband: now humorous 4. [L-] *a)* God (with *the* except in direct address) *b)* Jesus Christ (often with *Our*) 5. in Great Britain *a)* a nobleman holding the rank of baron, viscount, earl, or marquess; member of the House of Lords *b)* a man who

by courtesy or because of his office is given the title of Lord, as a bishop, the son of a duke, or a Lord Mayor **6.** [L-] [pl.] the House of Lords in the British Parliament (usually with *the*) **7.** [L-] in Great Britain, the title of a lord, variously used: as Earl of Leicester, John Doe would be called *Lord* Leicester; as a baron, John, *Lord* Doe; as the son of a marquess or duke, *Lord* John Doe —*interj.* [often L-] an exclamation of surprise or irritation —*vi.* to act like a lord; rule: chiefly in the phrase **lord it** (over), to act in an overbearing, dictatorial manner (toward) —*vt.* [Now Rare] to make a lord of

Lord (High) Chancellor the highest officer of state of Great Britain, Keeper of the Great Seal, privy councilor, presiding officer of the House of Lords, etc.

lord·ing (-iŋ) *n.* [ME. < OE. *hlafording*] [Obs.] **1.** *same as* LORDLING **2.** a lord: chiefly in pl. as a term of address

lord·ling (-liŋ) *n.* [ME.: see LORD & -LING¹] an unimportant or minor lord: usually contemptuous

lord·ly (-lē) *adj.* **-li·er, -li·est** [ME. < OE. *hlafordlic*] of, like, characteristic of, or suitable to a lord; specif., *a)* noble; grand *b)* haughty; overbearing —*adv.* in the manner of a lord —**lord′li·ness** *n.*

Lord Mayor the title of the mayor of London and of the mayor of any of several other British cities

Lord of hosts Jehovah; God

Lord of Misrule formerly, in England, a person who presided over revels and games, as at Christmas

lor·do·sis (lôr dō′sis) *n.* [ModL. < Gr. *lordōsis* < *lordos*, bent backward < IE. base *lerd-, to make crooked, whence Gael. *lorcach*, with a lame foot] forward curvature of the spine, producing a hollow in the back —**lor·dot′ic** (-dät′ik) *adj.*

Lord's day [transl. of LL.(Ec.) *dies Dominica* < Gr.(Ec.) *hē kyriakē hēmera* (cf. Rev. 1:10): from being the day of the resurrection of Christ] Sunday

lord·ship (lôrd′ship′) *n.* [OE. *hlafordscipe*: see -SHIP] **1.** the rank or authority of a lord **2.** rule; dominion **3.** the territory of a lord **4.** a title used in speaking of or to a lord: preceded by *his* or *your*

Lord's Prayer the prayer beginning *Our Father*, which Jesus taught his disciples: Matt. 6:9–13

lords spiritual the archbishops and bishops who are members of the British House of Lords

Lord's Supper 1. *same as* LAST SUPPER **2.** Holy Communion; Eucharist: so called because it commemorates the Last Supper

lords temporal those members of the British House of Lords who are not clergymen

lore¹ (lôr) *n.* [ME. < OE. *lar*, learning, teaching, akin to G. *lehre*, teaching: see LEARN] **1.** [Archaic] *a)* a teaching or being taught; instruction *b)* something taught **2.** knowledge or learning; specif., all the knowledge of a particular group or having to do with a particular subject, esp. that of a traditional nature

lore² (lôr) *n.* [ModL. *lorum* < L., thong < IE. *wloro- < base *wel-, whence Gr. *eulēra*, reins] the space between the eye and the upper edge of the bill of a bird or between the eye and the nostril of a snake or fish

Lor·e·lei (lôr′ə lī′) [G., altered by C. Brentano (1778-1842), Ger. poet < *Lurlei*, name of the rock (prob. lit., "ambush cliff") < MHG. *luren*, to watch, LOWER² + *lei*, a cliff, rock] in German literature and legend, a siren whose singing on a rock in the Rhine lured sailors to shipwreck on the reefs

Lo·rentz (lō′rents), **Hen·drik An·toon** (hen′drik än′tōn) 1853-1928; Du. physicist

Lo·ren·zo (lô ren′zō, lə-) a masculine name: see LAURENCE

Lo·ret·ta (lô ret′ə, lə-) [dim. of LAURA] a feminine name

lor·gnette (lôr nyet′) *n.* [Fr. < *lorgner*, to spy, peep, quiz < OFr. *lorgne*, squinting] **1.** a pair of eyeglasses attached to a handle **2.** opera glasses similarly mounted

†lor·gnon (lôr nyōn′) *n.* [Fr. < *lorgner*: see prec.] **1.** a single or double eyeglass, as a monocle or pince-nez **2.** *same as* LORGNETTE

lo·ri·ca (lə rī′kə) *n., pl.* **-cae** (-sē) [L., orig., corselet of thongs < *lorum*, a thong: see LORE²] **1.** in ancient Rome, the leather corselet, or cuirass, worn by a Roman legionary **2.** *Zool.* a hard, protective shell or other covering —**lor·i·cate** (lôr′ə kāt′, lär′-), **lor′i·cat′ed** *adj.*

LORGNETTE

Lor·ient (lôr yän′) seaport in W France, on the Bay of Biscay: pop. 61,000

lor·i·keet (lôr′ə kēt′, lär′-) *n.* [< LORY + (PARA)KEET] any of several small, brightly colored parakeets that feed on nectar, found in Australia and the East Indies

Lo·rin·da (lô rin′də, lə-) a feminine name: see LAURA

lo·ris (lôr′is) *n., pl.* **lo′ris** [ModL. < Fr., special use (by Buffon) of Du. *loeres*, a clown < *loer*, a clown] either of two small, slow-moving, large-eyed Asiatic lemurs that live in trees and are active at night; specif., *a)* the **slender loris** (*Loris gracilis*) *b)* the **slow loris** (*Nycticebus tardigradus*)

lorn (lôrn) *adj.* [ME., pp. of *losen, lesen*, to lose (see LOSE): the change of *s* to *r* is due to Verner's law] **1.** [Obs.] lost, ruined, or undone **2.** [Archaic] forsaken, forlorn, bereft, or desolate

Lor·na (lôr′nə) [apparently coined by R. D. Blackmore (1825-1900), Eng. novelist < title of the Marquis of *Lorne* (1845-1914)] a feminine name

Lorrain, Claude see CLAUDE LORRAIN

Lor·raine (lô rān′; *Fr.* lô ren′) [Fr.] **1.** a feminine name **2.** region & former province of NE France: see ALSACE-LORRAINE —**Cross of Lorraine** a cross having two horizontal arms, the lower one longer than the upper

lor·ry (lôr′ē, lär′-) *n., pl.* **-ries** [prob. < dial. *lurry, lorry*, to tug, pull] **1.** a low, flat wagon without sides **2.** any of various trucks fitted to run on rails **3.** [Brit.] a motor truck

lo·ry (lôr′e) *n., pl.* **-ries** [Malay *lūrī*] any of a number of small, brightly colored parrots, native to Australia and nearby islands and characterized by a fringed, brushlike tip of the tongue for feeding on soft fruits and nectar

Los Al·a·mos (lôs al′ə mōs′, läs) [Sp., lit., the poplars] town in NC N.Mex., near Santa Fe: site of atomic energy facility where the atomic bomb was developed: pop. 11,000

Los An·ge·les (lôs an′jə ləs, läs; aŋ′gə ləs; -lēz′) [Sp., lit., the angels, abbrev. of Queen of the Angels] city & seaport on the SW coast of Calif.: pop. 2,816,000 (met. area, incl. Long Beach, 7,032,000)

lose (lōōz) *vt.* **lost, los′ing** [ME. *losen, lesen*, merging OE. *losian*, to lose, be lost (< *los*, LOSS) + *leosan*, to lose, akin to OHG. *(vir)liosan*, Goth. *(fra)liusan* < IE. base *leu-, to cut off, separate, whence Gr. *lyein*, to dissolve, L. *luere*, to loose, release (from debt)] **1.** to bring to ruin or destruction [a ship *lost* in the storm] **2.** to become unable to find; mislay [to *lose* one's keys] **3.** *a)* to have taken from one by negligence, accident, death, removal, separation, etc.; suffer the loss of; be deprived of *b)* to suffer the miscarriage or stillbirth of (a baby) **4.** to get rid of (something undesirable) [to *lose* unwanted weight] **5.** to fail to keep or maintain [to *lose* one's temper, to *lose* speed] **6.** *a)* to fail to see, hear, or understand [she did not *lose* a word of his speech] *b)* to fail to keep in sight, mind, or existence **7.** to fail to have, get, take advantage of, etc.; miss [to *lose* one's chance] **8.** to fail to win or gain [to *lose* a game] **9.** to cause the loss of [it *lost* him his job] **10.** to cause to go astray, become bewildered, etc. **11.** to wander from and not be able to find (one's way, the right track, etc.) **12.** to fail or be unable to make proper use of; waste [to *lose* time] **13.** to leave behind; outdistance **14.** to engross or preoccupy: usually in the passive [to be *lost* in reverie] **15.** to go slower by [a watch that *loses* two minutes a day] —*vi.* **1.** to undergo or suffer loss **2.** to be defeated in a contest, etc. **3.** to be slow: said of a clock, etc. —**lose oneself 1.** to lose one's way; go astray; become bewildered **2.** to become absorbed **3.** to disappear from view or notice —☆**lose out** [Colloq.] to fail; be unsuccessful —☆**lose out on** [Colloq.] to fail to win, gain, or take advantage of —**los′a·ble** *adj.*

lo·sel (lō′z'l, lōō′-) *n.* [ME. *losel, lorel* < *losen*, pp. of *lesen*, LOSE] [Archaic or Dial.] a worthless person —*adj.* [Archaic or Dial.] worthless

los·er (lōō′zər) *n.* **1.** one that loses; esp., [Colloq.] one that seems doomed to lose **2.** a person who reacts to loss or defeat in a specified way [a poor *loser*] **3.** [Slang] a person who has been imprisoned for crime a (specified) number of times [a three-time *loser*]

los·ing (-ziŋ) *n.* **1.** the act of one that loses **2.** [pl.] losses by gambling —*adj.* **1.** that loses [a *losing* team] **2.** resulting in loss [a *losing* proposition]

loss (lôs, läs) *n.* [ME. *los* < pp. of *losen, lesen*, to LOSE (or < ? OE. *los*, ruin, dissolution < base of *leosan*)] **1.** a losing or being lost **2.** an instance of this **3.** the damage, trouble, disadvantage, deprivation, etc. caused by losing something **4.** the person, thing, or amount lost **5.** *Elec.* any reduction of voltage, current, or power between parts of a circuit or between different circuits, due to resistance of the elements **6.** *Insurance a)* death, injury, damage, etc. that is the basis for a valid claim for indemnity under the terms of the policy *b)* the amount paid by the insurer on this basis **7.** *Mil. a)* the losing of military personnel in combat by death, injury, or capture *b)* [pl.] those lost in this way *c)* [pl.] ships, aircraft, etc. lost in battle —**at a loss 1.** in an uncertain or perplexed state; puzzled **2.** so as to lose money [to operate a business *at a loss*] —**at a loss to** not able to; uncertain how to

☆**loss leader** any article that a store sells cheaply or below cost in order to attract customers

loss ratio the ratio between the losses incurred and the premiums earned by an insurance company during a specified time

lost (lôst, läst) *pt. & pp.* of LOSE —*adj.* **1.** destroyed or ruined physically or morally **2.** not to be found; missing **3.** no longer held or possessed; parted with **4.** no longer seen, heard, or known [a person *lost* in a crowd] **5.** not gained or won; attended with defeat **6.** having wandered from the way; uncertain as to one's location **7.** bewildered or ill at ease **8.** not spent profitably or usefully; wasted **9.** spent away from one's place of work, as because of illness [to make up *lost* time] —☆**get lost!** [Slang] go away! —**lost in** absorbed in; engrossed in —**lost on** without effect on; failing to influence —**lost to 1.** no longer in the possession or enjoyment of **2.** no longer available to **3.** having no sense of (shame, right, etc.); insensible to

☆**lost cause** an undertaking or movement that has failed or is certain to fail

lost motion the difference in the rate of motion of driving and driven parts of a machine, due to faulty fittings, etc.

lost tribes the ten tribes making up the kingdom of Israel that were carried off into Assyrian captivity about 722 B.C.: II Kings 17:6

lot (lät) *n.* [ME. < OE. *hlot*, akin to G. *los*, Du. *lot*, ON. *hlutr*, Goth. *hlauts* < IE. base **klēu-*, a hook, forked branch, whence L. *clavis*, key] **1.** an object used in deciding a matter by chance, a number of these being placed in a container and then drawn or cast out at random one by one **2.** the use of such an object or objects in determining a matter [to choose men by *lot*] **3.** the decision or choice arrived at by this means, regarded as the verdict of chance **4.** what a person receives as the result of such a decision; share **5.** one's portion in life; fortune [her unhappy *lot*] **6.** a plot of ground; specif., ☆*a*) a subdivision of a block in a town or city ☆*b*) a parcel of land in a cemetery **7.** *a*) a number of persons or things regarded as a group *b*) a quantity of material processed or manufactured at the same time **8.** [*often pl.*] [Colloq.] a great number or amount [a *lot* of cars, *lots* of money] **9.** Colloq.] sort (of person or persons) [he's a bad *lot*] ☆**10.** *Motion Pictures* a studio with the surrounding area belonging to it —*adv.* a great deal; very much [a *lot* happier]: also **lots** —*vt.* **lot′ted, lot′ting 1.** to divide into lots **2.** [Rare] to allot —*vi.* to draw or cast lots —**SYN.** see FATE —**cast** (or **throw**) **in one's lot with** to take one's chances in association with; share the fortunes of —**draw** (or **cast**) **lots** to decide an issue by using lots —**the lot** [Colloq.] the whole of a quantity or number

Lot (lät) [Heb. *Lōt*] *Bible* Abraham's nephew, who, warned by two angels, fled from the doomed city of Sodom: his wife looked back to see the destruction and was turned into a pillar of salt: Gen. 19:1–26

Lot (lôt) river in S France, flowing west into the Garonne: c. 300 mi.

lo·ta, lo·tah (lō′tə) *n.* [Hindi *lotā*] in India, a globe-shaped water pot, usually of brass

loth (lōth) *adj. alt. sp. of* LOATH

Lo·thar·i·o (lō ther′ē ō′) *n., pl.* **-i·os′** [name of young rake in Nicholas Rowe's play *The Fair Penitent* (1703)] [*often* l-] a gay seducer of women; rake

Lo·thi·ans (lō′thē ənz, -thē-), **The** region of SE Scotland made up of East Lothian, Midlothian, & West Lothian

Lo·ti (lō tē′), **Pierre** (pyer) (pseud. of *Louis Marie Julien Viaud*) 1850–1923; Fr. novelist

lo·tic (lōt′ik) *adj.* [< L. *lotus*, a washing (< *lautus*, pp. of *lavere*, to wash: see LATHER) + -IC] *Ecol.* designating, of, or living in flowing water, as rivers, streams, etc.: cf. LENTIC

lo·tion (lō′shən) *n.* [ME. *loscion* < L. *lotio* (gen. *lotionis*) < *lotus*, pp. of *lavare*, to wash, bathe: see LATHER] a liquid preparation used, as on the skin or eyes, for washing, soothing, healing, etc.

lo·tos (lōt′əs) *n. alt. sp. of* LOTUS

Lot·ta (lät′ə) a feminine name: see CHARLOTTE

lot·ter·y (lät′ər ē) *n., pl.* **-ter·ies** [MFr. *loterie* < MDu. *loterije* < *lot*, LOT] **1.** a game of chance in which people buy numbered tickets, and prizes are given to those whose numbers are drawn by lot: sometimes sponsored by a state or organization as a means of raising funds **2.** any undertaking that involves chance selections, as by the drawing of lots [military draft *lottery*]

Lot·tie, Lot·ty (lät′ē) a feminine name: see CHARLOTTE

lot·to (lät′ō) *n.* [It. < Fr. *lot* < MDu. *lot*, LOT] a game played with cards having squares numbered in rows, no two cards being numbered alike: counters are used to cover the numbered squares corresponding to the numbered disks drawn by lot from a bag or box and the player who first gets one row, etc. on his card covered is the winner: as a gambling game, usually called BINGO

lo·tus (lōt′əs) *n.* [L. < Gr. *lōtos* < Heb. *lōṭ*] **1.** *Gr. Legend a*) a fruit that was supposed to induce a dreamy languor and forgetfulness *b*) the plant bearing this fruit, variously supposed to be the date, the jujube, etc. **2.** any of several tropical African and Asiatic water lilies (genus *Nymphaea*) once held sacred to certain national deities, as the **white lotus** (*Nymphaea lotus*) of Egypt **3.** a representation of any of these plants in ancient, esp. Egyptian, sculpture and architecture **4.** any of a genus (*Lotus*) of plants of the legume family, with irregular, pinnate leaves and yellow, purple, or white pealike flowers

LOTUS (sense 2)

lo·tus-eat·er (-ēt′ər) *n.* in the *Odyssey*, one of a people who ate the fruit of the lotus and consequently became indolent, dreamy, and forgetful of duty

lotus position in yoga, an erect sitting posture with the legs crossed and with each foot, sole upturned, resting on the upper thigh of the opposite leg

‡**louche** (lōōsh) *adj.* [Fr., lit., squinting < L. *lusca*, fem. of *luscus*, one-eyed] of questionable character; disreputable

loud (loud) *adj.* [ME. < OE. *hlud*, akin to G. *laut* < IE. base **kleu-*, to hear, listen, whence L. *cluere*, to be called] **1.** striking with force on the organs of hearing; strongly audible: said of sound **2.** making a sound or sounds of great intensity [a *loud* bell] **3.** noisy **4.** clamorous; emphatic; insistent [*loud* denials] **5.** [Colloq.] too vivid; flashy [a *loud* pattern] **6.** [Colloq.] unrefined; vulgar **7.** [Dial.] strong or offensive, as in smell —*adv.* in a loud manner —**loud′ly** *adv.* —**loud′ness** *n.*

loud·en (-'n) *vt., vi.* to make or become loud or louder

loud-hail·er (-hāl′ər) *n. same as* BULLHORN

loud·ish (-ish) *adj.* somewhat loud

loud-mouthed (-moutht′, -mouthd′) *adj.* talking in a loud, irritating voice —**loud′mouth′** *n.*

loud·speak·er (-spē′kər) *n.* a device for converting electric current to sound waves and for amplifying this sound to the desired volume, as in a public-address system

lough (läkh) *n.* [ME., prob. < Gael. & OIr. *loch*, LOCH] [Ir.] **1.** a lake **2.** an arm of the sea

Lou·is (lōō′ē; *for* 1, *usually* lōō′is; Fr. lwē) [Fr. < OFr. *Loeis*; prob. via ML. *Ludovicus* < OHG. *Hluodowig* < Gmc. base **hluda-*, famous (< base of LOUD) + **wiga-*, war, hence, lit., famous in war; in the form *Lewis*, sometimes an adaptation of W. *Llewelyn*] **1.** a masculine name: dim. *Lou, Louie;* equiv. L. *Ludovicus,* Ger. *Ludwig,* It. *Luigi,* Sp. *Luis;* fem. *Louise* **2. Louis I** 778–840 A.D.; king of France & emperor of the Holy Roman Empire (814–840): son & successor of CHARLEMAGNE **3. Louis II de Bourbon** *see* Prince de CONDÉ **4. Louis IX** 1214–70; king of France (1226–70): canonized as **Saint Louis,** his day is Aug. 25 **5. Louis XI** 1423–83; king of France (1461–83): son of CHARLES VII **6. Louis XII** 1462–1515; king of France (1498–1515) **7. Louis XIII** 1601–43; king of France (1610–43): son of HENRY IV **8. Louis XIV** 1638–1715; king of France (1643–1715): his reign encompassed a period of flourishing Fr. culture: son of *prec.* **9. Louis XV** 1710–74; king of France (1715–74): great-grandson of *prec.* **10. Louis XVI** 1754–93; king of France (1774–92): reign marked by the French Revolution: guillotined: grandson of *prec.* **11. Louis XVII** 1785–95; titular king of France (1793–95): son of *prec.* **12. Louis XVIII** 1755–1824; king of France (1814–15; 1815–24): brother of *Louis XVI*

lou·is (lōō′ē) *n., pl.* **lou′is** (-ēz) *same as* LOUIS D'OR

Lou·is (lōō′is), **Joe** (born *Joseph Louis Barrow*) 1914– ; U.S. boxer: world heavyweight champion (1937–49)

Lou·i·sa (lōō wē′zə) [It.] a feminine name: see LOUISE

lou·is d'or (lōō′ē dôr′) [Fr., gold louis: orig. after LOUIS XIII] **1.** an old French gold coin of varying value, issued through the reigns of Louis XIII–Louis XVI **2.** a later French gold coin worth 20 francs

Lou·ise (lōō wēz′) [Fr., fem. of LOUIS] **1.** a feminine name: dim. *Lou, Lulu;* var. *Louisa, Eloise* **2. Lake,** small lake in SW Alberta, Canada, in Banff National Park

Lou·i·si·an·a (lōō wē′zē an′ə, lōō′ə zē-, lōō′zē-) [Fr. *La Louisianne,* name for the Mississippi valley, after LOUIS XIV] Southern State of the U.S., on the Gulf of Mexico: admitted 1812; 48,523 sq. mi.; pop. 3,643,000; cap. Baton Rouge: abbrev. **La., LA** —**Lou·i′si·an′i·an, Lou·i′si·an′an** *adj., n.*

☆**Louisiana Purchase** land bought by the U.S. from France in 1803 for $15,000,000: it extended from the Mississippi to the Rocky Mountains & from the Gulf of Mexico to Canada

LOUISIANA PURCHASE

Louis Napoleon *see Charles Louis Napoléon Bonaparte*) 1808–73; president of France (1848–52) &, as Napoleon III, emperor (1852–70): deposed: nephew of NAPOLEON I

Louis Phi·lippe (fi lēp′) 1773–1850; king of France (1830–48): abdicated in Revolution of 1848

Louis Qua·torze (kȧ tôrz′) designating or of the style of furniture, architecture, etc. of the time of Louis XIV of France, characterized by massive, baroque forms and lavish ornamentation

Louis Quinze (kanz) designating or of the style of furniture, architecture, etc. of the time of Louis XV of France, characterized by rococo treatment with emphasis on curved lines and highly decorative forms based on shells, flowers, etc.

Louis Seize (sez) designating or of the style of furniture, architecture, etc. of the time of Louis XVI of France, characterized by a return to straight lines, symmetry, and classic ornamental details

Louis Treize (trez) designating or of the style of furniture, architecture, etc. of the time of Louis XIII of France, characterized by Renaissance forms, rich inlays, etc.

Lou·is·ville (lōō′ē vil; *locally* lōō′ə vəl) [after LOUIS XVI] city in N Ky., on the Ohio River: pop. 361,000 (met. area 827,000)

lounge (lounj) *vi.* **lounged, loung′ing** [15th-c. Scot. dial. < ? *lungis*, laggard, drowsy person < OFr. *longis* < L. *Longinus*, apocryphal name of soldier who lanced Jesus in the side] **1.** to stand, move, sit, lie, etc. in a relaxed or lazy way; loll **2.** to spend time in idleness —*vt.* to spend by lounging [to *lounge* the summer away] —*n.* **1.** an act or time of lounging **2.** [Now Rare] a lounging gait or stroll **3.** *a)* a room, as in a hotel, equipped with comfortable furniture for lounging *b)* such a room, as in a theater, with an adjoining toilet or toilets **4.** a couch or sofa, esp. a backless one with a headrest at one end —**loung′er** *n.*

☆**lounge car** a railroad car where passengers may lounge in comfortable chairs and obtain light refreshments

☆**lounge lizard** [Slang] an indolent, pleasure-seeking man who frequents lounges, etc., often specif. as a gigolo

loup (loup, lōp, lōōp) *vi., vt.* [ME., akin to *leap, hleap:* see LEAP] [Scot.] to leap —*n.* [Scot.] a leap

loupe (lōōp) *n.* [Fr. < MFr., gem of imperfect transparency, shapeless iron lump, prob. < or akin to OHG. *luppa*, shapeless lumpy mass] a small, high-powered magnifying lens held close to the eye, used by jewelers, watchmakers, etc.

‡**loup-ga·rou** (lōō gà rōō′) *n., pl.* **loups-ga·rous** (lōō gà rōō′) [Fr. < *loup*, wolf (L. *lupus*) + *garou*, werewolf < OFr. *garolf* < Frank. *werwulf*, akin to OE. *werwulf*, WEREWOLF] *same as* WEREWOLF

lour (lour) *vi., n. same as* LOWER²

Lourdes (loord, loordz; *Fr.* lōōrd) town in SW France: the site of a famous Catholic shrine: pop. 16,000

Lou·ren·ço Mar·ques (lō ren′sō mär′kes; *Port.* lō ren′soo mär′kezh) capital of Mozambique; seaport on the Indian Ocean: pop. 447,000

louse (lous; *also, for v.,* louz) *n., pl.* **lice** [ME. *lous* < OE. *lus* (pl. *lys*), akin to G. *laus* < IE. **lūs*, whence W. *lleuen*, Bret. *laouen*] **1.** *a)* any of an order (Anoplura) of small, flat, wingless insects with sucking mouthparts, parasitic on the skin of man and some other mammals; esp., the human **body louse** (*Pediculus humanus corporis*) and **head louse** (*Pediculus humanus capitis*) *b)* any of various arthropods that suck blood or juice from other animals or plants **2.** *see* BIRD LOUSE **3.** any of various other small insects, arachnids, and crustaceans that are not parasitic, as the book louse, wood louse, etc. **4.** *pl.* **lous′es** [Slang] a person regarded as mean, contemptible, etc. —*vt.* **loused, lous′ing** [Rare] to delouse —☆**louse up** [Slang] to botch; spoil; ruin

louse·wort (-wurt′) *n.* [so called because sheep feeding on the plants were said to become infested with vermin] any of a genus (*Pedicularis*) of perennial plants of the figwort family, with pinnately divided leaves and spiked clusters of yellow, rose, or purple flowers

lous·y (lou′zē) *adj.* **lous′i·er, lous′i·est 1.** infested with lice **2.** covered with specks: said of silk **3.** [Slang] dirty, disgusting, or contemptible ☆**4.** [Slang] poor; inferior: a generalized epithet of disapproval ☆**5.** [Slang] well supplied or oversupplied (*with*) —**lous′i·ly** *adv.* —**lous′i·ness** *n.*

lout¹ (lout) *n.* [prob. < or akin to ME. *lutien*, to lurk < OE. *lutian*, akin to *lutan:* see ff.] a clumsy, stupid fellow; boor —*vt.* [Obs.] to treat with contempt; flout —**lout′ish** *adj.* —**lout′ish·ly** *adv.* —**lout′ish·ness** *n.*

lout² (lout) *vi., vt.* [ME. *louten* < OE. *lutan*, akin to ON. *luta:* for IE. base see LITTLE] [Archaic & Dial.] to bow or curtsy; bend; stoop

Lou·vain (lōō van′; *E.* lōō vān′) city in C Belgium: pop. 32,000

lou·ver (lōō′vər) *n.* [ME. *luver* < MFr. *lover* < MDu. *love*, gallery (in a theater), akin to OHG. *louba:* see LODGE, LEAF] **1.** an open turret or lantern on the roof of a medieval building **2.** *a)* a window or opening furnished with a series of sloping slats arranged so as to admit light and air but shed rain water outward *b)* any of these slats: also **louver board** *c)* any similar arrangement as of slats or fins, used to control ventilation, light intensity, etc. **3.** a ventilating slit Also **lou′vre** —**lou′vered** *adj.*

LOUVER

L'Ouverture *see* TOUSSAINT L'OUVERTURE

Lou·vre (lōō′vrə, lōōv; *Fr.* lōō′vr′) ancient royal palace in Paris, on the Seine, converted into an art museum in the 18th cent.

Louÿs (lwē), **Pierre** (pyer) (pseud. of *Pierre Louis*) 1870–1925; Fr. novelist & poet

lov·a·ble (luv′ə b'l) *adj.* inspiring love; easily loved; endearing: also sp. **love′a·ble** —**lov′a·bil′i·ty, lov′a·ble·ness** *n.* —**lov′a·bly** *adv.*

lov·age (luv′ij) *n.* [ME. *loveache*, altered (after ff. & *ache*, ACHE) < OFr. *levesche* < LL. *levisticum* for L. *ligusticum*, lovage, plant native to Liguria < *Ligusticus*, Ligurian, < *Liguria*, country in Cisalpine Gaul] a European plant (*Levisticum officinale*) of the parsley family, sometimes used as a potherb and formerly as a home medicine

lov·at (luv′ət) *n.* [prob. < *Lovat*, locality in the shire of

Inverness, Scotland] a variegated color, chiefly green, with shades of blue, gray, etc., characteristic of some tweeds

love (luv) *n.* [ME. < OE. *lufu*, akin to OHG. *luba*, Goth. *lubo* < IE. base **leubh-*, to be fond of, desire, whence LIBIDO, LIEF, LUST] **1.** a deep and tender feeling of affection for or attachment or devotion to a person or persons **2.** an expression of one's love or affection [give Mary my *love*] **3.** a feeling of brotherhood and good will toward other people **4.** *a)* a strong liking for or interest in something [a *love* of music] *b)* the object of such liking **5.** *a)* a strong, usually passionate, affection of one person for another, based in part on sexual attraction *b)* the person who is the object of such an affection; sweetheart; lover **6.** *a)* sexual passion *b)* sexual intercourse **7.** [L-] *a)* Cupid, or Eros, as the god of love *b)* [Rare] Venus **8.** [< phr. *play for love*, i.e., play for nothing] Tennis a score of zero **9.** Theol. *a)* God's benevolent concern for mankind *b)* man's devout attachment to God —*vt.* **loved, lov′ing 1.** to feel love for **2.** to show love for by embracing, fondling, kissing, etc. **3.** to delight in; take pleasure in [to *love* books] **4.** to gain benefit from [a plant that *loves* shade] —*vi.* to feel the emotion of love; be in love —**fall in love (with)** to begin to feel love (for) —**for love** as a favor or for pleasure; without payment —**for the love of** for the sake of; with loving regard for —**in love** feeling love; enamored —**make love 1.** to woo or embrace, kiss, etc. as lovers do **2.** to have sexual intercourse —**no love lost between** no liking or affection existing between —**not for love or money** not under any conditions

SYN.—**love** implies intense fondness or deep devotion and may apply to various relationships or objects [sexual *love*, brotherly *love*, *love* of one's work, etc.]; **affection** suggests warm, tender feelings, usually not as powerful or deep as those implied by love [he has no *affection* for children]; **attachment** implies connection by ties of affection, attraction, devotion, etc. and may be felt for inanimate things as well as for people [an *attachment* to an old hat]; **infatuation** implies a foolish or unreasoning passion or affection, often a transient one [an elderly man's *infatuation* for a young girl]

love affair 1. an amorous or romantic relationship or episode between two people not married to each other **2.** an intense or eager interest in something

love apple [transl. of Fr. *pomme d'amour*, G. *liebesapfel*, orig. prob. folk etym. for earlier It. *pomi dei Mori*, lit., apples of the Moors] [Archaic] the tomato

☆**love beads** a long strand of colorful beads worn by both men and women as a symbol of the counterculture

love·bird (-burd′) *n.* any of various small parrots, esp. of an African genus (*Agapornis*), often kept as cage birds: the mates appear to be greatly attached to each other

love feast 1. *a)* among the early Christians, a meal eaten together as a symbol of affection and brotherhood; agape *b)* a modern feast or gathering imitating this ☆**2.** any feast or gathering characterized by friendliness and good feeling

love game a game, as in tennis, in which the losing player or team scores no points

love-in-a-mist (-in ə mist′) *n.* an annual European plant (*Nigella damascena*) of the buttercup family, with finely cut leaves and blue or white flowers

love knot a knot of ribbon, etc. that serves as a token between lovers

Love·lace (luv′lās′), **Richard** 1618–58; Eng. poet

love·less (-lis) *adj.* without love; specif., *a)* feeling no love *b)* receiving no love; unloved —**love′less·ly** *adv.*

love-lies-bleed·ing (-līz′blēd′iɳ) *n.* a cultivated amaranth (*Amaranthus caudatus*) with drooping spikes of small, red flowers

love life [Colloq.] that part of one's life having to do with amorous or sexual relationships

Lov·ell (luv′əl), **Sir** (**Alfred Charles**) **Bernard** 1913– ; Eng. astronomer

love·lock (-läk′) *n.* a lock of hair lying apart from the rest of the hair; specif., such a long lock as formerly worn by courtiers

love·lorn (-lôrn′) *adj.* [see LORN] deserted by or pining for one's sweetheart; pining from love

love·ly (-lē) *adj.* **-li·er, -li·est** [ME. *luvelich* < OE. *luflic*] having those qualities that inspire love, affection, or admiration; specif., *a)* beautiful; exquisite *b)* morally or spiritually attractive; gracious *c)* [Colloq.] highly enjoyable [a *lovely* party] —*n.* [Colloq.] a lovely person or thing; esp., a beautiful young woman —**SYN.** see BEAUTIFUL —**love′li·ly** *adv.* —**love′li·ness** *n.*

love·mak·ing (-mā′kiɳ) *n.* the act of making love; specif., *a)* wooing or embracing, fondling, kissing, etc. *b)* sexual intercourse

love match a marriage for love only, not for wealth, social status, etc.

love potion a magic drink supposed to arouse love or passion for a certain person in the drinker; philter

lov·er (-ər) *n.* **1.** a person who loves; specif., *a)* a sweetheart *b)* [*pl.*] a couple in love with each other *c)* a man who has a sexual relationship with a woman without being married to her; paramour *d)* a person who greatly enjoys some (specified) thing [a *lover* of good music] —**lov′er·ly** *adj., adv.*

love seat a double chair or small sofa seating two persons

love set Tennis a set in which the loser wins no games

love·sick (-sik′) *adj.* **1.** so much in love as to be unable to act in a normal way **2.** expressive of such a condition *[a lovesick song]* —**love′sick′ness** *n.*

love·some (-səm) *adj.* [Archaic or Dial.] lovely

lov·ey-dov·ey (luv′ē duv′ē) *adj.* [LOVE + -Y² + DOVE¹ + -Y²] [Slang] very or excessively affectionate, amorous, or sentimental

lov·ing (-iŋ) *adj.* **1.** feeling love; devoted **2.** expressing love *[a loving act]* —**lov′ing·ly** *adv.* —**lov′ing·ness** *n.*

loving cup a large drinking cup of silver, etc., with two or more large handles by which it was formerly passed from guest to guest at banquets: now often given as a trophy in sports and games

lov·ing·kind·ness (-kīnd′nis) *n.* [earlier *loving kindness:* first use by COVERDALE, 1535] kindness or affectionate behavior resulting from or expressing love

low¹ (lō) *adj.* [ME. *lah* < ON. *lagr,* akin to MDu. *lage,* MLowG. *læge* < IE. base **legh-,* LIE¹] **1.** *a)* of little height or elevation; not high or tall *b)* not far above the ground *[low clouds]* **2.** depressed below the surrounding surface or normal elevation *[low land]* **3.** of little depth; shallow *[the river is low]* **4.** of little quantity, degree, intensity, value, etc. *[a low cost, low pressure]* **5.** of less than normal height, elevation, depth, quantity, degree, power, etc. **6.** below others in order, position, rating, etc. *[low man on the team, low marks]* **7.** near the horizon *[the sun was low]* **8.** near the equator *[a low latitude]* **9.** cut so as to expose the neck or part of the shoulders, chest, or back; décolleté *[a dress with a low neckline]* **10.** *a)* [Rare] prostrate or dead *b)* in hiding or obscurity *[to stay low]* **11.** deep; profound *[a low bow]* **12.** lacking energy; enfeebled; weak **13.** depressed in spirits; melancholy **14.** not of high rank; humble; plebeian *[a man of low origin]* **15.** vulgar; coarse; debased; undignified **16.** mean; despicable; contemptible *[a low trick]* **17.** poor; slight; unfavorable *[to have a low opinion of someone]* **18.** containing less than a normal amount of some usual element *[low in calories, a low-salt diet]* **19.** not advanced in evolution, development, complexity, etc.; inferior *[a low form of plant life]* **20.** relatively recent *[a manuscript of a low date]* ☆**21.** designating or of that gear ratio of a motor vehicle transmission which produces the lowest speed and the greatest power **22.** *a)* not well supplied with; short of (with *on*) *[low on ammunition]* *b)* [Colloq.] not having any or much money; short of ready cash **23.** of little intensity; not loud: said of a sound **24.** designating or producing tones made by relatively slow vibrations; deep in pitch **25.** very informal and permissive in matters of ceremony, doctrine, etc. **26.** *Phonet.* produced with the tongue held relatively low in the mouth: said of vowels, as (a, ä, ô) —*adv.* **1.** in, to, or toward a low position, level, direction, etc. *[hit them low]* **2.** in a low manner **3.** quietly; softly *[speak low]* **4.** with a deep pitch —*n.* something low; specif., ☆*a)* that gear of a motor vehicle, etc., producing the lowest speed and the greatest power: also, an arrangement similar to this in an automatic transmission *b)* a low level, point, degree, etc. *[the stock market low for the day]* ☆*c)* *Meteorol.* an area of low barometric pressure —*SYN.* see BASE² —**lay low 1.** to cause to fall by hitting **2.** to overcome or kill —**lie low** ☆**1.** to keep oneself hidden or inconspicuous ☆**2.** to wait patiently for an opportunity —**low′ness** *n.*

low² (lō) *vi.* [ME. *lowen* < OE. *hlowan,* akin to ON. *hloa,* to roar < IE. base **kel-,* to cry, cry out, whence L. *clamor]* to make the characteristic sound of a cow; moo —*vt.* to express by lowing —*n.* the characteristic sound of a cow

low³ (lō) *n., vi.* [ME. *loghe* < ON. *logi,* akin to MHG. *lohe,* flame: for IE. base see LIGHT¹] [Scot. or Brit. Dial.] flame or blaze

Low (lō) **1.** Sir **David,** 1891–1963; Brit. political cartoonist, born in New Zealand **2. Juliette,** (born *Juliette Gordon*) 1860–1927; U.S. founder of the Girl Scouts

Low Archipelago *same as* TUAMOTU ARCHIPELAGO

low blow 1. a blow below the belt, illegal in boxing ☆**2.** an unsportsmanlike or unfair action, attack, etc.

low·born (lō′bôrn′) *adj.* of humble birth

low·boy (-boi′) *n.* [LOW¹ + BOY] ☆a chest of drawers mounted on short legs to about the height of a table

low·bred (-bred′) *adj.* **1.** of inferior stock or breed **2.** ill-mannered; vulgar; crude; coarse

☆**low·brow** (-brou′) *n.* [Colloq.] a person lacking or considered to lack highly cultivated, intellectual tastes —*adj.* [Colloq.] of or for a lowbrow Often a term of contempt or of false humility

Low Church that party of the Anglican Church which attaches little importance to the priesthood and to traditional rituals, doctrines, etc. and is strongly evangelical: opposed to HIGH CHURCH, BROAD CHURCH —**Low′-Church′** *adj.* —**Low′-Church′man** *n., pl.* -men

low comedy comedy that gets its effect mainly from action and situation, as burlesque, farce, slapstick, and horseplay, rather than from witty dialogue and characterization: cf. HIGH COMEDY

low-cost (-kôst′) *adj.* available at a low cost

Low Countries the Netherlands, Belgium, & Luxembourg

☆**low-down** (lō′doun′; *for adj.* -doun′) *n.* [Slang] the true, pertinent facts; esp., secret or inside information (with *the*) —*adj.* [Colloq.] mean; contemptible; despicable

Low·ell (lō′əl) [after Francis C. *Lowell* (1775–1817), industrialist] city in NE Mass.: pop. 94,000

Low·ell (lō′əl) **1. Abbott Lawrence,** 1856–1943; U.S. educator **2. Amy,** 1874–1925; U.S. poet & critic: sister of *prec.* **3. James Russell,** 1819–91; U.S. poet, essayist, & editor **4. Percival,** 1855–1916; U.S. astronomer: brother of *Abbott & Amy* **5. Robert (Traill Spence, Jr.),** 1917– ; U.S. poet

low·er¹ (lō′ər) *adj. compar. of* LOW¹ **1.** in a place or on a level below another **2.** inferior in rank, authority, dignity, etc. **3.** less in quantity, degree, value, intensity, etc. **4.** being farther south, closer to a shore or to the mouth of a river, or below land of higher elevation **5.** [L-] *Geol.* earlier: used of a division of a period *[Lower Devonian]* —*n.* something below another similar thing; specif., ☆[Colloq.] a lower berth, as in a Pullman car —*vt.* **1.** to let or put down *[lower the window]* **2.** to reduce in height, elevation, amount, value, etc. *[to lower prices]* **3.** to weaken or lessen *[to lower one's resistance]* **4.** to bring down in respect, dignity, etc.; demean; degrade *[to lower oneself by accepting a bribe]* **5.** to reduce (a sound) in volume or in pitch —*vi.* to become lower; sink, fall, become reduced, etc.

low·er² (lou′ər) *vi.* [ME. *louren,* akin to LURK, G. *lauern,* to lurk] **1.** to scowl or frown **2.** to appear dark and threatening *[a lowering sky]* —*n.* a frowning or threatening look

lower bound *Math.* a number that is less than or equal to any number in a set

Lower California *same as* BAJA CALIFORNIA

Lower Canada *former name of* QUEBEC

low·er-case (lō′ər kās′) *adj. Printing* designating, of, or in lower case —*vt.* -**cased′,** -**cas′ing** to set up in, or to change to, lower case

lower case [from their being kept in the lower of two cases of type] small-letter type used in printing, as distinguished from capital letters (*upper case*)

lower class the social class below the middle class; working class, or proletariat

☆**low·er·class·man** (-klas′mən) *n., pl.* -**men** (-mən) a student in the freshman or sophomore class

lower criticism textual criticism of the Scriptures: see CRITICISM (sense 5)

lower fungus a fungus which lacks large, well-organized fruiting bodies and whose cells contain many nuclei, as the slime molds

Lower House [often l- h-] in a legislature having two branches, that branch which is usually larger and more representative, as the House of Representatives of the U.S. Congress

low·er·ing (lou′ər iŋ) *adj.* [prp. of LOWER²] **1.** scowling; frowning darkly **2.** dark, as if about to rain or snow; overcast —**low′er·ing·ly** *adv.*

low·er·most (lō′ər mōst′) *adj.* below all others; lowest

Lower Saxony state of N West Germany, on the North Sea: 18,296 sq. mi.; pop. 6,921,000; cap. Hanover: see SAXONY, map

Lower Silurian *same as* ORDOVICIAN

lower world 1. *same as* NETHER WORLD **2.** the earth

low·er·y (lou′ər ē) *adj.* [see LOWER² & -Y²] dark and cloudy

Lowes (lōz), **John Livingston** 1867-1945; U.S. scholar, critic, & educator

lowest common denominator 1. *same as* LEAST COMMON DENOMINATOR **2.** that which is accepted, understood, appreciated, etc. by the broadest mass of people

lowest common multiple *same as* LEAST COMMON MULTIPLE

Lowes·toft (lōs′täft, -təf) city in Suffolk, E England, on the North Sea: pop. 47,000 —*n.* a variety of porcelain formerly made there

low frequency any radio frequency between 30 and 300 kilohertz

Low German 1. *same as* PLATTDEUTSCH **2.** the West Germanic languages, other than High German, of the Germanic branch of the Indo-European family of languages, represented by Old Low Franconian, Old Saxon, Old Frisian, and Old English and their later stages, including Dutch, Plattdeutsch, English, Frisian, etc.: distinguished from HIGH GERMAN

low-grade (lō′grād′) *adj.* **1.** of inferior quality or value **2.** of little degree *[a low-grade fever]*

low-key (-kē′) *adj.* of low intensity, tone, etc.; subdued or restrained: also **low′-keyed′**

low·land (lō′lənd; *also, for n.,* -land′) *n.* land that is below the level of the surrounding land —*adj.* of, in, or from such a region —**the Lowlands** lowland region of SC Scotland, between the Highlands & the Southern Uplands —**low′land·er, Low′land·er** *n.*

Low Latin nonclassical Latin, esp. in the medieval period

low-lev·el (lō′lev′l) *adj.* **1.** of or by persons of low office or rank **2.** in a low office or rank

low·ly (-lē) *adj.* **-li·er, -li·est** 1. of or suited to a low position or rank 2. humble; meek 3. ordinary; commonplace —*adv.* 1. humbly; meekly 2. in a low manner, position, etc. 3. low in sound; softly; gently —SYN. see HUMBLE —**low′li·ness** *n.*

Low Mass a Mass said, not sung, and with less ceremonialism than High Mass: it is conducted by one priest, normally assisted by one or two servers

low-mind·ed (-mīn′did) *adj.* having or showing a coarse, vulgar mind —**low′-mind′ed·ly** *adv.* —**low′-mind′ed·ness** *n.*

low-necked (-nekt′) *adj.* having a low neckline; décolleté: said of a dress, etc.: also **low′-neck′**

low-pitched (-picht′) *adj.* 1. having a low tone or a low range of tone *[a low-pitched voice]* 2. having little pitch, or slope: said of a roof 3. of low intensity; subdued

low profile ☆an unobtrusive, barely noticeable presence, or concealed, inconspicuous activity

low-pres·sure (-presh′ər) *adj.* 1. *a)* having or using a low or relatively low pressure *b)* having or indicating a low barometric pressure 2. not energetic or forceful

low-priced (-prīst′) *adj.* costing relatively little

low-proof (-prōōf′) *adj.* low in alcohol content

low relief *same as* BAS-RELIEF

☆**low-rise** (-rīz′) *adj.* designating or of a building, esp. an apartment house, having only a few stories

low-spir·it·ed (-spir′i tid) *adj.* in low spirits; sad; depressed —**low′-spir′it·ed·ly** *adv.* —**low′-spir′it·ed·ness** *n.*

Low Sunday the first Sunday after Easter

low-ten·sion (-ten′shən) *adj.* having, carrying, or operating under a low voltage

low-test (-test′) *adj.* vaporizing at a relatively high temperature: said of gasoline

low tide 1. *a)* the lowest level reached by the ebbing tide *b)* the time when the tide is at this level 2. the lowest point reached by anything

low water 1. water at its lowest level, as in a stream 2. *same as* LOW TIDE

low-wa·ter mark (-wôt′ər, -wät′-) 1. a mark showing low water 2. the lowest point reached by anything

lox¹ (läks) *n.* [via Yid. < G. *lachs*, salmon, akin to OE. *leax*, salmon, Tocharian *lakṣi*, fish] a variety of salty smoked salmon

lox² (läks) *n.* [*l(iquid) ox(ygen)*] oxygen in a liquid state, used in a fuel mixture for rockets

lox·o·drom·ic (läk′sə dräm′ik) *adj.* [< Gr. *loxos*, oblique + *dromos*, a running] having to do with sailing or rhumb lines; of oblique sailing

lox·o·drom·ics (-iks) *n.pl.* [*with sing. v.*] the art or practice of oblique sailing

loy·al (loi′əl) *adj.* [Fr. < OFr. *loial, leial* < L. *legalis*: see LEGAL] 1. faithful to the constituted authority of one's country 2. faithful to those persons, ideals, etc. that one is under obligation to defend, support, or be true to 3. relating to or indicating loyalty —SYN. see FAITHFUL —**loy′al·ly** *adv.*

loy·al·ist (-ist) *n.* 1. a person who is loyal; esp., one who supports the established government of his country during times of revolt ☆2. [*often* L-] in the American Revolution, a colonist who was loyal to the British government 3. [L-] in the Spanish Civil War, one who remained loyal to the Republic, opposing Franco's revolt —**loy′al·ism** *n.*

loy·al·ty (-tē) *n.*, *pl.* **-ties** [ME. *loyaulte* < OFr. *loialte*] quality, state, or instance of being loyal; faithfulness or faithful adherence to a person, government, cause, duty, etc. —SYN. see ALLEGIANCE

Lo·yang (lō′yäŋ′) city in Honan province, EC China, near the Hwang Ho: pop. 600,000

Loy·o·la (loi ō′lə) see IGNATIUS (OF) LOYOLA

loz·enge (läz′nj) *n.* [ME. *losenge* < OFr., prob. < Gaul. *lausa*, stone slab: from the shape] 1. a plane figure with four equal sides and two obtuse angles; diamond 2. a cough drop, candy, etc., orig. in this shape

☆**LP** [*L(ong) P(laying)*] *a trademark for* a long-playing record —*n.* a long-playing record

LPG liquefied petroleum gas: also **LP-gas**

LPN, L.P.N. Licensed Practical Nurse

Lr *Chem.* lawrencium

L.R. Lloyd's Register

LS— *U.S. Navy* landing ship (following letter indicates type, as LST, Landing Ship-Tank)

L.S. 1. Licentiate in Surgery 2. [L. *locus sigilla*] place of the seal

LSD [*l(y)s(ergic acid) d(iethylamide)*] a crystalline compound, $C_{15}H_{15}N_2CON(C_2H_5)_2$, an amide of lysergic acid, used in the study of schizophrenia and other mental disorders and as a psychedelic drug: it produces hallucinations, delusions, etc. resembling those occurring in a psychotic state: also **LSD 25**

L.S.D., £.s.d., l.s.d. [L. *librae, solidi, denarii*] pounds, shillings, pence

Lt. Lieutenant

l.t. 1. local time 2. long ton

lt., lt *Football* left tackle

Lt. Col. Lieutenant Colonel

Lt. Comdr. Lieutenant Commander

Ltd., ltd. limited

Lt. Gen. Lieutenant General

Lt. Gov. Lieutenant Governor

Lu *Chem.* lutetium

Lu·a·la·ba (lōō′ä lä′bä) upper course of the Congo, rising in the SE Congo (sense 2) & flowing north

Lu·an·da (lōō än′də, -an′-) capital of Angola; seaport on the Atlantic: pop. 347,000

Lu·ang Pra·bang (lōō′ äŋ′ prə bäŋ′) royal capital of Laos, on the Mekong River: pop. c. 30,000

lu·au (lōō ou′, lōō′ou′) *n.* [Haw.] a Hawaiian feast, usually with entertainment

Lu·ba (lōō′bä) *n.* 1. *pl.* **-bas, -ba** any member of an agricultural people of the southern Congo (sense 2) 2. their Bantu language

lub·ber (lub′ər) *n.* [ME. *lobre* < *lobbe*- (see LOB)] 1. a big, slow, clumsy person 2. an inexperienced, clumsy sailor; landlubber —*adj.* big and clumsy —**lub′ber·li·ness** *n.* —**lub′ber·ly** *adj., adv.*

☆**lubber grasshopper** a flightless grasshopper (*Romalea microptera*) of the SE U.S., with a large, dark-brown body and clumsy movements

lubber line a vertical black mark or line inside a compass, which is aligned with the bow of a ship or aircraft

lub·ber's hole (lub′ərz) *Naut.* a hole in a top (of a lower mast) through which a sailor may go to reach the topmast rigging

Lub·bock (lub′ək) [after T. S. *Lubbock*, Confederate officer] city in NW Tex.: pop. 149,000

☆**lube** (lōōb) *n.* [contr. < *lubricating (oil)*] 1. a lubricating oil for machinery: also **lube oil** 2. [Colloq.] a lubrication

Lü·beck (lü′bek; *E.* lōō′-) city & port in N West Germany, in Schleswig-Holstein: pop. 240,000

Lub·lin (lyōō′blēn; *E.* lōō′blin) city in SE Poland: pop. 203,000

lu·bri·cant (lōō′brə kənt) *adj.* [L. *lubricans*, prp.: see ff.] reducing friction by providing a smooth film as a covering over parts that move against each other; lubricating —*n.* a substance for reducing friction in this way, as oil or grease

lu·bri·cate (-kāt′) *vt.* **-cat·ed, -cat·ing** [< L. *lubricatus*, pp. of *lubricare*, to make smooth or slippery < *lubricus*, smooth < IE. base **sleub*-, to slide, slip, whence SLIP¹, SLEEVE] 1. to make slippery or smooth 2. to apply a lubricant to —*vi.* to serve as a lubricant —**lu′bri·ca′tion** *n.* —**lu′bri·ca′tive** *adj.*

lu·bri·ca·tor (-kāt′ər) *n.* a person or thing that lubricates; specif., *a)* a lubricant *b)* an oil cup or similar device for supplying a lubricant to machinery

lu·bric·i·ty (lōō bris′ə tē) *n.*, *pl.* **-ties** [Fr. *lubricité* < LL. *lubricitas*] 1. slipperiness; smoothness; esp., effectiveness as a lubricant as indicated by this quality 2. trickiness; shiftiness 3. lewdness —**lu·bri′cious** (-brish′əs), **lu′bri·cous** (-bri kəs) *adj.*

Lu·bum·ba·shi (lōō′bōōm bä′shē) city in the SE Congo (sense 2), near the border of Zambia: pop. c. 200,000

Lu·can (lōō′kən) (L. name *Marcus Annaeus Lucanus*) 39–65 A.D.; Rom. poet, born in Spain

Lu·ca·ni·a (lōō kā′nē ə) 1. ancient district in S Italy, now the It. region of BASILICATA 2. Mount, mountain in the St. Elias range, SW Yukon, Canada: 17,150 ft.

lu·carne (lōō′kärn) *n.* [Fr., altered (after OFr. *luiserne*, lantern: see LUCERNE) < OFr. *lucanne* < ?] a dormer window

Lu·cas van Ley·den (lōō′käs vän lī′dən) (born *Lucas Jacobsz*) 1494?–1533; Du. painter & etcher

Luc·ca (lōōk′kä) city in Tuscany, W Italy: pop. 86,000

luce (lōōs) *n.* [ME. < OFr. *lus* < L. *lucius*, kind of fish] the pike, esp. when full-grown

Luce (lōōs), **Henry Robinson** 1898–1967; U.S. editor & publisher

lu·cent (lōō′s'nt) *adj.* [L. *lucens*, prp. of *lucere*, to shine: see LIGHT¹] 1. giving off light; shining 2. translucent or clear —**lu′cen·cy** *n.* —**lu′cent·ly** *adv.*

Lu·cerne (lōō surn′; *Fr.* lü sern′) 1. canton in C Switzerland: 577 sq. mi.; pop. 267,000 2. its capital: pop. 73,000 3. Lake (of), lake in C Switzerland: 44 sq. mi.

lu·cerne, lu·cern (lōō surn′) *n.* [Fr. *luzerne* < ModPr. *luzerno*, lit., glowworm < Pr. *luzerna*, lamp < VL. **lūcerna*, for L. *lucerna*, lamp < *lucere* (see LIGHT¹): so named because of the shiny seeds] [Chiefly Brit.] *same as* ALFALFA

lu·ces (lōō′sēz) *n. alt. pl. of* LUX

Lu·chou, Lu·chow (lōō′jō′) city in Szechwan province, SC China, on the Yangtze: pop. 289,000

Lu·cia (lōō′shə; *It.* lōō chē′ä) [It. < L.: see LUCIUS, LUCY] a feminine name

Lu·cian (lōō′shən) [L. *Lucianus*, lit., of Lucius] 1. a masculine name: equiv. Fr. *Lucien* 2. 2d cent. A.D.; Gr. satirist, born in Syria

lu·cid (lōō′sid) *adj.* [L. *lucidus* < *lucere*, to shine: see LIGHT¹] 1. [Poet.] bright; shining 2. transparent 3. designating an interval of sanity in a mental disorder 4. clear to the mind; readily understood *[lucid instructions]* 5. clearheaded; rational *[a lucid thinker]* —**lu·cid′i·ty, lu′cid·ness** *n.* —**lu′cid·ly** *adv.*

Lu·ci·fer (lōō′sə fər) [ME. < OE. < L., morning star (in ML., Satan), lit., light-bringing < *lux* (gen. *lucis*), LIGHT¹ + *ferre*, to BEAR¹] 1. [Poet.] the planet Venus when it is the morning star 2. *Theol.* Satan, esp. as leader of the revolt of the angels before his fall —*n.* [l-] an early type of friction match

lu·cif·er·ase (lōō sif′ə rās′) *n.* [LUCIFER(IN) + -ASE] an oxidizing enzyme that acts with luciferin to produce light

lu·cif·er·in (-ər in) *n.* [L. *lucifer* (see LUCIFER) + -IN¹] a

substance in luminescent organisms, as fireflies, that produces light by combining with oxygen in the presence of luciferase

lu·cif·er·ous (-əs) *adj.* [L. *lucifer* (see LUCIFER) + -OUS] [Now Rare] providing light or mental insight

Lu·cille, Lu·cile (loo sēl′) a feminine name: see LUCY

Lu·ci·na (loo sī′nə) *Rom. Myth.* the goddess of childbirth, variously identified with Juno, Diana, etc.

Lu·cin·da (loo sin′də) a feminine name: see LUCY

☆**Lu·cite** (loo′sīt) [< L. *lux* (gen. *lucis*), light + -ITE¹] a trademark for an acrylic resin or plastic that is cast or molded into transparent or translucent sheets, tubes, rods, etc.

Lu·cius (loo′shəs) [L. < *lux*, LIGHT¹] a masculine name: fem. *Lucia*.

luck (luk) *n.* [ME. *lucke*, prob. < MDu. *luk*, contr. < *gelucke* < ODu. *gilukki* (whence G. *glück*, fortune, good luck) < ? base *leug-*, to bend (cf. LEEK, LOCK): basic sense "what bends together," hence, "what occurs, what is fitting, lucky occurrence"] 1. the seemingly chance happening of events which affect one; fortune; lot; fate 2. good fortune; success, prosperity, advantage, etc. 3. an object believed to bring good luck —*vi.* [Colloq.] to be lucky enough to come (*into, on, through,* etc.) —☆**crowd** (or **push**) **one's luck** [Slang] to take superfluous risks in an already favorable situation —**down on one's luck** in misfortune; unlucky —**in luck** fortunate; lucky —☆**luck out** [Colloq.] to have things turn out favorably for one; be lucky —**out of luck** unfortunate; unlucky —**try one's luck** to try to do something without being sure of one's ability or of the outcome —**worse luck** unfortunately; unhappily

luck·less (-lis) *adj.* having no good luck; unlucky —**luck′less·ly** *adv.* —**luck′less·ness** *n.*

Luck·now (luk′nou) city in N India; capital of Uttar Pradesh: pop. 595,000

luck·y (-ē) *adj.* **luck′i·er, luck′i·est** 1. having good luck; fortunate 2. happening or resulting fortunately [a *lucky* change] 3. bringing or believed to bring good luck [a *lucky* coin] —**luck′i·ly** *adv.* —**luck′i·ness** *n.*

SYN.—**lucky** implies a favorable or advantageous event happening by mere chance, often unexpectedly, and not as the result of effort or merit [a *lucky* find, guess, etc.]; **fortunate**, a more formal word, is usually used of more important or serious matters [a *fortunate* choice of profession]; **providential** connotes the intervention of God or some higher agency in bringing about the favorable event [a *providential* escape from death]; **happy** emphasizes the pleasure felt by the person affected by the lucky event [marriage resulted from that *happy* encounter] —**ANT. unlucky, disastrous**

lu·cra·tive (loo′krə tiv) *adj.* [ME. *lucratif* < L. *lucrativus* < pp. of *lucrari*, to gain < *lucrum*: see ff.] producing wealth or profit; profitable; remunerative [a *lucrative* investment] —**lu′cra·tive·ly** *adv.* —**lu′cra·tive·ness** *n.*

lu·cre (loo′kər) *n.* [ME. < L. *lucrum*, gain, riches < IE. base *lau-*, to capture, whence Sans. *lótram*, booty, OE. *lean*, OHG. *lon*, reward] riches; money: now chiefly in a humorously derogatory sense, as in **filthy lucre** (cf. I Tim. 3:3)

Lu·cre·tia (loo krē′shə) [L., fem. of *Lucretius* < ? *lucrum*: see prec.] a feminine name: equiv. Fr. *Lucrèce*, It. *Lucrezia*

Lu·cre·tius (loo krē′shəs) (born *Titus Lucretius Carus*) 96?–55? B.C.; Rom. poet & Epicurean philosopher

lu·cu·brate (loo′kyoo brāt′) *vi.* **-brat·ed, -brat′ing** [< L. *lucubratus*, pp. of *lucubrare*, to work by candlelight < *lux* (gen. *lucis*), LIGHT¹] 1. to work, study, or write laboriously, esp. late at night 2. to write in a scholarly manner —**lu′cu·bra′tor** *n.*

lu·cu·bra·tion (loo′kyoo brā′shən) *n.* [L. *lucubratio*] 1. the act of lucubrating; laborious work, study, or writing, esp. that done late at night 2. something produced by such study, etc.; esp., a learned or carefully elaborated work 3. [often *pl.*] any literary composition: humorous usage suggesting pedantry

lu·cu·lent (loo′kyoo lənt) *adj.* [ME. < L. *luculentus* < *lux* (gen. *lucis*), LIGHT¹] 1. [Rare] bright; shining 2. clear to the understanding; lucid —**lu′cu·lent·ly** *adv.*

Lu·cul·lus (loo kul′əs), (**Lucius Licinius**) 110?–57? B.C.; Rom. general & consul: proverbial for his wealth & luxurious banquets —**Lu·cul′lan** (-ən), **Lu·cul′li·an** (-ē ən), **Lu·cul·le·an** (loo′kə lē′ən) *adj.*

Lu·cy (loo′sē) [prob. via Fr. *Lucie* < L. *Lucia*, fem. of *Lucius*: see LUCIUS] 1. a feminine name: var. *Lucille, Lucile, Lucinda*; equiv. It. & Sp. *Lucia* 2. Saint, ?–303? A.D.; It. martyr: her day is Dec. 13

☆**Lucy Ston·er** (stō′nər) [see Lucy STONE] a person who advocates that married women keep and use their maiden names

Lud·dite (lud′īt) *n.* [said to be after a Ned *Lud*, feeble-minded man who smashed two frames belonging to a Leicestershire employer (c. 1779)] any of a group of workers in England (1811–1816) who smashed new labor-saving textile machinery in protest against reduced wages and unemployment

Lu·den·dorff (loo′dən dôrf′), **E·rich** (**Friedrich Wilhelm**) **von** (ā′riH fôn) 1865–1937; Ger. general

Lu·dhi·a·na (loo′dē ä′nə) city in N India, in Punjab: pop. 244,000

lu·di·crous (loo′di krəs) *adj.* [L. *ludicrus* < *ludus*, a play, game < IE. base *leid-*, to play, tease, whence Gr. *loidorein*, to rail at, rebuke] causing laughter because absurd or ridiculous; laughably absurd —SYN. see ABSURD —**lu′di·crous·ly** *adv.* —**lu′di·crous·ness** *n.*

Lud·wigs·ha·fen (loot′viHs hä′fən; *E.* lood′vigz-) city in SW West Germany, in Rhineland-Palatinate, on the Rhine: pop. 176,000

lu·es (loo′ēz) *n.* [ModL. < L., a plague, decay < *luere*, to flow: see LOSE] same as SYPHILIS —**lu·et′ic** (-et′ik) *adj.*

luff (luf) *n.* [ME. *lof* < ODu. *loef*, weather side (of a ship), auxiliary oar for steering, akin to ON. *lōfi*, palm of the hand, IE. base *lēp-*, *lōp-*, flat object, flat hand, whence OHG. *lappo*, flat hand, rudder blade, Russ. *lopata*, a shovel, rudder blade] 1. the act of sailing close or closer to the wind 2. the forward edge of a fore-and-aft sail 3. the fullest part of a ship's bow —*vi.* 1. to turn the bow of a ship toward the wind; sail close or closer to the wind 2. to cause the luff of a sail to shake by turning too close to the wind 3. to raise or lower the jib of a crane

luf·fa (luf′ə) *n.* [ModL. < Ar. *lūf*] 1. same as DISHCLOTH GOURD 2. the fibrous, vascular skeleton of the pod of a dishcloth gourd, used as a sponge

‡**luft·mensch** (looft′mensh′) *n., pl.* **-mensch′en** (-men′shən) [Yid.: cf. G. *luft*, air (see ff.) + *mensch*, person] an impractical person who cannot apply himself realistically to ordinary work or everyday matters

‡**Luft·waf·fe** (looft′vä′fə) *n.* [G. < *luft*, air (akin to OE. *lyft*, air & ON. *lopt*: see LOFT) + *waffe*, WEAPON] the Nazi air force in World War II

lug¹ (lug) *vt.* **lugged, lug′ging** [ME. *luggen*, prob. < Scand., as in Sw. *lugga*, to pull, lit., pull by the hair < *lugg*, forelock] 1. to carry or drag (something heavy) 2. to introduce (a topic, story, etc.) without good reason into a conversation, discourse, etc. —*n.* [< ?] 1. [Scot.] an ear 2. an ear-like projection by which a thing is held or supported 3. a loop on the side of a harness through which the shaft passes 4. a heavy nut used with a bolt to secure a wheel to an axle ☆5. a shallow box in which fruit, as cherries, grapes, etc., is packed and shipped by growers ☆6. [Slang] money exacted for political purposes: chiefly in **put the lug on**, to exact a contribution from 7. [Slang] a fellow, esp. a stupid or loutish fellow 8. [Archaic] the act of lugging

lug² (lug) *n. clipped form of* LUGSAIL

lug³ (lug) *n.* [< ?] *clipped form of* LUGWORM

Lu·gansk (loo gänsk′) city in the E Ukrainian S.S.R., in the Donets Basin: pop. 339,000

luge (loozh) *n.* [Fr. < dial. (esp. in Savoy and Switzerland), prob. ult. < Gaul.] a racing sled for one or two persons —*vi.* **luged, luge′ing** to race with such a sled

Lu·ger (loo′gər) [G.] *a trademark for* a German semiautomatic pistol —*n.* [often l-] this pistol

lug·gage (lug′ij) *n.* [< LUG¹ + -AGE] suitcases, valises, trunks, etc.; baggage

lug·ger (lug′ər) *n.* a small vessel equipped with a lugsail or lugsails

lug·sail (lug′s'l, -sāl′) *n.* [< ? LUG¹, with reference to hauling sail around the mast in changing course] a four-sided sail without boom, or lower yard, attached to an upper yard which hangs obliquely on the mast

LUGSAIL

lu·gu·bri·ous (loo goo′brē əs, -gyoo′-) *adj.* [L. *lugubris* < *lugere*, to mourn + -OUS] very sad or mournful, esp. in a way that seems exaggerated or ridiculous —**lu·gu′bri·ous·ly** *adv.* —**lu·gu′bri·ous·ness** *n.*

lug·worm (lug′wurm′) *n.* [< ? + WORM] any of a genus (*Arenicola*) of segmented worms with bristly appendages, that burrow into sandy seashores and are used for bait

Lui·chow Peninsula (lā′jō′) peninsula in Kwangtung province, SE China, opposite Hainan island: c. 90 mi. long

Luik (loik, lük) *Fl. name of* LIÈGE

Luke (look) [LL.(Ec.) *Lucas* < Gr.(Ec.) *Loukas*, prob. contr. of *Loukanos*] 1. a masculine name 2. *Bible* a) one of the four Evangelists, a physician and companion of the apostle Paul and the reputed author of the third Gospel and the Acts of the Apostles: also *Saint Luke*: his day is Oct. 18 b) the third book of the New Testament, telling the story of Jesus' life

luke·warm (look′wôrm′) *adj.* [ME. *luke warme* < *luke*, tepid + *warm*, WARM: ME. forms < base of, or akin to, LowG. *luk*, Du. *leuk*, tepid < IE. *kleu-* < base *kel-*, warm, whence OE. *hleowe*, tepid, L. *calere*, to be warm] 1. barely or moderately warm: said of liquids 2. lacking warmth of feeling or enthusiasm [*lukewarm* praise] —**luke′warm′ly** *adv.* —**luke′warm′ness** *n.*

lull (lul) *vt.* [ME. *lullen*, of echoic orig.] 1. to calm or soothe by gentle sound or motion: chiefly in **lull to sleep**

2. to bring into a specified condition by soothing and reassuring [to *lull* people into a false sense of security] **3.** to make less intense; quiet; allay [to *lull* one's fears] —*vi.* to become calm —*n.* a short period of quiet or of comparative calm, lessened activity, etc.

lull·a·by (lul'ə bī') *n., pl.* **-bies'** [< *lulla* (< ME.), echoic + *-by*, as in BYE-BYE] **1.** a song for lulling a baby to sleep; cradlesong **2.** music for this —*vt.* **-bied'**, **-by'ing** to lull with or as with a lullaby

Lul·ly (lü lē'), **Jean Bap·tiste** (zhän bȧ tēst') (born *Giovanni Battista Lulli*) 1632–87; Fr. composer, chiefly of operas, born in Italy

Lu·lu (lōō'lōō) a feminine name: see LOUISE —*n.* [l-] ☆[Old Slang] any person or thing outstanding for some quality, as a beautiful girl, a difficult task, etc.

lum (lum) *n.* [< ?] [Scot. & N. Eng. Dial.] a chimney

lum·ba·go (lum bā'gō) *n.* [L. < *lumbus*, loin: see ff.] rheumatic pain in the lumbar region; backache, esp. in the lower part of the back

lum·bar (lum'bər, -bär) *adj.* [ModL. *lumbaris* < L. *lumbus*, loin < IE. *londhwos* < base *lendh-*, whence OE. *lendenu*, loins] of or near the loins; specif., designating or of the vertebrae, nerves, arteries, etc. in the part of the body just below the thoracic part

lum·ber[1] (lum'bər) *n.* [< ? LOMBARD: orig., pawnbroker's shop or storeroom, hence pawned articles in storage, hence stored articles, hence lumber] **1.** miscellaneous discarded household articles, furniture, etc. stored away or taking up room ☆**2.** timber sawed into beams, planks, boards, etc. of convenient sizes —*vt.* **1.** to fill or obstruct with useless articles or rubbish; clutter ☆**2.** to remove (timber) from an area; cut down (trees) —☆*vi.* to cut down timber and saw it into lumber —☆**lum'ber·er** *n.*

lum·ber[2] (lum'bər) *vi.* [ME. *lomeren* < ? Scand., as in Sw. *lomra*, to resound, *loma*, to walk heavily] **1.** to move heavily, clumsily, and, often, noisily [tanks *lumbering* up a slope] **2.** to rumble

lum·ber·ing[1] (lum'bər iŋ) *n.* ☆the occupation and business of cutting trees and preparing lumber

lum·ber·ing[2] (lum'bər iŋ) *adj.* **1.** moving heavily, clumsily, or noisily **2.** rumbling —**lum'ber·ing·ly** *adv.*

lum·ber·jack (lum'bər jak') *n.* **1.** a man whose work is cutting down timber and preparing it for the sawmill **2.** an earlier type of short, woolen or leather coat or jacket, of a kind worn by lumberjacks: also called **lumber jacket**

☆**lum·ber·man** (-mən) *n., pl.* **-men** (-mən) **1.** same as LUMBERJACK (sense 1) **2.** a person who deals in lumber

☆**lum·ber·yard** (-yärd') *n.* a place where lumber is kept for sale

lum·bo- (lum'bō, -bə) [< L. *lumbus*, loin: see LUMBAR] *a combining form meaning:* **1.** loin **2.** lumbar (and)

lum·bri·ca·lis (lum'bri kā'lis) *n., pl.* **-ca'les** (-kā'lēz) [ModL. < L. *lumbricus*, intestinal worm, earthworm: from the shape of the muscles] any of four small muscles in the palm of the hand and in the sole of the foot: also **lum'bri·cal** (-k'l)

lum·bri·coid (lum'bri koid') *adj.* [< L. *lumbricus* (see prec.) + -OID] resembling an earthworm

lu·men (lōō'mən) *n., pl.* **-mi·na** (-mi nə), **-mens** [ModL. < L., LIGHT[1]] **1.** a unit of measure for the flow of light, equal to the amount of flow through a unit solid angle from a uniform point source of one candle **2.** the bore of a hollow needle, catheter, etc. **3.** *Anat.* the passage within a tubular organ

lu·mi·naire (lōō'mə ner') *n.* [Fr., light, lighting < LL.(Ec.) *luminare*, a light, lamp: see LUMINARY] a floodlight fixture, with a lamp, reflector, etc.

lu·mi·nance (lōō'mə nəns) *n.* [< L. *lumen* (gen. *luminis*), LIGHT[1] + -ANCE] **1.** the quality or state of being luminous **2.** luminous intensity, expressed in candles per unit projected area for the luminous surface, measured as in square meters

lu·mi·nar·y (lōō'mə ner'ē) *n., pl.* **-nar'ies** [ME. < OFr. *luminarie* < LL.(Ec.) *luminarium*, pl. of *luminare* < L. *lumen*, LIGHT[1]] **1.** a body that gives off light, such as the sun or moon **2.** *a)* a person who sheds light on some subject or enlightens mankind; famous intellectual *b)* any famous or well-known person

lu·mi·nesce (lōō'mə nes') *vi.* **-nesced'**, **-nesc'ing** [backformation < LUMINESCENT] to be or become luminescent

lu·mi·nes·cence (-'ns) *n.* [< L. *lumen*, LIGHT[1] + -ESCENCE] any giving off of light caused by the absorption of radiant or corpuscular energy and not by incandescence; any cold light; specif., fluorescence or phosphorescence occurring in various chemical, biological, electrical, etc. processes at relatively low temperatures

lu·mi·nes·cent (-'nt) *adj.* [< L. *lumen*, LIGHT[1] + -ESCENT] of, exhibiting, or capable of exhibiting luminescence

lu·mi·nif·er·ous (lōō'mə nif'ər əs) *adj.* [< L. *lumen*, LIGHT[1] + -FEROUS] giving off or transmitting light

lu·mi·nos·i·ty (-näs'ə tē) *n., pl.* **-ties** [ML. *luminositas*] **1.** the quality or condition of being luminous **2.** something luminous **3.** brightness

lu·mi·nous (lōō'mə nəs) *adj.* [ME. < L. *luminosus* < *lumen*, LIGHT[1]] **1.** giving off light; shining; bright **2.** filled with light; illuminated **3.** glowing in the dark, as paint with a phosphor in it **4.** clear; readily understood **5.** intellectually brilliant —*SYN.* see BRIGHT —**lu'mi·nous·ly** *adv.* —**lu'mi·nous·ness** *n.*

luminous energy *same as* LIGHT[1] (sense 1 *a*)

luminous flux the rate of flow of light radiation

lum·mox (lum'əks) *n.* [< ?] [Colloq.] a clumsy, stupid person

lump[1] (lump) *n.* [ME. *lompe, lumpe*, akin ? to Dan. *lompe*, a mass, lump, Sw. dial. *lump*, a block, stump] **1.** a solid mass of no special shape, esp. one small enough to be taken up in the hand; hunk **2.** a small cube or oblong piece, specif. of sugar **3.** a swelling or protuberance, as one caused by a blow or formed by a tumor or cyst **4.** *a)* [Obs.] aggregate or collection *b)* a great mass, amount, number, etc. **5.** a dull, clodlike person ☆**6.** [*pl.*] [Colloq.] hard blows, punishment, criticism, or the like: usually in **get** (or **take**) **one's lumps** or **give someone his lumps** —*adj.* forming or formed into a lump or lumps [*lump* sugar] —*vt.* **1.** to put together in a lump or lumps **2.** to treat or deal with in a mass, or include in one group **3.** to make lumps in —*vi.* **1.** to become lumpy **2.** to move heavily and laboriously (usually with *along*) —**in the lump** in the mass or aggregate; all together —**lump in one's throat** a tight feeling in the throat, as from restrained emotion

lump[2] (lump) *vt.* [Early ModE., to look sour < ? prec., but infl. by GRUMP, MUMP] ☆[Colloq.] to dislike and have to put up with (something disagreeable) [if you don't like it, you can *lump* it]

‡**lump·en** (loom'pən; E. lum'-) *adj.* [< G. *lumpen-*, trashy < *lump*, a rascal, scoundrel, trash, lit., rag < MHG. *lumpe*: for IE. base see LIMP[1]] designating or of persons or groups regarded as belonging to a low or contemptible segment of their class or kind because of their unproductiveness, shiftlessness, alienation, degeneration, etc. —*n.* a person or group that is lumpen

lump·er (lum'pər) *n.* [LUMP[1], *vt.* + -ER] a laborer who helps to load and unload ships; longshoreman

lump·fish (lump'fish') *n., pl.* **-fish'**, **-fish'es:** see FISH[2] [prob. so called from its bulkiness] any of several bulky, sluggish fishes (family Cyclopteridae), esp. one of a species (*Cyclopterus lumpus*) found on both sides of the North Atlantic, with bony tubercles, or knobs, studding the skin: its pelvic fins unite to form a sucker: also **lump'suck'er** (-suk'ər)

lump·ish (-ish) *adj.* **1.** like a lump **2.** heavy, clumsy, dull, stupid, etc. —**lump'ish·ly** *adv.* —**lump'ish·ness** *n.*

lump sum a gross, or total, sum paid at one time

lump·y (lum'pē) *adj.* **lump'i·er**, **lump'i·est 1.** full of lumps [*lumpy* pudding] **2.** covered with lumps; having an uneven surface **3.** rough: said of water **4.** like a lump; heavy; clumsy —**lump'i·ly** *adv.* —**lump'i·ness** *n.*

☆**lumpy jaw** *same as* ACTINOMYCOSIS

Lu·na (lōō'nə) [ME. < L., the moon: see LIGHT[1]] **1.** *Rom. Myth.* the goddess of the moon, identified with the Greek Selene **2.** the moon personified **3.** [ML.] *alchemists' term for* silver

lu·na·cy (lōō'nə sē) *n., pl.* **-cies** [LUNA(TIC) + -CY] **1.** *a)* orig., intermittent insanity, formerly supposed to change in intensity with the phases of the moon *b)* mental unsoundness; insanity **2.** great folly or a foolish act —*SYN.* see INSANITY

☆**luna moth** a large N. American moth (*Tropaea luna*) with crescent-marked, pastel-green wings, the hind pair of which end in elongated tails

lu·nar (lōō'nər) *adj.* [L. *lunaris* < *luna*, the moon: see LIGHT[1]] **1.** of the moon **2.** like the moon; specif., *a)* pale; pallid *b)* round or crescent-shaped **3.** measured by the moon's revolutions [a *lunar* year] **4.** of or containing silver

lunar caustic fused silver nitrate, used in medicine for cauterizing

lunar eclipse *see* ECLIPSE (sense 1)

lu·nar·i·an (lōō nar'ē ən) *n.* [< L. *lunaris* (see LUNAR) + -IAN] **1.** a supposed inhabitant of the moon **2.** one who makes a study of the moon

lunar month *see* MONTH (sense 3)

lunar year *see* YEAR (sense 4)

lu·nate (lōō'nāt, -nit) *adj.* [L. *lunatus*, pp. of *lunare*, to bend like a half-moon < *luna*, the moon] crescent-shaped: also **lu'nat·ed** —**lu'nate·ly** *adv.*

lu·na·tic (lōō'nə tik) *adj.* [ME. *lunatik* < OFr. *lunatique* < LL. *lunaticus*, moon-struck, crazy < L. *luna*, the moon] **1.** suffering from lunacy; insane **2.** of or characterized by lunacy **3.** of or for insane persons **4.** utterly foolish —*n.* an insane person: Term seldom used now except in hyperbolic extension

☆**lunatic fringe** the minority considered foolishly extremist, fanatical, etc. in a political, social, religious, or other movement

lu·na·tion (lōō nā'shən) *n.* [ME. *lunacyon* < ML. *lunatio* < L. *luna*, the moon] the interval from one new moon to the next; lunar month

lunch (lunch) *n.* [earlier, a piece, thick piece < ?: first appears as rendering of Sp. *longja*, slice of ham, which it formerly paralleled in pronun.] **1.** any light meal; esp., the regular midday meal between breakfast and dinner **2.** the food prepared for such a meal —*vi.* to eat lunch —*vt.* to provide lunch for —**lunch'er** *n.*

lunch·eon (lun'chən) *n.* [earlier *lunchion, lunshin* < prec., prob. after dial. *nuncheon*, a snack, lunch < ME. *nonachenche*, lit., noon drink] a lunch; esp., a formal lunch with others

☆lunch·eon·ette (lun′chə net′) *n.* [see -ETTE] a place where light lunches can be had, usually in connection with soda fountain service

luncheon meat meat processed in loaves, sausages, etc. and ready to eat

☆lunch·room (lunch′rōōm′) *n.* a restaurant where light, quick meals, as lunches, are served

Lun·dy's Lane (lun′dēz) road near Niagara Falls, Ontario, Canada: site of an indecisive battle (1814) between Brit. & Am. forces

lune¹ (lōōn) *n.* [Fr. < L. *luna*, the moon] a crescent-shaped figure on a plane or spherical surface

lune² (lōōn) *n.* [var. of *loyn* < OFr. *loigne* < ML. *longia* < L. *longus*, LONG] a leash for a hawk

lunes (lōōnz) *n.pl.* [Fr., pl. of *lune*, whim, lit., moon: cf. LUNATIC] [Now Rare] fits of lunacy

lu·nette (lōō net′) *n.* [Fr., dim. of *lune*, the moon < L. *luna*] 1. a crescent-shaped figure or object 2. a crescent-shaped opening in a vaulted roof to admit light 3. a semicircular space, often containing a windowpane or a mural, above a door or window 4. *Mil.* a projecting fieldwork consisting of two faces and two flanks

Lu·né·ville (lü nā vēl′) city in NE France: treaty signed here (1801) between France & Austria: pop. 22,000

lung (lun) *n.* [ME. *lunge* < OE. *lungen*, akin to G. *lunge* < IE. base *legwh-*, light in weight and movement: the lungs were so named because of their lightness: cf. LIGHTS] 1. either of the two spongelike respiratory organs in the thorax of vertebrates, that oxygenate the blood and remove carbon dioxide from it 2. any analogous organ in invertebrates — at the top of one's lungs in one's loudest voice

lunge¹ (lunj) *n.* [contr. < *allonge* < Fr. *allonge*, lit., a lengthening < *allonger*, to lengthen, thrust < *a-* (L. *ad*), to + *long* (L. *longus*), LONG] 1. a sudden thrust with a sword or other weapon 2. a sudden plunge forward —*vi.* lunged, lung′ing [< the *n.*] to make a lunge or move with a lunge —*vt.* to cause to lunge; thrust with a lunge —lung′er *n.*

lunge² (lunj) *n., vt.* lunged, lung′ing same as LONGE

lung·er (lun′ər) *n.* [Old Slang] a person who has tuberculosis of the lungs

lung·fish (lun′fish′) *n., pl.* -fish′, -fish′es: see FISH² any of various fishes having lungs as well as gills, as a dipnoan, lepidosiren, etc.

lun·gi (lōōn′gē, lun′-) *n.* [Hind. & Per. *lungī*] in India, *a)* a long cloth used for loincloths, scarves, turbans, etc. *b)* a loincloth Also sp. lung′ee, lung′hi

Lung·ki (lōōn′kē′) former name of CHANGCHOU

lung·wort (lun′wurt′) *n.* [ME. *longwort* < OE. *lungenwyrt* (see LUNG & WORT²): from a fancied resemblance to human lungs] any of various plants formerly used in treating lung diseases; esp., any of a genus (*Pulmonaria*) of European plants of the borage family, with large, spotted, leaves and clusters of blue or purple flowers

lu·ni- (lōō′ni) [< L. *luna*, the moon: see LIGHT¹] a combining form meaning: 1. moon [*lunitidal*] 2. of the moon and [*lunisolar*]

lu·ni·so·lar (lōō′ni sō′lər) *adj.* [prec. + SOLAR] involving the mutual relationship or combined attraction of the moon and sun [*lunisolar* tides]

lu·ni·tid·al (-ti′d'l) *adj.* [LUNI- + TIDAL] of a tide or tidal movement caused by the moon's attraction

lunitidal interval the interval by which the lunar high tide lags behind the transit of the moon

☆lunk·er (lunk′ər) *n.* [< ?] [Colloq.] a big fish

☆lunk·head (lunk′hed′) *n.* [prob. echoic alteration of LUMP¹ (after HUNK) + HEAD] [Colloq.] a stupid person: also lunk —lunk′head′ed adj.

lunt (lunt, loont) *n.* [Du. *lont*, a match, earlier lamp wick] [Scot.] 1. a slow-burning match *b)* a torch 2. smoke —*vt., vi.* [Scot.] to kindle or smoke

lu·nu·la (lōō′nyoo lə) *n., pl.* -lae (-lē′) [ModL. < L., dim. of *luna*, the moon: see LIGHT¹] any structure or marking in the shape of a crescent, as the whitish half-moon at the base of a fingernail: also lu·nule (lōō′nyool) —lu′nu·lar adj.

lu·nu·late (-lit, -lāt′) *adj.* [< L. *lunula* (see LUNULA) + -ATE¹] 1. crescent-shaped 2. having crescent-shaped markings Also lu′nu·lat′ed

Lu·per·ca·li·a (lōō′pər kā′lē ə, -kal′yə) *n.pl.* [L. < *Lupercalis*, of Lupercus < *Lupercus* < *lupus*, a wolf: orig. meaning obscure] an ancient Roman festival with fertility rites, held on February 15 in honor of Lupercus, a pastoral god sometimes identified with Faunus: also Lu′per·cal′ (-kal′) *n.sing.* —Lu′per·ca′li·an adj.

lu·pine¹ (lōō′pin) *n.* [ME. < L. *lupinus* < *lupus*, WOLF: reason for name uncertain] 1. any of a genus (*Lupinus*) of plants of the legume family, with palmately compound leaves, racemes of white, rose, yellow, or blue flowers, and pods containing beanlike seeds: used for forage, green manure, etc. 2. the seed of the European lupine (*Lupinus albus*) used in some parts of Europe as food

lu·pine² (lōō′pin) *adj.* [L. *lupinus* < *lupus*, WOLF] 1. of a wolf or wolves 2. wolflike; fierce; ravenous

lu·pu·lin (lōō′pyoo lin) *n.* [< ModL. *lupulus*, the hop (dim. of L. *lupus*, hop plant, apparently identical with *lupus*, WOLF) + -IN¹] a resinous powder obtained from the strobiles of hops, formerly used in medicine as a sedative

Lu·pus (lōō′pəs) [L., WOLF] a S constellation near the Milky Way and east of Centaurus

lu·pus (lōō′pəs) *n.* [ModL. < L., a WOLF: from eating into the substance: cf. CANCER] any of various diseases with skin lesions, esp. LUPUS VULGARIS

lupus er·y·the·ma·to·sus (er′ə thē′mə tō′səs) [ModL., lit., erythematous lupus] a usually chronic skin disease of unknown cause, characterized by red, scaly patches that tend to produce scars, sometimes affecting connective tissue and involving the kidneys, spleen, etc.

lupus vul·gar·is (vul gar′is, -ger′-) [ModL., lit., common lupus: cf. VULGAR] tuberculosis of the skin, characterized by the appearance of reddish-brown nodules that tend to ulcerate and form scars

lur (loor) *n.* [Dan. & Norw. & Sw. < ON. *lūthr*, a war horn, hollow trunk] an S-shaped bronze horn or trumpet of prehistoric times, esp. in Scandinavia

lurch¹ (lurch) *vi.* [< ?] 1. to roll, pitch, or sway suddenly forward or to one side 2. to stagger —*n.* [earlier *lee-lurch* < ?] a lurching movement; sudden rolling, pitching, etc.

lurch² (lurch) *vi.* [ME. *lorchen*, var. of LURK] [Obs.] to remain furtively near a place; lurk —*vt.* 1. [Archaic] to prevent (a person) from getting his fair share of something 2. [Obs.] to get by cheating, robbing, tricking, etc. —*n.* [Obs.] the act of lurching —to lie at (or on) the lurch [Archaic] to lie in wait

lurch³ (lurch) *n.* [Fr. *lourche*, name of a 16th-c. game like backgammon, prob. < OFr. *lourche*, duped < MDu. *lurz*, left (hand), hence unlucky, akin to MHG. *lērz*, left, *lürzen*, to deceive] a situation in certain card games, as piquet, in which the winner has more than double the score of the loser —leave in the lurch to leave in a difficult situation; leave (a person) in trouble and needing help

lurch·er (lur′chər) *n.* 1. *a)* a person that lurches, or lurks *b)* a thief; poacher 2. [Brit.] a crossbred dog trained to hunt silently, used by poachers

lur·dan, lur·dane (lur′d'n) *n.* [ME. *lurdan* < OFr. *lourdin* < *lourd*, heavy, dull, stupid, prob. < VL. *lurdus* < L. *luridus*, LURID] [Archaic] a lazy, dull person —*adj.* [Archaic] lazy and dull

lure (loor) *n.* [ME. < MFr. *leurre* < OFr. *loirre*, prob. < Frank. or Goth. *lōthr*, akin to OE. *loder*, lure, OE. *lathian*, to invite] 1. a device consisting of a bunch of feathers on the end of a long cord, often baited with food: it is used in falconry to recall the hawk 2. *a)* the power of attracting, tempting, or enticing [the *lure* of the stage] *b)* anything that so attracts or tempts 3. a bait for animals; esp., an artificial one used in fishing —*vt.* lured, lur′ing 1. to recall (a falcon) with a lure 2. to attract, tempt, or entice (often with *on*) —lur′er *n.*

SYN.—lure suggests an irresistible force, as desire, greed, curiosity, etc., in attracting someone, esp. to something harmful or evil [*lured* on by false hopes]; entice implies a crafty or skillful luring [he *enticed* the squirrel to eat from his hand]; inveigle suggests the use of deception or cajolery in enticing someone [they *inveigled* him with false promises]; decoy implies the use of deceptive appearances in luring into a trap [artificial birds are used to *decoy* wild ducks]; beguile suggests the use of subtly alluring devices in leading someone on [*beguiled* by her sweet words]; tempt suggests the influence of a powerful attraction that tends to overcome scruples or judgment [I'm *tempted* to accept your offer]; seduce implies enticement to a wrongful or unlawful act, especially to loss of chastity —ANT. repel

Lur·ex (loor′eks) [arbitrary coinage, based on LURE + -ex, suffix of trade names] a trademark for a thread of aluminum coated with plastic —*n.* [l-] such thread, or fabric made of such thread

lu·rid (loor′id) *adj.* [L. *luridus*, pale yellow, ghastly] 1. [Rare] deathly pale; wan 2. glowing through a haze, as flames enveloped by smoke 3. *a)* vivid in a harsh or shocking way; startling; sensational *b)* characterized by violent passion or crime [a *lurid* tale] —lu′rid·ly adv. —lu′rid·ness *n.*

lurk (lurk) *vi.* [ME. *lurken*, akin to *louren* (see LOWER²), Norw. *lurka*, to sneak off] 1. to stay hidden, ready to spring out, attack, etc.; lie in wait 2. to exist undiscovered or unobserved; be present as a latent or not readily apparent threat 3. to move furtively

LUNGS
(A, trachea; B, bronchus; C, visceral pleura; D, parietal pleura; E, bronchiole; F, diaphragm; G, upper lobe; H, middle lobe; I, lower lobe)

SYN.—**lurk** implies a waiting in concealment or in the background, esp. with sinister or menacing intentions; **skulk** implies a lurking or moving about in a stealthy, sinister way, and also connotes cowardliness; **sneak** and **slink** suggest stealthy movement to avoid being seen or heard, but **sneak** more often implies an underhanded or cowardly purpose and **slink** suggests merely fear, guilt, etc.; **prowl** suggests a furtive, watchful roaming about, as in searching for prey or loot

Lu·sa·ka (loo sä′kä) capital of Zambia, in the C part: pop. 138,000

Lu·sa·ti·a (loo sā′shē ə, -sā′shə) region in E East Germany & SW Poland

Lu·sa·tian (-shən) n., adj. same as SORBIAN

lus·cious (lush′əs) adj. [ME. lucius, prob. var. of licious, aphetic form of DELICIOUS, infl. by lusch, LUSH¹] 1. highly gratifying to taste or smell, esp. because of a rich sweetness; delicious 2. a) delighting any of the senses b) having a strong sensual appeal; voluptuous 3. [Archaic] sickeningly sweet or full-flavored; cloying —**lus′cious·ly** adv. —**lus′cious·ness** n.

lush¹ (lush) adj. [ME. lusch, ? echoic var. of lassch, soft, flaccid < OFr. lasche, lax, loose < laschier, to loosen < LL. *lascare < L. *laxicare < laxare, to slacken, expand < laxus: see LAX] 1. tender and full of juice 2. of luxuriant growth [lush vegetation] 3. characterized by a rich growth of vegetation [lush fields] 4. characterized by richness, abundance, or extravagance, as in ornamentation, invention, etc., often tending to excess [lush writing] —SYN. see PROFUSE —**lush′ly** adv. —**lush′ness** n.

lush² (lush) n. [contr. < ? (City of) Lushington, name of actors' club at the Harp Tavern in London, dissolved 1895] [Slang] 1. alcoholic liquor 2. a person who drinks liquor habitually and to excess; esp., an alcoholic—vi., vt. [Slang] to drink (liquor)

Lü·shun (loo′shoon′) seaport in Liaoning province, NE China: pop. 135,000: see LÜTA

Lu·si·ta·ni·a (loo′sə tā′nē ə) 1. ancient Roman province in the Iberian Peninsula, corresponding to most of modern Portugal & part of W Spain 2. a British steamship that was torpedoed and sunk by a German submarine off Ireland on May 7, 1915

lust (lust) n. [ME. < OE., pleasure, delight, appetite, akin to G. lust, pleasure < IE. base *las-, to be eager, whence L. lascivus, playful, sportive (cf. LASCIVIOUS), larva, specter, ghost: sexual senses only in Eng. < rendering Vulgate concupiscentia carnis (I John 2:16) as "lusts of the flesh"] 1. a desire to gratify the senses; bodily appetite 2. a) sexual desire b) excessive sexual desire, esp. as seeking unrestrained gratification 3. a) overmastering desire [a lust for power] b) intense enthusiasm; zest 4. [Obs.] a) pleasure b) inclination —vi. to feel an intense desire, esp. sexual desire (often with after or for)

lus·ter¹ (lus′tər) n. [Fr. lustre < It. lustro < lustrare < L. lustrare, to light, illumine < lustrum, LUSTRUM] 1. the quality, condition, or fact of shining by reflected light; gloss; sheen 2. brightness; radiance; brilliance 3. a) radiant beauty b) great fame or distinction; glory 4. a) any of the glass pendants on a chandelier or candlestick b) a chandelier, etc. adorned with such pendants 5. a substance used to give luster to an object 6. a glossy fabric of cotton and wool 7. the reflecting quality and brilliance of the surface of a mineral 8. a metallic, sometimes iridescent, appearance given to pottery by a glaze —vt. 1. to give a lustrous finish or gloss to 2. to add glory or fame to —vi. to be or become lustrous

lus·ter² (lus′tər) n. same as LUSTRUM (sense 2)

lus·ter·ware (lus′tər wer′) n. highly glazed earthenware decorated by the application of metallic oxides to the glaze

lust·ful (lust′fəl) adj. 1. filled with or characterized by lust 2. [Archaic] lusty; vigorous —**lust′ful·ly** adv. —**lust′ful·ness** n.

lust·i·hood (-ē hood′) n. [Archaic] lustiness

lus·tral (lus′trəl) adj. [L. lustralis < lustrum, LUSTRUM] 1. of, used in, or connected with ceremonial purification 2. [Rare] of a lustrum, or five-year period

lus·trate (-trāt) vt. -trat·ed, -trat·ing [< L. lustratus, pp. of lustrare, to purify by means of a propitiatory sacrifice: see LUSTRUM] to purify by means of certain ceremonies —**lus·tra′tion** n.

lus·tre (lus′tər) n., vt., vi. -tred, -tring chiefly Brit. sp. of LUSTER¹

lus·tre·ware (-wer′) n. chiefly Brit. sp. of LUSTERWARE

lus·tring (lus′triŋ) n. [Fr. lustrine < It. lustrino < lustro, LUSTER¹] same as LUTESTRING

lus·trous (-trəs) adj. having luster; shining; bright; glorious —SYN. see BRIGHT —**lus′trous·ly** adv. —**lus′trous·ness** n.

lus·trum (lus′trəm) n., pl. -trums, -tra (-trə) [L., orig., prob. illumination < IE. *leukstrom, illumination < base *leuk-, to light, shine, whence lieg, fire, flame, OSlav. luča, ray (of light), LIGHT¹] 1. in ancient Rome, a purification of all the people by means of ceremonies held every five years, after the census 2. a five-year period

lust·y (lus′tē) adj. lust′i·er, lust′i·est full of vigor; strong, robust, hearty, etc. —**lust′i·ly** adv. —**lust′i·ness** n.

‡**lu·sus na·tu·rae** (loo′səs na tyoor′ē, -toor′-) [L.] a sport of nature; freak of nature

Lü·ta (loo′dä′) urban complex in NE China, at the tip of the Liaotung Peninsula: it consists of the seaports of

Talien (formerly Dairen) & Lüshun (formerly Port Arthur): pop. 3,600,000

lu·ta·nist (loot′'n ist) n. [ML. lutanista < lutana, a lute < MFr. lut, LUTE¹] a player on the lute

Lut Desert (loot) same as DASHT-I-LUT

lute¹ (loot) n. [ME. < MFr. lut < OFr. leüt < Ar. al′ūd, lit., the wood] an old stringed instrument related to the guitar, with a body shaped like half a pear and six to thirteen strings stretched along the fretted neck, which is often bent to form a sharp angle —vi., vt. lut′ed, lut′ing to play (on) a lute

lute² (loot) n. [OFr. lut < L. lutum, mud, clay < IE. base *leu-, dirt, whence Gr. lyma, filth, OIr. loth, dirt] a clayey cement used for making the joints of pipes airtight and as a sealing agent generally —vt. lut′ed, lut′ing to seal with lute

LUTE

lu·te·al (loot′ē əl) adj. of or pertaining to the corpus luteum

lu·te·ci·um (loo tē′shē əm) n. former sp. of LUTETIUM

lu·te·in (loot′ē in) n. [< (CORPUS) LUTE(UM) + -IN¹] 1. a yellow carotenoid pigment, $C_{40}H_{56}O_2$, found in green leaves, egg yolks, and in certain hormones 2. a preparation of dried and powdered corpus luteum

lu·te·in·ize (-īz′) vt. -ized′, -iz′ing to stimulate the production of the corpus luteum in —vi. to become part of the corpus luteum —**lu′te·in·i·za′tion** n.

luteinizing hormone a hormone, secreted by the anterior lobe of the pituitary gland, which stimulates ovulation and the development of the corpus luteum with its subsequent secretion of progesterone in females, and the development of interstitial tissue and the secretion of testosterone in the testes of males

lu·te·nist (loot′'n ist) n. var. sp. of LUTANIST

lu·te·o·lin (loot′ē ə lin) n. [Fr. luteoline < ModL. (Reseda) luteola, lit., yellowish (reseda) < L. luteolus, yellowish, dim. of luteus: see ff.] a yellow crystalline compound, $C_{15}H_{10}O_6$, extracted from weld

lu·te·ous (loot′ē əs) adj. [L. luteus, golden-yellow < lutum, weed used in dyeing yellow, akin to luridus, LURID] golden-yellow tinged with green

lute·string (loot′striŋ′) n. [altered (after LUTE²) < LUSTRING] a glossy silk cloth, formerly used for women's apparel

Lu·te·tia (loo tē′shə) ancient Rom. name of PARIS²

lu·te·ti·um (loo tē′shē əm) n. [ModL. < L. Lutetia (see prec.)] a metallic chemical element of the rare-earth group: symbol, Lu; at. wt., 174.97; at. no., 71; sp. gr., 9.84; melt. pt., 1652°C; boil. pt., 3330°C

Luth. Lutheran

Lu·ther (loo′thər) n. [G. < OHG. Chlothar, Hludher < Gmc. base *hluda-, famous (akin to LOUD) + OHG. hari, army, host: hence, lit., famous fighter] 1. a masculine name: equiv. Fr. Lothaire, It. Lotario 2. Martin, 1483-1546; Ger. theologian & translator of the Bible: leader of the Protestant Reformation in Germany

Lu·ther·an (-ən) adj. 1. of Martin Luther 2. of the Protestant denomination founded by Luther, or of its branches, doctrines, etc. —n. a member of a Lutheran Church —**Lu′ther·an·ism** n.

lu·thern (loo′thərn) n. [altered < ? Fr. lucarne] a dormer window: see DORMER

lu·thi·er (loo′tē ər) n. [Fr. < luth, lute (< OFr. leüt, LUTE¹) + -ier, -ER] a maker of stringed instruments, orig. of lutes

lut·ing (loot′iŋ) n. same as LUTE²

lut·ist (loot′ist) n. 1. a lute player 2. a maker of lutes

Lu·ton (loot′'n) city in Bedfordshire, SC England: pop. 136,000

Lu·wi·an (loo′ē ən) n. [< the native name] an extinct Anatolian language regarded as closely related to cuneiform and hieroglyphic Hittite —adj. of this language Also **Lu′vi·an** (-vē ən)

lux (luks) n., pl. lux, lux′es [L., LIGHT¹] Physics a unit of illumination, equal to one lumen per square meter or to the illumination of a surface uniformly one meter distant from a point source of one candle

Lux. Luxembourg

lux·ate (luk′sāt) vt. -at·ed, -at·ing [< L. luxatus, pp. of luxare, to dislocate, dislocated < IE. base *leug-, to bend, whence LOCK¹, Gr. loxos, slanting] to put out of joint; dislocate —**lux·a′tion** n.

luxe (looks, luks) n. [Fr. < L. luxus: see LUXURY] richness, elegance, luxury, or the like: see also DELUXE

Lux·em·bourg (luk′səm burg′; Fr. lük sän boor′) 1. grand duchy in W Europe, bounded by Belgium, Germany, & France: 998 sq. mi.; pop. 333,000 2. its capital, in the S part: pop. 79,000 3. province of SE Belgium: 1,706 sq. mi.; pop. 219,000: also **Lux′em·burg′**

Lux·em·burg (luk′səm burg′; G. look′səm burk′), **Rosa** 1870?-1919; Ger. socialist leader, born in Poland

Lux·or (luk′sôr, look′-) city in N Egypt, on the Nile, near the ruins of ancient Thebes: pop. 35,000

lux·u·ri·ant (lug zhoor′ē ənt, luk shoor′-) adj. [L. luxurians, prp. of luxuriare: see ff.] 1. [Rare] very productive;

fertile [*luxuriant* soil] 2. growing with vigor and in great abundance; lush; teeming 3. characterized by richness and extravagance, as in ornamentation, invention, etc., often tending to excess [a *luxuriant* imagination] 4. same as LUXURIOUS —*SYN.* see PROFUSE —lux·u′ri·ance, lux·u′ri·an·cy *n.* —lux·u′ri·ant·ly *adv.*

lux·u·ri·ate (-āt′) *vi.* -at′ed, -at′ing [< L. *luxuriatus,* pp. of *luxuriare,* to be too fruitful, be rank < *luxuria,* LUXURY] 1. to grow with vigor and in great abundance 2. to expand or develop greatly 3. to live in great luxury 4. to take great pleasure; revel (*in*) —lux·u′ri·a′tion *n.*

lux·u·ri·ous (-əs) *adj.* [ME. < OFr. *luxurius* < L. *luxuriosus*] 1. fond of or indulging in luxury 2. constituting or contributing to luxury; splendid, rich, comfortable, etc. —*SYN.* see SENSUOUS —lux·u′ri·ous·ly *adv.* —lux·u′ri·ous·ness *n.*

lux·u·ry (luk′shə rē, lug′zhə-) *n., pl.* -ries [ME. *luxurie* < OFr. < L. *luxuria* < *luxus,* extravagance, luxury, excess, prob. identical in origin with *luxus,* dislocated: see LUXATE] 1. the use and enjoyment of the best and most costly things that offer the most physical comfort and satisfaction 2. anything contributing to such enjoyment, usually something considered unnecessary to life and health 3. *a)* the unusual intellectual or emotional pleasure or comfort derived from some specified thing [to give in to the *luxury* of tears] *b)* something producing such pleasure or comfort —*adj.* characterized by luxury

Lu·zern (loō tsern′, E. loō zurn′) *Ger. name of* LUCERNE

Lu·zon (loō zän′) main island of the Philippines: 40,420 sq. mi.; chief city, Manila

lv. 1. leave(s) 2. livre(s)

Lvov (lvôf) city in W Ukrainian S.S.R.: pop. 502,000

L.W.M., l.w.m. low-water mark

Lwów (lvoōf) *Pol. name of* LVOV

LWS. Late West Saxon

LXX Septuagint

-ly¹ (lē) [ME. < OE. *-līc* < Gmc. **līka,* body, whence LIKE¹] *an adj.-forming suffix meaning:* 1. like, characteristic of, suitable to [*fatherly, manly*] 2. happening (once) every (specified period of time) [*hourly, monthly*]

-ly² (lē) [ME. < OE. *-lice* < *-līc*] *an adv.-forming suffix meaning:* 1. in a (specified) manner, to a (specified) extent or direction, in or at a (specified) time or place [*harshly, outwardly, hourly*] 2. in the (specified) order of sequence [*firstly, thirdly*]

Ly·all·pur (lī′əl poor′) city in NE West Pakistan, near Lahore: pop. 425,000

ly·can·thrope (lī′kən thrōp′, lī kan′thrōp) *n.* [< ModL. *lycanthropus* < Gr. *lykanthrōpos* < *lykos,* WOLF + *anthropos,* a man] 1. a person having lycanthropy 2. same as WEREWOLF

ly·can·thro·py (lī kan′thrə pē) *n.* [ModL. *lycanthropia* < Gr. *lykanthrōpia:* see prec.] 1. a form of mental disorder in which the patient imagines himself to be a wolf 2. *Folklore* the magical power to transform oneself or another into a wolf —ly·can·throp·ic (lī′kan thrāp′ik) *adj.*

‡ly·cée (lē sā′) *n.* [Fr. < L. *lyceum:* see ff.] in France, a secondary school maintained by the government for preparing students for a university

Ly·ce·um (lī sē′əm, lī′sē-) [L. < Gr. *Lykeion,* the Lyceum: so called from the neighboring temple of *Apollon Lykeios*] the grove at Athens where Aristotle taught —*n.* [l-] 1. a hall where public lectures or discussions are held 2. an organization presenting public lectures, concerts, etc. 3. same as LYCÉE

ly·chee (lē′chē) *n. same as* LITCHI

lych gate (lich) *same as* LICH GATE

lych·nis (lik′nis) *n.* [ModL. < L., a fiery red rose < Gr. *lychnis* < *lychnos,* lamp < IE. base **leuk-,* whence LIGHT¹] any of a genus (*Lychnis*) of plants of the pink family, with red, pink, or white flowers

Ly·ci·a (lish′ē ə) ancient country in SW Asia Minor, on the Mediterranean

Ly·ci·an (-ən) *adj.* of Lycia, its people, or their language —*n.* 1. a native or inhabitant of Lycia 2. the language of the Lycians, probably akin to cuneiform Hittite

ly·co·pod (lī′kə päd′) *n.* [see ff.] 1. any of a subphylum (Lycopsida) of living or fossil vascular plants with small leaves having a single vascular strand, and spores produced in cones at the tips of the stems or in leaf axils, including the club mosses and the quillworts 2. same as LYCOPODIUM (sense 1) 3. same as CLUB MOSS

ly·co·po·di·um (lī′kə pō′dē əm) *n.* [ModL. < Gr. *lykos,* WOLF + *-PODIUM*] 1. any of a genus (*Lycopodium*) of usually creeping, often evergreen, club mosses, very popular as Christmas decorations 2. the flammable yellow powder found in the spore cases of these plants, used in making fireworks and in medicine

Ly·cur·gus (lī kur′gəs) real or legendary Spartan lawgiver of about the 9th cent. B.C.

Lyd·da (lid′ə) *same as* LOD

lydd·ite (lid′īt) *n.* [< *Lydd,* village in Kent, England + -ITE¹: first made and tested at Lydd] a powerful explosive containing picric acid, used in shells

Lyd·gate (lid′gāt, -git), John 1370?–1450?; Eng. poet

Lyd·i·a (lid′ē ə) 1. [LL.(Ec.) < Gr.(Ec.) *Lydia,* orig. fem. of Gr. *Lydios,* Lydian: cf. Acts 16:14] a feminine name 2. ancient kingdom in W Asia Minor

Lyd·i·an (-ən) *adj.* 1. of Lydia, its people, or their language 2. *a)* soft; gentle; effeminate *b)* voluptuous; sensual —*n.* 1. a native or inhabitant of Lydia 2. their language, probably Anatolian

lye (lī) *n.* [ME. *lie* < OE. *leag,* akin to G. *lauge* < IE. base **lou-,* to wash, whence L. *lavare, lavere,* to wash: cf. LATHER] 1. orig., a strong, alkaline solution obtained by leaching wood ashes 2. any strongly alkaline substance, usually sodium or potassium hydroxide Lye is used in cleaning, making soap, etc. 3. any substance obtained by leaching

Ly·ell (lī′əl), Sir **Charles** 1797–1875; Brit. geologist

ly·gus bug (lī′gəs) [ModL. *lygus*] any of a genus (*Lygus*) of bugs including many that are injurious to plants

ly·ing¹ (lī′in) *prp. of* LIE¹

ly·ing² (lī′in) *prp. of* LIE² —*adj.* false; not truthful —*n.* the telling of a lie or lies —*SYN.* see DISHONEST

ly·ing-in (-in′) *n.* confinement in childbirth —*adj.* of or for childbirth [a *lying-in* hospital]

Lyle (līl) [< Brit. place name & surname] a masculine name

Lyl·y (lil′ē), **John** 1554?–1606; Eng. author & dramatist

Ly·man (lī′mən) [< Brit. surname] a masculine name

lymph (limf) *n.* [L. *lympha,* spring water, altered (after unrelated Gr. *nymphē:* see NYMPH) < OL. *limpa, lumpa*] 1. orig., a spring of clear water 2. a clear, yellowish fluid resembling blood plasma, found in intercellular spaces and in the lymphatic vessels of vertebrates 3. any of various colorless liquids similar to this; esp., the clear liquid given off from inflamed body tissues

lymph- (limf) *same as* LYMPHO-

lym·phad·e·ni·tis (lim fad′′n īt′əs) *n.* [ModL. < LYMPH- + -ADEN- + -ITIS] inflammation of the lymph nodes

lym·phan·gi·al (lim fan′jē əl) *adj.* [< LYMPH- + Gr. *angeion,* vessel + -AL] of the lymphatic vessels

lym·phan·gi·o- (lim fan′jē ō, -ə) *a combining form meaning* lymphangial; also, before a vowel, **lymphangi-**

lym·phan·gi·tis (lim′fan jīt′əs) *n.* [ModL. < prec. + -ITIS] inflammation of the lymphatic vessels

lym·phat·ic (lim fat′ik) *adj.* [ModL. *lymphaticus* < L. *lympha:* see LYMPH] 1. of, containing, or conveying lymph 2. of, or caused by improper functioning of, the lymph nodes 3. sluggish; without energy: a sluggish condition was formerly thought to be due to too much lymph in the body —*n.* a lymphatic vessel

lymph node any of many small compact structures lying in groups along the course of the lymphatic vessels and producing lymphocytes: also, esp. formerly, **lymph gland**

lym·pho- (lim′fə, -fō) *a combining form meaning* of lymph or the lymphatics [*lymphocyte*]

lym·pho·blast (lim′fə blast′) *n.* [prec. + -BLAST] a primitive cell that is a precursor of a lymphocyte

lym·pho·cyte (lim′fə sīt′) *n.* [LYMPHO- + -CYTE] a variety of leukocyte formed in lymphatic tissue, important in the synthesis of antibodies —lym′pho·cyt′ic (-sit′ik) *adj.*

lym·pho·cy·to·sis (lim′fə sī tō′sis) *n.* [ModL.: see prec. + -OSIS] a condition characterized by an increase in the number of lymphocytes in the blood, as in acute or chronic infection —lym′pho·cy·tot′ic (-tät′ik) *adj.*

lym·pho·gran·u·lo·ma (-gran′yoo lō′mə) *n., pl.* -mas, -ma·ta (-mə tə) [LYMPHO- + GRANULOMA] any of several diseases characterized by enlargement of specific lymph nodes; esp., a venereal disease (**lymphogranuloma venereum**) typically involving the lymph nodes in the groin

lymph·oid (lim′foid) *adj.* [LYMPH- + -OID] of or like lymph or the tissue of the lymph nodes

lym·pho·ma (lim fō′mə) *n.* [LYMPH- + -OMA] any of a group of diseases of unknown cause, characterized by painless, progressive enlargement of lymphoid tissue

lym·pho·poi·e·sis (lim′fō poi ē′sis) *n.* [ModL. < LYMPHO- + Gr. *poiesis,* a making: see POESY] the production of lymphocytes

lyn·ce·an (lin sē′ən) *adj.* [< L. *lynceus* (< Gr. *lynkeios* < *lynx,* LYNX) + -AN] [Rare] of or like a lynx; esp., having the keenness of sight attributed to the lynx

☆lynch (linch) *vt.* [< LYNCH LAW] to murder (an accused person) by mob action and without lawful trial, as by hanging —lynch′er *n.* —lynch′ing *n.*

Lynch·burg (linch′burg) [after John *Lynch,* reputed founder] city in C Va., on the James River: pop. 54,000

☆lynch law [formerly *Lynch's law,* after Capt. William

LYDIA (c. 7th cent. B.C.)

Lynch (1742-1820), member of a vigilance committee in Pittsylvania, Virginia, in 1780] the lawless practice of killing by lynching

Lynn (lin) [prob. < Brit. place name *Lynn* < Celt., as in W. *llyn*, a lake] 1. a masculine or feminine name 2. city in NE Mass., on Massachusetts Bay: suburb of Boston: pop. 90,000

Lyn·wood (lin′wood′) [ult. after Mrs. *Lynn Wood* Sessions, wife of a local dairy owner] city in SW Calif.: suburb of Los Angeles: pop. 43,000

lynx (liŋks) *n., pl.* **lynx′es, lynx:** see PLURAL, II, D, 1 [ME. < L. < Gr. *lynx* < IE. base *leuk-*, to shine, light, whence OE. *lox*, G. *luchs*, lynx: prob. so named from its shining eyes] 1. any of a genus (*Lynx*) of wildcats found throughout the Northern Hemisphere and characterized by a ruff on each side of the face, long legs, a short tail, long, usually tufted ears, and keen vision; specif., *a*) the Canada lynx and the bay lynx, or bobcat, of N. America *b*) the wildcat (*Lynx lynx*) of N Eurasia 2. the long, silky, tawny fur of the lynx —[L-] a N constellation lying between Auriga and Ursa Major

CANADA LYNX
(about 3 1/2 ft. long)

lynx-eyed (-īd′) *adj.* having very keen sight

Lyon (lyôn) city in EC France, at the juncture of the Rhone & Saône rivers: pop. 529,000

Ly·on (lī′ən), **Mary** 1797-1849; U.S. educator

Ly·on·nais (lē ô ne′) former province of EC France

ly·on·naise (lī′ə nāz′; *Fr.* lyô nez′) *adj.* [Fr., fem. of *Lyonnais*, of Lyon] prepared with finely sliced onions; esp., designating potatoes prepared with fried onions

Ly·on·nesse (lī′ə nes′) [OFr. *Leonois*, earlier *Loonois*, ult. < ? *Lothian*, former division of Scotland] *Arthurian Legend* a region in SW England, apparently near Cornwall, supposed to have sunk beneath the sea

Ly·ons (lī′ənz) *Eng. name of* LYON

ly·o·phil·ic (lī′ə fil′ik) *adj.* [*lyo-* < Gr. *lyein*, to loose (see LYSIS) + -PHIL + -IC] having a strong affinity for, and stabilized by, the liquid dispersing medium: said of a colloidal material: also **ly′o·phile′** (-fīl′)

ly·oph·i·lize (lī äf′ə līz′) *vt.* **-lized′, -liz′ing** [see prec. & -IZE] to freeze-dry (esp. biologicals) —**ly·oph′i·li·za′tion** *n.*

ly·o·pho·bic (lī′ə fō′bik) *adj.* [*lyo-* (see LYOPHILIC) + -PHOB(E) + -IC] having little affinity for the liquid dispersing medium: said of a colloidal material

Ly·ra (lī′rə) [L. < Gr. *Lyra:* see LYRE] a N constellation lying between Hercules and Cygnus: it contains the star Vega

ly·rate (lī′rāt) *adj.* [ModL. *lyratus*] shaped like or suggestive of a lyre: also **ly′rat·ed**

lyre (lir) *n.* [ME. *lire* < L. *lyra* < Gr. *lyra*] a small stringed instrument of the harp family, used by the ancient Greeks to accompany singers and reciters

lyre·bird (-burd′) *n.* either of two Australian songbirds (genus *Menura*): the long tail feathers of the male resemble a lyre when spread

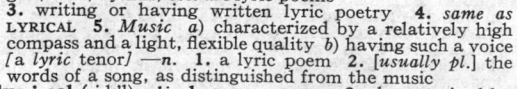

LYRE

lyr·ic (lir′ik) *adj.* [< Fr. or L.: Fr. *lyrique* < L. *lyricus* < Gr. *lyrikos*] 1. of a lyre 2. suitable for singing, as to the accompaniment of a lyre; songlike; specif., designating poetry or a poem mainly expressing the poet's emotions and thoughts: sonnets, elegies, odes, hymns, etc. are lyric poems 3. writing or having written lyric poetry 4. *same as* LYRICAL 5. *Music a*) characterized by a relatively high compass and a light, flexible quality *b*) having such a voice [a *lyric* tenor] —*n.* 1. a lyric poem 2. [*usually pl.*] the words of a song, as distinguished from the music

lyr·i·cal (-i k′l) *adj.* 1. *same as* LYRIC 2. characterized by or expressing rapture or great enthusiasm [a *lyrical* account of her trip] —**lyr′i·cal·ly** *adv.*

lyr·i·cism (lir′ə siz′m) *n.* 1. lyric quality, style, or character [Shelley's *lyricism*] 2. emotional and poetic expression of enthusiasm, etc.

lyr·i·cist (-sist) *n.* a writer of lyrics, esp. lyrics for popular songs

lyr·i·form (lī′rə fôrm′) *adj.* shaped like a lyre

lyr·ism (lir′iz′m; *for 2* lir′iz′m) *n.* [Fr. *lyrisme* < Gr. *lyrismos*] 1. the act of playing on a lyre 2. *same as* LYRICISM

lyr·ist (lir′ist; *for 2 & 3* lir′ist) *n.* [L. *lyristes* < Gr. *lyristēs* < *lyrizein*, to play on a lyre] 1. a player on a lyre 2. a lyric poet 3. *same as* LYRICIST

Lys (lēs) river in N France & W Belgium, flowing northeast into the Scheldt: c. 130 mi.

Ly·san·der (lī san′dər) ?-395 B.C.; Spartan naval and military commander

lyse (līs) *vt., vi.* **lysed, lys′ing** [back-formation < LYSIS] to cause or undergo lysis

-lyse (līz) *chiefly Brit. var. of* -LYZE

Ly·sen·ko·ism (lī seŋ′kō iz′m) *n.* [< T. D. *Lysenko* (1898-), Soviet agronomist who promoted it] a repudiated doctrine that characteristics acquired through environmental changes can be transmitted by heredity

ly·ser·gic acid (lī sur′jik) [< LYS(I)- + ERG(OT) + -IC] a monobasic acid, $C_{16}H_{16}N_2O_2$, extracted from ergot alkaloids or synthesized: see LSD

ly·si- (lī′si, lis′i) [ModL. < Gr. *lysi-* < *lysis:* see LYSIS] a combining form meaning freeing, loosening, dissolving [*lysimeter*]: also, before a vowel, **lys-**

Ly·sim·a·chus (lī sim′ə kəs) 361?-281 B.C.; Macedonian general; ruler of Thrace (323-281)

ly·sim·e·ter (lī sim′ə tər) *n.* [LYSI- + -METER] a device for determining the solubility of substances

ly·sin (lī′s′n) *n.* [< Gr. *lysis* (see LYSIS) + -IN[1]] any antibody capable of dissolving bacteria, blood corpuscles, etc.

ly·sine (lī′sēn) *n.* [LYS- + -INE[4]] an amino acid, $C_6H_{14}N_2O_2$, obtained synthetically or by the hydrolysis of certain proteins in digestion

Ly·sip·pus (lī sip′əs) 360?-316? B.C.; Gr. sculptor

ly·sis (lī′sis) *n.* [ModL. < Gr. *lysis*, a loosening < *lyein*, to loose < IE. base **lu-*, **leu-*, to cut, loosen, whence L. *luere*, to release (from debt), LOSE] 1. the process of cell destruction through the action of specific lysins 2. the gradual ending of disease symptoms

-ly·sis (lə sis) [< Gr. *lysis:* see LYSIS] a combining form meaning a loosing, dissolution, dissolving, destruction [*catalysis, paralysis*]

ly·so·some (lī′sə sōm′) *n.* [*lyso-*, pertaining to dissolving < Gr. *lysis* (see LYSIS) + -SOME[3]] a particle found in the cytoplasm of cells and containing a number of digestive enzymes capable of breaking down most of the constituents of living matter —**ly′so·so′mal** *adj.*

ly·so·zyme (lī′sə zīm′) *n.* [see prec. & ZYME] an enzyme present in egg white, tears, saliva, etc. that can kill certain bacteria by dissolving the cell walls

-lyte[1] (līt) [< Gr. *lytos* < *lyein:* see LYSIS] a combining form meaning a substance subjected to a process of decomposition (indicated by the corresponding noun ending in -LYSIS) [*hydrolyte*]

-lyte[2] (līt) *same as* -LITE

lyt·ic (lit′ik) *adj.* [see -LYTIC] 1. of a lysin 2. of or causing lysis

-lyt·ic (lit′ik) [Gr. *-lytikos* < *lytikos*, able to loose: see LYSIS] 1. a combining form used to form adjectives corresponding to nouns ending in -LYSIS [*catalytic, hydrolytic*] 2. *Biochem.* a suffix meaning undergoing hydrolysis by enzymes

lyt·ta (lit′ə) *n., pl.* **-tae** (-ē) [ModL. < L. < Gr. *lytta, lyssa* (lit., madness), thought to be a worm under a dog's tongue causing rabies] a band of cartilage lying along the underside of the tongue of dogs and certain other flesh-eating animals

Lytton *see* BULWER-LYTTON

-lyze (līz) [Fr. *-lyser* < nouns ending in *-lysis* + *-er*, inf. ending] a combining form used to form verbs corresponding to nouns ending in -LYSIS [*electrolyze*]

M

M, m (em) *n., pl.* **M's, m's** 1. the thirteenth letter of the English alphabet: from the Greek *mu*, derived ultimately from the Phoenician 2. the sound of *M* or *m:* in English, it is usually a voiced bilabial nasal 3. a type or impression for *M* or *m* 4. *a symbol for* the thirteenth in a sequence or group (or the twelfth if J is omitted) 5. *Printing* an em

—*adj.* 1. of *M* or *m* 2. thirteenth (or twelfth if J is omitted) in a sequence or group

M (em) *n.* 1. an object shaped like *M* 2. a Roman numeral for 1,000: with a superior bar (M̄), 1,000,000 3. *Chem. the symbol for* a metal or an electropositive radical 4. *Elec. the symbol for* mutual inductance (in henrys) 5. *Logic the*

symbol *for* the middle term of a syllogism —*adj.* shaped like *M*

m- *Chem* meta-

M'- (mə, mi) *same as* MAC- [*M'Coy*]

M. 1. Manitoba 2. Master 3. Medieval 4. *Music* mezzo 5. Monday 6. *pl.* MM. Monsieur

M., m. 1. majesty 2. male 3. manual 4. mark (a coin) 5. marquis 6. married 7. masculine 8. *Physics* mass 9. medicine 10. medium 11. meridian 12. mile(s) 13. mill(s) 14. minim 15. minute(s) 16. modulus 17. month 18. moon 19. morning 20. [L. *meridies*] noon [*A.M., P.M.*]

m., m meter; meters

ma (mä; *dial. often* mô) *n.* [Colloq.] mamma; mother

MA, M.A. *Psychol.* mental age

ma, mA milliampere; milliamperes

M.A. 1. [L. *Magister Artium*] Master of Arts 2. Military Academy

ma'am (mam, mäm; *unstressed* məm, 'm) *n.* [Colloq.] madam: used in direct address

Maas (mäs) *Du. name of the* MEUSE

Maas·tricht (mäs'triHt) city in SE Netherlands, on the Maas River: pop. 93,000

Mab (mab) *see* QUEEN MAB

Ma·bel (mā'b'l) [< *Amabel* < L. *amabilis*, lovable < *amare*, to love] a feminine name: dim. *Mab*

Mac (mak) *n.* [< MAC-, Mc-] [Slang] fellow: used as a general term of address for a man or boy

Mac- (mak, mək, mə) [< Ir. & Gael. *mac*, son < OCelt. **makkos*, akin to **makwos*, son, whence OW. *map*, W. *mab*, *ap*, son: for IE. base see MAIDEN] *a prefix meaning* son of: used in Scottish and Irish family names: also **Mc-, Mᶜ-, M'-**: in alphabetizing, all these forms are sometimes placed together

Mac. Maccabees

ma·ca·bre (mə käb'rə, mə käb', -kä'bər) *adj.* [Fr. < OFr. (*danse*) *Macabré*, (dance) of death, prob. altered < *Maccabeus*, Maccabee: semantic connection obscure] gruesome; grim and horrible; ghastly: also **ma·ca'ber** (-kä'bər) —*SYN.* see GHASTLY

ma·ca·co (mə kä'kō, -kä'-) *n., pl.* **-cos** [Port. < ?] any of several African and Asiatic lemurs; esp., the **black lemur** (*Lemur macaco*)

mac·ad·am (mə kad'əm) *n.* [after John L. *McAdam* (1756–1836), Scot. engineer who invented the process] 1. small broken stones used in making roads; esp., such stones combined with a binder such as tar or asphalt 2. a road made with layers of such stones

mac·a·dam·i·a nut (mak'ə dā'mē ə) [ModL. *Macadamia*, name of the genus: so named after John *Macadam* (d. 1865), Scot. chemist in Australia] a spherical, hard-shelled, edible nut from an Australian tree (*Macadamia ternifolia*) cultivated in Hawaii, etc.

mac·ad·am·ize (mə kad'ə mīz') *vt.* **-ized', -iz'ing** 1. to make (a road) by rolling successive layers of macadam on a dry earth roadbed 2. to repair or cover (a road) by this process

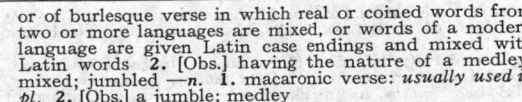

Ma·cao (mə kou') 1. Port. overseas territory in SE China, at the mouth of the Chu Kiang (Canton) River, opposite Hong Kong: it consists of the peninsula of an island belonging to China & two small adjacent islands: 6 sq. mi.; pop. 280,000 2. seaport at the tip of this peninsula Also, Port. sp., **Ma·cau'**

MACAO

ma·caque (mə käk') *n.* [Fr. < Port. *macaco*] any of a large group of monkeys (genus *Macaca*) of Asia, Africa, and the East Indies, with a long or short, nonprehensile tail, esp. the rhesus monkey

mac·a·ro·ni (mak'ə rō'nē) *n.* [It. *maccaroni, maccheroni*, pl. of *maccherone* < LGr. *makaria*, food of broth and barley groats, sacrificial cake made from such mixture, lit., blessed (cake) < Gr., bliss < *makar*, blessed] 1. pasta in the form of tubes or in various other shapes, often baked with cheese, ground meat, etc. 2. *pl.* **-nies** an English dandy in the 18th cent. who affected foreign mannerisms and fashions

PIG-TAILED MACAQUE
(2 1/2 ft. long)

mac·a·ron·ic (-rän'ik) *adj.* [Fr. *macaronique* < It. *maccaronico* < *maccaroni*, lit., macaroni] 1. involving or characterized by a mixture of languages; esp., designating or of burlesque verse in which real or coined words from two or more languages are mixed, or words of a modern language are given Latin case endings and mixed with Latin words 2. [Obs.] having the nature of a medley; mixed; jumbled —*n.* 1. macaronic verse: *usually used in pl.* 2. [Obs.] a jumble; medley

mac·a·roon (mak'ə rōōn') *n.* [Fr. *macaron* < It. *maccaroni*, MACARONI] a small cookie made chiefly of egg white, crushed almonds or coconut, and sugar

Mac·Ar·thur (mə kär'thər), **Douglas** 1880–1964; U.S. general: commander in chief of Allied forces in the SW Pacific, World War II

Macassar *same as* MAKASSAR

Ma·cau·lay (mə kô'lē) 1. Dame **Rose**, 1881–1958; Eng. novelist 2. **Thomas Bab·ing·ton** (bab'in tən), 1st Baron Macaulay of Rothley, 1800–59; Eng. historian, essayist, & statesman

ma·caw (mə kô') *n.* [Port. *macao*, prob. < the Braz. (Tupi) native name] any of a group of large, bright-colored, long-tailed, harsh-voiced parrots (esp. genus *Ara*) of Central and South America

Mac·beth (mək beth', mak-) 1. a tragedy (c. 1606) by Shakespeare 2. its title character, who, goaded by his ruthlessly ambitious wife, murders the king to gain the crown for himself

Macc. Maccabees

Mac·ca·bae·us (mak'ə bē'əs), **Judas** *see* MACCABEES

Mac·ca·be·an (mak'ə bē'ən) *adj.* of Judas Maccabaeus or the Maccabees

Mac·ca·bees (mak'ə bēz') [LL.(Ec.) *Machabaei*, pl. of *Machabaeus*, surname of Judas < Gr.(Ec.) *Makkabaios*, prob. < Aram. *maqqābā*, hammer: hence, lit., the hammerer] 1. family of Jewish patriots who, under Judas Maccabaeus, headed a successful revolt against the Syrians (175–164 B.C.) & ruled Palestine until 37 B.C. 2. *Bible* two books of the Old Testament Apocrypha that tell of this revolt

mac·ca·boy (mak'ə boi') *n.* [Fr. *macouba* < *Macouba*, district in Martinique where it is made] a kind of snuff, usually perfumed: also sp. **mac'co·boy'**

Mac·don·ald (mək dän'ld) 1. **George**, 1824–1905; Scot. novelist & poet 2. **Sir John Alexander**, 1815–91; Canad. statesman, born in Scotland

Mac·Don·ald (mək dän'ld), (**James**) **Ram·say** (ram'zē) 1866–1937; Brit. statesman & Labor Party leader: prime minister (1924; 1929–35)

Mac·Dow·ell (mək dou'əl), **Edward Alexander** 1861–1908; U.S. composer & pianist

Mace (mās) [< ff.] *a trademark* (in full **Chemical Mace**) *for* a chemical compound, prepared for use in aerosol containers, that has the combined effect of a tear gas and a nerve gas, temporarily stunning its victims

mace[1] (mās) *n.* [ME. < OFr. *masse* < VL. **mattea*, a club < L. **matea* < IE. base **mat-*, a hoe, club (whence Sans. *matyá-*, a club, harrow: cf. MATTOCK] 1. *a)* a heavy, armor-breaking club with a metal head, often spiked, used in the Middle Ages *b)* any similar weapon 2. *a)* a staff used as a symbol of authority by certain officials *b)* *same as* MACE-BEARER

mace[2] (mās) *n.* [ME., assumed as sing. of *macis*, mace < OFr. *macis* < ML. *macis*, prob. scribal error for L. *macir* < Gr. *makir*, a fragrant resin from India] a spice, usually ground, made from the dried outer covering of the nutmeg

mace·bear·er (-ber'ər) *n.* a person who carries a mace in ceremonial processions

ma·cé·doine (mas'i dwän'; *Fr.* mà sā dwän') *n.* [Fr., lit., Macedonia: ? referring to mixture of diverse races there] 1. a mixture of vegetables or fruits served as a salad, cocktail, etc., often in jelly 2. a medley

Mac·e·don (mas'ə dän') ancient Macedonia

Mac·e·do·ni·a (mas'ə dō'nē ə, -dōn'yə) 1. ancient kingdom in SE Europe, in the S Balkan Peninsula: now a region divided among Greece, Yugoslavia, & Bulgaria 2. division of N Greece, on the Aegean: 13,109 sq. mi.; pop. 1,891,000 3. republic of Yugoslavia, in the SE part: 9,928 sq. mi.; pop. 1,406,000; cap. Skopje

Mac·e·do·ni·an (-ən, -yən) *adj.* of Macedonia, its people, their language, etc. —*n.* 1. a native or inhabitant of Macedonia 2. the Indo-European language of the ancient Macedonians, akin either to Greek or to Illyrian 3. the South Slavic language of modern Macedonia and adjoining regions

MACEDONIA (c. 450 B.C.)

Ma·ce·ió (mä'sä yô') seaport in NE Brazil, on the Atlantic; capital of Alagoas state: pop. 170,000

mac·er (mā′sər) *n.* [ME. < OFr. *massier:* see MACE[1] & -ER] 1. *same as* MACEBEARER 2. in Scotland, an official in a law court

mac·er·ate (mas′ə rāt′) *vt.* **-at′ed, -at′ing** [< L. *maceratus,* pp. of *macerare,* to make soft or tender, weaken, harass < IE. base *māk-,* to knead, whence Lett. *màcu,* to squeeze] 1. to soften and break down into component parts by soaking in liquid for some time; specif., to soften and break down (food) in the digestive system 2. loosely, to break, tear, chop, etc. into bits 3. to cause to waste away or grow thin —*vi.* to undergo maceration; waste away; grow thin —**mac′er·a′tion** *n.* —**mac′er·a′tor** *n.*

Mach (mäk) *n. clipped form of* MACH NUMBER

mach. 1. machine 2. machinery 3. machinist

Mach·a·bees (mak′ə bēz′) *Douay Bible name for* MACCABEES

ma·che·te (mə shet′ē, -chet′ē; *Sp.* mä chā′tā) *n.* [Sp., dim. of *macho,* an ax, hammer < L. *marculus,* dim. of *marcus,* hammer] 1. a large, heavy-bladed knife used for cutting down sugar cane, dense underbrush, etc., esp. in Central and South America 2. a small Pacific tarpon (*Elops affinis*), sometimes found in fresh waters

Mach·i·a·vel·li (mä′kyä vel′lē; *E.* mak′ē ə vel′ē), **Nic·co·lò** (**di Bernardo**) (nē′kô lô′) 1469–1527; Florentine statesman & writer on government

MACHETE

Mach·i·a·vel·li·an (mak′ē ə vel′ē ən, -vel′yən) *adj.* 1. of Machiavelli 2. of, like, or characterized by the political principles and methods of expediency, craftiness, and duplicity advocated in Machiavelli's book, *The Prince;* crafty, deceitful, etc. —*n.* a follower of such principles and methods —**Mach′i·a·vel′li·an·ism** *n.*

ma·chic·o·late (mə chik′ə lāt′) *vt.* **-lat′ed, -lat′ing** [< ML. *machicolatus,* pp. of *machicolare* < MFr. *machicoler,* prob. < *macher,* to crush, beat (< L. *masticare:* see MASTICATE) + *col,* neck: from use of machicolations for dropping stones, etc.] to put machicolations in (a parapet, etc.)

ma·chic·o·la·tion (mə chik′ə lā′shən) *n.* [< prec.] 1. an opening in the floor of a projecting gallery or parapet, between the supports or corbels, or in the roof over an entrance, through which hot liquids, heavy stones, etc. could be dropped by the defenders of a fortress 2. a gallery, parapet, etc. with such openings

mach·i·nate (mak′ə nāt′; *now sometimes* mash′-) *vi., vt.* **-nat′ed, -nat′ing** [< L. *machinatus,* pp. of *machinari,* to devise, plan, plot < *machina,* MACHINE] to devise, plan, or plot artfully, esp. with evil intent —**mach′i·na′tor** *n.*

mach·i·na·tion (mak′ə nā′shən; *now sometimes* mash′-) *n.* [ME. *machinacion* < L. *machinatio*] 1. [Rare] the act of machinating 2. an artful or secret plot or scheme, esp. one with evil intent: *usually used in pl.* —SYN. see PLOT

ma·chine (mə shēn′) *n.* [Fr. < L. *machina* < Gr. *mēchanē,* a machine, engine < *mēchos,* a contrivance < IE. base *magh-,* to be able, help, whence MIGHT[2]] 1. formerly, a structure or built-up fabric of any kind 2. a vehicle, as an automobile, bicycle, etc.: an old-fashioned term 3. a structure consisting of a framework and various fixed and moving parts, for doing some kind of work; mechanism [a sewing *machine*] 4. *a)* a person or organization regarded as acting like a machine, without thought or will *b)* a complex organization coordinated to function in a smooth, effective way [the military *machine*] ☆5. *a)* the members of a political party or group who control policy and confer patronage *b)* the party organization generally 6. a device or apparatus, as in the ancient theater, for producing stage effects 7. a literary device for dramatic presentation, as a supernatural agent or force introduced into a poem 8. *Mech.* a device, as a lever or pulley, that transmits, or changes the application of, energy —*adj.* 1. of or for a machine or machines 2. made or done by machinery 3. standardized; stereotyped —*vt.* **-chined′, -chin′ing** to make, shape, finish, etc. by machinery —**ma·chin′a·ble** *adj.*

machine bolt a large bolt with usually a square or hexagonal head, and threads on the lower part for use with a nut

☆**machine gun** an automatic gun, usually mounted and with a cooling apparatus, firing a rapid and continuous stream of bullets fed into it now generally by a belt —**ma·chine′-gun′** (-gun′) *vt.* **-gunned′, -gun′ning**

machine language the system of characters, signs, or symbols, which represent instructions and information, used directly by a computer without translation

ma·chin·er·y (mə shēn′ər ē, -shēn′rē) *n., pl.* **-er·ies** 1. machines collectively 2. the working parts of a machine 3. any combination of things or persons by which something is kept in action or a desired result is obtained [the *machinery* of government] 4. apparatus used to produce stage effects 5. literary devices involving the introduction of supernatural beings or forces, as in epic poetry

machine screw a small screw designed for fastening metal parts having tapped holes

☆**machine shop** a workshop, factory, or part of a factory for making or repairing machines or machine parts

machine tool an automatic or semiautomatic power-driven tool, as an electric lathe, punch press, drill, or planer: machine tools are used in making machines or machine parts —**ma·chine′-tool′** *adj., vt.*

ma·chin·ist (-ist) *n.* 1. a person who makes or repairs

machinery 2. a worker skilled in using machine tools 3. a worker who operates a machine

☆**machinist's mate** *U.S. Navy* a petty officer trained to operate, repair, etc. ships' engines

‡**ma·chis·mo** (mä chēz′mō) *n.* [Sp. < *macho* (see MACHO) + *-ismo,* -ISM] strong or assertive masculinity, characterized by virility, courage, aggressiveness, etc.

Mach·me·ter (mäk′mēt′ər) *n.* [see ff. & -METER] an aircraft instrument that measures and indicates the ratio of airspeed to the speed of sound

Mach number [after Ernst *Mach* (1838–1916), Austrian physicist] [*also* m-] a number representing the ratio of the speed of an object to the speed of sound in the surrounding medium, as air, through which the object is moving

‡**ma·cho** (mä′chō) *n., pl.* **-chos** (-chōs) [Sp. < Port., ult. < L. *masculus,* MASCULINE] a strong, virile man —*adj.* masculine, virile, courageous, etc.

ma·chree (mə krē′, mə khrē′) *n.* [< Ir. *mo,* my + *croidhe* (OIr. *cride*), heart] literally, my heart: Anglo-Irish term of endearment [Mother *machree*]

Ma·chu Pic·chu (mä′chōō pēk′chōō) ruins of an ancient Incan city in SC Peru: also written **Machupicchu**

-ma·chy (mə ki) [< Gr. *machē,* a battle] *a combining form meaning* struggle, contest of [*gigantomachy*]

mac·in·tosh (mak′'n täsh′) *n. same as* MACKINTOSH

Mac·ken·zie (mə ken′zē) 1. river in W Mackenzie district, Canada, flowing from the Great Slave Lake northwest into the Beaufort Sea: 2,635 mi. 2. district of Northwest Territories, Canada: 527,490 sq. mi.; pop. 15,000

Mac·ken·zie (mə ken′zē) 1. **Sir Alexander,** 1763?–1820; Canad. explorer, born in Scotland 2. **William Lyon,** 1795–1861; Canad. journalist & politician, born in Scotland

mack·er·el (mak′ər əl, mak′rəl) *n., pl.* **-el, -els:** see PLURAL, II, D, 2 [ME. *makerel* < OFr. < ?] 1. an edible fish (*Scomber scombrus*) of the North Atlantic, that has a greenish, blue-striped back and a silvery belly 2. any of various other related fishes

mackerel sky a sky covered with rows of small, fleecy clouds, suggesting the streaks on a mackerel's back

Mack·i·nac (mak′ə nô′), **Straits of** [see MACKINAW] strait connecting Lake Huron & Lake Michigan, separating the upper & lower peninsulas of Mich.: c. 4 mi. wide

Mackinac Island [see ff.] small island in the Straits of Mackinac: a Mich. State park: 6 sq. mi.

Mack·i·naw (mak′ə nô′) *adj.* [CanadFr. *Mackinac* < AmInd. (Ojibway) *mitchimakinak,* large turtle] 1. of or from Mackinac Island, formerly a center of trade with the Indians of the Northwest 2. of or made of a heavy, napped woolen cloth, often plaid —*n.* [m-] *same as a)* MACKINAW BLANKET *b)* MACKINAW BOAT *c)* MACKINAW COAT

Mackinaw blanket a thick woolen blanket, often woven in bars of bright colors, much used by Indians, lumbermen, etc. in the American Northwest

Mackinaw boat a rowboat or sailboat with a flat bottom, sharp bow, and square or pointed stern, formerly used on and around the upper Great Lakes

Mackinaw coat a short, double-breasted coat made of heavy woolen cloth, usually plaid

mack·in·tosh (mak′in täsh′) *n.* [after Charles *Macintosh* (1766–1843), the Scot. inventor] 1. a waterproof outer coat; raincoat 2. the fabric used for this, orig. made by cementing layers of cloth with rubber See also MCINTOSH

mack·le (mak′'l) *n.* [Fr. *macule* < L. *macula,* a spot, stain] *Printing* 1. a blot or blur 2. a blurred sheet —*vt., vi.* **-led, -ling** *Printing* to print blurred or double; blur

ma·cle (mak′'l) *n.* [Fr. < OFr. *mascle,* prob. < ODu. *maske,* mesh, akin to OHG. *masca,* OE. *max:* see MESH] a twin crystal, as of a diamond

Mac·Leish (mə klēsh′), **Archibald** 1892– ; U.S. poet

Mac·leod (mə kloud′), **John James Rick·ard** (rik′ərd) 1876–1935; Scot. physiologist: co-discoverer of insulin

Mac·Ma·hon (mäk mä ôn′), **Comte Ma·rie Ed·mé Pa·trice Mau·rice de** (mä rē′ ed mā′ på trēs′ mô rēs′ də), Duke of Magenta, 1808–93; Fr. marshal & statesman: president of the Third Republic (1873–79)

Mac·Mil·lan (mak mil′ən), **Donald Baxter** 1874–1970; U.S. arctic explorer

Mac·Neice (mək nēs′), **Louis** 1907–63; Brit. poet & classical scholar, born in Ireland

Ma·con (mā′kən) [after Nathanael *Macon* (1758–1837), N.C. patriot] city in C Ga.: pop. 122,000

Mac·pher·son (mək fur′s′n), **James** 1736–96; Scot. poet: see OSSIAN

Mac·quar·ie (mə kwôr′ē, -kwär′-) river in SE Australia, flowing northwest into the Darling: c. 600 mi.

mac·ra·mé (mak′rə mā′) *n.* [Fr. < It. *macrame* < Turk. *makrama,* napkin < Ar. *miqramah,* a veil] a coarse fringe or lace of thread or cord knotted in designs, used for decorating furniture, pillows, etc.: also **macramé lace**

Mac·rea·dy (mə krē′dē), **William Charles** 1793–1873; Eng. actor

mac·ro- (mak′rō, -rə) [< Gr. *makros,* long < IE. *mekrós* < base *māk-,* long, slender, whence L. *macer,* MEAGER] *a combining form meaning* long (in extent or duration), large, enlarged or elongated (in a specified part) [*macrocyte, macrocephaly*]: also, before a vowel, *macr-*

mac·ro·bi·ot·ics (mak′rō bī ät′iks) *n.pl.* [with *sing. v.*] [see MACRO- & -BIOTIC] the art of prolonging life, as by a special diet —**mac′ro·bi·ot′ic** *adj.*

mac·ro·ceph·a·ly (mak'rə sef'ə lē) n. [MACRO- + CEPHAL- + -Y³] a condition in which the head or cranial capacity is abnormally large: opposed to MICROCEPHALY —**mac'·ro·ceph'a·lous, mac'ro·ce·phal'ic** (-si fal'ik) adj.

mac·ro·cli·mate (mak'rə klī'mət) n. [MACRO- + CLIMATE] the general climate over a large geographical area —**mac'ro·cli·mat'ic** (-kli mat'ik) adj.

mac·ro·cosm (-käz'm) n. [Fr. macrocosme < ML. macrocosmus: see MACRO- & COSMOS] 1. the great world; the universe 2. any large, complex entity Opposed to MICROCOSM —**mac'ro·cos'mic** (-käz'mik) adj.

mac·ro·cyst (-sist') n. [MACRO- + -CYST] a large or enlarged cyst; esp., an encysted mass of cytoplasm with many nuclei in a slime mold

mac·ro·cyte (-sīt') n. [MACRO- + -CYTE] an abnormally large red blood corpuscle occurring esp. in pernicious anemia —**mac'ro·cyt'ic** (-sit'ik) adj.

mac·ro·dont (-dänt') adj. having large teeth

mac·ro·e·co·nom·ics (mak'rō ē'kə näm'iks, -ek'ə-) n. a branch of economics dealing with all the forces at work in an economy or with the interrelationship of large sectors, as in total employment or income —**mac'ro·e'co·nom'ic** adj.

mac·ro·ev·o·lu·tion (-ev'ə lōō'shən) n. large-scale and long-range evolution involving the appearance of new genera, families, etc. of organisms

ma·cro·ga·mete (-gam'ēt, -gə mēt') n. [MACRO- + GAMETE] the larger of two conjugating cells in heterogamous sexual reproduction, considered to be female

mac·ro·mere (mak'rə mir') n. [MACRO- + -MERE] one of the large cells produced by unequal cell division during the early embryological development of many animals, as mollusks

mac·ro·mol·e·cule (mak'rə mäl'ə kyōōl') n. a very large molecule, as a protein or polymer molecule, composed of hundreds or thousands of atoms: also **mac'ro·mole'** (-mōl') —**mac'ro·mo·lec'u·lar** (-mə lek'yoo lər) adj.

ma·cron (mā'krän, -krən) n. [Gr. makron, neut. of makros, long (see MACRO-)] a short, straight mark (‾) placed horizontally over a vowel to indicate that it is long or is to be pronounced in a certain way

mac·ro·nu·cle·us (mak'rə nōō'klē əs) n. the larger of two types of nuclei present in the cells of ciliated protozoans —**mac'ro·nu'cle·ar** adj.

mac·ro·nu·tri·ent (-nōō'trē ənt) n. [MACRO- + NUTRIENT] any of the chemical elements, as carbon, required in relatively large quantities for plant growth

mac·ro·phage (mak'rə fāj') n. [MACRO- + -PHAGE] any of various phagocytic cells in connective tissue, lymphatic tissue, bone marrow, etc. of vertebrates —**mac'ro·phag'ic** (-faj'ik) adj.

mac·rop·ter·ous (ma kräp'tər əs) adj. [MACRO- + -PTEROUS] having unusually large wings or fins

mac·ro·scop·ic (mak'rə skäp'ik) adj. [MACRO- + -SCOP(E) + -IC] 1. visible to the naked eye: opposed to MICROSCOPIC 2. having to do with large groups or units Also **mac'ro·scop'i·cal**

mac·ro·spo·ran·gi·um (mak'rō spə ran'jē əm) n., pl. **-gi·a** (-ə) same as MEGASPORANGIUM

mac·ro·spore (mak'rə spôr') n. [MACRO- + SPORE] same as MEGASPORE

ma·cru·ran (mə kroor'ən) n. [ModL. Macrura (< MACRO- + Gr. oura, tail) + -AN] any of a suborder (Macrura) of ten-legged crustaceans with large abdomens, including the lobsters, shrimps, etc. —**ma·cru'rous, ma·cru'ral, ma·cru'roid** adj.

mac·u·la (mak'yoo lə) n., pl. **-lae** (-lē'), **-las** [L., a spot, stain] a spot, stain, blotch, etc.; esp., a) a discolored spot on the skin b) a dark spot on the sun —**mac'u·lar** adj.

macula lu·te·a (lōōt'ē ə) [ModL., lit., luteous spot] a small yellowish area of especially keen vision on the retina

mac·u·late (mak'yoo lāt'; for adj., -lit) vt. **-lat'ed, -lat'ing** [ME. maculaten < L. maculatus, pp. of maculare, to spot, speckle < macula, a spot, stain] [Archaic] to spot; stain; blemish; defile —adj. 1. spotted; blotched 2. defiled; impure

mac·u·la·tion (mak'yoo lā'shən) n. [L. maculatio: see prec.] 1. [Archaic] a spotting or being spotted 2. a spot; blemish 3. the pattern of spots on an animal or plant

mac·ule (mak'yōōl) n. [ME.] same as MACULA

‡**ma·cum·ba** (mə koom'bə) n. [Braz. Port.] a religious cult in Brazil, combining voodoo with elements of Christianity

mad (mad) adj. **mad'der, mad'dest** [ME. madd, aphetic < OE. gemæd, pp. of (ge)mædan, to make mad, akin to Goth. gamaiths, crippled, OS. gimēd, foolish < IE. *mait- < base *mai-, to hew, cut off, whence Gr. mitylos, dehorned, Goth. maitan, to hew] 1. mentally ill; insane 2. wildly excited or disorderly; frenzied; frantic [mad with fear] 3. showing or resulting from lack of reason; foolish and rash; unwise [a mad scheme] 4. blindly and foolishly enthusiastic or fond; infatuated [to be mad about clothes] 5. wildly amusing or gay; hilarious [a mad comedy] 6. having rabies [a mad dog] 7. a) angry or provoked (often with at) b) showing or expressing anger —vt., vi. **mad'ded,**

mad'ding [Archaic] to madden —n. an angry or sullen mood or fit —**have a mad on** [Colloq.] to be angry —**mad as a hatter** (or **March hare**) completely crazy

Mad·a·gas·car (mad'ə gas'kər) large island in the Indian Ocean, off the SE coast of Africa: coextensive with the republic of Malagasy —**Mad'a·gas'can** adj., n.

mad·am (mad'əm) n., pl. **mad'ams**; for 1, usually **mes·dames** (mā däm') [Fr. madame, orig. ma dame < L. mea domina, my lady] 1. a woman; lady: a polite term of address 2. the mistress of a household ☆3. a woman in charge of a brothel

mad·ame (mad'əm; Fr. må däm') n., pl. **mes·dames** (mā däm'; Fr. mā däm') [Fr.: see prec.] a married woman: French title equivalent to Mrs.: used in English as a title of respect for a distinguished woman or generally for any foreign married woman: abbrev. Mme., Mdme.

mad·cap (mad'kap') n. [MAD + CAP, fig. for head] a reckless, impulsive, or uninhibited person, orig. esp. a girl —adj. reckless and impulsive [madcap pranks]

mad·den (mad''n) vt., vi. to make or become mad; make or become insane, angry, or wildly excited —**mad'den·ing** adj. —**mad'den·ing·ly** adv.

mad·der¹ (mad'ər) n. [ME. mader < OE. mædere, akin to ON. mathra, Norw. modra < IE. base *modhro-, dye plant, whence Czech modrý, blue] 1. any of a genus (Rubia) of plants of the madder family, with petals fused to form a funnel-shaped corolla; esp., a perennial vine (Rubia tinctorum) with panicles of small, yellow flowers 2. a) the red root of this vine b) a red dye made from this: see also ALIZARIN 3. bright red; crimson —adj. designating a family (Rubiaceae) of chiefly tropical herbs, shrubs, and trees, including bedstraw, bluet, coffee, cinchona, etc.

mad·der² (mad'ər) adj. compar. of MAD

mad·ding (-in) adj. [Rare] 1. raving; frenzied ["the madding crowd"] 2. maddening; making mad

mad·dish (-ish) adj. somewhat mad

made (mād) pt. & pp. of MAKE¹ —adj. 1. constructed; shaped; formed [a well-made play] 2. produced artificially [made ground, from filling in a swamp] 3. invented; contrived [a made word] 4. prepared from various ingredients [a made dish] 5. sure of success [a made man] —☆**have (got) it made** [Slang] to be assured of success

Ma·dei·ra (mə dir'ə) 1. group of Port. islands in the Atlantic, off the W coast of Morocco, comprising the district of FUNCHAL 2. largest island of this group: 286 sq. mi. 3. river in NW Brazil, flowing northeast into the Amazon: c. 2,100 mi. —n. [also m-] a strong white wine made on the island of Madeira

mad·e·leine (mad'l in) n. [Fr., after Madeleine Paulnier, 19th-cent. Fr. cook who created the recipe] a type of small, rich cupcake

Mad·e·line (mad'l in, -ĭn') a feminine name: see MAGDALENE

ma·de·moi·selle (mad'ə mə zel', mam zel'; Fr. mád mwá zel') n., Fr. pl. **mesde·moi·selles** (mād mwá zel') [Fr. < ma, my + demoiselle, young lady: see DAMSEL] 1. an unmarried woman or girl: French title equivalent to Miss: abbrev. Mlle., Mdlle. 2. a French governess 3. same as SILVER PERCH (sense 1)

Ma·de·ro (mä de'rō), **Fran·cis·co In·da·le·cio** (frän sēs'kō ēn'dä le'syō) 1873–1913; Mex. revolutionist & statesman; president of Mexico (1911–13)

made-to-or·der (mād'tə ôr'dər) adj. 1. made to conform to the customer's specifications or measurements; custom-made 2. perfectly suitable or conformable

made-up (-up') adj. 1. put together; arranged [a made-up page of type] 2. invented; fabricated; false [a made-up story] 3. with cosmetics applied

Madge (maj) a feminine name: see MARGARET

mad·house (mad'hous') n. 1. a former kind of institution for the confinement of the mentally ill; insane asylum 2. any place of turmoil, noise, and confusion

Madh·ya Pra·desh (mud'yə prä'desh) state of C India: 171,217 sq. mi.; pop. 32,372,000; cap. Bhopal

Mad·i·son (mad'i s'n) [after James MADISON] capital of Wis., in the SC part: pop. 173,000

Mad·i·son (mad'i s'n) 1. **Dolly** or **Dolley** (born Dorothea Payne) 1768–1849; wife of ff. 2. **James,** 1751–1836; 4th president of the U.S. (1809–17)

Madison Avenue 1. a street in New York City, regarded as the center of the U.S. advertising industry 2. this industry, its practices, influence, etc.

Madison Heights city in SE Mich.: suburb of Detroit: pop. 39,000

mad·ly (mad'lē) adv. 1. insanely 2. wildly; furiously 3. foolishly 4. extremely

mad·man (mad'man', -mən) n., pl. **-men'** (-men', -mən) a demented or insane person; lunatic; maniac

mad money [Colloq.] a small amount of money carried by a woman for emergencies, as on a date to enable her to get home alone if she wishes

mad·ness (-nis) n. 1. dementia; insanity; lunacy 2. great anger; fury 3. great folly 4. wild excitement or enthusiasm 5. rabies

Ma·doe·ra (mä dōō'rä) Du. sp. of MADURA

ma·don·na (mə dän′ə) *n.* [It., my lady < *ma*, my (< L. *mea*) + *donna*, lady (< L. *domina*, fem. of *dominus*, lord: see DOMINATE)] **1.** a former Italian title for a woman, equivalent to *madam* **2.** [M-] *a*) Mary, mother of Jesus *b*) a picture or statue of Mary

☆**Madonna lily** a hardy lily (*Lilium candidum*) with white flowers

Ma·dras (mə dras′, -dräs′; mad′rəs, mäd′-) **1.** *former name of* TAMIL NADU **2.** capital of Tamil Nadu; seaport on the Coromandel Coast: pop. 1,729,000

ma·dras (mad′rəs, mäd′-; mə dras′, -dräs′) *n.* [< prec.] **1.** a fine, firm cotton cloth, usually striped or plaid, used for shirts, dresses, etc. **2.** a durable silk cloth, usually striped **3.** a figured cotton or rayon cloth in leno weave, used for draperies **4.** a large, bright-colored kerchief of silk or cotton —*adj.* made of madras

‡**ma·dre** (mä′dre) *n.* [Sp.] mother

Ma·dre de Di·os (mä′dre de dyôs′) river in SE Peru & N Bolivia, flowing east into the Beni: c. 900 mi.

mad·re·pore (mad′rə pôr′) *n.* [Fr. *madrépore* < It. *madrepora*, lit., mother-stone (from its rapid production) < *madre* (< L. *mater*, MOTHER[1]) + *poro*, a pore < L. *porus*, PORE[2]] any of various, usually branching, stony corals (order Madreporaria), which form reefs and islands in tropical seas —**mad′re·por′ic, mad′re·por′i·an** *adj.*

mad·re·por·ite (-pôr′īt) *n.* [prec. + -ITE[1]] a porous calcareous plate in most echinoderms, through which the sea water enters the vascular system

Ma·drid (mə drid′; *Sp.* mä thrēth′) capital of Spain, in the C part: pop. 2,559,000

mad·ri·gal (mad′ri gəl) *n.* [It. *madrigale* < ?] **1.** a short poem, usually a love poem, which can be set to music **2.** an often contrapuntal song with parts for several voices singing without accompaniment, popular in the 15th, 16th, and 17th cent. **3.** loosely, any song, esp. a part song —**mad′ri·gal·ist** *n.*

ma·dri·lène (mad′rə len′; *Fr.* mà drē len′) *n.* [Fr. (*consommé*) *Madrilène*, Madrid (consommé) < Sp. *Madrileño*, of Madrid] a highly seasoned consommé made with tomatoes

☆**ma·dro·ño** (mə drō′nyō) *n., pl.* **-ños** [Sp. < *maduro*: see MADURO] an evergreen tree (*Arbutus menziesii*) of the heath family, with smooth, red bark, leathery, oval leaves, and edible, red berries, native to W N. America: also **ma·dro′ne** (-nə), **ma·dro′ña** (-nya)

Ma·du·ra (mä door′ä) island of Indonesia, just off the NE coast of Java: 1,770 sq. mi.: see JAVA

Ma·du·rai (mä du rī′) city in S India, in Madras state: pop. 425,000: former name **Mad·u·ra** (maj′ oo rə)

ma·du·ro (mə door′ō) *adj.* [Sp., mature < L. *maturus*, MATURE] dark and strong: said of cigars

mad·wo·man (mad′woom′ən) *n., pl.* **-wo′men** (-wim′ən) a demented or insane woman

mad·wort (-wurt′) *n.* [MAD + WORT[2]: once a supposed remedy for rabies] *same as* ALYSSUM

Mae (mā) a feminine name: see MARY

mae (mā) *adj., n., adv. Scot. var. of* MORE

Mae·an·der (mē an′dər) *ancient name of* MENDERES (sense 1)

Mae·ce·nas (mi sē′nəs), (**Gaius Cilnius**) 70?–8 B.C.; Rom. statesman & patron of Horace & Virgil —*n.* any wealthy, generous patron, esp. of literature or art

Mael·strom (māl′strəm) [Early ModDu. (now *maalstroom*) < *malen*, to grind, whirl round + *stroom*, a stream: first applied by 16th-c. Du. geographers] a famous whirlpool off the W coast of Norway, hazardous to safe navigation —*n.* [m-] **1.** any large or violent whirlpool **2.** a violently confused or dangerously agitated state of mind, emotion, affairs, etc.

mae·nad (mē′nad) *n.* [L. *Maenas* (gen. *Maenadis*) < Gr. *mainas* (gen. *mainados*) < *mainesthai*, to rave < IE. *mnā*- var. of base *men*-, to think, whence MIND] **1.** [*often* M-] a female votary of Dionysus, who took part in the wild, orgiastic rites that characterized his worship; bacchante **2.** a frenzied or raging woman —**mae·nad′ic** (mi nad′ik) *adj.*

ma·es·to·so (mis tō′sō; *It.* mä′e stô′sō) *adj., adv.* [It.] *Music* with majesty or dignity: a direction to the performer

ma·es·tro (mis′trō; *also* mä es′trō) *n., pl.* **-tros, -tri** (-trē) [It. < L. *magister*, a MASTER] a master in any art; esp., a great composer, conductor, or teacher of music

Mae·ter·linck (māt′ər liŋk′, met′-.), Count **Maurice** 1862–1949; Belgian playwright, essayist, & poet

Mae West (mā′ west′) [after *Mae West* (1892–), shapely U.S. actress] an inflated life preserver vest for use as by aviators downed at sea

Maf·e·king (maf′ə kiŋ) city in NE Cape of Good Hope province, South Africa: former administrative headquarters (or capital) of Bechuanaland: pop. 8,000

maf·fick (maf′ik) *vi.* [back-formation < MAFEKING, where unrestrained celebration marked the successful Brit. stand against the Boers (1900)] [Chiefly Brit.] to celebrate in an exuberant, unrestrained manner

Ma·fi·a, Maf·fi·a (mä′fē ə) *n.* [It. *maffia*] **1.** in Sicily, *a*) [m-] an attitude of popular hostility to law and government *b*) any of the groups of brigands characterized by this attitude **2.** a secret society of criminals thought to exist in the U.S. and other countries, engaging in blackmail, illicit trade in narcotics, etc.

maf·ic (maf′ik) *adj.* [MA(GNESIUM) + L. *f(errum)*, iron + -IC] *Geol.* of or pertaining to igneous rocks rich in magnesium and iron and comparatively low in silica

Ma·fi·o·si (mä′fē ō′sē) *n.pl., sing.* **-so** (-sō′) [It.] **1.** members of the Mafia **2.** [m-] members of any exclusive group

mag (mag) *n. clipped form of:* **1.** MAGNETO **2.** MAGAZINE

mag. **1.** magazine **2.** magnetism **3.** magnitude

Ma·gal·la·nes (mä′gä yä′nes) *former name of* PUNTA ARENAS

mag·a·zine (mag′ə zēn′, mag′ə zēn′) *n.* [Fr. *magasin* < OFr. *magazin* < It. *magazzino* < Ar. *makhāzin*, pl. of *makhzan*, a storehouse, granary < *khazana*, to store up] **1.** a place of storage, as a warehouse, storehouse, or military supply depot **2.** a space in which explosives are stored, as a building or room in a fort, or a section of a warship **3.** a supply chamber, as a space in or container on a rifle or pistol from which cartridges are fed, or a space in or container on a camera from which a protected roll of film is fed **4.** the things kept in a magazine, as munitions or supplies **5.** [from the idea of "storehouse of information"] a publication, usually with a paper back and sometimes illustrated, that appears at regular intervals and contains stories, articles, etc. by various writers and, usually, advertisements

Mag·da·le·na (mäg′dä le′nä) river in W Colombia, flowing north into the Caribbean: c. 1,000 mi.

Mag·da·lene (mag′də lēn, -lin) [LL.(Ec.) < Gr.(Ec.) *Magdalēnē*, lit., of Magdala < *Magdala*, town on the Sea of Galilee] **1.** a feminine name: dim. *Lena*; var. *Magdalen, Madeline, Madelyn* **2.** (*also* mag′də lē′nē) Mary Magdalene: Luke 8:2 (identified with the repentant woman in Luke 7:37) —*n.* [m-] **1.** a reformed and repentant prostitute **2.** [Brit.] a reformatory for prostitutes Also **Mag′·da·len** (-lin)

Mag·da·le·ni·an (mag′də lē′nē ən) *adj.* [Fr. *magdalénien*, after *La Madeleine*, rock shelter in SW France, where many of the artifacts were found] designating or of a culture or late period of the Old Stone Age, characterized by cave art, bone engraving, and tools of polished stone and bone

Mag·de·burg (mäg′də boorkh; *E.* mag′də burg′) city & port in W East Germany, on the Elbe: pop. 266,000

mage (māj) *n.* [Fr. < L. *magus:* see MAGI] [Archaic] a magician; wizard

Ma·gel·lan (mə jel′ən), **Ferdinand** 1480?–1521; Port. navigator in the service of Spain: discovered the Strait of Magellan & the Philippine Islands —**Mag·el·lan·ic** (maj′ə lan′ik) *adj.*

Magellan, Strait of channel between the S. American mainland & Tierra del Fuego: c. 350 mi. long

Magellanic cloud [after Ferdinand MAGELLAN] *Astron.* either of two cloudlike, irregular galaxies visible in the southern heavens, that are the nearest of the external galaxies to the Milky Way

STRAIT OF MAGELLAN

Ma·gen Da·vid (mä gän′ dä vēd′, mô′gən dô′vid) [Heb.] *same as* STAR OF DAVID

ma·gen·ta (mə jen′tə) *n.* [< *Magenta*, town in Italy: so called because discovered about the time (1859) of the battle fought there] **1.** *same as* FUCHSIN **2.** purplish red —*adj.* purplish-red

Mag·gie (mag′ē) a feminine name: see MARGARET

Mag·gio·re (mə jôr′ē; *It.* mäd jô′re), **Lake** lake in NW Italy & S Switzerland: 82 sq. mi.

mag·got (mag′ət) *n.* [ME. *magotte*, prob. < earlier *mathek*, flesh worm (< ON. *mathkr* or OE. *matha*, a worm, maggot: cf. MAWKISH) after ? *Magot*, form of MARGARET] **1.** a wormlike insect larva, as the legless larva of the housefly: some maggots are found in filth and decaying matter **2.** an odd notion; whim —**mag′got·y** *adj.*

Ma·ghreb (mu′grəb) NW Africa, chiefly Morocco, Algeria, & Tunisia: the Arabic name

Ma·gi (mā′jī) *n.pl., sing.* **Ma′gus** (-gəs) [L., pl. of *magus* < Gr. *magos* < OPer. *magus* (or Iran. *magu*-), member of a priestly caste, magician < IE. base **magh*-, to be able, whence MIGHT[2], L. *machina*] **1.** the priestly caste in ancient Media and Persia, supposedly having occult powers **2.** *Douay Bible* the wise men from the East (in later tradition, three in number) who came bearing gifts to the infant Jesus: Matt. 2:1–13 —**Ma·gi·an** (-jē ən) *adj., n.*

mag·ic (maj′ik) *n.* [ME. *magike* < OFr. *magique* < L. *magice* < Gr. *magikē* (*technē*), magic (art), sorcery < *magikos*, of the Magi: see MAGI] **1.** *a*) the use of charms, spells, and rituals in seeking or pretending to cause or control events, or govern certain natural or supernatural forces; sorcery; witchcraft *b*) such charms, spells, etc. **2.** any mysterious, seemingly inexplicable, or extraordinary power or influence [the *magic* of love] **3.** the art or performing skill of producing baffling effects or illusions by sleight of hand, concealed apparatus, etc. —*adj.* [L.

magicus < Gr. *magikos*] **1.** of, produced by, used in, or using magic **2.** producing extraordinary results, as if by magic or supernatural means

SYN.—magic is the general term for any of the supposed arts of producing marvelous effects by supernatural or occult power and is figuratively applied to any extraordinary, seemingly inexplicable power; **sorcery** implies magic in which spells are cast or charms are used, usually for a harmful or sinister purpose; **witchcraft** (of women) and **wizardry** (of men) imply the possession of supernatural power by compact with evil spirits, **witchcraft** figuratively suggesting the use of womanly wiles, and **wizardry,** remarkable skill, cleverness, etc.

mag·i·cal (-'l) *adj.* magic (esp. in sense 2): used predicatively as well as attributively, whereas *magic* tends to be attributive only —**mag′i·cal·ly** *adv.*

ma·gi·cian (mə jish′ən) *n.* [ME. *magicien* < OFr.] an expert in magic; specif., *a)* a sorcerer; wizard *b)* a performer skilled in sleight of hand, illusions, etc.

magic lantern *old-fashioned term for* a projector for showing still pictures from transparent slides

Ma·gi·not line (mazh′ə nō′) [after André *Maginot* (1877–1932), Fr. minister of war] a system of heavy fortifications built before World War II on the E frontier of France: it failed to prevent invasion by the Nazi armies

mag·is·te·ri·al (maj′is tir′ē əl) *adj.* [ML. *magisterialis* < LL. *magisterius* < L. *magister*, a MASTER] **1.** of or suitable for a magistrate or master **2.** authoritative; official **3.** domineering; pompous —**SYN.** see MASTERFUL —**mag′is·te′ri·al·ly** *adv.*

mag·is·te·ri·um (maj′is tir′ē əm) *n.* [L. < *magister*, MASTER] the authority claimed by the R.C. Church, as divinely inspired, to teach true doctrine

mag·is·tra·cy (maj′is trə sē) *n., pl.* **-cies 1.** the position, office, function, or term of a magistrate **2.** magistrates collectively **3.** the district under a magistrate; magistrate's jurisdiction

mag·is·tral (-trəl) *adj.* [L. *magistralis*] **1.** [Rare] magisterial; authoritative **2.** guiding; principal *[a magistral* line in fortifications*]* **3.** [Obs.] prepared on prescription: said of medicines

mag·is·trate (-trāt, -trit) *n.* [ME. < L. *magistratus* < *magister*, MASTER] **1.** a civil officer empowered to administer the law: the President of the U.S. is sometimes called the *chief magistrate* **2.** a minor official with limited judicial powers, as a justice of the peace or judge of a police court —**mag′is·trat′i·cal** (-trat′i kəl) *adj.*

Mag·le·mo·se·an, Mag·le·mo·si·an (mag′lə mō′sē ən) *adj.* [after *Maglemose*, bog in Denmark] designating or of a mesolithic culture of N Europe

mag·ma (mag′mə) *n.* [L., the dregs of an unguent < Gr. *magma* < *massein*, to knead < IE. base **menk-*, to knead, crush, whence MINGLE] **1.** a pasty mixture of crude mineral or organic matter **2.** liquid or molten rock deep in the earth, which on cooling solidifies to produce igneous rock **3.** *Pharmacy* a suspension of precipitated matter in a watery substance —**mag·mat′ic** (-mat′ik) *adj.*

Mag·na Char·ta, Mag·na Car·ta (mag′nə kär′tə) [ML., lit., great charter] **1.** the great charter that King John of England was forced by the English barons to grant at Runnymede, June 15, 1215, traditionally interpreted as guaranteeing certain civil and political liberties **2.** any constitution guaranteeing such liberties

‡mag·na cum lau·de (mäg′nä koom lou′de, mag′nə kum lô′dē) [L.] with great praise: phrase used to signify graduation with high honors from a university or college: cf. CUM LAUDE, SUMMA CUM LAUDE

Mag·na Grae·ci·a (mag′nə grē′shē ə) ancient Gr. colonies in S Italy

mag·na·nim·i·ty (mag′nə nim′ə tē) *n.* [ME. *magnanimite*] **1.** the quality or state of being magnanimous **2.** *pl.* **-ties** a magnanimous act

mag·nan·i·mous (mag nan′ə məs) *adj.* [L. *magnanimus* < *magnus*, great (see MAGNI-) + *animus*, mind, soul (see ANIMAL)] noble in mind; high-souled; esp., generous in overlooking injury or insult; rising above pettiness or meanness —**mag·nan′i·mous·ly** *adv.*

mag·nate (mag′nāt) *n.* [ME. < LL. *magnas* (pl. *magnates*), great man < L. *magnus*, great: see MAGNI-] **1.** a very important or influential person in any field of activity, esp. in a large business **2.** formerly, in Hungary and Poland, a member of the upper branch of the Diet

Mag·ne·sia (mag nē′zhə, -shə) ancient name of MANISA

mag·ne·sia (mag nē′zhə, -shə) *n.* [ModL. *magnesia (alba)*, lit., (white) magnesia (in contrast to ML. *magnesia*, a black mineral < LGr. *magnēsia* < *Magnēsia*, MAGNESIA]: term suggested by F. Hoffmann (1660–1742), G. physician, for ModL. *magnes carneus*, lit., flesh-magnet (cf. MAGNET & CARNAL): so named from clinging to the lips] **1.** magnesium oxide, MgO, a white, tasteless powder, used as a mild laxative and antacid, and as an insulating substance, in firebrick, etc. **2.** hydrated magnesium carbonate, also used as a laxative —**mag·ne′sian, mag·ne′sic** (-sik) *adj.*

mag·ne·site (mag′nə sīt′) *n.* native magnesium carbonate, $MgCO_3$, a mineral occurring usually in white, compact

masses: used for furnace linings, in making carbon dioxide, etc.

mag·ne·si·um (mag nē′zē əm, -zhē əm, -zhəm) *n.* [ModL. < MAGNESIA] a light, silver-white metallic chemical element, malleable and ductile: used in making several alloys and, because it burns with a hot, white light, in photographic flash bulbs, incendiary bombs, etc.: symbol, Mg; at. wt., 24.312; at. no., 12; sp. gr., 1.74; melt. pt., 651°C; boil. pt., 1107°C

mag·net (mag′nit) *n.* [ME. *magnete* < OFr. < L. *magnes* (gen. *magnetis*) < Gr. *Magnētis* (*lithos*), (stone) of MAGNESIA] **1.** any piece of iron, steel, or, orig., magnetite (*lodestone*) that has the property of attracting iron or steel, etc.: this property may be naturally present or artificially induced: see ELECTROMAGNET **2.** a person or thing that attracts

mag·net·ic (mag net′ik) *adj.* **1.** having the properties of a magnet *[magnetic* needle*]* **2.** of, producing, caused by, or operating by magnetism **3.** of the earth's magnetism *[the magnetic* poles*]* **4.** that is or can be magnetized **5.** powerfully attractive: said of a person, personality, etc. —**mag·net′i·cal·ly** *adv.*

magnetic amplifier a tubeless, sensitive amplifier that controls the flow of current from an alternating voltage source by applying a weak signal to the control windings

magnetic axis the straight line joining the two poles of a magnet

☆**magnetic bottle** *Physics* a geometrical configuration whose extent is outlined by magnetic lines of force that will confine a hot plasma, and, in thermonuclear reactors, keep it away from the walls of the chambers

magnetic circuit a closed path of magnetic flux having the direction of the magnetic induction at every point

magnetic compass an instrument for indicating geographical directions magnetically, as by the action of the earth's magnetic field on a bar magnet (*magnetic needle*) suspended so as to swing freely on a pivot

magnetic course an airplane's course reckoned from the magnetic north

magnetic declination (or **deviation**) *same as* DECLINATION (sense 3)

magnetic equator *same as* ACLINIC LINE

magnetic field a region of space in which there is an appreciable magnetic force

magnetic flux the sum of all the lines of force in a magnetic field

magnetic force the attracting or repelling force between a magnet and a ferromagnetic material, between a magnet and a current-carrying conductor, etc.

magnetic induction the flux per unit area perpendicular to the direction of the flux: also **magnetic flux density**

magnetic meridian a continuous line on the earth's surface connecting the north and south magnetic poles

MAGNETIC FIELD
(F, direction of the magnetic flow; E, electromotive force; e-, current flow; SW, switch)

magnetic mine a naval mine designed to explode when the metal hull of a ship passing near it deflects a magnetic needle, closing an electric circuit and thus detonating the charge

magnetic moment 1. the ratio of the torque exerted on a magnet, a moving charge, or a current loop, to the strength of the magnetic field producing the torque **2.** a moment of electrons and nuclear particles caused by the intrinsic spin of a particle and the orbital motion of a particle, as around a nucleus

magnetic needle a slender bar of magnetized steel which, when mounted so as to swing freely on a pivot, will point along the line of the magnetic meridian toward the magnetic poles, approximately north and south: it is the essential part of a magnetic compass

magnetic north the direction toward which a magnetic needle points: in most places it is not true north

magnetic pickup a phonograph pickup in which a part of the stylus assembly vibrates in a magnetic field between two coils, thus inducing current in the coils

magnetic pole 1. either pole of a magnet, where the magnetic lines of force seem to be concentrated **2.** either point on the earth's surface toward which the needle of a magnetic compass points: the north and south magnetic poles do not precisely coincide with the geographical poles

magnetic recording the recording of electrical signals by means of changes in areas of magnetization on a tape, wire, or disc: used for recording sound, video material, digital computer data, etc.

mag·net·ics (mag net′iks) *n.pl.* [*with sing. v.*] the branch of physics dealing with magnets and magnetic phenomena

magnetic storm a worldwide disturbance of the earth's magnetic field, believed to be caused by sunspot activity

magnetic tape a thin plastic ribbon coated with a suspension of ferromagnetic iron oxide particles, used as a storage medium for magnetic recording

magnetic wire a fine wire of a ferromagnetic alloy, used as a storage medium for magnetic recording

mag·net·ism (mag′nə tiz′m) *n.* 1. the property, quality, or condition of being magnetic 2. the force to which this is due 3. the branch of physics dealing with magnets and magnetic phenomena; magnetics 4. power to attract; personal charm or allure 5. *former var. of* HYPNOTISM

mag·net·ite (-tīt′) *n.* [G. *magnetit:* see MAGNET & -ITE¹] a black iron oxide, Fe₃O₄, an important iron ore: called *lodestone* when magnetic

mag·net·ize (mag′nə tīz′) *vt.* -ized′, -iz′ing 1. to make into a magnet; give magnetic properties to (steel, iron, etc.) 2. [Rare] *same as* HYPNOTIZE 3. to attract or charm (a person) often in an almost hypnotic way —*vt.* to become magnetic —**mag′net·iz′a·ble** *adj.* —**mag′net·i·za′tion** *n.* —**mag′net·iz′er** *n.*

mag·ne·to (mag nēt′ō) *n., pl.* -tos a dynamo in which one or more permanent magnets produce the magnetic field; esp., a small machine of this sort connected with and run by an internal-combustion engine, used to generate the electric current providing a spark for the ignition

mag·ne·to- (mag nēt′ō, -ə; *also, occas.,* -net′ō) [see MAGNET] *a combining form meaning:* 1. magnetism, magnetic force [*magnetoelectric*] 2. magnetoelectric [*magnetohydrodynamics*]

mag·ne·to·e·lec·tric (-i lek′trik) *adj.* designating or of electricity produced by changing magnetic fields in the vicinity of electric conductors —**mag·ne′to·e·lec′tric′i·ty** (-tris′ə tē) *n.*

mag·ne·to·hy·dro·dy·nam·ics (-hī′drō dī nam′iks) *n.pl.* [*with sing. v.*] [MAGNETO- + HYDRODYNAMICS] the science that deals with the interaction of a magnetic field with an electrically conducting fluid, as a liquid metal or an ionized gas —**mag·ne′to·hy′dro·dy·nam′ic** *adj.*

mag·ne·tom·e·ter (mag′nə täm′ə tər) *n.* [MAGNETO- + -METER] an instrument for measuring magnetic forces, esp. the earth's magnetic field —**mag·ne′to·met′ric** (-nē′tō met′rik) *adj.* —**mag′ne·tom′e·try** (-ə trē) *n.*

mag·ne·to·mo·tive (mag nēt′ō mōt′iv) *adj.* [MAGNETO- + -MOTIVE] designating or of a force that gives rise to magnetic flux

mag·ne·ton (mag′nə tän′) *n.* a unit of the magnitude of the magnetic moment of atoms or other particles

mag·ne·to·re·sist·ance (mag nēt′ō ri zis′təns) *n.* [MAGNETO- + RESISTANCE] a change in the electrical resistance of a substance with the application of a magnetic field —**mag·ne′to·re·sis′tive** *adj.*

mag·ne·to·sphere (mag nēt′ə sfir′) *n.* [MAGNETO- + -SPHERE] that region surrounding a planet in which the planetary magnetic field is stronger than the interplanetary field: the earth's magnetosphere extends about 3.5 million miles in the direction away from the sun —**mag·ne′to·spher′ic** (-sfir′ik, -sfer′-) *adj.*

mag·ne·to·stric·tion (-strik′shən) *n.* [MAGNETO- + (CON)STRICTION] a small variation in the size of a ferromagnetic material when subjected to an applied magnetic field —**mag·ne′to·stric′tive** *adj.*

mag·ne·tron (mag′nə trän′) *n.* [MAGNE(T) + (ELEC)TRON] an electron tube in which the flow of electrons from the cathode to one or more anodes is controlled by an externally applied magnetic field parallel to the cathode: commonly used to generate alternating currents at microwave frequencies

mag·ni- (mag′nə) [< L. *magnus,* great, big < IE. base *meĝ(h)-,* whence Sans. *mahā-,* Gr. *megas,* big & MUCH] *a combining form meaning* great, big, large [*magnificent, magniloquence*]

mag·nif·ic (mag nif′ik) *adj.* [ME. *magnyfyque* < OFr. *magnifique* < L. *magnificus*] [Archaic] 1. magnificent 2. imposing in size, dignity, etc. 3. *a)* pompous *b)* grandiloquent 4. eulogistic Also **mag·nif′i·cal**

Mag·nif·i·cat (mag nif′i kat′, män yif′i kät′) *n.* [L.] 1. *a)* the hymn of the Virgin Mary in Luke 1:46–55, beginning *Magnificat anima mea Dominum,* "My soul doth magnify the Lord" *b)* any musical setting for this 2. [m-] any song, poem, or hymn of praise

mag·ni·fi·ca·tion (mag′nə fi kā′shən) *n.* [LL. *magnificatio*] 1. a magnifying or being magnified 2. the power of magnifying 3. a magnified image, model, or representation

mag·nif·i·cence (mag nif′ə s′ns) *n.* [ME. < OFr. < L. *magnificentia* < *magnificus,* noble < *magnus,* great (see MAGNI-) + *facere,* to DO¹] richness and splendor, as of furnishings, color, dress, etc.; stately or imposing beauty; grandeur

mag·nif·i·cent (-s′nt) *adj.* [OFr. < LL. *magnificens:* see prec.] 1. beautiful in a grand or stately way; rich or sumptuous, as in construction, decoration, form, etc. 2. exalted: said of ideas, etc., and also of some former rulers, as, Lorenzo the *Magnificent* 3. [Colloq.] exceptionally good; excellent —*SYN.* see GRAND —**mag·nif′i·cent·ly** *adv.*

mag·nif·i·co (-kō′) *n., pl.* -coes, -cos [It. < L. *magnificus:* see MAGNIFICENCE] 1. a nobleman of ancient Venice 2. a person of high rank or great importance

mag·ni·fi·er (mag′nə fī′ər) *n.* 1. a person who magnifies 2. a thing that magnifies; specif., a lens or combination of lenses for magnifying

mag·ni·fy (mag′nə fī′) *vt.* -fied′, -fy′ing [ME. *magnifien* < OFr. *magnifier* < L. *magnificare,* to make much of, esteem highly, LL.(Ec.), to worship < *magnus,* great (see MAGNI-) + *facere,* to make, DO¹] 1. [Rare] to make greater in size, status, or importance; enlarge 2. to cause to seem greater, more important, etc. than is really so; exaggerate [to *magnify* one's sufferings] 3. to cause to seem larger than is really so; increase the apparent size of, esp. by means of a lens or lenses 4. [Archaic] to glorify; praise; extol —*vi.* to have the power of increasing the apparent size of an object, as a microscope does

magnifying glass a lens or combination of lenses that increases the apparent size of an object seen through it

mag·nil·o·quent (mag nil′ə kwənt) *adj.* [prob. back-formation < *magniloquence* < L. *magniloquentia* < *magniloquus,* speaking in a lofty style < *magnus,* great (see MAGNI-) + *loqui,* to speak] 1. lofty, pompous, or grandiose in speech or style of expression 2. boastful or bombastic —**mag·nil′o·quence** *n.* —**mag·nil′o·quent·ly** *adv.*

Mag·ni·to·gorsk (mag′ni tō gôrsk′) city in the SW R.S.F.S.R., on the Ural River: pop. 352,000

mag·ni·tude (mag′nə tood′, -tyood′) *n.* [L. *magnitudo* < *magnus,* great] 1. greatness; specif., *a)* of size *b)* of extent *c)* of importance or influence *d)* [Obs.] of character 2. *a)* size or measurable quantity [the *magnitude* of a velocity] *b)* loudness (of sound) *c)* importance or influence 3. *Astron.* a number on an arbitrary scale by which the apparent brightness of a star is measured against the brightness of a selected group of standard stars and in which each whole magnitude represents a light ratio of 2.512 on a logarithmic scale: the brightest stars are of the first magnitude, and the faintest stars visible to the unaided eye are approximately of the sixth magnitude 4. *Math.* a number given to a quantity for purposes of comparison with other quantities of the same class —**of the first magnitude** of the greatest importance

☆**mag·no·li·a** (mag nōl′ē ə, -nōl′yə) *n.* [ModL., after Pierre *Magnol* (1638–1715), Fr. botanist] 1. any of a genus (*Magnolia*) of trees or shrubs of the magnolia family, with large, fragrant flowers of white, pink, or purple 2. the flower —*adj.* designating a family (Magnoliaceae) of trees, shrubs, and, sometimes, vines, including the magnolias, the cucumber tree, and the tulip tree

mag·num (mag′nəm) *n.* [L. *magnum,* neut. sing. of *magnus,* great (see MAGNI-)] a wine bottle holding twice as much as the usual bottle, or about 2/5 of a gallon

‡**mag·num o·pus** (mag′nəm ō′pəs) [L.] 1. a great work, esp. of art or literature; masterpiece 2. a person's greatest work or undertaking

mag·nus hitch (mag′nəs) [prob. < L. *magnus,* large] a kind of knot: see KNOT, illus.

Magog *see* GOG AND MAGOG

mag·pie (mag′pī′) *n.* [< *Mag,* dim. of MARGARET + PIE³] 1. any of a number of birds (genus *Pica*) of the crow family, related to the jays and characterized by black-and-white coloring, a long, tapering tail, and a habit of noisy chattering 2. a person who chatters 3. a person who collects odds and ends

M.Agr. Master of Agriculture

mag·uey (mag′wā; *Sp.* mä ge′ē) *n.* [Sp. < Taino] 1. any of a number of fleshy-leaved, fiber-yielding agaves of the SW U.S., Mexico, and Central America; esp., the century plant and species used in making rope, pulque, and tequila 2. any of several related plants (genus *Furcaea*) 3. any of several tough fibers from these plants

Ma·gus (mā′gəs) *n., pl.* -gi (-jī) [ME. < L.: see MAGI] 1. one of the Magi 2. [m-] a magician, sorcerer, or ancient astrologer: cf. SIMON MAGUS

Mag·yar (mag′yär; *Hung.* môd′yär) *n.* [Hung.] 1. a member of the people constituting the main ethnic group in Hungary 2. their Ugric language; Hungarian —*adj.* of the Magyars, their language, or culture

Ma·gyar·or·szag (môd′yär ōr′säg) *Hung. name of* HUNGARY

Ma·ha·bha·ra·ta (mə hä′bä′rə tə) [Sans. *Mahābhārata,* lit., the great story] one of the two great epics of India, written in Sanskrit about 200 B.C.: it combines stories and poems with history and mythology: also **Ma·ha′bha′·ra·tam** (-təm): cf. RAMAYANA

Ma·hal·la el Ku·bra (mä hä′lä el kōō′brä) city in N Egypt, in the Nile delta: pop. 178,000

Ma·han (mə han′), **Alfred Thay·er** (thā′ər) 1840–1914; U.S. naval officer & naval historian

ma·ha·ra·jah, ma·ha·ra·ja (mä′hə rä′jə) *n.* [Sans. *mahārāja < mahā,* great (see MAGNI-) + *rājā,* king: see REGAL] in India, a prince; formerly, the sovereign prince of any of the chief native states

ma·ha·ra·ni, ma·ha·ra·nee (-nē) *n.* [Hind. *mahārānī < mahā,* great (< Sans.: see MAGNI-) + *rani,* queen] in India, 1. the wife of a maharajah 2. a princess of equal rank with a maharajah

Ma·ha·rash·tra (mə hä′räsh′trə) state of W India: 118,717 sq. mi.; pop. 39,554,000; cap. Bombay

ma·hat·ma (mə hät′mə, -hat′-) *n.* [Sans. *mahātman < mahā,* great (see MAGNI-) + *ātmun,* ATMAN] *Theosophy & Buddhism* any of a class of wise and holy persons held in special regard or reverence: Mohandas Gandhi was often called *the Mahatma*

Ma·ha·ya·na (mä′hə yä′nə) *n.* [Sans. *mahāyāna,* lit., greater vehicle] a branch of Buddhism that stresses ideal-

ism, disinterested love, relief of the suffering of others, etc.: it developed mainly in China, Korea, and Japan

Mah·di (mä′dē) *n.* [Ar. *mahdīy*, one guided aright < *hadā*, to lead aright] a leader and prophet expected by Moslems to appear on earth before the world ends; Moslem Messiah —**Mah′dism** (-diz′m) *n.*—**Mah′dist** *n.*

Ma·hé (mä hā′) chief island of the Seychelles, in the Indian Ocean: 56 sq. mi.

Ma·hi·can (mə hē′kən) *n.* [AmInd. (Algonquian), lit., a wolf: cf. MOHEGAN] 1. a confederacy or tribe of Algonquian Indians who lived chiefly in the upper Hudson Valley 2. an Indian of this confederacy 3. *same as* MOHEGAN —*adj.* of this confederacy

mah·jongg, mah·jong (mä′jôŋ′, -jän′, -zhôŋ′, -zhäŋ′) *n.* [< dial. form of Chin. *ma-ch'iao*, lit., house sparrow, a figure on one of the tiles] a game of Chinese origin, played, usually by four persons, with 136 or 144 pieces resembling dominoes, marked in suits and called *tiles:* the object is to build combinations or sets by drawing, discarding, and exchanging tiles

Mah·ler (mä′lər), **Gus·tav** (goos′täf) 1860–1911; Austrian composer & conductor, born in Bohemia

mahl·stick (mäl′stik′, môl′-) *n.* [Du. *maalstok* < *malen*, to paint + *stok*, STICK] a long, light stick used by painters to rest and steady the brush hand while at work

ma·hog·a·ny (mə häg′ə nē, -hôg′-) *n., pl.* **-nies** [earlier *mohogeney* < ?] 1. *a)* any of a genus (*Swietenia*) of tropical trees of the mahogany family, with dark, heavy heartwood *b)* the wood of any of these trees; esp., the hard, reddish-brown to yellow wood of a tropical American tree (*Swietenia mahogani*), valued for furniture, interior finishing, and cabinetwork 2. *a)* any of various related trees, as the **African mahogany** (genus *Khaya*), or similar trees, as the **Australian red mahogany** (genus *Eucalyptus*) *b)* the wood of any of these trees 3. reddish brown —*adj.* 1. designating a family (Meliaceae) of chiefly tropical plants, including baywood, chinaberry, and mahogany 2. made of mahogany 3. reddish-brown

Ma·hom·et (mə häm′it) *same as* MOHAMMED —**Ma·hom′·et·an** *adj., n.*

☆**ma·ho·ni·a** (mə hō′nē ə) *n.* [ModL., after Bernard *McMahon* (c. 1775–1816), U.S. botanist] any of a genus (*Mahonia*) of low evergreen shrubs of the barberry family, with spiny-margined leaves and clusters of yellow flowers followed by blue berries

Ma·hound (mə hound′, -hōōnd′) [ME. *Mahun* < OFr. *Mahon,* contr. < *Mahomet*] 1. archaic var. of MOHAMMED 2. [Scot.] the Devil

ma·hout (mə hout′) *n.* [Hind. *mahāut, mahāvat* < Sans. *mahāmātra*, lit., great in measure, hence high officer] in India and the East Indies, an elephant driver or elephant keeper

Mah·rat·ta (mə rät′ə) *n. var. of* MARATHA

Mah·ra·ti, Mah·ra·ti (-ē) *n. var. of* MARATHI

mah·zor (mäkh zôr′, mäkh′zər) *n., pl.* **-zors′** Heb. **-zor′im** (-zôr′im) [Heb., cycle] the Jewish prayer book that contains the liturgy for festivals and holy days: cf. SIDDUR

Ma·ia (mā′ə, mī′-) [L. < Gr. *Maia*] 1. *Gr. Myth.* the eldest and loveliest of the Pleiades, mother of Hermes by Zeus 2. *Rom. Myth.* an earth goddess, sometimes identified with the Greek Maia: the month of May was named in her honor

maid (mād) *n.* [ME. *maide*, contr. < *maiden*] 1. *a)* a girl or young unmarried woman *b)* a virgin 2. [Now Rare] *same as* OLD MAID 3. a girl or woman servant: often in compounds [*barmaid, housemaid*] —**the Maid** *name for* JOAN OF ARC

Mai·da·nek (mī′də nek′) Nazi concentration camp & extermination center in E Poland, near Lublin

maid·en (mād′'n) *n.* [ME. < OE. *mægden*, dim. < base of *mægeth*, maid, virgin, akin to Goth. *magaths*, OHG. *magad* < IE. base *maghu-*, youngster, unmarried, whence OIr. *macc*, son (cf. MAC-)] 1. *a)* a girl or young unmarried woman *b)* a virgin 2. a race horse that has never won a race 3. [M-] a device like the guillotine, formerly used in Scotland for beheading criminals 4. *Cricket* an over in which no runs are scored: in full, **maiden over** —*adj.* 1. of, characteristic of, or suitable for a maiden 2. *a)* unmarried *b)* virgin 3. inexperienced; untried; unused; new; fresh 4. first or earliest [a *maiden* speech, a *maiden* voyage] 5. *a)* never having won a race [a *maiden* horse] *b)* for such horses [a *maiden* race]

maid·en·hair (-her′) *n.* any of a genus (*Adiantum*) of ferns with delicate brown to black fronds and slender stalks: also **maidenhair fern**

maidenhair tree *same as* GINKGO

maid·en·head (-hed′) *n.* 1. [Archaic] maidenhood; virginity 2. the hymen

maid·en·hood (-hood′) *n.* the state or time of being a maiden: also **maid′hood′**

maid·en·ly (-lē) *adj.* 1. of a maiden or maidenhood 2. like, characteristic of, or suitable for a maiden; modest, gentle, etc. —*adv.* [Archaic] in a maidenly manner —**maid′en·li·ness** *n.*

maiden name the surname that a woman had when not yet married

Maid Marian 1. a character in old May Day games and morris dances, variously a May queen, a boy dressed as a girl, or a buffoon 2. Robin Hood's sweetheart

maid of honor ☆1. an unmarried woman acting as chief attendant to the bride at a wedding: cf. MATRON OF HONOR 2. an unmarried woman, usually of noble birth, attending a queen or princess

Maid of Orléans *name for* JOAN OF ARC

maid·ser·vant (-sur′vənt) *n.* a girl or woman servant

Maid·stone (mād′stən, -stōn′) city in SE England; county seat of Kent: pop. 61,000

ma·ieu·tic (mā yōōt′ik, mī-) *adj.* [Gr. *maieutikos* < *maia*, midwife] designating or of the Socratic method of helping a person to bring forth and become aware of latent ideas or memories

mai·gre (mā′gər) *adj.* [Fr.: see MEAGER] [Rare] not made from flesh or its juices: said of food permissible to Roman Catholics, etc. on fast days

mai·hem (mā′hem) *n. earlier form of* MAYHEM

mail¹ (māl) *n.* [ME. *male* < OFr. < MHG. *malhe,* a traveling bag < OHG. *malaha,* wallet] 1. *a)* [Obs. except Scot.] a bag or piece of baggage *b)* [Archaic] a bag or packet of letters, etc. to be transported by post 2. *a)* letters, papers, packages, etc. handled, transported, and delivered by the post office ☆*b)* letters, papers, etc. received or sent by a person, company, etc. 3. [*also pl.*] the system of collection, transportation, and delivery of letters, packages, etc.; postal system 4. the collection or delivery of letters, packages, etc. at a certain time [late for the morning *mail*] 5. [Chiefly Brit.] a vehicle for mail —*adj.* of mail; esp., *a)* carrying, or used in the handling of, mail *b)* designating a person, or boat, train, etc. that transports letters, packages, etc. —*vt.* ☆to send by mail, as by putting into a mailbox; post —**mail′a·bil′i·ty** *n.* —**mail′a·ble** *adj.*

mail² (māl) *n.* [ME. *maille* < OFr. *maille,* a link, mesh < L. *macula,* a spot, mesh of a net] 1. a flexible body armor made of small, overlapping metal rings, loops of chain, or scales 2. the hard protective covering of some animals, as turtles —*vt.* to cover or protect with or as with mail —**mailed** *adj.*

mail³ (māl) *n.* [ME. *male,* rent, tribute: cf. BLACKMAIL] [Chiefly Scot.] rent or payment of any kind

☆**mail·bag** (māl′bag′) *n.* 1. a bag, as of leather, in which a mailman carries his deliveries: also **mail pouch** 2. a heavy canvas bag in which mail is transported: also **mail sack**

mail·box (-bäks′) *n.* ☆1. a box or compartment into which mail is put when delivered, as at one's home ☆2. a box, as on a street corner, into which mail is put for collection Also **mail box**

MAIL

☆**mail car** a railroad car equipped for handling mail

☆**mail carrier** a person whose work is carrying and delivering mail; mailman; postman

☆**mail·catch·er** (-kach′ər) *n.* a device for transferring bags of mail to or from a railroad train in motion: also **mail catcher**

mailed fist the use or threat of force, as between nations

☆**mail·er** (māl′ər) *n.* 1. a person who addresses and mails letters, etc. 2. an envelope or container in which something is to be mailed 3. an advertising leaflet for mailing out

mail·ing¹ (māl′iŋ) *n.* [see MAIL³ & -ING] [Scot.] a farm that is rented; also, the rent paid for it

☆**mail·ing²** (māl′iŋ) *n.* 1. *a)* the action of sending (something) by mail *b)* anything sent by mail 2. a batch of mail dispatched by a mailer at one time

☆**mailing list** 1. a list of members, contributors, etc. to whom an organization mails literature 2. a list of potential buyers to whom advertising matter is mailed

mailing tube a pasteboard cylinder in which printed matter or fragile objects are inserted for mailing

Mail·lol (mä yôl′), **A·ris·tide** (**Joseph Bonaventure**) (à rēs tēd′) 1861–1944; Fr. sculptor

mail·lot (mä yō′) *n.* [Fr., dim. < *maille,* knitted material, lit., mail: see MAIL²] 1. a swimming suit; esp., a one-piece swimming suit for women 2. a garment like this, worn by gymnasts, etc.

mail·man (māl′man′, -mən) *n., pl.* **-men** (-men′, -mən) *same as* MAIL CARRIER

☆**mail order** an order for goods to be sent by mail —**mail′-or′der** *adj.*

☆**mail-order house** a business establishment that takes mail orders and sends goods by mail

maim (mām) *vt.* [ME. *maymen* < OFr. *mahaigner, mayner*] to deprive of the use of some necessary part of the body; cripple; mutilate; disable —*n.* [ME. *mayme, maheym* < OFr. *mahaing, main*] [Obs.] an injury causing the loss or crippling of some necessary part of the body; mutilation; disablement: see MAYHEM —**maim′er** *n.*
SYN.—**maim** implies an injuring of a person's body so as to deprive him of some member or its use [*maimed* in an auto accident]; to **cripple** is to cause to be legless, armless, or lame in any member [*crippled* by rheumatism]; to **mutilate** is to remove

or severely damage a part of a person or thing essential to his or its completeness [a speech *mutilated* by censors]; **mangle** implies mutilation or disfigurement by or as by repeated tearing, hacking, or crushing [his arm was *mangled* in the press]; to **disable** is to make incapable of normal physical activity, as by crippling [*disabled* war veterans]

Mai·mon·i·des (mī män′ə dēz′) (born *Moses ben Maimon*) 1135–1204; Sp. rabbi, physician, & philosopher, in Egypt: also called *the Rambam*

Main (mīn; *E.* mān) river in S West Germany, flowing west into the Rhine at Mainz: 307 mi.

main[1] (mān) *n.* [ME. < OE. *mægen*, akin to ON. *magn*: for IE. base see MIGHT[2]] **1.** physical strength; force; power: now only in **with might and main**, with all one's strength **2.** [< the *adj.*] the principal or most important part or point: usually in the phrase **in the main**, mostly, chiefly **3.** a principal pipe, conduit, or line in a distributing system for water, gas, electricity, etc. **4.** [Poet.] the high, or open, sea; ocean **5.** [Archaic] the mainland: see SPANISH MAIN **6.** [Obs.] any broad expanse **7.** *Naut.* clipped form of: *a)* MAINMAST *b)* MAINSAIL —*adj.* [ME. *mayn* < OE. *mægen*- (in comp.) & ON. *meginn*, strong] **1.** orig., strong; powerful **2.** chief in size, extent, importance, etc.; principal; leading **3.** of, near, or connected with the mainmast or mainsail **4.** [Brit. Dial.] remarkable; considerable **5.** [Obs.] designating a broad expanse of land, sea, or space —*SYN.* see CHIEF —**by main force** (or **strength**) by sheer or utter force (or strength)

main[2] (mān) *n.* [prob. < prec., *adj.*, as in *main chance*] **1.** a number chosen by a dice player before he throws **2.** a series of matches between pairs of birds in cockfighting

main clause in a complex sentence, a clause that can function syntactically as a complete sentence by itself; independent clause: distinguished from SUBORDINATE CLAUSE (Ex.: *She will visit us* if she can)

main course the mainsail of a square-rigged vessel

main deck the topmost, principal deck of a ship

☆**main drag** [Slang] the principal street of a city or town

Maine (mān; *for 2, Fr.* men) [prob. from its being the *main* part of the New England region] **1.** New England State of the U.S.: admitted, 1820; 33,215 sq. mi.; pop. 992,000; cap. Augusta: abbrev. **Me., ME 2.** region & former province of W France **3.** a U.S. battleship blown up in the harbor of Havana, Cuba, February 15, 1898

Main·land (mān′land′, -lənd) **1.** largest of the Orkney Islands: c. 190 sq. mi. **2.** largest of the Shetland Islands: 407 sq. mi.

main·land (mān′land′, -lənd) *n.* the principal land or largest part of a continent, as distinguished from a relatively small island or peninsula —**main′land′er** *n.*

main·line (-līn′) *n.* the principal road, course, etc. —☆*vt.* **-lined′, -lin′ing** [Slang] to inject (a narcotic drug) directly into a large vein —**main′lin′er** *n.*

main·ly (-lē) *adv.* **1.** chiefly; principally; in the main **2.** [Obs.] *a)* strongly *b)* very much

main·mast (-məst, -mast′, -mäst′) *n.* the principal mast of a vessel: in a schooner, brig, bark, etc., the mast second from the bow; in a ketch or yawl, the mast nearer the bow

main·sail (-s′l, -sāl′) *n.* **1.** in a square-rigged vessel, the sail set from the main yard **2.** in a fore-and-aft-rigged vessel, the large sail set from the mainmast

main·sheet (-shēt′) *n.* the sheet of a mainsail; line controlling the angle at which a mainsail is set

main·spring (-sprin′) *n.* **1.** the principal spring in a clock, watch, or other mechanism; driving spring, by the steady uncoiling of which the mechanism is kept going **2.** the chief motive, incentive, or impelling cause

main·stay (-stā′) *n.* **1.** the stay of the mainmast; line extending forward from the mainmast, supporting it and holding it in position **2.** a chief support

☆**main stem** [Slang] same as: **1.** MAIN DRAG **2.** MAINLINE

main·stream (-strēm′) *n.* **1.** the middle of a stream, where the current is strongest **2.** the part of something considered to be the most active, productive, lively, busy, etc. [the *mainstream* of life] **3.** a major or prevailing trend or line of thought, action, etc.

☆**Main Street 1.** the principal street of any small town **2.** the typical inhabitants of a small town, regarded as provincial and conservative

main·tain (mān tān′) *vt.* [ME. *mainteinen* < OFr. *maintenir* < ML. *manutenere* < L. *manu tenere*, to hold in the hand < *manu*, abl. of *manus*, hand + *tenere*, to hold] **1.** to keep or keep up; continue in or with; carry on **2.** *a)* to keep in existence or continuance [food *maintains* life] *b)* to keep in a certain condition or position, esp. of efficiency, good repair, etc.; preserve [to *maintain* roads] **3.** to keep or hold (a place, position, etc.) against attack; defend **4.** *a)* to uphold or defend, as by argument; affirm *b)* to declare in a positive way; assert **5.** to support by aid, influence, protection, etc. **6.** to support by providing means of

existence; bear the expenses of [to *maintain* a family] —*SYN.* see SUPPORT —**main·tain′a·ble** *adj.* —**main·tain′er** *n.*

main·te·nance (mān′t'n əns) *n.* [ME. *maintenaunce* < OFr. *maintenance*] **1.** a maintaining or being maintained; upkeep, support, defense, etc.; specif., the work of keeping a building, machinery, etc. in a state of good repair **2.** means of support or sustenance; livelihood [a job that barely provides a *maintenance*] **3.** *Criminal Law* the act of interfering unlawfully in a suit between others by helping either party, as by giving money, etc., to carry it on

maintenance of membership in some union contracts, a provision by which all employees who are already members of the union, and all who join during the time covered by the contract, must remain members and pay dues or be discharged by the employer

Mainte·non (mant nōn′), marquise de (born *Françoise d'Aubigné*) 1635–1719; 2d wife of Louis XIV

main·top (mān′täp′) *n.* a platform at the head of the lower section of the mainmast

main·top·mast (mān′täp′məst) *n.* the section of the mainmast above the maintop

main·top·sail (-s′l, -sāl) *n.* the sail above the mainsail on the mainmast

main yard the lower yard on the mainmast; yard from which the mainsail is set

Mainz (mīnts) city in W West Germany, on the Rhine: capital of Rhineland-Palatinate: pop. 144,000

mair (mer) *adj.* [Scot.] more

‡**mair·ie** (me rē′) *n.* [Fr. < OFr. < *maire*, magistrate < L. *major*: see MAJOR] in France, a town hall or a similar building in an arrondissement

mai·son·ette (mā′zə net′) *n.* [Fr., dim of *maison*, house] **1.** a small house; cottage **2.** an apartment, esp. a duplex apartment

maist (māst) *adj.* [Scot.] most

Mait·land (māt′lənd), **Frederic William** 1850–1906; Eng. legal historian & jurist

mai·tre d' (mā′tər dē′) [< ff.] [Colloq.] a headwaiter

‡**mai·tre d'hô·tel** (me′tr′ dô tel′) [Fr., lit., master of the house] **1.** a butler or steward; major-domo **2.** a hotel manager **3.** a headwaiter **4.** (with) a sauce of melted butter, parsley, and lemon juice or vinegar

maize (māz) *n.* [Sp. *maíz* < WInd. (Taino) *mahiz*] **1.** same as CORN[1] (sense 3) **2.** the color of ripe corn; yellow —*adj.* yellow

Maj. Major

ma·jes·tic (mə jes′tik) *adj.* having or characterized by majesty; very grand or dignified; lofty; stately: also **ma·jes′ti·cal** —*SYN.* see GRAND —**ma·jes′ti·cal·ly** *adv.*

maj·es·ty (maj′is tē) *n., pl.* **-ties** [ME. *maiesty* < OFr. *majesté* < L. *majestas* < base of *major*, compar. of *magnus*, great: see MAGNI-] **1.** *a)* the dignity or power of a sovereign *b)* sovereign power [the *majesty* of the law] *c)* a sovereign **2.** [M-] a title used in speaking to or of a sovereign, preceded by *His, Her*, or *Your* **3.** grandeur or stateliness

Maj. Gen. Major General

ma·jol·i·ca (mə jäl′i kə, -yäl′-) *n.* [It. *maiolica* < *Maiolica*, MAJORCA, whence the first specimens came] **1.** a variety of Italian pottery, enameled, glazed, and richly colored and decorated **2.** pottery like this

ma·jor (mā′jər) *adj.* [ME. *maiour* < L. *major*, compar. of *magnus*, great: see MAGNI-] **1.** *a)* greater in size, amount, number, or extent *b)* greater in importance or rank **2.** of full legal age **3.** constituting the majority: said of a part, etc. ☆**4.** *Educ.* designating or of a field of study in which a student specializes and receives his degree **5.** *Logic* broader; more inclusive: see MAJOR PREMISE, MAJOR TERM **6.** *Music a)* designating an imperfect interval greater than the corresponding minor by a semitone *b)* characterized by major intervals, scales, etc. [the *major* key] *c)* designating a triad having a major third *d)* based on the scale pattern of the major mode: see MAJOR SCALE —*vi.* ☆*Educ.* to pursue a major subject or field of study; specialize [to *major* in physics] —*n.* **1.** [< the *adj.*] a superior in some class or group **2.** [Fr.] *U.S. Mil.* an officer ranking above a captain and below a lieutenant colonel ☆**3.** *Educ. a)* a major subject or field of study *b)* a student specializing in a (specified) subject **4.** *Law* a person who has reached his full legal age **5.** *Logic* a major term or premise **6.** *Music* a major interval, key, etc. —**the Majors** ☆*Baseball* the Major Leagues

Ma·jor·ca (mə jôr′kə) largest of the Balearic Islands: 1,405 sq. mi.: Sp. name, MALLORCA

ma·jor-do·mo (mā′jər dō′mō) *n., pl.* **-mos** [Sp. *mayordomo* or It. *maggiordomo* < LL. *major domus* < L. *major*, greater, an elder + gen. of *domus*, house] **1.** a man in charge of a great, royal, or noble household; chief steward **2.** any steward or butler: humorous usage

☆**ma·jor·ette** (mā′jər et′) *n.* short for DRUM MAJORETTE

major form class *Linguis.* a form class that contains a relatively large number of words: in English, nouns, verbs, adjectives, and adverbs are major form classes

major general *pl.* **major generals** *U.S. Mil.* an officer ranking below a lieutenant general and above a brigadier general

ma·jor·i·ty (mə jôr′ə tē, -jär′-) *n., pl.* **-ties** [Fr. *majorité* < ML. *majoritas* < L. *major*: see MAJOR] **1.** the greater part or larger number; more than half of a total ☆**2.** the excess of the larger number of votes cast for one candidate,

bill, etc. over all the rest of the votes: if candidate A gets 100 votes, candidate B, 200, and candidate C, 350, C has a majority of 50: cf. PLURALITY 3. the group, party, or faction with the larger number of votes 4. the condition or time of having reached full legal age, with full legal rights and responsibilities 5. the military rank or position of a major 6. [Obs.] the state or quality of being greater; superiority

☆**major league** a principal league in a professional sport; specif., [M- L-] [*pl.*] the two main leagues of professional baseball clubs in the U.S., the National League and the American League —**ma′jor-league′** adj.

major mode a progression, phrase, section, or composition of music predominantly using the intervals of the major scale

major order 1. *R.C.Ch.* the order of priest, deacon, or subdeacon 2. in certain other Christian churches, the order of bishop, priest, or deacon

major premise the premise (in a syllogism) that contains the major term

major scale one of the two standard diatonic musical scales, with half steps instead of whole steps after the third and seventh tones

major seminary *R.C.Ch.* a seminary offering usually the full six years of training for the priesthood

major suit *Bridge* spades or hearts: so called from their higher value in scoring

major term the predicate of the conclusion of a syllogism

ma·jus·cule (mə jus′kyōōl, maj′əs-) *n.* [Fr. < L. *majuscula* (*littera*), somewhat larger (letter), dim. < *major*: see MAJOR] 1. a large letter, capital or uncial, as in medieval manuscripts 2. writing in which such letters are used —*adj.* 1. of, like, or having the nature of, a majuscule 2. written in majuscules Cf. MINUSCULE —**ma·jus′cu·lar** adj.

Ma·kas·sar (mə kas′ər) seaport on the SW coast of Celebes, Indonesia: pop. 604,000

make¹ (māk) *vt.* **made**, **mak′ing** [ME. *maken* < OE. *macian*, akin to G. *machen* < IE. base **mag-*, to knead, press, stretch, whence Gr. *magis*, kneaded mass, paste, dough, *mageus*, kneader: cf. MASON] 1. to bring into being; specif., *a*) to form by shaping or putting parts or ingredients together, physically or mentally; build, construct, fabricate, fashion, create, compose, devise, formulate, etc. *b*) to fit or destine, as if by fashioning [they were made for each other] *c*) to cause; bring about; produce [to *make* corrections] *d*) to bring together materials for and start [to *make* a fire] *e*) to cause to be available; provide [to *make* change, to *make* room] 2. to bring into a specified condition; specif., *a*) to cause to be or become; specif., to elect or appoint [*make* him chairman] *b*) to cause to seem [the portrait *makes* him an old man] Sometimes used reflexively [*make* yourself comfortable] 3. to prepare for use; arrange [*make* the beds] 4. *a*) to amount to; form as a total [two pints *make* a quart] *b*) to count as; constitute [this *makes* his fifth novel] 5. to turn out to be; have, or prove to have, the essential qualities of [to *make* a fine leader] 6. to set up; establish [to *make* rules] 7. *a*) to get or acquire, as by one's behavior [to *make* friends] *b*) to get by earning, investing, etc. [to *make* a fortune] 8. to cause the success of [that venture *made* him] 9. to understand or regard as the meaning (of) [what do you *make* of the poem?] 10. to estimate to be; regard as [I *make* the distance about 500 miles] 11. *a*) to do or perform (a specified action); execute; accomplish [to *make* a quick turn] *b*) to engage in; carry on [to *make* war] 12. to deliver (a speech) or utter (remarks, etc.) 13. to cause or force: followed by an infinitive without *to* [make the machine work, *make* him behave] 14. *a*) to arrive at; reach [the ship *made* port] *b*) to arrive at in time [to *make* a train] 15. to go or travel; traverse [to *make* 500 miles the first day, to *make* 90 miles an hour] 16. [Colloq.] to succeed in getting membership in, a position on, the status of, recognition in, etc. [to *make* the team, to *make* the headlines] ☆17. [Slang] to succeed in becoming the lover of; seduce 18. [Archaic] to shut (a door) tight 19. *Card Playing a*) to win (tricks) or fulfill (one's bid) *b*) to take a trick with (a card) *c*) to shuffle (the cards) 20. *Elec.* to close (a circuit); effect (a contact) 21. *Games* to score; get as a score 22. *Law a*) to perform, execute, or sign (a will or other legal instrument) *b*) to do (what one has bound himself to do) To **make oath** is to swear in the legally prescribed form —*vi.* 1. to start (to do something) [she *made* to go] 2. to tend, extend, or point (*to*, *toward*, etc.) 3. to behave in a specified manner: with a following adjective [*make* bold, *make* merry, etc.] 4. to cause something to be in a specified condition [*make* ready, *make* fast, etc.] 5. to increase in depth or volume; rise or accumulate, as tide, snow, water in a ship, etc. 6. to mature: said of hay, etc. *Make* is widely and variously used in idiomatic phrases, many of which are entered in this dictionary under the key word, as *make fun of*, *make good*, *make the grade*, *make hay*, etc. —*n.* 1. the act or process of making; esp., manufacture 2. the amount made; output, esp. of manufacture 3. the way in which something is made; style; build 4. type, sort, or brand: with refer-

ence to the maker or the place, time, etc. of making [a foreign *make* of car] 5. disposition; character; nature [a man of this *make*] 6. *Elec.* the closing of a circuit by making contact —**make a fool** (or **ass**, etc.) **of** to cause to seem a fool (or ass, etc.) —**make after** to chase or follow —**make a meal on** (or **of**) to eat as a meal —**make as if** (or **as though**) to behave as if —**make away with** 1. to steal 2. to get rid of 3. to eat all of 4. to kill —**make believe** to pretend; act a part —**make for** 1. to head for; go toward 2. to charge at; attack 3. to tend toward; help effect —**make heavy weather** 1. *Naut.* to pitch and roll, as in rough water 2. to have difficulties —**make it** 1. [Colloq.] to do or achieve a certain thing ☆2. [Slang] to have sexual intercourse (*with*) —☆**make like** [Slang] to imitate; impersonate —**make off** to go away; run away —**make off with** to steal —**make or break** to cause the success or failure of —**make out** 1. to see with some difficulty; descry 2. to understand 3. to write out 4. to fill out (a blank form, etc.) 5. to show or prove to be 6. to try to show, affirm, or imply to be 7. to succeed; get along ☆8. [Slang] *a*) to kiss and caress as lovers *b*) to have sexual intercourse —**make over** 1. to change; renovate 2. to transfer the ownership of by or as by signing a legal document 3. [Colloq.] to be demonstrative toward or about —**make up** 1. to put together; compose; compound 2. to form; constitute 3. to invent; create 4. to complete by providing what is lacking 5. to compensate (*for*) 6. to arrange 7. *a*) to become friendly again after a disagreement or quarrel *b*) to settle (an argument or differences) in a friendly manner 8. *a*) to put on the required costume, cosmetics, etc. for a role in a play *b*) to put cosmetics on 9. to resolve or decide (one's mind) 10. to select and arrange type, illustrations, etc. for (a book, magazine, page, etc.) ☆11. *Educ.* to take again (an examination or course that one has failed) or to take (an examination that one has missed) —**make up to** to flatter, or try to be agreeable to, in order to become friendly or intimate with —**make with** [Slang] 1. to use, or do something with, in the way indicated or implied 2. to produce or supply [to *make with* the jokes] —**on the make** 1. [Colloq.] trying to succeed financially, socially, etc., esp. in an aggressive, single-minded way 2. [Slang] trying to get a lover —**mak′a·ble** adj.

SYN.—**make** is the general term meaning to bring into being and may imply a producing of something physically or mentally; **form** suggests a definite contour, structure, design, etc. in the thing made; **shape** suggests the imparting of a specific form as by molding, cutting, hammering, etc.; **fashion** implies inventiveness, cleverness of design, the use of skill, etc.; **construct** implies a putting of parts together systematically according to some design; **manufacture** implies a producing from raw materials, now especially by machinery and on a large scale; **fabricate** implies a building or manufacturing, often by assembling standardized parts, and, in extended use, connotes fictitious invention

make² (māk) *n.* [ME. < OE. *gemaca* (akin to G. *gemach*, fitting, suitable) < base of *macian*: see prec.] [Archaic] 1. an equal; peer 2. a mate, companion, or spouse

make-be·lieve (māk′bə lēv′) *n.* 1. pretense; feigning 2. a pretender —*adj.* pretended; feigned; sham

make·fast (-fast′, -fäst′) *n.* a buoy, post, pile, etc. to which a boat is fastened

make-peace (-pēs′) *n.* [Archaic] a peacemaker

mak·er (-ər) *n.* 1. a person or thing that makes (in various senses) 2. [M-] God 3. [Archaic] a poet 4. *Law* the signer of a promissory note —**meet one's Maker** to die

make·read·y (-red′ē) *n.* ☆*Printing* the final adjustment of the printing surfaces on a press by the use of leveling devices, overlays, underlays, etc.

make·shift (-shift′) *n.* a thing that will do for a while as a substitute; temporary expedient —*adj.* that will do for a while as a substitute —SYN. see RESOURCE

make-up, make·up (-up′) *n.* 1. the way in which something is put together; composition; construction 2. nature; disposition; constitution [to have a stolid *makeup*] 3. *a*) the way in which an actor is made up with a costume, cosmetics, etc. for a role *b*) the cosmetics, wigs, costumes, etc. used 4. *a*) cosmetics generally; rouge, lipstick, mascara, etc. *b*) the way in which these are applied or worn 5. the arrangement of type, illustrations, etc. in a book, newspaper, page, etc. ☆6. [Colloq.] a special test taken by a student to make up for a test that he has missed or failed to pass —*adj.* of or for making up

make·weight (-wāt′) *n.* 1. anything added to a scale to complete the required weight 2. an unimportant person or thing added to make up some lack

Ma·key·ev·ka (mä kā′yif kä′) city in SE Ukrainian S.S.R., in the Donets Basin: pop. 410,000

mak·ing (mā′kiŋ) *n.* 1. the act of one that makes or the process of being made; formation, construction, creation, production, composition, manufacture, development, performance, etc. 2. the cause or means of success or advancement [an experience that will be the *making* of him] 3. *a*) something made *b*) the quantity made at one time *c*) [*pl.*] earnings; profits 4. *a*) [often *pl.*] the material or qualities needed for the making or development of something [to

have the *making(s)* of a good doctor] ☆*b*) [*pl.*] [Old Colloq.] tobacco and paper for making one's own cigarettes

Mak·kah (mak′ə) *Arabic name of* MECCA

Ma·ku·a (mä kōō′ä) *n.* **1.** *pl.* **-kuʹas, -kuʹa** any member of a people of N Mozambique and adjacent Tanganyika **2.** their Bantu language

ma·ku·ta (mä kōō′tä) *n. pl. of* LIKUTA

mal- (mal) [Fr. < L. *male-* < *male*, badly, *malus*, bad, evil < ? IE. base *(s)mēlo-*, whence SMALL] *a prefix meaning* bad or badly, wrong, ill [*maladjustment*]

Mal. 1. Malachi **2.** Malay **3.** Malayan

Mal·a·bar Coast (mal′ə bär′) coastal region in SW India, extending from Cape Comorin to Goa & inland to the Western Ghats: c. 450 mi. long: also **Malabar**

Ma·lac·ca (mə lak′ə) **1.** state of W Malaya, on the strait of Malacca: 640 sq. mi.; pop. 384,000 **2.** seaport in this state: pop. 70,000 **3. Strait of,** strait between Sumatra & the Malay Peninsula: c. 500 mi. long

Malacca cane [< prec.] a lightweight walking stick of rattan, often mottled brown

Mal·a·chi (mal′ə kī′) [Heb. *malʹākhī*, lit., my messenger] *Bible* **1.** a Hebrew prophet of the 5th cent. B.C. **2.** the book containing prophecies attributed to him Also, in the Douay Bible, **Mal·a·chi·as** (mal′ə kī′əs)

mal·a·chite (mal′ə kīt′) *n.* [ME. *melochites* < L. *molochites* < Gr. *molochītēs*, a stone (? malachite) < Gr. *malachē*, *molochē*, mallow: its color is like that of mallow leaves] native basic copper carbonate, $CuCO_3 \cdot Cu(OH)_2$, a green mineral used as an ore of copper or for ornamental objects

mal·a·co- (mal′ə kō′, -kə) [< Gr. *malakos*, soft < IE. *mlāk-* < base *mel-*, to crush, grind, whence MILL[1]] *a combining form meaning:* **1.** soft [*malacopterygian*] **2.** mollusks [*malacology*]

mal·a·col·o·gy (mal′ə käl′ə jē) *n.* [Fr. *malacologie:* see prec. & -LOGY] the branch of zoology dealing with mollusks

mal·a·cos·tra·can (mal′ə käs′trə kən) *adj.* [< ModL. *Malacostraca*, the subclass < Gr. *malakostrakos*, soft-shelled < *malakos*, soft + *ostrakon*, shell + -AN] of a large subclass (Malacostraca) of highly evolved crustaceans comprising the lobsters, shrimps, crabs, etc., typically having 19 pairs of appendages: also **mal′a·cos′tra·cous** (-kəs) —*n.* such a crustacean

mal·ad·ap·ta·tion (mal′ad əp tā′shən) *n.* inadequate or faulty adaptation —**mal′a·dapʹtive** (-ə dap′tiv) *adj.*

mal·a·dapt·ed (mal′ə dap′tid) *adj.* not suited or properly adapted (to a function, situation, etc.)

mal·ad·just·ed (mal′ə jus′tid) *adj.* poorly adjusted, esp. to the environment; specif., unable to adjust properly to the circumstances of one's life —**mal′ad·justʹment** *n.*

mal·ad·jus·tive (-tiv) *adj.* not leading to proper adjustment

mal·ad·min·is·ter (-əd min′ə stər) *vt.* to administer badly; conduct (public affairs, etc.) corruptly or inefficiently —**mal′ad·min′is·tra′tion** (-ə strā′shən) *n.*

mal·a·droit (mal′ə droit′) *adj.* [Fr.: see MAL- & ADROIT] awkward; clumsy; bungling —*SYN.* see AWKWARD — **mal′a·droit′ly** *adv.* —**mal′a·droit′ness** *n.*

mal·a·dy (mal′ə dē) *n., pl.* **-dies** [ME. *maladie* < OFr. < *malade*, sick < VL. *male habitus*, badly kept, out of condition: see MAL- & HABIT] a disease; illness; sickness: often used figuratively —*SYN.* see DISEASE

‡**ma·la fi·de** (mä′lə fī′dē, mal′ə) [L.] in bad faith; with intent to deceive: opposed to BONA FIDE

Má·la·ga (mäl′ä gä′; *E.* mal′ə gə) seaport in S Spain, on the Mediterranean: pop. 325,000

Mal·a·ga (mal′ə gə) *n.* [after prec.] **1.** a large, white, oval, firm-fleshed grape **2.** a white, usually sweet, wine, orig. from Málaga

Mal·a·gas·y (mal′ə gas′ē) *n.* [< native name, var. of the base *Madagas-* in MADAGASCAR] **1.** *pl.* **-gas′y, -gas′ies** a native or inhabitant of the Malagasy Republic **2.** the Indonesian language of the Malagasy —*adj.* of the Malagasy or their language

Malagasy Republic country coextensive with the island of Madagascar: a member state of the French Community: 228,000 sq. mi.; pop. c. 6,643,000; cap. Tananarive

mal·a·gue·na (mal′ə gān′yə, -gwā′nə) *n.* [Sp. *malagueña*, orig. fem. of *malagueño*, of MÁLAGA] any of several Spanish folk tunes or dances, esp. one like the fandango

ma·laise (ma lāz′) *n.* [Fr. < *mal*, bad (see MAL-) + *aise*, EASE] **1.** a vague feeling of physical discomfort or uneasiness, as early in an illness **2.** a vague awareness of moral or social decline

☆**mal·a·mute** (mal′ə myōōt′, mäl′-) *n.* [< *Malemute*, name of an Eskimo tribe] *same as* ALASKAN MALAMUTE

mal·an·ders (mal′ən dərz) *n.pl.* [ME. *malawnder* < MFr. *malandre* < L. *malandria*, blisters or pustules on the neck, esp. of horses] a variety of eczema about the knee of a horse's foreleg

Ma·lang (mä län′) city in E Java, Indonesia: pop. 375,000

mal·a·pert (mal′ə purt′) *adj.* [ME. < OFr. < *mal*, badly (see MAL-) + *appert*, var. of *espert*, experienced, deft (see EXPERT)]: infl. by *apert*, open, bold (< L. *apertus:* see APERTURE)] [Archaic] saucy; impudent; pert —*n.* [Archaic] a saucy, impudent person —**mal′a·pert′ly** *adv.* —**mal′a·pert′ness** *n.*

mal·a·prop (mal′ə präp′) *adj.* [< ff.] using or characterized by malapropisms: also **mal′a·prop′i·an** (-ē ən) —*n. same as* MALAPROPISM

Mal·a·prop (mal′ə präp′), **Mrs.** [< MALAPROPOS] a character in Sheridan's play *The Rivals*, who makes ludicrous blunders in her use of words

mal·a·prop·ism (mal′ə präp iz′m) *n.* [< prec. + -ISM] **1.** ludicrous misuse of words, esp. through confusion caused by resemblance in sound **2.** an instance of this (Ex.: *progeny* for *prodigy*)

mal·ap·ro·pos (mal′ap rə pō′, mal ap′-) *adj.* [Fr. *mal à propos:* see MAL- & APROPOS] at an awkward or improper time or place; inopportune; inappropriate —*adv.* in an inopportune or inappropriate manner

ma·lar (mā′lər) *adj.* [ModL. < L. *mala*, the cheek] of the cheek, cheekbone, or side of the head —*n.* the cheekbone; zygomatic bone

Mäl·ar (mel′är) lake in SE Sweden: 440 sq. mi.: Swed. name **Mäl·ar·en** (mel′ä rən)

ma·lar·i·a (mə ler′ē ə) *n.* [It., contr. < *mala aria*, bad air: see MAL- & ARIA] **1.** [Archaic] unwholesome or poisonous air, as from marshy ground; miasma **2.** [from the former notion that it was caused by the bad air of swamps] an infectious disease, generally intermittent and recurrent, caused by any of various protozoans (genus *Plasmodium*) that are parasitic in the red blood corpuscles and are transmitted to man by the bite of an infected mosquito, esp. the anopheles: it is characterized by severe chills and fever —**ma·lar′i·al, ma·lar′i·an, ma·lar′i·ous** *adj.*

☆**ma·lar·key, ma·lar·ky** (mə lär′kē) *n.* [< ? Irish surname] [Slang] insincere, meaningless, or deliberately misleading talk; nonsense

mal·ate (mal′āt, māl′āt) *n.* a salt or ester of malic acid

☆**mal·a·thi·on** (mal′ə thī′än) *n.* [< MAL(IC) A(CID) + THION(IC)] an organic phosphate, $C_{10}H_{19}O_6S_2P$, of relatively low toxicity for mammals, used as an insecticide

Ma·la·tya (mä′lä tyä′) city in EC Turkey: pop. 84,000

Ma·la·wi (mä′lä wē) country in SE Africa, on Lake Nyasa: a member of the Brit. Commonwealth: 46,066 sq. mi.; pop. 4,530,000; cap. Zomba

Ma·lay (mā′lā, mə lā′) *n.* [Malay *malāyu*] **1.** a member of a large group of brown-skinned, short, black-haired peoples living in the Malay Peninsula, the Malay Archipelago, and nearby islands **2.** their Indonesian language, widely used in the Far East as a trade language —*adj.* of the Malays, their country, language, culture, etc.

Ma·lay·a (mə lā′ə) **1.** *same as* MALAY PENINSULA **2. Federation of,** former federation of states on the S end of the Malay Peninsula, now a part of the Federation of Malaysia, called *West Malaysia:* 50,700 sq. mi.; pop. 8,655,000; cap. Kuala Lumpur: see INDOCHINA, map

Mal·a·ya·lam (mal′ə yä′ləm) *n.* [Malayalam *malayālam*] a Dravidian language spoken on the Malabar Coast, SW India, dialectally related to Tamil

Ma·lay·an (mə lā′ən) *adj. same as* INDONESIAN (sense 2) —*n.* **1.** *same as* MALAY (sense 1) **2.** *same as* INDONESIAN (sense 3)

Malay Archipelago large group of islands between SE Asia & Australia, including Indonesia, the Philippines, &, sometimes, New Guinea

MALAY ARCHIPELAGO

Ma·lay·o- (mə lā′ō) *a combining form meaning* Malay and

Ma·lay·o-Pol·y·ne·sian (mə lā′ō päl′ə nē′zhən, -shən) *adj.* designating or of a family of languages spoken over a large area extending from Madagascar to Hawaii and in the S Pacific, including Indonesian, Melanesian, Micronesian, Polynesian, etc. —*n.* these languages

Malay Peninsula peninsula in SE Asia, extending from Singapore to the Isthmus of Kra: it includes the former Federation of Malaya & part of Thailand: c. 700 mi. long

Ma·lay·sia (mə lā′zhə, -shə) **1.** *same as* MALAY ARCHIPELAGO **2. Federation of,** country in SE Asia, consisting of the former Federation of Malaya, Sabah, & Sarawak: a member of the Brit. Commonwealth: 128,654 sq. mi.; pop. 10,190,000; cap. Kuala Lumpur —**Ma·lay′sian** *adj., n.*

Mal·colm (mal′kəm) [Celt. *Maolcolm*, lit., servant of (St.) Columba] a masculine name

mal·con·tent (mal′kən tent′) *adj.* [OFr.: see MAL- & CONTENT[1]] discontented, dissatisfied, or rebellious —*n.* a discontented, dissatisfied, or rebellious person: applied esp. to critics of the government

‡**mal de mer** (mȧl də mer′) [Fr.] seasickness

Mal·den (môl′dən) [after *Maldon*, town in England] city in E Mass.: suburb of Boston: pop. 56,000

Mal·dive Islands (mal′dīv) country on a group of islands in the Indian Ocean, southwest of Ceylon: 115 sq. mi.; pop. 104,000

male (māl) *adj.* [ME. < OFr. *male, masle* < L. *masculus*, dim. of *mas* (gen. *maris*), a male, man] **1.** designating or of the sex that fertilizes the ovum of the female and begets offspring: opposed to FEMALE: biological symbol, ♂ **2.** of, characteristic of, or suitable for members of this sex;

masculine; virile **3.** consisting of men or boys **4.** designating or having a part shaped to fit into a corresponding hollow part (called *female*): said of pipe fittings, electric plugs, etc. **5.** *Bot. a)* having stamens or antheridia and no carpels, archegonia, or oogonia *b)* designating or of a reproductive structure or part producing spermatozoids that can fertilize the female eggs —*n* **1.** a male person; man or boy **2.** a male animal or plant —**male′ness** *n.*
SYN.—male is the basic term applied to members of the sex that is biologically distinguished from the female sex and is used of animals and plants as well as of human beings; **masculine** is applied to qualities, such as strength, vigor, etc., characteristic of men, or to things appropriate to men; **manly** suggests the noble qualities, such as courage, independence, etc., that one associates with a man who has maturity of character; **mannish**, used chiefly of women, implies the possession or adoption of the traits, manners, etc. of a man; **virile** stresses qualities such as robustness, vigor, and, specif., sexual potency, that belong to a physically mature man
Male·branche (mȧl bränsh′), **Ni·co·las** (de) (nē kô lä′) 1638–1715; Fr. philosopher
mal·e·dict (mal′ə dikt′) *adj.* [L. *maledictus*, pp. of *maledicere*: see ff.] [Archaic] accursed; hateful —*vt.* [Archaic] to curse
mal·e·dic·tion (mal′ə dik′shən) *n.* [ME. *malediccioun* < OFr. *malediction* < LL.(Ec.) *maledictio* < L., abuse, reviling: see MAL- & DICTION] **1.** a calling down of evil on someone; curse **2.** evil talk about someone; slander —**mal′e·dic′to·ry** *adj.*
mal·e·fac·tion (mal′ə fak′shən) *n.* [LL. *malefactio* < pp. of *malefacere*: see ff.] wrongdoing; crime
mal·e·fac·tor (mal′ə fak′tər) *n.* [L. < pp. of *malefacere* < *male*, evil (see MAL-) + *facere*, to DO¹] an evildoer or criminal —[Now Rare] **mal′e·fac′tress** *n.fem.*
male fern a fern (*Dryopteris filix-mas*) of the Northern Hemisphere: source of an oleoresin used to expel tapeworms
ma·lef·ic (mə lef′ik) *adj.* [L. *maleficus* < *malefacere*: see MALEFACTOR] causing disaster; harmful; evil
ma·lef·i·cent (-ə s′nt) *adj.* [back-formation < L. *maleficentia* < *maleficus*: see prec.] harmful; hurtful; evil —**ma·lef′i·cence** *n.*
ma·le·ic acid (mə lē′ik) [< Fr. *maléique*, altered (by Pelouze, Fr. chemist, 1834) < *malique*, MALIC (ACID), to indicate a relationship between the two acids] a colorless, crystalline, poisonous acid, $C_4H_4O_4$, an isomer of fumaric acid, used in organic syntheses, in textile dyeing, etc.
maleic hydrazide a slightly soluble solid, $C_4H_4N_2O_2$, used to inhibit plant growth, to stop the sprouting of vegetables in storage, etc.
☆**ma·le·mute, ma·le·miut** (mal′ə myoot′, mäl′-) *n.* same as ALASKAN MALAMUTE
‡**mal·en·ten·du** (mål än tän dü′) *adj.* [Fr.] misunderstood; poorly conceived —*n.* a misunderstanding
ma·lev·o·lence (mə lev′ə ləns) *n.* [ME. *malyvolence* < OFr. *malivolence* < L. *malevolentia*] the quality or state of being malevolent; malice; spitefulness; ill will —*SYN.* see MALICE
ma·lev·o·lent (-lənt) *adj.* [OFr. *malivolent* < L. *malevolens* (gen. *malevolentis*) < *male*, evil (see MAL-) + *volens*, prp. of *velle*, to wish: see WILL²] wishing evil or harm to others; having or showing ill will; malicious —**ma·lev′o·lent·ly** *adv.*
mal·fea·sance (mal fē′z′ns) *n.* [obs. Fr. *malfaisance* < *malfaisant* < *mal*, evil (see MAL-) + *faisant*, prp. of *faire* < L. *facere*, to DO¹] wrongdoing or misconduct, esp. by a public official; commission of an act that is positively unlawful: distinguished from MISFEASANCE, NONFEASANCE —**mal·fea′sant** *adj.*
mal·for·ma·tion (mal′fôr mā′shən) *n.* faulty, irregular, or abnormal formation or structure of a body or part —**mal·formed′** (-fôrmd′) *adj.*
mal·func·tion (mal funk′shən) *vi.* [MAL- + FUNCTION] to fail to function as it should —*n.* the act or an instance of malfunctioning
Mal·gache (mål gåsh′) *Fr. name of* MALAGASY
‡**mal·gré lui** (mål grā lwē′) [Fr.] in spite of oneself
Ma·li (mä′lē) country in W Africa, south & east of Mauritania: 464,873 sq. mi.; pop. 4,745,000; cap. Bamako
mal·ic acid (mal′ik, mā′lik) [Fr. *acide malique* < L. *malum* < Gr. *mēlon*, apple] a colorless, crystallizable acid, $C_4H_6O_5$, occurring in apples and other fruits
mal·ice (mal′is) *n.* [ME. < OFr. < L. *malitia* < *malus*, bad: see MAL-] **1.** active ill will; desire to harm another or to do mischief; spite **2.** *Law* evil intent; state of mind shown by intention to do, or intentional doing of, something unlawful —**malice aforethought** (or **prepense**) a deliberate intention and plan to do something unlawful, as murder
SYN.—malice implies a deep-seated animosity that delights in causing others to suffer or in seeing them suffer; **ill will** and the more formal **malevolence** imply hostile or unfriendly feelings such as dispose one to wish evil to others; **spite** suggests a mean desire to hurt, annoy, or frustrate others, usually as displayed in petty, vindictive acts; **rancor** implies an intensely bitter ill will that rankles; **malignity** suggests extreme and virulent malevolence that is relentless in expressing itself; **grudge** implies ill will inspired by resentment over a grievance
ma·li·cious (mə lish′əs) *adj.* [ME. < OFr. *malicios* < L. *malitiosus* < *malitia*] having, showing, or caused by

malice; spiteful; intentionally mischievous or harmful —**ma·li′cious·ly** *adv.* —**ma·li′cious·ness** *n.*
malicious mischief the willful destruction of another's personal property
ma·lign (mə līn′) *vt.* [ME. *malignen* < OFr. *malignier*, to plot, deceive < LL. *malignare* < L. *malignus*, wicked, malicious < *male*, ill (see MAL-) + base of *genus*, born: see GENUS] to speak evil of; defame; slander; traduce —*adj.* **1.** showing ill will; malicious **2.** evil; baleful [a *malign* influence] **3.** very harmful; malignant —*SYN.* see SINISTER —**ma·lign′er** *n.*
ma·lig·nan·cy (mə lig′nən sē) *n.* **1.** the quality or condition of being malignant: also **ma·lig′nance 2.** *pl.* **-cies** a malignant tumor
ma·lig·nant (-nənt) *adj.* [LL. *malignans* (gen. *malignantis*), prp. of *malignare*: see MALIGN] **1.** having an evil influence; malign **2.** wishing evil; very malevolent or malicious **3.** very harmful **4.** very dangerous or virulent; causing or likely to cause death; not benign [a cancer is a *malignant* growth] **5.** [Obs.] malcontent; rebellious; disaffected —*n.* [Archaic] a malcontent —**ma·lig′nant·ly** *adv.*
ma·lig·ni·ty (-nə tē) *n.* [ME. *malignitee* < OFr. *malignite* < L. *malignitas*: see MALIGN] **1.** persistent, intense ill will or desire to harm others; great malice **2.** the quality of being very harmful or dangerous; malignancy **3.** *pl.* **-ties** a malignant act, event, or feeling —*SYN.* see MALICE
ma·li·hi·ni (mä′lə hē′nē) *n.* [Haw.] a newcomer to Hawaii
Ma·lines (mȧ lēn′) *Fr. name of* MECHELEN
ma·lines (mə lēn′; *Fr.* mȧ lēn′) *n.* [Fr. < prec.] **1.** same as MECHLIN **2.** a thin, somewhat stiff, silk net used in dressmaking, etc.: also **ma·line′**
ma·lin·ger (mə lin′gər) *vi.* [< Fr. *malingre*, sickly, infirm < *mal*, bad (see MAL-) + OFr. *heingre*, lean, haggard, prob. < Frank. form akin to ME. *hagger*: see HAGGARD] to pretend to be ill or otherwise incapacitated in order to escape duty or work; shirk —**ma·lin′ger·er** *n.*
Ma·lin·ke (mä′liṇ kā′) *n.,* **1.** *pl.* **-kes′, -ke′** any member of a Mande people of WC Africa **2.** their Mande language
Ma·li·now·ski, Bron·is·law (Kaspar) (brô nē′slȧf) 1884–1942; Pol. anthropologist; in the U.S
mal·i·son (mal′ə z′n, -s′n) *n.* [ME. < OFr. *maleison*: see MALEDICTION] [Archaic] a curse
mal·kin (mô′kin; *occas.* môl′kin, mal′-) *n.* [ME. *malkyn*, orig. dim. of *Malde*, Maud, itself dim. of *Matilda*] [Obs. or Brit. Dial.] **1.** a slovenly or sluttish woman **2.** a mop **3.** a scarecrow **4.** a hare **5.** a cat
mall (môl, mal) *n.* [var. of MAUL, esp. associated in 17th cent. with cognate (PALL)-MALL] **1.** orig., a) a large, heavy mallet, used in the game of pall-mall *b)* [< PALL-MALL] the game itself *c)* a lane or alley where the game was played **2.** a shaded walk or public promenade ☆**3.** a) a street for pedestrians only, with shops on each side, and often with decorative plantings, benches, etc. *b)* a completely enclosed, air-conditioned shopping center like this **4.** a median strip: see MEDIAN (*n.* 3)
mal·lard (mal′ərd) *n., pl.* **-lards, -lard:** see PLURAL, II, D, 1 [ME. < OFr. *malart* < **maslart* < *masle*: see MALE] the common wild duck (*Anas platyrhynchos*), from which the domestic duck is descended: the male has a green or bluishblack head and a band of white around the neck
Mal·lar·mé (mȧ lȧr mā′), **Sté·phane** (stā fȧn′) 1842–98; Fr. symbolist poet
mal·le·a·ble (mal′ē ə b′l) *adj.* [ME. *malliable* < ML. *malleabilis* < L. *malleare*, to beat with a hammer < *malleus*, a hammer] **1.** that can be hammered, pounded, or pressed into various shapes without breaking: said of metals **2.** capable of being changed, molded, trained, etc.; adaptable —*SYN.* see PLIABLE —**mal′le·a·bil′i·ty, mal′le·a·ble·ness** *n.*
malleable iron cast iron made from pig iron by long heating at a high temperature and slow cooling: it is especially strong and malleable: also **malleable cast iron**
mal·lee (mal′ē) *n.* [native name in Australia] **1.** any of several shrubby species of Australian eucalyptus (as *Eucalyptus dumosa* and *Eucalyptus oleosa*) **2.** in Australia, a dense thicket formed by such plants
mal·le·muck (mal′ə muk′) *n.* [Du. *mallemok* < *mal*, foolish + *mok*, a gull] any of several large ocean birds, as the petrel, fulmar, or albatross
mal·le·o·lus (mə lē′ə ləs) *n., pl.* **-li** (-lī′) [L. *malleolus*, dim. of *malleus*, a hammer] the rounded bony protuberance on each side of the ankle joint —**mal·le′o·lar** *adj.*
mal·let (mal′it) *n.* [ME. *malyet* < MFr. *maillet*, dim. of *mail* < OFr. *maile*: see MAUL] **1.** a kind of hammer, usually with a heavy wooden head and a short handle, for driving a chisel, etc. **2.** *a)* a longhandled hammer with a cylindrical wooden head, used in playing croquet *b)* a similar instrument, but with a longer, flexible handle, used in playing polo **3.** a small, light hammer, usually with a felt-covered head, used for playing a vibraphone, xylophone, etc.
mal·le·us (mal′ē əs) *n., pl.* **mal′le·i** (-ī′) [L., a hammer] the largest and

MALLET

outermost of the three small bones in the middle ear of mammals, shaped somewhat like a hammer

Mal·lor·ca (mäl yôr′kä, mä-) *Sp.* name of MAJORCA

mal·low (mal′ō) *n.* [ME. *malwe* < OE. *mealuwe* < L. *malva* (whence G. *malve*, Fr. *mauve*)] 1. any of a genus (*Malva*) of plants of the mallow family, with dissected or lobed leaves 2. any of various other plants of the mallow family, as the marsh mallow, rose mallow, etc. —*adj.* designating a family (Malvaceae) of plants, including the hollyhock, cotton, marsh mallow, and okra, typically having large, showy flowers with many stamens borne on a tube, and a sticky juice in their stems, leaves, and roots

mallow rose *same as* ROSE MALLOW

malm (mäm) *n.* [ME. *malme* < OE. *mealm-*, sand, akin to Goth. *malma*, sand, ON. *malmr*, ore < IE. base **mel-*, to crush, whence MILL¹] 1. [Brit.] *a)* a soft, crumbly, grayish-white limestone *b)* a soft, chalky loam formed from this 2. clay and chalk mixed for use in making bricks

Malmes·bury (mämz′ber ē, -ber′ē), **William of** *see* WILLIAM OF MALMESBURY

Malm·ö (mälm′ö; *E.* mal′mō) seaport in S Sweden, on the Öresund: pop. 249,000

malm·sey (mäm′zē) *n.* [ME. *malmesey* < ML. *malmasia* < *Malmasia* < Gr. *Monembasia*, Monemvasia, or Malvasia, small town on the coast of Laconia, Greece, formerly noted for exporting wine] 1. a strong, full-flavored, sweet white wine 2. the grape from which this is made

mal·nour·ished (mal nur′isht) *adj.* improperly nourished

mal·nu·tri·tion (mal′nōō trish′ən) *n.* faulty or inadequate nutrition; poor nourishment resulting from insufficient food, improper diet, etc.

mal·oc·clu·sion (-ə klōō′zhən) *n.* improper meeting of the upper and lower teeth; faulty occlusion

mal·o·dor (-ō′dər) *n.* a bad odor; stench

mal·o·dor·ous (-ō′dər əs) *adj.* having a bad odor; stinking —*SYN.* see STINKING —**mal·o′dor·ous·ly** *adv.* —**mal·o′dor·ous·ness** *n.*

Ma·lone (mə lōn′), **Edmund** (or **Edmond**) 1741–1812; Ir. literary critic & editor of Shakespeare's works

ma·lon·ic acid (mə län′ik, -lō′nik) [Fr. *malonique*, altered < *malique*: see MALIC ACID] a colorless, crystalline, dibasic acid, $CH_2(CO_2H)_2$, obtained from malic acid by oxidation and used in synthesizing barbiturates

Mal·o·ry (mal′ər ē), Sir **Thomas** ?–1471?; Eng. compiler & translator of *Morte d'Arthur*, Arthurian tales taken mostly from Fr. sources

Mal·pi·ghi (mäl pē′gē), **Mar·cel·lo** (mär chel′ō) 1628–94; It. physiologist & pioneer in microscopic anatomy — **Mal·pigh·i·an** (mal pig′ē ən) *adj.*

Malpighian body (or **corpuscle**) 1. any nodule of lymphatic tissue in the spleen 2. any of a number of small masses of blood vessels in the kidney, enclosed by a capsule that is an enlargement of the end of a tubule through which urine passes

Malpighian layer the soft, lowest layer of the epidermis, from which the outer layers are derived

Malpighian tubules a group of small, tubular, excretory and water-regulating glands that open into the hind part of the alimentary canal in most insects and spiders

mal·po·si·tion (mal′pə zish′ən) *n.* faulty or abnormal position, esp. of the fetus in the uterus

mal·prac·tice (mal prak′tis) *n.* 1. injurious or unprofessional treatment or culpable neglect of a patient by a physician or surgeon 2. misconduct or improper practice in any professional or official position —**mal′prac·ti′tion·er** (-tish′ən ər) *n.*

Mal·raux (mäl rō′), **An·dré** (än drā′) 1901–   ; Fr. writer & politician

malt (môlt) *n.* [ME. *malte* < OE. *mealt*, akin to G. *malz* < IE. **mel-d*, soft < base **mel-*, to crush, grind, whence MELT, MILL¹] 1. barley or other grain softened by soaking in water until it sprouts and then kiln-dried: used for brewing and distilling certain alcoholic beverages or liquors 2. a beverage or liquor made from malt, esp. beer, ale, or the like ☆3. [Colloq.] *same as* MALTED MILK —*adj.* made with malt —*vt.* 1. to change (barley, etc.) into malt or something maltlike 2. to treat or prepare (milk, etc.) with malt or malt extract —*vi.* 1. to be changed into malt or something maltlike 2. to change barley, etc. into malt

Mal·ta (môl′tə) 1. country on a group of islands in the Mediterranean, south of Sicily: a member of the Brit. Commonwealth: 122 sq. mi.; pop. 318,000; cap. Valletta 2. main island of this group: 95 sq. mi.

Malta fever [so named because prevalent in Malta and nearby areas] *same as* UNDULANT FEVER

malt·ase (môl′tās) *n.* [MALT + -ASE] an enzyme found in the small intestine, in yeast, etc., that hydrolyzes maltose into glucose

☆**malted milk** 1. a powdered preparation of dried milk

and malted cereals 2. a drink made by mixing this with milk and, usually, ice cream and flavoring

Mal·tese (môl tēz′) *adj.* 1. of Malta, its inhabitants, their language, etc. 2. of the medieval Knights of Malta —*n.* 1. *pl.* **Mal·tese′** a native or inhabitant of Malta 2. the Arabic language of Malta, strongly influenced by Italian 3. a variety of domestic cat with bluish-gray fur: in full, **Maltese cat** 4. a variety of toy spaniel with long, silky, white hair: in full, **Maltese dog**

Maltese cross [from its use as an emblem by the medieval Knights of Malta] 1. a cross whose arms look like arrowheads pointing inward: see CROSS, illus. 2. a perennial garden flower (*Lychnis chalcedonica*) of the pink family, having brilliant red five-parted flowers

malt extract a sticky, sugary substance obtained from malt soaked in water: it is used as a medicinal food

mal·tha (mal′thə) *n.* [L. < Gr., mixture of wax and pitch] 1. any of several black, semisolid bitumens between petroleum and asphalt in consistency 2. any of several natural, viscous hydrocarbon mixtures, as ozocerite

Mal·thus (mal′thəs), **Thomas Robert** 1766–1834; Eng. political economist

Mal·thu·sian (mal thōō′zhən, -zē ən) *adj.* of Malthus or his theory that the population of the world tends to increase faster than the food supply and that war, famine, and disease serve as natural restrictions of the increase —*n.* a supporter of this theory —**Mal·thu′sian·ism** *n.*

malt liquor beer, ale, or the like made from malt by fermentation

malt·ose (môl′tōs) *n.* [MALT + -OSE¹] a white, crystalline, dextrorotatory sugar, $C_{12}H_{22}O_{11} \cdot H_2O$, obtained by the action of the diastase of malt on starch

mal·treat (mal trēt′) *vt.* [Fr. *maltraiter*: see MAL- & TREAT] to treat roughly, unkindly, or brutally; abuse —**mal·treat′ment** *n.*

malt·ster (môlt′stər) *n.* one who makes or sells malt

malt sugar *same as* MALTOSE

malt·y (môl′tē) *adj.* **malt′i·er**, **malt′i·est** of, like, or containing malt —**malt′i·ness** *n.*

mal·va·si·a (mal′və sē′ə) *n.* [It.: see MALMSEY] *same as* MALMSEY —**mal′va·si′an** *adj.*

Mal·vern Hill (mal′vərn) [after *Malvern Hills*, England] plateau near Richmond, Va.: site of a battle (1862) of the Civil War

mal·ver·sa·tion (mal′vər sā′shən) *n.* [Fr. < *malverser*, to commit malpractices < L. *male*, badly + *versari*, to turn, occupy oneself: see MAL- & VERSE] [Chiefly Brit.] corrupt conduct or fraudulent practices in public office or other position of trust

mal·voi·sie (mal′voi zē, -və zē) *n.* [Fr.] [Archaic] *same as* MALMSEY

ma·ma (mä′mə; *now less freq.* mə mä′) *n. same as* MAMMA¹

mam·ba (mäm′bə) *n.* [Zulu *imamba*] any of several extremely poisonous, African tree snakes (genus *Dendraspis*), related to the cobras but not hooded; esp., a long South African snake (*Dendraspis angusticeps*) having a green and black phase

☆**mam·bo** (mäm′bō) *n.* [AmSp.: musicians' slang term equivalent to "riff"] 1. a rhythmic musical form, of Cuban Negro origin, in 4/4 syncopated time and with a heavy accent on the second and fourth beats 2. a ballroom dance to such music —*vi.* to dance the mambo

Mam·e·luke (mam′ə lōōk′) *n.* [obs. Fr. *mameluk* < Ar. *mamlūk*, slave, lit., one possessed < *malaka*, to possess] 1. a member of a military caste, orig. made up of slaves, that ruled in Egypt from 1250 until 1517 and remained powerful until 1811 2. [m-] in Moslem countries, a slave

mam·ma¹ (mä′mə; *now less freq.* mə mä′) *n.* [like L. *mamma*, mother, Sans. *mā*, Gr. *mammē* < baby talk] mother: a child's word, corresponding to *papa* for *father*

mam·ma² (mam′ə) *n., pl.* **-mae** (-ē) [L., breast, prob. identical with prec.] a gland for secreting milk, present in the female of all mammals; mammary gland: it is rudimentary in the male

mam·mal (-əl) *n.* [< ModL. *Mammalia* < LL. *mammalis*, of the breasts < L. *mamma*: see MAMMA²] any of a large class (Mammalia) of warm-blooded, usually hairy vertebrates whose offspring are fed with milk secreted by the female mammary glands —**mam·ma·li·an** (mə mā′lē ən, ma-) *adj., n.*

mam·mal·o·gy (mə mal′ə jē, ma-) *n.* the branch of zoology dealing with mammals —**mam·mal′o·gist** *n.*

mam·ma·ry (mam′ər ē) *adj.* designating or of the milk-secreting glands; of the mammae

mam·mee (mä mā′, -mē′) *n.* [Sp. *mamey* < Taino] 1. *a)* any of a genus (*Mammea*) of West Indian trees; specif., a tall, tropical, American tree (*Mammea americana*) bearing a large, russet, apricot-flavored fruit: also **mammee apple**, **Santo Domingo apricot** *b)* the fruit 2. *same as* MARMALADE TREE Also **ma·mey′, mam′mey′, ma·mie′**

mam·mer (mam′ər) *n. same as* MAUMET

mam·mif·er·ous (ma mif′ər əs, mə-) *adj.* [see -FEROUS] having mammae, or breasts

mam·mil·la (ma mil′ə, mə-) *n., pl.* **-lae** (-ē) [L. *mam(m)illa*, dim. of *mamma*: see MAMMA²] 1. a nipple 2. any nipple-shaped or breast-shaped protuberance —**mam′mil·lar′y** *adj.*

mam·mil·late (mam′ə lāt′) *adj.* 1. having mammillae 2. nipple-shaped Also **mam′mil·lat′ed** —**mam′mil·la′tion** *n.*

MALTA

mam·mock (mam′ək) *n.* [< ?] [Archaic or Dial.] a fragment; shred; scrap —*vt.* [Archaic or Dial.] to break or tear into fragments or shreds

mam·mog·ra·phy (mə mäg′rə fē) *n.* [< MAMMA² + -GRAPHY] an X-ray technique for the detection of breast tumors before they can be seen or felt

mam·mon (mam′ən) *n.* [ME. *mammon(as)* < LL.(Ec.) *mammon(as)* < Gr.(Ec.) *mammōnas* (cf. Matt. 6:24) < Aram. *māmōnā*, riches, prob. < *mā′mon*, that which is made secure or deposited < *′āman*, to trust] [*often* M-] riches regarded as an object of worship and greedy pursuit; wealth or material gain as an evil, more or less deified —**mam′mon·ism** *n.*

mam·moth (mam′əth) *n.* [Russ. *mamont*] any of a genus (*Mammuthus*) of extinct elephants with a hairy skin and long tusks curving upward: remains have been found in N. America, Europe, and Asia —*adj.* very big; huge; enormous —*SYN.* see ENORMOUS

HAIRY MAMMOTH
(to 13 ft. high at shoulder)

Mammoth Cave National Park national park in SW Ky., containing enormous caverns: 79 sq. mi.

mam·my (mam′ē) *n., pl.* **-mies** [dial. var. of MAMMA¹] **1.** mother: a child's word ☆**2.** a Negro woman who takes care of white children, esp. in the South

mammy wagon (or **bus**) a small, open, brightly decorated bus or truck used for public transportation in W Africa

Ma·mo·ré (mä′mō re′) river in NC Bolivia, flowing north to join the Beni & form the Madeira: c. 1,200 mi.

man (man) *n., pl.* **men** (men) [ME. < OE. *mann*, akin to G. *mann*, Goth. *manna* < IE. base *manu-* (whence Sans. *mānu-*, Russ. *muž*, man): akin ? to *men-*, to think (whence MIND)] **1.** a human being; person; specif., *a)* a primate (*Homo sapiens*) having an erect stance, an apposable thumb, the ability to make and use specialized tools, articulate speech, and a highly developed brain with the faculty of abstract thought: the only living species of a worldwide family (Hominidae) *b)* any member of several extinct species of this family, as Neanderthal man **2.** the human race; mankind: used without *the* or *a* **3.** *a)* an adult male human being *b)* sometimes, a boy **4.** *a)* an adult male servant, follower, attendant, or subordinate *b)* a male employee; workman *c)* [*usually pl.*] a soldier, sailor, etc.; esp., one of the rank and file *d)* [Archaic] a vassal **5.** *a)* a husband *b)* a lover **6.** *a)* a person with qualities conventionally regarded as manly, such as strength, courage, etc. *b)* manly qualities **7.** a player on a team **8.** any of the pieces used in chess, checkers, etc. **9.** [Slang] fellow; chap: used in direct address: see also *interj.* below **10.** *Naut.* a ship: used in compounds [*man-of-war, merchantman*] —*vt.* **manned, man′ning 1.** to furnish with men for work, defense, etc. [*to man a ship*] **2.** to take assigned places in, on, or at for work or defense [*man the guns!*] **3.** to strengthen; brace; fortify; nerve [*to man* oneself for an ordeal] **4.** *Falconry* to tame or accustom (a hawk) to the presence of men —*interj.* [Slang] an exclamation of emphasis: often used in a neutral way, as now in hippie talk; to preface or resume one's remarks —*adj.* male —**as a** (or **one**) **man** in unison; unanimously —**be one's own man 1.** to be free and independent **2.** to be in full control of one's powers, senses, etc. —**man and boy** first as a boy and then as a man —☆**the Man** [Slang] the person having power or authority over one; esp., as orig. used by U.S. Negroes, a white man, or a boss, policeman, etc. —**to a man** with no one as an exception; everyone

-man (mən, man) *a combining form meaning* man or person of a specified kind, in a specified activity, etc. [*Frenchman, sportsman*]

Man. 1. Manila (paper) **2.** Manitoba

man. manual

Man, Isle of one of the Brit. Isles, between Northern Ireland & England: 227 sq. mi.; pop. 48,000; cap. Douglas

ma·na (mä′nä) *n.* [native Polynesian term] the impersonal supernatural force to which certain primitive peoples attribute good fortune, magical powers, etc.

man about town a worldly man who spends much time in fashionable restaurants, clubs, etc.

man·a·cle (man′ə k'l) *n.* [ME. *manicle* < OFr. < L. *manicula*, dim. of *manus*, hand: see MANUAL] **1.** a handcuff; fetter or shackle for the hand **2.** any restraint *Usually used in pl.* —*vt.* **-cled, -cling 1.** to put handcuffs on; fetter **2.** to restrain; hamper —*SYN.* see HAMPER¹

Ma·na·do (mä nä′dō) seaport in NE Celebes, Indonesia: pop. 128,000

man·age (man′ij) *vt.* **-aged, -ag·ing** [It. *maneggiare* < *mano*, hand < L. *manus:* see MANUAL] **1.** orig., to train (a horse) in his paces; cause to do the exercises of the manège **2.** to control the movement or behavior of; handle; manipulate **3.** to have charge of; direct; administer [to *manage* a household] **4.** [Rare] to handle or use carefully;

husband **5.** to get (a person) to do what one wishes, esp. by skill, tact, flattery, etc.; make docile or submissive **6.** to bring about by contriving; contrive; succeed in accomplishing: often used ironically [he *managed* to make a mess of it] —*vi.* **1.** to conduct or direct affairs; carry on business **2.** to contrive to get along; succeed in handling matters —*n.* [It. *maneggio* < *maneggiare:* infl. by Fr. *ménage:* see MÉNAGE] [Archaic] same as: **1.** MANÈGE **2.** MANAGEMENT —*SYN.* see CONDUCT

man·age·a·ble (man′ij ə b'l) *adj.* that can be managed; controllable, tractable, contrivable, etc. —**man′age·a·bil′i·ty, man′age·a·ble·ness** *n.* —**man′age·a·bly** *adv.*

managed currency a currency regulated by various governmental agencies through procedures that alter the amount of money in circulation so as to control credit, the price structure, etc.

man·age·ment (man′ij mənt) *n.* **1.** the act, art, or manner of managing, or handling, controlling, directing, etc. **2.** skillful managing; careful, tactful treatment **3.** skill in managing; executive ability **4.** *a)* the person or persons managing a business, institution, etc. [the problems of labor and *management*] *b)* such persons collectively, regarded as a distinct social group with special interests, characteristic economic views, etc.

man·ag·er (-ij ər) *n.* a person who manages; esp., *a)* one who manages a business, institution, etc. *b)* one who manages affairs or expenditures, as of a household, a client (as an entertainer or athlete), an athletic team, etc. ☆*c)* *Baseball* the person who is in overall charge of a team and the strategy in games —**man′ag·er·ship′** *n.*

man·a·ge·ri·al (man′ə jir′ē əl) *adj.* **1.** of, like, or characteristic of a manager **2.** of management —**man′a·ge′ri·al·ism** *n.* —**man′a·ge′ri·al·ly** *adv.*

Ma·na·gua (mä nä′gwä) **1.** lake in W Nicaragua: c. 390 sq. mi. **2.** capital of Nicaragua, on this lake: pop. 318,000

man·a·kin (man′ə kin) *n.* [see MANIKIN] **1.** any of various brightly colored, small birds (family Pipridae) of Central and South America, with short beaks **2.** same as MANIKIN

‡ma·ña·na (mä nyä′nä) *n.* [Sp. < VL. *maneana* < L. (*cras*) *mane*, (tomorrow) morning] tomorrow —*adv.* **1.** tomorrow **2.** at some indefinite time in the future

Ma·nâos (mä nous′) *Port. name of* MANAUS

Ma·nas·sas (mə nas′əs) [< ?] town in NE Va., near Bull Run: site of two Civil War battles in which Union forces were defeated: pop. 9,200

Ma·nas·seh (mə nas′e) *n.* [Heb. *měnaşşeh*, lit., causing to forget] *Bible* **1.** the elder son of Joseph **2.** the tribe of Israel descended from him **3.** a king of Judah in the 7th cent. B.C.: II Kings 21:1-18 Douay sp. **Ma·nas′ses** (-ēz)

man-at-arms (man′ət ärmz′) *n., pl.* **men-at-arms** (men′-) formerly, a soldier; esp., a heavily-armed, medieval soldier on horseback

man·a·tee (man′ə tē′, man′ə tē′) *n.* [Sp. *manatí* < native (Carib) name] any of several large, plant-eating aquatic mammals (genus *Trichechus*) living in shallow tropical waters near the coasts of N. and S. America and W Africa, having flippers and a broad, flat, rounded tail; sea cow

MANATEE
(8-13 ft. long)

Ma·naus (mä nous′) city in NW Brazil, on the Negro River; capital of Amazonas state: pop. 175,000

Man·ches·ter (man′ches′tər, -chi stər) **1.** city & port in Lancashire, NW England, connected by canal (**Manchester Ship Canal**, 35 mi. long) with the Irish Sea: pop. 661,000 **2.** [after prec.] *a)* city in S N.H., on the Merrimack River: pop. 88,000 *b)* suburb of Hartford, in NC Conn.: pop. 48,000

Manchester terrier any of a breed of small terrier having glossy, short, black fur with tan markings

man·chet (man′chit) *n.* [ME. *manchete* < ? or akin ? to *maine* (same sense), aphetic < OFr. *paindemaine* (L. *panis dominicus*), lit., lord's bread] [Archaic or Brit. Dial.] **1.** white bread made of the finest wheat flour **2.** a roll or small loaf of such bread

man-child (man′chīld′) *n., pl.* **men′-chil′dren** (-chil′drən) a male child; boy; son

man·chi·neel (man′chə nēl′) *n.* [Fr. *mancenille* < Sp. *manzanillo* < *manzana*, apple < L. *matianum* (*pomum*), (apple) of *Matius*, Roman author of a cookery manual] **1.** a tropical American tree (*Hippomane mancinella*) of the spurge family, with a milky, irritant juice and plumlike, poisonous fruit **2.** its wood

Man·chu (man′chōō, man′chōō) *n.* [Manchu, lit., pure] **1.** *pl.* **-chus′, -chu′** a member of a Mongolian people of Manchuria: the Manchus conquered China in 1643–44 and set up a dynasty that ruled until 1912 **2.** the Tungusic language of the Manchus —*adj.* of Manchuria, the Manchus, their language, etc.

Man·chu·kuo (man chōō′kwō) former country (1932–45), a Japanese puppet state consisting mainly of Manchuria

Man·chu·ri·a (man choor′ē ə) region & former adminis-

trative division of NE China coextensive with the provinces of Heilungkiang, Kirin, & Liaoning, & the NE section of Inner Mongolia —**man·chu′ri·an** *adj.*, *n.*

man·ci·ple (man′si p'l) *n.* [ME. < OFr. < ML. *mancipium*, office of a purchaser < L., legal purchase, possession < *manceps*, buyer, contractor < *manus*, a hand + base of *capere*, to take] a steward or buyer of provisions, as for an English college, a monastery, etc.

Man·cu·ni·an (man kyōō′nē ən, -kyōōn′yən) *adj.* [< ML. *Mancunium*, Manchester] of Manchester, England —*n.* a native or inhabitant of Manchester, England

-man·cy (man′sē) [ME. < OFr. -*mancie* < LL. -*mantia* < Gr. *manteia*, divination < *mantis*, prophet: see MANTIS] *a combining form meaning* divination [*chiromancy*]

Man·dae·an (man dē′ən) *n.*, *adj. same as* MANDEAN

man·da·la (mun′də lə) *n.* [Sans. *maṇḍala*, a circle] a circular design containing concentric geometric forms, images of deities, etc. and symbolizing the universe, totality, or wholeness in Hinduism and Buddhism

Man·da·lay (man′də lā′, man′də lā′) city in C Burma, on the Irrawaddy River: pop. 322,000

man·da·mus (man dā′məs) *n.* [L., we command, 1st pers. pl., pres. indic., of *mandare*: see MANDATE] *Law* a writ commanding that a specified thing be done, issued by a higher court to a lower one, or to a private or municipal corporation, government agency, official, etc. —*vt.* [Colloq.] to serve with or command by such a writ

☆**Man·dan** (man′dan) *n.* [< Siouan] **1.** *pl.* **-dans, -dan** a member of a village tribe of Plains Indians who live in North Dakota **2.** their Siouan language

man·da·rin (man′də rin) *n.* [Port. *mandarim*, altered (after *mandar*, to command < L. *mandare*: see MANDATE) < Hind. *mantrī*, minister of state < Sans. *mantrin*, counselor < *mantra*, counsel < IE. base **men-*, to think, whence MIND] **1.** a high official of China under the Empire: each of the nine classes of mandarin was distinguished by a characteristic jeweled button worn on the cap **2.** a member of any elite group; leading intellectual, political figure, etc., sometimes one who is pompous, arbitrary, etc. **3.** [M-] the official or main dialect of Chinese, spoken in about nine tenths of mainland China and comprising a standard northern, a southwestern, and a southern variety **4.** [prob. from the color of a mandarin's robe] *a*) a small, sweet orange with a loose rind: in full, **mandarin orange** *b*) the tree (*Citrus reticulata*) of the rue family that it grows on **5.** a deep-orange color —*adj.* **1.** designating or of a Chinese style of dress, esp. a narrow, closefitting, stand-up collar parted in the front **2.** designating or of an elegant, over-refined literary style —**man′da·rin·ism** *n.*

mandarin duck a bright-colored, crested, Asian duck (*Aix galericulata*), sometimes domesticated

man·date (man′dāt) *n.* [L. *mandatum*, neut. pp. of *mandare*, lit., to put into one's hand, command, entrust < *manus*, a hand + pp. of *dare*, to give] **1.** an authoritative order or command, esp. a written one **2.** *a*) formerly, a commission from the League of Nations to a country to administer some region, colony, etc. *b*) the area so administered: cf. TRUSTEESHIP, TRUST TERRITORY **3.** the wishes of constituents expressed to a representative, legislature, etc., as through an election, and regarded as an order **4.** *Law a*) an order from a higher court or official to a lower one: a **mandate on remission** is a mandate from an appellate court to the lower court, communicating its decision in a case appealed *b*) in English law, a bailment of personal property with no consideration *c*) in Roman law, a commission or contract by which a person undertakes to do something for another, without recompense but with indemnity against loss *d*) any contract of agency —*vt.* **-dat·ed, -dat·ing** to assign (a region, etc.) as a mandate —**man·da′tor** *n.*

man·da·to·ry (man′də tôr′ē) *adj.* [L. *mandatorius*] **1.** of, having the nature of, or containing a mandate **2.** authoritatively commanded or required; obligatory **3.** having received a mandate over some territory —*n.*, *pl.* **-ries** a country assigned to administer a mandate: also **man′da·tar′y** (-ter′ē) —**man′da·to′ri·ly** *adv.*

Man·de (män′dā) *n.* **1.** *pl.* **-des, -de** any member of a group of Negroid peoples of W Africa, including the Malinkes, Susus, etc. **2.** a branch of the Niger-Congo subfamily of languages —*adj.* of the Mandes or their languages

Man·de·an (man dē′ən) *n.* [< Mandean *mandayyā*, lit., having knowledge (used as transl. of Gr. *gnōstikoi*, Gnostics) < *mandā*, knowledge + -AN] **1.** a member of an ancient Gnostic sect still extant in southern Iraq **2.** the Eastern Aramaic dialect used in Mandean writings: it was spoken along the Euphrates from the 7th to the 9th centuries A.D. —*adj.* **1.** of the Mandeans, their doctrines, etc. **2.** of Mandean

Man·de·ville (man′də vil) **1.** Bernard (de), 1670?–1733; Eng. satirist, born in the Netherlands **2.** Sir John, 14th cent.; putative English author of a romanticized travel book

man·di·ble (man′də b'l) *n.* [OFr. < LL. *mandibula* < *mandibulum*, a jaw < L. *mandere*, to chew < IE. base **menth-*, whence MOUTH] the jaw; specif., *a*) the lower jaw of a vertebrate *b*) either of a pair of frontmost biting jaws of an insect or other arthropod *c*) either jaw of a beaked animal, as a cephalopod —**man·dib′u·lar** (-dib′yōō lər) *adj.*

man·dib·u·late (man dib′yōō lit) *adj.* **1.** having a mandible or mandibles, as some insects **2.** adapted for chewing —*n.* a mandibulate insect

Man·din·go (man diŋ′gō) *n.*, *pl.* **-gos, -goes, -go** [< the native name] *same as* MANDE

man·do·lin (man′d'l in′, man′də lin′) *n.* [Fr. *mandoline* < It. *mandolino*, dim. of *mandola, mandora* < LL. *pandura*, kind of lute < LGr. *pandoura*, prob. < Ar. *ṭanbur*] a musical instrument with four or five pairs of strings stretched over a fretted neck and a deep, rounded sound box: it is played with a plectrum, which is moved rapidly back and forth to give a tremolo effect —**man′do·lin′ist** *n.*

man·drag·o·ra (man drag′ər ə) *n. same as* MANDRAKE (senses 1 & 2)

MANDOLIN

man·drake (man′drāk) *n.* [ME. *mondrake*, altered by folk etym. (after *man* + *drake*, dragon) < *mandrag(g)e* < OE. *mandragora* < LL. < L. *mandragoras* < Gr. *mandragoras*] **1.** a poisonous plant (*Mandragora officinarum*) of the nightshade family, found in Mediterranean regions: it has a short stem, purple or white flowers, and a thick root, often forked, formerly used in medicine for its narcotic and emetic properties **2.** the root, formerly thought to have magical powers because of the fancied resemblance to the human shape ☆**3.** *same as* MAY APPLE

man·drel, man·dril (man′drəl) *n.* [earlier *manderil*; prob. < Fr. *mandrin* < ModPr. *mandre*, spindle, winch, beam (of a balance) < L. *mamphur*, a bow drill < IE. base **menth-*, to twirl, whence ON. *mondull*, handle of a quern] **1.** a metal spindle or bar, often tapered, inserted into a lathe center to support work while it is being machined or turned **2.** a metal rod or bar used as a core around which metal, wire, glass, etc. is cast, molded, forged, or shaped

man·drill (man′dril) *n.* [MAN + DRILL⁴] a large, fierce, strong baboon (*Mandrillus sphinx*) of W Africa: the male has blue and scarlet patches on the face and rump

man·du·cate (man′joo kāt′) *vt.* **-cat·ed, -cat·ing** [< L. *manducatus*, pp. of *manducare*: see MANGER] [Rare] to chew; masticate —**man′du·ca′tion** *n.* —**man′du·ca·to′ry** (-kə tôr′ē) *adj.*

mane (mān) *n.* [ME. < OE. *manu*, akin to G. *mähne* < IE. base **mono-*, neck, whence Sans. *mányā*, nape of the neck, W. *mwn*, neck] **1.** the long hair growing from the top or sides of the neck of certain animals, as the horse, lion, etc. **2.** long, thick human hair —**maned** *adj.* —**mane′less** *adj.*

man-eat·er (man′ēt′ər) *n.* **1.** a cannibal **2.** an animal that eats, or is thought to eat, human flesh; specif., ☆*a*) any of certain sharks of tropical waters *b*) a lion, tiger, etc. with a taste for human flesh —**man′-eat′ing** *adj.*

ma·nège, ma·nege (ma nezh′, -nāzh′) *n.* [Fr. < It. *maneggio*: see MANAGE] **1.** the art of riding and training horses; horsemanship **2.** the paces and exercises of a trained horse **3.** a school for training horses and teaching riders; riding academy

Ma·nes (mā′nēz) *same as* MANI

ma·nes (mā′nēz) *n.pl.* [ME. < L. < IE. base **mā-*, good, whence OL. *manus*] [*often* M-] **1.** *Ancient Rom. Religion* the deified souls of the dead, esp. of dead ancestors **2.** [*with sing. v.*] the soul or spirit of a dead person

Ma·net (må nā′), É·douard (ā dwär′) 1832–83; Fr. impressionist painter

ma·neu·ver (mə nōō′vər, -nyōō′-) *n.* [Fr. *manœuvre*, orig., hand labor < VL. *manuopera* < L. *manu operare*, to work by hand < *manus*, a hand + *opera*, pl. of *opus*, a work: see OPUS] **1.** a planned and controlled tactical or strategic movement of troops, warships, aircraft, etc. **2.** [*pl.*] large-scale practice movements and exercises of troops, warships, aircraft, etc. under simulated combat conditions **3.** *a*) any change of movement by a flying aircraft *b*) a series of movements by an aircraft according to a specific pattern, as a roll, a loop, etc. **4.** any movement or procedure intended as a skillful or shrewd step toward some objective; stratagem; artifice; scheme —*vi.*, *vt.* **1.** to perform or cause to perform a maneuver or maneuvers **2.** to manage or plan skillfully or shrewdly; manipulate or scheme **3.** to move, lead, get, put, make, compel, etc. (a person or thing) by some stratagem or scheme —*SYN.* see TRICK —**ma·neu′ver·a·bil′i·ty** *n.* —**ma·neu′ver·a·ble** *adj.* —**ma·neu′ver·er** *n.*

man Friday *see* FRIDAY

man·ful (man′fəl) *adj.* manly; brave, resolute, strong, etc. —**man′ful·ly** *adv.* —**man′ful·ness** *n.*

man·ga·bey (maŋ′gə bā′) *n.* [< *Mangabey*, Madagascar] any of a genus (*Cercocebus*) of large African monkeys having a silky, gray coat, white eyelids, and a long tail

man·ga·nate (maŋ′gə nāt′) *n.* a salt of manganic acid

man·ga·nese (maŋ′gə nēs′, -nēz′) *n.* [Fr. *manganèse* < It. *manganese*, by metathesis < ML. *magnesia*: see MAGNESIA] a grayish-white, metallic chemical element, usually hard and brittle, which rusts like iron but is not magnetic: it is used in the manufacture of alloys of iron, aluminum, and copper: symbol, Mn; at. wt., 54.9380; at. no., 25; sp. gr., 7.20; melt. pt., 1220°C; boil. pt., 2152°C

manganese bronze an alloy of copper and zinc containing

up to about 3 percent manganese, used in making steamship propellers, toothed wheels, gears, etc.

manganese steel a hard, malleable and ductile steel containing 12 to 14 percent of manganese, used in drill bits, crushers, etc.

man·gan·ic (man gan′ik, maŋ-) *adj.* designating or of chemical compounds in which manganese has a valence of three

manganic acid an acid, H_2MnO_4, known only in the form of its salts

Man·ga·nin (maŋ′gə nin) [MANGAN(ESE) + -IN[1]] *a trademark for* an alloy consisting mainly of copper with some manganese and nickel: it is used in rheostats, very accurate resistors, etc.

man·ga·nite (-nīt′) *n.* **1.** hydrous manganese trioxide, $Mn_2O_3 \cdot H_2O$, a steel-gray or black, crystalline mineral with a metallic luster **2.** any of a series of salts that may be considered as derivatives of manganous acid, the hydroxide of tetravalent manganese

man·gan·ous (maŋ′gə nəs; man gan′əs, maŋ-) *adj.* designating or of chemical compounds in which manganese has a valence of two

mange (mānj) *n.* [ME. *manjewe* < OFr. *mangeue*, an itch, eating < *mangier* < L. *manducare:* see MANGER] any of various skin diseases of mammals caused by parasitic mites and characterized by intense itching, lesions and scabs, and a loss of hair

man·gel-wur·zel (maŋ′g'l wur′z'l, -wurt′-) *n.* [G., altered after *mangel*, lack < *mangoldwurzel* < *mangold*, beet + *wurzel*, a root] a variety of large beet, used as food for cattle, esp. in Europe: also **mangel**

man·ger (mān′jər) *n.* [ME. < OFr. *mangeure* < VL. *manducatoria*, feeding trough < pp. of L. *manducare*, to eat < *mandere*, to chew < IE. base *menth-*, to chew, whence MOUTH] a box or trough to hold hay, etc. for horses or cattle to eat

man·gle[1] (maŋ′g'l) *vt.* **-gled, -gling** [ME. *manglen* < AngloFr. *mangler*, prob. freq. of OFr. *mehaigner*, MAIM] **1.** to mutilate or disfigure by repeatedly and roughly cutting, tearing, hacking, or crushing; lacerate and bruise badly **2.** to spoil; botch; mar; garble [*to mangle a text*] —*SYN.* see MAIM —**man′gler** *n.*

man·gle[2] (maŋ′g'l) *n.* [Du. *mangel* < G. < MHG., dim. of *mange*, a mangle < L. *manganum* < Gr. *manganon*, war machine, orig. deceptive device < IE. base *meng-*, to embellish deceptively, whence MIr. *meng*, deceit, L. *mango*, falsifying dealer] a machine for pressing and smoothing cloth, esp. sheets and other flat pieces, between heated rollers —*vt.* **-gled, -gling** to press in a mangle —**man′gler** *n.*

man·go (maŋ′gō) *n., pl.* **-goes, -gos** [Port. *manga* < Malay *maṅga* < Tamil *mān-kāy* < *mān*, mango tree + *kāy*, fruit] **1.** a yellow-red, oblong tropical fruit with a thick rind, somewhat acid and juicy pulp, and a hard stone: it is eaten when ripe, or preserved or pickled when unripe **2.** the tropical, evergreen, Asiatic tree (*Mangifera indica*) of the cashew family on which it grows

man·go·nel (maŋ′gə nel′) *n.* [OFr., dim. < L. *manganum:* see MANGLE[2]] an obsolete military apparatus for hurling heavy stones and other missiles

man·go·steen (maŋ′gə stēn′) *n.* [Malay *mangustan*] **1.** an edible East Indian fruit somewhat like an orange, with a thick, reddish-brown rind and sweet, white, juicy, segmented pulp **2.** the tree (*Garcinia mangostana*) that it grows on

man·grove (maŋ′grōv) *n.* [altered (after GROVE) < earlier *mangrowe* < Port. *mangue* < Sp. *mangle* < the WInd. (Taino) name] **1.** any of a genus (*Rhizophora*) of tropical trees or shrubs of the mangrove family, growing in swampy ground along river banks, with branches that spread and send down roots, thus forming more trunks and causing a thick growth over a large area; esp., the **American mangrove** (*Rhizophora mangle*) that is important in building new land in Florida and on other tropical coasts **2.** a plant (*Avicennia nitida*) of the verbena family that grows in a similar way —*adj.* designating a family (Rhizophoraceae) of trees and shrubs that inhabit tidal marshes and river mouths in the tropics

man·gy (mān′jē) *adj.* **-gi·er, -gi·est** **1.** having, infected with, resembling, or caused by the mange **2.** shabby and filthy; sordid; squalid **3.** mean and low; despicable —**man′gi·ly** *adv.* —**man′gi·ness** *n.*

man·han·dle (man′han′d'l) *vt.* **-dled, -dling** **1.** [Rare] to move or do by human strength only, without mechanical aids **2.** to handle roughly

Man·hat·tan (man hat′'n, mən-) [< Du. < a native term < ?] **1.** island in SE N.Y., between the Hudson & East rivers, forming part of New York City: 13 mi. long: also **Manhattan Island** **2.** borough of New York City, consisting of this island, some small nearby islands, & a small bit of the mainland: 22 sq. mi.; pop. 1,525,000 —*n.* **1.** any member of a tribe of Algonquian Indians who lived on Manhattan Island ☆**2.** [*often* m-] a cocktail made of whiskey and sweet vermouth, usually with a dash of bitters and a maraschino cherry

Manhattan Beach [< *Manhattan* Island, N.Y.] city in SW Calif.: suburb of Los Angeles: pop. 35,000

Manhattan District a division of the U.S. Army Corps of Engineers, established in 1942, which produced the atomic bomb

man·hole (man′hōl′) *n.* a hole through which a man can get into a sewer, conduit, ship's tank, etc. for repair work or inspection

man·hood (man′hood′) *n.* **1.** the state or time of being a man (human being or, esp., adult male human being) **2.** manly character or qualities; virility, courage, resolution, etc. **3.** men collectively

man-hour (-our′) *n.* an industrial time unit equal to one hour of work done by one man

☆**man·hunt** (-hunt′) *n.* a hunt for a man, esp. for a fugitive: also **man hunt**

Ma·ni (mä′nē) 216?-276? A.D.; Persian prophet: see MANICHAEISM

ma·ni·a (mā′nē ə, mān′yə) *n.* [ME. < LL. < Gr. *mania*, madness < *mainesthai*, to rage < IE. base *men-*, to think, be mentally excited, whence MIND] **1.** wild or violent mental disorder; specif., the manic phase of manicdepressive psychosis, characterized generally by abnormal excitability, exaggerated feelings of well-being, flight of ideas, excessive activity, etc. **2.** an excessive, persistent enthusiasm, liking, craving, or interest; obsession; craze [*a mania for dancing*]

SYN.—**mania** in its basic sense (see definition above) describes the phase of manic-depressive psychosis that is distinguished from *depression;* **delirium** denotes a temporary state of extreme mental disturbance (marked by restlessness, incoherence, and hallucinations) that occurs during fevers, in alcoholic psychosis, etc.; **frenzy,** not used technically in psychiatry, implies extreme emotional agitation in which self-control is lost; **hysteria** is applied in psychiatry to certain psychogenic disorders characterized by excitability, anxiety, sensory and motor disturbances, and the involuntary simulation of blindness, deafness, etc. In extended use, **mania** suggests a craze for something [*a mania for surfing*], **delirium,** rapturous excitement [*a delirium of joy*], and **hysteria,** an outburst of wild, uncontrolled feeling [*she laughed and cried in her hysteria*]

-ma·ni·a (mā′nē ə, mān′yə) [see prec.] *a combining form meaning:* **1.** a (specified) type of mental disorder characterized by an abnormal preoccupation, compulsion, etc. [*kleptomania*] **2.** a continuing, intense enthusiasm, craving, or liking for (a specified thing) [*bibliomania*]

ma·ni·ac (mā′nē ak′) *adj.* [ML. *maniacus*] of, having, or showing mania; maniacal —*n.* a wildly or violently insane person; madman; lunatic

-ma·ni·ac (mā′nē ak′) *a combining form meaning* (a person) affected by a (specified) mania [*kleptomaniac*]

ma·ni·a·cal (mə nī′ə k'l) *adj.* of, having, or showing mania; wildly insane; raving —**ma·ni′a·cal·ly** *adv.*

man·ic (man′ik; *chiefly Brit.,* mā′nik) *adj. Psychiatry* having, characterized by, or like mania

man·ic-de·pres·sive (-di pres′iv) *adj.* designating, of, or having a psychosis characterized by alternating periods of mania and mental depression —*n.* a person who has this psychosis

Man·i·chae·ism, Man·i·che·ism (man′ə kē′iz'm) *n.* a religious philosophy taught from the 3d cent. to the 7th cent. A.D. by the Persian Mani, or Manichaeus, and his followers, combining Zoroastrian, Gnostic Christian, and pagan elements, and based on the doctrine of the two contending principles of good (light, God, the soul) and evil (darkness, Satan, the body): also **Man′i·chae′an·ism** —**Man′i·chae′an** *n., adj.* —**Man′i·chee′** *n.*

Man·i·chae·us, Man·i·che·us (man′ə kē′əs) *same as* MANI

man·i·cot·ti (man′i kät′ē; *It.* mä′nē kôt′tē) *n.* [It., lit., muffs, pl. of *manicotto*] pasta, in the form of long, broad tubes, usually boiled, stuffed with cheese, and baked with a tomato sauce

man·i·cure (man′ə kyoor′) *n.* [Fr. < L. *manus*, a hand + *cura*, care] the care of the hands; esp., a trimming, polishing, etc. of the fingernails —*vt.* **-cured′, -cur′ing** **1.** *a)* to trim, polish, etc. (the fingernails) *b)* to give a manicure to **2.** [Colloq.] to trim, clip, etc. meticulously [*to manicure a lawn*]

man·i·cur·ist (-ist) *n.* a person, usually a woman, whose work is giving manicures

man·i·fest (man′ə fest′) *adj.* [ME. < OFr. *manifeste* < L. *manifestus*, earlier *manufestus*, lit., struck by the hand, palpable, evident < *manus*, a hand + base akin to (*in*)*festus:* see INFEST] apparent to the senses, esp. that of sight, or to the mind; evident; obvious; clear; plain —*vt.* [ME. *manifesten* < OFr. *manifester* < L. *manifestare*] **1.** to make clear or evident; show plainly; reveal; evince **2.** to prove; be evidence of **3.** to enter in a ship's manifest —*vi.* to appear to the senses; show itself —*n.* **1.** *a)* an itemized list of a ship's cargo, telling the place of lading, destination, etc., to be shown to customs officials *b)* a waybill of lading *c)* a list of the passengers and cargo on an airplane **2.** [RARE] a manifestation —*SYN.* see EVIDENT —**man′i·fest′a·ble** *adj.* —**man′i·fest′ly** *adv.*

man·i·fes·ta·tion (man'ə fes tā'shən, -fəs-) n. [LL. *manifestatio*] 1. a manifesting or being manifested 2. something that manifests or is manifested / his smile was a *manifestation* of joy/ 3. any of the forms in which a being manifests or is thought to manifest itself 4. a public demonstration, as by a government, party, etc., for political effect

☆**Manifest Destiny** the 19th-cent. doctrine postulating the continued territorial expansion of the U.S. as its obvious destiny: term current during the annexation of territories in the Southwest and Northwest and of islands in the Pacific and Caribbean

man·i·fes·to (man'ə fes'tō) n., pl. **-toes** [It. < *manifestare*, to MANIFEST] a public declaration of motives and intentions by a government or by a person or group regarded as having some public importance

man·i·fold (man'ə fōld') adj. [ME. < OE. *manigfeald*: see MANY & -FOLD] 1. having many and various forms, features, parts, etc. [*manifold* wisdom] 2. of many sorts; many and varied; multifarious: used with a plural noun [*manifold* duties] 3. being such in many and various ways or for many reasons [a *manifold* villain] 4. comprising, consisting of, or operating several units or parts of one kind: said of certain devices —n. 1. something that is manifold 2. a pipe with one inlet and several outlets or with one outlet and several inlets, for connecting with other pipes, as, in an automobile, for conducting exhausts from each cylinder into a single exhaust pipe —vt. 1. to make manifold; multiply 2. to make more than one copy of [to *manifold* a letter with carbon paper] —**SYN.** see MANY —**man'i·fold'er** n. —**man'i·fold'ly** adv. —**man'i·fold'ness** n.

MANIFOLD
(A, manifold; B, cylinders)

man·i·kin (man'ə k'n) n. [Du. *manneken* < *man*, man + dim. suffix -*ken*] 1. a little man; dwarf 2. an anatomical model of the human body, usually with movable and detachable parts, used in medical schools, art classes, etc. 3. same as MANNEQUIN

Ma·nil·a (mə nil'ə) principal city & seaport of the Philippines, in SW Luzon, on an inlet (**Manila Bay**) of the South China Sea: pop. 1,300,000 —n. [often m-] same as: *a*) MANILA HEMP *b*) MANILA PAPER *c*) MANILA ROPE Also, for n., **Ma·nil'la**

Manila hemp [often m-] 1. a strong, tough fiber from the leafstalks of the abacá, used for making high-quality rope, paper, clothing, etc. 2. same as ABACÁ (sense 2)

Manila paper [often m-] buff or light brownish-yellow paper used for envelopes, wrapping paper, etc., orig. made of Manila hemp, now of various fibers

Manila rope [often m-] strong rope made of Manila hemp

man in the street the average man; ordinary person

man·i·oc (man'ē äk') n. [Fr. < Tupi *manioca*] same as CASSAVA

man·i·ple (man'ə p'l) n. [L. *manipulus*, orig., a handful, bundle < *manus*, a hand + base of *plere*, to fill: from use of bundles of hay as standards of the maniples] 1. a subdivision of the ancient Roman legion; one third of a cohort, consisting of either 60 or 120 men 2. [ME. *maniple* < MFr. < ML.(Ec.) *manipulus* < L.] a silk band worn hanging over the left forearm as a Eucharistic vestment

ma·nip·u·lar (mə nip'yoo lər) adj. [L. *manipularis*] 1. of a maniple (in the ancient Roman army) 2. of manipulation —n. a soldier of a maniple

ma·nip·u·late (mə nip'yə lāt') vt. **-lat'ed, -lat'ing** [backformation < ff.] 1. to work, operate, or treat with or as with the hand or hands; handle or use, esp. with skill 2. to manage or control artfully or by shrewd use of influence, often in an unfair or fraudulent way [to *manipulate* an election by bribing the voters] 3. to change or falsify (figures, accounts, etc.) for one's own purposes or profit; rig; specif., to cause (prices of stock, etc.) to fall or rise, as by wash sales, etc. —**SYN.** see HANDLE —**ma·nip'u·la·ble, ma·nip'u·lat'a·ble** adj. —**ma·nip'u·la'tive, ma·nip'u·la·to'ry** adj.

ma·nip·u·la·tion (mə nip'yə lā'shən) n. [Fr. < *manipule*, a bundle of herbs < L. *manipulus*: see MANIPLE] a manipulating or being manipulated; skillful handling or operation, artful management or control, etc.

ma·nip·u·la·tor (-lāt'ər) n. 1. a person or thing that manipulates ☆2. a mechanical device that is operated by remote control, as for handling radioactive materials

Man·i·pur (mun'ə poor') territory of NE India: 8,628 sq. mi.; pop. 780,000; cap. Imphal

Ma·ni·sa (mä'ni sä') city in W Turkey: as Magnesia, site of a battle (190 B.C.) in which the Romans defeated Antiochus the Great: pop. 60,000: also sp. **Ma'nis·sa'**

Man·i·to·ba (man'ə tō'bə) [< ? Ojibway *manito bau*, spirit strait: cf. MANITOU] 1. province of SC Canada: 251,000 sq. mi.; pop. 963,000; cap. Winnipeg: abbrev. **Man.** 2. Lake, lake in S Manitoba: 1,817 sq. mi. —**Man'i·to'ban** adj., n.

☆**man·i·tou** (man'ə tōō') n. [< AmInd. (Algonquian) name] any of various spirits or supernatural forces believed in by the Algonquian Indians and variously conceived of as nature spirits of both good and evil influence: also **man'i·tu', man'i·to'** (-tō')

Man·i·tou·lin Island (man'ə tōō'lin) Canadian island in N Lake Huron: 1,068 sq. mi.; pop. 10,000

Ma·ni·za·les (mä'nē sä'les) city in WC Colombia: pop. 176,000

man jack see phr. under JACK[1]

man·kind (man'kīnd'; also, & for 2 always, man'kīnd') n. [see MAN & -KIND] 1. all human beings; the human race 2. all human males; the male sex

man·like (man'līk') adj. 1. like or characteristic of a man or men 2. fit for a man; masculine

man·ly (-lē) adj. **-li·er, -li·est** [ME.: see MAN & -LY[1]] 1. having the qualities generally regarded as those that a man should have; virile; strong, brave, resolute, honorable, etc. 2. fit for a man; masculine [*manly* sports] —adv. in a manly way —**SYN.** see MALE —**man'li·ness** n.

man·made (-mād') adj. made by man; artificial or synthetic

Mann (man; for 2 män) 1. Horace, 1796–1859; U.S. educator 2. Thom·as (G. tō'mäs), 1875–1955; Ger. novelist in the U.S., etc.

man·na (man'ə) n. [ME. < OE. < LL.(Ec.) < Gr.(Ec.) *manna* < Aram. *mannā* < Heb. *mān*, orig., prob. *man hu*, lit., what is it?] 1. a) *Bible* food miraculously provided for the Israelites in the wilderness: Ex. 16:14–36 b) divine aid, spiritual sustenance, etc. 2. anything badly needed that comes unexpectedly 3. a) a sweet, gummy juice obtained from a European ash tree (*Fraxinus ornus*), formerly used as a laxative b) any of various similar substances exuded by certain plants and insects

Mann Act (man) [after James Robert *Mann* (1856–1922), U.S. Congressman] an act of Congress (June, 1910) prohibiting the interstate transportation of women for immoral purposes (*white slavery*)

man·ne·quin (man'ə kin) n. [Fr. < Du. *manneken*: see MANIKIN] 1. a model of the human body, used by tailors, window dressers, artists, etc. 2. a woman whose work is modeling clothes in stores, etc., for customers

man·ner (man'ər) n. [ME. *manere* < OFr. *maniere* < VL. *manaria* < L. *manuarius*, of the hand < *manus*, a hand] 1. a way or method in which something is done or happens; mode or fashion of procedure 2. a) a way of acting; personal, esp. customary, behavior or bearing [a sarcastic *manner*] b) distinguished bearing or behavior 3. [pl.] a) ways of social life; prevailing social conditions or customs [a comedy of *manners*] b) ways of social behavior; deportment, esp. with reference to polite conventions [good *manners*, bad *manners*] c) polite ways of social behavior; deportment conforming with polite conventions [a child who has no *manners*] 4. characteristic style or method in art, music, literature, etc. 5. a) kind; sort [what *manner* of man is he?] b) [with pl. v.] kinds; sorts [all *manner* of things] —**SYN.** see BEARING, METHOD —**by all manner of means** of course; surely —**by any manner of means** in any way; at all —**by no manner of means** in no way; definitely not —**in a manner of speaking** so to speak; in a certain sense or way —**to the manner born** 1. accustomed from birth to the way or usage spoken of 2. naturally fitted for a certain thing

man·nered (-ərd) adj. 1. having manners of a specified sort: used in hyphenated compounds [ill-*mannered*] 2. having or showing a specified manner [a solemnly *mannered* ceremony] 3. artificial, stylized, or affected [a *mannered* literary style]

man·ner·ism (man'ər iz'm) n. 1. excessive use of some distinctive, often affected, manner or style in art, literature, speech, or behavior 2. a peculiarity of manner in behavior, speech, etc. that has become a habit 3. [M-] a 16th-cent. style in art characterized by distortion of realistic proportions, contorted figures, an avoidance of classical balance, etc. —**SYN.** see POSE[1] —**man'ner·ist** n., adj. —**man'ner·is'tic** adj.

man·ner·less (-lis) adj. lacking good manners; impolite; unmannerly

man·ner·ly (-lē) adj. having or showing good manners; well-behaved; polite; courteous —adv. politely —**man'ner·li·ness** n.

Mann·heim (man'hīm; G. män'-) city in SW West Germany, on the Rhine, in Baden-Württemberg: pop. 328,000

man·ni·kin (man'ə kin) n. alt. sp. of MANIKIN

man·nish (man'ish) adj. of, like, or fit for a man: used in referring to a woman with masculine characteristics —**SYN.** see MALE —**man'nish·ly** adv. —**man'nish·ness** n.

man·nite (man'īt) n. [MANN(A) + -ITE[2]] same as MANNITOL —**man·nit'ic** (mə nit'ik) adj.

man·ni·tol (man'ə tōl', -tôl') n. [< prec. + -OL[1]] a colorless, crystalline alcohol, $C_6H_8(OH)_6$, occurring in various plants and animals, as the flowering ash, sponges, etc.

man·nose (man'ōs) n. [MANN(ITOL) + -OSE[1]] a sugar, $C_6H_{12}O_6$, formed by the oxidation of mannitol or found naturally in some plants

ma·noeu·vre (mə nōō'vər, -nyōō'-) n., vi., vt. **-vred, -vring** chiefly Brit. sp. of MANEUVER

Man of Galilee an epithet of JESUS

man of God 1. a holy man; saint, hermit, etc. 2. a clergyman; minister, priest, rabbi, etc.

man of letters a writer, scholar, editor, etc., esp. one whose work is in the field of literature

Man of Sorrows a person alluded to by Isaiah (Isa. 53:3) and interpreted as being the Messiah: regarded by Christians as a name for Jesus

man of the world a man familiar with and tolerant of various sorts of people and their ways; worldly man

man-of-war (man′əv wôr′, -ə wôr′) *n., pl.* **men′-of-war′** an armed naval vessel; warship

man-of-war bird *same as* FRIGATE BIRD

Ma·no·le·te (mä′nō le′te) (born *Manuel Rodríguez y Sánchez*) 1917–47; Sp. matador

ma·nom·e·ter (mə näm′ə tər) *n.* [Fr. *manomètre*, coined (1705) by Varignon, Fr. mathematician < Gr. *manos*, rare (taken in sense "thin, sparse") + Fr. *-mètre*, -METER] an instrument for measuring the pressure of gases or liquids —**man·o·met·ric** (man′ə met′rik), **man′o·met′ri·cal** *adj.*

man on horseback a military man with such influence and power over the people as to be, or seem to be, able to seize control and rule as a dictator

man·or (man′ər) *n.* [ME. *maner* < OFr. *manoir* < *manoir*, to stay, dwell < L. *manere*, to remain < IE. base *men-*, to remain (whence Sans. *man-*, to delay, stand still), prob. orig. identical with *men-*, to think (whence MIND): sense prob. from idea "stand in thought"] **1.** in England, *a)* in feudal times, the district over which a lord held authority and which was subject to the jurisdiction of his court *b)* more recently, a landed estate, usually with a main residence, the owner of which still holds some feudal rights over the land **2.** in the U.S. during colonial times, a district granted as a manor and leased to tenants at a set rental **3.** *a)* a mansion *b)* the main residence on an estate or plantation *c)* a lord's mansion with its land —**ma·no·ri·al** (mə nôr′ē əl) *adj.*

manor house the house of the lord of a manor

man·pow·er (man′pou′ər) *n.* **1.** power furnished by human physical strength **2.** a unit of power generally taken as equal to 1/10 horsepower **3.** the collective strength or availability for work of the people in any given area, nation, etc. Also **man power**

†man·qué (män kā′) *adj.* [Fr. < pp. of *manquer*, to fail, be lacking < It. *mancare* < *manco*, deficient < L. *mancus*, infirm, defective] **1.** that falls short of the goal; unsuccessful or defective **2.** potential but unrealized; would-be Placed after the noun it modifies [a scholar *manqué*] —**man·quée′** (-kā′) *adj.fem.*

man·rope (man′rōp′) *n. Naut.* a rope serving as a handrail along a gangway, ladder, etc.

man·sard (roof) (man′särd) [Fr. *mansarde*, after François *Mansard* (1598–1666), Fr. architect, who revived the use of such roofs] a roof with two slopes on each of the four sides, the lower steeper than the upper

manse (mans) *n.* [LME. *manss* < ML. *mansus* (or *mansum*, *mansa*), a dwelling < pp. of L. *manere*, to remain, dwell: see MANOR] **1.** the residence of a minister, esp. a Presbyterian minister; parsonage **2.** [Archaic] a large, imposing house; mansion

MANSARD ROOF

man·ser·vant (man′sur′vənt) *n., pl.* **men·ser·vants** (men′sur′vənts) a male servant: also **man servant**

Mans·field (manz′fēld′, mans′-) **1.** city in Nottinghamshire, NC England: pop. 53,000 **2.** [after Jared *Mansfield* (1759–1830), surveyor] city in NC Ohio: pop. 55,000

Mans·field (manz′fēld′, mans′-) **1. Katherine**, (born *Katherine Beauchamp*) 1888–1923; Brit. short-story writer, born in New Zealand **2. Richard**, 1854–1907; U.S. actor, born in Germany of Eng. parents

Man·ship (man′ship), **Paul** 1885–1966; U.S. sculptor

-man·ship (mən ship) [< (GAMES)MANSHIP] *a combining form* meaning talent or skill (esp. in gaining advantage) in connection with: freely used in coinages /"grantsmanship," "quotesmanship"]

man·sion (man′shən) *n.* [ME. *mansioun* < OFr. *mansion* < L. *mansio*, a sojourn, dwelling < pp. of *manere*, to remain, dwell: see MANOR] **1.** formerly, a manor house **2.** a large, imposing house; stately residence **3.** [Archaic] *a)* a dwelling place *b)* a separate dwelling place or lodging in a large house or structure: *usually used in pl.* **4.** [pl.] [Brit.] an apartment house **5.** [Obs.] a stay; sojourn **6.** *Astrol. a) same as* HOUSE (sense 11) *b)* any of the 28 parts of the moon's course occupied on successive days

man·sized (man′sīzd′) *adj.* [Colloq.] of a size fit for a man; large; big: also **man′-size′**

man·slaugh·ter (-slôt′ər) *n.* the killing of a human being by another; esp., such killing when unlawful but without malice: see also MURDER, HOMICIDE

man·slay·er (-slā′ər) *n.* a person who commits homicide or manslaughter —**man′slay′ing** *n., adj.*

man·sue·tude (man′swi tōōd′, -tyōōd′) *n.* [ME. < L. *mansuetudo* < pp. of *mansuescere*, to tame < *manus*, a hand + *suescere*, to accustom < IE. base *swedh-*, custom, habit: cf. ETHICAL] gentleness; tameness

Man·sur (man soor′) 712?–775 A.D.; Arab caliph (754–775): founder of Baghdad: called **al-Mansur**

man·ta (man′tə; *Sp.* män′tä) *n.* [Sp. < LL. *mantum*, a cloak, prob. back-formation < L. *mantellum*: see MANTLE]

☆**1.** *a)* coarse cotton cloth used for cheap shawls, capes, etc. in Spanish America *b)* a shawl, cape, etc. made of this ☆**2.** a horse blanket or horse cloth **3.** *Zool. same as* DEVILFISH (sense 1): also **manta ray**

man·teau (man′tō; *Fr.* män tō′) *n., pl.* **-teaus**, Fr. **-teaux** (-tō′) [Fr. < OFr. *mantel*: see MANTLE] a cloak or mantle, esp. one worn by a woman

Man·te·gna (män te′nyä), **An·dre·a** (än dre′ä) 1431–1506; It. painter & engraver

man·tel (man′t'l) *n.* [see MANTLE] **1.** the facing of stone, marble, etc. about a fireplace, including a projecting shelf or slab above it **2.** the shelf or slab

man·tel·et (man′t'l it, mant′lit) *n.* [ME. < OFr., dim. of *mantel*: see MANTLE] **1.** a short mantle, cape, or cloak **2.** a movable or stationary protective shelter or screen; esp., *a)* a movable roof or screen formerly used to protect besiegers from the enemy *b)* any of various bulletproof shields or screens

man·tel·let·ta (man′tə let′ə) *n.* [It., dim. < *mantello*: see MANTLE] *R.C.Ch.* a sleeveless vestment worn by cardinals, bishops, etc.

man·tel·piece (man′t'l pēs′) *n.* the projecting shelf of a mantel, or this shelf and the side elements framing the fireplace in front

man·tel·tree (-trē) *n.* **1.** a beam, stone, or arch above the opening of a fireplace, supporting the masonry above **2.** [Archaic] *same as* MANTELPIECE

man·tic (man′tik) *adj.* [Gr. *mantikos* < *mantis*, seer, soothsayer: see MANTIS] of, or having powers of, divination; prophetic

-man·tic (man′tik) [< Gr. *mantikos*: see MANTIC] *a combining form used to form adjectives corresponding to nouns ending in -MANCY [geomantic]*

man·til·la (man til′ə, -tē′ə) *n.* [Sp., dim. of *manta*: see MANTA] **1.** a woman's scarf, as of lace, worn over the hair and shoulders, as in Spain, Mexico, etc. **2.** a short mantle, cape, or cloak

MANTILLA

man·tis (man′tis) *n., pl.* **-tis·es**, **-tes** (-tēz) [ModL. < Gr. *mantis*, prophet, seer, kind of insect < IE. base *men-*, to think, whence MIND] any of various slender, elongated insects (family Mantidae) that feed on other insects and grasp their prey with stout, spiny forelegs often held up together as if praying

man·tis·sa (man tis′ə) *n.* [L., (useless) addition, makeweight < ? Etruscan] the decimal part of a logarithm as distinguished from the integral part (called the *characteristic*) [.7193] is the *mantissa* of the logarithm 4.7193]

mantis shrimp *same as* STOMATOPOD

MANTIS
(to 5 in. long)

man·tle (man′t'l) *n.* [ME. *mantel* < OE. *mentel* & OFr. *mantel*, both < L. *mantellum*, *mantelum*, a cloth, napkin, cloak, mantle < ?] **1.** a loose, sleeveless cloak or cape: sometimes used figuratively, in allusion to royal robes of state, as a symbol of authority or responsibility **2.** anything that cloaks, envelops, covers, or conceals [hidden under the *mantle* of night] **3.** a small hood or cap, usually cylindrical, of a meshwork substance, such as a thorium or cerium compound, which when placed over a flame becomes white-hot and gives off light **4.** the outer wall and casing of a blast furnace, above the hearth **5.** *same as* MANTEL **6.** *Anat.* old term *for* the cortex of the cerebrum **7.** *Geol. a)* the layer of the earth's interior between the crust and the core *b) same as* MANTLEROCK **8.** *Zool. a)* the glandular flap or folds of the body wall of a mollusk or similar organism, typically secreting a shell-forming fluid *b)* the soft outer body wall of a tunicate or barnacle *c)* the plumage on the back and folded wings of certain birds when the color markings are distinct —*vt.* **-tled**, **-tling** to cover with or as with a mantle; envelop; cloak; conceal —*vi.* **1.** to be or become covered, as a surface with scum or froth **2.** to spread like a mantle, as a blush over the face **3.** to blush or flush **4.** *Falconry* to spread first one wing, then the other, over the outstretched legs: said of a perched hawk

man·tle·rock (-räk′) *n.* the loose, unconsolidated material, residual or transported, that rests on the solid rock of the earth's crust

mant·let (mant′lit) *n. same as* MANTELET (sense 2)

Man·toux test (man tōō′, man′tōō) [after Charles *Mantoux*, Fr. physician (1877–1947)] a test for present or past tuberculosis, in which a small amount of protein from tuberculosis bacteria is injected into the skin

man·tra (mun′trə, man′-) *n.* [Sans., akin to *mantar*, thinker < IE. base *men-*, to think, whence MIND] *Hinduism* a hymn or portion of text, esp. from the Veda, chanted or intoned as an incantation or prayer

Man·tu·a (man′choo wə, -too wə) commune in Lombardy, N Italy: birthplace of Virgil: pop. 62,000: It. name **Man·to·va** (män′tô vä) —**Man′tu·an** *adj., n.*

man·tu·a (man′choo wə, -too wə) *n.* [altered (after prec.) < Fr. *manteau* < OFr. *mantel*, MANTEL] a mantle or loose gown or cloak formerly worn by women

man·u·al (man′yoo wəl) *adj.* [ME. *manuel* < OFr. < L. *manualis* < *manus*, a hand < IE. *mo-n-és, akin to *mntos, whence ON. & OE. *mund*, a hand] **1.** *a)* of or having to do with a hand or the hands *b)* made, done, worked, or used by the hands *c)* involving or doing hard physical work that requires use of the hands **2.** *Law* in actual possession —*n.* [ME. *manuele* < ML. *manuale*, manual, service book < LL., case or covering for a book < L. *manualis*: see the adj.] **1.** a handy book of facts, instructions, etc. for use as a guide, reference, or the like; handbook **2.** any of the separate keyboards of an organ console or harpsichord **3.** prescribed drill in the handling of a weapon, esp. a rifle: also **manual of arms** —**man′u·al·ly** *adv.*

☆**manual training** training in practical arts and crafts, as metalworking, etc.

ma·nu·bri·um (mə noo′brē əm, -nyoo′-) *n., pl.* **-bri·a** (-ə), **-bri·ums** [L., a handle, hilt, haft < *manus*, a hand] a handlelike structure, process, or part; esp., *a)* the portion of a jellyfish or other coelenterate that bears the mouth at its tip *b)* the uppermost of the three bony segments constituting the sternum, or breastbone, in mammals

Man·u·el (man′yoo wəl) a masculine name: see EMMANUEL

manuf., manufac. 1. manufacture **2.** manufactured **3.** manufacturer **4.** manufacturing

man·u·fac·to·ry (man′yə fak′tər ē) *n., pl.* **-ries** [< ff. + FACTORY] *same as* FACTORY (sense 1)

man·u·fac·ture (man′yə fak′chər) *n.* [Fr. < ML. *manufactura* < L. *manu*, abl. of *manus*, a hand + *factura*, a making < *factus*, pp. of *facere*, to make, DO[1]] **1.** the making of goods and articles by hand or, esp., by machinery, often on a large scale and with division of labor **2.** anything so made; manufactured product **3.** the making of something in any way, esp. when regarded as merely mechanical —*vt.* **-tured, -tur·ing 1.** to make by hand or, esp., by machinery, often on a large scale and with division of labor **2.** to work (wool, steel, etc.) into usable form **3.** to produce (art, literature, etc.) in a way regarded as mechanical and uninspired **4.** to make up (excuses, evidence, etc.); invent; fabricate; concoct —*SYN.* see MAKE[1]

man·u·fac·tur·er (-ər) *n.* a person or company in the business of manufacturing; esp., a factory owner

man·u·mis·sion (man′yə mish′ən) *n.* [ME. < OFr. < L. *manumissio* < pp. of *manumittere:* see ff.] a freeing or being freed from slavery; liberation; emancipation

man·u·mit (-mit′) *vt.* **-mit′ted, -mit′ting** [ME. *manumitten* < OFr. *manumitter* < L. *manumittere*, lit., to let go from the hand, free < *manu*, abl. of *manus*, a hand + *mittere*, to send] to free from slavery; liberate (a slave, serf, etc.)

ma·nure (mə noor′, -nyoor′) *vt.* **-nured′, -nur′ing** [ME. *manouren*, orig., to farm (land) < Anglo-Fr. *maynoberer* < OFr. *manouvrer*, to cultivate, lit., to work with the hands: see MANEUVER] to put manure on or into (soil); fertilize —*n.* [< the *v.*] animal excrement or other substance put on or into the soil to fertilize it —**ma·nur′er** *n.*

ma·nus (mā′nəs) *n., pl.* **ma′nus** [L., hand: see MANUAL] **1.** the terminal part of the forelimb of a vertebrate, as the hand of a person or the forefoot of a four-legged animal **2.** *Rom. Law* the authority of a husband over his wife

man·u·script (man′yə skript′) *adj.* [L. *manu scriptus*, written by hand < *manu*, abl. of *manus*, a hand + *scriptus*, pp. of *scribere*, to write] **1.** written by hand or with a typewriter, not printed **2.** designating writing that consists of unconnected letters resembling print; not cursive —*n.* [ML. *manuscriptum*] **1.** a book or document written by hand, esp. before the invention of printing: see CODEX **2.** a written or typewritten document or paper, esp. an author's copy of his work, as submitted to a publisher or printer **3.** writing as distinguished from print *[a novel still in manuscript]*

Ma·nu·ti·us (mə noo′shē əs, -nyoo′-), **Al·dus** (ôl′dəs, al′-) (It. name, *Aldo Manucci* or *Manuzio*) 1450–1515; Venetian printer: cf. ALDINE

man·ward (man′wərd) *adj., adv.* toward man; in relation to man: also **man′wards** *adv.*

man·wise (-wīz′) *adv.* [see -WISE] as a man would do; like a man

Manx (maŋks) *adj.* [by metathesis < obs. *Maniske* < ON. *manskr < *Man-*, inflectional base of *Mǫn*, Isle of Man < Celtic name, as in MW. *Manau*, OIr. *Manu*] of the Isle of Man, its people, or their language —*n.* the Goidelic language formerly spoken on the Isle of Man, but now nearly extinct —**the Manx** the people of the Isle of Man

Manx cat [*also* m-] a variety of domestic cat with a rudimentary tail

Manx·man (-mən) *n., pl.* **-men** (-mən) a native or inhabitant of the Isle of Man —**Manx′wom·an** *n.fem., pl.* **-wom′en**

man·y (men′ē) *adj.* **more, most** [ME. < OE. *manig*, akin to G. *manch* (OHG. *manag*) < IE. base **menegh-*, many, richly, whence Sans. *maghā-*, gift, OIr. *menicc*, abundant] **1.** consisting of some large, indefinite number (of persons or things); numerous **2.** relatively numerous (preceded by *as, too*, etc.) —*n.* a large number (of persons or things)

—*pron.* many persons or things **Many a** (or **an, another**) followed by a singular noun or pronoun is equivalent to *many* followed by the corresponding plural (e.g., *many a man has tried*) —**good many** [*with pl. v.*] a relatively large number (of persons or things) —**a great many** [*with pl. v.*] an extremely large number (of persons or things) —**as many** the same number of *[to read ten books in as many days]* —**be one too many for** to defeat; overwhelm —**the many 1.** the majority of people **2.** the people; the masses

SYN.—**many** is the simple, common word implying a relatively large number of units *[many children, excuses, bacteria, etc.];* **numerous**, a more formal equivalent for **many**, sometimes connotes a crowding of one unit upon another *[numerous complaints have come in];* **manifold** adds the connotation of great variety *[manifold problems]* or, in modifying a singular noun, great complexity in the component parts of the whole *[her manifold sorrow];* **multifarious** adds the connotation of great diversity, or even incongruity, in the variety *[multifarious interests];* **innumerable** implies a number too great to count and is often used hyperbolically *[innumerable instances of his kindness]* —*ANT.* **few**

man·y·plies (men′ē plīz′) *n.* [prec. + pl. of PLY[1], *n.*] *same as* OMASUM

man·y·sid·ed (-sīd′id) *adj.* **1.** having many sides or aspects **2.** having many possibilities, qualities, interests, or accomplishments —**man′y·sid′ed·ness** *n.*

☆**man·za·ni·ta** (man′zə nēt′ə) *n.* [AmSp. < Sp., dim. of *manzana*, apple: see MANCHINEEL] any of several shrubs or small trees (genus *Arctostaphylos*) of the heath family, found in the W U.S.

Man·zo·ni (män dzô′nē), **A·les·san·dro** (Francesco Tommaso Antonio) (ä′les sän′drô) 1785–1873; It. poet & novelist

Mao·ism (mou′iz′m) *n.* the communist theories and policies of Mao Tse-tung —**Mao′ist** *adj., n.*

Ma·o·ri (mou′rē, mä′ô rē; mä ôr′ē, mä-) *n.* [< Maori: said to mean "native, of the usual kind"] **1.** *pl.* **-ris, -ri** a member of a brown-skinned people native to New Zealand, of Polynesian origin **2.** their Polynesian language —*adj.* of the Maoris, their language, etc.

Mao Tse-tung (mou′ dzu′dŏŏŋ′) 1893– ; Chin. communist leader; chairman of the People's Republic of China (1949–59) & of the Chin. Communist Party (1949–)

map (map) *n.* [ML. *mappa (mundi)*, map (of the world) < L. *mappa*, napkin, cloth (on which maps were painted)] **1.** a drawing or other representation, usually on a flat surface, of all or part of the earth's surface, ordinarily showing countries, bodies of water, cities, mountains, etc. **2.** a similar representation of part of the sky, showing the relative position of the stars, planets, etc. **3.** any maplike representation or delineation **4.** [Slang] the face —*vt.* **mapped, map′ping 1.** to make a map or maps of; represent or chart on or as on a map **2.** to arrange or plan in detail (often with *out*) *[to map out a project]* **3.** to survey or explore for the purpose of making a map **4.** *Math.* to transform, as by a mapping —**put on the map** to make well known —☆**wipe off the map** to put out of existence —**map′per** *n.*

Map (map), **Walter** 1140?–1209?; Welsh poet & satirist: also, L. name, **Mapes** (māps, mä′pēz)

ma·ple (mā′p'l) *n.* [ME. < OE. *mapel(treo)*, akin to ON. *mǫpurr*] **1.** any of a large genus (*Acer*) of trees of the maple family, grown for wood, sap, or shade **2.** the hard, closegrained, light-colored wood of such a tree, used for furniture, flooring, etc. **3.** the reddish-yellow or yellowish color of the finished wood **4.** the flavor of maple syrup or of the sugar made from this **5.** [Slang] a bowling pin: *usually used in pl.* —*adj.* **1.** designating a family (Aceraceae) of trees and a few shrubs, characterized by opposite, often lobed leaves, small clusters of flowers, and two-winged fruits **2.** of or made of maple **3.** flavored with maple

☆**maple sugar** sugar made by a further boiling down of maple syrup

☆**maple syrup** syrup made by boiling down the sap of any of various maples, esp. the sugar maple

map·ping (map′iŋ) *n. Math.* a transformation taking the points of one space into the points of the same or another space

ma·quette (ma ket′) *n.* [Fr. < It. *macchietta*, lit., little spot, dim. of *macchia* < L. *macula*, a spot] a small model of a planned sculpture, building, etc.

ma·qui (mä′kē) *n.* [AmSp. < Chilean (Araucan) name] an ornamental plant (*Aristotelia chilensis*) of Chile: fiber from its bark is used for stringing native musical instruments, and its purple berries are made into a medicinal wine

‡**ma·quil·lage** (má kē yäzh′) *n.* [Fr. < *maquiller*, to make up, orig., to work, irreg. < OFr. *makier*, to do, make < ODu. *maken*, akin to MAKE[1]] makeup; cosmetics

ma·quis (mä kē′; Fr. má kē′) *n.* [Fr. < It. *macchia*, a thicket, orig. a spot < L. *macula*, a spot, stain] **1.** a zone of shrubby plants, chiefly evergreens, growing in the area around the Mediterranean, used as a hiding place by fugitives, guerrilla fighters, etc. **2.** [*often* M-] *pl.* **-quis′** (-kēz′; Fr. -kē′) a member of the French underground fighting against the Nazis in World War II

mar (mär) *vt.* **marred, mar′ring** [ME. *marren* < OE. *mierran*, to hinder, spoil, akin to Goth. *marzjan*, to offend < IE. base **mer-*, to disturb, anger, whence Sans. *mṛṣyate*,

(he) forgets, neglects] to injure or damage so as to make imperfect, less attractive, etc.; spoil; impair; disfigure —*n.* [Rare] something that mars; an injury or blemish

Mar. March

mar. 1. marine **2.** maritime **3.** married

mar·a·bou (mar′ə bōō′) *n.* [Fr., lit., MARABOUT: so named from its contemplative posture] **1.** any of several large storks (genus *Leptoptilus*); *esp., a)* a bare-headed, large-billed, dark-green species (*Leptoptilus crumeniferus*) of Africa *b)* the Indian adjutant **2.** soft feathers from the wing coverts and tail of the marabou, used in millinery **3.** *a)* a delicate, white raw silk thread that can be dyed with the natural gum still in it *b)* a fabric made of such thread

mar·a·bout (-bōōt′) *n.* [Fr. < Port. *marabuto* < Ar. *murābit*, hermit] **1.** a Moslem hermit or holy man, esp. among the Berbers and Moors **2.** the tomb or shrine of such a man **3.** *same as* MARABOU

ma·ra·ca (mə rä′kə) *n.* [Port. *maracá* < the Braz. native name] a percussion instrument consisting of a dried gourd or a gourd-shaped rattle with loose pebbles in it, shaken to beat out a rhythm

Mar·a·cai·bo (mar′ə ki′bō; *Sp.* mä′rä ki′bō) **1.** seaport in NW Venezuela: pop. 421,000 **2. Gulf of,** *same as* Gulf of VENEZUELA **3. Lake,** lake in NW Venezuela, connected by channel with the Gulf of Venezuela: c. 5,000 sq. mi.

Mar·a·can·da (mar′ə kan′də) *ancient name of* SAMARKAND

Ma·ra·cay (mä′rä ki′) city in N Venezuela: pop. 135,000

☆**mar·ag·ing steels** (mār′ä/jiŋ) [MAR(TENSITE) + *aging*, spontaneous hardening of metals during storage] nickel-iron alloys of extremely high strength, produced from martensite steel by spontaneous hardening at moderate temperatures without quenching

mar·a·nath·a (mer′ə nath′ə) *n.* [ME. < ML.(Ec.) < Gr.(Ec.) < Aram. *mārana thā*, O Lord, come] an invocation to the Lord, sometimes regarded as forming, with the preceding *anathema* (in I Cor. 16:22), an intensified curse or malediction

Ma·ra·nhão (mä′rə nyoun′) state of NE Brazil: 126,897 sq. mi.; pop. 2,493,000; cap. São Luiz

Ma·ra·ñón (mä′rä nyōn′) river in W & N Peru that joins the Ucayali to form the Amazon: c. 1,000 mi.

ma·ras·ca (mə ras′kə) *n.* [It.: see ff.] a wild cherry (*Prunus cerasus*) of the rose family, from which maraschino is made: the fruit is small, black, and bitter

mar·a·schi·no (mar′ə skē′nō, -shē′-) *n.* [It. < *marasca*, *amarasca*, kind of cherry < *amaro*, bitter < L. *umarus* < IE. base *om-, raw, bitter, whence OE. *ampre*, sorrel] a strong, sweet liqueur or cordial made from the fermented juice of the marasca

maraschino cherries cherries in a syrup flavored with maraschino or, now usually, imitation maraschino

ma·ras·mus (mə raz′məs) *n.* [ML. < Gr. *marasmos*, a wasting away < *marainein*, to quench, cause to waste away: for IE. base see MARE³] a condition of progressive emaciation, esp. in infants, as from inability to assimilate food —**ma·ras′mic** *adj.*

Ma·rat (mä rä′), **Jean Paul** (zhän pōl) 1743–93; Fr. Revolutionary leader, born in Switzerland: assassinated by Charlotte Corday

Ma·ra·tha (mə rä′tə) *n.* [Marathi *Marathā* < Sans. *Mahārāṣṭra*, lit., great country] a member of a people of Maharashtra state, in W India

Ma·ra·thi (mə rä′tē) *n.* the Indic language of the Marathas

Mar·a·thon (mar′ə thän′) ancient Greek village in E Attica, or a plain near by, where the Athenians under Miltiades defeated the Persians under Darius I (490 B.C.)

mar·a·thon (mar′ə thän′) *n.* **1.** a foot race of 26 miles, 385 yards, run over an open course, esp. as an event of the Olympic games: after the legend of the Greek runner who ran from Marathon to Athens to tell of the victory over the Persians (490 B.C.) **2.** any long-distance or endurance contest

MARATHON
(5th cent. B.C.)

ma·raud (mə rôd′) *vi.* [Fr. *marauder* < *maraud*, vagabond, prob. special use of dial. Fr. *maraud*, tomcat, echoic of cry] to rove in search of plunder; make raids —*vt.* to raid; plunder; pillage —*n.* [Archaic] the act of marauding —**ma·raud′er** *n.*

mar·a·ve·di (mar′ə vā′dē) *n.* [Sp. < Ar. *Murābitīn*, name of a Moorish dynasty at Córdoba (1086–1147) < *murābit*: see MARABOUT] **1.** a gold coin used by the Moors in Spain in the 11th & 12th cent. **2.** an obsolete Spanish copper coin

mar·ble (mär′b'l) *n.* [ME. *marble*, *marbre* < OFr. *marbre* < L. *marmor* < Gr. *marmaros*, white glistening stone, orig.

boulder (meaning infl. by cognate, *marmairein*, to shine) < IE. base *mer-, to rub, whence MARE³] **1.** a hard, crystalline or granular, metamorphic limestone, white or variously colored and sometimes streaked or mottled, which can take a high polish: it is much used in building and sculpture **2.** *a)* a piece or slab of this stone, used as a monument, inscribed record, etc. *b)* a piece of sculpture in marble **3.** anything resembling or suggesting marble in hardness, smoothness, coldness, coloration, etc. **4.** *a)* a little ball of stone, glass, or clay, used in games *b)* [*pl.*, *with sing. v.*] a children's game in which a marble is propelled by the thumb to hit other marbles, usually to drive them out of a marked circle **5.** a marbled pattern; marbling **6.** [*pl.*] [Slang] brains; good sense [to lose one's *marbles*] —*adj.* **1.** made of or consisting of marble **2.** like marble in some way; hard, cold, smooth, white, etc., or streaked, mottled, etc. —*vt.* **-bled, -bling 1.** to stain or color (book edges) to look mottled or streaked like marble **2.** to cause fat to be evenly distributed in narrow streaks through (meat) —**mar′bled, mar′bly** *adj.*

☆**marble cake** a cake made of light and dark batter mixed to give a streaked, marblelike appearance

Mar·ble·head (mär′b'l hed′) [after the large rocks (called "marble") there] resort town in NE Mass., near Boston: pop. 21,000

☆**mar·ble·ize** (-īz′) *vt.* **-ized′, -iz′ing** to make, color, grain, or streak in imitation of marble

mar·bling (mär′bliŋ) *n.* **1.** the art or process of staining or veining like marble, as the decoration of book edges in marblelike patterns **2.** a streaked, veined, or mottled appearance like that of marble [the *marbling* of fat in prime meat]

marc (märk) *n.* [Fr. < *marcher*, to tread, trample, march, press: see MARCH¹] **1.** refuse of grapes, seeds, fruits, etc. after pressing **2.** a brandy distilled from this **3.** any insoluble matter left after treating a substance, as a drug, with a solvent

Marc (märk), **Franz** (fränts) 1880–1916; Ger. painter

Marc Antony *see* ANTONY

mar·ca·site (mär′kə sīt′) *n.* [Fr. *marcassite* < ML. *marcasita* < Ar. *marqashīta*] **1.** a pale-colored pyrite (**white iron pyrite**) crystallized in orthorhombic form **2.** this mineral or polished steel cut in the form of brilliants and used as an ornament

Mar·ceau (mär sō′), **Marcel** 1923— ; Fr. pantomimist

Mar·cel (mär sel′) **1.** a masculine name: see MARCELLUS **2.** (mär sel′), **Ga·bri·el** (gä brē el′) 1889— ; Fr. philosopher

mar·cel (mär sel′) *n.* [after *Marcel* Grateau, early 20th-cent. Fr. hairdresser] a series of even waves put in the hair with a curling iron: also **marcel wave** —*vt.* **-celled′, -cel′ling** to put such waves in (hair)

Mar·cel·la (mär sel′ə) [L.] a feminine name: see MARCELLUS

Mar·cel·lus (mär sel′əs) [L., dim. of *Marcus*] **1.** a masculine name: var. *Marcel*; fem. *Marcella* **2.** (**Marcus Claudius**), 268?–208 B.C.; Rom. statesman & general

mar·ces·cent (mär ses′'nt) *adj.* [L. *marcescens*, prp. of *marcescere*, to wither, decay < *marcere*, to wither < IE. base *merk-, to grow soft, rot, akin to *mer-, whence OE. *mearu*, soft, tender] *Bot.* withering but not falling off —**mar·ces′cence** *n.*

March¹ (märch) *n.* [ME. < OFr. *march, marz* < L. *Martius* (*mensis*), (month) of Mars < *Mars*, MARS] the third month of the year, having 31 days: abbrev. **Mar.**

March² (märkh) Ger. name of MORAVA, Czechoslovakia

march¹ (märch) *vi.* [Fr. *marcher* < OFr., prob. < Frank. *markon < *marka, MARK¹: orig. sense prob. "to pace off the boundary"] **1.** to walk with regular, steady steps of equal length, usually in a group or military formation **2.** to walk in a grave, steady way **3.** to advance or progress steadily —*vt.* **1.** to cause (troops, etc.) to march **2.** to cause or force to go —*n.* **1.** the act of marching **2.** a regular forward movement; steady advance; progress [the *march* of events] **3.** a regular, steady step or pace **4.** the distance covered in a period of marching [a day's *march*] **5.** a long, tiring walk **6.** a piece of music, with a steady, even beat, suitable for marching **7.** an organized walk by a number of people demonstrating on some public issue [a peace *march*] —**on the march** marching —**steal a march on** to get an advantage over without being perceived

march² (märch) *n.* [ME. < OFr. < Frank. *marka, MARK¹] **1.** a boundary, border, or frontier **2.** a borderland, esp. one in dispute —*vi.* [Rare] to have a common border (*with*); border —**the Marches** borderlands between England & Scotland & between England & Wales

March. Marchioness

Marche (mårsh) region & former province of C France

Mar·che (mär′ke), **Le** (le) region of C Italy, on the Adriatic: 3,742 sq. mi.; pop. 1,347,000; chief city, Ancona: Eng. name (**The**) **Marches**

‡**Mär·chen** (mer′Hən) *n.*, *pl.* **-chen** [G.] a story or tale; esp., a fairy tale or folk tale

march·er¹ (mär′chər) *n.* a person who marches

march·er² (mär′chər) *n.* **1.** a person who lives in a march, or borderland **2.** a lord who governed or defended the Marches (see MARCH²) for England

---

fat, āpe, cär; ten, ēven; is, bīte; gō, hôrn, tōōl, look; oil, out; up, fur; get; joy; yet; chin; she; thin, then; zh, leisure; ŋ, ring; ə for *a* in *ago*, *e* in *agent*, *i* in *sanity*, *o* in *comply*, *u* in *focus*; ′ as in *able* (ā′b'l); Fr. bâl; ë, Fr. coeur; ö, Fr. feu; ô, Fr. mon; ō, Fr. coq; ü, Fr. duc; r, Fr. cri; H, G. ich; kh, G. doch. See inside front cover. ☆ Americanism; ‡foreign; *hypothetical; <derived from

mar·che·se (mär ke′ze) n., pl. -che′si (-zē) [It.: see MARQUIS] an Italian nobleman ranking above a count and below a prince; marquis —**mar·che′sa** (-ke′zä) n.fem., pl. -che′se (-ze)

March hare a hare in breeding time, proverbially regarded as an example of madness

marching orders orders to march, go, or leave

mar·chion·ess (mär′shə nis, mär′shə nes′) n. [ML. marchionissa, fem. of marchio, prefect of the marches < marcha, border < Frank. *marka, MARK¹] 1. the wife or widow of a marquess 2. a lady whose rank in her own right equals that of a marquess See also MARQUISE

march·pane (märch′pān′) n. same as MARZIPAN

Mar·cia (mär′shə) [L., fem. of Marcius, name of a Roman gens < Marcus, MARCUS] a feminine name

Mar·cion·ism (mär′shə niz′m) n. [< Marcion, Christian Gnostic of the 2d cent. A.D.] the doctrines of an ascetic Christian sect of the 2d & 3d cent. that rejected the Old Testament and much of the New Testament —**Mar′cion·ite′** (-nīt′) n.

Mar·co·ni (mär kō′nē; It. mär kō′nē), Marchese Gu·gliel·mo (gōō lyel′mō) 1874–1937; It. physicist: developed wireless telegraphy

mar·co·ni·gram (mär kō′ni gram′) n. earlier name of RADIOGRAM

☆**Marconi rig** a fore-and-aft rig of triangular sails for a yacht: also **Bermuda rig**

Marco Polo see POLO

Mar·cus (mär′kəs) [L. < Mars, MARS] a masculine name: var. Mark; fem. Marcia

Marcus Aurelius see AURELIUS

Mar·cy (mär′sē), **Mount** [after Wm. L. Marcy, governor (1833–39)] mountain in N N.Y.: highest peak of the Adirondacks: 5,344 ft.

☆**Mar·di gras** (mär′di grä′) [Fr., lit., fat Tuesday] Shrove Tuesday, the last day before Lent: it is a day of merry-making and carnival, as in New Orleans, often marking the climax of a carnival period

Mar·duk (mär′dook) [Bab.] the chief god of the ancient Babylonian religion, orig. a local sun god

mare¹ (mer) n. [ME. < OE. mere, fem. of mearh, akin to G. mähre, jade, prob. < IE. base *marko-, horse, seen only in Gmc. & Celt. (Ir. marc, W. march, horse)] a fully mature female horse, mule, donkey, burro, etc.; specif., a female horse that has reached the age of five

ma·re² (mer′ē, mär′ē) n., pl. -ri·a (-ē ə) [L., sea < IE. base *mori, whence Goth. marei, sea, OE. mere, sea, lake, W. mor, sea] 1. a sea 2. a large, dark area on the moon's surface or a similar area on Mars

mare³ (mer) n. [ME. < OE., akin to G. dial. mahr, ON. mar < IE. *mora, incubus < base *mer-, to rub, seize, whence OE. mearu, soft] [Obs.] the evil spirit that was once thought to produce nightmares

‡**ma·re clau·sum** (mer′ē klô′səm, mär′-) [L., closed sea] a sea under the jurisdiction of a single nation and not open to all others

Mare Island (mer) [said to be for a mare that swam to the island from a capsized boat] island at the N end of San Francisco Bay, Calif.: site of a U.S. navy yard

ma·re li·be·rum (mer′ē li′bər əm, mär′-; lē′-) [L., free sea] a sea open to all nations

ma·rem·ma (mə rem′ə) n., pl. -rem′me (-ē) [It. < L. maritimus: see MARITIME] low, unhealthful, but fertile marshy land near the sea, esp. in Italy

Ma·ren·go (mə ren′gō) village in the Piedmont, NW Italy: site of a victory (1800) by Napoleon over the Austrians

‡**ma·re nos·trum** (mer′ē näs′trəm, mär′-; nōs′-) [L.] our sea: Roman name for the Mediterranean

mare's-nest (merz′nest′) n. 1. something supposed to be a wonderful discovery but turning out to be a hoax or a delusion 2. a disorderly or confused condition; mess

mare's-tail (-tāl′) n. 1. long, narrow formations of cirrus cloud somewhat like a horse's tail in shape, supposed to be a sign of wind 2. a marsh plant (Hippuris vulgaris) with tiny flowers and narrow, hairlike leaves growing in thick whorls around the slender, erect stems

marg. 1. margin 2. marginal

Mar·ga·ret (mär′grit, -gər it) [ME. < OFr. Margarete < L. margarita, a pearl < Gr. margaritēs < margaron, a pearl, ult. < or akin to Sans. mañjaram, a pearl, orig., bud] a feminine name: dim. Greta, Madge, Maggie, Marge, Meg, Peg, Peggy; var. Margery, Marjory, Marjory; equiv. Fr. Marguerite, Ger. Margarete, Gretchen, It. Margherita, Sp. Margarita

Margaret of Anjou 1430–82; queen of Henry VI of England (1445–61; 1470–71)

Margaret of Navarre 1492–1549; queen of Navarre (1544–49); writer & patroness of literature: also **Margaret of An·gou·lême** (än gōō lem′)

Margaret of Valois 1553–1615; queen of Henry IV of France (1589–99): called Queen Margot

mar·gar·ic acid (mär gar′ik, -gär′-) [Fr. margarique < Gr. margaron, a pearl (see MARGARET): from the pearly luster of its crystals] a white, crystalline fatty acid, C₁₇H₃₄O₂, obtained from lichens or synthetically

mar·ga·rine (mär′jə rin) n. [Fr., from the erroneous notion that margaric acid was contained in all fats and oils] a spread or cooking fat made of refined vegetable oils

processed to the consistency of butter, often churned with pasteurized skim milk, and generally fortified with vitamins A and D: also **mar′ga·rin**

Mar·ga·ri·ta (mär′gə rēt′ə) island of Venezuela, just off the N coast: with small nearby islands it constitutes a state (Nueva Esparta), 444 sq. mi.: pop. 89,000 —n. ☆[often m-] a cocktail made with tequila, triple sec, and lemon or lime juice

mar·ga·rite (mär′gə rīt′) n. [ME. < OFr. < L. margarita: see MARGARET] 1. a hydrated silicate of calcium and aluminum, CaAl₂(Si₂Al₂)O₁₀(OH)₂, found as scales with a pearly luster 2. a crystalline material, occurring in some igneous rocks, consisting of strings of tiny, beadlike masses 3. [Obs.] a pearl

Mar·gate (mär′gāt, -git) seaport & summer resort in Kent, SE England: pop. 45,000

mar·gay (mär′gā) n. [Fr. < Port. maracajá < Braz. (Tupi) name] a spotted cat (Felis tigrina) of Central and South America, like the ocelot but smaller

marge (märj) n. [Fr. < L. margo, MARGIN] [Archaic or Poet.] a border; edge; margin

mar·gent (mär′jənt) n. [< MARGIN, with unhistoric -t] [Archaic] a margin, or edge

Mar·ger·y (mär′jər ē) [ME. Margerie < OFr. < L. margarita: see MARGARET] a feminine name: dim. Marge

mar·gin (mär′jən) n. [ME. margine < L. margo (gen. marginis): see MARK¹] 1. a border, edge, or brink [the margin of the pond] 2. the blank space around the printed or written area on a page or sheet 3. a limit to what is desirable or possible 4. a) an amount of money, supplies, etc. reserved or allowed beyond what is needed; extra amount for contingencies or emergencies b) provision for increase, addition, or advance 5. the amount by which something is higher or lower [to win by a wide margin] 6. Business, Finance a) the difference between the cost and the selling price of goods manufactured, produced, sold, etc. b) money or collateral deposited with a broker or other lender, either to meet legal requirements or to insure him against loss on contracts which he undertakes for the actual buyer or seller of stocks, commodities, etc. c) a customer's equity if his account is closed at the prevailing prices d) the difference between the face value of a loan and the market value of collateral put up to secure it 7. Econ. the minimum return, below which activities are not profitable enough to be continued 8. Psychol. the fringe of consciousness —vt. [L. marginare] 1. to provide with a margin or border; be a margin to; border 2. to enter, place, or summarize in the margin of a page or sheet 3. Business ☆a) to deposit a margin upon b) to hold by depositing or adding to a margin upon —SYN. see BORDER

mar·gin·al (-'l) adj. [ML. marginalis] 1. written or printed in the margin of a page or sheet 2. of or constituting a margin 3. at, on, or close to the margin or border 4. close to a margin or limit, esp. a lower limit [a marginal standard of living] 5. Econ. a) on the border between being profitable or nonprofitable [a marginal business, marginal land] b) of or from goods produced and sold at margin [marginal costs, marginal profits] —**mar′gin·al′i·ty** (-al′ə tē) n. —**mar′gin·al·ly** adv.

mar·gi·na·li·a (mär′jə nā′lē ə, -näl′yə) n.pl. [ModL. < neut. pl. of ML. marginalis] marginal notes

mar·gin·ate (mär′jə nāt′; also for adj., -nit) vt. -at′ed, -at′ing [< L. marginatus, pp. of marginare] to provide with a margin —adj. having a distinct margin: also **mar′gin·at′ed** —**mar′gin·a′tion** n.

Mar·got (mär′gō, -gət) [Fr.] a feminine name: see MARGARET

mar·gra·vate (mär′grə vāt′) n. [see ff. & -ATE²] the territory ruled over by a margrave: also **mar·gra·vi·ate** (mär grā′vē āt′)

mar·grave (mär′grāv) n. [MDu. markgrave < MHG. marcgrave < OHG. marcgravo < marc (see MARK¹), a march, border + graf, a count, earl] 1. orig., a military governor of a march, or border province, in Germany 2. the hereditary title of certain princes of the Holy Roman Empire or Germany —**mar·gra′vi·al** adj.

mar·gra·vine (mär′grə vēn′) n. [Du. markgravin, fem. of markgraaf] the wife of a margrave

Mar·gue·rite (mär′gə rēt′) [see ff.] a feminine name

mar·gue·rite (mär′gə rēt′) n. [Fr., a pearl, daisy: see MARGARET] 1. same as DAISY (sense 1) 2. any of several cultivated chrysanthemums with a single flower, esp. the **Paris daisy** (Chrysanthemum frutescens) 3. any of various daisy-like plants of the composite family

Ma·ri·a (mə rī′ə, -rē′-) a feminine name: see MARY

ma·ri·a (mer′ē ə, mär′-) n. pl. of MARE²

☆**ma·ri·a·chi** (mär′ē ä′chē) n., pl. -chis [MexSp. < ?] 1. a member of a strolling band of musicians in Mexico 2. such a band 3. their music

‡**ma·ri·age de con·ve·nance** (må ryàzh′ də kōnv näns′) [Fr.] same as MARRIAGE OF CONVENIENCE

Mar·i·an (mer′ē ən, mar′-) [var. of MARION, but spelled as if < MARY + ANNE] a feminine name: var. Marianne, Marianna —adj. 1. of the Virgin Mary 2. of Mary I of England 3. of Mary, Queen of Scots —n. 1. a worshiper or devotee of the Virgin Mary 2. a follower or defender of Mary, Queen of Scots

Ma·ri·an·a Islands (mer′ē an′ə, mar′-) group of islands

in the W Pacific, east of the Philippines: formerly (except Guam) a Jap. mandate & possession, since 1947 part of the U.S. Trust Territory of the Pacific Islands, pop. 11,000 Also **Ma·ri·an'as Islands**

Ma·ri·na·o (mä'ryä nä'ŏ) city in NW Cuba: suburb of Havana: pop. 230,000

Mar·i·anne (mer'ē an', mar'-) **1.** a feminine name: see MARIAN **2.** *a personification of* the French Republic: a woman in French Revolutionary costume

Maria Theresa 1717–80; queen of Bohemia & Hungary & archduchess of Austria (1740–80): mother of MARIE ANTOINETTE

Ma·rie (mə rē') a feminine name: see MARY

Marie An·toi·nette (an'twə net', -ta-), (**Joséphe Jeanne**) 1755–93; wife of Louis XVI; queen of France (1774–92): guillotined

Marie Byrd Land region in Antarctica, on the Amundsen Sea

Marie de Médicis *see* Maria de' MEDICI

Ma·rie Ga·lante (mȧ rē' gȧ länt') island dependency of Guadeloupe, in the Leeward group of the West Indies: 58 sq. mi.; pop. 16,000

Marie Louise 1791–1847; 2d wife of Napoleon I & empress of France (1810–15)

Mar·i·et·ta (mer'ē et'ə, mar'-) **1.** a feminine name: see MARY **2.** [after MARIE ANTOINETTE] city in SE Ohio, on the Ohio River: 1st permanent settlement (1788) in the Northwest Territory: pop. 17,000

mar·i·gold (mar'ə gōld') n. [ME. *marigolde* < *Marie* (prob. the Virgin Mary) + *gold*, GOLD] **1.** *a)* any of a genus (*Tagetes*) of annual plants of the composite family, with red, yellow, or orange flowers *b)* the flower of any of these plants **2.** any of several unrelated plants, as the pot marigold

☆**ma·ri·jua·na, ma·ri·hua·na** (mar'ə wä'nə, mär'-; -hwä'-) n. [AmSp. *marihuana, mariguana* < ? native word blended with pers. name *Maria Juana*, Mary Jane] **1.** *same as* HEMP (n. 1 *a)* **2.** its dried leaves and flowers, smoked, esp. in the form of cigarettes, for the psychological and euphoric effects

Mar·i·lyn (mar'ə lin) a feminine name: see MARY

ma·rim·ba (mə rim'bə) n. [Mbundu, a percussive instrument resembling the xylophone, akin to Tshiluba *madimba*] a musical instrument somewhat like a xylophone, consisting of a series of hard wooden bars, usually with resonators beneath, played by being struck with small mallets

Mar·in (mar'in), **John** (**Cheri**) 1870–1953; U.S. painter

ma·ri·na (mə rē'nə) n. [It. & Sp., seacoast < L. *marinus*: see MARINE] ☆a small harbor or boat basin providing dockage, supplies, and services for small pleasure craft

mar·i·nade (mar'ə nād') n. [Fr. < Sp. *marinada* < *marinar*, to pickle in brine < *marino* < L. *marinus*: see MARINE] **1.** a spiced pickling solution, esp. a mixture of oil, wine or vinegar, and spices, in which meat, fish, or salad is steeped, often before cooking **2.** meat or fish thus pickled or steeped —vt. **-nad'ed, -nad'ing** *same as* MARINATE

mar·i·nate (mar'ə nāt') vt. **-nat'ed, -nat'ing** [< It. *marinato*, pp. of *marinare*, to pickle in brine < *marino* < L. *marinus*: see MARINE] to steep (meat, fish, salad, etc.) in a marinade —**mar'i·na'tion** n.

ma·rine (mə rēn') adj. [ME. *maryne* < L. *marinus* < *mare*, the sea: see MARE²] **1.** *a)* of the sea or ocean *b)* inhabiting, found in, or formed by the sea **2.** *a)* of navigation on the sea; nautical *b)* of naval affairs; naval *c)* of shipping by sea; maritime **3.** used, or to be used, at sea [a *marine* engine] **4.** *a)* trained for service at sea, on land, etc., as certain troops *b)* of such troops —n. **1.** a member of a marine military force; specif., [*often* M-] a member of the MARINE CORPS **2.** naval or merchant ships collectively; seagoing ships of a nation; fleet [the merchant *marine*] **3.** in some countries, the department of government in charge of naval affairs **4.** a picture of a ship or sea scene

☆**Marine Corps** a branch of the U.S. armed forces, established by the Continental Congress in 1775, equipped and trained for land, sea, and aerial combat: the Commandant of the Marine Corps is responsible to the Secretary of the Navy

mar·i·ner (mar'ə nər) n. [ME. *marinere* < Anglo-Fr. *mariner* (OFr. *marinier*) < ML. *marinarius* < L. *marinus*, MARINE] a sailor; seaman

Mar·i·ol·a·try (mer'ē äl'ə trē, mar'-) n. [< Gr. *Maria*, Mary + -LATRY] veneration of the Virgin Mary, when regarded as carried to an idolatrous extreme

Mar·i·ol·o·gy (-äl'ə jē) n. [see prec. & -LOGY] study and beliefs concerned with the Virgin Mary

Mar·i·on¹ (mar'ē ən, mer'-) [Fr., orig. dim. of *Marie*, MARY] **1.** a masculine name: see MARY **3. Francis,** 1732?–95; Am. general in the Revolutionary War: called the *Swamp Fox*

Mar·i·on² (mar'ē ən, mer'-) [after Francis MARION] **1.** city in EC Ind.: pop. 40,000 **2.** city in C Ohio: pop. 39,000

mar·i·o·nette (mar'ē ə net') n. [Fr., dim. of *Marion*: see

MARION¹] a puppet or little jointed doll moved by strings or wires from above, often on a miniature stage

☆**Mar·i·po·sa lily** (or **tulip**) (mar'ə pō'zə, -sə) [AmSp. *mariposa* < Sp., butterfly: from the appearance of the blossoms] **1.** any of a genus (*Calochortus*) of plants of the lily family, found in W N. America, with tuliplike flowers of white, red, yellow, or violet **2.** the flower of any of these plants

mar·ish (mar'ish) n. [ME. *mareis* < OFr. < Frank. **marisk*, akin to OE. *merisc*, MARSH] [Archaic] a marsh; swamp —adj. [Archaic] marshy

Mar·ist (mar'ist, mer'-) adj. [Fr. *Mariste* < *Marie*, MARY] R.C.Ch. **1.** of or dedicated to the Virgin Mary **2.** of the Society of Mary (**Marist Fathers**), a congregation of missionary priests founded in 1816 —n. a member of this group

Ma·ri·tain (mȧ rē tan'), **Jacques** (zhȧk) 1882– ; Fr. philosopher

mar·i·tal (mar'ə t'l) adj. [L. *maritalis* < *maritus*, married, a husband < *mas* (gen. *maris*), male] **1.** orig., of a husband **2.** of marriage; matrimonial; connubial —**mar'i·tal·ly** adv.

mar·i·time (mar'ə tīm') adj. [L. *maritimus* < *mare*, the sea: see MARE²] **1.** on, near, or living near the sea [*maritime* provinces, a *maritime* people] **2.** of the sea in relation to navigation, shipping, etc. [*maritime* law] **3.** characteristic of sailors; nautical

Maritime Alps S division of the W Alps, along the French-Italian border: highest peak, 10,817 ft.

Maritime Provinces Canad. provinces of Nova Scotia, New Brunswick, & Prince Edward Island

Ma·ri·u·pol (mä'rē ōō'pôl) *former name of* ZHDANOV

Mar·i·us (mer'ē əs), **Gai·us** (gā'əs, gī'-) 157?–86 B.C.; Rom. general & statesman

mar·jo·ram (mär'jər əm) n. [ME. *majoran* < OFr. *majorane* < ML. *maiorana*, prob. altered < L. *amaracus* < Gr. *amarakos*, marjoram: of Oriental origin, akin to Sans. *maruva*-] any of a number of perennial plants of the mint family; esp., **sweet marjoram** (*Majorana hortensis*) grown as an annual for its aromatic leaves used in cooking

Mar·jo·rie, Mar·jo·ry (mär'jər ē) a feminine name: see MARGARET

Mark (märk) **1.** a masculine name: see MARCUS **2.** *Bible a)* one of the four Evangelists, the reputed author of the second Gospel: also *Saint Mark*: his day is Apr. 25 *b)* the second book of the New Testament, telling the story of Jesus' life

mark¹ (märk) n. [ME. < OE. *mearc*, orig., boundary, hence boundary sign, hence sign, akin to G. *mark*, boundary, boundary mark, *marke*, a token, mark < IE. base **mereĝ-*, edge, boundary, whence L. *margo*, MARGIN, OIr. *mruig*, borderland] **1.** a visible trace or impression on a surface; specif., *a)* a line, dot, or other distinctive feature produced by drawing, coloring, stamping, etc. *b)* a spot, stain, scratch, blemish, mar, bruise, dent, etc. **2.** a sign, symbol, or indication; specif., *a)* a printed or written sign or stroke [punctuation *marks*] *b)* a brand, label, seal, tag, etc. put on an article to show the owner, maker, etc. *c)* a sign or indication of some quality, character, etc. [politeness is a *mark* of good upbringing] *d)* a letter or figure used in schools, etc. to show quality of work or behavior; grade; rating [a *mark* of B in history] *e)* a cross or other sign made on a document as a substitute for a signature by a person unable to write **3.** a standard of quality, proficiency, propriety, etc. [failing to come up to the *mark*] **4.** importance; distinction; eminence [a man of *mark*] **5.** impression; influence [to leave one's *mark* in history] **6.** *a)* a visible object of known position, serving as a guide or point of reference [a tower as a *mark* for fliers] **7.** a line, dot, notch, etc. used to indicate position, as on a graduated scale **8.** *a)* an object aimed at; target *b)* an object desired or worked for; end; aim; goal **9.** *a)* a person against whom an attack, criticism, ridicule, etc. is directed *b)* [Slang] an intended victim of a swindle **10.** a taking notice; heed **11.** [Archaic] *a)* a boundary, border, or borderland; march *b)* among Germanic peoples in earlier times, land held or worked in common by a community **12.** *Naut. a)* one of the knots, bits of leather, or colored cloth placed at intervals on a lead line to indicate depths in fathoms *b)* *same as* PLIMSOLL MARK **13.** *Sports a)* the starting line of a race *b)* a spare or a strike in bowling —vt. **1.** to put or make a mark or marks on **2.** to identify or designate by or as by a mark or marks [abilities that *mark* one for success] **3.** to trace, make, or produce by or as by marks; draw, write, record, etc. **4.** to show or indicate by a mark or marks **5.** to show plainly; manifest; make clear or perceptible [a smile *marking* happiness] **6.** to set off as distinctive; distinguish; characterize [scientific discoveries that *marked* the 19th century] **7.** to observe; note; take notice of; heed [*mark* my words] **8.** to give a grade or grades to; rate [to *mark* examination papers] **9.** to put price tags on (merchandise) **10.** to keep (score, etc.); record —vi. **1.** to make a mark or marks **2.** to observe; take note **3.** *Games* to keep score —SYN. see SIGN —**beside the mark 1.** not striking the point aimed at **2.** not to the point; irrelevant —(**God**) **save the mark!** an

exclamation of humorous astonishment, irony, contempt, etc. —**hit the mark** 1. to achieve one's aim; be successful in one's attempt 2. to be accurate; be right —**make one's mark** to achieve success or fame —**mark down** 1. to make a note of; write down; record ☆2. to mark for sale at a reduced price —**mark off** (or **out**) to mark the limits of; demarcate —**mark out for** to select for or note as selected for —**mark time** 1. to keep time while at a halt by lifting the feet alternately as if marching 2. to suspend progress for a time, as while awaiting developments —**mark up** 1. to cover with marks ☆2. to mark for sale at an increased price 3. to add overhead and profit to the cost of in order to arrive at the selling price —**miss the mark** 1. to fail in achieving one's aim; be unsuccessful in one's attempt 2. to be inaccurate —**wide of the mark** 1. not striking the point aimed at 2. not to the point; irrelevant

mark² (märk) *n.* [ME. *marke* < OE. *marc* < ON. *mǫrk*, a half-pound of silver, mark, akin to prec.: orig. prob. in reference to symbol on the balance, later on the silver bar] 1. formerly, a European unit of weight for gold and silver, equal to about eight ounces 2. a coin or money of account, orig. equivalent in value to about eight ounces of silver; specif., *a*) an obsolete Scottish silver coin *b*) a monetary unit of the old German Empire, superseded by the reichsmark, and of East Germany: see MONETARY UNITS, table 3. *same as* DEUTSCHE MARK 4. *same as* MARKKA

Mark Antony *see* ANTONY

☆**mark·down** (märk′doun′) *n.* 1. a marking for sale at a reduced price 2. the amount of reduction in price

marked (märkt) *adj.* having a mark or marks (in various senses) 2. singled out to be watched or looked for as an object of suspicion, hostility, etc. [a *marked* man] 3. noticeable; obvious; appreciable; distinct; conspicuous [a *marked* change in behavior] —**mark·ed·ly** (mär′kid lē) *adv.* —**mark′ed·ness** *n.*

mark·er (mär′kər) *n.* a person or thing that marks; specif., *a*) a person who keeps score in a game *b*) a device for keeping score *c*) a device for marking lines, as on a tennis court *d*) a bookmark *e*) a memorial tablet or gravestone ☆*f*) a milestone or similar sign

mar·ket (mär′kit) *n.* [ME. < ONormFr. < L. *mercatus*, trade, marketplace, pp. of *mercari*, to trade < *merx* (gen. *mercis*), wares, merchandise < ? IE. base **merk-*, to seize] 1. *a*) a gathering of people for buying and selling things, esp. provisions or livestock *b*) the people gathered *c*) the time of such a gathering 2. an open space or a building where goods are shown for sale, usually with stalls or booths for the various dealers [a meat *market*] 4. a region in which goods can be bought and sold [the Latin American *market*] 5. *a*) buying and selling; trade in goods, stocks, etc. [an active *market*] *b*) trade in a specified commodity [the wheat *market*] *c*) a place where such trade is carried on *d*) the group of people associated in such trade 6. *short for* STOCK MARKET 7. opportunity to sell, or demand [for goods or services] [a good *market* for new products] 8. opportunity to buy, or supply (of goods or services) [reduced labor *market*] 9. *same as:* *a*) MARKET PRICE *b*) MARKET VALUE —*vt.* 1. to send or take to market 2. to offer for sale 3. to sell —*vi.* 1. to deal in a market; buy or sell 2. to buy provisions for the home —**be in the market for** to be seeking to buy —**be on the market** to be offered for sale —**buyer's market** a state of trade favorable to the buyer (relatively heavy supply and low prices) —**put on the market** to offer for sale —**seller's market** a state of trade favorable to the seller (relatively heavy demand and high prices) —**mar′ket·er** *n.* —**mar′ket·eer′** (-kə tir′) *n.*

mar·ket·a·ble (-ə b'l) *adj.* 1. *a*) that can be sold; fit for sale *b*) readily salable 2. of buying or selling [*marketable* value] —**mar′ket·a·bil′i·ty** *n.*

mar·ket·ing (-iŋ) *n.* 1. the act of buying or selling in a market 2. all business activity involved in the moving of goods from the producer to the consumer, including selling, advertising, packaging, etc.

market order an order to buy or sell goods, stock, etc. at the current market price

mar·ket·place (-plās′) *n.* 1. a place, esp. an open place, where goods are offered for sale 2. the world of trade, business, economic affairs, etc.: often used figuratively [the *marketplace* of ideas]

market price the price that a commodity brings when sold in a given market; prevailing price

market research the study of the demands or needs of consumers in relation to particular goods or services

market value the price that a commodity can be expected to bring when sold in a given market

Mark·ham (mär′kəm), (Charles) **Edwin** 1852–1940; U.S. poet

Mark·ham (mär′kəm), **Mount** mountain in Antarctica, near the SW edge of the Ross Ice Shelf: 14,270 ft.

mark·ing (mär′kiŋ) *n.* 1. the act of making a mark or marks 2. a mark or marks 3. the characteristic arrangement of marks or coloring, as of a plant or animal

mark·ka (märk′kä) *n., pl.* **-kaa** (-kä) [Finn. < Sw., *mark*: see MARK²] the monetary unit of Finland, equal to 100 pennia: see MONETARY UNITS, table

marks·man (märks′mən) *n., pl.* **-men** (-mən) a person who shoots, esp. one who shoots well —**marks′man·ship′** *n.*

☆**mark·up** (märk′up′) *n.* 1. a marking for sale at an in-

creased price 2. the amount of increase in price 3. the amount added to the cost to cover overhead and profit in arriving at the selling price

marl¹ (märl) *n.* [ME. < OFr. *marle* < ML. *margila* (whence G. *mergel*), dim. of L. *marga*, marl < Gaul.] 1. a mixture of clay, sand, and limestone in varying proportions, that is soft and crumbly and usually contains shell fragments 2. any loose, earthy, crumbly deposit 3. [Poet.] earth —*vt.* to cover or fertilize with marl —**marl′y** *adj.*

marl² (märl) *vt.* [Du. *marlen*, prob. freq. < MDu. *marren*, to lash, bind, akin to MHG. *merren*, to hinder, fasten < IE. base *mer-, to disturb, anger, whence MAR] to bind or wind (rope, etc.) with marline, taking a hitch at each turn

Marl·bor·ough (märl′bur′ō, -ə; *Brit.* môl′bər ə), 1st Duke of, (*John Churchill*) 1650–1722; Eng. general & statesman

mar·lin (mär′lin) *n., pl.* **-lin, -lins**: see PLURAL, II, D, 2 [< MARLINESPIKE: from the shape] any of several large, slender, deep-sea fishes (genus *Makaira*) related to the sailfish and spearfish, esp. the **blue marlin** (*Makaira nigricans*) of the Atlantic

mar·line (mär′lin) *n.* [Du. *marlijn*, altered (after *lijn*, LINE¹) < *marling* < *marlen*: see MARL²] a small cord of two loosely twisted strands, used for winding around the ends of ropes or cables to prevent fraying: also **mar′lin, mar′ling** (-liŋ)

mar·line·spike, mar·lin·spike (-spīk′) *n.* a pointed iron instrument for separating the strands of a rope in splicing or marling: also **mar′ling·spike′**

Mar·lowe (mär′lō) 1. **Christopher,** 1564–93; Eng. dramatist & poet 2. **Julia,** (born *Sarah Frances Frost; Mrs. E. H. Sothern*) 1865?–1950; U.S. actress, born in England

mar·ma·lade (mär′mə lād′) *n.* [OFr. *marmelade* < Port. *marmelada*, orig., confection of quinces < *marmelo*, quince < L. *melimelum* < Gr. *melimēlon*, sweet apple < *meli*, honey + *mēlon*, apple] a jamlike preserve made by boiling the pulp, and usually the sliced-up rinds, of oranges or some other fruits with sugar

marmalade tree a tropical American evergreen tree (*Calocarpum sapota*) of the sapodilla family, bearing a plumlike fruit used for preserving: also called **marmalade plum**

Mar·ma·ra (mär′mə rə), **Sea of** sea between European & Asiatic Turkey, connected with the Black Sea by the Bosporus & with the Aegean by the Dardanelles: c. 4,300 sq. mi.: also sp. **Marmora** See DARDANELLES, map

Mar·mo·la·da (mär′mō lä′dä) highest peak of the Dolomites, N Italy: 10,965 ft.

mar·mo·re·al (mär môr′ē əl) *adj.* [< L. *marmoreus* < *marmor*, marble + -AL] 1. of marble 2. like marble; cold, white, smooth, hard, etc. Also **mar·mo′re·an** —**mar·mo′re·al·ly** *adv.*

mar·mo·set (mär′mə zet′, -set′) *n.* [ME. < OFr. *marmouset*, grotesque figure < ?: form prob. infl. by *marmouser*, to mumble, grumble, of echoic orig.] any of various very small monkeys (family Callithricidae) of South and Central America, with thick, soft, variously colored fur and a nonprehensile tail

MARMOSET
(body to 15 in. long, tail to 17 in. long)

mar·mot (mär′mət) *n.* [Fr. *marmotte* < earlier *marmottaine*, prob. < L. *mus montanus*, mountain mouse] any of a group of thick-bodied, gnawing and burrowing rodents (genus *Marmota*) with coarse fur and a short, bushy tail, as the woodchuck

Marne (märn) river in NE France, flowing northwest into the Seine at Paris: scene of two World War I battles in which German offensives were checked

Ma·roc (må rôk′) *Fr.* name of MOROCCO

Mar·o·nite (mar′ə nīt′) *n.* [ML. *Maronita* < *Maro* (lit., master), 5th c. Syrian monk, founder of the sect] a member of a Christian Uniate sect, chiefly in Lebanon, with a patriarch recognized by the Pope

ma·roon¹ (mə rōōn′) *n., adj.* [Fr. *marron*, chestnut, chestnut color < It. *marrone*] dark brownish red

ma·roon² (mə rōōn′) *n.* [Fr. *marron* < AmSp. *cimarrón*, wild, unruly < OSp. *cimarra*, thicket] 1. in the West Indies and Surinam, *a*) orig., a fugitive Negro slave *b*) a descendant of such slaves 2. [Rare] a marooned person —*vt.* 1. to put (a person) ashore in some desolate place, as a desert island, and abandon him there, as pirates or mutineers sometimes did 2. to leave abandoned, isolated, or helpless —*vi.* ☆formerly, in the South, to camp out or picnic for several days

mar·plot (mär′plät′) *n.* a person or, sometimes, a thing that mars or spoils some plan by officious interference

Marq. 1. Marquess 2. Marquis

Mar·quand (mär′kwänd), **J(ohn) P(hillips)** 1893–1960; U.S. novelist

marque¹ (märk) *n.* [ME. *mark* < MFr. *marque* < Pr. *marca*, seizure, reprisal < *marcar*, to seize as a pledge < *marc*, token of pledge < Gmc.: see MARK¹] reprisal: obsolete except in **letters of marque**

marque² (märk) *n.* [Fr., a sign < *marquer*, to mark < OIt. *marcare* < *marca*, a mark < Gmc. *marka: see MARK¹] a distinctive nameplate or emblem used to identify an automobile

mar·quee (mär kē′) *n.* [false sing. < Fr. *marquise* (misunderstood as pl.), an awning, lit., marquise, orig. a canopy over an officer's tent: reason for name uncertain] **1.** [Chiefly Brit.] a large tent with open sides, esp. one used for some outdoor entertainment ☆**2.** a rooflike structure or awning projecting over an entrance, as to a theater

Mar·que·san (mär kā′z'n, -kā′s'n) *n.* **1.** any of the aboriginal people of the Marquesas Islands **2.** their Polynesian language —*adj.* **1.** of the Marquesas Islands or their people **2.** of Marquesan

Mar·que·sas Islands (mär kā′zəs, -səz) group of islands in French Polynesia, in E South Pacific: 492 sq. mi.; pop. 4,800: also *sp.* **Marquezas Islands**

mar·quess (mär′kwis) *n.* [see MARQUIS] **1.** a British nobleman ranking above an earl and below a duke **2.** same as MARQUIS —**mar′quess·ate** (-kwə zit) *n.*

Marquess of Queensbury rules [after 8th Marquess of *Queensbury* (1844–1900), who supervised their formulation, c. 1867] the basic rules of modern boxing, providing for the use of gloves, the division of a match into rounds, etc.

mar·que·try, mar·que·terie (mär′kə trē) *n.* [Fr. *marqueterie* < *marqueter*, to spot, inlay < *marque*, a mark: see MARK[1]] decorative inlaid work of wood, ivory, metal, etc., used in furniture and flooring

Mar·quette (mär kct′), **Jacques** (zhȧk) 1637–75; Fr. Jesuit missionary & explorer in N. America: called *Père Marquette*

mar·quis (mär′kwis; *Fr.* mȧr kē′) *n.*, *pl.* **-quis·es**; Fr. **-quis′** (-kē′) [ME. *markis* < OFr. *marchis* (later *marquis*) < ML. *marchisus*, prefect of a frontier town < *marca*, a borderland < Frank. *marka*: see MARK[1]] in some countries of Europe, a nobleman ranking above an earl or count and below a duke: cf. MARQUESS —**mar′quis·ate** (-kwə zit) *n.*

Mar·quis (mär′kwis), **Don**(**ald Robert Perry**) 1878–1937; U.S. humorist & journalist

mar·quise (mär kēz′; *Fr.* mȧr kēz′) *n.* [Fr., fem. of *marquis*] **1.** *a)* the wife or widow of a marquis *b)* a lady whose rank in her own right equals that of a marquis **2.** *same as* MARQUEE **3.** *a)* a ring with jewels set in the shape of a pointed oval *b)* a gem cut in this shape, esp. a diamond

mar·qui·sette (mär′ki zct′, -kwi-) *n.* [dim. of Fr. *marquise*, awning: cf. MARQUEE] a thin, meshlike fabric used for curtains, dresses, etc.

Mar·ra·kech, Mar·ra·kesh (mə rä′kesh, mar′ə kesh′) city in C Morocco; traditional S capital: pop. 265,000

Mar·ra·no (mə rä′nō) *n.*, *pl.* **-nos** [Sp., lit., swine (expression of contempt) < Ar. *muharram*, forbidden thing: or < ? Heb. *mar′ē*, appearance + Sp. ending] [*also* **m-**] in the Spanish Inquisition, a Jew forced to profess Christianity in order to escape death or persecution, often observing Judaism secretly

mar·riage (mar′ij) *n.* [ME. *mariage* < OFr. < *marier*: see MARRY[1]] **1.** the state of being married; relation between husband and wife; married life; wedlock; matrimony **2.** the act of marrying; wedding **3.** the rite or form used in marrying **4.** any close or intimate union **5.** the king and queen of a suit, as in pinochle

SYN.—**marriage** refers to the state of, or relation between, a man and woman who have become husband and wife or to the ceremony marking this union; **matrimony**, a formal word, applies specif. to the religious sacrament of marriage and stresses the rights and obligations of the marriage state *[the bonds of holy matrimony]*; **wedlock** now applies specif. to marriage as a legal relationship *[a child born out of wedlock]*; **wedding** refers specif. to the marriage ceremony and connotes festivities of one sort or another; **nuptials** is a highly formal, sometimes affected, term implying an elaborate ceremony, pomp, etc.

mar·riage·a·ble (mar′i jə b'l) *adj.* **1.** old enough to get married **2.** suitable for marriage *[of a marriageable age]* —**mar′riage·a·bil′i·ty** *n.*

marriage broker a person whose occupation is arranging marriages for others

marriage of convenience marriage entered into from calculated self-interest or expediency

marriage portion *same as* DOWRY

mar·ried (mar′ēd) *adj.* **1.** living together as husband and wife; joined in wedlock **2.** having a husband or wife **3.** of marriage or married people; connubial; conjugal **4.** closely or intimately joined —*n.* a married person: chiefly in **young marrieds**

mar·ron (mar′ən; *Fr.* mȧ rōn′) *n.* [Fr. < It. *marrone*, chestnut] a large, sweet European chestnut, often used in confectionery

‡**mar·rons gla·cés** (mȧ rōn′ glȧ sā′) [Fr.] marrons in syrup or glazed with sugar; candied chestnuts

mar·row (mar′ō) *n.* [ME. *merow* < OE. *mearg*, akin to G. *mark*, marrow < IE. base *moʒgho-*, marrow, brains, whence Sans. *majján-*, marrow] **1.** the soft, vascular, fatty tissue that fills the cavities of most bones **2.** the innermost, essential, or choicest part; pith **3.** vitality **4.** [Brit.] *same as* VEGETABLE MARROW —**mar′row·y** *adj.*

marrow bean a plump-seeded strain of the common field bean (*Phaseolus vulgaris*), grown for its dry, edible seeds

mar·row·bone (-bōn′) *n.* **1.** a bone containing marrow, esp. one used in cooking **2.** [*pl.*] the knees: humorous usage

mar·row·fat (-fat′) *n.* a variety of large, rich pea: also **marrowfat pea, marrow pea**

☆**marrow squash** any variety of oblong squash with a hard, smooth rind

Mar·rue·cos (mär′we′kôs) *Sp. name of* MOROCCO

mar·ry[1] (mar′ē) *vt.* **-ried, -ry·ing** [ME. *marien* < OFr. *marier* < L. *maritare* < *maritus*, a husband, married, prob. < IE. base *meri*, young wife, akin to *meryo*, young man, whence Sans. *márya-*, man, young man, suitor] **1.** *a)* to join as husband and wife; unite in wedlock *b)* to join (a man) to a woman as her husband, or (a woman) to a man as his wife **2.** to take as husband or wife; take in marriage **3.** to join closely or intimately; unite —*vi.* **1.** to get married; take a husband or wife **2.** to enter into a close or intimate relationship; unite —**marry off** to give in marriage: said of a parent or guardian —**mar′ri·er** *n.*

mar·ry[2] (mar′ē) *interj.* [euphemistic respelling of (the Virgin) MARY] [Archaic or Dial.] an exclamation of surprise, anger, etc., sometimes a mere intensive

Mar·ry·at (mar′ē ət), **Frederick** 1792–1848; Eng. naval officer & novelist

Mars (märz) [L.] **1.** *Rom. Myth.* the god of war: identified with the Greek Ares **2.** *a personification of* war **3.** a planet of the solar system, fourth in distance from the sun, notable for its red color: diameter, c. 4,200 mi.; diurnal rotation, 24 hrs., 37 min.; year, 687 days; symbol, ♂

Mar·sa·la (mär sä′lä) *n.* [< *Marsala*, seaport in W Sicily] a light, sweet white wine orig. from Sicily

Mar·seil·laise (mär′sə läz′; *Fr.* mȧr se yez′) [Fr., lit., of Marseille: first sung by Marseille volunteers] the national anthem of France, composed by Rouget de Lisle in 1792 during the French Revolution

Mar·seille (mȧr se′y′; *E.* mär sā′) seaport in SE France, on the Gulf of Lions: pop. 778,000

Mar·seilles (mär sā′; *chiefly Brit.*, -sälz′; *for n.*, -sālz′) *Eng. sp. of* MARSEILLE —*n.* a thick, strong, figured or striped cotton cloth with a raised weave, somewhat resembling piqué: originally made in Marseille

marsh (märsh) *n.* [ME. *mersch* < OE. *merisc*, akin to MLowG. *mersch, marsch* (whence G. *marsch*) < IE. base *mori*, sea, whence MARE[2]] a tract of low, wet, soft land; swamp; bog; morass; fen

Marsh (märsh), **Reginald** 1898–1954; U.S. painter

Mar·shal (mär′shəl) [< ff.] a masculine name

mar·shal (mär′shəl) *n.* [ME. *muresшul* < OFr. *mareschal* < Frank. *marhskalk* or OHG. *marahscalh*, lit., horse servant (whence ML. *marescalcus*) < *marah*, horse (akin to OE. *mearh*, horse: see MARE[1]) + *scalh*, servant < IE. base *skel-*, to spring] **1.** orig., a groom or, later, a master of the horse in a medieval royal household **2.** a high official of a royal household or court, as in medieval times, in charge of military affairs, ceremonies, etc. **3.** a military commander; specif., *a) same as* FIELD MARSHAL *b)* in various foreign armies, a general officer of the highest rank *c)* an officer of the highest rank in the British Royal Air Force **4.** an official in charge of ceremonies, processions, rank and order, etc. who arranges the order of march ☆**5.** an officer of various kinds in the U.S.; specif., *a)* a Federal officer appointed to a judicial district to carry out court orders and perform functions like those of a sheriff *b)* a minor officer of the law in some cities *c)* the head, or a high-ranking officer, of a police or fire department in some cities —*vt.* **-shaled** *or* **-shalled, -shal·ing** *or* **-shal·ling 1.** to arrange (troops, things, ideas, etc.) in order; array; dispose *[to marshal forces for battle]* **2.** *a)* to direct as a marshal; manage *b)* to lead or guide ceremoniously —**mar′shal·cy, mar′shal·ship′** *n.*

Mar·shall (mär′shəl) **1. George C**(**atlett**), 1880–1959; U.S. general & statesman; U.S. Army chief of staff (1939–45); secretary of state (1947–49) **2. John**, 1755–1835; U.S. jurist; chief justice of the U.S. (1801–35) **3. Thur·good** (thur′good), 1908– ; U.S. jurist; associate justice, Supreme Court (1967–)

Marshall Islands [after John *Marshall*, Brit. explorer (1788)] group of islands in the W Pacific, east of the Caroline Islands: formerly a Jap. mandate, since 1947 part of the U.S. Trust Territory of the Pacific Islands: c. 70 sq. mi.; pop. 18,000

Mar·shal·sea (mär′shəl sē′) [ME. *marschalcie* < Anglo-Fr. *mareschalcie* < ML. *marescalcia*: see MARSHAL] **1.** a British court of justice, abolished in 1849, under the marshal of the royal household **2.** a prison in Southwark, London, for debtors, etc., abolished in 1842

marsh elder ☆any of a genus (*Iva*) of N. American plants of the composite family, growing in salt marshes and moist soil

marsh gas a gaseous product, chiefly methane, formed from decomposing vegetable matter, as in marshes

marsh hawk a large, gray, American hawk (*Circus cyaneus*) that nests on the ground and preys on mice, frogs, snakes, etc.

marsh hen any of several birds, as the rail, coot, etc., living or feeding in marshy areas

marsh·mal·low (märsh′mel′ō, -mal′ō) *n.* **1.** orig., a confection made from the root of the marsh mallow **2.** a

---

fat, āpe, cär; ten, ēven; is, bīte; gō, hôrn, tōōl, look; oil, out; up, fur; get; joy; yet; chin; she; thin, *th*en; zh, leisure; ŋ, ring; ə for *a* in *ago*, *e* in *agent*, *i* in *sanity*, *o* in *comply*, *u* in *focus*; ' as in *able* (ā′b'l); Fr. bȧl; ë, Fr. coeur; ö, Fr. feu; Fr. mon; ὃ, Fr. coq; ü, Fr. duc; ʀ, Fr. cri; H, G. ich; kh, G. doch. See inside front cover. ☆ Americanism; ‡foreign; *hypothetical; <derived from

soft, spongy confection made of sugar, starch, corn syrup, and gelatin, coated with powdered sugar

marsh mallow 1. a pink-flowered, perennial, European plant (*Althaea officinalis*) of the mallow family: the root was formerly used for marshmallows and is sometimes used in medicine 2. *same as* ROSE MALLOW

marsh marigold a marsh plant (*Caltha palustris*) of the buttercup family, with bright-yellow flowers and shiny, circular leaves, sometimes used as greens

marsh·y (mär'shē) *adj.* **marsh'i·er, marsh'i·est** 1. of, consisting of, or containing a marsh or marshes 2. like a marsh; soft and wet; boggy; swampy 3. growing in marshes —**marsh'i·ness** *n.*

Mar·ston (mär'stən), **John** 1575?-1634; Eng. dramatist & satirist

Marston Moor moor in Yorkshire, N England: site of a battle (July, 1644) of the English civil war in which Royalist forces were routed by the Parliamentarians

mar·su·pi·al (mär sōō'pē əl) *adj.* 1. of or like a marsupium, or pouch 2. of an order (Marsupialia) of mammals that lack a placenta and have an external abdominal pouch containing the teats: the incompletely developed offspring nurses within the marsupium of the mother for several months after birth to complete its development —*n.* an animal of this kind, as a kangaroo, bandicoot, opossum, wombat, etc.

mar·su·pi·um (-əm) *n., pl.* **-pi·a** (-ə) [ModL. < L. < Gr. *marsypion*, dim. of *marsypos*, a pouch, bag] 1. a fold of skin on the abdomen of a female marsupial, forming a pouch in which the young are carried and complete their development 2. a structure like this, in some crustaceans, fishes, etc.

mart (märt) *n.* [ME. *marte* < MDu., var. of *markt*, MARKET] 1. a market, or trading center 2. [Obs.] *a*) a fair *b*) buying and selling; bargaining *c*) a bargain

Mar·ta·ban (mär'tə bän'), **Gulf of** part of the Andaman Sea, on the S coast of Burma

mar·ta·gon (mär'tə gən) *n.* [ME. < Fr. < Turk. *martagān*, a turban] a Turk's-cap lily (*Lilium martagon*) having white or purple flowers

Mar·tel (mär tel'), **Charles** 688?-741 A.D.; ruler of Austrasia (714-741) & of all the Franks (720-741): checked the Moorish invasion of Europe with a decisive victory near Tours (732): grandfather of CHARLEMAGNE

mar·tel·lo tower (mär tel'ō) [It. *martello*, a hammer, folk-etym. substitution for *mortella*, a tower < *Mortello*, in Corsica, where such a tower was attacked by the English fleet in 1794] [*occas.* M-] a circular fort of masonry, formerly built on coasts to protect against invaders: also **mar·tel'lo** *n.*

mar·ten (mär't'n) *n., pl.* **-tens, -ten**: see PLURAL, II, D, 1 [ME. *martren* < OFr. *martrine*, adj. < *martre*, marten < Frank. *martar*, akin to G. *marder*, OE. *mearth*] 1. any of several small, flesh-eating mammals (genus *Martes*) like a weasel but larger, that live chiefly in trees and have a long, slender body, short legs, and soft, thick, valuable fur 2. the fur

mar·tens·ite (mär't'nz it') *n.* [after A. *Martens* (?-1914), G. metallurgist] a very hard, brittle, solid solution of iron and carbon or the carbide of iron, Fe₃C, into which hot steel turns when suddenly chilled by cold water —**mar'ten·sit'ic** (-tən zit'ik) *adj.*

MARTEN
(body to 2 ft. long, tail to 1 ft. long)

Mar·tha (mär'thə) [LL.(Ec.) < Gr.(Ec.) < Aram. *Mārthā*, lit., lady] 1. a feminine name: equiv. Fr. *Marthe*, It. & Sp. *Marta* 2. *Bible* sister of Lazarus and Mary, rebuked by Jesus for doing housework while he talked with Mary: Luke 10:40

Martha's Vineyard [after a *Martha* Gosnold and the wild grapes there] island off the SE coast of Mass., south of Cape Cod: c. 100 sq. mi.; pop. 6,000

Mar·tí (mär tē'), **Jo·sé (Julian)** 1853-95; Cuban poet, essayist, & revolutionary patriot

Mar·tial (mär'shəl) (*Marcus Valerius Martialis*) 40?-104? A.D.; Rom. epigrammatist & poet, born in Spain

mar·tial (mär'shəl) *adj.* [ME. *martialle* < L. *martialis*, of Mars] 1. of or suitable for war [*martial songs*] 2. showing a readiness or eagerness to fight; warlike 3. of the army, navy, or military life; military [*martial law*] 4. [M-] under the dire influence of Mars —**mar'tial·ism** *n.* —**mar'tial·ist** *n.* —**mar'tial·ly** *adv.*

SYN.—**martial** refers to anything connected with or characteristic of war or armies, connoting esp. pomp, discipline, etc. [*martial music, martial law*]; **warlike** stresses the bellicose or aggressive nature or temperament that leads to war or results from preparations for war [a *warlike* nation]; **military** applies to anything having to do with armies or soldiers [*military* uniforms, police, etc.] —ANT. peacelike, pacifist

martial law temporary rule by the military authorities over the civilian population, as in an area of military operations in time of war, or when civil authority has broken down: distinguished from MILITARY LAW

Mar·tian (mär'shən) *adj.* [L. *Martius* + -AN] of Mars (god or planet) —*n.* an imagined inhabitant of the planet Mars, as in science fiction

Mar·tin (mär't'n) [Fr. < L. *Martinus* < *Mars* (gen. *Martis*), Mars: hence, lit., warlike] 1. a masculine name 2. Saint, 315?-397? A.D.; bishop of Tours: his day is MARTINMAS: also called St. **Martin of Tours** 3. **Homer Dodge**, 1836-97; U.S. painter

mar·tin (mär't'n) *n.* [Fr., prob. < prec.] 1. any of several birds (genus *Progne*) of the swallow family, with a stout bill 2. an old-world, swallowlike bird (*Delichon urbica*), with a deeply forked tail 3. any of various similar birds

Mar·ti·neau (mär't'n ō') 1. **Harriet**, 1802-76; Eng. writer 2. **James**, 1805-1900; Eng. theologian: brother of *prec.*

Mar·ti·nel·li (mär't'n el'ē), **Gio·van·ni** (jō vä'nē) 1885-1969; U.S. operatic tenor, born in Italy

mar·ti·net (mär't'n et', mär't'n et) *n.* [after Gen. Jean *Martinet*, 17th-c. Fr. drillmaster] 1. a very strict military disciplinarian 2. any very strict disciplinarian or stickler for rigid regulations

mar·tin·gale (mär't'n gāl') *n.* [Fr., prob. < Sp. *almártaga*, a check, rein < Ar.] 1. the strap of a horse's harness passing from the noseband to the girth between the forelegs, to keep the horse from rearing or throwing back its head 2. *a*) a lower stay for the jib boom or flying jib boom of a sailing vessel, to bear the strain of the head stays *b*) *same as* DOLPHIN STRIKER 3. any system of trying to make up one's losses in previous bets by doubling or otherwise increasing the amount bet Also **mar'tin·gal'** (-gal')

☆**mar·ti·ni** (mär tē'nē) *n., pl.* **-nis** [altered (prob. as assumed sing.) < earlier *Martines*: reason for name unc.] [*also* M-] a cocktail made of gin (or vodka) and dry vermouth, usually served with a green olive or a twist of lemon peel

Mar·ti·nique (mär'tə nēk') island in the Windward group of the West Indies; overseas department of France: 420 sq. mi.; pop. 325,000; cap. Fort-de-France

Mar·tin·mas (mär't'n məs) *n.* [see -MAS] Saint Martin's day, a church festival held on November 11

mart·let (märt'lit) *n.* [Fr. *martelet*, prob. < *martinet*, dim. of *martin*] 1. a martin 2. *Heraldry* a representation of a bird without feet, used as a crest or bearing

mar·tyr (mär'tər) *n.* [ME. *martir* < OE. < LL.(Ec.) < Gr. *martyr, martys*, a witness, in LGr.(Ec.), martyr < IE. base *(s)mer-*, to remember, care, whence L. *memor*, mindful, Sans. *smárati*, (he) remembers] 1. a person who chooses to suffer or die rather than give up his faith or his principles; person tortured or killed because of his beliefs 2. a person who suffers great pain or misery for a long time 3. a person who assumes an attitude of self-sacrifice or suffering in order to arouse feelings of pity, guilt, etc. in others —*vt.* 1. to put to death or torture for adherence to a belief 2. to torture; make suffer greatly; persecute

mar·tyr·dom (-dəm) *n.* [ME. *martirdom* < OE. *martyrdom*] 1. the state of being a martyr 2. the death or sufferings of a martyr 3. severe, long-continued suffering; torment; torture

mar·tyr·ize (mär'tə rīz') *vt.* **-ized', -iz'ing** [ME. *martirizen* < LL. *martyrizare*] to make a martyr of —*vi.* to be or become a martyr —**mar'tyr·i·za'tion** *n.*

mar·tyr·ol·o·gy (mär'tə räl'ə jē) *n., pl.* **-gies** [ML. *martyrologium* < LGr. *martyrologion*: see MARTYR & -LOGY] 1. a list of martyrs 2. a historical account of religious martyrs, esp. Christian martyrs 3. such accounts collectively 4. the branch of ecclesiastical history dealing with the lives of martyrs —**mar'tyr·ol'o·gist** *n.*

mar·tyr·y (mär'tər ē) *n., pl.* **-ies** [ME. *martyrye* < LL.(Ec.) *martyrium* < LGr.(Ec.) *martyrion*] a shrine built in memory of a martyr

mar·vel (mär'v'l) *n.* [ME. *mervaile* < OFr. *merveille*, a wonder < VL. *mirabilia*, wonderful things, orig. neut. pl. of L. *mirabilis*, wonderful < *mirari*, to wonder at, admire: for IE. base see SMILE] 1. a wonderful or astonishing thing; prodigy or miracle 2. [Archaic] astonishment —*vi.* -veled or -velled, -vel·ing or -vel·ling to be filled with admiring surprise; be amazed; wonder —*vt.* to wonder at or about (followed by a clause)

Mar·vell (mär'v'l), **Andrew** 1621-78; Eng. poet

mar·vel-of-Pe·ru (mär'v'l əv pə rōō') *n. same as* FOUR-O'-CLOCK

mar·vel·ous (mär'v'l əs) *adj.* [ME. *merveilous* < OFr. *merveillos* < *merveille*: see MARVEL] 1. causing wonder; surprising, astonishing, or extraordinary 2. so extraordinary as to be improbable, incredible, or miraculous 3. [Colloq.] very good; fine; splendid Also, chiefly Brit. sp., **mar'vel·lous** —**mar'vel·ous·ly** *adv.* —**mar'vel·ous·ness** *n.*

Mar·vin (mär'vin) [prob. ult. < Gmc. *mari*, sea + *winiz*, friend] a masculine name

Marx (märks), **Karl (Heinrich)** 1818-83; Ger. revolutionary leader, social philosopher, & political economist, in London after 1850; founder of modern socialism

Marx·ism (märk'siz'm) *n.* the system of thought developed by Karl Marx, his co-worker Friedrich Engels, and their followers: also **Marx'i·an·ism** See also SOCIALISM, COMMUNISM, DIALECTICAL MATERIALISM —**Marx'ist, Marx'i·an** *adj., n.*

Mar·y (mer'ē, mar'ē, mā'rē) [ME. *Marie* < OE. < LL.(Ec.) *Maria* < Gr. *Maria, Mariam* < Heb. *Miryām* or Aram. *Maryam*, lit., rebellion] 1. a feminine name: dim. *Mae, Muriella, May, Moll, Molly, Polly*; var. *Maria, Marie, Marilyn, Marion, Maureen, Miriam*; equiv. Fr. *Marie, Marion*, Ger., It., & Sp. *Maria*, Pol. *Marya* 2.

Mary I (*Mary Tudor*) 1516–58; queen of England (1553–58): daughter of HENRY VIII & CATHERINE OF ARAGON: wife of PHILIP II of Spain **3. Mary II** 1662–94; queen of England, Scotland, and Ireland (1689–94), ruling jointly with her husband, WILLIAM III: daughter of JAMES II **4.** *Bible a)* mother of Jesus: Matt. 1:18–25: often referred to as the (*Blessed*) *Virgin Mary, Saint Mary b)* sister of Martha and Lazarus: Luke 10:38–42 *c) same as* MARY MAGDALENE

Mary Janes ☆*a trademark for* low-heeled slippers, usually of patent leather with a strap across the instep, worn by little girls

Mar·y·land (mer′ə lənd) [after Queen Henrietta *Maria*, wife of CHARLES I] E State of the U.S., on the Atlantic: one of the 13 original States; 10,577 sq. mi.; pop. 3,922,000; cap. Annapolis: abbrev. **Md., MD**

Mary Magdalene *Bible* woman out of whom Jesus cast seven devils: Luke 8:2: usually identified with the repentant woman whom Jesus forgave: Luke 7:37 ff.

Mary, Queen of Scots (*Mary Stuart*) 1542–87; queen of Scotland (1542–67): beheaded

mar·zi·pan (mär′zi pan′) *n.* [G. < It. *marzapane*, confection, earlier, the small box containing it, small dry measure, certain weight < ML. *matapanus*, Venetian coin with figure of Christ on a throne < Ar. *mauthaban*, seated king (< *wathaba*, to sit)] a confection of ground almonds, sugar, and egg white made into a paste and variously shaped and colored

-mas (məs) *a combining form for* Mass *meaning* a (specified) festival or celebration [*Martinmas*]

Ma·sac·cio (mä sät′chō) (born *Tommaso Guidi*) 1401–29?; Florentine painter

Ma·sa·da (mə sä′də, mä sä dä′) ancient Jewish fortress in Israel, near the Dead Sea: site of a prolonged Roman siege (72–73 A.D.) resulting in a mass suicide by the Jews to avoid capture

Ma·sai (mä sī′) *n.* **1.** *pl.* **-sai′, -sais′** any member of a pastoral people of Kenya and Tanganyika **2.** their Eastern Sudanic language

Ma·sa·ryk (mä′sä rik; *E.* mas′ə rik) **1. Jan** (yän), 1886–1948; Czech statesman: son of *ff* **2. To·máš Gar·rigue** (tō′mäsh gå rēg′), 1850–1937; Czech statesman; 1st president of Czechoslovakia (1918–35)

Mas·ba·te (mäs bä′tē) island of the EC Philippines, west of Samar: 1,262 sq. mi.; pop. (with nearby small islands) 337,000

masc., mas. masculine

Mas·ca·gni (mäs kä′nyē), **Pie·tro** (pye′trō) 1863–1945; It. composer of operas

mas·ca·ra (mas kar′ə) *n.* [Sp. *máscara*, a mask < It. *maschera*: see MASK] a cosmetic preparation for coloring or darkening the eyelashes and eyebrows —*vt.* **-ca′raed, -ca′ra·ing** to put mascara on

Mas·ca·rene Islands (mas′kə rēn′) group of islands in the W Indian Ocean, east of Madagascar, including Mauritius & Réunion

mas·cle (mas′k'l) *n.* [ME. < OFr.: see MACLE] **1.** any of many small, diamond-shaped steel plates, linked together to make up a kind of 13th-cent. armor **2.** *Heraldry* a diamond-shaped figure with a diamond-shaped opening

☆**mas·con** (mäs′kän) *n.* [*mas*(*s*) *con*(*centration*)] a concentration of very dense material beneath the surface of the moon

mas·cot (mas′kät, -kət) *n.* [Fr. *mascotte* < Pr. *mascot*, dim. of *masco*, sorcerer (< ?): in pop. use < *La Mascotte* (1880), operetta by the Fr. composer Edmond Audran] any person, animal, or thing supposed to bring good luck by being present

mas·cu·line (mas′kyə lin) *adj.* [ME. *masculyn* < OFr. *masculin* < L. *masculinus* < *masculus*, male < *mas*, male] **1.** male; of men or boys **2.** having qualities regarded as characteristic of men and boys, as strength, vigor, boldness, etc.; manly; virile **3.** suitable to or characteristic of a man **4.** mannish: said of women **5.** *Gram.* designating or of the gender of words denoting or referring to males or things orig. regarded as male **6.** *Music* designating or of a cadence ending on an accented note or chord **7.** *Prosody* designating or of a rhyme of stressed final syllables (Ex.: hill, fill, enjoy, destroy) —*n. Gram.* **1.** the masculine gender **2.** a word or form in this gender —*SYN.* see MALE —**mas′cu·line·ly** *adv.* —**mas′cu·lin′i·ty** *n.*

mas·cu·lin·ize (-li nīz′) *vt.* **-ized′, -iz′ing** [< prec. + -IZE] to make masculine; esp., to produce male characteristics in (a female) —**mas′cu·lin′i·za′tion** *n.*

Mase·field (mās′fēld, māz′-), **John** 1878–1967; Eng. writer, esp. of poetry: poet laureate (1930–1967)

☆**ma·ser** (mā′zər) *n.* [*m*(*icrowave*) *a*(*mplification by*) *s*(*timulated*) *e*(*mission of*) *r*(*adiation*)] a device, operating at microwave, infrared, etc. frequencies, in which atoms in a crystal or a gas are concentrated, raised to a higher energy level by excitation, then radiation is emitted in a very narrow beam when the excited atoms return to their original energy level: see also LASER

Ma·se·ru (maz′ə rōō′) capital of Lesotho, in the NW part: pop. 10,000

mash (mash) *n.* [ME. *masshe-* < OE. *masc-*, in *mascwyrt*, mashwort, infused malt, akin to G. *meisch, maisch*, crushed grapes, infused malt < IE. base **meigh-*, to urinate, whence L. *mingere* (see MICTURATE)] **1.** crushed or ground malt or meal soaked in hot water for making wort, used in brewing beer **2.** a mixture of bran, meal, etc. in warm water, for feeding horses, cattle, etc. **3.** any soft mixture or mass —*vt.* [ME. *maschen* < the *n.*] **1.** to mix (crushed malt, etc.) in hot water for making wort **2.** to change into a soft or uniform mass by beating, crushing, etc. **3.** to crush and injure or damage ☆**4.** [Old Slang] to make sexual advances to; flirt with

mash·er (-ər) *n.* one that mashes; specif., *a*) a device for mashing vegetables, fruit, etc. ☆*b*) [Slang] a man who makes unwanted advances to women not acquainted with him, esp. in public places

Mash·had (mə shäd′) city in NE Iran: site of a Shiite shrine: pop. 312,000

mash·ie (mash′ē) *n.* [< ? Fr. *massue*, a club < VL. **mattiuca* < **mattea*: see MACE[1]] a golf club with a metal head and medium loft, for making shots of medium length: now usually called *number 5 iron*

Mas·i·nis·sa (mas′ə nis′ə) 238?–149? B.C.; Numidian king who fought as a Roman ally against Hannibal

mas·jid (mus′jid) *n.* [Ar.: see MOSQUE] a mosque

mask (mask, mäsk) *n.* [Fr. *masque* < It. *maschera, mascara*, a mask, prob. < Ar. *maskhara*, a clown, buffoonery] **1.** a covering for the face or part of the face, to conceal or disguise the identity **2.** anything that conceals or disguises **3.** a party, carnival, etc. where masks are worn; masquerade **4.** a person wearing a mask; masker **5.** a likeness of a person's face, or face and neck; specif., *a*) a sculptured or molded likeness of the face: cf. DEATH MASK *b*) a grotesque or comic representation of a face, worn to amuse or frighten, as at Halloween; falseface *c*) a sculptured head or face, often grotesque, used as an ornament on a building, gargoyle, etc. *d*) a figure of a head worn on the stage by an

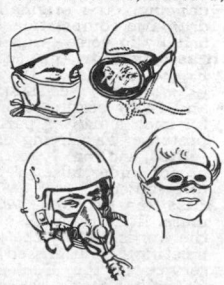

MASKS

ancient Greek or Roman actor to identify a character and amplify the voice **6.** a protective covering for the face or head, as a wire screen [fencer's *mask*] or respirator [gas *mask*] **7.** *a*) a covering for the mouth and nose used in administering an anesthetic or oxygen *b*) a piece of gauze, etc. worn over the mouth and nose to prevent infection of other people by exhaled matter **8.** the face or head of a dog, fox, etc. **9.** something serving to conceal artillery, military operations, etc. from observation; piece of camouflage **10.** an opaque border used to cover unwanted parts of a photograph or to alter its shape **11.** *same as* MASQUE (senses 2 & 3) **12.** *Zool.* a masklike formation about the head, as the enlarged lower lip of a dragonfly larva —*vt.* **1.** to conceal or cover with or as with a mask **2.** to conceal or disguise **3.** to make (a sound, smell, taste, etc.) less noticeable —*vi.* **1.** to put on a mask, as for a masquerade **2.** to hide or disguise one's true motives, character, etc.

masked (maskt, mäskt) *adj.* **1.** wearing a mask **2.** concealed, disguised, not apparent, etc. **3.** *Bot. same as* PERSONATE

masked ball a ball at which masks and fancy costumes are worn

mask·er (mas′kər, mäs′-) *n.* one who wears a mask; specif., a participant in a masque or masquerade

mask·ing tape (-kiŋ) an adhesive tape for covering and protecting margins, borders, etc., as during painting

mas·och·ism (mas′ə kiz'm, maz′-) *n.* [after Leopold von Sacher-*Masoch* (1835–95), Austrian writer in whose stories it is described] **1.** the getting of sexual pleasure from being dominated, mistreated, or hurt physically or otherwise by one's partner **2.** the getting of pleasure from suffering physical or psychological pain, inflicted by others or by oneself Cf. SADISM —**mas′och·ist** *n.* —**mas′och·is′tic** *adj.* —**mas′och·is′ti·cal·ly** *adv.*

ma·son (mā′s'n) *n.* [ME. < OFr. *maçon* < ML. *matio* < ? Frank. **mattjo* (akin to Sans. *matya*, club): see MATTOCK] **1.** a person whose work is building with stone, brick, concrete blocks, etc. **2.** [M-] *same as* FREEMASON —*vt.* to build of or reinforce with masonry

mason bee a solitary bee that builds its nest of clay, sand, mud, etc.

Ma·son-Dix·on line (mā′s'n dik′s'n) [after C. *Mason* & J. *Dixon*, who surveyed it, 1763–67] boundary line between Pa. & Md., regarded, before the Civil War, as separating the free States from the slave States or, now, the North from the South: also **Mason and Dixon's line**

Ma·son·ic (mə sän′ik) *adj.* [*also* m-] of Masons (Freemasons) or Masonry (Freemasonry)

☆**Ma·son·ite** (mā′s'n it′) [after W. H. *Mason* (1877–1947?), U.S. engineer] *a trademark for* a kind of hardboard

made from pressed wood fibers, used as building material, insulation, etc. —*n.* such hardboard

☆**Mason jar** [patented in 1858 by John L. *Mason* of New York] [*also* **m-**] a glass jar having a wide mouth and a screw top, used for preserving foods, esp. in home canning

ma·son·ry (mā′s'n rē) *n.*, *pl.* **-ries** [ME. *masonerie* < OFr. *maçonnerie* < *maçon*, MASON] **1.** the trade or art of a mason **2.** something built by a mason or masons; brickwork or stonework **3.** [*usually* M-] *same as* FREEMASONRY

mason wasp any of a number of solitary wasps (subfamily Eumeninae) that build urn-shaped nests of mud

Ma·so·ra, Ma·so·rah (mə sō′rə) *n.* [ModHeb. *māsōrāh*, tradition < LHeb. *māsōreth*] **1.** all the accumulated Jewish tradition concerning the correct Hebrew text of the Holy Scriptures **2.** the marginal notes on manuscripts of the Holy Scriptures embodying this tradition, compiled from the 2d to the 10th cent. A.D.

Mas·o·rete (mas′ə rēt′) *n.* [< LHeb. *māsōreth*] any of the Jewish scribes who compiled the Masora: also **Mas′o·rite′** (-rīt′) —**Mas′o·ret′ic** (-ret′ik) *adj.*

Mas·qaṭ (məs kät′) *Arabic name of* MUSCAT

masque (mask, mäsk) *n.* [see MASK] **1.** a masquerade; masked ball **2.** a form of dramatic entertainment popular among the aristocracy in England during the 16th and 17th cent., usually based on a mythical or allegorical theme, and emphasizing lavish costumes, scenery, music, dancing, etc.: originally it contained no dialogue **3.** a dramatic composition written for such an entertainment, usually in verse —**masqu′er** *n.*

mas·quer·ade (mas′kə rād′) *n.* [altered (after prec.) < Fr. *mascarade* < It. *mascarata*, dial. var. of *mascherata* (< *maschera*): see MASK] **1.** a ball or party at which masks and fancy costumes or disguises are worn **2.** a costume for such a ball or party **3.** *a)* a disguise, false show, or pretense *b)* a living or acting under false pretenses —*vi.* **-ad′ed, -ad′ing 1.** to take part in a masquerade **2.** to live or act under false pretenses; go about disguised —**mas′quer·ad′er** *n.*

Mass (mas) *n.* [ME. *masse* < OE. *mæsse* < LL.(Ec.) *missa*, mass, lit., dismissal, orig. pp. of L. *mittere*, to dismiss < the words said by the priest *ite, missa est* (*contio*), go, (the meeting) is dismissed [*also* **m-**] **1.** the celebration or service of the Eucharist, a sacrament of the Roman Catholic Church, consisting of a series of prayers and ceremonies: the term is also used in some High Anglican churches: see HIGH MASS, LOW MASS **2.** a musical setting for certain parts of this service See also BLACK MASS

mass (mas) *n.* [ME. *masse* < OFr. < L. *massa*, a lump, mass < Gr. *maza*, barley cake < *massein*, to knead < IE. base *mag̑-*, whence MAKE[1]] **1.** a quantity of matter forming a body of indefinite shape and size, usually of relatively large size; lump **2.** a large quantity or number [*a mass* of bruises] **3.** bulk; size; magnitude **4.** the main or larger part; majority **5.** *Painting* a large area or form of one color, shade, intensity, etc. **6.** *Pharmacy* the paste or plastic combination of drugs from which pills are made **7.** *Physics* the quantity of matter in a body as measured in its relation to inertia: mass is determined for a given body by dividing the weight of the body by the acceleration due to gravity: cf. MATTER (*n.* 2) —*adj.* **1.** *a)* of a large number of things; large-scale [*mass* production] *b)* of a large number of persons [*a mass* demonstration] **2.** of, characteristic of, or for the masses [*mass* education] —*vt., vi.* to gather or form into a mass —*SYN.* see BULK[1] —**in the mass** collectively; as a whole —**the masses** the great mass of common people; specif., the working people, or lower classes in the social order

Mass. Massachusetts

Mas·sa·chu·sett (mas′ə chōō′sit) *n.*, [Algonquian *Massa-adchu-es-et*, lit., at the big hill, with reference to the Blue Hills near Boston] **1.** *pl.* **-setts, -sett** a member of a tribe of Algonquian Indians who lived around Massachusetts Bay **2.** their Algonquian language Also **Mas′-sa·chu′set**

Mas·sa·chu·setts (-sits) New England State of the U.S.: one of the 13 original States; 8,257 sq. mi.; pop. 5,689,000; cap. Boston: abbrev. **Mass., MA**

Massachusetts Bay inlet of the Atlantic, on the E coast of Mass. See Cape COD, map

mas·sa·cre (mas′ə kər) *n.* [< OFr. *maçacre, macecle*, butchery, shambles < ?] **1.** *a)* the indiscriminate, merciless killing of a number of human beings *b)* a large-scale slaughter of animals **2.** [Colloq.] an overwhelming defeat, as in sports —*vt.* **-cred, -cring 1.** to kill indiscriminately and mercilessly and in large numbers **2.** [Colloq.] to defeat overwhelmingly —*SYN.* see SLAUGHTER —**mas′sa·crer** (-krər) *n.*

mas·sage (mə säzh′) *n.* [Fr. < *masser*, to massage < Ar. *massa*, to touch] a rubbing, kneading, etc. of part of the body, usually with the hands, as to stimulate circulation and make muscles or joints supple —*vt.* **-saged′, -sag′ing** to give a massage to —**mas·sag′er, mas·sag′ist** *n.*

mas·sa·sau·ga (mas′ə sô′gə) *n.* [< *Mississauga*, Ojibway name of river and Indian tribe in Ontario] a variety of small, gray or brownish rattlesnake (*Sistrurus catenatus*) found in swampy regions in the E and S U.S.

Mas·sa·soit (mas′ə soit′) 1580?-1661; chief of the Wampanoag Indians: signed a treaty with the Pilgrims at Plymouth in 1621

Mas·sa·wa (mäs sä′wä) seaport in Eritrea, N Ethiopia, on the Red Sea: pop. 25,000

☆**mass·cult** (mas′kult′) *n.* [MASS + CULT(URE)] [Colloq.] an artificial, commercialized culture popularized for the masses through the mass media

mass defect *Physics* the difference between the mass of an atom and the number of neutrons and protons in its nucleus (mass number): it can be either positive or negative and is expressed in atomic mass units

mas·sé (ma sā′) *n.* [Fr., pp. of *masser*, to make a massé shot < *masse*, billiard cue, lit., mace] a stroke in billiards made by hitting the cue ball off center with the cue held nearly vertically, usually so as to make the ball move in a curve around another ball before hitting the object ball: also **massé shot**

Mas·sé·na (ma sā nà′), **An·dré** (än drā′), prince d'Essling, 1758-1817; Fr. marshal under Napoleon I

Mas·se·net (mas′ə nā′, mäs ne′), **Jules** (**Émile Frédéric**) (zhül) 1842-1912; Fr. composer

mas·se·ter (ma sēt′ər) *n.* [ModL. < Gr. *masētēr*, a chewer < *masasthai*, to chew < IE. base **menth-*, whence MOUTH] either of a pair of large muscles in the angle of the lower jaw, which raise the jaw in chewing, etc. —**mas·se·ter·ic** (mas′ə ter′ik) *adj.*

mas·seur (ma sur′, mə-; Fr. mà sër′) *n.* [Fr. < *masser*: see MASSAGE] a man whose work is giving massages —**mas·seuse′** (-sooz′, -sooz′; Fr. -söz′) *n.fem.*

mas·si·cot (mas′i kät′) *n.* [ME. *masticote*, altered (after *mastik*, MASTIC) < MFr. < It. *marzacotto* < Sp. *mezacote* < Ar. *shabb qubṭi*, Coptic alum: see COPTIC] natural lead monoxide, PbO

mas·sif (ma sēf′, mas′if) *n.* [Fr., lit., solid: see MASSIVE] *Geol.* **1.** mountainous mass broken up into separate peaks and forming the backbone of a mountain range **2.** a diastrophic block of the earth's crust that is isolated by boundary faults and has shifted as a unit

Mas·sine (mà sēn′), **Lé·o·nide** (lā ô nēd′) 1896- ; U.S. ballet dancer & choreographer, born in Russia

Mas·sin·ger (mas′'n jər), **Philip** 1583-1640; Eng. dramatist

Mas·si·nis·sa (mas′ə nis′ə) *same as* MASINISSA

mas·sive (mas′iv) *adj.* [Fr. *massif*, with change of suffix (see -IVE), for OFr. *massiz* < VL. **massiceus* < L. *massa*, MASS] **1.** *a)* forming or consisting of a large mass; big and solid; bulky; ponderous *b)* larger or greater than normal [a *massive* dose of medicine] **2.** large and imposing or impressive; of considerable magnitude **3.** large-scale; extensive [*massive* retaliation] **4.** *Geol. a)* homogeneous in structure, without stratification, foliation, etc. [*massive* rock formations] *b)* occurring in thick beds, without minor joints and lamination: said of some stratified rocks **5.** *Med.* heavy and of wide extent [*massive* hemorrhage] **6.** *Mineralogy* irregular in form, though occasionally crystalline in internal structure —*SYN.* see HEAVY —**mas′sive·ly** *adv.* —**mas′sive·ness** *n.*

mass media those means of communication that reach and influence large numbers of people, esp. newspapers, popular magazines, radio, and television

☆**mass meeting** a large public meeting to discuss public affairs, demonstrate public approval or disapproval, etc.

☆**mass noun** a noun used to denote an abstraction or something that is uncountable, and not preceded by *a* or *an*: it is typically in a singular construction, but may be singular or plural in form (Ex.: *love, girlhood, logic, butter, savings*)

mass number *Physics, Chem.* the number of neutrons and protons in the nucleus of an atom: the approximate mass of a given nucleus is obtained by multiplying the mass number by the fundamental unit of mass, 1.6605×10^{-24} grams (1/12 the mass of C^{12} atom)

mass production the production or manufacture of goods in large quantities, esp. by machinery and division of labor —**mass′-pro·duce′** *vt.* **-duced′, -duc′ing**

mass spectrograph an instrument for sorting and analyzing streams of ionized particles by passing these through deflecting fields, typically designed to focus particles of equal mass on a fluorescent screen or photographic plate: used to detect various particles, to determine the relative abundance of isotopes in an element, etc.: also **mass spectrometer**

mass·y (mas′ē) *adj.* **mass′i·er, mass′i·est** [Now Rare] massive; weighty, bulky, etc. —**mass′i·ness** *n.*

mast[1] (mast, mäst) *n.* [ME. *maste* < OE. *mæst*, akin to G. *mast* < IE. **mazdos*, a pole, rod, whence L. *malus*, mast (< **madus* with Sabine *l* for *d*), Ir. *maide*, a stick] **1.** a tall spar or, now often, a hollow metal structure, sometimes in sections, rising vertically from the keel or deck of a vessel and used to support the sails, yards, radar and radio equipment, etc. **2.** a specified section of this [the *topmast*] **3.** any vertical pole, as in a crane or derrick **4.** a metal post for the support of a radio aerial or television antenna ☆**5.** [*also* M-] *U.S. Navy* a summary session held by a commanding officer to try minor offenses, hear requests, or give commendations: in full, **captain's mast** —*vt.* to put a mast or masts on —**before the mast** [quarters for common sailors were formerly located forward of the foremast] [Now Rare] as a common sailor

mast[2] (mast, mäst) *n.* [ME. *maste* < OE. *mæst*, akin to G. *mast* < IE. base **mad-*, moist, dripping (with fat, sap),

whence Gr. *mastos*, a breast & MEAT] beechnuts, acorns, chestnuts, etc., esp. as food for hogs

mast- *same as* MASTO-: used before a vowel

mas·ta·ba, mas·ta·bah (mas'tə bə) *n.* [Ar. *maṣṭabah*] an oblong structure with a flat roof and sloping sides, built over the opening of a mummy chamber or burial pit in ancient Egypt and used as a tomb

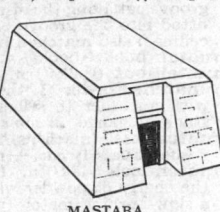

MASTABA

mast cell [< G. *mastzelle* < *mast*, food (see MAST²) + *zelle*, cell < OHG. *cella* < L.: see CELL] a cell containing large, basophilic granules, found in connective and other body tissues

mas·tec·to·my (mas tek'tə mē) *n., pl.* **-mies** [MAST- + -ECTOMY] the surgical removal of a breast

mas·ter (mas'tər, mäs'-) *n.* [ME. *maistre* < OE. *mægester*, magister & OFr. *maistre*, both < L. *magister*, a master, chief, leader, orig., double comparative < base of L. *magnus*, great < IE. base **meg-*, great, whence Gr. *megas*, large] **1.** a man who rules others or has control, authority, or power over something; specif., *a)* a man who is head of a household or institution *b)* an employer *c)* an owner of an animal or slave *d)* the captain of a merchant ship *e)* the one that excels in a contest, skill, etc.; victor or superior *f)* [Chiefly Brit.] a male schoolteacher or tutor *g)* a person whose teachings in religion, philosophy, etc. one follows or professes to follow *h)* [M-] Jesus Christ (with *our, the*, etc.) **2.** something regarded as having control, power, etc. **3.** a person very skilled and able in some work, profession, science, etc.; expert; specif., *a)* a highly skilled workman or craftsman qualified to follow his trade independently and, usually, to supervise the work of others *b)* an artist regarded as great *c)* *Games, Sports* a person recognized as having achieved the highest degree of skill [chess *master*, golf *master*] **4.** [M-] a title variously applied to *a)* orig., a man of high rank *b)* later, any man or youth: now superseded by the variant *Mister*, usually written *Mr. c)* a boy regarded as too young to be addressed as *Mr. d)* a man who heads some institution, group, activity, or place *e)* in Scotland, the heir apparent of a viscount or baron *f)* a person who is a MASTER OF ARTS, MASTER OF SCIENCE, etc. **5.** a metal matrix or mold made from the original recording and used to produce phonograph records in quantity **6.** *Law* any of several court officers appointed to assist the judge by hearing evidence, reporting on certain matters, etc. —*adj.* **1.** being a master **2.** of a master **3.** chief; main; controlling; specif., designating a mechanism or contrivance that controls others or sets a standard or norm [a *master* switch, a *master* test sheet] —*vt.* **1.** to become master of; control, conquer, etc. **2.** [Now Rare] to rule or govern as master **3.** to become an expert in (an art, science, etc.)

mas·ter-at-arms (-ət ärmz') *n., pl.* **mas'ters-at-arms'** any naval petty officer assigned responsibility for keeping order, maintaining discipline, taking charge of prisoners, etc. on a warship

master builder **1.** a person skilled in, or in charge of, building; esp., formerly, an architect: now often figurative **2.** a building contractor

mas·ter·dom (-dəm) *n.* [Now Rare] complete control; mastery

mas·ter·ful (-fəl) *adj.* · **1.** fond of acting the part of a master; arbitrary; imperious **2.** having or showing the ability of a master; expert; skillful —**mas'ter·ful·ly** *adv.* —**mas'ter·ful·ness** *n.*

SYN.—**masterful** implies such strength of personality as enables one to impose his will on others [a *masterful* orchestral conductor]; **domineering** implies the arrogant, tyrannical manner of one who openly tries to dominate another [a *domineering* mother]; **imperious** suggests the arbitrary ruling of an emperor, but connotes less arrogance than domineering [the *imperious* old dean of the college]; **magisterial**, while not suggesting an assumption of arbitrary powers, implies an excessive use or display of such inherent powers as a magistrate might have [he dismissed me with a *magisterial* air]

master hand **1.** an expert **2.** great ability or skill

master key a key that will open every one of a set of locks

mas·ter·ly (-lē) *adj.* showing the ability or skill of a master; expert [a *masterly* job of repair work] —*adv.* in a masterly manner —**mas'ter·li·ness** *n.*

master mason **1.** a highly skilled mason **2.** [often M- M-] a Freemason of the third degree

master mechanic a skilled mechanic, esp. one serving as foreman

mas·ter·mind (-mīnd') *n.* a very intelligent or clever person, esp. one with the ability to plan or direct a group project —*vt.* to be the mastermind of (a project)

Master of Arts (or ☆**Science**, etc.) **1.** a degree given by a college or university to a person who has completed a prescribed course of graduate study in the humanities or related studies (or in science, etc.): it ranks above the degree of *Bachelor* and below that of *Doctor* **2.** a person who has this degree

master of ceremonies **1.** a person who supervises a ceremony ☆**2.** a person who presides over an entertainment, as on a radio or television program or in a nightclub, at a banquet, etc., introducing the speakers or performers, filling in the intervals with jokes, etc.

mas·ter·piece (-pēs') *n.* [calque < G. *meisterstück*] **1.** a thing made or done with masterly skill; great work of art or craftsmanship **2.** the greatest work made or done by a person or group

Mas·ters (mas'tərz), **Edgar Lee** 1869-1950; U.S. poet

☆**master sergeant** *U.S. Mil.* a noncommissioned officer of high rank; in the Army, the rank just above sergeant first class; in the Air Force, the rank just above technical sergeant; in the Marine Corps, the rank just above gunnery sergeant

mas·ter·ship (-ship') *n.* **1.** the state of being a master; rule; control; dominion **2.** the position, duties, or term of office of a master **3.** masterly ability; expert skill or knowledge

mas·ter·sing·er (-siŋ'ər) *n.* [calque < G. *meistersinger*] *same as* MEISTERSINGER

mas·ter·stroke (-strōk') *n.* a masterly action, move, or achievement

mas·ter·work (-wurk') *n. same as* MASTERPIECE

mas·ter·y (mas'tər ē, mäs'-; -trē) *n., pl.* **-ter·ies** [ME. *maistrie* < OFr.: see MASTER] **1.** mastership; rule; control **2.** ascendancy or victory in struggle or competition; the upper hand **3.** masterly ability; expert skill or knowledge [his *mastery* of chess] **4.** the act of mastering (an art, science, etc.)

mast·head (mast'hed', mäst'-) *n.* **1.** the top part of a ship's mast, esp. of the lower mast ☆**2.** a box or section printed in each issue of a newspaper or magazine, giving the publishers, owners, and editors, the location of the offices, subscription rates, etc. **3.** *same as* NAMEPLATE (sense 2) —*vt.* **1.** to send (a sailor) to the masthead as a punishment **2.** to hoist to or display at the masthead

mas·tic (mas'tik) *n.* [ME. *mastik* < OFr. *mastic* < LL. *mastichum* < L. *mastiche* < Gr. *mastichē*, akin to *mastichan*: see ff.] **1.** a yellowish resin obtained from a small Mediterranean evergreen tree (*Pistacia lentiscus*) of the cashew family, used as an astringent and in making varnish, adhesives, etc. **2.** the tree: in full, **mastic tree 3.** any of various quick-drying, pasty cements used for cementing tiles to a wall, etc.

mas·ti·cate (mas'tə kāt') *vt.* **-cat'ed, -cat'ing** [< LL. *masticatus*, pp. of *masticare*, to chew < Gr. *mastichan*, to grind the teeth, gnash < *mastax*, a mouth, morsel < IE. base **menth-*, to chew, mouth, whence MOUTH, L. *mandere*, to chew] **1.** to chew up (food, etc.) **2.** to grind, cut, or knead (rubber, etc.) to a pulp —**mas'ti·ca'tion** *n.* —**mas'ti·ca'tor** *n.*

mas·ti·ca·to·ry (-kə tôr'ē) *adj.* of or for mastication; specif., adapted for chewing —*n., pl.* **-ries** any substance to be chewed but not swallowed, to increase saliva flow

mas·tiff (mas'tif) *n.* [ME. *mastif* < OFr. *mastin* < VL. **mansuetinus* < L. *mansuetus*, tame; ME. form infl. by OFr. *mestif*, a mongrel < L. *mixtus*, mixed: see MIX] any of a breed of large, powerful, smooth-coated dog with hanging lips and drooping ears, formerly used for hunting and as watchdogs

mas·ti·goph·o·ran (mas'tə gäf'ə rən) *n.* [< ModL. *Mastigophora* (< Gr. *mastix*, gen. *mastigos*, a whip + ModL. *-phora*, fem. of *-phorus*: see -PHORE) + -AN] any of a class (Mastigophora) of protozoans, sometimes parasitic, having flagella: some species are classed as algae by botanists —*adj.* of or relating to the mastigophorans —**mas'ti·goph'o·rous** (-rəs) *adj.*

mas·ti·tis (mas tīt'is) *n.* [MAST- + -ITIS] inflammation of the breast or udder

mas·to- (mas'tə, -tō) [< Gr. *mastos*, the breast: see MAST²] *a combining form meaning* of or like a breast, or mammary gland [mastodon]

mas·to·don (mas'tə dän') *n.* [ModL. < Fr. *mastodonte*, coined by Cuvier (1812) < Gr. *mastos*, a breast + *odous* (gen. *odontos*), a tooth: from the nipplelike processes on its molars] any of various large, extinct animals (genera *Mammut* and *Mastodon*) resembling the elephant but larger, and differing from it and the mammoth mainly in the structure of the molars —**mas'to·don'ic** *adj.* —**mas'to·dont** (-dänt') *adj., n.*

mas·toid (mas'toid) *adj.* [Gr. *mastoeidēs* < *mastos*, a breast (see MAST²) + *eidos*, form] **1.** shaped like a breast or nipple **2.** designating, of, or near a projection of the temporal bone behind the ear —*n.* **1.** the mastoid projection: see SKULL, illus. **2.** [Colloq.] *same as* MASTOIDITIS

mas·toid·ec·to·my (mas'toi dek'tə mē) *n., pl.* **-mies** [see -ECTOMY] the surgical removal of part or all of a mastoid

mas·toid·i·tis (-dīt'is) *n.* inflammation of the mastoid

mas·tur·bate (mas'tər bāt') *vi., vt.* **-bat'ed, -bat'ing** [< L. *masturbatus*, pp. of *masturbari*, altered (after *turbare*, to disturb) < **manstupro* < *manus*, hand (see MANUAL) + *stuprum*, defilement < IE. base **steup-*, to

strike, a stick, stump, whence STEEP¹] to manipulate one's own genitals, or the genitals of (another), for sexual gratification —**mas′tur·ba′tion** n. —**mas′tur·ba′tor** n. —**mas′tur·ba·to′ry** (-bə tôr′ē) adj.

Ma·su·ri·a (mə zoor′ē ə) region with many lakes, in NE Poland: formerly in East Prussia

ma·su·ri·um (mə soor′ē əm, -syoor′-) n. [ModL. < G. *Masuren*, Masuria, where the ore thought to contain the element was found] *former name for* TECHNETIUM

mat¹ (mat) n. [ME. *matte* < OE. *meatt* < LL. *matta* (whence also G. *matte*) < Phoen. word akin to Heb. *mittāh*, a cover] **1.** a flat, coarse fabric made of woven or plaited hemp, straw, rope, rushes, etc., often used as a floor covering **2.** a piece of this or of corrugated rubber, cocoa fiber, etc., used variously as a *a)* DOORMAT *b)* BATHMAT *c)* removable floor covering for a car **3.** *a)* a flat piece of cloth, woven straw, etc., put under a vase, dish, or the like, or used as an ornament, as on a table *b)* a pad, as of rubber or plastic, used to protect the surface of an oven, sink, drainboard, etc. **4.** a thickly padded floor covering, esp. one used in a gymnasium for tumbling, wrestling, etc. **5.** anything densely interwoven or felted, or growing in a thick tangle [a mat of hair] **6.** *Naut.* a thick web of rope yarn, used to protect rigging from wear —vt. **mat′ted, mat′ting 1.** to cover with or as with a mat or mats **2.** to interweave, felt, or tangle together into a thick mass —vi. to be interwoven, felted, or tangled together into a thick mass

mat² (mat) adj. [Fr. < OFr. *mat*, defeated, exhausted, prob. < L. *mattus*, drunk < *madidus*, soaked, drunk < *madere*, to be drenched, drunk < IE. base *mad-*, to be wet, drip, juicy, fat, whence MEAT] *same as* MATTE² —n. [Fr.] **1.** *same as* MATTE² **2.** a border, as of cardboard or cloth, put around a picture, either as the frame or, usually, between the picture and the frame —vt. **mat′ted, mat′ting 1.** to produce a dull surface or finish on (metal, glass, etc.) **2.** to frame (a picture) with a mat

mat³ (mat) n. [Colloq.] a matrix; printing mold

Mat·a·be·le (mat′ə bē′lē) n., pl. **-be′le, -be′les** [< Zulu name, lit., vanishing (or hidden) people: from "hiding" behind large oxhide shields in battle] any member of a Zulu tribe driven out of the Transvaal by the Boers in 1837 into Rhodesia

Ma·ta·di (mä tä′dē) main port of the Congo (sense 2), on the Congo River: pop. 59,000

mat·a·dor (mat′ə dôr′) n. [Sp., lit., killer < *matar*, to kill < *mate*, checkmate: see CHECKMATE] **1.** a bullfighter whose specialty is killing the bull with a sword thrust at the end of a bullfight after performing a series of formalized actions with a cape to anger and tire the animal **2.** one of the principal cards in certain card games

Ma·ta·mo·ros (mä′tä mô′rōs; E. mat′ə môr′əs) city in NE Mexico, on the Rio Grande, opposite Brownsville, Tex.: pop. 152,000

Mat·a·nus·ka (mat′ə nōōs′kə) [native name of river; ? lit., copper river] agricultural region in S Alas., in a river valley northeast of Anchorage: development begun (1935) by homesteaders with Federal aid

Ma·tan·zas (mə tan′zəs; Sp. mä tän′säs) seaport on the NW coast of Cuba: pop. 83,000

Ma·ta·pan (mat′ə pan′), **Cape** promontory of the S Peloponnesus, Greece

match¹ (mach) n. [ME. *macche* < OFr. *mesche* (Fr. *mèche*), wick of a candle, match < VL. *micca*, prob. altered (after *muccare*, to snuff a candle, orig., to blow one's nose < L. *mucus*, MUCUS) < L. *myxa* < Gr. *myxa*, lamp wick, lit., nasal discharge, akin to L. *mucus*] **1.** orig., a wick or cord prepared to burn at a uniform rate, used for firing guns or explosives **2.** a slender piece of wood, cardboard, waxed cord, etc. tipped with a composition that catches fire by friction, sometimes only when rubbed on a specially prepared surface

match² (mach) n. [ME. *macche* < OE. (ge)*mæcca*, one suited to another, mate < base of *macian*, to make, form: see MAKE¹] **1.** any person or thing equal or similar to another in some way; specif., *a)* a person, group, or thing able to cope with or oppose another as an equal in power, size, etc.; peer *b)* a counterpart or facsimile *c)* either of two corresponding things or persons; one of a pair **2.** two or more persons or things that go together in appearance, size, or other quality; pair [a purse and shoes that are a good *match*] **3.** a contest or game involving two or more contestants **4.** *a)* an agreement to marry or mate *b)* a marriage or mating [to make a good *match*] **5.** a person regarded as a suitable or possible mate —vt. **1.** to join in marriage; get a (suitable) match for; mate **2.** *a)* formerly, to meet as an antagonist *b)* to compete with successfully **3.** to put in opposition (with); pit (against) **4.** to be equal, similar, suitable, or corresponding to in some way [his looks *match* his character] **5.** to make, show, produce, or get a competitor, counterpart, or equivalent to [to *match* a piece of cloth] **6.** to suit or fit (one thing) to another **7.** to fit (things) together; make similar or corresponding **8.** to compare ☆**9.** *a)* to flip or reveal (coins) as a form of gambling or to decide something contested, the winner being determined by the combination of faces thus exposed *b)* to match coins with (another person), usually betting that the same faces will be exposed —vi. **1.** to be equal, similar, suitable, or corresponding in some way

2. [Obs.] to get married; mate —**match′a·ble** adj. —**match′er** n.

match·board (-bôrd′) n. any of a number of identical thin boards with a tongue formed along one edge and a groove cut along the other so that the tongue of one can be fitted into the groove of the next, as in making floors or ceilings: also **matched board**

match·book (-book′) n. ☆a folder of book matches

match·box (-bäks′) n. a small box for holding matches

☆**matched order 1.** the pairing of an order to buy stock with an order to sell stock by member brokers on the stock exchange **2.** *same as* WASH SALE

match·less (mach′lis) adj. having no equal; peerless —**match′less·ly** adv. —**match′less·ness** n.

match·lock (-läk′) n. **1.** an old type of gunlock in which the charge of powder was ignited by a slow-burning match (wick or cord) **2.** a musket with such a gunlock

match·mak·ing¹ (-mā′kiŋ) n. the work or business of making matches (for burning) —**match′mak′er** n.

match·mak·ing² (-mā′kiŋ) n. **1.** the act or occupation of arranging marriages for others **2.** the arranging of wrestling or boxing matches, etc. —**match′mak′er** n.

☆**match·mark** (-märk′) n. a mark put on parts, as of a machine, to distinguish them as an aid in assembling —vt. to put such a mark on

MATCHLOCK

match play 1. play in a match, as in tennis, etc. **2.** *Golf* a form of competitive play in which the score is calculated by counting holes won rather than strokes taken: distinguished from MEDAL PLAY

match point the final point needed to win the match, as in tennis

match·wood (-wood′) n. **1.** wood for making matches **2.** very small pieces; splinters

mate¹ (māt) n. [ME. < MDu., a companion < *gemate* < Gmc. *gamatan* < *ga-*, together (for IE. base see COM-) + *mad-*, food, MEAT: hence, orig., one who shares meals: sense translated in VL. *companio*, COMPANION¹] **1.** a companion, comrade, or fellow worker: often used in compounds [*classmate*] and, among sailors, British workingmen, etc., as a familiar form of address **2.** one of a pair, esp. of a matched pair **3.** *a)* a husband or wife; spouse *b)* the male or female of animals paired for propagation **4.** [Archaic] an equal; fit associate **5.** *Naut.* *a)* an officer of a merchant ship, ranking below the captain *b)* an assistant ☆**6.** *U.S. Navy* any of various petty officers [a boatswain's *mate*] —vt. **mat′ed, mat′ing 1.** to join as a pair; couple **2.** to join as mates; couple in marriage or sexual union **3.** to provide with a mate —vi. to become mated

mate² (māt) n., interj., vt. **mat′ed, mat′ing** [ME. *mat* < OFr.: see CHECKMATE] *same as* CHECKMATE

ma·té (mä′tā, mat′ā) n. [AmSp. *mate* < Quechua *mati*, calabash: in allusion to the gourd in which it is steeped] **1.** a beverage made from the dried leaves of a S. American evergreen tree (*Ilex paraguariensis*) of the holly family **2.** this tree **3.** the dried leaves of this tree Also sp. **mate**

ma·te·las·sé (mat′lə sā′; Fr. mät′l ä′sā) adj. [Fr., pp. of *matelasser*, to stuff, pad < *matelas*, mattress] having a surface with a raised design; embossed: said of fabrics —n. a fabric with such a surface

mat·e·lote (mat′'l ōt′) n. [Fr. < *matelot*, sailor] stewed fish in a sauce of wine, oil, onions, mushrooms, etc.

ma·ter (māt′ər, mät′-) n. [L., MOTHER¹] [Chiefly Brit. Colloq.] mother: often preceded by *the*

ma·ter·fa·mil·i·as (-fə mil′ē əs) n. [L.] the mother of a family; woman head of a household

ma·te·ri·al (mə tir′ē əl) adj. [LL. *materialis* < L. *materia*, MATTER] **1.** of matter; of substance; relating to or consisting of what occupies space; physical [a *material* object, *material* forces] **2.** *a)* of the body or bodily needs, satisfactions, etc.; corporeal, sensual, or sensuous [*material* pleasures] *b)* of or fond of comfort, pleasure, wealth, etc. rather than spiritual or intellectual values; worldly [*material* success] **3.** important, essential, or pertinent (to the matter under discussion) **4.** *Law* important enough to affect the outcome of a case, the validity of a legal instrument, etc. [a *material* witness] **5.** *Philos.* of the matter of reasoning, as distinguished from the formal element —n. **1.** what a thing is, or may be, made of; elements, parts, or constituents [raw *material*] **2.** ideas, notes, observations, sketches, etc. that may be worked up or elaborated; data **3.** cloth or other fabric **4.** [pl.] tools, implements, articles, etc. needed to make or do something [writing *materials*]

SYN.—**material** is applied to anything that is formed of matter and has substance [*material* objects, possessions, etc.]; **physical** applies either to material things as they are perceivable by the senses or to forces that are scientifically measurable [the *physical* world, the *physical* properties of sound]; **corporeal** applies only to such material objects as have bodily form and are tangible [*corporeal* property]; **sensible** is specifically applied to anything that can be known through the senses rather than through the intellect [a *sensible* phenomenon] —**ANT. spiritual, mental, psychical**

ma·te·ri·al·ism (-iz'm) *n.* [Fr. *matérialisme*] **1.** *a*) the philosophical doctrine that matter is the only reality and that everything in the world, including thought, will, and feeling, can be explained only in terms of matter: opposed to IDEALISM *b*) the doctrine that comfort, pleasure, and wealth are the only or highest goals or values **2.** the tendency to be more concerned with material than with spiritual or intellectual goals or values **3.** *same as* HISTORICAL MATERIALISM

ma·te·ri·al·ist (-ist) *n.* **1.** a person who believes in materialism (senses 1 & 3) **2.** a person characterized by materialism (sense 2) —*adj.* of materialism or materialists —**ma·te'ri·al·is'tic** *adj.* —**ma·te'ri·al·is'ti·cal·ly** *adv.*

ma·te·ri·al·i·ty (mə tir'ē al'ə tē) *n.* [ML. *materialitas*] **1.** the state or quality of being material, or physical **2.** matter; substance **3.** *pl.* **-ties** something material

ma·te·ri·al·ize (mə tir'ē ə līz') *vt.* **-ized'**, **-iz'ing 1.** to give material form or characteristics to; represent in material form **2.** to make (a spirit, etc.) appear in bodily form **3.** to make materialistic —*vi.* **1.** to become fact; develop into something real or tangible; be realized [*a plan that never materialized*] **2.** to take on, or appear in, bodily form: said of spirits, etc. **3.** to appear suddenly or unexpectedly —**ma·te'ri·al·i·za'tion** *n.*

ma·te·ri·al·ly (-lē) *adv.* **1.** with regard to the matter, substance, or content, and not the form **2.** with regard to material objects, interests, etc.; physically **3.** to a great extent; substantially; considerably

ma·te·ri·a med·i·ca (mə tir'ē ə med'i kə) [ML. < *materia*, matter, material + *medica*, fem. of *medicus*, MEDICAL] **1.** the drugs and other remedial substances used in medicine **2.** the branch of medical science that deals with such substances, their uses, etc.

ma·te·ri·el, ma·té·ri·el (mə tir'ē el') *n.* [Fr. *matériel*: see MATERIAL] **1.** materials and tools necessary to any work, enterprise, etc.; specif., weapons, equipment, supplies, etc. of armed forces: distinguished from PERSONNEL **2.** weapons and equipment of armed forces in combat

ma·ter·nal (mə tur'n'l) *adj.* [ME. < MFr. *maternel* < L. *maternus* < *mater*, MOTHER[1]] **1.** of, like, or characteristic of a mother or motherhood; motherly **2.** derived, received, or inherited from a mother **3.** related through the mother's side of the family [*maternal* grandparents] —**ma·ter'nal·ly** *adv.*

ma·ter·ni·ty (mə tur'nə tē) *n.*, *pl.* **-ties** [Fr. *maternité* < ML. *maternitas* < L. *maternus*, MATERNAL] **1.** the state of being a mother; motherhood **2.** the character or qualities of a mother; motherliness **3.** a maternity ward in a hospital —*adj.* **1.** for pregnant women [*a maternity* dress] **2.** for the care of women giving birth and of newborn babies [*a maternity* ward]

mate·y (māt'ē) *adj.* [MATE[1] + -Y[2]] [Brit. Colloq.] friendly; companionable —*n.* [Brit. Colloq.] a chum

math (math) *n. clipped form of* MATHEMATICS

math. 1. mathematical **2.** mathematics

math·e·mat·i·cal (math'ə mat'i k'l) *adj.* [ML. *mathematicalis* < L. *mathematicus* < Gr. *mathēmatikos*, inclined to learn, mathematical < *mathēma*, what is learned < *manthanein*, to learn < IE. base *mendh-*, to pay attention to, be alert, whence Av. *mazdā*, memory, G. *munter*, cheerful] **1.** of, having the nature of, or concerned with mathematics **2.** rigorously exact, precise, accurate, etc. Also **math'e·mat'ic** —**math'e·mat'i·cal·ly** *adv.*

mathematical logic *same as* SYMBOLIC LOGIC

math·e·ma·ti·cian (math'ə mə tish'ən, math'mə-) *n.* [ME. *mathematicien* < MFr. *mathematicien*] an expert or specialist in mathematics

math·e·mat·ics (math'ə mat'iks) *n.pl.* [with sing. v.] [see MATHEMATICAL & -ICS] the group of sciences (including arithmetic, geometry, algebra, calculus, etc.) dealing with quantities, magnitudes, and forms, and their relationships, attributes, etc., by the use of numbers and symbols

Math·er (math'ər) **1. Cot·ton** (kät'n), 1663–1728; Am. clergyman & writer **2. In·crease** (in'krēs), 1639–1723; Am. clergyman & writer: father of *prec.*

Math·ews (math'yōoz), **Mit·ford M(cLeod)** (mit'fərd) 1891– ; U.S. lexicographer & educator

Ma·thu·ra (mut'oo rə) city in N India, in Uttar Pradesh, on the Jumna River: sacred Hindu city, reputed birthplace of Krishna: pop. 125,000

Ma·til·da, Ma·thil·da (mə til'də) [ML. *Matilda*, *Mathildis* < OHG. *Mahthilda* < *maht*, might, power + *hiltia*, battle; hence, lit., powerful (in) battle] a feminine name: dim. *Matty, Maud, Tilda, Tilly*

mat·in (mat'n) *n.* [Early ME. *matyn* < OFr. *matin*, pl. *matines* < ML.(Ec.) *matulinae (vigiliae)*, morning (watches) < L. *matutinus*, of the morning < *Matuta*, goddess of dawn < IE. base *mā-*, good, in good time, hence early, whence L. *maturus*] **1.** [pl.] [often M-] *a*) R.C.Ch. the first of the seven canonical hours, properly recited at midnight, but often at daybreak, usually joined with lauds *b*) *Anglican Ch.* the order for, or the service of, public morning prayer **2.** [Poet.] a morning song, esp. of birds —*adj.* **1.** of matins **2.** of morning —**mat'in·al** *adj.*

mat·i·nee, mat·i·née (mat'n ā'; chiefly Brit., mat'n ā') *n.* [Fr. *matinée* < *matin*, morning: see MATIN] a reception or entertainment held in the daytime; esp., a performance, as of a play, held in the afternoon

matinee idol an actor whose looks and manner make him popular with women theatergoers

Ma·tisse (mà tēs'), **Hen·ri** (än rē') 1869–1954; Fr. painter

mat·jes herring (mät'yəs) *n.* [< Du. *maatjesharing*, altered < MDu. *medykens hering*, lit., maiden herring (because prepared from herrings that have never spawned)] a reddish herring, filleted and served or packed usually in a spiced wine sauce

Ma·to Gros·so (mät'oo grō'soo) state of W Brazil: 475,502 sq. mi.; pop. 910,000; cap. Cuiabá

mat·rass (mat'rəs) *n.* [Fr. *matras* < *matras*, kind of arrow, blunt borer < Gaul. *mataris*, javelin] a glass container with a rounded body and a long neck, formerly used in distilling, etc.

ma·tri- (mā'trē, mat'rē) [< L. *mater* (gen. *matris*), a mother] a combining form meaning mother [*matriarch*]

ma·tri·arch (mā'trē ärk') *n.* [prec. + -ARCH] a mother who rules her family or tribe; specif., a woman who is head of a matriarchy —**ma'tri·ar'chal** (-är'k'l) *adj.*

ma·tri·ar·chate (-är'kit, -kāt) *n.* **1.** a family, tribe, etc. ruled by a matriarch **2.** a matriarchal system

ma·tri·ar·chy (-trē är'kē) *n.*, *pl.* **-chies** [MATRI- + -ARCHY] **1.** a form of social organization in which the mother is recognized as the head of the family or tribe, descent and kinship being traced through the mother instead of the father **2.** government, rule, or domination by women —**ma'tri·ar'chic** *adj.*

mat·ri·ces (mā'trə sēz', mat'rə-) *n.* *alt. pl. of* MATRIX

mat·ri·cide (mat'rə sīd', mā'trə-) *n.* [L. *matricidium* < *mater*, MOTHER[1] + *caedere*, to kill: see -CIDE] **1.** the act of killing one's mother **2.** [L. *matricida*] a person who kills his mother —**mat'ri·ci'dal** *adj.*

ma·tric·u·lant (mə trik'yoo lənt) *n.* a person who has matriculated or is applying for matriculation

ma·tric·u·late (-lāt'; also, for n., -lit) *vt.*, *vi.* **-lat'ed**, **-lat'ing** [< ML. *matriculatus*, pp. of *matriculare*, to register < LL. *matricula*, dim. of *matrix*: see MATRIX] to enroll, esp. as a student in a college or university —*n.* a person so enrolled —**ma·tric'u·la'tion** *n.*

mat·ri·lin·e·al (mat'rə lin'ē əl, mā'trə-) *adj.* [MATRI- + LINEAL] designating or of descent, kinship, or derivation through the mother instead of the father —**ma'tri·lin'e·al·ly** *adv.*

mat·ri·mo·ni·al (mat'rə mō'nē əl) *adj.* [Fr. < LL. *matrimonialis*] of matrimony; marital; nuptial; conjugal —**mat'ri·mo'ni·al·ly** *adv.*

mat·ri·mo·ny (mat'rə mō'nē) *n.*, *pl.* **-nies** [ME. *matrimonye* < OFr. *matrimoine* < L. *matrimonium* < *mater* (gen. *matris*), MOTHER[1]] **1.** the act, rite, or sacrament of marriage **2.** the state of being husband and wife **3.** married life **4.** *a*) a card game with any number of players, who try to form certain pairs of cards *b*) a combination of the king and queen of trump in this game —*SYN.* see MARRIAGE

matrimony vine a plant (genus *Lycium*) of the nightshade family, with small flowers and reddish berries

ma·trix (mā'triks) *n.*, *pl.* **-tri·ces** (mā'trə sēz', mat'rə-), **-trix·es** [LL., womb, public register, origin < L., breeding animal < *mater* (gen. *matris*), MOTHER[1]] **1.** orig., the womb; uterus **2.** that within which, or within and from which, something originates, takes form, or develops; specif., *a*) a die or mold for casting or shaping *b*) an impression from which a large number of phonograph records can be duplicated **3.** *Geol.* the rock or earthy material in which a crystal, pebble, fossil, etc. is enclosed or embedded **4.** *Linguis.* an independent clause **5.** *Math.* a set of numbers or terms arranged in rows and columns between parentheses or double lines **6.** *Printing a*) a metal mold for casting the face of type *b*) a papier-mâché, plaster, or similar impression of type, etc., from which a plate can be made, as in stereotypy **7.** *Zool. a*) any nonliving, intercellular substance in which living cells are embedded, as in bone, cartilage, etc. *b*) the formative cells from which a nail, tooth, etc. grows

ma·tron (mā'trən) *n.* [ME. *matrone* < OFr. < L. *matrona* < *mater*, MOTHER[1]] **1.** a married woman or widow, esp. one who has a mature appearance and manner **2.** a woman superintendent or manager of the domestic arrangements of a hospital, prison, or other institution **3.** a woman attendant or guard in charge of women or children, as in an institution —**ma'tron·al** *adj.* —**ma'tron·hood'** *n.*

ma·tron·age (-ij) *n.* **1.** matrons collectively **2.** the state of being a matron **3.** matronly care or supervision

ma·tron·ize (mā'trə nīz') *vt.* **-ized'**, **-iz'ing 1.** to make matronly **2.** to chaperon

ma·tron·ly (-lē) *adj.* of, like, or suitable for a matron; dignified, sedate, etc. —**ma'tron·li·ness** *n.*

☆**matron of honor** a married woman acting as chief attendant to the bride at a wedding: cf. MAID OF HONOR

mat·ro·nym·ic (mat'rə nim'ik) *adj.* [Gr. *mētrōnymikos*, altered after L. *mater* (gen. *matris*), by analogy with PATRONYMIC] of or derived from the name of the mother or a female ancestor —*n.* a matronymic name

Mat·su (mät′sōō′, mat′-) island of a small group in Taiwan Strait, held by the Chinese Nationalist government on Taiwan: pop. 2,000

Ma·tsu·ya·ma (mä′tsoo yä′mə) seaport on W Shikoku, Japan, on the Inland Sea: pop. 283,000

Matt. Matthew

matte[1] (mat) *n.* [Fr. < dial. *mate*, a lump, prob. ult. < L. *matta*, MAT[1]] an impure mixture of sulfides that is produced in smelting the sulfide ores of copper, nickel, lead, etc.

matte[2] (mat) *n.* [var. of MAT[2]] a dull surface or finish, often roughened —*adj.* not shiny or glossy; dull Also sp. **matt**

mat·ted[1] (mat′id) *adj.* **1.** closely tangled together in a dense mass [*matted hair*] **2.** covered with a dense growth **3.** covered with or enclosed in matting or mats

mat·ted[2] (mat′id) *adj.* having a matte, or dull finish

mat·ter (mat′ər) *n.* [ME. *matiere* < OFr. < L. *materia*, material, stuff, wood (< base of *mater*, MOTHER[1]), orig., the growing trunk of a tree] **1.** what a thing is made of; constituent substance or material **2.** what all (material) things are made of; whatever occupies space and is perceptible to the senses in some way: in modern physics, matter and energy are regarded as equivalents, mutually convertible according to Einstein's formula, $E = mc^2$ (i.e., energy equals mass multiplied by the square of the velocity of light); in dualistic thinking, matter is regarded as the opposite of mind, spirit, etc. **3.** any specified sort of substance [*coloring matter*] **4.** material of thought or expression; what is spoken or written, regarded as distinct from how it is spoken or written; content, as distinguished from manner, style, or form **5.** an amount or quantity, usually indefinite [*a matter of a few days*] **6.** *a)* something that is the subject of discussion, concern, action, etc.; thing or affair [*business matters*] *b)* cause, occasion, or grounds [no *matter* for jesting] **7.** *a)* an important affair; thing of some moment or significance *b)* importance; moment; significance [it's of no *matter*] **8.** an unfavorable state of affairs; trouble; difficulty (with *the*) [something seems to be the *matter*] **9.** documents, letters, etc. sent, or to be sent, by mail; mail [second-class *matter*] **10.** a substance discharged by the body; specif., pus **11.** *Law* something that is to be proved **12.** *Philos.* that which has yet to take on form; undifferentiated substance of reality or experience **13.** *Printing a)* material set up, or to be set up, in type; copy *b)* type set up —*vi.* **1.** to be of importance or consequence; have significance [the things that *matter* to one] **2.** to form and discharge pus; suppurate —**as a matter of fact** in fact; in actuality; really —**for that matter** in regard to that; as far as that is concerned: also **for the matter of that** —**no matter 1.** it is of no importance **2.** regardless of

Mat·ter·horn (mat′ər hôrn′) mountain of the Pennine Alps, on the Swiss-Italian border: c. 14,700 ft.

mat·ter-of-course (-əv kôrs′) *adj.* **1.** coming as a natural or logical occurrence in the course of events; routine **2.** reacting to events in a calm and natural way

matter of course a thing to be expected as a natural or logical occurrence in the course of events

mat·ter-of-fact (-əv fakt′, -ə fakt′) *adj.* sticking strictly to facts; literal, unimaginative, unemotional, prosaic, etc. —**mat′ter-of-fact′ly** *adv.* —**mat′ter-of-fact′ness** *n.*

Mat·thew (math′yōō) [ME. *Matheu* < OFr. < LL.(Ec.) *Matthaeus* < Gr.(Ec.) *Matthaios, Matthias*, contr. < *Mattathias* < Heb. *mattĭthyāh*, lit., gift of God] **1.** a masculine name: dim. *Mat*(*t*); var. *Matthias*; equiv. Fr. *Mathieu*, Ger. & Sw. *Matthaus*, It. *Matteo*, Sp. *Mateo* **2.** *Bible a)* one of the four Evangelists, a customs collector and the reputed author of the first Gospel: also *Saint Matthew*: his day is Sept. 12 *b)* the first book of the New Testament, telling of Jesus' life

Matthew (of) Paris 1200?–59; Eng. monk & chronicler

Mat·thews (math′yōōz), (**James**) **Bran·der** (bran′dər) 1852–1929; U.S. scholar, writer, & critic

Mat·thi·as (mə thī′əs) [cf. MATTHEW] *Bible* one of the apostles, chosen by lot to replace Judas Iscariot: also called *Saint Matthias*: his day is Feb. 24

mat·ting[1] (mat′iŋ) *n.* **1.** a woven fabric of fiber, as straw or hemp, for mats, floor covering, wrapping, etc. **2.** mats collectively **3.** the making of mats

mat·ting[2] (mat′iŋ) *n.* [see MATTE[2]] **1.** the production of a dull surface or finish on metal, glass, etc. **2.** such a surface or finish **3.** a mat, or border

mat·tins (mat′′nz) *n.pl. Brit. var. of* MATINS (see MATIN, *n.* 1)

mat·tock (mat′ək) *n.* [ME. *mattok* < OE. *mattuc* < VL. *mattiuca* < *mattea*, back-formation < L. *mateola*, dim. < *matea* < IE. base *mat-*, hoe, club, whence Sans. *matyā-*, a harrow] a tool for loosening the soil, digging up and cutting roots, etc.: it is like a pickax but has a flat, adz-shaped blade on one or both sides

Matto Grosso former *sp.* of MATO GROSSO, Brazil

mat·toid (mat′oid) *n.* [It. *mattoide* < *matto*, mad < L. *mattus*, intoxicated: see MAT[2]] [Rare] a person of unbalanced mind verging on insanity

mat·tress (mat′ris) *n.* [ME. *materas* < OFr. < It. *materasso* < Ar. *matrah*, place where something is thrown or laid, cushion] **1.** *a)* a casing of strong cloth or other fabric filled with cotton, hair, foam rubber, etc., and usually coiled springs, often quilted or tufted at intervals, and used on or as a bed *b)* an inflatable pad used in the same way: in full **air mattress 2.** a mass or mat of interwoven brushwood, poles, etc. used to protect an embankment or dike from erosion, etc.

mat·u·rate (mach′oo rāt′, mat′yoo-) *vi.* **-rat′ed, -rat′ing** [< L. *maturatus*, pp. of *maturare*, to ripen, MATURE] **1.** to suppurate; discharge pus **2.** to ripen; mature —**ma·tur·a·tive** (mə tyoor′ə tiv, mach′oo rāt′iv, mat′yoo-) *adj.*

mat·u·ra·tion (mach′oo rā′shən) *n.* [Fr. < L. *maturatio* < pp. of *maturare*: see ff.] **1.** the formation or discharge of pus; suppuration **2.** the act or process of maturing, esp. of becoming full-grown or fully developed **3.** *Zool.* the final stages in the development of gametes in which, through meiosis, the normal number of chromosomes is reduced by half —**mat′u·ra′tion·al** *adj.*

ma·ture (mə toor′, -choor′, -tyoor′) *adj.* [ME. < L. *maturus*, seasonable, ripe, mature < IE. base **ma-*, good, in good time, whence L. *matuta* (cf. MATIN)] **1.** *a)* full-grown, as plants or animals *b)* ripe, as fruits *c)* fully developed, as a person, a mind, etc. **2.** fully or highly developed, perfected, worked out, considered, etc. [a *mature* scheme] **3.** of a state of full development [a person of *mature* age] **4.** due; payable: said of a note, bond, etc. **5.** *Geol.* having reached maximum development of topographical form or vigor of action, as with streams that have no plains and that have begun to widen rather than deepen their valleys —*vt.* **-tured′, -tur′ing 1.** to bring to full growth or development, or to ripeness **2.** to develop or work out fully —*vi.* **1.** to become fully grown, developed, or ripe **2.** to become due: said of a note, etc. —*SYN.* see RIPE —**ma·ture′ly** *adv.* —**ma·ture′ness** *n.*

ma·tu·ri·ty (-ə tē) *n.* [ME. *maturite* < L. *maturitas*] **1.** the state or quality of being mature; specif., *a)* a being full-grown, ripe, or fully developed *b)* a being perfect, complete, or ready **2.** *a)* a becoming due *b)* the time at which a note, etc. becomes due

ma·tu·ti·nal (mə tōōt′′n əl, -tyōōt′-; *chiefly Brit.*, mach′oo tī′n′l) *adj.* [L. *matutinalis* < *matutinus*, of morning < *Matuta*, goddess of morning: see MATIN] of or in the morning; early —**ma·tu′ti·nal·ly** *adv.*

mat·zo (mät′sə, -sō) *n., pl.* **mat′zot, mat′zoth** (-sōt), **mat′zos** [Heb. *matstsāh*, unleavened] flat, thin unleavened bread eaten by Jews during the Passover, or a piece of this: also **mat′sah**

maud (môd) *n.* [< ? ff.] **1.** a gray striped plaid, worn by shepherds in southern Scotland **2.** a shawl, wrap, or rug made of such plaid

Maud, Maude (môd) a feminine name: see MATILDA

maud·lin (môd′lin) *adj.* [< *Maudlin*, *Magdalene* < ME. *Maudeleyne* < OFr. *Madeleine*: Magdalene was often represented with eyes red from weeping] **1.** foolishly and tearfully or weakly sentimental **2.** tearfully sentimental from too much liquor —*SYN.* see SENTIMENTAL

Maugham (môm), (**William**) **Som·er·set** (sum′ər set′) 1874–1965; Eng. novelist & playwright

mau·gre, mau·ger (mô′gər) *prep.* [ME. < OFr. *maugre, malgré*, lit., with displeasure < *mal*, ill + *gré*, pleasure: see MAL- & AGREE] [Archaic] in spite of

Mau·i (mou′ē) [Haw. < ?] an island of Hawaii, southeast of Oahu: 728 sq. mi.; pop. 39,000

mau·kin (mô′kin) *n. var. of* MALKIN

maul (môl) *n.* [Early ModE. phonetic sp. of ME. *malle* < OFr. *maile* < L. *malleus*, a hammer] **1.** a very heavy hammer or mallet, often of wood, for driving stakes, wedges, etc. **2.** [Archaic] *a)* a mace *b)* a wooden club —*vt.* [ME. *mallen* < OFr. *mailler* < the *n.*] **1.** to injure by beating or tearing; bruise or lacerate **2.** to handle roughly or clumsily; manhandle; paw ☆**3.** to split (fence rails) with a maul and wedges —*SYN.* see BEAT —**maul′er** *n.*

maul·stick (môl′stik′) *n. same as* MAHLSTICK

Mau Mau (mou′ mou′) *pl.* **Mau Mau, Mau Maus** a member of a secret society of Kikuyu tribesmen in Kenya, organized c. 1951 to fight against white rule: both the movement and its suppression were marked by terrorism and violence

mau·met (mô′mit) *n.* [ME. < OFr. *mahumet*, lit., Mohammed] **1.** [Obs.] an idol: from the notion that Moslems worshiped Mohammed as a god **2.** [Brit. Dial.] a doll or puppet

maun (män, môn) *vi.* [MScot. *mane* < ON. *man*, pt. of *munu*, shall, will, lit., intend] [Scot.] must

Mau·na Ke·a (mou′nə kā′ə) [Haw., lit., ? white mountain] extinct volcano on the island of Hawaii: 13,796 ft.

Mauna Lo·a (lō′ə) [Haw., lit., long mountain] active volcano in Hawaii Volcanoes National Park, on the island of Hawaii: 13,680 ft.

maund (mônd) *n.* [Hind. & Per. *man* < Sans. *manā*, prob. < Sem.] a varying unit of weight used in Nepal, Pakistan, Aden, Saudi Arabia, and certain other Middle East countries, usually equal to 82.28 pounds

maun·der (môn′dər) *vi.* [Early ModE. *mander*, to grumble, growl, prob. freq. of obs. *maund*, to beg: sense prob. infl. by MEANDER] **1.** to move or act in a dreamy, vague, aimless way **2.** to talk in an incoherent, rambling way; drivel —**maun′der·er** *n.*

Maun·dy Thursday (môn′dē) [ME. *maunde*, ceremony of

MATTOCK

washing the feet of the poor < OFr. *mandé* < LL.(Ec.) *mandatum*, commandment of God < L. (see MANDATE): from use of *mandatum* at the beginning of the prayer for washing the feet, commemorating Jesus' washing of the disciples' feet: John 13:5, 34] the Thursday before Easter

Mau·pas·sant (mō′pə sänt′; *Fr.* mō pȧ sän′), **(Henri René Albert) Guy de** (gē də) 1850–93; Fr. writer of novels & short stories

Mau·reen (mô rēn′) [Ir. *Mairin*, dim. of *Maire*, MARY] a feminine name

Mau·re·ta·ni·a (môr′ə tā′nē ə, -tän′yə) ancient country & Roman province in NW Africa, including areas now in NE Morocco & W Algeria

Mau·riac (mōr′is, mär′-; mō rēs′) 1885–1970; Fr. novelist & essayist

Mau·rice (môr′is, mär′-; mō rēs′) [Fr. < LL. *Mauritius* < *Maurus*, a Moor] a masculine name: var. *Morris;* equiv. Ger. *Moritz,* It. *Maurizio,* Sp. *Mauricio*

Maurice of Nassau, Prince of Orange, 1567–1625; Du. statesman & military leader

Mau·ri·ta·ni·a (môr′ə tā′nē ə, -tän′yə) country in W Africa, on the Atlantic: 419,230 sq. mi.; pop. 1,120,000; cap. Nouakchott: official name, **Islamic Republic of Mauritania** —**Mau′ri·ta′ni·an** *adj., n.*

Mau·ri·ti·us (mō rish′ē əs, -rish′əs) **1.** island in the Indian Ocean, east of Madagascar: 720 sq. mi.; pop. 759,000 **2.** country consisting of this island & several nearby islands: a member of the Brit. Commonwealth: 809 sq. mi.; pop. 810,000; cap. Port Louis

Mau·rois (mō rwä′), **An·dré** (än drā′) (born *Émile Salomon Wilhelm Herzog*) 1885–1967; Fr. novelist & biographer

Mau·ry (môr′ē), **Matthew Fon·taine** (fän tān′) 1806–73; U.S. oceanographer & hydrographer

Mau·so·le·um (mô′sə lē′əm, -zə-) [L. < Gr. *Mausōleion*] the tomb of Mausolus, king of Caria, at Halicarnassus: included among the seven wonders of the ancient world —*n.* [m·] *pl.* -le′ums, -le′a (-lē′ə) a large, imposing tomb: humorously applied to any large, somber building or room —**mau′so·le′an** (-ən) *adj.*

mauve (mōv, môv) *n.* [Fr., mallow < L. *malva,* MALLOW: from the color of the mallow] **1.** a purple dye and pigment, a coal-tar dyestuff produced by oxidizing aniline **2.** any of several shades of delicate purple —*adj.* of such a color

☆**mav·er·ick** (mav′ər ik, mav′rik) *n.* [after Samuel *Maverick* (1803–70), Texas rancher who did not brand his cattle] **1.** an unbranded animal, esp. a strayed calf, formerly the legitimate property of the first person who branded it **2.** [Colloq.] a person who takes an independent stand, as in politics, refusing to conform to that of his party or group

ma·vis (mā′vis) *n.* [ME. < OFr. *mauvis,* prob. < MBret. *milhvid*] *same as* SONG THRUSH

ma·vour·neen, ma·vour·nin (mə voor′nēn, -vôr′-) *n.* [Ir. *mo muirnin*] my darling

maw¹ (mô) *n.* [ME. *mawe* < OE. *maga,* akin to G. *magen,* stomach < IE. base *mak-,* skin, bag, whence W. *megin,* bellows] **1.** *a)* orig., the stomach or its cavity *b)* the stomach of an animal; specif., the fourth stomach of a cud-chewing animal **2.** the throat, gullet, jaws, or oral cavity of a voracious animal **3.** anything thought of as consuming, devouring, etc. without end

maw² (mô) *n.* [Dial.] ma; mamma; mother

maw·kin (mô′kin) *n. var. of* MALKIN

mawk·ish (mô′kish) *adj.* [lit., maggoty < ME. *mawke,* maggot < ON. *mathkr* < IE. base *math-,* gnawing vermin, whence MOTH] **1.** having a sweet, weak, sickening taste; insipid or nauseating **2.** sentimental in a weak, insipid way, so as to be sickening —*SYN.* see SENTIMENTAL —**mawk′ish·ly** *adv.* —**mawk′ish·ness** *n.*

Maw·son (mô′s'n), Sir **Douglas** 1882–1958; Australian geologist & antarctic explorer, born in England

Max (maks) a masculine name: see MAXIMILIAN

max. maximum

☆**max·i-** (mak′sē) [< MAXI(MUM)] *a combining form meaning* maximum, very large, very long [*maxicoat*]: used freely to form nonce compounds, often hyphenated, meaning "of greater scope, extent, etc. than usual" [*maxi-power*]

max·il·la (mak sil′ə) *n., pl.* -lae (-ē) [L., dim., akin to *mala,* a jaw] **1.** in vertebrates, the upper jaw, or a major bone or cartilage of the upper jaw: see SKULL, illus. **2.** in most arthropods, as insects, crabs, etc., one of the first or second pair of accessory jaws or head appendages situated just behind the mandibles

max·il·lar·y (mak′sə ler′ē; *chiefly Brit.,* mak sil′ə rē) *adj.* [L. *maxillaris*] designating, of, or near the jaw or jawbone, esp. the upper one; relating to a maxilla or maxillae —*n., pl.* -lar′ies a maxillary bone; maxilla

max·il·li·ped (mak sil′i ped′) *n.* [< MAXILLA + -PED] any one limb of the three pairs of appendages lying behind the maxillae in crustaceans and modified for aid in feeding

max·im (mak′sim) *n.* [ME. *maxime* < MFr. < ML. *maxima* < LL. *maxima* (*propositio*), the greatest (premise), fem. of L. *maximus,* greatest, superl. of *magnus,* great: see MAGNI-] a concisely expressed principle or rule of conduct,

or a statement of a general truth; precept —*SYN.* see SAYING

Max·im (mak′sim) **1.** Sir **Hiram Stevens,** 1840–1916; Brit. engineer & inventor of weapons & explosives, born in the U.S. **2. Hudson,** 1853–1927; U.S. chemist & inventor of explosives: brother of *prec.*

max·i·ma (mak′sə mə) *n. alt. pl. of* MAXIMUM

max·i·mal (-m'l) *adj.* highest or greatest possible; of or constituting a maximum —**max′i·mal·ly** *adv.*

max·i·mal·ist (mak′sə m'l ist) *n.* [prec. + -IST] a person who favors direct or revolutionary action to achieve a goal

Maxim gun [after H. S. MAXIM, its inventor] an early, single-barreled, water-cooled machine gun

Max·i·mil·ian (mak′sə mil′yən) [? a blend of the L. names *Maximus & Aemilianus*] **1.** a masculine name: dim. *Max* **2.** (*Ferdinand Maximilian Joseph*), 1832–67; archduke of Austria; emperor of Mexico (1864–67): executed **3. Maximilian I** 1459–1519; emperor of the Holy Roman Empire (1493–1519) **4. Maximilian II** 1527–76; emperor of the Holy Roman Empire (1564–76)

☆**max·im·ite** (mak′sə mit′) *n.* [after Hudson MAXIM] a high explosive made with picric acid, formerly much used in armor-piercing projectiles

max·i·mize (mak′sə mīz′) *vt.* -mized′, -miz′ing to increase to the maximum; raise to the highest possible degree; enlarge, intensify, etc. as much as possible — **max′i·mi·za′tion** *n.* —**max′i·miz′er** *n.*

max·i·mum (-məm) *n., pl.* -mums, -ma (-mə) [L., neut. of *maximus,* superl. of *magnus,* great: see MUCH] **1.** the greatest quantity, number, or degree possible or permissible **2.** the highest degree or point (of a varying quantity, as temperature) reached or recorded; upper limit of variation **3.** *Math.* the largest of a specified set of real numbers —*adj.* **1.** greatest possible, permissible, or reached **2.** of, marking, or setting a maximum or maximums

Max·ine (mak sēn′) [fem. of MAX] a feminine name

max·well (maks′wel) *n.* [after ff.] the cgs electromagnetic unit of magnetic flux, equal to the flux through one square centimeter normal to a magnetic field with an intensity of one gauss

Max·well (maks′wel, -wəl), **James Clerk** (klärk) 1831–79; Scot. physicist

May¹ (mā) *n.* [ME. < OFr. *mai* < L. (*mensis*) *Maius,* (month) of *Maia,* goddess of increase < base of *magnus,* great: see MUCH] **1.** the fifth month of the year, having 31 days **2.** *a)* springtime *b)* the springtime of life; youth; prime **3.** [m·] *a)* the English hawthorn (*Crataegus oxyacantha*) with small, lobed leaves and white, pink, or red flowers *b)* its branches or flowers **4.** the festivities of May Day —*vi.* [*also* m-] to gather flowers in the spring: chiefly in the participle [to go *Maying*]

May² (mā) [contr. of MARY, MARGARET, often associated with the name of the month] a feminine name

may¹ (mā) *v.aux. pt.* **might** [ME. < OE. *mæg,* akin to G. *mag,* Goth. *magan,* lit., to be physically capable of doing < IE. base *māgh-,* to be able, whence Gr. *mēchanē,* a machine, Sans. *maghā-,* might] an auxiliary preceding an (expressed or implied) infinitive (without *to*) and expressing: **1.** orig., ability or power: now generally replaced by *can* **2.** possibility or likelihood [it *may* rain] **3.** permission or chance [you *may* go]: see also CAN¹ **4.** contingency, as in clauses of purpose, result, concession, or condition [they died that we *may* be free] **5.** wish, hope, or prayer: used in exclamations and apostrophes [*may* he rest in peace] **6.** *Law* shall; must —*SYN.* see CAN¹

may² (mā) *n.* [ME. < OE. *mæg,* kinswoman, woman (? merged with ON. *mær,* maiden) [Archaic] a maiden

May, Cape [after Cornelius J. *Mey,* Du. official] peninsula at the southernmost point of N.J.: c. 20 mi. long

Ma·ya¹ (mä′yə) *n.* [Sp. < native name] **1.** *pl.* **Ma′yas, Ma′ya** any member of a tribe of Indians found in Yucatan, British Honduras, and N Guatemala: the Mayas had a highly developed civilization when discovered by Europeans early in the 16th century **2.** *a)* their Mayan language *b)* one of several branches of the Mayan family of languages —*adj.* of the Mayas, their language, culture, etc.; Mayan

Ma·ya² (mä′yə) [Sans. *māyā*] *Hinduism* the goddess Devi, or Shakti, consort of Siva —*n.* [*also* m-] illusion, or the illusory world of the senses, often personified as a woman

Ma·ya·güez (mä′yä gwes′) seaport in W Puerto Rico: pop. 69,000

Ma·ya·kov·sky (mä′yä kôf′skē), **Vla·di·mir** (**Vladimirovich**) (vlä dē′mir′) 1894–1930; Russ. poet

Ma·yan (mä′yən) *adj.* **1.** designating or of an American Indian language family of Central America, consisting of about 25 languages that are grouped in several branches, as Maya, Huastec, etc. **2.** *same as* MAYA¹ —*n.* **1.** any member of the Indian peoples that speak a Mayan language **2.** the Mayan language family

☆**May apple 1.** a perennial woodland plant (*Podophyllum peltatum*) of the barberry family, with shield-shaped leaves and a single, large, white, cuplike flower, found in the E U.S. **2.** its edible, yellow, oval fruit

may·be (mā′bē) *adv.* [ME. (for *it may be*)] perhaps

May beetle ☆*same as* JUNE BUG (sense 1)

---

fat, āpe, cär; ten, ēven; is, bīte; gō, hôrn, tōōl, look; oil, out; up, fur; get; joy; yet; chin; she; thin, *then*; zh, leisure; ŋ, ring; ə for *a* in *ago, e* in *agent, i* in *sanity, o* in *comply, u* in *focus;* ′ as in *able* (ā′b'l); Fr. bȧl; ë, Fr. coeur; ö, Fr. feu; ô, Fr. mon; ö̃, Fr. coq; ü, Fr. duc; r, Fr. cri; H, G. ich; kh, G. doch. See inside front cover. ☆ Americanism; ‡foreign; *hypothetical; <derived from

May·day (mā'dā') *n.* [prob. short for Fr. (*venez*) *m'aider*, (come) help me] the international radiotelephonic signal for help, used by ships and aircraft in distress

May Day May 1: as a traditional spring festival, often celebrated by dancing around a Maypole, crowning a May queen, etc.; as a more recent international labor holiday, observed in many countries by parades, demonstrations, etc.

may·est (mā'ist, māst) *archaic 2d pers. sing., pres. indic., of* MAY[1]: *used with* thou

May·fair (mā'fer') [after an annual fair held there (prior to 1708) in May] a fashionable residential district of the West End, London

may·flow·er (-flou'ər) *n.* any of various plants that flower in May or early spring; esp., ☆a) in the U.S., the trailing arbutus, any of several anemones, etc. b) in England, the may, cowslip, marsh marigold, etc. —[M-] the ship on which the Pilgrims came to America (1620)

may·fly (-flī') *n., pl.* **-flies** 1. any of an order (Ephemeroptera) of delicate, soft-bodied insects with gauzy wings held vertically when at rest: in the adult stage, it lives only hours or a few days, but the aquatic larval stage may last for several years 2. an angler's artificial fly made to resemble this insect

MAYFLY
(body to 1 inch)

may·hap (mā'hap', mā'hap') *adv.* [< *it may hap(pen)*] [Archaic] perhaps; maybe: also **may'hap'pen**

may·hem (mā'hem, mā'əm) *n.* [see MAIM] 1. *Law* the offense of maiming a person; specif., a) the intentional mutilation of another's body b) injury inflicted on another so as to cause loss of a bodily part or function necessary for self-defense 2. loosely, any deliberate destruction or violence

May·ing (mā'iŋ) *n.* [*also* m-] the celebration of May Day, as by gathering flowers, dancing, etc.

May·nard (mā'nərd, -närd) [ME. < Anglo-Fr. *Mainard* < OHG. *Maganhard* < *magan*, power, strength (see MAY[1]) + *hart*, strong, HARD] a masculine name

may·n't (mā'ənt, mānt) may not

May·o (mā'ō) county in NW Ireland, in Connacht province: 2,084 sq. mi.; pop. 116,000

May·o (mā'ō), **Charles Horace**, 1865–1939, & his brother **William James**, 1861–1939; U.S. surgeons

Ma·yon (mä yōn') active volcano in SE Luzon, Philippines: c. 8,000 ft.

may·on·naise (mā'ə nāz', mā'ə nāz') *n.* [Fr., earlier *mahonnaise*, apparently fem. of *mahonais*, of *Mahón*, Minorca: reason for name unknown] 1. a creamy salad dressing or sauce made by beating together egg yolks, olive oil or other vegetable oil, lemon juice or vinegar, and seasoning 2. a dish of meat or fish made with this

may·or (mā'ər, mer) *n.* [ME. *mair* < OFr. *maire* < L. *major*, compar. of *magnus*, great: see MUCH] the chief administrative official of a city, town, or other municipality, or, under a city-manager plan, the titular, or formal, head —**may'or·al** *adj.* —[Rare] **may'or·ess** *n.fem.*

may·or·al·ty (-əl tē) *n., pl.* **-ties** [ME. *mairalte* < OFr. *mairalté*] the office or term of office of a mayor

May·pole (mā'pōl') *n.* a high pole wreathed with flowers, streamers, etc., around which merrymakers dance on May Day

may·pop (mā'päp') *n.* [altered < *maracock* < AmInd. (Algonquian)] 1. the small, yellow, edible fruit of a passionflower (*Passiflora incarnata*) growing in the S U.S. 2. the plant itself

May queen a girl chosen to be queen of the merrymakers on May Day and crowned with flowers

mayst (māst) *archaic 2d pers. sing., pres. indic., of* MAY[1]: *used with* thou

May·time (mā'tīm') *n.* the month of May: also **May'tide'** (-tīd')

may tree [Brit.] *same as* MAY[1] (sense 3)

may·weed (mā'wēd') *n.* [for *maidweed* < **maythe-weed* < OE. *magothe*, mayweed (prob. akin to *mægeth*, maiden) + WEED[1]] *same as* DOG FENNEL (sense 1)

May wine [after the month of May, when the woodruff blossoms] a punch made of white wine flavored with woodruff and slices of pineapple and orange

maz·ard (maz'ərd) *n.* [altered (after -ARD) < MAZER] [Obs.] 1. a mazer 2. a) the head or skull b) the face

Ma·za·rin (má zà ran'; E. maz'ər in), **Jules** (zhül), Cardinal, (born *Giulio Mazarini*) 1602–61; Fr. statesman & prelate, born in Italy

Ma·za·tlán (mä'sät län') seaport on the Pacific coast of Mexico, in the state of Sinaloa: pop. 75,000

Maz·da·ism (maz'də iz'm) *n.* [< Avestan *mazda* (see ORMAZD) + -ISM] *same as* ZOROASTRIANISM

maze (māz) *n.* [ME. *masen*, to confuse, puzzle < OE. **masian* < *amasian* (see AMAZE) & pp. *amasod*, puzzled, confused] 1. [Archaic] to stupefy; daze 2. to confuse; bewilder —*n.* 1. a confusing, intricate network of winding pathways; labyrinth; specif., such a network with one or more blind alleys, used in psycholog-

ical experiments and tests 2. a state of confusion or bewilderment

‡**maz·el tov** (mä'z'l tōv', tôf') [Heb. (often via Yid.) < *mãzal*, luck + *tōv*, good] good luck: an expression of congratulation: also **maz'el·tov', maz'zel tov**

ma·zer (mā'zər) *n.* [ME. *maser* < OFr. *masere*, maple wood < Gmc., as in OHG. *masar*, gnarled growth on oaks, ON. *mösurr*, maple, akin to OHG. *māsa*, a spot] a large drinking bowl or goblet, orig. of a hard wood, probably maple, later of metal

☆**ma·zu·ma** (mə zōō'mə) *n.* [Yid. *mezumon* < Heb. *mezũmānim*] [Slang] money

ma·zur·ka, ma·zour·ka (mə zur'kə, -zoor'-) *n.* [Pol. *mazurka*, woman from Mazovia (or Masovia), region of C Poland] 1. a lively Polish dance like the polka 2. music for this, generally in 3/4 or 3/8 time

ma·zy (mā'zē) *adj.* **-zi·er, -zi·est** like a maze; intricately winding; bewildering —**maz'i·ly** *adv.* —**maz'i·ness** *n.*

maz·zard (maz'ərd) *n.* [? var. of MAZER] *same as* SWEET CHERRY; esp., a wild sweet cherry whose young seedlings are used as a rootstock for cultivated varieties

Maz·zi·ni (mät tsē'nē, mäd dzē'nē), **Giu·sep·pe** (jōō zep' pe) 1805–72; It. patriot & revolutionist

mb millibar; millibars

M.B.A. Master of Business Administration

M·ba·ba·ne ('m bä bä'nä) capital of Swaziland in the NW part: pop. 14,000

MBS Mutual Broadcasting System

Mbun·du ('m bōōn'dōō) *n.* 1. *pl.* **-dus, -du** any member of a Bantu-speaking people of WC Angola 2. their language

Mc-, Mc- (mak, mək, mə) *same as* MAC-

mc. 1. megacycle(s) 2. millicurie(s)

M.C. 1. Master Commandant 2. Master of Ceremonies 3. Medical Corps 4. Member of Congress

Mc·Al·len (mə kal'ən) [after John *McAllen*, local rancher] city in S Tex., in the Rio Grande valley: pop. 38,000

☆**Mc·Car·thy·ism** (mə kär'thē iz'm) *n.* [after J. *McCarthy*, U.S. senator (1946–1957), to whom such practices were attributed] the use of indiscriminate, often unfounded, accusations, sensationalism, inquisitorial investigative methods, etc., ostensibly in the suppression of communism

Mc·Clel·lan (mə klel'ən), **George Brin·ton** (brin't'n) 1826–85; Union general in the Civil War

Mc·Cor·mack (mə kôr'mək), **John** 1884–1945; U.S. tenor, born in Ireland

Mc·Cor·mick (mə kôr'mik), **Cyrus Hall** 1809–84; U.S. inventor of the reaping machine

Mc·Coy (mə koi'), **the** (**real**) [altered (? after Kid *McCoy*, Am. boxer) < Scottish (*the real*) *Mackay*, name of a clan, later of a whisky) [Slang] the real person or thing, not a substitute

Mc·Guf·fey (mə guf'ē), **William Holmes** 1800–73; U.S. educator: editor of a series of school readers

Mc·In·tosh (mak/in täsh') *n.* [after John *McIntosh*, Ontario, who discovered and cultivated it (1796)] a late-n.autumn variety of red apple: also **McIntosh Red**

Mc·Kees·port (mə kēz'pôrt) [after David *McKee*, early land owner (c. 1770)] city in SW Pa., on the Monongahela River, near Pittsburgh: pop. 38,000

Mc·Kin·ley (mə kin'lē), **Mount** [after ff.] mountain of the Alaska Range, SC Alas.: highest peak in N. America: 20,320 ft.: in a national park (**Mount McKinley National Park**), 3,030 sq. mi.

McKinley, William 1843–1901; 25th president of the U.S. (1897–1901): assassinated

M.C.L. Master of Civil Law

Mc·Lu·han (mə klōō'ən), (**Herbert**) **Marshall** 1911– ; Canad. writer & educator

Mc·Mur·do Sound (mək mur'dō) arm of the Ross Sea, off the coast of Victoria Land, Antarctica

Md *Chem.* mendelevium

M/D, m/d month's date (i.e., months after date)

Md. Maryland

M.D. 1. [L. *Medicinae Doctor*] Doctor of Medicine 2. Medical Department

M-day (em'dā') *n.* [*m(obilization) day*] the day on which active mobilization for war is ordered

Mdlle., *pl.* **Mdlles.** Mademoiselle

Mdm., *pl.* **Mdms.** Madam

Mdme., *pl.* **Mdmes.** Madame

M.D.S. Master of Dental Surgery

mdse. merchandise

MDu. Middle Dutch

me (mē) *pron.* [ME. < OE., akin to G. *mich*, acc., *mir*, dat. < IE. base **me-*, whence L. *me*, acc., *mi(hi)*, dat.] *objective case of* I: also used colloquially as a predicate complement with a linking verb (Ex.: that's *me*)

Me methyl

ME. Middle English

Me. Maine

M.E. 1. Master of Education 2. Mechanical Engineer 3. Medical Examiner 4. Methodist Episcopal 5. Middle English 6. Military Engineer 7. Mining Engineer 8. Most Excellent

‡**me·a cul·pa** (mē'ə kul'pə, mā'ä kool'pä) [L.] (by) my fault; I am to blame

mead[1] (mēd) *n.* [ME. *mede* < OE. *meodu*, akin to G. *met* < IE. base **medhu-*, honey, whence Sans. *mādhu*, Gr. *methy*, wine, W. *medd*, mead] an alcoholic liquor made of

fermented honey and water, often with spices, fruit, malt, etc. added

mead² (mēd) *n.* [ME. *mede* < OE. *mæd*, MEADOW] *poet. var. of* MEADOW

Mead (mēd), **Lake** [after Elwood *Mead* (1858–1936), U.S. engineer] lake in SE Nev. & NW Ariz., formed by the Hoover Dam on the Colorado River: c. 250 sq. mi.

Mead (mēd), **Margaret** 1901– ; U.S. anthropologist

Meade (mēd), **George Gordon**, 1815–72; Union general in the Civil War

mead·ow (med′ō) *n.* [ME. *medowe* < OE. *mædwe*, oblique case of *mæd* < Gmc. base *mædwa- < IE. base *mē-, to MOW¹] **1.** a piece of grassland, esp. one whose grass is grown for use as hay **2.** low, level grassland near a stream, lake, etc. —**mead′ow·y** *adj.*

☆**meadow beauty** any of a genus (*Rhexia*) of perennial N. American plants of the melastome family, with pink or lavender flowers and large stamens

meadow fescue a tufted perennial grass (*Festuca elatior*) with narrow lustrous leaves, used for hay meadows and lawns, esp. in the E U.S.

☆**mead·ow·lark** (-lärk′) *n., pl.* **-larks′, -lark′:** see PLURAL, II, D, 1 either of two N. American songbirds (genus *Sturnella*) having upper parts streaked with black and brown and a bright yellow breast with a black V-shaped collar; specif., the **eastern meadowlark** (*Sturnella magna*) and the **western meadowlark** (*Sturnella neglecta*)

☆**meadow lily** *same as* CANADA LILY

meadow mouse *same as* FIELD MOUSE

meadow mushroom a common edible mushroom (*Agaricus campestris*) with pinkish or brown gills, found in open, grassy areas and often cultivated for the market

meadow nematode any of a number of roundworms (genus *Pratylenchus*), parasitic on the roots of various commercial crops and other plants

meadow rue any of a genus (*Thalictrum*) of perennial plants of the buttercup family, with leaves like those of rue

meadow saffron *same as* COLCHICUM (sense 1)

mead·ow·sweet (-swēt′) *n.* **1.** any of several spiraeas; esp., two common species (*Spiraea alba* and *Spiraea latifolia*) **2.** any of a genus (*Filipendula*) of plants of the rose family, with fragrant, white, pink, or purple flowers in clusters

mea·ger (mē′gər) *adj.* [ME. *megre* < OFr. < L. *macer*, lean, thin < IE. base *māk-, long and thin, whence Gr. *makros*, long, OE. *mæger*, meager] **1.** thin; lean; emaciated **2.** of poor quality or small amount; not full or rich; inadequate Also, Brit., **mea′gre** —**mea′ger·ly** *adv.* —**mea′ger·ness** *n.*

SYN.—**meager** literally implies an emaciated thinness and, hence, connotes a lack of those qualities which give something richness, vigor, strength, etc. [*meager* cultural resources]; **scanty** implies an inadequacy in amount, number, quantity, etc. of something essential [a *scanty* income]; **scant** is applied to a barely sufficient amount or a stinted quantity [the *scant* attendance at the concert]; **spare** implies less than a sufficient amount but does not necessarily connote great hardship [to live on *spare* rations]; **sparse** applies to a scanty quantity that is thinly distributed over a wide area [his *sparse* hair] —**ANT. ample, abundant, plentiful**

meal¹ (mēl) *n.* [ME. *mele* < OE. *mæl*, a measure, fixed time, meal, akin to G. *mal*, time, *mahl* < IE. base *mē-, to measure, whence Gr. *metron*, measure, L. *metiri*, to measure, whence *mensa*, dining table] **1.** any of the times, esp. the customary times, for eating, as breakfast, lunch, or dinner **2.** the food served or eaten at such a time

meal² (mēl) *n.* [ME. *mele* < OE. *melu*, akin to G. *mehl* < IE. base *mel-, to grind, soft, tender, whence L. *molere*, to grind, *molina*, MILL¹] **1.** any edible grain, or the edible part of any grain, coarsely ground and unbolted [*cornmeal*] **2.** any substance similarly ground or powdered

-meal (mēl) [ME. *-mele* < OE. *-mælum* < *mæl*, measure, time (see MEAL¹) + adv. dat. *-um*] an *adv.-forming suffix meaning* amount done or used at one time: obsolete except in *inchmeal, piecemeal*

meal·ie (mēl′ē) *n.* [Afrik. *milje* < Port. *milho*, millet, in *milho grande*, maize] in South Africa, **1.** [*pl.*] *same as* CORN¹ (sense 3) **2.** an ear of this

☆**meal ticket 1.** a ticket entitling the holder to a specified value in meals at a particular restaurant **2.** [Slang] a person, job, skill, etc. that one depends on as one's means of support

meal·time (mēl′tīm′) *n.* the usual time for serving or eating a meal

meal·worm (-wurm′) *n.* the wormlike larva of any of various beetles (genus *Tenebrio*) which infests granaries and bakeries, destroying flour, meal, etc.

meal·y (mēl′ē) *adj.* **meal′i·er, meal′i·est 1.** like meal; powdery, dry, soft, etc. **2.** of or containing meal **3.** sprinkled or covered with meal **4.** spotty or flecked: said of color, etc. **5.** floury in color; pale **6.** *same as* MEALY-MOUTHED —**meal′i·ness** *n.*

meal·y·bug (-bug′) *n.* any of a family (Pseudococcidae) of destructive, homopterous insects, having a soft body protected by a white, flourlike or cottony wax secretion

meal·y·mouthed (-mouthd′, -moutht′) *adj.* not out-

spoken or blunt; not willing to state the facts in simple, direct words; euphemistic and insincere

mean¹ (mēn) *vt.* **meant** (ment), **mean′ing** [ME. *menen* < OE. *mænan*, akin to G. *meinen*, to have in mind, have as opinion < IE. base *maino-, opinion, intent, whence OIr. *mian*, wish, desire] **1.** to have in mind; intend; purpose [he *means* to go] **2.** *a)* to intend or design for a certain person or purpose [a gift *meant* for you] *b)* to destine or seem to destine [he was *meant* to be a doctor] **3.** to intend to express, signify, or indicate [to say what one *means*] **4.** to be used to convey; signify; denote; import [the German word "ja" *means* "yes"] —*vi.* **1.** to have a purpose or intention in mind: chiefly in **mean well,** to have good intentions **2.** to have a (specified) degree of importance, effect, or influence [honors *mean* little to him] —**SYN.** see INTEND —**mean well by** to have good intentions or friendly, helpful feelings toward

mean² (mēn) *adj.* [ME. *mene*, common, hence mean < OE. (ge)*mæne*, akin to G. *gemein*, plentiful, common, vulgar: for IE. base see COMMON] **1.** low in quality, value, or importance; paltry; poor; inferior: now usually in negative constructions [paid no *mean* sum] **2.** [Rare] low in social status or rank; of humble origin **3.** poor in appearance; shabby [a *mean* dwelling] **4.** ignoble; base; small-minded; petty **5.** stingy; miserly; penurious ☆**6.** bad-tempered; vicious; unmanageable: said of a horse, etc. ☆**7.** pettily or contemptibly selfish, bad-tempered, disagreeable, malicious, etc. ☆**8.** humiliated or ashamed ☆**9.** [Colloq.] in poor health; not well; ill; indisposed ☆**10.** [Slang] *a)* hard to cope with; difficult [to throw a *mean* curve in baseball] *b)* skillful; expert [to play a *mean* game of chess] —**SYN.** see BASE² —**mean′ly** *adv.* —**mean′ness** *n.*

mean³ (mēn) *adj.* [ME. *mene* < OFr. *meien* (Fr. *moyen*) < L. *medianus*: see MEDIAN] **1.** halfway between extremes; in a middle or intermediate position as to place, time, quantity, quality, kind, value, degree, etc. **2.** medium; average; middling —*n.* **1.** what is between extremes; intermediate state, quality, course, or procedure **2.** avoidance of extremes or excess; moderation **3.** the middle term of a syllogism **4.** *Math. a)* a number between the smallest and largest values of a set of quantities, obtained by some prescribed method: unless otherwise qualified, *same as* ARITHMETIC MEAN *b)* the number obtained by multiplying each value of x by the probability (or probability density) of x and then summing (or integrating) over the range of x *c)* the second or third term of a four-term proportion See also GEOMETRIC MEAN, MEANS —**SYN.** see AVERAGE

Meander *same as* MAEANDER

me·an·der (mē an′dər) *n.* [L. *maeander* < Gr. *maiandros* < *Maiandros*, the MAEANDER (noted for its winding course)] **1.** [*pl.*] windings or convolutions, as of a stream **2.** an ornamental pattern of winding or crisscrossing lines **3.** an aimless wandering; rambling —*vi.* **1.** to take a winding or tortuous course: said of a stream **2.** to wander aimlessly or idly; ramble —**SYN.** see ROAM —**me·an′drous** (-drəs) *adj.*

mean deviation the average of the absolute values of a set of deviations or differences from a specified value, usually the arithmetic mean

mean distance the arithmetic mean of the greatest and least distances in the orbit of a body, as a planet, satellite, etc., from its focus

mean·ie, mean·y (mē′nē) *n., pl.* **mean′ies** [Colloq.] a person who is mean, selfish, cruel, etc.

mean·ing (mē′niŋ) *n.* **1.** what is meant; what is intended to be, or in fact is, signified, indicated, referred to, or understood; signification, purport, import, sense, or significance [the *meaning* of a word] **2.** [Archaic] intention; purpose —*adj.* **1.** that has meaning; significant; expressive **2.** intending; having purpose —**mean′ing·ly** *adv.*

SYN.—**meaning** is the general word for what is intended to be expressed or understood by something [the *meaning* of a sentence]; **sense,** in this connection, refers esp. to any of the various meanings conveyed by a word or phrase [this word has several *slang senses*]; **import** refers to the total implication of something said or done, including the subtle connotations [I didn't get the full *import* of his remark]; **purport** refers to the general meaning, or gist, of something [what was the *purport* of her letter?]; **signification** is applied esp. to the meaning conventionally understood by a sign, symbol, character, etc. [the *signification* of the ace of spades in fortunetelling]; **significance** refers to the subtle, hidden implications of something as distinguished from its openly expressed meaning [his "no!" had a special *significance* for us]

mean·ing·ful (-fəl) *adj.* full of meaning; having significance or purpose —**mean′ing·ful·ly** *adv.* —**mean′ing·ful·ness** *n.*

mean·ing·less (-lis) *adj.* having no meaning; without significance or purpose; senseless —**mean′ing·less·ly** *adv.* —**mean′ing·less·ness** *n.*

means (mēnz) *n.pl.* [< MEAN³, *n.*] **1.** [*with sing. or pl. v.*] that by which something is done or obtained; agency [the fastest *means* of travel] **2.** resources or available wealth; often, specif., great wealth; riches [a person of *means*] —**by all means 1.** without fail **2.** of course; certainly —**by any means** in any way possible; at all;

somehow —**by means of** by using; with the aid of; through —**by no (manner of) means** not at all; in no way —**means to an end** a method of getting or accomplishing what one wants

mean solar time time measured by the mean sun and having exactly equal divisions: also **mean time**

means test the investigation of his financial resources that a person who is unemployed or has a relatively low income must undergo in order to be eligible for welfare payments, low-cost housing, etc.

mean sun *Astron.* a hypothetical sun thought of as moving uniformly along the celestial equator at the average speed with which the true sun moves in the ecliptic and completing one circuit of the sky with respect to the vernal equinox in a tropical year

meant (ment) *pt. & pp.* of MEAN[1]

mean·time (mēn′tīm′) *adv.* 1. in or during the intervening time 2. at the same time —*n.* the intervening time Also, and for adv. now usually, **mean′while′** (-hwīl′)

Mean·y (mē′nē), **George** 1894– ; U.S. labor leader; president of the AFL-CIO (1955–)

meas. measure

mea·sled (mē′z'ld) *adj.* infected with measles (sense 2)

mea·sles (mē′z'lz) *n.pl.* [*with sing. v. in senses 1 & 2 a*] [ME. *maseles*, pl. of *masel*, measle, spot (? infl. by *mesel*, leper < OFr. < L. *misellus*, wretch < *miser*, wretched), akin to OHG. *māsa*, a spot, G. *masern*, measles] 1. *a*) an acute, infectious, communicable virus disease, characterized by small red spots on the skin, high fever, nasal discharge, etc., and occurring most frequently in childhood; rubeola *b*) any of various similar but milder diseases; esp., rubella (called *German measles*) 2. *a*) a disease of cattle and hogs caused by tapeworm larvae in the flesh *b*) these larvae

mea·sly (mēz′lē) *adj.* **-sli·er, -sli·est** 1. infected with measles (sense 1 or 2) 2. [Colloq.] contemptibly slight, worthless, or skimpy

meas·ur·a·ble (mezh′ər ə b'l) *adj.* [ME. *mesurable* < OFr.] that can be measured —**meas′ur·a·bil′i·ty, meas′ur·a·ble·ness** *n.* —**meas′ur·a·bly** *adv.*

meas·ure (mezh′ər, mā′zhər) *n.* [ME. *mesure* < OFr. < L. *mensura* < *mensus*, pp. of *metiri*, to measure < IE. base **mē*-, to measure, whence Gr. *metron*] 1. the extent, dimensions, capacity, etc. of anything, esp. as determined by a standard 2. the act or process of determining extent, dimensions, etc.; measurement 3. *a*) a standard for determining extent, dimensions, etc.; unit of measurement, as an inch, yard, or bushel *b*) any standard of valuation, comparison, judgment, etc.; criterion 4. a system of measurement [*dry measure, board measure*] 5. an instrument for measuring, or a container of standard capacity [*a quart measure*] 6. a definite quantity measured out or thought of as measured 7. an extent or degree not to be exceeded [*remain within measure*] 8. proportion, quantity, or degree [*in large measure*] 9. a procedure; course of action; step [*take measures to stop him*] 10. a legislative enactment; statute; law 11. *a*) rhythm in verse; meter *b*) a metrical unit; foot of verse 12. a dance or dance movement, esp. if slow or stately 13. [Poet.] a melody or tune 14. [*pl.*] *Geol.* [Rare] related beds or strata, as of coal 15. *Math.* a divisor that leaves no remainder 16. *Music a*) the notes or rests, or both, contained between two vertical lines on the staff, subdividing a part of a composition into equal groups of beats; bar *b*) musical time or rhythm 17. *Printing* the width of a column or page —*vt.* **-ured, -ur·ing** [ME. *mesuren* < OFr. *mesurer* < LL. *mensurare*, to measure < the L. *n.*] 1. to find out or estimate the extent, dimensions, etc. of, esp. by a standard 2. to get, take, set apart, or mark off by measuring (often with *off* or *out*) 3. to estimate by comparison; judge; appraise [*to measure one's foe*] 4. to bring into comparison or rivalry (*against*) [*to measure one's skill against another's*] 5. to be a measure of [*a clock measures time*] 6. to adjust or proportion by a standard [*to measure a speech by the listeners' reactions*] 7. to choose or weigh carefully (one's words or actions) 8. [Now Rare] to go over or through; traverse as if measuring —*vi.* 1. to find out or estimate extent, dimensions, etc.; get or take measurements 2. to be of a specified dimension, quantity, etc. when measured [*a pole that measures ten feet*] 3. to allow of measurement —**beyond** (or **above**) **measure** so much as not to be measurable; exceedingly; extremely —**for good measure** as a bonus or something extra —**in a measure** to some extent; somewhat —**made to measure** made to fit one's own measurements; custom-made: said of clothes —**measure one's length** to fall, lie, or be thrown down at full length —**measure out** to give out or allot by measuring —**measure swords** 1. to duel with swords 2. to fight or contend —**measure up** 1. to be considered, according to some standard 2. to prove to be competent or qualified —☆**measure up to** to come up to; meet (expectations, a standard, etc.) —**take measures** to take action; do things to accomplish a purpose —**take someone's measure** to make an estimate or judgment of someone's ability, character, etc. —**tread a measure** to dance —**meas′ur·er** *n.*

meas·ured (-ərd, -zhərd) *adj.* 1. determined, ascertained,

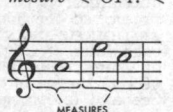

MEASURES

or proportioned by a standard 2. *a*) regular, steady, or uniform *b*) steady, slow, and deliberate [*to walk with a measured tread*] 3. *a*) rhythmical *b*) metrical 4. calculated, restrained, and deliberate; careful and guarded: said of speech, etc. —**meas′ured·ly** *adv.*

meas·ure·less (mezh′ər lis, mā′zhər-) *adj.* too large to be measurable; vast; immense —**meas′ure·less·ly** *adv.*

meas·ure·ment (-mənt) *n.* 1. a measuring or being measured; mensuration 2. extent, quantity, or size as determined by measuring; dimension [*a waist measurement of 32 inches*] 3. a system of measuring or of measures

measuring cup a standard cup, usually one holding either 8 oz. or 16 oz., with marks to show fractional amounts and with a lip for pouring, used to measure ingredients in cooking

☆**measuring worm** the caterpillar larva of any geometrid moth: it moves by alternately advancing the front end of its body and bringing the rear end forward to form a loop

meat (mēt) *n.* [ME. *mete* < OE., akin to Goth. *mats* < IE. base **mad*-, to be moist, trickle, whence MAST[2], Gr. *mastos*, breast] 1. food; esp., solid food, as distinguished from drink: now archaic or dialectal except in **meat and drink** 2. the flesh of animals used as food; esp., the flesh of mammals and, sometimes, of fowl 3. the edible, inner part [*the meat of a nut*] 4. the substance, meaning, or gist [*the meat of a story*] 5. one's quarry 6. [Archaic] a meal, esp. dinner —☆**one's meat** [Slang] something that one especially enjoys or is skillful at [*golf's my meat*]

meat·ball (-bôl′) *n.* 1. a small ball of ground meat, seasoned and cooked, often with sauce, gravy, etc. 2. [Slang] a stupid, awkward, or boring person

☆**meat·head** (-hed′) *n.* [Slang] a stupid person; blockhead

meat hooks ☆[Slang] the hands or fists

meat·less (-lis) *adj.* 1. having no meat or food 2. when no meat is to be eaten [*a meatless day*]

meat·man (-man′) *n., pl.* **-men** (-men′) a man who sells meat; butcher

☆**meat·pack·ing** (-pak′iŋ) *n.* the process or industry of slaughtering animals and preparing their meat for market —**meat′pack′er** *n.*

me·a·tus (mē āt′əs) *n., pl.* **-tus·es, -tus** [LL., avenue of sensation in the body < L., a passage, pp. of *meare*, to go, pass < IE. base **mei*-, to go] a natural passage or duct in the body, or its opening

meat·y (mēt′ē) *adj.* **meat′i·er, meat′i·est** 1. of, like, or having the flavor or quality of, meat 2. *a*) full of meat *b*) stout; heavy ☆3. full of substance; thought-provoking; pithy —**meat′i·ness** *n.*

Mec·ca (mek′ə) one of the two capitals of Saudi Arabia, near the Red Sea: birthplace of Mohammed & hence a holy city of Islam, to which Moslems make pilgrimages: pop. c. 200,000 —*n.* [*often m-*] *a*) any place visited by many people *b*) any place that one yearns to go to *c*) any goal that one is seeking to achieve —**Mec′can** *adj., n.*

mech. 1. mechanical 2. mechanics 3. mechanism

me·chan·ic (mə kan′ik) *adj.* [L. *mechanicus* < Gr. *mēchanikos* < *mēchanē*, MACHINE] *rare or archaic var.* of MECHANICAL —*n.* 1. a worker skilled in using tools or in making, operating, and repairing machines 2. [Archaic] a manual laborer

me·chan·i·cal (-i k'l) *adj.* 1. having to do with, or having skill in the use of, machinery or tools 2. produced or operated by machinery or a mechanism 3. of, in accordance with, or using the principles and terminology of, the science of mechanics 4. automatic, as if from force of habit; machinelike; lacking spontaneity, expression, warmth, etc. [*to greet someone in a mechanical way*] 5. [Archaic] of manual labor or manual laborers —*n. Printing* a pasted-up dummy that is photographed for making into a plate —**me·chan′i·cal·ly** *adv.*

mechanical advantage the ratio of the output force of a device that performs useful work to the input force: used in rating the performance of a machine

mechanical drawing 1. the art of drawing by the use of T squares, scales, compasses, etc. 2. a drawing so made

mechanical tissue a plant tissue made up of hard, thick-walled cells that add strength to an organ

mech·a·ni·cian (mek′ə nish′ən) *n.* a person skilled in the theory, design, operation, or care of machinery

me·chan·ics (mə kan′iks) *n.pl.* [*with sing. v. in senses 1, 2, and usually 3*] [see MECHANIC] 1. the branch of physics that deals with the motion of material bodies and the phenomena of the action of forces on bodies: cf. STATICS, DYNAMICS, KINEMATICS 2. theoretical and practical knowledge of the design, construction, operation, and care of machinery 3. the mechanical aspect; technical part [*the mechanics of writing*]

☆**mechanic's lien** a lien on a building, etc. given by statute to those who perform work or furnish materials in the improvement of that property

mech·a·nism (mek′ə niz'm) *n.* [ModL. *mechanismus* < Gr. *mēchanē*, MACHINE] 1. the working parts or arrangement of parts of a machine; works [*the mechanism of a clock*] 2. *a*) a system whose parts work together like those of a machine [*the mechanism of the universe*] *b*) any system or means for doing something; esp., a physical or mental process or processes, whether conscious or unconscious, by which some result is produced; machinery; cf. DEFENSE MECHANISM 3. the mechanical aspect; technical part 4. the theory

or doctrine that all the phenomena of the universe, particularly life, can ultimately be explained in terms of physics and chemistry

mech·a·nist (-nist) *n.* 1. a person who believes in the theory of mechanism 2. *rare var. of* MECHANICIAN

mech·a·nis·tic (mek′ə nis′tik) *adj.* 1. of or in accordance with the theory of mechanism 2. of mechanics or mechanical concepts —**mech′a·nis′ti·cal·ly** *adv.*

mech·a·nize (mek′ə nīz′) *vt.* **-nized′, -niz′ing** 1. to make mechanical 2. to do or operate by machinery, not by hand 3. to bring about the use of machinery in (an industry, etc.) 4. to equip (an army, etc.) with motor vehicles, tanks, self-propelled guns, etc., so as to increase mobility and striking power —**mech′a·ni·za′tion** *n.* —**mech′a·niz′er** *n.*

mech·a·no·ther·a·py (mek′ə nō ther′ə pē) *n.* [< Gr. *mēchanē*, MACHINE + THERAPY] the treatment of disease by mechanical means, such as massage —**mech′an·o·ther′a·pist** *n.*

Mech·e·len (mekh′ə lən) city in NC Belgium, in Antwerp province: pop. 65,000

Mech·lin (mek′lin) *Eng. name of* MECHELEN —*n.* a fine lace made there, with the design clearly outlined by a thread: also **Mechlin lace**

Meck·len·burg (mek′lən burg′; *G.* -boork′) region in N East Germany, on the Baltic: a former state & earlier a duchy

mec·li·zine (mek′lə zēn′) *n.* [ME(THYL BENZENE) + C(H)L(OROFORM) + *i* + (PIPERA)ZINE] an antihistamine, C₂₅H₂₇ClN₂, used for treating nausea and motion sickness

me·co·ni·um (mi kō′nē əm) *n.* [ModL. < L., meconium, orig. poppy juice < Gr. *mēkōnion* < *mēkōn*, poppy < IE. *mak(en)-,* whence OHG. *maho* (G. *mohn*), Russ. *mak*] the greenish fecal matter in a fetus, forming the first bowel movement of a newborn infant

me·cop·ter·an (mi käp′tər ən) *n.* [< Gr. *mēkos*, length (for IE. base see MEAGER) + PTER(O)- + -AN] any of an order (Mecoptera) of carnivorous insects, with a head that is greatly elongated into a beak with chewing mouthparts, and, usually, four long, narrow, membranous wings **me·cop′ter·ous** (-əs) *adj.*

med. 1. medical 2. medicine 3. medieval 4. medium

M.Ed. Master of Education

med·al (med′'l) *n.* [Fr. *médaille* < It. *medaglia* < VL. *medalia*, a small coin < *medalis* < LL. *medialis*, MEDIAL] 1. a small, flat piece of metal with a design or inscription stamped or inscribed on it, made to commemorate some event, or awarded for some distinguished action, merit, etc. 2. a disk bearing a religious symbol, blessed by the Church and worn as a religious token —*vt.* **-aled** or **-alled, -al·ing** or **-al·ling** [Rare] to honor with a medal

☆**Medal for Merit** a U.S. military decoration awarded civilians for exceptionally meritorious conduct in the performance of outstanding services

med·al·ist (-'l ist, -list) *n.* 1. a person who designs or makes medals 2. a person who has been awarded a medal 3. *Golf* the low scorer in a qualifying round of medal play preliminary to a match play tournament Also, Brit. sp., **med′al·list**

me·dal·lion (mə dal′yən) *n.* [Fr. *médaillon* < It. *medaglione* < *medaglia:* see MEDAL] 1. a large medal 2. an oval or circular design, portrait, relief carving, etc. resembling a medal in shape and used as a decorative form in architecture, textiles, etc.

☆**Medal of Freedom** a U.S. military decoration awarded to civilians for significant aid in prosecuting a war and, since 1963, to civilians or military persons for any of various achievements

☆**Medal of Honor** the highest U.S. military decoration, awarded by Congress for gallantry at the risk of life above and beyond the call of duty: established 1862

medal play *Golf* a form of competitive play in which the score is calculated by counting the total number of strokes taken to play the designated number of holes: distinguished from MATCH PLAY

Me·dan (me dän′) city in N Sumatra, Indonesia, near the Strait of Malacca: pop. 479,000

med·dle (med′'l) *vi.* **-dled, -dling** [ME. *medlen* < OFr. *medler, mesler,* to mix, hence "mix in," meddle < VL. *misculare* < L. *miscere,* to MIX] 1. to concern oneself with or take part in other people's affairs without being asked or needed; interfere (*in* or *with*) 2. to tamper (*with*) 3. [Obs.] to mingle; combine —*vt.* [Obs.] to mix; mingle —**med′dler** *n.*

med·dle·some (-səm) *adj.* meddling or inclined to meddle; interfering —SYN. see CURIOUS —**med′dle·some·ness** *n.*

Mede (mēd) *n.* [L. *Medus,* pl. *Medi* < Gr. *Mēdos,* pl. *Mēdoi*] a native or inhabitant of Media

Me·de·a (mi dē′ə) [L. < Gr. *Mēdeia*] *Gr. Myth.* a sorceress who helped Jason get the Golden Fleece and, later, when deserted by him, killed her own children

Me·del·lín (me′de yēn′) city in NW Colombia: pop. 773,000

Med·ford (med′fərd) [? for the meadlike marshes once there] city in E Mass.: suburb of Boston: pop. 64,000

MedGr. Medieval Greek

me·di- (mē′dē) *same as* MEDIO-: used before a vowel

Me·di·a (mē′dē ə) ancient kingdom in the part of SW Asia that is now NW Iran: cap. Ecbatana

me·di·a¹ (mē′dē ə) *n. alt. pl. of* MEDIUM (*n.,* 3)

me·di·a² (mē′dē ə) *n., pl.* **-di·ae′** (-ē′) [ModL. < fem. of L. *medius,* middle: see MID¹] 1. *Anat.* the middle coat of the wall of a blood or lymph vessel 2. [LL., used by Priscian for L. *littera media,* intermediate letter: so named as medial between aspirates and tenues] *Phonet.* formerly, a voiced stop

me·di·a·cy (mē′dē ə sē) *n.* the state or quality of being mediate

me·di·ad (mē′dē ad) *adv.* [MEDI- + -AD²] *Biol.* toward the median plane or axis of a body or part

me·di·ae·val (mē′dē ēr′v'l, med′ē-, mid′ē-) *adj. same as* MEDIEVAL —**me′di·ae′val·ism** *n.* —**me′di·ae′val·ist** *n.*

me·di·al (mē′dē əl) *adj.* [LL. *medialis* < L. *medius,* middle: see MID¹] 1. of or in the middle; neither beginning nor ending; median 2. nearer the median plane or axis of a body or part 3. *a)* of an average or mean *b)* average; ordinary —*n.* 1. a medial letter 2. in some alphabets, that form of a letter which is used as neither an initial nor final letter —**me′di·al·ly** *adv.*

Me·di·an (mē′dē ən) *adj.* of Media, its people (the Medes), their Iranian language (Medic), or their culture —*n.* a Mede

me·di·an (mē′dē ən) *adj.* [L. *medianus* < *medius,* middle: see MID¹] 1. middle; intermediate 2. *a)* designating a line extending from a vertex of a triangle to the middle of the opposite side *b)* designating a line joining the midpoints of the nonparallel sides of a trapezoid 3. *a)* designating the plane that divides a body or part into symmetrical parts *b)* situated in this plane 4. *Statistics a)* designating the middle number in a series containing an odd number of items (Ex.: 7 in the series 1, 4, 7, 16, 43) *b)* designating the number midway between the two middle numbers in a series containing an even number of items (Ex.: 10 in the series, 3, 1, 8, 12, 46, 72) Distinguished from AVERAGE, MEAN³, MODE —*n.* 1. a median number, point, or line 2. an artery, vein, nerve, etc. in the median plane ☆3. a strip of land of varying width separating the lanes of opposing traffic of a divided highway: in full, **median strip** —SYN. see AVERAGE —**me′di·an·ly** *adv.*

me·di·ant (-ənt) *n.* [It. *mediante* < LL. *medians,* prp. of *mediare:* see MEDIATE] the third tone of a musical scale, halfway between the tonic and the dominant

me·di·as·ti·num (mē′dē əs tī′nəm) *n., pl.* **-na** (-nə) [ModL. < ML. *mediastinus,* in the middle < L. *medius,* middle: see MID¹] 1. a membranous partition between two cavities of the body, esp. that separating the lungs or the two pleural sacs 2. the space between the pleural sacs, containing the heart and other chest viscera except the lungs —**me′di·as·ti′nal** *adj.*

me·di·ate (mē′dē āt′; *for adj.,* -it) *vi.* **-at′ed, -at′ing** [< LL. *mediatus,* pp. of *mediare,* to divide in the middle < L. *medius,* middle: see MID¹] 1. to be in an intermediate position or location 2. to be an intermediary or conciliator between persons or sides —*vt.* 1. to settle by mediation; bring about by conciliation 2. to be the medium for bringing about (a result), conveying (an object), communicating (information), etc. —*adj.* 1. [Now Rare] intermediate or intervening 2. dependent on, acting by, or connected through some intervening agency; related indirectly —SYN. see INTERPOSE —**me′di·ate·ly** *adv.* —**me′di·a′tor** *n.* —[Now Rare] **me′di·a′trix** (-ā′triks) *n.fem.*

me·di·a·tion (mē′dē ā′shən) *n.* [ME. *mediacioun* < ML. *mediatio*] 1. the act of mediating; friendly or diplomatic intervention, usually by consent or invitation, for settling differences between persons, nations, etc. 2. the state of being mediated —**me′di·a′tive** *adj.* —**me′di·a·to′ry** (-ə tôr′ē) *adj.*

me·di·a·tize (mē′dē ə tīz′) *vt.* **-tized′, -tiz′ing** [< Fr. or G.: Fr. *médiatiser* (< *médiat:* see MEDIATE), or G. *mediatisieren* < Fr.] to annex (a smaller state) to a larger one, leaving the ruler his title and some authority

Med·ic (med′ik) *n.* the language of the ancient Medes; Median

med·ic¹ (med′ik) *n.* [L. *medicus*] [Colloq.] 1. a physician or surgeon ☆2. a medical student or intern 3. a member of a military medical corps, esp. one who gives first aid in combat

med·ic² (med′ik) *n.* [ME. *medike* < L. *medica* < Gr. *mēdikē* (*poa*), Median (grass), kind of clover from Media < *Mēdikos,* of Media] any of a genus (*Medicago*) of leguminous plants, as alfalfa

med·i·ca·ble (med′i kə b'l) *adj.* [L. *medicabilis*] that can be cured, healed, or relieved by medical treatment

☆**Med·i·caid** (med′i kād′) *n.* [MEDIC(AL) + AID] [*also* m-] a public health program through which certain medical and hospital expenses of those having no income, or a low income, are paid for from State and Federal funds

med·i·cal (med′i k'l) *adj.* [Fr. *médical* < LL. *medicalis* < L. *medicus,* physician < IE. base *med-:* see MEASURE), to measure, consider, wise counselor, doctor, whence OE. *metan,* to measure] 1. of or connected with

medicine or the practice or study of medicine **2.** *rare var.* of MEDICINAL —**med′i·cal·ly** *adv.*

medical examiner **1.** a coroner or similar public officer **2.** a physician who performs medical examinations, as of applicants for life insurance

medical jurisprudence the application of medical knowledge to questions of law affecting life or property, including ascertaining and certifying the cause of death, proper medical practice, etc.

med·i·ca·ment (med′i kə mənt, mə dik′ə-) *n.* [Fr. *médicament* < L. *medicamentum*] *same as* MEDICATION (sense 2)

Med·i·care (med′i ker′) *n.* [MEDI(CAL) + CARE] [*also* m-] a national health program through which certain medical and hospital expenses of the aged are paid for from Federal, mostly social security, funds

med·i·cate (med′ə kāt′) *vt.* **-cat′ed, -cat′ing** [< L. *medicatus*, pp. of *medicari*, to heal] **1.** to treat with medicine **2.** to add a medicinal substance to; tincture or impregnate with medicine —**med′i·ca′tive** *adj.*

med·i·ca·tion (med′ə kā′shən) *n.* [L. *medicatio*] **1.** a medicating or being medicated **2.** a medicine; substance for curing or healing, or for relieving pain

Med·i·ci (med′ə chē′; *It.* me′dē chē′) family of rich, powerful bankers, merchants, & rulers of Florence & Tuscany in the 14th, 15th, & 16th cent., also noted as patrons of art & literature; specif., *a)* **Catherine de′,** 1519–89; queen of Henry II of France (1574–89): Fr. name **Catherine de Mé·di·cis** (də mā dē sēs′) *b)* **Cos·i·mo de′** (kô′zē mô′ de), 1389–1464; head of the Florentine Republic: called *the Elder c)* **Cosimo I de′,** 1519–74; grand duke of Tuscany (1569–74): called *the Great d)* **Giu·lio de′** (jōo′lyô de), *see* CLEMENT VII *e)* **Lo·ren·zo de′** (lô ren′tsô de), 1449–92; ruler of Florence (1469–92): called *the Magnificent f)* **Maria de′,** 1573–1642; queen of Henry IV of France (1600–10); queen regent (1610–17): Fr. name **Ma·rie de Mé·di·cis** (má rē′ də mā dē sēs′) —**Med′i·ce′an** (-sē′ən, -chē′ən) *adj.*

me·dic·i·nal (mə dis′'n 'l) *adj.* [ME. *medycinal* < OFr. < L. *medicinalis*] of, or having the properties of, medicine; curing, healing, or relieving: also [Archaic] **me·dic′i·na·ble** —**me·dic′i·nal·ly** *adv.*

med·i·cine (med′ə s'n; *Brit.* med′sin) *n.* [ME. < OFr. < L. *medicina* < *medicus*: see MEDICAL] **1.** the science and art of diagnosing, treating, curing, and preventing disease, relieving pain, and improving and preserving health **2.** the branch of this science and art that makes use of drugs, diet, etc., as distinguished esp. from surgery and obstetrics **3.** *a)* any drug or other substance used in treating disease, healing, or relieving pain *b)* [Obs.] a drug or other substance, as a poison, love potion, etc., used for other purposes ☆**4.** among N. American Indians *a)* any object, spell, rite, etc. supposed to have natural or supernatural powers as a remedy, preventive, protection, etc. *b)* magical power —*vt.* **-cined, -cin·ing** to give medicine to; treat medicinally —☆**take one's medicine** to endure just punishment or accept the results of one's action

☆**medicine ball** a large, heavy, leather-covered ball, tossed from one person to another for physical exercise

☆**medicine dance** among N. American Indians, etc., a ritual dance to drive out disease or make magic

☆**medicine man** among N. American Indians, etc., a man supposed to have supernatural powers of curing disease and controlling spirits; shaman

☆**medicine show** formerly, a show given by entertainers who traveled from town to town, in order to sell cure-alls and nostrums

med·ick (med′ik) *n. same as* MEDIC[2]

med·i·co (med′i kō′) *n., pl.* **-cos′** [It. < L. *medicus:* see MEDICAL] [Colloq.] **1.** a physician or surgeon; doctor **2.** a medical student

med·i·co- (med′i kō′) *a combining form meaning:* **1.** medical **2.** medical and

me·di·e·val (mē′dē ē′v'l, med′ē-, mid′ē-) *adj.* [< L. *medius*, middle (see MID[1]) + *aevum*, AGE + -AL] of, like, characteristic of, or suggestive of the Middle Ages — **me′di·e′val·ly** *adv.*

Medieval Greek the Greek language as it was used in the Middle Ages, from c. 600–c. 1500 A.D.

me·di·e·val·ism (-iz′m) *n.* **1.** medieval spirit, beliefs, customs, etc. **2.** devotion to or acceptance of medieval beliefs, habits, customs, etc. **3.** a belief, custom, etc. characteristic of or surviving from the Middle Ages

me·di·e·val·ist (-ist) *n.* **1.** a student of or specialist in medieval history, literature, art, etc. **2.** a person devoted to medieval customs, beliefs, etc.

Medieval Latin the Latin language as it was used throughout Europe in the Middle Ages, from c. 600–c. 1500 A.D., characterized by many Latinized borrowings from other languages

Me·di·na (mə dē′nə) city in Hejaz, NW Saudi Arabia: site of Mohammed's tomb & hence a holy city of Islam: pop. c. 50,000

me·di·na (mə dē′nə) *n.* [native term in N Africa, orig. lit., city < Ar. *medinat*, city] the old native quarter of a N African city

me·di·o- (mē′dē ō, -ə) [< L. *medius:* see MID[1]] *a combining form meaning* middle

me·di·o·cre (mē′dē ō′kər, mē′dē ō′kər) *adj.* [Fr. *médiocre* < L. *mediocris* < *medius*, middle (see MID[1]) + *ocris*, a

peak < IE. base *ak̑-*, sharp, whence L. *acer*] **1.** neither very good nor very bad; ordinary; average **2.** not good enough; inferior

me·di·oc·ri·ty (mē′dē äk′rə tē) *n., pl.* **-ties** [Fr. *médiocrité* < L. *mediocritas*] **1.** the quality or state of being mediocre **2.** mediocre ability or attainment **3.** a person of mediocre abilities or attainments

Medit. Mediterranean

med·i·tate (med′ə tāt′) *vt.* **-tat′ed, -tat′ing** [< L. *meditatus*, pp. of *meditari*, to meditate: for base see MEDICAL] **1.** [Rare] to reflect upon; study; ponder **2.** to plan or intend —*vi.* to think deeply and continuously; reflect; muse —*SYN.* see PONDER —**med′i·ta′tor** *n.*

med·i·ta·tion (med′ə tā′shən) *n.* **1.** act of meditating; deep, continued thought **2.** deep reflection on sacred matters as a devotional act **3.** [*often pl.*] oral or written material, as a sermon, based on meditation

med·i·ta·tive (med′ə tāt′iv) *adj.* **1.** meditating or inclined to meditate **2.** indicating meditation —*SYN.* see PENSIVE —**med′i·ta′tive·ly** *adv.*

med·i·ter·ra·ne·an (med′i tə rā′nē ən, -rān′yən) *adj.* [< L. *mediterraneus* < *medius*, middle (see MID[1]) + *terra*, land (see TERRAIN)] **1.** *a)* far from the coast; inland: said of land *b)* surrounded, or almost surrounded, by land; landlocked: said of water **2.** [M-] of the Mediterranean Sea or nearby regions **3.** [M-] designating or of a physical type of the Caucasoid peoples exemplified by the long-headed, short, olive-skinned people living around the Mediterranean Sea: see also ALPINE, NORDIC —*n.* [M-] a Mediterranean person See also MEDITERRANEAN SEA

Mediterranean climate a climate characterized by warm dry summers and rainy winters

Mediterranean fever *same as* UNDULANT FEVER

Mediterranean flour moth a small gray moth (*Ephestia kühniella*), whose larvae are serious pests in flour

Mediterranean fruit fly a small, gall-forming, two-winged fly (*Ceratitis capitata*), whose larvae infest and feed on many kinds of fruit

Mediterranean Sea large sea surrounded by Europe, Africa, & Asia: c. 2,300 mi. long; c. 965,000 sq. mi.

me·di·um (mē′dē əm) *n., pl.* **-di·ums;** also (except sense 7), and for sense 3 usually, **-di·a** (-ə) [L., the middle, neut. of *medius:* see MID[1]] **1.** *a)* something intermediate *b)* a middle state or degree; mean **2.** an intervening thing through which a force acts or an effect is produced [copper is a good *medium* for conducting heat] **3.** any means, agency, or instrumentality; specif., a means of communication that reaches the general public and carries advertising: in this sense, a singular form media (*pl.* medias) is now sometimes heard **4.** any surrounding or pervading substance in which bodies exist or move **5.** environment **6.** a sterilized nutritive substance, as agar, for cultivating bacteria, viruses, etc. ☆**7.** a person through whom communications are supposedly sent to the living from spirits of the dead **8.** any material or technique as used for expression or delineation in art **9.** a liquid mixed with pigments to give fluency **10.** a size of printing paper (18 x 23 inches) —*adj.* **1.** in a middle position; intermediate in quality, amount, degree, size, etc. **2.** neither rare nor well-done: said of cooked meat

medium frequency any radio frequency between 300 kilohertz and 3 megahertz

me·di·um·is·tic (mē′dē ə mis′tik) *adj.* of or like a medium (sense 7)

medium of exchange anything used as a measure of value in exchange for goods and services; currency, checks, etc.

me·di·um-sized (mē′dē əm sīzd′) *adj.* of a medium size; neither large nor small

MedL. Medieval Latin

med·lar (med′lər) *n.* [ME. *medler* < OFr. *medler, meslier* < *mesle*, the fruit < L. *mespilum* < Gr. *mespilon*] **1.** a small tree (*Mespilus germanica*) of the rose family, growing in Europe and Asia **2.** its small, brown, applelike fruit, hard and bitter when ripe and eaten or used in preserves when partly decayed

med·ley (med′lē) *n., pl.* **-leys** [ME. *medle* < OFr. *medlee*, a mixing < fem. pp. of *medler:* see MEDDLE] **1.** a mixture of things not usually placed together; heterogeneous assortment or collection; hodgepodge **2.** a musical piece made up of tunes or passages from various works **3.** [Archaic] *same as* MELEE —*adj.* [Archaic] made up of heterogeneous parts; mixed

medley race **1.** a relay race in which each contestant must cover a different distance: also **medley relay** **2.** a swimming race in which a different stroke must be used for each length of the pool

Mé·doc (mā dôk′; *E.* mā′däk, mā däk′) region in SW France, on the Gironde estuary —*n.* a red Bordeaux wine made there

me·dul·la (mi dul′ə) *n., pl.* **-dul′las, -dul′lae** (-ē) [L., the marrow] **1.** *Anat. a) same as* MEDULLA OBLONGATA *b)* the inner substance of an organ, as of the kidney, adrenal gland, etc. *c)* bone marrow **2.** *Bot. same as* PITH (sense 1) —**med·ul·lar·y** (med′ə ler′ē, mej′-; mi dul′ər ē) *adj.*

medulla ob·lon·ga·ta (äb′lôn gät′ə, -gät′-) [ModL., oblong medulla] the widening continuation of the spinal cord forming the lowest part of the brain and containing nerve centers that control breathing, circulation, etc.

medullary ray 1. *Anat.* extensions of the kidney tubules into the cortical substance 2. *Bot.* strands of parenchymatous tissue extending from the pith to the bark and separating the vascular bundles in the stems of certain plants (dicotyledons and gymnosperms)

medullary sheath 1. *Anat.* a layer of myelin forming a sheath around certain nerve fibers 2. *Bot.* a ring of primary xylem around the pith of some stems

med·ul·lat·ed (med′l āt′id, mej′-; mi dul′āt′id) *adj.* 1. covered with a medullary substance; having myelin sheaths 2. having a medulla

Me·du·sa (mə dōō′sə, -dyōō′-; -zə) [ME. *Meduse* < L. *Medusa* < Gr. *Medousa*] *Gr. Myth.* one of the three Gorgons, slain by Perseus —n. [m-] *pl.* **-sas, -sae** (-sē, -zē) [ModL.] *Zool.* same as JELLYFISH

me·du·san (-s′n, -z′n) *adj.* of a medusa, or jellyfish: also **me·du′sal** —n. a medusa, or jellyfish

me·du·soid (-soid, -zoid) *adj.* like a medusa, or jellyfish —n. a medusa-shaped gonophore of a hydrozoan

meed (mēd) *n.* [ME. *mede* < OE. *med*, a recompense, reward, akin to G. *miete*, pay, rent < IE. base *mizdhó-*, reward, pay, whence Sans. *mīdhá-*, prize] 1. [Archaic] a merited recompense or reward 2. [Obs.] *a)* a bribe *b)* merit; worth

meek (mēk) *adj.* [ME. *meke* (earlier *meoc*) < ON. *miukr*, pliant, soft < IE. base *meug-*, *meuk-*, to slip, slippery, whence L. *mucus*, Gr. *myxa* & MUCK] 1. patient and mild; not inclined to anger or resentment 2. too submissive; easily imposed on; spineless; spiritless 3. [Obs.] gentle or kind —*SYN.* see HUMBLE —**meek′ly** *adv.* —**meek′ness** *n.*

Meer (mer, mir) **Jan van der** same as VERMEER

meer·schaum (mir′shəm, -shôm) *n.* [G., lit., sea foam (< *meer*, sea + *schaum*, foam), transl. of ML. *spuma maris*, orig. used of coral: name transferred in 18th-cent. G. to a variety of lithomarge] 1. a soft, white, claylike, heat-resistant mineral, a hydrous magnesium silicate, $H_4Mg_2Si_3O_{10}$, used for tobacco pipes, etc. 2. a pipe made of this

Mee·rut (mē′rət) city in N India, in Uttar Pradesh: pop. 284,000

meet¹ (mēt) *vt.* **met, meet′ing** [ME. *meten* < OE. *metan* < base of *mot*, a coming together, meeting: see MOOT] 1. to come upon or encounter; esp., to come face to face with or up to (a person or thing moving from a different direction) 2. to be present at the arrival of [to *meet* a bus] 3. to come into contact, connection, or conjunction with [the ball *met* the bat] 4. *a)* to come into the presence or company of *b)* to be introduced to; get acquainted with *c)* to keep an appointment or engagement with 5. *a)* to encounter in or as in battle; contend with *b)* to deal with; face [to *meet* angry words with a laugh] *c)* to refute or deal with effectively [to *meet* an objection] 6. to experience [to *meet* disaster] 7. to come within the perception of (the eye, ear, etc.) 8. *a)* to comply with; satisfy (a demand, etc.) *b)* to pay (a bill, etc.) —*vi.* 1. to come together, as from different directions 2. to come into contact, connection, or conjunction 3. to become acquainted; be introduced 4. to be opposed in or as in battle; contend; fight 5. to be united 6. *a)* to assemble *b)* to come together for discussion, bargaining, etc. (*with*) —n. 1. a meeting, gathering, or assembling, as for a sporting event [a track *meet*] 2. the people who so meet or the place of meeting —**meet with** 1. to experience 2. to receive 3. to come upon or across; encounter: also **meet up with**

meet² (mēt) *adj.* [ME. *mete* < OE. (ge)*mæte*, fitting, akin to G. *gemäss*, commensurable < IE. base *med-*: see MEDICAL] [Now Rare] suitable; proper; fit —**meet′ly** *adv.*

meet·ing (mēt′iŋ) *n.* [see MEET¹] 1. a coming together of persons or things 2. an assembly; gathering of people, esp. to discuss or decide on matters 3. an assembly or place of assembly for purposes of worship, as among the Friends, or Quakers 4. a series of horse or dog races held during a period of days at a certain track 5. a point of contact or intersection; junction

meet·ing·house (-hous′) *n.* a building used for public meetings, esp. for public worship, as by Friends, or Quakers

meg. megohm; megohms

meg·a- (meg′ə) [Gr. *mega-* < *megas*, great, mighty: see MUCH] *a combining form meaning:* 1. large, great, powerful [*megaphone*] 2. a million, a million of (the specified unit); the factor 10^6 [*megahertz, megaton*] Also, before a vowel, **meg-**

☆**meg·a·buck** (meg′ə buk) *n.* [prec. + BUCK³] [Slang] a million dollars

meg·a·ce·phal·ic (meg′ə sə fal′ik) *adj.* [MEGA- + CEPHALIC] having a large head; esp., having a cranial capacity greater than the average: also **meg′a·ceph′a·lous** (-sef′ə ləs) —**meg′a·ceph′a·ly** (-ə lē) *n.*

meg·a·cy·cle (meg′ə si′k'l) *n. former name for* MEGAHERTZ

☆**meg·a·death** (-deth′) *n.* [MEGA- + DEATH] one million dead persons: a unit used in computing the hypothetical victims of a nuclear explosion

Meg·a·gae·a (meg′ə jē′ə) *n.* [ModL. < MEGA- + Gr. *gaia*, earth] one of the three primary zoogeographic areas of the earth including N. America, N Mexico, Europe, Africa, Asia, and certain islands SE of Asia —**Meg′a·gae′an** *adj.*

meg·a·ga·mete (-gam′ēt, -ga mēt′) *n.* same as MACROGAMETE

meg·a·hertz (meg′ə hurts′) *n., pl.* **-hertz′** [MEGA- + HERTZ] one million hertz: abbrev. **MHz** (sing. & pl.)

meg·a·lith (-lith′) *n.* [MEGA- + -LITH] a huge stone, esp. one used in prehistoric monuments or in the construction work of ancient peoples —**meg′a·lith′ic** *adj.*

meg·a·lo- (meg′ə lō, -lə) [ModL. < Gr. *megalo-* < *megas*, large: see MUCH] *a combining form meaning:* 1. large, great, powerful [*megalomania*] 2. abnormal enlargement [*megalocardia*] Also, before a vowel, **meg′al-**

meg·a·lo·car·di·a (meg′ə lō kär′dē ə) *n.* [ModL. < MEGALO- + Gr. *kardia*, HEART] abnormal enlargement of the heart

meg·a·lo·ma·ni·a (-mā′nē ə, -mān′yə) *n.* [ModL.: see MEGALO- & MANIA] 1. a mental disorder characterized by delusions of grandeur, wealth, power, etc. 2. a passion for, or for doing, big things 3. a tendency to exaggerate —**meg′a·lo·ma′ni·ac′** (-ak′) *adj., n.* —**meg′a·lo·ma·ni′a·cal** (-mə nī′ə k'l) *adj.* —**meg′a·lo·man′ic** (-man′ik) *adj.*

meg·a·lop·o·lis (meg′ə läp′ə ləs) *n.* [Gr. *megalopolis*, great city] an extensive, heavily populated, continuously urban area, including any number of cities —**meg′a·lo·pol′i·tan** (-lə päl′ə tən) *adj., n.*

meg·a·lops (meg′ə läps′) *n., pl.* **-lops′, -lop′ses** [ModL. < MEGAL(O)- + Gr. *ōps*, EYE] an advanced larval stage of the true crabs, just preceding the definitive adult stage —**meg′a·lop′ic** *adj.*

meg·a·lo·saur (meg′ə lə sôr′) *n.* [ModL. *megalosaurus*: see MEGALO- & -SAURUS] any of a genus (*Megalosaurus*) of huge, flesh-eating dinosaurs of the Jurassic Period —**meg′a·lo·sau′ri·an** (-sôr′ē ən) *adj., n.*

☆**meg·a·phone** (meg′ə fōn′) *n.* [MEGA- + -PHONE] a large, funnel-shaped device for increasing the volume of the voice and directing it —*vt., vi.* **-phoned′, -phon′ing** to magnify or direct (the voice) through or as through a megaphone —**meg′a·phon′ic** (-fän′ik) *adj.*

meg·a·pod (-päd′) *adj.* [MEGA- + -POD] large-footed —n. same as MEGAPODE

meg·a·pode (-pōd′) *n.* [see prec.] any of a family (Megapodiidae) of large-footed, mound-building birds of Australia and the East Indies

Meg·a·ra (meg′ər ə) city on the Isthmus of Corinth, C Greece: capital of ancient Megaris: pop. 15,000

Meg·a·ris (meg′ər is) ancient district on the Isthmus of Corinth

meg·a·scop·ic (meg′ə skäp′ik) *adj.* [MEGA- + -SCOP(E) + -IC] visible to the naked eye: opposed to MICROSCOPIC —**meg′a·scop′i·cal·ly** *adv.*

meg·a·spo·ran·gi·um (-spə ran′jē əm) *n., pl.* **-gi·a** (-ə) [ModL.: see MEGA- & SPORANGIUM] a sporangium, or spore case, containing only megaspores, as in some ferns

meg·a·spore (meg′ə spôr′) *n.* [MEGA- + SPORE] a haploid spore, usually larger than a microspore of the same plant, which gives rise to a female gametophyte: found in all seed plants and some vascular plants —**meg′a·spor′ic** *adj.*

meg·a·spo·ro·phyll (meg′ə spôr′ə fil′) *n.* a sporophyll bearing only megasporangia

me·gass, me·gasse (mə gas′, -gäs′) *n.* same as BAGASSE

meg·a·the·ri·um (meg′ə thir′ē əm) *n.* [ModL. < Gr. *megas* (see MEGA-) + *thērion*, beast: see FIERCE] an extinct genus (*Megatherium*) of very large, slothlike, plant-eating animals, whose remains have been found in the Pleistocene of America: also **meg′a·there′** (-thir′)

meg·a·ton (meg′ə tun′) *n.* [MEGA- + TON¹] the explosive force of a million tons of TNT: a unit for measuring the power of thermonuclear weapons —**meg′a·ton′nage** *n.*

Me·gid·do (mə gid′ō) ancient town in N Palestine, on the plain of Esdraelon, dating from c. 3500 B.C.: thought to be the Biblical Armageddon

me·gil·lah (mə gil′ə) *n.* [Yid. < Heb. *megillāh*, scroll, roll] [Slang] 1. a long or involved explanation, story, etc. 2. a complicated matter or affair

me·gilp (mə gilp′) *n.* [< ?] a mixture of linseed oil with mastic varnish or turpentine, etc., used in oil paints

meg·ohm (meg′ōm′) *n.* one million ohms

me·grim (mē′grəm) *n.* [LME. *migreime* < OFr. *migraine*: see MIGRAINE] 1. *obs. var. of* MIGRAINE 2. [Archaic] a whim, fancy, or fad 3. [*pl.*] [Rare] *a)* low spirits; the blues *b)* staggers: see STAGGER (*n.* 3)

Me·he·met A·li (me met′ ä lē′) 1769–1849; viceroy of Egypt (1805–48)

Mei·ji (mā′jē′) [Jap., lit., enlightened peace] the reign name of the emperor Mutsuhito of Japan

mein·ie, mein·y (mā′nē) *n.* [ME. *menie* < OFr. *meisniee*: see MENIAL] 1. [Obs.] feudal retainers or attendants, collectively; retinue or household 2. [Scot.] a crowd; throng; multitude

mei·o·sis (mī ō′sis) *n.* [ModL. < Gr. *meiōsis* < *meioun*, to make smaller < *meiōn*, less: see MINOR] 1. the process of two consecutive nuclear divisions in the formation of germ cells in animals and of spores in most plants, by which the number of chromosomes ordinarily is reduced from the diploid, or double, number found in somatic cells to the haploid, or halved, number found in gametes and in

spores: distinguished from MITOSIS **2.** same as LITOTES —**mei·ot′ic** (-ät′ik) adj. —**mei·ot′i·cal·ly** adv.

Meis·sen (mī′sən) city in E East Germany, on the Elbe: pop. 50,000: noted for its porcelain

Meis·so·nier (mā sō nyā′), **Jean Louis Er·nest** (zhän lwē er nest′) 1815–91; Fr. painter

Meis·ter·sing·er (mīs′tər siŋ′ər, -ziŋ′ər) n., pl. **-sing′er** [G., lit., master singer] a member of one of the guilds, mainly of workingmen, organized in the chief German cities in the 14th, 15th, and 16th cent. for the purpose of cultivating music and poetry

Meit·ner (mīt′nər), **Li·se** (lē′zə) 1878–1968; Austrian nuclear physicist, in U.S. & Sweden

Mé·ji·co (me′hē kô′) Sp. name of MEXICO

Mek·nès (mek′nes) city in NC Morocco: pop. 205,000

Me·kong (mā′käŋ′, -kôŋ′) river in SE Asia, flowing from Tibet through SW China & the Indochinese peninsula into the South China Sea: c. 2,600 mi.

mel (mel) n. [L.: see MILDEW] honey, esp. in the pure, clarified form used in pharmacy

mel·a·mine (mel′ə mēn′) n. [G. melamin < melam, an ammonium thiocyanate distillate < mel < ? + am(monium), AMMONIUM + -in, -INE] a white, crystalline, cyclic compound, $C_3H_6N_6$, containing three cyanamide molecules in its structure, used in making synthetic resins ☆**melamine resin** any of various thermosetting, synthetic resins made by condensing formaldehyde with melamine: used as molding and laminating compounds in making dishes, utensils, adhesives, etc.

mel·an- same as MELANO-: used before a vowel

mel·an·cho·li·a (mel′ən kō′lē ə, -kōl′yə) n. [ModL. < LL., MELANCHOLY] a mental disorder, often psychotic, characterized by extreme depression of spirits, brooding, and anxiety —**mel′an·cho′li·ac′** (-kō′lē ak′) adj., n.

mel·an·chol·y (mel′ən käl′ē) n., pl. **-chol′ies** [ME. malencoli < OFr. melancolie < LL. melancholia < Gr. melancholia < melas (gen. melanos), black (see MELANO-) + cholē, bile, gall: see YELLOW] **1.** [Obs.] a) orig., black bile: in medieval times considered to be one of the four humors of the body, to come from the spleen or kidneys, and to cause gloominess, irritability, or depression b) the condition of having, or the disorder supposed to result from having, too much black bile **2.** a) sadness and depression of spirits b) a tendency to be sad, gloomy, or depressed **3.** sad, sober musing; pensiveness —adj. **1.** sad and depressed; gloomy **2.** a) causing sadness, gloom, or depression b) lamentable; deplorable **3.** sadly or soberly musing; pensive **4.** [Obs.] having the disorder of melancholy —SYN. see SAD —**mel′an·chol′ic** adj. —**mel′an·chol′i·cal·ly** adv.

Me·lanch·thon (mə laŋk′thən), **Philipp** (born Philipp Schwarzerd) 1497–1560; Ger. Protestant reformer

Mel·a·ne·sia (mel′ə nē′zhə, -shə) [< Gr. melas, black + nēsos, island: in reference to the color of the natives] one of the three major divisions of the Pacific islands, south of the equator and including groups from the Bismarck Archipelago to the Fiji Islands

Mel·a·ne·sian (-zhən, -shən) adj. of Melanesia, its people, or their languages —n. **1.** a member of the dark-skinned native people of Melanesia **2.** a branch of the Malayo-Polynesian family of languages consisting of the languages of Melanesia

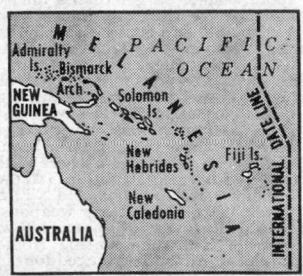

MELANESIA

mé·lange (mā länzh′, -länj′) n. [Fr. < mêler, to mix: see MEDDLE] a mixture or medley; hodgepodge

me·lan·ic (mə lan′ik) adj. of, characteristic of, or having melanism or melanosis

mel·a·nin (mel′ə nin) n. [MELAN- + -IN¹] a brownish-black pigment found in skin, hair, and other animal tissues

mel·a·nism (-niz′m) n. [MELAN- + -ISM] **1.** abnormal development of dark pigmentation in the skin, hair, feathers, etc. **2.** darkness of skin, hair, eyes, etc., resulting from a high degree of pigmentation —**mel′a·nis′tic** adj.

mel·a·nite (-nīt′) n. [G. melanit, coined (1799) by A. G. Werner (see WERNERITE) < Gr. melanos (see MELANO-) + G. -it, -ITE¹] a black variety of andradite garnet

mel·a·nize (-nīz′) vt. **-nized′, -niz′ing** [MELAN- + -IZE] **1.** to darken by the deposition of abnormal amounts of melanin in tissues **2.** to make dark

mel·a·no- (mel′ə nō′, -nə) [< Gr. melas (gen. melanos), black < IE. base *mel-, dark, dirty, whence MHG. mal, a spot] a combining form meaning black, very dark

Mel·a·noch·ro·i (mel′ə näk′rō i′) n.pl. [ModL. < MELAN- + Gr. ōchros, pale] members of the Caucasoid major group having dark hair and a light complexion: no longer in scientific usage —**Mel′a·noch′roid** (-roid) adj.

mel·a·no·cyte (mel′ə nō sīt′, mə lan′ə-) n. [MELANO- + -CYTE] a specialized cell containing melanin

mel·a·noid (mel′ə noid′) adj. **1.** pigmented black or dark **2.** of or like melanosis

mel·a·no·ma (mel′ə nō′mə) n., pl. **-mas, -ma·ta** (-mə tə) [ModL.: see MELANO- & -OMA] a tumor whose cells contain melanin

mel·a·no·sis (-sis) n. [ModL. < Gr. melanōsis, a becoming black < melanousthai, to become black < melas: see MELANO-] the abnormal production and deposition of melanin in the body tissues —**mel′a·not′ic** (-nät′ik) adj.

mel·a·nous (mel′ə nəs) adj. [MELAN- + -OUS] having black or dark skin and hair

mel·a·phyre (mel′ə fir′) n. [Fr. mélaphyre < Gr. melas, black + Fr. (por)phyre, porphyry] [Obs.] any dark-colored porphyritic igneous rock

mel·a·stome (mel′ə stōm′) adj. [< ModL. Melastoma, name of the type genus < Gr. melas, black + stoma, mouth: so named from the stain caused by the fruit] designating or of a family (Melastomataceae) of plants widespread in the tropics and characterized by showy flowers and leaves with strong longitudinal ribs, including the meadow beauty

mel·a·to·nin (mel′ə tō′nin) n. [MELA(NO)- + TON(IC) + -IN] a hormone produced by the pineal body, that regulates the activity of certain glands

Mel·ba (mel′bə), **Dame Nellie** (Helen Porter Mitchell Armstrong) 1861–1931; Australian soprano

Melba toast [after prec.] [also m-] slightly stale bread sliced thin and toasted until brown and crisp

Mel·bourne (mel′bərn) **1.** seaport in SE Australia; capital of Victoria: pop. 90,000 (met. area 2,108,000) **2.** [after prec.] city on the E coast of Fla.: pop. 40,000

Mel·bourne (-bərn), 2d Viscount, (William Lamb) 1779–1848; Eng. statesman; prime minister (1834; 1835–41)

Mel·chior (mel′kyôr), **Lau·ritz** (Lebrecht Hommel) (lou′rits) 1890– ; U.S. tenor, born in Denmark

Mel·chite (mel′kīt) n. [ModL. Melchita < MGr. melchitēs, lit., a royalist < Heb. melekh, king: cf. MOLOCH] an Arabic-speaking Catholic of the Byzantine rite in Egypt, Israel, and Syria: also **Mel′kite**

Mel·chiz·e·dek, Mel·chis·e·dech (mel kiz′ə dek′) [Heb. malkī-tsedheq, lit., king of righteousness] Bible the priest and king of Salem who blessed Abraham: Gen. 14:18 —adj. ☆designating or of the higher order of priests in the Mormon Church: cf. AARONIC

☆**meld¹** (meld) vt., vi. [G. melden, to announce, akin to OE. meldian, proclamation < IE. base *meldh-, to address a deity, whence OBulg. moliti, to ask] Card Games to declare (a combination of cards in one's hand), esp. by putting them face up on the table —n. **1.** the act of melding **2.** a combination of cards melded or to be melded

meld² (meld) vt., vi. [merging of MELT + WELD¹] to blend; merge; unite

Mel·e·a·ger (mel′ē ā′jər) [L. < Gr. Meleagros] Gr. Myth. one of the Argonauts, the son of Althea, queen of Calydon: he killed the Calydonian boar

me·lee, mê·lée (mā′lā, mā lā′) n. [Fr. mêlée < OFr. meslee: see MEDLEY] a noisy, confused fight or hand-to-hand struggle among a number of people

Me·li·an (mē′lē ən) adj. of or relating to Melos

mel·ic (mel′ik) adj. [L. melicus < Gr. melikos < melos, song, musical member, orig., limb < IE. base *mel-, a limb, whence Corn. mel, a knuckle] **1.** of song or poetry, esp. Greek poetry written in strophes **2.** meant to be sung; lyric

Me·li·lla (mə lē′ə) Sp. seaport in NW Africa; enclave in NE Morocco: pop. 80,000

mel·i·lot (mel′ə lät′) n. [ME. mellilot < OFr. melilot < L. melilotos < Gr. melilōtos, kind of clover < meli, honey (see MILDEW) + lōtos, lotus] same as SWEET CLOVER

mel·i·nite (mel′ə nīt′) n. [Fr. mélinite < Gr. mēlinos, quince-yellow < mēlon, quince, apple: from its color] a powerful explosive like lyddite, made by combining picric acid with guncotton

mel·io·rate (mēl′yə rāt′) vt., vi. **-rat′ed, -rat′ing** [< LL. melioratus, pp. of meliorare, to make better < L. melior, better < IE. base *mel-, strong, big, whence Gr. mala, very] to make or become better; improve; ameliorate —**mel′io·ra·ble** (-yər ə b′l) adj. —**mel′io·ra′tive** (-yə rāt′iv, -yər ə tiv) adj. —**mel′io·ra′tor** n.

mel·io·ra·tion (mēl′yə rā′shən) n. **1.** a meliorating or being meliorated; improvement **2.** Linguis. a change of meaning for the better

mel·io·rism (mēl′yə riz′m) n. [L. melior, better (see MELIORATE) + -ISM] **1.** the belief that the world naturally tends to get better and, esp., that this tendency can be furthered by human effort **2.** the betterment of society by improving people's health, living conditions, etc. —**mel′io·rist** n., adj. —**mel′io·ris′tic** adj.

me·lis·ma (mə liz′mə) n., pl. **-ma·ta** (-mə tə), **-mas** [Gr. melisma, song < melizein, to sing, modulate < melos, song (see MELIC)] a succession of different notes sung upon a single syllable, as orig. in plainsong or, now especially, in the ornamental phrases of Near Eastern and Asian music —**mel·is·mat·ic** (mel′iz mat′ik) adj.

Me·lis·sa (mə lis′ə) [Gr. Melissa, lit., a bee < meli, honey: see MILDEW] a feminine name

mell (mel) vt., vi. [ME. mellen < OFr. meller, var. of mesler: see MEDDLE] [Brit. Dial.] **1.** to mingle; mix **2.** to meddle

mel·lif·er·ous (mə lif′ər əs) *adj.* [L. *mellifer* < *mel*, honey (see MILDEW) + *-fer* (see -FEROUS) + -OUS] producing honey

mel·lif·lu·ent (-loo wənt) *adj.* [LL. *mellifluens*] *same as* MELLIFLUOUS —**mel·lif′lu·ence** *n.*

mel·lif·lu·ous (-loo wəs) *adj.* [L. *mellifluus* < *mel* (gen. *mellis*), honey (see MILDEW) + *fluere*, to flow] sounding sweet and smooth; honeyed [*mellifluous* tones] —**mel·lif′-lu·ous·ly** *adv.* —**mel·lif′lu·ous·ness** *n.*

Mel·lon (mel′ən), **Andrew William** 1855–1937; U.S. financier; secretary of the treasury (1921–32)

mel·low (mel′ō) *adj.* [ME. *melwe*, ripe, prob. < or akin to OE. *melu* (see MEAL²), Fl. *meluw*, soft, mellow] **1.** soft, sweet, and juicy because ripe: said of fruit **2.** full-flavored; matured; not acid or bitter: said of wine, etc. **3.** full, rich, soft, and pure; not harsh: said of sound, light, color, weather, etc. **4.** moist and rich; loamy: said of soil **5.** softened and made gentle, understanding, and sympathetic by age and experience **6.** [Colloq.] genial or convivial, as from drinking liquor —*vt.*, *vi.* to make or become mellow —SYN. see RIPE —**mel′low·ly** *adv.* —**mel′low·ness** *n.*

☆**mel·o·de·on** (mə lō′dē ən) *n.* [G. *melodion*, coined (1806) by J. C. Dietz, G. inventor, for another instrument < *melodic* < OFr., MELODY] a small keyboard organ in which the tones are produced by drawing air through metal reeds by means of a bellows operated by pedals: it is much like a harmonium

me·lo·di·a (-dē ə) *n.* [ModL. < LL., MELODY] an 8-foot organ stop with wooden pipes and a flutelike tone

me·lod·ic (mə lädʹik) *adj.* [Fr. *mélodique* < LL. *melodicus*] **1.** of, or having the nature of, melody **2.** *same as* MELODIOUS —**me·lod′i·cal·ly** *adv.*

me·lo·di·ous (mə lō′dē əs) *adj.* [ME. < OFr. *melodieus*] **1.** containing or producing melody **2.** pleasing to hear; sounding sweet; tuneful —**me·lo′di·ous·ly** *adv.* —**me·lo′-di·ous·ness** *n.*

mel·o·dist (mel′ə dist) *n.* a singer or composer of melodies

mel·o·dize (-dīz′) *vt.* **-dized**′, **-diz′ing** [ML. *melodizare*] **1.** to make melodious **2.** to set to melody —*vi.* to make melody or compose melodies —**mel′o·diz′er** *n.*

mel·o·dra·ma (mel′ə drä′mə, -dram′ə) *n.* [altered (after DRAMA) < Fr. *mélodrame* < Gr. *melos*, a song + Fr. *drame* < LL. *drama*] **1.** orig., a sensational or romantic stage play with interspersed songs and an orchestral accompaniment **2.** now, a drama with exaggerated conflicts and emotions, stereotyped characters, etc. **3.** any sensational, extravagantly emotional action, utterance, etc. —**mel′-o·dram′a·tist**′ (-dram′ə tist) *n.*

mel·o·dra·mat·ic (mel′ə drə mat′ik) *adj.* of, characteristic of, or like melodrama; sensational, violent, and extravagantly emotional —**mel′o·dra·mat′i·cal·ly** *adv.*

mel·o·dra·mat·ics (-iks) *n.pl.* melodramatic behavior

mel·o·dy (mel′ə dē) *n., pl.* **-dies** [ME. *melodie* < OFr. < LL. *melodia* < Gr. *melōidia* < *melos*, song (see MELIC) + *aeidein*, to sing: see ODE] **1.** *a)* pleasing sounds or arrangement of sounds in sequence *b)* musical quality, as in the arrangement of words **2.** *Music a)* a sequence of single tones, usually in the same key or mode, to produce a rhythmic whole; often, a tune, air, or song *b)* the element of form having to do with the arrangement of single tones in sequence: distinguished from HARMONY *c)* the leading part, or voice, in a harmonic composition; the air SYN.—**melody** refers to the rhythmic arrangement of tones in sequence to express a musical idea; **air**, in strict application, refers to the principal, or leading, melody of a harmonized composition, but it is sometimes used as an equivalent of **tune**, which is the popular term for any easily remembered melody that identifies a song, dance, etc.

mel·oid (mel′oid) *n.* [< ModL. *Meloidae*, name of the family < *meloe*, oil beetle] *same as* BLISTER BEETLE —*adj.* of such beetles

mel·o·lon·thid (mel′ə län′thid) *n.* [< Gr. *mēlolonthē*, cockchafer + -ID] any of various beetles (family Melolonthidae) including the cockchafers, June bugs, etc. whose larvae feed chiefly on roots —*adj.* of these beetles

mel·on (mel′ən) *n.* [ME. < OFr. < LL. *melo* (gen. *melonis*), for L. *melopepo* < Gr. *mēlopepōn*, apple-shaped melon < *mēlon*, apple + *pepōn*, melon] **1.** any of several large, juicy, thick-skinned, many-seeded fruits of certain trailing plants of the gourd family, as the watermelon, muskmelon, cantaloupe, etc. **2.** any of these plants ☆**3.** [Slang] profits, winnings, political spoils, or the like, for distribution among stockholders, etc.: chiefly in **cut a melon**, to distribute such profits, etc.

Me·los (mē′läs) *same as* MÍLOS

Mel·pom·e·ne (mel päm′ə nē′) [L. < Gr. *Melpomenē* < *melpein*, to sing] *Gr. Myth.* the Muse of tragedy

Mel·rose (mel′rōz) village in SE Scotland: site of the ruins of a Cistercian abbey

melt (melt) *vt.*, *vi.* **melt′ed**, **melt′ing**, archaic pp. **mol′ten** [ME. *melten* < OE. *meltan*, *vi.*, *mieltan*, *vt.*: for IE. see MILL¹] **1.** to change from a solid to a liquid state, generally by heat **2.** to dissolve; disintegrate **3.** to disappear or cause to disappear gradually (often with *away*) **4.** to merge gradually; blend [the sea *melting* into the sky] **5.** to soften; make or become gentle and tender [a story

to *melt* our hearts] —*n.* **1.** a melting or being melted **2.** something melted **3.** the quantity melted at one operation or during one period —**melt down** to melt (previously formed metal) so that it can be cast or molded again —**melt in one's mouth** **1.** to require little or no chewing: said of tender meat **2.** to taste especially delicious —**melt′a·bil′i·ty** *n.* —**melt′a·ble** *adj.* —**melt′er** *n.* —**melt′ing·ly** *adv.*

SYN.—**melt** implies the bringing of a substance from its solid to its liquid state, usually by heat [to *melt* butter]; **dissolve** refers specifically to the reduction of a solid to a liquid by placing it in another liquid so that its particles are evenly distributed among those of the solvent [to *dissolve* sugar in water]; **liquefy** is the general term meaning to change to a liquid state and may be applied to gases as well as solids; **thaw** implies the reducing of a frozen substance to its normal state, usually to a liquid or a semiliquid, by raising its temperature [the ice has *thawed*] —ANT. **solidify, freeze**

melt·age (-ij) *n.* **1.** the act of melting **2.** the thing or quantity resulting from melting

melting point the temperature at which a specified solid becomes liquid

melting pot **1.** a container in which metals or other substances are melted; crucible **2.** a country, place, etc. in which immigrants of various nationalities and races are assimilated

mel·ton (mel′t′n) *n.* [< *Melton* Mowbray in Leicestershire, England] a heavy woolen cloth with a smooth surface and a short nap, used for overcoats

melt. pt. melting point

melt·wa·ter (melt′wôt′ər, -wät′ər) *n.* water produced by the melting of snow or ice

Mel·ville (mel′vil) [< the surname: var. *Melvil* **2. Herman**, 1819–91; U.S. novelist

Melville Island **1.** island of Canada in the Arctic Ocean, north of Victoria Island: 16,141 sq. mi. **2.** island of Australia in the Timor Sea, off the NW coast of Northern Territory: c. 2,400 sq. mi.

Melville Peninsula peninsula in NE Canada, opposite Baffin Island: c. 250 mi. long

Mel·vin (mel′vin) [< ? OE. *mæl*, *mæthel*, council + *wine*, friend, protector] a masculine name

mem (mem) *n.* [Heb. *mēm*, lit., water: see M] the thirteenth letter of the Hebrew alphabet (מ, ם)

mem. **1.** member **2.** memoir **3.** memorandum; memoranda **4.** memorial **5.** [L. *memento*] remember

mem·ber (mem′bər) *n.* [ME. *membre* < OE. < L. *membrum* < IE. **mēmsro-*, var. of *mēmso-*, flesh, whence Sans. *māmsá-*, Goth. *mimz*, flesh] **1.** a part or organ of a human or animal body; specif., *a)* an arm or leg *b)* the penis **2.** a part of a plant considered with regard to structure or position rather than function **3.** *a)* a distinct part or element of a whole, as of a mathematical equation, a sentence, a syllogism, a series, a building, a bridge, etc. *b)* a part or division in a system of classification [species are *members* of a genus] **4.** a person belonging to some association, society, community, party, etc. **5.** [M-] ☆*a)* a Member of Congress, in the House of Representatives *b)* a Member of Parliament, in the House of Commons *c)* a Member of the Canadian Parliament —**mem′bered** *adj.*

mem·ber·ship (-ship′) *n.* **1.** the state of being, or status as, a member **2.** members collectively, as of an organization **3.** the number of members

mem·brane (mem′brān) *n.* [L. *membrana*, membrane, fine skin, parchment < *membrum*, member] a thin, soft, pliable sheet or layer, especially of animal or vegetable tissue, serving as a covering or lining, as for an organ or part —**mem′braned** *adj.*

membrane bone a bone developed in a connective tissue membrane rather than in cartilage

mem·bra·nous (mem′brə nəs) *adj.* [Fr. *membraneux* < L. *membraneus*] **1.** of, having the nature of, or like membrane **2.** characterized by the forming of a membrane: said of some diseases Also **mem′bra·na′ceous** (-nā′shəs) —**mem′bra·nous·ly** *adv.*

membranous labyrinth the soft tissue structure conforming to the bony labyrinth of the inner ear: see EAR¹

Me·mel (mā′məl; E. mem′əl) Ger. *name* of KLAIPEDA

me·men·to (mi men′tō, mə-) *n., pl.* **-tos**, **-toes** [L., imperative of *meminisse*, to remember: for IE. base see MIND] **1.** [M-] *R.C.Ch.* either of two prayers in the Canon of the Mass, one for the living and one for the dead, beginning "Memento" **2.** anything serving as a reminder or warning or, now esp., a souvenir

‡**me·men·to mo·ri** (mi men′tō mō′rī, -rē) [L., remember that you must die] any reminder of death

Mem·ling (mem′liŋ), **Hans** 1433?–94; Fl. painter, prob. born in Germany: also **Mem′linc** (-liŋk)

Mem·non (mem′nän) [L. < Gr. *Memnōn*] **1.** *Gr. Myth.* an Ethiopian king killed by Achilles in the Trojan War and made immortal by Zeus **2.** a gigantic statue of an Egyptian king at Thebes, said to have emitted a musical sound at sunrise —**Mem·no′ni·an** (-nō′nē ən) *adj.*

mem·o (mem′ō) *n., pl.* **-os** *clipped form of* MEMORANDUM

mem·oir (mem′wär) *n.* [Fr. *mémoire,* masc., a memorandum, memoir, fem., memory < L. *memoria,* MEMORY] **1.** a biography or biographical notice, usually written by a relative or personal friend of the subject **2.** [*pl.*] an autobiography, usually a full or highly personal account **3.** [*pl.*] a report or record of important events based on the writer's personal observation, special knowledge, etc. **4.** a report or record of a scholarly investigation, scientific study, etc. **5.** [*pl.*] the record of the proceedings of a learned society

mem·o·ra·bil·i·a (mem′ər ə bil′ē ə, -bil′yə; -bēl′-) *n.pl., sing.* **mem′o·rab′i·le** (-ə rab′ə lē) [L., neut. pl. of *memorabilis,* memorable] things worth remembering or recording, as a collection of anecdotes, accounts, etc., or of mementos, esp. about one subject, event, etc.

mem·o·ra·ble (mem′ər ə b′l, mem′rə-) *adj.* [L. *memorabilis*] worth remembering; notable; remarkable —**mem′o·ra·bil′i·ty** *n.* —**mem′o·ra·bly** *adv.*

mem·o·ran·dum (mem′ə ran′dəm) *n., pl.* **-dums, -da** (-də) [ME. < L. neut. of *memorandus,* to be remembered, gerundive of *memorare,* to remember: see MEMORY] **1.** *a)* a short note written to help one remember something or remind one to do something *b)* a record of events or observations, esp. one for future use **2.** an informal written communication, as from one department to another in an office **3.** in diplomacy, a summary or outline of a subject under discussion, reasons for or against some action, etc. **4.** *Business* a statement, made by the consignor, of the goods and terms of a consignment sent with the privilege of return **5.** *Law* a short written statement of the terms of an agreement, contract, or transaction

me·mo·ri·al (mə môr′ē əl) *adj.* [ME. < OFr. < L. *memorialis* < *memoria,* MEMORY] **1.** serving to help people remember some person or event; commemorative **2.** of memory —*n.* **1.** anything meant to help people remember some person or event, as a monument, trust fund, holiday, etc. **2.** an informal diplomatic paper **3.** a statement of facts, often with a petition that something be done, sent to a governing body, official, etc. —**me·mo′ri·al·ly** *adv.*

☆**Memorial Day** a legal holiday in the U.S. (the last Monday in May in most States) in memory of the dead servicemen of all wars; Decoration Day: in Southern States, **Confederate Memorial Day** is variously observed on April 26, May 10, June 3, etc.

me·mo·ri·al·ist (-ist) *n.* **1.** a person who draws up, signs, or presents a memorial **2.** a writer of a memoir

me·mo·ri·al·ize (-īz′) *vt.* **-ized′, -iz′ing 1.** to commemorate **2.** to present a memorial to; petition

mem·o·rize (mem′ə rīz′) *vt.* **-rized′, -riz′ing** ☆to commit to memory; learn by heart —**mem′o·ri·za′tion** *n.*

mem·o·ry (mem′ər ē, -rē) *n., pl.* **-ries** [ME. *memorie* < OFr. < L. *memoria* < *memor,* mindful, remembering < IE. **mimoro-,* redupl. of base **(s)mer-,* to remember, recall, whence Sans. *smaraṇa,* memory, OE. *mimorian,* to recall, *murnam,* MOURN] **1.** the power, act, or process of recalling to mind facts previously learned or past experiences **2.** the total of what one remembers **3.** a person, thing, happening, or act remembered **4.** the length of time over which remembering extends [a happening within the *memory* of living men] **5.** commemoration or remembrance [in *memory* of his father] **6.** the fact of being remembered; posthumous reputation **7.** *same as* PLASTIC MEMORY **8.** *Electronics* the components of a computer, guidance system, etc. designed to accept, store, and recall information or instructions

SYN.—memory refers specifically to the ability or power for retaining or reviving in the mind past thoughts, images, ideas, etc. [to have a good *memory*]; **remembrance** applies to the act or process of having such events or things come to mind again [the *remembrance* of things past]; **recollection** implies the voluntary and detailed remembering of a half-forgotten event [his *recollection* of the campaign is not too clear]; **reminiscence** implies the pensive or wistful recollection of long-past, usually pleasurable, events, or the narration of these [he entertained us with *reminiscences* of his childhood] —*ANT.* **forgetfulness, oblivion**

Mem·phis (mem′fis) **1.** capital of ancient Egypt, on the Nile just south of Cairo **2.** [after prec.] city in SW Tenn., on the Mississippi: pop. 624,000 (met. area 770,000) —**Mem′phi·an** (-fē ən) *adj., n.*

Mem·phre·ma·gog (mem′fri mā′gäg) [AmInd., lit., beautiful water] lake in N Vt. & S Quebec, Canada: c. 30 mi. long: 2–4 mi. wide

mem·sa·hib (mem sä′ib, -säb′) *n.* [Anglo-Ind.: *mem* for MA′AM + Hind. *ṣāhib,* SAHIB] in India, lady: formerly applied to a European married woman by servants, etc.

men (men) *n. pl. of* MAN

men·ace (men′is) *n.* [ME. < OFr. < L. *minacia* < *minax* (gen. *minacis*), projecting, threatening < *minari,* to threaten < *minae,* threats, orig. projecting points of walls < IE. base **men-,* to project, whence Corn. *meneth,* mountain] **1.** a threat or the act of threatening **2.** anything threatening harm or evil **3.** [Colloq.] a person who is a nuisance —*vt., vi.* **-aced, -ac·ing** to threaten or be a danger (to) —**men′ac·ing·ly** *adv.*

me·nad (mē′nad) *n. alt. sp. of* MAENAD

men·a·di·one (men′ə dī′ōn) *n.* [ME(THYL) + *na(phtho-quinone)* + DI-¹ + -ONE] a yellow, crystalline powder, $C_{11}H_8O_2$, possessing vitamin K activity and used in medicine

Me·na·do (me nä′dō) *same as* MANADO

mé·nage, me·nage (mā näzh′, mə-) *n.* [Fr. *ménage* & ME. *menage,* both < OFr. *manage* < *manoir* (see MANOR), infl. in form and sense by *maisniee,* family < VL. **mansionata* < L. *mansio:* see MANSION] **1.** a household; domestic establishment **2.** the management of a household; housekeeping

‡**mé·nage à trois** (mā näzh å trwä′) [Fr., lit., household of three] an arrangement by which a married couple and the lover of one of them live together

me·nag·er·ie (mə naj′ər ē, -nazh′-) *n.* [Fr. *ménagerie* < *ménage:* see MÉNAGE] **1.** a collection of wild or strange animals kept in cages or enclosures for exhibition **2.** a place where such animals are kept

Men·ai Strait (men′ī) narrow channel between the NW mainland of Wales & Anglesey island: 14 mi. long

Me·nam (me näm′) *same as* CHAO PHRAYA

Me·nan·der (mi nan′dər) 343?–291? B.C.; Athenian comic dramatist

men·ar·che (mə när′kē) *n.* [ModL. < Gr. *mēn,* month (see MOON) + *archē,* beginning] the first menstrual period of a girl in puberty

Men·ci·us (men′shē əs) (L. name of *Meng-tse*) 372?–289? B.C.; Chin. Confucian philosopher

Men·cken (men′k′n), **H**(enry) **L**(ouis) 1880–1956; U.S. writer, editor, & critic

mend (mend) *vt.* [ME. *menden,* aphetic < *amenden,* AMEND] **1.** to repair (something broken, torn, or worn); restore to good condition; make whole; fix **2.** to make better; improve; reform; set right [to mend one's manners] **3.** to atone for; make amends for: now only in least said, soonest mended —*vi.* **1.** to get better; improve, esp. in health **2.** to grow together again or heal, as a fracture —*n.* **1.** the act of mending; improvement **2.** a mended place, as on a garment —**on the mend** improving, esp. in health —**mend′a·ble** *adj.* —**mend′er** *n.*

SYN.—mend is the general word implying a making whole again something that has been broken, torn, etc. [to *mend* a toy, dress, etc.]; **repair,** often equivalent to mend, is preferred when the object is a relatively complex one that has become damaged or decayed through use, age, exhaustion, etc. [to *repair* an automobile, radio, etc.]; **patch** and **darn** imply the mending of a hole, tear, etc., the former by inserting or applying a piece of similar material [to *patch* a coat, a tire, etc.], the latter by sewing a network of stitches across the gap [to *darn* a sock]

men·da·cious (men dā′shəs) *adj.* [< L. *mendax* (gen. *mendacis*) < IE. base **mend-,* a flaw, shortcoming, whence L. *emendare,* AMEND] not truthful; lying or false —**men·da′cious·ly** *adv.* —**men·da′cious·ness** *n.*

men·dac·i·ty (men das′ə tē) *n., pl.* **-ties** [LL. *mendacitas* < L. *mendax*] **1.** the quality or state of being mendacious **2.** a lie; falsehood

Men·de (men′dē) *n.,* **1.** *pl.* **-des, -de** any member of a people living in Sierra Leone and Liberia **2.** their Niger-Congo language

Men·del (men′d′l), **Gre·gor Jo·hann** (grā′gôr yō′hän) 1822–84; Austrian monk & botanist: founder of genetics: see MENDEL'S LAWS

Men·de·le·ev (men′də lā′əf; *Russ.* men′di lyā′yef), **Dmi·tri I·va·no·vich** (d′mē′trē ē vä′nō vich) 1834–1907; Russ. chemist

Mendeleev's law *Chem. same as* PERIODIC LAW

☆**men·de·le·vi·um** (men′də lē′vē əm) *n.* [ModL., after D. I. MENDELEEV] a radioactive chemical element produced by bombarding einsteinium with high-energy alpha particles in a cyclotron: symbol, Md; at. wt., 258(?); at. no., 101

Men·de·li·an (men dē′lē ən, -dēl′yən) *adj.* **1.** of Gregor Mendel **2.** of, or inherited according to, Mendel's laws

Men·del·ism (men′d′l iz′m) *n.* the theory of heredity as formulated by Gregor Mendel —**Men′del·ist** *adj., n.*

Mendel's laws the four principles of hereditary phenomena discovered and formulated by Gregor Mendel: 1) the law of independent unit characters, which states that characters, as height, color, etc., are inherited separately as units 2) the law of segregation, which states that body cells and primordial germ cells contain pairs of such unit characters and that when gametes are produced, each gamete receives only one member of each such pair 3) the law of dominance, which states that in every individual there is a pair of determining factors (see GENE) for each unit character, one from each parent; if these factors are different (*heterozygous*), one character (the *dominant*) appears in the organism, the other (the *recessive*) being latent; the recessive character can appear in the organism only when the dominant is absent Hence in all crossbred generations, unit characters are shown in varying combinations, each appearing in a definite proportion of the total number of offspring 4) the law of independent assortment, which states that any one pair of characters is inherited independently, notwithstanding the simultaneous transmission of other traits: this principle has been modified by the discovery of linkage and pleiotropy

Men·dels·sohn (men′d′l sən; *G.* -dəls zōn′) **1. Fe·lix** (fā′liks), (full name *Jakob Ludwig Felix Mendelssohn-Bartholdy*) 1809–47; Ger. composer: grandson of *ff.* **2. Moses,** 1729–86; Ger. Jewish philosopher

Men·de·res (men′də res′) **1.** river in SW Asia Minor, flowing west into the Aegean: c. 250 mi.: ancient name, MEANDER **2.** river in SW Asia Minor, flowing west into the Dardanelles: 60 mi.: ancient name, SCAMANDER

men·di·cant (men′di kənt) *adj.* [L. *mendicans* (gen. *mendicantis*), prp. of *mendicare*, to beg < *mendicus*, needy: for base see MENDACIOUS] **1.** asking for alms; begging **2.** of or characteristic of a beggar **3.** designating or of any of various religious orders whose members originally held no personal or community property, living mostly on alms —*n.* **1.** a beggar; pauper **2.** one who begs for alms **2.** a mendicant friar —**men′di·can·cy, men·dic·i·ty** (mən dis′ə tē) *n.*

mend·ing (men′diŋ) *n.* **1.** the act of one who mends **2.** things to be repaired by sewing, darning, patching, etc.

Men·do·ci·no (men′də sē′nō), **Cape** [Sp., prob. < *Mendoza*, surname of a viceroy of New Spain] cape in NW Calif.: westernmost point of the State

Men·do·za (men dō′zə; *Sp.* men dô′sä) city in W Argentina: pop. 120,000

Men·e·la·us (men′ə lā′əs) [L. < Gr. *Menelaos*] *Gr. Myth.* a king of Sparta, son of Atreus, brother of Agamemnon, and husband of Helen of Troy

Men·e·lik II (men′ə lik) 1844-1913; emperor of Ethiopia (1889-1913)

‡**me·ne, me·ne, tek·el, u·phar·sin** (mē′nē mē′nē tek′′l yōō fär′sin) [Aram., prob. lit., numbered, numbered, weighed, and divided] *Bible* the writing on the wall, interpreted by Daniel to mean that God had weighed Belshazzar and his kingdom, found them wanting, and would destroy them: Dan. 5:25

Me·nén·dez de A·vi·lés (me nen′deth the ä′vē les′), **Pe·dro** (pā′thrō) 1519-74; Sp. naval officer & explorer: founded St. Augustine, Fla., in 1565

Me·nes (mē′nēz) fl. c. 3200 B.C.; traditionally, 1st king of the 1st dynasty of ancient Egypt

men·folk (men′fōk′) *n.pl.* [Dial. or Colloq.] men: also **men′folks′**

Meng·tse (meŋ′tsē′; *Chin.* muŋ′dzu′) *see* MENCIUS

☆**men·ha·den** (men hād′′n) *n., pl.* **-den, -dens:** see PLURAL, II, D, 2 [< AmInd. (Algonquian) name: orig. sense prob. "fertilizer"] a sea fish (*Brevoortia tyrannus*) of the herring family, common along the Atlantic coast from New England southward: it is used for bait or for making oil and fertilizer

men·hir (men′hir) *n.* [Fr. < Bret. *men*, stone + *hir*, long] a tall stone, usually rough, standing upright (either as part of a circle or row, or alone), erected probably as a prehistoric monument; megalith

me·ni·al (mē′nē əl, mēn′yəl) *adj.* [ME. *meynal* < Anglo-Fr. *meignal* < *meiniee*, a family retainer, servant < OFr. *meisniee*, household < L. *mansio:* see MANSION] **1.** of or fit for servants **2.** servile; low; mean —*n.* **1.** a domestic servant **2.** a servile, low person —*SYN.* see SERVILE —**me′ni·al·ly** *adv.*

Mé·nière's syndrome (or **disease**) (mān yerz′) [after Prosper *Ménière* (1799-1862), Fr. physician] a malfunctioning of the semicircular canal of the inner ear, characterized by dizziness, nausea, vomiting, a buzzing in the ear, etc.

me·nin·ges (mə nin′jēz) *n.pl., sing.* **me·ninx** (mē′niŋks) [ModL., pl. of *meninx* < Gr. *mēninx* (gen. *mēningos*), a membrane, akin to L. *membrum*, MEMBER] the three membranes that envelop the brain and the spinal cord: dura mater, arachnoid, and pia mater —**me·nin′ge·al** (-jē əl) *adj.*

men·in·gi·tis (men′in jīt′is) *n.* [ModL.: see MENINGES & -ITIS] inflammation of the meninges, esp. as the result of infection by bacteria or viruses —**men′in·git′ic** (-jit′ik) *adj.*

me·nin·go·coc·cus (mə niŋ′gō käk′əs) *n., pl.* **-coc′ci** (-käk′sī) the bacterium (*Neisseria meningitidis*) that is a common cause of meningitis —**me·nin′go·coc′cal** (-käk′′l), **me·nin′go·coc′cic** (-käk′sik) *adj.*

me·nis·cus (mi nis′kəs) *n., pl.* **-nis′cus·es, -nis′ci** (-nis′ī, -kī) [ModL. < Gr. *mēniskos*, dim. of *mēnē*, the MOON] **1.** a crescent or crescent-shaped thing **2.** a lens convex on one side and concave on the other **3.** fibrous cartilage within a joint, esp. of the knee **4.** *Physics* the curved upper surface of a column of liquid: as a result of capillarity it is convex when the walls of the container are dry, concave when they are wet

MENISCUS (left, mercury; right, water)

☆**Men·lo Park** (men′lō) [after *Menlo Park*, Calif., in turn after *Menlough*, town in Galway, Ireland] village in NE N.J. that was the site of Thomas Edison's workshop (1876-87)

Men·ning·er (men′iŋ ər), **Karl Augustus** 1893- ; U.S. psychiatrist

Men·non·ite (men′ə nīt′) *n.* [after *Menno* Simons (1496?-1561?), a leader] any member of an evangelical Protestant Christian sect founded in Friesland in the 16th cent. and still existing in America and Europe: Mennonites oppose the taking of oaths, infant baptism, military service, and the acceptance of public office, and favor plain dress and plain living

‡**me·no** (me′nō) *adv.* [It. < L. *minus*] *Music* less

me·nol·o·gy (mi näl′ə jē) *n., pl.* **-gies** [ModL. *menologium* < LGr. *mēnologion* < Gr. *mēn*, month, MOON + *logos*, an account: see LOGIC] **1.** a calendar of the months, with their events **2.** a register of the saints, with brief biographies, arranged in a calendar

☆**Me·nom·i·ni** (mə näm′ə nē) *n.* [Chippewa, lit., men of the wild rice] **1.** *pl.* **-nis, -ni** any member of an American Indian people now living in Wisconsin and formerly living also in the Upper Peninsula, Michigan **2.** their Algonquian language Also sp. **Me·nom′i·nee**

men·o·pause (men′ə pôz′) *n.* [< Gr. *mēn* (gen. *mēnos*), month, MOON + *pauein*, to cause to cease (see PAUSE)] the permanent cessation of menstruation, normally between the ages of 40 and 50, or the period during which this occurs; female climacteric, or change of life —**men′o·paus′al** *adj.*

men·o·rah (mə nō′rə, -nôr′ə) *n.* [Heb. *menōrah*, lamp stand; akin to Ar. *manārah:* see MINARET] a candelabrum; specif., *a)* one with seven branches, a traditional symbol of Judaism *b)* one with nine branches, used during the festival of Hanuka

Me·nor·ca (me nôr′kä) *Sp. name* of MINORCA

men·or·rha·gi·a (men′ə rā′jē ə) *n.* [< Gr. *mēn* (gen. *mēnos*), month, MOON + -RRHAGIA] excessive menstrual flow —**men′or·rha′gic** (-raj′ik) *adj.*

Me·not·ti (mə nät′ē), **Gian Car·lo** (jän kär′lō) 1911- ; U.S. operatic composer, born in Italy

Men·sa (men′sə) [L., table] a constellation near the S celestial pole

men·sal[1] (men′s′l) *adj.* [LL. *mensalis* < L. *mensa*, a table, prob. < *mensus:* see MEASURE] of or used at the table

men·sal[2] (men′s′l) *adj.* [< L. *mensis*, month (see MOON) + -AL] monthly

‡**mensch** (mensh, mench) *n., pl.* **mensch′en** (-′n) [Yid. < G., person] a sensible, mature, responsible person

men·ses (men′sēz) *n.pl.* [L., pl. of *mensis*, month: see MOON] the periodic flow of blood and sloughed-off tissue from the uterus, discharged through the genital tract: it normally occurs in nonpregnant women about every four weeks, from menarche to menopause

Men·she·vik (men′shə vik′) *n., pl.* **-viks′, -vik′i** (-vē′kē) [Russ. (1903) < *menshe*, the smaller, less, minority] [*also* m-] a member of the minority faction (*Mensheviki*) of the Social Democratic Party of Russia, which opposed the more radical majority faction (*Bolsheviki*) from 1903 on —*adj.* of, characteristic of, or like the Mensheviks —**Men′she·vism** *n.* —**Men′she·vist** *n., adj.*

‡**mens sa·na in cor·po·re sa·no** (menz sä′nə in kôr′pə rē sä′nō) [L.] a sound mind in a sound body

men·stru·al (men′stroo wəl, men′strəl) *adj.* [ME. *menstrual* < L. *menstrualis* < *menstruus*, monthly < *mensis*, month: see MOON] **1.** of the menses or menstruation **2.** [Now Rare] monthly

men·stru·ate (-stroo wāt′, -strāt) *vi.* **-at′ed, -at′ing** [< L. *menstruatus*, pp. of *menstruare*, to menstruate < *menstruus:* see prec.] to have a discharge of the menses

men·stru·a·tion (men′stroo wā′shən, -strā′shən) *n.* [ML. *menstruatio*] the discharge of the menses, or the period when this occurs

men·stru·ous (men′stroo wəs, men′strəs) *adj.* [ML. *menstruosus* < L. *menstruus*, monthly < *mensis*] of or having the menses

men·stru·um (-stroo wəm) *n., pl.* **-stru·ums, -stru·a** (-wə) [ML., orig. neut. of L. *menstruus* (see prec.): from an alchemical notion of the power of the menses as a solvent] a liquid that dissolves a solid; solvent

men·sur·a·ble (men′shər ə b′l, -sər-) *adj.* [Fr. < LL. *mensurabilis* < *mensurare:* see MENSURATION] **1.** that can be measured; measurable **2.** *Music* same as MENSURAL —**men′sur·a·bil′i·ty** *n.*

men·su·ral (-əl) *adj.* [LL. *mensuralis*] **1.** of measure **2.** *Music* designating or of polyphonic music in which each note is given a strictly determined value

men·su·ra·tion (men′shə rā′shən, -sə-) *n.* [LL. *mensuratio* < *mensuratus*, pp. of *mensurare*, to measure < L. *mensura*, MEASURE] **1.** the act, process, or art of measuring **2.** the branch of mathematics dealing with the determination of length, area, or volume —**men′su·ra′tive** (-rāt′iv) *adj.*

mens·wear (menz′wer′) *n.* clothing for men; haberdashery: also **men's wear**

-ment (mənt, mint) [ME. < OFr. < L. *-mentum*] a *n.-forming suffix meaning:* **1.** a result or product [*improvement, pavement*] **2.** a means, agency, or instrument [*adornment, escapement*] **3.** the act, fact, process, or art [*measurement, movement*] **4.** the state, condition, fact, or degree [*disappointment*] Final *y* after a consonant becomes *i* before *-ment* [*embodiment*]

men·tal[1] (men′t′l) *adj.* [ME. < MFr. < LL. *mentalis* < L. *mens* (*mentis*), MIND] **1.** of or for the mind or intellect [*mental* powers, *mental* aids] **2.** done by, or carried on in, the mind (i.e., without using written symbols) [*mental*

arithmetic/ **3.** having a mental disorder; mentally ill [a *mental* patient/ **4.** for the mentally ill [a *mental* hospital/ **5.** having to do with mind reading, telepathy, etc. —**men′tal·ly** *adv.*

men·tal² (men′t'l) *adj.* [< L. *mentum*, the chin < IE. base **men-*, to project (cf. MENACE) + -AL] of the chin

mental age an individual's degree of mental development measured in terms of the chronological age of the average individual of corresponding mental ability

mental deficiency *earlier term for* MENTAL RETARDATION

☆**mental healing** the treatment of diseases or disorders by mental concentration or hypnotic suggestion

men·tal·ism (men′t'l iz′m) *n.* a doctrine that material substances exist only when perceived by some mind —**men′tal·is′tic** *adj.* —**men′tal·is′ti·cal·ly** *adv.*

men·tal·ist (-ist) *n.* **1.** a person who believes in mentalism **2.** a person who professes to read minds or tell fortunes

men·tal·i·ty (men tal′ə tē) *n.*, *pl.* **-ties** mental capacity, power, or activity; mind

mental reservation a qualification (of a statement) that one makes to oneself but does not express

mental retardation lack since birth of some mental function or functions present in the normal individual; congenital subnormality of intelligence; amentia; feeble-mindedness: it ranges in degree from *mild* (IQ of 70–85) to *moderate* (IQ of 50–70) and *severe* (IQ below 50): this technical classification has generally replaced the older terms, moron, imbecile, and idiot: formerly called *mental deficiency*

men·ta·tion (men tā′shən) *n.* [< L. *mens* (gen. *mentis*), MIND + -ATION] the act or process of using the mind; thought

men·thene (men′thēn) *n.* [MENTH(OL) + -ENE] a colorless, oily hydrocarbon, $C_{10}H_{18}$, derived from oil of peppermint or from menthol by dehydration

men·thol (men′thōl, -thôl, -thäl) *n.* [G. < L. *mentha*, MINT² + -*ol*, -OL¹] a white, waxy, crystalline alcohol, $C_{10}H_{19}OH$, with a characteristic pungent odor and taste, obtained from oil of peppermint and used in medicine, cosmetics, cigarettes, etc.

men·tho·lat·ed (men′thə lāt′id) *adj.* containing menthol; treated or impregnated with menthol

men·tion (men′shən) *n.* [ME. *mencion* < OFr. *mention* < L. *mentio* < stem of *mens*, MIND] **1.** a brief, often incidental, reference or statement **2.** a citing for honor —*vt.* **1.** to refer to or speak about briefly or incidentally; specify, as by name **2.** to cite for honor —**make mention of** to mention —**not to mention** without even mentioning, or barely mentioning —**men′tion·a·ble** *adj.*

Men·ton (män tōn′) seaport & resort town on the French Riviera: pop. 20,000

Men·tor (men′tər, -tôr) [L. < Gr. *Mentōr*, lit., adviser] *Gr. Myth.* the loyal friend and adviser of Odysseus, and teacher of his son, Telemachus —*n.* [m-] **1.** a wise, loyal adviser **2.** a teacher or coach

Men·tor (men′tər) [prob. after prec., adviser of Odysseus] city in NE Ohio, near Cleveland: pop. 37,000

men·u (men′yōō, mān′-) *n.*, *pl.* **men′us** [Fr., small, detailed < L. *minutus*: see MINUTE²] **1.** a detailed list of the foods served at a meal or of the foods available at a restaurant; bill of fare **2.** the foods served

Men·u·hin (men′yōō win), **Ye·hu·di** (yə hōō′dē) 1916– ; U.S. violinist

Men·zies (men′zēz), **Robert Gordon** 1894– ; Australian statesman; prime minister (1939–41; 1949–66)

me·ow, me·ou (mē ou′, myou) *n.* [echoic] the characteristic vocal sound made by a cat —*vi.* to make such a sound

m.e.p. mean effective pressure

me·per·i·dine (mə per′ə dēn′) *n.* [ME(THYL) + (PI)PERIDINE] a synthetic, bitter-tasting, crystalline narcotic, $C_{15}H_{21}O_2N$, used as a sedative and analgesic

Me·phis·to·phe·le·an, Me·phis·to·phe·li·an (mef′is tə fē′lē ən, mə fis′tə-; -fēl′yən; mef′ə stäf′ə lē′ən) *adj.* **1.** of Mephistopheles **2.** like Mephistopheles; fiendish, diabolical, crafty, malevolent, sardonic, etc.

Meph·i·stoph·e·les (mef′ə stäf′ə lēz′) [G., earlier *Miphostophiles* < ?] a devil in medieval legend and later literary and operatic works, to whom Faust, or Faustus, sells his soul for knowledge and power —*n.* a crafty, powerful, sardonic person Also **Me·phis·to** (mə fis′tō)

me·phit·ic (mə fit′ik) *adj.* [LL. *mephiticus*] **1.** of or caused by mephitis **2.** a) bad-smelling *b)* poisonous; noxious

me·phi·tis (-fīt′is) *n.* [L., earlier *mefitis* < Oscan] **1.** a harmful, bad-smelling vapor from the earth, as the exhalation from decomposing organic matter or poisonous gas from a mine **2.** a bad smell; stench

☆**me·pro·ba·mate** (mə prō′bə māt′) *n.* [*me*(thyl) *pro*(pyl) (*dicar*)*bamate*] a bitter, white, crystalline powder, $C_9H_{18}N_2O_4$, used as a tranquilizer

meq. milliequivalent

mer. **1.** meridian **2.** meridional

☆**mer·bro·min** (mər brō′min) *n.* [*mer*(*curic acetate*) + (*di*)*brom*(*ofluoresce*)*in*] *generic name for* MERCUROCHROME

mer·can·tile (mur′kən til, -tīl′, -tēl′) *adj.* [Fr. < It. < *mercante*, a merchant < L. *mercans*, prp. of *mercari*: see MERCHANT] **1.** of or characteristic of merchants or trade; commercial **2.** of mercantilism

☆**mercantile paper** *same as* COMMERCIAL PAPER

mer·can·til·ism (-iz'm) *n.* **1.** the doctrine that arose in

Europe with the decline of feudalism, that the economic interests of the nation as a whole are of primary importance and that these interests could be strengthened by the government by protection of home industries, as through tariffs, by increased foreign trade, as through monopolies, and by a balance of exports over imports, with a consequent accumulation of bullion **2.** *same as* COMMERCIALISM —**mer′can·til·ist** *n.*, *adj.* —**mer′can·til·is′tic** *adj.*

mer·cap·tan (mər kap′tan) *n.* [G. < ML. *mercurium captans*, lit., seizing mercury < L. *mercurius* (see MERCURY) + *captans*, prp. of *captare*, to seize, freq. of *capere*: see CAPTURE] any of a class of chemical compounds analogous to the alcohols, characterized by the substitution of sulfur for oxygen in the OH radical and strong, unpleasant odors

mer·cap·tide (-tīd) *n.* a metallic salt of a mercaptan, characterized by the substitution of a metal for the hydrogen in the SH radical

mer·cap·to (-tō) *adj.* [< MERCAPTAN] containing the monovalent radical SH

Mer·ca·tor (mər kāt′ər), **Ger·har·dus** (jər här′dəs) [Latinized from *Gerhard Kremer*; G. *kremer* & L. *mercator* mean "dealer"] 1512–94; Fl. geographer & cartographer

Mercator projection a method of making maps in which the earth's surface is shown with the meridians as parallel straight lines spaced at equal intervals and the parallels of latitude as parallel straight lines intersecting the meridians at right angles but spaced farther apart as their distance from the equator increases: areas on such maps become increasingly distorted toward the poles

mer·ce·nar·y (mur′sə ner′ē) *adj.* [L. *mercenarius* < *merces*, pay, wages, akin to *merx*: see MARKET] **1.** working or done for payment only; motivated by a desire for money or other gain; venal; greedy **2.** designating a soldier serving for pay in a foreign army; hired —*n.*, *pl.* **-nar′ies** **1.** a professional soldier hired to serve in a foreign army **2.** any person who will do anything for money; hireling —**mer′ce·nar′i·ly** *adv.* —**mer′ce·nar′i·ness** *n.*

mer·cer (mur′sər) *n.* [ME. < OFr. *mercier* < *merz*, goods < L. *merx*, wares: see MARKET] [Brit.] a dealer in textiles; dry goods merchant

mer·cer·ize (mur′sə rīz′) *vt.* **-ized′, -iz′ing** [after John *Mercer* (1791–1866), Eng. calico dealer who invented the process] to treat (cotton thread or fabric) under tension with a caustic soda solution in order to strengthen it, give it a silky luster, and make it more receptive to dyes

mer·cer·y (mur′sər ē) *n.*, *pl.* **-cer·ies** [ME. *mercerie* < OFr.] [Brit.] **1.** goods sold by a mercer **2.** the business or shop of a mercer

mer·chan·dise (mur′chən dīz′; *for n.*, *also* -dīs′) *n.* [ME. *marchandise* < OFr. < *marchant*: see MERCHANT] **1.** things bought and sold; goods; commodities; wares **2.** [Obs.] buying and selling; trade —*vt.*, *vi.* **-dised′, -dis′ing** **1.** to buy and sell; carry on trade in (some kind of goods) **2.** to advertise, promote, and organize the sale of (a particular product) —**mer′chan·dis′er** *n.*

mer·chan·dize (-dīz′) *vt.*, *vi.* **-dized′, -diz′ing** *same as* MERCHANDISE —**mer′chan·diz′er** *n.*

mer·chant (mur′chənt) *n.* [ME. *marchant* < OFr. *marchant* < VL. **mercatans*, prp. of **mercatare*, for L. *mercari*, to trade, buy < *merx*, wares: see MARKET] **1.** a person whose business is buying and selling goods for profit; trader, esp. one in the wholesale trade who deals with foreign countries **2.** a person who sells goods at retail; storekeeper; shopkeeper —*adj.* **1.** of or used in trade; mercantile; commercial **2.** of the merchant marine —*vt.* to carry on trade in; deal in

mer·chant·a·ble (-ə b'l) *adj.* *same as* MARKETABLE

mer·chant·man (-mən) *n.*, *pl.* **-men** (-mən) **1.** a ship used in commerce **2.** [Archaic] a merchant

merchant marine **1.** all the ships of a nation that are used in commerce **2.** their personnel

Merchant of Venice, The **1.** a comedy (c. 1596) by Shakespeare **2.** Antonio, the merchant of the play

‡**mer·ci** (mer sē′) *interj.* [Fr.] thanks; thank you

Mer·cia (mur′shə) former Anglo-Saxon kingdom in C & S England

Mer·cian (mur′shən) *adj.* of Mercia, its people, or their dialects —*n.* **1.** a native or inhabitant of Mercia **2.** the Old English dialect of the Mercians **3.** sometimes, the Middle English dialects descended from these

mer·ci·ful (mur′si fəl) *adj.* full of mercy; having, feeling, or showing mercy; compassionate; lenient; clement —**mer′ci·ful·ly** *adv.* —**mer′ci·ful·ness** *n.*

mer·ci·less (mur′si lis) *adj.* without mercy; having, feeling, or showing no mercy; pitiless; cruel; implacable —**mer′ci·less·ly** *adv.* —**mer′ci·less·ness** *n.*

mer·cu·rate (mur′kyoo rāt′) *vt.* **-rat′ed, -rat′ing** to treat or combine with mercury or a compound of mercury —**mer′cu·ra′tion** *n.*

mer·cu·ri·al (mər kyoor′ē əl) *adj.* [ME. < L. *mercurialis*] **1.** [M-] of Mercury (the god or planet) **2.** of or containing mercury **3.** caused by the action or use of mercury **4.** having qualities attributed to the god Mercury or supposedly influenced by the planet Mercury; eloquent, clever, shrewd, thievish, etc. **5.** having qualities suggestive of mercury; quick, quick-witted, volatile, changeable, fickle, etc. —*n.* a drug or preparation containing mercury —**mer′cu′ri·al·ly** *adv.* —**mer′cu′ri·al·ness** *n.*

mer·cu·ri·al·ize (-īz′) *vt.* **-ized′, -iz′ing 1.** to make mercurial **2.** to treat with mercury or a compound of mercury —**mer·cu′ri·al·i·za′tion** *n.*

mer·cu·ric (mər kyoor′ik) *adj.* of or containing mercury, esp. with a valence of two

mercuric chloride a very poisonous, white, crystalline compound, HgCl₂: used in photography and as an insecticide, antiseptic, etc.

mercuric oxide a poisonous red powder, HgO, used as an oxidizing agent and a chemical reagent and in the manufacture of pigment, cosmetics, batteries, polishing compounds, etc.

☆**Mer·cu·ro·chrome** (mər kyoor′ə krōm′) [see MERCURY, n. & -CHROME] *a trademark for* merbromin, a green, iridescent compound, C₂₀H₈Br₂HgNa₂O₆, that forms a red solution in water: used as a mild antiseptic and germicide —*n.* [m-] this red solution

mer·cu·rous (mər kyoor′əs, mur′kyoo rəs) *adj.* of or containing mercury, esp. with a valence of one

Mer·cu·ry (mur′kyoo rē) [L. *Mercurius*, Mercury] **1.** *Rom. Myth.* the messenger of the gods, god of commerce, manual skill, eloquence, cleverness, travel, and thievery: identified with the Greek god Hermes **2.** the smallest planet in the solar system and the one nearest to the sun: diameter, c.3,000 mi.; period of revolution, 88 days; period of rotation, 59 days; symbol, ☿ —*n.* [m-] **1.** [ME. < ML. *mercurius* < L., Mercury: so named by the alchemists because of its fluidity: cf. QUICKSILVER] *a)* a heavy, silver-white metallic chemical element, liquid at ordinary temperatures, which sometimes occurs in a free state but usually in combination with sulfur; quicksilver: it is used in thermometers, air pumps, dentistry, pharmacy, etc.: symbol, Hg; at. wt. 200.59; at. no. 80; sp. gr., 13.594; melt. pt., −38.87°C; boil. pt., 356.58°C *b)* the mercury column in a thermometer or barometer **2.** *pl.* **-ries** [Now Rare] a messenger or guide **3.** *Bot. a)* any of a genus (*Mercurialis*) of plants of the spurge family *b)* an edible European plant (*Chenopodium bonus-henricus*) of the goosefoot family

mercury arc an electric discharge passed through mercury vapor inside a quartz tube

mercury chloride 1. *same as* MERCURIC CHLORIDE **2.** *same as* CALOMEL

☆**mer·cu·ry-va·por lamp** (-vā′pər) a discharge tube containing mercury vapor

mer·cy (mur′sē) *n., pl.* **-cies** [ME. < OFr. *merci* < L. *merces*, hire, payment, reward (in LL., mercy, pity, favor): see MARKET] **1.** a refraining from harming or punishing offenders, enemies, persons in one's power, etc.; kindness in excess of what may be expected or demanded by fairness; forbearance and compassion **2.** imprisonment rather than the death penalty imposed on those found guilty of capital crimes **3.** a disposition to forgive, pity, or be kind **4.** the power to forgive or be kind; clemency [to throw oneself on the *mercy* of the court] **5.** kind or compassionate treatment; relief of suffering **6.** a fortunate thing; thing to be grateful for; blessing [a *mercy* he wasn't killed] —*interj.* a mild exclamation expressing surprise, annoyance, emphasis, etc. —**at the mercy of** completely in the power of

SYN.—**mercy** implies a kindness or forbearance, as in punishing offenders, in excess of what may be demanded by fairness, or it may connote kindness and sympathy to those in distress; **clemency** refers to a tendency toward mercy in one whose duty it is to punish offenders; **lenity** usually implies excessive mercy or mildness toward offenders where greater strictness might be preferable; **charity**, in this connection, implies a kindly understanding and tolerance in judging others —*ANT.* severity, cruelty

mercy killing *same as* EUTHANASIA

mercy seat [transl. (by Tyndale, 1530) of G. *gnadenstuhl*, transl. (by Luther) of Gr.(Ec.) *hilastērion* (< Gr. *hilasia*, propitiation: for IE. base see SILLY), transl. (in LXX) of Heb. *kappōreth*] *Bible* the gold covering on the Ark of the Covenant regarded as the resting place of God: Ex. 25:17

mere¹ (mir) *adj. superl.* **mer′est** [ME. < L. *merus*, unmixed, pure < IE. base *mer-*, to sparkle, whence OE. *amerian*, to purify] **1.** nothing more or other than; only (as said to be) [a *mere* boy] **2.** [Obs.] unmixed; pure **3.** [Obs.] absolute; downright

mere² (mir) *n.* [ME. < OE.: see MARE²] **1.** [Poet.] a lake or pond **2.** [Brit. Dial.] a marsh **3.** [Obs.] *a)* the sea *b)* an arm of the sea

mere³ (mir) *n.* [ME. < OE. (ge)*mære* < IE. base *mei-*, to secure, a post, wooden wall, whence L. *murus*, wall] [Archaic or Brit. Dial.] a boundary

-mere (mir) [< Gr. *meros*, a part: see MERIT] *a combining form meaning* part [*blastomere*]

Mer·e·dith (mer′ə dith) **1.** [W., prob. < *mor*, sea + base of *differal*, I protect; lit. lit. sea protector] *a masculine name* **2. George,** 1828–1909; Eng. novelist & poet **3. Owen,** (pseud. of *Edward Robert Bulwer*, 1st Earl of Lytton) 1831–91; Eng. poet & diplomat

mere·ly (mir′lē) *adv.* [MERE¹ + -LY²] **1.** no more than; and nothing else; only **2.** [Obs.] absolutely; altogether

☆**mer·en·gue** (mə ren′gā) *n.* [AmSp. < Haitian Creole *méringue*, lit., meringue < Fr. *meringue*] **1.** a Haitian and Dominican ballroom dance, a kind of one-step **2.** music for this dance

mer·e·tri·cious (mer′ə trish′əs) *adj.* [L. *meretricius* < *meretrix* (gen. *meretricis*), a prostitute < *mereri*, to serve for hire, earn: see MERIT] **1.** orig., of, like, or characteristic of a prostitute **2.** alluring by false, showy charms; attractive in a flashy way; tawdry **3.** superficially plausible; specious —**mer′e·tri′cious·ly** *adv.* —**mer′e·tri′cious·ness** *n.*

mer·gan·ser (mər gan′sər) *n., pl.* **-sers, -ser:** see PLURAL, II, D, 1 [ModL. < L. *mergus*, diver (waterfowl) < *mergere* (see MERGE) + *anser*, GOOSE] any of several large, fish-eating, diving ducks with a long, slender, toothed beak hooked at the tip and, usually, a crested head, as the **American merganser** (*Mergus merganser*) and the **hooded merganser** (*Lophodytes cucullatus*)

merge (murj) *vi.,* *vt.* **merged, merg′ing** [L. *mergere*, to dip, plunge, sink < IE. base *megg-*, to plunge, whence Sans. *májjati*, (he) sinks under] **1.** to lose or cause to lose identity by being absorbed, swallowed up, or combined **2.** to join together; unite; combine —*SYN.* see MIX —**mer′gence** *n.*

Mer·gen·thal·er (mur′gən thäl′ər, -thôl′-), **Ott·mar** (ät′mär) 1854–99; U.S. inventor of the Linotype, born in Germany

merg·er (mur′jər) *n.* a merging; specif., ☆*a)* a combining of several companies, corporations, etc. in one, as by issuing stock of the controlling corporation to replace the greater part of that of the others *b)* the absorption of one estate, interest, obligation, contract, etc. in another, or of a lesser offense in a greater

Mé·ri·da (me′rē dä) city in SE Mexico; capital of Yucatán state: pop. 194,000

Mer·i·den (mer′i dən) [MERRY + DEN (in obs. sense of "valley")] city in C Conn.: pop. 56,000

Me·rid·i·an (mə rid′ē ən) [reason for name obscure] city in E Miss.: pop. 45,000

me·rid·i·an (mə rid′ē ən) *adj.* [ME. < OFr. *meridien* < L. *meridianus*, of noon, southern < *meridies*, noon, the south < older *medidies* < *medius*, MID¹ + *dies*, day: see DEITY] **1.** of or at noon **2.** of or passing through the highest point in the daily course of any heavenly body **3.** of or at the highest point of prosperity, splendor, power, etc. **4.** of or along a meridian **5.** [Rare] southern —*n.* **1.** orig., the highest apparent point reached by a heavenly body in its course **2.** *a)* the highest point of power, prosperity, splendor, etc.; zenith; apex *b)* the middle period of one's life, regarded as the highest point of health, vigor, etc.; prime **3.** [Obs.] noon **4.** *Astron.* an imaginary great circle passing through the poles of the celestial sphere and the zenith and nadir of any given point, and cutting the equator at right angles **5.** *Geog. a)* a great circle of the earth passing through the geographical poles and any given point on the earth's surface *b)* either half of such a circle between the poles *c)* any of the lines of longitude running north and south on a globe or map, representing such a half circle **6.** [Archaic] distinctive character of a particular place or situation

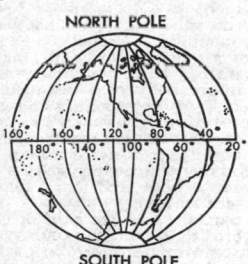

NORTH POLE

SOUTH POLE

MERIDIANS

me·rid·i·o·nal (mə rid′ē ə n'l) *adj.* [ME. < OFr. < LL. *meridionalis* < L. *meridianus:* see prec.] **1.** southern; southerly **2.** of or characteristic of the south or people living in the south, esp. of France **3.** of or like a meridian —*n.* [often M-] an inhabitant of the south, esp. of France —**me·rid′i·o·nal·ly** *adv.*

Mé·ri·mée (mā rē mā′), **Pros·per** (prôs per′), 1803–70; Fr. novelist, essayist, & historian

me·ringue (mə ran′) *n.* [Fr. < ?] **1.** egg whites beaten stiff and mixed with sugar, often browned in the oven and used as a covering for pies, cakes, etc. **2.** a baked shell made of this, often filled with fruit, etc.

me·ri·no (mə rē′nō) *n., pl.* **-nos** [Sp., prob. < (*Beni*) *Merin*, name of a Berber tribe of nomads and shepherds] **1.** one of a hardy breed of sheep with long, fine, silky wool, orig. from Spain **2.** the wool **3.** a fine, soft yarn made from this wool, often mixed with cotton **4.** a soft, thin cloth made of this yarn —*adj.* designating or of this sheep, wool, yarn or cloth

Mer·i·on·eth·shire (mer′ē än′ith shir′) county of NW Wales: 660 sq. mi.; pop. 38,000: also **Merioneth**

mer·i·stem (mer′ə stem′) *n.* [< Gr. *meristos*, divided < *merizein*, to divide < *meros*, a part (see MERIT) + *-ēm(a)*, *n.* suffix] undifferentiated plant tissue, as the growing tips of roots and stems, the cambium, etc., consisting of actively growing and dividing cells that give rise to various

permanent tissues —mer′i·ste·mat′ic (-stə mat′ik) *adj.* —mer′i·ste·mat′i·cal·ly *adv.*

mer·it (mer′it) *n.* [ME. < OFr. *merite* < L. *meritum* < *meritus*, pp. of *merere*, to deserve, earn < IE. base *(s)mer-*, to remember, care (hence provide for, allot a share to), whence Gr. *meros*, a part, *moira*, lot, fate] **1.** [*sometimes pl.*] the state, fact, or quality of deserving well or, sometimes, ill; desert **2.** worth; value; excellence **3.** something deserving reward, praise, or gratitude **4.** a reward or honor given for superior qualities or conduct; mark, badge, etc. awarded for excellence **5.** [*pl.*] intrinsic rightness or wrongness apart from formalities, emotional considerations, etc. [to decide a case on its *merits*] —*vt.* to deserve; be worthy of —mer′it·less *adj.*

mer·i·toc·ra·cy (mer′ə täk′rə sē) *n.* [MERIT + -o- + -CRACY] an intellectual elite, based on academic achievement —mer′i·to·crat′ *n.* —mer′i·to·crat′ic *adj.*

mer·i·to·ri·ous (mer′ə tôr′ē əs) *adj.* [ME. < L. *meritorius*, bringing in money < *meritus*: see MERIT] having merit; deserving reward, praise, etc. —mer′i·to′ri·ous·ly *adv.* —mer′i·to′ri·ous·ness *n.*

☆merit system a system of hiring and promoting people to civil service positions on the basis of merit as determined by competitive examinations

merl, merle (murl) *n.* [ME. *merle* < OFr. < L. *merulus*, prob. < IE. base *(a)mes-*, whence OE. *osle*, G. *amsel*] [Archaic or Poet.] the European blackbird

Merle (murl) [Fr., prob. < *merle*, blackbird: see prec.] a masculine or feminine name

Mer·lin (mur′lin) [ML. *Merlinus* < W. *Myrrdin* < Brythonic **Mori-dūnon* < **mori*, sea + PCelt. **dunom*, hill, fortified hill, fort, hence, lit., sea-hill or sea-fortress] **1.** a masculine name **2.** *Arthurian Legend* a magician and seer, helper of King Arthur

mer·lin (mur′lin) *n.* [ME. *merlion* < OFr. *esmerillon*, dim. of *esmeril*, merlin < OHG. *smirl*, merlin] **1.** a small, black and white European falcon (*Falco aesalon*) with a striped, brownish-red breast **2.** *same as* PIGEON HAWK

mer·lon (mur′lən) *n.* [Fr. < It. *merlone* < *merlo*, a battlement < ML. *merulus*: ? < or akin to L. *merulus*, MERL] the solid part of a battlement or parapet, between two openings, or crenels

mer·maid (mur′mād′) *n.* [ME. *mermayde*: see MERE² & MAID] **1.** an imaginary sea creature with the head and upper body of a beautiful woman and the tail of a fish **2.** a girl or woman who swims well

mer·man (mur′man′) *n., pl.* -men′ (-men′) [ME. *mereman*: cf. MERMAID] **1.** an imaginary sea creature with the head and upper body of a man and the tail of a fish **2.** a man or boy who swims well

mer·o·blas·tic (mer′ə blas′tik) *adj.* [< Gr. *meros*, part (see MERIT) + -BLAST + -IC] *Embryology* undergoing only partial cleavage: said of certain ova with much yolk, as bird's eggs: cf. HOLOBLASTIC —mer′o·blas′ti·cal·ly *adv.*

mer·o·crine (mer′ə krin, -krin′, -krēn′) *adj.* [< Gr. *meros*, part + *krinein*, to separate: see CRISIS] designating or of any gland which secretes its products without any obvious damage to its cells

Mer·o·ë (mer′ō ē′) ruined city in N Sudan, on the Nile: capital of ancient Ethiopia

mer·o·mor·phic (mer′ə môr′fik) *adj.* [< Gr. *meros*, part + -MORPHIC] *Math.* designating or of a function of a complex variable that is regular in a given domain except for a finite number of poles

mer·o·plank·ton (mer′ə plaŋk′tən) *n.* [< Gr. *meros*, part + PLANKTON] an organism that spends only a part of its life cycle as a member of the plankton community (e.g., the barnacle or starfish, in which only the larval stages are planktonic): cf. HOLOPLANKTON

-mer·ous (mər əs) [< Gr. *meros*, a part (see MERIT) + -OUS] *an adj.-forming suffix meaning* having (a specified number or kind of) parts; partite [trimerous (often written 3-merous)]

Mer·o·vin·gi·an (mer′ə vin′jē ən, -jən) *adj.* [Fr. *Mérovingien* < ML. *Merovingi*, descendants of *Merovaeus*, Latinized name of *Merowig*, grandfather of Clovis] designating or of the Frankish line of kings who reigned in Gaul (ancient France) from c. 500 to 751 A.D.: the line was founded by Clovis I —*n.* a king of this line

mer·o·zo·ite (mer′ə zō′it) *n.* [< Gr. *meros*, part (see MERIT) + ZO(O)- + -ITE¹] any of various cells produced by multiple fission in the asexual stage of certain protozoans, as the malaria parasite

Mer·ri·mac (mer′ə mak′) **1.** a U.S. frigate equipped by the Confederates with iron armor, engaged in battle (1862) by the Monitor, a Union ironclad, in the first battle between ironclads: Confederate name, *Virginia* **2.** *same as* MERRIMACK

Mer·ri·mack (mer′ə mak′) [< AmInd., ? place of swift current] river flowing from C N.H. through NE Mass. into the Atlantic: 110 mi.

mer·ri·ment (mer′i mənt) *n.* **1.** merrymaking; gaiety and fun; mirth; hilarity **2.** [Obs.] something that amuses or entertains —*SYN.* see MIRTH

mer·ry (mer′ē) *adj.* -ri·er, -ri·est [ME. *mery* < OE. *myrge*, pleasing, agreeable, akin to OHG. *murgi*, short < IE. base **mreĝhu-*, **mrĝhu-*, short, whence Gr. *brachys*, L. *brevis*, short: basic sense "lasting a short time, seeming brief"] **1.** full of fun and laughter; lively and cheerful; gay;

mirthful **2.** conducive to fun and laughter; festive [the *merry* month of May] **3.** [Archaic] pleasant or amusing —*SYN.* see HAPPY —make merry to be festive and full of gaiety; have fun —mer′ri·ly *adv.* —mer′ri·ness *n.*

mer·ry-an·drew (mer′ē an′drōō) *n.* [MERRY + ANDREW: orig. unc.] a buffoon; clown

mer·ry-go-round (mer′ē gō round′) *n.* **1.** a circular, revolving platform with wooden animals and seats on it, used at carnivals, amusement parks, etc.: it is turned by machinery, usually to music; carrousel **2.** a whirl or busy round, as of work or pleasure

mer·ry·mak·ing (-mā′kiŋ) *n.* **1.** a making merry, laughing, and having fun; conviviality; festivity **2.** a gay festival or entertainment —*adj.* taking part in merrymaking; gay and festive —mer′ry·mak′er *n.*

mer·ry·thought (-thôt′) *n.* [< the supposed granting of a wish to the person winning the wishbone contest: cf. WISHBONE] [Chiefly Brit.] the wishbone

Mer·sey (mur′zē) river in NW England, flowing into the Irish Sea through an estuary at Liverpool: 70 mi.

Mer·thi·o·late (mar thī′ə lāt′) [(sodium ethyl-)mer(curi-)thio(salicy)late] *a trademark for* THIMEROSAL

Mer·thyr Tyd·fil (mur′thər tid′vil) city in Glamorganshire, SE Wales: pop. 59,000

Mer·vin (mur′vin) [prob. var. of MARVIN] a masculine name: var. *Mervyn, Merwin, Merwyn*

mes- (mes) *same as* MESO-: used before a vowel

Me·sa (mā′sə) [see ff.] city in SC Ariz., on the Salt River, near Phoenix: pop. 63,000

☆me·sa (mā′sə) *n.* [Sp. < L. *mensa*, a table: see MENSAL¹] a small, high plateau or flat tableland with steep sides, esp. in the SW U.S.

Me·sa·bi Range (mə sä′bē) [< Ojibway *missabe wudjiu*, giant mountain] range of hills in NE Minn., containing rich iron ore deposits

mé·sal·li·ance (mā zal′ē əns, mā′zə li′əns; *Fr.* mā zȧ lyäns′) *n.* [Fr.] a marriage with a person of lower social status

mes·arch (mez′ärk, mes-) *adj.* [MES- + Gr. *archē*, beginning] **1.** *Bot.* having the primary xylem maturing from the center toward both the interior and exterior of the stem, as in certain ferns **2.** *Ecol.* beginning in a moderately moist habitat

Me·sa Ver·de National Park (mā′sə ver′dā, vur′dē, verd′) [Sp. *mesa verde*, green plateau] national park in SW Colo., containing ruins of early cliff dwellings: 80 sq. mi.

☆mes·cal (mes kal′) *n.* [Sp. *mezcal* < Nahuatl *mexcalli*] **1.** a colorless, alcoholic, Mexican liquor made from pulque or the fermented juice of various agaves **2.** any plant from which this liquor is made **3.** a small, spineless cactus (*Lophophora williamsii*) of N Mexico and the SW U.S., with rounded stems, whose buttonlike tops (mescal buttons) are chewed, specif. in religious ceremonies by Mexican Indians, for their hallucinogenic effects

mes·ca·line (mes′kə lēn′, -lin) *n.* [prec. + -INE⁴] a white, crystalline alkaloid, $C_{11}H_{17}O_3N$, a psychedelic drug obtained from mescal buttons

mes·dames (mā däm′; *Fr.* mā dȧm′) *n. pl. of* MADAME, MADAM (sense 1), *or* MRS.: abbrev. Mmes.

mes·de·moi·selles (mā′də mə zel′; *Fr.* mād mwȧ zel′) *n. pl. of* MADEMOISELLE: abbrev. Mlles.

me·seems (mē sēmz′) *v.impersonal pt.* me·seemed′[Archaic] (it) seems to me: also me·seem′eth

me·sem·bry·an·the·mum (me zem′brē an′thə məm) *n.* [ModL. < Gr. *mesēmbria*, midday (< *mesos*, middle + *hēmera*, day) + *anthemon*, flower < *anthos*, flower] **1.** *same as* FIG MARIGOLD ☆**2.** any of a large group of fleshy, succulent plants of the carpetweed family, sometimes grown for ornament in warm climates; esp., any of several species of a genus (*Carpobrotus*) growing wild in California

mes·en·ceph·a·lon (mez′en sef′ə län′, mes′-) *n., pl.* -la (-lə) [ModL.: see MESO- & ENCEPHALON] the middle of the three major subdivisions of the vertebrate brain —mes′en·ce·phal′ic (-sə fal′ik) *adj.*

mes·en·chyme (mez′'n kim′, -iŋ-; mes′-) *n.* [< MES- + ModL. -enchyma, suffix denoting a type of cell tissue: cf. PARENCHYMA] *Embryology* that part of the unspecialized mesoderm from which the connective tissues, cartilage, bone, blood, heart, and lymphatic vessels are derived —mes·en·chy·mal (mez en′ki məl, mes-) *adj.*

mes·en·ter·i·tis (mez en′tə rit′is, mes-) *n.* [see -ITIS] inflammation of the mesentery

mes·en·ter·on (mez en′tə rän′, mes-) *n., pl.* -ter·a (-ə) [ModL.: see MESO- & ENTERON] *same as* MIDGUT —mes·en′ter·on′ic *adj.*

mes·en·ter·y (mez′'n ter′ē, mes′-) *n., pl.* -ter′ies [ML. *mesenterium* < Gr. *mesenterion* < *mesos*, MID¹ + *enteron*, intestine: see ENTERO-] a supporting membrane or membranes enfolding some internal organ and attaching it either to the body wall or to another organ; esp., a double thickness of the peritoneum enfolding most of the small intestine and attaching it to the spinal wall of the abdominal cavity —mes·en·ter′ic *adj.*

mesh (mesh) *n.* [earlier *meash*, prob. < MDu. *maesche* < IE. base **mezg-*, to knit, entwine, whence Lith. *mezgu*, to knit together, OE. *max*, a net] **1.** any of the open spaces of a net, screen, sieve, etc.: a 50-mesh screen is one with 50 such open spaces per linear inch **2.** [*pl.*] the threads, cords, etc. forming these openings **3.** a net or network

4. a netlike, woven material, as that used for stockings **5.** a structure of interlocking metal links **6.** anything that entangles, snares, or entraps **7.** the engagement of the teeth of gears —*vt., vi.* **1.** to entangle or become entangled ☆**2.** to engage or become engaged: said of gears or gear teeth **3.** to fit closely together; interlock —**in mesh** in gear; interlocked —**mesh′y** *adj.*

Me·shach (mē′shak) [Heb. *mēshakh*] *Bible* one of the three captives who came out of the blazing furnace miraculously unharmed: Dan. 3

Mesh·ed (me shed′) same as MASHHAD

mesh knot same as SHEET BEND

‡**me·shu·ga** (mə shoog′ə) *adj.* [< Yid. < Heb. *meshuggāh*] crazy; mad; insane: also **meshugga, meshugah,** etc.

mesh·work (mesh′wurk′) *n.* meshes; network

me·si·al (mē′zē əl, -sē-; mez′ē-, mes′-) *adj.* [< Gr. *mesos*, MID¹ + -IAL] **1.** of, in, toward, or along the middle; middle; median; esp., designating or of a median plane or line **2.** *Dentistry* toward the midline of the face along the curve of the dental arch —**me′si·al·ly** *adv.*

me·sic (mez′ik, mes′-; mē′zik, -sik) *adj.* [MES- + -IC] **1.** *Bot.* requiring moderate amounts of moisture: said of plants **2.** *Ecol.* moderately moist: said of a habitat **3.** [MES(ON) + -IC] *Physics* of or pertaining to a meson

me·sit·y·lene (mi sit′'l ēn′) *n.* [*mesityl* (< Gr. *mesitēs*, mediator < *mesos*, MID¹ + -YL) -ENE] a colorless, aromatic hydrocarbon, C₉H₁₂, found in coal tar or made by distillation of a mixture of sulfuric acid and acetone

mes·mer·ism (mez′mər iz'm, mes′-) *n.* [Fr. *Mesmérisme*, after F. A. *Mesmer* (1734–1815), G. physician] **1.** hypnotism, esp. as practiced by Mesmer in connection with his theory of animal magnetism **2.** hypnotic or irresistible attraction; fascination —**mes·mer′ic** (-mer′ik) *adj.* —**mes·mer′i·cal·ly** *adv.* —**mes′mer·ist** *n.*

mes·mer·ize (-īz′) *vt.* -ized′, -iz′ing to hypnotize; esp., to spellbind, or fascinate —**mes′mer·i·za′tion** *n.* —**mes′mer·iz′er** *n.*

mesn·al·ty (mēn′əl tē) *n.* [Legal Fr. *mesnalte, menalte*] the estate or condition of a mesne lord

mesne (mēn) *adj.* [Legal Fr. form of Anglo-Fr. *meen* < OFr. *meien*: see MEAN³] *Law* middle; intermediate; intervening; **mesne profits** are profits accruing from the time possession of land has been improperly withheld from its rightful owner until his reinstatement in possession of the property —*n.* same as MESNE LORD

mesne lord a feudal lord holding land from a superior

mes·o- (mes′ō, mez′ō; -ə; *occas.* mē′sō, -sə) [< Gr. *mesos*, middle: see MID¹] *a combining form meaning* in the middle, intermediate [*mesocarp, mesozoic*]

mes·o·ben·thos (mes′ə ben′thäs, mez′-) *n.* [ModL.: see MESO- & BENTHOS] all the animals and plants living on the sea bottom at depths between 200 and 1,000 meters

mes·o·blast (mes′ə blast′, mez′-) *n.* [MESO- + -BLAST] same as MESODERM —**mes′o·blas′tic** *adj.*

mes·o·carp (-kärp′) *n.* [MESO- + -CARP] the middle layer of the wall of a ripened ovary or fruit, as the flesh of a plum —**mes′o·car′pic** *adj.*

mes·o·ce·phal·ic (mes′ō sə fal′ik, mez′-; mē′sō-, -zō-) *adj.* [MESO- + CEPHALIC] having a head form intermediate between brachycephalic and dolichocephalic; having a head whose width is from 76 to 80.9 percent of its length: also **mes′o·ceph′a·lous** (-sef′ə ləs): see also CEPHALIC INDEX —**mes′o·ceph′a·ly** (-sef′ə lē) *n.*

mes·o·cra·ni·al (mes′ə krā′nē əl, mez′-) *adj.* [MESO- + CRANIAL] having a skull of medium breadth, with a cranial index of between 76 and 80.9: also **mes′o·cra′nic** (-krā′nik) —**mes′o·cra′ny** (-krā′nē) *n.*

mes·o·crat·ic (-krat′ik) *adj.* [< MESO- + Gr. *kratein*, to rule + -IC] containing 30 to 60 percent of heavy, dark minerals: said esp. of igneous rocks

mes·o·derm (mes′ə durm′, mez′-) *n.* [MESO- + -DERM] the middle layer of cells of an embryo, from which the skeletal, reproductive, muscular, vascular, connective, etc. tissues develop —**mes′o·der′mal, mes′o·der′mic** *adj.*

mes·o·gas·tri·um (mes′ə gas′trē əm, mez′-) *n.*, *pl.* **-tri·a** (-ə) [ModL. < *meso-*, MESO- + Gr. *gastēr*, belly] **1.** either mesentery of the stomach of an embryo **2.** the region of the abdomen about the naval —**mes′o·gas′tric** *adj.*

mes·o·gle·a, mes·o·gloe·a (-glē′ə) *n.* [ModL. < Gr. *mesos*, middle + LGr. *gloia*, glue, akin to Gr. *gloios*, sticky oil: cf. GLUE] a jellylike layer in coelenterates and ctenophores, lying between the ectoderm and the endoderm —**mes′o·gle′al, mes′o·gloe′al** *adj.*

mes·o·lim·ni·on (-lim′nē ən) *n.* [ModL.: see MESO- & HYPOLIMNION] same as THERMOCLINE

mes·o·lith·ic (-lith′ik) *adj.* [MESO- + -LITHIC] designating or of an Old World cultural period between the paleolithic and the neolithic, during which certain animals and plants were domesticated

mes·o·morph (mes′ə môrf′, mez′-) *n.* a person of the mesomorphic physical type

mes·o·mor·phic (mes′ə môr′fik, mez′-) *adj.* **1.** [MESO- + -MORPHIC] of a state intermediate between the liquid and the crystalline **2.** [MESO(DERM) + -MORPHIC] designating or of the muscular or athletic physical type, characterized

by predominance of the structures developed from the mesodermal layer of the embryo (i.e., muscle, bone, and connective tissue): cf. ECTOMORPHIC & ENDOMORPHIC —**mes′o·mor′phism** *n.* —**mes′o·mor′phy** (-fē) *n.*

☆**mes·on** (mes′än, mez′-; mē′sän, -zän) *n.* [MES(OTR)ON] any of several unstable particles, first observed in cosmic rays, having a mass between that of the electron and the proton: mesons can exist in a variety of masses and half-lives and can have a neutral, positive, or negative charge —**me·son′ic** (me sän′ik, mez′-; mē-) *adj.*

mes·o·neph·ros (mes′ə nef′räs, mez′-) *n.* [ModL. < *meso-*, MESO- + Gr. *nephros*, kidney] the excretory organ serving as the adult kidney of fishes and amphibians and as the embryonic kidney of higher vertebrates: the mesonephros and its duct develop into the epididymis and vas deferens in the male of higher vertebrates —**mes′o·neph′ric** *adj.*

mes·o·pause (mes′ə pôz′, mez′-) *n.* [MESO(SPHERE) + PAUSE] a transition zone at the top of the mesosphere (an atmospheric zone above the stratosphere, extending between about 15 to 50 miles above the earth's surface), in which the temperature first rises and then decreases rapidly with height

mes·o·phyll (mes′ə fil′, mez′-) *n.* [ModL. *mesophyllum*: see MESO- & -PHYLL] the soft tissue (*green parenchyma*) inside a leaf, between the lower epidermis and the upper, chiefly concerned in photosynthesis —**mes′o·phyl′lic, mes′o·phyl′lous** *adj.*

mes·o·phyte (-fīt′) *n.* [MESO- + -PHYTE] any plant adapted to grow under medium conditions of moisture —**mes′o·phyt′ic** (-fit′ik) *adj.*

Mes·o·po·ta·mi·a (mes′ə pə tā′mē ə) ancient country in SW Asia, between the lower Tigris & Euphrates rivers: a part of modern Iraq —**Mes′o·po·ta′mi·an** *adj., n.*

mes·o·sphere (mes′ə sfir′, mez′-) *n.* [MESO- + SPHERE] see MESO-PAUSE

mes·o·the·li·um (mes′ə thē′lē əm, mez′-) *n.*, *pl.* **-li·a** (-ə) [ModL. < MESO- + (epi)thelium] epithelium of mesodermal origin; specif., the thin layer of mesodermal epithelial cells lining the serous cavities

MESOPOTAMIA (c. 2100 B.C.)

mes·o·tho·rax (-thôr′aks) *n.* the middle one of the three segments of an insect's thorax —**mes′o·tho·rac′ic** (-thō ras′ik) *adj.*

mes·o·tho·ri·um (-thôr′ē əm) *n.* [ModL.: see MESO- & THORIUM] **1.** a radioactive isotope of radium (**mesothorium 1**), formed from thorium **2.** a radioactive isotope of actinium (**mesothorium 2**), formed from this isotope

☆**mes·o·tron** (mes′ə trän′, mez′-) *n.* [MESO- + (ELEC)-TRON] earlier name for MESON —**mes′o·tron′ic** *adj.*

Mes·o·zo·ic (mes′ə zō′ik, mez′-) *adj.* [MESO- + ZO- + -IC] designating or of a geologic era after the Paleozoic and before the Cenozoic: it covered a period between c. 230,000,000 and 65,000,000 years ago and is characterized by the development and extinction of the dinosaurs, the appearance of flowering plants, grasses, birds, etc. —**the Mesozoic** the Mesozoic Era or its rocks: see GEOLOGY, chart

Mes·quite (mes kēt′) [after the *mesquite* trees found there] city in NE Tex.: suburb of Dallas: pop. 55,000

☆**mes·quite, mes·quit** (mes kēt′, mes′kēt) *n.* [Sp. *mezquite* < Nahuatl *mizquitl*] **1.** any of several thorny trees or shrubs (genus *Prosopis*) of the legume family, common in the SW U.S. and in Mexico: the sugary, beanlike, edible pods are used as fodder **2.** same as SCREWBEAN

mess (mes) *n.* [ME. *messe* < OFr. *mes* < L. *missus*, a course (at a meal), orig. pp. of *mittere*, to send, put: see MISSION] **1.** a portion or quantity of food for a meal or dish **2.** a portion of soft or semiliquid food, as porridge **3.** unappetizing food; disagreeable concoction **4.** *a)* a group of people who regularly have their meals together, as in the army *b)* the meal eaten by such a group *c)* the place where it is eaten **5.** a disorderly or confused collection or mass of things; jumble; hodgepodge **6.** *a)* a state of embarrassment, trouble, difficulty, or confusion; muddle *b)* a state of being disorderly, untidy, or dirty ☆*c)* [Colloq.] a person in either of these states —*vt.* **1.** to supply meals to **2.** to make a mess of; specif., to make dirty, soiled, or untidy; also, to bungle; muddle; botch: often with *up* —*vi.* **1.** to eat as one of a mess (sense 4 *a*) **2.** to make a mess **3.** to putter (*with*) **4.** to meddle (*in* or *with*) —☆**mess around** (*or about*) **1.** to be busy in a desultory way, without getting anything done; putter around **2.** [Colloq.] to become involved (*with*)

mes·sage (mes′ij) *n.* [ME. < OFr. < ML. *missaticum* < pp. of L. *mittere*, to send] **1.** a communication passed or

sent between persons by speech, in writing, by signals, etc. **2.** a formal, official communication [the President's *message* to Congress] **3.** a) an inspired communication, as of a prophet or philosopher b) the chief idea that an artist, writer, etc. seeks to communicate in a work **4.** [Archaic] the errand or function of a messenger —*vt.*, *vi.* **-saged, -sag·ing** to send (as) a message —**get the message** [Colloq.] to get the implications of a hint, insinuation, etc.

Mes·sa·li·na (mes'ə li'nə), **Valeria** ?–48 A.D.; Rom. empress: 3d wife of Claudius I: notorious for her dissolute life: executed

mes·sa·line (mes'ə lēn', mes'ə lēn') *n.* [Fr.] a thin, soft, lustrous twilled silk cloth

mes·sei·gneurs (mes'en yurz'; Fr. mā se nyër') *n. pl.* of MONSEIGNEUR

Mes·se·ne (me sē'nē) town in Messenia: it was the capital of the region in ancient times

mes·sen·ger (mes'′n jər) *n.* [ME. *messengere* (with unhistoric -n-) < OFr. *messagier:* see MESSAGE] **1.** a) a person who carries a message or goes on an errand b) a person whose work is delivering telegrams, official dispatches, or the like **2.** [Archaic] a harbinger; forerunner **3.** *Naut.* a light line tied to a heavier one and used in passing it, as from one ship to another

Mes·se·ni·a (mə sē'nē ə, -sēn'yə) **1.** ancient region in the SW Peloponnesus **2.** province of Greece in this region: 1,130 sq. mi.; pop. 211,000

☆**mess hall** a room or building where a group, as of soldiers, regularly have their meals

Mes·si·ah (mə sī'ə) [used by the Geneva translators (1560) for LL.(Ec.) *Messias* & ME. *Messie*, both (ME. via OFr. < LL.) < Gr.(Ec.) *Messias* < Aram. *mĕshīhā*, Heb. *māshīah*, lit., anointed] **1.** *Judaism* the promised and expected deliverer of the Jews **2.** *Christianity* Jesus, regarded as the realization of the Messianic prophecy, and hence called *the Christ* Also, esp. in the Douay Bible, **Mes·si'as** (-əs) —*n.* [m-] any expected savior or liberator of a people, country, etc. —**Mes·si'ah·ship'** *n.* —**Mes·si·an·ic** (mes'ē an'ik) *adj.* —**mes·si·a'nism** *n.*

mes·sieurs (mes'ərz; Fr. mā syö') *n. pl.* of MONSIEUR: abbrev. **MM.**: see also MESSRS.

Mes·si·na (mə sē'nə, me-) **1.** seaport in NE Sicily, on the Strait of Messina: site of devastating earthquake in 1908: pop. 265,000 **2. Strait of,** strait between Sicily & Italy: 2–12 mi. wide; 20 mi. long

mess jacket a man's short, closefitting jacket worn for semiformal dress, as by the military, or as part of the uniform of waiters, busboys, etc.

mess kit the compactly arranged metal or plastic plates and eating utensils carried by a soldier or camper for use in the field: also **mess gear**

mess·mate (mes'māt') *n.* [MESS, *n.* 4 + MATE[1]] a person with whom one regularly has meals, as in the army

Messrs. (mes'ərz) Messieurs: now used chiefly as the pl. of MR.

mes·suage (mes'wij) *n.* [ME. < Anglo-Fr. *mesuage*, prob. altered < OFr. *mesnage:* see MÉNAGE] *Law* a dwelling house with its outbuildings and adjacent land

mess·y (mes'ē) *adj.* **mess'i·er, mess'i·est** in, like, or characterized by a mess; untidy, disordered, dirty, etc. —**mess'i·ly** *adv.* —**mess'i·ness** *n.*

mes·ti·zo (mes tē'zō) *n.*, *pl.* **-zos, -zoes** [Sp. < LL.(Ec.) *misticius*, of mixed race (transl. of Gr. *symmiktos*, commingled) < pp. of L. *miscere*, MIX] a person of mixed parentage; esp., in the western U.S. and in Latin American countries, the offspring of a Spaniard or Portuguese and an American Indian —**mes·ti'za** (-zə) *n.fem.*

Meš·tro·vic (mesh'trə vich), **I·van** (ē'vän) 1883–1962; Yugoslav sculptor: U.S. citizen (1954)

met (met) *pt.* & *pp.* of MEET[1]

met. 1. metaphor **2.** metaphysics **3.** metropolitan

met·a- (met'ə) [< Gr. *meta*, along with, after, between, among < IE. **meta* < base **me-*, between: cf. MID[1]] a prefix meaning: **1.** changed in position or form, altered, transposed [*metamorphosis, metathesis*]: equivalent to TRANS- **2.** after [*metaphysics*]: sometimes, as in medical terms, equivalent to POST- **3.** behind, hinder, at the back [*metathorax*]: in anatomical terms, equivalent to DORSO- **4.** [< supposed analogy to *metaphysics*] going beyond, higher, transcending [*metapsychology*]: used in many nonce coinages, as "metacriticism," "metadiplomacy," etc. **5.** *Chem.* a) a polymer of [*metaldehyde*] b) a derivative of [*metaprotein*] c) an acid containing less water combined with the anhydride than other acids of the same nonmetallic element [*metaphosphoric* acid] d) characterized by substitutions in the 1, 3 position in the benzene ring Also, before a vowel, **met-**

met·a·bol·ic (met'ə bäl'ik) *adj.* [Gr. *metabolikos*] **1.** of, involving, characterized by, or resulting from metabolism **2.** *same as* METABOLOUS

me·tab·o·lism (mə tab'ə liz'm) *n.* [< Gr. *metabolē*, change < *meta*, beyond (see META-) + *ballein*, to throw (see BALL[2]) + -ISM] the chemical and physical processes continuously going on in living organisms and cells, comprising those by which assimilated food is built up (*anabolism*) into protoplasm and those by which protoplasm is used and broken down (*catabolism*) into simpler substances or waste matter, with the release of energy for all vital processes

me·tab·o·lite (-līt') *n.* any substance produced by or taking part in metabolism

me·tab·o·lize (-līz') *vt.*, *vi.* **-lized', -liz'ing** to change by or subject to metabolism —**me·tab'o·liz'a·ble** *adj.*

me·tab·o·lous (-ləs) *adj.* [< Gr. *metabolos*, changeable (< *metabolē:* see METABOLISM) + -OUS] of or undergoing metamorphosis

met·a·car·pal (met'ə kär'pəl) *adj.* of the metacarpus —*n.* any of the bones of the metacarpus

met·a·car·pus (-kär'pəs) *n.*, *pl.* **-pi** (-pī) [ModL., altered < *metacarpium* < Gr. *metakarpion:* see META- & CARPUS] **1.** the part of the hand consisting of the five bones between the wrist and the fingers: see SKELETON, illus. **2.** the corresponding part of a land vertebrate's forelimb, between the carpus and the phalanges

met·a·cen·ter (met'ə sen'tər) *n.* [Fr. *métacentre:* see META- & CENTER] that point in a floating body at which a vertical line drawn through its center of buoyancy when it is upright meets the vertical line drawn through its center of buoyancy when it is tipped; center of gravity of the unsubmerged part of a floating body: for stability the metacenter must be above the center of gravity —**met'a·cen'tric** (-trik) *adj.*

METACENTER
(C, center of gravity; A, center of buoyancy of a floating body; B, center of buoyancy when body is tipped; M, metacenter at point of intersection of verticals MA and MB)

met·a·chro·ma·tism (met'ə krō'mə tiz'm) *n.* [< META- + Gr. *chroma* (gen. *chrōmatos*), color + -ISM] a change of color, esp. as a result of a change in temperature —**met'a·chro·mat'ic** (-krō mat'ik) *adj.*

met·a·gal·ax·y (-gal'ək sē) *n.* *Astron.* the total recognized assemblage of galaxies and the matter in the spaces between the galaxies; measurable material universe —**met'a·ga·lac'tic** (-gə lak'tik) *adj.*

met·age (mēt'ij) *n.* [METE[1] + -AGE] **1.** official measurement of contents or weight of coal, grain, etc. **2.** the charge for this

met·a·gen·e·sis (met'ə jen'ə sis) *n.* [ModL.: see META- & -GENESIS] *Biol.* reproduction in which there is alternation of an asexual with a sexual generation, as in many coelenterates —**met'a·ge·net'ic** (-jə net'ik) *adj.*

me·tag·na·thous (mə tag'nə thəs) *adj.* [META- + -GNATHOUS] **1.** having the points of the mandibles crossed, as in the crossbills **2.** having larvae that feed by chewing and adults that feed by sucking, as in butterflies and moths —**me·tag'na·thism** *n.*

met·al (met'′l) *n.* [ME. < OFr. < L. *metallum*, metal, mine, quarry < Gr. *metallon*, mine, quarry] **1.** a) any of a class of chemical elements, as iron, gold, aluminum, etc., generally characterized by ductility, malleability, luster, and conductivity of heat and electricity: these elements act as cations in chemical reactions, form bases with the hydroxyl radical, and can replace the hydrogen of an acid to form a salt b) an alloy of such elements, as brass, bronze, etc. **2.** any substance or thing consisting of metal **3.** material or substance of which someone or something is made; stuff **4.** molten cast iron **5.** molten material for making glassware **6.** [Brit.] broken stones, cinders, etc. used in making roads, ballasting roadbeds, etc. **7.** *Heraldry* either of the tinctures gold (*or*) and silver (*argent*) **8.** *Printing* a) type metal b) composed type —*adj.* made of metal —*vt.* **-aled** or **-alled, -al·ing** or **-al·ling** to cover or supply with metal

metal., metall. 1. metallurgical **2.** metallurgy

☆**met·a·lin·guis·tics** (met'ə liŋ gwis'tiks) *n.pl.* [with sing. *v.*] the linguistic study dealing with relations between language and other elements of a culture

met·al·ist (met'′l ist) *n.* **1.** a person who works in metals **2.** an advocate of the use of metallic instead of paper money Also sp. **met'al·list**

met·al·ize (-īz') *vt.* **-ized', -iz'ing 1.** to treat, cover, or impregnate with metal or a compound of metal **2.** to make metallic Also sp. **met'al·lize'**

metal lath lath made of expanded metal or metal mesh

me·tal·lic (mə tal'ik) *adj.* [L. *metallicus* < Gr. *metallikos*] **1.** of, or having the nature of, metal **2.** containing, yielding, or producing metal **3.** like, characteristic of, or suggestive of metal [a *metallic* sound] —**me·tal'li·cal·ly** *adv.*

metallic soap a soaplike substance made by combining the salts of lead, aluminum, and some other metals with fatty acids: it is used in making paint, lubricants, cloth, etc.

☆**met·al·lid·ing** (met'′l īd'iŋ) *n.* [< METAL + -IDE + -ING] a method of creating alloy coatings on the surface of a wide variety of materials by electrolytically diffusing metals and metalloids into the surface

met·al·lif·er·ous (met'′l if'ər əs) *adj.* [L. *metallifer* < *metallum*, METAL + *ferre*, to BEAR[1] + -OUS] containing, yielding, or producing metal or ore

met·al·line (met'′l in, -īn') *adj.* [ME. *mettaline* < ML. *metallinus*] **1.** resembling metal; metallic **2.** containing metal or metallic salts

met·al·log·ra·phy (met'′l äg'rə fē) *n.* [Fr. *métallographie:* see METAL & -GRAPHY] the study of the structure and

physical properties of metals and alloys, esp. by the use of the microscope and X-rays —**met·al·lo·graph·ic** (mə tal′ə graf′ik) *adj.* —**met′al′lo·graph′i·cal·ly** *adv.*

met·al·loid (met′'l oid′) *n.* **1.** *same as* NONMETAL **2.** an element having some of, but not all, the properties of metals, as arsenic or silicon —*adj.* **1.** like a metal in appearance **2.** of, or having the nature of, a metalloid

met·al·lur·gy (met′'l ʉr′jē) *n.* [ModL. *metallurgia* < Gr. *metallourgein*, to work in metals or mines < *metallon*, metal, mine + *ergon*, WORK] the science of metals, esp. the science of separating metals from their ores and preparing them for use, by smelting, refining, etc. —**met′·al·lur′gi·cal**, **met′al·lur′gic** *adj.* —**met′al·lur′gi·cal·ly** *adv.* —**met′al·lur′gist** *n.*

met·al·ware (-wer) *n.* kitchenware, etc. made of metal
met·al·work (met′'l wʉrk′) *n.* **1.** things made of metal **2.** *same as* METALWORKING

met·al·work·ing (-wʉr′kiŋ) *n.* the act or process of making things of metal —**met′al·work′er** *n.*

met·a·math·e·mat·ics (met′ə math′ə mat′iks) *n.pl.* [*with sing.*] the logical study of the nature and validity of mathematical reasoning and proof

met·a·mer (met′ə mər) *n.* [< META- | Gr. *meros*, a part: see MERIT] *Chem.* a compound exhibiting metamerism with another or others

met·a·mere (met′ə mir′) *n.* [META- + -MERE] any of a longitudinal series of similar segments making up the body of a worm, crayfish, etc.

met·a·mer·ic (met′ə mer′ik) *adj.* **1.** *Chem.* of or exhibiting metamerism **2.** *Zool.* of or formed of metameres; segmented —**met′a·mer′i·cal·ly** *adv.*

me·tam·er·ism (mə tam′ər iz'm) *n.* **1.** [METAMER + -ISM] *Chem.* the type of isomerism in which chemical compounds have identical proportions of the same elements and the same molecular weight, but have the radicals differing in type or position, with resulting differences in chemical properties **2.** *Zool.* the condition of being made up of metameres

met·a·mor·phic (met′ə môr′fik) *adj.* of, characterized by, causing, or formed by metamorphism or metamorphosis

met·a·mor·phism (-môr′fiz'm) *n.* **1.** *same as* METAMORPHOSIS **2.** change in the mineralogical, structural, or textural composition of rocks under pressure, heat, chemical action, etc., which turns limestone into marble, granite into gneiss, etc.

met·a·mor·phose (-fōz, -fōs) *vt., vi.* **-phosed′, -phos·ing** [Fr. *métamorphoser*] to change in form or nature; transform; subject to or undergo metamorphosis or metamorphism —*SYN.* see TRANSFORM

met·a·mor·pho·sis (-môr′fə sis, -môr fō′sis) *n., pl.* **-ses** (-sēz) [L. < Gr. *metamorphōsis* < *metamorphoun*, to transform, transfigure < *meta*, over (see META-) + *morphē*, form, shape] **1.** *a)* change of form, shape, structure, or substance; transformation, as, in myths, by magic or sorcery *b)* the form resulting from such change **2.** a marked or complete change of character, appearance, condition, etc. **3.** *Biol.* a change in form, structure or function as a result of development; specif., the physical transformation, more or less sudden, undergone by various animals during development after the embryonic state, as of the larva of an insect to the pupa and the pupa to the adult, or of the tadpole to the frog **4.** *Med.* a pathological change of form of some tissues

met·a·neph·ros (met′ə nef′räs) *n., pl.* **-roi** (-roi) [ModL. < META- + Gr. *nephros*, kidney: see NEPHRO-] the excretory organ lying behind the mesonephros in an embryo, which in mammals, reptiles, and birds develops into the permanent, or adult, kidney —**met′a·neph′ric** *adj.*

metaph. **1.** metaphor **2.** metaphysics

met·a·phase (met′ə fāz′) *n.* [META- + PHASE] *Biol.* the stage in mitosis and meiosis, after the prophase and before the anaphase, during which the split chromosomes are arranged along the equatorial plane of the spindle

met·a·phor (met′ə fôr′, -fər) *n.* [Fr. *métaphore* < L. *metaphora* < Gr. *metaphora* < *metapherein*, to carry over < *meta*, over (see META-) + *pherein*, to BEAR¹] a figure of speech containing an implied comparison, in which a word or phrase ordinarily and primarily used of one thing is applied to another (Ex.: the curtain of night, "all the world's a stage"): cf. SIMILE —**mix metaphors** to use two or more inconsistent metaphors in a single expression (Ex.: the storm of protest was nipped in the bud) —**met′a·phor′i·cal**, **met′a·phor′ic** *adj.* —**met′a·phor′i·cal·ly** *adv.*

met·a·phos·phate (met′ə fäs′fāt) *n.* any salt of metaphosphoric acid

met·a·phos·phor·ic acid (-fäs fôr′ik) glacial phosphoric acid, HPO_3, a glassy, deliquescent solid obtained by heating orthophosphoric acid: used in dentistry and as an analytical reagent

met·a·phrase (met′ə frāz′) *n.* [ModL. *metaphrasis* < Gr. *metaphrasis* < *metaphrazein*: see META- & PHRASE] a translation; esp., a literal, word-for-word translation, as distinguished from a paraphrase —*vt.* **-phrased′, -phras′ing 1.** to translate, esp. literally **2.** to change the wording of —**met′a·phras′tic** (-fras′tik) *adj.*

met·a·phrast (-frast′) *n.* [Gr. *metaphrastēs:* see prec.] a person who puts a piece of writing into another literary form, as prose into verse

met·a·phys·ic (met′ə fiz′ik) *n.* **1.** *same as* METAPHYSICS **2.** [Obs.] a metaphysician —*adj.* [Rare] metaphysical

met·a·phys·i·cal (-fiz′i k'l) *adj.* [ML. *metaphysicalis*] **1.** of, or having the nature of, metaphysics; of the nature of being or essential reality **2.** very abstract, abstruse, or subtle: often a derogatory usage **3.** based on abstract reasoning **4.** beyond the physical or material; incorporeal, supernatural, or transcendental **5.** fond of or skilled in metaphysics **6.** designating or of the school of early 17th-cent. English poets, including esp. John Donne, George Herbert, Richard Crashaw, and Abraham Cowley, whose verse is characterized by very subtle, highly intellectualized imagery, sometimes deliberately fantastic and farfetched —**met′a·phys′i·cal·ly** *adv.*

met·a·phy·si·cian (-fə zish′ən) *n.* [Fr. *métaphysicien*] a person versed in metaphysics

met·a·phys·ics (met′ə fiz′iks) *n.pl.* [*with sing. v.*] [< ML. *metaphysica*, neut. pl. < Gr. (*ta*) *meta* (*ta*) *physika*, lit., (that) after (the) physics (in reference to location after the *Physics* in early collections of Aristotle's works)] **1.** the branch of philosophy that deals with first principles and seeks to explain the nature of being or reality (*ontology*) and of the origin and structure of the world (*cosmology*): it is closely associated with the study of the nature of knowledge (*epistemology*) **2.** speculative philosophy in general **3.** the theory or principles (of some branch of knowledge) **4.** popularly, any very subtle or difficult reasoning

met·a·pla·sia (met′ə plā′zhə) *n.* [META- + PLASIA] **1.** abnormal change of one type of adult tissue to another **2.** conversion of one tissue into another, as of cartilage into bone —**met′a·plas′tic** (-plas′tik) *adj.*

met·a·plasm (met′ə plaz′m) *n.* **1.** [META- + -PLASM] that part of the contents of a cell which consists of lifeless, nonprotoplasmic matter, as certain inclusions of fatty granules or carbohydrates **2.** [L. *metaplasmus*, an irregularity < Gr. *metaplasmes*, formation of cases of nouns from a missing nom. < *meta*, over (see META-) + *plassein*, to form: see PLASTIC] a change in a word by adding, leaving out, or transposing letters or syllables —**met′a·plas′mic** *adj.*

met·a·pro·tein (-prō′tēn, -prōt′ē in) *n.* any of a group of complex hydrolytic substances produced by the action of acids or alkalies on proteins and soluble in alkalies or weak acids, but insoluble in water

met·a·psy·chol·o·gy (-sī käl′ə jē) *n.* speculation about the origin, structure, function, etc. of the mind and about the relation between the mental and the physical, regarded as supplemental to psychology —**met′a·psy′cho·log′i·cal** (-kə läj′i k'l) *adj.*

☆**met·a·se·quoi·a** (-si kwoi′ə) *n.* [ModL.: see META- & SEQUOIA] *same as* DAWN REDWOOD

met·a·so·ma·tism (-sō′mə tiz'm) *n.* [META- + SOMAT- + -ISM] the process by which minerals of a rock or ore body are replaced by minerals of different chemical composition, usually as a result of action by ascending waters —**met′a·so·mat′ic** (-sō mat′ik) *adj.*

met·a·sta·ble (-stā′b'l) *adj.* changing readily either to a more stable or less stable condition, as certain electrons; unstable

me·tas·ta·sis (mə tas′tə sis) *n., pl.* **-ses′** (-sēz′) [ModL. < LL., a passing over, transition < Gr. *metastasis* < *methistanai*, to place in another way, change < *meta*, after (see META-) + *histanai*, to place: see STAND] **1.** [Rare] change of form or matter; transformation **2.** *Med.* the spread of disease from one part of the body to another unrelated to it, as in the transfer of the cells of a malignant tumor by way of the bloodstream or lymphatics —**met·a·stat·ic** (met′ə stat′ik) *adj.* —**met′a·stat′i·cal·ly** *adv.*

me·tas·ta·size (-sīz′) *vi.* **-sized′, -siz′ing** *Med.* to spread to other parts of the body by metastasis

met·a·tar·sal (met′ə tär′s'l) *adj.* of the metatarsus —*n.* any of the bones of the metatarsus

met·a·tar·sus (-tär′səs) *n., pl.* **-tar′si** (-sī) [ModL.: see META- & TARSUS] **1.** the part of the human foot consisting of the five bones between the ankle and toes: see SKELETON, illus. **2.** *a)* the corresponding part of a land vertebrate's hind limb, between the tarsus and phalanges *b)* the bone between the tibia and the phalanges in a bird's leg

me·tath·e·sis (mə tath′ə sis) *n., pl.* **-ses′** (-sēz′) [LL. < Gr. *metathesis*, transposition, a going over < *metatithenai*, to put over, transpose < *meta*, over (see META-) + *tithenai*, to place: see DO¹] transposition or interchange; specif., *a)* the transposition of letters or sounds in a word, or the result of this [*clasp* developed from Middle English *clapse* by *metathesis*] *b) Chem.* the interchange of elements or radicals between compounds, as when two compounds react with each other to form two new compounds —**met·a·thet·ic** (met′ə thet′ik), **met′a·thet′i·cal** *adj.*

met·a·tho·rax (met′ə thô′raks) *n., pl.* **-tho′rax·es, -tho′ra·ces** (-thôr′ə sēz′) [ModL.] the hindmost of the three

segments of an insect thorax —**met′a·tho·rac′ic** (-thô ras′ ik) *adj.*

met·a·xy·lem (met′ə zī′lem) *n.* [META- + XYLEM] the outer part, and last to be formed, of the primary xylem, or woody tissue of a plant, consisting of thick-walled or pitted cells

met·a·zo·an (met′ə zō′ən) *n.* [ModL. *metazoa* (see META- + -ZOA) + -AN] any of the very large subkingdom (Metazoa) made up of all animals whose bodies, originating from a single cell, are composed of many differentiated cells arranged into definite organs and organ systems —*adj.* of the metazoans

Metch·ni·koff (mech nē kôf′; *Russ.* myech′ni kôf′), **É·lie** (ā lē′) (Russ. *Ilya Ilyich Mechnikov*) 1845–1916; Russ. biologist & bacteriologist, in France

mete¹ (mēt) *vt.* **met′ed, met′ing** [ME. *meten* < OE. *metan,* akin to G. *messen* < IE. base *med-, to measure, whence L. *modus,* Gr. *metron:* cf. METER¹] 1. to allot; distribute; apportion (usually *with out*) 2. [Archaic or Poet.] to measure —*n.* [the *v.*] [Obs.] measure

mete² (mēt) *n.* [ME. < OFr. < L. *meta,* boundary, goal < LL. *-meit-* (var. of *-mei-*), post, stake, whence ON. *meithr,* a tree, MIr. *methos,* boundary mark: cf. MERE³] 1. a boundary; limit 2. a boundary mark or line

met·en·psy·cho·sis (mi temp′si kō′sis, -tem′-; met′əm si-) *n., pl.* **-ses** (-sēz) [LL. < Gr. *metempsychōsis* < *metempsychoun* < *meta,* over (see META-) + *empsychoun,* to put a soul into < *en,* IN + *psychē,* soul, life: see PSYCHE] the supposed passing of the soul at death into another body, either human or animal; transmigration

met·en·ceph·a·lon (met′en sef′ə län′) *n., pl.* **-la** (-lə) [ModL.: see META- & ENCEPHALON] 1. that part of the brain of an embryo from which the pons and cerebellum are derived 2. that part of the brain consisting of the pons and cerebellum Cf. HINDBRAIN —**met′en·ce·phal′ic** (-sə fal′ik) *adj.*

me·te·or (mēt′ē ər) *n.* [ME. < ML. *meteorum* < Gr. *meteōron,* pl. *meteōra,* things in the air < *meteōros,* lifted up, in air < *meta,* beyond (see META-) + *eōra,* a hovering in the air (akin to *aeirein,* to lift up)] 1. the flash and streak of light, the ionized trail, etc. occurring when a meteoroid is heated by its entry into the earth's atmosphere: popularly called *shooting* (or *falling*) *star* 2. loosely, a meteoroid or meteorite 3. *Meteorol.* any atmospheric phenomenon, as precipitation, lightning, a rainbow, etc.

me·te·or·ic (mēt′ē ôr′ik, -är′-) *adj.* [ML. *meteoricus:* also < METEOR + -IC] 1. atmospheric or meteorological [hail is a *meteoric* phenomenon] 2. of a meteor or meteors 3. like a meteor; momentarily dazzling or brilliant, flashing, or swift —**me′te·or′i·cal·ly** *adv.*

me·te·or·ite (mēt′ē ə rīt′) *n.* that part of a relatively large meteoroid that survives passage through the atmosphere and falls to the earth's surface as a mass of metal or stone —**me′te·or·it′ic** (-rit′ik) *adj.*

me·te·or·o·graph (mēt′ē ôr′ə graf′, -gräf′; mēt′ē ər ə-) *n.* [Fr. *météorographe:* see METEOR & -GRAPH] an apparatus for automatically recording various weather conditions, as moisture, temperature, etc., at the same time —**me′te·or′o·graph′ic** *adj.*

me·te·or·oid (mēt′ē ə roid′) *n.* any of the many small, solid bodies traveling through outer space, which are seen as meteors when they enter the earth's atmosphere

meteorol. 1. meteorological 2. meteorology

me·te·or·o·log·i·cal (mēt′ē ər ə läj′i k′l, -ôr′ə-) *adj.* 1. of the atmosphere or atmospheric phenomena; of weather or climate 2. of meteorology: also **me′te·or·o·log′ic** —**me′te·or·o·log′i·cal·ly** *adv.*

me·te·or·ol·o·gy (mēt′ē ə räl′ə jē) *n.* [Gr. *meteōrologia:* see METEOR & -LOGY] the science of the atmosphere and atmospheric phenomena; study of weather and climate —**me′te·or·ol′o·gist** *n.*

meteor shower the effect produced by a group of meteoroids entering the earth's atmosphere in nearly parallel paths

me·ter¹ (mēt′ər) *n.* [ME. *metre* < OFr. < L. *metrum* < Gr. *metron,* measure < IE. base *mē-,* to mark off, measure, whence L. *metiri,* Sans. *mātrā,* a measure, OE. *mæl:* cf. MEAL¹] 1. *a)* rhythm in verse; measured, patterned arrangement of syllables, primarily according to stress and length: see also FOOT (sense 9) *b)* the specific rhythm as determined by the prevailing foot and the number of feet in the line [iambic *meter*] *c)* the specific rhythmic pattern of a stanza as determined by the kind and number of lines 2. rhythm in music; esp., the division into measures, or bars, having a uniform number of beats; pattern of strong and weak beats in a measure [4/4 *meter* is also called *common time*] 3. [Fr. *mètre*] the basic unit of length in the metric system, equal to 39.37 inches: officially equal to 1,650,763.73 wavelengths of the orange-red radiation of an isotope of krypton (Kr⁸⁶)

me·ter² (mēt′ər) *n.* 1. [METE¹ + -ER] a person who measures; esp., an official who measures commodities 2. [< ff.] *a)* an instrument or apparatus for measuring; esp., an apparatus for measuring and recording the quantity or rate of flow of gas, electricity, or water passing through it ☆*b) same as* POSTAGE METER ☆*c) same as* PARKING METER —*vt.* 1. to measure or record with a meter or meters 2. to provide in measured quantities ☆3. to process (mail) in a postage meter

-me·ter (mēt′ər, mi tər) [Fr. *-mètre* or ModL. *-metrum,* both < Gr. *metron,* a measure: see METER¹] *a suffix meaning:* 1. a device for measuring (a specified thing) [*thermometer, barometer*] 2. *a)* (a specified number of) meters [*kilometer*] *b)* (a specified fraction of) a meter [*centimeter*] 3. having (a specified number of) metrical feet [*pentameter*]

me·ter·age (mēt′ər ij) *n.* [METER² + -AGE] measurement as by a meter, or the charge for this

me·ter-kil·o·gram-sec·ond (-kil′ə gram sek′ənd) *adj.* designating or of a system of measurement in which the meter, kilogram, and second are used as the units of length, mass, and time, respectively

☆**meter maid** a woman employed by a police traffic department to issue tickets for illegal or overtime parking, jaywalking, etc.

metes and bounds (mēts) [see METE²] *Law* the precisely described boundary lines of a parcel of land

met·es·trus (met es′trəs) *n.* [ModL.: see META- & ESTRUS] the quiescent period of the estrous cycle in mammals

Meth. Methodist

meth·ac·ry·late (meth ak′rə lāt′) *n.* a salt or ester of methacrylic acid

methacrylate resin any of several plastic substances formed by polymerizing esters of methacrylic acid

meth·a·cryl·ic acid (meth′ə kril′ik) [METH(YL) + ACRYLIC] a colorless liquid, $C_4H_6O_2$, prepared by treating acetone cyanohydrin with dilute sulfuric acid: it is readily polymerized and is used in making synthetic resins

meth·a·done (meth′ə dōn′) *n.* [< (*6 di*)*meth(yl)*a(*mino-4, 4-*)d(*iphenyl-3-heptan*)one] a synthetic narcotic drug, $C_{21}H_{27}ON$, used in medicine: it is more potent than morphine and less rapidly habit-forming

meth·ane (meth′ān) *n.* [METH(YL) + -ANE] a colorless, odorless, flammable gaseous hydrocarbon, CH_4, present in natural gas and formed by the decomposition of vegetable matter, as in marshes and mines, or produced artificially by heating carbon monoxide and hydrogen over a nickel catalyst: it is used as a fuel, a source of carbon black, etc.

methane series a series of saturated hydrocarbons of the open-chain type, having the general formula C_nH_{2n+2}: methane is the first member

☆**meth·a·nol** (meth′ə nôl′, -nōl′) *n.* [METHAN(E) + -OL¹] a colorless, volatile, flammable, poisonous liquid, CH_3OH, obtained by the destructive distillation of wood and synthesized chiefly from carbon monoxide and hydrogen: it is used in organic synthesis, as a fuel, solvent, and antifreeze, and in the manufacture of formaldehyde, smokeless powders, paints, etc.; methyl alcohol

me·than·the·line (me than′thə lēn′, -lin) *n.* [METH(YL) + (X)ANTHE(NE) (CARBOXY)L(ATE) + -INE⁴] a synthetic drug having an atropinelike action and used in the form of its bromide in treating peptic ulcers

Meth·e·drine (meth′ə dren′) [*meth*(*amphetamine*) + (*eph*)*edrine*] *a trademark for* methamphetamine hydrochloride, $C_{10}H_{15}N \cdot HCl$, used in medicine like amphetamine —*n.* [m-] this drug

me·theg·lin (mə theg′lin) *n.* [W. *meddyglyn* < *medd,* MEAD¹ + *llyn,* juice] an alcoholic liquor made of fermented honey; kind of mead

met·he·mo·glo·bin (met hē′mə glō′bin, -hem′ə-) *n.* [MET- + HEMOGLOBIN] a brownish, crystalline substance containing ferric iron, formed in the blood by the oxidation of hemoglobin, as by the action of certain drugs or in the decomposition of the blood, and no longer able to combine reversibly with oxygen

me·the·na·mine (mə thē′nə mēn′, -min) *n.* [*methen*(*e*) (< METHYL + -ENE) + AMINE] *same as* HEXAMETHYLENETETRAMINE

me·thinks (mi thiŋks′) *v.impersonal pt.* **me·thought′** [ME. *me thinketh* < OE. *me thyncth < me,* to me + *thyncth,* it seems < *thyncan,* to seem: see THINK²] [Archaic] it seems to me

me·thi·o·nine (mə thī′ə nēn′, -nin) *n.* [ME(THYL) + THION(IC) + -INE⁴] a sulfur-containing, essential amino acid, $C_5H_{11}NO_2S$, obtained from various proteins and used as a food supplement and in medicine

meth·o- (meth′ō, -ə) *a combining form meaning* methyl: also, before a vowel, **meth-**

meth·od (meth′əd) *n.* [Fr. *méthode* < L. *methodus* < Gr. *methodos,* a going after, pursuit, system < *meta,* after (see META-) + *hodos,* a way < IE. base *sed-,* to go, whence OBulg. *choditi,* L. *cedere*] 1. a way of doing anything; mode; procedure; process; esp., a regular, orderly, definite procedure or way of teaching, investigating, etc. 2. regularity and orderliness in action, thought, or expression; system in doing things or handling ideas 3. regular, orderly arrangement —*adj.* [*often* M-] using the Method —**the Method** a realistic style of acting originated by Stanislavsky, in which the actor strives for close personal identification with his role

SYN.—**method** implies a regular, orderly, logical procedure for doing something [a *method* of vulcanizing rubber]; **manner** applies to a distinctive, often personal, procedure or course [her *manner* of speech]; **mode** refers to a customary, established, or usual method or manner [their *mode* of dress]; **way** is a simple, common, but less explicit synonym for any of the preceding words [a *way* of talking, preparing something, etc.]; **fashion,** also a general term, often emphasizes currency of mode [it is the *fashion*

to wear bright colors/; **system**, in this comparison, implies a carefully developed, relatively complex method [a *system* of government/

me·thod·i·cal (mə thäd′i k'l) *adj.* [< LL. *methodicus* < Gr. *methodikos* + -AL] characterized by method; orderly; systematic: also **me·thod′ic** —*SYN.* see ORDERLY — **me·thod′i·cal·ly** *adv.* —**me·thod′i·cal·ness** *n.*

Meth·od·ism (meth′ə diz′m) *n.* 1. the doctrines, organization, and way of worship of the Methodists 2. [m-] excessive adherence to systematic procedure

Meth·od·ist (-dist) *n.* 1. a member of any branch of a Protestant Christian denomination that developed from the evangelistic teachings and work of John and Charles Wesley, George Whitefield, and others in the first half of the 18th cent.: so called from the methodical study and worship practiced by the founders in their "Holy Club" at Oxford University, England (1729) 2. [m-] [Rare] one who stresses or strictly adheres to method —*adj.* of or characteristic of the Methodists or Methodism: also **Meth·od·is′tic**

meth·od·ize (-dīz′) *vt.* -ized′, -iz′ing to make methodical; systematize —**meth′od·iz′er** *n.*

meth·od·ol·o·gy (meth′ə däl′ə jē) *n.* [ModL.: see METHOD & -LOGY] 1. the science of method, or orderly arrangement, specif., the branch of logic concerned with the application of the principles of reasoning to scientific and philosophical inquiry 2. a system of methods, as in any particular science —**meth′od·o·log′i·cal** (-də läj′i k'l) *adj.* —**meth′od·o·log′i·cal·ly** *adv.* —**meth′od·ol′o·gist** *n.*

meth·o·trex·ate (meth′ə trek′sāt) *n.* [METH(YL) + -trex- (< ?) + -ATE²] an orange-brown, crystalline powder, C₂₀H₂₂N₈O₅, that is a folic acid antagonist: used in medicine, esp. in treating leukemia and various tumors

me·thought (mi thôt′) *pt. of* METHINKS

meth·ox·ide (me thäk′sīd) *n.* [METH(YL) + OXIDE] *same as* METHYLATE

☆**meth·ox·y·chlor** (mə thäk′si klôr′) *n.* [METH(YL) + OXY-¹ + CHLOR-] a white solid, Cl₂C₁₆H₁₅O₂, used as an insecticide, esp. against mosquitoes and flies

Me·thu·en (mə thōō′ən, -thyōō′-) [after Sir Paul *Methuen* (1672–1757), Eng. diplomat] town in NE Mass., adjacent to Lawrence: pop. 35,000

Me·thu·se·lah (mə thōō′zə lə, -thyōō′-) [Heb. *methūshelaḥ*, lit., ? man of the dart, or ? man of Shelah (a Babylonian deity)] *Bible* one of the patriarchs, who lived 969 years: Gen. 5:27 —*n.* [*often* m-] a large wine bottle, esp. for champagne, holding 6 1/2 quarts

meth·yl (meth′əl) *n.* [Fr. *méthyle*, back-formation < *méthylène*: see 'METHYLENE] the monovalent hydrocarbon radical CH₃, normally existing only in combination, as in methanol —**me·thyl′ic** (me thil′ik) *adj.*

methyl acetate a colorless, volatile, flammable liquid, C₃H₆O₂, that smells like apples: it is a methyl ester of acetic acid, used as a solvent, in flavoring extracts, etc.

meth·yl·al (meth′ə lal′, meth′ə lal′) *n.* [Fr. *méthylal* < *méthyle*, methyl + *alcool*, alcohol] a colorless, volatile, flammable liquid, CH₂(OCH₃)₂, that smells like chloroform: it is produced by the incomplete oxidation of methanol and is used as a solvent, anesthetic, etc.

methyl alcohol *same as* METHANOL

meth·yl·a·mine (meth′ə lə mēn′, -ə lam′ēn) *n.* [METHYL + AMINE] a colorless, flammable gas, CH₃NH₂, that smells like ammonia and is usually prepared synthetically by heating methanol with ammonia under pressure in the presence of a catalyst: it is used in the manufacture of dyes, pharmaceuticals, insecticides, etc.

meth·yl·ate (meth′ə lāt′) *n.* a compound derived from methanol, in which the hydroxyl hydrogen is replaced by a metal —*vt.* -at′ed, -at′ing 1. to mix with methanol, often in order to make the resulting mixture undrinkable 2. to introduce a methyl group into (a compound) — **meth′yl·a′tion** *n.* —**meth′yl·a′tor** *n.*

methylated spirits (or **spirit**) ethyl alcohol made unfit to drink by the addition of methanol

methyl benzene *same as* TOLUENE

methyl bromide a colorless, poisonous gas, CH₃Br, with an odor resembling chloroform, used as a refrigerant, fumigant, and in organic synthesis

methyl chloride a colorless, poisonous gas, CH₃Cl, which when compressed becomes a sweet, transparent liquid: it is used as a refrigerant and local anesthetic

meth·yl·ene (meth′ə lēn′) *n.* [Fr. *méthylène* < Gr. *methy*, wine (see MEAD¹) + *hylē*, wood] the bivalent hydrocarbon radical CH₂, normally existing only in combination

methylene blue a bluish-green aniline dye, C₁₆H₁₈N₃ClS·3H₂O, used as a bacteriological stain, an antidote in cyanide poisoning, etc.

methyl violet *same as* GENTIAN VIOLET

me·tic·u·lous (mə tik′yoo ləs) *adj.* [L. *meticulosus*, fearful < *metus*, fear] extremely or excessively careful about details; scrupulous or finicky —*SYN.* see CAREFUL — **me·tic′u·lous·ly** *adv.* —**me·tic′u·lous·ness**, **me·tic′u·los′i·ty** (-läs′ə tē) *n.*

mé·tier (mā tyā′) *n.* [Fr. < OFr. *mestier*, ult. < L. *ministerium*: see MINISTRY] a trade, profession, or occupation; esp., the work that one is particularly suited for

☆**mé·tis** (mā tēs′, -tē′) *n., pl.* **-tis** [Fr. < LL.(Ec.) *misticius*, of mixed race, born of parents of different nations: present sense in Fr. infl. by Sp. *mestizo*: see MESTIZO] a person of mixed parentage; esp., the offspring of a French Canadian and an American Indian

Me·tol (mē′tôl, -tōl) [< *met*(hyl-amino-cres)ol(-sulfate)] *a trademark for* a white, soluble powder, C₇H₉ON, used in its hydrosulfate as a photographic developer

Me·ton·ic cycle [after *Meton*, Athenian astronomer (5th cent. B.C.)] a period of about 19 years (almost 235 lunar revolutions) at the end of which the phases of the moon repeat in the same order and on the same days: used for finding the date of Easter

met·o·nym (met′ə nim) *n.* [back-formation < ff.] a word used in metonymy, as a substitute for another

me·ton·y·my (mə tän′ə mē) *n., pl.* **-mies** [LL. *metonymia* < Gr. *metōnymia* < *meta*, other (see META-) + *onoma*, *onyma*, NAME] use of the name of one thing for that of another associated with or suggested by it (Ex.: "the White House" for "the President") —**met·o·nym·ic** (met′ə nim′ik), **met′o·nym′i·cal** *adj.*

☆**me-too** (mē′tōō′) *adj.* [Colloq.] designating or of policies or attitudes, esp. of a politician, adopted from a successful or powerful rival —**me′-too′ism** *n.*

met·o·pe (met′ə pē′, met′ōp) *n.* [Gr. *metopē* < *meta*, between (see META-) + *opē*, an opening, hole in frieze for beam, akin to *ōps*, EYE] any of the square areas, plain or decorated, between triglyphs in a Doric frieze

me·top·ic (mi täp′ik) *adj.* [< Gr. *metōpon*, forehead (akin to prec.) + -IC] of the forehead; frontal

met·o·pon hydrochloride (met′ə pän′) [< *met*(hyldi-hydr)o(*mor*)*p*(*hin*)*on*(*e*)] a narcotic drug, C₁₈H₂₁O₃N·HCl, derived from morphine, but more potent and producing fewer side effects

me·tral·gi·a (mi tral′jē ə) *n.* [ModL. < Gr. *mētra*, uterus (see METRO-²) + -ALGIA] pain in the uterus

☆**Met·ra·zol** (met′rə zôl′, -zōl′) [< (*penta*)*met*(*hylenetet*)-*razol*] *a trademark for* PENTYLENETETRAZOL

me·tre (mē′tər) *n. chiefly Brit. sp. of* METER

met·ric (met′rik) *adj.* 1. *same as* METRICAL 2. [Fr. *métrique*] *a*) of the meter (unit of length) *b*) designating or of the system of measurement based on the meter and the gram: see METRIC SYSTEM

met·ri·cal (-ri k'l) *adj.* [L. *metricus* < Gr. *metrikos* (see METER¹ & -IC) + -AL] 1. of or composed in meter or verse 2. of, involving, or used in measurement; metric — **met′ri·cal·ly** *adv.*

metric hundredweight a unit of weight equal to 50 kilograms

me·tri·cian (me trish′ən) *n.* [ME. < L. *metricus* (after ME. *phisician*, physician)] *same as* METRIST

met·rics (met′riks) *n.pl.* [*with sing. v. in senses 1 & 3*] 1. the science or art of writing in meter 2. metrical characteristics and details (of a poem, etc.) 3. the theory or a system of measurement

metric system a decimal system of weights and measures in which the gram (.0022046 pound), the meter (39.37 inches), and the liter (61.025 cubic inches) are the basic units of weight, length, and capacity, respectively: most names for the various other units are formed by the addition of the following prefixes to these three terms (but see also ARE², STERE):

deca- or *deka-* (ten), as, 1 decameter = 10 meters
hecto- (one hundred), as, 1 hectometer = 100 meters
kilo- (one thousand), as, 1 kilometer = 1,000 meters
deci- (one tenth), as, 1 decimeter = 1/10 meter
centi- (one hundredth), as, 1 centimeter = 1/100 meter
milli- (one thousandth), as, 1 millimeter = 1/1000 meter

Other prefixes sometimes used are *myria-* (ten thousand), *decimilli-* (one ten-thousandth), *mega-* (one million), *micro-* (one millionth), etc.

metric ton a measure of weight equal to 1,000 kilograms or 2,204.62 pounds

met·ri·fy (met′rə fī′) *vt., vi.* -fied′, -fy′ing to put into or write in meter; versify

met·rist (met′rist, mē′trist) *n.* [ML. *metrista*] 1. a person who writes in meter; writer of verse 2. an expert or specialist in metrics (sense 1)

me·tri·tis (mi trīt′əs) *n.* [ModL. < Gr. *mētra*, uterus: (see METRO-²) + -ITIS] inflammation of the uterus

met·ro¹ (met′rō) *adj., n. clipped form of* METROPOLITAN

met·ro² (met′rō) *n., pl.* **-ros** [Fr. *métro*, contr. < *chemin de fer métropolitain*: in England, taken as contr. for *Metropolitan District Railway*, in London] [*often* M-] an underground railway, as in European cities; subway

met·ro-¹ (met′rō, -rə) [< Gr. *metron*, measure: see METER¹] *a combining form meaning* measure [*metrology*]

met·ro-² (met′rō, -rə) [< Gr. *mētra*, uterus < *mētēr*, MOTHER] *a combining form meaning* uterus, womb [*metrorrhagia*]: also, before a vowel, **metr-**

me·trol·o·gy (me träl′ə jē) *n.* [METRO-¹ + -LOGY] 1. the science of weights and measures 2. *pl.* **-gies** a system of weights and measures —**met·ro·log′i·cal** (met′rə läj′i k'l) *adj.* —**met·ro·log′i·cal·ly** *adv.* —**me·trol′o·gist** *n.*

met·ro·nome (met'rə nōm') n. [< METRO-¹ + Gr. nomos, law: see -NOMY] 1. a clockwork device with an inverted pendulum that beats time at a rate determined by the position of a sliding weight on the pendulum: it is used esp. to help a person maintain regular tempo in practicing on the piano, etc. 2. an electrical device that makes an intermittent sound or flashing light for similar use —**met'ro·nom'ic** (-näm'ik) adj.

METRONOME

me·tro·nym·ic (mē'trə nim'ik, met'rə-) adj., n. same as MATRONYMIC

me·trop·o·lis (mə träp''l is) n., pl. -lis·es [LL. < Gr. mētropolis < mētēr, MOTHER¹ + polis, a state, city: see POLICE] 1. the main city, often the capital, of a country, state, or region 2. any large city or center of population, culture, etc. 3. in ancient Greece, the mother city or state of a colony 4. the seat, or see, of a metropolitan bishop; main diocese of an ecclesiastical province

met·ro·pol·i·tan (met'rə päl'it 'n) adj. [LL. metropolitanus] 1. of or constituting a metropolis (senses 1 & 2) 2. designating or of a metropolitan (sense 2) or metropolis (sense 4) ☆3. designating or of a population area consisting of a central city or adjacent cities and smaller surrounding communities 4. designating or of a mother country as distinguished from a colony, territory, etc. —n. 1. a person who lives in and knows a metropolis (senses 1 & 2) or one who has the characteristic attitudes and manners of such a person 2. [LL.(Ec.) Metropolitanus] a) an archbishop having authority over the bishops of a church province b) Orthodox Eastern Ch. a bishop ranking just below Patriarch 3. in ancient Greece, a citizen of a metropolis (sense 3)

met·ro·pol·i·tan·ize (-īz') vt. -ized', -iz'ing to cause to be metropolitan or have a metropolitan character —**met'ro·pol'i·tan·ism** n. —**met'ro·pol'i·tan·i·za'tion** n.

me·tror·rha·gi·a (mē'trə rā'jē ə, met'rə-) n. [ModL.: see METRO-² & -RRHAGIA] nonmenstrual bleeding from the uterus

-me·try (mə trē) [Gr. -metria < metron, MEASURE] a terminal combining form meaning the process, art, or science of measuring [anthropometry]

Met·ter·nich (met'ər nik; G. met'ər niH'), Prince (Klemens Wenzel Nepomuk Lothar) von 1773–1859; Austrian statesman & diplomat

met·tle (met''l) n. [var. of METAL, used figuratively] quality of character or temperament; esp., high quality of character; spirit; courage; ardor —**on one's mettle** roused or prepared to do one's best

met·tle·some (met''l səm) adj. full of mettle; spirited; ardent, brave, etc.: also **met'tled**

Metz (mets) city in NE France, on the Moselle River: pop. 103,000

meu·nière (mœ nyer') adj. [Fr. (à la) meunière, (in the style of) a miller's wife, fem. of meunier, a miller] designating fish prepared by being rolled in flour, etc., fried in butter, and sprinkled with lemon juice and chopped parsley

Meuse (myōōz; Fr. mœz) river flowing from NE France, through Belgium, & the Netherlands into the North Sea: c. 575 mi.: Du. name, MAAS

mev, Mev (mev) n., pl. **mev, Mev** [M(ILLION) E(LECTRON-)V(OLTS)] a unit of energy equal to one million (10⁶) electron-volts

mew¹ (myōō) n. [ME. mewe < OFr. mue < muer, to change, molt < L. mutare, to change: see MUTATE] 1. a cage, as for hawks while molting 2. a secret place or den 3. [Obs.] a place of confinement See also MEWS —vt. 1. [< the n.] to confine in or as in a cage; shut up or conceal (often with up) 2. [ME. mewen < OFr. muer] [Archaic] to shed or change (feathers); molt —vi. [Archaic] to molt

mew² (myōō) n. [echoic] the characteristic vocal sound made by a cat —vi. to make this sound

mew³ (myōō) n. [ME. mewe < OE. mæw, akin to G. möwe (< LowG.): echoic of its cry, as in IE. echoic base *mu-: cf. MOPE] a sea gull, esp. a common European gull

mewl (myōōl) vi. [freq. of MEW²] to cry weakly, like a baby; whimper or whine —**mewl'er** n.

mews (myōōz) n.pl. [usually with sing. v.] [< MEW¹] 1. the royal stables in London, built on the site where the royal hawks were mewed 2. [Chiefly Brit.] a) stables or carriage houses, now often converted into dwellings, grouped around a court or along an alley b) such an alley

Mex. 1. Mexican 2. Mexico

Mex·i·cal·i (mek'sə kal'ē) city in NW Mexico, on the U.S. border; capital of Baja California: pop. 350,000

Mex·i·can (mek'si kən) adj. of Mexico, its people, their dialect of Spanish, or their culture —n. 1. a native or inhabitant of Mexico 2. same as NAHUATL

☆**Mexican bean beetle** a species of spotted ladybug beetle (Epilachna varivestis) that eats the leaves and pods of bean plants

Mexican hairless any of a breed of small dog native to Mexico, hairless except for the end of the tail and a patch on the head

Mexican War a war between the U.S. and Mexico (1846–48)

Mex·i·co (mek'si kō') [< Sp. Méjico < Aztec Mexìtli, name of the war god] 1. country in N. America, south of the U.S.: 760,373 sq. mi.; pop. 45,671,000; cap. Mexico City 2. state of SC Mexico: 8,268 sq. mi.; pop. 2,576,000; cap. Toluca 3. Gulf of, arm of the Atlantic, east of Mexico & south of the U.S.: c. 700,000 sq. mi. Mexican sp. **Mé·xi·co** (me'hē kō'), Spanish sp., MÉJICO

Mexico City capital of Mexico, in a federal district (573 sq. mi.) in the SC part of Mexico: pop. 3,353,000 (met. area c. 5,100,000): official name **Mexico, D(istrito) F(ederal)**

MexSp. Mexican Spanish

Mey·er·beer (mī'ər bir', -ber'), **Gia·co·mo** (jä'kə mō) (born Jakob Liebmann Beer) 1791–1864; Ger. operatic composer

Mey·er·hof (mī'ər hôf'), **Otto (Fritz)** 1884–1951; U.S. physiologist & biochemist, born in Germany

mez·ca·line (mez'kə lēn', -lin) n. same as MESCALINE

me·ze·re·um (mə zir'ē əm) n. [ModL. < LME. mizerion < ML. mezereon < Ar. māzariyūn] 1. a low European shrub (Daphne mezereum) of the mezereum family, with clusters of pink or purple flowers in early spring 2. its dried bark, formerly used in liniments and in the treatment of some diseases —adj. designating a family (Thymelaeaceae) of plants including daphne and mezereum Also **me·ze're·on** (-ən)

me·zu·za (mə zoo'zə, -zoo'-) n., pl. -zot (-zōt), -zas [Heb. mĕzūzāh, doorpost] Judaism a small piece of parchment inscribed with the Shema, from Deuteronomy (6:4–9 & 11:13–21), rolled and put into a case and attached to the doorpost of the home, as commanded in the Biblical passages: also sp. **me·zu'zah**

mez·za·nine (mez'ə nēn', mez'ə nēn') n. [Fr. < It. mezzanino < mezzano, middle < L. medianus: see MEDIAN] 1. a low-ceilinged story between two main stories in a building, usually immediately above the ground floor and in the form of a balcony projecting only partly over the floor below it: also **mezzanine floor** 2. in some theaters, the first few rows of the balcony, separated from the others by an aisle

mez·zo (met'sō, med'zō, mez'ō) adj. [It. < L. medius, middle: see MID¹] Music medium; moderate; half —adv. Music moderately; somewhat —n., pl. -zos clipped form of: a) MEZZO-SOPRANO b) MEZZOTINT

mez·zo-re·lie·vo (-ri lē'vō) n., pl. -vos (-vōz) [It. mezzo rilievo < mezzo < L. medius, middle (see MID¹) + rilievo, relief] sculpture in which the figures project halfway from the background

mez·zo-so·pra·no (-sə pran'ō, -prä'nō) n., pl. -nos, -ni (-ē, -nē) [It.: see MEZZO & SOPRANO] 1. a woman's voice or part between soprano and contralto 2. a singer with such a voice —adj. of or for a mezzo-soprano

mez·zo·tint (-tint') n. [It. mezzotinto: see MEZZO & TINT] 1. a method of engraving on a copper or steel plate by scraping or polishing parts of a roughened surface so that an impression of light and shade can be produced 2. an engraving or print so produced —vt. to engrave by this method

MF, M.F. 1. machine finish 2. medium frequency

mf 1. Music mezzo forte 2. millifarad

M.F.A. Master of Fine Arts

mfd. manufactured

mfg. manufacturing

M.F.H. master of foxhounds

MFl. Middle Flemish

MFr. Middle French

mfr. pl. **mfrs.** 1. manufacture 2. manufacturer

Mg Chem. magnesium

MG 1. machine gun 2. military government

mg, mg. milligram; milligrams

MGr. Medieval (or Middle) Greek

Mgr. 1. Manager 2. Monseigneur 3. Monsignor

mh. millihenry

M.H. Medal of Honor

MHD magnetohydrodynamics

MHG Middle High German

mho (mō) n. [OHM spelled backward] the unit of electrical conductance, equal to the reciprocal of the ohm

M.H.R. Member of the House of Representatives

MHz, Mhz megahertz

mi (mē) n. [ML.: see GAMUT] Music a syllable representing the third tone of the diatonic scale: see SOLFEGGIO

mi. 1. mile(s) 2. mill(s)

M.I. 1. Military Intelligence 2. Mounted Infantry

MIA missing in action

Mi·am·i (mī am'ē, -ə) [< Fr., ? var. of Chippewa omaumeg, peninsula people] city on the SE coast of Fla.: pop. 335,000 (met. area 1,268,000) —n. 1. pl. **Mi·am'is, Mi·am'i** a member of a former tribe of Indians who migrated from Wisconsin to Indiana and nearby regions: also **Miami Indian** 2. their Algonquian dialect —**Mi·am'i·an** n.

Miami Beach resort city in SE Fla., on an island opposite Miami: pop. 87,000

mi·aow, mi·aou (mē ou', myou) n., vi. same as MEOW

mi·as·ma (mī az'mə, mē-) n., pl. -mas, -ma·ta (-mə tə) [ModL. < Gr. miasma, pollution < miainein, to pollute < IE. base *mai-, whence OE. mal, a spot] 1. a vapor rising as from marshes or decomposing animal or vegetable matter, formerly supposed to poison and infect the air, causing malaria, etc. 2. an unwholesome or befogging

atmosphere, influence, etc. —**mi·as′mal, mi′as·mat′ic** (-mat′ik), **mi′as′mic** *adj.*

☆**mib** (mib) *n.* [altered < MARBLE] [Dial.] 1. a marble 2. [*pl.*] the game of marbles

Mic. Micah

mi·ca (mī′kə) *n.* [ModL. < L., a crumb, grain (< IE. *(s)meik-*, var. of base *(s)mei-*, to smear, rub over, whence OE. *smitte*, a smudge): sense infl. by *micare*, to shine, glitter < IE. *meik-*, to flicker, blink] any of a group of minerals (complex silicates) that crystallize in thin, somewhat flexible, translucent or colored, easily separated layers: most are resistant to heat and electricity and the transparent form is often called ISINGLASS —**mi·ca·ceous** (mī kā′shəs) *adj.*

Mi·cah (mī′kə) [Heb. *mīkhā(yah)*, lit., who is like (God)?: cf. MICHAEL] 1. a masculine name 2. *Bible a)* a Hebrew prophet of the 8th cent. B.C. *b)* the book containing his prophecy

mice (mīs) *n. pl. of* MOUSE

mi·celle (mī sel′, mi-) *n.* [ModL. *micella*, dim. < L. *mica*, a grain, crumb: see MICA] 1. *Biol.* a hypothetical, sub-microscopic structural unit composed of a group of molecules, as in living protoplasm, starch grains, etc. 2. *Chem.* a structural unit, as *a)* a colloidal ion composed of an oriented arrangement of molecules *b)* an aggregate of polymerized molecules joined together Also **mi·cel′la** (-sel′ə), *pl.* **-lae** (-ē) —**mi·cel′lar** *adj.*

Mich. 1. Michaelmas 2. Michigan

Mi·chael (mī′k'l) [LL.(Ec.) < Gr.(LXX & NT.) *Michaēl* < Heb. *mikhā′ēl*, lit., who is like God?: cf. MICAH] 1. a masculine name: dim. *Mike, Mickey;* equiv. Fr. *Michel,* It. *Michele,* Sp. *Miguel;* fem. *Michelle* 2. *Bible* one of the archangels

Mich·ael·mas (-məs) *n.* [see -MAS] the feast of the archangel Michael, celebrated, chiefly in England, on September 29: also **Michaelmas Day**

Michaelmas daisy [Chiefly Brit.] any of various asters, wild or cultivated, that bloom in the fall

miche (mich) *vi.* **miched, mich′ing** [ME. *mychen* < OFr. *muchier* (Fr. *musser*) < Gaul. *mukyare,* to hide, akin to MIr. *muchaim,* I conceal < IE. base *meug-,* to spy upon: cf. MOOCH] [Brit. Dial.] 1. to skulk 2. to play truant

Mi·che·as (mī kē′əs) *Douay Bible name for* MICAH

Mi·chel·an·ge·lo (mī′k'l an′jə lō′, mik′'l-) (*Michelangelo Buonarroti*) 1475–1564; It. sculptor, painter, architect, & poet

Miche·let (mēsh le′), **Jules** (zhül) 1798–1874; Fr. historian

Mi·chel·son (mī′k'l s'n), **Albert Abraham** 1852–1931; U.S. physicist, born in Germany

Mich·i·gan (mish′ə gən) [< Fr. < Algonquian, lit., great water] 1. Middle Western State of the U.S.: admitted, 1837; 58,216 sq. mi.; pop. 8,875,000; cap. Lansing: abbrev. **Mich., MI** 2. Lake, one of the Great Lakes, between Mich. & Wis.: 22,178 sq. mi. —**Mich′i·gan′der** (-gan′dər) *n.* —**Mich′i·ga′ni·an** (-gā′nē ən), **Mich′i·gan·ite′** *adj., n.*

Michigan City city in NW Ind., on Lake Michigan: pop. 39,000

mick·ey¹ (mik′ē) *n.* [prob. < *Mickey,* nickname for MICHAEL] [Canad. Slang] a 13-oz. bottle of whisky

mick·ey² (mik′ē) *n.* [< *Mickey* (nickname for MICHAEL, taken as typical Irish name), slang for Irishman] [Brit. Slang] spirit; pride; brag: chiefly in the ff. phrases —**take the mickey** to make fun; mock —**take the mickey out of** to deflate (a person)

☆**Mick·ey Finn** (mik′ē fin′) [< ?] [*also* m- f-] [Slang] a drink of liquor to which a powerful narcotic or purgative has been added, given to an unsuspecting person: often shortened to **Mick′ey, mick′ey** *n., pl.* **-eys**

☆**Mickey Mouse** [< a trademark for a cartoon character created by Walt DISNEY] [Slang] [*also* m- m-] 1. designating dance-band music that is corny, unimaginative, bland, etc. 2. childish, oversimplified, unrelated to reality, etc. [*a Mickey Mouse* college course]

Mic·kie·wicz (mits kye′vich), **A·dam** (ä′däm) 1798–1855; Pol. poet

mick·le (mik′'l) *adj., adv., n.* [ME. (Northern) *mikel* < OE. *micel,* infl. by cognate ON. *mikell:* for IE. base see MUCH] [Archaic or Scot.] much

Mic·mac (mik′mak) *n.* [Algonquian, lit., allies] 1. *pl.* **-macs, -mac** any member of a tribe of Indians in Newfoundland and the Maritime Provinces of Canada 2. their Algonquian language

mi·cra (mī′krə) *n. alt. pl. of* MICRON

mi·cri·fy (mī′krə fī′) *vt.* **-fied′, -fy′ing** [< ff. + -FY] to make small or unimportant

mi·cro- (mī′krō, -krə) [Gr. *mikro-* < *mikros,* small < IE. *(s)meik-:* see MICA] *a combining form meaning:* 1. *a)* little, small, minute *b)* exceptionally little, abnormally small [*microcephalic*] 2. enlarging or amplifying [*microscope, microphone*] 3. involving microscopes, microscopic [*microchemistry*] 4. one millionth part of (a specified unit); the factor 10⁻⁶ [*microgram*]: symbol μ Also, before a vowel, **micr-**

mi·cro·a·nal·y·sis (mī′krō ə nal′ə sis) *n.* the chemical analysis and identification of very small quantities —**mi′cro·an′a·lyst** (-an′'l ist) *n.*

mi·cro·bar (mī′krə bär′) *n.* [MICRO- + BAR²] a metric unit of pressure, including acoustical pressure, equal to one dyne per square centimeter

mi·cro·bar·o·graph (mī′krō bar′ə graf′) *n.* a barograph for recording very small changes in atmospheric pressure

mi·crobe (mī′krōb) *n.* [Fr. < Gr. *mikro-* (see MICRO-) + *bios,* life (see BIO-)] a microscopic organism; esp., any of the bacteria that cause disease; germ —**mi·cro′bic, mi·cro′bi·al, mi·cro′bi·an** *adj.*

mi·cro·bi·cide (mī krō′bə sīd′) *n.* [< MICROBE + -CIDE] anything that kills microbes —**mi·cro′bi·ci′dal** *adj.*

mi·cro·bi·ol·o·gy (mī′krō bī äl′ə jē) *n.* the branch of biology that deals with microorganisms —**mi′cro·bi·o·log′i·cal** (-ə läj′ə k'l), **mi′cro·bi′o·log′ic** *adj.* —**mi′cro·bi·ol′o·gist** *n.*

☆**mi·cro·bus** (mī′krə bus′) *n.* [MICRO- + BUS] a small motorbus, like a station wagon but higher and roomier

mi·cro·ceph·a·ly (mī′krə sef′'l ē) *n.* [MICRO- + CEPHAL- + -Y³] a condition in which the head or cranial capacity is abnormally small: opposed to MACROCEPHALY —**mi′cro·ceph′a·lous, mi′cro·ce·phal′ic** (-si fal′ik) *adj.*

mi·cro·chem·is·try (-kem′is trē) *n.* the chemistry of microscopic or submicroscopic quantities or objects

mi·cro·cir·cuit (mī′krə sur′kit) *n.* [MICRO- + CIRCUIT] a highly miniaturized electronic circuit, used in computers, etc. —**mi′cro·cir′cuit·ry** *n.*

mi·cro·cli·mate (-klī′mit) *n.* [MICRO- + CLIMATE] the climate of a small, distinct area, as of a forest or city, or of a confined space, as of a building, cave, or greenhouse —**mi′cro·cli·mat′ic** (-kli mat′ik) *adj.*

mi·cro·cli·ma·tol·o·gy (mī′krə klī′mə täl′ə jē) *n.* the study of climate and its characteristics in a small area —**mi′cro·cli′ma·tol′o·gist** *n.*

mi·cro·cline (mī′krə klīn′) *n.* [G. *mikroklin* (< Gr. *mikros,* small + *klinein,* to incline): its cleavage angle differs slightly from 90°] a grayish, yellowish, greenish, or reddish triclinic, feldspar mineral, KAlSi₃O₈, having a glassy luster and good cleavage: it is common in some igneous rocks and resembles orthoclase

mi·cro·coc·cus (mī′krə käk′əs) *n., pl.* **-coc′ci** (-käk′sī) [ModL.: see MICRO- & -COCCUS] any of a genus (*Micrococcus*) of spherical or egg-shaped bacteria that occur in irregular masses or plates and feed on dead or living matter

mi·cro·cop·y (mī′krə käp′ē) *n., pl.* **-cop′ies** [MICRO- + COPY] a copy of printed matter, etc. produced by microfilming or other processes in very greatly reduced size

mi·cro·cosm (mī′krə käz′m) *n.* [ME. *microcosme* < ML. *microcosmus* < LGr. *mikros kosmos,* little world: see MICRO- & COSMOS] a little world; miniature universe; specif., *a)* man regarded as an epitome of the world *b)* a community, village, etc. regarded as a miniature or epitome of the world *c) Ecol.* a small ecosystem, as a pond, rotting log, etc. —**mi′cro·cos′mic** *adj.* —**mi′cro·cos′mi·cal·ly** *adv.*

microcosmic salt a white, crystalline salt, Na(NH₄)HPO₄·4H₂O, used as a reagent in blowpipe analysis because it forms characteristically colored compounds when fused with salts and oxides of metals

mi·cro·crys·tal·line (mī′krō kris′t'l in) *adj.* having crystalline structure that can be seen only with a microscope

mi·cro·cyte (mī′krə sīt′) *n.* [MICRO- + -CYTE] an abnormally small red blood corpuscle, occurring esp. in certain types of anemia —**mi′cro·cyt′ic** (-sit′ik) *adj.*

mi·cro·dont (-dänt′) *adj.* [MICR(O)- + -ODONT] having very small teeth: also **mi′cro·dont′ous** —**mi′cro·dont′ism** *n.*

mi·cro·dot (-dät′) *n.* [MICRO- + DOT¹] a copy, as of written or printed matter, reduced by microphotography to pinhead size, used in espionage, etc.

mi·cro·e·lec·tron·ics (mī′krō i lek′trän′iks) *n.pl.* [*with sing. v.*] [MICRO- + ELECTRONICS] the science dealing with the theory, design, and applications of microcircuits —**mi′cro·e·lec′tron′ic** *adj.*

☆**mi·cro·en·cap·su·la·tion** (-in kap′sə lā′shən, -syoo-) *n.* a process in which tiny particles or droplets of a substance are separately encapsulated for controlled release: used to prolong the action of drugs, solidify liquids, etc. —**mi′cro·en·cap′su·late′** *vt.* **-lat′ed, -lat′ing**

mi·cro·ev·o·lu·tion (-ev′ə lōō′shən) *n.* [MICRO- + EVOLUTION] small-scale hereditary changes in organisms through mutations and recombinations, resulting in the formation of slightly differing new varieties

mi·cro·far·ad (mī′krə far′ad, -əd) *n.* one millionth of a farad: symbol μf

mi·cro·fiche (mī′krə fēsh′) *n.* [Fr. < *micro-,* MICRO- + *fiche,* a small card, mark on a card, orig. a pin, peg < OFr. *ficher,* to attach: see FICHU] a sheet of microfilm, approximately 4 by 6 in., on which it is possible to record a number of pages of microcopy

mi·cro·film (-film′) *n.* 1. film on which documents, printed pages, etc. are photographed in a reduced size for convenience in storage and transportation: enlarged prints can be made from such film, or the film can be viewed by

projection **2.** reproduction on microfilm —*vt.*, *vi.* to photograph on microfilm

mi·cro·ga·mete (mī′krō gam′ēt, -ga mēt′) *n.* the smaller, usually the male, of a pair of conjugating gametes in heterogamous sexual reproduction

mi·cro·gram (mī′krə gram′) *n.* **1.** one millionth of a gram: also, chiefly Brit. sp., **mi′cro·gramme′**: symbol, μg **2.** *same as* MICROGRAPH (sense 2)

mi·cro·graph (-graf′, -gräf′) *n.* [MICRO- + -GRAPH] **1.** an apparatus for doing extremely small writing, drawing, or engraving **2.** a photograph or drawing of an object as seen through a microscope **3.** an apparatus by which, through the movements of a diaphragm, very slight movements can be recorded in magnified visual form and measured

mi·crog·ra·phy (mī kräg′rə fē) *n.* [MICRO- + -GRAPHY] **1.** the description, depiction, or study of microscopic objects **2.** the art or practice of writing in tiny characters —**mi′cro·graph′ic** *adj.*

☆**mi·cro·groove** (mī′krə grōōv′) *n.* a very narrow needle groove, as for a long-playing phonograph record, allowing for more recorded material than does a wider groove

mi·cro·lith (-lith′) *n.* [MICRO- + -LITH] any of various small flint tools flaked in two directions, characteristic of the mesolithic period

mi·crol·o·gy (mī kräl′ə jē) *n.* [ML. *micrologia*: see MICRO- & -LOGY] the discussion or study of trivial matters or petty differences

mi·cro·mere (mī′krə mir′) *n.* [MICRO- + -MERE] any of certain small cells produced by unequal cell division during early embryological development in many animals, as in mollusks, flatworms, etc.

mi·cro·me·te·or·ite (mī′krə mēt′ē ə rīt′) *n.* a microscopic meteorite, with a diameter measured in microns, that drifts through the earth's atmosphere to the ground without becoming incandescent

mi·cro·me·te·or·oid (-mēt′ē ə roid′) *n.* [MICRO- + METEOROID] an extremely small meteoroid

mi·cro·me·te·or·ol·o·gy (-mēt′ē ə räl′ə jē) *n.* [MICRO- + METEOROLOGY] the branch of meteorology that deals with the small-scale processes, physical conditions, and interactions that occur in the lowest part of the atmosphere, esp. in the first few hundred feet above the earth's surface —**mi′cro·me′te·or·ol′o·gist** *n.*

mi·crom·e·ter (mī kräm′ə tər) *n.* [Fr. *micromètre*: see MICRO- & -METER] **1.** an instrument for measuring very small distances, angles, diameters, etc., used on a telescope or microscope **2.** *same as* MICROMETER CALIPER

micrometer caliper (or **calipers**) calipers with a micrometer screw, for extremely accurate measurement

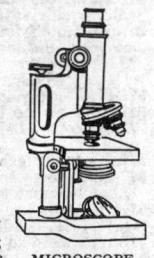

MICROMETER

micrometer screw a finely threaded screw of definite pitch, with a head graduated to show how much the screw has been moved in or out; used in micrometers, etc. to give fine measurements, as of thickness, sometimes to .0001 of an inch

mi·crom·e·try (-trē) *n.* measurement with micrometers

mi·cro·mi·cro- (mī′krō mī′krō) *same as* PICO-

mi·cro·mi·cron (-mī′krän) *n.* one millionth of a micron

mi·cro·mil·li- (-mil′ə) *same as* NANO-

mi·cro·min·i·a·ture (-min′ē ə chər, -min′i chər) *adj.* of or using extremely small electronic parts, circuits, etc.

mi·cro·min·i·a·tur·ize (-chə rīz′) *vt.* -**ized**′, -**iz′ing** to provide with electronic equipment of extremely small size —**mi′cro·min′i·a·tur·i·za′tion** *n.*

mi·cron (mī′krän) *n.*, *pl.* -**crons**, -**cra** (-krə) [ModL. < Gr. *mikron*, neut. of *mikros*, small, minute: see MICA] a unit of length equal to one millionth of a meter, or one thousandth of a millimeter

Mi·cro·ne·sia (mī′krə nē′zhə, -shə) one of the three major divisions of the Pacific islands, north of the equator, east of the Philippines, & west of the international date line

Mi·cro·ne·sian (-zhən, -shən) *adj.* of Micronesia, its people, or their languages —*n.* **1.** a native of Micronesia, which is inhabited by peoples of mixed Melanesian, Polynesian, and Malayan ancestry **2.** any of the Malayo-Polynesian languages spoken in Micronesia

☆**mi·cron·ize** (mī′krə nīz′) *vt.* -**ized**′, -**iz′ing** [MICRON + -IZE] to reduce to particles of only a few microns in diameter

mi·cro·nu·cle·us (mī′krō nōō′klē əs, -nyōō′-) *n.* the smaller of two types of nuclei present in the cells of ciliated protozoans, associated primarily with reproduction and genetics —**mi′cro·nu′cle·ar** *adj.*

mi·cro·nu·tri·ent (-nōō′trē ənt, -nyōō′-) *n.* [MICRO- + NUTRIENT] any of the chemical elements, as iron, required in minute quantities for growth of an organism

mi·cro·or·gan·ism (-ôr′gə niz′m) *n.* any microscopic or ultramicroscopic animal or vegetable organism; esp., any of the bacteria, protozoans, viruses, etc.

mi·cro·par·a·site (-par′ə sit′) *n.* a parasitic microorganism —**mi′cro·par′a·sit′ic** (-sit′ik) *adj.*

mi·cro·phone (mī′krə fōn′) *n.* [MICRO- + -PHONE] an instrument containing a transducer that converts the mechanical energy of sound waves into an electric signal:

microphones are used in telephony, radio, sound amplification, etc. —**mi′cro·phon′ic** (-fän′ik) *adj.*

mi·cro·phon·ics (mī′krə fän′iks) *n.pl.* [*with sing. v.*] [MICROPHON(E) + -ICS] noise in the output of various electronic devices, as a loudspeaker, caused by mechanical vibration of some part

mi·cro·pho·to·graph (-fōt′ə graf′, -gräf′) *n.* **1.** a very small photograph requiring enlargement to bring out the details **2.** *same as* PHOTOMICROGRAPH **3.** an enlarged photograph printed from a microfilm —**mi′cro·pho′to·graph′ic** *n.* —**mi′cro·pho·tog′ra·phy** (-fa täg′rə fē) *n.*

mi·cro·phyte (mī′krə fīt′) *n.* [MICRO- + -PHYTE] any microscopically small plant, esp. a parasitic one —**mi′cro·phyt′ic** (-fit′ik) *adj.*

mi·cro·print (-print′) *n.* a microphotograph of printed or written matter so greatly reduced that it can be read only through a magnifying device

mi·cro·pyle (-pīl′) *n.* [Fr. < Gr. *mikros*, small (see MICRO- + *pylē*, gate] **1.** *Bot.* *a)* a very small opening in the outer coats of an ovule, through which the pollen tube penetrates *b)* the corresponding opening in the developed seed **2.** *Zool.* a very small opening in the vitelline membrane of an ovum, through which spermatozoa can enter —**mi′cro·py′lar** (-pī′lər) *adj.*

mi·cro·py·rom·e·ter (mī′krō pī räm′ə tər) *n.* [MICRO- + PYROMETER] an optical instrument for determining temperature, etc. of minute bodies giving off light or heat

mi·cro·ra·di·o·graph (-rā′dē ə graf′, -gräf′) *n.* [MICRO- + RADIOGRAPH] an X-ray photograph showing very small details —**mi′cro·ra′di·o·graph′ic** *adj.* —**mi′cro·ra′di·og′ra·phy** (-rā′dē äg′rə fē) *n.*

☆**mi·cro·read·er** (mī′krō rēd′ər) *n.* a device for providing an enlarged image as of a microfilm on a screen so that it can be read

micros. microscopy

mi·cro·scope (mī′krə skōp′) *n.* [ModL. *microscopium*: see MICRO- & -SCOPE] an instrument consisting essentially of a lens or combination of lenses, for making very small objects, as microorganisms, look larger so that they can be seen and studied: see also ELECTRON MICROSCOPE

mi·cro·scop·ic (mī′krə skäp′ik) *adj.* **1.** so small as to be invisible or obscure except through a microscope; extremely small; minute **2.** of, with, or as if with a microscope **3.** like or suggestive of a microscope; searching; minutely observing Also **mi′cro·scop′i·cal** —**mi′cro·scop′i·cal·ly** *adv.*

mi·cros·co·py (mī kräs′kə pē; *occas.* mī′krə skō′pē) *n.* the use of a microscope; investigation by means of a microscope —**mi′cros′co·pist** *n.*

MICROSCOPE

mi·cro·sec·ond (mī′krə sek′ənd) *n.* [MICRO- + SECOND²] one millionth of a second

mi·cro·seism (mī′krə siz′m) *n.* [< MICRO- + Gr. *seismos*: see SEISMIC] a very slight tremor or quivering of the earth's crust —**mi′cro·seis′mic** (-siz′mik, -sis′mik) *adj.*

mi·cro·some (-sōm′) *n.* [MICRO- + -SOME³] any of a number of minute granules in the cytoplasm of an active cell, thought to be associated with protein synthesis —**mi′cro·so′mal** *adj.*

mi·cro·sphere (-sfir′) *n.* [MICRO- + -SPHERE] any of various minute globules, as an encapsulated isotope, a cell-like structure resembling a proteinoid, etc.

mi·cro·spo·ran·gi·um (mī′krō spə ran′jē əm) *n.*, *pl.* -**gi·a** (-ə) [ModL.] a sporangium containing microspores, as the pollen sac of the anther in seed plants

mi·cro·spore (mī′krə spôr′) *n.* a haploid spore, usually smaller than a megaspore of the same plant, which gives rise to a male gametophyte: found in all seed plants, where it is an immature pollen grain, and in many lower vascular plants —**mi′cro·spor′ic** *adj.*

mi·cro·spo·ro·phyll (mī′krə spôr′ə fil) *n.* a sporophyll bearing only microsporangia

mi·cro·stom·a·tous (-stäm′ə təs, -stō′mə-) *adj.* [MICRO- + -STOMATOUS] having a small mouth: also **mi·cros′to·mous** (-kräs′tə məs)

mi·cro·struc·ture (mī′krō struk′chər) *n.* the structure, as of a metal or alloy, seen under a microscope

mi·cro·tome (-tōm′) *n.* [MICRO- + -TOME] any of various precision instruments for cutting thin sections, as of organic tissue, for study under the microscope

mi·crot·o·my (mī krät′ə mē) *n.* the skill or work of using the microtome —**mi·crot′o·mist** *n.*

mi·cro·wave (mī′krō wāv′) *adj.* designating or of that part of the electromagnetic spectrum lying between the far infrared and some lower frequency limit: commonly regarded as extending from 300,000 megahertz to 300 megahertz —*n.* any electromagnetic wave of microwave frequency

mic·tu·rate (mik′choo rāt′) *vi.* -**rat′ed**, -**rat′ing** [see ff. & -ATE¹] *same as* URINATE

mic·tu·ri·tion (mik′choo rish′ən) *n.* [< L. *micturitus*, pp. of *micturire*, to desire to urinate < *mingere*, to urinate < *meiere*, to urinate < IE. base *meigh-*: cf. MASH, MISTLETOE] the act of urinating

mid¹ (mid) *adj.* [ME. *myd* < OE. *midd-*, akin to Goth.

midjis, ON. *mithr* < IE. base **medhjo-*, whence L. *medius*, Gr. *mesos*] **1.** *same as* MIDDLE **2.** *Phonet.* pronounced with the tongue in a position approximately midway between high and low: said of certain vowels, as the *e* in *set* or the *o* in *sold* —*n.* [Archaic] the middle

mid² (mid) *prep.* [Poet.] *also* '**mid**

mid- (mid) *a combining form meaning* middle or middle part of [*midbrain, midday*]

mid. **1.** middle **2.** midshipman

mid·air (-er′) *n.* any point in space, not in contact with the ground or other surface

Mi·das (mī′dəs) *Gr. Myth.* a king of Phrygia granted the power of turning everything that he touched into gold

mid·brain (mid′brān′) *n. same as* MESENCEPHALON

☆**mid·cult** (mid′kult′) *n.* [MID¹ + CULT(URE)] [Colloq.] a commercialized, pseudo-intellectual culture popularized for middlebrows through the mass media

mid·day (mid′dā′) *n.* [ME. *middai* < OE. *middæg*] the middle part of the day; noon —*adj.* of midday

mid·den (mid′'n) *n.* [ME. *midden*, prob. < Scand., as in Dan. *mögdynge* < *mög*, muck + *dynge*, a heap] **1.** [Brit.] a dunghill or refuse heap **2.** *short for* KITCHEN MIDDEN

mid·dle (mid′'l) *adj.* [ME. *middel* < OE., akin to G. *mittel*: see MID¹] **1.** halfway between two given points, times, limits, etc.; also, equally distant from all sides or extremities; in the center; mean **2.** in between; intermediate; intervening **3.** *Gr. Gram.* designating or of a voice of the verb, passive in form, in which the subject is represented as acting reflexively **4.** [M-] *Geol.* designating a division of a period or a formation between those called *Upper* and *Lower* **5.** [M-] *Linguis.* designating a stage in language development intermediate between those called *Old* and *Modern* [*Middle English*] **6.** *Logic* designating a term that appears in both premises of a syllogism but not in the conclusion —*n.* **1.** a point or part halfway between extremes; middle point, part, time, etc. **2.** something intermediate **3.** the middle part of the body; waist **4.** *Gr. Gram.* the middle voice **5.** *Logic* a middle term —*vt.*, *vi.* -**dled**, -**dling** **1.** to put in the middle **2.** to fold (a rope, etc.) in the middle; double

SYN.—**middle** refers to the point or part equally distant from either or all sides or extremities and may apply to space, time, etc. [*the middle* of the stage, the day, etc.]; **center** more precisely stresses the point equidistant from the bounding lines or surfaces of any plane or solid figure [*the center* of a circle, globe, etc.] and is sometimes used figuratively [*the center* of town, a trade *center*]; **midst**, usually used in prepositional phrases, denotes a middle part that is completely surrounded by persons or things or a middle point in some action [in the *midst* of a crowd, one's work, etc.]

middle age the time of life between youth and old age: now usually the years from about 40 to about 65

mid·dle-aged (mid′'l ājd′) *adj.* in, of, characteristic of, or suitable for middle age

Middle Ages the period of European history between ancient and modern times, 476 A.D.–c. 1450 A.D.

Middle America **1.** the part of America that includes Mexico, Central America, &, sometimes, the West Indies ☆**2.** the American middle class, characterized generally by moderate or conservative political attitudes and conventional social values; sometimes, specif., the middle class of Midwestern America

Middle Atlantic States New York, New Jersey, and Pennsylvania

☆**mid·dle-break·er** (mid′'l brā′kər) *n. same as* LISTER¹: *also* ☆**mid′dle-bust′er** (-bus′tər)

☆**mid·dle-brow** (-brou′) *n.* [Colloq.] a person regarded as having conventional, middle-class tastes or opinions, and as being anti-intellectual or pseudo-intellectual —*adj.* [Colloq.] of or for a middlebrow *Often a term of contempt or derision*

middle C **1.** the musical note on the first leger line below the treble staff and the first above the bass staff **2.** the corresponding tone or key

middle class the social class between the aristocracy or very wealthy and the lower working class: people in business and the professions, highly skilled workers, well-to-do farmers, etc. are now generally included in the middle class: see also BOURGEOISIE —**mid′dle-class′** *adj.*

middle distance the space between the foreground and the background in a picture

middle ear the part of the ear including the eardrum and the adjacent cavity containing three small bones (hammer, anvil, and stirrup); tympanum

Middle East **1.** orig., those regions between the Far East & the Near East **2.** area from Afghanistan to Egypt, including the Arabian Peninsula, Cyprus, & Asiatic Turkey **3.** sometimes, the Near East, excluding the Balkans —**Middle Eastern**

Middle English the English language as written and spoken between c.1100 and c.1500, preceded by Old English and followed by Early Modern English: it is characterized by the loss of most of the inflectional endings and of the grammatical gender of Old English, by the emergence of a syntax based on word order and function

words, by the attendant simplification of the pronominal system, and by extensive vocabulary borrowings from French, Latin, and Low German sources

Middle French the French language as written and spoken between the 14th and 16th centuries

Middle Greek *same as* MEDIEVAL GREEK

Middle High German the High German language as written and spoken between c.1100 and c.1500

Middle Irish the Irish language as written and spoken from the 11th to the 15th century

Middle Kingdom **1.** a kingdom of ancient Egypt, c. 2133–1786 B.C. (11th and 12th dynasties): also called **Middle Empire** **2.** formerly, *a)* the Chinese Empire, considered as the center of the world *b)* the 18 inner provinces of China proper

Middle Latin *same as* MEDIEVAL LATIN

Middle Low German the Low German language as written and spoken between c.1100 and c.1500

mid·dle·man (mid′'l man′) *n., pl.* -**men′** **1.** a trader who buys commodities from the producer and sells them to the retailer or, sometimes, directly to the consumer **2.** a go-between; intermediary

mid·dle·most (-mōst′) *adj. same as* MIDMOST (sense 1)

☆**mid·dle-of-the-road** (-əv thə rōd′) *adj.* avoiding extremes, esp. of the political left and right; uncommitted to either liberalism or conservatism

middle passage the passage across the Atlantic from West Africa to the West Indies or America that was the route of the former slave trade

Mid·dles·brough (mid′lz brə) city in Yorkshire, NE England, on the Tees River: pop. 156,000

middle school in some school systems, a school between elementary school and high school, usually having three or four grades, variously between grades 5 and 9

Mid·dle·sex (mid′'l seks′) county of SE England, containing the NW section of metropolitan London: 232 sq. mi.; pop. 2,235,000

mid·dle-sized (-sīzd′) *adj.* of medium size

Middle States those eastern States between the New England States and the South; New York, New Jersey, Pennsylvania, Delaware, and Maryland

Middle Temple *see* INN OF COURT

Mid·dle·ton (mid′'l tən), **Thomas** 1580–1627; Eng. dramatist

Mid·dle·town (mid′'l toun′) **1.** [after *Middletown*, in England] city in C Conn., on the Connecticut River: pop. 37,000 **2.** [because midway between Dayton & Cincinnati] city in SW Ohio: pop. 49,000

mid·dle-weight (-wāt′) *n.* **1.** one of average weight **2.** a boxer or wrestler between a welterweight and a light heavyweight (in boxing, 148–160 pounds)

Middle West region of the NC U.S. between the Rocky Mountains & the E border of Ohio, north of the Ohio River & the S borders of Kans. & Mo. —**Middle Western**

mid·dling (mid′liŋ) *adj.* [MID¹ + -LING¹] of middle size, quality, grade, state, etc.; medium; ordinary; mediocre —*adv.* [Colloq.] fairly; moderately; somewhat —*n.* ☆**1.** pork or bacon from between the ham and the shoulder **2.** [*pl.*] products of medium quality, grade, size, or price **3.** [*pl.*] particles of coarsely ground grain, often mixed with bran and used as feed —**fair to middling** [Colloq.] moderately good or well

Middx. Middlesex

mid·dy (mid′ē) *n., pl.* -**dies** **1.** [Colloq.] a midshipman ☆**2.** a loose blouse with a sailor collar, worn by women and children: in full, **middy blouse**

Mid·gard (mid′gärd′) [ON. *mithgarthr* < *mithr*, MID¹ + *garthr*, YARD²] *Norse Myth.* the earth, regarded as midway between heaven and hell and engirdled by a huge serpent: *also* **Mid′garth′** (-gärth′)

midge (mij) *n.* [ME. *migge* < OE. *mycg*, akin to G. *mücke* < IE. base **mu-*, echoic for fly, gnat, whence L. *musca*, a fly] **1.** any of a large number of small, two winged, gnat-like insects, esp. *a)* the true midge (family Tendipedidae) *b)* *same as* BITING MIDGE **2.** a very small person; midget

midg·et (mij′it) *n.* [dim. of prec.] **1.** a very small person **2.** anything very small of its kind —*adj.* very small of its kind; miniature —*SYN.* see DWARF

mid·gut (mid′gut′) *n.* **1.** the middle part of the alimentary canal in vertebrate embryos **2.** the endoderm-lined portion of the digestive tract of arthropods

Mi·di (mē dē′) [Fr., south, lit., midday < *mi-*, half (< L. *medius*, middle) + *di* (< L. *dies*), day] S France

mid·i- (mid′ē) [< MID, after MINI-] *a combining form meaning* of a length to the middle of the calf [*midiskirt*]

Mid·i·an·ite (mid′ē ə nīt′) *n.* [< Heb. *midhyān*, name of a son of Abraham (Gen. 25:2) + -ITE¹] *Bible* a member of a nomadic tribe of Arabs that fought the Israelites: Ex. 2:15–22, Numb. 31, Judg. 6–8

mid·i·nette (mid′'n et′) *n.* [Fr., blend of *midi*, midday + *dinette*, a little lunch < *diner*, to DINE + -*ette*, dim. suffix: in allusion to their customary light lunch] a young, Parisian shopgirl, esp. one who works in a dress shop

mid·i·ron (mid′ī′ərn) *n.* [MID- + IRON] a golf club with a

metal head and little loft, used for fairway shots of medium distance: now usually called *number 2 iron*

Mid·land (mid'lənd) **1.** [from being about midway between Fort Worth and El Paso] city in WC Tex.: pop. 59,000 **2.** [from its central location in the S peninsula of Mich.] city in C Mich.: pop. 35,000

mid·land (mid'lənd) *n.* **1.** the middle region of a country; interior **2.** [M-] a Midland dialect —*adj.* **1.** in or of the midland; inland **2.** [M-] of the Midlands **3.** [M-] *a)* designating dialects of English spoken or formerly spoken in the Midlands and divided into eastern and western groups *b)* designating a dialect of American English spoken in southern New Jersey, central and southern Pennsylvania, Ohio, Indiana, and Illinois, northern Delaware, the Shenandoah Valley, the southern Appalachians, the upper Piedmont of North and South Carolina, Kentucky, northern Tennessee, and southern Iowa —**the Midlands** region in WC England, around Birmingham

mid·leg (mid'leg') *n.* **1.** the middle of the leg **2.** one of the middle, or second, pair of legs of an insect —*adv.* to the middle of the leg

mid·line (-līn') *n.* a median line

Mid·lo·thi·an (mid lō'thē ən) county of SE Scotland: 366 sq. mi.; pop. 589,000; county seat, Edinburgh

mid·most (mid'mōst') *adj.* [ME. *mydmest* (with -*most* for -*mest* < 17th c. onward) < OE. *midmest* < *middjumo*, in the middle < IE. *medhiemo-*, superl. of base *medhi-*, middle) + superl. suffix -*est*, -EST] **1.** exactly in the middle, or nearest the middle; middlemost **2.** most secret; inmost —*adv.* in the middle or midst —*prep.* in the middle or midst of —*n.* the middle part

mid·night (-nīt') *n.* **1.** the middle of the night: twelve o'clock at night **2.** deep darkness —*adj.* **1.** of or at midnight **2.** like or suggestive of midnight; very dark [*midnight* blue] —**burn the midnight oil** to study or work very late at night

midnight sun the sun visible at midnight in the arctic or antarctic regions during the summer

mid·noon (-nōōn') *n.* [Rare] noon; midday

mid·point (-point') *n.* a point at or close to the middle or center, or equally distant from the ends

mid·rash (mid'räsh) *n., pl.* **mid·rash'im** (mid rä'shim), **mid·rash'oth** (-shōt) [Heb. *midrāsh*, explanation] any of the rabbinical commentaries and explanatory notes on the Scriptures, written between the beginning of the Exile and c.1200 A.D. —**the Midrash** these commentaries and notes collectively —**Mid·rash'ic** *adj.*

mid·rib (mid'rib') *n.* the central vein, or rib, of a leaf, usually running from the stem to the apex

mid·riff (-rif) *n.* [ME. *mydrif* < OE. *midhrif* < *midd* (see MID[1]) + *hrif*, belly (akin to OHG. *href*, body) < IE. base *krep-*, body, whence L. *corpus*] **1.** same as DIAPHRAGM (sense 1) **2.** *a)* the middle part of the torso, between the abdomen and the chest *b)* that part of a woman's garment that covers this part, or that is cut away to expose it —*adj.* designating or of a garment that bares this part

mid·sec·tion (-sek'shən) *n.* the section in the middle

mid·ship (mid'ship') *adj.* of the middle of a ship

mid·ship·man (-ship'mən) *n., pl.* **-men** (-mən) [for *amidshipmen*, from being *amidships* when on duty] **1.** a student in training for the rank of ensign; specif., such a student at the U.S. Naval Academy at Annapolis **2.** formerly, a junior British naval officer ranking between naval cadet and sublieutenant

mid·ship·mite (-mīt) *n.* [blend of prec. + MITE[1]] [Brit.] a midshipman: a sailors' humorous alteration

mid·ships (mid'ships') *adv.* same as AMIDSHIPS

midst[1] (midst, mitst) *n.* [ME. *middest*, prob. merging of *middes*, gen. of *mid* (with unhistoric -*t*) + *middest*, superl. of *mid*] the middle; central part: now mainly in phrases as below —*SYN.* see MIDDLE —**in our** (or **your, their**) **midst** among us (or you, them) —**in the midst of 1.** in the middle of; surrounded by **2.** in the course of; during

midst[2] (midst, mitst) *prep.* [Poet.] in the midst of; amidst; amid: also 'midst

mid·stream (mid'strēm') *n.* the middle of a stream

mid·sum·mer (-sum'ər) *n.* **1.** the middle of summer **2.** popularly, the time of the summer solstice, about June 21 —*adj.* of, in, or like midsummer

Midsummer Day June 24, feast of St. John the Baptist

mid·term (-turm') ☆*adj.* occurring in the middle of the term —*n.* ☆[Colloq.] a midterm examination, as in a college course

mid·Vic·to·ri·an (mid'vik tôr'ē ən) *adj.* **1.** of, like, or characteristic of the middle part of Queen Victoria's reign in Great Britain (c. 1850–1890) of the culture, morals, or art of this period **2.** old-fashioned, prudish, morally strict, stuffy, etc. —*n.* **1.** a person who lived during this period **2.** a person of mid-Victorian ideas, manners, attitudes, etc.

mid·way (mid'wā'; also, for adj. & adv., -wā') *n.* [ME. *midwei* < OE. *midweg*] **1.** orig., *a)* the middle of the way or distance *b)* a middle way or course ☆**2.** short for *Midway Plaisance*, the amusement area of the Columbian Exposition (1893), in Chicago] that part of a fair or exposition where sideshows and other amusements are located —*adj., adv.* in the middle of the way or distance; halfway

Midway Islands U.S. territory in the North Pacific, consisting of a coral atoll & two islets: 2 sq. mi.

mid·week (mid'wēk') *n.* **1.** the middle of the week **2.**

[M-] Wednesday: so called by the Friends (Quakers) —*adj.* in the middle of the week —**mid'week'ly** *adj., adv.*

Mid·west (mid'west') *n.* same as MIDDLE WEST —*adj.* same as MIDWESTERN

Midwest City city in C Okla.: suburb of Oklahoma City: pop. 48,000

Mid·west·ern (-ərn) *adj.* of, in, or characteristic of the Middle West; Middle Western —**Mid'west'ern·er** *n.*

mid·wife (mid'wīf') *n., pl.* **-wives'** (-wīvz') [ME. *midwyf* < *mid*, with < OE. (akin to G. *mit*) + *wif*, woman (see WIFE): basic sense "woman with, woman assisting"] a woman whose work is helping women in childbirth

mid·wife·ry (-wīf'rē) *n.* the work of a midwife

mid·win·ter (-win'tər) *n.* **1.** the middle of the winter **2.** popularly, the time of the winter solstice, about December 22 —*adj.* of, in, or like midwinter

mid·year (-yir') *adj.* ☆occurring in the middle of the (calendar or academic) year —*n.* ☆[Colloq.] a midyear examination, as in a college course

mien (mēn) *n.* [aphetic for DEMEAN[2], but altered after Fr. *mine*, look, air] **1.** a way of carrying and conducting oneself; manner **2.** a way of looking; appearance —*SYN.* see BEARING

Mies van der Ro·he (mēz' van dər rō'ə), **Ludwig** 1886–1969; U.S. architect, born in Germany

miff (mif) *n.* [prob. orig. cry of disgust] [Colloq.] a trivial quarrel or fit of the sulks; tiff or huff —*vt., vi.* [Colloq.] to offend or take offense; put or be put out of humor

MIG (mig) [after Artem *M*ikoyan & *M*ikhail *G*urevich, its Soviet designers] a small, fast, highly maneuverable jet military aircraft: also written MiG

☆**mig·gle** (mig'l) *n.* [dim. of dial. *mig*, a marble] [Dial.] **1.** a playing marble **2.** [*pl.*] the game of marbles

might[1] (mit) *v.* [ME. *mihte* < OE., akin to G. *möchte*] **1.** *pt.* of MAY[1] **2.** an auxiliary with present or future sense, generally equivalent to *may* in meaning and use, expressing esp. a shade of doubt or a smaller degree of possibility [it *might* rain] or permission [*might* I go?] or obligation [you *might* try to help]

might[2] (mit) *n.* [ME. *mighte* < OE. *miht*, akin to G. *macht* < IE. base *māgh-*, to be able: cf. MAY[1]] **1.** great or superior strength, power, force, or vigor **2.** strength or power of any degree —*SYN.* see STRENGTH

might·y (-ē) *adj.* **might'i·er**, **might'i·est** [ME. *myghty* < OE. *mihtig*] **1.** having might; powerful; strong **2.** remarkably large, extensive, etc.; great —*adv.* [Colloq.] very; extremely —**might'i·ly** *adv.* —**might'i·ness** *n.*

mi·gnon (min'yän; *Fr.* mē nyôn') *adj.* [Fr., for OFr. *mignot*, dainty < *min-*, echoic of a caressing cry: cf. IE. base *mī(n)-*, var. of *mei-*, gentle, soft, whence OIr. *min*, gentle] small, delicately formed, and pretty; dainty —**mi·gnonne** (min'yən; *Fr.* mē nyôn') *adj.fem.*

mi·gnon·ette (min'yə net') *n.* [Fr. *mignonnette*, dim. of *mignon*: see prec.] **1.** any of a genus (Reseda) of plants of a family (Resedaceae) with thick stems and coarse foliage, esp. an annual plant (*Reseda odorata*) bearing terminal spikes of small greenish, whitish, or reddish flowers **2.** any of several similar plants **3.** a pale, yellowish green

mignonette tree same as HENNA (*n.* 1)

mi·graine (mi'grān) *n.* [Fr. < OFr. < LL. *hemicrania* < Gr. *hēmikrania* < *hēmi-*, half + *kranion*, CRANIUM] a type of intense, periodically returning headache, usually limited to one side of the head and often accompanied by nausea, visual disorders, etc. —**mi·grain'ous** *adj.*

mi·grant (mi'grənt) *adj.* [L. *migrans*, prp. of *migrare*] migrating; migratory —*n.* a person, bird, or animal that migrates; ☆specif., a farm laborer who moves from place to place to harvest seasonal crops

mi·grate (mi'grāt) *vi.* **-grat·ed**, **-grat·ing** [< L. *migratus*, pp. of *migrare*, to move from one place to another, change < IE. *meigw-*, to change location < base *mei-*, to change, exchange: cf. COMMON] **1.** to move from one place to another; esp., to leave one's country and settle in another **2.** to move from one region to another with the change in seasons, as many birds and some fishes **3.** to move from place to place to harvest seasonal crops —**mi'gra·tor** *n.*

SYN.—**migrate** denotes a moving from one region or country to another and may imply, of people, intention to settle in a new land, or, of animals, a periodical movement influenced by climate, food supply, etc.; **emigrate** and **immigrate** are used only of people, **emigrate** specifically denoting the leaving of a country to settle in another, and **immigrate**, the coming into the new country

mi·gra·tion (mi grā'shən) *n.* [L. *migratio*] **1.** the act of migrating **2.** a group of people, or of birds, fishes, etc., migrating together **3.** *Chem. a)* the shifting of one or more atoms from one position in the molecule to another *b)* the movement of ions toward one electrode or the other, under the influence of electromotive force —**mi·gra'tion·al** *adj.*

mi·gra·to·ry (mi'grə tôr'ē) *adj.* **1.** migrating; characterized by migration **2.** of migration **3.** roving; wandering

mih·rab (mē'räb) *n.* [Ar. *mihrāb*] a niche in that wall of a mosque which faces toward Mecca

mi·ka·do (mi kä'dō) *n., pl.* **-dos** [Jap., lit., exalted gate (i.e., of the Imperial palace) < *mi*, exalted + *kado*, gate] [often M-] the emperor of Japan: title no longer used

☆**mike** (mik) *n.* [Colloq.] a microphone

mi·kron (mi'krän) *n.* [G.] same as MICRON

mil (mil) *n.* [L. *mille*, thousand] **1.** a unit of length, equal to 1/1000 inch (25.4001 microns), used in measuring the diameter of wire **2.** a milliliter, or cubic centimeter **3.** a unit of currency in Cyprus, equal to 1/1000 pound **4.** *Mil.* a unit of angle measurement for artillery fire, missile launching, etc., equal to the angle forming an arc that is 1/6400 of the circumference of a circle

mil. 1. military **2.** militia

mi·la·dy, mi·la·di (mi lā'dē) *n.* [Fr. < Eng. *my lady*] **1.** an English noblewoman or gentlewoman ☆**2.** a woman of fashion: shopkeepers' or advertisers' term

mil·age (mil'ij) *n. alt. sp.* of MILEAGE

Mi·lan (mi lan') commune in NW Italy, in Lombardy: pop. 1,673,000: It. name **Mi·la·no** (mē lä'nō) —*n.* [*also* m-] a fine kind of straw from Milan, or a hat made of it — **Mil·a·nese** (mil'ə nēz') *adj., n., pl.* **-nese'**

milch (milch) *adj.* [ME. *milche*, milk-giving < OE. *-milce*, akin to *milc*, MILK] giving milk; kept for milking [*milch cows*]

mild (mīld) *adj.* [ME. *milde* < OE., akin to G. *mild* < IE. *meldh-* < base *mel-*, to crush, rub fine, tender: cf. MELT, MILL[1]] **1.** *a*) gentle or kind in disposition, action, or effect; not severe, harsh, bitter, etc. *b*) not extreme in any way; moderate; temperate [a *mild* winter] **2.** having a soft, pleasant taste or flavor; not strong, sour, bitter, biting, or sharp: said of tobacco, cheese, etc. **3.** designating steel that is tough but malleable and contains only a small percentage of carbon —*SYN.* see SOFT —**mild'ness** *n.*

mild·en (mīl'd'n) *vt., vi.* to make or become mild or milder

mil·dew (mil'dōō', -dyōō') *n.* [ME. *mildewe* < OE. *meledeaw*, nectar, lit., "honeydew," akin to Goth. *milith*, honey < IE. base *melit-* (whence L. *mel*, Gr. *meli*, honey) + base of OE. *deaw*, DEW] **1.** any fungus (esp. families Peronosporaceae and Erysiphaceae) that attacks various plants or appears on organic matter, paper, leather, etc., esp. when exposed to damp, resulting in a thin, furry, whitish coating or discoloration **2.** any such coating or discoloration **3.** any plant disease caused by such fungus —*vt., vi.* to affect or become affected with mildew — **mil'dew'y** *adj.*

mild·ly (mīld'lē) *adv.* **1.** in a mild manner **2.** to a mild degree; somewhat —**to put it mildly** to state it with or as if with restraint

Mil·dred (mil'drid) [OE. *Myldthryth* < *milde*, mild + *thryth*, power, strength] a feminine name: dim. *Mil*, *Millie*, *Milly*

mile (mīl) *n., pl.* **miles**, dial. **mile** [ME. < OE. *mil*, pl. *mila* < WGmc. **milja* < L. *milia*, pl. of *mille*, thousand, in *milia passuum*, thousand paces, mile] a unit of linear measure, equal to 1,760 yards (5,280 feet or 1,609.35 meters), used in the U.S., Great Britain, etc.: in full, **statute mile** The **nautical mile** (replacing the earlier **geographical mile**) is equal to one minute of a great circle of the earth, by international agreement, 1,852 meters (6,076.11549 feet)

☆**mile·age** (-ij) *n.* **1.** an allowance for traveling expenses at a specified amount per mile **2.** aggregate distance in miles or total number of miles traveled, recorded, etc. **3.** rate per mile, as in allowing for travel expenses or in charging for the use of railroad freight cars **4.** the number of miles a motor vehicle will go on a gallon of fuel, a tire will run before it wears out, etc. **5.** the amount of use, service, or benefit one gets or can get from something

☆**mile·post** (-pōst') *n.* a signpost showing the distance in miles to or from a specified place

mil·er (-ər) *n.* one who competes in mile races

Miles (mīlz) [OFr. *Miles*, *Milon* < OHG. *Milo*, lit., mild, peaceful] a masculine name

‡**mi·les glo·ri·o·sus** (mī'lēz glôr'ē ō'səs, mē'lās) [L.] a braggart, swashbuckling soldier, esp. as a stock character in classical comedy

mile·stone (mīl'stōn') *n.* **1.** a stone or pillar set up to show the distance in miles to or from a specified place **2.** a significant or important event in history, in the career of a person, etc.

Mi·le·tus (mī lēt'əs) city in ancient Ionia, SW Asia Minor —**Mi·le·sian** (-lē'zhən) *adj., n.*

mil·foil (mil'foil') *n.* [ME. < OFr. < L. *millefolium* < *mille*, thousand + *folium*, leaf (see FOLIATE): from the finely divided leaves] **1.** *same as* YARROW **2.** *same as* WATER MILFOIL

Mil·ford (mil'fərd) city in SW Conn., on Long Island Sound, near Bridgeport: pop. 51,000

Milford Haven 1. inlet of the Atlantic, in Pembrokeshire, SW Wales **2.** seaport on this inlet: pop. 13,000

Mil·haud (mē yō'), **Da·rius** (dà ryüs') 1892– ; Fr. composer, at intervals in the U.S.

mil·i·a·ri·a (mil'ē er'ē ə) *n.* [ModL. < fem. of L. *miliarius*: see ff.] an acute skin disease resulting from inflammation of the sweat glands, as from exposure to heat, and characterized by small white or red eruptions

mil·i·ar·y (mil'ē er'ē, -yər ē) *adj.* [L. *miliarius* < *milium*, MILLET] **1.** like a millet seed or seeds **2.** *Med.* characterized or accompanied by lesions about the size of millet seeds: said specif. of a form of tuberculosis which spreads from a primary focus of infection to other parts of the body, forming many minute tubercles

Mil·i·cent (mil'ə s'nt) a feminine name: see MILLICENT

mi·lieu (mēl yoo'; Fr. mē lyö') *n., pl.* **-lieus'**; Fr. **-lieux'** (-lyö') [Fr., lit., middle < OFr. *mi* (< L. *medius*: see MID[1]) + *lieu*, a place < L. *locus* (see LOCUS)] environment; esp., social or cultural setting

milit. military

mil·i·tant (mil'i tənt) *adj.* [ME. < L. *militans*, prp. of *militare*, to serve as a soldier < *miles* (gen. *militis*), a soldier] **1.** at war; fighting **2.** ready and willing to fight; esp., vigorous or aggressive in support or promotion of a cause —*n.* a militant person —*SYN.* see AGGRESSIVE —**mil'i·tan·cy** *n.* —**mil'i·tant·ly** *adv.*

mil·i·ta·rism (mil'ə tər iz'm) *n.* [Fr. *militarisme*] **1.** military spirit; attitudes of professional soldiers **2.** the glorification or prevalence of such a spirit, attitudes, etc. in a nation, or the predominance of the military caste in government **3.** the policy of maintaining a strong military organization in aggressive preparedness for war

mil·i·ta·rist (-ist) *n.* **1.** a person who supports or advocates militarism **2.** [Now Rare] an expert or specialist in war and military affairs —**mil'i·ta·ris'tic** *adj.* —**mil'i·ta·ris'ti·cal·ly** *adv.*

mil·i·ta·rize (mil'i tə rīz') *vt.* **-rized'**, **-riz'ing 1.** to make military; equip and prepare for war **2.** to fill with warlike spirit —**mil'i·ta·ri·za'tion** *n.*

mil·i·tar·y (mil'ə ter'ē) *adj.* [Fr. *militaire* < L. *militaris* < *miles* (gen. *militis*), a soldier] **1.** of, characteristic of, for, fit for, or done by soldiers or the armed forces **2.** of, for, or fit for war **3.** of the army, as distinguished from the navy —**the military** the army; soldiers collectively; esp., army officers as an influential force —*SYN.* see MARTIAL —**mil'i·tar'i·ly** (*also* mil'ə ter'ə lē) *adv.*

military attaché an army officer attached to his nation's embassy or legation in a foreign country

military law the code of law concerned with the government and discipline of the armed forces, whether in time of war or in time of peace

military police soldiers assigned to carry on police duties for the army

mil·i·tate (mil'ə tāt') *vi.* **-tat'ed**, **-tat'ing** [< L. *militatus*, pp. of *militare*: see MILITANT] **1.** orig., to serve as a soldier; fight (*against*) **2.** to be directed (*against*); operate or work (*against* or, rarely, *for*): said of facts, evidence, actions, etc. [his youth *militated* against him]

mi·li·tia (mə lish'ə) *n.* [L., military service, soldiery < *miles* (gen. *militis*), a soldier] **1.** *a*) orig., any military force *b*) later, any army composed of citizens rather than professional soldiers, called out in time of emergency ☆**2.** in the U.S., all able-bodied male citizens between 18 and 45 years old who are not already members of the regular armed forces: members of the National Guard and of the Reserves (of the Army, Air Force, Coast Guard, Navy, and Marine Corps) constitute the **organized militia**; all others, the **unorganized militia** —**mi·li'tia·man** (-mən) *n., pl.* **-men** (-mən)

mil·i·um (mil'ē əm) *n., pl.* **-i·a** (-ə) [ModL. < L., MILLET] a small, whitish nodule of the skin, somewhat like a millet seed, resulting from retention of the secretion of a sebaceous gland

milk (milk) *n.* [ME. < OE. *meolc*, akin to ON. *mjolk*, G. *milch* < IE. base **melg̑-*, to stroke, press out, wipe off, hence to milk (an animal), whence Gr. *amelgein*, L. *mulgere*, to milk] **1.** a white or yellowish liquid secreted by the mammary glands of female mammals for suckling their young **2.** cow's milk, or, sometimes, that of goats, camels, etc., drunk by humans as a food or used to make butter, cheese, casein products, etc. **3.** any liquid like this, as the juice of various plants or fruits (e.g., coconut milk), or any of various emulsions —*vt.* **1.** to draw or squeeze milk from the mammary glands of (a cow, etc.) **2.** to draw (*out*) or drain off; extract as if by milking **3.** to drain off or extract money, ideas, strength, etc. from as if by milking; exploit **4.** to extract juice, sap, venom, etc. from **5.** to draw out (information, etc.) as if by milking —*vi.* **1.** to give milk **2.** to draw milk —**cry over spilt milk** to mourn or regret something that cannot be undone

milk-and-wa·ter (-ən wôt'ər, -wät'-) *adj.* insipid; weak; wishy-washy; namby-pamby

milk·er (mil'kər) *n.* **1.** a person who milks **2.** a machine for milking cows, etc. **3.** a cow or other animal that gives milk

milk fever 1. *a former term for* mild puerperal fever as erroneously attributed to an accumulation of milk in the breasts **2.** a disease often occurring in dairy cows shortly after calving, characterized by a drop in blood calcium, paralysis, etc.

milk·fish (-fish') *n., pl.* **-fish'**, **-fish'es**: see FISH[2] a large, silvery, toothless, herringlike fish (*Chanos chanos*) of the tropical Pacific and Indian oceans, important as a food fish in Hawaii

milk glass a translucent or nearly opaque whitish glass

milk·i·ness (mil'kē nis) *n.* a milky quality or state

milk leg *a former term for* a painful swelling of the leg,

caused by inflammation and clotting in the femoral veins, usually as a result of infection during childbirth

milk-liv·ered (-liv′ərd) *adj.* timid; cowardly

milk·maid (-mād′) *n.* a girl or woman who milks cows or works in a dairy; dairymaid

milk·man (-man′) *n., pl.* **-men′** (-men′) a man who sells or delivers milk for a dairy

milk of magnesia a milky-white fluid, a suspension of magnesium hydroxide, Mg(OH)₂, in water, used as a laxative and antacid

milk run [Slang] a routine mission, as of a bomber aircraft, that is not expected to be dangerous

☆**milk·shake** (-shāk′) *n.* a drink made of milk, flavoring, and, usually, ice cream, mixed or shaken until frothy

☆**milk·shed** (-shed′) *n.* [MILK + (WATER)SHED] all the dairy farm areas supplying milk for a given city

☆**milk sickness** a rare disease, formerly common in the W U.S., caused by consuming dairy products or flesh from cattle that have eaten any of various poisonous weeds, as white snakeroot: cf. TREMBLE (*n.* 2)

☆**milk snake** a harmless snake (*Lampropeltis triangulum*), gray or reddish with black-rimmed markings: it feeds on rodents, reptiles, etc. and is related to the king snake

milk·sop (-säp′) *n.* an unmanly man or boy; sissy

milk sugar *same as* LACTOSE

☆**milk toast** a dish consisting of toast in warm milk

milk tooth any of the temporary, first set of teeth in a child or the young of other mammals

milk vetch [from the notion that it increases the secretion of milk in goats] any of a genus (*Astragalus*) of plants of the legume family, with deeply cut leaves, flowers of various colors in spikes or racemes, and usually inflated pods

milk·weed (-wēd′) *n.* **1.** any of a genus (*Asclepias*) of perennial plants of the milkweed family, with a milky juice, or latex, and pods which when ripe burst to release plumed seeds **2.** any of various plants with similar milky juice —*adj.* designating a large family (Asclepiadaceae) of plants with a milky juice, including the milkweeds, anglepods, and stapelias

milk·wort (-wurt′) *n.* [from the former notion that it increases the secretion of milk in nursing women] any of a genus (*Polygala*) of plants of a family (Polygalaceae) with showy flowers of various colors

milk·y (mil′kē) *adj.* **milk′i·er, milk′i·est** **1.** like milk; esp., white as milk **2.** of, containing, or yielding milk **3.** timid, meek, mild, etc.

MILKWEED PODS

milky disease any of several bacterial diseases of the larvae of scarabaeid beetles, as a disease of Japanese beetle grubs caused by a bacillus (*Bacillus popilliae*), characterized by the milky-white appearance of the infected larvae

Milky Way a broad, faintly luminous band seen as an arch across the sky at night, created by many billions of stars and by clouds of interstellar gas lying near the plane of our galaxy

mill¹ (mil) *n.* [ME. *melle* < OE. *mylen*, akin to OHG. *mulin*, ON. *mylna*, all < 4th-c. Gmc. borrowing < LL. *molinae*, pl. of *molina*, mill < LL.(Ec.) *molina*, of a mill < L. *mola*, millstone < IE. base *mel-*, to grind, crush, whence Gr. *mylē*, mill & MEAL², MILD] **1.** *a)* a building with machinery for grinding grain into flour or meal *b)* the machine for grinding grain **2.** *a)* a machine for grinding or pulverizing any solid material [a coffee *mill*] *b)* a machine for grinding or crushing fruits or vegetables to press out the juice [a cider *mill*] **3.** *a)* any of various machines for stamping, shaping, polishing, or dressing metal surfaces, coins, etc., or for making something by some action done again and again ☆*b)* [Colloq.] an organization, establishment, etc. where things are done, produced, issued, etc. in a routine, rapid, mechanical way [a diploma *mill*, a divorce *mill*] **4.** a building or group of buildings with machinery for manufacturing or processing something; factory [a textile *mill*] **5.** a roller of hardened steel with a raised design on it, for making a die or printing plate by pressure **6.** *a) same as* MILLING CUTTER *b) same as* MILLING MACHINE **7.** a raised edge, ridged surface, etc. made by milling **8.** [< the *v.*] [Old Slang] a fist fight —*vt.* **1.** to grind, work, process, form, polish, etc. by, in, or as in a mill **2.** to raise and ridge the edge of (a coin), as a safeguard against wear and clipping; knurl **3.** [Now Rare] to beat or whip (chocolate, etc.) to a froth —*vi.* ☆**1.** to move slowly in a circle, as cattle, or aimlessly, as a confused crowd (often with *around* or *about*) **2.** [Old Slang] to fight with the fists; box —**in the mill** in preparation —**through the mill** [Colloq.] through a hard, painful, instructive experience, training, test, etc.

☆**mill²** (mil) *n.* [for L. *millesimus*, thousandth < *mille*, thousand: cf. CENT] one tenth of a cent; $.001: a monetary unit used in calculating but not as a coin

Mill (mil) **1.** **James**, 1773–1836; Scot. philosopher, historian, & political economist **2.** **John Stuart**, 1806–73; Eng. philosopher & political economist: son of *prec.*

☆**mil·lage** (mil′ij) *n.* [MILL² + -AGE] taxation in mills per dollar of valuation

Mil·lais (mi lā′), Sir **John Everett** 1829–96; Eng. painter

Mil·lay (mi lā′), **Edna St. Vincent** (*Mrs. Eugen Boissevain*) 1892–1950; U.S. poet

mill·board (-bôrd′) *n.* [contr. < *milled board*] a heavy, flexible pasteboard used in bookbinding, etc.

mill·cake (-kāk′) *n.* the residue left after the oil has been pressed from linseed

mill·dam (-dam′) *n.* **1.** a dam built across a stream to raise its level enough to provide water power for turning a mill wheel **2.** *same as* MILLPOND

milled (mild) *adj.* **1.** ground, cut, worked, etc. by or in a mill **2.** having the edges raised and ridged or grooved, as a coin; knurled

mille·fleurs (mēl′flur′) *adj.* [Fr. *mille fleurs*, a thousand flowers] having an allover, multicolored pattern of many flowers, as a tapestry

mil·le·nar·i·an (mil′ə ner′ē ən) *adj.* [< LL. *millenarius*, containing a thousand < L. *milleni*, a thousand each < *mille*, thousand + -AN] of a thousand years; of the millennium —*n.* a person who believes in the coming of the millennium

mil·le·nar·y (mil′ə ner′ē) *adj.* [LL. *millenarius*: see prec.] **1.** of or consisting of a thousand, esp. a thousand years **2.** of the millennium or millenarians —*n., pl.* **-nar′ies** **1.** a thousand **2.** a thousand years; millennium **3.** a thousandth anniversary **4.** a millenarian

mil·len·ni·um (mi len′ē əm) *n., pl.* **-ni·ums, -ni·a** (-ə) [ModL. < L. *mille*, thousand + *annus*, year (after L. *biennium*)] **1.** any period of 1,000 years [2000 B.C. through 1001 B.C. is the 2d *millennium* B.C.] **2.** *Theol.* the period of a thousand years during which Christ will reign on earth (with *the*): Rev. 20:1–5 **3.** any period of great happiness, peace, prosperity, etc.; imagined golden age —**mil·len′ni·al** *adj.* —**mil·len′ni·al·ism** *n.* —**mil·len′ni·al·ist** *n.*

mil·le·pede (mil′ə pēd′) *n. same as* MILLIPEDE

mil·le·pore (-pôr′) *n.* [Fr. *millépore* < *mille*, thousand + *pore* < L. *porus*, PORE²] any of a genus (*Millepora*) of coralline hydrozoans that form branching or leaflike calcareous masses with many very small openings on the surface

mill·er (mil′ər) *n.* [ME. *mylnere*] **1.** a person who owns or operates a mill, esp. a flour mill **2.** *a) same as* MILLING MACHINE *b)* a tool to be used in such a machine **3.** any of various moths with wings that look dusty or powdered, suggesting a miller's clothes

Mil·ler (mil′ər) **1.** **Arthur**, 1915– ; U.S. playwright **2.** **Henry**, 1891– ; U.S. writer **3.** **Joa·quin** (wä kēn′), (pseud. of *Cincinnatus Heine Miller*) 1839?–1913; U.S. poet **4.** **Joe**, 1684–1738; Eng. stage comedian: *Joe Miller's Jests* (1739), a book of jokes attributed to him, was published after his death

☆**Mill·er·ite** (mil′ər īt) *n.* a follower of William Miller (1782–1849), a U.S. preacher who declared that the end of the world and the second coming of Christ would occur in 1843

mill·er·ite (mil′ər īt′) *n.* [G. *millerit*, after W. H. *Miller*, 19th-c. Brit. mineralogist] native nickel sulfide, NiS, a brassy-yellow, crystalline mineral

mill·er's-thumb (mil′ərz thum′) *n.* **1.** any of several small freshwater fishes (genus *Cottus*) of N. America and Europe, with spiny fins and a broad, flat head **2.** in England, any of various unrelated small birds

Mil·les (mil′əs), **Carl** (born *Carl Wilhelm Emil Anderson*) 1875–1955; U.S. sculptor, born in Sweden

mil·les·i·mal (mi les′ə m'l) *adj.* [L. *millesimus* < *mille*, thousand + -AL] **1.** thousandth **2.** of or consisting of thousandths —*n.* a thousandth

mil·let (mil′it) *n.* see PLURAL, II, D, 3 [ME. *milet* < MFr., dim. of *mil* < L. *milium*, millet < IE. *melēi-* (var. of base *mel-*), to grind, whence Gr. *melinē*, millet] **1.** *a)* a cereal grass (*Panicum miliaceum*) whose small grain is used for food in Europe and Asia *b)* the grain **2.** any of several other similar grasses or their seed, as foxtail millet, pearl millet, etc.

Mil·let (mē le′; *E.* mi lā′), **Jean Fran·çois** (zhän frän swä′) 1814–75; Fr. painter

mil·li- (mil′ə, -i, -ē) [< L. *mille*, thousand] *a combining form meaning* a 1000th part of; the factor 10⁻³ [*millimeter*]

mil·li·am·pere (mil′ē am′pir) *n.* one thousandth of an ampere

mil·liard (mil′yərd, -yärd′) *n.* [Fr. < *million* (see MILLION) + -ard (see -ARD), orig., "large million"] [Brit.] 1,000 millions; billion

mil·li·ar·y (mil′ē er′ē) *adj.* [L. *milliarius*, containing a thousand < *mille*, thousand] of the ancient Roman mile, or 1,000 paces —*n., pl.* **-ar′ies** an ancient Roman milestone

mil·li·bar (mil′ə bär′) *n.* [< MILLI- + Gr. *baros*, weight] a unit of atmospheric pressure equal to 1/1000 bar, or 1,000 dynes per square centimeter

Mil·li·cent (mil′ə s'nt) [OFr. *Melisent* < OHG. *Amalaswind* < *amal*, work + *swind*-, strong, akin to Goth. *swinths*] a feminine name

mil·li·cu·rie (mil′ə kyoor′ē) *n.* one thousandth of a curie

mil·lieme (mēl yem′, mē-) *n.* [Fr. *millième*, a thousandth < MFr. < *mille*, a thousand < L.] a unit of currency in Egypt, Sudan, and Libya, equal to 1/1000 pound

mil·li·far·ad (mil′ə far′ad, -əd) *n.* one thousandth of a farad

mil·li·gal (-gal′) *n.* one thousandth of a gal

mil·li·gram (mil′ə gram′) *n.* [Fr. *milligramme*] one thousandth of a gram (.0154 grain): also, chiefly Brit. sp., **mil′li·gramme′**: abbrev. **mg.** (*sing. & pl.*)

mil·li·hen·ry (-hen′rē) *n.* one thousandth of a henry

Mil·li·kan (mil′ə kən), **Robert Andrews** 1868–1953; U.S. physicist

mil·li·li·ter (mil′ə lēt′ər) *n.* [Fr. *millilitre*] one thousandth of a liter (1.000027 cubic centimeters or .06102 cubic inch): also, chiefly Brit. sp., **mil′li·li′tre**: abbrev. **ml.** (*sing. & pl.*)

mil·lime (mil′ēm, -im) *n.* [Fr. < *millième*: see MILLIEME] a monetary unit and coin of Tunisia equal to 1/1000 dinar

mil·li·me·ter (mil′ə mēt′ər) *n.* [Fr. *millimetre*] one thousandth of a meter (.03937 inch): also, chiefly Brit. sp., **mil′li·me′tre**: abbrev. **mm.** (*sing. & pl.*)

mil·li·mi·cron (mil′ə mi′krän) *n.* one thousandth of a micron, one millionth of a millimeter, or ten angstroms: a unit of length for measuring waves of light, etc.

mil·line (mil′lin′) *n.* [MIL(LION) + LINE¹] 1. a unit of measurement equal to a one-column agate line (of an advertisement) in one million copies of a publication 2. the cost per milline of an advertisement

mil·li·ner (mil′ə nər) *n.* [< *Milaner*, inhabitant of Milan, importer of dress wares from Milan] a person who designs, makes, trims, or sells women's hats

mil·li·ner·y (mil′ə ner′ē; *chiefly Brit.*, -nər i) *n.* [< prec. + -ERY] 1. women's hats, headdresses, etc. 2. the work or business of a milliner

mill·ing (mil′in) *prp. of* MILL¹ —*n.* 1. the process or business of grinding grain into flour or meal 2. the grinding, cutting, or processing of metal, cloth, etc. in a mill 3. *a*) the process of ridging the edge of a coin, etc. *b*) the ridging thus produced; milled edge 4. circular or random motion of or as of a herd or crowd

milling cutter any of various rotating cutters used in a milling machine to cut, grind, or shape metal parts

milling machine a machine with a table on which material rests as it is fed against a milling cutter

mil·lion (mil′yən) *n.* [ME. *millioun* < OFr. *million* < It. *milione* < *mille*, thousand < L.] 1. a thousand thousands; 1,000,000 2. a million (unspecified but understood) monetary units, as dollars, pounds, francs, etc. 3. an indefinite but very large number: a hyperbolic use —*adj.* amounting to one million in number

mil·lion·aire (mil′yə ner′) *n.* [Fr. *millionnaire*] a person whose wealth comes to at least a million dollars, pounds, francs, etc.: also sp. **mil′lion·naire′**

mil·lionth (mil′yənth) *adj.* 1. coming last in a series of a million 2. designating any of the million equal parts of something —*n.* 1. the last in a series of a million 2. any of the million equal parts of something

mil·li·pede (mil′ə pēd′) *n.* [< L. *millepeda* < *mille*, thousand + *pes* (gen. *pedis*), a FOOT] any of various many-legged arthropods (class Diplopoda) with an elongated, cylindrical body having two pairs of walking legs on each apparent segment

mil·li·rad (-rad′) *n.* one thousandth of a rad

mil·li·sec·ond (-sek′ənd) *n.* one thousandth of a second

mil·li·volt (-vōlt′) *n.* one thousandth of a volt

mill·pond (mil′pänd′) *n.* a pond formed by a milldam, from which water flows for driving a mill wheel

mill·race (-rās′) *n.* 1. the current of water that drives a mill wheel 2. the channel in which it flows

mill·run (-run′) *n.* 1. same as MILLRACE ☆2. a quantity of ore whose quality or mineral content is tested by milling 3. the mineral obtained by such testing

mill-run (mil′run′) *adj.* ☆just as it comes out of the mill; ordinary; average; run-of-the-mill

mill·stone (-stōn′) *n.* 1. either of a pair of large, flat, round stones between which grain or other substances are ground 2. stone used for these, usually a hard sandstone or conglomerate 3. a heavy burden 4. something that grinds, pulverizes, or crushes

mill·stream (-strēm′) *n.* water flowing in a millrace

mill wheel the wheel, usually a water wheel, that drives the machinery in a mill

mill·work (-wurk′) *n.* 1. objects made in a mill; esp., doors, windows, etc. made in a planing mill 2. work done in a mill —**mill′work′er** *n.*

mill·wright (-rit′) *n.* 1. a person who designs, builds, or installs mills or their machinery 2. a worker who installs, maintains, or repairs the shafting, belting, and other machinery in a mill

Milne (miln), **A(lan) A(lexander)** 1882–1956; Eng. playwright, novelist, & writer of children's books

Mi·lo (mī′lō) a famous Greek athlete, c. 520 B.C.

☆**mi·lo** (mī′lō) *n.* [< Bantu (Sesuto) *maili*] any of a group of grain sorghums with somewhat juicy stalks and compact heads of white or yellow, soft grains

mi·lord (mi lôrd′) *n.* [Fr. < Eng. *my lord*] an English nobleman: used as a term of address

Mí·los (mē′lôs) Gr. island of the SW Cyclades, in the Aegean Sea: 61 sq. mi.: It. name **Mi·lo** (mē′lō)

☆**milque·toast** (milk′tōst′) *n.* [< Caspar *Milquetoast*, character of this sort in a comic strip by H. T. Webster (1885–1952), U.S. cartoonist: cf. MILK TOAST] a timid, shrinking, apologetic person

mil·reis (mil′rās′) *n., pl.* **mil·-reis′** [Port. *mil reis*, lit., a thousand reis] 1. a former Brazilian monetary unit and silver coin, equivalent to 1,000 reis: superseded in 1942 by the CRUZEIRO 2. a former Portuguese monetary unit and gold coin: superseded in 1911 by the ESCUDO

Mil·stein (mil′stīn), **Nathan** 1904–   ; U.S. violinist, born in Russia

milt (milt) *n.* [ME. *milte*, prob. < Scand. (as in Norw. *milt*, *mjelte*), altered (after ON. *milti*, spleen) < base of ON. *mjolk*, MILK] 1. the reproductive glands of male fishes, esp. when filled with germ cells and the milky fluid containing them 2. such cells and fluid; fish sperm —*adj.* breeding: said of male fishes —*vt.* to fertilize (fish roe) with milt —**milt′er** *n.*

Mil·ti·a·des (mil tī′ə dēz′) died c. 489 B.C.; Athenian general: defeated the Persians at Marathon in 490

Mil·ton (mil′t'n) [< surname or place name *Milton* < OE. *Middel-tun* (lit., Middletown) & OE. *Mylen-tun* (lit., Mill town)] 1. a masculine name: dim. *Milt, Miltie* 2. John, 1608–74; Eng. poet

Mil·ton·ic (mil tän′ik) *adj.* of or like John Milton or his writings; solemn, elevated, majestic, etc.: also **Mil·to′ni·an** (-tō′nē ən)

☆**Mil·town** (mil′toun) [arbitrary coinage] *a trademark for* MEPROBAMATE

Mil·wau·kee (mil wô′kē) [< Fr. < Algonquian, lit., good land, council place] city & port in SE Wis., on Lake Michigan: pop. 717,000 (met. area 1,404,000)

mim (mim) *adj.* [echoic of sound made with pursed lips: cf. MUM⁶] [Brit. Dial.] primly quiet or shy; demure

mime (mīm) *n.* [L. *mimus* < Gr. *mimos*, imitator, actor] 1. an ancient Greek or Roman farce, in which people and events were mimicked and burlesqued 2. the representation of an action, character, mood, etc. by means of gestures and actions rather than words 3. an actor who performs in mimes; specif., a mimic or pantomimist —*vt.* **mimed**, **mim′ing** to imitate, mimic, or act out as a mime —*vi.* to act as a mime; play a part with gestures and actions, but usually without words —**mim′er** *n.*

☆**mim·e·o·graph** (mim′ē ə graf′, mim′yə-) *n.* [a former trademark < Gr. *mimeomai*, I imitate + -GRAPH] a machine for making copies of written, drawn, or typewritten matter by means of a stencil placed around a drum containing ink —*vt.* 1. to make copies of on such a machine 2. to make (copies) on such a machine

mi·me·sis (mi mē′sis, mī-) *n.* [ModL. < Gr. *mimēsis*, imitation < *mimos*, imitator] imitation; specif., *a*) *Art & Literature* imitation or representation, as of human speech or behavior *b*) *Biol.* same as MIMICRY

mi·met·ic (mi met′ik, mī-) *adj.* [Gr. *mimētikos* < *mimeisthai*, to imitate, akin to *mimos*, actor] 1. of or characterized by imitation; imitative 2. of or characterized by mimicry —**mi·met′i·cal·ly** *adv.*

mim·ic (mim′ik) *adj.* [L. *mimicus* < Gr. *mimikos* < *mimos*, a mime] 1. inclined to copy; imitative 2. of, or having the nature of, mimicry or imitation 3. make-believe; simulated; mock [*mimic* tears] —*n.* a person or thing that imitates; esp., an actor skilled in mimicry —*vt.* **mim′icked**, **mim′ick·ing** 1. to imitate in speech or action, often so as to ridicule 2. to copy closely; imitate accurately 3. to resemble closely; have or take on the appearance of [animals that *mimic* their environment] —*SYN.* see IMITATE —**mim′ick·er** *n.*

mim·ic·ry (-rē) *n., pl.* **-ries** 1. the practice or art, or an instance or way, of mimicking 2. close resemblance, in color, form, or behavior, of one organism to another or to some object in its environment, as of some insects to the leaves or twigs of plants: it serves to disguise or conceal the organism from predators

Mi·mir (mē′mir) [ON. *Mimir*] *Norse Myth.* a giant guarding the spring of wisdom at the root of the tree Ygdrasil

mi·mo·sa (mi mō′sə) *n.* [ModL. < L. *mimus*: see MIME: from the apparent mimicry of the sensitivity of animal life] 1. any of a large genus (*Mimosa*) of trees, shrubs, and herbs of the legume family, growing in warm regions and usually having bipinnate leaves, and heads or spikes of small white, yellow, or pink flowers, including the sensitive plant 2. any of several similar leguminous trees, as the albizzia

min. 1. mineralogical 2. mineralogy 3. minim(s) 4. minimum 5. mining 6. minister 7. minor 8. minute(s)

mi·na¹ (mī′nə) *n., pl.* **-nae** (-nē), **-nas** [L. < Gr. *mna*, of Sem. origin, as in Heb. *māneh*] a varying unit of weight and money used in ancient Greece, Egypt, etc., generally equal to 1/60 talent or 100 drachmas

mi·na² (mī′nə) *n.* same as MYNA: also sp. **mi′nah**

min·a·ble, mine·a·ble (mīn′ə b'l) *adj.* that can be mined

mi·na·cious (mi nā'shəs) *adj.* [< L. *minax* (gen. *minacis*): see MENACE + -OUS] menacing; threatening —**mi·nac'i·ty** (-nas'ə tē) *n.*

min·a·ret (min'ə ret', min'ə ret') *n.* [Fr. < Turk. *menāret* < Ar. *manārah*, lamp, lighthouse, minaret < *minār*, candlestick, lighthouse < base of *nār*, fire] a high, slender tower attached to a Moslem mosque, with one or more projecting balconies from which a muezzin, or crier, calls the people to prayer

Mi·nas Basin (mī'nəs) E arm of the Bay of Fundy, Nova Scotia, Canada: c. 60 mi. long

Mi·nas Ge·rais (mē'nəs zhi rīs') state of EC Brazil: 225,192 sq. mi.; pop. 9,798,000; cap. Belo Horizonte

min·a·to·ry (min'ə tôr'ē) *adj.* [OFr. *minatoire* < LL. *minatorius* < pp. of L. *minari*, to threaten: for IE. base see MENACE] menacing; threatening

mince (mins) *vt.* **minced, minc'ing** [ME. *mincen* < OFr. *mincier* < VL. **minutiare* < L. *minutus*, small: see MINUTE²] 1. to cut up or chop up (meat, etc.) into very small pieces; hash 2. to subdivide minutely 3. to express or do with affected elegance or daintiness 4. to lessen the force of; weaken, as by euphemism [to *mince* no words] —*vi.* 1. to speak or act with affected elegance or daintiness 2. to walk with short steps or in an affected, dainty manner —*n. same as* MINCEMEAT —**not mince matters** to speak frankly —**minc'er** *n.*

mince·meat (-mēt') *n.* [< *minced meat*] 1. a mixture of chopped apples, spices, suet, raisins, etc., and sometimes meat, used as a pie filling 2. [Obs.] minced meat —**make mincemeat of** 1. to chop into small pieces 2. to defeat or refute completely

mince pie a pie with a filling of mincemeat

minc·ing (min'siŋ) *adj.* 1. affectedly elegant or dainty: of a person or his speech, manner, etc. 2. characterized by short steps or affected daintiness [a *mincing* walk] —**minc'ing·ly** *adv.*

mind (mīnd) *n.* [ME. *mynde* < OE. *(ge)mynd*, memory < IE. base **men-*, to think, whence Gr. *menos*, spirit, force, L. *mens*, mind] 1. memory; recollection or remembrance [to bring to *mind* a story] 2. what one thinks; opinion [speak your *mind*] 3. *a)* that which thinks, perceives, feels, wills, etc.; seat or subject of consciousness *b)* the thinking and perceiving part of consciousness; intellect or intelligence *c)* attention; notice *d)* all of an individual's conscious experiences *e)* the conscious and the unconscious together as a unit; psyche 4. the intellect in its normal state; reason; sanity [to lose one's *mind*] 5. a person having intelligence or regarded as an intellect [the great *minds* of today] 6. way, state, or direction of thinking and feeling [the reactionary *mind*] 7. [Rare] a Mass in memory of a dead person ☆8. [M-] God: in full, **Divine Mind:** so called in Christian Science 9. *Philos.* consciousness as an element in reality: contrasted with MATTER —*vt.* 1. to direct one's mind to; specif., *a)* [Now Dial.] to perceive; observe *b)* to pay attention to; heed *c)* to obey *d)* to attend to; apply oneself to (a task, etc.) *e)* to tend; take care of; watch over; look after [*mind* the baby] *f)* to be careful about; watch out for [*mind* those rickety stairs] 2. *a)* to care about; feel concern about *b)* to object to; dislike [to *mind* the cold] 3. [Dial.] to remember: sometimes used reflexively 4. [Dial.] to intend; purpose 5. [Dial. or Archaic] to remind —*vi.* 1. to pay attention; give heed 2. to be obedient 3. to be careful; watch out 4. *a)* to care; feel concern *b)* to object —**bear (or keep) in mind** to remember —**be in one's right mind** to be mentally well; be sane —**be of one mind** to have the same opinion or desire —**be of two minds** to be undecided or irresolute —☆**blow one's mind** [Slang] to undergo hallucinations, etc. caused by, or as by, psychedelic drugs —**call to mind** 1. to remember 2. to be a reminder of —**change one's mind** 1. to change one's opinion 2. to change one's intention, purpose, or wish —**give (someone) a piece of one's mind** to criticize or rebuke (someone) sharply —**have a (good or great) mind to** to feel (strongly) inclined to —**have half a mind to** to be somewhat inclined to —**have in mind** 1. to remember 2. to think of 3. to intend; purpose —**know one's own mind** to know one's own real thoughts, desires, etc. —**make up one's mind** to form a definite opinion or decision —**meeting of (the) minds** an agreement —**never mind** don't be concerned; it doesn't matter —**on one's mind** 1. occupying one's thoughts 2. worrying one —**out of one's mind** 1. mentally ill; insane 2. frantic (*with* worry, grief, etc.) —**put in mind** to remind —**set one's mind on** to be determined on or determinedly desirous of —**take one's mind off** to stop one from thinking about; turn one's attention from —**to one's mind** in one's opinion —**mind'er** *n.*

Min·da·na·o (min'də nou', -nä'ō) 2d largest island of the Philippines, at the S end of the group: 36,906 sq. mi.

mind·ed (mīn'did) *adj.* 1. having a (specified kind of) mind: used in hyphenated compounds [high-*minded*] 2. having a mind to; inclined; disposed

mind·ful (mīnd'f'l) *adj.* having in mind; aware, heedful, or careful (*of*) [to be *mindful* of the danger] —**mind'ful·ly** *adv.* —**mind'ful·ness** *n.*

mind·less (-lis) *adj.* 1. not using one's mind; showing little or no intelligence or intellect; senseless or thoughtless 2. taking no thought; heedless or careless (*of*); unmindful —**mind'less·ly** *adv.* —**mind'less·ness** *n.*

Min·do·ro (min dôr'ō) island of the Philippines, south of Luzon: 3,759 sq. mi.

mind reader a person who seems or professes to be able to perceive another's thoughts without apparent means of communication —**mind reading**

mind's eye the imagination

mine¹ (mīn) *pron.* [ME. *min* < OE., gen. sing. of *ic*, I, akin to G. *mein*: for base see ME] that or those belonging to me: the absolute form of *my*, used without a following noun, often after *of* [a friend of *mine*, that book is *mine*, *mine* are better] —*possessive pronominal adj.* [Mainly Archaic] my: formerly used before a word beginning with a vowel or *h* [*mine* eyes, *mine* honor], now used after a noun in direct address [daughter *mine*]

mine² (mīn) *n.* [ME. < MFr. < ? Celt., as in Ir. *mein*, vein of metal] 1. *a)* a large excavation made in the earth, from which to extract metallic ores, coal, precious stones, salt, or certain other minerals: distinguished from QUARRY³ *b)* the surface buildings, shafts, elevators, etc. of such an excavation *c)* a deposit of ore, coal, etc. 2. any great source of supply [a *mine* of information] 3. a kind of firework that explodes in the air and scatters a number of smaller fireworks 4. *Mil. a)* a tunnel dug under an enemy's trench, fort, etc., esp. one in which an explosive is placed to destroy the enemy or its fortifications *b)* an explosive charge in a container, buried in the ground for destroying enemy troops or vehicles on land, or placed in the sea for destroying enemy ships 5. *Zool.* the burrow of an insect —*vi.* **mined, min'ing** [ME. *minen* < OFr. *miner*] to dig a mine; specif., *a)* to dig ores, coal, etc. from the earth *b)* to dig or lay military mines —*vt.* 1. *a)* to dig in (the earth) for ores, coal, etc. *b)* to dig (ores, coal, etc.) from the earth 2. to take from (a source) 3. *a)* to dig a tunnel under (an enemy installation) *b)* to place explosive mines in or under (an area) 4. to make hollows under the surface of [leaves *mined* by larvae] 5. to undermine or ruin slowly by secret methods, plotting, etc.

mine detector an electromagnetic device for locating the position of hidden explosive mines

mine field an area on land or in water where explosive mines have been set

mine·lay·er (mīn'lā'ər) *n.* a ship especially equipped to lay explosive mines in the water

min·er (-ər) *n.* [ME. *minour* < OFr. < *miner*, to mine] 1. a person whose work is digging coal, ore, etc. in a mine 2. [Archaic] a soldier who mines enemy installations, etc.

min·er·al (min'ər əl, min'rəl) *n.* [ME. < OFr. < ML. *minerale*, neut. of *mineralis*, mineral < *minera*, a mine] 1. an inorganic substance occurring naturally in the earth and having a consistent and distinctive set of physical properties (e.g., a usually crystalline structure, hardness, color, etc.) and a composition that can be expressed by a chemical formula: sometimes applied to substances in the earth of organic origin, such as coal 2. *same as* ORE 3. any substance that is neither vegetable nor animal 4. any of certain elements, as iron, phosphorus, etc., essential to the physiology of animals and plants 5. [*pl.*] [Brit. Colloq.] aerated or carbonated drinks —*adj.* of, having the nature of, consisting of, or containing a mineral or minerals

mineral. 1. mineralogical 2. mineralogy

min·er·al·ize (min'ər ə līz', min'rə-) *vt.* **-ized', -iz'ing** 1. to convert (organic matter) into a mineral; petrify 2. to impregnate (water, etc.) with minerals 3. to convert (a metal) into an ore, as by oxidation —*vi.* [Rare] to collect minerals for study —**min'er·al·i·za'tion** *n.*

min·er·al·iz·er (-ər) *n.* 1. a substance, such as water, acid, or certain gases, which, when dissolved in magma, lowers the melting point and viscosity, promotes crystallization, and influences the formation of minerals 2. an element, as sulfur, arsenic, etc., that combines chemically with a metal to form an ore

☆**mineral jelly** *same as* PETROLATUM

min·er·al·o·gy (min'ə räl'ə jē, -ral'-) *n.* [< MINERAL + -LOGY] 1. the scientific study of minerals 2. *pl.* **-gies** a book about minerals —**min'er·a·log'i·cal** (-ər ə läj'i k'l) *adj.* —**min'er·a·log'i·cal·ly** *adv.* —**min'er·al'o·gist** *n.*

mineral oil any oil found in the rock strata of the earth; specif., *a)* petroleum *b)* any of various colorless, tasteless oils derived from petroleum and used as a laxative

mineral pitch natural asphalt

mineral spring any spring of natural mineral water

mineral tar *same as* MALTHA (sense 1)

mineral water water naturally or artificially impregnated with mineral salts or gases; esp., any such water alleged to have medicinal values

mineral wax *same as* OZOKERITE

☆**mineral wool** a fibrous material made from rock and melted slag and used as insulation in buildings

MINARET

Mi·ner·va (mi nur′və) [L., prob. of Etruscan origin] **1.** a feminine name **2.** the ancient Roman goddess of wisdom, technical skill, and invention: identified with the Greek goddess Athena

mi·ne·stro·ne (min′ə strō′nē; *occas.* -strōn′; *It.* mě′ne strō′ne) *n.* [It. < *minestra*, soup < *minestrare* < L. *ministrare*: see MINISTER, *v.*] a thick vegetable soup containing vermicelli, barley, etc. in a meat broth

mine sweeper a ship equipped for destroying enemy mines at sea

Ming (miŋ) [Chin., lit., luminous] Chin. dynasty (1368–1644): period noted for scholarly achievements & artistic works, esp. porcelains

min·gle (miŋ′g'l) *vt.* **-gled, -gling** [ME. *mengelen*, freq. of *mengen* < OE. *mengan*, to mix, akin to G. *mengen* < IE. base *menk-*, to knead, whence Gr. *massein*] **1.** to bring or mix together; combine; blend **2.** [Now Rare] to make by mixing ingredients; compound —*vi.* **1.** to be or become mixed, blended, etc. **2.** to join, unite, or take part with others —*SYN.* see MIX —**min′gler** *n.*

ming tree [MING + TREE] an artificial plant made in imitation of a bonsai

min·gy (min′jē) *adj.* **-gi·er, -gi·est** prob. altered < MANGY, after STINGY[1] [Colloq.] mean and stingy

min·i- (min′ē) [< MINI(ATURE)] *a combining form meaning* miniature, very small, very short [*miniskirt*]: used freely to form nonce compounds, often hyphenated, meaning "of lesser scope, extent, intensity, etc. than usual" [*mini-crisis, mini-culture*]

min·i·a·ture (min′ē ə chər, min′i chər) *n.* [It. *miniatura*, rubrication, illumination of manuscripts < ML. < pp. of L. *miniare*, to paint red < *minium*, red lead (see MINIUM): sense infl. by L. *minutus*, MINUTE[2]] **1.** a small painting or illuminated letter, as in a medieval manuscript **2.** *a)* a very small painting, esp. a portrait, done on ivory, vellum, etc. *b)* the art of making such paintings **3.** a copy or model on a very small scale —*adj.* on or done on a very small scale; diminutive; minute —*SYN.* see SMALL —**in miniature** on a small scale; greatly reduced

min·i·a·tur·ist (-chər ist) *n.* a painter of miniatures

min·i·a·tur·ize (-īz′) *vt.* **-ized′, -iz′ing** to make in a small and compact form —**min′i·a·tur′i·za′tion** *n.*

☆**min·i·bus** (min′ē bus′) *n.* [MINI- + BUS] a very small bus

Min·i·é ball (min′ē, min′ē ā) [after C. E. *Minié* (1814–79), its Fr. inventor] a cone-shaped rifle bullet with a cavity in its base, which expanded, when fired, to fit the rifling in the bore: used in the 19th cent.

min·i·fy (min′ə fī′) *vt.* **-fied′, -fy′ing** [< L. *minor*, less, after MAGNIFY] to make or make seem smaller or less important —**min′i·fi·ca′tion** *n.*

min·i·kin (min′i kin) *n.* [MDu. *minneken*, dim. of *minne*, love: see MINNESINGER & -KIN] **1.** [Obs.] a darling **2.** [Rare] anything very small and delicate —*adj.* [Archaic] **1.** diminutive **2.** affected or mincing

min·im (min′im) *n.* [ME. *mynym* (in sense 3) < L. *minimus*, least: see MINIMUM] **1.** the smallest liquid measure, equal to 1/60 fluid dram, or about a drop **2.** anything very small; tiny portion **3.** *Music* a half note (♩) —*adj.* smallest; tiniest

min·i·ma (min′ə mə) *n. alt. pl. of* MINIMUM

min·i·mal (-m'l) *adj.* smallest or least possible; of or constituting a minimum —**min′i·mal·ly** *adv.*

min·i·mal·ist (-m'l ist) *n.* [prec. + -IST] a person who advocates action of a minimal or conservative kind

min·i·mize (min′ə mīz′) *vt.* **-mized′, -miz′ing** **1.** to reduce to a minimum; decrease to the least possible amount, degree, etc. **2.** to estimate or make appear to be of the least possible amount, value, or importance —*SYN.* see DISPARAGE —**min′i·mi·za′tion** *n.* —**min′i·miz′er** *n.*

min·i·mum (-məm) *n., pl.* **-mums, -ma** (-mə) [L., neut. of *minimus*, least, superl. < base of *minor*, MINOR] **1.** the smallest quantity, number, or degree possible or permissible **2.** the lowest degree or point (of a varying quantity, as temperature) reached or recorded; lowest limit of variation **3.** *Math.* the smallest of a specified set of real numbers —*adj.* **1.** smallest possible, permissible, or reached **2.** of, marking, or setting a minimum or minimums

minimum wage 1. a wage established by contract or by law as the lowest that may be paid to employees doing a specified type of work **2.** *same as* LIVING WAGE

min·ing (mī′niŋ) *n.* **1.** the act, process, or work of removing ores, coal, etc. from a mine **2.** the act or process of laying explosive mines

min·ion (min′yən) *n.* [Fr. *mignon*, favorite, darling: see MIGNON] **1.** a favorite, esp. one who is a fawning, servile follower: term of contempt **2.** a subordinate official, deputy, or the like **3.** [Obs.] a mistress or paramour **4.** *Printing* a size of type, 7 point —*adj.* [Rare] delicate, dainty, etc.

minion of the law *same as* POLICEMAN

min·is·cule (min′ə skyo͞ol′) *adj.* erroneous *sp.* of MINUSCULE

min·ish (min′ish) *vt., vi.* [ME. *minusschen* < OFr. *menuisier*, to lessen, make small < VL. *minutiare* < L. *minutus*, MINUTE[2]] [Archaic] to make or become less, smaller, inferior, etc.; diminish

min·i·skirt (min′ē skurt′) *n.* [MINI- + SKIRT] a very short skirt ending well above the knee

min·is·ter (min′is tər) *n.* [ME. < OFr. *ministre* < L. *minister*, an attendant, servant, in LL.(Ec.), Christian preacher < base of L. *minor*, MINOR: formed prob. after *magister*, MASTER] **1.** a person acting for another as his agent and carrying out his orders or designs; specif., *a)* a person appointed by the head of a government to take charge of some department *b)* a diplomatic officer sent to a foreign nation to represent his government, usually one to a less important state and ranking below an ambassador **2.** *a)* anyone authorized to carry out the spiritual functions of a church, usually Protestant, conduct worship, administer sacraments, preach, etc.; clergyman; pastor *b)* R.C.Ch. the superior of certain religious orders **3.** any person or thing thought of as serving as the agent of some power, force, etc. [*a minister* of evil] —*vt.* [ME. *ministren* < OFr. *ministrer* < L. *ministrare*] [Archaic] **1.** to supply; provide **2.** to administer, as a sacrament —*vi.* **1.** to serve or act as a minister in a church **2.** to give help (*to*); attend to needs

min·is·te·ri·al (min′is tir′ē əl) *adj.* [Fr. *ministériel* < LL. *ministerialis*] **1.** of ministry, a minister, or ministers collectively **2.** serving as a minister, or agent; subordinate **3.** *a)* having the nature of or characteristic of the administrative functions of government; executive *b)* designating or of an administrative act carried out in a prescribed manner not allowing for personal discretion **4.** being a cause; instrumental —**min′is·te′ri·al·ly** *adv.*

min·is·te·ri·al·ist (-ist) *n.* [Brit.] a supporter of the government ministry in office

minister plenipotentiary *pl.* **ministers plenipotentiary** a diplomatic representative with full authority to negotiate

min·is·trant (min′is trənt) *adj.* [L. *ministrans*, prp.: see MINISTER, *v.*] serving as a minister; ministering —*n.* a person who ministers, or serves

min·is·tra·tion (min′is trā′shən) *n.* [ME. *ministracion* < L. *ministratio* < pp. of *ministrare*, to MINISTER] **1.** the act of serving as a minister or clergyman; performance of pastoral duties **2.** the act or an instance of giving help or care; service —**min′is·tra′tive** *adj.*

min·is·try (min′is trē) *n., pl.* **-tries** [ME. *mynystere* < L. *ministerium* < *minister*, MINISTER] **1.** *a)* the act of ministering, or serving; ministration *b)* that which serves as a means; agency **2.** *a)* the office, function, tenure, or service of a minister of religion *b)* such ministers collectively; clergy **3.** *a)* the department under a minister of government *b)* the term of office of such a minister *c)* the building or buildings of such a department *d)* the ministers of a particular government as a group

☆**min·i·track** (min′ə trak′) *n.* a system used to track the path of an artificial satellite in orbit by signals received from miniature transmitters in the satellite

min·i·um (min′ē əm) *n.* [L., of Iberian origin, as in Basque *arminea*] **1.** the color vermilion **2.** *same as* RED LEAD

min·i·ver (min′ə vər) *n.* [ME. *menyuere* < OFr. *menu ver*, miniver < *menu*, small (see MENU) + *vair*, VAIR] **1.** a white fur used for trimming garments, esp. ceremonial robes, as of royalty **2.** [Brit. Dial.] an ermine in winter when its fur is white

mink (miŋk) *n., pl.* **minks, mink:** see PLURAL, II, D, 1 [LME. *minke* < Scand., as in Sw. *menk*] **1.** any of several slim, carnivorous mammals (genus *Mustela*) with partly webbed feet; esp., a dark-brown weasel (*Mustela vison*) living in water part of the time and common in N. America **2.** its valuable fur, soft, thick, and white to brown in color

MINK
(17–28 in. long,
including tail)

Minn. Minnesota

Min·ne·ap·o·lis (min′ē ap′'l is) *n.* [< nearby *Minnehaha* Falls (< Sioux *minne*, water, and *haha*, waterfall) + Gr. *polis*, city] city in E Minn., on the Mississippi, adjacent to St. Paul: pop. 434,000 (met. area, with St. Paul, 1,814,000)

Min·ne·ha·ha (min′ē hä′hä) the girl Hiawatha marries, in Longfellow's *The Song of Hiawatha*

min·ne·sing·er (min′i siŋ′ər) *n.* [G., altered (after *singer* < *singen*, SING) < MHG. *minnesenger* < *minne*, love < OHG. *minna*, orig., loving recollection (< IE. base see MIND) + MHG. *senger*, a singer < OHG. *sangari* < *sang*, SONG + *-ari*, -ER] any of a number of German lyric poets and singers of the 12th to the 14th cent., corresponding to the minstrels or troubadours

Min·ne·so·ta (min′ə sōt′ə) [< Siouan river name, lit., milky blue water] Middle Western State of the U.S., adjoining the Canadian border: admitted, 1858; 84,068 sq. mi.; pop. 3,805,000; cap. St. Paul: abbrev. **Minn.**, **MN** —**Min′ne·so′tan** *adj., n.*

Min·ne·ton·ka (min′ə täŋ′kə) [< Siouan lake name, lit., big water] village in E Minn.: suburb of Minneapolis: pop. 36,000

Min·ne·wit (min′yoo wit, min′ə-), Peter same as MINUIT
min·now (min′ō) n., pl. **-nows, -now**: see PLURAL, II, D, 1 [ME. *menow* < or akin to OE. *myne*, akin to OHG. *muniwa*, prob. < IE. base **meni-*, a kind of fish, whence Gr. *mainē*, Russ. *men′*, eelpout] **1.** any of a large number of usually small freshwater fishes (family Cyprinidae), used commonly as bait **2.** any very small fish Also [Dial. or Colloq.] **min′ny** (-ē), pl. **-nies**
Mi·no·an (mi nō′ən) adj. [< MINOS + -AN] designating or of an advanced prehistoric culture that flourished in Crete from c.2800–c.1100B.C.
mi·nor (mī′nər) adj. [ME. *menour* < L. *minor* < IE. **minu-*, small < base **mei-*, to lessen, whence Gr. *meiōn*, less, ON. *minni*, smaller] **1.** a) lesser in size, amount, number, or extent b) lesser in importance or rank **2.** under full legal age (usually twenty-one years) **3.** constituting the minority: said of a part, etc. **4.** sad; melancholy; plaintive: from the identification in Occidental music of the minor key with such qualities ☆**5.** *Educ.* designating or of a field of study in which a student specializes, but to a lesser degree than in his major **6.** *Logic* narrower; less inclusive: see MINOR PREMISE, MINOR TERM **7.** *Music* a) designating an imperfect interval smaller than the corresponding major interval by a semitone b) characterized by minor intervals, scales, etc. [the *minor* key] c) designating a triad having a minor third d) based on the scale pattern of the minor mode: see MINOR SCALE —vi. ☆*Educ.* to specialize in a secondary degree in some subject or field of study [to *minor* in chemistry] —n. **1.** a person under full legal age, who has not yet acquired all civil rights ☆**2.** *Educ.* a minor subject or field of study **3.** *Logic* a minor term or premise **4.** *Music* a minor interval, key, etc. —**the minors** the minor leagues, esp. in baseball
Mi·nor·ca (mi nôr′kə) 2d largest island of the Balearic Islands, east of Majorca: 264 sq. mi.: Sp. name, MENORCA —n. any of a breed of large chicken with black, white, or buff feathers
Mi·nor·ite (mī′nə rīt′) n. [MINOR, adj. + -ITE[1]: they regarded themselves as a humbler rank than members of other orders] a Franciscan friar
mi·nor·i·ty (mə nôr′ə tē, mī-; -när′-) n., pl. **-ties** [ML. *minoritas* < L. *minor*, MINOR] **1.** the lesser part or smaller number; less than half of a total **2.** a group, party, or faction with a smaller number of votes or adherents than the majority **3.** a racial, religious, ethnic, or political group smaller than and differing from the larger, controlling group in a community, nation, etc. **4.** the period or condition of being under full legal age
☆**minor league** any league in a professional sport other than the major leagues —**mi·nor-league** (mī′nər lēg′) adj.
minor mode a progression, phrase, section, or composition of music predominantly using the intervals of the minor scale
minor order *R.C.Ch.* any of the four lower orders preceding the subdiaconate (doorkeeper, lector, exorcist, or acolyte), requisite for aspirants to major orders
minor premise the premise (in a syllogism) that contains the minor term
minor scale one of the two standard diatonic scales, with half steps instead of whole steps a) after the second and seventh tones in ascending and after the sixth and third tones in descending (**melodic minor scale**), or b) after the second, fifth, and seventh tones in ascending and after the eighth, sixth, and third tones in descending (**harmonic minor scale**)
minor seminary *R.C.Ch.* a seminary offering usually a high school education and the first two years of college
minor suit *Bridge* diamonds or clubs: so called from their lower value in scoring
minor term the subject of the conclusion of a syllogism
Mi·nos (mī′nəs, -näs) [Gr. *Minōs*] *Gr. Myth.* a king of Crete, son of Zeus by Europa: after he died he became one of the three judges of the dead in the lower world: see also MINOTAUR
Min·o·taur (min′ə tôr′) [ME. *Minotaure* < L. *Minotaurus* < Gr. *Minōtauros* < *Minōs*, Minos + *tauros*, a bull] *Gr. Myth.* a monster with the body of a man and the head of a bull (in some versions, with the body of a bull and head of a man), confined by Minos in a labyrinth built by Daedalus, and annually fed seven youths and seven maidens from Athens, until killed by Theseus: see also PASIPHAË
Minsk (minsk; *Russ.* mēnsk) capital of the Byelorussian S.S.R., in the C part: pop. 717,000
min·ster (min′stər) n. [ME. *mynstre* < OE. *mynster* < LL.(Ec.) *monasterium*, MONASTERY] **1.** the church of a monastery **2.** any of various large churches or cathedrals: often used in compounds [Westminster]
min·strel (min′strəl) n. [ME. *menestrel* < OFr., minstrel, servant, orig., official < LL. *ministerialis*, imperial officer < L. *ministerium*, MINISTRY] **1.** any of a class of lyric poets and singers of the Middle Ages, who traveled from place to place singing and reciting, usually to the accompaniment of a harp or lute **2.** [Poet.] a poet, singer, or musician ☆**3.** a performer in a minstrel show
☆**minstrel show** [< the Christy *Minstrels*, the first such troupe, organized (c. 1842) by Edwin P. Christy at Buffalo, New York] a comic variety show presented by a company of performers in blackface, who sing songs, tell jokes, etc.

min·strel·sy (-sē) n., pl. **-sies** [ME. *menestralcie* < OFr. *menestralsie*] **1.** the art or occupation of a minstrel **2.** a group of minstrels **3.** a collection of minstrels' ballads or songs
mint[1] (mint) n. [ME. *mynt* < OE. *mynet*, coin, akin to OHG. *munizza* < Gmc. **munita* < L. *moneta*, place for coining money < *Moneta*, epithet of Juno, in whose temple at Rome money was coined: cf. MONEY] **1.** a place where money is coined by authority of the government **2.** an apparently unlimited supply; large amount [a *mint* of ideas] **3.** a source of manufacture or invention —adj. new or in its original condition, as if freshly minted [a postage stamp in *mint* condition] —vt. **1.** to coin (money) by stamping metal **2.** to invent or create; fabricate —**mint′er** n.
mint[2] (mint) n. [ME. *mynte* < OE. *minte*, akin to OHG. *minza* < WGmc. **minta* < L. *menta* < or akin to Gr. *mintha*] **1.** any of various aromatic plants of the mint family, esp. any of a genus (*Mentha*) whose leaves are used for flavoring and in medicine **2.** any of various candies flavored with mint —adj. designating a family (Labiatae) of plants with fragrant foliage, volatile oil, and square stems, including spearmint, peppermint, basil, and bergamot
mint·age (min′tij) n. **1.** the act or process of minting money **2.** the act of inventing or making **3.** money produced in a mint **4.** the cost of minting money **5.** the impression made on a coin
mint jelly (or **sauce**) a jelly (or sauce) flavored with mint leaves, served esp. with lamb
☆**mint julep** a frosted drink consisting of whiskey or brandy, sugar, and mint leaves in a tall glass packed with crushed ice
min·u·end (min′yoo wend′) n. [L. *minuendum*, to be diminished, neut. gerundive of *minuere*: see MINUTE[2]] *Arith.* the number or quantity from which another (the subtrahend) is to be subtracted
min·u·et (min′yoo wet′) n. [Fr. *menuet*, orig., minute, tiny < OFr. < *menu* (see MENU): from the small steps taken] **1.** a slow, stately dance for groups of couples, introduced in France in the 17th cent. **2.** the music for this, in 3/4 time: often a movement of certain musical compositions
Min·u·it (min′yoo wit, min′ə-), Peter 1580?–1638; 1st Du. director general of New Netherland (1626–31)
mi·nus (mī′nəs) prep. [LME. < L., less, neut. sing. of *minor*, MINOR] **1.** reduced by the subtraction of; less [four *minus* two] **2.** [Colloq.] without; lacking [minus a toe] —adj. **1.** indicating or involving subtraction [a *minus* sign] **2.** negative [a *minus* quantity] **3.** somewhat less than [a grade of A *minus*] **4.** *Bot.* designating one of two strains of certain fungi and algae which only mate with the opposite (*plus*) strain ☆**5.** *Elec.* same as NEGATIVE —n. **1.** a minus sign **2.** a negative quantity
mi·nus·cule (mi nus′kyool, min′ə skyool′) n. [Fr. < L. *minusculus*, rather small, dim. < *minor*: see MINOR] **1.** a small cursive script developed from the uncial and used in medieval manuscripts **2.** a letter in this script **3.** any small, or lower-case, letter —adj. **1.** of, in, like, or having the nature of, minuscules **2.** very small; tiny; minute Cf. MAJUSCULE —**mi·nus′cu·lar** adj.
minus sign *Math.* a sign (−), indicating subtraction or negative quantity
min·ute[1] (min′it) n. [ME. < OFr. < ML. *minuta* < L. (*pars*) *minuta* (*prima*), (first) small (part), term used by Ptolemy for the sixtieth part of a unit in his system of fractions (of the circle, radius, day, later applied also to the hour): see ff.] **1.** the sixtieth part of any of certain units; specif., a) 1/60 of an hour; sixty seconds b) 1/60 of a degree of an arc; sixty seconds: indicated by the symbol (′) **2.** a very short period of time; moment; instant **3.** a specific point in time **4.** a measure of the distance usually covered in a minute [five *minutes* from downtown] **5.** a note or memorandum; specif., [pl.] an official record of what was said and done at a meeting, convention, etc. —vt. **-ut·ed, -ut·ing 1.** to time to the minute **2.** a) to make a minute, or memorandum, of; record b) to put in the minutes of a meeting, etc. —**the minute (that)** just as soon as —☆**up to the minute** in the latest style, fashion, etc.
mi·nute[2] (mī noot′, mi-; -nyoot′) adj. [ME. < L. *minutus*, little, small, pp. of *minuere*, to lessen, diminish < *minor*: see MINOR] **1.** very small; tiny **2.** of little importance or significance; petty; trifling **3.** of, characterized by, or attentive to tiny details; exact; precise —SYN. see SMALL —**mi·nute′ness** n.
minute gun a cannon firing at intervals of a minute, as a distress signal, or as part of a funeral ceremony
minute hand the longer hand of a clock or watch, which indicates the minutes and moves around the dial once every hour
min·ute·ly[1] (min′it lē) adj. **1.** occurring at intervals of a minute **2.** occurring very often or continually —adv. **1.** every minute **2.** often or continually
mi·nute·ly[2] (mī noot′lē, mi-; -nyoot′-) adv. **1.** in a minute manner or in minute detail **2.** into tiny pieces
☆**min·ute·man** (min′it man′) n., pl. **-men′** (-men′) [also M-] any of the members of the American citizen army at the time of the Revolution who volunteered to be ready for military service at a minute's notice

☆min·ute steak (min′it) a small, thin steak that can be cooked quickly

mi·nu·ti·ae (mi nōō′shi ē′, -nyōō′-) *n.pl., sing.* -ti·a (-shē ə, -shə) [L., pl. of *minutia,* smallness < *minutus,* MINUTE²] small or relatively unimportant details

minx (miŋks) *n.* [Early ModE., first used in sense "puppy" < ?] a pert, saucy girl or young woman

min·yan (min yän′, min′yən) *n., pl.* min′ya·nim′ (-yë nēm′), min′yans [Heb. *minyān,* number, quorum] a properly constituted group for a public Jewish prayer service, made up of at least ten Jewish males over thirteen years of age

Mi·o·cene (mī′ə sēn′) *adj.* [< Gr. *meiōn,* less (see MINOR) + *kainos,* recent] designating of the fourth epoch of the Tertiary Period in the Cenozoic Era, marked by the evolution of many mammals of relatively modern form —the Miocene the Miocene Epoch or its rocks: see GEOLOGY, chart

mi·o·sis (mī ō′sis) *n., pl.* -ses (-sēz) [ModL. < Gr. *myein,* to close + -OSIS] abnormal contraction of the pupil of the eye —mi·ot′ic (-ät′ik) *adj., n.*

Mi·que·lon (mik′ə län′; *Fr.* mē klôn′) island in the Atlantic, off the S coast of Newfoundland: part of the Fr. overseas territory of St. Pierre and Miquelon: 83 sq. mi.; pop. 600

mir (mir) *n.* [Russ., lit., world] in czarist Russia, a village community of peasant farmers

MIr. Middle Irish

Mi·ra·beau (mir′ə bō′; *Fr.* mē rà bō′), comte (Honoré Gabriel Riqueti) de 1749–91; Fr. revolutionist, orator, & statesman

mir·a·belle (mir′ə bel′, mir′ə bel′) *n.* [Fr., altered < L. *myrobalanum,* fruit of a kind of palm tree < Gr. *myrobalanan* < *myron,* unguent, perfume + *balanos,* acorn, date] 1. a European variety of plum tree 2. the sweet, small, golden fruit of this tree 3. a brandy made from these fruits

‡mi·ra·bi·le dic·tu (mə rä′bi lā′ dik′tōō) [L.] wonderful to tell

‡mi·ra·bi·li·a (mir′ə bil′ē ə) *n.pl.* [L.] marvels; miracles

mir·a·cle (mir′ə k′l) *n.* [ME. < OFr. < L. *miraculum,* a strange thing, in LL.(Ec.), miracle < *mirari,* to wonder at < *mirus,* wonderful < IE. base *(s)moi,* to smile, be surprised, whence Sans. *smáyati,* (he) smiles & SMILE] 1. an event or action that apparently contradicts known scientific laws and is hence thought to be due to supernatural causes, esp. to an act of God 2. a remarkable event or thing; marvel 3. a wonderful example [a *miracle* of tact] 4. *same as* MIRACLE PLAY

miracle play any of a class of medieval religious dramas dealing with events in the lives of the saints: cf. MYSTERY PLAY

mi·rac·u·lous (mi rak′yoo ləs) *adj.* [MFr. *miraculeux* < ML. *miraculosus* < L. *miraculum*] 1. having the nature of a miracle; supernatural 2. like a miracle; wonderful; marvelous 3. able to work miracles —mi·rac′u·lous·ly *adv.* —mi·rac′u·lous·ness *n.*

mi·ra·dor (mir′ə dôr′, mir′ə dôr′) *n.* [Sp. < *mirar,* to observe < L. *mirare,* to wonder at, akin to *mirari:* see MIRACLE] a balcony, turret, belvedere, etc. that affords a fine view

mi·rage (mi räzh′) *n.* [Fr. < (se) *mirer,* to be reflected < VL. *mirare,* to look at, for L. *mirari:* see MIRACLE] 1. an optical illusion in which the image of a distant object, as a ship or an oasis, is made to appear nearby, floating in air, inverted, etc.: it is caused by the refraction of light rays from the object through layers of air having different densities as the result of unequal temperature distributions 2. something that falsely appears to be real —SYN. see DELUSION

Mi·ran·da (mə ran′də) [L., fem. of *mirandus,* strange, wonderful < *mirari:* see MIRACLE] a feminine name

mire (mir) *n.* [ME. < ON. *myrr,* akin to OE. *mos,* MOSS] 1. an area of wet, soggy ground; bog 2. deep mud; wet, soggy earth; slush —*vt.* mired, mir′ing 1. to cause to get stuck in or as in mire 2. to soil or splatter with mud or dirt —*vi.* to sink or stick in mud

Mir·i·am (mir′ē əm) [Heb. *miryām*] 1. a feminine name: see MARY 2. *Bible* the sister of Moses and Aaron: Ex. 15:20

mir·i·ness (mir′ē nis) *n.* a miry quality or condition

mirk (murk) *n. alt. sp. of* MURK —mirk′y *adj.* mirk′i·er, mirk′i·est

Mi·ró (mē rō′), Joan (hwän) 1893– ; Sp. painter

mir·ror (mir′ər) *n.* [ME. *mirour* < OFr. *mireor* < VL. *miratorium* < *mirare:* see MIRAGE] 1. a smooth surface that reflects the images of objects; esp., a piece of glass coated on the reverse side as with silver or an amalgam; looking glass 2. anything that gives a true representation or description 3. [Rare] something to be imitated or emulated; model 4. [Archaic] a crystal used by fortunetellers, sorcerers, etc. —*vt.* to reflect, as in a mirror; give or show a likeness of

mirror image an image or view of someone or something as seen in a mirror, i.e., with the right side as though it were the left, and vice versa

mirth (murth) *n.* [ME. *myrthe* < OE. *myrgth,* pleasure, joy < base of *myrig,* pleasant (see MERRY)] joyfulness, gaiety, or merriment, esp. when characterized by laughter *SYN.*—mirth implies gaiety, gladness, or great amusement, esp. as expressed by laughter; glee implies exultant and demonstrative joy or it may suggest malicious delight over another's misfortunes; jollity and merriment imply exuberant mirth or joy and usually suggest convivial merrymaking; hilarity implies boisterous merriment and sometimes suggests an excessively noisy display of high spirits —ANT. sadness, melancholy

mirth·ful (-fəl) *adj.* full of, expressing, or causing mirth; merry —mirth′ful·ly *adv.* —mirth′ful·ness *n.*

mirth·less (-lis) *adj.* without mirth; humorless; sad; melancholy —mirth′less·ly *adv.* —mirth′less·ness *n.*

mir·y (mir′ē) *adj.* mir′i·er, mir′i·est 1. full of, or having the nature of, mire; boggy; swampy 2. covered or spattered with mire; muddy; dirty

mir·za (mir′zä) *n.* [Per. *mīrza,* contr. < *mīrzādah* < *mīr,* prince (< Ar. *amīr,* ruler) + *zād,* born] a Persian title of honor placed after the name of a royal prince or before the name of a high official, scholar, etc.

mis-¹ (mis) [ME. < OE. & OFr.: OE. *mis-,* akin to OHG. *missa,* Goth. *missa-* (for IE. base see MISS¹); OFr. *mes-* < Frank. **missi-,* akin to OHG. *missa-*] a prefix meaning: 1. wrong, wrongly, bad, badly [misplace, misread, misrule] 2. no, not [mistrust, misfire]

mis-² (mis) *same as* MISO-: used before a vowel

mis·ad·ven·ture (mis ad ven′chər) *n.* [ME. *mesaventure* < OFr.: see MIS-¹ & ADVENTURE] an unlucky accident; mishap; bad luck; mischance

mis·ad·vise (-əd vīz′) *vt.* -vised′, -vis′ing to advise badly —mis′ad·vice′ (-vīs′) *n.*

mis·al·li·ance (-ə lī′əns) *n.* [after Fr. *mésalliance*] an improper alliance; esp., an unsuitable marriage

mis·al·ly (-ə lī′) *vt.* -lied′, -ly′ing to ally unsuitably or inappropriately

mis·an·thrope (mis′ən thrōp′, miz′-) *n.* [Gr. *misanthrōpos,* hating mankind < *misein,* to hate + *anthrōpos,* a man] a person who hates or distrusts all people: also mis·an·thro·pist (mis an′thrə pist)

mis·an·throp·ic (mis′ən thräp′ik) *adj.* of or like a misanthrope: also mis′an·throp′i·cal —SYN. see CYNICAL —mis′an·throp′i·cal·ly *adv.*

mis·an·thro·py (mis an′thrə pē) *n.* [Gr. *misanthrōpia*] hatred or distrust of all people

mis·ap·ply (mis′ə plī′) *vt.* -plied′, -ply′ing 1. to use badly, incorrectly, or wastefully [to *misapply* one's energies] 2. to apply or handle dishonestly or illegally [to *misapply* an employer's money] —mis′ap·pli·ca′tion (-ap lə kā′shən) *n.*

mis·ap·pre·hend (-ap rə hend′) *vt.* to fail to apprehend correctly; misunderstand —mis′ap·pre·hen′sion (-hen′shən) *n.*

mis·ap·pro·pri·ate (mis′ə prō′prē āt′) *vt.* -at′ed, -at′ing to appropriate to a bad, incorrect, or dishonest use —mis′ap·pro′pri·a′tion *n.*

mis·ar·range (mis′ə ranj′) *vt.* -ranged′, -rang′ing to arrange wrongly or improperly —mis′ar·range′ment *n.*

mis·be·come (-bi kum′) *vt.* -came′, -come′, -com′ing to be unbecoming to; be unsuitable or unfit for

mis·be·got·ten (-bi gät′′n) *adj.* wrongly or unlawfully begotten; specif., born out of wedlock: also mis′be·got′

mis·be·have (-bi hāv′) *vi.* -haved′, -hav′ing to behave wrongly —*vt.* to conduct (oneself) improperly —mis′-be·hav′er *n.* —mis′be·hav′ior (-yər) *n.*

mis·be·lieve (-bə lēv′) *vi.* -lieved′, -liev′ing [Archaic] to hold unorthodox or heretical beliefs or opinions, esp. in religion —*vt.* rare var. of DISBELIEVE —mis′be·lief′ *n.* —mis′be·liev′er *n.*

mis·brand (mis brand′) *vt.* to brand or label improperly or falsely

misc. 1. miscellaneous 2. miscellany

mis·cal·cu·late (mis kal′kyə lāt′) *vt., vi.* -lat′ed, -lat′ing to calculate incorrectly; miscount or misjudge —mis′-cal·cu·la′tion *n.*

mis·call (-kôl′) *vt.* 1. to call by a wrong name; misname 2. [Obs. or Brit. Dial.] to revile or abuse

mis·car·riage (-kar′ij) *n.* 1. failure to carry out what was intended [a *miscarriage* of justice] 2. failure of mail, freight, etc. to reach its destination 3. the expulsion of a fetus from the womb before it is sufficiently developed to survive: see ABORTION

mis·car·ry (-kar′ē) *vi.* -ried, -ry·ing 1. a) to go wrong; fail: said of a plan, project, etc. b) to go astray; fail to arrive: said of mail, freight, etc. 2. a) to give birth prematurely to a fetus, so that it does not live b) [Obs.] to be born prematurely

mis·cast (-kast′, -käst′) *vt.* -cast′, -cast′ing 1. to cast (an actor) for a role not suited to him 2. to cast (a play) with actors unsuited to their roles

☆mis·ce·ge·na·tion (mis′i jə nā′shən, mi sej′ə-) *n.* [coined (c. 1863) < L. *miscere,* MIX + *genus,* race (see GENUS) + -ATION] marriage or sexual relations between a man and woman of different races, esp., in the U.S., between a white and a Negro

mis·cel·la·ne·a (mis′ ə lā′nē ə, -lān′yə) *n.pl.* [*often with sing. v.*] [L., neut. pl.: see ff.] a miscellaneous collection, esp. of literary works; miscellany

mis·cel·la·ne·ous (-əs, -yəs) *adj.* [L. *miscellaneus < miscellus*, mixed < *miscere*, MIX] **1.** consisting or formed of various kinds; varied; mixed [a box of *miscellaneous* candies] **2.** having various qualities, abilities, etc.; many-sided —**mis′cel·la′ne·ous·ly** *adv.* —**mis′cel·la′ne·ous·ness** *n.*

mis·cel·la·ny (mis′ə lā′nē; *Brit.* mi sel′ə nē) *n.*, *pl.* **-nies** [< Fr. *miscellanées*, pl. < L. *miscellanea*, neut. pl. of *miscellaneus*: see prec.] **1.** a miscellaneous collection, esp. of literary works **2.** [*often pl.*] such a collection of writings, as in a book

mis·chance (mis chans′, -chäns′) *n.* [ME. *mescheance* < OFr. *meschance*: see MIS-[1] & CHANCE] an unlucky accident; bad luck; misadventure

mis·chief (mis′chif) *n.* [ME. *meschief* < OFr. < *meschever*, to come to grief < *mes-* (see MIS-[1]) + *chief*, end, head (see CHIEF)] **1.** harm, damage, or injury, esp. that done by a person **2.** a cause or source of harm, damage, or annoyance; specif., *a*) action or conduct that causes damage or trouble *b*) a person causing damage or annoyance **3.** a tendency or disposition to annoy or vex with playful tricks **4.** *a*) a troublesome or annoying act; prank; playful, vexing trick *b*) playful, harmless spirits; gay teasing

mis·chief-mak·er (-mā′kər) *n.* a person who causes mischief; esp., one who creates trouble by gossiping or talebearing —**mis′chief-mak′ing** *n.*, *adj.*

mis·chie·vous (mis′chi vəs) *adj.* [ME. *mischevous* < Anglo-Fr.] **1.** causing mischief; specif., *a*) injurious; harmful *b*) prankish; teasing; full of tricks **2.** inclined to annoy or vex with playful tricks; naughty: said esp. of a child —**mis′chie·vous·ly** *adv.* —**mis′chie·vous·ness** *n.*

mis·ci·ble (mis′ə b'l) *adj.* [ML. *miscibilis* < L. *miscere*, to MIX] that can be mixed —**mis′ci·bil′i·ty** *n.*

mis·col·or (mis kul′ər) *vt.* **1.** to give a wrong color to **2.** to give a false account of; misrepresent

mis·con·ceive (mis′kən sēv′) *vt.*, *vi.* **-ceived′**, **-ceiv′ing** to conceive wrongly; interpret incorrectly; misunderstand —**mis′con·cep′tion** (-sep′shən) *n.*

mis·con·duct (mis kän′dukt; *for n.* mis kän′dukt) *vt.* **1.** to manage badly or dishonestly **2.** to conduct (oneself) improperly —*n.* **1.** unlawful, bad, or dishonest management, esp. by a governmental or military official; specif., malfeasance **2.** willfully improper behavior

mis·con·strue (-kən strōō′) *vt.* **-strued′**, **-stru′ing** to construe wrongly; misinterpret; misunderstand —**mis′con·struc′tion** (-struk′shən) *n.*

mis·count (mis kount′; & *for n.*, usually mis′kount) *vt.*, *vi.* to count incorrectly; miscalculate —*n.* an incorrect count, as of votes in an election

mis·cre·ant (mis′krē ənt) *adj.* [ME. < OFr., unbelieving < *mes-* (see MIS-[1]) + *creant*, prp. of *croire*, to believe < L. *credere*: see CREED] **1.** villainous; evil **2.** [Archaic] unbelieving or heretical —*n.* **1.** an evil person; criminal; villain **2.** [Archaic] an unbeliever or heretic —**mis′cre·an·cy** *n.*

mis·cre·ate (mis′krē āt′) *vt.*, *vi.* **-at′ed**, **-at′ing** to create amiss; form badly —*adj.* [Archaic] same as MISCREATED —**mis′cre·a′tion** *n.*

mis·cre·at·ed (-id) *adj.* improperly formed; misshapen

mis·cue (mis kyōō′) *n.* **1.** *Billiards* a shot spoiled by the cue's slipping off the ball **2.** [Colloq.] a mistake; error —*vi.* **-cued′**, **-cu′ing 1.** to make a miscue **2.** *Theater* to miss one's cue or answer the wrong cue

mis·date (-dāt′) *vt.* **-dat′ed**, **-dat′ing** to put a wrong date on (a document, letter, etc.) or assign a wrong date to (an event); date incorrectly —*n.* a wrong date

mis·deal (-dēl′) *vt.*, *vi.* **-dealt′**, **-deal′ing** to deal (playing cards) wrongly —*n.* a wrong deal —**mis′deal′er** *n.*

mis·deed (mis dēd′) *n.* a wrong or wicked act; crime, sin, etc.

mis·de·mean (mis′di mēn′) *vt.*, *vi.* [MIS-[1] + DEMEAN[1]] [Rare] to conduct (oneself) badly; misbehave

mis·de·mean·ant (-ənt) *n.* **1.** a person who has misbehaved **2.** *Law* a person guilty or convicted of a misdemeanor

mis·de·mean·or (-ər) *n.* [MIS-[1] + DEMEANOR] **1.** [Rare] the act of misbehaving **2.** *Law* any minor offense, as the breaking of a municipal ordinance, for which statute provides a lesser punishment than for a felony: the penalty is usually a fine or imprisonment for a short time (usually less than one year) in a local jail, workhouse, etc. Brit. sp. **mis′de·mean′our**

mis·di·rect (mis′di rekt′, -dī-) *vt.* to direct wrongly or badly; specif., *a*) to aim (a blow, etc.) badly *b*) to address (a letter) incorrectly *c*) to give incorrect instructions to, esp. as a judge to a jury —**mis′di·rec′tion** (-rek′shən) *n.*

mis·do (mis dōō′) *vt.* **-did′**, **-done′**, **-do′ing** [ME. *misdoen* < OE. *misdon*: see MIS-[1] & DO[1]] to do wrongly —*vi.* [Obs.] to do evil —**mis·do′er** *n.* —**mis·do′ing** *n.*

mis·doubt (-dout′) *vt.* [Archaic] **1.** to have doubt or suspicion about; distrust **2.** to fear —*vi.* [Archaic] to have doubts —*n.* [Archaic] suspicion; doubt

mise (mēz, miz) *n.* [LME. < Anglo-Fr. < OFr., a putting, placing (of expenses, etc.) < *mis*, pp. of *mettre*, to put, lay < L. *mittere*, to send: see MISSION] **1.** orig., an agreement or pact **2.** *Law* the issue in a writ of right

mis·ease (mis ēz′) *n.* [ME. *misese* < OFr. *mesaise*: see MIS-[1] & EASE] **1.** [Archaic] discomfort; distress **2.** [Obs.] poverty

‡**mise en scène** (mē zän sen′) [Fr.] **1.** the staging of a play, including the setting, arrangement of the actors, etc. **2.** general surroundings; environment

mis·em·ploy (mis′em ploi′) *vt.* to employ, or use, wrongly or badly; misuse —**mis′em·ploy′ment** *n.*

mi·ser (mī′zər) *n.* [L., wretched, unhappy, ill, worthless] **1.** a greedy, stingy person who hoards money for its own sake, even at the expense of his own comfort **2.** [Obs.] a miserable person; wretch

mis·er·a·ble (miz′ər ə b'l, miz′rə-) *adj.* [Fr. *misérable* < L. *miserabilis*, pitiable < *miserari*, to pity < *miser*, wretched] **1.** in a condition of misery; wretched, unhappy, suffering, etc. **2.** causing misery, discomfort, or suffering [*miserable* weather] **3.** bad; inferior; inadequate [a *miserable* performance] **4.** pitiable **5.** shameful; disgraceful —*n.* [Obs.] a miserable person —**mis′er·a·ble·ness** *n.* —**mis′er·a·bly** *adv.*

Mis·e·re·re (miz′ə rer′ē, -rir′-) *n.* [ME. < LL.(Ec.), have mercy (imper. of L. *misereri*, to feel pity < *miser*, wretched): first word of the psalm in the Vulgate] **1.** the 51st Psalm of the Bible (50th in the Douay Version), beginning, "Have mercy upon me, O God" **2.** a musical setting for this **3.** [m-] *same as* MISERICORD, sense 2

mis·er·i·cord, mis·er·i·corde (miz′ər i kôrd′, mi zer′ə kôrd′) *n.* [ME. *misericorde* < OFr. < L. *misericordia* < *misericors*, merciful < base of *misereri* (see prec.) + *cors*, HEART] **1.** formerly *a*) a relaxation of the strict observance of a rule or rules in a monastery *b*) a dining room in a monastery set aside for those who had received such relaxation from fasting **2.** a narrow ledge on the underside of a hinged seat, as in a choir stall, which, when the seat is turned up, furnishes support to one while standing **3.** a slender dagger used in the Middle Ages for giving the death stroke (*coup de grâce*) to a wounded knight

mi·ser·ly (mī′zər lē) *adj.* like or characteristic of a miser; greedy and stingy —*SYN.* see STINGY[1] —**mī′ser·li·ness** *n.*

mis·er·y (miz′ər ē) *n.*, *pl.* **-er·ies** [ME. *miserie* < OFr. < L. *miseria* < *miser*, wretched] **1.** a condition of great wretchedness or suffering, because of pain, sorrow, poverty, etc.; distress **2.** a cause of such suffering; pain, sorrow, poverty, squalor, etc. **3.** [Dial.] a pain (*in* some part of the body)

mis·es·teem (mis′ə stēm′) *vt.* to fail to have the proper esteem for —*n.* a lack of proper esteem

mis·es·ti·mate (mis es′tə māt′; *for n.* -mit) *vt.* **-mat′ed**, **-mat′ing** to estimate incorrectly —*n.* an incorrect estimate —**mis·es′ti·ma′tion** *n.*

mis·fea·sance (-fē′z'ns) *n.* [OFr. *mesfaisance* < *mesfaire*, to misdo: see MIS-[1] & FEASANCE] *Law* wrongdoing; specif., the doing of a lawful act in an unlawful or improper manner, so that there is an infringement on the rights of another or others: distinguished from MALFEASANCE, NONFEASANCE —**mis·fea′sor** (-zər) *n.*

mis·file (-fīl′) *vt.* **-filed′**, **-fil′ing** to file (papers, etc.) in the wrong place or order

mis·fire (mis fīr′) *vi.* **-fired′**, **-fir′ing** [MIS-[1] + FIRE, *v.*] **1.** to fail to ignite properly or at the right time: said of an internal-combustion engine **2.** to fail to go off, or be discharged: said of a firearm, missile, etc. **3.** to fail to achieve a desired effect —*n.* an act or instance of misfiring

mis·fit (mis fit′; *for n. also, & for 3 always*, mis′fit′) *vt.*, *vi.* **-fit′ted**, **-fit′ting** to fit badly —*n.* **1.** the act or condition of misfitting **2.** anything that misfits, as a badly fitting garment **3.** a person not suited to his position, associates, etc.; maladjusted person

mis·for·tune (mis fôr′chən) *n.* **1.** bad luck; ill fortune; trouble; adversity **2.** an instance of this; unlucky accident; mishap; mischance —*SYN.* see AFFLICTION

mis·give (-giv′) *vt.* **-gave′**, **-giv′en**, **-giv′ing** [MIS-[1] + GIVE] to cause fear, doubt, or suspicion in: said usually of the heart, mind, conscience, etc. [his heart *misgave* him] —*vi.* to feel fear, doubt, suspicion, etc.

mis·giv·ing (-giv′iŋ) *n.* [see prec.] [*often pl.*] a disturbed feeling of fear, doubt, apprehension, etc. —*SYN.* see QUALM

mis·gov·ern (-guv′ərn) *vt.* to govern, administer, or manage badly —**mis·gov′ern·ment** *n.*

mis·guide (-gīd′) *vt.* **-guid′ed**, **-guid′ing** to guide wrongly; lead into error or misconduct; mislead —**mis·guid′ance** *n.* —**mis·guid′ed·ly** *adv.* —**mis·guid′ed·ness** *n.* —**mis·guid′er** *n.*

mis·han·dle (mis han′d'l) *vt.* **-dled**, **-dling** to handle badly or roughly; abuse, maltreat, or mismanage

mi·shan·ter (mi shan′tər) *n.* [altered < MISADVENTURE] [Scot.] mishap; misadventure

mis·hap (mis′hap) *n.* [ME. (see MIS-[1] & HAP[1], prob. after OFr. *meschance*, mischance] **1.** an unlucky or unfortunate accident **2.** [Now Rare] bad luck; misfortune

Mish·a·wa·ka (mish′ə wô′kə) [name of an Indian village there < ?] city in N Ind., near South Bend: pop. 36,000

mis·hear (mis hir′) *vt.*, *vi.* **-heard′**, **-hear′ing** to hear incorrectly or poorly

mish·mash (mish′mash′, -mäsh′) *n.* [redupl. of MASH (parallel with G. *mischmasch*, LowG. *miskmask*)] a hodgepodge; jumble: also **mish′mosh′** (-mäsh′)

Mish·na, Mish·nah (mish nä′, mish′nə) *n.*, *pl.* **Mish·na-**

yot (mish'nä yōt') [ModHeb. *mishnāh*, (oral) instruction < Heb. *shānāh*, to repeat, (later) to learn, teach] **1.** the first part of the Talmud, containing traditional oral interpretations of scriptural ordinances (*halakhot*), compiled by the rabbis about 200 A.D. **2.** any of these interpretations **3.** the teachings of a distinguished rabbi —**Mish·na'ic** *adj.*

mis·in·form (mis'in fôrm') *vt.* to supply with false or misleading information —**mis'in·form'ant, mis'in·form'er** *n.* —**mis'in·for·ma'tion** *n.*

mis·in·ter·pret (-in tur'prit) *vt.* to interpret wrongly; understand or explain incorrectly —**mis'in·ter'pre·ta'tion** *n.* —**mis'in·ter'pre·ter** *n.*

mis·join·der (-join'dər) *n. Law* the improper joining together of parties or of different causes of action in one lawsuit or other legal proceeding

mis·judge (-juj') *vt., vi.* **-judged', -judg'ing** to judge wrongly or unfairly —**mis·judg'ment, mis·judge'ment** *n.*

Mis·kolc (mish'kōlts) city in NE Hungary: pop. 180,000

mis·la·bel (mis lā'b'l) *vt., vi.* **-beled or -belled, -bel·ing or -bel·ling** to label incorrectly or improperly

mis·lay (-lā') *vt.* **-laid', -lay'ing** [see MIS-[1] & LAY[1], v.] **1.** to put in a place afterward forgotten or not easily found **2.** to put down or install improperly [to *mislay* floor tiles]

mis·lead (-lēd') *vt.* **-led', -lead'ing 1.** to lead in a wrong direction; lead astray **2.** to lead into error (of judgment); deceive or delude **3.** to lead into wrongdoing; influence badly —*SYN.* see DECEIVE —**mis·lead'ing** *adj.* —**mis·lead'ing·ly** *adv.*

mis·like (mis līk') *vt.* **-liked', -lik'ing 1.** [Archaic] *same as* DISPLEASE **2.** [Now Rare] to be displeased at; dislike —*n.* [Now Rare] dislike; disapproval

mis·man·age (-man'ij) *vt., vi.* **-aged', -ag·ing** to manage or administer badly or dishonestly —**mis·man'age·ment** *n.*

mis·match (mis mach') *vt.* to match badly or unsuitably —*n.* a bad or unsuitable match

mis·mate (mis māt') *vt., vi.* **-mat'ed, -mat'ing** to mate badly or unsuitably

mis·name (-nām') *vt.* **-named', -nam'ing** to give or apply an inappropriate name to

mis·no·mer (mis nō'mər) *n.* [ME. *misnoumer* < OFr. *mesnoumer*, inf. used as n. < *mes-*, MIS-[1] + *nommer*, to name < L. *nominare*. see NOMINATE] **1.** *a*) the act of applying a wrong name or epithet to some person or thing *b*) such a name or epithet **2.** an error in naming a person or place in a legal document

mis·o- (mis'ō, -ə) [Gr. *misos* < *misein*, to hate] *a combining form meaning* hatred or hating [*misogyny*]

mi·sog·a·my (mi säg'ə mē) *n.* [MISO- + -GAMY] hatred of marriage —**mi·sog'a·mist** *n.*

mi·sog·y·ny (mi säj'ə nē) *n.* [Gr. *misogynia*: see MISO- & -GYNY] hatred of women, esp. by a man —**mi·sog'y·nist** *n.* —**mi·sog'y·nous, mi·sog'y·nic** *adj.*

mi·sol·o·gy (mi säl'ə jē) *n.* [Gr. *misologia*: see MISO- & -LOGY] hatred of argument, debate, or reasoning —**mi·sol'o·gist** *n.*

mis·o·ne·ism (mis'ō nē'iz'm) *n.* [It. *misoneismo* < Gr. *miso-*, MISO- + *neos*, NEW + It. *-ismo*, -ISM] hatred of innovation or change —**mis'o·ne'ist** *n.*

mis·per·ceive (mis'pər sēv') *vt.* **-ceived', -ceiv'ing** to perceive incorrectly —**mis'per·cep'tion** *n.*

mis·place (mis plās') *vt.* **-placed', -plac'ing 1.** to put in a wrong place **2.** to bestow (one's trust, affection, etc.) on an unsuitable or undeserving object **3.** *same as* MISLAY (sense 1) —**mis·place'ment** *n.*

mis·play (mis plā') *vt., vi.* to play wrongly or badly, as in games or sports —☆*n.* a wrong or bad play

mis·plead (-plēd') *vt., vi.* **-pled', -plead'ing** to plead incorrectly

mis·plead·ing (-iŋ) *n. Law* an incorrect statement or an omission in pleading, as a misstatement of a cause of action

mis·print (mis print'; *for n., usually* mis'print') *vt.* to print incorrectly —*n.* an error in printing

mis·pri·sion (mis prizh'ən) *n.* [ME. *mesprision* < OFr. < pp. of *mesprendre*, to take wrongly < *mes-*, MIS-[1] + *prendre* < L. *prehendere*, to take: see PREHENSILE] **1.** *Law a*) misconduct or neglect of duty, esp. by a public official *b*) act of contempt against a government or court **2.** [Archaic] a mistake

misprision of felony (or **treason**) *Law* the offense of concealing knowledge of a felony (or treason) by one who has not participated or assisted in it

mis·prize (mis prīz') *vt.* **-prized', -priz'ing** [ME. *mesprisen* < OFr. *mesprisier* < *mes-*, MIS-[1] + *prisier* < LL. *pretiare*, to value < L. *pretium*, a PRICE] to despise or undervalue

mis·pro·nounce (mis'prə nouns') *vt., vi.* **-nounced', -nounc'ing** to give (a word or words) a pronunciation different from any of the accepted standard pronunciations; pronounce incorrectly —**mis'pro·nun'ci·a'tion** (-nun'sē ā'shən) *n.*

mis·quote (mis kwōt') *vt., vi.* **-quot'ed, -quot'ing** to quote incorrectly —**mis'quo·ta'tion** *n.*

mis·read (-rēd') *vt., vi.* **-read'** (-red'), **-read'ing** (-rēd'iŋ) to read wrongly, esp. so as to misinterpret or misunderstand

mis·reck·on (-rek'ən) *vt.* to reckon or calculate incorrectly

mis·re·mem·ber (mis'ri mem'bər) *vt., vi.* **1.** to make an error in remembering **2.** [Dial.] to forget

mis·re·port (-ri pôrt') *vt.* to report incorrectly or falsely —*n.* an incorrect or false report

mis·rep·re·sent (mis'rep ri zent') *vt.* **1.** to represent falsely; give an untrue or misleading idea of **2.** to be an improper or bad representative of —**mis'rep·re·sen·ta'tion** *n.*

mis·rule (mis rōōl') *vt.* **-ruled', -rul'ing** to rule badly or unjustly; misgovern —*n.* **1.** misgovernment **2.** disorder or riot

miss¹ (mis) *vt.* [ME. *missen* < OE. *missan*, akin to G. *missen* < IE. base *meit(h)-*, to change, exchange, whence L. *mutare*, to change] **1.** to fail to hit or land on (something aimed at) **2.** to fail to meet, reach, attain, catch, accomplish, see, hear, perceive, understand, etc. **3.** to overlook; let (an opportunity, etc.) go by **4.** to escape; avoid [he just *missed* being struck] **5.** to fail or forget to do, keep, have, be present at, etc. [to *miss* an appointment] **6.** to notice the absence or loss of [to suddenly *miss* one's wallet] **7.** to feel or regret the absence or loss of; want [to *miss* one's friends] —*vi.* **1.** to fail to hit something aimed at; go wide of the mark **2.** to fail to be successful **3.** to misfire, as an engine **4.** [Archaic] to fail to obtain, receive, etc. (with *of* or *in*) —*n.* a failure to hit, meet, obtain, see, etc. —**a miss is as good as a mile** missing by a narrow margin is as conclusive as missing by a wide one

miss² (mis) *n., pl.* **miss'es** [contr. of MISTRESS] **1.** [M-] *a*) a title used in speaking to or of an unmarried woman or girl, placed before the name [*Miss* Smith, the *Misses* Smith] *b*) a title used in speaking to an unmarried woman or girl, used without the name ☆*c*) a title given to a girl winning a particular beauty contest or promoting a particular product [*Miss* Ohio, *Miss* Cotton] **2.** a young unmarried woman or girl **3.** [*pl.*] a series of sizes in clothing for women and girls of average proportions [coats in *misses*' sizes]

Miss. Mississippi

miss. 1. mission **2.** missionary

‡**mis·sa can·ta·ta** (mis'ä kän tä'tä, mē'sä) [L.] *same as* SUNG MASS

mis·sal (mis'l) *n.* [ME. *missale* < ML. (Ec.) neut. of *missalis*, of Mass < LL.(Ec.) *missa*, MASS] **1.** *R.C.Ch.* the official, liturgical book of the Roman rite containing all the prayers, rites, etc. used by a priest in celebrating the Mass throughout the year **2.** any of various forms of the missal prepared for use at Mass by the laity

mis·say (mis sā') *vt., vi.* **-said', -say'ing** [Chiefly Archaic] **1.** to say or speak wrongly **2.** to speak evil (of); vilify; abuse; slander

mis·shape (mis shāp') *vt.* **-shaped', -shaped' or archaic -shap'en, -shap'ing** [ME. *mysshapen*: see MIS-[1] & SHAPE] to shape badly; deform

mis·shap·en (-'n) *adj.* [ME.: see prec.] badly shaped; deformed —**mis·shap'en·ly** *adv.* —**mis·shap'en·ness** *n.*

mis·sile (mis'l) *adj.* [L. *missilis* < *missus*, pp. of *mittere*, to send: see MISSION] **1.** that can be, or is, thrown or shot, as from a gun **2.** [Rare] throwing or shooting missiles —*n.* a weapon or other object, as a spear, bullet, rocket, etc. designed to be thrown, fired, or launched toward a target; often, specif., a guided missile

☆**mis·sile·man** (-mən) *n., pl.* **-men** (-mən) one who builds or launches guided missiles: also **mis'sil·eer'** (-ir')

mis·sile·ry, mis·sil·ry (-rē) *n.* [cf. -RY] **1.** the science of building and launching guided missiles **2.** guided missiles collectively

miss·ing (mis'iŋ) *adj.* absent; lost; lacking; specif., absent after combat, but not definitely known to be dead or taken prisoner

missing link something necessary for completing a series; specif., a hypothetical form of animal believed to have existed in the evolutionary process intermediate between the anthropoid apes and man

mis·sion (mish'ən) *n.* [L. *missio*, a sending, sending away < *missus*, pp. of *mittere*, to send < IE. base *smeit-*, to throw, whence Avestan *hamista-*, cast down] **1.** a sending out or being sent out with authority to perform a special duty; specif., *a*) the sending out of persons by a religious organization to preach, teach, and proselytize *b*) the sending out of persons to a foreign government to conduct negotiations *c*) the work done by such persons **2.** *a*) a group of persons sent by a church to spread its religion, esp. in a foreign land *b*) its organization, headquarters, or place of residency *c*) [*pl.*] organized missionary work, esp. for spreading Christianity **3.** a group of persons sent to a foreign government to conduct negotiations; diplomatic delegation; embassy **4.** a group of technicians; specialists, etc. sent to a foreign country **5.** the special duty or function for which someone is sent as a messenger or representative; errand **6.** the special task or purpose for which a person is apparently destined in life; calling **7.** any charitable, educational, or religious organization for doing welfare work for the needy of a city or district **8.** a series of special religious exercises, sermons, etc. for proselytizing **9.** a district without a church of its own, served by the pastor or priest of a nearby parish **10.** *Mil.* a specific

combat operation assigned to an individual or unit; esp., a single combat flight by an airplane or group of airplanes —*adj.* **1.** of a mission or missions ☆**2.** of or in the style of the early Spanish missions in the SW U.S.; specif., designating a type of heavy, dark furniture with simple, square lines —*vt.* **1.** to send on a mission **2.** to establish a religious mission in (a district) or among (a people)

mis·sion·ar·y (-er′ē) *adj.* [ModL. (Ec.) *missionarius*] of or characteristic of religious missions or missionaries —*n., pl.* **-ar′ies** a person sent on a mission; specif., a person sent out by his church to preach, teach, and proselytize, as in a foreign country considered heathen: also **mis′sion·er** (-ər)

Missionary Ridge [after the Brainerd *Mission* there] ridge in Tenn. & Ga.: site of a Civil War battle

mis·sion·ize (-īz′) *vi., vt.* **-ized′, -iz′ing** to carry on missionary work (among); proselytize

mis·sis (mis′əz) *n.* [altered < MISTRESS, MRS.] [Colloq. or Dial.] **1.** one's wife: also used with *the* **2.** the mistress of a household (with *the*)

Mis·sis·sip·pi (mis′ə sip′ē) [< Fr. < Algonquian, lit., big river] **1.** river in C U.S., flowing from N Minn. south into the Gulf of Mexico: 2,348 mi.: cf. MISSOURI **2.** Southern State of the U.S., on the Gulf of Mexico: admitted, 1817; 47,716 sq. mi.; pop. 2,217,000; cap. Jackson: abbrev. **Miss., MS**

☆**Mis·sis·sip·pi·an** (-ən) *adj.* **1.** of the Mississippi River **2.** of the State of Mississippi **3.** designating or of the first coal-forming period of the Paleozoic Era in N. America, following the Devonian and preceding the Pennsylvanian —*n.* a native or inhabitant of Mississippi —**the Mississippian** the Mississippian Period or its rocks: see GEOLOGY, chart

mis·sive (mis′iv) *n.* [Fr. (*lettre*) *missive* < ML. *missivus* < L. *missus*, pp. of *mittere*, to send: see MISSION] a letter or written message

Mis·sour·i¹ (mi zoor′ē) *n.* [< Algonquian, lit., people of the big canoes] **1.** *pl.* **-ris, -ri** any member of a tribe of Indians who formerly lived on the Missouri River in N. Dakota and later in Nebraska **2.** their Siouan language

Mis·sour·i² (mi zoor′ē, -ə) [< prec.] **1.** river in WC U.S., flowing from NW Mont. southeast into the Mississippi: 2,466 mi.: length from its headwaters to the Gulf of Mexico, 3,860 mi. **2.** Middle Western State of the C U.S.: admitted, 1821; 69,686 sq. mi.; pop. 4,677,000; cap. Jefferson City: abbrev. **Mo., MO** —**from Missouri** [Colloq.] not easily convinced; skeptical until shown definite proof —**Mis·sour′i·an** *adj., n.*

mis·speak (mis spēk′) *vt., vi.* **-spoke′, -spok′en, -speak′ing** to speak or say incorrectly

mis·spell (-spel′) *vt., vi.* **-spelled′ or -spelt′, -spell′ing** to spell incorrectly

mis·spell·ing (-spel′iŋ) *n.* (an) incorrect spelling

mis·spend (-spend′) *vt.* **-spent′, -spend′ing** to spend improperly or wastefully

mis·state (-stāt′) *vt.* **-stat′ed, -stat′ing** to state incorrectly or falsely —**mis·state′ment** *n.*

☆**mis·step** (mis step′) *n.* **1.** a wrong or awkward step **2.** a mistake in conduct; faux pas

mis·sus (mis′əz) *n.* [Colloq. or Dial.] same as MISSIS

miss·y (mis′ē) *n., pl.* **miss′ies** [Colloq.] miss: diminutive form, used in speaking to or of a young girl

mist (mist) *n.* [ME. < OE., darkness, mist, akin to ON. *mistr*, dark weather < IE. base **meigh-*, to blink, be dim, whence Sans. **mēghá-*, cloud] **1.** a large mass of water vapor at or just above the earth's surface and like a fog, but less dense **2.** a thin film of moisture condensed on a surface in droplets **3.** *a)* a cloud of dust, smoke, gas, etc. *b)* a fine spray, as of medication or perfume **4.** a cloudiness or film before the eyes, dimming or blurring the vision [through a *mist* of tears] **5.** anything that dims or obscures the understanding, memory, etc. —*vt., vi.* to be, become, or make misty; dim or obscure with or as with a mist

SYN.—mist applies to a visible atmospheric vapor of rather fine density, that blurs the vision; **haze** suggests a thin dispersion of smoke, dust, etc. that makes objects indistinct; **fog** suggests a greater density of moisture particles than mist, sometimes suggesting a thickness impenetrable by the vision; **smog** is applied to a mixture of fog and smoke of a kind that sometimes appears in industrial centers The first three terms are also used figuratively [lost in the *mists* of the past, a mellow *haze* of intoxication, in a *fog* of doubt]

mis·take (mi stāk′) *vt.* **-took′, -tak′en** or obs. **-took′, -tak′ing** [ME. *mistaken* < ON. *mistaka*, to take wrongly: see MIS-¹ & TAKE] **1.** to understand or perceive wrongly; interpret or judge incorrectly [to *mistake* someone's motives] **2.** to take (someone or something) to be another; recognize or identify incorrectly [to *mistake* one twin for the other] —*vi.* to make a mistake —*n.* **1.** a fault in understanding, perception, interpretation, etc. **2.** an idea, answer, act, etc. that is wrong; blunder; error —*SYN.* see ERROR —**and no mistake** [Colloq.] without doubt; certainly —**mis·tak′a·ble** *adj.*

mis·tak·en (-tāk′'n) *adj.* **1.** wrong; having an incorrect understanding, perception, interpretation, etc.: said of persons **2.** incorrect; misunderstood; erroneous: said of ideas, etc. —**mis·tak′en·ly** *adv.*

Mis·tas·si·ni (mis′tə sē′nē) lake in C Quebec, Canada: 840 sq. mi.

mis·ter (mis′tər) *n.* [weakened form of MASTER] **1.** [M-]

a) a title used in speaking to or of a man, placed before the name or title of office and usually written *Mr.* ☆*b)* a title before a name of a place, occupation, activity, etc. to designate a certain man as eminently representative of a group [*Mr.* Television] ☆**2.** *Mil.* the official title of address for *a)* a warrant officer in the army *b)* a cadet in a U.S. service academy *c)* a naval officer below the rank of commander **3.** [Colloq.] sir: in direct address, not followed by a name **4.** [Colloq. or Dial.] one's husband: also used with *the*

☆**mist·flow·er** (mist′flou′ər) *n.* a perennial E American plant (*Eupatorium coelestinum*) of the composite family, with small, purple-flowered heads lacking ray flowers

mis·think (mis thiŋk′) *vi.* **-thought′, -think′ing** [Archaic] to think mistakenly —*vt.* [Archaic] to have a bad opinion of

Misti same as EL MISTI

mis·time (mis tīm′) *vt.* **-timed′, -tim′ing** **1.** to time wrongly; do or say at an inappropriate time **2.** to judge incorrectly the time of

mis·tle thrush (mis′'l) a variety of large, brown European thrush (*Turdus viscivorus*) with blackish-brown spots on the breast, that feeds on mistletoe berries

mis·tle·toe (mis′'l tō′) *n.* [OE. *misteltan* (akin to ON. *mistilteinn*) < *mistel*, mistletoe (prob. < Gmc. *mista, dung: from being propagated by seeds in bird dung) + *tan*, a twig] **1.** any of various evergreen plants (genera *Phoradendron* and *Viscum*) of a family (Loranthaceae) parasitic on deciduous or evergreen trees, with small, yellowish-green leaves, yellowish flowers, and waxy white, poisonous berries **2.** a sprig of such a plant, hung as a Christmas decoration: men are by custom privileged to kiss women standing under it

mis·took (mi stook′) *pt. & obs. pp.* of MISTAKE

mis·tral (mis′trəl, mis trāl′) *n.* [Fr. < Pr., lit., master-wind < L. *magistralis* < *magister*, MASTER] a cold, dry north wind that blows over the Mediterranean coast of France and nearby regions

Mis·tral (mē strāl′) **1.** Fré·dé·ric (frā dā rēk′), 1830–1914; Fr. Provençal poet **2.** Ga·bri·e·la (gä brē e′lä), (pseud. of *Lucila Godoy Alcayaga*) 1889–1957; Chilean poet

mis·trans·late (mis trans′lāt, -tranz′-) *vt.* **-lat·ed, -lat·ing** to translate incorrectly —**mis′trans·la′tion** *n.*

mis·treat (mis trēt′) *vt.* to treat wrongly or badly —**mis·treat′ment** *n.*

mis·tress (mis′tris) *n.* [ME. *maistresse* < OFr., fem. of *maistre*, MASTER] **1.** a woman who rules others or has control, authority, or power over something; specif., *a)* a woman who is head of a household or institution *b)* a woman in relation to an animal or slave that she owns *c)* [Chiefly Brit.] a woman schoolteacher **2.** a woman very skilled and able in some art, science, etc. **3.** [sometimes M-] something regarded as feminine that has control, power, etc. [England was *Mistress* of the seas] **4.** a woman who has sexual intercourse with and, often, is supported by a man for a period of time without being married to him; paramour **5.** [Archaic or Poet.] a sweetheart **6.** [M-] formerly, a title used in speaking to or of a woman, prefixed to the name: now replaced by *Mrs.* or *Miss*

mis·tri·al (mis trī′əl) *n.* *Law* a trial made void because of *a)* a prejudicial error in the proceedings or lack of jurisdiction by the court ☆*b)* the inability of the jury to agree upon a verdict

mis·trust (-trust′) *n.* lack of trust or confidence; suspicion; doubt —*vt., vi.* to have no trust or confidence in (someone or something); doubt —**mis·trust′ful** *adj.*

mist·y (mis′tē) *adj.* **mist′i·er, mist′i·est** [ME. *misti* < OE. *mistig*] **1.** of, or having the nature of, mist **2.** characterized by or covered with mist **3.** *a)* blurred or dimmed, as by mist; indistinct *b)* obscure or vague —**mist′i·ly** *adv.* —**mist′i·ness** *n.*

mis·un·der·stand (mis′un dər stand′, mis un′-) *vt.* **-stood′, -stand′ing** to fail to understand correctly; miscomprehend or misinterpret

mis·un·der·stand·ing (-stan′diŋ) *n.* **1.** a failure to understand; mistake of meaning or intention **2.** a quarrel or disagreement

mis·un·der·stood (-stood′) *adj.* **1.** not properly understood **2.** not properly appreciated

mis·us·age (mis yoō′sij, -zij) *n.* **1.** incorrect usage; misapplication, as of words **2.** bad or harsh treatment

mis·use (mis yoōz′; *for n.,* -yoōs′) *vt.* **-used′, -us′ing** **1.** to use incorrectly or improperly; misapply **2.** to treat badly or harshly; abuse —*n.* **1.** incorrect or improper use **2.** [Obs.] bad or harsh treatment

mis·us·er (-yoō′zər) *n.* **1.** a person who misuses **2.** *Law* abuse of some privilege, right, benefit, etc.

mis·val·ue (-val′yoō) *vt.* **-ued, -u·ing** to fail to value properly or adequately

mis·word (-wurd′) *vt.* to word incorrectly

mis·write (-rīt′) *vt.* **-wrote′, -writ′ten, -writ′ing** to write incorrectly

Mitch·ell (mich′əl) **1.** Maria, 1818–89; U.S. astronomer **2.** William, 1879–1936; U.S. army officer & aviation pioneer

Mitchell, Mount [after Elisha *Mitchell* (1793–1857)] mountain of the Black Mountains, W N.C.: highest peak of the E U.S.: 6,684 ft.

mite¹ (mīt) *n.* [ME. < OE., akin to OHG. *miza*, a gnat < IE. base **mai-*, to cut, cut off, whence MAD] any of a large number of tiny, sometimes microscopic, arachnids (order Acarina), often parasitic upon animals, insects, or plants,

or infesting prepared foods, and including many species that transmit diseases

mite² (mīt) *n*. [ME. < MDu., ult. same as prec.] **1.** *a)* a very small sum of money or contribution: see WIDOW'S MITE *b)* formerly a coin of very small value **2.** *same as* BIT² (*n*. 1 *b*) **3.** a very small creature or object

mi·ter¹ (mīt′ər) *n*. [ME. *mitre* < OFr. < L. *mitra* < Gr. *mitra*, a belt, fillet, headband, turban] **1.** a headdress; specif., *a)* a tall, ornamented cap with peaks in front and back, worn by the Pope, bishops, and abbots as a mark of office *b)* the official headdress of the ancient Jewish high priest *c)* in ancient Greece, a headband worn by women **2.** the office or rank of a bishop; bishopric —*vt*. to invest with the office of bishop by placing a miter on

MITER

mi·ter² (mīt′ər) *n*. [prob. < prec.] *Carpentry* **1.** a kind of joint formed by fitting together two pieces, beveled to a specified angle (usually 45°) to form a corner (usually a right angle): also **miter joint 2.** either of the facing surfaces of such a joint **3.** *same as* MITER SQUARE —*vt*. **1.** to fit together in a miter **2.** to bevel the edges of to form a miter

miter box a device used to guide the saw in cutting wood at an angle for a miter joint

miter square a tool used to mark out angles for miter joints, with two blades set at a 45° angle or adjustable to any angle

☆**mi·ter·wort** (mīt′ər wurt′) *n*. same as BISHOP'S-CAP

MITER JOINT

mith·er (mith′ər) *n. chiefly Scot. var. of* MOTHER¹

Mith·ra·ic (mith rā′ik) *adj*. of Mithras or Mithraism

Mith·ra·ism (mith′rə iz′m, -rā-) *n*. the ancient Persian religion based on worship of Mithras —**Mith′ra·ist** *n., adj.* —**Mith′ra·is′tic** *adj*.

Mith·ras (mith′ras) [L. < Gr. *Mithras* < OPer. *Mithra*] the ancient Persian god of light and truth, opponent of darkness and evil: also **Mith′ra** (-rə)

mith·ri·date (mith′ri dāt′) *n*. [ML. *mithridatum* < LL. *mithridatium* < *Mithridatius*, of Mithridates VI, said to have become immune to poisons by taking them in gradually increased doses] formerly, a substance supposed to be an antidote against all poisons

Mith·ri·da·tes VI (mith′ri dāt′ēz) 132?–63 B.C.; king of Pontus (120–63): called *the Great*

☆**mi·ti·cide** (mīt′i sīd′) *n*. [< MITE¹ + -CIDE] any substance used for destroying mites

mit·i·gate (mit′ə gāt′) *vt., vi. -gat′ed, -gat′ing* [ME. *mitigaten* < L. *mitigatus*, pp. of *mitigare*, to make mild, soft, or tender < *mitis*, mild, soft (for IE. base see MIGNON) + *agere*, to drive: see ACT] to make or become milder, less severe, less rigorous, or less painful; moderate —**mit′i·ga·ble** (-i gə b'l) *adj*. —**mit′i·ga′tion** *n*. —**mit′i·ga′tive** *adj*. —**mit′i·ga′tor** *n*. —**mit′i·ga·to·ry** (gə tôr′ē) *adj*.

Mit·i·li·ni (mīt′'l ē′nē) **1.** seaport & capital of Lesbos, on the SE coast; pop. 26,000 **2.** *same as* LESBOS

mi·to·chon·dri·on (mīt′ə kän′drē ən) *n., pl.* **-dri·a** (-ə) [ModL. < Gr. *mitos*, a thread + *chondrion*, a small cartilage < *chondros*: see CHONDRO-] any of various very small, usually rodlike structures found in the cytoplasm of most cells and serving as a center of intracellular enzyme activity —**mi′to·chon′dri·al** *adj*.

mi·to·sis (mī tō′sis, mi-) *n., pl.* **-ses** (-sēz) [ModL. < Gr. *mitos*, thread + -OSIS] *Biol.* the indirect and more common method of nuclear division of cells, consisting typically of prophase, metaphase, anaphase, and telophase: the nuclear chromatin first appears as long threads which shorten and thicken to form the typical number of chromosomes, each of which splits lengthwise to double in number with half of each set then moving toward opposite poles of the cell to become reorganized into two new nuclei with the normal number of chromosomes —**mi·tot′ic** (-tät′ik) *adj*. —**mi·tot′i·cal·ly** *adv*.

‡**mi·trail·leur** (mē trä yër′) *n*. [Fr. < *mitrailler*, to fire grapeshot < *mitraille*, grapeshot, orig. small coins < OFr. *mitre, mite*, small coin < MDu.: see MITE²] a soldier who operated a mitrailleuse

‡**mi·trail·leuse** (-yöz′) *n*. [Fr.: see prec.] an obsolete, breechloading machine gun with a cluster of barrels fired simultaneously or in rapid succession

mi·tral (mī′trəl) *adj*. [Fr. < ModL. *mitralis* < L. *mitra*, MITER¹] of or like a miter or the mitral valve

mitral valve the valve between the left atrium and left ventricle of the heart, preventing a flow of blood back into the atrium during systole

mi·tre (mīt′ər) *n., vt. -tred, -tring Brit. sp. of* MITER

mitt (mit) *n*. [contr. < MITTEN] **1.** a woman's glove, often of lace or net, covering part of the arm, the hand, and

sometimes part of the fingers **2.** *same as* MITTEN **3.** a padded glove or mitten for a specified use [dusting *mitt*] ☆**4.** [Slang] a hand ☆**5.** *a) Baseball* a padded glove, with a thumb but usually without separate fingers, worn for protection [catcher's *mitt*] *b)* a boxing glove

mit·ten (mit′n) *n*. [ME. *mytten* < OFr. *mitaine* < *mite* (in same sense), prob. metaphorical use of *mite*, cat] **1.** a glove with a thumb but no separately divided fingers **2.** *earlier var. of* MITT (sense 1) —**to give** (or **get**) **the mitten** [Colloq.] to reject (or be rejected) as a lover

mit·ti·mus (mit′i məs) *n*. [L., we send < *mittere*: see MISSION] *Law* **1.** a warrant or writ for putting into prison a person convicted of crime **2.** dismissal, as from office

mitz·vah (mits vä′, mits′və) *n., pl.* **mitz·voth′** (-vōt′), **mitz′vahs** [Heb. *mitswāh*] *Judaism* **1.** a commandment or precept, as in the Bible or from the rabbis **2.** an act fulfilling such a command or the spirit of such commands [an act of charity is a *mitzvah*]: also **mits·vah′**

mix (miks) *vt*. **mixed** or **mixt, mix′ing** [prob. back-formation < *mixt*, mixed, taken as pp. < Fr. *mixte* < L. *mixtus*, pp. of *miscere*, to mix (whence OE. *miscian*) < IE. base *mei-*, whence Gr. *mygnynai*, W. *mysgu*, to mix] **1.** to put or blend together in a single mass, collection, or compound **2.** to make by putting ingredients together [to *mix* a cake] **3.** to join; combine [to *mix* work and play] **4.** to cause to join or associate [to *mix* the boys with the girls in a school] **5.** to hybridize —*vi*. **1.** to be mixed or capable of being mixed; be blended; mingle **2.** to associate or get along [to *mix* with other people] **3.** to hybridize —*n*. **1.** a mixing or being mixed **2.** a muddle; state of confusion ☆**3.** *a)* a product of mixing; mixture [cement *mix*] *b)* a commercial mixture of ingredients for preparing a food, usually by adding liquid [cake *mix*] **4.** a beverage, as soda or ginger ale, for mixing with alcoholic liquor **5.** [Colloq.] a mixture of dissimilar components, elements, parts, ideas, etc. —**mix up 1.** to mix thoroughly; mingle together **2.** to confuse; specif., *a)* to cause confusion in *b)* to mistake for another (with *with*) **3.** to involve or implicate (*in* some matter) —**mix′a·ble** *adj*.

SYN.—**mix** implies a combining of things so that the resulting substance is uniform in composition, whether or not the separate elements can be distinguished [to *mix* paints]; **mingle** usually implies that the separate elements can be distinguished [*mingled* feelings of joy and sorrow]; **blend** implies a mixing of different varieties to produce a desired quality [a *blended* tea, whiskey, etc.] or the mingling of different elements to form a harmonious whole [a novel *blending* fact and fiction]; **merge** stresses the loss of distinction of elements by combination or may suggest the total absorption of one thing in another [the companies *merged* to form a large corporation]; **coalesce** implies a union or growing together of things into a single body or mass [the factions *coalesced* into a party of opposition]; **fuse** means to unite by melting together and stresses the indissoluble nature of the union

mixed (mikst) *adj*. [earlier *mixt*: see MIX] **1.** joined or mingled in a single mass or compound; blended **2.** made up of different or incongruous parts, groups, elements, classes, races, etc. **3.** consisting of or involving both sexes [a *mixed* class, *mixed* company] **4.** confused; muddled [to get one's dates *mixed*] **5.** *Phonet.* central: said of a vowel

☆**mixed bag** an assortment or mixture, esp. of diverse elements, types of people, etc. brought together at random

mixed bud a bud which produces both leaves and flowers

mixed marriage marriage between persons of different religions or races

mixed media 1. the simultaneous presentation of a series of effects in more than two media, as by combining acting, flashing colored lights, tape recordings, etc. **2.** *Painting* the use of different media, as water colors and crayon, in the same composition

mixed number a number consisting of a whole number and a fraction, as 3 2/3

mix·er (mik′sər) *n*. **1.** a person or thing that mixes; specif., ☆*a)* a person with reference to his ability to get along with others [a good *mixer*] *b)* an electric appliance for mixing ingredients or beating foods *c)* a machine for mixing [concrete *mixer*] ☆**2.** [Slang] a social gathering for getting people acquainted with one another **3.** *Electronics a)* a device or circuit for combining carriers of differing frequencies to produce a desired carrier *b)* an electrical apparatus in which signals from various audio sources are combined in desired proportions

☆**mix·ol·o·gist** (mik säl′ə jist) *n*. [MIX + -ologist, as in *biologist*] [Slang] a bartender

mix·o·lyd·i·an (mik′sə lid′ē ən) *adj*. [< Gr. *mixolydios* (< *mixis*, a mingling + *Lydios*, Lydian) + -AN] *Music* **1.** designating or of one of the ancient Greek modes **2.** designating or of a medieval church mode corresponding to the modern major mode with a minor seventh

mixt (mikst) *alt. pt. & pp. of* MIX

Mix·tec (mēs′tek) *n*. **1.** *pl.* **-tecs, -tec** any member of a large tribe of American Indians who live in the Mexican states of Oaxaca, Guerrero, and Puebla **2.** their Mixtecan language

Mix·tec·an (mēs tek′ən) *n*. any of a family of four American Indian languages spoken in Mexico

mix·ture (miks′chər) *n.* [LME. < L. *mixtura* < *mixtus:* see MIX] 1. a mixing or being mixed 2. something made by mixing; esp., *a*) a combination of ingredients, kinds, etc. *b*) a yarn or fabric made of two or more different fibers, often of different colors 3. *Chem.* a substance containing two or more ingredients: distinguished from COMPOUND¹ in that the constituents are not in fixed proportions, do not lose their individual characteristics, and can be separated by physical means

mix-up (miks′up′) *n.* 1. a condition or instance of confusion; tangle 2. [Colloq.] a fight

Mi·zar (mī′zär) [Ar. *mīzār*, lit., waist-cloth, apron] a double star at the middle of the handle of the Big Dipper

miz·zen, miz·en (miz′'n) *adj.* [LME. *meseyn* < or akin to MFr. *misaine* < It. *mezzana*, fem. of *mezzano*, middle < L. *medianus:* see MEDIAN] of the mizzenmast —*n.* 1. a fore-and-aft sail set on the mizzenmast 2. *clipped form of* MIZZENMAST

miz·zen·mast (-məst, -mast′, -mäst′) *n.* [see MIZZEN] the mast closest to the stern in a ship with two or three masts

miz·zle (miz′'l) *vt., vi.* **-zled, -zling** [LME. *misellen*, prob. < a LowG. source, as in Du. dial. *miezelen*. LowG. *miseln:* for base see MIST] [Dial.] to rain in a fine mist; drizzle —*n.* [Dial.] a misty rain; drizzle —**miz′zly** *adj.*

mk. *pl.* **mks.** 1. mark (the monetary unit) 2. markka

mks, m.k.s., M.K.S. meter-kilogram-second

mkt. market

ML. Medieval (or Middle) Latin

ml. 1. mail 2. milliliter(s)

M.L.A. Modern Language Association

MLD minimum (or minimal) lethal dose

Mlle. *pl.* **Mlles.** Mademoiselle

MLowG. Middle Low German

M.L.S. Master of Library Science

mm, mm. 1. millimeter(s) 2. [L. *millia*] thousands

MM. 1. Messieurs 2. Their Majesties

Mme. Madame

M.M.E. 1. Master of Mechanical Engineering 2. Master of Mining Engineering

Mmes. Mesdames

mmf m.m.f. magnetomotive force

Mn *Chem.* manganese

mne·mon·ic (nē măn′ik) *adj.* [Gr. *mnēmonikos* < *mnēmōn*, mindful < *mnasthai*, to remember: for IE. base see MIND] 1. helping, or meant to help, the memory 2. of mnemonics or memory —**mne·mon′i·cal·ly** *adv.*

mne·mon·ics (-iks) *n.pl.* [see prec.] 1. [*with sing. v.*] a technique or system of improving the memory by the use of certain formulas 2. such formulas

Mne·mos·y·ne (nē măs′ə nē′, -măz′-) [L. < Gr. *mnēmosynē*, memory < *mnasthai*, to remember: for IE. base see MIND] *Gr. Myth.* the goddess of memory, and mother (by Zeus) of the Muses

mo (mō) *n.* [Colloq.] *clipped form of* MOMENT (sense 1)

-mo (mō) [< ending of L. abl. forms of ordinals, after prep. *in*, as in *duodecimo* (< *duodecimus*, twelfth)] a suffix added to numerals or to words representing numerals, meaning having a (specified number of) leaves as a result of folding a sheet of paper [*12mo, duodecimo,* or *twelvemo*]

Mo *Chem.* molybdenum

Mo. 1. Missouri 2. Monday

mo. 1. money order 2. *pl.* **mos.** month

M.O., MO 1. Medical Officer 2. [L. *modus operandi*] mode of operation 3. money order

m.o. money order

mo·a (mō′ə) *n.* [< native (Maori) name] any of an extinct group (family Dinornithidae) of very large, flightless birds of New Zealand, resembling the ostrich

Mo·ab (mō′ab) [LL.(Ec.) < Gr.(Ec.) < Heb. *mō′ābh*] 1. *Bible* a son of Lot: Gen. 19:37 2. ancient kingdom east & south of the Dead Sea

Mo·ab·ite (mō′ə bīt′) *n.* [ME. < LL.(Ec.) *Moabita* < Gr.(Ec.) *mōabitis*] 1. a native or inhabitant of Moab 2. the extinct Semitic language of the Moabites —*adj.* of Moab or the Moabites: also **Mo′ab·it′ish** (-bīt′ish) —**Mo′ab·it′ess** *n.fem.*

moan (mōn) *n.* [ME. *mone*, prob. < base of OE. *mænan*, to complain: see MEAN¹] 1. formerly, a complaint; lamentation 2. a low, mournful sound of sorrow or pain 3. any sound like this [*the moan of the wind*] —*vi.* 1. to utter a moan or moans 2. to complain, lament, grieve, etc. —*vt.* 1. to say with a moan 2. to complain about; bewail [*to moan one's fate*] —*SYN.* see CRY

moat (mōt) *n.* [ME. *mote* < OFr., orig., mound, embankment, prob. < Gmc. *motta*, heap of earth] a deep, broad ditch dug around a fortress or castle, and often filled with water, for protection against invasion —*vt.* to surround with or as with a moat

mob (mäb) *n.* [< L. *mobile* (*vulgus*), movable (crowd)] 1. a disorderly and lawless crowd; rabble 2. any crowd 3. the masses; common people collectively: a contemptuous term 4. [Slang] a gang of criminals —*vt.* **mobbed, mob′bing** 1. to crowd around and attack 2. to crowd around and jostle, annoy, etc., as in curiosity or anger 3. to fill with many people; throng —*SYN.* see CROWD¹ —**mob′bish** *adj.*

mob·cap (mäb′kap′) *n.* [< MDu. *mop*, woman's cap + CAP] formerly, a woman's cap for indoor wear, with a high, puffy crown, often tied under the chin

Mo·bile (mō bēl′, mō′bēl) [< Fr. < AmInd. < ?] 1. seaport in SW Ala., on Mobile Bay: pop. 190,000 2. river in SW Ala., formed by the Alabama & Tombigbee rivers & flowing into Mobile Bay: c. 45 mi.

mo·bile (mō′b'l, -bil; *also, & for adj. 5 and n. usually,* -bēl) *adj.* [OFr. < L. *mobilis*, movable < *movere*, to MOVE] 1. *a*) moving, or capable of moving or being moved, from place to place *b*) movable by means of a motor vehicle or vehicles [*a mobile X-ray unit*] 2. very fluid, as mercury 3. that can change rapidly or easily, as in response to different moods, feelings, conditions, needs, or influences; flexible, adaptable, etc. 4. designating or of a society in which one may advance in social status, and in which social groups mingle freely 5. *Art* that is or has to do with a mobile or mobiles —*n.* a piece of abstract sculpture which aims to depict movement, i.e., kinetic rather than static rhythms, as by an arrangement of thin forms, rings, rods, etc. balanced and suspended in midair and set in motion by air currents —**mo·bil′i·ty** (mō bil′ə tē) *n.*

Mobile Bay arm of the Gulf of Mexico, extending into SW Ala.: c. 35 mi. long

☆**mobile home** a large trailer outfitted as a home meant to be parked more or less permanently at a location

mo·bi·lize (mō′bə līz′) *vt.* **-lized, -liz′ing** [Fr. *mobiliser*] 1. *a*) to make mobile, or movable *b*) to put into motion, circulation, or use 2. to bring into readiness for immediate active service in war 3. to organize (people, resources, etc.) for active service or use in any emergency, drive, etc. —*vi.* to become organized and ready, as for war —**mo′bi·liz′a·ble** *adj.* —**mo′bi·li·za′tion** *n.* —**mo′bi·liz′er** *n.*

Mö·bi·us strip (mā′bē əs, mō′-) [after A. F. *Möbius* (1790–1868), G. mathematician] a surface with only one side, formed by giving a half twist to a narrow, rectangular strip of paper and then pasting its two ends together

mob·oc·ra·cy (mäb äk′rə sē) *n., pl.* **-cies** [MOB + (DE-M)OCRACY] 1. rule or domination by a mob 2. the mob as ruler —**mob′o·crat′ic** *adj.*

mob·ster (mäb′stər) *n.* [Slang] a member of a criminal mob; gangster

Mo·çam·bi·que (mōō′səm bē′kə) *Port. name of* MOZAMBIQUE

☆**moc·ca·sin** (mäk′ə s'n) *n.* [< AmInd. (Algonquian), as in Narragansett *mokussin*, Massachusett *mohkisson*] 1. a heelless slipper of soft, flexible leather, worn orig. by N. American Indians 2. any slipper more or less like this but with a hard sole and heel 3. *same as* WATER MOCCASIN

☆**moccasin flower** *same as* CYPRIPEDIUM (sense 1)

Mo·cha (mō′kə) seaport in SW Yemen, on the Red Sea: pop. 6,000 —*n.* [m-] 1. a choice grade of coffee grown orig. in Arabia 2. [Colloq.] any coffee 3. a flavoring made from an infusion of coffee, or of coffee and chocolate 4. a soft, velvety leather of Egyptian sheepskin, used esp. for gloves 5. chocolate brown —*adj.* [m-] 1. flavored with coffee or coffee and chocolate 2. chocolate brown

mock (mäk) *vt.* [ME. *mokken* < OFr. *mocquer*, to mock] 1. to hold up to scorn or contempt; ridicule 2. to imitate or mimic, as in fun or derision; burlesque 3. to lead on and disappoint; deceive 4. to defy and make futile; defeat [*the fortress mocked the invaders*] —*vi.* to show or express scorn, ridicule, or contempt; jeer (often with *at*) —*n.* 1. an act of mocking; jibe; sneer 2. a person or thing receiving or deserving ridicule or derision 3. an imitation or counterfeit —*adj.* sham; false; imitation; pretended [*a mock battle*] —*SYN.* see IMITATE, RIDICULE —**mock′er** *n.* —**mock′ing·ly** *adv.*

mock·er·y (-ər ē) *n., pl.* **-er·ies** [ME. *moquerye* < OFr. *moquerie*] 1. a mocking (in various senses) 2. a person or thing receiving or deserving ridicule 3. a false, derisive, or impertinent imitation; travesty; burlesque 4. vain or disappointing effort; futility

mock-he·ro·ic (-hi rō′ik) *adj.* mocking, or burlesquing, heroic manner, action, or character —*n.* a mock-heroic literary work —**mock′-he·ro′i·cal·ly** *adv.*

☆**mock·ing·bird** (mäk′iŋ burd′) *n.* a widely distributed American bird (*Mimus polyglottos*) noted for its song and its ability to imitate the calls of many other birds

mock orange ☆ any of a genus (*Philadelphus*) of shrubs of the saxifrage family, with fragrant white flowers resembling those of the orange

mock turtle soup a soup made from calf's head, veal, etc., spiced so as to taste like green turtle soup

mock-up (mäk′up′) *n.* [altered (after MOCK & UP¹) < Fr. *maquette*, a sketch, mock-up < *maquiller*, to pretend, orig. a cant term, to work < dial. *makier*, to make, do < MDu. *maken*, akin to MAKE¹] a scale model, usually a full-sized replica, of a structure or apparatus used for instructional or experimental purposes

mod (mäd) *n.* [< MOD(ERN)] [*also* M-] any of the young people in England in the 1960's characterized, like the U.S. hippies, by rebellion against conventional society, the wearing of flamboyant clothes, long hair, etc. —*adj.* [*also* M-] of or characteristic of such young people

mod. 1. moderate 2. *Music* moderato 3. modern 4. modulus

mod·a·cryl·ic (mäd′ə kril′ik) *adj.* [*mod*(*ified*) *acrylic*] designating or of any of various manufactured fibers made from long-chain polymers composed primarily of acrylonitrile modified by other polymers: used in making wool substitutes, carpets, etc.

mod·al (mōd′'l) *adj.* [ML. *modalis* < L. *modus*, MODE] of or indicating a mode or mood; specif., *a) Gram.* of or expressing mood [a *modal* verb] *b) Logic* expressing or characterized by modality *c) Music* of or composed in any of the medieval church modes *d) Philos.* of mode, or form, as opposed to substance *e) Statistics* having to do with a statistical mode —**mod′al·ly** *adv.*

modal auxiliary an auxiliary verb used with another to indicate its mood: *can, may, might, must, should,* and *would* are *modal auxiliaries*

mo·dal·i·ty (mō dal′ə tē) *n., pl.* **-ties** [ML. *modalitas*] 1. the fact, state, or quality of being modal 2. a special attribute, emphasis, etc. that marks certain individuals, things, groups, etc. 3. *Logic* the qualification in a proposition affirming or denying possibility, impossibility, necessity, etc. 4. *Med.* [Rare] the employment of, or the method of employment of, a therapeutic agent

mode (mōd) *n.* [ME. *moede* < L. *modus*, measure, manner, mode < IE. base *med-*, to measure, whence METE[1], L. *medicus*] 1. a manner or way of acting, doing, or being; method or form 2. [Fr. < L. *modus*] customary usage, or current fashion or style, as in manners or dress 3. *Gram. same as* MOOD[2] 4. *Logic a)* modality or the form of a proposition with reference to its modality *b)* any of the various forms of valid syllogisms, as determined by the quantity and quality of their constituent propositions 5. *Metaphysics* the form, or way of being, of something, as apart from its substance 6. *Music a)* the selection and arrangement of tones and semitones in a scale, esp. any of such arrangements in medieval church music *b)* a rhythmical system of the 13th cent. *c)* either of the two forms of scale arrangement in later music (MAJOR MODE and MINOR MODE) 7. *Geol.* the actual mineral composition of an unaltered igneous rock 8. *Statistics* the value, number, etc. that occurs most frequently in a given series —SYN. see FASHION, METHOD

mod·el (mäd′'l) *n.* [Fr. *modèle* < It. *modello*, dim. of *modo* < L. *modus*, MODE] 1. *a)* a small copy or imitation of an existing object, as a ship, building, etc., made to scale *b)* a preliminary representation of something, serving as the plan from which the final, usually larger, object is to be constructed *c) same as* ARCHETYPE (sense 1) *d)* a hypothetical or stylized representation, as of an atom *e)* a piece of sculpture in wax or clay from which a finished work in bronze, marble, etc. is to be made 2. a person or thing considered as a standard of excellence to be imitated 3. a style or design; specif., any of a series of different styles or designs of a particular product [a two-door *model*, a 1969 *model*] 4. *a)* a person who poses for an artist or photographer *b)* any person or thing serving as a subject for an artist or writer *c)* a person, esp. a woman, employed to display clothes by wearing them; mannequin —*adj.* 1. serving as a model, pattern, or standard of excellence [a *model* student] 2. representative of others of the same kind, style, etc. [a *model* home] —*vt.* **-eled** or **-elled, -el·ing** or **-el·ling** 1. *a)* to make a model of *b)* to plan, form, or design after a model *c)* to make conform to a standard of excellence [to *model* one's behavior on that of one's father] 2. to shape or form in or as in clay, wax, etc. 3. to display (a dress, etc.) by wearing —*vi.* 1. to make a model or models [to *model* in clay] ☆2. to serve as a model (sense 4) 3. *Painting, Drawing,* etc. to take on a three-dimensional appearance as a result of contrast in lighting and color —**mod′el·er, mod′el·ler** *n.*

SYN.—**model** refers to a representation made to be copied or, more generally, to any person or thing to be followed or imitated because of his or its excellence, worth, etc.; **example** suggests that which is presented as a sample, or that which sets a precedent for imitation, whether good or bad; a **pattern** is a model, guide, plan, etc. to be strictly followed; **paradigm** is common now only in its grammatical sense of an example of a declension or conjugation, giving all the inflectional forms of a word; **archetype** applies to the original pattern serving as the model for all later things of the same kind; **standard** refers to something established for use as a rule or a basis of comparison in judging quality, etc.

mo·dem (mō′dem) *n.* [MO(DULATOR) + DEM(ODULATOR)] a device that converts data to a form that can be transmitted, as by telephone, to data-processing equipment, where a similar device reconverts it

Mo·de·na (mō′de nä′) commune in N Italy, in Emilia-Romagna: pop. 157,000

mod·er·ate (mäd′ər it; *for v.* -ə rāt′) *adj.* [ME. *moderat* < L. *moderatus,* pp. of *moderare,* to keep within bounds, restrain < *modus:* see MODE] 1. within reasonable limits; avoiding excesses or extremes; temperate or restrained 2. mild; calm; gentle; not violent [*moderate* weather] 3. of average or medium quality, amount, scope, range, etc. [*moderate* skills, *moderate* prices] —*n.* a person holding moderate views or opinions, as in politics or religion —*vt.* **-at·ed, -at·ing** 1. to cause to become moderate; make less extreme, violent, etc.; restrain 2. to preside over (a meeting, etc.) —*vi.* 1. to become moderate 2. to serve as a moderator; preside —**mod′er·ate·ly** *adv.* —**mod′er·ate·ness** *n.*

SYN.—**moderate** and **temperate** are often interchangeable in denoting a staying within reasonable limits, but in strict discrimination, **moderate** implies merely an absence of excesses or extremes, while **temperate** suggests deliberate self-restraint [*moderate* demands, a *temperate* reply] —ANT. EXCESSIVE, EXTREME

moderate breeze a wind whose speed is 13 to 18 miles per hour: see BEAUFORT SCALE

moderate gale a wind whose speed is 32 to 38 miles per hour: see BEAUFORT SCALE

mod·er·a·tion (mäd′ə rā′shən) *n.* 1. a moderating, or bringing within bounds 2. avoidance of excesses or extremes 3. absence of violence; calmness —**in moderation** to a moderate degree; without excess

mod·e·ra·to (-rät′ō) *adj., adv.* [It.] *Music* with moderation in tempo: a direction to the performer

mod·er·a·tor (mäd′ə rāt′ər) *n.* [ME. *moderatour* < L. *moderator*] a person or thing that moderates; specif., *a)* a person who presides at a town meeting, debate, assembly, etc. *b)* the presiding officer of a governing body, as of the Presbyterian Church *c)* a substance, as graphite or heavy water, used to slow down high-energy neutrons in a nuclear reactor —**mod′er·a′tor·ship′** *n.*

mod·ern (mäd′ərn) *adj.* [Fr. *moderne* < LL. *modernus* < L. *modo*, just now, orig. abl. of *modus:* see MODE] 1. of the present or recent times; specif., *a)* of or having to do with the latest styles, methods, or ideas; up-to-date *b)* designating or of certain contemporary trends and schools of art, music, literature, dance, etc. 2. of or relating to the period of history after the Middle Ages, from c.1450 A.D. to the present day 3. [often M-] designating the form of a language in its most recent stage of development —*n.* 1. a person living in modern times 2. a person having modern ideas, beliefs, standards, etc. 3. *Printing* a style of typeface characterized by heavy down strokes contrasting with narrow cross strokes —SYN. see NEW —**mod′ern·ly** *adv.* —**mod′ern·ness** *n.*

☆**modern dance** a form of dance as a performing art, variously developed in the 20th cent. by Mary Wigman, Martha Graham, etc., and characterized by bodily movements and rhythms less formalized than in classical ballet and less firmly bound to predetermined musical form

Modern English the English language since about the mid-15th cent.: cf. EARLY MODERN ENGLISH

Modern Greek the Greek language as spoken and written in Greece since about 1500

Modern Hebrew Hebrew as spoken and written in post-Biblical times; esp., the language of modern Israel

mod·ern·ism (-iz′m) *n.* 1. *a)* modern practices, trends, ideas, etc., or sympathy with any of these *b)* an instance of this; a modern idiom, practice, or usage 2. [M-] *Christianity* any of several movements variously attempting to redefine Biblical and Christian dogma and traditional teachings in the light of modern science, historical research, etc.: condemned in the Roman Catholic Church in 1907 as a negation of faith —**mod′ern·ist** *n., adj.*

mod·ern·is·tic (mäd′ər nis′tik) *adj.* 1. of or characteristic of modernism or modernists 2. modern: used esp. to designate certain contemporary trends and schools of art, music, etc., sometimes in a deprecatory sense —SYN. see NEW —**mod′ern·is′ti·cal·ly** *adv.*

mo·der·ni·ty (mä dur′nə tē, mə-) *n.* 1. the state or quality of being modern 2. *pl.* **-ties** something modern

mod·ern·ize (mäd′ər nīz′) *vt.* **-ized′, -iz′ing** [Fr. *moderniser*] to make modern; bring up to date in style, design, methods, etc. —*vi.* to adopt modern ways; become modern —**mod′ern·i·za′tion** *n.* —**mod′ern·iz′er** *n.*

Modern Latin the Latin that has come into use since about 1500, chiefly in scientific literature

mod·est (mäd′ist) *adj.* [Fr. *modeste* < L. *modestus,* keeping due measure, modest < *modus:* see MODE] 1. having or showing a moderate opinion of one's own value, abilities, achievements, etc.; not vain or boastful; unassuming 2. not forward; shy or reserved [*modest* behavior] 3. behaving, dressing, speaking, etc. in a way that is considered proper or decorous; decent 4. moderate or reasonable; not extreme [a *modest* request] 5. quiet and humble in appearance, style, etc.; not pretentious [a *modest* home] —SYN. see CHASTE, HUMBLE, SHY —**mod′est·ly** *adv.*

Mo·des·to (mə des′tō) [Sp., lit., modest: said to be with reference to Wm. C. Ralston's modest refusal to have the place named after him] city in C Calif.: pop. 62,000

mod·es·ty (mäd′is tē) *n.* [Fr. *modestie* < L. *modestia*] the quality or state of being modest; specif., *a)* unassuming or humble behavior *b)* lack of excesses or pretensions; moderation *c)* decency; decorum

ModGr. Modern Greek

ModHeb. Modern Hebrew

mod·i·cum (mäd′i kəm) *n.* [LME. < L., neut. of *modicus*, moderate < *modus:* see MODE] a small amount; bit

mod·i·fi·ca·tion (mäd′ə fi kā′shən) *n.* [MFr. < L. *modificatio* < pp. of *modificare*] a modifying or being modified; specif., *a)* a partial or slight change in form *b)* a product of such a change *c)* a slight reduction; moderation *d)* a qualification or limitation of meaning *e) Biol.* a change in an organism caused by its environment and not inheritable

---

f) Linguis. a change in the form of a phoneme within a particular construction —**mod′i·fi·ca′to·ry** *adj.*

mod·i·fi·er (mäd′ə fī′ər) *n.* a person or thing that modifies; esp., a word, phrase, or clause that limits the meaning of another word or phrase [adjectives and adverbs are *modifiers]*

mod·i·fy (mäd′ə fī′) *vt.* **-fied′, -fy′ing** [ME. *modifien* < MFr. < L. *modificare*, to limit, regulate < *modus*, measure (see MODE) + *facere*, to make: see FACT] **1.** to change or alter; esp., to change slightly or partially in character, form, etc. **2.** to limit or reduce slightly; moderate [to *modify* a penalty] **3.** *Gram.* to limit the meaning of; qualify [*"old" modifies "man"* in *old man*] **4.** *Linguis.* to change (a vowel) by umlaut —*vi.* to be modified —*SYN.* see CHANGE —**mod′i·fi′a·ble** *adj.*

Mo·di·glia·ni (mō′dē lyä′nē), **A·me·de·o** (ä′me de′ō) 1884–1920; It. painter, in France

mo·dil·lion (mō dil′yən) *n.* [It. *modiglione* < LL. *mutilio* < L. *mutulus*, modillion, prob. < Etruscan base *mut-*, a projection] *Archit.* an ornamental block or bracket placed under a projecting cornice, esp. in the Corinthian order

mo·di·o·lus (mō dī′ə ləs) *n., pl.* **-o·li** (-lī′) [ModL., dim. of L. *modius*, measure for grain < *modus*, measure: see MODE] the central bony axis of the cochlea of the ear

mod·ish (mōd′ish) *adj.* in the current mode; in the latest style; fashionable —**mod′ish·ly** *adv.* —**mod′ish·ness** *n.*

mo·diste (mō dēst′) *n.* [Fr. < *mode*: see MODE] a woman who makes or deals in fashionable clothes, hats, etc. for women: somewhat old-fashioned term

Mo·djes·ka (mə jes′kə), **He·le·na** (he lā′nə) 1840–1909; Pol. actress, in the U.S.

ModL. Modern Latin

ModPr. Modern Provençal

Mo·dred (mō′drid) *Arthurian Legend* treacherous nephew of King Arthur: they killed each other in battle

mod·u·lar (mäj′ə lər) *adj.* [ModL. *modularis*] **1.** of a module or modulus ☆**2.** designating or of units of standardized size, design, etc. that can be arranged or fitted together in a variety of ways

mod·u·late (-lāt′) *vt.* **-lat′ed, -lat′ing** [< L. *modulatus*, pp. of *modulari*, to regulate, measure off, arrange < *modulus*, dim. of *modus:* see MODE] **1.** to regulate, adjust, or adapt to the proper degree **2.** to vary the pitch, intensity, etc. of (the voice), often specif. to a lower degree **3.** *Radio* to vary the amplitude, frequency, or phase of (an oscillation, as a carrier wave) in accordance with some signal —*vi.* to shift from one key to another within a musical composition —**mod′u·la′tor** *n.* —**mod′u·la·to′ry** *adj.*

mod·u·la·tion (mäj′ə lā′shən) *n.* [ME. *modulacioun* < L. *modulatio*] **1.** a modulating or being modulated; specif., *a) Music* a shifting from one key to another *b) Radio* a variation in the amplitude, frequency, or phase of a wave in accordance with some signal **2.** a variation in stress or pitch in speaking, as in distinguishing between the merely auxiliary and lexical uses of a word (Ex.: "I've been there," as contrasted with "I *have* friends")

mod·ule (mäj′ōōl) *n.* [Fr. *module* < L. *modulus*, dim. of *modus:* see MODE] **1.** a standard or unit of measurement; specif., *a)* in classical architecture, the diameter, or one half the diameter, of a column at the base of the shaft, used to determine the proportions of the structure *b)* any of several standardized units of measurement used in architectural planning, in the construction of building materials, etc. [4-inch *module*, 2-foot *module]* ☆**2.** any of a set of units, as tiles, wall cabinets, shelves, etc., designed to be arranged or joined in a variety of ways *b)* a detachable section, compartment, or unit with a specific purpose or function, as in a spacecraft *c) Electronics* a compact assembly functioning as a component of a larger unit

mod·u·lus (mäj′ə ləs) *n., pl.* **-u·li** (-lī′) [ModL. < L.: see prec.] **1.** *Math. a) same as* ABSOLUTE VALUE: for a complex number, computed by adding the squares of each part and taking the positive square root of the sum (Ex.: the modulus of $a + bi$ is $\sqrt{a^2 + b^2}$) *b)* a given quantity which gives the same remainders when it is the divisor of two quantities *c)* the factor by which a logarithm to one base is multiplied to change it to a logarithm to another base **2.** *Physics* a positive number or quantity expressing the measure of a function, force, or effect, as of elasticity, resistance, etc., esp. in relation to a basic unit or to some other factor or factors

‡**mo·dus o·pe·ran·di** (mō′dəs äp′ə ran′dī, -dē) [L.] mode of operation; way of doing or making; procedure

‡**modus vi·ven·di** (vi ven′dī, -dē) [L.] **1.** manner of living or of getting along **2.** a temporary agreement in a dispute pending final settlement; compromise

Moe·si·a (mē′shē ə) ancient Roman province in SE Europe, between the Danube & the Balkan Mountains

Moe·so-Goth, Moe·so·goth (mē′sō gäth′) *n.* a member of a Gothic tribe that lived in Moesia (c. 300 A.D.)

Moe·so-Goth·ic, Moe·so·goth·ic (mē′sō gäth′ik) *adj.* of the Moeso-Goths or their extinct, East Germanic language

mo·fette, mof·fette (mō fet′) *n.* [Fr. < It. *muffare*, to be moldy < G. *muff*, mold] a vent or fissure in an area of recent volcanic activity, emitting steam, carbon dioxide, and, sometimes, other gases

mog (mäg) *vi.* **mogged, mog′ging** [< ?] [Dial.] **1.** to plod (*along*) steadily **2.** to decamp; move away

Mo·ga·di·shu (mō′gä dē′shōō) capital of Somalia; seaport on the Indian Ocean: pop. 100,000: It. name **Mo′ga·di′scio** (-shō)

Mogen David *same as* MAGEN DAVID

Mo·gi·lev (mō′gi lyôf′; *E.* mō′gi lef′) city in E Byelorussian S.S.R., on the Dnepr: pop. 164,000

Mo·gul (mō′gul, -g′l; mō gul′) *n.* [Per. *Mughul* < Mongol. *Mongol*, a Mongol] **1.** a Mongol, or Mongolian; esp., any of the Mongolian conquerors of India or their descendants **2.** [m-] a powerful or important person, esp. one with autocratic power

mo·gul (mō′g′l) *n.* [< prec.: reason for use unc.] *Skiing* a bump or ridge of closely packed snow, built up on a curve where skiers turn

mo·hair (mō′her) *n.* [altered (after HAIR) < earlier *mocayare* < OIt. *mocajarro* < Ar. *mukhayyar*] **1.** the long, silky hair of the Angora goat **2.** yarn, or any of several fabrics for clothing or upholstery, made from this hair, often mixed with other fibers —*adj.* made of or upholstered with mohair

Moham. Mohammedan

Mo·ham·med (mō ham′id) [Ar. *Muhammed*, lit., praised] **1.** 570?–632 A.D.; Arabian prophet: founder of the Moslem religion **2.** *Mohammed II* 1430–81; sultan of Turkey (1451–81): captured Constantinople (1453)

Mohammed Ali *same as* MEHEMET ALI

Mo·ham·med·an (mō ham′i d′n) *adj.* of Mohammed or the Moslem religion —*n. same as* MOSLEM: term used mainly by non-Moslems

Mo·ham·med·an·ism (-iz′m) *n. same as* ISLAM: term used mainly by non-Moslems

Mohammed Re·za Pah·la·vi (rē zä′ pä′lə vē) 1919– ; shah of Iran (1941–)

Mo·ha·ve (mō hä′vē) *n.* [< AmInd., prob. < Yuman *hamok*, three + *avi*, mountain] **1.** *pl.* **-ves, -ve** any member of a tribe of Indians who live along the Colorado River in Arizona **2.** their dialect of the Yuman language —*adj.* of this people

Mohave Desert *same as* MOJAVE DESERT

Mo·hawk[1] (mō′hôk) *n.* [AmInd. (Algonquian), as in Narragansett *mohowaůuck*, lit., they eat animate things, hence man-eaters: orig. so named by enemy tribes] **1.** *pl.* **-hawks, -hawk** a member of a tribe of Iroquoian Indians who lived in the Mohawk Valley, New York, and now live in Canada and New York: see FIVE NATIONS **2.** their language —*adj.* of the Mohawks

Mo·hawk[2] (mō′hôk) [< prec.] river in C & E N.Y., flowing into the Hudson: c. 140 mi.

Mo·he·gan (mō hē′gan) *n.* [AmInd. (Algonquian), lit., a wolf: cf. MAHICAN] **1.** *pl.* **-gans, -gan** a member of a Mahican tribe of Algonquian Indians who lived in Connecticut, along the Thames River **2.** *same as* MAHICAN —*adj.* of the Mohegans

Mo·hen·jo-Da·ro (mō hen′jō dä′rō) an archaeological site in the Indus valley of West Pakistan, containing ruins of cities from c.3000 to c.1500 B.C.

Mo·hi·can (mō hē′kən) *n., adj. same as* MAHICAN

Mo·ho (mō′hō) *clipped form of* MOHOROVIČIĆ DISCONTINUITY

Mo·hock (mō′häk) *n.* [var. of MOHAWK[1]] any of a gang of rowdy young men of fashion who attacked and terrorized people at night in the streets of London in the early 18th cent.

☆**Mo·hole** (mō′hōl′) *n.* [MO(HO) + HOLE] a proposed hole to be drilled beneath the sea through the earth's crust and the Mohorovičić discontinuity to the mantle

Mo·ho·ro·vi·čić discontinuity (mō hō rō′və chich) [after A. *Mohorovičić* (1857–1936), Yugoslavian geologist] *Geol.* an irregular dividing line separating the earth's crust from its underlying mantle, situated about 22 miles below the continents and 6 miles below the deep sea bottom

Mohs' scale (mōz) [after Friedrich *Mohs* (1773–1839), G. mineralogist] *Mineralogy* **1.** an arbitrary scale used to indicate relative hardness, arranged in 10 ascending degrees: 1, talc; 2, gypsum; 3, calcite; 4, fluorite; 5, apatite; 6, feldspar; 7, quartz; 8, topaz; 9, corundum; 10, diamond **2.** a modification of this scale, retaining its first six minerals and continuing: 7, vitreous pure silica; 8, quartz; 9, topaz; 10, garnet; 11, fused zirconia; 12, fused alumina; 13, silicon carbide; 14, boron carbide; 15, diamond

mo·hur (mō′hər) *n.* [Hind. *muhur, muhr* < Per. *muhr*, a seal, akin to Sans. *mudrā*, a seal] a former gold coin of India, equal to 15 rupees

moi·dore (moi′dôr) *n.* [Port. *moeda d'ouro*, lit., coin of gold < L. *moneta*, money + *aurum*, gold] a former gold coin of Portugal or Brazil

moi·e·ty (moi′ə tē) *n., pl.* **-ties** [ME. *moite* < OFr. < L. *medietas*, the middle (in LL., half, moiety) < *medius:* see MID[1]] **1.** a half; either of two equal, or more or less equal, parts **2.** an indefinite share or part **3.** *Anthropology* any of two or more primary subdivisions in some tribes

moil (moil) *vi.* [ME. *moillen*, to moisten, make wet < OFr. *moillier* < VL. *molliare*, to soften < L. *mollis*, soft] to toil; drudge —*vt.* [Archaic] to moisten or soil —*n.* **1.** drudgery; hard work **2.** confusion; turmoil —**moil′er** *n.*

Moi·ra (moi′rə) *Gr. Myth.* fate or destiny

moire (mwär, môr) *n.* [Fr., watered silk < E. MOHAIR] a

fabric, esp. silk, rayon, or acetate, having a watered, or wavy, pattern

moi·ré (mwä rā′, mô-; môr′ā) *adj.* [Fr., pp. of *moirer*, to water < *moire*: see prec.] having a watered, or wavy, pattern, as certain fabrics, stamps, or metal surfaces —*n.* 1. a watered pattern pressed into cloth, etc. with engraved rollers 2. *same as* MOIRE

moist (moist) *adj.* [ME. < OFr. *moiste* < VL. *muscidus*, altered (prob. after L. *musteus*, of new wine, fresh < *mustum*, MUST[3]) < L. *mucidus*, moldy < *mucus*, MUCUS] 1. slightly wet; damp 2. suggestive of the presence of liquid [a *moist* sound] 3. tearful —*SYN.* see WET —**moist′ly** *adv.* —**moist′ness** *n.*

mois·ten (mois′'n) *vt.*, *vi.* to make or become moist —**mois′ten·er** *n.*

mois·ture (-chər) *n.* [ME. < OFr. *moisteur* < *moiste*: see prec.] water or other liquid causing a slight wetness or dampness —**mois′ture·less** *adj.*

mois·tur·ize (-īz′) *vt.*, *vi.* -ized′, -iz′ing to add, provide, or restore moisture to (the skin, air, etc.) —**mois′tur·iz′er** *n.*

Mo·ja·ve (mō hä′vē) *n.*, *adj. same as* MOHAVE

Mojave Desert desert in SE Calif.: c. 15,000 sq. mi.

moke (mōk) *n.* [< ?] 1. *a)* [Brit. Slang] a donkey *b)* a stupid fellow 2. [Australian] an inferior horse; nag

MOL manned orbiting laboratory

mol (mōl) *n. same as* MOLE[4]

mol. 1. molecular 2. molecule

mo·la (mō′lə) *n.*, *pl.* **mo′las**, **mo′la**: see PLURAL, II, D, 1 [ModL. < L., a millstone (see MILL[1]): so named from its rough skin and round shape] *same as* OCEAN SUNFISH

mo·lal (mō′lal) *adj.* relating to the mole or gram-molecular weight; specif., designating a solution with a concentration equal to one mole of the solute in 1,000 grams of the solvent

mo·lar[1] (mō′lər) *adj.* [L. *molaris*, a mill < *mola*, millstone: for IE. base see MILL[1]] 1. used for or capable of grinding 2. designating or of a tooth or teeth adapted for grinding —*n.* a molar tooth: in man there are twelve molars, three on each side of each jaw behind the bicuspids

mo·lar[2] (mō′lər) *adj.* [MOL(E) + -AR] 1. *Chem.* relating to the mole, or gram-molecular weight; specif., designating a solution containing one mole of solute per liter of solution 2. [< L. *molos*, mass (see MOLE[3]) + -AR] *Physics* of a body (of matter) as a whole

mo·las·ses (mə las′iz) *n.* [< Port. *melaço* < LL. *mellaceum*, must < L. *mellaceus*, resembling honey < *mel*, honey: see MILDEW] a thick, usually dark brown syrup produced during the refining of sugar, or from sorghum, etc.

mold[1] (mōld) *n.* [ME. *moolde* < OFr. *molle*, earlier *modle* < L. *modulus*: see MODULE] 1. a pattern, hollow form, or matrix for giving a certain form to something in a plastic or molten state 2. a frame, shaped core, etc. on or around which something is modeled 3. a pattern after which something is formed; model 4. something formed or shaped in or on, or as if in or on, a mold; often, specif., a gelatin dessert, aspic, etc. so prepared 5. *a)* the form or shape given to a mold *b)* form or shape in general 6. distinctive character or nature [men of his *mold*] 7. *Archit.* a molding or group of moldings —*vt.* 1. to make or shape in or on, or as if in or on, a mold 2. to work into a certain form or shape; shape 3. to have a strong or important influence on (public opinion, thought, etc.) 4. to fit closely to the outline or contours of 5. to ornament by or with molding 6. to make a mold of or from in order to make a casting —**mold′a·ble** *adj.* —**mold′er** *n.*

mold[2] (mōld) *n.* [ME. *moul*, *mowlde*, mold, mildew: sp. prob. infl. by ff.] 1. a downy or furry growth on the surface of organic matter, caused by fungi, esp. in the presence of dampness or decay 2. any fungus producing such a growth —*vt.*, *vi.* [< ME. *moulen* (with unhistoric *-d-*), akin to Dan. *mulne*, ult. < IE. base *meu-*, moist, whence MOSS, MUD] to make or become moldy

mold[3] (mōld) *n.* [ME. *mold* < OE. *molde*, dust, ground, earth, akin to Goth. *mulda* < IE. base *mel-*, to rub away, grind, whence L. *molere*, to grind, MILL[1]] 1. loose, soft, easily worked soil, esp. when rich with decayed animal or vegetable matter and good for growing plants 2. [Archaic or Poet.] earth or ground

Mol·dau (mōl′dou) *Ger. name of* VLTAVA River

Mol·da·vi·a (mäl dā′vē ə, -dāv′yə) region & former principality in E Europe, east of the Carpathians: merged with Walachia (1861) to form Romania —**Mol·da′vi·an** *adj.*, *n.*

Moldavian Soviet Socialist Republic republic of the U.S.S.R., adjacent to the Romanian region of Moldavia: 13,000 sq. mi.; pop. 3,400,000; cap. Kishinev

mold·board (mōld′bôrd′) *n.* [MOLD[3] & BOARD] 1. a curved plate of iron attached to a plowshare, for turning over the soil ☆2. a plate like this at the front of a bulldozer or snowplow, angled to push material aside 3. one of the boards used in making a mold for concrete

mold·er (mōl′dər) *vi.* [freq. of obs. *mold, v.*, to molder: see MOLD[3] & -ER] to crumble into dust; decay; waste away (often with *away*) —*vt.* [Now Rare] to cause to molder —*SYN.* see DECAY

mold·ing (mōl′diŋ) *n.* 1. the act or process of one that molds 2. something molded 3. *a)* any of various orna-mental contours given to cornices, jambs, etc. *b)* a cornice, or other projecting or sunk ornamentation, of wood, stone, brick, etc. *c)* a shaped strip of wood, etc., used for finishing or decor-ating walls (esp. near the ceiling), furniture, etc.

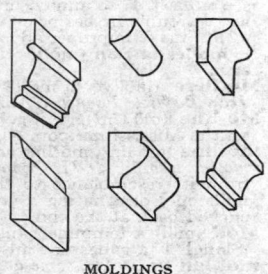

MOLDINGS

molding board *same as* BREADBOARD (sense 1)

mold·y (mōl′dē) *adj.* **mold′i·er**, **mold′i·est** [MOLD[2] + -Y[2]] 1. covered or over-grown with mold 2. musty or stale, as from age or decay —**mold′i·ness** *n.*

mole[1] (mōl) *n.* [ME. < OE. *mal*, akin to Goth. *mail* < IE. base *mai-*, to spot, whence Gr. *miainein*, to sully] a small, congenital spot on the human skin, usually dark-colored and slightly raised, often hairy; esp., a pigmented nevus

mole[2] (mōl) *n.* [ME. *molle*, akin to or < MDu. *mol*, altered (after *mul*, earth, MOLD[3]) < Gmc. base, whence MOW[2]: orig. sense, "mound maker"] any of a number of small, burrowing, insect-eating mammals (family Talpidae) with small eyes and ears, shovellike fore-feet, and soft fur: moles live mainly underground

mole[3] (mōl) *n.* [Fr. *môle* < LGr. *mōlos* < L. *moles*, a mass, dam, mole < IE. base *molo-*, to strive, whence Gr. *mōlos*, effort, G. *müde*, tired] 1. a barrier of stone, etc. built in the water to protect from the force of the waves, as a breakwater 2. a harbor or anchorage so formed or protected

MOLE
(5–8 in. long, including tail)

mole[4] (mōl) *n.* [G. *mol*, short for *molekulargewicht*, molecular weight] *Chem.* the quantity of a chemical substance having a weight in grams numerically equal to its molecular weight: one mole of a substance contains 6.02257×10^{23} molecules

mole[5] (mōl) *n.* [Fr. *môle* < L. *mola*, false conception, mill-stone: for IE. base see MILL[1]] 1. a marked growth of grapelike masses of fetal placental tissue 2. any of various fleshy or bloody masses in the uterus

Mo·lech (mō′lek) [LL.(Ec.) *Moloch* < Gr.(Ec.) *Moloch* (in LXX) < Heb. *mōlōkh*, *mōlekh*] *Bible* an ancient Phoe-nician and Ammonite god, to whom children were sacri-ficed by burning —*n.* anything demanding terrible sacrifice

mole cricket any of a family (Gryllotalpidae) of insects having large front legs specialized for burrowing, and feeding chiefly on plant roots

mo·lec·u·lar (mə lek′yə lər) *adj.* [MOLECUL(E) + -AR] of, consisting of, produced by, or existing between molecules —**mo·lec′u·lar′i·ty** (-lar′ə tē) *n.* —**mo·lec′u·lar·ly** *adv.*

molecular biology a branch of biology that deals with the chemical and physical composition and activities of the molecules making up living matter

molecular film *same as* MONOLAYER

molecular formula a formula which gives the kinds of atoms or radicals and the number of each kind in the molecule of a compound (Ex.: C_6H_6 for benzene)

molecular sieve any of a class of zeolites or similar mate-rials, natural or synthetic, having small, precisely uniform, pores in their crystal lattices that can absorb molecules small enough to pass through the pores: used as for sep-arating or drying gases and liquids

molecular weight the relative average weight of a molecule of a substance, expressed by a number equal to the sum of the atomic weights of all atoms in the molecule

mol·e·cule (mäl′ə kyool′) *n.* [Fr. *molécule* < ModL. *molecula*, dim. < L. *moles*, a mass: see MOLE[3]] 1. the smallest particle of an element or compound that can exist in the free state and still retain the characteristics of the element or compound: the molecules of elements consist of one atom or two or more similar atoms; those of compounds consist of two or more different atoms 2. a small particle

mole fraction the ratio of the number of moles of one constituent of a mixture or solution to the total number of moles of all the constituents

mole·hill (mōl′hil′) *n.* a small ridge or mound of earth, formed by a burrowing mole —**make a mountain out of a molehill** to regard or treat a trivial problem as a great or important one

mole·skin (-skin′) *n.* 1. the soft, dark-gray skin of the mole, used as fur 2. *a)* a strong, twilled cotton fabric with a soft nap, used for work clothes, etc. *b)* [*pl.*] trousers made of this fabric 3. soft fabric, often with an adhesive backing, used for foot bandages

mo·lest (mə lest′, mō-) *vt.* [ME. *molesten* < OFr. *molester*

< L. *molestare* < *molestus*, troublesome < *moles*, a burden: see MOLE³] **1.** to annoy, interfere with, or meddle with so as to trouble or harm, or with intent to trouble or harm ☆**2.** to make improper advances to, esp. of a sexual nature —**mo·les·ta·tion** (mō′les tā′shən, mäl′əs-) *n.* —**mo·lest′-er** *n.*

Mo·lière (mōl yer′, mō′lē er′; *Fr.* mô lyer′) (pseud. of *Jean Baptiste Poquelin*) 1622–73; Fr. dramatist

Mo·line (mō lēn′) [< Sp. *molino*, mill] city in NW Ill., on the Mississippi: pop. 46,000

mo·line (mō lin′, mō′lin) *adj.* [< AngloFr. *moliné* < OFr. *molin*, a mill < VL. *molinum*, for LL. *molina*, MILL¹: from its resemblance to the iron support for the upper millstone] designating a cross with each arm forked and curved back at the end

Moll (mäl) a feminine name: see MARY —*n.* [*usually* m-] [Slang] **1.** a gangster's mistress **2.** a prostitute

mol·lah (mäl′ə) *n. same as* MULLAH

mol·les·cent (mə les′'nt) *adj.* [L. *mollescens*, prp. of *mollescere*, to soften < *mollere*, to be soft < *mollis*, soft: see MOLLIFY] softening or tending to soften —**mol·les′-cence** *n.*

mol·li·fy (mäl′ə fī′) *vt.* -**fied′**, -**fy′ing** [ME. *molifien*, MFr. *mollifier* < LL. *mollificare*, to soften < L. *mollis*, soft (< IE. *mldu-*, soft < base *mel-*, to crush, whence MILL¹) + *facere*, to make, DO¹] **1.** to soothe the temper of; pacify; appease **2.** to make less intense, severe, or violent —*SYN.* see PACIFY —**mol′li·fi·ca′tion** *n.* —**mol′li·fi′er** *n.*

mol·lusc (mäl′əsk) *n. same as* MOLLUSK —**mol·lus·can** (mə lus′kən) *adj., n.*

mol·lus·coid (mə lus′koid) *adj.* **1.** of or like a mollusk or mollusks **2.** in some classifications, designating or of a group (Molluscoidea) of phyla comprising the brachiopods, phoronids, and bryozoans, all of which have a lophophore —*n.* a molluscoid animal

mol·lusk (mäl′əsk) *n.* [Fr. *mollusque* < ModL. *Mollusca*, coined by Cuvier < L. *mollusca*, a soft-shelled nut < *molluscus*, soft < *mollis*: see MOLLIFY] any of a large phylum (Mollusca) of invertebrate animals including the chitons, oysters, clams, mussels, snails, whelks, slugs, squids, octopuses, etc., characterized by a soft, usually unsegmented body, often enclosed wholly or in part in a mantle and a calcareous shell of one or more pieces, and usually having gills and a foot —**mol·lus·kan** (mə lus′kən) *adj., n.*

Moll·wei·de projection (mōl′vī də) [after Karl B. *Mollweide* (1774–1825), G. mathematician] an equal-area map projection with the whole earth on one map, showing the prime meridian and all parallels of latitude as straight lines and all other meridians as increasing in curvature toward the margins

Mol·ly (mäl′ē) a feminine name: see MARY

mol·ly (mäl′ē) *n., pl.* -**lies** [short for ModL. *Molliensia*, genus name < F. N. *Mollien* (1758–1850), Fr. statesman] any of a genus (*Molliensia*) of various brightly colored tropical and subtropical American fishes often kept in aquariums: also **mol′lie**

mol·ly·cod·dle (mäl′ē käd′'l) *n.* [MOLLY + CODDLE] a man or boy used to being coddled, or protected, pampered, etc.; milksop —*vt.* -**dled**, -**dling** to pamper; coddle —**mol′ly·cod′dler** *n.*

Molly Ma·guires (mə gwirz′) [its members were sometimes disguised as women] **1.** a secret society organized in Ireland in 1843 to prevent evictions by terrorizing agents of landlords ☆**2.** a secret society of Irish-American miners in E Pennsylvania (c. 1865–1875), which opposed oppressive industrial and social conditions, sometimes with physical force

Mol·nár (mōl′när), **Fe·renc** (fe′rents) 1878–1952; Hung. playwright & novelist, later in the U.S.

Mo·loch (mō′läk, mäl′ək) *same as* MOLECH —*n.* [m-] a spiny-headed Australian lizard (*Moloch horridus*)

Mo·lo·kai (mō′lō kī′) [Haw. < ?] island of Hawaii, southeast of Oahu: site of a leper colony: 259 sq. mi.; pop. 5,000

Mo·lo·tov (mô′lə täf), **V(yacheslav) M(ikhailovich)** (born *Vyacheslav Mikhailovich Skriabin*) 1890– ; Russ. statesman; foreign minister of the U.S.S.R. (1939–49; 1953–56)

Molotov cocktail [after prec.] [Slang] a bottle filled with gasoline, etc. and wrapped in a saturated rag or plugged with a wick, ignited, and hurled as an antitank grenade

molt (mōlt) *vi.* [ME. *mouten* (with unhistoric -*l*- after FAULT, in which the letter was orig. silent) < OE. (*be*)*mutian*, to exchange < L. *mutare*, to change: see MUTATE] to cast off or shed the hair, outer skin, horns, or feathers at certain intervals, prior to replacement of the castoff parts by a new growth: said of certain animals, as reptiles, birds, etc. —*vt.* to shed and replace by molting —*n.* **1.** the act or process of molting **2.** the parts so shed —**molt′-er** *n.*

mol·ten (mōl′t'n) [ME.] *archaic pp. of* MELT —*adj.* **1.** melted or liquefied by heat **2.** made by being melted and cast in a mold

Molt·ke (mōlt′kə) **1.** Count **Hel·muth (Johannes Ludwig) von** (hel′mŏŏt fôn), 1848–1916; Ger. general **2.** Count **Helmuth (Karl Bernhard) von**, 1800–91; Ger. field marshal: uncle of *prec.*

mol·to (mōl′tō) *adv.* [It. < L. *multum*, much] *Music* very; much: used in musical directions

Mo·luc·cas (mō luk′əz) group of islands constituting a province of Indonesia, between Celebes & New Guinea: c. 32,000 sq. mi.; pop. 790,000: also **Molucca Islands**

mol. wt. molecular weight

mo·ly¹ (mō′lē) *n.* [L. < Gr. *mōly*] **1.** *Classical Myth.* an herb of magic powers, as, in Homer's *Odyssey*, that given to Odysseus to protect him from Circe's incantation **2.** a European wild garlic (*Allium moly*)

mol·y² (mäl′ē) *n. clipped form of* MOLYBDENUM

mo·lyb·date (mō lib′dāt) *n.* a salt of molybdic acid

mo·lyb·de·nite (mə lib′də nit′) *n.* native molybdenum sulfide, MoS₂, a scaly or foliated, lead-gray mineral, the chief ore of molybdenum

mo·lyb·de·num (-nəm) *n.* [ModL. < *molybdena*, a lead ore, molybdenite, altered < L. *molybdaena*, lead, galena < Gr. *molybdaina* < *molybdos*, lead] a soft, lustrous, silver-white metallic chemical element, used in alloys, windings for electrical resistance furnaces, points for spark plugs, etc.: symbol, Mo; at. wt., 95.94; at. no., 42; sp. gr., 10.2; melt. pt., 2620°C; sublimes at 4507°C

mo·lyb·dic (mə lib′dik) *adj. Chem.* designating or of compounds in which molybdenum has a higher valence (usually 3 or 6) than in the corresponding molybdous compounds

mo·lyb·dous (-dəs) *adj. Chem.* designating or of compounds in which molybdenum has a lower valence than in the corresponding molybdic compounds

mom (mäm) *n.* [Colloq.] mother

☆**mom and pop store (stand**, etc.) a small retail business, typically family operated and now often franchised

Mom·ba·sa (mäm bä′sə, -bäs′ə) seaport on the SE coast of Kenya: pop. 180,000

mome (mōm) *n.* [< ?] [Archaic] a blockhead; fool

mo·ment (mō′mənt) *n.* [ME. < L. *momentum*, movement, impulse, brief space of time, importance < *movimentum* < *movere*, to MOVE] **1.** an indefinitely brief period of time; instant **2.** a definite point in time or in a series of events **3.** a brief time of being important or outstanding **4.** importance; consequence [news of great *moment*] **5.** *Mech.* a) the tendency to cause rotation about a point or axis b) a measure of this tendency c) the product of a (specified) force, mass, volume, etc. and its perpendicular distance from its axis, fulcrum, or plane **6.** *Philos.* any of the constituent elements of a complex entity —*SYN.* see IMPORTANCE —**the moment** the present or the immediate future

mo·men·tar·i·ly (mō′mən ter′ə lē) *adv.* **1.** for a moment or short time **2.** in an instant **3.** from moment to moment; at any moment

mo·men·tar·y (mō′mən ter′ē) *adj.* [L. *momentarius*] **1.** lasting for only a moment; passing; transitory **2.** [Now Rare] recurring every moment; constant **3.** likely to occur at any moment —*SYN.* see TRANSIENT —**mo′-men·tar′i·ness** *n.*

mo·ment·ly (mō′mənt lē) *adv.* **1.** from instant to instant; every moment **2.** at any moment **3.** for a single moment

mo·men·to (mō men′tō) *n. erroneous sp. of* MEMENTO

☆**moment of truth 1.** the point in a bullfight when the matador faces the bull for the kill **2.** a critical moment or time that tests and reveals one's true self or makes one face the truth

mo·men·tous (mō men′təs) *adj.* of great moment; very important [a *momentous* decision] —**mo·men′tous·ly** *adv.* —**mo·men′tous·ness** *n.*

mo·men·tum (mō men′təm) *n., pl.* -**tums**, -**ta** (-tə) [ModL. < L.: see MOMENT] **1.** the impetus of a moving object **2.** strength or force that keeps growing [a campaign that gained *momentum*] **3.** *Physics & Mech.* the quantity of motion of a moving object, equal to the product of its mass and its velocity

☆**mom·ism** (mäm′iz'm) *n.* [coined (1942) by Philip Wylie, U.S. writer: cf. MOM & -ISM] excessive devotion to mothers that gives them a domineering role over their children

Momm·sen (mäm′sən; *E.* mäm′s'n, -z'n), **The·o·dor** (tā′ō dôr) 1817–1903; Ger. historian

mom·my (mäm′ē) *n., pl.* -**mies** child's term for MOTHER¹

Mo·mus (mō′məs) [L. < Gr. *Mōmos*, lit., blame, ridicule] *Gr. Myth.* the god of mockery and censure —*n.* a faultfinder or caviling critic

Mon (mōn) *n.* **1.** *pl.* **Mons, Mon** any member of a people living in Burma east of Rangoon **2.** their Mon-Khmer language

mon (män) *n. Scot. & North Eng. var. of* MAN

mon- (män) *same as* MONO-: used before a vowel

Mon. 1. Monastery **2.** Monday **3.** Monsignor

mon. 1. monastery **2.** monetary

Mo·na (mō′nə) [Ir. *Muadhnait*, dim. of *muadh*, noble] a feminine name

mon·a·chal (män′ə k'l) *adj.* [ML.(Ec.) *monachalis* < LL.(Ec.) *monachus*: see MONK] *same as* MONASTIC —**mon′a·chism** (-kiz′m) *n.*

mon·a·cid (män as′id) *adj., n. same as* MONOACID

Mon·a·co (män′ə kō, mə nä′kō) independent principality on the Mediterranean; enclave in SE France: 1/2 sq. mi.; pop. 23,000

mo·nad (mō′nad, män′ad) *n.* [LL. *monas* (gen. *monadis*) < Gr. *monas* (gen. *monados*), a unit, unity < *monos*, alone: see MONO-] **1.** a unit; something simple and indivisible **2.** *Biol.* a) any simple, single-celled organism,

specif. a simple type of flagellated protozoan or protist *b)* any of the four nuclei formed at the completion of meiosis **3.** *Chem.* an atom, element, or radical with a valence of one **4.** *Philos.* an entity or elementary being thought of as a microcosm or ultimate unit —*adj.* of, consisting of, or having the nature of, a monad or monads —**mo·nad′ic, mo·nad′i·cal** *adj.*

mon·a·del·phous (män′ə del′fəs) *adj.* [< MON- + Gr. *adelphos*, brother + -OUS] having the stamens united by their filaments into one set or bundle, as some legumes and the members of the mallow family

mo·nad·ism (mō′nad iz′m, män′ad-) *n. Philos.* the theory that the universe consists of monads

☆**mo·nad·nock** (mə nad′näk) *n.* [after Mt. *Monadnock,* N.H.] *Geol.* an isolated rocky hill or mountain rising above a peneplain

Mon·a·ghan (män′ə gən) county in NE Ireland, in Ulster province: 499 sq. mi.; pop. 46,000

Mo·na Li·sa (mō′nə lē′sə, -zə) a famous portrait of a faintly smiling woman, by Leonardo da Vinci: also called *La Gioconda*

mo·nan·drous (mə nan′drəs) *adj.* [Gr. *monandros,* having one husband: see MON- & -ANDROUS] **1.** having but one husband at a time **2.** of or characterized by monandry **3.** having only one stamen, as some flowers

mo·nan·dry (-drē) *n.* **1.** the state or practice of having but one husband at a time **2.** *Bot.* a monandrous condition

mo·nan·thous (mə nan′thəs) *adj.* [MON- + -ANTHOUS] *Bot.* having only one flower, as some plants

mon·arch (män′ərk, -ärk) *n.* [LME. *monarcha* < LL. < Gr. *monarchēs* < *monos,* alone (see MONO-) + *archein,* to rule] **1.** the single or sole ruler of a state **2.** the hereditary (often constitutional) head of a state; king, queen, etc. **3.** a person or thing that surpasses others of the same kind **4.** a large, migrating butterfly (*Danaus plexippus*) of N. America, having reddish-brown, black-edged wings: the larvae feed on milkweed

mo·nar·chal (mə när′k′l) *adj.* of, like, suitable for, or characteristic of a monarch; royal; regal: also **mo·nar′chi·al** (-kē əl) —**mo·nar′chal·ly** *adv.*

Mo·nar·chi·an·ism (-kē ən iz′m) *n.* [see MONARCH, -AN, & -ISM] the doctrine of several Christian sects in the 2d and 3d cent. that the Three Persons of the Trinity are manifestations of one God, single in person —**Mo·nar′chi·an** *adj., n.*

mo·nar·chi·cal (-ki k′l) *adj.* **1.** of, characteristic of, or like a monarch or monarchy **2.** characterized by or favoring a monarchy Also **mo·nar′chic** —**mo·nar′chi·cal·ly** *adv.*

mon·ar·chism (män′ər kiz′m, -är-) *n.* [Fr. *monarchisme*] monarchical principles or the advocacy of these —**mon′ar·chist** *n., adj.* —**mon′ar·chis′tic** *adj.*

mon·ar·chy (män′ər kē, -är-) *n., pl.* -**ar·chies** [ME. *monarchie* < OFr. < LL. *monarchia* < Gr. *monarchia* < *monarchos:* see MONARCH] **1.** [Rare] rule by only one person **2.** a government or state headed by a monarch: called *absolute* (or *despotic*) when there is no limitation on the monarch's power, *constitutional* (or *limited*) when there is such limitation

mo·nar·da (mə när′də) *n.* [ModL., after N. *Monardes,* 16th c. Sp. botanist] ☆same as HORSEMINT

mon·as·ter·y (män′ə ster′ē) *n., pl.* -**ter′ies** [ME. *monasterie* < LL.(Ec.) *monasterium* < LGr.(Ec.) *monastērion* < Gr. *monazein,* to be alone < *monos,* alone: see MONO-] **1.** a place of residence occupied by a group of people, esp. monks, who have retired from the world under religious vows **2.** those living in such a place —*SYN.* see CLOISTER —**mon′as·te′ri·al** (-stir′ē əl) *adj.*

mo·nas·tic (mə nas′tik) *adj.* [ME. *monastik* < ML.(Ec.) *monasticus* < LGr.(Ec.) < Gr. *monastikos* < *monazein:* see prec.] **1.** of or characteristic of monasteries **2.** of or characteristic of monks or nuns or their way of life; ascetic; self-denying; austere Also **mo·nas′ti·cal** —*n.* a person living a monastic life; esp., a monk —**mo·nas′ti·cal·ly** *adv.*

mo·nas·ti·cism (-tə siz′m) *n.* the monastic system, state, or way of life

Mon·as·tir (mō′nä stir′) *Turk.* name of BITOLA

mon·a·tom·ic (män′ə täm′ik) *adj.* [MON- + ATOMIC] **1.** *a)* consisting of one atom: said of a molecule *b)* having one atom in the molecule **2.** containing one replaceable atom or atomic group **3.** *same as* UNIVALENT

mon·ax·i·al (-ak′sē əl) *adj.* having only one axis; uniaxial

mon·a·zite (män′ə zīt′) *n.* [G. *monazit* < Gr. *monazein,* to be alone (see MONASTERY) + G. -*it,* -ITE[1]: so named because of its isolated crystals] a brown or brownish-red native phosphate of the rare-earth metals, a major source of thorium, cerium, lanthanum, neodymium, and praseodymium

Mön·chen-Glad·bach (mön′khən glät′bäkh) city in W West Germany, in North Rhine-Westphalia: pop. 154,000

Monck, George *same as* George MONK

Monc·ton (muŋk′tən) [orig. *Monckton,* after Robert *Monckton* (1726–82), Lt.-Governor of Nova Scotia] city in SE New Brunswick, Canada: pop. 46,000

Mon·day (mun′dē, -dā) *n.* [ME. < OE. *monandæg,* moon's day < *monan,* gen. of *mona,* MOON + *dæg,* DAY, transl. of LL. *Lunae dies*] the second day of the week

☆**Monday morning quarterback** a person who, after the event, offers advice or criticism concerning decisions made by others; one who second-guesses

Mon·days (-dēz, -dāz) *adv.* on or during every Monday

‡**monde** (mōnd) *n.* [Fr. < L. *mundus*] the world; people; society

‡**mon Dieu** (mōn dyö′) [Fr.] my God: often used as an interjection

Mon·dri·an (môn′drē än′), **Piet** (pēt) (born *Pieter Cornelis Mondriaan*) 1872–1944; Du. painter, in France & the U.S.

mo·ne·cious (mə nē′shəs, mō-) *adj. same as* MONOECIOUS

☆**Mo·nel metal** (mō nel′) [after Ambrose *Monell* (d. 1921), U.S. manufacturer] *a trademark for* an alloy mainly of nickel and copper, very resistant to corrosion

Mo·net (mō nā′, mə-; *Fr.* mô ne′), **Claude** 1840–1926; Fr. painter

mon·e·tar·y (män′ə ter′ē, mun′-) *adj.* [LL. *monetarius,* of a mint < L. *moneta,* a MINT[1]] **1.** of or having to do with the coinage or currency of a country: see table of MONETARY UNITS on next page **2.** of money; pecuniary —*SYN.* see FINANCIAL —**mon′e·tar′i·ly** *adv.*

mon·e·tize (-tīz′) *vt.* -**tized′**, -**tiz′ing** [< L. *moneta,* a MINT[1] + -IZE] **1.** to coin into money **2.** to legalize as money —**mon′e·ti·za′tion** *n.*

mon·ey (mun′ē) *n., pl.* -**eys, -ies** [ME. < OFr. *moneie* < L. *moneta,* a MINT[1]] **1.** *a)* standard pieces of gold, silver, copper, nickel, etc., stamped by government authority and used as a medium of exchange and measure of value; coin or coins: also called **hard money** *b)* any paper note issued by a government or an authorized bank and used in the same way; bank notes; bills: also called **paper money** **2.** any substance or article used as money, as bank notes, checks, etc. **3.** any definite or indefinite sum of money **4.** property; possessions; wealth **5.** very wealthy persons or groups **6.** any form or denomination of legally current money **7.** *same as* MONEY OF ACCOUNT **8.** money won as a prize **9.** [*pl.*] sums of money: now used chiefly in law —**for one's money** [Colloq.] for one's choice; in one's opinion —**in the money** [Slang] **1.** among the winners, as in a contest, race, etc. **2.** prosperous; wealthy; successful —**make money** to gain profits; become wealthy —**one's money's worth** full value or benefit —**place** (or **put**) **money on** to bet on —**put money into** to invest money in —**mon′ey·less** *adj.*

mon·ey·bag (-bag′) *n.* **1.** a bag for holding money **2.** [*pl.,* with *sing. v.*] [Colloq.] a rich person

money belt a belt with a compartment to hold money

mon·ey·chang·er (-chān′jər) *n.* **1.** a person whose business is money-changing ☆**2.** a device holding stacked coins for making change quickly

mon·ey·chang·ing (-chān′jiŋ) *n.* the business or act of exchanging currency, usually of different countries, esp. at an established or official rate

mon·ey·eyed (mun′ēd) *adj.* **1.** having much money; rich; wealthy **2.** consisting of, derived from, or representing money *[moneyed interests]*

mon·ey·er (mun′ē ər) *n.* [ME. *moneyour* < OFr. *monoier* < L. *monetarius,* mint master < *moneta,* MINT[1]] **1.** [Obs.] a banker or capitalist **2.** [Archaic] a coiner of money

mon·ey·grub·ber (-grub′ər) *n.* a person who is greedily intent on accumulating money —**mon′ey·grub′bing** *adj., n.*

mon·ey·lend·er (-len′dər) *n.* a person whose business is lending money at interest

mon·ey·mak·er (-mā′kər) *n.* **1.** a person successful at acquiring money **2.** something that produces monetary gain, as a lucrative business —**mon′ey·mak′ing** *adj., n.*

money of account a monetary denomination used in keeping accounts, etc., esp. one not issued as a coin or piece of paper money (e.g., the U.S. mill)

money order an order for the payment of a specified sum of money, as one issued for a fee at one post office or bank and payable at another

mon·ey·wort (-wurt′) *n.* [MONEY + WORT[2], after the ModL. name *Nummularia* (see NUMMULAR): so called from its round leaves] a European creeping perennial plant (*Lysimachia nummularia*) of the primrose family, with yellow flowers and roundish leaves

Mong. 1. Mongolia 2. Mongolian

mon·ger (muŋ′gər, män′-) *n.* [ME. *mongere* < OE. *mangere* < L. *mango,* dealer in tricked-out wares < ? Gr. **mangōn* < *manganon,* device for deceiving (see MANGLE[2])] a dealer or trader: usually in compounds *[fishmonger]:* sometimes used figuratively and derogatorily *[scandalmonger]:* chiefly Brit. in literal uses

mon·go (mäŋ′gō) *n., pl.* -**gos** a unit of money in the Mongolian People's Republic, equal to 1/100 tugrik

Mon·gol (mäŋ′gəl, -gōl) *adj.* [Mongol.: cf. MOGUL] *same as* MONGOLIAN —*n.* **1.** a native of Mongolia (sense 1) or of a contiguous region in E Siberia **2.** *same as* MONGOLOID

fat, āpe, cär; ten, ēven; is, bīte; gō, hôrn, tōol, look; oil, out; up, fur; get; joy; yet; chin; she; thin, *then;* zh, leisure; ŋ, ring; ə for *a* in *ago, e* in *agent, i* in *sanity, o* in *comply, u* in *focus;* ′ as in *able* (ā′b′l); Fr. bål; ë, Fr. coeur; ö, Fr. feu; Fr. mon; ℧, Fr. coq; ü, Fr. duc; r, Fr. cri; H, G. ich; kh, G. doch. See inside front cover. ☆ Americanism; ‡foreign; *hypothetical; < derived from

Monetary Units of All Nations

(The exchange rates in this list are unofficial.)

Country	Basic Unit	Equiv. (1971) in U.S. Currency	Chief Fractional Unit	Country	Basic Unit	Equiv. (1971) in U.S. Currency	Chief Fractional Unit
Afghanistan	afghani	.022	pul	Laos	kip	.002	at
Albania	lek	.20	qintar	Lebanon	pound	.31	piaster
Algeria	dinar	.20	centime	Lesotho	rand	1.40	cent
Andorra	franc	.18	centime	Liberia	dollar	1.00	cent
	peseta	.014	centimo	Libya	pound	2.82	millieme
Argentina	peso	.003	centavo	Liechtenstein	franc	.232	rappen
Australia	dollar	1.12	cent	Luxembourg	franc	.02	centime
Austria	schilling	.04	groschen	Malagasy	franc	.004	centime
Bahrain	dinar	2.10	fils	Malawi	kwacha	1.20	tambala
Barbados	dollar	.50	cent	Malaysia	dollar	.33	cent
Belgium	franc	.02	centime	Maldive Is.	rupee	.17	cent
Bhutan	rupee	.131		Mali	franc	.002	centime
Bolivia	peso boliviano	.085	centavo	Malta	pound	2.40	penny
Botswana	rand	1.40	cent	Mauritania	franc	.004	centime
Brazil	cruzeiro	.21	centavo	Mauritius	rupee	.181	cent
Bulgaria	lev	.855	stotinka	Mexico	peso	.08	centavo
Burma	kyat	.21	pya	Monaco	franc	.18	centime
Burundi	franc	.012	centime	Mongolia	tugrik	.25	mongo
Cambodia	riel	.018	sen	Morocco	dirham	.20	franc
Cameroun	franc	.004	centime	Muscat & Oman	rupee	.21	paisa
Canada	dollar	.93	cent	Nauru	dollar	1.12	cent
Central African Republic	franc	.004	centime	Nepal	rupee	.10	pice
				Netherlands	guilder	.276	cent
Ceylon	rupee	.169	cent	New Zealand	dollar	1.12	cent
Chad	franc	.004	centime	Nicaragua	cordoba	.143	centavo
Chile	escudo	.085	centesimo	Niger	franc	.004	centime
China	yuan	.40	fen	Nigeria	pound	2.80	shilling
China (Taiwan)	dollar	.025	cent	Norway	krone	.14	øre
				Pakistan	rupee	.21	paisa
Colombia	peso	.055	centavo	Panama	balboa	1.00	centesimo
Congo (Brazzaville)	franc	.004	centime	Paraguay	guarani	.008	centimo
				Peru	sol	.023	centavo
Congo (Kinshasa)	zaire	2.00	likuta	Philippines	peso	.256	centavo
				Poland	zloty	.25	grosz
Costa Rica	colon	.151	centimo	Portugal	escudo	.035	centavo
Cuba	peso	1.00	centavo	Qatar	riyal	.21	dirham
Cyprus	pound	2.40	mil	Rhodesia	dollar	1.40	cent
Czechoslovakia	koruna	.14	haler	Romania	leu	.167	ban
Dahomey	franc	.004	centime	Rwanda	franc	.01	centime
Denmark	krone	.134	øre	San Marino	lira	.002	centesimo
Dominican Republic	peso	1.00	centavo	Saudi Arabia	riyal	.224	qursh
				Senegal	franc	.004	centime
Ecuador	sucre	.04	centavo	Sierra Leone	leone	1.20	cent
El Salvador	colon	.40	centavo	Singapore	dollar	.33	cent
Equatorial Guinea	peseta	.014	centimo	Somalia	shilling	.141	cent
Ethiopia	dollar	.40	cent	South Africa	rand	1.40	cent
Fiji	dollar	1.15	cent	Southern Yemen	dinar	2.42	fils
Finland	markka	.24	penni	Spain	peseta	.014	centimo
France	franc	.18	centime	Sudan	pound	2.87	piaster
Gabon	franc	.004	centime	Swaziland	rand	1.40	cent
Gambia	dalasi	.48	butut	Sweden	krona	.193	öre
Germany, East	mark	.450	pfennig	Switzerland	franc	.232	rappen
Germany, West	deutsche mark	.27	pfennig	Syria	pound	.233	piaster
Ghana	cedi	.98	pesewa	Tanzania	shilling	.140	cent
Greece	drachma	.034	lepton	Thailand	baht	.049	satang
Guatemala	quetzal	1.00	centavo	Togo	franc	.004	centime
Guinea	franc	.004	centime	Tonga	paanga	1.12	seniti
Guyana	dollar	.50	cent	Trinidad & Tobago	dollar	.50	cent
Haiti	gourde	.20	centime				
Honduras	lempira	.50	centavo	Tunisia	dinar	1.92	millime
Hungary	forint	.033	fillér	Turkey	lira	.066	piaster
Iceland	króna	.012	eyrir	Uganda	shilling	.140	cent
India	rupee	.134	paisa	United Arab Republic	pound	2.31	piaster
Indonesia	rupiah	.003	sen				
Iran	rial	.014	dinar	United Kingdom	pound	2.39	penny
Iraq	dinar	2.80	fils	United States	dollar	1.00	cent
Ireland	pound	2.39	penny	Upper Volta	franc	.004	centime
Israel	pound	.29	agora	Uruguay	peso	.004	centesimo
Italy	lira	.002	centesimo	USSR	ruble	1.11	kopeck
Ivory Coast	franc	.004	centime	Vatican City	lira	.002	centesimo
Jamaica	dollar	1.20	cent	Venezuela	bolívar	.223	centimo
Japan	yen	.003	sen	Vietnam, North	dong	.285	sau
Jordan	dinar	2.80	fils	Vietnam, South	piaster	.008	centime
Kenya	shilling	.14	cent	Western Samoa	dollar	1.12	cent
Korea, North	won	.013	chon	Yemen	riyal	.93	bugshah
Korea, South	won	.004	chon	Yugoslavia	dinar	.066	para
Kuwait	dinar	2.80	fils	Zambia	kwacha	1.40	ngwee

3. same as MONGOLIC (*n.* 2) **4.** Khalka, the main Mongolic language, and the official language of the Mongolian People's Republic **5.** [*often* m-] same as MONGOLIAN IDIOT

Mon·gol. Mongolian

Mon·go·li·a (män gō′lē ə, män-; -gōl′yə) **1.** region in EC Asia, consisting of Inner Mongolia & the Mongolian People's Republic **2.** same as MONGOLIAN PEOPLE'S REPUBLIC

Mon·go·li·an (-ən, -yən) *adj.* **1.** of Mongolia, its people, or their culture **2.** same as MONGOLOID (*adj.* 1 & 2) **3.** same as MONGOLIC (*adj.* 1) **4.** *Med.* having Mongolism —*n.* **1.** a native of Mongolia **2.** same as MONGOLOID **3.** same as MONGOLIC (*n.* 2)

Mongolian idiocy same as MONGOLISM

Mongolian (or **Mongoloid**) **idiot** a person having Mongolism

Mongolian People's Republic country in EC Asia, north of China: 592,600 sq. mi.; pop. 1,121,000; cap. Ulan Bator

Mon·gol·ic (män gäl′ik, män-) *adj.* **1.** designating or of a subfamily of Altaic languages spoken by the Mongols and probably related to the Turkic and Tungusic languages **2.** same as MONGOLIAN (*adj.* 1) **3.** same as MONGOLOID (*adj.* 1 & 2) —*n.* **1.** a branch of the Altaic language family including Kalmuck and Khalka **2.** any of the Mongolic languages

Mon·gol·ism (män′gə liz'm) *n.* [*often* m-] a congenital disease characterized by mental deficiency, a broad face, slanting eyes, a short fifth finger, etc.: the preferred term in technical literature is now DOWN'S SYNDROME

Mon·gol·oid (-loid′) *adj.* **1.** of or characteristic of the natives of Mongolia **2.** designating or of one of the three major groups of mankind: it includes most of the peoples of Asia, the Eskimos, the N. American Indians, etc., who are generally characterized by straight black hair, slanting eyes, a broad face, etc. **3.** [*often* m-] of or having Mongolism —*n.* a member of the Mongoloid group of mankind

mon·goose (män′gōōs) *n.*, *pl.* **-goos·es** [Marathi *mangūs*] any of various Old World, ferret-like, flesh-eating mammals, esp. any of several species (genus *Herpestes*) noted for their ability to kill poisonous snakes, rodents, etc. and frequently domesticated

MONGOOSE
(body 9–25 in. long; tail 9–20 in. long)

mon·grel (muŋ′grəl, mäŋ′-) *n.* [ME. *mengrell* < base of OE. *mengan*, to mix + dim. suffix *-rel* as in COCKEREL: form infl. by ME. *mong*, aphetic < OE. *gemong*, mixture: cf. AMONG] **1.** an animal or plant produced by the crossing of different breeds or varieties; esp., a dog of this kind **2.** anything produced by indiscriminate mixture —*adj.* of mixed breed, race, origin, or character Often a derogatory usage

mon·grel·ize (-īz′) *vt.* **-ized′**, **-iz′ing 1.** to mix the type, breed, class, etc. of **2.** to intermix in racial or ethnic character: a derogatory term used by racists —**mon′-grel·i·za′tion** *n.*

'mongst, mongst (muŋst) *prep.* archaic var. of AMONGST

Mon·i·ca (män′i kə) [LL. < ?] a feminine name

mon·ied (mun′ēd) *adj.* same as MONEYED

mon·ies (mun′ēz) *n. alt. pl. of* MONEY

mon·i·ker (män′i kər) *n.* [< ?] [Slang] a person's name or nickname: also sp. **mon′ick·er**

mo·nil·i·form (mō nil′ə fôrm′) *adj.* [< L. *monile* (gen. *monilis*), necklace < IE. base **mono-*, neck, whence MANE + -FORM] shaped somewhat like a string of beads; specif., *Biol.* consisting of, or having, a series of alternate swellings and constrictions, as some stems and some antennae

mon·ish (män′ish) *vt.* [Archaic] same as ADMONISH

mo·nism (mō′niz'm, män′iz'm) *n.* [ModL. *monismus* < Gr. *monos*, single: see MONO-] *Philos.* **1.** the doctrine that there is only one ultimate substance or principle, whether mind (*idealism*), matter (*materialism*), or some third thing that is the basis of both **2.** the doctrine that reality is an organic whole without independent parts Cf. DUALISM, PLURALISM —**mo′nist** *n.* —**mo·nis′tic, mo·nis′-ti·cal** *adj.* —**mo·nis′ti·cal·ly** *adv.*

mo·ni·tion (mō nish′ən) *n.* [ME. *monicion* < OFr. *monition* < L. *monitio* < pp. of *monere*, to warn: see ff.] **1.** admonition; warning; caution **2.** an official or legal notice; specif., a formal notice from a bishop requiring that an ecclesiastical offense be amended **3.** *Law* a summons to appear and answer in a suit or to contempt charges

mon·i·tor (män′ə tər) *n.* [L. < pp. of *monere*, to warn < IE. **moni-* < base **men-*, to think, whence MIND] **1.** [Rare] a person who advises, warns, or cautions **2.** in some schools, a student chosen to help keep order, record attendance, etc. **3.** something that reminds or warns **4.** any of several very large, flesh-eating lizards (family Varanidae) of Africa, S Asia, and Australia: from the notion that they warn of the presence of crocodiles ☆**5.** formerly, an armored warship, or ironclad, with a low freeboard, low flat deck, and heavy guns fitted in one or

more revolving turrets; specif., [M-] the Union ironclad that fought the Confederate Merrimac (March 9, 1862) in the first battle between ironclads ☆**6.** a mounting for a nozzle that allows a stream of water to be played in any direction, as in fire fighting **7.** a person who monitors a foreign broadcast, etc. **8.** any of various devices for checking or regulating the performance of machines, aircraft, guided missiles, etc. **9.** an instrument for measuring radioactive contamination by means of the ionizing radiation being emitted **10.** *Radio & TV* a receiver or speaker, as in the control room of a broadcasting studio, for checking the quality of the transmission —*vt.*, *vi.* **1.** to watch or check on (a person or thing) as a monitor **2.** to check on or regulate the performance of (a machine, airplane, etc.) **3.** to test for radioactive contamination with a monitor **4.** to listen in on (a foreign broadcast, telephone conversation, etc.) as for gathering political or military information **5.** *Radio & TV* to check the quality of (transmission) with or as with a monitor —**mon′i·tor·ship′** *n.*

mon·i·to·ri·al (män′ə tôr′ē əl) *adj.* **1.** of a monitor or using a monitor or monitors **2.** same as MONITORY

mon·i·to·ry (män′ə tôr′ē) *adj.* [LME. *manyterye* < L. *monitorius* < *monitor:* see MONITOR] giving or containing monition; admonishing —*n.*, *pl.* **-ries** a monitory letter, as from a bishop

monk (muŋk) *n.* [ME. *munec* < OE. *munuc* < LL.(Ec.) *monachus* < LGr.(Ec.) *monachos* < Gr., one who lives alone < Gr. *monos*, alone: see MONO-] **1.** orig., a man who retired from the world and lived in solitary self-denial for religious reasons **2.** a man who joins a religious order living in retirement according to a rule and generally under vows, as of poverty, obedience, and chastity —**monk′ish** *adj.* —**monk′ish·ly** *adv.*

Monk (muŋk), **George**, Duke of Albemarle, 1608–70; Eng. general & politician

monk·er·y (muŋk′ər ē) *n.*, *pl.* **-er·ies 1.** *a)* the way of life, condition, behavior, etc. of monks *b)* [*pl.*] monastic practices or beliefs Generally a hostile term **2.** a monastery

mon·key (muŋ′kē) *n.*, *pl.* **-keys** [Early ModE., prob. < or akin to MLowG. *Moneke*, name applied in the beast epic *Reynard the Fox* to the son of Martin the Ape < Fr. or Sp. *mona*, ape + LowG. *-ke*, -KIN] **1.** any of the primates except man and, usually, the lemurs; specif., any of the smaller, long tailed members of the primates, excluding the anthropoid apes **2.** the fur of some species of long-haired monkeys **3.** a person regarded as somehow like a monkey, as a mischievous or imitative child **4.** any of various mechanical devices, as the iron block raised and dropped in a pile driver —*vi.* ☆[Colloq.] to play, fool, trifle, or meddle (often followed by *around, with,* or *around with*) —*vt.* [Rare] to mimic; ape —☆**a monkey on one's back** [Slang] **1.** addiction to a drug **2.** any trying, burdensome obsession, problem, etc.

monkey bread 1. the fruit of the African baobab tree, eaten by monkeys **2.** same as BAOBAB

☆**monkey business** [Colloq.] foolish, mischievous, or deceitful tricks or behavior

monkey flower any of a genus (*Mimulus*) of plants of the figwort family, with snapdragonlike flowers in yellow, purple, or red, having a corolla whose appearance suggests a gape or grimace

monkey jacket [from the resemblance to coats worn by trained monkeys] [Colloq.] a short, tight jacket, as that formerly worn by sailors

mon·key·pot (-pät′) *n.* **1.** the large, bowl-shaped, woody seed vessel of any of various S. American trees (genus *Lecythis*) **2.** any of these trees

monkey puzzle a tall Chilean coniferous tree (*Araucaria araucana*) with stiff pointed leaves, edible nuts, and hard wood, widely grown as an ornamental

☆**mon·key·shine** (-shīn′) *n.* [Colloq.] a mischievous or playful trick, joke, or prank: *usually used in pl.*

monkey suit [see MONKEY JACKET] [Slang] **1.** a uniform **2.** a man's dress suit

monkey wrench a wrench with one movable jaw, adjusted by a screw to fit various sizes of nut, etc.: see WRENCH, illus. —☆**throw a monkey wrench into** [Colloq.] to disrupt the orderly functioning or realization of

Mon-Khmer (mōn′k'mer′) *adj.* designating or of a branch of the Austro-Asiatic family of languages, spoken mainly in Indochina and including Mon and Khmer

monk·hood (muŋk′hood′) *n.* **1.** the condition or profession of a monk **2.** monks collectively

monk's cloth 1. orig., a worsted cloth used for monks' garments **2.** now, a heavy cloth, as of cotton, with a basket weave, used for drapes, etc.

monks·hood (muŋks′hood′) *n. same as* ACONITE (sense 1)

Mon·mouth (män′məth), Duke of, (*James Scott*) 1649–85; pretender to the Eng. throne: led an insurrection against James II: executed

Mon·mouth·shire (-shir′) county between England & Wales, on the Severn estuary, once considered part of Wales: 542 sq. mi.; pop. 451,000; county seat, Newport: also called **Mon′mouth**

mon·o (män′ō) *adj. clipped form of* MONOPHONIC (sense 2) —*n. clipped form of* MONONUCLEOSIS

mon·o- (män′ə, -ō; *occas.* mō′nō) [Gr. *mono-* < *monos*, single, alone < IE. base *men-*, small, single, whence OIr. *menb*, small] *a prefix meaning:* **1.** one, alone, single [*monoclinic*] **2.** containing one atom or one group (of a specified element) [*monochloride*] **3.** [< *mono*-molecular] having a thickness of one molecule [*monolayer*]

mon·o·ac·id (män′ō as′id) *adj. same as* MONOACIDIC —*n.* an acid having only one replaceable hydrogen atom per molecule

mon·o·a·cid·ic (-ə sid′ik) *adj.* **1.** designating a base or alcohol one molecular weight of which can react with only one equivalent weight of an acid, or that has one hydroxyl group capable of replacing one acid hydrogen atom **2.** having only one acid hydrogen atom per molecule

mon·o·a·tom·ic (-ə täm′ik) *adj. same as* MONATOMIC

mon·o·bas·ic (män′ə bā′sik) *adj. Chem.* **1.** designating an acid the molecule of which contains one hydrogen atom replaceable by a metal or positive radical or capable of reacting with the hydroxyl group **2.** designating a compound in which a metal or positive radical has replaced one acid hydrogen atom —**mon′o·ba·sic′i·ty** (-bā sis′ə tē) *n.*

mon·o·car·box·yl·ic (-kär′bäk sil′ik) *adj.* having only one carboxylic acid group in the molecule

mon·o·car·pel·lar·y (-kär′pə ler′ē) *adj.* consisting of or having only a single carpel

mon·o·car·pic (-kär′pik) *adj.* [MONO- + -CARPIC] bearing fruit only once, and then dying: said of annuals, biennials, and some long-lived plants, as the bamboos and century plants: also **mon′o·car′pous**

Mo·noc·er·os (mə näs′ər əs) [L., the unicorn] a S constellation east of Orion

mon·o·cha·si·um (män′ə kā′zhē əm, -zē əm) *n., pl.* **-si·a** (-ə) [ModL. < MONO- + Gr. *chasis*, division, akin to *chainein*, to yawn, GAPE] *Bot.* a cymose or determinate inflorescence having only a single main axis —**mon′o·cha′si·al** *adj.*

mon·o·chla·myd·e·ous (-klə mid′ē əs) *adj.* [< ModL. *monochlamydeae*, name of the group < MONO- + Gr. *chlamyd-*, base of *chlamys*, a mantle + -OUS] having only one series of perianth parts, usually designated as sepals, in the flower

mon·o·chlo·ride (-klôr′īd) *n.* a chloride containing one chlorine atom per molecule

mon·o·chord (män′ə kôrd′) *n.* [ME. *monocorde* < MFr. < LL. *monochordon* < Gr. *monochordon*: see MONO- & CHORD[1]] an acoustical instrument consisting of a wooden sounding box with a single string and a movable bridge set on a graduated scale: used for determining musical intervals mathematically by dividing the string into separate parts whose vibrations can be measured

mon·o·chro·mat (män′ə krō′mat) *n.* [< L. *monochromatos*, one-colored < Gr. *monochrōmatos*: see MONO- & CHROMA] a person who has monochromatism

mon·o·chro·mat·ic (män′ə krō mat′ik) *adj.* [< L. *monochromatos* < Gr. *monochrōmatos*: see MONOCHROME & -IC] **1.** of or having one color: also **mon′o·chro′ic** (-krō′ik) **2.** of or producing light of one wavelength **3.** of, having, or having to do with monochromatism —**mon′o·chro·mat′i·cal·ly** *adv.*

mon·o·chro·ma·tism (-krō′mə tiz′m) *n.* [MONOCHROMAT-(IC) + -ISM] total colorblindness in which all objects appear as shades of gray

mon·o·chrome (män′ə krōm′) *n.* [ML. *monochroma* < Gr. *monochrōmos*, of one color < *monos*, single + *chrōma*, color] **1.** a painting, drawing, or photograph in one color or shades of one color **2.** the art or process of making these —**mon′o·chro′mic** *adj.* —**mon′o·chro′mist** *n.*

mon·o·cle (män′ə k'l) *n.* [Fr. < LL. *monoculus*, one-eyed < Gr. *monos*, single (see MONO-) + L. *oculus*, EYE] an eyeglass for one eye only —**mon′o·cled** *adj.*

mon·o·cli·nal (män′ə klī′n'l) *adj. Geol.* **1.** dipping in one direction: said of strata, or rock layers **2.** of strata dipping in the same direction —*n. same as* MONOCLINE

mon·o·cline (män′ə klīn′) *n.* [< MONO- + Gr. *klinein*, to incline: see LEAN[1]] a monoclinal rock fold or structure

mon·o·clin·ic (män′ə klin′ik) *adj.* [see prec. & -IC] designating or of a system of crystallization characterized by three axes of unequal length, two of which intersect obliquely and are perpendicular to the third

mon·o·cli·nous (-klī′nəs) *adj.* [ModL. *monoclinus* < MONO- + Gr. *klinē*, a bed, couch: see CLINIC] having stamens and pistils in the same flower

mon·o·coque (män′ə kōk′, -käk′) *adj.* [Fr. < *mono-*, MONO- + *coque*, a shell < L. *coccum*, scarlet berry < Gr. *kokkos*, a seed, gall of kermes oak] **1.** designating or of a kind of construction, as of an airplane fuselage, in which the skin or outer shell bears all or most of the stresses **2.** designating or of a kind of construction, as of an automobile, in which the body and chassis are one unit

mon·o·cot·y·le·don (män′ə kät′'l ē′d'n) *n. Bot.* any of a subclass (Monocotyledoneae) of flowering plants having an embryo containing only one seed leaf, and usually having parallel-veined leaves, flower parts in multiples of three, and no secondary growth in stems and roots, as lilies, orchids, grasses, etc.: sometimes clipped to **mon′o·cot′** —**mon′o·cot′y·le′don·ous** *adj.*

mo·noc·ra·cy (mə näk′rə sē) *n., pl.* **-cies** [MONO- + -CRACY] government by one person; autocracy —**mon′o·crat′ic** *adj.*

☆**mon·o·crat** (män′ə krat′) *n.* a person who favors monocracy, esp. monarchy: term applied by Thomas Jefferson c. 1790 to pro-English Federalists in the war between England and France

mo·noc·u·lar (mə näk′yə lər) *adj.* [< LL. *monoculus* (see MONOCLE) + -AR] **1.** having only one eye **2.** of, or for use by, only one eye —*n.* a field glass or telescopic device with a single eyepiece

mon·o·cul·ture (män′ə kul′chər) *n.* [MONO- + CULTURE] the raising of only one crop or product without using the land for other purposes

mon·o·cy·cle (-sī′k'l) *n. same as* UNICYCLE

mon·o·cy·clic (män′ə sī′klik) *adj.* **1.** of or forming one cycle, circle, whorl, etc. **2.** *Chem.* containing one ring of atoms in the molecule

mon·o·cyte (män′ə sīt′) *n.* [MONO- + -CYTE] a large, nongranular white blood cell with a relatively small kidney-shaped nucleus —**mon′o·cyt′ic** (-sit′ik) *adj.*

mon·o·dist (män′ə dist) *n.* a writer or singer of monody

mon·o·dra·ma (män′ə drä′mə, -dram′ə) *n.* drama acted, or written to be acted, by only one performer —**mon′o·dra·mat′ic** (-drə mat′ik) *adj.*

mon·o·dy (män′ə dē) *n., pl.* **-dies** [LL. *monodia* < Gr. *monōidia* < *monōidos*, singing alone < *monos*, alone (see MONO-) + *aeidein*, to sing: see ODE] **1.** in ancient Greek literature, an ode sung by a single voice, as in a tragedy; lyric solo, generally a lament or dirge **2.** a poem in which the poet mourns another's death ☆**3.** a monotonous sound or tone, as of waves **4.** *Music a)* a style of composition in which one part, or voice, predominates, and the others serve as accompaniment; homophony, as distinguished from polyphony *b)* a composition in this style —**mo·nod′ic** (mə näd′ik), **mo·nod′i·cal** *adj.* —**mo·nod′i·cal·ly** *adv.*

mo·noe·cious (mə nē′shəs, mō-) *adj.* [< MON- + Gr. *oikos*, a house + -IOUS] **1.** *Bot.* having separate male flowers and female flowers on the same plant, as in maize **2.** *Zool.* having both male and female reproductive organs in the same individual; hermaphroditic —**mo·noe′cism** (-siz′m) *n.*

mon·o·fil·a·ment (män′ə fil′ə mənt) *n.* a single, untwisted strand, of synthetic material: also **mon′o·fil′**

mo·nog·a·my (mə näg′ə mē) *n.* [Fr. *monogamie* < LL.(Ec.) *monogamia* < Gr. *monogamia*: see MONO- & -GAMY] **1.** the practice or state of being married to only one person at a time **2.** [Rare] the practice of marrying only once during life **3.** *Zool.* the practice of having only one mate —**mo·nog′a·mist** *n.* —**mo·nog′a·mous, mon·o·gam·ic** (män′ə gam′ik) *adj.*

mon·o·gen·e·sis (män′ə jen′ə sis) *n.* [ModL.: see MONO- & GENESIS] **1.** *Biol.* the hypothetical descent of all living organisms from a single original organism or cell **2.** *Zool.* asexual reproduction, as by budding or spore formation

mon·o·ge·net·ic (-ji net′ik) *adj.* **1.** of or pertaining to monogenesis **2.** designating or of animals without alternating asexual and sexual generations

mon·o·gen·ic (-jen′ik) *adj.* **1.** [MONO- + GEN(E) + -IC] *Biol.* designating or of a mode of inheritance in which a character is controlled by one pair of genes **2.** [MONO- + -GEN + -IC] *Zool.* producing offspring of one sex only, as females only in some species of aphids —**mo·nog′e·ny** (mə näj′ə nē) *n.*

mon·o·ge·nism (mə näj′ə niz′m) *n.* [MONO- + -GEN + -ISM] the doctrine that all human beings are descended from a single pair of ancestors

mon·o·glot (män′ə glät′) *adj.* [Gr. *monoglōttos:* cf. MONO- & (POLY)GLOT] speaking or writing only one language —*n.* a monoglot person

mon·o·gram (män′ə gram′) *n.* [LL. *monogramma* < Gr. *mono-*, MONO- + *gramma*, letter: see GRAM[1]] a character or figure made up of two or more letters, often initials of a name, combined in a single design: used on writing paper, ornaments, clothing, etc. —*vt.* **-grammed′, -gram′ming** to put a monogram on —**mon′o·gram·mat′ic** (-grə mat′ik) *adj.*

mon·o·graph (män′ə graf′, -gräf′) *n.* [MONO- + -GRAPH] **1.** orig., a treatise on a single genus, species, etc. of plant or animal **2.** a book, article, or paper written about a particular subject; esp., a scholarly writing on some detailed aspect of a subject —**mon′o·graph′ic** *adj.*

mo·nog·y·nous (mə näj′ə nəs) *adj.* **1.** of or characterized by monogyny **2.** *Bot.* having one style or pistil

mo·nog·y·ny (-nē) *n.* [MONO- + -GYNY] the practice or state of being married to only one woman at a time

mon·o·hy·drate (män′ə hī′drāt) *n.* a hydrate containing one molecule of water per molecule of combining compound

mon·o·hy·dric (-hī′drik) *adj.* [MONO- + -HYDRIC] **1.** *same as* MONOHYDROXY **2.** [Rare] having one atom of replaceable hydrogen

mon·o·hy·drox·y (-hī dräk′sē) *adj.* [MONO- + HYDROXY] having one hydroxyl group in the molecule

mo·nol·a·try (mə näl′ə trē) *n.* [MONO- + -LATRY] the worship of only one god, where several are believed to exist: distinguished from MONOTHEISM —**mo·nol′a·ter** *n.*

mon·o·lay·er (män′ə lā′ər) *n.* a layer or film one molecule thick

mon·o·lin·gual (män′ə lin′gwəl) *adj.* [MONO- + LINGUAL] using or knowing only one language

mon·o·lith (män′ə lith′) *n.* [Fr. *monolithe* < L. *monolithus* < Gr. *monolithos*, made of one stone < *monos*, single (see MONO-) + *lithos*, stone] **1.** a single large block or piece of stone, as in architecture or sculpture **2.** something made of a single block of stone, as an obelisk **3.** something like a monolith in size, unity of structure or purpose, unyielding quality, etc. —**mon′o·lith′ic** *adj.* —**mon′·o·lith′ism** *n.*

mon·o·logue, mon·o·log (män′ə lôg′, -läg′) *n.* [Fr. < Gr. *monologos*, speaking alone < *monos*, single (see MONO-) + *legein*, to speak (see LOGIC)] **1.** a long speech by one speaker, esp. one monopolizing the conversation **2.** a poem or other composition in the form of a soliloquy **3.** a part of a play in which one character speaks alone; soliloquy **4.** a play, skit, or recitation for one actor only —**mon′o·logu′ist, mo·nol·o·gist** (mə näl′ə jist) *n.*

mon·o·ma·ni·a (män′ə mā′nē ə) *n.* [ModL.: see MONO- & MANIA] **1.** an excessive interest in or enthusiasm for some one thing; craze **2.** a mental disorder characterized by irrational preoccupation with one subject —**mon′o·ma′ni·ac′** (-mā′nē ak′) —**mon′o·ma·ni′a·cal** (-mə nī′k′l) *adj.*

mon·o·mer (män′ə mər) *n.* [MONO- + Gr. *meros*, a part] a simple molecule that can form polymers by combining with identical or similar molecules —**mon′o·mer′ic** (-mer′ik) *adj.*

mo·nom·er·ous (mə näm′ər əs) *adj.* [ModL. *monomerus* < Gr. *monomerēs* < *monos*, alone: see MONO- + *meros*, a part) + -OUS] having one member, as a fruit of one carpel

mon·o·me·tal·lic (män′ō mə tal′ik) *adj.* **1.** of or using one metal **2.** of or based on monometallism

mon·o·met·al·lism (män′ə met′'l iz′m) *n.* **1.** the use of only one metal, usually gold or silver, as the monetary standard **2.** the doctrine or policies supporting this —**mon′·o·met′al·list** *n.*

mo·no·mi·al (mō nō′mē əl, mä-) *adj.* [MO(NO)- + (BI)-NOMIAL] **1.** *Algebra* consisting of only one term **2.** *Biol.* consisting of only one word: said of a taxonomic name —*n.* a monomial expression, quantity, or name

mon·o·mo·lec·u·lar (män′ə mə lek′yə lər) *adj.* **1.** of a single molecule **2.** designating or of a layer one molecule thick

mon·o·mor·phic (män′ə môr′fik) *adj.* [MONO- + -MORPHIC] **1.** having only one form **2.** having the same or an essentially similar type of structure Also **mon′o·mor′phous** (-fəs)

Mo·non·ga·he·la (mə nän′gə hē′lə) [< Algonquian < ?] river in N W.Va. & SW Pa., flowing north to join the Allegheny at Pittsburgh & form the Ohio: 128 mi.

mon·o·nu·cle·ar (män′ə nōō′klē ər, -nyōō′-) *adj.* **1.** *Bot.* having one nucleus in a cell **2.** *Chem. same as* MONOCYCLIC (sense 2)

mon·o·nu·cle·o·sis (-nōō′klē ō′sis, -nyōō′-) *n.* [MONO- + NUCLE(US) + -OSIS] **1.** *same as* INFECTIOUS MONONUCLE-OSIS **2.** the presence in the blood of an excessive number of cells having a single nucleus

mo·noph·a·gous (mə näf′ə gəs) *adj.* [MONO- + -PHAGOUS] *Biol.* feeding on only one kind of food, as on a certain plant

mon·o·pho·bi·a (män′ə fō′bē ə) *n.* [ModL.: see MONO- & -PHOBIA] an abnormal fear of being alone

mon·o·phon·ic (män′ə fän′ik) *adj.* **1.** of, or having the nature of, monophony **2.** designating or of sound reproduction using a single channel to carry and reproduce sounds through one or more loudspeakers

mo·noph·o·ny (mə näf′ə nē) *n.* [MONO- + -PHONY] **1.** music having a single melody without accompaniment or harmonizing parts **2.** *same as* MONODY

mon·oph·thong (män′əf thôŋ′) *n.* [< Gr. *monophthongos*, of or with one sound < *monos*, single (see MONO-) + *phthongos*, a sound, voice] a simple vowel sound during the utterance of which the vocal organs remain in a relatively unchanging position, as (ō) in *go* —**mon′oph·thong′al** *adj.*

mon·o·phy·let·ic (män′ə fi let′ik) *adj.* [see MONO- & PHYLETIC] **1.** of a single stock **2.** developed from a single ancestral type —**mon′o·phy′le·tism** (-fī′lə tiz′m) *n.*

mon·o·phyl·lous (män′ə fil′əs) *adj.* [Gr. *monophyllos* < *monos*, single (see MONO-) + *phyllon*, leaf (see BLOOM[1])] *Bot.* **1.** having or consisting of only one leaf **2.** having united sepals or petals

Mo·noph·y·site (mə näf′ə sīt′) *n.* [LGr.(Ec.) *monophysitēs* < Gr. *monos*, single (see MONO-) + *physis*, nature (see PHYSIC)] *Theol.* a person who believes that Christ had but one nature, or a composite nature of both the human and the divine, a tenet held as by members of the Coptic Church —**Mo·noph′y·sit′ic** (-sit′ik, män′ə fə-) *adj.*

mon·o·plane (män′ə plān′) *n.* an airplane with only one main supporting surface, or pair of wings

mon·o·ple·gi·a (män′ə plē′jē ə, -plē′jə) *n.* [ModL. < MONO- + Gr. *plēgē*, a stroke < IE. *pleg-*, var. of *plāk-*, to strike, whence L. *plangere*, FLAW?] paralysis of a single limb or part of the body —**mon′o·ple′gic** (-plē′jik, -plej′ik) *adj.*

mon·o·ploid (män′ə ploid′) *adj., n.* [MONO- + -PLOID] *Biol. same as* HAPLOID

mon·o·pode (män′ə pōd′) *adj.* [LL. *monopodius* < Gr. **monopodios*, for *monopous* < *monos*, single + *pous* (gen. *podos*), FOOT] having only one foot —*n.* **1.** a monopode creature; specif., a member of a fabled race of monopode men **2.** *same as* MONOPODIUM

mon·o·po·di·um (män′ə pō′dē əm) *n., pl.* **-di·a** (-ə) [ModL.: see MONO- & -PODIUM] *Bot.* a single main stem that continues to extend at the apex in its original line of growth, giving off lateral branches or axes, as the trunk of certain pine trees —**mon′o·po′di·al** *adj.*

mo·nop·o·list (mə näp′ə list) *n.* **1.** one who monopolizes or has a monopoly **2.** a person who favors or advocates monopoly —**mo·nop′o·lis′tic** *adj.* —**mo·nop′o·lis′ti·cal·ly** *adv.*

mo·nop·o·lize (-līz′) *vt.* **-lized′, -liz′ing** **1.** to get, have, or exploit a monopoly of **2.** to get full possession or control of; dominate completely [*to monopolize* a conversation] —**mo·nop′o·li·za′tion** *n.* —**mo·nop′o·liz′er** *n.*

mo·nop·o·ly (-lē) *n., pl.* **-lies** [L. *monopolium* < Gr. *monopōlion*, right of exclusive sale, *monopōlia*, exclusive sale < *monos*, single (see MONO-) + *pōlein*, to sell < IE. base **pel-*, whence Lith. *pelnas*, wages] **1.** exclusive control of a commodity or service in a given market, or control that makes possible the fixing of prices and the virtual elimination of free competition **2.** an exclusive privilege of engaging in a particular business or providing a service, granted by a ruler or by the state **3.** exclusive possession or control of something **4.** something that is held or controlled as a monopoly **5.** a company or combination that has a monopoly —☆[M-] *a trademark for* a game played on a special board by two or more players: they move according to the throw of dice, engaging in mock real estate transactions with play money

SYN.—**monopoly** applies to the exclusive control of a commodity, etc., as defined above; a **trust** is a combination of corporations, organized for the purpose of gaining a monopoly, in which stock is turned over to trustees who issue stock certificates to the stockholders: trusts are now illegal in the U.S.; **cartel**, the European term for a trust, now usually implies an international trust; a **syndicate** is now usually a group of bankers, corporations, etc. organized to buy large blocks of securities, afterwards selling them in small parcels to the public at a profit; a **corner** is a temporary speculative monopoly of some stock or commodity for the purpose of raising the price

☆**mon·o·pro·pel·lant** (män′ō prə pel′ənt) *n.* [MONO- + PROPELLANT] a liquid or solid propellant consisting of a single substance, or an intimate mixture of substances, which combines both fuel and oxidizer

mo·nop·so·ny (mə näp′sə nē) *n., pl.* **-nies** [MONO- + Gr. *opsōnia*, a purchase of fish, catering < *opsōnein*, to buy victuals < *opson*, cooked food, fish < *o-*, with + base of *psōmos*, a morsel, bit] *Econ.* a situation in which there is only one buyer for a particular commodity or service

mon·o·rail (män′ə rāl′) *n.* **1.** a single rail serving as a track for trucks or cars suspended from it or balanced on it **2.** a railway with such a track

mon·o·sac·cha·ride (män′ə sak′ə rīd′) *n.* [MONO- + SACCHARIDE] a carbohydrate not decomposable by hydrolysis; simple sugar, as glucose

mon·o·sep·al·ous (-sep′'l əs) *adj. Bot. same as* GAMO-SEPALOUS

mon·o·so·di·um glu·ta·mate (män′ə sō′dē əm glōō′tə māt′) a white crystalline powder, $C_5H_8O_4NaN$, derived from vegetable protein and used in foods as a flavor intensifier

mon·o·some (män′ə sōm′) *n.* [MONO- + -SOME[3]] an unpaired chromosome in an otherwise diploid cell; esp., an unpaired sex chromosome —**mon′o·so′mic** *adj.*

mon·o·sper·mous (män′ə spur′məs) *adj.* [MONO- + -SPER-MOUS] *Bot.* having only one seed

mon·o·sper·my (män′ə spur′mē) *n.* [MONO- + SPERM[1] + -y[3]] *Zool.* the system in which a single sperm cell fertilizes an ovum —**mon′o·sper′mic** *adj.*

mon·o·ste·le (män′ə stē′lē, män′ə stēl′) *n.* [MONO- + STELE] a stem or root having a single vascular cylinder —**mon′o·ste′lic** *adj.*

mon·o·stich (män′ə stik′) *n.* [LL. *monostichum* < Gr. *monostichon* < *monos*, single (see MONO-) + *stichos*, a line, verse: see STILE[1]] **1.** a poem or epigram consisting of one metrical line **2.** one line of poetry

mon·o·stome (-stōm′) *adj.* [MONO- + -STOME] having one mouth or sucker, as some flatworms: also **mo·nos·to·mous** (mə näs′tə məs)

mo·nos·tro·phe (mə näs′trə fē, män′ə strōf′) *n.* [< Gr. *monostrophos*: see MONO- & STROPHE] a poem in which all the stanzas have the same metrical form

mon·os·ty·lous (män′ə stī′ləs) *adj. Bot.* having only one style

mon·o·syl·lab·ic (-si lab′ik) *adj.* [ML. *monosyllabicus*] **1.** having only one syllable [a *monosyllabic* word] **2.** consisting of monosyllables **3.** using, or speaking in, monosyllables, often so as to seem terse or uncommunicative —**mon′o·syl·lab′i·cal·ly** *adv.*

mon·o·syl·la·ble (män′ə sil′ə b'l) *n.* [altered < ML. *monosyllaba*, ult. < Gr. *monosyllabos:* see MONO- & SYLLABLE] a word of one syllable

mon·o·sym·met·ric (män′ə si met′rik) *adj.* same as: **1.** MONOCLINIC **2.** ZYGOMORPHIC Also **mon′o·sym·met′ri·cal**

mon·o·the·ism (män′ə thē iz′m) *n.* [MONO- + THEISM] the doctrine or belief that there is only one God —**mon′o·the·ist** *n.* —**mon′o·the·is′tic, mon′o·the·is′ti·cal** *adj.* — **mon′o·the·is′ti·cal·ly** *adv.*

mon·o·tint (män′ə tint′) *n.* same as MONOCHROME

mon·o·tone (-tōn′) *n.* [< LL. *monotonus:* see ff.] **1.** uninterrupted repetition of the same tone; utterance of successive syllables or words without change of pitch or key **2.** monotony or sameness of tone, style, manner, color, etc. **3.** a single, unchanging musical tone **4.** recitation, chanting, or singing in such a tone **5.** a person who sings in such a tone —*adj.* same as MONOTONOUS — **mon′o·ton′ic** (-tän′ik) *adj.*

mo·not·o·nous (mə nät′'n əs) *adj.* [LL. *monotonus* < Gr. *monotonos:* see MONO- & TONE] **1.** going on in the same tone without variation **2.** having little or no variation or variety **3.** tiresome because unvarying —**mo·not′o·nous·ly** *adv.* —**mo·not′o·nous·ness** *n.*

mo·not·o·ny (-ē) *n.* [Fr. *monotonie* < Gr. *monotonia:* see prec.] **1.** sameness of tone or pitch, or continuance of the same tone without variation **2.** lack of variation or variety **3.** tiresome sameness or uniformity

mon·o·treme (män′ə trēm′) *n.* [< ModL. *Monotremata* < Gr. *monos,* single (see MONO-) + *trēma,* a hole < IE. base *ter-,* to rub, drill, whence THROW] any of the lowest order (Monotremata) of mammals, consisting of the platypus and the echidnas, which lay eggs and have a single opening for the digestive and urinary tracts and for the genital organs —**mon′o·trem′a·tous** (-trem′ə təs, -trē′mə-) *adj.*

mo·not·ri·chous (mə nä′tri kəs) *adj.* [MONO- + TRICH(O)- + -OUS] having a single flagellum at one end, as some bacteria

mon·o·type (män′ə tīp′) *n.* [MONO- + -TYPE] **1.** *Biol.* the only type of its group, as a single species constituting a genus, a single genus constituting a family, etc. **2.** *Printing a)* type produced by Monotype *b)* a unique print from a metal or glass plate on which a picture has been made, as with paint or ink *c)* the method of making such prints —☆[M-] *a trademark for* either of a pair of machines for casting and setting up type in separate characters on individual bodies: one, a casting machine, is controlled by a paper tape perforated on the other, a keyboard machine

mon·o·typ·ic (män′ə tip′ik) *adj.* **1.** having only one type, as a genus consisting of only one species **2.** having the nature of a monotype

mon·o·va·lent (-vā′lənt) *adj.* **1.** *Bacteriology* capable of resisting one strain of a given species of disease-producing organism because the right antibodies or antigens are present **2.** *Chem.* same as UNIVALENT (sense 2) —**mon′o·va′lence, mon′o·va′len·cy** *n.*

mon·ox·ide (mə näk′sīd, män äk′-) *n.* an oxide with one atom of oxygen in each molecule

Mon·roe (mən rō′) city in N La.: pop. 56,000

Mon·roe (mən rō′), **James** 1758-1831; 5th president of the U.S. (1817-25)

Monroe Doctrine the doctrine, essentially stated by President Monroe in a message to Congress (Dec., 1823), that the U.S. would regard as an unfriendly act any attempt by a European nation to interfere in the affairs of the American countries or increase its possessions on the American continents

Mon·ro·vi·a (mən rō′vē ə) capital of Liberia; seaport on the Atlantic: pop. 80,000

mons (mänz) *n., pl.* **mon·tes** (män′tēz) [ModL. < L., hill, MOUNT[1]] same as: **1.** MONS PUBIS **2.** MONS VENERIS

Mons. Monsieur

Mon·sei·gneur (män′scn yur′; *Fr.* mōn se nyër′) *n., pl.* **Mes·sei·gneurs** (mes′en yurz′; *Fr.* mā se nyër′) [Fr., lit., my lord < *mon,* my + *seigneur,* lord < L. *senior,* older: see SENIOR] **1.** a French title of honor given to persons of high birth or rank, as princes, or to important church officers, as bishops, cardinals, etc. **2.** [*often* m-] a person with this title

mon·sieur (mə syur′; *Fr.* mā syö′) *n., pl.* **mes·sieurs** (mes′ərz; *Fr.* mā syö′) [Fr., lit., my lord (see SIRE): orig. applied to men of high position] a man; gentleman: French title [M-], equivalent to *Mr.* or *Sir:* abbrev. **M., Mons.**

Monsig. **1.** Monseigneur **2.** Monsignor

Mon·si·gnor (män sēn′yər; *It.* mōn′sē nyōr′) *n., pl.* **-gnors** (-yərz) *It.* **-gno′ri** (-nyō′rē) [It., lit., my lord: cf. MONSEIGNEUR] a title given to certain dignitaries of the Roman Catholic Church **2.** [*often* m-] a person who has this title

mon·soon (män sōōn′) *n.* [MDu. *monssoen* < Port. *monção* < Ar. *mausim,* a time, a season] **1.** a seasonal wind of the Indian Ocean and S Asia, blowing from the southwest from April to October, and from the northeast during the rest of the year **2.** the season during which this wind blows from the southwest, characterized by heavy rains **3.** any wind that reverses its direction seasonally or blows constantly between land and adjacent water — **mon·soon′al** *adj.*

mons pu·bis (mänz′ pyōō′bis) [see MONS & PUBES[1]] the fleshy, rounded elevation, covered with pubic hair, at the lower part of the adult human abdomen

mon·ster (män′stər) *n.* [ME. *monstre* < OFr. < L. *monstrum,* divine portent of misfortune, monster < *monere,* to admonish, warn: see MONITOR] **1.** any plant or animal of abnormal shape or structure, as one greatly malformed or lacking some parts; monstrosity **2.** any imaginary creature part human and part animal in form, as a centaur, or made up of the parts of two or more different animals, as a unicorn **3.** something monstrous **4.** a person so cruel, wicked, depraved, etc. as to horrify others **5.** any huge animal or thing **6.** *Pathology* a malformed fetus, esp. one with an excess or deficiency of limbs or parts; teratism —*adj.* huge; enormous; monstrous

mon·strance (män′strəns) *n.* [ME. *munstraunce* < OFr. *monstrance* < ML. *monstrantia* < L. *monstrare,* to show, akin to *monstrum:* see prec.] *R.C.Ch.* a receptacle in which the consecrated Host is exposed for adoration

mon·stros·i·ty (män sträs′ə tē) *n.* [LL. *monstrositas*] **1.** the state or quality of being monstrous **2.** *pl.* **-ties** a monstrous thing or creature

mon·strous (män′strəs) *adj.* [LME. < OFr. *monstreux* < L. *monstrosus* < *monstrum:* see MONSTER] **1.** abnormally or prodigiously large; huge; enormous **2.** very unnatural or abnormal in shape, type, or character **3.** having the character or appearance of a monster **4.** horrible; hideous; shocking **5.** hideously wrong or evil; atrocious —*adv.* [Chiefly Dial.] very; extremely —*SYN.* see OUTRAGEOUS —**mon′strous·ly** *adv.* —**mon′strous·ness** *n.*

mons ven·er·is (mänz′ ven′ər is) [L., lit., mount of Venus] the mons pubis of the human female

Mont. Montana

mon·tage (män tāzh′, mōn-) *n.* [Fr., a mounting, setting together < *monter,* MOUNT[2]] **1.** *a)* the art or process of making a composite picture by bringing together into a single composition a number of different pictures or parts of pictures and arranging these, as by superimposing one on another, so that they form a blended whole while remaining distinct *b)* a picture so made **2.** *Motion Pictures a)* the art or process of producing a sequence of abruptly alternating scenes or images to convey associated ideas, or a sequence in which superimposed images are shown whirling about, flashing into focus, etc., as for emotional effect *b)* a part of a motion picture in which this is used **3.** *a)* any similar technique, as in literature or music, of juxtaposing discrete or contrasting elements *b)* anything that is or is like the result of such a process —*vt.* **-taged′, -tag′ing** to incorporate in a montage

Mon·ta·gnard (män′tən yärd′) *n.* [Fr., lit., mountaineer < *montagne,* MOUNTAIN + *-ard,* -ARD] **1.** a member of a people living in the hills of central Vietnam **2.** a member of an American Indian tribe living in the northern Rocky Mountains

Mon·ta·gu (män′tə gyōō′), **Lady Mary Wort·ley** (wurt′lē) (born *Mary Pierrepont*) 1689-1762; Eng. writer

Mon·ta·gue (män′tə gyōō′) the family name of Romeo in Shakespeare's *Romeo and Juliet*

Mon·taigne (män tān′; *Fr.* mōn ten′y′), **Mi·chel Ey·quem de** (mē shel′ e kem′ də) 1533-92; Fr. essayist

Mon·tan·a (män tan′ə) [L. *montana,* mountainous regions: see MOUNTAIN] Mountain State of the NW U.S.: admitted, 1889; 147,138 sq. mi.; pop. 694,000; cap. Helena: abbrev. **Mont., MT** —**Mon·tan′an** *adj., n.*

mon·tan wax (män′tan) [< L. *montanus,* of a mountain (see MOUNTAIN) + WAX[1]] a brown or whitish hydrocarbon wax extracted from lignite and peat, and used in making candles, polishes, phonograph records, etc.

Mon·tauk Point (män′tôk′) [< Algonquian tribal name < ? + POINT] promontory at the easternmost tip of Long Island, N.Y.

Mont Blanc *see* BLANC

Mont·calm (mōn kälm′; *E.* mänt käm′), **Louis Jo·seph de** (zhō zef′ də) (full name *Louis Joseph de Montcalm-Gozon,* marquis *de Saint Véran*) 1712-59; Fr. general defeated & killed by Brit. forces under Wolfe at Quebec

Mont Cervin *see* CERVIN

Mont·clair (mänt kler′) [Fr., clear mountain] suburb of Newark, in NE N.J.: pop. 44,000

†mont-de-pié·té (mōn də pyä tā′) *n., pl.* **monts-de-pié·té′** (mōn) [Fr. < It. *monte di pietà,* charitable bank, lit., mount of pity] a public pawnshop, authorized and controlled by the government, for lending money to the poor at a low rate of interest

☆**mon·te** (män′tē) *n.* [Sp. *monte,* lit., mountain, hence heap of cards (left after players have their shares) < L. *mons* (gen. *montis*), mountain] **1.** a gambling game of Spanish origin, played with a special deck of forty cards, in which the players bet against a banker on the color of cards to be turned up from the deck: also called **monte bank 2.** *see* THREE-CARD MONTE

Mon·te·bel·lo (män′tə bel′ō) [It., beautiful mountain] city in SW Calif.: suburb of Los Angeles: pop. 43,000

Mon·te Car·lo (män′ti kär′lō) town in Monaco: gambling resort: pop. 9,500

☆**Monte Carlo method** a technique for obtaining an approximate solution to certain mathematical and physical problems, characteristically involving the replacement of a probability distribution by sample values and usually done on a computer

mon·teith (män tēth′) *n.* [said to be named after a 17th-c. Scot who wore a coat with a notched hem] a large punch bowl, usually of silver, with a notched brim from which glasses and ladles are hung

Mon·te·ne·gro (män′tə nē′grō) republic of S Yugoslavia: formerly a kingdom: 5,333 sq. mi.; pop. 472,000; cap. Titograd —**Mon′te·ne′grin** (-grin) *adj., n.*

Mon·te·rey (män′tə rā′) [< Sp. *Puerto de Monterrey*, port of Monterrey (the viceroy of New Spain in 1602)] city on the coast of C Calif.: former capital (until 1846) of Calif. region: pop. 26,000

Monterey Park [see prec.] city in SW Calif.: suburb of Los Angeles: pop. 49,000

mon·te·ro (män ter′ō) *n., pl.* **-ros** [Sp., hunter, lit. mountaineer < *monte*, hill < L. *mons*, MOUNT¹] a round cap with a flap, of a style worn by Spanish huntsmen

Mon·ter·rey (män′tə rā′; *Sp.* mōn′ter rā′) city in NE Mexico; capital of Nuevo León: pop. 900,000

Mon·tes·quieu (mōn tes kyö′; *E.* män′təs kyoo′), (Baron **de la Brède et de**), (*Charles Louis de Secondat*) 1689–1755; Fr. philosophical writer on history

Mon·tes·so·ri (män′tə sōr′ē; *It.* mōn′tes sō′rē), **Maria** 1870–1952; It. educator

Montessori method (or **system**) a system of training and teaching young children, devised in 1907 by Maria Montessori, which emphasizes training of the senses and guidance rather than rigid control of the child's activity so as to encourage self-education

Mon·teux (mōn tö′), **Pierre** 1875–1964; U.S. orchestra conductor, born in France

Mon·te·ver·di (mōn′te ver′dē, **Clau·dio** (**Giovanni An·tonio**) (klou′dyō) 1567–1643; It. composer

Mon·te·vid·e·o (män′tə vi dā′ō, -vid′ē ō′; *Sp.* mōn′te vē the′ō) capital of Uruguay; seaport on the Rio de la Plata: pop. 1,204,000

Mon·te·zu·ma II (män′tə zōō′mə) 1479?–1520; Aztec emperor of Mexico (1502–20)

Mont·fort (mänt′fərt), **Simon de** **1.** 1160?–1218; Fr. crusader **2.** Earl of Leicester, 1208?–65; Eng. statesman & soldier: son of *prec.*

Mont·gom·er·y (mənt gum′ər ē, mänt-, mən-, -gum′rē) **1.** [after Gen. Richard *Montgomery* (1736–75)] capital of Ala., in the SC part, on the Alabama River: pop. 133,000 **2.** *same as* MONTGOMERYSHIRE

Mont·gom·er·y (mənt gum′ər ē, mänt-; mən-), **Bernard Law** (lô), 1st Viscount Montgomery of Alamein, 1887– ; Brit. field marshal in World War II

Mont·gom·er·y·shire (-shir′) county of C Wales: 797 sq. mi.; pop. 44,000

month (munth) *n.* [ME. < OE. *monath*, akin to G. *monat*, ON. *manuthr* < Gmc. **menôth-* < IE. **mēnôt*, month, moon, var. of *mēn*: see MOON] **1.** any of the main parts (usually twelve) into which the calendar year is divided: also **calendar month** **2.** *a)* the time from any day of one month to the corresponding day of the next *b)* a period of four weeks or 30 days **3.** the period of a complete revolution of the moon with reference to some fixed point (in full, **lunar month**); esp., the period from one new moon to the next (in full, **synodic month**): equivalent to 29 days, 12 hours, 44 minutes, and 2.7+ seconds **4.** one twelfth of the solar year (in full, **solar month**) —**month after month** every month —**month by month** each month —**month in, month out** every month

Mon·ther·lant (mōn′tər län′), **Hen·ri** (**Millon**) **de** (än rē′ də) 1896– ; Fr. novelist & playwright

month·ly (munth′lē) *adj.* **1.** continuing or lasting for a month **2.** done, happening, payable, etc. once a month, or every month [a *monthly* magazine] **3.** of a month, or of each month —*n., pl.* **-lies** **1.** a periodical published once a month **2.** [Colloq.] [*also pl.*] the menses —*adv.* once a month; every month

month's mind *R.C.Ch.* a Requiem Mass said for a person on the 30th day after death or burial

Mon·ti·cel·lo (män′tə sel′ō, -chel′ō) [It., little mountain] home of Thomas Jefferson, near Charlottesville, Va.

mon·ti·cule (män′tə kyōol′) *n.* [Fr. < LL. *monticulus*, dim. of L. *mons*, MOUNTAIN] **1.** a small mountain or hill **2.** a secondary cone of a volcano

Mont·lu·çon (mōn lü sōn′) city in C France, on the Cher: pop. 59,000

Mont·mar·tre (mōn mår′tr′) district of Paris, in N part, noted for its cafés and as an artists' quarter

mont·mo·ril·lon·ite (mänt′mə ril′ə nit′) *n.* [Fr. < *Montmorillon*, France + *-ite*, -ITE¹] any of a group of related clay minerals with the general formula, $Al_2Si_4O_{10}(OH)_2$, which swell greatly in the presence of water

Mont·par·nasse (mōn pår nås′) section of Paris, on the left bank of the Seine

Mont·pel·ier (mänt pēl′yər) [after ff.] capital of Vt., in the NC part: pop. 9,000

Mont·pel·lier (mōn pel yā′) city in S France, near the Gulf of Lions: pop.

Mont·re·al (män′trē ôl′, mun′-) **1.** [Fr. *Montréal* < *Mont Royal*, Mount Royal, at its center] seaport in SW Quebec, Canada, on an island in the St. Lawrence River: pop.

1,222,000 (met. area 2,437,000) **2.** this island: 201 sq. mi. Fr. name **Mont·ré·al** (mōn rä äl′)

Montreal North suburb of Montreal, on Montreal Island: pop. 68,000 Fr. name **Montréal Nord** (nōr)

Mont·treu·il (mōn trö′y′) city in NC France: suburb of Paris: pop. 92,000

Mont·rose (män trōz′), 1st Marquis of, (*James Graham*) 1612–50; Scot. supporter of Charles I: executed

Mont·ser·rat (mänt′sə rat′) **1.** Brit. island of the Leeward group, in the West Indies: 33 sq. mi.; pop. 14,000 **2.** mountain in NE Spain, near Barcelona: c. 4,070 ft.

Mont-St-Mi·chel (mōn san mē shel′) islet just off the NW coast of France, noted for its fortified abbey: also **Mont Saint Michel**

mon·u·ment (män′yə mənt) *n.* [ME. < OFr. < L. *monumentum* < *monere*, to remind, warn: see MONITOR] **1.** something set up to keep alive the memory of a person or event, as a tablet, statue, pillar, building, etc. **2.** a structure surviving from a former period **3.** a writing or the like serving as a memorial **4.** *a)* a work, production, etc. of enduring value or significance [*monuments* of learning] *b)* lasting or outstanding evidence or example ☆**5.** a stone shaft or other object set in the earth to mark a boundary **6.** [Obs.] *a)* a tomb; sepulcher *b)* a statue; effigy See also NATIONAL MONUMENT

mon·u·men·tal (män′yə men′t'l) *adj.* [LL. *monumentalis*] **1.** of, suitable for, or serving as a monument or monuments **2.** like a monument; massive, enduring, etc. **3.** historically notable, important, or of lasting value **4.** very great; colossal [*monumental* ineptitude] **5.** *Art* larger than life-size —**mon′u·men·tal′i·ty** (-tal′ə tē) *n.* —**mon′u·men′-tal·ly** *adv.*

mon·u·men·tal·ize (-iz′) *vt.* **-ized′, -iz′ing** to make a lasting memorial or record of, as by a monument

mon·y (män′ē) *adj., n.* [Scot. & N.Eng. Dial.] many

-mo·ny (mō′nē) [L. *-monia, -monium*] a *n.-forming suffix meaning* a resulting thing, condition, or state [*patrimony, sanctimony*]

Mon·za (mōn′tsä) commune in Lombardy, N Italy: pop. 74,000

mon·zo·nite (män′zə nit′) *n.* [G. *monzonit*, after Mt. *Monzoni* (in Tyrol), where it occurs] an igneous rock containing orthoclase and plagioclase feldspar in nearly equal quantities, a very small amount of quartz, some biotite, and often hornblende and diopside

moo (mōō) *n., pl.* **moos** [echoic] the characteristic vocal sound made by a cow; lowing sound —*vi.* **mooed, moo′ing** to make this sound; low

mooch (mōōch) *vi.* [ME. *mowchen*, dial. var. of *mychen*, to pilfer: see MICHE] [Slang] **1.** to skulk or sneak **2.** to loiter, loaf, or rove about **3.** to get food, money, etc. by begging or sponging —*vt.* [Slang] **1.** to steal; pilfer **2.** to get by begging or sponging; cadge —**mooch′er** *n.*

mood¹ (mōōd) *n.* [ME. < OE. *mod*, mind, soul, courage, akin to G. *mut*, mental disposition, spirit, courage < IE. base **mē-*, to strive strongly, be energetic, whence L. *mos*, custom, customary behavior (cf. MORAL)] **1.** a particular state of mind or feeling; humor, or temper **2.** a predominant or pervading feeling, spirit, or tone **3.** [*pl.*] fits of morose, sullen, or uncertain temper **4.** [Obs.] anger **SYN.**—**mood** is the broadest of these terms referring to a temporary state of mind and emphasizes the constraining or pervading quality of the feeling [she's a merry *mood*]; **humor** emphasizes the variability or capriciousness of the mood [he wept and laughed as his *humor* moved him]; **temper**, in this comparison, applies to a mood characterized by a single, strong emotion, esp. that of anger [my, he's in a nasty *temper*!]; **vein** stresses the transient nature of the mood [if I may speak in a serious *vein* for a moment]

mood² (mōōd) *n.* [< MODE, altered after prec.] **1.** *Gram. a)* in many languages, that aspect of verbs which has to do with the speaker's attitude toward the action or state expressed, indicating whether this is regarded as a fact (*indicative mood*), as a matter of supposition, desire, possibility, etc. (*subjunctive mood*), or as a command (*imperative mood*): mood is shown by inflection, as in Latin and Greek, or by auxiliaries, as English *may, might, should*, or by both *b)* a set of forms expressing this aspect *c)* any such form **2.** *Logic* *same as* MODE

mood·y (mōō′dē) *adj.* **mood′i·er, mood′i·est** [ME. *modi* < OE. *modig*] **1.** subject to or characterized by gloomy, sullen moods or changes of mood **2.** resulting from or indicating such a mood —**mood′i·ly** *adv.* —**mood′i·ness** *n.*

Moody (mōō′dē) **1.** Dwight Ly·man (li′mən), 1837–99; U.S. evangelist **2.** William Vaughn (vôn), 1869–1910; U.S. poet & playwright

☆**moo·la, moo·lah** (mōō′lə) *n.* [< ?] [Slang] money

moon (mōōn) *n.* [ME. *mone* < OE. *mona*, akin to Goth. *mēna* < IE. **mēn-*, month, moon (whence L. *mensis*, Gr. *mēn*, month, *mēnē*, moon) < base *mē-*, to measure] **1.** the heavenly body that revolves around the earth from west to east once in c. 27 1/3 days with reference to the stars or once in c. 29 1/2 days with

PHASES OF THE MOON

reference to the sun, and that accompanies the earth in its yearly revolution about the sun, reflecting the sun's light: the moon's diameter is c. 2,160 miles, its mean distance from the earth is c. 238,857 miles, its mean density is c. 3/5 that of the earth, its mass is c. 1/81, and its volume c. 1/49 **2.** this body as it appears during a particular lunar month or period of time, or at a particular time of the month: see NEW MOON, HALF-MOON, FULL MOON, OLD MOON, FIRST QUARTER, LAST QUARTER **3.** a month; esp., a lunar month **4.** same as MOONLIGHT **5.** anything shaped like the moon (i.e., an orb or crescent) **6.** any satellite of a planet —vi. [from the notion of behaving as if moonstruck] to behave in an idle, dreamy, or abstracted way, as when in love —vt. to pass (time) in mooning

moon·beam (-bēm′) n. a ray of moonlight

moon·blind (-blīnd′) adj. having moon blindness

moon blindness 1. night blindness: formerly attributed to the effects of moonlight **2.** a disease of horses, of undetermined cause, characterized by recurrent inflammation of the eyes and, eventually, blindness

moon·calf (-kaf′, -käf′) n. [from the notion of being influenced by the moon: cf. LUNATIC] **1.** a congenital idiot; born fool **2.** a person, esp. a youth, who spends time mooning about **3.** [Obs.] a monstrosity

☆**moon child** Astrol. a person born under the sign of Cancer

mooned (mōōnd) adj. **1.** round or crescent like the moon **2.** decorated with moon-shaped marks

moon-eyed (-īd′) adj. **1.** same as MOON-BLIND **2.** having the eyes wide open, as from fright or wonder

moon-faced (-fāst′) adj. having a round face

moon-fish (-fish′) n., pl. -fish′, -fish′es: see FISH² **1.** any of a number of deep-bodied, sharply compressed sea fishes (family Carangidae), usually silvery or white, found in the warmer coastal waters of N. and S. America **2.** any of various other fishes; esp., the opah

moon·flow·er (-flou′ər) n. any of a genus (Calonyction) of tropical American, perennial twining vines of the morning-glory family, with heart-shaped leaves and large, fragrant white or purple flowers that bloom at night

moon gate a large, circular opening in a wall, through which one can step: orig. a feature of Chinese architecture

moon·ish (-ish) adj. like the moon; changeable; fickle; capricious —**moon′ish·ly** adv.

moon·let (-lit) n. a small moon or artificial satellite

moon·light (-līt′) n. the light of the moon —adj. **1.** of moonlight **2.** lighted by the moon **3.** done or occurring by moonlight, or at night

moon·light·ing (-līt′iŋ) n. [from the usual night hours of such jobs] ☆the practice of holding a second regular job in addition to one's main job —**moon′light′er** n.

moon·lit (-lit′) adj. lighted by the moon

☆**moon·port** (-pôrt′) n. [MOON + -port, as in AIRPORT] an installation for launching rockets to the moon

☆**moon·quake** (-kwāk′) n. a trembling of the surface of the moon, thought to be caused by internal rock slippage or, possibly, meteorite impact

moon·rise (-rīz′) n. **1.** the rising of the moon above the horizon ☆**2.** the time of this

moon·scape (-skāp′) n. [MOON + (LAND)SCAPE] the surface of the moon or a representation of it

moon·seed (-sēd′) n. any of a genus (Menispermum) of twining vines of a family (Menispermaceae), with small clusters of purple berries and crescent-shaped seeds

moon·set (-set′) n. the setting or time of setting of the moon below the horizon

moon·shine (-shīn′) n. **1.** same as MOONLIGHT **2.** foolish or empty talk, notions, plans, etc.; nonsense **3.** [Colloq.] a) smuggled whiskey ☆b) whiskey unlawfully distilled

moon·shin·er (-shīn′ər) n. [Colloq.] ☆a person who makes and sells alcoholic liquor unlawfully

moon·shin·y (-shī′nē) adj. **1.** lighted by the moon **2.** like or suggestive of moonlight **3.** unreal, unsubstantial, visionary, foolish, etc.

☆**moon·shot** (-shät′) n. the launching of a rocket to the moon

moon·stone (-stōn′) n. a milky-white, translucent feldspar with a pearly luster, used as a gem

moon·struck (-struk′) adj. affected mentally in some way, supposedly by the influence of the moon; specif., a) crazed; lunatic; insane b) romantically dreamy or sentimental c) dazed or distracted Also **moon′strick′en** (-strik′'n)

moon·wort (-wurt′) n. **1.** any of a genus (Botrychium) of ferns bearing a leafy part each year that is divided into separate sterile and fertile segments **2.** same as HONESTY (sense 2)

moon·y (-ē) adj. **moon′i·er, moon′i·est 1.** of or characteristic of the moon **2.** like the moon, esp. in shape; round or crescent-shaped **3.** lighted by the moon **4.** like moonlight **5.** mooning; listless; dreamy

Moor (moor) n. [ME. More < OFr. More, Maure < L. Maurus, a Moor, Mauritanian < Gr. Mauros] **1.** a member of a Moslem people of mixed Arab and Berber descent living in NW Africa **2.** a member of a group of this people that invaded and occupied Spain in the 8th cent. A.D. —**Moor′ish** adj.

moor¹ (moor) n. [ME. more < OE. mor, wasteland, akin to LowG. mor < IE. base *mori-, sea, whence L. mare, sea & MARSH, MERE²: basic sense "swampy coastland"] [Brit.]

1. a tract of open, rolling wasteland, usually covered with heather and often marshy or peaty; heath **2.** a tract of land with game preserves

moor² (moor) vt. [Early ModE. < or akin to MDu. maren, LowG. moren, to tie] **1.** to hold (a ship, etc.) in place by cables or chains to the shore, or by anchors, etc. **2.** to cause to be held in place; secure —vi. **1.** to moor a ship, etc. **2.** to be secured as by cables

moor·age (-ij) n. **1.** a mooring or being moored **2.** a place for mooring **3.** a charge for the use of such a place

moor cock [Brit.] the male moorfowl, or red grouse

Moore (moor, môr) **1. George (Augustus),** 1852–1933; Ir. novelist, playwright, & critic **2. G(eorge) E(dward),** 1873–1958; Eng. philosopher **3. Henry,** 1898– ; Eng. sculptor **4. Marianne (Craig),** 1887– ; U.S. poet **5. Thomas,** 1779–1852; Ir. poet

moor·fowl (-foul′) n. [Brit.] same as RED GROUSE

moor·hen (-hen′) n. **1.** [Brit.] the female moorfowl, or red grouse **2.** a common gallinule (Gallinula chloropus) of Europe and the E U.S.

moor·ing (-iŋ) n. **1.** the act of a person or thing that moors **2.** [often pl.] the lines, cables, etc. by which this is done **3.** [pl.] a place where a ship, etc. is or can be moored **4.** [often pl.] beliefs, habits, ties, etc. that can make one feel secure

moor·land (-land′) n. [Brit.] same as MOOR¹

moor·wort (-wurt′) n. either of two hardy, evergreen shrubs (genus Andromeda); esp., a species (Andromeda glaucophylla) native to peaty bogs in N. America

☆**moose** (mōōs) n., pl. moose [< AmInd. (Algonquian), as in Massachusett moos, lit., eats off] **1.** the largest animal (Alces americana) of the deer family, native to the N U.S. and Canada: the male has huge palmate antlers and weighs up to 1,800 lbs. **2.** same as ELK (sense 1)

moose·bird (-burd′) n. [Canad.] same as CANADA JAY

Moose·head Lake (mōōs′hed′) [transl. of AmInd. name] lake in WC Me.: 117 sq. mi.

MOOSE
(4 1/2–6 ft. high at shoulder)

moot (mōōt) n. [ME. mote < OE. mot, gemot, a meeting & prob. ON. mot, both < IE. base *mōd-, to encounter] **1.** an early English assembly of freemen to administer justice, decide community problems, etc. **2.** a discussion or argument, esp. of a hypothetical law case, as in a law school —adj. **1.** subject to or open for discussion or debate; debatable **2.** so hypothetical as to be meaningless —vt. **1.** to debate or discuss **2.** to propose or bring up for discussion or debate **3.** [Archaic] to argue or plead (a case, etc.), esp. in a mock court

moot court a mock court in which hypothetical cases are tried as an academic exercise for law students

mop¹ (mäp) n. [Early ModE. mappe, nautical term < ? Wal. mappe < L. mappa, napkin (see MAP)] **1.** a bundle of loose rags, yarns, a sponge, etc. fastened to the end of a stick, as for washing or wiping floors **2.** anything suggestive of this, as a thick head of hair —vt. mopped, mop′ping to wash, rub, wipe, or remove with or as with a mop —mop up **1.** [Colloq.] a) to bring or come to an end; finish b) to defeat completely **2.** Mil. to clear out or round up isolated or scattered remnants of beaten enemy forces from (a town, battle area, etc.) —mop (up) the floor with [Slang] to defeat decisively —mop′per n.

mop² (mäp) n., vi. mopped, mop′ping [< or akin to MDu. moppen, MHG. muffen, to grimace: for base see MOPE] [Archaic] same as GRIMACE

☆**mop·board** (mäp′bôrd′) n. same as BASEBOARD (sense 1)

mope (mōp) vi. moped, mop′ing [akin to MDu. mopen, Sw. dial. mopa < IE. base *mu-, echoic of sound produced with tightly closed lips, whence MUTTER] to be gloomy, dull, apathetic, and dispirited —vt. **1.** to make gloomy, dull, etc.: used reflexively and in the passive **2.** to pass in gloom, dullness, etc. (with away) —n. **1.** a person who mopes or is inclined to mope **2.** [pl.] low spirits —mop′er n. —mop′ey, mop′y, mop′ish adj. —mop′ish·ly adv.

mo·ped (mō′ped′) n. [< MO(TOR) + PED(AL)] a bicycle propelled by a small motor

☆**mo·per·y** (mō′pər ē) n. [MOP(E) + -ERY] [Slang] a trivial or imaginary violation of law

mop·pet (mäp′it) n. [dim. of ME. moppe, rag doll < ?] [Colloq.] a little child: a term of affection

mop-up (mäp′up′) n. a clearing out or rounding up of isolated or scattered remnants of beaten enemy forces in an area

mo·quette (mō ket′) n. [Fr.] a kind of carpet or upholstery fabric with a thick, soft, napped surface

mor (môr) n. [Dan., humus < or akin to ON. morth, a quantity, mass < IE. base *mer-, to rub, grind: see MORDANT] a layer of humus, usually matted or compact, just above the mineral soil

Mor. Morocco

mo·ra (môr′ə) n., pl. -rae (-ē), -ras [L. mora, delay < IE. base *(s)mer-, to reflect: cf. MOURN] **1.** Linguis. an arbitrary unit of syllabic length **2.** Prosody the unit of metrical time, equal to the ordinary short syllable, usually indicated by a breve (˘)

Mo·rad·a·bad (mō′rä dä bäd′) city in N India, in Uttar Pradesh: pop. 192,000

mo·raine (mə rān′, mô-) *n.* [Fr. < dial. *morêna* < *morre*, muzzle, akin to Sp. *morro*, snout, headland < VL. *murru*, echoic word for snout] a mass of rocks, gravel, sand, clay, etc. carried and deposited directly by a glacier, along its side (**lateral·moraine**), at its lower end (**terminal moraine**), or beneath the ice (**ground moraine**) —**mo·rain′ic** *adj.*

mor·al (môr′əl, mär′-; *for n.* 4, mə ral′) *adj.* [ME. < L. *moralis*, of manners or customs < *mos* (gen. *moris*), pl. *mores*, manners, morals (see MOOD¹): transl. of Gr. *ēthikos*] 1. relating to, dealing with, or capable of making the distinction between, right and wrong in conduct 2. relating to, serving to teach, or in accordance with, the principles of right and wrong 3. good or right in conduct or character; sometimes, specif., virtuous in sexual conduct 4. designating support, etc. that involves approval and sympathy without action 5. being virtually such because of its effect on thoughts, attitudes, etc., or because of its general results [a moral victory] 6. based on strong probability [a moral certainty] 7. *Law* based on general observation of people, on analogy, etc. rather than on what is demonstrable [moral evidence] —*n.* 1. a moral implication or moral lesson taught by a fable, event, etc. 2. the conclusion of a fable or story containing a moral lesson 3. [pl.] principles, standards, or habits with respect to right or wrong in conduct; ethics, sometimes, specif., standards of sexual behavior 4. [Rare] *same as* MORALE —**mor′al·ly** *adv.*

SYN.—**moral** implies conformity with the generally accepted standards of goodness or rightness in conduct or character, sometimes, specif., in sexual conduct [a moral woman]; **ethical** implies conformity with an elaborated, ideal code of moral principles, sometimes, specif., with the code of a particular profession [an *ethical* lawyer]; **virtuous** implies a morally excellent character, connoting justice, integrity, and often, specif., chastity; **righteous** implies a being morally blameless or justifiable [righteous anger] —*ANT.* immoral

mo·rale (mə ral′, mô-) *n.* [Fr., fem. *of moral* < L. *moralis:* see prec.] 1. moral or mental condition with respect to courage, discipline, confidence, enthusiasm, willingness to endure hardship, etc. within a group, in relation to a group, or within an individual 2. [Rare] *same as* MORALITY

moral hazard risk (to an insurance company) arising from the possible dishonesty or imprudence of the insured

mor·al·ism (môr′əl iz′m, mär′-) *n.* 1. moral teaching; moralizing 2. a moral maxim 3. belief in or practice of a system of ethics apart from religion

mor·al·ist (-ist) *n.* 1. a teacher of or writer on morals; person who moralizes 2. a person who adheres to a system of moralism 3. a person who seeks to impose his morals on others

mor·al·is·tic (môr′ə lis′tik, mär′-) *adj.* 1. moralizing 2. of moralism or moralists —**mor′al·is′ti·cal·ly** *adv.*

mo·ral·i·ty (mə ral′ə tē, mô-) *n.*, *pl.* **-ties** [ME. *moralite* < OFr. < LL. *moralitas* < *moralis*] 1. moral quality or character; rightness or wrongness, as of an action 2. the character of being in accord with the principles or standards of right conduct; right conduct; sometimes, specif., virtue in sexual conduct 3. principles of right and wrong in conduct; ethics 4. a particular system of such principles 5. moral instruction or lesson 6. a narrative with a moral lesson 7. *same as* MORALITY PLAY

morality play any of a class of allegorical dramas of the 15th and 16th cent., the characters of which personify abstractions, as Everyman, Vice, Virtue, etc.

mor·al·ize (môr′ə līz′, mär′-) *vi.* **-ized′**, **-iz′ing** [Fr. *moraliser* < LL. *moralizare* < L. *moralis*] to think, write, or speak about matters of right and wrong, often in a self-righteous or tedious way —*vt.* 1. *a)* to interpret or explain in terms of right and wrong *b)* to point out the moral in or draw a moral from 2. to improve the morals of —**mor′al·i·za′tion** *n.* —**mor′al·iz′er** *n.*

moral philosophy *same as* ETHICS

mo·rass (mə ras′, mô-) *n.* [Du. *moeras*, a marsh, fen; earlier *marasch* < OFr. *maresc* < Frank. *marisk*, a swamp, akin to MARSH] a tract of low, soft, watery ground; bog; marsh; swamp: often used figuratively of a difficult, troublesome, or perplexing state of affairs

mor·a·to·ri·um (môr′ə tôr′ē əm, mär′-) *n.*, *pl.* **-ri·ums**, **-ri·a** (-ə) [ModL. < neut. of LL. *moratorius*, delaying < L. *morari*, to delay < *mora*, a delay: for IE. base see MOURN] 1. a legal authorization, usually by a law passed in an emergency, to delay payment of money due, as by a bank or debtor nation 2. the effective period of such an authorization 3. any authorized delay or stopping of some specified activity

mor·a·to·ry (môr′ə tôr′ē, mär′-) *adj.* [LL. *moratorius:* see prec.] *Law* delaying or postponing; esp., designating or of a law authorizing a moratorium

Mo·ra·va (mō′rä vä) 1. *Czech name of* MORAVIA 2. river in Moravia flowing south along the Austrian border, into the Danube: c. 230 mi. 3. river in E Yugoslavia, flowing north into the Danube: 134 mi.

Mo·ra·vi·a (mô rā′vē ə, mə-) region, formerly a province, of C Czechoslovakia: chief city, Brno

Mo·ra·vi·a (mô rā′vyä; E. mô rā′vē ə), **Al·ber·to** (äl ber′tô) (pseud. of *Alberto Pincherle*) 1907– ; It. writer

MORAVIA

Mo·ra·vi·an (mô rā′vē ən, mə-) *adj.* 1. of Moravia, its people, etc. 2. of the religious sect of Moravians —*n.* 1. a native or inhabitant of Moravia 2. the Czech dialect of Moravia 3. a member of a Protestant sect founded in Saxony (c.1722) by disciples, from Moravia, of John Huss

Mo·rav·ská Os·tra·va (mô′räf skä ôs′trä vä) *same as* OSTRAVA

Mor·ay (mur′ē) county on the coast of NE Scotland: 476 sq. mi.; pop. 51,000: also **Mor′ay·shire′** (-shir′)

☆**mo·ray** (môr′ā; mô rā′, mə-) *n.* [Port. *moreia* < L. *muraena*, kind of fish < Gr. *myraina*] any of a number of voracious eels (family Muraenidae) of warm seas, characterized by brilliant coloring and found esp. among coral reefs: the Mediterranean moray is valued as a food fish: in full, **moray eel**

Moray Firth inlet of the North Sea, on the NE coast of Scotland

mor·bid (môr′bid) *adj.* [L. *morbidus*, sickly, diseased < *morbus*, disease < IE. base *mer-, to wear away, destroy, whence OIr. *meirb*, lifeless] 1. of, having, or caused by disease; unhealthy; diseased 2. resulting from or as from a diseased state of mind; esp., having or showing an unwholesome tendency to dwell on gruesome or gloomy matters 3. gruesome; grisly; horrible [the morbid details of a story] 4. of diseased parts; pathological [morbid anatomy] 5. [Rare] causing disease —**mor′bid·ly** *adv.* —**mor′bid·ness** *n.*

mor·bid·i·ty (môr bid′ə tē) *n.*, *pl.* **-ties** 1. state, quality, or instance of being morbid 2. the rate of disease or proportion of diseased persons in a given locality, nation, etc.

mor·bif·ic (môr bif′ik) *adj.* [Fr. *morbifique* < LL. *morbificare*, to produce disease < L. *morbus*, disease (see MORBID) + *facere*, to make: see FACT] causing or leading to disease: also **mor·bif′i·cal**

mor·bil·li (môr bil′ī) *n.pl.* [ML., pl. of *morbillus*, dim. of L. *morbus*, disease] *older term for* MEASLES

‡**mor·ceau** (môr sō′) *n.*, *pl.* **-ceaux** (-sō′) [Fr.: see MORSEL] 1. a morsel; bit; fragment 2. a short composition, passage, or excerpt, as of poetry or music

mor·da·cious (môr dā′shəs) *adj.* [< L. *mordax* (gen. *mordacis*), biting < base of *mordere*, to bite: see ff. + -OUS] biting, sharp, acrid, or caustic —**mor·da′cious·ly** *adv.* —**mor·dac′i·ty** (-das′ə tē) *n.*

mor·dant (môr′d'nt) *adj.* [ME. *mordent* < OFr. *mordant*, prp. *of mordre*, to bite < L. *mordere* < IE. *merd-*, var. of base *mer-:* see MORBID] 1. biting, cutting, caustic, or sarcastic, as speech, wit, etc. 2. *same as* CORROSIVE 3. acting as a mordant —*n.* 1. a substance used in dyeing to fix the coloring matter, as a metallic compound that combines with the organic dye to form an insoluble colored compound, or lake, in the fiber of the fabric 2. an acid or other corrosive substance used in etching to bite lines, areas, etc. into the surface —*vt.* to treat or impregnate with a mordant —**mor′dan·cy** *n.* —**mor′dant·ly** *adv.*

Mor·de·cai (môr′də kī′) [Heb. *mordĕkhai*] 1. a masculine name: dim. *Mordy* 2. *Bible* the cousin of Esther (in the Book of Esther), who saved the Jews from the destruction planned by Haman: cf. PURIM

mor·dent (môr′d'nt) *n.* [G. < It. *mordente*, prp. of *mordere* < L., to bite: see MORDANT] *Music* an ornament made by a single rapid alternation of a principal tone with a subsidiary tone a half step or whole step below: in a **double mordent** there are two alternations: in an **inverted mordent** the subsidiary tone is a half step or whole step above the principal tone

MORDENTS

Mor·dred (môr′drid) *n. same as* MODRED

Mo·ré (mô rā′) *n. same as* MOSSI

more (môr) *adj. superl.* MOST [ME. < OE. *mara*, greater, used as compar. *of micel*, big, much (cf. MUCH): akin to Goth. *maiza* < IE. base *mē-, more, *mō-, big] 1. greater in amount, quantity, or degree: used as the comparative of MUCH 2. greater in number: used as the comparative of MANY 3. additional; further [take more tea] —*n.* 1. a

greater amount, quantity, or degree 2. [*with pl. v.*] *a*) a greater number (*of* persons or things) [*more* of us are going] *b*) a greater number of persons or things 3. something additional or further [*more* can be said] 4. something of greater importance —*adv. superl.* MOST [< the above, replacing earlier *mo* (OE. *ma*) < IE. positive **me-ro-s, *mō-ro-s < *mē-, *mō-*] 1. in or to a greater degree or extent: used with many adjectives and adverbs (regularly with those of three or more syllables) to form the comparative degree [*more* satisfying, *more* intensely] 2. in addition; further; again; longer —**more and more** 1. to an increasing degree; increasingly 2. a constantly increasing amount, quantity, degree, or number (of persons or a specified thing) —**more or less** 1. to some extent 2. approximately
More (môr) 1. Hannah, 1745–1833; Eng. writer, esp. of religious tracts 2. Sir Thomas, 1478–1535; Eng. statesman & writer: executed: canonized in 1935: also called **Saint Thomas More**
Mo·re·a (mô rē′ə) *former name of* PELOPONNESUS
Mo·reau (mô rō′), **Jean Vic·tor** (zhän vēk tôr′) 1763–1813; Fr. general: opponent of Napoleon
mo·reen (mə rēn′, mô-) *n.* [prob. < MOIRÉ + *-een,* as in VELVETEEN] a strong fabric, as of wool or cotton, having, esp. formerly, a moiré, or watered, finish
mo·rel (mə rel′, mô-) *n.* [Fr. *morille* < MDu. *morilhe* < OHG. *morhila,* dim. of *morha,* carrot, akin to OE. *more*] any of a genus (*Morchella*) of edible ascomycete mushrooms resembling a sponge on a stalk
Mo·re·lia (mô re′lyä) city in C Mexico; capital of Michoacán; pop. 140,000
mo·rel·lo (mə rel′ō) *n., pl.* **-los** [Fl. *marelle,* aphetic < *amarelle* < G.: see AMARELLE] a cultivated cherry with dark-red skin and juice
Mo·re·los (mô re′lôs) state in SC Mexico: 1,917 sq. mi.; pop. 546,000
more·o·ver (môr ō′vər) *adv.* in addition to what has been said; besides; further; also: used with conjunctive force
☆**mo·res** (môr′ēz, -āz) *n.pl.* [L., pl. of *mos,* custom: see MORAL] folkways that are considered conducive to the welfare of society and so, through general observance, develop the force of law, often becoming part of the formal legal code

MOREL

Mo·resque (mô resk′, mə-) *adj.* [Fr. < Sp. *morisco* < *Moro* < L. *Maurus,* MOOR] Moorish in design or decoration, etc. —*n.* Moorish design or decoration, characterized by intricate tracery, bright colors, gilt, etc.
Mor·gan[1] (môr′gən) 1. [W., lit., sea dweller] a masculine name 2. **Daniel,** 1736–1802; Am. Revolutionary general 3. **Sir Henry,** 1635?–88; Welsh buccaneer in the Spanish Main 4. **John Hunt,** 1825–64; Confederate general in the Civil War 5. **J(ohn) P(ierpont),** 1837–1913; U.S. financier 6. **John Pier·pont** (pir′pänt), 1867–1943; U.S. financier: son of *prec.* 7. **Lewis Henry,** 1818–81; U.S. anthropologist 8. **Thomas Hunt,** 1866–1945; U.S. zoologist
Mor·gan[2] (môr′gən) *n.* [after Justin *Morgan* (1747–98), New Englander who owned the sire of the breed] ☆any of a breed of strong, light harness or saddle horses
mor·ga·nat·ic (môr′gə nat′ik) *adj.* [< ML. (*matrimonium ad*) *morganaticam,* (marriage with) morning gift < *morganaticum,* altered < OHG. *morgengeba,* morning gift, gift given to the wife on the day after marriage (in lieu of any share in the husband's property)] designating or of a form of marriage in which a man of royalty or nobility marries a woman of inferior social status with the provision that, although children of the marriage, if any, will be legitimate, neither they nor the wife may lay claim to his rank or property —**mor′ga·nat′i·cal·ly** *adv.*
☆**mor·gan·ite** (môr′gə nīt′) *n.* [after J. P. MORGAN] a transparent, rose-colored variety of beryl, used as a gem
Mor·gan le Fay (môr′gən lə fā′) [OFr. *Morgain la fée,* lit., Morgan the fairy < Celt.: ? akin to OIr. *Morrigain,* queen of the incubi, sorceress < **mor-* < IE. **mora* (see MARE[3]) + OIr. *rigain,* queen < IE. base **reg-,* to rule (see REGAL)] *Arthurian Legend* the evil fairy half sister of King Arthur: in other legends, variously a water spirit, lake fairy, etc.
mor·gen (môr′gən) *n., pl.* **-gen, -gens** [Du. & G., lit., MORNING: hence area plowed in one morning] 1. a land measure formerly used in the Netherlands and its possessions, and still used in South Africa, equal to about 2 acres 2. a land measure formerly used in Prussia, Denmark, and Norway, equal to about 2/3 acre
Mor·gen·thau (môr′gən thô′), **Henry, Jr.** 1891–1967; U.S. public official: secretary of the treasury (1934–45)
morgue (môrg) *n.* [Fr., morgue, earlier, identification room of a prison: orig., "haughty air" < dial. *morre,* snout: see MORAINE] 1. a place where the bodies of unknown dead persons or those dead of unknown causes are kept to be examined, identified, etc. before burial ☆2. *Journalism a*) the reference library of back numbers, photographs, clippings, etc. kept by a newspaper, magazine, etc. *b*) the room in which this is kept
mor·i·bund (môr′ə bund′) *adj.* [L. *moribundus,* dying < *mori,* to die: see MORTAL] 1. dying 2. coming to an end 3. having little or no vital force left —**mor′i·bund′i·ty** *n.*
mo·ri·on[1] (môr′ē än′) *n.* [OFr. < Sp. *morrión < morra,* crown of the head: see MORAINE] a hatlike, crested helmet

without beaver or visor and with a curved brim coming to a peak in front and in back, worn in the 16th and 17th cent.
mo·ri·on[2] (môr′ē än′) *n.* [misreading of L. *mormorion* (in early editions of Pliny)] a variety of quartz, dark-brown to black in color
Mo·ris·co (mə ris′kō, mô-) *adj.* [Sp. < *Moro* < L. *Maurus,* MOOR] Moorish —*n., pl.* **-cos, -coes** a Moor; esp., one of the Moors of Spain
Mor·i·son (môr′i sən), **Samuel Eliot** 1887– ; U.S. historian
☆**Mor·mon** (môr′mən) *n.* a member of the Church of Jesus Christ of Latter-day Saints (commonly called the *Mormon Church*), founded in the U.S. in 1830 by Joseph Smith: among its holy books is the Book of Mormon, represented by Smith as being his translation of an account of some ancient American peoples by a prophet among them named Mormon —*adj.* of the Mormons or their religion —**Mor′mon·ism** *n.*
morn (môrn) *n.* [ME. *morne* < OE., contr. of *morgene,* dat. of *morgen,* MORNING] [Poet.] morning
Mor·nay (môr nā′), **Phi·lippe de** (fē lēp′ də), seigneur du Plessis-Marly, 1549–1623; Fr. diplomat & Huguenot leader: also *Duplessis-Mornay*
morn·ing (môr′niŋ) *n.* [ME. *morweninge* (by analogy with EVENING) < OE. *morgen,* morning, akin to G. *morgen* < IE. base **mer(e)k-,* to glimmer, twilight, whence OCzech *mrkati,* to dawn, grow dark] 1. the first or early part of the day, from midnight, or esp. dawn, to noon 2. the first or early part [the *morning* of life] 3. the dawn; daybreak —*adj.* of, suited to, or occurring, appearing, etc. in the morning
morning after [Colloq.] a hangover, or painful awakening
morning dress formal daytime dress for men, including a cutaway (**morning coat**)
☆**morn·ing-glo·ry** (-glôr′ē) *adj.* designating a family (Convolvulaceae) of twining vines and some erect shrubs and trees with flowers having five sepals and a funnel-shaped corolla, including the morning glories, bindweeds, jalaps, and sweet potatoes
☆**morning glory** any of a genus (*Ipomoea*) of plants of the morning-glory family; esp., a twining annual vine (*Ipomoea purpurea*), with heart-shaped leaves and trumpet-shaped flowers of lavender, blue, pink, or white
morning prayer *Anglican Church* the worship service assigned to the morning
morn·ings (-niŋz) *adv.* during every morning or most mornings
morning sickness nausea and vomiting occurring in the morning during the first months of pregnancy
morning star a planet, esp. Venus, visible in the eastern sky before sunrise
Mo·ro (môr′ō) *n.* [Sp., lit., Moor < L. *Maurus*] 1. *pl.* **-ros, -ro** a member of a group of Moslem Malay tribes living in the S Philippines 2. any of the Malayo-Polynesian languages of the Moros —*adj.* of the Moros
Mo·roc·co (mə rä′kō) kingdom on the NW coast of Africa: c. 171,300 sq. mi.; pop. c. 14,140,000: cap. Rabat —*n.* [m-] *a*) a fine, soft leather made, orig. in Morocco, from goatskins tanned with sumac *b*) any similar leather, as one made from sharkskin Also **morocco leather** —**Mo·roc′can** *adj., n.*
☆**mo·ron** (môr′än) *n.* [arbitrary use (by H. H. Goddard, 1866–1957, U.S. psychologist) of Gr. *mōron,* neut. of *mōros,* foolish, akin to Sans. *mūrá-,* stupid] 1. a mentally retarded person with an intelligence quotient ranging from 50 to 70; adult person mentally equal to a child between eight and twelve years old: an obsolescent term: see MENTAL RETARDATION 2. a very foolish or stupid person —**mo·ron·ic** (mô rän′ik, mə-) *adj.* —**mo·ron′i·cal·ly** *adv.* —**mo·ron′i·ty, mo′ron·ism** *n.*
mo·rose (mə rōs′, mô-) *adj.* [L. *morosus,* peevish, fretful, fastidious < *mos* (gen. *moris*), manner: see MOOD[1]] 1. ill-tempered; gloomy, sullen, etc. 2. characterized by gloom —SYN. see SULLEN —**mo·rose′ly** *adv.* —**mo·rose′ness** *n.*
morph (môrf) *n.* [< Gr. *morphē,* form] *Linguis.* 1. same as ALLOMORPH 2. a representation of an occurrence of a morpheme 3. a sequence of phonemes isolated from surrounding sequences but not yet assigned to a particular morpheme
-morph (môrf) [see prec.] *a combining form meaning* one having a (specified) form [*pseudomorph*]
morph. morphology
morph·al·lax·is (môr′fə lak′sis) *n., pl.* **-lax′es** (-sēz) [ModL. < Gr. *morphē,* form + *allaxis,* an exchange < *allassein,* to change, exchange < *allos,* other: see ELSE] *Zool.* the transformation of one part into another during regeneration, as in the growth of an antennule from the stump of an eye in some crustaceans
mor·pheme (môr′fēm) *n.* [Fr. *morphème* < Gr. *morphē,* form + Fr. *-ème,* as in *phonème,* PHONEME] *Linguis.* the smallest meaningful unit or form in a language: it may be an affix (Ex.: *un-* in *undo* or *-er* in *doer*), a base (Ex.: *do* in *undo*), or an inflectional form (Ex.: *-ing* in *doing* or *-s* in *girls*) —**mor·phe′mic** *adj.* —**mor·phe′mi·cal·ly** *adv.*
mor·phe·mics (môr fē′miks) *n.pl.* [*with sing. v.*] that part of linguistic analysis concerned with the description of morphemes
Mor·pheus (môr′fē əs, -fyo͞os) [ME. < L. < Gr. *Mor-*

pheus, prob. < *morphē*, form: hence, orig., one who shapes (dreams)] *Gr. Myth.* the god of dreams, son of Hypnos
-mor·phic (môr′fik) [< Gr. *morphē*, form + -IC] *a combining form meaning* having a (specified) form or shape [*anthropomorphic*]
mor·phine (môr′fēn) *n.* [G. *morphin* or Fr. *morphine* < ModL. *morphium*, so named (1811) by F. W. A. Sertürner (1783–1841), G. pharmacist < L. *Morpheus*: see MORPHEUS] a bitter, white or colorless, crystalline alkaloid, $C_{17}H_{19}O_3N \cdot H_2O$, derived from opium and used in medicine to relieve pain: also **mor′phi·a** (-fē ə) —**mor·phin′ic** (-fē′nik, -fin′ik) *adj.*
mor·phin·ism (môr′fin iz′m) *n.* a diseased condition resulting from the habitual or excessive use of morphine 2. addiction to the use of morphine
mor·pho·gen·e·sis (môr′fō jen′ə sis) *n.* [ModL.: see -MORPH & -GENESIS] *Zool.* the structural changes occurring during the development of an organism, organ, or part —**mor′pho·ge·net′ic** (-jə net′ik) *adj.*
morphol. morphology
mor·phol·o·gy (môr fäl′ə jē) *n.* [G. *morphologie*, coined (1822) by J. W. von GOETHE < Gr. *morphē*, form + -logie, -LOGY] 1. the branch of biology that deals with the form and structure of animals and plants 2. *a*) the branch of linguistics that deals with the internal structure and forms of words: with syntax, it forms a division of grammar *b*) the study of the structure, classification, and relationships of morphemes 3. any scientific study of form and structure, as in physical geography 4. form and structure, as of an organism, regarded as a whole —**mor′pho·log′i·cal** (-fə läj′i k′l), **mor′pho·log′ic** *adj.* —**mor′pho·log′i·cal·ly** *adv.* —**mor·phol′o·gist** *n.*
mor·pho·pho·ne·mics (môr′fō fə nē′miks) *n.pl.* [*with sing. v.*] [ModL. < Gr. *morphē*, form + PHONEMICS] *Linguis.* 1. the study of phonemic differences in given morphemes 2. the study of the distribution of phonemes within one morpheme 3. the total class of such differences in a particular language —**mor′pho·pho·ne′mic** *adj.*
mor·pho·sis (môr fō′sis) *n., pl.* -ses (-sēz) [ModL. < Gr. *morphōsis*, form < *morphoun*, to form < *morphē*, form] the mode of developmental formation of an organism or any of its parts —**mor·phot′ic** (-fät′ik) *adj.*
-mor·phous (môr′fəs) [Gr. -*morphos* < *morphē*, form] *same as* -MORPHIC
Mor·ris (môr′is, mär′-) [var. of MAURICE] 1. a masculine name: dim. *Morrie, Morry* 2. **Gouv·er·neur** (guv′ər nir′), 1752–1816; Am. statesman & diplomat 3. **Robert**, 1734–1806; Am. financier & patriot 4. **William**, 1834–96; Eng. poet, artist, craftsman, & socialist
mor·ris (môr′is, mär′-) *adj.* [< ME. *morys*, MOORISH] designating or of an old folk dance formerly common in England, esp. on May Day, in which fancy costumes were worn, often those associated with characters in the Robin Hood legends —*n.* this dance
Morris chair [after Wm. MORRIS, who popularized it] an armchair with an adjustable back and removable cushions
Morris Jes·sup (jes′əp), **Cape** cape at the N tip of Greenland: northernmost point of land in the world
mor·ro (mär′ō; Sp. môr′ō) *n., pl.* -ros (-ōz; Sp. -rōs) [Sp.: see MORAINE] a rounded hill or point of land
mor·row (mär′ō, môr′-) *n.* [ME. *morwe, morwen* < OE. *morgen*, MORNING] [Archaic or Poet.] 1. morning 2. the next day 3. the time just after some particular event
Mors (môrz) [L.] *Rom. Myth.* death personified as a god: identified with the Greek god Thanatos
Morse[1] (môrs) *adj.* [after ff.] [*often* m-] designating or of a code, or alphabet, consisting of a system of dots and dashes, or short and long sounds or flashes, used to represent letters, numerals, etc. in telegraphy, signaling, and the like: the *international* (or *continental*) *code* has been adapted from the original, esp. for use in radiotelegraphy —*n.* the Morse code
Morse[2] (môrs), **Samuel F(inley) B(reese)** 1791–1872; U.S. artist & inventor of the telegraph
mor·sel (môr′s′l) *n.* [ME. < OFr., dim. of *mors* < L. *morsum*, a bite, piece < pp. of *mordere*, to bite: see MORDANT] 1. a small bite or portion of food 2. a small piece or amount; bit 3. a tasty dish —*vt.* to divide into or distribute in small portions
mort[1] (môrt) *n.* [ME. < OFr. < L. *mors* (gen. *mortis*), death: see MORTAL] 1. [Obs.] death 2. a note sounded on a hunting horn to announce the killing of the quarry
mort[2] (môrt) *n.* [< : MORTAL, used as intens.] [Dial.] a great quantity or number
mor·ta·del·la (môr′tə del′ə) *n.* [It. < L. *murtatum* (*farcimen*), (sausage) spiced with myrtle, neut. of *myrtatus* < *myrtus*, MYRTLE] a type of Italian bologna
mor·tal (môr′t′l) *adj.* [ME. < OFr. < L. *mortalis* < *mors* (gen. *mortis*), death, akin to *mori*, to die < IE. base *mer-*, to die, be worn out, whence Sans. *marati*, (he) dies & MURDER] 1. that must eventually die [all *mortal* beings] 2. of man as a being who must eventually die 3. of this world 4. of death 5. causing death; deadly; fatal 6. to the death [*mortal* combat] 7. not to be pacified [a *mortal* enemy] 8. very intense; grievous [*mortal* terror]

[Colloq.] *a*) extreme; very great *b*) very long and tedious *c*) conceivable; possible [of no *mortal* good to anyone] 10. *Theol.* that can cause death of the soul: said of sin: distinguished from VENIAL —*n.* a being who must eventually die; esp., a human being; person —*adv.* [Dial.] extremely —SYN. see FATAL —**mor′tal·ly** *adv.*
mor·tal·i·ty (môr tal′ə tē) *n.* [ME. *mortalite* < OFr. < L. *mortalitas* < *mortalis*, MORTAL] 1. the condition of being mortal; esp., the nature of man, as having eventually to die 2. death on a large scale, as from disease or war 3. *a*) the proportion of deaths to the population of a region, nation, etc.; death rate *b*) the death rate from a particular disease 4. the number or proportion than fail 5. human beings collectively; mankind 6. [Obs.] death
mortality table a statistical table, based on a sample group of the population, stating the percentage of people who live to any given age and the life expectancy at any given age
mor·tar (môr′tər) *n.* [ME. *mortere* < OE. *mortere* & OFr. *mortier*, both < L. *mortarium*, mixing vessel or trough < IE. **mrtos*, pulverized < base **mer-*, to rub, whence OE. *mearu*, tender, soft] 1. a very hard bowl in which softer substances are ground or pounded to a powder with a pestle 2. any machine in which materials are ground or pounded 3. [Fr. *mortier*] a short-barreled cannon with a low muzzle velocity, which hurls shells in a high trajectory 4. any of various similar devices, for shooting lifelines, flares, etc. 5. [ME. *morter* < MFr. *mortier* < L. *mortarium*, a mixture of sand and lime: so called from the vessel in which it was made] a mixture of cement or lime with sand and water, used between bricks or stones in building, or as plaster —*vt.* 1. to plaster or bind together with mortar 2. to attack with mortar shells

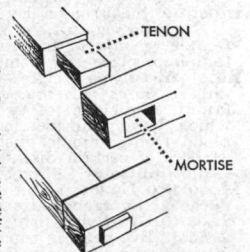

PESTLE
MORTAR

mor·tar·board (-bôrd′) *n.* 1. a square board with a handle beneath, on which mortar is carried by masons 2. an academic cap with a square, flat, horizontal top, worn at commencements, etc. in schools and colleges
mort·gage (môr′gij) *n.* [ME. < OFr. *morgage, mort gage*, lit., dead pledge < *mort*, dead (acc MORT[1]) + *gage*, GAGE[1]] *Law* 1. the pledging of property to a creditor as security for the payment of a debt 2. the deed by which this pledge is made 3. the claim of the mortgagee on the property —*vt.* **-gaged, -gag·ing** 1. *Law* to pledge (property) by a mortgage 2. to put an advance claim or liability on [to mortgage one's future]
mort·ga·gee (môr′gə jē′) *n.* a person to whom property is mortgaged
mort·ga·gor, mort·gag·er (môr′gi jər) *n.* a person who mortgages property
mor·tice (môr′tis) *n., vt. alt. sp.* of MORTISE
☆**mor·ti·cian** (môr tish′ən) *n.* [< L. *mors*, death (see MORTAL) + -ICIAN] *same as* UNDERTAKER (sense 2)
mor·ti·fi·ca·tion (môr′tə fi kā′shən) *n.* [ME. *mortificacioun* < LL.(Ec.) *mortificatio* < pp. of *mortificare*] 1. a mortifying or being mortified; specif., *a*) the control of physical desires and passions by self-denial, fasting, etc. *b*) shame, humiliation, chagrin, etc.; loss of self-respect 2. something causing shame, humiliation, etc. 3. *old term for* GANGRENE
mor·ti·fy (môr′tə fī′) *vt.* **-fied′, -fy′ing** [ME. *mortifien* < OFr. *mortifier* < LL.(Ec.) *mortificare*, to kill; destroy < L. *mors*, death (see MORTAL) + *facere*, to make: see FACT] 1. to punish (one's body) or control (one's physical desires and passions) by self-denial, fasting, etc., as a means of religious or ascetic discipline 2. to cause to feel shame, humiliation, chagrin, etc.; injure the pride or self-respect of 3. [Now Rare] to cause (body tissue) to decay or become gangrenous 4. [Obs.] to destroy the vitality or vigor of —*vi.* 1. to practice mortification (sense 1 *a*) 2. [Now Rare] to decay or become gangrenous —**mor′ti·fi′er** *n.*
Mor·ti·mer (môr′tə mər) [< Norm. surname < place name] a masculine name: dim. *Mort, Morty*
mor·tise (môr′tis) *n.* [ME. *mortays* < MFr. *mortaise*, a mortise < Ar. *murtazza*, joined, fixed in] a notch, hole, or space cut, as in a piece of wood, to receive a projecting part (*tenon*) shaped to fit —*vt.* **-tised, -tis·ing** 1. to join or fasten securely, esp. with a mortise and tenon 2. to cut a hole or mortise in

TENON

MORTISE

mort·main (môrt′mān′) *n.* [ME. *morte-mayne* < OFr. *mortemain* < ML. *mortua manus*, lit., dead hand < fem. of L. *mortuus*, pp. of *mori*, to die (see MORTAL) + *manus*, hand: see MANUAL] *Law* 1. a transfer of lands or houses to a corporate body, such as a school, church,

or charitable organization, for perpetual ownership **2.** such ownership

Mor·ton (môr′t'n) [orig. surname & place name < OE. *Mor-tun* < *mor*, a swamp, MOOR[1] + *tun*, TOWN] a masculine name: dim. **Mort, Morty**

Mor·ton (môr′t'n), **William Thomas Green** 1819–68; U.S. dentist: introduced the use of ether for anesthesia (1846)

mor·tu·ar·y (môr′choo wer′ē) *n.*, *pl.* **-ar′ies** [< LL. *mortuarius*, of the dead < L. *mortuus*, pp. of *mori*, to die: see MORTAL] a place where dead bodies are kept before burial or cremation, as a morgue or funeral home —*adj.* **1.** of or having to do with the burial of the dead **2.** of or connected with death

mor·u·la (môr′yoo lə, mär′-; -oo lə) *n.*, *pl.* **-lae** (-lē′) [ModL., dim. of L. *morum*, mulberry] a solid mass of cells, somewhat like a mulberry in shape, formed by cleavage of an ovum in the early stages of embryonic development —**mor′u·lar** *adj.* —**mor′u·la′tion** *n.*

MOS military occupational specialty

mos. months

Mo·sa·ic (mō zā′ik) *adj.* [LL.(Ec.) *Mosaicus* < Gr.(Ec.) *Mōsaikos*] of Moses or the writings, principles, etc. attributed to him

mo·sa·ic (mō zā′ik) *n.* [LME. *musycke* < OFr. *musique* < ML. *musaicum*, altered < LL. *musivum*, mosaic, orig. neut. of L. *musivus*, artistic, of a muse < L. *musa*, MUSE: sp. altered after Fr. *mosaïque* < It. *mosaico* < same ML. source] **1.** the process of making pictures or designs by inlaying small bits of colored stone, glass, tile, etc. in mortar **2.** inlaid work made by this process **3.** a picture or design so made **4.** anything resembling this, as, a number of aerial photographs pieced together to show a continuous area **5.** *Biol.* same as CHIMERA (*n.* 3) **6.** *Bot.* any of the virus diseases that cause wrinkling or mottling of leaves **7.** *TV* the photosensitive plate in an iconoscope or other television camera tube —*adj.* of or resembling mosaic or a mosaic —*vt.* **-icked, -ick·ing 1.** to make by or as by mosaic **2.** to decorate with mosaics —**mo·sa′i·cal·ly** *adv.* —**mo·sa′i·cist** (-ə sist) *n.*

mosaic gold 1. a yellow, crystalline powder, stannic sulfide, SnS_2, used as a pigment **2.** same as ORMOLU

mosaic image the image produced by a compound eye in which each element (*ommatidium*) focuses and forms a very small part of the total view

mo·sa·i·cism (mō zā′ə siz′m) *n.* [MOSAIC, *n.* 5 + -ISM] the condition existing when tissues of different genetic makeup occur in the same organism

Mosaic law the ancient law of the Hebrews, ascribed to Moses and contained mainly in the Pentateuch

mos·chate (mäs′kāt, -kit) *adj.* [ModL. *moschatus* < ML. *moschus*, musk] having the smell of musk; musky

Mos·cow (mäs′kou, -kō) capital of the U.S.S.R. & the R.S.F.S.R., in W R.S.F.S.R.: pop. 6,464,000: Russ. name, MOSKVA

Mo·selle (mō zel′; *Fr.* mō zel′) river in NE France & W West Germany, flowing north into the Rhine at Koblenz: c. 320 mi.: Ger. name **Mo·sel** (mō′zəl) —*n.* a variety of white wine made in the valley of this river or any wine like this

Mo·ses (mō′ziz) [LL.(Ec.) < Gr.(Ec.) *Mōsēs* < Heb. *mōsheh*, prob. < Egypt. *mes, mesu*, child, son] **1.** a masculine name: dim. **Mo, Mose 2.** *Bible* the leader who brought the Israelites out of slavery in Egypt and led them to the Promised Land, received the Ten Commandments from God, and gave laws to the people —*n.* a leader; lawgiver

Mo·ses (mō′ziz), **Anna Mary Robertson** (called *Grandma Moses*) 1860–1961; U.S. primitive painter

☆mo·sey (mō′zē) *vi.* [< VAMOSE] [Slang] **1.** to stroll, amble, or shuffle along **2.** to go away; move along

‡mo·shav (mō shäv′) *n.*, *pl.* **mo·sha·vim** (mō′shä vēm′) [ModHeb. *mōshābh* < Heb., a dwelling] in Israel, a type of settlement consisting of individual leaseholds farmed cooperatively: cf. KIBBUTZ

Mos·kva (môs kvä′) *Russ. name of* MOSCOW

Mos·lem (mäz′ləm, muz′-, mäs′-) *n.* [Ar. *muslim*, true believer < *aslama*, to resign oneself (to God)] an adherent of Islam —*adj.* of Islam or the Moslems: also **Mos·lem′ic** (-lem′ik) —**Mos′lem·ism** *n.*

mosque (mäsk) *n.* [Early ModE. *muskey* < MFr. *mosquez* < It. *moschea*, ult. < Ar. *masjid*, place of adoration, temple < *sajada*, to prostrate oneself, pray] a Moslem temple or place of worship

mos·qui·to (mə skēt′ō, -ə) *n.*, *pl.* **-toes, -tos** [Sp. & Port., dim. of *mosca* < L. *musca*, a fly: see MIDGE] any of a large family (Culicidae) of two-winged insects, the females of which have skin-piercing mouthparts used to extract blood from animals, including man: some varieties are carriers of certain diseases, as malaria and yellow fever —**mos·qui′to·ey** (-ē) *adj.*

Mosquito Coast region on the Caribbean coast of Honduras & Nicaragua: also **Mos·qui·ti·a** (môs kē′tē ä)

☆mos·qui·to·fish (-fish′) *n.*, *pl.* **-fish′, -fish′es:** see FISH[2] a small, live-bearing topminnow (*Gambusia affinis*), often introduced into a body of water to control mosquito larvae

☆mosquito hawk *same as:* **1.** DRAGONFLY **2.** NIGHTHAWK (sense 1)

☆mosquito net (*or* **netting**) a very fine cloth mesh or a curtain made of this, for keeping out mosquitoes

moss (môs mäs) *n.* [ME. *mos*, a bog, moss < OE. *mos*, a swamp, akin to ON. *mosi*, G. *moos*, a bog, moss < IE. **meus-* (whence L. *muscus*, moss) < base **meu-*, moist] **1.** *a)* any of a class (Musci) of very small, green, bryophytic plants having stems with leaflike structures and growing in velvety clusters on rocks, trees, moist ground, etc. *b)* a growth of these **2.** any of various similar plants, as some lichens, algae, etc. —*vt.* to cover with a growth of moss —**moss′like′** *adj.*

moss agate a kind of agate with black, brown, or green, mosslike markings

☆moss·back (-bak′) *n.* **1.** an old fish, shellfish, turtle, etc. that develops a greenish growth of algae, etc. over the back **2.** [Colloq.] an old-fashioned or very conservative person

Möss·bau·er effect (môs′bou ər) [after R. L. *Mössbauer* (1929–), G. physicist in the U.S.] the phenomenon in which gamma rays from the nuclei of certain radioactive isotopes maintain an unvarying wavelength and frequency if the emitting nuclei are bound in the lattice of a crystal

☆moss·bunk·er (môs′bun′kər, mäs′-) *n.* [altered < Du. *marsbanker* < ?] *same as* MENHADEN

moss-grown (-grōn′) *adj.* **1.** overgrown with moss **2.** old-fashioned; antiquated

Mos·si (mäs′ē) *n.* **1.** *pl.* **Mos′sis, Mos′si** any member of several peoples of WC Sudan (sense 1) **2.** their Niger-Congo language

☆moss pink a hardy, perennial phlox (*Phlox subulata*) forming sprawling mats with bristly, narrow leaves and white, pink, or lavender flowers

moss rose 1. *same as* PORTULACA **2.** a variety of the cabbage rose (*Rosa centifolia*) with a roughened, mossy flower stalk and calyx

moss-troop·er (-trōō′pər) *n.* [< Scot. *moss*, a swamp < ME. *mos*: see MOSS] **1.** any of the raiders who infested the swampy borderland between England and Scotland in the 17th cent. **2.** a raider; marauder

moss·y (-ē) *adj.* **-i·er, -i·est 1.** full of or covered with moss or a mosslike growth **2.** as if covered with moss **3.** like moss —**moss′i·ness** *n.*

most (mōst) *adj. compar.* MORE [ME. < OE. *mast*, used as superl. of *micel*, big (cf. MUCH): akin to Goth. *maists:* for base see MORE] **1.** greatest in amount, quantity, or degree: used as the superlative of MUCH **2.** greatest in number: used as the superlative of MANY **3.** in the greatest number of instances [*most* fame is fleeting] —*n.* **1.** the greatest amount, quantity, or degree [to take *most* of the credit] **2.** [*with pl. v.*] *a)* the greatest number (*of* persons or things) [*most* of us are going] *b)* the greatest number of persons or things —*adv.* **1.** *compar.* MORE in or to the greatest degree or extent: used with many adjectives and adverbs (regularly with those of three or more syllables) to form the superlative degree [*most* horrible, *most* quickly] **2.** very (often preceded by *a*) [a *most* beautiful morning] **3.** [for ALMOST] [Colloq.] almost; nearly —**at** (**the**) **most** at the very limit; not more than —**make the most of** to make the greatest use of; take fullest advantage of —**the most** [Slang] the best or most exciting, attractive, etc. of its kind

-most (mōst) [ME., altered (after prec.) < ME. *-mest* < OE. < older superl. suffixes, *-ma* + *-est*] *a suffix used in forming superlatives* [foremost, hindmost]

most·ly (mōst′lē) *adv.* **1.** for the most part **2.** chiefly; principally **3.** usually; generally

Mo·sul (mō sōōl′) city in N Iraq, on the Tigris, opposite the site of ancient Nineveh: pop. 180,000

mot (mō) *n.* [Fr., a word, saying < L. *muttum*, a grunt, muttering < IE. echoic base **mu-*, whence MOPE, MEW[3]] a witticism or pithy remark; bon mot

mote[1] (mōt) *n.* [ME. < OE. *mot*, akin to Du. *mot*, sawdust, grit] a speck of dust or other tiny particle

mote[2] (mōt) *vi.* [ME. *moten* < OE. *motan*, akin to G. *müssen:* basic sense "it is permitted"; *must* (OE. *moste*) is the pt. of this v.] [Archaic] may; might

☆mo·tel (mō tel′) *n.* [MO(TORIST) + (HO)TEL] a hotel intended primarily for those traveling by car, usually with direct access from each room to an area for cars

mo·tet (mō tet′) *n.* [ME. < OFr. dim. of *mot*, a word: see MOT] *Music* a contrapuntal, polyphonic song of a sacred nature, generally unaccompanied

moth (môth) *n.*, *pl.* **moths** (môthz, môths) [ME. *motthe* < OE. *moththe*, akin to G. *motte* < IE. base **math-*, gnawing vermin] **1.** any of a group of four-winged, chiefly night-flying insects (order Lepidoptera) related to the butterflies but generally smaller, less brightly colored, and not having the antennae knobbed **2.** *same as* CLOTHES MOTH

moth·ball (-bôl′) *n.* a small ball of naphthalene or, sometimes, camphor, the fumes of which repel moths, as from woolens, furs, etc. —*vt.* to store with protective covering or set aside indefinitely for possible future use —*adj.* in storage or reserve [a *mothball* fleet] —**in** (*or* **out of**) **mothballs** put into (*or* taken from) a condition of being stored or in reserve

moth-eat·en (-ēt′'n) *adj.* **1.** gnawed away in patches by moths, as cloth **2.** decayed or decrepit in appearance; worn-out **3.** outdated

moth·er[1] (muth′ər) *n.* [ME. *moder* < OE. *modor*, akin to G. *mutter* < IE. **mater-*, mother (whence L. *mater*, Gr.

mēt̲ēr, OIr. *māthir*] < *ma-, echoic of baby talk] **1.** a woman who has borne a child; esp., a woman as she is related to her child or children **2.** *a)* a stepmother *b)* a mother-in-law **3.** the female parent of a plant or animal **4.** that which gives birth to something, is the origin or source of something, or nurtures in the manner of a mother **5.** *a)* a woman having the responsibility and authority of a mother *b)* a woman who is the head (*mother superior*) of a religious establishment **6.** an elderly woman: used as a title of affectionate respect **7.** the qualities of a mother —*adj.* **1.** of, like, or like that of a mother **2.** derived or learned from one's mother; native [*mother* tongue] **3.** designating a company, institution, etc. from which another or others originated as an offshoot [*mother* church] —*vt.* **1.** to be the mother of; give birth to: often used figuratively **2.** to look after or care for as a mother does **3.** to acknowledge or admit that one is the mother, author, or originator of —**moth′er·less** *adj.*

moth·er² (mu*th*′ər) *n.* [altered (after prec.) < MDu. *moeder*, akin to MLowG. *modder*: for IE. base see MUD] **1.** *same as* MOTHER OF VINEGAR **2.** [Obs.] dregs

Mother Car·ey's chicken (ker′ēz) [< ?] any of various oceanic petrels; esp., *same as* STORMY PETREL (sense 1)

mother country *same as* MOTHERLAND

Mother Goose 1. the imaginary narrator of a collection of tales (c. 1697) by Charles Perrault **2.** the imaginary creator of a collection of nursery rhymes first published in London c. 1765

moth·er·hood (mu*th*′ər hood′) *n.* **1.** the state of being a mother; maternity **2.** the qualities or character of a mother **3.** mothers collectively

Mother Hub·bard (hub′ərd) **1.** the subject of an old nursery rhyme **2.** [from the costume in old illustrations of the rhyme] a full, loose gown for women

mother image (or **figure**) a person substituted in one's mind for one's mother and often the object of emotions felt toward the mother

moth·er-in-law (-ən lô′) *n., pl.* **moth′ers-in-law′ 1.** the mother of one's husband or wife **2.** [Rare] a stepmother

moth·er·land (land′) *n.* **1.** a person's native land or, sometimes, the land of his ancestors **2.** a country thought of as originator or source

☆**mother lode** the main lode, or vein of ore, in a particular region or district

moth·er·ly (-lē) *adj.* of, like, or befitting a mother; maternal —*adv.* in a motherly manner —**moth′er·li·ness** *n.*

moth·er-na·ked (-nā′kid) *adj.* as naked as when one was born; completely naked

Mother of God *a title of* VIRGIN MARY

moth·er-of-pearl (-əv pʉrl′) *n.* [transl. of ML. *mater perlarum*: orig. applied to the marine animal, later to the shell] the hard, pearly internal layer of certain marine shells, as of the pearl oyster, abalone, etc., used in the arts and in the manufacture of pearl buttons; nacre —*adj.* of mother-of-pearl

mother of vinegar [see MOTHER²] a stringy, gummy, slimy substance formed by bacteria (genus *Acetobacter*) in vinegar or on the surface of fermenting liquids: used as a starter to make vinegar

☆**Mother's Day** the second Sunday in May, a day set aside (in the U.S.) in honor of mothers

mother superior the woman head of a convent

mother tongue 1. one's native language **2.** a language in its relation to another derived from it

Moth·er·well and Wi·shaw (mu*th*′ər wel′ 'nd wish′ô) city in Lanark, S Scotland: pop. 76,000

mother wit native intelligence; common sense

moth·er·wort (-wʉrt′) *n.* [ME. *moderwort* (see MOTHER¹ & WORT²]: from the notion that it was helpful in curing diseases of the womb] any of a genus (*Leonurus*) of weedy plants of the mint family; esp., an Old-World perennial (*Leonurus cardiaca*) with pink or purplish flowers and a spiny, toothed calyx

moth·proof (môth′prōōf′) *adj.* treated chemically so as to repel the clothes moth —*vt.* to make mothproof

moth·y (môth′ē) *adj.* **moth′i·er, moth′i·est 1.** infested with moths **2.** moth-eaten

mo·tif (mō tēf′) *n.* [Fr.: see MOTIVE] **1.** a main element, idea, feature, etc.; specif., *a)* a main theme or subject to be elaborated on or developed, as in a piece of music, a book, etc. *b)* a repeated figure in a design **2.** *same as* MOTIVE (sense 1)

mo·tile (mōt′'l) *adj.* [< L. *motus*, pp. of *movere*, to MOVE + -ILE] *Biol.* capable of or exhibiting spontaneous motion —**mo·til·i·ty** (mō til′ə tē) *n.*

mo·tion (mō′shən) *n.* [ME. *mocioun* < L. *motio* (gen. *motionis*), a moving < *motus*, pp. of *movere*, MOVE] **1.** the act or process of moving; passage of a body from one place to another; movement **2.** the act of moving the body or any of its parts **3.** a meaningful movement of the hand, eyes, etc.; gesture **4.** the ability to move **5.** an impulse; inclination [of one's own *motion*] **6.** a proposal; suggestion; esp., a proposal formally made in an assembly or meeting **7.** *Law* an application to a court for a ruling, order, etc. **8.** *Mech.* a combination of moving parts;

mechanism **9.** *Music* melodic progression, as a change from one pitch to another in a voice part —*vi.* to make a meaningful movement of the hand, head, etc.; gesture —*vt.* to direct or command by a meaningful gesture —**go through the motions** to do something from habit or according to formalities, but without purpose, meaning, etc. —**in motion** moving; traveling or in operation —**mo′tion·al** *adj.* —**mo′tion·less** *adj.* —**mo′tion·less·ly** *adv.* —**mo′tion·less·ness** *n.*

motion picture 1. a sequence of photographs or drawings projected on a screen in such rapid succession that they create the optical illusion (because of the persistence of vision) of moving persons and objects **2.** a play or story photographed as a motion picture

motion sickness sickness characterized by nausea, vomiting, and dizziness, and caused by the motion of an aircraft, boat, etc.

motion study *see* TIME STUDY

mo·ti·vate (mōt′ə vāt′) *vt.* **-vat′ed, -vat′ing** to provide with, or affect as, a motive or motives; incite or impel —**mo′ti·va′tion** *n.* —**mo′ti·va′tion·al** *adj.* —**mo′ti·va′tive** *adj.* —**mo′ti·va′tor** *n.*

☆**motivational research** a systematic and scientific analysis of the forces influencing people so as to control the making of their decisions: applied in advertising, marketing, etc.

mo·tive (mōt′iv) *n.* [ME. *motif* < OFr. *motif* (adj.) < ML. *motivus*, moving < L. *motus*, pp. of *movere*, to MOVE] **1.** some inner drive, impulse, intention, etc. that causes a person to do something or act in a certain way; incentive; goal **2.** *same as* MOTIF (sense 1) —*adj.* [ML. *motivus*] **1.** of, causing, or tending to cause motion **2.** [Rare] of, or having the nature of, a motive or motives —*vt.* **-tived, -tiv·ing** to supply a motive for; motivate —**mo′tive·less** *adj.* SYN.—**motive** refers to any impulse, emotion, or desire that moves one to action [greed was his only *motive* for stealing]; **incentive** applies to a stimulus, often a reward, that encourages or inspires one to action [he needs no *incentive* other than the desire to be useful]; **inducement** always refers to an outer stimulus, rather than an inner urge, that tempts or entices one to do something [the money was an added *inducement*]; a **spur** is an impulse or incentive that pricks one on to greatly increased activity or endurance [security for his family was the *spur* that drove him on] See also CAUSE

-mo·tive (mōt′iv) [< prec. (adj.)] a suffix meaning moving, of motion [*automotive, locomotive*]

motive power 1. any power, as steam, electricity, etc., used to impart motion; any source of mechanical energy **2.** an impelling force

mo·tiv·i·ty (mō tiv′ə tē) *n.* the power of moving or causing motion

‡**mot juste** (mō zhüst′) *pl.* **mots justes** (mō zhüst′) [Fr.] the right word; exact, appropriate word or phrase

mot·ley (mät′lē) *adj.* [ME. *mottley* < ?] **1.** of many colors or patches of color **2.** wearing many-colored garments [a *motley* fool] **3.** having or composed of many different or clashing elements; heterogeneous [a *motley* group] —*n.* **1.** cloth of mixed colors **2.** a garment of various colors, worn by a clown or jester **3.** [Rare] a fool or jester **4.** a combination of diverse or clashing elements

Mot·ley (mät′lē), **John Lo·throp** (lō′thrəp) 1814-77; U.S. historian & diplomat

mot·mot (mät′mät) *n.* [AmSp., echoic of its note] any of a group of long-tailed, chiefly green, jaylike birds (family Motmotidae) of tropical and subtropical America, related to the kingfishers and usually nesting in tunnels they make along river banks

mo·to·neu·ron (mō′tə noor′än, -nyoor′-) *n.* [MOTO(R) + NEURON] a motor nerve cell: see MOTOR (adj. 5)

mo·tor (mōt′ər) *n.* [L., a mover < *motus*, pp. of *movere*, MOVE] **1.** anything that produces or imparts motion **2.** an engine; esp., an internal-combustion engine for propelling a vehicle **3.** *same as* MOTOR VEHICLE **4.** *Elec.* a machine for converting electrical energy into mechanical energy —*adj.* **1.** producing or imparting motion **2.** of or powered by a motor or motors [a *motor* bicycle] **3.** of, by, or for motor vehicles [a *motor* trip] **4.** for motorists [a *motor* inn] **5.** designating of a nerve carrying impulses from the central nervous system to a muscle producing motion **6.** of, manifested by, or involving muscular movements [a *motor* reflex, *motor* skills] —*vi.* to ride in a motor vehicle; esp., to travel by automobile —*vt.* [Chiefly Brit.] to convey by automobile

☆**mo·tor·bike** (-bīk′) *n.* [Colloq.] **1.** a bicycle propelled by a motor **2.** a light motorcycle

mo·tor·boat (-bōt′) *n.* a boat propelled by an internal-combustion engine or other kind of motor

mo·tor·bus (-bus′) *n.* a passenger bus propelled by a motor, usually an internal-combustion engine: also **motor coach**

☆**mo·tor·cade** (-kād′) *n.* [MOTOR + (CAVAL)CADE] a procession of automobiles

mo·tor·car (-kär′) *n.* **1.** *same as* AUTOMOBILE ☆**2.** a small, open car propelled by a motor and used on a railroad by workmen: also **motor car**

mo·tor·cy·cle (-sī′k'l) *n.* [MOTOR + (BI)CYCLE] a two-wheeled (or, if equipped with a sidecar, three-wheeled) vehicle propelled by an internal-combustion engine and resembling a bicycle, but usually larger and heavier, and often having two saddles —*vi.* **-cled, -cling** to ride a motorcycle —**mo′tor·cy′clist** (-sī′klist) *n.*

motor drive an electric motor and other parts of a mechanical system for operating a machine or machines

mo·tor·drome (-drōm′) *n.* [MOTOR + -DROME] a rounded track or course for racing or testing automobiles or motorcycles

mo·tored (mōt′ərd) *adj.* having a motor or motors: usually used in compounds [bimotored]

motor generator an apparatus consisting of one or more electric motors coupled to one or more generators, for transforming or converting electrical energy

☆**motor hotel** *same as* MOTEL: also **motor court, motor inn, motor lodge**

mo·tor·ic (mō tôr′ik) *adj. same as* MOTOR (*adj.* 6)

mo·tor·ist (mōt′ər ist) *n.* a person who drives an automobile or travels by automobile

mo·tor·ize (mōt′ə rīz′) *vt.* **-ized′, -iz′ing 1.** *a)* to equip with motor-driven vehicles (as in place of horses and horse-drawn vehicles) *b)* to make mobile by designing as part of a motor vehicle or mounting on a motor vehicle **2.** to equip (vehicles, machines, etc.) with a motor or motors **3.** *Mil.* to provide (troops) with motor vehicles for transportation, as to a combat area —**mo′tor·i·za′tion** *n.*

☆**mo·tor·man** (mōt′ər mən) *n., pl.* **-men** (-mən) **1.** a person who drives an electric streetcar or electric locomotive **2.** a person who operates a motor

☆**motor pool** a group of motor vehicles kept, as at a military installation or government center, for use as needed by personnel

motor scooter *see* SCOOTER

motor ship a ship propelled by diesels or other internal-combustion engines

☆**motor torpedo boat** a high-speed motorboat equipped with torpedoes and machine guns

motor truck a motor-driven truck for hauling loads

motor vehicle a vehicle on wheels having its own motor and not running on rails or tracks, for use on streets or highways; esp., an automobile, truck, or bus

☆**Mo·town** (mō′toun′) *adj.* [< *Mo*(tor) *Town*, nickname for Detroit, Mich., where it originated] designating or of a style of rhythm and blues characterized by a strong, even beat

Mott (mät), **Lucretia** (born *Lucretia Coffin*) 1793–1880; U.S. abolitionist & women's rights advocate

☆**motte, mott** (mät) *n.* [AmSp. *mata* < LL. *matta*, a cover, MAT¹] [Southwest & West] a small grove of trees

mot·tle (mät′'l) *vt.* **-tled, -tling** [back-formation < *mottled* < MOTLEY + -ED] to mark with blotches, streaks, and spots of different colors or shades —*n.* **1.** such a blotch, streak, or spot **2.** a mottled pattern or coloring, as of marble —**mot′tled** *adj.*

mot·to (mät′ō) *n., pl.* **-toes, -tos** [It., a word < L. *muttum*: see MOT] **1.** a word, phrase, or sentence chosen as expressive of the goals or ideals of a nation, group, etc. and inscribed or marked on a seal, banner, coin, etc. **2.** a maxim adopted as a principle of behavior —*SYN.* see SAYING

‡**moue** (mōō) *n., pl.* **moues** (mōō) [Fr.: see MOW³] a pouting grimace; wry face

mouf·lon, mouf·flon (mōōf′län) *n., pl.* **-lons, -lon:** see PLURAL, II, D, 1 [Fr. *mouflon* < It. dial. *muffolo*, for *muffione* < LL. dial. *mufro*] 1. a wild sheep (*Ovis musimon*) native to the mountainous regions of Corsica and Sardinia: the male has large, curving horns 2. the wool of this sheep

mouil·lé (mōō yā′) *adj.* [Fr., pp. of *mouiller*, to moisten < VL. *molliare* < L. *mollis*, soft: see MOLLIFY] *Phonetics* palatalized, as Spanish *ñ* in *cañon* or French *ll* in *fille*

mou·jik (mōō zhēk′, mōō′zhik) *n. same as* MUZHIK

mou·lage (mōō läzh′) *n.* [Fr. < MFr., a molding < *mouler*, to mold < OFr. *modle*: see MOLD¹] **1.** the science or practice of making a mold, as in plaster of Paris, of an object, footprint, etc., for use in crime detection **2.** such a mold

mould (mōld) *n., vt., vi. chiefly Brit. sp.* of MOLD (all terms and senses) —**mould′y** *adj.* **mould′i·er, mould′i·est**

mould·board (-bôrd′) *n. chiefly Brit. sp.* of MOLDBOARD

mould·er (mōl′dər) *vt., vi. chiefly Brit. sp.* of MOLDER

mould·ing (mōl′diŋ) *n. chiefly Brit. sp.* of MOLDING

mou·lin (mōō lan′) *n.* [Fr., lit., a mill < LL. *molinum, molina*, MILL¹] a nearly vertical shaft through a glacier, down which a stream of surface water plunges

Moul·mein (mool mān′, mōl-) seaport in S Burma, on the Gulf of Martaban: pop. 190,000

moult (mōlt) *n., vt., vi. chiefly Brit. sp.* of MOLT

mound¹ (mound) *n.* [< ? MDu. *mond*, protection, infl. by MOUNT¹] **1.** a heap or bank of earth, sand, etc. built over a grave, in a fortification, etc. **2.** a natural elevation like this; small hill **3.** any heap or pile ☆**4.** *Baseball* the slightly raised area on which the pitcher must stand when pitching —*vt.* **1.** [Archaic] to enclose or fortify with a mound **2.** to heap up in a mound

mound² (mound) *n.* [Fr. *monde* < L. *mundus*, the world] *same as* ORB (sense 4)

☆**Mound Builders** the early Indian peoples who built the burial mounds, fortifications, and other earthworks found in the Middle West and the Southeast

mount¹ (mount) *n.* [ME. < OE. *munt* & OFr. *mont*, a mount, both < L. *mons* (gen. *montis*), hill, mountain < IE. base *men-*, to project, whence W. *meneth*, mountain] **1.** a mountain or hill: now poetic except before a proper name [*Mount* McKinley] **2.** [Obs.] a raised fortification **3.** *Palmistry* any of the fleshy raised parts on the palm of the hand

mount² (mount) *vi.* [ME. *mounten* < OFr. *munter* < VL. *montare*, lit., to go uphill < L. *mons:* see prec.] **1.** to climb; ascend (often with *up*) **2.** to climb up on something; esp., to get on the back of a horse, on a bicycle, etc. for riding **3.** to increase in amount [profits are *mounting*] —*vt.* **1.** to go up; ascend; climb [to *mount* stairs] **2.** *a)* to get up on (a horse, bicycle, etc.) for riding *b)* to set on a horse *c)* to climb or get up on (a platform, stool, etc.) **3.** to provide with a horse or horses **4.** to mount (a female) for copulation: said of a male animal **5.** to place on something raised (with *on*) [*mount* the statue on a pedestal] **6.** to place, fix, or fasten on or in the proper support, backing, etc. for the required purpose; specif., *a)* to fix (a jewel) in a setting *b)* to fix (a specimen) on (a slide) for microscopic study *c)* to arrange (a skeleton, dead animal, etc.) for exhibition *d)* to affix (a picture) to a mat or other backing **7.** to furnish the necessary costumes, settings, etc. for producing (a play) **8.** to prepare for and undertake (an expedition, campaign, etc.) **9.** *Mil. a)* to raise or adjust (a gun) into proper position for use *b)* to be armed with (cannon) [a ship that *mounts* six cannon] *c)* to post (a guard) on sentry duty *d)* to go on (guard) as a sentry —*n.* **1.** the act or manner of mounting (a horse, etc.) **2.** a horse, bicycle, etc. for mounting and riding **3.** the opportunity for riding a horse, etc., esp. in a race **4.** the support, setting, etc. on or in which something is mounted, as the support for a microscopic slide or setting for a jewel —**mount′a·ble** *adj.* —**mount′er** *n.*

moun·tain (moun′t'n) *n.* [ME. *montaine* < OFr. *montaigne* < VL. *montanea*, for L. *montana* < *montanus*, mountainous < *mons:* see MOUNT¹] **1.** a natural raised part of the earth's surface, usually rising more or less abruptly, and larger than a hill **2.** [pl.] a chain or group of such elevations **3.** a large pile, heap, or mound **4.** a very large amount —*adj.* **1.** of a mountain or mountains **2.** situated, living, or used in the mountains **3.** like a mountain; esp., very large —**the Mountain** [transl. of Fr. *la Montagne*] the extreme revolutionary party of Danton and Robespierre, which occupied the highest seats in the National Assembly of 1793

mountain ash any of a genus (*Sorbus*) of small trees or shrubs of the rose family, with compound leaves and clusters of white flowers and red or orange berries

mountain avens 1. a small evergreen plant (*Dryas octopetala*) of the rose family, found on mountains and in arctic regions **2.** a perennial plant (*Geum triflorum*) of the rose family, with reddish flowers and elongated, plumy styles

mountain cat any of various animals, as the cougar, bobcat, cacomistle, etc.

mountain chain 1. a mountain range **2.** two or more relatively adjacent mountain ranges

☆**mountain cranberry** *same as* COWBERRY

☆**mountain dew** [Colloq.] **1.** orig., Scotch whisky **2.** any whiskey, esp. when illegally distilled, as by mountaineers

moun·tain·eer (moun′t'n ir′) *n.* **1.** a person who lives in a mountainous region **2.** a mountain climber —*vi.* to climb mountains, as for sport

☆**mountain goat** *same as* ROCKY MOUNTAIN GOAT

☆**mountain laurel 1.** an evergreen shrub (*Kalmia latifolia*) of the heath family, with pink and white flowers and poisonous, shiny leaves, native to E N. America **2.** *same as* CALIFORNIA LAUREL

☆**mountain lion** *same as* COUGAR

☆**mountain mahogany** any of a genus (*Cercocarpus*) of W N. American shrubs or small trees of the rose family, with lobed leaves and single dry fruits

moun·tain·ous (moun′t'n əs) *adj.* **1.** having or full of mountains **2.** having the nature of or like a mountain; esp., very large —**moun′tain·ous·ly** *adv.*

mountain range a series of connected mountains considered as a single system because of geographical proximity or common origin

☆**mountain sheep** any of various wild sheep found in mountain regions; esp., *same as* BIGHORN

mountain sickness a feeling of weakness, nausea, etc. brought on at high altitudes by the rarefied air

moun·tain·side (-sīd′) *n.* the side of a mountain

☆**Mountain Standard Time** a standard time used in a zone which includes the Rocky Mountain region of the U.S., corresponding to the mean local time of the 105th meridian west of Greenwich, England: it is seven hours behind Greenwich time: see TIME ZONES, chart

Mountain State any of the eight States of the W U.S. through which the Rocky Mountains pass; Mont., Ida., Wyo., Nev., Utah, Colo., Ariz., & N.Mex.

moun·tain·top (-täp′) *n.* the top of a mountain

Mountain View city in W Calif., near San Jose: pop. 51,000

Mount·bat·ten (mount'bat''n), **Louis** (*Francis Albert Victor Nicholas*), 1st Earl Mountbatten of Burma (orig. family name *Battenberg*) 1900– ; Brit. admiral

Mount Desert Island island off the S coast of Me.: resort: c. 100 sq. mi.

moun·te·bank (moun'tə baŋk') *n.* [It. *montambanco* < *montare,* MOUNT[2] + *in,* on + *banco,* a bench: see BANK[1]] **1.** orig., a person who mounted a bench, or platform, in a public place and sold quack medicines, usually attracting an audience by tricks, stories, etc. **2.** any charlatan, or quack —*vi.* to act as a mountebank —SYN. see QUACK[2] —**moun·te·bank'er·y** *n.*

mount·ed (moun'tid) *adj.* **1.** seated on horseback, a bicycle, etc. **2.** serving on horseback [*mounted* police] **3.** set up and ready for use [a *mounted* gun] **4.** fixed on or in the proper backing, support, setting, etc. **5.** *Mil.* regularly equipped with a means of transportation, as with horses, tanks, armored vehicles, etc.

Mount·ie, Mount·y (moun'tē) *n., pl.* **-ies** [Colloq.] a member of the Royal Canadian Mounted Police

mount·ing (moun'tiŋ) *n.* **1.** the act of a person or thing that mounts **2.** something serving as a backing, support, setting, etc.

Mount McKinley National Park see McKINLEY

Mount Prospect [after a high ridge in the area] village in NE Ill.: suburb of Chicago: pop. 35,000

Mount Rainier National Park see RAINIER

Mount Vernon 1. [after Brit. Admiral Edward *Vernon* (1684–1757)] home & burial place of George Washington in N Va., on the Potomac, near Washington, D.C. **2.** [after prec.] city in SE N.Y.: suburb of New York City: pop. 73,000

mourn (môrn) *vi.* [ME. *mournen* < OE. *murnan;* akin to Goth. *maúrnan,* to be anxious < IE. base *(s)mer-,* to remember, think of, whence Sans. *smárati,* (he) remembers, L. *memor,* mindful of] **1.** to feel or express sorrow; lament; grieve **2.** to grieve for someone who has died; specif., to manifest the conventional signs of such grief, as by wearing black clothes **3.** to make the low, continuous sound of a dove —*vt.* **1.** to feel or express sorrow for (something regrettable) **2.** to grieve for (someone who has died) **3.** to utter in a manner expressing sorrow

mourn·er (môr'nər) *n.* **1.** *a)* a person who is in mourning *b)* any of the persons attending a funeral **2.** a person who makes a public profession of penitence at a revival meeting

☆**mourners' bench** a front row of seats at a revival meeting, reserved for those who are to make professions of penitence

mourn·ful (-fəl) *adj.* **1.** of or characterized by mourning; feeling or expressing grief or sorrow **2.** causing sorrow or depression; melancholy —**mourn'ful·ly** *adv.* —**mourn'ful·ness** *n.*

mourn·ing (môr'niŋ) *n.* **1.** the actions or feelings of one who mourns; specif., the expression of grief at someone's death **2.** black clothes, drapery, etc., worn or displayed as a conventional sign of grief for the dead **3.** the period during which one mourns the dead —*adj.* of or expressing mourning —**mourn'ing·ly** *adv.*

mourning band a strip of black cloth or crape worn, usually around the arm, to show mourning

mourning cloak a common butterfly (*Nymphalis antiopa*) having purplish-brown wings with a wide yellow border, found throughout Europe and N. America

☆**mourning dove** a small, gray wild dove (*Zenaidura macroura*) of the U.S.: so called because of its cooing, regarded as mournful

mouse (mous; *for v., usually* mouz) *n., pl.* **mice** [ME. *mous* < OE. *mus;* akin to G. *maus* < IE. **mūs,* a mouse, whence L. *mus,* mouse & *musculus,* MUSCLE] **1.** any of a large number of small rodents (as genera *Mus* and *Microtus*) found throughout the world; esp., the **house mouse** (*Mus musculus*) which infests human dwellings **2.** *a)* a girl or young woman: a term of endearment *b)* a timid or spiritless person **3.** [Slang] a dark, swollen bruise under the eye; black eye **4.** *Naut.* [Rare] a knot made on a rope to keep a running eye or loop from slipping —*vi.* **moused, mous'ing 1.** to hunt for or catch mice **2.** to seek about or search for something busily and stealthily —*vt.* **1.** to hunt for **2.** [Obs.] to tear or rend as a cat does a mouse

mouse·bird (-bʉrd') *n.* same as COLY

mouse deer same as CHEVROTAIN

mouse-ear (-ir') *n.* any of various plants with short, hairy leaves resembling the ear of a mouse, as the hawk-weed, chickweed, etc.

mous·er (mou'zər, -sər) *n.* a cat, dog, etc., with reference to its ability to catch mice [a poor *mouser*]

mouse·tail (mous'tāl') *n.* any of a genus (*Myosurus*) of plants of the buttercup family, with a slender spike resembling the tail of a mouse

mouse·trap (-trap') *n.* a trap for catching mice —*vt.* **-trapped', -trap'ping** ☆to trick or ensnare by means of a feint or stratagem

mous·ey (mou'sē, -zē) *adj.* **mous'i·er, mous'i·est** same as MOUSY

mous·ing (mou'ziŋ, -siŋ) *n.* **1.** the act of hunting or

catching mice **2.** *Naut.* a turn of yarn or rope or a metal fastening between the point of a hook and its shank to keep it from coming unhooked

‡**mous·que·taire** (mōōs kə ter') *n.* [Fr.] a musketeer

mous·sa·ka (mōō sä'kə) *n.* [ModGr.] a Greek dish consisting typically of sliced eggplant and ground meat arranged in layers, covered with a white sauce and cheese, and baked

mousse (mōōs) *n.* [Fr., foam, prob. < L. *mulsa,* kind of mead < *mulsus,* mixed with honey < *mel,* honey: see MILDEW] any of various light chilled or frozen foods made with egg white, gelatin, whipped cream, etc., combined with fruit or flavorings for desserts, or with fish, meat, etc. as an aspic

‡**mousse·line** (mōōs lēn') *n.* [Fr.] **1.** *a)* muslin *b)* a sheer, somewhat stiff fabric made of rayon, etc. **2.** a fine, blown glass with a lacy pattern

‡**mousse·line de laine** (də len') [Fr., lit., muslin of wool] a lightweight woolen cloth, often printed, used for dresses

‡**mousse·line de soie** (də swä') [Fr., lit., muslin of silk] a gauzelike silk or rayon cloth with a plain weave, used for wedding gowns, etc.

Moussorgsky *var. sp.* of MUSSORGSKY

mous·tache (mə stash', mus'tash) *n. var.* of MUSTACHE

mous·ta·chio (mə stä'shō) *n. var.* of MUSTACHIO

Mous·te·ri·an (mōōs tir'ē ən) *adj.* [Fr. *moustérien:* remains were found at Le *Moustier,* cave in S France] designating or of a late paleolithic culture, believed to be that of Neanderthal men

mous·y (mou'sē, -zē) *adj.* **mous'i·er, mous'i·est 1.** of, characteristic of, or like a mouse, in any of various ways; quiet, timid, drab, etc. **2.** full of or infested with mice —**mous'i·ness** *n.*

mouth (mouth; *for v.,* mouth) *n., pl.* **mouths** (mouthz) [ME. < OE. *muth,* akin to G. *mund* < IE. base **menth-,* to chew, whence Gr. *masasthai,* L. *mandere,* to chew] **1.** the opening through which an animal takes in food; specif., the cavity, or the entire structure, in the head of any of the higher animals which contains the teeth and tongue and through which sounds are uttered **2.** *a)* the mouth regarded as the organ of chewing and tasting *b)* the mouth regarded as the organ of speech **3.** a person or animal regarded as a being needing food [six *mouths* to feed] **4.** the lips, or the part of the face surrounding the lips **5.** a wry expression of the face; grimace **6.** any opening regarded as like the mouth; specif., *a)* the part of a river, stream, etc. where the water empties into another body of water *b)* the opening into the earth of a cave, volcano, tunnel, etc. *c)* the opening of a container, through which it is filled or emptied *d)* the front opening in the muzzle of a firearm *e)* the opening between the jaws of a vise *f)* the opening between the lips of an organ pipe *g)* the opening in a flute across which the player blows —*vt.* **1.** *a)* to say, esp. in an affected, oratorical, or insincere manner; declaim *b)* to form (a word) with the mouth soundlessly **2.** to take or put into the mouth **3.** to caress or rub with the mouth or lips **4.** to train (a horse) to become accustomed to the bit —*vi.* **1.** to speak in an affected or oratorical manner; declaim **2.** [Rare] to make a wry face by twisting the mouth; grimace —**down in** (or **at**) **the mouth** [Colloq.] depressed; unhappy; discouraged —**give mouth to** to express in speech; say —**have a big mouth** [Slang] to talk loudly, excessively, indiscreetly, or impudently —**mouth'er** (mouth'-) *n.* —**mouth'less** *adj.*

mouth·breed·er (-brē'dər) *n.* any of a number of small fishes that carry their eggs and young in the mouth

-mouthed (mouthd) *a combining form meaning* having a (specified kind of) mouth, voice, etc. [loudmouthed]

mouth·ful (mouth'fool') *n., pl.* **-fuls' 1.** as much as the mouth can hold **2.** as much as is usually taken into the mouth at one time **3.** a small amount, esp. of food **4.** [Colloq.] a long word or group of words hard to say ☆**5.** [Slang] a pertinent, important, or correct remark: chiefly in **say a mouthful**

mouth organ same as: ☆**1.** HARMONICA (sense 3) **2.** PANPIPE

mouth·part (-pärt') *n.* any of various structures, organs, or appendages around the mouth in arthropods, modified for biting, piercing, sucking, chewing, grasping, etc.: usually used in *pl.*

mouth·piece (-pēs') *n.* **1.** a part placed at, or forming, a mouth [the *mouthpiece* of a telephone, a pipe, a horse's bit, etc.] **2.** the part of a musical instrument held in or to the mouth **3.** a person, periodical, etc. used by another or others to express their views, ideas, etc. **4.** [Slang] a lawyer who defends criminals

☆**mouth-to-mouth** (mouth'tə mouth') *adj.* designating a method of resuscitation in which the rescuer forces his breath directly into the mouth and lungs of a person who has stopped breathing

mouth·wash (-wôsh', -wäsh') *n.* a flavored, often antiseptic liquid used for rinsing the mouth or for gargling

mouth·wa·ter·ing (-wôt'ər iŋ, -wät'ər-) *adj.* appetizing enough to make the mouth water; tasty

mouth·y (mou'*th*ē, -thē) *adj.* **mouth'i·er, mouth'i·est** overly talkative, esp. in a bombastic or rude way — **mouth'i·ly** *adv.* —**mouth'i·ness** *n.*

mou·ton (mōō'tän) *n.* [Fr., sheep: see MUTTON] lambskin, processed and dyed to resemble beaver, seal, etc.

mou·ton·née (mōōt'n ā') *adj.* [Fr., fem. pp. of *moutonner*, make sheeplike < *mouton*, sheep: see MUTTON] rounded like the back of a sheep, as by glacial action: said of rock formations —*n. same as* ROCHE MOUTONNÉE

mov·a·ble (mōō'və b'l) *adj.* **1.** that can be moved from one place to another; not fixed; specif., *Law* designating or of personal property as distinguished from real property **2.** changing in date from one year to the next [Thanksgiving is a *movable* holiday] —*n.* **1.** something movable **2.** *Law* a piece of property that is movable, as furniture; personal property: *usually used in pl.* Also **move'a·ble** —**mov'a·bil'i·ty** *n.* —**mov'a·bly** *adv.*

move (mōōv) *vt.* **moved, mov'ing** [ME. *moven* < Anglo-Fr. *mover* < OFr. *movoir* < L. *movere* < IE. base *mew-*, to push away, whence Sans. *mīvati*, (he) shoves] **1.** to change the place or position of; push, carry, or pull from one place or position to another **2.** to set or keep in motion; actuate, impel, turn, stir, etc. **3.** to cause or persuade (*to act, do, say, speak*, etc.); prompt **4.** to arouse or stir the emotions, passions, or sympathies of **5.** to propose or suggest; esp., to propose formally, as in a meeting **6.** to cause (the bowels) to evacuate **7.** *Commerce* to dispose of (goods) by selling —*vi.* **1.** to change place or position; go (*to* some place) **2.** to change one's place of residence **3.** to live or be active in a specified milieu or setting [to *move* in artistic circles] **4.** to make progress; advance **5.** to take action; begin to act **6.** *a)* to be, or be set, in motion *b)* to operate in a certain fixed motion; turn, revolve, etc.: said of machines **7.** to make a formal appeal or application (*for*) [*move* for a new trial] **8.** to evacuate: said of the bowels **9.** [Colloq.] to start leaving; depart (often with *on*) [time to be *moving on*] **10.** *Chess, Checkers*, etc. *a)* to change the position of a piece *b)* to be put in another position: said of a piece **11.** *Commerce* to be disposed of by sale: said of goods —*n.* **1.** act of moving; movement **2.** one of a series of actions toward some goal **3.** a change of residence **4.** *Chess, Checkers*, etc. the act of moving or one's turn to move —☆**get a move on** [Slang] **1.** to start moving **2.** to hurry; go faster —☆**move in on** [Slang] **1.** to draw near, with the intention of capturing **2.** to attempt to take over control of (something) from (someone) —**move up** to promote or be promoted —**on the move** [Colloq.] moving about from place to place; very busy **SYN.**—**move**, the broadest in scope of these terms, means merely to change from one place or position to another [to *move* a rock, one's foot, a house, etc.]; **remove** stresses the departure of the thing moved from its original or usual place or position [to *remove* one's hat, a cause of strife, etc.]; **shift** emphasizes the change in position or location and, hence, often connotes instability, unrest, etc. [to *shift* in one's opinions]; **transfer** implies a change from one container, vehicle, ownership, etc. to another [we *transferred* to a cross-town bus] See also AFFECT[1]

move·ment (-mənt) *n.* [ME. < OFr.] **1.** the act or process of moving; specif., *a)* a motion or action of a person or group *b)* a shift in position *c)* an evacuation (of the bowels); also, the matter evacuated *d)* *Mil.* a change in the location of troops, ships, etc., as part of a maneuver **2.** a particular manner of moving **3.** *a)* a series of organized activities by people working concertedly toward some goal *b)* the organization consisting of those active in this way **4.** a tendency or trend in some particular sphere of activity **5.** the progress of events in a literary work; action **6.** the effect or representation of motion in painting, sculpture, etc. **7.** *Commerce* a change in the price of some stock or commodity **8.** *Mechanics* the moving parts of a mechanism; esp., a series of connected moving parts [the *movement* of a clock] **9.** *Music a)* any of the principal divisions of a symphony, sonata, or other extended composition *b) same as* TEMPO or RHYTHM *c) same as* MOTION (*n.* 9) **10.** *Prosody* rhythmic flow; cadence

mov·er (-ər) *n.* a person or thing that moves; specif., ☆a person whose work or business is moving furniture, etc. for those changing residence

☆**mov·ie** (mōō'vē) *n.* [contr. < MOVING PICTURE] **1.** a motion picture **2.** a motion-picture theater —**the movies 1.** the motion-picture industry **2.** a showing of a motion picture [an evening at the *movies*]

☆**mov·ie·go·er** (-gō'ər) *n.* a person who goes to see motion pictures, esp. often or regularly

mov·ing (mōō'vin) *adj.* **1.** that moves; specif., *a)* changing, or causing to change, place or position *b)* causing motion *c)* causing to act; impelling, instigating, influencing, etc. *d)* arousing or stirring the emotions or feelings; esp., arousing pathos **2.** involving a moving motor vehicle [a *moving* violation (of a traffic law)] —**mov'ing·ly** *adv.* **SYN.**—**moving** implies a general arousing or stirring of the emotions or feelings, sometimes, specif., of pathos [her *moving* plea for help]; **poignant** is applied to that which is sharply painful to the feelings [the *poignant* cry of a lost child]; **affecting** applies to that which stirs the emotions, as to tears [the *affecting* scene of their reunion]; **touching** is used of that which arouses tender feelings, as of sympathy, gratitude, etc. [her *touching* little gift to me]; **pathetic** applies to that which arouses pity or compassion, sometimes pity mingled with contempt [his *pathetic* attempt at wit]

moving picture *same as* MOTION PICTURE

☆**moving sidewalk** (or **walk**) a moving surface formed by an endless belt extending along a level stretch, for conveying pedestrians who step onto it

☆**moving staircase** (or **stairway**) *same as* ESCALATOR

☆**Mov·i·o·la** (mōō'vē ō'lə) *a trademark for* a small machine for viewing and editing motion-picture film —*n.* [m-] such a machine: also **mov'ie·o'la**

mow[1] (mō) *vt., vi.* **mowed, mowed** or **mown, mow'ing** [ME. *mowen* < OE. *mawan*, akin to G. *mähen* < IE. base *mē-*, *met-*, whence L. *metere*, to mow] **1.** to cut down (standing grass or grain) with a sickle, scythe, lawn mower, etc. **2.** to cut grass or grain from (a lawn, field, etc.) —**mow down 1.** to cause to fall like grass or grain being cut; knock down **2.** to kill or destroy as with swift, sudden strokes, gunfire, etc. **3.** to overwhelm (an opponent) —**mow'er** *n.*

mow[2] (mou) *n.* [ME. *mowe* < OE. *muga*, a heap, pile, akin to ON. *mūgi*, a crowd, swath < IE. base *muk-*, heap, whence Gr. *mykōn*] **1.** a stack or heap of hay, grain, etc., esp. in a barn **2.** the part of a barn where hay or grain is stored; haymow or hayloft

mow[3] (mou, mō) *n., vi.* [ME. *mowe* < OFr. *moue* < Frank. *mauwa*, akin to MDu. *mouwe*: for IE. base see MOPE] [Archaic] *same as* GRIMACE

mow·ing (mō'in) *n.* **1.** the act of cutting down grass or grain **2.** the quantity of grass or grain mowed at one time ☆**3.** a field on which grass is grown for hay

☆**mowing machine** a farm machine with a reciprocating blade for mowing standing grain or grass

mown (mōn) *alt. pp. of* MOW[1]

mox·a (mäk'sə) *n.* [altered < Jap. *mogusa*, a caustic < *moe kusa*, burning herb] **1.** a soft, downy material, burned on the skin as a cauterizing agent or counterirritant, esp. in traditional Chinese and Japanese medicine **2.** any of various plants yielding such material, as a Chinese wormwood (*Artemisia chinensis*) or a basidiomycete fungus (*Polyporus fomentarius*)

mox·i·bus·tion (mäk'si bus'chən) *n.* [< prec. + COMBUSTION] the burning of moxa on the skin in treating various diseases or disorders

☆**mox·ie** (mäk'sē) *n.* [< *Moxie*, trademark for a soft drink] [Slang] courage, pluck, daring, perseverance, etc.; guts

†**moy·en âge** (mwȧ'ye'näzh') [Fr.] the Middle Ages

Moz. Mozambique

Mo·zam·bique (mō'zəm bēk') Port. overseas territory in SE Africa, on Mozambique Channel: c. 302,300 sq. mi.; pop. 6,998,000; cap. Lourenço Marques

Mozambique Channel part of the Indian Ocean, between Mozambique & Madagascar: c. 1,000 mi. long

Moz·ar·ab (mō zar'əb) *n.* [Sp. *mozárabe* < Ar. *musta'rib*, would-be Arab] any of the Spanish Christians who were permitted to practice their religion in a modified form during the Moorish domination —**Moz·ar'a·bic** *adj.*

Mo·zart (mō'tsärt), **Wolf·gang A·ma·de·us** (vôlf'gäŋk' ä'mä dā'oos) 1756–91; Austrian composer

moz·za·rel·la (mät'sə rel'ə) *n.* [It., dim. of *mozza*, a kind of cheese < *mozzare*, to cut off < *mozzo*, blunt < VL. *muttius*, blunted] a soft, white Italian cheese with a mild flavor, used esp. in cooking

moz·zet·ta, mo·zet·ta (mō zet'ə) *n.* [It. *mozzetta* < *mozzo*, shortened < VL. *mutius*] a short cape with a small hood, worn over the rochet by the Pope and other high dignitaries of the Roman Catholic Church

MP, M.P. Military Police

mp [It. *mezzo piano*] *Music* moderately soft

M.P. 1. Member of Parliament **2.** Metropolitan Police (London) **3.** Mounted Police

M.P., m.p. melting point

mpg, m.p.g. miles per gallon

mph, m.p.h. miles per hour

MR motivational research

Mr. (mis'tər) *pl.* **Messrs.** (mes'ərz) mister: used before the name or title of a man: see MISTER

Mrs. (mis'iz) *pl.* **Mmes.** (mā däm') mistress: now used as a title before the name of a married woman

MS 1. motor ship **2.** multiple sclerosis

MSS., ms, ms *pl.* **MSS., mss.**, **mss** manuscript

M.S. 1. Master of Science **2.** Master of Surgery **3.** [L. *memoriae sacrum*] sacred to the memory of

M.Sc. Master of Science

MScand. Middle Scandinavian

MScot. Middle Scottish

msec. millisecond; milliseconds

MSG monosodium glutamate

Msgr. Monsignor

MSgt, M/Sgt Master Sergeant

m'sieur (mə syœr'; *Fr.* mə syö') *n.* monsieur

m.s.l. mean sea level

MST, M.S.T. Mountain Standard Time

Msth *Chem.* mesothorium: also **Ms-Th**

Mt., mt. *pl.* **mts. 1.** mount **2.** mountain

M.T. 1. Masoretic Text **2.** mean time **3.** metric ton

mtg. 1. meeting **2.** mortgage: also **mtge.**

mtn. mountain

Mt. Rev. Most Reverend

mu (myōō, mōō) *n.* [Gr. *my*] the twelfth letter of the Greek alphabet (M, μ)

muc- (myōōk) *same as* MUCO-: used before a vowel

much (much) *adj.* **more, most** [ME. *muche* < *muchel*, large, much < OE. *mycel*, large in size or quantity < IE. base *meǥ(h)-*, large, whence Gr. *megas*, L. *magnus*] **1.** [Obs.] many in number **2.** great in quantity, amount, degree, etc. —*adv.* **1.** to a great degree or extent [*much happier*] **2.** just about; almost; nearly [*much the same as yesterday*] **3.** at frequent intervals; often [*do you dine out much?*] —*n.* **1.** a great amount or quantity [*much to be done*] **2.** something great, unusual, or outstanding [*not much to look at*] —**as much as 1.** to the degree that **2.** practically; virtually; in effect —**make much of** to treat or consider as of great importance —**much as 1.** almost as **2.** however; although —**not much of a** not particularly good as a

‡**mu·cha·cha** (moo chä′chä) *n., pl.* **-chas** [Sp.] a girl or young woman —**mu·cha′cho** (-chō) *n.masc.*

much·ness (much′nis) *n.* greatness, as of quantity, degree, etc.; magnitude

mu·cic acid (myōō′sik) [Fr. *mucique* < L. *mucus* (see MUCUS) + *-ique*, -IC] a colorless, crystalline acid, $C_6H_{10}O_8$, formed by oxidizing lactose, gums, etc.

mu·cid (-sid) *adj.* [L. *mucidus* < *mucere*, to be moldy, akin to *mucus*, MUCUS] [Archaic] moldy; musty

mu·cif·er·ous (myōō sif′ər əs) *adj.* [MUC(US) + -*i*- + -FEROUS] producing or secreting mucus

mu·ci·lage (myōō′s'l ij) *n.* [ME. *muscilage* < MFr. *mucilage* < LL. *mucilago*, musty juice < L. *mucere*: see MUCID] **1.** any of various thick, sticky substances produced in certain plants ☆**2.** any watery solution of gum, glue, etc. used as an adhesive

mu·ci·lag·i·nous (myōō′sə laj′ə nəs) *adj.* [MFr. *mucilagineux* < ML. *mucilaginosus*] **1.** of or like mucilage; slimy; sticky **2.** producing or secreting mucilage

mu·cin (myōō′sin) *n.* [Fr. *mucine*: see MUCUS & -IN[1]] any of various glycoproteins present in connective tissue, saliva, mucus, etc. —**mu′cin·oid**, **mu′cin·ous** *adj.*

mu·cin·o·gen (myōō sin′ə jən) *n.* [MUCIN + -o- + -GEN] any of a group of substances from which mucins are derived

muck (muk) *n.* [ME. *muk* < or akin to ON. *myki*, dung < IE. base *meuk-*, slippery, viscous, whence L. *mucus*] **1.** moist manure **2.** black earth containing decaying matter, used as a fertilizer **3.** *a)* mire; mud *b)* anything unclean or degrading; dirt; filth —*vt.* **1.** to fertilize with muck **2.** [Colloq.] to dirty with or as with muck (often with *up*) **3.** [Chiefly Brit.] Slang] to make a mess of; bungle (often with *up*) **4.** Mining, etc. to remove muck from —**muck about** (or **around**) [Chiefly Brit. Slang] to waste time; putter

muck·er (muk′ər) *n.* [prob. < G. *mucker*, low person < *mucken*, to grumble] [Slang] a coarse or vulgar person, esp. one without honor; cad

muck·le (muk′'l) *adj., adv., n. var. OF* MICKLE

muck·rake (muk′rāk′) *vi.* **-raked′, -rak′ing** [inspired by the allusion by T. ROOSEVELT in a speech (1906) to the man with the *muck rake* in Bunyan's *Pilgrim's Progress*] ☆to search for and publicize in newspapers, etc. real or alleged corruption by public officials, businessmen, etc. —**muck′rak′er** *n.*

muck·worm (-wurm′) *n.* **1.** a grub, or larva, that lives and develops in muck, or manure **2.** a miser

muck·y (-ē) *adj.* **muck′i·er, muck′i·est** of or like muck; esp., dirty, filthy, etc.

mu·co- (myōō′kō, -kə) a combining form meaning mucus or mucous membrane [*mucoprotein*]

mu·coid (myōō′koid) *n.* [MUC(IN) + -OID] any of a group of mucoproteins found in connective tissue, in certain types of cysts, etc. —*adj.* like mucus

mu·co·pol·y·sac·cha·ride (myōō′kō päl′ē sak′ə rīd′) *n.* [MUCO- + POLYSACCHARIDE] one of a class of carbohydrates containing a small amount of protein in the molecule, and found throughout the body, esp. in tissue

mu·co·pro·tein (myōō′kō prō′tēn, -prōt′ē in) *n.* any of various glycoproteins with a nitrogen-containing carbohydrate group, found in animal tissues and fluids

mu·co·pu·ru·lent (-pyoor′yə lənt) *adj.* containing both mucus and pus

mu·co·sa (myōō kō′sə) *n., pl.* **-sae** (-sē), **-sas** [ModL. < fem. of L. *mucosus*, MUCOUS] *same as* MUCOUS MEMBRANE —**mu·co′sal** *adj.*

mu·cous (myōō′kəs) *adj.* [L. *mucosus*, slimy < *mucus*, MUCUS] **1.** of, containing, or secreting mucus **2.** like mucus or covered with or as with mucus; slimy —**mu·cos′i·ty** (-käs′ə tē) *n.*

mucous membrane a mucus-secreting membrane lining body cavities and canals connecting with the external air, as the alimentary canal and respiratory tract

mu·cro (myōō′krō) *n., pl.* **-cro′nes** (myōō krō′nēz) [ModL. < L., sharp point < IE. base *meuk-*, to scratch, whence Gr. *amychē*, a scratch] *Bot., Zool.* a short, sharp point, tip, or process projecting abruptly from certain parts and organs, as at the end of a leaf

mu·cro·nate (myōō′krə nit, -nāt′) *adj.* [ModL. < L. *mucronatus*] ending in a mucro, or sharp point: also **mu′cro·nat′ed** —**mu′cro·na′tion** *n.*

mu·cus (myōō′kəs) *n.* [L. < IE. base *meuk-, *meug-*, slippery, slime, to slide, whence Gr. *myxa*; cf. MEEK, MUCK] the thick, slimy secretion of the mucous membranes, that moistens and protects them

mud (mud) *n.* [ME., prob. < a LowG. source as in LowG. *mudde* < IE. *meut* < base *meu-*, wet, musty, whence MOSS, MOTHER[2]] **1.** wet, soft, sticky earth **2.** defamatory remarks; libel or slander —*vt.* **mud′ded, mud′ding** to cover or soil with or as with mud; muddy

☆**mud·cat** (-kat′) *n.* any of several catfishes living in muddy waters

mud crack a crack formed in mud beds in the course of drying and shrinking, sometimes filled in and preserved when the beds are changed to rock

☆**mud dauber** any of a variety of narrow-waisted wasps (family Sphecidae) that build cells of hard, caked mud for their larvae

☆**mud·der** (mud′ər) *n.* a race horse that performs especially well on a wet, muddy track

mud·dle (mud′'l) *vt.* **-dled, -dling** [< MUD + -LE] **1.** to mix up in a confused manner; jumble; bungle **2.** to mix or stir (a drink, etc.) **3.** to make (water, etc.) turbid **4.** to confuse mentally; befuddle, as with alcoholic liquor **5.** to confuse (the brain, mind, etc.); befog —*vi.* to act or think in a confused way —*n.* **1.** a confused or disordered condition; mess, jumble, etc. **2.** mental confusion —*SYN.* see CONFUSION —**muddle through** [Chiefly Brit.] to manage to succeed in spite of apparent blunders or confusion

mud·dle·head·ed (-hed′id) *adj.* stupid; blundering; confused —**mud′dle·head′ed·ness** *n.*

☆**mud·dler** (mud′lər) *n.* a stick for stirring mixed drinks

mud·dy (mud′ē) *adj.* **-di·er, -di·est 1.** full of or spattered with mud **2.** *a)* not clear; containing sediment; cloudy [*muddy coffee*] *b)* not light or bright; dull [*a muddy complexion*] **3.** confused, obscure, vague, etc. [*muddy thinking*] —*vt., vi.* **-died, -dy·ing** to make or become muddy —**mud′di·ly** *adv.* —**mud′di·ness** *n.*

mud eel ☆a small, slime-coated, eellike amphibian (*Siren lacertina*) with no hind legs, two short front legs, internal lungs, and external gills: it lives in swamps, ditches, and ponds in the SE U.S.

mud·fish (-fish′) *n., pl.* **-fish′, -fish′es:** see FISH[2] ☆any of various unrelated fishes that live in mud or muddy water, as the bowfin and killifish

mud flat low, muddy land that is flooded at high tide and left uncovered at low tide

mud·guard (-gärd′) *n. older name for* FENDER (sense *a*)

mud hen any of various birds that live in marshes, as the coot, gallinule, etc.

☆**mud·hole** (-hōl′) *n.* a hole or low place, as in a field or road, full of mud

mud·lark (-lärk′) *n. Brit. colloq. for* STREET URCHIN

mud·pack (-pak′) *n.* a paste made up of fuller's earth, astringents, etc., used as a facial

☆**mud puppy** any of various N. American salamanders (esp. genera *Necturus* and *Cryptobranchus*) that live in mud under water

mu·dra (mə drä′) *n.* [Sans., a seal, sign] **1.** in ancient India, any identifying symbol or seal **2.** a stylized, symbolic gesture used in dances, rituals, etc. of India; specif., an intricate movement or positioning of the hands or fingers

mud·sill (mud′sil′) *n.* the lowest sill in the foundation of a structure, placed in or on the ground

mud·skip·per (-skip′ər) *n.* any of a group of fishes (genus *Periophthalmus*) that are able to leave the water for a time and that skip over the mud flats and even climb mangrove roots in search of food

mud·sling·ing (-slin′in) *n.* the practice of making unscrupulous, malicious attacks against an opponent, as in a political campaign —**mud′sling′er** *n.*

☆**mud snake** a long, bluish-black snake (*Farancia abacura*) with a red belly, and a nonpoisonous spine at the tip of the tail, found in the SE U.S.

mud·stone (-stōn′) *n.* a hardened sedimentary rock consisting of clay and similar to shale, but not distinctly laminated

☆**mud turtle** any of a large group of small turtles (genus *Kinosternon*) of North and Central America that live in muddy ponds, streams, etc.

Muen·ster (mun′stər, moon′-) *n.* [first made near *Munster*, in E France] a semisoft, light-yellow, mild cheese

mu·ez·zin (myoo ez′in) *n.* [Ar. *mu'adhdhin*, prp. of *adhdhana*, freq. of *adhana*, to proclaim < *udhn*, an ear] in Moslem countries, a crier, as in a minaret, who calls the people to prayer at the proper hours

muff (muf) *n.* [Du. *mof* < Wal. *moufe*, shortened < Fr. *moufle*, a mitten < ML. *muffula*] **1.** a cylindrical covering of fur or other soft material into which the hands are placed from either end for keeping them warm **2.** a tuft of feathers on the sides of the head, or on the legs, of certain fowl **3.** *a) Baseball,* etc. a failure to hold the ball when catching it *b)* any bungling action —*vt., vi.* to do (something) badly or awkwardly; specif., *Baseball,* etc. to miss (a catch) or bungle (a play)

muf·fin (muf′'n) n. [< dial. *mouffin, moufin,* ? akin to OFr. *moufflet,* soft, as in *pain moufflet,* soft bread] a quick bread made with eggs, baked in a small cup-shaped mold and usually eaten hot See also ENGLISH MUFFIN

muf·fin·eer (muf′ə nir′) n. a shaker for sprinkling sugar, spices, etc. on muffins, fruit, etc.

muf·fle (muf′'l) vt. **-fled, -fling** [ME. *muflen,* prob. akin to OFr. *enmoufle,* muffled < *moufle,* a mitten: cf. MUFF] **1.** to wrap up in a shawl, blanket, cloak, etc. so as to hide, keep warm, or protect **2.** to keep (a person) from seeing or speaking by wrapping up the head **3.** to wrap or cover in order to deaden or prevent sound **4.** to deaden (a sound), as by wrapping **5.** to prevent the expression of; stifle —n. **1.** a wrap, covering, etc. used for muffling **2.** an oven in which pottery, etc. can be fired without being exposed directly to the flame **3.** the fleshy bare part of the upper lip and nose of ruminants and certain other mammals

muf·fler (-lər) n. **1.** a scarf worn around the throat, as for warmth **2.** any of various devices for silencing noises, as☆ a larger section with a baffle or baffles in the exhaust pipe of an internal-combustion engine

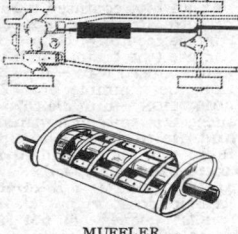

MUFFLER

muf·ti (muf′tē) n., pl. **-tis** [Ar., one who gives a decisive response < *āftā,* to judge; sense 2 ? in allusion to the Moslemlike dressing gown and tasseled cap worn by an officer off duty in the early 19th cent.] **1.** in Moslem countries, an interpreter or expounder of religious law **2.** ordinary clothes, esp. when worn by one who normally wears, or has long worn, a military or other uniform

mug (mug) n. [prob. < Scand., as in Sw. *mugg*] **1.** a heavy drinking cup of earthenware or metal, having a handle and formerly often ornamented with a human face **2.** as much as a mug will hold **3.** [Slang] *a)* the face *b)* the mouth *c)* a grimace *d)* a rough, ugly person; ruffian, thug, etc. ☆*e)* a photograph of the face of a criminal or suspect: also **mug shot** —vt. **mugged, mug′ging 1.** to assault, esp. from behind and usually with intent to rob ☆**2.** [Slang] to photograph; esp., to photograph (a criminal or suspect) for police records —vi. **1.** to assault a person, esp. from behind and usually with intent to rob him **2.** [Slang] to make a grimace; esp., *Theater* to overact by exaggerated facial expressions

mug·ger¹ (-ər) n. one who mugs; esp., *a)* a robber who assaults his victim from behind *b) Theater* one who overacts, esp. by exaggerated facial expressions

mug·ger² (mug′ər) n. [Hind. *magar* < Sans. *makara,* sea monster] a large, relatively timid crocodile (*Crocodylus palustris*) of India and Malaysia, with a broad, wrinkled snout

mug·gins (mug′'nz) n. [< personal name *Muggins,* associated with slang *mug,* cardsharper's dupe] **1.** a practice in some versions of dominoes, cribbage, etc. by which a player may take his opponent's points if the latter neglects to do so at the proper time **2.** any of various simple card games **3.** [Brit. Slang] a dupe; fool

mug·gy (mug′ē) adj. **-gi·er, -gi·est** [< dial. *mug,* mist, drizzle, prob. < or akin to ON. *mugga* < IE. base *meuk-*: cf. MUCUS] hot and damp, with little or no stirring of the air [*muggy* weather] —**mug′gi·ness** n.

mu·gho pine (myōō′gō) [prob. via Fr. *mugho,* mugho pine < It. *mugo*] a Swiss mountain pine (*Pinus mugo*), esp. a shrubby spreading form often used as an ornamental

☆**mug·wump** (mug′wump′) n. [Algonquian *mugquomp,* chief] **1.** a Republican who refused to support the party ticket in 1884 **2.** any independent, esp. in politics

Mu·ham·mad (mōō ham′əd) *same as* MOHAMMED — **Mu·ham′mad·an** adj., n. —**Mu·ham′mad·an·ism** n.

Muir (myoor), **John** 1838-1914; U.S. naturalist, explorer, & writer; born in Scotland

mu·jik (mōō zhēk′, mōō′zhik) n. *same as* MUZHIK

Muk·den (mook′dən, mook den′) *former name of* SHEN-YANG

☆**muk·luk** (muk′luk′) n. [Esk. *muklok,* a large seal] **1.** an Eskimo boot made of sealskin or reindeer skin **2.** a boot like this, made of canvas, rubber, etc.

mu·lat·to (mə lat′ō, myoo-) n., pl. **-toes** [Sp. & Port. *mulato,* mulatto, of mixed breed, orig. young mule < *mulo,* mule < L. *mulus*] **1.** a person who has one Negro parent and one white parent **2.** popularly, any person with mixed Negro and Caucasoid ancestry —adj. **1.** of a mulatto **2.** of the light-brown color of a mulatto's skin

mul·ber·ry (mul′ber′ē, -bər ē) n., pl. **-ries** [ME. *mulberie,* dissimilated var. of *murberie* < OE. *morberie* < L. *morum,* mulberry, blackberry + OE. *berie,* BERRY] **1.** any of a genus (*Morus*) of shrubs and trees of the mulberry family, with milky juice and multiple false fruits which resemble the fruits of the raspberry **2.** the edible fruit **3.** purplish red —adj. designating a family (Moraceae) of plants of wide horticultural and economic importance, including the mulberry, fig, and breadfruit trees

mulch (mulch) n. [ME. *molsh,* soft, akin to G. dial. *molsch,* soft: for prob. IE. base see MOLD³] leaves, straw, peat moss, etc., spread on the ground around plants to prevent evaporation of water from soil, freezing of roots, etc. —vt. to apply mulch to

mulct (mulkt) vt. [L. *mulctare* < *mulcta, multa,* a fine] **1.** to punish by a fine or by depriving of something **2.** to extract (money, etc.) from (someone), as by fraud or deceit —n. a fine or similar penalty

mule¹ (myōōl) n. [ME. < OFr., fem. of *mul* < L. *mulus,* mule] **1.** the offspring of a donkey and a horse; esp., the offspring of a jackass and a mare: cf. HINNY: mules are nearly always sterile **2.** a small tractor or electric engine used to tow boats along a canal **3.** a machine for drawing and spinning cotton fibers into yarn and winding the yarn on spindles **4.** a hybrid; esp., a sterile hybrid: among bird fanciers, esp. the offspring of a canary and some other finch **5.** [Colloq.] a stubborn person

mule² (myōōl) n. [Fr., ult. < L. *mulleus,* red or purple shoe < IE. base *mel-,* dark-colored, whence Gr. *melas,* black] a lounging slipper that does not cover the heel

☆**mule deer** a long-eared deer (*Odocoileus hemionus*) of the W U.S. with a black tail

☆**mule skinner** [Colloq.] a driver of mules

mu·le·ta (mōō lāt′ə, -let′ə) n. [Sp., muleta, crutch, orig. dim. of *mula,* a she-mule < L. *mulus,* MULE¹] a red flannel cloth draped over a stick and manipulated by the matador in his series of passes

mu·le·teer (myōō′lə tir′) n. [OFr. *muletier* < *mulet,* dim. of *mule*] a driver of mules

mul·ey (myōō′lē, mool′ē) adj. [Scot. *moiley* < Celt., as in W. *moel,* Gael. *maol,* hornless, bald < IE. base *mai-,* to cut off, whence MAD] hornless; polled: said of cattle —n. **1.** a hornless cow **2.** any cow

☆**muley saw** [prob. < prec.] a mechanical ripsaw, with a stiff, vertical blade that is not stretched in a frame but is guided by clamps at either end

Mul·ha·cén (mool′ä then′) highest mountain in Spain, in the S part, near Granada: 11,420 ft.

Mül·heim (mül′him′) city in W West Germany, in North Rhine-Westphalia, on the Ruhr: pop. 191,000: also **Mülheim an der Ruhr** (än der rŏŏr′)

Mul·house (mü lōōz′) city in E France, near the Rhine: pop. 109,000

mu·li·eb·ri·ty (myōō′lē eb′rə tē) n. [LL. *muliebritas* < L. *muliebris,* womanly, womanish < *mulier,* a woman, prob. < IE. *mlyési,* (the) softer (one), compar. of *mldwis* (whence L. *mollis*) < base *mel-*: cf. MILL¹] **1.** the condition of being a woman; womanhood **2.** the qualities characteristic of a woman; womanliness; femininity

mul·ish (myōō′lish) adj. like or characteristic of a mule; stubborn, obstinate, balky, etc. —**mul′ish·ly** adv. — **mul′ish·ness** n.

Mull (mul) island of the Inner Hebrides, Scotland: 367 sq. mi.; pop. (with small nearby islands) 1,700

mull¹ (mul) vt., vi. [ME. *mullen,* to grind < *mul,* dust < OE. *myl,* dust: for IE. base see MOLD³] [Colloq.] to cogitate or ponder (usually with *over*)

mull² (mul) vt. [< ?] to heat, sweeten, and flavor with spices (ale, cider, wine, etc.)

mull³ (mul) n. [contr. < *mulmul* < Hind. & Per. *malmal*] a thin, soft muslin

mul·lah, mul·la (mul′ə, mool′-) n. [Turk., Per. & Hind. *mulla* < Ar. *mawlā,* a master, sir] a Moslem teacher or interpreter of the religious law: used as a general title of respect for a learned man

mul·lein (mul′in) n. [ME. *moleyne* < OFr. *moleine* < *mol,* soft < L. *mollis*: see MOLLIFY] any of a genus (*Verbascum*) of tall plants of the figwort family, with spikes of yellow, lavender, or white flowers

mullein pink a perennial woolly plant (*Lychnis coronaria*) of the pink family, with reddish flowers

mull·er (mul′ər) n. [ME. *molour,* prob. < *mullen,* to grind: see MULL¹] any of various mechanical or hand devices for grinding; specif., a flat-bottomed pestle of stone, etc., as for grinding paints or drugs

Mül·ler (mü′lər; E. mul′ər, mil′-), **(Friedrich) Max** (mäks) 1823-1900; Eng. philologist, mythologist, & Orientalist, born in Germany

Mul·ler (mul′ər), **H**(ermann) **J**(oseph) 1890-1967; U.S. biologist & geneticist

mul·let (mul′it) n., pl. **-lets, -let:** see PLURAL, II, D, 1 [ME. *molet* < OFr. *mulet,* dim. < L. *mullus,* red mullet < Gr. *myllos,* kind of fish < IE. base *mel-*: see MULE²] **1.** any of a family (Mugilidae) of edible, spiny-rayed fishes found in fresh and salt waters and having a small mouth and feeble teeth, as the **striped** (or **gray**) **mullet** (*Mugil cephalus*) **2.** *same as* GOATFISH, esp. the **red goatfish** (*Mullus barbatus*) with reddish or golden scales and two chin barbels

mul·ley (mool′ē, mōō′lē) adj., n. *same as* MULEY

☆**mul·li·gan** (mul′i g'n) n. [prob. < personal name *Mulligan*] **1.** [Slang] a stew made of odd bits of meat and vegetables, esp. as prepared by hobos: also **mulligan stew 2.** *Golf* in informal play, a free drive, esp. off the first tee after a poor shot

mul·li·ga·taw·ny (mul′i gə tô′nē) n. [Tamil *milagutannir,* lit., pepper water] an East Indian soup of meat, etc., flavored with curry

mul·lion (mul'yən) *n.* [prob. altered < OFr. *moienel* < *moien*, median < L. *medianus*, middle: see MID¹] a slender vertical dividing bar between the lights of windows, panels, etc. —*vt.* to furnish with or divide by mullions —**mul'lioned** *adj.*

mul·lite (mul'īt) *n.* [< *Mull*, island off W coast of Scotland, where the ore is found + -ITE¹] a heat-resistant mineral, 3Al₂O₃·2SiO₂, a silicate of aluminum, used in furnace linings, etc.

mul·lock (mul'ək) *n.* [ME. *mulloc* < *mul*, small particles, dust, (see MULL¹) + -oc, -OCK] in Australia, the refuse earth or rock left over in mining

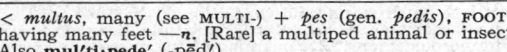

MULLIONS

Mul·tan (mool tän') city in NE West Pakistan, near the Chenab River: pop. 358,000

mul·tan·gu·lar (mul taŋ'gyoo lər) *adj.* having many angles: also **mul'ti·an'gu·lar** (mul'tē aŋ'-)

mul·ti- (mul'ti, -tə, -tē; *occas.* -tĭ) [L. < *multus*, much, many < IE. base *mel-*, strong, big, whence Gr. *mala*, very] *a combining form meaning:* 1. having, consisting of, or affecting many [*multicolored*] 2. more than one (or sometimes one) [*multilateral, multicylinder*] 3. many times more than [*multimillionaire*] Also, before a vowel, **mult-** The meanings of the following words can be determined by combining the meanings of their component elements:

multicellular	multimolecular
multichannel	multinational
multicircuit	multiovular
multicoil	multiphase
multicolored	multipinnate
multicostate	multipolar
multicylinder	multipurpose
multidentate	multiracial
multidimensional	multisegmented
multidirectional	multispeed
multifaceted	multispermous
multifamily	multispiculate
multifilament	multispinous
multifoliate	multispiral
multihued	multistaminate
multilayered	multistoried
multilevel	multistory
multilinear	multivalve
multilingual	multivitamin
multilobate	multivoiced
multilocular	multivolume

mul·ti·dis·ci·pli·nar·y (mul'ti dis'ə pli ner'ē) *adj.* of or combining the disciplines of many different branches of learning or research

mul·ti·far·i·ous (mul'tə far'ē əs, -fer'-) *adj.* [L. *multifarius*, manifold < *multus*, many (see MULTI-) + base of *facere*, to make (see FACT)] having many kinds of parts or elements; of great variety; diverse; manifold —*SYN.* see MANY —**mul'ti·far'i·ous·ly** *adv.* —**mul'ti·far'i·ous·ness** *n.*

mul·ti·fid (mul'tə fid) *adj.* [L. *multifidus*: see MULTI- & -FID] cut into many divisions or lobes, as a leaf — **mul'ti·fid'ly** *adv.*

mul·ti·flo·ra rose (mul'tə flôr'ə) a rose (*Rosa multiflora*) with thick clusters of small flowers, grown esp. for hedges

mul·ti·fold (mul'tə fōld') *adj.* [MULTI- + -FOLD] 1. doubled or folded many times 2. same as MANIFOLD

mul·ti·form (-fôrm') *adj.* [< Fr. or L.: Fr. *multiforme* < L. *multiformis* < *multus*, many (see MULTI-) + *forma*, FORM] having many forms, shapes, etc. —**mul'ti·for'mi·ty** *n.*

mul·ti·lat·er·al (mul'ti lat'ər əl) *adj.* [MULTI- + LATERAL] 1. many-sided 2. participated in by more than two parties, nations, etc.; multipartite [a *multilateral* treaty] —**mul'ti·lat'er·al·ly** *adv.*

mul·ti·me·di·a (-mē'dē ə) *n.* same as MIXED MEDIA

☆**mul·ti·mil·lion·aire** (-mil'yə ner') *n.* a person whose wealth amounts to many millions of dollars, francs, pounds, etc.

mul·ti·nu·cle·ate (-nōō'klē it, -āt'; -nyōō'-) *adj.* having more than two nuclei: also **mul'ti·nu'cle·at'ed**, **mul'ti·nu'cle·ar**

mul·tip·a·ra (mul tip'ər ə) *n., pl.* **-ras, -rae** (-rē') [ModL. < fem. of *multiparus*: see ff.] a woman who is bearing her second child or has borne two or more children

mul·tip·a·rous (-əs) *adj.* [ModL. *multiparus*: see MULTI- & -PAROUS] 1. of or being a multipara 2. *Zool.* designating or of a species of animal that normally bears more than one offspring at a birth

mul·ti·par·tite (mul'ti pär'tīt) *adj.* [L. *multipartitus* < *multus*, many (see MULTI-) + *pars* (gen. *partis*), PART] 1. divided into many parts 2. participated in by more than two parties, nations, etc.; multilateral

mul·ti·ped (mul'ti ped) *n.* [L. *multipes* (gen. *multipedis*),

< *multus*, many (see MULTI-) + *pes* (gen. *pedis*), FOOT] having many feet —*n.* [Rare] a multiped animal or insect Also **mul'ti·pede'** (-pēd')

mul·ti·ple (mul'tə p'l) *adj.* [Fr. < L. *multiplex* < *multus* (see MULTI-) + -*plex*, -fold: see DUPLEX] 1. having or consisting of many parts, elements, etc.; more than one or once; manifold or complex 2. shared by or involving many 3. *Elec.* designating or of a circuit having two or more conductors connected in parallel —*n.* 1. *Elec.* a group of terminals so arranged that connection with the circuit can be made at any of a number of points 2. *Math.* a number which is a product of some specified number and another number [10 is a *multiple* of 5]

☆**mul·ti·ple-choice** (-chois') *adj.* designating a question for which one of several proposed answers is to be selected, or a test made up of such questions

multiple factors *Genetics* a series of two or more pairs of allelic genes, considered to act as a single unit with a cumulative effect in the transmission of certain characters, such as size, pigmentation, etc.

multiple fruit a false fruit formed by a fused cluster of the ovaries of several flowers, as a pineapple or mulberry

multiple sclerosis a chronic disease in which there is scattered demyelination of the central nervous system: it is characterized by speech defects, loss of muscular coordination, etc.

multiple shop (or **store**) [Brit.] *same as* CHAIN STORE

multiple star *Astron.* three or more stars appearing close together in the sky, often forming a system with a single gravitational center: cf. BINARY STAR

mul·ti·plet (mul'tə plet) *n.* [MULTIPL(E) + -ET] *Physics* 1. a set of particles or particle states related to each other whose single atomic energy level can be split into a specific number of energy levels 2. a line in a spectrum composed of a group of related lines

mul·ti·plex (mul'tə pleks') *adj.* [L. *multiplex*, MULTIPLE] 1. multiple, or manifold 2. designating or of a system for transmitting or receiving simultaneously two or more messages or signals over a common circuit, carrier wave, etc. —*vt.* to send (messages or signals) by a multiplex system

mul·ti·pli·a·ble (mul'tə plī'ə b'l) *adj.* that can be multiplied: also **mul'ti·plic'a·ble** (-plik'ə b'l)

mul·ti·pli·cand (mul'tə pli kand') *n.* [L. *multiplicandus*, to be multiplied, gerundive of *multiplicare*, MULTIPLY¹] *Math.* the number that is, or is to be, multiplied by another (the *multiplier*)

mul·ti·pli·cate (mul'tə pli kāt') *adj.* [ME. < L. *multiplicatus*, pp. of *multiplicare*, to MULTIPLY¹] [Now Rare] multiple; manifold

mul·ti·pli·ca·tion (mul'tə pli kā'shən) *n.* [ME. *multiplicacioun* < OFr. *multiplication* < L. *multiplicatio*] a multiplying or being multiplied; specif., *Math.* the process of finding the number or quantity (*product*) obtained by repeating a specified number or quantity (*multiplicand*) a specified number of times (*multiplier*), indicated in arithmetic by the symbol ×

multiplication factor (or **constant**) the ratio of the number of neutrons in a generation to the number of neutrons in the next generation: when the multiplication factor is equal to or greater than one, a chain reaction is possible

multiplication table a table for memorization showing the results of multiplying each number of a series, usually 1 to 12, by each of the numbers in succession

mul·ti·pli·ca·tive (mul'tə pli kāt'iv) *adj.* [LL. *multiplicativus* < L. *multiplicatus*, pp.: see MULTIPLY¹] tending to multiply or capable of multiplying —**mul'ti·pli·ca'tive·ly** *adv.*

mul·ti·plic·i·ty (mul'tə plis'ə tē) *n.* [LL. *multiplicitas* < L. *multiplex*, MULTIPLE] 1. the quality or condition of being manifold or various 2. a great number

mul·ti·pli·er (mul'tə plī'ər) *n.* 1. a person or thing that multiplies or increases 2. *Econ.* the ratio between the total increase in income resulting from the stimulating effect of an initial expenditure and the initial expenditure itself 3. *Math.* the number by which another number (the *multiplicand*) is, or is to be, multiplied 4. *Physics* any device for multiplying, or intensifying, some effect

mul·ti·ply¹ (mul'tə plī') *vt.* **-plied'**, **-ply'ing** [ME. *multiplien* < OFr. *multiplier* < L. *multiplicare* < *multiplex*, MULTIPLE] 1. to cause to increase in number, amount, extent, or degree 2. *Math.* to find the product of by multiplication —*vi.* 1. to increase in number, amount, extent, or degree; specif., to increase by procreation 2. *Math.* to perform multiplication —*SYN.* see INCREASE

mul·ti·ply² (mul'tə plē) *adv.* in multiple ways

mul·ti·stage (mul'ti stāj') *adj.* having, or operating in, more than one stage; specif., having several propulsion systems, used and discarded in sequence: said of a rocket or missile

mul·ti·tude (mul'tə tōōd', -tyōōd') *n.* [ME. < OFr. < L. *multitudo* < *multus*, many: see MULTI-] 1. the quality or state of being numerous, or many 2. a large number of persons or things, esp. when gathered together or considered as a unit; host, myriad, etc. 3. the masses (preceded by *the*) —*SYN.* see CROWD

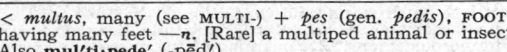

MULTIFID LEAF

mul·ti·tu·di·nous (mul′tə tōōd′′n əs, -tyōōd′-) *adj.* [< L. *multitudo* (gen. *multitudinis*), multitude + -OUS] **1.** very numerous; many **2.** consisting of many parts, elements, etc.; manifold **3.** [Rare or Poet.] holding a multitude; crowded —**mul′ti·tu′di·nous·ly** *adv.*

mul·ti·va·lent (mul′ti vā′lənt, mul tiv′ə lənt) *adj.* Chem. same as POLYVALENT (sense 2) —**mul′ti·va′lence** *n.*

☆**mul·ti·ver·si·ty** (mul′ti vur′sə tē) *n., pl.* -ties [MULTI- + (UNI)VERSITY: coined by Clark Kerr (1911–), U.S. educator] the modern large and complex university with its many colleges, schools, extensions, etc., characteristically regarded as being impersonal, bureaucratic, etc.

mul·ture (mul′chər) *n.* [ME. *multer* < OFr. *molture* < VL. **molitura* < pp. of L. *molere*, to grind < *mola*, MILL[1]] formerly, a fee paid to the owner of a mill for the privilege of having one's grain ground there, usually a percentage of the grain or of the ground flour

mum[1] (mum) *n.* [G. *mumme*: said to be named after Christian *Mumme*, 15th-c. G. brewer] a strong beer

mum[2] (mum) *vi.* mummed, mum′ming [< OFr. *momer* < *momo*, echoic for grimace (as in Sp. *momo*)] to wear a mask or costume in fun; specif., to act as a mummer at Christmas time: also sp. **mumm**

☆**mum**[3] (mum) *n.* [Colloq.] a chrysanthemum

mum[4] (mum) *n.* [Chiefly Brit. Colloq.] mother

mum[5] (mum) *adj.* [ME. *momme*, echoic of sound made with the lips closed] silent; not speaking —*interj.* be silent! do not speak! —**mum's the word** say nothing; remain secretive

mum·ble (mum′b'l) *vt., vi.* -bled, -bling [ME. *momelen*, like G. *mummeln*, Du. *mommelen*, of echoic origin] **1.** to speak or say indistinctly and in a low voice, as with the mouth partly closed; mutter **2.** [Rare] to chew gently and ineffectively, as with toothless gums —*n.* a mumbled sound or utterance —*SYN.* see MURMUR —**mum′bler** *n.* —**mum′- bling·ly** *adv.*

mum·ble·ty·peg (mum′b'l tē peg′) *n.* [altered < *mumble- the-peg* < *mumble*, to bite] a boy's game in which a jack-knife is tossed in various ways to make it land with the blade in the ground, the loser originally having to draw a peg from the ground with his teeth

mum·bo jum·bo (mum′bō jum′bō) [of Afr. orig.: meaning, form, & dialect unc.] **1.** [M- J-] among certain West African tribes, an idol or god supposed to protect the people from evil and terrorize the women into subjection **2.** *a*) any idol or fetish *b*) any object of fear or dread **3.** meaningless ritual or show of activity **4.** unintelligible expression, gibberish, etc.

Mum·ford (mum′fərd), **Lewis** 1895– ; U.S. social philosopher & architectural critic

mum·mer (mum′ər) *n.* [MFr. *momeur* < OFr. *momer:* see MUM[2]] **1.** a person who wears a mask or disguise for fun; specif., in England, any of the masked and costumed persons who travel about, as at Christmas time, acting out short pantomimes **2.** any actor

mum·mer·y (-ē) *n., pl.* -mer·ies [MFr. *mommerie* < OFr. *momer:* see MUM[2]] **1.** performance by mummers **2.** any display or ceremony regarded as pretentious or hypocritical

mum·mi·fy (mum′ə fi′) *vt.* -fied′, -fy′ing [MUMMY + -FY] to make into or like a mummy —*vi.* to shrivel or dry up —**mum′mi·fi·ca′tion** *n.*

mum·my (mum′ē) *n., pl.* -mies [Fr. *momie* < ML. *mumia* < Ar. *mumiya*, embalmed body, mummy < Per. *mum*, wax] **1.** a dead body preserved by embalming, as by the ancient Egyptians **2.** any dead body that has been naturally well preserved **3.** any thin, withered person regarded as looking like a mummy —*vt.* -mied, -my·ing [Rare] same as MUMMIFY

mump (mump) *vt., vi.* [echoic, or < ? Du. *mompelen*, var. of *mommelen*, to mumble] **1.** [Dial.] to mumble; mutter **2.** [Du. *mompen*, to cheat, prob. akin to *mompelen*] [Old Slang] *a*) to beg *b*) to cheat

mumps (mumps) *n.pl.* [with *sing. v.*] [pl. of obs. *mump*, a grimace: prob. from patient's appearance] an acute communicable disease, usually of childhood, caused by a virus and characterized by swelling of the salivary glands, esp. the parotid, and, in adults, often complicated by inflammation of the testes, ovaries, etc.

mu·mu, mu-mu (mōō′mōō′) *n.* same as MUUMUU

mun. municipal

munch (munch) *vt., vi.* [ME. *monchen*, prob. echoic alteration of *mangen*, to feast < OFr. *manger* < L. *manducare:* see MANGER] to chew steadily, often with a crunching sound —**munch′er** *n.*

Mun·chau·sen (mun′chou′zən, moon′-; -chô′-), **Baron** (*Karl Friedrich Hieronymus von Münchhausen*) 1720–97; Ger. soldier & adventurer known for his exaggerated tales of his exploits, esp. as collected by Rudolf Erich Raspe (1737–94), Ger. writer in England

Mün·chen (mün′Hən) *Ger. name of* MUNICH

Mün·chen-Glad·bach (mün′Hən glät′bäkh) *same as* MÖNCHEN-GLADBACH

Mun·cie (mun′sē) [after the *Munsee* (Delaware) Indians] city in EC Ind.: pop. 69,000

Mun·da (moon′dä) *adj.* designating or of a branch of the Austro-Asiatic family of languages, spoken in areas of EC and S India

mun·dane (mun dān′, mun′dān) *adj.* [LME. *mondeyne* < OFr. *mondain* < L. *mundanus* < *mundus*, world] **1.** of the

world; esp., worldly, as distinguished from heavenly, spiritual, etc. **2.** commonplace, everyday, ordinary, etc. —*SYN.* see EARTHLY —**mun·dane′ly** *adv.*

mun·dun·gus (mun dun′gəs) *n.* [orig. facetious use of Sp. *mondongo*, tripe] [Archaic] a dark tobacco with a disagreeable smell

mung bean (mun) [*mung*, short for *mungo* < Tamil *mūngu* < Hind. *mug* < Sans. *mudga*] an annual bean (*Phaseolus aureus*) grown for green manure and forage, and as a source of bean sprouts

mun·go (mun′gō) *n., pl.* -gos [< Yorkshire dial. < ?] the waste of milled wool used to make a cheap cloth: cf. SHODDY

Mu·nich (myōō′nik) city in SE West Germany; capital of Bavaria: pop. 1,215,000: Ger. name, MÜNCHEN

Munich Pact (or **Agreement**) a pact signed in 1938 at Munich by Great Britain and France, ceding the Czech Sudetenland to Nazi Germany: regarded as the epitome of political appeasement

mu·nic·i·pal (myoo nis′ə p'l) *adj.* [L. *municipalis* < *municeps*, inhabitant of a free town < *munia*, official duties, functions < IE. base **mei-*, to exchange (cf. COMMON, MEAN[2]) + *capere*, to take] **1.** *a*) of or having to do with a city, town, etc. or its local government *b*) having self-government locally **2.** of the internal, as distinguished from the international, affairs of a state or nation —**mu·nic′i·pal·ly** *adv.*

mu·nic·i·pal·ism (-iz'm) *n.* **1.** self-government by a municipality **2.** the principle that such government should be fostered —**mu·nic′i·pal·ist** *n.*

mu·nic·i·pal·i·ty (myoo nis′ə pal′ə tē) *n., pl.* -ties [Fr. *municipalité* < *municipal* < L. *municipalis*, MUNICIPAL] **1.** a city, town, etc. having its own incorporated government for local affairs **2.** the officials governing such a community

mu·nic·i·pal·ize (myoo nis′ə pə līz′) *vt.* -ized′, -iz′ing **1.** to bring under the control or ownership of a municipality **2.** to make a municipality of —**mu·nic′i·pal·i·za′tion** *n.*

mu·nif·i·cent (myoo nif′ə s'nt) *adj.* [L. *munificens* < *munificus*, bountiful < *munus*, a gift (akin to *munia:* see MUNICIPAL) + *facere*, to make: see FACT] **1.** very generous in giving; lavish **2.** characterized by great generosity [a *munificent* reward] —**mu·nif′i·cence** *n.* —**mu·nif′i·cent·ly** *adv.*

mu·ni·ment (myōō′ni mənt) *n.* [ME. < Anglo-Fr. < OFr. < L. *munimentum*, a fortification, defense, protection < *munire*, to furnish with walls, fortify: see MUNITIONS] **1.** [Now Rare] a means of protection or defense **2.** [*pl.*] [ML. *munimentum*] *Law* a document or documents serving as evidence of inheritances, title to property, etc.

mu·ni·tion (myoo nish′ən) *vt.* [< ff.] to provide with munitions

mu·ni·tions (-ənz) *n.pl.* [< MFr. *munition* < L. *munitio*, a fortifying, defending < *munire*, to fortify < *moenia*, fortifications < IE. base **mei-*, to fortify, whence L. *murus*, wall & MERE[3]] war supplies; esp., weapons and ammunition

mun·nion (mun′yən) *n.* archaic var. of MULLION

Mun·ro (mən rō′), **H**(ector) **H**(ugh) *see* SAKI

Mun·ster (mun′stər) province of SW Ireland: 9,315 sq. mi.; pop. 859,000

Mün·ster (mün′stər) city in NW West Germany, in North Rhine-Westphalia: pop. 196,000

munt·jac, munt·jak (munt′jak) *n.* [< Jav. & Malay *mĕnjaṅan*] any of various small, jungle deer (genus *Muntiacus*) of SE Asia and the East Indies: the males have horns and long, sharp, tusklike, canine teeth

mu·on (myōō′än) *n.* [MU + (MES)ON] a positively or negatively charged meson with a mass 207 times that of an electron: it decays into an electron and two neutrinos with a mean life of 2.2×10^{-6} seconds and interacts very weakly with matter —**mu·on′ic** *adj.*

mu·ral (myoor′əl) *adj.* [Fr. < L. *muralis*, of a wall < *murus:* see MUNITIONS] **1.** of, on, in, or for a wall **2.** like a wall —*n.* a picture, esp. a large one, painted directly on a wall or ceiling, or a large photograph, etc. attached directly to a wall

mu·ral·ist (-ist) *n.* a painter of murals

Mu·ra·sa·ki Shi·ki·bu (mōō′rä sä′kē shē′kē bōō′), **Lady** 978?–1031? A.D.; Jap. novelist & poet

Mu·rat (mü rä′), **Jo·a·chim** (zhô á kēm′) 1767?–1815; Fr. marshal under Napoleon; king of Naples (1808–15)

Mur·ci·a (mur′shə, -shē·ə; *Sp.* mōōr′thyä) **1.** region & former kingdom of SE Spain **2.** city in this region: pop. 256,000

☆**Mur·cott** (mur′kät) *n.* [after Charles *Murcott* Smith, Florida citrus grower, who developed the strain c. 1922] a citrus fruit with a deep-orange pulp, probably a cross between a tangerine and a sweet orange hybrid, easily peeled and segmented for eating: also **Mur′cot** (**orange**)

mur·der (mur′dər) *n.* [ME. *murthir, mordre* < OE. & OFr.: OE. *morthor*, akin to ON. *morth*, Goth. *maurthr*; OFr. *mordre* < cognate Frank. **morth:* all ult. < IE. **mrtóm* < base **mer-:* cf. MORTAL] **1.** the unlawful and malicious or premeditated killing of one human being by another; also, any killing done while committing some other felony, as rape or robbery ☆**2.** [Colloq.] something very hard, unsafe, or disagreeable to do or deal with —*vt.* **1.** to kill (a person) unlawfully and with malice **2.** to kill

inhumanly or barbarously, as in warfare **3.** to spoil, mar, etc., as in performance [a song *murdered* in the rendition] —*vi.* to commit murder —*SYN.* see KILL[1] —☆**get away with murder** [Slang] to escape detection of or punishment for a blameworthy act —**murder will out 1.** a murder or murderer will always be revealed **2.** any secret or wrong-doing will be revealed sooner or later —**mur′der·er** *n.* —**mur′der·ess** *n.fem.*

mur·der·ous (-əs) *adj.* **1.** of, having the nature of, or characteristic of murder; brutal [a *murderous* act] **2.** capable or guilty of, or intending, murder ☆**3.** [Colloq.] very difficult, disagreeable, dangerous, trying, etc. —**mur′der·ous·ly** *adv.* —**mur′der·ous·ness** *n.*

mure (myoor) *vt.* **mured, mur′ing** [ME. *muren* < MFr. *murer* < LL.(Ec.) *murare*, to provide with walls < *murus*, wall: see MURAL] *same as* IMMURE

Mu·res (moo resh′) river flowing west from the Carpathian Mountains through C & W Romania, into the Tisza in SE Hungary: 470 mi.

mu·rex (myoor′eks) *n.*, *pl.* **-ri·ces′** (-ə sēz′), **-rex·es** [ModL., name of the genus < L., the purple fish < IE. base *mus, whence MOUSE, Gr. *myax*, sea mussel] any of a genus (*Murex*) of flesh-eating snails, found in warm salt waters and having a rough, spiny shell: some species yield a purple substance formerly valued as a dye

Mur·frees·bor·o (mur′frēz bur′ō, -ə) [after Col. Hardy *Murfree* (1752–1809)] city in C Tenn.: site of a Civil War battle (1863): pop. 26,000

mu·ri·ate (myoor′ē āt′, -it) *n.* [Fr. < *muriatique:* see MURIATIC ACID] [Now Rare] a salt of hydrochloric acid; chloride; esp., potassium chloride, used as a fertilizer

mu·ri·at·ic acid (myoor′ē at′ik) [Fr. *muriatique* < L. *muriaticus*, pickled < *muria*, brine < IE. *meuro- base *meu-, damp, musty, whence MOSS, MIRE] hydrochloric acid: now only a commercial term

mu·ri·cate (myoor′ə kāt′) *adj.* [< L. *muricatus*, pointed, shaped like a purple fish < *murex*, MUREX] rough, with short, sharp points: also **mu′ri·cat′ed**

mu·rid (myoor′id) *n.* [< ModL. *Muridae* < *Mus* (gen. *Muris*), type genus < L., MOUSE] any of a family (*Muridae*) of rodents, including the old-world rats and mice

Mu·ri·el (myoor′ē əl) [prob. < Celt., as in Ir. *Muirgheal* < *muir*, the sea + *geal*, bright] a feminine name

Mu·ril·lo (mōō rē′lyō; E. myoo ril′ō), **Bar·to·lo·mé Es·te·ban** (bär′tō lō me′ es te′bän) 1617–82; Sp. painter

mu·rine (myoor′in, -in) *adj.* [L. *murinus* < *mus* (gen. *muris*), MOUSE] of the murids, or family of rodents including the rats and mice —*n.* a murine rodent

murk (murk) *n.* [ME. *mirke* < ON. *myrkr*, dark, akin to OE. *mirce*, dark] darkness; gloom —*adj.* [Archaic] dark or dim

murk·y (mur′kē) *adj.* **murk′i·er, murk′i·est** [ME. *mirky*] **1.** dark or gloomy **2.** heavy and obscure with smoke, mist, etc. [the *murky* air] —*SYN.* see DARK —**murk′i·ly** *adv.* —**murk′i·ness** *n.*

Mur·mansk (moor mänsk′) seaport on the NW coast of Kola Peninsula, U.S.S.R., on the Barents Sea: pop. 279,000

mur·mur (mur′mər) *n.* [ME. *murmure* < OFr. < L., a murmur, roar, muttering < IE. echoic base *mormor-, *murmur-, whence Sans. *marmara*-, Gr. *mormurein*] **1.** a low, indistinct, continuous sound, as of a stream, far-off voices, etc. **2.** a mumbled or muttered complaint **3.** *Med.* any abnormal sound heard by auscultation of various parts of the body; esp., such a sound in the region of the heart —*vi.* **1.** to make a murmur **2.** to mumble or mutter a complaint —*vt.* to say in a murmur —**mur′mur·er** *n.* —**mur′mur·ing** *adj.*

SYN.—**murmur** implies a continuous flow of words or sounds in a low, indistinct voice and may apply to utterances of satisfaction or dissatisfaction [to *murmur* a prayer]; **mutter** usually suggests angry or discontented words or sounds of this kind [to *mutter* curses]; to **mumble** is to utter almost inaudible or inarticulate sounds in low tones, with the mouth nearly closed [an old woman *mumbling* to herself]

mur·mur·ous (-əs) *adj.* characterized by or making a murmur or murmurs —**mur′mur·ous·ly** *adv.*

mur·phy (mur′fē) *n.*, *pl.* **-phies** [< *Murphy*, Ir. surname] [Old Slang] a potato

☆**Mur·phy bed** (mur′fē) [after W. L. *Murphy*, its U.S. inventor (c. 1900)] a bed that swings up or folds into a closet or cabinet when not in use

Murphy's Law a facetious or satirical proposition stating that if there is a possibility for something to go wrong, it will go wrong

mur·rain (mur′in) *n.* [ME. *moreine* < OFr. *morine* < L. *mori*, to die: see MORTAL] **1.** any of various infectious diseases of cattle **2.** [Archaic] a pestilence; plague

Mur·ray (mur′ē) [< the surname *Murray* < ? Celt., as in W. *mor*, the sea] **1.** a masculine name **2. (George) Gilbert (Aimé)**, 1866–1957; Brit. classical scholar & statesman, born in Australia **3. Sir James Augustus Henry**, 1837–1915; Brit. lexicographer, born in Scotland **4. Lind·ley** (lind′lē), 1745–1826; Eng. grammarian, born in America

Mur·ray (mur′ē) river in SE Australia, flowing from the Australian Alps into the Indian Ocean: 1,596 mi.

murre (mur) *n.*, *pl.* **murres, murre:** see PLURAL, II, D, 1 [< ?] any of several swimming and diving birds (genus *Uria*) related to the guillemots and auks

murre·let (-lit) *n.* [prec. + -LET] any of a number of small auklike birds found chiefly on N Pacific islands

mur·rey (mur′ē) *n.* [ME. *murry* < OFr. *moree*, a dark-red color < ML. *moratum* < L. *morum*, a mulberry] a purplish-red color; mulberry —*adj.* of this color

mur·rhine (mur′in, -in) *adj.* [L. *murr(h)inus* < *murr(h)a* < Iran., as in Per. *mori*, glass ball] of an ancient Roman semiprecious stone, variously believed to be jade, fluorite, etc., used for making vases and drinking cups

Mur·rum·bidg·ee (mur′əm bij′ē) river in SE Australia, flowing west into the Murray: c. 1,000 mi.

mur·ther (mur′thər) *n.*, *vt.*, *vi.* *obs.* or *dial.* *var.* *of* MURDER

mus. 1. museum 2. music 3. musical 4. musician

Mus. B., Mus. Bac. [L. *Musicae Baccalaureus*] Bachelor of Music

Mus·ca (mus′kə) [L., a fly: see MIDGE] a S constellation

mus·ca·dine (mus′kə din, -dīn′) *n.* [altered < *muscadel*, var. of MUSCATEL] an American grape (*Vitis rotundifolia*) growing in the SE U.S., with small leaves, simple tendrils, and small clusters of large, spherical, musky grapes

‡**mus·cae vo·li·tan·tes** (mus′ē väl′ə tan′tēz, mus′kē) [L., flying flies] specks that appear to float before the eyes, caused by defects or impurities in the vitreous humor

mus·ca·rine (mus′kə rin, -rēn′) *n.* [< ModL. (*Amanita) muscaria*, fly (agaric) < L. *muscarius*, of flies < *musca*, a fly: see MIDGE] an extremely poisonous alkaloid, $C_8H_{19}O_3N$, found in certain mushrooms, rotten fish, etc.

Mus·cat (mus kat′) capital of Muscat and Oman; seaport on the Gulf of Oman: pop. 7,500

mus·cat (mus′kət, -kat) *n.* [Fr. < Pr. < It. *moscato*, musk, wine, lit., having the smell or flavor of musk < LL. *muscus*, MUSK] **1.** a variety of sweet European grape from which muscatel and raisins are made **2.** *same as* MUSCATEL (sense 1)

Muscat and Oman independent sultanate in SE Arabia: 82,000 sq. mi.; pop. c. 600,000; cap. Muscat

mus·ca·tel (mus′kə tel′) *n.* [ME. *muscadelle* < OFr. *muscadel* < Pr. or < It. *moscadello*, orig. dim of Pr. *muscat*, It. *muscato*, MUSCAT] **1.** a rich, sweet wine made from the muscat **2.** *same as* MUSCAT (sense 1) Also **mus′ca·del′** (-del′)

mus·cid (mus′id) *adj.* [< ModL. *Muscidae*, name of the family < L. *musca*, a fly: see MIDGE] of the family (Muscidae) of two-winged insects that includes the common housefly —*n.* a muscid insect

mus·cle (mus′'l) *n.* [Fr. < L. *musculus*, a muscle, lit., little mouse (from the fancied resemblance between the movements of a mouse and muscle), dim. of *mus*, MOUSE] **1.** any of the body organs consisting of bundles of cells or fibers that can be contracted and expanded to produce bodily movements **2.** the tissue making up such an organ **3.** muscular strength; brawn ☆**4.** [Colloq.] power or influence, esp. when based on force or threats of force —*vi.* **-cled, -cling** ☆[Colloq.] to make one's way or take control by sheer strength or force or threats of force (usually with *in*)

mus·cle-bound (-bound′) *adj.* **1.** having some of the muscles enlarged and less elastic, as from too much exercise **2.** not flexible or adaptive; rigid

muscle sense *same as* KINESTHESIA

mus·co·va·do (mus′kə vā′dō, -vä′-) *n.* [Sp. *mascabado* (or Port. *mascavado*), unrefined, of inferior quality < Sp. *mascabar*, to depreciate] the dark raw sugar that remains after the molasses has been extracted from the juice of the sugar cane

Mus·co·vite (mus′kə vīt′) *n.* **1.** a native or inhabitant of Muscovy; Russian **2.** an inhabitant of Moscow —*adj.* **1.** of Muscovy; Russian **2.** of Moscow

mus·co·vite (mus′kə vīt′) *n.* [formerly called *Muscovy glass:* see -ITE[2]] the common, light colored mica, $KAl_3Si_3O_{10}(OH)_2$, used as an electrical insulator

Mus·co·vy (mus′kə vē) **1.** former grand duchy surrounding and including Moscow, that expanded into the Russian Empire under Ivan IV **2.** *former name of* RUSSIA

Muscovy duck [altered (after prec.) < MUSK DUCK] any of a number of varieties of domestic duck (*Cairina moschata*) characterized by a large crest, red wattles, and its wheezy sound

mus·cu·lar (mus′kyə lər) *adj.* [< L. *musculus* (see MUSCLE) + -AR] **1.** of, consisting of, or accomplished by a muscle or muscles **2.** having well-developed or prominent muscles; strong; brawny **3.** suggestive of great physical strength; vigorous; powerful —**mus′cu·lar′i·ty** (-lar′ə tē) *n.* —**mus′cu·lar·ly** *adv.*

muscular dystrophy a chronic, noncontagious disease characterized by a progressive wasting of the muscles

mus·cu·la·ture (mus′kyə lə chər) *n.* [Fr. < L. *musculus*] the arrangement of the muscles of a body or of some part of the body; muscular system

mus·cu·lo- (mus′kyə lō, -lə) [< L. *musculus*, MUSCLE] *a combining form meaning* muscle or the muscles (and): also, before a vowel, **mus′cul-**

Mus. D., Mus. Doc., Mus. Dr. [L. *Musicae Doctor*] Doctor of Music

Muse (myōōz) *n.* [ME. < OFr. < L. *musa* < Gr. *mousa*, a Muse, music, eloquence < ? IE. base *mendh-*, to pay attention to, be lively, whence ON. *munda*, to strive] **1.** *Gr. Myth.* any of the nine goddesses who presided over literature and the arts and sciences; Calliope, Clio, Euterpe, Melpomene, Terpsichore, Erato, Polyhymnia (or Polymnia), Urania, or Thalia **2.** [m-] *a)* the spirit that is thought to inspire a poet or other artist; source of genius or inspiration *b)* [Now Rare] a poet

muse (myōōz) *vi.* **mused, mus′ing** [ME. *musen* < OFr. *muser*, to ponder, loiter, orig., ? to stand with muzzle in the air (< *musel*, MUZZLE)] to think deeply and at length; meditate —*vt.* to think or say meditatively —*n.* a musing; deep meditation —*SYN.* see PONDER

muse·ful (-fəl) *adj.* [MUSE + -FUL] [Archaic] meditative

mu·sette (myōō zet′) *n.* [ME. < OFr. < *muser*, to play music, MUSE] **1.** a small French bagpipe of the 17th and 18th cent. **2.** a soft pastoral melody, in imitation of the tunes played on this **3.** *same as* MUSETTE BAG

musette bag *Mil.* a small bag of canvas or leather for toilet articles, etc., worn suspended from a shoulder strap, as by soldiers or hikers

mu·se·um (myōō zē′əm) *n.* [L. < Gr. *mouseion*, place for the Muses or for study < *mousa*, MUSE] an institution, building, or room for preserving and exhibiting artistic, historical, or scientific objects

mush¹ (mush) *n.* [prob. var. of MASH] **1.** a thick porridge made by boiling meal, esp. cornmeal, in water or milk **2.** any thick, soft, yielding mass **3.** [Colloq.] maudlin sentimentality —*vt.* [Chiefly Brit. Dial.] to make into mush; crush

mush² (mush) *interj.* [prob. < *mush on*, altered < Fr. *marchons*, let's go < *marcher*, to go, move forward] in Canada and Alaska, a shout commanding sled dogs to start or to go faster —*vi.* to travel on foot over snow, usually with a dog sled —*n.* a journey by mushing

mush·room (mush′rōōm′, -room′) *n.* [ME. < OFr. *moisseron* < LL. *mussirio* (gen. *mussirionis*)] **1.** any of various rapid-growing, fleshy fungi (esp. class Basidiomycetes), typically having a stalk capped with an umbrellalike top; esp., in popular use, any edible variety, as distinguished from the poisonous ones (*toadstools*) **2.** anything like a mushroom in shape or rapid growth —*adj.* **1.** of or made with mushrooms **2.** like a mushroom in shape or rapid growth —*vi.* **1.** to grow or spread rapidly **2.** to flatten out at the end so as to resemble a mushroom

mush·y (mush′ē) *adj.* **mush′i·er, mush′i·est 1.** like mush; thick, soft, and yielding **2.** [Colloq.] affectionate or sentimental in a maudlin fashion —**mush′i·ly** *adv.*

mu·sic (myōō′zik) *n.* [ME. *musike* < OFr. *musique* < L. *musica* < Gr. *mousikē* (*technē*), musical (art), orig. an art of the Muses < *mousa*, MUSE] **1.** the art and science of combining vocal or instrumental sounds or tones in varying melody, harmony, rhythm, and timbre, esp. so as to form structurally complete and emotionally expressive compositions **2.** the sounds or tones so arranged, or the arrangement of these **3.** any rhythmic sequence of pleasing sounds, as of birds, water, etc. **4.** *a)* a particular form, style, etc. of musical composition or a particular class of musical works or pieces [folk *music*] *b)* the body of musical works of a particular style, place, period, or composer **5.** the written or printed score of a musical composition **6.** ability to respond to or take pleasure in music [no *music* in his soul] **7.** [Rare or Obs.] a group of musical performers —☆**face the music** [Colloq.] to accept the consequences of one's actions, however unpleasant —**set to music** to compose music for (a poem, etc.)

mu·si·cal (-zi k′l) *adj.* [ME. < ML. *musicalis* < L. *musica*] **1.** of or for the creation, production, or performance of music **2.** having the nature of music; melodious or harmonious **3.** fond of, sensitive to, or skilled in music **4.** set to music; accompanied by music —*n.* ☆**1.** a theatrical or film production, often elaborately costumed and staged, with dialogue developing the story line and an integrated musical score featuring songs and dances in a popular idiom: in full, variously, **musical comedy, musical play, musical drama 2.** [Archaic] *same as* MUSICALE —**mu′si·cal′i·ty** (-kal′ə tē) *n.* —**mu′si·cal·ly** *adv.*

musical chairs a game in which the players march to music around a row of empty chairs (always containing one fewer than the number of players) and rush to find a seat each time the music stops: one player is eliminated in each round

☆**mu·si·cale** (myōō′zə kal′) *n.* [Fr.] a party or social affair featuring a musical program

musical saw a handsaw held upright between the knees and variously flexed and stroked with a violin bow to produce musical tones

music box a mechanical musical instrument consisting of a case containing a bar with tuned steel teeth that are struck by pins so arranged on a revolving cylinder as to produce a certain tune or tunes

music drama a form of opera, specif. as developed by Richard Wagner, characterized by a continuous flow of orchestral music, with an integrative use of musical themes (*leitmotifs*), and singing that is free from formal division into arias, recitative, etc.

music hall 1. an auditorium for musical or theatrical productions **2.** [Brit.] a vaudeville theater

mu·si·cian (myōō zish′ən) *n.* [ME. < MFr. *musicien*] a person skilled in music; esp., a professional performer, composer, or conductor of music —**mu·si′cian·ly** *adj.* —**mu·si′cian·ship′** *n.*

music of the spheres an ethereal music supposed by Pythagoras and other early mathematicians to be produced by the movements of the heavenly bodies

mu·si·col·o·gy (myōō′zi käl′ə jē) *n.* [It. *musicologia:* see MUSIC & -LOGY] the systematized study of the science, history, forms, and methods of music —**mu′si·co·log′i·cal** (-kə läj′i k′l) *adj.* —**mu′si·col′o·gist** *n.*

music stand a rack to hold sheets of music for a performer or conductor

mus·ing (myōō′zin) *adj.* that muses; meditative —*n.* meditation; reflection —**mus′ing·ly** *adv.*

‡**mu·sique con·crète** (mü zēk kōn kret′) [Fr., concrete (as opposed to abstract) music] a musiclike art form composed directly on magnetic tape by the electronic manipulation, distortion, or transformation of natural sounds and noises, as of musical instruments, rain, etc.

mus·jid (mus′jid) *n. same as* MASJID

musk (musk) *n.* [ME. < OFr. *musc* < LL. *muscus* < Gr. *moschos* < Per. *mušk*, musk < Sans. *muṣka*, testicle, dim. of *mus*, MOUSE] **1.** a substance with a strong, penetrating odor, obtained from a small sac (**musk bag**) under the skin of the abdomen in the male musk deer: used as the basis of numerous perfumes **2.** a similar substance secreted by certain other animals, as the alligator, musk ox, etc. **3.** the odor of any of these substances, now often created synthetically **4.** any of several plants having a musky scent

musk deer a small, hornless deer (*Moschus moschiferus*) of the uplands of C Asia: the male secretes musk

musk duck 1. an Australian duck (*Biziura lobata*) with an inflatable leathery pouch beneath the lower jaw, spikelike tail feathers, and a musklike odor during the breeding season **2.** *same as* MUSCOVY DUCK

mus·keg (mus′keg) *n.* [< AmInd. (Ojibway) native name] a kind of bog or marsh containing thick layers of decaying vegetable matter, mosses, etc., found esp. in Canada and Alaska and often overgrown with moss

Mus·ke·gon (məs kē′gən) [< Algonquian tribal name *Maskegon*, lit., marsh dwellers] city in W Mich., on Lake Michigan: pop. 45,000

☆**mus·kel·lunge** (mus′kə lunj′) *n., pl.* **-lunge′** [< AmInd. (Ojibway) *maskinoje* < *mas*, great + *kinoje*, a pike (fish)] a very large pike (*Esox masquinongy*) of the Great Lakes and upper Mississippi drainages, valued as a game and food fish: also called **mus′kie** (-kē)

mus·ket (mus′kit) *n.* [MFr. *mosquet* < It. *moschetto*, musket, orig., fledged arrow < *mosca*, a fly < L. *musca:* see MIDGE] a smooth-bore, long-barreled firearm, fired from the shoulder and used esp. by infantry soldiers before the invention of the rifle

mus·ket·eer (mus′kə tir′) *n.* [Fr. *mousquetaire*] formerly, a soldier armed with a musket: cf. MOUSQUETAIRE

mus·ket·ry (mus′kə trē) *n.* [Fr. *mousqueterie*] **1.** the skill of firing muskets or other small arms **2.** *a)* muskets collectively *b)* musketeers collectively

musk·mel·on (musk′mel′ən) *n.* [MUSK + MELON] **1.** *a)* any of several round or oblong fruits growing on a trailing vine (*Cucumis melo*) of the gourd family, as the cantaloupe: they have a thick, ribbed rind, sweet, juicy flesh, and a musky odor *b)* this plant **2.** popularly, any of various other melons, as the casaba

☆**Mus·ko·ge·an** (mus kō′gē ən, -jē·) *adj.* [< MUSKOGEE] designating or of a N. American Indian language family of the SE U.S., consisting of four languages each of which is represented by two dialects (as the dialects Choctaw and Chickasaw): also **Mus·kho′ge·an**

Mus·ko·gee (mus kō′gē) [< *n.*] city in E Okla.: pop. 37,000 —*n., pl.* **-gees, -gee** [< AmInd. (? Algonquian) < ?] *same as* CREEK

musk ox a hardy ox (*Ovibos moschatus*) of arctic America and Greenland, with a long, coarse, hairy coat, large, curved horns, and a musklike odor

musk plant a perennial N. American plant (*Mimulus moschatus*) of the figwort family, with yellow tubular flowers and, sometimes, a musky odor

☆**musk·rat** (musk′rat′) *n., pl.* **-rats′, -rat′:** see PLURAL, II, D, 1 **1.** a N. American rodent (*Ondatra zibethica*) living in water and having a glossy brown fur, a long, flattened tail, webbed hind feet, and a musklike odor **2.** its fur

musk rose a Mediterranean rose (*Rosa moschata*) with fragrant, usually white, flowers

☆**musk turtle** any of several small, aquatic turtles (genus *Sternotherus*), found in E N. America and having a heavy, musky scent

musk·y (mus′kē) *adj.* **musk′i·er, musk′i·est** of, like, or smelling of musk —**musk′i·ness** *n.*

MUSKRAT
(body 9–13 in. long; tail 7–11 in. long)

Mus·lim (muz′ləm, mooz′-) *n., adj.* same as MOSLEM

mus·lin (muz′lin) *n.* [Fr. *mousseline* < It. *mussolino* < *mussolo*, muslin < *Mussolo* (< Ar. *Mōsul*), Mosul, city in Iraq, where it was made] any of various strong, often sheer cotton cloths of plain weave; esp., a heavy variety used for sheets, pillowcases, etc.

muslin delaine same as DELAINE

☆**mus·quash** (mus′kwäsh, -kwôsh) *n., pl.* **-quash·es, -quash:** see PLURAL, II, D, 1 [< AmInd. (Algonquian), akin to Abnaki *muskwessu*, it is red] same as MUSKRAT

muss (mus) *n.* [prob. var. of MESS] 1. [Now Rare] a mess; disorder 2. [Old Slang or Dial.] a squabble; row; commotion —*vt.* to make messy or disordered; disarrange (often with *up*)

mus·sel (mus′l) *n.* [ME. *muscle* < OE., akin to OHG. *muscula*, both < VL. *muscula*, for L. *musculus*, mussel, MUSCLE] any of various bivalve mollusks; specif., *a*) any of several often edible, saltwater genera (esp. *Mytilus* and *Modiolaria*) attached to rocks, ships, etc. by threadlike secretions *b*) any of many large, freshwater mollusks (as family Unionidae), found esp. in rivers of the C U.S. and having a shell with a pearly inner surface, formerly made into buttons

Mus·set (mü se′), (**Louis Charles**) **Al·fred de** (ál fred′ də) 1810–57; Fr. poet. & writer

Mus·so·li·ni (mōōs′sō lē′nē; E. moos′ə lē′nē, mus′-), **Be·ni·to** (be nē′tō) 1883–1945; It. dictator; Fascist prime minister of Italy (1922–43): executed

Mus·sorg·sky (moo sôrg′skē), **Mo·dest Pe·tro·vich** (mô dyest′ pyi trô′vich) 1839–81; Russ. composer

Mus·sul·man (mus′′l mən) *n., pl.* **-mans** [Per. *musulmān*, a Moslem < Ar. *muslim*] [Now Rare] a Moslem

muss·y (mus′ē) *adj.* **muss′i·er, muss′i·est** [Colloq.] messy; disordered, untidy, rumpled, etc.

must[1] (must; *unstressed* məst) *v.aux. pt.* **must** [ME. *moste*, pt., had to < OE., pt. of *motan*, may, akin to Goth. (*ga*)*mot*, (I) find room, am permitted, prob. < IE. **mōt-*, var. of base **med-*, to measure, whence METE] an auxiliary used with the infinitive of various verbs (without *to*) to express: 1. compulsion, obligation, requirement, or necessity [I *must* pay her] 2. probability [then you *must* be my cousin] 3. certainty or inevitability [all men *must* die] *Must* is sometimes used elliptically, the verb being understood [shoot if you *must*] —*n.* [Colloq.] something that must be done, had, read, seen, etc. [this book is a *must*] —*adj.* [Colloq.] that must be done, etc.; necessary; essential

must[2] (must) *n.* [Hind. *mast*, intoxicated < Per. *mast*] a state of frenzy in animals, esp. in the male elephant, usually associated with sexual heat —*adj.* in must

must[3] (must) *n.* [ME. < OE. < L. *mustum*, new wine, neut. of *mustus*, new, fresh < IE. base **meu-*, moist, whence MOSS] the juice pressed from grapes or other fruit before it has fermented; new wine

must[4] (must) *n.* [back-formation < MUSTY] a musty quality or state; mustiness

mus·tache (mə stash′, mus′tash) *n.* [Fr. *moustache* < It. *mostacchio*, mustache < MGr. *mustaki* < Gr. *mystax*, upper lip, mustache < *mastax*, a mouth, jaws < IE. base **menth-*, whence MOUTH] 1. the hair on the upper lip of men: sometimes used in the plural in reference to the two halves of the upper lip 2. the hair or bristles growing about the mouth in some animals

mus·ta·chio (məs tä′shō, -shē ō′) *n., pl.* **-chios** [< Sp. *mostacho* or It. *mostaccio*] a mustache, esp. a large, bushy one —**mus·ta′chioed** *adj.*

Mus·ta·fa Ke·mal (moos′tä fä ke mäl′) same as KEMAL ATATURK

☆**mus·tang** (mus′taŋ) *n.* [AmSp. *mestengo* < Sp. *mesteño*, belonging to the graziers, wild < *mesta*, company of graziers, orig. a group < ML. *mixta*, a mixture < fem. of L. *mixtus*, a mingling, orig. pp. of *miscere*, MIX] a small wild or half-wild horse of the SW plains of the U.S.

mus·tard (mus′tərd) *n.* [ME. *mustarde* < OFr. *moustarde* < *moust*, must < L. *mustum* (see MUST[3]): orig. prepared with must as an ingredient] 1. any of several annual plants (genus *Brassica*) of the mustard family, with yellow flowers and slender pods containing round seeds 2. the ground or powdered seeds of some species (as *Brassica nigra*) of these plants, often prepared as a paste, used as a pungent seasoning for foods, or as a counter-irritant in medicine 3. the color of ground mustard, a dark yellow —*adj.* designating or of a family (Cruciferae) of plants with cross-shaped flowers, pointed pods, and strong, cabbagelike odors, including cabbage, turnip, broccoli, radish, horseradish, alyssum, etc. —☆**cut the mustard** [Colloq.] to come up to expectation or to the required standard

mustard gas [from its odor, like that of ground mustard] an oily, volatile liquid, (CH₂ClCH₂)₂S, used in warfare as a poison gas because of its extremely irritating, blistering, and disabling effects

mustard oil an oil extracted from mustard seed, used in making soap

mustard plaster a paste made with powdered mustard, spread on a cloth and applied to the skin as a counter-irritant and rubefacient

mus·tee (mus tē′, mus′tē) *n.* [altered < MESTIZO] 1. same as OCTOROON 2. any person of mixed ancestry

mus·te·line (mus′tə lin′, -lin) *adj.* [L. *mustelinus* < *mustela*, a weasel, akin to *mus*, MOUSE] designating or of a large family (Mustelidae) of fur-bearing mammals, including the weasel, marten, polecat, mink, etc.

mus·ter (mus′tər) *vt.* [ME. *mousteren* < OFr. *moustrer*, to exhibit, show < ML. *mustrare* < L. *monstrare*, to show < *monere*, to warn, admonish: see MONITOR] 1. to assemble or summon (troops, etc.), as for inspection, roll call, or service 2. to put through a roll call 3. to gather together and display; collect; summon (often with *up*) [to *muster* up strength] 4. to have in number; amount to —*vi.* to come together or gather; specif., to assemble as for inspection or roll call —*n.* 1. a gathering together or assembling, as of troops for inspection 2. *a*) the persons or things assembled; assemblage *b*) the sum of these 3. the roll, or list, of men in a military or naval unit: also **muster roll** —*SYN.* see GATHER —☆**muster in** (or out) to enlist in (or discharge from) military service —**pass muster** to measure up to the required standards

musth (must) *n.* same as MUST[2]

must·n't (mus′nt) must not

mus·ty (mus′tē) *adj.* **-ti·er, -ti·est** [< ? earlier *moisty* < MOIST] 1. having a stale, moldy smell or taste, as an unused room, food kept in a damp place, etc. 2. stale or trite; worn-out; antiquated [musty ideas] 3. dull; apathetic —*SYN.* see STINKING —**mus′ti·ly** *adv.* —**mus′ti·ness** *n.*

mu·ta·ble (myōōt′ə b'l) *adj.* [ME. < L. *mutabilis*, changeable < *mutare*, to change: see MISS[1]] 1. that can be changed 2. tending to frequent change; inconstant; fickle 3. subject to mutation —**mu′ta·bil′i·ty, mu′ta·ble·ness** *n.* —**mu′ta·bly** *adv.*

mu·ta·gen (myōōt′ə jən) *n.* [MUTA(TION) + -GEN] *Biol.* any agent or substance, as X-rays, mustard gas, etc., capable of noticeably increasing the frequency of mutation —**mu′ta·gen′ic** (-jen′ik) *adj.* —**mu′ta·gen′i·cal·ly** *adv.*

mu·ta·gen·e·sis (myōōt′ə jen′ə sis) *n.* [MUTA(TION) + GENESIS] the occurrence or production of mutation

mu·tant (myōōt′nt) *adj.* [< L. *mutans*, prp. of *mutare*: see MISS[1]] having to do with or undergoing mutation —*n.* an animal or plant with inheritable characteristics that differ from those of the parents; sport

mu·tate (myōō′tāt) *vi., vt.* **-tat·ed, -tat·ing** [< L. *mutatus*, pp. of *mutare*, to change: see MISS[1]] to change; specif., to undergo or cause to undergo mutation

mu·ta·tion (myōō tā′shən) *n.* [ME. *mutacioun* < OFr. *mutacion* < L. *mutatio* < *mutare*, to change: see MISS[1]] 1. a changing or being changed 2. a change, as in form, nature, qualities, etc. 3. *Biol. a*) a sudden variation in some inheritable characteristic in a germ cell of an individual animal or plant, as distinguished from a variation resulting from generations of gradual change *b*) an individual resulting from such variation; mutant *c*) an abrupt and relatively permanent change in somatic cells that is transmitted only to daughter cells and can be inherited only in plants that reproduce asexually 4. *Linguis.* umlaut —**mu·ta′tion·al** *adj.* —**mu·ta′tion·al·ly** *adv.*

‡**mu·ta·tis mu·tan·dis** (myoo tāt′is myoo tan′dis, -tät′-) [L.] the necessary changes having been made

mu·ta·tive (myōōt′ə tiv) *adj.* [ML. *mutativus*] of, tending to, or characterized by mutation

mutch·kin (much′k'n) *n.* [ME. *muchekyn* < obs. Du. *mudseken*, a measure of capacity] [Scot.] a measure of liquid volume, equal to a little less than a pint

mute (myōōt) *adj.* [ME. *mewet* < OFr. *muet* < *mu* < L. *mutus*, silent: for IE. base see MOPE] 1. not speaking; voluntarily silent: often used figuratively 2. unable to speak 3. not spoken [a *mute* appeal] 4. not pronounced; silent, as the *e* in *mouse* 5. *Law* refusing to plead when arraigned: used esp. in **stand mute**, to refuse to plead guilty or not guilty —*n.* 1. a person who does not speak; specif., one who, deaf from infancy, has not learned to speak; deaf-mute 2. [Obs.] a hired mourner at a funeral 3. a letter that is not pronounced 4. *Law* a defendant who refuses to plead when arraigned 5. *Music* any of various devices used to soften or muffle the tone of an instrument, as a block placed within the bell of a brass instrument or a piece set onto the bridge of a violin —*vt.* **mut′ed, mut′ing** 1. to soften or muffle the sound of (a musical instrument, etc.), as with a mute 2. to subdue the intensity of (a color) —*SYN.* see VOICELESS —**mute′ly** *adv.* —**mute′ness** *n.*

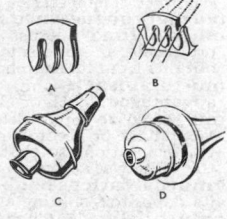

MUTES
(A, violin mute; B, on violin bridge; C, trumpet mute; D, in bell of trumpet)

mu·ti·cous (myōōt′i kəs) *adj.* [L. *muticus*, curtailed,

docked] **1.** *Bot.* lacking a point or awn; blunt **2.** *Zool.* lacking defensive structures, as teeth, claws, etc. Also **mu′ti·cate′** (-kāt′)

mu·ti·late (myōōt′'l āt′) *vt.* **-lat′ed, -lat′ing** [< L. *mutilatus*, pp. of *mutilare*, to maim, mutilate < *mutilus*, maimed] **1.** to cut off or damage a limb or other important part of (a person or animal) **2.** to damage, injure, or otherwise make imperfect, esp. by removing an essential part or parts [to *mutilate* a book by censorship] —*SYN.* see MAIM —**mu′ti·la′tion** *n.* —**mu′ti·la′tive** *adj.* —**mu′ti·la′tor** *n.*

mu·ti·neer (myōōt′'n ir′) *n.* [Fr. *mutinier* < *mutin:* see MUTINY] a person guilty of mutiny

mu·ti·nous (myōōt′'n əs) *adj.* **1.** of, engaged in, or inclined to mutiny **2.** like or characteristic of mutiny —**mu′ti·nous·ly** *adv.* —**mu′ti·nous·ness** *n.*

mu·ti·ny (myōōt′'n ē) *n., pl.* **-nies** [< earlier *mutine*, to rebel < Fr. *mutiner* < OFr. *mutin*, mutinous < *meute*, a revolt < LL. *movita*, movement, ult. < L. *movere*, MOVE] revolt against and, often, forcible resistance to constituted authority; esp., rebellion of soldiers or sailors against their officers —*vi.* **-nied, -ny·ing** to participate in a mutiny; revolt against constituted authority —*SYN.* see REBELLION

mut·ism (myōōt′iz'm) *n.* [Fr. *mutisme* < L. *mutus*, MUTE] the condition of being mute; esp., a refusal to speak, as a manifestation of a psychotic disorder

Mu·tsu·hi·to (mōōt′sə hēt′ō) 1852–1912; emperor of Japan (1867–1912): see MEIJI

☆**mutt** (mut) *n.* [prob. contr. < MUTTONHEAD] [Slang] **1.** a stupid person; blockhead **2.** a mongrel dog; cur

mut·ter (mut′ər) *vi.* [ME. *moteren*, akin to G. *muttern*, ult. < IE. echoic base **mu-* (see MOPE), whence L. *muttire*] **1.** to speak in low, indistinct tones without much movement of the lips, as in complaining or in speaking to oneself **2.** to complain or grumble **3.** to make a low, rumbling, threatening sound, as thunder —*vt.* to say in low, indistinct, often angry or discontented, tones —*n.* **1.** the act of muttering **2.** something muttered; esp., a complaint or grumble —*SYN.* see MURMUR —**mut′ter·er** *n.*

mut·ton (mut′'n) *n.* [ME. *moton* < OFr. *moton*, a ram < ML. *multo*, sheep, prob. of Celt. origin as in W. *mollt*, Ir. *molt*] **1.** the flesh of a sheep, esp. a grown sheep, used as food **2.** [Rare] a sheep —**mut′ton·y** *adj.*

mutton chop 1. a piece cut from the rib of a sheep for broiling or frying **2.** [pl.] side whiskers shaped like mutton chops (i.e., narrow at the top, and broad and rounded at the bottom), with a clean-shaven chin separating the two whiskers; burnsides

mut·ton·head (-hed′) *n.* [Slang] a stupid person

Mut·tra (mut′rə) former name of MATHURA

mu·tu·al (myōō′choo wəl) *adj.* [LME. *mutuall* < MFr. *mutuel* < L. *mutuus*, mutual, reciprocal < *mutare*, to change, exchange: see MISS¹] **1.** *a)* done, felt, etc. by each of two or more for or toward the other or others; reciprocal [*mutual* admiration] *b)* of, or having the same relationship toward, each other or one another [*mutual* enemies] **2.** shared in common; joint [our *mutual* friend] **3.** designating or of a type of insurance in which the policyholders elect the directors, share in the profits, and agree to indemnify one another against loss —**mu·tu·al′i·ty** (-wal′ə tē) *n., pl.* **-ties** —**mu′tu·al·ly** *adv.*

SYN.—**mutual** may be used for an interchange of feeling between two persons [John and Joe are *mutual* enemies] or may imply a sharing jointly with others [the *mutual* efforts of a group]; **reciprocal** implies a return in kind or degree by each of two sides of what is given or demonstrated by the other [a *reciprocal* trade agreement], or it may refer to any inversely corresponding relationship [the *reciprocal* functions of two machine parts]; **common** simply implies a being shared by others or by all the members of a group [our *common* interests]

mutual conductance same as TRANSCONDUCTANCE

mutual fund a trust or corporation formed to invest, ordinarily in diversified securities, the funds which it obtains from its shareholders

mu·tu·al·ism (-iz'm) *n. Biol.* symbiosis with mutual advantage to both or all organisms involved

mu·tu·al·ize (myōō′choo wə līz′) *vt., -i.,* **-ized, -iz′ing** **1.** to make or become mutual **2.** to organize or reorganize (a corporation) so that a majority of shares are held by the employees or customers —**mu′tu·al·i·za′tion** *n.*

☆**mutual savings bank** a savings bank that has no capital, its depositors sharing all the net profits

☆**mu·tu·el** (myōō′choo wəl) *n.* same as PARIMUTUEL

mu·tule (myōō′chool) *n.* [Fr. < L. *mutulus:* see MODILLION] *Archit.* a flat block projecting beneath, and supporting, the corona of a Doric cornice

☆**muu-muu** (mōō′mōō) *n.* [< Haw., lit., cut off] a full, long, loose garment for women, usually in a bright print as orig. worn in Hawaii

☆**Mu·zak** (myōō′zak) *a trademark for* a system of transmitting recorded background music by telephone line or radio to restaurants, stores, factories, etc. —*n.* the music so transmitted, variously regarded as unobtrusive but pervasive, bland and monotonous, etc.

‡**mu·zhik, mu·zjik** (mōō zhēk′, mōō′zhik) *n.* [Russ.] in czarist Russia, a peasant

muz·zle (muz′'l) *n.* [ME. *mosel* . < OFr. *musel*, snout, muzzle, dim. of *mus* < ML. *musum* < ?] **1.** the projecting part of the head of a dog, horse, etc., including the mouth, nose, and jaws; snout **2.** a device, as of straps, fastened over the mouth of an animal to prevent its biting or eating **3.** anything that prevents free speech or discussion **4.** the front end of the barrel of a firearm —*vt.* **-zled, -zling** **1.** to put a muzzle on (an animal) **2.** to prevent from talking or expressing an opinion; gag —**muz′zler** *n.*

muz·zle·load·er (-lōd′ər) *n.* any firearm loaded through the muzzle —**muz′zle·load′ing** *adj.*

muzzle velocity the velocity of a projectile as it leaves the muzzle of a firearm: expressed in feet per second

muz·zy (muz′ē) *adj.* **-zi·er, -zi·est** [prob. < MU(DDY) + (FU)ZZY] [Colloq.] **1.** confused; befuddled **2.** blurred

Mv *Chem.* mendelevium

mv millivolt; millivolts

m.v. 1. market value **2.** mean variation **3.** motor vessel

mw milliwatt; milliwatts

Mwe·ru (mwä′rōō) lake between SE Congo (sense 2) & NE Zambia: c. 1,700 sq. mi.

my (mī; *unstressed, often* mə) *possessive pronominal adj.* [ME. *mi*, shortened form of *min* used before consonants < OE. *min*, of me, my, mine: see MINE¹, ME] of, belonging to, or done by me: also used before some formal title of address [*my* lord, *my* dear Mr. Brown] —*interj.* an exclamation of surprise, dismay, disbelief, etc.: often in combination with other words [Oh, *my! my* goodness! *my* eye!]

my- (mī) same as MYO-: used before a vowel

my·al·gi·a (mī al′jē ə, -jə) *n.* [ModL.: see MYO- & -ALGIA] pain in a muscle or muscles —**my·al′gic** *adj.*

my·as·the·ni·a (mī′əs thē′nē ə) *n.* [ModL.: see MYO- & ASTHENIA] muscular weakness or fatigue —**my′as·then′ic** (-then′ik) *adj.*

myasthenia gra·vis (grā′vis) a disease of faulty nerve conduction characterized by weakness and quick fatigue of muscles, esp. of the face and neck

myc- same as MYCO-: used before a vowel

my·ce·li·um (mī sē′lē əm) *n., pl.* **-li·a** (-ə) [ModL. < Gr. *mykēs*, a mushroom (see MYCO-) + *-lium*, as in EPITHELIUM] the thallus, or vegetative part, of a fungus, made of a mass or network of threadlike tubes —**my·ce′li·al** *adj.*

My·ce·nae (mī sē′nē) ancient city in Argolis, in the NE Peloponnesus

My·ce·nae·an (mī′sə nē′ən) *adj.* **1.** of Mycenae **2.** designating or of a civilization which existed in Greece, Crete, Asia Minor, etc. from c. 1500 to c. 1100 B.C.

-my·cete (mī′sēt, mī sēt′) [< ff.] a combining form meaning one of a specified class of fungi [schizomycete]

-my·ce·tes (mī sēt′ēz) [ModL. < Gr. *mykētes*, pl. of *mykēs*, a mushroom (see MYCO-)] a combining form used in forming the names of classes of fungi [Basidiomycetes]

my·ce·to- (mī sēt′ə) [< Gr. *mykētes:* see prec.] a combining form meaning fungus [mycetoma]

my·ce·to·ma (mī′si tō′mə) *n.* [MYCET(O)- + -OMA] a chronic infection of the skin and subcutaneous tissues, characterized by a tumorous mass consisting mostly of fungi, occurring esp. in warm climates, and usually affecting the foot

my·ce·to·zo·an (mī sēt′ə zō′ən) *n.* [MYCETO- + -ZO(A) + -AN] same as MYXOMYCETE: term used when classified as an animal —*adj.* same as MYXOMYCETOUS

-my·cin (mīs′'n) [< Gr. *mykēs*, fungus (see ff.) + -IN¹] a combining form meaning an antibiotic derived from a fungus [aureomycin]

my·co- (mī′kō, mī′kə) [< Gr. *mykēs*, fungus < IE. base **meuk-*, slippery, whence MUCK, L. *mucus*] a combining form meaning fungus [mycology]

my·co·bac·te·ri·um (mī′kō bak tir′ē əm) *n., pl.* **-ri·a** (-ə) [ModL.: see prec. & BACTERIA] any of a genus (*Mycobacterium*) of rod-shaped, Gram-positive bacteria, including those causing tuberculosis and leprosy

my·col·o·gy (mī käl′ə jē) *n.* [ModL. *mycologia:* see MYCO- & -LOGY] **1.** the branch of botany dealing with fungi **2.** all the fungi of a region —**my·co·log·ic** (mī′kə läj′ik), **my′co·log′i·cal** *adj.* —**my′co·log′i·cal·ly** *adv.*

my·co·plas·ma (mī′kō plaz′mə) *n.* [ModL.: see MYCO- & PLASMA] any of a genus (*Mycoplasma*) of tiny microorganisms, smaller than bacteria but larger than viruses, seemingly the causative agents of many diseases, esp. of the joints and lungs, in man and domestic animals

my·cor·rhi·za (mī′kō rī′zə) *n., pl.* **-zae** (-zē), **-zas** [< MYCO- + Gr. *rhiza*, ROOT¹] an intimate symbiotic association of the mycelium of certain fungi with the root cells of some vascular plants, as certain orchids, in which the hyphae often function as root hairs —**my′cor·rhi′zal** *adj.*

my·co·sis (mī kō′sis) *n., pl.* **-ses** (-sēz) [ModL.: see MYCO- & -OSIS] **1.** the growth of parasitic fungi in any part of the body **2.** a disease caused by such fungi —**my·cot′ic** (-kät′ik) *adj.*

my·dri·a·sis (mi drī′ə sis, mī-) *n.* [LL. < Gr.] prolonged or excessive dilatation of the pupil of the eye, as the result of disease or the administration of a drug

myd·ri·at·ic (mid′rē at′ik) *adj.* of or causing mydriasis —*n.* any drug causing mydriasis

my·e·len·ceph·a·lon (mī′ə len sef′ə län′) *n., pl.* **-la** (-lə) [ModL.: see MYELO- & ENCEPHALON] the posterior part of the embryonic hindbrain

my·e·lin (mī′ə lin) *n.* [G. < Gr. *myelos*, marrow: see MYELO- & -INE⁴] the white, fatty substance forming a sheath about certain nerve fibers —**my′e·lin′ic** *adj.*

my·e·li·tis (mī′ə līt′is) *n.* [ModL.: see MYELO- & -ITIS] inflammation of the spinal cord or the bone marrow

my·e·lo- (mī′ə lō′) [< Gr. *myelos,* marrow, akin to *mys,* MOUSE] *a combining form meaning* the bone marrow, the spinal cord, or myelin: also, before a vowel, **myel-**

my·e·lo·gen·ic (mī′ə lō jen′ik) *adj.* [prec. + -GENIC] produced in or by the bone marrow: also **my′e·log′e·nous** (-läj′ə nəs)

my·e·lo·gram (mī′ə lō gram′) *n.* [MYELO- + -GRAM] an X-ray of the spinal cord, taken after the injection of a substance that will show contrast on the developed photograph —**my′e·log′ra·phy** (-läg′rə fē) *n.*

my·e·loid (mī′ə loid′) *adj.* [MYEL(O)- + -OID] 1. of, like, or derived from bone marrow 2. of the spinal cord

my·e·lo·ma (mī′ə lō′mə) *n., pl.* **-mas, -ma·ta** (-mə tə) [MYEL(O)- + -OMA] a malignant tumor of the bone marrow, consisting generally of abnormal plasma cells —**my′e·lom′a·tous** (-läm′ə təs, -lō′mə-) *adj.*

myg myriagram; myriagrams

my·i·a·sis (mī ī′ə sis) *n.* [< Gr. *myia,* fly + -ASIS] infestation of a body area or cavity by fly maggots

myl myrialiter; myrialiters

☆**My·lar** (mī′lär) *a trademark for* a polyester made in extremely thin sheets of great tensile strength and used for recording tapes, insulating film, fabrics, etc. —*n.* [m-] this substance

mym myriameter; myriameters

my·na, my·nah (mī′nə) *n.* [Hind. *mainā*] any of a group of tropical birds of SE Asia related to the starling; esp., the HILL MYNA

Myn·heer (min her′, -hir′) *n.* [Du. *mijn heer,* lit., my lord] Sir; a Dutch title of address

my·o- (mī′ō, -ə) [< Gr. *mys* (gen. *myos*), a muscle, MOUSE] *a combining form meaning* muscle [*myograph*]

my·o·car·di·o·graph (mī′ə kär′dē ə graf′, gräf′) *n.* [prec. + CARDIOGRAPH] an instrument for recording the movements of the heart muscle

my·o·car·di·tis (-kär dīt′is) *n.* [ModL.: see -ITIS] inflammation of the myocardium

my·o·car·di·um (-kär′dē əm) *n.* [ModL.: see MYO & CARDIO-] the muscular substance of the heart —**my′o·car′di·al** *adj.*

my·oc·lo·nus (mī äk′lə nəs) *n.* [MYO- + CLONUS] involuntary twitching or spasm of a muscle or muscles —**my′o·clon′ic** (mī′ə klän′ik) *adj.*

my·o·e·lec·tric (mī′ō i lek′trik) *adj.* [MYO- + ELECTRIC] designating or of potential developed in a muscle or muscles which is then picked up, amplified, and used to operate various attached prosthetic devices —**my′o·e·lec′tri·cal·ly** *adv.*

my·o·gen·ic (mī′ə jen′ik) *adj.* [MYO- + -GENIC] originating in or produced by a muscle

my·o·glo·bin (mī′ə glō′bin, mī′ə glō′bin) *n.* [MYO- + GLOBIN] an iron-containing protein, similar to hemoglobin, found in muscle and serving as a reservoir for oxygen and carbon dioxide

my·o·graph (mī′ə graf′, -gräf′) *n.* [MYO- + -GRAPH] an instrument for recording muscular contractions

my·ol·o·gy (mī äl′ə jē) *n.* [ModL. *myologia:* see MYO- & -LOGY] the branch of anatomy dealing with the muscles —**my′o·log′ic** (-ə läj′ik), **my′o·log′i·cal** *adj.*

my·o·ma (mī ō′mə) *n., pl.* **-mas, -ma·ta** (-mə tə) [ModL.: see MYO- & -OMA] any tumor consisting of muscular tissue —**my·om′a·tous** (-äm′ə təs, -ō′mə-) *adj.*

my·o·neu·ral (mī′ə noor′əl, -nyoor′-) *adj.* [MYO- + NEURAL] pertaining to both muscle and nerve, esp. to the ending of a nerve of a muscle fiber

my·op·a·thy (mī äp′ə thē) *n.* [MYO- + -PATHY] any disease of a muscle

my·ope (mī′ōp) *n.* [Fr. < LL. *myops* < Gr. *myōps,* shortsighted, blinking < *myein,* to close + *ōps,* EYE] a person having myopia; nearsighted person

my·o·pi·a (mī ō′pē ə) *n.* [ModL. < Gr. *myōpia:* see prec.] 1. an abnormal eye condition in which light rays from distant objects are focused in front of the retina instead of on it, so that the objects are not seen distinctly; nearsightedness 2. lack of foresight —**my·op′ic** (-äp′ik) *adj.* —**my·op′i·cal·ly** *adv.*

my·o·sin (mī′ə sin) *n.* [< Gr. *mys* (gen. *myos*), a muscle, MOUSE + -IN¹] a protein in muscles: see ACTOMYOSIN

my·o·so·tis (mī′ə sōt′is) *n.* [ModL. *Myosotis,* name of the genus < L., mouse ear < Gr. *myosōtis* < *mys* (gen. *myos*), MOUSE + *ōtos,* gen. of *ous,* EAR¹] any of a genus (*Myosotis*) of plants of the borage family, including the forget-me-not, having light-green leaves and white, blue, or pink flowers

my·o·tome (mī′ə tōm′) *n.* [MYO- + -TOME] 1. the bodywall musculature in a single segment of a chordate 2. one of the paired mesodermal masses in a vertebrate embryo from which the musculature develops

my·o·to·ni·a (mī′ə tō′nē ə) *n.* [MYO- + TON(IC) + -IA] prolonged muscular spasm, often a manifestation of certain diseases of muscles —**my′o·ton′ic** (-tän′ik) *adj.*

My·ra¹ (mī′rə) [< ? Ir. *Moira, Moyra*] a feminine name

My·ra² (mī′rə) seaport in ancient Lycia, SW Asia Minor

Myr·dal (mür′däl; E. mʉr′däl), (**Karl**) **Gun·nar** (goon′är) 1898– ; Swed. economist & sociologist

myr·i·a- (mir′ē ə) [< Gr. *myrias:* see ff.] *a combining form meaning:* 1. many, numerous [*myriapod*] 2. ten thousand; the factor 10⁴ [*myriameter*]

myr·i·ad (mir′ē əd) *n.* [< Gr. *myrias* (gen. *myriados*), the number ten thousand < *myrios,* countless] 1. orig., ten thousand 2. any indefinitely large number 3. a great number of persons or things —*adj.* 1. of an indefinitely large number; countless; innumerable 2. of a highly varied nature

myr·i·a·pod (mir′ē ə päd′) *adj.* [< ModL. *Myriapoda,* name of the class: see MYRIA- & -POD] having many legs; specif., of or belonging to those classes of arthropods having a long body consisting of many segments, each of which bears one or more pairs of jointed legs, as the millipedes and centipedes —*n.* any animal of the class

myr·me·co- (mʉr′mə kō, -kə) [Gr. *myrmēko- < myrmēx,* ant < IE. base **morwi-,* whence OIr. *moirb,* OE. *myre,* (PIS)MIRE] *a combining form meaning* ant [*myrmecology*]

myr·me·col·o·gy (mʉr′mə käl′ə jē) *n.* [MYRMECO- + -LOGY] the branch of entomology dealing with ants —**myr′me·co·log′i·cal** (-kə läj′i k'l) *adj.* —**myr′me·col′o·gist** *n.*

myr·me·coph·a·gous (-käf′ə gəs) *adj.* [MYRMECO- + -PHAGOUS] feeding on ants

Myr·mi·don (mʉr′mə dän′, -dən) *n., pl.* **-dons,** **Myr·mid·o·nes** (mər mid′ə nēz′) [ME. *mirmidones* < L. *Myrmidones,* pl. < Gr. *Myrmidones,* the Myrmidons] 1. any of a tribe of Thessalian warriors who, according to Greek legend, fought under Achilles, their king, in the Trojan War 2. [m-] an unquestioning follower or subordinate

my·rob·a·lan (mī räb′ə lən, mi-) *n.* [Fr. < L. *myrobalanum* < Gr. *myrobalanon < myron,* plant juice (for base see SMEAR) + *balanos,* a nut, acorn: see GLAND¹] 1. any of the dried prunelike fruits of various tropical trees (genus *Terminalia*), containing tannin and used for dyeing and tanning 2. same as CHERRY PLUM

My·ron (mī′rən) 1. [prob. < Gr. *Myrōn*] a masculine name 2. Gr. sculptor of the 5th cent. B.C.

myrrh (mʉr) *n.* [ME. *mirre* < OE. *myrre* & OFr. *mirre,* both < L. *myrrha* < Gr. *myrrha* < Ar. *murr,* myrrh, bitter] 1. a fragrant, bitter-tasting gum resin exuded from any of several plants of Arabia and E. Africa, used in making incense, perfume, etc. 2. any of these plants; esp., any of several small trees (genus *Commiphora*)

Myr·tle (mʉr′t'l) [< ff.] a feminine name

myr·tle (mʉr′t'l) *n.* [ME. *mirtille* < OFr. *myrtille* < ML. *myrtillus,* dim. < L. *myrtus* < Gr. *myrtos,* myrtle, prob. < Sem.] 1. any of a genus (*Myrtus*) of plants of the myrtle family, with evergreen leaves, white or pinkish flowers, and dark, fragrant berries 2. any of various other plants, as the periwinkle and the California laurel —*adj.* designating a family (Myrtaceae) of evergreen trees and shrubs, including myrtle, eucalyptus, guava, clove, and blue gum

my·self (mi self′, mə-) *pron.* [ME. *meself* < OE. *me sylf:* see ME & SELF] a form of the 1st pers. sing. pronoun, used: *a)* as an intensive [I went *myself*] *b)* as a reflexive [I hurt *myself*] *c)* as a quasi-noun meaning "my real, true, or actual self" [I am not *myself* today]: in this construction *my* may be considered as a possessive pronominal adjective and *self* a noun, and they may be separated [*my* own sweet *self*]

My·si·a (mish′ē ə) ancient region in NW Asia Minor

my·sid (mī′sid) *n.* [< ModL. *Mysidacea,* name of the order] any of an order (Mysidacea) of small, shrimplike crustaceans with a carapace over most of the thorax, which has two-branched appendages

My·sore (mī sôr′) 1. state of SW India: 74,210 sq. mi.; pop. 23,587,000; cap. Bangalore 2. city in S part of this state: pop. 254,000

mys·ta·gogue (mis′tə gäg′, -gôg′) *n.* [Fr. < L. *mystagogus* < Gr. *mystagōgos < mystēs* (see MYSTERY¹) + *agōgos,* leader < *agein:* see ACT] a person who interprets religious mysteries or initiates others into them —**mys′ta·gog′ic** (-gäj′ik) —**mys′ta·go′gy** (-gō′jē) *n.*

mys·te·ri·ous (mis tir′ē əs) *adj.* [< L. *mysterium* (see ff.) + -OUS] of, containing, implying, or characterized by mystery —**mys·te′ri·ous·ly** *adv.* —**mys·te′ri·ous·ness** *n.*

SYN.—**mysterious** is applied to that which excites curiosity, wonder, etc. but is impossible or difficult to explain or solve [*a mysterious murder*]; that is **inscrutable** which is completely mysterious and is altogether incapable of being searched out, interpreted, or understood [the *inscrutable* ways of God]; **mystical** applies to that which is occult or esoteric in connection with religious rites or spiritual experience

mys·ter·y¹ (mis′tə rē, -trē) *n., pl.* **-ter·ies** [ME. *mysterye* < L. *mysterium* (in NT., supernatural thing) < Gr. *mystērion,* a secret rite (in NT., divine secret) < *mystēs,* one initiated into the mysteries < *myein,* to initiate into the mysteries, orig., to close (eyes or mouth) < IE. echoic base **mu-,* sound made with closed lips, whence MUTTER, MEW³] 1. something unexplained, unknown, or kept secret [the *mystery* of life] 2. *a)* any thing or event

that remains so secret or obscure as to excite curiosity [a murder *mystery*] *b*) a novel, story, or play involving such an event, esp. a crime and the gradual discovery of who committed it **3**. the quality of being inexplicable; obscurity or secrecy [an air of *mystery* surrounding the affair] **4**. [*pl.*] secret rites or doctrines known only to a small, esoteric group; specif., in ancient Greece, religious ceremonies or doctrines revealed only to the initiated **5**. [*pl.*] any of the ancient cults characterized by such ceremonies [the Eleusinian *mysteries*] **6**. [? influenced by MYSTERY²] *same as* MYSTERY PLAY **7**. *Christianity a*) a sacrament; esp., the Eucharist *b*) any of fifteen events in the lives of Jesus and Mary serving as a subject for meditation during the saying of the rosary **8**. *Theol.* any religious truth known to man only through divine revelation and to be accepted on faith

SYN.—**mystery** is applied to something beyond human knowledge or understanding, or it merely refers to any unexplained or seemingly inexplicable matter; **enigma** specifically applies to that whose meaning is hidden by cryptic or ambiguous allusions, and, generally, to anything very difficult to explain; a **riddle** is an enigma (usually in the form of a question in guessing games) that involves paradoxes; a **puzzle** is a situation, problem, or, often, a contrivance, that requires some ingenuity to solve or explain; **conundrum** is specifically applied to a riddle whose answer is a pun, and generally, to any puzzling question or problem

mys·ter·y² (mis′tə rē) *n., pl.* **-ter·ies** [ME. *misterie*, a trade, craft < ML. *misterium*, altered < L. *ministerium*, office, occupation (see MINISTER), by confusion with *mysterium* (see prec.)] [Archaic] **1**. a craft or trade **2**. *same as* GUILD (sense 1)

mystery play any of a class of medieval dramatic representations of Biblical events, esp. of the life and death of Jesus: they originated in the church liturgy but were later presented by craft guilds in marketplaces, etc.: cf. MIRACLE PLAY, MORALITY PLAY

mys·tic (mis′tik) *adj.* [ME. *mistik* < L. *mysticus* < Gr. *mystikos*, belonging to secret rites < *mystēs*, one initiated: see MYSTERY¹] **1**. of mysteries, or esoteric rites or doctrines **2**. *same as* MYSTICAL **3**. of obscure or occult character or meaning [*mystic* powers] **4**. beyond human comprehension; mysterious or enigmatic **5**. filling one with wonder or awe **6**. having magic power —*n.* **1**. a person initiated into esoteric mysteries **2**. a believer in mysticism; specif., one who professes to undergo mystical experiences by which he intuitively comprehends truths beyond human understanding

mys·ti·cal (-ti k′l) *adj.* **1**. spiritually significant or symbolic; allegorical [the *mystical* rose, a symbol of the Virgin Mary] **2**. of mystics or mysticism; esp., relating to or based on intuition, contemplation, or meditation of a spiritual nature **3**. *same as* MYSTIC (sense 3) **4**. [Rare] mysterious; enigmatic —SYN. see MYSTERIOUS —**mys′ti·cal·ly** *adv.* —**mys′ti·cal·ness** *n.*

mys·ti·cism (-tə siz′m) *n.* **1**. the doctrines or beliefs of mystics; specif., the doctrine that it is possible to achieve communion with God through contemplation and love without the medium of human reason **2**. any doctrine that asserts the possibility of attaining knowledge of spiritual truths through intuition acquired by fixed meditation **3**. vague, obscure, or confused thinking or belief

mys·ti·fy (mis′tə fi′) *vt.* **-fied′, -fy′ing** [Fr. *mystifier* < *mystère*, mystery (< L. *mysterium*) + *-fier*, -FY] **1**. *a*) to puzzle or perplex *b*) to bewilder deliberately; play on the credulity of; hoax **2**. to involve in mystery, or obscurity; make obscure or hard to understand —**mys′ti·fi·ca′tion** *n.*

mys·tique (mis tēk′) *n.* [Fr., mystic] a complex of quasi-mystical attitudes and feelings surrounding some person, institution, activity, etc.

myth (mith) *n.* [LL. *mythos* < Gr. *mythos*, a word, speech, story, legend] **1**. a traditional story of unknown authorship, ostensibly with a historical basis, but serving usually to explain some phenomenon of nature, the origin of man, or the customs, institutions, religious rites, etc. of a people: myths usually involve the exploits of gods and heroes: cf. LEGEND **2**. such stories collectively; mythology **3**. any fictitious story, or unscientific account, theory, belief, etc. **4**. any imaginary person or thing spoken of as though existing

myth. mythology

myth·i·cal (-i k′l) *adj.* **1**. of, or having the nature of, a myth or myths **2**. existing only in a myth or myths [a *mythical* creature] **3**. imaginary, fictitious, or not based on facts or scientific study Also **myth′ic** —SYN. see FICTITIOUS —**myth′i·cal·ly** *adv.*

myth·i·cize (-ə sīz′) *vt.* **-cized′, -ciz′ing** to make into, or explain as, a myth —**myth′i·ciz′er** *n.*

myth·o- (mith′ə, -ō) [< Gr. *mythos*, myth] a combining form meaning myth [*mythology*]

my·thog·ra·pher (mi thäg′rə fər) *n.* a person who collects or writes about myths

myth·o·log·i·cal (mith′ə läj′i k′l) *adj.* **1**. of mythology **2**. mythical; imaginary Also **myth′o·log′ic** —**myth′o·log′i·cal·ly** *adv.*

my·thol·o·gist (mi thäl′ə jist) *n.* **1**. an expert in mythology **2**. a writer or compiler of myths

my·thol·o·gize (-jīz′) *vi.* **-gized′, -giz′ing** [Fr. *mythologiser*] **1**. to relate or construct a myth or myths **2**. to compile, classify, or write about myths —*vt. same as* MYTHICIZE —**my·thol′o·giz′er** *n.*

my·thol·o·gy (-jē) *n., pl.* **-gies** [ME. *methologie* < LL. *mythologia* < Gr. *mythologia*, a telling of tales or legends < *mythos*, myth + *-logia*, -LOGY] **1**. the science or study of myths **2**. a book of or about myths **3**. myths collectively; esp., all the myths of a specific people or about a specific being

myth·o·ma·ni·a (mith′ə mā′nē ə, -mān′yə) *n.* [ModL.: see MYTHO- & -MANIA] *Psychiatry* an abnormal tendency to lie or exaggerate —**myth′o·ma′ni·ac′** *adj., n.*

myth·o·poe·ia (mith′ə pē′ə) *n.* [< Gr. *mythopoios* < *mythos*, myth + *poiein*, to make] the making of myths —**myth′o·poe′ic** (-ik), **myth′o·po·et′ic** (-pō et′ik) *adj.*

myth·os (mith′äs, mi′thäs) *n.* [see MYTH] **1**. *same as* MYTH (senses 1, 2, & 3) **2**. the complex of attitudes, beliefs, etc. most characteristic of a particular group or society

Myt·i·le·ne (mit′′l ē′nē) *same as* MITILÍNI

myx·e·de·ma (mik′sə dē′mə) *n.* [ModL.: see ff. & EDEMA] a disease caused by failure of the thyroid gland and characterized by a drying and thickening of the skin and a slowing down of physical and mental activity —**myx′·e·de′ma·tous** (-təs) *adj.*

myx·o- (mik′sō, -sə) [< Gr. *myxa*, MUCUS] a combining form meaning slime or mucus [*myxomycete*]

myx·o·ma (mik sō′mə) *n., pl.* **-mas, -ma·ta** (-mə tə) [MYX(O)- + -OMA] a tumor of connective tissue cells containing a mucuslike material —**myx·o′ma·tous** (-təs) *adj.*

myx·o·ma·to·sis (mik′sə mə tō′sis) *n.* [see prec. & -OSIS] **1**. the presence of many myxomas **2**. an infectious virus disease in rabbits, transmitted by mosquitoes and characterized by tumorous growths resembling myxomas

myx·o·my·cete (mik′sō mī′sēt, -mi sēt′) *n.* [MYXO- + -MYCETE] any of a class (Myxomycetes) of primitive organisms, the slime molds, whose juvenile stages consist of masses of naked protoplasm and have some characteristics of both plants and animals, but which are generally classified as plants (fungi): usually found on decaying vegetation: see MYCETOZOAN —**myx′o·my·ce′tous** (-sē′təs) *adj.*

N

N, n (en) *n., pl.* **N's, n's** **1**. the fourteenth letter of the English alphabet: from the Greek *nu*, a borrowing from the Phoenician **2**. the sound of *N* or *n*: normally, in English, it is a voiced apical nasal continuant **3**. a type or impression for *N* or *n* **4**. *a symbol for* the fourteenth (or the thirteenth if J is omitted) in a sequence or group **5**. *Printing* an en (half an em) —*adj.* **1**. of *N* or *n* **2**. fourteenth (or thirteenth if J is omitted) in a sequence or group

N (en) *n.* **1**. an object shaped like *N* **2**. *Chem.* nitrogen —*adj.* shaped like *N*

n (en) *n.* **1**. *Math. the symbol for* an indefinite number: see NTH **2**. *Physics the symbol for* neutron

n- negative

N, N., n, n. **1**. north **2**. northern

N. **1**. National(ist) **2**. Navy **3**. Norse **4**. November

N., n. **1**. [L. *natus*] born **2**. nail **3**. name **4**. navy **5**. neuter **6**. new **7**. nominative **8**. noon **9**. *Chem.* normal **10**. noun

n. **1**. nephew **2**. net **3**. note **4**. number

na (nə) *adv.* [cf. OE. *ne*, not & *a*, ever] [Chiefly Scot.] **1**. no **2**. not: usually with auxiliary verbs [*wouldna*] —*conj.* [Chiefly Scot.] nor

Na [L. *natrium*] *Chem.* sodium

n/a *Banking* no account

N.A. **1**. National Academician **2**. National Academy **3**. National Army **4**. North America

NAACP, N.A.A.C.P. National Association for the Advancement of Colored People

nab (nab) *vt.* **nabbed, nab′bing** [< thieves' slang (16th-17th c.), prob. var. of dial. *nap*, to snatch < Scand., as in Dan. *nappe*, Sw. *nappa*, to snatch] [Colloq.] **1.** to seize suddenly; snatch or steal **2.** to arrest or catch (a felon or wrongdoer) —*SYN.* see CATCH

Nab·a·te·a, Nab·a·tae·a (nab′ə tē′ə) ancient Arab kingdom in SW Asia, in what is now W Jordan —**Nab′a·te′an, Nab′a·tae′an** *adj., n.*

☆**nabe** (nāb) *n.* [altered < NEIGHB(ORHOOD)] a neighborhood movie theater

Nab·lus (nä blōōs′) city in W Jordan; capital (as *Shechem*) of ancient Samaria: pop. 202,000

na·bob (nā′bäb) *n.* [Hind. *nawwāb* < Ar. *nuwwāb*, pl. of *nā'ib*, deputy, viceroy] **1.** a native provincial deputy or governor of the old Mogul Empire in India **2.** a European who has become rich in India **3.** a very rich or important man —**na′bob·ish** *adj.*

Na·bo·kov (nä bô′kôf, nä′bə kôf′), **Vladimir** 1899–   ; U.S. writer & teacher, born in Russia

Na·both (nā′bäth) [Heb. *nābhōth*] *Bible* the owner of a vineyard, killed at the behest of Jezebel so that Ahab could seize the vineyard: I Kings 21

Na·bu·cho·don·o·sor (nab′ə kə dän′ə sôr′) *Douay Bible* name for NEBUCHADNEZZAR

na·celle (nə sel′) *n.* [Fr. < LL. *navicella*, dim. of L. *navis*, a ship: see NAVE¹] a streamlined enclosure on an aircraft, esp. that which houses an engine

‡**nach·as, nach·es** (näkh′əs) *n.* [< Yid. < Heb. *nakhās*, lit., a coming to rest, ease] pleasurable pride, esp. in another or in his achievements

na·cre (nā′kər) *n.* [Fr. < It. *naccaro* < Ar. *naqqārah*, small kettledrum] *same as* MOTHER-OF-PEARL

na·cre·ous (-krē əs) *adj.* **1.** of or like nacre **2.** yielding nacre **3.** iridescent; lustrous

☆**Na-De·ne** (nä′di nē′, -dä ; nā′) *n.* [neologism < Haida *na*, to dwell and Tlingit *na*, people + Athapascan *dene*, person, people] a proposed grouping of American Indian languages, including the Athapascan family and the perhaps very remotely related Tlingit and Haida languages

Na·dine (nə dēn′, nä-) [Fr. < Russ. *nadevhda*, hope] a feminine name

na·dir (nā′dər, -dir) *n.* [ME. < MFr. < ML. < Ar. *nazir*, in *nazir as-samt*, lit., opposite to the zenith < *nazir*, opposite + *as-samt*, zenith] **1.** that point of the celestial sphere directly opposite to the zenith and directly below the observer **2.** the lowest point; time of greatest depression or dejection

nae (nā) *adv.* [Scot.] no; not —*adj.* no

nae·vus (nē′vəs) *n., pl.* **-vi** (-vī) *chiefly Brit. sp.* of NEVUS —**nae′void** *adj.*

Na·fud (ne fōōd′) desert in the N Arabian Peninsula: c. 180 mi. long; 140 mi. wide

nag¹ (nag) *vt.* **nagged, nag′ging** [< Scand. (as in Sw. *nagga*, obs. Dan. *nagge*, to nibble, gnaw, nag) < ON. *gnaga*: for base see GNAW: for sense development cf. FRET¹] **1.** to annoy by continual scolding, faultfinding, complaining, urging, etc. **2.** to keep troubling, worrying, etc. [nagged by a thought] —*vi.* **1.** to urge, scold, find fault, etc. constantly **2.** to cause continual discomfort, pain, etc. [a nagging toothache] —*n.* a person, esp. a woman, who nags: also **nag′ger** —**nag′ging·ly** *adv.* —**nag′gy** *adj.* **-gi·er, -gi·est**

nag² (nag) *n.* [ME. *nagge*, akin to obs. Du. *negghe* < ?] **1.** orig., a small saddle horse; pony **2.** a mediocre or poor horse, esp. an old one ☆**3.** [Slang] a racehorse, esp. an inferior one

Na·ga·land (nä′gə land′) state of NE India, on the Burma border: 6,366 sq. mi.; pop. 369,000

na·ga·na (nə gä′nə) *n.* [< Zulu *u(lu)-nakane*] an infectious disease affecting horses and cattle in tropical Africa, caused by a trypanosome (*Trypanosoma brucei*) transmitted by the bite of infected tsetse flies

Na·ga·sa·ki (nä′gə sä′kē) seaport on the W coast of Kyushu, Japan: partly destroyed (Aug. 9, 1945) by a U.S. atomic bomb, the second ever used in warfare (cf. HIRO-SHIMA): pop. 405,000

Na·go·ya (nä′gô yä′) seaport in S Honshu, Japan, on an inlet of the Pacific: pop. 1,935,000

Nag·pur (näg′poor) city in C India, in Maharashtra state: pop. 690,000

Na·gy·vá·rad (nädʹy′ vä′räd) *Hung. name of* ORADEA

Na·ha (nä′hä′) seaport on Okinawa: pop. 257,000

Na·huat (nä′wät) *n.* [Nahuatl] **1.** *pl.* **Na′huats, Na′huat** a member of a tribe of Indians of Mexico **2.** their Nahuatl language

Na·hua·tl (nä′wät 'l) *n.* [Nahuatl] **1.** *pl.* **Na′hua·tls, Na′hua·tl** a member of any of a number of Uto-Aztecan tribes of Mexico **2.** their language, spoken in numerous dialects in Mexico **3.** a branch of the Uto-Aztecan language family, spoken in Mexico, El Salvador, Guatemala, and Honduras, and including Nahuatl, Nahuat, etc.

Na·hua·tlan (-lən) *adj.* of the Nahuatl branch of the Uto-Aztecan language family —*n. same as* NAHUATL

Na·hum (nä′əm, -həm) [Heb. *nahūm*, lit., comfort] *Bible* **1.** a Hebrew prophet of the 7th cent. B.C. **2.** the book containing his prophecies: abbrev. **Nah.**

nai·ad (nā′ad, nī′-; -əd) *n., pl.* **-ads, -a·des′** (-ə dēz′) [Fr. *naiade* < L. *Naias* (gen. *Naiadis*) < Gr. *naias* (pl. *Naïades*) < *naein*, to flow < IE. base *(s)na-*, to flow, whence L. *natare*, to swim] **1.** [*also* N-] *Gr. & Rom. Myth.* any of the nymphs living in and giving life to springs, fountains, rivers, and lakes **2.** a girl or woman swimmer **3.** *Bot.* any of a number of submerged aquatic plants (genus *Naias*) of a family (Naiadaceae), with linear opposite leaves, common in lakes and ponds **4.** *Zool.* a) the aquatic nymph of certain insects, as the dragonfly and mayfly b) any of various freshwater mussels

na·if, na·ïf (nä ēf′) *adj.* [Fr.] *same as* NAIVE

nail (nāl) *n.* [ME. < OE. *naile* < OE. *nægl*, akin to G. *nagel* < IE. base *onogh*, nail, whence Sans. *ánghri-*, foot, Gr. *onyx*, nail, L. *unguis*, finger-nail] **1.** a) the thin, horny substance growing out at the ends of the fingers and toes of man, monkeys, etc. b) a similar growth on the toes of a bird or animal; claw **2.** a tapered piece of metal, commonly pointed and having a flattened head, driven with a hammer, and used for holding pieces as of wood together, as a peg, or for decoration **3.** an old cloth measure, equal to 2 1/4 inches —*vt.* [ME. *nailen* < OE. *mæglan*] **1.** to attach or fasten together or onto something else with or as with nails **2.** to secure, hold, or fasten shut with nails **3.** to fix (the eyes, attention, etc.) steadily on an object **4.** to discover or expose (a lie, etc.) **5.** [Colloq.] to catch, capture, seize, or intercept **6.** [Colloq.] to hit squarely —**hard as nails** callous, unfeeling, remorseless, etc. —**hit the nail on the head** to do or say whatever is exactly right or to the point —**nail down 1.** to fasten tightly with nails, as a lid on a box **2.** to settle definitely; make sure [to nail down an agreement] —**nail up 1.** to fasten to a wall or at some height **2.** to fasten tightly with nails, as a door no longer used

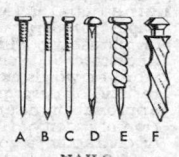

NAILS
(A, common wire; B, flooring; C, finishing; D, boat; E, screw; F, masonry)

nail·brush (-brush′) *n.* a small, stiff brush for cleaning the fingernails

☆**nail file** a small, flat file for trimming the fingernails

nail·head (-hed′) *n.* **1.** the flattened or, sometimes, rounded head of a nail **2.** a decoration resembling the rounded head of a nail, as on a leather belt

nail polish a kind of lacquer, usually colored, applied to the fingernails or toenails as a cosmetic

nail set a tool for sinking the head of a nail so that it is below the surface of the wood

nain·sook (nān′sook) *n.* [Hind. *nainsukh* < *nain*, the eye + *sukh*, pleasure] a thin, plain-woven, lightweight cotton fabric

Nairn (nern) county of NE Scotland: 163 sq. mi.; pop. 8,300: also **Nairn′shire** (-shir)

Nai·ro·bi (nī rō′bē) capital of Kenya, in the SW part: pop. 297,000

na·ïve, na·ive (nä ēv′) *adj.* [Fr., fem. of *naïf* < L. *nativus*, natural, NATIVE] **1.** unaffectedly, or sometimes foolishly, simple; childlike; unsophisticated **2.** not suspicious; credulous —**na·ive′ly, na·ïve′ly** *adv.*

SYN.—**naive** implies a genuine, innocent simplicity or lack of artificiality but sometimes connotes an almost foolish lack of worldly wisdom [his *naive* belief in the kindness of others]; **ingenuous** implies a frankness or straightforwardness that suggests the simplicity of a child [her *ingenuous* smile at my discomfiture]; **artless** suggests a lack of artificiality or guile that derives from indifference to the effect one has upon others [her *artless* beauty]; **unsophisticated**, like **naive**, implies a lack of worldly wisdom but connotes that this is the result merely of a lack of experience [an *unsophisticated* freshman] —*ANT.* sophisticated, artful

na·ive·té, na·ïve·té (nä ēv tā′, -ēv′tā) *n.* [Fr.] **1.** the quality or state of being naive; simplicity; artlessness **2.** a naive action or remark Also **na·ive′ness, na·ïve′ness, na·ive′ty** (-tē), **na·ïve′ty**

na·ked (nā′kid) *adj.* [ME. < OE. *nacod*, akin to G. *nackt* < IE. base *nogw-*, naked, whence Sans. *nagnā-*, L. *nudus*] **1.** a) completely unclothed; bare; nude b) uncovered; exposed: said of parts of the body **2.** lacking clothing, means of support, etc.; destitute **3.** without protection or defense **4.** without conventional or usual covering; specif., a) out of its sheath [a *naked* sword] b) without grass, vegetation, etc. c) without furnishing, decoration, etc. [a *naked* wall] **5.** without additions, ornaments, disguises, or embellishments; plain; stark [the *naked* truth] **6.** without the aid of a microscope, telescope, etc. [the *naked* eye] **7.** *Bot.* without leaves, corolla, ovary, perianth, etc. **8.** *Law* without objective support; lacking a necessary condition; invalid [a *naked* contract] **9.** *Zool.* without hair, scales, feathers, shell, etc. —*SYN.* see BARE¹ —**na′ked·ly** *adv.* —**na′ked·ness** *n.*

NAM, N.A.M. National Association of Manufacturers

Na·ma (nä′mä) *n.* [< the native name] **1.** the chief tribe of the Hottentots **2.** a Hottentot **3.** the Khoisan language of the Hottentots

Na·ma·qua·land (nə mä′kwə land′) region in SW Africa,

inhabited by Hottentots: divided by the Orange River into a region (**Great Namaqualand**) in South West Africa & a region (**Little Namaqualand**) in W South Africa Also **Na·ma·land** (nä′mə land′)

‡**na·mast·e** (nä′mə stā′) n. [Hind. < Sans. *námas*-, a bow < IE. base *nem-*, to bend, bow] a Hindu gesture of salutation made by placing the palms together, thumbs against the chest, and nodding the head slightly

nam·by-pam·by (nam′bē pam′bē) adj. [orig. satirical nickname of *Ambrose Philips*, 18th-c. Eng. poet: in ridicule of his sentimental pastorals] weakly sentimental; wishy-washy; without vigor; insipidly pretty or nice —n., pl. -bies 1. a namby-pamby talk or writing 2. a namby-pamby person

name (nām) n. [ME. < OE. nama, akin to G. name < IE. base *(o)nomn̥*, whence L. nomen, Gr. onoma] 1. a word or phrase by which a person, thing, or class of things is known, called, or spoken to or of; appellation; title 2. a word or words expressing some quality considered characteristic or descriptive of a person or thing, often showing approval or disapproval; epithet 3. the sacred designation of a deity [his ineffable name] 4. a) fame, reputation, or character [a good name] b) good reputation 5. a family or clan [the last of his name] 6. appearance only, not reality; semblance [chief in name only] 7. a distinguished or famous person [the greatest name in science] 8. Logic a word or symbol for a concept; term —adj. ☆1. having a good reputation; well-known [a name brand] 2. carrying a name [a name tag] —vt. named, nam′ing 1. to give a name or title to; entitle; style 2. to designate, mention, or refer to by name 3. to identify by the right name [name all the oceans] 4. to nominate or appoint to a post, situation, or office 5. to set or fix; specify (a date, price, etc.) 6. to speak about; mention —call names to mention in an abusive manner; swear at —in the name of 1. in appeal or reference to 2. by the authority of; as the representative of 3. as belonging to —know only by name to be familiar with the name of but not know personally —name names to identify specific persons, esp. as doing wrong —to one's name belonging to one —name′a·ble, nam′a·ble adj. —nam′er n.

name-call·ing (-kôl′iŋ) n. the use of disparaging or abusive names in attacking another —name′-call′er n.

name day 1. the feast day of the saint after whom one is named 2. day of baptism

name-drop·per (-dräp′ər) n. a person who seeks to impress others by frequently mentioning famous or important persons in a familiar way —name′-drop′ping n.

name·less (-lis) adj. 1. not having or bearing a name 2. left unnamed; anonymous [a rogue who shall be nameless] 3. not publicly known; obscure 4. lacking a legal name; illegitimate 5. that cannot be described; indescribable [nameless dread] 6. too horrid or painful to specify [nameless crimes] —name′less·ly adv. — name′less·ness n.

name·ly (-lē) adv. [ME.: see NAME & -LY²] that is to say; specifically; to wit

name·plate (-plāt′) n. 1. a piece of metal, wood, etc. on which a name is inscribed 2. the name of a newspaper as it appears across the top of the front page

name·sake (-sāk′) n. [earlier name's sake] a person with the same name as another, esp. if named after the other

Na·mib·i·a (nä mib′ē ə) official (U.N.) name for SOUTH WEST AFRICA

Na·mi·er (nā′mē ər), Sir **Lewis Bernstein** 1888–1960; Brit. historian, born in Russia

Nam Tso (or **Tsho**) (näm′ tsō′) large salt lake in E Tibet: c. 15,180 ft. above sea level; c. 950 sq. mi.

Na·mur (nȧ mür′) 1. province of S Belgium: 1,413 sq. mi.; pop. 378,000 2. its capital, on the Meuse River: pop. 33,000 Fl. name **Na·men** (nä′mən)

nance (nans) n. [< NANCY (fem. name)] [Slang] an effeminate or homosexual man: also **nan·cy** (nan′sē)

Nan·chang (nän′chäŋ′) city in SE China; capital of Kiangsi province: pop. 520,000

Nan·cy (nan′sē; also, for 2, Fr. nän sē′) 1. [prob. by faulty division of MINE¹ + Ancy, dim. form of ME. Annis, AGNES, confused with ANNE: cf. ANNA] a feminine name 2. city in NE France: pop. 129,000

Nan·da De·vi (nun′dä dā′vē) mountain of the Himalayas, in N Uttar Pradesh, India: 25,645 ft.

Nan·ga Par·bat (nun′gä pär′but′) mountain of the Himalayas, in W Kashmir: 26,660 ft.

nan·keen, nan·kin (nan kēn′) n. [< ff., whence orig. imported] 1. a buff-colored, durable cotton cloth, orig. from China 2. [pl.] trousers made of this cloth

Nan·king (nan′kiŋ′, nän′-) city in E China, on the Yangtze; capital of Kiangsu province: pop. 2,700,000

Nan·nette, Na·nette (na net′) a feminine name: see ANNA

Nan·ning (nän′niŋ′) city in S China; capital of Kwangsi-Chuang autonomous region: pop. 260,000

nan·no·plank·ton (nan′ō plaŋk′tən) n. [< NANO- + PLANKTON] planktonic organisms smaller than 40 microns in diameter: also **na′no·plank′ton**

nan·ny (nan′ē) n., pl. -nies [< Nan, dim. of ANN(A)] [Brit.] a child's nurse

nanny goat [see prec.] [Colloq.] a female goat

na·no- (nan′ō, -ə) [< Gr. nanos, dwarf, akin to nanna, aunt: see NUN¹] a combining form meaning a 1,000,000,000th

part of (a specified unit); the factor 10⁻⁹ [nanosecond]

na·no·sec·ond (-sek′ənd) n. one billionth of a second

Nan·sen (nän′sən; E. nan′s'n), **Fridt·jof** (frit′yäf) 1861–1930; Norw. arctic explorer, naturalist, & statesman

Nansen bottle [after prec.] an oceanographic instrument used to obtain water samples and temperature readings at various depths in the seas

Nan Shan (nän′ shän′) mountain system in NW China, in N Tsinghai & S Kansu provinces: highest peak, c. 20,000 ft.

Nan·terre (nän ter′) city in NC France: suburb of Paris: pop. 84,000

Nantes (nänt; E. nants) 1. city in W France, on the Loire River: pop. 240,000 2. **Edict of**, a decree issued in 1598 by Henry IV of France, giving political equality to the Huguenots: it was revoked in 1685

Nan·tuck·et (nan tuk′it) [AmInd., lit., ? faraway land] island of Mass., south of Cape Cod: summer resort: 46 sq. mi.; pop. 3,800

Na·o·mi (nā ō′mē, na-; nā′ə mī′) [Heb. nā′omī, lit., my delight] 1. a feminine name 2. Bible the mother-in-law of Ruth: Ruth 1

na·os (nā′äs, nä′-) n., pl. **na′oi** (-oi) [Gr. naos < IE. base *nes-*, to unite, be protected, whence OE. nerian, G. nähren, to protect, support] 1. an ancient temple 2. the enclosed part of such a temple; cella

nap¹ (nap) vi. napped, nap′ping [ME. nappen < OE. hnappian, akin to OHG. hnaffezan] 1. to doze or sleep lightly for a short time 2. to be careless or unprepared —n. a brief, light sleep; doze

nap² (nap) n. [ME. noppe < or akin to MDu. & MLowG. noppe (G. noppe), Dan. nappe < IE. *kenebh-* < base *ken*, to scratch, rub, whence Gr. knaptein, to scratch, tear apart] 1. the downy or hairy surface of cloth formed by short hairs or fibers, esp. when artificially raised by brushing, etc.; pile of velvet, etc. 2. any downy surface like this, as that raised on the flesh side of leather —vt. napped, nap′ping to raise a nap on (fabric or leather) by brushing, etc. —nap′less adj. —napped adj.

nap³ (nap) n. clipped form of NAPOLEON (senses 1 & 2)

Nap·a (nap′ə) [< AmInd. < ?] city in W Calif., north of Oakland: pop. 36,000

☆**na·palm** (nā′päm) n. [NA(PHTHENE) + PALM(ITATE), constituents used in its manufacture] 1. sodium palmitate or an aluminum soap added to gasoline or oil to form a jellylike substance 2. this substance, used in flame throwers and bombs —vt. to attack or burn with napalm

nape (nāp, nap) n. [ME. < ?] the back of the neck

na·per·y (nā′pər ē) n. [ME. naprye < MFr. naperie < OFr. nappe: see NAPKIN] household linen; esp., table linen

Naph·ta·li (naf′tə lī′) [Heb. < naphtulim; wrestlings: see Gen. 30:8] Bible 1. the sixth son of Jacob: Gen. 30:7,8 2. the tribe of Israel descended from him: Num. 1:15, 43

naph·tha (naf′thə, nap′-) n. [L. < Gr. naphtha, naphtha, bitumen < Per. neft, pitch, prob. < IE. base *nebh-*, damp, water, whence Gr. nephelē, cloud, fog] 1. a flammable, volatile, oily liquid produced by the fractional distillation of petroleum: it is the fraction that boils between gasoline and kerosine and is used as a fuel, solvent, and illuminant 2. same as PETROLEUM 3. any of several flammable, volatile liquids produced by the distillation of coal tar, wood, coal, and other carbonaceous materials

naph·tha·lene (-lēn′) n. [earlier naphthaline < prec. + -l- + -INE⁴] a white, crystalline, aromatic hydrocarbon, C₁₀H₈, produced in the fractional distillation of coal tar: it is used in moth repellents and in the manufacture of certain dyes and other organic compounds: also **naph′-tha·lin′** —**naph′tha·len′ic** (-lē′nik, -len′ik) adj.

naph·thene (naf′thēn, nap′-) n. [NAPHTH(A) + -ENE] any of a group of cyclic hydrocarbons of the general formula CₙH₂ₙ, found in petroleums from various sources —**naph-then′ic** (-thē′nik, -then′ik) adj.

naph·thol (naf′thôl, -thōl; nap′-) n. [NAPHTH(ALENE) + -OL¹] either of two white, crystalline isomeric compounds, C₁₀H₇OH, derived from naphthalene and used as antiseptics and in dyes, pharmaceuticals, etc.

naph·thyl (-thil) n. [NAPHTH(ALENE) + -YL] a univalent radical, C₁₀H₇−, derived from naphthalene

Na·pi·er (nā′pē ər, nə pir′) 1. Sir **Charles James**, 1782–1853; Brit. general 2. **John**, 1550–1617; Scot. mathematician: inventor of logarithms

Na·pier·i·an logarithm (nə pir′ē ən) [after John NAPIER] same as NATURAL LOGARITHM

na·pi·form (nā′pə fôrm′) adj. [< L. napus, turnip (see NEEP) + -FORM] large and round at the top, tapering sharply below; turnip-shaped: said of roots

nap·kin (nap′kin) n. [ME. nappekyn, dim. < OFr. nappe, cloth, tablecloth < L. mappa: cf. MAP] 1. a small piece of cloth or paper, usually square, used at table for protecting the clothes and wiping the fingers or lips 2. any small cloth, towel, etc.; esp., a) [Brit.] a diaper b) [Brit. Dial.] a handkerchief c) [Scot.] a kerchief or neckerchief

Na·ples (nā′p'lz) 1. seaport in S Italy, on the Bay of Naples: pop. 1,236,000 2. former kingdom occupying the S half of Italy 3. **Bay of**, inlet of the Tyrrhenian Sea, on the S coast of Italy: c. 10 mi. wide

na·po·le·on (nə pō′lē ən, -pōl′yən) n. [after ff.] 1. a former gold coin of France, equivalent to 20 francs, with a portrait of Napoleon I (or III) on it 2. a) a card game

similar to euchre b) a bid to take all five tricks in this game ☆3. a layered puff pastry with a custardlike cream filling

Na·po·le·on I (nə pōʹlē ən, -pōlʹyən) (full Fr. name *Napoléon Bonaparte*) 1769–1821; Fr. military leader & emperor of France (1804–15), born in Corsica: see also BONAPARTE

Napoleon II (born *François Charles Joseph Napoléon Bonaparte*), Duke of Reichstadt, 1811–32; titular emperor of France: son of *prec.* & MARIE LOUISE

Napoleon III see LOUIS NAPOLEON

Na·po·le·on·ic (nə pōʹlē änʹik) *adj.* of, characteristic of, or like Napoleon I, his campaigns, period, etc.

Na·po·li (näʹpō lē′) *It.* name of NAPLES

nap·per¹ (napʹər) *n.* a person who naps or is in the habit of taking naps

nap·per² (napʹər) *n.* a person, device, or machine that raises a nap on cloth

nap·py¹ (napʹē) *n., pl.* -pies [dim. of obs. *nap*, a drinking cup, bowl < ME. *nap*, *hnap* < OE. *hnæp*, akin to G. *napf*] a shallow, flat-bottomed, rounded dish with sloping sides, used for serving food

nap·py² (napʹē) *adj.* -pi·er, -pi·est covered with nap; hairy, downy, shaggy, etc. —**napʹpi·ness** *n.*

nap·py³ (napʹē) *adj.* -pi·er, -pi·est [prob. < *prec.*] [Brit.] foaming; heady; strong: said of ale —*n.* [Brit.] ale

nap·py⁴ (napʹē) *n., pl.* -pies [< NAPKIN + -Yⁱ] *Brit. term for* DIAPER (*n.* 2)

Nar·bad·a (nur budʹə) river in C India, flowing west into the Arabian Sea: c. 800 mi.

nar·ce·ine (närʹsē ēn′, -in) *n.* [Fr. *narcéine* < Gr. *narkē*, numbness: see NARCOTIC] a bitter, white, crystalline alkaloid, $C_{23}H_{27}O_8N$, obtained from opium: it is a narcotic

nar·cis·sism (närʹsə siz′m; *chiefly Brit.*, när sisʹiz′m) *n.* [G. *Narzissismus* (< *Narziss*, NARCISSUS) + -ISM] 1. self-love; excessive interest in one's own appearance, comfort, importance, abilities, etc. 2. *Psychoanalysis* arrest at or regression to the first stage of libidinal development, in which the self is an object of erotic pleasure Also **narʹcism** —**narʹcis·sist** *n.*, *adj.* —**narʹcis·sisʹtic** *adj.*

Nar·cis·sus (när sisʹəs) [L. < Gr. *Narkissos*] *Gr. Myth.* a beautiful youth who, after Echo's death (see ECHO), is made to pine away for love of his own reflection in a spring and changed into the narcissus —*n.* [n-] *pl.* -cisʹsus, -cisʹsus·es, -cisʹsi (-ī) [ModL., name of the genus < L. < Gr. *narkissos*, ? akin to *narkē*, stupor (see NARCOTIC), in reference to the plant's narcotic properties] any of a genus (*Narcissus*) of bulb plants of the amaryllis family with smooth, linear leaves and clusters of white, yellow, or orange flowers, including the daffodils and jonquils

nar·co- (närʹkō, -kə) [< Gr. *narkē*: see NARCOTIC] *a combining form meaning* narcosis, sleep, stupor: also, before a vowel, **narc-**

nar·co·a·nal·y·sis (närʹkō ə nalʹə sis) *n.* [NARCO- + ANALYSIS] psychotherapy using the method of narcosynthesis but in a slower, gentler, and more extensive manner

nar·co·lep·sy (närʹkə lep′sē) *n.* [NARCO- + -LEPSY] a condition of frequent and uncontrollable desire for sleep; paroxysmal sleep —**narʹco·lepʹtic** *adj.*

nar·co·sis (när kōʹsis) *n.* [ModL. < Gr. *narkōsis* < *narkoun*: see NARCOTIC] a condition of deep stupor which passes into unconsciousness and paralysis, caused by a narcotic or certain chemicals

nar·co·syn·the·sis (närʹkō sin′thə sis) *n.* [NARCO- + SYNTHESIS] a method of treating an acute traumatic neurosis by working with a patient while he is under the influence of a hypnotic drug, as thiopental sodium

nar·cot·ic (när kätʹik) *n.* [ME. *narcotyke* < OFr. *narcotique*, orig. adj. < ML. *narcoticus* < Gr. *narkoun*, to benumb < *narkē*, numbness, stupor < IE. **nerk-* < base **(s)ner-*, to twist, entwine, whence SNARE, NARROW] 1. a drug, as opium or any of its derivatives (morphine, heroin, codeine, etc.), used to relieve pain and induce sleep: narcotics are often addictive and in excessive doses can cause stupor, coma, or death 2. anything that has a soothing, lulling, or dulling effect —*adj.* 1. of, like, or capable of producing narcosis 2. of, by, or for narcotic addicts

nar·co·tism (närʹkə tiz′m) *n.* 1. the condition induced by a narcotic; narcosis 2. a method or influence producing narcosis 3. addiction to narcotics

nar·co·tize (närʹkə tīz′) *vt.* -tized′, -tizʹing 1. to subject to a narcotic; stupefy 2. to lull or dull the senses of —narʹco·ti·zaʹtion *n.*

nard (närd) *n.* [ME. *narde* < OFr. < L. *nardus* < Gr. *nardos* < Sem., as in Heb. *nērd*, Per. *nārdēn* < Sans.] *same as* SPIKENARD (sense 2)

nar·es (nerʹēz) *n.pl., sing.* **narʹis** (-is) [L.: see NOSE] the nasal passages; esp., the nostrils —**narʹi·al** (-ē al), **narʹine** (-in, -īn) *adj.*

Na·rew (näʹref) river in NE Poland, flowing west & southwest into the Bug River, near Warsaw: c. 270 mi.

nar·ghi·le (närʹgə lē′, -lā′) *n.* [Turk. & Per. *nārgīleh* < Per. *nargīl*, coconut tree, prob. < Sans. *nārikera*, coconut: orig. made of coconut shell] *same as* HOOKAH: also sp. **narʹgi·le, narʹgi·leh**

nark (närk) *n.* [< Romany *nāk*, a nose, akin to Avestan *nāh-*, nose: for IE. base see NOSE] [Brit. Slang] an informer; stool pigeon —*vt., vi.* [Brit. Slang] 1. to inform on (a person) 2. to make, be, or become annoyed, angry, grumbly, etc. —**nark it** [Brit. Slang] stop it; keep quiet —**narkʹy** *adj.*

Nar·ra·gan·sett (narʹə gan′sit) *n., pl.* **-setts, -sett** [< Algonquian, lit., on a small cape] a member of an extinct tribe of Algonquian Indians who lived around Narragansett Bay —*adj.* of this tribe Also sp. **Narʹra·gan′set**

Narragansett Bay [see *prec.*] inlet of the Atlantic, extending into R.I.: c. 30 mi.

nar·rate (narʹāt, na rātʹ) *vt., vi.* -rat·ed, -rat·ing [< L. *narratus*, pp. of *narrare*, to tell, akin to *gnarus*, acquainted with < IE. **ĝnoro-* < base **ĝen-*, to KNOW] 1. to tell (a story) in writing or speech 2. to give an account of (happenings, etc.) —*SYN.* see TELL

nar·ra·tion (na räʹshən) *n.* [ME. *narracion* < OFr. < L. *narratio*] 1. the act or process of narrating; the telling of a story or of happenings 2. a story or account; narrative 3. writing or speaking that narrates, as history, biography, or fiction —**narʹraʹtion·al** *adj.*

nar·ra·tive (narʹə tiv) *adj.* [L. *narrativus*] 1. of, or having the nature of, narration; in story form 2. occupied or concerned with narration [a *narrative* poet] —*n.* 1. a story; account; tale 2. the art or practice of relating stories or accounts; narration —*SYN.* see STORY¹ —**narʹra·tive·ly** *adv.*

nar·ra·tor (narʹāt ər, -ət-; na rātʹər) *n.* [L. < *narratus*: see NARRATE] 1. a person who relates a story or account 2. a person who reads descriptive or narrative passages, as between scenes of a play

nar·row (narʹō, nerʹō) *adj.* [ME. *narwe* < OE. *nearu*, akin to MDu. *nare*, OS. *naru* < IE. base **(s)ner-*, to turn, twist, whence Gr. *narkē*, stupor (cf. NARCOTIC)] 1. small in width as compared to length; esp., less wide than is customary, standard, or expected; not wide 2. limited in meaning, size, amount, extent [a *narrow* majority] 3. limited in outlook; without breadth of view or generosity; not liberal; prejudiced [a *narrow* mind] 4. close; careful; minute; thorough [a *narrow* inspection] 5. with limited margin; with barely enough space, time, etc.; barely successful [a *narrow* escape] 6. limited in means; with hardly enough to live on [*narrow* circumstances] ☆7. having a relatively high proportion of protein: said of livestock feed 8. [Dial.] stingy; parsimonious 9. *Phonetics* tense: said of the tongue —*vi.* to decrease in width; contract [the river *narrows*] —*vt.* to decrease or limit in width, extent, or scope; restrict [to *narrow* an argument] —*n.* 1. a narrow part or place, esp. in a valley, mountain pass, road, etc. 2. [*usually pl.*] a narrow passage, as between two bodies of water; strait —**The Narrows** strait between Upper & Lower New York Bay, separating Staten Island & Long Island —**narʹrow·ly** *adv.* —**narʹrow·ness** *n.*

narrow gauge 1. a width (between the rails of a railroad) less than standard gauge (56 1/2 inches) ☆2. a narrow-gauge railroad or car —**narʹrow-gauge′, narʹrow-gauged′** *adj.*

nar·row-mind·ed (-mīnʹdid) *adj.* limited in outlook; not liberal; bigoted; prejudiced —**narʹrow-mindʹed·ly** *adv.* —**narʹrow-mindʹed·ness** *n.*

nar·thex (närʹtheks) *n.* [Gr. *narthēx*, giant fennel (in LGr., a court, exterior portico): from a fancied resemblance of the porch to the hollow stem] 1. in early Christian churches, a porch or portico at the west end for penitents and others not admitted to the church itself 2. any church vestibule leading to the nave

nar·whal (närʹwəl, -hwəl) *n.* [< Scand., as in Norw. & Dan. *narhval* < ON. *nahvalr*, lit., corpse whale < *nār*, corpse + *hvalr*, WHALE¹ (with reference to the whitish underside)] an arctic cetacean (*Monodon monoceros*) valued for its oil and ivory: the male has a long, spiral tusk extending from the upper jaw: also **narʹwal** (-wəl), **narʹwhale** (-hwāl)

nar·y (nerʹē) *adj.* [altered < *ne'er a*, never a] [Dial.] not any; no (with *a* or *an*) [*nary* a doubt]

NAS, N.A.S. 1. National Academy of Sciences 2. Naval Air Station

NASA (nasʹə) National Aeronautics and Space Administration

na·sal (nāʹz'l) *adj.* [ModL. *nasalis* < L. *nasus*, NOSE] 1. of the nose 2. produced by stopping all or part of the breath in the mouth and permitting it to pass through the nose, as the sounds of *m, n, ng* (ŋ), and the French nasalized vowels 3. characterized by such production of sounds [a *nasal* voice] —*n.* 1. a nasal sound or a letter representing such a sound 2. *Anat.* a bone or plate of the

NARWHAL
(body 11–16 ft. long;
tusk to 9 ft. long)

fat, āpe, cär; ten, ēven; is, bīte; gō, hôrn, tōōl, look; oil, out; up, fur; get; joy; yet; chin; she; thin, then; zh, leisure; ŋ, ring; ə for a in ago, e in agent, i in sanity, o in comply, u in focus; ' as in able (āʹb'l); Fr. bâl; ë, Fr. coeur; ö, Fr. feu; Fr. mon; ô, Fr. coq; ü, Fr. duc; r, Fr. cri; H, G. ich; kh, G. doch. See inside front cover. ☆Americanism; ‡foreign; *hypothetical; < derived from

nose **3.** [ME. < OFr. *nasal, nasel* < L. *nasus*] the protective nosepiece of a helmet —**na·sal·i·ty** (nā zal/ə tē) *n.* —**na′sal·ly** *adv.*

nasal index 1. in cephalometry, the ratio of the greatest breadth of the nose to its greatest height multiplied by 100 **2.** in craniometry, the ratio of the greatest breadth of the nasal aperture (of the skull) to its greatest height multiplied by 100

na·sal·ize (nā/zə līz/) *vt.* **-ized′, -iz′ing** to pronounce with a nasal sound —*vi.* to speak with nasal sounds; talk through the nose —**na′sal·i·za′tion** *n.*

Nas·by (naz/bē), **Pe·tro·le·um V.** (pə trō/lē əm) (pseud. of *David Ross Locke*) 1833–88; U.S. humorist

nas·cent (nas/′nt, nā/s′nt) *adj.* [L. *nascens,* prp. of *nasci,* to be born: see NATURE] **1.** coming into being; being born **2.** beginning to form, start, grow, or develop: said of ideas, cultures, etc. **3.** *Chem.* designating or of the state of an element just released from a compound and having unusual chemical activity because atoms of the element have not combined to form molecules [*nascent* chlorine] —**nas′cence,** **nas′cen·cy** *n.*

nase·ber·ry (nāz/ber/ē) *n., pl.* **-ries** [Sp. *níspero,* medlar tree, *néspero,* medlar < L. *mespilus:* see MEDLAR] *same as* SAPODILLA

Nase·by (nāz/bē) village in Northamptonshire, England: site of a decisive Royalist defeat (1645)

Nash (nash), **Ogden** 1902–71; U.S. writer of humorous verse

Nashe (nash), **Thomas** 1567–1601; Eng. satirist & pamphleteer: also sp. **Nash**

Nash·u·a (nash/oo wə) [< Algonquian, lit., ? the land between] city in S N.H., on the Merrimack River: pop. 56,000

Nash·ville (nash/vil; *locally* -vəl) [after Gen. Francis *Nash* (1720–77)] capital of Tenn., on the Cumberland River, in Davidson county, with which it constitutes a metropolitan government (**Nashville-Davidson**): pop. 448,000

na·si·on (nā/zē än/) *n.* [ModL. < L. *nasus,* NOSE] in craniometry, the point in the skull at which the suture between the two nasal bones meets the suture between these and the frontal bone —**na′si·al** *adj.*

na·so- (nā/zō, -zə) [< L. *nasus,* NOSE] *a combining form meaning:* **1.** nose, nasal **2.** nasal and [*nasofrontal*]

na·so·fron·tal (nā/zō frun/t′l) *adj.* of the nose and the frontal bone

na·so·phar·ynx (-far/iŋks) *n.* the part of the pharynx lying directly behind the nasal passages and above the soft palate —**na′so·pha·ryn′ge·al** (-fə rin/jē əl) *adj.*

Nas·sau (nas/ô) **1.** capital of the Bahamas, on New Providence Island: pop. (of the island) 55,000 **2.** region in C West Germany: formerly a duchy **3.** princely family of this former duchy, which, as the House of Orange, has ruled the Netherlands since 1815

Nas·ser (nas/ər), **Ga·mal Ab·del** (gä mäl/ äb/dəl) 1918–70; Egypt. president of the United Arab Republic (1958–70)

Nast (nast), **Thomas** 1840–1902; U.S. political cartoonist & illustrator, born in Germany

nas·tic (nas/tik) *adj.* [< Gr. *nastos,* pressed close < *nasein,* to press, squeeze close + -IC] designating, of, or exhibiting movement or change in position of a plant or its parts, as in the opening and closing of flowers, in response to a stimulus but independent of the direction of the stimulus and caused by unequal growth of certain cells, changes in light intensity, etc.

-nas·tic (nas/tik) *a combining form meaning* nastic by some (specified) means or in some (specified) direction [*photonastic*]

na·stur·tium (nə stur/shəm, na-) *n.* [L., kind of cress < **nasitortium,* lit., nose-twist < *nasus,* NOSE + pp. of *torquere,* to turn, twist: from the pungent odor of the plant] **1.** any of a genus (*Tropaeolum*) of related garden plants of a family (Tropaeolaceae) with shield-shaped leaves, and showy, trumpet-shaped, usually red, yellow, or orange spurred flowers **2.** the flower of this plant

nas·ty (nas/tē) *adj.* **-ti·er, -ti·est** [ME. < ? or akin to Du. *nestig,* dirty] **1.** very dirty; filthy **2.** offensive in taste or smell; nauseating **3.** morally offensive; indecent **4.** very unpleasant; objectionable [*nasty* weather] **5.** mean; malicious; ill-humored [a *nasty* temper] **6.** very harmful or troublesome [a *nasty* bruise] —**nas′ti·ly** *adv.* —**nas′ti·ness** *n.*

nat. 1. national **2.** native **3.** natural **4.** naturalist

Na·tal (nə tal/, -täl/) **1.** province of E South Africa, on the Indian Ocean: 33,578 sq. mi.; pop. 2,933,000; cap. Pietermaritzburg **2.** seaport on the NE coast of Brazil: pop. 163,000

na·tal (nāt/′l) *adj.* [ME. < L. *natalis* < *natus,* pp. of *nasci,* to be born: see NATURE] **1.** of or connected with one's birth **2.** dating from birth **3.** native: said of a place

Nat·a·lie (nat/′l ē) [Fr. < LL. *Natalia* < L. *natalis* (*dies*), natal (day), name given to children born on Christmas Day] a feminine name

na·tal·i·ty (nā tal/ə tē, nə-) *n.* [Fr. *natalité*] *same as* BIRTHRATE

na·tant (nāt/′nt) *adj.* [L. *natans,* prp. of *natare,* to swim < IE. **(s)net-* < base **(s)na-,* to flow, whence L. *nare,* to swim, OIr. *snām,* swimming] swimming or floating; esp., floating on the surface of water

na·ta·tion (nā tā/shən) *n.* [L. *natatio* < pp. of *natare:* see prec.] the act or art of swimming —**na·ta′tion·al** *adj.*

na·ta·to·ri·al (nāt/ə tôr/ē əl) *adj.* [< LL. *natatorius* < L. *natator,* swimmer (see NATANT) + -AL] of, characterized by, or adapted for swimming: also **na′ta·to′ry**

☆**na·ta·to·ri·um** (-əm) *n., pl.* **-ri·ums, -ri·a** (-ə) [LL. < *natatorius:* see prec.] a swimming pool, esp. one indoors

☆**natch** (nach) *adv.* [Slang] naturally; of course

Natch·ez (nach/iz) *n.* [orig. a Natchez place name] **1.** *pl.* **Natch′ez** any member of an extinct tribe of Indians who lived in SW Mississippi **2.** their language, the sole known member of its family

Natchez Trace early 19th-cent. road following an old Indian trail from Natchez, Miss., to Nashville, Tenn.

na·tes (nā/tēz) *n.pl.* [L., pl. of *natis,* akin to Gr. *nōton,* the back] the buttocks

Na·than (nā/thən) [Heb. *nāthān,* lit., gift] **1.** a masculine name: dim. *Nat, Nate* **2.** *Bible* a prophet who rebuked David for the death of Uriah: II Sam. 12:1–14 **3. George Jean,** 1882–1958; U.S. drama critic & editor

Na·than·a·el (nə than/yəl, -ē əl) [LL.(Ec.) < Gr.(Ec.) *Nathanaēl* < Heb. *nĕthan′ēl,* lit., gift of God] **1.** a masculine name: dim. *Nat:* also sp. **Nathaniel 2.** *Bible* one of the disciples of Jesus: John 1:45–51

nathe·less (nāth/lis, nath/-) *adv.* [ME. *natheles* < OE. < *na,* never + *the* (for *thy,* instrumental case of def. art.) + *læs,* less) [Archaic] nevertheless —*prep.* [Archaic] notwithstanding Also **nath′less** (nath/-)

na·tion (nā/shən) *n.* [ME. *nacion* < OFr. < L. *natio* < *natus,* born: see NATURE] **1.** a stable, historically developed community of people with a territory, economic life, distinctive culture, and language in common **2.** the people of a territory united under a single government; country; state **3.** *a*) a people or tribe; esp., ☆a tribe of N. American Indians, sometimes one belonging to a confederation ☆*b*) [N-] the territory of a particular Indian tribe or tribes —**the nations 1.** *Bible* the non-Jewish nations; Gentiles **2.** [Poet.] all the peoples of the earth —**na′tion·hood′** (-hood′) *n.*

Na·tion (nā/shən), **Carry** (born *Carry Amelia Moore*) 1846–1911; U.S. agitator for temperance

na·tion·al (nash/ə n′l) *adj.* [Fr.] **1.** of or having to do with a nation or the nation **2.** affecting a (or the) nation as a whole; nationwide in scope, involvement, representation, etc. **3.** patriotic or nationalist **4.** established, maintained, or owned by the federal government [a *national* park] —*n.* **1.** a person under the protection of a (specified) country; citizen or subject **2.** the national headquarters or administration of an organization —*SYN.* see CITIZEN —**na′tion·al·ly** *adv.*

national bank 1. a bank or system of banks owned and operated by a government, as in some foreign countries ☆**2.** in the U.S., a member bank of the Federal Reserve System, chartered by the Federal government: national banks formerly issued bank notes secured by government bonds

National City [located on part of Rancho de la Nacion, whence *National* Ranch, *National* City] city in SW Calif.: suburb of San Diego: pop. 43,000

national debt the total debt incurred by the central government of a nation, specif. by the Federal government of the U.S.

☆**National Guard** in the U.S., the organized militia forces of the individual States, a component of the Army of the U.S. when called into active Federal service

☆**National Guard of the United States** those members and units of the National Guard that have been accorded Federal recognition as a reserve component part of the Army or Air Force of the U.S.

national income the total income of a nation, including all profits, rents, interest, wages, salaries, etc., during a specified period, usually a year: equal in total to the net national product minus indirect business taxes and business transfer payments

na·tion·al·ism (nash/ə n′l iz′m) *n.* **1.** *a*) devotion to one's nation; patriotism *b*) excessive, narrow, or jingoist patriotism; chauvinism **2.** the doctrine that national interest, security, etc. are more important than international considerations **3.** the desire for or advocacy of national independence

na·tion·al·ist (-ist) *n.* a person who believes in or advocates nationalism —*adj.* of nationalism or nationalists: also **na′tion·al·is′tic** —**na′tion·al·is′ti·cal·ly** *adv.*

na·tion·al·i·ty (nash/ə nal/ə tē) *n., pl.* **-ties 1.** national quality or character **2.** the status of belonging to a particular nation by birth or naturalization; identification as to national origin **3.** the condition or fact of being a nation **4.** a nation or national group

na·tion·al·ize (nash/ə nə līz/) *vt.* **-ized′, -iz′ing 1.** to make national in character **2.** to transfer ownership or control of (land, resources, industries, etc.) to the national government —**na′tion·al·i·za′tion** *n.* —**na′tion·al·iz′er** *n.*

National Liberation Front a revolutionary, political front or party working for national independence in any of various countries; specif., such a front organized in South Vietnam in 1961

☆**national monument** a natural geographic feature or historic site, as a mountain, canyon, old fort, etc., maintained and preserved by the Federal government for the public to visit

☆**national park** an area of scenic beauty, historical and scientific interest, etc. maintained and preserved by the Federal government for the public to visit

☆**National Weather Service** the division of the Department of Commerce that gathers and compiles data on weather conditions over the U.S., on the basis of which weather forecasts are made

nation-state (nā′shən stāt′) *n.* the independent nation as the representative unit of political organization in modern times

na·tion·wide (-wīd′) *adj.* by or throughout the whole nation; national

na·tive (nāt′iv) *adj.* [ME. *natyf* < MFr. *natif* < L. *nativus* < *natus*, born: see NATURE] **1.** inborn or innate rather than acquired **2.** belonging to a locality or country by birth, production, or growth; indigenous [a native Bostonian, *native* industry, *native* plants] **3.** related to one as, or in connection with, the place of one's birth or origin [one's *native* land, one's *native* language] **4.** simple; natural; free from affectation **5.** as found in nature; natural and not refined, adorned, or altered by man **6.** occurring in a pure state in nature [*native* gold] **7.** of or characteristic of the natives, or indigenous inhabitants, of a place *n.* **1.** a person born in the place or country indicated **2.** *a)* an original or indigenous inhabitant of a region, as distinguished from an invader, explorer, colonist, etc. *b)* an indigenous plant or animal **3.** a permanent resident, as distinguished from a temporary resident or visitor **4.** *Astrol.* a person born under a certain sign —**go native** to adopt a simple, uncomplicated mode of life —**na′tive·ly** *adv.* —**na′tive·ness** *n.*

SYN.—**native** applies to a person born, or thing originating, in a certain place or country [a *native* Italian, *native* fruits]; **indigenous**, which also suggests natural origin in a particular region, is applied to races or species rather than to individuals [the potato is *indigenous* to South America]; **aboriginal** applies to the earliest known inhabitants (or, rarely, animals or plants) of a region [the Indians are the *aboriginal* Americans]; **endemic**, applied esp. to plants and diseases, implies prevalence in or restriction to a particular region [typhus is *endemic* in various countries] See also CITIZEN —*ANT.* **alien, foreign**

na·tive-born (-bôrn′) *adj.* of a specified place by birth

☆**native son** a man native to a particular place [the Ohio delegation nominated a *native son*]

☆**na·tiv·ism** (nāt′iv iz′m) *n.* ☆**1.** the practice or policy of favoring native-born citizens as against immigrants **2.** the revival or preservation of a native culture **3.** *Philos.* the doctrine of innate ideas —**na′tiv·ist** *adj., n.* —**na′-tiv·is′tic** *adj.*

na·tiv·i·ty (nə tiv′ə tē, nā-) *n., pl.* **-ties** [ME. *natiuite* < OFr. *nativite* < LL. *nativitas* < L. *nativus*, NATIVE] **1.** birth, esp. with reference to place, time, or accompanying conditions **2.** *Astrol.* the horoscope for one's birth —**the Nativity 1.** the birth of Jesus **2.** a representation of this **3.** Christmas Day

natl. national

NATO (nā′tō) North Atlantic Treaty Organization

nat·ro·lite (nat′rə līt′, nā′trə-) *n.* [G. *natrolith* (< Fr.: see NATRON) + *-lith*, -LITE] a hydrous silicate of sodium and aluminum, $Na_2Al_2Si_3O_{10} \cdot 2H_2O$, a member of the zeolite group of minerals

na·tron (nā′trän) *n.* [Fr. < Sp. *natrón* < Ar. *naṭrūn* < Gr. *nitron*: see NITER] hydrated sodium carbonate, $Na_2CO_3 10H_2O$

nat·ter (nat′ər) *vi.* [var. of dial. *gnatter* < Gmc. echoic base whence ON. *gnata*, to crash noisily & G. *knattern*, to clatter] [Chiefly Brit.] **1.** to chatter idly; talk on at length **2.** to find fault; scold —*n.* [Chiefly Brit.] a chat or talk

nat·ty (nat′ē) *adj.* **-ti·er, -ti·est** [< ? NEAT¹] trim and smart in appearance or dress [a *natty* suit] —**nat′ti·ly** *adv.* —**nat′ti·ness** *n.*

Na·tu·fi·an (nə tōō′fē ən) *adj.* [after Wady en-*Natuf*, valley in Palestine + -IAN] designating or of a mesolithic culture of SW Asia, characterized by microlith assemblages and the first evidences of the reaping of cereals

nat·u·ral (nach′ər əl, nach′rəl) *adj.* [ME. < OFr. < L. *naturalis*, by birth, according to nature] **1.** of or arising from nature; in accordance with what is found or expected in nature **2.** produced or existing in nature; not artificial or manufactured **3.** dealing with nature as an object of study [a *natural* science] **4.** in a state provided by nature, without man-made changes; wild; uncultivated **5.** of the real or physical world as distinguished from a spiritual, intellectual, or imaginary world **6.** *a)* present by virtue of nature; innate; not acquired [*natural* abilities] *b)* having certain qualities, abilities, etc. innately [a *natural* comedian] **7.** innately felt to be right; based on instinctive moral feeling [*natural* rights] **8.** true to nature; lifelike [a *natural* likeness] **9.** normal or usual; in the ordinary course of events [a *natural* outcome] **10.** customarily expected or accepted [a *natural* courtesy] **11.** free from affectation or artificiality; at ease [a *natural* smile] **12.** without a legal relationship; specif., *a)* illegitimate [a *natural* child] *b)* relating biologically rather than by adoption [*natural* parents] **13.** *Math. a)* designating or of an

integer or any number referred to 1 as the base *b)* designating or of an actual number as distinguished from a logarithm [a *natural* sine, cosine, etc.] **14.** *Music a)* without flats or sharps, as the key of C major *b)* modified in pitch by the sign (♮) *c)* neither sharped nor flatted —*n.* **1.** a person without normal intelligence; fool; idiot **2.** [Colloq.] a person who is or seems to be naturally expert ☆**3.** [Colloq.] a thing that is, or promises to be, immediately successful ☆**4.** [Colloq.] a winning cast of 7 or 11 on the first throw in craps **5.** *Music a)* the sign (♮), used to remove the effect of a preceding sharp or flat within the measure in which it occurs: in full, **natural sign** *b)* the note so changed *c)* a white key on a piano —*SYN.* see NORMAL —**nat′u·ral·ness** *n.*

☆**natural bridge** a natural rock formation suggestive of a bridge; esp., *a)* [N- B-] a limestone formation in WC Va., over a tributary of the James River: 215 ft. high; span c. 90 ft. *b)* any of three such formations in SE Utah, the main features of a national monument (**Natural Bridges National Monument**), 4 sq. mi.

natural childbirth a method of childbirth in which the expectant mother is prepared emotionally and physically for labor as a relaxed, relatively painless process, so that a normal delivery will require little or no anesthesia

natural gas a mixture of gaseous hydrocarbons, chiefly methane, occurring naturally in the earth, often in association with petroleum deposits, and piped to cities, etc., to be used as a fuel

natural history the study of zoology, botany, mineralogy, geology, and other subjects dealing with the physical world, esp. in a popular, nontechnical manner

nat·u·ral·ism (-iz′m) *n.* **1.** action or thought based on natural desires or instincts **2.** *Literature, Art,* etc. *a)* faithful adherence to nature; realism; specif., the principles and methods of a group of 19th-cent. writers, including Émile Zola, Gustave Flaubert, and Guy de Maupassant, who believed that the writer or artist should apply scientific objectivity and precision in his observation and treatment of life, without idealizing, imposing value judgments, or avoiding what may be regarded as repulsive *b)* the quality resulting from the use of such realism **3.** *Ethics* the theory that distinctions between good and bad can be reduced to nonnormative or factual terms and statements, according to psychology, biology, etc. **4.** *Philos.* the belief that the natural world, known and experienced scientifically, is all that exists and that there is no supernatural or spiritual creation, control, or significance **5.** *Theol.* the doctrine that religion does not depend on supernatural experience, divine revelation, etc., and that all religious truth may be derived from the natural world

nat·u·ral·ist (-ist) *n.* [Fr. *naturaliste*] **1.** a person who studies nature, esp. by direct observation of animals and plants **2.** a person who believes in or practices naturalism in any form —*adj.* same as NATURALISTIC

nat·u·ral·is·tic (nach′ər ə lis′tik) *adj.* **1.** of natural history or naturalists **2.** of or characterized by naturalism in any form **3.** in accordance with, or in imitation of, nature —**nat′u·ral·is′ti·cal·ly** *adv.*

nat·u·ral·ize (nach′ər ə līz′, nach′rə-) *vt.* **-ized′, -iz′ing** [Fr. *naturaliser*: see NATURAL & -IZE] **1.** to confer the rights of citizenship upon (an alien) **2.** to adopt and make common (a custom, word, etc.) from another country or place **3.** to adapt (a plant or animal) to a new environment; acclimate **4.** to explain (occurrences) by natural law, rejecting supernatural influence **5.** to make natural or less artificial; free from conventionality —*vi.* **1.** to become naturalized, or as if native **2.** to study nature —**nat′u·ral·i·za′tion** *n.*

natural law 1. rules of conduct supposedly inherent in the relations between human beings and discoverable by reason; law based upon man's innate moral sense **2.** a law of nature: see LAW (sense 8 *a)* **3.** the laws of nature, collectively

natural logarithm a logarithm to the base *e*

nat·u·ral·ly (nach′ər əl ē, nach′rə lē) *adv.* **1.** in a natural manner **2.** by nature; innately **3.** as one might expect; of course

natural number any positive integer, as 1, 2, 3, etc.

natural philosophy *earlier name for* NATURAL SCIENCE (specif., physics)

natural resources those actual and potential forms of wealth supplied by nature, as coal, oil, water power, arable land, etc.

natural science 1. the systematized knowledge of nature and the physical world, including zoology, botany, chemistry, physics, geology, etc. **2.** any of these branches of knowledge

natural selection in evolution, the process by which those individuals (of a species) with characters that help them to become adapted to their specific environment tend to leave more progeny and transmit their characters, while those less able to become adapted tend to leave fewer progeny or die out, so that in the course of generations there is a progressive tendency in the species to a greater degree of adaptation: see also DARWINIAN THEORY

natural theology theology that is based on observation of natural processes and not on divine revelation

na·ture (nā′chər) *n.* [ME. < OFr. < L. *natura* < *natus*, born, produced, pp. of *nasci*, to be born < IE. base **gen-*, to give birth to, produce, whence Gr. *genetē*, birth, L. *gens*, family] **1.** the essential character of a thing; quality or qualities that make something what it is; essence **2.** inborn character; innate disposition; inherent tendencies of a person **3.** the vital functions, forces, and activities of the organs: often used as a euphemism **4.** kind; sort; type [things of that *nature*] **5.** any or all of the instincts, desires, appetites, drives, etc. of a person or animal **6.** what is regarded as normal or acceptable behavior **7.** the sum total of all things in time and space; the entire physical universe **8.** [*sometimes* N-] the power, force, principle, etc. that seems to regulate this: often personified **9.** the primitive state of man **10.** a simple way of life close to or in the outdoors **11.** natural scenery, including the plants and animals that are part of it **12.** [Archaic] affectionate or kindly feeling **13.** *Theol.* the state of man unredeemed by grace —*SYN.* see TYPE —**by nature** naturally; inherently —**in a state of nature 1.** completely naked **2.** not cultivated or tamed; wild **3.** uncivilized —**of** (or **in**) **the nature of** having the essential character of; like

-na·tured (nā′chərd) *a combining form meaning* having or showing a (specified kind of) nature, disposition, or temperament [*good-natured*]

nature study the study of plant and animal life by direct observation, esp. in an elementary, nontechnical manner

nature worship 1. worship of natural forces as gods **2.** poetic love for nature

na·tur·o·path (nā′chər ə path′) *n.* a person who practices naturopathy

na·tur·op·a·thy (nā′chər äp′ə thē) *n.* [< NATURE + -*o-* + -PATHY] a system of treating diseases, largely employing natural agencies, such as air, water, sunshine, etc., and rejecting the use of drugs and medicines —**na′tur·o·path′-ic** (-ə path′ik) *adj.*

Nau·cra·tis (nô′krə tis) Gr. city in the Nile delta in ancient Egypt

☆**Naug·a·hyde** (nôg′ə hīd′) [arbitrary coinage] *a trademark for* a kind of imitation leather, used for upholstery —*n.* [n-] this material

naught (nôt) *n.* [ME. < OE. *nawiht* < *na* (see NA, NO¹) + *wiht* (see WIGHT, WHIT)] **1.** nothing **2.** *Arith.* the figure zero (0) —*adj.* [Archaic or Obs.] **1.** worthless; useless **2.** wicked; evil —**set at naught** to defy; scorn

naugh·ty (nôt′ē) *adj.* **-ti·er, -ti·est** [ME. *naugti*: see NAUGHT] **1.** [Obs.] wicked; bad; evil **2.** not behaving properly; mischievous or disobedient: used esp. of children or their behavior **3.** showing lack of decorum; improper, indelicate, or obscene —*SYN.* see BAD¹ —**naugh′ti·ly** *adv.* —**naugh′ti·ness** *n.*

nau·ma·chi·a (nô mā′kē ə) *n., pl.* **-chi·as, -chi·ae′** (-ē′) [L. < Gr. *naumachia* < *naus*, ship (see NAVY) + *machē*, battle] **1.** in ancient Rome, a mock sea battle **2.** a place constructed for this Also **nau·ma·chy** (nô′mə kē), *pl.* **-chies**

nau·pli·us (nô′plē əs) *n., pl.* **-pli·i′** (-ī′) [L., kind of shellfish < Gr. *nauplios*, kind of shellfish said to sail in its shell as in a ship < *naus*, ship (see NAVY) + *pleiein*, to sail] the first larval stage in the development of certain crustaceans, typically unsegmented with only three pairs of appendages, all on the head, and an unpaired median eye

Na·u·ru (nä ōō′rōō) country on an island in the W Pacific, just south of the equator: formerly, a UN trust territory (1947–68): 8 sq. mi.; pop. 5,500

nau·se·a (nô′shə, -sē ə, -zē ə, -zhə) *n.* [L. < Gr. *nausia*, *nautia*, seasickness < *naus*, a ship, *nautēs*, sailor: see NAVY] **1.** a feeling of sickness at the stomach, with an impulse to vomit **2.** disgust; loathing —**nau′se·ant** *adj., n.*

nau·se·ate (-shē āt′, -sē-, -zē-, -zhē-) *vt.* **-at′ed, -at′ing** [< L. *nauseatus*, pp. of *nauseare*, to be seasick: see NAUSEA] **1.** to cause to feel nausea; make sick **2.** [Rare] to feel nausea at; loathe —*vi.* to feel nausea; become sick —**nau′se·at′ing·ly** *adv.* —**nau′se·a′tion** *n.*

nau·seous (nô′shəs, -zē əs, -sē-) *adj.* [L. *nauseosus*] **1.** causing nausea; specif., *a)* sickening *b)* disgusting **2.** [Colloq.] feeling nausea; nauseated —**nau′seous·ly** *adv.* —**nau′seous·ness** *n.*

Nau·sic·a·ä (nô sik′ā ə, -ē ə) in Homer's *Odyssey*, King Alcinoüs's daughter, who discovers, and secures safe passage for, the shipwrecked Odysseus

naut. nautical

nautch (nôch) *n.* [Hind. *nāc* < Prakrit *nacca* < Sans. *nṛtya*, dancing < *nṛt*, to dance] in India, a performance by professional dancing girls (**nautch girls**)

nau·ti·cal (nôt′i k'l) *adj.* [Fr. *nautique* < L. *nauticus* < Gr. *nautikos* < *nautēs*, sailor, seaman < *naus*, a ship: see NAVY] of or having to do with sailors, ships, or navigation —**nau′ti·cal·ly** *adv.*

nautical mile any of various units of distance for sea and air navigation: in the U.S. since 1959, an international unit of linear measure equal to one minute of arc of a great circle of the earth, 6,076.11549 ft. (1,852 meters)

nau·ti·loid (nôt′'l oid′) *n.* [< ModL. *Nautiloidea*: see NAUTILUS & -OIDEA] any of a suborder (Nautiloidea) of shelled cephalopods, including as the only living representatives the nautiluses

nau·ti·lus (-əs) *n., pl.* **-lus·es, -li′** (-ī′) [ModL., name of the genus < L. < Gr. *nautilos*, sailor, nautilus < *naus*, a ship: see NAVY] **1.** any of a genus (*Nautilus*) of tropical, cephalopod mollusks with a many-chambered, spiral shell, having a pearly interior **2.** *same as* PAPER NAUTILUS —[N-] a U.S. Navy submarine, the first to be powered by atomic energy

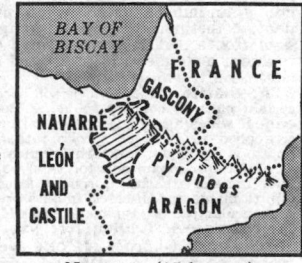

NAUTILUS
(shell to 10 in.
in diameter)

nav. 1. naval **2.** navigable **3.** navigation **4.** navigator **5.** navy

Nav·a·ho (nav′ə hō′) *n.* [< Sp. (*apaches de*) *Navajó* < AmInd. (Tewa) *Navahú*, lit., great fields, name of the Tewa pueblo near which the Spaniards first met Navahos] **1.** *pl.* **-hos, -ho, -hoes** any member of the largest Indian tribe in the U.S., who live in Arizona, New Mexico, and Utah **2.** their Apache language Also sp. **Nav′a·jo′**

na·val (nā′v'l) *adj.* [< Fr. or L.: Fr. *naval* < L. *navalis* < *navis*, a ship: see NAVY] **1.** [Obs.] of ships or shipping **2.** of, having, characteristic of, or for a navy, its ships, personnel, etc.

Na·varre (nə vär′) region in NE Spain & SW France: formerly a kingdom: Sp. name **Na·va·ra** (nä vär′rä)

nave¹ (nāv) *n.* [ML. *navis* < L., ship: see NAVY] that part of a church which is between the side aisles and extends from the chancel to the principal entrance, forming the main part of the building

nave² (nāv) *n.* [ME. < OE. *nafu*, akin to G. *nabe*: see ff.] the hub of a wheel

na·vel (nā′v'l) *n.* [ME. < OE. *nafela*, akin to G. *nabel* < IE. base **ombh-*, **nōbh-*, navel, whence L. *umbilicus*, Gr. *omphalos* & NAVE²] **1.** the small scar, usually a depression in the middle of the abdomen, marking the place where the umbilical cord was attached to the fetus; umbilicus **2.** any centrally located point, part, or place

☆**navel orange** a seedless orange having at its apex a depression like a navel, containing a small, undeveloped secondary fruit

nav·i·cert (nav′ə surt′) *n.* [*navi*(gation) *cert*(*ificate*)] a document issued by a nation at war exempting a ship of a friendly or neutral nation from search or seizure of goods as it moves through that belligerent's blockade

na·vic·u·lar (nə vik′yoo lər) *adj.* [LL. *navicularis* < L. *navicula*, dim. of *navis*, a ship: see NAVY] shaped like a boat: said esp. of certain bones —*n.* any of various boat-shaped bones; esp., *a)* the outer bone of the first row of carpals in the wrist *b)* a bone on the inner side of the human foot, in front of the anklebone

navig. 1. navigation **2.** navigator

nav·i·ga·ble (nav′i gə b'l) *adj.* [L. *navigabilis* < *navigare*: see ff.] **1.** wide or deep enough, or free enough from obstructions, to be traveled on by vessels [a *navigable* river] **2.** that can be steered, or directed [a *navigable* balloon] —**nav′i·ga·bil′i·ty** *n.* —**nav′i·ga·bly** *adv.*

nav·i·gate (nav′ə gāt′) *vi.* **-gat′ed, -gat′ing** [< L. *navigatus*, pp. of *navigare*, to sail < *navis*, a ship (see NAVY) + *agere*, to lead, go (see ACT)] **1.** to steer, or direct, a ship or aircraft ☆**2.** [Colloq.] to make one's way; walk **3.** [Rare] to travel by ship —*vt.* **1.** to travel through or over (water, air, or land) in a ship or aircraft **2.** to steer, or direct (a ship or aircraft) **3.** to plot the course for (a ship or aircraft) **4.** [Colloq.] to walk or make one's way on or through

nav·i·ga·tion (nav′ə gā′shən) *n.* [L. *navigatio*] **1.** the act or practice of navigating; esp., the science of locating the position and plotting the course of ships and aircraft **2.** traffic by ship —**nav′i·ga′tion·al** *adj.* —**nav′i·ga′tion·al·ly** *adv.*

nav·i·ga·tor (nav′ə gāt′ər) *n.* [L.] **1.** a person who navigates; esp., one skilled or employed in navigation, either of a ship or an aircraft **2.** an explorer by ship **3.** [Brit.] *same as* NAVVY

nav·vy (nav′ē) *n., pl.* **-vies** [abbrev. of prec.] [Brit.] an unskilled laborer, as on canals, roads, etc.

na·vy (nā′vē) *n., pl.* **-vies** [ME. *navie* < OFr. < VL. **navia* < L. *navis*, a ship < IE. base **naus*, boat (prob. dugout), whence Sans. *nâuh*, boat, Gr. *naus*, ship, ON. *nōr*, ship] **1.** [Archaic or Poet.] a fleet of ships **2.** all the warships of a nation **3.** [*often* N-] *a)* the entire sea force of a nation, including vessels, officers, men, stores, yards, etc. *b)* the governmental department in charge of this **4.** *same as* NAVY BLUE

☆**navy bean** [from common use in the U.S. *Navy*] a small, white variety of kidney bean, dried for use as a food

navy blue [from the color of the Brit. naval uniform] very dark, purplish blue

☆**Navy Cross** a decoration awarded to members of the U.S. Navy, Marine Corps, or Coast Guard for extraordinary heroism in military action against an armed enemy

navy yard a dockyard for building and repairing naval ships, storing naval supplies, etc.

na·wab (nə wäb′, -wôb′) *n.* [Hindi *navāb*: see NABOB] *same as* NABOB

Nax·os (nak′säs; *Gr.* näk′sôs) largest island of the Cyclades, in the SC Aegean: c. 170 sq. mi.

nay (nā) *adv.* [ME. < ON. *nei* < *ne*, not + *ei*, ever (see AYE)] **1.** no: now seldom used except in voting by voice **2.** not that only, but also: used to reinforce a statement [I permit, *nay*, encourage it] —*n.* **1.** a refusal or denial **2.** a negative vote or a person voting in the negative **3.** a negative answer —**say (someone) nay** to refuse or forbid (someone)

Na·ya·rit (nä′yä rēt′) state of W Mexico: 10,445 sq. mi.; pop. 532,000; cap. Tepic

nay·say·er (nā′sā′ər) *n.* [NAY + SAY + -ER] one who opposes, refuses, or denies, esp. habitually

Naz·a·rene (naz′ə rēn′, naz′ə rēn′) *adj.* [ME. *Nazaren* < LL.(Ec.) *Nazarenus* < Gr.(Ec.) *Nazarēnos*, the Nazarene] of Nazareth or the Nazarenes —*n.* **1.** a native or inhabitant of Nazareth **2.** any member of an early sect of Christians of Jewish origin who continued to observe much of the Mosaic law ☆**3.** a member of the Church of the Nazarene, a Protestant evangelical sect **4.** [Obs.] a Christian: term formerly used by Moslems, Jews, etc. —**the Nazarene** Jesus

Naz·a·reth (naz′ər əth) town in Galilee, N Israel, where Jesus lived as a child: pop. 26,000

Naz·a·rite, Naz·i·rite (naz′ə rīt′) *n.* [LL.(Ec.) *Nazaraeus* < Gr.(Ec.) *Nazaraios*, for Heb. *nāzīr* < *nāzar*, to separate, consecrate] **1.** among the ancient Hebrews, a person who voluntarily assumed certain strict religious vows, such as abstaining from wine, not cutting his hair, etc. **2.** *rare var. of* NAZARENE

Na·zi (nät′sē, nat′-) *adj.* [G. < *Nati*(*onalsozialistische Deutsche Arbeiterpartei*), party name] designating, of, or characteristic of the German fascist political party (*National Socialist German Workers' Party*), founded in 1919 and abolished in 1945: under Hitler it seized control of Germany in 1933, systematically eliminated opposition, and put into effect its program of nationalism, racism, rearmament, aggression, etc. —*n.* **1.** a member of this party **2.** [*often* n-] a supporter or follower of this or any similar party; fascist —**Na′zism** (-siz′m), **Na′zi·ism** (-sē iz′m) *n.*

Na·zi·fy (-sə fī′) *vt.* -**fied′, -fy′ing** [*also* n-] to place under Nazi control or influence; cause to be Nazi or like the Nazis —**Na′zi·fi·ca′tion** *n.*

Nb *Chem.* niobium

N.B. New Brunswick

N.B., n.b. [L. *nota bene*] note well

NBA, N.B.A. 1. National Basketball Association **2.** National Boxing Association

NBC National Broadcasting Company

NbE north by east

NBS, N.B.S. National Bureau of Standards

NbW north by west

NC, N.C. 1. nitrocellulose **2.** no charge **3.** nurse corps

N.C. 1. New Caledonia **2.** North Carolina

NCAA, N.C.A.A. National Collegiate Athletic Association

NCO, N.C.O. noncommissioned officer

NCTE, N.C.T.E. National Council of Teachers of English

Nd *Chem.* neodymium

N.D., n.d. no date

N.Dak., N.D. North Dakota

ne- (nē) *same as* NEO-: used before a vowel

Ne *Chem.* neon

NE, N.E., n.e. 1. northeast **2.** northeastern

N.E. 1. Naval Engineer **2.** New England

NEA, N.E.A. 1. National Education Association **2.** Newspaper Enterprise Association

Neal (nēl) [ME. *Nel, Neel, Nele*, prob. < Ir. *Niul* (Gael. *Niall*) < *niadh*, a champion] a masculine name

Ne·an·der·thal (nē an′dər thôl′, -täl′) *adj.* [G., lit., Neander valley (G. *thal, tal*, valley, akin to DALE), named after Joachim *Neander* (1650-80), G. hymn writer] **1.** designating, of, or from a valley in the Rhine Province, Germany **2.** designating or of a form of primitive man (*Homo sapiens neanderthalensis*) of the paleolithic period whose skeletal remains were first found in this valley

neap[1] (nēp) *adj.* [ME. *neep* < OE. *nep-* in *nepflod*, neap tide] designating the tide occurring just after the first and third quarters of the lunar month: at these times the difference between high and low tides is smallest —*n.* neap tide

neap[2] (nēp) *n.* [prob. < ON., as in Norw. dial. *neip*, forked pole] [Dial.] the tongue of a wagon drawn by two animals

Ne·a·pol·i·tan (nē′ə päl′ə t'n) *adj.* [L. *Neapolitanus* < *Neapolites*, a citizen of Naples < *Neapolis*, Naples < Gr. *Neapolis*, lit., new town] of Naples —*n.* a native or inhabitant of Naples

☆**Neapolitan ice cream** brick ice cream containing several flavors and colors in layers, often chocolate, strawberry, and vanilla

near (nir) *adv.* [ME. *nere* < ON. & OE.: ON. *nær*, near (orig. compar. of *nā*-): OE. *near*, nearer, compar. of *neah*, NIGH] **1.** at or to a relatively short distance in space or time [summer draws *near*] **2.** relatively close in degree; almost [*near* right]: now usually **nearly 3.** closely; intimately **4.** [Rare] in a stingy manner; thriftily —*adj.* **1.** close in distance or time; not far **2.** close in relationship; akin **3.** close in feelings, desires, etc.; close in friendship; intimate **4.** *a)* close in degree; narrow [a *near* escape] *b)* almost happening [a *near* accident] **5.** on the left side, facing forward: said of animals, wheels, etc. [the *near* horse]: opposed to OFF **6.** short or direct [take the *near* way] **7.** stingy; niggardly **8.** somewhat resembling; approximating [a *near* likeness] —*prep.* at a relatively short distance from in space, time, degree, etc.; close to —*vt., vi.* to come or draw near (to); approach —**near at hand** very close in time or space —**near′ness** *n.*

near·by (nir′bī′) *adj., adv.* near; close at hand

Ne·arc·tic (nē ärk′tik, -är′-) *adj.* [NE- + ARCTIC] designating or of the biogeographic subregion that includes the arctic and temperate parts of N. America and Greenland

Near East 1. countries near the E end of the Mediterranean, including those of SW Asia, the Arabian Peninsula, NE Africa, &, sometimes, the Balkans **2.** *a)* formerly, the lands occupied by the Ottoman Empire, including the Balkans *b)* [Brit.] the Balkans —**Near Eastern**

near·ly (-lē) *adv.* **1.** almost; not quite; all but [*nearly* finished] **2.** [Now Rare] closely; intimately [to be *nearly* related] **3.** [Archaic] parsimoniously; stingily —**not nearly** not at all; far from

near miss *Mil.* **1.** a shell, aerial bomb, etc. that does not score a direct hit on the target but comes close enough to inflict some damage **2.** any result that is nearly but not quite successful

near·sight·ed (-sīt′id) *adj.* having better vision for near objects than for distant ones; myopic —**near′sight′ed·ly** *adv.* —**near′sight′ed·ness** *n.*

neat[1] (nēt) *adj.* [Fr. *net* < L. *nitidus*, shining, elegant, smart, trim < *nitere*, to shine < IE. base *nei*-, to be active, shine, whence MIr. *nīam*, luster, beauty] **1.** unmixed with anything; undiluted; straight: said esp. of liquor drunk without a mixer or chaser **2.** [Rare] free of deductions; net **3.** *a)* clean and in good order; trim; tidy *b)* characterized by tidiness, skill, and precision [a *neat* worker] *c)* without anything superfluous; simple **4.** well-proportioned; shapely **5.** cleverly or smartly phrased or done; adroit **6.** [Slang] nice, pleasing, fine, etc.: a generalized term of approval —**neat′ly** *adv.* —**neat′ness** *n.* SYN.—**neat** suggests cleanness and orderliness and, hence, connotes a lack of superfluous or confusing details [a *neat* house, design, etc.]; **tidy** emphasizes painstaking, orderly arrangement rather than cleanliness [a *tidy* closet]; **trim** adds to the sense of **neat** connotations of smartness, dapperness, good proportion, etc. [a *trim* figure, ship, etc.] —ANT. slovenly, sloppy

neat[2] (nēt) *n., pl.* **neat** [ME. *nete* < OE. *neat* (akin to ON. *naut*, Du. *noot*) < base of *neotan*, to enjoy, possess < IE. base *neud*-, to make use of, whence Lith. *naudà*, benefit, possessions] [Now Rare] a bovine animal; ox, cow, etc.

neat·en (nēt′'n) *vt.* [NEAT + -EN] to make neat; cause to be clean, tidy, orderly, or trim (often with *up*)

'neath, neath (nēth) *prep. poet. var. of* BENEATH

neat·herd (nēt′hʉrd′) *n.* [ME. *netherd*: see NEAT[2] & HERD[2]] *rare var. of* COWHERD

neat's-foot oil (nēts′foot′) a light-yellow oil obtained by boiling the feet and shinbones of cattle, used mainly as a dressing for leather

neb (neb) *n.* [ME. < OE. *nebb*, akin to MDu. *nebbe*, ON. *nef*] [Now Chiefly Brit. Dial.] **1.** *a)* the bill of a bird *b)* the snout of an animal **2.** the nose or mouth of a person **3.** a projecting end or point; nib; tip

☆**neb·bish** (neb′ish) *n.* [< Yid. *nebekh*, pity, pitiably] a person who is pitifully inept, ineffective, shy, dull, etc.

NEbE northeast by east

Ne·bi·im (nə vē ēm′; *E.* neb′i ēm′) *n.pl.* [Heb. *nebī'īm*, pl. of *nābī*, prophet] *Bible* the books of the Prophets

NEbN northeast by north

Ne·bo (nē′bō), **Mount** *Bible* mountain from which Moses saw the Promised Land; summit of Pisgah (Deut. 34:1)

Ne·bras·ka (nə bras′kə) [< Siouan name of Platte River, lit., flat water] Middle Western State of the NC U.S.: admitted, 1867; 77,227 sq. mi.; pop. 1,484,000; cap. Lincoln: abbrev. **Nebr., Neb., NB** —**Ne·bras′kan** *adj., n.*

Neb·u·chad·nez·zar (neb′yə kəd nez′ər, neb′ə-) (626?-562 B.C.; king of Babylonia (605?-562), who conquered Jerusalem, destroyed the Temple, & deported many Jews into Babylonia (586 B.C.): II Kings 24; Dan. 1-4 Also **Neb′u·chad·rez′zar** (-rez′ər)

neb·u·la (neb′yə lə) *n., pl.* -**lae′** (-lē′), -**las** [ModL. < L., vapor, fog, mist < IE. base *nebh*-, moist, vapor, cloud, whence Gr. *nephelē*, cloud, OE. *nifol*, mist, darkness] **1.** any of several vast, diffuse, cloudlike patches seen in the night sky, consisting of groups of stars too far away to

be seen singly, or of masses of gaseous matter, or of external galaxies **2.** *Med. a)* a small, cloudy opacity on the cornea *b)* a liquid preparation used as a spray —**neb′u·lar** *adj.*

nebular hypothesis the theory that the solar system was once a nebula which condensed to form the sun and planets

neb·u·lize (neb′yə līz′) *vt.* **-lized′, -liz′ing** [< L. *nebula*, mist (see NEBULA) + -IZE] **1.** to reduce (a liquid) to a fine spray **2.** to spray (a diseased or injured surface) with a medicated liquid —**neb′u·li·za′tion** *n.* —**neb′u·liz′er** *n.*

neb·u·los·i·ty (neb′yə läs′ə tē) *n.* [Fr. *nébulosité* < LL. *nebulositas*] **1.** the quality or condition of being nebulous **2.** *pl.* **-ties** same as NEBULA (sense 1)

neb·u·lous (neb′yə ləs) *adj.* [ME. < L. *nebulus* < L. *nebulosus*] **1.** of or like a nebula or nebulae **2.** [Rare] cloudy; misty **3.** unclear; vague; indefinite Also **neb′u·lose′** (-lōs′) —**neb′u·lous·ly** *adv.* —**neb′u·lous·ness** *n.*

nec·es·sar·i·ly (nes′ə ser′ə lē, nes′ə ser′-) *adv.* **1.** because of necessity; by or of necessity **2.** as a necessary result; inevitably

nec·es·sar·y (nes′ə ser′ē) *adj.* [ME. < L. *necessarius* < *necesse*, unavoidable, necessary < *ne-*, not + *cedere*, to give way: see CEDE] **1.** that cannot be dispensed with; essential; indispensable [the nutriments *necessary* to life] **2.** resulting from necessity; inevitable [a *necessary* result] **3.** *a)* that must be done; mandatory; not voluntary, required *b)* not free to choose; compelled by circumstances [a *necessary* agent] **4.** inherent in the situation; undeniable; unavoidable from the premises **5.** [Archaic] rendering some essential and intimate service —*n.*, *pl.* **-sar′ies** **1.** a necessary thing; thing essential to life, some purpose, etc.: *often used in pl.* **2.** [Dial.] a privy or toilet **3.** [*pl.*] *Law* those things essential to maintaining a dependent or incompetent in comfort and well-being —*SYN.* see ESSENTIAL

necessary condition 1. *Logic* a consequent whose denial implies the denial of the antecedent **2.** *Philos.* an indispensable antecedent of an event or proposition

ne·ces·si·tar·i·an·ism (nə ses′ə ter′ē ən iz′m) *n.* the theory that every event is determined by causal necessity and that the action of the human will is not free, but is caused by previous actions and experiences; determinism —**ne·ces′si·tar′i·an** *n.*, *adj.*

ne·ces·si·tate (nə ses′ə tāt′) *vt.* **-tat′ed, -tat′ing** [< ML. *necessitatus*, pp. of *necessitare* < L. *necessitas*, necessity] **1.** to make (something) necessary or unavoidable; involve or imply as a necessary condition, outcome, etc. **2.** [Now Rare] to compel; require; force [he was *necessitated* to agree] —**ne·ces′si·ta′tion** *n.*

ne·ces·si·tous (-təs) *adj.* [Fr. *nécessiteux*: see ff. & -OUS] **1.** in great need; destitute; needy **2.** that is necessary or essential **3.** calling for action; urgent —**ne·ces′si·tous·ly** *adv.* —**ne·ces′si·tous·ness** *n.*

ne·ces·si·ty (-tē) *n.*, *pl.* **-ties** [ME. *necessite* < OFr. *nécessité* < L. *necessitas* < *necesse*: see NECESSARY] **1.** the power of natural law that cannot be other than it is; natural causation; physical compulsion placed on man by nature; fate **2.** anything that is inevitable, unavoidable, etc. as a result of natural law; that which is necessary in natural sequence **3.** *a)* the compulsion or constraint of man-made circumstances, habit, custom, law, etc.; logical or moral conditions making certain actions inevitable or obligatory [faced by the *necessity* to earn a living] *b)* what is required by this social or legal compulsion **4.** great or imperative need **5.** something that cannot be done without; necessary thing: *often used in pl.* **6.** the state or quality of being necessary **7.** want; poverty —*SYN.* see NEED —**of necessity** necessarily; inevitably

Nech·es River (nech′əz) river in E Tex., flowing southeast into Sabine Lake: 415 mi.: see SABINE[1]

neck (nek) *n.* [ME. *nekke* < OE. *hnecca*, akin to G. *nacken* < IE. base *ken-*, to bend, squeeze, whence NOOK, NUT] **1.** that part of man or animal joining the head to the body, including the part of the backbone between the skull and the shoulders **2.** a narrow part between the head, or end, and the body, or base, of any object [the *neck* of a violin, the *neck* of a goblet] **3.** that part of a garment which covers, encircles, or is nearest the neck **4.** the narrowest part of any object, considered to be like a neck; specif., *a)* a narrow strip of land *b)* the narrowest part of an organ [the *neck* of the uterus, the *neck* of a tooth] *c)* the narrowest or tapering part of a bottle, vase, etc. *d)* a strait or channel **5.** *Geol.* a vertical column of hardened igneous rock, formerly plugging a volcanic conduit and later exposed by erosion —*vt.* **1.** to kill (a fowl) by twisting its neck ☆**2.** [Slang] to hug, kiss, and caress in making love —☆*vi.* [Slang] to engage in such lovemaking —*SYN.* see CARESS —☆**get it in the neck** [Slang] to be severely reprimanded or punished —**neck and crop** completely; entirely —**neck and neck** so close together in a race or contest that the outcome hangs in the balance —**neck of the woods** ☆a region or locality [not from this *neck of the woods*] —**risk one's neck** to put one's life, career, reputation, etc. in danger —**stick one's neck out** to expose oneself to possible failure, ridicule, loss, etc. by taking a chance —**win (or lose) by a neck 1.** *Horse Racing* to win (or lose) by the length of a horse's head and neck **2.** to win (or lose) any contest by a narrow margin —**neck′er** *n.*

...·band (-band′) *n.* **1.** a band worn around the neck

2. the part of a garment that encircles the neck; esp., the part to which the collar is fastened

neck·cloth (-klôth′, -kläth′) *n.* [Archaic] same as CRAVAT

Neck·er (ne ker′; *E.* nek′ər), **Jacques** (zhȧk) **1732–1804**; Fr. statesman & financier, born in Switzerland: father of Madame de STÄEL

neck·er·chief (nek′ər chif, -chēf′) *n.* [ME. *nekkyrchefe*: see NECK & KERCHIEF] a handkerchief or scarf worn around the neck

neck·ing (nek′iŋ) *n.* **1.** *Archit.* any small molding around the top of a column below the capital ☆**2.** [see NECK, *v.*] [Slang] the act of kissing and caressing in making love

neck·lace (nek′lis) *n.* [NECK + LACE, 1] a string of beads, jewels, etc. or a fine chain of gold, silver, etc., worn around the neck as an ornament

neck·line (-līn′) *n.* the line formed by the edge of a garment around or nearest the neck

neck·piece (-pēs′) *n.* **1.** a decorative scarf, esp. of fur **2.** a piece of armor for the neck

☆**neck·rein** (-rān′) *vi.* to go to the right if the left rein is lightly pressed against the neck or to the left if the right rein is so pressed: said of a saddle horse —*vt.* to guide (a horse) by such pressure of the reins

neck·tie (-tī′) *n.* **1.** a band worn around the neck under a collar and tied in front as a four-in-hand or in a bow **2.** a decorative piece clipped onto the collar to resemble this

☆**necktie party** [Slang] a hanging; esp., a lynching

neck·wear (-wer′) *n.* articles worn about the neck, as neckties, scarfs, etc.

nec·ro- (nek′rō, -rə) [< Gr. *nekros*, dead body < IE. base *nek-*, physical death, corpse, whence L. *nex*, death, *nocere*, to injure, *necere*, to kill] *a combining form meaning* death, corpse, dead tissue [*necrology*]: also, before a vowel, **necr-**

nec·ro·bi·o·sis (nek′rō bī ō′sis) *n.* [ModL. < prec. + -BIOSIS] the process of decay and death of body cells

ne·crol·a·try (ne kräl′ə trē) *n.* [NECRO- + -LATRY] worship of, or excessive reverence for, the dead

ne·crol·o·gy (-ə jē) *n.*, *pl.* **-gies** [ModL.: see NECRO- & -LOGY] **1.** a list of people who have died within a certain period, as that in a newspaper **2.** a death notice; obituary —**nec·ro·log·i·cal** (nek′rə läj′i k'l) *adj.* —**nec′ro·log′i·cal·ly** *adv.* —**ne·crol′o·gist** *n.*

nec·ro·man·cy (nek′rə man′sē) *n.* [ME. *nigromancie* < OFr. *nigromance* < ML. *nigromantia* (altered by association with L. *niger*, black) < L. *necromantia* < Gr. *nekromanteia* < *nekros*, corpse (see NECRO-) + *manteia*, divination] **1.** the practice of claiming to foretell the future by alleged communication with the dead **2.** black magic; sorcery —**nec′ro·man′cer** *n.* —**nec′ro·man′tic** *adj.*

nec·ro·pha·gi·a (nek′rə fā′jē ə) *n.* [ModL.: see NECRO- & -PHAGY] the eating of dead bodies; esp., the practice of feeding on carrion —**ne·croph·a·gous** (ne kräf′ə gəs) *adj.*

nec·ro·phil·i·a (-fil′ē ə) *n.* [< NECRO- + Gr. *philos*, loving + -ISM] an abnormal fascination with death and the dead; esp., an erotic attraction to corpses: also **ne·croph·i·lism** (ne kräf′ə liz′m) —**nec′ro·phile′** (-fīl′) *n.* —**nec′ro·phil′·i·ac, ne·croph′i·lous** *adj.*

nec·ro·pho·bi·a (nek′rō fō′bē ə) *n.* [NECRO- + -PHOBIA] an abnormal fear of death or of dead bodies

ne·crop·o·lis (nə kräp′ə lis) *n.*, *pl.* **-lis·es, -leis′** (-līs′) [Gr. *nekropolis* < *nekros* (see NECRO-) + *polis*, city: see POLICE] a cemetery, esp. one belonging to an ancient city

nec·rop·sy (nek′räp sē) *n.*, *pl.* **-sies** [see NECRO- & -OPSIS] an examination of a dead body; post-mortem: also **ne·cros·co·py** (ne kräs′kə pē)

ne·cro·sis (ne krō′sis) *n.*, *pl.* **-ses** (-sēz) [ModL. < LL., a killing < Gr. *nekrōsis* < *nekroun*, to make dead, mortify < *nekros*, dead body: see NECRO-] **1.** the death or decay of tissue in a particular part of the body, as from loss of blood supply, burning, etc. **2.** *Bot.* death of plant tissue, as from disease, frost, etc. —**ne·crose** (ne krōs′, nek′rōs) *vt.*, *vi.* **-crosed′, -cros′ing** —**ne·crot′ic** (-krät′ik) *adj.*

ne·crot·o·my (ne krät′ə mē) *n.*, *pl.* **-mies** [NECRO- + -TOMY] **1.** the dissection of corpses **2.** the surgical removal of dead bone

nec·tar (nek′tər) *n.* [L. < Gr. *nektar* < base of *necros*, dead body (see NECRO-) + *tar*, who overcomes (akin to Sans. *tarati*, he overcomes): hence, death-overcoming: the drink was held to confer immortality] **1.** *Gr. Myth.* the drink of the gods **2.** any very delicious beverage **3.** *Bot.* the sweetish liquid in many flowers, used by bees for the making of honey —**nec·tar′e·an** (-ter′ē ən), **nec·tar′e·ous** (-ē əs), **nec′tar·ous** *adj.*

nec·tar·ine (nek′tə rēn′, nek′tə rēn′) *n.* [orig. adj., of *nectar*] a variety (*Prunus persica* var. *nectarina*) of peach, having a smooth skin without down and often a mutation of the common peach

nec·ta·ry (nek′tər ē) *n.*, *pl.* **-ries** [ModL. *nectarium*] an organ or part (of a flower) that secretes nectar —**nec·tar′i·al** (-ter′ē əl) *adj.*

Ned (ned) [by faulty division of *mine Ed*] a masculine name: see EDGAR, EDMUND, EDWARD

N.E.D., NED New English Dictionary

Ne·der·land (nā′dər länt′) *Du.* name of the NETHERLANDS

nee, née (nā; *now often* nē) *adj.* [Fr., fem. of *né*, pp. of *naître* < L. *nasci*, to be born: see NATURE] born: used to indicate the maiden name of a married woman [Mrs. Helen Jones, *nee* Smith]

need (nēd) *n.* [ME. *nede* < OE. *nied*, akin to G. *not*, Goth. *nauths* < IE. **neuti-* < base *neu-*, to collapse with weariness, whence W. *newyn*, starvation] **1.** necessity or obligation created by some situation *[no need to worry]* **2.** a lack of something useful, required, or desired *[to have need of a rest]* **3.** something useful, required, or desired that is lacking; want; requirement *[list your daily needs]* **4.** *a)* a condition in which there is a deficiency of something, or one requiring relief or supply *[a friend in need] b)* a condition of poverty, or extreme want —*vt.* to have need of; want or lack; require *Need* is often used as an auxiliary, either uninflected and followed by an infinitive without *to,* or inflected and followed by an infinitive with *to,* meaning "to be obliged, must" *[he need not come, he needs to be careful]* —*vi.* **1.** [Archaic] to be necessary: chiefly in impersonal constructions *[it needs not]* **2.** to be in need   See also NEEDS —**have need to** to be compelled or required to; must —**if need be** if it is required; if the occasion demands —**need'er** *n.*
SYN.—**need** refers to an urgent requirement of something essential or desirable that is lacking; **necessity,** a more formal word, suggests an imperative need for something indispensable but lacks the emotional connotations of **need** *[they are in need of food, food is a necessity for all living things];* **exigency** refers to a necessity created by some emergency, crisis, or compelling circumstances *[the exigencies created by the flood];* **requisite** applies to something that is indispensable to a particular end or goal *[a sense of rhythm is a requisite in a dancer]* See also LACK

need·ful (-fəl) *adj.* **1.** necessary; needed; required **2.** [Archaic] characterized by great need or distress; needy —**need'ful·ly** *adv.* —**need'ful·ness** *n.*

need·i·ness (-ē nis) *n.* the fact or state of being needy; poverty; indigence; want

nee·dle (nēd'']) *n.* [ME. *nedle* < OE. *nædl,* akin to G. *nadel* < IE. base **(s)nē-, *(s)nēi-,* to sew, spin, whence L. *nere,* Gr. *nein,* to spin & SNOOD] **1.** *a)* a small, slender piece of steel with a sharp point at one end and a hole for thread at the other, used for sewing by hand or for surgical sutures *b)* a similar implement with a hole for thread near the pointed end, used esp. on sewing machines **2.** *a)* a slender rod of steel, bone, wood, etc. with a hook at one end, used for crocheting *b)* a similar rod, usually larger and without a hook, used in knitting **3.** the short, pointed piece of metal, often tipped as with diamond, that moves in the grooves of a phonograph record and transmits vibrations **4.** a pointed instrument used in etching or engraving **5.** *a)* the magnetized pointer of a compass *b)* the indicator or pointer of a speedometer or other gauge **6.** the thin, short, pointed leaf of such trees as the pine, spruce, etc. **7.** the thin rod which, when moved, opens or closes a passage in a valve and permits close adjustment **8.** *a)* the sharp, very slender metal tube at the end of a hypodermic syringe, that is introduced into the blood vessel, muscle, etc. ☆*b)* [Colloq.] a hypodermic injection **9.** *same as* ELECTRIC NEEDLE **10.** any object roughly resembling a needle or its point in shape, as the sharp point of some crystals, a narrow, pointed rock, an obelisk, spire, etc. —*vt.* **-dled, -dling 1.** to sew, puncture, etc. with a needle **2.** [Colloq.] *a)* to provoke into doing something; goad; prod *b)* to tease or heckle ☆**3.** [Slang] to strengthen by adding alcohol *[to needle beer]* —*vi.* **1.** to work with a needle; sew, embroider, etc. **2.** to form needles in crystallization —☆**on the needle** [Slang] addicted to narcotics —**nee'dle·like'** *adj.* —**nee'dler** *n.*

nee·dle·fish (-fish') *n., pl.* **-fish', -fish'es:** see FISH² any of a group of long, pipelike, voracious marine fishes (family Belonidae) with elongated jaws and many sharp teeth

nee·dle·point (-point') *n.* **1.** an embroidery of woolen threads upon canvas, used for upholstery, tapestries, etc. **2.** a lace made on a paper pattern, with a needle instead of a bobbin: in full, **needlepoint lace**

need·less (nēd'lis) *adj.* not needed; unnecessary —**need'less·ly** *adv.* —**need'less·ness** *n.*

needle valve a type of valve in which a needlelike device controls the flow of fluid through a cone-shaped opening: used esp. in carburetors

nee·dle·wom·an (nēd''l woom'ən) *n., pl.* **-wom'en** a woman who does needlework; esp., a seamstress

nee·dle·work (-wurk') *n.* **1.** work done with a needle; sewing or fancywork **2.** the art or practice of such work —**nee'dle·work'er** *n.*

need·n't (nēd''nt) need not

needs (nēdz) *adv.* [ME. *nedes* < OE. *nedes, nydes* < *nied* (see NEED) + *-s,* gen. & adv. suffix] of necessity; necessarily (with *must*) *[he must needs obey]*

need·y (nēd'ē) *adj.* **need'i·er, need'i·est** in, or characterized by, need; not having enough to live on; very poor; destitute; indigent

neep (nēp) *n.* [ME. *nepe* < OE. *næp* < L. *napus,* prob.

< Gr. *napy,* mustard] [Scot. & Brit. Dial.] a turnip

ne'er (ner) *adv.* [Poet.] never

ne'er-do-well (-dōo wel') *n.* a person who never does anything worthwhile; one who cannot make a living, get things done, etc. —*adj.* lazy, inadequate, etc.

ne·far·i·ous (ni fer'ē əs) *adj.* [L. *nefarius* < *nefas,* crime, wrong < *ne-,* not + *fas,* lawful: for IE. base see FAME] very wicked; villainous; iniquitous —*SYN.* see VICIOUS —**ne·far'i·ous·ly** *adv.* —**ne·far'i·ous·ness** *n.*

Nef·er·ti·ti (nef'ər tē'tē) 14th cent. B.C.; queen of Egypt & wife of Ikhnaton: also **Nef're·te'te** (-rə-)

Ne·fud (ne fōod') *same as* NAFUD

neg. 1. negative **2.** negatively

ne·gate (ni gāt') *vt.* **-gat'ed, -gat'ing** [< L. *negatus:* see ff.] **1.** to deny the existence or truth of **2.** to make ineffective —*SYN.* see NULLIFY —**ne·ga'tor, ne·gat'er** *n.*

ne·ga·tion (ni gā'shən) *n.* [< Fr. or L.; Fr. *négation* < L. *negatio* < *negatus,* pp. of *negare,* to deny < *ne-, *neg-,* not (see NO¹)] **1.** the act or an instance of denying; negative answer; denial **2.** the lack or opposite of some positive character or quality *[death is the negation of life]* **3.** something negative; nonentity —**ne·ga'tion·al** *adj.*

neg·a·tive (neg'ə tiv) *adj.* [ME. *negatife* < OFr. or L.: OFr. *négatif* < L. *negativus* < *negatus:* see prec.] **1.** containing, expressing, or implying a denial or refusal; that says "no" *[a negative reply]* **2.** opposite to something regarded as positive; specif., *a)* lacking in positive character or quality; lacking evidence, affirmation, etc.; having the effect of diminishing, depriving, or denying *[a negative personality] b) Biol.* directed away from the source of a stimulus *[negative tropism] c) Logic* denying the subject or predicate of a proposition *d) Math.* designating a quantity less than zero, or one to be subtracted; minus *e) Med.* not demonstrating or proving the presence or existence of symptoms, bacteria, etc. *f) Photog.* reversing the relation of light and shade of the original subject ☆**3.** *Elec. a)* of negative electricity *b)* of, generating, or charged with negative electricity *c)* having an excess of electrons —*adv.* no; not so: so used in radio communication —*n.* **1.** a word, affix, phrase, etc. that denies, rejects, or refuses (Ex.: *no, not, by no means*) **2.** a statement of denial, refusal, or rejection **3.** the point of view that denies or attacks the positive or affirmative *[the negative won the debate]* **4.** [Obs.] the right of veto **5.** an impression of something, as a sculpture, that shows it in reverse **6.** the plate in a voltaic battery where the lower potential is **7.** *Math.* a quantity less than zero, or one to be subtracted; minus quantity **8.** *Photog.* an exposed and developed photographic film or plate on which light and shadow are the reverse of what they are in the positive printed from this —*vt.* **-tived, -tiv·ing 1.** *a)* to refuse; reject ☆*b)* to veto (a candidate, motion, or bill) **2.** to deny; contradict **3.** to prove false; disprove **4.** to counteract; neutralize —**in the negative 1.** in refusal or denial of a plan, suggestion, etc. **2.** with a denial or negative answer —**neg'a·tive·ly** *adv.* —**neg'a·tive·ness, neg'a·tiv'i·ty** *n.*

☆**negative electricity** the kind of electricity that predominates as in a body of resin after it has been rubbed with wool and has accumulated an excess of electrons

negative sign *Math.* the sign (−), used to indicate a negative quantity

neg·a·tiv·ism (neg'ə tiv iz'm) *n.* **1.** an attitude or system of thought characterized by doubt and question, rather than approval and acceptance **2.** *Psychol.* an attitude characterized by ignoring, resisting, or opposing suggestions or orders coming from other people —**neg'a·tiv·ist** *n., adj.* —**neg'a·tiv·is'tic** *adj.*

neg·a·to·ry (neg'ə tôr'ē) *adj.* [LL. *negatorius*] negative

neg·a·tron (neg'ə trän') *n.* [NEGA(TIVE) + (ELEC)TRON] *rare var. of* ELECTRON

Ne·gev (neg'ev) region in S Israel of partially reclaimed desert: c. 4,000 sq. mi.: also **Ne'geb** (-eb)

neg·lect (ni glekt') *vt.* [< L. *neglectus,* pp. of *neglegere,* not to heed, be regardless of < *neg-,* not + *legere,* to gather (see LOGIC)] **1.** to ignore or disregard *[to neglect the advice of others]* **2.** to fail to care for or attend to sufficiently or properly; slight *[to neglect one's family]* **3.** to fail to carry out (an expected or required action) through carelessness or by intention; leave undone —*n.* **1.** the action of neglecting **2.** lack of sufficient or proper care; negligence; disre-

NEGEV

gard **3.** the state of being neglected —**neg·lect'er, neg·lec'tor** n.
SYN. —**neglect** implies a failure to carry out some expected or required action, either through carelessness or by intention [I *neglected* to wind the clock]; **omit**, in this connection, implies a neglecting through oversight, absorption, etc. [she should not *omit* to visit the Louvre]; **overlook** suggests a failure to see or to take action, either inadvertently or indulgently [I'll *overlook* your errors this time]; **disregard** implies inattention or neglect, usually intentional [she always *disregards* his wishes]; **ignore** suggests a deliberate disregarding, sometimes through stubborn refusal to face the facts [but you *ignore* the necessity for action]; **slight** implies a disregarding or neglecting in an indifferent or disdainful way [he seems to *slight* the newer writers]; **forget**, in this connection, implies an intentional disregarding or omitting [after his election he *forgot* the wishes of the voters]
neg·lect·ful (-fəl) adj. characterized by neglect; heedless; negligent (often with of) —**SYN.** see REMISS —**neg·lect'ful·ly** adv. —**neg·lect'ful·ness** n.
neg·li·gee (neg'lə zhā', neg'lə zhā') n. [Fr. *négligée*, fem. of *négligé*, pp. of *négliger*, to neglect < L. *negligere*: see NEGLECT] **1.** a woman's loosely fitting dressing gown, usually decorative and of a soft, flowing material **2.** any informal, careless, or incomplete attire —adj. carelessly or incompletely dressed
neg·li·gence (neg'li jəns) n. [ME. *neglygence* < OFr. *négligence* < L. *negligentia*] **1.** the quality or condition of being negligent; specif., *a*) habitual failure to do the required thing *b*) carelessness in manner or appearance; indifference **2.** an instance of such failure, carelessness, or indifference **3.** *Law* failure to use a reasonable amount of care when such failure results in injury or damage to another
neg·li·gent (-jənt) adj. [ME. < OFr. *négligent* < L. *negligens*, prp. of *negligere*: see NEGLECT] **1.** habitually failing to do the required thing; neglectful **2.** careless, lax, inattentive, or indifferent —**SYN.** see REMISS —**neg'li·gent·ly** adv.
neg·li·gi·ble (neg'li jə b'l) adj. [< L. *negligere* (see NEGLECT) + -IBLE] that can be neglected or disregarded because small, unimportant, etc.; trifling —**neg'li·gi·bil'·i·ty** n. —**neg'li·gi·bly** adv.
ne·go·ti·a·ble (ni gō'shē ə b'l, -shə b'l) adj. that can be negotiated; specif., *a*) legally transferable to another by endorsement or by proper delivery: said of promissory notes, checks, etc. *b*) that can be passed, crossed, surmounted, etc. —**ne·go'ti·a·bil'i·ty** n.
ne·go·ti·ate (-shē āt') vi. **-at'ed, -at'ing** [< L. *negotiatus*, pp. of *negotiari*, to carry on business < *negotium*, business < *neg-*, not (see NO[1]) + *otium*, ease] to confer, bargain, or discuss with a view to reaching agreement —vt. **1.** to make arrangements for, settle, or conclude (a business transaction, treaty, etc.) **2.** to transfer, assign, or sell (negotiable paper) **3.** to succeed in crossing, surmounting, moving through, etc. [to *negotiate* a deep river] —**ne·go'·ti·a·tor** n.
ne·go·ti·a·tion (ni gō'shē ā'shən) n. [L. *negotiatio*] a negotiating; specif., [often pl.] a conferring, discussing, or bargaining to reach agreement —**ne·go'ti·a·to·ry** (-ə tôr'ē) adj.
Ne·gress (nē'gris) n. [Fr. *négresse*, fem. of *nègre* < Sp. or Port. *negro*, NEGRO[1]] a Negro woman or girl: term avoided by those who regard the -*ess* suffix as patronizing or discriminatory
Ne·gril·lo (nə gril'ō) n., pl. **-los, -loes** [Sp., dim. of *negro*, NEGRO[1]] an African Pygmy
Ne·gri Sem·bi·lan (nā'grē sem'bē län') state of W Malaya: 2,565 sq. mi.; pop. 480,000; cap. Seremban
Ne·gri·to (nə grēt'ō) n., pl. **-tos, -toes** [Sp., dim. of *negro*, NEGRO[1]] a member of any of various groups of dwarfish Negroid peoples living in the East Indies, the Philippines, and Africa —**Ne·grit'ic** (-grit'ik) adj.
ne·gri·tude (neg'rə tōōd', nē'grə-; -tyōōd') n. [Fr. *négritude*, coined (prob. in 1939 by Aimé Césaire, poet of Martinique) < *nègre*, black (< Sp. or Port. *negro*, NEGRO[1]) + -i- + -tude (see -TUDE)] [also N-] the consciousness in Negroes, esp. African Negroes, of their cultural heritage, together with an affirmation of the distinctive qualities and values of this heritage
Ne·gro[1] (nē'grō) n., pl. **-groes** [Sp. & Port. *negro*, black, black person < L. *niger*, black] **1.** a member of the dominant group of mankind in Africa, living chiefly south of the Sahara, and characterized generally by a dark skin **2.** same as NEGROID **3.** any person with some Negro ancestors —adj. of, for, or being a Negro or Negroes Other terms, as *black* or *Afro-American* (for U.S. Negroes) are preferred by some
Ne·gro[2] (nā'grō; Port. nā'grōō; Sp. nā'grō) **1.** river in N Brazil, flowing southeast into the Amazon, near Manaus: c. 1,400 mi. **2.** river in SC Argentina, flowing east into the Atlantic: c. 700 mi.
Ne·groid (nē'groid) adj. designating or of one of the three major groups of mankind: it includes the majority of the peoples of Africa, and peoples of Melanesia, New Guinea, etc. who are generally characterized by a dark skin, black, frizzly hair, a broad, flat nose, etc. —n. any member of the Negroid group of mankind
Ne·gro·phile (nē'grə fīl', -grō-) n. [NEGRO[1] + -PHILE] [sometimes n-] a person who admires, likes, or champions

Negroes, their culture, etc. —**Ne·groph·i·lism** (ni gräf'ə liz'm) n.
Ne·gro·phobe (-fōb') n. [NEGRO[1] + -PHOBE] [sometimes n-] a person who hates or fears Negroes —**Ne'gro·pho'bi·a** (-fō'bē ə) n.
Neg·ro·pon·te (ne'grō pōn'te) It. name of CHALCIS & EVVOIA
Ne·gros (nā'grōs; Sp. ne'grōs) island of the C Philippines, between Cebu & Panay: 4,905 sq. mi.
Ne·gus (nē'gəs) n. [Amharic *nĕgŭš*, king] the title of the ruler of Ethiopia
ne·gus (nē'gəs) n. [after Col. Francis Negus (d. 1732), who concocted it] a beverage of hot water, wine, and lemon juice, sweetened and spiced
Ne·he·mi·ah (nē'ə mī'ə) [Heb. *neḥemyāh*, lit., comfort of *Jah* (God)] *Bible* **1.** a Hebrew leader of about the 5th cent. B.C. **2.** the book that tells about his work: abbrev. **Neh.** In the Douay Bible, Ne'he·mi'as (-əs)
Neh·ru (nā'rōō), **Ja·wa·har·lal** (jə wä'hər läl') 1889–1964; Hindu leader in India's movement for independence; prime minister (1947–64)
neigh (nā) vi. [ME. *neyen* < OE. *hnægan*, akin to MDu. *neyen*, of echoic orig.] to utter the loud, characteristic cry of a horse; whinny —n. this cry; a whinny
neigh·bor (nā'bər) n. [ME. *neighbour* < OE. *neahgebur* (akin to G. *nachbar*) < *neah* (see NIGH) + *gebur*, freeholder, peasant (cf. BOOR, BOER)] **1.** a person who lives near another **2.** a person, country, or thing situated near another **3.** a fellow man [love thy *neighbor*] **4.** any person: used as a term of direct address —adj. nearby; adjacent —vt. **1.** to live or be situated near (someone or something) **2.** [Rare] to bring near or into close association with —vi. **1.** to live or be situated nearby **2.** to have friendly relations; associate on friendly terms (with) Also, Brit. sp., **neighbour**
neigh·bor·hood (-hood') n. **1.** orig., friendly relations, as of neighbors; neighborliness **2.** the state or quality of being neighbors **3.** a community, district, or area, esp. with regard to some characteristic or point of reference [an old *neighborhood*] **4.** the people living near one another; community **5.** *Math.* the set of all points which lie within a stated distance of a given point —☆**in the neighborhood of** [Colloq.] **1.** near; close to (a place) **2.** about; approximately (the age, amount, etc. specified)
neigh·bor·ing (-in) adj. nearby; adjacent; close together; in the same region —**SYN.** see ADJACENT
neigh·bor·ly (nā'bər lē) adj. like, characteristic of, or appropriate to neighbors; kind, friendly, sociable, etc. —**neigh'bor·li·ness** n.
Neil (nēl) a masculine name: see NEAL
Neil·son (nēl'sən), **William Allan** 1869–1946; U.S. educator & editor, born in Scotland
Neis·se (nī'sə) river in N Europe, flowing from NW Czechoslovakia into the Oder River on the Polish-German border: c. 140 mi.: see ODER
nei·ther (nē'thər, nī'-) adj., pron. [ME. *naither*, altered (after *eyther*, EITHER) < *nauther* < OE. *na-hwæther*, lit., not whether (cf. NA, NO[1], WHETHER), not either of two] not one or the other (of two); not either [*neither* boy went, *neither* of them was invited] —conj. **1.** not either: the first element of the pair of correlatives *neither . . . nor*, implying negation of both parts of the statement [I could *neither* laugh nor cry] **2.** nor yet; and . . . not [he doesn't smoke, *neither* does he drink] —adv. [Dial. or Colloq.] any more than the other; also [following negative expressions) [if she won't go, I won't *neither*]
Nejd (nezhd) district in C & E Saudi Arabia, formerly a sultanate & now administered as a viceroyalty: c. 450,000 sq. mi.; pop. c. 4,000,000; cap. Riyadh
nek·ton (nek'tän) n. [ModL. < Gr. *nēkton*, neut. of *nēktos*, swimming] all the larger, aquatic, free-swimming animals in lakes, seas, ponds, etc. whose movement is largely independent of currents and waves, including shrimps, fishes, and whales
Nell (nel) a feminine name: see HELEN, ELEANOR
Nel·lie, Nel·ly (nel'ē) a feminine name: see HELEN, ELEANOR
Nel·son[1] (nel's'n) [< the surname *Nelson* < ME. *Nel* (see NEAL) + *son*, SON] **1.** a masculine name **2.** **Horatio,** Viscount Nelson, 1758–1805; Eng. admiral
Nel·son[2] (nel's'n) river in Manitoba, Canada, flowing from Lake Winnipeg northeast into Hudson Bay: 400 mi.
nel·son (nel's'n) n. [< personal name *Nelson*] a hold in wrestling: see FULL NELSON, HALF NELSON
ne·lum·bo (ni lum'bō) n., pl. **-bos** [ModL. < Singhalese *nelumbu*] any of a genus (*Nelumbo*) of waterlilies with large, dish-shaped leaves and flowers of white to dark red: also **ne·lum'bi·um** (-bē əm)
ne·ma (nē'mə) n. *clipped form of* NEMATODE
Ne·man (nye'mən; E. nem'ən) river in W U.S.S.R., flowing west through the Byelorussian S.S.R. & Lithuanian S.S.R. into the Baltic: 597 mi.
nem·a·thel·minth (nem'ə thel'minth) n. [ff. + HELMINTH] in some classifications, any of a large phylum (Nemathelminthes) of round, unsegmented worms, many of which are parasitic, as the hookworm, heartworm, meadow nematode, etc.
ne·mat·ic (ni mat'ik) adj. [NEMAT(O)- + -IC] designating or of a phase of the mesomorphic state in which the

liquid is characterized by a low viscosity and a threadlike structure with a diffuse X-ray pattern

nem·a·to- (nem′ə tō′, -tə) [< Gr. *nēma* (gen. *nēmatos*), what is spun, thread, akin to *nein*: see NEEDLE] *a combining form meaning* thread, threadlike [*nematocyst*]: also, before a vowel, **nemat-**

nem·a·to·cyst (nem′ə tō sist′) *n.* [NEMATO- + -CYST] any of the intracellular stinging structures characteristic of all coelenterates, as the jellyfish: it contains a threadlike sting —**nem′a·to·cys′tic** *adj.*

nem·a·tode (nem′ə tōd′) *n.* [< ModL. *Nematoda*, name of the phylum: see NEMATO- & -ODE²] any of a phylum (Nematoda) of worms, often parasites of animals and plants, with long, cylindrical, unsegmented bodies and a heavy cuticle, as the hookworm, pinworm, etc.

nem·a·tol·o·gy (nem′ə täl′ə jē) *n.* [NEMATO(DE) + -LOGY] the branch of zoology that deals with nematodes

☆**Nem·bu·tal** (nem′byə tôl′, -tal′) [N(A) + E(THYL) + M(ETHYL) + BU(TYL) + (BARBI)TAL] *a trademark for* PENTOBARBITAL SODIUM

nem. con. [L. *nemine contradicente*] (with) no one contradicting; unanimously

nem. diss. [L. *nemine dissentiente*] (with) no one dissenting; unanimously

Ne·me·a (nē′mē ə) valley in Argolis, Greece, in the NE Peloponnesus —**Ne·me·an** (ni mē′ən, nē′mē-) *adj.*

Nemean games a Greek festival held in ancient times every other year at Nemea, consisting chiefly of athletic and musical contests

Nemean lion *Gr. Myth.* a fierce lion killed by Hercules as the first of his twelve labors

ne·mer·te·an (ni mur′tē ən) *n.* [< ModL. *Nemertea*, name of the phylum < Gr. *Nēmertēs*, name of a sea nymph < *nēmertēs*, unerring] any of a phylum (Nemertea) of usually very elongate, unsegmented marine worms with no body cavity and with a protrusible proboscis, living mostly in coastal mud or sand —*adj.* of or belonging to these worms: also **nem·er·tine** (nem′ər tin, -tīn′), **nem′er·tin′e·an** (-tin′ē ən)

Nem·e·sis (nem′ə sis) [L. < Gr. *Nemesis* < *nemein*, to distribute, deal out < IE. base *nem-*, to allot, whence L. *numerus*, number, Gr. *nomos*, order] *Gr. Myth.* the goddess of retributive justice, or vengeance —*n.* [*usually* n-] *pl.* **-ses′** (-sēz′) 1. *a)* just punishment; retribution *b)* one who imposes retribution 2. anyone or anything by which, it seems, one must inevitably be defeated or frustrated

ne·moph·i·la (ni mäf′ə lə) *n.* [ModL. < Gr. *nemos*, a wooded pasture, orig. wooded valley (< IE. base *nem-*, to bend, form a hollow, whence NAMASTE) + ModL. *-phila*, suffix indicating attraction toward < L., neut. pl. of *-philus*, -PHILOUS] any of a genus (*Nemophila*) of annual W American plants of the waterleaf family, cultivated for garden ornament

ne·ne (nā′nā′) *n.* [Haw. *nēnē*] a grayish-brown Hawaiian goose related to the Canada goose: now nearly extinct

N.Eng. 1. New England 2. North England

ne·o- (nē′ō, -ə) [ModL. < Gr. *neos*, NEW] *a combining form meaning:* 1. [*often* N-] *a)* new, recent, latest [*neolithic*, *Neozoic*] *b)* in a new, different, or modified way [*neocolonialism*] *c)* the New World [*Neotropical*] 2. *Chem. a)* designating a compound related in some way to an older one *b)* indicating a hydrocarbon having at least one carbon atom joined to four other carbon atoms

ne·o·an·throp·ic (nē′ō an thräp′ik) *adj.* [NEO- + ANTHROP- + -IC] of, pertaining to, or resembling modern forms of man: also **ne′an·throp′ic**

ne·o·ars·phen·a·mine (nē′ō ärs fen′ə mēn′) *n.* a sodium compound of arsphenamine, formerly used in the treatment of syphilis instead of arsphenamine because less toxic and more soluble

Ne·o·Cath·o·lic (-kath′ə lik, -kath′lik) *adj.* designating or of a group in the Anglican Church that tends toward Roman Catholic doctrine and practice —*n.* a member of this group

Ne·o·cene (nē′ə sēn′) *adj.* [NEO- + -CENE] formerly, designating or of the later of two epochs of the Tertiary, including the Miocene and the Pliocene, when mammals evolved to relatively modern types

ne·o·clas·sic (nē′ō klas′ik) *adj.* designating or of a revival of classic style and form in art, literature, etc., as in England from c. 1660 to c. 1740: also **ne′o·clas′si·cal** —**ne′o·clas′si·cism** *n.* —**ne′o·clas′si·cist** *n.*

ne·o·co·lo·ni·al·ism (-kə lō′nē əl iz′m) *n.* the survival or revival of coloniallike exploitation by a foreign power, as by the imposition of a puppet government, of a region that has ostensibly achieved independence —**ne′o·co·lo′ni·al** *adj.* —**ne′o·co·lo′ni·al·ist** *n.*, *adj.*

Ne·o·Dar·win·ism (-där′win iz′m) *n.* a biological theory which maintains that natural selection is the main factor in the evolution of animals and plants and adjusts this concept to modern genetics

ne·o·dym·i·um (nē′ə dim′ē əm) *n.* [ModL. < NEO- + (DI)DYMIUM] a metallic chemical element of the rare-earth group: symbol, Nd; at. wt., 144.24; at. no., 60; sp. gr., 7.00; melt. pt., 1024°C; boil. pt., 3030°C

Ne·o·gae·a (nē′ə jē′ə) *n.* [ModL. < NEO- + Gr. *gaia*, earth] one of the three primary zoogeographic areas of the earth, coextensive with the Neotropical realm —**Ne′o·gae′an** *adj.*

ne·o·gen·e·sis (nē′ō jen′ə sis) *n.* [NEO- + -GENESIS] regeneration, esp. of tissue —**ne′o·ge·net′ic** (-jə net′ik) *adj.*

Ne·o·He·bra·ic (nē′ō hi brā′ik) *n.*, *adj.* same as MODERN HEBREW

ne·o·im·pres·sion·ism (-im presh′ən iz′m) *n.* a late 19th-cent. theory and practice of painting, based on a strict scientific application of impressionist techniques, esp. pointillism —**ne′o·im·pres′sion·ist** *adj.*, *n.*

Ne·o·La·marck·ism (-lə märk′iz′m) *n.* a theory of inheritance based on a modification and extension of Lamarckism, essentially maintaining the principle that genetic changes can be influenced and directed by environmental factors

Ne·o·Lat·in (-lat′n) *n.* same as MODERN LATIN

ne·o·lith (nē′ə lith′) *n.* a neolithic stone tool

ne·o·lith·ic (nē′ə lith′ik) *adj.* [NEO- + -LITH + -IC] designating or of an Old World cultural period in the later part of the Stone Age, during which man developed polished stone tools, metal tools, pottery, weaving, stock rearing, and agriculture

ne·ol·o·gism (nē äl′ə jiz′m) *n.* [Fr. *néologisme:* see NEO-, -LOGY, & -ISM] 1. a new word or a new meaning for an established word 2. the use of new words or of new meanings for established words —**ne·ol′o·gis′tic** *adj.* —**ne·ol′o·gis′ti·cal** *adj.*

ne·ol·o·gize (-jiz′) *vi.* -gized′, -giz′ing [Fr. *néologiser:* see ff. & -IZE] to invent, or make a practice of using, neologisms —**ne·ol′o·gist** *n.*

ne·ol·o·gy (-jē) *n.*, *pl.* -gies [Fr. *néologie:* see NEO- & -LOGY] same as NEOLOGISM —**ne·o·log·i·cal** (nē′ə läj′i k'l) *adj.* —**ne′o·log′i·cal·ly** *adv.*

ne·o·my·cin (nē′ə mī′sin) *n.* [NEO- + MYC- + -IN¹] a broad-spectrum antibiotic obtained from an actinomycete (*Streptomyces fradiae*) and used in the treatment of various infections, esp. of the skin and eye

ne·on (nē′än) *n.* [ModL. < Gr. *neon*, neut. of *neos*, NEW] a rare, colorless, and inert gaseous chemical element, found in small quantities in the earth's atmosphere and used in discharge tubes: symbol, Ne; at. wt., 20.183; at. no., 10; density, 0.9002 g/l (0°C); melt. pt., -248.67°C; boil. pt., -245.92°C

ne·o·nate (nē′ə nāt′) *n.* [ModL. *neonatus* < *neo-*, NEO- + L. *natus*, born: see NATURE] a newly-born individual, esp. an infant during its first month of life —**ne′o·na′tal** *adj.* —**ne′o·na′tal·ly** *adv.*

neon lamp a discharge tube containing neon, which ionizes and glows with a red light when an electric current is sent through it: used esp. in advertising signs

neon tetra a popular tetra (*Hyphessobrycon innesi*) with blue or green back, white belly, and a posterior, red, lateral stripe

ne·o·orth·o·dox·y (nē′ō ôr′thə däk′sē) *n.* a movement in 20th-cent. Protestantism stressing traditional doctrines of the Reformation in reaction to theological liberalism —**ne′o·orth′o·dox** *adj.*

ne·o·phyte (nē′ə fīt′) *n.* [LL.(Ec.) *neophytus* < Gr. *neophytos*, newly planted (in I Tim. 3:6, a new convert) < *neos*, NEW + *phytos* < *phyein*, to produce, grow: see BONDAGE] 1. a new convert; esp., a newly baptized member of the early Christian Church 2. a newly ordained priest or new member of a convent 3. any beginner; novice —*SYN.* see AMATEUR

ne·o·pla·sia (nē′ə plā′zhə, -zhē ə) *n.* [NEO- + -PLASIA] the growth of new tissue, esp. the formation of neoplasms

ne·o·plasm (nē′ə plaz′m) *n.* [NEO- + -PLASM] an abnormal growth of tissue, as a tumor

ne·o·plas·tic (nē′ə plas′tik) *adj.* 1. of or relating to neoplasia or a neoplasm 2. of or relating to neoplasticism

ne·o·plas·ti·cism (nē′ō plas′tə siz′m) *n.* [NEO- + PLASTIC + -ISM] the principles and methods of the de Stijl movement in painting: see DE STIJL

ne·o·plas·ty (nē′ə plas′tē) *n.* [NEO- + -PLASTY] the restoration or repair of a part of the body by plastic surgery

Ne·o·pla·to·nism (nē′ō plāt′n iz′m) *n.* any of various schools of philosophy based on a modified Platonism; esp., a school developed by Plotinus in Alexandria, postulating a single source from which all forms of existence emanate and with which the soul seeks mystical union —**Ne·o·pla·ton·ic** (-plə tän′ik) *adj.* —**Ne′o·pla′ton·ist** *n.*

☆**ne·o·prene** (nē′ə prēn′) *n.* [NEO- + (CHLORO)PRENE] a synthetic rubber produced by the polymerization of chloroprene: it is highly resistant to oil, heat, light, and oxidation

Ne·o·Scho·las·ti·cism (nē′ō skə las′tə siz′m) *n.* a philosophical system based on scholasticism but incorporating new elements, particularly emphasis on the discoveries of science and on research, to make it applicable to contemporary life

ne·ot·e·ny (nē ät′ə nē, nē′ə tē′nē) *n.* [ModL. *neotenia* < *neo-*, NEO- + Gr. *teinein*, to stretch: see TEND²] *Zool.* 1. the retention of juvenile characteristics in the adult 2. the development of adult features in the juvenile, as the

attainment of sexual maturity in some larvae —**ne·o·te·nic** (nē'ə tē'nik, -ten'ik) adj.

ne·o·ter·ic (nē'ə ter'ik) adj. [LL. neotericus < Gr. neōterikos < neōteros, compar. of neos, NEW] recent; new; newly invented —n. a modern person; one accepting new ideas and practices —**ne'o·ter'i·cal·ly** adv.

Ne·o·trop·i·cal (-träp'i k'l) adj. [NEO- + TROPICAL] designating or of the zoogeographical region that includes South America, the West Indies, Central America, and tropical Mexico: also **Ne'o·trop'ic**

Ne·o·zo·ic (-zō'ik) adj. [< NEO- + Gr. zōē, life + -IC] Geol. former name for CENOZOIC

NEP, N.E.P., Nep New Economic Policy

Ne·pal (ni pôl', ne-; -päl') country in the Himalayas, between India & Tibet: 54,362 sq. mi.; pop. 10,294,000; cap. Katmandu: see INDIA, map —**Nep·a·lese** (nep'ə lēz') adj., n., pl. -**lese'**

Ne·pal·i (ni pôl'ē, -päl'-) n. the Indic language of Nepal

ne·pen·the (ni pen'thē) n. [L. nepenthes < Gr. nepenthēs, removing sorrow < ne-, not (see NO[1]) + penthos, sorrow, grief < IE. base *kwenth-, to suffer, bear, whence OIr. cessaim, (I) suffer] 1. a drug supposed by the ancient Greeks to cause forgetfulness of sorrow 2. anything causing such forgetfulness Also **ne·pen'thes** (-thēz) —**ne·pen'the·an** (-thē ən) adj.

neph·a·nal·y·sis (nef'ə nal'ə sis) n., pl. -**ses'** (-sēz') [NEPH(O)- + ANALYSIS] the analysis of the data on a map or chart that pertains to clouds and precipitation; also, such a map or chart

neph·e·line (nef'ə lēn', -lin) n. [Fr. néphéline < Gr. nephelē, a cloud (see NEBULA) + -ine, -INE[1]] a hexagonal mineral, (NaK)AlSiO₄, common in some igneous rocks that are relatively deficient in silica: also **neph'e·lite'** (-līt')

neph·e·lin·ite (nef'ə li nīt') n. [< prec. + -ITE[1]] a dark, granular igneous rock composed mainly of nepheline and pyroxene

neph·e·lom·e·ter (nef'ə läm'ə tər) n. [< Gr. nephelē, a cloud (see NEBULA) + -METER[2]] an apparatus for measuring the concentration of a suspension, as of bacteria or some substance in solution, by comparing the brightness of light passed through it with that passed through a set of standard solutions of barium chloride

neph·ew (nef'yoō; chiefly Brit., nev'-) n. [ME. neveu < OFr. < L. nepos < IE. base *nepot-, grandson, nephew, whence Sans. napat, OE. nefa] 1. a) the son of one's brother or sister b) the son of one's brother-in-law or sister-in-law 2. an illegitimate son, as of a medieval prelate: a euphemism 3. [Obs.] a) a grandson b) a descendant

neph·o- (nef'ō, -ə) [< Gr. nephos, cloud (see NEBULA)] a combining form meaning cloud, clouds [nephology]

neph·o·gram (nef'ə gram') n. [prec. + -GRAM] a photograph of a cloud

ne·phol·o·gy (ni fäl'ə jē) n. [NEPHO- + -LOGY] the branch of meteorology dealing with clouds —**neph·o·log·i·cal** (nef'ə läj'i k'l) adj. —**ne·phol'o·gist** n.

neph·o·scope (nef'ə skōp') n. [NEPHO- + -SCOPE] an instrument for determining the direction and velocity of the movement of clouds

nephr- same as NEPHRO-: used before a vowel

ne·phral·gi·a (ne fral'jē ə, -jə) [prec. + -ALGIA] pain in the kidneys

ne·phrec·to·my (ne frek'tə mē) n., pl. -**mies** [NEPHR- + -ECTOMY] surgical removal of a kidney

ne·phrid·i·um (ne frid'ē əm) n., pl. -**phrid'i·a** (-ə) [ModL. < Gr. nephridion, dim. of nephros, kidney: see NEPHRO-] 1. a waste-discharging tubule with an external excretory pore, found in many invertebrates, as worms, mollusks, etc. 2. any of the excretory tubules of the pronephros of a vertebrate embryo —**ne·phrid'i·al** adj.

neph·rite (nef'rīt) n. [G. nephrit < Gr. nephritēs, of the kidneys < nephros, kidney: see NEPHRO-: formerly worn as a supposed remedy for kidney ailments] a kind of amphibole, a variety of jade, compact in structure and varying in color from white to dark green

ne·phrit·ic (ne frit'ik) adj. [LL. nephriticus < Gr. nephritikos < nephros, kidney] 1. of a kidney or the kidneys; renal 2. of or having nephritis

ne·phri·tis (ne frīt'əs) n. [LL. < Gr. nephritis: see ff. & -ITIS] an acute or chronic disease of the kidneys, characterized by inflammation, degeneration, fibrosis, etc.: certain types were formerly called Bright's disease

neph·ro- (nef'rō, -rə) [< Gr. nephros, kidney < IE. base *neguhros, kidney, testicle, whence ME. nere] a combining form meaning kidney [nephrotomy]

neph·ro·gen·ic (nef'rə jen'ik) adj. [prec. + -GENIC] 1. arising in the kidneys 2. producing kidney tissue

neph·ron (nef'rän) n. [G. < Gr. nephros (see NEPHRO-)] a single urinary tubule in the vertebrate kidney

ne·phro·sis (ne frō'sis) n. [NEPHR- + -OSIS] a degenerative disease of the kidneys, characterized by generalized edema, protein in the urine, and an increase in serum cholesterol —**ne·phrot'ic** (-frät'ik) adj.

ne·phrot·o·my (ne frät'ə mē) n., pl. -**mies** [NEPHRO- + -TOMY] surgical incision into the kidney, as for removing a stone

ne plus ul·tra (nē plus ul'trə) [L., lit., no more beyond] 1. the utmost limit, or the highest point of perfection 2. [Now Rare] (go) no further

nep·o·tism (nep'ə tiz'm) n. [Fr. népotisme < It. nepotismo

< nepote, nephew < L. nepos (gen. nepotis), grandson, NEPHEW: from favoritism shown to "nephews" by medieval prelates] favoritism shown to relatives, esp. in appointment to desirable positions —**nep'o·tist** n. —**nep'o·tis'tic** adj.

Nep·tune (nep'toōn, -tyoōn) [ME. < L. Neptunus] 1. Rom. Myth. the god of the sea: identified with the Greek god Poseidon 2. the sea personified 3. [ModL.] a planet of the solar system, eighth in distance from the sun: diameter, c.29,425 mi.; period of revolution, c.165.951 years; period of rotation, c.12 hrs., 43 min.; symbol, Ψ

Nep·tu·ni·an (nep toō'nē ən, -tyoō'-) adj. 1. of the sea god Neptune 2. of the planet Neptune 3. [often n-] formerly, designating or of water-formed strata

☆**nep·tu·ni·um** (-əm) n. [ModL. < Neptunus: so named because next to uranium, as the planet Neptune comes next to Uranus] a radioactive chemical element produced by irradiating uranium atoms with neutrons: symbol, Np; at. wt., 237.00; at. no., 93; sp. gr., 20.45; melt. pt., 630°C

neptunium series the radioactive series of nuclides starting with neptunium 237, with a half-life of 2.2 x 10⁶ years, and ending with stable bismuth 209: many radionuclides, as plutonium 241, uranium 237, etc., eventually decay into neptunium 237 and could be considered members of the neptunium series

Ne·re·id (nir'ē id) n. [L. Nereis (gen. Nereidis) < Gr. Nērēis (gen. Nērēidos) < Nēreus, Nereus] Gr. Myth. any of the sea nymphs, the fifty daughters of Nereus

ne·re·is (nir'ē is) n., pl. **ne·re·i·des** (nə rē'ə dēz') [ModL. Nereis, name of the genus: see prec.] any of a genus (Nereis) of relatively large carnivorous marine worms

Ne·re·us (nir'ōōs, -ē əs) [L. < Gr. Nēreus] Gr. Myth. a benevolent sea god, father of the fifty Nereids

ne·rit·ic (nə rit'ik) adj. [< Gr. nēritēs, a sea snail (< Nereus, NEREUS) + -IC] designating or of that part of the sea adjoining the coast and extending to a depth of c. 200 meters

Nernst (nernst), **Wal·ther Her·mann** (väl'ter her'män) 1864–1941; Ger. physicist & chemist

Ne·ro (nir'ō) (Nero Claudius Caesar Drusus Germanicus, born Lucius Domitius Ahenobarbus) 37–68 A.D.; emperor of Rome (54–68): notoriously cruel & depraved —**Ne·ro'ni·an** (-nē ən), **Ne·ron'ic** (-rän'ik) adj.

ner·o·li (ner'ə lē) n. [Fr. néroli < It. neroli, nerolo, after the Princess of Nerole (17th cent.) said to have discovered it] an oil distilled from orange flowers and used in perfumery: in full, **neroli oil**

Ne·ru·da (ne rōō'thä; E. nə rōō'də), **Pa·blo** (pä'blō) (pseud. of Ricardo Eliezer Neftalí Reyes Basoalto) 1904–   ; Chilean poet

nerv·ate (nur'vāt) adj. Bot. having nerves, or veins

ner·va·tion (nər vā'shən) n. [< NERVE + -ATION] same as VENATION

nerve (nurv) n. [ME. nerfe < OFr. nerf < L. nervus, sinew, nerve, string < IE. base *(s)nēu-, to twist, wind, whence Gr. neuron, tendon, nerve, OE. sneowan, to hurry] 1. orig., a sinew or tendon: now chiefly in phr. **strain every nerve,** to try as hard as possible 2. any of the cordlike fibers or bundles of fibers connecting the body organs with the central nervous system (the brain and the spinal cord) and parts of the nervous system with each other, and carrying impulses to and from the brain or a nerve center 3. emotional control; coolness in danger; courage [a man of nerve] 4. strength; energy; vigor 5. [pl.] the nervous system regarded as indicating health, emotional stability, endurance, etc. 6. [pl.] a) nervousness b) an attack of this; hysteria 7. [Colloq.] impudent boldness; audacity; brazenness 8. Biol. a rib or vein in a leaf or insect's wing —vt. **nerved, nerv'ing** to give strength or courage to — SYN. see TEMERITY —**get on one's nerves** [Colloq.] to make one irritable or exasperated —**nerve oneself** to collect one's energies or courage for an effort

nerve block a method of local anesthesia in which the passage of impulses through a particular nerve is stopped by the injection of an anesthetic into or near the nerve

nerve cell 1. same as NEURON 2. occasionally, a nerve cell body without its processes

nerve center 1. any group of nerve cells that function together in controlling some specific sense or bodily activity, as breathing 2. a control center for any complex activity; headquarters

nerve fiber any of the threadlike elements, either dendrites or axons, making up a nerve

nerve gas any of several poisonous, odorless, colorless, and tasteless liquids that volatile readily and are rapidly absorbed through the eyes, lungs, or skin, that inactivate the enzyme cholinesterase, causing paralysis of the respiratory and central nervous systems

nerve impulse an electrical wave transmitted along a nerve that has been stimulated

nerve·less (nurv'lis) adj. 1. without strength, vigor, force, or courage; weak; inert; unnerved 2. not nervous; cool; controlled 3. Biol. without nerves —**nerve'less·ly** adv. —**nerve'less·ness** n.

nerve-rack·ing, nerve-wrack·ing (-rak'in) adj. very trying to one's patience or equanimity; causing irritation or exasperation

nerv·ing (nur'vin) n. Veterinary Med. removal of part of a nerve trunk, as when it is chronically inflamed

nerv·ous (nur'vəs) *adj.* [ME. *neruous* < L. *nervosus*] **1.** orig., strong; sinewy **2.** vigorous in expression; animated **3.** of the nerves **4.** made up of or containing nerves **5.** characterized by or having a disordered state of the nerves **6.** characterized by or showing emotional tension, restlessness, agitation, etc. **7.** fearful; apprehensive —**ner'vous·ly** *adv.* —**ner'vous·ness, ner·vos'i·ty** (-väs'ə tē) *n.*

☆**nervous breakdown** a psychotic or neurotic disorder that impairs the ability to function normally: a popular, nontechnical term

☆**nervous Nellie** [orig. used of high-strung racehorses: in reference to *old Nell*, jocular name for a nag] [Slang] a timid person who is easily upset and is hesitant to act

nervous system all the nerve cells and nervous tissues in an organism, including, in the vertebrates, the brain, spinal cord, ganglia, nerves, and nerve centers: it coordinates and controls responses to stimuli and conditions behavior and consciousness

ner·vure (nur'vyoor) *n.* [Fr.: see NERVE & -URE] *Zool.* same as VEIN (*n.* 2)

nerv·y (nur'vē) *adj.* **nerv'i·er, nerv'i·est 1.** [Rare] strong; vigorous; sinewy **2.** [Brit.] nervous; excitable; jittery **3.** full of courage; bold ☆**4.** [Colloq.] rudely bold; brazen; impudent —**nerv'i·ly** *adv.* —**nerv'i·ness** *n.*

n.e.s. not elsewhere specified

nes·ci·ent (nesh'ənt, -ē ənt) *adj.* [L. *nesciens,* prp. of *nescire,* to be ignorant of: see NICE] **1.** lacking knowledge; ignorant **2.** same as AGNOSTIC —**nes'ci·ence** *n.*

ness (nes) *n.* [ME. *nesse* < OE. *næs* & ON. *nes,* akin to OE. *nosu,* NOSE] a promontory; headland: now chiefly in place names [*Inverness*]

-ness (nis, nəs) [ME. *-nesse* < OE. *-nes(s),* akin to G. *-niss,* Goth. *-nassus* (for *-assus,* with *n-* < end of the base of weak verbs ending in *-atjan*)] a *n.-forming suffix meaning* state, quality, or instance of being [*greatness, sadness, togetherness*]

Nes·sel·rode (nes'l rōd') *n.* [after ff.] a mixture of preserved fruits, chopped nuts, etc., used in ice cream, puddings, pies, or the like

Nes·sel·rode (nes'l rōd'; *Russ.* nyes'sil rô'dye), Count **Karl Robert** 1780-1862; Russ. statesman & diplomat

nest (nest) *n.* [ME. < OE., akin to G. *nest* < IE. *nizdos* < base *ni-,* down + *sed-,* to sit, whence L. *nidus,* W. *nyth*] **1.** the structure made or the place chosen by birds for laying their eggs and sheltering their young **2.** the place used by turtles, hornets, fish, etc. for spawning or breeding **3.** a cozy or snug place to live or rest; retreat **4.** *a)* a resort, haunt, or den: used esp. in an unfavorable sense *b)* the people who frequent such a place [a nest of criminals] **5.** a brood, swarm, or colony of birds, insects, etc. **6.** a set or series of similar things, each fitting within the one next larger —*vi.* **1.** to build or live in or as in a nest **2.** to fit one into another **3.** to hunt for birds' nests: usually in the present participle —*vt.* **1.** to make a nest for **2.** to place or settle in or as in a nest **3.** to fit (an object) closely within another —**nest'a·ble** *adj.* —**nest'er** *n.*

‡**n'est-ce pas?** (nes pä') [Fr., lit., is it not?] isn't that so?

nest egg 1. an artificial or real egg left in a nest to induce a hen to lay more eggs there **2.** money, etc. put aside as a reserve or to establish a fund

nes·tle (nes'l) *vi.* **-tled, -tling** [ME. *nestlen* < OE. *nestlian:* see NEST & -LE] **1.** orig., to nest **2.** to settle down comfortably and snugly **3.** to draw or press close for comfort or in affection **4.** to lie sheltered or partly hidden, as a house among trees —*vt.* **1.** to rest or press (a baby, one's head, etc.) in a snug, affectionate manner **2.** to settle or house as in a nest; shelter —**nes'tler** *n.*

nest·ling (nest'liŋ, nes'-) *n.* [ME. (akin to G. *nestling):* see NEST & -LING[1]] **1.** a young bird not yet ready to leave the nest **2.** a young child

Nes·tor (nes'tər) [L. < Gr. *Nestōr*] **1.** a masculine name **2.** *Gr. Myth.* a wise old counselor who fought with the Greeks at Troy —*n.* [also **n-**] any wise old man

Nes·to·ri·an·ism (nes tôr'ē ən iz'm) *n.* the doctrine attributed to Nestorius (patriarch of Constantinople, 428-431 A.D.) that the divine and the human existed as two distinct natures in Jesus: declared heretical in 431 —**Nes·to'ri·an** *n., adj.*

net[1] (net) *n.* [ME. < OE. *nett,* akin to G. *netz* (Goth. *nati*) < IE. base *ned-,* to twist together, whence L. *nodus,* a knot] **1.** a fabric made from string, cord, etc., loosely knotted or woven in an openwork pattern and used to trap or snare birds, fish, etc. **2.** anything that catches or entraps; trap; snare **3.** any of various devices made of meshed fabric, used to hold, protect, or mark off something [a hairnet, tennis net] **4.** a fine, meshed lacelike cloth, used to make curtains, trim garments, etc. **5.** same as NETWORK (sense 2) **6.** *Tennis, Badminton,* etc. a ball or shuttlecock that hits the net, whether or not it goes over: in full, **net ball** —*vt.* **net'ted, net'ting 1.** to make into net or a net **2.** to make with net **3.** to trap or snare with or as with a net **4.** to protect, shelter, or enclose with or as with a net **5.** *Tennis,* etc. to drive (the ball) into the net —*vi.* to make nets or network —*adj.* **1.** of or like net **2.** caught in a net; netted —**net'like'** *adj.*

net[2] (net) *adj.* [ME., trim, clean < Fr.: see NEAT[1]] **1.** remaining after certain deductions or allowances have been made, as for expenses, weight of containers or waste materials, nonessential considerations, etc. **2.** after all considerations; final [net loss] —*n.* a net amount, profit, weight, price, result, etc. —*vt.* **net'ted, net'ting** to get or bring in as a net; clear as profit, etc.

Neth. Netherlands

neth·er (neth'ər) *adj.* [ME. *nethere* < OE. *neothera,* akin to G. *nieder* < IE. base *ni-,* down (cf. NEST) + compar. suffix] **1.** lying, or thought of as lying, below the earth's surface [the *nether* world] **2.** lower or under [the *nether* tip of a crescent]

Neth·er·lands (neth'ər ləndz) **1.** country in W Europe, on the North Sea: 12,978 sq. mi.; pop. 12,597,000; cap. Amsterdam; seat of govt. The Hague **2.** kingdom consisting of the independent states of the Netherlands, Surinam, & Netherlands Antilles Du. name, NEDERLAND —**Neth'er·land'er** (-lan'dər, -lən dər) *n.*

Netherlands Antilles islands in the West Indies, constituting a part of the kingdom of the Netherlands & comprising two of the Leeward Islands & part of another & three islands off the coast of Venezuela: 394 sq. mi.; pop. 210,000; cap. Willemstad

Netherlands (East) Indies former island possessions of the Netherlands, in the East Indies: now part of Indonesia

Netherlands Guiana former name of SURINAM

Netherlands New Guinea former name of WEST IRIAN

neth·er·most (neth'ər mōst') *adj.* [ME. *nethermest:* see NETHER & -MOST] lowest; farthest down

neth·er·ward (-wərd) *adv.* in a downward course, or direction: also **neth'er·wards**

nether world *Theol. & Myth.* the world of the dead or of punishment after death; hell

Né·thou (nā tōō'), **Pic de** (pēk də) *Fr. name of* Pico de ANETO

net national product a country's total output of goods and services during a specified period of time, valued at current market prices and after allowance for replacement of capital goods

net·su·ke (net'soo kā', -kē) *n.* [Jap.] an ornamental button or figure of ivory, wood, etc., once used to attach a purse or other article to a kimono sash

Net·tie, Net·ty (net'ē) a feminine name: see ANTOINETTE, HENRIETTA, JEANNETTE

net·ting (net'iŋ) *n.* **1.** the act or process of making nets **2.** the action or right of fishing with nets **3.** netted material

netting knot same as SHEET BEND: see KNOT, illus.

net·tle (net'l) *n.* [ME. *netle* < OE. *netele,* akin to G. *nessel* < IE. base *ned-,* to twist together, whence NET[1]: from the use of such plants as a source of spinning fiber] **1.** any of a genus (*Urtica*) of annual and perennial weeds of the nettle family with stinging hairs **2.** any of various other stinging or spiny plants —*adj.* designating a family (Urticaceae) of chiefly tropical plants usually covered with stinging hairs, including the ramie and the nettle —*vt.* **-tled, -tling 1.** to sting with or as with nettles **2.** to irritate; annoy; vex —SYN. see IRRITATE —**net'tler** *n.*

nettle rash same as URTICARIA

net·tle·some (-səm) *adj.* that nettles or irritates

net ton same as SHORT TON

net-winged (-wiŋd') *adj.* having a network of veins in the wings: said of insects

net·work (net'wurk') *n.* [NET[1] + WORK] **1.** any arrangement or fabric of parallel wires, threads, etc. crossed at regular intervals by others fastened to them so as to leave open spaces; netting; mesh **2.** a thing resembling this in some way; specif., *a)* a system of roads, canals, veins, etc. that connect with or cross one another *b)* *Radio & TV* a chain of transmitting stations controlled and operated as a unit *c)* a group, system, etc. of interconnected or cooperating individuals **3.** the making of nets or netted fabric —*adj.* broadcast over all or most of the stations of a network

Neu·châ·tel (nö shā tel') **1.** canton of W Switzerland, on the Fr. border: 308 sq. mi.; pop. 157,000 **2.** its capital, on the Lake of Neuchâtel: pop. 51,000 **3.** Lake of, lake in W Switzerland: 84 sq. mi.

Neu·en·burg (noi'ən boorkh') *Ger. name of* NEUCHÂTEL

Neuf·châ·tel (cheese) (nöö'shə tel', nyoo'-; *Fr.* nö shä tel') [Fr., after *Neufchâtel,* town in N France] a soft, white cheese prepared from whole milk or skim milk and eaten fresh or cured

Neuil·ly-sur-Seine (nö yē sür sen') city in NC France: suburb of Paris: pop. 73,000

neuk (nyōōk) *n.* [Scot.] a nook; corner

neume, neum (nyōōm, nōōm) *n.* [Fr. < ML. *neuma,* prob. ult. < Syriac *ne'mo,* a sound, tone, song, altered in form and sense by association with Gr. *neuma,* a sign & *pneuma,* a breath] any of a set of signs used in medieval church music before the invention of an exact music notation and placed over words in order to aid the memory by indicating direction of melody, manner of performance, etc. —**neu·mat'ic** *adj.*

neur- same as NEURO-: used before a vowel

neu·ral (noor′əl, nyoor′-) *adj.* [prec. + -AL] of a nerve, nerves, or the nervous system

neural arch a bony or cartilaginous arch resting on the chief part of each vertebra and forming a tunnel through which the nerve cord passes

neu·ral·gia (noo ral′jə, nyoo-) *n.* [ModL.: see NEURO- & -ALGIA] severe pain along the course of a nerve or in its area of distribution —**neu·ral′gic** (-jik) *adj.*

neural tube a tubular, primitive, dorsal structure formed from ectodermal tissue in the early vertebrate embryo, that develops into the brain and spinal cord

neu·ras·the·ni·a (noor′as thē′nē ə, nyoor′-) *n.* [ModL.: see NEURO- & ASTHENIA] a type of neurosis, usually the result of emotional conflicts, characterized by irritability, fatigue, weakness, anxiety, and, often, localized pains or distress without apparent physical causes: formerly thought to result from weakness or exhaustion of the nervous system —**neu′ras·then′ic** (-then′ik) *adj., n.*

neu·rec·to·my (noo rek′tə mē, nyoo-) *n., pl.* -mies [NEUR- + -ECTOMY] surgical removal of a nerve or part of a nerve

neu·ri·lem·ma (noor′ə lem′ə, nyoor′-) *n.* [ModL., altered (after Gr. *lemma,* skin, peel) < *neurilema* < Gr. *neuron,* NERVE + *eilēma,* a covering < *eilyein,* to wind, wrap: for IE. base see WALK] the thin outer sheath covering a nerve fiber

neu·rine (noor′ēn, nyoor′-) *n.* [NEUR- + -INE⁴] a ptomaine poison, $CH_2:CHN(CH_3)_2OH$, formed by the dehydration of choline, as during the putrefaction of flesh

neu·ri·tis (noo rīt′əs, nyoo-) *n.* [ModL.: see NEURO- & -ITIS] inflammation of a nerve or nerves, often associated with a degenerative process, and accompanied by changes in sensory and motor activity in the region of the affected nerve —**neu·rit′ic** (-rit′ik) *adj.*

neu·ro- (noor′ō, nyoor′-; -ə) [< Gr. *neuron,* NERVE] a combining form meaning of a nerve, nerves, or the nervous system [*neuropath*]

neu·ro·blast (-blast′) *n.* [prec. + -BLAST] any of the embryonic cells from which the nerve cells develop

neu·ro·coel, neu·ro·coele (-sēl′) *n.* [NEURO- + -COELE] the cavity of the chordate cerebrospinal system, consisting of the ventricles of the brain and the central canal of the spinal cord, regarded as a unit

neu·ro·ep·i·the·li·um (noor′ō ep′ə thē′lē əm, nyoor′-) *n.* a highly specialized structure of epithelial origin, serving as the ending of a nerve of special sense, including the gustatory cells, the olfactory cells, the rods and cones of the retina, etc. —**neu′ro·ep′i·the′li·al** *adj.*

neu·ro·fi·bril (-fī′bril) *n.* a fibril comprising part of a nerve cell —**neu′ro·fi′bril·lar′y** (-er ē) *adj.*

neu·ro·gen·ic (-jen′ik) *adj.* 1. originating in nervous tissue 2. stimulated or induced by nervous factors 3. controlled by nerve impulses —**neu·ro·gen′i·cal·ly** *adv.*

neu·rog·li·a (noo räg′lē ə, nyoo-) *n.* [ModL.: < NEURO- + MGr. *glia,* for Gr. *gloios,* GLUE] the connective tissue, consisting of a special type of branched cells, that binds together and supports the nerve tissue of the central nervous system —**neu·rog′li·al** *adj.*

neu·ro·hu·mor (noor′ə hyoo′mər, nyoor′-) *n.* [NEURO- + HUMOR] a hormone secreted by part of the nervous system, that activates a neighboring structure —**neu′ro·hu′mor·al** *adj.*

neu·rol·o·gy (noo räl′ə jē, nyoo-) *n.* [ModL. *neurologia:* see NEURO- & -LOGY] the branch of medicine dealing with the nervous system, its structure, and its diseases —**neu·ro·log·i·cal** (noor′ə läj′i k′l, nyoor′-) *adj.* —**neu′ro·log′i·cal·ly** *adv.* —**neu·rol′o·gist** *n.*

neu·rol·y·sis (-ə sis) *n.* [ModL.: see NEURO- & -LYSIS] 1. destruction of nerve tissue or its exhaustion from excessive stimulation 2. the freeing of a nerve from adhesions —**neu·ro·lyt·ic** (noor′ə lit′ik, nyoor′-) *adj.*

neu·ro·ma (noo rō′mə, nyoo-) *n., pl.* -mas, -ma·ta (-mə tə) [ModL.: see NEURO- & -OMA] a tumor derived from nervous tissue, consisting of nerve cells and fibers

neu·ro·mast (noor′ə mast′, nyoor′-) *n.* [NEURO- + Gr. *mastos,* breast: see MAST²] 1. any of various small, sensory projections or papillae found in many vertebrates and invertebrates 2. any of the elongated sensory cells having a projecting hairlike process, found along the lateral line system of fishes

neu·ro·mus·cu·lar (noor′ō mus′kyə lər, nyoor′-) *adj.* of or involving both nerves and muscles

neu·ron (noor′än, nyoor′-) *n.* [ModL. < Gr. *neuron,* NERVE] the structural and functional unit of the nervous system, consisting of the nerve cell body and all its processes, including an axon and one or more dendrites: also **neu′rone** (-ōn) —**neu′ro·nal** (-ə nəl), **neu·ron′ic** (noo rän′ik, nyoo-) *adj.*

neu·ro·path (noor′ə path′, nyoor′-) *n.* [< NEUROPATHIC] *earlier term for* NEUROTIC

neu·ro·pa·thol·o·gy (noor′ō pə thäl′ə jē, nyoor′-) *n.* the branch of pathology dealing with diseases of the nervous system —**neu′ro·pa·thol′o·gist** *n.*

neu·rop·a·thy (noo räp′ə thē, nyoo-) *n.* [NEURO- +

SPINAL CORD
MOTOR NEURON
SENSORY NEURON
END ORGAN
CELL BODY OF NEURON

NEURON

-PATHY] any disease of the nervous system —**neu·ro·path·ic** (noor′ə path′ik, nyoor′-) *adj.*

neu·ro·phys·i·ol·o·gy (noor′ō fiz′ē äl′ə jē, nyoor′-) *n.* the physiology of the nervous system

neu·ro·psy·chi·a·try (-sə kī′ə trē) *n.* a branch of medicine dealing with disorders of both the mind and the nervous system —**neu·ro·psy′chi·at′ric** (-sī′kē at′rik) *adj.*

neu·rop·ter·an (noo räp′tər ən, nyoo-) *n.* [< ModL. *Neuroptera,* name of the order (< NEURO- + Gr. *pteron,* wing, FEATHER) + -AN] any of an order (Neuroptera) of carnivorous insects, including the lacewings and ant lions, with four finely veined, membranous wings and biting mouthparts —**neu·rop′ter·ous** *adj.*

neu·ro·sis (noo rō′sis, nyoo-) *n., pl.* -ses (-sēz) [ModL.: see NEURO- & -OSIS] any of various psychic, or mental, functional disorders characterized by one or several of the following reactions: anxiety, compulsions and obsessions, phobias, depression, dissociations, and conversion; psychoneurosis

neu·ro·sur·ger·y (noor′ō sur′jər ē, nyoor′-) *n.* the branch of surgery involving some part of the nervous system, including the brain and the spinal cord

neu·rot·ic (noo rät′ik, nyoo-) *adj.* of, characteristic of, or having a neurosis —*n.* a neurotic person —**neu·rot′i·cal·ly** *adv.* —**neu·rot′i·cism** (-ə siz′m) *n.*

neu·rot·o·my (-ə mē) *n., pl.* -mies [NEURO- + -TOMY] the surgical severing of a nerve, as for relieving pain

neu·ro·tox·in (noor′ō täk′sin, nyoor′-) *n.* a toxin that destroys nerves or nervous tissue —**neu′ro·tox′ic** *adj.*

neu·ro·trop·ic (noor′ō träp′ik, nyoor′-) *adj.* [NEURO- + -TROPIC] having an affinity for nervous tissue, as certain viruses and poisons

neus·ton (noo̅s′stän, nyoo̅s′-) *n.* [Gr., neut. of *neustos,* swimming (verbal of *nein,* to swim < IE. base *(s)neu-,* whence SNOT)] minute organisms, as mosquito larvae, existing in or dependent upon the surface film of a body of water —**neus′tic** *adj.*

Neu·stri·a (noo̅s′strē ə, nyoo̅s′-) W part of the kingdom of the Merovingian Franks in what is now N & NW France

neut. neuter

neu·ter (noo̅t′ər, nyoo̅t′-) *adj.* [ME. *neutre* < MFr. or L.: MFr. *neutre* < L. *neuter,* neither < *ne-,* not (see NO¹) + *uter,* either] 1. [Archaic] taking neither side; neutral 2. *Biol. a)* having no sexual organ; asexual *b)* having undeveloped or imperfect sexual organs in the adult, as the worker bee 3. *Gram. a)* in many highly inflected languages, designating or of that one of the three genders of words that are neither masculine nor feminine *b)* neither active nor passive; intransitive: said of verbs —*n.* 1. a castrated or spayed animal 2. [Archaic] a neutral person or group 3. *Biol.* a plant or animal lacking, or having undeveloped, sexual organs 4. *Gram. a)* the neuter gender *b)* a neuter word —*vt.* to castrate or spay (an animal)

neu·tral (noo̅′trəl, nyoo̅′-) *adj.* [Fr. < ML. *neutralis* < L., of neuter gender < *neuter:* see prec.] 1. *a)* not taking part in either side of a dispute or quarrel *b)* not taking part in a war; giving no active aid to any belligerent 2. of, belonging to, or characteristic of a nation not taking part in a war or not aligning itself with either side in a power struggle 3. belonging to neither extreme in type, kind, etc.; without strongly marked characteristics; indefinite, indifferent, middling, etc. 4. *a)* having little or no decided color; not vivid *b)* free from mixture of other colors 5. *Biol.* same as NEUTER 6. *Chem.* giving neither acid nor alkaline reaction 7. *Elec.* neither negative nor positive; uncharged 8. *Phonet.* pronounced with the tongue in the relaxed, mid-central position, as the vowel in most unstressed syllables, which tends to become (ə) —*n.* 1. a nation not taking part in a war; neutral power 2. a neutral person or a citizen of a neutral country 3. a neutral color 4. *Mechanics* a disengaged position of gears, in which they do not transmit power from the engine to the operating parts —**neu′tral·ly** *adv.*

neu·tral·ism (-iz′m) *n.* a policy, or the advocacy of a policy, of remaining neutral, esp. in international power conflicts —**neu′tral·ist** *adj., n.* —**neu′tral·is′tic** *adj.*

neu·tral·i·ty (noo̅ tral′ə tē, nyoo̅-) *n.* 1. the quality, state, or character of being neutral 2. the status or policy of a nation not participating directly or indirectly in a war between other nations 3. neutral status, as of a seaport in wartime

neu·tral·ize (noo̅′trə līz′, nyoo̅′-) *vt.* -ized′, -iz′ing [Fr. *neutraliser*] 1. to declare (a territory, nation, etc.) neutral in war; declare open to all nations under international law and exempt from attack 2. to make ineffective; destroy or counteract the effectiveness, force, disposition, etc. of 3. *Chem.* to destroy the distinctive or active properties of [an alkali *neutralizes* an acid] 4. *Elec.* to make electrically neutral —**neu′tral·i·za′tion** *n.* —**neu′tral·iz′er** *n.*

neutral spirits ethyl alcohol of 190 proof or over, esp. as used for blending with aged whiskeys, or with flavorings to make liqueurs, cordials, etc.

neu·tri·no (noo̅ trē′nō, nyoo̅-) *n., pl.* -nos [It., coined by E. FERMI < *neutrone* (< NEUTRON) + dim. suffix -*ino*] *Physics* a neutral particle, difficult to detect, having a mass approaching zero and no charge: it has almost no interaction with matter

neu·tron (noo̅′trän, nyoo̅′-) *n.* [NEUTR(AL) + -*on,* as in ELECTRON] one of the elementary particles of an atom:

neutrons are uncharged, have approximately the same mass as protons, interact strongly with nuclei, and are readily absorbed: a free neutron decays into a proton, an electron, and a neutrino with a half-life of c. 13 minutes

neutron number the number of neutrons in a given nucleus: it is the difference between the mass number and the atomic number

☆**neutron star** a heavenly object hypothesized to be a collapsed star consisting of immense numbers of densely packed neutrons: often equated with PULSAR

neu·tro·phil (n$\overline{oo}$′trə fil, ny$\overline{oo}$′-) n. [< NEUTRAL + -PHIL] a type of phagocytic white blood cell in vertebrate blood, stainable by neutral dyes —adj. easily stained by neutral dyes Also **neu′tro·phile′** (-fīl′)

Ne·va (nē′və; Russ. nyi vä′) river in NW R.S.F.S.R., flowing from Lake Ladoga through Leningrad into the Gulf of Finland: 46 mi.

Ne·vad·a (nə vad′ə, -vä′də) [< (SIERRA) NEVADA] Mountain State of the W U.S.: admitted, 1864; 110,540 sq. mi.; pop. 489,000; cap. Carson City: abbrev. Nev., NV —**Ne·vad′an** adj., n.

né·vé (nā vā′) n. [Fr. (Swiss dial.), glacier, ult. < L. nix (gen. nivis), snow: for base see SNOW] 1. same as FIRN 2. the area above or at the head of a glacier that accumulates more snow than is dissipated during the summer

nev·er (nev′ər) adv. [ME. nevere < OE. næfre < ne, not (see NO) + æfre, EVER] 1. not ever; at no time 2. not at all; by no chance; in no case; under no conditions

nev·er·more (nev′ər môr′) adv. never again; at no future time

nev·er-nev·er (nev′ər nev′ər) n. [Brit. Slang] the installment plan —adj. imaginary, fantasized, unrealistic, etc.

never-never land [after the fairyland in J. M. Barrie's Peter Pan] an unreal, unrealistic, or fantasized place, state, or situation

nev·er·the·less (-thə les′) adv. in spite of that; however; nonetheless: often used as a conjunctive adverb

Nev·il, Nev·ile (nev′'l) [< Norman surname Nevil, Néville < Neuville, town in Normandy (lit., new city)] a masculine name: also sp. **Nev′ile, Nev′ill**

Ne·vis (nē′vis, nev′is) Brit. island in the Leeward group of the West Indies: 50 sq. mi.; pop. 13,000: see ANGUILLA

Nevski, Alexander see ALEXANDER NEVSKI

ne·vus (nē′vəs) n., pl. **ne′vi** (vī) [ModL. < L. naevus, prob. akin to genus, gnatus (cf. GENUS)] a colored spot on the skin, usually congenital —**ne′void** (-void) adj.

new (n$\overline{oo}$, ny$\overline{oo}$) adj. [ME. newe < OE. niwe, akin to G. neu < IE. *newos, new, whence L. novus, Gr. neos, W. newydd, new] 1. never existing before; appearing, thought of, developed, made, produced, etc. for the first time 2. a) existing before, but known or discovered for the first time [a new planet] b) recently observed, experienced, manifested, etc.; different [a new understanding of the problem] c) strange; unfamiliar; foreign [languages new to one] 3. not yet familiar or accustomed; inexperienced [new to the work] 4. a) designating the more or most recent of two or more things of the same class, though both may be old [New York] b) taking the place of the previous one; recently appointed, acquired, etc. [a new regime] 5. recently grown; fresh [new potatoes] 6. not previously used or worn 7. modern; recent; fashionable; recently current 8. more; additional [two new inches of snow] 9. beginning again; starting as a repetition of a cycle, series, etc.; making another start [the new moon, the new year] 10. having just reached a position, rank, place, etc. [a new arrival] 11. refreshed in spirits, health, etc. [a new man] 12. [N-] same as MODERN (sense 3) —n. something new (with the) —adv. 1. again 2. newly; recently —**new′ness** n.

SYN.—**new** is applied to that which has never existed before or which has only just come into being, possession, use, etc. [a new coat, plan, etc.]; **fresh** implies such newness that the original appearance, quality, vigor, etc. have not been affected by time or use [fresh eggs, a fresh start]; **novel** implies a newness that is strikingly unusual or strange [a novel idea, combination, etc.]; **modern** and **modernistic** apply to that which is of the present time, as distinguished from earlier periods, and connotes up-to-dateness, the latter word, sometimes, with derogatory implications; **original** is used of that which is not only new but is also the first of its kind [an original plan, melody, etc.] —**ANT.** old

New Albany city in S Ind., on the Ohio, opposite Louisville, Ky.: pop. 38,000

New Amsterdam Du. colonial town on Manhattan Island: renamed (1664) New York by the British

New·ark (n$\overline{oo}$′ərk, ny$\overline{oo}$′-) [after Newark, in England] 1. city in NE N.J.: pop. 382,000 (met. area 1,857,000) 2. city in C Ohio: pop. 42,000

New Bedford [after Wm. Russell, Duke of Bedford (1639–83)] seaport in SE Mass.: pop. 102,000

new blood new people, regarded as a potential source of fresh ideas, renewed vigor, etc.

new-born (-bôrn′) adj. [ME.] 1. recently born 2. reborn

New Britain 1. largest island of the Bismarck Archipelago, east of New Guinea: (with small nearby islands) 14,100 sq. mi.; pop. 115,000; chief city, Rabaul 2. city in C Conn.: pop. 83,000

New Brunswick [after GEORGE II, Duke of Brunswick] 1. province of SE Canada, on the Gulf of St. Lawrence: 28,354 sq. mi.; pop. 617,000; cap. Fredericton: abbrev. N.B. 2. city in NC N.J.: pop. 42,000

New·burg (-bərg) adj. ☆served in a rich, creamy sauce made with butter, egg yolks, and wine

New Caledonia Fr. island in the SW Pacific, west of Australia: with nearby islands an overseas territory of France: 7,218 sq. mi.; pop. 87,000; cap. Nouméa

new candle see CANDLE (n. 3 a)

New Castile see CASTILE

New·cas·tle (n$\overline{oo}$′kas′'l, ny$\overline{oo}$′-; -käs′-) 1. seaport in N England, county seat of Northumberland: pop. 254,000: in full, **New′cas′tle-up·on-Tyne′** (-tīn′) 2. city in Staffordshire, WC England: pop. 77,000: in full, **New′cas′tle-under-Lyme′** (-līm′) 3. seaport in E New South Wales, Australia, on the Pacific: pop. (with suburbs) 222,000 —**carry coals to Newcastle** 1. to take things to a place where they are plentiful or not needed: Newcastle (sense 1) was a center for coal 2. to do an unnecessary or redundant thing

New Castle [prob. after prec. (sense 1)] city in W Pa.: pop. 39,000

Newcastle disease [< NEWCASTLE(-UPON-TYNE)] an acute viral disease of poultry and other birds, characterized by pneumonia and encephalomyelitis

New·comb (n$\overline{oo}$′kəm, ny$\overline{oo}$′-), **Simon** 1835–1909; U.S. astronomer, born in Canada

new·com·er (-kum′ər) n. a person who has come recently; recent arrival

New Criticism ☆a method of literary analysis, in vogue in the 20th cent., stressing close examination of the text itself, its language, symbolism, structure, etc.

☆**New Deal** 1. the economic and political principles and policies adopted by President Franklin D. Roosevelt in the 1930's to advance economic recovery and social welfare 2. the Roosevelt administration —**New Dealer**

New Delhi capital of India, in Delhi territory, adjacent to the old city of Delhi: pop. 261,000

New Egyptian 1. same as COPTIC 2. the Egyptian language from c. 1600–c. 1000 B.C.

new·el (n$\overline{oo}$′əl, ny$\overline{oo}$′-) n. [ME. nowelle < OFr. nuel, a nut, fruit pit < LL. nucalis, like a nut < L. nux (gen. nucis), NUT] 1. the central upright pillar around which the steps of a winding staircase turn 2. the post at the top or bottom of a flight of stairs, supporting the handrail: also **newel post**

New England [so named (1616) by Captain John SMITH] ☆the six NE States of the U.S.: Me., Vt., N.H., Mass., R.I., & Conn.: abbrev. **New Eng.** —**New Englander**

☆**New England aster** a native aster (Aster novae-angliae) with purplish ray flowers, growing in E N. America

☆**New England boiled dinner** a dish consisting of meat, often corned beef, and whole potatoes, onions, carrots, cabbage, etc. cooked by boiling

New English [term popularized by H. SWEET after G. neuhochdeutsch, New High German] Modern English (c. 1750 to the present) as distinguished from Early Modern English, Middle English, and Old English

New English Bible a British translation of the Bible, published in 1970 (New Testament in 1961)

new-fan·gled (n$\overline{oo}$′fan′g'ld, ny$\overline{oo}$′-) adj. [ME. < newefangel < newe, NEW + -fangel < base of OE. fon, to take: see FANG] 1. newly done, made, etc.; new; novel: a humorously derogatory term 2. [Now Rare] tending toward or fond of novelty or new things

new-fash·ioned (-fash′ənd) adj. 1. recently come into fashion 2. made in a new and different form or style

New Forest partially wooded rural district in Hampshire, England: 144 sq. mi.; pop. 62,000

New·found·land (n$\overline{oo}$′fənd land′, -lənd; ny$\overline{oo}$′-; ny$\overline{oo}$ found′land′) 1. island of Canada, off the E coast: 42,734 sq. mi. 2. province of Canada, including this island & Labrador: 156,185 sq. mi.; pop. 493,000; cap. St. John's: abbrev. **Nfld.** —**New′found·land′er** n.

Newfoundland dog [< prec.] any of a North American breed of large, powerful, usually black, shaggy-haired dogs

Newfoundland Standard Time a standard time used in Newfoundland, Canada: it is three hours and thirty minutes behind Greenwich time

New France Fr. possessions in N. America, from the end of the 16th cent. to 1763, including E Canada, the Great Lakes region, & the Mississippi valley

New·gate (n$\overline{oo}$′gāt, ny$\overline{oo}$′-) former prison in London: torn down in 1902

New Georgia 1. group of islands in the Brit. Solomon Island Protectorate, in the SW Pacific: c. 2,500 sq. mi. 2. largest island of this group: c. 1,300 sq. mi.

New Granada 1. former Sp. possessions, mostly in NW S. America, including what is now Colombia, Venezuela, Ecuador, & Panama 2. former country consisting of present-day Colombia & Panama

New Guinea large island in the East Indies, north of Australia: divided between West Irian (in Indonesia), and two territories (North-East New Guinea & Papua) jointly

administered by Australia: c. 330,000 sq. mi.: Indonesian name, IRIAN **2. Trust Territory of,** Australian trust territory (administered jointly with the *Territory of Papua*) including North-East New Guinea, the Bismarck Archipelago, Bougainville, Buka, & smaller adjacent islands of the Solomons: 93,000 sq. mi.; pop. 1,582,000; cap. Port Moresby

New Hampshire [after HAMPSHIRE] New England State of the U.S.: one of the 13 original States; 9,304 sq. mi.; pop. 738,000; cap. Concord: abbrev. N.H., NH

New Haven city in S Conn., on Long Island Sound: pop. 138,000

New Hebrides group of islands in the SW Pacific, west of the Fiji Islands: Brit. & Fr. condominium: 5,700 sq. mi.; pop. 68,000: see FIJI ISLANDS, map

New High German *see* GERMAN, HIGH GERMAN

New Ireland island in the Bismarck Archipelago, north of New Britain: 3,340 sq. mi.; pop. (with small nearby islands) 41,000

new·ish (nōō′ish, nyōō′-) *adj.* somewhat new

New Jersey [after JERSEY (the Channel Island)] Eastern State of the U.S. on the Atlantic: one of the 13 original States; 7,836 sq. mi.; pop. 7,168,000; cap. Trenton: abbrev. N.J., NJ —New Jer′sey·ite′

New Jerusalem *Bible* the holy city of heaven: Rev. 21:2

New Jerusalem, Church of the the church of the Swedenborgians: also **New Church**

☆**New Left** a U.S. political movement that developed in the 1960's as a loose coalition of various organizations, mainly of young people, seeking radical social and economic change

New London city in SE Conn., on Long Island Sound: site of U.S. Coast Guard Academy: pop. 32,000

new·ly (nōō′lē, nyōō′-) *adv.* **1.** recently; lately **2.** anew; afresh **3.** in a new way or style

new·ly·wed (-wed′) *n.* a recently married person

New·man (nōō′mən, nyōō′-), **John Henry,** Cardinal Newman, 1801–90; Eng. theologian & writer

New·mar·ket (-mär′kit) rural district in Cambridgeshire, E England: scene of many horse-racing events: pop. 21,000

new·mar·ket (-mär′kit) *n.* [< prec.: orig. worn for riding at Newmarket races] **1.** formerly, a long, closefitting coat: also **Newmarket coat 2.** [*often* N-] a kind of card game

☆**new math** an ordered system for teaching fundamental concepts of mathematics by the use of set theory

New Mexico [transl. of Sp. *Nuevo Méjico*] Mountain State of the SW U.S.: admitted, 1912; 121,666 sq. mi.; pop. 1,016,000; cap. Santa Fe: abbrev. **N.Mex., NM —New Mexican**

new moon 1. that phase of the moon when it is between the earth and the sun, with the dark side of its disk toward the earth: after two or three days it reappears as a thin crescent curving toward the right **2.** the time of the new moon

new-mown (nōō′mōn′, nyōō′-) *adj.* freshly mown or cut: said of hay or grass

New Netherland Du. colony (1613–64) on Manhattan Island & along the Hudson River: taken by England & divided into the colonies of New York & New Jersey

New Or·le·ans (ôr′lē ənz, ôr lēnz′; *chiefly Southern* ôr′lənz) [< Fr. *Nouvelle Orléans,* in honor of the Duke of ORLÉANS[1], and of ORLÉANS[2], France] city & port in SE La., on the Mississippi: pop. 593,000 (met. area 1,046,000)

New·port (nōō′pôrt′, nyōō′-) **1.** seaport in SE Wales; county seat of Monmouthshire: pop. 113,000 **2.** [on the analogy of Eng. towns of the same name] city in SE R.I., on Narragansett Bay: pop. 35,000

Newport Beach [see prec.] city in SW Calif., on the Pacific, near Long Beach: pop. 49,000

Newport News [origin obscure] seaport in SE Va., on the James River at Hampton Roads: pop. 138,000

New Providence island of the NC Bahamas: 58 sq. mi.: see NASSAU

New Ro·chelle (rə shel′) [after *La Rochelle,* in France] city in SE N.Y., on Long Island Sound, north of New York City: pop. 75,000

news (nōōz, nyōōz) *n.pl.* [*with sing. v.*] [ME. *newes,* novelties (pl. of *newe,* adj.), after OFr. *noveles* or ML. *nova,* pl. of *novum,* what is new: see NEW] **1.** new information about anything; information previously unknown **2.** *a)* reports, collectively, of recent happenings, esp. those broadcast over radio or TV, printed in a newspaper, etc. *b)* any person or thing thought to merit special attention in such reports **3.** *clipped form of* NEWSCAST —**make news** to do something that is apt to be reported as news

☆**news agency** an organization that supplies news to newspapers, radio and television stations, etc. that subscribe to its services

news agent *chiefly Brit. var. of* NEWSDEALER

news·boy (-boi′) *n.* a boy who sells or delivers newspapers

☆**news·cast** (-kast′, -käst′) *n.* [NEWS + (BROAD)CAST] a program of news broadcast over radio or television —**news′cast′er** *n.* —**news′cast′ing** *n.*

☆**news conference** *same as* PRESS CONFERENCE

☆**news·deal·er** (-dēl′ər) *n.* a person who sells newspapers, magazines, etc., esp. as a retailer

☆**news·hawk** (-hôk′) *n.* [Slang] a newspaper reporter —**news′hen′** (-hen′) *n.fem.*

New Siberian Islands group of islands of the R.S.F.S.R., in the Arctic Ocean, between the Laptev & East Siberian seas: c. 11,000 sq. mi.

news·let·ter (nōōz′let′ər, nyōōz′-) *n.* **1.** a bulletin issued at regular intervals to subscribers, containing recent news, often of interest to a special group and usually including interpretations and predictions **2.** any similar report issued by a firm, governmental agency, etc. to keep employees or the public informed

news·man (-man′, -mən) *n., pl.* **-men** (-men′, -mən) **1.** *same as* NEWSDEALER **2.** one who gathers and reports news for a newspaper, radio or TV station, etc.

news·mon·ger (-muŋ′gər, -mäŋ′gər) *n.* a person who spreads news; esp., a gossip; tattler

New South Wales state of SE Australia, on the Pacific: 309,433 sq. mi.; pop. 4,235,000; cap. Sydney

New Spain former Sp. viceroyalty (1535–1821) including, at its greatest extent, Mexico, SW U.S., Central America north of Panama, the West Indies, & the Philippines

news·pa·per (nōōz′pā′pər, nyōōz′-) *n.* **1.** a publication regularly printed and distributed, usually daily or weekly, containing news, opinions, advertisements, and other items of general interest **2.** *same as* NEWSPRINT

news·pa·per·man (-man′) *n., pl.* **-men** (-men′) **1.** a man who works for a newspaper, esp. as a reporter, editor, writer, etc. **2.** a person who owns or publishes a newspaper —**news′pa′per·wom′an** *n.fem., pl.* **-wom′en**

new·speak (nōō′spēk′, nyōō′-) *n.* [coined (< NEW + SPEAK) by G. ORWELL in his novel *1984*] [*sometimes* N-] the deliberate use of ambiguous and deceptive talk, as by government officials, in seeking to mold public opinion

news·print (nōōz′print′, nyōōz′-) *n.* a cheap, low-grade paper made mainly from wood pulp and used chiefly for newspapers

☆**news·reel** (-rēl′) *n.* a short motion picture of news events

news room ☆a room in a newspaper office, or in a radio or television station, where the news is written and edited

☆**news·stand** (-stand′) *n.* a stand at which newspapers, magazines, etc. are sold: also [Brit.] **news stall**

New Style the method of reckoning time in accordance with the Gregorian calendar

news·wor·thy (nōōz′wur′thē, nyōōz′-) *adj.* having the qualities of news; timely and important or interesting

news·y (-ē) *adj.* **news′i·er, news′i·est** [Colloq.] containing much news —*n., pl.* **news′ies** [Old Colloq.] a newsboy

newt (nōōt, nyōōt) *n.* [ME. *neute,* for *eute,* by syllabic merging < *an eute* < OE. *efeta,* EFT[1]] any of various small salamanders (family Salamandridae) that can live both on land and in water

New Testament *Christian Theol.* **1.** the promises of God to man that are embodied in the life and teachings of Jesus **2.** the part of the Bible that contains the life and teachings of Jesus and his followers, including the four Gospels, the Acts of the Apostles, the Epistles, and the Revelation of Saint John

NEWT
(3–4 in. long)

New Thought a modern religious philosophy emphasizing the power of the mind in achieving health and happiness

New·ton[1] (nōōt′'n, nyōōt′'n) [< *New Towne,* orig. name of Cambridge, Mass.] city in E Mass.: suburb of Boston: pop. 91,000

New·ton[2] (nōōt′'n, nyōōt′'n) [< surname *Newton* < common Eng. place name *Newton* < OE. *neowa tun,* new town] **1.** a masculine name **2.** Sir **Isaac,** 1642–1727; Eng. mathematician & natural philosopher: formulated the laws of gravity & motion & the elements of differential calculus —**New·to′ni·an** (-tō′nē ən) *adj., n.*

new·ton (nōōt′'n, nyōōt′'n) *n.* [after Sir Isaac NEWTON[2]] the unit of force in the mks system; force which imparts to a mass of one kilogram an acceleration of one meter per second per second

New Town 1. any of a number of comprehensively planned, self-contained communities built in Great Britain since World War II under government direction **2.** [*often* n- t-] any large-scale public or private housing development like this

New Westminster seaport in S British Columbia, Canada, on the Fraser River: pop. 38,000

New World the Western Hemisphere —**new′-world′, New′-World′** *adj.*

new year [*also* N- Y-] **1.** the year just about to begin or just begun (usually with *the*) **2.** the first day or days of the new year

New Year's (Day) January 1, the first day of a calendar year, usually celebrated as a legal holiday

New Year's Eve the evening before New Year's Day

New York [after the Duke of *York* and Albany] **1.** State of the NE U.S.: one of the 13 original States; 49,576 sq. mi.; pop. 18,191,000; cap. Albany: abbrev. **N.Y., NY 2.** city & port in SE N.Y., at the mouth of the Hudson: divided into five boroughs (the Bronx, Brooklyn, Manhattan, Queens, Richmond): often **New York City:** 365 sq. mi.; pop. 7,868,000 (met. area, incl. four other counties of N.Y., 11,529,000) —**New York′er**

New York Bay inlet of the Atlantic, south of Manhattan,

divided by the Narrows into a N section (**Upper Bay**) & a S section (**Lower Bay**)

New York State Barge Canal system of waterways connecting Lake Erie & the Hudson River, with branches to Lakes Ontario, Champlain, Cayuga, & Seneca: c. 525 mi. Cf. ERIE CANAL

New Zea·land (zē′lənd) country made up of two large & several small islands in the S Pacific, southeast of Australia: a member of the Brit. Commonwealth: 103,736 sq. mi.; pop. 2,726,000; cap. Wellington —**New Zea′land·er**

Nex·ø (nik′sö), **Mar·tin An·der·sen** (mär′tĕn ȧn′ər s'n) 1869–1954; Dan. novelist

next (nekst) adj. older superl. of NIGH [ME. nexte < OE. neahst, niehst, superl. of neah, NIGH] just before or after in time, space, degree, or rank; nearest; immediately preceding or following —adv. 1. in the time, place, degree, or rank nearest, or immediately preceding or following 2. on the first subsequent occasion [when next we meet] —prep. beside; nearest to [sit next the tree] —n. 1. the one immediately following 2. [Colloq.] one's turn to be next, as in being served —☆**get next to** [Slang] to ingratiate oneself with; become friendly or intimate with —**next door (to)** 1. in, at, or to the next house, building, etc. (adjacent to) 2. almost; nearly

next-door (neks′dôr′) adj. in or at the next house, building, etc.

next friend Law a person who, though not appointed as a guardian, acts for another legally unable to act for himself

next of kin 1. a person's nearest relative or relatives 2. Law a) the blood relatives who may be entitled to share in the estate of a person who dies without a will b) sometimes, the nearest relative by blood as defined in the law of the various States

nex·us (nek′səs) n., pl. **-us·es, nex′us** [L. < pp. of nectere, to bind: cf. ANNEX] 1. a connection, tie, or link between individuals of a group, members of a series, etc. 2. the group or series connected

Ney (nā), **Mi·chel** (mē shel′), duc d'Elchingen, Prince de La Moskova, 1769–1815; Fr. military leader under Napoleon I: executed

Nez Per·cé (nez′ pər sā′, purs′) [Fr., lit., pierced nose, though there is no evidence that this tribe practiced nose piercing] 1. pl. Nez Per·cés′, Nez Per·cé′ a member of a tribe of N. American Indians living in Idaho, Washington, and Oregon 2. their Sahaptin language

N.F. 1. Newfoundland 2. Norman French

N.F., n/f Banking no funds

Nfld., Nfd. Newfoundland

NG, N.G. National Guard

N.G. New Guinea

N.G., n.g. [Slang] no good

ngwee (ŋ gwē′) n., pl. **ngwee** [native term, lit., bright] a monetary unit of Zambia, equal to 1/100 of a kwacha

N.H. New Hampshire

N.Heb. New Hebrides

NHG., N.H.G. New High German

NHI [Brit.] National Health Insurance

Ni Chem. nickel

N.I. Northern Ireland

☆**ni·a·cin** (nī′ə sin) n. [NI(COTINIC) AC(ID) + -IN¹] same as NICOTINIC ACID

Ni·ag·a·ra (nī ag′rə, -ər ə) [< Fr. < Iroquoian town name < ?] river between W N.Y. & SE Ontario, Canada, flowing from Lake Erie into Lake Ontario: c. 36 mi. —n. a torrent, or flood [a Niagara of junk mail]

Niagara Falls 1. large waterfall on the Niagara River: it is divided by an island into two falls, Horseshoe, or Canadian, Falls (c. 160 ft. high) & American Falls (c. 167 ft. high) 2. city in W N.Y., near Niagara Falls: pop. 86,000 3. city in SE Ontario, opposite Niagara Falls, N.Y.: pop. 57,000

Nia·mey (nyä mā′) capital of Niger, in the SW part, on the Niger River: pop. 42,000

nib (nib) n. [var. of NEB] 1. the bill or beak of a bird 2. a) orig., the split and sharpened end of a quill pen b) the point of a pen 3. the projecting end of anything; point; sharp prong —vt. **nibbed, nib′bing** 1. orig., to sharpen and split the end of (a quill) to make a pen 2. to mend (a pen point)

nib·ble (nib′'l) vt. **-bled, -bling** [LME. nebyllen, prob. akin to MLowG. nibbelen: for base see NIP¹] 1. to eat (food) with quick bites, taking only a small amount at a time, as a mouse does 2. to bite at with small, gentle bites —vi. 1. to take small, cautious, or gentle bites (usually with at) 2. to show little interest in food by taking only small bites intermittently (usually with at) —n. 1. a small bite, morsel, or quantity 2. the act or an instance of nibbling —**nib′bler** n.

Ni·be·lung (nē′bə loon′) n. [G.] 1. Germanic Legend a) any of a race of dwarfs, the children of the mist, who owned a magic ring and a hoard of gold, taken from them by Siegfried b) any of Siegfried's followers 2. in the Nibelungenlied, any of the Burgundian kings

Ni·be·lung·en·lied (nē′bə loon′ən lēt′) [G., song of the Nibelungs] a Middle High German epic poem by an un-

known author, written in the first decade of the 13th cent. and based on Germanic legends: see SIEGFRIED

nib·lick (nib′lik) n. [< ?] a golf club with a metal head and much loft, used in sand and for short shots in which the ball must stop close to the point where it lands: now usually called number 9 iron

nibs (nibz) n. [< ?] [Colloq.] an important, or esp. self-important, person (with his)

Ni·cae·a (nī sē′ə) ancient city in Bithynia, NW Asia Minor: the Nicene Creed was formulated here in 325 A.D. —**Ni·cae′an** adj., n.

Nicar. Nicaragua

Nic·a·ra·gua (nik′ə rä′gwə) 1. country in Central America, on the Caribbean & the Pacific: 54,342 sq. mi.; pop. 1,984,000; cap. Managua 2. Lake, lake in S Nicaragua: c. 3,100 sq. mi. —**Nic′a·ra′guan** adj., n.

nic·co·lite (nik′ə līt′) n. [< ModL. niccolum (see NICKEL) + -ITE¹] a pale-red native arsenide of nickel, NiAs

Nice (nēs) seaport & resort in SE France: pop. 293,000

nice (nīs) adj. **nic′er, nic′est** [ME., strange, lazy, foolish < OFr. nice, nisce, stupid, foolish < L. nescius, ignorant, not knowing < nescire, to be ignorant < ne-, not (see NO¹) + scire, to know: see SCIENCE] 1. difficult to please; fastidious; refined 2. delicate; precise; discriminative; subtle [a nice distinction] 3. calling for great care, accuracy, tact, etc., as in handling or discrimination [a nice problem] 4. a) able to make fine or delicate distinctions; delicately skillful; finely discriminating b) minutely accurate, as an instrument 5. having high standards of conduct; scrupulous 6. a generalized term of approval meaning variously: a) agreeable; pleasant; delightful b) attractive; pretty c) courteous and considerate d) conforming to approved social standards; respectable e) in good taste f) good; excellent 7. [Obs.] a) ignorant; foolish b) wanton c) coy; shy —adv. well, pleasingly, attractively, etc.: variously regarded as substandard, dialectal, or colloquial —SYN. see DAINTY —**nice and** [Colloq.] altogether, in a pleasing way [likes his tea nice and hot] —**nice′ly** adv. —**nice′ness** n.

Ni·cene (nī′sēn, nī sēn′) adj. of Nicaea

Nicene Council either of two church councils that met at Nicaea in 325 A.D. and 787 A.D.; esp., the first of these, that condemned Arianism and adopted the Nicene Creed

Nicene Creed a confession of faith for Christians, orig. adopted at the first Nicene Council (325 A.D.) and later expanded to various forms accepted by most Christian denominations

☆**nice Nelly** a prudish or affectedly modest person, who uses euphemisms: also **nice Nellie** —**nice′-Nel′ly** adj. —**nice′-Nel′ly·ism** n.

ni·ce·ty (nī′sə tē) n., pl. **-ties** [ME. nicete < OFr. nicete, folly < nice: see NICE] 1. the quality or state of being nice; specif., a) scrupulosity b) precision; accuracy; exactness, as of discrimination or perception c) fastidiousness; refinement; delicacy of taste 2. the quality of calling for delicacy, accuracy, or precision in handling, discrimination, or adjustment 3. anything involving or calling for delicacy, accuracy, or precision; subtle or minute detail, distinction, etc. 4. something choice, dainty, or elegant —**to a nicety** to a precise degree; exactly

niche (nich) n. [Fr. < OFr. nichier, to nest < VL. *nidicare < L. nidus, nest] 1. a recess or hollow in a wall, as for a statue, bust, or vase 2. a place or position particularly suitable to the person or thing in it 3. Ecol. a) the particular role of an individual species or organism in its community and its environment, including its position in the food cycle, its behavior, etc. b) the specific space occupied by an organism within its habitat —vt. **niched, nich′ing** to place in or as in a niche

STATUE IN NICHE

Nich·o·las (nik′l əs) [ME. < OFr. Nicolas < L. Nicolaus < Gr. Nikolaos < nikē, victory + laos, the people] 1. a masculine name: dim. Nick; equiv. L. Nicolaus, Fr. & Sp. Nicolas, Ger. Nikolaus, It. Niccolo 2. Nicholas I a) (Nikolai Pavlovich) 1796–1855; czar of Russia (1825–55) b) Saint, 800?–867 A.D.; Pope (858–867): his day is Nov. 13: called the Great 3. Nicholas II (Nikolai Aleksandrovich) 1868–1918; last czar of Russia (1894–1917): forced to abdicate; executed 4. Saint, 4th cent. A.D.; bishop of Myra: patron saint of Russia, of Greece, & of young people, sailors, etc.: his day is Dec. 6: cf. SANTA CLAUS

‡**nicht wahr?** (niHt vär′) [G., lit., not true?] isn't that so?

Nic·i·as (nish′ē əs) ?–413 B.C.; Athenian general & statesman: defeated at Syracuse

Nick (nik) 1. a masculine name: see NICHOLAS 2. same as OLD NICK

nick (nik) n. [LME. nyke, prob. akin to nocke, notch] 1. a small notch or slit; esp., a small cut, indention, or chip made on the edge or surface of wood, metal, china, etc. 2. a notch in the lower side of the shank of a printing type, for identification 3. [Brit. Slang] prison; jail —vt. 1. to

make a nick or nicks in **2.** [Now Rare] to score or tally by means of notches **3.** *a)* to wound superficially *b)* to strike lightly and glancingly **4.** to strike or catch at the exact or proper time; hit, guess, grasp, etc. exactly **5.** [Slang] *a)* to fine *b)* to overcharge or cheat **6.** [Brit. Slang] *a)* to arrest; nab *b)* to steal —**in the nick of time** exactly when needed; just before it is too late

nick·el (nik'l) *n.* [Sw., contr. < *kopparnickel* < G. *kupfernickel*, copper nickel < *kupfer*, copper + *nickel*, demon (assumed to be < *Nikolaus*, NICHOLAS, but prob. altered < *nix*, goblin: see NIX[1]): in spite of its copperlike appearance the ore contained no copper] **1.** a hard, silver-white, malleable metallic chemical element, used extensively in alloys and for plating because of its resistance to oxidation: symbol, Ni; at. wt., 58.71; at. no., 28; sp. gr., 8.90; melt. pt., 1455°C; boil. pt., 2730°C ☆**2.** a U.S. or Canadian coin made of an alloy of nickel and copper and equal to five cents —*vt.* **-eled** or **-elled, -el·ing** or **-el·ling** to plate with nickel

nickel bloom *same as* ANNABERGITE
nick·el·ic (nik'l ik, ni kel'ik) *adj.* of or containing nickel, esp. trivalent nickel
nick·el·if·er·ous (nik'ə lif'ər əs) *adj.* [see NICKEL & -FEROUS] containing nickel: said of ore, etc.
☆**nick·el·o·de·on** (nik'ə lō'dē ən) *n.* [NICKEL + *odeon* (< Fr. *odéon*), ODEUM] **1.** formerly, a motion-picture theater, variety show, etc. where admission was five cents **2.** [NICKEL + (MEL)ODEON] a player piano or an early type of jukebox operated by the insertion of a nickel in a slot
nick·el·ous (nik'l əs) *adj.* containing nickel, esp. divalent nickel
nickel plate a thin layer of nickel placed by electrolysis on objects made of other metal, to improve the finish and prevent rust —**nick'el-plate'** *vt.* **-plat'ed, -plat'ing**
nickel silver a hard, tough, ductile, malleable, silver-white alloy composed essentially of nickel, copper, and zinc: used in the manufacture of tableware, electric-resistance wire, etc.
nickel steel a steel alloy made harder, stronger, and more resistant to corrosion than ordinary steel by the addition of up to five percent of nickel
nick·er[1] (nik'ər) *vi.* [prob. var. of *nicher, neigher*, freq. of NEIGH] to utter a low whinnying sound: said of a horse —*n.* this sound
nick·er[2] (nik'ər) *n.*, *pl.* **-er** [orig. underworld cant < ?] [Brit. Slang] one pound sterling
nick·nack (nik'nak') *n. same as* KNICKKNACK
nick·name (nik'nām') *n.* [by syllabic merging < *an ekename* < ME. *ekename*, surname: see EKE[1] & NAME] **1.** an additional or substitute name given to a person, place, or thing: usually descriptive and given in fun, affection, or derision, as "Doc," "Shorty," etc. **2.** a familiar, often shorter, form of a proper name, as "Dick" for "Richard" —*vt.* **-named', -nam'ing 1.** to give a nickname to **2.** [Now Rare] to call by a wrong name; misname
Nic·o·bar Islands (nik'ə bär', nik'ə bär') group of islands in the Bay of Bengal, south of the Andaman Islands: 635 sq. mi.: see ANDAMAN ISLANDS
Nic·o·las (nik'l əs) a masculine name: see NICHOLAS
Nic·ol prism (nik'əl) [after Wm. *Nicol*, its Brit. inventor (1828)] a prism consisting of two crystals of clear calcite cemented together, used for obtaining polarized light: also **Nic'ol**
Ni·cop·o·lis (ni käp'ə lis) city in ancient Epirus, near the Ionian Sea
Nic·o·si·a (nik'ə sē'ə) capital of Cyprus, in the NC part: pop. 104,000
ni·co·ti·a·na (ni cō'shē ā'nə, -an'ə, -än'ə) *n.* [< ModL. *nicotiana* (*herba*): see NICOTINE] any of a genus (*Nicotiana*) of new-world plants of the nightshade family, including tobacco and several species with fragrant flowers, grown as ornamentals
nic·o·tin·am·ide (nik'ə tin'ə mīd', -mid') *n.* a white crystalline powder, $C_6H_5N_2O$, the amide of nicotinic acid: found in the heart, liver, and muscles and used in treating pellagra
nic·o·tine (nik'ə tēn', -tin) *n.* [Fr. < *nicotiane*, the tobacco plant < ModL. *nicotiana* (*herba*), Nicot's plant), after Jean *Nicot*, Fr. ambassador at Lisbon, who first introduced tobacco into France (1560)] a poisonous, water-soluble alkaloid, $C_{10}H_{14}N_2$, found in tobacco leaves and used, ordinarily in an aqueous solution of its sulfate, as an insecticide —**nic'o·tin'ic** (-tin'ik, -tē'nik) *adj.*
nicotinic acid a white, odorless, crystalline substance, $C_6H_5O_2N$, found in protein foods or prepared synthetically: it is a member of the vitamin B complex and is used in the treatment of pellagra
nic·o·tin·ism (nik'ə tēn'iz'm, -tin-) *n.* a diseased condition caused by the ingestion of nicotine, as from tobacco; nicotine poisoning
nic·tate (nik'tāt) *vi.* **-tat·ed, -tat·ing** *same as* NICTITATE —**nic·ta'tion** *n.*
nic·ti·tate (nik'tə tāt') *vi.* **-tat·ed, -tat'ing** [< ML. *nictitatus*, pp. of *nictitare*, freq. < L. *nictare*, to wink, blink < *nicere*, to beckon: see CONNIVE] to wink or blink rapidly, as birds and animals with a nictitating membrane —**nic'ti·ta'tion** *n.*
nictitating membrane a transparent third eyelid hinged

at the inner side or lower lid of the eye of various animals, serving to keep the eye clean and moist: it is vestigial in man
nid·der·ing, nid·er·ing (nid'ər iŋ) *n.* [popularized by Sir W. SCOTT < error in printed text (1596) of William of Malmesbury, for ME. *nithing* (< ON. *nithingr*), mean person, coward] [Archaic] coward; wretch —*adj.* [Archaic] base; cowardly
nide (nīd) *n.* [< L. *nidus*, NEST] [Chiefly Brit.] a nest or brood, esp. of pheasants
ni·dic·o·lous (nī dik'ə ləs) *adj.* [< L. *nidus*, NEST + -COLOUS] **1.** remaining in the nest for some time after hatching, as some birds **2.** living in the nest of another species
ni·dif·u·gous (nī dif'yə gəs) *adj.* [< L. *nidus*, NEST + *fugere*, to flee (see FUGITIVE) + -OUS] leaving the nest almost immediately after hatching, as chickens
nid·i·fy (nid'ə fī') *vi.* **-fied', -fy'ing** [L. *nidificare* < *nidus*, NEST + *facere*, to make: see FACT] to build a nest: also **nid'i·fi·cate'** (-fi kāt') **-cat'ed, -cat'ing —nid'i·fi·ca'tion** *n.*
ni·dus (nī'dəs) *n.*, *pl.* **-di** (-dī), **-dus·es** [L., NEST] **1.** a nest, esp. one in which insects or spiders deposit their eggs **2.** a breeding place; specif., *a)* a place where spores or seeds germinate *b)* a focus of infection —**ni'dal** *adj.*
Nie·buhr (nē'boor; G. nē'bōōr) **1. Bar·thold Ge·org** (bär'tôlt gā ôrkh'), 1776–1831; Ger. historian, born in Denmark **2. Rein·hold** (rīn'hōld), 1892–1971; U.S. clergyman & Protestant theologian
niece (nēs) *n.* [ME. *nece* < OFr. *niece* < LL. *neptia* < L. *neptis*, granddaughter, niece, akin to *nepos*, NEPHEW] **1.** the daughter of one's brother or sister **2.** the daughter of one's brother-in-law or sister-in-law **3.** an illegitimate daughter, as of a medieval prelate: a euphemism
Nie·der·sach·sen (nē'dər zäkh'zən) *Ger. name of* LOWER SAXONY
ni·el·lo (nē el'ō) *n.*, *pl.* **-li** (-ē), **-los** [It. < VL. *nigellum* < L. *nigellus*, somewhat black, dark < *niger*, black] **1.** any of a number of alloys of sulfur with silver, lead, copper, etc., characterized by a deep-black color and used to decorate metallic objects by means of inlay **2.** the process of decorating with niello **3.** something decorated in this way —*vt.* **-loed, -lo·ing** to decorate with niello —**ni·el'·list** *n.*
Nie·men (nye'men) *Pol. name for* NEMAN River
Nie·möl·ler (nē'mö lər), **(Friedrich Gustav Emil) Mar·tin** (mär'tēn) 1892– ; Ger. Protestant leader
Nier·stein·er (nir'stī nər; G. nir'shtīn ər) *n.* [G. < *Nierstein*, town on the Rhine, in Germany, where it is made] a variety of white Rhine wine
Nie·tzsche (nē'chə), **Frie·drich Wil·helm** (frē'driH vil'helm) 1844–1900; Ger. philosopher —**Nie'tzsche·an** (nē'chē ən) *adj., n.* —**Nie'tzsche·an·ism** *n.*
nieve (nēv) *n.* [ME. *neve* < ON. *hnefi*] [Now Scot. & Brit. Dial.] a fist or hand
nif·fer (nif'ər) *vt., vi., n.* [< ?] [Scot.] barter; trade
Ni·fl·heim (nivʼl hām') [ON. *Niflheimr*] Norse Myth. the region of darkness and cold, or realm of the dead
☆**nif·ty** (nif'tē) *adj.* **-ti·er, -ti·est** [orig. theatrical slang, prob. < MAGNIFICENT] [Slang] attractive, smart, stylish, enjoyable, etc.: a generalized term of approval —*n., pl.* **-ties** [Slang] a nifty person or thing; esp., a clever remark
Ni·ger (nī'jər) **1.** river in W Africa, flowing from Guinea through Mali, Niger, & Nigeria into the Gulf of Guinea: c. 2,600 mi. **2.** country in WC Africa, north of Nigeria: c. 458,500 sq. mi.; pop. 4,016,000; cap. Niamey
Ni·ger-Con·go (-käŋ'gō) *adj.* designating a subfamily of the Congo-Kordofanian family of African languages, including the Kwa, Mande, and Voltaic branches
Ni·ger·i·a (nī jir'ē ə) country in WC Africa, on the Gulf of Guinea: a member of the Brit. Commonwealth (see CAMEROONS & BIAFRA): 327,186 sq. mi.; pop. 61,450,000; cap. Lagos —**Ni·ger'i·an** *adj., n.*
nig·gard (nig'ərd) *n.* [ME. *negarde*, prob. < Scand., as in ON. *hnøggr*, Norw. dial. *nøgg*, afraid, stingy < IE. base *kneu-* (var. of *ken-*, to scrape), whence OE. *hneaw*, sparse, stingy] a stingy person; miser —*adj.* stingy; miserly
nig·gard·ly (-lē) *adj.* **1.** like or characteristic of a niggard; stingy; miserly **2.** small, few, or scanty, as if given by a niggard [a *niggardly* sum] —*adv.* in the manner of a niggard; stingily —*SYN.* see STINGY[1] —**nig'gard·li·ness** *n.*
nig·gle (nig'l) *vi.* **-gled, -gling** [North Brit. dial., prob. akin to Norw. dial. *nigla* in same sense] to work fussily; pay too much attention to petty details; be finicky —**nig'gler** *n.* —**nig'gling** *adj., n.*
nigh (nī) *adv.* [ME. *neih* < OE. *neah*, akin to G. *nahe*] [Chiefly Archaic or Dial.] **1.** near in time, place, etc. **2.** nearly; almost —*adj.* **nigh'er, nigh'est** or, older, **next** [Chiefly Archaic or Dial.] **1.** near; close **2.** direct or short **3.** on the left: said of animals, vehicles, etc. —*prep.* [Chiefly Archaic or Dial.] near; near to —*vi., vt.* [Archaic] to draw near; approach
night (nīt) *n.* [ME. *niht* < OE., akin to G. *nacht* < IE. base *nekwt-*, whence Gr. *nyx* (gen. *nyktos*), L. *nox* (gen. *noctis*), night] **1.** *a)* the period from sunset to sunrise *b)* the period of actual darkness after sunset and before sunrise; also, a part of this period before bedtime [a *night* at the opera] or the part between bedtime and morning [a sleepless *night*] **2.** the evening following a specified day

[*Christmas night*] **3.** the darkness of night **4.** any period or condition of darkness or gloom; specif., *a*) a period of intellectual or moral degeneration *b*) a time of grief *c*) death —*adj.* **1.** of, for, or at night **2.** active, working, or in use at night —**make a night of it** to celebrate all or most of the night —**night and day** continuously or continually

night blindness imperfect vision in the dark or in dim light: a symptom of vitamin A deficiency

night-bloom·ing cereus (-blōō′miŋ) any of various cactuses that bloom at night, esp. any of many specie (genera *Hylocereus, Selenicereus,* etc.), often grown as house plants

night·cap (-kap′) *n.* **1.** a cap worn in bed, esp. formerly, to protect the head from cold **2.** [Colloq.] an alcoholic drink taken just before going to bed ☆**3.** *Baseball* [Colloq.] the second game of a double-header

night clothes clothes to be worn in bed, as pajamas

night·club (-klub′) *n.* a place of entertainment open at night for eating, drinking, dancing, etc., and usually having a floor show

☆**night crawler** any large earthworm that comes to the surface at night, commonly used as fish bait

night·dress (-dres′) *n. same as:* **1.** NIGHTGOWN **2.** NIGHT CLOTHES

night·fall (-fôl′) *n.* the close of the day; dusk

night·gown (-goun′) *n.* **1.** a loose gown, usually long, worn in bed by women or girls **2.** *same as* NIGHTSHIRT **3.** [Obs.] a dressing gown

night·hawk (-hôk′) *n.* ☆**1.** any of a group of new-world night birds (genus *Chordeiles*) related to the goatsuckers and the whippoorwill, and having brown, mottled feathers and a broad, deeply cleft bill **2.** *same as* NIGHTJAR ☆**3.** *same as* NIGHT OWL (sense 2)

night heron any of several herons most active at night or twilight

night·ie (nīt′ē) *n. colloq. dim.* of NIGHTGOWN

night·in·gale (nīt′'n gāl′, -iŋ-) *n.* [ME. *nigtingale,* for earlier *nihtegale* < OE. *nihtegale* (akin to G. *nachtigall*) < *niht,* night + base of *galan,* to sing, akin to *giellan,* YELL] any of various small European thrushes (genus *Luscinia*) with a russet back and buff to white underparts: the male is known for its varied, melodious singing, esp. at night during the breeding season

Night·in·gale (nīt′'n gāl′, -iŋ-), **Florence** 1820–1910; Eng. nurse in the Crimean War: regarded as the founder of modern nursing

night·jar (nīt′jär′) *n.* [NIGHT + JAR¹: from the whirring noise made by the male] the European goatsucker (*Caprimulgus europaeus*)

night latch a door latch with a bolt opened from the outside by a key, and from the inside by a knob

☆**night letter** a telegram with a minimum charge for 100 words or fewer, sent at night to be delivered the next morning, and cheaper than a regular telegram

☆**night life** attendance at theaters or nightclubs, or similar pleasure-seeking activity, at night

night light a small, dim light kept burning all night, as in a hallway, bathroom, sickroom, etc.

night·long (-lôŋ′) *adj.* lasting the entire night —*adv.* during the entire night

night·ly (-lē) *adj.* **1.** of, like, or characteristic of the night **2.** done or occurring every night —*adv.* **1.** at night **2.** night after night; every night

night·mare (-mer′) *n.* [ME. *nihtmare:* see NIGHT & MARE³] **1.** formerly, an evil spirit believed to haunt and suffocate sleeping people **2.** a frightening dream, often accompanied by a sensation of oppression and helplessness **3.** any experience like a nightmare in its frightening or oppressing aspects —**night′mar′ish** *adj.*

night owl 1. an owl active chiefly at night ☆**2.** a person who works at night or otherwise stays up late

night raven [Poet.] any of various birds, esp. the night heron, that are most active at night

☆**night·rid·er** (-rīd′ər) *n.* any of a band of masked, mounted men who perform lawless acts of violence and terror at night to intimidate, terrorize, etc.; esp., any of such a band of white men in the S U.S. after the Civil War

nights (nīts) *adv.* on every night or most nights

night school a school held in the evening, esp. one for those, usually adults, unable to attend by day

night·shade (nīt′shād′) *n.* [ME. *nichtheschode* < OE. *nihtscada* (see NIGHT & SHADE): ? with reference to narcotic qualities] **1.** any of a large genus (*Solanum*) of chiefly tropical plants of the nightshade family, with five-lobed leaves and flowers of various colors, including BLACK NIGHTSHADE **2.** *same as* BELLADONNA (sense 1) **3.** *same as* HENBANE —*adj.* designating a large family (Solanaceae) of poisonous and nonpoisonous plants chiefly of warm regions, generally having a round stem, rank smell, and watery sap, and including the tobaccos, red peppers, potatoes, petunias, and eggplant

night·shirt (-shʉrt′) *n.* a long, loose, shirtlike garment worn in bed, esp. formerly, by men or boys

night soil [from being collected at night] excrement removed from a cesspool or privy and used as fertilizer

☆**night·spot** (nīt′spät′) *n. colloq. var.* of NIGHTCLUB
☆**night stand** a small table at the bedside
☆**night stick** a long, heavy club carried by a policeman
night·tide (-tīd′) *n. archaic var.* of NIGHTTIME
night·time (-tīm′) *n.* the period of darkness from sunset to sunrise
night·walk·er (-wôk′ər) *n.* [Rare] a person who goes about at night, as a thief, prostitute, etc.
night watch 1. a watching or guarding during the night **2.** the person or persons doing such guarding **3.** the time of their guarding **4.** any of the periods into which the night was formerly divided for such guarding: *usually used in pl.*
night watchman a watchman hired for duty at night
night·wear (-wer′) *n. same as* NIGHT CLOTHES
night·y (-ē) *n., pl.* **night′ies** *alt. sp.* of NIGHTIE
night·y-night (nīt′ē nīt′) *interj. colloq. var.* of GOOD NIGHT
ni·gres·cent (nī gres′'nt) *adj.* [L. *nigrescens,* prp. of *nigrescere,* to grow black < *niger,* black] becoming or tending to become black —**ni·gres′cence** *n.*
nig·ri·fy (nig′rə fī′) *vt.* -**fied′,** -**fy′ing** [L. *nigrificare* < *niger,* black + *facere,* to make: see FACT] to make black —**nig′ri·fi·ca′tion** *n.*
nig·ri·tude (-tōōd′, -tyōōd′) *n.* [L. *nigritudo* < *niger,* black] blackness or darkness
ni·gro·sine (nig′rə sēn′, -sin) *n.* [< L. *niger,* black + -OS(E)¹ + -INE⁴] any of a group of blue-black or black dyes used as pigments in inks, dyes, shoe polish, etc.
NIH, N.I.H. National Institutes of Health
ni·hil (nī′hil, nī′-) *n.* [L., contr. < *nihilum* < *nehilum* < *ne-,* not (see NO¹) + *hilum,* little thing, trifle] nothing
ni·hil·ism (nī′ə liz′m, nē′-, nĭ′hi-) *n.* [< L. *nihil* (see NIHIL) + -ISM] **1.** *Philos. a*) the denial of the existence of any basis for knowledge or truth *b*) the general rejection of customary beliefs in morality, religion, etc.: also **ethical nihilism 2.** the belief that there is no meaning or purpose in existence **3.** *Politics a*) the doctrine that existing social, political, and economic institutions must be completely destroyed in order to make way for new institutions *b*) [N-] a movement in Russia (c. 1860–1917) which advocated such revolutionary reform and attempted to carry it out through the use of some terrorism and assassination *c*) loosely, any violent revolutionary movement involving the use of terrorism —**ni′hil·ist** *n.* —**ni′hil·is′tic** *adj.*
ni·hil·i·ty (nī hil′ə tē) *n.* [ML. *nihilitas*] nothingness
‡**nihil ob·stat** (äb′stat) [L., lit., nothing obstructs] **1.** *R.C.Ch.* certification by an official censor that he has examined a given book and found nothing in it contrary to the teachings of the Church concerning faith and morals **2.** any official sanction
Ni·hon (nē′hän′) *a Jap. name for* JAPAN
Ni·i·ga·ta (nē′ē gä′tä) seaport in N Honshu, Japan, on the Sea of Japan: pop. 356,000
Ni·i·ha·u (nē′ē hä′ōō, nē′hou) [Haw. < ?] an island of Hawaii, west of Kauai: 72 sq. mi.; pop. 250
Ni·jin·sky (ni zhēn′ski; *E.* nə jin′skē), **Vas·lav** (väs läf′) 1890–1950; Russ. ballet dancer
Nij·me·gen (nī′mā′gan; *Du.* nī′mā′khən) city in the E Netherlands, on the Waal River: pop. 142,000
-nik (nik) [< Russ. (chiefly via Yid.) *nik,* equivalent to -ER] *a suffix used to form slang or colloquial words, meaning* one who is or has to do with
Ni·ke (nī′kē) [Gr. *Nikē*] *Gr. Myth.* the winged goddess of victory
Nik·ko (nēk′kō) town in C Honshu, Japan: Buddhist religious center: pop. 33,000
Ni·ko·la·ev (nē′kō lä′yef) seaport in the S Ukrainian S.S.R., on the Bug River: pop. 289,000
nil (nil) *n.* [L., contr. of NIHIL] nothing
‡**nil de·spe·ran·dum** (nil′ des′pə ran′dəm) [L.] nothing should be despaired of; never despair
Nile (nīl) river in NE Africa, formed at Khartoum, Sudan, by the juncture of the Blue Nile (flowing from N Ethiopia, c. 1,000 mi.) & the White Nile (flowing from Lake Victoria, c. 1,650 mi.), & flowing north through Egypt into the Mediterranean: with the White Nile & a headstream south of Lake Victoria, over 4,000 mi.
Nile green yellowish green —**Nile′-green′** *adj.*
nil·gai (nil′gī) *n., pl.* -**gais,** -**gai:** see PLURAL, II, D, 1 [Per. *nīlgāw,* lit., blue cow < Per. *nīl,* blue + *gāw,* cow: for IE. base see COW¹] a large, gray, Indian antelope (*Boselaphus tragocamelus*): the male has short, straight horns and a black mane: also **nil′gau** (-gô)
nill (nil) *vt., vi.* [ME. *nillen* < OE. *nyllan* < *ne,* not (see NO¹) + *wyllan* (see WILL¹)] [Archaic] not to will (something); refuse [will I, *nill I*]: see also WILLY-NILLY
nil ni·si bo·num (nil′ nī′sī bō′nəm) [L.] *short for* DE MORTUIS NIL NISI BONUM
Ni·lo-Ham·it·ic (nī′lō ha mit′ik) *adj.* designating or of the eastern branch of the Nilotic group of Sudanic languages, including Masai
Ni·lo-Sa·ha·ran (-sə her′ən) *adj.* designating a large family of African languages including the Chari-Nile subfamily
Ni·lot·ic (ni lät′ik) *adj.* [L. *Niloticus* < Gr. *Neilōtikos* < *Neilos,* the Nile] **1.** of the Nile or the Nile Valley **2.**

designating or of the peoples who live in the valley of the White Nile, including the Dinkas **3.** *a)* designating or of a group of languages spoken in the upper Nile valley from Khartoum southeast into Kenya and Tanganyika *b)* designating or of the western branch only of this group of languages, including Dinka: cf. NILO-HAMITIC

Ni·lus (nī′ləs) [L.] *Rom. name for* NILE

nim (nim) *vt., vi.* **nam** (näm) *or* **nimmed, no·men** (nō′mən) *or* **nome** (nōm), **nim′ming** [ME. *nimen* < OE. *niman*, akin to G. *nehmen*, to take: see -NOMY] [Archaic] to steal or pilfer

nim·ble (nim′b'l) *adj.* **-bler, -blest** [with intrusive *-b-* < ME. *nimmel* < OE. *numol* < *niman*, to take, seize (cf. prec.): basic sense "capable of taking"] **1.** mentally quick; quick-witted; alert *[a nimble mind]* **2.** showing mental quickness *[a nimble reply]* **3.** moving or acting quickly and lightly —*SYN.* see AGILE —**nim′ble·ness** *n.* —**nim′bly** *adv.*

nim·bo·stra·tus (nim′bō strāt′əs, -strat′əs) *n.* [ModL.: see ff. & STRATUS] an extensive, dark, low-level cloud, commonly the source of persistent rain or snow

nim·bus (nim′bəs) *n., pl.* **-bi** (-bī), **-bus·es** [L., violent rain, black rain cloud < IE. base **enebh-, *nebh-*, whence L. *nebula*] **1.** orig., any rain-producing cloud **2.** a bright cloud supposedly surrounding gods or goddesses appearing on earth **3.** an aura of splendor about any person or thing **4.** a halo or bright disk surrounding the head of a divinity, saint, or sovereign on pictures, medals, etc.

Nîmes (nēm) city in S France: pop. 100,000

ni·mi·e·ty (ni mī′ə tē) *n.* [L. *nimietas* < *nimius*, adj., *nimis*, adv., too much] excess; redundancy

nim·i·ny-pim·i·ny (nim′ə nē pim′ə nē) *adj.* [imitative of mincing speech] fussily dainty or refined; mincing

Nim·itz (nim′its), **Chester William** 1885-1966; U.S. admiral in World War II

Nim·rod (nim′räd) [Heb. *nimrōdh*] *Bible* the son of Cush, referred to as a mighty hunter: Gen. 10:8-9 —*n.* [*often* n-] a hunter

nin·com·poop (nin′kəm pōōp′, niŋ′-) *n.* [< ?] a stupid, silly person; fool; simpleton

nine (nīn) *adj.* [ME. *nine* < OE. *nigon*, akin to G. *neun* < IE. **enewen* (whence Gr. *ennea*, L. *novem*, nine), prob. extension of base **newo-*, new (cf. NEW), indicating a new division of the numeral system commencing with 9] totaling one more than eight —*n.* **1.** the cardinal number between eight and ten; 9; IX **2.** any group of nine persons or things; esp., a baseball team **3.** something numbered nine or having nine units, as a playing card, throw of dice, etc. —**the Nine** the nine Muses —**to the nines 1.** to perfection **2.** in the most elaborate or showy manner *[dressed to the nines]*

nine days' wonder anything that arouses great excitement and interest, but for only a short time

nine·fold (-fōld′) *adj.* **1.** having nine parts **2.** having nine times as much or as many —*adv.* nine times as much or as many

nine·pence (-pəns) *n.* **1.** the sum of nine British pennies **2.** a 16th-cent. English coin for use in Ireland

nine·pins (-pinz′) *n.pl.* **1.** [*with sing. v.*] a British version of the game of tenpins, in which nine wooden pins are used **2.** the pins used in this game

nine·teen (-tēn′) *adj.* [ME. *nynetene* < OE. *nigontyne*: see NINE & -TEEN¹] nine more than ten —*n.* the cardinal number between eighteen and twenty; 19; XIX

nine·teenth (-tēnth′) *adj.* [ME. *nyntenthe* < OE. *nigonteotha*: see prec. & -TH²] **1.** preceded by eighteen others in a series; 19th **2.** designating any of the nineteen equal parts of something —*n.* **1.** the one following the eighteenth **2.** any of the nineteen equal parts of something; 1/19

☆**nineteenth hole** [Colloq.] any place, as the bar of a clubhouse, where golfers meet for drinks and conviviality after playing a round of golf

nine·ti·eth (nīn′tē ith) *adj.* [ME. *nyntithe* < OE. *nigenteothan*: see NINETY & -TH²] **1.** preceded by eighty-nine others in a series; 90th **2.** designating any of the ninety equal parts of something —*n.* **1.** the one following the eighty-ninth **2.** any of the ninety equal parts of something; 1/90

nine·ty (nīn′tē) *adj.* [ME. *nigenty* < OE. *nigontig*: see NINE & -TY²] nine times ten —*n., pl.* **-ties** the cardinal number between eighty-nine and ninety-one; 90; XC (or LXXXX) —**the nineties** the numbers or years, as of a century, from ninety through ninety-nine

Nin·e·veh (nin′ə və) capital of ancient Assyria, on the Tigris, opposite modern Mosul in N Iraq

Ning·po (niŋ′pō′) city in Chekiang province, E China: pop. 280,000

Ning·sia-Hui (niŋ′shyä′wē′) autonomous region in NW China, on the border of Inner Mongolia: 25,630 sq. mi.; pop. 1,810,000; cap. Yinchuan: also sp. **Ninghsia-Hui**

nin·ny (nin′ē) *n., pl.* **-nies** [prob. by syllabic merging and contr. of *an innocent*] a fool; dolt

ni·non (nē′nän; *Fr.* nē nôn′) *n.* [Fr. < ?] a sheer fabric of rayon or other synthetic material, used chiefly for curtains

ninth (nīnth) *adj.* [ME. *ninthe* < OE. *nigonthe*: see NINE & -TH²] **1.** preceded by eight others in a series; 9th **2.** designating any of the nine equal parts of something —*n.* **1.** the one following the eighth **2.** any of the nine equal parts of something; 1/9 **3.** *Music a)* an interval in pitch of an octave and a second *b)* a tone separated from another by such an interval *c)* the combination of two such tones —**ninth′ly** *adv.*

ninth chord *Music* a chord consisting of the third, fifth, seventh, and ninth above the root

Ni·nus (nī′nəs) *Latin name for* NINEVEH

Ni·o·be (nī′ə bē′) [L. < Gr. *Niobē*] *Gr. Myth.* a queen of Thebes, daughter of Tantalus, who, weeping for her slain children, was turned into a stone from which tears continued to flow

ni·o·bic (nī ō′bik) *adj. Chem.* of or containing niobium with a valence of five

ni·o·bi·um (nī ō′bē əm) *n.* [ModL. < L. *Niobe*, NIOBE: from association with tantalum: see TANTALUM] a gray or white metallic chemical element, somewhat ductile and malleable, used in chrome steels, in jet engines and rockets, etc.: symbol, Nb; at. wt., 92.906; at. no., 41; sp. gr., 8.57; melt. pt., 2415°C; boil. pt., c. 3300°C

ni·o·bous (nī ō′bəs) *adj. Chem.* of or containing niobium with a valence of three

Ni·o·brar·a (nī′ə brer′ə) [< Siouan (Omaha), lit., broad, flat river] river flowing from E Wyo. east through N Nebr. into the Missouri: 431 mi.

nip¹ (nip) *vt.* **nipped, nip′ping** [ME. *nippen*, prob. < MLowG. *nippen* or ON. *hnippa* < IE. **kneib-* (< base **ken-*, to scrape), whence Gr. *kniptos*, stingy] **1.** to catch or squeeze between two surfaces, points, or edges; pinch or bite **2.** to sever (shoots, buds, etc.) by pinching or clipping **3.** to check the growth or development of **4.** to have a painful or injurious effect on because of cold *[frost nipped the plants]* **5.** [Slang] *a)* to snatch *b)* to steal —*vi.* **1.** to give a nip or nips **2.** [Brit. Colloq.] to move quickly or nimbly (with *off, away, along*, etc.) —*n.* **1.** the act of nipping; pinch; bite **2.** a piece nipped off; small bit **3.** a stinging quality, as in cold or frosty air **4.** stinging cold; frost **5.** a stinging remark **6.** a strong flavor; tang —☆**nip and tuck** so close, even, or critical as to leave the outcome in doubt; neck and neck

nip² (nip) *n.* [prob. contr. < *nipperkin* < Du. *nippertje*, small measure for liquors < base of *nippen*, to sip, prob. akin to prec.] a small drink of liquor; dram; sip —*vt., vi.* **nipped, nip′ping** to drink (liquor) in nips

ni·pa (nē′pə, nī′-) *n.* [Sp. < Malay *nipah*] **1.** an Asiatic palm (*Nipa fruticans*) with feathery leaves used in thatching and large bunches of edible fruit **2.** thatch or fruit from the nipa **3.** a liquor made from its sap

Nip·i·gon (nip′ə gän′), **Lake** lake in WC Ontario, Canada, north of Lake Superior: 1,870 sq. mi.

Nip·is·sing (nip′ə siŋ), **Lake** [< Fr. < Algonquian, lit., at the little lake] lake in SE Ontario, Canada, between Georgian Bay & the Ottawa River: 350 sq. mi.

nip·per (nip′ər) *n.* **1.** anything that nips, or pinches **2.** [*pl.*] any of various tools for grasping or severing wire, etc., as pliers, pincers, or forceps **3.** any of certain organs of animals, used in biting, grasping, holding, etc.; specif., *a)* an incisor tooth of a horse *b)* the pincerlike claw of a crab or lobster; chela **4.** [Chiefly Brit. Colloq.] a small boy; lad **5.** [*pl.*] [Slang] handcuffs or leg irons

nip·ping (-iŋ) *adj.* **1.** that nips, or pinches **2.** sharp; biting; nippy **3.** sarcastic —**nip′ping·ly** *adv.*

nip·ple (nip′'l) *n.* [earlier *neble*, prob. dim. of NEB] **1.** the small protuberance on a breast or udder through which, in the female, the milk passes in suckling the young; teat; pap **2.** an artificial teatlike part, as of rubber, in the cap of a baby's nursing bottle **3.** any projection, part, or thing resembling the nipple of a breast in shape or function; specif., *a)* a threaded piece of pipe at the end of a water line, to which is fastened a nozzle, faucet, etc. *b)* a short piece of pipe with both ends threaded *c)* a projection with a small opening through which a liquid or grease can be forced

Nip·pon (nēp′pôn′; *E.* nip′än, ni pän′) *a Jap. name for* JAPAN

Nip·pon·ese (nip′ə nēz′) *adj., n., pl.* **-ese′** [< prec.] *same as* JAPANESE

Nip·pur (ni poor′) ancient Sumerian city of Babylonia, on the Euphrates, in what is now SE Iraq

nip·py (nip′ē) *adj.* **-pi·er, -pi·est 1.** nipping or tending to nip, or pinch **2.** cold in a stinging way **3.** [Brit. Colloq.] quick or nimble —**nip′pi·ness** *n.*

nip-up (nip′up′) *n.* the acrobatic feat of springing to one's feet from a position flat on one's back

nir·va·na (nir vä′nə, nər-; -van′ə) *n.* [Sans. *nirvāṇa* < *nirvā*, to blow] [*also* N-] **1.** *Hinduism* a blowing out, or extinction, of the flame of life through reunion with Brahma **2.** *Buddhism* the state of perfect blessedness achieved by the extinction of individual existence and by the absorption of the soul into the supreme spirit, or by the extinction of all desires and passions **3.** any place or condition of great peace or bliss

Niš (nēsh) city in Serbia, E Yugoslavia: pop. 85,000

Ni·san (nē sän′, nis′ən) *n.* [Heb. *nīsān*] the seventh month of the Jewish year: see JEWISH CALENDAR

☆**ni·sei** (nē′sā) *n., pl.* **ni′sei, ni′seis** [Jap., lit., second generation] [*also* N-] a native U.S. or Canadian citizen born of immigrant Japanese parents and educated in America: distinguished from ISSEI, KIBEI

Ni·sha·pur (nē′shä poor′) town in NE Iran: birthplace of Omar Khayyám: pop. 30,000

ni·si (nī′sī) *conj.* [L. < *ne-*, not (see NO[1]) + *si*, if (see SO[1])] unless: used in law after *decree, order*, etc. to indicate that it shall take permanent effect at a specified time unless cause is shown why it should not, or unless it is changed by further proceedings

nisi pri·us (prī′əs) [L., unless before: used orig. in a writ directing a sheriff to summon a jury to Westminster on a certain date "unless before" that date the trial had been held in his own county] any of various courts in which a cause of action is originally tried and heard

Nis·sen hut (nis′′n) [after P. N. Nissen (1871–1930), engineer in the Canadian army] a prefabricated shelter of corrugated metal shaped like a cylinder cut vertically in two and resting on its flat surface: first used by the British Army in World War I

ni·sus (nī′səs) *n., pl.* **ni′sus** [L. < *nisus*, pp. of *niti*, to strive: for IE. base see CONNIVE] effort; endeavor; impulse

nit (nit) *n.* [ME. *nite* < OE. *hnitu*, akin to G. *niss* < IE. base *knid-*, louse, nit, prob. < *ken-*, to scratch] 1. the egg of a louse or similar insect 2. a young louse, etc.

ni·ter (nīt′ər) *n.* [ME. *nitre* < MFr. < L. *nitrum* < Gr. *nitron*, native soda, akin to Heb. or Egypt.: Heb. *netr* < Egypt. *ntr*] *same as:* 1. POTASSIUM NITRATE 2. SODIUM NITRATE Also, chiefly Brit., **ni′tre**

Ni·te·rói (nē′tə roi′) capital of Rio de Janeiro state, a seaport in SE Brazil: pop. 245,000

☆**nit·er·y** (nīt′ər ē) *n., pl.* **-er·ies** [*nite* (for NIGHT) + -ERY] [Slang] *same as* NIGHTCLUB

ni·ton (nī′tän) *n.* [ModL. < L. *nitere*, to shine + -on as in ARGON] *former name of* RADON

☆**nit-pick·ing** (nit′pik′iŋ) *adj., n.* paying too much attention to petty details; niggling —**nit′-pick′er** *n.*

nitr- *same as* NITRO-: used before a vowel

ni·trate (nī′trāt) *n.* [Fr. < *nitre*, NITER] 1. a salt or ester of nitric acid 2. potassium nitrate or sodium nitrate, used as a fertilizer —*vt.* **-trat·ed, -trat·ing** to treat or combine with nitric acid or a nitrate; esp., to make into a nitrate

ni·tra·tion (nī trā′shən) *n.* the process of nitrating; esp., the introduction of the NO₂ group into an organic compound

ni·tric (nī′trik) *adj.* [Fr. *nitrique*: see NITER & -IC] 1. of or containing nitrogen 2. designating or of compounds in which nitrogen has a higher valence than in the corresponding nitrous compounds

nitric acid a colorless, fuming acid, HNO_3, that is highly corrosive: prepared by the action of sulfuric acid on nitrates and by the oxidation of ammonia

nitric bacteria soil and water bacteria (genus *Nitrobacter*, etc.) that convert nitrites into nitrates

nitric oxide a colorless gas, NO, prepared by the action of nitric acid on copper or directly from the air by various processes

ni·tride (nī′trīd) *n.* [NITR- + -IDE] a compound of nitrogen with a more electropositive element, as boron

ni·tri·fy (nī′trə fī′) *vt.* **-fied′, -fy′ing** [Fr. *nitrifier*: see NITER & -FY] 1. to combine with nitrogen or nitrogen compounds 2. to impregnate (soil, etc.) with nitrates 3. to cause the oxidation of (ammonium salts, atmospheric nitrogen, etc.) to nitrites and nitrates, as by the action of soil bacteria, etc. —**ni′tri·fi·ca′tion** *n.* —**ni′tri·fi′er** *n.*

ni·trile (nī′tril, -tril) *n.* [NITR- + -ile, n. suffix used in chem.] an organic cyanide of the general formula $R \cdot C \colon N$, yielding the corresponding acid and ammonia on hydrolysis

ni·trite (nī′trīt) *n.* [NITR- + -ITE[1]] a salt or ester of nitrous acid

ni·tro- (nī′trō) *adj.* [< ff.] 1. designating certain compounds containing nitrogen and produced by the action of nitric or nitrous acid 2. designating the NO₂ radical or compounds in which one or more NO₂ radicals have replaced atoms of hydrogen

ni·tro- (nī′trō, -trə) [see NITER] *a combining form used to indicate:* 1. the presence of nitrogen compounds made by the action of nitric or nitrous acid and other substances [*nitrocellulose*] 2. the presence of the NO₂ radical [*nitrobenzene*] 3. niter [*nitrobacteria*]

ni·tro·bac·te·ri·a (nī′trō bak tir′ē ə) *n.pl., sing.* **-ri·um** (-əm) [ModL.: see prec. & BACTERIA] bacteria in the soil that oxidize ammonia compounds into nitrites, or nitrites into nitrates: see NITRIC BACTERIA, NITROUS BACTERIA

ni·tro·ben·zene (-ben′zēn) *n.* a poisonous yellow liquid, $C_6H_5NO_2$, prepared by treating benzene with nitric acid, used in making aniline, as a solvent, etc.

ni·tro·cel·lu·lose (-sel′yoo lōs′) *n.* any ester of nitric acid and cellulose; esp., a pulplike substance produced by the action of nitric acid upon wood, cotton, etc. in the presence of concentrated sulfuric acid: used in making smokeless explosives, plastics, lacquers, etc. —**ni′tro·cel′lu·los′ic** *adj.*

ni·tro·fu·ran (-fyoor′an, -fyoo ran′) *n.* [NITRO- + FURAN] a furan derivative, $C_4H_3O \cdot NO_2$, used to treat bacterial infections

ni·tro·gen (nī′trə jən) *n.* [Fr. *nitrogène*: see NITRO- & -GEN] a colorless, tasteless, odorless gaseous chemical element forming nearly four fifths of the atmosphere: it is a component of all living things: symbol, N; at. wt., 14.0067; at. no., 7; density, 1.2506 g/l (0°C); melt. pt., −209.9°C; boil. pt., −195.8°C

nitrogen cycle the cycle of natural processes through which atmospheric nitrogen is converted by nitrogen fixation and nitrification into compounds used by plants and animals in the formation of proteins and is eventually returned by decay and denitrification to its original state

nitrogen dioxide a poisonous, reddish-brown gas, NO₂, used in making nitric acid, as a rocket-fuel oxidizer, etc.

nitrogen fixation 1. the conversion of atmospheric nitrogen into nitrates by soil bacteria (**nitrogen fixers**) found in the nodules of certain legumes 2. the conversion of free nitrogen into nitrogenous compounds of commercial value by any of various processes —**ni′tro·gen-fix′ing** *adj.*

ni·trog·e·nize (nī träj′ə niz′, nī′trə jə nīz′) *vt.* **-nized′, -niz′ing** to combine or impregnate with nitrogen or its compounds

nitrogen mustard any of a class of compounds similar to mustard gas, but having an amino nitrogen in place of a sulfur atom: used experimentally in the treatment of cancers, etc.

nitrogen narcosis reduction in the ability to think clearly and react quickly, caused by the inhalation of too much nitrogen, as by deep-sea divers

ni·trog·e·nous (nī träj′ə nəs) *adj.* of or containing nitrogen or nitrogen compounds

ni·tro·glyc·er·in, ni·tro·glyc·er·ine (nī′trə glis′ər in, -trō-) *n.* a thick, pale-yellow, flammable, explosive oil, $C_3H_5(ONO_2)_3$, prepared by treating glycerin with a mixture of nitric and sulfuric acids: used in medicine and in making dynamites and propellants

ni·tro·hy·dro·chlo·ric acid (-hī′drə klôr′ik) *same as* AQUA REGIA

ni·trol·ic acid (nī träl′ik) [NITR- + -OL + -IC] any of a series of acids with the general formula $RC(\colon NOH)NO_2$, formed by the action of nitrous acid on nitroparaffin

ni·trom·e·ter (nī träm′ə tər) *n.* [NITRO- + -METER] an apparatus for measuring the amount of nitrogen, or certain of its gaseous compounds, emitted during a chemical reaction

ni·tro·par·af·fin (nī′trə par′ə fin, -trō-) *n.* a nitrogen compound derived from any member of the methane, or paraffin, series of hydrocarbons and containing an NO₂ group in place of one or more of the hydrogen atoms

ni·tros·a·mine (nī′trōs ə mēn′, -am′in) *n.* [< NITROSO- + AMINE] any of a series of organic compounds derived from amines and containing the divalent $=N \cdot NO$ radical

ni·tro·so (nī trō′sō) *adj.* [see ff.] designating or containing the NO radical, or group

ni·tro·so- (nī trō′sō) [< L. *nitrosus*, full of natron < *nitrum*: see NITER] *a combining form meaning* of or containing the NO radical

ni·tro·syl (nī′trə sil, -sēl′; nī trō′sil) *n.* [< prec. + -YL] the nitroso radical, or group

ni·trous (nī′trəs) *adj.* [L. *nitrosus*: see NITROSO-] 1. of, like, or containing niter 2. designating or of compounds in which nitrogen has a lower valence than in the corresponding nitric compounds

nitrous acid an acid, HNO₂, known only in solution or in the form of its salts (*nitrites*)

nitrous bacteria soil and water bacteria (genus *Nitrosomonas*, etc.) that convert ammonia into nitrites

nitrous oxide a colorless, nonflammable gas, N₂O, used as an anesthetic and in aerosols

nit·ty (nit′ē) *adj.* **-ti·er, -ti·est** full of nits

☆**nit·ty-grit·ty** (-grit′ē) *n.* [rhyming extension of GRITTY] [Slang] the actual, basic facts, elements, issues, etc.

☆**nit·wit** (nit′wit′) *n.* [*nit* (< G. dial. for G. *nicht*, not) or ? NIT + WIT[1]] a stupid or silly person

Ni·u·e (nē ōō′ā) island in the SC Pacific, east of Tonga, belonging to the Cook Islands of New Zealand: 100 sq. mi.; pop. 5,000

ni·val (nī′v′l) *adj.* [L. *nivalis* < *nix* (gen. *nivis*), SNOW] of, or growing under, snow

niv·e·ous (niv′ē əs) *adj.* [L. *niveus*, snowy: see prec.] snowy; snowlike

Ni·ver·nais (nē ver ne′) region & former province of C France

nix[1] (niks) *n., pl.* **nix′es**, G. **nix′e** (nik′sə) [G. *nix*, masc., *nixe*, fem. < OHG. *nihhus*, sea beast, *nicchussa*, water sprite, akin to OE. *nicor*, ON. *nykr*, water sprite < Gmc. *nik-*, *nikwus-*, water spirit < IE. base *neigw-*, to wash, whence Sans. *nénēkti*, (he) washes] *Germanic Myth.* a water sprite, usually small and of human or partly human form —**nix′ie** (nik′sē) *n.fem.*

☆**nix**[2] (niks) *adv.* [G. *nichts*] [Slang] 1. no 2. not at all —*interj.* [Slang] an exclamation meaning: 1. stop! 2. I forbid, refuse, disagree, etc. —*n.* [Slang] 1. nothing 2. refusal or rejection —*vt.* [Slang] to disapprove of or put a stop to

Nix·on (nik′s′n), **Richard M**(ilhous) 1913– ; 37th president of the U.S. (1969–)

Ni·zam (ni zäm′, ni zam′) *n.* [Hindi & Per. *nizām* < Ar. *nizām*, to order, arrange < *nazama*, to govern] 1. the title of the former native ruler in Hyderabad, India 2. [n-] *pl.* **ni·zam′** a soldier in the Turkish regular army —**ni·zam′-ate** *n.*

Nizh·ni Ta·gil (nēzh′ni tä gēl′) city in the W R.S.F.S.R., in the C Urals: pop. 375,000

N.J. New Jersey

Njorth (nyôrth) [ON. *Njörthr*] *Norse Myth.* a Vanir, the father of Frey and Freya: also **Njord** (nyôrd)

Nkru·mah (′n krōō′mə), **Kwa·me** (kwä′mē) 1909– ; president of Ghana (1960–66)

n.l. 1. [L. *non liquet*] it is not clear 2. [L. *non licet*] it is not lawful 3. *Printing* new line

N.Lat., N.lat. north latitude

N.L.F., NLF National Liberation Front (of South Vietnam)

NLRB, N.L.R.B. National Labor Relations Board

N.Mex. New Mexico: also **N.M.**

NMI no middle initial

NMR nuclear magnetic resonance

NNE, N.N.E., n.n.e. north-northeast

NNW, N.N.W., n.n.w. north-northwest

no[1] (nō) *adv.* [ME. < OE. *na* < *ne a*, lit., not ever < IE. base *ne*, *nē*, negative particle, whence Sans. *ná*, Gr. *ne-*, L. *ne-*, Goth. & OHG. *ni*, OIr. *no*: see AYE[1]] 1. [Scot. or Rare] not [whether or no] 2. not in any degree; not at all [*no worse*] 3. nay; not so: the opposite of YES, used to deny, refuse, or disagree *No* is also used to give force to a negative that follows, to precede a fuller or more specific statement, or, interjectionally, to express surprise, disbelief, dismay, etc. —*adj.* [ME., form of *non, none* (cf. NONE[1]) used only before a consonant < OE. *nan* < *ne an*, lit., not one (cf. ONE)] not any; not a; not a; not one [*no errors*] —*n., pl.* **noes, nos**] 1. an utterance of *no*; refusal or denial 2. a negative vote, or a person voting in the negative

no[2] (nō) *n., pl.* **no** [Jap. *nō*] [*often* N-] a classic form of Japanese drama with choral music and dancing, using set themes, simple symbolic scenery, elaborately masked and costumed performers, and stylized acting

No *Chem.* nobelium

No. 1. north 2. northern 3. number: also **no.**

no-ac·count (nō′ə kount′) *adj.* [Colloq.] of no account; worthless; good-for-nothing —*n.* a shiftless person

No·a·chi·an (nō ā′kē ən) *adj.* 1. of Noah or his time 2. ancient; antique: also **No·ach′ic** (-ak′ik)

No·ah (nō′ə) [Heb. *nōaḥ*, lit., rest, comfort] 1. a masculine name 2. *Bible* the patriarch commanded by God to build the ark on which he, his family, and two of every kind of creature survived the Flood: Gen. 5:28–10:32

nob[1] (näb) *n.* [later form of KNOB] 1. [Slang] the head 2. *Cribbage* the jack of the same suit as the card cut from the pack: it counts one point for the holder

nob[2] (näb) *n.* [< ? prec.] [Chiefly Brit. Slang] a person of wealth and high social status

no-ball (nō′bôl′) *n. Cricket* a ball improperly bowled

nob·ble (näb′′l) *vt.* **-bled, -bling** [? freq. of NAB] [Brit. Slang] 1. to disable or harm (a horse), as by drugging, etc. to keep it from winning a race 2. to win over by bribery or other underhanded methods 3. to cheat or swindle —**nob′bler** *n.*

nob·by (näb′ē) *adj.* **-bi·er, -bi·est** [< NOB[2]] [Chiefly Brit. Slang] of or for nobs; stylish —**nob′bi·ly** *adv.*

No·bel (nō bel′), **Al·fred Bern·hard** (ál′fred ber′näṙd) 1833–96; Swed. industrialist, philanthropist, & inventor of dynamite: established the Nobel prizes

no·bel·i·um (nō bel′ē əm) *n.* [after *Nobel* Institute in Stockholm, where discovered] a radioactive chemical element produced by the nuclear bombardment of curium: symbol, No; at. wt., 255(?); at. no., 102

Nobel prizes annual international prizes given by the Nobel Foundation for distinction in physics, chemistry, medicine or physiology, and literature, and for the promotion of peace

no·bil·i·ar·y (nō bil′ē er′ē) *adj.* [Fr. *nobiliaire*: see NOBLE & -ARY] of nobles or nobility

no·bil·i·ty (nō bil′ə tē) *n., pl.* **-ties** [ME. *nobilite* < OFr. *nobilité* < L. *nobilitas*] 1. the quality or state of being noble 2. high station or rank in society, esp. when accompanied by a title 3. the class of people of noble rank or having hereditary titles: usually limited in Great Britain to the peerage (usually with *the*)

no·ble (nō′b′l) *adj.* **-bler, -blest** [ME. < OFr. < L. *nobilis*, lit., well-known < base of (g)*noscere*, KNOW] 1. having eminence, renown, fame, etc.; illustrious 2. having or showing high moral qualities or ideals, or greatness of character; lofty 3. having excellent qualities; superior 4. grand; stately; splendid; magnificent [*a noble view*] 5. of high hereditary rank or title; aristocratic 6. chemically unreactive, esp. with acids and air; precious; pure: said of metals, esp. gold, platinum, etc.: also said of rare gases such as helium, neon, radon, etc., several of which were at one time considered to be completely inert —*n.* 1. a person having hereditary rank or title; nobleman; peer 2. a former gold coin of England ☆3. [Old Slang] the head of a gang of strikebreakers —**no′ble·ness** *n.*

☆**noble fir** a very large fir (*Abies procera*) of the W U.S.

no·ble·man (-mən) *n., pl.* **-men** (-mən) a member of the nobility; peer —**no′ble·wom′an** *n.fem.,* **-wom′en**

no·blesse (nō bles′) *n.* [ME. *noblesce* < OFr. < ML. *nobilitia*] *same as* NOBILITY

no·blesse o·blige (nō bles′ ō blēzh′; *Fr.* nō bles′ ô blēzh′) [Fr., lit., nobility obliges] the inferred obligation of people of high rank or social position to behave nobly or kindly toward others

no·bly (nō′blē) *adv.* 1. with noble courage or spirit; gallantly 2. *a)* idealistically; loftily *b)* excellently; splendidly 3. of titled birth; of the peerage

no·bod·y (nō′bud′ē, -bäd′ē, -bəd ē) *pron.* not any person; not anybody; no one —*n., pl.* **-bod′ies** a person of no influence, authority, or importance

no·cent (nō′s′nt) *adj.* [LME. < L. *nocens*, prp. of *nocere*, to harm: see NOXIOUS] [Obs. or Rare] 1. causing harm or injury; hurtful 2. guilty or criminal

no·ci·cep·tive (nō′si sep′tiv) *adj.* [< L. *noce* to harm & (RE)CEPTIVE] of, causing, or reacting to pain

nock (näk) *n.* [ME. *nocke* < Scand., as in Sw. dial. *nokke*, notch < IE. *kneug-* < base *ken-*, to pinch, whence NOOK, NUT] 1. a notch for holding the string at either end of a bow 2. a similar notch in the end of an arrow, for the insertion of the bowstring —*vt.* 1. to make a notch in (a bow or arrow) 2. to set (an arrow) into the bowstring

noc·tam·bu·lism (näk tam′byoo liz′m) *n.* [Fr. *noctambulisme* < L. *nox* (gen. *noctis*), NIGHT + *ambulare*, to walk + *-isme*, -ISM] walking in one's sleep; somnambulism: also **noc·tam′bu·la′tion** —**noc·tam′bu·list** *n.*

noc·ti- (näk′tə) [< L. *nox* (gen. *noctis*), NIGHT] *a combining form meaning* night: also, before a vowel, **noct-**

noc·ti·lu·ca (näk′tə lōō′kə) *n.* [ModL., name of the genus < L., something that shines at night < *nox* (gen. *noctis*), NIGHT + *lucere*, to shine < *lux*, LIGHT[1]] any of a genus (*Noctiluca*) of large, spherical, reddish, luminescent protozoans that occur in vast numbers in the sea, causing parts of it to appear luminous at night

noc·ti·lu·cent (näk′tə lōō′s′nt) *adj.* [NOCTI- + LUCENT] designating or of a luminous cloud of unknown composition, visible at night in the polar regions at an altitude of c. 50 miles

noc·tu·id (näk′choo wid) *n.* [< ModL. *Noctuidae*, name of the family < L. *noctua*, night owl < *nox* (gen. *noctis*), NIGHT] any of a large family (*Noctuidae*) of mostly dull-colored moths which fly at night, including many of those flying into lighted houses, as the cutworm moth, dagger moth, etc.: their larvae often are very destructive

noc·tule (näk′chōōl) *n.* [Fr. < VL. *noctula*, night owl, dim. < L. *noctua* (see prec.)] a variety of large brown bat (*Nyctalus noctula*) of Europe and the British Isles

noc·turn (näk′tərn) *n.* [ME. *nocturne* < OFr. < ML.(Ec.) *nocturna* < L. *nocturnus*: see ff.] any of the divisions, usually three, of the office of matins

noc·tur·nal (näk tur′n′l) *adj.* [LME. < LL. *nocturnalis* < L. *nocturnus < nox* (gen. *noctis*), NIGHT] 1. of, done, or happening in the night 2. functioning or active during the night 3. having blossoms that open at night, as some flowers —**noc·tur′nal·ly** *adv.*

noc·turne (näk′tərn) *n.* [Fr. < L. *nocturnus*: see prec.] 1. a painting of a night scene 2. a musical composition, esp. for the piano, of a romantic or dreamy character thought appropriate to night

noc·u·ous (näk′yoo wəs) *adj.* [L. *nocuus < nocere*, to do hurt to: see NOXIOUS] harmful; poisonous; noxious —**noc′u·ous·ly** *adv.* —**noc′u·ous·ness** *n.*

nod (näd) *vi.* **nod′ded, nod′ding** [ME. *nodden*, prob. in basic sense "to shake the head," akin to G. *notten*, to move about, OHG. *hnoton*, to shake, OE. *hnossian*, to knock < IE. *kneudh* < base *ken-*, to scratch, scrape, whence NIP[1]] 1. to bend the head forward slightly and raise it again quickly, as a sign of greeting, command, acknowledgment, invitation, or, specif., of agreement or assent 2. to let the head fall forward involuntarily because of drowsiness; be very sleepy 3. to be inattentive or careless; make a slip 4. to sway back and forth or up and down, as the tops of trees, flowers, plumes, etc. —*vt.* 1. to bend (the head) forward slightly and raise it again quickly 2. to signify (assent, approval, agreement, etc.) by doing this 3. to invite or dismiss by a nod —*n.* 1. a nodding, as of the head, treetops, etc. 2. a sign of affirmation, assent, favorable decision, etc. [to give or get the *nod*] 3. *see* LAND OF NOD —**nod′der** *n.*

nod·al (nōd′′l) *adj.* of or like a node or nodes —**no·dal·i·ty** (nō dal′ə tē) *n.* —**nod′al·ly** *adv.*

nod·ding acquaintance 1. a slight, not intimate, acquaintance with a person or thing 2. a person whom one knows slightly

nod·dle (näd′′l) *n.* [ME. *nodle* < ?] [Old Colloq.] the head; pate: a humorous term —*vt., vi.* **-dled, -dling** [Now Rare] to nod (the head)

nod·dy (näd′ē) *n., pl.* **-dies** [< ? NOD] 1. a fool; simpleton 2. any of several kinds of tropical sea birds (genus *Anous*), with dark feathers and a short tail

node (nōd) *n.* [L. *nodus*, a knot: for IE. base see NET[1]] 1. a dilemma or complication, as of a story or play 2. a knot; knob; swelling 3. a point of concentration; central point 4. *Anat.* a knotty, localized swelling; protuberance 5. *Astron.* either of the two diametrically opposite points at which the orbit of a heavenly body intersects a fundamental plane, as the plane of the ecliptic 6. *Bot.* that part, or joint, of a stem from which a leaf starts to grow

VIBRATING STRING

NODES
(N, nodes formed when vibrating string is stopped at intervals along its length; L, loops between nodes)

7. *Geom.* the point where a continuous curve crosses or meets itself **8.** *Physics* the point, line, or surface of a vibrating object, as a string, where there is comparatively no vibration

nod·i·cal (nō′di k'l, näd′i-) *adj. Astron.* of the nodes

no·dose (nōd′ōs, nō dōs′) *adj.* [L. *nodosus*] having nodes; knotty: said of roots, etc. —**no·dos′i·ty** (-däs′ə tē) *n.*

nod·ule (näj′ōōl) *n.* [L. *nodulus*, dim. of *nodus*, a knot: see NODE] **1.** a small knot or irregular, rounded lump **2.** *Anat.* a small node **3.** *Bot.* a small knot or node on a stem or root, esp. one containing nitrogen-fixing bacteria **4.** *Geol.* a small, usually rounded, concreted body harder than the surrounding material —**nod′u·lar, nod′u·lose, nod′u·lous** *adj.*

no·dus (nō′dəs) *n., pl.* **-di′** (-dī′) [ME. < L., a knot, NODE] complication; difficulty; knotty situation, as in a play

No·e (nō′ə) *var.* (*esp. Douay Bible*) of NOAH

No·el (nō′ə) [OFr. *Nouel, Noel, Noel*, lit., natal: see ff.: cf. NATALIE] a masculine or feminine name

no·el, no·ël (nō el′) *n.* [< Fr. *noël* < OFr. *nowel, nouel* < L. *natalis*, NATAL] **1.** a Christmas carol **2.** [N-] *same as* CHRISTMAS

no·et·ic (nō et′ik) *adj.* [Gr. *noētikos* < *noēsis* < *noein*, to perceive < *nous*, the mind] **1.** of, or existing or originating in, the intellect **2.** given to or involving purely intellectual speculation —**no·e′sis** (-ē′sis) *n.*

nog[1] (näg) *n.* [< ?] any of various wooden pins or blocks, esp. one set in a brick or masonry wall to hold nails —*vt.* **nogged, nog′ging** to fill in space in a wall, as between studs, with bricks

nog[2], **nogg** (näg) *n.* [< East Anglian dial. < ?] **1.** [Brit.] a kind of strong ale **☆2.** *same as* EGGNOG

nog·gin (näg′in) *n.* [prob. < NOG[2]] **1.** a small cup or mug **2.** one fourth of a pint: a measure for ale or liquor **☆3.** [Colloq.] the head

nog·ging (näg′in) *n.* [< NOG[1]] brick masonry built up between wooden frames

no-good (nō′good′) *adj.* [Slang] contemptible; despicable

No·gu·chi (nō gōō′chē), **Hi·de·yo** (hē′de yō′) 1876-1928; Jap. bacteriologist in the U.S.

noh (nō) *n. same as* NO[2]

☆no-hit·ter (nō′hit′ər) *n.* a baseball game in which the pitcher allows the opposing team no base hits —**no′-hit′** *adj.*

no·how (nō′hou′) *adv.* [Dial.] in no manner; not at all

noil (noil) *n.* [< SW. Yorkshire dial. < ?] short or knotted textile fibers combed from the long staple or, sometimes, spun in with longer staple to make yarn

noise (noiz) *n.* [ME. < OFr., noise, quarreling, clamor < L. *nausea* (see NAUSEA)] **1.** *a)* loud or confused shouting; din of voices; clamor *b)* any loud, discordant, or disagreeable sound or sounds **2.** a sound of any kind [the *noise* of the rain] **3.** [Obs.] common gossip; rumor; scandal **4.** *Electronics* any unwanted electrical signal within a communication system that interferes with the sound or image being communicated —*vt.* **noised, nois′ing** to spread about (a report, rumor, etc.): usually with *about, around, abroad,* etc. —*vi.* [Now Rare] **1.** to talk much or loudly **2.** to make noise or a noise

SYN.—**noise** is the general word for any loud, unmusical, or disagreeable sound; **din** refers to a loud, prolonged, deafening sound, painful to the ears [the *din* of the steeple bells]; **uproar** applies to a loud, confused sound, as of shouting, laughing, etc., and connotes commotion or disturbance [his remarks threw the audience into an *uproar*]; **clamor** suggests loud, continued, excited shouting, as in protest or demand [the *clamor* of an aroused people]; **hubbub** implies the confused mingling of many voices [the *hubbub* of a subway station]; **racket** refers to a loud, clattering combination of noises regarded as annoyingly excessive [he couldn't work for the *racket* next door] See also SOUND[1] —*ANT.* quiet

noise·less (-lis) *adj.* with little or no noise; very quiet; silent —*SYN.* see STILL[1] —**noise′less·ly** *adv.* —**noise′less·ness** *n.*

noise·mak·er (-mā′kər) *n.* a person or thing that makes noise; specif., a horn, cowbell, etc. used for making noise in celebration, as on New Year's Eve

noi·some (noi′səm) *adj.* [ME. *noyesum* < *noy*, aphetic of *anoy* < OFr. *anoi*: see ANNOY & -SOME[1]] **1.** injurious to health; noxious; harmful **2.** having a bad odor; foulsmelling; offensive —*SYN.* see STINKING —**noi′some·ly** *adv.* —**noi′some·ness** *n.*

nois·y (noi′zē) *adj.* **nois′i·er, nois′i·est** **1.** making, or accompanied by, noise **2.** making more sound than is expected or customary **3.** full of noise; clamorous [the *noisy* city] —**nois′i·ly** *adv.* —**nois′i·ness** *n.*

‡no·lens vo·lens (nō′lenz vō′lenz) [L.] unwilling (or) willing; whether or not one wishes it; willy-nilly

no·li me tan·ge·re (nō′lī mē tan′jə rē) [L., lit., touch me not] **1.** a warning against touching or meddling **2.** *same as* JEWELWEED

nol·le pros·e·qui (näl′ē präs′ə kwī′) [L., to be unwilling to prosecute] *Law* **1.** formal notice by the prosecutor that prosecution in a criminal case will be ended as to one or more counts, one or more defendants, or altogether **2.** similar formal notice by the plaintiff in a civil suit

no-load (nō′lōd′) *adj.* designating or of mutual funds charging no commissions on sales

no·lo con·ten·de·re (nō′lō kən ten′də rē) [L., I do not wish to contest (it)] *Law* a plea by the defendant in a criminal case declaring that he will not make a defense, but not admitting guilt: it leaves him open to conviction but does not prejudice his case in collateral proceedings

☆nol-pros (näl′präs′) *vt.* **-prossed′, -pros′sing** [< abbrev. of NOLLE PROSEQUI] to abandon (all or part of a suit) by entering a nolle prosequi on the court records

nom. nominative

no·ma (nō′mə) *n.* [ModL. < Gr. *nomē*, a spreading (of sores), lit., feeding < *nemein*, to distribute, pasture: see -NOMY] a severe ulcerous condition of the mouth, occurring esp. in young children, as after debilitating disease, and usually resulting in gangrene

no·mad (nō′mad) *occas.* näm′ad) *n.* [L. *nomas* (gen. *nomadis*) < Gr. *nomas*, orig., roaming about for pasture < *nemein*, to pasture, orig., to distribute: see -NOMY] **1.** a member of a tribe or people having no permanent home, but moving about constantly in search of food, pasture, etc. **2.** any wanderer who has no fixed home —*adj.* nomadic; wandering —**no′mad·ism** *n.*

no·mad·ic (nō mad′ik) *adj.* of, characteristic of, or like nomads or their way of life —*SYN.* see ITINERANT —**no·mad′i·cal·ly** *adv.*

no man's land **1.** a piece of land, usually wasteland, to which no one has a recognized title **2.** the area on a battlefield separating the combatants **3.** an indefinite area of operation, involvement, jurisdiction, etc.

nom·arch (näm′ärk) *n.* [Gr. *nomarchēs*: see NOME & -ARCH] the governor of a nome, or nomarchy

nom·arch·y (-är kē) *n., pl.* **-arch·ies** [Gr. *nomarchia*] *same as* NOME

nom·bles (num′b'lz) *n.pl.* [Archaic] *same as* NUMBLES

nom·bril (näm′brəl) *n.* [Fr., the navel, for OFr. *lombril* < LL. *umbiliculus, dim. < L. *umbilicus*, NAVEL] the point on an escutcheon just below the true center and above the center of the base; navel point

nom de guerre (näm′ də ger′; Fr. nōn də ger′) *pl.* **noms′ de guerre′** (näm′ də ger′) [Fr., lit., a war name] a pseudonym

nom de plume (näm′ də plōōm′; Fr. nōn də plüm′) *pl.* **noms′ de plume′** (Fr. nōn) [Fr.] a pen name; pseudonym —*SYN.* see PSEUDONYM

Nome (nōm) [< nearby Cape *Nome*, prob. < *? name*, query on an early map, misread as *C. Nome*] city in W Alas., on S coast of Seward Peninsula: pop. 2,500

nome (nōm) *n.* [Gr. *nomos* < *nemein*, to divide: see -NOMY] **1.** a province of ancient Egypt **2.** a major political subdivision of modern Greece; prefecture

no·men (nō′mən) *n., pl.* **nom′i·na** (näm′i nə) [L., NAME] the second of the three names of an ancient Roman, following the praenomen and preceding the cognomen (Ex.: Marcus *Tullius* Cicero)

no·men·cla·tor (nō′mən klāt′ər) *n.* [L. < *nomen*, NAME + *calator*, caller, crier < pp. of *calare*, to call: for IE. base see CLAMOR] **1.** a person, specif. a slave in ancient Rome, who announces the names of guests, etc. **2.** a person who invents names for, or assigns them to, things, as in scientific classification

no·men·cla·ture (nō′mən klā′chər, nō men′klə-) *n.* [L. *nomenclatura*: see prec.] **1.** the system or set of names used in a specific branch of learning or activity, as in biology for plants and animals, or for the parts of a particular mechanism **2.** the act or a system of naming

nom·i·nal (näm′i n'l) *adj.* [ME. *nominalle* < L. *nominalis*, of a name < *nomen*, NAME] **1.** of, consisting of, having the nature of, or giving a name or names **2.** of or having to do with a noun or nouns **3.** in name only, not in fact [the *nominal* leader] **4.** very small compared to usual expectations; slight [a *nominal* fee] —*n. Linguis.* a noun or other word or word group, including adjective and verb forms, that occurs in positions typically occupied by nouns

nom·i·nal·ism (-iz'm) *n.* [Fr. *nominalisme:* see prec. & -ISM] a doctrine of the late Middle Ages that all universal or abstract terms are mere necessities of thought or conveniences of language and therefore exist as names only and have no general realities corresponding to them —**nom′i·nal·ist** *n., adj.* —**nom′i·nal·is′tic** *adj.*

nom·i·nal·ly (-ē) *adv.* **1.** in a nominal way **2.** in name only **3.** by name

nominal value *same as* PAR VALUE

nominal wages wages stated in terms of money paid, not in terms of purchasing power

nom·i·nate (näm′ə nāt′) *vt.* **-nat·ed, -nat′ing** [< L. *nominatus*, pp. of *nominare*, to name < *nomen*, NAME] **1.** orig., to name, call, or designate **2.** to name or appoint to an office or position **3.** *a)* to name as a candidate for election or appointment; propose for office *b)* to propose as a candidate for a specific award or honor —**nom′i·na′tor** *n.*

nom·i·na·tion (näm′ə nā′shən) *n.* [ME., a calling by name < OFr. < L. *nominatio* < pp. of *nominare:* see prec.] the act of nominating or the fact of being nominated

nom·i·na·tive (näm'ə nə tiv; *for adj. 1 & 2, also* -nāt'iv) *adj.* [ME. *nomenatyf* < OFr. *nominatif* < L. *nominativus*, belonging to a name < pp. of *nominare:* see NOMINATE] **1.** named or appointed, rather than elected, to a position or office **2.** having the name of a person on it, as a stock certificate **3.** *Gram.* in inflected languages, designating or of the case of the subject of a finite verb and the words (appositives, predicate nouns or adjectives, and nouns of direct address) that agree with it; active or actor case —*n.* [L. *nominativus* (*casus*)] **1.** the nominative case **2.** a word in this case

nom·i·nee (näm'ə nē') *n.* [NOMIN(ATE) + -EE¹] a person who is nominated, esp. a candidate for election

no·mism (nō'miz'm) *n.* [< Gr. *nomos*, law (see -NOMY) + -ISM] the basing of conduct upon adherence to a religious law or holy scripture —**no·mis'tic** *adj.*

no·mo- (näm'ə, nō'mə) [< Gr. *nomos*, law: see -NOMY] *a combining form meaning* law or custom [*nomology*]

no·mo·graph (näm'ə graf', nō'mə-; -gräf') *n.* [prec. + -GRAPH] a set of scales for the variables in a problem which are so distorted and so placed that a straight line connecting the known values on some scales will provide the unknown values at its intersections with other scales: also **no'mo·gram'** (-gram')

no·mog·ra·phy (nō mäg'rə fē) *n.* [Gr. *nomographia* < *nomos*, law (see -NOMY) + *graphein*, to write: see GRAPHIC] **1.** the art of drafting laws **2.** a treatise on law or on the drafting of laws **3.** *a)* the science of making nomographs *b)* the laws for constructing such charts —**nom·o·graph·ic** (näm'ə graf'ik, nō'mə-) *adj.* —**nom'o·graph'i·cal·ly** *adv.*

no·mol·o·gy (nō mäl'ə jē) *n.* [NOMO- + -LOGY] **1.** the science of law and lawmaking **2.** the branch of a science, as of psychology, that investigates and formulates the principles governing its phenomena —**nom·o·log·i·cal** (näm'ə läj'i k'l, nō'mə-) *adj.*

nom·o·thet·ic (näm'ə thet'ik) *adj.* [Gr. *nomothetikos* < *nomothetēs*, lawgiver < *nomos*, law (see -NOMY) + *tithenai*, to make, DO¹] **1.** giving or enacting laws **2.** based on law **3.** of a science of general or universal laws Also **nom'o·thet'i·cal**

-no·my [Gr. *-nomia* < *nomos*, law < *nemein*, to distribute, govern < IE. base *nem-, to assign, take, arrange, whence L. *numerus* (cf. NUMBER), OE. *niman*, G. *nehmen*, to take] *a combining form meaning* the systematized knowledge of [*astronomy*]

non- (nän; *occas.* nun) [< L. *non*, not < OL. *noenum* < *ne-*, negative particle (see NO¹) + *oinom*, ONE] *a prefix meaning* not: used to give a negative force, esp. to nouns, adjectives, and adverbs [*nonresident*]: non- is less emphatic than *in-* and *un-*, which often give a word an opposite or reverse meaning or force (Ex.: *nonhuman, inhuman; non-American, un-American*); a hyphen may be used after *non-* and is generally used when the base word begins with a capital letter The list below includes the more common compounds formed with *non-* that do not have special meanings; they will be understood if *not* is used before the meaning of the base word

non·age (nän'ij, nō'nij) *n.* [ME. < Anglo-Fr. *nounage* < OFr. *nonage:* see NON- & AGE] **1.** *Law* the state of being under the lawful age for doing certain things, as making contracts, marrying, etc.; usually, the state of being under twenty-one **2.** the period of immaturity

non·a·ge·nar·i·an (nän'ə ji ner'ē ən, nō'nə-) *adj.* [L. *nonagenarius* < *nonageni*, ninety each < *nonaginta*, ninety < base of *novem*, NINE + *-ginta*, -TY²] ninety years old, or between the ages of ninety and one hundred —*n.* a person of this age

non·ag·gres·sion pact (nän'ə gresh'ən) an agreement between two nations not to attack each other, usually for a specified period of years

non·a·gon (nän'ə gän') *n.* [< L. *nonus*, ninth (see NOON) + -GON] a plane figure having nine angles and nine sides

non·a·ligned (nän'ə lind') *adj.* ☆not aligned with either side in a conflict of power, especially power politics —**non'a·lign'ment** *n.*

non·ap·pear·ance (-ə pir'əns) *n.* a failure to appear, esp. in court

non·be·ing (nän'bē'iŋ) *n.* same as NONEXISTENCE

☆**non·book** (-book') *n.* a book of little intrinsic worth, published merely to exploit some current vogue or consumer demand

nonce (näns) *n.* [ME. (*for the*) *nones*, formed by syllabic merging < (*for then*) *ones*, lit., the once: *then* is the dat. sing. of the def. art.] the present use, occasion, or time; time being: chiefly in **for the nonce**

nonce word a word coined and used for a single or particular occasion

non·cha·lance (nän'shə läns', nän'shə ləns) *n.* the state or quality of being nonchalant —*SYN.* see EQUANIMITY

non·cha·lant (-länt', -lənt) *adj.* [Fr. < *non* (L. *non*), not + *chaloir*, to care for < L. *calere*, to be warm or ardent: for IE. base see CALDARIUM] **1.** without warmth or enthusiasm; not showing interest **2.** showing cool lack of concern; casually indifferent —*SYN.* see COOL —**non'cha·lant'ly** *adv.*

non·com (nän'käm') *n. colloq. clipped form of* NON-COMMISSIONED OFFICER

non·com·bat·ant (nän käm'bə tənt, nän'kəm bat'ənt) *n.* **1.** a member of the armed forces whose activities do not include actual combat, as a chaplain **2.** any civilian in wartime —*adj.* **1.** not involving combat **2.** of noncombatants

non·com·mis·sioned officer (nän'kə mish'ənd) an enlisted person of any of various grades in the armed forces, as, in the U.S. Army, from corporal to sergeant major inclusive: see also PETTY OFFICER

☆**non·com·mit·tal** (-kə mit''l) *adj.* **1.** not committing one to any point of view or course of action; not revealing one's position or purpose **2.** having no definite quality, meaning, etc. —**non'com·mit'tal·ly** *adv.*

non·com·pli·ance (-kəm plī'əns) *n.* failure to comply; refusal to yield, agree, etc. —**non'com·pli'ant** *adj.*

non com·pos men·tis (nän' käm'pəs men'tis) [L.] *Law* not of sound mind; mentally incapable of handling one's own affairs: often **non compos**

non·con·duc·tor (nän'kən duk'tər) *n.* a substance that does not readily transmit certain forms of energy, as sound, heat, and, esp., electricity

non·con·form·ist (-kən fôr'mist) *n.* a person who does not act in conformity with generally accepted beliefs and practices; esp., [N-], a Protestant in England who is not a member of the Anglican Church; Dissenter —*adj.* not following established customs, beliefs, etc. —**non'con·form'ism** *n.*

---

nonabrasive	non-Arab	noncalcareous	noncollectible
nonabsorbent	non-Arabic	noncaloric	noncollegiate
nonacademic	nonaristocratic	noncancelable	noncolloid
nonacceptance	nonarithmetical	noncancerous	noncombat
nonacid	nonartistic	noncanonical	noncombining
nonactinic	non-Aryan	noncapitalistic	noncombustible
nonactive	non-Asiatic	noncapsizable	noncommercial
nonaddictive	nonassertive	noncarbohydrate	noncommissioned
nonadjacent	nonassessable	noncarbonated	noncommunicable
nonadjectival	nonassignable	noncarnivorous	noncommunicant
nonadjustable	nonassimilable	noncategorical	noncommunicating
nonadministrative	nonassimilation	non-Catholic	non-Communist
nonadvantageous	nonassociative	non-Caucasian	noncompensating
nonadverbial	nonathletic	noncellular	noncompetency
nonaesthetic	nonatmospheric	noncensored	noncompetent
nonaffiliated	nonattendance	noncereal	noncompeting
non-African	nonattributive	noncertified	noncompetitive
nonaggression	nonauthoritative	nonchargeable	noncomplacent
nonaggressive	nonautomatic	nonchemical	noncompletion
nonagreement	nonautomotive	non-Chinese	noncomplying
nonagricultural	nonbacterial	non-Christian	noncomprehending
nonalcoholic	nonbasic	nonchurch	noncompressible
nonalgebraic	nonbeliever	noncitizen	noncompression
nonallergenic	nonbelieving	noncivilized	noncompulsory
nonallergic	nonbelligerency	nonclassical	nonconciliating
nonalphabetic	nonbelligerent	nonclassifiable	nonconclusive
nonamendable	non-Biblical	nonclerical	nonconcurrence
non-American	nonblooming	nonclinical	noncondensing
nonanalytic	nonbreakable	noncoagulating	nonconducive
non-Anglican	non-British	noncoalescing	nonconducting
nonantagonistic	non-Buddhist	noncoercive	nonconductive
nonapologetic	nonbudding	noncognitive	nonconferrable
nonapostolic	nonbureaucratic	noncohesive	nonconfidential
nonappearing	nonburnable	noncollaborative	nonconflicting
nonapplicable	nonbusiness	noncollapsible	nonconformance
nonaquatic	noncaking	noncollectable	nonconforming

non·con·form·i·ty (-kən fôr′mə tē) *n.* **1.** failure or refusal to act in conformity with generally accepted beliefs and practices; esp., [N-], refusal to accept the doctrines or follow the practices of the Anglican Church **2.** [N-] the doctrines and rites of Nonconformists **3.** lack of agreement or harmony

non·co·op·er·a·tion (-kō äp′ə rā′shən) *n.* **1.** failure to work together or in unison with a person, group, or organization **2.** refusal to cooperate with a government through various acts of civil disobedience, as by nonpayment of taxes: used as a form of protest, as by Mohandas Gandhi against the former British government in India —**non′co·op′er·a′tion·ist** *n.* —**non′co·op′er·a·tive** *adj.* —**non′co·op′er·a′tor** *n.*

non·de·script (nän′di skript′) *adj.* [< L. *non*, not + *descriptus*, pp. of *describere*, DESCRIBE] so lacking in recognizable character or qualities as to belong to no definite class or type; hard to classify or describe —*n.* a nondescript person or thing

non·dis·junc·tion (nän′dis junk′shən) *n. Biol.* the failure of paired chromosomes to pass to separate cells in meiosis

non·du·ra·ble (-door′ə b'l, -dyoor′-) *adj.* not durable —*n.* [*pl.*] same as NONDURABLE GOODS —**non′du·ra·bil′i·ty** *n.*

nondurable goods goods that remain usable for, or must be replaced within, a relatively short period of time, as food, apparel, or fabrics

none¹ (nun) *pron.* [ME. < OE. *nan* < *ne*, not (see NO¹) + *an*, ONE] **1.** no one; not anyone [*none* but Jack can do it] **2.** [*usually with pl. v.*] no persons or things; not any [*there are none* on the table] —*n.* not any (of); no part; nothing [I want *none* of it] —*adv.* in no way; not at all [*none* the worse for wear] —*adj.* [Archaic] not any: used before a vowel [of *none* effect]

none² (nōn) *n.* [OE. *non*: see NOON] *Eccles.* [*often* N-] the fifth of the canonical hours

non·e·go (nän ē′gō) *n., pl.* **-gos** **1.** anything or everything that is not the self **2.** the external world

non·en·ti·ty (-en′tə tē) *n., pl.* **-ties** **1.** the state of not existing **2.** something that exists only in the mind or imagination **3.** a person or thing of little or no importance

nones (nōnz) *n.pl.* [ME. < L. *nonae* < *nonus*, ninth: see NOON] **1.** in the ancient Roman calendar, the ninth day before the ides of a month **2.** same as NONE²

non·es·sen·tial (nän′i sen′shəl) *adj.* **1.** not essential; of relatively no importance; unnecessary **2.** *Biochem.* designating or of those amino acids required by man that can be synthesized in the body from other constituents —*n.* a nonessential person or thing

none·such (nun′such′) *n.* **1.** a person or thing unrivaled or unequaled; something or someone unique; nonpareil **2.** same as BLACK MEDIC

none·the·less (nun′*th*ə les′) *adv.* in spite of that; nevertheless: also **none the less**

non-Eu·clid·e·an (nän′yōo klid′ē ən) *adj.* designating or of a geometry that rejects any of Euclid's postulates, esp. his postulate that through a given point only one line can be drawn parallel to another line

non·ex·ist·ence (-ig zis′təns) *n.* **1.** the condition of not existing **2.** something that does not exist —**non′ex·ist′ent** *adj., n.*

non·fea·sance (nän fē′z'ns) *n. Law* failure to do what duty requires to be done: distinguished from MALFEASANCE, MISFEASANCE

non·fer·rous (-fer′əs) *adj.* **1.** not made of or containing iron **2.** designating or of metals other than iron

non·he·ro (nän′hir′ō) *n.* same as ANTIHERO

noncongealing	nondefilement	noneducable	nonfatal
noncongenital	nondefining	noneducational	nonfatalistic
noncongestion	nondehiscent	noneffective	nonfattening
non-Congressional	nondelivery	noneffervescent	nonfederal
nonconnective	nondemand	nonefficacious	nonfederated
nonconscious	nondemocratic	nonefficient	nonfertile
nonconsecutive	nondenominational	nonelastic	nonfestive
nonconsent	nondepartmental	nonelective	nonfeudal
nonconservative	nondeparture	nonelectric	nonfiction
nonconstitutional	nondependence	nonelectrical	nonfictional
nonconstructive	nondepletion	nonelectrolyte	nonfiduciary
nonconsultative	nondepositor	nonelementary	nonfigurative
noncontagious	nondepreciating	nonemotional	nonfilterable
noncontemporary	nonderivative	nonemphatic	nonfinancial
noncontentious	nonderogatory	nonempirical	nonfireproof
noncontiguous	nondespotic	nonencyclopedic	nonfiscal
noncontinental	nondestructive	nonendemic	nonfissionable
noncontinuance	nondetachable	nonenforceable	nonflammable
noncontinuous	nondetonating	nonenforcement	nonflowering
noncontraband	nondevelopment	non-English	nonflowing
noncontradiction	nondevotional	nonentailed	nonfluctuating
noncontradictory	nondialectal	nonephemeral	nonflying
noncontributing	nondictatorial	nonepiscopal	nonfocal
noncontributory	nondidactic	nonequal	nonforfeiture
noncontrollable	nondifferentiation	nonequivalent	nonformal
noncontrolled	nondiffractive	nonequivocating	nonfraudulent
noncontroversial	nondiffusible	nonerotic	nonfreezing
nonconventional	nondiffusing	noneternal	non-French
nonconvergent	nondilatable	nonethical	nonfricative
nonconvertible	nondiplomatic	noneugenic	nonfulfillment
nonconviction	nondirectional	non-European	nonfunctional
noncoordinating	nondirective	nonevangelical	nonfundamental
noncorporate	nondisappearing	nonevasion	nongaseous
noncorrective	nondischarging	noneviction	nongelatinous
noncorresponding	nondisciplinary	nonevolutionary	nongenerative
noncorrodible	nondiscrimination	nonexchangeable	nongenetic
noncorroding	nondiscriminatory	nonexclusive	non-Gentile
noncorrosive	nondisfranchised	nonexcusable	non-German
noncreative	nondisparaging	nonexecution	non-Germanic
noncredible	nondispersion	nonexecutive	nongovernmental
noncriminal	nondisposal	nonexempt	nongranular
noncritical	nondistinctive	nonexisting	non-Greek
noncrucial	nondistributive	nonexotic	nongregarious
noncrystalline	nondivergent	nonexpansive	nonhabitable
nonculpable	nondivisible	nonexpendable	nonhabitual
noncultivated	nondoctrinaire	nonexperienced	nonhabituating
noncultivation	nondoctrinal	nonexperimental	nonharmonious
noncumulative	nondocumentary	nonexpert	nonhazardous
noncurrent	nondogmatic	nonexplosive	nonheathen
noncyclic	nondomesticated	nonexportable	non-Hellenic
non-Czech	nondramatic	nonextended	nonhereditary
nondamageable	nondrinker	nonextension	nonheritable
non-Darwinian	nondriver	nonexternal	nonhistoric
nondecaying	nondrying	nonextraditable	nonhomogeneous
nondeceptive	nondutiable	nonextraneous	nonhostile
nondeciduous	nondynastic	nonfactual	nonhuman
nondeductible	nonearning	nonfading	nonhumorous
nondefamatory	nonecclesiastical	nonfanatical	nonidentical
nondefensive	noneconomic	nonfanciful	nonidiomatic
nondeferential	nonedible	non-Fascist	nonidolatrous
nondeferrable	noneditorial	nonfat	nonignitible

no·nil·lion (nō nil′yən) *n.* [Fr. < L. *nonus*, ninth (see NOON) + Fr. *million*] **1.** in the U.S. and France, the number represented by 1 followed by 30 zeros **2.** in Great Britain and Germany, the number represented by 1 followed by 54 zeros —*adj.* amounting to one nonillion in number

non·in·duc·tive (nän′in duk′tiv) *adj. Elec.* not inductive [a *noninductive* resistance]

non·in·ter·ven·tion (-in tər ven′shən) *n.* the state or fact of not intervening; esp., a refraining by one nation from interference in the affairs of another —**non′in·ter·ven′tion·ist** *adj., n.*

non·join·der (nän join′dər) *n. Law* failure to include some person in a suit, when such person should have been included either as a plaintiff or defendant

non·ju·ror (-joor′ər) *n.* a person who refuses to take an oath of allegiance to his ruler or government; specif., [N-] any of the clergymen of the Church of England who refused to take such an oath at the accession of William and Mary in 1689 —**non·ju′ring** *adj.*

non·met·al (-met′'l) *n.* any of those elements lacking the characteristics of a metal; specif., any of the electro-negative elements (e.g., oxygen, carbon, nitrogen, fluorine, phosphorous, sulfur) whose oxides form acids —**non′me·tal′lic** *adj.*

non·mor·al (-môr′əl, -mär′-) *adj.* not connected in any way with morality or ethical concepts; not moral and not immoral

non·ni·trog·e·nous (nän′nī träj′ə nəs) *adj.* having no nitrogen

non·nu·cle·ar (nän nōō′klē ər) *adj.* not nuclear; specif., not characterized by the use of, or operated by, nuclear energy

non·ob·jec·tive (nän′əb jek′tiv) *adj. same as* NONREPRE-SENTATIONAL —**non′ob·jec′tiv·ism** *n.* —**non′ob·jec′tiv·ist** *n.*

‡non ob·stan·te (nän äb stan′tē) [L. < *non*, not + *obstans* (gen. *obstantis*), prp. of *obstare*: see OBSTACLE: from use in medieval legal clauses permitting to the king certain actions notwithstanding statutes to the contrary] notwithstanding; despite (a law, ruling, etc.)

no-non·sense (nō nän′sens) *adj.* not indulging in or tolerating nonsense, impracticality, etc.; matter-of-fact; practical and serious

non·pa·reil (nän′pə rel′) *adj.* [Fr. < *non*, not + *pareil*, equal < VL. **pariculus*, dim. of L. *par*, equal, PAR] un-equaled; unrivaled; peerless —*n.* **1.** someone or something unequaled or unrivaled ☆**2.** *same as* PAINTED BUNTING **3.** a small, rounded wafer of chocolate covered with tiny pellets of sugar **4.** [Fr. *nonpareille*] *Printing* a size of type between agate and minion; 6 point

non·par·ous (nän per′əs) *adj.* [NON- + -PAROUS] having borne no children

non·par·tic·i·pat·ing (nän′pər tis′ə pāt′iŋ, -pär-) *adj.* not participating; specif., *Insurance* not giving the right to participate in the dividends from the profits or surplus of the company —**non′par·tic′i·pa′tion** *n.*

non·par·ti·san (nän pär′tə z′n) *adj.* not partisan; esp., not controlled or influenced by, or supporting, any single political party: also **non·par′ti·zan** —**non·par′ti·san·ship′** *n.*

‡non pla·cet (nän plā′sət) [L.] it does not please: used in casting a negative vote

non·plus (nän plus′, nän′plus′) *n.* [L. *non*, not + *plus*, more, further] a condition of perplexity in which one is unable to go, speak, or act further —*vt.* **-plused′** or **-plussed′, -plus′ing** or **-plus′sing** to put in a nonplus; bewilder —*SYN.* see PUZZLE

‡non pos·su·mus (nän päs′yə məs) [L.] we cannot: signifying the impossibility of doing a particular thing

non·pro·duc·tive (nän′prə duk′tiv) *adj.* not productive; specif., *a)* not resulting in the production of the goods sought or the realization of the effects expected [a *nonproductive* plan] *b)* not directly related to the production of goods, as clerks, salesmen, etc. —**non′pro·duc′tive·ness** *n.*

non·prof·it (nän präf′it) *adj.* not intending or intended to earn a profit [a *nonprofit* organization]

non·pro·lif·er·a·tion (nän′prō lif′ə rā′shən) *n.* a not proliferating; specif., the limitation of the production of nuclear weapons, as by international agreement

non-pros (-präs′) *vt.* **-prossed′, -pros′sing** to enter a judgment of non prosequitur against (a plaintiff or his suit)

non pro·se·qui·tur (nän′ prō sek′wi tər) [L., he does not prosecute] *Law* a judgment entered against a plaintiff who fails to appear at the court proceedings of his suit or fails to do any other thing procedurally necessary to his suit: abbrev. **non pros.**

---

nonimaginary	non-Latin	nonmystical	nonperformance
nonimitative	nonlegal	nonmythical	nonperforming
nonimmune	nonlethal	nonnarcotic	nonperiodical
nonimmunized	nonlicensed	nonnational	nonperishable
nonimperative	nonlife	nonnative	nonperishing
nonimperial	nonlimiting	nonnatural	nonpermanent
nonimportation	nonlinear	nonnautical	nonpermeable
nonimpregnated	nonliquefying	nonnaval	nonpermissible
noninclusive	nonliquid	nonnavigable	nonperpendicular
nonindependent	nonliquidating	nonnecessity	nonpersecution
non-Indian	nonliterary	nonnegotiable	nonpersistent
nonindictable	nonliterate	non-Negro	nonphilosophical
nonindividualistic	nonliturgical	nonneutral	nonphysical
non-Indo-European	nonliving	nonnormative	nonphysiological
nonindustrial	nonlocal	nonnucleated	nonplastic
noninfallible	nonluminous	nonnutritious	nonplausible
noninfected	nonlustrous	nonnutritive	nonpoetic
noninfectious	non-Lutheran	nonobedience	nonpoisonous
noninflammable	nonmagnetic	nonobligatory	nonpolitical
noninflammatory	nonmailable	nonobservance	nonporous
noninflationary	nonmaintenance	nonobservant	nonpossession
noninflectional	nonmalignant	nonobstructive	nonpredatory
noninformative	nonmalleable	nonoccupational	nonpredictable
noninheritable	nonmarital	nonoccurrence	nonpreferential
noninjurious	nonmaritime	nonodorous	nonprejudicial
noninstructional	nonmarketable	nonofficial	nonprescriptive
noninstrumental	nonmarrying	nonoperating	nonpreservative
nonintegrated	nonmartial	nonoperational	nonpresidential
nonintellectual	nonmaterial	nonoperative	nonprevalent
nonintelligent	nonmaterialistic	nonoptional	nonpriestly
noninterchangeable	nonmaternal	nonoriental	nonproducer
nonintercourse	nonmathematical	non-Oriental	nonprofessional
noninterference	nonmatrimonial	nonorthodox	nonprofessorial
nonintermittent	nonmechanical	nonoxidizing	nonproficient
noninternational	nonmechanistic	nonoxygenated	nonprogressive
nonintersecting	nonmedicinal	nonpacific	nonprohibitive
nonintoxicant	nonmelodious	nonpagan	nonprolific
nonintoxicating	nonmember	nonpalatal	nonprophetic
nonintuitive	nonmembership	nonpalatalization	nonproportional
noninvolvement	nonmercantile	nonpapal	nonproprietary
noniodized	nonmetaphysical	nonpapist	nonproscriptive
nonionized	nonmetropolitan	nonparallel	nonprotective
non-Irish	nonmigratory	nonparasitic	nonprotein
nonirradiated	nonmilitant	nonparental	non-Protestant
nonirrigated	nonmilitary	nonparishioner	nonproven
nonirritant	nonmineral	nonparliamentary	nonpsychic
nonirritating	nonministerial	nonparochial	nonpublic
non-Islamic	nonmobile	nonparticipant	nonpuncturable
non-Israelite	non-Mormon	nonparty	nonpunishable
non-Italian	nonmortal	nonpasserine	nonpurulent
non-Japanese	non-Moslem	nonpaying	nonracial
non-Jew	nonmotile	nonpayment	nonradiating
non-Jewish	nonmunicipal	nonperceptual	nonradical
nonjudicial	nonmuscular	nonperforated	nonradioactive

non·rat·ed (nän rāt′id) *adj.* not rated; specif., *U.S. Navy* designating an enlisted man who is not a petty officer

non·rep·re·sen·ta·tion·al (nän′rep ri zən tā′shən 'l) *adj.* not representational; specif., designating or of art that does not attempt to represent in recognizable form any object in nature; abstract; nonobjective —**non′rep·re·sen·ta′tion·al·ism** *n.*

non·res·i·dent (nän rez′ə dənt) *adj.* not residing in a specified place; esp., having one's home in some locality other than where one works, attends school, etc. —*n.* **1.** a person whose permanent home is not where he is staying **2.** a person who lives away from the locality of his business, school, etc. —**non·res′i·dence, non·res′i·den·cy** *n.* —**non′res·i·den′tial** *adj.*

non·re·sist·ant (nän rez′i stənt) *adj.* not resistant; esp., submitting to force or arbitrary authority —*n.* **1.** a person who believes that force and violence should not be used to oppose arbitrary authority, however unjust **2.** a person who refuses to use force even to defend himself —**non′re·sist′ance** *n.*

non·re·straint (-ri strānt′) *n.* the absence of restraint; esp., *Psychiatry* the management of psychotic persons without the use of a straitjacket or other physical restraint

non·re·stric·tive (-ri strik′tiv) *adj.* not restrictive; specif., *Gram.* designating a clause, phrase, or word felt as not essential to the sense, or purely descriptive, and hence usually set off by commas (Ex.: John, *who is six feet tall*, is younger than Bill)

☆**non·sched·uled** (nän skej′ool d) *adj.* designating or of an airline, plane, etc. licensed for commercial flights as warranted by demand rather than on a regular schedule

non·sec·tar·i·an (nän′sek ter′ē ən) *adj.* not sectarian; not confined to or affiliated with any specific religion

non·sense (nän′sens, -səns) *n.* [NON- + SENSE] **1.** words or actions that convey an absurd meaning or no meaning at all **2.** things of relatively no importance or value; trivialities **3.** impudent, foolish, or evasive behavior —*adj.* designating or of syllables or words constructed arbitrarily of sounds or symbols so as to have no meaning —*interj.* how foolish! how absurd!: an exclamation of impatience, contradiction, contempt, etc.

non·sen·si·cal (nän sen′si k'l) *adj.* unintelligible, foolish, silly, absurd, etc. —**non·sen′si·cal·ly** *adv.* —**non·sen′si·cal·ness, non·sen′si·cal′i·ty** (kal′ə tē) *n.*

non se·qui·tur (nän′ sek′wi tər) [L., lit., it does not follow] **1.** *Logic* a conclusion or inference which does not follow from the premises: abbrev. *non seq.* **2.** a remark having no bearing on what has just been said

☆**non-sked** (-sked) *adj.* [Colloq.] *same as* NONSCHEDULED —*n.* [Colloq.] a nonscheduled airline, plane, etc.

non·skid (nän′skid′) *adj.* having the tread so constructed as to reduce skidding: said of a tire, etc.

non·so·cial (nän sō′shəl) *adj.* not social —*SYN.* see UNSOCIAL

non·stand·ard (-stan′dərd) *adj.* not standard; specif., designating or of locutions, grammatical constructions, pronunciations, etc. that do not fall into the category of standard speech, as slang or cant usages, obscenities, etc.: cf. SUBSTANDARD

non·stop (-stäp′) *adj., adv.* without a stop

non·stri·at·ed muscle (nän strī′āt id) *same as* SMOOTH MUSCLE

non·such (nun′such′) *n. same as* NONESUCH

non·suit (nän′sōōt′) *n.* [ME. *noun suyt* < Anglo-Fr. *nonsule*: see NON- & SUIT] *Law* **1.** a judgment against a plaintiff because of his failure to proceed to trial, to establish that he has a valid case, or to produce adequate evidence **2.** the ending of a lawsuit by the voluntary withdrawal of the plaintiff —*vt.* to bring a nonsuit against (a plaintiff or his case)

non·sup·port (nän′sə pôrt′) *n.* failure to provide for a legal dependent

non trop·po (nän trō′pō; *It.* nôn trôp′pô) [It.] *Music* not too much; moderately: a direction to the performer, as in *allegro non troppo*, fast, but not too fast

non·un·ion (nän yōōn′yən) *n.* failure to mend or unite: said of a broken bone —*adj.* **1.** not belonging to a labor union **2.** not made or serviced by union workers or under conditions required by a labor union **3.** refusing to recognize, or sign a contract with, a labor union —**non·un′ion·ism** *n.* —**non·un′ion·ist** *n.*

non·vi·o·lence (-vī′ə ləns) *n.* an abstaining from violence or from the use of physical force, as in efforts to obtain civil rights or in opposing government policy: see also CIVIL DISOBEDIENCE, PASSIVE RESISTANCE —**non·vi′o·lent** *adj.*

non·vot·er (nän vōt′ər) *n.* a person who does not vote or is not permitted to vote —**non·vot′ing** *adj.*

---

nonratable	nonrival	nonsparing	nontherapeutic
nonrational	non-Roman	nonspeaking	nonthinking
nonreactive	nonromantic	nonspecialist	nontoxic
nonreader	nonrotating	nonspecialized	nontraditional
nonrealistic	nonroyal	nonspecializing	nontragic
nonreality	nonrural	nonspecific	nontransferable
nonreceiving	non-Russian	nonspectral	nontransitional
nonreciprocal	nonsacred	nonspeculative	nontransparent
nonreciprocating	nonsacrificial	nonspherical	nontreasonable
nonrecognition	nonsalable	nonspiritual	nontributary
nonrecoverable	nonsalaried	nonspirituous	nontropical
nonrecurrent	nonsalutary	nonspottable	nontuberculous
nonrecurring	nonsaturated	nonstaining	nontypical
nonredeemable	non-Scandinavian	nonstandardized	nontyrannical
nonrefillable	nonscholastic	nonstarter	nonulcerous
nonregenerating	nonscientific	nonstarting	nonunderstandable
nonregimented	nonscoring	nonstatic	nonuniform
nonregistered	nonseasonal	nonstationary	nonuniversal
nonregistrable	nonsecret	nonstatistical	nonusable
nonregulation	nonsecretory	nonstatutory	nonuse
nonreigning	nonsectional	nonstrategic	nonuser
nonrelative	nonsecular	nonstretchable	nonuterine
nonreligious	nonsedentary	nonstriker	nonutilitarian
nonremission	nonseditious	nonstriking	nonutilized
nonremovable	nonsegregated	nonstructural	nonvascular
nonremunerative	nonsegregation	nonsubmissive	nonvegetative
nonrenewable	nonselective	nonsubscriber	nonvenereal
nonrepayable	non-Semitic	nonsuccessful	nonvenomous
nonrepentance	nonsensitive	nonsuccessive	nonvenous
nonrepresentative	nonsensitized	nonsupporting	nonverbal
nonreproductive	nonsensory	nonsuppurative	nonvernacular
nonresidual	nonsensuous	nonsustaining	nonvertical
nonresonant	nonserious	nonsymbolic	nonvesicular
nonrestricted	nonservile	nonsymmetrical	nonviable
nonretentive	nonsexual	nonsympathizer	nonvibratory
nonretiring	non-Shakespearean	nonsymphonic	nonvicarious
nonretraceable	nonsharing	nonsymptomatic	nonviolation
nonretractile	nonshattering	nonsynchronous	nonvirulent
nonretroactive	nonshrinkable	nonsyntactic	nonviscous
nonreturnable	nonshrinking	nonsynthesized	nonvisual
nonrevealing	nonsinkable	nonsystematic	nonvitreous
nonreversible	nonslaveholding	nontarnishable	nonvocal
nonrevertible	non-Slavic	nontaxable	nonvocational
nonrevolting	nonsmoker	nonteachable	nonvolatile
nonrevolving	nonsmoking	nontechnical	nonvolcanic
nonrhetorical	nonsocialist	nonterrestrial	nonvoluntary
nonrhyming	nonsolid	nonterritorial	nonwhite
nonrhythmic	nonsolvent	nontestamentary	nonworker
nonrigid	nonsovereign	nontheatrical	nonwoven
nonritualistic	non-Spanish	nontheological	nonyielding

---

fat, āpe, cär; ten, ēven; is, bīte; gō, hôrn, tōōl, look; oil, out; up, fur; get; joy; yet; chin; she; thin, then; zh, leisure; ŋ, ring; ə for a in ago, e in agent, i in sanity, o in comply, u in focus; ' as in able (ā′b'l); Fr. bal; ë, Fr. coeur; ö, Fr. feu; Fr. mon; ô, Fr. coq; ü, Fr. duc; r, Fr. cri; H, G. ich; kh, G. doch. See inside front cover. ☆ Americanism; ‡foreign; *hypothetical; < derived from

non·yl (nä′nil′, nō′-) *n.* [*non(ane)*, a paraffin hydrocarbon from which it is derived + -YL] a monovalent alkyl radical C₉H₁₉; esp., the normal radical CH₃(CH₂)₇CH₂-

noo·dle¹ (nōō′d′l) *n.* [prob. < NODDLE¹] 1. a simpleton; fool 2. [Slang] the head

☆**noo·dle²** (nōō′d′l) *n.* [G. *nudel*] a flat, narrow strip of dry dough, usually made with egg and served in soup, baked in casseroles, etc.

noo·dle³ (nōō′d′l) *vi.* -**dled, -dling** [prob. echoic var. of DOODLE] [Colloq.] 1. to play idly or improvise loosely on a musical instrument 2. to explore an idea; think something up, through, etc.

nook (nook) *n.* [ME. (chiefly Northern) *nok*, akin to Norw. *nakke*, a hook, ON. *hnekkja*, to hem in, drive back, OE. *hnecca*, the NECK] 1. a corner, esp. of a room 2. a small recess or secluded spot; retreat

noon (nōōn) *n.* [ME. < OE. *non*, orig., the ninth hour (by the Roman method, reckoning from sunrise) < L. *nona* (*hora*), ninth (hour) < *novem*, NINE] 1. twelve o'clock in the daytime; midday 2. the highest point or culmination; time of greatest power, etc. 3. [Rare or Poet.] midnight: now only in **noon of night** —*adj.* of or occurring at noon (midday)

noon·day (-dā′) *n., adj.* noon (midday)

no one no person; not anybody; nobody

noon·ing (nōōn′iŋ) *n.* [Archaic or Dial.] 1. noon (midday) ☆2. a stop at midday for rest or food 3. a meal or refreshment at noon

noon·time (-tīm′) *n., adj.* noon (midday): also **noon′tide′**

Noord·bra·bant (nōrt′brä bänt′) *Du. name of* NORTH BRABANT

Noord·hol·land (-hō′länt) *Du. name of* NORTH HOLLAND

noose (nōōs) *n.* [ME. *nose*, prob. via Pr. *nous* < L. *nodus*, knot, NODE] 1. a loop formed in a rope, cord, etc. by means of a slipknot so that the loop tightens as the rope is pulled 2. anything that restricts one's freedom; tie, bond, snare, trap, etc. —*vt.* **noosed, noos′ing** 1. to catch or hold in or as in a noose; trap, ensnare, etc. 2. to form a noose in or of (a rope, cord, etc.) —**the noose** death by hanging

Noot·ka (nōōt′kə, nōōt′-) *n. 1. pl.* **-kas, -ka** a member of a tribe of Indians who live chiefly on Vancouver Island 2. their Algonquian language

n.o.p. not otherwise provided for

no·pal (nō′pəl, nō päl′) *n.* [Sp. < Nahuatl *nopalli*] any of a genus (*Nopalea*) of cactuses with red flowers, esp. a tropical prickly pear (*Nopalea cochinellifera*) formerly grown as a host plant for the cochineal insect and for its edible fruit

no-par (nō′pär′) *adj.* having no stated par value [a *no-par* certificate of stock]

☆**nope** (nōp) *adv.* [Slang] no: a negative reply

nor¹ (nôr; *unstressed* nər) *conj.* [ME., contr. of *nother*, akin to OFris. *noer*: see NEITHER] and not; and not either: usually as the second of the correlatives *neither . . . nor*, implying negation of both parts of the statement [I can *neither* go *nor* stay]: also used after some other negative, as *not, no, never* [he doesn't smoke, *nor* does he drink], or poetically as the first in a pair or series of negative correlatives [*nor* flood *nor* fire], or to introduce a reinforcing negative after an affirmative statement [he works from dawn to dusk, *nor* does he pause for rest]

nor² (nôr) *conj.* [Northern ME.] [Dial.] than

nor′, nor (nôr) north: used especially in compounds [*nor′western*]

nor- (nôr) [< NOR(MAL)] *Chem. a combining form meaning normal:* used to indicate a parent compound from which another compound may be regarded as derived [*norepinephrine*]

Nor. 1. Norman 2. North 3. Norway 4. Norwegian

No·ra (nôr′ə) [Ir., contr. of *Honora, Eleanor, Leonora*] a feminine name: see ELEANOR, LEONORA

Nor·dau (nôr′dou), **Max Simon** (born *Max Simon Südfeld*) 1849–1923; Ger. writer, physician, & Zionist leader, born in Hungary

Nor·den·skjöld (noor′dən shüld′), **Baron Nils A·dolf E·rik** (nils ä′dôlf ā′rik) 1832–1901; Swed. arctic explorer, born in Finland

Nor·den·skjöld Sea (noor′dən shüld′) *former name of* LAPTEV SEA

Nor·dic (nôr′dik) *adj.* [ModL. *Nordicus* < Fr. *nordique* < *nord*, north < OE. *north*, NORTH] designating or of a physical type of the Caucasoid peoples exemplified by the long-headed, tall, blond people of Scandinavia: see also ALPINE, MEDITERRANEAN

Nord·kyn (nôr′kün′), **Cape** cape in NE Norway: northernmost point of the European mainland

nor·ep·i·neph·rine (nôr′ep′ə nef′rin, -rēn) *n.* [see NOR-] a hormone, C₈H₁₁NO₃, related to epinephrine: it is secreted by the adrenal medulla, assists in transmitting nerve impulses, and is used medically to constrict blood vessels and to stop bleeding

Nor·folk (nôr′fək) 1. [after the ff.] seaport in SE Va., on Hampton Roads & Chesapeake Bay: pop. 308,000 (met. area, incl. adjacent Portsmouth, 681,000) 2. county of E England, on the North Sea: 2,054 sq. mi.; pop. 569,000; county seat, Norwich

Norfolk Island Australian island in the SW Pacific, east of New South Wales: 13 sq. mi.; pop. c. 1,000

Norfolk Island pine an evergreen tree (*Araucaria excelsa*) with small needles and branches arranged in regular whorls, commonly grown as a pot plant or outdoors in warm climates

Norfolk jacket (or **coat**) a loose-fitting, single-breasted, belted jacket with a pocket on each side and box pleats in front and back

Nor·ge (nôr′gə) *Norw. name of* NORWAY

no·ri·a (nôr′ē ə) *n.* [Sp. < Ar. *nā′ūrah*] a water wheel with buckets at its circumference, used in Spain and the Orient to raise and discharge water

Nor·i·cum (nôr′i kəm) ancient Rom. province south of the Danube, in the region of modern Austria

norm (nôrm) *n.* [L. *norma*, carpenter's square, rule, prob. via Etruscan < Gr. *gnōmōn*, carpenter's square, lit., one that knows: see GNOMON] a standard, model, or pattern for a group; esp., *a*) such a standard of achievement as represented by the median or average achievement of a large group *b*) a standard of conduct that should or must be followed *c*) a way of behaving typical of a certain group —*SYN.* see AVERAGE

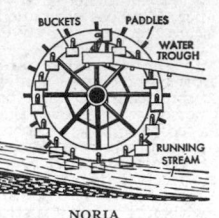

NORIA

Norm. Norman

Nor·ma (nôr′mə) 1. [< ? L. *norma*: see NORM] a feminine name 2. [L.: see NORM] a S constellation in the Milky Way between Lupus and Ara

nor·mal (nôr′m′l) *adj.* [L. *normalis* < *norma*, a rule: see NORM] 1. conforming with or constituting an accepted standard, model, or pattern; esp., corresponding to the median or average of a large group in type, appearance, achievement, function, development, etc.; natural; usual; standard; regular 2. *Biol.* occurring naturally [*normal* immunity] 3. *Chem. a*) designating or of a salt formed by replacing all the replaceable hydrogen of an acid with a metal or metals *b*) designating or of a solution which contains an amount of the dissolved substance chemically equivalent to one gram atom of hydrogen per liter of solution *c*) designating or of a fatty hydrocarbon, the chain of which is continuous rather than branched, in which no carbon atom is united directly to more than two others 4. *Math.* perpendicular; at right angles 5. *Med., Psychol. a*) free from disease, disorder, or malformation; specif., average in intelligence or development *b*) mentally sound —*n.* 1. anything normal 2. the usual state, amount, degree, etc.; esp., the median or average 3. *Math.* a perpendicular; esp., a perpendicular to a line tangent to a curve, at its point of tangency —**nor′mal·cy** (-sē), **nor·mal′i·ty** (-mal′ə tē) *n.*

SYN.—**normal** implies conformity with the established norm or standard for its kind [*normal* intelligence]; **regular** implies conformity with the prescribed rule or accepted pattern for its kind [the *regular* working day]; **typical** applies to that which has the representative characteristics of its type or class [a *typical* Southern town]; **natural** implies behavior, operation, etc. that conforms with the nature or innate character of the person or thing [a *natural* comedian]; **usual** applies to that which conforms to the common or ordinary use or occurrence [the *usual* price]; **average**, in this connection, implies conformity with what is regarded as normal or ordinary [the *average* man] —*ANT.* abnormal, unusual

normal distribution *Statistics* a frequency distribution whose graphical representation is a bell-shaped curve symmetrical about the mean

normal (frequency) curve *same as* GAUSSIAN CURVE

nor·mal·ize (nôr′mə līz′) *vt.* -**ized′, -iz′ing** to make normal; specif., *a*) to bring to the natural, or usual, state *b*) to bring into conformity with a standard, pattern, model, etc. —*vi.* to become normal —**nor′mal·i·za′tion** *n.* —**nor′mal·iz′er** *n.*

nor·mal·ly (-lē) *adv.* 1. in a normal manner 2. under normal circumstances; ordinarily

normal school [after Fr. *école normale*] esp. formerly, a school for training high-school graduates, usually in a two-year program, to become teachers

normal state *same as* GROUND STATE

Nor·man¹ (nôr′mən) [< OE. *Northman*, OHG. *Nordemann*, lit., Northman] 1. a masculine name: dim. *Norm* 2. [ult. after Aubrey *Norman*, railroad surveyor] city in C Okla., near Oklahoma City: pop. 52,000

Nor·man² (nôr′mən) *n.* [ME. < OFr. *Normant* or ML. *Normannus*, both < Frank. **nortman* < **nort*, akin to OE. *north*, NORTH + **man*, akin to MAN] 1. any of the Scandinavians who occupied Normandy in the 10th cent. A.D. 2. a descendant of the Normans and French who conquered England in 1066 3. *same as* NORMAN FRENCH 4. a native or inhabitant of Normandy —*adj.* 1. of Normandy, the Normans, their language, or culture 2. designating or of the Romanesque style of architecture as it flourished in Normandy and, after the Norman Conquest, as developed in England: characterized by massive construction, round arches over recessed doors and windows, and carving —**Nor′man·esque′** (-esk′) *adj.*

Norman Conquest the conquest of England by the Normans under William the Conqueror in 1066

Nor·man·dy (nôr′mən dē) region & former province in NW France, on the English Channel: chief city, Rouen

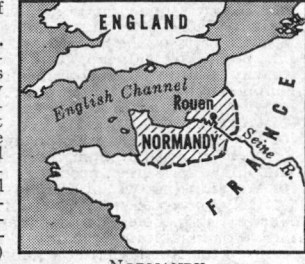

NORMANDY

Norman French 1. the French of the Normans or Normandy, as spoken in England by the Norman conquerors; Anglo-French: it was not imposed on the English as an official language at the Conquest, but gained legal and administrative currency after the accession of Eleanor of Aquitaine as queen (1152) **2.** the form of this language used as the legal jargon of England until the late 17th cent. **3.** the modern French dialect of Normandy —**Nor′man-French′** *adj.*

Nor·man·ize (nôr′mə nīz′) *vi., vt.* **-ized′, -iz′ing** to make or become Norman in style, character, language, customs, law, etc.

norm·a·tive (nôr′mə tiv) *adj.* **1.** of or establishing a norm, or standard **2.** having to do with usage norms [*normative* grammar] —**norm′a·tive·ly** *adv.*

Norn (nôrn) *n.* [ON. *nor n* < IE. base *(s)ner-, *(s)nur-, to snarl, mutter, whence SNEER, ME. *nyrnen*, to utter] *Norse Myth.* any of three goddesses, representing the past, present, and future, who determine the destiny of gods and men

Nor·ris (nôr′is, när′-) **1. Frank**, (born *Benjamin Franklin Norris, Jr.*) 1870–1902; U.S. novelist **2. George William**, 1861–1944; U.S. senator (1913–43)

Nor·ris·town (nôr′is toun′) [after Isaac *Norris* (1671–1736), local landowner] city in SE Pa., on the Schuylkill River: suburb of Philadelphia: pop. 38,000

Norr·kö·ping (nôr′chö′piŋ) seaport in SE Sweden, on an inlet of the Baltic Sea: pop. 94,000

Norse (nôrs) *adj.* [prob. < Du. *Noorsch*, a Norwegian, var. of *Noordsch* < *noord*, NORTH + -*sch*, -ISH] **1.** *same as* SCANDINAVIAN **2.** West Scandinavian (Norwegian, Icelandic, and Faroese) —*n.* **1.** the Scandinavian group of languages **2.** the West Scandinavian group of languages **3.** *same as* NORWEGIAN See OLD NORSE, ICELANDIC —**the Norse 1.** the Scandinavians **2.** the West Scandinavians

Norse·man (-mən) *n., pl.* **-men** (-mən) a member of the ancient Scandinavian people; Northman

north (nôrth) *n.* [ME. < ON. *noord*, G. *nord*, ON. *northr* < IE. base *ner-*, beneath, below, whence Gr. *nerteros*, lower] **1.** the direction to the right of a person facing the sunset; direction of the North Pole from any other point on the earth's surface: the needle of a compass points to the *magnetic north pole* rather than to the geographic pole **2.** the point on a compass at 0° or 360°, directly opposite south **3.** a region or district in or toward this direction **4.** [*often* N-] the northern part of the earth, esp. the arctic regions —*adj.* **1.** in, of, to, toward, or facing the north **2.** from the north [a *north* wind] **3.** [N-] designating the northern part of a continent, country, etc. [*North Africa*] —*adv.* in or toward the north; in a northerly direction —**the North** ☆that part of the U.S. which is bounded on the south by Maryland, the Ohio River, and Missouri; specif., the States opposed to the Confederacy in the Civil War

North, Frederick, 2d Earl of Guilford; 1732–92; Eng. statesman; prime minister of Great Britain (1770–82): called *Lord North*

North America N continent in the Western Hemisphere: c. 9,330,000 sq. mi. (excl. adjacent islands, c. 8,400,000); pop. 312,000,000 —**North American**

North·amp·ton (nôr thamp′tən) **1.** *same as* NORTHAMPTONSHIRE **2.** county seat of Northamptonshire: pop. 105,000

North·amp·ton·shire (-shir′) county of C England: 914 sq. mi.; pop. 411,000; county seat, Northampton

Northants. Northamptonshire

North Babylon [prob. ult. after BABYLON] suburb of New York City, on E Long Island: pop. 40,000

North Borneo *former name of* SABAH

☆**north·bound** (-bound′) *adj.* bound north; going northward

North Brabant province of the S Netherlands, between the Meuse River & the Belgian border: 1,903 sq. mi.; pop. 1,671,000; cap. 's Hertogenbosch

north by east the direction, or the point on a mariner's compass, halfway between due north and north-northeast; 11°15′ east of due north

north by west the direction, or the point on a mariner's compass, halfway between due north and north-northwest; 11°15′ west of due north

North Canadian River river flowing from NE N.Mex. east & southeast into the Canadian River in E Okla.: 760 mi.

North Carolina [see CAROLINA] Southern State of the SE U.S.: one of the 13 original States; 52,712 sq. mi.; pop. 5,082,000; cap. Raleigh: abbrev. **N.C., NC** —**North Carolinian**

North Cascades National Park national park in the N Cascade Range, N Wash.: 789 sq. mi.

North Channel strait between Northern Ireland & SW Scotland: c. 80 mi. long

North Chicago city in NE Ill., on Lake Michigan: suburb of Chicago: pop. 47,000

North·cliffe (nôrth′klif), Viscount, (*Alfred Charles William Harmsworth*) 1865–1922; Eng. newspaper publisher, born in Ireland

North Dakota [see DAKOTA] Middle Western State of the NC U.S.: admitted, 1889; 70,665 sq. mi.; pop. 618,000; cap. Bismarck: abbrev. **N.Dak., ND** —**North Dakotan**

North Downs *see* THE DOWNS (at entry DOWN³)

north·east (nôrth′ēst′; *in nautical usage*, nôr-) *n.* **1.** the direction, or the point on a mariner's compass, halfway between north and east; 45° east of due north **2.** a region or district in or toward this direction —*adj.* **1.** in, of, to, toward, or facing the northeast **2.** from the northeast, as a wind —*adv.* in, toward, or from the northeast —☆**the Northeast** the northeastern part of the U.S., esp. New England, but sometimes including New York City and its environs

northeast by east the direction, or the point on a mariner's compass, halfway between northeast and east-northeast; 11°15′ east of northeast

northeast by north the direction, or the point on a mariner's compass, halfway between northeast and north-northeast; 11°15′ north of northeast

☆**north·east·er** (nôrth′ēs′tər; *in nautical usage*, nôr-) *n.* a storm or strong wind from the northeast

north·east·er·ly (-tər lē) *adj., adv.* **1.** in or toward the northeast **2.** from the northeast [a *northeasterly* wind]

north·east·ern (-tərn) *adj.* **1.** in, of, or toward the northeast **2.** from the northeast [a *northeastern* wind] ☆**3.** [N-] of or characteristic of the Northeast or New England —**North′east′ern·er** *n.*

North East Frontier Agency (or **Tract**) territory of NE India, on the border of Tibet, administered as part of Assam state: 31,438 sq. mi.; pop. 337,000

North-East New Guinea NE section of the island of New Guinea (see NEW GUINEA): 70,200 sq. mi.

Northeast Passage water route from the Atlantic to the Pacific through the seas north of Europe & Asia

north·east·ward (nôrth′ēst′wərd; *in nautical usage*, nôr-) *adv., adj.* toward the northeast —*n.* a northeastward direction, point, or region

north·east·ward·ly (-wərd lē) *adj., adv.* **1.** toward the northeast **2.** from the northeast, as a wind

north·east·wards (-wərdz) *adv. same as* NORTHEASTWARD

☆**north·er** (nôr′thər) *n.* a storm or strong wind from the north; esp., such a wind in the area of or about the Gulf of Mexico or of the Southwestern plains

north·er·ly (-lē) *adj.* **1.** in, of, or toward the north **2.** from the north [a *northerly* wind] —*adv.* **1.** toward the north **2.** from the north

north·ern (nôr′thərn) *adj.* [ME. *northerne* < OE. *northerna*] **1.** in, of, toward, or facing the north **2.** from the north [a *northern* wind] **3.** [N-] of or characteristic of the North ☆**4.** [N-] designating a dialect area of American English, including New England, New York, N New Jersey and Pennsylvania, the N counties of Ohio, Indiana, Illinois, Iowa, and South Dakota, and Michigan, Wisconsin, Minnesota, and North Dakota

Northern Cross six stars in Cygnus forming a cross

Northern Crown *same as* CORONA BOREALIS

Northern Dvina *see* DVINA

north·ern·er (nôr′thər nər, -thə nər) *n.* **1.** a native or inhabitant of the north ☆**2.** [N-] a native or inhabitant of the northern part of the U.S.

Northern Hemisphere that half of the earth north of the equator

Northern Ireland division of the United Kingdom, in the NE part of the island of Ireland: 5,462 sq. mi.; pop. 1,487,000; cap. Belfast

northern lights *same as* AURORA BOREALIS

north·ern·most (nôr′thərn mōst′) *adj.* farthest north

Northern Rhodesia *former name of* ZAMBIA

Northern Sporades group of islands in the NW Aegean, included in the Gr. provinces of Thessaly & Euboea

☆**Northern Spy** a yellowish-red winter apple

Northern Territory territory of N Australia, on the Arafura Sea: 523,620 sq. mi.; pop. 55,000; cap. Darwin

North Holland province of the W Netherlands, on the North Sea: 1,038 sq. mi.; pop. 2,181,000; cap. Haarlem

north·ing (nôr′thiŋ, -thin) *n.* **1.** northerly movement **2.** the distance covered sailing or traveling northward

North Island N island of the two main islands of New Zealand: 44,297 sq. mi.; pop. 1,894,000

north·land (nôrth′land′, -lənd) *n.* [*also* N-] **1.** the northern region of a country **2.** land in the north **3.** the Scandinavian Peninsula —**north′land′er** *n.*

North Las Vegas city in SE Nev.: suburb of Las Vegas: pop. 36,000

North Little Rock city in C Ark., on the Arkansas River opposite Little Rock; pop. 60,000

North·man (-mən) *n., pl.* **-men** (-mən) [OE. *Northmanna:* see NORTH & MAN] *same as* NORSEMAN

North Miami city on the SE coast of Fla.: suburb of Miami: pop. 35,000

north-north·east (nôrth′nôrth′ēst′; *in nautical usage,* nôr′nôr-) *n.* the direction, or the point on a mariner's compass, halfway between due north and northeast; 22°30′ east of due north —*adj., adv.* **1.** in or toward this direction **2.** from this direction, as a wind

north-north·west (-west′) *n.* the direction, or the point on a mariner's compass, halfway between due north and northwest; 22°30′ west of due north —*adj., adv.* **1.** in or toward this direction **2.** from this direction, as a wind

North Platte river flowing from N Colo. north into Wyo. & then southeast through W Nebr., joining the South Platte to form the Platte: 618 mi.

North Pole 1. the northern end of the earth's axis: its zenith (called the **north pole of the heavens**) is slightly more than 1° from Polaris, the North Star **2.** [n- p-] that end of a straight magnet that points to the north when the magnet hangs free

North Rhine-West·pha·li·a (rīn′west fā′lē ə, -fāl′yə) state of W West Germany: 13,119 sq. mi.; pop. 16,735,000; cap. Düsseldorf

North Riding administrative division of Yorkshire county, NE England: 2,128 sq. mi.; pop. 571,000

North River lower course of the Hudson River, between New York City & NE N.J.

North Saskatchewan river flowing from SW Alberta east through Saskatchewan, joining the South Saskatchewan to form the Saskatchewan: 760 mi.

North Sea arm of the Atlantic, between Great Britain & the N European mainland: c. 222,000 sq. mi.

North Star Polaris, the bright star almost directly above the northern end of the earth's axis; polestar

North Ton·a·wan·da (tän′ə wän′də) [after *Tonawanda,* Seneca form of Iroquoian stream name] city in W N.Y., on the Niagara River: suburb of Buffalo: pop. 36,000

North·um·ber·land (nôr thum′bər lənd) northernmost county of England: 2,019 sq. mi.; pop. 826,000; county seat, Newcastle-upon-Tyne:abbrev. **North., Northumb.**

North·um·bri·a (nôr thum′brē ə) former Anglo-Saxon kingdom in Great Britain, between the Humber estuary & the Firth of Forth

North·um·bri·an (-ən) *adj.* **1.** of Northumbria, its people, or their dialect **2.** of Northumberland, its people, or their dialect —*n.* **1.** a native or inhabitant of Northumbria **2.** the Old English dialect of Northumbria **3.** a native or inhabitant of Northumberland **4.** the modern English dialect of Northumberland

north·ward (nôrth′wərd; *in nautical usage,* nôr′thərd) *adv., adj.* toward the north —*n.* a northward direction, point, or region

north·ward·ly (-lē) *adj., adv.* **1.** toward the north **2.** from the north [a *northwardly* wind]

north·wards (-wərdz) *adv. same as* NORTHWARD

north·west (nôrth′west′; *in nautical usage,* nôr-) *n.* **1.** the direction, or the point on a mariner's compass, halfway between north and west; 45° west of due north **2.** a district or region in or toward this direction —*adj.* **1.** in, of, toward, or facing the northwest **2.** from the northwest [a *northwest* wind] —*adv.* in, toward, or from the northwest —☆the Northwest **1.** *same as* NORTHWEST TERRITORY **2.** the northwestern part of the U.S. esp. Wash., Oreg., and Ida. **3.** the northwestern part of Canada

northwest by north the direction, or the point on a mariner's compass, halfway between northwest and north-northwest; 11°15′ north of northwest

northwest by west the direction, or the point on a mariner's compass, halfway between northwest and west-northwest; 11°15′ west of northwest

north·west·er (nôrth′wes′tər; *in nautical usage,* nôr-) *n.* a storm or strong wind from the northwest

north·west·er·ly (-tər lē) *adj., adv.* **1.** in or toward the northwest **2.** from the northwest [a *northwesterly* wind]

north·west·ern (-tərn) *adj.* **1.** in, of, or toward the northwest **2.** from the northwest [a *northwestern* wind] ☆**3.** [N-] of or characteristic of the Northwest —**North′-west′ern·er** *n.*

Northwest Passage water route from the Atlantic to the Pacific, through the arctic islands of Canada

Northwest Territories division of N Canada, subdivided into the Districts of Mackenzie, Keewatin, & Franklin: 1,304,903 sq. mi.; pop. 29,000; cap. Yellowknife: abbrev. **N.W.T.**

☆**Northwest Territory** region north of the Ohio River, between Pa. & the Mississippi (established 1787): it now forms Ohio, Ind., Ill., Mich., Wis., & part of Minn.

north·west·ward (nôrth′west′wərd; *in nautical usage,* nôr-) *adv., adj.* toward the northwest —*n.* a northwestward direction, point, or region

north·west·ward·ly (-wərd lē) *adj., adv.* **1.** toward the northwest **2.** from the northwest, as a wind

north·west·wards (-wərdz) *adv. same as* NORTHWESTWARD

Norw. 1. Norway **2.** Norwegian

Nor·walk (nôr′wôk′) **1.** [prob. after ff.] city in SW Calif.: suburb of Los Angeles: pop. 92,000 **2.** [< AmInd. < ?] city in SW Conn., on Long Island Sound: pop. 79,000

Nor·way (nôr′wā′) country in N Europe, occupying the W & N parts of the Scandinavian Peninsula: 125,064 sq. mi.; pop. 3,769,000; cap. Oslo: Norw. name, NORGE

Norway maple a European maple (*Acer platanoides*), commonly grown in the U.S. for shade

Norway pine *same as* RED PINE

Norway rat *see* RAT

Norway spruce a common, evergreen, ornamental spruce (*Picea abies*) with drooping branchlets, large, brown cones, and shiny, dark-green needles

Nor·we·gian (nôr wē′jən) *adj.* [< ML. *Norwegia,* Norway (< ON. *Norvegr < northr,* NORTH + *vegr,* WAY) + -AN] of Norway, its people, their language, or culture —*n.* **1.** a native or inhabitant of Norway **2.** either of two official forms of the North Germanic language of the Norwegians, one ("Book Language") derived from Danish, or the other ("New Norwegian") created c. 1850 from Norwegian dialects

Norwegian elkhound any of a Norwegian breed of medium-sized dog with a short, compact body, a thick, gray coat, and a tail that curves over the back

Norwegian Sea part of the Atlantic between Norway & Iceland

Nor·wich (nôr′ij, -ich; när′-; *for 2* -wich) **1.** county seat of Norfolk, E England: known for its cathedral (founded 1096): pop. 119,000 **2.** [after prec.] city in SE Conn.: pop. 41,000

Nos., nos. numbers

n.o.s. not otherwise specified

nose (nōz) *n.* [ME. < OE. *nosu,* akin to G. *nase,* orig. a dual, meaning "the two nostrils" < IE. base *nas-,* nostril, whence Sans. *nāsā,* the nose, lit., pair of nostrils, L. *nasus,* nose & *naris,* nostril] **1.** the part of the human face between the mouth and the eyes, having two openings and cavities behind them for breathing and smelling **2.** the part that corresponds to this in animals; snout, muzzle, etc. **3.** the sense of smell **4.** the power of tracking or perceiving by or as if by scent [a *nose* for news] **5.** anything resembling a nose in shape or position; projecting or foremost part, as a nozzle, spout, prow of a ship, front of an airplane, etc. **6.** the nose regarded as a symbol of prying or meddling [to poke one's *nose* into another's affairs] **7.** [Slang] a police spy or informer —*vt.* **nosed, nos′ing 1.** to discover or perceive by or as if by the sense of smell **2.** to touch or rub with the nose **3.** to push with the nose (with *aside, open,* etc.) **4.** to make or push (a way, etc.) with the front forward [the ship *nosed* its way into the harbor] —*vi.* **1.** to smell; sniff **2.** to pry inquisitively **3.** to advance; move forward —☆**by a nose 1.** by the length of the animal's nose in horse racing, etc. **2.** by a very small margin —**count noses** to count the number of people present, voting, etc. —**cut off one's nose to spite one's face** to injure one's own interests, in a fit of anger, resentment, etc. —**follow one's nose** to go straight forward —**lead by the nose** to dominate completely —**look down one's nose at** [Colloq.] to be disdainful of —**nose out 1.** to defeat by a very small margin **2.** to discover, as by smelling —**nose over** to turn over on its nose: said of an airplane moving on the ground —**on the nose** [Slang] **1.** that (a specified horse, etc.) will finish first in a race **2.** precisely; exactly —**pay through the nose** to pay an unreasonable price —**put someone's nose out of joint 1.** to replace someone in another's affection, regard, etc. **2.** to ruin one's plans, hopes, etc. —**turn up one's nose at** to sneer at; scorn —**under one's (very) nose** in plain view

nose bag *same as* FEED BAG

nose·band (nōz′band′) *n.* that part of a bridle or halter which passes over the animal's nose

nose·bleed (-blēd′) *n.* a bleeding from the nose; nasal hemorrhage; epistaxis

nose cone the cone-shaped foremost part of a rocket or missile, usually housing the payload, instruments, etc. and made to withstand intense heat

nose dive 1. a swift, steep downward plunge of an airplane, with the nose toward the earth **2.** any sudden, sharp drop, as in profits or prices —**nose′-dive′** *vi.* **-dived′, -div′ing**

nose drops medication administered through the nose with a dropper

☆**no-see-um** (nō sē′əm) *n.* [pseudo-AmInd. term, altered < *no see (th)em:* in reference to its very small size] *same as* BITING MIDGE

nose·gay (nōz′gā′) *n.* [NOSE + GAY (in obs. sense of "gay object")] a bunch of flowers; small bouquet, esp. for carrying in the hand

nose·piece (-pēs′) *n.* **1.** that part of a helmet which covers and protects the nose **2.** *same as* NOSEBAND **3.** anything like a nose in form or position, as the nozzle of a hose or lower end of a microscope **4.** the bridge of a pair of eyeglasses

nose ring 1. a metal ring passed through the nose of an animal for leading it about **2.** a ring of bone or metal worn in the nose as an ornament

nos·ey (nō′zē) *adj.* **nos′i·er, nos′i·est** *same as* NOSY

nosh (näsh) *vt., vi.* [< Yid. < G. *naschen,* to nibble, taste] [Slang] to eat (a snack) —*n.* [Slang] a snack —**nosh′er** *n.*

☆**no-show** (nō′shō′) *n.* [Colloq.] a person who makes a reservation, as for an airline flight, but fails to claim or cancel it

nos·ing (nō′ziŋ) *n.* [NOSE + -ING] **1.** the projecting edge of a step; that part of the tread which extends beyond the riser **2.** a strip, as of metal, for protecting this edge from wear **3.** any projection like a stair nosing

nos·o- (nō′sō) [< Gr. *nosos*, disease] *a combining form meaning* disease [*nosology*]: also, before a vowel, **nos-**

no·sog·ra·phy (nō säg′rə fē) *n.* [prec. + -GRAPHY] the systematic description of diseases

no·sol·o·gy (nō säl′ə jē) *n.* [ModL. *nosologia:* see NOSO- & -LOGY] **1.** classification of diseases **2.** the branch of medicine dealing with this —**nos·o·log·ic** (näs′ə läj′ik), **nos′o·log′i·cal** *adj.* —**nos′o·log′i·cal·ly** *adv.*

nos·tal·gia (näs tal′jə, nəs-, nôs-; -jē ə) *n.* [ModL. < Gr. *nostos*, a return + -ALGIA] **1.** a longing to go back to one's home, home town, or homeland; homesickness **2.** a longing for something far away or long ago or for former happy circumstances —**nos·tal′gic** (-jik) *adj.* —**nos·tal′gi·cal·ly** *adv.*

nos·toc (näs′täk) *n.* [ModL., coined by Paracelsus] any of a genus (*Nostoc*) of blue-green algae, having twisted, coiled filaments embedded in a gelatinous material and forming spherical colonies

nos·tol·o·gy (näs täl′ə jē) *n.* [< Gr. *nostos*, a return + -LOGY] *earlier term for* GERONTOLOGY —**nos′to·log′ic** (-tə läj′ik) *adj.*

nos·to·ma·ni·a (näs′tə mā′nē ə, -mān′yə) *n.* [ModL. < Gr. *nostos*, a return + -MANIA] *Psychiatry* excessive or abnormal nostalgia

Nos·tra·da·mus (näs′trə dā′məs, nō′strə dä′məs) (born *Michel de Notredame*) 1503–66; Fr. astrologer

nos·tril (näs′trəl) *n.* [ME. *nosethirl* < OE. *nosthyrl* < *nos*, for *nosu*, the nose + *thyrel*, a hole < *thurh*, through: see NOSE & THROUGH] **1.** either of the external openings of the nose **2.** the fleshy wall on either side of the nose [with flaring *nostrils*]

nos·trum (näs′trəm) *n.* [L., neut. of *noster*, ours: ? so called from the seller's calling it "our" remedy] **1.** *a)* a medicine prepared by the person selling it *b)* a patent medicine of a kind sold with exaggerated claims; quack medicine **2.** a pet scheme for solving some social or political problem; panacea

nos·y (nō′zē) *adj.* **nos′i·er, nos′i·est** [NOS(E) + -Y²] [Colloq.] given to prying; inquisitive —**nos′i·ly** *adv.* —**nos′i·ness** *n.*

Nosy Parker (pär′kər) [NOSY + proper name *Parker:* reason for use uncertain] [*also* **n- p-, n- P-**] [Colloq.] a nosy person; busybody

not (nät) *adv.* [ME. *not*, unstressed form of *noht, nought, naught:* see NOUGHT] in no manner; to no degree: a particle of negation, or word expressing the idea of *no*, often implying refusal, affirmation of the opposite, etc.: sometimes used elliptically [whether you like it or *not*]

not- (nōt) *same as* NOTO-: used before a vowel

‡**no·ta·be·ne** (nō′tə be′nē, nō′tä be′nä) [L.] note well; take particular notice

no·ta·bil·i·a (-bil′ē ə, -bil′yə) *n.pl.* [L., neut. pl. of *notabilis:* see ff.] things worthy of notice

no·ta·bil·i·ty (nōt′ə bil′ə tē) *n.* **1.** *pl.* **-ties** a person who is notable or prominent **2.** the quality of being notable

no·ta·ble (nōt′ə b'l; *for adj. 2, also* nāt′-) *adj.* [ME. < OFr. < L. *notabilis* < *notare*, to mark, note < *nota*, a mark: see NOTE] **1.** worthy of notice; remarkable; outstanding **2.** [Archaic] industrious and capable, as in housekeeping —*n.* **1.** a person of distinction; famous or well-known person **2.** [N-] formerly in France, any of the persons of authority, rank, etc. summoned by the king as a deliberative assembly in emergencies —**no′ta·bly** *adv.*

no·tar·i·al (nō ter′ē əl) *adj.* **1.** of or characteristic of a notary public **2.** drawn up or executed by a notary public —**no·tar′i·al·ly** *adv.*

☆**no·ta·rize** (nōt′ə rīz′) *vt.* **-rized′, -riz′ing** to certify or attest (a document) as a notary public, esp. with a signature seal —**no′ta·ri·za′tion** *n.*

no·ta·ry (nōt′ər ē) *n., pl.* **-ries** [ME. *notarye* < OFr. *notaire* < L. *notarius* < *notare*, to NOTE] *clipped form of* NOTARY PUBLIC

notary public *pl.* **notaries public, notary publics** an official authorized to certify or attest documents, take depositions and affidavits, etc.

no·ta·tion (nō tā′shən) *n.* [L. *notatio* < *notare*, to NOTE] **1.** the use of a system of signs or symbols to represent words, phrases, numbers, quantities, etc. **2.** any such system of signs or symbols, as in mathematics, chemistry, music, etc. **3.** a brief note jotted down, as to remind one of something, explain something, etc. **4.** the act of noting something in writing —**no·ta′tion·al** *adj.*

notch (näch) *n.* [prob. by syllabic merging of ME. *an oche* < OFr. *oche, osche*, a notch < *oschier*, to notch] **1.** a concave or V-shaped cut or indentation in an edge or across a surface ☆**2.** a narrow pass with steep sides; defile; gap **3.** [Colloq.] a step; grade; degree; peg [a *notch* below average] —*vt.* **1.** to cut a notch or notches in; indent with notches **2.** to record or tally, as by means of notches —**notched** *adj.* —**notch′er** *n.*

note (nōt) *n.* [ME. < OFr. < L. *nota*, a mark, sign, character, letter < *notus*, pp. of *noscere*, to know < *gnoscere:* for IE. base see KNOW] **1.** a mark of some quality, condition, or fact; distinguishing or characteristic feature, mood, tone, etc. [a *note* of sadness] **2.** importance, distinction, or eminence [a person of *note*] **3.** *a)* a brief statement of a fact, experience, etc. written down for review, as an aid to memory, or to inform someone else; memorandum *b)* [*pl.*] a record of experiences, etc. [the *notes* of a journey] **4.** a comment, explanation, or elucidation, as at the foot of a page; annotation **5.** notice; heed; observation [worthy of *note*] **6.** any of certain types of correspondence; specif., *a)* a short, informal letter *b)* a formal diplomatic or other official communication **7.** *a)* any of certain commercial papers, some of which are negotiable, relating to the owing of debts or payment of money [a promissory *note*] *b)* a piece of paper currency [a Federal Reserve *note*] **8.** a cry or call, as of a bird **9.** a signal or intimation [a *note* of admonition] **10.** [Archaic or Poet.] a melody, tune, or song **11.** *Music a)* a tone of definite pitch, as made by a voice or musical instrument *b)* a symbol for a tone, indicating the duration by its form and the pitch by its position on the staff *c)* a key of a piano or the like —*vt.* **not′ed, not′ing** [ME. *noten* < OFr. *noter* < L. *notare* < *nota*] **1.** to pay close attention to; heed; notice; observe **2.** to set down in writing; make a note of **3.** to mention particularly **4.** to denote, signify, or indicate **5.** to set down in musical notes —**compare notes** to exchange views; discuss —**strike the right note** to say, write, or do what is specially apt or pleasing —**take notes** to write down notes, as during a lecture or interview, for later reference

NOTES
(A, whole; B, half; C, quarter; D, eighth; E, sixteenth; F, thirty-second; G, sixty-fourth)

note·book (nōt′book′) *n.* a book in which notes, or memorandums, are kept

note·case (-kās′) *n.* [Brit.] *same as* BILLFOLD

not·ed (nōt′id) *adj.* distinguished; well-known; renowned; eminent —*SYN.* see FAMOUS —**not′ed·ly** *adv.* —**not′ed·ness** *n.*

note·less (nōt′lis) *adj.* **1.** not noted; unnoticed; undistinguished **2.** unmusical

note of hand *same as* PROMISSORY NOTE

note paper paper for writing notes, or letters

note·wor·thy (-wur′thē) *adj.* worthy of note; deserving notice; outstanding; remarkable; notable —**note′wor′thi·ly** *adv.* —**note′wor′thi·ness** *n.*

noth·ing (nuth′iŋ) *n.* [ME. < OE. *na thing, nan thing*] **1.** *a)* no thing; not anything; nought *b)* no part, element, trace, etc. [*nothing* of kindness in him] **2.** *a)* nonexistence; nothingness *b)* insignificance; unimportance **3.** a thing that does not exist **4.** *a)* something of little or no value, seriousness, importance, etc.; triviality or trifle *b)* a person considered of no value or importance **5.** a nought; zero; cipher —*adv.* not at all; in no manner or degree [*nothing* daunted] —**for nothing 1.** free; at no cost **2.** in vain; uselessly **3.** without reason —☆**have nothing on** to have no implicating evidence, information, etc. about —☆**in nothing flat** [Colloq.] in almost no time at all —**make nothing of 1.** to treat as of little importance **2.** to fail to understand —**nothing but** only; nothing other than —**nothing doing** [Colloq.] **1.** no: used as a refusal of a request **2.** no result, accomplishment, etc.: an exclamation of disappointment —**nothing less than** no less than; just the same as: also **nothing short of** —**think nothing of 1.** to attach no importance to **2.** to regard as easy to do

noth·ing·ness (-nis) *n.* **1.** the quality or condition of being nothing or not existing; nonexistence or extinction **2.** lack of value, worth, meaning, etc.; uselessness, insignificance, etc. **3.** unconsciousness or death **4.** anything that is nonexistent, worthless, insignificant, useless, etc.

no·tice (nōt′is) *n.* [LME. < MFr. < L. *notitia < notus:* see NOTE] **1.** information, announcement, or warning; esp., formal announcement or warning, as in a newspaper [a legal *notice*] **2.** a brief mention or critical review of a work of art, book, play, etc. **3.** a written or printed sign giving some public information, warning, or rule **4.** *a)* the act of observing; attention; regard; heed; cognizance *b)* courteous attention; civility **5.** a formal announcement or warning of intention to end an agreement, relation, or contract at a certain time [to give a tenant *notice*] —*vt.* **-ticed, -tic·ing 1.** *a)* to mention; refer to; comment on *b)* to review briefly **2.** *a)* to regard; observe; pay attention to *b)* to be courteous or responsive to **3.** [Rare] to serve with a formal notice —*SYN.* see DISCERN —**serve notice** to give formal warning or information, as of intentions; announce —**take notice** to become aware; pay attention; observe

no·tice·a·ble (-ə b'l) *adj.* 1. readily noticed; conspicuous 2. worth noticing; significant —**no'tice·a·bly** *adv.*
SYN.—**noticeable** is applied to that which must inevitably be noticed [a *noticeable* coolness in his manner]; **remarkable** applies to that which is noticeable because it is unusual or exceptional [*remarkable* beauty]; **prominent** refers to that which literally or figuratively stands out from its background [a *prominent* nose, a *prominent* author]; an **outstanding** person or thing is remarkable as compared with others of its kind [an *outstanding* sculptor]; **conspicuous** applies to that which is so obvious or manifest as to be immediately perceptible [*conspicuous* gallantry]; **striking** is used of something so out of the ordinary that it leaves a sharp impression on the mind [a *striking* epigram]

no·ti·fi·a·ble (nōt'ə fī'ə b'l) *adj.* that must be reported to health authorities [*notifiable* diseases]

no·ti·fi·ca·tion (nōt'ə fi kā'shən) *n.* [ME. *notificacioun* < MFr. *notification*] 1. a notifying or being notified 2. the notice given or received 3. the letter, form, etc. used to convey such a notice

no·ti·fy (nōt'ə fī') *vt.* -**fied'**, -**fy'ing** [ME. *notifien* < MFr. *notifier* < L. *notificare* < *notus* (see NOTE) + *facere*, to make (see FACT)] 1. to give notice to; inform; announce to 2. [Chiefly Brit.] to give notice of; announce; make known —**no'ti·fi'er** *n.*
SYN.—**notify** implies a sending of a formal notice imparting required or pertinent information [*notify* me when you are ready]; **inform** implies a making aware of something by giving knowledge of it [he *informed* me of your decision to join us]; **acquaint** suggests a making familiar with something hitherto unknown to one [she *acquainted* me with her problems]; **apprise** implies a notifying someone of something that has particular interest for him [I have *apprised* him of your arrival]

no·tion (nō'shən) *n.* [Fr. < L. *notio* < *notus*, pp. of *noscere*: see NOTE] 1. *a)* a mental image; general idea *b)* a vague thought 2. a belief; opinion; view 3. a desire; inclination; whim 4. a plan or intention ☆5. [*pl.*] small, useful articles, as needles, thread, etc., sold in a store —*SYN.* see IDEA

no·tion·al (-'l) *adj.* [ML. *notionalis*] 1. of, expressing, or consisting of notions, or concepts 2. imaginary; not actual [to inhabit a *notional* world] ☆3. having visionary ideas; given to whims; fanciful 4. *Gram.* having full lexical, as distinguished from relational, meaning —**no'tion·al·ly** *adv.*

no·to- (nōt'ə, nōt'ō) [ModL. < Gr. *nōton*, the back, akin to L. *nates*, buttocks] *a combining form meaning* the back, dorsum [*notochord*]

no·to·chord (nōt'ə kôrd') *n.* [prec. + CHORD[1]] 1. an elongated, rod-shaped structure composed of cells, forming the primitive supporting axis of the body in the lowest chordates and lying between the digestive tract and the central nervous system 2. a similar structure in the embryonic stages of higher vertebrates, which later is surrounded and replaced by the vertebral column —**no'to·chord'al** *adj.*

No·to·gae·a (nōt'ə jē'ə) *n.* [ModL. < Gr. *notos*, south, south wind + *gaia*, earth, land] one of three primary zoogeographic areas of the earth, including Australia, New Zealand, New Guinea, Celibes, and nearby islands —**No'to·gae'an** *adj.*

no·to·ri·e·ty (nōt'ə rī'ə tē) *n.* [Fr. *notorieté* < ML. *notorietas* < *notorius*] 1. the quality or state of being notorious 2. *pl.* -**ties** [Chiefly Brit.] a prominent or well-known person

no·to·ri·ous (nō tôr'ē əs) *adj.* [ML. *notorius* < LL. *notoria*, news, information < pp. of *noscere*: see NOTE] 1. well-known; publicly discussed 2. widely but unfavorably known or talked about —*SYN.* see FAMOUS —**no·to'ri·ous·ly** *adv.* —**no·to'ri·ous·ness** *n.*

no·tor·nis (nō tôr'nis) *n.* [ModL. < Gr. *notos*, the south + *ornis*, bird] any of a recently extinct genus (*Notornis*) of nonflying birds of New Zealand, related to the coot and rail

no·to·un·gu·late (nōt'ō uŋ'gyoo lit, -lāt') *n.* [< ModL. *Notoungulata*, name of the order: see NOTO- & UNGULATE] any of an extinct order (Notoungulata) of plant-eating mammals, once widespread in S. America: also **no·tun'-gu·late** (nō tun'-)

No·tre Dame (nō'trə däm', nōt'ər däm'; *Fr.* nô tr' dåm') [Fr., lit., Our Lady (Mary, mother of Jesus)] a famous early Gothic cathedral in Paris, built 1163-1257: in full, **Notre Dame de Paris**

no-trump (nō'trump') *adj.* 1. without trumps 2. *Bridge* designating or of a bid to play with no suit being trumps —*n.* 1. a bid in bridge to play with no suit being trumps 2. the hand so played

Not·ting·ham (nät'iŋ əm) 1. *same as* NOTTINGHAMSHIRE 2. county seat of Nottinghamshire: pop. 315,000

Not·ting·ham·shire (-shir') county of C England: 844 sq. mi.; pop. 926,000; county seat, Nottingham

no·tum (nōt'əm) *n.*, *pl.* -**ta** (-ə) [ModL. < Gr. *nōton*, the back: cf. NATES] the back or dorsal portion of an insect segment

not·with·stand·ing (nät'with stan'diŋ, -with-) *prep.* in spite of [he flew on, *notwithstanding* the storm]: sometimes in an inverted construction [he flew on, the storm *notwithstanding*] —*adv.* all the same; nevertheless [he must be told, *notwithstanding*] —*conj.* in spite of the fact that; although

Nouak·chott (nwäk shät') capital of Mauritania, in the W part: pop. 10,000

nou·gat (nōō'gət) *n.* [Fr. < Pr. *nogat* < *noga*, *nuga*, nut < L. *nux*, NUT] a confection of sugar paste with almonds or other nuts, and, sometimes, fruit

nought (nôt) *n.* [ME. < OE. *nowiht* < *ne*, not (see NO[1]) + *owiht*, *awiht*, AUGHT] 1. nothing 2. *Arith.* the figure zero (0) —*adj.* [Archaic or Obs.] 1. worthless; useless 2. wicked; evil —*adv.* [Archaic] in no way; not at all —**set at nought** to defy; scorn

Nou·mé·a (nōō'mā ä') capital of New Caledonia; seaport on the SE coast: pop. 35,000

nou·me·nal·ism (nōō'mə n'l iz'm, nou'-) *n.* the doctrine maintaining the existence of noumena —**nou'me·nal·ist** *n.*

nou·me·non (nōō'mə nän, nou'-) *n.*, *pl.* -**me·na** (-nə) [G. < Gr. *nooumenon*, neut. of *nooumenos*, prp. pass. of *noein*, to perceive < *noos*, the mind] in Kantian philosophy, an object reached by intellectual intuition, without the aid of the senses: opposed to PHENOMENON —**nou'me·nal** *adj.* —**nou'me·nal·ly** *adv.*

noun (noun) *n.* [ME. *nowne* < OFr. *noun*, *nom* < L. *nomen*, NAME] *Gram.* 1. any of a class of words naming or denoting a person, thing, place, action, quality, etc. (Ex.: *boy*, *water*, and *truth* are nouns) 2. any word, phrase, or clause similarly used; substantive —**noun'al** *adj.*

nour·ish (nur'ish) *vt.* [ME. *norischen* < OFr. extended stem of *norrir* < L. *nutrire*: see NURSE] 1. to feed or sustain (any plant or animal) with substances necessary to life and growth 2. to foster; develop; promote (a feeling, attitude, habit, etc.) —**nour'ish·er** *n.*

nour·ish·ing (-iŋ) *adj.* contributing to health or growth; nutritious —**nour'ish·ing·ly** *adv.*

nour·ish·ment (-mənt) *n.* [ME. *norysshement* < OFr. *norissement*] 1. a nourishing or being nourished 2. something that nourishes; food; nutriment

nous (nōōs, nous) *n.* [Gr. *nous*, *noos*] *Philos.* mind; understanding; reason; intellect

nou·veau riche (nōō'vō rēsh') *pl.* **nou·veaux riches** (nōō' vō rēsh') [Fr., newly rich] a person who has only recently become rich: often connoting tasteless ostentation, lack of culture, etc.

nou·veau ro·man (nōō vō rô män') *pl.* **nou·veaux ro·mans** (nōō vō rô män') [Fr., new novel] a type of antinovel developed in France since the 1950's in which physical objects and setting are described minutely and objectively with no psychological interpretation of setting or action

‡**nou·veau·té** (nōō vō tā') *n.* [Fr.] a novelty

‡**nou·velle** (nōō vel') *n.* [Fr., new] a short novel; novella

Nov. November

nov. novelist

no·va (nō'və) *n.*, *pl.* -**vas**, -**vae** (-vē) [ModL. < L. *nova* (*stella*), new (star) < *novus*, NEW] *Astron.* a type of variable star that suddenly increases in brightness by thousands to millions of times its original intensity and then decreases in brightness over a period of months to years

no·vac·u·lite (nō vak'yoo līt') *n.* [< L. *novacula*, razor + -ITE[1]] a hard, extremely fine-grained siliceous rock: it is used for whetstones

No·va·ra (nō vä'rä) commune in the Piedmont, NW Italy: pop. 86,000

No·va Sco·tia (nō'və skō'shə) [ModL., New Scotland] province of SE Canada, consisting of a peninsula on the Atlantic & Cape Breton Island: 21,425 sq. mi.; pop. 756,000; cap. Halifax: abbrev. N.S. —**No'va Sco'tian**

no·va·tion (nō vā'shən) *n.* [LL. *novatio* < L. *novare*, to make new < *novus*, NEW] *Law* the substitution of a new obligation or contract for an old one by the mutual agreement of all parties concerned

No·va·ya Zem·lya (nō'vä yä zem lyä') archipelago of two large islands & several small ones in NW R.S.F.S.R., between the Barents & Kara seas: c. 36,000 sq. mi.

nov·el (näv'l) *adj.* [ME. *novell* < OFr. *novel* < L. *novellus*, dim. of *novus*, NEW] new and unusual; esp., being the first of its kind —*n.* [It. *novella* < L. *novella*, neut. pl. of *novellus* (see the *adj.*), hence, orig., new things, news] 1. orig., a novella (sense 1): *usually used in pl.* 2. a relatively long fictional prose narrative with a more or less complex plot or pattern of events, about human beings, their feelings, thoughts, actions, etc. 3. the type or form of literature represented by such narratives (with *the*) 4. [< LL. *novellae* (*constitutiones*)] *Roman Law* a new law or decree, specif. one made by Justinian supplementary to the Justinian code: *usually used in pl.* —*SYN.* see NEW —**nov'el·is'tic** *adj.* —**nov'el·is'ti·cal·ly** *adv.*

nov·el·ette (näv'ə let') *n.* a short novel; novella

nov·el·ist (näv'l ist) *n.* a person who writes novels

nov·el·ize (näv'ə līz') *vt.* -**ized'**, -**iz'ing** to give the form or characteristics of a novel to; make into or like a novel —**nov'el·i·za'tion** *n.*

no·vel·la (nō vel'ə; *It.* nô vel'lä) *n.*, *pl.* -**las**, -**le** (-ē; *It.* -lē) [It.: see NOVEL, *n.*] 1. a short prose narrative, usually with a moral and often satiric, as any of the tales in Boccaccio's *Decameron* 2. a short novel; novelette

nov·el·ty (näv'l tē) *n.*, *pl.* -**ties** [ME. *novelte* < OFr. *noveleté* < LL. *novellitas*] 1. the quality of being novel; newness; freshness 2. something new, fresh, or unusual; change; innovation 3. a small, often cheap, cleverly made article, usually for play or adornment: *usually used in pl.*

No·vem·ber (nō vem'bər) *n.* [ME. & OFr. *Novembre* < L. *November* < *novem*, NINE (+ -*ber* < ?): so named as the ninth month of the ancient Roman year, which began

with March] the eleventh month of the year, having 30 days: abbrev. **Nov., N.**

no·ve·na (nō vē′nə) *n.* [ML. < fem. sing. of L. *novenus*, nine each < *novem*, NINE] *R.C.Ch.* the recitation of prayers and the practicing of devotions on nine days, usually to seek some special favor

no·ver·cal (nō vur′k'l) *adj.* [L. *novercalis* < *noverca*, a stepmother, prob. < *novus*, NEW] [Rare] of, like, or befitting a stepmother

Nov·go·rod (nŏv′gŏ rôt′) city in NW R.S.F.S.R.: former political & commercial center: pop. 61,000

nov·ice (näv′is) *n.* [ME. *novis* < OFr. *novice* < L. *novicius*, new, fresh < *novus*, NEW] **1.** a person on probation in a religious group or order before taking the final vows; neophyte **2.** a person new to a particular occupation, activity, etc.; apprentice; beginner; tyro —**SYN.** see AMATEUR

No·vi Sad (nŏ′vē säd′) city in NE Yugoslavia, on the Danube; capital of Vojvodina: pop. 111,000

no·vi·ti·ate (nō vish′ē it, -āt′, -vish′it) *n.* [Fr. *noviciat* < ML. *novitiatus*] **1.** the period or state of being a novice **2.** one who is a novice **3.** the quarters assigned to religious novices Also, chiefly Brit. sp., **no·vi′ci·ate**

☆**No·vo·cain** (nō′və kān′) [L. *nov(us)*, NEW + (C)OCAINE] *a trademark for* PROCAINE: also sp. **Novocaine**

No·vo·kuz·netsk (nŏ′vō kōoz nyetsk′) city in SE Ukrainian S.S.R., in the Donets Basin: pop. 484,000

No·vo·si·birsk (-si birsk′) city in the S R.S.F.S.R., on the Ob River: pop. 1,049,000

now (nou) *adv.* [ME. < OE. *nu*, akin to ON. Goth., OHG. *nu* < IE. base **nu*, whence Gr. *nu*, L. *nunc*] **1.** *a)* at the present time; at this moment *b)* at once **2.** at the time referred to; then; next [*now* his joy began] **3.** at a time very close to the present; specif., *a)* very recently; not long ago (with *just*) [he left just *now*] *b)* very soon (often with *just*) [they are leaving just *now*] **4.** given the situation; with things as they are [*now* we'll never know what happened] *Now* is often used without any definite meaning for emphasis or to preface or resume one's remarks [*now* look here] —*conj.* since; seeing that [*now* that you know] —*n.* the present time [that's all for *now*] —*adj.* of the present or current time [the *now* generation] —*interj.* an exclamation expressing warning, reproach, etc. —**now and then** sometimes; occasionally: also **now and again**

now·a·days (nou′ə dāz′) *adv.* [ME. *nou adaies* < *now* + *on* + *day* + *-s*, adv. suffix] in these days; at the present time —*n.* the present time

no·way (nō′wā′) *adv.* in no manner; by no means; not at all; nowise: also **no′ways′** (-wāz′)

now·el, now·ell (nō el′) *n. archaic sp. of* NOEL

no·where (nō′hwer′, -wer′) *adv.* [ME. *nowher* < OE. *nahwær*] not in, at, or to any place; not anywhere: also [Dial. or Colloq.] **no′wheres** —*n.* **1.** a place that is nonexistent, unknown, very primitive or remote, etc. **2.** a place or state of obscurity —**nowhere near** not nearly; not by a wide margin

no·whith·er (-hwith′ər, -with′-) *adv.* [ME. *nowhider* < OE. *nahwider*] in, at, or to no place; nowhere

no·wise (-wīz′) *adv.* in no manner; noway

nowt (nout) *n.pl., sing.* **nowt** [ME. < ON. *naut*, cattle, akin to OE. *neat*: see NEAT²] [Chiefly Scot.] cattle; oxen

Nox (näks) [L., NIGHT] *Rom. Myth.* the goddess of night: identified with the Greek goddess Nyx

nox·ious (näk′shəs) *adj.* [L. *noxius* < *noxa*, injury, hurt < *nocere*, to hurt, injure: see NECRO-] **1.** harmful to the health; injurious [a *noxious* gas] **2.** morally injurious; corrupting; unwholesome —*SYN.* see PERNICIOUS — **nox′ious·ly** *adv.* —**nox′ious·ness** *n.*

no·yade (nwä yäd′) *n.* [Fr. < *noyer*, to drown < L. *necare*, to kill (in LL., to drown): see NECRO-] a mass execution of persons by drowning, as practiced at Nantes, France, during the Reign of Terror (1794)

Noyes (noiz), **Alfred** 1880–1958; Eng. poet

noz·zle (näz′'l) *n.* [dim. of NOSE] **1.** a spout at the end of a hose, pipe, bellows, etc., by which a stream of liquid or gas may be directed and controlled **2.** [Slang] the nose

NP neuropsychiatric

Np *Chem.* neptunium

N.P., n.p. 1. new paragraph **2.** nisi prius **3.** no protest **4.** Notary Public

NRA, N.R.A. National Recovery Administration

NRC; N.R.C. National Research Council

NS nuclear ship

N/S, n/s *Banking* not sufficient funds: also **N.S.F.**

N.S. 1. New Series **2.** New Style **3.** not specified: also **n.s. 4.** Nova Scotia **5.** Numismatic Society

NSA National Shipping Authority

NSC, N.S.C. National Security Council

NSF N.S.F. National Science Foundation

N.S.W. New South Wales

-n't a contracted and enclitic form of *not* [aren't]

NT., NT, N.T. New Testament

N.T. Northern Territory

nth (enth) *adj.* **1.** expressing the ordinal equivalent to *n* **2.** of the indefinitely large or small quantity represented by *n* —**to the nth degree** (or **power**) **1.** to an indefinite degree or power **2.** to an extreme

NTP normal temperature (0°C) and pressure (760 mm)

nt. wt. net weight

nu (nōō, nyōō) *n.* [Gr. *ny* < Sem., as in Heb. *nūn*] the thirteenth letter of the Greek alphabet (N, ν)

nu·ance (nōō′äns, nyōō′-; nōō äns′) *n.* [Fr. < *nuer*, to shade < *nue* < VL. **nuba*, for L. *nubes*, a cloud < IE. base **sneudh-*, fog, whence W. *nudd*] a slight or delicate variation in tone, color, meaning, etc.; shade of difference —**nu′anced** *adj.*

nub (nub) *n.* [var. of *knub*, for KNOB] **1.** *a)* a knob or lump *b)* small piece ☆**2.** [Colloq.] the point of a story or gist of a matter

Nu·ba (nōō′bə) *n.* **1.** *pl.* **-bas, -ba** a member of a Negroid people living in C Sudan (sense 2) **2.** their Kordofanian language

nub·bin (nub′in) *n.* [dim. of NUB] ☆**1.** a small or imperfect ear of Indian corn **2.** anything small or undeveloped [*nubbins* of coal]

nub·ble (nub′'l) *n.* [dim. of NUB] a small knob or lump —**nub′bly** *adj.* **-bli·er, -bli·est**

nub·by (-ē) *adj.* **-bi·er, -bi·est** covered with small nubs, or lumps; having a rough, knotted surface; nubbly [a *nubby* fabric] —**nub′bi·ness** *n.*

Nu·bi·a (nōō′bē ə, nyōō′-) region & former kingdom in NE Africa, between the Red Sea & the Sahara, in Egypt & Sudan

Nu·bi·an (-ən) *adj.* of Nubia, its people, or their language —*n.* **1.** a member of a Negroid people with some Caucasoid admixture, living in Nubia **2.** their Eastern Sudanic language

Nubian Desert desert in NE Sudan, between the Nile & the Red Sea

nu·bile (nōō′b'l, nyōō′-; -bil) *adj.* [Fr. *nubile* < L. *nubilis* < *nubere*, to veil oneself, marry < IE. base **sneubh-*, to woo, marry, whence Gr. *nymphē*, bride, nymph, Czech *snoubiti*, to woo] marriageable: said of a young woman with reference to her age or physical development—**nu·bil′i·ty** *n.*

nu·bi·lous (nōō′b'l əs, nyōō′-) *adj.* [LL. *nubilosus*, cloudy, for L. *nubilus* < *nubes*, a cloud: see NUANCE] **1.** cloudy; misty; foggy **2.** obscure; indefinite

nu·cel·lus (nōō sel′əs, nyōō-) *n., pl.* **-cel·li** (-ī) [ModL. < L. *nucella*, dim. of *nux* (gen. *nucis*), NUT] *Bot.* the central part of an ovule, containing the embryo sac —**nu·cel′lar** *adj.*

nu·cha (nōō′kə, nyōō′-) *n., pl.* **-chae** (-kē) [ME. < ML. < Ar. *nukhā′*, spinal marrow] *Zool.* **1.** the nape of the neck **2.** in insects, the back part of the thorax —**nu′chal** *adj.*

nu·cle·ar (nōō′klē ər, nyōō′-) *adj.* **1.** of, like, or forming a nucleus **2.** of or relating to atomic nuclei [*nuclear* energy] **3.** of, characterized by, or operated by the use of atomic energy [*nuclear* weapons] **4.** of, having, or involving nuclear weapons [*nuclear* warfare]

nuclear bomb an explosive device that generates its energy by nuclear fission or fusion: see ATOMIC BOMB, HYDROGEN BOMB

nuclear emulsion any of various specialized photographic emulsions for recording the characteristic tracks of ionizing particles as specific arrangements of developed silver grains

nuclear energy *same as* ATOMIC ENERGY

nuclear fission the splitting of the nuclei of atoms into two fragments of approximately equal mass, accompanied by conversion of part of the mass into energy: the principle of the atomic bomb

nuclear forces the short-range, strongly attractive, saturated forces that act between nucleons and bind them together in the nucleus

nuclear fusion the fusion of lightweight atomic nuclei, as of deuterium or tritium, into a nucleus of heavier mass, as of helium, with a resultant loss in the combined mass, which is converted into energy: the principle of the hydrogen bomb

nuclear magnetic resonance a method for determining the number and distribution of hydrogen atoms in a molecule by measuring the frequency and amount of energy absorbed and emitted by the hydrogen nucleus in an electromagnetic field

nuclear physics the branch of physics dealing with the structure of atomic nuclei, nuclear forces, the interaction between particles and nuclei, the fission process, the study of radioactive decay, etc.

nuclear reactor a device for initiating and maintaining a controlled nuclear chain reaction in a fissionable fuel for the production of energy or additional fissionable material

nuclear sap *same as* KARYOLYMPH

nu·cle·ase (nōō′klē ās′, nyōō′-) *n.* [NUCLE(O)- + -ASE] any of various enzymes that speed up the hydrolysis of nucleic acids

nu·cle·ate (-it; *also, & for v. always,* -āt′) *adj.* [L. *nucleatus*, having a kernel, pp. of *nucleare*, to become like a kernel < *nucleus*: see NUCLEUS] having a nucleus —*vt.* **-at′ed, -at′ing** [< L. *nucleatus*] to form into or around a nucleus

—*vi.* to form a nucleus —**nu′cle·a′tion** *n.* —**nu′cle·a′tor** *n.*

nu·cle·i (nōō′klē ī′, nyōō′-) *n. pl. of* NUCLEUS

nu·cle·ic acid (nōō klē′ik, nyōō-) any of a group of complex organic acids found esp. in the nucleus of all living cells and essential to life: each consists of a combination of phosphoric acid, a carbohydrate, and a base derived from purine or pyrimidine, bound in helical chains by hydrogen bonds between the bases

nu·cle·in (nōō′klē in, nyōō′-) *n.* [NUCLE(US) + -IN¹] any of a group of substances rich in phosphorus and composed of a protein molecule united to one nucleic acid: obtained by hydrolysis of nucleoproteins

nu·cle·o- (nōō′klē ō′, nyōō′-; -ə) *a combining form meaning:* 1. nucleus 2. nuclear 3. nucleic acid Also, before a vowel, **nu′cle-**

nu·cle·o·lat·ed (nōō klē′ə lāt′id, nyōō-) *adj.* having a nucleolus or nucleoli: also **nu′cle′o·late′**

nu·cle·o·lus (nōō klē′ə ləs, nyōō-) *n., pl.* **-li** (-lī′) [ModL. < LL., dim. of L. *nucleus*] a conspicuous body, mainly of protein with some RNA and usually spherical, found in the nucleus of most cells: also **nu′cle·ole′** —**nu·cle·o·lar** *adj.*

nu·cle·on (nōō′klē än′, nyōō′-) *n.* [NUCLE(US) + (PROT)ON] a neutron or proton, either of the fundamental particles making up the atomic nucleus —**nu′cle·on′ic** *adj.*

nu·cle·on·ics (nōō′klē än′iks, nyōō′-) *n.pl.* [*with sing. v.*] [prec. + -ICS] the branch of physics dealing with nucleons or with nuclear phenomena and esp. with practical applications of nuclear physics

nu·cle·o·phile (nōō′klē ə fīl′, nyōō′-) *n.* [NUCLEO- + -PHILE] an atom or molecule that has an affinity for atomic nuclei or that donates or shares electrons with atomic nuclei —**nu′cle·o·phil′ic** (-fil′ik) *adj.*

nu·cle·o·plasm (-plaz′m) *n.* [NUCLEO- + -PLASM] the protoplasm that composes the nucleus of a cell —**nu′cle·o·plas′mic** *adj.*

nu·cle·o·pro·te·in (nōō′klē ō prō′tēn, nyōō′-; -prōt′ē in) *n.* [NUCLEO- + PROTEIN] any of a class of compound proteins consisting of nucleic acid linked to protein, found in the nuclei and surrounding cytoplasm of living cells

nu·cle·o·side (nōō′klē ə sīd′, nyōō′-) *n.* [< NUCLEO- + -OSE¹ + -IDE] any of various compounds consisting of a purine or pyrimidine base linked to a carbohydrate

nu·cle·o·tide (-tīd′) *n.* [altered < prec.] 1. any of several phosphate esters of nucleosides 2. any of several compounds not found in nucleic acids which function as coenzymes

nu·cle·us (nōō′klē əs, nyōō′-) *n., pl.* **-cle·i** (-ī′), **-cle·us·es** [ModL. < L., a nut, kernel, for **nuculeus*, dim. < *nux* (gen. *nucis*), NUT] 1. a thing or part forming the center around which other things or parts are grouped or collected; core 2. anything serving as a center of growth or development [the *nucleus* of a library] 3. *Anat.* a group of nerve cells in the brain or spinal column 4. *Astron.* the bright central part of the head of a comet 5. *Biol.* the central, usually spherical or oval mass of protoplasm present in most plant and animal cells, containing most of the hereditary material and necessary to such functions as growth, reproduction, etc. 6. *Bot.* the central point in a starch grain 7. *Chem., Physics* the central part of an atom, the fundamental particles of which are the proton and neutron, except for hydrogen, which is composed of one proton only: it carries a positive charge and constitutes almost all of the mass of the atom 8. *Organic Chem.* a fundamental, stable arrangement of atoms (e.g., the benzene ring) that may occur in many compounds by atomic substitution without structural change

nu·clide (-klīd) *n.* [< NUCL(EUS) + -ide < Gr. *eidos*, form (cf. -OID)] a specific type of atom that has a measurable mean life and is characterized by its nuclear properties, such as the number of neutrons and protons and the energy state of its nucleus —**nu·clid′ic** (-klid′ik) *adj.*

nude (nōōd, nyōōd) *adj.* [L. *nudus*, NAKED] 1. completely unclothed or uncovered; naked; bare 2. *Law* without consideration or other legal essential: said of contracts, etc. —*n.* 1. a nude person 2. a representation of a nude human figure in painting, sculpture, etc. 3. the condition of being nude; nakedness [in the *nude*] —SYN. see BARE¹ —**nude′ly** *adv.* —**nude′ness** *n.*

nudge (nuj) *vt.* **nudged**, **nudg′ing** [prob. akin to Norw. dial. *nygga*, to push, shove, MLowG. *nucke*, a sudden push, ult. < IE. base **nue-*, to jerk, shove: see INNUENDO] to push or poke gently, esp. with the elbow, in order to get the attention of, hint slyly, etc. —*n.* a gentle push with the elbow, etc.; jog —**nudg′er** *n.*

nu·di- (nōō′də, nyōō′-) [< L. *nudus*, NAKED] *Biol.* a combining form meaning nude, bare [nudibranch]

nu·di·branch (-braŋk′) *n.* [< ModL. *Nudibranchia:* see NUDI- & BRANCHIAE] any of a suborder (Nudibranchia) of marine gastropods without a shell and with external gills, often beautifully colored —**nu′di·bran′chi·ate** (-braŋ′kē it, -āt′) *adj., n.*

nu·di·caul (nōō′də kôl′, nyōō′-) *adj.* [< NUDI- + L. *caulis*, a stem] *Bot.* having stems without leaves: also **nu′di·cau′lous** (-kô′ləs)

☆**nud·ie** (nōō′dē, nyōō′-) *n.* [Slang] a cheap motion picture exploiting nudity and sex

nud·ism (-diz′m) *n.* the practice or cult of going nude for hygienic reasons —**nud′ist** *n., adj.*

nu·di·ty (-də tē) *n.* [Fr. *nudité* < L. *nuditas*] 1. the state, quality, or fact of being nude; nakedness 2. *pl.* **-ties** a nude figure, as in art

☆**nud·nik** (nood′nik) *n.* [< Yid. < Russ. < *nudniy*, tiresome + -nik, -NIK] [Slang] a dull, tiresome, annoying person

Nu·e·ces (nōō ā′sās) [Sp., nut, esp. the pecan] river in S Tex., flowing SE into the Gulf of Mexico at Corpus Christi: 315 mi.

Nu·er (nōō′ər) *n.* 1. *pl.* **Nu′ers, Nu′er** any member of a pastoral Nilotic people in Sudan and on the border of Ethiopia 2. their Eastern Sudanic language

Nue·vo La·re·do (nwe′vō lä re′dō) city in N Mexico, on the Rio Grande, opposite Laredo, Tex.: pop. 129,000

Nue·vo Le·ón (nwe′vō le ōn′) state in NE Mexico: 25,136 sq. mi.; pop. 1,535,000; cap. Monterrey

nu·ga·to·ry (nōō′gə tôr′ē, nyōō′-) *adj.* [L. *nugatorius* < pp. of *nugari*, to trifle < *nugae*, trifles] 1. trifling; worthless 2. not operative; invalid

nug·get (nug′it) *n.* [prob. dim. of Eng. dial. *nug*, a lump] a lump; esp., a lump of native gold

nui·sance (nōō′s'ns, nyōō′-) *n.* [ME. *nusance* < OFr. < *nuisir, noisir* < L. *nocere*, to annoy: see NECRO-] 1. an act, condition, thing, or person causing trouble, annoyance, or inconvenience 2. *Law* a thing or condition causing danger or annoyance either to a limited number of persons (**private nuisance**) or to the general public (**public nuisance**), or, because of its attraction, to children who will be unlikely to recognize its dangerous quality (**attractive nuisance**)

nuisance tax a tax considered a nuisance because it is paid in very small amounts by the consumer

null (nul) *adj.* [MFr. *nul* < L. *nullus*, not any, none < *ne-*, not (see NO¹) + *ullus*, any, dim. of *unus*, ONE] 1. without legal force; not binding; invalid: usually in the phrase **null and void** 2. amounting to nought; nil 3. of no value, effect, or consequence; insignificant 4. *Math.* designating, of, or being zero, as: *a)* having all zero elements [null matrix] *b)* having a limit of zero [null sequence] *c)* having no members whatsoever [null set]

nul·lah (nul′ə) *n.* [Hind. *nālā*, brook, ravine] in India, etc., a watercourse, esp. one that is often dry; gully

nul·li·fi·ca·tion (nul′ə fi kā′shən) *n.* [LL.(Ec.) *nullificatio*, a despising] 1. a nullifying or being nullified ☆2. in U.S. history, the refusal of a State to recognize or enforce within its territory any Federal law held to be an infringement on its sovereignty

nul·li·fid·i·an (-fid′ē ən) *n.* [< L. *nullus*, none + *fides*, faith + -IAN] a person having no religious faith

nul·li·fy (nul′ə fī′) *vt.* **-fied′, -fy′ing** [LL.(Ec.) *nullificare*, to despise < L. *nullus*, none (see NULL) + *facere*, to make: see FACT] 1. to make legally null; make void; annul 2. to make valueless or useless; bring to nothing 3. to cancel out —☆**nul′li·fi′er** *n.*

SYN. —to **nullify** is literally to bring to nought, as by depriving of effectiveness, validity, etc. [the bad weather *nullified* whatever advantage we'd had]; **invalidate** and **void** specifically imply a depriving of legal force or authority [to *invalidate*, or *void*, a contract]; **negate** implies a bringing to a state of nonexistence, as by destroying or denying [good *negates* evil]

nul·lip·a·ra (nu lip′ər ə) *n., pl.* **-a·ras, -a·rae′** (-ə rē′) [ModL. < L. *nullus*, none (see NULL) + *parere*, to bring forth, bear: see -PAROUS] a woman who has never given birth to a child —**nul·li·par·i·ty** (nul′ə par′ə tē) *n.* —**nul·lip′a·rous** *adj.*

nul·li·pore (nul′ə pôr′) *n.* [< L. *nullus*, none (see NULL) + *porus,* PORE²] any of several red-spored, coralline algae (family Rhodophyceae) that secrete lime

nul·li·ty (nul′ə tē) *n.* [Fr. *nullité* < ML. *nullitas*] 1. the state or fact of being null 2. *pl.* **-ties** anything that is null, as an act that has no legal force

☆**nul·lo** (nul′ō) *n.* [extension of NULL] *Card Games* a bid to take no tricks

Num. (the book of) Numbers

num. 1. number 2. numeral(s)

Nu·man·ti·a (nōō man′shē ə, nyōō-; -shə) ancient Celtic city in what is now NC Spain: besieged & captured by Scipio the Younger (133 B.C.)

numb (num) *adj.* [< ME. *nome, nomen*, pp. of *nimen*, to take (with unhistoric *-b*): see -NOMY] 1. weakened in or deprived of the power of feeling or moving; benumbed; deadened; insensible [numb with cold, numb with grief] 2. having the nature of numbness [a numb feeling] —*vt.* to make numb —**numb′ly** *adv.* —**numb′ness** *n.*

num·ber (num′bər) *n.* [ME. *nombre* < OE. < L. *numerus* < IE. base **nem-*, to distribute: see -NOMY] 1. a symbol or word, or a group of either of these, showing how many or which one in a series: 1, 2, 10, 101 (one, two, ten, one hundred and one) are called **cardinal numbers**; 1st, 2d, 10th, 101st (first, second, tenth, one hundred and first) are called **ordinal numbers** 2. [*pl.*] *same as* ARITHMETIC 3. the sum or total of persons or units; aggregate 4. a collection of persons or things; company; assemblage [a small *number* of people] 5. *a)* [often *pl.*] a large group; many [cut down *numbers* of trees] *b)* [*pl.*] numerical superiority [safety in *numbers*] 6. quantity, as consisting of units [a *number* of errors] 7. one of a series or group that is numbered or thought of as numbered; specif., *a)* a single issue of a periodical [the winter *number* of a quarterly] *b)* a single song, dance, skit, etc. in a program of entertainment

8. [Colloq.] a person or thing singled out [this hat is a smart *number*]: see also OPPOSITE NUMBER **9.** *Gram. a)* a differentiation of form to show whether one or more than one is meant *b)* the form itself See SINGULAR, DUAL, PLURAL **10.** [*pl.*] *a)* metrical form; meter *b)* metrical lines; verses *c)* [Archaic] musical notes or groups of notes; measures —*vt.* [ME. *nombren* < OFr. *nombrer* < L. *numerare*, to count < *numerus*] **1.** to total the number of persons or things in; count; enumerate **2.** to give a number to; designate by number **3.** to include as one of a group, class, collection, etc. (*among*) **4.** to fix or limit the number or the duration of [his days are *numbered*] **5.** to have or comprise; total [a library *numbering* 10,000 volumes] —*vi.* **1.** to total; count; enumerate **2.** to be numbered; be included —**a number of** an unspecified number of; several or many —**beyond number** too numerous to be counted —☆**by the numbers 1.** *Mil.* in prescribed sequence of movements and accompanied by a count **2.** in a mechanical, unthinking way —☆**get** (or **have**) **one's number** to discover (or know) one's true character or motives —☆**have one's number on it** [Slang] to be assumed to have been marked by fate for the person whom it kills: said of a bullet, etc. —**one's number is up** [Slang] one's time to die, suffer punishment, etc. has arrived —☆**the numbers** an illegal lottery in which small bets are placed on the order of certain numbers, usually the last three, in some tabulation of game scores, financial reports, etc. published in the daily newspapers: also called **numbers pool** (or **racket**, etc.) —**without number** too numerous to be counted —**num'ber·er** *n.*

num·ber·less (-lis) *adj.* **1.** innumerable; countless **2.** without a number or numbers

number one [Colloq.] **1.** oneself ☆**2.** the first, usually the very best, quality or grade

Num·bers (num'bǝrz) [transl. of Gr. *Arithmoi* (cf. ARITHMETIC): from containing the census of the Hebrews after the Exodus] the fourth book of the Pentateuch in the Bible

numb·fish (num'fish') *n., pl.* -**fish', -fish'es:** see FISH² *same as* ELECTRIC RAY

num·bles (num'b'lz) *n.pl.* [ME. *noumbles* < OFr. *nombles*, by dissimilation < L. *lumbulus*, dim. of *lumbus*, loin: see LUMBAR] [Archaic] the heart, lungs, liver, etc. of a deer, etc., used for food: cf. HUMBLE PIE

numb·skull (num'skul') *n. same as* NUMSKULL

nu·men (nōō'men, nyōō'-) *n., pl.* -**mi·na** (-mi nǝ) [L., akin to *-nuere*, to nod: see INNUENDO] **1.** *Rom. Myth.* a presiding spirit; guardian deity **2.** an indwelling, guiding force or spirit

nu·mer·a·ble (nōō'mǝr ǝ b'l, nyōō'-) *adj.* [L. *numerabilis*] that can be numbered or counted

nu·mer·al (-ǝl) *adj.* [LL. *numeralis* < L. *numerus*, NUMBER] of, expressing, or denoting a number or numbers —*n.* **1.** a figure, letter, or word, or a group of any of these, expressing a number: see ARABIC NUMERALS, ROMAN NUMERALS **2.** [*pl.*] the numerals of the year of graduation of one's class in college, etc., awarded for participation in sports, etc.

nu·mer·ar·y (nōō'mǝ rer'ē, nyōō'-) *adj.* [ML. *numerarius*] of a number or numbers

nu·mer·ate (-rāt') *vt. -at'ed, -at'ing* [< L. *numeratus*, pp. of *numerare*: see NUMBER] **1.** *same as* ENUMERATE **2.** to read as words (numbers expressed in figures)

nu·mer·a·tion (nōō'mǝ rā'shǝn, nyōō'-) *n.* [ME. *numeracioun* < L. *numeratio* < *numerare*: see NUMBER] **1.** a numbering or counting; calculation **2.** a system of numbering or of reading as words numbers expressed in figures

nu·mer·a·tor (nōō'mǝ rāt'ǝr, nyōō'-) *n.* [LL. < L. *numerare*: see NUMBER] **1.** a person or thing that numbers **2.** *Math.* the term above or to the left of the line in a fraction, indicating how many of the specified parts of a unit are taken [6 is the *numerator* of 6/7]

nu·mer·i·cal (nōō mer'i k'l, nyōō-) *adj.* **1.** of, or having the nature of, number **2.** in or by numbers **3.** denoting (a) number **4.** expressed by a number or numbers, not by a letter or letters **5.** *Math.* designating or of value regardless of sign [the *numerical* value of −3 is less than that of −7] —**nu·mer'i·cal·ly** *adv.*

nu·mer·ol·o·gy (nōō'mǝ räl'ǝ jē, nyōō'-) *n.* [< L. *numerus*, a number + -LOGY] a system of occultism built around numbers, esp. those giving birth dates, those which are the sum of the letters in one's name, etc.; divination by numbers

nu·mer·ous (nōō'mǝr ǝs, nyōō'-) *adj.* [L. *numerosus* < *numerus*, NUMBER] **1.** consisting of many persons or things [a *numerous* collection] **2.** very many —*SYN.* see MANY —**nu'mer·ous·ly** *adv.* —**nu'mer·ous·ness** *n.*

Nu·mid·i·a (nōō mid'ē ǝ, nyōō'-) ancient country in N Africa, mainly in what is now E Algeria

Nu·mid·i·an (-ǝn) *adj.* of Numidia, its people, or their language —*n.* **1.** a native or inhabitant of Numidia **2.** the Afro-Asiatic language of the Numidians

Numidian crane *same as* DEMOISELLE (sense 2)

nu·min·ous (nōō'mǝ nǝs, nyōō'-) *adj.* [< L. *numen* (gen. *numinis*), a deity (see NUMEN) + -OUS] **1.** of or characteristic of a numen; supernatural; divine **2.** having a deeply spiritual or mystical effect

numis., numism. numismatic(s)

nu·mis·mat·ic (nōō'miz mat'ik, nyōō'-; -mis-) *adj.* [Fr. *numismatique* < L. *numisma* (gen. *numismatis*), a coin < Gr. *nomisma*, a coin, lit., what is sanctioned by law < *nomizein*, to sanction < *nomos*, law: see -NOMY] **1.** of coins or medals **2.** of or having to do with currency **3.** of numismatics —**nu'mis·mat'i·cal·ly** *adv.*

nu·mis·mat·ics (-iks) *n.pl.* [*with sing. v.*] [see prec.] the study or collection of coins, medals, paper money, etc.: also **nu·mis·ma·tol·o·gy** (nōō miz'mǝ täl'ǝ jē, nyōō-; -mis'-')

nu·mis·ma·tist (nōō miz'mǝ tist, nyoo-; -mis'-) *n.* [Fr. *numismatiste*: see NUMISMATIC] a specialist in or collector of coins, medals, paper money, etc.

num·mu·lar (num'yoo lǝr) *adj.* [L. *nummularius* < *nummulus*, dim. of *nummus*, a coin < Gr. *nomimos*, legal, customary, akin to *nomos*, law: see -NOMY] coin-shaped; circular or oval

num·mu·lite (-līt') *n.* [< L. *nummus*, a coin (see prec.) + -LITE] any of a genus (*Nummulites*) of nearly extinct foraminifers with a somewhat coin-shaped shell —**num'mu·lit'ic** (-lit'ik) *adj.*

num·skull (num'skul') *n.* [NUM(B) + SKULL] **1.** a stupid person; dolt; dunce **2.** [Archaic] the head of such a person

nun¹ (nun) *n.* [ME. *nunne* < OE. < LL.(Ec.) *nonna*, nun, orig., child's nurse: like Gr. *nanna*, aunt, Sans. *nanā*, mother, ult. < baby talk] **1.** a woman devoted to a religious life; esp., a member of a convent living under vows of poverty, chastity, and obedience **2.** any of various birds; esp., any of a domesticated breed of pigeon **3.** a cone-shaped buoy: in full, **nun buoy**

nun² (nōōn, noon) *n.* [Heb. *nūn*, lit., fish] the fourteenth letter of the Hebrew alphabet (נ)

nun·a·tak (nun'ǝ tak') *n.* [prob. via Dan. < Esk.] *Geol.* an isolated mountain peak protruding through glacial ice

Nunc Di·mit·tis (nuŋk' di mit'is, noonk'-) [L., now thou lettest depart: first words of the L. version] **1.** the song of Simeon, sung as a canticle in various liturgies: Luke 2:29-32 **2.** [**n- d-**] *a)* departure or farewell, esp. from life *b)* permission to depart; dismissal

nun·ci·a·ture (nun'shē ǝ chǝr, -sē-) *n.* [It. *nunziatura*] the office or term of office of a nuncio

nun·ci·o (nun'shē ō', -sē-) *n., pl.* -**ci·os'** [It. *nuncio, nunzio* < L. *nuntius*, messenger] the permanent official representative of the Pope to a foreign government; papal ambassador

nun·cle (nuŋ'k'l) *n.* [by syllabic merging of *mine* (or *an*) *uncle*] *Brit. dial. or obs. var. of* UNCLE

nun·cu·pa·tive (nuŋ'kyoo pāt'iv, nuŋ kyōō'pǝ tiv) *adj.* [LL. *nuncupativus*, so-called, nominal < L. *nuncupare*, to name before witnesses as one's heir < *nomen*, NAME + *capere*, to take] oral, not written: said esp. of wills

nun·na·tion (nu nā'shǝn) *n.* [ModL. *nunnatio* < Ar. *nūn*, the letter *n*: cf. NUN²] the addition of final, unhistoric *n* to a word, as in the declension of certain Arabic nouns: also **nun·a'tion**

nun·ner·y (nun'ǝr ē) *n., pl.* -**ner·ies** [ME. *nonnerie* < OFr.] *a former name for* CONVENT —*SYN.* see CLOISTER

nun's veiling a soft, loosely woven material, usually of worsted or silk, used for veils, dresses, etc.

nup·tial (nup'shǝl, -chǝl) *adj.* [LME. *nupcyalle* < L. *nuptialis* < *nuptiae*, marriage < *nuptus*, pp. of *nubere*, to marry: see NUBILE] **1.** of marriage or a wedding **2.** of or having to do with mating —*n.* [*pl.*] a wedding; marriage ceremony

Nu·rem·berg (noor'ǝm burg', nyoor'-) city in NC Bavaria, West Germany: site of international trials (1945-46) of Nazi war criminals: pop. 472,000: Ger. name **Nürn·berg** (nürn'berkh')

Nu·ris·tan (noor'is tan') mountainous district of E Afghanistan

nurse (nurs) *n.* [ME. *norse* < OFr. *norice* < LL. *nutricia* < L. *nutricius*, that suckles or nourishes < *nutrix* (gen. *nutricis*), wet nurse < *nutrire*, to nourish < IE. **sneu-*, var. of base **snā-*, to flow, whence Sans. *snāuti*, (she) gives milk, Gr. *naein*, to flow] **1.** *same as* WET NURSE **2.** a woman hired to take full care of another's young child or children; nursemaid **3.** a person trained to take care of the sick, injured, or aged, to assist surgeons, etc.: specif., *same as: a)* REGISTERED NURSE *b)* PRACTICAL NURSE **4.** a person or thing that nourishes, fosters, protects, etc. **5.** *Zool.* a sexually incomplete worker bee or ant that cares for the young —*vt.* **nursed, nurs'ing 1.** to give milk from the breast to (an infant); suckle **2.** to suck milk from the breast of **3.** to take care of (a child or children) **4.** to bring up; rear **5.** to tend (the sick, injured, or aged) **6.** to cause to continue, grow, or develop; nourish or foster [to *nurse* a grudge] **7.** to treat, or try to cure [to *nurse* a cold] **8.** *a)* to use, operate, or handle cautiously or carefully, so as to avoid injury, pain, exhaustion, etc. [to *nurse* an injured leg] *b)* to consume, spend, etc. slowly or carefully so as to conserve [to *nurse* a highball] **9.** to clasp; hold carefully; fondle **10.** *Billiards* to keep (the balls) close together for a series of caroms —*vi.* **1.** to be suckled; feed at the breast **2.** to suckle a child **3.** to tend the sick, injured, etc. as a nurse —**nurs'er** *n.*

nurse·maid (-mād') *n.* a woman hired to take care of a child or children: also **nurs'er·y·maid'**

nurs·er·y (nur'sə rē, nurs'rē) *n., pl.* **-er·ies** [ME. *norcery*: see NURSE] **1.** *a)* an infant's bedroom *b)* a room or apartment in a home, set apart for the children as a playroom, study, dining room, etc. **2.** a place where parents may temporarily leave children with trained attendants; specif., *same as: a)* NURSERY SCHOOL *b)* DAY NURSERY **3.** a place where young trees or other plants are raised for experimental purposes, for transplanting, or for sale **4.** anything that nourishes, protects, develops, or fosters

nurs·er·y·man (-mən) *n., pl.* **-men** (-mən) a person who owns, operates, or works for a nursery for growing and transplanting trees, plants, etc.

nursery rhyme a short, rhymed poem for children

nursery school a prekindergarten school for young children, usually between the ages of 3 and 5

nursing bottle a bottle with a rubber nipple, for feeding liquids to babies

nursing home 1. a residence equipped and staffed to provide care for the infirm, chronically ill, disabled, etc. **2.** [Chiefly Brit.] a small private hospital

nurs·ling (nurs'liŋ) *n.* **1.** a young baby still being nursed **2.** anything that is being carefully tended or cared for Also **nurse'ling**

nur·ture (nur'chər) *n.* [ME. < OFr. *norreture* < LL. *nutritura*, pp. of L. *nutrire*, to nourish: see NURSE] **1.** anything that nourishes; food; nutriment **2.** the act or process of raising or promoting the development of; training, rearing, upbringing, fostering, etc.: also **nur'tur·ance 3.** all the environmental factors, collectively, to which the individual is subjected from conception onward, as distinguished from his nature or heredity —*vt.* **-tured, -tur·ing 1.** to feed or nourish **2.** to raise or promote the development of; train, educate, rear, foster, etc. —**nur'tur·ant, nur'tur·al** *adj.* —**nur'tur·er** *n.*

Nu·sa Teng·ga·ra (nōō'sä teŋ'gä rä) *Indonesian name of* the Lesser Sunda Islands (see SUNDA ISLANDS)

nut (nut) *n.* [ME. *nutte* < OE. *hnutu*, akin to G. *nuss* < IE. **kneu-*, lump, nut (< base **ken-*, to squeeze together), whence L. *nux*, MIr. *cnū*] **1.** the dry, one-seeded fruit of any of various trees or shrubs, consisting of a kernel, often edible, in a hard and woody or tough and leathery shell, more or less separable from the seed itself, as the walnut, pecan, chestnut, acorn, etc. **2.** the kernel, or meat, of such a fruit **3.** loosely, any hard-shelled fruit that will keep more or less indefinitely, as a peanut, almond, cashew, etc. **4.** a small block, usually of metal, with a threaded hole through the center, for screwing onto a bolt, etc. **5.** *a)* a ridge of wood, ebony, etc. at the top of the fingerboard of a stringed instrument, over which the strings pass *b)* the small knob at the end of a violin bow, for tightening or loosening the hairs **6.** [Colloq.] the initial cost of an undertaking, or the amount of money it is necessary to take in before a profit is realized on it **7.** [Slang] *a)* the head *b)* [*pl.*] the testicles: a vulgar usage **8.** [Slang] *a)* a foolish, crazy, or eccentric person *b)* a devotee; fan **9.** *Printing same as* EN (sense 2) See also NUTS —*vi.* **nut'ted, nut'ting** to hunt for or gather nuts —**hard** (or **tough**) **nut to crack** a person, problem, or thing difficult to understand or deal with —**off one's nut** [Slang] foolish, silly, or crazy

nu·tant (nōōt'nt, nyōōt'-) *adj.* [L. *nutans*, prp. of *nutare*, to nod, freq. of *nuere*: see NUDGE] with the top bent downward; drooping; nodding: said of plants

nu·ta·tion (nōō tā'shən, nyōō-) *n.* [L. *nutatio* < *nutare*, to nod: see prec.] **1.** the act or instance of nodding the head **2.** a periodic variation in the inclination from the vertical of the rotation axis of a spinning body, as a top; specif., *Astron.* such a small, periodic oscillation of the earth's axis superimposed on the precessional motion **3.** *Bot.* a slight rotatory movement, as in the stem of a growing plant, due to the varying rates of growth in its parts —**nu·ta'tion·al** *adj.*

nut-brown (nut'broun') *adj.* dark-brown, like some ripe nuts

nut·crack·er (-krak'ər) *n.* **1.** an instrument for cracking the shells of nuts, usually consisting of two hinged metal levers, between which the nut is squeezed **2.** *a)* a white-spotted, dark-brown European bird (*Nucifraga caryocatactes*) of the crow family, that feeds on nuts *b)* a similar bird, **Clark's nutcracker** (*Nucifraga columbiana*) of W N. America, with grayish plumage

nut·gall (-gôl') *n.* a small, nut-shaped gall on the oak and other trees

nut·hatch (-hach') *n.* [ME. *notehach* < *note*, NUT + **hache* < MFr., HATCHET] any of various small, nut-eating birds (family Sittidae) related to the creepers and titmice, having a sharp beak and a short tail

nut·let (-lit) *n.* **1.** a small nut or nutlike fruit **2.** the pit, or stone, of a cherry, peach, plum, etc. **3.** any of the segments of an ovary which splits into parts, as in plants of the borage and mint families

nut·meat (-mēt') *n.* the kernel of a nut, esp. if edible

nut·meg (nut'meg') *n.* [ME. *notemygge*, partial transl. of OFr. *noix muscade* < Pr. *noz muscade*, lit., musky nut < L. *nux*, NUT + LL. *muscus*, MUSK] **1.** the hard, aromatic seed of an East Indian tree (*Myristica fragrans*): it is grated and used as a spice, and its outer covering yields the spice mace **2.** the tree itself

☆**nut·pick** (nut'pik') *n.* a small, sharp instrument for digging out the kernels of cracked nuts

☆**nut pine** any of several pines with edible seeds; esp., *same as* PIÑON (sense 1)

NUTMEG

☆**nu·tri·a** (nōō'trē ə, nyōō'-) *n.* [Sp. < L. *lutra*, otter, altered (with *l-* after *lutum*, mire) < IE. **udro-*, water animal (see OTTER)] **1.** a S. American water-dwelling rodent (*Myocastor coypus*), with webbed feet and a long, almost hairless tail; coypu **2.** its short-haired, soft, brown fur, often dyed to look like beaver

nu·tri·ent (nōō'trē ənt, nyōō'-) *adj.* [L. *nutriens*, prp. of *nutrire*, to nourish: see NURSE] nutritious; nourishing —*n.* anything nutritious

nu·tri·ment (-trə mənt) *n.* [L. *nutrimentum* < *nutrire*, to nourish: see NURSE] **1.** anything that nourishes; food **2.** anything that promotes growth or development —**nu'tri·men'tal** (-men't'l) *adj.*

nu·tri·tion (nōō trish'ən, nyōō-) *n.* [< L. *nutrire*, to nourish: see NURSE] **1.** a nourishing or being nourished; esp., the series of processes by which an organism takes in and assimilates food for promoting growth and replacing worn or injured tissues **2.** anything that nourishes; nourishment; food **3.** the science or study of proper, balanced diet to promote health, esp. in human beings —**nu·tri'tion·al** *adj.* —**nu·tri'tion·al·ly** *adv.*

nu·tri·tion·ist (-ist) *n.* a specialist in nutrition

nu·tri·tious (nōō trish'əs, nyōō-) *adj.* [L. *nutricius*: see NURSE] nourishing; of value as food —**nu·tri'tious·ly** *adv.* —**nu·tri'tious·ness** *n.*

nu·tri·tive (nōō'trə tiv, nyōō'-) *adj.* [ME. *nutritiff* < OFr. *nutritif* < ML. *nutritivus*] **1.** having to do with nutrition **2.** promoting nutrition; nutritious —**nu·tri·tive·ly** *adv.*

nuts (nuts) *adj.* [see NUT, 7, 8] ☆[Slang] crazy; foolish —☆*interj.* [Slang] an exclamation of disgust, scorn, disappointment, refusal, etc.: often in the phrase **nuts to (someone** or **something)** —**be nuts about** [Slang] **1.** to be greatly in love with **2.** to be very enthusiastic about

nut·shell (nut'shel') *n.* the shell enclosing the kernel of a nut —**in a nutshell** in brief or concise form; in a few words

nut·ting (nut'iŋ) *n.* the act or process of gathering or hunting for nuts —**nut'ter** *n.*

nut·ty (-ē) *adj.* **-ti·er, -ti·est 1.** containing or producing many nuts **2.** having a nutlike flavor **3.** [Slang] *a)* enthusiastic, often to excess *b)* queer, foolish, crazy, etc. —**nut'ti·ly** *adv.* —**nut'ti·ness** *n.*

nux vom·i·ca (nuks' väm'i kə) [ML. < L. *nux*, NUT + *vomere*, to vomit] **1.** the poisonous, disklike seed of an Asiatic tree (*Strychnos nux-vomica*) of the logania family, containing strychnine, brucine, and other alkaloids **2.** the tree bearing these seeds **3.** a medicine made from the seed, formerly used as a heart stimulant

nuz·zle (nuz'l) *vt.* **-zled, -zling** [ME. *noselen* < *nose*, NOSE + freq. *-elen*] **1.** to push against or rub with the nose, snout, muzzle, etc. **2.** to root up with the nose or snout: said of a pig, etc. —*vi.* **1.** to push or rub with the nose, etc. against or into something **2.** to lie close; nestle; snuggle —**nuz'zler** *n.*

NW, N.W., n.w. 1. northwest **2.** northwestern

NWbN northwest by north

NWbW northwest by west

N.W.T. Northwest Territories (Canada)

N.Y. New York

nya·la (nyä'lə) *n., pl.* **-la, -las:** see PLURAL, II, D, 2 [< EAfr. name] any of several antelopes (genus *Strepsiceros*) of E Africa, with large, spiral horns

Nya·sa (nyä'sä, ni as'ə), **Lake** lake in SE Africa, between Malawi & Mozambique: c. 11,000 sq. mi.

Nya·sa·land (-land') *former name of* MALAWI

N.Y.C. New York City

nyc·ta·lo·pi·a (nik'tə lō'pē ə) *n.* [LL. < Gr. *nyktalōps* < *nyx* (gen. *nyktos*), NIGHT + *alaos*, blind + *ōps*, EYE] *same as* NIGHT BLINDNESS: cf. HEMERALOPIA —**nyc'ta·lop'ic** (-läp'ik) *adj.*

nyc·ti- (nik'tə) [< Gr. *nyx* (gen. *nyktos*), NIGHT] *a combining form meaning* of or at night [*nyctitropic*]: also, before a vowel, **nyct-**

nyc·tit·ro·pism (nik tit'rə piz'm) *n.* [prec. + -TROPISM] the tendency of the leaves or petals of certain plants to assume a different position at night —**nyc'ti·trop'ic** (-träp'ik) *adj.*

nyc·to- (nik'tə, -tō) *same as* NYCTI-

nyc·to·pho·bi·a (nik'tə fō'bē ə) *n.* [prec. + -PHOBIA] an unnatural or excessive fear of darkness or night

Nye (nī), **Edgar Wilson** (pseud. *Bill Nye*) 1850–96; U.S. humorist

‡**nyet** (nyet) *adv.* [Russ.] no

nyl·ghai (nil'gī) *n. same as* NILGAI

NUTS
(A, square neckline; B, hexagon machine; C, wing; D, snap-on)

☆**ny·lon** (nī′län) *n.* [arbitrary coinage, prob. based on (VI)NYL + (RAY)ON] **1.** any of a group of synthetic long-chain polymeric amides with recurring amide groups, made into fiber, yarn, bristles, sheets, molded plastics, etc. that have great strength and elasticity **2.** any of the materials made from nylon; specif., [*pl.*] stockings of nylon yarn

nymph (nimf) *n.* [ME. *nimphe* < OFr. < L. *nympha* < Gr. *nymphē:* see NUBILE] **1.** *Gr. & Rom. Myth.* any of a group of minor nature goddesses, represented as beautiful maidens living in rivers, mountains, trees, etc. **2.** *a)* a lovely young woman *b)* a young woman; maiden: literary or playful usage **3.** *Entomology a)* the young of an insect with incomplete metamorphosis, differing from the adult primarily in size and structural proportions *b)* any of a genus (*Satyrus*) of N. American butterflies, having brown wings with yellowish bands —**nymph′al, nymph′e·an** *adj.*

nym·pha·lid (nim′fə lid) *n.* [< ModL. *Nymphalidae*, name of the family < *Nymphalis*, name of the type genus < Gr. *nymphē*, nymph: see NUBILE] any of a family (*Nymphalidae*) of brightly colored butterflies with very short forelegs that cannot be used for walking, including the monarch, mourning cloak, and viceroy —*adj.* of this family

nymph·et (nim′fət, nim fet′) *n.* [Fr. *nymphette*, dim. of *nymphe:* see NYMPH] a pubescent girl, esp. one who is sexually precocious —**nym·phet′ic** *adj.*

nym·pho·lep·sy (nim′fə lep′sē) *n.* [< *nympholept* (< ML. *nympholeptus* < Gr. *nympholēptos*, seized by nymphs < *nymphē* - *lēptos*, seized < *lambanein*, to take, seize) + -LEPSY] **1.** in ancient times, a state of frenzy that was believed to seize any man who looked at a nymph **2.** a violent emotional state arising as from frustrated idealism —**nym′pho·lept′** *n.* —**nym′pho·lep′tic** *adj.*

nym·pho·ma·ni·a (nim′fə mā′nē ə, -mān′yə) *n.* [ModL. < Gr. *nymphē*, bride + -MANIA] abnormal and uncontrollable desire by a woman for sexual intercourse: cf. SATYRIASIS —**nym′pho·ma′ni·ac′** (-ak′) *adj., n.*

Ny·sa (nis′ə) *Pol. name of the* NEISSE *River*

NYSE New York Stock Exchange

nys·tag·mus (nis tag′məs) *n.* [ModL. < Gr. *nystagmos*, drowsiness < *nystazein*, to be sleepy < IE. base *sneud-*, to sleep] an involuntary, rapid movement of the eyeball, usually from side to side —**nys·tag′mic** *adj.*

Nyx (niks) [Gr., NIGHT] *Gr. Myth.* the goddess of night

N.Z., N.Zeal. New Zealand

O

O, o (ō) *n., pl.* **O's, o's** **1.** the fifteenth letter of the English alphabet: from the Greek *omega* and *omicron*, both borrowed from the Phoenician **2.** a sound of O or o: in English, the mid-back vowel (ō) of *cold*, the low central vowel (ä) of *hot*, or the low back vowel (ô) of *wrong* **3.** a type or impression for O or o **4.** the numeral zero; a cipher **5.** an object shaped like O or o **6.** *a symbol for* the fifteenth (or the fourteenth if J is omitted) in a sequence or group **7.** *Physics the symbol for* ohm —*adj.* **1.** *of* O or o **2.** circular or oval in shape **3.** fifteenth (or fourteenth if J is omitted) in a sequence or group

O (ō) *interj.* an exclamation variously used: **1.** in direct address [*O* Lord!] **2.** to express surprise, fear, wonder, pain, etc.: now usually *oh* **3.** at the end of a line in some ballads —*n., pl.* **O's** a use of this exclamation *O* and *oh* are now often interchangeable

o' (ə, ō) *prep. an abbreviated form of:* **1.** of [*o'clock*] **2.** [Archaic or Dial.] on

O' (ō) [Ir. ō, descendant] *a prefix of some Irish surnames, meaning* a descendant of [*O'Reilly*]

o- *Chem.* ortho-

O 1. *Linguis.* Old [*OFr.*] **2.** *Chem.* oxygen

O. 1. Ocean **2.** October **3.** Ohio **4.** Ontario

O., o. 1. octavo **2.** old **3.** [L. *octarius*] *Pharmacy* pint

o. 1. off **2.** only **3.** *Baseball* outs

oaf (ōf) *n.* [earlier *auf, ouphe* < ON. *alfr*, ELF] **1.** orig., a changeling **2.** [Rare] a misshapen or idiotic child **3.** a stupid, clumsy fellow; lout —**oaf′ish** *adj.* —**oaf′ish·ly** *adv.* —**oaf′ish·ness** *n.*

O·a·hu (ō ä′hōō) [Haw. < ?] chief island of Hawaii: 598 sq. mi.; pop. 629,000; chief city, Honolulu

oak (ōk) *n.* see PLURAL, II, D, 3 [ME. *oke* < OE. *ac*, akin to G. *eiche* < IE. base *aig-*, oak, whence Gr. *aigilōps*, a kind of oak] **1.** any of a number of large hardwood trees and bushes (genus *Quercus*) of the beech family, bearing nuts called *acorns* **2.** the wood of an oak **3.** any of various plants resembling an oak in some way **4.** a wreath of oak leaves **5.** woodwork, furniture, etc. made of oak —*adj.* of oak; oaken

oak apple an applelike gall on oak trees

oak·en (ōk′kən) *adj.* made of the wood of the oak

Oak·land (ōk′lənd) [after the oak groves orig. there] seaport in W Calif., on San Francisco Bay, opposite San Francisco: pop. 362,000

Oak Lawn [after the many *oak* trees there] village in NE Ill.: suburb of Chicago: pop. 60,000

☆**oak-leaf cluster** a small bronze cluster of oak leaves and acorns awarded to the holder of a U.S. Army or Air Force decoration for each new award of that decoration: a silver cluster equals five bronze clusters

Oak Park [see OAK LAWN] **1.** village in NE Ill.: suburb of Chicago: pop. 63,000 **2.** city in SE Mich.: suburb of Detroit: pop. 37,000

Oak Ridge [see OAK LAWN] city in E Tenn., near Knoxville: center for atomic research: pop. 28,000

oa·kum (ō′kəm) *n.* [ME. *okom* < OE. *acumba*, tow, oakum < *a-*, away, out + *camb*, COMB¹: lit., what is combed out] loose, stringy, hemp fiber got by taking apart old ropes: used in caulking boat seams, etc.

Oak·ville (ōk′vil) town in SE Ontario, Canada, on Lake Ontario, near Toronto: pop. 53,000

☆**oak wilt** a disease of oaks which plugs the vessels of the wood and makes the leaves wilt, caused by an ascomycete fungus (*Ceratocystis fagacearum*)

oar (ôr) *n.* [ME. *ore* < OE. *ar*, akin to ON. *ār*] **1.** a long wooden pole with a broad, thin blade at one end, used in rowing or, sometimes, in steering a boat **2.** a person who uses an oar; rower —*vt., vi.* to row —**put one's oar in** to be meddlesome; interfere —**rest on one's oars** to stop to rest or relax

OAr. Old Arabic

oared (ôrd) *adj.* equipped with oars: often used in hyphenated compounds [two-*oared*]

oar·fish (ôr′fish′) *n., pl.* **-fish′, -fish′es:** see FISH² any of several large, long, narrow, deep-sea fishes (genus *Regalecus*), having a fin along the length of the back and a manelike crest behind the head: some reach a length of 30 ft. and are responsible for many reports of sea serpents

oar·lock (-läk′) *n.* a device, often U-shaped, for holding the oar in place in rowing or steering

oars·man (ôrz′mən) *n., pl.* **-men** (-mən) a man who rows; esp., an expert at rowing —**oars′man·ship′** *n.*

oar·y (ôr′ē) *adj.* [Poet.] having or like oars

OAS, O.A.S. Organization of American States

o·a·sis (ō ā′sis; *occas.* ō′ə sis) *n., pl.* **-ses** (-sēz) [L. < Gr. *oasis*, fertile spot: orig. Coptic] **1.** a fertile place in a desert, due to the presence of water **2.** any place or thing offering welcome relief from difficulty, dullness, etc.

oast (ōst) *n.* [ME. *ost* < OE. *ast* < Gmc. **aist-* < IE. base **aidh-*, to burn, whence L. *aestus*, a heat, *aestas*, summer] a kiln for drying hops, malt, or tobacco

oat (ōt) *n.* [ME. *ote* < OE. *ate:* not found in other Gmc. languages: prob. < IE. base **oid-*, to swell, whence Russ. *jádrica*, groats] **1.** [*usually pl.*] *a)* a hardy, widely grown cereal grass (*Avena sativa*) *b)* the edible grain of this grass **2.** any of various related grasses (genus *Avena*), esp. the wild oat **3.** [Obs. or Poet.] a simple musical pipe made of an oat stalk —☆**feel one's oats** [Slang] **1.** to be in high spirits; be frisky **2.** to feel and act important

oat·cake (-kāk′) *n.* a thin, flat cake made of oatmeal

oat·en (-'n) *adj.* of or made of oats, oatmeal, or oat straw

Oates (ōts), **Titus** 1649–1705; Eng. conspirator who fabricated the Popish Plot, a supposed Roman Catholic plot (1678) to massacre Protestants, burn London, & kill the king: convicted of perjury (1685) & imprisoned, but later (1689) pardoned & pensioned

oat grass any of various oatlike grasses; esp., any of several grasses (genera *Arrhenatherum* and *Danthonia*) growing on hillsides and in woods

oath (ōth) *n., pl.* **oaths** (ōthz, ōths) [ME. *oth* < OE. *ath*, akin to G. *eid*, prob. < IE. base **ei-*, to go (basic sense: ? to advance to take an oath), whence L. *ire*, to go] **1.** *a)* a ritualistic declaration, typically based on an appeal to God or a god or to some revered person or object, that

one will speak the truth, keep a promise, remain faithful, etc. b) the ritual form used in making such a declaration c) the thing promised or declared in this way **2.** the irreverent or profane use of the name of God or of a sacred thing to express anger or emphasize a statement **3.** a swearword; curse —**take oath** to promise or declare by making an oath; swear solemnly

oat·meal (ōt′mēl′) n. **1.** oats ground or rolled into meal or flakes **2.** a porridge made from such oats

Oa·xa·ca (wä hä′kä) **1.** state of SE Mexico: 36,374 sq. mi.; pop. 2,072,000 **2.** its capital: pop. 72,000

Ob (ōb; Russ. ôb′y′) **1.** river in W Siberia, flowing from the Altai Mountains northwest & north into the Gulf of Ob: 2,495 mi. **2.** Gulf of, arm of the Kara Sea, in NW Siberia: c. 600 mi. long

ob- (äb, əb) [< L. ob, toward, for, about, before < IE. base *epi-, *opi, near, at, toward, after, whence Gr. epi] a prefix meaning: **1.** to, toward, before [object] **2.** opposed to, against [obnoxious] **3.** upon, over [obfuscate] **4.** completely, totally [obsolete] **5.** inversely, oppositely [objurgate] In words of Latin origin, ob- assimilates to oc- before c [occur]; of- before f [offer]; and op- before p, [oppress]; it becomes o- before m [omit]

OB, O.B. 1. obstetrician **2.** obstetrics

ob. 1. [L. obiit] he (or she) died **2.** [L. obiter] in passing **3.** oboe

O·ba·di·ah (ō′bə dī′ə) [ult. < Heb. 'ôbhadhyāh, lit., servant of the Lord] **1.** a masculine name **2.** Bible a) one of the minor Hebrew prophets b) the book containing his prophecies: abbrev. **Ob., Obad.**

obb. obbligato

ob·bli·ga·to (äb′lə gät′ō) adj. [It., lit., obliged < L. obligatus, pp. of obligare: see OBLIGE] Music not to be left out; indispensable: said earlier of an accompaniment essential to the proper performance of a piece, but now usually of one that can be omitted —n., pl. -tos, -ti (-ē) such a musical accompaniment

ob·con·ic (äb kän′ik) adj. [OB- + CONIC] Bot. conical but attached by the point: also **ob·con′i·cal**

ob·cor·date (äb′kôr′dāt) adj. [OB- + CORDATE] Bot. heart-shaped and joined to the stem at the apex: said of certain leaves

obdt. obedient

ob·du·rate (äb′door ət, -dyoor-) adj. [ME. < L. obduratus, pp. of obdurare, to harden < ob-, intens. + durare, to harden < durus, hard: see DURESS] **1.** not easily moved to pity or sympathy; hardhearted **2.** hardened and unrepenting; impenitent **3.** not giving in readily; stubborn; obstinate; inflexible —SYN. see INFLEXIBLE —**ob′du·ra·cy** (-ə sē) n. —**ob′du·rate·ly** adv.

O.B.E. Officer (of the Order of the) British Empire

☆**o·be·ah** (ō′bē ə) n. [of WAfr. orig.] **1.** [often O-] a form of witchcraft or magic practiced by some Negroes in Africa, and formerly also in parts of the South and in the West Indies **2.** a talisman or fetish used in such witchcraft

o·be·di·ence (ō bē′dē əns, ə-) n. [ME. < OFr. < L. obedientia < obediens] **1.** the state, fact, or an instance of obeying, or a willingness to obey; submission **2.** R.C.Ch. a) the Church's jurisdiction b) all those who submit to this jurisdiction

o·be·di·ent (-ənt) adj. [ME. < OFr. < L. obediens, prp. of obedire, OBEY] obeying or willing to obey; submissive —**o·be′di·ent·ly** adv.

SYN.—obedient suggests a giving in to the orders or instructions of one in authority or control [an obedient child]; **docile** implies a temperament that submits easily to control or that fails to resist domination[a docile wife]; **tractable** implies ease of management or control but does not connote the submissiveness of **docile** and applies to things as well as people [silver is a tractable, i.e., malleable, metal]; **compliant** suggests a weakness of character that allows one to yield meekly to another's request or demand [army life had made him compliant]; **amenable** suggests such amiability or desire to be agreeable as would lead one to submit readily [he is amenable to discipline] —ANT. **disobedient, refractory**

o·bei·sance (ō bā′s′ns, -bē′-) n. [ME. obeisaunce < OFr. obeissance < obeissant, prp. of obeir, OBEY] **1.** a gesture of respect or reverence, such as a bow, curtsy, etc. **2.** the attitude shown by this; homage; deference —**o·bei′sant** adj.

ob·e·lisk (äb′ə lisk, ō′bə-) n. [L. obeliscus < Gr. obeliskos, a small spit, obelisk, dim. of obelos: see OBELUS] **1.** a tall, four-sided stone pillar tapering toward its pyramidal top **2.** same as OBELUS

ob·e·lize (äb′ə līz′) vt. -lized′, -liz′ing [Gr. obelizein] to mark with an obelus

ob·e·lus (äb′ə ləs) n., pl. -li (-lī′) [ME. < L., a spit, obelus (in LL., obelisk) < Gr. obelos, a spit, needle, obelus] **1.** a mark (— or ÷) used in ancient manuscripts to indicate questionable passages or readings **2.** same as DAGGER (sense 2)

O·ber·am·mer·gau (ō′bər äm′ər gou′) village in Bavaria, S West Germany, site of a Passion play performed usually every ten years: pop. 4,700

O·ber·hau·sen (ō′bər hou′z′n) city in W West Germany, in North Rhine-Westphalia: pop. 260,000

O·ber·land (ō′bər länt′) same as BERNESE ALPS

OBELISK

O·ber·on (ō′bə rän′, -bər ən) [Fr. < OFr. Auberon < Gmc. base of ELF, OAF] in early folklore, the king of fairyland and husband of Titania

o·bese (ō bēs′) adj. [L. obesus, pp. of obedere, to devour < ob- (see OB-) + edere, EAT] very fat; stout; corpulent —**o·be′si·ty** n.

o·bey (ō bā′, ə-) vt. [ME. obeien < OFr. obeir < L. obedire, to obey < OL. oboedire < ob- (see OB-) + audire, to hear: see AUDIENCE] **1.** to carry out the instructions or orders of **2.** to carry out (an instruction, order, etc.) **3.** to be guided by; submit to the control of [to obey one's conscience] —vi. to be obedient —**o·bey′er** n.

ob·fus·cate (äb′fus kāt′, äb fus′kāt) vt. -cat′ed, -cat′ing [< L. obfuscatus, pp. of obfuscare, to darken < ob- (see OB-) + fuscare, to obscure < fuscus, dark < IE. base *dhus-, whence DUSK, DOZE, DUST] **1.** to cloud over; obscure; make dark or unclear **2.** to muddle; confuse; bewilder —**ob′fus·ca′tion** n.

☆**o·bi¹** (ō′bē) n. same as OBEAH

o·bi² (ō′bē) n. [Jap.] the broad sash with a bow in the back, worn with a Japanese kimono

o·bit (ō′bit, äb′it) n. [ME. obite < OFr. obit < L. obitus, death < pp. of obire, to fall, die < ob- (see OB-) + ire, to go: see YEAR] same as OBITUARY

ob·i·ter dic·tum (äb′i tər dik′təm, ō′bi-) pl. **ob′i·ter dic′ta** (-tə) [L., (something) said incidentally] **1.** an incidental opinion expressed by a judge, having no bearing upon the case in question, hence not binding **2.** any incidental remark

o·bit·u·ar·y (ō bich′oo wer′ē, ə-) n., pl. -ar·ies [ML. obituarius < L. obitus: see OBIT] a notice of someone's death, as in a newspaper, usually with a brief biography —adj. of or recording a death or deaths

obj. 1. object **2.** objection **3.** objective

ob·ject (äb′jikt; for v., əb jekt′, äb-) n. [ME. < ML. objectum, something thrown in the way < L. objectus, a casting before, that which appears, orig. pp. of objicere < ob- (see OB-) + jacere, to throw: see JET¹] **1.** a thing that can be seen or touched; material thing that occupies space **2.** a) a person or thing to which action, thought, or feeling is directed b) [Old Colloq.] a person or thing that excites pity or ridicule **3.** what is aimed at; purpose; end; goal **4.** Gram. a noun or substantive that directly or indirectly receives the action of a verb, or one that is governed by a preposition: in "Give me the book," book is the direct object and me is the indirect object **5.** Philos. anything that can be known or perceived by the mind —vt. **1.** formerly, a) to oppose b) to thrust in; interpose c) to expose d) to bring forward as a reason, instance, etc.; adduce **2.** to put forward in opposition; state by way of objection [it was objected that the new tax law was unfair] —vi. **1.** to put forward an objection or objections; enter a protest; be opposed **2.** to feel or express disapproval or dislike —**ob′ject·less** adj. —**ob·jec′tor** n.

SYN.—object implies opposition to something because of strong dislike or disapproval [I object to her meddling]; **protest** implies the making of strong, formal, often written objection to something [they protested the new tax increases]; **remonstrate** implies protest and argument in demonstrating to another that he is wrong or blameworthy [he remonstrated against her hostile attitude]; **expostulate** suggests strong, earnest pleading or argument to change another's views or actions [I expostulated with him about his self-sacrifice]; **demur** implies the raising of objections or the taking of exception so as to delay action [I demurred at her proposal to dine out] See also INTENTION —ANT. **agree, consent, acquiesce**

object ball Billiards & Pool any ball other than the cue ball

object glass same as OBJECTIVE (n. 4)

ob·jec·ti·fy (əb jek′tə fī′, äb-) vt. -fied′, -fy′ing [OBJECT + -i- + -FY] to give objective form to; make objective or concrete; externalize —**ob·jec′ti·fi·ca′tion** n.

ob·jec·tion (əb jek′shən, äb-) n. [ME. objeccioun < LL. objectio < pp. of L. objicere: see OBJECT] **1.** the act of objecting **2.** a feeling or expression of opposition, disapproval, or dislike **3.** a cause for objecting; reason for opposing, disapproving, or disliking

ob·jec·tion·a·ble (-ə b'l) adj. **1.** open to objection **2.** disagreeable; offensive —**ob·jec′tion·a·bly** adv.

ob·jec·tive (əb jek′tiv, äb-) adj. [ML. objectivus] **1.** of or having to do with a known or perceived object as distinguished from something existing only in the mind of the subject, or person thinking **2.** being, or regarded as being, independent of the mind; real; actual **3.** determined by and emphasizing the features and characteristics of the object, or thing dealt with, rather than the thoughts, feelings, etc. of the artist, writer, or speaker [an objective painting, description, etc.] **4.** without bias or prejudice; detached; impersonal **5.** being the aim or goal [an objective point] ☆**6.** designating a kind of test, as a multiple-choice or true-false test, that minimizes subjective factors in answering and grading **7.** Gram. designating or of the case of an object of a preposition or transitive verb **8.** Med. designating or of a symptom or condition perceptible to others besides the patient —n. **1.** anything external to or independent of the mind; something objective; reality **2.** something aimed at or striven for **3.** Gram. a) the objective case b) a word in this case **4.** Optics the lens or lenses nearest to the object observed, as in a microscope or telescope, that focuses light to form the image

of the object —SYN. see FAIR[1], INTENTION —ob·jec'tive·ly
adv. —ob·jec'tive·ness n.

objective complement a word or group of words used in the predicate as a modifier or qualifier of the direct object (Ex.: *a stimulating and provocative teacher* in *we found him a stimulating and provocative teacher*)

ob·jec·tiv·ism (-tiv iz'm) n. 1. any of various philosophical doctrines that stress the external, independent existence of what is perceived or known 2. an ethical theory equating ethical assertions with assertions about natural or social processes 3. the use of objective methods in art or literature —ob·jec'tiv·ist n., adj. —ob·jec'tiv·is'tic adj.

ob·jec·tiv·i·ty (äb'jek tiv'ə tē) n. 1. the state or quality of being objective 2. objective reality

ob·jec·tiv·ize (əb jek'tə viz', äb-) vt. -ized', -iz'ing same as OBJECTIFY —ob·jec'ti·vi·za'tion n.

object lesson an actual or practical demonstration or exemplification of some principle

ob·jet d'art (äb'zhā där', ub'-) pl. **ob·jets d'art** (äb'zhā, ub'-) [Fr., lit., object of art] a relatively small object of artistic value, as a figurine, vase, etc.

‡**ob·jet trou·vé** (ôb zhe trōō vā') pl. **ob·jets trou·vés** (ôb zhe trōō vā') [Fr., lit., found object] an ordinary object, as a piece of driftwood, a shell, or a manufactured article, that is treated as an object of art by one who finds it aesthetically pleasing

ob·jur·gate (äb'jər gāt', əb jur'gāt) vt. -gat·ed, -gat·ing [< L. objurgatus, pp. of objurgare, to rebuke, chastise < ob- (see OB-) + jurgare, to chide, orig., to sue at law < jus (gen. juris: see JURY[1]) + agere, to do, ACT] to chide vehemently; upbraid sharply; rebuke; berate —ob'jur·ga'tion n. —ob'jur·ga'tor n. —ob·jur'ga·to·ry (-gə tôr'ē) adj.

obl. 1. oblique 2. oblong

ob·lan·ce·o·late (äb lan'sē ə lit, -lāt') adj. [OB- + LANCEOLATE] lance-shaped, with the broad end at the top: said of a leaf

ob·last (äb'last) n. [Russ. oblast'] an administrative subdivision, or region, of a republic in the U.S.S.R.

ob·late[1] (äb'lāt, äb lāt') adj. [ModL. oblatus < OB- + -latus as in prolatus (see PROLATE): from being thrust forward at the equator] Geom. flattened at the poles [an oblate spheroid]

ob·late[2] (äb'lāt) n. [ML. oblatus, offered, thrust forward < pp. of L. offerre: see OFFER] R.C.Ch. a person dedicated to the religious life; esp., a person living in or associated with a religious community but not bound by vows

ob·la·tion (ä blā'shən, ə-) n. [ME. oblacioun < OFr. oblation < L. oblatio, an offering < oblatus: see OBLATE[2]] 1. an offering of a sacrifice, thanksgiving, etc. to God or a god 2. the thing or things offered; esp., the bread and wine of the Eucharist —ob·la'tion·al, ob·la·to·ry (äb'lə tôr'ē) adj.

ob·li·gate (äb'lə gāt'; for adj., -git) vt. -gat·ed, -gat·ing [< L. obligatus, pp. of obligare: see OBLIGE] to bind by a contract, promise, sense of duty, etc.; put under obligation —adj. [ME. < L. obligatus] 1. bound; obliged 2. Biol. limited to a certain condition of life, as some parasites

ob·li·ga·tion (äb'lə gā'shən) n. [ME. obligacioun < OFr. obligation < L. obligatio] 1. an obligating or being obligated 2. a binding contract, promise, moral responsibility, etc. 3. a duty imposed legally or socially; thing that one is bound to do by contract, promise, moral responsibility, etc. 4. the binding power of a contract, promise, etc. 5. a) the condition or fact of being indebted to another for a favor or service received b) a favor or service 6. Law a) an agreement or duty by which one person (the obligor) is legally bound to make payment or perform services for the benefit of another (the obligee) b) the bond, contract, or other document setting forth the terms of this agreement —SYN. see DUTY —ob'li·ga'tion·al adj.

ob·li·ga·to (äb'lə gät'ō) adj., n., pl. -tos, -ti (-ē) same as OBBLIGATO

ob·lig·a·to·ry (ə blig'ə tôr'ē, äb'lig ə-) adj. [LL. obligatorius] 1. legally or morally binding; constituting, or having the nature of, an obligation; required 2. Biol. same as OBLIGATE —ob·lig'a·to'ri·ly adv.

o·blige (ə blij', ō-) vt. o·bliged', o·blig'ing [ME. obligen < OFr. obligier < L. obligare, to bind, oblige < ob- (see OB-) + ligare, to bind: see LIGATURE] 1. to compel by moral, legal, or physical force; constrain 2. to make indebted for a favor or kindness done; do a favor for —vi. to do a favor or service —o·blig'er n.

ob·li·gee (äb'lə jē') n. [< OBLIGE + -EE[1]] 1. a person obliged to do something for another 2. Law a person to whom another is bound by contract

o·blig·ing (ə blī'jiŋ, ō-) adj. ready to do favors; helpful; courteous; accommodating —SYN. see AMIABLE —o·blig'ing·ly adv.

ob·li·gor (äb'lə gôr', äb'lə gôr') n. [< OBLIGE + -OR] Law a person who binds himself to another by contract

ob·lique (ə blēk', ō-; also, esp. in mil. use, -blīk') adj. [ME. oblike < L. obliquus < ob- (see OB-) + liquis, awry < IE. base *leik-, var. of elei, to bend, whence ELL[2]] 1. having a

slanting position or direction; neither perpendicular nor horizontal; not level or upright; inclined 2. not straight to the point; not straightforward; indirect 3. evasive, disingenuous, underhand, etc. 4. indirectly aimed at or attained [oblique results] 5. Anat. designating or of any of certain muscles obliquely placed and attached 6. Bot. having the sides unequal, as some leaves 7. Geom. with its axis not perpendicular to its base [an oblique cone] 8. Gram. designating or of any case except the nominative and the vocative (and, sometimes, the accusative) —n. an oblique angle, muscle, etc. —vi. ob·liqu'ing 1. to veer from the perpendicular; slant 2. Mil. to change the direction of march by approximately 45 degrees —adv. Mil. at an angle of 45 degrees —ob·lique'ly adv. —ob·lique'ness n.

oblique angle any angle other than a right angle; acute or obtuse angle

oblique sailing a ship's movement in sailing on a course that forms an oblique angle with the meridian

ob·liq·ui·ty (ə blik'wə tē, ō-) n., pl. -ties [ME. obliquitee < L. obliquitas] 1. the state or quality of being oblique 2. an oblique statement, action, etc. 3. a turning aside from moral conduct or sound thinking 4. Astron. the angle between the planes of the earth's equator and its orbit about the sun, approximately 23° 27' and decreasing at the rate of 0.47'' a year 5. Math. a) deviation of a line or plane from the perpendicular or parallel b) the degree of this —ob·liq'ui·tous adj.

ob·lit·er·ate (ə blit'ə rāt', ō-) vt. -at·ed, -at·ing [< L. obliteratus, pp. of obliterare, to blot out < ob- (see OB-) + litera, LETTER[1]] 1. to blot out or wear away, leaving no traces; erase; efface 2. to do away with as if by effacing; destroy —SYN. see ERASE —ob·lit'er·a'tion n. —ob·lit'er·a'tive adj. —ob·lit'er·a'tor n.

ob·liv·i·on (ə bliv'ē ən, ō-) n. [ME. < OFr. < L. oblivio < oblivisci, to forget < ob- (see OB-) + (prob.) levis, smooth < IE. base *lei-, slippery, whence LIME[1]] 1. a forgetting or having forgotten; forgetfulness 2. the condition or fact of being forgotten 3. official overlooking of offenses; pardon

ob·liv·i·ous (-əs) adj. [ME. oblivyous < L. obliviosus < oblivio: see prec.] 1. forgetful or unmindful (usually with of or to) 2. causing forgetfulness —ob·liv'i·ous·ly adv. —ob·liv'i·ous·ness n.

ob·long (äb'lôŋ) adj. [ME. oblonge < L. oblongus, rather long < ob- (see OB-) + longus, LONG[1]] longer than broad; elongated; specif., a) rectangular and longer in one direction than in the other, esp. longer horizontally b) elliptical —n. an oblong figure

ob·lo·quy (äb'lə kwē) n., pl. -quies [ME. obliqui < LL. obloquium < L. obloqui, to speak against < ob- (see OB-) + loqui, to speak] 1. verbal abuse of a person or thing; censure or vituperation, esp. when widespread or general 2. ill repute, disgrace, or infamy resulting from this

ob·nox·ious (əb näk'shəs, äb-) adj. [L. obnoxiosus < obnoxius, subject or exposed to danger < ob- (see OB-) + noxa, harm < base of nocere, to hurt: see NECRO-] 1. orig., a) exposed or liable to injury, evil, or harm b) liable to punishment; censurable 2. very unpleasant; objectionable; offensive —SYN. see HATEFUL —ob·nox'ious·ly adv. —ob·nox'ious·ness n.

o·boe (ō'bō; now rarely -boi) n. [It. < Fr. hautbois: see HAUTBOY] 1. a double-reed woodwind instrument having a range of nearly three octaves and a high, penetrating, melancholy tone 2. an organ stop producing an oboelike sound —o'bo·ist n.

ob·o·lus (äb'l əs) n., pl. -li (-ī') [L. < Gr. obolos] 1. in ancient Greece a) a coin valued at 1/6 drachma b) a weight equal to 11 1/4 grains 2. any of several small coins formerly current in Europe Also ob'ol

ob·o·vate (äb ō'vāt) adj. inversely ovate; having the shape of the longitudinal section of an egg, with the broad end at the top, as some leaves

ob·o·void (-void) adj. [OB- + OVOID] egg-shaped, with the broad end at the top: said of some fruits, etc.

O·bre·gón (ō'bre gôn'), Ál·va·ro (äl' vä rō') 1880–1928; Mex. statesman; president (1920–24): assassinated

OBOE

Obs., obs. 1. obsolete 2. observation 3. observatory

ob·scene (äb sēn', əb-) adj. [Fr. obscène < L. obscenus, obscaenus < obs-, var. of ob- (see OB-) + caenum, filth] 1. offensive to one's feelings, or to prevailing notions, of modesty or decency; lewd 2. disgusting; repulsive —SYN. see COARSE —ob·scene'ly adv.

ob·scen·i·ty (əb sen'ə tē; also, -sē'nə-) n. [Fr. obscénité < L. obscenitas] 1. the state or quality of being obscene 2. pl. -ties an obscene remark, act, event, etc.

ob·scu·rant (äb skyoor'ənt, əb-) n. [< L. obscurans] a person or thing that obscures, esp. one that opposes or tends to prevent human progress and enlightenment

—*adj.* that obscures; of or constituting an obscurant: also **ob·scu·ran·tic** (äb′skyoo ran′tik)

ob·scu·rant·ism (-iz′m) *n.* 1. opposition to human progress or enlightenment 2. the practice of being deliberately obscure or vague —**ob·scu′rant·ist** *n., adj.*

ob·scu·ra·tion (äb′skyoo rā′shən) *n.* [L. *obscuratio*] an obscuring or being obscured

ob·scure (əb skyoor′, äb-) *adj.* [ME. < OFr. *obscur* < L. *obscurus*, lit., covered over < *ob-* (see OB-) + IE. *skuro- < base *skeu-*, to cover, conceal, whence HIDE[1], SKY] 1. lacking light; dim; dark; murky [the *obscure* night] 2. not easily perceived; specif., *a)* not clear or distinct; faint or undefined [an *obscure* figure or sound] *b)* not easily understood; vague; cryptic; ambiguous [an *obscure* explanation] *c)* in an inconspicuous position; hidden [an *obscure* village] 3. not well-known; not famous [an *obscure* scientist] 4. *Phonet.* reduced; weakened: said of a vowel pronounced as (ə) or (i) —*vt.* **-scured′, -scur′ing** [L. *obscurare* < the *adj.*] 1. to make obscure; specif., *a)* to darken; make dim *b)* to conceal from view; hide *c)* to make less conspicuous; overshadow [a success that *obscured* earlier failures] *d)* to make less intelligible; confuse [testimony that *obscures* the issue] 2. *Phonet.* to make (a vowel) obscure —*n.* [Rare] *same as* OBSCURITY —**ob·scure′ly** *adv.* —**ob·scure′ness** *n.*

SYN.—**obscure** applies to that which is perceived with difficulty either because it is concealed or veiled or because of obtuseness in the perceiver [his reasons remain *obscure*]; **vague** implies such a lack of precision or exactness as to be indistinct or unclear [a *vague* idea]; **enigmatic** and **cryptic** are used of that which baffles or perplexes, the latter word implying deliberate intention to puzzle [his *enigmatic* behavior, a *cryptic* warning]; **ambiguous** applies to that which puzzles because it allows of more than one interpretation [an *ambiguous* title]; **equivocal** is used of something ambiguous that is deliberately used to mislead or confuse [an *equivocal* answer]—**ANT.** clear, distinct, obvious

ob·scu·ri·ty (-skyoor′ə tē) *n.* 1. the quality or condition of being obscure 2. *pl.* **-ties** an obscure person or thing

ob·se·crate (äb′sə krāt′) *vt.* **-crat′ed, -crat′ing** [< L. *obsecratus*, pp. of *obsecrare*, to beseech (on religious grounds) < *ob-* (see OB-) + *sacrare:* see SACRED] [Rare] to beg for (something) or supplicate (someone); entreat —**ob·se·cra′tion** *n.*

ob·se·quies (äb′sə kwēz) *n.pl.* [< obs. sing. *obsequy* < ME. < OFr. *obseques* < ML. *obsequiae* (pl.) (< L. *obsequium*, compliance: see ff.), substituted for L. *exsequiae* (see EXEQUIES)] funeral rites or ceremonies

ob·se·qui·ous (əb sē′kwē əs, äb-) *adj.* [ME. *obsequyouse* < L. *obsequiosus < obsequium*, compliance < *obsequi*, to comply with < *ob-* (see OB-) + *sequi*, to follow: see SEQUENT] 1. much too willing to serve or obey; overly submissive; fawning 2. [Archaic] compliant; devoted; dutiful —*SYN.* see SERVILE —**ob·se′qui·ous·ly** *adv.* —**ob·se′qui·ous·ness** *n.*

ob·serv·a·ble (əb zur′və b′l, äb-) *adj.* [L. *observabilis*] 1. that can be observed; visible; discernible; noticeable 2. deserving of attention; noteworthy 3. that can or must be kept or celebrated [an *observable* holiday] —**ob·serv′a·bly** *adv.*

ob·serv·ance (-vəns) *n.* [ME. *observaunce* < OFr. *observance* < L. *observantia*, attention, regard, in LL.(Ec.), divine worship] 1. the act or practice of observing, or keeping, a law, duty, custom, rule, etc. 2. a customary act, rite, ceremony, etc. 3. the act of observing, or noting; observation 4. [Archaic] respectful attention; deference 5. *R.C.Ch. a)* the rule or constitution to be observed by a religious order *b)* an order observing such a rule

ob·serv·ant (-vənt) *adj.* [Fr., prp. of *observer*, OBSERVE] 1. strict in observing, or keeping, a law, custom, duty, rule, etc. (often with *of*) [*observant* of the rules of etiquette] 2. paying careful attention; keenly watchful 3. perceptive or alert —*n.* [O-] *former name for* FRIAR MINOR —**ob·serv′ant·ly** *adv.*

ob·ser·va·tion (äb′zər vā′shən) *n.* [ME. *observacioun* < L. *observatio*, in LL.(Ec.), reverence, outward display] 1. orig., observance, as of laws, customs, etc. 2. *a)* the act, practice, or power of noticing *b)* something noticed 3. the fact of being seen or noticed [seeking to avoid *observation*] 4. *a)* the act or practice of noting and recording facts and events, as for some scientific study *b)* the data so noted and recorded 5. a comment or remark based on something observed 6. *a)* the act of determining the altitude of the sun, a star, etc., in order to find a ship's position at sea *b)* the result obtained —*adj.* for observing —*SYN.* see REMARK

ob·ser·va·tion·al (-′l) *adj.* of or based on observation rather than experimentation

☆**observation car** a railway car with extra-large windows or a transparent dome for facilitating a view of the scenery

observation post an advanced military position from which movements of the enemy can be observed, artillery fire directed, etc.

ob·serv·a·to·ry (əb zur′və tôr′ē, äb-) *n., pl.* **-ries** [ModL. *observatorium* < pp. of L. *observare:* see ff.] 1. *a)* a building equipped for scientific observation, esp. such a building with a large telescope for astronomical research *b)* an institution for such research 2. any building or place providing an extensive view of the surrounding terrain

ob·serve (əb zurv′, äb-). *vt.* **-served′, -serv′ing** [ME.

observen < OFr. *observer* < L. *observare*, to watch, note < *ob-* (see OB-) + *servare*, to keep or hold < IE. base *ser-*, to watch over, guard, whence Sans. *haraiti*, (he) guards] 1. to adhere to, follow, keep, or abide by (a law, custom, duty, rule, etc.) 2. to celebrate or keep (a holiday, etc.) according to custom 3. *a)* to notice or perceive (something) *b)* to pay special attention to 4. to arrive at as a conclusion after study 5. to say or mention casually; remark 6. to examine and study scientifically —*vi.* 1. to take notice 2. to comment or remark (*on* or *upon*) 3. to act as an observer —*SYN.* see CELEBRATE, DISCERN —**ob·serv′ing·ly** *adv.*

ob·serv·er (-zur′vər) *n.* 1. a person who observes something; specif., *a)* a soldier manning an observation post *b)* a person who attends an assembly, convention, etc., not as an official delegate but only to observe and report the proceedings *c)* an official, usually a member of a group, sent by a UN committee to collect and report facts on the situation in a special area 2. a member of an aircraft crew, other than a pilot, with certain specialized duties and a special rating (**aircraft observer**)

ob·sess (əb ses′, äb-) *vt.* [< L. *obsessus*, pp. of *obsidere*, to besiege < *ob-* (see OB-) + *sedere*, SIT[1]] to haunt or trouble in mind, esp. to an abnormal degree; preoccupy greatly

ob·ses·sion (-sesh′ən) *n.* [L. *obsessio*] 1. orig., the act of an evil spirit in possessing or ruling a person 2. *a)* the fact or state of being obsessed with an idea, desire, emotion, etc. *b)* such a persistent idea, desire, emotion, etc., esp. one that cannot be got rid of by reasoning —**ob·ses′sion·al** *adj.*

obsessional neurosis a psychoneurosis characterized by compulsive ideas or irresistible urges and often manifested in the ritualistic performance of certain acts

ob·ses·sive (əb ses′iv, äb-) *adj.* of, having the nature of, or causing an obsession or obsessions —**ob·ses′sive·ly** *adv.* —**ob·ses′sive·ness** *n.*

ob·sid·i·an (əb sid′ē ən, äb-) *n.* [ModL. *obsidianus* < L. *Obsidianus (lapis)*, a faulty reading in Pliny (altered after L. *obsidium*, a siege < *obsidere:* see OBSESS) for *Obsianus (lapis)*, stone of Obsius, the finder of a similar stone in Ethiopia] a hard, usually dark-colored or black, volcanic glass with conchoidal fracture, often used as a gemstone

ob·so·lesce (äb′sə les′) *vi.* **-lesced′, -lesc′ing** [L. *obsolescere:* see OBSOLETE] to be or become obsolescent

ob·so·les·cent (-les′′nt) *adj.* [L. *obsolescens*] in the process of becoming obsolete —**ob′so·les′cence** *n.* —**ob′so·les′cent·ly** *adv.*

ob·so·lete (äb′sə lēt′, äb′sə lēt′) *adj.* [L. *obsoletus*, pp. of *obsolescere*, to go out of use < *ob-* (see OB-) + *solere*, to become accustomed] 1. no longer in use or practice; discarded 2. no longer in fashion; out-of-date; passé 3. *Biol.* rudimentary or poorly developed as compared with its counterpart in other individuals of a related species, the opposite sex, etc.; vestigial: said as of an organ —*vt.* **-let′ed, -let′ing** to make obsolete, as by replacing with something newer —*SYN.* see OLD —**ob′so·lete′ly** *adv.* —**ob′so·lete′ness** *n.*

ob·sta·cle (äb′sti k'l) *n.* [ME. < OFr. < L. *obstaculum*, obstacle < *obstare*, to withstand < *ob-* (see OB-) + *stare*, to STAND] anything that gets in the way or hinders; impediment; obstruction; hindrance

SYN.—**obstacle** is used of anything which literally or figuratively stands in the way of one's progress [her father's opposition remained their only *obstacle*]; **impediment** applies to anything that delays or retards progress by interfering with the normal action [a speech *impediment*]; **obstruction** refers to anything that blocks progress or some activity as if by stopping up a passage [your interference is an *obstruction* of justice]; **hindrance** applies to anything that thwarts progress by holding back or delaying [lack of supplies is the greatest *hindrance* to my experiment]; **barrier** applies to any apparently insurmountable obstacle that prevents progress or keeps separate and apart [language differences are often a *barrier* to understanding]

obstet. 1. obstetrical 2. obstetrician 3. obstetrics

ob·stet·ric (əb stet′rik, äb-) *adj.* [ModL. *obstetricus*, for L. *obstetricius*, belonging to a midwife < *obstetrix*, midwife, lit., she who stands before < *ob-* (see OB-) + *stare*, to STAND] of childbirth or obstetrics: also **ob·stet′ri·cal** —**ob·stet′ri·cal·ly** *adv.*

ob·ste·tri·cian (äb′stə trish′ən) *n.* a medical doctor who specializes in obstetrics

ob·stet·rics (əb stet′riks, äb-) *n.pl.* [with sing. *v.*] [< OBSTETRIC] the branch of medicine concerned with the care and treatment of women during pregnancy, childbirth, and the period immediately following

ob·sti·na·cy (äb′stə nə sē) *n.* [ME. *obstinacie* < ML. *obstinatia*, for L. *obstinatio*] 1. the state or quality of being obstinate; specif., *a)* stubbornness *b)* resistance to treatment; persistence, as of a disease 2. *pl.* **-cies** an obstinate act, attitude, etc.

ob·sti·nate (äb′stə nit) *adj.* [ME. < L. *obstinatus*, pp. of *obstinare*, to resolve on < *obstare*, to stand against, oppose < *ob-* (see OB-) + *stare*, to STAND] 1. unreasonably determined to have one's own way; not yielding to reason or plea; stubborn; dogged; mulish 2. resisting remedy or treatment [an *obstinate* fever] 3. not easily subdued, ended, etc. —*SYN.* see STUBBORN —**ob′sti·nate·ly** *adv.* —**ob′sti·nate·ness** *n.*

ob·sti·pa·tion (äb′stə pā′shən) *n.* [L. *obstipatio* < L. *ob-* (see OB-) + *stipans,* prp. of *stipare,* to cram, pack] [Rare] *Med.* severe and persistent constipation

ob·strep·er·ous (əb strep′ər əs, äb-) *adj.* [L. *obstreperus* < *obstrepere,* to roar at < *ob-* (see OB-) + *strepere,* to roar < IE. base *(s)trep-,* to make a loud noise, whence OE. *thræft,* strife] noisy, boisterous, or unruly, esp. in resisting or opposing —*SYN.* see VOCIFEROUS —**ob·strep′er·ous·ly** *adv.* —**ob·strep′er·ous·ness** *n.*

ob·struct (əb strukt′, äb-) *vt.* [< L. *obstructus,* pp. of *obstruere,* to block up, build against < *ob-* (see OB-) + *struere,* to pile up: for IE. base see STREW] 1. to block or stop up (a passage) with obstacles or impediments; dam; clog 2. to hinder (progress, an activity, etc.); impede 3. to cut off from being seen; block (the view) —*SYN.* see HINDER —**ob·struct′er, ob·struc′tor** *n.*

ob·struc·tion (əb struk′shən, äb-) *n.* [L. *obstructio*] 1. an obstructing or being obstructed 2. anything that obstructs; hindrance —*SYN.* see OBSTACLE

ob·struc·tion·ist (-ist) *n.* anyone who obstructs progress; esp., a member of a legislative group who hinders the passage of legislation by various technical maneuvers —*adj.* of obstructionists or obstructionism: also **ob·struc′tion·is′tic** —**ob·struc′tion·ism** *n.*

ob·struc·tive (əb struk′tiv, äb-) *adj.* obstructing or tending to obstruct —**ob·struc′tive·ly** *adv.* —**ob·struc′tive·ness** *n.*

ob·stru·ent (äb′strσo wənt) *adj.* [L. *obstruens,* prp. of *obstruere,* to block up] [Rare] obstructing; esp., blocking a passage of the body —*n.* [Rare] something, as a kidney stone, that blocks a passage of the body

ob·tain (əb tān′, äb-) *vt.* [ME. *obteinen* < OFr. *obtenir* < L. *obtinere,* to obtain, prevail, maintain < *ob-* (see OB-) + *tenere,* to hold: see TENANT] 1. to get possession of, esp. by some effort; procure 2. [Archaic] to arrive at; reach or achieve —*vi.* 1. to be in force or in effect; prevail [a law that no longer *obtains*] 2. [Archaic] to succeed —*SYN.* see GET —**ob·tain′a·ble** *adj.* —**ob·tain′er** *n.* —**ob·tain′ment** *n.*

ob·tect (äb tekt′) *adj* [< L. *obtectus,* pp. of *obtegere,* to cover over < *ob-* (see OB-) + *tegere,* to cover: see THATCH, *v.*] pertaining to an insect pupa in which the appendages and wings are glued down against the body by a secretion: also **ob·tect′ed**

ob·test (äb test′) *vt.* [L. *obtestari* < *ob-* (see OB-) + *testari,* to witness < *testis,* a witness: see TESTIFY] 1. to beg for; beseech; supplicate 2. to call to witness —**ob′tes·ta′tion** (-tes tā′shən) *n.*

ob·trude (əb trσod′, äb-) *vt.* **-trud′ed, -trud′ing** [L. *obtrudere* < *ob-* (see OB-) + *trudere,* to thrust] 1. to thrust forward; push out; eject 2. to offer or force (oneself, one's opinions, etc.) upon others unasked or unwanted —*vi.* to obtrude oneself (*on* or *upon*) —*SYN.* see INTRUDE — **ob·trud′er** *n.* —**ob·tru′sion** *n.*

ob·tru·sive (-trσo′siv) *adj.* [< L. *obtrusus,* pp. of *obtrudere* + -IVE] 1. inclined to obtrude 2. obtruding itself; esp., calling attention to itself in a displeasing way —**ob·tru′sive·ly** *adv.* —**ob·tru′sive·ness** *n.*

ob·tund (əb tund′) *vt.* [ME. *obtunden* < L. *obtundere,* to strike at, blunt < *ob-* (see OB-) + *tundere,* to strike < IE. *(s)teud-,* to strike, whence STOKE, STOCK] to make blunt or dull; make less acute; deaden

ob·tu·rate (äb′tσo rāt′, -tyσo-) *vt.* **-rat′ed, -rat′ing** [< L. *obturatus,* pp. of *obturare,* to stop up < *ob-* (see OB-) + base akin to *turgere,* to swell: see TURGID] [Rare] to close (an opening); stop up; obstruct —**ob′tu·ra′tion** *n.* —**ob′tu·ra′tor** *n.*

ob·tuse (äb tσos′, -tyσos′; also, -tyσos′) *adj.* [L. *obtusus,* blunted, dull, pp. of *obtundere:* see OBTUND] 1. not sharp or pointed; blunt 2. greater than 90 degrees and less than 180 degrees [an *obtuse* angle] 3. slow to understand or perceive; dull or insensitive 4. not producing a sharp impression; not acute [an *obtuse* pain] —*SYN.* see DULL — **ob·tuse′ly** *adv.* —**ob·tuse′ness, ob·tu′si·ty** *n.*

OBTUSE ANGLES
(ABE, DBE, CBE)

ob·verse (äb vurs′, əb-; *also, & for n. always,* äb′vurs) *adj.* [L. *obversus,* pp. of *obvertere,* to turn toward < *ob-* (see OB-) + *vertere,* to turn: see VERSE] 1. turned toward the observer 2. narrower at the base than at the top [an *obverse* leaf] 3. forming a counterpart —*n.* 1. the side, as of a coin or medal, bearing the main design: opposed to REVERSE 2. the front or main surface of anything 3. a counterpart 4. *Logic* the negative counterpart of an affirmative proposition, or the affirmative counterpart of a negative [''no one is infallible'' is the *obverse* of ''everyone is fallible''] —**ob·verse′ly** *adv.*

ob·ver·sion (äb vur′zhən, əb-) *n.* [LL. *obversio* < L. *obversus:* see OBVERSE] 1. the act of obverting 2. *Logic* inference of the obverse

ob·vert (-vurt′) *vt.* [L. *obvertere:* see OBVERSE] 1. to turn so that the main surface or a different surface is shown 2. *Logic* to state the obverse of (a proposition)

ob·vi·ate (äb′vē āt′) *vt.* **-at′ed, -at′ing** [< LL. *obviatus,* pp. of *obviare,* to prevent < *obvius:* see OBVIOUS] to do away with or prevent by effective measures; make unnecessary —*SYN.* see PREVENT —**ob′vi·a′tion** *n.*

ob·vi·ous (äb′vē əs) *adj.* [L. *obvius,* in the way, meeting: see *ob-* + VIA] 1. easy to see or understand; plain; evident 2. [Obs.] being in the way —*SYN.* see EVIDENT —**ob′vi·ous·ly** *adv.* —**ob′vi·ous·ness** *n.*

ob·vo·lute (äb′və lσot′) *adj.* [L. *obvolutus,* pp. of *obvolvere,* to wrap around < *ob-* (see OB-) + *volvere,* to roll: see WALK] having overlapping margins: said of leaves or petals: also **ob′vo·lu′tive** —**ob′vo·lu′tion** *n.*

oc- *same as* OB-: used before *c*

o/c overcharge

Oc., oc. ocean

O.C. 1. Officer Commanding 2. Old Catholic 3. *Philately* original cover

o.c. [L. *opere citato*] in the work cited

oc·a·ri·na (äk′ə rē′nə) *n.* [It., dim. of *oca,* a goose < LL. *auca,* a goose (< *avica,* back-formation < L. *avicula,* dim. of *avis,* bird): from its fancied resemblance in shape] a small, simple wind instrument shaped like a sweet potato and usually made of terra cotta, with finger holes and a mouthpiece: it produces soft, hollow tones

OCARINA

O.Carm. Order of Carmelites

O.Cart. Order of Carthusians

O'Ca·sey (ō kā′sē), **Sean** (shôn) 1880–1964; Ir. playwright

Occam, William *see* OCKHAM

occas. 1. occasion 2. occasional 3. occasionally

oc·ca·sion (ə kā′zhən) *n.* [ME. *occasioun* < OFr. < L. *occasio,* accidental opportunity, fit time < *occasus,* pp. of *occidere,* to fall < *ob-* (see OB-) + *cadere,* to fall] 1. a favorable time or juncture; opportunity 2. a fact, event, or state of affairs that makes something else possible [a chance meeting was the *occasion* of the renewal of their friendship] 3. *a)* a happening; occurrence *b)* the time at which something happens; particular time [on the *occasion* of our last meeting] 4. a special time or event, suitable for celebration 5. need arising from circumstances 6. [*pl.*] *a)* [Obs.] needs; requirements *b)* [Archaic] affairs; business —*vt.* to be the occasion of; give occasion to; cause —**on occasion** once in a while; sometimes; occasionally —**rise to the occasion** to do whatever suddenly becomes necessary; meet an emergency —**take (the) occasion** to use the opportunity (to do something)

oc·ca·sion·al (-'l) *adj.* 1. occurring on a particular occasion 2. of or for a special occasion [*occasional* verse] 3. acting only on special occasions 4. of irregular occurrence; happening now and then; infrequent 5. designating chairs, tables, etc. intended for occasional or auxiliary use 6. being the occasion, or incidental cause

oc·ca·sion·al·ism (-'l iz′m) *n.* in post-Cartesian philosophy, the doctrine that mind and matter cannot interact and that God intervenes in each instance where an act of mind is coordinated with a movement of the body

oc·ca·sion·al·ly (-'l ē) *adv.* now and then; sometimes; on occasion

oc·ci·dent (äk′sə dənt) *n.* [ME. < OFr. < L. *occidens,* direction of the setting sun < prp. of *occidere,* to fall, set < *ob-* (see OB-) + *cadere,* to fall: cf. ORIENT] [Poet.] the west —[O-] the part of the world west of Asia, esp. Europe and the Americas

oc·ci·den·tal (äk′sə den′t'l) *adj.* [ME. *occidentale*] 1. [Poet.] western 2. [O-] of the Occident, its people, or their culture; Western —*n.* [*usually* O-] a native of the Occident, or a member of a people native to that region

Oc·ci·den·tal·ism (-iz′m) *n.* the character, culture, customs, etc. of the Occident —**Oc′ci·den′tal·ist** *n.*

Oc·ci·den·tal·ize (-īz′) *vt., vi.* **-ized′, -iz′ing** to make or become Occidental in character, culture, customs, etc.

oc·cip·i·tal (äk sip′ə t'l) *adj.* [ML. *occipitalis*] of the occiput or the occipital bone —*n. same as* OCCIPITAL BONE —**oc·cip′i·tal·ly** *adv.*

occipital bone the bone that forms the back part of the skull

oc·ci·put (äk′si put′) *n., pl.* **oc·cip′i·ta** (-sip′ə tə), **-puts′** [ME. < MFr. < L. < *ob-* (see OB-) + *caput,* [head: see CHIEF] the back part of the skull or head

oc·clude (ə klσod′, ä-) *vt.* **-clud′ed, -clud′ing** [L. *occludere* < *ob-* (see OB-) + *claudere,* to CLOSE²] 1. to close, shut, or block (a passage) 2. to prevent the passage of; shut in or out 3. *Chem.* to retain or absorb (a gas, liquid, or solid) —*vi. Dentistry* to meet with the cusps fitting close together: said of the upper and lower teeth —**oc·clud′ent** *adj.*

☆**occluded front** *Meteorol.* the front formed when a warm front is overtaken by a cold front and the original air mass is forced aloft up the warm-front or cold-front surface

oc·clu·sion (ə klσo′zhən, ä-) *n.* 1. an occluding or being occluded 2. *Dentistry* the fitting together of the upper and lower teeth, or the way in which these fit together when

the jaws are closed **3.** *Meteorol.* same as OCCLUDED FRONT **4.** *Phonet.* the complete closing of the air passages in pronunciation, as of a stop —**oc·clu′sive** *adj.*

oc·cult (ə kult′, ä′kult) *adj.* [L. *occultus*, concealed, pp. of *occulere*, to cover over < *ob-* (see OB-) + *celare*, to hide (see CONCEAL)] **1.** hidden; concealed **2.** secret; esoteric **3.** beyond human understanding; mysterious **4.** designating or of certain alleged mystic arts, such as magic, alchemy, astrology, etc. —*vt.*, *vi.* to hide or become hidden from view; specif., *Astron.* to hide by occultation —**the occult** the occult arts or studies —**oc·cult′ly** *adv.* —**oc·cult′ness** *n.*

oc·cul·ta·tion (äk′ul tā′shən) *n.* [ME. *occultacioun* < L. *occultatio*, a hiding < *occultus*: see prec.] **1.** the state of becoming hidden or of disappearing from view **2.** *Astron.* an eclipse in which the apparent size of the eclipsed body is much smaller than that of the eclipsing body

oc·cult·ism (ə kul′tiz'm, äk′əl-) *n.* **1.** belief in occult forces and powers **2.** preoccupation with occult arts —**oc·cult′ist** *n.*

oc·cu·pan·cy (äk′yə pən sē) *n.*, *pl.* **-cies** [< ff.] **1.** *a)* an occupying; a taking or keeping in possession *b)* the period during which a house, etc. is occupied **2.** the condition of being occupied **3.** *Law* the taking possession of a previously unowned object, thus establishing ownership

oc·cu·pant (-pənt) *n.* [< L. *occupans*, prp. of *occupare*, OCCUPY] **1.** a person who occupies a house, post, etc. **2.** a person who acquires title to anything by occupancy

oc·cu·pa·tion (äk′yə pā′shən) *n.* [ME. < OFr. < L. *occupatio*] **1.** an occupying or being occupied; specif., the seizure and control of a country or area by military forces **2.** that which chiefly engages one's time; (one's) trade, profession, or business —**oc′cu·pa′tion·al** *adj.* —**oc′cu·pa′tion·al·ly** *adv.*

☆**occupational disease** a disease commonly acquired by people in a particular occupation [silicosis is an *occupational disease* of miners]

☆**occupational therapy** therapy by means of work, as arts and crafts, designed to divert the mind or to correct a particular physical defect

oc·cu·py (äk′yə pī′) *vt.* **-pied′**, **-py′ing** [ME. *occupien* < OFr. *occuper* < L. *occupare*, to take possession of, possess < *ob-* (see OB-) + *capere*, to seize] **1.** to take possession of by settlement or seizure **2.** to hold possession of by tenure; specif., *a)* to dwell in *b)* to hold (a position or office) **3.** to take up or fill up (space, time, etc.) **4.** to employ, busy, or engage (oneself, one's attention, mind, etc.) —**oc′cu·pi′er** *n.*

oc·cur (ə kur′) *vi.* **-curred′**, **-cur′ring** [L. *occurrere*, to run, come up to, meet < *ob-* (see OB-) + *currere*, to run: see CURRENT] **1.** to be found; exist [fish *occur* in most waters] **2.** to present itself; come to mind [an idea *occurred* to him] **3.** to take place; happen —*SYN.* see HAPPEN

oc·cur·rence (-əns) *n.* **1.** the act or fact of occurring **2.** something that occurs; event; incident —**oc·cur′rent** *adj.* *SYN.*—**occurrence** is the general word for anything that happens or takes place [an unforeseen *occurrence*]; an **event** is an occurrence of relative significance, especially one growing out of earlier happenings or conditions [the *events* that followed the surrender]; an **incident** is an occurrence of relatively minor significance, often one connected with a more important event [the award was just another *incident* in his career]; an **episode** is a distinct event that is complete in itself but forms part of a larger event or is one of a series of events [an *episode* of his childhood]; a **circumstance** is an event that is either incidental to, or a determining factor of, another event [the *circumstances* surrounding my decision]

OCD Office of Civil Defense

o·cean (ō′shən) *n.* [ME. *occean* < OFr. < L. *oceanus* < Gr. *Ōkeanos*, the outer sea (in contrast to the Mediterranean), orig. thought of as a great river flowing around the earth] **1.** the great body of salt water that covers approximately 71% of the surface of the earth **2.** any of its five principal geographical divisions: the Atlantic, Pacific, Indian, Arctic, or Antarctic Ocean **3.** any great expanse or quantity

☆**o·cean·ar·i·um** (ō′shən er′ē əm) *n.*, *pl.* **-i·ums**, **-i·a** (-ə) [OCEAN + -*arium* < L., neut. of -*arius*, -*ary*] a large salt-water aquarium for ocean fish and animals

☆**o·cean·aut** (ō′shən ôt′) *n.* [< OCEAN + Gr. *nautēs*, sailor] same as AQUANAUT

o·cean·go·ing (ō′shən gō′iŋ) *adj.* of, having to do with, or made for travel on, the ocean

O·ce·an·i·a (ō′shē an′ē ə) islands in the Pacific, including Melanesia, Micronesia, & Polynesia &, sometimes, Australia, New Zealand, & the Malay Archipelago: also **O′ce·an′i·ca** (-i kə) —**O′ce·an′i·an** *adj.*, *n.*

o·ce·an·ic (ō′shē an′ik) *adj.* **1.** of, living in, or produced by the ocean **2.** like the ocean; vast

O·ce·a·nid (ō sē′ə nid) *n.*, *pl.* **O·ce·a·ni·des** (-an′ə dēz′) [Gr. *Ōkeanis* (gen. *Ōkeanidos*)] *Gr. Myth.* any of three thousand ocean nymphs, daughters of Oceanus and Tethys

oceanog. oceanography

o·ce·a·nog·ra·phy (ō′shə näg′rə fē, ō′shē ə-) *n.* [< G. *oceanographie* < Fr. *océanographie*: see OCEAN & -GRAPHY] the study of the environment in the oceans, including the waters, depths, beds, animals, plants, etc. —**o′ce·a·nog′ra·pher** *n.* —**o′ce·a·no·graph′ic** (-nə graf′ik), **o′ce·a·no·graph′i·cal** *adj.*

☆**o·ce·an·ol·o·gy** (-näl′ə jē) *n.* [OCEAN + -o- + -LOGY] **1.** the study of the sea in all its aspects, including oceanog-

raphy, geophysical phenomena, undersea exploration, economic and military uses, etc. **2.** same as OCEANOGRAPHY —**o′ce·an·ol′o·gist** *n.*

O·cean·side (ō′shən sid′) **1.** city in SW Calif., near San Diego: pop. 40,000 **2.** suburb of New York City, on the SW coast of Long Island: pop. 35,000

ocean sunfish a large, sluggish, oceanic fish (*Mola mola*) with a greatly truncated tail

O·ce·an·us (ō sē′ə nəs) [L. < Gr. *Ōkeanos*: cf. OCEAN] *Gr. Myth.* **1.** a Titan who was god of the sea before Poseidon and father of the Oceanids **2.** the great outer stream supposedly encircling the earth

oc·el·late (äs′ə lāt′, ō sel′it) *adj.* **1.** resembling an ocellus **2.** having an ocellus or ocelli **3.** spotted Also, for senses 2 & 3, **oc′el·lat′ed**

oc·el·la·tion (äs′ə lā′shən) *n.* an eyelike spot

o·cel·lus (ō sel′əs) *n.*, *pl.* **-li** (-ī) [L., dim. of *oculus*, EYE] **1.** the simple eyespot of certain invertebrates, as distinguished from the compound eye of an insect or the camera-type eye of vertebrates and cephalopods **2.** an eyelike spot, as on a peacock's feathers —**o·cel′lar** *adj.*

o·ce·lot (äs′ə lät′, ō′sə-) *n.*, *pl.* **-lots, -lot**: see PLURAL, II, D, 1 [Fr., use (by Buffon) of Nahuatl *ocelotl*, jaguar] a large cat (*Felis pardalis*) of N. and S. America, with a yellow or gray coat marked with black spots

OCelt. Old Celtic

o·cher (ō′kər) *n.* [ME. *ocra* < L. *ochra* < Gr. *ōchra* < *ōchros*, pale, pale-yellow] **1.** an earthy clay colored by iron oxide, usually yellow or reddish brown: used as a pigment in paints **2.** the color of ocher; esp., dark yellow —*vt.* to color or mark with ocher —**o′cher·ous** *adj.*

och·loc·ra·cy (äk läk′rə sē) *n.* [Fr. *ochlocratie* < Gr. *ochlokratia* < *ochlos*, a mob, populace + -*kratia*, -CRACY] government by the mob; mob rule —**och·lo·crat** (äk′lə krat′) *n.* —**och′lo·crat′ic** *adj.*

och·one (ə khōn′) *interj.* [Scot. & Ir.] alas! woe!

o·chre (ō′kər) *n.*, *vt.* **o′chred, o′chring** *alt. sp.* of OCHER —**o′chre·ous** (-kər əs, -krē əs) *adj.*

o·chroid (ō′kroid) *adj.* [Gr. *ōchroeidēs*: see OCHER & -OID] resembling ocher; of a dark-yellow color

Ochs (äks), **Adolph Simon** 1858–1935; U.S. newspaper publisher

-ock (ək) [ME. *-ok* < OE. *-oc, -uc*, dim.] *a suffix used orig. to form the diminutive [hillock]*: it has lost its meaning in such words as *buttock, tussock*

Ock·ham (äk′əm), **William of** 1300?–49?; Eng. philosopher

o′clock (ə kläk′, ō-) *adv.* **1.** of or according to the clock [nine *o'clock* at night] **2.** as if on a clock dial, with the number 12 straight ahead or directly overhead: used to indicate direction, as of an approaching aircraft

O′Con·nell (ō kän′'l), **Daniel** 1775–1847; Ir. nationalist leader

O′Con·nor (ō kän′ər), **Thomas Power** 1848–1929; Ir. journalist & nationalist leader

☆**o·co·til·lo** (ō′ka tēl′ō; *Sp.* ô′kô tē′yô) *n.*, *pl.* **-los** (-yōz; *Sp.* -yôs) [AmSp., dim. of *ocote*, Mexican pine < Nahuatl *ocotl*] a spiny, desert candlewood (*Fouquieria splendens*) with scarlet flowers, found in the SW U.S.

oc·re·a (äk′rē ə, ō′krē ə) *n.*, *pl.* **-re·ae′** (-ē′) [ModL. < L., a legging, greave < Gr. *okris*, a projection, peak, edge] *Bot.* a tubelike covering around some stems, formed of the united stipules: found esp. in the buckwheat family —**o′cre·ate′** (-āt′, -it) *adj.*

OCS, O.C.S. Officer Candidate School

O.C.S.O. Order of Cistercians of the Strict Observance

oct- *same as:* **1.** OCTA- **2.** OCTO- Used before a vowel

Oct. October

oct. octavo

oc·ta- (äk′tə) [Gr. *okta-* < *oktō*, EIGHT] *a combining form meaning eight [octagon]*

oc·ta·chord (äk′tə kôrd′) *n.* [L. *octachordus* < Gr. *oktachordos*, eight-stringed: see prec. & CHORD[1]] *Music* **1.** a series of eight tones; esp., an octave of the diatonic scale **2.** any eight-stringed musical instrument

oc·tad (äk′tad) *n.* [Gr. *oktas* (gen. *oktados*) < *oktō*, EIGHT] **1.** a series or group of eight **2.** *Chem.* an element, atom, or radical with a valence of eight

oc·ta·gon (äk′tə gän′) *n.* [L. *octagonum* < Gr. *oktagōnos*, eight-cornered: see OCTA- & -GON] a plane figure with eight angles and eight sides —**oc·tag′o·nal** (-tag′ə n'l) *adj.* —**oc·tag′o·nal·ly** *adv.*

oc·ta·he·drite (äk′tə hē′drīt) *n.* [< LL. *octaedros* (< Gr. *oktaedros*: see ff.) + -ITE[1]] orig. thought to crystallize in octahedrons] a tetragonal mineral, titanium dioxide, TiO₂

oc·ta·he·dron (-drən) *n.*, *pl.* **-drons, -dra** (-drə) [Gr. *oktaedron*: see OCTA- & -HEDRON] a solid figure with eight plane surfaces —**oc′ta·he′dral** *adj.*

oc·tal (äk′t'l) *adj.* [OCT- + -AL] **1.** of or based on the number eight **2.** designating an electronic tube base or its matching socket designed to hold eight equally spaced pins

oc·tam·er·ous (äk tam′ər əs) *adj.* [OCTA- + -MEROUS] having eight parts in each whorl: said of flowers: also **8-merous**

oc·tam·e·ter (-ə tər) *n.* [LL., having eight feet < Gr. *oktametros*: see OCTA-

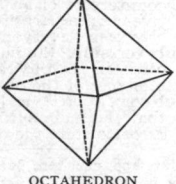

OCTAHEDRON

& -METER] a line of verse with eight metrical feet —*adj.* containing eight metrical feet

oc·tan (äk′tən) *adj.* [< L. *octo*, EIGHT + -AN] occurring every eighth day (counting both days of occurrence) —*n.* an octan fever, etc.

oc·tane (äk′tān) *n.* [OCT- + -ANE] an oily paraffin hydrocarbon, C_8H_{18}, occurring in petroleum, or any of a group of isomers of this substance

☆**octane number** (or **rating**) a number representing the antiknock properties of a gasoline, fuel mixture, etc., determined by the percentage of isooctane that must be mixed with normal heptane to produce the knocking quality of the fuel being tested: the higher the number, the greater the antiknock properties

oc·tan·gle (äk′taŋ g′l) *n.* [OCT- + ANGLE¹] *same as* OCTAGON

oc·tan·gu·lar (äk taŋ′gyə lər) *adj.* having eight angles

oc·ta·nol (äk′tə nôl′) *n.* [OCTAN(E) + -OL] any of four colorless, liquid alcohols, $C_8H_{17}OH$, used in perfumery and as solvents, foam control agents, etc.

Oc·tans (äk′tanz) [ModL.: see OCTANT] a S constellation containing the south celestial pole

oc·tant (äk′tənt) *n.* [LL. *octans*, eighth part < L. *octo*, EIGHT] **1.** an eighth of a circle; 45° angle or arc **2.** an instrument like the sextant, for measuring angles **3.** *Astron.* the position of one heavenly body when it is 45° distant from another **4.** *Math.* any of the eight parts into which a space is divided by three planes intersecting at a single point and at right angles to one another

oc·tarch·y (äk′tär kē) *n.*, *pl.* **-tarch·ies** [OCT- + -ARCHY] **1.** government by eight rulers **2.** a group of eight governments or kingdoms: sometimes applied to the Heptarchy of Anglo-Saxon England: see HEPTARCHY

oc·tave (äk′tiv, -tāv) *n.* [ME. < OFr. < L. *octava*, fem. of *octavus*, eighth < *octo*, EIGHT] **1.** *a)* the eighth day following a church festival, counting the festival day as the first *b)* the entire period between the festival and this day **2.** a group of eight lines of verse; specif., *a)* the first eight lines of a sonnet, esp. the Petrarchan sonnet *b)* *same as* OTTAVA RIMA **3.** any group of eight **4.** *Fencing* a position of thrust or parry in which the hand is rotated with the palm up **5.** *Music a)* the eighth full tone above a given tone, having twice as many vibrations per second, or below a given tone, having half as many vibrations per second *b)* the interval of eight diatonic degrees between a tone and either of its octaves *c)* the series of tones contained within this interval, or the keys of an instrument producing such a series *d)* a tone and either of its octaves sounded together *e)* an organ stop producing tones an octave above those ordinarily produced by the keys struck —*adj.* **1.** consisting of eight, or an octave **2.** *Music* producing tones an octave higher [an *octave* key] —**oc·ta·val** (äk tā′v′l, äk′tə v′l) *adj.*

Oc·ta·vi·a (äk tā′vē ə) [L., fem. of *Octavius*] **1.** a feminine name **2.** ?–11 B.C.; wife of Mark Antony

Oc·ta·vi·an (-ən) *see* AUGUSTUS (sense 2)

Oc·ta·vi·us (-əs) [L. < *octavus*, eighth] a masculine name: fem. *Octavia*

oc·ta·vo (äk tā′vō, -tä′-) *n.*, *pl.* **-vos** [< L. (*in*) *octavo*, (*in*) eight, abl. of *octavus*: see OCTAVE] **1.** the page size of a book made up of printer's sheets folded into eight leaves: the usual size of each leaf is 6 by 9 inches **2.** a book consisting of pages of this size: also called **eightvo**, and written **8vo** or **8°** —*adj.* consisting of pages of this size

oc·ten·ni·al (äk ten′ē əl) *adj.* [< LL. *octennium*, period of eight years (< L. *octo*, eight + *annus*, year) + -AL] **1.** happening every eight years **2.** lasting for eight years —**oc·ten′ni·al·ly** *adv.*

oc·tet, oc·tette (äk tet′) *n.* [OCT- + (DU)ET] **1.** any group of eight; esp., an octave (sense 2 *a*) **2.** *Music a)* a composition for eight voices or eight instruments *b)* the eight performers of this

oc·til·lion (äk til′yən) *n.* [Fr. < L. *octo*, eight + Fr. *(m)illion*] ☆**1.** in the U.S. and France, the number represented by 1 followed by 27 zeros **2.** in Great Britain and Germany, the number represented by 1 followed by 48 zeros —*adj.* amounting to one octillion in number

oc·to- (äk′tō, -tə) [L. *oktō-* < *oktō*, EIGHT] *a combining form meaning* eight [octopod]

Oc·to·ber (äk tō′bər) *n.* [ME. < OE. < L. < *octo*, EIGHT (+ -ber < ?): so named as the eighth month of the ancient Roman year, which began with March] **1.** the tenth month of the year, having 31 days: abbrev. **Oct., O. 2.** [Brit.] ale brewed in October

October Revolution *see* RUSSIAN REVOLUTION

oc·to·dec·i·mo (äk′tō des′ə mō′) *adj.*, *n.*, *pl.* **-mos** [< L. (*in*) *octodecimo*, (*in*) eighteen, abl. of *octodecimus*, eighteenth] *same as* EIGHTEENMO

oc·to·ge·nar·i·an (äk′tə ji ner′ē ən) *adj.* [L. *octogenarius*, containing eighty < *octogeni*, eighty each < *octoginta*, eighty: see OCTO- & -TY²] eighty years old, or between the ages of eighty and ninety —*n.* a person of this age

oc·to·nar·y (äk′tə ner′ē) *adj.* [L. *octonarius* < *octo*, EIGHT] of or consisting of eight or groups of eight —*n.*, *pl.* **-nar′ies 1.** a group of eight **2.** a stanza of eight lines; octave

---

oc·to·pod (äk′tə päd′) *n.* [< Gr. *oktōpous* (gen. *octōpodos*): see ff.] any animal with eight limbs; specif., any of a suborder (Octopoda) of cephalopod mollusks, including the octopus and the paper nautilus —**oc·top′o·dan** (-täp′ə dən) *adj.*, *n.* —**oc·top′o·dous** (-dəs) *adj.*

oc·to·pus (äk′tə pəs) *n.*, *pl.* **-pus·es, -pi′** (-pī′), **oc·top·o·des** (äk täp′ə dēz′) [ModL., name of the genus < Gr. *oktōpous*, eight-footed < *oktō*, EIGHT + *pous* (gen. *podos*), FOOT] **1.** any of a genus (*Octopus*) of cephalopod mollusks having a soft, saclike body, a large head with a mouth on the undersurface, and eight arms covered with suckers **2.** anything suggesting an octopus; esp., an organization with branches that reach out in a powerful and influential manner

OCTOPUS (diameter, with outspread arms, from 1 in. to 25 ft.)

☆**oc·to·roon** (äk′tə rōōn′) *n.* [OCTO- + (QUAD)ROON] a person who is the offspring of a white and a quadroon

oc·to·syl·lab·ic (äk′tə si lab′ik) *adj.* **1.** containing eight syllables, as a line of verse **2.** containing lines of eight syllables —*n.* an octosyllabic line or verse

oc·to·syl·la·ble (äk′tə sil′ə b′l) *n.* a line or word of eight syllables —*adj. same as* OCTOSYLLABIC

oc·troi (äk′troi; *Fr.* ôk trwä′) *n.*, *pl.* **-trois** (-troiz; *Fr.* -trwä′) [Fr. < *octroyer*, for earlier *ottroyer, otreier*, to grant < VL. *auctoricare* < L. *auctor*: see AUTHOR] **1.** a tax on certain goods entering a town **2.** the place where this tax is collected **3.** the official or officials collecting this tax

oc·tu·ple (äk′tōō p′l, -tyōō-; äk tōō′-, -tyōō′-) *adj.* [L. *octuplus* < *octo*, EIGHT + *-plus*: see DOUBLE] **1.** eightfold **2.** consisting of eight parts —*n.* something eight times as great as something else —*vt.* **-pled, -pling** to multiply by eight

oc·u·lar (äk′yə lər) *adj.* [LL. *ocularis* < *oculus*, EYE] **1.** of, for, or like the eye **2.** by eyesight [an *ocular* demonstration] —*n.* the lens or lenses constituting the eyepiece of an optical instrument —**oc′u·lar·ly** *adv.*

oc·u·list (-list) *n.* [Fr. *oculiste* < L. *oculus*, EYE] *earlier term for* OPHTHALMOLOGIST

oc·u·lo- (äk′yə lō, -lə) [< L. *oculus*, EYE] *a combining form meaning* the eye

oc·u·lo·mo·tor (äk′yə lō mōt′ər) *adj.* [prec. + MOTOR] moving the eyeball; specif., designating or of either nerve of the third pair of cranial nerves, arising in the midbrain and supplying four of the six muscles that move each eyeball

Od, ’Od (äd) *interj.* [*often* o-] [Archaic] a euphemism for *God*, used in oaths, etc.

od (äd) *n.*, *pl.* **od** [G., coined by K. v. Reichenbach (1788–1869), G. scientist] a hypothesized force in nature formerly thought to manifest itself in such phenomena as hypnotism, magnetism, light, etc. —**od′ic** *adj.*

OD, O.D. 1. Officer of the Day **2.** olive drab **3.** outside diameter **4.** overdraft **5.** overdrawn **6.** [L. *oculus dexter*] right eye

O.D. Doctor of Optometry

o·da·lisque, o·da·lisk (ōd′l isk) *n.* [Fr. *odalisque* < Turk. *ōdalik*, chambermaid < *ōdah*, chamber + -*lik*, suffix expressing function] **1.** a female slave or concubine in an Oriental harem **2.** a conventionalized painting of a reclining odalisque as variously by Matisse

ODan. Old Danish

Odd (äd) *interj. same as* OD

odd (äd) *adj.* [ME. *odde* < ON. *oddi*, point of land, triangle, hence (from the third angle) odd number, akin to OE. *ord*, a point] **1.** *a)* being one of a pair of which the other is missing [an *odd* glove] *b)* being the one remaining after the others are paired, grouped, taken, etc. *c)* being one or more of a set, series, or group separated from the others [a few *odd* volumes of Dickens] **2.** having a remainder of one when divided by two; not even: said of numbers **3.** numbered with an odd number [the *odd* months] **4.** *a)* in addition to that mentioned in a round number [ten dollars and some *odd* change] *b)* with a relatively small number over that specified [thirty *odd* years ago] **5.** not the usual, regular, habitual, accounted for, etc.; occasional; incidental [*odd* jobs, at *odd* moments] **6.** *a)* not usual or ordinary; singular; peculiar; strange *b)* queer; eccentric **7.** out-of-the-way [in *odd* corners] —*n.* an odd, or additional, thing; specif., *Golf a)* a stroke more than one's opponent has played *b)* [Brit.] a stroke taken from a player's total score for a hole, to give him odds —*SYN.* see STRANGE —**odd man** out a person left out when others pair off or form into groups —**odd′ly** *adv.* —**odd′ness** *n.*

☆**odd·ball** (-bôl) *n.* [ODD + BALL¹] [Slang] an eccentric, unconventional, or nonconforming person —*adj.* strange or unconventional

Odd Fellow a member of the Independent Order of Odd

Fellows, a fraternal and benevolent secret society, originated in England in the 18th cent.

odd·i·ty (äd/ə tē) *n.* **1.** the state or quality of being odd; queerness; peculiarity; strangeness **2.** *pl.* **-ties** an odd person or thing

☆**odd lot** an amount smaller than the usual unit of trading; specif., a quantity of less than 100 shares of stock in a transaction —**odd'-lot'** *adj.*

odd·ment (-mənt) *n.* [ODD + -MENT] **1.** any of various miscellaneous items **2.** a scrap or remnant

odd-pin·nate (äd'pin'āt) *adj. Bot.* pinnate with an odd, or single, terminal leaflet

odds (ädz) *n.pl.* [*sometimes, esp. formerly, with sing. v.*] **1.** formerly, inequalities **2.** [Now Rare] difference or amount of difference **3.** difference in favor of one side over the other; advantage **4.** an equalizing advantage given by a bettor or competitor in proportion to the assumed chances in his favor —**at odds** in disagreement; quarreling —**by (all) odds** by far; unquestionably —**the odds are** the likelihood is

odds and ends scraps; remnants; oddments

odds-on (-än') *adj.* having better than an even chance of winning [*an odds-on bet, favorite, etc.*]

ode (ōd) *n.* [Fr. < LL. *oda* < Gr. *ōidē*, song, contr. < *aoidē* < *aeidein*, to sing < IE. *aweid*- < base *aw*-, to speak, whence Sans. *vádati*, (he) speaks] **1.** orig., a poem written to be sung **2.** in modern use, a lyric poem, rhymed or unrhymed, typically addressed to some person or thing and usually characterized by lofty feeling, elaborate form, and dignified style —**od·ic** (ō'dik) *adj.*

-ode[1] (ōd) [< Gr. *hodos*, path, way < IE. base *sed*-, to go, whence L. *cedere*] *a suffix meaning* way, path [*anode, cathode*]

-ode[2] (ōd) [Gr. *-ōdēs, -ōdes* < *-ō*-, ending of base or thematic vowel + *-eidēs*, like, -OID] *a suffix meaning* like or something like [*phyllode*]

O·den·se (ō'ʻthən sə, -dən-) seaport on N Fyn island, Denmark: pop. 133,000

O·der (ō'dər) river in C Europe, flowing northeast through Czechoslovakia & Poland, into the Baltic: c. 560 mi.: it forms, with the Neisse, the boundary (**Oder-Neisse Line**) between East Germany & Poland

O·des·sa (ō des'ə) **1.** seaport in S Ukrainian S.S.R., on the Black Sea: pop. 753,000 **2.** city in WC Tex.: pop. 78,000

O·dets (ō dets'), **Clifford** 1906–63; U.S. playwright

o·de·um (ō dē'əm) *n., pl.* **o·de'ums, o·de'a** (-ə) [LL. < Gr. *ōideion* < *ōidē*: see ODE] **1.** in ancient Greece and Rome, a roofed building' for musical performances **2.** a modern concert hall

O·din (ō'din) [Dan. < ON. *Othinn*, akin to OE. *Woden*] *Norse Myth.* the chief deity, god of art, culture, war, and the dead: identified with the Teutonic Woden

o·di·ous (ō'dē əs) *adj.* [ME. < OFr. *odieus* < L. *odiosus* < *odium*, hatred: see ff.] arousing or deserving hatred or loathing; disgusting; offensive —*SYN.* see HATEFUL —**o'di·ous·ly** *adv.* —**o'di·ous·ness** *n.*

o·di·um (-əm) *n.* [L. *odium*, hatred, ill will < *odi*, I hate < IE. base *od*-, hatred, whence Gr. *odyssasthai*, to be angry, ON. *atall*, frightful] **1.** *a)* hatred, esp. of a person or thing regarded as loathsome *b)* the state or fact of being hated **2.** the disgrace brought on by hateful action; opprobrium —*SYN.* see DISGRACE

O·do·a·cer (ō'dō ā'sər) 435?–493 A.D.; 1st barbarian ruler of Italy (476–493)

o·do·graph (ō'də graf', -gräf') *n.* [< Gr. *hodos*, way (see -ODE[1]) + -GRAPH] a device for measuring distance traveled

☆**o·dom·e·ter** (ō däm'ə tər) *n.* [Fr. *odomètre* < Gr. *hodometros* < *hodos*, way (see -ODE[1]) + *metron*, MEASURE] an instrument for measuring the distance traveled by a vehicle

-o·dont (ə dänt') [< Gr. *odōn* (gen. *odontos*), TOOTH] *a combining form meaning* tooth [*macrodont*]

o·don·tal·gi·a (ō'dän tal'jē ə, -tal'jə) *n.* [Gr. *odontalgia*: see ff. & -ALGIA] pain in a tooth; toothache

o·dont·o- (ō dän'tə, -tō) [< Gr. *odōn* (gen. *odontos*), TOOTH] *a combining form meaning* tooth or teeth [*odontoblast, odontology*]: also, before a vowel, **odont-**

o·don·to·blast (ō dän'tə blast') *n.* [prec. + -BLAST] any of the cells forming the outer surface of the pulp of a tooth and secreting a substance which develops into dentin —**o·don'to·blas'tic** *adj.*

o·don·to·glos·sum (ō dän'tə gläs'əm) *n.* [ModL. < ODONTO- + Gr. *glōssa*, a tongue: see GLOSS[2]] any of a genus (*Odontoglossum*) of tropical American, epiphytic orchids with clustered flowers of various colors

o·don·to·graph (ō dän'tə graf', -gräf') *n.* [ODONTO- + -GRAPH] **1.** an instrument for laying out or marking gear teeth **2.** an instrument for recording the surface irregularities of a tooth

o·don·toid (ō dän'toid) *adj.* [Gr. *odontoeidēs*: see ODONTO- & -OID] **1.** toothlike **2.** designating or of a toothlike or peg-shaped process projecting from the second vertebra of the neck, on which the top vertebra moves and rotates

o·don·tol·o·gy (ō'dän täl'ə jē) *n.* [Fr. *odontologie*: see ODONTO- & -LOGY] the science dealing with the structure, growth, and diseases of the teeth; dentistry —**o·don'to·log'i·cal** (-tə läj'i k'l) *adj.* —**o·don'to·log'i·cal·ly** *adv.* —**o'don·tol'o·gist** *n.*

o·don·to·phore (ō dän'tə fôr') *n.* [ODONTO- + -PHORE] a muscular structure of most mollusks, usually protrusible, supporting the radula —**o·don·toph·o·ral** (ō dän täf'ər əl) *adj.*

o·dor (ō'dər) *n.* [ME. < OFr. < L. < IE. base *od*-, to smell, odor, whence Gr. *odmē*, (var. of *osmē*), scent, Sw. *os*, smell, suffocating gas] **1.** *a)* that characteristic of a substance which makes it perceptible to the sense of smell *b)* a smell, whether pleasant or unpleasant; fragrance, stench, etc. **2.** a pervasive atmosphere or quality [*an odor of intolerance*] **3.** [Archaic] a perfume or other sweet-smelling substance —*SYN.* see SMELL —**be in bad (or ill) odor** to have a poor reputation; be in ill repute —**o'dor·less** *adj.*

o·dor·ant (-ənt) *n.* [ODOR + -ANT] any substance or thing that produces a perceptible odor

o·dor·if·er·ous (ō'də rif'ər əs) *adj.* [ME. < L. *odorifer*: see ODOR & -FEROUS] giving off an odor, often specif. a fragrant one —**o'dor·if'er·ous·ly** *adv.* —**o'dor·if'er·ous·ness** *n.*

o·dor·ous (ō'dər əs) *adj.* having an odor; esp., fragrant —**o'dor·ous·ly** *adv.* —**o'dor·ous·ness** *n.*

o·dour (ō'dər) *n. Brit. sp.* of ODOR

O·do·va·car (ō'dō vā'kər) *same as* ODOACER

O·dra (ō'drä) *Pol. name of the* ODER *River*

-o·dus (ə dəs) [ModL. < Gr. *-odous* < *odōn*, TOOTH] *a combining form meaning* having teeth, toothed

od·yl, od·yle (äd'il, ōd'-) *n.* [< *od* + Gr. *hylē*, matter] *same as* OD

-o·dyn·i·a (ə din'ē ə, -din'-) [ModL. < Gr. *-odynia* < *odynē*, a pain] *a combining form meaning* pain in (a specified organ or part) [*osteodynia*]

O·dys·se·us (ō dis'yōōs, -dis'ē əs) [Gr. *Odysseus*] the hero of the *Odyssey*, a king of Ithaca and one of the Greek leaders in the Trojan War: L. name, *Ulysses*

Od·ys·sey (äd'ə sē) [L. *Odyssea* < Gr. *Odysseia*] an ancient Greek epic poem, ascribed to Homer, about the wanderings of Odysseus during the ten years after the fall of Troy —*n.* [*sometimes* o-] *pl.* **-seys** any extended wandering or journey —**Od'ys·se'an** *adj.*

oe (ō) *n.* [< Faeroese *othi* < *othur*, raging < ON. *other* < PGmc. *wōtha*, whence WOOD[2]] a whirlwind near the Faeroe Islands

oe- an earlier variant spelling for many words of Gr. and L. origin, now usually written with *e-*

OE., OE, O.E. Old English

o.e. omissions excepted

oec·u·men·i·cal (ek'yoo men'i k'l; *chiefly Brit.* ē'kyoo-) *adj. alt. sp. of* ECUMENICAL

OED, O.E.D. Oxford English Dictionary

oe·de·ma (ē dē'mə) *n. chiefly Brit. sp. of* EDEMA

Oed·i·pal (ed'ə pəl, ē'də-) *adj.* [*also* o-] of or relating to the Oedipus complex

Oed·i·pus (-pəs) [L. < Gr. *Oidipous* (< *oidein*, to swell + *pous*, foot: lit. swollen foot] *Gr. Myth.* the son of Láius and Jocasta, king and queen of Thebes, who, raised by the king of Corinth, later returned to Thebes and unwittingly killed his father and married his mother

Oedipus complex *Psychoanalysis* the unconscious tendency of a child to be attached to the parent of the opposite sex and hostile toward the other parent: its persistence in adult life results in neurotic disorders: orig. restricted to a son's attachment: cf. ELECTRA COMPLEX

‡**oeil-de-boeuf** (ë y' də bëf') *n., pl.* **oeils-de-boeuf'** (ë y'-) [Fr., lit., eye of an ox,] a round or oval window

‡**oeil·lade** (ë yàd') *n.* [Fr. < *oeil*, an eye < L. *oculus*, EYE] an amorous or flirting glance; ogle

oe·nol·o·gy (ē näl'ə jē) *n.* [< Gr. *oinos*, wine + -LOGY] *alt. sp. of* ENOLOGY —**oe·nol'o·gist** *n.*

oe·no·mel (ē'nə mel') *n.* [LL. *oenomeli* < Gr. *oinomeli* < *oinos*, WINE + *meli*, honey: see MEL] **1.** a beverage of wine and honey, drunk by the ancient Greeks **2.** [Poet.] strong, sweet speech, etc.

Oe·no·ne (ē nō'nē) [L. < Gr. *Oinōnē*] *Gr. Myth.* a nymph who became the wife of Paris and was deserted by him for Helen of Troy

o'er (ôr) *prep., adv. chiefly poet. contr. of* OVER

oer·sted (ʉr'sted) *n.* [after Hans Christian *Oersted* (1777–1851), Dan. physicist] **1.** the cgs electromagnetic unit of magnetic intensity, or magnetizing force, equal to a force of one dyne acting upon a unit magnetic pole in a vacuum **2.** formerly, the cgs unit of magnetic reluctance

oe·soph·a·gus (i säf'ə gəs) *n. chiefly Brit. sp. of* ESOPHAGUS

oestrous, oestrus, etc. *Brit. sp.* of ESTROUS, ESTRUS, etc.

‡**oeu·vre** (ë'vr') *n., pl.* **oeu·vres** (ë'vr') [Fr.] **1.** all the works, usually of a lifetime, of a particular writer, artist, or composer **2.** any single artistic work

of (uv, äv; *unstressed* əv *or sometimes before consonants,* ə) *prep.* [ME. < OE., unstressed var. of *af, æf,* away (from); akin to G. *ab* < IE. base *apo*-, from, away from, whence L. *ab* (cf. AB-), Gr. *apo*-] **1.** from; specif., *a)* coming from [*men of Ohio*] *b)* as relates to [*how wise of her*] *c)* resulting from; caused by; through [*to die of fever*] *d)* at a distance from; apart from [*east of the city*] *e)* proceeding as a product from; by [*the poems of Poe*] *f)* deprived, relieved, or separated from [*cured of cancer, robbed of his money*] *g)* from the whole, or total number, constituting [*part of the time, one of her hats*] *h)* made from; using (a specified substance) as the material [*a

sheet *of* paper, made *of* tin] **2.** belonging to [pages of a book, the square root *of* a number] **3.** *a)* having; possessing [a man *of* property] *b)* containing [a bag *of* nuts] **4.** *a)* that is; having the designation; specified as [the State *of* Utah, a height *of* six feet] **5.** as a kind of [a prince of a fellow] **6.** with (something specified) as object, goal, etc. [a reader *of* books] **7.** having as a distinguishing quality or attribute; characterized by [a man *of* honor, a year *of* plenty] **8.** with reference to; concerning; about [think well *of* me] **9.** set aside for; dedicated to [a day *of* rest] **10.** *a)* during [*of* late years] *b)* on (a specified time) [he came *of* a Friday] **11.** before: used in telling time [ten *of* nine] **12.** [Archaic] by [rejected *of* men] *Of* is also used in various idiomatic expressions (as in *of course*), many of which are entered in this dictionary under the key words
of- (ôf, äf, əf) *same as* OB-: used before *f* [*offer*]
OF., O.F. Old French
off (ôf) *adv.* [a LME. var. of *of*, OF, later generalized for all occurrences of *of* in stressed positions] **1.** so as to be or keep away, at a distance, to a side, etc. [to move *off*, to ward *off*] **2.** so as to be measured, divided, etc. [to pace *off*, to mark *off*] **3.** so as to be no longer on, attached, united, covering, in contact, etc. [take *off* your hat, the paint wore *off*] **4.** (a specified distance) away: *a)* in space [a town ten miles *off*] *b)* in time [a date two weeks *off*] **5.** *a)* so as to be no longer in operation, function, continuance, etc. [turn the motor *off*] *b)* to the point of completion, extinction, or exhaustion [drink it *off*] **6.** so as to be less, smaller, fewer, etc. [to allow 5% *off* for cash] **7.** so as to lose consciousness [to doze *off*] **8.** away from one's work or usual activity [to take a week *off*] —*prep.* **1.** (so as to be) no longer (or not) on, attached, united, covering, in contact, etc. [it blew *off* the desk, a car *off* the road] **2.** away from [to live *off* the campus] **3.** from the substance of; on [to live *off* an inheritance] *b)* at the expense of **4.** coming or branching out from [an alley *off* Main Street] **5.** free or relieved from [*off* duty] **6.** not up to the usual level, standard, etc. of [*off* one's game] **7.** [Colloq.] no longer using, engaging in, supporting, etc.; abstaining from [to be *off* liquor] **8.** [Colloq.] from [to buy something *off* another] —*adj.* **1.** not on, attached, united, etc. [his hat is *off*] **2.** not in operation, function, continuance, etc. [the motor is *off*] **3.** gone away; on the way [be *off* to bed] **4.** less, smaller, fewer, etc. [sales are *off*] **5.** away from work, etc.; absent [the maid is *off* today] **6.** not up to what is usual, normal, standard, etc. [an *off* day] **7.** more remote; further [on the *off* chance, the *off* side] **8.** designating the horse on the right in double harness, etc. **9.** in (specified) circumstances [to be well *off*] **10.** not correct; in error; wrong [his figures are *off*] **11.** *Cricket* designating the side of the field facing the batsman **12.** *Naut.* toward the sea; seaward —*n.* **1.** the fact or condition of being *off* [turn the switch from *off* to on] **2.** *Cricket* the off side —*interj.* go away! stay away! *Off* is also used in various idiomatic expressions, many of which are entered in this dictionary under the key words —**off and on** now and then; intermittently —**off with!** put off! take off! remove! —**off with you!** go away! depart!
off. **1.** offered **2.** office **3.** officer **4.** official **5.** official
of-fal (ôf′l, äf′-) *n.* [ME. *ofall*, lit., off-fall] **1.** [*with sing. or pl. v.*] waste parts; esp., the entrails, etc. of a butchered animal **2.** refuse; garbage
off-beat (ôf′bēt′) *n. Music* any of the beats of a measure that have weak, or secondary, accents —*adj.* ☆**1.** *Jazz* having the strong, or primary, accent on the second and fourth beats in 4/4 time [*offbeat* rhythm] **2.** [Colloq.] not conforming to the usual pattern or trend; unconventional, unusual, strange, etc.
☆**off-Broad-way** (-brôd′wā′) *adj.* designating, of, or produced in any theater located outside the main theatrical district in New York City and presenting professional productions that are often unconventional, experimental, low-cost, etc. —*adv.* in an off-Broadway theater or theaters —*n.* off-Broadway theaters and their productions collectively *Also written* **Off Broadway**
off-cast (-kast′, -käst′) *adj., n. same as* CASTOFF
off-col-or (-kul′ər) *adj.* **1.** varying from the usual, standard, or required color ☆**2.** not quite proper; in rather poor taste; risqué [an *off*-color joke]
Of-fen-bach (ôf′ən bäkh′) city in C West Germany, on the Main River, in Hesse state: pop. 117,000
Of-fen-bach (ôf′n bäk′; *Fr.* ôf ən bäk′), **Jacques** (zhäk) (born *Jakob Eberscht*) 1819?-80; Fr. composer of operettas, born in Germany
of-fence (ə fens′) *n. Brit. sp. of* OFFENSE
of-fend (ə fend′) *vi.* [ME. *offenden* < OFr. *offendre* < L. *offendere*, to strike against < *ob*- (see OB-) + *-fendere*, to hit, strike: see DEFEND] **1.** to break a law, religious commandment, etc.; commit a sin or crime **2.** to create resentment, anger, or displeasure; give offense —*vt.* **1.** to hurt the feelings of; cause to feel resentful, angry, or displeased; insult **2.** to be displeasing to (the taste, sense, etc.) **3.** [Obs.] *a)* to transgress; violate *b)* to cause to sin —**of-fend′er** *n.*

SYN.—offend implies a causing displeasure or resentment in another, intentionally or unintentionally, by wounding his feelings or by a breach of his sense of propriety [he will be *offended* if he is not invited]; **affront** implies open and deliberate disrespect or offense [to *affront* one's modesty]; **insult** implies an affront so insolent or contemptuously rude as to cause deep humiliation and resentment [to *insult* someone by calling him a liar]; **outrage** implies an extreme offense against one's sense of right, justice, propriety, etc. [he was *outraged* by the offer of a bribe]
of-fense (ə fens′, ôf′ens, äf′-) *n.* [ME. < MFr. < L. *offensa* < pp. of *offendere:* see prec.] **1.** an offending; specif., *a)* the act of breaking a law; sin or crime; transgression *b)* the act of creating resentment, hurt feelings, displeasure, etc. **2.** the condition of being offended, esp. of feeling hurt, resentful, or angry; umbrage **3.** [Rare] something that causes sinning or wrongdoing **4.** something that causes resentment, anger, etc. **5.** the act of attacking or assaulting; aggression **6.** the person, army, etc. that is attacking ☆**7.** the side that is seeking to score in any contest —**give offense** to offend; anger, insult, etc. —**take offense** to become offended; feel hurt, angry, etc.
SYN.—offense implies displeased or hurt feelings as the result of a slight, insult, etc. [don't take *offense* at my criticism]; **resentment** adds implications of indignation, a brooding over an injury, and ill will toward the offender [a *resentment* cherished for days]; **umbrage** implies offense or resentment at being slighted or having one's pride hurt [he took *umbrage* at the tone of her letter]; **pique** suggests a passing feeling of ruffled pride, usually over a trifle; **displeasure** may describe a feeling varying from dissatisfaction or disapproval to anger and indignation
of-fense-less (ə fens′lis) *adj.* **1.** not offending **2.** lacking or incapable of offense
of-fen-sive (ə fen′siv) *adj.* [ML. *offensivus* < L. *offensa*, OFFENSE] **1.** attacking; aggressive **2.** of or for attack ☆**3.** designating or of the side that is seeking to score in any contest **4.** unpleasant, as to the senses; disgusting; repugnant [an *offensive* odor] **5.** causing resentment, anger, etc.; insulting —*n.* **1.** attitude or position of attack (often with *the*) **2.** an attack or hostile action, esp. by armed forces —**of-fen′sive-ly** *adv.* —**of-fen′sive-ness** *n.*
of-fer (ôf′ər, äf′-) *vt.* [ME. *offren* < OE. & OFr.: OE. *offrian* < LL.(Ec.) *offerre*, to offer to God, sacrifice; OFr. *offrir:* both < L. *offerre*, to bring before, present, show < *ob*- (see OB-) + *ferre*, to BEAR] **1.** to present to God or a god in an act of worship (often with *up*) [to *offer* prayers, *offer* up sacrifices] **2.** to present for approval or acceptance; proffer; tender [to *offer* one's services] **3.** to present for consideration; suggest; propose [to *offer* a plan] **4.** to indicate or express one's willingness or intention (to do something) [to *offer* to go] **5.** to show or give signs of [to *offer* resistance] **6.** *a)* to present for sale *b)* to bid (a price, etc.) —*vi.* **1.** to make a presentation or sacrifice in worship **2.** to occur; present itself [when the opportunity *offers*] **3.** [Rare] to make a proposal, as of marriage **4.** [Archaic] to make an attempt (*at*) —*n.* **1.** the act of offering **2.** something offered; presentation, proposal, suggestion, bid, etc. **3.** *Law* a proposal supported by adequate consideration, the full and complete acceptance of which constitutes a contract —**of′fer-er** *n.*, esp. *Law* **of′fer-or** *n.*
SYN.—offer is the general term meaning to hold out before one for acceptance or refusal [to *offer* money, help, etc.]; **proffer**, a literary term, is usually used of something intangible [she accepted the *proffered* assistance]; **tender** is a formal or polite synonym [to *tender* one's thanks, resignation, etc.] and is specifically applied to something offered in payment of an obligation; **present** often adds to **offer** the idea of outward show, formality, or ceremony [to *present* a petition to Congress, to *present* a new play]
of-fer-ing (-iŋ) *n.* **1.** the act of making an offer **2.** something offered; specif., *a)* a gift or contribution *b)* presentation in worship; oblation ☆*c)* something offered for sale *d)* a theatrical presentation
of-fer-to-ry (ôf′ər tôr′ē, äf′-) *n., pl.* -**ries** [ME. *offertorie* < ML.(Ec.) *offertorium* < LL.(Ec.), place for offerings < *offerre*, to OFFER] [*often* O-] **1.** that part of Holy Communion during which the Eucharistic bread and wine are offered to God: in the Anglican Church, alms are collected at this time **2.** any collection of money at a church service, or the part of the service for this **3.** the prayers, anthem, or music that accompany the offertory
off-glide (ôf′glīd′) *n.* a glide coming immediately after a speech sound in which the vocal organs resume their normal inactive position or take the position for articulating a following sound
off-hand (ôf′hand′) *adv.* without prior preparation or study; at once; extemporaneously —*adj.* **1.** said or done offhand; extemporary; unpremeditated **2.** casual, curt, informal, brusque, etc. *Also* **off′hand′ed** —**off′hand′ed-ly** *adv.* —**off′hand′ed-ness** *n.*
of-fice (ôf′is, äf′-) *n.* [ME. < OFr. < L. *officium* < *opus*, a work (see OPUS) + *facere*, to DO] **1.** something performed or intended to be performed for another; (specified kind of) service [done through someone's good (or ill) *offices*] **2.** *a)* a function or duty assigned to someone, esp. as an essential part of his work or position *b)* the function or characteristic action of a particular thing **3.** a position of

authority or trust, esp. in a government, business, institution, etc. [the *office* of president] **4.** ☆a) any of the branches of the U.S. Government ranking next below the departments [the Printing *Office*] b) [Chiefly Brit.] a governmental department [the Foreign *Office*] **5.** *a)* the building, room, or series of rooms in which the affairs of a business, professional person, branch of government, etc. are carried on b) all the people working in such a place; staff **6.** [*pl.*] [Chiefly Brit.] the rooms or buildings of a house or estate in which the servants carry out their duties **7.** [ME. < ML.(Ec.) *officium*, divine rite < L., ceremonial observance] a religious ceremony or rite; specif., a) [O-] *clipped form of* DIVINE OFFICE, LITTLE OFFICE b) the Morning and Evening Prayer of the Anglican Church c) [*often pl.*] prayers or rites for any special purpose —*SYN.* see FUNCTION, POSITION

☆**office boy** a boy who works in an office, doing odd jobs and errands

of·fice·hold·er (-hōl′dər) *n.* a government official, esp. one holding office through political patronage

office hours the hours during which an office is normally open for business or consultation

of·fi·cer (ôf′ə sər, äf′-) *n.* [ME. < Anglo-Fr. & OFr. *officier* < ML. *officiarius* < L. *officium*, OFFICE] **1.** anyone elected or appointed to an office or position of authority in a government, business, institution, society, etc. **2.** a policeman or constable **3.** a person appointed to a position of authority in the armed forces; specif., *same as* COMMISSIONED OFFICER **4.** the captain or any of the mates of a nonnaval ship **5.** in certain honorary societies, a member of any grade above the lowest —*vt.* **1.** to provide with officers. **2.** to command; direct; manage

officer of the day *Mil.* the officer in overall charge of the interior guard and security of his garrison for any given day

officer of the deck the officer in charge of a naval ship during a given watch

officer of the guard *Mil.* an officer detailed under the officer of the day to be in immediate command of the interior guard of a garrison

office seeker a person who tries to get himself appointed to public office

of·fi·cial (ə fish′əl) *adj.* [ME. < OFr. < LL. *officialis*] **1.** of or holding an office, or position of authority **2.** by, from, or with the proper authority; authorized or authoritative [an *official* request] **3.** in a formal or ceremonious manner, often involving persons of authority [an *official* welcome to the city] **4.** formally set or prescribed [the *official* date of publication] **5.** *Med., Pharmacy* contained in the current pharmacopoeia; authorized for use in medicine —*n.* **1.** a person holding office, esp. public office ☆**2.** *Sports* one who supervises an athletic contest, as a referee, umpire, etc. —**of·fi′cial·ly** *adv.*

of·fi·cial·dom (-dəm) *n.* **1.** officials collectively **2.** the domain or position of officials

of·fi·cial·ese (ə fish′ə lēz′) *n.* [see -ESE] the pompous, wordy, and involved language typical of official communications and reports

of·fi·cial·ism (ə fish′əl iz′m) *n.* **1.** the characteristic practices and behavior of officials; esp., excessive adherence to official routine and regulations; red tape **2.** officials collectively; officialdom

of·fi·ci·ant (ə fish′ē ənt) *n.* [< ML.(Ec.) *officians*] an officiating priest, minister, etc.

of·fi·ci·ar·y (-er′ē) *n., pl.* -**ar′ies** [ML. *officiarius*] ☆a group of officials —*adj.* connected with or resulting from the holding of an office

of·fi·ci·ate (-āt′) *vi.* -**at′ed**, -**at′ing** [< ML. *officiatus*, pp. of *officiare*] **1.** to perform the duties of an office; act as an officer **2.** to perform the functions of a priest, minister, rabbi, etc. at a religious ceremony **3.** *Sports* to act as referee, umpire, etc. —**of·fi′ci·a′tion** *n.* —**of·fi′ci·a′tor** *n.*

of·fic·i·nal (ə fis′i n′l) *adj.* [ML. *officinalis* < *officina*, storeroom (of a monastery) < L., workshop, contr. of *opificina* < *opifex*, worker < *opus*, a work (see OPUS) + *facere*, to DO¹] [Obs.] commonly kept in stock in a pharmacy: said of products or drugs dispensed without prescription —*n.* [Obs.] an officinal drug or preparation

of·fi·cious (ə fish′əs) *adj.* [L. *officiosus* < *officium*, OFFICE] **1.** orig., ready to serve; obliging **2.** offering unnecessary and unwanted advice or services; meddlesome, esp. in a highhanded or overbearing way **3.** in diplomacy, unofficial or informal —**of·fi′cious·ly** *adv.* —**of·fi′cious·ness** *n.*

off·ing (ôf′iŋ) *n.* [< OFF] **1.** the distant part of the sea visible from the shore **2.** distance, or position at a distance, from the shore —**in the offing** **1.** at some distance but in sight **2.** at some indefinite time in the future

off·ish (ôf′ish) *adj.* [Colloq.] *same as* STANDOFFISH

off-key (ôf′kē′) *adj.* **1.** not on the right note; flat or sharp **2.** not quite in accord with what is normal, fitting, etc.

off-lim·its (-lim′its) *adj.* ruled to be a place or area that cannot be entered, visited, or patronized by a specified group

off-line (-līn′) *adj.* designating or of equipment not directly controlled by the central processor of a computer system

off·load (-lōd′) *vt., vi.* [OFF + LOAD, prob. orig. transl. of Afrik. *aflaai* < Du. *afladen*] *same as* UNLOAD

☆**off-off-Broad·way** (ôf′ôf′brôd′wā′) *adj.* of or having to do with noncommercial, highly experimental theatrical

productions, presented in small halls, churches, cafés, etc. in New York City —*adv.* in such productions or locations —*n.* off-off-Broadway productions collectively Also written **Off-Off-Broadway**

off·print (-print′) *n.* a separate reprint of an article, etc. that first appeared in a magazine or other larger publication —*vt.* to reprint (an excerpt, etc.) separately

off-put·ting (-poot′iŋ) *adj.* [Chiefly Brit.] tending to put one off; distracting, annoying, etc.

off·scour·ing (-skour′iŋ) *n.* [*usually pl.*] **1.** something scoured off; rubbish; refuse **2.** an outcast from society

off·set (ôf′set′; *for v., usually* ôf set′) *n.* **1.** something that is set off, or has sprung or developed, from something else; offshoot; extension; branch; spur **2.** anything that balances, counteracts, or compensates for something else; compensation **3.** *rare var. of* OUTSET **4.** *Archit.* a ledge or recess formed in a wall by a reduction in its thickness above **5.** *Bot.* a side shoot that takes root and starts a new plant **6.** *Elec.* a branch off a main power line **7.** *Mech.* a curve or bend in a metal bar, pipe, etc. to permit it to pass an obstruction **8.** *Printing a) same as* OFFSET PRINTING *b)* an impression made by this process *c)* an ink smudge transferred from a freshly printed sheet to the one next to it **9.** *Surveying* a short distance measured at right angles from the main line to help in computing the area of an irregular plot of ground —*adj.* **1.** of, relating to, or being an offset **2.** that is offset, off center, or at an angle —*vt.* -**set′**, -**set′ting** **1.** to balance, complement, counteract, compensate for, etc. **2.** to make an offset in **3.** *Printing a)* to make (an impression) by offset printing *b)* to smudge with an offset —*vi.* **1.** to come out or develop as an offset **2.** *Printing* to make an offset

offset printing a lithographic printing process in which the inked impression is first made on a rubber-covered roller, then transferred to paper

off·shoot (ôf′shōōt′) *n.* anything that branches off, or derives from, a main source; specif., a shoot or stem growing laterally from the main stem of a plant

off·shore (-shôr′) *adj.* **1.** moving off or away from the shore **2.** situated or in operation at some distance from shore —*adv.* away or far from the shore; seaward

off·side (-sīd′) *adj. Sports* not in the proper position for play; specif., a) *Football* over the line of scrimmage or otherwise ahead of the ball before the play has begun, and hence subject to penalty b) *Ice Hockey* moving into the attacking zone ahead of the puck —*n.* an offside play

off·spring (-spriŋ′) *n., pl.* -**spring′**, -**springs′** [ME. *ofspring* < OE.: see OFF & SPRING] **1.** a child or animal as related to its parent **2.** a descendant or descendants collectively; progeny **3.** a product, outcome, or result

off·stage (-stāj′) *n.* that part of a stage, as the wings, not visible to the audience —*adj.* in or from the offstage [an *offstage* whisper] —*adv.* **1.** to the offstage [to go *offstage*] **2.** when not actually appearing before the public

off-the-shelf (-*th*ə shelf′) *adj.* designating commercial products that are ready for use, esp. by the military, without modification

off-white (-hwīt′, -wīt′) *adj.* of any of various shades of grayish-white or yellowish-white

☆**off year** **1.** a year in which a major, esp. presidential, election does not take place **2.** a year of little production, poor crops, etc. —**off′-year′** *adj.*

OFr. Old French

OFris. Old Frisian

oft (ôft) *adv.* [ME. < OE. akin to G. *oft*, Dan. *ofte*, Sw. *ofta*, Goth. *ufta*] *chiefly poet. var. of* OFTEN

of·ten (ôf′'n, ôf't'n) *adv.* [ME. var. of prec.] many times; repeatedly; frequently —*adj.* [Archaic] frequent

of·ten·times (-timz′) *adv. same as* OFTEN: also [Chiefly Poet.] **oft′times′**

O.G. **1.** Officer of the Guard **2.** *Philately* original gum: also **o.g.**

O·ga·sa·wa·ra Gun·to (ō gä′sä wä′rä goon′tō) *Jap. name of* BONIN ISLANDS

Og·bo·mo·sho (äg′bə mō′shō) city in SW Nigeria: pop. 342,000

Og·den (äg′dən, ôg′-) [after P. S. *Ogden*, local fur trader] city in N Utah: pop. 69,000

Og·den (äg′dən, ôg′-), C(harles) K(ay) 1889-1957; Eng. educator & linguist: devised BASIC ENGLISH

og·do·ad (äg′dō ad′) *n.* [LL.(Ec.) *ogdoas* (gen. *ogdoadis*) < Gr. *ogdoas* < *oktō*, EIGHT] **1.** the number eight **2.** any group or series of eight

o·gee (ō′jē, ō jē′) *n.* [ME. (pl.) *oggez* < OFr. *ogive*, OGIVE] **1.** a molding having an S-shaped curve in profile **2.** any S-shaped curve or line **3.** an ogee arch

ogee arch a pointed arch formed with the curve of an ogee on each side

O·gel·thorpe (ō′g'l thôrp′), **James Edward** 1696-1785; Eng. general: founder of the colony of Georgia (1733)

og·ham (äg′əm) *n.* [Ir. < OIr. *ogam*] an alphabetic system of writing Old Irish developed in the 5th and 6th centuries A.D. in which the letters are represented by various combinations of lines or notches as along the edge of a memorial stone: also **og′am**

OGEE ARCH

o·give (ō′jīv, ō jīv′) *n.* [Fr. < OFr.,

prob. < Sp. *aljibe*, a cistern < Ar. *al-ğubb*, a well] **1.** the diagonal rib or groin of a Gothic vault **2.** a pointed, or Gothic, arch —**o·gi′val** *adj.*

o·gle (ō′g'l, ä′-) *vi.*, *vt.* **o′gled**, **o′gling** [prob. < LowG. *oegeln* (akin to G. *äugeln*) < *oog*, EYE] to keep looking (at) boldly and with obvious desire; make eyes (at) —*n.* an ogling look —**o′gler** *n.*

o·gre (ō′gər) *n.* [Fr., altered < ? L. *Orcus*, Pluto, Hades] **1.** in fairy tales and folklore, a man-eating monster or giant **2.** a hideous, coarse, or cruel man —**o′gre·ish**, **o′grish** *adj.* —**o′gress** *n.fem.*

O·gyg·i·a (ō jij′ē ə) [L. < Gr. *Ōgygia*] in Homer's *Odyssey*, the island of the sea nymph Calypso

oh (ō) *interj.* **1.** an exclamation expressing surprise, fear, wonder, pain, etc. **2.** a word used in direct address, as to attract attention [*oh*, waiter!] —*n.*, *pl.* **oh's**, **ohs** any instance of this exclamation

O. Henry *see* HENRY

OHG, OHG., O.H.G. Old High German

O'Hig·gins (ō hig′ənz; *Sp.* ō ē′gēns), **Ber·nar·do** (ber när′dō) 1778–1842; Chilean revolutionary leader; 1st president of Chile (1817–23)

O·hi·o (ō hī′ō) **1.** [after the river] Middle Western State of the NC U.S.: admitted, 1803; 41,222 sq. mi.; pop. 10,652,000; cap. Columbus: abbrev. **O.**, **OH 2.** [< Fr. < Iroquoian, lit., fine (or large) river] river formed by the junction of the Monongahela & the Allegheny at Pittsburgh, flowing southwestward into the Mississippi: 981 mi. —**O·hi′o·an** (-ə wən) *adj.*, *n.*

ohm (ōm) *n.* [after Georg Simon *Ohm* (1789–1854), G. physicist] the practical mks unit of electrical resistance, equal to the resistance of a circuit in which an electromotive force of one volt maintains a current of one ampere

ohm·ic (ō′mik) *adj.* **1.** of the ohm **2.** measured in ohms **3.** designating or of any device that uses the principles of Ohm's law

ohm·me·ter (ōm′mēt′ər) *n.* [OHM + -METER] an instrument for measuring directly electrical resistance in ohms

Ohm's law [see OHM] a law which states that the steady current through certain electric circuits is directly proportional to the applied electromotive force

o·ho (ō hō′) *interj.* [ME. *o ho!*: cf. O & HO] an exclamation expressing surprise, taunting, triumph, etc.

-oid (oid) [Gr. *-o-eidēs* < *-o-*, termination of prec. element + *-eidēs*, *-oid* < *eidos*, a form, shape < IE. base *wedi*, to see, whence WISE[1], L. *videre*] *an adj.-forming and n.-forming suffix meaning* like, resembling [*crystalloid*, *metalloid*]

-oi·de·a (oi′dē ə) [ModL.: see -OID] *a combining form used to form the name* of a zoological class or superfamily [*Hominoidea* (a primate superfamily)]

oil (oil) *n.* [ME. *oile* < OFr. < L. *oleum*, oil, olive oil < Gr. *elaion*, (olive) oil, akin to *elaia*, olive] **1.** any of various kinds of greasy, combustible substances obtained from animal, vegetable, and mineral sources: oils are liquid at ordinary temperatures and soluble in certain organic solvents, as ether, but not in water **2.** *same as* PETROLEUM **3.** any of various substances having the consistency of oil. **4.** *same as*: *a)* OIL COLOR *b)* OIL PAINTING **5.** [Colloq.] smooth, hypocritical flattery —*vt.* **1.** to smear, lubricate, or supply with oil **2.** to bribe —*adj.* of, from, like, or yielding oil, or having to do with the production or use of oil —**pour oil on troubled waters** to settle quarrels, differences, etc. by calm, soothing methods —☆**strike oil 1.** to discover oil under the ground by drilling a shaft for it **2.** to become suddenly wealthy —**oiled** *adj.*

oil beetle any of various small beetles (esp. genus *Meloë*) which, when disturbed, produce an oily secretion from glands on the legs

oil·bird (-bʉrd′) *n. same as* GUACHARO

oil cake a cake or mass of crushed linseed, rapeseed, cottonseed, etc. from which the oil has been extracted, used as livestock feed and as a fertilizer

oil·can (-kan′) *n.* a can for holding oil, esp. one with a spout, used for lubricating machinery, etc.

oil·cloth (-klôth′, -kläth′) *n.* cloth made waterproof with oil or, now especially, with heavy coats of paint: used to cover tables, shelves, etc.

oil color a color or paint made by grinding a pigment in oil, esp. linseed oil

oil·cup (-kup′) *n.* a container (in a machine) for releasing oil gradually as lubrication for moving parts

oil·er (-ər) *n.* **1.** a person or thing that oils machinery, engines, etc. **2.** an oilcan **3.** a ship for transporting oil; tanker ☆**4.** [Old Colloq.] an oilskin coat

☆**oil field** a place where oil deposits of value are found

oil of turpentine *same as* TURPENTINE (sense 3)

oil of vitriol [so called because green vitriol was its source] *same as* SULFURIC ACID

oil painting 1. a picture painted in oil colors **2.** the art of painting in oil colors

oil palm a tropical African palm (*Elaeis guineensis*) whose seeds yield palm oil

oil·pa·per (-pā′pər) *n.* paper made transparent and waterproof by treatment with oil

oil shale shale containing hydrocarbons which can be extracted, esp. by distillation

oil·skin (-skin′) *n.* **1.** cloth made waterproof by treatment with oil **2.** [*often pl.*] a garment or outfit made of this, as a coat, or a suit of jacket and trousers

☆**oil slick** a film of oil on water, forming a smooth area

oil·stone (-stōn′) *n.* a whetstone treated with oil

☆**oil well** a well bored through layers of rock, etc. to a supply of petroleum

oil·y (-ē) *adj.* **oil′i·er**, **oil′i·est 1.** of, like, consisting of, or containing oil **2.** covered with oil; fat; greasy **3.** too smooth; slippery; unctuous —**oil′i·ly** *adv.* —**oil′i·ness** *n.*

☆**oink** (oink) *n.* the grunt of a pig, or a sound in imitation of it —*vi.* to grunt as or like a pig

oint·ment (oint′mənt) *n.* [ME. *oignement* < OFr. < VL. **unguimentum*, for L. *unguentum* (see UNGUENT): the *-t-* in Eng. from association with obs. v. *oint*, to anoint] a fatty substance applied to the skin for healing or cosmetic purposes; salve; unguent

OIr. Old Irish

Oir·each·tas (er′əkh təs) *n.* [Ir.] the legislature of Ireland, consisting of the Dail Eireann (lower house) and the Seanad Eireann (upper house)

Oise (wäz) river flowing from S Belgium southwest through N France into the Seine: 186 mi.

Oi·strakh (oi′sträkh), **David (Fyodorovich)** 1908– ; Russ. violinist

OIT Office of International Trade

OIt. Old Italian

oi·ti·ci·ca (oit′i sē′kə) *n.* [Port. < native (Tupi) name] a tree (*Licania rigida*) of the rose family, found in NE Brazil and yielding hard, heavy wood and large seeds rich in a drying oil (**oiticica oil**) similar to tung oil

☆**O·jib·wa** (ō jib′wā, -wä, -wə) *n.* [Algonquian *ojibway*, to roast till puckered (< *ojib*, to pucker + *uh-way*, to roast): from the puckered seam on their moccasins] **1.** *pl.* **-was**, **-wa** any member of a group of N. American Indian tribes living in Michigan, Wisconsin, Minnesota, and North Dakota **2.** their Algonquian language —*adj.* of these tribes Also **O·jib′way** (-wā)

☆**OK**, **O.K.** (ō′kā′; also, & for v. & n. usually, ō′kā′) *adj.*, *adv.*, *interj.* [orig. U.S. colloq.: first known use (March 23, 1839) by C. G. Greene, editor, in the Boston *Morning Post*, as if abbrev. for "oll korrect," facetious misspelling of *all correct* (cf. *Am. Speech*, Vol. XXXVIII, No. 1): popularized by use in name of Democratic *O.K.* Club (1840), in allusion to *Old Kinderhook*, native village of Martin Van Buren, whom the Club supported for a 2d term] all right; correct —*n.*, *pl.* **OK's**, **O.K.'s** approval; endorsement —*vt.* **OK'd**, **O.K.'d**, **OK'ing**, **O.K.'ing** to put an OK on; approve; endorse

O·ka (ō kä′) river in C European R.S.F.S.R., flowing northeast into the Volga: c. 950 mi.

o·ka·pi (ō kä′pē) *n.*, *pl.* **-pis**, **-pi**: see PLURAL, II, D, 1 [native Afr. name] an African animal (*Okapia johnstoni*) related to the giraffe, but having a much shorter neck

O·ka·van·go (ō′kə vän′gō) *same as* OKOVANGGO River

☆**o·kay** (ō′kā′) *adj.*, *adv.*, *interj.*, *n.*, *vt. colloq. var. of* OK

O·ka·ya·ma (ō′kä yä′mä) seaport in SW Honshu, Japan, on the Inland Sea: pop. 292,000

oke[1] (ōk) *n.* [< Turk. *ōqah* < Ar. *ūqīyah* < Gr. *oungia*: see OUNCE[1]] in Cyprus, Lebanon, Libya, Saudi Arabia, and Syria, a unit of weight equal to about 2 3/4 lbs.; also, in Cyprus, a unit of liquid measure equal to about 1 1/10 qt.

☆**oke[2]** (ōk) *interj. slang var. of* OK

O·kee·cho·bee (ō′kē chō′bē), **Lake** [< AmInd. < ?] lake in SE Fla. at the N edge of the Everglades: 700 sq. mi.: main element of a system (**Okeechobee Waterway**) of connected canals, rivers, & lakes across the Fla. peninsula, 155 mi. See EVERGLADES, map

O'Keeffe (ō kēf′), **Georgia** 1887– ; U.S. painter

O·ke·fe·no·kee Swamp (ō′kə fə nō′kē) [< AmInd. name, lit., trembling earth + SWAMP] swamp in SE Ga. & NE Fla.: c. 700 sq. mi.

O'Kel·ly (ō kel′ē), **Sean T(homas)** (shôn) 1882–1966; Ir. nationalist leader; president of Ireland (1945–59)

☆**o·key-doke** (ō′kē dōk′) *adj.*, *interj. slang var. of* OK: also **o′key-do′key** (-dō′kē)

O·khotsk (ō kätsk′; *Russ.* ō khôtsk′), **Sea of** arm of the Pacific, off the E coast of Siberia: 590,000 sq. mi.

☆**O·kie** (ō′kē) *n.* [OK(LAHOMA) + -IE] a migratory agricultural worker, esp. one forced to migrate from Oklahoma or other areas of the Great Plains because of drought, farm foreclosure, etc., in the late 1930's

O·ki·na·wa (ō′kə nä′wä) largest island of the Ryukyus, in the W Pacific northeast of Taiwan: 454 sq. mi.; pop. 759,000; cap. Naha City —**O′ki·na′wan** *adj.*, *n.*

OKAPI
(to 5 ft. high at shoulder)

---

ok·ka (äk′ə) n. [var. of OKE¹] in Turkey and Jordan, a unit of weight equal to about 2 3/4 lbs.

☆**O·kla·ho·ma** (ō′klə hō′ma) [< Choctaw *okla*, people + *homma*, red] State of the SC U.S.: admitted, 1907; 69,919 sq. mi.; pop. 2,559,000; cap. Oklahoma City: abbrev. **Okla., OK** —**O′kla·ho′man** adj., n.

Oklahoma City capital of Okla., in the C part: pop. 366,000 (met. area 641,000)

O·ko·vang·go (ō′kə väŋ′gō) river in SW Africa, flowing from C Angola southeast into a marshy basin (**Okovanggo Basin**) in N Botswana: c. 1,000 mi.

o·kra (ō′krə) n. [< WAfr. name] 1. a tall annual plant (*Hibiscus esculentus*) of the mallow family, grown for its slender, ribbed, sticky green pods 2. the pods, used as a cooked vegetable and in soups, stews, etc. 3. *same as* GUMBO (sense 2)

Ok·to·ber·fest (äk tō′bər fest′; G. ŏk tō′bər fest′) n. 1. a beer-drinking festival held in Munich, Germany, in the fall 2. a similar festival held elsewhere

-ol¹ (ōl, ôl) [< (ALCOH)OL] *a suffix used in chemistry to mean* an alcohol or phenol [*menthol, thymol*]

-ol² (ōl, ôl) var. of -OLE

OL., O.L. Old Latin

O·laf (ō′läf, -läf) 1. **Olaf I** (*Olaf Tryggvesson*) 965?-1000; king of Norway (995-1000): subject of many legends 2. **Olaf II**, Saint, (*Olaf Haraldsson*) 995?-1030; king of Norway (1015-28): patron saint of Norway: his day is July 29 3. **Olaf V** 1903- ; king of Norway (1957-): son of HAAKON VII Also sp. **Olav**

Ö·land (ö länd′) Swed. island in the Baltic Sea, off the SE coast of Sweden: c. 520 sq. mi.

OKRA

old (ōld) adj. **old′er** or **eld′er**, **old′est** or **eld′est** [ME. < OE. (Anglian) *ald*, WS. *eald*, akin to G. *alt* < IE. base *al*-, to grow, whence L. *alere*, to nourish: basic sense "grown"] 1. having lived or been in existence for a long time; aged 2. of, like, or characteristic of aged people; specif., mature in judgment, wise, etc. 3. of a certain or specified age or duration [a boy ten years *old*] 4. made or produced some time ago; not new 5. familiar or known from the past; accustomed [up to his *old* tricks] 6. [often O-] designating the form of a language in its earliest stage of development [*Old* English] 7. having been in use for a long time; worn out by age or use; shabby 8. that was at one time; former [his *old* teacher] 9. having had long experience or practice [an *old* hand at this work] 10. belonging to the remote past; having existed long ago; ancient [an *old* civilization] 11. dating or continuing from some period long before the present; of long standing [an *old* tradition] 12. designating the earlier or earliest of two or more [the *Old* World] 13. [Colloq.] dear: a term of affection or cordiality [*old* boy] 14. Geol. having reached the stage of greatly decreased activity or showing extensive reduction of topographical form: said of streams, mountain ranges, etc. Also used as a colloquial intensive, esp. after certain favorable adjectives [a fine *old* time, good *old* Al] —n. 1. time long past; yore [days of *old*] 2. a person of a specified age: used in hyphenated compounds [a six-year-*old*] 3. something old (with *the*) —**old′ness** n.

SYN.—**old** implies a having been in existence or use for a relatively long time [*old* shoes, *old* civilizations]; **ancient** specifically implies reference to times long past [*ancient* history]; **antique** is applied to that which dates from ancient times, or, more commonly, from a former period [*antique* furniture]; **antiquated** is used to describe that which has become old-fashioned or outdated [*antiquated* notions of decorum]; **archaic**, in this connection, applies to that which is marked by the characteristics of an earlier period [an *archaic* iron fence surrounded the house]; **obsolete** is applied to that which has fallen into disuse or is out-of-date [*obsolete* weapons] —**ANT. new, modern**

old age the advanced years of human life, when strength and vigor decline: cf. MIDDLE AGE

Old Bai·ley (bā′lē) historic criminal court in London on Old Bailey Street

Old Boy [often o- b-] [Chiefly Brit. Colloq.] an alumnus, esp. of a boys' preparatory school

Old Castile see CASTILE

Old·cas·tle (ōld′kas′'l), Sir **John**, Lord Cobham, 1378?-1417; Eng. Lollard leader: executed as a heretic

Old Catholic a member of a religious sect organized by Roman Catholics who, in 1870, refused to accept the doctrine of papal infallibility

Old Church Slavic the South Slavic language used in the 9th century Bible translation by Cyril and Methodius and still used as a liturgical language by Orthodox Slavs but extinct as a vernacular: also called **Old Church Slavonic, Old Bulgarian**

☆**old country** the country from which an immigrant came: said esp. of a country in Europe

Old Delhi same as DELHI (sense 2)

☆**Old Dominion** nickname of VIRGINIA (State)

Old Dutch the Dutch language in its oldest stage: it is actually recorded only on fragmentary relics, but may be

reconstructed from Middle Dutch and from loan words in related languages: cf. OLD LOW FRANCONIAN

old·en (ōl′d'n) adj. [ME., inflected form of *old*] [Poet.] old; ancient; of old, or of former times

Ol·den·burg (ōl′d'n burg′; G. ōl′dən boorkh′) 1. former state of NW Germany, earlier a grand duchy 2. city in NW West Germany, in Lower Saxony: pop. 128,000

Old English 1. the West Germanic, Low German language of the Anglo-Saxons, comprising West Saxon, the major literary dialect, and the Kentish, Northumbrian, and Mercian dialects: it was spoken in England from c. 400 to c. 1100 A.D. 2. *same as* BLACK LETTER

Old English sheep·dog (shēp′dôg′, -däg′) any of an English breed of strong, medium-sized dog, with long, shaggy, gray or bluish hair

☆**Old Faithful** a noted geyser in Yellowstone National Park, which erupts about every 67 minutes

old-fan·gled (ōld′faŋ′g'ld) adj. [OLD + (NEW)FANGLED] *same as* OLD-FASHIONED

old-fash·ioned (ōld′fash′ənd) adj. suited to or favoring the styles, methods, manners, or ideas of past times; esp., out-of-date; antiquated; outmoded —☆n. [also O- F-] an iced cocktail containing whiskey, a dash of soda, bitters, sweetening, and bits of fruit

old fogy, old fogey see FOGY

Old French the French language from c. 800 to c. 1550 A.D., esp. French from the 9th to the 14th century: cf. MIDDLE FRENCH

Old Frisian a West Germanic language, closely related to Old English, preserved in documents from the 13th to the 16th century

☆**Old Glory** the flag of the United States

old gold a soft, yellowish, metallic color

Old Guard [transl. of Fr. *Vieille Garde*: so named in contrast to the Young Guard, formed in 1810] 1. the imperial guard, organized by Napoleon I in 1804 2. any group that has long defended a cause 3. the most conservative element of a group, party, etc.

Old·ham (ōl′dəm) city in Lancashire, NW England: pop. 111,000

old hand a person with much skill or experience

Old Harry the Devil; Satan

old hat [Slang] 1. old-fashioned; out-of-date 2. well-known or familiar to the point of being trite or commonplace Used predicatively

☆**Old Hickory** nickname of Andrew JACKSON

Old High German the High German language from the 8th to the 12th century

Old Icelandic the North Germanic language of Iceland from the 9th to the 16th century

☆**old·ie, old·y** (ōl′dē) n., pl. **old′ies** [Colloq.] an old joke, saying, song, movie, etc.

Old Indic 1. the Indo-European languages of ancient India including early and classical Sanskrit, as well as Pali and the oldest vernaculars (*Prakrits*) 2. Sanskrit and Vedic

Old Ionic a dialect of ancient Greek, fundamentally the language of Homer

Old Irish Irish Gaelic from the earliest period to the 11th century

☆**Old I·ron·sides** (ī′ərn sīdz′) the U.S. frigate Constitution, active in the War of 1812

old·ish (ōl′dish) adj. somewhat old

old lady [Slang] 1. one's mother 2. one's wife

Old Latin the Latin language before c. 75 B.C.

old-line (ōld′līn′) adj. 1. with an old, well-established history 2. following tradition; conservative

Old Low Franconian the West Germanic language of the Franks of the lower Rhine before c. 1100 A.D., the ancestor of Dutch and Flemish: also called **Old Low Frankish**

Old Low German the Low German language from its earliest period to the 12th century A.D.

old maid 1. a woman, esp. an older woman, who has never married; spinster 2. a prim, prudish, fussy person 3. a simple card game in which the players draw cards from one another to match pairs —**old′maid′ish** adj.

old man [Slang] 1. one's father 2. one's husband 3. [usually O- M-] any man in authority, as the head of a company, captain of a vessel, military commander, etc.: with *the* 4. old Mr. ——: often used to distinguish the father from the son

Old Man of the Sea 1. in the *Arabian Nights*, an old man who clung to the back of Sinbad for many days and nights 2. any person or thing hard to shake off or get rid of

☆**Old Man River** nickname for the MISSISSIPPI River

old master 1. any of the great European painters before the 18th cent. 2. a painting by one of these

old moon the moon in its last quarter, when it appears as a crescent curving toward the left

Old Nick [prob. contr. < NICHOLAS, but perhaps < Gmc. *niġ-, water sprite, goblin: see NIX¹, NICKEL] the Devil; Satan

Old Norman French same as NORMAN FRENCH (sense 1)

Old Norse 1. the North Germanic language of the Scandinavian peoples before the 14th century 2. *same as* OLD ICELANDIC

Old North French the dialects of Old French spoken in N France, esp. those of Picardy and Normandy

Ol·do·wan (äl′də wən) *adj.* [< *Olduvai* Gorge, Tanzania, where remains have been found] designating or of the oldest known Stone Age culture, characterized by pebble tools usually flaked in two directions to form simple cutters, choppers, scrapers, etc.

Old Persian the oldest form of Persian, preserved in stone inscriptions dating from the 7th to the 4th century B.C.

Old Pretender *epithet of* James Francis Edward STUART

Old Prussian a Baltic language which became extinct in the 17th century

old rose a grayish or purplish red —**old′-rose′** *adj.*

Old Saxon a West Germanic language, the oldest type of Low German, known chiefly from manuscripts of the 9th and 10th centuries A.D.

old school a group of people who cling to traditional or conservative ideas, methods, etc.

old school tie 1. a necktie striped in the distinctive colors of any of the exclusive English public schools **2.** loyalties, traditions, attitudes, etc. of, or like those of, the graduates of such a school

Old Slavic *same as* OLD CHURCH SLAVIC

☆**old sledge** *same as* SEVEN-UP

☆**Old South** the South before the Civil War

Old Spanish the Spanish language from c. 1145 to the 16th century

☆**old squaw** a sea duck (*Clangula hyemalis*) of northern regions, with mostly black and white coloration and a long, pointed tail

old·ster (ōld′stər) *n.* [Colloq.] a person who is no longer a youngster; old or elderly person

old style 1. an old style of type with narrow, light letters having slanted strokes at the top **2.** [O- S-] the old method of reckoning time according to the Julian calendar, which was off one day every 128 years —**old′-style′** *adj.*

Old Testament *Christian designation for* the Holy Scriptures of Judaism, the first of the two general divisions of the Christian Bible: cf. BIBLE

old-time (ōld′tīm′) *adj.* **1.** of, like, or characteristic of past times. **2.** of long standing or experience [an *old-time* journalist]

old-tim·er (ōld′tī′mər) *n.* [Colloq.] **1.** a person who has been a resident, employee, member, etc. for a long time **2.** a person who is old-fashioned

Old Welsh the Welsh language from the earliest period to c. 1150

old·wife (-wīf′) *n., pl.* **-wives′** (-wīvz′) **1.** an old woman ☆**2.** *same as* OLD SQUAW **3.** any of various sea fishes

old wives' tale a silly story or superstitious belief such as might be passed around by gossip old women

old-wom·an·ish (-woom′ən ish) *adj.* like, characteristic of, or suitable for an old woman; fussy

Old World the Eastern Hemisphere; Europe, Asia, and Africa: often used specifically with reference to European culture, customs, etc. —**old′-world′, Old′-World′** *adj.*

‡**o·lé** (ō lā′) *interj.*, *n.* [Sp., prob. < *hola*, hollo, echoic of shout] a shout of approval, triumph, joy, etc., as at bullfights or flamenco dances

-ole (ōl) [< L. *oleum*, OIL] *a suffix used in chemistry to indicate:* **1.** a closed-chain compound with five members [*pyrrole*] **2.** a chemical compound without hydroxyl, esp. any of certain aldehydes and ethers [*anisole*]

o·le·ag·i·nous (ō′lē aj′i nəs) *adj.* [Fr. *oléagineux* < L. *oleaginus* < *olea*, olive tree (< Gr. *elaia*, olive, olive tree)] oily; greasy; unctuous —**o′le·ag′i·nous·ly** *adv.* —**o′le·ag′i·nous·ness** *n.*

o·le·an·der (ō′lē an′dər, ō′lē an′dər) *n.* [ML., earlier also *lorandrum*: altered < ? L. *rhododendron*] a poisonous evergreen shrub (*Nerium oleander*) of the dogbane family, with fragrant flowers of white, pink, or red and narrow, leathery leaves

o·le·as·ter (ō′lē as′tər) *n.* [ME. *oliaster* < L. < *olea*: see OLEAGINOUS] any of several plants (genus *Elaeagnus*) of the oleaster family, often grown for ornament; esp., *same as* RUSSIAN OLIVE —*adj.* designating a family (Elaeagnaceae) of plants, including buffalo berry and Russian olive

o·le·ate (ō′lē āt′) *n.* a salt or ester of oleic acid

o·lec·ra·non (ō lek′rə nän′, ō′li krā′nän) *n.* [ModL. < Gr. *ōlekranon* for *ōlenokronon*) < *ōlenē*, elbow (see ELL²) + *kranion*, the head: see CRANIUM] the part of the ulna projecting behind the elbow joint

o·le·fin (ō′lə fin) *n.* [< Fr. (*gaz*) *oléfiant* < L. *oleum*, OIL + prp. of Fr. *fier*, to make < L. *facere*: see FACT] any of a series of unsaturated open-chain hydrocarbons containing one double bond and corresponding in composition to the general formula C_nH_{2n}, including ethylene, propylene, etc.: also **o·le·fine** (-fin, -fēn′) —**o′le·fin′ic** (-fin′ik) *adj.*

o·le·ic (ō lē′ik, ō′lē-) *adj.* [< L. *oleum*, OIL + -IC] **1.** of or obtained from oil **2.** of or pertaining to oleic acid

oleic acid an oily acid, $C_{17}H_{33}COOH$, present in the form of the glyceryl ester in most animal and vegetable fats and oils, used in making soap, ointments, etc.

o·le·in (ō′lē in) *n.* [Fr. *oléine* < L. *oleum*, OIL] **1.** a liquid glyceride, $(C_{17}H_{33}CO_2)_3C_3H_5$, present in olive oil and certain other oils and fats **2.** the liquid part of any fat, as distinguished from the solid part

☆**o·le·o** (ō′lē ō′) *n.* *clipped form of* OLEOMARGARINE

o·le·o- (ō′lē ō, -ə) [L. < *oleum*, OIL] *a combining form meaning* oil, olein, or oleic [*oleomargarine*]

o·le·o·graph (ō′lē ə graf′, -gräf′) *n.* [prec. + -GRAPH] a chromolithograph finished so that its surface resembles that of an oil painting on canvas —**o′le·o·graph′ic** *adj.* —**o′le·og′ra·phy** (-äg′rə fē) *n.*

☆**o·le·o·mar·ga·rine, o·le·o·mar·ga·rin** (ō′lē ō mär′jə rin) *n.* [Fr. *oléomargarine*: see OLEO- & MARGARINE] *full name of* MARGARINE

☆**oleo oil** a butterlike oil obtained from animal fat

o·le·o·res·in (ō′lē ō rez′′n) *n.* **1.** a mixture of a resin and an essential oil, as turpentine, occurring naturally in various plants **2.** a prepared mixture of an essential oil holding resin in solution

☆**oleo strut** a shock-absorbing strut in the landing gear of some airplanes, consisting of a telescopic cylinder containing oil

ol·fac·tion (äl fak′shən, ōl-) *n.* [< L. *olfacere*: see OLFACTORY] **1.** the sense of smell **2.** the act of smelling

ol·fac·tom·e·ter (äl′fak täm′ə tər) *n.* [OLFACTO(RY) + -METER] a device for measuring the acuteness of the sense of smell —**ol·fac′to·met′ric** (-tə met′rik) *adj.* —**ol′fac·tom′e·try** *n.*

ol·fac·to·ry (äl fak′tər ē, -trē; ōl-) *adj.* [< L. *olfactus*, pp. of *olfacere*, to smell < *olere*, to have a smell (akin to *odor*, ODOR) + *facere*, to make: see FACT] of the sense of smell: also **ol·fac′tive** —*n., pl.* **-ries** [*usually pl.*] an organ of smell

olfactory nerve either of the first pair of cranial nerves that arise in the mucous membranes within the upper part of the nose (**olfactory organ**) and transmit impulses concerned with the sense of smell to the forebrain

ol·fac·tron·ics (äl′fak trän′iks, ōl′-) *n.pl.* [*with sing. v.*] [< OLFACT(O)R(Y) + (ELECTR)ONICS] the science that deals with the detection and measurement by instruments of vapors and particles given off by different substances

OLG, OLG., O.L.G. Old Low German

Ol·ga (äl′gə, ōl′-, ōl′-) [Russ. < ? *Oleg*, holy, or < ON. *Helga*, holy] a feminine name

o·lib·a·num (ō lib′ə nəm) *n.* [ME. < ML. < Ar. *al-luban*, frankincense, akin to Heb. *lebōnā*, whence Gr. *libanos*] *same as* FRANKINCENSE

ol·i·garch (äl′ə gärk′) *n.* [Gr. *oligarchēs*: see OLIGO- & ARCH] any of the rulers of an oligarchy

ol·i·gar·chy (-gär′kē) *n., pl.* **-gar′chies** [Gr. *oligarchia*: see OLIGO- & -ARCHY] **1.** a form of government in which the ruling power belongs to a few persons **2.** a state governed in this way **3.** the persons ruling such a state —**ol′i·gar′chic, ol′i·gar′chi·cal, ol′i·gar′chal** (-k′l) *adj.*

ol·i·go- (äl′ə gō) [Gr. *oligo-* < *oligos*, small, akin to *loigos*, destruction, death < IE. base *(o)leig-, wretched, illness, whence Lith. *ligà*, disease] *a combining form meaning* few, scant, small, a deficiency of [*oligochaete*]: also, before a vowel, **olig-**

Ol·i·go·cene (äl′ə gō sēn′) *adj.* [OLIGO- + -CENE] designating or of the third epoch of the Tertiary Period in the Cenozoic Era between the Eocene and the Miocene —**the Oligocene** the Oligocene Epoch or its rocks: see GEOLOGY, chart

ol·i·go·chaete (-kēt′) *n.* [see OLIGO- & CHAETA] any of a class (Oligochaeta) of segmented worms, as the earthworm, lacking a definite head and having relatively few body bristles: found chiefly in moist soil and fresh water —**ol′i·go·chae′tous** *adj.*

ol·i·go·clase (-klās′) *n.* [G. *oligoklas* < Gr. *oligos* (see OLIGO-) + *klasis*, a fracture (see CLASTIC), in contrast to ORTHOCLASE, because cleavage differs slightly from 90°] a plagioclase feldspar whose composition corresponds to 70 to 90 percent albite

ol·i·goph·a·gous (äl′ə gäf′ə gəs) *adj.* [OLIGO- + -PHAGOUS] feeding upon a limited variety of food, as certain caterpillars whose diet is restricted to a few related plants

ol·i·gop·o·ly (äl′ə gäp′ə lē) *n., pl.* **-lies** [OLIG(O)- + (MON)OPOLY] control of a commodity or service in a given market by a small number of companies or suppliers —**ol′i·gop′o·list** *n.* —**ol′i·gop′o·lis′tic** *adj.*

ol·i·gop·so·ny (-sə nē) *n., pl.* **-nies** [OLIG(O)- + Gr. *opsōnia*, a purchase of food, catering < *opsōnein*: see OPSONIN] control of the purchase of a commodity or service in a given market by a small number of buyers —**ol′i·gop′so·nist** *n.* —**ol′i·gop′so·nis′tic** *adj.*

ol·i·go·sac·cha·ride (äl′ə gō sak′ə rīd′) *n.* [OLIGO- + SACCHARIDE] any of a group of carbohydrates consisting of a small number (2 to 6) of simple sugar molecules

ol·i·go·tro·phic (-träf′ik, -trō′fik) *adj.* [OLIGO- + TROPHIC] designating or of a lake, pond, etc. poor in plant nutrient minerals and organisms and rich in oxygen at all depths —**ol·i·got·ro·phy** (äl′ə gät′rə fē) *n.*

ol·i·gu·ri·a (äl′ə gyoor′ē ə) *n.* [ModL.: see OLIGO- & -URIA] a condition characterized by an abnormally small amount of urine secretion

o·li·o (ō′lē ō′) *n., pl.* **o′li·os′** [< Sp. *olla*: see OLLA] **1.** a highly spiced stew of meat and vegetables; olla **2.** a medley or miscellany as of musical numbers

---

ol·i·va·ceous (äl′ə vā′shəs) *adj.* [ModL. *olivaceus:* see OLIVE & -ACEOUS] of or like the olive, esp. in color; olive-green

ol·i·var·y (äl′ə ver′ē) *adj.* [L. *olivarius*] *Anat.* **1.** shaped like an olive **2.** designating of or either of two oval bodies protruding from the sides of the medulla oblongata

Ol·ive (äl′iv) [ME. *oliva* < L., an olive] a feminine name: var. *Olivia*

ol·ive (äl′iv) *n.* [ME. < OFr. < L. *oliva* < Gr. *elaia*] **1.** *a)* an evergreen tree (*Olea europaea*) of the olive family, native to S Europe and the Near East, with leathery leaves, yellow flowers, and an edible fruit *b)* the small, oval fruit of this tree, eaten green or ripe as a relish, or pressed to extract olive oil **2.** the wood of this tree **3.** any of various plants resembling the olive **4.** an olive branch or wreath **5.** the dull, yellowish-green color of the unripe olive fruit —*adj.* **1.** of the olive **2.** *a)* olive-colored *b)* having a dark complexion tinged with this color **3.** designating a family (Oleaceae) of trees and shrubs with loose clusters of four-parted flowers, including the olives, ashes, lilacs, jasmines, and forsythias

olive branch **1.** the branch of the olive tree, traditionally a symbol of peace **2.** any peace offering

olive drab **1.** any of various shades of greenish brown, much used as a camouflage color in the armed forces **2.** woolen cloth dyed this color and used for uniforms by the U.S. Army **3.** [*pl.*] a uniform of this cloth —**ol′ive-drab′** *adj.*

olive green the color of the unripe olive

o·liv·en·ite (ō liv′ə nīt′, äl′ə və-) *n.* [G. *oliven(erz)*, olive (ore) + -ITE¹] a native copper arsenate, Cu₂(OH)AsO₄, olive-green to dark-green in color

olive oil a light-yellow oil pressed from ripe olives, used in cooking, salad dressings, liniments, soap, etc.

Ol·i·ver (äl′ə vər) [Fr. *Olivier:* form assimilated to OFr. *olivier*, olive tree < L. *olivarius*, but prob. < MLowG. *alfihar*, lit., elf-army < *alf*, elf + *hari*, a host, army] **1.** a masculine name **2.** one of Charlemagne's twelve peers, a friend of Roland: see ROLAND

Olives, Mount of ridge of hills east of Jerusalem: also **Mount Ol·i·vet** (äl′ə vet′, -vət)

O·liv·i·a (ō liv′ē ə, ə-) a feminine name: see OLIVE

ol·i·vine (äl′ə vēn′) *n.* [OLIV(E) + -INE⁴] an orthorhombic silicate of magnesium and iron, (Mg,Fe)₂SiO₄, existing usually as green crystals in many highly basic igneous rocks, used esp. in refractories —**ol′i·vin′ic** (-vin′ik) *adj.*

ol·la (äl′ə; *Sp.* ōl′yä) *n.* [Sp. < L., a pot: see OVEN] ☆**1.** a large-mouthed pot or jar of earthenware **2.** a highly spiced stew of meat and vegetables

ol·la-po·dri·da (äl′ə pō drē′də; *Sp.* ō′lyä pō thrē′thä) *n.* [Sp., lit., rotten pot < *olla*, pot (< L.) + *podrida*, rotten < L. *putridus:* see PUTRID] **1.** an olla (stew) **2.** any assortment, medley, or miscellany; olio

Ol·mec (äl′mek) *n., pl.* **-mecs, -mec** any member of an ancient Indian people centered in the Mexican states of Tabasco and Veracruz —*adj.* designating or of the culture of this people, characterized by a highly developed system of agriculture, huge sculptured heads, and carved jade

ol·o·gy (äl′ə jē) *n., pl.* **-gies** [properly a suffix (see -LOGY) with -o- of prec. element] a branch of learning; science: a humorous usage

-ol·o·gy (äl′ə jē) [< -LOGY + an initial medial -o-] a combining form meaning the science or study of [*endocrinology*]

Ol·o·mouc (ô′lô mōts′) city in N Moravia, Czechoslovakia: pop. 77,000

O·lym·pi·a (ō lim′pē ə, ə-) [L. < Gr. *Olympia*, fem. of *Olympios*, lit., of Olympus] **1.** a feminine name **2.** plain in ancient Elis, W Peloponnesus: site of the ancient Olympic games: see GREECE, map **3.** [< OLYMPIC MOUNTAINS] capital of Wash.: seaport on Puget Sound: pop. 23,000

O·lym·pi·ad (-ad′) *n.* [Fr. *olympiade* < Gr. *Olympias* (gen. *Olympiados*) < *Olympia*, OLYMPIA (sense 2)] [*often* **o-**] **1.** in ancient Greece, any of the four-year periods between Olympic games: used by the Greeks in computing time **2.** a celebration of the modern Olympic games

O·lym·pi·an (-ən) *n.* [< LL. *Olympianus*, Olympic] **1.** *Gr. Myth.* any of the twelve major gods supposed to live on the slopes of Mount Olympus **2.** a native of Olympia **3.** any participant in the ancient or modern Olympic games —*adj.* **1.** of Olympia or Mount Olympus **2.** like an Olympian god; exalted; celestial; majestic **3.** designating or of the Olympic games of ancient Greece

O·lym·pic (ō lim′pik, ə-) *adj.* [L. *Olympicus* < Gr. *Olympikos*] *same as* OLYMPIAN —*n.* **1.** an Olympic game **2.** [*pl.*] the Olympic games (preceded by *the*)

Olympic games **1.** an ancient Greek festival consisting of contests in athletics, poetry, and music, held every four years at Olympia to honor Zeus **2.** a modern international athletic competition generally held every four years in a selected city: it includes track and field events, swimming, team games, etc., and, at another site and time, various winter sports

Olympic Mountains one of the Coast Ranges on Olympic Peninsula, NW Wash.: highest peak, Mt. OLYMPUS

Olympic National Park national park in NW Wash., around Mount Olympus: 1,389 sq. mi.

Olympic Peninsula peninsula in NW Wash., between Puget Sound & the Pacific

O·lym·pus (ō lim′pəs, ə-), **Mount** [L. < Gr. *Olympos*] **1.** mountain in N Greece, between Thessaly & Macedonia:

c. 9,800 ft.: in Greek mythology, the home of the gods **2.** heaven; the sky **3.** mountain on the Olympic Peninsula: 7,954 ft.

O·lyn·thus (ō lin′thəs) city in ancient Greece, on the Chalcidice Peninsula

O.M. (British) Order of Merit

-o·ma (ō′mə) [ModL. < Gr. *-ōma*] a suffix meaning tumor [*lymphoma, sarcoma*]

O·ma·ha (ō′mə hô, -hä) [< Fr. < Siouan tribal name; lit., ? upstream people] city in E Nebr., on the Missouri River: pop. 347,000 (met. area 541,000) —*n.* **1.** *pl.* **-has, -ha** any member of a tribe of Indians in NE Nebraska, who migrated from the Ohio River Valley **2.** their Siouan language

O·man (ō män′) **1.** SE coastal region of Arabia, between Qatar & Aden: see also MUSCAT AND OMAN **2. Gulf of,** arm of the Arabian Sea, between Iran & Muscat and Oman in Arabia: c. 350 mi. long

O·mar Khay·yám (ō′mär kī yäm′, ō′mər kī yam′) ?–1123?; Persian poet & mathematician: author of The *Rubáiyát,* translated into English by Edward FitzGerald

o·ma·sum (ō mā′səm) *n., pl.* **o·ma′sa** (-sə) [ModL. < L., bullock's tripe < Gaul.] the third division in the stomach of a cud-chewing animal, as the cow

O·may·yad (ō mī′ad) *n., pl.* **-yads, -ya·des′** (-ə dēz′) [< *Omayya,* great-grandfather of the first caliph in the dynasty] any of a dynasty of Moslem caliphs who ruled at Damascus (661–750 A.D.), or of a closely related branch ruling in Spain (756–1031)

om·ber, om·bre (äm′bər) *n.* [< Fr. or Sp.: obs. Fr. *ombre* < Sp. *hombre* < L. *homo,* a man: see HOMAGE] **1.** a card game of Spanish origin, played with forty cards by three players: popular in England in the 17th and 18th cent. **2.** the player attempting to win the pool in this game

om·bré (äm′brā) *adj.* [Fr., pp. of *ombrer,* to shade < L. *umbrare* < *umbra,* shade] shaded or graduated in tone: said of a color

om·buds·man (äm′bədz mən) *n., pl.* **-men** (-mən) [Sw. < *ombud,* a deputy, representative (< ON. *umboth* < *um, umbe,* about < IE. **mbhi-:* cf. AMBI- + ON. *bjotha,* to offer, bid, akin to OE. *beodan:* see BID¹) + *man,* MAN] a public official appointed to investigate citizens' complaints against local or national government agencies that may be infringing on the rights of individuals

Om·dur·man (äm′door män′) city in WC Sudan, on the Nile, opposite Khartoum: pop. 167,000: see also KHARTOUM

o·me·ga (ō mā′gə, -meg′ə, -mē′gə) *n.* [Gr. *ō* + *mega,* great: lit., great (i.e., long) *o,* to distinguish from *o mikron* (see OMICRON)] **1.** the twenty-fourth and final letter of the Greek alphabet (Ω, ω) **2.** the last (of any series); end

om·e·let, om·e·lette (äm′lit, äm′ə let) *n.* [Fr. *omelette,* earlier *amelette,* by metathesis < *alemette < alemelle* < L. *lamella,* small plate: see LAMELLA] eggs beaten up, often with milk or water, cooked as a pancake in a frying pan, and served usually folded over and often with a filling, as of jelly, cheese, mushrooms, etc.

o·men (ō′mən) *n.* [< OL. *osmen*] a thing or happening supposed to foretell a future event, either good or evil; augury —*vt.* to be an omen of; augur

o·men·tum (ō men′təm) *n., pl.* **-ta** (-tə), **-tums** [L.: **o-* (< IE. base **eu-,* to put on, whence L. *exuere,* to strip off) + *-mentum,* -MENT] a free fold of the peritoneum connecting the stomach and certain other visceral organs: the **great omentum** covers the stomach and intestines like an apron over their anterior surfaces, while the **lesser omentum** forms a partial covering of the stomach and common bile duct —**o·men′tal** *adj.*

o·mer (ō′mər) *n.* [Heb. *'ōmer*] **1.** an ancient Hebrew dry measure equal to one tenth of an ephah **2.** [*usually* **O-**] *Judaism* the period of 49 days from the second day of Passover through the day before Shavuot

‡o·mer·tà (ō mer′tä) *n.* [It. dial. < ?] in Sicily, a policy or code of keeping silent about crimes and refusing to cooperate with the police

om·i·cron, om·i·kron (äm′ə krän′, ō′mə-; *Brit.* ō mī′ krən) *n.* [Gr. *o mikron,* lit., small *o:* cf. OMEGA] the fifteenth letter of the Greek alphabet (O, o)

om·i·nous (äm′ə nəs) *adj.* [L. *ominosus*] of or serving as an omen; esp., having the character of an evil omen; threatening; sinister; menacing —**om′i·nous·ly** *adv.* —**om′i·nous·ness** *n.*

SYN.—ominous implies a threatening character but does not necessarily connote a disastrous outcome [*his request was met by an ominous silence*]; **portentous** literally implies a foreshadowing, especially of evil, but is now more often used of that which arouses awe or amazement because of its prodigious or marvelous character [*a portentous event*]; **fateful** may imply a fatal character or control by fate, but is now usually applied to that which is of momentous or decisive significance [*a fateful truce conference*]; **foreboding** implies a portent or presentiment of something evil or harmful [*a foreboding anxiety*]

o·mis·si·ble (ō mis′ə b'l) *adj.* that can be omitted

o·mis·sion (ō mish′ən) *n.* [ME. *omissioun* < LL. *omissio*] **1.** an omitting or being omitted; specif., failure to do as one should **2.** anything omitted

o·mis·sive (ō mis′iv) *adj.* [< L. *omissus,* pp. of *omittere* + -IVE] failing to do or include; omitting —**o·mis′sive·ly** *adv.*

o·mit (ō mit′) *vt.* **o·mit′ted, o·mit′ting** [ME. *omitten* < L. *omittere < ob-* (see OB-) + *mittere,* to send: see MISSION] **1.** to fail to include; leave out **2.** to fail to do; neglect

3. [Obs.] *a)* to take no notice of *b)* to let go —*SYN.* see NEGLECT —**o·mit'ter** *n.*

om·ma·tid·i·um (äm'ə tid'ē əm) *n., pl.* **-i·a** (-ə) [ModL., dim. < Gr. *omma* (gen. *ommatos*), the eye, akin to *ōps*, EYE] any of the structural elements forming the compound eye of an insect, some crustaceans, etc.: each element is a complete photoreceptor in itself, having a lens, pigment, light-sensitive cells, etc. —**om'ma·tid'i·al** *adj.*

om·mat·o·phore (ə mat'ə fôr') *n.* [< Gr. *ommatos* (see prec.) + -PHORE] *same as* EYESTALK

Om·mi·ad (ō mī'ad) *n., pl.* **-ads, -a·des'** (-ə dēz') *same as* OMAYYAD

om·ni- (äm'ni, -nə) [L. < *omnis*, all] *a combining form meaning* all, everywhere [*omniscient*]

om·ni·bus (äm'nə bəs, -ni bus') *n., pl.* **-bus·es** [Fr. < (*voiture*) *omnibus*, lit., (carriage) for all < L., dat. pl. of *omnis*, all] **1.** *same as* BUS (sense 1) **2.** a collection in a single, large volume of previously published works, as by a single author or related in theme, etc. —*adj.* providing for many things at once; having a variety of purposes or uses

☆**omnibus bill** a legislative bill containing many miscellaneous provisions, appropriations, etc.

om·ni·di·rec·tion·al (äm'ni də rek'shən 'l) *adj.* [OMNI- + DIRECTIONAL] for sending or receiving radio or sound waves in or from any direction

om·ni·far·i·ous (äm'nə fer'ē əs) *adj.* [L. *omnifarius*, of all sorts < *omnis*, all + *-farius:* see BIFARIOUS] of all kinds, varieties, or forms

om·nif·ic (äm nif'ik) *adj.* [ML. *omnificus* < L. *omnis*, all + *facere*, to make, DO¹] creating all things: also **om·nif'·i·cent** (-ə s'nt)

om·nip·o·tence (äm nip'ə təns) *n.* [MFr. < LL. *omnipotentia*] **1.** the state or quality of being omnipotent **2.** an omnipotent force; specif., [O-] God

om·nip·o·tent (-tənt) *adj.* [ME. < OFr. < L. *omnipotens* < *omnis*, all + *potens*, able: see POTENT] having unlimited power or authority; all-powerful —**the Omnipotent** God —**om·nip'o·tent·ly** *adv.*

om·ni·pres·ent (äm'ni prez'n't) *adj.* [ML. *omnipraesens* < L. *omnis*, all + *praesens*, PRESENT] present in all places at the same time —**om'ni·pres'ence** *n.*

SYN.—omnipresent, strictly applicable only to the Deity in its implication of presence in all places at the same time, is loosely used of anything that is always present within a given sphere [the *omnipresent* spirit of competition in business]; **ubiquitous** implies a being present, or seeming to be present, everywhere but not always at the same time or place [the trillium is a *ubiquitous* spring wildflower]

☆**om·ni·range** (äm'nə rānj') *n.* [< *omni*(*directional radio*) *range*] a system of navigation by means of a radio transmitter on the ground that sends signals in all directions, from which an airplane pilot can receive his bearing

om·nis·cience (äm nish'əns) *n.* [ME. < ML. *omniscientia*] **1.** the state or quality of being omniscient **2.** [O-] the omniscient being; God

om·nis·cient (-ənt) *adj.* [ML. *omnisciens* < L. *omnis*, all + *sciens*, knowing: see SCIENCE] having infinite knowledge; knowing all things —**the Omniscient** God —**om·nis'·cient·ly** *adv.*

om·ni·um-gath·er·um (äm'nē əm gath'ər əm) *n.* [L. *omnium*, gen. pl. of *omnis*, all + Latinized form of GATHER] a miscellaneous collection of persons or things

om·ni·vore (äm'nə vôr') *n.* [< ModL. *omnivora* (pl.), old designation for the group containing the pig < L., neut. pl. of *omnivorus*, OMNIVOROUS] an omnivorous person or animal

om·niv·o·rous (äm niv'ər əs) *adj.* [L. *omnivorus:* see OMNI- & -VOROUS] **1.** eating any sort of food, esp. both animal and vegetable food **2.** taking in everything indiscriminately, as with the intellect [an *omnivorous* reader] —**om·niv'o·rous·ly** *adv.* —**om·niv'o·rous·ness** *n.*

o·mo·pha·gi·a (ō'mə fā'jē ə, -fā'jə) *n.* [Gr. *ōmophagia* < *ōmos*, raw + *phagein*, to eat: see -PHAGOUS] the eating of raw flesh —**o·moph·a·gist** (ō mäf'ə jist) *n.* —**o·moph'a·gous** (-gəs), **o'mo·phag'ic** (-faj'ik) *adj.*

Om·pha·le (äm'fə lē') *Gr. Myth.* a queen of Lydia in whose service Hercules, dressed as a woman, did womanly tasks for three years to appease the gods

om·pha·lo- (äm'fə lō, -lə) [< Gr. *omphalos*, the NAVEL] *a combining form meaning* the navel, umbilicus: also, before a vowel, **omphal-**

om·pha·los (-ləs) *n.* [see prec.] **1.** *same as* NAVEL **2.** a central point **3.** a rounded stone in Apollo's temple at Delphi, regarded as the center of the world by the ancients

om·pha·lo·skep·sis (äm'fə lō skep'sis) *n.* [OMPHALO- + Gr. *skepsis*, a viewing: for base see SKEPTIC] the act of contemplating one's navel, as an exercise for mystics

Omsk (ōmsk) city in W Siberia, on the Irtysh River: pop. 746,000

O·mu·ta (ō'mōō tä') seaport in NW Kyushu, Japan, on an inlet of the East China Sea: pop 221,000

On (än) *Biblical name of* HELIOPOLIS

on (än, ôn) *prep.* [ME. < OE. *on, an*, akin to G. *an*, Goth. *ana*, ON. *ā* < IE. base *an, *anō*, prob. meaning "ob-

liquely toward, slanting toward," whence Gr. *ana*] **1.** in a position above, but in contact with and supported by; upon **2.** in contact with (any surface); covering or attached to **3.** so as to be supported by [to lean on one's elbow] **4.** in the surface of [a scar on the body] **5.** near to; by [a cottage *on* the lake, seated *on* my right] **6.** at or during the time of [*on* entering, on the first day] **7.** with (something specified) as the ground or basis [based *on* his diary, *on* purpose] **8.** connected with, as a part [*on* the faculty] **9.** engaged in [*on* a trip] **10.** in a condition or state of [*on* parole] **11.** as a result of [a profit *on* the sale] **12.** in the direction or vicinity of [light shone *on* us] **13.** so as to affect [to put a curse *on* someone] **14.** through the use or medium of [to live *on* bread, to act *on* TV] **15.** with regard to; concerning [an essay *on* war] **16.** coming after: used to indicate repetition [to suffer insult *on* insult] ☆**17.** [Colloq.] chargeable to; at the expense of [a drink *on* the house] ☆**18.** [Slang] using; addicted to [to be *on* drugs] **19.** [Slang] carried by [to have no money *on* one] **20.** [Dial.] *used variously for* OF, AT, ABOUT, FOR, IN —*adv.* **1.** in or into a situation or position of contacting, being supported by, or covering [put your shoes *on*] **2.** in a direction to or toward [he looked *on*] **3.** in advance; forward; ahead [move *on*] **4.** lastingly; continuously [she sang *on*] **5.** into operation, performance, or action [switch on the light] ☆**6.** *Baseball* on base **7.** *Theater* on stage —*adj.* **1.** in action, operation, or occurrence [the TV is *on*] **2.** near or nearer **3.** arranged or planned for [tomorrow's game is still *on*] **4.** *Cricket* designating that side of the field, or of the wicket, where the batsman stands —*n.* **1.** the fact or state of being on **2.** *Cricket* the on side —**and so on** and more like the preceding; and so forth —☆**have something on someone** [Colloq.] to have unfavorable evidence against someone —**on and off** not continuously; intermittently —**on and on** continuously; at great length —☆**on** to [Slang] aware of or familiar with, esp. aware of the real nature or meaning of

ON., ON, O.N. Old Norse

-on *a n.-forming suffix designating:* **1.** [< *-on* in *argon*] an inert gas [*radon*] **2.** [< *-on* in *ion*] a subatomic particle [*neutron*] **3.** [< *-ONE*] a chemical compound that is not a ketone or has no ketone group [*cupferron*]

on·a·ger (än'ə jər) *n., pl.* **-gri'** (-grī'), **-gers** [ME. < L. < Gr. *onagros*, wild ass < *onos*, ass + *agrios*, wild < *agros*, field: see ACRE] **1.** a wild ass (*Equus onager*) of C Asia **2.** a catapult for throwing stones, used in ancient and medieval warfare

o·nan·ism (ō'nə niz'm) *n.* [< *Onan*, son of Judah (cf. Gen. 38:9) + -ISM] **1.** withdrawal in sexual intercourse before ejaculation **2.** *same as* MASTURBATION —**o'nan·ist** *n.* —**o'nan·is'tic** *adj.*

once (wuns) *adv.* [ME. *ones*, gen. of *on*, ONE] **1.** one time; one time only [to eat *once* a day] **2.** at any time; at all; ever [he'll succeed if *once* given a chance] **3.** at some time in the past; formerly [a *once* famous man] **4.** by one degree or grade [a cousin *once* removed] —*conj.* as soon as; if ever; whenever [*once* he is tired, he will quit] —*adj.* former; quondam —*n.* one time [go this *once*] —**all at once** **1.** all at the same time **2.** suddenly —**at once** **1.** immediately **2.** at the same time —**for once** for at least one time —**once and again** time after time; repeatedly —**once (and) for all** finally; decisively; conclusively —**once in a while** now and then; occasionally —**once or twice** not often; a few times —**once upon a time** a long time ago

☆**once-o·ver** (wuns'ō'vər) *n.* [Colloq.] **1.** a quick, comprehensive look or examination; swiftly appraising glance **2.** a quick, cursory or light cleaning or going-over

on·cid·i·um (än sid'ē əm) *n.* [ModL. < Gr. *onkos*, barbed hook (for IE. base see ANKLE) + ModL. *-idium* (< Gr. *-idion*, dim. suffix): from form of the labellum] any of a genus (*Oncidium*) of tropical American orchids

on·col·o·gy (äŋ käl'ə jē, än-) *n.* [< Gr. *onkos*, a mass + -LOGY] the branch of medicine dealing with tumors —**on'co·log'ic** (kə läj'ik) *adj.* —**on·col'o·gist** *n.*

on·com·ing (än'kum'iŋ) *adj.* **1.** coming nearer in position or time; approaching **2.** coming forth; emerging —*n.* an approach

one (wun) *adj.* [ME. < OE. *an*, akin to G. *ein*, Goth. *ains* < IE. *oinos* (whence Gr. *oinē*, L. *unus*, OIr. *ōen*) < *e-, *ei-*, prefixed pronominal stem meaning "the, this, this one"] **1.** being a single thing or unit; not two or more **2.** characterized by unity; forming a whole; united; undivided [with *one* accord] **3.** designating a person or thing as contrasted with or opposed to another or others [from *one* day to another] **4.** being uniquely or strikingly the person or thing specified [the *one* solution to the problem] **5.** single in kind; the same [all of *one* mind] **6.** designating a single, but not clearly specified, person or thing; a certain [*one* day last week]: also used as an intensive substitute for the indefinite article [she's *one* beautiful girl] —*n.* **1.** the number expressing unity or designating a single unit: the lowest cardinal number and the first used in counting a series; 1; I **2.** a single person or thing **3.** something numbered one or marked with one pip, as the face of a die or domino ☆**4.** [Colloq.]

a one-dollar bill —*pron.* **1.** a certain person or thing; some person or thing *[one* of us must go*]* **2.** any person or thing; anybody or anything: sometimes used affectedly in place of the first personal or second personal pronoun **3.** the person or thing previously mentioned —**all one** making no difference; of no importance —**at one** of the same opinion; in accord —**one and all** everybody —**one another** each one the other; each other: see EACH OTHER —**one by one** individually in succession —**one of those things** something that cannot be avoided, helped, changed, etc. —☆**tie one on** [Slang] to go on a drinking spree

-one [arbitrary use of Gr. *-ōnē*, used to signify a female descendant of] *a suffix used in chemistry, meaning* a ketone *[acetone, butanone]*

☆**one-armed bandit** (-ärmd′) [Slang] a slot machine for gambling with coins, having a lever that is pulled down to spin disks and turn up the symbols that determine the results

☆**one-base hit** (wun′bās′) *Baseball* a hit by which the batter can reach first base without benefit of an error: also [Slang] **one′-bag′ger** (-bag′ər)

O·ne·ga (ō nē′ga; *Russ.* ô nye′gä), **Lake** lake in NW European R.S.F.S.R., between Lake Ladoga & the White Sea: c. 3,800 sq. mi.

Onega Bay S arm of the White Sea, extending into NW European R.S.F.S.R.: c. 100 mi. long

one-horse (wun′hôrs′) *adj.* **1.** drawn by or using a single horse ☆**2.** [Colloq.] having little importance; limited in resources, scope, etc.; petty; inferior

O·nei·da (ō nī′də) *n.* [< Iroquois *Oneiute,* lit., standing rock] **1.** *pl.* **-das, -da** any member of a tribe of Indians originally living near Oneida Lake and now also in Wisconsin and Ontario **2.** their Iroquoian language

Oneida Lake lake near Syracuse, N.Y.: part of the New York State Barge Canal system: c. 80 sq. mi.

O'Neill (ō nēl′), **Eugene (Gladstone)** 1888–1953; U.S. playwright

o·nei·ric (ō nī′rik) *adj.* [< Gr. *oneiros,* a dream + -IC] of or having to do with dreams

o·nei·ro·crit·ic (ō nī′rə krit′ik) *n.* [< Gr. *oneirokritikos,* concerning the interpretation of dreams < *oneiros,* a dream + *kritikos,* critical: see CRITIC] a person who interprets dreams —**o·nei′ro·crit′i·cal** *adj.*

o·nei·ro·man·cy (ō nī′rə man′sē) *n.* [< Gr. *oneiros,* a dream + -MANCY] the practice of claiming to foretell the future by the interpretation of dreams

☆**one-lin·er** (wun′lin′ər) *n.* a short, witty remark

one·ness (wun′nis) *n.* **1.** the quality or state of being one; singleness; unity **2.** unity of mind, feeling, or purpose **3.** sameness; identity

☆**one-night stand** (wun′nīt′) a single appearance in one town by a traveling show, lecturer, etc.

on·er·ous (än′ər əs, ō′nər-) *adj.* [ME. < MFr. *onereus* < L. *onerosus* < *onus,* a load: see ONUS] **1.** burdensome; laborious **2.** *Law* involving a legal obligation that equals or exceeds the benefits *[onerous lease]* —**on′er·ous·ly** *adv.* —**on′er·ous·ness** *n.*

SYN.—**onerous** applies to that which is laborious or troublesome, often because of its annoying or tedious character *[the onerous duties of a janitor]*; **burdensome** applies to that which is wearisome or oppressive to the mind or spirit as well as to the body *[burdensome responsibilities]*; **oppressive** stresses the overbearing cruelty of the person or thing that inflicts hardship, or emphasizes the severity of the hardship itself *[oppressive weather, an oppressive king]*; **exacting** suggests the making of great demands on the attention, skill, care, etc. *[an exacting supervisor, exacting work]*

one·self (wun′self′, wunz′-) *pron.* a person's own self; himself or herself: also **one's self** —**be oneself 1.** to function physically and mentally as one normally does **2.** to be natural or sincere —**by oneself** alone; unaccompanied; withdrawn —**come to oneself 1.** to recover one's senses **2.** to recover one's capacity for sound judgment

one-shot (wun′shät′) *adj.* [Slang] **1.** happening, appearing, etc. one time only **2.** being the only instance; not part of a series

one-sid·ed (wun′sīd′id) *adj.* **1.** on, having, or involving only one side **2.** larger or more developed on one side; leaning to one side **3.** favoring one side; uneven or unfair; prejudiced **4.** uneven or unequal *[a one-sided race]* —**one′-sid′ed·ly** *adv.* —**one′-sid′ed·ness** *n.*

one-step (-step′) *n.* **1.** an old ballroom dance characterized by quick walking steps in 2/4 time **2.** music for this dance —*vi.* **-stepped′, -step′ping** to dance the one-step

one-time (-tīm′) *adj.* at some past time; former

one-to-one (wun′tə wun′) *adj.* **1.** permitting the pairing of an element of one group uniquely with a corresponding element of another group **2.** *Math.* designating a correspondence such that each member of one set has a partner in another set, and no element in either set is without a partner

one-track (wun′trak′) *adj.* **1.** having a single track ☆**2.** [Colloq.] able or willing to deal with only one thing at a time; limited in scope *[a one-track mind]*

one-up (-up′) *adj.* [Colloq.] having an advantage (over another): often in the phrase **be one-up on** —*vt.* **-upped′, -up′ping** [Colloq.] to have or seize an advantage over

one-up·man·ship (-mən ship′) *n.* [*one-up* + (GAMES)-MANSHIP] [Colloq.] the practice of, or skill in, seizing an advantage or gaining superiority over others

one-way (-wā′) *adj.* **1.** moving, or providing for movement, in one direction only *[a one-way* street, a *one-way* ticket*]* **2.** without any reciprocal action or obligation *[a one-way* contract*]*

on-glide (än′glīd′, ôn′-) *n.* a glide coming before a speech sound in which the vocal organs take the position for forming that sound, either from their normal inactive position or from their position in articulating a preceding sound

on·go·ing (än′gō′iŋ) *adj.* that is going on, or actually in process; continuing, progressing, etc.

ONI Office of Naval Intelligence

on·ion (un′yən) *n.* [ME. *oynon* < OFr. *oignon* < L. *unio* (gen. *unionis*), oneness, unity, also a kind of single onion: see UNION] **1.** a biennial plant (*Allium cepa*) of the lily family, having an edible bulb with a strong, sharp smell and taste **2.** the bulb of this plant, formed of close, concentric layers of leaf bases **3.** any of various related plants

On·ions (un′yənz), **C(harles) T(albut)** 1873–1965; Eng. lexicographer

on·ion·skin (un′yən skin′) *n.* **1.** the thin, translucent outer coating of an onion **2.** a tough, thin, translucent, glossy paper, often used for carbon copies

-on·i·um (ō′nē əm) [< (AMM)ONIUM] *a n.-forming suffix* designating any of a group of compounds that are isologues of ammonium *[sulfonium]*

on-line (än′līn′, ôn′-) *adj.* designating or of instruments, equipment, or devices directly connected to and controlled by the computer unit that interprets and executes instructions

on·look·er (än′look′ər) *n.* a person who watches without taking part; spectator —**on′look′ing** *adj., n.*

on·ly (ōn′lē) *adj.* [ME. < OE. *anlic* < *an,* ONE + *-lic,* -LY¹] **1.** alone of its or their kind; by itself or by themselves; sole **2.** alone in its or their superiority; best; finest —*adv.* **1.** and no other; and no (or nothing) more; solely; exclusively *[drink water only]* **2.** (but) in what follows or in the end *[to* meet one crisis, *only* to face another*]* **3.** as recently as *[elected only* last fall*]* —*conj.* [Colloq.] were it not that; except that; but *[I'd have gone, only* it rained*]* —**if . . . only** would that; I wish that —**only too** very; exceedingly

on·o·mas·tic (än′ə mas′tik) *adj.* [Gr. *onomastikos* < *onomazein,* to name < *onoma,* NAME] **1.** of or having to do with a name or names **2.** *Law* designating a signature in a handwriting different from that in the body of the instrument to which it is appended

on·o·mas·tics (-tiks) *n.pl.* [*with sing. v.*] **1.** the study of the origin, form, meaning, and use of names, esp. proper names **2.** a pattern or system serving as a basis for the formation and use of names and terms within a field or category

on·o·mat·o·poe·ia (än′ə mat′ə pē′ə, -mät′-) *n.* [LL. < Gr. *onomatopoiia* < *onoma* (gen. *onomatos*), NAME + *poiein,* to make: see POET] **1.** the formation of a word by imitating the natural sound associated with the object or action involved; echoism (Ex.: *tinkle, buzz, chickadee,* etc.) **2.** the use of such words, as in poetry or rhetoric —**on′o·mat′o·poe′ic, on′o·mat′o·po·et′ic** (-pō et′ik) *adj.* —**on′o·mat′o·po·et′i·cal·ly, on′o·mat′o·poe′i·cal·ly** *adv.*

On·on·da·ga (än′ən dô′gə, ôn′-; -dä′-) *n.* [< AmInd. (Iroquois) *Ononta′ge′,* lit., on top of the hill (name of the chief Onondaga village)] **1.** *pl.* **-gas, -ga** any member of a tribe of Indians who formerly lived near Onondaga Lake and now live in Ontario as well as New York **2.** their Iroquoian language —**On′on·da′gan** *adj.*

Onondaga Lake [see prec.] salt lake on the W border of Syracuse, N.Y.: c. 5 sq. mi.

ONormFr. Old Norman French

on·rush (än′rush′, ôn′-) *n.* a headlong dash forward; strong onward rush —**on′rush′ing** *adj.*

on·set (-set′) *n.* **1.** an attack; assault **2.** a setting out; beginning; start

on·shore (-shôr′) *adj.* **1.** moving onto or toward the shore **2.** situated or operating on land *[an onshore* patrol*]* —*adv.* toward the shore; landward

on·side (-sīd′) *adv. Sports* in the proper position for play; not offside —*adj.* **1.** not offside ☆**2.** *Football* designating a kickoff that is deliberately short in the hope that the receiver will fumble the ball

on·slaught (-slôt′) *n.* [altered (after SLAUGHTER) < Du. *annslag* < *slagen,* to strike] a violent, intense attack

Ont. Ontario

On·tar·i·o (än ter′ē ō) **1.** [after the lake, below] province of SC Canada, between the Great Lakes & Hudson Bay: 412,582 sq. mi.; pop. 6,961,000; cap. Toronto: abbrev. **Ont. 2.** [after prec.] city in S Calif.: pop. 64,000: see SAN BERNARDINO **3. Lake,** [< Fr. < Iroquoian, lit., fine lake] smallest & easternmost of the Great Lakes between N.Y. & Ontario, Canada: 7,313 sq. mi. —**On·tar′i·an** *adj., n.*

on·tic (än′tik) *adj.* [ONT(O)-] having the status of real and ultimate existence —**on′ti·cal·ly** *adv.*

on·to (än′tōō, ôn′-; -tə) *prep.* **1.** to and upon; to a position on ☆**2.** [Slang] aware of the real nature or meaning of *[he's onto* our schemes*]* Also **on to**

on·to- (än′tə, -tō) [< Gr. *ōn* (gen. *ontos*), prp. of *einai,* to be < IE. base **es-,* whence IS] *a combining form meaning:* a) being, existence *[ontology]* b) organism *[ontogeny]*

on·tog·e·ny (än täj′ə nē) n. [prec. + -GENY] the life cycle of a single organism; biological development of the individual: distinguished from PHYLOGENY: also **on′to·gen′e·sis** (än′tə jen′ə sis) —**on′to·ge·net′ic** (-jə net′ik), **on′to·gen′ic** adj.

ontological argument Metaphysics an a priori argument for the existence of God, asserting that the conception of a perfect being implies that being's existence outside man's mind

on·tol·o·gy (än täl′ə jē) n. [ModL. ontologia: see ONTO- & -LOGY] 1. the branch of metaphysics dealing with the nature of being, reality, or ultimate substance: cf. PHENOMENOLOGY 2. pl. **-gies** a particular theory about being or reality —**on·to·log·i·cal** (än′tə läj′i k'l) adj. —**on′to·log′i·cal·ly** adv. —**on·tol′o·gist** n.

o·nus (ō′nəs) n. [L., a load, burden < IE. base *enos- or *onos-, whence Sans. ánah, freight cart] 1. a difficult or unpleasant task, duty, etc.; burden 2. responsibility for a wrong; blame 3. [clip of L. onus probandi, burden of proving] same as BURDEN OF PROOF

on·ward (än′wərd) adv. [ME.: see ON & -WARD] toward or at a position or point ahead in space or time; forward: also **on′wards** —adj. moving or directed onward or ahead; advancing [an onward trend]

on·yx (än′iks; occas. ō′niks) n. [ME. onix < OFr. < L. onyx < Gr. onyx, the nail: its color resembles that of the fingernail] 1. a variety of agate with alternate colored layers, used as a semiprecious stone, esp. in making cameos 2. a translucent, finely crystalline, stalagmitic calcite, often banded, found in cave deposits: also called **onyx marble**

o·o- (ō′ə) [< Gr. ōion, EGG¹] a combining form meaning egg or ovum [oogenesis]: also written **oö-**

o·o·cyte (ō′ə sīt′) n. [OO- + -CYTE] Embryology an egg that has not yet undergone maturation

oo·dles (ōō′d'lz) n.pl. [< ? HUDDLE] [Colloq.] a great amount; very many

o·og·a·mous (ō äg′ə məs) adj. [OO- + -GAMOUS] characterized by the uniting of a large, nonmotile egg and a small, active sperm for reproduction —**o·og′a·my** (-mē) n.

o·o·gen·e·sis (ō′ə jen′ə sis) n. [OO- + -GENESIS] Biol. the process by which the ovum is formed in preparation for its fertilization and development —**o·o·ge·net′ic** (-jə net′ik) adj.

o·o·go·ni·um (-gō′nē əm) n., pl. **-ni·a** (-ə), **-ums** [ModL., dim. < OO- + -GONIUM] 1. the female reproductive organ in algae and fungi, consisting of a large cell in which the eggs (oospheres) are developed 2. Embryology any of the cells from which the oocytes derive

o·o·lite (ō′ə līt′) n. [Fr. oölithe: see OO- & -LITE] 1. a tiny, spherical or ellipsoid particle with concentric layers, usually of calcium carbonate, formed in wave-agitated sea waters: also **o′o·lith** (-lith) 2. a rock composed chiefly of oolites —**o′o·lit′ic** (-lit′ik) adj.

o·ol·o·gy (ō äl′ə jē) n. [OO- + -LOGY] that branch of ornithology concerned with the study of birds' eggs —**o·o·log·i·cal** (ō′ə läj′i k'l) adj. —**o·ol′o·gist** n.

oo·long (ōō′lôn) n. [Chin. dial. form of wulung, lit., black dragon] a dark tea from China and Taiwan that is partly fermented before being dried

oo·mi·ac, oo·mi·ak (ōō′mē ak′) n. same as UMIAK

☆**oom·pah, oom-pah** (ōōm′pä′) n. [echoic] the sound of a repeated, rhythmic bass figure played as by a tuba in a marching band —adj. of or characterized by this sound Also **oom′-pah′-pah′**

☆**oomph** (ōōmf) n. [echoic of involuntary expression of approval] [Old Slang] 1. sex appeal 2. vigor; energy

o·o·phore (ō′ə fôr′) n. [OO- + -PHORE] same as OOPHYTE

o·o·pho·rec·to·my (ō′ə fə rek′tə mē) n., pl. **-mies** [OOPHOR(O)- + -ECTOMY] the surgical removal of one or both ovaries

o·o·pho·ri·tis (-rīt′is) n. [ModL.: see ff. + -ITIS] inflammation of an ovary or the ovaries

o·o·phor·o (ō′ə fə rō′) [< ModL. oöphoron, ovary < Gr. ōion, EGG¹ + -phoros, bearing < pherein, to BEAR¹] a combining form meaning ovary or ovaries: also, before a vowel, **oophor-**

o·o·phyte (ō′ə fīt′) n. [OO- + -PHYTE] in plants undergoing alternation of generations, as ferns, mosses, etc., that generation in which the reproductive organs are developed —**o′o·phyt′ic** (-fit′ik) adj.

oops (ōōps, oops) interj. same as WHOOPS

o·o·sperm (ō′ə spurm′) n. [OO- + -SPERM] obs. var. of: 1. OOSPORE 2. ZYGOTE

o·o·sphere (-sfir′) n. [OO- + -SPHERE] Bot. any of the large, spherical, nonmotile, unfertilized eggs that develop in an oogonium

o·o·spore (-spôr′) n. [OO- + SPORE] Bot. a thick-walled, resting spore produced by the fertilization of an oosphere —**o′o·spor′ic** adj.

Oost·en·de (ōs ten′də) Fl. name of OSTEND

o·o·the·ca (ō′ə thē′kə) n., pl. **-cae** (-sē) [ModL. < OO- + Gr. thēkē, a case] an egg case, as of certain mollusks and insects —**o′o·the′cal** adj.

o·o·tid (ō′ə tid) n. [OO- + -t- + -ID] a large, haploid cell

produced at the second meiotic division, that quickly becomes an egg cell

ooze¹ (ōōz) n. [ME. wose < OE. wos, sap, juice, akin to MLowG. wose, scum < IE. base *wes-, wet: meaning influenced by OE. wase, mire, dirt] 1. an infusion of oak bark, sumac, etc., used in tanning leather 2. [< the v.] a) an oozing; gentle flow b) something that oozes —vi. **oozed, ooz′ing** 1. to flow or leak out slowly, as through very small holes; seep 2. to give forth moisture, as through pores 3. to escape or disappear gradually [hope oozed away] —vt. 1. to give forth, or exude (a fluid) 2. to seem to radiate [to ooze confidence]

ooze² (ōōz) n. [ME. wose < OE. wase < IE. base *weis-, to flow away, whence L. virus] 1. soft mud or slime; esp., the deep layers of sediment at the bottom of a lake, ocean, etc. 2. an area of muddy ground; bog

ooze leather leather of calfskin, sheepskin, or goatskin with a velvety or suede finish on the flesh side

oo·zy¹ (ōō′zē) adj. **-zi·er, -zi·est** oozing; giving forth moisture —**oo′zi·ly** adv. —**oo′zi·ness** n.

oo·zy² (ōō′zē) adj. **-zi·er, -zi·est** full of or like ooze; slimy —**oo′zi·ly** adv. —**oo′zi·ness** n.

op- (äp, əp) same as OB-: used before p [oppose]

OP observation post

op. 1. opera 2. operation 3. opposite 4. opus

O.P. Order of Preachers (Dominicans)

O.P., OP, o.p., op 1. out of print 2. Philately overprint 3. overproof

OPA, O.P.A. Office of Price Administration

o·pac·i·ty (ō pas′ə tē) n. [Fr. opacité < L. opacitas < opacus, shady] 1. the state, quality, or degree of being opaque 2. pl. **-ties** something opaque

o·pah (ō′pə) n. [WAfr. (Ibo) úbá] a very large, brightly spotted, silvery fish (Lampris regius) of the Atlantic and Pacific oceans

o·pal (ō′p'l) n. [L. opalus < Gr. opallios < Sans. upala, precious stone] a hydrated amorphous silica, $SiO_2 \cdot nH_2O$, of various colors, capable of refracting light and then reflecting it in a play of colors: the translucent milky or colored varieties, as the **fire opal**, are used as semiprecious stones

o·pal·es·cent (ō′pə les′'nt) adj. [OPAL + -ESCENT] showing a play of colors like that of the opal; iridescent —**o′pal·esce′** vi. **-esced′, -esc′ing** —**o′pal·es′cence** n.

o·pal·ine (ō′p'l in, -ēn′, -īn′) adj. [OPAL + -INE¹] of or like opal —n. a translucent, milky variety of glass

o·paque (ō pāk′) adj. [ME. opake < L. opacus, shady] 1. not letting light pass through; not transparent or translucent 2. not reflecting light; not shining or lustrous; dull or dark 3. not allowing electricity, heat, etc. to pass through 4. hard to understand; obscure 5. slow in understanding; obtuse —n. 1. anything opaque 2. Photog. an opaque liquid used in blocking out parts of a negative —vt. **o·paqued′, o·paqu′ing** 1. to make opaque 2. Photog. to apply opaque to (a negative) —**o·paque′ly** adv. —**o·paque′ness** n.

☆**opaque projector** a projector for throwing images on a screen by reflecting light from opaque objects

☆**op (art)** (äp) [< OP(TICAL)] a style of abstract painting utilizing geometrical patterns or figures to create various optical effects, such as the illusion of movement

op. cit. [L. opere citato] in the work cited

ope (ōp) adj., vt., vi. **oped, op′ing** [ME. < open(en)] earlier poet. var. of OPEN

o·pen (ō′p'n) adj. [ME. < OE., akin to G. offen < PGmc. *upana: for IE. base see UP¹] 1. in a state which permits access, entrance, or exit; not closed, covered, clogged, or shut [open doors] 2. a) in a state which permits freedom of view or passage; not enclosed, fenced in, sheltered, screened, etc.; unobstructed; clear [open fields] b) having few or no trees, houses, etc. [open country] 3. unsealed; unwrapped 4. a) not covered over; without covering, top, etc. b) vulnerable to attack, etc.; unprotected or undefended: see also OPEN CITY 5. spread out; unfolded; unclosed; expanded [an open book] 6. having spaces between; having gaps, holes, interstices, etc. [open ranks] 7. free from ice [the lake is open] 8. having relatively little snow or frost; mild [an open winter] 9. a) free to be entered, used, competed in, shared, visited, etc. by all [an open meeting] b) ready to admit customers, clients, etc. 10. free to be argued or contested; not settled or decided [an open question] 11. a) free from prejudice or bigotry; not closed to new ideas, etc. [an open mind] b) liberal; generous 12. ☆a) free from legal restrictions [an open season on deer] ☆b) free from discriminatory restrictions based on race, religion, etc. [open housing] ☆c) free from effective regulation with respect to drinking, gambling, etc. [the city is wide open] 13. characterized by social mobility, political freedom, diversity of opinion, etc. [an open society] 14. in force or operation [an open account] 15. a) not already taken, occupied, or engaged [the job is still open] b) free to be accepted or rejected 16. not closed against access; accessible; available 17. not hidden or secret; generally known; public [an open quarrel] 18. frank; candid; direct; honest [an open manner]

19. *Math.* of a set whose every point has a neighborhood completely contained in the set **20.** *Music a)* not stopped by the finger: said of a string *b)* not closed at the top: said of an organ pipe *c)* produced by an open string or pipe, or, in wind instruments, brasses, etc., without a slide or key: said of a tone *d)* not muted **21.** *Phonetics a)* pronounced with the tongue as low as possible; low: said of a vowel, as (e) and (ô) *b)* pronounced with the organs of speech not in close contact; fricative: said of a consonant *c)* ending in a vowel or diphthong: said of a syllable **22.** *Printing a)* designating of a style of type the letters of which are cast in outline so that the inside of letters shows white *b)* widely spaced with lead separators between lines of type; not solid **23.** *Sports* designating a stance, as of a golfer, in which the front of the body is turned slightly forward —*vt.* **1.** to make or cause to be open; specif., *a)* to unclose; unfasten [*open* the door] *b)* to remove obstructions from [to *open* a drain] **2.** *a)* to make an opening or openings in [to *open* an abscess] *b)* to make or produce (a hole, way, etc.) **3.** to make spaces between; spread out; expand [to *open* ranks] **4.** to unclose, unfold, or unroll [to *open* a book] **5.** to make accessible or subject (to an influence or action); expose **6.** to make available for use, competition, or participation, without restriction, taxation, fee, etc. **7.** to free from prejudice and bigotry; make liberal and generous [to *open* one's mind] **8.** to make known, public, etc.; reveal; disclose **9.** to begin; enter upon; start; commence [to *open* the bidding, a session, etc.] **10.** to cause to start operating, going, etc. [to *open* a new shop] **11.** to undo, recall, or set aside (a judgment, settlement, etc.), so as to leave the matter open to further action —*vi.* **1.** to become open **2.** to spread out; expand; unroll; unfold **3.** to become free from prejudice, etc.; become liberal and generous **4.** to become revealed, disclosed, etc.; come into view **5.** to be or act as an opening; give access (with *to, into, on,* etc.) **6.** to begin; start **7.** to start operating, going, bidding, etc.; specif., in the stock exchange, to show an indicated price level at the beginning of the day [steel *opened* high] **8.** to begin a series of performances, games, etc. —*n.* [*usually* O-] any of various golf tournaments open to both professionals and amateurs —*SYN.* see FRANK¹ —**open out 1.** to make or become extended or larger **2.** to develop **3.** to disclose to view; reveal —**open to 1.** glad or willing to receive, discuss, etc. **2.** liable to; subject to **3.** available or accessible to or for —**open up 1.** to make or become open **2.** to spread out; unfold **3.** to start; begin **4.** [Colloq.] to begin firing a gun or guns **5.** [Colloq.] to speak freely or with great feeling **6.** [Colloq.] to go or make go faster or as fast as possible —**the open 1.** any open, unobstructed space on land or water **2.** an unenclosed area; the outdoors **3.** public knowledge ☆**4.** [O-] *Golf* an annual U.S. tournament open to both professionals and amateurs: in full, the **National Open** or **U.S. Open** —**o'pened** *adj.* —**o'pen·ly** *adv.* —**o'pen·ness** *n.*

open air the outdoors —**o'pen-air'** *adj.*

☆**o·pen-and-shut** (ō'p'n 'n shut') *adj.* that can be clearly and easily determined or decided; very simple or obvious [an *open-and-shut* case]

open chain a molecular formation shown by a structural formula in which the chain of atoms does not form a ring

open circuit an electrical circuit that is broken and thus carries no current —**o'pen-cir'cuit** *adj.*

open city a city which is a military objective but is completely demilitarized and left open to enemy occupation in order to gain immunity, under international law, from bombardment and attack

open door 1. unrestricted admission or access **2.** equal opportunity for all nations to trade with a given nation, without restrictive terms —**o'pen-door'** *adj.*

o·pen-end (-end') *adj.* **1.** of or pertaining to an investment company that has no fixed limit to the number of shares issued, so that the shares are sold and redeemed at their net asset value as the demand requires **2.** allowing the borrowing of additional funds over a period of time on the original security **3.** *same as* OPEN-ENDED

o·pen-end·ed (-en'did) *adj.* **1.** having no set limits as to duration, direction, amount, number, etc.; broad, unlimited, or unrestricted [an *open-ended* discussion] **2.** open to change; allowing for modifications as things develop **3.** designating or of a question allowing for a freely formulated answer rather than one made by a choice from among predetermined answers —**o'pen-end'ed·ness** *n.*

o·pen·er (-ər) *n.* **1.** a person or thing that opens **2.** any of several devices for opening bottles, cans, etc. **3.** the first game in a series, the first act in a vaudeville show, etc. ☆**4.** [*pl.*] *Poker* cards of sufficient value to allow a player to open the betting

o·pen-eyed (-īd') *adj.* **1.** having the eyes open or wide-open; awake, aware, watchful, discerning, amazed, etc. **2.** done with the eyes open

o·pen-faced (-fāst') *adj.* **1.** with the face uncovered **2.** having a frank, honest face ☆**3.** designating a sandwich without a top slice of bread: also **o'pen-face'**

o·pen-hand·ed (-han'did) *adj.* generous —**o'pen-hand'ed·ly** *adv.* —**o'pen-hand'ed·ness** *n.*

o·pen-heart·ed (-härt'id) *adj.* **1.** not reserved; frank; candid **2.** kindly; generous —**o'pen-heart'ed·ly** *adv.* —**o'pen-heart'ed·ness** *n.*

o·pen-hearth (-härth') *adj.* **1.** designating a furnace with a wide, saucer-shaped hearth and a low roof, used in making steel **2.** using a furnace of this kind [the *open-hearth* process]

o·pen-heart surgery (-härt') surgery done on the heart when the chest has been opened and the blood recirculated and oxygenated by mechanical means

open house 1. an informal reception at one's home, with visitors freely coming and going **2.** an occasion when a school, institution, etc. is open to visitors for inspection and observation of activities

OPEN-HEARTH FURNACE (A, lining; B, metal; C, heater ports; D, gas; E, air: fired alternately from either end)

o·pen·ing (-iŋ) *n.* [ME. *openyng*] **1.** a becoming open or causing to be open **2.** an open place or part; hole; gap; aperture ☆**3.** a clearing in the midst of a wooded area **4.** *a)* a beginning; first part; commencement *b)* start of operations; formal beginning *c)* a first performance, as of a play **5.** a favorable chance or occasion; opportunity **6.** an unfilled position or office for which a person is wanted **7.** *Chess, Checkers,* etc. the series of moves at the beginning of a game

open letter a letter written as to a specific person, often in attack, criticism, etc., but published in a newspaper or magazine for everyone to read

open market *same as* FREE MARKET

o·pen-mind·ed (-mīn'did) *adj.* having a mind open to new ideas; free from prejudice or bias —**o'pen-mind'ed·ly** *adv.* —**o'pen-mind'ed·ness** *n.*

o·pen-mouthed (-mouthd', -moutht') *adj.* **1.** having the mouth open **2.** gaping, as in astonishment **3.** clamorous

o·pen-pol·li·na·tion (-päl'ə nā'shən) *n.* the pollination of flowers by insects, the wind, etc. without human action

☆**open primary** a primary election in which the voter need not declare party affiliation

open punctuation punctuation characterized by the use of relatively few commas or other marks

open sea 1. the expanse of sea away from any coastlines, bays, inlets, etc. **2.** *same as* HIGH SEAS

open secret something supposed to be secret but known to almost everyone

open sesame 1. magic words spoken to open the door of the robbers' den in the story of Ali Baba in the *Arabian Nights* **2.** any unfailing means of gaining admission or achieving some end

☆**open shop 1.** a factory, business, etc. employing workers without regard to whether or not they are members of a union with which it may have a contract **2.** formerly, a factory, business, etc. refusing to employ union members, and following an antiunion policy

open stock merchandise, as dishes, available in sets, with individual pieces kept in stock for replacements or additions

o·pen·work (-wʉrk') *n.* ornamental work, as in cloth, metal, etc., with openings in the material

OPer. Old Persian

op·er·a¹ (äp'ər ə, äp'rə) *n.* [It. < L., a work, labor, akin to *opus:* see OPUS] **1.** a play having all or most of its text set to music, with arias, recitatives, choruses, duets, trios, etc. sung to orchestral accompaniment, usually characterized by elaborate costuming, scenery, and choreography: see GRAND OPERA, COMIC OPERA **2.** the branch of art represented by such plays **3.** the score, libretto, or performance of such a play **4.** a theater in which operas are given

op·er·a² (äp'ər ə) *n. pl. of* OPUS

op·er·a·ble (äp'ər ə b'l) *adj.* [ML. *operabilis:* see OPERATE & -ABLE] **1.** practicable or feasible **2.** that can be treated by a surgical operation —**op'er·a·bil'i·ty** *n.* —**op'er·a·bly** *adv.*

‡**o·pé·ra bouffe** (ô pā rä bōōf'; *E.* äp'ər ə bōōf') [Fr.] comic, esp. farcical, opera: also [It.] **o·pe·ra buf·fa** (ô'pe rä bōōf'fä)

‡**o·pé·ra co·mique** (ô pā rà' kô mēk') [Fr., lit., comic opera] French opera with some spoken dialogue: it may or may not be comic

opera glasses a small binocular telescope used at the opera, in theaters, etc.

opera hat a man's tall, collapsible silk hat

opera house a theater chiefly for the performance of operas

op·er·and (äp'ə rand') *n.* [< L. *operandum,* neut. gerundive of *operari,* to work (see OPERATE)] *Math.* that which is operated upon by an operator

op·er·ant (-ənt) *adj.* [< L. *operans,* prp. of *operari:* see OPERATE] **1.** operating, or producing an effect or effects ☆**2.** *Psychol. a)* designating behavior defined by the resulting stimulus rather than the stimulus which elicits it *b)* designating conditioning in which the desired response, when it occurs, is reinforced by a stimulus

‡**o·pe·ra se·ri·a** (ô'pe rä se'rē ä; *E.* äp'ər ə sir'ē ə) [It. lit., serious opera] 18th-cent. opera characterized by the stylized treatment of mythological or classical subjects and the extensive use of arias

op·er·ate (äp'ə rāt') *vi.* -at'ed, -at'ing [< L. *operatus,*

pp. of *operari*, to work < *opus* (gen. *operis*): see OPUS]
1. to be in action so as to produce an effect; act; function;
work **2.** to bring about a desired or appropriate effect;
have a certain influence **3.** to carry on strategic military
movements (usually with *against*) **4.** to perform a surgical
operation —*vt.* **1.** [Now Rare] to bring about as an effect
2. *a)* to put or keep in action; work (a machine, etc.) *b)*
to conduct or direct the affairs of (a business, etc.);
manage **3.** [Colloq.] to perform a surgical operation on
op·er·at·ic (äp′ə rat′ik) *adj.* [OPERA¹ + (DRAMA)TIC] of
or like the opera —**op′er·at′i·cal·ly** *adv.*
op·er·a·tion (äp′ə rā′shən) *n.* [ME. *operacion* < OFr. <
L. *operatio*] **1.** the act, process, or method of operating
2. the condition of being in action or at work **3.** a process
or action that is part of a series in some work **4.** *a)* any
movement or series of movements made in carrying out
strategic military plans; also, [*pl.*] a center where such
activities are monitored or supervised, as at an air base
b) any specific plan, project, venture, etc. *[Operation
Cleanup]* **5.** any surgical procedure performed, usually
with the aid of instruments, to remedy a physical ailment
or defect **6.** *Math.* any process, as addition, division, etc.,
involving a change or transformation in a quantity —**in
operation 1.** in the act or process of making, working,
etc. **2.** having an influence or effect; in force
op·er·a·tion·al (-′l) *adj.* **1.** of, having to do with, or
derived from the operation of a device, system, process,
etc. **2.** *a)* that can be used or operated *b)* in use; operating
3. of or ready for use in a military operation —**op′er·
a′tion·al·ly** *adv.*
op·er·a·tion·al·ism (-′l iz′m) *n. Philos.* the view that
concepts or terms of purportedly factual statements must
be definable in terms of identifiable and repeatable
activities, experimental performances, etc.: also **op′er·
a′tion·ism** —**op′er·a′tion·al·ist** *n.* —**op′er·a′tion·al·is′tic**
adj.
op·er·a·tion·al·ize (-′l īz′) *vt.* **-ized′, -iz′ing** to make
operational; put into operation —**op′er·a′tion·al·i·za′·
tion** *n.*
operations research the systematic and scientific analysis
and evaluation of problems, as in government, military,
or business operations: also **operations analysis**
op·er·a·tive (äp′ə rā′tiv, äp′ər ə-) *adj.* [Fr. *opératif* <
LL.(Ec.) *operativus*] **1.** capable of, characterized by, or in
operation **2.** accomplishing what is desired; effective
3. connected with physical work or mechanical action
4. *Surgery* of or resulting from a surgical operation —*n.*
1. a worker, esp. one skilled in industrial work ☆**2.** a
detective or spy —**op′er·a′tive·ly** *adv.*
op·er·a·tor (äp′ə rāt′ər) *n.* [LL.] **1.** a person who
operates; specif., *a)* a person who effects something;
agent ☆*b)* a person who works some machine *[a telephone
operator] c)* a person who performs surgical operations
☆*d)* a person engaged in financial, commercial, or industrial
operations; owner or manager of a mine, railroad, factory,
etc. ☆**2.** [Slang] a clever, persuasive person who generally
manages to achieve his ends **3.** *Math.* any symbol or
term conventionally indicating that a certain process,
substitution, etc. is to be carried out
o·per·cu·lar (ō pur′kyoo lər) *adj.* of, or having the nature
of, an operculum
o·per·cu·late (-lit, -lāt′) *adj.* [L. *operculatus*] having an
operculum: also **o·per′cu·lat′ed**
o·per·cu·lum (-ləm) *n., pl.* **-la** (-lə), **-lums** [ModL. < L.,
lid, dim. < *operire*, to close, shut: for IE. bases see OB-
& APERTURE] any of various covering flaps or lidlike structures in plants and animals; specif., *a)* the bony covering
protecting the gills of fishes *b)* in many gastropods, the
horny plate serving to close the shell when the animal is
retracted *c)* the lid of the spore cases in mosses *d)* the
lid of a pitcher-shaped leaf
op·er·et·ta (äp′ə ret′ə) *n.* [It., dim. of *opera*, OPERA¹] a
light, amusing opera with spoken dialogue
op·er·on (äp′ə rän′) *n.* [< L. *operare*, to work (see
OPERATE) + -ON] a cluster of genes, with related functions
acting as a coordinated unit controlled by a regulatory
gene
op·er·ose (äp′ə rōs′) *adj.* [L. *operosus* < *opus* (gen. *operis*),
work: see OPUS] [Archaic] **1.** done with or requiring much
toil **2.** very busy; industrious
O·phe·lia (ō fēl′yə) [prob. < Gr. *ōphelia*, a help, succor]
1. a feminine name **2.** in Shakespeare's *Hamlet*, Polonius's
daughter, in love with Hamlet
oph·i·cleide (äf′i klīd′) *n.* [Fr. *ophicléide* < Gr. *ophis*,
serpent + *kleis*, a key: for IE. base see LOT] an early
brass-wind instrument consisting of a long tube doubled
back on itself, with keys for fingering
o·phid·i·an (ō fid′ē ən) *n.* [< ModL. *Ophidia*, former name
of the suborder *Serpentes* (< Gr. *ophis*) + -AN] a snake or
serpent —*adj.* of or like a snake
oph·i·ol·a·try (äf′ē äl′ə trē) *n.* [< Gr. *ophis*, a snake +
-LATRY] the worship of serpents
oph·i·ol·o·gy (-ə jē) *n.* [< Gr. *ophis*, a snake + -LOGY] the
branch of zoology dealing with snakes —**oph′i·o·log′ic**
(-ə läj′ik), **oph′i·o·log′i·cal** *adj.*—**oph′i·ol′o·gist** *n.*

O·phir (ō′fər) [Heb. *ōphīr*] *Bible* a land rich in gold:
I Kings 9:28; 10:11; II Chr. 8:18
o·phit·ic (ō fit′ik) *adj.* [< L. *ophites* < Gr. *ophitēs* (*lithos*),
snake (stone) < *ophis*, a snake + -IC] designating a texture
of rock, characteristic of dolerites, in which long, flat,
narrow crystals of plagioclase feldspar are embedded in
augite
Oph·i·u·chus (äf′ē yōō′kəs, ō′fē-) [L. < Gr. *ophiouchos*,
lit., holding a serpent] a large constellation south of
Hercules
ophthal. ophthalmology
oph·thal·mi·a (äf thal′mē ə) *n.* [ME. *obtalmia* < LL.
ophthalmia < Gr. *ophthalmia* < *ophthalmos*, the eye, akin
to *ōps*, EYE] a severe inflammation of the eyeball or
conjunctiva: also **oph·thal·mi·tis** (äf′thəl mīt′is)
oph·thal·mic (-mik) *adj.* [LL. *ophthalmicus* < Gr. *oph-
thalmikos* < *ophthalmos*: see prec.] of or connected with
the eyes
oph·thal·mo- (äf thal′mō, -mə; äp-) [< Gr. *ophthalmos*,
the eye] *a combining form meaning* the eye or eyes *[oph-
thalmoscope]:* also, before a vowel, **oph·thalm′-**
oph·thal·mol·o·gy (äf′thal mäl′ə jē, äp′-; -thə-) *n.* [OPH-
THALMO- + -LOGY] the branch of medicine dealing with
the structure, functions, and diseases of the eye —
oph′thal·mo·log′i·cal (-mə läj′i k′l) *adj.* —**oph′thal·mol′-
o·gist** *n.*
oph·thal·mo·scope (äf thal′mə skōp′, äp-) *n.* [OPHTHAL-
MO- + -SCOPE] an instrument used to
examine the interior of the eye: it consists
of a perforated mirror arranged to reflect
light from a small bulb into the eye
—**oph·thal′mo·scop′ic** *adj.* —
oph·thal·mos·co·py (äf′thəl mäs′kə pē,
äp′-) *n.*
-o·pi·a (ō′pē ə) [Gr. *-ōpia* < *ōps*, EYE] *a
combining form meaning* a (specified kind
of) eye defect *[diplopia]*
o·pi·ate (ō′pē it; *also, & for v. always,*
-āt′) *n.* [ML. *opiatum:* see OPIUM] **1.**
any medicine containing opium or
any of its derivatives, and acting as a
sedative and narcotic **2.** anything
tending to quiet, soothe, or deaden —*adj.*
1. containing opium **2.** bringing sleep,
quiet, or ease; narcotic —*vt.* **-at′ed,
-at′ing** [Rare] **1.** to treat with an opiate
2. to dull; deaden

OPHTHALMO-
SCOPE

o·pine (ō pīn′) *vt., vi.* **o·pined′, o·pin′ing** [MFr. *opiner* <
L. *opinari*, to think: see ff.] to hold or express (an opinion);
think; suppose: now usually humorous
o·pin·ion (ə pin′yən) *n.* [ME. *opinioun* < OFr. < L.
opinio < *opinari*, to think, akin to *optare*, to select, desire:
see OPTION] **1.** a belief not based on absolute certainty
or positive knowledge but on what seems true, valid, or
probable to one's own mind; judgment **2.** an evaluation,
impression, or estimation of the quality or worth of a
person or thing **3.** the formal judgment of an expert on a
matter in which his advice is sought **4.** *Law* the formal
statement by a judge, court referee, etc. of the law bearing
on a case
SYN.—**opinion** applies to a conclusion or judgment which, while
it remains open to dispute, seems true or probable to one's own
mind *[it's my opinion that he'll agree]*; **belief** refers to the mental
acceptance of an idea or conclusion, often a doctrine or dogma
proposed to one for acceptance *[religious beliefs]*; a **view** is an
opinion affected by one's personal manner of looking at things
[she gave us her views on life]; a **conviction** is a strong belief
about whose truth one has no doubts *[I have a conviction of his
innocence]*; **sentiment** refers to an opinion that is the result of
deliberation but is colored with emotion; **persuasion** refers to a
strong belief that is unshakable because one wishes to believe
in its truth
o·pin·ion·at·ed (-āt′id) *adj.* holding unreasonably or
obstinately to one's own opinions —**o·pin′ion·at′ed·ly**
adv. —**o·pin′ion·at′ed·ness** *n.*
o·pin·ion·a·tive (-āt′iv, -ə tiv) *adj.* **1.** of, or having the
nature of, opinion **2.** same as OPINIONATED —**o·pin′ion·
a′tive·ly** *adv.* —**o·pin′ion·a′tive·ness** *n.*
op·is·thog·na·thous (äp′is thäg′nə thəs) *adj.* [< Gr. *opis-
then*, behind (< IE. *opi-*: cf. OB-) + -GNATHOUS] having
receding jaws
o·pi·um (ō′pē əm) *n.* [L. < Gr. *opion* < *opos*, vegetable
juice] **1.** a yellow to dark brown, addicting, narcotic
drug prepared from the juice of the unripe seed capsules
of the opium poppy: it contains such alkaloids as morphine,
codeine, and papaverine, and is used as an intoxicant
and medicinally to relieve pain and produce sleep **2.**
anything that has a tranquilizing or stupefying effect
o·pi·um·ism (-iz′m) *n.* **1.** opium addiction **2.** the condition resulting from this
opium poppy an annual poppy (*Papaver somniferum*)
with grayish-green leaves and large, white or purple
flowers, the source of opium
O·por·to (ō pôr′tō) seaport in N Portugal, on the Douro
River: pop. 305,000: Port. name, PÔRTO

fat, āpe, cär; ten, ēven; is, bīte; gō, hôrn, tōōl, look; oil, out; up, fur; get; joy; yet; chin; she; thin, *th*en; zh, leisure; ŋ, ring;
ə for a in ago, e in agent, i in sanity, o in comply, u in focus; ′ as in able (ā′b'l); Fr. bâl; ë, Fr. coeur; ö, Fr. feu; Fr. mon; ō, Fr. coq;
ü, Fr. duc; r, Fr. cri; H, G. ich; kh, G. doch. See inside front cover. ☆Americanism; ‡foreign; *hypothetical; <derived from

☆o·pos·sum (ə päs′əm) n., pl. -sums, -sum: see PLURAL, II, D, 1 [< AmInd. (Algonquian) name, lit., white beast] 1. any of several American marsupials (family Didelphidae); esp., the American (or Virginian) opossum, a small, omnivorous, tree-dwelling mammal (Didelphis virginiana), with a rat-like, prehensile tail, the female of which carries its young in a pouch: it is active at night and pretends to be dead when trapped 2. any of various Australian phalangers

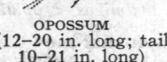

OPOSSUM
(12–20 in. long; tail 10–21 in. long)

opossum shrimp a shrimplike crustacean (order Mysidacea), the female of which carries her eggs in a pouch between the legs

opp. 1. opposed 2. opposite

Op·pen·heim (äp′′n hīm′), E(d-ward) Phillips 1866–1946; Eng. novelist

Op·pen·heim·er (äp′′n hī′mər), J(ulius) Robert 1904–1967; U.S. nuclear physicist

op·pi·dan (äp′i dən) adj. [L. oppidanus < oppidum, town] of a town; urban —n. a person living in a town

op·pi·late (äp′ə lāt′) vt. -lat′ed, -lat′ing [< L. oppilatus, pp. of oppilare, to stop up < ob- (see OB-) + pilare, to ram down < pilum, pestle] [Rare] to block or obstruct (the pores, bowels, etc.) —op′pi·la′tion n.

op·po·nen·cy (ə pō′nən sē) n. opposition; resistance

op·po·nent (ə pō′nənt) n. [< L. opponens, prp. of opponere < ob- (see OB-) + ponere, to place: see POSITION] a person who opposes; person against one in a fight, game, debate, argument, etc.; adversary —adj. 1. [Rare] opposite, as in position 2. opposing; adverse; antagonistic 3. Anat. bringing parts into opposition: said of a muscle
SYN.—opponent, an unemotional word, refers to anyone who is opposed to one, as in a fight, game, debate, etc.; antagonist implies more active opposition, especially in a struggle for control or power; adversary usually suggests actual hostility in the conflict; enemy may imply actual hatred in the opponent and a desire to injure, or it may simply refer to any member of the opposing group, nation, etc., whether or not there is personal animosity or hostility involved; foe, now a somewhat literary synonym for enemy, connotes more active hostility —ANT. ally, confederate

op·por·tune (äp′ər tōōn′, -tyōōn′) adj. [ME. < MFr. < L. opportunus, lit., at or before the port < ob- (see OB-) + portus, PORT¹] 1. right for the purpose; fitting in regard to circumstances: said of time 2. happening or done at the right time; seasonable; well-timed; timely —SYN. see TIMELY —op′por·tune′ly adv. —op′por·tune′ness n.

op·por·tun·ism (-iz′m) n. [< prec., after Fr. opportunisme] the practice or policy of adapting one's actions, judgments, etc. to circumstances, as in politics, in order to further one's immediate interests, without regard for basic principles or eventual consequences —op′por·tun′ist n., adj. —op′por·tun·is′tic adj. —op′por·tun·is′ti·cal·ly adv.

op·por·tu·ni·ty (äp′ər tōō′nə tē, -tyōō′-) n., pl. -ties [ME. opportunite < OFr. opportunité < L. opportunitas < opportunus: see OPPORTUNE] 1. a combination of circumstances favorable for the purpose; fit time 2. a good chance or occasion, as to advance oneself

op·pos·a·ble (ə pō′zə b'l) adj. 1. that can be opposed 2. that can be placed opposite something else —op·pos′a·bil′i·ty n.

op·pose (ə pōz′) vt. -posed′, -pos′ing [ME. opposen < OFr. opposer, altered (after poser: see POSE¹) < L. opponere: see OB- & POSITION] 1. to set against; place opposite, in balance or contrast 2. to contend with in speech or action; resist; withstand —vi. to act in opposition —op·pos′er n.
SYN.—oppose implies offensive action taken against something that threatens or interferes with one; resist implies defensive action taken against something that is already in active opposition to one [one opposes legislative action under consideration, one resists a measure already passed by refusing to comply with it]; withstand usually implies resistance that successfully thwarts or frustrates the attack [can they withstand the new onslaught?] —ANT. submit, succumb, comply

op·po·site (äp′ə zit) adj. [ME. < OFr. < L. oppositus, pp. of opponere: see OB- & POSITION] 1. set against, facing, or back to back; at the other end or side; in a contrary position or direction (often with to) 2. characterized by hostility or resistance 3. different in every way; exactly contrary; antithetical 4. Bot. a) growing in pairs, but separated by a stem b) having one part on the same radius as another, as a stamen in front of a petal —n. anything opposed or opposite —adv. on opposing sides or in an opposite position —prep. 1. fronting; across from 2. Theater in a complementary role (of the opposite sex) to [he played opposite her] —op′po·site·ly adv. —op′po·site·ness n.
SYN.—opposite is applied to things that are symmetrically opposed in position, direction, etc. [they sat at opposite ends of the table]; contrary adds to this connotations of conflict or antagonism [they hold contrary views]; antithetical implies diametrical opposition so that the contrasted things are as far apart or as different as is possible [our interests are completely antithetical]; reverse applies to that which moves or faces in the opposite direction [the reverse side of a fabric]; antonymous is

used specifically of words that are so opposed in meaning that each contradicts, reverses, or negates the other [good and bad are antonymous terms] —ANT. same, identical, like

opposite number a person with reference to another having a comparable position, rank, etc. but in a different place, organization, or situation

op·po·si·tion (äp′ə zish′ən) n. [ME. opposicioun < OFr. opposition < L. oppositio < oppositus, pp. of opponere: see OPPOSITE] 1. the act of opposing 2. an opposed condition; resistance, contradiction, contrast, hostility, etc. 3. any person, group, or thing that opposes; specif., [often O-] a political party opposing, and serving as a check on, the party in power 4. Astrol., Astron. the position of two heavenly bodies when their celestial longitudes differ by 180°; esp., the position of a planet or the moon when either is on the opposite side of the earth from the sun 5. Law the refusal of a creditor to assent to a debtor's release under the bankruptcy law 6. Logic the relation of exclusion or inclusion which exists between propositions having the same subject and predicate but differing in quality, quantity, or both —op′po·si′tion·al adj. —op′po·si′tion·ist n., adj.

op·press (ə pres′) vt. [ME. < OFr. oppresser < ML. oppressare < L. oppressus, pp. of opprimere, to press against < ob- (see OB-) + premere, PRESS¹] 1. to weigh heavily on the mind, spirits, or senses of; worry; trouble 2. to keep down by the cruel or unjust use of power or authority; rule harshly; tyrannize over 3. [Obs.] a) to crush; trample down b) to overpower; subdue —SYN. see WRONG —op·pres′sor n.

op·pres·sion (ə presh′ən) n. [ME. < OFr. < L. oppressio] 1. an oppressing or being oppressed 2. a thing that oppresses 3. a feeling of being weighed down, as with worries or problems; physical or mental distress

op·pres·sive (ə pres′iv) adj. [ME. oppressivus < L. oppressus: see OPPRESS] 1. hard to put up with; causing great discomfort or fatigue 2. cruelly overbearing; tyrannical 3. weighing heavily on the mind, spirits, or senses; distressing —SYN. see ONEROUS —op·pres′sive·ly adv. —op·pres′sive·ness n.

op·pro·bri·ous (ə prō′brē əs) adj. [ME. < LL. opprobriosus] 1. expressing opprobrium; abusive; disrespectful 2. [Now Rare] deserving opprobrium; disgraceful —op·pro′bri·ous·ly adv. —op·pro′bri·ous·ness n.

op·pro·bri·um (ə prō′brē əm) n. [L. < opprobrare, to reproach < ob- (see OB-) + probrum, a disgrace < pro- (see PRO-²) + base of ferre, BEAR¹] 1. the disgrace or infamy attached to conduct viewed as grossly shameful 2. anything bringing shame or disgrace 3. reproachful contempt for something regarded as inferior

op·pugn (ə pyōōn′) vt. [ME. oppugnen < L. oppugnare < ob- (see OB-) + pugnare < pugna, a fight: see PUGNACIOUS] to oppose with argument; criticize adversely; call in question; controvert —op·pugn′er n.

op·pug·nant (ə pug′nənt) adj. [L. oppugnans, prp.: see OPPUGN] [Rare] hostile; antagonistic —op·pug′nan·cy n.

Ops (äps) [L., lit., strength, riches: for base see OPUS] Rom. Myth. the wife of Saturn and goddess of the harvest: identified with the Greek goddess Rhea

-op·sis (äp′sis) [Gr. -opsis < opsis, a sight < ōps, EYE] a combining form meaning sight or view [stereopsis]

opsonic index [see OPSONIN] the ratio of the number of bacteria destroyed by phagocytes in an individual's blood serum to the number destroyed in a normal blood serum

op·son·i·fy (äp sän′ə fī′) vt. -fied′, -fy′ing same as OPSONIZE —op·son′i·fi·ca′tion n.

op·so·nin (äp′sə nin) n. [obs. opson(ium), relish (< L. < Gr. opsōnion, food, provisions < opsōnein, to buy food < opson, meat or any food eaten with bread < o-, together with + *psōn, food, bread, akin to psōmos, mouthful) + -IN¹] a substance in blood serum acting on bacteria and foreign cells to make them more liable to destruction by phagocytes —op·son′ic (-sän′ik) adj.

op·so·nize (-nīz′) vt. -nized′, -niz′ing [see prec.] to make bacteria more liable to destruction by phagocytes —op′so·ni·za′tion n.

opt (äpt) vi. [Fr. opter < L. optare: see OPTION] to make a choice (often with for) —opt out (of) to choose not to be or continue in (some activity, organization, etc.)

opt. 1. optical 2. optician 3. optics 4. optional

op·ta·tive (äp′tə tiv) adj. [Fr. optatif < LL. optativus: see OPTION] 1. expressing wish or desire 2. designating or of the grammatical mood, as in Greek, which expresses wish or desire —n. 1. the optative mood 2. a verb in this mood —op′ta·tive·ly adv.

op·tic (äp′tik) adj. [MFr. optique < ML. opticus < Gr. optikos: for ult. base see EYE] of the eye or sense of sight —n. an eye: a pretentiously humorous usage, generally in the pl.

op·ti·cal (-'l) adj. 1. of or connected with the sense of sight; visual; ocular 2. of the relation between light and vision 3. having to do with optics 4. for aiding vision [optical instruments] —op′ti·cal·ly adv.

optical activity the ability of certain substances to rotate the plane of polarization when transmitting polarized light

optical double (star) same as DOUBLE STAR (sense 2)

optical isomerism a type of isomerism in which isomeric compounds differ only in the direction in which they rotate the plane of polarized light

optic axis in a crystal not having the same properties in all directions with regard to light, a direction along which there is no apparent double refraction since both components of the light ray have the same velocity

optic disk *same as* BLIND SPOT (sense 1)

op·ti·cian (äp tish′ən) *n.* [Fr. *opticien*] a person who makes or deals in optical instruments, esp. one who prepares and dispenses eyeglasses

optic nerve either of the second pair of cranial nerves, which connect the retina of the eye with the brain

op·tics (äp′tiks) *n.pl.* [*with sing. v.*] [< OPTIC] the branch of physics dealing with the nature and properties of light and vision

op·ti·mal (äp′tə məl) *adj.* [OPTIM(UM) + -AL] most favorable or desirable; best; optimum —**op′ti·mal·ly** *adv.*

op·ti·mism (-miz′m) *n.* [Fr. *optimisme* < L. *optimus*, best (see OPTIMUM)] **1.** *Philos. a)* the doctrine held by Leibniz and others that the existing world is the best possible *b)* the doctrine or belief that good ultimately prevails over evil **2.** the tendency to take the most hopeful or cheerful view of matters or to expect the best outcome; practice of looking on the bright side of things —**op′ti·mist** (-mist) *n.* —**op′ti·mis′tic** (-mis′tik), **op′ti·mis′ti·cal** *adj.* —**op′ti·mis′ti·cal·ly** *adv.*

op·ti·mize (-mīz′) *vi.* **-mized′**, **-miz′ing** to be given to optimism —*vt.* to make the most of; develop or realize to the utmost extent; obtain the most efficient or optimum use of —**op′ti·mi·za′tion** *n.*

op·ti·mum (-məm) *n.*, *pl.* **-mums**, **-ma** (-mə) [L., neut. of *optimus*, best < *ops*, power, riches: for base see OPUS] **1.** the best or most favorable degree, condition, amount, etc. **2.** *Biol.* the amount of heat, light, moisture, food, etc. most favorable for growth and reproduction —*adj.* most favorable or desirable; best; optimal

op·tion (äp′shən) *n.* [Fr. < L. *optio* < *optare*, to wish, desire, ult. < IE. base *op-*, to choose, prefer] **1.** the act of choosing: choice **2.** the power, right, or liberty of choosing **3.** something that is or can be chosen; choice **4.** the right, acquired for a consideration, to buy, sell, or lease something at a fixed price, sign or renew a contract, etc. within a specified time —*vt. Sports* to transfer (a player) to a minor league with the option of recalling him —*SYN.* see CHOICE

op·tion·al (-′l) *adj.* left to one's option, or choice; not compulsory; elective —**op′tion·al·ly** *adv.*

op·tom·e·ter (äp täm′ə tər) *n.* [see OPTIC & -METER] an instrument for determining error in the refractive power of the eye

☆**op·tom·e·trist** (-trist) *n.* a specialist in optometry

op·tom·e·try (-trē) *n.* [see OPTIC & -METRY] **1.** measurement of the range and power of vision **2.** the profession of examining the eyes and measuring errors in refraction and of prescribing glasses to correct these defects —**op′to·met′ric** (äp′tə met′rik), **op′to·met′ri·cal** *adj.*

op·u·lent (äp′yə lənt) *adj.* [L. *opulentus* or *opulens* < *ops*: see OPUS] **1.** having much wealth or property; rich **2.** characterized by abundance or profusion; luxuriant —*SYN.* see RICH —**op′u·lence**, **op′u·len·cy** *n.* —**op′u·lent·ly** *adv.*

o·pun·ti·a (ō pun′shē ə, -shə) *n.* [ModL. < L. (*herba*) *Opuntia*, (plant) of Opus, city in Locris, Greece] any of a large genus (*Opuntia*) of cactus plants with red, purple, or yellow flowers, pulpy or dry berries, and fleshy, jointed stems, including the prickly pears and chollas

o·pus (ō′pəs) *n.*, *pl.* **o·pe·ra** (ō′pə rə, äp′ər ə), **o′pus·es** [L., a work < IE. *ops* < base *op-*, to work, riches, whence L. *ops*, riches, Sans. *ápas-*, work, OE. *efnan*, to work, do] a work; composition; esp., any of the musical works of a composer numbered in order of composition or publication

o·pus·cule (ō pus′kyōol) *n.* [Fr. < L. *opusculum*, dim. of *opus*: see prec.] a small or trivial work or composition —**o·pus′cu·lar** *adj.*

-o·py (ō′pē) *same as* -OPIA

☆**o·quas·sa** (ō kwas′ə) *n.* [< *Oquassa* Lake, in Maine] a small trout (*Salvelinus oquassa*) of lakes of W Maine

or[1] (ôr; *unstressed* ər) *conj.* [ME., in form a contr. of *other*, *auther*, either, but actually < OE. *oththe* (in *äther* . . . *oththe*, either . . . or)] a coordinating conjunction introducing an alternative; specif., *a)* introducing the second of two possibilities [*beer or wine*] *b)* introducing any of the possibilities in a series, but usually used only before the last [*apples*, (*or*) *pears*, *or plums*] *c)* introducing a synonymous word or phrase [*botany*, *or* the science of plants] *d)* introducing the second of two possibilities when the first is introduced by *either or whether* [*either go or stay*, whether to go *or* stay] *e)* *Poetry* substituted for *either* as the first correlative ["*or* in the heart *or* in the head"]

or[2] (ôr) *conj.*, *prep.* [ME. < OE. *ār*, var. of *ær*, *ere*: cf. ERE] [Archaic or Dial.] before; ere

or[3] (ôr) *n.* [Fr. < L. *aurum*, gold: for IE. base see EAST] *Heraldry* gold or yellow, represented in engraving by small dots powdered over a plain field

-or (ər; *occas.* ôr) **1.** [ME. -*our* < OFr. -*our*, -*or*, -*eur* < L.

-*or*, -*ator*] *a n.-forming suffix meaning* a person or thing that [*inventor*, *objector*] **2.** [ME. -*our* < OFr. < L. -*or*] *a n.-forming suffix meaning* quality or condition [*horror*, *error*]: in Brit. usage, often **-our**

o.r. owner's risk

☆**o·ra** (ôr′ə) *n. pl.* of OS[2]

or·ach, or·ache (ôr′ach, är′-) *n.* [ME. *orage* < Anglo-Fr. *orache* < OFr. *arroche* < VL. *atrapica* (for L. *atriplex*) < Gr. *atraphaxys*] any of a genus (*Atriplex*) of plants of the goosefoot family, widespread in salty or alkaline areas, having usually silvery foliage and small green flowers; esp., **garden orach** (*Atriplex hortensis*), cultivated as a potherb, chiefly in France

or·a·cle (ôr′ə k′l, är′-) *n.* [ME. < OFr. < L. *oraculum*, divine announcement, oracle < *orare*, to speak, pray, beseech < *os* (gen. *oris*), the mouth: see ORAL] **1.** among the ancient Greeks and Romans, *a)* the place where, or medium by which, deities were consulted *b)* the revelation or response of a medium or priest **2.** *a)* any person or agency believed to be in communication with a deity *b)* any person of great knowledge or wisdom *c)* opinion or statements of any such oracle **3.** the holy of holies of the ancient Jewish Temple: I Kings 6:16, 19–23

o·rac·u·lar (ō rak′yōo lər) *adj.* **1.** of, or having the nature of, an oracle **2.** like an oracle; wise, prophetic, mysterious, etc. —**o·rac′u·lar′i·ty** (-yə lar′ə tē) *n.* —**o·rac′u·lar·ly** *adv.*

o·rad (ôr′ad) *adv.* [< L. *os* (gen. *oris*), the mouth + -AD[2]] toward the mouth or oral region

O·ra·dea (ô räd′yä) city in NW Romania, near the Hungarian border: pop. 112,000

o·ral (ôr′əl) *adj.* [< L. *os* (gen. *oris*), the mouth < IE. base *ōus-*, mouth, edge, whence Sans. *ā-h*, mouth, ON. *ōss*, mouth of a stream] **1.** uttered by the mouth; spoken **2.** of speech; using speech **3.** of, at, or near the mouth **4.** *Phonet.* having mouth resonance only: distinguished from NASAL **5.** *Psychoanalysis a)* designating or of the earliest stage of psychosexual development in which interest centers around sucking, feeding, and biting *b)* designating or of such traits in the adult as friendliness, generosity, and optimism or aggressiveness and pessimism, regarded as unconscious psychic residues of that stage: cf. ANAL, GENITAL **6.** *Zool.* on or of the same side as the mouth —*n.* an examination that is oral and not written, as in a college —**o′ral·ly** *adv.*

SYN.—**oral** refers to that which is spoken, as distinguished from that which is written or otherwise communicated [*an oral promise, request, etc.*]; **verbal**, though sometimes synonymous with **oral**, in strict discrimination refers to anything using words, either written or oral, to communicate an idea or feeling [*a verbal image, caricature, etc.*]

O·ran (ō ran′; *Fr.* ô rän′) seaport in N Algeria, on the Mediterranean: pop. 430,000

o·rang (ō raŋ′, -ə) *n. same as* ORANGUTAN

Or·ange[1] (ôr′inj, är′-) ruling family of the Netherlands: see NASSAU —*adj.* of or having to do with Orangemen

Or·ange[2] (ôr′inj, är′-; *also, for* 3 & 4, *Fr.* ô ränzh′) **1.** [prob. after the *orange* groves there] city in SW Calif.: suburb of Los Angeles: pop. 77,000 **2.** river in South Africa, flowing from NE Lesotho west into the Atlantic: c. 1,300 mi. **3.** former principality of W Europe, now in SE France **4.** city in SE France: former cap. of *prec.*: pop. 21,000

or·ange (ôr′inj, är′-) *n.* [ME. < OFr. *orenge* < Pr. *auranja* (with sp. influenced by L. *aurum*, gold & loss of initial *n* through faulty separation of art. *un*) < Sp. *naranja* < Ar. *nāranj* < Per. *nārang* < Sans. *naranga*, prob. akin to Tamil *naru*, fragrant] **1.** a reddish-yellow, round, edible citrus fruit, with a sweet, juicy pulp **2.** any of various evergreen trees (genus *Citrus*) of the rue family producing this fruit, having white, fragrant blossoms, often carried by brides, and hard, yellow wood **3.** any of several plants or fruits resembling the orange **4.** reddish yellow —*adj.* **1.** reddish-yellow **2.** made with or from orange **3.** having a flavor more or less like that of oranges —**or′ang·y** (-in jē) *adj.*

☆**or·ange·ade** (-ād′) *n.* [Fr.: see ORANGE & -ADE] a drink made of orange juice and water, usually sweetened

Orange Free State province of South Africa, west of Lesotho: formerly a Boer republic (1854–1900) & then a Brit. colony (**Orange River Colony**, 1900–10): 49,866 sq. mi.; pop. 1,387,000; cap. Bloemfontein

☆**orange hawkweed** *same as* DEVIL'S PAINTBRUSH

Or·ange·ism (ôr′inj iz′m, är′-) *n.* the principles and practices of the Orangemen

Or·ange·man (-mən) *n.*, *pl.* **-men** (-mən) [after the Prince of *Orange*, later WILLIAM III] a member of a secret society organized in northern Ireland in 1795 to support Protestantism

orange pekoe a black tea grown in Ceylon and India: see PEKOE

or·ange·ry (ôr′inj rē, är′-) *n.*, *pl.* **-ries** [Fr. *orangerie* < *oranger*, orange tree < *orange*] a hothouse or other sheltered place for growing orange trees in cooler climates

☆**orange stick** a pointed stick of orangewood, used in manicuring

or·ange·wood (-wood′) *n.* the wood of the orange tree, used in carving, etc. —*adj.* of orangewood

o·rang·u·tan (ô raṅ′oo tan′, ə-; -taṅ′) *n.* [Malay *oraṅ utan*, lit., man of the forest < *oraṅ*, man + *utan*, forest: first applied to the ape by Europeans] a manlike ape (*Pongo satyrus*) with shaggy, reddish-brown hair, very long arms, small ears, and a hairless face: it is smaller than the gorilla and is found only in the swampy, coastal jungles of Borneo and Sumatra: also sp. **o·rang′ou·tang′** (-taṅ′)

ORANGUTAN
(standing height
to 60 in.)

o·rate (ô rāt′, ôr′āt) *vi.* **o·rat′ed, o·rat′ing** [back-formation < ff.] to make an oration; speak in a pompous or bombastic manner: a humorously derogatory term

o·ra·tion (ô rā′shən) *n.* [ME. *oracion* < L. *oratio* < *orare*, to speak < IE. base *ōr-*, to speak, call, whence Gr. *ara*, prayer] a formal public speech, esp. one given in connection with a ceremony —*SYN.* see SPEECH

or·a·tor (ôr′ət ər, är′-) *n.* [ME. *oratour* < OFr. *orateur* < L. *orator*] 1. a person who delivers an oration 2. a skilled, eloquent public speaker 3. [Obs.] *Law* a petitioner; plaintiff

Or·a·to·ri·an (ôr′ə tôr′ē ən) *n.* a member of an Oratory

or·a·tor·i·cal (ôr′ə tôr′i k'l) *adj.* 1. of or characteristic of orators or oratory 2. given to oratory —**or′a·tor′i·cal·ly** *adv.*

or·a·tor·i·o (ôr′ə tôr′ē ō′, är′-) *n., pl.* **-os′** [It., lit., small chapel (< LL.(Ec.) *oratorium*: see ff., sense 2): from the performance of such compositions at the oratory of Saint Philip Neri in Rome] a long, dramatic musical composition, usually on a religious theme, consisting of arias, recitatives, duets, trios, choruses, etc. sung to orchestral accompaniment: it is presented without stage action, scenery, or costumes

or·a·tor·y (ôr′ə tôr′ē, är′-) *n., pl.* **-ries** [ME. *oratorie* < L. *oratoria*] 1. the art of an orator; skill or eloquence in public speaking 2. [ME. *oratorie* < LL.(Ec.) *oratorium*, place of prayer < L. *oratorius*, of an orator (in Ec. use, of praying) < *orator*] a small chapel, esp. one for private prayer 3. [O-] *R.C.Ch.* a religious society of secular priests, esp. that founded by Saint Philip Neri in 1564: its members live under obedience but not under vows

orb (ôrb) *n.* [L. *orbis*, a circle] 1. a sphere, or globe 2. *a)* any of the heavenly spheres, as the sun, moon, etc. *b)* [Obs.] the earth *c)* [Obs.] the orbit of a planet, etc. 3. [Poet.] the eye or eyeball 4. a small globe with a cross on top, as a symbol of royal power 5. [Archaic] *a)* a sphere of activity; province *b)* rank; status 6. [Archaic] a collective body; organized whole 7. [Rare] anything circular in form; circle 8. *Astrol.* the sphere of influence of a planet, star, or house —*vt.* 1. to form into a sphere or circle 2. [Poet.] to enclose or encircle —*vi.* 1. [Rare] to move in an orbit 2. [Poet.] to take on the shape of an orb —**orbed** *adj.* —**orb′y** *adj.*

or·bic·u·lar (ôr bik′yoo lər) *adj.* [ME. *orbiculer* < LL. *orbicularis* < L. *orbiculus*, dim. of *orbis*, a circle] 1. in the form of an orb; spherical or circular 2. *Bot.* round and flat, as some leaves Also **or·bic′u·late** (-lit, -lāt′), **or·bic′u·lat′ed** (-lāt′id) —**or·bic′u·lar′i·ty** (-lar′ə tē) *n.* —**or·bic′u·lar·ly** *adv.*

or·bit (ôr′bit) *n.* [MFr. *orbite* < ML. *orbita* < L., path, track < *orbis*, a circle, wheel] 1. the bony cavity containing the eye; eye socket 2. [L. *orbita*] *a)* the path taken by a heavenly body during its periodic revolution around another body *b)* the path taken by an artificial satellite or spacecraft around a heavenly body 3. the range of one's experience or activity; ordinary course of life 4. *Zool.* the skin around the eye of a bird —*vi.* to move in an orbit or circle —*vt.* 1. to put (a satellite or spacecraft) into an orbit in space 2. to move in an orbit around —**or′bit·al** *adj.* —**or′bit·er** *n.*

orbital index the ratio of the greatest breadth of the orbital cavity to its greatest height, times 100

orc (ôrk) *n.* [Fr. *orque* < L. *orca*, kind of whale, altered (after *orca*, a large tub) < Gr. *oruga*, acc. of *oryx*, a large fish] a grampus, killer whale, or other cetacean identified by early writers as a "sea monster"

O.R.C., ORC 1. Officers' Reserve Corps 2. Organized Reserve Corps

or·ce·in (ôr′sē in) *n.* [ORC(IN) + -*e*- + -IN¹] a brownish-red, crystalline dye, $C_{28}H_{24}O_7N_2$, the main coloring matter of archil, obtained from lichens or by treating orcinol with ammonia and oxygen, and used as a biological stain, reagent, etc.

orch. orchestra

or·chard (ôr′chərd) *n.* [ME. < OE. *ortgeard* < VL. *orto*, for L. *hortus*, a garden + OE. *geard*, YARD²] 1. an area of land devoted to the cultivation of fruit trees or nut trees 2. such a stand of trees

or·chard·ist (-ist) *n.* a person skilled or engaged in the cultivation of orchards: also **or′chard·man** (-mən), *pl.* **-men** (-mən)

or·ches·tra (ôr′kis trə, -kes′-) *n.* [L. < Gr. *orchēstra* < *orcheisthai*, to dance < IE. base *ergh-*, extension of *er-*, swift movement, rise abruptly, whence Sans. *r̥ghāyati*, (he) rages, G. *arg*, bad] 1. in ancient Greek theaters, the semicircular space in front of the stage, used by the chorus 2. in modern theaters, the space in front of and below the stage, where the musicians sit: in full, **orchestra pit** ☆3. *a)* the section of seats on the main floor of a theater, esp. the front section *b)* the main floor of a theater 4. *a)* a group of musicians playing together; esp., same as SYMPHONY ORCHESTRA *b)* the instruments of such a group

or·ches·tral (ôr kes′trəl) *adj.* of, for, by, or like an orchestra —**or·ches′tral·ly** *adv.*

or·ches·trate (ôr′kis trāt′) *vt., vi.* **-trat′ed, -trat′ing** 1. to compose or arrange (music) for an orchestra 2. to furnish (a ballet, etc.) with an orchestral score 3. to combine in a harmonious way —**or′ches·tra′tion** *n.* —**or′ches·tra′tor, or′ches·trat′er** *n.*

or·ches·tri·on (ôr kes′trē ən) *n.* a large, mechanical music box, somewhat like a barrel organ, that produces an effect imitative of that of an orchestra

or·chi- (ôr′ki) *same as* ORCHIDO-

or·chid (ôr′kid) *n.* [< ModL. *Orchideae*, name of the order: so named (1751) by Linnaeus < *orchid-*, mistaken as stem of L. *orchis*: see ORCHIS] 1. any of a family (Orchidaceae) of perennial plants that grow in the ground or as epiphytes and are characterized by a bulbous root system, three petals of which one is lip-shaped with many distinctive forms, waxy pollen masses, and minute seeds 2. the flower of such a plant; esp., any of the brightly colored tropical varieties cultivated for wear as a corsage 3. a light bluish red, or pale purple —*adj.* of this color

or·chi·do- (ôr′ki dō) [< *orchidos*, mistaken as gen. of Gr. *orchis*, testicle: see ORCHIS] *a combining form meaning:* 1. testicle [orchidotomy] 2. orchid [orchidology] Also, before a vowel, **orchido-**

or·chid·ol·o·gy (ôr′ki däl′ə jē) *n.* [prec. + -LOGY] the branch of horticulture dealing with orchids

or·chid·ot·o·my (-dät′ə mē) *n., pl.* **-mies** [ORCHIDO- + -TOMY] the surgical incision of a testicle

or·chi·ec·to·my (ôr′kē ek′tə mē) *n., pl.* **-mies** [ORCHI- + -ECTOMY] the surgical removal of one or both testicles; castration

or·chil (ôr′kil, -chil) *n. same as* ARCHIL

or·chis (ôr′kis) *n.* [ModL., name of the genus < L., orchid < Gr. *orchis*, orchid, lit., testicle (< IE. base *orĝhi-*, whence Lith. *aržùs*, lustful): from the shape of the roots] an orchid; specif., any of a genus (*Orchis*) with small purplish or white flowers growing in spikes

or·cin·ol (ôr′sə nōl′, -nôl′) *n.* [< It. *orcello*, ARCHIL + -IN¹ + -OL¹] a colorless, crystalline compound, $C_6H_3 \cdot CH_3(OH)_2$, that becomes red in air, obtained from aloes, lichens, etc. and used as a medicine, in dyes, etc.: also **or′cin** (-sin)

Or·cus (ôr′kəs) [L.] *Rom. Myth.* 1. the lower world; Hades 2. Pluto, or Dis

ord. 1. ordained 2. order 3. ordinal 4. ordinance 5. ordinary 6. ordnance

or·dain (ôr dān′) *vt.* [ME. *ordeinen* < OFr. *ordener* < L. *ordinare*, in LL.(Ec.), to ordain (as a priest) < L. *ordo* (gen. *ordinis*), ORDER] 1. orig., to put in order; arrange; prepare 2. *a)* to decree; order; establish; enact *b)* to predetermine; predestine 3. to invest with the functions or office of a minister, priest, or rabbi —*vi.* to command; decree —**or·dain′er** *n.* —**or·dain′ment** *n.*

or·deal (ôr dēl′, -dē′əl; ôr′dēl) *n.* [ME. *ordal* < OE., akin to G. *urteil*, judgment < WGmc. *uzdailjo-*, what is dealt out < *uzdailjan*, to deal out, allot, adjudge < *uz-*, out + *dailjan*, whence DEAL¹] 1. an ancient method of trial in which the accused was exposed to physical dangers, from which he was supposed to be divinely protected if he was innocent 2. any difficult, painful, or trying experience; severe trial

or·der (ôr′dər) *n.* [ME. < OFr. *ordre* < L. *ordo* (gen. *ordinis*), straight row, regular series, akin to *ordiri*, to lay the warp, hence begin, set in order, prob. < IE. base *ar-*, to join, fit, whence ARM¹, ART¹] 1. social position; rank in the community 2. a state of peace and serenity; observance of the law; orderly conduct 3. the sequence or arrangement of things or events; series; succession 4. a fixed or definite plan; system; law of arrangement 5. a group or class set off from others by some trait or quality 6. a group of men constituting a military, monastic, or social brotherhood [the *Order* of Knights Templars, the Franciscan *Order*, the Masonic *Order*] 7. *a)* a group of persons distinguished by having received a certain award or citation, as for outstanding service to a state [the *Order* of the Garter] *b)* the insignia of such a group 8. *a)* a state or condition in which everything is in its right place and functioning properly 9. condition or state in general [not in working *order*] 10. a command, direction, or instruction, usually backed by authority 11. a distinctive or unique group; class; kind; sort [sentiments of a high *order*] 12. an established method or system, as of conduct or action in meetings, worship, court, etc. 13. *a)* a request or commission to make or supply something [an *order* for merchandise or services] *b)* the goods so made or supplied [to deliver a grocery *order*] ☆*c)* a single portion of some

food, as served in a restaurant /an *order* of cole slaw/ **14.** *Archit. a)* any of several classical styles of structure, determined chiefly by the type of column and entablature: see DORIC, IONIC, CORINTHIAN *b)* a style of building **15.** *Biol.* a classification of a group of related plants or animals ranking above a family and below a class **16.** *Finance* written instructions to pay money or surrender property **17.** *Gram.* the arrangement of elements within a grammatical unit **18.** *Law* a direction or command of a court, judge, public body, etc. **19.** *Math. a)* a whole number describing the degree or stage of complexity of an algebraic expression *b)* an established sequence of numbers, letters, events, units, etc. *c)* the number of elements in a given group *d)* the number of rows or columns in a determinant **20.** *Theol. a)* any of the nine ranks or grades of angels *b)* any rank or grade in the Christian clergy *c)* [*pl.*] the position of ordained minister /to take holy *orders*/ *d)* [*often pl.*] the ceremony of ordaining a minister —*vt.* **1.** to put or keep in order; organize; arrange **2.** *a)* to instruct to do something; give an order to; command *b)* to command to go (*to, out of,* etc. a specified place) **3.** to request or direct (something to be supplied) /to *order* merchandise/ **4.** [Archaic] *Eccles.* to ordain (a priest, etc.) —*vi.* **1.** to give a command **2.** to request that something be supplied —SYN. see COMMAND —**by order of** according to the command of —**call to order** to request to be quiet, as in order to start (a meeting) —**in** (or **out of**) **order 1.** in (or not in) proper sequence or position **2.** in (or not in) good condition **3.** in (or not in) accordance with the rules, as of parliamentary procedure ☆**4.** being (or not being) suitable to the occasion —**in order that** so that; to the end that —**in order to** for the purpose of; as a means to; to —**in short order** without delay; quickly —**on order** ordered, or requested, but not yet supplied —**on the order of 1.** somewhat resembling; similar to **2.** approximately; roughly —☆**tall order** [Colloq.] a difficult task or requirement —**to order** in accordance with the buyer's specifications —**or'der-er** *n.*

order arms *Mil.* **1.** to bring the rifle to an upright position with its butt on the ground beside the right foot, and remain at attention **2.** a command to do this

or-der-ly (ôr′dər lē) *adj.* **1.** *a)* neat or tidy in arrangement; in good order *b)* arranged in, conforming to, or exhibiting some regular order; systematic **2.** well-behaved; law-abiding; peaceful **3.** having to do with the recording and transmission of military orders, records, etc. /the *orderly* room/ —*adv.* in regular or proper order; methodically —*n., pl.* **-lies 1.** *Mil.* an enlisted man assigned to perform personal services for an officer or officers or to carry out a specific task /latrine *orderly*/ **2.** a male hospital attendant —**or'der-li-ness** *n.*

SYN.—**orderly** implies freedom from disorder or confusion as by observing a proper arrangement, a set rule, etc. /an *orderly* desk, crowd, meeting, etc./; **methodical** implies a following closely and regularly a definite procedure that is carefully planned in detail /a *methodical* investigation, worker, etc./; **systematic** often adds the implications of thoroughness and elaborateness and stresses the overall purpose, design, pattern, etc. /a *systematic* suppression of the opposition, etc./ —ANT. **disorderly, haphazard, chaotic**

Order of the Garter the highest order of British knighthood, instituted c. 1344 by Edward III

or-di-nal (ôr′d′n əl) *adj.* [ME. *ordynal,* conforming to order < LL. *ordinalis* < L. *ordo,* ORDER] **1.** expressing order or succession, specif. of a number in a series: see ORDINAL NUMBER **2.** of an order of animals or plants —*n.* **1.** same as ORDINAL NUMBER **2.** [often O-] any book of prescribed forms used in ordaining priests, deacons, etc., consecrating churches, or the like

ordinal number any number used to indicate order (e.g., second, ninth, 25th, etc.) in a particular series: distinguished from CARDINAL NUMBER

or-di-nance (ôr′d′n əns) *n.* [ME. < OFr. *ordenance* < *ordener:* see ORDAIN] **1.** a direction or command of an authoritative nature **2.** that which is held to be a decree of fate or of a deity **3.** an established or prescribed practice or usage, esp. a religious rite ☆**4.** a governmental, now esp. municipal, statute or regulation —SYN. see LAW

or-di-nar-i-ly (ôr′d′n er′ə lē) *adv.* **1.** usually; as a rule **2.** in an ordinary manner or to an ordinary degree

or-di-nar-y (ôr′d′n er′ē) *n., pl.* **-nar'ies** [ME. < OFr. & ML.: OFr. *ordinarie* < ML.(Ec.) *ordinarius* < L., an overseer, orig., orderly, regular < *ordo,* ORDER] **1.** *a)* an official of church or court whose power or jurisdiction is original and not that of a deputy ☆*b)* in some States, a judge of probate *c)* [Obs.] a prison chaplain **2.** [Brit.] *a)* a set meal served regularly at the same price *b)* an inn, tavern, etc. where such meals are served **3.** an early type of bicycle with one large wheel, and a smaller one behind **4.** *Eccles.* [often O-] *a)* the form for Mass, or a book containing this *b)* the relatively unchangeable part of the Mass **5.** *Heraldry* any one of the major devices used as heraldic distinctions —*adj.* [ME. *ordinarie* < L. *ordinarius*] **1.** customary; usual; regular; normal **2.** *a)* familiar; unexceptional; common *b)* relatively poor or

inferior **3.** having immediate, not delegated, jurisdiction, as a judge —SYN. see COMMON —**in ordinary** in regular, permanent service —**out of the ordinary** unusual; extraordinary —**or'di·nar'i·ness** *n.*

ordinary seaman a sailor of less experience than, and ranking below, an able-bodied seaman

or-di-nate (ôr′d′n it, -āt′) *n.* [< ModL. (*linea*) *ordinate* (*applicata*), line applied in ordered manner] *Math.* the vertical Cartesian coordinate on a plane, measured from the x-axis along a line parallel with the y-axis: cf. ABSCISSA

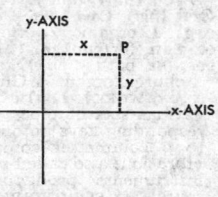

ORDINATE
(X, the abscissa of P;
Y, the ordinate of P)

or-di-na-tion (ôr′d′n ā′shən) *n.* [ME. *ordinacioun* < L. *ordinatio* < *ordinare:* see ORDAIN] **1.** the act of ordaining **2.** a being ordained, as to the ministry

ord-nance (ôrd′nəns) *n.* [contr. < ORDINANCE, in restricted meaning] **1.** cannon or artillery **2.** all military weapons together with ammunition, combat vehicles, etc. and the equipment and supplies used in servicing these **3.** military branch or unit that orders, stores, and supplies ordnance

or-do (ôr′dō) *n., pl.* **-dos, -di-nes′** (-də nēz′) [L., ORDER] *R.C.Ch.* an annual calendar that gives directions for each day's Mass and Office

or-don-nance (ôr′d′n əns; *Fr.* ôr dô näns′) *n.* [Fr. < OFr. *ordenance:* see ORDINANCE] **1.** the proper or orderly arrangement of parts, as in a painting, literary work, etc. **2.** in France, an ordinance, law, or decree

Or-do-vi-cian (ôr′də vish′ən) *adj.* [< L. *Ordovices,* ancient Celtic tribe in Wales] designating or of the second period of the Paleozoic Era immediately following the Cambrian and preceding the Silurian, characterized by an abundance of invertebrate life of many different kinds —**the Ordovician** the Ordovician Period or its rocks: see GEOLOGY, chart

or-dure (ôr′jər, -dyoor) *n.* [ME. < OFr. < *ord,* filthy < L. *horridus,* HORRID] dung; filth; manure; excrement

Or-dzho-ni-kid-ze (ôr′jô ni kêd′ze) city in the S European R.S.F.S.R., in the Caucasus: pop. 212,000

ore (ôr) *n.* [ME. *or* < OE. *ar,* brass, copper (< IE. base *ayos,* metal, copper, bronze, iron, whence Sans. *áyas,* metal, L. *aes,* copper) identified with *ora,* unwrought metal (akin to ON. *aurr,* ferrous sand, gravel)] **1.** any natural combination of minerals, esp. one from which a metal or metals can be profitably extracted **2.** a natural substance from which a nonmetallic material, such as sulfur, can be extracted

ö·re (ö′rə) *n., pl.* **ö′re** [Sw. < ON. *aurar,* a unit of weight, coin < L. *aureus,* a gold coin, orig. adj., golden < *aurum,* gold] **1.** the 100th part of a Swedish krona **2.** a coin of this value

ø·re (ö′rə) *n., pl.* **ø′re** [Dan. & Norw. < ON. *aurar:* see prec.] **1.** the 100th part of a Danish krone or a Norwegian krone **2.** a coin of either of these values

o-re-ad (ôr′ē ad′) *n.* [< L. *oreas* (gen. *oreadis*) < Gr. *oreias* (gen. *oreiados*) < *oros,* mountain: see ORIENT] *Gr. & Rom. Myth.* a mountain nymph

Ö-re-bro (ö′rə brȫō′) city in SC Sweden: pop. 82,000

o-rec-tic (ō rek′tik, ô-) *adj.* [Gr. *orektikos* < *orektos,* stretched out < *oregein,* to reach for, desire < IE. base *reĝ̑-,* to make straight, stretch, whence L. *regere,* to direct] *Philos.* of or characterized by appetite or desire

o-reg-a-no (ō reg′ə nō, ə-) *n.* [Sp. *orégano* < L. *origanum* < Gr. *origanon*] any of a number of plants (esp. *Origanum vulgare*) of the mint family, the fragrant leaves of which are used for seasoning

Or-e-gon (ôr′i gən, är′-; *also, but not locally,* -gän′) [prob. < AmInd. *ouragan* (lit., birch-bark dish), native name of the Columbia River] NW coastal State of the U.S.: admitted, 1859; 96,981 sq. mi.; pop. 2,091,000; cap. Salem: abbrev. Oreg., OR —**Or'e-go'ni-an** (-gō′nē ən) *adj., n.*

☆**Oregon fir** same as DOUGLAS FIR: also **Oregon pine**
☆**Oregon grape** same as MAHONIA
☆**Oregon Trail** former route extending from the Missouri River in Mo., northwest to the Columbia River in Oreg., much used by westward migrants (c. 1840-60): c. 2,000 mi.

Or-el (ō rel′; *Russ.* är yō̄l′) city in C European R.S.F.S.R., on the Oka River: pop. 183,000

O-ren-burg (ôr′yən boorkh′) city in SE European R.S.F.S.R., on the Ural River: pop. 316,000

OREGON TRAIL

fat, āpe, cär; ten, ēven; is, bīte; gō, hôrn, tōōl, look; oil, out; up, fur; get; joy; yet; chin; she; thin, *then;* zh, leisure; ŋ, ring; ə for *a* in *ago, e* in *agent, i* in *sanity, o* in *comply, u* in *focus;* ′ as in *able* (ā′b'l); Fr. bâl; ë, Fr. coeur; ö, Fr. feu; Fr. mon; ô, Fr. coq; ü, Fr. duc; r, Fr. cri; H, G. ich; kh, G. doch. See inside front cover. ☆ Americanism; ‡foreign; *hypothetical; <derived from

O·res·tes (ô res'tēz, ə-) [L. < Gr. *Orestēs* < *oros*, mountain: see ORIENT] *Gr. Myth.* son of Agamemnon and Clytemnestra, who, with the aid of his sister Electra, avenged the murder of his father by killing his mother and her lover Aegisthus

O·re·sund (*Swed.* ö're sund') strait between Sweden and the Danish island of Zealand: c. 80 mi. long Dan. sp. **Ø're·sund** ('-soon')

Orff (ôrf), **Carl** 1895– ; Ger. composer

org. 1. organic **2.** organization **3.** organized

or·gan (ôr'gən) *n.* [ME. *organe* < OE. *organa* & OFr. *organe*, both < L. *organum*, a tool, implement, in LL.(Ec.), a church organ < Gr. *organon*, an implement, engine < *ergon*, WORK] **1.** *a)* a large wind instrument consisting of various sets of pipes which, as they are opened by corresponding keys on one or more keyboards, allow passage to a column of compressed air that causes sound by vibration: also called **pipe organ** *b)* any of several musical instruments producing similar or somewhat similar sounds: cf. ELECTRONIC ORGAN, REED ORGAN, BARREL ORGAN *c)* [Archaic] any musical instrument; esp., a wind instrument **2.** in animals and plants, a part composed of specialized tissues and adapted to the performance of a specific function or functions **3.** a means or instrument for the performance of some action [an *organ* of local government] **4.** a means of communicating ideas or opinions, as a periodical

or·gan·dy, or·gan·die (ôr'gən dē) *n., pl.* **-dies** [Fr. *organdi* < ?: cf. ORGANZINE] a very sheer, crisp cotton fabric used for dresses, curtains, etc.

or·gan·elle (ôr'gə nel') *n.* [G. < ModL. *organella* < L. *organum* (< Gr. *organon*: see ORGAN) + *-ella*, fem. of *-ellus*, dim. suffix] a discrete structure within a cell, as a chloroplast, cilium, centriole, etc., characterized by having specialized functions, a usually distinctive chemical composition, and an identifying molecular structure: often found in large numbers in a particular cell

organ grinder a person who makes a living by playing a barrel organ in the streets

or·gan·ic (ôr gan'ik) *adj.* [L. *organicus* < Gr. *organikos*] **1.** of or having to do with a bodily organ **2.** of or involving the basic makeup of a thing; inherent; inborn; constitutional **3.** made up of systematically interrelated parts; organized **4.** *a)* designating or of any chemical compound containing carbon: some of the simple compounds of carbon, as carbon dioxide, are frequently classified as inorganic compounds *b)* designating or of the branch of chemistry dealing with carbon compounds **5.** of, having the characteristics of, or derived from living organisms ☆**6.** grown with only animal or vegetable fertilizers, as manure, bone meal, compost, etc. ☆**7.** *Law* designating or of the fundamental, or constitutional, law of a state **8.** *Med.* producing or involving alteration in the structure of an organ [an *organic* disorder]: cf. FUNCTIONAL — **or·gan'i·cal·ly** *adv.*

or·gan·i·cism (-ə siz'm) *n.* **1.** holism as applied to a living organism **2.** the theory that the entire, coordinated, autonomous system of an organism, rather than any of its parts, constitutes the living process — **or·gan'i·cist** *n., adj.*

or·gan·ism (ôr'gə niz'm) *n.* **1.** any individual animal or plant having diverse organs and parts that function together as a whole to maintain life and its activities **2.** anything resembling a living thing in its complexity of structure or functions —**or'gan·is'mic, or'gan·is'mal** *adj.* —**or'gan·is'mi·cal·ly** *adv.*

or·gan·ist (ôr'gə nist) *n.* [< MFr. *organiste* or ML. *organista*] one who plays the organ

or·gan·i·za·tion (ôr'gə ni zā'shən, -nī-) *n.* [ME. *organizacion* < ML. *organizatio*] **1.** an organizing or being organized **2.** the manner of being organized; organic structure **3.** [Rare] *same as* ORGANISM **4.** any unified, consolidated group of elements; systematized whole; esp., *a)* a body of persons organized for some specific purpose, as a club, union, or society *b)* the administrative personnel or executive structure of a business *c)* all the functionaries, committees, etc. of a political party —**or'gan·i·za'tion·al** *adj.* —**or'gan·i·za'tion·al·ly** *adv.*

☆**organization man** an employee, esp. of a large corporation, who has adapted so completely to what is expected in attitudes, ideas, behavior, etc. by the corporation as to have lost his sense of personal identity or independence

or·gan·ize (ôr'gə nīz') *vt.* **-ized', -iz'ing** [ME. *organyzen* < ML. *organizare* < L. *organum*] **1.** to provide with an organic structure; esp., *a)* to arrange in an orderly way [to *organize* office records] *b)* to make into a whole with unified and coherent relationships [to *organize* an essay] *c)* to make plans or arrange for [to *organize* a campaign] **2.** to bring into being; establish; institute [to *organize* a corporation] **3.** to persuade to join in some common cause or enlist in some organization; specif., *a)* to enlist in, or cause to form, a labor union ☆*b)* to enlist the employees of (an industry, business, etc.) in a labor union **4.** [Colloq.] to set (oneself) into an orderly state of mind —*vi.* **1.** to become organized ☆**2.** to join in some common cause or form some organization, esp. a labor union —**or'gan·iz'a·ble** *adj.*

or·gan·iz·er (-ər) *n.* **1.** a person who organizes; specif., ☆a labor-union official whose work is enlisting and orienting members **2.** *Embryology* any portion of a developing embryo, or any substance produced by it, capable of inducing differentiation in other portions

or·ga·no- (ôr'gə nō, -nə) [< Gr. *organon*, ORGAN] a combining form meaning organ or organic [*organography*]

or·ga·no·gen·e·sis (ôr'gə nō jen'ə sis) *n.* [ModL.: see prec. & -GENESIS] *Biol.* the origin and development of organs —**or'ga·no·ge·net'ic** (-jə net'ik) *adj.*

or·ga·nog·ra·phy (ôr'gə näg'rə fē) *n.* [ORGANO- + -GRAPHY] *Biol.* the descriptive study of the organs of animals and plants, esp. the outer parts of plants —**or'ga·no·graph'ic** (-nō graf'ik) *adj.*

or·ga·no·lep·tic (ôr'gə nō lep'tik) *adj.* [Fr. *organoleptique* < Gr. *organon*, ORGAN + *lēptikos*, disposed to accept < *lēptos*, verbal of *lambainein*, to seize] **1.** affecting or involving an organ, esp. a sense organ as of taste, smell, or sight **2.** responsive to sensory stimuli

or·ga·nol·o·gy (ôr'gə näl'ə jē) *n.* [ORGANO- + -LOGY] that branch of science dealing with the form, structure, development, and functions of plant or animal organs —**or'ga·no·log'ic** (-nə läj'ik), **or'ga·no·log'i·cal** *adj.* —**or'ga·nol'o·gist** *n.*

or·ga·no·me·tal·lic (ôr'gə nō mə tal'ik) *adj.* [ORGANO- + METALLIC] *Chem.* designating or of a compound containing carbon and a metal, specif. one in which the metal atom is firmly attached to one or more carbon atoms

or·ga·non (ôr'gə nän') *n., pl.* **-na** (-nə), **-nons'** [Gr.: see ORGAN] **1.** a method, means, or agency for communicating knowledge **2.** *Philos.* a system of principles used in investigation

or·ga·no·ther·a·py (ôr'gə nō ther'ə pē) *n.* [ORGANO- + THERAPY] the treatment of disease with extracts of animal organs, as of the glands of internal secretion

or·ga·no·trop·ic (-träp'ik) *adj.* [ORGANO- + -TROPIC] **1.** designating or of a substance or virus that travels predominantly to a specific organ **2.** having an affinity for tissues

or·ga·num (ôr'gə nəm) *n., pl.* **-nums, -na** (-nə) [L. < Gr. *organon*: see ORGAN] **1.** *same as* ORGANON **2.** *Music a)* an early type of harmony in which the voices are separated by an interval of a fourth or fifth *b)* such a voice part

☆**or·gan·za** (ôr gan'zə) *n.* [? akin to ff.] a thin, stiff fabric of rayon, silk, etc., used for hats, bridal gowns, as an underlining for sheer materials, etc.

or·gan·zine (ôr'gən zēn') *n.* [Fr. *organsin* < It. *organzino*, prob. < *Urgang*, name of a town in Russian Turkestan, famous as a silk market in medieval times] **1.** a strong raw silk thread made of twisted strands **2.** a fabric made of such threads

or·gasm (ôr'gaz'm) *n.* [Fr. *orgasme* < Gr. *orgasmos* < *organ*, to swell with moisture, lust < IE. base *werg-, to swell with sap or anger, whence Sans. *ūrjā*, violence, vigor, sap] a frenzy; great excitement; esp., the climax of sexual excitement, as in intercourse, usually accompanied in the male by ejaculation —**or·gas'mic** (-gaz'mik), **or·gas'tic** (-gas'tik) *adj.*

or·geat (ôr'zhat; *Fr.* ôr'zhȧ') *n.* [Fr. < Pr. *orjat* < *orge*, barley < L. *hordeum* < IE. base *ĝhrzd*, barley, whence G. *gerste*] a syrup or beverage, orig. made from barley, flavored with almonds and orange flowers

or·gi·as·tic (ôr'jē as'tik) *adj.* [Gr. *orgiastikos* < *orgiastēs*, one who celebrates orgies < *orgiazein*, to celebrate orgies: see ORGY] having to do with or resembling an orgy

☆**or·gone** (ôr'gōn) *n.* [coined by Wilhelm Reich (1897–1957), Austrian psychiatrist in the U.S., prob. < ORGASM + *-one*, as in OZONE] a postulated energy permeating the universe and allegedly restorable to a person suffering from various emotional or physical ills by his sitting in a small special cabinet (**orgone box**) in which this energy was supposed to accumulate

or·gy (ôr'jē) *n., pl.* **-gies** [earlier chiefly in pl. < Fr. *orgies* < L. *orgia*, pl. < Gr. *orgia*, pl., secret rites, akin to *ergon*, WORK] **1.** [*usually pl.*] in ancient Greece and Rome, feasting and wild celebration in worship of certain gods, esp. Dionysus **2.** any wild, riotous, licentious merrymaking; debauchery **3.** unrestrained indulgence in any activity

or·i·bi (ôr'ə bē) *n.* [Afrik. < Nama *arab*] an African pygmy antelope (*Ourebia ourebia*), having a long tuft of hair growing from each knee and slender, straight horns

o·ri·el (ôr'ē əl) *n.* [ME. < OFr. *oriol* < ? ML. *oriolum*, porch, gallery] a large window built out from a wall and resting on a bracket or a corbel; bay window

o·ri·ent (ôr'ē ənt; *also, and for v. usually,* -ent') *n.* [ME. < OFr. < L. *oriens*: see the *adj.*] **1.** [Poet.] the east **2.** *a)* the quality that determines a pearl's value; luster *b)* a pearl of high quality —[O-] the East, or Asia; esp., the Far East —*adj.* [L. *oriens*, direction of the rising sun, prp. of *oriri*, to arise < IE. base *er-*, to set in motion, elevate, whence Gr. *oros*, mountain, RISE, RUN] **1.** brilliant; shining; precious: orig. of pearls, now more general **2.** [Poet.] *a)* eastern; oriental *b)* rising, as the sun —*vt.* [Fr. *orienter* < the *adj.*] **1.** to arrange with reference to the east; esp., to build (a church) with the chief altar at the eastern end **2.** to set (a map or chart) in agreement with the points

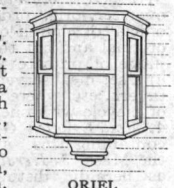
ORIEL

of the compass 3. to adjust with relation to facts or principles; correct 4. to adjust or adapt to a particular situation (often used reflexively)

o·ri·en·tal (ôr′ē en′t'l) *adj.* [ME. *orientale* < OFr. *oriental* < L. *orientalis*] 1. [Poet.] eastern 2. being corundum of gemstone quality, but resembling another gem [*oriental topaz*] 3. [O-] of the Orient, its people, or their culture; Eastern 4. [O-] designating or of the zoogeographical region that includes SE Asia south of the Himalayas, the Philippines, Sumatra, Java, Borneo, and other associated, continental islands —*n.* [*usually* O-] a native of the Orient or a member of a people native to that region

O·ri·en·tal·ism (-iz′m) *n.* [prec. + -ISM] 1. any trait, quality, mannerism, etc. usually associated with people of the East 2. study of Eastern culture —**O′ri·en′tal·ist** *n.*

O·ri·en·tal·ize (-īz′) *vt., vi.* **-ized′, -iz′ing** to make or become Oriental in character, culture, customs, etc.

Oriental poppy a perennial poppy (*Papaver orientale*) with bristly foliage, often cultivated for its large red, pink, or white flowers

Oriental roach a cockroach (*Blatta orientalis*) with a very dark, brown body

Oriental rug any of various kinds of carpets made in the Orient, hand-woven in one piece, usually with intricate, colorful designs: also **Oriental carpet**

o·ri·en·tate (ôr′ē ən tāt′, -en-) *vt.* **-tat′ed, -tat′ing** [ORIENT + -ATE¹, after Fr. *orienter*] *same as* ORIENT —*vi.* 1. to face east, or in any specified direction 2. to adjust to a situation

o·ri·en·ta·tion (ôr′ē ən tā′shən, -en-) *n.* 1. an orienting or being oriented 2. *a)* position with relation to the points of the compass *b)* the planning of church architecture so that the altar is in the east end 3. familiarization with and adaptation to a situation or environment; specif., *a)* *Psychol.* awareness of one's environment as to time, space, objects, and persons *b)* a period or process of introduction and adjustment 4. *Biol.* the position or change of position of an organism or part under a stimulus, such as gravity, light, etc. 5. *Chem. a)* the position and arrangement of atoms or radicals in a molecule *b)* the ordering of molecules, crystals, etc. so that the axes point in a particular direction 6. *Zool.* the homing faculty of certain animals

o·ri·fice (ôr′ə fis, är′-) *n.* [Fr. < LL. *orificium* < L. *os* (gen. *oris*), a mouth (see ORAL) + -*facere*, to make, DO¹] a mouth or aperture of a tube, cavity, etc.; opening —**or′i·fi′cial** (-fish′əl) *adj.*

or·i·flamme (ôr′ə flam′, är′-) *n.* [Fr. < OFr. *orieflambe* < L. *aurea flamma* < *aurum*, gold + *flamma*, a flame] 1. the ancient royal standard of France, a red silk banner split at one end to form flame-shaped streamers 2. any battle standard 3. any symbol of courage or devotion

orig. 1. origin 2. original 3. originally

o·ri·ga·mi (ôr′ə gä′mē) *n.* [Jap.] 1. a traditional Japanese art of folding paper to form flowers, animal figures, etc. 2. an object so made

Or·i·gen (ôr′i jən, är′-; -jen′) (L. name *Origenes Adamantius*) 185?–254? A.D.; Christian theologian & scholar, born in Alexandria

or·i·gin (ôr′ə jin, är′-) *n.* [ME. *origyne* < MFr. *origine* < L. *origo* (gen. *originis*) < *oriri*, to rise: see ORIENT] 1. a coming into existence or use; beginning 2. parentage; birth; lineage 3. that in which something has its beginning; source; root; cause 4. *Anat.* the less movable of the two points of attachment of a muscle, usually the end attached to the more rigid part of the skeleton 5. *Math. a)* in a system of Cartesian coordinates, the point at which the axes intersect; base point where the abscissa and ordinate equal zero *b)* any zero reference point from which measurement begins

SYN.—**origin** is applied to that from which a person or thing has its very beginning [the *origin* of a word]; **source** is applied to the point or place from which something arises, comes, or develops [the sun is our *source* of energy]; **beginning** is the basic general term for a starting point or place [the *beginning* of a quarrel]; **inception** is specifically applied to the beginning of an undertaking, organization, etc. [Smith headed the business from its *inception*]; **root** suggests an origin so deep and basic as to be the ultimate cause from which something stems [to go to the *root* of the matter]

o·rig·i·nal (ə rij′ə n'l) *adj.* [ME. < OFr. < L. *originalis*] 1. having to do with an origin; initial; first; earliest 2. never having occurred or existed before; not copied; fresh; new; novel 3. capable of or given to inventing or creating something new, or thinking or acting in an independent, individual, fresh way 4. coming from someone as the originator, maker, author, etc. 5. being that or those from which reproductions, copies, etc. have been made —*n.* [Fr. < the *adj.*] 1. a pristine form or primary type that has given rise to varieties 2. an original work, as of art or literature, in contradistinction to any reproduction, copy, etc. 3. the person or thing represented in a painting or the like 4. *a)* a person of original mind and unusual creativity *b)* [Archaic] an eccentric person 5. [Archaic] an originator —*SYN.* see NEW

o·rig·i·nal·i·ty (ə rij′ə nal′ə tē) *n.* [Fr. *originalité*] 1. the quality or condition of being original 2. the ability to be original, inventive, or creative

o·rig·i·nal·ly (ə rij′ə n'l ē) *adv.* 1. with reference to origin, or beginning 2. in the first place; initially 3. in an original, independent, or novel manner

original sin a tendency to sin and depravity which, in Christian theology, is held to be inherent in mankind as a direct result of Adam's sin of rebellion and which, in Roman Catholicism, is held to have resulted in the loss of sanctifying grace

o·rig·i·nate (ə rij′ə nāt′) *vt.* **-nat′ed, -nat′ing** [< ML. *originatus*, pp. of *originari*, to begin] to bring into being; esp., to create (something original); invent —*vi.* to come into being; begin; start —*SYN.* see RISE —**o·rig′i·na′tion** *n.* —**o·rig′i·na′tive** *adj.* —**o·rig′i·na′tor** *n.*

o·ri·na·sal (ôr′ə nā′z'l) *adj.* [< L. *os* (gen. *oris*), a mouth (see ORAL) + NASAL] *Phonet.* sounded with breath passing through the mouth and the nose at the same time —*n.* an orinasal sound, as some French vowels

O·ri·no·co (ôr′ə nō′kō) river in Venezuela, flowing from the Brazil border into the Atlantic: c. 1,700 mi.

o·ri·ole (ôr′ē ōl′) *n.* [OFr. *oriol* < ML. *aureolus* < L., golden, dim. of *aureus* < *aurum*, gold: for IE. base see EAST] 1. any of a family (Oriolidae) of chiefly yellow and black birds related to the crows, including the **golden oriole** (*Oriolus oriolus*), found from Europe to Australia ☆2. any of a genus (*Icterus*) of American birds, including the Baltimore oriole, that have bright-orange (or yellow) and black plumage and build hanging nests

O·ri·on (ō rī′ən, ô-) [ME. < L. < Gr. *Orion*] 1. *Gr. & Rom. Myth.* a hunter whom Diana loved but accidentally killed, placed in the heavens by her as a constellation 2. *Astron.* an equatorial constellation near Taurus, containing the bright stars Rigel and Betelgeuse

o·ri·son (ôr′i z'n, är′-; -s'n) *n.* [ME. *oreisun* < OFr. *oreison* < LL.(Ec.) *oratio*, a prayer < L., a speech: see ORATION] a prayer

O·ris·sa (ō ris′ə) state of E India, on the Bay of Bengal: 60,164 sq. mi.; pop. 17,549,000; cap. Dhubaneswar

O·ri·za·ba (ô′rē sä′bä) 1. volcanic mountain in SE Mexico, highest mountain in Mexico: 18,700 ft. 2. city at the foot of this mountain, in Veracruz state: pop. 56,000

Ork·ney Islands (ôrk′nē) group of islands north of Scotland, constituting a county (**Orkney**) of Scotland: 376 sq. mi.; pop. 18,000

Or·lan·do (ôr lan′dō; *also, for 2, It.* ôr län′dô) [It.] 1. a masculine name: see ROLAND 2. **Vit·to·rio E·ma·nue·le** (vēt tô′ryô e′mä nwe′le), 1860–1952; It. statesman; premier of Italy (1917–19)

Orlando [after *Orlando* Reeves, an Indian runner] city in C Fla.; pop. 99,000

orle (ôrl) *n.* [Fr. < OFr. *ourle, urle,* dim. < L. *ora,* margin, border: for base see ORAL] *Heraldry* the inner border on an escutcheon, following the outline of the edge of the shield

Or·lé·a·nais (ôr lā à ne′) region (former province) in NC France: chief city, Orléans

Or·le·an·ist (ôr′lē ə nist) *n.* a supporter of the house of Orléans' claim to the French throne through the Duke of Orléans, a younger brother of Louis XIV

Or·lé·ans¹ (ôr lā än′; *E.* ôr′lē ənz) 1. a branch of the house of Bourbon, one of whose members (LOUIS PHILIPPE) ruled France, 1830–48 2. **Louis Phi·lippe Jo·seph** (lwē′ fē lēp′ zhô zef′), duc d', 1747–93; Fr. revolutionist: guillotined: father of LOUIS PHILIPPE

Or·lé·ans² (ôr lā än′; *E.* ôr′lē ənz) city in NC France, on the Loire: under a siege (1429) by the English, which Joan of Arc was instrumental in lifting, thereby leading to French independence: pop. 84,000

☆**Or·lon** (ôr′län) [arbitrary coinage, after (NYL)ON] a trademark for a synthetic acrylic fiber somewhat like nylon, or a fabric made from this fiber —*n.* [o-] this fiber or fabric

or·lop (ôr′läp) *n.* [ME. *ouerlop* < Du. *overloop* < *over,* over + *loopen,* to run (see LEAP): so called because it covers the hold] the lowest deck of a ship, esp. of a warship

Or·mazd (ôr′mazd) [Per. *Ormazd* < OPer. *Auramazda* < Av. *Ahuro-Mazdao,* wise lord] *Zoroastrianism* the supreme deity and creator of the world, or the spirit of good: also sp. **Or′muzd:** cf. AHRIMAN

or·mer (ôr′mər) *n.* [Fr. dial. (Channel Islands) < Fr. *ormier* < L. *auris maris,* ear of the sea: from the shape] *Brit. dial. term for* ABALONE

or·mo·lu (ôr′mə lōō′) *n.* [Fr. *or moulu,* lit., ground gold < *or* (see OR³) + pp. of *moudre* < L. *molere,* to grind: see MILL¹] 1. an imitation gold made of an alloy of copper and tin, used in making ornaments, moldings, cheap jewelry, etc. 2. imitation gold leaf

Or·muz (ôr′muz′), **Gulf of** *same as* Gulf of HORMUZ

or·na·ment (ôr′nə ment; *for v.,* -ment′) *n.* [ME. < OFr. *ornement* < L. *ornamentum* < *ornare,* to adorn (akin to *ordinare:* see ORDAIN)] 1. anything serving to adorn; decoration; embellishment 2. a person whose character or talent adds luster to his surroundings, society, etc.

3. an adorning or being adorned; ornamentation **4.** mere external display **5.** [Archaic exc. Eccles.] an adjunct, accessory, or article of equipment **6.** *Music* a tone or tones used to embellish a principal melodic tone —*vt.* to furnish with ornaments or be an ornament to; decorate; beautify —*SYN.* see ADORN —**or'na·ment'er** *n.*

or·na·men·tal (ôr'nə men't'l) *adj.* serving as or pertaining to an ornament; decorative —*n.* something ornamental; specif., a plant or shrub grown for its decorative effect —**or'na·men'tal·ly** *adv.*

or·na·men·ta·tion (-men tā'shən) *n.* **1.** an ornamenting or being ornamented **2.** ornaments collectively; decoration

or·nate (ôr nāt') *adj.* [ME. < L. *ornatus*, pp. of *ornare*: see ORNAMENT] **1.** heavily ornamented or adorned, often to excess **2.** showy or unnatural, as some literary styles —**or·nate'ly** *adv.* —**or·nate'ness** *n.*

or·ner·y (ôr'nər ē) *adj.* [altered < ORDINARY] [Chiefly Dial.] **1.** having an ugly or mean disposition **2.** obstinate **3.** base; low **4.** ordinary —☆**or'ner·i·ness** *n.*

or·nis (ôr'nis) *n.* [G. < Gr. *ornis*, bird] *same as* AVIFAUNA

ornith. **1.** ornithological **2.** ornithology

or·nith·ic (ôr nith'ik) *adj.* [Gr. *ornithikos* < *ornis* (gen. *ornithos*), bird] of or characteristic of birds

or·ni·thine (ôr'nə thēn', -thin) *n.* [< Gr. *ornis* (gen. *ornithos*), bird + -INE⁴] a nonessential amino acid, $C_5H_{12}O_2N_2$, found in the animal body as a product of urea formation from proteins and in the excrement of birds

or·ni·tho- (ôr'nə thō, -thə) [< Gr. *ornis* (gen. *ornithos*), bird < IE. base *er-*, to set in motion, whence ORIGIN] *a combining form meaning* a bird or birds [*ornithology*]: also, before a vowel, **ornith-**

☆**or·ni·thoid** (ôr'nə thoid') *adj.* [< prec. + -OID] like a bird in appearance or structure

ornithol. **1.** ornithological **2.** ornithology

or·ni·thol·o·gy (ôr'nə thäl'ə jē) *n.* [ModL. *ornithologia*: see ORNITHO- & -LOGY] the branch of zoology dealing with birds —**or·ni·tho·log·i·cal** (ôr'ni thə läj'i k'l) *adj.* —**or'ni·tho·log'i·cal·ly** *adv.* —**or'ni·thol'o·gist** *n.*

or·ni·tho·pod (ôr'ni thə päd', ôr nith'ə-) *n.* [< ModL. *Ornithopoda*, name of the group: see ORNITHO- & -POD] any of a suborder (Ornithopoda) of plant-eating dinosaurs that walked upright on digitigrade hind feet

or·ni·thop·ter (ôr'nə thäp'tər) *n.* [< ORNITHO- + Gr. *pteron*, wing, FEATHER] an experimental type of aircraft designed to be propelled by the flapping of the wings

or·ni·tho·rhyn·chus (ôr'nə thō riŋ'kəs) *n.* [< ORNITHO- + Gr. *rhynchos*, bill, snout] *same as* PLATYPUS

or·ni·tho·sis (ôr'nə thō'sis) *n.* [ModL. < ORNITH(O)- + -OSIS] a virus disease, such as psittacosis, transmitted by birds

o·ro- (ôr'ō, -ə) [< Gr. *oros*, mountain: see ORIENT] *a combining form meaning* mountain [*orography*]

o·rog·e·ny (ô räj'ə nē) *n.* [ORO- + -GENY] the formation of mountains through structural disturbance of the earth's crust, esp. by folding and faulting: also **or·o·gen·e·sis** (ôr'ə jen'ə sis) —**or·o·gen·ic** (-jen'ik), **or·o·ge·net·ic** (-jə net'ik) *adj.*

o·rog·ra·phy (ô räg'rə fē) *n.* [ORO- + -GRAPHY] the branch of physical geography dealing with mountains —**or·o·graph·ic** (ôr'ə graf'ik), **or·o·graph'i·cal** *adj.*

☆**o·ro·ide** (ôr'ō id') *n.* [< Fr. *oréide*: see OR³ & -IDE] an alloy, mainly of copper, tin, and zinc, resembling gold, used in cheap jewelry

o·rol·o·gy (ô räl'ə jē) *n.* [ORO- + -LOGY] the study of mountains —**or·o·log·i·cal** (ôr'ə läj'i k'l) *adj.*

O·ron·tes (ō rän'tēz) river in SW Asia, flowing from Lebanon through Syria & Turkey into the Mediterranean: c. 240 mi.

o·ro·tund (ôr'ə tund') *adj.* [< L. *ore rotundo*, lit., with a round mouth: see ORAL & ROTUND] **1.** clear, strong, and deep; resonant: said of the voice **2.** bombastic or pompous: said of a style of speaking or writing —**o'ro·tun'di·ty** (-tun'də tē) *n.*

O·roz·co (ō rôs'kō), **Jo·sé Cle·men·te** (hō se' kle men'te) 1883-1949; Mex. painter

or·phan (ôr'fən) *n.* [LL.(Ec.) *orphanus* < Gr. *orphanos* < IE. base *orbho-*, orphan, whence L. *orbus*, bereft, G. *erbe*, inheritance, *arbeit*, work, Czech *robotnik*, serf] a child whose father and mother are dead: sometimes applied to a child who has lost only one parent by death —*adj.* **1.** being an orphan **2.** of or for orphans [an *orphan* home] —*vt.* to cause to become an orphan [*orphaned* by the war] —**or'phan·hood'** *n.*

or·phan·age (-ij) *n.* **1.** the condition of being an orphan **2.** an institution that is a home for orphans **3.** [Rare] orphans collectively

Or·phe·us (ôr'fē əs, -fyōos) [L. < Gr. *Orpheus*] *Gr. Myth.* a poet-musician with magic musical powers who descended to the underworld and tried to lead his wife, Eurydice, back from the dead but failed because he broke the injunction not to look back at her until they reached the upper world

Or·phic (-fik) *adj.* [L. *Orphicus* < Gr. *Orphikos*] **1.** of or characteristic of Orpheus or the mystic doctrines and rites in worship of Dionysus ascribed to him **2.** [also o-] *a)* like the music attributed to Orpheus; entrancing *b)* mystic; occult; oracular

Or·phism (-fiz'm) *n.* the rites and religion ascribed to Orpheus as founder

or·phrey (ôr'frē) *n.* [ME. *orferay*, taken as sing. of *orfreis*, orphrey < OFr. < ML. *aurifrigium* < L. *aurum*, gold + ML. *frisium*, FRIEZE¹] a richly embroidered decorative band on the front of some ecclesiastical robes

or·pi·ment (ôr'pi mənt) *n.* [ME. < OFr. < L. *auripigmentum*, pigment of gold: see AURIC & PIGMENT] arsenic trisulfide, As_2S_3, having a lemon-yellow color and a resinous luster: it is used as a pigment

or·pine (ôr'pin) *n.* [ME. *orpin* < MFr. < *orpiment* (see prec.): orig. used of a yellow-flowered plant] any of a number of related plants (esp. genus *Sedum*) of the orpine family, with fleshy leaves and stems, and white, yellow, or purple flowers —*adj.* designating a family (Crassulaceae) of succulent plants, including the sempervivums and sedums

Or·ping·ton (ôr'piŋ tən) *n.* [after *Orpington*, village in Kent, England] any of a breed of heavy, full-bodied chickens having black, white, buff, or blue plumage, single combs, and featherless legs

or·rer·y (ôr'ər ē) *n., pl.* **-rer·ies** [after Charles Boyle, Earl of *Orrery* (1676-1731) for whom one was made] a mechanical apparatus which illustrates with balls of various sizes the relative motions and positions of the bodies in the solar system

or·ris (ôr'is, är'-) *n.* [prob. altered < MIt. *ireos* < L. *iris*, IRIS] any of several European irises, esp. a white-flowered species (*Iris florentina*) whose rootstocks yield orrisroot

or·ris·root (-rōōt') *n.* the rootstock of the orris: used, when pulverized, in perfumery, tooth powders, etc.

Orsk (ôrsk) city in SE European R.S.F.S.R., on the Ural River: pop. 212,000

Or·son (ôr's'n) [< Fr. *ourson*, dim. of *ours*, a bear (< L. *ursus*)] a masculine name

ort (ôrt) *n.* [LME. *ortus*, pl., prob. < LowG.] [Dial. or Archaic] a scrap or fragment of food left from a meal: *usually used in pl.*

Or·te·gal (ôr'te gäl'), **Cape** cape in NW Spain, extending into the Bay of Biscay

Or·te·ga y Gas·set (ôr te'gä ē gä set'), **Jo·sé** (hō se') 1883-1955; Sp. essayist & philosopher

☆**or·thi·con** (ôr'thi kän') *n.* [ORTH(O)- + ICON(OSCOPE)] a television camera tube, an improved form of the iconoscope, in which the charges on a photosensitive plate are scanned by a low-velocity electron beam which is reflected and which delivers the signal current to an output electrode: also **or'thi·con'o·scope'** (-ə skōp')

or·tho- (ôr'thō, -thə) [< Gr. *orthos*, straight < IE. base *werdh-*, to grow, climb, high, whence Sans. *várdhati*, (he) grows] *a combining form meaning:* **1.** straight, regular, upright [*orthognathous*] **2.** right angle [*orthorhombic*] **3.** proper, correct, standard [*orthography*] **4.** *Chem. a)* that acid (of a group containing the same nonmetallic element) which has the largest number of OH groups per atom of the nonmetal [*orthophosphoric* acid] *b)* characterized by substitutions in the 1, 2 position in the benzene ring **5.** *Med.* correction of deformities [*orthopedics*] Also, before a vowel, **orth-**

or·tho·ce·phal·ic (ôr'thō sə fal'ik) *adj.* [prec. + -CEPHAL-IC] having a skull whose height is 70.1 to 75 percent of its length: also **or'tho·ceph'a·lous** (-sef'ə ləs) —**or'tho·ceph'a·ly** *n.*

or·tho·chro·mat·ic (-krō mat'ik) *adj.* [ORTHO- + CHRO-MATIC] designating or of photographic film that registers the correct visual brightness of a subject, apart from color: such film is sensitive to all colors except red

or·tho·clase (ôr'thə klās', -klāz') *n.* [G. *orthoklas* < Gr. *orthos* (see ORTHO-) + *klasis*, fracture (see CLASTIC), because of 90° cleavage] potassium feldspar, $KAlSi_3O_8$, a monoclinic mineral that is a common constituent of many granitic rocks

or·tho·don·tics (ôr'thə dän'tiks) *n.pl.* [*with sing. v.*] [ModL.: see ORTH-, -ODONT, & -ICS] the branch of dentistry concerned with correcting and preventing irregularities of the teeth and poor occlusion: also **or'tho·don'ti·a** (-dän'shə, -shē ə) —**or'tho·don'tic** *adj.* —**or'tho·don'tist** *n.*

or·tho·dox (ôr'thə däks') *adj.* [< Fr. or LL.: Fr. *orthodoxe* < LL. *orthodoxus* < LGr.(Ec.) *orthodoxos*, orthodox (in religion) < Gr. *orthos* (see ORTHO-) + *doxa*, opinion < *dokein*, to think: see DOCTOR] **1.** conforming to the usual beliefs or established doctrines, as in religion, politics, etc.; approved or conventional [*orthodox* ideas]; specif., *a)* conforming to the Christian faith as formulated in the early ecumenical creeds and confessions **[O-]** strictly observing the rites and traditions of Judaism, such as kashrut, the Sabbath, etc., as formulated in the Torah and Talmud **2. [O-]** designating or of any of the churches comprised in the Orthodox Eastern Church

Orthodox Eastern Church the Christian church dominant in E Europe, W Asia, and N Africa, orig. made up of four patriarchates (Constantinople, Alexandria, Antioch, Jerusalem) rejecting the authority of the Roman See in 1054 and now also including certain autonomous churches of the Soviet Union, Greece, Romania, Bulgaria, etc.

or·tho·dox·y (ôr'thə däk'sē) *n., pl.* **-dox'ies** [Gr. *orthodoxia*] **1.** the quality or fact of being orthodox **2.** an orthodox belief, doctrine, custom, etc.

or·tho·e·py (ôr thō'ə pē, ôr'thō-) *n.* [ModL. *orthoepia* < Gr. *orthoepeia* < *orthos*, right + *epos*, a word (see ORTHO-

& EPIC)] **1.** the study of pronunciation; phonology **2.** the standard pronunciations of cultivated speakers of a language —**or·tho·ep·ic** (ôr′thō ep′ik), **or′tho·ep′i·cal** *adj.* —**or·tho′e·pist** *n.*

or·tho·gen·e·sis (ôr′thə jen′ə sis) *n.* [ModL.: see ORTHO- & -GENESIS] **1.** *Biol.* progressive evolution of certain organisms in a restricted direction throughout successive generations, so that variation is consistently limited to definite trends independent of outside influences **2.** *Sociology* the theory that every culture follows the same fixed course of evolution, uninfluenced by differing environmental factors —**or′tho·ge·net′ic** (-jə net′ik) *adj.*

or·thog·na·thous (ôr thäg′nə thəs) *adj.* [ORTHO- + -GNATHOUS] having the jaws straight or in line, with the lower jaw neither projecting nor receding —**or·thog′na·thism** *n.*

or·thog·o·nal (ôr thäg′ə n'l) *adj.* [Fr. < orthogone, right-angled < L. orthogonius < Gr. orthogōnios: see ORTHO- & -GON] having to do with right angles; rectangular —**or·thog′o·nal·ly** *adv.*

or·tho·grade (ôr′thə grād′) *adj.* [ORTHO- + -GRADE] *Zool.* walking with the body upright

or·thog·ra·pher (ôr thäg′rə fər) *n.* a person skilled in orthography; expert speller

or·tho·graph·ic (ôr′thə graf′ik) *adj.* **1.** of or characterized by orthography **2.** *Geom.* of right angles and perpendicular lines; orthogonal Also **or′tho·graph′i·cal** —**or′tho·graph′i·cal·ly** *adv.*

orthographic projection *Archit., Geom.* a projection in which the projecting lines are perpendicular to the plane of projection

or·thog·ra·phy (ôr thäg′rə fē) *n., pl.* **-phies** [ME. *or-tografye* < MFr. *ortographie* < L. *orthographia* < Gr. *orthographia*: see ORTHO- & -GRAPHY] **1.** spelling in accord with accepted usage **2.** any style or method of spelling **3.** spelling as a subject for study **4.** *same as* ORTHOGRAPHIC PROJECTION

or·tho·pe·dics, or·tho·pae·dics (ôr′thə pē′diks) *n.pl.* [*with sing. v.*] [< Fr. *orthopédique*, orthopedic < *orthopédie* < Gr. *orthos*, straight (see ORTHO-) + *paideia*, training of children < *pais* (gen. *paidos*), child: see PEDO-¹] the branch of surgery dealing with the treatment of deformities, diseases, and injuries of the bones, joints, muscles, etc. —**or′tho·pe′dic, or′tho·pae′dic** *adj.* —**or′tho·pe′dist, or′tho·pae′dist** *n.*

or·tho·phos·phate (ôr′thə fäs′fāt) *n.* [ORTHO- + PHOS-PHATE] a salt or ester of orthophosphoric acid

or·tho·phos·phor·ic acid (-fäs fôr′ik, -fär′-) [ORTHO- + PHOSPHORIC] a clear, colorless, syrupy liquid or a colorless crystalline solid, H_3PO_4, produced from phosphorus or phosphate rock and used in the manufacture of fertilizers, textiles, etc.

or·tho·psy·chi·a·try (-sī kī′ə trē) *n.* [ORTHO- + PSY-CHIATRY] the study and treatment of disorders of behavior and personality, with emphasis on prevention through a clinical approach —**or′tho·psy′chi·at′ric** (-sī′kē at′rik) *adj.* —**or′tho·psy·chi′a·trist** *n.*

or·thop·ter (ôr thäp′tər) *n. same as* ORNITHOPTER

or·thop·ter·an (ôr thäp′tər ən) *n.* [< ORTHO- + Gr. *pteron*, feather, wing] any of a large order (Orthoptera) of mostly plant-eating insects, including cockroaches, crickets, grasshoppers, locusts, etc., having chewing mouthparts and narrow, hard forewings that cover longitudinally folded membranous hind wings in most species and undergoing gradual metamorphosis —**or·thop′ter·ous** *adj.*

or·thop·tic (ôr thäp′tik) *adj.* [ORTH- + OPTIC] correcting any deviations of the visual axis of the eye, esp. by exercises to strengthen the eye muscles

or·tho·rhom·bic (ôr′thə räm′bik) *adj.* [ORTHO- + RHOM-BIC] designating or of a system of crystallization characterized by three axes unequal in length and at right angles to one another

or·tho·scope (ôr′thə skōp′) *n.* [ORTHO- + -SCOPE] an instrument containing a layer of water which is held in contact with the eye, allowing an examination of the interior of the eye without the distortion due to corneal refraction

or·tho·scop·ic (ôr′thə skäp′ik) *adj.* [< ORTHO- + Gr. *skopein*, to view + -IC] giving a true flat image without distortion

or·tho·stat·ic (-stat′ik) *adj.* [ORTHO- + STATIC] of or caused by an upright position [*orthostatic* hypotension]

or·tho·ti·chy (ôr thäs′ti kē) *n., pl.* **-chies** [< ORTHO- + Gr. *stichos*, a row (see STILE¹) + -Y²] a vertical arrangement of leaves or flowers on a stem —**or·thos′ti·chous** *adj.*

or·thot·ics (ôr thät′iks) *n.pl.* [*with sing. v.*] [ORTH(O)- + -OT(IC) + -ICS] the science of developing and fitting surgical devices designed to activate or supplement a weakened or atrophied limb or function —**or·thot′ic** *adj.* —**or·tho·tist** (ôr′thə tist) *n.*

or·tho·trop·ic (ôr′thə träp′ik) *adj.* [ORTHO- + -TROPIC] **1.** designating or of a design for bridges in which the structural supporting units also form the deck, or road surface, thus reducing weight and cost of construction

2. *Bot.* designating, of, or showing vertical growth, as most main stems and roots

or·thot·ro·pism (ôr thät′rə piz′m) *n.* [ORTHO- + -TROPISM] growth, or a tendency to grow, in a vertical direction or position

or·thot·ro·pous (-pəs) *adj.* [ORTHO- + -TROPOUS] *Bot.* growing straight: said of an ovule with its hilum and micropyle in a straight line

Ort·les (ôrt′läs) range of the E Alps, in N Italy: highest peak (**Ortles**), 12,792 ft.: Ger. name **Ort·ler** (ôrt′lər)

or·to·lan (ôr′t'l ən) *n.* [Fr. < Pr. < It. *ortolana*, gardener, ortolan < L. *hortulanus*, dim. of *hortus*, a garden (see YARD²): from its frequenting gardens] **1.** an old-world bunting (*Emberiza hortulana*), prized as a choice food ☆**2.** *same as* BOBOLINK ☆**3.** *same as* SORA

O·ru·ro (ō rōō′rō) city in W Bolivia: pop. 90,000

Or·ville (ôr′vil) [Fr.; orig. place name] a masculine name

Or·well (ôr′wel, -wəl), **George** (pseud. of *Eric Arthur Blair*) 1903–50; Eng. writer —**Or·well′i·an** *adj.*

-o·ry (ôr′ē, ər ē) **1.** [ME. -orie < OFr. -oire < L. -orius, -oria, -orium] an *adj.*-forming suffix meaning of, having the nature of [*hortatory, contradictory*] **2.** [ME. -orie < OFr. -oire, -orie < L. -orium] a *n.*-forming suffix meaning a place or thing for [*laboratory*]

o·ryx (ôr′iks, är′-) *n., pl.* **o′ryx·es, o′ryx:** see PLURAL, II, D, 1 [ModL., name of the genus < L., wild goat, gazelle < Gr. *oryx*, lit., pickax (< *oryssein*, to dig: for base see RIP¹): from its pointed horns] any of a genus (*Oryx*) of large African and Asian antelopes, including the gemsbok, with long, straight horns

‡**os¹** (äs) *n., pl.* **os′sa** (-ə) [L.: see OSSIFY] a bone

‡**os²** (äs) *n., pl.* **o·ra** (ō′rə) [L.: see ORAL] a mouth; opening

os³ (ōs) *n., pl.* **o·sar** (ō′sär) [Sw. *ås*, ridge, pl. *åsar* < ON. *āss* < I.E. base **omso-*, shoulder, whence Gr. *ōmos*, L. *umerus*, shoulder] *same as* ESKER

Os *Chem.* osmium

OS, O.S. **1.** [L. *oculus sinister*] left eye **2.** old series **3.** Old Style **4.** ordinary seaman

OS., OS, O.S. Old Saxon

O/S, o/s Old Style

O.S., OS, O/S, o.s. out of stock

O·sage (ō sāj′, ō′sāj) *n.* [< Osage *Wazhazhe*] **1.** *pl.* **O·sag′es, O·sage′** any member of a tribe of Indians who migrated from the Ohio River Valley to the Osage River in Missouri and now live in Oklahoma **2.** their Siouan language

☆**Osage orange 1.** a small thorny tree (*Maclura pomifera*) of the mulberry family, with hard, yellow wood, native to the C U.S. and often used for hedges, railroad ties, and fence posts **2.** its greenish-yellow, orange-shaped, inedible fruit

Osage River river in C Mo. & E Kans., flowing east into the Missouri: c. 500 mi.

O·sa·ka (ō′sä kä′; *E.* ō sä′kə) seaport in S Honshu, Japan: pop. 3,156,000

O.S.B. Order of St. Benedict

Os·born (äz′bərn), **Henry Fairfield** 1857–1935; U.S. paleontologist & biologist

Os·borne (äz′bərn, -bôrn) **1. John (James)**, 1929– ; Eng. playwright **2. Thomas Mott** (mät), 1859–1926; U.S. prison reformer

Os·can (äs′kən) *n.* [< L. *Oscus*, Oscan + -AN] **1.** a member of an ancient people who lived in Campania, Italy **2.** their Italic language —*adj.* of the Oscans or their language

Os·car (äs′kər) [OE. *Osgar* < *os*, a god + *gar*, a spear] **1.** a masculine name **2.** Oscar II 1829–1907; king of Norway & Sweden (1872–1905), then of Sweden alone —*n.* ☆[Slang] [said to be so named from comment ("He reminds me of my Uncle Oscar") made by an Academy official on first seeing the statuette] any of the statuettes awarded annually in the U.S. for achievements in motion pictures: see ACADEMY AWARD

Os·ce·o·la (äs′ē ō′lə) 1804?–38; leader of the Seminole Indians

os·cil·late (äs′ə lāt′) *vi.* **-lat′ed, -lat′ing** [< L. *oscillatus*, pp. of *oscillare*, to swing < *oscillum*, a swing] **1.** to swing or move regularly back and forth **2.** to be indecisive in purpose or opinion; vacillate **3.** *Physics* to vary regularly between maximum and minimum values, as an electric current —*vt.* to cause to oscillate —*SYN.* see SWING —**os′cil·la·to′ry** (-lə tôr′ē) *adj.*

os·cil·la·tion (äs′ə lā′shən) *n.* [L. *oscillatio*] **1.** the act of oscillating **2.** fluctuation; instability; variation **3.** *Physics a)* regular variation between maximum and minimum values, as of current or voltage *b)* a single swing of an oscillating object between the two extremes of its arc

os·cil·la·tor (äs′ə lāt′ər) *n.* **1.** a person or thing that oscillates **2.** *Physics* an apparatus, as an electron tube, for

ORYX
(3–7 ft. high at shoulder; horns 2–4 ft. long)

establishing and maintaining oscillations of a frequency determined by its physical constants

os·cil·lo·gram (ä sil′ə gram′, ə-) *n.* [see -GRAM] a record obtained from an oscillograph

os·cil·lo·graph (-graf′, -gräf′) *n.* [< L. *oscillare*, to swing + -GRAPH] an instrument for displaying or recording in the form of a curve the instantaneous values of rapidly varying electrical quantities —**os·cil′lo·graph′ic** *adj.*

os·cil·lo·scope (-skōp′) *n.* [< L. *oscillare*, to swing + -SCOPE] a type of oscillograph that visually displays an electrical wave on a fluorescent screen, as of a cathode-ray tube —**os·cil′lo·scop′ic** (-skäp′ik) *adj.*

os·cine (äs′in, -in) *adj.* [< ModL. *Oscines*, name of the group < L., pl. of *oscen*, bird whose notes were used in divining < *obs*-, var. of *ob*- (see OB-) + *canere*, to crow, sing (see CHANT, *v.*)] designating or of a suborder (Oscines) of perching birds, as the finches, shrikes, larks, buntings, etc., with highly developed vocal organs: some do not sing —*n.* a bird of this group

os·ci·tan·cy (äs′i tən sē) *n.* [< L. *oscitans*, prp. of *oscitare*, to yawn < *os*, a mouth + *citare*, to move] drowsiness, dullness, apathy, etc.

Os·co-Um·bri·an (äs′kō um′brē ən) *n.* a branch of the Italic subfamily of languages consisting of Oscan and Umbrian

os·cu·lant (äs′kyə lənt) *adj.* [L. *osculans*, prp. of *osculari*: see OSCULATE] 1. *Biol.* intermediate; linking; shared: said of a characteristic common to two or more groups, genera, etc. 2. *Zool.* gripping or adhering together

os·cu·lar (-lər) *adj.* [L. *osculum* (see ff.) + -AR] 1. of the mouth or kissing 2. *Zool.* of an osculum

os·cu·late (-lāt′) *vt., vi.* -lat′ed, -lat′ing [< L. *osculatus*, pp. of *osculari*, to kiss < *osculum*, little mouth, kiss, dim. of *os*, mouth: see ORAL] 1. to kiss: a pretentious or facetious usage 2. to touch closely 3. *Biol.* to have (characteristics) in common —**os′cu·la′tion** *n.* —**os′cu·la·to′ry** (-lə tôr′ē) *adj.*

os·cu·lum (äs′kyə ləm) *n., pl.* -la (-lə) [L., dim. of *os*, a mouth: see ORAL] any of the openings of a sponge through which water passes out

-ose[1] (ōs) [Fr. < (*gluc*)*ose*: see GLUCOSE] a suffix designating: 1. a carbohydrate [*cellulose, sucrose*] 2. the product of a protein hydrolysis [*protease*]

-ose[2] (ōs) [L. *-osus*] a suffix meaning full of, having the qualities of, like [*bellicose, verbose*]

O·see (ō′sē, -zē) Douay Bible name for HOSEA

OSerb. Old Serbian

Osh·a·wa (äsh′ə wə, -wô) city in SE Ontario, Canada, on Lake Ontario: pop. 78,000

Osh·kosh (äsh′käsh) [after *Oshkosh* (1795-1850), Menomini chief] city in E Wis., on Lake Winnebago: pop. 53,000

o·sier (ō′zhər) *n.* [ME. *osiere* < OFr. < ML. *ausaria*, bed of willows] 1. any of a number of related willows (esp. *Salix viminalis* and *Salix purpurea*) whose lithe branches or stems are used for baskets and furniture 2. a willow branch used for wickerwork ☆3. any of several N. American dogwoods

O·si·ris (ō si′ris) [L. < Gr. *Osiris* < Egypt. *Us-âr*] the ancient Egyptian god of the lower world and judge of the dead, brother and husband of Isis

-o·sis (ō′sis) [L. < Gr. *-ōsis* < *-ō-*, *-o-*, ending of preceding verbal or substantive stem + *-sis*] a suffix meaning: 1. state, condition, action [*osmosis*] 2. an abnormal or diseased condition [*neurosis*]

-os·i·ty (äs′ət ē) [< Fr. or L.: Fr. *-osité* < L. *-ositas*: cf. -OSE[2], -ITY] a n.-forming suffix corresponding to -OSE[2] or -OUS

OSlav. Old Slavic

Os·ler (ōs′lər), Sir **William** 1849-1919; Canad. physician & medical writer

Os·lo (äs′lō, äz′-; *Norw.* oos′loo) capital of Norway; seaport on an inlet (**Oslo Fjord**) of the Skagerrak: pop. 483,000

Os·man (äz′mən, äs′-; *Turk.* äs män′) 1259-1326; Turkish leader & founder of the Ottoman Empire

Os·man·li (äz man′lē, äs-) *n.* [Turk. < *Osman* < Ar. ′*Uthmân*, Osman] 1. *pl.* -**lis** an Ottoman Turk 2. *same as* TURKISH (sense 1) —*adj. same as* TURKISH

os·mic (äz′mik) *adj.* designating or of chemical compounds in which osmium has a higher valence than in the corresponding osmous compounds

os·mics (äz′miks) *n.pl.* [*with sing. v.*] [< Gr. *osmē*, Attic var. of *odmē*, odor (akin to L. *odor*, ODOR) + -ICS] the science dealing with smells and the sense of smell

os·mir·i·di·um (äz′mə rid′ē əm) *n.* [OSM(IUM) + IRIDIUM] *same as* IRIDOSMINE

os·mi·um (äz′mē əm) *n.* [ModL.: so named (1804) by its discoverer, S. Tennant, Eng. chemist < Gr. *osmē*, ODOR, from the odor of one of its oxides] a very hard, bluish-white, amorphous, metallic chemical element of the platinum group: it occurs in the form of an alloy with platinum and iridium and is used in pen points, electric light filaments, etc., and as a catalyst: symbol, Os; at. wt., 190.2; at. no., 76; sp. gr., 22.48; melt. pt., 2700°C; boil. pt., >530°C

os·mom·e·ter (äs mäm′ə tər, äz-) *n.* [< Gr. *ōsmos* (see OSMOSIS) + METER[2]] an instrument for measuring osmotic pressure

os·mose (äs′mōs, äz′-) *vt., vi.* -mosed, -mos·ing [back-formation < ff.] to subject to, or undergo, osmosis

os·mo·sis (äs mō′sis, äz-) *n.* [ModL., ult. < Gr. *ōsmos*,

impulse < *ōthein*, to push] 1. the tendency of a solvent to pass through a semipermeable membrane, as the wall of a living cell, into a solution of higher concentration, so as to equalize concentrations on both sides of the membrane 2. the diffusion of fluids through a membrane or porous partition —**os·mot′ic** (-mät′ik) *adj.* —**os·mot′i·cal·ly** *adv.*

osmotic pressure the force exerted by a solvent passing through a semipermeable membrane in osmosis, equal to the pressure that must be applied to the solution in order to prevent passage of the solvent into it

os·mous (äz′məs) *adj.* designating or of chemical compounds in which osmium has a lower valence than in the corresponding osmic compounds

os·mun·da (äz mun′də) *n.* [ModL. < ML., a flowering fern < OFr. *osmonde* < ?] any of a genus (*Osmunda*) of ferns having specialized nonleafy fronds or portions of fronds bearing dense masses of spore cases

os·mun·dine (äz′mən dēn′) *n.* [< ModL. *Osmunda* (see prec.) + -INE[4]] a fibrous mass of dried fern roots, used as a rooting medium for orchids or other air plants

Os·na·brück (ôs′nä brük′; *E.* äz′nə brook′) city in NW West Germany, in Lower Saxony state: pop. 143,000

os·na·burg (äz′nə burg′) *n.* [altered < prec. (where orig. made)] a type of coarse, heavy cloth, orig. of linen and now of cotton, used in making sacks, work clothes, etc.

O·sor·no (ô sôr′nô) city in SC Chile: pop. 94,000

OSp. Old Spanish

os·prey (äs′prē) *n., pl.* -preys [LME. *ospray*, ult. < L. *ossifraga*, osprey, lit., the bone-breaker < *os*, a bone (see OSSIFY) + *frangere*, to BREAK[1]] a large diving bird of prey (*Pandion haliaetus*) of the hawk family, that feeds solely on fish: its plumage is blackish on top and whitish underneath

OSS, O.S.S. Office of Strategic Services

Os·sa (äs′ə) mountain in Thessaly, NE Greece: 6,490 ft.: see PELION

‡**os·sa** (äs′ə) *n., pl. of* OS[2]

os·se·in (äs′ē in) *n.* [< L. *osseus*, bony < *os*, a bone (see OSSIFY) + -IN[1]] *Biochem.* the organic basis of bone, the part left after the mineral matter is dissolved in dilute acids

OSPREY (20-24 in. long)

os·se·ous (-əs) *adj.* [L. *osseus* < *os*, a bone (see OSSIFY)] composed of, containing, or like bone; bony

Os·set (äs′it) *n.* any of a people of Ossetia: also **Os′sete** (-ēt) —**Os·se′tian** (ä sē′shən) *adj., n.*

Os·se·tia (ä sē′shə; *Russ.* ô se′tyä) region in the N Caucasus, U.S.S.R.: 4,593 sq. mi.; pop. 622,000

Os·set·ic (ä set′ik) *adj.* of the Ossets; Ossetian —*n.* the Iranian language of the Ossets

Os·sian (äsh′ən, äs′ē ən) [Gael. *Oisīn*, dim. of *os*, a fawn] *Gaelic Folklore* a bard and hero of the 3d cent.: James Macpherson wrote and published poems (1761-65) which he falsely claimed were his translations of Ossian's poetry from old Gaelic manuscripts —**Os·si·an·ic** (äs′ē an′ik, äsh′-) *adj.*

os·si·cle (äs′i k′l) *n.* [< L. *ossiculum*, dim. of *os*, a bone: see OSSIFY] a small bone or bonelike structure; esp., any of the three small bones in the tympanic cavity of the ear —**os·sic·u·lar** (ä sik′yə lər), **os·sic′u·late** (-lit) *adj.*

Os·si·etz·ky (ôs′ē et′skē), **Carl von** (kärl fôn) 1889-1938; Ger. journalist & pacifist

os·sif·er·ous (ä sif′ər əs) *adj.* [< L. *os*, a bone (see OSSIFY) + -FEROUS] containing bones, as a geological deposit

os·si·frage (äs′ə frij) *n.* [L. *ossifraga*, OSPREY] *same as:* 1. LAMMERGEIER 2. OSPREY

os·si·fy (äs′ə fī′) *vt., vi.* -fied′, -fy′ing [< L. *os* (gen. *ossis*), a bone (< IE. base *ost-, whence Sans. *ásthi*, Gr. *osteon*, bone) + -FY] 1. to change or develop into bone 2. to settle or fix rigidly in a practice, custom, attitude, etc. —**os′si·fi·ca′tion** *n.*

Os·si·ning (äs′ə nin) [< Delaware *ossingsing*, lit., at the standing stone] village in SE N.Y., on the Hudson: site of Sing Sing, State prison: pop. 22,000

‡**os·so bu·co** (ôs′sô boo′kô) [It.] an Italian dish of braised veal shanks

os·su·ar·y (äsh′oo wer′ē, äs′yoo-) *n., pl.* -ar·ies [LL. *ossuarium* < *ossuarius*, of or for bones < L. *os*: see OSSIFY] a container, as an urn, vault, etc., for the bones of the dead

os·te·al (äs′tē əl) *adj.* [< Gr. *osteon*, a bone (see OSSIFY) + -AL] osseous; bony

os·te·i·tis (äs′tē īt′əs) *n.* [< Gr. *osteon* (see OSSIFY) + -ITIS] inflammation of the bone or bony tissue

Ost·end (äs tend′, äs′tend) seaport & summer resort in NW Belgium, on the North Sea: pop. 57,000: Fr. name **Ost·ende** (ô stäṅd′)

os·ten·si·ble (äs ten′sə b′l, əs-) *adj.* [Fr. < ML. *ostensibilis* < L. *ostendere*, to show < *ob*(*s*)-, against (see OB-) + *tendere*, to stretch: see TEND[2]] 1. apparent; seeming; professed 2. [Rare] clearly evident; conspicuous —**os·ten′si·bly** *adv.*

os·ten·sive (äs ten′siv) *adj.* [Fr. *ostensif* < ML. *ostensivus*] 1. directly pointing out; clearly demonstrative 2. *same as* OSTENSIBLE (sense 1) —**os·ten′sive·ly** *adv.*

os·ten·ta·tion (äs′tən tā′shən) *n.* [ME. *ostentacioun* < L. *ostentatio* < *ostentare* < *ostendere*: see OSTENSIBLE] showy display, as of wealth, knowledge, etc.; pretentiousness —**os′ten·ta′tious** *adj.* —**os′ten·ta′tious·ly** *adv.* —**os′ten·ta′tious·ness** *n.*

os·te·o- (äs′tē ō′, -ə) [ModL. < Gr. *osteon*, a bone: see OSSIFY] *a combining form meaning* a bone or bones [*osteopath*]: also, before a vowel, **oste-**

os·te·o·ar·thri·tis (äs′tē ō′är thrīt′əs) *n.* [prec. + ARTHRITIS] a slowly progressive, degenerative joint disease, found chiefly in elderly persons, causing pain, swelling, stiffness, etc.

os·te·o·blast (äs′tē ə blast′) *n.* [OSTEO- + -BLAST] any cell which develops into bone or secretes substances producing bony tissue —**os′te·o·blas′tic** *adj.*

os·te·oc·la·sis (äs′tē äk′lə sis) *n.* [ModL. < OSTEO- + Gr. *klasis*, a breaking < *klan*, to break] 1. the breaking down and absorption of bony tissue 2. the breaking of a bone to correct a deformity, esp. after a badly healed previous fracture

os·te·o·clast (äs′tē ə klast′) *n.* [< OSTEO- + Gr. *klastos*, broken < *klan*, to break] 1. any of the large multinuclear cells in bone which absorb or break down bony tissue 2. an instrument used to perform osteoclasis

os·te·oid (äs′tē oid′) *adj.* [OSTE- + -OID] like bone

os·te·ol·o·gy (äs′tē äl′ə jē) *n.* [ModL.: see OSTEO- & -LOGY] the study of the structure and function of bones —**os′te·o·log′i·cal** (-ə läj′i k'l) *adj.* —**os′te·ol′o·gist** *n.*

os·te·o·ma (äs′tē ō′mə) *n., pl.* **-mas, -ma·ta** (-mə tə) [ModL.: see OSTEO- & -OMA] a tumor composed of bony tissue

os·te·o·ma·la·ci·a (äs′tē ō mə lā′shə, -shē ə) *n.* [ModL.< OSTEO- + *malacia*, a softening of tissue < Gr. *malakia*, softness < *malakos*, soft] a bone disease characterized by a softening of the bones, resulting from a deficiency in calcium salts, found chiefly in adult women

os·te·o·my·e·li·tis (-mī′ə līt′is) *n.* [ModL.: see OSTEO- & MYELITIS] infection of bone marrow or bone structures, usually caused by a bacterium (genus *Staphylococcus*) that produces pus

☆**os·te·o·path** (äs′tē ə path′) *n.* a doctor who practices osteopathy

☆**os·te·op·a·thy** (äs′tē äp′ə thē) *n.* [ModL.: see OSTEO- & -PATHY] a school of medicine and surgery employing various methods of diagnosis and treatment, but placing special emphasis on the interrelationship of the musculoskeletal system to all other body systems —**os′te·o·path′ic** (-ə path′ik) *adj.* —**os′te·o·path′i·cal·ly** *adv.*

os·te·o·phyte (äs′tē ə fīt′) *n.* [OSTEO- + -PHYTE] a small bony outgrowth —**os′te·o·phyt′ic** (-fit′ik) *adj.*

os·te·o·plas·tic (äs′tē ō plas′tik) *adj.* [OSTEO- + -PLASTIC] 1. *Anat.* of or pertaining to bone formation 2. *Surgery* of or based on the replacement of bone by restorative operations —**os′te·o·plas′ty** *n.*

os·te·o·po·ro·sis (-pō rō′sis) *n.* [ModL. < OSTEO- + *porosis*, a porous condition < L. *porus*, a PORE² + -OSIS] a bone disease characterized by a reduction in bone density accompanied by increasing porosity and brittleness, associated with loss of calcium from the bones

os·te·o·sis (äs′tē ō′sis) *n.* [ModL.: see OSTEO- & -OSIS] the formation of bone

os·te·o·tome (äs′tē ə tōm′) *n.* [OSTEO- + -TOME] a surgical instrument for cutting or dividing bone

os·te·ot·o·my (äs′tē ät′ə mē) *n., pl.* **-mies** [OSTEO- + -TOMY] a surgical operation of dividing a bone or cutting out a piece of bone

Ös·ter·reich (ös′tər rīH′) *Ger. name of* AUSTRIA

Os·ti·a (äs′tē ə) ancient city in Latium, at the mouth of the Tiber, that was the port of Rome

Os·ti·ak (äs′tē ak′) *n. same as* OSTYAK

os·ti·ar·y (äs′tē er′ē) *n., pl.* **-ar′ies** [L. *ostiarius* < *ostium*, door, entrance, os, mouth: see ORAL] *same as* PORTER¹

os·ti·na·to (äs′tə nät′ō; *It.* ōs′tē nä′tō) *n., pl.* **-tos** (-ōz; *It.* -tōs) [It., lit., obstinate] *Music* a short melodic phrase persistently repeated by the same voice or instrument and in the same pitch

os·ti·ole (äs′tē ōl′) *n.* [< ModL. *ostiolum* < L., dim. of *ostium*: see OSTIARY] a small opening or orifice, as a pore —**os·ti·o·lar** (äs′tē ə lər, -ō′lər) *adj.*

os·ti·um (äs′tē əm) *n., pl.* **-ti·a** (-ə) [L. *ostium*: see OSTIARY] *Anat.* an opening or orifice

ost·ler (äs′lər) *n.* [ME. *osterler*, var. of *hostelere*: see HOSTLER] *same as* HOSTLER (sense 1)

os·to·sis (äs tō′sis) *n. same as* OSTEOSIS

os·tra·cism (äs′trə siz′m) *n.* [Gr. *ostrakismos* < *ostrakizein*: see ff.] 1. in ancient Greece, the temporary banishment of a citizen by popular vote 2. a rejection or exclusion by general consent, as from a group or from acceptance by society

os·tra·cize (-sīz′) *vt.* **-cized′, -ciz′ing** [Gr. *ostrakizein*, to exile by votes written on tiles or potsherds < *ostrakon*, a shell, potsherd, akin to *os*, bone (see OSSIFY) to banish, bar, exclude, etc. by ostracism —SYN. see BANISH

os·tra·cod (äs′trə käd′) *n.* [< ModL. *Ostracoda*, name of the subclass < Gr. *ostrakon*: see prec.] any of a subclass (Ostracoda) of small crustaceans, having a bivalve carapace that covers the entire body, found in fresh and salt waters and as fossils

Os·tra·va (ôs′trä vä) city in N Moravia, Czechoslovakia: pop. 265,000

os·trich (ôs′trich, äs′-) *n., pl.* **-trich·es, -trich**: see PLURAL, II, D, 1 [ME. < OFr. *ostrusce* < VL. *avis·truthius* < L. *avis*, bird + *struthio*, ostrich, altered < Gr. *strouthos*] 1. a large, swift-running bird (*Struthio camelus*) of Africa and the Near East, the largest and most powerful of living birds; it has a long neck, very long legs with two toes on each foot, and small, useless wings: the white tail and wing feathers of the male are used in millinery and as trimming 2. *same as* RHEA (*see* RHEA *n.*)

OSTRICH (to 8 ft. high)

Os·tro·goth (äs′trə gäth′) *n.* [LL. *Ostrogothus*, earlier *Austrogoti* (pl.) < Gmc. *austra-*, EAST + LL. *Gothi*: see GOTH] an East Goth; esp., a member of the tribe which conquered Italy in the 5th cent. A.D. —**Os′tro·goth′ic** *adj.*

Ost·wald (ôst′vält), **Wil·helm** (vil′helm) 1853–1932; Ger. chemist, born in Latvia

Os·ty·ak (äs′tē ak′) *n.* 1. a member of a Finno-Ugric people living in W Siberia 2. their Ugric language

Os·wald, Os·wold (äz′wôld, -wəld) [OE. *Osweald* < *os*, a god + *weald*, power] a masculine name

☆**Os·we·go tea** (äs wē′gō) [after the *Oswego* River, in N.Y.] 1. a N. American mint (*Monarda didyma*) with dense terminal heads of brilliant red flowers 2. the tea brewed from its leaves

Oś·wię·cim (ôsh vyän′tsim) *Pol. name of* AUSCHWITZ

ot- *same as* OTO-: used before a vowel

OT, o.t. overtime

OT., OT, O.T. 1. occupational therapy 2. Old Testament

o·tal·gi·a (ō tal′jē ə, -jə) *n.* [ModL. < Gr. *ōtalgia*: see OTO- & -ALGIA] an earache; pain in the ear

O·ta·ru (ô′tä rōō′) seaport on the W coast of Hokkaido, Japan: pop. 197,000

‡**O tem·po·ra! O mo·res!** (ō tem′pər ə ō môr′ēz) [L.] O the times! O the customs!: a quotation from Cicero

O·thel·lo (ə thel′ō, ô-) a tragedy (1604?) by Shakespeare in which the title character, a noble Moor, made madly jealous by the villainous Iago, kills his faithful and loving wife, Desdemona

oth·er (u*th*′ər) *adj.* [ME. < OE., akin to G. *ander*, Goth. *anthar* < IE. *anteros*, the other of two (< base *an*, there + compar. suffix), whence Sans. *ántara-*] 1. being the remaining one or ones of two or more [Bill and the *other* boy(s)] 2. different or distinct from that or those referred to or implied [use your *other* foot, not Jane but some *other* girl] 3. different in nature or kind [it is *other* than you think] 4. further or additional [to have no *other* coat] 5. former [the customs of *other* times] —*pron.* 1. the *other* one [each loved the *other*] 2. another or some other person or thing [how many *others* are there?] —*n.* the opposite [hate is the *other* of love] —*adv.* otherwise; differently [he can't do *other* than go] —**of all others** above all others —**the other day** (or **night,** etc.) not long ago; recently —**oth′er·ness** *n.*

☆**oth·er·di·rect·ed** (-də rek′tid) *adj.* guided by or concerned with goals or ideals determined by others rather than by oneself; conformist

oth·er·guess (-ges′) *adj.* [var. of dial. *othergates*, otherwise] [Obs.] of another kind; different

oth·er·where (-hwer′, -wer′) *adv.* [Archaic] in or to another place; elsewhere

oth·er·while (-hwīl′, -wīl′) *adv.* [Archaic or Dial.] 1. at some other time or times 2. at times; sometimes Also **oth′er·whiles′**

oth·er·wise (-wīz′) *adv.* [ME. *othre wise* < OE. *on othre wisan*] 1. in another manner; differently [to believe *otherwise*] 2. in all other points or respects [an *otherwise* intelligent man] 3. in other circumstances Often used as a conjunctive adverb meaning "or else" —*adj.* in another condition; different [his answer could not be *otherwise*]

other world 1. a supposed world after or beyond death 2. an ideal or imagined world

oth·er·world·ly (-wurld′lē) *adj.* being apart from material or earthly interests; spiritual or concerned with life in a future or imaginary world —**oth′er·world′li·ness** *n.*

O·thin (ō′thin) *same as* ODIN

Oth·man (äth′män, -mən; *for 1, also Ar.* ooth män′) *same as:* 1. OSMAN 2. OTTOMAN

o·tic (ōt′ik, ät′-) *adj.* [Gr. *ōtikos* < *ous* (gen. *ōtos*), EAR¹] of or connected with the ear

-ot·ic (ät′ik) [Gr. -*ōtikos*] an *adj.*-forming suffix corresponding to -OSIS, meaning: 1. of or affected with [*sclerotic*] 2. producing [*narcotic*]

o·ti·ose (ō′shē ōs′, ōt′ē-) *adj.* [L. *otiosus* < *otium*, leisure] 1. at leisure; idle; indolent 2. ineffective; futile; sterile 3. useless; superfluous —SYN. see VAIN —**o′ti·ose′ly** *adv.* —**o′ti·os′i·ty** (-äs′ə tē) *n.*

O·tis (ōt′əs) 1. [orig. family name: popularized as given name in honor of ff.] a masculine name 2. **James,** 1725–83; Am. Revolutionary patriot

o·ti·tis (ō tīt′əs) *n.* [ModL.: see OTO- & -ITIS] inflammation of the ear, esp. (**otitis media**) of the middle ear

o·to- (ōt′ō, -ə) [< Gr. *ous* (gen. *ōtos*), EAR¹] *a combining form meaning* the ear [*otology, otoscope*]

o·to·cyst (ōt′ə sist′) *n.* [prec. + -CYST] 1. *Embryology* the hollow chamber of ectoderm that develops into the vertebrate inner ear 2. *Zool.* same as STATOCYST (sense 2) —**o′to·cys′tic** *adj.*

o·to·lar·yn·gol·o·gy (ōt′ə lar′in gäl′ə jē) *n.* [OTO- + LARYNGOLOGY] the branch or practice of medicine dealing with disorders of the ear, nose, and throat —**o′to·lar′yn·gol′o·gist** *n.*

o·to·lith (ōt′ə lith′) *n.* [OTO- + -LITH] 1. a tiny, bonelike particle or stony, platelike structure in the internal ear of lower vertebrates 2. a similar calcareous concretion in the statocyst of many invertebrates —**o′to·lith′ic** *adj.*

☆**o·tol·o·gy** (ō täl′ə jē) *n.* [OTO- + -LOGY] the branch of medicine dealing with the ear and its disorders —**o·to·log·i·cal** (ōt′ə läj′i k'l) *adj.* —**o·tol′o·gist** *n.*

o·to·scle·ro·sis (ōt′ō skli rō′sis) *n.* [OTO- + SCLEROSIS] a growth of spongy bone in the inner ear causing progressive deafness —**o′to·scle·rot′ic** (-skli rät′ik) *adj.*

o·to·scope (ōt′ə skōp′) *n.* [OTO- + -SCOPE] an instrument for examining the tympanic membrane and external canal of the ear

O·tran·to (ō trän′tō; *It.* ō trän′tō), **Strait of** strait between Albania & Italy, connecting the Adriatic & Ionian seas: c. 45 mi. wide

‡**ot·ta·va** (ōt tä′vä) *adv., adj.* [It.] same as ALL'OTTAVA

ot·ta·va ri·ma (ō tä′və rē′mə, ə-) [It.: same as OCTAVE & RHYME] a stanza of eight lines with the rhyme scheme *ababbcc:* the Italian form has eleven syllables in a line, the English, ten or eleven

Ot·ta·wa¹ (ät′ə wə, -wä′) *n.* [< CanadFr. *Otaua* < Algonquian: cf. Cree *atâweu,* trader] 1. *pl.* **-was, -wa** any member of a tribe of N. American Indians who lived near the mouth of the Ottawa River, on Manitoulin Island, and in Michigan 2. their Algonquian language —*adj.* of the Ottawas

Ot·ta·wa² (ät′ə wə, -wä′) 1. river in SE Canada, forming the border between Ontario & Quebec, flowing southeast into the St. Lawrence: 696 mi. 2. capital of Canada, in SE Ontario, on the Ottawa River: pop. 291,000

ot·ter (ät′ər) *n., pl.* **-ters, -ter** see PLURAL, II, D, 1 [ME. *oter* < OE., akin to ON. *otr* < IE. **udros,* a water animal (whence Sans. *udrá-h*) < base **wed-,* to make wet, whence WATER] 1. any of a genus (*Lutra*) of furry, flesh-eating mammals related to the weasel and mink, with webbed feet used in swimming and a long, slightly flattened tail; often, specif., the **American otter** (*Lutra canadensis*) 2. the short, thick, lustrous fur of this animal 3. same as SEA OTTER

Ot·to (ät′ō) [OHG. *Otho, Odo* < *auda,* rich] 1. a masculine name 2. **Otto I** 912–973 A.D.; king of Germany (936–973) & emperor of the Holy Roman Empire (962–973): called *the Great*

ot·to (ät′ō) *n.* same as ATTAR

Ot·to·man (ät′ə mən) *adj.* [Fr. < It. *Ottomano* < ML. *Ottomanus* < Ar. *'Uthmāni,* of *'Uthmān* (Osman)] same as TURKISH —*n., pl.* **-mans** 1. a Turk, esp. one belonging to the tribe or family of Osman; Othman 2. [Fr. *ottomane* < fem. of *adj.*] [o-] *a*) a low, cushioned seat without a back or arms *b*) a kind of couch or divan, with or without a back *c*) a low, cushioned footstool *d*) a corded fabric of silk, rayon, etc., with wide, flat ribs

Ottoman Empire empire (c. 1300–1918) of the Turks, including at its peak much of SE Europe, SW Asia, & NE Africa: cap. (after 1453) Constantinople

Ot·way (ät′wā), **Thomas** 1652–85; Eng. dramatist

Ötz·tal Alps (öts′täl) division of the E Alps, along the Austro-Italian border: highest peak, 12,379 ft.

oua·ba·in (wä bā′in) *n.* [Fr. *ouabaine* < *ouabaio,* name of an African tree from which the substance is obtained (< Somali *waba yo*) + *-ine,* -INE⁴] a poisonous glycoside, $C_{29}H_{44}O_{12} \cdot 8H_2O$, made chiefly from the seeds of an African plant (*Strophanthus gratus*): it is a constituent of a Zulu arrow poison and is used in medicine as a substitute for digitalis

Ouach·i·ta (wäsh′i tô, wôsh′-) [< Fr. < AmInd. tribal name < ?] river flowing from W Ark. southeast & south into the Red River in La.: 605 mi.

Oua·ga·dou·gou (wä′gə dōō′gōō) capital of Upper Volta, in the C part: pop. 51,000

oua·na·niche (wä′nə nēsh′) *n., pl.* **-niche′** [CanadFr. < Algonquian *wananish*] a small, landlocked salmon (*Salmo ouananiche*) of SE Canada

ou·bli·ette (ōō′blē et′) *n.* [Fr. < *oublier,* to forget < VL. **oblitare* < pp. of *oblivisci,* to forget: see OBLIVION] a concealed dungeon having a trap door in the ceiling as its only opening

OTTOMAN EMPIRE
(16th cent.)

ouch¹ (ouch) *interj.* [echoic of natural cry] an exclamation expressing sudden pain

ouch² (ouch) *n.* [altered by faulty separation of ME. *a nouche* < OFr. *nousche* < Frank. **nuskja,* brooch] [Archaic] 1. a clasp or buckle; specif., an ornament with a clasp, esp. when set with precious stones 2. a setting, as of gold, for a precious stone —*vt.* [Archaic] to ornament with or as with ouches

oud (ōōd) *n.* [Ar. *'ud,* orig. wood, hence wooden instrument] a stringed instrument of the Middle East and northern Africa, like a lute

Oudh (oud) region of India that with *Agra* formed United Provinces: cf. UTTAR PRADESH

ought¹ (ôt) *v.aux.* [orig., pt. of OWE: ME. *aughte* < OE. *ahte,* pp. of *agan,* OWE] an auxiliary used with infinitives and meaning: 1. to be compelled by obligation or duty [he *ought* to pay his debts] or by desirability [you *ought* to eat more] 2. to be expected or likely [it *ought* to be over soon] Past time is expressed by combining *ought* with the perfect infinitive of the verb being used [I *ought* to have told you] —*n.* obligation or duty

ought² (ôt) *n.* [var. of AUGHT] anything whatever; aught —*adv.* [Archaic] to any degree; at all; aught

ought³ (ôt) *n.* [by faulty division of *a nought*] a nought; the figure zero (0)

ought·n't (-'nt) ought not

‡**oui** (wē) *adv.* [Fr.] yes

☆**Oui·ja** (wē′jə, -jē) [Fr. *oui,* yes + G. *ja,* yes] *a trademark for* a device consisting of a planchette and a board bearing the alphabet and various other symbols, used in spiritualistic séances, etc., supposedly to convey and record messages from the spirits

Ouj·da (ōōj dä′) city in NE Morocco: pop. 150,000

ounce¹ (ouns) *n.* [ME. < OFr. *unce* < L. *uncia,* a twelfth, twelfth part of a foot or pound, orig., unit, akin to L. *unus,* ONE] 1. a unit of weight equal to 1/16 pound avoirdupois, or 1/12 pound troy 2. same as FLUID OUNCE 3. any small amount [an *ounce* of care] Abbrev. *oz.* (*sing. & pl.*)

ounce² (ouns) *n.* [ME. *once* < OFr. < *l'once,* mistaken for *lonce* < VL. < LL. **luncea* < L. *lynx,* LYNX] same as SNOW LEOPARD

ouphe, ouph (ouf, ōōf) *n.* [var. of OAF] an elf; goblin

our (our, är) *possessive pronominal adj.* [ME. *ure* < OE. *ure,* earlier *user,* gen. of *us* (see US), akin to G. *unser*] of, belonging to, made, or done by us

ou·ra·ri (ōō rä′rē) *n.* [see CURARE] same as CURARE

Our Father same as LORD'S PRAYER

Our Lady Mary, the mother of Jesus; Virgin Mary

ours (ourz, ärz) *pron.* [ME. *ures* < *ure,* OUR + gen. *-s,* hence, in form, a double possessive] that or those belonging to us: the absolute form of OUR, used without a following noun, often after *of* [a friend of *ours,* that book is *ours, ours* are better]

our·self (our self′, är-) *pron.* a form corresponding to OURSELVES, used, as in royal proclamations, by one person who refers to himself as *we:* cf. WE (for I)

our·selves (-selvz′) *pron.* [LME. *ure selves,* for Midland *ure selven,* replacing *us selven,* lit., us selves] a form of the 1st pers. pl. pronoun, used: *a*) as an intensive [we went *ourselves*] *b*) as a reflexive [we hurt *ourselves*] *c*) as a quasi-noun meaning "our real, true, or actual selves" [we are not *ourselves* when we are upset]: in this construction *our* may be considered a possessive pronominal adjective and *selves* a noun, and they may be separated [our own sweet *selves*]

-ous (əs) [ME. < L. *-us* & OFr. *-ous, -eus* < L. *-osus*] an adj.-forming suffix meaning: 1. having, full of, characterized by [hazardous, dangerous] 2. *Chem.* having a lower valence than is indicated by the suffix *-ic* [nitrous]

Ouse (ōōz) 1. river in E England, flowing north into The Wash: 156 mi.: also **Great Ouse** 2. river in Yorkshire, N England, flowing southeast to join the Trent & form the Humber: 45 mi.

ou·sel (ōō′z'l) *n.* same as OUZEL

oust (oust) *vt.* [Anglo-Fr. *ouster* < OFr. *ouster* (Fr. *ôter*) < L. *ostare,* to obstruct < *ob-,* against (see OB-) + *stare,* to STAND] to force or drive out; expel, dispossess, eject, etc. —*SYN.* see EJECT

oust·er (ous′tər) *n.* [Anglo-Fr., inf. used as n.: see prec.] 1. a person or thing that ousts 2. *Law* an ousting or being ousted, esp. from real property; legal eviction or unlawful dispossession

out (out) *adv.* [ME. < OE. *ut,* akin to ON. *ūt,* G. *aus* < IE. base **ud-,* up, up away, whence Sans. *úd-,* L. *us(que)*] 1. *a*) away from, forth from, or removed from a place, position, or situation [they live ten miles *out*] *b*) away from home [to go *out* for dinner] *c*) away from shore *d*) on strike 2. into or in the open air [come *out* and play] 3. into or in existence or activity [disease broke *out*] 4. *a*) to a conclusion or result [argue it *out*] *b*) completely, fully, or to the point of exhaustion [tired *out,* dry *out*] *c*) in full bloom, or in leaf 5. into sight or notice [the moon came *out*] 6. *a*) into or in circulation [to put *out* a new style] *b*) into or in society [debutantes who come *out*] 7. from existence, operation, or activity [fade *out,* burn *out,* die *out*] 8. so as to remove from power or office [vote them *out*] 9. forcefully; aloud [sing *out,* speak *out*] 10. beyond a regular or normal surface, condition, or

position [stand *out*, eke *out*, lengthen *out*] 11. away from the interior, center, or midst [spread *out*, reach *out*, branch *out*]: sometimes implying sharing or dividing [deal *out*, sort *out*] 12. from one state, as of composure, harmony, or agreement, into another, as of annoyance, discord, or disagreement [to feel put *out*, friends may fall *out*] 13. into or in disuse, discard, or obsolescence [long skirts went *out*] 14. from a number, group, or stock [pick *out*] 15. [Slang] into or in unconsciousness [to pass *out*] ☆16. *Baseball*, etc. in a manner that results in an out [to fly *out*] —*adj.* 1. external: usually in combination [*outpost, outfield*] 2. beyond regular limits 3. outlying; remote 4. going or directed outward [an *out* flight] 5. away from work, school, etc. [*out* because of sickness] 6. bared because of torn clothing, etc. [*out* at the elbow] 7. deviating from what is accurate or right [*out* in one's estimates] 8. *a*) not in effective use, operation, etc. *b*) turned off; extinguished 9. not to be considered; not possible 10. in disagreement; at variance 11. that is not successful or in power ☆12. [Colloq.] having suffered a financial loss [*out* fifty dollars] 13. [Colloq.] no longer smart, popular, fashionable, etc.; outmoded ☆14. *Baseball* failing or having failed to get on base —*prep.* 1. out of; through to the outside [walk *out* the door] 2. along the way of [to drive *out* a driveway] 3. [Poet.] forth from: usually after *from* —*n.* 1. something that is out 2. a person, group, etc. that is not in power, in office, or in a favored position: *usually used in pl.* ☆3. [Slang] a way out; means of avoiding; excuse ☆4. *Baseball* the failure of a batter or runner to reach base safely ☆5. *Printing a*) the omission of a word or words *b*) the word or words omitted 6. *Tennis, Squash*, etc. a service or return that lands out of bounds —*vi.* to come out; esp., to become known [the truth will *out*] —*vt.* to put out —*interj.* 1. get out! begone! 2. communication completed: term used in radio communication —**all out** completely; wholeheartedly —**on the outs** [Colloq.] on unfriendly terms: also, esp. formerly, **at outs** —**out and away** by far; without comparison —**out and out** completely; thoroughly —☆**out for** making a determined effort to get or do —**out from under** [Colloq.] away from difficulty or danger —**out of** 1. from inside of 2. from the number of 3. past the boundaries or scope of; beyond 4. from (material, etc.) [made *out of* stone] 5. because of [*out of* spite] 6. given birth by: said of animals 7. not in possession of; having no [*out of* money, *out of* gas] 8. not in a condition of [*out of* order, *out of* focus] 9. so as to deprive or be deprived of [cheat *out of* money] —**out one's way** [Colloq.] in, to, or near one's neighborhood —☆**out on one's feet** 1. dazed or stunned, but still standing, as a boxer 2. completely exhausted —**out** to making a determined effort to

out- (out) [< OUT] *a combining form meaning:* 1. situated at or coming from a point away, outside, external [*outbuilding, outpatient*] 2. going away or forth, outward [*outbound, outcast*] 3. better, greater, or more than [*outrun, outdo, outsell, outshoot*]: a frequent usage in such self-explanatory terms as the following:

outact	outdrink	outproduce
outargue	outeat	outquote
outbluff	outfight	outrace
outboast	outhit	outscore
outbox	outleap	outshout
outbrag	outmarch	outspend
outclimb	outperform	outswim
outdance	outpitch	outwalk

☆**out·age** (out′ij) *n.* [OUT- + -AGE] an interruption; accidental suspension of operation, as of electric power

out-and-out (out′'n out′) *adj.* complete; thorough

out·back (out′bak) *n.* [*also* O-] 1. the sparsely settled, flat, arid inland region of Australia 2. any remote, sparsely settled region thought of as uncivilized —*adj.* [*also* O-] of such a region

out·bal·ance (out′bal′əns) *vt.* -anced, -anc·ing to be greater than in weight, value, etc.

out·bid (-bid′) *vt.* -bid′, -bid′ding to bid or offer more than (someone else)

out·board (out′bôrd′) *adj., adv.* 1. outside the hull or bulwarks of a ship or boat ☆2. away from or farther from the hull or fuselage of an aircraft ☆3. outside the main body of a spacecraft —*n.* 1. same as OUTBOARD MOTOR ☆2. a boat with an outboard motor

☆**outboard motor** a portable gasoline engine mounted outboard on a boat to propel it

out·bound (-bound′) *adj.* outward bound

out·brave (out′brāv′) *vt.* -braved′, -brav′ing 1. to surpass in bravery 2. to face defiantly

out·break (out′brāk′) *n.* 1. a breaking out; sudden occurrence, as of disease, war, anger, etc. 2. an insurrection or riot

out·breed·ing (-brēd′in) *n.* 1. the breeding of unrelated stocks or individuals 2. *Sociology* a marrying outside the family or tribe —**out′breed′** *vt., vi.* -bred′, -breed′ing

out·build·ing (-bil′din) *n.* a structure, as a garage or barn, separate from the house or main building

out·burst (-burst′) *n.* a sudden release, as of feeling, energy, etc.

out·cast (-kast′, -käst′) *adj.* driven out; rejected —*n.* a person or thing cast out or rejected, as by society

out·caste (-kast′, -käst′) *n.* in India, a person expelled from his caste, or one who belongs to no caste

out·class (out′klas′, -kläs′) *vt.* to surpass in excellence by a wide margin

out·come (out′kum′) *n.* [ME. *utcome*] result; consequence; aftermath —*SYN.* see EFFECT

out·crop (out′kräp′; *for v.,* -kräp′) *n.* 1. a breaking forth; specif., the emergence of a mineral from the earth so as to be exposed on the surface 2. the mineral that so emerges —*vi.* -cropped′, -crop′ping 1. to emerge from the earth in this way 2. to break forth

☆**out·cross** (-krôs′) *vt.* to subject to outcrossing —*n.* an individual produced by outcrossing

out·cross·ing (-krôs′in) *n.* the producing of offspring from individuals usually of the same breed but of different strains

out·cry (-krī′) *n., pl.* -cries′ 1. a crying out 2. a strong protest or objection

☆**out·curve** (-kurv′) *n. Baseball earlier term for* CURVE

out·dat·ed (out′dāt′id) *adj.* no longer current or popular; behind the times; antiquated

out·dis·tance (-dis′təns) *vt.* -tanced, -tanc·ing to leave behind or get ahead of, as in a race

out·do (-dⁿ′) *vt.* -did′, -done′, -do′ing to exceed or surpass —*SYN.* see EXCEL —**outdo oneself** 1. to do something better than one ever did before or thought one could do 2. to make a supreme effort

out·door (out′dôr′) *adj.* 1. being or taking place outdoors 2. of, relating to, or fond of the outdoors

☆**out·doors** (-dôrz′) *adv.* in or into the open; outside a building or shelter —*n.* 1. any area or place outside a building or shelter 2. countryside, forests, etc. where there are few or no houses

out·er (out′ər) *adj.* [ME. *outter;* new form < *out* + -*er*, replacing *uttre*, UTTER[1]] 1. located farther without; exterior; external 2. relatively far out or far removed [the *outer* regions]

Outer Banks chain of long, narrow, sandy islands along the E coast of N.C.

out·er·coat (-kōt′) *n.* a topcoat, overcoat, etc.

Outer Hebrides *see* HEBRIDES

Outer Mongolia *former name of* MONGOLIAN PEOPLE'S REPUBLIC

out·er·most (-mōst′) *adj.* located farthest without

Outer Seven a group of European countries (Britain, Norway, Sweden, Denmark, Switzerland, Austria, Portugal) making up a trading bloc outside the European Economic Community: Finland is an associate member

outer space 1. space beyond the atmosphere of the earth 2. space outside the solar system

out·er·wear (-wer′) *n.* outer garments worn over the usual clothing; specif., topcoats, raincoats, etc.

out·face (out′fās′) *vt.* -faced′, -fac′ing 1. to overcome or subdue with a look or stare; stare down 2. to defy or resist

out·fall (out′fôl′) *n.* the outlet of a river, sewer, etc.

out·field (out′fēld′) *n.* 1. the outlying land of a farm ☆2. *a*) the playing area of a baseball field beyond the infield *b*) the outfielders collectively

☆**out·field·er** (-ər) *n. Baseball* a player whose position is in the outfield; right fielder, center fielder, or left fielder

out·fit (-fit′) *n.* 1. *a*) a set of articles for fitting out, or equipping *b*) the equipment used in any craft or activity; paraphernalia [a mason's *outfit*, camping *outfit*] ☆2. articles of clothing worn together; ensemble [a fall *outfit*] ☆3. a group of people associated in some undertaking or activity, as a military unit, business, ranch, etc. 4. a fitting out; equipping —*vt.* -fit′ted, -fit′ting to furnish or equip, as with an outfit; fit out —*vi.* to obtain an outfit —*SYN.* see FURNISH

out·fit·ter (-fit′ər) *n.* a person who furnishes, sells, or makes outfits

out·flank (out′flank′) *vt.* 1. to go around and beyond the flank of (a body of enemy troops) 2. to thwart; outwit

out·flow (out′flō′) *n.* 1. the act of flowing out 2. *a*) that which flows out *b*) the amount flowing out

out·foot (out′foot′) *vt.* 1. to walk, run, etc. faster than 2. to sail faster than (another ship)

☆**out·fox** (-fäks′) *vt.* to outwit; outsmart

out·gas (-gas′) *vi.* -gassed′, -gas′sing 1. to liberate gaseous elements from a planet's interior into its atmosphere 2. to evaporate minute portions of its substance in the form of gas molecules

out·gen·er·al (-jen′ər əl) *vt.* -aled or -alled, -al·ing or -al·ling to surpass in leadership or management

out·go (out′gō′; *for n.,* out′gō′) *vt.* -went′, -gone′, -go′ing to surpass, as in achievement; go beyond; outdo —*n., pl.* -goes′ 1. the act of going out 2. that which goes or is paid out; outflow or expenditure

out·go·ing (out′gō′in) *adj.* 1. *a*) going out; leaving *b*) retiring from office 2. expansive, sociable, friendly, etc.

[an outgoing personality*]* —*n.* **1.** the act of going out **2.** *[usually pl.]* [Brit.] an outlay; expenses

out-group (-grōōp′) *n.* all the people not belonging to a specific in-group

out·grow (out′grō′) *vt.* **-grew′, -grown′, -grow′ing 1.** to grow faster or larger than **2.** to lose or get rid of in the process of growing or maturing *[to outgrow* one's credulity*]* **3.** to grow too large for *[to outgrow* a suit*]*

out·growth (out′grōth′) *n.* **1.** the act of growing out **2.** a result; consequence; development **3.** that which grows out; offshoot or excrescence

out·guess (out′ges′) *vt.* to outwit in anticipating

out·haul (out′hôl′) *n. Naut.* a rope used to haul the corners of a sail out to the end of a boom

out-Her·od (out′her′əd) *vt.* to surpass in excess, as in violence or cruelty: usually in the phrase **out-Herod Herod,** Hamlet's reference to the usual characterization of Herod Antipas in the old mystery plays

out·house (out′hous′) *n.* a building separate from but located near a main building or dwelling; ☆specif., a small structure used for defecating or urinating, typically having a seat with a hole over a deep pit

out·ing (-iŋ) *n.* **1.** a pleasure trip or holiday outdoors or away from home **2.** an outdoor walk, ride, etc.

☆**outing flannel** a soft, warm cotton fabric in a plain or twill weave with a nap on both sides

out·land (-land′; *also, for adj.,* -lənd) *n.* [ME. < OE. *utland*] **1.** *[usually pl.]* [Obs.] outlying or remote areas; hinterland **2.** [Archaic] a foreign land —*adj.* **1.** outlying **2.** [Archaic] foreign

out·land·er (-lan′dər) *n.* [prec. + -ER, in part after Du. *uitlander,* foreigner] a foreigner; alien; stranger

out·land·ish (out lan′dish) *adj.* [ME. *utlandisch* < OE. *utlendisc* < *utland* + *-isc,* -ISH] **1.** [Archaic] foreign; alien **2.** very odd, strange, or peculiar; fantastic; bizarre **3.** remote; out-of-the-way —*SYN.* see STRANGE —**out·land′-ish·ly** *adv.* —**out·land′ish·ness** *n.*

out·last (out last′, -lăst′) *vt.* **1.** to endure longer than **2.** to outlive —*SYN.* see OUTLIVE

out·law (out′lô′) *n.* [ME. *outlawe* < OE. *utlaga* < ON. *utlagr,* lit., outlawed: see OUT & LAW] **1.** orig., a person declared by a court of law to be deprived of legal rights and protection, generally for the commission of some crime: the killing of such a person was not a legal offense **2.** a habitual or notorious criminal who is a fugitive from the law ☆**3.** a fierce or uncontrollable horse or other animal —*vt.* **1.** orig., to declare to be an outlaw **2.** in the U.S., to remove the legal force of (contracts, etc.) **3.** to declare unlawful or illegal **4.** to bar, or ban

out·law·ry (-rē) *n., pl.* **-ries 1.** an outlawing or being outlawed **2.** the state or condition of being an outlaw **3.** disregard or defiance of the law

out·lay (out′lā′; *for v., usually* out′lā′) *n.* **1.** a spending (of money, energy, etc.) **2.** money, etc. spent —*vt.* **-laid′, -lay′ing** to spend (money)

out·let (out′let′) *n.* **1.** a passage or vent for letting something out **2.** a means of expression *[an outlet* for the emotions*]* **3.** a stream, river, etc. that flows out from a lake **4.** *a)* a market for goods *b)* a store, agency, etc. that sells the goods of a specific manufacturer or wholesaler ☆**5.** *Elec.* any point in a wiring system at which current may be taken for consumption by inserting a plug

out·li·er (-lī′ər) *n.* any person or thing that lies, dwells, exists, etc. away from the main body or expected place; specif., *a)* a person who resides away from his place of work or business *b)* a person who is excluded, or excludes himself, from some group; outsider *c) Geol.* a mass of untransported rock, usually of large size, separated by erosion from the main mass

out·line (-līn′) *n.* **1.** a line bounding the limits of an object, showing its shape; contour line **2.** a sketch showing only the contours of an object, without use of shading **3.** *[also pl.]* an undetailed general plan **4.** a summary of a subject, consisting of a systematic listing of its most important points —*vt.* **-lined′, -lin′ing 1.** to draw a profile of; draw in outline **2.** to give or write an outline, or the main points, of —**out′lin′er** *n.*

SYN.—**outline** is used of the line bounding the limits of an object *[the sketch shows only the* outline *of the skyscrapers];* **contour,** specifically applied to the configuration of a land mass, in extension stresses the shape of an object or mass as determined by its outline *[the soft* contour *of her waist];* **profile** is used of the outline or contour of the face in a side view or of the outline of any object as it is seen against a background *[the* profile *of the trees against the sky];* **silhouette** applies to a profile portrait, esp. of the head and usually in solid black, or it may be used of any dark shape seen against a light background *[the* silhouette *of a house against the moonlight]* See also FORM

out·live (out′liv′) *vt.* **-lived′, -liv′ing 1.** to live or endure longer than **2.** to live through; outlast

SYN.—**outlive, outlast,** and **survive** all imply a continuing to exist longer than others or after a specified occasion, **outlive** stressing one's power to endure, as in competition with others or in overcoming a difficulty *[to* outlive *one's enemies, a disgrace, etc.],* **outlast,** a remaining existent for a longer time *[to* outlast *one's usefulness],* and **survive,** a remaining alive after another's death *[two sons* survive *the deceased]* or after a perilous incident *[they* survived *the tornado]*

out·look (out′look′) *n.* **1.** *a)* a place for watching or looking out *b)* the view from such a place **2.** the act of looking out **3.** mental view or attitude **4.** expectation or prospect; probable outcome

out·ly·ing (-lī′in) *adj.* relatively far out from a certain point or center; remote

out·man (out′man′) *vt.* **-manned′, -man′ning** to surpass in number of men; outnumber

out·ma·neu·ver, out·ma·noeu·vre (-mə nōō′vər) *vt.* **-vered** or **-vred, -ver·ing** or **-vring** to maneuver with better effect than; outwit

out·match (-mach′) *vt.* to be superior to; outdo

out·mi·grant (out′mī′grənt) *adj.* leaving one district, region, etc. to go to another —*n.* an out-migrant person or animal —**out′-mi′grate** (-grāt) *vi.* **-grat·ed, -grat·ing** —**out′-mi·gra′tion** *n.*

out·mod·ed (out′mōd′id) *adj.* no longer in fashion or accepted; obsolete

out·most (out′mōst′) *adj.* [ME., altered (after *out*) < *utemest,* UTMOST] most remote; outermost

out·num·ber (out′num′bər) *vt.* to exceed in number

out-of-date (out′əv dāt′) *adj.* no longer in style or use; not current; outmoded; old-fashioned

out-of-door (-dôr′) *adj. same as* OUTDOOR

out-of-doors (-dôrz′) *adv., n. same as* OUTDOORS

out-of-pock·et (-päk′it) *adj.* designating unbudgeted expenses, or ready cash paid out, as for miscellaneous items

out-of-the-way (-*th*ə wā′) *adj.* **1.** not near a frequented road or populous place; secluded **2.** not common; unusual **3.** not conventional or proper

out-of-town·er (-toun′ər) *n.* a visitor from another town or city

out·pace (out′pās′) *vt.* **-paced′, -pac′ing** to surpass; exceed

out·pa·tient (out′pā′shənt) *n.* a patient receiving treatment or care at a hospital without being an inmate

out·play (out′plā′) *vt.* to play better than

out·point (-point′) *vt.* **1.** to score more points than **2.** *Naut.* to get into a position closer to the wind than (another vessel)

out·port (out′pôrt′) *n.* [Canad.] an isolated fishing village on the Newfoundland coast

out·post (-pōst′) *n.* **1.** *Mil. a)* a small group stationed at a distance from the main force in order to prevent an enemy surprise attack *b)* the place or station occupied by such a group *c)* any military base away from the home country **2.** a settlement on a frontier or border

out·pour (out′pôr′; *for the v.,* out′pôr′) *n.* **1.** the action of pouring out **2.** that which pours out; outflow Also **out′pour′ing** (-iŋ), *vi.* to pour out

out·put (out′poot′) *n.* **1.** *a)* the work done or amount produced by a person, machine, production line, manufacturing plant, etc., esp. over a given period *b)* the act of producing **2.** in computers, *a)* information transferred from internal storage to external storage by a computer or delivered in response to instructions *b)* any of various devices involved in transferring or recording this information *c)* the act or process of transferring or delivering this information **3.** *Elec. a)* the useful voltage, current, or power delivered by amplifiers, generators, receivers, etc. or by a circuit *b)* the terminal where such energy is delivered

out·rage (out′rāj′) *n.* [ME. < OFr. < *outre,* beyond < L. *ultra* (see ULTRA): meaning infl. by association with OUT] **1.** an extremely vicious or violent act **2.** a deep insult or offense **3.** great anger, indignation, etc. aroused by such an act or offense —*vt.* **-raged′, -rag′ing 1.** to commit an outrage upon or against; specif., *a)* to offend, insult, or wrong grievously *b)* to rape **2.** to cause great anger, indignation, etc. in —*SYN.* see OFFEND

out·ra·geous (out rā′jəs) *adj.* [ME. < OFr. *outrageus:* see prec. & -OUS] **1.** having the nature of, involving, or doing great injury or wrong **2.** exceeding all bounds of decency or reasonableness; very offensive or shocking **3.** violent in action or disposition; unrestrained —**out·ra′geous·ly** *adv.* —**out·ra′geous·ness** *n.*

SYN.—**outrageous** applies to that which so exceeds all bounds of right, morality, decency, etc. as to be intolerable *[an* outrageous *insult];* **flagrant** implies a glaringly bad or openly evil character in persons or their acts *[a* flagrant *sinner, a* flagrant *violation];* **monstrous** and **atrocious** are applied to that which is extremely or shockingly wrong, bad, evil, cruel, etc. *[a* monstrous *vice, lie, etc.,* atrocious *cruelty, manners, etc.];* **heinous** implies such extreme wickedness as to arouse the strongest hatred and revulsion *[a* heinous *crime]*

ou·trance (ōō träns′) *n.* [Fr.; also, in earlier use, ME. < MFr. < *outrer,* to pass beyond < *outre* (see OUTRAGE)] the extreme limit; utmost extremity

out·range (out′rānj′) *vt.* **-ranged′, -rang′ing 1.** to have a greater range than **2.** to range beyond

☆**out·rank** (-raŋk′) *vt.* to exceed in rank

‡**out·ré** (ōō trā′; E. -trā′) *adj.* [Fr. (cf. OUTRAGE)] **1.** exaggerated; eccentric; bizarre

out·reach (out′rēch′) *vt., vi.* **1.** to reach farther (than); exceed; surpass **2.** to reach out; extend —*n.* **1.** the act of reaching out **2.** the extent of reach —☆*adj.* designating or of a branch office of a social agency, governmental department, etc. set up to accommodate those who cannot or will not utilize the services of the main offices

out·ride (out′rīd′) *vt.* **-rode′, -rid′den, -rid′ing 1.** to surpass or outstrip in riding **2.** to withstand or endure successfully; ride out

out·rid·er (out'rīd'ər) *n.* **1.** an attendant on horseback who rides out ahead of or beside a carriage, stagecoach, etc. **2.** a person who rides out or forth; specif., ☆a cowboy who rides over a range to prevent cattle from straying **3.** a trailblazer; forerunner

out·rig·ger (-rig'ər) *n.* **1.** any temporary support extending out from a main structure **2.** *Naut. a)* any of a variety of frameworks extended beyond the rail of a ship for various purposes *b)* a brace holding an oarlock out from the side of a boat, to give the rower more leverage *c)* a timber rigged out from the side of certain native canoes to prevent tipping; also, a canoe of this type **3.** a projection for supporting the lesser airfoils of an airplane

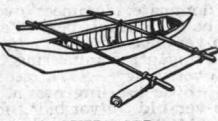

OUTRIGGER

out·right (out'rīt'; *for adj.* out'rīt') *adj.* **1.** without reservation; downright **2.** straightforward **3.** complete; total; whole —*adv.* **1.** entirely; wholly **2.** without reservation; openly **3.** at once **4.** [Obs.] straight ahead —**out'right'ness** *n.*

out·root (out'root') *vt.* **1.** *same as* UPROOT **2.** to wipe out; destroy; eradicate

out·run (-run') *vt.* **-ran'**, **-run'**, **-run'ning** **1.** to run faster, farther, or better than **2.** to exceed **3.** to escape (a pursuer) by or as by running

out·run·ner (out'run'ər) *n.* **1.** a person or thing that runs out **2.** an attendant running beside or before a carriage **3.** the leading dog of a team of sled dogs

out·sell (out'sel') *vt.* **-sold'**, **-sell'ing** **1.** to sell in greater amounts than **2.** to excel in salesmanship **3.** [Rare] to sell for a higher price than

out·set (out'set') *n.* a setting out; beginning; start

out·shine (out'shīn') *vt.* **-shone'** or **-shined'**, **-shin'ing** **1.** to shine brighter or longer than (another) **2.** to surpass; excel —*vi.* to shine forth

out·shoot (out'shoot'; *for n.*, out'shoot') *vt.* **-shot'**, **-shoot'ing** **1.** to shoot more effectively than **2.** to shoot out —*vi.* to shoot out; protrude —*n.* **1.** a shooting or being shot out **2.** that which shoots out or protrudes ☆**3.** *Baseball. earlier term for* CURVE

out·side (out'sīd', out'-; -sīd') *n.* **1.** the outer side, part, or surface; exterior **2.** *a)* outward aspect or appearance; that part of anything that is presented to view *b)* that which is obvious or superficial **3.** any place or area not inside —*adj.* **1.** of or on the outside; outer **2.** *a)* originating, coming from, or situated beyond given limits; from some other place, person, group, etc. *[*to accept no *outside* help*] b)* leading to the outside **3.** extreme; maximum *[an outside estimate]* **4.** mere; slight *[an outside chance]* —*adv.* **1.** on or to the outside **2.** beyond certain limits **3.** in or into the open air —*prep.* **1.** on or to the outer side of **2.** beyond the limits of **3.** [Colloq.] except —**outside the** at the most; at the absolute limit —**outside of 1.** outside **2.** [Colloq.] other than; with the exception of

out·sid·er (out'sīd'ər) *n.* **1.** one who is outside or not included; esp., one not a member of or in sympathy with a given group **2.** a contender given little chance of winning a race or contest

out·sit (-sit') *vt.* **-sat'**, **-sit'ting** **1.** to sit longer than (another) **2.** to sit beyond the time of

out·size (out'sīz') *n.* **1.** a size varying from the usual standard; odd size; esp., an unusually large size **2.** a garment or other article of such a size —*adj.* of nonstandard size; esp., unusually large: also **out'sized'** (-sīzd')

out·skirt (-skurt') *n.* [*usually pl.*] part or district remote from the center or midst, as of a city

☆**out·smart** (out'smärt') *vt.* [Colloq.] to overcome by cunning or cleverness; outwit

out·soar (-sôr') *vt.* to soar beyond or higher than

out·span (out'span'; *for n.*, out'span') *vt., vi.* **-spanned'**, **-span'ning** [Afrik. *uitspannen* < Du. *uit*, OUT + *spannen*, to harness, SPAN[1]] in South Africa, to unyoke or unharness (animals) —*n.* the act or place of outspanning

out·speak (-spēk') *vt.* **-spoke'**, **-spo'ken**, **-speak'ing** **1.** to speak better or more forcefully than **2.** to say boldly or candidly —*vi.* to speak out boldly or candidly

out·spo·ken (out'spō'kən) *adj.* **1.** unrestrained in speech; frank **2.** spoken boldly or candidly —*SYN.* see FRANK[1] —**out'spo'ken·ly** *adv.* —**out'spo'ken·ness** *n.*

out·spread (out'spred'; *for adj. & n.*, out'spred') *vt., vi.* **-spread'**, **-spread'ing** to spread out; extend; expand —*n.* a spreading out; extension; expansion —*adj.* spread out; extended; expanded

out·stand (out'stand') *vi.* **-stood'**, **-stand'ing** **1.** to stand out plainly; project **2.** *Naut.* to leave port; sail out to sea —*vt.* **1.** [Archaic] to endure or stay beyond **2.** [Dial.] to withstand

out·stand·ing (-iŋ) *adj.* **1.** projecting **2.** prominent; distinguished; conspicuous **3.** unfulfilled; unsettled **4.** unpaid; uncollected **5.** that have been issued and sold: said of stocks and bonds —*SYN.* see NOTICEABLE —**out'stand'ing·ly** *adv.*

out·stare (out'ster') *vt.* **-stared'**, **-star'ing** to outdo in staring; stare down; outface

out·sta·tion (out'stā'shən) *n.* a post or station in a remote or unsettled area

out·stay (out'stā') *vt.* **1.** to stay longer than **2.** to stay beyond the time of; overstay

out·stretch (-strech') *vt.* **1.** to stretch out; extend **2.** to stretch beyond

out·strip (-strip') *vt.* **-stripped'**, **-strip'ping** **1.** to go at a faster pace than; pass or leave behind; get ahead of **2.** to excel; surpass

out·talk (-tôk') *vt.* to talk more skillfully, loudly, or forcibly than; surpass in talking

out·think (-think') *vt.* **-thought'**, **-think'ing** **1.** to think deeper, faster, or more cunningly than **2.** to outwit by such thinking

out·turn (out'turn') *n. same as* OUTPUT (sense 1 *a*)

out·vote (out'vōt') *vt.* **-vot'ed**, **-vot'ing** to defeat or surpass in voting

out·ward (out'wərd) *adj.* [ME. *utward* < OE. *utweard:* see OUT & -WARD] **1.** having to do with the outside or exterior; outer **2.** clearly apparent; observable; visible **3.** away from the interior; to or toward the outside **4.** having to do with the physical or the body as opposed to the mind or spirit **5.** concerning the surface only; superficial —*adv.* **1.** away from the interior or from port; toward the outside **2.** visibly; openly; publicly **3.** [Obs.] on the outside; externally —*n.* **1.** the outward part; exterior **2.** the material or external world **3.** outward form or appearance —**out'ward·ness** *n.*

out·ward·ly (-lē) *adv.* **1.** toward or on the outside **2.** in regard to external appearance or action

out·wards (-wərdz) *adv. same as* OUTWARD

☆**out·wash** (-wôsh', -wäsh') *n.* sand and gravel deposited by meltwater streams in front of glacial ice

out·wear (out'wer') *vt.* **-wore'**, **-worn'**, **-wear'ing** **1.** to wear out; use up **2.** to be more lasting than; outlast **3.** to outgrow or outlive **4.** to exhaust, as in strength

out·weigh (-wā') *vt.* **1.** to weigh more than **2.** to be more important, valuable, etc. than

out·wit (-wit') *vt.* **-wit'ted**, **-wit'ting** **1.** to overcome, or get the better of, by cunning or cleverness **2.** [Archaic] to be more intelligent than

out·work (out'wurk'; *for v.*, out'wurk') *n. Mil.* a lesser trench or fortification built out beyond the main defenses —*vt.* **-worked'** or **-wrought'**, **-work'ing** **1.** to work better, faster, or harder than **2.** to work out to completion

ouz·el (ōō'z'l) *n.* [ME. *osul* < OE. *osle*, akin to OHG. *amsala*, prob. < IE. base *ames-*, whence L. *merula*, W. *mwyalch*] **1.** *same as* RING OUZEL **2.** any of several heavy-bodied, perching birds (family Cinclidae) including the dippers, found in mountainous areas of Europe, Asia, and the New World; esp., *same as* WATER OUZEL **3.** [Archaic] a European blackbird

ou·zo (ōō'zō) *n.* [ModGr. *ouzon* < ?] a colorless Greek cordial flavored with aniseed

o·va (ō'və) *n. pl. of* OVUM

o·val (ō'v'l) *adj.* [Fr. *ovale* < L. *ovum*, EGG[1]] **1.** shaped like the longitudinal cross section of an egg; elliptical **2.** having the form of an egg; ellipsoid —*n.* anything oval —**o'val·ly** *adv.* —**o'val·ness** *n.*

o·var·i·ec·to·my (ō ver'ē ek'tə mē) *n., pl.* **-mies** [see -ECTOMY] the surgical removal of one or both ovaries

o·var·i·ot·o·my (-ät'ə mē) *n., pl.* **-mies** [see -TOMY] **1.** a surgical incision into an ovary **2.** *same as* OVARIECTOMY

o·va·ri·tis (ō'və rīt'is) *n.* [see -ITIS] inflammation of an ovary

o·va·ry (ō'vər ē) *n., pl.* **-ries** [ModL. *ovarium* < L. *ovum*, EGG[1]] **1.** *Anat., Zool.* either of the pair of female reproductive glands producing eggs and, in vertebrates, sex hormones **2.** *Bot.* the enlarged hollow part of the pistil or gynoecium in angiosperms, containing ovules —**o·var·i·an** (ō ver'ē ən) *adj.*

o·vate (ō'vāt) *adj.* [L. *ovatus* < *ovum*, EGG[1]] **1.** egg-shaped **2.** *Bot.* having the shape of the longitudinal section of an egg, esp. with the broader end at the base, as some leaves: see LEAF, illus. —**o'vate·ly** *adv.*

o·va·tion (ō vā'shən) *n.* [L. *ovatio* < *ovare*, to celebrate a triumph, akin to Gr. *euaxein*, to rejoice, *euai*, a cry of Bacchic joy] **1.** in ancient Rome, a lesser ceremonial tribute to a hero whose deeds were not great enough to justify a full triumph **2.** an enthusiastic outburst of applause or an enthusiastic public welcome

ov·en (uv'ən) *n.* [ME. < OE. *ofen*, akin to G. *ofen* < IE. base *auqw-*, cooking vessel, whence L. *aulla*, *olla* (cf. OLLA)] a compartment or receptacle for baking or roasting food or for heating or drying things

ov·en·bird (-burd') *n.* **1.** any of several S. American perching birds (genus *Furnarius*) that build a two-chambered, dome-shaped, ovenlike nest from clay and dried leaves ☆**2.** a N. American ground warbler (*Seiurus aurocapillus*) that builds a domelike nest on the ground in the woods

o·ver (ō'vər) *prep.* [ME. *ouer* < OE. *ofer*, akin to G. *über*, *ober* < IE. *uper* (orig. a compar. of *upo*, up) whence L.

super, Gr. *hyper*] **1.** *a)* in, at, or to a position up from; higher than; above [a canopy *over* the bed] *b)* across and down from [to fall *over* a cliff] **2.** while occupied or engaged in [to discuss a matter *over* dinner] **3.** upon the surface of [to spread icing *over* a cake] **4.** so as to cover or close [shutters *over* the windows] **5.** upon, as an effect or influence [to cast a spell *over* someone] **6.** so as to show care, concern, etc. for [to watch *over* a flock] **7.** above in authority, position, power, etc. [to rule *over* a land] **8.** in a course leading along or across, or above and to the other side of [fly *over* the lake] **9.** on the other side of [a city *over* the border] **10.** here and there in, or through all parts of [*over* the whole city] **11.** during; through [*over* the past ten years] **12.** more than, or above in degree, amount, number, etc. [costing *over* five dollars] **13.** up to and including; until after [stay *over* Easter] **14.** in preference to [chose red *over* blue] **15.** concerning; about; regarding [a quarrel *over* politics] **16.** through the medium of; on [*over* the telephone] —*adv.* **1.** *a)* above, across, or to the other side *b)* across the brim or edge **2.** more; in excess; beyond [three hours or *over*] **3.** longer or till a time later [please stay *over*] **4.** throughout or covering the entire area [the wound healed *over*] **5.** from start to finish; through [talk it *over*] **6.** *a)* from an upright position [to fall *over*] *b)* upside down; into an inverted position [turn the cup *over*] **7.** again; another time [do it *over*] **8.** at or on the other side, as of an intervening space, or at or to a specified place [*over* in England, come *over* here] **9.** from one side, belief, viewpoint, etc. to another [they won him *over*] **10.** from one person, etc. to another [hand *over* the money] See also phrases GET OVER, PUT OVER —*adj.* **1.** upper, outer, superior, excessive, or extra: often in combination [*overcoat*, *overseer*, *oversupply*] **2.** done with; finished; past [his life is *over*] **3.** having reached the other side; having got across **4.** [Colloq.] as a surplus; in excess; extra [to be three hours *over* for the week] —*n.* **1.** something in addition; excess; surplus **2.** *Cricket* *a)* the set number of balls bowled during a single turn at one end of the wicket *b)* the period of time during which this takes place **3.** *Mil.* a shot that hits or explodes beyond the target —*vt.*, *vi.* [Poet.] to pass above and across —*interj.* **1.** turn the page, etc. over **2.** communication turned over to you for reply: used in radio communication —**over again** again; another time; anew —**over all** over the whole extent; from end to end —**over and above** in addition to; more than; besides —**over and over (again)** repeatedly; time after time

o·ver- (ō′vər) *a combining form meaning:* **1.** above in position, outer, upper, superior, eminent [*overhead*, *over-bearing*, *overlord*] **2.** passing across or beyond [*overshoot*, *overpass*, *overrun*] **3.** denoting a movement downward from above [*overflow*] **4.** excessive, too much, beyond the normal [*overrate*, *oversell*, *oversleep*]: the list below includes some of the more common compounds formed with *over-* that can be understood if *too much* or *excessively* is added to the meaning of the base word

overactive	overgreedy
overambitious	overhasty
overanxious	overindulge
overattentive	overorganize
overbold	overpraise
overbusy	overprecise
overcareful	overprize
overcareless	overrefined
overcautious	overreligious
overconscientious	overripe
overconservative	oversensitive
overcook	oversentimental
overcritical	oversolicitous
overdependent	overspecialize
overeager	overstimulate
overemotional	overstretch
overemphasize	overstrict
overenthusiastic	oversubtle
overexercise	oversufficient
overexpansion	oversuspicious
overfed	overtire
overfond	overvalue
overgenerous	overzealous

o·ver·a·bun·dance (ō′vər ə bun′dəns) *n.* more than an abundance; superfluity; excess —**o′ver·a·bun′dant** *adj.*
o·ver·act (-akt′) *vt.*, *vi.* to act with exaggeration
o·ver·age[1] (-āj′) *adj.* **1.** over the age fixed as a standard **2.** so old as to be of no use
o·ver·age[2] (ō′vər ij) *n.* [OVER- + -AGE] a surplus or excess, as of goods
o·ver·all (ō′vər ôl′; *for adv.*, -ôl′) *adj.* **1.** from end to end **2.** including everything; total —*adv.* **1.** from end to end **2.** in general
☆**o·ver·alls** (-ôlz′) *n.pl.* **1.** loose-fitting trousers of some strong cotton cloth, often with a part extending up over the chest, worn, usually over other clothing, to protect against dirt and wear **2.** [*sing.*] [Brit.] a smock or other protective outer garment
o·ver·arch (ō′vər ärch′) *vt.*, *vi.* to form an arch over (something)
o·ver·arm (ō′vər ärm′) *adj.* performed by raising the arm above the shoulder, as a swimming stroke

o·ver·awe (ō′vər ô′) *vt.* -awed′, -aw′ing to overcome or subdue by inspiring awe
o·ver·bal·ance (ō′vər bal′əns; *for n.*, ō′vər bal′əns) *vt.* -anced, -anc·ing **1.** *same as* OUTWEIGH **2.** to throw off balance —*n.* something that outweighs or overbalances
o·ver·bear (ō′vər ber′) *vt.* -bore′, -borne′, -bear′ing **1.** to press or bear down by weight or physical power **2.** to dominate, domineer over, overrule, or subdue —*vi.* to be too fruitful; bear to excess
o·ver·bear·ing (-iŋ) *adj.* **1.** acting in a dictatorial manner; arrogant; domineering **2.** of transcending importance; overriding —SYN. see PROUD —**o′ver·bear′ing·ly** *adv.* —**o′ver·bear′ing·ness** *n.*
o·ver·bid (ō′vər bid′; *for n.*, ō′vər bid′) *vt.*, *vi.* -bid′, -bid′ding **1.** to outbid (another person) **2.** to bid more than the worth of (a thing, as one's hand in bridge) —*n.* a higher or excessive bid
o·ver·bite (ō′vər bīt′) *n.* faulty occlusion of the teeth in which the upper incisors and canines project over the lower to an abnormal extent
o·ver·blouse (-blous′) *n.* a blouse for women, extending below the waist and worn outside the skirt, etc.
o·ver·blow (ō′vər blō′) *vt.* -blew′, -blown′, -blow′ing **1.** to blow across, away, or down **2.** to cover with something blown, as sand **3.** *Music* to blow (a wind instrument) so as to produce overtones
o·ver·blown[1] (-blōn′) *adj.* past the stage of full bloom
o·ver·blown[2] (-blōn′) *adj.* **1.** stout; obese **2.** *a)* overdone; excessive *b)* pompous or bombastic
o·ver·board (ō′vər bôrd′) *adv.* [ME. *ouer bord* < OE. *ofor bord:* see OVER & BOARD] **1.** over a ship's side **2.** from a ship into the water —**go overboard** [Colloq.] ☆to go to extremes; esp., to be wildly enthusiastic —**throw overboard** to discard
o·ver·build (ō′vər bild′) *vt.*, *vi.* -built′, -build′ing **1.** to build over or on top of (something) **2.** to build too elaborately **3.** to erect more buildings than are needed or desirable in (an area)
o·ver·bur·den (ō′vər bur′d'n; *for n.*, ō′vər bur′d'n) *vt.* to burden oppressively; weigh down —*n.* **1.** something that overburdens **2.** *Geol.* soil overlying bedrock, or soil, rock, or other naturally occurring material overlying a useful deposit, as coal
o·ver·buy (-bī′) *vt.*, *vi.* -bought′, -buy′ing to buy more than is needed or justified by ability to pay
o·ver·call (-kôl′) *vt.*, *vi.* *Bridge* to make a higher bid than (an opponent or his bid) when there has been no intervening bid —*n.* such a bid
o·ver·cap·i·tal·ize (-kap′ə tə līz′) *vt.*, *vi.* -ized′, -iz′ing **1.** to capitalize beyond what is warranted by the state of the business, etc.; furnish too much capital for or overestimate the capital value of (a business) **2.** to set the nominal value of the capital of (a corporation) higher than is lawful or justifiable —**o′ver·cap′i·tal·i·za′tion** *n.*
o·ver·cast (ō′vər kast′, -käst′; *for v. 1, usually* ō′vər kast′, -käst′) *n.* **1.** a covering, esp. of clouds **2.** an arch in a mine, supporting an overhead passage —*adj.* **1.** cloudy; dark: said of the sky or weather **2.** *Sewing* made with overcasting —*vt.*, *vi.* -cast′, -cast′ing **1.** to overcloud; darken **2.** *Sewing* to sew over (an edge) with long, loose stitches so as to prevent raveling
o·ver·charge (ō′vər chärj′; *for n.*, ō′vər chärj′) *vt.*, *vi.* -charged′, -charg′ing **1.** to charge too high a price **2.** to overload or fill too full **3.** to exaggerate —*n.* **1.** an excessive charge **2.** a load that is too full or heavy
o·ver·clothes (ō′vər klōz′, -klōthz′) *n.pl.* *same as* OUTERWEAR
o·ver·cloud (ō′vər kloud′) *vt.*, *vi.* **1.** to darken or cover over with clouds; dim **2.** to make or become gloomy, angry, etc. in appearance
☆**o·ver·coat** (ō′vər kōt′) *n.* a coat, esp. a heavy coat, worn over the usual clothing for warmth
o·ver·come (ō′vər kum′) *vt.* -came′, -come′, -com′ing [ME. *ouercomen* < OE. *ofercuman*] **1.** to get the better of in competition, struggle, etc.; conquer **2.** to master, prevail over, or surmount [to *overcome* obstacles] **3.** to make helpless; overpower or overwhelm [*overcome* by laughter] **4.** [Archaic] to spread over or overrun —*vi.* to be victorious; win —SYN. see CONQUER
o·ver·com·pen·sate (-kam′pən sāt′) *vt.* -sat′ed, -sat′ing to give an excessive compensation to —*vi.* *Psychol.* to react to a real or imagined physical or psychological defect by a conscious or unconscious exaggerated drive to compensate for it —**o′ver·com′pen·sa′tion** *n.* —**o′ver·com·pen′sa·to·ry** (-kəm pen′sə tôr′ē) *adj.*
o·ver·con·fi·dent (-kän′fə dənt) *adj.* confident without adequate reason; too confident —**o′ver·con′fi·dence** *n.* —**o′ver·con′fi·dent·ly** *adv.*
o·ver·cor·rec·tion (-kə rek′shən) *n.* ☆an improper usage resulting from an overly conscious effort to avoid an error, as in the case form of personal pronouns (Ex.: between you and I)
o·ver·crop (-kräp′) *vt.* -cropped′, -crop′ping to deplete the fertility of (land) by overproduction of crops
o·ver·crowd (-kroud′) *vt.* to crowd with too many people or things
o·ver·de·vel·op (-di vel′əp) *vt.* **1.** to develop too much **2.** *Photog.* to develop (a film, plate, etc.) too long or with too strong a developer —**o′ver·de·vel′op·ment** *n.*

o·ver·do (-dōō′) *vt.* **-did′, -done′, -do′ing** **1.** to do too much, or to excess **2.** to spoil the effect of by exaggeration [to *overdo* an apology] **3.** to cook too long; overcook **4.** to overwork; exhaust; tire —*vi.* to do too much; esp., to exhaust oneself by doing too much

o·ver·dose (ō′vər dōs′; *for v.*, ō′vər dōs′) *n.* too large a dose —*vt.* **-dosed′, -dos′ing** to dose to excess

o·ver·draft (ō′vər draft′, -dräft′) *n.* **1.** *a)* a withdrawal of money from a bank in excess of the amount credited to the drawer *b)* the amount withdrawn in excess **2.** a draft, or current of air, passed over a fire, as in a furnace, or passing down through a kiln

o·ver·draw (ō′vər drô′) *vt.* **-drew′, -drawn′, -draw′ing 1.** to spoil the effect of by exaggeration; overdo **2.** to draw on in excess of the amount credited to the drawer **3.** to draw (a bow, etc.) too far or too much

o·ver·dress (-dres′) *vt., vi.* to dress too warmly, too showily, or too formally for the occasion

o·ver·drive (ō′vər drīv′) *n.* a gear that at a certain speed automatically reduces an engine's power output without reducing its driving speed: used to lessen fuel consumption and engine wear

o·ver·due (ō′vər dōō′, -dyōō′) *adj.* **1.** past the time for payment **2.** delayed in arrival or occurrence beyond the time set or anticipated **3.** that should have come about sooner [overdue reforms] —*SYN.* see TARDY

o·ver·dye (-dī′) *vt.* **-dyed′, -dye′ing 1.** to subject too long to the dyeing process so as to make too dark **2.** to dye over (a color previously dyed)

o·ver·eat (-ēt′) *vi.* **-ate′, -eat′en, -eat′ing** to eat too much or to the point of surfeit

o·ver·es·ti·mate (-es′tə māt′; *for n.*, -mit) *vt.* **-mat′ed, -mat′ing** to set too high an estimate on or for —*n.* an estimate that is too high —**o′ver·es′ti·ma′tion** *n.*

o·ver·ex·ert (-ig zurt′) *vt.* to exert too much or too long: often used reflexively —**o′ver·ex·er′tion** *n.*

o·ver·ex·pose (-ik spōz′) *vt.* **-posed′, -pos′ing** to expose too much or too long —**o′ver·ex·po′sure** (-spō′zhər) *n.*

o·ver·ex·tend (-ik stend′) *vt.* to extend beyond reasonable limits or beyond one's capacity to meet obligations or commitments —**o′ver·ex·ten′sion** (-ik sten′shən) *n.*

o·ver·flow (ō′vər flō′; *for n.*, ō′vər flō′) *vt.* **1.** to flow or spread over or across; flood **2.** to flow over the brim or edge of **3.** to cause to overflow by filling beyond capacity —*vi.* **1.** to flow or spread beyond the limits; run over **2.** to be more than full or complete; be superabundant —*n.* **1.** an overflowing or being overflowed **2.** the amount that overflows; surplus **3.** an outlet for overflowing liquids

o·ver·fly (ō′vər flī′) *vt.* **-flew′, -flown′, -fly′ing** to fly an aircraft over (a specified area) or beyond (a specified place); esp., to fly over (foreign territory) for reconnaissance —**o′ver·flight′** *n.*

o·ver·gar·ment (ō′vər gär′mənt) *n.* an outer garment

☆**o·ver·glaze** (ō′vər glāz′; *for v.*, ō′vər glāz′) *n. Ceramics* **1.** a second glaze applied over the first **2.** a decoration applied over a glaze —*vt.* **-glazed′, -glaz′ing** to cover with a glaze or an overglaze

o·ver·grow (ō′vər grō′) *vt.* **-grew′, -grown′, -grow′ing 1.** to overspread with growth or foliage so as to cover **2.** to grow too large for; outgrow —*vi.* **1.** to grow too large or too fast **2.** to grow beyond normal size —**o′ver·growth′** *n.*

o·ver·grown (-grōn′) *adj.* **1.** overspread with foliage **2.** grown excessively or beyond normal size

o·ver·hand (ō′vər hand′) *adj.* **1.** with the hand over the object it grasps **2.** performed with the hand raised above the elbow or the arm above the shoulder [an *overhand* pitch] **3.** designating or of a style of sewing, or a seam, in which the stitches are passed over two edges to sew them together —*adv.* in an overhand manner —*vt.* ☆to sew overhand —*n. Sports* an overhand stroke

overhand knot a kind of knot: see KNOT, illus.

o·ver·hang (ō′vər haŋ′; *for n.*, ō′vər haŋ′) *vt.* **-hung′, -hang′ing 1.** to hang or project over or beyond **2.** to impend; threaten —*vi.* to hang over; project or jut out over something —*n.* **1.** *a)* the projection of one thing over or beyond another *b)* the amount of such projection *c)* an overhanging or projecting part, as the part of a ship's stern projecting beyond the stern post **2.** *Aeron.* one half the difference in span of two wings **3.** *Archit.* a projection of one part of a structure over another

o·ver·haul (ō′vər hôl′; *also, & for n. always,* ō′vər hôl′) *vt.* **1.** to haul over, as for examination **2.** *a)* to check thoroughly for needed repairs *b)* to make the repairs, adjustments, etc. needed to restore (a motor, etc.) to good working order **3.** to gain on, catch up with, or overtake —*n.* an overhauling; thorough examination or restoration to good working order

o·ver·head (ō′vər hed′; *for adv.*, ō′vər hed′) *adj.* **1.** *a)* located or operating above the level of the head ☆*b)* designating a door, as of a garage, that moves into place overhead when opened **2.** in the sky **3.** on a higher level, with reference to related objects [a machine with an *overhead* drive] **4.** having to do with the overhead of a business **5.** *Sports* made with a downward motion from above the head [an *overhead* stroke] —*n.* **1.** the general,

continuing costs involved in running a business, as of rent, maintenance, utilities, taxes, etc. **2.** *Navy* the ceiling of a compartment —*adv.* above the level of the head; aloft

o·ver·hear (ō′vər hir′) *vt.* **-heard′, -hear′ing** to hear (something spoken or a speaker) without the speaker's knowledge or intention

o·ver·heat (-hēt′) *vt., vi.* to make or become too hot

o·ver·in·dul·gence (-in dul′jəns) *n.* excessive indulgence —**o′ver·in·dul′gent** *adj.* —**o′ver·in·dul′gent·ly** *adv.*

o·ver·is·sue (ō′vər ish′ōō) *n.* an issue, as of bonds or stocks, that exceeds authorization, credit limits, etc.

o·ver·joy (ō′vər joi′) *vt.* to give great joy to; delight

☆**o·ver·kill** (ō′vər kil′) *n.* the capacity of a nation's nuclear weapon stockpile to kill many times the total population of any given nation

o·ver·lad·en (ō′vər lād′n) *adj.* having too heavy a load

o·ver·land (ō′vər land′, -lənd) *adv., adj.* by, on, or across land

O·ver·land Park (ō′vər lənd) [after the *Overland*, or *Santa Fe, Trail* which passed through the area] city in NE Kans.: suburb of Kansas City: pop. 77,000

o·ver·lap (ō′vər lap′; *for n.*, ō′vər lap′) *vt., vi.* **-lapped′, -lap′ping 1.** to lap over; lie upon and extend beyond a part of (something or each other) **2.** to extend over part of (a period of time, sphere of activity, etc.); coincide in part (with) —*n.* **1.** an overlapping **2.** a part that overlaps **3.** the amount or extent of overlapping **4.** the place of overlapping

o·ver·lay (ō′vər lā′; *for n.*, ō′vər lā′) *vt.* **-laid′, -lay′ing 1.** to lay or spread over **2.** to cover or overspread, as with a decorative layer of something **3.** [Archaic] to put too much upon; weigh down; burden; oppress **4.** *Printing* to place an overlay upon —*n.* **1.** anything laid over another thing; covering **2.** a decorative layer or the like, applied in overlaying **3.** a transparent flap showing additional details, areas of color, etc. placed over a map, art work, etc. **4.** *Printing* the paper affixed to the impression surface of a press to help make a uniform impression

o·ver·leaf (ō′vər lēf′) *adj., adv.* on the other side of the page or sheet

o·ver·leap (ō′vər lēp′) *vt.* **1.** to leap over or across **2.** to omit; pass over; ignore **3.** to overreach (oneself) by leaping too far

o·ver·lie (-lī′) *vt.* **-lay′, -lain′, -ly′ing 1.** to lie on or over **2.** to stifle or smother by lying on

o·ver·live (-liv′) *vt.* **-lived′, -liv′ing** [Archaic] to outlive or outlast —*vi.* [Archaic] to continue living; endure

o·ver·load (ō′vər lōd′; *for n.*, ō′vər lōd′) *vt.* to put too great a load in or on —*n.* too great a load

o·ver·long (ō′vər lôŋ′) *adj., adv.* too long

o·ver·look (ō′vər look′; *for n.*, ō′vər look′) *vt.* **1.** to look at from above **2.** to give a view of from above **3.** to rise above; overtop **4.** *a)* to look over or beyond and not see; fail to notice *b)* to ignore; neglect **5.** to pass over indulgently; excuse **6.** *a)* to oversee; supervise *b)* [Now Rare] to inspect; look over **7.** [Archaic] to bewitch by looking at —*n.* ☆a height from which to view surroundings; also, the view —*SYN.* see NEGLECT

o·ver·lord (ō′vər lôrd′) *n.* a lord ranking above other lords, esp. in the feudal system

o·ver·ly (-lē) *adv.* [ME. *ouerly, ouerliche:* see OVER & -LY²] too or too much; excessively

o·ver·man (ō′vər mən; *for v.*, ō′vər man′) *n., pl.* **-men** (-mən) a man above others in power or authority; leader; foreman —*vt.* **-manned′, -man′ning** to supply with more men than necessary

o·ver·mas·ter (ō′vər mas′tər, -mäs′-) *vt.* [ME. *overmaistren*] to overcome; conquer; subdue

o·ver·match (-mach′) *vt.* **1.** to be more than a match for **2.** to match against a superior opponent

o·ver·much (ō′vər much′) *adj., adv.* too much —*n.* too great a quantity; excessive amount

o·ver·nice (-nīs′) *adj.* too nice; too fastidious, precise, etc. —**o′ver·nice′ly** *adv.* —**o′ver·nice′ness** *n.*

o·ver·night (ō′vər nīt′; *for adj.*, ō′vər nīt′) *adv.* **1.** during or through the night **2.** on or during the previous evening **3.** very suddenly —*adj.* **1.** done, happening, or going on during the night **2.** of the previous evening **3.** of or for only one night [an *overnight* guest] ☆**4.** of or for a brief trip [an *overnight* bag]

o·ver·night·er (-nīt′ər) *n.* a small piece of luggage for use on a brief trip

o·ver·pass (ō′vər pas′, -päs′; *for v.*, ō′vər pas′, -päs′) ☆*n.* a bridge or other passageway over or across a road, railway, etc. —*vt.* [Now Rare] **1.** to pass over, across, or through **2.** to surpass; exceed; outdo **3.** to overlook; ignore **4.** to transgress

o·ver·pay (ō′vər pā′) *vt., vi.* **-paid′, -pay′ing 1.** to pay too much, or more than (the due amount) **2.** to pay too much to (someone) —**o′ver·pay′ment** *n.*

o·ver·per·suade (-pər swād′) *vt.* **-suad′ed, -suad′ing** [Rare] to win over by persuading; esp., to persuade (someone) against his natural inclinations

o·ver·play (-plā′) *vt.* **1.** to overact, overdo, or overemphasize **2.** *Card Games* to overestimate the strength of (one's

hand) and be defeated as a result **3.** *Golf* to hit (the ball) beyond the green

o·ver·plus (ō'vər plus'), *n.* [ME. *overe-plus*, partial transl. of MFr. *surplus*, SURPLUS] **1.** an amount left over; surplus ☆**2.** too great an amount; excess

o·ver·pop·u·late (ō'vər päp'yə lāt') *vt.* **-lat'ed, -lat'ing** to populate (an area) too heavily for the available sustaining resources —**o'ver·pop'u·la'tion** *n.*

o·ver·pow·er (-pou'ər) *vt.* **1.** to get the better of by superior power; make helpless **2.** to subdue or overwhelm **3.** to supply with more power than is needed —**o'ver·pow'er·ing** *adj.* —**o'ver·pow'er·ing·ly** *adv.*

o·ver·print (ō'vər print'; *for n.,* ō'vər print') *vt.* to print over or on top of (a previously printed surface) —*n.* **1.** anything overprinted **2.** *a)* anything officially printed over the original design on a stamp *b)* a stamp so overprinted

o·ver·pro·duce (ō'vər prə dōōs', -dyōōs') *vt., vi.* **-duced', -duc'ing** to produce in a quantity that exceeds the need or demand —**o'ver·pro·duc'tion** *n.*

o·ver·proof (ō'vər prōōf') *adj.* containing more alcohol than proof spirit does

o·ver·pro·tect (-prə tekt') *vt.* to protect more than is necessary or desirable; specif., to exercise excessive, damaging control over (one's child, etc.) in seeking to shield from hurt, conflict, disappointment, etc. —**o'ver·pro·tec'tive** *adj.*

o·ver·rate (-rāt') *vt.* **-rat'ed, -rat'ing** to rate, assess, or estimate too highly

o·ver·reach (-rēch') *vt.* **1.** to reach or stretch beyond or above; extend beyond **2.** to reach too far for and miss **3.** to get the better of by cunning or cheating; outwit —*vi.* **1.** to reach too far **2.** to strike the forefoot with the hind foot: said of hoofed animals —**overreach oneself 1.** to fail because of trying to do more than one can **2.** to fail because of being too crafty or eager —**o'ver·reach'er** *n.*

o·ver·re·act (-ri akt') *vi.* to react in a highly emotional way, beyond what seems called for, as by undue use of force

o·ver·ride (-rīd') *vt.* **-rode', -rid'den, -rid'ing 1.** to ride over **2.** to trample down **3.** to suppress or prevail over **4.** to disregard, overrule, or nullify **5.** to fatigue (a horse, etc.) by riding too long **6.** to pass or extend over ☆**7.** *same as* OVERWRITE (*vt.* 3) **8.** *Surgery* to overlap —☆*n. same as* OVERWRITE

o·ver·rule (ō'vər rōōl') *vt.* **-ruled', -rul'ing 1.** to set aside or decide against by virtue of higher authority; rule against or rule out; annul or reverse **2.** to have a dominant influence over; prevail over

o·ver·run (ō'vər run'; *for n.,* ō'vər run') *vt.* **-ran', -run', -run'ning 1.** to run or spread out over so as to cover **2.** to infest or swarm over, as vermin, or rove over and ravage, as an invading army **3.** to invade, defeat, or conquer by a rapid, broad advance **4.** to spread swiftly throughout, as ideas, a fad, etc. **5.** to run or extend beyond (certain limits) [*to overrun* second base] **6.** [Archaic] to outrun **7.** *Printing* to rearrange (lines of type, columns, or pages) by shifting words or letters from one line to another —*vi.* **1.** to overflow **2.** to run over or beyond certain limits —*n.* **1.** the act or an instance of overrunning **2.** the amount that overruns

o·ver·score (ō'vər skôr'; *for n.,* ō'vər skôr') *vt.* **-scored', -scor'ing** to draw a line over or through (a word, sentence, etc.) —*n.* a line over or through a word, sentence, etc.

o·ver·seas (ō'vər sēz') *adv.* abroad; over or beyond the sea —*adj.* **1.** of, from, or to countries across the sea; foreign **2.** over or across the sea Also, chiefly Brit., **o'ver·sea'**

☆**overseas cap** a soft cap without a visor or brim, worn by U.S. forces since World War I

overseas department any of several French possessions, formerly French colonies, having since 1947 the status of departments of metropolitan France

overseas territory any of several French or Portuguese possessions, formerly colonies or protectorates, having administrative autonomy and an appointed governor or high commissioner

o·ver·see (ō'vər sē') *vt.* **-saw', -seen', -see'ing** [ME. *overseen* < OE. *oferseon:* see OVER & SEE[1]] **1.** to watch over and manage; supervise; superintend **2.** to catch sight of (a person or persons in some action) secretly or accidentally **3.** to survey; watch **4.** [Archaic] to examine; inspect

o·ver·se·er (ō'vər sē'ər) *n.* one who watches over and directs the work of others; supervisor

o·ver·sell (ō'vər sel') *vt.* **-sold', -sell'ing 1.** to sell more than can be supplied ☆**2.** to promote, try to persuade, etc. to such an extreme degree as to defeat one's purposes

o·ver·set (ō'vər set'; *for n.,* ō'vər set') *vt.* **-set', -set'ting 1.** to overcome or upset **2.** to overturn or overthrow **3.** to set too great an amount of (type or copy), or too much type for (a given space) —*vi.* to overturn; tip over —*n.* **1.** an overturning **2.** type matter set and not used

o·ver·sew (ō'vər sō', ō'vər sō') *vt.* **-sewed'** or **-sewn', -sew'ing** to sew together (two pieces of material) by passing small, close stitches over their coinciding edges; sew overhand

o·ver·sexed (ō'vər sekst') *adj.* characterized by an exceptional sexual drive or preoccupation with sexual matters

o·ver·shade (ō'vər shād') *vt.* **-shad'ed, -shad'ing** *same as* OVERSHADOW

o·ver·shad·ow (-shad'ō) *vt.* [ME. *ouerschadewen* < OE. *ofersceadwian* (see OVER & SHADOW), transl. of LL. *obumbrare* in NT. (cf. Luke 9:34)] **1.** *a)* to cast a shadow over *b)* to darken; obscure **2.** to be more significant or important than by comparison

☆**o·ver·shoe** (ō'vər shōō') *n.* a kind of shoe or boot of rubber or fabric, worn over the regular shoe to protect against cold or dampness; galosh; rubber

o·ver·shoot (ō'vər shōōt') *vt.* **-shot', -shoot'ing 1.** to shoot or pass over or beyond (a target, mark, etc.); specif., to fly an aircraft beyond (a runway, landing field, etc.) while trying to land **2.** to go farther than (an intended or normal limit); exceed —*vi.* to shoot or go too far

o·ver·shot (ō'vər shät') *adj.* **1.** with the upper part or half extending past the lower [an *overshot* jaw] **2.** driven by water flowing onto the upper part [an *overshot* water wheel]

o·ver·sight (-sīt') *n.* **1.** a superintendence; supervision **2.** an unintentional, careless mistake or omission

o·ver·sim·pli·fy (ō'vər sim'plə fī') *vt., vi.* **-fied', -fy'ing** to simplify to the point of distortion, as by ignoring essential details —**o'ver·sim'pli·fi·ca'tion** *n.*

o·ver·size (ō'vər sīz') *adj.* **1.** too large **2.** larger than the normal or usual; outsize Also **o'ver·sized'** —*n.* a size larger than regular sizes; outsize

☆**o·ver·skirt** (-skurt') *n.* an outer skirt

o·ver·slaugh (ō'vər slô') *vt.* [< Du. *overslaan,* to pass over, omit < *over* (akin to OVER) + *slaan,* to beat, strike (for IE. base *see* SLAY)] ☆**1.** to pass over (one person) by preferring or promoting another ☆**2.** to bar or hinder —*n.* ☆a sand bar or other obstacle to river navigation

o·ver·sleep (-slēp') *vi.* **-slept', -sleep'ing** to sleep past the intended time for getting up

☆**o·ver·soul** (ō'vər sōl') *n.* the spirit which inspires and motivates all living things: a concept in the transcendentalist philosophy of Emerson and others

o·ver·spend (ō'vər spend') *vt.* **-spent', -spend'ing 1.** [Rare] to use till worn out; exhaust **2.** to spend more than —*vi.* to spend more than one can afford

o·ver·spread (-spred') *vt.* **-spread', -spread'ing** to spread over; cover the surface of

o·ver·state (-stāt') *vt.* **-stat'ed, -stat'ing** to give an extravagant or magnified account of (facts, truth, etc.); exaggerate —**o'ver·state'ment** *n.*

o·ver·stay (-stā') *vt.* to stay beyond the time, duration, or limit of

o·ver·step (-step') *vt.* **-stepped', -step'ping** to go beyond the limits of; exceed

o·ver·stock (ō'vər stäk'; *for n.,* ō'vər stäk') *vt.* to stock more of than can be readily used —*n.* too large a stock

o·ver·strain (-strān') *vt.* to put under very great strain; overwork —*vi.* to exert great effort

o·ver·stride (-strīd') *vt.* **-strode', -strid'den, -strid'ing 1.** to stride across or over; go beyond **2.** to outdo; surpass **3.** *same as* BESTRIDE

o·ver·strung (-strun') *adj.* too highly strung; tense

o·ver·stud·y (ō'vər stud'ē) *vt., vi.* **-stud'ied, -stud'y·ing** to study too hard or too much —*n.* too much study

o·ver·stuff (ō'vər stuf') *vt.* **1.** to stuff with too much of something **2.** to upholster (furniture) with deep stuffing —**o'ver·stuffed'** *adj.*

o·ver·sub·scribe (-səb skrīb') *vt., vi.* **-scribed', -scrib'ing** to subscribe for more (of) than is available or asked —**o'ver·sub·scrip'tion** (-skrip'shən) *n.*

o·ver·sup·ply (-sə plī') *vt.* **-plied', -ply'ing** to supply in excess —*n., pl.* **-plies** too great a supply

o·vert (ō vurt', ō'vurt) *adj.* [ME. *overte* < MFr. *overt,* pp. of *ovrir,* to open < VL. **operire* < L. *aperire,* to open: see APERTURE] **1.** not hidden; open; observable; apparent; manifest **2.** *Law* done openly and publicly, without attempt at concealment and with evident intent —**o·vert'ly** *adv.*

o·ver·take (ō'vər tāk') *vt.* **-took', -tak'en, -tak'ing 1.** to catch up with and, often, go beyond **2.** to come upon unexpectedly or suddenly

o·ver·task (-task', -täsk') *vt.* to impose too great or heavy a task or tasks upon

o·ver·tax (-taks') *vt.* **1.** to tax too heavily **2.** to make excessive demands on

o·ver-the-count·er (ō'vər thə koun'tər) *adj.* **1.** sold directly to buyers rather than on the floor of a stock exchange, as unlisted stocks and bonds **2.** *Pharmacy* sold legally without prescription, as some drugs

o·ver·throw (ō'vər thrō'; *for n.,* ō'vər thrō') *vt.* **-threw', -thrown', -throw'ing 1.** to throw or turn over; upset **2.** to overcome; conquer; end **3.** to throw a ball or the like beyond (the intended receiver or target) —*n.* **1.** an overthrowing or being overthrown **2.** destruction; ruin; end —*SYN.* see CONQUER

o·ver·time (ō'vər tim'; *for v.,* -tīm') *n.* **1.** time beyond the established limit, as of working hours **2.** pay for work done in such time **3.** *Sports* an extra time period added to the game to decide a tie —*adj., adv.* of, for, or during a period of overtime —*vt.* **-timed', -tim'ing** to allow too much time for (a photographic exposure, etc.)

o·ver·tone (ō'vər tōn') *n.* [transl. of G. *oberton,* contr. < *oberpartialton,* upper partial tone] **1.** any of the attendant

higher tones heard with a fundamental tone produced by the vibration of a given string or column of air, having a frequency of vibration that is an exact multiple of the frequency of the fundamental **2.** an implication; nuance: *usually used in pl.* [a reply full of *overtones*]

o·ver·top (ō'vər tāp') *vt.* **-topped'**, **-top'ping 1.** to rise above; exceed in height; tower over **2.** to excel; surpass

o·ver·trade (-trād') *vi.* **-trad'ed**, **-trad'ing** to trade beyond one's financial means or the market demand

o·ver·train (-trān') *vt.*, *vi.* to train too long or too hard

o·ver·trick (ō'vər trik') *n.* *Card Games* a trick taken in excess of the number bid

o·ver·trump (ō'vər trump') *vt.*, *vi.* *Card Games* to trump with a higher trump than has been played

o·ver·ture (ō'vər chər, ō'və-) *n.* [ME., an opening < OFr. < VL. *opertura* < L. *apertura*, APERTURE] **1.** an introductory proposal or offer; indication of willingness to negotiate **2.** *a)* a musical introduction to an opera or other large musical work *b)* an independent orchestral composition of varying form **3.** in Presbyterian churches, a proposal or question submitted as by the general assembly to the presbyteries **4.** an introductory section, as of a poem —*vt.* **-tured, -tur·ing** to present as an overture

o·ver·turn (ō'vər turn'; *for n.*, ō'vər turn') *vt.* **1.** to turn or throw over; upset **2.** to conquer; defeat; ruin —*vi.* to turn or tip over; capsize —*n.* an overturning or being overturned —*SYN.* see UPSET

☆**o·ver·un·der** (ō'vər un'dər) *adj.* designating a double-barreled firearm with one barrel over the other

o·ver·use (ō'vər yoōs'; *for v.*, ō'vər yoōz') *n.* too much use —*vt.* **-used', -us'ing** to use too much or too often

o·ver·view (-vyoō') *n.* a general review or survey

o·ver·watch (ō'vər wäch', -wôch') *vt.* **1.** to watch over **2.** [Archaic] to make weary by long watching

o·ver·wea·ry (-wer') *vt.* **-wore', -worn', -wear'ing** to wear out or exhaust

o·ver·wea·ry (-wir'ē) *adj.* weary to the point of exhaustion —*vt.* **-ried, -ry·ing** to make overweary; exhaust

o·ver·ween·ing (-wē'niŋ) *adj.* [ME. *oferweninge*, prp. of *oferwenen* < OE. *oferwenian*: see OVER- & WEEN] **1.** arrogant; excessively proud **2.** exaggerated; excessive —**o'ver·ween'ing·ly** *adv.*

o·ver·weigh (-wā') *vt.* **1.** *same as* OUTWEIGH **2.** to burden; oppress; weigh down

o·ver·weight (ō'vər wāt'; *for adj. & v.*, ō'vər wāt') *n.* more weight than is needed, desired, or allowed; extra or surplus weight —*adj.* above the normal, desirable, or allowed weight —*vt. same as* OVERWEIGH

o·ver·whelm (ō'vər hwelm', -welm') *vt.* [ME. see OVER- & WHELM] **1.** to pour down upon and cover over or bury beneath **2.** to make helpless, as with greater force or deep emotion; overcome; crush; overpower **3.** [Obs.] to overthrow or overturn —**o'ver·whelm'ing** *adj.* —**o'ver·whelm'ing·ly** *adv.*

o·ver·wind (-wind') *vt.* **-wound', -wind'ing** to wind (a watch spring, etc.) too far or too tightly

o·ver·win·ter (-win'tər) *vi.* to pass the winter

o·ver·word (ō'vər wurd') *n.* a much-repeated word or phrase; refrain

o·ver·work (ō'vər wurk'; *for n.*, ō'vər wurk') *vt.* **1.** to work or use to excess [to *overwork* a horse, to *overwork* an excuse] **2.** to decorate the surface of **3.** to make very excited or nervous —*vi.* to work too hard or too long —*n.* **1.** work that is severe or burdensome **2.** work beyond the amount agreed upon; extra work

o·ver·write (ō'vər rīt'; *for n.*, ō'vər rīt') *vt.*, *vi.* **-wrote', -writ'ten, -writ'ing 1.** *a)* to write (something) over other writing *b)* to write over (other writing) **2.** to write too much, or in too flowery or labored a style, about (some subject) **3.** to receive a commission on the sales made by (a subagent) —*n.* the commission paid an agent or manager on sales made by his representatives

o·ver·wrought (ō'vər rôt') *adj.* **1.** formerly, overworked; fatigued **2.** very nervous or excited **3.** with the surface adorned **4.** too elaborate; ornate

o·vi- (ō'vi) [< L. *ovum*, EGG¹] *a combining form meaning* egg or ovum [oviduct, oviform]

Ov·id (äv'id) (L. name, *Publius Ovidius Naso*) 43 B.C.–17? A.D.; Rom. poet

ov·i·duct (ō'vi dukt') *n.* [ModL. *oviductus*: see OVI- & DUCT] a duct or tube through which the ova pass from an ovary to the uterus or to the outside

O·vie·do (ō vye'thō) city in NW Spain: pop. 134,000

o·vif·er·ous (ō vif'ər əs) *adj.* [OVI- + -FEROUS] bearing, producing, or carrying ova

o·vi·form (ō'vi fôrm') *adj.* [OVI- + -FORM] egg-shaped

o·vig·er·ous (ō vij'ər əs) *adj.* [OVI- + -GEROUS] *same as* OVIFEROUS

o·vine (ō'vīn) *adj.* [LL. *ovinus* < L. *ovis*, sheep: for IE. base see EWE] of, or having the nature of, sheep

o·vip·a·rous (ō vip'ər əs) *adj.* [L. *oviparus*: see OVI- & -PAROUS] **1.** producing eggs which hatch after leaving the body of the female **2.** designating or of this type of reproduction Opposed to VIVIPAROUS —**o·vi·par·i·ty** (ō'vi par'ə tē), **o·vip'a·rous·ness** *n.* —**o·vip'a·rous·ly** *adv.*

o·vi·pos·it (ō'vi päz'it, ō'vi päz'it) *vi.* [< OVI- + L. *positus*, pp. of *ponere*, to place: see POSITION] to deposit or lay eggs, esp. by means of an ovipositor —**o'vi·po·si'tion** (-pə zish'ən) *n.*

o·vi·pos·i·tor (ō'vi päz'i tər) *n.* [ModL. < OVI- + L. *positor*, one who places < *ponere*: see prec.] **1.** a special organ of many female insects, usually at the end of the abdomen, for depositing eggs in a suitable place, often in a host **2.** an extension of the female genital orifice of certain fishes

o·vi·sac (ō'vi sak') *n.* [OVI- + SAC] **1.** *same as* OOTHECA **2.** an egg receptacle

o·void (ō'void) *adj.* [OV(I)- + -OID] egg-shaped; ovate: also **o·void'al** —*n.* anything of ovoid form

o·vo·lo (ō'və lō') *n.*, *pl.* **-li'** (-lē') [obs. It. (now *uovolo*), dim. of *ovo* < L. *ovum*, EGG¹] a convex molding, in cross section a quarter of a circle or an ellipse

o·vo·tes·tis (ō'vō tes'tis) *n.* [< OVI- + TESTIS] a single reproductive organ that produces both sperm and ova, usually at different times, as in many mollusks

o·vo·vi·vip·a·rous (ō'vō vi vip'ər əs) *adj.* [< OVI- + VIVIPAROUS] designating various animals, as some reptiles, fishes, and snails, which produce eggs with enclosing membranes, that are hatched within the female's body so that the young are born alive —**o'vo·vi'vi·par'i·ty** (-ō'və par'ə tē), **o'vo·vi·vip'a·rous·ness** *n.* —**o'vo·vi·vip'a·rous·ly** *adv.*

o·vu·lar (ō'vyə lər, äv'yə-) *adj.* [ModL. *ovularis* < *ovulum*: see OVULE] of or having to do with an ovule

o·vu·late (-lāt') *vi.* **-lat'ed, -lat'ing** [back-formation < ff.] to produce and discharge ova from the ovary

o·vu·la·tion (ō'vyə lā'shən, äv'yə-) *n.* [OVUL(E) + -ATION] the process by which a mature ovum escapes from a ruptured Graafian follicle —**o'vu·la·to'ry** (-lə tôr'ē) *adj.*

o·vule (ō'vyoōl, äv'yoōl) *n.* [Fr. < ModL. *ovulum*, dim. < L. *ovum*, EGG¹] a small egg or seed, esp. one in an early stage of development; specif., *a) Bot.* a structure in seed plants consisting of a nucellus that contains an embryo sac: it develops into a seed after fertilization *b) Zool.* the immature ovum while still in the Graafian follicle

o·vum (ō'vəm) *n.*, *pl.* **o·va** (ō'və) [L., EGG¹] **1.** *Biol.* a mature female germ cell which, generally only after fertilization, develops into a new member of the same species **2.** *Archit.* an egg-shaped ornament

ow (ou) *interj.* a cry of pain

OW. Old Welsh

owe (ō) *vt.* **owed, ow'ing** [ME. *owen* < OE. *agan*, to own, possess, have, akin to Goth. *aigan*, OHG. *eigan* < IE. base *eik-*, to have as one's own, be capable (of), whence Sans *īśé*, (he) possesses] **1.** to have an obligation to pay; be indebted to the amount of **2.** to have or feel the need to do, give, etc., as because of gratitude **3.** to have or cherish (a certain feeling) toward another: now only in **owe a grudge 4.** to be indebted (*to*) for the existence of **5.** [Obs.] to own; have —*vi.* to be in debt

Ow·en (ō'ən) [W. < *Owein*, earlier *Ewein* < Celt. *Esuganyos*, akin to Gr. *Eugenios*: see EUGENE¹] **1.** a masculine name **2. Robert**, 1771–1858; Brit. industrialist & socialist **3. Wil·fred** (wil'frid), 1893–1918; Eng. poet

O·wens·bor·o (ō'ənz bur'ō) [after a Col. A. Owen (1769–1811)] city in NW Ky., on the Ohio: pop. 50,000

Owen Stanley Range mountain range in SE New Guinea, in the Territory of Papua: highest peak, 13,363 ft.

ow·ing (ō'iŋ) *adj.* [ME. *owynge*] **1.** that owes **2.** due; unpaid [ten dollars *owing* on a bill] —**owing to** because of; as a result of

owl (oul) *n.* [ME. *owle* < OE. *ule*, akin to G. *eule* < echoic base, whence L. *ulula*, owl, *ululare*, to howl] any of an order (Strigiformes) of night birds of prey found throughout the world, distinguished by a large, flat face, eyes surrounded by stiff-feathered disks, a short, hooked beak, feathered legs with sharp talons, and soft plumage which permits noiseless flight: applied figuratively to a person of nocturnal habits, solemn appearance, etc. —**owl'like'** *adj.*

owl·et (-it) *n.* any young or small owl

owl·ish (-ish) *adj.* like or characteristic of an owl —**owl'ish·ly** *adv.* —**owl'ish·ness** *n.*

owl parrot *same as* KAKAPO

☆**owl's-clo·ver** (oulz'klō'vər) *n.* any of a genus (Orthocarpus) of plants of the figwort family of W N. and S. America; esp., a California species (Orthocarpus purpurascens) with red or purple upper leaves and yellow or purple flowers

own (ōn) *adj.* [ME. *owen* < OE. *agen*, pp. of *agan*, to possess: see OWE] belonging, relating, or peculiar to oneself or itself: used to strengthen a preceding possessive [his *own* book, her *own* idea] —*n.* that which belongs to oneself [the car is his *own*] —*vt.* **1.** to possess; hold as personal property; have **2.** to admit; recognize; acknowledge —*vi.* to confess (*to*) —*SYN.* see ACKNOWLEDGE, HAVE —**come into one's own** to receive what properly belongs to one, esp. acclaim or recognition —**of one's own** belonging strictly to oneself —**on one's own** [Colloq.] *a)* by one's own efforts or on one's own initiative *b)* in-

dependent of help from others —**own up** (**to**) to confess (to) —**own′er** n. —**own′er·less** adj.

own·er·ship (ō′nər ship′) n. **1.** the state or fact of being an owner **2.** legal right of possession; lawful title (to something); proprietorship

ox (äks) n., pl. **ox′en**, rarely **ox**: see PLURAL, II, D, 1 [ME. < OE. *oxa*, akin to G. *ochse* < IE. *ukwsen*, a bull < base *wegw-*, *ūgw-*, wet, sprinkle, whence L. *umere*, to be moist & HUMOR, HUMID] **1.** any of several bovid mammals (genus *Bos* or closely related genera), as the buffalo, bison, gaur, yak, etc. **2.** a castrated bull of a domesticated breed (esp. *Bos taurus*), used as a draft animal

ox- *same as* OXY-

Ox. 1. Oxford **2.** Oxfordshire

ox·a- (äk′sə) [var. < OXY-¹] *Chem.* *a prefix indicating* oxygen, esp. as replacing carbon in a ring

ox·a·late (äk′sə lāt′) n. [Fr.: see ff. & -ATE²] a salt or ester of oxalic acid

ox·al·ic acid (äk sal′ik) [Fr. *oxalique* < L. *oxalis*: see ff.] a colorless, poisonous, crystalline acid, $(COOH)_2$, found in oxalis and other plants or prepared synthetically and used in dyeing, bleaching, etc.

ox·a·lis (äk′sə lis) n. [L., garden sorrel < Gr. *oxalis*, *oxys*, acid, sour (see OXY-²)] *same as* WOOD SORREL

ox·a·zine (-zēn′, -zin) n. [OX- + AZINE] any of thirteen compounds having a composition corresponding to the formula C_4H_5NO and composed of molecules which contain four atoms of carbon and one atom each of oxygen and nitrogen united in a ring structure

ox·blood (äks′blud′) n. a deep red color

ox·bow (-bō′) n. [ME. *oxboue*: see OX & BOW²] **1.** the U-shaped part of an ox yoke which passes under and around the neck of the animal ☆**2.** *a)* something shaped like this, as a bend in a river *b)* the land within such a bend

Ox·bridge (äks′brij) n. [Ox(FORD) + (CAM)BRIDGE] Oxford and Cambridge universities thought of as forming a single entity in terms of their similar organization, traditions, and prestige —adj. of or relating to Oxbridge

OXBOWS

ox·en (äk′s'n) n. pl. of OX

ox·eye (äks′ī′) n. [ME. *oxie*: see OX & EYE] **1.** any of several composite plants, ☆as a sunflowerlike perennial plant (*Heliopsis helianthoides*) of E N. America **2.** any of various birds, as the dunlin

ox-eyed (-īd′) adj. having large, full eyes

☆**oxeye daisy** *same as* DAISY (sense 1)

Oxf. 1. Oxford **2.** Oxfordshire

Ox·ford (äks′fərd) **1.** city in SC England; county seat of Oxfordshire & the site of Oxford University: pop. 110,000 **2.** *same as* OXFORDSHIRE

ox·ford (äks′fərd) n. [after prec.] [*sometimes* O-] **1.** a type of low shoe laced over the instep: also **oxford shoe 2.** a cotton or rayon fabric with a basketlike weave, used for men's shirts, etc.: also **oxford cloth**

Oxford gray a very dark gray, approaching black

Oxford movement a High-Church, anti-liberal movement within the Anglican Church, begun at Oxford University in 1833: see TRACTARIANISM

Ox·ford·shire (äks′fərd shir′) county of SC England: 749 sq. mi.; pop. 324,000; county seat, Oxford

ox·heart (äks′härt′) n. ☆a large, heart-shaped cherry

ox·i·dant (äk′sə dənt) n. an oxidizing agent

ox·i·dase (-dās′, -dāz′) n. [OXID(IZE) + -ASE] any of a group of enzymes which catalyze oxidations, as in the transfer of hydrogen ions to oxygen —**ox′i·da′sic** (-dā′sik, -zik) adj.

ox·i·da·tion (äk′sə dā′shən) n. [Fr.: see OXIDE & -ATION] **1.** orig., the union of a substance with oxygen **2.** the process of increasing the positive valence or of decreasing the negative valence of an element or ion **3.** the process by which electrons are removed from atoms or ions Cf. REDUCTION —**ox′i·da′tive** adj.

ox·i·da·tion-re·duc·tion (-ri duk′shən) n. a chemical reaction in which one of the reactants is reduced (gains one or more electrons) and another reactant is oxidized (loses one or more electrons)

ox·ide (äk′sīd) n. [Fr. < Gr. *oxys*, acid, sour (see OXY-²) + Fr. *(ac)ide*, acid] a binary compound of oxygen with some other element or with a radical

ox·i·dize (äk′sə dīz′) vt. -**dized′**, -**diz′ing** [< OXIDE + -IZE] **1.** to unite with oxygen, as in burning or rusting **2.** to increase the positive valence or decrease the negative valence of (an element or ion) **3.** to remove electrons from (an atom or ion) —vi. to become oxidized —**ox′i·diz′a·ble** adj. —**ox′i·diz′er** n.

ox·ime (äk′sēm, -sim) n. [< OX- + IM(IDE)] any of a series of compounds formed by the action of hydroxylamine on an aldehyde or ketone, in which the oxygen atom of the CHO group of the aldehyde, or of the CO group of the ketone, is replaced by the :NOH group

ox·lip (äks′lip′) n. [OE. *oxanslyppe* < *oxan*, gen. of *oxa* (see OX) + *slyppe*, dropping: cf. COWSLIP] a perennial plant (*Primula elatior*) of the primrose family, having yellow flowers in early spring

Ox·nard (äks′närd) [after Henry T. *Oxnard*, local businessman] city in SW Calif., between Los Angeles & Santa Barbara: pop. 71,000

Oxon. 1. [L. *Oxoniensis*] of Oxford **2.** [L. *Oxonia*] Oxford or Oxfordshire

Ox·o·ni·an (äk sō′nē ən) adj. [< ML. *Oxonia*, Oxford] of Oxford (England) or Oxford University —n. **1.** a student or alumnus of Oxford University **2.** a native or inhabitant of Oxford, England

ox·peck·er (äks′pek′ər) n. any of a group of African starlings that feed on the parasitic ticks found on the hides of large mammals, esp. oxen

ox·tail (-tāl′) n. the tail of an ox or steer, esp. when skinned and used in soup, stew, etc.

ox·ter (äk′stər) n. [Early ModE. *oxtere*, altered < OE. *ohsta*, akin to G. *achsel*, shoulder < IE. base *aks-*: see AXIS¹] [Scot. & Brit. Dial.] the armpit

ox·tongue (äks′tuŋ′) n. [Obs.] any of a number of plants, as alkanet, with rough, tongue-shaped leaves

Ox·us (äk′səs) *ancient name of the* AMU DARYA

ox·y-¹ (äk′si, -sə, -sē) [< OXY(GEN)] *a combining form* *meaning:* **1.** containing oxygen **2.** containing the hydroxyl radical: in this sense *hydroxy-* is preferred

ox·y-² (äk′si, -sə) [< Gr. *oxys*, sharp, acid < IE. *aks-* < base *ak-*, whence Gr. *akmē*, a point, L. *acus*, a needle] *a combining form meaning* sharp, pointed, acute, or acid [*oxycephaly*, *oxymoron*, *oxygen*]

ox·y·a·cet·y·lene (äk′sē ə set′'l ēn′) adj. [OXY-¹ + ACET-YLENE] of or using a mixture of oxygen and acetylene, as for producing an extremely hot flame used in welding or cutting metals [*oxyacetylene* torch]

ox·y·ac·id (-as′id) n. an acid containing oxygen

ox·y·ceph·a·ly (äk′si sef′ə lē) n. [< OXY-² + Gr. *kephalē*, head: see CEPHALIC] a condition in which the skull has a peaked or somewhat conical shape, specif. as a result of the premature closing of the skull sutures —**ox′y·ce·phal′ic** (-sə fal′ik), **ox′y·ceph′a·lous** (-sef′ə ləs) adj.

ox·y·gen (äk′si jən) n. [Fr. *oxygène*, altered (1786) < earlier *oxygine*: both coinages by Lavoisier < Gr. *oxys* (see OXY-²) + Fr. *-gène*, -GEN or *-gine* < L. *gignere*, to beget] a colorless, odorless, tasteless, gaseous chemical element, the most abundant of all elements: it occurs free in the atmosphere, forming one fifth of its volume, and in combination in water, sandstone, limestone, etc.; it is very active, being able to combine with nearly all other elements, and is essential to life processes and to combustion: symbol, O; at. wt., 15.9994; at. no., 8; density, 1.429 g/l (0°C); melt. pt., -218.4°C; boil. pt., -182.96°C —**ox′y·gen′ic** (-jen′ik), **ox′y·ge·nous** (äk sij′ə nəs) adj.

oxygen acid *same as* OXYACID

ox·y·gen·ate (äk′si jə nāt′) vt. -**at′ed**, -**at′ing** [< Fr. *oxygéner* + -ATE¹] to mix, treat, or combine with oxygen —**ox′y·gen·a′tion** n. —**ox′y·gen·a′tor** n.

ox·y·gen·ize (-nīz′) vt. -**ized′**, -**iz′ing** *same as:* **1.** OXIDIZE **2.** OXYGENATE

oxygen tent a transparent enclosure into which oxygen is released, fitted around a bed patient to facilitate his breathing

ox·y·hem·o·glo·bin (äk′si hē′mə glō′bin) n. [OXY-¹ + HEMOGLOBIN] the bright-red substance found in the arterial blood, formed in the lungs by the loose union of hemoglobin with oxygen, which is thus carried to the body tissues

ox·y·hy·dro·gen (-hī′drə jən) adj. [OXY-¹ + HYDROGEN] of or using a mixture of oxygen and hydrogen, as for producing a hot flame used in welding or cutting metals [*oxyhydrogen* torch]

ox·y·mo·ron (äk′si môr′än) n., pl. -**mo′ra** (-ə) [LGr. *oxymōron* < neut. of *oxymōros*, acutely silly: see OXY-² & MORON] a figure of speech in which opposite or contradictory ideas or terms are combined (Ex.: thunderous silence, sweet sorrow)

ox·y·phil (äk′si fil) n. [OXY-² + -PHIL] *same as* ACIDOPHIL: also **ox′y·phile′** (-fīl′) —**ox′y·phil′ic** adj.

ox·y·salt (äk′si sôlt′) n. any salt of an oxyacid

ox·y·sul·fide (äk′si sul′fīd) n. a compound formed of an element or positive radical with oxygen and sulfur, in which oxygen may be thought of as replacing a part of the sulfur

ox·y·tet·ra·cy·cline (äk′si tet′rə sī′klin, -klin) n. [OXY-¹ + TETRA- + CYCL(IC) + -INE⁴] an antibiotic, $C_{22}H_{24}N_2O_9$, derived from cultures of a soil fungus (*Streptomyces rimosus*)

ox·y·to·cic (äk′si tō′sik, -täs′ik) adj. [< Gr. *oxytokion*, medicine for speeding childbirth < *oxys*, sharp, quick (see OXY-²) + *tokos*, birth < *tiktein*, to bear (for base see THANE) + -IC] hastening the process of childbirth, as oxytocin does —n. any oxytocic substance

ox·y·to·cin (-tō′sin, -täs′in) n. [< prec. + -IN¹] a hormone of the posterior pituitary gland, serving to increase the contractions of the smooth muscle of the uterus and facilitate the secretion of milk

ox·y·tone (äk′si tōn′) adj. [Gr. *oxytonos* < *oxys*, sharp (see OXY-²) + *tonos*, TONE] with an acute accent on the last syllable —n. an oxytone word

o·yer (ō′yər) n. [ME. < Anglo-Fr., inf. used as n. < L. *audire*, to hear (see AUDIENCE)] a copy of a bond or other instrument that is the subject of a suit, given to the opposite party instead of being read aloud, as formerly

oyer and ter·mi·ner (tur'mi nər) [ME., for Anglo-Fr. *oyer et terminer*, lit., to hear and determine] 1. a commission issued to English judges authorizing them to hear and determine criminal cases at the assizes 2. formerly in the U.S., the higher criminal courts

o·yez, o·yes (ō'yez', -yes', -yā') *interj.* [ME. < Anglo-Fr. hear ye, pl. imper. of *oyer*: see OYER] hear ye! attention!: usually cried out three times by court or public officials to command silence before a proclamation is made —*n.* a cry of "oyez"

oys·ter (oi'stər) *n.* [ME. < OFr. *oistre* < L. *ostrea* < Gr. *ostreon*, oyster; akin to *osteon*, a bone (see OSSIFY)] 1. any of a genus (*Ostrea*) of marine mollusks with an irregularly shaped, unequal, bivalve shell, attached to objects, esp. at the bottom of the sea, and widely used as food 2. any of several similar or related bivalve mollusks 3. the oyster-shaped bit of meat contained in a depression on each side of the pelvic bone of a fowl 4. something from which profit or advantage can be extracted /the world is his *oyster*/ 5. [Colloq.] a taciturn person

oyster bed a place on the ocean floor naturally suited to, or artificially prepared for, the breeding and cultivation of oysters

oyster catcher any of a family (Hacmatopodidae) of wading birds with a strong, wedge-shaped beak and stout legs, feeding chiefly on bivalve mollusks; esp., an American species (*Haematopus palliatus*), mostly black above and white below

oyster crab any of a family (Pinnotheridae) of small, thin-shelled crabs that live as commensals in the gill cavities of oysters, clams, etc.

☆**oyster cracker** a small, round, salted soda cracker eaten with oyster stews, soups, etc.

oyster farm a place where oyster beds are maintained

oys·ter·man (-mən) *n., pl.* -**men** (-mən) 1. a person who gathers, sells, or raises oysters 2. a vessel used in gathering oysters

oyster plant ☆*same as* SALSIFY

☆**oyster rake** a rake with a long handle and curved teeth for gathering in oysters from shallow waters

☆**oyster stew** a dish consisting of whole oysters in a soup of heated milk or cream, butter, and seasoning

oyster white an off-white color with a creamy or yellowish cast

oz. *pl.* **oz., ozs.** ounce

☆**Oz·a·lid** (äz'ə lid) [arbitrary coinage] *a trademark for* a machine or process for producing positive prints made directly from original drawings or printed material and developed dry in the presence of ammonia vapor —*n.* such a print

O·zark Mountains (ō'zärk) [< Fr. *aux Arcs*, to the (region of the) Arc (Arkansa) Indians] highland region in NW Ark., SW Mo., & NE Okla.: 1,500–2,500 ft. high

O·zarks (ō'zärks) 1. *same as* OZARK MOUNTAINS 2. Lake of the, artificial lake in C Mo., formed by a dam on the Osage River: 130 mi. long

o·zo·ke·rite, o·zo·ce·rite (ə zō'kə rīt', ō'zō kir'īt) *n.* [G. *ozokerit* < Gr. *ozein* (see ff.) + *kēros*, wax] a yellowish-brown to green mineral wax occurring naturally as a mixture of solid hydrocarbons: used in making candles, insulation, etc. and as a substitute for beeswax

o·zone (ō'zōn) *n.* [Fr. < Gr. *ozein*, to smell < IE. base *od-*, whence L. *odor*] 1. an unstable, pale-blue gas, O₃, with a penetrating odor: it is an allotropic form of oxygen, formed usually by a silent electrical discharge in air, and is used as an oxidizing, deodorizing, and bleaching agent and in the purification of water 2. [Slang] pure, fresh air —**o·zon'ic** (-zän'ik, -zō'nik), **o'zo·nous** (-zō nəs) *adj.*

o·zon·ide (ō'zō nīd') *n.* any of a series of compounds formed by the action of ozone on unsaturated organic compounds

o·zon·ize (-nīz') *vt.* -**ized'**, -**iz'ing** 1. to change (oxygen) into ozone 2. to treat or impregnate with ozone — **o'zon·i·za'tion** *n.* —**o'zon·iz'er** *n.*

o·zo·no·sphere (ō zō'nə sfir') *n.* [< OZONE + -SPHERE] the atmospheric layer, extending from a height of c. 6 mi. to c. 30 mi., in which there is an appreciable concentration of ozone, absorbing much ultraviolet radiation and preventing some heat loss from the earth

ozs. ounces

P

P, p (pē) *n., pl.* **P's, p's** 1. the sixteenth letter of the English alphabet: from the Greek *pi*, a borrowing from the Phoenician 2. the sound of *P* or *p*, normally a voiceless bilabial stop 3. a type or impression for *P* or *p* 4. *a symbol for* the sixteenth in a sequence or group (or the fifteenth if J is omitted) —*adj.* 1. of *P* or *p* 2. sixteenth in a sequence or group (or fifteenth if J is omitted) — **mind one's p's and q's** to be careful of one's words and actions

P (pē) *n.* 1. an object shaped like *P* 2. *Chem.* phosphorus 3. *the symbol for:* a) *Genetics* parental generation b) *Physics* power or pressure —*adj.* shaped like *P*

p- 1. *Chem.* para- 2. positive

P 1. *Chess* pawn 2. police 3. *Mil.* prisoner 4. purl

p [Brit.] penny; pennies

P., p. 1. pastor 2. pitcher 3. post 4. power 5. president 6. pressure 7. priest 8. prince

p. 1. *pl.* **pp.** page 2. part 3. participle 4. past 5. penny 6. per 7. peseta 8. peso 9. piano 10. pint 11. pipe 12. pole 13. population 14. pro

pa (pä; *dial. often* pô) *n.* [Colloq.] father; papa

Pa *Chem.* protactinium

Pa. Pennsylvania

P.A. 1. Passenger Agent 2. Post Adjutant 3. power of attorney: also **P/A** 4. press agent 5. public address (system) 6. Purchasing Agent

p.a. 1. participial adjective 2. per annum

PABA para-aminobenzoic acid

☆**Pab·lum** (pab'ləm) [contr. < PABULUM] *a trademark for* a soft, bland cereal food for infants —*n.* [p-] any oversimplified or tasteless writing, ideas, etc.

pab·u·lum (pab'yoo ləm) *n.* [L.] 1. food or sustenance 2. nourishment for the mind 3. *same as* PABLUM

☆**pac** (pak) *n.* [< AmInd. (Lenape) *pacu*, a kind of shoe] 1. orig., a high moccasin; larrigan 2. a high, insulated, waterproof, laced boot, for wear in very cold weather

Pac. Pacific

pa·ca (pä'kə, pak'ə) *n.* [Port. & Sp. < Tupi *páca*] any of a genus (*Cuniculus*) of short-tailed or tailless, burrowing, vegetarian rodents of South and Central America, with spotted brown fur and hooflike toes

pace¹ (pās) *n.* [ME. *pas* < OFr. < L. *passus*, a step, lit., a stretching out of the leg < pp. of *pandere*, to stretch out < IE. base *pet-*, to stretch out, whence FATHOM] 1. a step in walking, running, etc.; stride 2. a unit of length, equal to the length of a step or stride, variously estimated at from 30 in. to 40 in.: the regulation **military pace** is 30 in., or 36 in. for double time The **Roman pace**, measured from the heel of one foot to the heel of the same foot in the next stride, was 5 Roman ft., or 58.1 in., now known as a **geometric pace**, about 5 ft. 3. the rate of speed in walking, running, etc. 4. rate of movement, progress, development, etc. 5. a particular way of walking, running, etc. (of a person or animal); gait; walk 6. the gait of a horse in which both legs on the same side are raised together —*vt.* **paced, pac'ing** 1. to walk or stride back and forth across 2. to measure by paces (often with *off*) 3. to train, develop, or guide the pace of (a horse) 4. to set the pace for (a runner, horse, etc.) 5. to go before and lead 6. to cover (a certain distance) —*vi.* 1. to walk with slow or regular steps 2. to raise both legs on the same side at the same time in moving: said of a horse —**change of pace** 1. variation in tempo or mood, in the presentation of acts in a variety show, etc. 2. *Sports* variation of speed in delivery, as in pitching a slow ball with the same arm movement as a fast ball —**go through one's paces** to show one's abilities, skills, etc. —**keep pace (with)** 1. to go at the same speed (as) 2. to maintain the same rate of progress, etc. (as) —**off the pace** behind the leader; out of first place —**put through one's paces** to test one's abilities, skills, etc. —**set the pace** 1. to go at a speed that others try to equal, as in a race 2. to do or be something for others to emulate

‡**pa·ce²** (pā'sē, pä'che) *prep.* [L., abl. of *pax*, PEACE] with all due respect to: used in expressing polite disagreement

paced (pāst) *adj.* 1. having a specified pace: used in hyphenated compounds /fast-*paced*/ 2. measured by paces or pacing 3. *Horse Racing* having its pace set by a pacemaker

pace·mak·er (pās'māk'ər) *n.* **1.** *a)* a runner, horse, automobile, etc. that sets the pace for others, as in a race *b)* a person, group, or thing that leads the way or serves as a model Also **pace'set'ter 2.** *Anat. a)* a dense network of interwoven fibers in the right atrium of the heart where the stimulus that initiates the heartbeat begins *b)* any of several similar sources of stimulus **3.** *Med.* an electronic device implanted into the body and connected to the wall of the heart, designed to provide regular, mild, electric shock that stimulates contraction of the heart muscles and restores normalcy to the heartbeat —**pace'mak'ing** *n.*

pac·er (pā'sər) *n.* **1.** one who paces **2.** a horse whose normal gait is a pace **3.** *same as* PACEMAKER (sense 1)

pa·cha (pə shä', pä'shə, pash'ə) *n. var. of* PASHA

pa·cha·lic (pə shä'lik) *n. var. of* PASHALIK

pa·chin·ko (pə chin'kō) *n.* [Jap.] a Japanese gambling device like a pinball machine

pa·chi·si (pə chē'zē) *n.* [Hind. *pacīsī* < *pacīs*, twenty-five: so named from the highest throw] **1.** in India, a game for four players in which the moves of the pieces around a board are determined by the throwing of cowrie shells **2.** *same as* PARCHEESI

Pa·chu·ca (pä chōō'kä) city in EC Mexico; capital of Hidalgo state: pop. 65,000

☆**pa·chu·co** (pə chōō'kō) *n., pl.* **-cos** [MexSp. < ?] a member of a Mexican-American neighborhood gang, usually having a small tattoo, as on the wrist

pach·y·derm (pak'ə durm') *n.* [Fr. *pachyderme* < Gr. *pachydermos*, thick-skinned < *pachys*, thick (< IE. base *bhengh-*, thick, dense, whence Sans. *bahú-*, dense, much) + *derma*, a skin (see DERMA[1])] **1.** any of certain large, thick-skinned, hoofed animals, as the elephant, rhinoceros, and hippopotamus, formerly classified together **2.** a thick-skinned, insensitive, stolid person —**pach'y·der'mal, pach'y·der'mic** *adj.*

pach·y·der·ma·tous (pak'ə dur'mə təs) *adj.* **1.** of, or having the nature of, a pachyderm **2.** thick-skinned; insensitive to criticism, insult, etc.: also **pach'y·der'mous** —**pach'y·der'ma·tous·ly** *adv.*

☆**pach·y·san·dra** (-san'drə) *n.* [ModL., name of the genus < Gr. *pachys* (see PACHYDERM) + ModL. *-andrus*, -AN-DROUS] any of a genus (*Pachysandra*) of low, dense-growing, hardy evergreen plants of the box family, often used for a ground cover in the shade

Pa·cif·ic (pə sif'ik) [< ff.: so called by Magellan because of its tranquil appearance] largest of the earth's oceans, between Asia and the American continents: c. 64,000,000 sq. mi.; greatest known depth, 37,782 ft. —*adj.* designating of, in, on, or near this ocean

pa·cif·ic (pə sif'ik) *adj.* [Fr. *pacifique* < L. *pacificus* < *pacificare*, PACIFY] **1.** making or tending to make peace; appeasing; conciliatory **2.** of a peaceful nature or disposition; not warlike; mild; tranquil; calm Also [Rare] **pa·cif'i·cal** —**pa·cif'i·cal·ly** *adv.*

Pa·cif·i·ca (pə sif'ə kə) city in W Calif., on the Pacific: suburb of San Francisco: pop. 36,000

pa·cif·i·cate (-ə kāt') *vt.* **-cat'ed, -cat'ing** *same as* PACIFY —**pa·cif'i·ca'tor** *n.* —**pa·cif'i·ca·to'ry** (-kə tôr'ē) *adj.*

pac·i·fi·ca·tion (pas'ə fi kā'shən) *n.* [Fr. < L. *pacificatio*] a pacifying or being pacified

Pacific Islands, Trust Territory of the U.S. trust territory in the W Pacific, consisting of the Caroline, Marshall, & Mariana islands: 700 sq. mi.; pop. 92,000

pa·cif·i·cism (pə sif'ə siz'm) *n. chiefly Brit. var. of* PACIFISM —**pa·cif'i·cist** *n., adj.*

☆**Pacific Standard Time** a standard time used in a zone which includes the W States of the U.S., corresponding to the mean local time of the 120th meridian west of Greenwich, England: it is eight hours behind Greenwich time: see TIME, chart

pac·i·fi·er (pas'ə fī'ər) *n.* **1.** a person or thing that pacifies ☆**2.** a nipple or teething ring for babies

pac·i·fism (-fiz'm) *n.* [Fr. *pacifisme*: see PACIFIC & -ISM] opposition to the use of force under any circumstances; specif., refusal for reasons of conscience to participate in war or any military action —**pac'i·fist** *n., adj.* —**pac'i·fis'tic** *adj.* —**pac'i·fis'ti·cal·ly** *adv.*

pac·i·fy (pas'ə fī') *vt.* **-fied', -fy'ing** [ME. *pacifien* < OFr. *pacefier* < L. *pacificare* < *pax* (gen. *pacis*), PEACE + *facere*, to make: see FACT] **1.** to make peaceful or calm; appease; tranquilize **2.** *a)* to establish or secure peace in (a nation, etc.) *b)* to seek to neutralize or win over (people in occupied areas) —**pac'i·fi'a·ble** *adj.*

SYN.—**pacify** implies a making quiet and peaceful that which has become noisy or disorderly [to *pacify* a crying child]; **appease** suggests a pacifying by gratifying or giving in to the demands of [to *appease* one's hunger]; **mollify** suggests a soothing or an allaying of wounded feelings or an allaying of indignation [his compliments failed to *mollify* her]; **placate** implies the changing of a hostile or angry attitude to a friendly or favorable one [to *placate* an offended colleague]; **propitiate** implies an allaying or forestalling of hostile feeling by winning the good will of [to *propitiate* a deity]; **conciliate** implies the use of arbitration, concession, persuasion, etc. in an attempt to win over —ANT. anger, enrage

pack[1] (pak) *n.* [ME. *pakke* < MDu. *pak* < MFl. *pac*: term carried throughout Europe via the Low Countries' wool trade (as in Fr. *pacque*, It. *pacco*, Ir. *pac*, ML. *paccus*)] **1.** a large bundle of things wrapped or tied up for carrying, as on the back of a man or animal; load; burden **2.** a

container in which something may be stored compactly [parachute *pack*] **3.** a number of similar or related persons or things; specif., *a)* a group or collection [a *pack* of lies] *b)* a package of a standard number [a *pack* of cigarettes] *c)* same as FILM PACK *d)* a set of playing cards; deck *e)* a set of hunting hounds *f)* a number of wild animals living and hunting together *g)* combat craft moving together [submarine *pack*] *h)* a united group; gang; set **4.** *same as* ICE PACK **5.** *a)* treatment by wrapping a patient in blankets or sheets that are wet or dry and hot or cold *b)* the blankets or sheets used **6.** any of various cosmetic pastes applied to the skin and left to dry [mudpack] **7.** *a)* the amount of food put in cans, etc. in a season or year *b)* a method of packing or canning [cold *pack*] —*vt.* [ME. *pakken*] **1.** to make a pack, or bundle, of **2.** *a)* to put together compactly in a box, trunk, etc. for carrying or storing *b)* to fill (a box, bag, trunk, etc.) for carrying or storing **3.** to put (food) in (cans, boxes, etc.) for preservation or sale **4.** *a)* to fill closely; crowd; cram [a hall *packed* with people] *b)* to crowd or press (people) together **5.** to fill in or surround tightly for protection, prevention of leaks, etc. [to *pack* valves] **6.** to press together firmly [*packed* earth] **7.** to load (an animal) with a pack **8.** to carry (goods, equipment, etc.) in or as in a pack: said of an animal **9.** to treat with a pack (sense 5 *a)* **10.** to send (*off*), usually in haste [to *pack* a boy off to school] ☆**11.** [Slang] to wear or carry (a gun, etc.) as part of one's regular equipment **12.** [Slang] *a)* to deliver or be able to deliver (a blow, punch, etc.) with force *b)* to provide or contain [a play that *packs* a message] —*vi.* **1.** to make up packs **2.** to put one's clothes, belongings, etc. into luggage for a trip [an hour in which to *pack*] **3.** to press, crowd, or throng together in a small space **4.** to admit of being folded compactly, put in a container, etc. [a suit that *packs* well] ☆**5.** to settle into a compact or solid mass **6.** to go away in haste (sometimes with *off*) —*adj.* **1.** *a)* used in packing *b)* suitable for packing **2.** formed in a pack or packs **3.** used for carrying packs, loads, etc. [a *pack* animal] —SYN. see BUNDLE, GROUP —**send packing** to dismiss (a person) abruptly —**pack'a·ble** *adj.*

pack[2] (pak) *vt.* [orig. unc., but infl. by prec.] **1.** to choose or arrange (a jury, court, etc.) in such a way as to get desired decisions, results, etc. **2.** to cheat by prearranging (a deck of playing cards)

pack[3] (pak) *adj.* [prob. altered < *pact*, ult. < L. *pactus*: see PACT] [Scot.] closely acquainted; intimate

☆**-pack** (pak) *a combining form meaning* a carton of (a specified number of) bottles or cans, as of beer

pack·age (pak'ij) *n.* **1.** orig., the act or process of packing **2.** a wrapped or boxed thing or group of things; parcel **3.** a container, wrapping, etc., esp. one in which a commodity is packed for sale ☆**4.** a number of items, plans, etc. offered or proposed as an inseparable unit **5.** a self-contained component or unit, usually one that is pre-assembled —*vt.* **-aged, -ag·ing 1.** to wrap or box, as for transporting, carrying, etc. **2.** to wrap or seal (a commodity) in a container, wrappings, etc. designed to attract purchasers **3.** to put together or offer as a unit —*adj.* ☆designating or of a plan, offer, etc. by which a number of items are offered for acceptance as an inseparable unit [*package* deal, *package* tour] —SYN. see BUNDLE —**pack'ag·er** *n.*

☆**package store** a retail store where alcoholic beverages are sold by the bottle to be drunk off the premises

pack·er (-ər) *n.* a person or thing that packs; specif., *a)* a person who packs goods for preservation, transportation, or sale ☆*b)* a person who owns or manages a packing house ☆*c)* a person who transports goods on pack animals

pack·et (-it) *n.* [MFr. *paquet*, dim. of *pacque*, PACK[1]] **1.** orig., a parcel of letters **2.** a small package or parcel **3.** same as PACKET BOAT **4.** [Brit. Slang] a large amount of money —*vt.* to make up into a packet

packet boat [so called from orig. carrying mail] a boat that travels a regular route, as along a coast or on a river, carrying passengers, freight, and mail

pack ice *same as* ICE PACK (sense 1)

pack·ing (-in) *n.* **1.** the act or process of a person or thing that packs; specif., *a)* the large-scale, esp. commercial, processing and packaging of meats, fruits, or vegetables *b)* *Med.* the filling of a wound or cavity with gauze, etc. to permit drainage and prevent closure **2.** any material used to pack, as excelsior, cardboard, etc. used in packages to cushion and brace the contents, a substance put around valves to make them watertight, etc.

packing box (or **case**) a large crate or box for storing or shipping goods

packing fraction the ratio of the mass defect of an isotope to its mass number, equal to $M - A \div A$, where M is the atomic mass and A is the mass number: usually expressed as parts per 10,000

☆**packing house** a plant where meats are processed and packed for sale; also, a similar plant for packing fruits and vegetables

pack·man (-mən) *n., pl.* **-men** (-mən) a peddler

☆**pack rat** any of a genus (*Neotoma*) of N. American rats that often carry off and hide small articles in their nests

☆**pack·sack** (-sak') *n.* a traveling sack of canvas or leather, usually carried strapped on the shoulders

pack·sad·dle (-sad''l) *n.* a saddle with fastenings to secure and balance the load carried by a pack animal

pack·thread (-thred') *n.* strong, thick thread or twine for tying bundles, packages, etc.

☆**pack train** a train, or procession, of pack animals

pact (pakt) *n.* [ME. < OFr. < L. *pactum*, neut. of *pactus*, pp. of *paciscere*, to agree < *pax*, PEACE] an agreement between persons, groups, or nations; compact; covenant

pad[1] (pad) *n.* [echoic, but infl. by PAD[2]] the dull sound made by a footstep or staff on the ground

pad[2] (pad) *n.* [? var. of POD[1]] **1.** a soft, stuffed saddle **2.** anything made of or stuffed with soft material to fill out a shape, protect against friction, pressure, jarring, or blows, etc.; cushion [a shoulder *pad*, seat *pad*] **3.** a piece of folded gauze, compressed cotton, etc. used as a dressing or protection on a wound, etc. **4.** *a)* the foot or footprint of certain animals, as the wolf, fox, etc. *b)* any of the cushionlike parts on the underside of the foot of some animals ☆**5.** the floating leaf of a water plant, as the water lily **6.** a number of sheets of paper for writing or drawing, glued together along one edge; tablet **7.** an absorbent cushion soaked with ink for inking a rubber stamp: in full, **stamp pad** or **ink pad 8.** *same as* LAUNCH PAD **9.** [Slang] *a)* a pallet or bed *b)* the room, apartment, etc. where one lives —*vt.* **pad'ded, pad'ding 1.** to stuff, cover, or line with a pad or padding **2.** to lengthen (a speech or piece of writing) by inserting unnecessary or irrelevant material ☆**3.** to fill (an expense account, etc.) with invented or inflated entries

pad[3] (pad) *vi.* **pad'ded, pad'ding** [< ff., akin to LowG. *padden*] **1.** to travel on foot; walk; tramp **2.** to walk or run with a soft, almost soundless, step

pad[4] (pad) *n.* [Du. *pad*, PATH] **1.** [Brit. Dial.] a path; road; way **2.** a horse with an easy, slow pace **3.** [Now Rare] a highwayman or footpad

Pa·dang (pä däŋ') seaport on the W coast of Sumatra, Indonesia: pop. 144,000

pa·dauk (pä douk') *n.* [< native name in Burma] a reddish wood obtained from various trees (genus *Pterocarpus*) of the legume family, native to Asia and Africa

padded cell a cell, or room, for the confinement of violently deranged patients or prisoners, lined with heavy, soft material as a protection against injury

pad·ding (pad'iŋ) *n.* **1.** the action of a person who pads **2.** any soft material used to pad, as cotton, felt, etc. **3.** material, often unnecessary or irrelevant, inserted in a speech, writing, etc. to make it longer

Pad·ding·ton (pad'iŋ tən) metropolitan borough of London: pop. 114,000

pad·dle[1] (pad'l) *n.* [ME. *padell*, small spade < ?] **1.** a relatively short oar with a wide blade at one end or both ends, used, without an oarlock, to propel a canoe **2.** any of various implements shaped like this; specif., *a)* a metal tool for stirring iron in a furnace *b)* a small, flat, wooden instrument for working butter, stirring clay, etc. ☆*c)* a flat stick used for beating clothes in washing them by hand, as in a stream *d)* a flat, wooden stick for administering punishment by beating ☆*e)* a flat, rounded piece of wood with a short handle, used to hit a ball, as in table tennis **3.** any of the propelling boards in a water wheel or paddle wheel —*vi.* **-dled, -dling 1.** to propel a canoe, etc. by means of a paddle **2.** to row slowly and gently —*vt.* **1.** to propel (a canoe, etc.) by means of a paddle or paddles **2.** to punish by beating as with a paddle; spank **3.** to stir, work, etc. with a paddle —☆**paddle one's own canoe** to depend entirely on oneself —**pad'dler** *n.*

pad·dle[2] (pad'l) *vi.* **-dled, -dling** [prob. freq. < PAD[3]] **1.** to move the hands or feet about in the water, as in playing; dabble **2.** to walk like a small child; toddle **3.** [Archaic] to play idly with the fingers (*on, in,* etc.) —**pad'dler** *n.*

☆**paddle ball** a game similar to squash racquets, played in a walled court with short-handled rackets

☆**pad·dle·fish** (-fish') *n., pl.* **-fish', -fish'es:** see FISH[2] any of a family (Polyodontidae) of large fishes of the Mississippi and Yangtse rivers, with a paddle-shaped snout

☆**paddle tennis** an outdoor game played with paddles and a rubber ball on a raised platform surrounded by a screen, combining elements of tennis, handball, and squash

paddle wheel a wheel with paddles set at right angles about its circumference for propelling a steamboat

pad·dock[1] (pad'ək) *n.* [ME. *paddoke* < *padde* (< OE. *pad*, frog, toad) + *-ok, -OCK*] **1.** [Scot.] a frog **2.** [Archaic] a toad

pad·dock[2] (pad'ək) *n.* [phonetic alteration of earlier *parrock* < ME. *parrok*, an enclosed field < OE. *pearruc*, enclosure: see PARK] **1.** a small field or enclosure near a stable, in which horses are exercised **2.** an enclosure at a race track, where horses are saddled and walked before a race **3.** in Australia, an enclosed piece of land —*vt.* to shut in a paddock

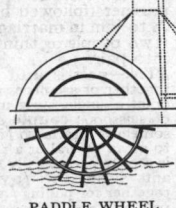

PADDLE WHEEL

Pad·dy (pad'ē) *n., pl.* **-dies** [< *Pádraig*, Ir. form of PATRICK] *a nickname for* IRISHMAN

pad·dy (pad'ē) *n., pl.* **-dies** [Malay *padi*] **1.** rice in the husk, growing or gathered **2.** rice in general **3.** a rice field: often **rice paddy**

☆**paddy wagon** [prob. < PADDY: cf. ff.] *slang name for* PATROL WAGON

pad·dy·whack (-hwak', -wak') *n.* [orig., an Irishman (PADDY + WHACK: cf. "get one's Irish up")] **1.** [Brit. Dial.] a rage; temper **2.** [Colloq.] a beating or spanking —*vt.* [Colloq.] to beat or spank

Pa·de·rew·ski (pä'de ref'skē; *E.* pad'ə ref'skē), **I·gnace Jan** (ē'nyäs' yän) 1860–1941; Pol. pianist & composer; prime minister of Poland (1919)

pa·di·shah (pä'dē shä') *n.* [Per. *pädshäh* < *pati,* master + *shäh,* SHAH] **1.** a great king; emperor **2.** [*often* P-] *a former title of: a)* the shah of Iran *b)* the sultan of Turkey *c)* the British sovereign as emperor of India

pad·lock (pad'läk') *n.* [ME. *padlocke* < *pad* (< ?) + *lokke,* LOCK[1]] a removable lock with a hinged or pivoted link to be passed through a staple, chain, or eye —*vt.* **1.** to fasten with or as with a padlock **2.** to close (a building) against entrance

Pa·do·va (pä'dô vä) *It. name of* PADUA

pa·dre (pä'drā, -drē; *Sp.* -*three*) *n., pl.* **-dres** (-dräz, -drēz; *Sp.* -*three*s); *It.* **pa'dri** (-drē) [Sp., Port., It. < L. *pater,* FATHER] **1.** father: the title of a priest in Italy, Spain, Portugal, and Latin America **2.** [Slang] a priest or chaplain

pa·dro·ne (pə drō'nē; *It.* pä drô'ne) *n., pl.* **-nes;** *It.* **-ni** (-nē) [It. < L. *patronus,* PATRON] **1.** patron; master; boss **2.** in Italy *a)* a master of a Mediterranean trading ship *b)* an innkeeper ☆**3.** formerly, a contractor for immigrant Italian laborers in America

Pad·u·a (paj'ōō ə, pad'yōō ə) commune in N Italy, in Veneto: pop. 214,000: It. name, PADOVA

pad·u·a·soy (paj'oo wə soi') *n.* [altered (after prec.) < earlier *poudesoy* < Fr. *pou-de-soie*] **1.** a rich, corded silk cloth of a kind used in hangings, vestments, etc. **2.** a garment made of this

Pa·dus (pä'dəs) *ancient name of the* Po

pae·an (pē'ən) *n.* [L. < Gr. *paian,* hymn < *Paian,* epithet of Apollo] **1.** in ancient Greece, a hymn of thanksgiving to the gods, esp. to Apollo **2.** a song of joy, triumph, praise, etc.

pae·do- (pē'də, ped'ə) *same as* PEDO-: also **paed-**

pae·do·gen·e·sis (pē'də jen'ə sis) *n.* [PAEDO- + -GENESIS] reproduction by larval or juvenile animal forms —**pae'do·gen'ic** (-jen'ik), **pae'do·ge·net'ic** (-jə net'ik) *adj.*

pa·el·la (pä yel'ə; *Sp.* pä e'lyä) *n.* [Catal., lit., cooking pot < OFr. *paelle* < L. *patella,* a small pan: see PATELLA] a Spanish dish of rice cooked with chicken, seafood, etc. and seasoned with saffron

pae·on (pē'ən) *n.* [L. < Gr. (Attic) *paiōn,* PAEAN] *Gr. & Latin Prosody* a foot of three short syllables and one long syllable occurring in any order

pae·sa·no (pī sä'nō, -zä'-) *n., pl.* **-ni** (-nē), **-nos** [It. < LL. *pagensis:* see PEASANT] a fellow countryman; esp., a fellow Italian: also **pae·san'**

Paes·tum (pes'təm) ancient Greek city in S Italy

pa·gan (pā'gən) *n.* [ME. < LL.(Ec.) *paganus,* a heathen, pagan (contrasted with Christian or Jew) < L., a peasant, rustic < *pagus,* country < IE. base *pak-,* to join, enclose, fasten, whence L. *pax* & *FANG*] **1.** a person who is not a Christian, Moslem, or Jew; heathen: formerly, sometimes applied specif. to a non-Christian by Christians **2.** a person who has no religion —*adj.* **1.** of pagans or paganism; not Christian, Moslem, or Jewish **2.** not religious; heathen —**pa'gan·dom** *n.* —**pa'gan·ish** *adj.* —**pa'gan·ism** *n.*

SYN.—**pagan** and **heathen** are both applied to nonmonotheistic peoples, but **pagan** specifically refers to one of the ancient polytheistic peoples, esp. the Greeks and Romans, and **heathen** is applied to any of the peoples regarded as primitive idolaters; **gentile** (often **Gentile**) is applied to one who is not a Jew, or, among Mormons, one who is not a Mormon

Pa·ga·ni·ni (pä'gä nē'nē; *E.* pag'ə nē'nē), **Ni·co·lò** (nē'kô lô') 1782–1840; It. violinist & composer

pa·gan·ize (pā'gə nīz') *vt., vi.* **-ized', -iz'ing** [ML. *paganizare*] to make or become pagan —**pa'gan·iz'er** *n.*

page[1] (pāj) *n.* [Fr. < L. *pagina,* a page < base of *pangere,* to fasten: see PEACE] **1.** *a)* one side of a leaf of a book, newspaper, letter, etc. *b)* the printing or writing on such a leaf, often with reference to the particular contents [the sports *pages*] *c)* an entire leaf in a book, etc. **2.** [*often pl.*] a record of events [the *pages* of history] **3.** an event or series of events that might fill a page [a colorful *page* in his life] **4.** *Printing* the type set for printing a page —*vt.* **paged, pag'ing 1.** to number the pages of **2.** to make up (copy set in type) into pages —*vi.* to turn pages as in scanning [to *page* through a book]

page[2] (pāj) *n.* [ME. < OFr. < It. *paggio*] **1.** formerly, a boy training for knighthood, who attended a knight **2.** a boy attendant or servant, esp. one serving a person of high rank, as in court **3.** a boy, often in uniform, who runs errands, carries messages, etc., as in a hotel, legisla-

ture, etc. —*vt.* **paged, pag′ing** 1. to attend as a page ☆2. to try to find, summon, or notify (a person) by calling his name, as a hotel page does

Page (pāj), **Walter Hines** (hīnz) 1855–1918; U.S. journalist, editor, & diplomat

pag·eant (paj′ənt) *n.* [ME. *pagent* (with unhistoric -*t*) < earlier *pagyn* < Anglo-L. *pagina,* scene displayed on a stage, stage < L., PAGE¹] 1. orig., *a)* an individual scene in a medieval mystery play *b)* any of a series of movable outdoor platforms on which a mystery play was performed 2. a spectacular exhibition, elaborate parade, etc., as a procession with floats 3. an elaborate drama, often staged outdoors, celebrating a historical event or presenting the history of a community 4. empty pomp or display; mere show

pag·eant·ry (-ən trē) *n., pl.* **-ries** 1. pageants collectively 2. grand spectacle; gorgeous display 3. empty show or display

page·boy (pāj′boi′) *n.* [from its resemblance to the groomed hair of knights' pages] a woman's hair style in which the hair is worn straight and close to the head in a long bob, with the ends rolled under

Pag·et (paj′ət), **Sir James** 1814–99; Eng. surgeon & pathologist

pag·i·nal (paj′ə n'l) *adj.* [LL. *paginalis*] 1. of or consisting of pages 2. page for page

pag·i·nate (-nāt′) *vt.* **-nat′ed, -nat′ing** [back-formation < ff.] to number the pages of (a book, etc.)

pag·i·na·tion (paj′ə nā′shən) *n.* [< L. *pagina,* PAGE¹ + -TION] 1. the act of numbering the pages of a book, etc. 2. the marks or figures with which pages are numbered in sequence 3. the arrangement and number of pages, as noted in a catalog

pa·go·da (pə gō′də) *n.* [Port. *pagode,* prob. < Per. *butkadah,* house of idols < *but,* idol + *kadah,* house, dwelling, prob. infl. by Prakrit *bhagodī,* divine, holy < Sans. *bhaga-vatī,* divine, deity] in India and the Far East, a temple in the form of a pyramidal tower of several stories, usually an odd number, commonly built over a sacred relic or as a work of devotion

PAGODA

Pa·go Pa·go (päŋ′ō päŋ′ō, pä′gō pä′gō) seaport on the S coast of Tutuila Island, American Samoa: pop. 2,500

pa·gu·rid (pə gyoor′id, pag′yoo rid) *n.* [< L. *pagurus,* kind of crab < Gr. *pagouros* < base of *pagos,* hard object + *oura,* tail + -ID] any of a family (Paguridae) of ten-legged, marine crustaceans, including most of the hermit crabs, that have a soft, asymmetrical abdomen and inhabit empty snail shells —*adj.* of or pertaining to the pagurids Also **pa·gu′ri·an** (-ē ən)

pah (pä, pa, pə) *interj.* an exclamation expressing disgust, contempt, or disbelief

Pa·hang (pä häŋ′) state of the Federation of Malaya, on the South China Sea: 13,873 sq. mi.; pop. 399,000

Pah·la·vi (pä′lə vē) *n.* same as PEHLEVI

pah·la·vi (pä′lə vē) *n., pl.* **-vi** [Per. *pahlawī,* orig., belonging to Riza Khan *Pahlawi* (1877–1944), Shah of Persia] a former gold coin of Iran

☆**pa·ho·e·ho·e** (pä hō′ē hō′ē) *n.* [Haw.] solidified lava with a smooth, billowy, or ropy surface: cf. AA

paid (pād) *pt. & pp.* of PAY¹

pail (pāl) *n.* [ME. *paile* < OE. *pægel,* small measure, wine vessel < LL. *pagella* (dim. of L. *pagina,* PAGE¹), a small page, in VL., a measure of area, later a measure of volume: infl. by OFr. *paele,* a pan < L. *patella,* dim. of *patina:* see PATEN] 1. a more or less cylindrical container, usually with a hoop-shaped handle, for holding and carrying liquids, etc.; bucket 2. the amount held by a pail: also **pail′ful′,** *pl.* **-fuls′**

pail·lasse (pal yas′, pal′yas) *n.* same as PALLIASSE

pail·lette (pal yet′; Fr. pá yet′) *n.* [Fr., dim. of *paille,* straw: see PALLET²] a small, shiny ornament, as a metal disk, used in decorating women's dresses, etc.; spangle

pain (pān) *n.* [ME. *peine* < OFr. < L. *poena,* penalty, punishment < Gr. *poinē,* penalty: see PENAL] 1. orig., penalty or punishment 2. a sensation of hurting, or strong discomfort, in some part of the body, caused by an injury, disease, or functional disorder, and transmitted through the nervous system 3. the distress or suffering, mental or physical, caused by great anxiety, anguish, grief, disappointment, etc. 4. [*pl.*] the labor of childbirth 5. [*pl.*] great care or effort [to take *pains* with one's work] 6. [Slang] an annoyance: often used in phrases specifying a part of the body (e.g., **pain in the neck**) —*vt.* to cause pain to; cause to suffer; hurt; distress —*vi.* to have or cause pain —**feel no pain** [Slang] to be drunk —**on** (or **upon** or **under**) **pain of** at the risk of bringing upon oneself (punishment, death, etc.)

Paine (pān) 1. **Robert Treat** (trēt), 1731–1814; Am. jurist & statesman 2. **Thomas,** 1737–1809; Am. Revolutionary patriot, writer, & political theorist, born in England

pained (pānd) *adj.* 1. hurt or distressed; having the feelings hurt; offended 2. showing hurt feelings or resentment [a *pained* expression]

pain·ful (pān′fəl) *adj.* 1. causing pain; hurting; distressing 2. full of or suffering with pain; aching [a *painful* finger] 3. requiring trouble and care; exacting and difficult 4. annoying or tedious [a long, *painful* lecture] 5. [Archaic] painstaking —**pain′ful·ly** *adv.* —**pain′ful·ness** *n.*

☆**pain·kill·er** (-kil′ər) *n.* [Colloq.] a medicine that relieves pain; analgesic

pain·less (-lis) *adj.* 1. free from or without pain 2. not causing or involving pain [*painless* childbirth] —**pain′less·ly** *adv.* —**pain′less·ness** *n.*

pains·tak·ing (pānz′tā′kiŋ) *n.* the act of taking pains; great care or diligence —*adj.* 1. taking pains; very careful; diligent 2. characterized by great care —**pains′tak′ing·ly** *adv.*

paint (pānt) *vt.* [ME. *peinten* < OFr. *peint,* pp. of *peindre* < L. *pingere,* to paint, embroider < IE. base *peig-,* to mark by scratching or coloring, whence Gr. *pikros,* sharp, OE. *fag,* stained] 1. *a)* to make (a picture, design, etc.) in colors applied to a surface *b)* to depict or portray with paints [to *paint* a landscape] 2. to describe colorfully or vividly; depict in words 3. to cover or decorate with paint; color [to *paint* a wall] 4. to apply cosmetics to; adorn; beautify 5. *a)* to apply (a medicine, etc.) with a brush or swab *b)* to treat (a wound, etc.) in this way —*vi.* 1. to practice the art of painting pictures 2. to use cosmetics —*n.* 1. *a)* a mixture of a pigment with oil, water, etc., in liquid or paste form, applied as with a brush, roller, or spray gun, and used for protective covering or coloring of a surface or for making pictures on canvas, paper, etc. *b)* dry pigment for such use 2. a dried coat of paint 3. *a)* coloring matter, such as lipstick, rouge, etc., used as a cosmetic *b)* same as GREASEPAINT ☆4. [Dial.] a piebald horse; pinto —**paint out** to cover up with or as with a coat of paint —☆**paint the town (red)** [Slang] to go on a boisterous spree; carouse —**paint′a·ble** *adj.*

paint·brush (-brush′) *n.* 1. a brush used for applying paint ☆2. same as: *a)* INDIAN PAINTBRUSH *b)* DEVIL'S PAINTBRUSH

☆**painted bunting** a brightly colored blue, green, red, and brown variety of finch (*Passerina ciris*) found in the SE U.S.

painted cup ☆same as INDIAN PAINTBRUSH

Painted Desert [so named from the colorful rock strata] desert plateau in NC Ariz., east of the Colorado River

paint·er¹ (pānt′ər) *n.* 1. an artist who paints pictures 2. a person whose work is covering surfaces, as walls, with paint

paint·er² (pānt′ər) *n.* [LME. *paynter* < OFr. *pentour,* ult. < L. *pendere,* to hang: see PEND] a rope attached to the bow of a boat for tying it to a wharf, mooring, etc.

☆**paint·er³** (pānt′ər) *n.* [altered < PANTHER] *dial. var.* of COUGAR

paint·er·ly (-lē) *adj.* 1. orig., of or characteristic of a painter 2. characterized by those qualities related to a painter's techniques in applying colors in masses, esp. with a thick, rough surface texture, as distinguished from linear qualities that emphasize outline and contour

painter's colic same as LEAD COLIC

paint·ing (pānt′iŋ) *n.* 1. the act or occupation of covering surfaces with paint 2. *a)* the act, art, or occupation of applying paints to canvases, paper, etc. in producing pictures and compositions *b)* a picture or composition so painted

paint·y (-ē) *adj.* **paint′i·er, paint′i·est** 1. of, smeared, or covered with paint 2. having more paint than necessary: said of a picture

pair (per) *n., pl.* **pairs;** sometimes, after a number, **pair** [ME. *paire* < OFr. < L. *paria,* neut. pl. of *par,* equal: see PAR] 1. two similar or corresponding things joined, associated, or used together [a *pair* of gloves] 2. a single thing made up of two corresponding parts that are used together [a *pair* of pants] 3. two persons or animals; specif., *a)* a married, engaged, or courting couple *b)* two mated animals *c)* any two people considered as having something in common [a *pair* of thieves] *d)* a brace; span [a *pair* of oxen] *e)* two legislators on opposing sides of some question who agree to withhold their vote so as to offset each other; also, such an agreement 4. two playing cards of the same denomination 5. [Rare or Dial.] a set or series [a *pair* of stairs, a *pair* of beads] —*vt.* 1. to make a pair of (two persons or things) by matching, joining, mating, etc. 2. to arrange in pairs 3. to provide with a partner (followed by *with*) —*vi.* 1. to form a pair; match 2. to join in marriage; mate —**pair off** 1. to join or arrange (two people or things) in a pair 2. to go apart or separate into pairs

SYN.—**pair** is used of two similar things that are associated together or are necessary in twos for proper use [a *pair* of socks] or of a single thing made up of two corresponding parts [a *pair* of scissors]; **couple** applies to any two similar things that are somehow associated [a *couple* of dollars] or it is used colloquially to mean several or a few [I must buy a *couple* of things]; a **brace** is a couple, especially of certain birds or animals [a *brace* of pheasants, hounds, etc.]; **yoke** applies to a pair of animals harnessed together for pulling [a *yoke* of oxen]; **span** is used especially of a pair of horses harnessed together

pair·ing (-iŋ) *n.* 1. the act of grouping contestants or teams in a tournament into competing pairs 2. [*pl.*] the list of such pairs

pair-oar (-ôr′) *n.* a racing shell rowed by two persons

who sit one behind the other, each using one oar: also **pair-oared shell**

pair production a process whereby a gamma ray having an energy greater than 1.02 mev is converted into an electron and positron pair in the strong electric field of a nucleus

pai·sa (pī′sa) n., pl. **pai′se** (-se) [Hindi paisā] a unit of money in India, Pakistan, Qatar, & Muscat and Oman, equal to 1/100 of a rupee

pai·san·o (pi sä′nō, -zä′-) n., pl. **-os** [Sp. < Fr. paysan < OFr. paisent: see PEASANT] 1. a fellow countryman 2. [Slang] a comrade; pal Also **pai·san′** — **pai·san′a** (-nä) n.fem.

Pais·ley (pāz′lē) city in SC Scotland, near Glasgow: pop. 96,000

pais·ley (pāz′lē) adj. [after prec., where a wool shawl in this pattern was orig. made] [also P-] 1. designating, of, or having an elaborate, colorful pattern of intricate figures 2. made of cloth having such a pattern —n. [also P-] a paisley cloth, shawl, necktie, etc.

Pai·ute (pī′yōōt, pī yōōt′) n. [< Shoshonean pah-ute, lit., water Ute] 1. pl. **-utes, -ute** any member of any of various bands of N. American Indians living in Nevada, E California, S Utah, and NW Arizona 2. any of their Shoshonean dialects

pa·ja·mas (pə jam′əz, -jä′məz) n.pl. [Hind. pājāmā < Per. pāi, a leg + jāma, garment] 1. in the Orient, a pair of loose silk or cotton trousers 2. a loosely fitting sleeping or lounging suit consisting of jacket (or blouse) and trousers —**pa·ja′ma** adj.

PAISLEY PATTERN

Pak. Pakistan

Pa·ki·stan (pä′ki stän′, pak′i stan′) country in S Asia, consisting of two provinces (EAST PAKISTAN, WEST PAKISTAN) separated by India: a member of the Brit. Commonwealth: 365,529 sq. mi.; pop. 107,258,000; cap. Rawalpindi

Pa·ki·stan·i (pä′ki stä′nē, pak′i stan′ē) adj. of Pakistan or its people —n. a native or inhabitant of Pakistan

pal (pal) n. [Eng. Romany, brother, mate (for prāl, phrāl, in dial. on European continent) < Sans. bhrātr, BROTHER] [Colloq.] an intimate friend; comrade; chum —vi. **palled, pal′ling** [Colloq.] 1. to associate as pals 2. to be a pal (with another)

pal·ace (pal′is) n. [ME. palais < OFr. < L. palatium < Palatium, one of the seven hills of Rome, where Augustus lived] 1. the official residence of a king, emperor, bishop, etc. 2. any large, magnificent house or building 3. a large, ornate place of entertainment

pal·a·din (pal′ə din) n. [Fr. < It. paladino < L. palatinus, officer of a palace < palatium: see prec.] 1. any of the twelve legendary peers, or douzepers, of Charlemagne's court 2. a knight or a heroic champion

pa·lae·o- (pā′lē ō, pal′ē ō) same as PALEO-: also **pa′lae- pa·laes·tra** (pə les′trə) n., pl. **-trae** (-trē), **-tras** same as PALESTRA

pal·an·quin, pal·an·keen (pal′ən kēn′) n. [Port. palanquim < Jav. pĕlangki < Sans. palyaṅka, paryaṅka] formerly in E Asia, a covered litter, usually for one person, carried by poles on the shoulders of two or more men

pal·at·a·ble (pal′it ə b'l) adj. [PALAT(E) + -ABLE] 1. pleasant or acceptable to the taste; fit to be eaten or drunk 2. acceptable to the mind —**pal′at·a·bil′i·ty, pal′at·a·ble·ness** n. —**pal′at·a·bly** adv.

pal·a·tal (pal′it 'l) adj. [Fr. < L. palatum, palate] 1. of the palate 2. Phonet. a) pronounced with the front of the tongue raised against or near the hard palate: said of certain consonants, as y in yes, ch in German ich (iH) b) designating a stop, fricative, etc. whose point of articulation is on or near the hard or soft palate, as (ch, j, sh, zh) c) [Rare] front: said of a vowel —n. a palatal sound —**pal′a·tal·ly** adv.

pal·a·tal·ize (-īz′) vt. **-ized′, -iz′ing** Phonet. to pronounce as a palatal; specif., to change (a nonpalatal) into a palatal (the t in nature is now invariably palatalized to ch] —**pal′a·tal·i·za′tion** n. [ML. palati-

pal·ate (pal′it) n. [ME. < L. palatum] 1. the roof of the mouth, consisting of a hard bony forward part (the hard palate) and a soft fleshy back part (the soft palate, or velum) 2. sense of taste: the palate was incorrectly thought to be the organ of taste 3. intellectual taste; liking

PALATE

pa·la·tial (pə lā′shəl) adj. [< L. palatium, PALACE] 1. of, suitable for, or like a palace 2. large and ornate; magnificent; stately —**pa·la′tial·ly** adv.

Pa·lat·i·nate (pə lat′'n āt′, -it) a former division of Bavaria: see RHINELAND-PALATINATE —n. [ML. palati-

natus] 1. [p-] the territory ruled by a palatine 2. a native or inhabitant of the Palatinate

pal·a·tine¹ (pal′ə tīn′, -tin) adj. [ME. < OFr. palatin < L. palatinus < palatium, PALACE] 1. of a palace 2. having royal privileges (a count palatine) 3. of or belonging to a count palatine or earl palatine 4. [P-] of the Palatinate —n. 1. an officer of an imperial palace 2. a medieval vassal lord having the rights of royalty in his own territory, or palatinate 3. a fur piece covering the shoulders 4. [P-] a native or inhabitant of the Palatinate 5. [P-] see SEVEN HILLS OF ROME

pal·a·tine² (pal′ə tīn′, -tin) adj. [Fr. palatin: see PALATE & -INE¹] having to do with the palate —n. either of the two bones forming the hard palate

Pa·lau Islands (pä lou′) island group in the Caroline Islands, east of Mindanao: 188 sq. mi.; pop. 11,000

pa·lav·er (pə lav′ər) n. [Port. palavra, a word, speech < LL.(Ec.) parabola, PARABLE] 1. a conference or discussion, as orig. between African natives and European explorers or traders 2. talk; esp., idle chatter 3. flattery; cajolery —vi. 1. to talk, esp. idly or flatteringly 2. to confer —vt. to flatter or wheedle

Pa·la·wan (pä lä′wän) island in the W Philippines, southwest of Mindoro: 4,550 sq. mi.

‡**pa·laz·zo** (pä lät′sō) n., pl. **pa·laz·zi** (-sē) [It.] a palace or palatial building

pale¹ (pāl) adj. [ME. < OFr. < L. pallidus, pale < pallere, to be pale < IE. base *pel-, gray, pale, whence FALLOW²] 1. of a whitish or colorless complexion; pallid; wan 2. lacking intensity or brilliance: said of color, light, etc.; faint; dim 3. feeble; weak (a pale imitation) —vi. **paled, pal′ing** 1. to become pale; lose color 2. to seem weaker or less important —vt. to make pale —**pale′ly** adv. —**pale′ness** n.

SYN.—**pale**, in this comparison the least connotative of these words, implies merely an unnatural whiteness or colorlessness, often temporary, of the complexion; **pallid** suggests a paleness resulting from exhaustion, faintness, emotional strain, etc.; **wan** suggests the paleness resulting from an emaciating illness; **ashen** implies the grayish paleness of the skin as in death; **livid** refers to a grayish-blue complexion, as of one in great rage or fear —ANT. ruddy, rosy

pale² (pāl) n. [ME. < MFr. pal < L. palus, a stake < IE. base *pak-, to fasten (as by ramming into the ground), whence Gr. passalos, a peg, stake, L. pax, peace] 1. a narrow, upright, pointed stake used in fences; picket 2. a fence; enclosure; boundary; restriction: now chiefly figurative (outside the pale of the law, beyond the pale (of respectability)) 3. a territory or district enclosed within bounds 4. Bot. a chaffy bract or scale; esp., a bract at the base of a floret of a composite flower 5. Heraldry a vertical third of the field; an ordinary

pa·le- (pā′lē, pal′ē) same as PALEO-: used before a vowel

pa·le·a (pā′lē ə) n., pl. **-le·ae** (-ē′) [ModL. < L., chaff < IE. base *pel-, to cover, a skin, whence FELL⁴, FILM] 1. the upper, or inner, thin, membranous bract enclosing the flower in grasses 2. same as PALE² (sense 4) —**pa′le·a′ceous** (-ā′shəs) adj.

Pa·le·arc·tic (pā′lē ärk′tik, -är′-) adj. [PALE- + ARCTIC] designating or of the biogeographic subregion that includes Europe, Africa and Arabia north of the Tropic of Cancer, and Asia north of the Himalayas

pa·le·eth·nol·o·gy (-eth näl′ə jē) n. [PALE- + ETHNOLOGY] the study of prehistoric races of man —**pa′le·eth′no·log′i·cal** (-nə läj′i k'l) adj.

☆**pale·face** (pāl′fās′) n. a white person: a term alleged to have been first used by N. American Indians

Pa·lem·bang (pä′lem bäŋ′) seaport in SE Sumatra, Indonesia: pop. 723,000

Pa·len·que (pä leŋ′kā) village in N Chiapas state, Mexico: site of ancient Mayan ruins

pa·le·o- (pā′lē ō, pal′ē ō) [< Gr. palaios, ancient < IE. base *kwel-, remote, whence Sans. caramá-, the last, Gr. tēle, far, W. pell, far] a combining form meaning: 1. the Old World (Paleotropical) 2. ancient, early, prehistoric, primitive, etc. (Paleozoic, paleolithic]: used widely to form compounds, as below, meaning "involving or dealing with (specified) forms, conditions, phenomena, fossils, etc. of remote, esp. geologic, eras

    paleoanthropology   paleoecology
    paleobotany   paleogeography
    paleobiology   palĕomagnetism
    paleoclimate   paleopathology
    paleoclimatology   paleozoology

pa·le·o·an·throp·ic (pā′lē ō an thräp′ik, pal′ē-) adj. [< prec. + ANTHROP(O)- + -IC] of or pertaining to early forms of fossil man, as Neanderthal

Pa·le·o·cene (pā′lē ō sēn′, pal′ē-) adj. [PALEO- + -CENE] designating or of the first or earliest epoch of the Tertiary Period in the Cenozoic Era, preceding the Eocene —the Paleocene the Paleocene Epoch or its rocks: see GEOLOGY, chart

pa·le·og·ra·phy (pā′lē äg′rə fē, pal′ē-) n. [ModL. palaeographia: see PALEO- & -GRAPHY] 1. ancient writing or

forms of writing, collectively **2.** the study of describing or deciphering ancient writings —**pa'le·og'ra·pher** *n.* —**pa'le·o·graph'ic** (-ə graf'ik), **pa'le·o·graph'i·cal** *adj.*

pa·le·o·lith (pā'lē ə lith', pal'ē-) *n.* [PALEO- + -LITH] a Pleistocene stone tool

pa·le·o·lith·ic (pā'lē ə lith'ik, pal'ē-) *adj.* [PALEO- + -LITHIC] designating or of an Old World cultural period of the early Stone Age, during which man developed flint, stone, and bone tools and lived by hunting, fishing, and gathering wild fruits

paleolithic man any of the types of man of the paleolithic period, including Heidelberg, Neanderthal, and Cro-Magnon man

paleon., paleontol. paleontology

pa·le·on·tog·ra·phy (pā'lē än täg'rə fē, pal'ē-) *n.* [PALE(O)- + ONTO- + -GRAPHY] the description of fossils —**pa'le·on'to·graph'i·cal** (-tə graf'i k'l), **pa'le·on'to·graph'ic** *adj.*

pa·le·on·tol·o·gy (-än täl'ə jē) *n.* [Fr. *paléontologie*: see PALEO- & ONTO- & -LOGY] **1.** the branch of geology that deals with prehistoric forms of life through the study of plant and animal fossils **2.** a treatise on this subject —**pa'le·on'to·log'i·cal** (-tə läj'i k'l), **pa'le·on'to·log'ic** *adj.* —**pa'le·on·tol'o·gist** *n.*

Pa·le·o·zo·ic (-ə zō'ik) *adj.* [PALEO- + ZO- + -IC] designating or of the geologic era between the Proterozoic and the Mesozoic: it covered the period between c. 600,000,000 and 230,000,000 years ago and was characterized by the development of the first fishes, amphibians, reptiles, and land plants —**the Paleozoic** the Paleozoic Era or its rocks: see GEOLOGY, chart

Pa·ler·mo (pə lur'mō; *It.* pä ler'mô) capital of Sicily; seaport on the N coast: pop. 634,000

Pal·es·tine (pal'əs tīn') **1.** region on the E coast of the Mediterranean, the country of the Jews in Biblical times **2.** Brit. mandated territory in this region, west of the Jordan River, from 1923 to the establishment of the state of Israel in 1948 by the United Nations —**Pal'es·tin'i·an** (-tin'ē ən) *adj., n.*

pa·les·tra (pə les'trə) *n., pl.* **-trae** (-trē), **-tras** [L. < Gr. *palaistra* < *palaiein*, to wrestle < IE. base *pel-*, to shake, swing, whence ON. *fæla*, to frighten] in ancient Greece, a public place for exercise in wrestling and athletics

Pal·es·tri·na (pal'es trē'nä; *Eng.* päl'əs strē'nə), **Gio·van·ni Pier·lu·i·gi da** (jô vän'nē pyer lōō ē'jē dä) 1525?-94; It. composer

pal·e·tot (pal'ə tō') *n.* [Fr. < OFr. *palletoc* < ME. *paltok*, akin to *pal*: see PALL²] formerly, a man's overcoat or a loose jacket worn by women and children

pal·ette (pal'it) *n.* [Fr., dim. of *pale*, a shovel < L. *pala*, a spade, shovel] **1.** a thin board with a hole for the thumb at one end, on which an artist arranges and mixes his paints **2.** the colors used by a particular artist or for a particular painting

palette knife a thin, flexible steel blade with a blunt edge and a wooden handle, used by artists to mix oil colors and clean the palette, and, sometimes, to apply paint

Pa·ley (pā'lē), **William** 1743-1805; Eng. theologian & philosopher

pal·frey (pôl'frē) *n., pl.* **-freys** [ME. < OFr. *palefrei* < ML. *palafredus*, for LL. *paraveredus*, extra post horse < Gr. *para*, beside + L. *veredus*, post horse < Gaul. **voredos* (akin to W. *gorwydd*, horse): **redos* < IE. base **reidh-*, whence RIDE] [Archaic] a saddle horse, esp. a gentle one for a woman

Pal·grave (pôl'grāv, pal'-), **Francis Turner** 1824-97; Eng. poet & anthologist

Pa·li (pä'lē) *n.* [Sans. *pāli*, lit., a row, line, canon, short for *pāli bhāsā*, canon language] the Old Indic Prakrit, or dialect, of the southern Buddhist scriptures, which has become the religious language of Buddhism

pal·imp·sest (pal'imp sest') *n.* [L. *palimpsestus* < Gr. *palimpsēstos*, lit., rubbed again < *palin*, again (see ff.) + *psēn*, to rub smooth < IE. base **bhes-*, to rub off, pulverize, whence L. *sabulum*, SAND] a parchment, tablet, etc. that has been written upon or inscribed two or three times, the previous text or texts having been imperfectly erased and remaining, therefore, still partly visible

pal·in·drome (pal'in drōm') *n.* [Gr. *palindromos*, running back < *palin*, again < IE. base **kwel-*, to turn, whence WHEEL) + *dramein*, to run: see DROMEDARY] a word, phrase, or sentence which reads the same backward or forward (Ex.: name no one man)

pal·ing (pāl'iŋ) *n.* **1.** the action of making a fence of pales **2.** a fence made of pales **3.** pales collectively **4.** a strip of wood used in making a fence; pale

pal·in·gen·e·sis (pal'in jen'ə sis) *n.* [ModL. < Gr. *palin*, again (see PALINDROME) + *genesis*, birth, GENESIS] **1.** birth over again; regeneration **2.** the doctrine of successive rebirths; metempsychosis **3.** that phase in the development of an individual plant or animal which theoretically repeats the evolutionary history of the taxonomic group to which it belongs; recapitulation: cf. CENOGENESIS —**pal'in·ge·net'ic** (-jə net'ik) *adj.*

pal·i·node (pal'ə nōd') *n.* [MFr. *palinod* < LL. *palinodia* < Gr. *palinōidia* < *palin*, again (see PALINDROME) + *ōidē*, song: see ODE] **1.** an ode or poem written to retract something said in a previous poem **2.** a retraction

pal·i·sade (pal'ə sād', pal'ə sād') *n.* [Fr. *palissade* < Pr. *palisada* < *palisa*, a pale < L. *palus*, a stake, PALE²] **1.** any one of a row of large pointed stakes set in the ground to form a fence used for fortification or defense **2.** a fence of such stakes ☆**3.** [*pl.*] a line of very steep cliffs, usually along a river —*vt.* **-sad'ed**, **-sad'ing** to fortify or defend with a palisade —**the Palisades** the line of steep cliffs in NE N.J. & SE N.Y. on the west shore of the Hudson: c. 15 mi. long

palisade parenchyma a layer of cylindrical cells containing chloroplasts, lying just below the upper epidermis of many leaves with their long axes at right angles to the epidermis

pal·ish (pāl'ish) *adj.* somewhat pale

pall¹ (pôl) *vi.* **palled**, **pall'ing** [ME. *pallen*, aphetic for *appallen*, APPALL] **1.** to become cloying, insipid, boring, wearisome, etc. **2.** to become satiated or bored —*vt.* to satiate, bore, or disgust

pall² (pôl) *n.* [ME. *pal* < OE. *pæll* < L. *pallium*, a cover (akin to *palla*, a robe, mantle)] **1.** a black, purple, or white piece of velvet, etc. used to cover a coffin, hearse, or tomb **2.** a dark or gloomy covering [a *pall* of smoke] **3.** a piece of cloth, or cardboard covered with cloth, used to cover the chalice in some Christian churches **4.** *same as* PALLIUM (sense 3) **5.** [Archaic] an altar cloth **6.** [Obs.] a rich cloth or coverlet **7.** [Obs.] a cloak or mantle —*vt.* **palled**, **pall'ing** to cover with or as with a pall

Pal·la·di·an¹ (pə lā'dē ən) *adj.* [< L. *Palladius* (< *Pallas*) + -AN] **1.** of Pallas Athena: see PALLAS **2.** [*occas.* **p-**] of wisdom or learning

Pal·la·di·an² (pə lā'dē ən, -lä'-) *adj.* of or in the classical Roman style of Andrea Palladio

pal·lad·ic (pə lad'ik, -lā'dik) *adj.* designating or of chemical compounds containing palladium with a valence of four

Pal·la·dio (päl lä'dyô), **An·dre·a** (än dre'ä) (born *Andrea di Pietro*) 1518-80; It. architect

Pal·la·di·um (pə lā'dē əm), *pl.* **-di·a** (-ə) [L. < Gr. *palladion*, sacred statue or image < *Pallus*] **1.** in ancient Greece and Rome, any statue of the Greek goddess Pallas Athena; specif., the legendary statue in Troy on the preservation of which the safety of the city was supposed to depend **2.** [**p-**] anything supposed to ensure the safety of something; safeguard

pal·la·di·um (pə lā'dē əm) *n.* [ModL. < *Pallas*, the asteroid < Gr. *Pallas*, the goddess] a rare, silvery-white, ductile, malleable, metallic chemical element of the platinum group: it is used as a catalyst, esp. in hydrogenation processes, or in alloys with gold, silver, and other metals: symbol, Pd; at. wt., 106.4; at. no., 46; sp. gr., 11.97; melt. pt., 1549.4°C; boil. pt., c. 2200°C

pal·la·dous (pə lā'dəs, pal'ə dəs) *adj.* designating or of chemical compounds containing palladium with a valence of two

Pal·las (pal'əs) [L. < Gr. *Pallas*] *Gr. Myth.* a name for Athena, the goddess of wisdom: also **Pallas Athena** —*n.* [ModL. < L., Athena] one of the asteroids, between Jupiter and Mars

pall·bear·er (pôl'ber'ər) *n.* [PALL² + BEARER: formerly, one who held the edges of the pall] one of the persons who attend or bear the coffin at a funeral

pal·let¹ (pal'it) *n.* [MFr. *palette*: see PALETTE] **1.** a wooden tool consisting of a flat blade with a handle; esp., such a tool used by potters for smoothing and rounding **2.** *same as* PALETTE (sense 1) **3.** a low, portable platform, usually double-faced, on which materials are stacked for storage or transportation, as in a warehouse **4.** *Bookbinding* a tool used for stamping letters on the binding of a book **5.** *Mech.* a part of a machine that changes back-and-forth motion to circular motion, or vice versa, by engaging the teeth of a ratchet wheel; pawl; click; esp., any of the clicks or pawls in the escapement of a clock or watch, which regulate the speed by releasing one tooth of a ratchet wheel at each swing of the pendulum or turn of the balance wheel

pal·let² (pal'it) *n.* [ME. *pailet* < MFr. *paillet* < OFr. *paille*, straw < L. *palea*, chaff: see PALEA] a small, inferior bed or a mattress or pad filled as with straw and used directly on the floor

pal·let³ (pal'it) *n.* [ME. *palet* < MFr., dim. of *pal*, PALE²] *Heraldry* a vertical stripe on an escutcheon, half as wide as a pale

pal·let·ize (pal'ə tīz') *vt.* **-ized'**, **-iz'ing** to store or transport (materials) on pallets

pal·lette (pal'it) *n.* [Fr. *palette*: see PALETTE] a plate in the armpit of a suit of armor

pal·liasse (pal yas', pal'yas) *n.* [< Fr. *paillasse* < It. *pagliaccio* < VL. **paleaceum* < L. *palea*, straw, chaff] a mattress filled with straw, sawdust, etc.

pal·li·ate (pal'ē āt') *vt.* **-at'ed**, **-at'ing** [< pp. of LL. *palliare*, to conceal, cloak, back-formation < L. *palliatus*, cloaked < *pallium*, a cloak] **1.** to lessen the pain or severity of without actually curing; alleviate; ease **2.** to make appear less serious or offensive; excuse; extenuate —**pal'li·a'tion** *n.* —**pal'li·a'tor** *n.*

PALETTE

pal·li·a·tive (pal′ē āt′iv, -ə tiv) *adj.* serving or tending to palliate; specif., *a)* alleviating *b)* excusing; extenuating — *n.* a thing that palliates

pal·lid (pal′id) *adj.* [L. *pallidus*, PALE[1]] faint in color; pale; wan —*SYN.* see PALE[1] —**pal′lid·ly** *adv.* —**pal′lid·ness** *n.*

pal·li·um (pal′ē əm) *n., pl.* **-li·ums, -li·a** (-ə) [L., a cloak, mantle] **1.** in ancient Greece, a large, oblong mantle worn by men; himation **2.** *Anat.* the cerebral cortex with its adjacent white matter **3.** *R.C.Ch.* a circular white wool band with pendants, worn over the shoulders by a pope or archbishop **4.** *Zool.* the mantle, or shell gland, of mollusks and brachiopods

pall-mall (pel′mel′) *n.* [MFr. *palemail* < It. *pallamaglio* < *palla* (< Lombard *palla*, akin to OHG. *balla*, BALL[1]) + *maglio* < L. *malleus*, a hammer, MALL < IE. base *mel*-, to crush, grind, whence MILL[1]] an old game in which a boxwood ball was struck by a mallet through an iron ring hung at the end of an alley; also, the alley in which this game was played

Pall Mall (pel′ mel′, pal′ mal′, pôl′ môl′) a London street, noted for its clubs, built on the site of an old pall-mall alley

pal·lor (pal′ər) *n.* [L. < base of *pallere*, to be pale: see PALE[1]] lack of color; unnatural paleness, as of the face, associated with poor health, fear, etc.

palm[1] (päm; *occas.* pälm) *n.* [ME. *palme* < OE. *palm* < L. *palma*: so named because its leaf somewhat resembles the palm of the hand] **1.** any of a family (Palmae) of tropical or subtropical monocotyledonous trees or shrubs, having usually a woody, branchless trunk and large, evergreen, featherlike or fan-shaped leaves growing in a bunch at the top **2.** a leaf of such a tree carried or worn as a symbol of victory, triumph, joy, etc. **3.** victory; triumph **4.** a representation of a palm leaf or frond given in lieu of a second award of the same military decoration —*adj.* designating or of a family of plants including the coconut palm, betel nut palm, date palm, etc. —**bear** (or **carry off**) **the palm** to be the winner; take the prize —**yield the palm to** to acknowledge the superiority of; admit to defeat by —**pal·ma′ceous** (pal mā′shəs, pä-) *adj.*

palm[2] (päm; *occas.* pälm) *n.* [altered (after L.) < ME. *paume* < OFr. < L. *palma*, palm of the hand < IE. base *pele*-, broad, flat, spread out, whence FLOOR, FIELD] **1.** the inner part or surface of the hand between the fingers and wrist **2.** the part of a glove, etc. that covers the palm **3.** the broad, flat part of an antler, as of a moose **4.** a unit of measure based either on the width of the hand (3 to 4 inches) or on its length (7 to 9 inches) **5.** any broad, flat part at the end of an arm, handle, etc., as the blade of an oar **6.** a metal disk used by sailmakers over the palm of the hand to push a needle through canvas —*vt.* **1.** to hide (something) in the palm or between the fingers, as in a sleight-of-hand trick **2.** to touch with the palm —**have an itching palm** [Colloq.] to desire money greedily —**palm off** to pass off by fraud or deceit

Pal·ma (päl′mä) seaport on Majorca; capital of Baleares province, Spain: pop. 171,000: in full, **Palma de Mal·lor·ca** (*the* mä lyôr′kä)

pal·mar (pal′mər, pä′-) *adj.* [L. *palmaris*] of, in, or corresponding to the palm of the hand

pal·ma·ry (-mə rē) *adj.* [L. *palmarius*] bearing or worthy to bear the palm; preeminent; victorious

pal·mate (pal′māt, pä′-) *adj.* [L. *palmatus* < *palma*, PALM[1]] shaped like a hand with the fingers spread; specif., *a) Bot.* having veins or lobes radiating from a common center: said of some leaves *b) Zool.* web-footed, as many water birds Also **pal′mat·ed** —**pal′mate·ly** *adv.*

pal·mat·i·fid (pal mat′ə fid) *adj.* [< L. *palmatus*, PALMATE + -FID] having leaves cleft about halfway to the base, but not into separate leaflets

pal·ma·tion (pal mā′shən) *n.* **1.** the state or quality of being palmate; palmate formation or structure **2.** a part or division of a palmate formation

Palm Beach town in SE Fla., on the Atlantic: winter resort: pop. 9,000

palm crab a large tropical land crab (*Birgus latro*) that feeds esp. on coconuts, found on islands in the S Pacific and Indian oceans

palm·er (päm′ər, pälm′ər) *n.* [ME. *palmere* < Anglo-Fr. *palmer* < OFr. *palmier* < ML. *palmarius* < L. *palma*, PALM[1]] **1.** a pilgrim who carried a palm leaf as a sign that he had been to the Holy Land **2.** any pilgrim

Pal·mer Peninsula (päm′ər) *former name of* ANTARCTIC PENINSULA

Palm·er·ston (päm′ər stən) **,** 3d Viscount, (*Henry John Temple*) 1784–1865; Brit. statesman; prime minister (1855–58; 1859–65)

palm·er·worm (päm′ər wurm′, päl′mər-) *n.* any of various unrelated wandering caterpillars feeding on plants

pal·mette (pal met′) *n.* [Fr. < *palme*, palm < L. *palma*, PALM[1]] *Archit.* a conventionalized ornament somewhat resembling a palm leaf

pal·met·to (pal met′ō) *n., pl.* **-tos, -toes** [Sp. *palmito*, dim. < *palma* < L., PALM[1]] **1.** any of a few small-sized palms (*Sabal*) of fan palms; esp., a species (*Sabal palmetto*) of

the SE U.S. with an edible terminal bud **2.** loosely, any of various palms with fan-shaped leaves

palm·is·try (päm′is trē, päl′mis-) *n.* [altered (after PALM[2]) < ME. *paumestrie*, prob. contr. < *paume*, PALM[2] + *maistrie*, mastery] the pretended art of telling a person's character or fortune by the lines and marks of the palm of his hand —**palm′ist** *n.*

pal·mi·tate (pal′mə tāt′, pä′-) *n.* a salt or ester of palmitic acid

pal·mit·ic acid (pal mit′ik, pä-) [Fr. *palmitique*: see PALM[1] & -ITE[1] & -IC] a colorless, crystalline fatty acid, $C_{16}H_{32}O_2$, found uncombined in palm oil and as the glyceryl ester in other vegetable and animal fats and oils

pal·mi·tin (pal′mə tin, pä′-) *n.* [Fr. *palmitine*] a colorless crystalline compound, $C_{51}H_{98}O_6$, found in palm oil and many other fats: it is the glyceryl ester of palmitic acid

palm leaf the leaf of a palm tree, esp. of one of the palmettos, used to make fans, hats, etc.

palm oil a yellow or reddish, semisolid oil obtained from the fruit of several kinds of palms, esp. the oil palm (*Elaeis guineensis*): used in making soap, candles, etc.

Palm Springs resort city in S Calif.: pop. 21,000

palm sugar *same as* JAGGERY

Palm Sunday the Sunday before Easter, commemorating in Christian churches Jesus' entry into Jerusalem, when palm branches were strewn before him

palm·y (päm′ē, päl′mē) *adj.* **palm′i·er, palm′i·est 1.** abounding in or shaded by palm trees **2.** of or like a palm or palms **3.** flourishing; prosperous [*palmy* days]

Pal·my·ra (pal mī′rə) ancient city in C Syria: now the site of a village, pop. 2,000

pal·my·ra (pal mī′rə) *n.* [altered (after prec.) < Port. *palmeira* < *palma* < L., PALM[1]] a fan palm (*Borassus flabellifer*) grown in India, Ceylon, and tropical Africa for its durable wood, its sap that yields jaggery and toddy, its edible fruits, and its leaves used for thatching, etc.

Pal·o Al·to (pal′ō al′tō) [Sp., lit., tall tree (the redwood)] city in W Calif., near San Francisco: pop. 56,000

☆**pal·o·mi·no** (pal′ə mē′nō) *n., pl.* **-nos** [AmSp. < Sp., dove-colored < L. *palumbinus* < *palumbes*, a pigeon, ringdove < IE. base *pel*-, gray, pale (whence PALE[1], FALLOW[2]): form prob. infl. by L. *columba*: cf. COLUMBARIUM] a cream, golden, or light-chestnut horse that has a silvery-white or ivory mane and tail

☆**pa·loo·ka** (pə lōō′kə) *n.* [coined by Jack Conway (died 1928), U.S. baseball player and sports writer] [Old Slang] a clumsy or oafish fellow; esp., an inept athlete

Pa·los (pä′lôs) village & former port in SW Spain, from which Columbus embarked on his 1st voyage

Pa·los Ver·des Peninsula (pal′ōs vur′dəs) [see *ff.*] suburb of Los Angeles, on the Pacific: pop. 40,000

☆**pa·lo·ver·de** (pal′ō vur′dē, -verd′) *n.* [MexSp., lit., green tree < Sp. *palo*, a stick, log (< L. *palus*, a stake, PALE[2]) + *verde*, green < L. *viridis*: cf. VERDURE] any of several trees or shrubs (genus *Cercidium*) of the legume family, with spiny branches, green bark, and bright yellow flowers, found in the SW U.S. and Mexico

palp (palp) *n. same as* PALPUS —**pal′pal** *adj.*

pal·pa·ble (pal′pə b'l) *adj.* [ME. < LL. *palpabilis* < L. *palpare*, to touch, prob. < IE. base *pel*-, to make move, shake, whence FEEL] **1.** that can be touched, felt, or handled; tangible **2.** easily perceived by the senses; audible, recognizable, perceptible, noticeable, etc. **3.** clear to the mind; obvious; evident; plain —*SYN.* see EVIDENT, PERCEPTIBLE —**pal′pa·bil′i·ty** *n.* —**pal′pa·bly** *adv.*

pal·pate[1] (pal′pāt) *vt.* **-pat·ed, -pat·ing** [< L. *palpatus*, pp. of *palpare*, to touch: see PALPABLE] to examine by touching, as for medical diagnosis —**pal·pa′tion** *n.*

pal·pate[2] (pal′pāt) *adj.* [ModL. *palpatus*: see PALPUS & -ATE[1]] having a palpus or palpi

pal·pe·bral (pal′pə brəl) *adj.* [LL. *palpebralis* < L. *palpebra*, eyelid, akin to *palpare*: see PALPABLE] of or having to do with the eyelids

pal·pi (pal′pī) *n. pl. of* PALPUS

pal·pi·tate (pal′pə tāt′) *vi.* **-tat·ed, -tat·ing** [< L. *palpitatus*, pp. of *palpitare*, freq. of *palpare*, to feel, stroke: see PALPABLE] **1.** to beat rapidly or flutter: said esp. of heart action that one is conscious of **2.** to throb; quiver; tremble —**pal′pi·tant** (-tənt) *adj.* —**pal′pi·ta′tion** *n.*

pal·pus (pal′pəs) *n., pl.* **pal′pi** (-pī) [ModL. < L. *palpus*, the soft palm of the hand, akin to *palpare*: see PALPABLE] **1.** a jointed organ or feeler for touching or tasting, attached to one of the head appendages of insects, lobsters, etc. **2.** a fleshy, sensory structure in the oral region of some polychaete worms

pals·grave (pôlz′grāv′, palz′-) *n.* [Du. *paltsgrave* < *palts* (< L. *palatium*), palace + *graaf*, count, akin to G. *pfalzgraf*] formerly, in Germany, a count palatine —**pals′gra·vine** (-grə vēn′) *n.fem.*

pal·sy (pôl′zē) *n., pl.* **-sies** [ME. *palesie, parlesie* < OFr. *paralisie* < L. *paralysis*, PARALYSIS] paralysis of any voluntary muscle as a result of some disorder in the nervous system, sometimes accompanied with involuntary tremors —*vt.* **-sied, -sy·ing** to afflict with or as with palsy; paralyze

pal·sy-wal·sy (pal′zē wal′zē) *adj.* [reduplication of *palsy* < *pals,* pl. of PAL + -Y²] [Slang] very friendly; intimate

pal·ter (pôl′tər) *vi.* [freq. formation < dial. *palt,* rag, piece of cloth (< a LowG. source): orig. ? with reference to haggling over cloth prices] **1.** to talk or act insincerely; prevaricate **2.** to deal with facts, decisions, etc. lightly or carelessly; trifle **3.** to quibble, as in bargaining —**pal′-ter·er** *n.*

pal·try (pôl′trē) *adj.* -tri·er, -tri·est [prob. < LowG. *paltrig,* ragged < *palte,* a rag] practically worthless; trifling; insignificant; contemptible; petty —**SYN.** see PETTY —**pal′tri·ness** *n.*

pa·lu·dal (pə lōō′d'l, pal′yoo d'l) *adj.* [ML. *paludalis* < L. *palus* (gen. *paludis*), marsh < IE. base *pel-,* whence Gr. *pēlos,* clay, mud, bog] **1.** of a marsh or marshes; marshy **2.** [Archaic] malarial

pal·u·dism (pal′yoo diz'm) *n.* [< L. *palus* (see prec.) + -ISM] *archaic term for* MALARIA

pal·y¹ (pā′lē) *adj.* [Archaic] somewhat pale

pal·y² (pā′lē) *adj.* [Late ME. < MFr. *palé* < *pal,* PALE²] *Heraldry* divided into four or more vertical stripes, or pales, of equal width, in alternating colors: said of the field of an escutcheon

pal·y·nol·o·gy (pal′ə näl′ə jē) *n.* [< Gr. *palynein,* to strew, sprinkle < *palē,* fine meal, dust < IE. base *pel-,* dust, meal, whence L. *pollen*) + -LOGY] the study of living or fossil plant spores and pollen —**pal′y·no·log′i·cal** (-nə läj′i k'l) *adj.* —**pal′y·nol′o·gist** *n.*

pam. pamphlet

Pam·e·la (pam′ə lə) [apparently coined by Sir Philip Sidney for a character in his *Arcadia* (1590)] a feminine name

Pa·mir·i (pä mir′ē) *n., pl.* -mir′i any member of various, mainly nomadic peoples living in the Pamirs

Pa·mirs (pä mirz′) mountain system mostly in the Tadzhik S.S.R.: highest peak, c. 25,000 ft.: also **Pa·mir′**

Pam·li·co Sound (pam′li kō′) [< Algonquian tribal name < ?] sound between the coast of N.C. and narrow offshore islands: c. 80 mi. long See Cape HATTERAS, map

pam·pas (pam′pəz; *for adj. usually* -pəs; *Sp.* päm′päs) *n.pl.* [AmSp., pl. of *pampa* < Quechua, plain, field] the extensive treeless plains of Argentina and some other parts of S. America —*adj.* of the pampas

pampas grass any of several giant S. American grasses (genera *Cortaderia* and *Gynerium*), grown for their large, plumelike, silvery or pinkish panicles, which are used for bouquets, often after dyeing

pam·pe·an (pam′pē ən, pam pē′-) *adj.* of the pampas or their Indian natives —*n.* a pampean Indian

pam·per (pam′pər) *vt.* [ME. *pampren* < LowG. source, akin to WFl. *pampren* in the same sense] **1.** orig., to feed too much; gratify to excess; glut **2.** to be overindulgent with; give in easily to the wishes of; coddle [to *pamper* a child] —**SYN.** see INDULGE —**pam′per·er** *n.*

pam·pe·ro (päm per′ō, pam-) *n., pl.* -ros [AmSp. < *pampa:* see PAMPAS] a strong, cold wind that blows from the Andes across the S. American pampas

pamph. pamphlet

pam·phlet (pam′flit) *n.* [ME. *pamfilet* < OFr. *Pamphilet,* dim. of ML. *Pamphilus,* short for *Pamphilus, seu de Amore,* Pamphilus, or on Love, title of 12th-c. ML. amatory poem] **1.** a small, thin, unbound book made up of sheets of paper stapled or stitched together and usually having a paper cover **2.** something published in this form, usually on some topic of current interest

pam·phlet·eer (pam′flə tir′) *n.* a writer or publisher of pamphlets; esp., one who writes pamphlets dealing polemically with political or social issues —*vi.* to write or publish pamphlets

Pam·phyl·i·a (pam fil′ē ə) ancient region in S Asia Minor, on the Mediterranean

Pam·plo·na (päm plō′nä) city in Navarre, NE Spain: pop. 115,000

Pan (pan) [L. < Gr.] *Gr. Myth.* a god of fields, forests, wild animals, flocks, and shepherds, represented with the legs (and, sometimes, horns and ears) of a goat: identified with the Roman god Faunus

pan¹ (pan) *n.* [ME. *panne* < OE., akin to G. *pfanne,* early Gmc. loan word < VL. *panna,* prob. < L. *patina,* a pan: see PATELLA] **1.** any of many kinds of containers, usually broad, shallow, without a cover, and made of metal, used for domestic purposes: often in combination [a frying *pan,* *saucepan,* *dishpan*] **2.** any object or part shaped like a pan; specif., *a)* an open container for washing out gold, tin, etc. from gravel or the like, in mining *b)* either receptacle in a pair of scales *c)* a container for heating, evaporating, etc. **3.** the amount a pan will hold; panful **4.** any area suggestive of a pan; esp., a hollow, natural or artificial depression in the ground **5.** a layer of hard soil, impervious to water; hardpan **6.** a small ice floe **7.** the part of the flintlock that held the firing powder in old guns and pistols ☆**8.** [Slang] a face —*vt.* **panned, pan′ning 1.** to cook in a pan ☆**2.** [Colloq.] to criticize unfavorably, as in reviewing [to *pan* a play] ☆**3.** *Mining a)* to wash (gravel, etc.) in a pan,

as for separating gold *b)* to separate (gold, etc.) from gravel by washing in a pan —*vi. Mining* ☆**1.** to wash gravel in a pan, searching for gold ☆**2.** to yield gold in this process —☆**pan out 1.** *Mining* to yield gold, as gravel, a mine, etc. **2.** [Colloq.] to turn out (as specified); transpire; esp., to turn out well; succeed —☆**put on the pan** to criticize severely

pan² (pän) *n.* [Hind. *pān* < Sans. *parna,* a leaf, feather: cf. FERN] **1.** a leaf of the betel palm **2.** a substance made of this leaf, betel nut, lime, and spices, used like chewing gum

pan³ (pan) *vt., vi.* **panned, pan′ning** [< PAN(ORAMA)] to move (a motion-picture or television camera) so as to get a panoramic effect or to follow a moving object —*n.* the act of panning

pan- (pan) [< Gr. *pan,* neut. of *pas,* all, every, universal < IE. base *keu-,* to swell, arch, whence L. *cavus,* hollow] *a combining form meaning:* **1.** all [*panchromatic, pantheism*] **2.** [P-] *a)* of, comprising, embracing, or common to all or every [*Pan-American*] *b)* (belief in) the cooperation, unity, or union of all members of (a specified nationality, race, church, etc.) [*Pan-Americanism*] In sense 2, usually followed by a hyphen, as in the following words:

Pan-African	**Pan-European**
Pan-Arabic	**Pan-Islamic**
Pan-Asiatic	**Pan-Slavic**

PAN peroxyacetyl nitrate

Pan. Panama

pan·a·ce·a (pan′ə sē′ə) *n.* [L. < Gr. *panakeia* < *pan,* all + *akeisthai,* to cure < ? IE. base *yēk-,* to cure, whence prob. W. *iach,* healthy, OIr. *hícc,* cure] a supposed remedy, cure, or medicine for all diseases or ills; cure-all —**pan′-a·ce′an** *adj.*

pa·nache (pə nash′, -näsh′) *n.* [Fr. < OFr. *pannache* < OIt. *pennacchio* < LL. *pinnaculum,* tuft, plume: see PINNACLE] **1.** a plume of feathers; esp., such a plume on a helmet **2.** dashing elegance of manner; carefree, spirited self-confidence or style; flamboyance

pa·na·da (pə nä′də, -nä′-) *n.* [Sp. < *pan* < L. *panis,* bread < IE. base *pāt-,* to feed, whence FOOD, L. *pastor*] **1.** orig., a dish made of bread boiled to a pulp and flavored **2.** a paste made of flour boiled in water or milk, and used as a binding agent, esp. in forcemeats

Pan·a·ma (pan′ə mä′, -mô′) [< AmSp. *Panamá* < native Indian word < ?] **1.** country in Central America, on the Isthmus of Panama: 29,201 sq. mi.; pop. 1,329,000 **2.** its capital; seaport on the Gulf of Panama: pop. 344,000 **3. Gulf of,** arm of the Pacific, on the S coast of Panama: c. 115 mi. wide **4. Isthmus of,** strip of land connecting South America & Central America: 31 mi. wide at its narrowest point —**Pan·a·ma′ni·an** (-mä′nē ən) *adj., n.*

Panama Canal ship canal across the Isthmus of Panama, connecting the Caribbean Sea (hence, Atlantic Ocean) and the Pacific Ocean: 50.7 mi. long

Panama Canal Zone *same as* CANAL ZONE

Panama City *same as* PANAMA (sense 2)

Panama (hat) [after *Panama* (city), once a main distributing center] [*also* p-] **1.** a fine, hand-plaited hat made from select leaves of the jipijapa plant **2.** any similar straw hat

Panama hat plant *popular name for* JIPIJAPA (sense 1)

☆**Pan-A·mer·i·can** (pan′ə mer′ə kən) *adj.* of North America, South America, and Central America, collectively

☆**Pan-A·mer·i·can·ism** (-iz′m) *n.* any theory or policy of, or movement toward, political and economic cooperation, mutual social and cultural understanding, international alliance, etc. among the Pan-American nations

☆**Pan American Union** the official agency of the Organization of American States (OAS) through which the twenty-three member American republics work to develop closer cooperation among themselves: renamed (1970) *General Secretariat of the OAS*

Pan·a·mint Range (pan′ə mint) [< name of a division of the Shoshonean Indians < ?] mountain range in SE Calif., forming the W rim of Death Valley: highest peak, 11,045 ft.

☆**pan·a·tel·a, pan·a·tel·la** (pan′ə tel′ə) *n.* [AmSp. *panatela,* orig., a long, narrow biscuit < It., dim. of *pane,* bread: see PANETTONE] a cigar of a long, slender shape

Pa·nay (pä nī′; *E. pə nī′*) island of the C Philippines, between Mindoro & Negros: 4,446 sq. mi.

pan·broil (pan′broil′) *vt.* to fry in a pan with little or no fat

pan·cake (pan′kāk′) *n.* **1.** a thin, flat cake of batter fried on a griddle or in a pan; griddlecake; flapjack **2.** a landing in which the airplane levels off higher than for a normal landing, stalls, then drops almost vertically: in full, **pancake landing** ☆**3.** *clipped form of* PANCAKE MAKEUP —*vi., vt.* -caked′, -cak′ing to make, or cause (an airplane) to make, a pancake landing

☆**pancake makeup** [< *Pan-Cake Make-Up,* a trademark] a cosmetic or theatrical makeup made of a soluble, matte powder compressed into a thin cake and typically applied with a damp sponge

pan·chax (pan′kaks) *n.* [ModL.] any of various brilliantly colored killifishes (genus *Aplocheilus*) often kept in tropical fish aquariums

‡**pan·cha·yat** (pən chī′ət) *n.* [Hindi *pañcāyat* < Sans. *pāñca,* FIVE] in India, an elective village council

PAN

pan·chro·mat·ic (pan′krō mat′ik) *adj.* [PAN- + CHRO-MATIC] sensitive to light of all colors *[panchromatic film]* —**pan·chro·ma·tism** (pan krō′mə tiz′m) *n.*

pan·cra·ti·um (pan krā′shē əm) *n., pl.* **-ti·a** (-ə) [L. < Gr. *pankration* < *pan*, all (see PAN-) + *kratos*, strength: see -CRAT] in ancient Greece and Rome, an athletic contest combining boxing and wrestling —**pan·crat′ic** *adj.*

pan·cre·as (pan′krē əs, paŋ′-) *n.* [ModL. < Gr. *pankreas* < *pan*, all (see PAN-) + *kreas*, flesh (see CRUDE)] a large, elongated gland situated behind the stomach and secreting a digestive juice (*pancreatic juice*) into the small intestine: groups of differentiated cells (*islets of Langerhans*) in the gland produce the hormone insulin; the pancreas of animals, used as food, is usually called *sweetbread* —**pan′cre·at′ic** (-at′ik) *adj.*

pancreatic juice the clear, alkaline juice secreted by the pancreas into the small intestine, where its constituent enzymes act on food passed down from the stomach

pan·cre·a·tin (pan′krē ə tin, paŋ′-) *n.* **1.** any of the pancreatic enzymes or a mixture of these **2.** a commercial preparation of pancreas extract from cattle or hogs, used as an aid to digestion

pan·cre·a·ti·tis (pan′krē ə tīt′əs, paŋ′-) *n.* [< ff. + -ITIS] inflammation of the pancreas

pan·cre·a·to- (pan′krē ə tō′, paŋ′-) *a combining form meaning of the pancreas [pancreatotomy]:* also, before a vowel, **pancreat-**

pan·da (pan′də) *n.* [Fr. < native name in Nepal] *clipped form of:* **1.** GIANT PANDA **2.** LESSER PANDA

pan·da·nus (pan dā′nəs) *n.* [ModL. < Malay *pandan*] same as SCREW PINE

Pan·da·rus (pan′dər əs) [L. < Gr. *Pandaros*] a leader of the Lycians in the Trojan War: in medieval romances and in Boccaccio, Chaucer, and Shakespeare, he acts as the go-between for Troilus and Cressida

Pan·de·an (pan dē′ən) *adj.* of Pan

Pandean pipes same as PAN PIPE

pan·dect (pan′dekt) *n.* [Fr. *pandecte* < LL. *Pandectae*, the Pandects < L., pl. of *pandectes*, an all-inclusive book < Gr. *pandektēs*, lit., all receiving < *pan*, all (see PAN-) + *dechesthai*, to contain, receive < IE. base *dek-*, to take, receive, whence L. *decere*, to be fitting] **1.** *[often pl.]* a complete body of laws; legal code **2.** a complete or comprehensive digest —**the Pandects** a digest of Roman civil law in fifty books, compiled for the emperor Justinian in the 6th cent. A.D.; the Digest

pan·dem·ic (pan dem′ik) *adj.* [< LL. *pandemus* < Gr. *pandēmos* < *pan*, all (see PAN-) + *dēmos*, the people: see DEMOCRACY] prevalent over a whole area, country, etc.; universal; general; specif., epidemic over a large region: said of a disease —*n.* a pandemic disease

Pan·de·mo·ni·um (pan′də mō′nē əm) [ModL. < Gr. *pan*, all (see PAN-) + *daimōn*, DEMON] the abode of all demons: in *Paradise Lost* it is the palace built by Satan's orders as the capital of Hell —*n.* **1.** same as HELL **2.** [p-] *a)* any place or scene of wild disorder, noise, or confusion *b)* wild disorder, noise, or confusion

pan·der (pan′dər) *n.* [< ME. *Pandare*, PANDARUS < L. *Pandarus*] **1.** a go-between in a sexual intrigue; esp., a procurer; pimp **2.** a person who provides the means of helping to satisfy the ignoble ambitions or desires, vices, etc. of another Also **pan′der·er** —*vt.* [Archaic] to be a pander for —*vi.* to act as a pander (*to*)

pan·dit (pun′dit, pan′-) *n.* [var. of PUNDIT] in India, a learned man; scholar: used [P-] as a title of respect

P. and L., P. & L. profit and loss

Pan·do·ra (pan dôr′ə) [L. < Gr. *Pandōra* < *pan*, all (see PAN-) + *dōron*, a gift] *Gr. Myth.* the first mortal woman, who in curiosity opened a box, letting out all human ills into the world (or, in a later version, letting all human blessings escape and to be lost, leaving only hope)

pan·do·ra (pan dôr′ə) *n.* [It. < LL. *pandura*: see BANDORE] same as BANDORE —**pan·dore′** (-dôr′)

pan·dour (pan′door) *n.* [< Fr. < or G. *pandur*, both < Croatian *pândûr*, constable, prob. < ML. *banderius*, one who follows a banner: see BANNER] **1.** a member of a force of 18th-cent. Croatian soldiers in the Austrian army, noted for their brutality **2.** any brutal soldier

☆**pan·dow·dy** (pan dou′dē) *n., pl.* **-dies** [prob. < obs. Somersetshire dial. *pandoulde*, custard < PAN¹ + *doulde* < ?] deep-dish apple pie or pudding, having a top crust only

pan·du·rate (pan′door it, -dyoor-; -āt′) *adj.* [< LL. *pandura*, PANDORA + -ATE¹] *Bot.* shaped somewhat like a

violin, as some leaves: also **pan·dur·i·form** (pan door′ə fôrm′, -dyoor′-)

pan·dy (pan′dē) *n., pl.* **-dies** [L. *pande*, open (your hand), imperative of *pandere*, to extend < IE. base *pand-*, var. of *pet-*, to stretch out, whence FATHOM] [Scot.] a stroke on the palm of the hand with a strap or cane, as a punishment —*vt.* **-died, -dy·ing** [Scot.] to punish by such a stroke or strokes

pane (pān) *n.* [ME. *pan* < OFr. < L. *pannus*, a piece of cloth < IE. base *pan-*, fabric, whence Gr. *pēnos*, cloth, OE. *fana*, banner] **1.** a piece or division, esp. if flat and rectangular; specif., *a)* a single division of a window, etc., consisting of a sheet of glass in a frame *b)* such a sheet of glass **2.** a panel, as of a door, wall, etc. **3.** any of the flat sides, or faces, as of a nut, bolt head, cut diamond, etc. **4.** *Philately a)* a separate section of stamps, variously a quarter, half, or full sheet, as cut for sale *b)* any of the small block of stamps sold in a booklet: in full, **booklet pane**

pan·e·gyr·ic (pan′ə jir′ik) *n.* [Fr. *panégyrique* < L. *panegyricus* < Gr. *panēgyris*, public meeting < *pan*, all (see PAN-) + *ageirein*, to bring together] **1.** a formal speech or writing praising a person or event **2.** high or hyperbolic praise; laudation —*SYN.* see TRIBUTE — **pan′e·gyr′i·cal** *adj.* —**pan′e·gyr′i·cal·ly** *adv.* —**pan′e·gyr′ist** *n.* —**pan′e·gy·rize′** (-jə rīz′) *vt., vi.* **-rized′, -riz′ing**

pan·el (pan′l) *n.* [ME. < OFr. < VL. *pannellus*, dim. of L. *pannus*, piece of cloth: see PANE] **1.** *a)* a piece of cloth placed under a saddle; saddle lining *b)* a soft saddle **2.** a section or division of a wall, ceiling, or other surface; specif., *a)* a section of a fence or railing between two posts *b)* a flat piece, usually rectangular, forming a part of the surface of a wall, door, cabinet, etc., and usually raised, recessed, framed, etc. *c)* a similar piece used for enclosing or covering something or serving as a light diffuser, a built-in heating element in space heating, etc. *d)* a compartment or pane of a window *e)* an insulated board, or flat surface, for instruments or controls, as of an electric circuit, airplane, etc. **3.** *a)* a thin board used for oil painting *b)* a painting on such a board *c)* any picture very much longer than it is wide **4.** [< piece of parchment on which orig. recorded] *a)* a list of persons summoned for jury duty *b)* the persons summoned or the jury itself **5.** a group of persons selected for a specific purpose, as judging a contest, discussing an issue publicly, performing on a radio or TV quiz show, etc. **6.** *Aeron. a)* any of the sections of a wing *b)* in dirigibles, the quadrilateral area bounded by two adjacent longerons and transverses **7.** *Dressmaking* a lengthwise strip, as of contrasting material, in a skirt or dress **8.** *Mining* a compartment of a mine —*vt.* **-eled** or **-elled, -el·ing** or **-el·ling 1.** to cover, provide, fit, or decorate with panels **2.** *Law* to impanel (a jury) **3.** *Scottish Law* to indict

panel discussion a discussion carried on by a selected group of speakers before an audience

pan·el·ing, pan·el·ling (-iŋ) *n.* **1.** the action of a person who panels **2.** panels collectively; series of panels in a wall, etc. **3.** sections of plastic, wood, or other material from which to cut panels

pan·el·ist (-ist) *n.* a member of a panel (*n.* 5)

☆**panel truck** a small, enclosed pickup truck

☆**pan·e·tel·a, pan·e·tel·la** (pan′ə tel′ə) *n.* same as PANATELA

pan·et·to·ne (pan′i tō′nē; *It.* pä′net tō′ne) *n.* [It. < *panetto*, dim. of *pane*, bread < L. *panis*: for IE. base see FOOD] a rich, light, Italian coffeecake containing raisins, citron, nuts, etc.

☆**pan fish** any small fish that can be fried whole in a pan

pan-fry (pan′frī′) *vt.* **-fried′, -fry′ing** to fry in a shallow skillet or frying pan

pang (paŋ) *n.* [< ?] a sudden, sharp, and brief pain, physical or emotional; spasm of distress

pan·ga (päŋ′ga) *n.* [< native name in E Africa] a long knife with a broad, hooked, sharp blade used in Africa as a cutting tool or as a weapon

pan·gen·e·sis (pan jen′ə sis) *n.* [ModL.: see PAN- & -GENESIS] a former hypothesis of heredity in which each unit or cell of the body throws off very minute particles (**pangenes**) into the blood which circulate freely, undergo division, and are collected in the reproductive cells as the units of hereditary transmission —**pan′ge·net′ic** (-jə net′ik) *adj.*

Pang·fou (päŋ′fou′) city in Anhwei province, EC China: pop. 330,000

pan·go·lin (paŋ gō′lin) *n.* [Malay *pĕngulin*, roller < *gulin*, to roll] any of a number of related, toothless, scaly mammals (order Pholidota) of Asia and Africa, feeding on ants and termites and able to roll into a ball when attacked

Pang·o Pang·o (päŋ′ō päŋ′ō) same as PAGO PAGO

pan·gram (pan′gram) *n.* [PAN- + -GRAM] a sentence that uses every letter of the alphabet, ideally only once

pan·han·dle¹ (pan′han′d'l) *n.* **1.** the handle of a pan ☆**2.** *[often P-]* a strip of land projecting like the handle of a pan, as the northern extension of W.Va. (the **Panhandle State**) between Ohio and Pa.

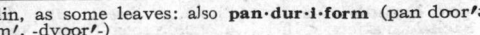

PANCREAS
(A, pancreas; B, right kidney; C, left kidney; D, duodenum; E, spleen; F, interior vena cava; G, aorta; H, ureter; I, ascending colon; J, descending colon; K, right adrenal gland; L, left adrenal gland; M, superior mesenteric artery; N, esophagus; O, diaphragm)

☆**pan·han·dle²** (pan′han′d'l) *vt.*, *vi.* **-dled, -dling** [prob. back-formation < ff.] [Colloq.] to beg (from), esp. on the streets

☆**pan·han·dler** (-dlər) *n.* [PAN¹ + HANDLER] [Colloq.] a beggar, esp. one who begs on the streets

Pan·hel·len·ic (pan′hə len′ik) *adj.* 1. of all the Greek peoples 2. of Panhellenism 3. of all Greek-letter fraternities and sororities

Pan·hel·len·ism (pan hel′ən iz′m) *n.* [see PAN-, HELLENE, & -ISM] formerly, the theory of, or a movement toward, the political unification of all the Greek peoples

pan·ic¹ (pan′ik) *n.* [ME. *panyk* < L. *panicum*, kind of millet < *panus*, ear of millet, a swelling < IE. base *pank-, to swell, whence Pol. *pąk*, a bud] any of several related grasses (genus *Panicum*), as millet, used as fodder: also **panic grass**

pan·ic² (pan′ik) *adj.* [Fr. *panique* < Gr. *panikos*, of Pan < *Pan*] 1. literally of Pan 2. of sudden fear, as supposedly inspired by Pan 3. having the nature of, or showing or resulting from, panic —*n.* 1. a sudden, unreasoning, hysterical fear, often spreading quickly 2. a widespread fear of the collapse of the financial system, resulting in unreasoned attempts to turn property into cash, withdraw money, etc. 3. [Slang] a person or thing considered extremely humorous or entertaining —*vt.* **-icked, -ick·ing** 1. to affect with panic 2. [Slang] to convulse (a listener, audience, etc.) with laughter, delight, etc. —*vi.* to give way to or show panic —SYN. see FEAR —**push** (or **press, hit,** etc.) **the panic button** [Slang] to panic; specif., to react to a crisis by some frantic, often disastrous action —**pan′ic·al·ly** *adv.* —**pan′ick·y** *adj.*

pan·i·cle (pan′i k'l) *n.* [L. *panicula*, tuft on plants, panicle, dim. of *panus*, a swelling, ear of millet: see PANIC¹] a loose, irregularly branched, indeterminate flower cluster; compound raceme — **pan′i·cled, pa·nic·u·late** (pa nik′yə lit, -lāt′), **pa·nic′u·lat′ed** *adj.*

pan·ic-strick·en (pan′ik strik″'n) *adj.* stricken with panic; badly frightened; hysterical and out of control from fear: also **pan′ic-struck′** (-struk′)

Pan·ja·bi (pən jä′bē) *n. same as* PUNJABI

pan·jan·drum (pan jan′drəm) *n.* [arbitrary formation from a nonsense passage by Samuel Foote (1721–77), Eng. actor & playwright] a self-important, pompous official: a satirical title

Pank·hurst (paŋk′hurst′), **Emmeline** (born *Emmeline Goulden*) 1858–1928; Eng. suffragist

panne (pan) *n.* [Fr. < OFr. *penne*, fur lining, a soft substance < L. *penna*, a feather: see PEN²] a soft cloth resembling velvet, but having a longer nap and a lustrous finish

pan·nier, pan·ier (pan′yər, -ē ər) *n.* [ME. *panier* < MFr. < L. *panarium*, breadbasket < *panis*, bread: see PANADA] 1. a large basket; specif., *a*) a wicker basket for carrying loads on the back *b*) either of a pair of baskets hung across the back of a donkey, horse, etc. for carrying market produce 2. *a*) a framework, as of whalebone, wire, etc., used as formerly to puff out a skirt at the hips *b*) a skirt extended or puffed at the hips to give the effect of a pannier

pan·ni·kin (pan′ə kin) *n.* [dim. of PAN¹: see -KIN] [Chiefly Brit.] 1. a small pan 2. a metal cup

Pan·no·ni·a (pə nō′nē ə) ancient Roman province in C Europe, between the Danube & Sava rivers

☆**pa·no·cha** (pə nō′chə) *n.* [AmSp. < Sp. *pan*, bread: see PANADA] 1. a coarse sugar made in Mexico 2. *var.* of PENUCHE: also **pa·no′che** (-chē)

pan·o·ply (pan′ə plē) *n.*, *pl.* **-plies** [Gr. *panoplia* < *pan*, all (see PAN-) + *hopla*, arms, pl. of *hoplon*, tool (see HOPLITE)] 1. a complete suit of armor 2. any protective covering 3. any complete or magnificent covering or array —**pan′o·plied** *adj.*

pan·op·tic (pan äp′tik) *adj.* [PAN- + OPTIC] including in one view everything within sight

pan·o·ra·ma (pan′ə ram′ə, -rä′mə) *n.* [coined (c. 1789) by Robert Barker (by whom the first was painted) < PAN- + Gr. *horama*, a view < *horan*, to see < IE. base *wer-*, to heed, whence WARD, GUARD] 1. *a*) a picture or series of pictures of a landscape, historical event, etc., presented on a continuous surface encircling the spectator; cyclorama *b*) a picture unrolled before the spectator in such a way as to give the impression of a continuous view 2. an unlimited view in all directions 3. a comprehensive survey of a subject 4. a continuous series of scenes or events; constantly changing scene —**pan′o·ram′ic** *adj.* —**pan′o·ram′i·cal·ly** *adv.*

panoramic sight a kind of periscopic gun sight that provides a greatly enlarged field of view

PANICLE OF OATS

PANNIERS

pan·pipe (pan′pīp′) *n.* [PAN + PIPE] [also P-] a primitive musical instrument made of a row or rows of reeds or tubes of graduated lengths bound together and played by blowing across the open upper ends: also **panpipes, Pan's pipes**

PANPIPE

pan·so·phism (pan′sə fiz′m) *n.* [< Gr. *pansophos*, all-wise (< *pan*, all + *sophos*, wise) + -ISM] pretension to universal wisdom or knowledge —**pan′so·phist** *n.*

pan·so·phy (-fē) *n.* [ModL. *pansophia* < Gr. *pan*, all (see PAN-) + *sophia*, wisdom] 1. universal knowledge or wisdom 2. *pl.* **-phies** a system or work embracing all knowledge —**pan·soph′ic** (-säf′ik), **pan·soph′i·cal** *adj.*

pan·sy (pan′zē) *n.*, *pl.* **-sies** [Fr. *pensée*, a thought < *penser*, to think < L. *pensare*: see PENSIVE] 1. a small garden plant (*Viola tricolor*) of the violet family, with flat, broad, velvety petals in many colors ☆2. [Slang] an effeminate man; esp., a male homosexual

pant¹ (pant) *vi.* [ME. *panten*, prob. shortened < OFr. *pantaisier* < VL. *phantasiare*, to suffer from a nightmare < L. *phantasia*, idea, notion, nightmare: see FANTASY] 1. to breathe rapidly and heavily; gasp, as from running fast 2. to beat rapidly, as the heart; throb; pulsate 3. to feel strong desire; yearn eagerly (with *for* or *after*) 4. to give off steam, smoke, etc. in loud puffs, as an engine —*vt.* to utter hurriedly and breathlessly; gasp out —*n.* 1. any of a series of rapid, heavy breaths, as from exertion; gasp 2. a throb, as of the heart 3. a puff, as of an engine

pant² (pant) *n.*, *adj. see* PANTS

Pan·tag·ru·el (pan tag′roo wel′, pan′tə groō′əl; *Fr.* pän tà grü el′) [Fr., coined by Rabelais < Gr. *panta*, all (see PANTO-) + "Hagarene" (i.e., Arabic) *gruel*, athirst, hence, lit., all-thirsty] the boisterous, young giant son of Gargantua in Rabelais' *Gargantua and Pantagruel*: he is a jovial drunkard characterized by rough, extravagant humor —**Pan′ta·gru·el′i·an** (-tə groō wel′ē ən, -tag′roo wel′ē ən) *adj.* —**Pan·tag·ru·el·ism** (pan′tə groō′əl iz′m, pan tag′roo wəl iz′m) *n.*

pan·ta·lets, pan·ta·lettes (pan′t'l ets′) *n.pl.* [dim. of ff.] 1. long, loose drawers frilled at the ankle and showing beneath the skirt, worn by women during the middle of the 19th cent. 2. detachable ruffles for the legs of drawers

pan·ta·loon (pan′t'l ōōn′) [Fr. *Pantalon* < It. *Pantalone*, name of a character in Italian comedy, from the Venetian patron saint *Pantalone* or *Pantaleone*: also, the garment worn by this character] [P-] 1. a stock character in an old Italian comedy, usually a slender, foolish old man wearing tight trousers extending to the feet 2. a similar figure in modern pantomime, the butt of the clown's jokes —*n.* [*pl.*] 1. *orig.*, tight trousers fastened below the calf or strapped under the boots 2. later, any trousers: see PANTS

pant-dress (pant′dres′) *n.* a women's one-piece garment with the lower part like pants instead of a skirt

pan·tech·ni·con (pan tek′ni kän′, -kən) *n.* [PAN- + Gr. *technikon* (neut. adj.), of the arts < *technē*, art] [Brit.] 1. *orig.*, a bazaar where all kinds of things were sold 2. a warehouse 3. a furniture van: also **pantechnicon van**

Pan·tel·le·ri·a (pän tel′le rē′ä) It. island in the Mediterranean, between Sicily & Tunisia: 32 sq. mi.

pan·the·ism (pan′thē iz′m) *n.* [Fr. *panthéisme* < E. *pantheist*, coined (1705) by J. Toland, Eng. deist: see PAN-, THEO-, & -ISM] 1. the doctrine that God is not a personality, but that all laws, forces, manifestations, etc. of the self-existing universe are God 2. the worship, or toleration of worship, of all gods of various cults —**pan′the·ist** *n.* —**pan′the·is′tic, pan′the·is′ti·cal** *adj.* —**pan′the·is′ti·cal·ly** *adv.*

pan·the·on (pan′thē än′, -ən) *n.* [ME. *Panteon* < L. < Gr. *pantheion* < *pan*, all (see PAN-) + *theos*, a god] 1. a temple for all the gods; esp., [P-] a temple built by Agrippa in Rome in 27 B.C., and rebuilt in the 2d cent. A.D. by Hadrian: used since 609 A.D. as a Christian church 2. all the gods of a people 3. [often P-] a building in which famous dead persons of a nation are entombed or commemorated, as the church of Sainte-Geneviève in Paris

pan·ther (pan′thər) *n.*, *pl.* **-thers, -ther:** see PLURAL, II, D, 1 [ME. *pantere* < OFr. *pantère* < L. *panthera* < Gr. *panthēr*] 1. a leopard; specif., *a*) a leopard of the black varieties *b*) a leopard larger or fiercer than the average 2. *same as: a*) COUGAR *b*) JAGUAR —**pan′ther·ess** *n.fem.*

☆**pant·ies** (pan′tēz) *n.pl.* women's or children's short underpants: also **pant′ie** (-tē)

pan·tile (pan′tīl′) *n.* [PAN¹ + TILE] a roofing tile having an S curve, laid with the large curve of one tile overlapping the small curve of the next

pan·to- (pan′tō, -tə) [< Gr. *pantos*, gen. of *pan*] *a combining form meaning* all or every [*pantograph*]: also, before a vowel, **pant-**

PANTILES

pan·to·fle (pan′tə f'l; pan tä′f'l, -tōf′-) *n.* [LME. *pantufle* < MFr. *pantoufle* < ?] *same as* SLIPPER

pan·to·graph (pan′tə graf′, -gräf′) *n.* [Fr. *pantographe*: see PANTO- & -GRAPH] 1. a mechanical device for reproducing a map, drawing, etc. on the same or a

different scale, consisting of a framework of jointed rods in a roughly parallelogram form **2.** any similar framework, as an extensible arm for a telephone, a trolley on an electric locomotive, etc. —**pan′to·graph′ic** adj.

pan·to·mime (pan′tə mīm′) n. [L. pantomimus < Gr. pantomimos < pantos (see PANTO-) + mimos, a mimic] **1.** in ancient Rome a) an actor who played his part by gestures and action without words b) a drama played in action and gestures to the accompaniment of music or of words sung by a chorus **2.** a) any dramatic presentation played without words, using only action and gestures b) the art of acting in this way **3.** action or gestures without words as a means of expression **4.** in England, a type of entertainment presented at Christmas time, ending in a harlequinade —adj. of or like pantomime —vt., vi.-**mimed′**, -**mim′ing** to express or act in pantomime —**pan′to·mim′ic** (-mim′ik) adj. —**pan′to·mim′ist** (-mī′mist, -mim′ist) n.

pan·to·then·ate (pan′tə then′āt, pan tä′th′ə nāt′) n. a salt or ester of pantothenic acid

pan·to·then·ic acid (pan′tə then′ik) [Gr. pantothen, from every side < pantos (see PANTO-) + -IC] a yellow, viscous oil, $C_9H_{17}O_5N$, a member of the vitamin B complex, widely distributed in animal and plant tissues and prepared synthetically: thought to be essential for cell growth and used in treating certain anemias

pan·toum (pan tōōm′) n. [Fr. < Malay pantun] a verse form made up of quatrains rhyming abab, bcbc, cdcd, etc., with the second and fourth lines of one quatrain recurring as the first and third lines of the next and with the first and third lines of the first quatrain recurring as the second and fourth lines of the last

pan·try (pan′trē) n., pl. -**tries** [ME. paneterie < OFr. < ML. panetaria < L. panis, bread] **1.** a small room or closet off the kitchen, where cooking ingredients and utensils, china, etc. are kept **2.** a small room between the kitchen and dining room for storing tableware and for serving **3.** a larder or buttery

☆**pants** (pants) n.pl. [abbrev. of PANTALOONS] **1.** an outer garment extending from the waist to the knees or ankles and divided into separate coverings for the legs: more formally called trousers **2.** drawers or panties As an adjective or in compounds, usually **pant** [pant legs, pantdress]

pant·suit (pant′sōōt′) n. a woman's outfit consisting of a matched jacket and pants: also **pants suit**

pan·tun (pan tōōn′) n. [Malay] the Malayan verse form from which the pantoum originated

☆**pan·ty** (pan′tē) n., pl. -**ties** same as: **1.** PANTIES **2.** PANTY GIRDLE

panty girdle a girdle with a crotch or legs like panties

panty hose a woman's one-piece undergarment combining panties with hose

☆**pan·ty·waist** (-wāst′) n. **1.** orig., a child's two-piece undergarment that buttoned together at the waist **2.** [Slang] a man or youth considered as like a child in lacking strength, courage, etc.; sissy

Pan·urge (pan urj′; Fr. pá nürzh′) [Fr. < Gr. panourgos, knavish, ready for anything < pan (see PAN-) + -ourgos, worker < ergon, WORK] the gay, cowardly companion of Pantagruel in Rabelais' Gargantua and Pantagruel

Panza, Sancho see SANCHO PANZA

pan·zer (pan′zər; G. pän′tsər) adj. [G., armor < MHG. panzier < OFr. pancier < It. pancia, belly < L. pantex: see PAUNCH] armored [a panzer division]

Pa·o·lo (pä′ō lō) see FRANCESCA DA RIMINI

Pao·ting (bou′din′) city in Hopei province, NE China: pop. 250,000

Pao·tou (bou′dō′) city in the SW Inner Mongolian Autonomous Region: pop. 1,500,000: also sp. **Pao′tow′**

pap[1] (pap) n. [ME. pappe, prob. orig. < baby talk] **1.** [Archaic] a nipple or teat **2.** something shaped like a nipple or teat, as a cone-shaped hill

pap[2] (pap) n. [ME., orig. < baby talk (as in L. papa)] **1.** a) any soft or semiliquid food for babies or invalids b) any mash, paste, or pulp **2.** any oversimplified or tasteless writing, ideas, etc. ☆**3.** money, favors, etc. received because of association with public office

pa·pa (pä′pə; now less freq. pə pä′) n. [< baby talk, as also in Fr. & L. papa, Gr. pappas, father, pappos, grandfather] father: a child's word, corresponding to mamma for mother

pa·pa·cy (pä′pə sē) n., pl. -**cies** [ME. papacie < ML.(Ec.) papatia < LL.(Ec.) papa, bishop, POPE] **1.** the position, authority, or rank of the Pope **2.** the period of time during which a pope rules **3.** the succession of popes; popes collectively **4.** [also P-] the government of the Roman Catholic Church, headed by the Pope

Pa·pa·go (pä′pə gō′) n. [< Papago, lit., bean people] **1.** pl. -**gos′, -go′** a member of a tribe of N. American Indians living mostly south of Tucson, Ariz. **2.** their Uto-Aztecan language

pa·pa·in (pə pā′in, -pī′in) n. [PAPA(YA) + -IN[1]] a proteinsplitting enzyme obtained from the juice of unripe papaya and used as an aid to digestion, as a meat tenderizer, in pharmacy, etc.

pa·pal (pā′pəl) adj. [ME. < MFr. < ML.(Ec.) papalis: see POPE & -AL] **1.** of the Pope or the papacy **2.** of the Roman Catholic Church —**pa′pal·ly** adv.

Papal States former territory in C & NC Italy, ruled by the papacy from the 8th cent. until 1870

‡**pa·pa·raz·zi** (pä′pä rät′tsē) n.pl., sing. -**raz′zo** (-tsō) [It., prob. < Fr. paperassier, a scribbler, rummager in old papers < paperasse, old paper, waste paper < papier, PAPER] photographers, esp. free-lance ones, who take candid shots of celebrities for newspapers or magazines

pa·pav·er·ine (pə pav′ə rēn′, -ər in) n. [L. papaver, poppy + -INE[4]] a white, crystalline alkaloid, $C_{20}H_{21}NO_4$, derived from opium and used in medicine to relax muscles in spasms and as a local anesthetic

pa·paw (pô′pô, pə pô′) n. [prob. < ff.] **1.** same as PAPAYA ☆**2.** a) a tree (Asimina triloba) of the custard-apple family, growing in the C and S U.S. and having an oblong, yellowish, edible fruit with many seeds b) its fruit

pa·pa·ya (pə pä′yə) n. [Sp. < native name in a Caribbean Indian language] **1.** a tropical American tree (Carica papaya) of the papaya family, resembling a palm, having a bunch of large leaves at the top, and bearing a large, oblong, yellowish-orange fruit like a melon **2.** its fruit, eaten raw or cooked, and also valued for its juice —adj. designating a family (Caricaceae) of tropical and subtropical trees and shrubs including the papaya

Pa·pe·e·te (pä′pē ā′tā) seaport & chief town on Tahiti; capital of French Polynesia: pop. 20,000

pa·per (pā′pər) n. [ME. papir < OFr. papier < L. papyrus < Gr. papyros, PAPYRUS] **1.** a thin, flexible material made usually in sheets from a pulp prepared from rags, wood, or other fibrous material, and used for writing or printing on, for packaging, as structural material, as a fabric substitute, etc. **2.** a single piece or sheet of paper **3.** a printed or written sheet; specif., a) an official document b) an essay, monograph, or dissertation, as read before a learned society, published in a scholarly journal, etc. c) a written examination, report, theme, etc. **4.** same as: a) COMMERCIAL PAPER b) PAPER MONEY **5.** clipped form of: a) NEWSPAPER b) WALLPAPER **6.** a small wrapper or card of paper, usually including its contents [a paper of pins] **7.** any material like paper, as papyrus **8.** [pl.] a) documents identifying a person; credentials b) a collection of documents, letters, writings, etc., esp. of one person [the Lincoln papers] **9.** [Slang] a) a free pass or passes to a theater, etc. b) the people admitted by free passes —adj. **1.** of paper; made of paper **2.** like paper; thin **3.** existing only in written or printed form; theoretical; not real [paper profits] —vt. **1.** to cover or line with paper; specif., to cover or decorate with wallpaper **2.** to wrap or enclose in paper **3.** [Slang] to help to fill (a theater, etc.) by issuing free passes **4.** [Archaic] to describe in writing —vi. to hang wallpaper —**on paper 1.** in written or printed form **2.** in theory —**pa′per·er** n.

pa·per·back (-bak′) n. a book bound in paper instead of cloth, leather, etc. —**pa′per·backed′** adj.

☆**paper birch** the N. American birch (Betula papyrifera), having white or ash-colored, paperlike bark

pa·per·board (-bôrd′) ☆n. a relatively stiff, heavy material, thicker than paper, made from paper pulp

pa·per·bound (-bound′) adj. designating or of a book bound in paper; paperbacked

pa·per·boy (-boi′) n. a boy or man who sells or delivers newspapers

☆**paper clip** a flexible clasp, typically of metal wire, for holding loose sheets of paper together by pressure

paper cutter 1. same as PAPER KNIFE **2.** a device or machine for cutting and trimming a number of sheets of paper at a time

pa·per·hang·er (-haŋ′ər) n. **1.** a person whose work is covering walls with wallpaper ☆**2.** [Slang] a person who passes forged checks or counterfeit paper money —**pa′per·hang′ing** n.

paper knife a knifelike blade of metal, wood, ivory, etc., used to cut folded paper, as sealed envelopes or the uncut pages of books; paper cutter

☆**paper money** noninterest-bearing notes, as dollar bills, issued by a government or its banks, circulating as legal tender: the term sometimes includes checks, drafts, money orders, etc.

paper mulberry an Asiatic tree (Broussonetia papyrifera) with deeply lobed leaves and red, fleshy, compound fruits: grown for ornament in mild climates

paper nautilus an eight-armed, cephalopod mollusk (genus Argonauta) related to the octopus: the female inhabits a thin, paperlike, spiral shell which she can leave at will and in which the young develop

paper tiger a person, nation, etc. that seems to pose a threat but is actually ineffective or powerless

pa·per·weight (-wāt′) n. any small, heavy object set on papers to keep them from being blown away or otherwise scattered

☆**pa·per·white** (-hwīt′) n. same as POLYANTHUS (sense 2)

paper work the keeping of records, filing of reports, etc. incidental to some work or task

pa·per·y (pā'pər ē) *adj.* thin, light, etc., like paper
pap·e·terie (pap'ə trē) *n.* [MFr. < *papelier*, paper maker, stationer < *papier*, PAPER] a box of stationery
Pa·phi·an (pā'fi ən) *adj.* [< L. *Paphius* + -AN] 1. of Paphos 2. [in reference to the worship of Aphrodite in Paphos] of sexual love; erotic
Paph·la·go·ni·a (paf'lə gō'nē ə) ancient region of N Asia Minor, on the Black Sea
Pa·phos (pā'fäs) ancient city in SW Cyprus, founded by the Phoenicians
Pa·pia·men·to (pä'pyä men'tō) *n.* [Sp. < Papiamento *papia*, talk, prob. (? via Port. *papear*, to jabber) of echoic orig. + Sp. *-mento*, -ment] a creolized Spanish with admixtures of Dutch, Portuguese, etc., spoken on Curaçao and Aruba
‡**pa·pier col·lé** (på pyä kô lā') *pl.* **pa·piers col·lés** (-pyä kô lā') [Fr., lit., pasted paper: see COLLAGE] a kind of collage in which the pasted objects are grouped for pattern rather than for symbolism
pa·pier-mâ·ché (pā'pər mə shā') *n.* [Fr. *papier*, paper + *mâché*, pp. of *mâcher* (L. *masticare*), to chew] a material made of paper pulp mixed with size, glue, etc., that is easily molded when moist and that dries strong and hard —*adj.* made of papier-mâché
pa·pil·i·o·na·ceous (pə pil'ē ə nā'shəs) *adj.* [< L. *papilio*, butterfly (< redupl. of IE. base *pel-, to fly, flutter, swim, whence OE. *fifealde*, butterfly) + -ACEOUS] *Bot.* shaped like a butterfly: said of certain flowers, esp. those of some legumes, as the pea
pa·pil·la (pə pil'ə) *n.*, *pl.* **-lae** (-ē) [L., dim. of *papula*, pimple: see PAPULE] 1. *a)* any small nipplelike projection or process of connective tissue, as the small elevations at the root of a developing tooth, hair, feather, etc. or the many and variously shaped elevations on the surface of the tongue *b)* [Rare] the nipple of the breast 2. *Bot.* a tiny, protruding cell —**pa·pil·late** (pap'ə lāt', pə pil'it), **pa·pil·lose** (pap'ə lōs') *adj.*
pap·il·lar·y (pap'ə ler'ē, pə pil'ər ē) *adj.* 1. of, or having the nature of, a papilla 2. provided with, consisting of, or affecting papillae
pap·il·lo·ma (pap'ə lō'mə) *n.*, *pl.* **-ma·ta** (-mə tə), **-mas** [ModL.: see PAPILLA & -OMA] 1. a benign tumor of the skin or mucous membrane, consisting of a thickened and enlarged papilla or group of papillae, as a corn or wart 2. such a tumor caused by a virus —**pap·il·lo·ma·tous** (-təs) *adj.*
pa·pil·lon (pap'ə län'; Fr. pä pē yōn') *n.* [Fr., a butterfly (< L. *papilio:* see PAPILIONACEOUS): from the shape of the ears] any of a breed of toy spaniel: one type has erect; fringed ears
pa·pist (pā'pist) *n.* [ModL. *papista* < LL.(Ec.) *papa*, POPE] 1. a person who believes in papal supremacy 2. a Roman Catholic —*adj.* Roman Catholic: A hostile term
pa·pist·ry (pā'pis trē) *n.* [see PAPIST & -(E)RY] Roman Catholic beliefs and practices: a hostile term
☆**pa·poose** (pa pōōs', pə-) *n.* [< AmInd. (Algonquian) *papoos*] a North American Indian baby
pap·pose (pap'ōs) *adj.* having or being a pappus: also **pap'pous** (-əs)
pap·pus (pap'əs) *n.*, *pl.* **pap'pi** (-ī) [ModL. < L. < Gr. *pappos*, old man, grandfather (see PAPA) hence substance resembling gray hairs] *Bot.* a group or tuft of prongs, bristles, scales, or simple or branched hairs, as on the achenes of the dandelion, forming the modified calyx of the composite and certain other families and serving in the dispersal of the fruit
pap·py¹ (pap'ē) *n.*, *pl.* **-pies** [Dial. or Colloq.] father
pap·py² (pap'ē) *adj.* **-pi·er, -pi·est** [PAP² + -Y²] like pap; mushy
pa·pri·ka (pa prē'kə, pə-; pap'ri kə) *n.* [Hung. < Serb. *påprika* < *påpar*, pepper < Gr. *peperi*, PEPPER] a mild, red, powdered condiment ground from the fruit of certain strains of the chili pepper, grown esp. in C Europe and the American tropics
☆**Pap test** (pap) [after George *Papanicolaou* (1883–1962), U.S. anatomist who developed the test] the microscopic examination of cells taken as a smear (**Pap smear**) from the cervix of a woman, used as a test for uterine cancer in its early, curable stage
Pa·pu·a (pap'yoo wə, pä'poo wə) 1. *same as* NEW GUINEA 2. Gulf of, arm of the Coral Sea, on the SE coast of New Guinea: c. 225 mi. wide 3. Territory of, Australian territory consisting of the SE section of the island of New Guinea, & nearby islands: 90,540 sq. mi.; pop. 601,000; cap. Port Moresby: see Trust Territory of NEW GUINEA
Pap·u·an (-wən) *adj.* of Papua, its people, or their languages —*n.* 1. a member of a Negroid people living in New Guinea and nearby islands 2. a member of any of the dark-skinned peoples of Oceania 3. *a)* any of a group of languages of uncertain relationship spoken in New Guinea, New Caledonia, and elsewhere in the SW Pacific *b)* this group
pap·ule (pap'yōol) *n.* [L. *papula* < IE. base *pap-*, to swell, whence Sans. *pippalah*, berry] a small, usually inflammatory, elevation of the skin; pimple —**pap'u·lar** (-lər) *adj.* —**pap'u·lose** (-lōs') *adj.*
pap·y·ra·ceous (pap'ə rā'shəs) *adj.* [L. *papyraceus:* see ff. & -ACEOUS] like paper; papery

pa·py·rus (pə pī'rəs) *n.*, *pl.* **-ri** (-rī), **-rus·es** [ME. *papirus* < L. *papyrus* < Gr. *papyros*, prob. < Egypt.] 1. a tall water plant (*Cyperus papyrus*) of the sedge family, abundant in the Nile region of Egypt and widely cultivated as an ornamental 2. a writing material made from this plant by the ancient Egyptians, Greeks, and Romans, by soaking, pressing, and drying thin slices of its pith laid crosswise 3. any ancient document or manuscript on papyrus

PAPYRUS
(to 8 ft. high)

par (pär) *n.* [L., an equal, orig. *adj.* < IE. base *per-*, to sell, barter, hence, make equal, whence Sans. *pûrtá*, reward] 1. the established or recognized value of the money of one country in terms of the money of another country, based on a metal accepted as the common standard of value 2. an equal or common status, standing, footing, level, etc.: usually in phrase **on a par (with)** 3. the average or normal state, condition, degree, etc. [work that is above *par*] 4. *Commerce* the nominal, or face, value of stocks, bonds, etc. 5. *Golf* the number of strokes established as a skillful score for any given hole or for a whole course —*adj.* 1. of or at par 2. average; normal —*vt.* **parred, par'ring** *Golf* to score par on (a given hole or course)
par- *same as* PARA-¹
par. 1. paragraph 2. parallel 3. parenthesis 4. parish
Pa·rá (pä rä') 1. river in NE Brazil, forming the estuary of the Tocantins & a S estuary of the Amazon: c. 200 mi. 2. state of N Brazil, on the Atlantic: 481,800 sq. mi.; pop. 1,551,000; cap. Belém 3. *same as* BELÉM
pa·ra (pä rä', pär'ə) *n.* [Turk. < Per. *pārah*, a piece] 1. formerly, a Turkish copper coin equal to 1/40 piaster 2. a Yugoslavian unit of currency equal to 1/100 dinar, or a coin of this value
par·a-¹ (par'ə) [Gr. *para-* < *para*, at the side of, alongside < IE. *pera-*, var. of *per-*, a going beyond, whence FAR, FORE] *a prefix meaning:* 1. by the side of, beside, alongside of, by, past, beyond, to one side, aside from, amiss [*parapsychology*] 2. *Chem.* an isomer, modification, polymer, derivative, etc. of (a specified substance): used especially to designate a derivative of benzene in which two atoms or radicals are substituted in positions directly opposite each other in the ring [*paradichlorobenzene*] 3. *Med.* *a)* in a secondary or accessory capacity *b)* functionally disordered, abnormal [*parafunctional*] *c)* like or resembling [*paracholera*]
par·a-² (par'ə, per'ə) [Fr. < It. *para*, imperative of *parare*, to ward off < L. *parare*, to prepare] *a combining form meaning:* 1. a protection against [*parasol*] 2. [< PARA- (CHUTE)] using a parachute [*paratrooper*]
Para. Paraguay
par·a-a·mi·no·ben·zo·ic acid (par'ə ə mē'nō ben zō'ik, -am'ə nō'-) [PARA-¹ + AMINO- + BENZOIC] a yellowish crystalline compound, $C_7H_7NO_2$, considered a member of the vitamin B complex, widely distributed in nature, esp. in yeast, and commercially prepared: required by many organisms as a growth vitamin
par·a·bi·o·sis (-bī ō'sis) *n.* [PARA-¹ + -BIOSIS] 1. the union of two animals, naturally or experimentally, as by blood circulatory connections 2. the temporary and reversible suspension of a vital life process 3. the living together of two or more different species, as in mixed flocks of animals or birds or in mixed colonies of ants —**par·a·bi·ot·ic** (-ät'ik) *adj.*
par·a·blast (par'ə blast') *n.* [PARA-¹ + -BLAST] *Embryology* 1. the nutritive yolk of a meroblastic ovum 2. the portion of a mesoblast that gives rise to vascular and lymphatic tissues —**par·a·blas'tic** *adj.*
par·a·ble (par'ə b'l) *n.* [ME. < MFr. *parabole* < LL.(Ec.) *parabola*, an allegorical relation, parable < L., a comparison < Gr. *parabolē*, an analogy (< *paraballein*, to throw beside: see PARA-¹ & BALL²), in NT. & LXX, a parable: transl. of Heb. *māshāl*, a comparison] a short, simple story, usually of an occurrence of a familiar kind, from which a moral or religious lesson may be drawn
pa·rab·o·la (pə rab'ə lə) *n.* [ModL. < Gr. *parabolē*, lit., application, comparison (see prec.): it is produced by the "application" of a given area to a given straight line] *Geom.* a plane curve which is the path, or locus, of a moving point that remains equally distant from a fixed point (*focus*) and from a fixed straight line (*directrix*); curve formed by the intersection of a cone with a plane parallel to its side

PARABOLA
(X, x-axis; Y, y-axis; A, vertex; F, focus; DD', directrix; P, point on parabola; PQ=PF)

par·a·bol·ic[1] (par′ə bäl′ik) *adj.* [LL. *parabolicus* < LGr. *parabolikos*] of, in the form of, or expressed by a parable: also **par′a·bol′i·cal** —**par′a·bol′i·cal·ly** *adv.*

par·a·bol·ic[2] (par′ə bäl′ik) *adj.* 1. of or like a parabola 2. bowl-shaped, as a reflector, antenna, or microphone, so that sections parallel to the plane of symmetry are parabolas —**par′a·bol′i·cal·ly** *adv.*

pa·rab·o·lize (pə rab′ə līz′) *vt.* -**lized′**, -**liz′ing** 1. to tell in a parable or parables 2. to make parabolic in shape —**pa·rab′o·liz′er** *n.*

pa·rab·o·loid (-loid′) *n.* a surface or solid formed so that sections parallel to the plane of symmetry are parabolas and sections perpendicular to it are ellipses (**elliptic paraboloid**), hyperbolas (**hyperbolic paraboloid**), or circles (**paraboloid of revolution**) —**pa·rab·o·loi′dal** *adj.*

Par·a·cel·sus (par′ə sel′səs), **Phi·lip·pus Au·re·o·lus** (fi lip′əs ô rē′ə ləs) (born *Theophrastus Bombastus von Hohenheim*) 1493–1541; Swiss physician & alchemist

par·a·chute (par′ə shoot′) *n.* [Fr. < *para*- (see PARA-[2]) + *chute*, a fall: see CHUTE[2]] 1. a large cloth contrivance shaped like an umbrella when expanded, and used to retard the falling speed of a person or thing dropping from an airplane, etc.: it is generally carried folded in a pack, from which it is released by a rip cord or other device 2. something shaped like or having the effect of a parachute 3. *Zool.* same as PATAGIUM (sense 1) —*vt.* -**chut′ed**, -**chut′ing** to drop by parachute —*vi.* to descend by parachute

par·a·chut·ist (-shoot′ist) *n.* a person who descends by parachute: also **par′a·chut′er**

par·a·clete (par′ə klēt′) *n.* [ME. *paraclit* < OFr. *paraclet* < LL.(Ec.) *paracletus* < Gr. *paraklētos* (in NT., the Holy Spirit) < *parakalein*, to call, summon (in NT.), to comfort) < *para*-, PARA-[1] + *kalein*, to call: see CLAMOR] 1. an advocate; intercessor; pleader 2. [P-] *Christianity* the Holy Spirit, considered as comforter, intercessor, or advocate

pa·rade (pə rād′) *n.* [Fr. < Sp. *parada*, a parade, place for the exercise of troops < *parar*, to stop (a horse), prepare < L. *parare*, PREPARE] 1. ostentatious or pompous display 2. *a)* a military display or assembly; esp., a review of marching troops *b)* a place where troops assemble regularly for parade; parade ground 3. any organized procession or march, as for display 4. *a)* a public walk or promenade *b)* persons promenading; strollers —*vt.* -**rad′ed**, -**rad′ing** 1. to bring together (troops, etc.) for inspection or display 2. to march or walk through, as for display [a band *parading* the streets] 3. to make a display of; show off [to *parade* one's knowledge] —*vi.* 1. to march in a parade or procession 2. to walk about ostentatiously; show off 3. to assemble in military formation for review or display —**on parade** on display —**pa·rad′er** *n.*

parade rest *Mil.* 1. a formal position of rest, distinguished by its prescribed, motionless stance from the informal position of *at ease* (see under EASE) 2. the command to assume this position

par·a·di·chlo·ro·ben·zene (par′ə dī klôr′ə ben′zēn, -ben zēn′) *n.* [PARA-[1] + DI-[1] + CHLORO- + BENZENE] a white crystalline compound, $C_6H_4Cl_2$, used as an insecticide, esp. in protecting clothes from moths, as a deodorant, disinfectant, etc.

par·a·did·dle (par′ə did′'l) *n.* [echoic] a pattern of beats on a snare drum executed with alternate strokes of the sticks

par·a·digm (par′ə dim, -dīm′) *n.* [Fr. *paradigme* < LL. *paradigma* < Gr. *paradeigma* < *para*-, PARA-[1] + *deigma*, example < *deiknynai*, to show: for IE. base see DICTION] 1. a pattern, example, or model 2. *Gram.* an example of a declension or conjugation, giving all the inflectional forms of a word —*SYN.* see MODEL —**par′a·dig·mat′ic** (-dig mat′ik) *adj.* —**par′a·dig·mat′i·cal·ly** *adv.*

par·a·di·sa·ic (par′ə di sā′ik) *adj.* same as PARADISIACAL: also **par′a·dis′al** (-dī′s'l), **par′a·di·sa′i·cal**

par·a·dise (par′ə dīs′) *n.* [ME. *paradis* < OE. & OFr., both < LL.(Ec.) *paradisus*, heaven, abode of the blessed < L., park, orchard < Gr. *paradeisos*, park, garden (in NT. & LXX, Paradise) < MIran. *pardez*, akin to Av. *pairi-daēza*, an enclosure < *pairi*, around (see PERI-) + *daēza*, a wall < IE. base *dheigh*-, to knead clay, build a wall, whence Gr. *teichos*, wall: cf. DOUGH] 1. [P-] the garden of Eden: see EDEN 2. same as: *a)* HEAVEN *b)* LIMBO[1] 3. *a)* any place of great beauty and perfection *b)* any place or condition of great happiness

par·a·di·si·a·cal (par′ə di sī′ə k'l) *adj.* [LL.(Ec.) *paradisiacus*] of, like, or fit for paradise: also **par′a·dis′i·ac′** (-dis′ē ak′) —**par′a·di·si′a·cal·ly** *adv.*

par·a·dos (par′ə däs′) *n.* [Fr. < *para*-, PARA-[2] + *dos* < L. *dorsum*, back] an embankment of earth along the back of a trench as to protect against fire from the rear

par·a·dox (par′ə däks′) *n.* [L. *paradoxum* < Gr. *paradoxon*, neut. of *paradoxos*, paradoxical < *para*- (see PARA-[1]) + *doxa*, opinion < *dokein*, to think, suppose: see DOCTOR] 1. formerly, a statement contrary to common belief 2. a statement that seems contradictory, unbelievable, or absurd but that may actually be true in fact 3. a statement that is self-contradictory in fact and, hence, false

4. a person, situation, act, etc. that seems to have contradictory or inconsistent qualities

par·a·dox·i·cal (par′ə däk′si k'l) *adj.* 1. of, having the nature of, or expressing, a paradox or paradoxes 2. fond of using paradoxes —**par′a·dox′i·cal·ly** *adv.* —**par′a·dox′i·cal·ness** *n.*

par·a·drop (par′ə dräp′) *n., vt.* -**dropped′**, -**drop′ping** [PARA-[2] + DROP] same as AIRDROP

par·aes·the·si·a (par′es thē′zhə, -zhē ə) *n. var. of* PARESTHESIA

par·af·fin (par′ə fin) *n.* [G. < L. *parum*, too little + *affinis*, akin: from its chemical inertia] 1. a white, waxy, odorless, tasteless solid substance consisting of a mixture of straight-chain, saturated hydrocarbons: it is obtained chiefly from the distillation of petroleum and is used for making candles, sealing preserving jars, waterproofing paper, etc. 2. *Chem.* any hydrocarbon of the methane series 3. [Brit.] same as KEROSENE —*vt.* to coat or impregnate with paraffin —**par′af·fin′ic** *adj.*

par·af·fine (-fin, -fēn′) *n., vt.* -**fined**, -**fin·ing** *var. of* PARAFFIN

paraffin series same as METHANE SERIES

paraffin wax same as PARAFFIN (n. 1)

par·a·gen·e·sis (par′ə jen′ə sis) *n.* [ModL.: see PARA-[1] & -GENESIS] the order in which closely associated minerals in rocks, veins, etc. have been formed, including their interactions with one another from contact —**par′a·ge·net′ic** (-jə net′ik) *adj.*

par·a·go·ge (par′ə gō′jē) *n.* [LL. < Gr. *paragōgē*, a drawing out < *paragein*, to draw out < *para*-, PARA-[1] + *agein*, to lead: see ACT] the adding of a letter or syllable to the end of a word, either grammatically, as in *drowned*, or unnecessarily, as in nonstandard *drownded* (droun′did), or for ease in pronunciation, as in *amidst*, etc. —**par′a·gog′ic** (-gäj′ik) *adj.*

par·a·gon (par′ə gän′, -gən) *n.* [MFr. (now *parangon*) < It. *paragone*, a comparison, test, lit., touchstone < *paragonare*, to test, compare < Gr. *parakonan*, to whet < *para*-, PARA-[1] + *akonē*, whetstone: for IE. base see ACID] 1. a model or pattern of perfection or excellence 2. a perfect diamond weighing a hundred carats or more 3. a perfectly round, large pearl —*vt.* 1. [Poet.] *a)* to put side by side; compare *b)* to be equal to; match 2. [Obs.] *a)* to surpass *b)* to set forth as a paragon

pa·rag·o·nite (pə rag′ə nīt′) *n.* [G. *paragonit* < Gr. *paragōn*, prp. of *paragein*, to mislead < *para*-, PARA-[1] + *agein*, to lead (see ACT) + -ITE[1]] a kind of mica distinguished from muscovite by containing sodium instead of potassium —**pa·rag′o·nit′ic** (-nit′ik) *adj.*

par·a·graph (par′ə graf′, -gräf′) *n.* [MFr. < ML. *paragraphus*, orig., sign marking separation of parts, as of a chapter < Gr. *paragraphos* < *para*-, beside (see PARA-[1]) + *graphein*, to write (see GRAPHIC)] 1. a distinct section or subdivision of a chapter, letter, etc., usually dealing with a particular point: it is begun on a new line, often indented 2. a mark (¶) used as by proofreaders to indicate the beginning of a paragraph or as a sign marking material referred to elsewhere 3. a brief article, item, or note in a newspaper or magazine —*vt.* 1. to mention in a paragraph or paragraphs 2. to separate or arrange in paragraphs —*vi.* to write paragraphs, esp. for a newspaper —**par′a·graph′er**, **par′a·graph′ist** *n.* —**par′a·graph′ic** *adj.*

par·a·graph·i·a (par′ə graf′ē ə) *n.* [ModL. < Gr. *para*-, PARA-[1] + *graphein*, to write: see GRAPHIC] a form of aphasia, usually due to cerebral injury, characterized by the unintentional omission, transposition, or insertion of letters or words in writing

Par·a·guay (par′ə gwā′, -gwī′; *Sp.* pä rä gwī′) 1. inland country in SC S. America: 157,042 sq. mi.; pop. 2,161,000; cap. Asunción 2. river in SC S. America, flowing from S Brazil south through Paraguay into the Paraná: c. 1,500 mi. —**Par′a·guay′an** *adj., n.*

Paraguay tea same as MATÉ

Pa·ra·í·ba (pä rä ē′bä) state of NE Brazil: 21,750 sq. mi.; pop. 2,018,000; cap. João Pessoa

par·a·keet (par′ə kēt′) *n.* [MFr. *paroquet*, prob. < *perrot*, PARROT] any of various small, slender parrots with a long, tapering tail

par·al·de·hyde (pə ral′də hīd′) *n.* [PAR- + ALDEHYDE] a colorless liquid, $C_6H_{12}O_3$, produced by the polymerization of acetaldehyde, having a strong, nauseating smell and used in medicine as a hypnotic and sedative

PARAKEET
(to 8 in. long, including tail)

par·a·leip·sis (par′ə līp′sis) *n.* [Gr. *paraleipsis*, omission < *para*-, PARA-[1] + *leipein*, to leave: for IE. base see LOAN] a rhetorical device in which a point is stressed by suggesting that it is too obvious or well-known to mention, as in the phrase, "not to mention the expense involved": also **par′a·lep′sis** (-lep′-), **par′a·lip′sis** (-lip′-)

Par·a·li·pom·e·non (par′ə li päm′ə nän′) *Douay Bible name for* CHRONICLES

par·al·lax (par′ə laks′) *n.* [Fr. *parallaxe* < Gr. *parallaxis* < *parallassein*, to vary, decline, wander < *para-*, PARA-[1] + *allassein*, to change < *allos*, other: see ELSE] 1. the apparent change in the position of an object resulting from the change in the direction or position from which it is viewed 2. the amount of angular degree of such change; specif., *Astron.* the apparent

PARALLAX
(P, star; R, point on earth's surface; A, center of the earth; angle RPA, parallax)

difference in the position of a heavenly body with reference to some point on the surface of the earth and some other point, as the center of the earth (**diurnal**, or **geocentric, parallax**) or a point on the sun (**annual**, or **heliocentric, parallax**): the parallax of an object may be used in determining its distance from the observer 3. the difference between the area taken in by a camera lens and the area seen in the viewfinder —**par′al·lac′tic** (-lak′tik) *adj.*

par·al·lel (par′ə lel′, -ləl) *adj.* [Fr. *parallèle* < L. *parallelus* < Gr. *parallēlos* < *para-*, side by side (see PARA-[1]) + *allēlos*, one another < *allos*, other: see ELSE] 1. extending in the same direction and at the same distance apart at every point, so as never to meet, as lines, planes, etc. 2. having parallel parts or movements, as some machines, tools, etc. 3. *a)* closely similar or corresponding, as in purpose, tendency, time, or essential parts *b)* characterized by a balanced or coordinated arrangement of elements, esp. of phrases or clauses [*parallel* structure] 4. *Elec.* designating, of, or pertaining to a circuit in parallel 5. *Music* having consistently equal intervals in pitch, as two parts of harmony′, a series of chords, etc. —*adv.* in a parallel manner —*n.* 1 something parallel to something else, as a line or surface 2. any person or thing essentially the same as, or closely corresponding to, another; counterpart 3. the condition of being parallel; conformity in essential points 4. any comparison showing the existence of similarity or likeness 5. *a)* any of the imaginary lines parallel to the equator and representing degrees of latitude on the earth′s surface *b)* such a line drawn on a map or globe: in full, **parallel of latitude** 6. [*pl.*] a sign (‖) used in printing as a reference mark 7. *Elec.* a method of circuit interconnection in which two or more components in the system have their negative terminals joined to one conductor and their positive to another, so that an identical potential difference is applied to each component: usually in the phrase, **in parallel** —*vt.* **-al·leled′** or **-al·lelled′**, **-al·lel′ing** or **-al·lel′ling** 1. *a)* to make (one thing) parallel to another *b)* to make parallel to each other 2. to be parallel with; extend parallel to [a road that *parallels* the river] 3. to compare (things, ideas, etc.) in order to show similarity or likeness 4. to be or find a counterpart for; match; equal

parallel bars two bars parallel to each other, set horizontally on adjustable upright posts from 15 to 18 inches apart and used in gymnastics

par·al·lel·e·pi·ped (par′ə lel′ə pī′pid, -pip′id) *n.* [Gr. *parallēlepipedon* < *parallēlos*, parallel + *epipedos*, on the ground, plane < *epi*, upon (see EPI-) + *pedon*, the ground < IE. *pedom* (whence Sans. *padám*, footstep) < base *ped-*, FOOT] a solid with six faces, each of which is a parallelogram: also **par′al·lel′-e·pip′e·don′** (-pip′ə dän′)

par·al·lel·ism (par′ə lel iz′m, -ləl-) *n.* [Gr. *parallēlismos*] 1. the state of being parallel 2. close resemblance; similarity 3. the use of parallel structure in writing 4. *Philos.* the theory that mind and matter, though independent, function together in a parallel, but without an interactive causal relationship

PARALLEL BARS

par·al·lel·o·gram (par′ə lel′ə gram′) *n.* [Fr. *parallélo-gramme* < L. *parallelogrammum* < Gr. *parallēlogrammon* < *parallēlos*, PARALLEL + *grammē*, stroke in writing < *graphein*, to write: see GRAPHIC] a plane figure with four sides, having the opposite sides parallel and equal

pa·ral·o·gism (pə ral′ə jiz′m) *n.* [MFr. *paralogisme* < LL. *paralogismus* < Gr. *paralogismos* < *paralogizesthai*, to reason illogically < *para-*, beyond (see PARA-[1]) + *logizesthai*, to reason < *logos*, a discourse, reason: see LOGIC] reasoning contrary to the rules of logic; faulty argument —**pa·ral′o·gis′tic** *adj.*

pa·ral·o·gize (pə ral′ə jiz′) *vi.* **-gized′, -giz′ing** [ML. *paralogizare* < Gr. *paralogizesthai*: see prec.] to reason falsely or illogically

pa·ral·y·sis (pə ral′ə sis) *n., pl.* **-ses′** (-sēz′) [L. < Gr. *paralysis* < *paralyein*, to loosen, dissolve, or weaken at the side: see PARA-[1] & LYSIS] 1. partial or complete loss, or temporary interruption, of a function, esp. of voluntary motion or of sensation in some part or all of the body 2. any condition of helpless inactivity or of inability to act

paralysis a·gi·tans (aj′i tənz) *same as* PARKINSON'S DISEASE

par·a·lyt·ic (par′ə lit′ik) *adj.* [ME. *paraletik* < OFr. *paralytique* < L. *paralyticus* < Gr. *paralytikos*] 1. of, or having the nature of, paralysis 2. having or subject to paralysis —*n.* a person having paralysis

par·a·lyze (par′ə līz′) *vt.* **-lyzed′, -lyz′ing** [Fr. *paralyser*, back-formation < *paralysie* < L. *paralysis*] 1. to cause paralysis in; make paralytic 2. to bring into a condition of helpless inactivity; make ineffective or powerless —SYN. see SHOCK[1] —**par′a·ly·za′tion** *n.* —**par′a·lyz′er** *n.*

par·a·mag·net·ic (par′ə mag net′ik) *adj.* designating or of a material, as aluminum, platinum, etc., having a magnetic permeability slightly greater than unity and varying to only a small extent with the magnetizing force —**par′a·mag′net·ism** (-mag′nə tiz′m) *n.*

Par·a·mar·i·bo (par′ə mar′i bō′) seaport & capital of Surinam: pop. 123,000

par·a·mat·ta (par′ə mat′ə) *n.* [after *Parramatta*, city in SE Australia] a soft, lightweight dress fabric with a cotton warp and a filling of fine wool

par·a·me·ci·um (par′ə mē′shē əm, -sē əm) *n., pl.* **-ci·a** (-ə) [ModL. < Gr. *paramēkēs*, oval < *para-*, PARA-[1] + *mēkos*, length, akin to *makros*, long: see MACRO-] any of a genus (*Paramecium*) of one-celled, elongated, slipper-shaped protozoans moving by means of cilia and having a backward-curving oral groove that ends with the mouth

☆**par·a·med·ic¹** (par′ə med′ik) *n.* [PARA-[2] + MEDIC[1]] a medic, esp. a medical corpsman, who parachutes to combat or rescue areas

☆**par·a·med·ic²** (par′ə med′ik) *n.* [back-formation < ff.] a person in paramedical work

☆**par·a·med·i·cal** (par′ə med′i k′l) *adj.* [PARA-[1] + MEDICAL] designating of or auxiliary medical personnel, such as midwives, corpsmen, laboratory technicians, nurses′ aides, etc.

par·a·ment (par′ə ment′) *n., pl.* **-ments′, -men′ta** (-men′tə) [ME. < ML. *paramentum* < L. *parare*, to PREPARE + *-mentum*, -ment] *Eccles.* an ornamental hanging, covering, or vestment

pa·ram·e·ter (pə ram′ə tər) *n.* [ModL. *parametrum* < Gr. *para-*, PARA-[1] + *metron*, MEASURE] 1. *Math.* a quantity or constant whose value varies with the circumstances of its application, as the radius line of a group of concentric circles, which varies with the circle under consideration 2. any constant, with variable values, used as a referent for determining other variables —**par·a·met·ric** (par′ə met′rik) *adj.*

par·a·mil·i·tar·y (par′ə mil′ə ter′ē) *adj.* [PARA-[1] + MILITARY] 1. designating or of forces working along with, or in place of, a regular military organization, often as a semiofficial or secret auxiliary 2. designating or of a private, often secret, quasimilitary organization

par·am·ne·sia (par′am nē′zhə) *n.* [PAR- + AMNESIA] *Psychol.* 1. distortion of memory with confusion of fact and fantasy 2. *same as* DÉJÀ VU

pa·ra·mo (par′ə mō′) *n., pl.* **-mos′** [AmSp. < Sp. *páramo* < Celt. *paramus*, a plain] any high, barren plain in the S. American tropics, esp. in the Andes

par·a·morph (par′ə môrf′) *n.* a mineral that has undergone paramorphism

par·a·mor·phism (par′ə môr′fiz′m) *n.* [PARA-[1] + -MORPH + -ISM] the process by which one sort of mineral may change into another by change in the crystal structure of the molecule without change of its chemical composition —**par′a·mor′phic, par′a·mor′phous** *adj.*

par·a·mount (par′ə mount′) *adj.* [Anglo-Fr. *paramont* < OFr. *par* (L. *per*), by + *amont*, à *mont* (< L. *ad montem*, to the hill), uphill] ranking higher than any other, as in power or importance; chief; supreme —*n.* supreme ruler; overlord —SYN. see DOMINANT —**par′a·mount′cy** (-sē) *n.* —**par′a·mount′ly** *adv.*

par·a·mour (par′ə moor′) *n.* [ME. < *par amur* < OFr. *par amour*, with love < *par* (L. *per*), by + *amour* (L. *amor*), love] 1. a lover or mistress; esp., the illicit sexual partner of a married man or woman 2. [Archaic or Poet.] a sweetheart

Pa·ra·ná (pä′rä nä′) 1. state of S Brazil: 77,040 sq. mi.; pop. 4,278,000; cap. Curitiba 2. river port in NE Argentina, on the Paraná River: pop. 174,000 3. river in S S. America, flowing from S Brazil along the SE boundary of Paraguay, through NE Argentina into the Río de la Plata: c. 2,000 mi.

pa·rang (pä räŋ′) *n.* [Malay] a heavy knife used by the Malays as a tool and weapon

par·a·noi·a (par′ə noi′ə) *n.* [ModL. < Gr. *paranoia*, derangement < *para-*, beside (see PARA-[1]) + *nous*, the mind] *Psychiatry* a mental disorder characterized by systematized delusions, as of grandeur or, esp., persecution, often, except in a schizophrenic state, with an otherwise relatively intact personality

par·a·noid (par′ə noid′) *adj.* 1. of or like paranoia 2. characterized by oversuspiciousness, grandiose delusions, or delusions of persecution: also **par′a·noi′dal** —*n.* a person afflicted with paranoia Also **par′a·noi′ac** (-noi′ak)

par·a·nor·mal (par′ə nôr′məl) *adj.* [PARA-[1] + NORMAL] designating of or psychic or mental phenomena outside the range of the normal

par·a·nymph (par′ə nimf′) *n.* [LL. *paranymphus* < Gr.

paranymphos < para-, beside (see PARA-¹) + nymphē, bride: see NUBILE] **1.** in ancient Greece, a groomsman who escorted the bridegroom when he went to bring his bride home, or a bridesmaid who escorted the bride to the bridegroom **2.** a best man or bridesmaid

par·a·pet (par'ə pit, -pet') n. [Fr. < It. parapetto < parare, to guard (< L., PREPARE) + petto, breast < L. pectus] **1.** a wall or bank used to screen troops from frontal enemy fire, sometimes placed along the top of a rampart **2.** a low wall or railing, as along a balcony or bridge —**par'a·pet'ed** adj.

par·aph (par'əf) n. [ME. parafe < MFr. < ML. paraphus, contr. < paragraphus, PARAGRAPH] a flourish made after a signature, orig. as a safeguard against forgery

par·a·pher·na·li·a (par'ə fər nāl'yə, -fə nāl'-; -nā'lē ə) n.pl. [often with sing. v.] [ML., short for paraphernalia bona, wife's own goods < LL. parapherna < Gr. parapherna, bride's possessions beyond her dower < para-, beyond (see PARA-¹) + phernē, a dowry, portion < pherein, to BEAR¹] **1.** personal belongings **2.** any collection of articles, usually things used in some activity; equipment; apparatus; trappings; gear **3.** Law formerly, property or possessions (other than dower) given over to the control and possession of a wife

par·a·phrase (par'ə frāz') n. [Fr. < L. paraphrasis < Gr. paraphrasis < paraphrazein, to say in other words: see PARA-¹ & PHRASE] **1.** a rewording of the meaning expressed in something spoken or written **2.** the use or process of paraphrase as a literary or teaching device —vt., vi. -phrased', -phras'ing to express in a paraphrase —SYN. see TRANSLATION —**par'a·phras'er, par'a·phrast'** (-frast') n.

par·a·phras·tic (par'ə fras'tik) adj. [ML. paraphrasticus < Gr. paraphrastikos] **1.** of, having the nature of, or forming a paraphrase **2.** using paraphrase —**par'a·phras'ti·cal·ly** adv.

pa·raph·y·sis (pə raf'ə sis) n., pl. -ses (-sēz') [ModL. < Gr., an offshoot, sucker < para- (see PARA-¹) + physis, a growth < phyein, to grow: see PHYSIC] a sterile, threadlike part found with the spore-bearing organs of some ferns and mosses

par·a·ple·gi·a (par'ə plē'jē ə, -jə) n. [ModL. < Gr. paraplēgia, a stroke at one side: see PARA-¹ & -PLEGIA] motor and sensory paralysis of the entire lower half of the body —**par'a·ple'gic** (-plē'jik, -plej'ik) adj., n.

par·a·prax·is (-prak'sis) n., pl. -es (-sēz) [PARA-¹ + PRAXIS] an action in which one's conscious intention is not fully carried out, as in the mislaying of objects, slips of the tongue and pen, etc.: thought to be generally due to a conflicting unconscious intention: also **par'a·prax'i·a** (-sē ə)

par·a·psy·chol·o·gy (-sī käl'ə jē) n. [PARA-¹ + PSYCHOLOGY] the branch of psychology that investigates psychic phenomena, as telepathy, extrasensory perception, clairvoyance, etc. —**par'a·psy'cho·log'i·cal** (-sī'kə läj'i k'l) adj. —**par'a·psy·chol'o·gist** n.

☆**par·a·res·cue** (par'ə res'kyōō) n. [PARA-² + RESCUE] the rescue of a person or persons, as from a dangerous or risky situation, by parachutists

par·a·ros·an·i·line (par'ə rō zan'¹l in) n. [PARA-¹ + ROSANILINE] a red aniline dye, $C_{19}H_{19}N_3O$, used in coloring fabrics, paper, etc. and as a biological stain

Pará rubber crude rubber obtained from several tropical S. American trees (genus Hevea), esp. a species (Hevea brasiliensis), of the spurge family

par·a·sail, par·a·sail (par'ə sāl') n. a type of parachute used in the sport of sailing through the air while being towed as by a powerboat —vi. to engage in this sport

par·a·sang (par'ə saŋ') n. [L. parasanga < Gr. parasangēs < OPer., whence Per. farsang] an ancient Persian measure of distance, equal to about 3 1/2 mi.

par·a·se·le·ne (par'ə sə lē'nē) n., pl. -nae (-nē) [ModL.: see PARA-¹ & SELENE] a bright moonlike spot on a lunar halo —**par'a·se·len'ic** (-len'ik) adj.

par·a·shah (pär'ə shä') n., pl. **par'a·shoth'** (-shōt') [Heb. pārāshāh, lit., an explanation] any of the sections into which the Pentateuch is annually divided for reading in the synagogue on each Sabbath; also, any of various selections from the Pentateuch for reading as on holy days

par·a·site (par'ə sīt') n. [L. parasitus < Gr. parasitos, one who eats at the table of another, parasite, toady < para-, beside (see PARA-¹) + sitos, food, grain] **1.** a person, as in ancient Greece, who flattered and amused his host in return for free meals **2.** a person who lives at the expense of another or others without making any useful contribution or return; hanger-on **3.** Biol. a plant or animal that lives on or in an organism of another species from which it derives sustenance or protection without benefiting the host and usually doing harm

SYN.—parasite refers to one who derives advantage or sustenance from another and gives nothing in return; a sycophant is one who seeks advantage or favor from the wealthy or powerful by flattery, fawning, etc.; toady suggests the servility and snobbery of one who seeks familiarity with those whom he regards as his superiors; hanger-on is applied to anyone regarded contemptuously for his close adherence to and dependence on another; leech is applied to

a parasite who clings closely to another and extracts whatever he can for his own advantage; sponge (or sponger) is a colloquial term for a parasite and stresses his total dependence, disinclination to work, etc.

parasite drag Aeron. the drag caused by the nonlifting parts of an aircraft, as nacelles, the fuselage, etc.

par·a·sit·ic (par'ə sit'ik) adj. [L. parasiticus < Gr. parasitikos] **1.** of or like a parasite; living at the expense of others **2.** caused by parasites, as a disease Also **par'a·sit'i·cal** —**par'a·sit'i·cal·ly** adv.

par·a·sit·i·cide (par'ə sit'ə sid') n. [< PARASITE + -CIDE] a substance or agent used to destroy parasites —**par'a·sit'i·ci'dal** adj.

par·a·sit·ism (par'ə sīt'iz'm) n. **1.** the state or condition of being a parasite **2.** the habits of a parasite **3.** Biol. a symbiotic association of two kinds of organisms in which the parasite is benefited and the host is usually harmed **4.** Med. the condition of being infested with parasites

par·a·sit·ize (-sī tīz', -sī-) vt. -ized', -iz'ing **1.** to live on, in, or with as a parasite **2.** to infest with parasites

par·a·sit·oid (-sī toid') n. [PARASIT(E) + -OID] a parasite that ultimately destroys its host, as any of various wasp larvae which feed progressively on the tissues of an immature stage of a host species

par·a·si·tol·o·gy (par'ə sī täl'ə jē, -sī-) n. the science dealing with parasites and parasitism —**par'a·si'to·log'i·cal** (-sīt'ə läj'i k'l) adj. —**par'a·si·tol'o·gist** n.

par·a·sit·o·sis (-sī tō'sis, -sī-) n. [PARASIT(E) + -OSIS] Med. any disease caused by parasites

par·a·sol (par'ə sôl', -säl') n. [Fr. < It. parasole < parare, to ward off (< L., PREPARE) + sole (< L. sol), the sun] a lightweight umbrella carried by women as a sunshade

par·a·sym·pa·thet·ic (par'ə sim'pə thet'ik) adj. [PARA-¹ + SYMPATHETIC] Anat., Physiol. designating or of that part of the autonomic nervous system whose nerves originate in the midbrain, the hindbrain, and the sacral region of the spinal cord and whose functions include the constriction of the pupils of the eyes, the slowing of the heartbeat, and the stimulation of certain digestive glands: cf. SYMPATHETIC

par·a·sym·pa·tho·mi·met·ic (-sim'pə thō'mi met'ik) adj. [< prec. + MIMETIC] having an effect similar to that produced when the parasympathetic nervous system is stimulated: said of drugs, chemicals, etc.

par·a·syn·ap·sis (-si nap'sis) n. [ModL.: see PARA-¹ & SYNAPSIS] the conjugation of chromosomes side by side

par·a·syn·the·sis (-sin'thə sis) n. [ModL.: see PARA-¹ & SYNTHESIS] Linguis. the process of forming words by both derivation and composition (Ex.: big-hearted < big heart + -ed, not < big + hearted) —**par'a·syn·thet'ic** (-sin thet'ik) adj.

par·a·tax·is (-tak'sis) n. [ModL. < Gr. parataxis, a placing beside < para-, beside (see PARA-¹) + tassein, to place: see TACTICS] the placing of related clauses, etc. in a series without the use of connecting words (Ex.: "I came, I saw, I conquered") —**par'a·tac'tic** (-tak'tik), **par'a·tac'ti·cal** adj. —**par'a·tac'ti·cal·ly** adv.

☆**par·a·thi·on** (par'ə thī'än) n. [PARA-¹ + THION(IC)] a highly poisonous compound, $C_{10}H_{14}O_5NPS$, commercially a colorless to dark-brown liquid, used as an agricultural insecticide

par·a·thy·roid (-thī'roid) adj. [PARA-¹ + THYROID] **1.** situated alongside or near the thyroid gland **2.** designating or of any of usually four small, oval glands on or near the thyroid gland: they secrete a hormone important in the control of the calcium-phosphorus balance of the body —n. a parathyroid gland

par·a·troops (par'ə trōōps') n.pl. [< PARA(CHUTE) + TROOP] troops trained and equipped to parachute into a combat area —**par'a·troop'** adj. —**par'a·troop'er** n.

par·a·ty·phoid (par'ə tī'foid) adj. [PARA-¹ + TYPHOID] designating, of, or causing an infectious disease closely resembling typhoid fever but usually milder and caused by various bacteria (genus Salmonella) —n. paratyphoid fever

par·a·vane (par'ə vān') n. [PARA-¹ + VANE] either of a pair of torpedo-shaped devices towed by cables from the bow of a ship and equipped to cut the moorings of submerged mines, allowing them to float and be destroyed

‡**par·a·vion** (pår à vyōn') [Fr., lit., by airplane] by air mail

☆**par·a·wing** (par'ə wiŋ') n. [< PARA(CHUTE) + WING] a winglike, maneuverable parachute that can be steered over short distances to a preselected landing site

par·a·zo·an (par'ə zō'ən) n. [ModL.: see PARA-¹ & -ZOA] any of the subkingdom (Parazoa) containing a single phylum (Porifera), the sponges, made up of animals having two tissue layers only and lacking a nervous system and true digestive cavity —adj. of the parazoans

par·boil (pär'boil') vt. [ME. parboilen < OFr. parboullir < par (< L. per), through, thoroughly + boullir (< L. bullire), to BOIL¹: meaning infl. in ME. & ModE. by association of par with PART] **1.** to boil (meat or vegetables) until partly cooked, as in preparation for roasting, etc. **2.** to make uncomfortably hot; overheat

par·buck·le (pär′buk′'l) *n.* [altered (after BUCKLE[1]) < Early ModE. *parbunkel*] **1.** a sling for a log, barrel, etc., made by passing a doubled rope around the object and pulling the rope ends through the loop **2.** a device consisting of a doubled rope, the middle of which is attached at a given height and the ends passed around a cylindrical object which may then be raised or lowered by hauling in or paying out the rope ends —*vt.* **-led, -ling** to raise or lower by using a parbuckle

Par·cae (pär′sē) *n.pl.* [L., pl. of *Parca*, one of the Fates, orig., a birth-goddess < *parere*, to give birth: see -PAROUS] *Rom. Myth.* the three Fates: see FATE

par·cel (pär′s'l) *n.* [ME. < MFr. *parcelle* < LL. *particella*, for L. *particula*: see PARTICLE] **1.** a small, wrapped bundle; package **2.** a quantity or unit of some commodity put up for sale **3.** a group or collection; pack; bunch [*a parcel of fools*] **4.** a piece, as of land, usually a specific part of a large acreage or estate **5.** a portion or part: now only in **part and parcel**, an inseparable or essential part —*vt.* **-celed** or **-celled, -cel·ing** or **-cel·ling 1.** to separate into parts and distribute; apportion (with *out*) **2.** to make up in or as a parcel **3.** *Naut.* to wrap in parceling —*adj., adv.* [Archaic] partly; partly —SYN. see BUNDLE

par·cel·ing, par·cel·ling (pär′s'l in) *n.* **1.** the act of separating into parts and distributing **2.** *Naut.* canvas strips, usually covered with tar, wrapped around a rope to protect it

parcel post 1. a mail service and system for carrying and delivering parcels not over a specified weight and size **2.** mail handled by this service; fourth-class mail

par·ce·nar·y (pär′sə ner′ē) *n.* [Anglo-Fr. *parcenerie* < OFr. *parçonerie* < ML. *partionaria* < *partionarius*: see ff.] *same as* COPARCENARY (n. 1)

par·ce·ner (pär′sə nər) *n.* [ME. < Anglo-Fr. *parcenier* < OFr. *parçonnier* < ML. *partionarius*, contr. of *partitionarius* < L. *partitio*: see PARTITION] *same as* COPARCENER

parch (pärch) *vt.* [ME. *perchen* < ?] **1.** to expose (corn, peas, etc.) to great heat so as to dry or roast slightly **2.** to dry up with heat; make hot and dry **3.** to make very thirsty **4.** to dry up and shrivel with cold —*vi.* to become very dry, hot, thirsty, etc.

Par·chee·si (pär chē′zē) *a trademark for* a game like pachisi in which the moves of pieces on a board are determined by the throwing of dice —*n.* [p-] *same as* PACHISI: also sp. **par·che′si, par·chi′si**

parch·ment (pärch′mənt) *n.* [ME. *parchemin* < OFr. < LL. *pergamina* < L. (*charta*) *Pergamenum*, (paper) of PERGAMUM, where used as a substitute for papyrus: altered in OFr. after *parche*, parchment < LL. *parthica* (*pellis*), lit., Parthian (leather)] **1.** the skin of an animal, usually a sheep or goat, prepared as a surface on which to write or paint **2.** paper specially treated to resemble parchment, and used for lampshades, stationery, etc. **3.** a document, manuscript, or diploma on parchment

pard[1] (pärd) *n.* [ME. *parde* < OFr. < L. *pardus* < Gr. *pardos*] [Archaic or Poet.] a leopard, or panther

☆**pard**[2] (pärd) *n. clipped form of* PARDNER

par·die, par·di (pär dē′) *adv., interj.* [ME. *parde* < OFr. *par dé* (Fr. *pardieu*), by God!] [Archaic] verily; indeed: a mild oath: also sp. **par·dy′**

☆**pard·ner** (pärd′nər) *n.* [altered < PARTNER] [Chiefly Dial.] a partner; companion

par·don (pär′d'n) *vt.* [ME. *pardonen* < OFr. < LL. *perdonare* < L. *per-*, through, quite (see PER-) + *donare*, to give: see DONATION] **1.** to release (a person) from further punishment for a crime **2.** to cancel or not exact penalty for (an offense); forgive **3.** *a)* to excuse or forgive (a person) for some minor fault, discourtesy, etc. *b)* to overlook (a discourtesy, etc.) —*n.* [ME. < OFr.] **1.** a pardoning or being pardoned; forgiveness **2.** an official document granting a pardon **3.** *R.C.Ch. same as* INDULGENCE —**I beg your pardon** excuse me: a polite formula of apology, disagreement, etc. —SYN. see ABSOLVE —**par′don·a·ble** *adj.* —**par′don·a·bly** *adv.*

par·don·er (-ər) *n.* [ME. < Anglo-Fr.] **1.** in the Middle Ages, a person authorized to sell ecclesiastical pardons, or indulgences **2.** a person who pardons

pare (per) *vt.* **pared, par′ing** [ME. *paren* < OFr. *parer* < L. *parare*, to PREPARE] **1.** to cut or trim away (the rind, skin, covering, rough surface, etc.) of (anything); peel **2.** to reduce or diminish (costs, etc.) gradually (often with *down*)

Pa·ré (pȧ rā′), **Am·broise** (än brwȧz′) 1517?-90; Fr. surgeon

par·e·gor·ic (par′ə gôr′ik, -gär′-) *adj.* [LL. *paregoricus* < Gr. *parēgorikos* < *parēgoros*, speaking, consoling, soothing < *para-*, on the side of (see PARA-[1]) + *agora*, assembly] [Archaic] soothing or lessening pain —*n.* **1.** orig., a medicine that soothes or lessens pain **2.** a camphorated tincture of opium, containing benzoic acid, anise oil, etc., used to relieve diarrhea

pa·rei·ra (bra·va) (pə rer′ə brä′və) [Port. *parreira brava*, wild vine < *parreira*, vine + *brava*, wild] the root of a S. American plant (*Chondrodendron tomentosum*) which is

a source of curare, formerly used as a diuretic and tonic

paren., *pl.* **parens.** parenthesis

pa·ren·chy·ma (pə ren′ki mə) *n.* [ModL. < Gr. *parenchyma*, anything poured in beside < *para-*, beside (see PARA-[1]) + *enchyma*, infusion < *enchein*, to pour in < *en-*, in + *cheein*, to pour (see FOUND[2])] **1.** *Anat.* the essential or functional tissue of an organ, as distinguished from its connective tissue, blood vessels, etc. **2.** *Bot.* a soft tissue made up of thin-walled, undifferentiated living cells with air spaces between them, constituting the chief substance of plant leaves and roots, the pulp of fruits, the central portion of stems, etc. **3.** *Zool.* a spongy mass of tissue packing the spaces between the organs of some invertebrates —**pa·ren′chy·mal, par·en·chym·a·tous** (par′en kim′ə təs) *adj.* —**par′en·chym′·a·tous·ly** *adv.*

par·ent (per′ənt, par′-) *n.* [ME. < OFr. < L. *parens*, parent, orig. prp. of *parere*, to beget: see -PAROUS] **1.** a father or mother **2.** a progenitor or ancestor **3.** any animal, organism, or plant in relation to its offspring **4.** anything from which other things are derived; source; origin —*adj.* ☆designating a corporation in relation to a subsidiary that it owns and controls —**par′ent·hood′** *n.*

par·ent·age (-ij) *n.* [LME. < MFr.] **1.** descent or derivation from parents or ancestors; lineage; origin **2.** the position or relation of a parent; parenthood

pa·ren·tal (pə ren′t'l) *adj.* [L. *parentalis*] **1.** of or characteristic of a parent or parents **2.** constituting the source or origin of something **3.** *Biol.* designating or of the generation in which fertilization produces hybrids —**pa·ren′tal·ly** *adv.*

par·en·ter·al (pa ren′tər əl) *adj.* [PAR- + ENTER(O)- + -AL] **1.** outside the intestine **2.** brought into the body through some way other than the digestive tract, as by subcutaneous or intravenous injection —*n.* a substance for parenteral injection —**par·en′ter·al·ly** *adv.*

pa·ren·the·sis (pə ren′thə sis) *n., pl.* **-ses′** (-sēz′) [LL. < Gr. *parenthesis* < *parentithenai*, to put beside < *para-*, beside (see PARA-[1]) + *entithenai*, to insert < *en-*, in + *tithenai*, to put, place: see DO[1]] **1.** an additional word, clause, etc. placed as an explanation or comment within an already complete sentence: in writing or printing it is usually marked off by curved lines, dashes, or commas **2.** either or both of the curved lines ( ), used to mark off parenthetical words, etc. or to enclose mathematical or logical symbols that are to be treated as a single term **3.** an episode or incident, often an irrelevant one; interlude

pa·ren·the·size (-sīz′) *vt.* **-sized′, -siz′ing 1.** *a)* to insert (a word, phrase, etc.) as a parenthesis *b)* to put into parentheses (sense 2) **2.** to place a parenthesis within [*to parenthesize a talk with jokes*]

par·en·thet·i·cal (par′ən thet′i k'l) *adj.* [ML. *parentheticus*] **1.** *a)* of, or having the nature of, a parenthesis *b)* marked off or placed within parentheses **2.** interjected as qualifying information or explanation **3.** using or containing parentheses Also **par′en·thet′ic** or **par′en·thet′i·cal·ly** *adv.*

Pares (perz), **Sir Bernard** 1867-1949; Eng. historian

pa·re·sis (pə rē′sis, par′ə sis) *n., pl.* **-ses** (-sēz) [ModL. < Gr. *paresis* < *parienai*, to relax < *para-* (see PARA-[1]) + *hienai*, to go] **1.** partial or slight paralysis **2.** a disease of the brain caused by syphilis of the central nervous system and characterized by inflammation of the meninges, dementia, paralytic attacks, etc.: in full, **general paresis** —**pa·ret′ic** (-ret′ik, -rē′tik) *adj.*

par·es·the·si·a (par′is thē′zhə, -zhē ə) *n.* [ModL.: see PARA-[1] & ESTHESIA] an abnormal sensation, as of burning, prickling, etc. on the skin —**par′es·thet′ic** (-thet′ik) *adj.*

Pa·re·to (pä re′tō), **Vil·fre·do** (vēl fre′dō) 1848-1923; It. economist & sociologist in Switzerland

pa·re·u (pä′rä ōō′) *n.* [Tahitian] a long, colorful, wraparound skirt worn by Polynesian men and women

par·eve (pär′ə və, -ve) *adj.* [Yid. *parev*] *Judaism* prepared without either meat or milk products, hence permissible to be eaten with either meat or dairy dishes, in accordance with the laws of kashrut

par ex·cel·lence (pär ek′sə läns′; *Fr.* pȧr ek se läns′) [Fr., lit., by way of excellence] in the greatest degree of excellence; beyond comparison; preeminently

par·fait (pär fā′) *n.* [Fr., lit., perfect] **1.** a dessert made of rich cream, eggs, syrup, etc. frozen together and served in a tall, slender, short-stemmed glass **2.** a dessert of ice cream with crushed fruit or syrup, served in layers in a similar glass

par·fleche (pär′flesh, pär flesh′) *n.* [CanadFr. *parflèche*, prob. < Fr. *parer*, PARRY + *flèche*, arrow: see FLECHE] **1.** a rawhide with the hair removed by soaking it in water and lye **2.** something made of this, as a case or robe

parge (pärj) *vt.* **parged, parg′ing** [< ff.] to apply a thin coat of mortar or plaster to brickwork, stonework, etc., to seal the surface —**parg′ing** *n.*

par·get (pär′jit) *vt.* **-get·ed** or **-get·ted, -get·ing** or **-get·ting** [ME. *pargeten, pargetten* < MFr. *pargeter, parjeter* < *par-* (see PER-), completely + *jeter*, to throw: see JET[1]] to put plaster on, esp. in a decorative way —*n.* **1.** plaster or any similar wall coating **2.** raised ornamental plasterwork formerly used on walls or ceilings Also, for n., **par′get·ing, par′get·ting**

par·he·lic (pär hē′lik, -hel′ik) *adj.* of or like a parhelion or parhelia: also **par′he·li·a·cal** (-hi lī′ə k'l)]

parhelic circle a bright circular band or halo that appears to intersect the sun in a plane parallel to the horizon: also **parhelic ring**

par·he·li·on (-hē′lē ən, -hēl′yən) *n., pl.* **-li·a** (-ə, -yə) [L. *parelion* < Gr. *parēlion* < *para*-, beside (see PARA-[1]) + *hēlios*, the sun: see HELIOS] a bright, colored spot of light sometimes seen on the ring of a solar halo

par·i- (par′i) [< L. *par* (gen. *paris*): see PAR] *a combining form meaning* equal *[paripinnate]*

pa·ri·ah (pə rī′ə; *chiefly Brit.,* par′ē ə) *n.* [Tamil *paṟaiyan*, drummer < *paṟai*, a drum: the pariah was a hereditary drumbeater] **1.** a member of one of the lowest social castes in India **2.** any person despised or rejected by others; outcast

Par·i·an (per′ē ən, par′-) *adj.* **1.** of Paros **2.** *a)* designating a fine, white marble found in Paros *b)* like this marble **3.** designating a fine, white porcelain (**Parian ware**) that resembles Parian marble —*n.* a native or inhabitant of Paros

Pa·ri·cu·tín (pä rē kōō tēn′) volcanic mountain in WC Mexico, formed by eruptions starting 1943 & now dormant: c. 9,000 ft. Also **Pa·ri·cu·tin** (pä rē′kōō tēn)

pa·ri·es (per′ē ēz′, par′-) *n., pl.* **pa·ri·e·tes** (pə rī′ə tēz′) [ModL. < L., a wall < IE. base *(s)per-*, a bar, spear, whence SPAR[2], SPEAR] *Biol.* a wall, as of a hollow organ, cavity, cell, etc.: *usually used in pl.*

pa·ri·e·tal (pə rī′ə t'l) *adj.* [Fr. *pariétal* < LL. *parietalis* < L. *paries:* see prec.] ☆**1.** of or having to do with life within a college *[parietal* regulations] **2.** *Anat.* of, pertaining to, or forming the walls of a cavity or hollow structure; esp., designating either of the two bones between the frontal and occipital bones, forming part of the top and sides of the skull: see SKULL, illus. **3.** *Bot.* attached to the wall of the ovary, as the placenta in some plants

parietal lobe the part of each hemisphere of the brain between the frontal and the occipital lobes

par·i·mu·tu·el (par′ə myōō′choo wəl) *n.* [Fr. *pari mutuel* < *pari*, a bet (< *parier*, to bet, orig., to equalize < LL. *pariare*, to make equal < L. *par:* acc PAR) + *mutuel*, MUTUAL] **1.** a system of betting on races in which those backing the winners divide, in proportion to their wagers, the total amount bet, minus a percentage for the track operators, taxes, etc. **2.** a machine for recording such bets and computing payoffs; totalizator

par·ing (per′iŋ) *n.* **1.** the act of one who pares something **2.** a thin piece or strip pared off, as of the skin of a potato

‡**pa·ri pas·su** (per′ē pas′ōō, par′-) [L.] **1.** with equal pace; with equal speed **2.** in equal proportion **3.** *Law* without preference or priority

par·i·pin·nate (par′i pin′āt) *adj.* [PARI- + PINNATE] *Bot.* having an equal number of leaflets on either side of the central stalk: said of compound leaves

Par·is[1] (par′is) [L. < Gr. *Paris*] *Gr. Legend* a son of Priam, king of Troy: his kidnapping of Helen, wife of Menelaus, caused the Trojan War

Par·is[2] (par′is; *Fr.* på′rē′) capital of France, in the NC part, on the Seine: pop. 2,790,000 (urbanized area, 7,369,000)

Paris, Matthew *see* MATTHEW (OF) PARIS

Paris green [after PARIS[1]] a poisonous, bright-green powder made by reacting sodium arsenite with copper sulfate and acetic acid: used chiefly as an insecticide

par·ish (par′ish) *n.* [ME. *parissche* < OFr. *parroche* < LL.(Ec.) *parochia*, for *paroecia* < LGr.(Ec.) *paroikia*, a diocese < Gr., a sojourning (in a foreign land, or, by early Christians, on earth) < *paroikos*, a stranger < *para*- (see PARA-[1]) + *oikos*, dwelling] **1.** orig., a British church district with its own church and clergyman **2.** a district of British local civil government, often identical with the original church parish **3.** an administrative district of various churches, esp. a part of a diocese, under the charge of a priest or minister **4.** *a)* the members of the congregation of any church *b)* the territory in which they live ☆**5.** a civil division in Louisiana, corresponding to a county

pa·rish·ion·er (pə rish′ə nər) *n.* [ME. *parisshoner* < *parishion* < OFr. *paroissien* < *paroiche*, PARISH) + -ER] a member of a parish

parish register a book for recording every baptism, marriage, and death of the members of a parish

Pa·ri·sian (pə rizh′ən, -rē′zhən) *adj.* of or like Paris, its people, or culture —*n.* a native or inhabitant of Paris

par·i·ty[1] (par′ə tē) *n., pl.* **-ties** [Fr. *parité* < L. *paritas* < *par*, equal: see PAR] **1.** the state or condition of being the same in power, value, rank, etc.; equality **2.** resemblance; similarity **3.** equivalence in value of one currency expressed in terms of another country's currency **4.** equality of value at a given ratio between different kinds of money, commodities, etc. ☆**5.** a price for certain farm products, usually maintained by government price supports, designed to keep the purchasing power of the farmer at the level of a designated base period **6.** *Math.* the condition existing between two integers that are both odd or both even **7.** *Physics* a symmetry property of a wave function: expressed as +1 if no difference can be detected between

the wave function and its mirror image, and as −1 if the wave function is changed only in sign

par·i·ty[2] (par′ə tē) *n.* [< L. *parere*, to bear (see PARTURIENT) + -ITY] *Med.* the state or fact of having borne offspring

park (pärk) *n.* [ME. *parc* < OFr. < ML. *parricus*] **1.** *English Law* an enclosed area of land, held by authority of the king or by prescription, stocked and preserved for hunting **2.** an area of land containing pasture, woods, lakes, etc., surrounding a large country house or private estate **3.** an area of public land; specif., *a)* an area in or near a city, usually laid out with walks, drives, playgrounds, etc., for public recreation *b)* an open square in a city, with benches, trees, etc. *c)* same as AMUSEMENT PARK *d)* a large area known for its natural scenery and preserved for public recreation by a State or national government ☆**4.** *same as* BALLPARK ☆**5.** [Western] a level, open area surrounded by mountains or forest **6.** that arrangement in an automatic transmission of a motor vehicle that holds the vehicle in place when it is parked **7.** a space set aside for parking motor vehicles **8.** *Mil.* an area for storing and servicing vehicles and other equipment —*vt.* **1.** to enclose in or as in a park **2.** to assemble (military equipment) in a park ☆**3.** to leave (a vehicle) in a certain place temporarily ☆**4.** to maneuver (a vehicle) into a space where it can be left temporarily ☆**5.** [Colloq.] to put or leave in a particular place; deposit —*vi.* to park a vehicle —**park′er** *n.*

Park (pärk), **Mun·go** (muŋ′gō) 1771–1806; Scot. explorer in Africa

☆**par·ka** (pär′kə) *n.* [Aleutian < Russ., a skin shirt, fur coat] **1.** a hip-length pullover fur garment with a hood, worn in arctic regions **2.** a hooded jacket like this, often with fleece or pile lining

Park Avenue a wealthy residential street in New York City: a symbol of high society, fashion, etc.

Par·ker (pär′kər) **1. Charlie,** (born *Charles Christopher Parker, Jr.*) 1920–55; U.S. jazz musician **2. Sir Gilbert,** (born *Horatio Gilbert George Parker*) 1862–1932; Canad. novelist in England **3. Theodore,** 1810–60; U.S. clergyman, social reformer, & abolitionist

☆**par·ker·house roll** (pär′kər hous′) [< *Parker House,* hotel in Boston where first served] a yeast roll shaped by folding over a flat, round piece of buttered dough

Par·kers·burg (pär′kərz burg′) [after A. *Parker,* early owner of the site] city in NW W.Va., on the Ohio River: pop. 44,000

☆**parking lot** an area for parking motor vehicles

☆**parking meter** a coin-operated timing device installed near a parking space for indicating the length of time that a parked vehicle may continue to occupy that space

☆**parking orbit** a temporary orbit of an artificial satellite or spacecraft around the earth or some other heavenly body, prior to carrying out a further maneuver

par·kin·son·ism (pär′kin sən iz'm) *n.* [see ff.] **1.** any of various brain disorders characterized by muscle rigidity as in Parkinson's disease, with or without tremor **2.** same as PARKINSON'S DISEASE

Par·kin·son's disease (pär′kin sənz) [after James *Parkinson* (1755–1824), Eng. physician who first described it] a degenerative disease of later life, characterized by a rhythmic tremor and muscular rigidity, caused by degeneration in the basal ganglia of the brain

Parkinson's Law [propounded by C. *Parkinson* (1909–), Brit. economist] any of several satirical statements expressed as economic laws, as one to the effect that work expands to fill the time allotted to it

Park·man (pärk′mən), **Francis** 1823–93; U.S. historian

Park Range range of the Rockies, in NC Colo. & S Wyo.: highest peak, 14,284 ft.

Park Ridge city in NE Ill.: suburb of Chicago: pop. 42,000

☆**park·way** (pärk′wā′) *n.* **1.** a broad roadway bordered or divided with plantings of trees, bushes, and grass **2.** the landscaped center strip or border

Parl. 1. Parliament **2.** Parliamentary

par·lance (pär′ləns) *n.* [Anglo-Fr. *parlaunce* < OFr. < *parler:* see PARLEY] **1.** [Archaic] conversation; esp., parley or debate **2.** a style or manner of speaking or writing; language; idiom *[military parlance]*

par·lan·do (pär län′dō) *adj., adv.* [It.] *Music* to be sung in a style suggesting or approximating speech

☆**par·lay** (pär′lā, -lē; *for v., also* pär lā′) *vt., vi.* [altered < earlier *paroli* < Fr. < It. < *paro,* an equal, pair < L. *par:* see PAR] **1.** to bet (an original wager plus its winnings) on another race, contest, etc. **2.** to exploit (an asset) successfully *[to parlay* one's voice into fame] —*n.* a bet or series of bets made by parlaying

par·ley (pär′lē) *vi.* [< Fr. *parler,* to speak < LL.(Ec.) *parabolare,* to speak < *parabola,* a speech, PARABLE] to have a conference or discussion, esp. with an enemy; confer —*n., pl.* **-leys** a talk or conference for the purpose of discussing a specific matter or of settling a dispute, as a military conference with an enemy, under a truce, for discussing terms

par·lia·ment (pär′lə mənt) *n.* [ME. *parlament* < OFr.

parlement < *parler*: see prec.] **1.** an official or formal conference or council, usually concerned with government or public affairs **2.** [P-] the national legislative body of Great Britain, composed of the House of Commons and the House of Lords **3.** [P-] any of several similar bodies in other countries **4.** any of several high courts of justice in France before 1789

par·lia·men·tar·i·an (pär′lə men ter′ē ən, -mən-) *n.* **1.** [P-] a supporter of the Long Parliament in opposition to Charles I of England; Roundhead **2.** a person skilled in parliamentary rules, practice, or debate

par·lia·men·ta·ry (pär′lə men′tər ē, -trē) *adj.* **1.** of or like a parliament **2.** decreed or established by a parliament **3.** based on or conforming to the customs and rules of a parliament or other public assembly [*parliamentary procedure*] **4.** having or governed by a parliament; specif., designating or of a government in which a prime minister or premier holds office only so long as he commands a majority in the parliament

par·lor (pär′lər) *n.* [ME. *parlour* < OFr. *parleor* < *parler*: see PARLEY] **1.** *a*) orig., a room set aside for the entertainment of guests; formal sitting room *b*) any living room: an old-fashioned term **2.** a small, semiprivate sitting room apart from the main lounges in a hotel, inn, etc. **3.** *a*) orig., a business establishment elegantly furnished to resemble a private sitting room [an ice-cream *parlor*] *b*) now, a shop or business establishment, often with some special equipment or furnishings for personal services [a beauty *parlor*] Brit. sp. **par′lour**

☆**parlor car** *same as* CHAIR CAR

par·lor·maid (-mād′) *n.* a maid who serves at table, answers the door, etc.

par·lous (pär′ləs) *adj.* [ME., contr. of *perilous*] [Chiefly Archaic] **1.** perilous; dangerous; risky **2.** dangerously clever; cunning, mischievous, shrewd, etc. —*adv.* [Chiefly Archaic] extremely; very

Par·ma (pär′mə; *for* 1, *also It.* pär′mä) **1.** *a*) commune in N Italy, in Emilia-Romagna: pop. 163,000 *b*) former duchy (1545–1860) in this region **2.** [ult. after prec.] city in NE Ohio: suburb of Cleveland: pop. 100,000

Par·men·i·des (pär men′ə dēz′) 5th cent. B.C.; Gr. Eleatic philosopher

Par·me·san (pär′mə zän′, -zən, -zan′) *adj.* [Fr. *parmesan* < It. *parmegiano* < *Parma*, city in Italy] of or from Parma, Italy —*n. same as* PARMESAN CHEESE

Parmesan cheese a very hard, dry Italian cheese made from skim milk and usually grated for sprinkling on spaghetti, soup, etc.

Par·na·í·ba (pär′nä ē′bə) river in NE Brazil, flowing north into the Atlantic: c. 800 mi.

Par·nas·si·an (pär nas′ē ən) *adj.* [L. *Parnassius*] **1.** of Mount Parnassus **2.** of the Parnassians **3.** of the art of poetry —*n.* [Fr. *parnassien* < *Le Parnasse contemporain*, title of their first collection (1866)] a member of a school of late 19th-cent. French poets concerned with form primarily

Par·nas·sus (pär nas′əs) [L. < Gr. *Parnasos*] mountain in C Greece, near the Gulf of Corinth: 8,061 ft.: sacred to Apollo and the Muses in ancient times —*n.* **1.** poetry or poets collectively **2.** any center of poetic or artistic activity

Par·nell (pär′n'l, pär nel′), **Charles Stewart** 1846–91; Ir. nationalist leader

pa·ro·chi·al (pə rō′kē əl) *adj.* [ME. *parochiele* < OFr. *parochial* < ML.(Ec.) *parochialis* < LL.(Ec.) *parochia*: see PARISH] **1.** of or in a parish or parishes **2.** restricted to a small area or scope; narrow; limited; provincial [a *parochial* outlook] —**pa·ro′chi·al·ism** *n.* —**pa·ro′chi·al·ist** *n.* —**pa·ro′chi·al·ly** *adv.*

☆**parochial school** a school supported and controlled by a church

par·o·dist (par′ə dist) *n.* a writer of parodies —**par′o·dis′tic** *adj.*

par·o·dy (-dē) *n., pl.* **-dies** [Fr. *parodie* < L. *parodia* < Gr. *parōidia, countersong* < *para-*, beside (see PARA-[1]) + *ōidē*, song (see ODE)] **1.** literary or musical composition imitating the characteristic style of some other work or of a writer or composer, but treating a serious subject in a nonsensical manner, as in ridicule **2.** a poor or weak imitation —*vt.* **-died, -dy·ing** to make a parody of —SYN. see CARICATURE —**pa·rod·ic** (pə räd′ik), **pa·rod′i·cal** *adj.*

pa·rol (pə rōl′) *n.* [MFr. *parole* < OFr.: see ff.] a word; speech; specif., *Law* spoken evidence given in court by a witness: now only in the phrase **by parol** —*adj.* oral or verbal

pa·role (pə rōl′) *n.* [Fr., a word, formal promise < LL.(Ec.) *parabola*, a speech, PARABLE] **1.** word of honor; promise; esp., the promise of a prisoner of war that, in exchange for full or partial freedom, he will abide by certain conditions, often specif., that he will take no further part in the fighting **2.** the condition of being on parole ☆**3.** *a*) the release of a prisoner before his sentence has expired, on condition of future good behavior: the sentence is not set aside and he remains under the supervision of a parole board *b*) the conditional freedom granted by such release, or the period of it **4.** *Mil.* formerly, a special password used only by certain authorized persons —*vt.* **-roled′, -rol′ing** ☆to release on parole —**on parole** at liberty under conditions of parole

☆**pa·rol·ee** (pə rō′lē′) *n.* [PAROL(E) + -EE[1]] a person who has been released from prison on parole

par·o·no·ma·si·a (par′ə nō mā′zhə, -zhē ə) *n.* [L. < Gr. *paronomasia* < *para-*, beside (see PARA-[1]) + *onomasia*, naming < *onomazein*, to name < *onoma*, NAME] the act or practice of punning —**par′o·no·mas′tic** (-mas′tik) *adj.*

par·o·nym (par′ə nim) *n.* [Gr. *parōnymon*, orig. neut. of *parōnymos*: see ff.] a paronymous word

pa·ron·y·mous (pə rän′ə məs) *adj.* [Gr. *parōnymos* < *para-*, beside (see PARA-[1]) + *onyma*, NAME] derived from the same root; cognate, as the words *differ* and *defer*

Par·os (per′äs; *Gr.* pä′rôs) island of the Cyclades, in the SC Aegean, west of Náxos: 81 sq. mi.

pa·rot·ic (pə rät′ik, -rōt′-) *adj.* [ModL. *paroticus* < Gr. *para-*, beside (see PARA-[1]) + *ous* (gen. *ōtos*), EAR[1]] situated near the ear

pa·rot·id (pə rät′id) *adj.* [ML. *parotidus* < L. *parotis* (gen. *parotidis*), a tumor near the ear < Gr. *parōtis* < *para-*, beside (see PARA-[1]) + *ous* (gen. *ōtos*), EAR[1]] situated near or beside the ear; esp., designating or of either of the salivary glands below and in front of each ear —*n.* [ML. *parotida*] a parotid gland

par·o·ti·tis (par′ə tīt′əs) *n.* [see -ITIS] inflammation of the parotid gland; esp., the mumps —**par′o·tit′ic** (-tit′ik) *adj.*

-pa·rous (pər əs) [L. *-parus* < *parere*, to bring forth, bear < IE. base *per-*, to give birth to, whence FARROW[1], PORK] *a combining form meaning* bringing forth, producing, bearing [*viviparous*]

Pa·rou·si·a (pə roo̅′sē ə, pə roo̅′zē ə) *n.* [Gr.(Ec.) *parousia* < Gr., lit., presence, arrival < *para-*, PARA-[1] + *ousia*, a being, substance < stem of *ōn*, prp. of *einai*, to be: see ONTO-] *same as* SECOND COMING

par·ox·ysm (par′ək siz′m) *n.* [Fr. *paroxysme* < ML. *paroxysmus* < Gr. *paroxysmos* < *paroxynein*, to excite, sharpen < *para-*, beyond (see PARA-[1]) + *oxynein*, to sharpen < *oxys*, sharp: see OXY-[2]] **1.** a sudden attack, or intensification of the symptoms, of a disease, usually recurring periodically **2.** a sudden convulsion or outburst, as of laughter, rage, sneezing, etc.; fit; spasm —**par·ox·ys·mal** (par′ək siz′m'l) *adj.*

par·ox·y·tone (par äk′sə tōn′) *adj.* [ModL. *paroxytonus* < Gr. *paroxytonos* < *para-* (see PARA-[1]) + *oxytonos*, having the acute accent < *oxys*, sharp + *tonos*, a sound: see OXY-[2] & TONE] *Gr. Gram.* having an acute accent on the next to the last syllable —*n.* a paroxytone word

par·quet (pär kā′) *n.* [Fr. < MFr. *parchet*, dim. of *parc*, PARK), a small enclosed section] ☆**1.** the main floor of a theater, esp. that part from the orchestra pit to the parquet circle: usually called *orchestra* **2.** a flooring of parquetry —*vt.* **-queted′** (-kād′), **-quet′ing** (-kā′iŋ) **1.** to use parquetry to make (a floor, etc.) **2.** to decorate the floor of (a room) with parquetry

☆**parquet circle** the part of a theater beneath the balcony and behind the parquet on the main floor

par·quet·ry (pär′kə trē) *n.* [Fr. *parqueterie*: see PARQUET] inlaid woodwork in geometric forms, usually of contrasting woods, used esp. in flooring

parr (pär) *n., pl.* **parrs, parr:** see PLURAL, II, D, 1 [< ?] **1.** a young salmon before it enters salt water **2.** the young of certain other fish

Parr (pär), **Catherine** 1512–48; 6th & last wife of Henry VIII of England

par·ra·keet (par′ə kēt′) *n. alt. sp. of* PARAKEET

par·ra·mat·ta (par′ə mat′ə) *n. alt. sp. of* PARAMATTA

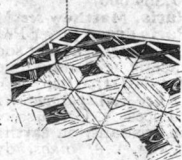

PARQUETRY

par·rel, par·ral (par′əl) *n.* [ME. *perell*, var. of *parail*, aphetic for *aparail*, equipment (see APPAREL)] *Naut.* a loop of rope, chain, etc. or a metal collar used to fasten a yard to a mast

par·ri·cide (par′ə sīd′) *n.* [Fr. < L. *parricida*, earlier *paricida* < IE. base *pāsos*, a relative (whence Gr. *pēos*, one related by marriage) + L. *-cida*, -CIDE] **1.** a person who murders his parent, someone standing in a similar relationship, or a close relative **2.** [L. *parricidium*] the act of a parricide —**par′ri·ci′dal** *adj.*

Par·ring·ton (par′iŋ tən), **Vernon Louis** 1871–1929; U.S. literary historian

Par·rish (par′ish), **Max·field** (maks′fēld) 1870–1966; U.S. illustrator & painter

par·rot (par′ət) *n.* [Fr. dial. *perrot*, prob. < *Perrot*, dim. of *Pierre*, Peter] **1.** any of a number of related tropical or subtropical birds (order Psittaciformes) with a hooked bill, brightly colored feathers, and feet having two toes pointing forward and two backward: some parrots can learn to imitate human speech **2.** a person who mechanically repeats the words or acts of others, usually without full understanding —*vt.* to repeat or imitate, esp. without understanding

parrot fever *same as* PSITTACOSIS

parrot fish any of a number of related, brightly colored, tropical ocean fishes (family Scaridae), with parrotlike jaws

par·ry (par′ē) *vt.* **-ried, -ry·ing** [prob. < imper. of Fr. *parer* < It. *parare*, to ward off < L. *parare*, to PREPARE] **1.** to ward off or deflect (a blow, the thrust of a sword,

etc.) 2. to turn aside (a question, criticism, etc.) as by a clever or evasive reply or remark —*vi*. to make a parry or evasion —*n*., *pl*. **-ries** 1. a warding off or a turning aside of a blow, thrust, etc., as in fencing 2. an evasion; evasive reply

Par·ry (par′ē), Sir **William Edward** 1790–1855; Eng. naval officer & arctic explorer

parse (pärs) *vt*., *vi*. **parsed, pars′ing** [< L. *pars*, a part, in *quae pars orationis?* what part of speech?] [Now Rare] 1. to separate (a sentence) into its parts, explaining the grammatical form, function, and interrelation of each part 2. to describe the form, part of speech, and function of (a word) in a sentence

par·sec (pär′sek′) *n*. [PAR(ALLAX) + SEC(OND)²] a unit of measure of astronomical distance, corresponding to that distance at which an object has an annual parallax of one second of arc, equal to 206,265 astronomical units, or 3.26 light years, or 19,200,000,000,000 miles

Par·see, Par·si (pär′sē, pär sē′) *n*. [Per. *Pārsī*, a Persian < *Pārs*, Persia] a member of a Zoroastrian religious sect in India descended from a group of Persian refugees who fled from the Moslem persecutions of the 7th and 8th cent. —**Par′see·ism, Par′si·ism** *n*.

Par·si·fal (pär′si fäl′, -fal) [G. < MHG. *Parzival* < OFr. *Perceval*: cf. PERCIVAL] the title character in Wagner's music drama (1882) of the knights of the Holy Grail

par·si·mo·ni·ous (pär′sə mō′nē əs) *adj*. characterized by parsimony; miserly; close —*SYN*. see STINGY¹ —**par′si·mo′ni·ous·ly** *adv*. —**par′si·mo′ni·ous·ness** *n*.

par·si·mo·ny (pär′sə mō′nē) *n*. [ME. *parcimony* < L. *parcimonia* < *parcere*, to spare] a tendency to be over-careful in spending; unreasonable economy; stinginess; extreme frugality

pars·ley (pärs′lē) *n*. [ME. *parseli* < OE. *petersilie* & OFr. *persil*, both < VL. *petrosilium* < L. *petroselinum* < Gr. *petroselinon*, rock parsley < *petros*, a rock + *selinon*, celery] a cultivated plant (*Petroselinum hortense*) of the parsley family, with greenish-yellow flowers and aromatic, often curled leaves used to flavor or garnish some foods —*adj*. designating a family (Umbelliferae) of hollow-stemmed, herbaceous plants, whose inflorescences are umbels, including the celery, parsnip, asafetida, caraway, carrot, etc.

pars·nip (pär′snip) *n*. [ME. *pusnepe*, altered (after *nepe*, turnip) < OFr. *pasnaie* < L. *pastinaca* < *pastinare*, to dig up < *pastinum*, two-forked dibble] 1. a biennial plant (*Pastinaca sativa*) of the parsley family, with yellow flowers and a long, thick, sweet, white root used as a vegetable 2. its root

par·son (pär′s′n) *n*. [ME. *persone* < OFr. < ML. *persona*, a beneficed priest, orig., person < L.: see PERSON] 1. a clergyman in charge of a parish 2. any clergyman or minister

par·son·age (-ij) *n*. [ME. *personage* < OFr. < ML.(Ec.) *personagium*, ecclesiastical benefice: see prec. & -AGE] 1. the dwelling provided by a church for the use of its parson 2. *Eng. Eccles. Law* the land or income provided by a parish for its parson

part (pärt) *n*. [ME. < OE. & OFr., both < L. *pars* (gen. *partis*) < IE. base *per-*, to sell, hand over in sale, whence L. *par*, equal, *parare*, to equate] 1. a portion or division of a whole; specif., *a*) any of several equal portions, quantities, numbers, pieces, etc. of which something is composed or into which it can be divided [a cent is a 100th *part* of a dollar] *b*) an essential element or constituent; integral portion which can be separated, replaced, etc. [automobile *parts*] *c*) a portion detached or cut from a whole; fragment; piece *d*) a certain amount but not all [to lose *part* of one's fortune] *e*) a certain amount or section regarded as a separate division *f*) a segment or organ of the body of men and animals *g*) a division of a literary work *h*) *Math*. an aliquot part 2. a portion assigned or given; share; specif., *a*) something a person must do; share of work or duty [to do one's *part*] *b*) interest or concern [to have some *part* in a matter] *c*) [usually *pl*.] talent; ability [a man of *parts*] *d*) a character or role in a theatrical presentation; also, the words, actions, etc. of a character in a play *e*) *Music* the score for a particular voice or instrument in a concerted piece; also, any of the voices or instruments in a musical ensemble 3. a region; area; esp., [usually *pl*.] a portion of a country; district 4. one of the different sides or parties in a transaction, dispute, conflict, etc. ☆5. the dividing line formed by combing the hair in different directions —*vt*. [ME. *parten* < OFr. *partir* < L. *partire*, to divide, separate < the *n*.] 1. to break or divide into separate parts 2. to comb (the hair) in different directions so as to leave a dividing line 3. to break up (a connection or relationship) by separating those involved 4. to separate (two or more persons or things); break or hold apart 5. to separate (substances) as by a chemical process 6. [Archaic] to distribute; share; apportion 7. *Naut*. to break or incur the breaking of (a hawser, chain, etc.) —*vi*. 1. to break or divide into two or more pieces 2. to separate and go different ways, as branches of a river

3. to separate; leave each other; cease associating 4. *a*) to go away; leave; depart (with *from*) *b*) to die —*adj*. of or having to do with only a part; partial —*adv*. partly; in part —**for one's part** so far as one is concerned —**for the most part** in the greatest part or to the greatest extent; mostly; generally —**in good part** good-naturedly; without offense —**in part** to a certain extent or degree; partly —**on the part of one** 1. as far as one is concerned 2. by or coming from one Also **on one's part** —**part with** to give up; let go; relinquish —**play a part** 1. to behave unnaturally in an attempt to deceive 2. to participate or share: also **take part** —**take someone's part** to support someone in a struggle or disagreement; side with someone —*SYN*.—**part** is the general word for any of the components of a whole [a *part* of one's life]; a **portion** is specifically a part allotted to someone or something [his *portion* of the inheritance]; a **piece** is either a part separated from the whole [a *piece* of pie] or a single standardized unit of a collection [a *piece* of statuary]; a **division** is a part formed by cutting, partitioning, classifying, etc. [the fine-arts *division* of a library]; **section** is equivalent to **division** but usually connotes a smaller part [a *section* of a bookcase]; **segment** implies a part separated along natural lines of division [a *segment* of a tangerine]; a **fraction** is strictly a part contained by the whole an integral number of times, but generally it connotes an insignificant part [he received only a *fraction* of the benefits]; a **fragment** is a relatively small part separated by or as by breaking [a *fragment* of rock] See also SEPARATE —*ANT*. whole

part. 1. participial 2. participle 3. particular

part. adj. participial adjective

par·take (pär tāk′) *vi*. **-took′, -tak′en, -tak′ing** [back-formation < *partaker*, contr. of *part taker*, translating L. *particeps* < *pars*, PART + *capere*, to take] 1. to take part (in an activity); participate 2. to take a portion or take some; specif., to eat or drink something, esp. in company with others (usually with *of*) 3. to have or show a trace (*of*); have some of the qualities (*of*) —*vt*. [Rare] to take or have a part or share in —*SYN*. see SHARE¹ —**par·tak′er** *n*.

par·tan (pär′t′n) *n*. [Scot.] a crab

part·ed (pär′tid) *adj*. 1. divided; separated 2. [Archaic] dead 3. *Bot*. divided almost to the base, as some leaves

par·terre (pär ter′) *n*. [Fr. < *par*, on + *terre* (L. *terra*), earth] 1. an ornamental garden area in which the flower beds and path form a pattern ☆2. *same as* PARQUET CIRCLE

par·the·no·car·py (pär′thə nō kär′pē) *n*. [G. *partheno karpie* < Gr. *parthenos*, a virgin + *karpos*, fruit] the development of a ripe fruit without fertilization of the ovules, as in the banana and pineapple —**par′the·no·car′pic** *adj*. —**par′the·no·car′pi·cal·ly** *adv*.

par·the·no·gen·e·sis (pär′thə nō jen′ə sis) *n*. [ModL. < Gr. *parthenos*, maiden, virgin + *genesis*, origin] reproduction by the development of an unfertilized ovum, seed, or spore, as in certain polyzoans, insects, algae, etc.: **artificial parthenogenesis** is the development of an ovum stimulated by chemical or mechanical means —**par′the·no·ge·net′ic** (-jə net′ik) *adj*. —**par′the·no·ge·net′i·cal·ly** *adv*.

Par·the·non (pär′thə nän′, -nən) [L. < Gr. *Parthenōn* < *parthenos*, a virgin (i.e., Athena)] the Doric temple of Athena built (5th cent. B.C.) on the Acropolis in Athens sculpture is attributed to Phidias

Par·then·o·pe (pär then′ə pē′) [L. < Gr. *Parthenopē*] *Gr. Myth.* the siren who threw herself into the sea after her songs failed to lure Ulysses into a shipwreck

Par·the·nos (pär′thə näs′) *n*. [< Gr. *parthenos*, a virgin] a virgin: an epithet of several Greek goddesses, esp. of Athena

Par·thi·a (pär′thē ə) ancient country southeast of the Caspian Sea —**Par′thi·an** *adj*., *n*.

Parthian shot any hostile gesture or remark made in leaving: Parthian cavalrymen usually shot at the enemy while retreating or pretending to retreat

par·tial (pär′shəl) *adj*. [ME. *parcial* < MFr. *partial* < ML. *partialis* < L. *pars*, PART] 1. favoring one person, faction, etc. more than another; biased; prejudiced 2. of, being, or affecting only a part; not complete or total —*n*. 1. *same as* PARTIAL TONE 2. a partial denture —**partial to** fond of; having a liking for —**par′tial·ly** *adv*.

partial fractions the fractions into which a given fraction may be separated and whose sum equals the given fraction
$$\left[\frac{1}{2xy} \text{ and } \frac{a}{xy} \text{ are the } \textit{partial fractions of } \frac{3a}{2xy} \right]$$

par·ti·al·i·ty (pär′shē al′ə tē, pär shal′-) *n*. [ME. *parcialitee* < MFr. *partialité*] 1. the state or quality of being partial; tendency to favor unfairly; bias 2. particular fondness or liking —*SYN*. see PREJUDICE

partial tone *Acoustics, Music* any of the pure, or harmonic, tones forming a complex tone

par·ti·ble (pär′tə b′l) *adj*. [LL. *partibilis* < L. *partiri*, to divide < *pars*, PART] that can be divided, separated, or parted; divisible

‡**par·ti·ceps cri·mi·nis** (pär′ti seps′ krim′i nis) [L.] a partner in crime; accomplice

par·tic·i·pant (pär tis′ə pənt, pər-) *adj*. [L. *participans*, prp. of *participare*] participating —*n*. a person who participates or shares in something

par·tic·i·pate (-pāt′) *vi.* **-pat′ed, -pat′ing** [< L. *participatus*, pp. of *participare* < *pars,* PART + *capere*, to take] to have or take a part or share with others (*in* some activity, enterprise, etc.) —*vt.* [Rare] to have or take a part or share in —*SYN.* see SHARE¹ —**par·tic′i·pa′tion, par·tic′i·pance** *n.* —**par·tic′i·pa′tive** *adj.* —**par·tic′i·pa·to′ry** (-pə·tô′rē) *adj.*

par·ti·cip·i·al (pär′tə·sip′ē·əl) *adj.* [L. *participialis*] of, based on, or having the nature and use of a participle —**par′ti·cip′i·al·ly** *adv.*

par·ti·ci·ple (pär′tə·sip′′l) *n.* [ME. < OFr. < L. *participium* < *particeps*, participating, partaking < *pars,* PART + *capere*, to take: from participating in the nature of both *v.* & *adj.*] a verbal form basically having the qualities of both verb and adjective: in English, the present participle most commonly ends in *-ing* (*asking*) and the past participle most commonly ends in *-ed* or *-en* (*asked, spoken*) Participles are used: *a)* in verb phrases (*are asking, was carried*) *b)* as verbs (*seeing* the results, he stopped) *c)* as adjectives (a *laughing* boy, the *beaten* path) *d)* as nouns, i.e., gerunds (*seeing* is *believing*) *e)* as adverbs (*raving* mad) *f)* as connectives (*saving* those present)

par·ti·cle (pär′ti k′l) *n.* [ME. *partycle* < MFr. *particule* < L. *particula*, dim. of *pars,* PART] **1.** *a)* an extremely small piece; tiny fragment [a dust *particle*] *b)* the slightest trace; speck [not a *particle* of truth] **2.** [Archaic] a clause or article in a document **3.** *Gram. a)* a short, usually uninflected and invariable part of speech, as an article, or any of certain prepositions, conjunctions, or interjections: used to show syntactical relationships *b)* an uninflected stem **4.** *Physics* a piece of matter so small as to be considered without magnitude though having inertia and the force of attraction **5.** *R.C.Ch.* a small piece of the consecrated Host or any of the small Hosts given to lay communicants

☆**par·ti·cle·board** (-bôrd′) *n.* a flexible board made by compressing sawdust or wood particles with a resin binder

par·ti·col·ored (pär′tē kul′ərd) *adj.* [< ME. *party*, particolored (< Fr. *parti*, pp. of *partir:* see PARTY) + COLORED] **1.** having different colors in different parts **2.** diversified; variegated

par·tic·u·lar (pər tik′yə lər, pär-) *adj.* [ME. *particuler* < MFr. < LL. *particularis* < L. *particula*, PARTICLE] **1.** of or belonging to a single, definite person, part, group, or thing; not general; distinct **2.** apart from any other; regarded separately; specific [to want a *particular* color] **3.** out of the ordinary; unusual; noteworthy; special [no *particular* reason for going] **4.** dealing with particulars; itemized; detailed **5.** not satisfied with anything considered inferior; exacting; extremely careful; fastidious **6.** *Logic* designating a proposition which affirms or denies its predicate to a part of, but not to the whole of, a subject; not universal ["some people have red hair" is a *particular* proposition] —*n.* **1.** a separate and distinct individual, fact, item, or instance which may be included under a generalization; single case **2.** a detail; item of information; point **3.** *Logic* a particular proposition —*SYN.* see DAINTY, ITEM, SINGLE, SPECIAL —**in particular** particularly; especially

par·tic·u·lar·ism (-iz′m) *n.* **1.** the Calvinist doctrine that redemption is possible only for particular persons, not all **2.** undivided adherence or devotion to one particular party, system, interest, theory, etc. **3.** the policy of allowing each member or state in a federation to govern independently without regard to the interests of the whole —**par·tic′u·lar·ist** *adj., n.* —**par·tic′u·lar·is′tic** *adj.*

par·tic·u·lar·i·ty (pər tik′yə lar′ə tē, pär-) *n., pl.* **-ties** [MFr. *particularité* < LL. *particularitas*] **1.** the state, quality, or fact of being particular; specif., *a)* individuality, as opposed to generality *b)* the quality of being detailed, as a description *c)* attention to detail; painstaking care *d)* the quality of being fastidious or hard to please **2.** something particular; specif., *a)* an individual characteristic; peculiarity *b)* a minute detail

par·tic·u·lar·ize (-tik′yə lə rīz′) *vt.* **-ized′, -iz′ing** [MFr. *particulariser*] to state or name individually or in detail; itemize —*vi.* to give particulars or details —**par·tic′u·lar·i·za′tion** *n.*

par·tic·u·lar·ly (-tik′yə lər lē) *adv.* **1.** so as to be particular; in detail **2.** especially; unusually; extraordinarily **3.** specifically

par·tic·u·late (-tik′yə lit, -lāt′) *adj.* [< L. *particula*, PARTICLE + -ATE¹] of, pertaining to, or consisting of very small, separate particles —*n.* a very minute particle

particulate inheritance *Genetics* inheritance by offspring of distinctive characters from both the father and the mother

part·ing (pärt′in) *adj.* **1.** dividing; separating **2.** departing **3.** given, spoken, done, etc. at parting —*n.* **1.** the act of breaking, dividing, or separating **2.** a place of division or separation; parting point or line **3.** something that separates or divides **4.** a leave-taking or departure **5.** death

parting strip a thin strip of wood, metal, etc. for separating adjoining parts of a structure

‡**par·ti pris** (pàr tē′ prē′) [Fr.] preconceived opinion

par·ti·san¹ (pär′tə z′n, -s′n) *n.* [MFr. < It. *partigiano* < *parte* < L. *pars,* PART] **1.** a person who takes the part of or strongly supports one side, party, or person; often,

specif., an unreasoning, emotional adherent **2.** any of a group of guerrilla fighters; esp., a member of an organized civilian force fighting covertly to drive out occupying enemy troops —*adj.* **1.** of, like, or characteristic of a partisan **2.** blindly or unreasonably devoted **3.** of or having to do with military partisans —*SYN.* see FOLLOWER —**par′ti·san·ship′** *n.*

par·ti·san² (pärt′ə z′n, -s′n) *n.* [MFr. *partisane* < It. *partigiana*, prob. < *pertugiare*, to pierce] a kind of halberd used by infantry in the 16th and 17th cent.

par·ti·ta (pär·tē′tə) *n.* [It. < fem. pp. of *partire*, to divide < L.: see PART, *v.*] *Music* **1.** a kind of suite, esp. of the 18th cent. **2.** an air with variations

par·tite (pär′tīt) *adj.* [L. *partitus*, pp. of *partire*, to PART] parted; having divisions; divided into parts: often in compounds [*bipartite, tripartite*]

par·ti·tion (pär tish′ən, pər-) *n.* [ME. *particioune* < L. *partitio*] **1.** a parting or being parted; division into parts; separation; apportionment **2.** something that separates or divides, as an interior wall dividing one room from another **3.** a part or section; portion; compartment **4.** *Law* the process of dividing property and giving separate title to those who previously had joint or common title **5.** *Logic* the separation of a class into its elements or parts: a method of analysis —*vt.* **1.** to divide into parts or shares; apportion **2.** to set off or divide by a partition —**par·ti′tioned** *adj.* —**par·ti′tion·er** *n.*

par·ti·tive (pärt′ə tiv) *adj.* [ML. *partitivus:* see PARTITE & -IVE] **1.** used in setting off or separating; making a division **2.** *Gram.* restricting to or involving only a part of a whole [the *partitive* genitive] —*n.* a partitive word or form —**par′ti·tive·ly** *adv.*

par·ti·zan (pärt′ə z′n, -s′n) *n., adj.* var. of PARTISAN¹

part·let (pärt′lit) *n.* [earlier *patelet* < MFr. *patelette*, band of stuff, orig., dim. of *pate*, a paw] a covering for the neck and upper chest, worn chiefly by women in the 16th cent.

part·ly (pärt′lē) *adv.* in some measure or degree; in part; not fully or completely

part·ner (pärt′nər) *n.* [ME. *partener*, altered (after *part,* PART) < *parcener* (see PARCENER)] **1.** a person who takes part in some activity in common with another or others; associate; specif., *a)* one of two or more persons engaged in the same business enterprise and sharing its profits and risks: each is an agent for the other or others and is liable, except when limited to his own investment, for the debts of the firm *b)* a husband or wife *c)* either of two persons dancing together *d)* either of two players on the same side or team playing or competing against two others, as in bridge or tennis **2.** *Naut.* one of the reinforcing timbers used to support a mast, capstan, etc. and to strengthen the deck at that point —*vt.* **1.** to join (others) together as partners **2.** to be or provide a partner for

part·ner·ship (-ship′) *n.* **1.** the state of being a partner; participation **2.** the relationship of partners; joint interest; association **3.** *a)* an association of two or more partners in a business enterprise *b)* a contract by which such an association is created *c)* the people so associated

part of speech any of the classes of words of a given language to which a word can be assigned: different kinds of grammar have different bases for classifying words, as form, function, meaning, etc., or combinations of these: in traditional English grammar, patterned after Latin grammar, the parts of speech are noun, verb, adjective, adverb, pronoun, preposition, conjunction, and interjection: see also MAJOR FORM CLASS

par·took (pär took′) *pt.* of PARTAKE

par·tridge (pär′trij) *n., pl.* **-tridg·es, -tridge:** see PLURAL, II, D, 1 [ME. *partriche* < OFr. *perdriz*, earlier *perdiz* < L. *perdix* < Gr. *perdix*, prob. akin to *perdesthai*, to break wind (< IE. base *perd-*, whence FART): from whirring sound made by wings on rising to fly] **1.** a European quaillike game bird (*Perdix perdix*) with an orange-brown head, a grayish neck, and a rust-colored tail: successfully introduced into N. America **2.** any of various game birds resembling the partridge, as the ruffed grouse, pheasant, etc.

Par·tridge (pär′trij), **Eric** (Honeywood) 1894— ; Brit. lexicographer & writer, born in New Zealand

☆**par·tridge·ber·ry** (-ber′ē) *n., pl.* **-ries** **1.** a trailing N. American evergreen (*Mitchella repens*) of the madder family with opposite, rounded leaves, pinkish flowers, and red berries **2.** its berry

part song a homophonic song for several voices singing in harmony, generally without accompaniment: also **part′-song′** *n.*

part-time (pärt′tīm′) *adj.* designating, of, or engaged in work, study, etc. for specified periods regarded as taking less time than a regular or full schedule

part time as a part-time employee, student, etc. [to work *part time*]

par·tu·ri·ent (pär tyoor′ē ənt, -toor′-) *adj.* [L. *parturiens*, prp. of *parturire*, to be in labor < *parere*, to bring forth:

PARTRIDGE
(to 14 in. long; wingspread to 13 in.)

see -PAROUS] **1.** giving birth or about to give birth to young **2.** of childbirth, or parturition **3.** on the point of coming forth with a discovery, idea, etc. —**par·tu′ri·en·cy** n.

par·tu·ri·fa·cient (pär tyoor′i fā′shənt, -toor′-) adj. [< L. parturire (see prec.) + -FACIENT] inducing or easing labor in childbirth —n. a parturifacient medicine

par·tu·ri·tion (pär′choo rish′ən, -tyoo-, -too-) n. [L. parturitio < parturire: see PARTURIENT] the act of bringing forth young; childbirth

part·way (pärt′wā′) adv. to some point, degree, or extent less than full, complete, final, etc. [partway done]

par·ty (pär′tē) n., pl. -ties [ME. partie < OFr. < partir, to divide < L. partiri < pars, PART] **1.** a) a group of people working together to establish or promote particular theories or principles of government which they hold in common; esp., an organized political group which seeks to elect its candidates to office and thus to direct government policies b) the political practice of forming and supporting such groups **2.** any group of persons acting together; specif., a) a group sent out on a task or mission [a surveying party] b) a group meeting together socially to accomplish a task [a quilting party] c) a group assembled for amusement or recreation [a fishing party] **3.** a gathering for social entertainment, or the entertainment itself, often of a specific nature [a birthday party, cocktail party] **4.** a person who participates in or is concerned in an action, proceeding, plan, etc. (often with to) [to be a party to a conspiracy] **5.** either of the persons or sides concerned in a legal matter **6.** [Colloq.] a person [the party who telephoned] —adj. **1.** of or having to do with a political party [a party leader] **2.** for a social gathering [party clothes] —vi. -tied, -ty·ing ☆to attend or hold social parties —vt. ☆to be host to at a party

par·ty-col·ored (-kul′ərd) adj. same as PARTI-COLORED

party line 1. a line marking the boundary between adjoining properties ☆**2.** a single circuit connecting two or more telephone users with the exchange ☆**3.** [usually pl.] a political tenet regarded as a line, or boundary, beyond which a political party or its members are not supposed to go **4.** the line of policy followed by a political party, esp. a communist party —**par′ty-lin′er** n.

party man a faithful supporter of a political party

party politics political acts and principles directed toward the interests of one political party or its members without reference to the common good

☆**party poop·er** (poo′pər) [PARTY + POOP² + -ER] [Slang] a spoilsport, esp. one who is too tired or lethargic to participate in the fun of a party: also **party poop**

party wall a wall separating and common to two buildings or properties: each owner has a partial right in its use

pa·rure (pə roor′; Fr. pả rür′) n. [Fr. < OFr. < LL. paratura, a preparation < parare, PREPARE] a matched set of jewelry, as earrings, bracelet, and necklace

par value the nominal value of a stock, bond, etc. fixed at the time of its issue; face value: distinguished from MARKET VALUE

par·ve (pär′və, -ve) adj. same as PAREVE

par·ve·nu (pär′və noo′, -nyoo′) n. [Fr., pp. of parvenir < L. pervenire, to arrive < per, through (see PER) + venire, COME] a person who has suddenly acquired wealth or power, esp. one who is not fully accepted socially by the class into which he has risen; person considered an upstart —adj. **1.** being a parvenu **2.** like or characteristic of a parvenu

par·vis (pär′vis) n. [ME. < OFr. parevis < L. paradisus, lit., PARADISE: name of the court before St. Peter's in Rome] **1.** an enclosed court or yard in front of a building, esp. a church **2.** a portico or single line of columns in front of a church

par·vo·line (pär′və lēn′, -lin) n. [< L. parvus, small, after (QUIN)OLINE: so named because of its low volatility] any of the isomeric, liquid, basic compounds, $C_9H_{13}N$, derived from pyridine and found in decaying fish or meat

pas (pä) n., pl. pas (päz; Fr. pä) [Fr. < L. passus, a step: see PASS²] **1.** the right to precede; precedence **2.** a step or series of steps in dancing

Pas·a·de·na (pas′ə dē′nə) **1.** [< Chippewa, lit., valley town] city in SW Calif., near Los Angeles: pop. 113,000 **2.** [after prec.] city in SE Tex., near Houston: pop. 89,000

Pa·sar·ga·dae (pə sär′gə dē′) ancient capital of Persia, built by Cyrus the Great: near modern Shiraz, Iran

Pa·say (pä′sī) city in S Luzon, the Philippines, on Manila Bay: pop. 133,000

Pas·cal (pås käl′; E. pas kal′), **Blaise** (blez) 1623-62; Fr. mathematician, physicist, & philosopher

Pas·cal celery (pas′k'l) [< ?] any of several large, high-yielding, dark-green varieties of celery with firm, crisp stalks

Pasch (pask) n. [ME. pasche < OFr. < LL.(Ec.) pascha < Gr.(Ec.) pascha (in NT. & LXX) < Heb. pesaḥ, usually interpreted "passage," as if < pāsaḥ, to pass over, but prob. < base akin to Assyr. pasāhu, to propitiate] same as: **1.** PASSOVER **2.** EASTER —**pas′chal** (pas′k'l) adj.

paschal lamb 1. among the ancient Hebrews, the lamb slain and eaten at the Passover **2.** [P- L-] Christianity

a) an epithet for JESUS b) any of several symbolic representations of Jesus, as an Agnus Dei

pasch flower (pask) same as PASQUEFLOWER

Pas·cua (päs′kwä), **Is·la de** (ēs′lä thä) Sp. name of EASTER ISLAND

pas de chat (pä′ də shä′; Fr. pät shä′) [Fr., lit., step of the cat] Ballet a catlike, springing leap

pas de deux (pä′ də doo′; Fr. päd dö′) pl. **pas′ de deux′** (dooz′; Fr. dö′) [Fr., step for two] Ballet a dance or figure for two performers: a **pas de trois** (pät trwä′) is for three performers, a **pas de qua·tre** (pät kä′tr′) is for four performers, etc.

‡**pa·se·o** (pä se′ō) n. [Sp. < pasear, to walk < paso, a step < L. passus: see PACE¹] **1.** a leisurely walk, esp. in the evening; stroll **2.** a street or plaza for strolling **3.** the parade of bullfighters into the arena preceding the bullfights

pash¹ (pash) vt., vi. [ME. passchen, prob. echoic] [Obs. or Dial.] to hurl or be hurled violently so as to break; smash —n. [Obs. or Dial.] a smashing blow

pash² (päsh) n. [< ?] [Brit. Dial.] the head

pa·sha (pə shä′, pä′shə, pash′ə) n. [Turk. pasha] formerly, in Turkey, **1.** a title of rank or honor placed after the name **2.** a high civil or military official

pa·sha·lik, pa·sha·lic (pə shä′lik) n. [Turk. pashalik < pasha + -lik, suffix of condition] the jurisdiction of or area governed by a pasha

Push·to (push′tō, päsh′-) n. a language of the Iranian branch of the Indo-European language family, spoken in Afghanistan and West Pakistan: one of the official languages of Afghanistan

Pa·siph·a·ë (pə sif′ə ē′) [L. < Gr. Pasiphaē] Gr. Myth. the wife of Minos and mother of the Minotaur by a white bull belonging to Minos

‡**pa·so·do·ble** (pä′sō dō′ble) n., pl. **pa′so·do′bles** (bles) [Sp., lit., double step] **1.** spirited music played at bullfights during the entrance (paseo) of the bullfighters or during the passes (faena) just before the kill **2.** a dance based on this: also **pa′so do′ble**

pasque·flow·er (pask′flou′ər) n. [earlier passeflower < MFr. passefleur < passer, PASS² + fleur, FLOWER, altered after Fr. pasque, PASCH] any of several plants (genus Anemone) of the buttercup family; esp., a N. American wildflower (Anemone patens) of early spring, having silky, hairy foliage and cup-shaped, bluish, solitary flowers

pas·quin·ade (pas′kwə nād′) n. [Fr. < It. pasquinata < Pasquino, classical statue in Rome to which it was the custom in the 16th cent. to attach satirical verses] a satire or sarcastic squib posted in a public place; lampoon: also **pas′quil** (-kwil) —vt. -ad′ed, -ad′ing to criticize or ridicule with such satire; lampoon

pass¹ (pas, päs) n. [ME. pas: see PACE¹] a narrow passage or opening, esp. between mountains; gap; defile

pass² (pas, päs) vi. [ME. passen < OFr. passer < VL. *passare < L. passus, a step: see PACE¹] **1.** to go or move forward, through, or out **2.** to extend; lead [a road passing around the hill] **3.** to be handed on or circulated from person to person **4.** to go, change, or be conveyed from one place, form, condition, circumstance, possession, etc. to another **5.** to be spoken or exchanged between persons, as greetings **6.** a) to cease; come to an end (often with away) [the fever passed] b) to go away; depart **7.** to die (usually with away, on, or out) **8.** to go by; move by or past **9.** to slip by or elapse [an hour passed] **10.** to get or make a way (with through or by) **11.** a) to go, take place, or be accepted without question, dispute, or challenge b) to gain acceptance as a member of a group by assuming an identity with it in denial of one's ancestry, background, etc. **12.** to be sanctioned, ratified, or approved by some authority, as a legislative body **13.** a) to go through a trial, test, or examination successfully; satisfy given requirements or standards b) to be barely acceptable as a substitute **14.** to happen; take place; occur **15.** a) to sit in inquest or judgment b) to give a judgment, opinion, or sentence; decide (on or upon a matter) **16.** to be rendered or pronounced [the judgment passed against us] **17.** to be expelled, as from the bowels **18.** Card Games to decline a chance to bid, play a round, etc. **19.** Sports to attempt or complete a pass of the ball, puck, etc. —vt. **1.** to go by, beyond, past, over, or through; specif., a) to leave behind [to pass others in a race] b) to undergo; experience (usually with through) c) to go by without noticing; disregard; ignore [to pass one's bus stop] ☆d) to omit the payment of (a regular dividend) e) to go through (a trial, test, examination, course of study, etc.) successfully; satisfy the requirements or standards of f) to go beyond or above the powers or limits of; surpass; excel g) [Archaic] to cross; traverse **2.** to cause or allow to go, move, or proceed; specif., a) to send; dispatch b) to cause to move in a certain way; direct the movement of [to pass a comb through one's hair] c) to guide into position [to pass a rope around a stake] d) to cause to go through, or penetrate e) to cause to move past [to pass troops in review] f) to cause or allow to get by an obstacle, obstruction, etc. g) to cause or allow to stand approved;

ratify; sanction; enact; approve *h*) to cause or allow to go through an examination, test, etc. successfully *i*) to allow to go by or elapse; spend (often with *away*) [to *pass* a pleasant hour] *j*) to discharge or expel from the bowels, bladder, etc.; excrete; void ☆*k*) Baseball to walk (a batter) **3.** to cause to move from place to place or person to person; transport or transmit; specif., *a*) to hand to another [*pass* the salt] *b*) to cause to be in circulation [to *pass* a bad check] *c*) to hand, throw, or hit (a ball, puck, etc.) from one player to another *d*) to hit a tennis ball past (an opponent) so as to score a point **4.** [Rare] to pledge **5.** *a*) to pronounce or give (an opinion or judgment) *b*) to utter (a remark) **6.** to manipulate (cards, etc.) or trick (a person), as by sleight of hand —*n.* [Fr. *passe* < *passer* (see the *v.*); partly < the ModE. *v.*] **1.** an act of passing; passage **2.** *a*) the successful completion of a scholastic course or examination, esp. if without honors *b*) a mark, etc. indicating this **3.** condition or situation [a strange *pass*] **4.** *a*) a ticket, certificate, etc. giving permission or authorization to come or go freely or without charge *b*) a ticket at a fixed price that permits unlimited rides on a bus, train, etc. for a specified period *c*) *Mil.* a written leave of absence for a brief period **5.** a motion of the hands that is meant to deceive, as in card tricks or magic; sleight of hand **6.** a motion or stroke of the hand, as in mesmerism or hypnotism **7.** *a*) a motion of the hand as if to strike *b*) a tentative attempt **8.** [Slang] an attempt to embrace, caress, or kiss, esp. in seeking sexual intimacy **9.** *Aeron.* a flight over a specified point or at a target **10.** *Card Games* a declining of a chance to bid, play a round, etc. **11.** *Sports a*) an intentional transfer of the ball, puck, etc. to another player during play *b*) a lunge or thrust made in fencing ☆*c*) a walk in baseball —**bring to pass** to cause to come about or happen —**come to pass** to come about or happen —**pass current 1.** to have a certain accepted value, as money **2.** to be commonly known or accepted; circulate widely, as a rumor —**pass for** to be accepted or looked upon as: usually said of an imitation or counterfeit —**pass off 1.** to come to an end; cease **2.** to take place; go through, as a transaction **3.** to be accepted or cause to be accepted as genuine, true, etc., esp. through deceit —**pass one's lips 1.** to be eaten or drunk by one **2.** to be said by one —**pass out 1.** to distribute **2.** to become unconscious; faint —**pass over 1.** to disregard; ignore; omit **2.** to leave (someone) out of consideration in promotions, appointments, etc. —☆**pass up** [Colloq.] to reject, refuse, or let go by, as an opportunity

pass. 1. passage **2.** passenger **3.** passim **4.** passive
pass·a·ble (-ə b'l) *adj.* [ME. < MFr. < *passer*, PASS²] **1.** that can be passed, traveled over, or crossed **2.** that can be circulated; genuine, as coin **3.** barely satisfactory for the purpose; adequate; fair **4.** that can be enacted, as a proposed law —**pass'a·ble·ness** *n.*
pass·a·bly (-ə blē) *adv.* **1.** well enough; acceptably **2.** moderately; somewhat
pass·a·ca·glia (päs'ə käl'yə, pas'-) *n.* [pseudo-It. < Sp. *pasacalle* < *pasar* (< VL. *passare*, PASS²) + *calle*, street < L. *callis*: so named from often being performed in the streets] **1.** formerly, a slow, stately Italian dance similar to the chaconne **2.** the music for this dance **3.** a musical form based on this dance, in 3/4 time and with a continuous ground bass
pas·sade (pə säd') *n.* [Fr. < It. *passata* < *passare*, PASS²] *Horsemanship* the movement of a horse backward and forward over the same ground
pas·sa·do (pə sä'dō) *n., pl.* **-dos, -does** [altered < Fr. *passade* < It. *passata*: see prec.] *Fencing* a thrust or lunge with one foot advanced
pas·sage (pas'ij) *n.* [ME. < OFr. < *passer*: see PASS² & -AGE] **1.** the act of passing; specif., *a*) movement from one place to another; migration [birds of *passage*] *b*) change or progress from one process or condition to another; transition *c*) the enactment of a law by a legislative body **2.** permission, right, or a chance to pass **3.** a journey, esp. by water; voyage **4.** *a*) passenger accommodations, esp. on a ship *b*) the charge for this **5.** a way or means of passing; specif., *a*) a road or path *b*) a channel, duct, etc. *c*) a hall or corridor that is an entrance or exit or onto which several rooms open; passageway **6.** that which happens or takes place between persons; interchange, as of blows or words **7.** *a*) a noted sentence, paragraph, etc. of a written work or speech [a Bible *passage*] *b*) a section or detail of a painting, drawing, etc. **8.** *Med.* a bowel movement **9.** *Music a*) a run consisting of the tones of a scale or chord *b*) a short section of a composition —*vi.* **-saged, -sag·ing** [Rare] **1.** to make a passage, or voyage; journey **2.** to take part in a fight or quarrel
pas·sage·way (-wā') *n.* a narrow way for passage, as a hall, corridor, or alley; passage
Pas·sa·ic (pə sā'ik) [< Delaware *passajeck*, valley] **1.** river in NE N.J., flowing south into Newark Bay: c. 100 mi. **2.** city on this river: pop. 55,000: see CLIFTON
Pas·sa·ma·quod·dy Bay (pas'ə mə kwäd'ē) [< Algonquian, plenty of pollack] arm of the Bay of Fundy between Maine & New Brunswick, Canada: c. 15 mi. long
pas·sant (pas'ənt) *adj.* [ME. (only in sense "excelling, passing") < OFr. *passant* < prp. of *passer*, PASS²] *Heraldry*

walking with the head forward and the forepaw farther from the viewer raised [a lion *passant*]
pass-band filter (pas'band', päs'-) *same as* BAND-PASS FILTER
pass·book (pas'book', päs'-) *n.* **1.** *same as* BANKBOOK **2.** a customer's record in which a merchant or dealer records items bought on credit
pas·sé (pa sā', pas'ā) *adj.* [Fr., lit., past] **1.** out-of-date; old-fashioned **2.** not youthful; rather old
☆**passed ball** *Baseball* a pitch that gets by the catcher when he could be expected to catch it, so that a man on base advances to any other base
pas·sel (pas'l) *n.* [altered < PARCEL] [Colloq. or Dial.] a group or collection, esp. a fairly large one
passe·men·terie (pas men'trē) *n.* [Fr. < *passement*, lace < *passer*: see PASS² & -MENT] trimming made of gimp, cord, beads, braid, etc.
pas·sen·ger (pas'n jər) *n.* [ME. *passager* < MFr. < OFr. *passage*, PASSAGE: the *n* is unhistoric, as in *messenger*] **1.** [Rare] a person passing by or through, usually on foot **2.** a person traveling in a train, bus, boat, automobile, etc., esp. a person having no part in the operation of the conveyance
☆**passenger pigeon** a variety of N. American pigeon (*Ectopistes migratorius*) with a narrow tail longer than its wings: formerly abundant, but slaughtered wholesale by man and extinct since c. 1914
passe-par·tout (pas'pär tōō', päs'-) *n.* [Fr., lit., passes everywhere] **1.** that which passes or allows passage everywhere **2.** a passkey or master key **3.** a mat used in mounting pictures **4.** a picture mounting in which glass, picture, backing, and often a mat are bound together, as by strips of gummed paper along the edges **5.** the gummed paper used for such a mounting
‡**passe·pied** (päs pyā') *n.* [Fr. < *passer*, PASS² + *pied* (< L. *pes*), FOOT] **1.** a lively, 17th-cent. French dance, similar to the minuet but faster in tempo: now sometimes a movement in ballet **2.** the music for this
pass·er-by (pas'ər bī', päs'-) *n., pl.* **pass'ers-by'** a person who passes by
pas·ser·ine (pas'ər in, -ə rīn') *adj.* [L. *passerinus* < *passer*, a sparrow] of or pertaining to an order (Passeriformes) of small or medium-sized, chiefly perching songbirds having grasping feet with the first toe directed backward: more than half of all birds belong to this group —*n.* any bird of this group
‡**pas seul** (pä söl') [Fr., lit., solo dance] *Ballet* a dance performed by one person
pas·si·ble (pas'ə b'l) *adj.* [ME. < OFr. < LL.(Ec.) < pp. of L. *pati*, to suffer: see PASSION] that can feel or suffer —**pas'si·bil'i·ty** *n.*
‡**pas·sim** (pas'im) *adv.* [L.] here and there; in various parts (of a book, etc.)
pass·ing (pas'iŋ, päs'-) *adj.* [ME.] **1.** going by, beyond, past, over, or through **2.** lasting only a short time; short-lived; fleeting; momentary **3.** casual; cursory; incidental [a *passing* remark] **4.** satisfying given requirements or standards [a *passing* grade] **5.** that is happening; current **6.** [Chiefly Archaic] surpassing; extreme; very —*adv.* [Chiefly Archaic] exceedingly; unusually; very —*n.* **1.** the act of one that passes; specif., death **2.** a means or place of passing —**in passing 1.** without careful thought; casually **2.** incidentally; by the way
passing note (or **tone**) *Music* a note not part of a harmonic scheme but introduced for ornamentation or for smoother transition from one tone or chord to another
pas·sion (pash'ən) *n.* [ME. < OFr. < LL.(Ec.) *passio*, a suffering, esp. that of Christ (< L. *passus*, pp. of *pati*, to endure < IE. base *pē-*, to harm, whence Gr. *pēma*, destruction, L. *paene*, scarcely): transl. of Gr. *pathos* (see PATHOS)] **1.** orig., suffering or agony, as of a martyr **2.** [P-] *a*) the agony and sufferings of Jesus during the Crucifixion or during the period following the Last Supper *b*) any of the Gospel descriptions of this *c*) an artistic or musical work based on this **3.** *a*) any one of the emotions, as hate, grief, love, fear, joy, etc. *b*) [*pl.*] all such emotions collectively **4.** extreme, compelling emotion; intense emotional drive or excitement; specif., *a*) great anger; rage; fury *b*) enthusiasm or fondness [a *passion* for music] *c*) strong love or affection *d*) sexual drive or desire; lust **5.** the object of any strong desire or fondness **6.** [Obs.] the condition of being acted upon, esp. by outside influences
SYN.—**passion** usually implies a strong emotion that has an overpowering or compelling effect [his *passions* overcame his reason]; **fervor** and **ardor** both imply emotion of burning intensity, **fervor** suggesting a constant glow of feeling [religious *fervor*], and **ardor**, a restless, flamelike emotion [the *ardors* of youth]; **enthusiasm** implies strongly favorable feelings for an object or cause and usually suggests eagerness in the pursuit of something [his *enthusiasm* for golf]; **zeal** implies intense enthusiasm for an object or cause, usually as displayed in vigorous and untiring activity in its support [a *zeal* for reform] See also FEELING
pas·sion·al (-'l) *adj.* of, characterized by, or due to passion —*n.* a book describing the sufferings of saints and martyrs: usually read during their festivals
pas·sion·ate (-it) *adj.* [ME. *passionat* < ML. *passionatus*] **1.** having or showing strong feelings; full of passion **2.** easily angered; hot-tempered **3.** resulting from, expressing, or tending to arouse strong feeling; ardent; intense;

impassioned [a *passionate* speech] **4.** readily aroused to sexual activity; sensual **5.** strong; vehement: said of an emotion —**pas′sion·ate·ly** *adv.*

SYN.—**passionate** implies strong or violent emotion, often of an impetuous kind [a *passionate* rage]; **impassioned** suggests an expression of emotion that is deeply and sincerely felt [an *impassioned* plea for tolerance]; **ardent** and **fervent** suggest a fiery or glowing feeling of eagerness, enthusiasm, devotion, etc. [an *ardent* pursuit of knowledge, a *fervent* prayer]; **fervid** differs from **fervent** in often suggesting an outburst of intense feeling that is at a fever pitch [a *fervid*, *fervid* hatred]

pas·sion·flow·er (-flou′ər) *n.* [from the supposed resemblance of parts of the flowers to Jesus' wounds, crown of thorns, etc.] any of a genus (*Passiflora*) of mostly climbing plants of the passionflower family, with red, yellow, green, white, or purple flowers and usually small, edible, yellow or purple, egglike fruit —*adj.* designating a family (Passifloraceae) of mostly tendril-climbing, tropical plants, including the maypop and passionflower

passion fruit the fruit of a passionflower

pas·sion·less (-lis) *adj.* free from passion or emotion; impassive; calm —**pas′sion·less·ly** *adv.*

Passion play a religious play representing the Passion of Jesus

Passion Sunday [cf. PASSION, 2a] the fifth Sunday in Lent, two weeks before Easter Sunday

Pas·sion·tide (-tīd′) *n.* the two weeks preceding Easter

Passion Week **1.** the week beginning with Passion Sunday **2.** formerly, the week before Easter; Holy Week

pas·si·vate (pas′ə vāt′) *vt.* **-vat′ed, -vat′ing** [PASSIV(E) + -ATE] *Metallurgy* to treat (a metal) so as to form a protective coating on its surface and reduce its chemical activity —**pas′si·va′tion** *n.* —**pas′si·va′tor** *n.*

pas·sive (pas′iv) *adj.* [ME. *passif* < L. *passivus* < *passus*: see PASSION] **1.** influenced or acted upon without exerting influence or acting in return; inactive, but acted upon **2.** offering no opposition or resistance; submissive; yielding; patient **3.** taking no active part; inactive **4.** *Business, Finance* non-interest-bearing, as certain bonds, but having some other stated or implicit benefit **5.** *Chem. a)* same as INERT *b)* resistant to corrosion **6.** *Gram. a)* denoting the voice or form of a verb whose subject is the receiver (object) of the action of the verb: opposed to ACTIVE *b)* in or of the passive voice (Ex.: in "the tree was struck by lightning," *was struck* is a passive construction) —*n. Gram.* **1.** the passive voice **2.** a verb in this voice —**SYN.** see INACTIVE —**pas′sive·ly** *adv.* —**pas′sive·ness** *n.*

passive immunity **1.** immunity to a disease acquired by the injection of antibodies from an animal or person who has acquired active immunity **2.** temporary immunity acquired by a child in the womb from antibodies transferred from the mother

passive resistance opposition to a government or occupying power by refusal to comply with orders, or by such nonviolent acts as voluntary fasting, public demonstrations, etc.

pas·siv·ism (pas′iv iz′m) *n.* **1.** passive behavior or characteristics **2.** the principle of or belief in being passive —**pas′siv·ist** (-ist) *n.*

pas·siv·i·ty (pa siv′ə tē) *n.* [LL. *passivitas*] the state or quality of being passive; esp., inaction, inertia, submissiveness, etc.

pass·key (pas′kē′, päs′-) *n.* **1.** same as: *a)* MASTER KEY *b)* SKELETON KEY **2.** any private key

Pass·o·ver (pas′ō′vər, päs′-) *n.* [PASS² + OVER, used to translate Heb. *pesah*: see PASCH] **1.** a Jewish holiday (*Pesach*) celebrated for eight (or seven) days beginning on the 14th of Nisan and commemorating the deliverance of the ancient Hebrews from slavery in Egypt: Ex. 12 **2.** [p-] formerly, the paschal lamb

pass·port (-pôrt′) *n.* [Fr. *passeport*, safe-conduct, orig., permission to leave or enter a port < *passer*, PASS² + PORT¹] **1.** a government document issued to a citizen for travel abroad, subject to visa requirements, certifying his identity and citizenship: it entitles the bearer to the protection of his own country and that of the countries visited **2.** same as SAFE-CONDUCT (*n.* 1 & 2) **3.** a government document permitting a vessel to leave or enter a port **4.** anything that enables a person to be accepted, admitted, etc.

☆**pass-through** (-thrōō′) *n.* an opening in a wall, as between a kitchen and dining room, often with a shelf, for passing food, etc.

pas·sus (pas′əs) *n., pl.* **-sus, -sus·es** [L., a step: see PACE¹] a part or section of a poem or story

pass·word (pas′wurd′, päs′-) *n.* **1.** a secret word or phrase used for identification, as by a soldier wishing to pass a guard **2.** any means of gaining entrance, etc.

Pas·sy (på sē′) **1. Fré·dé·ric** (frā dā rēk′), 1822-1912; Fr. economist **2. Paul É·douard** (pōl ā dwȧr′), 1859-1940; Fr. phonetician: principal originator of the International Phonetic Alphabet: son of *prec.*

past (past, päst) *rare pp.* of PASS² —*adj.* **1.** gone by; ended; over [his *past* troubles] **2.** of a former time; bygone **3.** immediately preceding; just gone by [the *past* week]

4. having served formerly [a *past* chairman] **5.** *Gram.* indicating a time or condition gone by or an action completed or in progress at a former time —*n.* **1.** the time that has gone by; days, months, or years gone by **2.** what has happened; the history, former life, or experiences of a person, group, or institution: often used to indicate a hidden or questionable past [a woman with a *past*] **3.** *Gram. a)* the past tense *b)* a verb form in this tense —*prep.* **1.** beyond in time; later than **2.** beyond in space; farther on than **3.** beyond in amount or degree **4.** beyond the extent, power, limits, scope, etc. of [*past* belief] —*adv.* to and beyond a point in time or space; by; so as to pass —**not put it past someone** to believe someone is likely (to do something specified)

pas·ta (päs′tə) *n.* [It. < LL. < Gr. *pastē*: see ff.] **1.** the flour paste or dough used in making spaghetti, macaroni, ravioli, etc. **2.** any food or foods made of this

paste (pāst) *n.* [ME. *past* < OFr. *paste* < LL. *pasta* < Gr. *pastē*, mess of barley porridge < *passein*, to sprinkle] **1.** *a)* dough used in making rich pastry *b)* same as PASTA **2.** any of various soft, moist, smooth-textured substances [toothpaste] **3.** a foodstuff, pounded or ground until fine and made creamy, soft, etc. [almond *paste*] **4.** a jellylike candy **5.** a mixture of flour or starch, water, and occasionally alum, resin, etc., used as an adhesive for paper or other light materials **6.** the moistened clay used in manufacturing pottery and porcelain **7.** *a)* a hard, brilliant glass containing oxide of lead, used in making artificial gems; strass *b)* such a gem or gems **8.** [Slang] a blow, or punch, as with the fist —*vt.* **past′ed, past′ing** **1.** to fasten or make adhere with or as with paste **2.** to cover with pasted material [to *paste* a wall with posters] **3.** [Slang] to hit; punch

paste·board (-bôrd′) *n.* **1.** a stiff material made of layers of paper pasted together or of pressed and dried paper pulp **2.** [Slang] something made of pasteboard, as a playing card, ticket, etc. —*adj.* **1.** of or like pasteboard **2.** flimsy; sham

pas·tel (pas tel′) *n.* [Fr. < It. *pastello* < VL. *pastellum*, dim. of *pasta*, PASTE] **1.** *a)* ground coloring matter mixed with gum and formed into a crayon *b)* such a crayon **2.** a picture drawn with such crayons **3.** drawing with pastels as an art form or medium **4.** a light, brief prose work **5.** a soft, pale shade of any color —*adj.* **1.** soft and pale: said of colors **2.** of pastel **3.** drawn with pastels —**pas·tel′ist, pas·tel′list** *n.*

past·er (pās′tər) *n.* **1.** a person or thing that pastes ☆**2.** a slip of gummed paper used to paste on or over something; sticker

pas·tern (pas′tərn) *n.* [ME. *pastron* < MFr. *pasturon* < *pasture*, tether for cattle < VL. *pastoria*, foot shackle, tether < L. *pastorius*, pastoral < *pastor*: see PASTOR] the part of a horse's foot between the fetlock and the hoof

PASTERN

paste-up (pāst′up′) *n.* same as MECHANICAL

Pas·teur (pas tur′; *Fr.* pȧs′tër′), **Louis** 1822-95; Fr. chemist & bacteriologist

pas·teur·ism (pas′tər iz′m) *n.* the theories or methods of Louis Pasteur; specif., *a)* same as PASTEURIZATION *b)* the Pasteur treatment for rabies

pas·teur·i·za·tion (pas′chər i zā′shən, pas′tər-) *n.* [Fr.: see ff. & -ATION] a method of destroying disease-producing bacteria and checking the activity of fermentative bacteria, as in milk, beer, cider, etc., by heating the liquid to a prescribed temperature for a specified period of time

pas·teur·ize (pas′chə rīz′, pas′tə-) *vt.* **-ized′, -iz′ing** [Fr. *pasteuriser* < L. PASTEUR + -ISER, -IZE] to subject (milk, beer, etc.) to pasteurization —**pas′teur·iz′er** *n.*

Pasteur treatment Pasteur's method of preventing certain diseases, esp. rabies, by successive inoculations with the specific virus in increasing strength

pas·tic·cio (päs tē′chō) *n., pl.* **-tic′ci** (-chē), **-tic′cios** [It. < ML. *pasticius* < VL. *pasticius*, composed of paste < LL. *pasta*, a paste] same as PASTICHE

pas·tiche (pas tēsh′, päs-) *n.* [Fr. < It. *pasticcio*] **1.** *a)* a literary, artistic, or musical composition made up of bits from various sources; potpourri *b)* such a composition intended to imitate or ridicule another artist's style **2.** a jumbled mixture; hodgepodge

pas·tie (pas′tē) *n.* same as PASTY²

pas·ties¹ (pas′tēz) *n. pl.* of PASTY²

past·ies² (pās′tēz) *n.pl.* a pair of small adhesive coverings for the nipples, worn by stripteasers, exotic dancers, etc.

pas·tille (pas tēl′) *n.* [Fr. < L. *pastillus*, little roll, lozenge < base of *pascere*, to feed: for IE. base see FOOD] **1.** a small tablet or lozenge containing medicine, flavoring, etc. **2.** a pellet of aromatic paste, burned for fumigating or deodorizing **3.** pastel for crayons **4.** a crayon of pastel Also **pas·til** (pas′til)

pas·time (pas′tīm′, päs′-) *n.* [LME. *passe tyme*, transl. of Fr. *passe-temps*] a way of spending spare time pleasantly; anything done for recreation or diversion

past·i·ness (pās′tē nis) *n.* a pasty state or quality

pas·tis (päs tēs′) *n.* [Fr. < ?] a colorless French cordial flavored with licorice and aniseed

past master 1. a person who formerly held the position of master, as in a lodge or club 2. a person who has had long experience in some occupation, art, etc.; expert —**past mistress** *fem.*

Pas·to (päs′tō) city in SW Colombia, in the Andes: pop. 124,000

pas·tor (pas′tər, päs′-) *n.* [ME. *pastour* < OFr. < L. *pastor,* shepherd, in LL.(Ec.) minister of a congregation < *pascere,* to feed: for IE. base see FOOD] 1. orig., a shepherd 2. a clergyman or priest in charge of a church or congregation

pas·to·ral (-əl) *adj.* [ME. *pastoralle* < L. *pastoralis* < *pastor,* a shepherd: see prec.] 1. of shepherds or their work, way of life, etc. 2. of or portraying rural life, esp. a conventionalized form of former rustic life among shepherds, dairymaids, etc. 3. of pastoral literature or a pastoral 4. characteristic of rural life, idealized as peaceful, simple, and natural 5. of a pastor or his duties —*n.* 1. a piece of literature dealing with life in the country; esp., a poem, play, etc. treating the rustic lives and loves of shepherds in a conventionalized, artificial manner 2. such writing as a literary form 3. a pastoral picture or scene 4. a book treating of the functions of a pastor 5. a letter from a pastor to his congregation or from a bishop to his clergy 6. *same as* CROSIER 7. *Music same as* PASTORALE —SYN. see RURAL —**pas′to·ral·ism** *n.* —**pas′to·ral·ly** *adv.*

pas·to·rale (pas′tə ral′, -räl′, -rä′lē; *It.* päs′tō rä′le) *n., pl.* **-rales′** [*It.* **-ra′li** (-lē) [It., lit., pastoral] *Music* 1. a composition in simple and idyllic style suggesting rural scenes 2. an opera or cantata with a rural theme or subject

pas·tor·ate (pas′tər it, päs′-) *n.* 1. *a)* the position, rank, or duties of a pastor *b)* a pastor's term of office, esp. with one church or parish: also **pas′tor·ship′** 2. a group of pastors, or pastors collectively

☆**pas·to·ri·um** (pas tôr′ē əm) *n.* [< neut. of L. *pastorius,* of a shepherd < *pastor:* see PASTOR] [South] a Protestant, esp. Baptist, parsonage

past participle a participle used: *a)* with auxiliaries and typically expressing completed action or a time or state gone by (as *started* in "he has started") *b)* as an adjective (as *grown* in "a grown man")

past perfect 1. a tense indicating an action or state as completed before a specified or implied time in the past; pluperfect 2. a verb form in this tense (Ex.: had gone)

pas·tra·mi (pə strä′mē) *n.* [Yid. < Romanian *pastrama* < *pastra,* to preserve < VL. **parsitare,* to save < pp. of L. *parcere,* to spare, preserve] highly spiced, smoked beef, esp. from a shoulder cut

pas·try (pās′trē) *n., pl.* **-tries** [see PASTE & -ERY] 1. flour dough or paste made with shortening and used for the crust of pies, tarts, etc. 2. foods made with this, as pies, tarts, etc. 3. broadly, all fancy baked goods, including cakes, sweet rolls, etc. 4. a single pie, cake, etc.

pas·tur·a·ble (pas′chər ə b'l, päs′-) *adj.* that can be used for pasture

pas·tur·age (-ij) *n.* [OFr.: see ff. & -AGE] 1. *same as* PASTURE 2. the pasturing of cattle

pas·ture (pas′chər, päs′-) *n.* [ME. < OFr. < LL. *pastura* < L. *pascere,* to feed: for IE. base see FOOD] 1. grass or other growing plants used as food by grazing animals 2. *a)* ground suitable for grazing *b)* a field, plot, etc. set aside for this —*vt.* **-tured, -tur·ing** 1. to put (cattle, etc.) out to graze in a pasture 2. to graze or feed on (grass, etc.) 3. to provide with pasture: said of land —*vi.* to feed on growing grass or herbage —**put out to pasture** 1. to put in a pasture to graze 2. to allow or compel to retire from work —**pas′tur·er** *n.*

past·y[1] (pās′tē) *adj.* **past′i·er, past′i·est** of or like paste in color or texture

pas·ty[2] (pas′tē, päs′-; päs′tē *is a sp. pronun.*) *n., pl.* **pas′ties** [ME. *pastee* < OFr. *pastée* < *paste,* PASTE] [Chiefly Brit.] a pie, esp. a meat pie

pat[1] (pat) *adj.* [prob. < ff.] 1. apt; timely; opportune 2. exactly suitable [a *pat* hand in poker] 3. so glibly plausible as to seem contrived —*adv.* in a *pat* manner —**have (down) pat** [Colloq.] to know or have memorized thoroughly —☆**stand pat** 1. to refuse to turn aside from an opinion, course of action, etc. 2. *Poker* to draw no further cards and play the hand as dealt —**pat′ness** *n.*

pat[2] (pat) *n.* [ME. *patte,* prob. echoic] 1. a quick, gentle tap, touch, or stroke with the hand or other flat surface 2. the sound made by this 3. a small lump or mass, as of butter —*vt.* **pat′ted, pat′ting** 1. *a)* to tap, touch, or stroke quickly or gently, esp. with the hand, as in affection, sympathy, or encouragement *b)* to tap or stroke lightly with a flat surface 2. to flatten, shape, apply, etc. by patting —*vi.* 1. to pat a surface 2. to move along with a patting sound, as in running —**pat on the back** 1. a compliment or encouragement 2. to compliment or praise

pat. 1. patent 2. patented

pat-a-cake (pat′ə kāk′) *n.* 1. the opening words of a nursery rhyme 2. a game played by clapping the hands in rhythm to this rhyme

pa·ta·gi·um (pə tā′jē əm) *n., pl.* **-gi·a** (-ə) [ModL. < L., gold edging of a tunic, border < Gr. *patageion < patagein,* to rustle] 1. a fold of skin between the fore and hind limbs of bats, flying squirrels, etc., enabling them to fly or

glide through the air 2. a fold of skin between the shoulder and forepart of a bird's wing —**pa·ta′gi·al** *adj.*

Pa·ta·go·ni·a (pat′ə gō′nē ə, -gōn′yə) dry grassy region in S S. America, east of the Andes, including the S parts of Argentina and Chile: often restricted to the portion (c. 250,000 sq. mi.) in Argentina

Pat·a·go·ni·an (-ən, -yən) *adj.* of Patagonia, its people, or their culture —*n.* 1. a native or inhabitant of Patagonia 2. *same as* TEHUELCHE

PATAGONIA

patch[1] (pach) *n.* [ME. *pacche,* prob. var. of *peche,* a piece < OFr. *pieche,* PIECE] 1. a piece of material applied to cover or mend a hole or tear or to strengthen a weak spot 2. a dressing applied to a wound or sore 3. a pad or shield worn over an injured eye 4. a surface area differing from its surroundings in nature or appearance [*patches* of blue sky] 5. a small plot of ground [a potato *patch*] 6. *a)* a small piece of any material; scrap; bit; remnant *b) same as* BEAUTY SPOT 7. *Mil.* a cloth insignia of unit identification worn high on the sleeve —*vt.* 1. to put a patch or patches on 2. to serve as a patch for 3. to form or make by the use of patches [to *patch* a quilt] 4. to produce or piece together roughly, crudely, or hurriedly (often with *up* or *together*) —SYN. see MEND —**patch up** to bring to an end or settle (differences, a quarrel, etc.) —**patch′er** *n.*

patch[2] (pach) *n.* [prob. < It. *paccheo,* dial. var. of *pazzo,* crazy (< ? L. *patiens,* sick: see PATIENT): altered after prec.] [Archaic] a court jester 2. any clown or fool

patch·ou·li, patch·ou·ly (pach′oo lē, pə choo′lē) *n.* [Fr., altered < E. *patch leaf,* part transl. of Tamil *paccili,* lit., green leaf < *paccu,* green + *ilai,* a leaf] 1. an East Indian mint (*Pogostemon patchouli*) that yields a heavy, darkbrown, fragrant oil 2. a perfume made from this oil

patch pocket a pocket made by sewing a patch of shaped material to the outside of a garment

patch reef a relatively small, isolated coral reef

patch test *Med.* a test for determining allergy to a specific substance, made by attaching a sample of it, often a small piece of material saturated with the substance, to the skin and observing the reaction

patch·work (pach′wurk′) *n.* 1. anything formed of irregular, incongruous, odd, or miscellaneous parts; jumble 2. needlework, as a quilt, made of odd patches of cloth, etc. sewn together at the edges 3. any design or used like this

patch·y (pach′ē) *adj.* **patch′i·er, patch′i·est** 1. *a)* made up of or characterized by patches *b)* forming or like patches 2. giving the effect of patches; not consistent or uniform in quality; irregular —**patch′i·ly** *adv.* —**patch′i·ness** *n.*

patd. patented

pate (pāt) *n.* [ME. < ?] 1. the head, esp. the top of the head 2. the brain or intellect A humorous or derogatory term

pâte (pät) *n.* [Fr.] paste; esp., the clay paste used in making pottery or porcelain

pâ·té (pä tā′) *n.* [Fr.] 1. a pie 2. a meat paste

-pat·ed (pāt′id) *a combining form meaning* having a (specified kind of) pate, or head [bald-*pated*]

pâ·té de foie gras (pä tā′ də fwä′ grä′, pät′ā) [Fr.] a paste made of the livers of fattened geese

pa·tel·la (pə tel′ə) *n., pl.* **-las, -lae** (-ē) [L., dim. of *patina,* a pan < Gr. *patanē* < IE. base **pet-,* to spread out, whence FATHOM] 1. a small, shallow pan 2. *same as* KNEECAP (sense 1) 3. *Bot., Zool.* any panlike formation —**pa·tel′lar** *adj.*

patellar reflex *Med.* a normal reflex kick with extension of the leg at the knee, produced by sharply tapping the tendon below the patella

pa·tel·late (-it, -āt) *adj.* having or resembling a patella

pa·tel·li·form (pə tel′ə fôrm′) *adj.* [< PATELLA + -FORM] 1. having the form of a flattened cone 2. having the shape of a limpet shell

pat·en (pat′n) *n.* [ME. < OFr. *patene* < L. *patina:* see PATELLA] 1. a metal plate; esp., the plate holding the bread in the Eucharist 2. a metallic disk

pa·ten·cy (pāt′n sē, pat′n-) *n.* [ML. *patentia*] 1. the state or quality of being patent, or obvious 2. *Med.* the state of being open or unobstructed

pat·ent (pat′nt; *Brit. & for adj.* 2, 3, 4 & 8, *usually* pāt′-) *adj.* [ME. < MFr. & L.: MFr. *patent* < L. *patens,* prp. of *patere,* to be open: for IE. base see PATELLA] 1. *a)* open to examination by the public: said of a document granting some right or rights, as to land, a franchise, an office, or now esp., an invention [letters *patent*] *b)* granted or appointed by letters patent 2. open to all; generally accessible or available 3. obvious; plain; evident [a *patent* lie] 4. open or unobstructed 5. *a)* protected by a

patent; patented *b)* of or having to do with patents or the granting of patents *[patent law]* 6. produced or sold as a proprietary product: cf. PATENT MEDICINE 7. new, unusual, individual, etc.: also **patented** 8. *Bot., Zool.* spreading out or open; patulous —*n.* 1. an official document open to public examination and granting a certain right or privilege; letters patent; esp., a document granting the monopoly right to produce, sell, or get profit from an invention, process, etc. for a specific number of years 2. *a)* the right so granted *b)* the thing protected by such a right; patented article or process 3. public land, or title to such land, granted to a person by letters patent 4. any exclusive right, title, or license —*vt.* 1. to grant a patent to or for 2. to secure exclusive right to produce, use, and sell (an invention or process) by a patent; get a patent for —**pat'ent·a·ble** *adj.*

patent ambiguity *Law* uncertainty existing where language employed in an instrument is unclear on its face and is thus capable of more than one meaning: see LATENT AMBIGUITY

pat·ent·ee (pat'n tē') *n.* a person who has been granted a patent

☆**patent leather** leather with a hard, glossy, usually black finish: made by a process formerly patented

pa·tent·ly (pāt'n't lē, pat') *adv.* in a patent manner; clearly; obviously; openly

patent medicine a trademarked medical preparation that can be bought without a physician's prescription

Patent Office ☆an office in the Department of Commerce which administers the patent and trademark laws

pat·en·tor (pat'n tər) *n.* the grantor of a patent

patent right an exclusive right established by patent, esp. the right to an invention

pa·ter (pāt'ər; *for 2*, pät'ər, pä'ter) *n.* [L., FATHER] 1. [Chiefly Brit. Colloq.] father 2. [P-] same as PATERNOSTER (sense 1)

Pa·ter (pāt'ər), **Walter (Horatio)** 1839–94; Eng. essayist & critic

pa·ter·fa·mil·i·as (pāt'ər fə mil'ē əs, pät'-) *n., pl.* **pa'tres·fa·mil'i·as** (pā'trēz-) [L.] the father of a family; male head of a household

pa·ter·nal (pə tur'n'l) *adj.* [ML. *paternalis* < L. *paternus* < *pater,* FATHER] 1. of, like, or characteristic of a father or fatherhood; fatherly 2. derived, received, or inherited from a father 3. related through the father's side of the family *[paternal* grandparents] —**pa·ter'nal·ly** *adv.*

pa·ter·nal·ism (-iz'm) *n.* [prec. + -ISM] the principle or system of governing or controlling a country, group of employees, etc. in a manner suggesting a father's relationship with his children —**pa·ter'nal·ist** *n., adj.* —**pa·ter'nal·is'tic** *adj.* —**pa·ter'nal·is'ti·cal·ly** *adv.*

pa·ter·ni·ty (pə tur'nə tē) *n.* [OFr. *paternité* < LL. *paternitas* < L. *paternus,* paternal] 1. the state of being a father; fatherhood 2. male parentage; paternal origin 3. origin or authorship in general

pa·ter·nos·ter (pāt'ər nôs'tər; pat'ər näs'tər, pāt'-) *n.* [ME. —ML.(Ec.) < LL.(Ec.) *Pater noster,* opening words of the Lord's Prayer < L. *pater,* FATHER + *noster,* our] 1. the Lord's Prayer, esp. in Latin: often **Pater Noster** 2. *a)* each large bead of a rosary on which this prayer is said *b)* [Archaic] a rosary 3. a muttered prayer or incantation

Pat·er·son (pat'ər s'n) [after Wm. *Paterson* (1745–1806), State governor] city in NE N.J., on the Passaic River: pop. 145,000: see CLIFTON

path (path, päth) *n.* [ME. < OE. *pæth,* akin to G. *pfad,* prob. early Gmc. loan word < Iranian (as in Avestan *path-*) < IE. base **pent(h)-,* to step, go, whence L. *pons,* bridge & FIND] 1. a track or way worn by footsteps; trail 2. a walk or way for the use of people on foot, as in a park or garden 3. a line of movement; course taken *[the path* of the meteor] 4. a course or manner of conduct, thought, or procedure —**path'less** *adj.*

path. 1. pathological 2. pathology

Pa·than (pə tän', pət hän') *n.* [Hindi *pathān* < Afghan *pēstānē,* pl. of *pēstūn,* an Afghan] a member of a Moslem, Indo-Iranian, Pashto-speaking people of Afghanistan and N West Pakistan

pa·thet·ic (pə thet'ik) *adj.* [LL. *patheticus* < Gr. *pathētikos,* akin to *pathos,* suffering, PATHOS] 1. expressing, arousing, or intended to arouse pity, sorrow, sympathy, or compassion; pitiful 2. pitifully unsuccessful, ineffective, etc. *[a pathetic* performance] 3. of the emotions: now only in PATHETIC FALLACY Also **pa·thet'i·cal** —*SYN.* see MOVING —**pa·thet'i·cal·ly** *adv.*

pathetic fallacy the literary device of portraying inanimate nature as having human feelings and character (Ex.: the angry sea, a stubborn door)

☆**path·find·er** (path'fīn'dər, päth'-) *n.* one who makes a path or way where none had existed, as in an unknown region, wilderness, etc.

-path·i·a (path'ē ə) [ModL.] same as -PATHY

-path·ic (path'ik) [see -PATHY & -IC] *a combining form used to form adjectives corresponding to nouns ending in* -PATHY *[osteopathic, psychopathic]*

path·o- (path'ō, -ə) [< Gr. *pathos:* see PATHOS] *a combining form meaning* suffering, disease, feeling *[pathology]:* also, before a vowel, **path-**

path·o·gen (path'ə jən) *n.* [prec. + -GEN] any microorganism or virus that can cause disease: also **path'o·gene'** (-jēn')

path·o·gen·e·sis (path'ə jen'ə sis) *n.* [ModL.: see PATHO- & -GENESIS] the production or development of a disease: also **pa·thog·e·ny** (pə thäj'ə nē) —**path'o·ge·net'ic** (-jə net'ik) *adj.*

path·o·gen·ic (-jen'ik) *adj.* producing disease —**path'o·gen'i·cal·ly** *adv.*

pa·thog·no·mon·ic (pə thäg'nə män'ik) *adj.* [Gr. *pathognōmonikos* < PATHOS, disease (see PATHOS) + *gnōmonikos,* able to judge < *gnōmon,* one who knows: see GNOMON] indicating or typical of a particular disease

pathol. 1. pathological 2. pathology

path·o·log·i·cal (path'ə läj'i k'l) *adj.* 1. of pathology; of or concerned with diseases 2. due to or involving disease 3. governed by a compulsion; compulsive *[a pathological* liar] Also **path'o·log'ic** —**path'o·log'i·cal·ly** *adv.*

pa·thol·o·gy (pə thäl'ə jē, pa-) *n., pl.* **-gies** [< Fr. *pathologie* or ModL. *pathologia* < Gr. *pathologia:* see ff. & -LOGY] 1. the branch of medicine that deals with the nature of disease, esp. with the structural and functional changes caused by disease 2. all the conditions, processes, or results of a particular disease 3. any abnormal variation from a sound or proper condition —**pa·thol'o·gist** *n.*

pa·thos (pā'thäs, -thôs) *n.* [Gr. *pathos,* suffering, disease, feeling, akin to *pathein, paschein,* to suffer, feel < IE. base **kwenth-,* to suffer, endure, whence OIr. *cessaim,* I suffer] 1. [Rare] suffering 2. the quality in something experienced or observed which arouses feelings of pity, sorrow, sympathy, or compassion 3. the feeling aroused *SYN.*—**pathos** names that quality, in a real situation or in a literary or artistic work, which evokes sympathy and a sense of sorrow or pity; **bathos** applies to a false or overdone pathos that is absurd in its effect; **poignancy** implies an emotional quality that is keenly felt, often to the point of being sharply painful

path·way (path'wā', päth'-) *n.* same as PATH

pa·thy (pə thē) [ModL. < *-pathia* < Gr. *-patheia* < *pathos:* see PATHOS] *a combining form meaning:* 1. feeling, suffering *[antipathy]* 2. disease, treatment of disease *[osteopathy]*

Pat·i·a·la (put'ē ä'lə) 1. former state of N India: since 1956, part of Punjab 2. city in Punjab; former capital of Patiala state: pop. 125,000

pa·tience (pā'shəns) *n.* [ME. *pacience* < OFr. < L. *patientia* < *pati,* to suffer: see PASSION] 1. the state, quality, or fact of being patient; specif., *a)* the will or ability to wait or endure without complaint *b)* steadiness, endurance, or perseverance in performing a task 2. [Chiefly Brit.] any of a number of card games, usually for one player; solitaire

SYN.—**patience** implies the bearing of suffering, provocation, delay, tediousness, etc. with calmness and self-control *[her patience* with children]; **endurance** stresses the capacity to bear suffering or hardship *[Job's endurance* of his afflictions]; **fortitude** suggests the resolute endurance that results from firm, sustained courage *[the fortitude* of the pioneers]; **forbearance** implies restraint under provocation or a refraining from retaliation for a wrong *[he acted* with *forbearance* toward the hecklers]; **stoicism** suggests such endurance of suffering without flinching as to indicate an almost austere indifference to pain or pleasure —*ANT.* impatience

pa·tient (pā'shənt) *adj.* [ME. *pacient* < OFr. < L. *patiens,* patient, prp. of *pati:* see PASSION] 1. bearing or enduring pain, trouble, etc. without complaining or losing self-control 2. refusing to be provoked or angered, as by an insult; forbearing; tolerant 3. calmly tolerating delay, confusion, inefficiency, etc. 4. able to wait calmly for something desired 5. showing or characterized by patience *[a patient* face] 6. steady; diligent; persevering *[a patient* worker] 7. [Rare] receiving action; passive —*n.* 1. a person receiving care or treatment, esp. from a doctor 2. [Rare] a person who receives action or is affected — **patient of** 1. capable of bearing (fatigue, thirst, etc.) 2. admitting of or having (a certain meaning) —**pa'tient·ly** *adv.*

pat·i·na¹ (pat'ə n ə) *n., pl.* **-nae** (-nē') [L.] same as PATEN

pat·i·na² (pat'n ə, pə tē'nə) *n.* [Fr. < It., orig., tarnish (on a metal plate), prob. < L., pan: see PATELLA] 1. a fine crust or film on bronze or copper, usually green or greenish-blue, formed by natural oxidation and often valued as being ornamental 2. any thin coating or color change resulting from age, as on old wood or silver

pat·i·nate (pat'n āt') *vt.* **-nat'ed, -nat'ing** to produce a patina on —*vi.* to take on a patina Also **pat'i·nize' -nized', -niz'ing**

pat·ine (pat'n; *for 2, usually* pə tēn') *n.* same as: 1. PATEN 2. PATINA²

pa·ti·o (pat'ē ō', pät'-) *n., pl.* **-ti·os'** [Sp., a court yard] ☆1. a courtyard or inner area open to the sky, as in Spanish and Spanish-American architecture ☆2. a paved area, as one adjacent to a house, with chairs, tables, etc. for outdoor lounging, dining, or the like

pa·tis·se·rie (pə tis'ə rē; *Fr.* pä tēs rē') *n.* [Fr. *pâtisserie*

< MFr. < OFr. *pastiz, pastry (< VL. *pasticium < LL. pasta, dough, PASTE) + -erie, -ERY] 1. fancy pastry 2. a shop where such pastry is made and sold

Pat·more (pat′môr), **Cov·en·try (Kersey Dighton)** (kuv′ən trē) 1823–96; Eng. poet

Pat·mos (pat′məs, pät′-) island of the Dodecanese, in the SE Aegean (Bible, see Rev. 1:9): 13 sq. mi.

Pat·na (put′nə, pat′-) city in NE India, on the Ganges; capital of Bihar state: pop. 364,000

pat·ois (pat′wä; Fr. på twä′) n., pl. -ois (-wäs; Fr. -twä′) [Fr. < OFr., uncultivated speech, akin to patoier, to shake paws, behave crudely < pate, paw, akin to Frank. *pauta, whence G. pfote, PAW¹] 1. a form of a language differing generally from the accepted standard, as a provincial or local dialect 2. same as JARGON¹ (sense 4)

Pa·ton (pāt′'n), **Alan (Stewart)** 1903– ; South African novelist

pat. pend. patent pending

Pa·tras (pä träs′) 1. seaport in W Greece, on the Gulf of Patras: pop. 95,000 2. Gulf of, arm of the Ionian Sea, in the NW Peloponnesus Gr. name **Pá·trai** (pä′trī)

pat·ri- (pat′rə, pāt′-; -ri) [L. < Gr. patri- < patēr, FATHER] a combining form meaning father [patrimony]

pa·tri·arch (pā′trē ärk′) n. [ME. patriarche < OFr. < LL.(Ec.) patriarcha < Gr.(Ec.) patriarchēs (transl. of Heb. rōshē abōth) < Gr. patria, family < patēr, FATHER + -archēs < archein, to rule] 1. the father and ruler of a family or tribe, as one of the founders of the ancient Hebrew families: in the Bible, Abraham, Isaac, Jacob, and Jacob's twelve sons were patriarchs 2. a person regarded as the founder or father of a colony, religion, business, etc. 3. a man of great age and dignity 4. the oldest individual of a class or group 5. [often P-] a) a bishop in the early Christian Church, esp. a bishop of Rome, Constantinople, Alexandria, Antioch, or Jerusalem b) R.C.Ch. the Pope (**Patriarch of the West**), or any of certain bishops ranking immediately after him, as the bishops of Constantinople, Alexandria, Antioch, and Jerusalem c) Orthodox Eastern Ch. the highest-ranking bishop at Constantinople, Alexandria, Antioch, Jerusalem, Moscow, Bucharest, etc. d) the jurisdictional head of any of certain other churches, as the Coptic, Nestorian, Armenian, etc. e) a high-ranking member of the Melchizedek priesthood in the Mormon Church —**pa′tri·ar′chal** adj.

pa·tri·ar·chate (-är′kit, -kāt) n. [ML.(Ec.) patriarchatus] 1. the position, rank, jurisdiction, territory, etc. of a patriarch 2. same as PATRIARCHY

pa·tri·ar·chy (-är′kē) n., pl. -ar·chies [Gr. patriarchia: see PATRIARCH] 1. a form of social organization in which the father or the eldest male is recognized as the head of the family or tribe, descent and kinship being traced through the male line 2. government, rule, or domination by men —**pa′tri·ar′chic** adj.

Pa·tri·cia (pə trish′ə, -trē′shə) [L., fem. of patricius: see PATRICK] a feminine name: dim. **Pat, Patty**

pa·tri·cian (pə trish′ən) n. [ME. patricion < MFr. patricien < L. patricius < patres, senators, lit., fathers, pl. of pater, FATHER] 1. in ancient Rome a) orig., a member of any of the ancient Roman citizen families b) later, a member of the nobility: opposed to PLEBEIAN c) a member of a class of honorary nobility of the later Empire d) a chief administrator in the Roman provinces in Africa and Italy 2. a person of high rank in some medieval Italian republics and in certain free cities of the German Empire 3. any person of high social rank; aristocrat —adj. [MFr. patricien] 1. of or characteristic of patricians 2. noble; aristocratic

pa·tri·ci·ate (pə trish′ē it, -āt′) n. [ML. patriciatus < L. patricius] 1. the rank or position of a patrician 2. the patrician class; aristocracy

pat·ri·cide (pat′rə sīd′) n. [ML. patricida: see PATRI- & -CIDE] 1. the act of killing one's father 2. a person who kills his father —**pat′ri·ci′dal** adj.

Pat·rick (pat′rik) [L. patricius, a patrician] 1. a masculine name: dim. **Paddy, Pat;** fem. **Patricia** 2. Saint, 385?–461? A.D.; Brit. missionary in, and patron saint of, Ireland: his day is Mar. 17

pat·ri·lin·e·al (pat′rə lin′ē əl, pā′trə-) adj. [PATRI- + LINEAL] designating or of descent, kinship, or derivation through the father instead of the mother —**pat′ri·lin′e·al·ly** adv.

pat·ri·mo·ny (pat′rə mō′nē) n., pl. -nies [ME. patrimoigne < OFr. patrimoine < L. patrimonium < pater, FATHER] 1. property inherited from one's father or ancestors 2. property endowed to an institution, as a church 3. anything inherited, as a trait or character —SYN. see HERITAGE —**pat′ri·mo′ni·al** adj.

pa·tri·ot (pā′trē ət, -ät′; chiefly Brit. pat′rē-) n. [Fr. patriote < LL. patriota, fellow countryman < Gr. patriōtēs < patris, fatherland < patēr, FATHER] a person who loves and loyally or zealously supports his own country —**pa′tri·ot′ic** adj. —**pa′tri·ot′i·cal·ly** adv.

pa·tri·ot·ism (-ə tiz′m) n. [PATRIOT + -ISM] love and loyalty or zealous support of one's own country

☆**Patriots' Day** April 19, a legal holiday in Maine and Massachusetts commemorating the battles of Lexington and Concord (1775)

pa·tris·tic (pə tris′tik) adj. [G. patristisch < L. patres, pl.

of pater, FATHER] of the early leaders, or fathers, of the Christian Church or the writings and doctrines attributed to them: also **pa·tris′ti·cal** —**pa·tris′ti·cal·ly** adv.

Pa·tro·clus (pə trō′kləs) [L. < Gr. Patroklos] Gr. Myth. a Greek warrior and friend of Achilles in the Trojan War, slain by Hector

pa·trol (pə trōl′) vt., vi. -trolled′, -trol′ling [Fr. patrouiller, altered < OFr. patouiller, to paddle, puddle, patrol < pate, paw: see PATOIS] to make a regular and repeated circuit of (an area, town, camp, etc.) in guarding or inspecting —n. [Fr. patrouille < the v.] 1. the act of patrolling 2. a person or persons patrolling 3. a) a small group of soldiers sent on a mission, as for reconnaissance b) a group of ships, airplanes, etc. used in guarding 4. a subdivision of a troop of Boy Scouts or Girl Scouts —**pa·trol′er** n.

☆**pa·trol·man** (-mən) n., pl. -men (-mən) a man who patrols; esp., a policeman assigned to patrol a specific beat

☆**patrol wagon** a small, enclosed truck used by the police in transporting prisoners

pa·tron (pā′trən) n. [ME. patroun < OFr. patrun < ML. & L.: ML.(Ec.) patronus, patron saint, patron < L., a protector, defender < pater, FATHER] 1. a person empowered with the granting of an English church benefice 2. same as PATRON SAINT 3. a person corresponding in some respects to a father; protector; benefactor 4. a person, usually a wealthy and influential one, who sponsors and supports some person, activity, institution, etc. [the patrons of the orchestra] 5. a regular customer, as of a store 6. in ancient Rome, a person who had freed his slave but still retained a certain paternal control over him —SYN. see SPONSOR —**pa′tron·ess** n.fem.

pa·tron·age (pā′trən ij, pat′rən-) n. [ME. < OFr.: see PATRON & -AGE] 1. a) the function or status of a patron b) support, encouragement, sponsorship, etc. given by a patron 2. the power to grant an English church benefice 3. good will, favor, courtesy, etc. shown to people considered inferior; condescension 4. a) patrons collectively; clientele b) business; trade; custom 5. a) the power to appoint to office or grant other favors, esp. political ones b) the distribution of offices or other favors through this power c) the offices, etc. thus distributed

pa·tron·al (-'l) adj. [Fr. < LL. patronalis] of or characteristic of a patron or patron saint; protective

pa·tron·ize (pā′trə nīz′, pat′rə-) vt. -ized′, -iz′ing 1. to act as a patron toward; sponsor; support 2. to treat or deal with in a condescending manner 3. to be a regular customer of (a store, merchant, etc.)

patron saint a saint looked upon as the special guardian of a person, place, institution, etc.

pat·ro·nym·ic (pat′rə nim′ik) adj. [LL. patronymicus < Gr. patrōnymikos < patēr, FATHER + onyma, NAME] 1. derived from the name of a father or ancestor 2. showing such descent [a patronymic suffix] —n. 1. a name showing descent from a given person as by the addition of a prefix or suffix (e.g., Stevenson, son of Steven, O'Brien, descendant of Brien) 2. a family name; surname

pa·troon (pə trōōn′) n. [Du., protector < Fr. patron, PATRON] ☆a person who held a large estate with manorial rights under a grant from the old Dutch governments of New York and New Jersey

pat·sy (pat′sē) n., pl. -sies [prob. altered (after Patsy, nickname for PATRICK) < It. pazzo, an insane person] ☆[Slang] a person easily imposed upon or victimized

pat·ten (pat′'n) n. [ME. patyn < MFr. patin < pate, a paw: see PATOIS] any of various thick wooden sandals or clogs formerly worn for walking over wet or muddy ground

pat·ter¹ (pat′ər) vi. [freq. of PAT²] 1. to make a patter 2. to move so as to make a patter —n. a series of quick, light taps [the patter of rain on leaves]

pat·ter² (pat′ər) vt., vi. [ME. pateren < pater, in paternoster, as pronounced in rapid, mechanical recitation] to speak or mumble rapidly or glibly; recite (prayers, etc.) mechanically or thoughtlessly —n. 1. language peculiar to a group, class, etc., and not generally understood by outsiders; cant; jargon 2. the glib, rapid speech of salesmen, comedians, magicians, etc. 3. idle, meaningless chatter —**pat′ter·er** n.

pat·ter³ (pat′ər) n. a person or thing that pats

pat·tern (pat′ərn) n. [ME. patron < OFr., patron, hence something to be imitated, pattern: see PATRON] 1. a person or thing considered worthy of imitation or copying 2. a model or plan used as a guide in making things; set of forms to the shape of which material is cut for assembly into the finished article [a dress pattern] 3. the full-scale model used in making a sand mold for casting metal 4. something representing a class or type; example; sample 5. an arrangement of form; disposition of parts or elements; design [wallpaper patterns, the pattern of a novel] 6. a regular, mainly unvarying way of acting or doing [behavior patterns] 7. a predictable or prescribed route, movement, etc. [traffic pattern, landing pattern] 8. a) grouping or distribution, as of a number of bullets fired at a mark b) something, as a diagram, showing such distribution ☆9. [Now Rare] sufficient material for making a garment —vt. 1. to make, do, shape, or plan in imitation of a model or pattern (with on, upon, or after) 2. to supply with a pattern or design; mark or decorate with a pattern —SYN. see MODEL

pat·tern·mak·er (-mā′kər) *n.* a person who makes patterns, as for molds or for various articles to be mass-produced: also **pattern maker**

patter song a musical comedy song with a simple tune and comic lyrics sung with great rapidity

Pat·ti (pät′tē; *E.* pat′ē), **A·de·li·na** (ä′de lē′nä) (born *Adela Juana Maria Patti*) 1843–1919; It. operatic soprano, born in Spain

pat·ty (pat′ē) *n., pl.* **-ties** [Fr. *pâté:* see PÂTÉ] **1.** a small pie **2.** a small, flat cake of ground meat, fish, etc., usually fried **3.** any disk-shaped piece, as of candy

pat·ty-cake (pat′ē kāk′) *n. same as* PAT-A-CAKE

patty shell a pastry case in which individual portions of creamed foods, etc. are served

pat·u·lous (pach′oo ləs) *adj.* [L. *patulus* < *patere,* to be open: see PATELLA] *Bot.* standing open, or spreading —**pat′u·lous·ly** *adv.* —**pat′u·lous·ness** *n.*

Pau (pō) city in SW France: pop. 60,000

P.A.U., PAU Pan American Union

pau·ci·ty (pô′sə tē) *n.* [ME. *paucyte* < MFr. or L.: MFr. *paucité* < L. *paucitas* < *paucus,* FEW] **1.** fewness; small number **2.** scarcity; dearth; insufficiency

Paul (pôl) [L. *Paulus* (or Gr. *Paulos*), Rom. surname, prob. < or akin to *paulus,* small] **1.** a masculine name: equiv. L. *Paulus,* It. *Paolo,* Sp. *Pablo;* fem. *Paula, Pauline* **2.** *Bible* (original name *Saul*) a Jew of Tarsus who became the apostle of Christianity to the Gentiles: author of several Epistles in the New Testament; lived ?-67? A.D.: also *Saint Paul:* his day is June 29 **3.** **Paul I** (*Pavel Petrovich*) 1754–1801; czar of Russia (1796–1801): son of CATHERINE II & PETER III **4.** **Paul III** (*Alessandro Farnese*) 1468–1549; Pope (1534–49) **5.** **Paul VI** (*Giovanni Montini*) 1897– ; Pope (1963–)

Paul·a (-ə) [G., fem. of *Paul,* PAUL] a feminine name

☆**Paul Bun·yan** (bun′yən) *American Folklore* a giant lumberjack who, with the help of his blue ox, Babe, performed various superhuman feats

paul·dron (pôl′drən) *n.* [ME. *polrond,* aphetic < MFr. *espauleron* < *espaule,* the shoulder: see EPAULET] a piece of plate armor to protect the shoulder: see ARMOR, illus.

Pau·li (pou′lē), **Wolf·gang** (vôlf′gäŋk′) 1900–58; Austrian physicist, in the U.S. & Switzerland

Pauli exclusion principle [after prec.] the principle that no two electrons can occupy the same orbit in the electron structure of an atom, i.e., have the same set of quantum numbers

Pau·line[1] (pô lēn′) [L. *Paulina,* fem. of *Paulinus:* see ff.] a feminine name

Paul·ine[2] (pôl′in, -ēn) *adj.* [ModL. *Paulinus*] of or characteristic of the Apostle Paul, his writings, or doctrines

Paul·ing (pôl′iŋ), **Li·nus** (Carl) (lī′nəs) 1901– ; U.S. chemist

Paul·ist (-ist) *n.* ☆a Roman Catholic priest belonging to the Missionary Society of St. Paul the Apostle, founded in New York in 1858

pau·low·ni·a (pô lō′nē ə) *n.* [< ModL., name of the genus, after Anna *Pavlovna* (?–1865), daughter of Czar PAUL I] any of a genus (*Paulownia*) of Asiatic trees of the figwort family, with large, heart-shaped leaves and large, erect clusters of violet flowers; esp., a tree (*Paulownia tomentosa*) having fragrant, violet flowers like those of foxglove

paunch (pônch) *n.* [ME. *paunche* < MFr. *panche* < L. *pantex* (gen. *panticis*), belly < IE. base **pank-,* to swell, whence Russ. *puk,* a bundle] **1.** the abdomen, or belly; esp., a large, protruding belly; potbelly **2.** the first and largest stomach of a cud-chewing animal; rumen —**paunch′i·ness** *n.* —**paunch′y** *adj.*

pau·per (pô′pər) *n.* [L., poor person, POOR] **1.** a person who lives on charity, esp. on tax-supported charity **2.** any person who is extremely poor

pau·per·ism (-iz′m) *n.* **1.** the condition of being a pauper **2.** paupers collectively Also **pau′per·dom** (-dəm)

pau·per·ize (pô′pə rīz′) *vt.* **-ized′, -iz′ing** to make a pauper of —**pau′per·i·za′tion** *n.*

pau·ro·me·tab·o·lous (pôr′ō mə tab′ə ləs) *n.* [< Gr. *pauros,* small (< IE. base **pōu-:* see FEW) + *metabolos,* changeable < *metabolē,* change: see METABOLISM] designating or of a group of insect orders in which metamorphosis to the adult state from the juvenile state is gradual and without any sudden radical change of body form: also **pau′ro·met′a·bol′ic** (-met′ə bäl′ik) —**pau′ro·me·tab′o·lism** *n.*

Pau·sa·ni·as (pô sā′nē əs) 2d cent. A.D.; Gr. historian & geographer, probably born in Lydia

pause (pôz) *n.* [ME. *pawse* < MFr. *pause* < L. *pausa* < Gr. *pausis,* a stopping < *pauein,* to bring to an end < IE. base **paus-,* to let go, whence OPrus. *pausto,* wild] **1.** a short period of inaction; temporary stop, break, or rest, as in speaking or reading **2.** hesitation; interruption; delay [pursuit without *pause*] **3.** *a)* a stop or break in speaking or reading to clarify meaning *b)* any mark of punctuation indicating this **4.** *Music same as* FERMATA **5.** *Prosody* a rhythm break or caesura —*vi.* **paused, paus′ing 1.** to make a pause; be temporarily inactive; stop; hesitate **2.** to dwell or linger (with *on* or *upon*) —**give one**

pause to make one hesitant or uncertain —**paus′er** *n.*

pav·ane (pə vän′, -van′) *n.* [Fr. < OIt. *pavana* < (danza) *Pavana,* lit., Paduan (dance) < dial. *Pava,* for *Padua:* associated by folk etym. with Fr. *pavaner,* to strut, walk like a peacock] **1.** a slow, stately court dance of Spanish or Italian origin, performed by couples **2.** the music for this Also **pav·an** (pav′ən)

pave (pāv) *vt.* **paved, pav′ing** [ME. *paven* < OFr. *paver* < VL. **pavare,* for L. *pavire,* to ram, beat < IE. base **pēu-,* to strike, chop, whence Lith. *piauti,* L. *putare,* to cut] **1.** to cover over the surface of (a road, etc.), as with concrete, asphalt, or brick **2.** to be the top surface or covering of **3.** to cover closely or thickly; overlay —**pave the way (for)** to prepare the way (for); facilitate the introduction (of) —**pav′er** *n.*

pa·vé (pä vā′) *n.* [Fr., orig. pp. of *paver,* PAVE] **1.** pavement **2.** a setting of jewelry in which the gems are placed close together so that no metal shows

pave·ment (pāv′mənt) *n.* [ME. < OFr. < L. *pavimentum* < *pavire,* to beat down: see PAVE] **1.** a paved surface or covering, as of concrete, brick, etc.; specif., *a)* a paved street or road *b)* [Chiefly Brit.] a sidewalk **2.** the material used in paving

Pa·vi·a (pä vē′ä) commune in NW Italy, on the Ticino River: pop. 74,000

pav·id (pav′id) *adj.* [L. *pavidus* < *pavere,* to be afraid, akin to *pavire:* see PAVE] [Rare] fearful; afraid; timid

pa·vil·ion (pə vil′yən) *n.* [ME. *pavilon* < OFr. *pavillon* < L. *papilio,* butterfly, also tent (from its shape): see PAPILIONACEOUS] **1.** a large tent, usually with a peaked top **2.** *a)* a building or part of a building, often partly open and highly ornamented, used for entertainment, exhibits, etc., as at a fair or park *b)* a decorative shelter or summer-house **3.** part of a building jutting out from the main part and often ornamented **4.** any of the separate or connected parts of a group of related buildings, as of a hospital or sanitarium **5.** the part of a brilliant-cut gem between the girdle and the culet —*vt.* to furnish with or shelter in or as in a pavilion

pav·in (pav′ən) *n. same as* PAVANE

pav·ing (pā′viŋ) *n.* **1.** a pavement **2.** material for a pavement

pav·ior, pav·iour (pāv′yər) *n.* [altered < ME. *pavier* < *paven,* PAVE] a person or thing that paves; paver

pav·is (pav′is) *n.* [ME. *puveis* < MFr. *puvaiz* < It. *pavese* < *Pavia,* Italy, where first made] in medieval times, a large shield for protecting the entire body

Pav·lov (päv′lôf; *E.* päv′lôv), **I·van Pe·tro·vich** (i vän′ pye trō′vich) 1849–1936; Russ. physiologist —**Pav·lov·i·an** (pav lō′vē ən) *adj.*

Pav·lo·va (päv′lô vä; *E.* päv lō′və), **An·na** (Matveyevna) (än′ä) 1885?–1931; Russ. ballet dancer

Pa·vo (pā′vō) [L., PEACOCK] a constellation near the S. celestial pole

pav·o·nine (pav′ə nīn′, -nin) *adj.* [L. *pavoninus* < *pavo,* PEACOCK] **1.** of or resembling a peacock **2.** rainbowlike in color, as a peacock's tail; iridescent

paw[1] (pô) *n.* [ME. *paue* < OFr. *poue* < Frank. **pauta,* a paw, whence G. *pfote*] **1.** the foot of a four-footed animal having claws. **2.** [Colloq.] a hand —*vi.* **1.** to touch, dig, hit, strike at, etc. with the paws or feet [a horse *pawing* the air] **2.** to handle clumsily or roughly, or caress overintimately —**paw′er** *n.*

paw[2] (pô) *n.* [Dial.] pa; papa; father

pawk·y (pô′ki) *adj.* **pawk′i·er, pawk′i·est** [Chiefly Brit.] shrewd and witty; crafty; sly —**pawk′i·ly** *adv.* —**pawk′i·ness** *n.*

pawl (pôl) *n.* [akin ? to Du. *pal,* pawl, stake, pole] a mechanical device allowing rotation in only one direction: one type consists of a hinged tongue, the tip of which engages the notches of a ratchet wheel, preventing backward motion

HANDLE
PAWL
PAWL SPRING
RATCHET WHEEL
PAWL

pawn[1] (pôn) *n.* [LME. *paun* < MFr. *pan,* akin to G. *pfand* < ?] **1.** anything given as security, as for a debt, performance of an action, etc.; pledge; guaranty **2.** a hostage **3.** the state of being pledged [to put a ring in *pawn*] **4.** the act of pawning —*vt.* **1.** to give as security; put in pawn **2.** to stake, wager, or risk [to *pawn* one's honor] —*SYN.* see PLEDGE —**pawn′age** *n.* —**pawn′er, pawn′nor** *n.*

pawn[2] (pôn) *n.* [ME. *poun* < OFr. *peon* < ML. *pedo* (gen. *pedonis*), foot soldier < LL., one who has flat feet < L. *pes* (gen. *pedis*), FOOT] **1.** a chessman of the lowest value: it can be moved only forward and but one square at a time (or two squares on its first move), but it captures with a diagonal move **2.** a person used to advance another's purposes; tool

pawn·bro·ker (-brō′kər) *n.* [PAWN[1] + BROKER] a person licensed to lend money at a legally specified rate of interest on an article or articles of personal property left with him as security —**pawn′bro′king** *n.*

☆**Paw·nee** (pô nē′) *n.* [< ? Algonquian *pani*, slave] **1.** *pl.* **-nees′, -nee′** a member of a confederacy of N. American Plains Indians, formerly living in the valley of the Platte River, Nebraska, and now in N Oklahoma **2.** their Caddoan language —*adj.* of this tribe or their language

pawn·shop (pôn′shäp′) *n.* a pawnbroker's shop

pawn ticket a receipt for goods in pawn

paw-paw (pô′pô′) *n.* same as PAPAW

Paw·tuck·et (pô tuk′it) [< Algonquian, little falls] city in R.I.: pop. 77,000: see PROVIDENCE

pax (paks) *n.* [ME. < ML.(Ec.) < L., PEACE] **1.** a small tablet representing the Crucifixion, the Virgin, a saint, etc.: formerly kissed during the Roman Catholic Eucharistic service **2.** in certain High Masses, a formalized bow and greeting that follows the Agnus Dei and that is exchanged among the celebrant, assistants, and often the congregation: also called **kiss of peace** —[P-] the Roman goddess of peace, identified with the Greek goddess Irene

Pax Ro·man·a (päks rō mä′nä, paks rō mā′nə) [L., Roman peace] **1.** the terms of peace imposed by Rome on any of its dominions **2.** any peace dictated to a subjugated people by a conquering nation

‡**pax vo·bis·cum** (paks vō bis′kəm, päks wō bis′kŏŏm) [L.] peace (be) with you

pax·wax (paks′waks′) *n.* [ME., earlier *faxwax* < OE. *feax*, hair (< IE. base *pek-*, to pull hair, whence L. *pecten*, a comb) + *weaxan*, to grow, WAX²] [Brit. Dial.] a strong, elastic ligament in the back of the neck in many mammals, serving to support the head; nuchal ligament

pay¹ (pā) *vt.* **paid** or obs. (except in phrase *pay out*, sense 2) **payed, pay′ing** [ME. *paien*, to pay, satisfy < OFr. *paier*, L. *pacare*, to pacify < *pax*, PEACE] **1.** to give to (a person) what is due, as for goods received, services rendered, etc.; remunerate; recompense **2.** to give (what is due or owed) in return, as for goods or services **3.** to make a deposit or transfer of (money) [*paid* $50 into the credit union] **4.** to discharge or settle (a debt, obligation, expenses, etc.) by giving something in return **5.** *a)* to give or offer (a compliment, respects, attention, etc.) *b)* to make (a visit, call, etc.) **6.** to yield as a recompense or return [a job that *pays* $90] **7.** to be worthwhile or profitable to [it will *pay* him to listen] —*vi.* **1.** to give due compensation; make payment **2.** to be profitable or worthwhile **3.** to yield return or compensation as specified [a stock that *pays* poorly] —*n.* **1.** a paying or being paid; payment **2.** money paid, esp. for work or services; wages or salary **3.** anything, good or bad, given or done in return **4.** [Now Rare] a person regarded as a credit risk —*adj.* **1.** rich enough in minerals, etc. to make mining profitable [*pay* gravel] **2.** operated or made available by depositing a coin or coins [a *pay* telephone, *pay* toilet] **3.** designating a service, facility, etc. paid for by subscription, fees, etc. [*pay* TV] —**in the pay of** employed and paid by —☆**pay as you go** to pay expenses as they arise —**pay back 1.** to repay **2.** to retaliate upon —**pay down 1.** to pay in cash **2.** to pay (part of the purchase price) at the time of purchase: used in installment buying —**pay for 1.** to suffer or undergo punishment because of **2.** to atone or make amends for —**pay off 1.** to pay all that is owed on (a debt, etc.) or to (a person, as in discharging from employment) **2.** to take revenge on (a wrongdoer) or for (a wrong done) **3.** to yield full recompense or return, for either good or evil **4.** [Colloq.] to bring about a desired result; succeed **5.** *Naut.* to veer or cause to veer to leeward: said of the bow of a vessel —**pay one's way** to pay one's share of the expenses —**pay out 1.** to give out (money, etc.); expend **2.** to let out (a rope, cable, etc.) —**pay up** to pay in full or on time

SYN.—**pay** is the simple, direct word meaning to give money, etc. due for services rendered, goods received, etc.; **compensate** implies a return, whether monetary or not, thought of as equivalent to the service given, the effort expended, or the loss sustained [he could never be *compensated* for the loss of his son]; **remunerate** stresses the idea of payment for a service rendered, but it often also carries an implication of reward [a bumper crop *remunerated* the farmer for his labors]; to **reimburse** is to pay back what has been expended [the salesman was *reimbursed* for his traveling expenses]; to **indemnify** is to pay for what has been lost or damaged [they were *indemnified* for the war destruction]; **repay** implies a paying back of money given to one or it may refer to a doing or giving of anything in requital [how can I *repay* you for your kindness?]; **recompense** stresses the idea of compensation or requital See also WAGE

pay² (pā) *vt.* **payed, pay′ing** [ONormFr. *peier* < L. *picare*, to cover with pitch < *pix* (gen. *picis*), pitch < IE. base *pi-*, whence FAT] to coat (the seams of a vessel, etc.) as with tar, in order to make waterproof

pay·a·ble (pā′ə b'l) *adj.* **1.** that can be paid **2.** that is to be paid (*on* a specified date); due **3.** that is or can be profitable, as a mine or business venture

☆**pay·check** (-chek′) *n.* a check in payment of wages or salary

pay·day (-dā′) *n.* the day on which wages are paid

☆**pay dirt** soil, gravel, ore, etc. rich enough in minerals to make mining profitable —**hit** (or **strike**) **pay dirt** [Colloq.] to discover a source of wealth, success, etc.

pay·ee (pā ē′) *n.* the person to whom a check, note, money, etc. is payable

pay·er (pā′ər) *n.* the person who pays or is to pay

pay·grade (-grād′) *n. Mil.* the grade of a serviceman according to a scale of increasing amounts of base pay

pay·load (-lōd′) *n.* **1.** a cargo, or the part of a cargo, producing income: also **pay load 2.** *a)* the warhead of a ballistic missile, the instruments of an artificial satellite, etc., along with the compartment or final stage carrying these *b)* the weight of such a load or of the load and its container

pay·mas·ter (-mas′tər, -mäs′-) *n.* the official in charge of paying employees —**pay′mis′tress** (-mis′tris) *n.fem.*

pay·ment (-mənt) *n.* **1.** a paying or being paid **2.** something that is paid **3.** penalty or reward

pay·nim (pā′nim) *n.* [ME. *painim* < OFr. *paienime*, heathendom < LL.(Ec.) *paganismus*, paganism] [Archaic] **1.** a pagan; heathen **2.** a non-Christian; esp., a Moslem **3.** the pagan world

☆**pay·off** (pā′ôf′) *n.* **1.** the act, event, or time of payment **2.** a settlement or reckoning **3.** that which is paid off; return; recompense **4.** [Colloq.] a bribe **5.** [Colloq.] something coming as a climax or culmination to a series of events, esp. when unexpected or improbable

☆**pay·o·la** (pā ō′lə) *n.* [PAY¹ + -ola, as in *Pianola* (trademark for a player piano), whence Tin Pan Alley *pianola*, slang term for the music business] [Slang] **1.** the practice of paying bribes or graft for commercial advantage or special favors, as to a disk jockey for promoting a song unfairly **2.** such a bribe or graft

☆**pay phone** (or **station**) a public telephone, usually coin-operated

☆**pay·roll** (-rōl′) *n.* **1.** a list of employees to be paid, with the amount due to each **2.** the total amount needed, or the money on hand, for this for a given period

payt., pay't payment

pa·zazz (pə zaz′) *n.* same as PIZAZZ

Pb [L. *plumbum*] *Chem.* lead

P.B. **1.** [L. *Pharmacopoeia Britannica*] British Pharmacopoeia **2.** Prayer Book

PBS Public Broadcasting Service

PBX, P.B.X. [< *p(rivate) b(ranch) ex(change)*] a telephone system operating within one building, company, etc. and having outside telephone lines

pc. **1.** piece **2.** price(s)

P/C, p/c 1. petty cash **2.** prices current

P.C. 1. Past Commander **2.** Police Constable **3.** Post Commander **4.** Privy Council (or Councilor)

p.c. 1. percent **2.** postal card **3.** post card

pct. percent

Pd *Chem.* palladium

pd. paid

P.D. 1. per diem: also **p.d. 2.** Police Department **3.** postal district **4.** potential difference

P.D.Q. [*p(retty) d(amn) q(uick)*] [Old Slang] quickly or immediately

pe (pā) *n.* same as PEH

P.E. 1. Physical Education **2.** *Statistics* probable error **3.** Professional Engineer **4.** Protestant Episcopal

pea (pē) *n., pl.* **peas,** archaic or Brit. dial. **pease** [back-formation < ME. *pese*, *pees*, a pea, taken as pl. < OE. *pise* < LL. *pisa* < L. *pisa*, pl. of *pisum*, a pea < Gr. *pison*, a pea] **1.** an annual, tendril-climbing plant (*Pisum sativum*) of the legume family, with white or pinkish flowers and green seedpods **2.** its small, round, smooth or wrinkled seed, used as a vegetable **3.** *a)* any of a number of related plants *b)* the seed of any of these —**as like as two peas (in a pod)** exactly alike

pea bean any of various kidney beans; esp., same as NAVY BEAN

Pea·bod·y (pē′bäd′ē, -bəd ē) [after ff.] city in NE Mass.: suburb of Boston: pop. 48,000

Pea·bod·y (pē′bäd′ē, -bəd ē), **George** 1795–1869; U.S. merchant & philanthropist, in England

☆**Peabody bird** [echoic of its note] [also **p-**] same as WHITE-THROATED SPARROW

peace (pēs) *n.* [ME. *pais* < OFr. < L. *pax* (gen. *pacis*) < IE. base *pak-*, to fasten, whence L. *pacisci*, to confirm an agreement, *pangere*, to fasten & FANG] **1.** freedom from or a stopping of war **2.** a treaty or agreement to end war or the threat of war **3.** freedom from public disturbance or disorder; public security; law and order **4.** freedom from disagreement or quarrels; harmony; concord **5.** an undisturbed state of mind; absence of mental conflict; serenity: in full, **peace of mind 6.** calm; quiet; tranquillity —*vi.* [Obs. except in imperative] to be or become silent or quiet —**at peace 1.** free from war **2.** quiet; in repose —**hold** (or **keep**) **one's peace** to be silent; keep quiet —**keep the peace** to avoid or prevent violation of law and good order —**make one's peace with** to effect a reconciliation with —**make peace** to end hostilities, settle arguments, etc.

peace·a·ble (-ə b'l) *adj.* [ME. *peisible* < OFr.] **1.** fond of, inclined toward, or promoting peace; not quarrelsome **2.** at peace; peaceful —**peace′a·ble·ness** *n.* —**peace′a·bly** *adv.*

peace conference a conference for the purpose of ending a war or for seeking ways to establish lasting peace

☆**Peace Corps** an agency of the U.S. Department of State, established in 1961 to provide volunteers skilled in teaching, construction, etc. to assist the people of underdeveloped areas abroad

peace·ful (-fəl) *adj.* **1.** not quarrelsome; peaceable **2.** characterized by peace; free from disturbance or disorder;

calm; quiet; tranquil **3.** of or characteristic of a time of peace —*SYN.* see CALM —**peace′ful·ly** adv. —**peace′ful·ness** n.

peace·mak·er (-mā′kər) n. a person who makes peace, as by settling the disagreements or quarrels of others —**peace′mak′ing** n., adj.

☆**peace·nik** (-nik) n. [PEACE + -NIK] a person demonstrating against war or a war: a hostile or derogatory term

peace offering [used to translate Heb. *shelem*, lit., thank-offering] **1.** an offering or sacrifice in thanksgiving to God **2.** an offering made to maintain or bring about peace

peace officer an officer entrusted with maintaining law and order, as a sheriff, constable, or policeman

☆**peace pipe** a ceremonial pipe smoked by American Indians as part of a peace conference; calumet

Peace River [after *Peace Point*, where Cree & Beaver Indians made a peace pact] river in W Canada, flowing from N British Columbia east & northeast into the Slave River in NE Alberta: 1,195 mi.

peace·time (-tīm′) n. a time of peace —adj. of or characteristic of such a time

peach[1] (pēch) n. [ME. *peche* < OFr. *pesche* < VL. *persica* < pl. of L. *persicum* < *Persicum* (*malum*), Persian (apple)] **1.** a small tree (*Prunus persica*) of the rose family, with lance-shaped leaves, pink flowers, and round, juicy, orange-yellow fruit, with a fuzzy skin and a single, rough pit **2.** its fruit **3.** the orange-yellow color of this fruit ☆**4.** [Slang] any person or thing well liked

peach[2] (pēch) vt. [ME. *pechen*, aphetic for *apechen*, via Anglo-Fr. < OFr. *empechier*, IMPEACH] [Obs.] to name in an indictment; impeach —vi. [Old Slang] to give evidence against another; turn informer

peach-blow (-blō′) n. [PEACH[1] + BLOW[3]] **1.** a delicate purplish-pink color **2.** a porcelain glaze of this color

peach·y (pē′chē) adj. **peach′i·er**, **peach′i·est 1.** peachlike, as in color or texture ☆**2.** [Old Slang] fine, excellent, beautiful, etc. —**peach′i·ness** n.

☆**pea·coat** (pē′kōt′) n. same as PEA JACKET

pea·cock (pē′käk′) n., pl. **-cocks′**, **-cock′**: see PLURAL, II, D, 1 [ME. *pacok* < *pa*, peacock (< OE. *pea* < early WGmc. borrowing < L. *pavo*, peacock, prob. akin to Gr. *taōs*, ? of Oriental orig.) + *cok*, COCK[1]] **1.** the male of a species (*Pavo cristatus*) of peafowls, with a crest of plumules and long, brightly colored upper tail coverts bearing rainbow-colored, eyelike spots: these coverts can be erected and spread out like a fan **2.** any male peafowl **3.** a vain, strutting person —vi. to display vanity in behavior, dress, etc.; strut —**pea′cock′ish**, **pea′cock′y** adj.

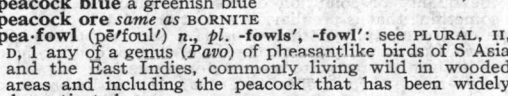
PEACOCK
(to 6 ft. long, including 4 ft. of train)

Pea·cock (pē′käk′), **Thomas Love** 1785–1866; Eng. novelist & poet

peacock blue a greenish blue

peacock ore same as BORNITE

pea·fowl (pē′foul′) n., pl. **-fowls′**, **-fowl′**: see PLURAL, II, D, 1 any of a genus (*Pavo*) of pheasantlike birds of S Asia and the East Indies, commonly living wild in wooded areas and including the peacock that has been widely domesticated

☆**peag, peage** (pēg) n. [< AmInd. (Algonquian) *wampumpeage*: see WAMPUM] same as WAMPUM

pea green a light yellowish green

pea·hen (-hen′) n. a female peafowl

☆**pea jacket** [altered by folk etym. (after PEA) < Du. *pijjekker* < *pij*, coarse, thick cloth + *jekker*, jacket < *jak* < OFr. *jaque*: see JACK[2]] a hip-length, double-breasted coat of heavy woolen cloth, worn as by seamen

peak[1] (pēk) vi. [< ?] to become sickly; waste away; droop

peak[2] (pēk) n. [var. of PIKE[3]] **1.** a tapering part that projects; pointed end or top, as of a cap, roof, etc. **2.** part of the hairline coming to a point on the forehead; widow's peak **3.** [Rare] a promontory **4.** *a)* the crest or summit of a hill or mountain ending in a point *b)* a mountain with such a pointed summit **5.** the highest or utmost point of anything; height; maximum [the *peak* of production] **6.** *Elec.* the maximum value of a varying quantity during a specified period **7.** *Naut. a)* the top rear corner of a fore-and-aft sail *b)* the upper end of the gaff *c)* the narrowed part of the hull, front or rear —adj. maximum [peak production] —vt., vi. **1.** to bring or come to a vertical position; tilt up, as a sail yard or spar **2.** to come or cause to come to a peak; reach or bring to a high, or the highest, point —*SYN.* see SUMMIT

peaked[1] (pēkt; occas. pēk′id) adj. having or ending in a peak; pointed

peak·ed[2] (pē′kid) adj. [< PEAK[1]] thin and drawn, or weak and wan, as from illness —**peak′ed·ness** n.

peal (pēl) n. [ME. *pele*, aphetic for *apele*, APPEAL] **1.** the loud ringing of a bell or set of bells **2.** *a)* a set of tuned bells; chimes; carillon *b)* the ringing of changes on such

a set of bells **3.** any loud, prolonged sound, as of gunfire, thunder, laughter, etc. —vi., vt. to sound in a peal; resound; ring

Peale (pēl), **Charles Will·son** (wil′sən) 1741–1827; Am. portrait painter

pe·an (pē′ən) n. *alt. sp.* of PAEAN

☆**pea·nut** (pē′nut′) n. [PEA + NUT] **1.** a spreading, annual vine (*Arachis hypogaea*) of the legume family, with yellow flowers and brittle pods ripening underground and containing one to three edible seeds **2.** the pod or any of its seeds **3.** [pl.] [Slang] a trifling or relatively small sum of money

☆**peanut butter** a food paste or spread made by grinding roasted peanuts

☆**peanut gallery** [Slang] the topmost balcony section in a theater, where the cheaper seats are located

pear (per) n. [ME. *pere* < OE. *peru* < VL. *pira* < L. *pira*, pl. of *pirum*, pear] **1.** a tree (*Pyrus communis*) of the rose family, with glossy leaves and greenish-yellow, brownish, or reddish fruit **2.** the soft, juicy fruit, round at the base and narrowing toward the stem

PEANUT PLANT

Pearl (purl) [< ff.] a feminine name

pearl[1] (purl) n. [ME. *perle* < MFr. < VL. *perla*, *perula*, altered (? after L. *sphaerula*, SPHERULE) < L. *perna*, a sea mussel, lit., a ham: from its shape] **1.** a smooth, hard, usually white or bluish-gray, abnormal nacreous growth of various, usually roundish, shapes, formed around a grain of sand, a parasite, or other foreign body within the shell of some oysters and certain other mollusks: it is used as a gem **2.** same as MOTHER-OF-PEARL **3.** anything pearllike in size, shape, color, beauty, value, etc. **4.** the color of some pearls, a bluish gray **5.** *Printing* a size of type, 5 point —vt. **1.** to adorn or cover with pearls or pearllike drops **2.** to make like a pearl in shape or color —vi. to fish for pearl-bearing mollusks, esp. oysters —adj. **1.** of or having pearls **2.** like a pearl in shape or color **3.** made of mother-of-pearl [pearl buttons] —**cast pearls before swine** [cf. Matt. 7:6] to present something of great interest or value to someone incapable of appreciating it —**pearl′er** n.

pearl[2] (purl) vt., vi., n. obs. var. of PURL[2]

pearl ash a refined potash, potassium carbonate

pearl barley barley seed rubbed down into small, round grains: also **pearled barley**

pearl diver (or **fisher**) a person who dives for pearl-bearing mollusks

pearl gray a pale bluish gray

Pearl Harbor [after the *pearl* oysters once there] inlet on the S coast of Oahu, Hawaii, near Honolulu: site of a U.S. naval base bombed by Japan, Dec. 7, 1941

pearl·ite (-īt) n. [Fr. *perlite* < *perle*, PEARL[1] + -ite, -ITE[1]] *Metallurgy* a mixture of iron and carbon alloys which crystallize on the slow cooling of high-temperature steel and cast iron —**pearl·it′ic** (-it′ik) adj.

pearl·ized (-īzd) adj. resembling mother-of-pearl

☆**pearl millet** a tall cereal and forage grass (*Pennisetum glaucum*) having pearly white seeds borne in dense spikes

Pearl River 1. river in C Miss., flowing into Lake Borgne: 490 mi. **2.** same as CHU KIANG

pearl·y (pur′lē) adj. **pearl′i·er**, **pearl′i·est 1.** of or like a pearl, as in color or luster **2.** adorned or covered with pearls or mother-of-pearl —**pearl′i·ness** n.

Pearly Gates [Colloq.] the gates of heaven: cf. Rev. 21:21

pearly nautilus same as NAUTILUS (sense 1)

pear·main (per′mān) n. [ME. *parmayn* < OFr. *parmain*, associated by folk etym. with *Parma*, Italy, but prob. < OFr. *parmaindre*, to remain (< L. *permanere*: see PERMANENT], from its long-keeping qualities: cf. WARDEN] a variety of apple

pear-shaped (per′shāpt′) adj. **1.** shaped like a pear **2.** full, clear, even, and resonant: said of sung tones

Pear·son (pir′s′n), **Lester Bowles** (bōlz) 1897– ; Canad. statesman; prime minister (1963–68)

peart (pirt) adj. [var. of PERT] [Dial.] lively, chipper, sprightly, smart, etc. —**peart′ly** adv.

Pear·y (pir′ē), **Robert Edwin** 1856–1920; U.S. arctic explorer, the first to reach the North Pole

peas·ant (pez′nt) n. [LME. *paissaunt* < Anglo-Fr. *paisant* < MFr. *paisent* < OFr. *paisenc* < *pais*, country < LL. *pagensis*, belonging to the district < *pagus*, district: see PAGAN] **1.** any person of the class of small farmers or of farm laborers, as in Europe or Asia **2.** a person regarded as coarse, boorish, ignorant, etc.

peas·ant·ry (-′n trē) n. **1.** peasants collectively **2.** a peasant's rank or condition

pease (pēz) n. [see PEA] **1.** pl. **peas′es**, **peas′en** (-′n) [Obs.] a pea **2.** archaic or Brit. dial. pl. of PEA

pease·cod, peas·cod (pēz'käd') n. [ME. *pesecod:* see PEASE & COD²] [Archaic] the pod of the pea plant

pea·shoot·er (pē'shōōt'ər) n. a toy consisting of a tube through which dried peas, etc. are blown

pea soup 1. a heavy soup made from dried split peas or, sometimes, fresh peas 2. [Colloq.] a dense, yellowish fog: also, esp. Brit., **pea'soup'er**

peat (pēt) n. [ME. *pete* < ML. *peta,* piece of turf, prob. specialized var. of *petia,* a piece (cf. PIECE) < Celt.] 1. partly decayed, moisture-absorbing plant matter found in ancient bogs and swamps, used as a plant covering or fuel 2. a dried block of this used as fuel —**peat'y** adj. **peat'i·er, peat'i·est**

peat moss 1. any moss which forms peat; specif., same as SPHAGNUM 2. any peat composed of residues of mosses, used chiefly as a mulch 3. [Brit. Dial.] a peat bog

peau de soie (pō' də swä') [Fr., lit., skin of silk] a soft, rich silk or rayon cloth with a dull, satiny finish

☆**pea·vey** (pē'vē) n., pl. **-veys** [prob. after a Joseph *Peavey,* said to be its inventor, c. 1872] a heavy wooden lever with a pointed metal tip and a hinged hook near the end: used by lumbermen in handling logs: also sp. **pea'vy,** pl. **-vies**

peb·ble (peb'l) n. [ME. *pobble* < OE. *papol-(stan), popol-(stan),* pebble (stone), prob. of echoic origin] 1. a small stone worn smooth and round, as by the action of water 2. clear, transparent quartz or a lens made from it 3. a surface grain of pebbly appearance, artificially produced on leather (**pebble leather**), paper, etc. —vt. **-bled, -bling** 1. to cover with pebbles or objects that look like pebbles 2. to stamp (leather) so as to produce a pebbly appearance

peb·bly (peb'lē) adj. **-bli·er, -bli·est** 1. having many pebbles 2. having a pebble surface or grain

☆**pe·can** (pi kän', -kan'; pē'kan, -kän) n. [< AmInd. (Algonquian) *pakan,* a hard-shelled nut, akin to Ojibway *pagân*] 1. an olive-shaped, edible nut with a thin, smooth shell 2. the N. American tree (*Carya illinoensis*) of the walnut family on which it grows

pec·ca·ble (pek'ə b'l) adj. [ML. *peccabilis* < L. *peccare,* to sin] liable to or capable of sin —**pec·ca·bil'i·ty** n.

pec·ca·dil·lo (pek'ə dil'ō) n., pl. **-loes, -los** [Sp. *pecadillo,* dim. < *pecado* < L. *peccatum,* a sin < *peccare,* to sin] a minor or petty sin; slight fault

pec·can·cy (pek'ən sē) n. [LL.(Ec.) *peccantia* < L. *peccare,* to sin] 1. sinfulness 2. pl. **-cies** a sin

pec·cant (pek'ənt) adj. [L. *peccans,* prp. of *peccare,* to sin] 1. sinful; sinning 2. breaking or disregarding a rule or practice; faulty 3. [OFr.] [Rare] diseased or causing disease —**pec'cant·ly** adv.

pec·ca·ry (pek'ər ē) n., pl. **-ries, -ry:** see PLURAL, II, D, 1 [AmSp. *pecari* < native Carib name] either of two related grayish, piglike animals (family Tayassuidae) of N. and S. America, with a musk gland, sharp tusks, and porklike flesh, as the **collared peccary** (*Tayassu tajaçu*) with a white band around the throat, and the **white-lipped peccary** (*Tayassu pecari*) with a white strip across the chin

‡**pec·ca·vi** (pe kä'wē, -vē; pe kā'vi) [L.] I have sinned —n., pl. **-vis** a confession of sin or guilt

Pe·cho·ra (pe chôr'ə; Russ. pye chô'rä) river in N European R.S.F.S.R., flowing from the Urals north into the Barents Sea: 1,110 mi.

peck¹ (pek) vt. [ME. *pecken,* var. of *pikken,* PICK³, in specialized senses] 1. to strike with a pointed object, as with a beak 2. to make by doing this (to peck a hole) 3. to pick up with the beak; get by pecking —vi. to make strokes as with a pointed object —n. 1. a stroke so made, as with the beak 2. a mark made as by pecking 3. [Colloq.] a quick, casual kiss —**peck at** 1. to make a pecking motion at 2. [Colloq.] to eat very little of; eat carelessly or sparingly 3. [Colloq.] to criticize or find fault with constantly

peck² (pek) n. [ME. *pek* < OFr., prob. akin to *piche,* a dry measure, ult. < L. *pica,* a wine jar (see BEAKER)] 1. a unit of dry measure equal to 1/4 bushel or eight quarts 2. any container with a capacity of one peck 3. [Colloq.] a large amount, as of trouble

peck·er (pek'ər) n. 1. a person or thing that pecks 2. [Brit. Colloq.] courage; spirits: chiefly in the phrase **keep one's pecker up**

☆**peck·er·wood** (-wood') n. [inversion of WOODPECKER] [Dial.] same as: 1. WOODPECKER 2. POOR WHITE

☆**peck·ing order** (-in) [transl. < G. *hackordnung*] 1. a hierarchy among birds, as a flock of hens, in which the most aggressive pecks, and the least aggressive is pecked by, all the others 2. social organization in which status is determined by aggressive awareness of rank, income, etc. Also **peck order**

peck·ish (-ish) adj. [PECK¹ + -ISH] 1. [Chiefly Brit. Colloq.] somewhat hungry 2. [Colloq.] cross; irritable —**peck'ish·ly** adv. —**peck'ish·ness** n.

Peck·sniff·i·an (pek snif'ē ən) adj. [after *Pecksniff,* unctuous hypocrite in Dickens' *Martin Chuzzlewit*] falsely moralistic; hypocritical; insincere

☆**peck·y** (pek'ē) adj. [PECK¹ (n. 2) + -Y²] showing or marked by spots or holes caused by decay (pecky cypress)

Pe·cos (pā'kōs, -kəs) [< native name of a pueblo near the upper river < ?] river in SW U.S., flowing from N N.Mex. through Tex. into the Rio Grande: 735 mi.

☆**Pecos Bill** *American Folklore* a legendary frontier cowboy, who performed such superhuman feats as digging the Rio Grande

Pécs (pāch) city in SW Hungary: pop. 130,000

pec·tase (pek'tās) n. [PECT(IN) + -ASE] an enzyme in fruits that converts pectin into pectic acid

pec·tate (-tāt) n. a salt or ester of pectic acid

pec·ten (pek'tən) n., pl. **pec'ti·nes** (-tə nēz') [L. *pecten,* a comb < *pectere,* to comb < IE. base *pek-,* to pull wool or hair, shorn animal: cf. FEE] *Zool.* 1. a) a comblike tissue around the transparent, jellylike part of the eye in many birds and reptiles b) any comblike structure, as a part of the stridulating organ of some spiders 2. same as SCALLOP (n. 1)

pec·tic (pek'tik) adj. [Fr. *pectique* < Gr. *pēktikos,* congealing < *pēktos,* congealed < *pēgnynai,* to fix: for IE. base see PEACE] of, containing, or derived from pectin

pectic acid a water-insoluble acid, $C_{17}H_{24}O_{16}$, formed by hydrolysis of the methyl ester groups of pectin

pec·tin (pek'tin) n. [< Gr. *pēktos* (see PECTIC) + -IN¹] a water-soluble carbohydrate, obtained from certain ripe fruits, which yields a gel that is the basis of jellies and jams —**pec'tin·ous** adj.

pec·ti·nate (pek'tə nāt') adj. [L. *pectinatus,* pp. of *pectinare,* to comb < *pecten:* see PECTEN] having toothlike projections like those on a comb: also **pec'ti·nat'ed**

pec·ti·na·tion (pek'tə nā'shən) n. [see PECTINATE & -ION] 1. an interlocking or being fitted together, as the teeth of two combs 2. a comblike part

pec·to·ral (pek'tər əl) adj. [< L. *pectoralis* < *pectus* (gen. *pectoris*), breast] 1. of or located in or on the chest or breast 2. worn on the chest or breast (a bishop's *pectoral cross*) 3. influenced by or resulting from personal feelings; subjective —n. [ME. < MFr. < L. *pectorale*] 1. something worn on the breast, as an ornamental plate 2. a pectoral fin or muscle

pectoral fin either of a pair of fins, associated with the pectoral girdle, just behind the head of a fish, corresponding to the forelimbs of a higher vertebrate

pectoral girdle *Anat., Zool.* the bony or cartilaginous structures to which the forelimbs (or arms) of a vertebrate are attached

☆**pectoral sandpiper** a large, grayish-brown, American sandpiper (*Erolia melanotos*) with a pale, streaked, buff-colored breast

pec·u·late (pek'ya lāt') vt., vi. **-lat'ed, -lat'ing** [< L. *peculatus,* pp. of *peculari,* to embezzle < *peculium,* private property < *pecus,* cattle: for IE. base see FEE] to steal or misuse (money or property entrusted to one's care, esp. public funds); embezzle —**pec'u·la'tion** n. —**pec'u·la'tor** n.

pe·cul·iar (pi kyōōl'yər) adj. [ME. *peculier* < L. *peculiaris* < *peculium:* see PECULATE] 1. of only one person, thing, group, country, etc.; distinctive; exclusive 2. particular; unique; special (a matter of *peculiar* interest) 3. out of the ordinary; queer; odd; strange —n. 1. something belonging to one only, as a privilege 2. a church or parish under a jurisdiction other than that of the diocese in which it is located —*SYN.* see STRANGE —**pe·cul'iar·ly** adv.

pe·cul·i·ar·i·ty (pi kyōō'lē ar'ə tē, -kyōōl'yar'-) n. 1. the quality or condition of being peculiar 2. pl. **-ties** something that is peculiar, as a trait or habit

pe·cul·i·um (pi kyōō'lē əm) n. [L.: see PECULATE] 1. *Rom. Law* property given to a slave, wife, or child to hold as his own 2. a private property or possession

pe·cu·ni·ar·y (pi kyōō'nē er'ē) adj. [L. *pecuniarius* < *pecunia,* money < *pecus,* cattle: see FEE] 1. of or involving money 2. involving a money penalty, or fine (a *pecuniary* offense) —*SYN.* see FINANCIAL —**pe·cu'ni·ar'i·ly** adv.

ped- (ped, pēd) same as: 1. PEDO-. 2. PEDI-. Used before a vowel

-ped (ped) same as -PEDE

ped. 1. pedal 2. pedestal

ped·a·gog·ic (ped'ə gäj'ik, -gō'jik) adj. [Gr. *paidagōgikos* < *paidagōgos:* see PEDAGOGUE] of or characteristic of teachers or of teaching: also **ped'a·gog'i·cal** —**ped'a·gog'i·cal·ly** adv.

☆**ped·a·gog·ics** (-gäj'iks, -gō'jiks) n.pl. [with sing. v.] same as PEDAGOGY

ped·a·gogue, ped·a·gog (ped'ə gäg', -gôg') n. [ME. *pedagoge* < OFr. < L. *paedagogus* < Gr. *paidagōgos* < *pais,* child (see PEDO-¹) + *agein,* to lead: see ACT] a teacher; often specif., a pedantic, dogmatic teacher

ped·a·go·gy (ped'ə gō'jē, -gäj'ē) n. [Fr. *pédagogie* < LL. *paedagogia* < Gr. *paidagōgia:* see prec.] 1. the profession or function of a teacher; teaching 2. the art or science of teaching; esp., instruction in teaching methods

ped·al (ped'l; also, for adj. 1, pēd'-) adj. [L. *pedalis* < *pes* (gen. *pedis*), FOOT] 1. of or having to do with the foot or feet 2. of or operated by a pedal or pedals —n. [MFr. *pédale* < It. *pedale* < L. *pedalis:* see the adj.] a lever operated by the foot, used in transmitting motion, as in a bicycle or sewing machine, or in changing the tone or volume of a musical instrument, as an organ or harp —vt., vi. **-aled** or **-alled, -al·ing** or **-al·ling** to move or operate by a pedal or pedals; use the pedals (of)

pe·dal·fer (pi dal'fər) n. [Gr. *ped(on),* ground (see PEDO-²) + L. *al(umen),* ALUM + L. *fer(rum),* iron] soil containing much alumina and iron oxide and lacking calcium and magnesium carbonates: usually found in forested areas of the tropics characterized by high humidity and temperature —**ped·al·fer·ic** (ped'əl fer'ik) adj.

ped·al·o (ped′ə lō′) *n., pl.* **-os** [arbitrary extension of PEDAL] a small watercraft for one or two persons, on pontoons, with a paddle wheel propelled by foot pedals: also **ped′al·lo′, pedal boat**

pedal point *Music* a single continuous tone, usually in the bass, held against the changing figures or harmonies of the other parts

☆**pedal pushers** calf-length pants for women or girls, used originally for bicycle riding

ped·ant (ped′nt) *n.* [Fr. *pédant*, pedant, schoolmaster < It. *pedante*, ult. < Gr. *paidagōgos*: see PEDAGOGUE] **1.** a person who lays unnecessary stress on minor or trivial points of learning, displaying a scholarship lacking in judgment or sense of proportion **2.** a narrow-minded teacher who insists on exact adherence to a set of arbitrary rules **3.** [Obs.] a schoolmaster —**pe·dan·tic** (pi dan′tik) *adj.* —**pe·dan′ti·cal·ly** *adv.*

ped·ant·ry (ped′n trē) *n., pl.* **-ries** [Fr. *pédanterie* < It. *pedanteria* < *pedante*: see PEDANT] **1.** the qualities, practices, etc. of a pedant; ostentatious display of knowledge, or an instance of this **2.** an arbitrary adherence to rules and forms

ped·ate (ped′āt) *adj.* [L. *pedatus* < *pes* (gen. *pedis*), FOOT] **1.** *Bot.* palmately divided into three main divisions, the two outer divisions forked into smaller ones **2.** *Zool.* a) having a foot or feet b) like a foot; footlike

pe·da·ti- (pi dat′ə, -dāt′ə) *a combining form meaning* pedately [*pedatifid*]

pe·dat·i·fid (pi dat′ə fid, -dāt′-) *adj.* [prec. + -FID] *Bot.* cleft pedately, but not into entirely separate leaflets

ped·dle (ped′'l) *vi.* **-dled, -dling** [back-formation < PEDDLER] **1.** to go from place to place selling small articles **2.** [infl. by PIDDLE] to spend time on trifles; piddle —*vt.* **1.** to carry from place to place and offer for sale **2.** to deal out or circulate (gossip, ideas, etc.)

ped·dler (ped′lər) *n.* [ME. *pedlare, pedlere* < ? *peddare*, peddler < *ped, pedde*, a basket, via dim. *pedle*] a person who peddles

ped·dler·y (-ē) *n.* **1.** the business or trade of a peddler **2.** wares sold by a peddler

ped·dling (ped′liŋ) *adj.* [see PEDDLE, *vi.* 2] busy with trifles; trifling; petty

-pede (pēd) [< L. *pes* (gen. *pedis*), FOOT] *a combining form meaning* foot or feet [*centipede*]

ped·er·ast (ped′ə rast′, pē′də-) *n.* [Fr. *pédéraste* < Gr. *paiderastēs*] a man who practices pederasty —**ped′er·as′tic** *adj.* —**ped′er·as′ti·cal·ly** *adv.*

ped·er·as·ty (ped′ə ras′tē, pē′də-) *n.* [ModL. *paederastia* < Gr. *paiderastia* < *paiderastēs*, lover of boys < *pais* (gen. *paidos*), boy (see PEDO-¹) + *eran*, to love] sodomy between males, esp. as practiced by a man with a boy

ped·es·tal (ped′is t'l) *n.* [Fr. *piédestal* < It. *piedestallo* < *piè* (L. *pes*, gen. *pedis*), FOOT + *di*, of + *stal* (< Gmc. *stal*, STALL¹), a rest, place] **1.** the foot or bottom support of a column, pillar, vase, lamp, statue, etc. **2.** any foundation, base, support, etc. —*vt.* **-taled** or **-talled**, **-tal·ing** or **-tal·ling** to place on or furnish with a pedestal —**put (**or **set) on a pedestal** to regard with great or excessive admiration; idolize

pe·des·tri·an (pə des′trē ən) *adj.* [< L. *pedester*, on foot < *pes* (gen. *pedis*), FOOT + -IAN] **1.** going or done on foot; walking **2.** of or for pedestrians [a *pedestrian* crossing] **3.** lacking interest or imagination; prosaic; ordinary and dull: said of a literary style, a speech, etc. —*n.* one who goes on foot; walker —**pe·des′tri·an·ism** *n.*

ped·i- (ped′i) [< L. *pes* (gen. *pedis*), FOOT] *a combining form meaning* foot or feet [*pedicure*]

pe·di·a·tri·cian (pē′dē ə trish′ən) *n.* a specialist in pediatrics: also **pe′di·at′rist** (-at′rist)

pe·di·at·rics (pē′dē at′riks) *n.pl.* [*with sing. v.*] [< PED(O)-¹ + -IATRICS] the branch of medicine dealing with the development and care of infants and children, and with the treatment of their diseases —**pe′di·at′ric** *adj.*

ped·i·cab (ped′i kab′) *n.* [PEDI- + CAB¹] a three-wheeled passenger vehicle, esp. in SE Asia, which the driver propels by pedaling like a bicycle

ped·i·cel (ped′i s'l) *n.* [ModL. *pedicellus*, dim. of L. *pediculus*, dim. of *pes* (gen. *pedis*), FOOT] **1.** *Bot.* a) the stalk of a single flower, fruit, leaf, etc. b) the stalk of a grass spikelet **2.** *Zool.* a) a small, stalklike structure or support, as the stalk of a sessile organism, the second segment of an insect's antenna, etc. b) a small, footlike organ or part —**ped′i·cel′late** (-sel′it, -āt) *adj.*

ped·i·cle (ped′i k'l) *n.* [L. *pediculus*] same as PEDICEL

pe·dic·u·lar (pi dik′yə lər) *adj.* [L. *pedicularis < pediculus*, dim. of *pedis*, a louse] **1.** of lice **2.** infested with lice; lousy

pe·dic·u·late (-lit, -lāt′) *adj.* [< L. *pediculus* (see PEDICEL) + -ATE¹] of or belonging to an order (Pediculati) of bony fishes, including the anglers, having pectoral fins attached to an armlike base and a reduced dorsal fin whose first flexible ray, attached to the head, often serves as a lure —*n.* any fish of this order

pe·dic·u·lo·sis (pi dik′yə lō′sis) *n.* [< L. *pediculus* (see PEDICULAR) + -OSIS] infestation with lice —**pe·dic′u·lous** (-ləs) *adj.*

☆**ped·i·cure** (ped′i kyoor′) *n.* [Fr. *pédicure* < L. *pes* (gen. *pedis*), FOOT + *curare*, to care for < *cura*: see CURE] **1.** *early term for* PODIATRIST **2.** [by analogy with MANICURE] care of the feet, esp. a trimming, polishing, etc. of the toenails —**ped′i·cur′ist** *n.*

ped·i·gree (ped′ə grē′) *n.* [ME. *pedegru, pe de gre* < MFr. *pié de grue*, lit., crane's foot < L. *pes*, FOOT + *grus*, a crane: from the lines in the genealogical tree] **1.** a list of ancestors; record of ancestry; family tree **2.** descent; lineage; ancestry **3.** a recorded or known line of descent, esp. of a purebred animal —**ped′i·greed′** *adj.*

ped·i·ment (ped′ə mənt) *n.* [altered (after L. *pes*, gen. *pedis*, FOOT) < earlier *periment*, prob. altered < PYRAMID] **1.** a low-pitched gable on the front of some buildings in the Grecian style of architecture **2.** any similar triangular piece used ornamentally, as over a doorway, fireplace, etc. —**ped′i·men′tal** *adj.*

PEDIMENT

ped·i·men·ted (-men′tid) *adj.* having a pediment

ped·i·palp (ped′i palp′) *n.* [ModL. *pedipalpus*: see PEDI- & PALPUS] either of the second pair of appendages of spiders and other arachnids, variously developed for grasping, sensing, fertilizing, etc.

ped·lar, ped·ler (ped′lər) *n.* same as PEDDLER —**ped′lar·y, ped′ler·y** *n.*

pe·do-¹ (pē′dō, -də) [< Gr. *pais* (gen. *paidos*), a child < IE. *pōu-*, small, small animal, child: cf. FEW, FOAL] *a combining form meaning* child, children, offspring [*pedodontics*]

ped·o-² (ped′ə) [< Gr. *pedon*, the ground < IE. *ped*-, FOOT] *a combining form meaning* ground, soil, earth [*pedogenesis*]

pe·do·bap·tism (pē′dō bap′tiz'm) *n.* [ModL. *paedobaptismus*: see PEDO-¹ & BAPTISM] baptism of infants

ped·o·cal (ped′ə kal′) *n.* [< PEDO-² + L. *calx* (gen. *calcis*), lime] soil containing much lime, commonly formed in prairie regions characterized by low humidity and temperature —**ped′o·cal′ic** *adj.*

☆**pe·do·don·tics** (pē′də dän′tiks) *n.* [ModL.: see PEDO-¹, -ODONT, & -ICS] the branch of dentistry concerned with the care and treatment of children's teeth —**pe′do·don′tist** *n.*

ped·o·gen·e·sis (ped′ə jen′ə sis) *n.* [PEDO-² + -GENESIS] soil formation —**ped′o·gen′ic** (-jen′ik), **ped′o·ge·net′ic** (-jə net′ik) *adj.*

☆**pe·dol·o·gy¹** (pi däl′ə jē) *n.* [PEDO-¹ + -LOGY] the systematic study of the behavior and development of children —**pe·do·log·ic** (pē′də läj′ik), **pe′do·log′i·cal** *adj.* —**pe′do·log′i·cal·ly** *adv.* —**pe·dol′o·gist** *n.*

pe·dol·o·gy² (pi däl′ə jē) *n.* [PEDO-² + -LOGY] the scientific study of soils —**ped·o·log·ic** (ped′ə läj′ik), **ped′o·log′i·cal** *adj.* —**ped′o·log′i·cal·ly** *adv.* —**pe·dol′o·gist** *n.*

pe·dom·e·ter (pi däm′ə tər) *n.* [Fr. *pédomètre* < L. *pes* (gen. *pedis*), FOOT + Gr. *metron*, MEASURE] an instrument carried by a walker, which measures approximately distance covered in walking by recording the number of steps

pe·do·phil·i·a (pē′də fil′ē ə, -fil′yə) *n.* [PEDO-¹ + -PHILIA] abnormal sexual desire in an adult for children

☆**pe·dro** (pē′drō, pā′-) *n., pl.* **-dros** [Sp. *Pedro*, Peter < LL. *Petrus*: see PETER] **1.** a variety of the card game seven-up in which the five of trumps counts five **2.** the five of trumps in this game

pe·dun·cle (pi duŋ′k'l, pē′duŋ k'l) *n.* [ModL. *pedunculus*, dim. of L. *pes* (gen. *pedis*), FOOT] **1.** *Anat.* a stalklike bundle of nerve fibers connecting various parts of the brain **2.** *Bot.* a) the stalk of a flower cluster or inflorescence b) the stalk of a solitary flower which is regarded as a reduced inflorescence, as in the narcissus **3.** *Med.* a narrow, stalklike base of a tumor or polyp **4.** *Zool.* a slender, stalklike part, as between the abdomen and middle section of an insect, or the stalk of a goose barnacle; pedicel —**pe·dun′cu·lar** (pi duŋ′kyə lər) *adj.*

pe·dun·cu·late (pi duŋ′kyə lit, -lāt′) *adj.* growing on or having a peduncle: also **pe·dun′cu·lat′ed**

pee (pē) *vi., vt.* [orig. euphemistic use of P(ISS)] to urinate —*n.* urine Now a somewhat vulgar usage

Pee·bles (pē′b'lz) county of SC Scotland: 347 sq. mi.; pop. 14,000: also called **Pee′bles·shire′** (-shir′)

Pee Dee (pē′ dē′) [< AmInd. tribal name < ?] river flowing through N.C. & S.C. into the Atlantic: with its upper course (the *Yadkin*), which rises in NW N.C., 435 mi.

peek (pēk) *vi.* [ME. *piken* < ?] to glance or look quickly and furtively, esp. through an opening or from behind something —*n.* such a glance —*SYN.* see LOOK

peek·a·boo (pēk′ə boo′) *n.* a game to amuse a young child, in which someone hides his face, as behind his hands, and then suddenly reveals it, calling "peekaboo!" —☆*adj.* made of openwork or sheer fabric, as a blouse

peel¹ (pēl) *vt.* [ME. *pelen* < OFr. *peler*, to strip, pare < L. *pilare*, to make bald < *pilus*, a hair: see PILE²] to cut

away or strip off (the rind, skin, covering, surface, etc.) of (anything); pare —*vi.* 1. to shed skin, bark, etc. 2. to come off in layers or flakes, as old paint 3. [Slang] to undress —*n.* the rind or skin of fruit —*SYN.* see SKIN —**peel off** *Aeron.* to veer away from a flight formation in an abrupt maneuver —☆**peel rubber** (or **tires**) [Slang] to accelerate an automobile quickly, as in a drag race —**peel′er** *n.*

peel² (pēl) *n.* [ME. *pele* < OFr. < L. *pala*, a spade] a long shovellike tool used by bakers for moving bread into and out of the ovens

peel³ (pēl) *n.* [ME. *pel* < Anglo-Fr. < OFr., a fort, stake < L. *palus:* see PALE²] a fortified house or tower of a type built on the Scottish border during the 16th cent.

Peel (pēl), Sir **Robert** 1788–1850; Brit. statesman; prime minister (1834–35; 1841–46)

Peele (pēl), **George** 1558?–97?; Eng. dramatist

peel·er (pēl′ər) *n.* [after Sir Robert PEEL, who first organized the Irish constabulary] [Old Brit. Slang] a policeman

peel·ing (pēl′iŋ) *n.* a peeled-off strip, as of apple skin

peen (pēn) *n.* [prob. < Scand., as in Norw. *pænn*, sharpened end of a hammer, Sw. *pæna*, to beat out] the part of the head of certain hammers opposite to the flat striking surface: it is often ball-shaped (**ball peen**) or wedge-shaped —*vt.* to hammer, bend, etc. with a peen

peep¹ (pēp) *vi.* [ME. *pepen:* orig. echoic] 1. to make the short, high-pitched cry of a young bird or chick; chirp; cheep 2. to utter a sound or speak in a small, weak voice, as from fear —*n.* 1. a short, high-pitched sound; chirp; cheep 2. the slightest vocal sound

peep² (pēp) *vi.* [ME. *pepen*, ? akin to *piken*, PEEK] 1. to look through a small opening or from a place of hiding 2. to peer slyly or secretly; take a hasty, furtive look 3. to come into view; show or appear gradually or partially, as though from hiding [stars *peeped* through the clouds] —*vt.* to cause to appear or protrude —*n.* 1. a brief, hasty look or restricted view; secret or furtive glimpse or glance 2. the first appearance; crack, as of dawn

peep·er¹ (-ər) *n.* 1. a person who peeps or pries 2. [Slang] *a*) [*pl.*] the eyes ☆*b*) a private detective

peep·er² (pēp′ər) *n.* 1. a person or thing that peeps, cheeps, chirps, etc. ☆2. any of various tree frogs (esp. family Hylidae) that peep in early spring

peep·hole (-hōl′) *n.* a hole to peep through

Peeping Tom 1. *Eng. Legend* the Coventry tailor who was struck blind after peeping at Lady Godiva 2. [p- T-] a person who gets pleasure, esp. sexual pleasure, from watching others, esp. furtively

peep show a pictured scene or group of objects, as in a box, viewed through a small opening, sometimes with a magnifying lens

peep sight a rear sight for a firearm usually consisting of an adjustable disk with a small opening in the center through which the front sight and target are lined up

pee·pul (pē′pəl) *n. same as* PIPAL

peer¹ (pir) *n.* [ME. *peir* < OFr. *per* < L. *par*, an equal: see PAR] 1. a person or thing of the same rank, value, quality, ability, etc.; equal; specif., an equal before the law 2. a noble; esp., a British duke, marquess, earl, viscount, or baron —*vt.* 1. [Archaic] to match or equal 2. [Brit.] to make a nobleman of —**peer of the realm** any of the class of British peers entitled to a seat in the House of Lords

peer² (pir) *vi.* [? aphetic < APPEAR] 1. to look closely and searchingly, or squint, as in trying to see more clearly 2. to come out or show slightly; come partly into sight 3. [Poet.] to appear —*SYN.* see LOOK

peer·age (pir′ij) *n.* 1. all the peers of a particular country 2. the rank or dignity of a peer 3. a book or list of peers with their lineage

peer·ess (-is) *n.* 1. the wife of a peer 2. a woman having the rank of peer in her own right

peer group all those people of about the same age, status, etc. in a society, regarded as forming a sociological group with a homogeneous system of values

peer·less (-lis) *adj.* without equal; unrivaled —**peer′less·ly** *adv.* —**peer′less·ness** *n.*

☆**peet-weet** (pēt′wēt′) *n.* [echoic] *same as* SPOTTED SANDPIPER

☆**peeve** (pēv) *vt.* **peeved, peev′ing** [back-formation < PEEVISH] [Colloq.] to make peevish or bad-tempered —*n.* [Colloq.] 1. an object of dislike; annoyance 2. a peevish state —*SYN.* see IRRITATE

☆**peeved** (pēvd) *adj.* [pp. of prec.] irritated; annoyed

☆**pee·vish** (pē′vish) *adj.* [ME. *pevische* < ?] 1. hard to please; irritable; fretful; cross 2. showing ill humor or impatience, as a glance or remark —**pee′vish·ly** *adv.* —**pee′vish·ness** *n.*

☆**pee-wee** (pē′wē′) *n.* [prob. echoic redupl. of WEE] 1. [Colloq.] a person or thing that is unusually small 2. *var. of* PEWEE

pee-wit (pē′wit) *n. var. of* PEWIT

peg (peg) *n.* [ME. *pegge*, prob. < LowG. source, as in Du. *peg*, wooden plug < IE. base **bak-*, staff, whence L. *baculum*, stick] 1. a short, usually tapering or pointed piece used to hold parts together or in place, or to close an opening, as in a barrel 2. a projecting pin or bolt used to hang things on, fasten ropes to, mark degrees of measure-

ment or the score in a game, etc. 3. *a*) the distance between pegs *b*) a step or degree *c*) a fixed level, as for a price 4. any of the pins which hold, and are used in regulating the tension of, the strings of a violin or other stringed instrument 5. a point or prong for tearing, hooking, etc. 6. a point of reference, esp. an excuse or reason 7. [Colloq.] the foot or leg 8. [Colloq.] an act or instance of throwing 9. [Brit.] *same as* CLOTHESPIN 10. [Brit. Colloq.] a drink, esp. brandy or whiskey and soda —*vt.* **pegged, peg′ging** 1. to put a peg or pegs into so as to fasten, secure, mark, etc. 2. to mark (a boundary, claim, etc.) with pegs (usually with *out*) 3. to strike with a peg so as to pierce or hook 4. to maintain (prices, etc.) at a fixed level 5. to score (points) in cribbage during the play of a hand 6. [Colloq.] to give support, relevance, or perspective to (an idea, news story, etc.) by relating to something else 7. [Colloq.] to identify or categorize [*pegged* him as a man of action] 8. [Colloq.] to throw [to *peg* a ball to first base] —*vi.* 1. to keep score with pegs, as in cribbage 2. to move energetically or quickly (usually with *down, along*, etc.) —**off the peg** [Chiefly Brit.] ready-made; directly off the rack: said of clothing —**peg away (at)** to work steadily and persistently (at) —**round peg in a square hole** a person in a position, situation, etc. for which he is unfitted or unqualified: also **square peg in a round hole** —**take down a peg** to lower the pride or conceit of; humble or dispirit

Peg·a·sus (peg′ə səs) [L. < Gr. *Pēgasos*] 1. *Gr. Myth.* a winged horse which sprang from the body of Medusa at her death: a stamp of his hoof caused Hippocrene, the fountain of the Muses, to issue from Mount Helicon 2. a large northern constellation near the vernal equinox

peg·board (peg′bôrd′) *n.* a board with holes for inserting pegs; specif., *a*) a small board used for scoring in cribbage ☆*b*) boardlike material, or a piece of this, perforated with rows of holes, for arranging pegs or hooks to hold displays, tools, etc.: as a trademark, **Peg-Board** *c*) a game in which pegs are arranged in patterns on a small, perforated board

Peg·gy (peg′ē) a feminine name: see MARGARET

peg leg [Colloq.] 1. a wooden leg 2. a person with a wooden leg

peg·ma·tite (peg′mə tīt′) *n.* [< Gr. *pēgma* (gen. *pēgmatos*), a framework, something fastened (< IE. base **pak-:* see PEACE, FANG) + -ITE¹: from its closeness of texture] a relatively coarsegrained, intrusive, igneous rock, usually granitic, containing large crystals of quartz, feldspar, and mica, and sometimes rare minerals: usually found in fissures and cracks of other igneous rocks — **peg′ma·tit′ic** (-tit′ik) *adj.*

peg-top (peg′täp′) *adj.* pear-shaped like a peg top; esp., designating trousers that are full at the hips and narrow at the cuffs

peg top 1. a child's spinning top having a metal tip on which it spins 2. [*pl.*] peg-top trousers

peh (pā) *n.* [Heb. *peh*, lit., mouth] the seventeenth letter of the Hebrew alphabet (פ, ף)

Peh·le·vi (pā′lə vē′) *n.* [< Per. *pahlawī* < Pahlav., Parthia < OPer. *Parthava*] an Iranian language spoken and written in Persia from about the 3d to the 8th century A.D.; Middle Persian: the name is often restricted to the literary language of the Zoroastrian books, written c. 224–651 A.D.

P.E.I. Prince Edward Island

peign·oir (pān wär′, pen-; pān′wär, pen′-) *n.* [Fr. < *peigner*, to comb < L. *pectinare* < *pecten*, comb: see PECTEN] a woman's loose, full dressing gown, like a negligee but typically shorter

Pei·ping (bā′piŋ′) *former name of* PEKING

Peip·si (pāp′sē) *Estonian name of* CHUDSKOYE Lake

Pei·pus (pī′poos) *Ger. name of* CHUDSKOYE Lake

Pei·rai·évs (pē′re efs′) *Gr. name of* PIRAEUS

Peirce (purs), **Charles San·ders** (san′dərz) 1839–1914; U.S. philosopher & mathematician

pe·jo·ra·tion (pē′jə rā′shən, pej′ə-) *n.* [ML. *pejoratio:* see ff.] 1. a worsening; depreciation 2. *Linguis.* a change of meaning for the worse

pe·jo·ra·tive (pi jôr′ə tiv, -jär′-; pē′jə rāt′iv, pej′ə-) *adj.* [< L. *pejoratus*, pp. of *pejorare*, to make worse < *pejor*, worse, orig., inclined downward < IE. base **ped-*, FOOT] 1. declining; making or becoming worse: applied to words whose basic meaning has changed for the worse (Ex.: *knave, cretin*) 2. disparaging or derogatory —*n.* a pejorative word or form —**pe·jo′ra·tive·ly** *adv.*

pek·an (pek′ən) *n.* [CanadFr. < AmInd. (Algonquian) name, as in Abnaki *pékané*] *same as* FISHER (sense 3)

Pe·kin (pē′kin) *former var. of* PEKING

pe·kin (pē′kin′) *n.* [Fr. *pékin* < *Pékin*, Peking] a striped silk material, orig. from China

Pekin (duck) a large, white domesticated duck of a breed originating in China: also **Peking (duck)**

Pe·king (pē′kiŋ′; *Chin.* bā′jiŋ′) capital of the People's Republic of China, in the NE part: pop. c. 4,000,000 (met. area, 6,100,000)

Pe·king·ese (pē′kiŋ ēz′; *for n. 3, usually* -kə nēz′) *adj.* of Peking, China, or its people —*n., pl.* **Pekingese** 1. a native or inhabitant of Peking 2. the Chinese dialect of Peking 3. a small dog with long, silky hair, protruding eyes, short legs, and a pug nose: orig. bred in China Also **Pe′kin·ese′** (-kə nēz′)

Peking man a type of early man (*Homo erectus pekinensis*) of the Pleistocene age, known from fossil remains found near Peking, China

pe·koe (pē′kō; *Brit.* often pek′ō) *n.* [< Chin. dial. *pek-ho*, lit., white down: from being picked while leaves still have the down on them] a fine grade of black tea of Ceylon and India, made from the small leaves at the tips of the stem

pel·age (pel′ij) *n.* [Fr. < OFr. *pel*, hair < L. *pilus*, hair: see PILE²] the coat, or covering, of a mammal, as hair, fur, etc.

Pe·la·gi·an (pi lā′jē ən) *n.* [LL.(Ec.) *Pelagianus*] a follower of Pelagius, who denied the doctrine of original sin and maintained that man has freedom of will —*adj.* of Pelagius or his followers —**Pe·la′gi·an·ism** *n.*

pe·lag·ic (pi laj′ik) *adj.* [L. *pelagicus* < Gr. *pelagikos* < *pelagos*, the sea < IE. *plāg-*, broad, flat < base *plā-*, whence L. *planus*, flat] of the ocean surface or the open sea, esp. as distinguished from coastal waters

Pe·la·gi·us (pə lā′jē əs) 360?–420? A.D.; *Brit.* monk & theologian

pel·ar·gon·ic acid (pel′är gän′ik, -gō′nik) a monobasic fatty acid, $C_8H_{17}COOH$, obtained from the leaves of a pelargonium or by oxidation of oleic acid: used in lacquers, pharmaceuticals, etc.

pel·ar·go·ni·um (pel′är gō′nē əm) *n.* [ModL. *Pelargonium*, name of the genus < Gr. *pelargos*, stork (after ModL. *Geranium*: see GERANIUM), because the carpels resemble a stork's bill] any of a genus (*Pelargonium*) of mostly South African plants of the geranium family, having circular or lobed, often aromatic, leaves and variously colored flowers

Pe·las·gi (pə laz′jī) *n.pl.* the Pelasgians

Pe·las·gi·an (pə laz′jē ən) *n.* any of a prehistoric people believed to have lived in Greece, Asia Minor, and the Aegean Islands —*adj.* of the Pelasgians: also **Pe·las′gic** (-jik) *adj.*

pe·lec·y·pod (pə les′ə päd′) *n., adj.* [< Gr. *pelekys*, an ax + -POD] same as LAMELLIBRANCH

Pe·lée (pə lā′), **Mount** volcanic mountain on Martinique, in the West Indies: 5,100 ft.

pel·er·ine (pel′ə rēn′) *n.* [Fr. *pèlerine* < *pèlerin*, a pilgrim < L. *peregrinus*: see PILGRIM] a woman's cape, usually of fur, tapering to long points in the front

Pele's hair (pē′lēz, pā′lāz) [transl. of Haw. *lauoho-o Pele*, after *Pele*, goddess of volcanoes] a kind of mineral wool formed when the wind blows molten lava into glassy fibers

Pe·leus (pēl′yoos, pē′lē əs) *Gr. Myth.* a king of the Myrmidons, father of Achilles

pelf (pelf) *n.* [ME., akin to (< ?) MFr. *pelfre*, booty] **1.** orig., ill-gotten gains; booty **2.** money or wealth regarded with contempt

Pe·li·as (pē′lē əs, pel′ē-) [L. < Gr. *Pelias*] *Gr. Myth.* a king of Thessaly and the uncle and guardian of Jason, whom he sent in search of the Golden Fleece

pel·i·can (pel′i kən) *n.* [ME. < OE. *pellicane* < LL.(Ec.) *pelicanus* < Gr. *pelekan* (used in LXX to translate Heb. *kā′ath*, a bird of prey), akin to *pelekas*, woodpecker, prob. < *pelekys*, an ax (from the shape of the bill)] any of a genus (*Pelecanus*) of water birds with completely webbed feet and a distensible pouch which hangs from the large lower bill and is used to scoop up or store fish

☆**pelican hook** a hinged hook that can be quickly secured or released by a sliding ring

Pe·li·on (pē′lē ən) mountain in E Thessaly, NE Greece: 5,417 ft.: in Greek mythology, the Titans piled Pelion on Ossa & both on Olympus in a futile attempt to reach & attack the gods in heaven

PELICAN
(to 5 ft. long; wingspread 6–9 ft.)

pe·lisse (pə lēs′) *n.* [Fr. < OFr. < VL. *pellicia*, for *pellicia* (*vestis*) < L. *pellicius*, made of skins < *pellis*, a skin: for IE. base see FELL⁴] a long cloak or outer coat, esp. one made, lined, or trimmed with fur

pel·la·gra (pə lag′rə, -lā′grə) *n.* [It. < *pelle* (L. *pellis*, the skin + -agra < Gr. *agra*, seizure, akin to *agein*: see ACT] a chronic disease caused by a deficiency of nicotinic acid in the diet and characterized by gastrointestinal disturbances, skin eruptions, and mental disorders: it is endemic in some parts of the world —**pel·la′grous** *adj.*

pel·la·grin (-rin, -grin) *n.* a person who has pellagra

pel·let (pel′ət) *n.* [ME. *pelote* < OFr. < VL. *pilotta*, dim. of L. *pila*, a ball, orig., knot of hair: see PILE²] **1.** a little ball or rounded mass, as of clay, paper, medicine, compressed food for animals, etc. **2.** *a*) a crude projectile of stone, etc., as used in a catapult or early cannon *b*) a bullet, or an imitation bullet for a popgun *c*) any of various pieces of small, usually lead, shot —*vt.* **1.** to make pellets of **2.** to shoot or hit with pellets

pel·let·ize (-īz′) *vt.* **-ized′, -iz′ing** to form (a substance) into pellets; specif., to make pellets of the iron-containing particles recovered from pulverized low-grade iron (ore) —**pel′let·i·za′tion** *n.*

pel·li·cle (pel′i k'l) *n.* [L. *pellicula*, dim. of *pellis*, skin: for IE. base see FELL⁴] **1.** a thin skin or film, as on a photographic emulsion or on a liquid **2.** *Zool.* a thin non-living membrane secreted by animal cells, as the envelope covering many protozoans —**pel·lic′u·lar** (pə lik′yə lər), **pel·lic′u·late** (-lit, -lāt′) *adj.*

pel·li·to·ry (pel′i tôr′ē) *n., pl.* **-ries** [altered < ME. *peritorie* < OFr. *paritoire* < L. *parietaria* < *parietarius*, of walls < *paries*: see PARIES] **1.** any of a genus (*Parietaria*) of plants of the nettle family, containing niter and formerly used as a diuretic: in full **wall pellitory 2.** a Mediterranean plant (*Anacyclus pyrethrum*) of the composite family, whose root was formerly used to relieve toothache: in full **pellitory of Spain**

pell-mell, pell·mell (pel′mel′) *adv., adj.* [Fr. *pêle-mêle* < OFr. *pesle mesle*, redupl. < *mesler*, to mix] **1.** in a jumbled, confused mass or manner; without order or method **2.** in wild, disorderly haste; with reckless speed; headlong —*n.* a jumble; confusion; disorder

pel·lu·cid (pə lōō′sid) *adj.* [L. *pellucidus* < *pellucere*, to shine through < *per*, through (see PER) + *lucere*, to shine < *lux*, LIGHT¹] **1.** transparent or translucent; clear **2.** easy to understand; clear and simple in style [a *pellucid* explanation] —SYN. see CLEAR —**pel·lu·cid·i·ty** (pel′oo sid′ə tē, -yoo-), **pel·lu′cid·ness** *n.* —**pel·lu′cid·ly** *adv.*

pel·met (pel′mət) *n.* [? altered < Fr. *palmette*, a palm-leaf ornament on a cornice < *palme*, PALM¹] a decorative cornice or valence for concealing the fixtures of curtains or drapes

Pe·lop·i·das (pi läp′ə dəs) ?–364 B.C.; Theban general

Peloponnesian War a war between Athens and Sparta (431–404 B.C.) ending with the victory of Sparta

Pel·o·pon·ne·sus, Pel·o·pon·ne·sos (pel′ə pə nē′səs) peninsula forming the S part of the mainland of Greece: 8,130 sq. mi.; pop. 1,096,000 —**Pel′o·pon·ne′sian** (-shən, -zhən) *adj., n.*

Pe·lops (pē′läps) [L. < Gr. *Pelops*, prob. < *pellos*, dark + *ops*, face: see EYE] *Gr. Myth.* the son of Tantalus: served up to the gods as food by his father and later restored to life by them

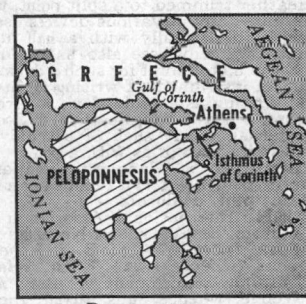

PELOPONNESUS

pe·lo·ri·a (pi lôr′ē ə) *n.* [ModL. < Gr. *pelōros*, monstrous < *pelōr*, monster] an abnormal regularity of form in a flower normally irregular —**pe·lo′ric** *adj.*

pe·lo·rus (pə lôr′əs) *n.* [? after L. *Pelorus*, pilot of Hannibal's ship] *Naut.* a device for taking bearings, consisting of a stand containing a gyrocompass over which sighting vanes are mounted

pe·lo·ta (pə lōt′ə; *Sp.* pe lô′tä) *n.* [Sp., lit., a ball < VL. *pilotta*: see PELLET] Spanish name for JAI ALAI

pelt¹ (pelt) *vt.* [LME. *pelten*, ? var. of *pulten*, to thrust, hasten < L. *pultare*, freq. of *pillare*, to drive] **1.** to throw things at; strike with or as with missiles **2.** to beat or pound heavily and repeatedly **3.** to throw or cast (missiles) —*vi.* **1.** to beat or strike heavily or steadily, as hard rain **2.** to rush or hurry —*n.* **1.** the act of pelting **2.** a blow —(at) **full pelt** at full speed —**pelt′er** *n.*

pelt² (pelt) *n.* [ME., prob. back-formation < OFr. *peleterie*: see PELTRY] **1.** the skin of a fur-bearing animal, esp. after it has been stripped from the carcass **2.** the human skin: a humorous usage SYN. see SKIN

pel·tast (pel′tast) *n.* [L. *peltasta* < Gr. *peltastēs* < *peltē*, light shield < IE. *pelto-*, a cover < base *pel-*, to cover, whence FILM] in ancient Greece, a soldier carrying a light shield

pel·tate (pel′tāt) *adj.* [< L. *pelta* < Gr. *peltē*: see prec.) + -ATE¹] *Bot.* shield-shaped; specif., having the stalk attached to the lower surface within the margin: said of a leaf —**pel′tate·ly** *adv.*

pelt·er (pel′tər) *vt., vi.* same as PELT¹

Pel·tier effect (pel′tyā) [after Jean *Peltier* (1785–1845), Fr. physicist] *Elec.* the liberation or absorption of heat at a junction of two unlike metals through which an electric current is passing

pelt·ing (pel′tin) *adj.* [prob. < obs. *pelt*, to haggle: cf. PALTRY] [Archaic] mean; miserly; paltry

pelt·ry (pel′trē) *n., pl.* **-ries** [ME. < OFr. *peleterie* < *peletier*, furrier < *pel* (L. *pellis*), a skin: for base see PELTAST] pelts, or fur-bearing skins, collectively

pel·vic (pel′vik) *adj.* of or near the pelvis

pelvic fin either of a pair of fins corresponding to the hind

limbs of a higher vertebrate and associated with the pelvic girdle in fishes

pelvic girdle the bony or cartilaginous structures to which the hind limbs or fins of a vertebrate are attached

pel·vis (pel′vis) *n., pl.* **-vis·es, -ves** (-vēz) [ModL. < L., a basin < IE. base *pel-, a container, whence ON., OE. *full*, a cup] *Anat., Zool.* any basinlike or funnel-shaped structure; specif., *a)* the basinlike cavity formed by the ring of bones of the pelvic girdle in the posterior part of the trunk in many vertebrates: in man, it is formed by the ilium, ischium, pubis, and sacrum, supporting the spinal column and resting upon the legs *b)* these bones collectively; pelvic girdle *c)* the funnel-shaped part of the kidney leading into the ureter

Pem·ba (pem′bə) island of Tanzania in the Indian Ocean, off the E coast of Africa: 380 sq. mi.

Pem·broke (pem′brook; *also, & for n. always*, -brōk) *same as* PEMBROKESHIRE —*n. see* WELSH CORGI

Pem·broke·shire (-shir′) county of SW Wales: 614 sq. mi.; pop. 95,000

pem·mi·can (pem′i kən) *n.* [< AmInd. (Cree) *pemikkân*, fat meat < *pimiy*, fat] **1.** dried lean meat, pounded into a paste with fat and preserved in the form of pressed cakes **2.** dried beef, suet, dried fruit, etc., prepared as a concentrated high-energy food, used for emergency rations, as on arctic expeditions

pem·phi·gus (pem′fi gəs, pem fī′-) *n.* [ModL. < Gr. *pemphix* (gen. *pemphigos*), bubble] a disease characterized by the formation of watery blisters on the skin, sometimes with itching

pen[1] (pen) *n.* [ME. < OE. *penn*: for IE. base see PIN] **1.** a small yard or enclosure for domestic animals **2.** the animals so confined **3.** any small enclosure —*vt.* **penned** or **pent, pen′ning** to confine or enclose in or as in a pen

pen[2] (pen) *n.* [ME. *penne* < OFr., a pen, feather < L. *pinna*, var. of *penna*, a feather < *petna < IE. base *pet-, to fly, go, whence FEATHER] **1.** orig., a heavy quill or feather trimmed to a split point, used for writing with ink **2.** now, any of various devices used in writing or drawing with ink, usually with a half-tubular metal point split into two nibs: see also BALL POINT PEN, FOUNTAIN PEN **3.** the metal point for such a device **4.** *a)* the pen regarded as an instrument of writing *b)* literary style or expression *c)* writing as a profession **5.** [Archaic] a feather or quill; esp., a heavy wing feather **6.** *Zool.* the long, pen-shaped, internal, horny shell of a squid —*vt.* **penned, pen′ning** to write with or as with a pen

☆**pen**[3] (pen) *n.* [Slang] a penitentiary

pen[4] (pen) *n.* [< ?] a female swan

Pen., pen. peninsula

P.E.N. International Association of Poets, Playwrights, Editors, Essayists, and Novelists

pe·nal (pē′n′l) *adj.* [ME. < L. *poenalis* < *poena*, punishment (whence PAIN) < Gr. *poinē*, penalty, fine < IE. *kwoina, punishment < base *kwei-, to heed, respect, avenge, whence Sans. *cáyatē*, (he) avenges, Lith. *káina*, price] **1.** of, for, or constituting punishment, esp. legal punishment **2.** specifying or prescribing punishment [a *penal* code] **3.** making a person liable to punishment [a *penal* offense] —**pe′nal·ly** *adv.*

penal code a body of law dealing with various crimes or offenses and their legal penalties

pe·nal·ize (pē′n′l īz′, pen′′l-) *vt.* **-ized′, -iz′ing** **1.** to make punishable; set a penalty for (an offense, etc.) **2.** to impose a penalty on; specif., to subject to a handicap in a contest as penalty for the infraction of a rule **3.** to put at a disadvantage —**pe′nal·i·za′tion** *n.*

penal servitude imprisonment, usually at hard labor: the legal punishment for conviction of certain crimes

pen·al·ty (pen′′l tē) *n., pl.* **-ties** [LME. *penalyte* < ML. *poenalitas* < L. *poenalis*: see PENAL] **1.** a punishment fixed by law, as for a crime or breach of contract **2.** the disadvantage, suffering, handicap, etc. imposed upon an offender or one who does not fulfill a contract or obligation, as a fine or forfeit **3.** any unfortunate consequence or result of an act or condition **4.** *Sports* any disadvantage, as a loss of yardage or the removal of a player, imposed because of infraction of a rule

penalty box *Hockey* an enclosure off the rink for players temporarily removed from the game as a penalty

pen·ance (pen′əns) *n.* [ME. < OFr. *penance* < L. *paenitentia, poenitentia < paenitens: see* PENITENT] **1.** *R.C.Ch. & Orthodox Eastern Ch.* a) a sacrament involving the confession of sin, repentance, and submission to the satisfaction imposed, followed by absolution by a priest *b)* the satisfaction so imposed, as the recital of certain prayers **2.** any voluntary act of reparation, self-punishment, etc. to show repentance for a sin or wrongdoing —*vt.* **-anced, -anc·ing** to impose a penance on —**do penance** to perform an act of penance

Pe·nang (pi naŋ′) **1.** island off the NW coast of the Malay Peninsula: 110 sq. mi. **2.** state of the Federation of Malaya, including this island & a section of the mainland opposite it: 398 sq. mi.; pop. 714,000 **3.** seaport on the NE coast of Penang island: pop. 235,000

pe·na·tes (pi nāt′ēz) *n.pl.* [L., akin to *penus*, inner part of temple of Vesta: for IE. base see PENETRATE] the household gods of the ancient Romans: see LARES AND PENATES

pence (pens; *in compounds*, pəns) *n.* [ME. *pens*, contr. of

penies, pl. of *peny*, PENNY [Brit.] *pl. of* PENNY: used also in compounds [*twopence*]

pen·cel (pen′s′l) *n.* [ME. < Anglo-Fr., contr. < OFr. *penoncel*, dim. of *penon*, PENNON] [Archaic] a small pennon, or narrow flag

pen·chant (pen′chənt; *Fr.* pän shän′) *n.* [Fr. < *pencher*, to incline < VL. *pendicare < L. *pendere*, to hang: see PEND] a strong liking or fondness; inclination; taste

Pen·chi (bun′chē′) city in Liaoning province, NE China, near Shenyang: pop. 449,000

pen·cil (pen′s′l) *n.* [ME. *pencel* < MFr. *pincel* < VL. *penicellus < L. *penicillus*, a brush < dim. of *penis*, a tail, PENIS: mod. sense & form infl. by PEN[2]] **1.** orig., an artist's small, fine brush **2.** the individual style or ability of an artist **3.** a pointed, rod-shaped instrument of wood, metal, etc. with a center stick of graphite, crayon, etc. that is sharpened to a point for marking, writing, and drawing **4.** something shaped or used like a pencil; specif., *a)* a small cosmetic stick as for touching up the eyebrows *b)* a stick of some medicated substance [a styptic *pencil*] **5.** a series of lines or rays coming to or spreading out from a point **6.** *Math.* a set of lines or planes passing through a given point or points and satisfying a given equation; as *a)* all the lines passing through a given point *b)* all the planes passing through a given line *c)* all the circles lying in a given plane and passing through two fixed points —*vt.* **-ciled** or **-cilled, -cil·ing** or **-cil·ling** **1.** to mark, write, or draw with or as with a pencil **2.** to use a pencil on —**pen′cil·er, pen′cil·ler** *n.*

pend (pend) *vi.* [OFr. *pendre* < L. *pendere*, to hang] **1.** to await judgment or decision **2.** [Dial.] to depend

pend·ant (pen′dənt) *n.* [ME. *pendaunt* < OFr. *pendant*, prp. of *pendre* < L. *pendere*, to hang < base *(s)pen(d)-, to pull, stretch, whence SPIN] **1.** an ornamental hanging object, as from an earring **2.** the stem and ring of a pocket watch **3.** either of a pair; match or companion piece **4.** anything hanging, as the pull chain on a lamp **5.** *Archit.* a decorative piece suspended from a ceiling or roof: used esp. in Gothic architecture —*adj. same as* PENDENT —**pend′ant·ly** *adv.*

Pen·del·i·kón (pen del′ē kôn′) mountain in Attica, Greece, northeast of Athens: known for its fine marble: 3,638 ft.

pend·en·cy (pen′dən sē) *n.* the state or condition of being pendent or pending

pend·ent (-dənt) *adj.* [ME. *pendaunt*: see PENDANT] **1.** hanging; suspended **2.** overhanging **3.** undecided; pending —*n. same as* PENDANT —**pend′ent·ly** *adv.*

pen·den·tive (pen den′tiv) *n.* [Fr. *pendentif* < L. *pendens*, prp. of *pendere*, to hang: see PENDANT] *Archit.* one of the triangular pieces of vaulting springing from the corners of a rectangular area, serving to support a rounded or polygonal dome: usually supported by a single pier

pend·ing (pen′diŋ) *adj.* [prp. of PEND, after Fr. *pendant*, L. *pendens*] **1.** not decided, determined, or established [a *pending* lawsuit, patent *pending*] **2.** about to happen; impending —*prep.* **1.** throughout the course or process of; during [*pending* the review] **2.** while awaiting; until [*pending* his arrival]

Pend O·reille (pän′də rā′) **1.** river in N Ida. & NE Wash., flowing from Pend Oreille Lake into the Columbia River: see CLARK FORK **2.** lake in N Ida.: 148 sq. mi.

pen·drag·on (pen drag′ən) *n.* [LME. < W. < *pen*, head + *dragon*, dragon symbol, war standard, hence leader < L. *draco* (gen. *draconis*), a cohort's standard] supreme chief or leader: a title used in ancient Britain

pen·du·lous (pen′joo ləs, -dyoo-) *adj.* [L. *pendulus* < *pendere*, to hang: see PENDANT] **1.** hanging freely or loosely; suspended so as to swing **2.** hanging or bending downward; drooping **3.** [Now Rare] vacillating; uncertain —**pen′du·lous·ly** *adv.* —**pen′du·lous·ness** *n.*

pen·du·lum (pen′joo ləm, -dyoo-, -d′l əm) *n.* [ModL. < neut. of L. *pendulus*: see prec.] a body hung from a fixed point so as to swing freely to and fro under the combined forces of gravity and momentum: often used in regulating the movement of clocks —**pen′du·lar** *adj.*

Pe·nel·o·pe (pə nel′ə pē) [L. < Gr. *Pēnelopē*] **1.** a feminine name: dim. *Penny* **2.** Ulysses' wife, who waited faithfully for his return

☆**pe·ne·plain, pe·ne·plane** (pē′nə plān′) *n.* [L. *pene*, *paene*, almost (see PASSION) + PLAIN[1], PLANE[2]] land worn down by erosion almost to a level plain

pen·e·tra·ble (pen′i trə b′l) *adj.* [ME. < L. *penetrabilis*] that can be penetrated —**pen′e·tra·bil′i·ty** *n.* —**pen′e·tra·bly** *adv.*

pen·e·tra·li·a (pen′ə trā′lē ə) *n.pl.* [L., neut. pl. of *penetralis*, penetrating, inward] **1.** the innermost parts, as of a temple **2.** things kept private or secret

pen·e·trance (pen′ə trəns) *n.* [< PENETR(ATE) + -ANCE] *Genetics* the degree of regularity with which a gene produces its specific effect in its carriers in a population

pen·e·trant (pen′ə trənt) *adj.* [L. *penetrans*, prp. of *penetrare*] sharp; acute; penetrating —*n.* a thing that penetrates

pen·e·trate (-trāt′) *vt.* **-trat′ed, -trat′ing** [< L. *penetratus*, pp. of *penetrare*, to pierce into, penetrate < base of *penitus*, inward, far within (< *penus*, store of food, storeroom, sanctuary of temple of Vesta < IE. base *pen-, to feed, food) + (*in*)*trare*, ENTER] **1.** to pass into; find or force a way into or through; enter by or as by piercing

2. to see into the interior of **3.** to have an effect throughout; spread through; permeate **4.** to affect or move deeply; imbue **5.** to grasp mentally; understand —*vi.* **1.** to make a way into or through something; pierce **2.** to have a marked effect on the mind or emotions

pen·e·trat·ing (-trāt′iŋ) *adj.* **1.** that can penetrate [a *penetrating* oil] **2.** sharp; piercing [a *penetrating* sound or smell] **3.** that has entered deeply [a *penetrating* wound] **4.** keen or acute; discerning [a *penetrating* mind] Also **pen′e·tra′tive** (-trāt′iv) —**pen′e·trat′ing·ly, pen′e·trat′ive·ly** *adv.*

pen·e·tra·tion (pen′ə trā′shən) *n.* [LL. *penetratio*] **1.** the act or power of penetrating **2.** the depth to which something penetrates, as a projectile into a target, or a military force into enemy territory **3.** the extension of the influence of a country over a weaker one by means of commercial investments, loans, diplomatic maneuvers, etc. **4.** keenness of mind; discernment; insight

☆**pen·e·trom·e·ter** (pen′ə träm′ə tər) *n.* [< PENETR(ATE) + -o- + -METER] **1.** an instrument used to measure the hardness of a substance **2.** an instrument that measures the penetrating power of X-rays

Pe·ne·us (pi nē′əs) *ancient name of* PINIÓS

pen·gö (pen′gö) *n., pl.* **-gö, -gös** [Hung.] the former monetary unit of Hungary, replaced by the forint (1946)

pen·guin (peŋ′gwin, pen′-) *n.* [prob. < W. *pen gwyn,* lit., white head (or cognate Bret. *pen gouin*): ? in reference to a white headland on a N Atlantic island, near which they were found] **1.** *former name of* GREAT AUK **2.** any of an order (Sphenisciformes) of flightless birds found in the Southern Hemisphere, having webbed feet and paddlelike flippers for swimming and diving

pen·hold·er (pen′hōl′dər) *n.* **1.** the handle or holder into which a pen point fits **2.** a container or rack for a pen or pens

pen·i·cil·late (pen′ə sil′it, -āt) *adj.* [< L. *penicillus* (see PENCIL) + -ATE¹] *Biol.* **1.** pencil-shaped **2.** having a tufted tip of fine hairs Also **pen′i·cil′li·form′** (-form′) —**pen′i·cil·late·ly** *adv.* —**pen′i·cil·la′tion** *n.*

pen·i·cil·lin (-in) *n.* [< ff. + -IN¹] any of a group of isomeric, antibiotic compounds with the general formula $C_9H_{11}N_2O_4SR$, obtained from the filtrates of certain molds (esp., *Penicillium notatum* and *Penicillium chrysogen*) or produced synthetically

pen·i·cil·li·um (-ē əm) *n., pl.* **-li·ums, -li·a** (-ə) [ModL. < L. *penicillus* (see PENCIL): from the tuftlike ends of the conidiophores] any of a genus (*Penicillium*) of imperfect fungi growing as green mold on stale bread, ripening cheese, decaying fruit, etc.: penicillin is derived from some species

pen·in·su·la (pə nin′sə lə, -syoo-) *n.* [L. *paeninsula* < *paene*, almost (see PASSION) + *insula*, an ISLE] **1.** a land area almost entirely surrounded by water and connected with the mainland by an isthmus **2.** any land area projecting out into water —**pen·in′su·lar** *adj.*

pe·nis (pē′nis) *n., pl.* **-nis·es, -nes** (-nēz) [L. *penis,* tail, penis < IE. base **pes-,* whence Sans. *pásas,* Gr. *peos,* OE. *fæsl,* penis] the male organ of sexual intercourse: in mammals it is also the organ through which urine is ejected —**pe′nile** (-nīl, -nil) *adj.*

pen·i·tence (pen′ə təns) *n.* [ME. < OFr. < L. *paenitentia*] the state of being penitent; repentance
SYN.—**penitence** implies sorrow over having sinned or done wrong; **repentance** implies full realization of one's sins or wrongs and a will to change one's ways; **contrition** implies a deep, crushing sorrow for one's sins, with a true purpose of amendment; **compunction** implies a pricking of the conscience and therefore suggests a sharp but passing feeling of uneasiness about wrongdoing; **remorse** implies a deep and torturing sense of guilt; **regret** may refer to sorrow over any unfortunate occurrence as well as over a fault or act of one's own

pen·i·tent (-tənt) *adj.* [ME. < OFr. < L. *paenitens,* prp. of *paenitere,* to repent, prob. akin to *paene,* scarcely: see PASSION] sorry or ashamed for having done wrong and willing to atone; repentant —*n.* **1.** a penitent person **2.** *R.C.Ch.* a person undergoing the sacrament of penance —**pen′i·tent·ly** *adv.*

pen·i·ten·tial (pen′ə ten′shəl) *adj.* [ML.(Ec.) *penitentialis*] of, constituting, or expressing penitence or penance —*n.* **1.** a penitent **2.** a list or book of rules governing religious penance —**pen′i·ten′tial·ly** *adv.*

pen·i·ten·tia·ry (pen′ə ten′shə rē) *adj.* [ML. *penitentiarius, poenitentiarius* (form and meaning infl. by association with L. *poena:* see PENAL) < L. *paenitentia < paenitens,* PENITENT] **1.** of or for penance **2.** used in punishing, disciplining, and reforming **3.** making one liable to imprisonment in a penitentiary **4.** of or in a penitentiary —*n., pl.* **-ries** **1.** [ML. *penitentiaria < the adj.*] a prison;

specif., *a)* [Brit.] *same as* REFORMATORY ☆*b)* a State or Federal prison for persons convicted of serious crimes **2.** [ML.(Ec.) *penitentiarius < the adj.*] *R.C.Ch.* an office or tribunal headed by a cardinal (**Grand Penitentiary**) and dealing with matters of penance, confession, dispensation, absolution, etc.

Pen·ki (bun′chē′) *same as* PENCHI

pen·knife (pen′nīf′) *n., pl.* **-knives′** (-nīvz′) a small pocketknife; orig., one used in making quill pens

☆**pen·light, pen·lite** (pen′līt′) *n.* a flashlight that is about as small and slender as a fountain pen

pen·man (pen′mən) *n., pl.* **-men** (-mən) **1.** a person employed to write or copy; scribe **2.** a person skilled in penmanship **3.** an author

pen·man·ship (-ship′) *n.* **1.** handwriting considered as an art or skill **2.** a style of handwriting

Penn (pen), **William** 1644–1718; Eng. Quaker leader: founder of Pennsylvania

Penn., Penna. Pennsylvania

pen·na (pen′ə) *n., pl.* **-nae** (-ē) [L.: see PEN²] any of the feathers forming the general outer covering, or contour, of a bird —**pen·na·ceous** (pe nā′shəs) *adj.*

pen name a name used by an author in place of his true name; nom de plume —*SYN.* see PSEUDONYM

pen·nant (pen′ənt) *n.* [< PENNON, altered after PENDANT] **1.** any long, narrow, usually triangular flag, as used for naval signaling, a school banner, etc. **2.** any such flag symbolizing a championship, esp. in baseball

pen·nate (pen′āt) *adj.* [L. *pennatus,* winged < *penna,* quill, wing: see PEN²] *Bot. same as* PINNATE

Pen·nel (pen′l), **Joseph** 1857–1926; U.S. etcher, book illustrator, & writer

pen·ni (pen′ē) *n., pl.* **-ni·a** (-ə), **-nis, -ni** [Finn. < OFris. *penni* or LG. *pennig,* PENNY] a copper Finnish coin equal to 1/100 markka

pen·ni·less (pen′i lis) *adj.* without even a penny; extremely poor —**pen′ni·less·ness** *n.*

Pen·nine Alps (pen′īn, -in) division of the W Alps, along the Swiss-Italian border, northeast of the Graian Alps: highest peak, c. 15,200 ft.

Pennine Chain range of hills in N England, extending from the Cheviot Hills southward to Derbyshire & Staffordshire: highest point, c. 3,000 ft.

pen·non (pen′ən) *n.* [ME. *penon* < OFr. < *penne,* a feather: see PEN²] **1.** a long, narrow, triangular or swallow-tailed flag borne on a lance as an ensign, as formerly by knights and lancers **2.** any flag or pennant **3.** a pinion; wing

pen·non·cel (-sel′) *n. same as* PENCEL

Penn·syl·va·ni·a (pen′s'l vān′yə, -vā′nē ə) [after Wm. PENN or his father + L. *sylvania,* wooded (land), fem. of *sylvanus < sylva* (silva), forest] Middle Atlantic State of the NE U.S.: one of the 13 original States; 45,333 sq. mi.; pop. 11,794,000; cap. Harrisburg: abbrev. **Pa., PA**

☆**Pennsylvania Dutch** **1.** the descendants of early German immigrants, principally from the Palatinate, who settled mainly in E Pennsylvania **2.** their High German dialect: also called **Pennsylvania German** **3.** their form of folk art, characterized by carved or painted, stylized decorations of flowers, fruits, birds, etc., as on furniture —**Penn′syl·va′ni·a-Dutch** *adj.*

☆**Penn·syl·va·ni·an** (pen′s'l vān′yən, -vā′nē ən) *adj.* **1.** of Pennsylvania **2.** designating or of the sixth period of the Paleozoic Era in N. America following the Mississippian and preceding the Permian —*n.* a native or inhabitant of Pennsylvania —**the Pennsylvanian** the Pennsylvanian Period or its rocks: see GEOLOGY, chart

pen·ny (pen′ē) *n., pl.* **-nies;** for 1 (esp. collectively), **pence** [ME. *peny* < OE. *penig, pening,* akin to G. *pfennig:* < ? early WGmc. borrowing < L. *pannus,* cloth (used as medium of exchange)] **1.** in the United Kingdom and certain Commonwealth countries, *a)* a unit of currency equal to one twelfth of a shilling: abbrev. **d.** *b)* a unit in the new decimal monetary system (Feb., 1971), equal to one 100th part of a pound, or to 2.4 old penny: in full, **new penny:** abbrev. **p** ☆**2.** a U.S. or Canadian cent **3.** any of several other low-value coins, as a denarius **4.** a sum of money: now chiefly in the following phrases —**a pretty penny** [Colloq.] a large sum of money —**turn an honest penny** to earn money fairly and honestly

-pen·ny (pen′ē; *chiefly Brit.,* pə nē) *a combining form meaning* costing (a specified number of) pennies [*sixpenny*]: formerly applied to nails to indicate the cost per hundred, but now simply a measure of their length

☆**penny ante** **1.** a game of poker in which the ante is limited to one cent **2.** any trifling undertaking

penny arcade a public amusement hall with various coin-operated game and vending machines

penny dreadful [Brit. Colloq.] a cheap book or magazine containing stories of crime, terror, etc.

penny pincher a person who is extremely frugal or stingy —**pen′ny-pinch′ing** *n., adj.*

pen·ny·roy·al (pen′ē roi′əl) *n.* [altered < earlier *pulyol ryal* < Anglo-Fr. *puliol real* < OFr. *poliol, pouliol* (< L. *pulegium,* fleabane) + *real,* ROYAL] **1.** a strongly scented,

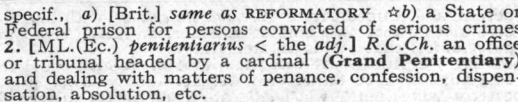

PENGUIN
(to 4 ft. high)

perennial European mint (*Mentha pulegium*) with bluish-lavender flowers **2.** a similar N. American mint (*Hedeoma pulegioides*) that yields an aromatic oil

pen·ny·weight (pen′ē wāt′) *n.* a unit of weight, equal to 24 grains or 1/20 ounce troy avoir.: abbrev. dwt., pwt.

pen·ny-wise (pen′ē wīz′) *adj.* careful or thrifty in regard to small matters —**penny-wise and pound-foolish** careful or thrifty in small matters but careless or wasteful in major ones

pen·ny·wort (-wurt′) *n.* [ME. *penywort:* see PENNY & WORT²] any of various plants with small round leaves growing in crevices of rocks and walls or in marshy places, as any of a genus (*Hydrocotyle*) of perennial plants of the parsley family and a small N. American plant (*Obolaria virginica*) of the gentian family

pen·ny·worth (-wurth′) *n.* **1.** the amount that can be bought for one penny **2.** the value of something bought, with regard to the price paid **3.** a small amount

Pe·nob·scot (pə näb′skät, -skət) [< Algonquian name, lit., ? it forks on the white rocks] river in C Me., flowing south into an arm (**Penobscot Bay**) of the Atlantic: c. 350 mi. —*n.* **1.** *pl.* **-scots, -scot** a member of a tribe of Indians living around this river **2.** their Algonquian dialect —*adj.* of the Penobscots

pe·nol·o·gy (pē näl′ə jē) *n.* [< L. *poena* or Gr. *poinē*, punishment (see PENAL) + -LOGY] the study of the reformation and rehabilitation of criminals and of the management of prisons —**pe·no·log·i·cal** (pē′nə läj′i k'l) *adj.* —**pe·nol′o·gist** *n.*

pen pal a person, esp. a stranger in another country, with whom one arranges a regular exchange of letters

Pen·sa·co·la (pen′sə kō′lə) [< Choctaw, hair people < *pansha*, hair + *okla*, people: cf. OKLAHOMA] seaport in NW Fla., on an inlet (**Pensacola Bay**) of the Gulf of Mexico: pop. 60,000

pen·sile (pen′sil) *adj.* [L. *pensilis* < pp. of *pendere*, to hang: see PENDANT] **1.** hanging **2.** having or building a hanging nest, as the Baltimore oriole

pen·sion (pen′shən; *for n.* 3, pän′sē än′, *Fr.* pän syōn′) *n.* [ME. *pensioun* < MFr. < L. *pensio*, a paying < pp. of *pendere*, to weigh, pay, orig., to hang, weigh: see PENDANT] **1.** a payment, not wages, made regularly to a person (or to his family) who has fulfilled certain conditions of service, reached a certain age, etc. [a soldier's *pension*, an old-age *pension*] **2.** a regular payment, not a fee, given to an artist, etc. by his patron; subsidy **3.** in France and other continental countries *a)* a boarding house *b)* room and board —*vt.* to grant a pension to —**pension off** to dismiss from service with a pension —**pen′sion·a·ble** *adj.*

pen·sion·ar·y (-er′ē) *adj.* [ML. *pensionarius*] **1.** of or constituting a pension **2.** receiving a pension **3.** dependent; hireling —*n., pl.* **-ar′ies** **1.** a pensioner **2.** a hireling; tool; puppet

‡pen·si·o·ne (pen syō′ne) *n., pl.* **-ni** (-nē) [It.] *same as* PENSION (*n.* 3)

pen·sion·er (pen′shən ər) *n.* [ME. < MFr. *pensionnier* < ML. *pensionarius*] **1.** a person who receives a pension; pensionary **2.** a student who pays his own expenses at Cambridge University, England **3.** [Obs.] a gentleman-at-arms

pen·sive (pen′siv) *adj.* [ME. *pensif* < OFr. < *penser*, to think, reflect < L. *pensare*, to weigh, consider, freq. of *pendere*, to weigh: see PENDANT] **1.** thinking deeply or seriously, often of sad or melancholy things **2.** expressing deep thoughtfulness, often with some sadness —**pen′-sive·ly** *adv.* —**pen′sive·ness** *n.*

SYN.—**pensive** suggests a dreamy, often somewhat sad or melancholy concentration of thought [the *pensive* look in her eye]; **contemplative** implies intent concentration of thought as on some abstract matter, often connoting this as a habitual practice [a *contemplative* scholar]; **reflective** suggests an orderly, often analytical turning over in the mind with the aim of reaching some definite understanding [after a *reflective* pause he answered]; **meditative**, on the other hand, implies a quiet and sustained musing, but with no definite intention of understanding or reaching a conclusion [a *meditative* walk in the cloister]

☆pen·ste·mon (pen stē′mən, pen′stə-) *n.* [ModL. < Gr. *penta-*, five + *stēmōn*, warp: see STAMEN] any of a large genus (*Pentstemon*) of chiefly N. American plants of the figwort family, having five stamens, the fifth of which is bearded and sterile, and bearing tubular, showy, white, pink, red, blue, or purple flowers

pen·stock (pen′stäk′) *n.* [PEN¹ + STOCK] **1.** a gate or sluice used in controlling the flow of water ☆**2.** a tube or trough for carrying water to a water wheel

pent (pent) *alt. pt. & pp.* of PEN¹ —*adj.* held or kept in; confined; penned (often with *up*)

pen·ta- (pen′tə) [Gr. *penta-* < *pente*, FIVE] *a combining form meaning* five [*pentamerous*]: also, before a vowel, **pent-**

pen·ta·chlo·ro·phe·nol (pen′tə klōr′ə fē′nōl, -nōl) *n.* [PENTA- + CHLORO- + PHENOL] a white powder, C₆Cl₅OH, produced by chlorinating phenol: used as a herbicide, fungicide, wood preservative, etc.

pen·ta·cle (pen′tə k'l) *n.* [MFr. < ML. *pentaculum* < Gr. *penta-*, five + L. *-culum*, dim. suffix] a symbol, usually a five-pointed star, formerly used in magic

pen·tad (-tad) *n.* [Gr. *pentas* (gen. *pentados*) < *pente*, FIVE] **1.** the number five **2.** a series or group of five **3.** a five-

year period **4.** *Chem.* an element or radical with a valence of five

pen·ta·dac·tyl (pen′tə dak′t'l) *adj.* [L. *pentadactylus* < Gr. *pentadaktylos:* see PENTA- & DACTYL] having five fingers or toes on each hand or foot

pen·ta·e·ryth·ri·tol (pen′tə i rith′rə tōl′) *n.* [PENTA- + ERYTHRITOL] a colorless, crystalline compound, C(CH₂OH)₄, prepared by reacting acetaldehyde with formaldehyde: used in the manufacture of alkyd resins, explosives, insecticides, etc.

pen·ta·gon (pen′tə gän′) *n.* [L. *pentagonum* < Gr. *pentagonon:* see PENTA- & -GON] a plane figure with five angles and five sides —☆**the Pentagon** a five-sided building in Arlington, Virginia, in which the main offices of the U.S. Department of Defense are located; hence, the U.S. military establishment —**pen·tag·o·nal** (pen tag′ə n'l) *adj.* —**pen·tag′o·nal·ly** *adv.*

pen·ta·gram (-gram′) *n.* [Gr. *pentagrammon*, neut. of *pentagrammos*, having five lines: see PENTA- & -GRAM] **1.** *same as* PENTACLE **2.** any figure with five lines

pen·ta·he·dron (pen′tə hē′drən) *n., pl.* **-drons, -dra** (-drə) [ModL.: see PENTA- & -HEDRON] a solid figure with five plane surfaces —**pen′ta·he′dral** *adj.*

pen·tam·er·ous (pen tam′ər əs) *adj.* [PENTA- + -MEROUS] *Biol.* made up of five parts or divisions: also written **5-merous**

pen·tam·e·ter (-ə tər) *n.* [L. < Gr. *pentametros:* see PENTA- & METER¹] **1.** a line of verse containing five metrical feet or measures; esp., English iambic pentameter (Ex.: "Hĕ jĕsts | ăt scȧrs | whŏ nēv | ĕr fēlt | ă woúnd") **2.** verse consisting of pentameters; heroic verse —*adj.* having five metrical feet or measures

pen·tane (pen′tān) *n.* [PENT- + -ANE] any of three known isomeric, colorless hydrocarbons, C₅H₁₂, of the methane series, occurring in petroleum, etc.: used as a solvent, in low-temperature thermometers, etc.

pen·tan·gu·lar (pen taŋ′gyə lər) *adj.* [PENT- + ANGULAR] having five angles

pen·ta·nol (pen′tə nōl′) *n.* [PENTAN(E) + -OL] *same as* AMYL ALCOHOL

pen·ta·ploid (-ploid′) *adj.* [PENTA- + -PLOID] *Biol.* having five times the haploid number of chromosomes —*n.* a pentaploid cell or organism —**pen′ta·ploi′dy** *n.*

pen·ta·quine (pen′tə kwēn′, -kwin) *n.* [PENTA- + QUIN-(OLIN)E] a synthetic antimalarial drug, C₁₈H₂₇N₃O, used chiefly in the form of its phosphate

pen·tar·chy (pen′tär kē′) *n., pl.* **-chies** [Gr. *pentarchia:* see PENTA- & -ARCHY] **1.** a federation of five states, each under an individual leader or ruler **2.** government by five rulers

pen·ta·stich (pen′tə stik′) *n.* [Gr. *pentastichos:* see PENTA- & STICH] a poem or stanza of five lines

Pen·ta·teuch (-tōōk′, -tyōōk′) *n.* [LL.(Ec.) *Pentateuchus* < Gr.(Ec.) *pentateuchos*, composed of five books < *penta-*, FIVE + *teuchos*, an implement, book: for IE. base see DOUGHTY] the first five books of the Bible

pen·tath·lon (pen tath′län, -lən) *n.* [Gr. *pentathlon* < *penta-*, five + *athlon*, a contest] **1.** an athletic contest in which each contestant takes part in five events (long jump, javelin throw, 200-meter dash, discus throw, and 1500-meter run) **2.** in the Olympic games, a contest consisting of five events (5000-meter cross-country horseback ride, 4000-meter cross-country run, 300-meter swim, foil fencing, and pistol shooting): in full **modern pentathlon**

pen·ta·ton·ic (pen′tə tän′ik) *adj.* [see PENTA- & TONIC] designating or of a musical scale having only five tones

pen·ta·va·lent (pen tə vā′lənt) *adj.* **1.** having a valence of five **2.** *same as* QUINQUEVALENT (sense 1)

☆pen·ta·zo·cine (-zō′sēn) *n.* [PENTA- + (A)Z(O)- + -ocin, suffix for an 8-membered ring + -e] a pain-killing, synthetic drug derived from coal tar: used in place of morphine because it is nonaddictive

Pen·te·cost (pen′tə kôst′, -käst′) *n.* [ME. < LL.(Ec.) *pentecoste* < Gr.(Ec.) *pentēkostē* (*hēmera*), the fiftieth (day) after Passover < *pentēkonta*, fifty < *pente*, FIVE] **1.** *same as* SHAVUOT **2.** a Christian festival on the seventh Sunday after Easter, celebrating the descent of the Holy Spirit upon the Apostles; Whitsunday

Pen·te·cos·tal (pen′tə kôs′t'l, -käs′-) *adj.* **1.** of or relating to Pentecost ☆**2.** designating or of any of various Protestant fundamentalist sects often stressing direct inspiration by the Holy Spirit, as in glossolalia

Pen·tel·i·cus (pen tel′i kəs) L. *name of* PENDELIKÓN

Pen·tel·i·kon (pen tel′i kän′) *same as* PENDELIKÓN

pent·house (pent′hous′) *n.* [altered (after HOUSE) < *pentice* < ME. *pentis*, penthouse < MFr. *apentis* < ML. *appenticium* < LL. *appendicium*, lit., an appendage < L. *appendere:* see APPEND] **1.** a small structure, esp. one with a sloping roof, attached to a larger building **2.** a sloping roof, or, sometimes, an awning, etc. extending out from a wall or building **3.** an apartment or other houselike structure built on the roof of a building

Pent·land Firth (pent′lənd) channel between the mainland of Scotland & the Orkney Islands: 6-8 mi. wide

pent·land·ite (pent′lən dīt′) *n.* [Fr., after J. B. *Pentland*, 19th-c. Ir. mineralogist] an isometric mineral, (Fe,Ni)₉S₈, the principal ore of nickel

pen·to·bar·bi·tal sodium (pen′tə bär′bi tôl′) [PENTO- for PENTA- (because of methylbutyl five-carbon group) + BARBITAL] an odorless, white, crystalline powder,

$C_{11}H_{17}N_2O_3Na$, soluble in water: used in medicine as a sedative, hypnotic, and analgesic

pen·tode (pen′tōd) *n.* [PENT(A)- + -ODE[1]] an electron tube containing five electrodes, usually a cathode, anode, and three grids: used as a voltage amplifier

☆**pen·tom·ic** (pen tăm′ik) *adj.* [PEN(TA)- + (A)TOMIC] designating or of a military force organized primarily in units of five, esp. for nuclear warfare

pen·to·san (pen′tə san′) *n.* [PENTOS(E) + -AN] any of a group of plant carbohydrates which form pentoses upon undergoing hydrolysis

pen·tose (pen′tōs) *n.* [PENT- + -OSE[1]] any of a group of monosaccharides having a composition corresponding to the formula $C_5H_{10}O_5$, including ribose, arabinose, etc.

pen·to·side (pen′tə sid′) *n.* [PENT(OSE) + (GLYC)OSIDE] a sugar derivative that yields a pentose on hydrolysis

☆**Pen·to·thal Sodium** (-thal′) [*pento-* for PENTA- (because of methylbutyl five-carbon group) + *th*(iobarbiturate) + -AL (as in VERONAL, BARBITAL)] *a trademark for* THIOPENTAL SODIUM: often clipped to **Pentothal**

pent·ox·ide (pen tăk′sid) *n.* [PENT- + OXIDE] an oxide that contains five oxygen atoms in its molecule

☆**pent·ste·mon** (pent stē′mən, pent′stə-) *n. same as* PENSTEMON

pent-up (pent′up′) *adj.* held in check; curbed; confined [*pent-up* emotion]

pen·tyl (pent′'l) *n.* [PENT(A)- + -YL] *same as* AMYL

pen·tyl·ene·tet·ra·zol (pen′t'l ēn tet′rə zôl′, -zōl′) *n.* [*pent(a-meth)ylene-tetrazol(e)*] a white, crystalline powder, $C_6H_{10}N_4$, used as a circulatory and respiratory stimulant and formerly in shock therapy

☆**pe·nu·che, pe·nu·chi** (pə nōō′chē) *n.* [var. of PANOCHA] a candy resembling fudge, made of brown sugar, milk, butter, and, sometimes, nuts

☆**pe·nuch·le, pe·nuck·le** (pē′nuk′'l) *n. same as* PINOCHLE

pe·nult (pē′nult, pi nult′) *n.* [L. *paenultima* < *paene*, almost (see PASSION) + *ultima*, fem. of *ultimus*, last: see ULTIMATE] the one next to the last; specif., the second last syllable in a word: also **pe·nul′ti·ma** (pi nul′tə mə)

pe·nul·ti·mate (pi nul′tə mit) *adj.* [< prec., after ULTIMATE] 1. next to the last 2. of the penult —*n.* the penult —**pe·nul′ti·mate·ly** *adv.*

pe·num·bra (pi num′brə) *n., pl.* **-brae** (-brē), **-bras** [ModL. < *paene*, almost (see PASSION) + *umbra*, shade] 1. the partly lighted area surrounding the complete shadow of a body, as the moon, in full eclipse: see ECLIPSE, illus. 2. the less dark region surrounding the dark central area of a sunspot 3. a vague, indefinite, or borderline area —**pe·num′bral** *adj.*

pe·nu·ri·ous (pə nyoor′ē əs, -noor′-) *adj.* [ML. *penuriosus* < L. *penuria*: see ff.] 1. unwilling to part with money or possessions; mean; miserly; stingy 2. characterized by extreme poverty; impoverished —*SYN.* see STINGY[1] —**pe·nu′ri·ous·ly** *adv.* —**pe·nu′ri·ous·ness** *n.*

pen·u·ry (pen′yə rē) *n.* [ME. *pennury* < L. *penuria*, want, scarcity < *paene*, scarcely: see PASSION] lack of money, property, or necessities; extreme poverty; destitution —*SYN.* see POVERTY

☆**Pe·nu·ti·an** (pə nōōt′ē ən, pə nōō′shən) *n.* [arbitrary coinage < AmInd. (Wintun) *pen*, two + (Miwok) *uti*, two + -AN] a linguistic phylum or group of remotely related language families, including the Chinook, Sahaptin, etc. and various isolated languages, in W N. America

Pen·za (pen′zä) city in the SW R.S.F.S.R., southeast of Moscow: pop. 324,000

Pen·zance (pen zans′) city in SW Cornwall, England, on the English Channel: pop. 19,000

pe·on (pē′än, -ən; *for 3, Brit.* pyōōn) *n.* [< Sp. *peón* or (in sense 2) Port. *peão*, both < ML. *pedo*, foot soldier: see PAWN[2]] 1. in Latin America, *a)* a person of the laboring class *b)* formerly, a person forced to work off a debt or to perform penal servitude ☆2. in the SW U.S., a person forced into servitude to work off a debt 3. in India, *a)* a foot soldier *b)* a native policeman *c)* an attendant or footman 4. an unskilled or exploited laborer

pe·on·age (pē′ə nij) *n.* [see -AGE] 1. the condition of a peon 2. the system by which debtors or legal prisoners are held in servitude to labor for their creditors or for persons who lease their services from the state

pe·o·ny (pē′ə nē) *n., pl.* **-nies** [ME. *pione* < OE. *peonie* & OFr. *peoine*, both < L. *paeonia* < Gr. *paiōnia* < *Paiōn*, epithet of Apollo, physician of the gods: from its former medicinal use] 1. any of a genus (*Paeonia*) of perennial, often double-flowered, plants of the buttercup family, with large pink, white, red, or yellow, showy flowers 2. the flower

peo·ple (pē′p'l) *n., pl.* **-ple**; *for 1 & 10,* **-ples** [ME. *peple* < Anglo-Fr. *poeple, people* < OFr. *pople* < L. *populus*, nation, crowd < ?] 1. *a)* all the persons of a racial, national, religious, or linguistic group; nation, race, etc. [the *peoples* of the world] *b)* a group of persons with common traditional, historical, or cultural ties, as distinct from racial or political unity [the Jewish *people*] 2. the persons belonging to a certain place, community, or class [the *people* of Iowa, *people* of wealth] 3. the members of a

group under the leadership, influence, or control of a particular person or body, as a number of servants, royal subjects, etc. 4. the members of (someone's) class, occupation, set, race, tribe, etc. [the miner spoke for his *people*] 5. one's relatives or ancestors; family 6. persons without wealth, influence, privilege, or distinction; populace 7. the citizens or electorate of a state 8. persons considered indefinitely [what will *people* say?] 9. human beings, as distinct from other animals 10. a group of creatures [the ant *people*] —*vt.* **-pled, -pling** [Fr. *peupler* < the *n.*] to fill with or as with people; populate; stock

people's front *same as* POPULAR FRONT

☆**People's party** *see* POPULIST

Pe·or·i·a (pē ôr′ē ə) [< Fr. *Peouarea,* a tribal name < Algonquian *piwarea,* ? he carries a pack] city in C Ill., on the Illinois River: pop. 127,000

☆**pep** (pep) *n.* [< PEPPER] [Colloq.] energy; vigor; liveliness; spirit —*vt.* **pepped, pep′ping** [Colloq.] to fill with pep; invigorate; stimulate (with *up*)

pep·er·o·ni (pep′ə rō′nē) *n. same as* PEPPERONI

Pep·in the Short (pep′in) 715?–768 A.D.; king of the Franks (751–768): father of CHARLEMAGNE

pep·los, pep·lus (pep′ləs) *n.* [Gr. *peplos*] a large shawl or scarf worn draped about the body by women in ancient Greece

pep·lum (pep′ləm) *n., pl.* **-lums, -la** (-lə) [L. < Gr. *peplos*: cf. prec.] 1. orig., a peplos 2. a flounce or short, flared flap attached at the waist of a dress, blouse, coat, etc. and extending around the hips

pe·po (pē′pō) *n., pl.* **-pos** [L., species of large melon: see PUMPKIN] any fleshy gourd fruit with a hard rind and many seeds, as the melon, squash, etc.

pep·per (pep′ər) *n.* [see PLURAL, II, D, 3 [ME. *peper* < OE. *pipor* < WGmc. borrowing < L. *piper* < Gr. *peperi,* via Per. < Sans. *pippali,* peppercorn] 1. *a)* a pungent condiment obtained from the small, dried fruits of an East Indian plant (*Piper nigrum*) of the pepper family: **black pepper** is ground from the entire fruits, including the fleshy coverings; **white pepper,** from the internal tissues only *b)* the plant itself, a vine with smooth, soft stems 2. any of various plants (families Myrtaceae, Zingiberaceae, etc.) possessing aromatic and pungent properties, used in flavoring foods 3. *a) same as* CAPSICUM *b)* the fruit of the capsicum: see RED PEPPER, GREEN PEPPER, SWEET PEPPER 4. any of various pungent spices, as cayenne pepper ☆5. *Baseball* a warm-up or practice session in which the ball is repeatedly thrown to a batter close by, who bunts it back to be fielded: in full **pepper game** —*adj.* designating a family (Piperaceae) of plants, including cubeb and pepper (*n.* 1 *b*) —*vt.* 1. to sprinkle or flavor with ground pepper 2. to sprinkle freely or thickly 3. to shower or pelt with many small objects [a roof *peppered* with hailstones] 4. to beat or hit with short, quick jabs

PEPPER

pep·per-and-salt (-'n sôlt′) *adj.* dotted or speckled with contrasting colors, esp. black and white

pep·per·box (-bäks′) *n. same as* PEPPER SHAKER

pep·per·corn (-kôrn′) *n.* [ME. *pepercorn* < OE. *piporcorn*] 1. the dried berry of the black PEPPER (*n.* 1) 2. something insignificant or trifling

pep·per·grass (-gras′, -gräs′) *n.* any of a genus (*Lepidium*) of small plants of the mustard family, with small whitish flowers and flattened pods; esp., *same as* GARDEN CRESS

pep·per·idge (-ij) *n.* [var. of Brit. dial. *pipperidge,* the barberry] ☆*same as* BLACK GUM

pepper mill a hand mill used to grind peppercorns

pep·per·mint (-mint′, -mənt) *n.* 1. an aromatic, perennial plant (*Mentha piperita*) of the mint family, with lance-shaped leaves and whitish or purplish flowers in dense terminal spikes 2. the pungent oil it yields, used for flavoring 3. a candy or lozenge flavored with this oil

☆**pep·per·o·ni** (pep′ə rō′nē) *n., pl.* **-nis, -ni** [< It. *peperoni* (sing. *peperone*), cayenne peppers] a hard, highly spiced Italian sausage

pepper pot 1. *same as* PEPPER SHAKER 2. a West Indian stew of vegetables and meat or fish, flavored with cassava juice, red pepper, etc. ☆3. a hotly seasoned stew of vegetables, dumplings, tripe, etc. 4. a soup of meat and vegetables flavored with hot spices

pepper shaker a container with a perforated top, for sprinkling ground pepper

pepper tree a S. American ornamental tree (*Schinus molle*) of the cashew family, with panicles of yellowish flowers, pinnately compound leaves, and pinkish-red berries

pep·per·wort (-wurt′) *n.* 1. *same as* PEPPERGRASS 2. any of a genus (*Marsilea*) of water ferns having long-stalked leaves with four leaflets

pep·per·y (-ē) *adj.* 1. of, like, or highly seasoned with pepper 2. sharp or fiery, as speech or writing 3. hot-tempered; irritable —**pep′per·i·ness** *n.*

☆**pep pill** [Slang] any of various pills or tablets containing a stimulant, esp. amphetamine

---

fat, āpe, cär; ten, ēven; is, bīte; gō, hôrn, tōōl, look; oil, out; up, fur; get; joy; yet; chin; she; thin, then; zh, leisure; ŋ, ring; ə for *a* in ago, *e* in agent, *i* in sanity, *o* in comply, *u* in focus; ′ as in able (ā′b'l); Fr. bâl; ë, Fr. coeur; ö, Fr. feu; Fr. mon; ȟ, Fr. coq; ü, Fr. duc; r, Fr. cri; H, G. ich; kh, G. doch. See inside front cover. ☆ Americanism; ‡foreign; *hypothetical; <derived from

☆**pep·py** (pep′ē) *adj.* **-pi·er, -pi·est** [Colloq.] full of pep, or energy; brisk; vigorous; spirited —**pep′pi·ly** *adv.* — **pep′pi·ness** *n.*

pep·sin (pep′s'n) *n.* [G. < Gr. *pepsis*, digestion < *peptein*, earlier *pessein*, to cook, digest < IE. base **pekw-*, whence L. *coquere*, COOK] **1.** an enzyme secreted in the stomach, aiding in the digestion of proteins by splitting them into the less complex proteoses and peptones **2.** an extract of pepsin from the stomachs of calves, pigs, etc., formerly used as a digestive aid

pep·sin·ate (pep′sə nāt′) *vt.* **-at′ed, -at′ing** to treat, mix, or infuse with pepsin

pep·sin·o·gen (pep sin′ə jən) *n.* [< PEPSIN + -O- + -GEN] a zymogen, or precursor substance, in the cells of the gastric glands of the stomach, from which pepsin is produced by the action of hydrochloric acid

☆**pep talk** a talk, as to an athletic team by its coach, designed to instill enthusiasm, determination, etc.

pep·tic (pep′tik) *adj.* [L. *pepticus* < Gr. *peptikos* < *peptein*, to digest: see PEPSIN] **1.** of or aiding digestion **2.** of or relating to pepsin **3.** related to, or caused to some extent by, digestive secretions [a *peptic* ulcer]

pep·ti·dase (pep′ti dās′) *n.* [PEPTID(E) + -ASE] any of a class of enzymes, as erepsin, that split peptides into amino acids

pep·tide (-tīd) *n.* [PEPT(ONE) + -IDE] any of a group of compounds formed from two or more amino acids by the linkage of amino groups of some of the acids with carboxyl groups of others, or by the hydrolysis of proteins

peptide bond (or **linkage**) the bond formed when a carboxyl group of one molecule of an amino acid is condensed with an amino group of a second molecule; the bivalent radical —CO—NH—

pep·tize (-tīz) *vt., vi.* **-tized, -tiz·ing** [PEPT(ONE) + -IZE] to change into a colloid, usually through the action of an added chemical; esp., to change (a gel) into a sol

pep·tone (-tōn) *n.* [G. *pepton* < Gr. *pepton*, neut. of *peptos*, digested: see PEPSIN] any of a group of soluble and diffusible derived proteins formed by the action of enzymes on proteins, as in the process of digestion, or by acid hydrolysis of proteins —**pep·ton′ic** (-tän′ik) *adj.*

pep·to·nize (-tə nīz′) *vt.* **-nized′, -niz′ing 1.** to change (proteins) into peptones **2.** to subject to the action of pepsin or other protein-converting agents —**pep′to·ni·za′tion** *n.*

Pepys (pēps; *occas.* peps, pep′is, pē′pis), **Samuel** 1633–1703; Eng. government official, known for his diary

☆**Pe·quot** (pē′kwät) *n.* [< AmInd. (Algonquian) *paquatanog*, destroyers] **1.** *pl.* **-quots, -quot** any member of a tribe of Indians dominant in Connecticut until dispersed in 1637 **2.** their Algonquian language —*adj.* of this tribe

per (pur; *unstressed* pər) *prep.* [L. < IE. base **per*, a going beyond, whence FAR, FOR] **1.** through; by; by means of **2.** for each; for every [fifty cents *per* yard] **3.** [Colloq.] according to [*per* your instructions]

per- (pur; *unstressed* pər) [L. < *per*, through: see prec.] *a prefix meaning:* **1.** through, throughout, away [*perceive, percolate*] **2.** thoroughly, completely, very [*persuade*] **3.** *Chem. a)* containing a specified element or radical in its maximum, or a relatively high, valence [*perchlorate*] *b)* containing the maximum amount of the indicated element [*perfluoropropane* (completely fluorinated propane, C₃F₈)]

Per. 1. Persia **2.** Persian

per. 1. period **2.** person

per·ac·id (pur′as′id) *n.* **1.** an acid containing a larger proportion of oxygen than other acids containing the same elements, as perboric acid, perchloric acid, etc. **2.** an acid that contains one or more —O—O— groups, as hydrogen peroxide

per·ad·ven·ture (pur′əd ven′chər) *adv.* [ME. *perauenture* < OFr. *par'aventure* < *par* (L. *per*), by + *aventure*, a chance, ADVENTURE] [Archaic] **1.** perhaps; possibly **2.** by chance —*n.* chance; question; doubt [beyond *peradventure*]

Pe·rae·a (pə rē′ə) in Roman times, a region in Palestine east of the Jordan, roughly the same as ancient Gilead

Pe·rak (pā′rak; *Malay* pā′rä) W state of the Federation of Malaya: 7,980 sq. mi.; pop. 1,547,000

per·am·bu·late (pər am′byoo lāt′) *vt.* **-lat′ed, -lat′ing** [< L. *perambulatus*, pp. of *perambulare* < *per*, through (see PER) + *ambulare*, to walk] **1.** to walk through, over, around, etc., esp. in examining or inspecting **2.** to walk around so as to officially inspect and maintain the boundary of (a forest, estate, etc.) —*vi.* to walk or move about; stroll —**per·am′bu·la′tion** *n.* —**per·am′bu·la·to′ry** (-lə tôr′ē) *adv.*

per·am·bu·la·tor (-lāt′ər) *n.* **1.** a person who perambulates **2.** [Chiefly Brit.] a baby carriage; buggy **3.** a large wheel with a calibrated mechanism, pushed along on the ground to measure distances, like an odometer

per an., per ann. per annum

per an·num (pər an′əm) [L.] by the year; annually

per·bo·rate (pər bôr′āt) *n.* a salt of perboric acid

per·bor·ic acid (-ik) [PER- + BORIC] the hypothetical acid, HBO₃, whose salts, the perborates, are formed by the action of hydrogen peroxide on borates

per·cale (pər kāl′, -kal′) *n.* [Fr. < Per. *pargāla*] fine, closely woven cotton cloth, used for sheets, etc.

per·ca·line (pur′kə lēn′, pur′kə lēn′) *n.* [Fr. < *percale*: see prec.] a fine cotton cloth, usually with a glazed or watered finish, used for linings

per cap·i·ta (pər kap′ə tə) [ML., lit., by heads, for L. *in capita*] for each person

per·ceive (pər sēv′) *vt., vi.* **-ceived′, -ceiv′ing** [ME. *perceyven* < OFr. *perceivre* < L. *percipere*, to take hold of, feel, comprehend < *per*, through + *capere*, to take] **1.** to grasp mentally; take note (of); recognize; observe **2.** to become aware (of) through sight, hearing, touch, taste, or smell —*SYN.* see DISCERN —**per·ceiv′a·ble** *adj.* — **per·ceiv′a·bly** *adv.* —**per·ceiv′er** *n.*

per·cent (pər sent′) *adv., adj.* [< It. *per cento* < L. *per centum*] per hundred; in, to, or for every hundred [a 20 *percent* rate means 20 in every 100]: symbol, %: also **per cent** or, now rare, **per cent., per cen·tum** (sen′təm) —*n.* **1.** a hundredth part **2.** [Colloq.] percentage **3.** [*pl.*] bonds, securities, etc. bearing regular interest of a (stated) percentage [the four *percents*]

per·cent·age (-ij) *n.* **1.** a given part or amount in every hundred **2.** any number or amount, as of interest, tax, etc., stated in percent **3.** part; portion; share [a *percentage* of the audience] ☆**4.** [Colloq.] *a)* use; advantage; profit [no *percentage* in worrying] *b)* [usually *pl.*] a risk based on favorable odds

per·cen·tile (pər sen′til, -sent′l) *n.* [PERCENT + -ILE] *Statistics* **1.** any of the values in a series dividing the distribution of the individuals in the series into one hundred groups of equal frequency **2.** any of these groups —*adj.* of a percentile or division into percentiles

per·cept (pur′sept) *n.* [back-formation (after CONCEPT) < PERCEPTION] a recognizable sensation or impression received by the mind through the senses

per·cep·ti·ble (pər sep′tə b'l) *adj.* [LL. *perceptibilis* < pp. of L. *percipere*] that can be perceived —**per·cep′ti·bil′i·ty** *n.* —**per·cep′ti·bly** *adv.*

SYN.—**perceptible** is applied to anything that can be apprehended by the senses but often connotes that the thing is just barely visible, audible, etc. [a *perceptible* smell of coffee]; **sensible** applies to that which can clearly be perceived [a *sensible* difference in their size]; **palpable** refers to anything that can be perceived by or as by the sense of touch [a *palpable* fog]; **tangible** applies to that which can be grasped, either with the hand or the mind [*tangible* property, ideas, etc.]; **appreciable** is used of that which is sufficiently perceptible to be measured, estimated, etc. or to have significance [an *appreciable* amount] —*ANT.* **imperceptible**

per·cep·tion (-shən) *n.* [L. *perceptio* < pp. of *percipere*: see PERCEIVE] **1.** *a)* the act of perceiving or the ability to perceive; mental grasp of objects, qualities, etc. by means of the senses; awareness; comprehension *b)* insight or intuition, or the faculty for these **2.** the understanding, knowledge, etc. got by perceiving, or a specific idea, concept, impression, etc. so formed —**per·cep′tion·al** *adj.*

per·cep·tive (-tiv) *adj.* [ML. *perceptivus*] **1.** of or capable of perception **2.** able to perceive quickly and easily; having keen insight or intuition; penetrating —**per·cep′tive·ly** *adv.* —**per·cep′tive·ness, per·cep·tiv·i·ty** (pur′sep tiv′ə tē) *n.*

per·cep·tu·al (-choo əl) *adj.* of, by means of, or involving perception —**per·cep′tu·al·ly** *adv.*

Per·ce·val (pur′sə v'l) **1.** a masculine name: see PERCIVAL **2.** same as PERCIVALE

perch¹ (purch) *n., pl.* **perch, perch′es:** see PLURAL, II, D, 2 [ME. *perche* < OFr. < L. *perca* < Gr. *perkē* < IE. base **perk-*, speckled, colorful, whence G. *farbe*, color, OE. *forn*, trout] **1.** any of a genus (*Perca*) of small, spiny-finned, freshwater, food fishes; esp., the **yellow perch** (*Perca flavescens*) of N. America and a closely related species (*Perca fluviatilis*) of Europe **2.** any of various bony, spiny-rayed, usually saltwater, fishes

perch² (purch) *n.* [ME. *perche* < OFr. < L. *pertica*, a pole, staff] **1.** a horizontal rod, pole, etc. provided as a roost for birds **2.** anything, as a branch or wire, upon which a bird rests **3.** any resting place or position, esp. a high or insecure one **4.** *a)* a measure of length, equal to 5 1/2 yards; rod *b)* a measure of area, equal to 30 1/4 square yards *c)* a cubic measure for stone, usually equal to 24 3/4 cubic feet **5.** a pole connecting the front and hind gear of a spring carriage —*vi.* [Fr. *percher*] to alight and rest on or as on a perch —*vt.* to place or set on or as on a perch

per·chance (pər chans′, -chäns′) *adv.* [ME. *par chance* < OFr. *par* (L. *per*), by + *chance*, CHANCE] [Archaic or Poet.] **1.** by chance; accidentally **2.** perhaps; possibly

Perche (persh) region in NW France, in Maine & Normandy

perch·er (pur′chər) *n.* a person or thing that perches; specif., a bird having feet adapted for perching

Per·che·ron (pur′chə rän′, -shə-) *n.* [Fr. < PERCHE, where bred] any of a breed of large, fast-trotting draft horses: also **Percheron Norman**

per·chlo·rate (pər klôr′āt) *n.* a salt of perchloric acid

per·chlo·ric acid (-ik) [PER- + CHLORIC] a colorless, liquid acid, HClO₄, that is a strong oxidizing agent: its concentrated solutions can form explosive mixtures with reducing agents: used in analytical chemistry, in making solid propellants, etc.

per·chlo·ride (-īd) *n.* any chloride in which the amount of chlorine is greater than that present in the ordinary chloride of the same element

per·cip·i·ent (pər sip′ē ənt) *adj.* [L. *percipiens*, prp. of *percipere*: see PERCEIVE] perceiving, esp. keenly or readily —*n.* a person who perceives —**per·cip′i·ence, per·cip′i·en·cy** *n.* —**per·cip′i·ent·ly** *adv.*

Per·ci·val (pur′sə v′l) [OFr. *Perceval*, prob. < *perce val*, pierce valley: apparently coined by CHRÉTIEN DE TROYES (12th c.)] 1. a masculine name: dim. *Percy* 2. *same as* PERCIVALE

Per·ci·vale (-v′l) [see prec.] a knight in Arthurian legend, who saw the Holy Grail

per·coid (pur′koid) *adj.* [< L. *perca*, PERCH¹ + -OID] of or belonging to a very large order (Percomorphi) of bony fishes found in fresh and salt water, including the perches, basses, sunfishes, etc. —*n.* a fish of this order

per·co·late (pur′kə lāt′; *also, for n.,* -lit) *vt.* **-lat′ed, -lat′ing** [< L. *percolatus*, pp. of *percolare*, to strain < *per*, through + *colare*, to strain: see COLANDER] 1. to pass (a liquid) gradually through small spaces or a porous substance; filter 2. to drain or ooze through (a porous substance); permeate 3. to brew (coffee) in a percolator —*vi.* 1. *a*) to pass or ooze through a porous substance *b*) to spread throughout; permeate 2. to become active or start bubbling up, as coffee in a percolator —*n.* a liquid produced by percolating —**per′co·la′tion** *n.*

per·co·la·tor (-lāt′ər) *n.* 1. a thing that percolates 2. a kind of coffeepot in which the boiling water repeatedly bubbles up through a tube and filters back to the bottom through the coffee grounds, which are held in a perforated container

per con·tra (pər kän′trə) [L.] on the contrary

per cu·ri·am (pər kyoor′ē am′) [L.] *Law* by the court: said of a judicial opinion presented as that of the entire court rather than that of any one judge

per·cuss (pər kus′) *vt.* [< L. *percussus*, pp. of *percutere*, to strike < *per-*, PER- + *quatere*, to shake: see QUASH²] to rap gently and firmly, as in medical diagnosis —**per·cus′sor** *n.*

per·cus·sion (pər kush′ən) *n.* [L. *percussio* < *percussus:* see prec.] 1. the hitting or impact of one body against another, as the hammer of a firearm against a powder cap 2. the shock, vibration, etc. resulting from this 3. the impact of sound waves on the ear 4. percussion instruments collectively 5. *Med.* the striking or tapping of the chest, back, etc. with the fingertips so as to determine from the sound produced the condition of internal organs

percussion cap a small paper or metal container holding a charge that explodes when struck: in certain earlier firearms, a cap containing fulminating powder was used as a primer

percussion instrument a musical instrument in which the tone or a sound is produced when some part is struck, as the drums, cymbals, tambourine, triangle, bells, xylophone, etc. and, broadly, the piano

per·cus·sion·ist (-ist) *n.* a musician who plays percussion instruments

percussion lock a gunlock on a firearm that fires by percussion

per·cus·sive (-kus′iv) *adj.* of or characterized by percussion —**per·cus′sive·ly** *adv.* —**per·cus′sive·ness** *n.*

per·cu·ta·ne·ous (pur′kyoo tā′nē əs) *adj.* [PER- + CUTANEOUS] effected or introduced through the skin, as by rubbing, injection, etc. —**per′cu·ta′ne·ous·ly** *adv.*

Per·cy (pur′sē) 1. a masculine name: see PERCIVAL 2. Sir Henry, 1364-1403; Eng. soldier & rebel against Henry IV: called *Hotspur* 3. Thomas, 1729-1811; Eng. bishop & collector of early English & Scottish ballads

Per·di·do (per *th*ē′*th*ō), Mon·te (mōn′te) mountain in the C Pyrenees, NE Spain: 11,007 ft.

per·die (pər dē′) *adv., interj. same as* PARDIE

per di·em (dē′əm, dī′əm) [L.] 1. by the day; daily ☆2. a daily allowance, as for expenses

per·di·tion (pər dish′ən) *n.* [ME. *perdicioun* < OFr. *pordicioun* < LL.(Ec.) *porditio* < L. *porditus*, pp. of *pordoro*, to lose, ruin < *per-*, PER- + *dare*, to give] 1. [Archaic] complete and irreparable loss; ruin 2. *Theol. a*) the loss of the soul; damnation *b*) *same as* HELL

per·du, per·due (pər doo′, -dyoo′) *adj.* [Fr. *perdu*, masc., *perdue*, fem., pp. of *perdre*, to lose < L. *perdere:* see prec.] out of sight; in hiding; concealed, as in military ambush —*n.* [< the *adj.*; also contr. of Fr. *sentinelle perdue*, advanced (lit., lost) sentry, or *enfants perdus*, forlorn hope] [Obs.] a soldier or group of soldiers on an especially dangerous assignment

Per·du (per dü′), Mont (mōn) *Fr.* name of Monte PERDIDO

per·dur·a·ble (pər door′ə b′l, -dyoor′-) *adj.* [ME. < OFr. < LL. *perdurabilis* < L. *perdurare*, to last, endure < *per-*, intens. + *durare:* see DURABLE] extremely durable or lasting; everlasting; permanent —**per′dur′a·bly** *adv.*

per·dure (-door′, -dyoor′) *vi.* **-dured′, -dur′ing** [ME. *perduren* < L. *perdurare*, to continue, endure < *per-*, intens. + *durare*, to last (see PER- & DURABLE] to remain in existence; continue; last

per·e·gri·nate (per′ə gri nāt′) *vt.* **-nat′ed, -nat′ing** [< L. *peregrinatus*, pp. of *peregrinari* < *peregrinus:* see PILGRIM] to follow (a route, etc.); travel, esp. walk, along or through —*vi.* to journey or travel —**per′e·gri·na′tion** *n.* —**per′e·gri·na′tor** *n.*

per·e·grine (per′ə grin, -grin′, -grēn′) *adj.* [L. *peregrinus:* see PILGRIM] traveling or migratory

peregrine (falcon) *same as* DUCK HAWK

Perel·man (purl′mən), S(idney) J(oseph) 1904- ; U.S. humorist

per·emp·to·ry (pə remp′tər ē) *adj.* [LL. *peremptorius*, decisive, final < L., destructive, deadly < *peremptus*, pp. of *perimere*, to destroy < *per-*, intens. + *emere*, to take, buy: see REDEEM] 1. *Law a*) barring further action, debate, question, etc.; final; absolute; decisive *b*) not requiring that any cause be shown [a *peremptory* challenge of a juror] 2. that cannot be denied, changed, delayed, opposed, etc., as a command 3. intolerantly positive; dictatorial; dogmatic; imperious [a *peremptory* manner] —**per·emp′to·ri·ly** *adv.* —**per·emp′to·ri·ness** *n.*

per·en·nate (per′ə nāt′) *vi.* **-nat′ed, -nat′ing** [< L. *perennatus*, pp. of *perennare*, to last for many years, endure < *perennis*, PERENNIAL] to survive from year to year for a number of years; be perennial —**per′en·na′tion** *n.*

per·en·ni·al (pə ren′ē əl) *adj.* [< L. *perennis*, lasting through the year < *per-*, through + *annus*, a year: see PER & ANNUAL] 1. lasting or active throughout the whole year 2. lasting or continuing for a long time [a *perennial* youth] 3. returning or becoming active again and again; perpetual 4. having a life cycle of more than two years: said esp. of herbaceous plants that produce flowers and seed from the same root structure year after year —*n.* a perennial plant —**per·en′ni·al·ly** *adv.*

perf. 1. perfect 2. perforated

per·fect (pur′fikt; *for v., usually* pər fekt′) *adj.* [ME. *perfit* < OFr. *parfit* < L. *perfectus*, pp. of *perficere*, to finish < *per-*, through (see PER-) + *facere*, to make, DO¹: mod. sp. is Latinized] 1. complete in all respects; without defect or omission; sound; flawless 2. in a condition of complete excellence, as in skill or quality; faultless; most excellent: sometimes used comparatively ["to create a more *perfect* union"] 3. completely correct or accurate; exact; precise [a *perfect* copy] 4. without reserve or qualification; pure; utter; sheer; absolute [a *perfect* fool, *perfect* stranger] 5. designating a binding of books in which pages are glued to cloth or paper at the spine rather than having the signatures sewn together 6. *Bot. same as* MONOCLINOUS 7. *Gram.* expressing or showing a state or action completed at the time of speaking or at the time indicated: verbs have three perfect tenses; simple (or present) perfect, past perfect (or pluperfect), and future perfect 8. *Music* designating an interval (i.e., the fourth, fifth, or octave) whose character is not altered by inversion and which has no alternative major and minor forms, but becomes augmented when raised, or diminished when lowered, by a semitone —*vt.* 1. to bring to completion 2. to make perfect or more nearly perfect according to a given standard, as by training or improvement —*n.* 1. the perfect tense 2. a verb form in this tense —**per·fect′er** *n.* —**per′fect·ness** *n.*

perfect cadence *Music* a cadence, immediately preceded by some form of dominant harmony, and consisting of the tonic triad of the key of the particular section or of the composition in its beginning, with the keynote appearing in both the highest and lowest voice

per·fect·i·ble (pər fek′tə b′l) *adj.* [ML. *perfectibilis*] that can become, or be made, perfect or more nearly perfect —**per·fect′i·bil′i·ty** *n.*

☆**perfecting press** a press that prints both sides of a sheet or web of paper at the same time

per·fec·tion (pər fek′shən) *n.* [ME. *perfeccioun* < OFr. < L. *perfectio*] 1. the act or process of perfecting 2. the quality or condition of being perfect; extreme degree of excellence according to a given standard 3. a person or thing that is the perfect embodiment of some quality —**to perfection** completely; perfectly

☆**per·fec·tion·ism** (-iz′m) *n.* 1. any doctrine that holds that moral, religious, or social perfection can and should be attained in this life 2. extreme or obsessive striving for absolute perfection, as in one's work —**per·fec′tion·ist** *n., adj.* —**per·fec′tion·is′tic** *adj.*

per·fec·tive (pər fek′tiv) *adj.* [LL. *perfectivus*] 1. [Now Rare] tending to bring to or achieve perfection 2. *Gram.* designating an aspect of verbs, as in Russian, expressing completion of the action or state —*n.* 1. the perfective aspect 2. a verb in this aspect —**per·fec′tive·ly** *adv.* —**per·fec′tive·ness** *n.*

per·fect·ly (pur′fikt lē) *adv.* 1. so as to be perfect; to a perfect degree 2. completely; fully

perfect number a positive integer which is equal to the sum of all its factors, excluding itself

☆**per·fec·to** (pər fek′tō) *n., pl.* **-tos** [Sp. < L. *perfectus*, PERFECT] a cigar of a standard shape, thick in the center and tapering to a point at each end

perfect participle *same as* PAST PARTICIPLE

perfect pitch *a popular term for* ABSOLUTE PITCH (sense 2)

perfect rhyme a rhyme of two words or syllables spelled or pronounced alike but differing in meaning, as *dear* and *deer*; rich rhyme

perfect square a quantity which is the exact square of another quantity; e.g., 25 is a *perfect square* of 5, $x^2 + 2xy + y^2$ of $(x + y)$

per·fer·vid (pər fur′vid) *adj.* [ModL. *perfervidus:* see PER- & FERVID] extremely fervid; ardent

per·fid·i·ous (pər fid′ē əs) *adj.* [L. *perfidiosus*] characterized by perfidy; treacherous —*SYN.* see FAITHLESS —**per·fid′i·ous·ly** *adv.*

per·fi·dy (pur′fə dē) *n., pl.* **-dies** [Fr. *perfidie* < L. *perfidia* < *per fidem* (*decipi*), (to deceive) through faith < *per* (see PER) + *fides*, FAITH] the deliberate breaking of faith; betrayal of trust; treachery

per·fo·li·ate (pər fō′lē it, -āt′) *adj.* [ModL. *perfoliatus* < L. *per-* < L. *folium*, a leaf: see FOLIATE] having a base surrounding the stem which bears it so that the stem seems to pass through it: said of a leaf —**per·fo′li·a′tion** *n.*

PERFOLIATE LEAVES
(left, bellwort; right, honeysuckle)

per·fo·rate (pur′fə rāt′; *for adj.*, *usually* -rit) *vt., vi.* **-rat′ed**, **-rat′ing** [< L. *perforatus*, pp. of *perforare* < *per*, through + *forare*, to BORE¹] 1. to make a hole or holes through, as by punching or boring; pierce; penetrate 2. to pierce with holes in a row, as a pattern, computer tape, sheet of stamps, etc. —*adj.* pierced with holes, esp. a row of holes, so as to facilitate tearing: also **per′fo·rat′ed** —**per′fo·ra·ble** *adj.* —**per′fo·ra′tor** *n.*

per·fo·ra·tion (pur′fə rā′shən) *n.* 1. a perforating or being perforated 2. a hole made by piercing, ulceration, etc. 3. any of a series of holes punched or drilled, as between postage stamps on a sheet

per·fo·ra·tive (pur′fə rāt′iv) *adj.* [Fr. *perforatif* < ML. *perforativus*] that perforates readily

per·force (pər fôrs′) *adv.* [ME. *par force* < OFr.: see PER & FORCE] by or through necessity; necessarily

per·form (pər fôrm′) *vt.* [ME. *performen* < Anglo-Fr. *parformer*, altered (after *forme*, FORM) < OFr. *parfournir*, to perform, consummate < *par* (< L. *per-*, intens.) + *fornir*, to accomplish, FURNISH] 1. to act on so as to accomplish or bring to completion; execute; do, as a task, process, etc. 2. to carry out; meet the requirements of; fulfill (a promise, command, etc.) 3. to give a performance of; render or enact (a piece of music, a dramatic role, etc.) —*vi.* to carry out or execute an action or process; esp., to take part in a musical program, act in a play, dance, etc. before an audience —**per·form′a·ble** *adj.* —**per·form′er** *n.*

SYN.—**perform**, often a more formal equivalent for **do**, is usually used of a more or less involved process rather than a single act [to *perform* an experiment]; **execute** implies a putting into effect or completing that which has been planned or ordered [to *execute* a law]; **accomplish** suggests effort and perseverance in carrying out a plan or purpose [to *accomplish* a mission]; **achieve** implies the overcoming of obstacles in accomplishing something of worth or importance [to *achieve* a lasting peace]; **effect** also suggests the conquering of difficulties but emphasizes what has been done to bring about the result [his cure was *effected* by the use of certain drugs]; **fulfill**, in strict discrimination, implies the full realization of what is expected or demanded [to *fulfill* a promise]

per·form·ance (-fôr′məns) *n.* [LME. *parfourmaunce* < MFr.] 1. the act of performing; execution, accomplishment, fulfillment, etc. 2. operation or functioning, usually with regard to effectiveness, as of a machine 3. something done or performed; deed or feat 4. *a)* a formal exhibition or presentation before an audience, as a play, musical program, etc.; show *b)* one's part in this

performing arts arts, such as drama, dance, and music, that involve performance before an audience

perf. part. perfect participle

per·fume (pər fyōōm′; *for n., usually* pur′fyōōm) *vt.* **-fumed′**, **-fum′ing** [MFr. *parfumer* < It. *perfumare* < L. *per-*, intens. + *fumare*, to smoke < *fumus*, smoke: see FUME] 1. to fill with a fragrant or pleasing odor; scent 2. to put perfume on; dab, spray, etc. with perfume —*n.* [MFr. *parfum* < the *v.*] 1. a pleasing smell or odor; sweet scent, as of flowers; fragrance 2. a substance producing a fragrant or pleasing odor; esp., a volatile oil, as that extracted from flowers, or a substance like this prepared synthetically —*SYN.* see SCENT

per·fum·er (pər fyōō′mər) *n.* 1. a person who makes or sells perfumes 2. a person or thing that perfumes

per·fum·er·y (-ē) *n., pl.* **-er·ies** [PERFUM(E) + -ERY] 1. the trade or art of a perfumer 2. a perfume, or perfumes collectively 3. a place where perfume is made or sold

per·func·to·ry (pər funk′tər ē) *adj.* [LL. *perfunctorius* < L. *perfunctus*, pp. of *perfungi*, to get rid of, discharge < *per-*, intens. + *fungi*, to perform: see FUNCTION] 1. done without care or interest or merely as a form or routine; superficial [a *perfunctory* examination] 2. without concern or solicitude; indifferent [a *perfunctory* teacher] —**per·func′to·ri·ly** *adv.* —**per·func′to·ri·ness** *n.*

per·fuse (pər fyōōz′) *vt.* **-fused′**, **-fus′ing** [< L. *perfusus*, pp. of *perfundere* < *per*, through + *fundere*, to pour: see FOUND³] 1. to sprinkle, cover over, or permeate with or as with a liquid; suffuse 2. to pour or spread (a liquid, etc.) through or over something —**per·fu′sion** *n.* —**per·fu′sive** (-fyōō′siv) *adj.*

Per·ga·mum (pur′gə məm) 1. ancient Greek kingdom occupying most of W Asia Minor, later a Roman province 2. ancient capital of this kingdom, the present site of Bergama, Turkey

per·go·la (pur′gə lə) *n.* [It., arbor < L. *pergula*, arbor, projecting cover] an arbor, esp. one with an open roof of cross rafters or latticework supported on posts or columns, usually with climbing vines

Per·go·le·si (per′gō le′zē, -sē), **Gio·van·ni Bat·tis·ta** (jô vän′nē bät tēs′tä) 1710–36; It. composer

per·haps (pər haps′, -aps′) *adv.* [PER + *haps*, pl. of HAP¹] possibly; maybe

pe·ri (pir′ē) *n.* [Per. *parī* < MPer. *parīk* < Avestan *pairika*, woman who misleads the faithful by seduction] 1. *Persian Myth.* a fairy or elf descended from evil angels and barred from paradise until penance has been done 2. any fairylike or elfin being

per·i- (per′ə, -ē) [Gr. *peri-* < *peri*, around < IE. base *per-*, a going beyond, whence Avestan *pairi* & FAR, FARE] *a prefix meaning:* 1. around, about, surrounding, enclosing [*periscope, pericardium*] 2. near [*perigee*]

per·i·anth (per′ē anth′) *n.* [ModL. *perianthium* < Gr. *peri-* (see prec.) + *anthos*, a flower: see ANTHO-] the outer envelope of a flower, including the calyx and corolla

per·i·apt (-apt′) *n.* [Fr. *périapte* < Gr. *periapton* < *periaptein*, to fit about, tie about < *peri-* (see PERI-) + *aptein*, to fasten] *same as* AMULET

per·i·blem (per′ə blem′) *n.* [G. < Gr. *periblēma*, a robe < *periballein*, to surround < *peri-* (see PERI-) + *ballein*, to throw: see BALL²] in older botanical theory, undifferentiated embryonic tissue at the growth points of plant stems and roots, which develop into the cortex

per·i·car·di·tis (per′ə kär dīt′is) *n.* [see -ITIS] inflammation of the pericardium

per·i·car·di·um (-kär′dē əm) *n., pl.* **-di·a** (-ə) [ModL. < Gr. *perikardion* < *perikardios*, around the heart < *peri-*, around + *kardia*, HEART] in vertebrates, the thin, closed, membranous sac surrounding the heart and the roots of the great blood vessels and containing a clear serous liquid —**per′i·car′di·al, per′i·car′di·ac′** *adj.*

per·i·carp (per′ə kärp′) *n.* [ModL. *pericarpium* < Gr. *perikarpion:* see PERI- & -CARP] *Bot.* the wall of a ripened ovary, sometimes consisting of three distinct layers, the endocarp, mesocarp, and exocarp —**per′i·car′pi·al** *adj.*

per·i·chon·dri·um (per′ə kän′drē əm) *n., pl.* **-dri·a** (-ə) [ModL. < PERI- + Gr. *chondros*, cartilage, grain: for IE. base see GRIND] the membrane of white, fibrous connective tissue covering cartilage, except at the joints —**per′i·chon′dri·al, per′i·chon′dral** *adj.*

Per·i·cle·an (per′ə klē′ən) *adj.* 1. of Pericles 2. of the period of great commercial, intellectual, and artistic achievement in Athens during the Age of Pericles

Per·i·cles (per′ə klēz′) 495?–429 B.C.; Athenian statesman & general

per·i·cli·nal (per′ə klī′n'l) *adj.* [see ff. & -AL] *Bot.* 1. running parallel to the surface of a plant organ or part: said of cell walls 2. designating or of a chimera having one kind of tissue completely enclosed by another kind

per·i·cline (per′ə klīn′) *n.* [< Gr. *periklinēs*, sloping on all sides < *peri*, around + *klinein*, to slope, INCLINE] a kind of albite found in white, crystalline form

pe·ric·o·pe (pə rik′ə pē) *n.* [LL.(Ec.) < Gr. *perikopē*, orig., a cutting all around < *peri-*, around (see PERI-) + *kopē*, a cutting < base of *koptein*, to cut: for IE. base see SHAFT] a passage, usually short, from a written work; esp., *same as* LECTION (sense 2)

per·i·cra·ni·um (per′ə krā′nē əm) *n., pl.* **-ni·a** (-ə) [ModL. < Gr. *perikranion*, orig. neut. adj., around the skull < *peri-*, around + *kranion*, skull: see CRANIUM] the periosteum of the external surface of the skull —**per′i·cra′ni·al** *adj.*

per·i·cy·cle (per′ə sī′k'l) *n.* [Fr. *péricycle* < Gr. *perikyklos*, spherical < *peri-*, around < *kyklos*, a ring, circle] the outer layer of the stele in the root and stem of most plants —**per′i·cy′clic** (-sī′klik, -sik′lik) *adj.*

per·i·derm (per′ə durm′) *n.* [ModL. *peridermis:* see PERI- & DERMIS] the outer bark and the layer of soft, growing tissue between the bark and the wood in plants —**per′i·der′mal, per′i·der′mic** *adj.*

pe·rid·i·um (pə rid′ē əm) *n., pl.* **-i·a** (-ə) [ModL. < Gr. *pēridion*, dim. of *pēra*, leather sack, wallet] the outer coat of the spore-bearing organ in certain fungi —**pe·rid′i·al** *adj.*

per·i·dot (per′ə dät′) *n.* [Fr. *péridot* < MFr. *peritot* < ?] a variety of yellowish-green olivine, used as a gem —**per′i·dot′ic** *adj.*

per·i·do·tite (per′ə dōt′īt, pə rid′ə tīt′) *n.* [Fr. *péridotite* < *péridot*, PERIDOT] any of several coarsegrained, dark igneous rocks consisting mainly of olivine and other ferromagnesian minerals —**per·i·do·tit·ic** (per′ə də tit′ik, pə rid′ə-) *adj.*

per·i·gee (per′ə jē′) *n.* [Fr. *périgée* < ModL. *perigeum* < LGr. *perigeion* < Gr. *perigeios*, around the earth < *peri-*,

around + *gē*, the earth] **1.** the point nearest to the earth in the orbit of the moon or of a man-made satellite: see APOGEE, illus. **2.** the lowest or nearest point —**per′i·ge′an, per′i·ge′al** *adj.*

pe·rig·y·nous (pǝ rij′ǝ nǝs) *adj.* [ModL. *perigynus:* see PERI- & -GYNOUS] *Bot.* having the sepals, petals, and stamens attached to the rim of a cup or tube which surrounds the ovary but is not attached to it, as in the rose, spiraea, etc. —**pe·rig′y·ny** (-nē) *n.*

per·i·he·li·on (per′ǝ hē′lē ǝn, -hēl′yǝn) *n.*, *pl.* **-li·ons, -li·a** (-ǝ) [ModL. < Gr. *peri-*, around + *hēlios*, the sun: see SOL¹] the point nearest the sun in the orbit of a planet or comet, or of a man-made satellite in orbit around the sun: see APHELION, illus.

per·il (per′ǝl) *n.* [ME. < OFr. < L. *periculum*, a danger < base *per-* (as in *experiri*, to try) < IE. base *per-*, to try, risk, whence FEAR] **1.** exposure to harm or injury; danger; jeopardy **2.** something that may cause harm or injury —*vt.* **-iled** or **-illed, -il·ing** or **-il·ling** to expose to danger; jeopardize; imperil —*SYN.* see DANGER

per·il·ous (-ǝs) *adj.* [ME. < OFr. *perilleus* < L. *periculosus*] involving peril or risk; dangerous —**per′il·ous·ly** *adv.* —**per′il·ous·ness** *n.*

per·i·lune (per′ǝ lōōn′) *n.* [< PERI- + LUNE¹] the point nearest to the moon in the elliptical orbit of a man-made satellite in orbit around it

pe·rim·e·ter (pǝ rim′ǝ tǝr) *n.* [L. *perimetros* < Gr. *perimetros* < *peri-*, around + *metron*, MEASURE] **1.** the outer boundary of a figure or area **2.** the total length of this **3.** an optical instrument for testing the scope of vision and the visual powers of various parts of the retina **4.** *Mil.* a boundary strip where defenses are set up —*SYN.* see CIRCUMFERENCE

per·i·met·ric (per′ǝ met′rik) *adj.* **1.** of a perimeter, or boundary **2.** of or by a perimeter or perimetry Also **per′i·met′ri·cal** —**per′i·met′ri·cal·ly** *adv.*

pe·rim·e·try (pǝ rim′ǝ trē) *n.* the testing of the scope of vision by means of a perimeter

per·i·morph (per′ǝ môrf′) *n.* [PERI- + -MORPH] a mineral of one kind enclosing one of another kind

per·i·my·si·um (per′ǝ miz′ē ǝm) *n.*, *pl.* **-si·a** (-ǝ) [ModL. < *peri-*, PERI- + Gr. *mys*, a muscle + ModL. *-ium*, -IUM] connective tissue covering and binding together bundles of muscle fibers

per·i·na·tal (per′ǝ nāt′'l) *adj.* [PERI- + NATAL] of, involving, or occurring during the period closely surrounding the time of birth

per·i·neph·ri·um (per′ǝ nef′rē ǝm) *n.* [ModL. < Gr. *perinephros*, fat about the kidneys < *peri-*, around + *nephros*, kidney: see NEPHRO-] the envelope of connective and fatty tissue surrounding the kidney

per·i·ne·um (-nē′ǝm) *n.*, *pl.* **-ne′a** (-ǝ) [ModL. < LL. *perinaeon* < Gr. *perineon* < *peri-*, around + *inein*, to discharge, defecate] the region of the body between the thighs, at the outlet of the pelvis; specif., the small area between the anus and the vulva in the female or between the anus and the scrotum in the male —**per′i·ne′al** *adj.*

per·i·neu·ri·um (-nyoor′ē ǝm) *n.*, *pl.* **-ri·a** (-ǝ) [ModL. < PERI- + Gr. *neuron*, NERVE] the sheath of dense connective tissue that envelops a bundle of nerve fibers composing a peripheral nerve —**per′i·neu′ri·al** *adj.*

pe·ri·od (pir′ē ǝd) *n.* [ME. *paryode* < MFr. *periode* < L. *periodus* < Gr. *periodos*, a going around, cycle < *peri-*, around + *hodos*, way: see CEDE] **1.** the interval between the successive occurrences of an astronomical event, as between two full moons **2.** the interval between certain happenings [a ten-year *period* of peace] **3.** a portion of time, often indefinite, characterized by certain events, processes, conditions, etc.; stage [a *period* of change, the present *period*] **4.** any of the portions of time into which an event of fixed duration, as a game or a school day, is divided **5.** the full course, or one of the stages, of a disease **6.** the time of menstruation; menses **7.** an end, completion, or conclusion, or a point of time marking this [death put a *period* to his plans] **8.** a subdivision of a geologic era corresponding to a rock system: periods are combined to form eras and subdivided into epochs: see GEOLOGY, chart **9.** *Gram., Rhetoric a)* a sentence, esp. a balanced, well-constructed, complex sentence *b)* the natural pause in speaking, or a mark of punctuation (.) in writing, used to indicate the end of a declarative sentence *c)* the dot (.) following many abbreviations **10.** *Math.* the interval from one repetition to the next of a recurrent or self-duplicating function **11.** *Music* a group of measures, usually eight or sixteen, arranged in two phrases and forming a complete statement ending with a cadence **12.** *Physics* the interval of time necessary for a regularly recurring motion to make a complete cycle **13.** *Prosody* a rhythm group of two or more cola in the Greek system —*adj.* of or like that of an earlier period or age [*period* furniture] —*interj.* an exclamation used colloquially to emphasize a completed statement [he hates cats, *period!*]

SYN.—**period** is the general term for any portion of time; **epoch** and **era** are often used interchangeably, but in strict discrimination **epoch** applies to the beginning of a new period marked by radical changes, new developments, etc. and **era**, to the entire period [the steam engine marked an *epoch* in transportation, an *era* of revolution]; **age** is applied to a period identified with some dominant personality or distinctive characteristic [the Stone *Age*]; **eon** refers to an indefinitely long period [it all happened *eons* ago]

pe·ri·o·date (pǝ rī′ǝ dāt′) *n.* a salt of periodic acid containing the IO₄ radical

pe·ri·od·ic (pir′ē äd′ik) *adj.* [MFr. *periodique* < L. *periodicus* < Gr. *periodikos*] **1.** occurring, appearing, or recurring at regular intervals [a *periodic* fever] **2.** occurring from time to time; intermittent **3.** of or characterized by a period or periods [the *periodic* motion of a planet] **4.** of or characterized by periodic sentences —*SYN.* see INTERMITTENT

per·i·od·ic acid (pur′ī äd′ik) [PER- + IODIC] a colorless solid, H₅IO₆, containing iodine in its highest valence: the simpler form of periodic acid, HIO₄, is unstable, but its salts are known

pe·ri·od·i·cal (pir′ē äd′i k'l) *adj.* **1.** *same as* PERIODIC **2.** published at regular intervals, as weekly, monthly, etc. **3.** of a periodical —*n.* a periodical publication

pe·ri·od·i·cal·ly (-ik 'l ē, -ik lē) *adv.* **1.** at regular intervals **2.** from time to time; recurrently

pe·ri·o·dic·i·ty (pir′ē ǝ dis′ǝ tē) *n.*, *pl.* **-ties** [Fr. *périodicité* < *période:* see PERIOD] **1.** the tendency, quality, or fact of recurring at regular intervals **2.** *Chem.* the occurrence of similar properties in elements occupying similar positions in the periodic table

periodic law the principle that the physical and chemical properties of the chemical elements recur periodically when the elements are arranged in increasing order of their atomic numbers

periodic sentence a sentence in which the essential elements are withheld until the end (Ex.: Because he was ill, he couldn't work.)

periodic system the system governing the classification of the elements: see PERIODIC LAW

periodic table an arrangement of the chemical elements according to their atomic numbers, to exhibit the periodic law: see chart on next page

per·i·o·don·tal (per′ē ǝ dän′t'l) *adj.* [PERI- + -ODONT + -AL] *Anat.* **1.** situated or occurring around a tooth **2.** affecting the gums, connective tissues, etc. surrounding the teeth

per·i·o·don·tics (-tiks) *n.pl.* [*with sing. v.*] [see prec. & -ICS] the branch of dentistry concerned with diseases of the bone and tissue supporting the teeth: also **per′i·o·don′ti·a** (-dän′shǝ, -shē ǝ) —**per′i·o·don′tic** *adj.* —**per′i·o·don′tist** *n.*

per·i·o·nych·i·um (per′ē ō nik′ē ǝm) *n.*, *pl.* **-i·a** (-ǝ) [ModL. < Gr. *peri-*, around (see PERI-) + *onych-*, nail (< *onyx:* see ONYX) + ModL. *-ium*, -IUM] the epidermis forming the border around a fingernail or toenail

per·i·os·te·um (per′ī äs′tē ǝm) *n.*, *pl.* **-te·a** (-ǝ) [ModL. < L. *periosteon* < Gr. *periosteon* < *peri-*, around + *osteon*, a bone: see OSTEO-] the membrane of tough, fibrous connective tissue covering all bones except at the joints —**per′i·os′te·al** (-ǝl) *adj.*

per·i·os·ti·tis (-äs tīt′ǝs) *n.* [ModL.] inflammation of the periosteum —**per′i·os·tit′ic** (-tit′ik) *adj.*

per·i·os·tra·cum (-äs′trǝ kǝm) *n.*, *pl.* **-tra·ca** (-kǝ) [ModL. < Gr. *peri-*, around (see PERI-) + *ostrakon*, a shell: see OSTRACIZE] a horny covering, secreted as the outermost layer of most mollusk shells, that protects the underlying shell from erosion

per·i·o·tic (per′ē ōt′ik, -ät′ik) *adj.* [PERI- + -OTIC] *Anat., Zool.* surrounding the inner ear; specif., of the bony structure (**periotic bone**) forming a capsule enclosing the labyrinth in mammals

per·i·pa·tet·ic (per′i pǝ tet′ik) *adj.* [Fr. *péripatétique* < L. *peripateticus* < Gr. *peripatētikos* < *peripatein*, to walk about < *peri-*, around + *patein*, to walk < IE. base *pent-*, to step, go, whence FIND] **1.** [P-] of the philosophy or the followers of Aristotle, who walked about in the Lyceum while he was teaching **2.** moving from place to place; walking about; itinerant —*n.* [ME. *parypatetik*] **1.** [P-] a follower of Aristotle **2.** a person who walks from place to place —*SYN.* see ITINERANT —**per′i·pa·tet′i·cal·ly** *adv.*

per·i·pe·tei·a (per′ǝ pi tē′ǝ, -tī′-) *n.* [Gr. *peripeteia*, a reversal < *peripetēs*, falling in with, changing suddenly < *peri-*, around (see PERI-) + *piptein*, to fall (see FEATHER)] a sudden change of fortune or reversal of circumstances, as in a drama: also **per′i·pe·ti′a, pe·rip·e·ty** (pǝ rip′ǝ tē)

pe·riph·er·al (pǝ rif′ǝr ǝl) *adj.* **1.** of, belonging to, or forming a periphery **2.** lying at the outside or away from the central part; outer; external; specif., *Anat.* of, at, or near the surface of the body **3.** only slightly connected with what is essential or important; merely incidental; tangential [of peripheral interest] —**pe·riph′er·al·ly** *adv.*

peripheral vision the area of vision lying just outside the line of direct sight

pe·riph·er·y (-ē) *n.*, *pl.* **-er·ies** [MFr. *peripherie* < LL. *peripheria* < Gr. *periphereia* < *peripherēs*, moving around < *peri-*, around + *pherein*, to BEAR¹] **1.** a boundary line,

PERIODIC TABLE OF THE ELEMENTS

GROUP	I	II	III	IV	V	VI	VII	VIII	O
SUBGROUP	A B	A B	B A	B A	B A	B A	B A		
Type of Hydride	RH	RH₂	RH₃	RH₄	RH₃	RH₂	RH		
Type of Oxide	R₂O	RO	R₂O₃	RO₂	R₂O₅	RO₃	R₂O₇	RO₄	

(Hydride/Oxide types shown as printed: RH, RH_2, RH_3, RH_4, RH_3, RH_2, RH; R_2O, RO, R_2O_3, RO_2, R_2O_5, RO_3, R_2O_7, RO_4)

Period 1

Z	Symbol	Atomic weight	Shells (K L M N O P Q)
1	H	1.00797	K 1
2	He	4.0026	K 2

Period 2

Z	Symbol	Atomic weight	Shells (L/K)
3	Li	6.939	1 / 2
4	Be	9.0122	2 / 2
5	B	10.811	3 / 2
6	C	12.01115	4 / 2
7	N	14.0067	5 / 2
8	O	15.9994	6 / 2
9	F	18.9984	7 / 2
10	Ne	20.183	8 / 2

Period 3

Z	Symbol	Atomic weight	Shells (M L K)
11	Na	22.9898	1 8 2
12	Mg	24.312	2 8 2
13	Al	26.9815	3 8 2
14	Si	28.086	4 8 2
15	P	30.9738	5 8 2
16	S	32.064	6 8 2
17	Cl	35.453	7 8 2
18	Ar	39.948	8 8 2

Period 4

Z	Symbol	Atomic weight	Shells (N M L K)
19	K	39.102	1 8 8 2
20	Ca	40.08	2 8 8 2
21	Sc	44.956	2 9 8 2
22	Ti	47.90	2 10 8 2
23	V	50.942	2 11 8 2
24	Cr	51.996	1 13 8 2
25	Mn	54.9380	2 13 8 2
26	Fe	55.847	2 14 8 2
27	Co	58.9332	2 15 8 2
28	Ni	58.71	2 16 8 2
29	Cu	63.546	1 18 8 2
30	Zn	65.37	2 18 8 2
31	Ga	69.72	3 18 8 2
32	Ge	72.59	4 18 8 2
33	As	74.9216	5 18 8 2
34	Se	78.96	6 18 8 2
35	Br	79.909	7 18 8 2
36	Kr	83.80	8 18 8 2

Period 5

Z	Symbol	Atomic weight	Shells (O N M L K)
37	Rb	85.47	1 8 18 8 2
38	Sr	87.62	2 8 18 8 2
39	Y	88.905	2 9 18 8 2
40	Zr	91.22	2 10 18 8 2
41	Nb	92.906	1 12 18 8 2
42	Mo	95.94	1 13 18 8 2
43	Tc	(97)	2 13 18 8 2
44	Ru	101.07	1 15 18 8 2
45	Rh	102.905	1 16 18 8 2
46	Pd	106.4	0 18 18 8 2
47	Ag	107.868	1 18 18 8 2
48	Cd	112.40	2 18 18 8 2
49	In	114.82	3 18 18 8 2
50	Sn	118.69	4 18 18 8 2
51	Sb	121.75	5 18 18 8 2
52	Te	127.60	6 18 18 8 2
53	I	126.9044	7 18 18 8 2
54	Xe	131.30	8 18 18 8 2

Period 6

Z	Symbol	Atomic weight	Shells (P O N M L K)
55	Cs	132.905	1 8 18 18 8 2
56	Ba	137.34	2 8 18 18 8 2
57*	La	138.91	2 9 18 18 8 2
72	Hf	178.49	2 9 32 18 8 2
73	Ta	180.948	2 11 32 18 8 2
74	W	183.85	2 12 32 18 8 2
75	Re	186.2	2 13 32 18 8 2
76	Os	190.2	2 14 32 18 8 2
77	Ir	192.2	2 15 32 18 8 2
78	Pt	195.09	1 17 32 18 8 2
79	Au	196.967	1 18 32 18 8 2
80	Hg	200.59	2 18 32 18 8 2
81	Tl	204.37	3 18 32 18 8 2
82	Pb	207.19	4 18 32 18 8 2
83	Bi	208.980	5 18 32 18 8 2
84	Po	210.05	6 18 32 18 8 2
85	At	(210)	7 18 32 18 8 2
86	Rn	222.00	8 18 32 18 8 2

Period 7

Z	Symbol	Atomic weight	Shells (Q P O N M L K)
87	Fr	(223)	1 8 18 32 18 8 2
88	Ra	226.00	2 8 18 32 18 8 2
89**	Ac	(227)	2 9 18 32 18 8 2
104			2 10 18 32 18 8 2

*58–71 RARE EARTHS (LANTHANIDE SERIES)

Shells listed as (P O N M L K):

Z	Symbol	Atomic weight	Shells
58	Ce	140.12	2 8 20 18 8 2
59	Pr	140.907	2 8 21 18 8 2
60	Nd	144.24	2 8 22 18 8 2
61	Pm	(145)	2 8 23 18 8 2
62	Sm	150.35	2 8 23 18 8 2
63	Eu	151.96	2 8 24 18 8 2
64	Gd	157.25	2 9 25 18 8 2
65	Tb	158.924	2 8 27 18 8 2
66	Dy	162.50	2 8 28 18 8 2
67	Ho	164.930	2 8 29 18 8 2
68	Er	167.28	2 8 30 18 8 2
69	Tm	168.934	2 8 31 18 8 2
70	Yb	173.04	2 8 32 18 8 2
71	Lu	174.97	2 9 32 18 8 2

**90–103 ACTINIDE SERIES

Shells listed as (Q P O N M L K):

Z	Symbol	Atomic weight	Shells
90	Th	232.038	2 10 18 32 18 8 2
91	Pa	231.10	2 9 20 32 18 8 2
92	U	238.03	2 9 21 32 18 8 2
93	Np	237.00	2 9 23 32 18 8 2
94	Pu	239.05	2 8 24 32 18 8 2
95	Am	243.13	2 8 25 32 18 8 2
96	Cm	(247)	2 9 25 32 18 8 2
97	Bk	(248)	2 8 27 32 18 8 2
98	Cf	(251)	2 8 28 32 18 8 2
99	Es	(252)	2 8 29 32 18 8 2
100	Fm	(257)	2 8 30 32 18 8 2
101	Md	(258)	2 8 31 32 18 8 2
102	No	(255)	2 8 31 32 18 8 2
103	Lr	(256)	2 8 32 32 18 8 2

Key at element 1, H   *a* atomic number   *b* chemical symbol   *c* atomic weight   *d* electrons in shells   ( ) encloses mass number of longest half-life isotope (if no exact atomic weight has been determined)

esp. that of a rounded figure; perimeter **2.** an outside surface, esp. that of a rounded object or body **3.** surrounding space or area; outer parts; environs or outskirts **4.** *Anat.* the area surrounding a nerve ending —*SYN.* see CIRCUMFERENCE

pe·riph·ra·sis (pə rif'rə sis) *n.*, *pl.* **-ses** (-sēz') [L. < Gr. *periphrasis* < *peri-*, around + *phrazein*, to speak] **1.** the use of many words where one or a few would do; roundabout way of speaking; circumlocution **2.** a periphrastic expression Also **per·i·phrase** (per'ə frāz')

per·i·phras·tic (per'ə fras'tik) *adj.* [ML. *periphrasticus* < Gr. *periphrastikos*] **1.** of, like, or expressed in periphrasis **2.** *Gram.* formed with a particle or auxiliary verb instead of by inflection, as the phrase *did sing* used for *sang* —**per'i·phras'ti·cal·ly** *adv.*

☆**pe·rique** (pə rēk') *n.* [AmFr., supposedly after *Pierre Chenet*, said to have introduced tobacco-growing in Louisiana, but prob. < Fr. pronun. of E. *prick*, vulgar for *penis* (from the shape of the dried, compacted plug)] a strong, rich black tobacco grown in Louisiana and used mainly in blending

per·i·sarc (per'ə särk) *n.* [< PERI- + Gr. *sarx* (gen. *sarkos*), flesh: see SARCO-] the tough, nonliving, outer skeleton layer of many hydroid colonies

per·i·scope (per'ə skōp) *n.* [PERI- + -SCOPE] **1.** a periscopic lens **2.** an optical instrument consisting of a tube holding a system of lenses and mirrors or prisms, so arranged that a person looking through the eyepiece at one end can see objects reflected at the other end: used on submerged submarines, etc.

per·i·scop·ic (per'ə skäp'ik) *adj.* **1.** providing clear lateral or oblique range of view, as certain lenses **2.** of or by a periscope

per·ish (per'ish) *vi.* [ME. *perischen* < extended stem of OFr. *perir* < L. *perire*, to go through, perish < *per-*, through (see PER) + *ire*, to go: see YEAR] **1.** to be destroyed, ruined, or wiped out **2.** to die; esp., to die a violent or untimely death —*SYN.* see DIE[1] —**perish the thought!** do not even consider such a possibility!

per·ish·a·ble (-ə b'l) *adj.* that may perish; esp., liable to spoil or deteriorate, as some foods —*n.* something, esp. a food, liable to spoil or deteriorate —**per'ish·a·bil'i·ty, per'ish·a·ble·ness** *n.*

pe·ris·so·dac·tyl (pə ris'ə dak'til) *adj.* [ModL. *perissodactylus* < Gr. *perissos*, uneven (< *peri-*, over) + *daktylos*, finger: see DACTYL] having an uneven number of toes on each foot —*n.* any of an order (Perissodactyla) of hoofed mammals with an uneven number of toes on each foot and a simple stomach, including the horse, tapir, etc. —**pe·ris'so·dac'ty·lous** *adj.*

per·i·stal·sis (per'ə stôl'sis, -stal'-) *n.*, *pl.* **-ses** (-sēz) [ModL. < Gr. *peristaltikos* < *peristellein*, to surround, involve < *peri-*, around + *stallein*, to place: for IE. base see STALK] the rhythmic, wavelike motion of the walls of the alimentary canal and certain other hollow organs, consisting of alternate contractions and dilations of transverse and longitudinal muscles that move the contents of the tube onward —**per'i·stal'tic** *adj.* —**per'i·stal'ti·cal·ly** *adv.*

per·i·stome (per'ə stōm') *n.* [ModL. *peristoma* < *peri-* + Gr. *stoma*, a mouth: see STOMACH] **1.** *Bot.* the fringe of teeth around the opening of the spore case in mosses **2.** *Zool.* the area or parts surrounding the mouth or a mouthlike part of various invertebrates —**per'i·sto'mi·al** (-stō'mē əl) *adj.*

per·i·style (per'ə stīl') *n.* [Fr. *péristyle* < L. *peristylum* < Gr. *peristylon* < *peri-*, around + *stylos*, a column: see STEER[1]] **1.** a row of columns forming an enclosure or supporting a roof **2.** any area or enclosure so formed as a court —**per'i·styl'ar** (-lər) *adj.*

per·i·the·ci·um (per'ə thē'shē əm, -sē-) *n.*, *pl.* **-ci·a** (-ə) [ModL. < *peri-* + Gr. *thēkē*, a case, box: see THECA] in certain ascomycetous fungi, a flasklike case containing the spore sacs (*asci*) —**per'i·the'ci·al** *adj.*

per·i·to·ne·um (per'it 'n ē'əm) *n.*, *pl.* **-ne'a** (-ə), **-ne'ums** [LL. < Gr. *peritonaion* < *peri-*, around + *teinein*, to stretch: see TENANT] the transparent serous membrane lining the abdominal cavity and reflected inward at various places to cover the visceral organs —**per'i·to·ne'al** *adj.*

per·i·to·ni·tis (-īt'əs) *n.* [see -ITIS] inflammation of the peritoneum

pe·rit·ri·chous (pə rit'ri kəs) *adj.* [PERI- + TRICH(O)- + -OUS] **1.** *Bot.* having flagella evenly distributed over the entire surface of the cell: said of bacteria **2.** *Zool.* having a wreath of cilia around the mouth: said of protozoans —**pe·rit'ri·chous·ly** *adv.*

‡**pe·ri·tus** (pā rē'tŏŏs; *E.* pə rēt'əs) *n.*, *pl.* **-ti** (-tē; *E.* -ē) [L.] an expert; specif., a skilled theologian used as a consultant

per·i·wig (per'ə wig') *n.* [earlier *perwyke*, altered < Fr. *perruque*: see PERUKE] a wig; specif., one of the type worn by men in the 17th and 18th cent., usually powdered and having the hair gathered together at the back with a ribbon

per·i·win·kle[1] (per'ə win'k'l) *n.* [ME. *pervinke* < OE. *peruince* < L. *pervinca*, periwinkle < *pervincire*, to entwine, bind < *per-* (see PER) + *vincire*, to bind, fetter: for IE. base see WEAK] any of a genus (*Vinca*) of trailing or erect, evergreen plants of the dogbane family; esp., a European creeper (*Vinca minor*) with blue, white, or pink flowers, grown as a ground cover

per·i·win·kle[2] (per'ə win'k'l) *n.* [< OE. *pinewincle* < L. *pina*, a mussel (< Gr. *pina*) + *-wincle*, akin to Dan. dial. *vinkel*, snail shell, OE. *winkel*, corner: for IE. base see WINK] **1.** any of a genus (*Littorina*) of small, related, intertidal saltwater snails having a thick, brown or yellowish, cone-shaped shell with dark spiral bands: some species are edible **2.** the shell of such a snail

per·jure (pur'jər) *vt.* **-jured, -jur·ing** [ME. *parjuren* < OFr. *parjurer* < L. *perjurare* < *per*, through + *jurare*, to swear: see JURY[1]] to make (oneself) guilty of perjury —**per'jur·er** *n.*

per·jured (-jərd) *adj.* **1.** guilty of perjury [a *perjured* witness] **2.** characterized by perjury [*perjured* testimony]: also **per·jur·i·ous** (pər jur'ē əs)

per·ju·ry (-jər ē) *n.*, *pl.* **-ries** [ME. < OFr. *parjurie* < L. *perjurium* < *perjurus*, false, breaking oath < *per*, through + *jus* (gen. *juris*), a right, justice: see JURY[1]] **1.** the willful telling of a lie while under lawful oath or affirmation to tell the truth in a matter material to the point of inquiry **2.** the breaking of any oath or formal promise

perk[1] (purk) *vt.* *perken* < ? ONormFr. *perquer*, to perch] **1.** to raise (the head, ears, etc.) briskly or spiritedly (often with *up*) **2.** to make jaunty or smart in appearance (often with *up* or *out*) **3.** to give or restore freshness, vivacity, etc. to (usually with *up*) —*vi.* **1.** to lift one's head, straighten one's posture, etc. jauntily **2.** to become lively or animated; esp., to recover one's spirits (with *up*) —*adj.* same as PERKY

perk[2] (purk) *vt.*, *vi.* *colloq.* clip of PERCOLATE

perk[3] (purk) *n.* [Chiefly Brit. Colloq.] *clipped form of* PERQUISITE

Per·kins (pur'kinz), **Frances** 1882–1965; U.S. social worker; secretary of labor (1933–45)

perk·y (pur'kē) *adj.* **perk'i·er, perk'i·est 1.** self-confident; aggressive **2.** gay or lively; saucy; jaunty —**perk'i·ly** *adv.* —**perk'i·ness** *n.*

Per·lis (per'lis) NW state of the Federation of Malaya: 310 sq. mi.; pop. 112,000

per·lite (pur'līt) *n.* [Fr. *perle*, PEARL[1]] **1.** *Geol.* a glassy volcanic rock, similar to obsidian, with a pearly luster and showing many minute concentric cracks: used as insulation, and in concrete, plaster, etc. **2.** *same as* PEARLITE —**per·lit·ic** (pər lit'ik) *adj.*

Perm (perm) city in E European R.S.F.S.R., on the Kama River: pop. 785,000

perm (purm) *n. colloq. clip of* PERMANENT WAVE —*vt.* [Colloq.] to give a permanent wave to

per·ma·frost (pur'mə frôst', -fräst') *n.* [PERMA(NENT) + FROST] permanently frozen subsoil

☆**Perm·al·loy** (purm'al'oi, pur'mə loi') [PERM(EABILITY) + ALLOY] a *trademark for* any of a series of alloys of iron and nickel with high magnetic permeability: used in magnetic cores, for wrapping underwater cables, etc. —*n.* [p-] such an alloy

per·ma·nence (pur'mə nəns) *n.* [ME. < ML. *permanentia*] the state or quality of being permanent

per·ma·nen·cy (-nən sē) *n.* **1.** same as PERMANENCE **2.** *pl.* **-cies** something permanent

per·ma·nent (-nənt) *adj.* [ME. < MFr. < L. *permanens*, prp. of *permanere* < *per*, through + *manere*, to remain: see MANOR] **1.** lasting or intended to last indefinitely without change **2.** lasting a relatively long time —*n. colloq. clip of* PERMANENT WAVE —**per'ma·nent·ly** *adv.*

permanent magnet a magnet, usually of hard steel, which keeps most of its magnetism after it has once been magnetized

permanent tooth any of the 32 adult human teeth including those that replace the milk teeth

permanent wave a hair wave that is produced by applying heat or chemical preparations and that remains even after the hair is washed

per·man·ga·nate (pər maŋ'gə nāt') *n.* a salt of permanganic acid, generally dark purple in color and a strong oxidizing agent

per·man·gan·ic acid (pur'man gan'ik) [PER- + MANGANIC] an unstable acid, $HMnO_4$, that is a strong oxidizing agent in aqueous solution

per·me·a·bil·i·ty (pur'mē ə bil'ət ē) *n.* **1.** the state or quality of being permeable **2.** *Physics a)* the measure of the ease with which magnetic lines of force are carried by a particular material *b)* the rate of diffusion of a fluid through a porous body under standard conditions of area, thickness, and pressure

per·me·a·ble (pur′mē ə b'l) *adj.* [ME. < L. *permeabilis*] that can be permeated; open to passage or penetration, esp. by fluids —**per′me·a·bly** *adv.*

per·me·ance (pur′mē əns) *n.* **1.** a permeating or being permeated **2.** the reciprocal of magnetic reluctance

per·me·ant (-ənt) *adj.* that permeates

per·me·ate (-āt′) *vt.* **-at′ed, -at′ing** [< L. *permeatus*, pp. of *permeare* < *per*, through + *meare*, to glide, flow, pass < IE. base *mei-*, to go, travel, whence Czech *mijeti*, to pass by] to pass into or through and affect every part of; penetrate and spread through [ink *permeates* blotting paper, a society *permeated* with idealism] —*vi.* to spread or diffuse; penetrate (with *through* or *among*) —**per′me·a′tion** *n.* —**per′me·a′tive** (-āt′iv) *adj.*

‡**per men·sem** (pər men′səm) [L.] by the month

Per·mi·an (pur′mē ən) *adj.* [after PERM] *Geol.* designating or of the seventh and last period of the Paleozoic Era, following the Pennsylvanian Period and characterized by increased reptile life, major mountain building, as in the Appalachians, and glaciation in the S Hemisphere —**the Permian** the Permian Period or its rocks: see GEOLOGY, chart

per mill [< PER + L. *mille*, thousand] for every thousand

per·mis·si·ble (pər mis′ə b'l) *adj.* [ME. *permyssyble* < MFr. < ML. *permissibilis* < L. *permissus*, pp. of *permittere*] that can be permitted; allowable —**per·mis·si·bil′i·ty** *n.* —**per·mis′si·bly** *adv.*

per·mis·sion (pər mish′ən) *n.* [ME. < MFr. < L. *permissio* < pp. of *permittere*] the act of permitting; esp., formal consent; leave; license [*permission* to go]

per·mis·sive (-mis′iv) *adj.* [ME. *permyssyue* < MFr. *permissif* < ML. *permissivus* < pp. of L. *permittere*] **1.** giving permission; that permits **2.** allowing freedom; esp., tolerant of behavior or practices disapproved of by others; indulgent; lenient **3.** [Archaic] allowable and at one's option —**per·mis′sive·ly** *adv.* —**per·mis′sive·ness** *n.*

per·mit¹ (pər mit′; for n., usually pur′mit) *vt.* **-mit′ted, -mit′ting** [LME. *permitten* < L. *permittere* < *per*, through + *mittere*, to send: see MISSION] **1.** to allow; consent to; tolerate [smoking is not *permitted*] **2.** to give permission to; authorize [to *permit* women to vote] **3.** to give opportunity for [to *permit* light to enter] —*vi.* to give opportunity or possibility [if the weather *permits*] —*n.* **1.** same as PERMISSION **2.** a document granting permission to do something; license; warrant —*SYN.* see LET¹ —**per·mit′ter** *n.*

☆**per·mit²** (pur′mit) *n.* [altered (after prec.) < Sp. *palometa*, orig. dim. of *paloma*, dove: see PALOMINO] an Atlantic pompano (*Trachinotus falcatus*), found esp. in the Caribbean

☆**per·mit·tiv·i·ty** (pur′mi tiv′ə tē) *n.* [< PERMIT¹ + -IVE + -ITY] the ratio of the capacitance of a capacitor in which a substance is the dielectric to its capacitance with a vacuum between the plates; dielectric constant

per·mu·ta·tion (pur′myōō tā′shən) *n.* [ME. *permutacion* < MFr. < L. *permutatio* < *permutare*: see ff.] **1.** any radical alteration; total transformation **2.** a complete rearrangement, esp. by interchanging; specif., *Math.* any of the total number of groupings, or subsets, into which a group, or set, of elements can be arranged in a particular order: the permutations of 1, 2, and 3 taken two at a time are 12, 21, 13, 31, 23, 32: cf. COMBINATION —**per′mu·ta′tion·al** *adj.*

per·mute (pər myōōt′) *vt.* **-mut′ed, -mut′ing** [ME. *permuten* < L. *permutare*, to change thoroughly < *per-*, intens. + *mutare*, to change: see MUTATE] **1.** to make different; alter **2.** to rearrange the order or sequence of —**per·mut′a·ble** *adj.*

Per·nam·bu·co (pur′nəm bōō′kō; *Port.* per′nänm bōō′koo) **1.** state of NE Brazil: 37,940 sq. mi.; pop. 4,137,000; cap. Recife **2.** same as RECIFE

per·ni·cious (pər nish′əs) *adj.* [Fr. *pernicieux* < L. *perniciosus* < *pernicies*, destruction < *pernecare*, to kill < *per*, thoroughly + *necare*, to kill: see NECRO-] **1.** causing great injury, destruction, or ruin; fatal; deadly **2.** [Rare] wicked; evil —**per·ni′cious·ly** *adv.* —**per·ni′cious·ness** *n.*

SYN.—**pernicious** applies to that which does great harm by insidiously undermining or weakening [*pernicious* anemia, a *pernicious* dogma]; **baneful** implies a harming by or as by poisoning [a *baneful* superstition]; **noxious** refers to anything that is injurious to physical or mental health [*noxious* fumes]; **deleterious** implies slower, less irreparable injury to the health [the *deleterious* effects of an unbalanced diet]; **detrimental** implies a causing of damage, loss, or disadvantage to something specified [his interference was *detrimental* to our cause] —*ANT.* **harmless, innocuous**

pernicious anemia a form of anemia characterized by a gradual reduction in the number of the red blood cells, gastrointestinal and nervous disturbances, etc.

per·nick·et·y (pər nik′ə tē) *adj.* same as PERSNICKETY

Per·nik (per′nik) city in W Bulgaria, on the Struma River: pop. 80,000

Per·nod (per nō′) [Fr.] *a trademark for* a green, anise-flavored French liqueur —*n.* [p-] a drink of this

per·o·ne·al (per′ə nē′əl) *adj.* [< ModL. *peroneus* (< *perone*, fibula < Gr. *peronē*, a pin, fibula) + -AL] of or near the fibula

per·o·ral (pər ôr′əl) *adj.* [PER- + ORAL] by, through, or around the mouth

per·o·rate (per′ə rāt′) *vt.* **-rat′ed, -rat′ing** [< L. *peroratus*: see ff.] **1.** to make a speech, esp. a lengthy oration **2.** to sum up or conclude a speech

per·o·ra·tion (per′ə rā′shən) *n.* [L. *peroratio* < *peroratus*, pp. of *perorare* < *per*, through + *orare*, to pray, speak: see ORATION] **1.** the concluding part of a speech, in which there is a summing up and emphatic recapitulation **2.** a high-flown or bombastic speech —**per′o·ra′tion·al** *adj.*

per·ox·i·dase (pə räk′sə dās′, -dāz′) *n.* [PER- + OXIDASE] any of the group of enzymes which catalyze reactions in which hydrogen peroxide or organic peroxides are reduced

per·ox·ide (pə räk′sīd) *n.* [PER- + OXIDE] any oxide containing the O_2 group in which the two atoms of oxygen are linked by a single bond; specif., hydrogen peroxide —*vt.* **-id·ed, -id·ing** to treat with a peroxide; esp., to bleach (hair, etc.) with hydrogen peroxide —*adj.* bleached with hydrogen peroxide

per·ox·y·ac·e·tyl nitrate (pə räk′sē ə set′'l) [PER- + OXY-¹ + ACETYL] an unstable nitrogen compound found in certain types of smog, that is an irritant, esp. to the eyes and to plants

per·pend¹ (pur′pənd) *n.* [ME. *perpoynt* < MFr. *parpain* < ?] a large stone extending through a wall from one side to the other, used as a binder: also **per′pent** (-pənt)

per·pend² (pər pend′) *vt., vi.* [L. *perpendere*: see ff.] [Archaic] to ponder or consider

per·pen·dic·u·lar (pur′pən dik′yə lər) *adj.* [ME. *perpendiculer* < OFr. < L. *perpendicularis* < *perpendiculum*, plumb line < *perpendere*, to weigh carefully < *per-*, intens. + *pendere*, to hang: see PENDANT] **1.** at right angles to a given plane or line **2.** exactly upright; vertical; straight up or down **3.** very steep **4.** [P-] of or designating the third and latest style of English Gothic architecture of the 14th to the 16th cent., characterized by vertical lines in its tracery —*n.* **1.** a device used in finding or marking the vertical line from any point **2.** a line at right angles to the plane of the horizon **3.** a line or plane at right angles to another line or plane **4.** a perpendicular or upright position —*SYN.* see VERTICAL —**per′pen·dic′u·lar′i·ty** (-lar′ət ē) *n.* —**per′pen·dic′u·lar·ly** *adv.*

per·pe·trate (pur′pə trāt′) *vt.* **-trat′ed, -trat′ing** [< L. *perpetratus*, pp. of *perpetrare*, to commit, perpetrate, orig., to bring about, achieve < *per*, thoroughly + *patrare*, to effect, prob. orig. a ritual term < *pater*, FATHER, priest] **1.** to do or perform (something evil, criminal, or offensive); be guilty of **2.** to commit (a blunder), impose (a hoax), etc. —**per′pe·tra′tion** *n.* —**per′pe·tra′tor** *n.*

per·pet·u·al (pər pech′ōō wəl) *adj.* [ME. *perpetuel* < OFr. < L. *perpetualis* < *perpetuus*, constant < *perpes* (gen. *perpetis*), continuous < *per-*, through + *petere*, to strive: for IE. base see FEATHER] **1.** lasting or enduring forever or for an indefinitely long time; eternal; permanent **2.** continuing indefinitely without interruption; unceasing; constant [a *perpetual* nuisance] **3.** blooming continuously throughout the growing season —*n.* a perpetual plant; esp., a variety of perpetual hybrid rose —*SYN.* see CONTINUAL —**per·pet′u·al·ly** *adv.*

perpetual calendar 1. a calendar mathematically so arranged that the correct day of the week can be determined for any given date over a wide range of years **2.** a desk calendar adjustable for each of many years

perpetual motion the motion of a hypothetical device which, once set in motion, would operate indefinitely by creating its own energy in excess of that dissipated

per·pet·u·ate (pər pech′ōō wāt′) *vt.* **-at′ed, -at′ing** [< L. *perpetuatus*, pp. of *perpetuare*] to make perpetual; cause to continue or be remembered; preserve from oblivion —**per·pet′u·a′tion** *n.* —**per·pet′u·a′tor** *n.*

per·pe·tu·i·ty (pur′pə tōō′ə tē, -tyōō′-) *n., pl.* **-ties** [ME. *perpetuite* < OFr. *perpetuité* < L. *perpetuitas*] **1.** the state or quality of being perpetual **2.** something perpetual, as an annuity or pension to be paid indefinitely or, often specif., for life **3.** unlimited time; eternity **4.** *Law* a) a limitation upon the transference of an estate: it is valid only for a legally specified period *b)* an estate so limited —**in perpetuity** forever or for an indefinite period with no stated limit

Per·pi·gnan (per pē nyän′) city in S France, near the Gulf of Lions & the Sp. border: pop. 83,000

per·plex (pər pleks′) *vt.* [< ME. *perplex*, perplexed < MFr. *perplexe* < L. *perplexus*, entangled, confused, involved < *per*, through + *plexus*, pp. of *plectere*, to twist, plait: see PLY¹] **1.** to make (a person) uncertain, doubtful, or hesitant; confuse; puzzle **2.** to make intricate or complicated; make confusing or hard to understand [to *perplex* an issue] —*n.* archaic or rare var. of PERPLEXITY —*SYN.* see PUZZLE —**per·plex′ing** *adj.* —**per·plex′ing·ly** *adv.*

per·plexed (-plekst′) *adj.* **1.** full of doubt or uncertainty; puzzled **2.** hard to understand; confusing —**per·plex′ed·ly** (-plek′sid lē) *adv.*

per·plex·i·ty (-plek′sə tē) *n.* [ME. *perplexite* < MFr. *perplexité* < LL. *perplexitas*] **1.** the condition of being perplexed; bewilderment; confusion **2.** *pl.* **-ties** something that perplexes or is perplexed, as a complication or intricacy

per pro. [L. *per procurationem*] by proxy

per·qui·site (pur′kwə zit) *n.* [ME. *perquysite* < ML. *perquisitum*, something acquired < neut. pp. of *perquirere*, to obtain, purchase < L., to search diligently for < *per-*,

intens. + *quaerere*, to seek: see QUERY] **1.** something additional to regular profit or pay, resulting from one's position or employment, esp. something customary or expected **2.** a tip or gratuity **3.** a privilege or benefit to which a person, institution, etc. is entitled by virtue of status, position, or the like; prerogative; right

Per·rault (pe rō′), **Charles** (shärl) 1628–1703; Fr. writer & compiler of fairy tales

Per·rin (pe ran′), **Jean Bap·tiste** (zhän bá·tēst′) 1870–1942; Fr. physicist

per·ron (per′ən; Fr. pe rōn′) n. [ME. *peroun* < OFr. *perron* < *pierre*, a stone < L. *petra*] an outside staircase, as up the slope of a terrace, leading to a platform at the front entrance of a building; also, the platform

Per·ry (per′ē) **1.** [? orig. a dim. of *Pers* < Fr. *Piers* < L. *Petrus*, PETER] a masculine name **2. Matthew Cal·braith** (kal′breth), 1794–1858; U.S. naval officer: negotiated U.S.-Japanese trade treaty (1854) **3. Oliver Haz·ard** (haz′ərd), 1785–1819; U.S. naval officer: defeated the Brit. fleet in the Battle of Lake Erie (1813): brother of *prec.* **4. Ralph Barton,** 1876–1957; U.S. philosopher & educator

per·ry (per′ē) n. [ME. *pereye* <MFr. *peré* < VL. **piratum*, for LL. *piracium* < L. *pirum*, pear] a fermented drink like cider, made from pear juice, esp. in England

Pers. 1. Persia **2.** Persian

pers. 1. person **2.** personal

per·salt (pur′sôlt′) n. a salt of a peracid

perse (purs) n. [ME. *pers* < OFr. < ML. *persus* < ? L. *Persa*, Persian] dark grayish blue

per se (per′ sē′, sā′) [L.] by (or in) itself; intrinsically

per second per second for each second every second: used of a rate of acceleration: e.g., a body accelerating from rest at 20 ft. per second per second would travel 120 ft. in 3 seconds, since it would travel 20 ft. in the first second, 40 ft. in the second, and 60 ft. in the third

per·se·cute (pur′sə kyōōt′) vt. -cut′ed, -cut′ing [LME. *persecuten* < MFr. *persécuter*, back-formation < *persécuteur* < L. *persecutor* < *persequi*, to pursue < *per-*, through + *sequi*, to follow: see SEQUENT] **1.** to afflict or harass constantly so as to injure or distress; oppress cruelly, esp. for reasons of religion, politics, or race **2.** to trouble or annoy constantly [*persecuted* by mosquitoes] —SYN. see WRONG —**per′se·cu′tive, per·se·cu·to·ry** (pur′sə kyōō tôr′ē, pər sek′yə-) adj. —**per′se·cu′tor** n.

per·se·cu·tion (pur′sə kyōō′shən) n. [ME. *persecucion* < OFr. < L. *persecutio*] a persecuting or being persecuted —**per′se·cu′tion·al** adj.

Per·se·ids (pur′sē idz) n.pl. [< ModL. *Perseis* (pl. *Perseïdes*) < Gr. *Perseïs*, sprung from Perseus] meteors of a major meteoric shower visible annually about August 12, appearing to radiate from the constellation Perseus

Per·seph·o·ne (pər sef′ə nē) [L. < Gr. *Persephonē*] *Gr. Myth.* the daughter of Zeus and Demeter, abducted by Hades (Pluto) to be his wife in the lower world: identified with the Roman goddess Proserpina

Per·sep·o·lis (pər sep′ə lis) capital of the ancient Persian Empire, near the modern city of Shiraz, Iran

Per·seus (pur′syōōs, -sē əs) [L. < Gr. *Perseus*] **1.** *Gr. Myth.* the son of Zeus and Danae and slayer of Medusa: he married Andromeda after rescuing her from a sea monster **2.** a N constellation between Taurus and Cassiopeia

per·se·ver·ance (pur′sə vir′əns) n. [ME. < OFr. < L. *perseverantia* < *perseverans*, prp. of *perseverare*: see ff.] **1.** the act of persevering; continued, patient effort **2.** the quality of one who perseveres; persistence **3.** *Calvinist Theol.* the continuance in grace of people elected to eternal salvation —**per′se·ver′ant** adj.

SYN.—**perseverance** implies a continuing to do something in spite of difficulties, obstacles, etc.; **persistence**, in a favorable sense, implies steadfast perseverance; in an unfavorable sense, annoyingly stubborn continuance; **tenacity** and **pertinacity** imply firm adherence to some purpose, action, belief, etc., the former word in a favorable sense, and the latter, with the unfavorable connotation of annoying obstinacy

per·sev·er·ate (pər sev′ə rāt′) vi. -at′ed, -at′ing [< L. *perseveratus*, pp. of *perseverare*, to PERSEVERE] to experience or display perseveration

per·sev·er·a·tion (pər sev′ə rā′shən) n. [L. *perseveratio* < *perseveratus*: see prec.] the tendency of an idea, impression, experience, etc. to persist or recur or of an individual to continue a particular mental activity without the ability to shift easily to another at a change in stimulus; specif., *Psychiatry* the persistent and pathological repetition of a verbal or motor response, often seen in organic brain disease and schizophrenia —**per·sev′er·a′tive** (-rāt′iv) adj.

per·se·vere (pur′sə vir′) vi. -vered′, -ver′ing [ME. *perseveren* < OFr. *perseverer* < L. *perseverare* < *perseverus*, very severe, strict < *per-*, intens. + *severus*, SEVERE] to continue in some effort, course of action, etc. in spite of difficulty, opposition, etc.; be steadfast in purpose; persist —**per′se·ver′ing·ly** adv.

Per·shing (pur′shin), **John Joseph** 1860–1948; U.S. general: commander in chief of American Expeditionary Forces, World War I

Per·sia (pur′zhə, -shə) **1.** *former official name of* IRAN **2.** *same as* PERSIAN EMPIRE

Per·sian (-zhən; -shən) adj. of Persia, ancient or modern, its people, their language, or culture; Iranian —n. **1.** a native or inhabitant of Persia **2.** the Iranian language of Iran; esp., its modern form developed after Old Persian and Pehlevi and spoken in Iran and Afghanistan

Persian blinds *same as* PERSIENNES

Persian cat a variety of domestic cat with long, silky hair

Persian Empire ancient empire in SW Asia, including at its peak (c. 500 B.C.) the area from the Indus River to the W borders of Asia Minor & Egypt: it was founded by Cyrus the Great (6th cent. B.C.) & conquered by Alexander the Great (c. 328 B.C.)

PERSIAN EMPIRE
(500 B.C.)

Persian Gulf arm of the Arabian Sea, between SW Iran & Arabia: c. 90,000 sq. mi.

Persian Gulf States group of independent Arab sheikdoms, including Bahrain, Qatar, and the Trucial States, under Brit. protection

Persian lamb 1. the lamb of the karakul sheep that supplies durable fur pelts **2.** the black or gray, glossy pelt of newborn karakul lambs, having small, tight curls

Persian rug (or **carpet**) an Oriental rug made in Persia (Iran), having rich, soft colors in any of various intricate, often floral, patterns

per·si·ennes (pur′zē enz′; Fr. per syen′) n.pl. [Fr., fem. pl. of *persien*, Persian] outside shutters for windows, having adjustable, horizontal slats like those on Venetian blinds

per·si·flage (pur′sə fläzh′) n. [Fr. < *persifler*, to banter < *per-* (see PER-) | *siffler*, to whistle, hiss < L. *sifilare*, var. of *sibilare*: see SIBILANT] **1.** a light, frivolous or flippant style of writing or speaking **2.** talk or writing of this kind; banter

☆**per·sim·mon** (pər sim′ən) n. [< AmInd. (Algonquian), as in Cree *pasiminan*, dried fruit] **1.** any of a genus (*Diospyros*) of trees of the ebony family with white, cup-shaped flowers, hard wood, and yellow or orange-red, plumlike fruit **2.** the fruit, sour and astringent when green, but sweet and edible when thoroughly ripe

per·sist (pər sist′, -zist′) vi. [MFr. *persister* < L. *persistere* < *per-*, through + *sistere*, to cause to stand, redupl. of base of *stare*, to STAND] **1.** to refuse to give up, esp. when faced with opposition or difficulty; continue firmly or steadily **2.** to continue insistently, as in repeating a question **3.** to continue to exist or prevail; endure; remain —SYN. see CONTINUE

per·sist·ence (-sis′təns, -zis′-) n. [Fr. *persistance*] **1.** the act of persisting; stubborn or enduring continuance **2.** a persistent or lasting quality; tenacity: also **per·sist′en·cy** (-tən sē) **3.** the continuance of an effect after the removal of its cause [*persistence* of vision causes visual impressions to continue upon the retina for a brief time] —SYN. see PERSEVERANCE

per·sist·ent (-tənt) adj. [L. *persistens*, prp. of *persistere*: see PERSIST] **1.** refusing to relent; continuing, esp. in the face of opposition, interference, etc.; stubborn; persevering **2.** continuing to exist or endure; lasting without change **3.** constantly repeated; continued **4.** *Bot.* remaining attached permanently or for a longer than normal time, as some leaves, perianths, etc. **5.** *Zool. a)* remaining essentially unchanged over a long period of geologic time, as a species *b)* remaining for life: said of such parts retained in the adult that normally disappear or wither at an early stage —**per·sist′ent·ly** adv.

per·snick·e·ty (pər snik′ə tē) adj. [< *pernickety* < Scot. dial., altered < ? *pertickie*, child's word for PARTICULAR] [Colloq.] **1.** too particular or precise; fastidious; fussy **2.** showing or requiring extremely careful treatment

per·son (pur′s'n) n. [ME. *persone* < OFr. < L. *persona*, lit., actor's face mask, hence a character, person, prob. < Etruscan *phersu*, a mask] **1.** a human being, esp. as distinguished from a thing or lower animal; individual man, woman, or child **2.** [Chiefly Brit.] an individual regarded slightingly, as one of a lower status **3.** *a)* a living human body *b)* bodily form or appearance [to be neat about one's *person*] **4.** personality; self; being **5.** *Gram. a)* division into three sets of pronouns and, in most languages, corresponding verb forms, the use of which indicates and is determined by the identity of the subject: see FIRST PERSON, SECOND PERSON, THIRD PERSON *b)* any of these sets **6.** [Archaic] a role in a play; character **7.** *Law* any individual or incorporated group having certain legal rights and responsibilities **8.** *Theol.* any of the three modes of being (Father, Son, and Holy Ghost) in the Trinity —**in person** in the flesh; in bodily presence

per·so·na (pər sō′nə) n., *pl.* -nae (-nē); for sense 2, -nas

[L.: see prec.] **1.** [*pl.*] the characters of a drama, novel, etc. **2.** *Psychol.* the outer personality or façade presented to others by an individual

per·son·a·ble (pur′s'n ə b'l) *adj.* [ME. *personabilis*] having a pleasing appearance and personality; attractive —**per′son·a·ble·ness** *n.* —**per′son·a·bly** *adv.*

per·son·age (-ij) *n.* [MFr.: see PERSON & -AGE] **1.** a person of importance or distinction; notable **2.** any person **3.** a character in history, a play, novel, etc.

‡**per·so·na gra·ta** (pər sō′nə grät′ə, grät′ə) [L.] a person who is acceptable or welcome; esp., a foreign diplomat acceptable to the government to which he is sent

per·son·al (pur′s'n əl) *adj.* [ME. < OFr. < L. *personalis*] **1.** of or peculiar to a certain person; private; individual **2.** done in person or by oneself without the use of another person or outside agency *[a personal interview]* **3.** involving persons or human beings *[personal relationships]* **4.** of the person, body, or physical appearance *[personal hygiene]* **5.** *a)* having to do with the character, personality, intimate affairs, conduct, etc. of a certain person *[a personal remark] b)* tending to make personal, esp. derogatory, remarks *[to get personal in an argument]* **6.** of, like, or having the nature of a person, or rational, self-conscious being **7.** *Gram.* indicating grammatical person, as the inflectional endings of verbs in Latin and Greek: see also PERSONAL PRONOUN **8.** *Law* of or constituting personal property —*n.* ☆**1.** a local news item about a person or persons ☆**2.** a classified advertisement about a personal matter

personal effects personal or intimate belongings of an individual, esp. those worn or carried on the person

personal equation 1. variation in judgment, observation, etc. between individuals, or in relation to a norm, often resulting in error **2.** an allowance for this

☆**personal foul** in certain team games, a foul involving body contact with an opponent, as unwarranted roughness or hindering

per·son·al·ism (-iz'm) *n.* any doctrine or movement which emphasizes the rights and centrality of the individual human being in his social, political, intellectual, etc. milieu —**per′son·al·ist** *n., adj.* —**per′son·al·is′tic** *adj.*

per·son·al·i·ty (pur′sə nal′ə tē) *n., pl.* **-ties** [ME. *personalite* < LL. *personalitas* < *personalis,* personal] **1.** the quality or fact of being a person **2.** the quality or fact of being a particular person; personal identity; individuality **3.** *a)* habitual patterns and qualities of behavior of any individual as expressed by physical and mental activities and attitudes; distinctive individual qualities of a person, considered collectively *b)* such qualities applied to a group, nation, etc. or to a place **4.** *a)* the sum of such qualities as impressing or likely to impress others *b)* personal attractiveness **5.** a person; esp., a notable person; personage **6.** [*pl.*] remarks, usually of an offensive or disparaging nature, aimed at or referring to a person —*SYN.* see DISPOSITION

per·son·al·ize (pur′s'n ə līz′) *vt.* **-ized′, -iz′ing 1.** to apply or understand as applied to a particular person, esp. to oneself **2.** *same as* PERSONIFY **3.** to have marked with one's name or initials *[personalized checks]*

per·son·al·ly (-lē) *adv.* **1.** without the help of others; in person *[to attend a matter personally]* **2.** as a person *[to dislike someone personally,* but admire his art*]* **3.** in one's own opinion; speaking for oneself **4.** as though directed at oneself *[to take a remark personally]*

personal pronoun any of a group of pronouns referring to the speaker(s), the person(s) spoken to, or any other person(s) or thing(s): the English personal pronouns, nominative case form, are: I², YOU, HE¹, SHE, IT, WE, THEY

personal property any property that is not real property and that is movable or not attached to the land

per·son·al·ty (pur′s'n al tē) *n., pl.* **-ties** [Anglo-Fr. *personaltie* < LL. *personalitas,* PERSONALITY] *same as* PERSONAL PROPERTY: opposed to REALTY

‡**per·so·na non gra·ta** (pər sō′nə nän grät′ə, grät′ə) [L.] a person who is not acceptable or welcome; esp., a foreign diplomat unacceptable to the government to which he is sent

per·son·ate (pur′sə nāt′; *for adj., usually* -s′n it) *vt.* **-at′ed, -at′ing** [< L. *personatus,* masked < *persona:* see PERSON] **1.** to act or play the part of, as in a drama or masquerade; portray **2.** to personify, as in poetry **3.** *Law* to assume the character or identity of with intent to defraud; impersonate —*adj. Bot.* having two lips and a projection in its throat: said of a tubular corolla, as in the snapdragon —**per′son·a′tion** *n.* —**per′son·a′tive** (-nāt′iv) *adj.* —**per′son·a′tor** *n.*

per·son·i·fi·ca·tion (pər sän′ə fi kā′shən) *n.* **1.** a personifying or being personified **2.** a person or thing thought of as representing some quality, thing, or idea; embodiment; perfect example *[Cupid is the personification of love]* **3.** a figure of speech in which a thing, quality, or idea is represented as a person

per·son·i·fy (pər sän′ə fī′) *vt.* **-fied′, -fy′ing** [Fr. *personnifier:* see PERSON & -FY] **1.** to think or speak of (a thing) as having life or personality; represent as a person *[to personify a ship by referring to it as "she"]* **2.** to symbolize (an abstract idea) by a human figure, as in art **3.** to be a symbol or perfect example of (some quality, thing, or idea); typify; embody —**per·son′i·fi′er** *n.*

per·son·nel (pur′sə nel′) *n.* [Fr. (lit., PERSONAL), prob. after G. *personal,* earlier *personale* < ML., orig. neut. of L. *personalis*] **1.** persons employed in any work, enterprise, service, establishment, etc.: distinguished in military usage from MATERIEL **2.** a personnel department or office, for hiring employees, etc. —*adj.* of or in charge of personnel *[personnel department]*

per·spec·tive (pər spek′tiv) *adj.* [ME. < LL. *perspectivus* < L. *perspicere,* to look through < *per,* through + *specere,* to look: see SPECTACLE] **1.** of perspective **2.** drawn in perspective —*n.* [ME. *perspectif* < ML. (*ars*) *perspectiva,* perspective (art)] **1.** the art of picturing objects or a scene in such a way, e.g. by converging lines (**linear perspective**), as to show them as they appear to the eye with reference to relative distance or depth **2.** *a)* the appearance of objects or scenes as determined by their relative distance and positions *b)* the effect of relative distance and position **3.** the relationship or proportion of the parts of a whole, regarded from a particular standpoint or point in time **4.** *a)* a specific point of view in understanding or judging things or events, esp. one that shows them in their true relations to one another *b)* the ability to see things in a true relationship **5.** a picture in perspective **6.** a distant view; vista **7.** [Obs.] an optical device, as a telescope glass —**per·spec′tive·ly** *adv.*

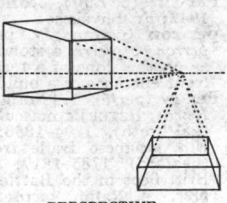

PERSPECTIVE

Per·spex (pur′speks) *Brit. trademark for* a hard, transparent plastic, an acrylic resin similar to Plexiglas —*n.* [**p-**] this plastic

per·spi·ca·cious (pur′spə kā′shəs) *adj.* [< L. *perspicax* (gen. *perspicacis*) < *perspicere,* to see through: see PERSPECTIVE] **1.** having keen judgment or understanding; acutely perceptive **2.** [Archaic] having keen vision —*SYN.* see SHREWD —**per′spi·ca′cious·ly** *adv.* —**per′spi·cac′i·ty** (-kas′ə tē), per′spi·ca′cious·ness *n.*

per·spic·u·ous (pər spik′yoo wəs) *adj.* [ME., transparent < L. *perspicuus* < *perspicere,* to see through: see PERSPECTIVE] clear in statement or expression; easily understood; lucid —**per·spi·cu·i·ty** (pur′spə kyōō′ə tē), **per·spic′u·ous·ness** *n.* —**per·spic′u·ous·ly** *adv.*

per·spi·ra·tion (pur′spə rā′shən) *n.* [Fr.] **1.** the act of perspiring; sweating **2.** salty moisture given off in perspiring; sweat

per·spir·a·to·ry (pər spir′ə tôr′ē) *adj.* of, relating to, or causing perspiration

per·spire (pər spir′) *vt., vi.* **-spired′, -spir′ing** [Fr. *perspirer* < L. *perspirare,* to breathe everywhere < *per-,* through + *spirare,* to breathe: see PER- & SPIRIT] to give forth (a characteristic salty moisture) through the pores of the skin; sweat

per·suade (pər swād′) *vt.* **-suad′ed, -suad′ing** [MFr. *persuader* < L. *persuadere* < *per-,* intens. + *suadere,* to urge: see SUASION] **1.** to cause to do something, esp. by reasoning, urging, or inducement; prevail upon **2.** to induce to believe something; convince —**per·suad′a·ble, per·sua′si·ble** (-swā′sə b'l) *adj.* —**per·sua′si·bil′i·ty** *n.* *SYN.*—**persuade** implies an influencing of a person to an action, belief, etc. by an overt appeal to his reason or emotions *[after some coaxing, pleading, and arguing, we persuaded him to go]*; **induce** suggests a subtler leading of a person to a course of action so that the decision seems finally to come from him *[he was induced to accept the position]*; **prevail on,** interchangeable with either of the preceding, often suggests stronger resistance overcome only after considerable argument, etc. *[he could not be prevailed on to change his mind]*

per·suad·er (-swā′dər) *n.* a person or thing that persuades; specif., [Colloq.] something used to intimidate or deter, as a weapon or punishment

per·sua·sion (pər swā′zhən) *n.* [ME. < L. *persuasio* < pp. of *persuadere*] **1.** a persuading or being persuaded **2.** power of persuading **3.** a strong belief; conviction **4.** *a)* a particular religious belief or system; religion *b)* a particular sect, party, group, etc. **5.** [Colloq.] kind, sort, sex, etc.: used jocularly —*SYN.* see OPINION

per·sua·sive (-siv) *adj.* [Fr. *persuasif* < ML. *persuasivus* < L. *persuasus,* pp. of *persuadere*] having the power, or tending, to persuade —**per·sua′sive·ly** *adv.* —**per·sua′sive·ness** *n.*

per·sul·fate (pər sul′fāt) *n.* [PER- + SULFATE] a salt containing the S₂O₈ radical, produced by the electrolysis of a sulfate solution

☆**PERT** (purt) [< P(*rogram*) E(*valuation and*) R(*eview*) T(*echnique*)] a system of planning, scheduling, controlling, and reviewing a series of interdependent events in order to follow a proper sequence and complete a project as quickly and inexpensively as possible

pert (purt) *adj.* [ME., aphetic for *apert* < OFr. < L. *apertus,* open: see APERTURE] **1.** bold or impudent in speech or behavior; saucy; forward **2.** chic and jaunty **3.** [Dial.] in good spirits or health; lively; brisk **4.** [Obs.] clever —**pert′ly** *adv.* —**pert′ness** *n.*

pert. pertaining

per·tain (pər tān′) *vi.* [ME. *partenen* < OFr. *partenir* <

L. *pertinere*, to stretch out, reach < *per-*, intens. + *tenere*, to hold: see TENANT] **1.** to belong; be connected or associated; be a part, accessory, etc. *[lands pertaining to an estate]* **2.** to be appropriate or suitable *[conduct that pertains to a lady]* **3.** to have reference or relevance; be related *[laws pertaining to the case]* —**pertaining to** having to do with; belonging to

Perth (purth) **1.** county of C Scotland: 2,493 sq. mi.; pop. 125,000: also **Perth′shire** (-shir) **2.** its county seat, on the Tay: pop. 41,000 **3.** capital of Western Australia, in the SW part: pop., met. area, 558,000

Perth Am·boy (am′boi) [after the Earl of *Perth* (1648–1716) + *Amboy* < Algonquian *ompage*, level area] seaport in NE N.J., on Raritan Bay: pop. 39,000

per·ti·na·cious (pur′tə nā′shəs) *adj.* [< L. *pertinax* (gen. *pertinacis*), firm < *per-*, intens. + *tenax*, holding fast < *tenere*, to hold: see TENANT] **1.** holding firmly to some purpose, belief, or action, often stubbornly or obstinately **2.** hard to get rid of; unyielding; persistent —*SYN.* see STUBBORN —**per′ti·na′cious·ly** *adv.*

per·ti·nac·i·ty (-nas′ə tē) *n.* [MFr. *pertinacité*] the quality or condition of being pertinacious; stubborn persistence; obstinacy —*SYN.* see PERSEVERANCE

per·ti·nence (purt′'n əns) *n.* the quality of being pertinent or appropriate; relevance: also **per′ti·nen·cy**

per·ti·nent (-ənt) *adj.* [ME. < MFr. < L. *pertinens*, prp. of *pertinere*: see PERTAIN] having some connection with the matter at hand; relevant; to the point —*SYN.* see RELEVANT —**per′ti·nent·ly** *adv.*

per·turb (pər turb′) *vt.* [ME. *perturben* < MFr. *perturber* < L. *perturbare* < *per-*, intens. + *turbare*, to disturb: see TURBID] **1.** to cause to be alarmed, agitated, or upset; disturb or trouble greatly **2.** to cause disorder or confusion in; unsettle **3.** *Astron.* to cause perturbations in (a heavenly body) —*SYN.* see DISTURB —**per·turb′a·ble** *adj.* —**per·turb′ed·ly** *adv.* —**per·turb′er** *n.*

per·tur·ba·tion (pur′tər bā′shən) *n.* [ME. < MFr. *perturbacion* < L. *perturbatio*] **1.** a perturbing or being perturbed **2.** something that perturbs; disturbance **3.** *Astron.* an irregularity in the orbit of a heavenly body, caused by the attraction of a body or bodies other than the one around which it orbits —**per′tur·ba′tion·al**, **per′tur·ba′tive** *adj.*

per·tus·sis (pər tus′is) *n.* [ModL. < L. *per-*, intens. + *tussis*, a cough] *same as* WHOOPING COUGH —**per·tus′sal**, **per·tus′soid** *adj.*

Pe·ru (pə rōō′) country in W S. America, on the Pacific: 496,222 sq. mi.; pop. 13,586,000; cap. Lima

Pe·ru·gia (pe rōō′jä) commune in Umbria, C Italy: pop. 121,000

Pe·ru·gi·no (pe′rōō jē′nō), **Il** (ēl) (born *Pietro Vannucci*) 1446?–1523?; It. painter

pe·ruke (pə rōōk′) *n.* [Fr. *perruque* < It. *perruca*, *parruca*] *same as* PERIWIG

pe·rus·al (pə rōō′z'l) *n.* the act of perusing

pe·ruse (pə rōōz′) *vt.* **-rused′**, **-rus′ing** [LME. *perusen*, to use up, prob. < L. *per-*, intens. + ME. *usen*, to USE] **1.** orig., to examine in detail; scrutinize **2.** to read carefully or thoroughly; study **3.** to read: a pretentious use, now often connoting a casual or leisurely reading —**pe·rus′er** *n.*

Pe·ru·vi·an (pə rōō′vē ən) *adj.* of Peru, its people, or their culture —*n.* a native or inhabitant of Peru

Peruvian bark *same as* CINCHONA (sense 2)

per·vade (pər vād′) *vt.* **-vad′ed**, **-vad′ing** [L. *pervadere* < *per*, through + *vadere*, to go: see EVADE] **1.** to pass through; spread or be diffused throughout **2.** to be prevalent throughout —**per·va′sion** (-vā′zhən) *n.*

per·va·sive (-vā′siv) *adj.* tending to pervade or spread throughout —**per·va′sive·ly** *adv.* —**per·va′sive·ness** *n.*

per·verse (pər vurs′) *adj.* [ME. *pervers* < OFr. < L. *perversus*, pp. of *pervertere*: see PERVERT] **1.** deviating from what is considered right or good; wrong, improper, etc. or corrupt, wicked, etc.; perverted **2.** persisting in error or fault; stubbornly contrary **3.** obstinately disobedient or difficult; intractable **4.** characterized by or resulting from obstinacy or contrariness —*SYN.* see CONTRARY —**per·verse′ly** *adv.* —**per·verse′ness** *n.*

per·ver·sion (pər vur′zhən, -shən) *n.* [ME. *peruersion* < L. *perversio* < pp. of *pervertere*] **1.** a perverting or being perverted **2.** something perverted; abnormal form **3.** any of various sexual acts or practices deviating from what is considered normal; sexual deviation

per·ver·si·ty (-sə tē) *n.* [OFr. *perversité* < L. *perversitas* < *perversus*] **1.** the quality or condition of being perverse **2.** *pl.* **-ties** an instance of this

per·ver·sive (-siv) *adj.* [ML. *perversivus*: see PERVERSE & -IVE] that perverts or is marked by perversion

per·vert (pər vurt′; *for n.*, pur′vurt) *vt.* [ME. *perverten* < OFr. *pervertir* < L. *pervertere*, to overturn, corrupt < *per-*, intens. + *vertere*, to turn: see VERSE] **1.** to cause to turn from what is considered right, good, or true; misdirect; lead astray; corrupt **2.** to turn to an improper use; misuse **3.** to change or misapply the meaning of; misinterpret; distort; twist **4.** to bring into a worse condition; debase —*n.* a perverted person; esp., a person who

practices sexual perversion —*SYN.* see DEBASE —**per·vert′er** *n.* —**per·vert′i·ble** *adj.*

per·vert·ed (pər vur′tid) *adj.* **1.** deviating from what is considered right, good, or true; misdirected, corrupted, etc. **2.** of or practicing sexual perversion **3.** misinterpreted; distorted —**per·vert′ed·ly** *adv.* —**per·vert′ed·ness** *n.*

per·vi·ous (pur′vē əs) *adj.* [L. *pervius* < *per*, through + *via*, way: see VIA] **1.** allowing passage through; that can be penetrated or permeated **2.** having a mind open to influence, argument, or suggestion —**per′vi·ous·ness** *n.*

pes (pēz, pās) *n.*, *pl.* **pe·des** (pē′dēz, ped′ās) [ModL. < L., FOOT] *Zool.* a foot or footlike structure in land vertebrates

Pe·sach (pā′säkh) *n.* [Heb. *pesah*: see PASCH] *same as* PASSOVER

pe·sade (pə säd′, -zäd′) *n.* [Fr., altered (prob. after *peser*, to weigh) < *posade* < It. *posata*, a halt < *posare*, to halt < L. *pausare* < *pausa*, PAUSE] *Horsemanship* a maneuver in which a horse is made to rear

Pes·ca·do·res (pes′kə dôr′ēz, -is) group of islands in Taiwan Strait, a dependency of Taiwan: c. 50 sq. mi.

pe·se·ta (pə sāt′ə; *Sp.* pe se′tä) *n.* [Sp., dim. of *peso*, PESO] the monetary unit and a coin of Spain and Equatorial Guinea: see MONETARY UNITS, table

pes·e·wa (pes′ə wä) *n.*, *pl.* **pes′e·was**, **pes′e·wa** a unit of money in Ghana, equal to 1/100 of a cedi

Pe·sha·war (pe shä′wər) city in N West Pakistan, near the Khyber Pass: pop. 219,000

Pe·shi·to (pə shēt′ō) *n.* [Syr. *peshitto*, lit., plain, simple] the standard translation of the Old and New Testaments in ancient Syriac: also **Pe·shit′ta** (pə shēt′tä)

pes·ky (pes′kē) *adj.* **-ki·er**, **-ki·est** [prob. var. of *pesty* < PEST + -Y²] [Colloq.] annoying; disagreeable; troublesome —**pes′ki·ly** *adv.* —**pes′ki·ness** *n.*

pe·so (pā′sō; *Sp.* pe′sō) *n.*, *pl.* **-sos** (-sōz; *Sp.* -sōs) [Sp., lit., a weight < L. *pensum*, something weighed < neut. pp. of *pendere*: see PENSION] the monetary unit and a coin of Argentina, Colombia, Cuba, the Dominican Republic, Mexico, the Philippines, and Uruguay: see MONETARY UNITS, table

peso boliviano *pl.* **pesos bolivianos** the monetary unit of Bolivia: see MONETARY UNITS, table

pes·sa·ry (pes′ər ē) *n.*, *pl.* **-ries** [ME. *pessarie* < LL. *pessarium* < L. *pessum* < Gr. *pessos*, oval pebble] a device worn in the vagina to support a displaced uterus or to prevent conception

pes·si·mism (pes′ə miz'm) *n.* [Fr. *pessimisme* < L. *pessimus*, worst, superl. of *pejor*, worse (see PEJORATIVE)] **1.** *Philos.* *a)* the doctrine or belief that the existing world is the worst possible *b)* the doctrine or belief that the evil in life outweighs the good **2.** the tendency to expect misfortune or the worst outcome in any circumstances; practice of looking on the dark side of things —**pes′si·mist** *n.*

pes·si·mis·tic (pes′ə mis′tik) *adj.* of or characterized by pessimism; expecting the worst —*SYN.* see CYNICAL —**pes′si·mis′ti·cal·ly** *adv.*

pest (pest) *n.* [Fr. *peste* < L. *pestis*, a plague] **1.** a person or thing that causes trouble, annoyance, discomfort, etc.; nuisance; specif., any destructive or troublesome insect, small animal, weed, etc. **2.** [Now Rare] a fatal epidemic disease; esp., bubonic plague

Pes·ta·loz·zi (pes′tä lôt′tsē), **Jo·hann Hein·rich** (yō′hän hin′riH) 1746–1827; Swiss educational reformer

pes·ter (pes′tər) *vt.* [< obs. *impester* < OFr. *empestrer*, orig., to hobble a horse at pasture, entangle < VL. **impastoriare* < L. *in-*, IN-¹ + VL. **pastoria*, shackle (see PASTERN): meaning infl. by PEST] **1.** to annoy constantly or repeatedly with petty irritations; bother; vex **2.** [Obs.] to overcrowd; cram —**pes′ter·er** *n.*

pest·hole (pest′hōl′) *n.* [PEST + HOLE] a place infested or likely to be infested with an epidemic disease

pest·house (-hous′) *n.* [PEST + HOUSE] [Archaic] a hospital for the isolation of people with contagious or epidemic diseases

pes·ti·cide (pes′tə sīd′) *n.* [< PEST + -CIDE] any chemical used for killing insects, weeds, etc. —**pes′ti·ci′dal** *adj.*

pes·tif·er·ous (pes tif′ər əs) *adj.* [ME. < L. *pestiferus* < *pestis*, a plague + *ferre*, to BEAR¹] **1.** orig., *a)* bringing or carrying disease *b)* infected with an epidemic disease **2.** dangerous to morals or to the welfare of society; noxious; evil **3.** [Colloq.] annoying; mischievous; bothersome —**pes·tif′er·ous·ly** *adv.* —**pes·tif′er·ous·ness** *n.*

pes·ti·lence (pes′t'l əns) *n.* [ME. < OFr. < L. *pestilentia* < *pestilens*: see ff.] **1.** any virulent or fatal contagious or infectious disease, esp. one of epidemic proportions, as bubonic plague **2.** anything, as a doctrine, regarded as harmful or dangerous

pes·ti·lent (-ənt) *adj.* [ME. < L. *pestilens* < *pestis*, plague] **1.** likely to cause death; deadly **2.** [Rare] contagious; pestilential **3.** dangerous to the security and welfare of society; pernicious *[the pestilent threat of war]* **4.** annoying; troublesome —**pes′ti·lent·ly** *adv.*

pes·ti·len·tial (pes′tə len′shəl) *adj.* [ME. *pestilencial* < ML. *pestilentialis*] **1.** of, causing, or likely to cause pestilence or infection **2.** like or constituting a pestilence;

widespread and deadly 3. pernicious; dangerous; harmful —**pes′ti·len′tial·ly** *adv.*

pes·tle (pes′'l) *n.* [ME. *pestel* < OFr. < L. *pistillum* < *pinsere*, to pound, beat < IE. base **pis-*, to pound, crush, whence Gr. *ptissein*, to stamp] 1. a tool, usually club-shaped, used to pound or grind substances, esp. in a mortar: see MORTAR, illus. 2. a heavy bar for pounding or stamping, as in a mill —*vt.*, *vi.* **-tled, -tling** to pound, grind, crush, etc. with or as with a pestle

pet[1] (pet) *n.* [orig. Scot. dial., prob. back-formation < ME. *pety*, small: see PETTY] 1. an animal that is tamed or domesticated and kept as a companion or treated with fondness 2. a person who is treated with particular affection or indulgence; favorite; darling —*adj.* 1. kept or treated as a pet [a *pet* duck] 2. especially liked; favorite 3. greatest; especial; particular [one's *pet* peeve] 4. showing fondness or affection [a *pet* name] —*vt.* **pet′ted, pet′ting** 1. to stroke or pat gently; fondle; caress 2. to be indulgent toward; pamper —☆*vi.* [Colloq.] to kiss, embrace, fondle intimately, etc. in making love —*SYN.* see CARESS —**pet′ter** *n.*

pet[2] (pet) *n.* [< earlier phr. *to take the pet* < ?] a state of sulky peevishness or ill humor —*vi.* **pet′ted, pet′ting** to be in a pet; sulk

Pet. Peter

Pé·tain (pā tan′), **Hen·ri Phi·lippe** (än rē′ fē lēp′) 1856-1951; Fr. general; premier of Fr. government at Vichy (1940-44): convicted of treason (1945)

pet·al (pet′'l) *n.* [ModL. *petalum* < Gr. *petalon*, a leaf < *petalos*, outspread < IE. base **pet-*, to spread out, whence L. *patere*, to be open & FATHOM] any of the component parts, or leaves, of a corolla —**pet′aled, pet′alled** (-'ld) *adj.* —**pet′al·like′** *adj.*

-pe·tal (pə t'l) [< ModL. *-petus* (< L. *petere*, to rush at, seek: see PETITION) + *-AL*] a combining form meaning moving toward, seeking [centripetal]

pet·al·if·er·ous (pet′'l if′ər əs) *adj.* [< PETAL + -FEROUS] having petals

pet·al·o·dy (pet′'l ō′dē) *n.* [< PETAL + Gr. *-ōdia*, a becoming like < *-ōdes*: see -ODE[2]] *Bot.* the conversion of stamens or other organs into petals

pet·al·oid (-oid′) *adj.* [PETAL + -OID] *Biol.* resembling a petal

pet·al·ous (-əs) *adj.* with petals

pe·tard (pi tärd′) *n.* [Fr. *pétard* < *péter*, to break wind < *pet*, fart < L. *peditum* < *peditus*, pp. of *pedere*, to break wind < IE. base **pezd-*, of echoic origin] 1. a metal cone filled with explosives, fastened in ancient warfare to walls and gates and exploded to force an opening 2. a kind of firecracker —**hoist with (or by) one's own petard** destroyed by the very devices with which one meant to destroy others: *Hamlet*, III, iv

pet·a·sos, pet·a·sus (pet′ə səs) *n.* [L. *petasus* < Gr. *petasos* < *petannynai*, to spread out: see PETAL] 1. a flat, wide-brimmed hat worn in ancient Greece 2. the winged hat of Hermes (Mercury)

pet·cock (pet′käk′) *n.* [< obs. *pet* (< Fr.: see PETARD) + COCK[1]] a small faucet or valve used in draining unwanted or excess water or air from pipes, radiators, boilers, etc.

pe·te·chi·a (pə tē′kē ə) *n.*, *pl.* **-chi·ae** (-ē′) [ModL. < It. *petecchia* < ?] a small hemorrhagic spot in the skin, mucous membrane, etc. —**pe·te′chi·al** *adj.*

Pe·ter (pēt′ər) [ME. < LL.(Ec.) < Gr. *Petros* (< *petros*, a stone, *petra*, a rock) used as transl. of Aram. *kēphā*, a rock] 1. a masculine name: dim. *Pete;* equiv. L. *Petrus*, Fr. *Pierre*, It. *Pietro*, Sp. *Pedro*, Russ. *Pëtr* 2. *Bible a)* (original name *Simon*) ?-64? A.D.; one of the twelve apostles, a fisherman; reputed author of the Epistles of Peter: considered the 1st Pope: also called *Simon Peter*, *Saint Peter:* his day is June 29 *b)* either of the two Epistles of Peter 3. **Peter I** (*Pëtr Alekseyevich*) 1672-1725; czar of Russia (1682-1725): called **Peter the Great** 4. **Peter II** (*Peter Karageorgevich*) 1923-70; king of Yugoslavia (1934-45): son of ALEXANDER I 5. **Peter III** (*Pëtr Feodorovich*) 1728-62; czar of Russia (1762): assassinated, & succeeded by his wife, CATHERINE II —**rob Peter to pay Paul** to take from one person, enterprise, etc. to pay or give to another

pe·ter (pēt′ər) *vi.* [< ?] [Colloq.] ☆to become gradually smaller, weaker, etc. and then cease or disappear (with *out*)

Pe·ter·bor·ough (pē′tər bur′ō, -ə) 1. county seat of the Soke of Peterborough: pop. 64,000. 2. city in SE Ontario, Canada, near Toronto: pop. 56,000 3. Soke of, administrative county in EC England, within Northamptonshire: 84 sq. mi.; pop. 78,000

Peter Pan the title character of J. M. Barrie's play (1904), a little boy who ran away to "Never-Never Land" and never grew up

Peter Pan collar [< traditional costume of prec.] a small, closefitting collar with ends rounded in front, used on women's and children's dresses, blouses, etc.

Pe·ters·burg (pē′tərz burg′) [after a Capt. *Peter* Jones] city in SE Va., near Richmond: scene of Civil War battles: pop. 36,000

Pe·ter·sham (pēt′ər shəm) *n.* [after Lord *Petersham*, who set the fashion (c. 1812)] 1. a rough, heavy, woolen cloth 2. formerly, an overcoat made of this

Peter's pence 1. an annual tax, orig. of one penny, paid to the papal see by certain English property owners before the Reformation 2. an annual voluntary donation made by Catholics everywhere to the papal see Also **Peter pence**

pet·i·o·lar (pet′ē ə lar) *adj.* of or attached to the petiole

pet·i·o·late (-lāt′, -lit) *adj.* [PETIOL(E) + -ATE[1]] *Biol.* having a stalk or petiole

pet·i·ole (pet′ē ōl′) *n.* [ModL. *petiolus* < L., a little foot, little leg, stalk, dim. < *pes*, FOOT] 1. *Bot.* same as LEAF-STALK 2. *Zool.* same as PEDUNCLE (sense 4)

pet·i·o·lule (pet′ē al yōōl′, -ə lōōl′) *n.* [ModL. *petiolulus* < *petiolus*, PETIOLE + *-ulus*, -ULE] the stalk of a leaflet in a compound leaf

pet·it (pet′ē; *Fr.* pə tē′) *adj.* [ME. < OFr.: see PETTY] small or of less importance; petty: now used only in law

petit bourgeois (pə tē′) a member of the petite bourgeoisie —**pe·tit′-bour·geois′** *adj.* —**petite bourgeoise** *fem.*

pe·tite (pə tēt′) *adj.* [Fr., fem. of *petit*] small and trim in figure: said of a woman —*SYN.* see SMALL —**pe·tite′ness** *n.*

petite bourgeoisie [Fr.] members of the bourgeoisie of lowest income or status, as small shopkeepers, routine office workers, etc., the lower middle class

pe·tit four (pet′ē fôr′; *Fr.* pə tē fōōr′) *pl.* **pe·tits fours** (pet′ē fôrz′; *Fr.* pə tē fōōr′), **pe·tit fours** (pet′ē fôrz′) [Fr., small cake < *petit*, small + *four*, lit., oven < L. *furnus:* see FURNACE] a small cake cut from spongecake, etc. in any of various shapes and decorated with icing

pe·ti·tion (pə tish′ən) *n.* [ME. < OFr. < L. *petitio* (gen. *petitionis*) < *petere*, to seek, ask < IE. base **pet-*, to rush at, fall upon, whence FEATHER] 1. a solemn, earnest supplication or request to a superior or deity or to a person or group in authority; prayer or entreaty 2. a formal writing or document embodying such a request, addressed to a specific person or group and often signed by a number of petitioners 3. something that is asked or entreated [to grant a *petition*] 4. *Law* a written request or plea in which specific court action is asked for [a *petition* for rehearing] —*vt.* 1. to address a petition to; ask formally or earnestly 2. to ask for; solicit —*vi.* to make a petition or entreaty —*SYN.* see APPEAL —**pe·ti′tion·ar′y** *adj.* —**pe·ti′tion·er** (-ər) *n.*

‡**pe·ti·ti·o prin·ci·pi·i** (pi tish′ē ō′ prin sip′ē ī′) [L., lit., a begging of the question] *Logic* the fallacy of assuming in the premise of an argument the conclusion which is to be proved

petit jury a group of twelve citizens picked to weigh the evidence in and decide the issues of a trial in court: distinguished from GRAND JURY

petit larceny theft in which the property stolen has a value less than a certain amount fixed by law: see GRAND LARCENY

pe·tit mal (pə tē′ mal′; *Fr.* pə tē mȧl′) [Fr., lit., small ailment] a type of epilepsy in which there are attacks of momentary unconsciousness without convulsions: distinguished from GRAND MAL

pet·it point (pet′ē) 1. a small needlepoint stitch over one vertical and one horizontal canvas thread 2. work done with this stitch, as a picture on canvas

‡**pe·tits pois** (pə tē pwä′) [Fr., little peas] small green peas

☆**pet·nap·ping, pet·nap·ing** (pet′nap′iŋ) *n.* [PET[1] + (KID)NAPPING] the stealing of pets, esp. dogs or cats, in order to sell them, as for use in laboratory experiments

Pe·tö·fi (pe′tö fē), **Sán·dor** (shän′dôr) 1823-49; Hung. poet & patriot

Pe·tra (pē′trə) ancient Edomite city in SW Jordan

Pe·trarch (pē′trärk) (It. name *Francesco Petrarca*) 1304-74; It. lyric poet & scholar

Pe·trar·chan sonnet (pi trär′kən) a sonnet composed of a group of eight lines (*octave*) with two rhymes *abba, abba,* and a group of six lines (*sestet*) with two or three rhymes variously arranged, typically *cdc dcd* or *cde cde:* the thought or theme is stated and developed in the octave, and expanded, contradicted, etc. in the sestet; Italian sonnet

pet·rel (pet′rəl) *n.* [earlier *pitteral:* orig. ? a dim. of PETER, in allusion to St. Peter's walking on the sea] any of various related small, dark, sea birds (order Procellariiformes) with long wings; esp., same as STORMY PETREL

pe·tri dish (pē′trē) [after Julius R. *Petri* (1852-1921), G. bacteriologist] [*also* **P- d-**] a very shallow, cylindrical, transparent glass or plastic dish with an overlapping cover, used for the culture of microorganisms

Pe·trie (pē′trē), Sir (**William Matthew**) **Flin·ders** (flin′dərz) 1853-1942; Eng. archaeologist & Egyptologist

pet·ri·fac·tion (pet′rə fak′shən) *n.* [< PETRIFY] 1. a petrifying or being petrified 2. something petrified Also **pet′ri·fi·ca′tion** (-fi kā′shən) —**pet′ri·fac′tive** *adj.*

Petrified Forest National Park national park in EC Ariz., containing petrified trunks of several coniferous forests dating from the Triassic Period: 147 sq. mi.

pet·ri·fy (pet′rə fī′) *vt.* **-fied′, -fy′ing** [Fr. *pétrifier* < L. *petra*, a stone, rock (< Gr. *petra*) + *facere*, to make: see DO[1]] 1. to replace the normal cells of (organic matter) with silica or other mineral deposits; re-form as a stony substance 2. to make rigid, inflexible, or inert; harden or deaden 3. to paralyze or make numb, as with fear; stupefy; stun —*vi.* to become petrified

Pe·trine (pē′trīn, -trin) *adj.* [< L. *Petrus*, PETER + -INE[1]] of, like, or attributed to the Apostle Peter

pet·ro- (pet′rō, -rə) [< Gr. *petra*, a rock, or *petros*, a stone] *a combining form meaning* rock or stone [petrography]: also, before a vowel, **petr-**

pet·ro·chem·i·cal (pet'rō kem'i k'l) *n.* [PETRO(LEUM) + CHEMICAL] a chemical derived ultimately from petroleum or natural gas, as ethylene glycol, the paraffin and aromatic hydrocarbons, etc. —**pet'ro·chem'is·try** (-is trē) *n.*

petrog. petrography

pet·ro·glyph (pet'rə glif') *n.* [Fr. *pétroglyphe* < Gr. *petra*, a rock + *glyphē*, carving: see GLYPH] a rock carving, esp. a prehistoric one —**pet'ro·glyph'ic** *adj.* —**pe·trog·ly·phy** (pi träg'lə fē) *n.*

Pet·ro·grad (pet'rə grad; *Russ.* pyet'rô grät') *former name (1914–24)* of LENINGRAD

pe·trog·ra·phy (pi träg'rə fē) *n.* [ModL. *petrographia:* see PETRO- + -GRAPHY] the science dealing with the description or classification of rocks —**pe·trog'ra·pher** *n.* —**pet·ro·graph·ic** (pet'rə graf'ik), **pet'ro·graph'i·cal** *adj.* —**pet'ro·graph'i·cal·ly** *adv.*

pet·rol (pet'rəl) *n.* [Fr. *pétrole* < ML. *petroleum:* see PETROLEUM] 1. *Brit.* term for GASOLINE 2. *obs. var.* of PETROLEUM

petrol. petrology

☆**pet·ro·la·tum** (pet'rə lāt'əm, -lät'-) *n.* [ModL. < PETROLEUM + L. *-atum*, neut. of *-atus:* see -ATE²] a greasy, jellylike substance consisting of a mixture of semisolid hydrocarbons obtained from petroleum: it is used as a base for ointments, in leather dressing, etc.

pe·tro·le·um (pə trō'lē əm) *n.* [ML. < L. *petra*, rock (< Gr. *petra*) + *oleum*, OIL] an oily, flammable, liquid solution of hydrocarbons, yellowish-green to black in color, occurring naturally in the rock strata of certain geological formations: when fractionally distilled, it yields paraffin, fuel oil, kerosine, naphtha, gasoline, benzine, etc.

☆**petroleum jelly** *same as* PETROLATUM

pe·trol·ic (pə träl'ik) *adj.* of or produced from petroleum

pe·trol·o·gy (pi träl'ə jē) *n.* [PETRO- + -LOGY] the study of the classification, location, composition, structure, and origin of rocks —**pet·ro·log·ic** (pet'rə läj'ik), **pet'ro·log'i·cal** *adj.* —**pet'ro·log'i·cal·ly** *adv.* —**pe·trol'o·gist** *n.*

pet·ro·nel (pet'rə nəl) *n.* [Fr. *petrinal* < OFr. *peitrine* (Fr. *poitrine*), breast, chest < L. *pectus*, chest: it was rested against the chest in firing] a carbinelike firearm of heavy caliber, used in the 15th to 17th cent.

Pe·tro·ni·us (pə trō'nē əs), **(Gaius)** 1st cent. A.D.; Rom. satirist: often called *Petronius Arbiter*

pe·tro·sal (pi trō's'l) *adj.* [< L. *petrosus*, rocky: see PETROUS & -AL] 1. very hard or stony 2. [< ModL. *petrosa* < ML. (*os*) *petrosus*, petrosal (bone)] *Anat.* of or located near the petrous part of the temporal bone

pet·rous (pet'rəs, pē'trəs) *adj.* [L. *petrosus*, rocky < *petra*, a rock (< Gr. *petra*)] 1. of or like rock; hard; stony 2. [ML. *petrosus*] designating or of that part of the temporal bone which surrounds and protects the internal ear

pet·ti·coat (pet'i kōt') *n.* [ME. *petycote:* see PETTY & COAT] 1. a skirt, now esp. an underskirt often trimmed at the hemline as with lace or ruffles, worn by women and girls 2. something resembling a petticoat 3. [Colloq.] a woman or girl —*adj.* of or by women; female [*petticoat government*]

pet·ti·fog·ger (pet'ē fäg'ər, -fôg'-) *n.* [PETTY + obs. *fogger* < ?] 1. a lawyer who handles petty cases, esp. one who uses unethical methods in conducting trumped-up cases 2. a trickster; cheater 3. a quibbler; caviler —**pet'ti·fog'** *vi.* -**fogged'**, -**fog'ging** —**pet'ti·fog'ger·y** *n.*

☆**pet·ti·pants** (pet'i pants) *n.* [PETTI(COAT) + PANTS] women's underpants extending partway down the thigh

pet·tish (pet'ish) *adj.* [PET² + -ISH] peevish; petulant; cross —**pet'tish·ly** *adv.* —**pet'tish·ness** *n.*

pet·ti·toes (pet'i tōz') *n.pl.* [prob. < MFr. *petite oye*, goose giblets < fem. of *petit* (see PETTY) + *oye*, goose < LL. *auca* (see OCARINA): form and meaning infl. by association with TOE] 1. pigs' feet, as an article of food 2. feet or toes, esp. a child's

‡**pet·to** (pet'tō) *n., pl.* -**ti** (-tē) [It. < L. *pectus*] the breast —**in petto** in one's breast; kept secret

pet·ty (pet'ē) *adj.* -**ti·er**, -**ti·est** [ME. *pety* < OFr. *petit* < **pit-*, little < baby talk] 1. relatively worthless or unimportant; trivial; insignificant 2. small-scale; minor 3. having or showing a tendency to make much of small matters; small-minded; mean; narrow, etc. 4. relatively low in rank; subordinate —**pet'ti·ly** *adv.* —**pet'ti·ness** *n.* SYN.—**petty** is applied to that which is comparatively small, minor, unimportant, etc. of its kind, and it is often used to imply small-mindedness [*petty* cash, a *petty* grudge]; **trivial**, in strict usage, applies to that which, because it is both petty and commonplace, is quite insignificant [a *trivial* remark]; **trifling** applies to something so small and unimportant as to be negligible or of very little account [a *trifling* matter]; **paltry** is applied to something contemptibly small or worthless [a *paltry* wage]; **picayune** is used of a person or thing considered small, mean, or insignificant [a *picayune* objection] —ANT. **important, significant**

petty bourgeois *same as* PETIT BOURGEOIS

petty cash a cash fund from which small incidental expenses are paid

petty jury *same as* PETIT JURY

petty larceny *same as* PETIT LARCENY

petty officer a naval enlisted man whose rank corresponds to that of a noncommissioned officer in the army

pet·u·lant (pech'ōō lənt) *adj.* [L. *petulans* (gen. *petulantis*), forward, petulant < base of *petere*, to make for, aim at, attack: see PETITION] 1. [Obs.] *a)* forward; immodest *b)* pert; insolent 2. impatient or irritable, esp. over a petty annoyance; peevish —**pet'u·lance, pet'u·lan·cy** *n.* —**pet'u·lant·ly** *adv.*

pe·tu·ni·a (pə tōōn'yə, -tyōōn'-; -ē ə) *n.* [ModL. < Fr. *petun* < Braz. (Tupi) *petun*, tobacco] any of a genus (*Petunia*) of plants of the nightshade family, with funnel-shaped flowers of various colors and patterns, esp. a common garden annual (*Petunia hybrida*)

Pevs·ner (pefs'nər), **An·toine** (än twän') 1886–1962; Fr. sculptor & painter, born in Russia: brother of Naum GABO

pew (pyōō) *n.* [ME. *pewe* < OFr. *puie*, balcony, balustrade < L. *podia*, pl. of *podium*, balcony < Gr. *podion* < *pous*, FOOT] 1. any of the benches with a back that are fixed in rows in a church 2. any of several boxlike enclosures with seats, in some churches, for the use of a particular family, etc.

☆**pe·wee** (pē'wē) *n.* [echoic of its call] any of several small flycatchers; esp., the **wood pewee** (genus *Contopus*)

pe·wit (pē'wit, pyōō'it) *n.* [echoic of its call] *same as:* 1. LAPWING ☆2. PEWEE

pew·ter (pyōōt'ər) *n.* [ME. *peutre* < OFr. *peautre*, akin to It. *peltro* < ?] 1. a dull, silvery-gray alloy of tin with brass, copper, or, esp., lead 2. articles made of pewter —*adj.* made of pewter

☆**pe·yo·te** (pā ōt'ē; *Sp.* pe yô'te) *n.* [AmSp. < Nahuatl *peyotl*, caterpillar, with reference to the down in the center] *same as* MESCAL (sense 3): also **pe·yo'tl** (-'l; *Sp.* -t'l)

pf. 1. perfect 2. pfennig 3. pianoforte 4. preferred

p.f. [It. *piu forte*] *Music* a little louder

Pfalz (pfälts) *see* RHEINLAND-PFALZ

Pfc, Pfc., PFC Private First Class

pfd. preferred

pfen·nig (fen'ig; *G.* pfen'iH) *n., pl.* -**nigs**; *G.* -**ni·ge** (-i gə) [*G.:* see PENNY] a German unit of currency equal to 1/100 Deutsche mark or 1/100 mark

pfft (*unvoiced* f't) *interj.* an exclamation expressing a sudden ending or fizzling out

pfg. pfennig

pfu·i (fōō'ē) *interj.* [G.] *same as* PHOOEY

Pg. 1. Portugal 2. Portuguese

pg. page

P.G. 1. Past Grand 2. paying guest 3. Postgraduate

PGA Professional Golfers Association

PH Purple Heart

Ph phenyl

pH (pē'āch') [< Fr. *p(ouvoir)* *h(ydrogène)*, lit., hydrogen power] *a symbol for* the degree of acidity or alkalinity of a solution; orig., and still often, expressed as the logarithm of the reciprocal of the hydrogen ion concentration in gram equivalents per liter of solution, and now, in some cases, given other operational definitions: pH7 (.0000001 gram atom of hydrogen ion per liter), the value for pure distilled water, is regarded as neutral; pH values from 0 to 7 indicate acidity, and pH values from 7 to 14 indicate alkalinity

ph. phase

PHA Public Housing Administration

Phae·dra (fē'drə) [L. < Gr. *Phaidra*] *Gr. Myth.* daughter of Minos and wife of Theseus: she killed herself after her stepson, Hippolytus, rejected her advances

Phae·drus (fē'drəs) 1st cent. A.D.; Rom. writer of fables and reputed translator of some of Aesop's fables

Pha·ë·thon (fā'ə thən) [L. *Phaethon* < Gr. *Phaethōn*, lit., shining (< *phaethein*, to shine)] *Gr. & Rom. Myth.* son of Helios, the sun god: he unsuccessfully tried to drive his father's sun chariot and would have set the world on fire if Zeus had not struck him down with a thunderbolt

pha·e·ton, pha·ë·ton (fā'ət'n) *n.* [Fr. *phaéton* < L. *Phaethon:* see prec.] 1. a light, four-wheeled carriage, drawn by one or two horses, with front and back seats and, usually, a folding top ☆2. *same as* TOURING CAR

phage (fāj) *n. shortened form of* BACTERIOPHAGE

-phage (fāj) [< Gr. *phagein*, to eat: see -PHAGOUS] *a combining form meaning* eating or destroying [*bacteriophage*]

phag·e·de·na, phag·e·dae·na (faj'ə dē'nə) *n.* [L. *phagedaenos* < Gr. *phagedaina* < *phagein*, to eat: see -PHAGOUS] a rapidly spreading ulcer accompanied by sloughing, or the separation of dead tissue —**phag'e·den'ic** (-den'ik) *adj.*

phag·o- (fag'ō, -ə) [< Gr. *phagein*, to eat: see -PHAGOUS] *a combining form meaning:* 1. eating or destroying [*phagocyte*] 2. phagocyte Also, before a vowel, **phag-**

phag·o·cyte (fag'ə sit') *n.* [prec. + -CYTE] any leucocyte that ingests and destroys other cells, microorganisms, or other foreign matter in the blood and tissues —**phag'o·cyt'ic** (-sit'ik) *adj.*

phagocytic index the average number of bacteria ingested per leucocyte in an incubated mixture of normal or immune serum, bacteria, and normal leucocytes

phag·o·cy·to·sis (fag′ō sĭ tō′sis) *n.* [ModL.: see PHAG-OCYTE & -OSIS] the ingestion and destruction by phago-cytes of cells, microorganisms, etc. —**phag′o·cy·tot′ic** (-tät′ik) *adj.*

-pha·gous (fə gəs) [< Gr. *-phagos* < *phagein,* to eat < IE. base *bhag-,* to allot, receive as share, whence Sans. *bhajati,* (he) allots] *a combining form meaning* that eats (something specified) [*anthropophagous*]

-pha·gy (fə jē) [ModL. *-phagia* < Gr. *phagein:* see prec.] *a combining form meaning* the practice of eating (some-thing specified) [*geophagy*]: also **-pha·gi·a** (fā′jē ə, -jə)

phal·ange (fal′ənj, fāl′-; fə lanj′) *n.* [Fr. < Gr. *phalanges.* pl. of *phalanx*] *same as* PHALANX (sense 5)

pha·lan·ge·al (fə lan′jē əl) *adj.* [< ModL. *phalangeus* + -AL] of a phalanx or the phalanges: also **pha·lan′gal** (-lang′l)

pha·lan·ger (fə lan′jər) *n.* [ModL. < Gr. *phalanx,* bone between two joints of the fingers or toes (see PHALANX): from the structure of the 2d and 3d phalanges of the hind feet] any of a large number of small, pouched, plant-eating Australian animals (family Phalangeridae) with a long, bushy tail: they are related to the cuscuses and koalas and live chiefly in trees

pha·lan·ges (fə lan′jēz) *n. alt. pl. of* PHALANX

phal·an·ster·y (fal′ən ster′ē) *n., pl.* **-ster′ies** [Fr. *phalan-stère* < *phalange,* phalange + (mona)*stère,* monastery] 1. a socialistic community of the type planned by F. M. C. Fourier 2. any communal association 3. the buildings housing such a community —**phal′an·ste′ri·an** (-stir′ē ən) *adj., n.*

pha·lanx (fā′laŋks; *chiefly Brit.,* fal′aŋks) *n., pl.* **-lanx·es**; also, & for 5 always, **pha·lan·ges** (fə lan′jēz) [L. < Gr. *phalanx,* line of battle, bone between fingers, orig., log < IE. base *bhel-,* log, whence BALK] 1. an ancient military formation of infantry in close and deep ranks with shields joined together and spears overlapping 2. a massed group of individuals; compact body 3. a group of individuals united for a common purpose 4. the people forming a phalanstery 5. *Anat.* any of the bones forming the fingers or toes: see SKELETON, illus.

phal·a·rope (fal′ə rōp′) *n.* [Fr. < ModL. *phalaropus,* name of the type genus < Gr. *phalaris,* coot (akin to *phalos,* white: from its white head) + *pous,* FOOT] any of a number of related small swimming and wading birds (family Phalaropodidae) of fresh and salt waters, that resemble the sandpiper: the male is less brightly colored than the female

phal·lic (fal′ik) *adj.* [Gr. *phallikos*] 1. of, like, or relating to the phallus 2. of or relating to phallicism 3. *same as* GENITAL (sense 2 *a*)

phal·li·cism (fal′ə siz′m) *n.* worship of the phallus as a symbol of the male generative power: also **phal′lism** —**phal′li·cist, phal′list** *n.*

phal·lus (fal′əs) *n., pl.* **-li** (-ī), **-lus·es** [L. < Gr. *phallos* < IE. base *bhel-,* to swell, whence L. *follis,* leather sack, *flare,* to blow] 1. a representation or image of the penis as the reproductive organ, worshiped as a symbol of genera-tive power, as in the Dionysiac festivals of ancient Greece 2. the penis or clitoris

-phane (fān) [< Gr. *phainein,* to appear: see FANTASY] *a combining form meaning* resembling, appearing like [*allophane*]

phan·er·o·gam (fan′ər ə gam′) *n.* [Fr. *phanérogame* < Gr. *phaneros,* visible (< *phainein:* see FANTASY) + *gamos,* marriage (see -GAMY)] *an earlier name for* a seed plant or flowering plant —**phan′er·o·gam′ic, phan′er·og′a·mous** (-ə räg′ə məs) *adj.*

phan·er·o·phyte (-fīt′) *n.* [< Gr. *phaneros,* visible (< base of *phainein,* to appear: see FANTASY) + -PHYTE] *Bot.* a perennial plant with its resting buds located well above the ground and exposed to the air

Pha·ner·o·zo·ic (fan′ər ə zō′ik) *adj.* designating or of a geologic eon that includes the Paleozoic, Mesozoic, and Cenozoic eras

phan·tasm (fan′taz′m) *n.* [ME. *fantasme* < OFr. < L. *phantasma* < Gr. *phantasma* < *phantazein,* to show < stem of *phainein,* to show: see FANTASY] 1. a perception of something that has no physical reality; figment of the mind; esp., a specter, or ghost: also **phan·tas·ma** (fan taz′mə), *pl.* **-ma·ta** (-mə tə) 2. a deceptive likeness 3. *Philos.* a mental image of a real person or thing — **phan·tas′mal** (-taz′m′l), **phan·tas′mic** *adj.*

phan·tas·ma·go·ri·a (fan taz′mə gôr′ē ə) *n.* [Fr. *fantas-magorie* < Gr. *phantasma,* phantasm + *agoreuein,* to speak in public < *ageirein,* to assemble (see GREGARIOUS): prob. infl. by Fr. *allegorie,* ALLEGORY] 1. an early type of magic-lantern show consisting of various optical illusions in which objects rapidly change size, blend into one another, etc. 2. a rapidly changing series of things seen or imagined, as the figures or events of a dream 3. any rapidly changing scene Also **phan·tas′ma·go·ry,** *pl.* **-ries** —**phan·tas′ma-go′ri·al, phan·tas′ma·go·ric, phan·tas′ma·go′ri·cal** *adj.*

phan·ta·sy (fan′tə sē) *n., pl.* **-sies** *same as* FANTASY

phan·tom (fan′təm) *n.* [ME. *fantome, fantosme* < OFr. *fantosme* < L. *phantasma* < Gr.: see FANTASY] 1. some-thing that seems to appear to the sight but has no physical existence; apparition; vision; specter 2. something feared or dreaded 3. something that exists only in the mind; illusion 4. a person or thing that is something in appear-

ance but not in fact [a *phantom* of a leader] 5. any mental image or representation [the *phantoms* of things past] —*adj.* of, like, or constituting a phantom; not really existing; illusory

Phar., phar. 1. pharmaceutical 2. pharmacopeia 3. pharmacy

Phar·aoh (fer′ō) *n.* [ME. *Pharaon* < OE. < LL.(Ec.) *Pharao* (gen. *Pharaonis*) < LGr. *Pharaō* < Heb. *par′ōh* < Egypt. *pr-′o,* great house] the title of the rulers of ancient Egypt: often used as a proper name in the Bible —**Phar′-a·on′ic** (-ā än′ik), **Phar′a·on′i·cal** *adj.*

pharaoh ant a common, tiny, red ant (*Monomorium pharaonis*) that is a household pest in most of the world

Phar·i·sa·ic (far′ə sā′ik) *adj.* [LL.(Ec.) *Pharisaicus* < Gr.(Ec.) *pharisaikos* < *pharisaios:* see PHARISEE] 1. of the Pharisees 2. [p-] [from the notion promulgated in the NT. that Pharisees were generally so characterized] emphasizing or observing the letter but not the spirit of religious law; self-righteous; sanctimonious 3. [p-] pre-tending to be highly moral or virtuous without actually being so; hypocritical: also **phar′i·sa′i·cal** —**phar′i·sa′-i·cal·ly** *adv.*

Phar·i·sa·ism (far′ə sā′iz′m) *n.* [ModL. *Pharisaïsmus* < Gr.(Ec.) *pharisaios* (see PHARISEE)] 1. the beliefs and practices of the Pharisees 2. [p-] pharisaic behavior, character, principles, etc.

Phar·i·see (far′ə sē′) *n.* [ME. *pharise* < OE. *fariseus* & OFr. *pharisé,* both < LL.(Ec.) *Pharisaeus* < Gr.(Ec.) *pharasaios* < Aram. *pĕrishaiyā,* pl. of *pĕrīsh* < Heb. *pārūsh,* separated < *parash,* to cleave, divide, separate] 1. a member of an ancient Jewish party or fellowship that carefully observed the written law but also accepted the oral, or traditional, law, advocated democratization of religious practices, etc.: opposed to SADDUCEE 2. [p-] a pharisaic person —**Phar′i·see′ism** *n.*

Pharm., pharm. 1. pharmaceutical 2. pharmacist 3. pharmacopeia 4. pharmacy

phar·ma·ceu·ti·cal (fär′mə sōōt′i k′l, -syōōt′-) *adj.* [LL. *pharmaceuticus* < Gr. *pharmakeutikos* < *pharmakeuein,* to practice witchcraft, use medicine < *pharmakon,* a poison, medicine] 1. of pharmacy or pharmacists 2. of or by drugs Also **phar′ma·ceu′tic** —*n.* a pharmaceutical product; drug —**phar′ma·ceu′ti·cal·ly** *adv.*

phar·ma·ceu·tics (-iks) *n.pl.* [*with sing. v.*] [< LL.] *same as* PHARMACY (sense 1)

phar·ma·cist (fär′mə sist) *n.* a person licensed to practice pharmacy; druggist

phar·ma·co- (fär′mə kō′) [< Gr. *pharmakon,* drug] *a combining form meaning* drug or drugs [*pharmacodynamics*]

phar·ma·co·dy·nam·ics (-di nam′iks) *n.pl.* [*with sing. v.*] [prec. + DYNAMICS] the branch of pharmacology that deals with the effect and the reactions of drugs within the body —**phar′ma·co·dy·nam′ic** *adj.*

phar·ma·cog·no·sy (fär′mə käg′nə sē) *n.* [< Gr. *phar-makon,* a drug + *-gnōsia < gnōsis,* knowledge: see GNOSIS] the science that deals with medicinal products of plant, animal, or mineral origin in their crude or unprepared state

phar·ma·col·o·gy (fär′mə käl′ə jē) *n.* [ModL. *pharma-cologia* < Gr. *pharmakon,* a drug] 1. orig., the study of the preparation, qualities, and uses of drugs 2. the science dealing with the effect of drugs on living organisms —**phar′ma·co·log′i·cal** (-kə läj′i k′l), **phar′ma·co·log′ic** *adj.* —**phar′ma·co·log′i·cal·ly** *adv.* —**phar′ma·col′o·gist** *n.*

phar·ma·co·pe·ia, phar·ma·co·poe·ia (fär′mə kə pē′ə) *n.* [ModL. < Gr. *pharmakopoiïa* < *pharmakon,* a drug + *poiein,* to make (see POET)] 1. an authoritative book containing a list and description of drugs and medicinal products together with the standards established under law for their production, dispensation, use, etc. 2. [Obs.] a stock of drugs —**phar′ma·co·pe′ial, phar′ma·co·poe′ial** *adj.*

phar·ma·cy (fär′mə sē) *n., pl.* **-cies** [ME. *fermacie,* a medicine < MFr. *farmacie* < LL. *pharmacia* < Gr. *pharmakeia* < *pharmakon,* a drug] 1. the art or profession of preparing and dispensing drugs and medicines 2. a place where pharmacy is practiced; drugstore

Pha·ros (fer′äs) 1. small peninsula at Alexandria, Egypt: in ancient times it was an island with a large lighthouse on it 2. this lighthouse, one of the Seven Wonders of the World —*n.* [p-] any lighthouse or marine beacon

Phar·sa·li·a (fär sā′lē ə) district in ancient Thessaly, surrounding Pharsalus

Phar·sa·lus (fär sā′ləs) city in S Thessaly, Greece: site of an ancient city near which Caesar decisively defeated Pompey (48 B.C.): pop. 6,000: modern name, **Phar·sa·la** or **Far·sa·la** (fär′sə lä)

pha·ryn·ge·al (fə rin′jē əl, far′ən jē′əl) *adj.* [< ModL. *pharyngeus*] of, or in the region of, the pharynx: also **pha·ryn′gal** (-gəl)

phar·yn·gi·tis (far′in jīt′əs) *n.* [ModL.: see ff. & -ITIS] inflammation of the mucous membrane of the pharynx; sore throat

pha·ryn·go- (fə riŋ′gō) [< Gr. *pharynx* (gen. *pharyngos*)] *a combining form meaning* pharynx, or the pharynx and [*pharyngology*]: also, before a vowel, **pharyng-**

phar·yn·gol·o·gy (far′in gäl′ə jē) *n.* [prec. + -LOGY] the branch of medicine dealing with the pharynx and its diseases

pha·ryn·go·scope (fə riŋ'gə skōp') *n.* [PHARYNGO- + -SCOPE] an instrument for examining the pharynx — **phar·yn·gos·co·py** (far'iŋ gäs'kə pē) *n.*

phar·ynx (far'iŋks) *n.*, *pl.* **phar'ynx·es, pha·ryn·ges** (fə rin'jēz) [ModL. < Gr. *pharynx* (gen. *pharyngos*), throat < IE. base *bher-*, to scratch, cut, whence L. *forare*, to BORE[1]] the muscular and membranous cavity of the alimentary canal leading from the mouth and nasal passages to the larynx and esophagus

PHARYNX

phase (fāz) *n.* [ModL. *phasis* < Gr. *phasis* < *phainesthai*, to appear, akin to *phainein:* see FANTASY] **1.** any of the recurring stages of variation in the illumination and apparent shape of the moon or a planet **2.** any of the stages or forms in any series or cycle of changes, as in development **3.** any of the ways in which something may be observed, considered, or presented; aspect; side; part [a problem with many *phases*] **4.** *Chem.* a solid, liquid, or gaseous homogeneous form existing as a distinct part in a heterogeneous system [ice is a *phase* of H_2O] **5.** *Physics* the fractional part of a cycle through which a periodic wave, as of light, sound, etc., has advanced at any instant, measured from an arbitrary starting point or assumed moment of starting **6.** *Zool.* any of the characteristic variations in color of the skin, fur, plumage, etc. of an animal, according to season, age, etc. —*vt.* **phased, phas'ing 1.** to plan, introduce, carry out, etc. in phases, or stages (often with *in, into,* etc.) **2.** to put in phase —*vi.* to move by phases —**in (or out of) phase** in (or not in) a state of exactly parallel movements, oscillations, etc.; in (or not in) synchronization —☆**phase out** to bring or come to an end, or withdraw from use, by stages —**pha·sic** (fā'zik) *adj.*

SYN.—**phase** applies to any of the ways in which something may be observed, considered, or presented and often refers to a stage in development, in a cycle of changes, etc. [the *phases* of the moon]; **aspect** emphasizes the appearance of a thing as seen or considered from a particular point of view [to consider a problem from all *aspects*]; **facet** literally or figuratively applies to any of the faces of a many-sided thing [the *facets* of a diamond, a personality, etc.]; **angle** suggests a specific aspect seen from a point of view sharply limited in scope, or, sometimes, an aspect seen only by a sharply acute intellect [he knows all the *angles*]

phase-con·trast microscope (fāz'kän'trast) a compound microscope that uses special lenses, diaphragms, etc. to alter slightly the paths of light waves from an object, thus producing a diffraction pattern that allows the viewing of transparent parts: also **phase microscope**

phase modulation *Radio* variation in the phase of a carrier wave in accordance with some signal, as speech

☆**phase-out** (fāz'out') *n.* a phasing out; gradual termination, withdrawal, etc.

phase rule *Physical Chem.* a generalization in the study of equilibria between two or more phases of a system stating that the number of degrees of freedom is equal to the number of components minus the number of phases plus the constant 2, or $F = C - P + 2$

-pha·si·a (fā'zhə, -zhē ə, -zē ə) [ModL. < Gr. *phanai*, to speak: for IE. base see BAN[1]] *a combining form meaning* a (specified) speech disorder [*aphasia*]: also **-pha·sy** (fə sē)

pha·sis (fā'sis) *n.*, *pl.* **-ses** (-sēz) [ModL.] a phase; aspect; way; stage

phas·mid (faz'mid) *n.* [< ModL. *Phasmida* < *Phasma*, the type genus (< Gr. *phasma*, an apparition, akin to *phainein*, to show: see FANTASY) + *-ida* < neut. pl. of L. *-ides*: see -ID] any of an order (Phasmida) of sticklike or leaflike insects, including the walking sticks and leaf insects

phat·ic (fat'ik) *adj.* [< Gr. *phatos*, spoken (< *phanai*, to speak: for IE. base see FAME) + -IC] of, constituting, or given to formulistic talk, meaningless sounds, etc. used merely to establish social contact rather than to communicate ideas [*phatic* noises] —**phat'i·cal·ly** *adv.*

Ph.B. [L. *Philosophiae Baccalaureus*] Bachelor of Philosophy

Ph.C. Pharmaceutical Chemist

Ph.D. [L. *Philosophiae Doctor*] Doctor of Philosophy

pheas·ant (fez'n't) *n.*, *pl.* **-ants, -ant:** see PLURAL, II, D, 1 [ME. *fesant* < Anglo-Fr. < OFr. *faisan* < L. *phasianus* < Gr. *phasianos* < *Phasis*, river of Colchis: the birds are said to have been numerous near its mouth] **1.** any of a number of related chickenlike game birds (family Phasianidae) with a long, sweeping tail and brilliant feathers ☆**2.** any of a number of birds resembling the pheasant, as the ruffed grouse

Phe·be (fē'bē) a feminine name: see PHOEBE

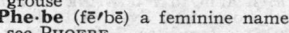
RING-NECKED PHEASANT
(to 35 in. long, including beak and tail)

Phei·dip·pi·des (fī dip'ə dēz') [prob. altered (by Herodotus) < *Philippides*] 5th cent. B.C.; Athenian courier who ran to Sparta to seek aid against the Persians before the battle of Marathon

phel·lem (fel'em) *n.* [< Gr. *phellos*, cork + E. -*em*, as in PHLOEM] the layer of dead, corky cells produced externally by the cork cambium in the bark of woody plants; cork

phel·lo·derm (fel'ə durm') *n.* [< Gr. *phellos*, a cork (akin to *phloos*, bark: see PHLOEM) + -DERM] the layer of soft, living cells developed on the inner side by the phellogen —**phel'lo·der'mal** *adj.*

phel·lo·gen (fel'ə jən) *n.* [< Gr. *phellos* (see PHELLODERM) + -GEN] *same as* CORK CAMBIUM —**phel'lo·ge·net'ic** (-jə net'ik) *adj.*

phen- (fen) [Fr. *phén*- < Gr. *phainein*, to show, shine (see FANTASY): term first used to indicate derivation from coal tar, a byproduct in manufacturing illuminating gas] *a combining form meaning* of or derived from benzene [*phenazine*]

phe·na·caine (fē'nə kān', fen'ə-) *n.* [*phen*(etidyl)a(*cet-phenetidine*) + (CO)CAINE] **1.** an organic, crystalline substance, $C_{18}H_{22}O_2N_2$, derived from coal tar **2.** its hydrochloride, a local anesthetic, esp. for the eyes

phe·nac·e·tin (fi nas'ə tin) *n.* [PHEN- + ACETIN] *same as* ACETOPHENETIDIN

phen·a·kite (fen'ə kīt') *n.* [< Gr. *phenax* (gen. *phenakos*), cheat + -ITE[1]: from being mistaken for quartz] a silicate of beryllium, $BeSiO_4$: it is colorless or red, yellow, or brown with white streaks and has been used as a gem: also **phen'a·cite'** (-sīt')

phe·nan·threne (fə nan'thrēn) *n.* [< PHEN- + ANTHRACENE] a colorless, crystalline hydrocarbon, $C_{14}H_{10}$, an isomer of the anthracene present in coal tar, used in making dyes, explosives, etc.

phe·nate (fē'nāt) *n.* [PHEN(OL) + -ATE[2]] a salt of carbolic acid (phenol in a dilute aqueous solution)

phen·a·zine (fen'ə zēn', -zin) *n.* [PHEN- + AZ- + -INE[4]] a tricyclid, yellow, crystalline base, $C_6H_4:N_2:C_6H_4$, from which many dyes are derived

phe·net·i·dinc (fə nct'ə dēn', -din) *n.* [PHENET(OLE) + AMID(O) + -INE[4]] any of three isomeric compounds, $C_2H_5OC_6H_4NH_2$, esp. the para form, used in manufacturing phenacetin and dyes

phen·e·tole (fen'ə tōl') *n.* [PHEN(OL) + ET(HYL) + -OLE] a colorless liquid, $C_6H_5OC_2H_5$, the ethyl ether of phenol

Phe·ni·cia (fə nish'ə, -nē'shə) *same as* PHOENICIA

phe·nix (fē'niks) *n.* *same as* PHOENIX

phe·no- (fē'nō, -nə; fen/ō, -ə) *same as* PHEN-

phe·no·bar·bi·tal (fē'nə bär'bə tôl', fē'nō-; -tal') *n.* [PHENO- + BARBITAL] an odorless, white crystalline powder, $C_{12}O_3N_2H_{12}$, used as a sedative and antispasmodic

phe·no·cop·y (fē'nə käp'ē) *n.*, *pl.* **-ies** [PHENO(TYPE) + COPY] *Genetics* an environmentally induced change in an organism that is similar to a mutation but is nonhereditary

phe·no·cryst (fē'nə krist, fen'ə-) *n.* [Fr. *phénocryste* < Gr. *phainein*, to show (see FANTASY) + *krystallos*, CRYSTAL] a relatively large and usually conspicuous crystal found in a fine-grained matrix in porphyritic igneous rock

phe·nol (fē'nōl, -nôl, -näl) *n.* [PHEN- + -OL[1]] **1.** a white crystalline compound, C_6H_5OH, produced from coal tar or by the hydrolysis of chlorobenzene, and used in making explosives, synthetic resins, etc.: it is a strong, corrosive poison with a characteristic odor, and its dilute aqueous solution, commonly called carbolic acid, is used as an antiseptic **2.** any of a group of aromatic hydroxyl derivatives of benzene, similar in structure and composition to phenol —**phe·no·lic** (fi nō'lik; -nôl'ik, -näl'-) *adj.*

phe·no·late (fē'nə lāt') *n. same as* PHENATE

phenolic resin any of a group of thermosetting resins formed by condensing phenol with various aldehydes, as formaldehyde: used to form molded and cast plastic items

phe·nol·o·gy (fi näl'ə jē) *n.* [contr. < PHENOMENOLOGY] the study of natural phenomena that recur periodically, as migration, blossoming, etc., and of their relation to climate and changes in season —**phe·no·log·i·cal** (fē'nə läj'i k'l) *adj.* —**phe'no·log'i·cal·ly** *adv.* —**phe·nol'o·gist** *n.*

phe·nol·phthal·ein (fē'nōl thal'ēn, -nôl-; -fthal'-; -ē ən) *n.* [PHENOL + PHTHALEIN] a white to pale-yellow, crystalline powder, $C_{20}H_{14}O_4$, used as a laxative, in making dyes, and as an acid-base indicator in chemical analysis: it is red in a solution containing a base and colorless in a solution containing an acid

phenol red a red, crystalline substance, $C_{19}H_{14}O_5S$, used, in dilute solution, as an acid-base indicator and as a test of renal function

phe·nom·e·na (fi näm'ə nə) *n. pl. of* PHENOMENON

phe·nom·e·nal (fi näm'ə n'l) *adj.* **1.** of or constituting a phenomenon or phenomena **2.** extremely unusual; extraordinary; highly remarkable **3.** *Philos.* apparent to or perceptible by the senses —**phe·nom'e·nal·ly** *adv.*

phe·nom·e·nal·ism (-iz'm) *n.* the philosophic theory that knowledge is limited to phenomena, either because there is no reality beyond phenomena or because such reality is unknowable —**phe·nom'e·nal·ist** *n.* —**phe·nom'e·nal·is'tic** *adj.* —**phe·nom'e·nal·is'ti·cal·ly** *adv.*

phe·nom·e·nol·o·gy (fi näm′ə näl′ə jē) n. [< ff. + -LOGY] 1. the philosophical study of phenomena, as distinguished from ontology 2. the branch of a science that classifies and describes its phenomena without any attempt at metaphysical explanation —**phe·nom′e·no·log′i·cal** (-nə läj′i k′l) adj. —**phe·nom′e·no·log′i·cal·ly** adv.

phe·nom·e·non (fi näm′ə nän′, -nən) n., pl. -na (-nə); also, esp. for 3 and usually for 4, -nons′ [LL. phaenomenon < Gr. phainomenon, neut. prp. of phainesthai, to appear, akin to phainein: see FANTASY] 1. any fact, circumstance, or experience that is apparent to the senses and that can be scientifically described or appraised, as an eclipse 2. the appearance or observed features of something experienced as distinguished from reality or the thing in itself 3. any extremely unusual or extraordinary thing or occurrence 4. [Colloq.] a person with an extraordinary quality, aptitude, etc.; prodigy

phe·no·thi·a·zine (fē′nō thī′ə zēn′) n. [PHENO- + THIA-ZINE] a yellowish crystalline substance, C₁₂H₉NS, used as an insecticide, in the treatment of worms and urinary infections in livestock, and as a tranquilizer

phe·no·type (fē′nə tīp′) n. [G. phänotypus < phänomen (< LL.: see PHENOMENON) + typus, TYPE] Biol. 1. the manifest characteristics of an organism collectively, including anatomical, psychological, etc. traits, that result from both its heredity and its environment 2. a) a group of organisms having a like phenotype b) an individual of such a group —**phe′no·typ′ic** (-tip′ik), **phe′no·typ′i·cal** adj. —**phe′no·typ′i·cal·ly** adv.

phe·nox·ide (fi näk′sīd) n. same as PHENATE

phe·nox·y (fi näk′sē) adj. [PHEN- + OXY-¹] containing the monovalent radical C₆H₅O—, derived from phenol

phen·yl (fen′il, fē′nil) n. [PHEN- + -YL] the monovalent radical C₆H₅, forming the basis of phenol, benzene, aniline, and various other aromatic compounds

phen·yl·al·a·nine (fen′il al′ə nēn′, fē′nil-) n. an essential amino acid, C₉H₁₁O₂N, occurring in proteins

phen·yl·am·ine (-ə mēn′, -am′ēn) n. [PHENYL + AMINE] same as ANILINE

phen·yl·bu·ta·zone (-byōōt′ə zōn′) n. [PHENYL + BU-T(YRIC) + az(al)one] a white powder, C₁₉H₂₀N₂O₂, used as an analgesic, as for the relief of rheumatoid arthritis

phen·yl·ene (fen′ə lēn′, fē′nə-) n. [PHENYL + -ENE] the bivalent radical —C₆H₄—, derived from benzene by displacement of two hydrogen atoms

phen·yl·ke·to·nu·ri·a (fen′il kēt′ə nyoor′ē ə, fē′nil-) n. [PHENYL + KETONURIA] a genetic disorder of phenylalanine metabolism, which, if untreated, causes severe mental retardation in infants through the accumulation of toxic metabolic products —**phen′yl·ke′to·nu′ric** adj.

pher·o·mone (fer′ə mōn′) n. [< Gr. pherein, to BEAR¹ + E. -o- + (HOR)MONE] any of various chemical substances secreted externally by certain animals, as ants, moths, etc., which convey information to and produce specific responses in other individuals of the same species

phew (fyōō, fyoo: conventionalized pronun., often unvoiced) interj. a breathy sound expressing disgust, surprise, relief, etc.

phi (fī, fē) n. [MGr. phi < Gr. phei] the 21st letter of the Greek alphabet (Φ, φ)

phi·al (fī′əl) n. [ME. fiole < OFr. fiole < Pr. fiola < ML. < L. phiala < Gr. phialē, broad, shallow drinking vessel] a small glass bottle; vial

☆**Phi Be·ta Kap·pa** (fī′ bāt′ə kap′ə, bēt′ə) [< the initial letters of the Gr. motto philosophia biou kybernētēs, philosophy the guide of life] 1. an honorary society of U.S. college students of high scholastic rank: founded 1776 2. a member of this society

Phid·i·as (fid′ē əs) 5th cent. B.C.; Gr. sculptor: see PARTHENON —**Phid′i·an** (-ən) adj.

Phi·dip·pi·des (fi dip′ə dēz′) same as PHEIDIPPIDES

phil- (fil) same as PHILO-: used before a vowel

-phil (fil) same as -PHILE

Phil. 1. Philippians 2. Philippine

phil. 1. philology 2. philosophy

Phil·a·del·phi·a (fil′ə del′fē ə, -fyə) [Gr. philadelphia, brotherly love < philos, loving + adelphos, brother] 1. city & port in SE Pa., on the Delaware River: pop. 1,949,000 (met. area 4,818,000) 2. ancient city in Lydia, W Asia Minor —**Phil′a·del′phi·an** adj., n.

☆**Philadelphia lawyer** [Colloq.] a clever, shrewd, or tricky lawyer, esp. one skilled in taking advantage of legal technicalities

phil·a·del·phus (fil′ə del′fəs) n. [ModL. < Gr. philadel-phon, mock orange < philadelphos, loving one's brother < philein, to love + adelphos, brother] same as MOCK ORANGE

phi·lan·der (fi lan′dər) n. [< Gr. philandros, fond of men < philos, loving + anēr, a man (see ANDRO-): used in fiction as a name for a lover] [Rare] a man who philanders —vi. to engage lightly in passing love affairs; make love insincerely: said of a man —**phi·lan′der·er** n.

phil·an·throp·ic (fil′ən thräp′ik) adj. [Fr. philanthropique] of, showing, or constituting philanthropy; charitable; benevolent; humane: also **phil′an·throp′i·cal** —**phil′an·throp′i·cal·ly** adv.

SYN.—**philanthropic** implies interest in the general human welfare, esp. as shown in large-scale gifts to charities, the endowment of institutions for human advancement, etc.; **humanitarian** implies more direct concern with promoting the welfare of human-ity, esp. through reducing pain and suffering; **charitable** implies the giving of money or other help to those in need; **altruistic** implies a putting of the welfare of others before one's own interests and therefore stresses freedom from selfishness

phi·lan·thro·pist (fi lan′thrə pist) n. a person, esp. a wealthy one, who practices philanthropy

phi·lan·thro·pize (-pīz′) vt. -pized′, -piz′ing to deal with philanthropically —vi. to practice philanthropy

☆**phi·lan·thro·poid** (-poid′) n. [jocular blend < PHILAN-THROP(IST) + (ANTHROP)OID] [Colloq.] any of the executive officers of various philanthropic foundations

phi·lan·thro·py (-pē) n. [LL. philanthropia < Gr. phi-lanthrōpia < philein, to love + anthrōpos, man] 1. a desire to help mankind, esp. as shown by gifts to charitable or humanitarian institutions; benevolence 2. pl. -pies a philanthropic act, gift, institution, etc.

phi·lat·e·ly (fi lat′′l ē) n. [Fr. philatélie, coined (1864) < Gr. philos, loving + ateleia, exemption from (further) tax taken as equivalent of "postage prepaid"] the collection and study of postage stamps, postmarks, stamped envelopes, etc., usually as a hobby —**phil·a·tel·ic** (fil′ə tel′ik) adj. —**phil′a·tel′i·cal·ly** adv. —**phi·lat′e·list** n.

-phile (fīl, fil) [< Gr. philos, loving] a combining form meaning loving, liking, favorably disposed to [Anglophile]

Phi·le·mon (fi lē′mən, fī-) [L. < Gr. Philēmōn, lit., affectionate] 1. a masculine name 2. a book of the New Testament which was an epistle from the Apostle Paul to his friend Philemon: abbrev. **Philem.** 3. Gr. Myth. the husband of Baucis: see BAUCIS

phil·har·mon·ic (fil′här män′ik, fil′ər-) adj. [Fr. philhar-monique, after It. filarmonico < Gr. philos, loving + harmonia, HARMONY] loving or devoted to music: often used in the title of a symphony orchestra, the society sponsoring it, etc. —n. 1. a society formed to sponsor a symphony orchestra 2. [Colloq.] an orchestra or concert sponsored by such a society

phil·hel·lene (fil hel′ēn) n. [see PHILO- & HELLENE] a friend or supporter of the Greeks or Greece —**phil′hel-len′ic** (-hə len′ik) adj. —**phil·hel′len·ism** (-ən iz′m) n. —**phil·hel′len·ist** n.

-phil·i·a (fil′ē ə, fil′yə) [< Gr. philos, loving] a combining form meaning: 1. tendency toward [hemophilia] 2. abnormal attraction to [coprophilia]

Phil·ip (fil′əp) [L. Philippus < Gr. Philippos, lit., fond of horses < philos, loving + hippos, a horse] 1. a masculine name: dim. Phil; equiv. L. Philippus, Fr. Philippe, Ger. Philipp, It. Filippo, Sp. Felipe; fem. Philippa 2. Bible one of the twelve apostles: also called Saint Philip: his day is May 1 3. (Ind. name Metacomet) ?-1676; chief of the Wampanoag Indians (1662-76): led a war against New England colonists: called King Philip: son of MASSASOIT 4. Prince, 1921- ; Duke of Edinburgh, born in Greece; husband of Elizabeth II of England 5. Saint, 1st cent. A.D.; evangelist & a deacon of the early Christian church: his day is June 6 6. **Philip II** a) 382-336 B.C.; king of Macedonia (359-336): father of ALEXANDER THE GREAT b) 1165-1223; king of France (1180-1223): also called **Philip Augustus** c) 1527-98; king of Spain (1556-98) & (as Philip I) of Portugal (1580-98): sent the Armada against England (1588) 7. **Philip IV** 1268-1314; king of France (1285-1314): moved the papacy to Avignon (1309): called the Fair 8. **Philip V** 1683-1746; 1st Bourbon king of Spain (1700-46)

Phi·lip·pa (fi lip′ə) [fem. of PHILIP] a feminine name

Phi·lip·pi (fi lip′ī) ancient city in Macedonia, where, in 42 B.C., Mark Antony & Octavius defeated Brutus & Cassius: site of an early Christian community established by Paul (Acts 16:12) —**Phi·lip′pi·an** adj., n.

Phi·lip·pi·ans (-ē ənz) [with sing. v.] a book of the New Testament which was an epistle from the Apostle Paul to the Christians of Philippi

Phi·lip·pic (fi lip′ik) n. [L. Philippicus < Gr. Philippikos, belonging to Philip < Philippos, Philip] 1. any of the orations of Demosthenes against Philip, king of Macedon 2. [p-] any bitter verbal attack

Phil·ip·pine (fil′ə pēn′) adj. of the Philippine Islands or their people

Philippine mahogany the light to dark reddish wood of various trees (esp. genera Shorea, Dipterocarpus, and Pentacme) of the Philippines and SE Asia

Phil·ip·pines (fil′ə pēnz′) country occupying a group of c. 7,100 islands (**Philippine Islands**) in the SW Pacific off the SE coast of Asia: 114,830 sq. mi.; pop. 38,613,000; cap. Quezon City

Philippine Sea part of the W Pacific, between the Philip-pines & the Mariana Islands, south of Japan

Phil·ip·pop·o·lis (fil′ə päp′ə lis) Gr. name of PLOVDIV

Philip the Good 1396-1467; duke of Burgundy (1419-67)

Phi·lis·ti·a (fə lis′tē ə) country of the Philistines (fl. 12th-4th cent. B.C.), in ancient SW Palestine

Phil·is·tine (fil′is tēn′; fi lis′tin, -tēn) n. [ME. < LL. (Ec.) Philistinus, usually pl. Philistini < LGr. (Josephus) philistinoi < Heb. p'lishtim, akin to PALESTINE] 1. a member of a non-Semitic people who lived in Philistia and repeatedly warred with the Israelites 2. [adapted < Gr. Philister, orig. student slang for townspeople] [often p-] a person regarded as smugly narrow and conventional in his views and tastes, lacking in and indifferent to cul-tural and aesthetic values, etc. —adj. 1. of the ancient

Philistines **2.** smugly conventional, lacking in culture, etc. —**Phil′is·tin·ism** *n.*

Phil·lip (fil′əp) a masculine name: see PHILIP

Phil·lips (fil′əps) **1.** Stephen, 1868–1915; Eng. poetic dramatist **2.** Wendell, 1811–84; U.S. abolitionist, reformer, & orator

Phil·lips (fil′əps) [after Henry F. *Phillips* (?–1958), its U.S. developer] ☆*a trademark for* a screwdriver (**Phillips screwdriver**) with a cross-shaped, pointed tip: used on a screw (**Phillips screw**) that has two slots crossing at the center of the head

Phil·lis (fil′is) a feminine name: see PHYLLIS

phil·o- (fil′ə, -ō) [< Gr. *philos*, loving] *a combining form meaning* loving, liking, having a predilection for [*philology*]

Phil·oc·te·tes (fil′äk tē′tēz) *Gr. Legend* the Greek warrior who killed Paris in the Trojan War with a poisoned arrow given him by Hercules

phil·o·den·dron (fil′ə den′drən) *n.* [ModL. < neut. of Gr. *philodendros*, loving trees < *philos*, loving + *dendron*, TREE] **1.** any of a genus (*Philodendron*) of tropical American vines of the arum family, often with leathery, heart-shaped leaves **2.** loosely, any similar plant

phi·log·y·ny (fi läj′ə nē) *n.* [Gr. *philogynia* < *philein*, to love + *gynē*, woman: see GYNO-] love of or fondness for women —**phi·log′y·nist** *n.* —**phi·log′y·nous** *adj.*

Phi·lo (Ju·dae·us) (fī′lō jōō dē′əs) 20? B.C.–50? A.D.; Hellenistic Jewish philosopher of Alexandria

philol. philology

phi·lol·o·gy (fi läl′ə jē) *n.* [Fr. *philologie* < L. *philologia*, love of learning < Gr. *philologia*, love of literature < *philein*, to love + *logos*, a word: see LOGIC] **1.** orig., the love of learning and literature; study; scholarship **2.** the study of written records, esp. literary texts, in order to determine their authenticity, meaning, etc. **3.** *earlier term for* LINGUISTICS —**phil·o·log·i·cal** (fil′ə läj′i k′l), **phil′o·log′ic** *adj.* —**phil′o·log′i·cal·ly** *adv.* —**phi·lol′o·gist** *n.*

phil·o·mel (fil′ə mel′) *n.* [altered (after L.) < ME. *Philomene* < ML. *Philomena*, for L. *Philomela*: see ff.] *poetic term for* NIGHTINGALE

Phil·o·me·la (fil′ə mē′lə) [L. < Gr. *Philomela* < *philein*, to love + *melos*, song] *Gr. Myth.* a princess of Athens raped by Tereus, husband of her sister Procne: the gods changed Philomela into a nightingale, Procne into a swallow, and Tereus into a hawk —*n.* [p-] *same as* PHILOMEL

☆**phil·o·pe·na** (fil′ə pē′nə) *n.* [altered < Fr. *philippine*, transl. of G. *Philippchen*, little Philip, folk-etym. or jocular corruption of *vielliebchen*, lit., sweetheart (pop. name for the joined kernels of nuts) dim. < *viel*, much + *lieb*, dear: infl. by association with Gr. *philos*, loving & L. *poena*, a penalty, because of the forfeit paid] **1.** a nut with two kernels **2.** *a)* a game in which the two kernels of a nut are shared by two people, one of whom, if failing to fulfill a given condition, must pay a forfeit to the other *b)* the forfeit, usually a gift

phil·o·pro·gen·i·tive (fil′ə prō jen′ə tiv) *adj.* [PHILO- + PROGENITIVE] **1.** productive of offspring; prolific **2.** *a)* loving offspring, esp. one's own *b)* of such love

philos. philosophy

†**phi·lo·sophe** (fē lô zôf′) *n., pl.* -**sophes′** (-zôf′) [Fr.] a philosopher: in English contexts often a somewhat derogatory term suggesting pretension

phi·los·o·pher (fi läs′ə fər) *n.* [ME. *philosophre* < OFr. *philosophe* < L. *philosophus* < Gr. *philosophos* < *philos*, loving + *sophos*, wise] **1.** a person who studies or is learned in philosophy **2.** a person who lives and thinks according to a system of philosophy **3.** *a)* a person who meets difficulties with calmness and composure *b)* a person given to philosophizing **4.** [Obs.] an alchemist, magician, etc.

philosophers′ (or **philosopher's**) **stone** an imaginary substance sought for by alchemists in the belief that it would change base metals into gold or silver

phil·o·soph·ic (fil′ə säf′ik) *adj.* [L. *philosophicus* < Gr. *philosophikos*] **1.** of or according to a philosophy or a philosopher **2.** devoted to or learned in philosophy **3.** like or suited for a philosopher **4.** sensibly composed or calm, as in a difficult situation; rational Also **phil′o·soph′i·cal** —**phil′o·soph′i·cal·ly** *adv.*

phi·los·o·phism (fi läs′ə fiz′m) *n.* [Fr. *philosophisme* < *philosophe*: see PHILOSOPHER] false or faulty philosophy or philosophic argument; sophistry

phi·los·o·phize (-fīz′) *vi.* -**phized′**, -**phiz′ing** **1.** to deal philosophically with abstract matter; think or reason like a philosopher **2.** to express superficial philosophic ideas, truisms, etc.; esp., to moralize —**phi·los′o·phiz′er** *n.*

phi·los·o·phy (-fē) *n., pl.* -**phies** [ME. *philosophie* < OFr. < L. *philosophia* < Gr. *philosophia* < *philosophos*: see PHILOSOPHER] **1.** orig., love of, or the search for, wisdom or knowledge **2.** theory or logical analysis of the principles underlying conduct, thought, knowledge, and the nature of the universe: included in philosophy are ethics, aesthetics, logic, epistemology, metaphysics, etc. **3.** the general principles or laws of a field of knowledge, activity, etc. [the *philosophy* of economics] **4.** *a)* a particular system of principles for the conduct of life *b)* a treatise covering

such a system **5.** *a)* a study of human morals, character, and behavior *b)* mental balance or composure thought of as resulting from this; calmness **6.** [Obs.] *same as* NATURAL PHILOSOPHY

-**phi·lous** (fi ləs) [< Gr. *philos*, loving] *a combining form meaning* loving, liking [*photophilous*]

phil·ter (fil′tər) *n.* [MFr. *philtre* < L. *philtrum* < Gr. *philtron* < *philein*, to love] **1.** a potion or charm thought to arouse sexual love, esp. toward a specific person **2.** any magic potion —*vt.* to charm or arouse with a philter Also, chiefly Brit., **phil′tre** (-tər) -**tred**, -**tring**

phi·mo·sis (fī mō′sis) *n.* [ModL. < Gr. *phimōsis*, a muzzling < *phimos*, a muzzle] an abnormal condition in which the foreskin of the penis is so tight that it cannot be drawn back over the glans —**phi·mot′ic** (-mät′ik) *adj.*

Phin·e·as (fin′ē əs) [LL. *Phinees* < Gr. *Phinees* < Heb. *pīnĕhās*, prob. < Egypt. *pe-nehase*] a masculine name

phiz (fiz) *n.* [contr. < PHYSIOGNOMY] [Old Slang] a face or facial expression

phle·bi·tis (fli bīt′is) *n.* [ModL.: see ff. & -ITIS] inflammation of a vein or veins —**phle·bit′ic** (-bit′ik) *adj.*

phleb·o- (fleb′ō, -ə) [< Gr. *phleps* (gen. *phlebos*), a vein < IE. *bhlegw-*, to swell < base *bhel-*, to blow up, swell, whence L. *flare*, to BLOW[1]] *a combining form meaning* vein [*phlebotomy*]: also, before a vowel, **phleb-**

phleb·o·scle·ro·sis (fleb′ō skli rō′sis) *n.* [ModL.: see prec. & SCLEROSIS] hardening of the walls of the veins

phle·bot·o·mize (fli bät′ə mīz′) *vt., vi.* -**mized′**, -**miz′ing** to practice phlebotomy (on); bleed

phle·bot·o·my (-mē) *n.* [ME. *flebotomie* < OFr. *flebothomie* < LL. *phlebotomia* < Gr. *phlebotomia*: see PHLEBO- & -TOMY] the act or practice of bloodletting as a therapeutic measure —**phle·bot′o·mist** *n.*

Phleg·e·thon (fleg′ə thän, flej′-) [L. < Gr. *Phlegethōn*, orig. prp. of *phlegethein*, to blaze: for IE. base see FLAGRANT] *Gr. Myth.* a river of fire in Hades

phlegm (flem) *n.* [ME. *fleume* < MFr. < LL. *phlegma*, clammy humor of the body < Gr. *phlegma*, inflammation, hence, humors caused by inflammation < *phlegein*, to burn: for IE. base see FLAGRANT] **1.** the thick, stringy mucus secreted by the mucous glands of the respiratory tract and discharged from the throat, as during a cold **2.** [Obs.] that one of the four imaginary humors of the body which was believed in medieval times to cause sluggishness or dullness **3.** *a)* sluggishness or apathy *b)* calmness or composure —**phlegm′y** *adj.* -**i·er**, -**i·est**

phleg·mat·ic (fleg mat′ik) *adj.* [ME. *fleumatike* < OFr. < LL. *phlegmaticus* < Gr. *phlegmatikos* < *phlegma*: see prec.] **1.** hard to rouse to action; specif., *a)* sluggish; dull; apathetic *b)* calm; cool; stolid **2.** [Obs.] of, like, or producing the humor phlegm Also **phleg·mat′i·cal** —*SYN.* see IMPASSIVE —**phleg′mat′i·cal·ly** *adv.*

phlo·em (flō′em) *n.* [G. < Gr. *phloos*, bark, akin to *phloiein*, to swell: for base see PHLEBO-] the vascular tissue serving as a path for the distribution of food material in a plant, made up chiefly of sieve tubes and parenchyma cells, sometimes with companion cells and fibers

phloem ray the portion of a vascular ray in a stem which traverses the phloem

phlo·gis·tic (flō jis′tik) *adj.* [< ModL. *phlogiston* (see ff.) + -IC] **1.** of phlogiston **2.** [Obs.] fiery; flaming **3.** *Med.* of inflammation; inflammatory

phlo·gis·ton (-tän, -tən) *n.* [ModL. < Gr. *phlogistos* < *phlogizein*, to burn, inflame < *phlegein*, to burn: for IE. base see FLAGRANT] an imaginary element formerly believed to cause combustion and to be given off by anything burning; matter or principle of fire

phlog·o·pite (fläg′ə pīt′) *n.* [G. *phlogopit* < Gr. *phlogōpos*, fiery (< *phlox*, a flame: see PHLOX + *ōps*, a face, EYE) + G. -*it*, -ITE[1]] a kind of magnesium mica, usually light brown in color

phlor·i·zin (flôr′ə zin, flə rī′zin) *n.* [< Gr. *phloos*, bark (see PHLOEM) + *rhiza*, ROOT[1] + -IN[1]] a bitter, white, crystalline substance, $C_{21}H_{24}O_{10}$, found in the root and bark of certain fruit trees: used experimentally to produce glycosuria: also **phlo·rid′zin** (-rid′zin), **phlo·rhi′zin** (-rī′zin)

phlox (fläks) *n.* [ModL., name of the genus < L., a flower, flame < Gr. *phlox*, wallflower, lit., flame < *phlegein*, to burn (for IE. base see FLAGRANT] any of a genus (*Phlox*) of chiefly N. American plants of the phlox family, with opposite leaves and white, pink, red, or bluish flowers —*adj.* designating a family (Polemoniaceae) of plants including phlox, Jacob's ladder, etc.

PHLOX

phlyc·te·na (flik tē′nə) *n., pl.* -**nae** (-nē) [ModL. < Gr. *phlyktaina*, a blister < *phlyein*, bubble up: for IE. base see PHLEBO-] a small blister or pustule —**phlyc·te′nar** *adj.*

phlyc·ten·ule (-ten′yool) *n.* [ModL. *phlyctenula*: see prec. & -ULE] a small phlyctena —**phlyc·ten′u·lar** *adj.*

Phnom Penh (p'nôm′ pen′) capital of Cambodia, at the junction of the Mekong & Tonle Sap rivers: pop. 403,000: also sp. **Pnom-Penh**

-phobe (fōb) [Fr. < L. *-phobus* < Gr. *-phobos* < *phobos*, a fear < IE. base *bhegw-*, to flee, whence Hindi *bhāg-*, Lett. *bēgu*, to flee] *a n.-forming suffix meaning* one who fears or hates [*Francophobe*]

pho·bi·a (fō′bē ə) *n.* [ModL. < Gr. *phobos*, a fear: see prec.] an irrational, excessive, and persistent fear of some particular thing or situation —**pho′bic** *adj.*

-pho·bi·a (fō′bē ə, fōb′yə) [Gr. *-phobia* < *phobos*, fear: see -PHOBE] *a combining form meaning* fear, dread, hatred [*claustrophobia, Anglophobia*]

Pho·cae·a (fō sē′ə) ancient Ionian city in W Asia Minor, on the Aegean

pho·cine (fō′sīn, -sin) *adj.* [< L. *phoca*, a seal (< Gr. *phōkē*) + -INE¹] *Zool.* of or relating to the seals

Pho·ci·on (fō′shē än′, -ən) 402?–317? B.C.; Athenian statesman & general

Pho·cis (fō′sis) ancient region in C Greece, on the Gulf of Corinth: chief city, Delphi

pho·co·me·li·a (fō′kō mē′lē ə, -mēl′yə) *n.* [ModL. < Gr. *phōkē*, a seal + ModL. *-melia*, a condition of limbs < Gr. *melos*, a limb] the congenital absence or abnormal shortening of arms or legs, often with only short, flipperlike limbs projecting from the body —**pho′co·me′lic** (-mē′lik) *adj.*

Phoe·be (fē′bē) [L. < Gr. *Phoibē*, fem. of *Phoibos*: see PHOEBUS] 1. a feminine name 2. *Gr. Myth.* Artemis, goddess of the moon: identified with the Roman goddess Diana 3. [Poet.] the moon personified

☆**phoe·be** (fē′bē) *n.* [echoic, with sp. after prec.] any of several American flycatchers (genus *Sayornis*) with a gray or brown back and a short crest

Phoe·bus (fē′bəs) [ME. *Phebus* < L. *Phoebus* < Gr. *Phoibos*, bright one < *phoibos*, bright] 1. *Gr. Myth.* Apollo, god of the sun 2. [Poet.] the sun personified

Phoe·ni·cia (fə nish′ə, -nē′shə) ancient region of city-states at the E end of the Mediterranean, in the region of present-day Syria & Lebanon

Phoe·ni·cian (-ən, -shən) *adj.* of Phoenicia, its people, their language, or culture —*n.* 1. a native of Phoenicia 2. the extinct Semitic language of the Phoenicians, closely related to Moabite and Hebrew

Phoe·nix (fē′niks) [in allusion to the ff.] capital of Arizona, in the SC part, near the Salt River: pop. 582,000 (met. area 968,000)

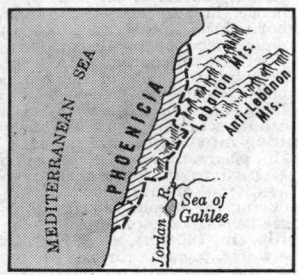

PHOENICIA

phoe·nix (fē′niks) [altered (after L.) < OE. & OFr. *fenix* < L. *phoenix* < Gr. *phoinix*, phoenix, dark red, Phoenician, akin to *phoinos*, blood-red, deadly] 1. *Egyptian Myth.* a beautiful, lone bird which lived in the Arabian desert for 500 or 600 years and then consumed itself in fire, rising renewed from the ashes to start another long life: a symbol of immortality 2. [P-] a S constellation near Eridanus

phon (fän) *n.* [< Gr. *phōnē*, a sound: see PHONO-] a measure of the apparent loudness level of a sound with respect to a 1000 cycle-per-second pure tone: based on the subjective judgment of the human ear or on objective comparisons of acoustical measurements

phon- (fōn) *same as* PHONO-: used before a vowel

phon. phonetics

pho·nate (fō′nāt) *vi.* **-nat·ed, -nat·ing** [PHON- + -ATE¹] to utter a voiced sound —**pho·na′tion** *n.*

phone¹ (fōn) *n.* [Gr. *phōnē*, a sound: see PHONO-] *Phonet.* any single speech sound: a phoneme is composed of various phones or allophones

☆**phone²** (fōn) *n., vt., vi.* **phoned, phon′ing** colloq. shortened form of TELEPHONE

-phone (fōn) [< Gr. *phōnē*, a sound: see PHONO-] *a combining form meaning:* 1. a device producing or transmitting sound [*saxophone, megaphone*] 2. a telephone [*interphone, radiophone*]

pho·neme (fō′nēm) *n.* [Fr. *phonème* < Gr. *phōnēma*, a sound < *phōnein*, to sound < *phōnē*, a voice: see PHONO-] *Linguis.* a set of phonetically similar but slightly different sounds in a language that are heard as the same sound by native speakers and are represented in phonemic transcription by the same symbol, as, in English, the phonetically differentiated sounds represented by *p* in *pin*, *spin*, and *tip*

pho·ne·mic (fə nē′mik, fō-) *adj.* 1. of, characterized by, or based on, phonemes 2. of phonemics —**pho·ne′mi·cal·ly** *adv.*

pho·ne·mi·cist (-mə sist) *n.* an expert in phonemics

pho·ne·mi·cize (-mə sīz′) *vt.* **-cized′, -ciz′ing** to transcribe in phonemic symbols —**pho·ne′mi·ci·za′tion** *n.*

pho·ne·mics (-miks) *n.pl.* [with sing. v.] 1. the branch of language study dealing with the phonemic systems of

languages 2. the description and classification of the phonemes of a specific language

phonet. phonetics

pho·net·ic (fə net′ik, fō-) *adj.* [ModL. *phoneticus* < Gr. *phōnētikos* < *phōnētos*, to be spoken < *phōnein*, to speak < *phōnē*, a sound: see PHONO-] 1. of speech sounds or the production or transcription of these 2. of phonetics 3. conforming to pronunciation [*phonetic* spelling] 4. of or involving detailed, nonsignificant distinctions in the production of speech sounds —**pho·net′i·cal·ly** *adv.*

phonetic alphabet a set of symbols used in phonetic transcription, having a separate symbol for every speech sound that can be distinguished

pho·ne·ti·cian (fō′nə tish′ən) *n.* an expert in phonetics

pho·net·ics (fə net′iks, fō-) *n.pl.* [with sing. v.] [see PHONETIC] 1. the branch of language study dealing with speech sounds, their production and combination, and their representation by written symbols 2. the system of sounds of a particular language

pho·ne·tist (fō′nə tist) *n.* [< Gr. *phōnētos*, to be spoken (see PHONETIC) + -IST] 1. *same as* PHONETICIAN 2. a person who advocates or uses a system of phonetic spelling

☆**pho·ney** (fō′nē) *adj., n.* [Colloq.] *same as* PHONY

-pho·ni·a (fō′nē ə) *same as* -PHONY

phon·ic (fän′ik; *occas.* fō′nik) *adj.* [PHON- + -IC] 1. of, or having the nature of, sound; esp., of speech sounds 2. of or relating to phonics —**phon′i·cal·ly** *adv.*

phon·ics (-iks, -niks) *n.pl.* [with sing. v.] [< prec.] 1. the science of sound; acoustics 2. a method of teaching beginners to read or enunciate by learning the usual sounds of certain letters or groups of letters

pho·no- (fō′nə, -nō) [< Gr. *phōnē*, a sound, voice, akin to *phanai*, to say < IE. base *bhā-*, to speak, whence BAN¹, FAME] *a combining form meaning* sound, tone, speech [*phonology*]

pho·no·gram (fō′nə gram′) *n.* [prec. + -GRAM] a sign or symbol representing a word, syllable, or sound, as in shorthand —**pho′no·gram′ic, pho′no·gram′mic** *adj.* —**pho′no·gram′i·cal·ly, pho′no·gram′mi·cal·ly** *adv.*

pho·no·graph (fō′nə graf′, -gräf′) *n.* [PHONO- + -GRAPH] ☆an instrument for reproducing sound that has been mechanically transcribed in a spiral groove on a circular disk or cylinder: a needle or stylus following the groove in the revolving disk or cylinder picks up and transmits the sound vibrations

pho·no·graph·ic (fō′nə graf′ik) *adj.* ☆1. of a phonograph or the sounds made by one 2. of phonography —**pho′no·graph′i·cal·ly** *adv.*

pho·nog·ra·phy (fō näg′rə fē) *n.* [PHONO- + -GRAPHY] 1. a written or printed representation of the sounds of speech; phonetic spelling or transcription 2. any system of shorthand based on a phonetic transcription of speech; esp., the system invented by Isaac PITMAN

pho·no·lite (fō′nə līt′) *n.* [Fr. *phonolithe* < *phono-* (see PHONO-) + -lithe (see -LITE): transl. of G. *klingstein* < *klingen*, to ring, clink + *stein*, STONE] a fine-grained, extrusive, igneous rock consisting chiefly of alkali feldspar and nepheline: it rings when struck —**pho′no·lit′ic** (-lit′ik) *adj.*

pho·nol·o·gy (fō näl′ə jē, fə-) *n.* [PHONO- + -LOGY] 1. phonetics or phonemics or, esp., both considered as a unified system of the speech sounds of a language 2. the study of the changes in speech sounds in the development of a language or dialect —**pho·no·log·i·cal** (fō′nə läj′i k'l), **pho′no·log′ic** *adj.* —**pho′no·log′i·cal·ly** *adv.* —**pho·nol′o·gist** *n.*

pho·nom·e·ter (fō näm′ə tər) *n.* [PHONO- + -METER] an instrument used to measure the intensity and vibration frequency of sound —**pho·nom′e·try** *n.*

pho·non (fō′nän) *n.* [PHONO- + -on, as in PHOTON] a quantum of sound energy that is a carrier of heat: cf. PHOTON

pho·no·scope (fō′nə skōp′) *n.* [PHONO- + -SCOPE] an instrument used to observe or exhibit the properties of a sounding body; esp., such an instrument for testing the quality of strings for musical instruments

pho·no·type (fō′nə tīp′) *n.* [PHONO- + -TYPE] a phonetic symbol or character, as used in printing

☆**pho·ny** (fō′nē) *adj.* **-ni·er, -ni·est** [altered < Brit. thieves' argot *fawney*, a gilt ring (passed off as gold by swindlers) < Ir. *fáinne*] [Colloq.] not genuine; false, counterfeit, spurious, pretentious, etc. —*n., pl.* **-nies** [Colloq.] 1. something not genuine; sham; fake 2. a person who is not what he pretends to be; one who deceives, dissembles, is insincere, etc.; fraud —**pho′ni·ness** *n.*

-pho·ny (fə nē, fō′nē) [< Gr. *phōnē*, a sound: see PHONO-] *a combining form meaning* a (specified kind of) sound

phoo·ey (fōō′ē) *interj.* [echoic of spitting sound, like (or ? <) G. *pfui*: cf. FIE] an exclamation expressing contempt, scorn, or disgust

-phore (fôr) [ModL. *-phorus, -phorum* < Gr. *-phoros, -phoron* < *pherein*, to BEAR¹] *a combining form. meaning* bearer, producer [*carpophore*]

pho·ro·nid (fə rō′nid) *n.* [< ModL. *Phoronidea* < *Phoronis*, name of the genus (prob. < L. *Phoronis*, Io) + *-idea*, neut. pl. suffix] any member of a small phylum (Phoronidea) of unsegmented, wormlike marine animals, with a U-shaped digestive tract and a lophophore —*adj.* of or belonging to the phoronids

-phor·ous (fər əs) [ModL. *-phorus* < Gr. *-phorus* <

pherein, BEAR[1]] *a combining form meaning* bearing, producing [*sporophorus*]

phos·gene (fäs′jēn) *n*. [so named (1812) < Gr. *phōs*, light (see PHOSPHORUS) + *-gene* (for -GEN)] a colorless, volatile, highly poisonous liquid, $COCl_2$, prepared by the reaction of carbon monoxide with chlorine in the presence of activated charcoal or, orig., in sunlight: used as a poison gas, in organic synthesis, in making dyes, etc.

phosph- *same as* PHOSPHO-: used before a vowel

phos·pha·tase (fäs′fə tās′) *n*. [< ff. + -ASE] any of various enzymes found in body tissues and fluids, that hydrolyze phosphoric acid esters of organic compounds, liberating phosphate ions

phos·phate (-fāt) *n*. [Fr. < (*acide*) *phosphorique* < -*ate*, -ATE²] 1. a salt or ester of phosphoric acid 2. any substance containing phosphates, used as a fertilizer ☆3. a soft drink made with soda water, syrup, and, orig., a few drops of phosphoric acid

☆**phosphate rock** sedimentary rock containing calcium phosphate in commercial quantity, used as a raw material for making fertilizers, phosphorous chemicals, etc.

phos·phat·ic (fäs fat′ik) *adj*. of or containing phosphoric acid or phosphates

phos·pha·tide (fäs′fə tīd′) *n*. [PHOSPHAT(E) + -IDE] any of a group of fatty compounds, as lecithin, found in animal and plant cells: they are complex triglyceride esters containing long chain fatty acids, phosphoric acid, and nitrogenous bases —**phos′pha·tid′ic** (-tid′ik) *adj*.

phos·pha·tize (-tīz′) *vt*. **-tized′, -tiz′ing** 1. to change into, or treat with, a phosphate or phosphoric acid 2. to treat with phosphoric acid —**phos′pha·ti·za′tion** *n*.

phos·pha·tu·ri·a (fäs′fə toor′ē ə, -tyoor′-) *n*. [ModL.: see PHOSPHATE & -URIA] an excess of phosphates in the urine —**phos′pha·tu′ric** *adj*.

phos·phene (fäs′fēn) *n*. [< Gr. *phōs*, light (see PHOSPHORUS) + *phainein*, to show (see FANTASY)] a sensation of light produced by mechanical stimulation of the retina, as by pressure on the eyeball through the closed eyelid

phos·phide (-fīd) *n*. a compound consisting of trivalent phosphorus with another element or a radical

phos·phine (-fēn, -fin) *n*. [PHOSPH- + -INE¹] 1. hydrogen phosphide, PH_3, a colorless, poisonous, flammable gas with a garliclike odor 2. a synthetic yellow dye

phos·phite (-fīt) *n*. [Fr.: see PHOSPH- & -ITE¹] a salt or ester of phosphorous acid

phos·pho- (fäs′fō, -fə) [< PHOSPHORUS] *a combining form meaning* phosphorus or phosphoric acid [*phosphoprotein*]

phos·pho·cre·a·tine (fäs′fō krē′ə tēn′, -tin) *n*. [prec. + CREATINE] a compound, $C_4H_{10}O_5N_3P$, containing a high-energy phosphate bond and involved in vertebrate muscular contraction

phos·pho·lip·id (-lip′id) *n*. [PHOSPHO- + LIPID] *same as* PHOSPHATIDE: also **phos′pho·lip′ide** (-īd)

phos·pho·ni·um (fäs fō′nē əm) *n*. [ModL.: see PHOSPHO- & (AMM)ONIUM] the monovalent radical PH_4, which is related to PH_3 as the ammonium radical NH_4 is related to NH_3

phos·pho·pro·tein (fäs′fō prō′tēn, -tē in) *n*. any of a group of proteins in which the protein molecule is combined with some phosphorous compound other than lecithin or a nucleic acid, as casein in milk

Phos·phor (fäs′far) [L. *Phosphorus*: see PHOSPHORUS] [Poet.] the morning star, esp. Venus —*n*. [p-] 1. *same as* PHOSPHORUS: now esp. in **phosphor bronze**, a bronze having a very small amount of phosphorus in it 2. a phosphorescent or fluorescent substance

phos·pho·rate (-fə rāt′) *vt*. **-rat′ed, -rat′ing** [PHOSPHOR(US) + -ATE¹] to combine or impregnate with phosphorus

phos·pho·resce (fäs′fə res′) *vi*. **-resced′, -resc′ing** [prob. back-formation < PHOSPHORESCENT] to produce, show, or undergo phosphorescence

phos·pho·res·cence (-res′′ns) *n*. [Fr.: see PHOSPHORUS & -ESCENT] 1. *a*) the condition or property of a substance of giving off a lingering emission of light after exposure to radiant energy, as light, X-rays, etc. *b*) the light thus given off 2. a continuing luminescence without noticeable heat, as from phosphorus when it is slowly oxidized —**phos′pho·res′cent** *adj*.

phos·pho·ret·ed, phos·pho·ret·ted (fäs′fə ret′id) *adj*. [< ModL. *phosphoretum*, phosphide < *phosphorus* + -ED] combined or impregnated with phosphorus: also **phos′phu·ret′ed** (-fyoo-), **phos′phu·ret′ted**

phos·phor·ic (fäs fôr′ik, -fär′-) *adj*. [Fr. *phosphorique*] of, like, or containing phosphorus, esp. with a valence of five

phosphoric acid any of several oxygen acids of phosphorus: see ORTHOPHOSPHORIC ACID, METAPHOSPHORIC ACID, PYROPHOSPHORIC ACID

phos·pho·rism (fäs′fər iz′m) *n*. chronic phosphorus poisoning

phos·pho·rite (fäs′fə rīt′) *n*. 1. natural calcium phosphate, similar chemically to apatite but without crystal form 2. *same as* PHOSPHATE ROCK —**phos′pho·rit′ic** (-rit′ik) *adj*.

phos·pho·ro- (fäs′fər ō, fäs fôr′ə) *a combining form meaning* phosphorus or phosphorescence [*phosphoroscope*]: also, before a vowel, **phosphor-**

phos·phor·o·scope (fäs fôr′ə skōp′, -fär′-) *n*. [PHOSPHORO- + -SCOPE] a device used in observing and measuring the persistence of phosphorescence after the source of light has been removed

phos·pho·rous (fäs′fər əs, fäs fôr′əs) *adj*. 1. [PHOSPHOR(US) + -OUS] *rare var. of* PHOSPHORESCENT 2. [Fr. *phosphoreux*] of, like, or containing phosphorus, esp. with a valence of three

phosphorous acid a white or yellowish, crystalline acid, H_3PO_3, that absorbs oxygen readily: used as a chemical reducing agent and as an analytical reagent

phos·pho·rus (fäs′fər əs) *n*. [ModL. < L. *Phosphorus*, morning star < Gr. *phōsphoros*, bringer of light < *phōs*, a light, contr. < *phaos* < IE. base **bhā-*, to shine, whence Gr. *phainein*, to show (cf. FANTASY)] 1. orig., any phosphorescent substance or object 2. a nonmetallic chemical element, normally a white, phosphorescent, waxy solid, becoming yellow when exposed to light: it is poisonous and unites easily with oxygen so that it ignites spontaneously at room temperature: when heated in sealed tubes it is converted into a red form which is nonpoisonous, and less flammable than the white: when heated under a pressure of 15,000 atmospheres it is converted into a black powder: symbol, P; at. wt., 30.9738; at. no., 15; sp. gr., 1.82; melt. pt., 44.1°C; boil. pt., 280.5°C: a radioactive isotope of phosphorus (**phosphorus 32**) is used in the diagnosis and treatment of certain diseases, as a tracer in chemical and biochemical research, etc.

phos·pho·ryl·ase (fäs′fər ə lās′, fäs fôr′-) *n*. [PHOSPHOR(O)- + -YL + -ASE] any of a class of enzymes widely distributed in plant and animal tissues, which catalyze reversibly the synthesis and decomposition of glucose monophosphates and aid in the synthesis of various polysaccharides

phos·pho·ryl·ate (-lāt′) *vt*. **-at′ed, -at′ing** [PHOSPHOR(O)- + -YL + -ATE¹] to add phosphate to an organic compound —**phos′pho·ryl·a′tion** *n*.

phot (fōt, fät) *n*. [< Gr. *phōs* (gen. *phōtos*), a light: see PHOSPHORUS] the cgs unit of illumination, equal to one lumen per square centimeter

phot. 1. photograph 2. photographic 3. photography

pho·tic (fōt′ik) *adj*. [< Gr. *phōs* (gen. *phōtos*), a light (see PHOSPHORUS) + -IC] 1. of light 2. *Biol*. having to do with the effect of light upon, or the production of light by, organisms

photic zone the uppermost layer in a body of water into which daylight penetrates in sufficient amounts to influence living organisms, esp. by permitting photosynthesis

pho·to (fōt′ō) *n*., *pl*. **-tos** *clipped form of* PHOTOGRAPH

pho·to- (fōt′ō, -ə) *a combining form meaning*: 1. [< Gr. *phōs* (gen. *phōtos*), a light: see PHOSPHORUS] of or produced by light [*photograph, photosynthesis*] 2. [< PHOTOGRAPH] of a photograph or photography [*photomontage*]

pho·to·ac·tin·ic (fōt′ō ak tin′ik) *adj*. [prec. + ACTINIC] that can produce actinic effect, as ultraviolet rays

pho·to·au·to·tro·phic (-ôt′ə träf′ik) *adj*. [PHOTO- + AUTOTROPHIC] able to manufacture organic foodstuffs from inorganic materials in the presence of light, as green plants and certain bacteria

pho·to·bi·ot·ic (-bī ät′ik) *adj*. [PHOTO- + BIOTIC] *Biol*. dependent upon light for existence

pho·to·cath·ode (-kath′ōd) *n*. a cathode that emits electrons when activated by radiation, as light

pho·to·cell (fōt′ə sel′) *n*. *same as* PHOTOELECTRIC CELL

pho·to·chem·is·try (fōt′ō kem′is trē) *n*. [PHOTO- + CHEMISTRY] the branch of chemistry having to do with the effect of light or other radiant energy in producing chemical action, as in photography —**pho′to·chem′i·cal** (-i k′l) *adj*.

pho·to·chro·mic (-krō′mik) *adj*. [PHOTO- + CHROMIC] designating or of a material, as certain glass or film, which turns dark when exposed to light and returns to its normal transparency with the removal of the light source —**pho′to·chro′mism** *n*.

pho·to·chron·o·graph (-krän′ə graf′, -gräf′) *n*. [PHOTO- + CHRONOGRAPH] 1. *a*) formerly, a device for recording motion in a series of photographs taken at regular, extremely brief, intervals *b*) a photograph so taken 2. an instrument for recording the exact time of an event by exposing a moving photographic plate to the tracing of a thin beam of light synchronized with the event

pho·to·co·ag·u·la·tion (-kō ag′yoo lā′shən) *n*. [PHOTO- + COAGULATION] a technique using intense light energy, as from a laser, to produce scar tissue: used in treating certain eye disorders, in medical and biological research, etc. —**pho′to·co·ag′u·la′tor** *n*.

pho·to·com·po·si·tion (-käm′pə zish′ən) *n*. any of various methods of composing matter for printing, in which light images of the letters are projected in succession onto a photosensitive surface to produce a negative from which plates can be prepared —**pho′to·com·pose′** (-kəm pōz′) *vt*. **-posed′, -pos′ing**

pho·to·con·duc·tive (-kən duk′tiv) *adj*. designating or of a substance, as selenium, which exhibits changed electrical conductivity under varying amounts of radiation —**pho′to·con′duc·tiv′i·ty** (-kän′dək tiv′ə tē) *n*. —**pho′to·con′duc′tor** *n*.

pho·to·cop·y (fōt'ə käp'ē) *n.*, *pl.* **-cop'ies** a copy of printed or other graphic material made by a device (**photocopier**) which photographically reproduces the original —*vt.* **-cop'ied -cop'y·ing** to make a photocopy of

pho·to·cur·rent (-kur'ənt) *n.* a stream of electrons released from a photoelectric cell by the action of light

pho·to·de·tec·tor (fōt'ō di tek'tər) *n.* [PHOTO- + DETECTOR] *Electronics* a light-sensitive device containing one or more photodiodes and capable of converting photons to electrons

pho·to·di·ode (-dī'ōd) *n.* [PHOTO- + DIODE] *Electronics* a light-sensitive, solid-state, semiconductor diode, used as a photoelectric cell

pho·to·dis·in·te·gra·tion (-dis in'tə grā'shən) *n.* *Physics* a nuclear reaction induced by the action of a photon of radiant energy

pho·to·dis·so·ci·a·tion (-di sō'sē ā'shən, -shē-) *n.* the breaking up of a substance, esp. a chemical compound, into simpler components by the action of radiant energy

pho·to·dy·nam·ic (-dī nam'ik) *adj.* of or pertaining to the energy of light; esp., designating a fluorescent substance

pho·to·dy·nam·ics (-dī nam'iks) *n.pl.* [*with sing. v.*] [PHOTO- + DYNAMICS] **1.** the activating effect of light on living organisms, as in causing phototropism in plants **2.** the science dealing with this

pho·to·e·las·tic·i·ty (-i las'tis'ə tē) *n.* [PHOTO- + ELASTICITY] the property shown by certain transparent solids, esp. glass and plastics, of producing double refraction when put under tension or compression, thus permitting stress analysis of models of parts —**pho'to·e·las'tic** (-tik) *adj.*

pho·to·e·lec·tric (-i lek'trik) *adj.* [PHOTO- + ELECTRIC] of or having to do with the electric effects produced by light or other radiation, esp. as in the emission of electrons by certain substances when subjected to light or radiation of suitable wavelength

☆**photoelectric cell** a cell whose electrical state is changed by the effect of light; specif., any device in which light controls the electron emission from a cathode, the electrical resistance of an element, or the electromotive force produced by a cell: usually incorporated in an electric circuit and used in mechanical devices, as for opening doors, setting off burglar alarms, etc.; electric eye

pho·to·e·lec·tron (-i lek'trän) *n.* an electron ejected from a system by a photon striking it, or emitted as a result of radiation

pho·to·e·mis·sion (-i mish'ən) *n.* [PHOTO- + EMISSION] the ejection of one or more electrons from a substance, usually a metal, when subjected to light or other suitable radiation —**pho'to·e·mis'sive** (-mis'iv) *adj.*

pho·to·en·grav·ing (-in grā'viŋ) *n.* **1.** a photomechanical process by which photographs are reproduced on relief printing plates **2.** a printing plate so made **3.** a print from such a plate —**pho'to·en·grave'** *vt.* **-graved', -grav'ing** —**pho'to·en·grav'er** *n.*

photo finish 1. a race finish so close that the winner can be determined only from a photograph of the contestants as they cross the finish line **2.** any close finish of a game, competition, etc.

pho·to·fin·ish·ing (-fin'ish iŋ) *n.* the process or work of developing exposed photographic film, making prints, etc. —**pho'to·fin'ish·er** *n.*

pho·to·flash (fōt'ə flash') *adj.* *Photog.* designating, of, or using a lamp or light, esp. a flashbulb, electrically synchronized with the shutter —*n.* a photoflash bulb, lamp, photograph, etc.

pho·to·flood (-flud') *adj.* *Photog.* designating, of, or using a high-intensity electric lamp or light used for sustained illumination —*n.* a photoflood bulb, lamp, photograph, etc.

pho·to·flu·o·rog·ra·phy (fōt'ə floo räg'rə fē, -flōō'ə-) *n.* the use of photography to record fluoroscopic images on film —**pho'to·flu'o·ro·graph'ic** (-floor'ə graf'ik) *adj.*

photog. 1. photographic **2.** photography

pho·to·gel·a·tin process (fōt'ə jel'ə t'n) *same as* COLLOTYPE (sense 1)

pho·to·gene (fōt'ə jēn') *n.* [see PHOTO- & -GEN] *same as* AFTERIMAGE

pho·to·gen·ic (fōt'ə jen'ik) *adj.* [PHOTO- + -GENIC] **1.** [Rare] due to or produced by light **2.** produced or giving off light; phosphorescent **3.** that looks or is likely to look attractive in photographs: said especially of a person —**pho'to·gen'i·cal·ly** *adv.*

pho·to·gram·me·try (-gram'ə trē) *n.* [*photogram* (var., after -GRAM, of PHOTOGRAPH) + -METRY] the art or process of surveying or measuring, as in map making by taking photographs, esp. aerial photographs —**pho'to·gram·met'·ric** (-grə met'rik) *adj.* —**pho'to·gram·met'ri·cal·ly** *adv.* —**pho'to·gram·me'trist** *n.*

pho·to·graph (fōt'ə graf', -gräf') *n.* [PHOTO- + -GRAPH] an image or picture made by photography —*vt.* to take a photograph of —*vi.* **1.** to take photographs **2.** to appear (as specified) in photographs [*to photograph well*]

pho·tog·ra·pher (fə täg'rə fər) *n.* a person who takes photographs, esp. as an occupation

pho·to·graph·ic (fōt'ə graf'ik) *adj.* **1.** of or like a photograph or photography **2.** used in or made by photography **3.** retaining or recalling in precise detail [*a photographic memory*] —**pho'to·graph'i·cal·ly** *adv.*

pho·tog·ra·phy (fə täg'rə fē) *n.* [PHOTO- + -GRAPHY] the art or process of producing images of objects upon a

photosensitive surface (as film in a camera) by the chemical action of light or other radiant energy

pho·to·gra·vure (fōt'ə grə vyoor') *n.* [Fr. < *photo* (contr. < *photographe* < E. PHOTOGRAPH) + *gravure*, engraving < *graver:* see ENGRAVE] **1.** a photomechanical process by which photographs are reproduced on intaglio printing plates or cylinders **2.** a plate or cylinder so made **3.** a print from such a plate, usually with a velvety, satinlike finish

pho·to·i·on·i·za·tion (-ī'ə nə zā'shən) *n.* ionization that occurs in a gaseous medium and as a result of radiation

pho·to·jour·nal·ism (-jur'n'l iz'm) *n.* journalism in which news stories, etc. are presented mainly through photographs —**pho'to·jour'nal·ist** *n.*

pho·to·ki·ne·sis (fōt'ō ki nē'sis) *n.* [ModL. < PHOTO- + *kinesis*, motion < Gr. *kinēsis* < *kinein*, to move] *Physiol.* movement in response to light —**pho'to·ki·net'ic** (-net'ik) *adj.*

pho·to·lith·o·graph (fōt'ə lith'ə graf', -gräf') *n.* a print made by photolithography —*vt.* to make a photolithograph of —**pho'to·lith·og'ra·pher** (-li thäg'rə fər) *n.*

pho·to·li·thog·ra·phy (-li thäg'rə fē) *n.* a process of printing from a plate, etc. prepared by methods combining photography and lithography —**pho'to·lith'o·graph'ic** (-lith'ə graf'ik) *adj.*

pho·to·lu·mi·nes·cence (-lōō'mə nes''ns) *n.* luminescence in response to excitation by light, as in fluorescence and phosphorescence —**pho'to·lu'mi·nes'cent** *adj.*

pho·tol·y·sis (fō tāl'ə sis) *n.* [ModL.: see PHOTO- & -LYSIS] chemical decomposition due to the action of light —**pho·to·lyt'ic** (fōt'ə lit'ik) *adj.*

photom. photometry

pho·to·map (fōt'ə map') *n.* a map made by imposing a grid on one or more aerial photographs, adding place names, etc. —**pho'to·map'** *vt.*, *vi.* **-mapped'**, **-map'ping**

pho·to·me·chan·i·cal (fōt'ō mə kan'i k'l) *adj.* [PHOTO- + MECHANICAL] designating or of any process by which printing plates are made by a photographic method —**pho'to·me·chan'i·cal·ly** *adv.*

pho·tom·e·ter (fō täm'ə tər) *n.* [PHOTO- + -METER] an instrument used in measuring the intensity of light, esp. in determining the relative intensity of light from different sources

pho·tom·e·try (-trē) *n.* [ModL. *photometria:* see PHOTO- & -METRY] **1.** the measurement of the intensity of light **2.** the branch of optics dealing with this —**pho·to·met·ric** (fōt'ə met'rik) *adj.* —**pho'to·met'ri·cal·ly** *adv.*

pho·to·mi·cro·graph (fōt'ō mī'krə graf', -gräf') *n.* [PHOTO- + MICROGRAPH] a photograph taken through a microscope —**pho'to·mi'cro·graph'ic** *adj.* —**pho'to·mi·crog'·ra·phy** (-mī kräg'rə fē) *n.*

pho·to·mon·tage (-män täzh', -mōn-) *n.* montage done in or with photographs

pho·to·mul·ti·pli·er (-mul'tə plī'ər) *n.* a photoemissive photoelectric cell which amplifies the emitted electrons and converts them into brighter light, an electric signal, etc.

pho·to·mu·ral (-myoor'əl) *n.* a very large photograph used as a mural

☆**pho·ton** (fō'tän) *n.* [PHOT(O)- + (ELECTR)ON] **1.** a quantum of electromagnetic energy having both particle and wave behavior: it has no charge or mass but possesses momentum: the energy of light, X-rays, gamma rays, etc. is carried by photons **2.** a unit of retinal illumination equal to the illumination from a surface having a brightness of one candle per sq. meter seen through a pupil area of one sq. millimeter

pho·to·neg·a·tive (fōt'ə neg'ə tiv) *adj.* *Biol.* responding negatively to light, as an earthworm

pho·to·neu·tron (-noo'trän, -nyoo'-) *n.* a neutron given off in the photodisintegration of an atomic nucleus

pho·to·off·set (fōt'ō ôf'set') *n.* a method of offset printing in which the pictures or text are photographically transferred to a metal plate from which inked impressions are made on the rubber roller

pho·to·pe·ri·od (-pir'ē əd) *n.* the number of daylight hours best suited to the growth and maturation of an organism —**pho'to·pe'ri·od'ic** (-pir'ē äd'ik) *adj.*

pho·to·pe·ri·od·ism (-iz'm) *n.* *Biol.* the behavioral and physiological reaction of an organism to variations in the intensity of light, as, in plants, by flowering or ceasing to flower, or, in certain animals, by changing the daily cycle of activities: also **pho'to·pe'ri·o·dic'i·ty** (-ə dis'ə tē)

pho·toph·i·lous (fō täf'ə ləs) *adj.* [PHOTO- + -PHILOUS] *Biol.* thriving in light: also **pho·to·phil·ic** (fōt'ə fil'ik) —**pho·toph'i·ly** (-lē) *n.*

pho·to·pho·bi·a (fōt'ə fō'bē ə) *n.* [ModL.: see PHOTO- & -PHOBIA] **1.** an abnormal fear of light **2.** an abnormal sensitivity to light, esp. of the eyes as in measles and certain eye conditions —**pho'to·pho'bic** (-fō'bik, -fäb'ik) *adj.*

pho·to·phore (fōt'ə fôr') *n.* [PHOTO- + -PHORE] a light organ in bioluminescent animals containing reflective tissue and light-producing cells

pho·to·pi·a (fō tō'pē ə) *n.* [< PHOTO- + -OPIA] adjustment of the eye to bright light —**pho·to'pic** (-tō'pik, -täp'ik) *adj.*

☆**pho·to·play** (fōt'ə plā') *n.* [PHOTO- + PLAY] *early name for* MOTION PICTURE (sense 2)

pho·to·pos·i·tive (fōt′ə päz′ə tiv) *adj. Biol.* responding positively to light, as a moth

pho·to·re·cep·tor (fōt′ō ri sep′tər) *n. Biol.* a sense organ specialized to detect light, as the eye or any of the elements of a compound eye —**pho′to·re·cep′tion** *n.* — **pho′to·re·cep′tive** *adj.*

pho·to·re·con·nais·sance (-ri kän′ə səns) *n. Mil.* reconnaissance by means of aerial photographs

pho·to·sen·si·tive (-sen′sə tiv) *adj.* reacting or sensitive to radiant energy, esp. to light —**pho′to·sen′si·tiv′i·ty** *n.*

pho·to·sen·si·tize (-sen′sə tiz′) *vt.* **-tized′, -tiz′ing** to make photosensitive —**pho′to·sen′si·ti·za′tion** *n.*

pho·to·set (fōt′ə set′) *vt.* **-set′, -set′ting** to set (matter for printing) by photocomposition

pho·to·sphere (-sfir′) *n.* [PHOTO- + SPHERE] the visible surface of the sun —**pho′to·spher′ic** (-sfer′ik) *adj.*

☆**Pho·to·stat** (-stat′) [PHOTO- + -STAT] *a trademark for* a device used in making photographic copies of printed matter, drawings, etc., directly as positives upon special paper —*n.* [p-] a copy so made —*vt.* [p-] **-stat′ed** or **-stat′ted, -stat′ing** or **-stat′ting** to make a photostat or photostats of —**pho′to·stat′ic** *adj.*

pho·to·syn·the·sis (fōt′ə sin′thə sis) *n.* [ModL.: see PHOTO- & SYNTHESIS] 1. the biological synthesis of chemical compounds in the presence of light 2. the production of organic substances, chiefly sugars, from carbon dioxide and water occurring in green plant cells supplied with enough light to allow chlorophyll to aid in the transformation of the radiant energy into a chemical form —**pho′to·syn·thet′ic** (-sin thet′ik) *adj.* —**pho′to·syn·thet′i·cal·ly** *adv.*

pho·to·syn·the·size (-siz′) *vt., vi.* **-sized′, -siz′ing** to carry on, or produce by, photosynthesis

pho·to·tax·is (-tak′sis) *n.* [ModL.: see PHOTO- & -TAXIS] the movement of an organism in response to stimulus from light —**pho′to·tac′tic** (-tik) *adj.*

☆**pho·to·tel·e·gra·phy** (fōt′ō tə leg′rə fē) *n.* 1. communication by means of a heliograph 2. *same as* TELEPHOTOGRAPHY (sense 2)

pho·to·ther·mic (fōt′ə thur′mik) *adj.* [PHOTO- + THERMIC] of or involving both light and heat

pho·tot·o·nus (fō tät′'n əs) *n.* [ModL.: see PHOTO & TONE] *Biol.* the state of being responsive to or irritated by exposure to light —**pho·to·ton·ic** (fōt′ə tän′ik) *adj.*

☆**pho·to·tran·sis·tor** (fōt′ō tran zis′tər, -sis′-) *n. Electronics* a device combining the function of a photodiode with the amplifying function of a transistor

pho·tot·ro·pism (fō tät′rə piz′m) *n.* [PHOTO- + TROPISM] *Bot.* movement of a part of a plant toward or away from light sources: see HELIOTROPISM —**pho·to·trop·ic** (fōt′ə träp′ik) *adj.*

pho·to·tube (fōt′ə tōōb′, -tyōōb′) *n.* [PHOTO(ELECTRIC) + TUBE] a vacuum tube in which one of the electrodes emits electrons in response to radiation

pho·to·type·set·ting (fōt′ə tip′set′iŋ) *n. same as* PHOTOCOMPOSITION —**pho′to·type′set′ter** *n.*

pho·to·vol·ta·ic (-väl tā′ik) *adj.* [PHOTO- + VOLTAIC] of or having to do with the generation of an electromotive force at the junction of two different materials in response to visible or other radiation

phr. phrase

phras·al (frā′z′l) *adj.* of, like, or consisting of a phrase or phrases —**phras′al·ly** *adv.*

phrase (frāz) *n.* [L. *phrasis,* diction < Gr. *phrasis* < *phrazein,* to speak] 1. a manner or style of speech or expression; phraseology 2. a short, colorful or forceful expression 3. a connected series of movements in a formal dance 4. *Gram.* a sequence of two or more words conveying a single thought or forming a distinct part of a sentence but not containing a subject and predicate: cf. CLAUSE 5. *Linguis.* a linguistic unit consisting of two or more words spoken between two distinguished pauses and having a single primary stress 6. *Music* a short, distinct part or passage, usually of two, four, or eight measures —*vt., vi.* **phrased, phras′ing** 1. to express in words or in a phrase 2. *Music* to mark off or divide (notes) into phrases

phra·se·o·gram (frā′zē ə gram′) *n.* [PHRASEO(LOGY) + -GRAM] a mark or symbol representing an entire phrase, as in Pitman shorthand

phra·se·ol·o·gist (frā′zē äl′ə jist) *n.* a person skilled at formulating well-turned phrases or one given to using catchy but trite phrases

phra·se·ol·o·gy (-jē) *n., pl.* **-gies** [ModL. *phraseologia:* see PHRASE & -LOGY] choice and pattern of words; way of speaking or writing; diction —**phra′se·o·log′i·cal** (-ə läj′i k′l) *adj.* —**phra′se·o·log′i·cal·ly** *adv.*

phras·ing (frā′ziŋ) *n.* 1. the act or manner of formulating phrases; phraseology 2. the manner in which one phrases musical passages

phra·try (frā′trē) *n., pl.* **-tries** [Gr. *phratria* < *phratēr,* akin to L. *frater,* BROTHER] 1. a subdivision of an ancient Greek phyle 2. any of the similar units, as a group of clans, of a primitive tribe —**phra′tric, phra′tral** *adj.*

phre·at·o·phyte (frē at′ə fīt′) *n.* [< Gr. *phrear* (gen. *phreatos*), a well < IE. *bh(e)reu-,* to boil up (cf. FERVENT)

+ -PHYTE] a long-rooted plant that absorbs its water from the water table or other permanent ground supply — **phre′at·o·phyt′ic** (-fit′ik) *adj.*

phren., phrenol. phrenology

phre·net·ic (fri net′ik) *adj.* [ME. *frenetik* < OFr. *frenetique* < L. *phreneticus* < Gr. *phrenētikos,* mad, suffering with inflammation of the brain < *phrenitis,* delirium < *phrēn* (see PHRENO-) + -itis, -ITIS] *earlier sp. of* FRENETIC

phren·ic (fren′ik) *adj.* [see PHRENO- & -IC] 1. of the diaphragm 2. of the mind; mental

phren·o- (fren′ə, -ō) [< Gr. *phrēn* (gen. *phrenos*), midriff, heart, also mind, mental capacity] *a combining form meaning:* 1. the diaphragm or the diaphragm and 2. the mind Also, before a vowel, **phren-**

☆**phre·nol·o·gy** (fri näl′ə jē) *n.* [PHRENO- (sense 2) + -LOGY] a system, now rejected, by which an analysis of character and of the development of the faculties can allegedly be made by studying the shape and protuberances of the skull —**phren·o·log′i·cal** (fren′ə läj′i k′l) *adj.* —**phre·nol′o·gist** *n.*

phren·sy (fren′zē) *n., pl.* **-sies,** *vt.* **-sied, -sy·ing** *earlier sp. of* FRENZY

Phryg·i·a (frij′ē ə) ancient country in WC Asia Minor

Phryg·i·an (-ən) *adj.* of Phrygia, its people, their language, etc. —*n.* 1. a native or inhabitant of Phrygia 2. the extinct Indo-European language of the ancient Phrygians, preserved only in fragmentary inscriptions

PHS, P.H.S. Public Health Service

phthal·ein (thal′ēn, thal′-; -ē ən) *n.* [< ff. + -IN¹] any of a group of synthetic dyes manufactured from phenols and phthalic anhydride

phthal·ic acid (-ik) [(NA)PHTHAL(ENE) + -IC] any of three isomeric acids, $C_6H_4(CO_2H)_2$; specif., orthophthalic acid which is produced by the oxidation of naphthalene and is used in the manufacture of dyes, medicines, phenolphthalein, synthetic perfumes, etc.

phthalic anhydride a white, solid substance, $C_6H_4(CO)_2O$, produced by the oxidation of naphthalene and used to make the phthalein dyes, certain synthetic resins, etc.

phthal·in (in) *n.* [PHTHAL(EIN) + -IN¹] any of a series of compounds produced by the reduction of the phthaleins

phthal·o·cy·a·nine (thal′ə sī′ə nēn′, fthal′-) *n.* [< PHTHALIC (ACID) + CYAN- + -INE⁴] 1. a blue-green organic compound, $(C_8H_4C_2N)_4N_4$ 2. any of a group of brilliant, green or blue pigments that are metal, esp. copper, derivatives of this compound

phthi·ri·a·sis (thə rī′ə sis) *n.* [L. < Gr. *phtheiriasis* < *phtheir,* a louse + -iasis, -IASIS] *same as* PEDICULOSIS; esp., infestation by the crab louse

phthi·sis (thī′sis, tī′-, fthī′-) *n.* [L. < Gr. *phthisis,* a decay < *phthiein,* to waste away < IE. base *gwhthei-,* to disappear, be destroyed, whence Sans. *kṣáyati,* (he) destroys] *old term for* any wasting disease, esp. tuberculosis of the lungs —**phthis·ic** (tiz′ik) *adj., n.* —**phthis′i·cal, phthis′ick·y** *adj.*

-phy·ce·ae (fī′sē ē′, fis′ē ē′) [ModL. < Gr. *phykos,* seaweed, orchil, rouge < Sem., as in Heb. *pūk,* rouge] *a combining form meaning* seaweed: used in forming the botanical names of the classes of algae

-phy·ceous (fish′əs) *a combining form used to form adjectives derived from nouns ending in* -PHYCEAE

phy·col·o·gy (fī käl′ə jē) *n.* [< Gr. *phykos,* seaweed (see -PHYCEAE) + -LOGY] *same as* ALGOLOGY

phy·co·my·cete (fī′kō mī′sēt, -mī sēt′) *n.* [< Gr. *phykos,* seaweed (see -PHYCEAE) + -MYCETE] any of a class (Phycomycetes) of fungi, including the downy mildews, black molds, etc., closely resembling the algae and producing small asexual spores, usually in sporangia —**phy′co·my·ce′tous** (-mī sēt′əs) *adj.*

Phyfe (fīf), **Duncan** (born *Duncan Fife*) 1768-1854; U.S. cabinetmaker & furniture designer, born in Scotland

phy·la (fī′lə) *n. pl. of* PHYLUM

phy·lac·ter·y (fi lak′tər ē, -trē) *n., pl.* **-ter·ies** [ME. *filaterie* < ML. *phylaterium* < LL. (Ec.) *phylacterium* (used for Heb. *tefillīn* < *tefillāh,* prayer) < Gr. *phylaktērion,* a safeguard < *phylassein,* to defend, guard < *phylax,* a watchman] 1. either of two small, leather cases holding slips inscribed with Scripture passages: one is fastened with leather thongs to the forehead and one to the left arm by Orthodox or Conservative Jewish men during morning prayer on weekdays: see Deut. 6:4-9 2. [Rare] something worn as a charm or safeguard

PHYLACTERIES

phy·le (fī′lē) *n., pl.* **-lae** (-lē) [ModL. < Gr. *phylē,* tribe: for IE. base see BE] the largest political subdivision in the ancient Athenian state

phy·let·ic (fī let′ik) *adj.* [ModL. *phyleticus* < Gr. *phyletikos* < *phyletēs,* tribesman < *phylē:* see prec.] *Biol.* of or pertaining to a phylum or to an evolutionary line of descent —**phy·let′i·cal·ly** *adv.*

-phyll (fil) [ModL. < Gr. *phyllon,* a leaf: for IE. base see BLOOM¹] *a combining form meaning* leaf [*sporophyll*]

Phyl·lis (fil'is) [L. < Gr. *Phyllis*, lit., leaf: see prec.] 1. a feminine name 2. a country maiden in Virgil's *Eclogues*

phyl·lo- (fil'ə, -ō) [ModL. < Gr. *phyllon*, a leaf: see -PHYLL] *a combining form meaning* leaf [*phyllotaxis*]: also, before a vowel, **phyll-**

phyl·lo·clad (fil'ə klad') *n.* same as CLADOPHYLL: also **phyl'lo·clade'** (-klād')

phyl·lode (fil'ōd) *n.* [ModL. *phyllodium* < Gr. *phyllōdes*, leaflike: see PHYLLO- & -ODE²] *Bot.* a flat leafstalk that functions as a leaf —**phyl·lo·di·al** (fə lō'dē əl) *adj.*

phyl·loid (-oid) *adj.* [ModL. *phylloides*: see PHYLLO- & -OID] like a leaf; leaflike

phyl·lome (-ōm) *n.* [ModL. *phylloma* < Gr. *phyllōma*, foliage < *phylloun*, to cover with leaves < *phyllon*, a leaf] *Bot.* a leaf or analogous member —**phyl·lom·ic** (fi läm'ik, -lō'mik) *adj.*

phyl·loph·a·gous (fi läf'ə gəs) *adj.* [PHYLLO- + -PHAGOUS] feeding on leaves

phyl·lo·pod (fil'ə päd') *n.* [ModL. *Phyllopoda*, name of the subclass: see PHYLLO- & -POD] any of a subclass (Phyllopoda) of primitive crustaceans with leaflike, swimming feet, as the fairy shrimp, brine shrimp, etc. —*adj.* of the phyllopods —**phyl·lop·o·dan** (fi läp'ə dən) *n., adj.* —**phyl·lop'o·dous** (-dəs) *adj.*

phyl·lo·tax·is (fil'ə tak'sis) *n.* [ModL. *phyllotaxis*: see PHYLLO- & -TAXIS] *Bot.* 1. the arrangement of leaves on a stem 2. the study or principles of such arrangement Also **phyl'lo·tax'y** (-sē) —**phyl'lo·tac'tic** (-tik) *adj.*

-phyl·lous (fil'əs) [see PHYLLO- & -OUS] *a combining form meaning* having (a specified number or kind of) leaves, leaflets, etc. [*heterophyllous*]

phyl·lox·e·ra (fil'ək sir'ə, fi läk'sər ə) *n., pl.* **-rae** (-ē), **-ras** [ModL. < Gr. *phyllon*, a leaf + *xēros*, dry: see PHYLLO- & SERENE] any of a number of related plant lice (family Phylloxeridae) that attack the leaves and roots of certain plants, including grapevines

phy·lo- (fi'lō, -lə) [< Gr. *phylon*, tribe: for IE. base see BE] *a combining form meaning* tribe, race, phylum, etc. [*phylogeny*]: also, before a vowel, **phyl-**

phy·log·e·ny (fi läj'ə nē) *n., pl.* **-nies** [G. *phylogenie*, coined (1866) by E. H. HAECKEL: see PHYLO- & -GENY] 1. the lines of descent or evolutionary development of any plant or animal species 2. the origin and evolution of a division, group, or race of animals or plants: distinguished from ONTOGENY 3. the historical development of a nonliving thing, as a group of languages Also **phy·lo·gen·e·sis** (fi'lə jen'ə sis) —**phy'lo·ge·net'ic** (-jə net'ik), **phy'lo·gen'ic** (-jen'ik) *adj.* —**phy'lo·ge·net'i·cal·ly** *adv.*

phy·lum (fi'ləm) *n., pl.* **-la** (-lə) [ModL. < Gr. *phylon*, tribe: for IE. base see BE] 1. any of the broad, principal divisions of the animal kingdom: sometimes, but not officially, used as a synonym for a plant subkingdom 2. *a)* a language stock *b)* loosely, a language family

-phyre (fir) [Fr. < *porphyre*: see PORPHYRY] *a combining form meaning* a porphyritic rock [*granophyre*]

phys. 1. physical 2. physician 3. physics

phys. ed. physical education

phys·i·at·rics (fiz'ē at'riks) *n.pl.* [*with sing. v.*] [PHYS(IO)- + -IATRICS] the branch of medicine that deals with physical therapy: also **phys'i·at'ry** (-rē) —**phys'i·at'rist** *n.*

phys·ic (fiz'ik) *n.* [ME. *fisike* < OFr. *fisique* < L. *physica*, natural science (in ML., medicine) < Gr. *physikē* < *physis*, nature < *phyein*, to produce: for IE. base see BE] 1. *rare var. of* PHYSICS 2. [Archaic] the art or science of healing; medical science 3. a medicine or remedy, esp. a laxative or cathartic —*vt.* **-icked**, **-ick·ing** 1. to dose with medicine, esp. with a cathartic 2. to have a curative effect on; heal **SYN.**—*physic* is the general word for anything taken to relieve constipation or to effect a bowel movement; *laxative* and *aperient* usually refer to milder physics of a kind that are ordinarily taken to promote discharge from the bowels, such as mineral oil, agar-agar, certain fruit juices, etc.; *purgative* and *cathartic* apply to stronger physics, such as castor oil, Epsom salts, calomel, etc., that are more drastic in their action

phys·i·cal (fiz'i k'l) *adj.* [ME. *phisical*, having to do with medicine < ML. *physicalis* < L. *physica*: see PHYSIC] 1. of nature and all matter; natural; material 2. of natural science or natural philosophy 3. of or according to the laws of nature 4. of, or produced by the forces of, physics 5. *a)* of the body as opposed to the mind [*physical exercise*] *b)* preoccupied with bodily or sexual pleasures; carnal —*n.* ☆a general medical examination: in full **physical examination** —**SYN.** see BODILY, MATERIAL —**phys'i·cal·ly** *adv.*

physical chemistry the branch of chemistry dealing with the physical properties of substances as they relate to the chemical properties and changes

☆**physical education** instruction in the exercise, care, and hygiene of the human body; esp., a course in gymnastics, athletics, etc., as in a school or college

physical geography the study of the features and nature of the earth's solid surface and oceans, atmosphere and climate, distribution of plant and animal life, etc.

phys·i·cal·ism (-iz'm) *n.* the theory that all referential terms in scientific or meaningful statements are reducible to terms connected with physical objects or events, or with their properties —**phys'i·cal·ist** *n.*

phys·i·cal·i·ty (fiz'ə kal'ə tē) *n.* 1. the quality or condition of being physical 2. preoccupation with physical, esp. bodily or carnal, matters

physical science any of the sciences that deal with inanimate matter or energy, as physics, chemistry, geology, astronomy, etc.

physical therapy the treatment of disease, injury, etc. by physical means rather than with drugs, as by exercise, massage, infrared or ultraviolet light, electrotherapy, hydrotherapy, or heat; physiotherapy

phy·si·cian (fə zish'ən) *n.* [ME. & OFr. *fisicien* < L. *physica*: see PHYSIC] 1. a person licensed to practice medicine; doctor of medicine 2. any medical doctor other than one specializing in surgery 3. any person or thing that heals, relieves, or comforts

phys·i·cist (fiz'ə sist) *n.* an expert or specialist in physics

phys·i·co- (fiz'ə kō) [< PHYSICAL] *a combining form meaning* physical or physical and

phys·i·co·chem·i·cal (fiz'ə kō kem'i k'l) *adj.* [prec. + CHEMICAL] 1. of or pertaining to both physical and chemical properties, changes, and reactions 2. of or according to physical chemistry —**phys'i·co·chem'i·cal·ly** *adv.*

phys·ics (fiz'iks) *n.pl.* [*with sing. v. in senses 1 & 2*] [transl. of L. *physica*, physics < Gr. (*ta*) *physika* (lit., natural things), a name given to the physical treatises of Aristotle: see PHYSIC] 1. orig., natural science or natural philosophy 2. *a)* the science dealing with the properties, changes, interactions, etc. of matter, and energy in which energy is considered to be continuous (**classical physics**), including electricity, heat, optics, mechanics, etc., and now also dealing with the atomic scale of nature in which energy is considered to be discrete (**quantum physics**), including such branches as atomic, nuclear, and solid-state physics *b)* a specific system of physics 3. a book or treatise on any of these 4. physical properties or processes [*the physics of flight*]

phys·i·o- (fiz'ē ō, -ə) [< Gr. *physis*, nature: see PHYSIC] *a combining form meaning:* 1. nature; natural [*physiography*] 2. physical [*physiotherapy*] Also, before a vowel, **physi-**

phys·i·o·crat (fiz'ē ə krat') *n.* [Fr. *physiocrate:* see PHYSIO- & -CRAT] a believer in the 18th-cent. French economic theory that land and its products are the only true sources of wealth and hence the only logical basis of revenue and that freedom of opportunity and trade and security of person and property are essential to prosperity —**phys'i·o·crat'ic** *adj.*

phys·i·og·no·my (fiz'ē äg'nə mē; *chiefly Brit.*, -än'ə-) *n.* [ME. *fisonomie* < MFr. *phisonomie* < ML. *physonomia* < Gr. *physiognōmonia* < *physis*, nature (see PHYSIC) + *gnōmōn*, one who knows < base of *gignōskein*, to KNOW] 1. the practice of trying to judge character and mental qualities by observation of bodily, esp. facial, features 2. facial features and expression, esp. as supposedly indicative of character; the face 3. apparent characteristics; outward features or appearance —**SYN.** see FACE — **phys'i·og·nom'ic** (-äg näm'ik, -ə näm'-), **phys'i·og·nom'i·cal** *adj.* —**phys'i·og·nom'i·cal·ly** *adv.* —**phys'i·og'no·mist** *n.*

phys·i·og·ra·phy (fiz'ē äg'rə fē) *n.* [PHYSIO- + -GRAPHY] 1. a description of the features and phenomena of nature 2. same as PHYSICAL GEOGRAPHY 3. same as GEOMORPHOLOGY —**phys'i·og'ra·pher** *n.* —**phys'i·o·graph'ic** (-ə graf'ik), **phys'i·o·graph'i·cal** *adj.*

physiol. 1. physiological 2. physiology

phys·i·o·log·i·cal (fiz'ē ə läj'i k'l) *adj.* 1. of physiology 2. characteristic of or promoting normal, or healthy, functioning Also **phys'i·o·log'ic** —**phys'i·o·log'i·cal·ly** *adv.*

physiological saline *Biochem., Med.* a salt solution that has the same osmotic pressure as that found in the blood or tissues

phys·i·ol·o·gy (fiz'ē äl'ə jē) *n.* [Fr. *physiologie* < L. *physiologia* < Gr. *physiologia:* see PHYSIO- & -LOGY] 1. the branch of biology dealing with the functions and vital processes of living organisms or their parts and organs 2. the functions and vital processes, collectively (*of an* organism, or of an organ or system of organs) —**phys'·i·ol'o·gist** *n.*

phys·i·o·ther·a·py (fiz'ē ō ther'ə pē) *n.* same as PHYSICAL THERAPY —**phys'i·o·ther'a·pist** *n.*

phy·sique (fi zēk') *n.* [Fr.: see PHYSIC] the structure, constitution, strength, form, or appearance of the body

phy·so·stig·mine (fi'sō stig'mēn, -min) *n.* [< ModL. *Physostigma*, name of the genus including the Calabar bean < Gr. *physa*, a bellows (< IE. *phus-, var. of pu-, phu-*, to blow, whence L. *pustula*) + *stigma*, a prick (see STICK) + -INE⁴] a colorless or pinkish crystalline alkaloid, $C_{15}H_{21}O_2N_3$, extracted from the Calabar bean, used in medicine for stimulating intestinal muscles, contracting the pupils of the eyes, etc.

phy·sos·to·mous (fi säs'tə məs) *adj.* [< Gr. *physa* (see prec.) + -STOMOUS] *Zool.* having the air bladder connected to the digestive tract by a tube, as certain fishes: also **phy·so·stom·a·tous** (fi'sə stäm'ə təs)

-phyte (fit) [< Gr. *phyton*, a plant, akin to *phyein*, to grow: see BE] *a combining form meaning:* 1. a plant growing in a (specified) way or place [*microphyte, sporophyte*] 2. plantlike [*zoophyte*] 3. *Med.* a (specified) kind of growth [*osteophyte*]

Phy·tin (fit''n) [< Gr. *phyton* (see prec.) + -IN¹] *a trademark for* a calcium-magnesium salt derived from various

seeds, potatoes, etc., and used as a dietary calcium supplement and in the manufacture of inositol

phy·to- (fīt′ō, -ə) [< Gr. *phyton* (see -PHYTE)] a *combining form meaning* a plant, flora, vegetation [*phytogeography*]: also, before a vowel, **phyt-**

phy·to·chrome (-krōm′) *n.* [prec. + -CHROME] a bluish-green plant protein that, in response to variations in red light, regulates the growth of plants

phy·to·flag·el·late (fīt′ə flaj′ə lāt′, -lit) *n.* [PHYTO- + FLAGELLATE] a flagellated microorganism with plantlike characteristics, as in the possession of cell walls and chlorophyll

phy·to·gen·e·sis (fīt′ə jen′ə sis) *n.* [PHYTO- + -GENESIS] the science of the origin and development of plants: also **phy·tog·e·ny** (fī täj′ə nē) —**phy′to·ge·net′ic** (-jə net′ik), **phy′to·ge·net′i·cal** *adj.*

phy·to·gen·ic (-jen′ik) *adj.* of plant origin, as peat or coal: also **phy·tog·e·nous** (fī täj′ə nəs)

phy·to·ge·og·ra·phy (fīt′ō jē äg′rə fē) *n.* the geography of the distribution of plant life

phy·tog·ra·phy (fī täg′rə fē) *n.* [ModL. *phytographia*: see PHYTO- & -GRAPHY] the branch of botany dealing with the description of plants

phy·to·he·mag·glu·ti·nin (fīt′ō hē′mə glōōt′'n in) *n.* [PHYTO- + HEMAGGLUTININ] a protein, obtained from the red kidney bean, that stimulates human lymphocytes to an increase in metabolic activity and cell size, cell division, etc.

phy·to·hor·mone (-hôr′mōn) *n.* same as PLANT HORMONE

phy·to·lith (fīt′ə lith) *n.* [PHYTO- + -LITH] a small opaline rock consisting chiefly of fossil plant remains

phy·tol·o·gy (fī täl′ə jē) *n.* [ModL. *phytologia*: see PHYTO- & -LOGY] an early term for BOTANY —**phy′to·log′ic** (-tə läj′ik), **phy′to·log′i·cal** *adj.*

phy·to·pa·thol·o·gy (fīt′ō pa thäl′ə jē) *n.* [PHYTO- + PATHOLOGY] the study of plant diseases and their control —**phy′to·path′o·log′ic** (-path′ə läj′ik), **phy′to·path′o·log′i·cal** *adj.*

phy·toph·a·gous (fī täf′ə gəs) *adj.* [PHYTO- + -PHAGOUS] *Zool.* feeding on plants; herbivorous

phy·to·plank·ton (fīt′ə plaŋk′tən) *n.* [PHYTO- + PLANK-TON] plankton consisting of plants, as algae —**phy′to·plank·ton′ic** (-tän′ik) *adj.*

phy·to·so·ci·ol·o·gy (-sō′sē äl′ə jē, -shē-) *n.* [PHYTO- + SOCIOLOGY] a division of ecology concerned particularly with the origin, composition, classification, distribution, etc. of plant communities

phy·tos·ter·ol (fī täs′tə rôl′, -rōl′) *n.* [PHYTO- + STEROL] 1. any of several steroid alcohols found in plants 2. an isomer of cholesterol found in plants

phy·to·tox·ic (fīt′ə täk′sik) *adj.* toxic to plants —**phy′to·tox·ic′i·ty** (-täk sis′ə tē) *n.*

☆**phy·to·tron** (fīt′ə trän′) *n.* [PHYTO- + Gr. *-tron*, suffix of instrument, akin to L. *-trum*] any of various chambers, etc. designed to provide a controlled environment for the study of plant growth

pi¹ (pī) *n., pl.* **pies** [see PIE²] 1. a mixed, disordered collection of printing type 2. any jumble or mixture —*vt.* **pied, pie′ing** or **pi′ing** to make jumbled or disordered; mix up (type)

pi² (pī) *n.* [Gr. *pi*, earlier *pei* < Sem., as in Heb. *pē*] 1. the sixteenth letter of the Greek alphabet (Π, π) 2. *a)* the symbol (π) designating the ratio of the circumference of a circle to its diameter *b)* the ratio itself, equal to 3.14159265+

Pia·cen·za (pyä chen′tsä) commune in N Italy, in Emilia-Romagna, on the Po River: pop. 88,000

pi·ac·u·lar (pī ak′yə lər) *adj.* [L. *piacularis* < *piaculum*, expiatory sacrifice < *piare*, to appease, expiate, akin to *pius*, pious] 1. making atonement; expiatory 2. calling for expiation or atonement; sinful; wicked

piaffe (pyaf) *n.* [Fr. < *piaffer*, to strut, paw the ground, prob. of echoic origin] a movement in horsemanship in which the animal executes the motions of a slow trot in place —*vi.* **piaffed, piaff′ing** to perform the piaffe

pi·al (pī′əl) *adj.* of the pia mater

pi·a ma·ter (pī′ə māt′ər, pē′ə mät′ər) [ME. < ML. (lit., gentle mother < fem. of L. *pius*, tender + *mater*, MOTHER¹]: used as transl. of Ar. *umm raqīqah*] the vascular membrane immediately enveloping the brain and spinal cord and surrounded by the arachnoid and dura mater

pi·an·ism (pē an′iz'm, pyan′-, pē′ən-) *n.* the art, technique, or performance of a pianist —**pi′an·is′tic** *adj.*

pi·a·nis·si·mo (pē′ə nis′ə mō′) *adj., adv.* [It., superl. of *piano*: see PIANO², *adj.* & *adv.*] *Music* very soft: a direction to the performer: opposed to FOR-TISSIMO —*n., pl.* **-mos′,** It. **-mi′** (-mē′) a passage to be performed pianissimo

pi·an·ist (pē an′ist, pyan′-, pē′ən-) *n.* [Fr. *pianiste*] a person who plays the piano, esp. a skilled or professional performer

pi·an·o¹ (pē an′ō, pyan′ō) *n., pl.* **-os** [It., contr. < *piano-forte*] a large, stringed percussion instrument played from a keyboard, each key of which operates a small, felt-covered hammer that strikes and vibrates a corresponding

rigid steel wire or set of wires stretched on a metal frame, typically harp-shaped, enclosed in a wooden case of various forms: the wires produce tones ranging over seven octaves

pi·a·no² (pē ä′nō, pyä′-) *adj., adv.* [It., soft, smooth < L. *planus*, smooth, PLANE²] *Music* soft: a direction to the performer —*n., pl.* **-os** a passage to be performed piano

pi·an·o·for·te (pē an′ə fôrt′, pyan′ə-; pē an′ə fôr′tē, -tā) *n.* [It. < *piano*, soft (see prec.) + *forte*, loud, strong (< L. *fortis:* see FORT)]: from its gradation of tone in contrast with the harpsichord] same as PIANO¹

☆**Pi·a·no·la** (pē′ə nō′lə) a trademark for a kind of player piano —*n.* [p-] such a piano

pi·as·sa·va (pē′ə sä′və) *n.* [Port. *piassaba* < Tupi *piaçába*] 1. a stiff, elastic fiber obtained from any of various palms and used in making brushes, brooms, etc. 2. a palm yielding piassava; esp., any of several Brazilian palms (as *Leopoldinia piassaba* and *Attalea funifera*)

pi·as·ter (pē as′tər) *n.* [Fr. *piastre* < It. *piastra*, thin plate of metal, dollar, ult. < L. *emplastrum:* see PLASTER] 1. [Rare] the Spanish dollar 2. a unit of currency equal to 1/100 of a pound in the United Arab Republic, Lebanon, Syria, and Sudan 3. the principal monetary unit in South Vietnam 4. a unit of money in Turkey, equal to 1/100 of a lira Also, Brit. sp., **pi·as′tre**

Piau·í (pyou ē′) state of NE Brazil: 96,886 sq. mi.; pop. 1,263,000; cap. Terezina

pi·az·za (pē az′ə; *for 1, usually* -at′sə; *It.* pyät′tsä) *n., pl.* **-zas;** It. **-ze** (-tse) [It. < L. *platea:* see PLACE] 1. in Italy, an open public square, surrounded by buildings 2. a covered gallery or arcade ☆3. a large, covered porch; veranda

☆**pi·bal** (pī′bal) *n.* [PI(LOT) BAL(LOON)] 1. same as PILOT BALLOON 2. observation by means of pilot balloon

pi·broch (pē′bräk; *Scot.* pē′bräkh) *n.* [Gael. *piobaireachd*, pipe music < *piobair*, piper < *piob* (< PIPE), a pipe, bag-pipe] a piece of music for the bagpipe, consisting of a theme with variations, usually martial but sometimes dirgelike

pi·ca¹ (pī′kə) *n.* [< ? ML.(Ec.), a directory, church manual (see PIE⁴): perhaps in reference to type used in printing it] 1. a size of type, 12 point 2. the height of this type, about 1/6 inch: used as a typographical unit of measure

pi·ca² (pī′kə) *n.* [ModL. < L., magpie: see PIE³] an abnormal craving to eat clay, paint, chalk, or similar substances not fit for food

pic·a·dor (pik′ə dôr′; *Sp.* pē′kä thôr′) *n., pl.* **-dors′;** Sp. **-dor′es** (-thô′res) [Sp. < *picar*, to prick < VL. *piccare* < *piccus*, for L. *picus*, woodpecker: see PIE³] in bullfighting, any of the horsemen who weaken the neck muscles of the bull by pricking with a lance

Pic·ar·dy (pik′ər dē) region & former province of N France: Fr. **Pi·car·die** (pē kàr dē′)

pic·a·resque (pik′ə resk′) *adj.* [Sp. *picaresco* < *picaro*, a rascal] 1. designating or of sharp-witted vagabonds and their roguish adventures 2. designating a kind of fiction originating in Spain and dealing episodically with the adventures of a picaresque hero

pic·a·ro (pē′kä rō′) *n., pl.* **-ros** [see prec.] an adventurous rogue or vagabond

pic·a·roon (pik′ə rōōn′) *n.* [Sp. *picaron* < *picaro*, a rogue] 1. same as PICARO 2. a pirate or pirate ship — *vi.* to act as a pirate

Pi·cas·so (pi kä′sō, -kas′ō), **Pa·blo** (pä′blō) 1881– ; Sp. painter & sculptor in France

☆**pic·a·yune** (pik′ē ōōn′, -ə yōōn′) *n.* [Fr. *picaillon*, small coin, halfpenny < Pr. *picaioun* < *picaio*, money, prob. < *pica*, to ring, jingle, strike < VL. *piccare:* see PICADOR] 1. a coin of small value, as a former Spanish real of Louisiana, etc. 2. anything trivial or worthless —*adj.* trivial or petty; small or small-minded: also **pic′a·yun′ish** —*SYN.* see PETTY

Pic·ca·dil·ly (pik′ə dil′ē) street in London, a traditional center of fashionable shops, clubs, & hotels

pic·ca·lil·li (pik′ə lil′ē) *n.* [prob. < PICKLE: formerly also *piccalillo*] a relish, orig. East Indian, of chopped vegetables, mustard, vinegar, and hot spices

Pic·card (pē′kär′; *E.* pi kärd′) 1. **Au·guste** (ō′güst′), 1884–1962; Swiss physicist in Belgium: known for balloon ascents into the stratosphere & descents in a bathyscaph 2. **Jean Fé·lix** (zhän fā lēks′), 1884–1963; U.S. chemist & aeronautical engineer, born in Switzerland: also known for balloon ascents: twin brother of *prec.*

pic·co·lo (pik′ə lō′) *n., pl.* **-los′** [It., small] a small instrument of the flute family, pitched an octave above the ordinary flute —**pic′co·lo′ist** *n.*

pice (pīs) *n., pl.* **pice** [Hind. *paisā*] 1. a former monetary unit and small coin of India, equal to 1/4 of a rupee 2. a monetary unit and small coin equal to 1/100 of a rupee in Pakistan and Nepal

pic·e·ous (pis′ē əs, pī′sē-) *adj.* [L. *piceus* < *pix*, PITCH¹] of or like pitch; specif., *Zool.* black as pitch

pich·i·ci·e·go (pich′ə sē ā′gō) *n., pl.* **-gos** [AmSp., prob. < native name in Argentina: ending after Sp. *ciego* (L. *caecus*), blind] a burrowing S. American animal (genus *Chlamyphorus*) related to the armadillo but smaller: also **pich′i·ci·a′go** (-ä′gō, -ā′gō)

pick¹ (pik) *vt.* [ME. *pykken*, var. of *picchen*, to PITCH²] *Weaving* to throw (a shuttle) —*n.* **1.** one passage or throw of the shuttle of a loom **2.** one of the weft threads, or filling yarns

pick² (pik) *n.* [ME. *pike* < OE. *pic*, PIKE⁴] **1.** a heavy tool used in breaking up soil, rock, etc.: the metal head is long, narrow, and slightly curved, and pointed at one or both ends, with a wooden handle fitted into its center **2.** any of several pointed tools or instruments for picking: usually in combination [*toothpick*] **3.** *same as* PLECTRUM **4.** a slender, plastic pin used to hold hair rollers in place

pick³ (pik) *vt.* [ME. *picken* < OE. *pician (akin to ON. *pikka*) & (?) OFr. *piquer*, to pierce: see PIKE²] **1.** to break up, pierce, or dig up (soil, rock, etc.) with something sharply pointed; use a pick on **2.** to make or form (a hole) with something pointed **3.** *a)* to dig, probe, or scratch at with the fingers or with something pointed in an attempt to remove *b)* to clear something from (the teeth, etc.) in this way **4.** to remove by pulling as with the fingers; specif., to pluck or gather (flowers, berries, etc.) **5.** to clear (something) in this way; specif., *a)* to prepare (a fowl) by removing the feathers *b)* to remove the fruit from (a tree, orchard, etc.) **6.** *a)* to take up (food, etc.) in small pieces, as a bird with its bill; peck *b)* to eat sparingly or daintily **7.** to pull (fibers, rags, etc.) apart **8.** to choose; select; cull **9.** to look for and find excuse or occasion for (a quarrel or fight) **10.** to look for purposefully and find [to *pick* flaws] ☆**11.** *a)* to pluck (the strings on a guitar, banjo, etc.) *b)* to play (a guitar, banjo, etc.) in this way **12.** to open (a lock) with a wire, etc. instead of a key, esp. in a stealthy manner **13.** to steal from (another's pocket, purse, etc.) —*vi.* **1.** to eat sparingly or fussily **2.** to thieve or pilfer **3.** to use a pick **4.** to gather growing berries, flowers, etc. **5.** to be picked [grapes *pick* easily] **6.** to select or choose, esp. in a careful or fussy manner ☆**7.** to play the guitar, banjo, etc. —*n.* **1.** the act of picking; stroke or blow with something pointed **2.** *a)* the act or right of choosing *b)* the person or thing chosen; choice **3.** the best or most desirable one or ones **4.** the amount of a crop picked at one time —*SYN.* see CHOOSE —**pick and choose** to choose or select carefully —**pick apart** (or **to pieces**) **1.** to separate or tear into many parts **2.** to find flaws in by examining critically —**pick at 1.** to eat small portions of, esp. in a dainty or fussy manner **2.** [Colloq.] to nag at; find fault with **3.** to toy or meddle with; finger —**pick off 1.** to remove by picking or plucking **2.** to hit with a carefully aimed shot ☆**3.** *Baseball* to throw out (a base runner taking a lead) —**pick on 1.** to choose; select **2.** [Colloq.] to single out for abuse, criticism, etc.; annoy; tease —**pick one's way** to progress slowly, choosing each move with care —**pick out 1.** to choose; select **2.** to single out from or recognize among a group; distinguish **3.** to make out (meaning or sense) **4.** to play (a tune) note by note, as on a piano —**pick over** to examine (a number of things) item by item; sort out —**pick up 1.** to grasp and raise or lift; take up **2.** to get, gain, find, or learn, esp. by chance or in a casual manner **3.** to stop for and take or bring along **4.** to take into custody; arrest **5.** to accelerate; gain (speed) **6.** to regain (health, power, efficiency, etc.); improve **7.** to resume (an activity, etc.) after a pause **8.** to bring into range of sight, hearing, radio or TV reception, etc. **9.** to find and travel along (a route, trail, etc.) ☆**10.** to make a room, etc. tidy **11.** [Colloq.] to become acquainted with casually or informally, esp. for purposes of lovemaking

pick·a·back (pik′ə bak′, pik′ē-) *adv., adj.* [var. of *pickapack, pickpack,* redupl. of PACK¹] *same as* PIGGYBACK

pick·ax, pick·axe (pik′aks′) *n.* [altered (after AX) < ME. *pikois* < OFr. *picquois*, pickax < *pic*, PIKE²] a pick with a point at one end of the head and a chisellike edge at the other —*vt., vi.* **-axed′, -ax′ing** to use a pickax (on)

picked¹ (pikt) *adj.* [< PICK³] **1.** selected with care [*picked* men] **2.** gathered from plants rather than from the ground, as berries, apples, etc.

pick·ed² (pik′id, pikt) *adj.* [ME. < PICK²] [Archaic or Dial.] having a sharp end; pointed

pick·er¹ (pik′ər) *n.* a person or thing that picks; esp., a machine for picking fibers

pick·er² (pik′ər) *n.* [PICK¹ + -ER] a device that throws the shuttle through the warp in weaving

PICKAX

pick·er·el (pik′ər əl, pik′rəl) *n., pl.* **-el, -els:** see PLURAL, II, D, 2 [ME. < *pik*, PIKE³ + -*rel*, dim. suffix] **1.** any of a number of relatively small, N. American freshwater fishes (genus *Esox*) including the **chain pickerel** (*Esox niger*), the **grass pickerel** (*Esox vermiculatus*), and the **redfin pickerel** (*Esox americanus*) **2.** a local name for WALLEYED PIKE **3.** [Brit.] a young pike

pick·er·el·weed (-wēd′) *n.* ☆any of a genus (*Pontederia*) of N. American aquatic plants, esp. any of a species (*Pontederia cordata*) with arrow-shaped leaves and spikes of blue-violet flowers, found in shallow waters

Pick·er·ing (pik′ər iŋ) **1.** **Edward Charles,** 1846–1919; U.S. astronomer & physicist **2.** **William Henry,** 1858–1938; U.S. astronomer: brother of *prec.*

pick·et (pik′it) *n.* [Fr. *piquet,* dim. of *pic,* PIKE²] **1.** a stake or slat, usually pointed, used as an upright in a fence, a hitching post for animals, a marker, etc. **2.** a group of soldiers or a single soldier stationed, usually at an outpost, to guard a body of troops from surprise attack **3.** a ship or airplane that patrols a defense perimeter **4.** a person, as a member of a labor union on strike, stationed outside a factory, store, public building, etc., often carrying a sign, to demonstrate protest, keep strikebreakers from entering, dissuade people from buying, etc. —*vt.* **1.** to enclose, shut in, or protect with a picket fence or palisade **2.** to hitch (an animal) to a picket **3.** *a)* to post as a military picket *b)* to guard (a body of troops) with a picket **4.** to place pickets, or serve as a picket, at (a factory, etc.) —*vi.* to serve as a picket (sense 4) —**pick′et·er** *n.*

☆**picket fence** a fence made of upright pales or stakes

picket line a line or cordon of people serving as pickets

Pick·ett (pik′it), **George Edward** 1825–75; Confederate general

pick·ing (pik′iŋ) *n.* **1.** the act of a person who picks **2.** [*usually pl.*] something that is or may be picked, or the amount of this; specif., *a)* small scraps or remains that may be gleaned *b)* something got by effort, often in a dishonest way; returns or spoils

pick·le (pik′'l) *n.* [ME. *pikil* < MDu. *pekel* < ? *pikken,* to prick, in sense "that which pricks, or is piquant"] **1.** any brine, vinegar, or spicy solution used to preserve or marinate food **2.** a vegetable, specif. a cucumber, preserved in such a solution **3.** a chemical bath used to clear metal of scale, preserve wood, etc. **4.** [Colloq.] an awkward or difficult situation; plight —*vt.* **-led, -ling** to treat with or preserve in a pickle solution —*SYN.* see PREDICAMENT

pick·led (-'ld) *adj.* [Slang] intoxicated; drunk

pick·lock (pik′läk′) *n.* **1.** a person, esp. a thief, who picks locks **2.** an instrument for picking locks

☆**pick-me-up** (pik′mē up′) *n.* [Colloq.] an alcoholic drink taken to raise one's spirits

pick·pock·et (-päk′it) *n.* a thief who steals from the pockets of persons, as in crowds

Pick's disease [after Arnold Pick (1851–1924), Czech physician] a condition characterized by progressive deterioration of the brain with atrophy of the cerebral cortex, esp. the frontal lobes, and evidenced in loss of memory, emotional instability, etc.

pick·up (pik′up′) *n.* **1.** the act of picking up, as in fielding a rapidly rolling baseball **2.** the process or power of increasing in speed; acceleration ☆**3.** a small, open truck with low sides, for hauling light loads **4.** [Colloq.] *a)* a casual or informal acquaintance, as one formed for purposes of lovemaking *b)* a person with whom such an acquaintance is formed ☆**5.** [Colloq.] improvement or recovery, as in trade ☆**6.** [Colloq.] *a)* a stimulant; bracer *b)* stimulation **7.** *a)* in an electric phonograph, a device that produces audiofrequency currents from the vibrations of a needle or stylus moving in a record groove *b)* the pivoted arm holding this device **8.** *Radio & TV a)* the reception of sound or light for conversion into electrical energy in the transmitter *b)* the apparatus used for this *c)* any place outside a studio where a broadcast originates *d)* the electrical system connecting the program from this place to the broadcasting station —*adj.* [Colloq.] assembled, organized, etc. informally or hastily [a *pickup* jazz band]

Pick·wick (pik′wik), **Mr. (Samuel)** the naive, benevolent president of the Pickwick Club in Dickens' *Pickwick Papers* (1836)

pick·wick·i·an (pik wik′ē ən) *adj.* **1.** of or characteristic of Mr. Pickwick or the Pickwick Club **2.** used with a special or esoteric sense: said of a word or phrase

☆**pick·y** (pik′ē) *adj.* **pick′i·er, pick′i·est** [PICK³ + -Y²] [Colloq.] overly fastidious or exacting; fussy

pic·nic (pik′nik) *n.* [Fr. *piquenique,* prob. < *piquer,* to pick + *nique,* a trifle < OFr. *niquier,* to nod] **1.** a pleasure outing at which a meal is eaten outdoors ☆**2.** a shoulder cut of pork, cured like ham: also **picnic ham, picnic shoulder 3.** [Slang] *a)* a pleasant experience *b)* an easy task —*vi.* **-nicked, -nick·ing** to hold or attend a picnic —**pic′nick·er** *n.*

pi·co- (pī′kō, pē′-; -kə) [prob. < It. *piccolo,* small (cf. PICCOLO)] *a combining form meaning* one trillionth; the factor 10⁻¹² [*picocurie*]

Pi·co del·la Mi·ran·do·la (pē′kō del′lä mē rän′dō lä), **Count Gio·van·ni** (jō vän′nē) 1463–94; It. humanist & philosopher

pic·o·line (pik′ə lēn′, -lin) *n.* [< L. *pix* (gen. *picis*), PITCH¹ + -OL² + -INE⁴] any of three isomeric, colorless, strong-smelling, liquid bases, $C_6H_4(CH_3)N$, found in the oil produced by the dry distillation of bones and coal: used in insecticides, pharmaceuticals, resins, etc.

Pi·co Ri·ver·a (pē′kō rə ver′ə) [after Pío *Pico,* last governor of Mexican Calif.: *Rivera,* in allusion to its being between two rivers] city in SW Calif.: suburb of Los Angeles: pop. 54,000

pi·cot (pē′kō) *n., pl.* **-cots** [Fr. < OFr., dim. of *pic,* a point: see PIKE²] any of a number of small, threadlike loops forming an ornamental edging on lace, ribbon, etc. —*vt., vi.* **-coted** (-kōd), **-cot·ing** (-kō in) to trim or edge with such ⸺ps

pic·o·tee (pik′ə tē′) *n.* [Fr. *picoté,* pp. of *picoter,* to mark with dots or pricks < *picot:* see prec.] a variety of carnation

whose light-colored petals are bordered with another, usually darker, color

pic·rate (pik′rāt) *n.* a salt or ester of picric acid, usually
highly explosive and sensitive to shock

pic·ric acid (-rik) [Fr. *picrique*: see PICRO- & -IC] a poisonous, yellow, crystalline, bitter acid, $C_6H_3O_7N_3$: used in
making dyes and explosives and in analytical chemistry

pic·rite (-rīt) *n.* [Fr.: see ff. & -ITE¹] a dark, olivine-rich
igneous rock —**pic·rit′ic** (-rit′ik) *adj.*

pic·ro- (pik′rō, -rə) [Fr. < Gr. *pikros*, bitter < IE. base
*peik-, colorful, sharp, whence L. *pingere*, to PAINT] *a
combining form meaning:* 1. bitter 2. picric acid Also,
before a vowel, **picr-**

pic·ro·tox·in (pik′rə täk′sin) *n.* [PICRO + TOXIN] a white,
bitter, poisonous, crystalline compound, $C_{30}H_{34}O_{13}$, resembling strychnine in its properties: used as a stimulant
in cases of barbiturate poisoning

Pict (pikt) *n.* [LME. *Pictes*, pl. < LL. *Picti* (lit. ? painted
people), whence OE. *Peohtas*] any of an ancient people of
Great Britain, driven into Scotland by the Britons and
Romans

Pict·ish (pik′tish) *adj.* of the Picts, their language, or their
culture —*n.* the language of the Picts: its relationship is
not established

pic·to·graph (pik′tə graf′, -gräf′) *n.* [< L. *pictus* (see
PICTURE) + -GRAPH] 1. a picture or picturelike symbol
representing an idea, as in primitive writing; hieroglyphic
2. same as PICTOGRAPHY 3. a diagram or graph using
pictured objects to convey ideas, information, etc. —**pic′-
to·graph′ic** *adj.*

pic·tog·ra·phy (pik täg′rə fē) *n.* writing by the use of
pictographs; picture writing

Pic·tor (pik′tər) [L., painter: see ff.] a S constellation
between Carina and Dorado

pic·to·ri·al (pik tôr′ē əl) *adj.* [LL. *pictorius* < L. *pictor*,
painter < pp. of *pingere*, to PAINT] 1. [Rare] of a painter
or painting 2. of, containing, or expressed in pictures
3. evoking or suggesting a mental image or picture; vivid;
graphic, as a description —☆*n.* a periodical featuring many
pictures —*SYN.* see GRAPHIC —**pic·to′ri·al·ly** *adv.* —**pic-
to′ri·al·ize** *vt.* -ized′, -iz′ing —**pic·to′ri·al·i·za′tion** *n.*

pic·ture (pik′chər) *n.* [ME. *pycture* < L. *pictura* < *pictus*,
pp. of *pingere*, to PAINT] 1. *a)* an image or likeness of an
object, person, or scene produced on a flat surface, esp. by
painting, drawing, or photography *b)* a printed reproduction of this 2. anything closely resembling or strikingly
typifying something else; perfect likeness or image [to be
the *picture* of one's mother, the *picture* of health] 3. anything regarded as having the compositional beauty of a
painting or drawing 4. a mental image or impression; idea
5. a vivid or detailed description [a *picture* of the times]
6. all the facts or conditions of an event, collectively;
situation 7. same as TABLEAU 8. same as MOTION PICTURE
9. the image on a television screen —*vt.* -tured, -tur·ing
1. to make a picture of by painting, drawing, photographing, etc. 2. to make visible; show clearly; reflect 3. to
describe or explain 4. to form a mental picture or impression of; imagine —**in** (or **out of**) **the picture** considered
(or not considered) as involved in a situation

picture card *same as* FACE CARD

picture hat a woman's wide-brimmed hat with plumes,
flowers, etc., like those seen in some famous paintings

☆**picture show** a motion picture or motion-picture theater:
an old-fashioned term

pic·tur·esque (pik′chə resk′) *adj.* [altered (after PICTURE)
< Fr. *pittoresque* < It. *pittoresco* < *pittore*, painter < L.
pictor, painter < pp. of *pingere*, to PAINT] 1. like or suggesting a picture; specif., *a)* having a wild or natural beauty,
as mountain scenery *b)* pleasantly unfamiliar or strange;
quaint [a *picturesque* Indian village] 2. suggesting or calling up a mental picture; striking; vivid [a *picturesque*
description] —*SYN.* see GRAPHIC —**pic′tur·esque′ly** *adv.*
—**pic′tur·esque′ness** *n.*

☆**picture tube** *same as* KINESCOPE (sense 1)

picture window a large window, esp. in a living room, that
seems to frame the outside view

picture writing 1. writing consisting of pictures or figures
representing ideas 2. the pictures or figures so used;
pictographs; hieroglyphics

pic·tur·ize (pik′chə rīz′) *vt.* -ized′, -iz′ing to portray in a
picture, esp. a motion picture —**pic′tur·i·za′tion** *n.*

pic·ul (pik′′l) *n., pl.* -**ul**, -**uls** [Jav. & Malay *pikul*, a man's
load < *pikul*, to carry on one's back] a unit of weight,
varying between 132 and 133 pounds, used in various
countries of southeast Asia

pid·dle (pid′′l) *vi., vt.* -dled, -dling [prob. euphemistic dim.
< base of PISS] 1. to urinate: child's term 2. to dawdle or
trifle (sometimes with *away*) [to *piddle* the time away]
—**pid′dler** *n.*

pid·dling (pid′liŋ) *adj.* insignificant; trifling; petty

pid·dock (pid′ək) *n.* [< ?] any of a number of bivalve
mollusks (genus *Pholas* or similar forms) which bore holes
in wood, clay, and soft rocks

pidg·in (pij′in) *n.* [a supposed Chin. pronun. of BUSINESS]
a mixed language, or jargon, originally developed for pur-

poses of trade, incorporating the vocabulary of one or more
languages with a very simplified form of the grammatical
system of one of these; pidgin English, bêche-de-mer, or
any similar jargon

pidgin English [see prec.] 1. a simplified form of English
used by Orientals and South Pacific natives in dealing with
foreigners: there are two forms, Chinese pidgin and Melanesian pidgin, the former based on the syntax of Chinese,
the latter on the syntax of certain aboriginal languages of
Melanesia and N Australia 2. any jargon intermixed with
English in a similar way, as W African pidgin

pi-dog (pī′dôg′, -däg′) *n.* [prob. Anglo-Indian contr. of
pariah dog] an undomesticated Asian dog, often roaming
in packs in and around villages

pie¹ (pī) *n.* [ME., akin ? to PIE³] 1. a baked dish consisting
of fruit, meat, etc., with either an under crust, an upper
crust, or both 2. a layer cake with a filling of custard,
cream, jelly, etc. ☆3. [Slang] *a)* something extremely good
or easy *b)* political graft *c)* a total amount to be divided in
shares —**(as) easy as pie** [Colloq.] extremely easy

pie² (pī) *n., vt.* [< ? prec.] *chiefly Brit. sp. of* PI¹

pie³ (pī) *n.* [ME. < OFr. < L. *pica*, magpie, akin to *picus*,
woodpecker < IE. base **(s)piko-*, woodpecker, whence
G. *specht*] *same as* MAGPIE

pie⁴ (pī) *n.* [transl. of ML.(Ec.) *pica*, prob. < or akin to
prec.] in England, a form or table of rules used before the
Reformation in selecting the correct church service or
office for the day

pie⁵ (pī) *n.* [Hind. *pā′ī*] formerly, a small bronze coin of
India, equal to 1/12 of an anna

pie·bald (pī′bôld′) *adj.* [PIE³ + BALD] covered with patches
or spots of two colors, esp. with white and black —*n.* a
piebald horse or other animal

piece (pēs) *n.* [ME. *pece* < OFr. < VL. **pettia*, prob. <
Gaul. **pettis*, akin to W. *peth*, a part, Bret. *pez*, a piece]
1. a part or fragment broken or separated from the whole
2. a section, division, or quantity regarded as complete
in itself and distinct from the whole of which it is a part
3. any single thing, amount, specimen, example, etc.;
specif., *a)* an artistic work or composition, as of music,
writing, painting, drama, etc. *b)* an action or its result
[a *piece* of nonsense, business, etc.] *c)* a firearm; specif., a
rifle *d)* a coin or token [a fifty-cent *piece*] *e)* one of a set
or class, as of silver, china, furniture, etc. *f)* a counter
or man, as used in various games; specif., *Chess* any man
other than a pawn 4. the quantity or size, as of cloth
or wallpaper, that is manufactured as a unit 5. an amount
or unit of work constituting a single job 6. [Archaic or
Dial.] an amount of time or space, esp. a small amount;
bit 7. [Archaic or Dial.] a person; individual ☆8. [Slang]
a financial interest; share 9. [Slang] a woman regarded as
a sexual partner; also, an instance of sexual intercourse: a
vulgar usage —*vt.* pieced, piec′ing 1. to add a piece or
pieces to, as in repairing or enlarging 2. to join or put
(*together*) the pieces of, as in mending 3. to join or unite
—*vi.* [Dial. or Colloq.] to eat a snack between meals —*SYN.*
see PART —**go to pieces** 1. to break into pieces; fall apart
2. to lose all self-control, morally or emotionally —**of a**
(or **one**) **piece** of the same sort; alike; consistent (*with*)
—☆**speak one's piece** to vent one's views or opinions
—**piec′er** *n.*

‡**pièce de ré·sis·tance** (pyes′ də rā zēs täns′) [Fr., piece
of resistance] 1. the principal dish of a meal 2. the main
item or event in a series

piece-dyed (pēs′dīd′) *adj.* dyed after being woven or
knitted: said of cloth

piece goods *same as* YARD GOODS

piece·meal (pēs′mēl′) *adv.* [ME. *pecemel* < *pece* (see
PIECE) + -mele (< OE. -*mæl*: see MEAL¹): modernized in
ME. < OE. *styccemæl*] 1. piece by piece; in small amounts
or degrees 2. into pieces or parts —*adj.* made or done in
pieces or one piece at a time

piece of eight the obsolete Spanish and Spanish-American
silver dollar, equal to eight reals

piece·work (-wurk′) *n.* work paid for at a fixed rate
(**piece rate**) per piece of work done —**piece′work′er** *n.*

pie chart a graph in the form of a circle divided into
sectors in which relative quantities are indicated by the
proportionately different sizes of the sectors

pied (pīd) *adj.* [ME. *pyed*, orig., black and white like a
magpie: see PIE³] 1. covered with patches or spots of two
or more colors; piebald; variegated 2. wearing a garment
of this description

‡**pied-à-terre** (pye tà ter′) *n., pl.* **pied-à-terre** (pye-) [Fr.,
lit., foot on the ground] a lodging or dwelling, esp. one
used only part time or temporarily

☆**pied·billed grebe** (pīd′bild′) *same as* DABCHICK (sense 2)

Pied·mont (pēd′mänt) 1. hilly, upland region of the E
U.S., between the Atlantic coastal plain & the Appala-
chians, stretching from SE N.Y. to C Ala. 2. region of
NW Italy, on the borders of Switzerland & France:
9,807 sq. mi.; pop. 3,890,000; chief city, Turin: It. name
Pie·mon·te (pye mŏn′te)

pied·mont (pēd′mänt) *adj.* [< *Piedmont*, Italy (< L.
Pedimontium < *pes* (gen. *pedis*), FOOT + *mons* (gen.

fat, āpe, cär; ten, ēven; is, bīte; gō, hôrn, tōōl, look; oil, out; up, fur; get; joy; yet; chin; she; thin, *t*hen; zh, leisure; ŋ, ring;
ə for *a* in *ago*, *e* in *agent*, *i* in *sanity*, *o* in *comply*, *u* in *focus*; ′ as in *able* (ā′b′l); Fr. bäl; ë, Fr. coeur; ö, Fr. feu; Fr. mon; ô, Fr. coq;
ü, Fr. duc; r, Fr. cri; H, G. ich; kh, G. doch. See inside front cover. ☆ Americanism; ‡ foreign; * hypothetical; < derived from

montis), MOUNT¹)] at the base of a mountain or mountains [a *piedmont* stream] —*n.* a piedmont area, plain, etc.
Pied·mon·tese (pēd/män tēz/) *adj.* of Piedmont, Italy, its people, or culture —*n.*, *pl.* **-tese'** a native or inhabitant of Piedmont, Italy
‡**pied noir** (pye nwàr/) *pl.* **pieds noirs'** (pye nwàr/) [Fr., lit., black foot] a French settler in or native of Algeria
Pied Piper (of Hamelin) Ger. *Legend* a musician who rid Hamelin of its rats by leading them with his piping to the river, where they drowned: in revenge for not being paid, he led the village children to a mountain, where they disappeared
☆**pie-eyed** (pī/īd/) *adj.* [Slang] intoxicated; drunk
Pie·gan (pē/gən) *n., pl.* **-gans, -gan** any member of a subtribe of the Blackfoot Indians
☆**pie in the sky** [Slang] 1. a promise of benefits or a reward in an afterlife or in the remote future 2. an unrealistically Utopian plan or project
☆**pie-plant** (pī/plant/) *n.* [PIE¹ + PLANT] the rhubarb: so called from its use in pies
pier (pir) *n.* [ME. *per* < ML. *pera*, ult. < ? or akin to L. *petra*, stone] 1. a heavy structure supporting the spans of a bridge, esp., as distinguished from an abutment, one supporting the adjacent ends of two center spans of a long bridge 2. a structure built out over the water and supported by pillars or piles: used as a landing place, pleasure pavilion, etc. 3. *Archit.* a) a heavy column, usually square, used to support weight, as at the end of an arch b) the part of a wall between windows or other openings c) a reinforcing part built out from the surface of a wall
pierce (pirs) *vt.* **pierced, pierc'ing** [ME. *percen* < OFr. *percer* < VL. **pertusiare* < L. *pertusus*, pp. of *pertundere*, to thrust through < *per*, through + *tundere*, to strike: see STOCK] 1. to pass into or through as a pointed instrument does; penetrate; stab 2. to affect sharply the senses or feelings of 3. to make a hole in or through; perforate; bore 4. to make (a hole), as by boring or stabbing 5. to force a way into or through; break through 6. to sound sharply through [a shriek *pierced* the air] 7. to penetrate with the sight or mind [to *pierce* a mystery] —*vi.* to penetrate (*to, into,* or *through* something) —**pierc'er** *n.* — **pierc'ing·ly** *adv.*
Pierce (pirs), **Franklin** 1804–69; 14th president of the U.S. (1853–57)
pier glass a tall mirror set in the pier, or wall section, between windows
Pi·er·i·a (pī ir/ē ə) province of Macedonia, N Greece: 593 sq. mi.; pop. 98,000
Pi·er·i·an (-ən) *adj.* 1. of Pieria, where the Muses were anciently worshiped 2. of the Muses or the arts
pi·er·i·dine (pī er/ə din/, -din) *adj.* [< ModL. *Pieridinae*, name of a subfamily < *Pieris*, type genus < Gr. *Pieris*, any of the Muses] of a large family (Pieridae) of small or medium-sized butterflies, usually white or yellow with dark markings, including the common cabbage butterflies
pie·ro·gi (pi rō/gē) *n.pl. Pol. var.* of PIROGI
Pi·erre¹ (pē er/; *Fr.* pyer) [Fr.: see PETER] a masculine name
Pierre² (pir) [after *Pierre* Chouteau, early fur trader] capital of S. Dak., on the Missouri River: pop. 10,000
Pi·er·rot (pē/ə rō/; *Fr.* pye rō/) [Fr., dim. of *Pierre*, PETER] a stock comic character in old French pantomime, having a whitened face and wearing loose white pantaloons and a jacket with large buttons
pier table a low table set in the pier, or wall section, between windows, often below a pier glass
Pie·tà (pyä tä/, pē ät/ə) *n.* [It., lit., pity < L. *pietas*, PIETY] a representation in painting, sculpture, etc. of Mary, the mother, grieving over the body of Jesus after the Crucifixion
Pie·ter·mar·itz·burg (pē/tər mer/its bʉrg/) capital of Natal province, South Africa: pop. 129,000
pi·e·tism (pī/ə tiz'm) *n.* [G. *pietismus*: see ff.] 1. a system that stresses the devotional ideal in religion 2. [P-] the principles and practices of the Pietists 3. exaggerated pious feeling or attitude —**pi'e·tis'tic, pi'e·tis'ti·cal** *adj.* —**pi'e·tis'ti·cal·ly** *adv.*
Pie·tist (-tist) *n.* [G. < ModL. *(Collegia) pietatis*, lit., (fellowship) of piety] 1. a member of a group of Germans who advocated a revival of the devotional ideal in the Lutheran Church 2. [p-] a pious person
pi·e·ty (pī/ə tē) *n., pl.* **-ties** [OFr. *pieté* < LL.(Ec.) *pietas*, duty to God < L., dutiful conduct, scrupulousness < *pius*: see PIOUS] 1. devotion to religious duties and practices 2. loyalty and devotion to parents, family, etc. 3. a pious act, statement, belief, etc.
pi·e·zo- (pē ā/zō, pī ē/-) [< Gr. *piezein*, to press < IE. **pised-*, to sit on, press < base **epi-*, on + **sed-*, SIT] a combining form meaning pressure [*piezometer*]
pi·e·zo·chem·is·try (pē ā/zō kem/is trē, pī ē/-) *n.* [prec. + CHEMISTRY] the branch of chemistry dealing with the effects of high pressure on chemical reactions
piezoelectric effect *Physics* the property exhibited by certain crystals of generating voltage when subjected to pressure and, conversely, undergoing mechanical stress when subjected to an electric field (e.g., alternately expanding and contracting in response to an alternating electric field), as in crystal oscillators, microphones, etc.
pi·e·zo·e·lec·tric·i·ty (pē ā/zō ə lek/tris/ə tē) *n.* [PIEZO-

+ ELECTRICITY] electricity resulting from the piezoelectric effect —**pi·e·zo'e·lec'tric, pi·e·zo'e·lec'tri·cal** *adj.* —**pi·e'zo·e·lec'tri·cal·ly** *adv.*
pi·e·zom·e·ter (pē/ə zäm/ə tər, pī/-) *n.* [PIEZO- + -METER] any of various instruments used in measuring pressure or compressibility —**pi·e·zo·met·ric** (pē ā/zə met/rik, pī ē/-) *adj.* —**pi'e·zom'e·try** (-ə trē) *n.*
pif·fle (pif/'l) *n.* [< Brit. dial.: cf. PIDDLE] [Colloq.] talk, writing, action, etc. regarded as insignificant or non-sensical —*interj.* nonsense! —**pif'fling** *adj.*
pig (pig) *n., pl.* **pigs, pig:** see PLURAL, II, D, 1 [ME. *pigge*, orig., young pig (replacing OE. *swin*) < OE., as in *picg-bread*, mast, pig's food] 1. a domesticated animal (*Sus scrofa*) with a long, broad snout and a thick, fat body covered with coarse bristles; swine; hog 2. a young hog of less than c. 100 lbs. 3. meat from a pig; pork 4. a) a person regarded as acting or looking like a pig; greedy or filthy person *b)* [Slang] a slatternly or sluttish woman 5. [from the shape or size] a) an oblong casting of iron or other metal poured from the smelting furnace b) any of the molds in which these are cast c) clipped form of PIG IRON —*vi.* **pigged, pig'ging** 1. to bear pigs 2. to live in filth, like a pig (usually with *it*) —**buy a pig in a poke** to buy, get, or agree to something without sight or knowledge of it in advance
pig bed the sand bed into which molten iron is poured in molding pigs
☆**pig·boat** (-bōt/) *n.* [from resembling suckling pigs when nosed against a tender] [Slang] a submarine
pi·geon¹ (pij/ən) *n., pl.* **-geons, -geon:** see PLURAL, II, D, 1 [ME. *pejon* < MFr. *pijon* < LL. *pipio* (gen. *pipionis*), chirping bird, squab < *pipire*, to chirp, of echoic orig.: cf. PEEP¹] 1. any of a number of related birds (family Columbidae) with a small head, plump body, long, pointed wings, and short legs, and characteristically larger than the doves ☆2. *same as* CLAY PIGEON 3. a girl or young woman 4. [Slang] a person easily deceived or gulled; dupe
pi·geon² (pij/ən) *n. same as* PIDGIN —**one's pigeon** [Chiefly Brit. Slang] one's special concern, or business
pigeon breast a deformity of the human chest occurring in rickets, etc., and characterized by a sharply projecting sternum like that of a pigeon—**pi'geon-breast'ed** *adj.*
pigeon hawk ☆a small, brownish or grayish, N. American falcon (*Falco columbarius*), with a light tan breast having brownish, longitudinal stripes
pi·geon-heart·ed (-härt/id) *adj.* cowardly or timid
pi·geon·hole (-hōl/) *n.* 1. a small recess or hole for pigeons to nest in, usually in a compartmented structure 2. a small open compartment, as in a desk, for filing papers —*vt.* **-holed', -hol'ing** 1. to put in the pigeonhole of a desk, etc. 2. to put aside indefinitely, as if intending to ignore or forget; shelve 3. to assign to a category or categories; classify
pi·geon-liv·ered (-liv/ərd) *adj.* [Rare] meek or gentle
pigeon pea 1. a tropical plant (*Cajanus cajan*) of the legume family, with yellow flowers, widely grown for its edible seed 2. its seed
pi·geon-toed (-tōd/) *adj.* having the toes or feet turned in
pi·geon wing (-wiŋ/) *n.* ☆1. a fancy dance step performed by jumping and striking the legs together ☆2. a figure in skating, outlining a pigeon wing
☆**pig·fish** (pig/fish/) *n., pl.* **-fish', -fish'es:** see FISH² any of a number of saltwater fishes (family Pomadasyidae) that make a grunting noise when taken out of water; esp., an Atlantic grunt (*Orthopristis chrysopterus*) abundant off the E coast of the U.S. and in the Gulf of Mexico
pig·ger·y (pig/ər ē) *n., pl.* **-ger·ies** *chiefly Brit. var.* of PIGPEN
pig·gin (pig/in) *n.* [< ?] a small wooden pail with one stave extended above the rim to serve as a handle
pig·gish (pig/ish) *adj.* like a pig; gluttonous or filthy —**pig'gish·ly** *adv.* —**pig'gish·ness** *n.*
pig·gy (pig/ē) *n., pl.* **-gies** a little pig: also sp. **pig'gie** —*adj.* **-gi·er, -gi·est** *same as* PIGGISH
pig·gy·back (pig/ē bak/) *adv., adj.* [alt. of PICKABACK] 1. on the shoulders or back [to carry a child *piggyback*] ☆2. of or by a transportation system in which loaded truck trailers are carried on railroad flatcars 3. fixed to, carried by, or connected with something else —☆*vt.* to carry or transport piggyback
☆**piggy bank** any small savings bank, often one in the form of a pig, with a slot for receiving coins
pig·head·ed (-hed/id) *adj.* stubborn; obstinate; mulish —**pig'head'ed·ly** *adv.* —**pig'head'ed·ness** *n.*
pig iron [see PIG, *n.* 5] crude iron, as it comes from the blast furnace
pig Latin a playful code in speaking, in which each word is begun with its first vowel and any preceding consonants are moved to the end to form a new syllable with the vowel sound (ā), as "oybay" for *boy*
pig·let (pig/lit) *n.* a little pig, esp. a suckling
pig·ment (pig/mənt) *n.* [ME. < L. *pigmentum* < base of *pingere*, to PAINT] 1. coloring matter, usually in the form of an insoluble powder, mixed with oil, water, etc. to make paints 2. any coloring matter in the cells and tissues of plants or animals —*vi., vt.* to take on or cause to take on pigment; color or become colored: also **pig'ment·ize' -ized', -iz'ing** —**pig'men·tar'y** (-mən ter/ē) *adj.*
pig·men·ta·tion (pig/mən tā/shən) *n.* [< LL. *pigmentatus*,

colored (< L. *pigmentum*) + -ION] coloration in plants or animals due to the presence of pigment in the tissue

Pig·my (pig′mē) *adj., n., pl.* **-mies** same as PYGMY

pi·gno·li·a (pēn yō′lē ə) *n.* [altered < It. *pignolo* < VL. *pineolus*, dim. of L. *pineus*, of pine < *pinus*, a pine tree] the edible seed of any of various nut pines: also **pi·gno′li** (-lē)

pig·nus (pig′nəs) *n., pl.* **-no·ra** (-nə rə) [L.] Civil Law a pledge; pawn

pig·nut (pig′nut′) *n.* ☆1. any of several bitter, astringent hickory nuts ☆2. any of the trees (genus *Carya*) on which these grow

pig·pen (-pen′) *n.* a pen where pigs are confined

pig·skin (-skin′) *n.* 1. the skin of a pig 2. leather made from this ☆3. [Colloq.] a football

pig·stick·ing (-stik′iŋ) *n.* the hunting of wild boars, esp. on horseback and using spears —**pig′stick′er** *n.*

pig·sty (-stī′) *n., pl.* **-sties** same as PIGPEN

pig·tail (-tāl′) *n.* 1. tobacco in a twisted roll 2. a long braid of hair hanging at the back of the head

pig·weed (-wēd′) *n.* ☆1. any of several coarse weeds (genus *Amaranthus*) of the amaranth family, with dense, bristly clusters of small green flowers 2. any of several goosefoots; esp., same as LAMB'S-QUARTERS

pi·ka (pī′kə) *n.* [< E. Siberian (Tungusic) name] any of various small, rabbitlike, short-legged mammals (family Ochotonidae), with a rudimentary tail, rounded ears, and two pairs of upper incisors: found in rocky areas, usually at high altitudes, in W. N. America and in Asia

pike¹ (pīk) *n.* clipped form of TURNPIKE —*vi.* **piked, pik′ing** [Old Slang] to move quickly (usually with *along*)

pike² (pīk) *n.* [Fr. *pique* < *piquer*, to pierce, prick < VL. *piccare*, prob. < *piccus*, for L. *picus*: see PIE³] a weapon, formerly used by foot soldiers, consisting of a metal spearhead on a long wooden shaft —*vt.* **piked, pik′ing** to pierce or kill with or as with a pike

pike³ (pīk) *n., pl.* **pike, pikes:** see PLURAL, II, D, 2 [ME. *pik*, prob. < *pike* (see ff.), from the pointed head] 1. a slender, voracious, freshwater game fish (*Esox lucius*) with a narrow, pointed head and conspicuous, sharp teeth, found throughout the northern parts of the N Hemisphere: also called **northern pike** 2. any of several related fishes (family Esocidae), as the muskellunge and the pickerel 3. any of various fishes resembling the true pikes, as the walleyed pike

pike⁴ (pīk) *n.* [ME. *pike* < OE. *pic*, a pickax, prob. akin to OFr. *pic*, a pick, pickax < VL. *piccus*: see PIKE²] a spike; point, as the pointed tip of a spear

pike⁵ (pīk) *n.* [ME., prob. < ON. *pik*, akin to OE. *pic*: see prec.] [Brit. Dial.] 1. a peaked summit 2. a mountain or hill with a peaked summit

Pike (pīk), **Zeb·u·lon Montgomery** (zeb′yoo lən) 1779–1813; U.S. general & explorer

pike·man (pīk′mən) *n., pl.* **-men** (-mən) a soldier armed with a pike

pike·perch (-purch′) *n., pl.* **-perch′, -perch′es:** see PLURAL, II, D, 2 a fish of the perch family resembling a pike, as the walleyed pike or the sauger

pik·er (pī′kər) *n.* [orig., prob. one from *Pike* County, Missouri, then applied to Missourians generally: reason for later uses obscure] ☆[Slang] a person who does things in a petty or niggardly way; esp., one who gambles or speculates in an overly cautious way

Pikes Peak (pīks) [after Zebulon M. PIKE] mountain of the Front Range, C Colo.: 14,110 ft.

pike·staff (pīk′staf′, -stäf′) *n., pl.* **-staves** (-stāvz′) 1. the shaft of a pike 2. a traveler's staff with a sharp iron or steel point

pi·laf, pi·laff (pi läf′, pē′läf) *n.* [Per. & Turk. *pilāw*] a dish of rice boiled in a seasoned liquid, and usually containing meat or fish

pi·las·ter (pi las′tər) *n.* [Fr. *pilastre* < It. *pilastro* < L. *pila*, a pile, column] a rectangular support or pier projecting partially from a wall and treated architecturally as a column, with a base, shaft, and capital

Pi·late (pī′lət), **Pon·tius** (pän′shəs, -chəs, -tē əs) 1st cent. A.D.; Rom. procurator of Judaea, Samaria, & Idumaea (26?–36?) who condemned Jesus to be crucified

pi·lau, pi·law (pi lô′) *n.* same as PILAF

pil·chard (pil′chərd) *n.* [earlier *pilcher* < ?] 1. a small, saltwater fish (*Sardinia pilchardus*) of the herring family, the commercial sardine of W Europe 2. any of several related fishes; esp., the **Pacific sardine** (*Sardinops sagax*) found off the western coast of the U.S.

Pil·co·ma·yo (pēl′kō mä′yō) river flowing from S Bolivia southeast along the Argentine-Paraguay border into the Paraguay River, near Asunción: c. 1,000 mi.

pile¹ (pīl) *n.* [ME. < MFr. < L. *pila*, a pillar] 1. a mass of things heaped together; heap 2. a heap of wood or other combustible material on which a corpse or sacrifice is burned 3. a large building or group of buildings 4. [Colloq.] *a)* a large amount or number ☆*b)* a lot of money; fortune

PILASTER

5. *Elec. a)* orig., a series of alternate plates of dissimilar metals with acid-saturated cloth or paper between them, for making an electric current *b)* any similar arrangement that produces an electric current; battery ☆6. *an earlier name for* NUCLEAR REACTOR —*vt.* **piled, pil′ing** 1. to put or set in a pile; heap up 2. to cover with a pile; load 3. to accumulate Often with *up* —*vi.* 1. to form a pile or heap 2. to move confusedly in a mass; crowd (with *in, into, out, on, off,* etc.) —SYN. see BUILDING

pile² (pīl) *n.* [ME. *pile,* bird's down < L. *pilus,* a hair < IE. base *pilo-,* whence Gr. *pilos,* felt] 1. a soft, velvety, raised surface on a rug, fabric, etc., produced by making yarn loops on the body of the material and, often, shearing them 2. soft, fine hair, as on wool, fur, etc. —**piled** *adj.*

pile³ (pīl) *n.* [ME. *pil* < OE., akin to G. *pfeil* < WGmc. borrowing < L. *pilum,* a javelin] 1. a long, heavy timber or beam driven into the ground, sometimes under water, to support a bridge, dock, etc. 2. any similar supporting member, as of concrete 3. the head of an arrow, usually of metal 4. *Heraldry* a wedge-shaped charge with the point usually downward —*vt.* **piled, pil′ing** 1. to drive piles into 2. to support or strengthen with piles

pi·le·ate (pī′lē it, pil′ē-; -āt′) *adj.* [L. *pileatus* < *pileus*] 1. having a pileus 2. having a crest extending from the bill to the nape, as some birds Also **pi′le·at′ed** (-āt′id)

☆**pileated woodpecker** a large N. American woodpecker (*Dryocopus pileatus*) with a black and white body and a red crest

pile driver (or **engine**) a machine with a drop hammer for driving piles

pi·le·ous (pī′lē əs, pil′ē-) *adj.* [< L. *pilus,* hair (see PILE²) + -EOUS] hairy or furry

piles (pīlz) *n.pl.* [ME. *pylys* < L. *pilae,* pl. of *pila,* a ball, orig. prob. a knot of hair: see PILE³] same as HEMORRHOIDS

pi·le·um (pī′lē əm, pil′ē-) *n., pl.* **-le·a** (-ə) [ModL. < L. *pilleum,* felt cap: see PILEUS] the top of a bird's head from the bill to the nape

pile-up (pīl′up′) *n.* 1. an accumulation as of burdensome tasks 2. [Colloq.] a collision involving several vehicles

pi·le·us (pī′lē əs, pil′ē-) *n., pl.* **-le·i** (-ī′) [< L. *pilleus* (or *pilleum*), felt cap, akin to *pilus,* hair: see PILE²] 1. a type of brimless cap worn in ancient Rome 2. *Bot.* the cap of a mushroom, or the uppermost part of the fruiting body of other fungi 3. *Zool. a)* the umbrella-shaped disk of a jellyfish *b)* same as PILEUM

pile·wort (pīl′wurt′) *n.* 1. same as CELANDINE 2. any of several plants reputed to have medicinal properties

pil·fer (pil′fər) *vt., vi.* [< MFr. *pelfrer* < *pelfre,* booty: cf. PELF] to steal (esp. small sums or petty objects); filch —SYN. see STEAL —**pil′fer·er** *n.*

pil·fer·age (-ij) *n.* 1. the act or practice of pilfering 2. something pilfered

pil·gar·lic (pil gär′lik) *n.* [altered < *pilled* (peeled) *garlic*] [Obs. exc. Dial.] 1. a bald head or a baldheaded man 2. a person regarded with mild contempt or feigned pity

pil·grim (pil′grəm) *n.* [ME. *pelegrim* < OFr. *pelegrin* < LL.(Ec.) *pelegrinus* < L. *peregrinus,* foreigner < *peregre,* from abroad < *per,* through + *ager,* field, country: see ACRE] 1. a person who travels about; wanderer 2. a person who travels to a shrine or holy place as a religious act ☆3. [P-] any member of the band of English Puritans who founded Plymouth Colony in 1620

pil·grim·age (-ij) *n.* [ME. *pilgrymage* < OFr. *pelegrinage* < *pelegrin,* PILGRIM] 1. a journey made by a pilgrim, esp. to a shrine or holy place 2. any long journey, as to a place of historical interest

☆**Pilgrim Fathers** the Pilgrims (of Plymouth Colony)

Pilgrim's Progress a religious allegory by John Bunyan (1678)

pi·li (pē lē′) *n.* [Tag.] 1. the edible nut, somewhat like an almond, of a tropical tree (*Canarium ovatum*) of the Philippines 2. the tree itself

pil·i- (pil′ə, pil′ə) [< L. *pilus,* a hair: see PILE²] *a combining form meaning* hair [*piliform*]

pi·lif·er·ous (pī lif′ər əs) *adj.* [prec. + -FEROUS] having or bearing hair or hairs

pil·i·form (pil′ə fôrm′) *adj.* [ModL. *piliformis:* see PILI- & -FORM] in the form of a hair; hairlike

pil·ing (pīl′iŋ) *n.* 1. piles collectively 2. a structure of piles

Pi·li·pi·no (pil′ə pē′nō) *n.* [Tag., altered < obs. Sp. *Philippino,* FILIPINO] same as TAGALOG (sense 2): under this name, proclaimed (1962) the official national language of the Philippines: also *Filipino*

pill¹ (pil) *n.* [LME. *pylle,* contr. < L. *pilula,* dim. of *pila,* a ball: see PILES] 1. a small ball or tablet (or, popularly, a capsule) of medicine to be swallowed whole 2. anything unpleasant but unavoidable 3. something like a pill in shape; specif., [Slang] a baseball, golf ball, etc. 4. [Slang] an unpleasant or boring person —*vt.* 1. to dose with pills 2. to form into pills 3. [Slang] to blackball —*vi.* to form into small balls, as fuzz on a fabric —**the pill** (or **Pill**) ☆[Colloq.] any contraceptive drug for women, taken in the form of a pill

pill² (pil) *vt., vi.* [ME. *pillen* < OE. *pylian,* to peel (prob. < L. *pilare,* to make bare of hair < *pilum:* see PILE²) &

MFr. *piller*, to rob < LL. **piliare*, for L. *pilare* < ? *pilum*, a spear] **1.** [Archaic] to pillage; plunder **2.** [Archaic or Dial.] to peel, skin, etc. **3.** [Obs.] to become or cause to become bald

pil·lage (pil′ij) *n.* [ME. *pilage* < MFr. < *piller:* see prec.] **1.** the act of plundering **2.** that which is plundered; booty; loot —*vt.* **-laged, -lag·ing 1.** to deprive of money or property by violence; loot **2.** to take as booty or loot —*vi.* to engage in plunder; take loot —*SYN.* see RAVAGE, SPOIL —**pil′lag·er** *n.*

pil·lar (pil′ər) *n.* [ME. *piler* < OFr. < VL. **pilare* < L. *pila*, a column] **1.** a long, slender, vertical structure used to support a superstructure; column **2.** such a column standing alone as a monument **3.** anything like a pillar in form or function, as a formation of ore left standing as a support in a mine **4.** a person who is a main support of an institution, movement, etc. —*vt.* to support or brace with or as with pillars —**from pillar to post** from one predicament, place of appeal, etc. to another, usually under harassment

pillar box [Brit.] a mail collection box

Pillars of Hercules two headlands on either side of the Strait of Gibraltar, one at Gibraltar (ancient CALPE) & the other at Ceuta (ancient ABYLA) or Jebel Musa, on the coast of Africa

pill·box (pil′bäks) *n.* **1.** a small, shallow box, often cylindrical, for holding pills **2.** a low, enclosed gun emplacement of concrete and steel **3.** a woman's short, cylindrical hat with a flat top

☆**pill bug** any of a number of related land crustaceans (order Isopoda) with a flat body, capable of rolling up into a ball, as a common species (*Armadillidium vulgare*) found in damp places

pil·lion (pil′yən) *n.* [Gael. *pillean* < *peall*, a hide, skin, ult. < L. *pellis:* see FELL⁴] **1.** a cushion attached behind a saddle for an extra rider, esp. a woman, as in medieval times **2.** an extra saddle behind the driver's on a motorcycle

pil·lo·ry (pil′ər ē) *n.*, *pl.* **-ries** [ME. *pilory* < OFr. *pilori*] **1.** a device consisting of a wooden board with holes for the head and hands, in which petty offenders were formerly locked and exposed to public scorn **2.** any exposure to public scorn, etc. —*vt.* **-ried, -ry·ing 1.** to punish by placing in a pillory **2.** to lay open to public ridicule, scorn, or abuse

PILLORY

pil·low (pil′ō) *n.* [ME. *pylwe* < OE. *pyle*, akin to G. *pfühl* < WGmc. borrowing of L. *pulvinus*, a cushion] **1.** a cloth case filled with feathers, down, foam rubber, air, etc., used in sleeping **2.** any object used as a headrest **3.** anything like a pillow or cushion, as a pad on which certain laces are made **4.** anything that supports like a pillow, as the block supporting the inner end of a bowsprit —*vt.* **1.** to rest on or as on a pillow **2.** to be a pillow for —*vi.* to rest the head on or as on a pillow

pillow block a block that supports the journal of a shaft, spindle, etc.

pil·low·case (-kās′) *n.* a removable, usually cotton case used to cover a pillow: also **pil′low·slip′** (-slip′)

pillow lace same as BOBBIN LACE

☆**pillow sham** a decorative cover laid over a bed pillow

pil·low·y (-ē) *adj.* like a pillow; soft; yielding

pi·lo·car·pine (pī′lə kär′pēn, -pin) *n.* [< ModL. *Pilocarpus*, type genus (< Gr. *pilos*, felt + *karpos*, a fruit: see PILE² & CARPO-) + -INE⁴] an alkaloid, C₁₁H₁₆N₂O₂, extracted from the leaves of the jaborandi plant and used in medicine to stimulate sweating or to contract the pupil of the eye

pi·lose (pī′lōs) *adj.* [L. *pilosus* < *pilus*, a hair: see PILE²] covered with hair, esp. fine, soft hair —**pi·los·i·ty** (pī läs′ə tē) *n.*

pi·lot (pī′lət) *n.* [MFr. *pilote* < It. *pilota*, *pedoto* < MGr. **pēdōtēs* < Gr. *pēdon*, oar blade (in pl., rudder), akin to *pous*, FOOT] **1.** a steersman; specif., a person licensed to direct or steer ships into or out of a harbor or through difficult waters **2.** a person qualified to operate the controls of an aircraft **3.** a guide; leader **4.** a device that guides the action of a machine or machine part **5.** same as: ☆*a*) COWCATCHER *b*) PILOT LIGHT *c*) PILOT FILM (or TAPE) —*vt.* **1.** to act as a pilot of, on, in, or over **2.** to guide; conduct; lead —*adj.* **1.** that serves as a guide or guiding device **2.** that serves as an activating device **3.** that serves as a trial unit for experimentation or testing —*SYN.* see GUIDE —**pi′lot·less** *adj.*

pi·lot·age (-ij) *n.* [Fr.: see prec. & -AGE] **1.** the action or occupation of piloting **2.** the fee paid to a pilot **3.** aircraft navigation by observation of ground features and the use of charts and maps

pilot balloon a small balloon sent up to determine the direction and velocity of the wind

☆**pilot biscuit** (or **bread**) same as HARDTACK

pilot engine a locomotive sent on in front to see that the line is clear

pilot film (or **tape**) a film (or videotape) of a single segment of a projected series of television shows, prepared for showing to prospective commercial sponsors

pilot fish 1. a narrow, spiny-finned fish (*Naucrates ductor*) with a widely forked tail, often seen swimming near sharks ☆**2.** a N. American whitefish (*Prosopium cylindraceum*), found in deep, cold, freshwater lakes from the Great Lakes to Alaska **3.** any of various fishes that seemingly act as pilots, as the remora

☆**pi·lot·house** (-hous′) *n.* an enclosed place on the upper deck of a ship, in which the helmsman stands while steering and from which the ship is usually conned

pi·lot·ing (-iŋ) *n.* the directing of a ship's movements near land, using landmarks, buoys, soundings, etc.

pilot lamp 1. an electric lamp which indicates the location of a switch or circuit breaker **2.** an electric lamp placed in an electric circuit to indicate when the current is on

pilot light 1. a small gas burner which is kept lighted to rekindle a principal burner when needed: also **pilot burner 2.** same as PILOT LAMP

pi·lous (pī′ləs) *adj.* same as PILOSE

Pil·sen (pil′z'n) Ger. name of PLZEŇ

Pil·sener, Pil·sner (pilz′nər, pils′-) *adj.* [after Pilsen (PLZEŇ), where first made] [*often* p-] designating a light, Bohemian lager beer, traditionally served in a tall, conical, footed glass (**Pilsener glass**)

Pilt·down man (pilt′doun′) a supposed species of prehistoric man whose existence was presumed on the basis of bone fragments found in Piltdown (Sussex, England) in 1911 and exposed as a hoax in 1953

pil·u·lar (pil′yoo lər) *adj.* of or like a pill or pills

pil·ule (pil′yool) *n.* [Fr. < L. *pilula:* see PILL¹] a small pill

☆**Pi·ma** (pē′mə) *n.* [< Sp. < a Piman word for "no," misunderstood and misapplied by missionaries] **1.** *pl.* **-mas**, **-ma** any member of a tribe of N. American Indians living in the Gila and Salt river valleys, Arizona **2.** their Uto-Aztecan language

☆**Pima cotton** [< *Pima* County, Ariz.] a tough, strong, smooth, long-staple cotton grown in the SW U.S.

☆**Pi·man** (pē′mən) *n.* a branch of the Uto-Aztecan family of languages —*adj.* **1.** of Piman **2.** of the Pimas

pi·men·to (pi men′tō) *n.*, *pl.* **-tos** [Sp. *pimiento* < L. *pigmentum*, lit., PIGMENT (in VL. & ML., plant juice, spiced drink, spice)] **1.** a sweet variety of the capsicum pepper, or its red, bell-shaped fruit, used as a relish, for stuffing olives, etc. **2.** same as ALLSPICE

pimento cheese a processed cheese containing pimentos

pi·mien·to (pi myen′tō, -men′-) *n.* same as PIMENTO

pimp (pimp) *n.* [prob. < or akin to MFr. *pimper*, to allure, dress smartly] a man who is an agent for a prostitute or prostitutes and lives off their earnings; procurer —*vi.* to act as a pimp

pim·per·nel (pim′pər nel′, -nəl) *n.* [ME. *pympernelle* < OFr. *piprenelle* < LL. *pimpinella*, an herb with medicinal uses, prob. altered < **piperinella*, ult. < *piper*, PEPPER: its fruit resembles small peppercorns] any of a genus (*Anagallis*) of plants of the primrose family, esp. the **scarlet pimpernel** (*Anagallis arvensis*), with red, white, or blue, starlike flowers which close in bad weather

pimp·ing (pim′piŋ) *adj.* [< dial., prob. akin to Du. *pimpel*, weak man, G. *pimpelig*, womanish] **1.** petty; mean **2.** sickly; puny

pim·ple (pim′p'l) *n.* [ME. *pinplis* (pl.), prob. < or akin to OE. *piplian*, to break out in pimples] any small, rounded, usually inflamed swelling of the skin; papule or pustule

pim·ply (pim′plē) *adj.* **-pli·er, -pli·est** having pimples: also **pim′pled** (-p'ld)

pin (pin) *n.* [ME. *pyn* < OE. *pinn*, akin to MHG. *pfinne*, a nail, prob. < IE. base **bend-*, a projecting point, whence MIr. *benn*, a peak] **1.** a peg of wood, metal, etc., used for fastening or holding things together, as a support on which to hang things, etc. **2.** a little piece of stiff wire with a pointed end and flattened or rounded head, for fastening things together **3.** something worthless or insignificant; trifle **4.** a pointed instrument for holding the hair, a hat, etc. in place **5.** *clipped form of* CLOTHESPIN, SAFETY PIN, COTTER PIN, etc. **6.** anything like a pin in form, use, etc. **7.** an ornament, badge, or emblem having a pin or clasp with which it is fastened to the clothing **8.** [Colloq.] the leg: *usually used in pl.* **9.** *Bowling* any of the bottle-shaped clubs of wood, or wood coated with plastic, at which the ball is rolled **10.** *Golf* a pole with a flag attached, placed in the hole of a green to mark its location **11.** *Med.* a metal rod used to hold a broken bone together **12.** *Music* any of the pegs for regulating the tension of the strings of a piano, harp, etc. **13.** *Naut. a*) same as THOLE¹ *b*) any of various pegs or bolts used in fastening the rigging —*vt.* **pinned, pin′ning 1.** to fasten with or as with a pin **2.** to pierce with a pin **3.** to hold firmly in one place or position ☆**4.** [Slang] to give one's fraternity pin to, as an informal token of betrothal —**pin down 1.** to get (someone) to commit himself as to his opinion, plans, etc. **2.** to determine or confirm (a fact, details, etc.); establish —☆**pin someone's ears back** [Colloq.] to beat, defeat, or scold someone soundly —**pin (something) on someone** [Colloq.] to lay the blame for (something) on someone

pi·na·ceous (pī nā′shəs) *adj.* [PIN(E)¹ + -ACEOUS] of the pine family of trees, including the pine, cedar, fir, etc.

pi·ña cloth (pēn′yə) [< Sp. *piña*, pineapple, orig., pine

cone < L. *pinea* < *pineus*, of pine < *pinus*, PINE[1] a fabric made of the fibers of pineapple leaves

pin·a·fore (pin'ə fôr') *n*. [PIN + AFORE] **1.** a sleeveless, apronlike garment worn by little girls over the dress **2.** a sleeveless housedress worn by women, as over a blouse

pi·nas·ter (pī nas'tər, pi-) *n*. [L., wild pine < *pinus*, PINE[1]] a Mediterranean pine (*Pinus pinaster*) with paired needles and prickly cones: also called **cluster pine**

‡**pi·ña·ta** (pē nyä'tä) *n*. [Sp., orig., a pot < It. *pignatta*, ult. < L. *pinea*, a pine cone < *pinus*, a pine tree] in Mexico, a clay or papier-mâché container of various forms and shapes, hung from the ceiling on certain festivals and broken in a game by children with a stick so as to release its contents of toys and candy

☆**pin·ball machine** (pin'bôl') a game machine with an inclined board that contains a number of pins, springs, holes, etc. and is variously marked with scores automatically recorded as the spring-driven ball released by the player makes various contacts on it

☆**pin boy** *Bowling* a boy or man who sets up the pins after each frame and returns the balls to the bowlers

pince-nez (pans'nā', pins'-; *Fr.* pans nā') *n*., *pl.* **pince-nez'** (-nāz'; *Fr.* -nā') [Fr. < *pincer*, to pinch + *nez*, nose] eyeglasses without temples, kept in place by a spring gripping the bridge of the nose

pin·cers (pin'sərz) *n.pl.* [*occas. with sing. v.*] [ME. *pinsours* < OFr. *pincier*, to pinch] **1.** a tool with two parts pivoted together to form two handles and two jaws, used in gripping or nipping things **2.** *Zool.* a grasping claw, as of a crab or lobster; chela —**pin'cer·like'** *adj*.

pincers movement a military maneuver in which simultaneous flank movements are used to converge upon an enemy force or stronghold and cut it off from support and supplies

PINCERS

pinch (pinch) *vt*. [ME. *pinchen* < ONormFr. **pincher* < OFr. *pincier*] **1.** to squeeze between a finger and the thumb or between two surfaces, edges, etc. **2.** to nip off the end of (a plant shoot), as for controlling bud development **3.** to press painfully upon (some part of the body) **4.** to cause distress or discomfort to **5.** to cause to become thin, cramped, etc., as by hunger, pain, cold, etc. **6.** to restrict closely; straiten; stint: usually in the passive voice **7.** [Slang] *a)* to steal *b)* to arrest **8.** *Naut.* to sail closehauled —*vi*. **1.** to squeeze painfully **2.** *a)* to be stingy or niggardly *b)* to be frugal with expenses; economize ☆**3.** *Mining* to become narrower; hence, to give (*out*): said of a vein of ore —*n*. **1.** a pinching; squeeze or nip **2.** the quantity that may be grasped between the finger and thumb; small amount **3.** distress; hardship; difficulty **4.** an emergency; urgent situation or time **5.** [Slang] *a)* a theft *b)* an arrest or police raid —**pinch pennies** to be very frugal or economical —*SYN.* see STEAL —**pinch'er** *n*.

pinch bar a kind of crowbar with a pointed, projecting end, used to roll heavy wheels, etc.

pinch·beck (pinch'bek') *n*. [after Christopher *Pinchbeck*, Eng. jeweler who invented it c. 1725] **1.** an alloy of copper and zinc used to imitate gold in cheap jewelry **2.** anything cheap or imitation —*adj*. **1.** made of pinchbeck **2.** cheap; imitation; spurious

pinch·cock (-käk') *n*. [PINCH + COCK[1]] a clamp on a flexible tube for controlling the flow of fluid through it

pinch effect *Physics* the constriction, or compression, of plasma by the action of the magnetic field of a strong electric current flowing through the plasma

pinch·ers (pin'chərz) *n.pl.* same as PINCERS

☆**pinch-hit** (pinch'hit') *vi.* -**hit'**, -**hit'ting** **1.** *Baseball* to bat in place of the batter whose turn it is, esp. when a hit is particularly needed **2.** to act as a substitute in an emergency (*for*) —**pinch hitter**

Pinck·ney (piŋk'nē), **Charles Cotes·worth** (kōts'wərth) 1746–1825; Am. statesman & diplomat

pin curl a strand of hair formed into a curl and held in place with a bobby pin while it sets

pin·cush·ion (pin'koosh'ən) *n*. a small cushion in which pins and needles are stuck to keep them handy

Pin·dar (pin'dər) 522?–438? B.C.; Gr. lyric poet

Pin·dar·ic (pin dar'ik) *adj*. [L. *Pindaricus* < Gr. *Pindarikos*] **1.** of, characteristic of, or in the style of, Pindar **2.** elaborate or regular in metrical structure **3.** designating an ode in which the strophe and antistrophe have the same form, in contrast to the epode, which has a different form —*n*. a Pindaric ode

pin·dling (pin'dlin) *adj*. [prob. var. of PIDDLING] ☆[Dial.] weak and undersized; puny

Pin·dus (pin'dəs) mountain range in C & NW Greece: highest peak, 8,650 ft.

pine[1] (pin) *n*. see PLURAL, II, D, 3 [ME. < OE. *pin* < L. *pinus*, pine tree < IE. **pitsnus* < base **pi-*, fat, whence L. *pix*, pitch, OE. *fǣted*, FAT] **1.** any of a genus (*Pinus*) of gymnospermous evergreen trees of the pine family, with

hard, woody cones and bundles of two to five needle-shaped leaves: many pines are valuable for their wood and their resin, from which turpentine, tar, etc. are obtained **2.** the wood of such a tree **3.** *clipped form of* PINEAPPLE —*adj*. designating a family (Pinaceae) of trees having needlelike leaves and, usually, woody cones and valuable wood, including the pines, larches, spruces, firs, hemlocks, etc.

pine[2] (pin) *vi*. **pined, pin'ing** [ME. *pinen* < OE. *pinian*, to torment < *pin*, pain < L. *poena*: see PENAL] **1.** to waste (*away*) through grief, pain, longing, etc. **2.** to have an intense longing or desire; yearn (with *for, after,* or an infinitive) —*vt*. [Archaic] to mourn for

pin·e·al (pin'ē əl) *adj*. [Fr. *pinéal* < L. *pinea*, a pine cone < *pinus*, PINE[1]] **1.** shaped like a pine cone **2.** of or pertaining to the pineal body

pineal body a small, reddish, cone-shaped body on the dorsal portion of the brain of all vertebrates: its function is obscure, though, in lampreys and in some lizards and salamanders, it is connected to a median eyelike structure on the dorsal surface of the head

pine·ap·ple (pin'ap''l) *n*. [ME. *pinappel*, pine cone (see PINE[1] & APPLE): mod. sense from shape of the fruit] **1.** a juicy, edible tropical plant somewhat resembling a pine cone: it consists of the fleshy inflorescence of a collective fruit developed from a spike of flowers **2.** the plant (*Ananas comosus*) of the pineapple family on which it grows, having a short stem and spiny-edged recurved leaves **3.** [Slang] a hand grenade shaped like a small pineapple —*adj*. designating a large family (Bromeliaceae) of tropical and subtropical, mostly epiphytic plants including the pineapple, Spanish moss, etc.

PINEAPPLE

Pine Bluff city in C Ark., on the Arkansas River: pop. 57,000

pine cone the cone of a pine tree: see CONE, illus.

☆**pine·drops** (-dräps') *n*., *pl.* -**drops'** a purplish-red, leafless plant (*Pterospora andromedea*) of the heath family, with white flowers: it is parasitic on the roots of pines

pi·nene (pi'nēn) *n*. [PINE[1] + -ENE] either of two isomeric terpenes, $C_{10}H_{16}$, occurring in oil of turpentine and other essential oils: used as a solvent, in synthetic resins, etc.

pine needle the needlelike leaf of a pine tree

pine nut ☆the sweet, edible seed of any of several pines found chiefly in the SW U.S. and in Mexico

Pi·ner·o (pi ner'ō, -nir'ō), **Sir Arthur Wing** 1855–1934; Eng. playwright

pin·er·y (pi'nər ē) *n*., *pl.* -**er·ies** [see PINE[1] + -ERY] ☆**1.** a forest of pine trees **2.** a pineapple plantation or hothouse

Pines, Isle of Cuban island south of W Cuba: c. 1,200 sq. mi.

☆**pine·sap** (pin'sap') *n*. any of a number of related whitish or reddish plants (genus *Monotropa*) of the heath family, including the Indian pipe, that live on dead vegetable material or as parasites on roots

☆**pine siskin** a small, brown finch (*Spinus pinus*) of N. America, with yellow markings on the wings and tail: also called **pine finch**

☆**pine snake** same as: **1.** BULL SNAKE (sense 1) **2.** FOX SNAKE

☆**pine straw** pine needles, esp. dried ones

pine tar a viscid, blackish-brown liquid prepared by the destructive distillation of pine wood and used in the preparation of expectorants, disinfectants, tar paints, roofing materials, etc.

pi·ne·tum (pi nēt'əm) *n*., *pl.* -**ne'ta** (-ə) [L. < *pinus*, PINE[1]] an arboretum of pine trees, etc.

☆**pine warbler** a variety of small, dull-green and brown or gray warbler (*Dendroica pinus*) living in the pine forests of the E U.S.

pin·ey (pi'nē) *adj*. **pin'i·er, pin'i·est** **1.** abounding in pines **2.** of or like pines; esp., having the odor of pines

pin·feath·er (pin'feth'ər) *n*. an undeveloped feather that is just emerging through the skin

☆**pin·fish** (-fish') *n*., *pl.* -**fish'**, -**fish'es**: see FISH[2] any of several fishes with sharp dorsal spines; esp., a small porgy (*Lagodon rhomboides*) found along the Atlantic coast of the U.S.

pin·fold (-fōld') *n*. [ME. *pynfold* < OE. *pundfald* < *pund*, POUND[3] + *fald*, FOLD[2]] a place where stray animals are confined; animal pound

ping (pin) *n*. [echoic] **1.** the sound made by a bullet striking something sharply **2.** any sound somewhat similar to this, as an engine knocking, a sonar echo, etc. —*vi., vt.* to make or cause to make such a sound

Ping-Pong (pin'pôn', -pän') [echoic reduplication] *a trademark for* table tennis equipment —*n.* [p- p-] same as TABLE TENNIS

pin·guid (pin'gwid) *adj*. [L. *pinguis*, fat + -*id*, as in TORPID] fat; oily; greasy —**pin·guid'i·ty** *n*.

pin·head (pin'hed') *n*. **1.** the head of a pin **2.** anything very small or trifling ☆**3.** a stupid or silly person

---

fat, āpe, cär; ten, ēven; is, bīte; gō, hôrn, to͞ol, look; oil, out; up, fur; get; joy; yet; chin; she; thin, *then*; zh, leisure; ŋ, ring; ə for *a* in *ago*, *e* in *agent*, *i* in *sanity*, *o* in *comply*, *u* in *focus*; ' as in *able* (ā'b'l); Fr. bāl; ë, Fr. coeur; ö, Fr. feu; Fr. mon; ö, Fr. coq; ü, Fr. duc; r, Fr. cri; H, G. ich; kh, G. doch. See inside front cover. ☆Americanism; ‡foreign; *hypothetical; < derived from

☆**pin·head·ed** (-id) *adj.* stupid or silly —**pin′head′ed·ness** *n.*

pin·hole (-hōl′) *n.* 1. a tiny hole made by or as by a pin 2. a hole into which a pin or peg goes

pin·ion[1] (pin′yən) *n.* [Fr. *pignon* < VL. *pinnio < L. *pinna*, bucket of a paddle wheel, lit., feather, var. of *penna* (see PEN[2]): associated in MFr. with *peigner*, to comb (see PEIGNOIR)] a small cogwheel the teeth of which fit into those of a larger gearwheel or those of a rack: see RACK, illus.

pin·ion[2] (pin′yən) *n.* [ME. *pynyon* < OFr. *pignon*, var. of *penon* < L. *pinna, penna*: see PEN[2]] 1. the end joint of a bird's wing 2. a wing 3. any wing feather 4. the anterior border of an insect's wing —*vt.* 1. to cut off or bind the pinions of (a bird) to keep it from flying 2. to bind (the wings) 3. to disable or impede by binding the arms of 4. to confine or shackle

Pi·niós (pēn yôs′) river in Thessaly, E Greece, flowing eastward to the Gulf of Salonika: 125 mi.

pin·ite (pin′īt, pī′nīt) *n.* [G. *pinit* < *Pini*, mine in Saxony] a hydrous silicate of aluminum and potassium, occurring as an amorphous mineral

pi·ni·tol (pī′ni tôl′, pin′i-; -tōl′) *n.* [< obs. *pinite*, pinitol < Fr. < *pin*, pine (< L. *pinus*) + *-ite*, -ITE[1] + *-ol*, -OL[2]] a sweet crystalline compound, $C_7H_{14}O_6$, occurring in the resin of the sugar pine

pink[1] (piŋk) *n.* [< ?] 1. any of a genus (*Dianthus*) of annual and perennial plants of the pink family with white, pink, or red flowers, often clove-scented 2. the flower 3. its pale-red color 4. the highest or finest example, degree, etc. [the *pink* of perfection] 5. [Colloq.] a person whose political or economic views are somewhat radical: a derogatory term 6. [Brit.] *a)* the scarlet worn by a fox hunter *b)* a fox hunter —*adj.* 1. designating a family (*Caryophyllaceae*) of widely distributed plants with bright-colored flowers, including the carnation, sweet william, etc. 2. pale-red 3. [Colloq.] somewhat radical —**in the pink** [Colloq.] in good physical condition; healthy; fit —**pink′ish** *adj.* —**pink′ness** *n.*

pink[2] (piŋk) *vt.* [ME. *pynken*, akin ? to OE. *pyngan*, to prick] 1. to ornament (cloth, paper, etc.) by making perforations in a pattern 2. to cut a saw-toothed edge on (cloth, etc.) so as to prevent unraveling or for decorative purposes 3. to prick or stab 4. to hurt or irritate, as by criticism 5. to adorn; embellish —**pink′er** *n.*

pink[3] (piŋk) *n.* [LME. *pynk* < MDu. *pinke*] a ship with a narrow stern

pink·en (piŋk′'n) *vi.* to become pink

Pink·er·ton (piŋk′ər t'n), **Allan** 1819–84; U.S. private detective, born in Scotland

pink·eye (piŋk′ī′) *n.* an acute, contagious form of conjunctivitis in which the eyeball and the lining of the eyelid become red and inflamed

pink gin a British cocktail made of gin and bitters

pink·ie[1] (piŋ′kē) *n.* [prob. < Du. *pinkje*, dim. of *pink*, little finger] the fifth, or smallest, finger

☆**pink·ie**[2] (piŋ′kē) *n. same as* PINK[3]

pink·ing shears shears with notched blades, used for pinking the edges of cloth, etc.

pink·o (piŋ′kō) *n., pl.* **-os** [Slang] *same as* PINK[1] (*n.* 5)

☆**pink·root** (piŋk′rōōt′, -root′) *n.* a plant (*Spigelia marilandica*) of the logania family, with tufted stems and red flowers with yellow throats, native to the SE U.S.

☆**pink salmon** a widespread species (*Onchorhynchus gorbuscha*) of salmon: see HUMPBACK (sense 4)

☆**pink slip** [from the sometime use of *pink* paper for the employee's carbon of the dismissal notice] [Colloq.] notice to an employee of termination of employment

☆**Pink·ster** (piŋk′stər) *n.* [Du., prob. via Goth. *paintēkuste* < Gr.(Ec.) *pentēkostē*: see PENTECOST] Whitsuntide: name formerly used in New Netherland

☆**pink·ster flower** (piŋk′stər) *same as* PINXTER FLOWER

☆**pink tea** [Colloq.] any frivolous social gathering, esp. one attended largely by women

pink·y[1] (piŋ′kē) *n., pl.* **pink′ies** *same as* PINKIE[1]

☆**pink·y**[2] (piŋ′kē) *n., pl.* **pink′ies** *same as* PINK[3]

pin money 1. orig., an allowance of money given to a wife for small personal expenses 2. any small sum of money, as for incidental minor expenses

pin·na (pin′ə) *n., pl.* **-nae** (-ē) **-nas** [L., a feather: see PEN[2]] 1. *Anat.* the external ear; auricle 2. *Bot.* a primary division of a pinnately compound leaf, esp. of a fern leaf 3. *Zool.* a feather, wing, fin, or similar structure —**pin′nal** *adj.*

pin·nace (pin′is) *n.* [Fr. *pinasse* < Sp. *pinaza* < VL. *pinacea < L. *pinus*, PINE[1]] 1. a small sailing ship formerly used as a tender, scout, etc. 2. a ship's boat

pin·na·cle (pin′ə k'l) *n.* [ME. *pinacle* < MFr. < LL.(Ec.) *pinnaculum*, dim. < L. *pinna*, pinnacle, wing: see PEN[2]] 1. a small turret or spire on a buttress or an angle pier 2. a slender, pointed formation, as at the top of some mountains; peak 3. the highest point; culmination; acme —*vt.* **-cled, -cling** 1. to set on a pinnacle 2. to furnish or ornament with pinnacles 3. to form the pinnacle of — SYN. see SUMMIT

pin·nate (pin′āt, -it) *adj.* [ModL. *pinnatus* < L. < *pinna*, a feather, fin: see PEN[2]] 1. resembling a feather 2. *Bot.* with leaflets on each side of a common axis in a featherlike arrangement: see LEAF, illus. —**pin′nate·ly** *adv.* —**pin·na′tion** *n.*

pin·nat·i- (pi nat′ə) [< ModL. *pinnatus*, PINNATE] a combining form meaning pinnately [*pinnatifid*]

pin·nat·i·fid (pi nat′ə fid) *adj.* [prec. + -FID] having leaves in a featherlike arrangement, with narrow lobes whose clefts extend more than halfway to the axis

pin·nat·i·sect (-sekt′) *adj.* [PINNATI- + -SECT] pinnatifid but with the clefts reaching to or almost to the axis

pin·ner (pin′ər) *n.* 1. a person or thing that pins 2. a cap-like headdress with a long, hanging flap pinned on either side, formerly worn by women

pin·ni·ped (pin′ə ped′) *adj.* [< ModL. *Pinnipedia*, name of the suborder < L. *pinnapes, pinnipes*, having winged feet < *pinna*, a feather, fin (see PEN[2]) + *pes*, FOOT] 1. having finlike feet or flippers 2. belonging to a suborder (Pinnipedia) of aquatic animals having flippers, including the seals and walruses —*n.* a pinniped animal Also **pin′ni·pe′di·an** (-pē′dē ən)

pin·nule (pin′yōōl) *n.* [ModL. *pinnula* < L., dim. of *pinna*, a wing, feather: see PEN[2]] 1. any of the smallest divisions of a leaf which is doubly compound, esp. in ferns 2. any of the lateral branches of the arm of a crinoid —**pin′nu·late′** (-yoo lāt′), **pin′nu·lat′ed** *adj.*

☆**pi·noch·le, pi·noc·le** (pē′nuk′'l, -näk′'l) *n.* [earlier *binochle* < G. dial. (Swiss) *binokel* < Fr. *binocle*, eyeglasses (<ModL. *binoculus*, binoculars: see BINOCULAR), taken as synonym for *bésigue*, BEZIQUE, wrongly identified with *besicles*, spectacles (prob. because the game is played with a double deck)] 1. a card game for two, three, or four persons, played with a deck of 48 cards, made up of two of every card above the eight, including the ace 2. the combination of the queen of spades and the jack of diamonds in this game

☆**pi·no·le** (pi nō′lē; *Sp.* pē nō′le) *n.* [AmSp. < Nahuatl *pinolli*] [Southwest] flour made of ground corn, mesquite beans, etc.

☆**pi·ñon** (pin′yən, -yōn; *Sp.* pē nyōn′) *n., pl.* **-ñons;** Sp. **-ño·nes** (-nyō′nes) [AmSp. *piñón* < Sp., pine nut < *piña*, pine cone < L. *pinea* < *pinus*, PINE[1]] 1. any of several small pines (as *Pinus cembroides, Pinus monophylla, Pinus parryana*, etc.) with large, edible seeds, widely distributed in W N. America 2. the seed

pin·point (pin′point′) *vt.* 1. to show the location of (a place on a map, etc.) by sticking in a pin 2. to locate, define, or focus on precisely —*n.* 1. the point of a pin 2. something trifling or insignificant —*adj.* minute, exact, precise, etc.

pin·prick (-prik′) *n.* 1. any tiny puncture made by or as by a pin 2. a minor irritation or annoyance

pins and needles a tingling and prickling feeling in some part of the body, esp. in a limb that has been numb —**on pins and needles** in a state of anxious suspense or nervous anticipation

☆**pin·set·ter** (-set′ər) *n.* 1. *same as* PIN BOY 2. a device that automatically sets up and spots bowling pins on the alley Also **pin′spot′ter** (-spät′ər)

Pinsk (pēnsk; *E.* pinsk) city in the W Byelorussian S.S.R.: pop. 39,000

pin stripe 1. a very narrow stripe, as in the fabric of some suits 2. a pattern of such stripes in parallel

pint (pint) *n.* [ME. *pynte* < MFr. *pinte* < ML. *pinta*, prob. < VL. *pincta, for L. *picta*, fem. pp. of *pingere*, to PAINT: orig. prob. a spot marking the level in a measure] 1. a measure of capacity (liquid or dry) equal to 1/2 quart 2. any container with a capacity of one pint Abbrev. **pt., p.**

pin·ta (pin′tə) *n.* [AmSp. < Sp., a spot < VL. *pincta: see prec.] a contagious skin disease of the tropics, characterized by patches of various colors and caused by a spirochete (*Treponema carateum*)

pin·ta·do (pin tä′dō) *n., pl.* **-dos, -does** [Port., painted, pp. of *pintar*, to paint < VL. *pinctare < *pinctus, for L. *pictus*, pp. of *pingere*, to PAINT] a long, silvery food and game fish (*Scomberomorus maculatus*) with orange spots and a widely forked tail: it is common in the waters off Florida and Cuba

pin·tail (pin′tāl′) *n., pl.* **-tails′, -tail′:** see PLURAL, II, D, 1 1. any of several ducks; esp., a species (*Anas acuta*) with a long neck, white belly, and long, pointed middle tail feathers ☆2. any variety of grouse with a long, pointed tail —**pin′tailed′** (-tāld′) *adj.*

pin·ta·no (pin tä′nō) *n., pl.* **-nos** [AmSp.] any of several brightly colored fishes (genus *Abudefduf*); esp., a small, striped fish (*Abudefduf saxatilis*) with bright green and black bands around its body, found near coral reefs

pin·tle (pin′t'l) *n.* [ME. *pintil*, penis < OE. *pintel*: for IE. base see PIN] a pin or bolt upon which some other part pivots or turns

☆**pin·to** (pin′tō) *adj.* [AmSp. < Sp., spotted < VL. *pinctus: see PINTADO] marked with patches of white and some other color; piebald or skewbald —*n., pl.* **-tos** 1. a pinto horse or pony 2. *same as* PINTO BEAN

☆**pinto bean** a kind of mottled kidney bean grown in the SW U.S. for food and fodder

PINTLE

PINTLE

Pintsch gas (pinch) [after R. *Pintsch* (1840–1919), G. inventor of the process] a gas obtained by the destructive distillation of petroleum, formerly used for lighting

pint-size (pīnt'sīz') *adj.* ☆small; tiny: also **pint'-sized'**

pin·up (pin'up') *adj.* **1.** that is or can be pinned up or otherwise fastened to a wall *[a pinup lamp]* ☆**2.** [Colloq.] designating a girl whose sexual attractiveness makes her a subject for the kind of pictures often pinned up on walls —*n.* [Colloq.] a pinup girl, picture, etc.

pin·wale (pin'wāl') *adj.* having a fine wale, as some corduroy

☆**pin·weed** (-wēd') *n.* any of a genus (*Lechea*) of perennial plants of the rockrose family, with thin stems and leaves, and small purplish or greenish flowers

pin·wheel (-hwēl', -wēl') *n.* **1.** a small wheel with variously colored vanes of paper, etc. pinned to a stick so as to revolve in the wind. **2.** a firework that revolves and throws off colored lights when set off

pin·worm (-wurm') *n.* a small nematode worm (*Enterobius vermicularis*) with an unsegmented body, sometimes found as a parasite in the human rectum and large intestine, esp. in children

pin wrench a type of wrench with a projecting polygonal pin that fits into a corresponding hole in a nut, etc. so as to secure a firm hold

‡**pinx·it** (piŋk'sit) [L.] he (or she) painted (it): placed, esp. formerly, after the artist's name on a painting: abbrev. **pinx.**

☆**pinx·ter flower** (piŋk'stər) [< PINKSTER + FLOWER] a variety of azalea (*Rhododendron nudiflorum*) with pink, sweet-smelling flowers, purplish-red at the base

pin·y (pī'nē) *adj.* **pin'i·er, pin'i·est** *same as* PINEY

Pin·zón (pēn thôn') **1. Mar·tín A·lon·so** (mär tēn' ä lôn'sô), 1440?–93; Sp. navigator with Columbus; commanded the *Pinta* **2. Vi·cen·te Yá·ñez** (vē then'te yä'nyeth), 1460?–1524?; Sp. navigator with Columbus; commanded the *Niña:* brother of *prec.*

pi·on (pī'än') *n.* [PI² + (MES)ON] any of three mesons that are positive, negative, or neutral, have a mass approximately 270 times that of an electron, and play an important role in the binding forces within the nucleus of an atom

pi·o·neer (pī'ə nir') *n.* [Fr. *pionnier* < OFr. *peonier,* foot soldier < *peon:* see PEON] **1.** orig., a member of a military engineer unit trained to construct or demolish bridges, roads, trenches, etc. ☆**2.** a person who goes before, preparing the way for others, as an early settler or a scientist doing exploratory work **3.** a plant, animal, etc. that starts a new cycle of life in a barren area —*adj.* **1.** being one of the first of its kind **2.** of or characteristic of the settlers of a new territory —*vi.* to be a pioneer —*vt.* **1.** to prepare or open (a way, etc.) ☆**2.** to be a pioneer in or of

pi·os·i·ty (pī äs'ə tē) *n.* the quality of being excessively or insincerely pious

pi·ous (pī'əs) *adj.* [L. *pius,* pious, devout, affectionate, good, prob. < IE. *pwiyos* < base *peu-,* to clean, whence L. *purus,* PURE] **1.** having or showing religious devotion; zealous in the performance of religious obligations **2.** springing from actual or pretended religious devotion or moral motives **3.** seemingly virtuous; affecting virtue hypocritically **4.** sacred, as distinguished from secular or profane **5.** [Archaic] having or showing a sense of duty and loyalty to parents, family, friends, etc. —*SYN.* see DEVOUT —**pi'ous·ly** *adv.* —**pi'ous·ness** *n.*

pip¹ (pip) *n.* [contr. < PIPPIN] **1.** a small seed, as of an apple, pear, orange, etc. **2.** [Old Slang] a person or thing much admired

pip² (pip) *n.* [earlier *peep* < ?] **1.** any of the figures or spots on playing cards, dominoes, dice, etc. **2.** a starlike shoulder insignia worn by certain officers in the British army **3.** any of the diamond-shaped divisions of the skin of a pineapple **4.** a single rootstock or flower of the lily of the valley, peony, etc. **5.** *same as* BLIP (sense 1)

pip³ (pip) *vi.* **pipped, pip'ping** [prob. var. of PEEP²] to peep or chirp, as a young bird —*vt.* to break through (the shell): said of a hatching bird

pip⁴ (pip) *n.* [ME. *pippe* < MDu. < WGmc. *pipit* < VL. *pipita,* for L. *pituita,* phlegm, pip: see PITUITARY] **1.** a contagious disease of fowl, characterized by the secretion of mucus in the throat and the formation of a scab on the tongue **2.** [Colloq.] any unspecified human ailment: a jocular usage

pip·age (pip'ij) *n.* **1.** transportation, as of water, gas, oil, etc., by pipes **2.** the charge for such transportation **3.** a system of such pipes

pi·pal (pē'pəl) *n.* [Hind. *pīpal* < Sans. *pippala*] an Indian fig tree (*Ficus religiosa*): see BO TREE

pipe (pīp) *n.* [ME. < OE. < WGmc. *pipa* < VL. *pipa* < L. *pipare,* to cheep, chirp, peep, of echoic orig.] **1.** a cylindrical tube, as of reed, straw, wood, or metal, into which air is blown as by the mouth for making musical sounds by the vibration of an air column; specif., [*pl.*] *same as: a)* PANPIPE *b)* BAGPIPE **2.** any of the tubes in an organ that produce the tones **3.** a boatswain's whistle used to signal the ship's crew **4.** a high, shrill sound, as of a voice, birdcall, etc. **5.** [*often pl.*] the vocal organs, esp. as used in singing **6.** a long tube of clay, concrete, metal, wood, etc., for conveying water, gas, oil, etc. or for use in construction **7.** a tubular organ or canal of the body; esp.,

[*pl.*] the respiratory organs **8.** *a)* a somewhat cylindrical deposit of ore *b)* an opening into a volcano's crater **9.** anything tubular in form **10.** *a)* a tube with a small bowl at one end, in which tobacco, etc. is smoked *b)* enough tobacco, etc. to fill such a bowl **11.** *a)* a large cask for wine, oil, etc., having a capacity of about two hogsheads, or 126 gallons *b)* this volume as a unit of measure *c)* such a cask with its contents ☆**12.** [Slang] something regarded as easy to accomplish —*vi.* **piped, pip'ing 1.** to play on a pipe **2.** to utter shrill, reedy sounds or tones **3.** *Metallurgy* to develop longitudinal cavities, as steel sometimes does in ingots and castings during solidification **4.** *Naut.* to signal a ship's crew by sounding the boatswain's pipe —*vt.* **1.** to play (a tune, etc.) on a pipe **2.** to utter in a shrill, reedy voice or tone **3.** to affect or bring to some place or condition by or as by playing pipes *[to pipe the clan to battle]* ☆**4.** to convey (water, gas, oil, etc.) by means of pipes ☆**5.** to provide with pipes **6.** to trim (a dress, etc.) with piping **7.** [Slang] to look at or notice **8.** *Naut.* to call together (the crew) or signal the arrival aboard or the departure of (someone) by sounding the boatswain's pipe —**pipe down** ☆[Slang] to become quiet or quieter; stop shouting, talking, etc. —**pipe in** to convey (esp. transcribed or remote music or speech) by an electric or electronic system —**pipe up 1.** to begin to play or sing (music) **2.** to speak up or say, esp. in a piping voice

pipe-clay (pip'klā') *vt.* to whiten with pipe clay

pipe clay a white, plastic clay used for making clay tobacco pipes or pottery, for whitening leather, etc.

pipe cleaner a short length of thin wires twisted so as to hold tiny tufts of yarn and used to clean the stem of a tobacco pipe, etc.

pipe cutter a tool for cutting steel or iron pipes, with a curved jaw containing one or more sharp disks, the whole tool being rotated around the pipe

☆**pipe dream** [Colloq.] a fantastic idea, vain hope or plan, etc., such as an opium smoker might have

pipe·fish (-fish') *n., pl.* **-fish', -fish'es:** see FISH² any of a number of related long, narrow, bony-scaled fishes (family Syngnathidae), with a tubelike snout, related to the sea horses

pipe fitter a mechanic who specializes in the installation and maintenance of plumbing pipes, etc.

pipe fitting 1. a coupling, elbow, etc. used to connect sections of pipe **2.** the work of a pipe fitter

pipe·ful (-fool') *n., pl.* **-fuls'** the amount (of tobacco, etc.) put in a pipe at one time

☆**pipe·line** (-līn') *n.* **1.** a line of pipes for conveying water, gas, oil, etc. **2.** any channel or means whereby something is conveyed *[a pipeline of information]* —*vt.* **-lined', -lin'ing 1.** to convey by a pipeline **2.** to supply with a pipeline

☆**pipe of peace** *same as* PEACE PIPE

☆**pipe organ** *same as* ORGAN (sense 1 *a*)

pip·er (-ər) *n.* [ME. *pipere* < OE.] a person who plays on a pipe; esp., a bagpiper —**pay the piper** to pay for one's pleasures or undertakings; bear the consequences of one's actions

pi·per·a·zine (pi per'ə zēn', pī-, pip'ər'-; -zin) *n.* [PIPER(INE) + AZ- + -INE⁴] a crystalline compound, $(C_2H_4NH)_2$, used in treating worm infestations, in insecticides, etc.

pi·per·i·dine (-dēn', -din) *n.* [< PIPER(INE) + -IDE + -INE⁴] a colorless, liquid hydrocarbon, $(CH_2)_5NH$, found in many alkaloids and obtained by reducing pyridine or by treating piperine with alkali: used in making rubber, oils, fuels, etc.

pip·er·ine (pip'ə rēn', -ər in) *n.* [L. *piper,* PEPPER + -INE⁴] a colorless, crystalline alkaloid, $C_{17}H_{19}O_3N$, found in pepper

pi·per·o·nal (pi per'ə nal', pī-, pip'ər-) *n.* [G. < *piperin,* piperine (see prec.) + *-on,* -ONE + *-al,* -AL] an aldehyde, $C_8H_6O_3$, obtained from piperine and having a strong smell like that of heliotrope: used in making perfume

pipe·stem (pip'stem') *n.* **1.** the stem of a tobacco pipe through which the smoke is drawn **2.** anything like this in form, as a very thin leg

☆**pipe·stone** (-stōn') *n.* a hard, reddish, claylike stone used by the American Indians to make tobacco pipes

pi·pette, pi·pet (pī pet', pi-) *n.* [Fr., dim. of *pipe,* pipe < VL. *pipa:* see PIPE] a slender pipe or tube into which small amounts of liquids are taken up by suction, as for measuring or transferring —*vt.* **-pet'ted, -pet'ting** to remove, transfer, or measure (liquid) by means of a pipette

pip·ing (pip'in) *n.* **1.** the act of a person who pipes **2.** the music made by pipes **3.** a shrill voice or sound **4.** a system of pipes **5.** material that resembles or can be used for pipes **6.** a pipelike fold of material with which edges or seams are trimmed **7.** *Cooking* ornamental, pipelike lines of icing, as on a cake —*adj.* **1.** playing on a pipe **2.** characterized by the music of the "peaceful" pipe rather than of the "warlike" drums, trumpets, etc.; hence, peaceful or tranquil **3.** sounding high and shrill —**piping hot** so hot as to hiss or sizzle; very hot

pip·is·trelle, pip·is·trel (pip'i strel', pip'i strel') *n.* [Fr. *pipistrelle* < It. *pipistrello,* altered < OIt. *vipistrello* < L.

vespertilio, bat < *vesper*, evening: see VESPER] any of a genus (*Pipistrellus*) of small bats that characteristically fly early in the evening: found in N. America and in most of the Eastern Hemisphere

pip·it (pip′it) *n.* [echoic of its cry] either of two small, N. American singing birds (genus *Anthus*) with a slender bill, streaked breast, and the habit of constantly moving the tail

pip·kin (pip′kin) *n.* [? dim. of PIPE, 11] 1. a small earthen-ware pot 2. *dial. var.* of PIGGIN

pip·pin (pip′in) *n.* [ME. *pipyn* < OFr. *pepin*, seed, pip] 1. any of a number of varieties of apple, esp. those valued as dessert 2. [Brit. Dial.] a small pip, or seed 3. [Old Slang] a person or thing much admired

☆**pip·sis·se·wa** (pip sis′ə wə) *n.* [< AmInd. (Algonquian), as in Cree *pipisisikweu*, lit., breaks it (i.e., gallstone) into fragments] any of a genus (*Chimaphila*) of N.American evergreen plants of the heath family, with pink or white flowers and jagged, leathery leaves formerly used as a diuretic and tonic

pip·squeak (pip′skwēk′) *n.* [PIP³ + SQUEAK] [Colloq.] any-thing or anyone regarded as small or insignificant

pip·y (pī′pē) *adj.* pip′i·er, pip′i·est 1. pipelike; tubular 2. sounding like a pipe; shrill —**pip′i·ness** *n.*

pi·quant (pē′kənt, -känt; *now occas.* -kwənt) *adj.* [Fr., prp. of *piquer*, to prick, sting: see PIKE²] 1. agreeably pungent or stimulating to the taste; pleasantly sharp or biting 2. exciting agreeable interest or curiosity; stimu-lating; provocative 3. [Archaic] piercing or stinging; bitter —SYN. see PUNGENT —**pi′quan·cy** (-kən sē), **pi′quant-ness** *n.* --**pi′quant·ly** *adv.*

pique¹ (pēk) *n.* [Fr. < *piquer*: see prec.] 1. resentment at being slighted or disdained; ruffled pride 2. a fit of dis-pleasure —*vt.* **piqued**, **piqu′ing** [Fr. *piquer*] 1. to arouse resentment in, as by slighting; offend; ruffle the pride of 2. to excite; arouse; provoke —SYN. see OFFENSE, PRO-VOKE —**pique oneself on** (or **upon**) [Archaic] to be proud of

pi·qué, pi·que² (pē kā′) *n.* [Fr., pp. of *piquer*, to prick: see PIKE²] a firmly woven cotton fabric with ribbed, corded, or ridged wales —*adj.* designating fine seams that have been turned under before sewing, as on women's gloves

pi·quet (pi ket′, -kā′) *n.* [Fr. < *pic*, term in piquet, orig., prick, sting < *piquer*: see PIKE²] a game of cards for two persons, played with 32 cards

pi·ra·cy (pī′rə sē) *n., pl.* **-cies** [ML. *piratia* < Gr. *peirateia* < *peiratēs*, PIRATE] 1. robbery of ships on the high seas 2. the unauthorized publication or use of a copyrighted or patented work

Pi·rae·us (pī rē′əs) seaport in SE Greece, on the Saronic Gulf: part of Athens metropolitan area: pop. 184,000: ModGr. name **Pei·rai·évs** (pē′re efs′)

pi·ra·gua (pi räg′wə, -rag′wə) *n.* [Sp.: see PIROGUE] 1. *Sp. name for* PIROGUE (sense 1) 2. a flat-bottomed, two-masted sailing boat

Pi·ran·del·lo (pir′ən del′ō; *It.* pē′rän del′lô), **Lu·i·gi** (lōō ē′jē) 1867–1936; It. playwright & novelist

pi·ra·nha (pi rän′yə, -ran′-) *n.* [Braz. Port. < Tupi *piranha*, toothed fish < *piro*, a fish + *sainha*, a tooth] any of several small, voracious, freshwater, S. American fishes that in schools attack any animal, including man; esp., any of a genus (*Serrasalmus*) with strong jaws and very sharp teeth

pi·ra·ru·cu (pi rär′oo kōō′) *n.* [Port. < Tupi *pirá-rucú*, lit., red fish] *same as* ARAPAIMA

pi·rate (pī′rət) *n.* [ME. < L. *pirata* < Gr. *peiratēs* < *peirān*, to attempt, attack < IE. base *per-*, to bring through, penetrate, whence FARE] 1. a person who practices piracy; esp., a robber of ships on the high seas 2. a ship used by pirates in attacking other vessels —*vt., vi.* **-rat·ed, -rat·ing** 1. to practice piracy (upon) 2. to take (something) by piracy 3. to publish or reproduce without authorization (a literary work, musical recording, etc.), esp. in violation of a copyright —**pi·rat·i·cal** (pī rat′i k'l), **pi·rat′i·cal·ly** *adv.*

pirn (pʉrn, pirn) *n.* [ME. *pyrne*, by metathesis < ? dial. *prin*, a pin, pointed twig] [Scot.] 1. the bobbin or spool of a weaver's shuttle 2. a fishing reel

pi·ro·gen (pi rō′gən) *n.pl.* [Yid. < Russ. *pirogi*] *same as* PIROGI

pi·ro·gi (pi rō′gē) *n.pl.* [Russ. *pirogi*, pl. of *pirog*, pie] small pastry turnovers with a filling, as of meat, cheese, mashed potatoes, etc.: also **pi·rosh′ki** (-räsh′kē)

pi·rogue (pi rōg′) *n.* [Fr. < Sp. *piragua* < the WInd. (Carib) name] 1. a canoe made by hollowing out a large log 2. any canoe-shaped boat

pir·ou·ette (pir′oo wet′) *n.* [Fr., spinning top; prob. < dial. *piroue*, a top, prob. < VL. *piro*, a plug, peg < Gr. *peiron*, a peg] a whirling around on one foot or the point of the toe, esp. in ballet —*vi.* **-et′ted, -et′ting** [Fr. *pirouetter* < the *n.*] to do a pirouette

Pi·sa (pē′zə; *It.* pē′sä) commune in Tuscany, W Italy, on the Arno River: famous for its Leaning Tower: pop. 100,000 —**Pi′san** (-zən) *adj., n.*

‡**pis-al·ler** (pē zà lā′) [Fr., lit., to go worse] last resort; last expedient

Pi·sa·no (pē sä′nô), **Ni·co·la** (nē kô′lä) 1220?–78?; It. sculptor & architect

pis·ca·ry (pis′kə rē) *n., pl.* **-ries** [ML. *piscaria* < L. *pis-carius*, of fish, of fishing < *piscis*, FISH²] 1. *Law* the right

of fishing in waters owned by another: now only in **common of piscary** 2. a place for fishing

pis·ca·tol·o·gy (pis′kə täl′ə jē) *n.* [< L. *piscatus*, pp. of *piscari*, to fish (< *piscis*, FISH²) + -LOGY] [Rare] the art or science of fishing

Pis·ca·tor (pis kä′tôr), **Erwin** 1893– ; Ger. theatrical director & producer, in the U.S. (1939–58)

pis·ca·to·ri·al (pis′kə tôr′ē əl) *adj.* [L. *piscatorius* < *piscator*, fisherman < *piscatus*: see PISCATOLOGY] of fishes, fishermen, or fishing: also **pis′ca·to′ry** —**pis′ca·to′ri·al·ly** *adv.*

Pis·ces (pī′sēz, pis′ēz) [ME. < L., pl. of *piscis*, FISH²] 1. a constellation south of Andromeda 2. the twelfth sign of the zodiac (✶), entered by the sun about February 21: see ZODIAC, illus. —*n.* the superclass of vertebrates that includes all the classes of fishes

pis·ci- (pis′i, pī′si) [< L. *piscis*, FISH²] *a combining form meaning* fish [*piscivorous*]

pis·ci·cul·ture (pis′i kul′chər) *n.* [prec. + CULTURE] the breeding and rearing of fish as a science or industry

pis·ci·na (pi sī′nə, -sē′-, -shē′-) *n.* [L., a tank, cistern, orig., fishpond < *piscis*, FISH²] a basin with a drain, formerly near the altar, now usually in the sacristy, for the disposal of holy water, etc.; sacrarium

pis·cine (pis′īn, -ēn, -in; pī′sēn) *adj.* [ModL. *piscinus* < L. *piscis*, FISH²] of or resembling fish

Pis·cis Aus·tri·nus (pī′sis ôs trī′nəs, pis′is) a S constella-tion west of Sculptor and containing Fomalhaut: also **Piscis Aus·tra·lis** (ôs trā′lis)

pis·civ·o·rous (pi siv′ər əs, pī-) *adj.* [PISCI- + -VOROUS] fish-eating

pis·co (pis′kō) *n.* [after *Pisco*, town in Peru] a brandy made in Peru

Pis·gah (piz′gə) [Heb. *pisgāh*, lit., prob., cleft] *Bible* mountain ridge east of the N end of the Dead Sea: Deut. 3:27: see NEBO

pish (psh, pish) *interj., n.* an exclamation of disgust or impatience —*vi., vt.* to make this exclamation (at)

Pi·sid·i·a (pi sid′ē ə) ancient country, later a Roman province, in SC Asia Minor, south of Phrygia

pi·si·form (pī′sə fôrm′) *adj.* [< L. *pisum*, PEA + -FORM] resembling a pea in shape and size —*n.* a small bone on the inner side of the wrist that resembles half a pea

Pi·sis·tra·tus (pī sis′trə təs, pi-) 600?–527 B.C.; tyrant of Athens (variously from 560 to 527)

pis·mire (pis′mīr′, piz′-) *n.* [ME. *pissemire* < *pisse*, urine + *mire*, ant (< Scand., as in Dan. *myre*, Sw. *myra* < IE. base *morwi-*, ANT, whence L. *formica*): from the odor of formic acid, discharged by ants] an ant

☆**pis·mo clam** (piz′mō) [after *Pismo* Beach, Calif.] a heavy-shelled, edible clam (*Tivela stultorum*) found on sandy beaches along the coast of California and Mexico

pi·so·lite (pī′sə līt′) *n.* [< Gr. *pison*, a pea + -LITE] 1. a small, pealike body more than 2 mm. in diameter, common-ly composed of calcium carbonate 2. a sedimentary rock, as limestone, containing many such bodies —**pi′so·lit′ic** (-lit′ik) *adj.*

piss (pis) *vi.* [ME. *pissen* < OFr. *pissier*, prob. of echoic origin] to urinate —*vt.* to discharge as or with the urine —*n.* urine Now vulgar in all uses

Pis·sar·ro (pē sà rō′; *E.* pi sär′ō), **Ca·mille** (kà mē′y′) 1830–1903; Fr. painter, born in the Virgin Islands

‡**pis·soir** (pē swàr′) *n.* [Fr. < MFr. < *pisser*, to urinate < OFr. *pissier*: see PISS] a public urinal for men, of a kind formerly common on streets of Paris

pis·ta·chi·o (pi stä′shē ō′, -stash′ē ō′, -stash′ō) *n., pl.* **-chi·os′** [It. *pistacchio* < L. *pistacium* < Gr. *pistakion* < *pistakē*, pistachio tree < OPer. *pistah*] 1. a small tree (*Pistacia vera*) of the cashew family 2. its edible, greenish seed (**pistachio nut**) 3. the flavor of this nut 4. a light yellow-green color

☆**pis·ta·reen** (pis′tə rēn′) *n.* [prob. orig. < dim. of PESETA] a former Spanish silver coin of the American colonies and the West Indies —*adj.* [Obs.] petty; trifling

‡**piste** (pēst) *n.* [Fr. < It. *pista* < *pistare*, to beat: see PISTON] a ski run of hard-packed snow

pis·til (pis′t'l) *n.* [Fr. < L. *pistillum*, PESTLE] the seed-bearing organ of a flowering plant, con-sisting of one carpel or of several united carpels

pis·til·late (pis′tə lit, -lāt′) *adj. Bot.* having a pistil or pistils; specif., having pistils but no stamens

Pis·to·ia (pē stô′yä) commune in Tus-cany, W Italy: pop. 82,000

pis·tol (pis′t'l) *n.* [Fr. *pistole* < G. < Czech *píšt'al*, a pistol, orig., pipe, prob. < *písk*, echoic word for a whistling sound] 1. a small firearm made to be held and fired with one hand 2. such a firearm in which the chamber is part of the barrel: distinguished from REVOLVER —*vt.* **-toled** or **-tolled**, **-tol·ing** or **-tol·ling** to shoot with a pistol

pis·tole (pis tōl′) *n.* [Fr., earlier *pistolet*, dim. of *pistole* (see prec.): so named in Fr. after a debasement of the coin, in punning allusion to a double use of the original name of the coin, *écu*, which also meant "shield"] 1. a former Spanish gold coin 2. any of various similar obsolete gold coins of Europe

PISTIL

pis·to·leer, pis·to·lier (pis′tə lir′) *n.* [Fr. *pistolier*] formerly, a soldier armed with a pistol

☆**pis·tol-whip** (-hwip′, -wip′) *vt.* **-whipped′, -whip′ping** to beat with a pistol, esp. about the head

pis·ton (pis′t'n) *n.* [Fr. < It. *pistone* < *pistare*, to pound, crush < LL., freq. of L. *pinsere*, to pound, beat: see PESTLE] **1.** a disk or short cylinder closely fitted in a hollow cylinder and moved back and forth by the pressure of a fluid so as to transmit reciprocating motion to the piston rod attached to it, or moved by the rod so as to exert pressure on the fluid **2.** *Music* a sliding valve moved in the cylinder of a brass-wind instrument to change the pitch

Pis·ton (pis′t'n), **Walter** 1894– ; U.S. composer

piston ring a split, expansible metal ring placed around a piston to make it fit the cylinder closely and thus prevent the fluid from escaping

piston rod a rod which moves, or is moved by, the piston to which it is attached

☆**pit**[1] (pit) *n.* [Du. < MDu. *pitte*, akin to PITH] the hard stone, as of the plum, peach, cherry, etc., which contains the seed —*vt.* **pit′ted, pit′ting** to remove the pit from

pit[2] (pit) *n.* [ME. < OE. *pytt* < early WGmc. & NGmc. *puttia* (whence ON. *pyttr*, G. *pfütze*) < L. *puteus*, a well, prob. < IE. base *peu-*, to chop, cut, whence L. *pavire*, to beat, strike] **1.** a hole or cavity in the ground **2.** an abyss **3.** hell: used with *the* **4.** a covered hole used to trap wild animals; pitfall **5.** any concealed danger; trap; snare **6.** an enclosed area in which animals are kept or made to fight [a bear *pit*] **7.** *a)* the shaft of a coal mine *b)* the coal mine itself **8.** a hollow or depression on a part of the human body [armpit] **9.** a small hollow in a surface; specif., a depressed scar on the skin, as that resulting from smallpox **10.** an area below floor level or ground level **11.** [Brit.] *a)* the ground floor of a theater, esp. the part at the rear *b)* the spectators in that section **12.** the section, often below floor level, in front of the stage, where the orchestra sits ☆**13.** the part of the floor of an exchange where a special branch of business is transacted [corn *pit*] ☆**14.** *a)* an area in a garage, often below floor level, for repairing and servicing automobiles *b)* an area off the side of a speedway for servicing racing cars **15.** *Bot.* a tiny depression in a plant cell wall —*vt.* **pit′ted, pit′ting 1.** to put, cast, or store in a pit **2.** to make pits in **3.** to mark with small scars [*pitted* by smallpox] **4.** to set (cocks, etc.) in a pit to fight **5.** to set in competition (*against*) —*vi.* to become marked with pits

pi·ta (pēt′ə) *n.* [Sp. < Quechua *pita*, fine thread] **1.** any of a number of related agave plants yielding a fiber used in paper, cord, etc. **2.** the fiber

pit·a·pat (pit′ə pat′) *adv.* [redupl. of PAT[2]] with rapid and strong beating; palpitatingly —*n.* a rapid succession of beats or taps —*vi.* **-pat′ted, -pat′ting** to go pitapat; palpitate

Pit·cairn Island (pit′kern) Brit. island in Polynesia, South Pacific: settled by mutineers of the Brit. ship *Bounty* in 1790: 1-3/4 sq. mi.; pop. 86

pitch[1] (pich) *n.* [ME. *pich* < OE. *pic* < L. *pix* (gen. *picis*) < IE. base *pi-*, to be fat, whence FAT] **1.** a black, sticky substance formed in the distillation of coal tar, wood tar, petroleum, etc. and used for waterproofing, roofing, pavements, etc. **2.** any of certain bitumens, as asphalt, asphaltite, etc. **3.** a resin found in certain evergreen trees **4.** any of various synthetic substances having pitchlike properties —*vt.* to cover or smear with or as with pitch

pitch[2] (pich) *vt.* [ME. *picchen*, ? form of *picken*, to PICK[2]] **1.** to set up; erect [*pitch* a tent] **2.** to throw; cast, fling, or toss **3.** to toss (coins, quoits, etc.) as at a mark in a contest **4.** to set in order for battle: obsolete except in PITCHED BATTLE **5.** to fix or set at a particular point, level, degree, etc. ☆**6.** *Baseball a)* to throw (the ball) to the batter *b)* to assign (a player) to pitch *c)* to serve as pitcher for (a game) **7.** *Golf* to loft (a ball), esp. in making an approach **8.** *Music* to determine or set the key of (a tune, an instrument, or the voice) —*vi.* **1.** to encamp **2.** to take up one's position; settle **3.** to hurl or toss anything, as hay, a baseball, etc. **4.** to fall or plunge headlong **5.** to incline downward; dip **6.** to plunge or toss with the bow and stern rising and falling: said of a ship **7.** to move in a like manner in the air: said of an aircraft **8.** to plunge forward; lurch, as when off balance **9.** to act as pitcher in a ball game **10.** to loft a golf ball, as in making an approach —*n.* **1.** act or manner of pitching **2.** a throw; fling; toss **3.** *a)* the rising and falling of the bow and stern of a ship in a rough sea *b)* the movement up or down of the nose and tail of an airplane **4.** anything pitched **5.** the amount pitched **6.** a point or degree [emotion was at a high *pitch*] **7.** the degree of slope or inclination ☆**8.** a card game in which the suit of the first card led becomes trump ☆**9.** [Slang] a line of talk, such as a salesman uses to persuade customers **10.** [Chiefly Brit.] a place where a street hawker or carnival hawker sets up his stand **11.** *Aeron. a)* the

blade angle of the propeller or rotor blade *b)* the distance advanced by a propeller in one revolution **12.** *Archit.* the slope by the sides of a roof, expressed by the ratio of its height to its span **13.** *Geol., Mining* the dip of a stratum or vein **14.** *Golf* a short, lofted shot, usually to the green **15.** *Machinery a)* the distance between corresponding points on two adjacent gear teeth *b)* the distance between corresponding points on two adjacent threads of a screw, measured along the axis **16.** *Music, Acoustics a)* that quality of a tone or sound determined by the frequency of vibration of the sound waves reaching the ear: the greater the frequency, the higher the pitch *b)* a standard of pitch for tuning instruments: see CONCERT PITCH — SYN. see THROW —☆**in there pitching** [Colloq.] working hard and enthusiastically —☆**make a pitch for** [Slang] to speak in favor or promotion of —**pitch in** [Colloq.] **1.** to set to work energetically **2.** to make a contribution — **pitch into** [Colloq.] to attack physically or verbally — **pitch on** (or **upon**) to select; decide on

pitch-black (pich′blak′) *adj.* very black

pitch·blende (-blend′) *n.* [G. *pechblende* < *pech* (< L. *pix*), PITCH[1] + *blende*, BLENDE] a brown to black lustrous mineral, the massive variety of uraninite

pitch circle a circle touching the teeth of a gearwheel at points where they mesh with the teeth of another gearwheel

pitch-dark (-därk′) *adj.* very dark

pitched battle (picht) **1.** a battle in which placement of troops and the line of combat are relatively fixed before the action **2.** a closely fought battle of great intensity

pitch·er[1] (pich′ər) *n.* [ME. *picher* < OFr. *pichier* < VL. *piccarium*, var. of *bicarium*, a jug, cup: see BEAKER] **1.** *a)* a container, usually with a handle and lip, for holding and pouring liquids *b)* as much as a pitcher will hold: also **pitch′er·ful′** (-fool′) **2.** *Bot.* same as ASCIDIUM; esp., a pitcherlike leaf that traps insects

pitch·er[2] (pich′ər) *n.* [PITCH[2] + -ER] a person who pitches; specif., *Baseball* the player who pitches the ball to the opposing batters

pitcher plant any of a number of plants with pitcherlike leaves which attract and trap insects, that become decomposed and are absorbed as nutrients by the plant cells; esp., any of a genus (*Sarracenia*) of such N. American plants usually growing in bogs and swamps

pitch·fork (pich′fôrk′) *n.* a large, long-handled fork used for lifting and tossing hay, straw, etc. —*vt.* to lift and toss with or as with a pitchfork

☆**pitch·man** (pich′mən) *n.*, *pl.* **-men** (-mən) **1.** a person who hawks novelties, jewelry, etc. from a stand on a city street or at a carnival, etc. **2.** [Slang] any high-pressure salesman or advertiser, as on radio

☆**pitch·out** (-out′) *n.* **1.** *Baseball* a ball pitched deliberately away from the plate in anticipation of a play by the catcher to throw out a runner who has moved away from the base **2.** *Football* a lateral pass behind the line of scrimmage, usually from the quarterback to another back

PITCHER PLANT

☆**pitch pine** any of several resinous pines from which pitch or turpentine is obtained; esp., a pine (*Pinus rigida*) of the E U.S.

pitch pipe a small metal pipe which produces a fixed tone used as a standard in tuning an instrument or establishing the pitch for singers

pitch·stone (pich′stōn′) *n.* [transl. of G. *pechstein* < *pech* (< L. *pix*), PITCH[1] + *stein*, STONE] a lustrous volcanic rock with a pitchy appearance

pitch·y (-ē) *adj.* **pitch′i·er, pitch′i·est 1.** full of pitch; smeared with pitch **2.** resembling pitch in consistency or stickiness **3.** black; very dark —**pitch′i·ness** *n.*

pit·e·ous (pit′ē əs) *adj.* [ME. *piteus* < MFr. < OFr. *pitous* < LL.(Ec.) *pietosus* < *pietas:* see PIETY] **1.** arousing or deserving pity or compassion **2.** [Archaic] having or showing pity; compassionate —*SYN.* see PITIFUL —**pit′e·ous·ly** *adv.* —**pit′e·ous·ness** *n.*

pit·fall (pit′fôl′) *n.* [ME. *pitfalle* < *pit*, PIT[2] + *falle*, a trap < OE. *fealle* < *feallan*, to FALL] **1.** a lightly covered pit used as a trap for animals **2.** an unsuspected difficulty, danger, or error that one may fall into —*SYN.* see TRAP

pith (pith) *n.* [ME. *pithe* < OE. *pitha*, akin to MDu. *pitte*, pit of a fruit, kernel, pith of a tree] **1.** the soft, spongy tissue in the center of certain plant stems **2.** the soft core of various other things, as of a bone, feather, etc. **3.** the spongy, fibrous tissue lining the rind and surrounding the sections of an orange, grapefruit, etc. **4.** the essential part; substance; gist **5.** importance: now usually in the phr. **of great pith and moment 6.** [Archaic] strength; vigor; force —*vt.* **1.** to remove the pith from (a plant stem) **2.** to pierce or sever the spinal cord of (an animal) in order to kill it or make it insensible for experimental purposes

pith·e·can·thro·pine (pith′ə kan′thrə pīn′) *adj.* [see ff. & -INE[1]] of, belonging to, or resembling a genus (*Pithecanthropus*, now often classified in *Homo*) of extinct

early men, including Java and Peking man: also **pith´e-can´thro·poid´** (-poid´) —*n.* a pithecanthropine man

Pith·e·can·thro·pus e·rec·tus (pith´ə kan´thrə pəs i rek´təs, -kan thrō´pəs) [ModL. < Gr. *pithēkos*, ape (< IE. **bhidh-*, dreadful, var. of base **bhōi-*, to be afraid, whence L. *foedus*, ugly) + *anthrōpos*, man (see ANTHROPO-)] *an earlier name for* JAVA MAN

pith·y (pith´ē) *adj.* **pith´i·er**, **pith´i·est** 1. of, like, or full of pith 2. terse and full of substance or meaning —*SYN.* see CONCISE —**pith´i·ly** *adv.* —**pith´i·ness** *n.*

pit·i·a·ble (pit´ē ə b'l) *adj.* [ME. *piteable* < MFr. < *pitier*: see PITY] arousing or deserving pity, sometimes mixed with scorn or contempt —*SYN.* see PITIFUL —**pit´i·a·ble·ness** *n.* —**pit´i·a·bly** *adv.*

pit·i·er (-ər) *n.* a person who pities

pit·i·ful (pit´i fəl) *adj.* 1. exciting or deserving pity 2. deserving contempt; despicable; mean 3. [Archaic] full of pity or compassion —**pit´i·ful·ly** *adv.* —**pit´i·ful·ness** *n.* *SYN.*—**pitiful** applies to that which arouses or deserves pity because it is sad, pathetic, etc. [the suffering of the starving natives was *pitiful*]; **pitiable** is the preferred term when a greater or lesser degree of contempt is mingled with commiseration [the opposition shrank to a *pitiable* minority]; **piteous** stresses the nature of the thing calling for pity rather than its influence on the observer [*piteous* groans].

pit·i·less (-lis) *adj.* without pity; unfeeling —*SYN.* see CRUEL —**pit´i·less·ly** *adv.* —**pit´i·less·ness** *n.*

pit·man (pit´mən) *n.* 1. *pl.* **-men** (-mən) a person who works in a pit; esp., a coal miner ☆2. *pl.* **-mans** (-mənz) *same as* CONNECTING ROD

Pit·man (pit´mən), Sir **Isaac** 1813–97; Eng. inventor of a system of shorthand

pi·ton (pē´tän; Fr. pē tōn´) *n.*, *pl.* **-tons** (-tänz; Fr. -tōn´) [Fr. < MFr., a spike, pointed object, akin to OIt. *pizza*, a point] a metal spike with an eye to which a rope can be secured: it is driven into rock or ice for support in mountain climbing

Pi·tot-stat·ic tube (pē´tō stat´ik) [*also* p- t-] an instrument combining a Pitot tube and a static tube, that measures the difference between the pressures in the two tubes to obtain the relative velocity of a fluid in motion

Pi·tot tube (pē´tō, pē tō´) [after Henri *Pitot* (1695–1771), Fr. physicist, who invented it] [*also* p- t-] 1. a small, L-shaped tube which, when inserted vertically into a flowing fluid with its open end facing upstream, measures the total pressure of the fluid and hence, indirectly, the velocity of its flow 2. *same as* PITOT-STATIC TUBE

pit saw a large saw worked by two men, one standing above the log, the other in a pit below it: also **pit´saw´**

Pitt (pit), **William** 1. 1st Earl of Chatham, 1708–78; Eng. statesman; prime minister (1766–68): called the *Great Commoner* 2. 1759–1806; Eng. statesman; prime minister (1783–1801; 1804–06): son of *prec.*

pit·tance (pit´ns) *n.* [ME. *pitaunce* < OFr. *pitance*, portion of food allowed a monk < ML. *pietantia* < LL.(Ec.) *pietas*: see PIETY] 1. a small or barely sufficient allowance of money 2. any small amount or share, as of income

pit·ted[1] (pit´id) *adj.* having had the pits removed

pit·ted[2] (pit´id) *adj.* marked with pits or hollows

pit·ter-pat·ter (pit´ər pat´ər) *n.* [ME. *pyter-pater*: echoic] a rapid succession of light beating or tapping sounds, as of raindrops —*adv.* with a pitter-patter —*vi.* to fall, move, etc. with a pitter-patter

Pitts·burgh (pits´bərg) [after Wm. PITT (the father)] city in SW Pa., at the juncture of the Allegheny & Monongahela rivers: pop. 520,000 (met. area, 2,401,000)

Pitts·field (pits´fēld´) [after Wm. PITT (the father)] city in W Mass.: pop. 57,000

pi·tu·i·tar·y (pi tōō´ə ter´ē, -tyōō´-) *adj.* [L. *pituitarius* < *pituita*, phlegm, rheum < IE. **pitu-*, juice, food < base **pei-*, to be fat: cf. PITCH[1], FAT] 1. orig., of or secreting mucus 2. of the pituitary gland —*n.*, *pl.* **-tar´ies** 1. *same as* PITUITARY GLAND 2. any of various preparations made from extracts of either of the lobes of the pituitary gland

pituitary gland (or **body**) a small, oval endocrine gland attached by a stalk to the base of the brain and consisting of an anterior and a posterior lobe: it secretes hormones influencing body growth, metabolism, the activity of other endocrine glands, etc.

pit viper any of a family (Crotalidae) of poisonous snakes, as the rattlesnake, copperhead, etc., with a prominent, heat-sensitive pit on each side of the head

pit·y (pit´ē) *n.*, *pl.* **pit´ies** [ME. *pite* < OFr. *pitet* < L. *pietas*: see PIETY] 1. sorrow felt for another's suffering or misfortune; compassion; sympathy 2. the ability to feel such compassion 3. a cause for sorrow or regret —*vt.*, *vi.* **pit´ied**, **pit´y·ing** to feel pity (for) —**have** (or **take**) **pity on** to show pity or compassion for —**pit´y·ing·ly** *adv.* *SYN.*—**pity** implies sorrow felt for another's suffering or misfortune, sometimes connoting slight contempt because the object is regarded as weak or inferior [he felt *pity* for a man so ignorant]; **compassion** implies pity accompanied by an urge to help or spare [moved by *compassion*, I did not press for payment]; **commiseration** implies deeply felt and openly expressed feelings of pity [she wept with her friend in *commiseration*]; **sympathy**, in this connection, implies such kinship of feeling as enables one to really understand or even to share the sorrow, etc. of another [he always turned to his wife for *sympathy*]; **condolence** now

usually implies a formal expression of sympathy with another in sorrow [a letter of *condolence*]

pit·y·ri·a·sis (pit´ə rī´ə sis) *n.* [ModL. < Gr. *pityriasis* < *pityrion*, bran, scale] 1. any of various skin diseases characterized by the shedding of scaly flakes of epidermis 2. a skin disease of domestic animals, characterized by the formation of dry scales

‡**più** (pyōō) *adv.* [It. < L. *plus*: see PLUS] more: a direction in music, as in *più allegro*, more quickly

Pi·us (pī´əs) name of twelve popes; esp., 1. **Pius II** (born *Enea Silvio de Piccolomini*) 1405–64; Pope (1458–64) 2. **Pius VII** (born *Luigi Barnaba Chiaramonti*) 1740–1823; Pope (1800–23) 3. **Pius IX** (born *Giovanni Maria Mastai-Ferretti*) 1792–1878; Pope (1846–78) 4. **Pius X**, Saint (born *Giuseppe Sarto*) 1835–1914; Pope (1903–14): his day is Sept. 3 5. **Pius XI** (born *Achille Ratti*) 1857–1939; Pope (1922–39) 6. **Pius XII** (born *Eugenio Pacelli*) 1876–1958; Pope (1939–58)

piv·ot (piv´ət) *n.* [Fr., prob. akin to Pr. *pua*, tooth of a comb] 1. a point, shaft, pin, etc. on which something turns 2. a person or thing on or around which something turns or depends, etc.; central point 3. a pivoting movement —*adj.* *same as* PIVOTAL —*vt.* to provide with, attach by, or mount on a pivot or pivots —*vi.* to turn on or as if on a pivot

piv·ot·al (-'l) *adj.* 1. of or acting as a pivot 2. on which something turns or depends; central, crucial, critical, etc. —**piv´ot·al·ly** *adv.*

pix[1] (piks) *n. obs. var.* of PYX

☆**pix**[2] (piks) *n.pl.* [< PIC(TURE)S] [Slang] 1. motion pictures 2. photographs

pix·ie, pix·y (pik´sē) *n.*, *pl.* **pix´ies** [SW Brit. dial. *pixey*, *pisky*] a fairy or sprite, esp. one that is puckish —**pix´ie·ish**, **pix´y·ish** *adj.*

☆**pix·i·lat·ed** (pik´sə lāt´id) *adj.* [altered < *pixy-led*, lost, lit., led astray by pixies, after pp. of verbs in -*late* (as *elated*, *titillated*)] eccentric, daft, whimsical, puckish, etc.

Pi·zar·ro (pē thär´rō; *E.* pi zär´rō), **Fran·cis·co** (frän thēs´kō) 1470?–1541; Sp. conqueror of Peru

☆**pi·zazz, piz·zazz** (pə zaz´) *n.* [prob. echoic of exuberant cry] [Slang] 1. energy, vigor, vitality, spirit, etc. 2. smartness and dash; style, sparkle, flair, flash, etc. —**pi·zaz´zy, piz·zaz´zy** *adj.*

pizz. *Music* pizzicato

☆**piz·za** (pēt´sə) *n.* [It., prob. substitution of *pizza*, a point, edge, for ModGr. *pitta*, a cake] an Italian dish made by baking a thin layer of dough covered with a spiced preparation of tomatoes, cheese, and often sausage, mushrooms, anchovies, etc.

☆**piz·ze·ri·a** (pēt´sə rē´ə) *n.* [It. < prec. + -*eria*, -ERY] a place where pizzas are prepared and sold

piz·zi·ca·to (pit´sə kät´ō; *It.* pēt´tsē kä´tō) *adj.* [It., pp. of *pizzicare*, to pluck, pinch] *Music* plucked: a direction to performers on stringed instruments to pluck the strings with the fingers instead of bowing —*adv.* in a pizzicato manner —*n.*, *pl.* **-ca´ti** (-ē; *It.* -tē) a note or passage played in this way

piz·zle (piz´'l) *n.* [prob. < LowG. *pesel* or Fl. *pezel*, dim. akin to Du. *pees*, a tendon, sinew] the penis of an animal, esp. that of a bull as formerly made into a whip

☆**pj's** (pē´jāz´) *n.pl.* [< P(A)J(AMA)S] *colloq. var.* of PAJAMAS

PK psychokinesis

pk. *pl.* **pks.** 1. pack 2. park 3. peak 4. peck

pkg. package; packages

pkt. packet

PKU phenylketonuria

pkwy. parkway

pl. 1. place 2. plate 3. plural

plac·a·ble (plak´ə b'l, plā´kə-) *adj.* [ME. < OFr. < L. *placabilis* < *placare*, to quiet, soothe: see PLEASE] capable of being placated; readily pacified; forgiving —**plac·a·bil´i·ty** *n.* —**plac´a·bly** *adv.*

plac·ard (plak´ärd, -ərd) *n.* [LME. *placquart* < MFr. *plackart* < MDu. *placke*, a piece, spot, patch] 1. a notice for display in a public place; poster 2. a small card or plaque —*vt.* 1. to place placards on or in 2. to advertise or give notice of by means of placards 3. to display as a placard —*vi.* to set up placards

pla·cate (plā´kāt, plak´āt) *vt.* **-cat·ed**, **-cat·ing** [< L. *placatus*, pp. of *placare*, to appease: see PLEASE] to stop from being angry; appease; pacify; mollify —*SYN.* see PACIFY —**pla´cat·er** *n.* —**pla·ca´tion** *n.* —**pla·ca·tive** (plā´kāt/iv, -kət-; plak´ät/-) *adj.* —**pla´ca·to´ry** *adj.*

place (plās) *n.* [ME. < OFr. < L. *platea*, a broad street (in LL., an open space) < Gr. *plateia*, a street < *platys*, broad (see PLATY-)] 1. a square or court in a city 2. a short, usually narrow, street 3. space; room 4. a particular area or locality; region 5. a) the part of space occupied by a person or thing b) situation or state [if I were in his *place*] 6. a city, town, or village 7. a residence; dwelling; house and grounds 8. a building or space devoted to a special purpose [a *place* of amusement] 9. a particular spot on or part of the body or a surface [a sore *place* on the leg] 10. a particular passage or page in a book, magazine, etc., esp. the point where one has temporarily stopped reading [to mark one's *place*] 11. position or standing, esp. one of importance, accorded to one [one's *place* in history] 12. a step or point in a sequence [in the first *place*] 13. the customary, proper, or natural position, time, or character

14. a space used, reserved, or customarily occupied by a person, as a seat in a theater, at a table, etc. **15.** an office; employment; position **16.** official position **17.** the duties of any position **18.** the duty or business (of a person) **19.** *Arith.* the position of an integer, as in noting decimals [the third decimal *place*] **20.** *Racing* the first, second, or third position at the finish, specif. the second position —*vt.* **placed, plac′ing** [Fr. *placer*] **1.** *a)* to put in a particular place, condition, or relation *b)* to put in an assigned or proper place, as in a sequence or series ☆*c)* to identify by associating with the correct place or circumstances [to *place* someone's face] **2.** to find employment or a position for; appoint to an office **3.** to arrange for a desired handling, treatment, or allocation of [to *place* a shipment, to *place* a child for adoption] **4.** to assign (a value) **5.** to make or give as an estimate **6.** to offer (a proposal, problem, etc.) to be considered **7.** to repose (confidence, trust, hope, etc.) *in* a person or thing **8.** to adjust (the voice) to head or chest register **9.** to finish in (a specified position) in a competition [to *place* last] —*vi. Sports* to finish among the first three in a contest; specif., to finish second in a horse or dog race —**give place 1.** to make room **2.** to yield —☆**go places** [Slang] to achieve success —**in** (or **out of**) **place 1.** in (or out of) the customary, proper, or assigned place **2.** that is (or is not) fitting, proper, or timely—**in place of** as a substitute for; instead of —**know one's place** to be conscious of one's (inferior) position or rank in life and act accordingly —**put someone in his place** to humble someone who is overstepping bounds —**take place** to come into being; happen; occur —**take the place of** to be a substitute for

pla·ce·bo (plə sē′bō) *n., pl.* **-bos, -boes** [ME. < L., I shall please] **1.** *R.C.Ch.* the first antiphon of the vespers for the dead, beginning with the word *placebo* **2.** a harmless, unmedicated preparation given as a medicine to a patient merely to humor him, or used as a control in testing the efficacy of another, medicated substance **3.** something said or done to win the favor of another

☆**place card** a small card bearing the name of a guest and set at the place that he is to occupy at a table

place kick *Football* a kick made while the ball is held in place on the ground, as in kicking off or attempting a field goal —**place′-kick′** *vi.*

place·man (plās′mən) *n., pl.* **-men** [Rare Brit.] a person appointed to a government position or the like as a political reward: usually a contemptuous term

place mat a small mat of cloth, paper, etc. serving as an individual table cover for a person at a meal

place·ment (-mənt) *n.* **1.** a placing or being placed **2.** the finding of employment for a person **3.** location or arrangement **4.** *Football a)* the setting of the ball on the ground in position for a place kick *b)* this position of the ball *c) same as* PLACE KICK

pla·cen·ta (plə sen′tə) *n., pl.* **-tas, -tae** (-tē) [ModL. < L., lit., a cake < Gr. *plakounta*, acc. of *plakous*, a flat cake < *plax* (gen. *plakos*), a flat object < IE. base *plāk-*, flat, whence L. *placere*, to PLEASE] **1.** *Anat., Zool. a)* a vascular organ, developed within the uterus of most mammals during gestation from the chorion of the embryo and a part of the maternal uterine wall, that is connected to the embryo by the umbilical cord and that is discharged shortly after birth: it serves as the structure through which nourishment for the fetus is received from, and wastes of the fetus are eliminated into, the circulatory system of the mother *b)* any similar structure in other animals **2.** *Bot. a)* that part of the lining of the ovary which bears the ovules *b)* any mass of tissue that bears sporangia or spores —**pla·cen′tal** *adj.*

pla·cen·tate (-tāt) *adj.* having a placenta

plac·en·ta·tion (plas′′n tā′shən) *n.* **1.** *Anat., Zool. a)* the formation or structure of a placenta *b)* the manner in which the placenta is attached to the uterus **2.** *Bot.* the manner in which the placentas are arranged in an ovary

plac·er¹ (plās′ər) *n.* a person who places

☆**plac·er**² (plas′ər) *n.* [AmSp. (for Sp. *placel*) < Catal., lit. sandbank < *plassa*, a place < L. *platea*: see PLACE] a waterborne or glacial deposit of gravel or sand containing heavy ore minerals, as gold, platinum, etc., which have been eroded from their original bedrock and concentrated as small particles that can be washed out

☆**plac·er mining** (plas′ər) mining of placer deposits by washing, dredging, or other hydraulic methods

place setting the china, silverware, etc. for setting one place at a table for a meal

pla·cet (plā′sit) *n.* [L., it pleases] a vote of assent expressed by saying *placet*

plac·id (plas′id) *adj.* [L. *placidus*, akin to *placere*, to PLEASE] undisturbed; tranquil; calm; quiet —*SYN.* see CALM —**pla·cid·i·ty** (plə sid′ə tē), **plac′id·ness** *n.* —**plac′id·ly** *adv.*

Plac·id (plas′id), **Lake** lake in NE N.Y., in the Adirondacks: resort center: c. 4 mi. long

plack·et (plak′it) *n.* [prob. altered < PLACARD, in obs. sense "breastplate, top of skirt"] **1.** a finished slit with a fastener at the waist of a skirt or dress to make it easy to put on and take off **2.** [Archaic] *a)* a pocket, esp. in a woman's skirt *b)* a petticoat

plac·oid (plak′oid) *adj.* [< Gr. *plax*, flat plate, tablet (see PLACENTA) + -OID] *Zool.* of or having horny scales consisting of a dentine base and an enamel-covered, toothlike spine, found in cartilaginous fishes, as the sharks, rays, skates, etc.

‡**pla·fond** (plȧ fōn′) *n.* [Fr., earlier *platfond* < *plat*, flat (< VL. *plattus* < Gr. PLATY-) + *fond*, background < L. *fundus*, BOTTOM] **1.** a decorated ceiling **2.** a painted or carved design on a ceiling

pla·gal (plā′gəl) *adj.* [ML. *plagalis* < *plaga*, plagal mode < MGr. *plagios*, plagal (in Gr., oblique, slanting) < Gr. *plagos*, a side, akin to *pelagos*, the sea: for IE. base see PELAGIC] *Music* **1.** with its keynote in the middle of the compass, as a mode **2.** designating a cadence with the subdominant chord immediately preceding the tonic chord

‡**plage**¹ (plȧzh) *n.* [Fr. < It. *piaggia* < LL. *plagia*, shore < *plagius*, slanting < Gr. *plagios*, oblique, akin to *pelagos*, sea surface] a sandy beach at a seaside resort area

plage² (plāzh) *n.* [< *prec.*] a bright area on the sun, visible in the light of hydrogen or ionized calcium

pla·gia·rism (plā′jə riz′m; -jē ə riz′m) *n.* [< L. *plagiarius*, kidnapper: see PLAGIARY & -ISM] **1.** the act of plagiarizing **2.** an idea, plot, etc. that has been plagiarized —**pla′gia·rist** *n.* —**pla′gia·ris′tic** *adj.*

pla·gia·rize (-riz′) *vt., vi.* **-rized′, -riz′ing** [see ff.] to take (ideas, writings, etc.) from (another) and pass them off as one's own —**pla′gia·riz′er** *n.*

pla·gia·ry (-rē) *n., pl.* **-ries** [L. *plagiarius*, kidnapper, literary thief < *plagium*, a kidnapping < Gr. *plagios*, oblique: see ff.] **1.** *archaic var.* OF PLAGIARIST **2.** *same as* PLAGIARISM

pla·gio- (plā′jē ə) [< Gr. *plagios*, oblique < *plagos*, a side: see PLAGAL] *a combining form meaning* oblique, slanting [*plagiotropic*]: also **pla′gi-**

pla·gi·o·clase (plā′jē ə klās′) *n.* [G. *plagioklas* < Gr. *plagios* (see *prec.*) + *klasis*, a cleaving, fracture < *klaein*, to break: see CLASTIC] any of a series of triclinic minerals of the feldspar family, ranging in composition from albite to anorthite and found in many rocks

pla·gi·o·trop·ic (plā′jē ə träp′ik) *adj.* [PLAGIO- + -TROPIC] *Bot.* having the longer axes of roots or branches slanting from the vertical line —**pla′gi·o·trop′i·cal·ly** *adv.* —**pla·gi·ot′ro·pism** (-ät′rə piz′m) *n.*

plague (plāg) *n.* [ME. < MFr. < L. *plaga*, a blow, misfortune, in LL.(Ec.), a plague < Gr. *plēgē*, *plaga* < IE. *plaga*, a blow < base *plag-*, to strike, whence FLAW²] **1.** anything that afflicts or troubles; calamity; scourge **2.** any contagious epidemic disease that is deadly; specif., *same as* BUBONIC PLAGUE **3.** [Colloq.] a nuisance; annoyance **4.** *Bible* any of various calamities sent down as divine punishment: Ex. 9:14; Num. 16:46 —*vt.* **plagued, plagu′ing 1.** to afflict with a plague **2.** to vex; harass; trouble; torment —*SYN.* see ANNOY —**plagu′er** *n.*

pla·guy, pla·guey (plā′gē) *adj.* [Dial. or Colloq.] annoying; vexatious; disagreeable —*adv.* [Dial. or Colloq.] annoyingly; disagreeably: also **pla′gui·ly**

plaice (plās) *n., pl.* **plaice, plaic′es:** see PLURAL, II, D, 2 [ME. *plais* < OFr. *plais* < LL. *platessa*, flatfish < Gr. *platys*, broad: see PLATY-] any of a number of related American and European flatfishes (esp. genera *Pleuronectes* and *Hippoglossoides*)

plaid (plad) *n.* [Gael. *plaide*, a blanket, plaid, contr. < ? *peallaid*, sheepskin] **1.** a long piece of twilled woolen cloth with a crossbarred pattern, worn over the shoulder by Scottish Highlanders **2.** a fabric with stripes or bars of various colors and widths that cross at right angles **3.** any pattern of this kind —*adj.* having a pattern of plaid

plaid·ed (plad′id) *adj.* **1.** wearing a plaid **2.** made, or having a pattern, of plaid

plain¹ (plān) *adj.* [ME. < OFr. < L. *planus*, flat, level < IE. base *plā-*, broad, flat, whence FLOOR, FIELD] **1.** orig., flat; level; plane **2.** free from obstructions; open; clear [in *plain* view] **3.** clearly understood; evident; obvious [to make one's meaning *plain*] **4.** *a)* outspoken; frank; straightforward [*plain* talk] *b)* downright; thoroughgoing [*plain* nonsense] **5.** not luxurious or ornate; unembellished [a *plain* coat] **6.** not complicated; simple [*plain* sewing] **7.** not good-looking; homely [a *plain* face] **8.** unfigured, undyed, or untwilled [*plain* cloth] **9.** pure; unmixed [*plain* soda] **10.** not of high rank or position; such as characterizes the common people; ordinary [a *plain* man] —*n.* an extent of level country —*adv.* clearly or simply [just *plain* tired] —*SYN.* see EVIDENT —**the Plain** the less radical party in the French legislature during the Revolution —**plain′ly** *adv.* —**plain′ness** *n.*

plain² (plān) *vi.* [ME. *pleynen* < OFr. *plaindre* < L. *plangere*: see PLAINT] [Archaic or Dial.] to complain

plain·chant (plān′chant) *n.* [Fr.] *same as* PLAINSONG

plain·clothes man (plān′klōz′, -klōthz′) a detective or policeman who wears civilian clothes on duty: also **plain′clothes′man** (-mən) *n., pl.* **-men**

plain dealing straightforward dealing with others

Plain·field (plān′fēld′) [after a local resident's estate] city in NE N.J.: suburb of Newark: pop. 47,000

fat, āpe, cär; ten, ēven; is, bīte; gō, hôrn, tōōl, look; oil, out; up, fur; get; joy; yet; chin; she; thin, *th*en; zh, leisure; ŋ, ring; ə for *a* in *ago*, *e* in *agent*, *i* in *sanity*, *o* in *comply*, *u* in *focus*; ' as in *able* (ā′b'l); Fr. bȧl; ë, Fr. coeur; ö, Fr. feu; ô, Fr. mon; ü, Fr. duc; r, Fr. cri; H, G. ich; kh, G. doch. See inside front cover. ☆Americanism; ‡foreign; *hypothetical; < derived from

plain-laid (plān′lād′) *adj.* made of three strands laid together with a right-handed twist: said of a rope

Plain People ☆the Mennonites, Dunkers, and Amish people: from their plain dress and simple way of life

plain sailing 1. sailing on a smooth, clear course 2. a smooth, clear course of action

☆**Plains Indian** a member of any of the American Indian tribes formerly inhabiting the prairie region of the U.S.: they were of various linguistic stocks but shared certain culture traits in common, esp. the nomadic following of bison herds

☆**plains·man** (plānz′mən) *n., pl.* **-men** (-mən) an inhabitant of the plains; esp., a frontiersman on the Great Plains

Plains of Abraham a plain near Quebec: site of a battle (1759) of the French and Indian War, in which the British under Wolfe defeated the French under Montcalm

plain·song (plān′sôŋ′) *n.* [transl. of ML. *cantus planus*] early Christian church music, still used in Roman Catholic and Anglican services, in free rhythm and the limited Gregorian scale, sung in unison

plain-spo·ken (plān′spō′k'n) *adj.* speaking or spoken plainly or frankly —**plain′-spo′ken·ness** *n.*

plaint (plānt) *n.* [ME. < OFr. < L. *planctus*, lamentation, a loud banging < pp. of *plangere*, to beat the breast in grief, lament < IE. base *plag-*, to strike, whence Gr. *plēssein*, to strike] 1. [Poet.] lamentation; lament 2. a complaint or grievance

plain·tiff (plān′tif) *n.* [ME. *plaintif* < OFr., mournful, making complaint < *plaindre*: see PLAINT] a person who brings a suit into a court of law; complainant

plain·tive (-tiv) *adj.* [ME. *pleintif* < OFr. *plaintif*: see prec.] expressing sorrow or melancholy; mournful; sad —**plain′tive·ly** *adv.* —**plain′tive·ness** *n.*

plais·ter (plās′tər) *n. obs. var.* OF PLASTER

plait (plāt; *chiefly Brit.*, plat) *n.* [ME. *pleit* < OFr. < VL. *plicta* < pp. of L. *plicare*, to fold: see PLY¹] 1. *same as* PLEAT 2. a braid of hair, ribbon, etc. —*vt.* [ME. *playten* < the *n.*] 1. *same as* PLEAT 2. to braid or interweave 3. to make by braiding —**plait′er** *n.*

plan (plan) *n.* [Fr., plan, plane, foundation: merging of *plan* (< L. *planus*: see PLAIN¹) with MFr. *plant* < It. *pianta* < L. *planta*, sole of the foot: see PLANT] 1. a drawing or diagram showing the arrangement in horizontal section of a structure, piece of ground, etc. 2. *a*) a scheme or program for making, doing, or arranging something; project, design, schedule, etc. *b*) a method of proceeding 3. any outline or sketch 4. in perspective, any of several planes thought of as perpendicular to the line of sight and between the eye and the object —*vt.* **planned, plan′ning** 1. to make a plan of (a structure, piece of ground, etc.) 2. to devise a scheme for doing, making, or arranging 3. to have in mind as a project or purpose —*vi.* to make plans

SYN.—**plan** refers to any detailed method, formulated beforehand, for doing or making something [vacation *plans*]; **design** stresses the final outcome of a plan and implies the use of skill or craft, sometimes in an unfavorable sense, in executing or arranging this [it was his *design* to separate us]; **project** implies the use of enterprise or imagination in formulating an ambitious or extensive plan [a housing *project*]; **scheme**, a less definite term than the preceding, often connotes either an impractical, visionary plan or an underhanded intrigue [a *scheme* to embezzle the funds]

plan- (plan) *same as* PLANO-: used before a vowel

pla·nar (plā′nər) *adj.* of or pertaining to a point on a surface at which the curvature is zero; of or lying in one plane

pla·nar·i·an (plə ner′ē ən) *n.* [< ModL. *Planaria*, name of the genus < LL. *planarius*, flat < L. *planus*, PLANE²] any of a family (Planariidae) or order (Tricladida) of related small, soft-bodied, free-living, turbellarian flatworms moving by means of cilia

pla·na·tion (plā nā′shən) *n.* [PLANE² + -ATION] the reduction of a land area by erosion to a nearly flat surface

planch (planch, plänch) *n.* [ME. *plaunche* < OFr. *planche*: see PLANK] [Obs. or Brit. Dial.] a plank, board, or floor

plan·chet (plan′chit) *n.* [Fr. *planchette*, dim. of *planche*, PLANK] a disk of metal to be stamped as a coin

plan·chette (plan chet′, -shet′) *n.* [Fr.: see prec.] a small, three-cornered device, often having as one of its supports a pencil, that is supposed to write out a message or, as with a Ouija board, point to letters or words, as it moves with the fingers resting lightly on it

Planck (pläŋk), **Max** (**Karl Ernst Ludwig**) (mäks) 1858-1947; Ger. physicist

Planck's constant [after prec.] *Physics* a universal constant (*h*) which gives the ratio of a quantum of radiant energy (*E*) to the frequency (*v*) of its source: it is expressed by the equation $E = hv$ and its approximate numerical value is 6.625 × 10⁻²⁷ erg second

plane¹ (plān) *n.* [ME. < MFr. *plasne* < L. *platanus* < Gr. *platanos* < *platys*, broad (see PLATY¹): from its broad leaves] any of a genus (*Platanus*) of trees of the plane-tree family having maplelike leaves, spherical dry fruits, and bark that comes off in large patches

plane² (plān) *adj.* [L. *planus*: see PLAIN¹] 1. flat; level; even 2. *Math. a*) lying on a surface that is a plane *b*) of such surfaces —*n.* [L. *planum*] 1. a surface that wholly contains every straight line joining any two points lying in it 2. a flat, level, or even surface 3. a level of development, achievement, existence, etc. 4. *clipped form of* AIRPLANE 5. any airfoil; esp., a wing of an airplane —**SYN.** see LEVEL

plane³ (plān) *n.* [ME. < OFr. *plaine* < LL. *plana* < *planare*, to plane, make level < L. *planus*: see PLAIN¹] a carpenter's tool for shaving a wood surface in order to make it smooth, level, etc. —*vt.* **planed, plan′ing** 1. to make smooth or level with or as with a plane 2. to remove with or as with a plane (with *off* or *away*) —*vi.* 1. to work with a plane 2. to do the work of a plane

plane⁴ (plān) *vi.* **planed, plan′ing** [Fr. *planer* < OFr. (term used in falconry, in reference to position of bird's wings while soaring) < LL. *planare*, to make level: see prec.] 1. to soar or glide 2. to rise partly out of the water while in motion at a high speed, as a hydroplane does 3. to travel by airplane

plane angle an angle made by two straight lines that lie in the same plane

plane geometry the branch of geometry dealing with plane figures

plan·er (plā′nər) *n.* 1. a person or thing that planes ☆2. a machine that smooths or finishes the surface of wood or metal by planing 3. *Printing* a block of wood used with a mallet to level type in a chase

☆**pla·ner tree** (plā′nər) [after J. J. Planer (d. 1787), G. botanist] a small tree (*Planera aquatica*) of the elm family, with ovate leaves and a nutlike fruit, found in the SE U.S.

plan·et (plan′it) *n.* [ME. *planete* < OFr. < LL. *planeta* < Gr. *planētēs*, wanderer < *planan*, to lead astray, wander < IE. base *pla-*, flat, spread out, whence (via Gmc.) Fr. *flâner*, to stroll] 1. *orig.*, any of the heavenly bodies with apparent motion (as distinguished from the fixed stars), including the sun, moon, Mercury, Venus, Mars, Jupiter, and Saturn 2. now, any heavenly body that shines by reflected sunlight and revolves about the sun: the major planets, in their order from the sun, are Mercury, Venus, Earth, Mars, Jupiter, Saturn, Uranus, Neptune, and Pluto; the minor planets are the asteroids, or planetoids, which move in orbits between Mars and Jupiter 3. *Astrol.* any heavenly body thought of as influencing human lives

plane table a surveying device for plotting maps in the field: it consists of a drawing board mounted on a tripod with an alidade pivoted over its center

plan·e·tar·i·um (plan′ə ter′ē əm) *n., pl.* **-i·ums, -i·a** (-ə) [ModL. < LL. *planeta*, PLANET + L. (*sol*)*arium*, SOLARIUM] 1. a model of the solar system in which, by means of clockwork, the relative motion of the planets around the sun can be demonstrated 2. *a*) an arrangement for projecting the images of the sun, moon, planets, and stars on the inside of a large hemispherical dome by means of a large, complex optical instrument which is revolved to show the principal celestial motions *b*) the room or building in which this is contained

plan·e·tar·y (plan′ə ter′ē) *adj.* [Fr. *planetaire*] 1. of or having to do with a planet or the planets 2. terrestrial; global 3. wandering; erratic 4. moving in an orbit, like a planet 5. designating or of an epicyclic train of gears, as in an automobile transmission 6. *Astrol.* under the influence of a planet

plan·e·tes·i·mal (plan′ə tes′i m'l) *adj.* [PLANET + (IN-FINIT)ESIMAL] of very small bodies in space that move in planetary orbits —*n.* any of these small bodies

planetesimal hypothesis a hypothesis that the planets were formed by the uniting of planetesimals created by the tidal eruptions caused on the sun by the passage of a star close to it

plan·et·oid (plan′ə toid′) *n.* [PLANET + -OID] *same as* ASTEROID (n. 1)

plane-tree (plān′trē′) *adj.* designating a family (Platanaceae) of deciduous trees variously called *buttonwood*, *buttonball*, *sycamore*

plane tree *same as* PLANE¹

plan·et-strick·en (plan′it strik′'n) *adj.* [Archaic] 1. supposedly influenced adversely by the planets 2. *same as* PANIC-STRICKEN Also **plan′et-struck′** (-struk′)

planet wheel a gearwheel that meshes with and revolves around another wheel in an epicyclic train

plan·gent (plan′jənt) *adj.* [L. *plangens*, prp. of *plangere*, to beat: see PLAINT] 1. beating with a loud or deep sound, as breaking waves, etc. 2. loud or resonant, and, often, mournful-sounding —**plan′gen·cy** (-jən sē) *n.* —**plan′-gent·ly** *adv.*

pla·ni- (plā′nə) [< L. *planus*, flat: see PLAIN¹] *a combining form meaning* plane, level, flat [*planisphere*]

pla·nim·e·ter (plə nim′ə tər, plā-) *n.* [Fr. *planimètre*: see prec. & -METER] an instrument for measuring the area of a regular or irregular plane figure by tracing the perimeter of the figure —**pla·ni·met·ric** (plā′nə met′rik, plan′ə-) *adj.* —**pla·nim′e·try** *n.*

☆**planing mill** a mill in which lumber is dressed and finished by being passed through planers, edgers, etc.

plan·ish (plan′ish) *vt.* [< MFr. *planiss-*, extended stem of *planir*, to flatten < *plan*, flat: see PLAN] to toughen, smooth, or polish (metal) by hammering or rolling —**plan′ish·er** *n.*

plan·i·sphere (plan′ə sfir′) *n.* [ML. *planisphaerium*: see PLANI- & SPHERE] 1. a map or chart that is the projection on a plane of all or part of a sphere 2. a projection on a plane of the celestial sphere, with the zenith of the North

PLANE

Pole or of the South Pole as the center —**plan′i·spher′ic** (-sfer′ik) *adj.*

plank (plaŋk) *n.* [ME. *planke* < ONormFr. < OFr. *planche* < LL. *planca*, a board, plank < VL. *palanca* < Gr. *phalangai* < *phalanx* (gen. *phalangos*): see PHALANX] 1. a long, broad, thick board 2. timber cut into planks; planking 3. something that supports or forms a foundation ☆4. any of the articles or principles making up the platform or stated program of a political party —*vt.* 1. to cover, lay, or furnish with planks ☆2. to broil and serve (steak, fish, etc.) on a board or wooden platter 3. [Colloq.] *a)* to lay or set (*down*) with force or emphasis ☆*b)* to pay (usually with *down* or *out*) —**walk the plank** to walk blindfold and manacled off a plank projecting over the water from the side of a ship, as the victims of pirates were sometimes forced to do

plank·ing (-iŋ) *n.* 1. the act of laying planks 2. planks in quantity 3. the planks of a structure

plank-sheer (-shir′) *n.* [altered < *plancher*, a plank < ME. *planchour* < OFr. *planchier* < *planche*, PLANK] a timber extending around the hull of a ship at the line of junction with the deck

plank·ter (plaŋk′tər) *n.* [Gr. *planktēr*, a wanderer < *planktos*, wandering: see PLANKTON] an individual planktonic organism

plank·ton (plaŋk′tən) *n.* [G. < Gr. *planktos*, wandering < *plazesthai*, to wander, akin to *planan*: see PLANET] the usually microscopic animal and plant life found floating or drifting in the ocean or in bodies of fresh water, used as food by fish —**plank·ton′ic** (-tän′ik) *adj.*

☆**planned parenthood** the planning of the number and spacing of the births of one's children, as through the use of birth-control measures

plan·ner (plan′ər) *n.* a person who plans

pla·no- (plā′nō) [< L. *planus*, level, flat: see PLAIN¹] *a combining form meaning:* 1. plane, flat [*planography*] 2. having one side plane and (the other as specified) [*plano*-concave]

pla·no·con·cave (plā′nō kän kāv′, -kän′kāv) *adj.* having one side plane and the other concave: see LENS, illus.

pla·no·con·vex (-kän veks′, -kän′veks) *adj.* having one side plane and the other convex: see LENS, illus.

pla·nog·ra·phy (plə näg′rə fē) *n.* [PLANO- + -GRAPHY] any method of printing from a flat surface, as lithography —**pla·no·graph·ic** (plā′nə graf′ik) *adj.*

☆**pla·nom·e·ter** (plə näm′ə tər) *n.* [PLANO- + -METER] a device, as a flat plate of iron, for gauging the accuracy of a plane surface

pla·no·sol (plā′nə sôl), -säl′) *n.* [< PLANO- + L. *solum*, SOIL] any of an intrazonal group of soils underlain by B-horizons strongly compacted by material leached from surface horizons, developed on nearly flat uplands in humid or subhumid climates

plan position indicator a circular radarscope on which signals are shown at radial distances from the center, which represents the location of the transmitter

plant (plant, plänt) *n.* [ME. *plante* < OE. L. *planta*, a sprout, twig, prob. back-formation < **plantare*, to smooth the soil for planting < *planta*, sole of the foot < IE. **plat-*, var. of base **pla-*, broad, flat, whence FLAT¹] 1. a living organism that, unlike an animal, cannot move voluntarily, has the ability to synthesize food from carbon dioxide, possesses cellulose cell walls, and lacks centrosomes, specialized sense organs, and digestive, nervous, and circulatory systems 2. a young tree, shrub, or herb, ready to put into other soil for growth to maturity; a slip, cutting, or set 3. a soft-stemmed organism of this kind, as distinguished from a tree or shrub 4. the tools, machinery, buildings, grounds, etc. of a factory or business 5. the equipment, buildings, etc. of any institution, as a hospital, school, etc. 6. the apparatus or equipment for a certain mechanical operation or process [the *power plant* of a ship] 7. [Slang] a person placed, or thing planned or used, to trick, mislead, or trap —*vt.* [ME. *planten* < OE. *plantian* & OFr. *planter*, both < L. *plantare* < the *n.*] 1. *a)* to put into soil, esp. into the ground, to grow *b)* to set plants in (a piece of ground) 2. to set firmly as into the ground; fix in position 3. to fix in the mind; implant (an idea, etc.) 4. to settle (a colony, colonists, etc.); found; establish 5. to furnish or stock with animals ☆6. to put a stock of (oysters, young fish, etc.) in a body of water 7. [Slang] to deliver (a punch, blow, etc.) with force 8. [Slang] *a)* to place (a person or thing) in such a way as to trick, trap, etc. *b)* to place (an ostensible news item) in a newspaper, etc. with some ulterior motive, as in order to mold public opinion 9. [Slang] *a)* to hide or conceal *b)* to place (something) surreptitiously where it is certain to be found or discovered —**plant′like′** *adj.*

Plan·tag·e·net (plan taj′ə nit) the ruling family of England (1154–1399), or any member of this family

plan·tain¹ (plan′tin) *n.* [ME. < OFr. < L. *plantago* < *planta*, sole of the foot (see PLANT): from the shape of the leaves] any member of a genus (*Plantago*) of plants of a family (Plantaginaceae), usually with rosettes of basal leaves and spikes of tiny greenish flowers

plan·tain² (plan′tin) *n.* [< Sp. *plá(n)tano*, banana tree, lit., plane tree (prob. misapplied to the plantain) < L. *platanus*: see PLANE¹] 1. a tropical banana plant (*Musa paradisiaca*) yielding a coarse fruit eaten as a cooked vegetable 2. this fruit

plantain lily any of several perennial plants (genus *Hosta*) of the lily family, with broad, strongly ribbed basal leaves and clusters or racemes of trumpet-shaped, white or bluish flowers

plan·tar (plan′tər) *adj.* [L. *plantaris* < *planta*, sole of the foot: see PLANT] of or on the sole of the foot

plan·ta·tion (plan tā′shən) *n.* [L. *plantatio* < *plantare*, to PLANT] 1. formerly, a colony or new settlement ☆2. an area growing cultivated crops 3. an estate, as in a tropical or semitropical region, cultivated by workers living on it [a sugar *plantation*] 4. a large, cultivated planting of trees [a rubber *plantation*]

plant·er (plan′tər, plän′-) *n.* ☆1. the owner of a plantation 2. a person or machine that plants 3. a container, usually decorative, for potted or unpotted house plants 4. [Archaic] a colonist or pioneer

planter's punch [prob. because served by planters (sense 1)] a chilled alcoholic drink made of Jamaica rum, lemon or lime juice, and sugar

plant hormone an organic chemical, as auxin, produced by plant cells and functioning at various sites to regulate growth, turning, metabolic processes, etc.

plan·ti·grade (plan′tə grād′) *adj.* [Fr. < L. *planta*, sole (see PLANT) + Fr. -*grade*, -GRADE] walking on the whole sole of the foot, as man, a bear, etc. —*n.* a plantigrade animal

plant louse *same as* APHID

plan·u·la (plan′yoo lə) *n.*, *pl.* -**u·lae′** (-lē′) [ModL. < LL., little plane, dim. < L. *planus*, flat: see PLAIN¹] the young, ciliated, usually free-swimming larva of a coelenterate —**plan′u·loid′** (-loid′) *adj.*

plaque (plak) *n.* [Fr. < MDu. *placke*, a disk, spot, patch] 1. *a)* any thin, flat piece of metal, wood, etc. with a picture, design in relief, etc., hung as on a wall for ornamentation *b)* a wall tablet inscribed to commemorate an event, identify a building, etc. 2. a platelike brooch worn as a badge or ornament 3. *a)* an abnormal patch on the skin, mucous membrane, etc. *b)* a thin, transparent film on a tooth surface, containing mucin, bacteria, etc., and, if not removed, hardening into tartar *c)* a deposit of fatty or fibrous material in a blood vessel wall

plash¹ (plash) *n.* [ME. *plasche* < OE. *plæsc*, akin to MDu. & MFl. *plasch*, pool: prob. echoic] a shallow pool, or puddle

plash² (plash) *vt.*, *vi.*, *n.* [echoic] *same as* SPLASH

plash³ (plash) *vt.* [LME. *plashen* < OFr. *plaissier* < VL. **plaxum*, hedge, for L. *plexum*, neut. pp. of *plectere*, to weave: for IE. base see FLAX] 1. to bend and intertwine (branches, stems, etc.) so as to form a hedge 2. to make or trim (a hedge) in this way

plash·y (plash′ē) *adj.* **plash′i·er, plash′i·est** 1. full of puddles; marshy; wet 2. splashing

-pla·si·a (plā′zhə, -zhē ə) [ModL. < Gr. *plasis*, a molding < *plassein*, to mold: see PLASTIC] *a combining form meaning change, development* [cataplasia]

plasm (plaz′m) *n.* *same as* PLASMA (senses 1, 2, 3)

plasm- *same as* PLASMO-: used before a vowel

-plasm (plaz′m) [< Gr. *plasma*: see ff.] *a terminal combining form meaning:* 1. the fluid substances of an animal or vegetable cell 2. protoplasm [ectoplasm]

plas·ma (plaz′mə) *n.* [G. < Gr. *plasma*, something molded < *plassein*, to form: see PLASTIC] 1. a green, somewhat translucent variety of quartz 2. the fluid part of blood, lymph, milk, or intramuscular liquid; esp., the fluid part of blood, as distinguished from the corpuscles, used for transfusions 3. *same as* PROTOPLASM 4. a high-temperature, ionized gas composed of electrons and positive ions in such relative numbers that the gaseous medium is essentially electrically neutral: confinement of plasma for thermonuclear reactions is achieved by magnetic fields —**plas·mat′ic** (-mat′ik) *adj.*

plas·ma·gel (plaz′mə jel′) *n.* [PLASMA + GEL] protoplasm in its more firm and jellylike state

plas·ma·gene (-jēn′) *n.* [PLASMA + GENE] any cytoplasmic structure or substance thought to carry inherited characteristics to a subsequent generation but not in a Mendelian manner —**plas′ma·gen′ic** (-jen′ik) *adj.*

plasma membrane a very thin living membrane surrounding the cytoplasm of a plant or animal cell

plas·ma·sol (plaz′mə sôl′, -säl′) *n.* [PLASMA + SOL³] protoplasm in its more liquid or fluid state

plas·min (plaz′min) *n.* [PLASM(A) + -IN¹] a proteolytic enzyme in blood plasma, which is capable of dissolving blood clots

plas·mo- (plaz′mō, -mə) *a combining form meaning* plasma [plasmolysis]

plas·mo·di·um (plaz mō′dē əm) *n.*, *pl.* -**di·a** (-ə) [ModL.: see PLASMA & -ODE²] 1. a mass of protoplasm with many nuclei and no definite size or shape, formed by the fusion of a number of one-celled organisms; esp., the nonreproductive stage of a slime mold 2. any of a genus (*Plasmo-*

dium) of unicellular parasites found in red blood corpuscles, including the parasite that causes malaria

plas·mol·y·sis (plaz mäl′ə sis) *n.* [ModL.: see PLASMO- & -LYSIS] *Biol.* a shrinking of the protoplasm of a living cell due to loss of water by osmosis

plas·mo·lyze (plaz′mə līz′) *vt., vi.* -lyzed′, -lyz′ing to subject to or undergo plasmolysis

Plas·sey (plä′sē) village in West Bengal, India, north of Calcutta: scene of a decisive victory (1757) by which the British established their rule in India

-plast (plast) [< Gr. *plastos*, formed < *plassein*, to form: see PLASTIC] *a combining form meaning* a unit of protoplasm [*chromoplast*]

plas·ter (plas′tər, pläs′-) *n.* [ME. < OE. *plaster* & OFr. *plastre*, both < LL. *plastrum*, for L. *emplastrum* < Gr. *emplastron*, plaster < *emplassein*, to daub over < *en*, on, in + *plassein*, to form: see PLASTIC] **1.** a pasty mixture of lime, sand, and water, which hardens on drying, for coating walls, ceilings, and partitions **2.** *same as* PLASTER OF PARIS **3.** a pasty preparation spread on cloth and applied to the body, used medicinally as a curative or counter-irritant —*vt.* **1.** to cover, smear, overlay, etc. with or as with plaster **2.** to apply or affix like a plaster [to *plaster* posters on walls] **3.** to make lie smooth and flat **4.** to apply plaster of Paris as a treatment **5.** [Colloq.] to affect or strike with force —**plas′ter·er** *n.* —**plas′ter·y** *adj.*

☆**plas·ter·board** (-bôrd′) *n.* thin board formed of layers of gypsum plaster and paper, used in wide sheets as a lath or substitute for plaster in walls, partitions, etc.

plaster cast 1. a copy or mold of a statue or other object, cast in plaster of Paris **2.** *Surgery* a rigid cast to hold a fractured bone in place and prevent movement, made by wrapping the limb or part with a bandage of gauze soaked in wet plaster of Paris

plas·tered (plas′tərd, pläs′-) *adj.* [pp. of PLASTER: orig. military slang] [Slang] intoxicated; drunk

plas·ter·ing (-tər iŋ) *n.* **1.** the act or process of applying plaster **2.** a coating of plaster as on a wall

plaster of Paris [from use of gypsum from Montmartre in Paris, France, in its manufacture] a heavy white powder, calcined gypsum, which, when mixed with water, forms a thick paste that sets quickly: used for casts, moldings, statuary, etc.

plas·tic (plas′tik) *adj.* [L. *plasticus* < Gr. *plastikos* < *plassein*, to form, prob. < IE. base *pla-*, to smooth out, whence L. *planus*, level] **1.** molding or shaping matter; formative **2.** *a)* capable of being molded or shaped *b)* made of a plastic **3.** in a flexible or changing state; impressionable **4.** dealing with molding or modeling, as in sculpture **5.** *Biol.* capable of readily changing or adapting in form, physiology, or behavior **6.** *Med. a)* of or helpful in the renewal of destroyed or injured tissue *b)* that can be so renewed **7.** *Physics* capable of continuous and permanent change of shape in any direction without breaking apart —*n.* **1.** any of various nonmetallic compounds, synthetically produced, usually from organic compounds by polymerization, which can be molded into various forms and hardened, or formed into pliable sheets or films, for commercial use **2.** any article made of plastic —SYN. see PLIABLE —**plas′ti·cal·ly** *adv.* —**plas·tic′i·ty** (-tis′ə tē) *n.*

-plas·tic (plas′tik) [< Gr. *plastikos:* see prec.] *a combining form:* **1.** *meaning* forming, developing [*cytoplastic*] **2.** *used to form adjectives corresponding to nouns ending in* -plasty, -plasm, *or* -plast [*neoplastic*]

plastic arts any of the arts concerned with molding or modeling, as sculpture, ceramics, etc.

plastic bomb a puttylike substance containing explosives, that will adhere to walls, etc. and is detonated by fuse or electricity, as in acts of terrorism

Plas·ti·cine (plas′tə sēn′) [PLASTIC + -INE⁴] *a trademark for* an oil-base modeling paste, used as a substitute for clay or wax —*n.* [p-] this paste: also **plas′ti·cene′** (-sēn′)

plas·ti·cize (plas′tə sīz′) *vt., vi.* -cized′, -ciz′ing to make or become plastic —**plas′ti·ci·za′tion** *n.*

plas·ti·ciz·er (-sī′zər) *n.* any of various substances added to a plastic material to keep it soft and viscous

plastic memory the tendency of certain plastics after being deformed to resume their original form when heated

plastic surgery surgery dealing with the repair or restoration of injured, deformed, or destroyed parts of the body, esp. by transferring tissue, as skin or bone, from other parts or from another individual —**plastic surgeon**

Plastic Wood *a trademark for* a cellulose product which dries and hardens to the consistency of wood when exposed to the air: used as a filler in cracks, etc.

plas·tid (plas′tid) *n.* [G. *plastiden* (pl.) < Gr. *plastides*, pl. of *plastis*, fem. of *plastēs*, molder < *plassein*, to form: see PLASTIC] any of several specialized protoplasmic structures occurring in the cytoplasm of some plant cells, in which starch, oil, protein, pigment, etc. are stored

‡**plas·tique** (plås tēk′) *n.* [Fr.] **1.** *same as* PLASTIC BOMB **2.** the technique or action of making very slow movements in dancing or pantomime, like a statue in motion

plas·ti·sol (plas′tə sôl′, -säl′) *n.* [PLASTI(C) + SOL³] a liquid dispersion consisting of very small particles of resin and a plasticizer; when heated, the mass first gels and then fuses to become a thermoplastic used as a coating, for molding, etc.

plas·to·gene (plas′tə jēn′) *n.* [< Gr. *plastos*, formed (<

plassein, to form: see PLASTIC) + E. -*gene*, -GEN] a separate genetic particle associated with the plastids and held responsible in part for their activities

plas·tron (plas′trən) *n.* [Fr. < It. *piastrone* < *piastra:* see PLASTER] **1.** a metal breastplate worn under a coat of mail **2.** a padded protector worn over the chest by fencers **3.** a trimming like a dickey, worn on the front of a woman's dress **4.** a starched shirt front **5.** the under shell of a turtle or tortoise

-plas·ty (plas′tē) [Gr. -*plastia* < *plastos*, formed < *plassein*, to form: see PLASTIC] *a terminal combining form meaning* plastic surgery involving a (specified) part [*thoracoplasty*], a (specified) source of tissue [*autoplasty*], or a (specified) purpose [*neoplasty*]

-pla·sy (plā′sē) *same as* -PLASIA

plat¹ (plat) *vt.* **plat′ted, plat′ting** [ME. *platten*, var. of *playten:* see PLAIT] [Dial.] to plait or braid —*n.* [Dial.] a plait or braid

plat² (plat) *n.* [var. of PLOT, infl. by ME. *plat*, flat < OFr.: see PLATE] **1.** a small piece of ground **2.** a map or plan, esp. of a piece of land divided into building lots —*vt.* **plat′ted, plat′ting** to make a map or plan of

plat- (plat) *same as* PLATY-

plat. 1. plateau **2.** *Mil.* platoon

Pla·ta (plä′tä), **Rí·o de la** (rē′ô de lä) estuary of the Paraná & Uruguay rivers, between Argentina & Uruguay: c. 200 mi.: Eng. name **River Plate**

Pla·tae·a (plə tē′ə) city in ancient Greece: site of a battle (479 B.C.) in which the Greeks defeated the Persians: also **Pla·tae′ae** (-ē)

plat·an, plat·ane (plat′'n) *n. same as* PLANE¹

‡**plat du jour** (plå dü zhōōr′) *n., pl.* **plats du jour** (plå) [Fr., dish of the day] the featured dish of the day in a restaurant

plate (plāt) *n.* [ME. < OFr., flat object < fem. of *plat*, flat < VL. **plattus* < Gr. *platys*, broad, flat: see PLATY-] **1.** a smooth, flat, relatively thin piece of metal or other material **2.** sheet metal made by beating, rolling, or casting **3.** *a)* any of the thin sheets of metal used in one kind of armor (**plate armor**) *b)* such armor **4.** *a)* a thin flat piece of metal on which an engraving is, or is to be, cut *b)* an impression taken from the engraved metal **5.** a print of a woodcut, lithograph, etc., esp. when used in a book **6.** a full page book illustration of any kind, printed on paper of a stock different from that of the text **7.** *a)* dishes, utensils, etc. of silver or gold, collectively *b)* metal dishes, utensils, etc., or any metallic ware, plated with gold or silver **8.** a shallow dish, usually circular, from which food is eaten **9.** *same as* PLATEFUL **10.** the food in a dish; a course [a *fruit plate*] **11.** food and service for an individual at a meal [*dinner at three dollars a plate*] **12.** a dish or other container passed in churches, etc. for donations of money **13.** *a)* a prize, orig. a gold or silver cup, given to the winner of a race or contest *b)* a contest, esp. a horse race, for such a prize, rather than for stakes: also called **plate race 14.** *same as* PETRI DISH **15.** a thin cut of beef from the forequarter, just below the short ribs: see BEEF, illus. **16.** *Anat., Zool.* a thin layer, plate, or scale, as of bone, horny tissue, etc.; lamina; scute **17.** *Archit.* a horizontal wooden girder that supports the trusses or rafters of a roof ☆**18.** *Baseball short for* HOME PLATE **19.** *Dentistry a)* that part of a denture which fits to the mouth and holds the teeth *b)* [*often pl.*] loosely, a full set of false teeth **20.** *Elec. same as* ANODE (senses 1 & 2) **21.** *Philately* the impression surface from which a sheet of postage stamps is printed **22.** *Photog.* a sheet of glass, metal, etc., coated with a film sensitive to light, upon which the image is formed **23.** *Printing* a cast, to be printed from, made from a mold of set type by the electrotype or stereotype process —*vt.* **plat′ed, plat′ing 1.** to overlay or coat with gold, silver, tin, etc. by a mechanical, chemical, or electrical process **2.** to cover with metal plates for protection **3.** *Printing* to make a stereotype or electrotype plate of

pla·teau (pla tō′) *n., pl.* **-teaus′, -teaux′** (-tōz′) [Fr. < OFr. *platel*, dim. < *plat:* see PLATE] **1.** an elevated tract of more or less level land; tableland; mesa **2.** a period, level, etc. that is relatively stable, or during which there is little change, as represented by a flat extent in a graph, etc.; specif., a period when there is an absence of progress in an individual's learning rate

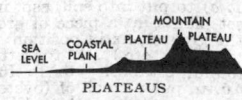

PLATEAUS

plate block *Philately* a block of postage stamps with a serial number (**plate number**) in the margin

plat·ed (plāt′id) *adj.* **1.** covered or protected with plates, as of armor **2.** knitted of two kinds of yarn, one forming the face and the other the back **3.** overlaid or coated with a metal, esp. a precious one, by a plating process [*silver-plated*]

plate·ful (plāt′fool′) *n., pl.* **-fuls′** as much as a plate will hold

plate glass ground and polished, clear glass in thick sheets, used for shop windows, mirrors, etc.

plate·let (plāt′lit) *n.* [PLATE + -LET] **1.** any of certain round or oval, nonnucleated disks, smaller than a red blood cell and containing no hemoglobin, found in the

blood of mammals and associated with the process of blood clotting **2.** *same as* THROMBOCYTE (sense 1)

plat·en (plat'n) *n.* [ME. *plateyne* < OFr. *platine*, flat plate, metal plate < *plat:* see PLATE] **1.** a flat metal plate, as that in a printing press which presses the paper against the inked type ☆**2.** in a typewriter, the roller against which the keys strike

plat·er (plāt'ər) *n.* **1.** a person or thing that plates **2.** [cf. PLATE, n. 13 b] an inferior race horse

plate rail a shelflike molding along the upper part of the wall of a room to hold ornamental plates, etc.

plat·form (plat'fôrm') *n.* [Fr. *plate-forme*, lit., flat form: see PLATE & FORM] **1.** a raised horizontal surface of wood, stone, or metal; specif., *a*) a raised stage or flooring beside railroad tracks or the like ☆*b*) a vestibule at the end of a railway car *c*) a raised flooring or stage for performers, speakers, etc. ☆**2.** a statement of principles and policies, esp. of a political party —*adj.* **1.** *a*) designating a thick sole of cork, leather, etc. for a woman's shoe *b*) designating a shoe with such a sole ☆**2.** designating a rocking chair (**platform rocker**) that rocks atop an attached, stationary base

☆**platform car** *same as* FLATCAR

☆**platform scale(s)** a weighing machine with a platform for holding whatever is to be weighed

plat·ing (plāt'iŋ) *n.* **1.** the act or process of a person or thing that plates **2.** an external layer of metal plates **3.** a thin coating of gold, silver, tin, etc.

pla·tin·ic (plə tin'ik) *adj.* of, like, or containing platinum, esp. with a valence of four

plat·i·nize (plat'n īz') *vt.* **-nized', -niz'ing** to coat or combine with platinum —**plat'i·ni·za'tion** *n.*

plat·i·no·cy·a·nide (plat'n ō sī'ə nīd') *n.* a double salt of platinous cyanide and another cyanide: used in photography, etc.

plat·i·noid (plat'n oid') *adj.* [PLATIN(UM) + -OID] resembling platinum —*n.* **1.** an alloy of copper, nickel, zinc, and tungsten: used in electrical resistance coils, etc. **2.** any metal associated with platinum

plat·i·no·type (plat'n ō tīp') *n.* **1.** a process of printing photographs in platinum black by using a platinum salt in the sensitizing solution or developer **2.** a print produced by this process

plat·i·nous (plat'n əs) *adj.* of, like, or containing platinum, esp. with a valence of two

plat·i·num (plat'n əm) *n.* [ModL. < Sp. *platina* < *plata*, silver, orig. thin plate of metal, coin < VL. *plattus*, flat: see PLATE] a steel-gray, malleable, ductile metallic chemical element, highly resistant to corrosion and electrochemical attack: used as a chemical catalyst, for acid-proof containers, ignition fuses, jewelry, dental alloys, etc.: symbol, Pt; at. wt., 195.09; at. no., 78; sp. gr., 21.45; melt. pt., 1773.5°C; boil. pt., 4300°C

platinum black a black powder of finely divided metallic platinum, made by reduction of platinum salts: used as a catalyst, as in organic synthesis

☆**platinum blonde 1.** a girl or woman with very light, silvery blonde hair, natural or bleached **2.** such a color

plat·i·tude (plat'ə tōōd', -tyōōd') *n.* [Fr. < *plat*, flat (see PLATE), after *latitude*, *rectitude*] **1.** a commonplace, flat, or dull quality, as in speech or writing **2.** a commonplace or trite remark, esp. one uttered as if it were fresh or original —**plat'i·tu·di·nous** (-tōōd'n əs) *adj.* —**plat'i·tu'di·nous·ly** *adv.*

SYN.—a **platitude** is a trite remark or idea, esp. one uttered as if it were novel or momentous; a **commonplace** is any obvious or conventional remark or idea; a **truism** is a statement whose truth is widely known and whose utterance, therefore, seems superfluous; a **cliché** is an expression or idea which, though once fresh and forceful, has become hackneyed and weak through much repetition; **bromide** is an informal term for a platitude that is especially dull, tiresome, or annoying

plat·i·tu·di·nize (plat'ə tōōd'n īz', -tyōōd'-) *vi.* **-nized', -niz'ing** to write or speak platitudes

Pla·to (plāt'ō) 427?-347? B.C.; Gr. philosopher

Pla·ton·ic (plə tän'ik, plā-) *adj.* [L. *Platonicus* < Gr. *Platōnikos* < *Platōn*, Plato] **1.** of or characteristic of Plato or his philosophy **2.** idealistic, visionary, or impractical **3.** [*usually* p-] designating or of a relationship, or love, between a man and a woman that is purely spiritual or intellectual and without sexual activity —**pla·ton'i·cal·ly** *adv.*

Pla·to·nism (plāt'n iz'm) *n.* [ModL. *platonismus*] **1.** the philosophy of Plato or his school; esp., the doctrine holding that objects of perception are real insofar as they imitate or participate in an independent realm of immutable essences, ideas, or logical forms which constitute the world of essential reality: see IDEALISM **2.** a doctrine or saying typical of Platonic philosophy **3.** the theory or practice of platonic love —**Pla'to·nist** *n.* —**Pla'to·nis'tic** *adj.*

Pla·to·nize (-īz') *vi.* **-nized', -niz'ing** to follow the philosophy of Plato; philosophize in a Platonic manner —*vt.* to make Platonic

pla·toon (plə tōōn') *n.* [Fr. *peloton*, a ball, group, platoon

< *pelote*, a ball: see PELLET] **1.** a military unit composed of two or more squads or sections, normally under the command of a lieutenant: it is a subdivision of a company, troop, etc. **2.** a group or unit like this [*a platoon of police*] ☆**3.** *Sports* any of the specialized squads (as the offensive and defensive squads in professional football) constituting a single team —*vt.* to divide into, or use as or on, a platoon

platoon sergeant *U.S. Army* the senior noncommissioned officer in a platoon, equal in grade to a sergeant first class

Platt·deutsch (plät'doich', plät'-) *n.* [G. < Du. *platduitsch* < *plat*, plain, clear, lit., flat (< OFr. *plat:* see PLATE) + *duitsch*, German, Dutch: see DEUTSCHLAND] the Low German vernacular dialects of N Germany

Platte (plat) [< Fr. *Rivière Platte*, lit., flat river] river formed in C Nebr. by the junction of the North Platte & the South Platte, & flowing eastward into the Missouri: 310 mi.

plat·ter (plat'ər) *n.* [ME. *plater* < Anglo-Fr. < OFr. *plat:* see PLATE] **1.** a large, shallow dish, usually oval, for serving food, esp. meat or fish ☆**2.** [Slang] *same as* HOME PLATE ☆**3.** [Slang] a phonograph record

Platt National Park (plat) [after O. H. Platt (1827-1905), U.S. senator from Conn.] national park in S Okla., containing sulfur springs: c. 1 1/2 sq. mi.

Platts·burgh (plats'bərg) [after Z. *Platt*, early settler, c. 1784] city in NE N.Y., on Lake Champlain: scene of a British invasion (1814) repulsed by U.S. forces: pop. 19,000: formerly sp. **Plattsburg**

plat·y¹ (plāt'ē) *adj.* Geol. composed of plates, sheets, or slabs, as certain lavas, muds, rocks, etc.

plat·y² (plat'ē) *n.*, *pl.* **plat'y**, **plat'ys** *or* **plat'ies** [clipped < ModL. *Platypoecilus*, name of a genus of fishes < PLATY- + Gr. *poikilos*, many-colored] any of a number of brightly colored, viviparous freshwater fishes (genus *Xiphophorus*) of Central America: used in tropical aquariums and in genetics research

plat·y- (plat'ē) [< Gr. *platys*, broad, flat < IE. **plat-*, var. of base **plā-*, whence L. *planus*, flat] a combining form meaning broad or flat [*platypus*]

plat·y·hel·minth (plat'ē hel'minth) *n.* [prec. + HELMINTH] any of a phylum (Platyhelminthes) of flattened worms, such as the planarians, tapeworms, liver flukes, etc., with a soft, unsegmented body and a flame cell system: many are parasitic —**plat'y·hel·min'thic** *adj.*

plat·y·pus (plat'ə pəs) *n.*, *pl.* **-pus·es, -pi'** (-pī') [ModL. < Gr. *platypous*, flatfooted < *platys*, flat (see PLATY-) + *pous*, FOOT] a small, aquatic, egg-laying monotreme mammal (*Ornithorhynchus anatinus*) of Australia and Tasmania, with webbed feet, a tail like a beaver's, and a bill like a duck's: in full **duckbill platypus**

PLATYPUS
(16-24 in. long, including tail)

plat·yr·rhine (plat'ə rīn', -rin) *adj.* [ModL. *platyrrhinus* < Gr. *platyrrhin*, broad-nosed < *platys* (see PLATY-) + *rhis* (gen. *rhinos*), nose] having a broad, flat nose with a wide, flat space between the nostrils —*n.* a platyrrhine creature, as a new-world monkey: Distinguished from CATARRHINE

plau·dit (plô'dit) *n.* [L. *plaudite*, pl. imper. of *plaudere*, to applaud] [*usually pl.*] **1.** an applauding or round of applause **2.** any expression of approval or praise

Plau·en (plou'ən) city in S East Germany: pop. 79,000

plau·si·ble (plô'zə b'l) *adj.* [L. *plausibilis* < *plaudere*, to applaud] **1.** seemingly true, acceptable, etc.: often implying disbelief **2.** seemingly honest, trustworthy, etc.: often implying distrust —**plau'si·bil'i·ty, plau'si·ble·ness** *n.* —**plau'si·bly** *adv.*

SYN.—**plausible** applies to that which at first glance appears to be true, reasonable, valid, etc. but which may or may not be so, although there is no connotation of deliberate deception [*a plausible argument*]; **credible** is used of that which is believable because it is supported by evidence, sound logic, etc.; [*a credible account*]; **specious** applies to that which is superficially reasonable, valid, etc. but is actually not so, and it connotes intention to deceive [*a specious excuse*] —ANT. **genuine, actual**

plau·sive (plô'siv) *adj.* **1.** [Rare] applauding or showing praise **2.** obs. var. of PLAUSIBLE

Plau·tus (plô'təs), (**Titus Maccius**) 254?-184 B.C.; Rom. writer of comic dramas

play (plā) *vi.* [ME. *pleien* < OE. *plegan*, to play, be active] **1.** to move lightly, rapidly, or erratically; flutter [*playing on the waves*] **2.** to amuse oneself, as by taking part in a game or sport; engage in recreation **3.** to take active part in a game or sport [*not playing because of an injury*] **4.** to engage in a game for stakes; gamble **5.** *a*) to act, deal, or touch carelessly or lightly; trifle (*with* a thing or person) *b*) to make love sportively; dally **6.** to perform on a musical instrument **7.** to give out sounds, esp. musical sounds: said of an instrument, phonograph or tape recorder, etc. **8.** to lend itself to performance [*a drama that does not play well*] **9.** to act in a specified way;

esp., to pretend to be [to *play* dumb] **10.** to act in or as in a drama; perform on the stage **11.** to be performed in a theater, on the radio, etc. [what movie is *playing*?] **12.** to move freely within limits, as parts of a machine **13.** to be ejected, discharged, or directed repeatedly or continuously, as a fountain, a spotlight, etc. (with *on*, *over*, or *along*) **14.** to impose unscrupulously (*on* another's feelings or susceptibilities) —*vt.* **1.** *a)* to take part in (a game or sport) *b)* to be stationed at (a specified position) in a sport **2.** to oppose (a person, team, etc.) in a game or contest **3.** to enter or use (a player, etc.) in a game or contest **4.** to do (something), as in fun or to deceive [*play* tricks] **5.** *a)* to bet ☆*b)* to bet on [*play* the horses] ☆*c)* to act on the basis of [*play* a hunch] ☆**6.** to speculate in (the stock market) **7.** to cause to move, act, operate, etc.; wield; ply **8.** to put (a specified card) into play [to *play* an ace] **9.** to cause or effect [to *play* havoc] **10.** to perform (music) **11.** *a)* to perform on (a musical instrument) *b)* to cause (a phonograph, phonograph record, etc.) to give out sounds, esp. of music **12.** to accompany or lead (someone) with music (with *in*, *off*, etc.) **13.** to perform (a drama or dramatic passage) **14.** to act the part of [to *play* Iago, to *play* the fool] **15.** to imitate the activities of, as children do for amusement [to *play* teacher, to *play* house] ☆**16.** to give performances in [to *play* Boston for a week] **17.** to eject, discharge, or direct (water, light, etc.) repeatedly or continuously (*on*, *over*, or *along*) **18.** to let (a hooked fish) tire itself by tugging at the line ☆**19.** to use or exploit (a person) [*played* him for a fool] —*n.* **1.** action, motion, or activity, esp. when free, rapid, or light [the *play* of muscles] **2.** freedom or scope for motion or action, esp. of a mechanism **3.** activity engaged in for amusement or recreation; sport, games, etc.; often, specif., the natural activities of children **4.** fun; joking [to do a thing in *play*] **5.** *a)* the playing of a game *b)* the way or technique of playing a game **6.** *a)* a maneuver, move, or act in a game *b)* a turn at playing **7.** the act of gambling **8.** a dramatic composition or performance; drama **9.** [Obs.] sexual activity; dalliance —**in** (or **out of**) **play** *Sports* in (or not in) the condition for continuing play: said of a ball, etc. —**make a play for** [Colloq.] **1.** to employ one's arts and wiles in order to attract, esp. sexually **2.** to use all one's skill in order to obtain —**play along** (**with**) to join in or cooperate (with) —**play around** to engage in some activity, as lovemaking, in a frivolous way —**play at 1.** to participate in **2.** to pretend to be engaged in **3.** to perform or work at halfheartedly —☆**play both ends against the middle 1.** to maneuver alternatives in order to win something no matter what the outcome **2.** to play off opposing factions, etc. against one another to one's own profit —**play down** to attach little importance, or give little publicity, to; minimize —**played out 1.** finished **2.** worn out; exhausted **3.** out-of-date —**play fair 1.** to play according to the rules **2.** to behave honorably —**play for time** to maneuver so as to delay an outcome, gain a respite, etc. —**play into** (**someone's**) **hands** to act in such a way as to give the advantage to (someone) —**play it** to act in a (specified) manner [to *play it* smart] —**play off 1.** to pit (a person or thing) against another ☆**2.** in games, to break (a tie) by playing once more **3.** [Archaic] to palm off —**play one's cards well** (or **right**) to use one's resources in the most effective manner —**play out 1.** to play to the finish; end **2.** to pay out or gradually release (a rope, etc.) —☆**play up** [Colloq.] to give prominence to; advertise —**play up to** [Colloq.] to try to please by flattery, etc. —**play'a·ble** *adj.*

SYN.—**play**, the general verb, implies activity, physical or mental, whose sole aim is diversion or amusement; **sport**, in this connection now somewhat literary, implies active physical play out-of-doors [children *sporting* in the woods]; **frolic** implies light-hearted, carefree gaiety in playing [*frolicking* at a New Year's Eve party]; **romp** suggests active, boisterous play that involves running about and jumping [youth *romping* on the beach]; **gambol** suggests the skipping about of lambs or young children in play [let them *gambol* on the lawn]

☆**pla·ya** (plä'ya) *n.* [Sp., beach < Pr. < VL. *plagia*, coast, side < akin to Gr. *plagia*, sides < *plagos*, side < IE. base *plāg-*, flat, whence FLAKE¹] a desert basin that temporarily becomes a shallow lake after heavy rains

play·act (plā'akt') *vi.* **1.** to act in a play **2.** to pretend; make believe **3.** to behave in an affected or dramatic manner —**play'act'ing** *n.*

play·back (-bak') *n.* the playing of a disc or tape just after recording material on it, as for checking the quality of performance or reproduction

play·bill (-bil') *n.* **1.** a poster or circular advertising a play **2.** a program of a play, listing the cast, staff, etc.

play·boy (-boi') *n.* ☆[Colloq.] a man, esp. a man of means, who is given to pleasure-seeking, sexual promiscuity, etc.

☆**play-by-play** (-bī plā') *adj.* recounting each play of a game or incident of a happening as it occurs or occurred

play·er (-ər) *n.* **1.** a person who plays a game [a football *player*] **2.** a performer in a drama; actor **3.** a person who plays a musical instrument **4.** a gambler ☆**5.** *a)* an apparatus attached to a musical instrument, as to a piano, for playing it automatically *b)* same as RECORD PLAYER

☆**player piano** a piano that can play automatically by means of a built-in pneumatic mechanism that depresses the keys in response to signals on a perforated roll

play·fel·low (plā'fel'ō) *n. same as* PLAYMATE

play·ful (-fəl) *adj.* **1.** fond of play or fun; frisky; frolicsome **2.** said or done in fun; jocular —**play'ful·ly** *adv.* —**play'·ful·ness** *n.*

play·go·er (-gō'ər) *n.* a person who goes to the theater frequently or regularly —**play'go'ing** *n., adj.*

play·ground (-ground') *n.* **1.** a place, often part of a schoolyard, for outdoor games and recreation **2.** a popular resort area

☆**play hook·y** (hook'ē) [*hooky* prob. < *hook it,* to run away] to stay away from school without permission; be a truant

play·house (plā'hous') *n.* [OE. *pleghus* < *plega,* a play + *hus,* HOUSE] **1.** a theater for live dramatic productions ☆**2.** a small house for children to play in **3.** a child's toy house or doll house

playing cards cards used in playing various games, arranged in decks of four suits (spades, hearts, diamonds, and clubs): a standard deck has 52 cards

playing field ground for playing games on, esp. as marked out for the playing of a particular game

play·let (-lit) *n.* a short drama

play·mate (-māt') *n.* a companion in games and recreation; playfellow

play-off (-ôf') *n.* a contest or any of a series of contests played to break a tie or to decide a championship, as between the top finishers in the divisions of a league

play on words a pun or punning

play·pen (-pen') *n.* a small, portable enclosure in which an infant can be left safely to play, crawl, etc.

☆**play·room** (-rōōm') *n.* a recreation room, esp. for children

play·suit (-sōōt') *n.* a woman's or child's outfit for sports or play, consisting usually of shorts or pants and a shirt

play·thing (-thiŋ') *n.* a thing to play with; toy

play·time (-tim') *n.* time for play or recreation

play·wright (-rit') *n.* [see WRIGHT] a person who writes plays; dramatist

pla·za (plä'zə, plaz'ə) *n.* [Sp. < L. *platea:* see PLACE] **1.** a public square or marketplace in a city or town **2.** a complex of shops or buildings, esp. a shopping center **3.** a service area along a superhighway, with a restaurant, gas station, etc.: also **service plaza**

plea (plē) *n.* [ME. *plai* < OFr. *plaid,* a suit, plea < L. *placitum,* an opinion, order, orig. that which is pleasing, orig. neut. pp. of *placere,* to PLEASE] **1.** a statement in defense or justification; excuse **2.** an earnest and urgent request; appeal; entreaty **3.** *Law a)* a pleading or allegation *b)* a statement made by, or on behalf of, a defendant, either answering the charges or showing why he should not be required to answer

pleach (plēch) *vt.* [ME. *plechen* < ONormFr. *plechier,* for OFr. *plessier, plaissier,* to weave, plait: see PLASH³] to bend and interlace (branches); plait

plead (plēd) *vi.* **plead'ed** or (colloq. or dial.) **pled** (pled), **plead'ing** [ME. *pleden* < OFr. *plaidier* < *plaid:* see PLEA] **1.** *a)* to present a case in a law court; argue the case of either party *b)* to present a plea (sense 3 *b*) **2.** to make an earnest appeal; supplicate; beg [to *plead* for mercy] —*vt.* **1.** to discuss or defend (a law case) by argument **2.** to declare oneself to be (guilty or not guilty) in answer to a charge **3.** to offer as an excuse or defense [to *plead* ignorance] —SYN. see APPEAL —**plead'a·ble** *adj.* —**plead'er** *n.*

plead·ings (-iŋz) *n.pl.* the statements setting forth the claims or allegations of the plaintiff and the answer of the defendant

pleas·ance (plez''ns) *n.* [ME. *plesaunce* < MFr. *plaisance* < *plaisant:* see ff.] **1.** orig., pleasure; joy **2.** a pleasure ground or garden, usually part of an estate: also sp. **pleas'aunce**

pleas·ant (-'nt) *adj.* [ME. *plesaunte* < MFr. *plaisant,* prp. of *plaisir,* to PLEASE] **1.** agreeable to the mind or senses; pleasing; delightful **2.** having an agreeable manner, appearance, etc.; amiable **3.** [Obs.] gay; merry; playful —**pleas'ant·ly** *adv.* —**pleas'ant·ness** *n.*

SYN.—**pleasant** and **pleasing** both imply the producing of an agreeable effect upon the mind or senses, but the former word stresses the effect produced [a *pleasant* smile] and the latter, the ability to produce such an effect [her *pleasing* ways]; **agreeable** is used of that which is in accord with one's personal likes, mood, etc. [*agreeable* music]; **enjoyable** implies the ability to give enjoyment or pleasure [an *enjoyable* picnic]; **gratifying** implies the ability to give satisfaction or pleasure by indulging the wishes, hopes, etc. [a *gratifying* experience] —ANT. unpleasant, disagreeable

pleas·ant·ry (plez'′n trē) *n., pl.* **-ries** [Fr. *plaisanterie*] **1.** the quality or state of being pleasant, or playful, in conversation; jocularity **2.** *a)* a humorous remark or action; joke *b)* a polite social remark [to exchange *pleasantries*] **3.** [Archaic] pleasure

please (plēz) *vt.* **pleased, pleas'ing** [ME. *plaisen* < MFr. *plaisir* < L. *placere,* to please, akin to *placidus,* gentle, mild, *placare,* to calm, soothe < IE. base *plāk-*, flat, smooth, whence FLAKE²] **1.** to be agreeable to; give pleasure to; satisfy **2.** to be the will or wish of [it *pleased* him to remain] —*vi.* **1.** to be agreeable; give pleasure; satisfy [to aim to *please*] **2.** to have the will or wish; like [to do as one *pleases*]: also used passively [you are *pleased* to scoff] *Please* is also used for politeness in requests or commands to mean "be obliging enough (to)" [*please* sit

down/ —**if you please** if you wish or like; if you will; if you permit: sometimes used in ironic exclamation —**please God** if it pleases God; if it is God's will —**please oneself** to do as one wishes

pleas·ing (plē′ziŋ) *adj.* giving pleasure; pleasant; agreeable; gratifying —*SYN.* see PLEASANT —**pleas′ing·ly** *adv.* —**pleas′ing·ness** *n.*

pleas·ur·a·ble (plezh′ər ə b'l) *adj.* pleasant; enjoyable; agreeable —**pleas′ur·a·bil′i·ty** (-bil′ə tē), **pleas′ur·a·ble·ness** *n.* —**pleas′ur·a·bly** *adv.*

pleas·ure (plezh′ər, plā′zhər) *n.* [ME., altered < *plesir* < MFr. *plaiser*, orig. inf.: see PLEASE] 1. a pleased feeling; enjoyment; delight; satisfaction 2. one's wish, will, or choice [what is your *pleasure?*] 3. a thing that gives delight or satisfaction 4. gratification of the senses; sensual satisfaction 5. amusement; fun —*vt., vi.* **-ured, -ur·ing** [Archaic, exc. Dial.] to give pleasure to or take pleasure (in) —**pleas′ure·ful** *adj.*

SYN.—**pleasure** is the general term for an agreeable feeling of satisfaction, ranging from a quiet sense of gratification to a positive sense of happiness; **delight** implies a high degree of obvious pleasure, openly and enthusiastically expressed [a child's *delight* with a new toy]; **joy** describes a keenly felt, exuberant, often demonstrative happiness [their *joy* at his safe return]; **enjoyment** suggests a somewhat more quiet feeling of satisfaction with that which pleases [our *enjoyment* of the recital] —*ANT.* displeasure, sorrow, vexation

pleasure principle *Psychoanalysis* the automatic adjustment of the mental activity to secure pleasure, or gratification, and avoid pain, or unpleasantness

pleat (plēt) *n.* [ME. *pleten*, var. of *playten*: see PLAIT] a flat double fold in cloth or other material, of uniform width and pressed or stitched in place —*vt.* to lay and press (cloth) in a pleat or series of pleats

pleat·er (-ər) *n.* a person or thing that pleats; specif., a sewing-machine attachment for making pleats

pleb (pleb) *n.* same as: 1. PLEBEIAN ☆2. PLEBE (sense 3)

plebe (plēb) *n.* [Fr. *plèbe* < L. *plebs*] 1. the plebs in ancient Rome 2. [Obs.] the common people of any nation ☆3. [short for PLEBEIAN] a member of the freshman class at the U.S. Military Academy or Naval Academy

ple·be·ian (pli bē′ən) *n.* [< L. *plebeius* < *plebs*, PLEBS] 1. a member of the ancient Roman lower class: opposed to PATRICIAN 2. one of the common people 3. a vulgar, coarse person —*adj.* 1. of or characteristic of the lower class in ancient Rome or of the common people in any country 2. vulgar, coarse, or common —**ple·be′ian·ism** *n.* —**ple·be′ian·ly** *adv.*

pleb·i·scite (pleb′ə sīt′; *chiefly Brit.*, -sit) *n.* [Fr. *plébiscite* < L. *plebiscitum* < *plebs*, PLEBS + *scitum*, decree, neut. pp. of *scire*, to know: see SCIENCE] an expression of the people's will by direct ballot on a political issue, as in choosing between independent nationhood or affiliation with another nation —**ple·bis·ci·tar·y** (plə bis′ə ter′ē) *adj.*

plebs (plebz) *n., pl.* **ple·bes** (plē′bēz) [L., akin to *plere*, to fill: for IE. base see PLENTY] 1. the lower class in ancient Roman society 2. the common people; the masses

plec·tog·nath (plek′täg nath′) *n.* [< ModL. Plectognathi, name of the order < Gr. *plektos*, twisted (< *plekein*, to braid: for IE. base see FLAX) + *gnathos*, a jaw] any of an order (Plectognathi) of bony fishes, including the triggerfishes, trunkfishes, etc., found in warm seas and having a small mouth with powerful jaws and bony or spiny scales —*adj.* of the plectognaths

plec·trum (plek′trəm) *n., pl.* **-trums, -tra** (-trə) [L. < Gr. *plēktron*, device for plucking the lyre < *plēssein*, to strike: see PLAINT] a thin piece of metal, bone, plastic, etc., used for plucking the strings of a guitar, mandolin, etc.: also **plec′tron** (-trän), *pl.* **-tra** (-trə)

pled (pled) *colloq. or dial. pt. & pp.* of PLEAD

pledge (plej) *n.* [ME. *plegge* < OFr. *plege* (or ML. *plegium*), prob. < OS. *plegan*, to guarantee, with form & meaning infl. by L. *praebere*, to offer] 1. the condition of being given or held as security for a contract, payment, etc. [a thing held in *pledge*] 2. a person or thing given or held as security for the performance of a contract, as a guarantee of faith, etc.; something pawned; hostage 3. a token or earnest 4. a drinking of someone's health to express good will or allegiance; toast 5. a promise or agreement 6. something promised, esp. money to be contributed in regular payments ☆7. a person undergoing a trial period before formal initiation into a fraternity —*vt.* **pledged, pledg′ing** 1. to present as security or guarantee, esp. for the repayment of a loan; pawn 2. to drink a health to; toast 3. to bind by a promise or agreement 4. to promise to give [to *pledge* allegiance, *pledge* money to a fund] ☆5. *a)* to accept tentative membership in (a fraternity) *b)* to accept as a pledge (*n.*) —**take the pledge** to take a vow not to drink alcoholic liquor

SYN.—**pledge** applies to anything given as security for the performance of an act or contract or for the payment of a debt [he gave her a ring as a *pledge*]; **earnest**, in current usage, applies to anything given or done as an indication, promise, or assurance of more to follow [his early triumphs were an *earnest* of his success]; **token** is used of anything serving or given as evidence of authority, genuineness, good faith, etc. [this watch is a *token* of our gratitude];

pawn now usually refers to an article left as security for the money lent on it by a pawnbroker; **hostage** is applied to a person handed over as a pledge for the fulfillment of certain terms or one seized and kept to force others to comply with demands

pledg·ee (plej′ē′) *n.* a person to whom a pledge is delivered: distinguished from PLEDGOR

pledg·er (plej′ər) *n.* a person who pledges

pledg·et (plej′it) *n.* [< ?] a small compress, sometimes medicated, used as a dressing for a wound or sore

pledg·or (plej′ər, plej′ôr′) *n. Law* a person who delivers something as security: distinguished from PLEDGEE

-ple·gia (plē′jē ə, -jə) [ModL. < Gr. *-plēgia* < *plēgē*, a stroke, akin to *plēssein*, to strike: see PLAINT] *a combining form meaning* paralysis [paraplegia]

Plé·iade (plā yàd′) [Fr.: see ff.] a group of seven French poets of the 16th cent. who favored the use of classical forms —*n.* a small group, usually seven, of brilliant persons: also **ple·iad, Ple·iad** (plē′ad)

Ple·ia·des (plē′ə dēz′; *chiefly Brit.*, plī′-) *n.pl., sing.* **Ple′iad** (-ad) [ME. *Pliades* < L. *Pleiades* < Gr., pl. of *Pleias*] 1. *Gr. Myth.* the seven daughters of Atlas and Pleione, placed by Zeus among the stars 2. *Astron.* a cluster of stars in the constellation Taurus, six of which are readily visible and represent the daughters of Atlas, the seventh being "lost" (the **Lost Pleiad**)

plein-air (plān′er′) *adj.* [Fr., lit., open air] designating, of, or in the manner of certain schools of French impressionist painting of the late 19th cent. engaged mainly in representing observed effects of outdoor light and atmosphere —**plein′-air′ism** *n.* —**plein′-air′ist** *n.*

plei·o- (plī′ə, -ō) *same as* PLEO-

Plei·o·cene (plī′ə sēn′) *adj. same as* PLIOCENE

plei·o·tax·y (plī′ə tak′sē) *n.* [PLEIO- + -TAXY] *Bot.* an increase in the number of whorls in a flower

plei·ot·ro·py (plī ät′rə pē) *n.* [PLEIO- + -TROPY] *Genetics* the condition in which a single gene exerts simultaneous effects on more than one character in the offspring: also **plei·ot′ro·pism** —**plei·o·trop·ic** (plī′ə träp′ik) *adj.* — **plei′o·trop′i·cal·ly** *adv.*

Pleis·to·cene (plīs′tə sēn′) *adj.* [< Gr. *pleistos*, most, superl. of *polys*, much (see POLY-) + -CENE] designating or of the first epoch of the Quaternary Period in the Cenozoic Era, characterized by the spreading and recession of continental ice sheets and by the appearance of modern man —**the Pleistocene** the Pleistocene Epoch or its rocks: see GEOLOGY, chart

ple·na·ry (plē′nə rē, plen′ə-) *adj.* [LL. *plenarius* < L. *plenus*, FULL[1]] 1. full; complete; absolute [*plenary* power] 2. for attendance by all members [a *plenary* session] —**ple′na·ri·ly** (-rə lē) *adv.*

plenary indulgence *R.C.Ch.* an indulgence remitting in full the temporal punishment incurred by a sinner

plen·i·po·ten·ti·ar·y (plen′i pə ten′shē er′ē, -shə rē) *adj.* [ML. *plenipotentiarius* < LL. *plenipotens*, possessing full power < L. *plenus*, full + *potens*, powerful] having or conferring full power or authority [an ambassador *plenipotentiary*] —*n., pl.* **-ar′ies** a person, esp. a diplomatic agent, given full authority to act as representative of a government

plen·ish (plen′ish) *vt.* [ME. *plenissen* < MFr. *pleniss-*, prp. stem of *plenir*, to fill < L. *plenus*, FULL[1]] [Scot.] to fill up; furnish; stock

plen·i·tude (plen′ə tōōd′, -tyōōd′) *n.* [ME. < OFr. < L. *plenitudo* < *plenus*, FULL[1]] 1. fullness; completeness 2. abundance; plenty

plen·i·tu·di·nous (plen′ə tōōd′'n əs, -tyōōd′-) *adj.* 1. marked by plenitude; abundant; full 2. stout; obese

plen·te·ous (plen′tē əs) *adj.* [ME. *plentevous* < OFr. *plentevous* < *plente*, PLENTY] 1. marked by or being in abundance; plentiful; copious 2. producing abundantly; fruitful; productive —**plen′te·ous·ly** *adv.* —**plen′te·ous·ness** *n.*

plen·ti·ful (plen′ti fəl) *adj.* 1. having or yielding plenty 2. sufficient or more than enough; abundant —**plen′ti·ful·ly** *adv.* —**plen′ti·ful·ness** *n.*

SYN.—**plentiful** implies a large or full supply [a *plentiful* supply of food]; **abundant** implies a very plentiful or very large supply [a forest *abundant* in wild game]; **copious**, now used chiefly with reference to quantity produced, used, etc., implies a rich or flowing abundance [a *copious* harvest, discharge, etc.]; **profuse** implies a giving or pouring forth abundantly or lavishly, often to excess [*profuse* in his thanks]; **ample** applies to that which is large enough to meet all demands [his savings are *ample* to see him through this crisis] —*ANT.* scarce, scant

plen·ty (plen′tē) *n., pl.* **-ties** [ME. *plente* < MFr. *plenté* < L. *plenitas* < *plenus*, FULL[1]] 1. prosperity; opulence 2. a sufficient supply; enough: in earlier use, with the article [a *plenty* of food] 3. a large number; many [*plenty* of errors] —*adj.* [Colloq.] plentiful; enough; ample [*plenty* time] —*adv.* [Colloq.] fully; sufficiently; quite [*plenty* good]

ple·num (plē′nəm) *n., pl.* **-nums, -na** (-nə) [ModL. < L., neut. of *plenus*, FULL[1]] 1. space filled with matter: opposed to VACUUM 2. fullness 3. a full or general assembly, as of all members of a legislative body 4. *a)* an enclosed volume of gas under greater pressure than that surrounding the container *b)* the state of this

---

fat, āpe, cär; ten, ēven; is, bīte; gō, hôrn, tōōl, look; oil, out; up, fur; get; joy; yet; chin; she; thin, *then*; zh, leisure; ŋ, ring; ə for *a* in *ago*, *e* in *agent*, *i* in *sanity*, *o* in *comply*, *u* in *focus*; ′ as in *able* (ā′b'l); Fr. bàl; ë, Fr. coeur; ö, Fr. feu; Fr. mon; ô, Fr. coq; ü, Fr. duc; r, Fr. cri; H, G. ich; kh, G. doch. See inside front cover. ☆ Americanism; ‡foreign; *hypothetical; < derived from

ple·o- (plē′ə, -ō) [< Gr. *pleon*, more: see PLEONASM] *a combining form meaning* more [*pleochroism*]

pleochroic halo a dark-colored, microscopic ring around a minute radioactive particle in certain mineral crystals, used in estimating the age of the rocks containing them

ple·och·ro·ism (plē äk′rō iz′m) n. [< PLEO- + Gr. *chroos*, color + -ISM] the property of some minerals of absorbing selectively various wavelengths of light and of displaying different colors when looked at in the directions of the different crystal axes —**ple′o·chro′ic** (-ə krō′ik) adj.

ple·o·mor·phism (plē′ə môr′fiz′m) n. [PLEO- + -MORPH(IC) + -ISM] **1.** *Bot.* the occurrence of two or more forms in one life cycle **2.** *Zool.* same as POLYMORPHISM (sense 2) —**ple′o·mor′phic, ple′o·mor′phous** (-fəs) adj.

ple·o·nasm (plē′ə naz′m) n. [LL. *pleonasmus* < Gr. *pleonasmos* < *pleonazein*, to be in excess < *pleon*, neut. of *pleōn*, more, compar. of *polys*, much: see POLY-] **1.** the use of more words than are necessary for the expression of an idea; redundancy (Ex.: "plenty enough") **2.** an instance of this **3.** the redundant word or expression —**ple′o·nas′tic** adj. —**ple′o·nas′ti·cal·ly** adv.

ple·o·pod (plē′ə päd′) n. [< Gr. *pleon*, prp. of *plein*, to swim + -POD] *Zool.* any of the biramous appendages attached to the abdomen of higher crustaceans; swimmeret

ple·si·o·saur (plē′sē ə sôr′) n. [ModL. *plesiosaurus* < Gr. *plēsios*, close, near + *sauros*, lizard: see -SAURUS] any of an extinct order (Plesiosauria) of large water reptiles of the Mesozoic Era, characterized by a small head, long neck, short tail, and four paddlelike limbs

ples·sor (ples′ər) n. *same as* PLEXOR

pleth·o·ra (pleth′ə rə) n. [ML. < Gr. *plēthōrē* < *plēthein*, to be full < *plēthos*, fullness < IE. *plē-*, var. of base *pel-*, to FILL] **1.** the state of being too full; overabundance; excess **2.** an abnormal condition characterized by an excess of blood in the circulatory system or in some part of it —**ple·thor·ic** (plə thôr′ik, -thär′-; pleth′ə rik) adj. —**ple·thor′i·cal·ly** adv.

ple·thys·mo·graph (plə thiz′mə graf′, -gräf′) n. [< Gr. *plēthysmos*, a multiplying < *plēthymein*, to increase < *plēthys*, a crowd < IE. *plē-*, var. of base *pel-*, to FILL) + -GRAPH] any of several instruments for measuring and recording various body functions, as the velocity or volume of blood flow, heart rate or breathing rate, changes in the size of organs or limbs, etc. —**ple·thys′mo·graph′ic** adj. —**pleth·ys·mog·ra·phy** (pleth′iz måg′rə fē) n.

pleu·ra (ploor′ə) n., pl. **-rae** (-ē) [ML. < Gr. *pleura*, a rib, side] the thin serous membrane that covers a lung and lines that half of the chest cavity in mammals —**pleu′ral** adj.

pleu·ri·sy (ploor′ə sē) n. [ME. *pleresye* < MFr. *pleurisie* < LL. *pleurisis*, for L. *pleuritis* < Gr. *pleuritis* < *pleura*, a rib, side: see PLEURA] inflammation of the pleura, characterized by difficult, painful breathing and often accompanied by the exudation of liquid into the chest cavity —**pleu·rit·ic** (ploo rit′ik) adj.

☆**pleurisy root 1.** *same as* BUTTERFLY WEED **2.** the root of this plant, formerly used as a cure for pleurisy

pleu·ro- (ploor′ə, -ō) [< Gr. *pleura*, a rib, side] *a combining form meaning:* **1.** on or near the side [*pleurodont*] **2.** of, involving, or near the pleura [*pleurotomy*] Also, before a vowel, **pleur-**

pleu·ro·dont (ploor′ə dänt′) adj. [prec. + -ODONT] having teeth growing from the inside of the jawbone instead of from separate sockets, as some lizards —n. a pleurodont animal

pleu·ron (ploor′än) n., pl. **pleu·ra** (-ə) [ModL. < Gr. *pleuron*, a rib] either of the lateral plates on the thoracic and abdominal segments of an arthropod

pleu·ro·pneu·mo·ni·a (ploor′ō nōō mōn′yə, -nyōō-; -mō′nē ə) n. [PLEURO- + PNEUMONIA] pneumonia complicated by pleurisy

pleu·rot·o·my (ploo rät′ə mē) n., pl. **-mies** [PLEURO- + -TOMY] surgical incision of the pleura to permit drainage of exuded liquids

pleus·ton (ploo′stän) n. [< Gr. *pleustikos*, fit for sailing < *plein*, to sail (< IE. base *pleu-*, FLOW) + -ton, as in NEUSTON, PLANKTON] small organisms, as algae, gastropods, etc., floating on or near the surface of a body of water —**pleus·ton′ic** adj.

Plev·en (plev′ən) city in N Bulgaria: pop. 79,000: also **Plev′na** (-nä)

plew (ploo) n. [< CanadFr. *pelu*, hairy < Fr. < L. *pilus*, hair: see PILE²] [Western & Canad.] a beaver skin

plex·i·form (plek′sə fôrm′) adj. [< PLEXUS + -FORM] like, or in the form of, a plexus or network; complex

☆**Plex·i·glas** (-glas′, -gläs′) n. [< L. *plexus*, a twining (see PLEXUS) + GLASS] a trademark for a lightweight, transparent, thermoplastic synthetic resin, used for aircraft canopies, lenses and windows, etc. —n. this material: also **plex′i·glass**

plex·or (plek′sər) n. [ModL. < Gr. *plēxis*: see prec.] *Med.* a small hammer with a soft head, as of rubber, formerly used in percussion

plex·us (plek′səs) n., pl. **-us·es, -us** [ModL. < L., a twining, braid < pp. of *plectere*, to twine, braid, akin to *plicare*: see PLY¹] a complexly interconnected arrangement of parts; network; specif., *Anat.* a network of blood vessels, lymphatic vessels, nerves, etc. [the solar *plexus* (of nerves) in the abdomen]

pli·a·ble (plī′ə b'l) adj. [LME. *plyable* < MFr. < *plier*, to bend, fold < L. *plicare*, to fold, bend: see PLY¹] **1.** easily bent or molded; flexible **2.** easily influenced or persuaded; tractable **3.** adjusting readily; adaptable —**pli′a·bil′i·ty, pli′a·ble·ness** n. —**pli′a·bly** adv.

SYN.—**pliable** and **pliant** both imply capability of being easily bent, suggesting the suppleness of a wooden switch and, figuratively, a yielding nature or adaptability; **plastic** is used of substances, such as plaster or clay, that can be molded into various forms which are retained upon hardening, and figuratively suggests an impressionable quality; **ductile** literally and figuratively suggests that which can be finely drawn or stretched out [copper is a *ductile* metal]; **malleable** literally or figuratively suggests that which can be hammered, beaten, or pressed into various forms [copper is *malleable* as well as ductile] —ANT. **inflexible, rigid, brittle**

pli·ant (plī′ənt) adj. [ME. *plyande* < MFr., prp. of *plier*: see PLIABLE] **1.** easily bent; pliable **2.** adaptable or compliant —SYN. see PLIABLE —**pli′an·cy, pli′ant·ness** n. —**pli′ant·ly** adv.

pli·ca (plī′kə) n., pl. **-cae** (-sē) [ML., a fold < L. *plicare*, to fold: see PLY¹] *Anat.* a fold or folding, esp. of the skin or mucous membrane

pli·cate (plī′kāt) adj. [L. *plicatus*, pp. of *plicare*, to fold: see PLY¹] folded or plaited; esp., having parallel folds like a fan [a *plicate* leaf]: also **pli′cat·ed**

pli·ca·tion (plī kā′shən) n. [ME. *plicacioun* < OFr. < L. *plicare*, to fold: see PLY¹] **1.** a folding or being folded **2.** a fold **3.** *Geol.* a fold or crumpling in layered rocks

plic·a·ture (plik′ə chər) n. *same as* PLICATION (senses 1 & 2)

pli·é (plē ā′) n. [Fr. < pp. of *plier*, to bend: see PLY¹] *Ballet* a movement in which the knees are bent outward, with the back held straight

pli·er (plī′ər) n. a person or thing that plies

pli·ers (-ərz) n.pl. [< PLY¹] small pincers in any of various forms, often with serrated jaws, for gripping small objects, bending wire, etc.

plight¹ (plīt) n. [ME. *plit*, a state, condition < Anglo-Fr. *plit*, for OFr. *pleit*, a fold, way of folding, condition (see PLAIT): sense infl. by ME. *plight* < OE. *pliht*: see ff.] a condition or state of affairs; esp., now, an awkward, sad, or dangerous situation —SYN. see PREDICAMENT

plight² (plīt) vt. [ME. *plihten* < OE. *plihtan*, to pledge, expose to danger < *pliht*, a pledge, danger, akin to *pleon*, to risk, G. *pflicht*, duty] to pledge or promise, or bind by a pledge —n. [Archaic] a pledge —**plight one's troth 1.** orig., to pledge one's truth, or one's word **2.** to make a promise of marriage

A　　B　　C
PLIERS
(A, slip joint; B, needle nose; C, arc joint)

Plim·soll mark (or **line**) (plim′səl, -säl, -sôl) [after Samuel *Plimsoll* (1824–98), Brit. advocate of legislation against overloading vessels] a line or set of lines on the outside of merchant ships, showing the water level to which they may legally be loaded

plim·solls (-səlz, -sälz, -sôlz) n.pl. [prob. from some fancied resemblance to a PLIMSOLL MARK] [Brit.] lightweight canvas shoes with rubber soles; sneakers: also **plim′soles** (-sōlz)

☆**plink** (pliŋk) n. [echoic] a light, sharp, ringing or clinking sound —vt., vi. **1.** to make such sounds on (a piano, banjo, etc.) **2.** to shoot at (tin cans or similar targets) —**plink′er** n.

plinth (plinth) n. [L. *plinthus* < Gr. *plinthos*, a brick, tile] **1.** the square block at the base of a column, pedestal, etc. **2.** the base on which a statue is placed **3.** a course of brick or stone along the base of a wall: also **plinth course 4.** a flat block at the base of door trim, an architrave, etc.

PLINTH

Plin·y (plin′ē) **1.** (L. name *Gaius Plinius Secundus*) 23–79 A.D.; Rom. naturalist & writer: called *the Elder* **2.** (L. name *Gaius Plinius Caecilius Secundus*) 62?–113? A.D.; Rom. writer & statesman: called *the Younger:* nephew of *prec.*

pli·o- (plī′ə, -ō) *same as* PLEO-

Pli·o·cene (plī′ə sēn′) adj. [< Gr. *pleon*, more (see PLEONASM) + -CENE] designating or of the last epoch of the Tertiary Period in the Cenozoic Era, during which many modern plants and animals developed —**the Pliocene** the Pliocene Epoch or its rocks: see GEOLOGY, chart

☆**Pli·o·film** (plī′ə film′) [< PLIABLE + FILM] a trademark for a transparent sheeting of rubber hydrochloride used for raincoats, as a packaging film, etc.

plis·sé, plis·se (pli sā′) n. [Fr. *plisse* < pp. of *plisser*, to pleat < MFr. < *pli*, PLY¹, n.] **1.** a crinkled finish given to cotton, nylon, etc. by treatment with a caustic soda solution **2.** a fabric with this finish

plod (pläd) vi. **plod′ded, plod′ding** [origin prob. echoic] **1.** to walk or move heavily and laboriously; trudge **2.** to work steadily and monotonously; drudge —n. **1.** the act of plodding **2.** the sound of a heavy step —**plod′der** n. —**plod′ding·ly** adv.

Plo·eşti (plô yesht′) city in SC Romania, north of Bucharest: pop. 137,000: also sp. **Ploieşti**

-ploid (ploid) [< Gr. *-ploos*, -fold + -OID] *a combining form meaning* of or being a (specified) multiple of the basic (haploid) number of chromosomes characteristic of a group of related organisms [*diploid*]

ploi·dy (ploi′dē) *n.* [prec. + -Y³] the condition of having or lacking one or more chromosomes than the number found in the normal diploid set

plonk (pläŋk, plunk) *vt.*, *vi.*, *n.* same as PLUNK

plop (pläp) *vt.*, *vi.* **plopped**, **plop′ping** [echoic] **1.** to drop with a sound like that of something flat falling into water without splashing **2.** to drop, or allow to drop, heavily —*n.* the act of plopping or the sound made by this —*adv.* with a plop

plo·sion (plō′zhən) *n.* [< (EX)PLOSION] *Phonet.* **1.** the articulation of a plosive sound **2.** loosely, the final stage, or sudden release of breath, in the articulation of a plosive

plo·sive (-siv) *adj.* [< (EX)PLOSIVE] *Phonet.* produced by the complete stoppage and sudden release of the breath, as the sounds of *k*, *p*, and *t* when used initially —*n.* a plosive sound

plot (plät) *n.* [ME. < OE., a piece of land: some meanings infl. by COMPLOT] **1.** a small area of ground marked off for some special use [*garden plot*, *cemetery plot*] **2.** a chart or diagram, as of a building or estate **3.** a secret, usually evil, project or scheme; conspiracy **4.** the plan of action of a play, novel, poem, short story, etc. —*vt.* **plot′ted**, **plot′ting 1.** *a)* to draw a plan or chart of (a ship's course, etc.) *b)* to mark the position or course of on a map **2.** to make secret plans for [*to plot* someone's destruction] **3.** to plan the action of (a story, etc.) **4.** *Math. a)* to determine or mark the location of (a point) on a graph by means of coordinates *b)* to represent (an equation) by locating points on a graph and joining them to form a curve *c)* to draw (the curve thus determined) —*vi.* to scheme or conspire —**plot′less** *adj.* —**plot′less·ness** *n.* —**plot′ter** *n.*
SYN.—**plot** is used of a secret, usually evil, project or scheme the details of which have been carefully worked out [*the plot* to deprive him of his inheritance failed]; **intrigue**, implying more intricate scheming, suggests furtive, underhanded maneuvering often of an illicit nature [*the intrigues* at the royal court]; **machination** stresses deceit and cunning in devising plots or schemes intended to harm someone [*the machinations* of the villain]; **conspiracy** suggests a plot in which a number of people plan and act together secretly for an unlawful or harmful purpose [*a conspiracy* to seize the throne]; **cabal** suggests a small group of persons involved in political intrigue

Plo·ti·nus (plō tī′nəs) 205?–270 A.D.; Rom. Neoplatonic philosopher, born in Egypt

plot·age (plät′ij) *n.* the area of a plot of land

plough (plou) *n.*, *vt.*, *vi. chiefly Brit. sp. of* PLOW

Plov·div (plôv′div) city in SC Bulgaria: pop. 224,000

plov·er (pluv′ər, plō′vər) *n.*, *pl.* **plov′ers**, **plov′er:** see PLURAL, II, D, 1 [ME. < OFr. *plovier*, lit., rain bird < VL. **pluviarius* < L. *pluvia*, rain (see PLUVIAL): reason for name obscure] **1.** any of a number of related wading and shore birds (family Charadriidae) having a short tail, long, pointed wings, a short, stout beak, and, usually, brown or gray feathers mixed with white **2.** any of various similar birds

plow (plou) *n.* [ME. *ploh* < Late OE., akin to G. *pflug*, ON. *plōgr*] **1.** a farm implement used to cut, turn up, or break up the soil ☆**2.** any implement like this; specif., *a) same as* SNOWPLOW *b)* any of various tools for cutting a groove or furrow —[P-] *Astron. same as: a)* URSA MAJOR *b)* BIG DIPPER —*vt.* **1.** to cut and turn up (soil) with a plow **2.** to make furrows in with or as with a plow **3.** to make by or as if by plowing [*to plow* one's way through a crowd] **4.** to cut a way through (water) [a ship *plowing* the waves] —*vi.* **1.** to till the soil with a plow; use a plow **2.** to take plowing as specified [a field that *plows* easily] **3.** to cut a way (*through* water, snow, etc.) **4.** to advance laboriously; plod **5.** to begin work vigorously (with *into*) **6.** to collide forcefully (with *into*) —**plow back** to reinvest (profits) in the same business enterprise —**plow under 1.** to bury (crops or vegetation) by plowing, so as to enrich the soil or in seeking to prevent overproduction **2.** [Colloq.] to destroy; obliterate —**plow up 1.** to remove with a plow **2.** to till (soil) thoroughly —**plow′a·ble** *adj.* —**plow′er** *n.*

plow·boy (-boi′) *n.* **1.** formerly, a boy who led a team drawing a plow **2.** a country boy

plow·man (-mən) *n.*, *pl.* **-men** (-mən) **1.** a man who guides a plow **2.** a farm worker; rustic

plow·share (-sher′) *n.* the share, or cutting blade, of a moldboard plow

ploy (ploi) *n.* [? < (EM)PLOY] an action or maneuver intended to outwit or disconcert another person

pluck (pluk) *vt.* [ME. *plukken* < OE. *pluccian*, akin to G. *pflücken* < VL. **piluccare*, to pull out (whence Fr. *éplucher*), for L. *pilare*, to deprive of hair < *pilus*, hair: see PILE²] **1.** to pull off or out; pick **2.** to drag or snatch; grab **3.** to pull feathers or hair from [*to pluck* a chicken, *pluck* eyebrows] **4.** to pull at (the strings of a musical instrument) and release quickly with little jerking move-

ments of the fingers **5.** [Slang] to rob or swindle **6.** [Brit. Slang] to reject (a candidate) in an examination —*vi.* **1.** to pull; tug; snatch (often with *at*) **2.** to pluck a musical instrument —*n.* **1.** an act of pulling; tug **2.** an animal's heart, liver, and lungs, used for food **3.** courage to meet danger or difficulty; fortitude —*SYN.* see FORTITUDE —**pluck up** to rouse one's (courage); take heart —**pluck′er** *n.*

pluck·y (-ē) *adj.* **pluck′i·er**, **pluck′i·est** [PLUCK, *n.* 3 + -Y²] brave; spirited; resolute —*SYN.* see BRAVE —**pluck′i·ly** *adv.* —**pluck′i·ness** *n.*

plug (plug) *n.* [MDu. *plugge*, a bung, plug, block, akin to G. *pflock*] **1.** an object used to stop up a hole, gap, outlet, etc. **2.** a natural concretion or formation that stops up a passage, duct, etc. **3.** a small wedge or segment cut from something, as from a melon to test its ripeness **4.** *a)* a cake of pressed tobacco *b)* a piece of chewing tobacco **5.** an electrical device, as with projecting prongs, to be fitted into an outlet, etc., thus making contact or closing the circuit **6.** a kind of fishing lure **7.** *same as: a)* SPARK PLUG *b)* FIREPLUG ☆*c)* PLUG HAT **8.** [Colloq.] a defective or shopworn article ☆**9.** [Slang] an old, worn-out horse ☆**10.** [Colloq.] a boost, advertisement, etc., esp. one inserted gratuitously in the noncommercial parts of a radio or TV program, magazine article, etc. for someone or something **11.** *Geol.* igneous rock which has filled in the vent of a dead volcano and hardened: it is often exposed by erosion —*vt.* **plugged**, **plug′ging 1.** to stop up or fill (a hole, gap, etc.) by inserting a plug (often with *up*) **2.** to insert a plug of (something) *in* a hole or gap ☆**3.** to cut a plug from (a melon) to test its ripeness **4.** [Colloq.] *a)* to publicize or boost (a song) by frequent performance ☆*b)* to advertise or publicize, esp. gratuitously in the noncommercial parts of a radio or TV program **5.** [Slang] to shoot a bullet into **6.** [Slang] to hit with the fist —*vi.* **1.** [Colloq.] to work or study hard and steadily; plod **2.** [Slang] to shoot or hit (at) —**plug in 1.** to connect (an electrical device) with an outlet, etc. by inserting a plug in a socket or jack **2.** to be so connected —**plug′ger** *n.*

☆**plug hat** [Old Slang] a man's high silk hat

☆**plug-ug·ly** (-ug′lē) *n.*, *pl.* **-lies** [cf. PLUG, *vt.* 6] [Old Slang] a city ruffian or gangster; rowdy

plum (plum) *n.* [ME. < OE. *plume*, akin to G. *pflaume* < WGmc. **pruma* < VL. *pruna:* see PRUNE¹] **1.** *a)* any of various small trees (genus *Prunus*) of the rose family, bearing a smooth-skinned, edible drupaceous fruit with a flattened stone *b)* the edible fruit **2.** any of various trees bearing plumlike fruits **3.** a raisin, when used in pudding or cake [*plum* pudding] **4.** the dark bluish-red or reddish-purple color of some plums **5.** something choice or desirable; esp., a well-paying job requiring little work or ability

plum·age (plōō′mij) *n.* [ME. < MFr. < *plume*, a feather: see PLUME] a bird's feathers, collectively

plu·mate (-māt, -mit) *adj.* [ModL. *plumatus* < L., pp. of *plumare*, to cover with feathers < *pluma:* see PLUME] *Zool.* resembling a feather, esp. in structure

plumb (plum) *n.* [ME. < MFr. *plomb* < L. *plumbum*, lead² < non-IE. source whence Gr. *molybdos*] a lead weight (**plumb bob**) hung at the end of a line (**plumb line**), used to determine how deep water is or whether a wall, etc. is vertical —*adj.* perfectly vertical; straight down —*adv.* **1.** in a vertical direction; straight down; directly **2.** [Colloq.] entirely; wholly; absolutely [*plumb* tired out] —*vi.* [ME. *plumben*] [Colloq.] to work as a plumber —*vt.* **1.** to test or sound with a plumb **2.** to discover the facts or contents of; fathom; solve; understand **3.** to make vertical **4.** to weight or seal with lead **5.** [Colloq.] to work on (pipes, etc.) as a plumber —*SYN.* see VERTICAL —**out of** (or **off**) **plumb** not vertical

PLUMB

plum·ba·go (plum bā′gō) *n.*, *pl.* **-gos** [L. *plumbago* < *plumbum*, lead²] *same as:* **1.** GRAPHITE **2.** *Bot.* LEADWORT —**plum·bag′i·nous** (-baj′i nəs) *adj.*

plumb bob see PLUMB, *n.*

plum·be·ous (plum′bē əs) *adj.* [L. *plumbeus* < *plumbum* (see PLUMB)] of, like, or containing lead; leaden

plumb·er (plum′ər) *n.* [ME. < MFr. *plummier* < L. *plumbarius*, lead worker < *plumbum*, lead: see PLUMB] a skilled worker who installs and repairs pipes, fixtures, etc., as of water, drainage, or gas systems in a building

☆**plumber's helper** [Colloq.] *same as* PLUNGER (sense 2)

plumb·er·y (-ē) *n. rare var. of* PLUMBING (sense 2)

plum·bic (plum′bik) *adj.* [PLUMB(UM) + -IC] of, like, or containing lead, esp. with a valence of four

plum·bif·er·ous (pləm bif′ər əs) *adj.* [< PLUMBUM + -FEROUS] that contains or yields lead

plumb·ing (plum′iŋ) *n.* **1.** the act of using a plumb **2.** the work or trade of a plumber **3.** the pipes and fixtures with which a plumber works

plum·bism (plum′biz'm) *n.* [PLUMB(UM) + -ISM] *same as* LEAD POISONING

plumb line 1. see PLUMB, *n.* **2.** a vertical line

plum·bous (-bəs) *adj.* [L. *plumbosus* < *plumbum*, lead: see PLUMB] of, like, or containing lead, esp. with a valence of two

plumb rule a narrow rule equipped with a plumb line and bob, used by carpenters, masons, etc.

plum·bum (plum′bəm) *n.* [L.] *same as* LEAD²

plume (plōōm) *n.* [ME. < OFr. < L. *pluma*, downy part of a feather, small soft feather, prob. < IE. base *pleus*, to pluck out, fluff of wool, hair, whence FLEECE] **1.** *a*) a feather, esp. a large, fluffy or showy one *b*) a cluster of such feathers **2.** an ornament made of a large feather or feathers, or of a feathery tuft of hair, esp. when worn on a hat, helmet, etc. as a mark of distinction **3.** any token of worth or achievement; prize **4.** plumage or down **5.** something like a plume in shape or lightness [a *plume* of smoke] **6.** *Bot., Zool.* a featherlike formation or part —*vt.* **plumed, plum′ing 1.** to provide, cover, or adorn with plumes **2.** *a*) to smooth the feathers of (itself) *b*) to preen (its feathers): said of a bird **3.** to pride (oneself)

plume·let (-lit) *n.* a small plume or tuft

plum·met (plum′it) *n.* [ME. *plomet* < MFr. *plommet*, dim. of *plomb*: see PLUMB] **1.** *same as: a*) PLUMB BOB *b*) PLUMB, *n.* **2.** a thing that weighs heavily —*vi.* to fall or drop straight downward; plunge

plum·my (plum′ē) *adj.* **-mi·er, -mi·est 1.** full of or tasting of plums **2.** [Brit. Colloq.] good or desirable **3.** [Colloq.] rich, full, and mellow: said of a sound or voice

plu·mose (plōō′mōs) *adj.* [L. *plumosus* < *pluma*, a feather: see PLUME] **1.** having feathers; feathered **2.** like a feather —**plu′mose·ly** *adv.* —**plu·mos·i·ty** (plōō mäs′ə tē) *n.*

plump¹ (plump) *adj.* [LME. < MDu. *plomp*, unwieldy, bulky, dull: orig. echoic] full and rounded in form; chubby —*vt., vi.* to make plump; fill out (sometimes with *up* or *out*) —**plump′ish** *adj.* —**plump′ly** *adv.* —**plump′ness** *n.*

plump² (plump) *vi.* [ME. *plumpen* < MDu. *plompen*: orig. echoic] **1.** to fall suddenly or with full impact **2.** to come in contact abruptly or heavily (*against* something) **3.** to vote (*for* only one candidate when two or more are to be chosen) **4.** to offer strong support (*for* someone or something) —*vt.* to drop, throw, or put down heavily or all at once —*n.* **1.** a falling, plunging, or colliding suddenly or heavily **2.** the sound of this —*adv.* **1.** with a plump; suddenly; heavily **2.** straight down **3.** in plain words; bluntly —*adj.* blunt; direct

plump³ (plump) *n.* [cf. PLUMP², *v.* & CLUMP] [Archaic exc. Brit. Dial.] a compact group; cluster

plump·er¹ (plum′pər) *n.* a person or thing that plumps, or fattens; specif., formerly, something carried in the mouth to plump out hollow cheeks

plump·er² (plum′pər) *n.* **1.** a plumping, or dropping heavily **2.** a vote for only one candidate when two or more are to be chosen

plum pudding [orig. made with PLUMS] a rich pudding made of raisins, currants, flour, spices, suet, etc., boiled or steamed, as in a linen bag

plu·mule (plōōm′yōōl) *n.* [ModL. < L. *plumula*, dim. of *pluma*, a feather: see PLUME] **1.** *Bot.* the growing stem tip of the embryo of a seed, above the place of attachment of the cotyledons **2.** *Ornithology* a soft down feather of young birds, persisting in some adults

plum·y (plōō′mē) *adj.* **plum′i·er, plum′i·est 1.** covered or adorned with plumes **2.** like a plume; feathery

plun·der (plun′dər) *vt.* [G. *plündern* < *plunder*, trash, baggage] **1.** to rob or despoil (a person or place) by force, esp. in warfare **2.** to take (property) by force or fraud —*vi.* to engage in plundering —*n.* **1.** the act of plundering; pillage; robbery **2.** goods taken by force or fraud; loot; booty ☆**3.** [Dial.] personal belongings or household furnishings —*SYN.* see RAVAGE, SPOIL —**plun′der·er** *n.* —**plun′der·ous** *adj.*

plun·der·age (-ij) *n.* [see -AGE] **1.** robbery; esp., an embezzling of property on shipboard **2.** the property embezzled

plunge (plunj) *vt.* **plunged, plung′ing** [ME. *plungen* < OFr. *plongier* < VL. *plumbicare* < L. *plumbum*, lead: see PLUMB] to thrust, throw, or force suddenly (*into* a liquid, hole, condition, etc.) [to *plunge* an oar into the water, to *plunge* a country into debt] —*vi.* **1.** to throw oneself, dive, or rush, as into water, a fight, etc. **2.** to move violently and rapidly downward or forward **3.** to pitch, as a ship **4.** to slope steeply, as a road **5.** to extend far down in a revealing way [a *plunging* neckline or back] **6.** [Colloq.] to spend, gamble, or speculate heavily or rashly —*n.* **1.** *a*) a dive or downward leap *b*) a swim **2.** any sudden, violent plunging motion **3.** a place for plunging, or swimming **4.** [Colloq.] a heavy, rash investment or speculation —**take the plunge** to start on a new and seemingly uncertain enterprise, esp. after some hesitation

plung·er (plun′jər) *n.* **1.** a person who plunges, or dives **2.** a large, rubber suction cup with a long handle, used to free clogged drains **3.** any cylindrical device that operates with a plunging motion, as a piston **4.** [Colloq.] a person who acts hastily or recklessly; esp., a rash gambler or speculator

plunk (plunk) *vt.* [echoic] **1.** to pluck or strum (a banjo, guitar, etc.) **2.** to throw or put down heavily; plump —*vi.* **1.** to give out a twanging sound: said of a banjo, etc. **2.** to fall or sink heavily **3.** [Colloq.] *same as* PLUMP² (*vi.* 3) —*n.* **1.** the act of plunking or the sound made by

this **2.** [Colloq.] a hard blow —*adv.* with a twang or thud —☆**plunk down** [Colloq.] to give in payment —**plunk′er** *n.*

plu·per·fect (plōō pur′fikt) *adj.* [LL. *plusquamperfectus* < L. *plus quam perfectum*, lit., more than perfect] designating a tense in any of certain languages corresponding to the past perfect in English —*n.* the pluperfect tense or a form in this tense

plupf. pluperfect

plur. 1. plural **2.** plurality

plu·ral (ploor′əl) *adj.* [ME. < L. *pluralis* < *plus* (gen. *pluris*), more: see PLUS] **1.** of or including more than one **2.** of, involving, or being one of, a plurality of persons or things [*plural* marriage, a *plural* mate] **3.** *Gram.* designating or of that category of number referring to more than one, or in languages having dual number, more than two —*n. Gram.* **1.** the plural number **2.** a plural form of a word **3.** a word in plural form

The plurals of nouns are formed in English according to the principles listed below. Words with alternative plurals in the regular -(*e*)s form are marked (*).

I. REGULAR ENGLISH PLURALS

A. By *sound:*
1. Add (iz) or (əz) after (s), (sh), (z), (zh), (ch), (j): *glasses, flashes, roses, rouges, matches, bridges*
2. Add (z) after all other voiced sounds: *heads, legs, pills, trees*
3. Add (s) after all other voiceless sounds: *lips, bats, rocks*

B. By *spelling:*
1. Add -*s* in all cases except as noted below
2. Add -*es* after final -*ss*, -*sh*, -*ch*, -*s*, -*x*, -*z*, and -*zz*: *glass-es, ash-es, witch-es, gas-es, box-es, adz-es, buzz-es*
3. Add -*es* after -*y* preceded by a consonant or by -*qu*-, and change the -*y* to -*i*: *fly, fli-es; army, armi-es; soliloquy, soliloqui-es,* etc. (Add -*s* after -*y* preceded by a vowel: *day, day-s; monkey, monkey-s,* etc.)
4. Add -*s* to most words ending in -*o* preceded by a consonant, and to all words ending in -*o* preceded by a vowel: *piano-s, radio-s, studio-s,* etc. (Add -*es* to some words ending in -*o* preceded by a consonant: *buffalo-s, *domino-s, echo-es, hero-es, potato-es,* etc.)

II. OTHER ENGLISH PLURALS

A. Regular plural with change in preceding consonant:
1. Change *f* to *v* in many words, and add -*es* (z): *half, self, life, leaf, *scarf, *wharf,* etc.
2. Change (th) to (*th*) in many words, and add -*s* (z): *path, mouth, sheath, wreath, truth, youth,* etc.
3. Change (s) to (z) and add -*s* (iz) or (əz) for *house*

B. Plural formed by:
1. -*en* ('n): *ox-en*
2. -*ren* (-rən) with prior vowel change: *child, children; brother, breth-ren*
3. Vowel change: *man, men; foot, feet; mouse, mice,* etc.

C. Plural the same as the singular: *alms, barracks, Chinese, deer* (occas. *deers*), *forceps, gross, Iroquois, Japanese, means, moose, sheep, Swiss,* etc.

D. Plural either different from or the same as the singular:
1. Plural usually different, but sometimes the same, esp. in the usage of hunters and fishermen:

addax	crappie	heron
agouti	croppie	herring
albacore	curlew	hind²
albatross	dhole	hippopotamus
alligator	doe	hog
alpaca	dog	horse
anchovy	dotterel	ibex
antelope	dowitcher	ibis
argali	duck¹	inconnu
badger	duiker	jack¹
bear²	dunlin	jackal
beaver¹	eel	jacksnipe
bighorn	egret	jaguar
bittern¹	eider	kangaroo
blackcock	elephant	killdeer
blenny	ermine	kittiwake
boar	fisher	klipspringer
bobcat	flounder²	kokanee
bobwhite	fowl	kudu, koodoo
bonito	fox	lemming
brant	gadwall	leopard
buck¹	gannet	lion
buffalo	gazelle	llama
canvasback	giraffe	lobster
carabao	gnu	lynx
caribou	goat	mallard
cat	goby	marten
char³	goldeneye	meadowlark
charr	goral	merganser
chub	grebe	mink
clam¹	grouper	minnow
coot	guanaco	mola
cougar	gull¹	mouflon, moufflon
coyote	gurnard	mullet
coypu	hare	murre
crake	hart	muskrat
crane	hartebeest	musquash

nilgai	rail	surmullet
ocelot	rhinoceros	swan[1]
okapi	robalo	tapir
opossum	roebuck	tarpon
oryx	sable	teal
ostrich	sambar, sambur	tench
otter	sandpiper	tiger
ox	sardine	tortoise
panther	scaup	tunny
parr	scoter	turkey
partridge	seal[2]	turtle
peacock	serval	vicuña
peafowl	shanny	wallaby
peccary	sheldrake	walrus
pheasant	shiner	wapiti
pig	shrimp	waterfowl
pigeon[1]	skate[2]	weasel
pintail	skipjack	whale
plover	skunk	whippoorwill
pochard	smelt[1]	whiting
polecat	snapper	widgeon, wigeon
porcupine	snipe	wildcat
porgy	squid	wildebeest
porpoise	squirrel	willet
pronghorn	stag	wolverine
ptarmigan	stilt	woodcock
puma	stint[2]	yak
quail	stoat	yellowtail
rabbit	stork	zebra
raccoon, racoon	sturgeon	zebu

2. Plural usually the same, but different if referring to different kinds, species, varieties, etc. /the *fishes* of the South Pacific/:

barracuda	elk	quagga
barramunda	fish[2] (and its com-	quillback
barramundi	pounds, as,	reedbuck
bass[2]	bluefish)	roach[2]
beluga	gar	roe[2]
blaubok	gemsbok	salmon
bleak[2]	grayling	scad
blesbok, blesbuck	grilse	scup
bontebok	haddock	shad
boschbok, boshbok	hake	sheepshead
bream[1]	halibut	sild
brill	ling[1]	springbok
burbot	lingcod	springbuck
bushbuck	mackerel	steelhead
capelin	marlin	steenbok
carp[1]	menhaden	steinbock
cavalla	nyala	steinbok
cero	perch[1]	torsk
cisco	pickerel	trout
cod[1]	pike[3]	trout-perch
codling[1]	pikeperch	tuna
cusk	plaice	turbot
dace	pollack, pollock	vendace
eelpout	pompano	warmouth
eland	pout[2]	waterbuck

3. Plural usually lacking, but given in *-(e)s* form when different kinds are referred to /the many *steels* produced/: the following list is typical but not exhaustive:

barley	iron	rye
brass	linen	silk
coffee	millet	steel
copper	oak	tea
corn[1]	pepper	wheat
fruit	pine[1]	wool

4. Plural and collective singular interchangeable: *seeds, seed*, etc.

III. FORMS SINGULAR OR PLURAL ONLY
A. Singular only (or when a generalized abstraction): *chess[1], clearness, fishing, information, knowledge, luck, music, nonsense, truth*, etc.
B. Plural only (even when singular in meaning), including certain senses of nouns otherwise singular: *Balkans, blues* (depression), *bowels, glasses, lodgings, overalls, pliers, remains* (corpse), *scissors, tongs, trousers*, etc.
C. Plural in form but used with singular verbs: *cards* (game), *checkers* (game), *measles, mumps, news*, etc.
D. Nouns ending in *-ics* are singular when they denote scientific subjects, as *mathematics, physics*, etc., and plural when they denote activities or qualities, as *acrobatics, acoustics*, etc.

IV. LATIN AND GREEK PLURALS
A. With Latin suffix *-i* replacing singular ending *-us*: *alumnus, alumn-i; *focus, foc-i; *nucleus, nucle-i; *radius, radi-i*, etc.
B. With Latin suffix *-ae* replacing singular ending *-a*: *alumna, alumn-ae; *formula, formul-ae*, etc.
C. With suffix *-a* replacing singular ending:
1. Latin nouns in *-um*: *agendum, agenda-a; datum, dat-a; *medium, medi-a*, etc.

2. Greek nouns in *-on*: *criterion, criteri-a; phenomenon, phenomen-a*, etc.
D. With suffix *-es* (ēz):
1. Latin suffix *-ex* or *-ix* replaced by *-ices* (-ə sēz, -i sēz): *appendix, append-ices; *index, ind-ices*, etc.
2. Latin or Greek suffix *-is* replaced by *-es*: *analysis, analys-es; axis, ax-es*, etc.
E. Miscellaneous Latin and Greek plurals: *phalanx, phalang-es; *stigma, stigma-ta; corpus, corp-ora; genus, gen-era*, etc.
V. OTHER FOREIGN PLURALS
A. Hebrew: *cherub, cherub-im; kibbutz, kibbutz-im; *matzo, matzo-t(h)
B. Italian: *bandit, bandit-ti; *dilettante, dilettant-i; *virtuoso, virtuos-i*, etc.
C. French: *bijou, bijou-x; *château, château-x; *portmanteau, portmanteau-x*, etc.
VI. PLURALS OF NUMBERS, LETTERS, SIGNS, WORDS (when thought of as things), etc. add *-'s* (or now often *-s*): *8's* (or *8s*), *B's* (or *Bs*), *&'s* (or *&s*), *but's* (or *buts*)

plu·ral·ism (-iz'm) *n.* **1.** the quality or condition of being plural, or of existing in more than one part or form **2.** the holding by one person of more than one office or church benefice at the same time **3.** *a)* the existence within a nation or society of groups distinctive in ethnic origin, cultural patterns, religion, or the like *b)* a policy of favoring the preservation of such groups within a given nation or society **4.** *Philos.* *a)* the theory that reality is composed of a multiplicity of ultimate beings, principles, or substances: cf. DUALISM, MONISM *b)* the theory that ultimate reality has more than one true explanation —**plu'ral·ist** *n., adj.* —**plu'ral·is'tic** *adj.* —**plu'ral·is'ti·cal·ly** *adv.*

plu·ral·i·ty (ploo ral'ə tē) *n., pl.* **-ties** [ME. *pluralite* < MFr. *pluralité* < LL. *pluralitas*] **1.** the condition of being plural or numerous **2.** a great number; multitude **3.** *a)* the holding of two or more church benefices at the same time *b)* any of the benefices so held **4.** ☆*a)* the number of votes in an election that the leading candidate obtains over the next highest candidate /if candidate A gets 65 votes, B gets 40, and C gets 35, then A has a *plurality* of 25/ *b)* same as MAJORITY

plu·ral·ize (ploor'ə līz') *vt., vi.* **-ized', -iz'ing** [Fr. *pluraliser*] to make or become plural in form or number —**plu'ral·i·za'tion** *n.* —**plu'ral·iz'er** *n.*
plu·ral·ly (-əl ē) *adv.* in the plural number
plu·ri- (ploor'i, -ə) [L. < *plus* (gen. *pluris*), several: see PLUS] a combining form meaning several or many
plu·ri·ax·i·al (ploor'i ak'sē əl) *adj.* [prec. + AXIAL] *Bot.* having several axes; specif., having flowers on secondary shoots

plus (plus) *prep.* [L., more < IE. *plēyos*, compar. of *pelu-*, much < base *pel-*, to FILL] **1.** added to /2 plus 2 equals 4/ **2.** increased by; in addition to /salary *plus* bonus/ **3.** [Colloq.] with the addition of /he returned wiser and *plus* $300/ —*adj.* **1.** indicating or involving addition /a *plus* sign/ **2.** positive /a *plus* quantity/ **3.** somewhat higher than /a grade of B *plus*/ **4.** involving extra gain or advantage /*plus* sales, a *plus* factor/ **5.** [Colloq.] and more /she has personality *plus*/ **6.** *Bot.* designating one of two strains of certain fungi and algae which only mate with the opposite (*minus*) strain ☆**7.** *Elec.* same as POSITIVE /the *plus* terminal/ —*adv.* [Colloq.] moreover; in addition: used with conjunctive force /he has the time *plus* he has the money/ —*n., pl.* **plus'es, plus'ses 1.** a plus sign **2.** an added or favorable quantity or thing **3.** a positive quantity

plus fours [orig. a tailoring term indicating an added four inches of material for overlap below the knee] loose knickerbockers worn, esp. formerly, for active sports

plush (plush) *n.* [Fr. *pluche* < *peluche* < OFr. *peluchier*, to pluck < VL. *piluccare*: see PLUCK] a fabric with a soft, thick, deep pile —*adj.* **1.** of or made of plush **2.** [Slang] luxurious, as in furnishings
plush·y (plush'ē) *adj.* **plush'i·er, plush'i·est 1.** of or like plush ☆**2.** [Slang] luxurious; plush —**plush'i·ly** *adv.* —**plush'i·ness** *n.*
plus sign *Math.* a sign (+), indicating addition or positive quantity
Plu·tarch (ploo'tärk) 46?-120? A.D.; Gr. biographer & historian
plu·te·us (ploot'ē əs) *n., pl.* **-te·i'** (-ī') [ModL. < L., a shelf, backrest: from being shaped like a painter's easel] *Zool.* the free-swimming, ciliated, larval stage of most echinoderms, characterized by elongated, slender arms
Plu·to (ploot'ō) [L. < Gr. *Ploutōn*] **1.** *Gr. & Rom. Myth.* the god ruling over the lower world: also called *Hades* by the Greeks and *Dis* or *Orcus* by the Romans **2.** the outermost planet of the solar system, discovered in 1930, ninth in distance from the sun: diameter, c.3,700 mi.; period of revolution, c.248 tropical yrs.; period of rotation, 6.39 days; symbol, B
plu·toc·ra·cy (ploo täk'rə sē) *n., pl.* **-cies** [Gr. *ploutokratia* < *ploutos*, wealth, akin to *plein*, to float, swim (for IE. base see PLUVIAL) + *kratein*, to rule] **1.** government

by the wealthy **2.** a group of wealthy people who control or influence a government

plu·to·crat (plōōt′ə krat′) *n.* [< Gr. *ploutos*, wealth (see prec.) + -CRAT] **1.** a member of a wealthy ruling class **2.** a person whose wealth gives him control or great influence —**plu′to·crat′ic** *adj.* —**plu′to·crat′i·cal·ly** *adv.*

Plu·to·ni·an (plōō tō′nē ən) *adj.* [L. *Plutonius* < Gr. *Ploutōnios*] of or like Pluto or the infernal regions

Plu·ton·ic (plōō tän′ik) *adj.* [< L. *Pluto* (gen. *Plutonis*) + -IC] **1.** *same as* PLUTONIAN **2.** [p-] *Geol. a)* formed far below the surface of the earth by intense heat, great pressure, and slow cooling: plutonic rocks are typically crystalline with a granitelike texture *b)* [Rare] of igneous origin

☆**plu·to·ni·um** (plōō tō′nē əm) *n.* [ModL., after PLUTO (planet): it is the second element beyond uranium: cf. NEPTUNIUM] a radioactive, metallic chemical element similar to uranium and neptunium and found in trace quantities in native uranium ores: its most important isotope, plutonium 239, is produced by irradiating uranium 238 with slow neutrons and is used in nuclear weapons and as a reactor fuel: symbol, Pu; at. wt., 239.05; at. no., 94; sp. gr. (alpha form), 19.84 (25°C); melt. pt., 639.5°C; boil. pt., 3235°C

Plu·tus (plōōt′əs) [L. < Gr. *Ploutos* < *ploutos*, wealth: see PLUTOCRACY] *Gr. Myth.* the blind god of wealth

plu·vi·al (plōō′vē əl) *adj.* [L. *pluvialis* < *pluvia*, rain < IE. **pleu-*, to flow, pour < base **pel-*, to pour, fill, whence FULL¹] **1.** *a)* of or having to do with rain *b)* having much rain **2.** *Geol.* formed by the action of rain

plu·vi·om·e·ter (plōō′vē äm′ə tər) *n.* [< L. *pluvia*, rain (see prec.) + -METER] a gauge for measuring the depth of a rainfall —**plu′vi·o·met′ric** (-ə met′rik) *adj.* —**plu′vi·om′e·try** *n.*

plu·vi·ose (plōō′vē ōs′) *adj.* [L. *pluviosus* < *pluvia*: see PLUVIAL] characterized by much rain; rainy: also **plu′vi·ous** (-əs) —**plu′vi·os′i·ty** (-äs′ə tē) *n.*

ply¹ (plī) *vt.* **plied, ply′ing** [ME. *plien* < OFr. *plier* < L. *plicare*, to fold < IE. base **plek-*, to entwine, whence FLAX] [Now Rare] to bend, twist, fold, or mold —*vi.* [Obs.] to bend or submit —*n., pl.* **plies** [MFr. *pli* < the *v.*] **1.** a single thickness, fold, or layer, as of doubled cloth, plywood, etc. **2.** one of the twisted strands in a rope, yarn, etc. **3.** *a)* the state of being bent or twisted *b)* bias or inclination —*adj.* having a (specified number of) layers, thicknesses, or strands: usually in hyphenated compounds [*three-ply*]

ply² (plī) *vt.* **plied, ply′ing** [ME. *plien*, aphetic for *applien*, APPLY] **1.** to do work with; wield or use (a tool, faculty, etc.), esp. with energy **2.** to work at (a trade) **3.** to address (someone) urgently and constantly (*with* questions, etc.) **4.** to keep supplying (*with* gifts, food, drink, etc.) **5.** to sail regularly back and forth across (*boats ply* the channel) —*vi.* **1.** to keep busy or work (*at* something or *with* a tool, etc.) **2.** to sail or travel regularly back and forth (*between* places): said of ships, buses, etc. **3.** [Poet.] to steer a course **4.** *Naut. same as* TACK —*SYN.* see HANDLE

Ply·mouth (plim′əth) **1.** seaport in Devonshire, SW England, on the English Channel: pop. 214,000 **2.** village on the SE coast of Mass.: settled by the Pilgrims (1620) as the 1st permanent colonial settlement (**Plymouth Colony**) in New England: pop. 19,000

☆**Plymouth Rock 1.** boulder at Plymouth, Mass., where the Pilgrims who sailed on the *Mayflower* are said to have landed in 1620 **2.** any of a breed of American chickens with feathers that are usually gray with bluish-black stripes

ply·wood (plī′wood′) *n.* [PLY¹ + WOOD¹] a construction material made of thin layers of wood glued and pressed together, usually with their grains at right angles to one another

Plzeň (p'l′zen y′) city in W Bohemia, Czechoslovakia: pop. 142,000

Pm *Chem.* promethium

pm. 1. phase modulation **2.** premium

P.M. 1. Past Master **2.** Paymaster **3.** Police Magistrate **4.** Postmaster **5.** Prime Minister **6.** Provost Marshal

P.M., p.m., PM [L. *post meridiem*] after noon: used to designate the time from noon to midnight

p.m. post-mortem

P.M.G. 1. Paymaster General **2.** Postmaster General

pmk. postmark

P/N, p.n. promissory note

pneum- (nōōm) *same as* PNEUMO-: used before a vowel

pneu·ma (nōō′mə, nyōō′-) *n.* [Gr. *pneuma* < *pnein*, to breathe < IE. echoic base **pneu-*, to wheeze, breathe, whence OE. *fneosan*, to SNEEZE] the soul or spirit

pneu·mat·ic (nōō mat′ik, nyōō-) *adj.* [L. *pneumaticus* < Gr. *pneumatikos* < *pneuma*, breath: see prec.] **1.** of or containing wind, air, or gases **2.** *a)* filled with compressed air [*pneumatic* tire] *b)* worked by compressed air [*pneumatic* drill] **3.** *Theol.* having to do with the spirit or soul **4.** *Zool.* having hollows filled with air, as certain bones in birds —**pneu·mat′i·cal·ly** *adv.*

pneu·mat·ics (-iks) *n.pl.* [*with sing. v.*] the branch of physics that deals with the mechanical properties, such as pressure, density, etc., of air and other gases

pneu·ma·to- (nōō′mə tō, nyōō′-; nōō mat′ə, nyōō-) [< Gr. *pneuma* (gen. *pneumatos*), air, spirit, breath < *pnein*, to breathe: see PNEUMA] *a combining form meaning:* **1.** air, vapor [*pneumatolysis*] **2.** breathing [*pneumatometer*] **3.** spirits [*pneumatology*]

pneu·ma·tol·o·gy (nōō′mə täl′ə jē, nyōō′-) *n.* [prec. + -LOGY] *Theol.* **1.** the study of spirits or spiritual phenomena **2.** any doctrine on the Holy Spirit —**pneu′ma·to·log′ic** (-tə läj′ik), **pneu′ma·to·log′i·cal** *adj.*

pneu·ma·tol·y·sis (-täl′ə sis) *n.* [ModL.: see PNEUMATO- & -LYSIS] the process of rock alteration and mineral formation by the action of gases emitted from solidifying igneous rocks —**pneu′ma·to·lyt′ic** (-tə lit′ik) *adj.*

pneu·ma·tom·e·ter (nōō′mə täm′ə tər, nyōō′-) *n.* [PNEUMATO- + -METER] *Physiol.* an instrument for measuring the capacity or force of the lungs in respiration

pneu·ma·to·phore (noo mat′ə fôr′, nyoo-; nōō′mə tō-, nyōō′-) *n.* [PNEUMATO- + -PHORE] **1.** *Bot.* a porous, woody, specialized branch growing upright into the air from the buried roots of certain swamp trees, as the mangrove, and providing access to the atmosphere **2.** *Zool.* a polyp with a gas-filled cavity in siphonophore hydrozoans, serving as a float for the colony

pneu·mec·to·my (nōō mek′tə mē, nyōō-) *n., pl.* **-mies** [PNEUM- + -ECTOMY] the surgical removal of all or part of a lung

pneu·mo- (nōō′mō, nyōō′-; -mə) [ModL., contr. < PNEUMONO-] *a combining form meaning* lung or lungs [*pneumococcus*]

pneu·mo·ba·cil·lus (nōō′mō bə sil′əs, nyōō′-) *n., pl.* **-cil′li** (-ī) [ModL.: see prec. & BACILLUS] a bacillus (*Klebsiella pneumoniae*) associated with one form of pneumonia

pneu·mo·coc·cus (nōō′mō käk′əs, nyōō′-) *n., pl.* **-coc′ci** (-käk′sī) [ModL.: see PNEUMO- & COCCUS] a bacterium (*Diplococcus pneumoniae*) that is a causative agent of pneumonia and of certain other diseases —**pneu′mo·coc′cal** (-käk′'l), **pneu′mo·coc′cic** (-käk′sik) *adj.*

pneu·mo·co·ni·o·sis (-kō′nē ō′sis) *n.* [ModL. < PNEUMO- + Gr. *konia*, dust + -OSIS] a disease of the lungs, characterized by fibrosis and caused by the chronic inhalation of mineral dusts, esp. silica and asbestos

pneu·mo·en·ceph·a·lo·gram (-en sef′ə lō gram′) *n.* [PNEUMO- + ENCEPHALOGRAM] an X-ray photograph of the brain made after the cerebrospinal fluid has been replaced with air or oxygen

pneu·mo·gas·tric (-gas′trik) *adj.* [PNEUMO- + GASTRIC] of the lungs and stomach —*n. earlier term for* VAGUS

pneu·mo·graph (nōō′mə graf′, nyōō′-; -gräf′) *n.* [PNEUMO- + -GRAPH] a device for measuring and recording the depth and rate of movement of the chest in respiration

pneu·mo·nec·to·my (nōō′mə nek′tə mē, nyōō′-) *n., pl.* **-mies** [see PNEUMONO- & -ECTOMY] the surgical removal of an entire lung

pneu·mo·ni·a (noo mōn′yə, nyoo-; -mō′nē ə) *n.* [ModL. < Gr. *pneumonia* < *pneumōn*, a lung < *pnein*, to breathe: see PNEUMA] inflammation or infection of the alveoli of the lungs of varying degrees of severity and caused by any of a number of agents, such as bacteria or viruses —**pneu·mon′ic** (-män′ik) *adj.*

pneu·mo·no- (nōō′mə nō′, nyōō′-) [< Gr. *pneumōn*, a lung < *pnein*, to breathe: see PNEUMA] *same as* PNEUMO-

pneu·mo·tho·rax (nōō′mō thôr′aks, nyōō′-) *n.* [ModL.: see PNEUMO- & THORAX] the presence of air or gas in a pleural cavity, esp. as a result of perforation or rupture of the lung tissue

p-n junction *Electronics* the boundary between two regions in a single crystal of a semiconductor: one region contains an electron acceptor and the other an electron donor

Pnom-Penh (p'nōm′pen′) *same as* PHNOM PENH

pnxt. [L. *pinxit*] he (or she) painted it

Po (pō) river in N Italy, flowing from the Cottian Alps east into the Adriatic: 405 mi.

Po *Chem.* polonium

po, p.o. *Baseball* putout; putouts

P.O., p.o. 1. petty officer: also **PO 2.** postal order **3.** post office **4.** post office box

poach¹ (pōch) *vt.* [ME. *pochen* < MFr. *pochier*, to pocket < *poche*, a pouch, pocket (< Frank. **pokka*, pocket: for IE. base see POKE²): the yolk is "pocketed" in the white] to cook (fish, an egg without its shell, etc.) in water or other liquid near boiling point, or in a small receptacle put over boiling water

poach² (pōch) *vt.* [Fr. *pocher* < OFr. *pochier*, to tread upon, poach into < MHG. *bochen, puchen*, to strike upon, plunder, akin to POKE¹] **1.** to soften, tear up, or make holes in (ground) by stamping; trample **2.** to mix with water until smooth **3.** *a)* to trespass on (private property), esp. for hunting or fishing *b)* to hunt or catch (game or fish) illegally, esp. by trespassing **4.** to take (anything) by unfair or illegal methods; steal —*vi.* **1.** to sink into soft or wet earth when walking **2.** to become soggy or full of holes when trampled; turn into mud **3.** to hunt or fish illegally, esp. by trespassing or —**poach′er** *n.*

poach·y (-ē) *adj.* **poach′i·er, poach′i·est** [POACH² + -Y²] soggy or swampy; sodden: said of land

POB, P.O.B. Post Office Box

Po·ca·hon·tas (pō′kə hän′təs) 1595?-1617; Am. Indian princess: reputed to have saved Captain John Smith from execution: daughter of POWHATAN

Po·ca·tel·lo (pō′kə tel′ō) [after an Indian chief who helped railroad builders] city in SE Ida.: pop. 40,000

po·chard (pō′chərd, -kərd) n., pl. **-chards, -chard:** see PLURAL, II, D, 1 [< ? Fr. pocher, to pocket: see POACH[1]] 1. a European, diving sea duck (Aythya ferina) with a brownish-red head: it is related to the redhead 2. any of various similar ducks (esp. genus Aythya)

pock (päk) n. [ME. pocke < OE. pocc: for IE. base see POKE[2]] 1. a pustule caused by smallpox or some other disease 2. same as POCKMARK See POX **—pocked** adj.

pock·et (päk′it) n. [ME. poket < Anglo-Fr. pokete, for ONormFr. poquette, dim. of poque, poche: see POKE[2]] 1. [Brit.] a sack, esp. when used to measure something 2. a) a little bag or pouch, now usually sewn into or on clothing, for carrying money and small articles b) any usually small container, compartment, enclosure, etc. 3. a cavity that holds or can hold something 4. a small area or group of a specified type [a pocket of poverty] 5. a confining or frustrating situation 6. financial resources; funds; means [a drain on one's pocket] 7. Aeron. same as AIR POCKET ☆8. Baseball a hollow in a baseball mitt where the ball can be securely caught and held 9. Billiards any of the pouches at the sides and corners of a billiard or pool table 10. Bowling the space between two pins, esp. the head pin and the pin next to it 11. Geol. a) a cavity filled with ore, oil, gas, or water b) a small deposit of ore, etc. 12. Racing a position of being hemmed in by other contestants so as to be held back 13. Zool. a sac or pouch in an animal's body —adj. 1. a) that is or can be carried in a pocket b) smaller than standard 2. not widespread; contained; isolated [pocket resistance] —vt. 1. to put into a pocket 2. to provide with a pocket or pockets 3. to envelop; enclose 4. to take dishonestly; appropriate (money, profits, etc.) for one's own use 5. to put up with (an insult, gibe, etc.) without answering or showing anger 6. to hide, suppress, or set aside [pocket one's pride] ☆7. Politics to prevent passage of (a bill) by the pocket veto **—in one's pocket** completely under one's influence **—in pocket** gained or available **—out of pocket** from money at hand

pocket battleship small battleship within the limits as to tonnage and guns set by the Treaty of Versailles

☆**pocket billiards** same as POOL[2] (n. 2 a)

pock·et·book (-book′) n. 1. a) a case or folder, as of leather, for carrying money and papers in one's pocket; billfold ☆b) esp. formerly, a man's pocket purse ☆2. a woman's purse or handbag 3. monetary resources

pocket book a book small enough to be carried in one's pocket

pocket borough in Great Britain before 1832, a borough whose representation in Parliament was controlled by one family or person

pock·et·ful (-fool′) n., pl. **-fuls** as much as a pocket will hold

☆**pocket gopher** same as GOPHER (sense 1)

pock·et·knife (-nīf′) n., pl. **-knives** (-nīvz′) a knife with a blade or blades that fold into the handle

pocket money cash for small expenses; small change

☆**pocket mouse** any of a genus (Perognathus) of small, nocturnal, long-tailed mice with fur-lined cheek pouches for carrying food to their burrows: found in unforested areas of W N. America

pocket rat same as KANGAROO RAT (sense 1)

pock·et·size (-sīz′) adj. of a relatively small size; esp., of a size to fit in the pocket: also **pock′et·sized′**

☆**pocket veto** 1. the indirect veto by the President of the U.S. of a bill presented to him by Congress within ten days of its adjournment, by failing to sign and return the bill before Congress adjourns 2. any action similar to this in defeating a measure

pock·mark (päk′märk′) n. 1. a scar or pit in the skin left by a pustule, as of smallpox 2. any pit or mark suggestive of this —vt. to pit, cover, or scar with pockmarks — **pock′marked′** adj.

pock·y (-ē) adj. **pock′i·er, pock′i·est** 1. of, like, or covered with pocks or pockmarks 2. of or having the pox

po·co (pō′kō) adv. [It.] Music somewhat: used in musical directions

po·co a po·co (pō′kō ä pō′kō) [It.] Music little by little; gradually: used in directions

po·co·cu·ran·te (pō′kō koo ran′tē, -kyoo-) adj. [It. poco curante < poco (< L. paucus, little: see FEW) + curante, prp. of curare, to care < L. cura, care: see CURE] caring little; indifferent; apathetic —n. an indifferent or apathetic person **—po′co·cu·ran′te·ism** (-tē iz′m), **po′co·cu·ran′tism** (-tiz′m) n.

Po·co·no Mountains (pō′kə nō′) [Pocono < AmInd. < ?] ridge of the Appalachians, in E Pa.: resort area: c. 2,000 ft. high

☆**po·co·sin** (pə kō′s'n) n. [< AmInd. (Delaware) pakwesen < pakw-, shallow + suffix of location] a low, flat, swampy region in savannas of the SE U.S.

pod[1] (päd) n. [Early ModE. < ?] 1. a dry fruit or seed vessel developed from a single carpel enclosing one or more seeds and usually splitting along two sutures at maturity, as a legume 2. a podlike container, as a cocoon, an egg capsule of an insect or fish, etc. ☆3. a contoured enclosure,

as a streamlined housing for a jet engine attached to an aircraft —vi. **pod′ded, pod′ding** 1. to bear pods 2. to swell out into a pod **—pod′like′** adj.

☆**pod**[2] (päd) n. [? special use of prec.] a small group of animals, esp. of seals, whales, etc. —vt. **pod′ded, pod′ding** to herd (animals) together

pod[3] (päd) n. [< ?] 1. a sharp groove in certain augers and other tools 2. the socket for the bit in a brace

-pod (päd) [< Gr. pous (gen. podos), FOOT] a combining form meaning: 1. foot [pleopod] 2. (one) having (a specified number or kind of) feet [tripod] Also **-pode** (pōd)

P.O.D. 1. pay on delivery 2. Post Office Department

-pod·a (pə də) pl. of -POD: used chiefly in zoological taxonomic names

po·dag·ra (pə dag′rə, päd′ə grə) n. [L. < Gr. < pous (gen. podos), FOOT + agra, a seizure] gout, esp. in the big toe **—po·dag′ral, po·dag′ric** adj.

po·des·ta (pō des′tə; It. pō′de stä′) n. [It. podestà < L. potestas, power < potis, able: see POTENT] 1. a chief magistrate of a medieval Italian town 2. a minor official in an Italian town

podg·y (päj′ē) adj. **podg′i·er, podg′i·est** var. of PUDGY

☆**po·di·a·try** (pō dī′ə trē, pə-) n. [< Gr. pous (gen. podos), FOOT + -IATRY] the profession dealing with the specialized care of the feet and, esp., with the treatment and prevention of foot disorders **—po·di′a·trist** n. **—po·di′a·tric** adj.

pod·ite (päd′īt) n. [< -POD + -ITE[1]] Zool. 1. an arthropod appendage 2. a clearly defined segment of such an appendage **—po·dit′ic** (pä dit′ik) adj.

po·di·um (pō′dē əm) n., pl. **-di·a** (-ə); also, and for 4 usually, **-di·ums** [L. < Gr. podion, dim. of pous (gen. podos), FOOT] 1. a low wall serving as a pedestal or foundation 2. a low wall separating the seats from the arena in an ancient amphitheater 3. a continuous bench projecting from the walls of a room 4. a low platform, esp. for the conductor of an orchestra; dais 5. Zool. a hand or foot, or a footlike structure

-po·di·um (pō′dē əm) [ModL. < Gr. pous (gen. podos), FOOT] a combining form meaning footstalk, supporting part [monopodium]

pod·o·car·pus (päd′ə kär′pəs) n. [< Gr. pous (gen. podos), FOOT + karpos, fruit (see HARVEST)] any of a genus (Podocarpus) of evergreen trees and shrubs with fernlike leaves, small flowers, and pulpy fruits

pod·o·phyl·lin (-fil′in) n. [< ModL. Podophyllum, name of the genus < Gr. pous (gen. podos), FOOT + phyllon, a leaf + -IN[1]] a yellow cathartic resin with a bitter taste, taken from the rootstock of the mandrake

-pod·ous (pə dəs) [see -POD & -OUS] a combining form meaning having (a specified number or kind of) feet

Po·dunk (pō′duŋk′) [after a village of that name in Mass. or one in Conn.: of AmInd. origin] [Colloq.] any hypothetical or actual small town in the U.S., regarded as typically dull, insignificant, etc.

pod·zol (päd′zôl, -zäl) n. [Russ., lit., ashlike] a type of light-colored, relatively infertile soil, poor in lime and iron, found typically in coniferous forests in cool, humid regions: also sp. **pod′sol** (-sôl), **pod·zol′ic** (-zäl′ik) adj.

pod·zol·i·za·tion (päd′zôl i zā′shən, -zäl-) n. [see prec.] a process of soil formation, esp. in cool, humid regions, in which the upper layers are leached of iron, lime, and alumina, which are then concentrated in underlying layers: also sp. **pod′sol·i·za′tion** (-sôl-) **—pod′zol·ize′** vt. -ized′, -iz′ing

POE, P.O.E. 1. port of embarkation 2. port of entry

Poe (pō), **Edgar Allan** 1809–49; U.S. poet, short-story writer, & critic

po·em (pō′əm) n. [MFr. poeme < L. poema < Gr. poiēma, anything made, poem < poiein, to make < IE. base *kwei-, to heap up, build, make, whence Sans. cinōti, (he) arranges, OBulg. činiti, to arrange, form] 1. an arrangement of words written or spoken, traditionally a rhythmical composition, sometimes rhymed, expressing experiences, ideas, or emotions in a style more concentrated, imaginative, and powerful than that of ordinary speech or prose: some poems are in meter, some in free verse 2. anything suggesting a poem in its effect

po·e·sy (pō′ə sē′, -zē′) n., pl. **-sies** [ME. poesie < OFr. < L. poesis < Gr. poiēsis < poiein, to make: see POEM] 1. old-fashioned var. of POETRY 2. [Obs.] a) a poem b) a motto c) a nosegay See POSY

po·et (pō′ət) n. [ME. < OFr. poete < L. poeta < Gr. poiētēs, one who makes, poet < poiein, to make: see POEM] 1. a person who writes poems or verses 2. a person who writes or expresses himself with imaginative power and beauty of thought, language, etc. **—po′et·ess** n.fem. (now rare)

SYN.—poet, the general term for a writer of poems or verses, is sometimes used specifically to designate a writer of verse, or, in extended use, of elevated prose, who has great powers of imagination, intuition, and expression; **rhymer, rhymester,** and **versifier** do not in themselves carry the special favorable connotations of **poet** and, when used in contrast to it, specifically suggest a lack of true poetic powers; **poetaster** is always a term of contempt for a writer of inferior or trashy verse

poet. 1. poetic 2. poetry

po·et·as·ter (pō′ə tas′tər) *n.* [ModL.: see POET & -ASTER²] a writer of mediocre verse; rhymester; would-be poet —*SYN.* see POET

po·et·ic (pō et′ik) *adj.* [MFr. *poétique* < L. *poeticus* < Gr. *poiētikos*] 1. of, characteristic of, like, or fit for a poet or poetry 2. skilled in or fond of poetry 3. written in verse 4. having the beauty, imagination, etc. of good poetry 5. imaginative or creative —*n. same as* POETICS

po·et·i·cal (-i k'l) *adj. same as* POETIC: now used chiefly in reference to form, whereas *poetic* refers to the basic qualities of poetry —**po·et′i·cal·ly** *adv.*

po·et·i·cize (-ə sīz′) *vt.* -**cized′**, -**ciz′ing** 1. to make poetic 2. to express, or deal with, in poetry —*vi.* to write poetry

poetic justice justice, as in some plays, stories, etc., in which good is properly rewarded and evil punished; justice as one might wish it to be

poetic license 1. disregard of strict fact or of conventional rules of form, style, etc., as by a poet, for artistic effect 2. freedom to do this

po·et·ics (pō et′iks) *n.pl.* [*with sing. v.*] 1. *a*) the theory or structure of poetry *b*) a treatise on this; specif., [P-] a famous treatise on poetic drama by Aristotle 2. the poetic theory or practice of a specific poet

po·et·ize (pō′ə tīz′) *vt., vi.* -**ized′**, -**iz′ing** [Fr. *poétiser*] *same as* POETICIZE

poet laureate *pl.* **poets laureate, poet laureates** 1. the court poet of England, appointed for life by the monarch to write poems celebrating official occasions, national events, etc. 2. the official or most respected poet of any specific nation, region, etc.

po·et·ry (pō′ə trē) *n.* [ME. *poetrie* < OFr. < ML. *poetria* < L. *poeta*, POET] 1. the art, theory, or structure of poems 2. poems; poetical works 3. *a*) poetic qualities; the rhythm, feelings, spirit, etc. of poems *b*) the expression or embodiment of such qualities

po·go·ni·a (pə gō′nē ə, -gōn′yə) *n.* [ModL., name of the genus < Gr. *pōgōn*, a beard] 1. a small American orchid (*Pogonia ophioglossoides*) with a single white or pinkish flower having a lip tufted with yellow-brown hairs 2. the flower

☆**pog·o·nip** (päg′ə nip′) *n.* [< AmInd. (Shoshonean)] a heavy winter fog containing ice particles, occurring in the valleys of the Sierra Nevada Mountains and in other mountain valleys of the western U.S.

☆**po·go stick** (pō′gō) [arbitrary coinage] a stilt with pedals and a spring at one end, used as a toy to move along in a series of bounds

po·grom (pō gräm′, -grum′; pō′grəm) *n.* [< Russ., desolation, earlier, riot, storm < *po-*, on, at, by (< IE. *po-*, aphetic < *apo-*, away: see AB-) + *grom*, thunder < IE. base *ghrem-*, whence GRIM] an organized persecution and massacre, often officially prompted, of a minority group, esp. of Jews (as in Czarist Russia) —*SYN.* see SLAUGHTER

☆**po·gy** (pō′gē) *n., pl.* -**gies** [prob. contr. < AmInd. (Algonquian) *pauhaugen*] 1. *same as* MENHADEN 2. a surfperch (*Amphistichus rhodoterus*)

Po Hai (bō′ hī′) arm of the Yellow Sea, north of Shantung peninsula in NE China: c. 300 mi. long

☆**poi** (poi, pō′ē) *n.* [Haw.] a Hawaiian food made of taro root mixed with water, cooked, pounded into a paste, and slightly fermented

-**po·et·ic** (poi et′ik) [< Gr. *poiētikos* < *poiētēs*: see POET] a combining form meaning making, producing, forming [galactopoietic]

poign·ant (poin′yənt; *chiefly Brit.*, -ənt) *adj.* [ME. *poynant* < MFr. *poignant*, prp. of *poindre* < L. *pungere*, to prick: see POINT] 1. *a*) sharp or pungent to the smell or, formerly, the taste *b*) keenly affecting the other senses [*poignant* beauty] 2. *a*) sharply painful to the feelings; piercing *b*) evoking pity, compassion, etc.; emotionally touching or moving 3. sharp, biting, penetrating, pointed, etc. [*poignant* wit] —*SYN.* see MOVING —**poign′an·cy** *n.* —**poign′ant·ly** *adv.*

poi·kil·o·ther·mal (poi kil′ō thur′m'l, poi′kə lō-) *adj.* < Gr. *poikilos*, variegated (< IE. *poiko-*, var. of base *peik-*, colorful (whence L. *pingere*, to PAINT) + THERMAL] *Zool. same as* COLDBLOODED (sense 1): also **poi·kil′o·ther′·mic** —**poi·kil′o·ther′mism** *n.*

poi·lu (pwä′lōō; *Fr.* pwȧ lü′) *n.* [Fr., hairy, virile < *poil*, hair < L. *pilus*: see PILE²] [Slang] a soldier in the French army: term used esp. in World War I

Poin·ca·ré (pwȧn kȧ rā′) 1. **Jules Hen·ri** (zhül′ än rē′), 1854–1912; Fr. mathematician 2. **Ray·mond** (rȧ môn′), 1860–1934; Fr. statesman; prime minister (1912–13; 1922–24; 1926–29); president (1913–20): cousin of *prec.*

poin·ci·a·na (poin′sē an′ə, -ā′nə, -än′ə) *n.* [ModL., name of the genus, after M. de *Poinci*, early governor of the Fr. West Indies] 1. any of a genus (*Poinciana*) of small tropical trees and shrubs of the legume family, growing in dry, sandy soil and having showy red, orange, or yellow flowers 2. *same as* ROYAL POINCIANA

☆**poin·set·ti·a** (poin set′ē ə, -set′ə) *n.* [ModL., after Joel R. *Poinsett* (d. 1851), U.S. ambassador to Mexico] a Mexican and Central American plant (*Euphorbia pulcherrima*) of the spurge family, with yellow flowers surrounded by tapering red leaves resembling petals

point (point) *n.* [ME. < OFr., a dot, prick < L. *punctum*, a dot, neut. of *punctus*, pp. of *pungere*, to prick (< IE. base *peug-*, *peuk-*, to prick, jab, whence G. *fichte*, spruce

tree, L. *pugil*, a boxer, *puguus*, fist); also < OFr. *pointe*, sharp end < ML. *puncta* < L. *punctus*] 1. a minute mark or dot 2. a dot in print or writing, as a period, decimal point, vowel point, etc. 3. *a*) an element in geometry having definite position, but no size, shape, or extension [a line between two *points*] *b*) a particular or precisely specified position, location, place, or spot [*points* on an itinerary] 4. *a*) any of certain positions a player is stationed at in cricket, lacrosse, and other games *b*) the player at such a position 5. a particular time; exact moment [the *point* of death] 6. a stage, condition, level, or degree reached or indicated [a boiling *point*] 7. a particular detail or element; item [to explain a problem *point* by *point*] 8. *a*) a distinguishing feature; characteristic *b*) a physical characteristic or quality of an animal, used as a standard in judging breeding 9. a unit, as of measurement, value, game scores, etc. 10. *a*) a sharp or projecting end of something; tip *b*) something with a sharp end 11. needlepoint lace 12. a projecting or tapering piece of land; promontory; cape 13. [*pl.*] a horse's extremities 14. a branch of a deer's antler [a ten-*point* buck] 15. *a*) the exact or essential fact or idea under consideration *b*) the main idea, striking feature, or effective twist of a joke, story, etc. 16. a purpose; aim; object; use [no *point* in complaining] 17. *a*) an impressive or telling argument, fact, or idea [he has a *point* there!] ☆*b*) a helpful hint or suggestion 18. the posture of a hunting dog to show the presence and position of game ☆19. the number that the thrower must make in order to win in craps 20. a unit used in rationing commodities, as in time of war 21. [Archaic] a cord with metal tips, formerly used to lace up articles of clothing 22. *Ballet* the position of being on the tips of the toes 23. *Boxing* a scoring unit used when the bout is not ended by a knockout [to win on *points*] ☆24. *Education* a unit of academic credit based on grades and class hours 25. *Elec.* *a*) either of the two contacts, tipped with tungsten or platinum, that make or break the circuit in a distributor *b*) [Brit.] an outlet or socket 26. *Finance* *a*) a standard unit of value, equal to $1, used in quoting variations in current prices of stocks, commodities, etc. *b*) a unit, equal to one percent of the total mortgage, sometimes paid in advance by the borrower as a premium 27. *Heraldry* any of certain subdivisions on a shield or escutcheon 28. *Jewelry* a unit of weight, equal to 1/100 carat [a 10-*point* diamond] 29. *Mil.* a small party before an advance guard or behind a rear guard 30. *Navigation* *a*) any of the 32 marks showing direction on the circumference of a compass card *b*) the corresponding position on the horizon *c*) the angle between two successive compass points, equal to 11 1/4° 31. *Printing* a measuring unit for type bodies and printed matter, equal to about 1/72 of an inch: there are 12 points in a pica 32. [Brit.] *Railroading* a tapering rail at a switch: *usually used in pl.* —*vt.* 1. *a*) to put punctuation marks or pauses in *b*) to put vowel points on (Hebrew characters) *c*) to mark off (sums or numbers) with points, as esp. a decimal fraction from a whole number (with *off*) 2. to sharpen to a point, as a pencil 3. to give (a story, remark, anecdote, action, etc.) extra force or special emphasis, as by repetition or elaboration (usually with *up*) 4. to show or call attention to (usually with *out*) [to *point* the way, to *point* out a person's shortcomings] 5. to aim or direct (a gun, finger, etc.) 6. to extend the foot so as to bring (the toe) more nearly in line with the leg 7. to show the presence and location of (game) by standing still and facing toward it: said of hunting dogs 8. *Masonry* to rake out set or crumbling mortar from the joints of (brickwork) and finish or refinish with fresh mortar —*vi.* 1. to direct one's finger or the like (at or to something) 2. to call attention or allude (to something); hint (at something) 3. to aim or be directed (to or toward something); extend in a specified direction 4. to point game: said of a hunting dog 5. [Brit.] to come to a head, as an abscess 6. *Naut.* to sail close to the wind —**at the point of** very close to; on the verge of —**beside the point** not pertinent; irrelevant —**in point** appropriate; pertinent; apt [a case in *point*] —**in point of** in the matter of; as concerns [in *point* of fact] —**make a point of** 1. to make (something) one's strict rule, habit, or practice 2. to call special attention to —**on** (or **upon**) **the point of** almost in the act of; on the verge of —**stretch** (or **strain**) **a point** to make an exception or concession —**to the point** pertinent; apt —**point′a·ble** *adj.*

point-blank (-blaŋk′) *adj.* [POINT + BLANK, *n.*, sense 4] 1. *Gunnery* *a*) aimed horizontally, straight at a mark, at such close range that rise and fall in the projectile's flight need not be considered *b*) of or suitable for such fire [*point-blank* range] 2. straightforward; plain; blunt [a *point-blank* answer] —*adv.* 1. in a direct line; straight 2. without hesitation or quibbling; directly; bluntly [to refuse *point-blank*]

‡**point d'ap·pui** (pwan dȧ pwē′) [Fr.] point of support, or base, as for a military operation

point-de·vice, point-de·vise (point′di vīs′) *adj.* [ME. at *point devis*, to an exact point: see DEVICE] [Archaic] completely correct; precise —*adv.* [Archaic] to perfection; meticulously

‡**pointe** (pwant) *n., pl.* **pointes** (pwant) [Fr., point] *Ballet* (the position of being on) the tip of the toe

point·ed (poin'tid) *adj.* **1.** *a*) having a point, or sharp end *b*) tapering to a point, as a Gothic arch **2.** sharp; incisive; to the point, as an epigram **3.** clearly aimed at, or referring to, someone [a *pointed* remark] **4.** very evident; emphasized; conspicuous —**point'ed·ly** *adv.* —**point'ed·ness** *n.*

Pointe-Noire (pwȧnt nwȧr') seaport in the Congo (sense 3), on the Atlantic: pop. 57,000

point·er (poin'tər) *n.* **1.** a person or thing that points **2.** a long, tapered rod used by teachers and lecturers for pointing to things on a map, blackboard, etc. **3.** an indicator on a clock, meter, scales, etc. **4.** any of a breed of large, lean hunting dog with a smooth coat, usually white with brown spots: it smells out game and then points until the hunter is ready to fire **5.** [Colloq.] a helpful hint or suggestion —**the Pointers** *Astron.* the two stars in the Big Dipper that are almost in a direct line with the North Star

POINTER
(26 in. high at shoulder)

poin·til·lism (pwȧn't'l iz'm, -tē iz'm; point'l-) *n.* [Fr. *pointillisme* < *pointiller*, to mark with dots < *pointille*, a dot < It. *puntiglio*, dim. of *punto* < L. *punctus*: see POINT] the method of painting of certain French impressionists, in which a white ground is systematically covered with tiny points of pure color that blend together when seen from a distance, producing a luminous effect —**poin'til·list** *n.*, *adj.* —**poin'til·lis'tic** *adj.*

point lace needlepoint lace

point·less (point'lis) *adj.* **1.** without a point **2.** without meaning, relevance, or force; senseless; inane —**point'less·ly** *adv.* —**point'less·ness** *n.*

point of honor a matter affecting a person's honor

point of no return 1. the point on an overseas flight when there is no longer enough fuel to return to the starting point **2.** a point in an enterprise, adventure, etc. when participants are too deeply involved or committed to withdraw

point of order a question as to whether the rules of parliamentary procedure are being observed

point of view 1. the place from which, or way in which, something is viewed or considered, standpoint **2.** a mental attitude or opinion **3.** the viewpoint from which a story is narrated [omniscient *point of view*]

point system ☆**1.** a system of averaging a student's letter grades by giving them equivalent numerical value in points: the average attained is called the **grade-point average 2.** a system of graduating the sizes of type on a uniform scale of points: see POINT (*n.* 31) **3.** any system of writing or printing for the blind, as Braille, in which raised points in certain combinations are used ☆**4.** a system of penalizing drivers of automotive vehicles a given number of points for certain driving offenses, and suspending the driver's license if a specified number of points accumulate

point·y (poin'tē) *adj.* **point'i·er, point'i·est 1.** that comes to a sharp point **2.** having many points

poise¹ (poiz) *n.* [ME. *pois*, weight < OFr. *pois* < VL. *pesum* < L. *pensum*, something weighed < *pendere*, to weigh: see PENDANT] **1.** balance; stability **2.** ease and dignity of manner; self-assurance; composure **3.** the condition of being calm or serene **4.** carriage; bearing, as of the body or head **5.** [Now Rare] *a*) a suspension of activity in a condition of balance *b*) suspense; irresolution; indecision —*vt.* **poised, pois'ing** [ME. *poisen* < OFr. *poiser* < *peise*, inflected form of *peser*, to weigh < VL. *pesare* < L. *pensare*, to weigh out < *pensus*, pp. of *pendere*] **1.** to balance; keep steady **2.** to suspend (usually passive or reflexive) **3.** [Rare] to weigh —*vi.* **1.** to be suspended or balanced **2.** to hover —*SYN.* see TACT

poise² (poiz) *n.* [Fr., after J. L. M. *Poiseuille*, 19th-c. anatomist] the cgs unit of viscosity of a liquid, equal to one dyne-second per square centimeter

poi·son (poi'z'n) *n.* [ME. < OFr. < L. *potio*, POTION] **1.** a substance causing illness or death when eaten, drunk, or absorbed even in relatively small quantities **2.** anything harmful or destructive to happiness or welfare, such as an idea, emotion, etc. **3.** in a nuclear reactor, a substance, as boron, that absorbs thermal neutrons from a chain reaction, thereby decreasing the reactivity of a reactor core: it is used for safety or control **4.** *Chem.* a substance that inhibits or destroys the activity of a catalyst, enzyme, etc. or that interferes with or checks a reaction —*vt.* **1.** to give poison to; harm or destroy by means of poison **2.** to put poison on or into **3.** to influence wrongfully; corrupt [to *poison* one's mind] —*adj.* poisonous or poisoned —**poi'son·er** *n.*

☆**poison dogwood** *same as* POISON SUMAC

poison gas any toxic chemical agent, in the form of a gas or vapor-forming liquid or solid, esp. one used in chemical warfare to kill or harass through inhalation or contact

☆**poison hemlock** *same as* HEMLOCK (sense 1)

☆**poison ivy 1.** any of several plants (genus *Toxicodendron*) of the cashew family, having leaves of three leaflets, greenish flowers, and ivory-colored berries: it can cause a severe rash on contact **2.** a rash so caused

☆**poison oak** *name variously used for:* **1.** POISON IVY **2.** POISON SUMAC

poi·son·ous (poi'z'n əs) *adj.* capable of injuring or killing by or as by poison; containing; or having the effects of, a poison; toxic; venomous —**poi'son·ous·ly** *adv.* —**poi'son·ous·ness** *n.*

POISON IVY

poi·son-pen (-pen') *adj.* [Slang] designating or of an abusive letter written out of spite or malice, usually anonymously, for the purpose of harassing the recipient

☆**poison sumac** a swamp plant (*Toxicodendron vernix*) of the cashew family, with greenish-white flowers, hanging clusters of small grayish fruit, and leaves made up of 7 to 13 leaflets: it can cause a severe rash on contact

Pois·son distribution (pwä sōn') [after S. D. *Poisson* (1781–1840), Fr. mathematician] *Statistics* a frequency distribution that may be regarded as an approximation of the binomial distribution when the number of events becomes large and the probability of success becomes small

Poisson's ratio [see prec.] *Physics* an elastic constant of a material equal to the ratio of contraction sidewise to expansion lengthwise when the material is stretched

Poi·tiers (pwä tyā') city in WC France: pop. 62,000

Poi·tou (pwä tōō') region & former province of WC France

‡**poi·trine** (pwä tren') *n.* [Fr.] the breast or chest; esp., a woman's bosom, when full and shapely

poke¹ (pōk) *vt.* **poked, pok'ing** [ME. *poken* < MDu. or LowG. *poken*] **1.** *a*) to push or jab with a stick, finger, etc.; prod *b*) [Slang] to hit with the fist **2.** to make by poking [to *poke* a hole in a bag] **3.** to stir up (a fire) by jabbing the coals with a poker **4.** to thrust (something) forward; intrude [to *poke* one's head out a window] —*vi.* **1.** to make jabs with a stick, poker, etc. (*at* something) **2.** to intrude; meddle **3.** to pry or search (sometimes with *about* or *around*) **4.** to stick out; protrude **5.** to live or move slowly or lazily; loiter; putter; dawdle (often with *along*) —*n.* **1.** *a*) the act of poking; jab; thrust; nudge *b*) [Slang] a blow with the fist **2.** *same as* SLOWPOKE **3.** a poke bonnet, or its projecting front brim —**poke fun (at)** to ridicule or deride, esp. satirically or slyly

poke² (pōk) *n.* [ME. < OFr. *poke, poque* < Frank. **pokka* < IE. base **beu-*, to blow up, swell, whence PUCK²] **1.** [Dial.] a sack or bag **2.** [Archaic] a pocket **3.** [Slang] *a*) a wallet or purse *b*) money, esp. all that one has

☆**poke³** (pōk) *n.* [earlier *pocan* < AmInd. (Virginian) *puccoon*, weed used for staining] *same as* POKEWEED

☆**poke·ber·ry** (-ber'ē) *n.*, *pl.* **-ries** *same as* POKEWEED

poke bonnet a bonnet with a projecting front brim

☆**pok·er¹** (pō'kər) *n.* [< ? Fr. *poque* < ?] a card game in which the players bet on the value of their hands (of five cards), the bets forming a pool to be taken by the player who has not dropped out of the betting and who holds the highest hand: there are several varieties See DRAW POKER, STUD POKER

pok·er² (pō'kər) *n.* **1.** a person or thing that pokes **2.** a bar, usually of iron, for stirring a fire

☆**poker face** [Colloq.] an expressionless face, as of a poker player trying to conceal the nature of his hand

☆**poke·root** (pōk'rōōt', -root') *n. same as* POKEWEED

☆**poke·weed** (pōk'wēd') *n.* [see POKE³] a N. American plant (*Phytolacca americana*) with clusters of purplish-white flowers, reddish-purple berries, and smooth leaves and stems: the roots and berry seeds are poisonous

pok·ey (pō'kē) *n.*, *pl.* **pok'eys, pok'ies** [< ?] [Slang] a jail: also **pok'y**

pok·y (pō'kē) *adj.* **pok'i·er, pok'i·est** [POKE¹ + -Y²] **1.** not lively; slow, dull, dilatory, etc. **2.** small and uncomfortable; stuffy [a *poky* room] **3.** shabbily dressed; dowdy Also **pok'ey** —**pok'i·ly** *adv.* —**pok'i·ness** *n.*

POL *Mil.* petroleum, oil, and lubricants

pol (päl) *n.* [Slang] an experienced politician

Pol. 1. Poland **2.** Polish

pol. 1. political **2.** politics

Po·la (pō'lä) *It. name of* PULA

Po·land (pō'lənd) country in C Europe, on the Baltic Sea: 120,625 sq. mi.; pop. 31,944,000; cap. Warsaw: Pol. name, POLSKA

☆**Poland China** any of an American breed of large hogs, usually black and white

po·lar (pō'lər) *adj.* [ML. *polaris* < L. *polus*: see POLE²] **1.** *a*) of, relating to, or near the North or South Pole *b*) coming from the region near the North or South Pole **2.** of a pole or poles **3.** having polarity **4.** opposite in character, nature, direction, etc. **5.** central and guiding, like the earth's pole or the polestar

polar bear a large, white bear (*Thalarctos maritimus*) of the arctic regions

polar body a minute cell cast off when a primary oocyte undergoes meiotic division to produce a secondary oocyte and again when the secondary oocyte divides to produce an ovum

polar circle *same as:* **1.** ARCTIC CIRCLE **2.** ANTARCTIC CIRCLE

polar coordinate either of two numbers that locate a point in a plane: one is the distance of the point from a fixed point on a fixed line, and the other is the angle made by the fixed line with the line connecting the two points

polar distance *Astron.* the complement of the angle of declination

polar front *Meteorol.* the boundary or transition region between the cold air of a polar region and the warmer air of the middle or tropical regions

po·lar·im·e·ter (pō′lə rim′ə tər) *n.* [POLARI(ZE) + -METER] **1.** an instrument for measuring the degree of polarization of light, or the amount of polarized light in a ray **2.** a polariscope made esp. for measuring the optical activity of a substance, esp. a liquid —**po·lar·i·met·ric** (pō lar′ə met′rik) *adj.* —**po′lar·im′e·try** (-trē) *n.*

Po·la·ris (pō lar′is) [ModL. < ML. (*stella*) *polaris*, polar (star): see POLE²] *same as* NORTH STAR —☆*n.* a U.S. ballistic missile with a nuclear warhead, esp. for launching from a submarine

po·lar·i·scope (pō lar′ə skōp′) *n.* [POLARI(ZE) + -SCOPE] **1.** an instrument for detecting or demonstrating the polarization of light, or for looking at things in polarized light **2.** *same as* POLARIMETER (sense 2) —**po·lar′i·scop′ic** (-skäp′ik) *adj.*

po·lar·i·ty (pō lar′ə tē) *n., pl.* -ties **1.** the property possessed by bodies having opposite magnetic poles of placing themselves so that their two extremities point to the two magnetic poles of the earth **2.** any tendency to turn, grow, think, feel, etc. in a certain way or direction, as if because of magnetic attraction or repulsion **3.** the having or showing of contrary qualities, powers, tendencies, forms, etc. as in the opposite extremities of a plant or animal, the two electrodes of a battery, etc. **4.** the condition of being positive or negative with respect to some reference point or object

po·lar·i·za·tion (pō′lər i zā′shən) *n.* [< ff. + -ATION] **1.** the producing of polarity in something, or the acquiring of polarity **2.** *Elec.* a condition in which gases produced during electrolysis accumulate on and around the electrodes of an electric cell and reduce the flow of current by setting up an opposing potential **3.** [Fr. *polarisation*] *Optics* a) the condition of light or radiant energy in which the transverse vibrations of the waves are confined to one plane or one direction only b) the production of this condition

po·lar·ize (pō′lə rīz′) *vt.* -ized′, -iz′ing [Fr. *polariser* < *polaire*, POLAR] to give polarity to; produce polarization in —*vi.* to acquire polarity; specif., to separate into diametrically opposed, often antagonistic, groups, viewpoints, etc. —**po′lar·iz′a·ble** *adj.* —**po′lar·iz′er** *n.*

polar lights *same as:* **1.** AURORA BOREALIS **2.** AURORA AUSTRALIS

Po·lar·o·graph (pō lar′ə graf′, -gräf′) *a trademark for* an apparatus used in polarography, usually having a cathode formed by mercury dropping at a fixed rate

po·lar·og·ra·phy (pō′lə räg′rə fē) *n.* [< POLARIZE + -GRAPHY] an electrochemical technique of analyzing solutions that measures the current flowing between two electrodes in the solution as well as the gradually increasing applied voltage to determine respectively the concentration of a solute and its nature —**po·lar·o·graph·ic** (pō lar′ə graf′ik) *adj.* —**po·lar′o·graph′i·cal·ly** *adv.*

☆**Po·lar·oid** (pō′lə roid′) [POLAR + -OID] *a trademark for:* **1.** a transparent material containing embedded crystals capable of polarizing light: used in optics, photography, etc. **2.** [short for *Polaroid Land camera*] a portable camera that develops the film negative internally and produces a print within seconds after the process is initiated: in full **Polaroid (Land) camera**

pol·der (pōl′dər) *n.* [Du., prob. akin to POOL¹] an area of low-lying land reclaimed from a sea, lake, or river, as by the building of dikes

Pole (pōl) *n.* a native or inhabitant of Poland

pole¹ (pōl) *n.* [ME. < OE. *pal* < L. *palus*, PALE²] **1.** a long, slender piece of wood, metal, etc. usually rounded [a tent *pole*, *flagpole*, fishing *pole*] **2.** a tapering wooden shaft extending from the front axle of a wagon or carriage and attached by chains or straps to the collars of a span of horses **3.** a unit of measure, equal to one rod in linear measure or one square rod in square measure **4.** the position on the innermost side of a race track —*vt., vi.* poled, pol′ing ☆**1.** to propel (a boat or raft) with a pole **2.** to manipulate, impel, support, etc. with or as with a pole —**under bare poles 1.** with all sails furled because of the force of a gale **2.** naked; stripped

pole² (pōl) *n.* [ME. < L. *polus*, pole of the heavens, heavens < Gr. *polos*, axis of the sphere, firmament < *pelein*, to be in motion < IE. base *kwel-*, to turn, whence WHEEL] **1.** either end of any axis, as of the earth, of the celestial sphere, of a mitotic spindle in an animal cell or plant cell, etc. **2.** the region around the North Pole or that around the South Pole **3.** either of two opposed or differentiated

forces, parts, or principles, such as the ends of a magnet, the terminals of a battery, motor, or dynamo, or two extremes of opinion, etc. **4.** *Embryology* either of the two differentiated regions in the early embryo of many animals; specif., the **animal pole** containing little yolk and the **vegetal pole** containing most of the yolk **5.** *Math.* a point or points with characteristic properties, as the point of origin of polar coordinates —**poles apart** widely separated; having opposite natures, opinions, etc.; at opposite extremes

Pole (pōl), **Reginald** 1500-58; Eng. cardinal; last Roman Catholic archbishop of Canterbury (1556-58)

pole·ax, pole·axe (pōl′aks′) *n., pl.* -ax′es (-ak′siz) [altered (after POLE²) < ME. *pollax* < *pol*, POLL + *ax*, AX] **1.** a long-handled battle-ax **2.** any ax with a spike, hook, or hammer opposite the blade —*vt.* -axed′, -ax′ing to attack or fell with or as with a poleax

☆**pole bean** any of various strains of the common garden bean that grow as vines twining about poles or other supports: cf. BUSH BEAN

pole·cat (pōl′kat′) *n., pl.* -cats′, *-cat:* see PLURAL, II, D, 1 [ME. *polcat*, prob. < OFr. *poule:* see POULTRY & CAT] **1.** a small, weasellike carnivore (*Mustela putorius*) of Europe, closely related to the domesticated ferret ☆**2.** *same as* SKUNK

☆**pole horse** a horse harnessed alongside the pole of a wagon or carriage

po·lem·ic (pə lem′ik, pō-) *adj.* [Fr. *polémique* < Gr. *polemikos* < *polemos*, a war < IE. *pelem-*, base *pel-*, to shake, cause to tremble, whence L. *palpitare*, to tremble] **1.** of or involving dispute; controversial **2.** argumentative; disputatious Also, esp. for 2, **po·lem′i·cal** —*n.* **1.** an argument or controversial discussion **2.** a person inclined to engage in argument or disputation —**po·lem′i·cal·ly** *adv.*

po·lem·i·cist (-ə sist) *n.* a person skilled, or inclined to engage, in polemics: also **po·lem′ist** (-ist, päl′ə mist)

po·lem·ics (-iks) *n.pl.* [*with sing. v.*] [see POLEMIC & -ICS] the art or practice of disputation or controversy

po·len·ta (pō len′tə) *n.* [It. < L. *pollenta*, peeled or pearl barley: for IE. base see POLLEN] an Italian dish, a mush made of barley, chestnut meal, or, now esp., cornmeal

pol·er (pō′lər) *n.* ☆**1.** *same as* POLE HORSE ☆**2.** a person who poles a boat

pole·star (pōl′stär′) *n.* **1.** Polaris, the North Star **2.** a guiding principle **3.** a center of attraction

pole vault *Track and Field* **1.** an event in which the contestant leaps for height, vaulting over a bar with the aid of a long, flexible pole **2.** a leap so performed Also, Brit., **pole jump** —**pole′-vault′** *vi.* —**pole′-vault′er** *n.*

po·lice (pə lēs′) *n.* [Fr. < LL. *politia*, administration of the commonwealth (in L., the state) < Gr. *politeia*, the state, citizenship < *politēs*, citizen < *polis*, city < IE. base *pel-*, fortress, whence Sans. *pūr*, town] **1.** the regulation within a community of morals, safety, sanitation, etc.; public order; law enforcement **2.** the governmental department (of a city, state, etc.) organized for keeping order, enforcing the law, and preventing, detecting, and prosecuting crimes **3.** a) a governmental force, or body of persons, established and maintained for keeping order, etc. b) a private organization like this [security *police* at a college] c) [*with pl. v.*] the members of any such force ☆**4.** *U.S. Army* a) the work or duty of keeping a camp, etc. clean and orderly b) [*with pl. v.*] the soldiers charged with such duty [kitchen *police*] —*vt.* -liced′, -lic′ing **1.** to control, protect, or keep orderly with or as police or a similar force [to *police* the streets] ☆**2.** to make or keep (a military camp, post, etc.) clean and orderly

police court in some States, an inferior court with jurisdiction over minor offenses and misdemeanors, and the power to hold for trial those charged with felonies

police dog a dog specially trained to assist police; esp., in popular use, a German shepherd dog

po·lice·man (-mən) *n., pl.* -men (-mən) a member of a police force —**po·lice′wom′an** *n.fem., pl.* -wom′en

police state a government that seeks to intimidate and suppress political opposition by means of police, esp. a secret national police organization

police station the headquarters of a local or district police force

pol·i·clin·ic (päl′i klin′ik) *n.* [G. *poliklinik* < Gr. *polis*, city + G. *klinik* < Fr. *clinique*, CLINIC] the department of a hospital where outpatients are treated: cf. POLYCLINIC

pol·i·cy¹ (päl′ə sē) *n., pl.* -cies [ME. *policie* < OFr. < L. *politia* < Gr. *politeia:* see POLICE] **1.** a) orig., government or polity b) [Now Rare] political wisdom or cunning **2.** wise, expedient, or prudent conduct or management **3.** a principle, plan, or course of action, as pursued by a government, organization, individual, etc. [foreign *policy*] **4.** *same as* INSURANCE POLICY ☆**5.** *see* POLICY (RACKET)

pol·i·cy² (päl′ə sē) *n., pl.* -cies [altered (after prec.) < MFr. *police* < It. *polizza* < ML. *apodixa* < MGr. *apodeixis* < Gr., proof < *apodeiknynai*, to display, make known] **1.** a written contract in which one party guarantees to insure another against a specified loss, damage, injury, etc. in consideration of payments, usually periodic, called premiums: in full **insurance policy 2.** *see* POLICY (RACKET)

pol·i·cy·hold·er (-hōl′dər) *n.* a person to whom an insurance policy is issued

☆**policy (racket)** *same as* THE NUMBERS (see phrase under NUMBER)

po·li·o (pō′lē ō′) *n. clipped form of* POLIOMYELITIS

po·li·o·my·e·li·tis (pō′lē ō mī′ə līt′əs) *n.* [ModL. < Gr. *polios*, gray + MYELITIS] an acute infectious disease, esp. of children, caused by a virus inflammation of the gray matter of the spinal cord: it is accompanied by paralysis of various muscle groups that sometimes atrophy, often with resulting permanent deformities: also **acute anterior poliomyelitis**

po·lis (pō′lis, päl′is) *n., pl.* **po′leis′** (-lās′, -ās′) [Gr. *polis:* see POLICE] in ancient Greece, a city-state

Pol·ish (pōl′ish) *adj.* of Poland, its people, their language, or culture —*n.* the West Slavic language of the Poles

pol·ish (päl′ish) *vt.* [ME. *polischen* < inflected stem of OFr. *polir* < L. *polire*, to polish, prob. < IE. base **pel-*, to drive, impel, whence FELT[1]] **1.** *a)* to smooth and brighten, as by rubbing *b)* to coat with polish, wax, etc. and make bright or glossy **2.** to improve or refine (a person, his manners, appearance, etc.) as by removing crudeness or vulgarity **3.** to complete or embellish (a piece of writing, etc.); finish; perfect —*vi.* to take a polish; become glossy, elegant, or refined —*n.* **1.** a surface gloss **2.** elegance, refinement, cultivation, finish, or the like **3.** a substance used for polishing **4.** the act of polishing or condition of being polished —**polish off** [Colloq.] **1.** to finish (a meal, job, etc.) completely and quickly **2.** to overcome or get rid of (a competitor, enemy, etc.) —**polish up** [Colloq.] to improve (something) —**pol′ish·er** *n.*

SYN.—**polish** implies a rubbing, as with a cloth or tool and, often, an abrasive, paste, etc., to produce a smooth or glossy surface [to *polish* silver, glass, furniture, etc.]; **burnish** specifically suggests a rubbing of metals to make them bright and lustrous [*burnished* steel]; **buff** implies polishing with a stick or tool covered with specially treated leather (originally buffalo hide) or other material [to *buff* the fingernails]; **shine** implies a making bright and clean by polishing [to *shine* shoes]

Polish Corridor strip of Poland, between Germany & East Prussia, giving Poland an outlet to the Baltic Sea (1919–39): c. 120 mi. long; 20–70 mi. wide

pol·ished (päl′isht) *adj.* **1.** *a)* made smooth and shiny, as by rubbing *b)* having a naturally smooth and shiny surface **2.** elegant; refined; cultivated **3.** without error or flaw, finished [a *polished* performance]

polit. **1.** political **2.** politics

Po·lit·bu·ro (päl′it byoor′ō, pō′lit-; pə lit′-) *n.* [< Russ. *Politbyuro* < *Polit(icheskoe) Byuro*, political bureau] the executive committee of the Communist Party of the Soviet Union

po·lite (pə līt′) *adj.* [L. *politus*, pp. of *polire*, to POLISH] **1.** having or showing culture or good taste; polished; cultured; refined [*polite* society, *polite* letters] **2.** having or showing good manners; esp., courteous, considerate, tactful, etc. —**po·lite′ly** *adv.* —**po·lite′ness** *n.*

pol·i·tesse (päl′ə tes′; Fr. pō lē tes′) *n.* [Fr. < It. *politezza*, cleanliness, courtliness < *pulito*, clean < L. *politus:* see prec.] politeness; courtesy

pol·i·tic (päl′ə tik) *adj.* [ME. *polytyk* < MFr. *politique* < L. *politicus* < Gr. *politikos*, of a citizen < *politēs:* see POLICE] **1.** having practical wisdom; prudent; shrewd; diplomatic **2.** crafty; unscrupulous **3.** prudently or artfully contrived; expedient, as a plan, action, remark, etc. **4.** *same as* POLITICAL: rare except in BODY POLITIC —*vi.* **-ticked, -tick·ing** to engage in political campaigning, vote-getting, etc. SEE SUAVE —**pol′i·tic·ly** *adv.*

po·lit·i·cal (pə lit′i k'l) *adj.* [< L. *politicus* (see prec.) + -AL] **1.** of or concerned with government, the state, or politics **2.** having a definite governmental organization **3.** engaged in or taking sides in politics [*political* parties] **4.** of or characteristic of political parties or politicians [*political* pressure] —**po·lit′i·cal·ly** *adv.*

political economy *earlier name for* ECONOMICS

po·lit·i·cal·ize (-īz′) *vt.* **-ized′, -iz′ing** to make political; organize politically —**po·lit′i·cal·i·za′tion** *n.*

political liberty the right to participate in determining the form, choosing the officials, making the laws, and carrying on the functions of one's government

political science the science of political institutions, or of the principles, organization, and methods of government —**political scientist**

pol·i·ti·cian (päl′ə tish′ən) *n.* [POLITIC & -IAN] **1.** a person actively engaged in politics, esp. party politics, professionally or otherwise; often, a person holding or seeking political office: frequently used in a derogatory sense, with implications of seeking personal or partisan gain, scheming, opportunism, etc.: cf. STATESMAN **2.** a person skilled or experienced in practical politics or political science

pol·i·ti·cize (pə lit′ə sīz′) *vi.* **-cized′, -ciz′ing** to talk about, or engage in, politics —*vt.* to make political in tone, character, etc. —**po·lit′i·ci·za′tion** *n.*

pol·i·tick·ing (päl′ə tik′iŋ) *n.* political activity; esp., the process of campaigning for support, votes, etc.

po·lit·i·co (pə lit′i kō′) *n., pl.* **-cos′** [Sp. *politico* or It. *politico*, both < L. *politicus:* see POLITIC] *same as* POLITICIAN

po·lit·i·co- (pə lit′ə kō′) a *combining form meaning* political and [*politico*-economic]

pol·i·tics (päl′ə tiks) *n.pl.* [*with sing. or pl. v.*] [POLIT(IC) + -ICS] **1.** the science and art of political government; political science **2.** political affairs **3.** the conducting of or participation in political affairs, often as a profession **4.** political methods, tactics, etc.; sometimes, specif., crafty or unprincipled methods **5.** political opinions, principles, or party connections **6.** factional scheming for power and status within a group [office *politics*]

pol·i·ty (päl′ə tē) *n., pl.* **-ties** [MFr. *politie* < L. *politia:* see POLICY[1]] **1.** political or governmental organization **2.** a society or institution with an organized government; state; body politic **3.** a specific form of church government

Polk (pōk), **James Knox** 1795–1849; 11th president of the U.S. (1845–49)

pol·ka (pōl′kə) *n.* [Czech, Polish dance, lit., Polish woman < Pol., fem. of *Polak*, a Pole] **1.** a fast dance for couples, developed in Bohemia in the early 19th cent.: the basic step is a hop followed by three small steps **2.** music for this dance, in fast duple time —*vi.* to dance the polka

☆**pol·ka dot** (pō′kə) [< prec.: from the popularity of the dance in the late 19th c., term applied to various garments, materials, etc.] **1.** one of the small round dots regularly spaced to form a pattern on cloth **2.** a pattern or cloth with such dots —**pol′ka-dot′** *adj.*

poll (pōl) *n.* [ME. *pol* < or akin to MDu. *pol*, top of the head, head] **1.** the head; esp., the crown, back, or hair of the head **2.** an individual person, esp. one among several, as one of twelve jurors **3.** a counting, listing, or register of persons, esp. of voters **4.** a voting or expression of opinion by individuals **5.** the amount of voting; number of votes recorded ☆**6.** [*pl.*] a place where votes are cast and recorded ☆**7.** *a)* a canvassing of a selected or random group of people to collect information, or to attempt to discover public opinion *b)* a report or résumé of the results of this **8.** the blunt or flat end as of a hammer —*vt.* [ME. *pollen*] **1.** to cut off or cut short **2.** to cut off or trim the wool, hair, horns, or branches of; specif., to pollard (a tree) **3.** *a)* to take or register the votes of [to *poll* a county] ☆*b)* to require each member of (a jury, committee, etc.) to declare his vote individually **4.** to receive (a specified number or proportion of votes) **5.** to cast (a vote) **6.** to canvass in a poll (sense 7) —*vi.* to vote in an election —**poll′er** *n.*

pol·lack (päl′ək) *n., pl.* **-lack, -lacks:** see PLURAL, II, D, 2 [for early Scot. *podlok* < ?] any of several related saltwater food fishes (genera *Pollachius* and *Theragra*) of the cod family, having tiny scales and a projecting lower jaw: also sp. **pollock**

pol·lard (päl′ərd) *n.* [POLL, *v.* + -ARD] **1.** a hornless goat, deer, ox, etc. **2.** a tree with its top branches cut back to the trunk, so as to cause a dense growth of new shoots —*vt.* to change into a pollard

poll·book (pōl′book′) *n.* a book or list of registered voters in a precinct, county, etc.

polled (pōld) *adj.* **1.** orig., with the wool, hair, etc. cut off or trimmed **2.** lacking horns; hornless

☆**poll·ee** (pōl′ē′) *n.* a person questioned in a poll

pol·len (päl′ən) *n.* [ModL. < L., fine flour, dust < IE. base **pel-*, dust, meal, whence L. *pulvis*, dust, Gr. *palē*, dust] the yellow, powderlike male sex cells formed in the anther of the stamen of a flower

pol·len·ate (-āt′) *vt.* **-at′ed, -at′ing** *same as* POLLINATE

pollen count the number of grains of a specified variety of pollen, usually ragweed, present in a given volume of air, usually a cubic yard, at a specified time and place

pol·len·o·sis (päl′ə nō′sis) *n.* [POLLEN + -OSIS] *same as* HAY FEVER: also sp. **pol′li·no′sis**

pol·lex (päl′eks) *n., pl.* **pol′li·ces′** (-ə sēz′) [L., thumb, big toe] the innermost digit of a forelimb; esp., the thumb —**pol′li·cal** (-i k'l) *adj.*

pol·li·nate (päl′ə nāt′) *vt.* **-nat′ed, -nat′ing** to transfer pollen from a stamen to the upper tip of the pistil of (a flower) —**pol′li·na′tion** *n.* —**pol′li·na′tor** *n.*

pol·li·nif·er·ous (päl′ə nif′ər əs) *adj.* [< L. *pollen* (gen. *pollinis*) + -FEROUS] **1.** bearing or yielding pollen **2.** adapted for carrying pollen

pol·lin·i·um (pə lin′ē əm) *n., pl.* **-i·a** (-ə) [ModL. < L. *pollen:* see POLLEN] *Bot.* a mass of pollen grains stuck together and transferred as a whole in pollination, often by an insect

pol·li·nize (päl′ə nīz′) *vt.* **-nized′, -niz′ing** *same as* POLLINATE —**pol′li·niz′er** *n.*

pol·li·wog (päl′ē wäg′, -wôg′) *n.* [ME. *polwygle*, prob. < *pol*, POLL + *wigelen*, to WIGGLE] *same as* TADPOLE

Pol·lock (päl′ək) **1.** Sir **Frederick**, 3d Baronet, 1845–1937; Eng. jurist & writer on law **2. Jackson**, 1912–56; U.S. abstract painter

☆**poll·ster** (pōl′stər) *n.* a person whose work is taking public opinion polls

poll tax a tax per head: in some States payment of a poll tax is a prerequisite for voting in State or local elections, but such a prerequisite is barred in Federal elections by Constitutional Amendment

pol·lu·tant (pə loot′nt) *n.* [POLLUT(E) + -ANT] something that pollutes; esp., a harmful chemical or waste material discharged into the water or atmosphere

---

fat, āpe, cär; ten, ēven; is, bīte; gō, hôrn, tōōl, look; oil, out; up, fʉr; get; joy; yet; chin; she; thin, *then*; zh, leisure; ŋ, ring; ə for *a* in *ago*, *e* in *agent*, *i* in *sanity*, *o* in *comply*, *u* in *focus*; ' as in *able* (ā′b'l); Fr. bál; ë, Fr. coeur; ö, Fr. feu; Fr. mon; ō, Fr. coq; ü, Fr. duc; r, Fr. cri; H, G. ich; kh, G. doch. See inside front cover. ☆ Americanism; ‡foreign; *hypothetical; <derived from

pol·lute (pə lo͞ot′) *vt.* **-lut′ed, -lut′ing** [ME. *poluten* < L. *pollutus*, pp. of *polluere*, to pollute < *por-, for *per-*, intens. + *-luere*, to soil < IE. base *leu-, dirt, whence Gr. *lyma*, dirt] to make unclean, impure, or corrupt; defile; contaminate; dirty —*SYN.* see CONTAMINATE —**pol·lut′er** *n.* —**pol·lu′tion** *n.*

Pol·lux (päl′əks) [L., earlier *Polluces* < Gr. *Polydeukēs*] **1.** *Gr. & Rom. Myth.* the immortal twin of Castor: see DIOSCURI **2.** the brightest star in the constellation Gemini

Pol·ly (päl′ē) a feminine name: see MARY

☆**Pol·ly·an·na** (päl′ē an′ə) *n.* [name of the young heroine of novels by Eleanor H. Porter (1868–1920), U.S. writer] an excessively or persistently optimistic person

polly seeds [< *Polly*, a pet name for parrots, who eat the seeds] [Colloq.] sunflower seeds

po·lo (pō′lō) *n.* [prob. < Tibet. dial. *polo*, var. of *pulu*, properly, the name of the ball] **1.** a game played on horseback by two teams of four players each, who attempt to drive a small wooden ball through the opponents' goal with a mallet having a long, flexible handle **2.** *same as* WATER POLO —**po′lo·ist** *n.*

Po·lo (pō′lō), **Mar·co** (mär′kō) 1254?–1324?; Venetian traveler in E Asia

po·lo·naise (päl′ə nāz′, pō′lə-) *n.* [Fr. < fem. of *polonais*, Polish] **1.** an 18th-cent. dress with the skirt divided in front and worn looped back over an elaborate underskirt, orig. in Poland **2.** a stately Polish dance in triple time, almost processional in character **3.** music for this dance

po·lo·ni·um (pə lō′nē əm) *n.* [ModL.: so named by its co-discoverer, Marie CURIE, after her native land, Poland (ML. *Polonia*)] a radioactive chemical element formed naturally by the disintegration of radium or synthetically by the neutron irradiation of bismuth followed by beta decay: used as a power source in space satellites, as an aid in inducing electric discharges, etc.: symbol, Po; at. wt., 210.05; at. no., 84; sp. gr., 9.4; melt. pt., 254°C; boil. pt., 962°C

Po·lo·ni·us (pə lō′nē əs) in Shakespeare's *Hamlet*, a voluble, sententious old courtier, lord chamberlain to the king and father of Ophelia and Laertes

☆**polo shirt** a knitted pullover sport shirt

Pol·ska (pōl′skä) *Pol. name of* POLAND

Pol·ta·va (pōl tä′vä) city in EC Ukrainian S.S.R.: scene of a battle (1709) in which the Russians under Peter the Great defeated Sweden: pop. 177,000

pol·ter·geist (pōl′tər gīst′) *n.* [G. < *poltern*, to make noise, rumble (< IE. base *bhel-, whence BELLOW) + *geist*, GHOST] a ghost supposed to be responsible for table rappings and other mysterious noisy disturbances

pol·troon (päl tro͞on′) *n.* [Fr. *poltron* < It. *poltrone*, coward < *poltro*, colt < VL. *pulliter, prob. < *pullus*, young animal, chick: see POULTRY] a thorough coward; craven —*adj.* cowardly —**pol·troon′er·y** (-ər ē) *n.*

poly- (päl′i, -ə; *also, & before vowels usually*, -ē) [ModL. < Gr. *poly-* < *polys*, much, many < IE. *pelu, large amount < base *pel-, to pour, fill, whence FULL] *a combining form meaning:* **1.** much, many, more than one [*polychromatic, polyandry*] **2.** more than usual, excessive [*polyphagia*] **3.** in or of many kinds or parts [*polymorphous*] **4.** polymer of; polymerized [*polyvinyl*]

pol·y·a·del·phous (päl′ē ə del′fəs) *adj.* [< Gr. *polyadelphos*, with many brothers < *polys-*, many (see POLY-) + *adelphos*, brother + -OUS] *Bot.* having stamens joined by their filaments into a number of clusters

pol·y·am·ide (-am′īd) *n.* [POLY- + AMIDE] any of various compounds having two or more amide groups; esp., a polymeric amide, as nylon

pol·y·an·drous (-an′drəs) *adj.* [Gr. *polyandros*] **1.** practicing polyandry **2.** of or characterized by polyandry **3.** *Bot.* having many stamens

pol·y·an·dry (päl′ē an′drē, päl′ē an′drē) *n.* [Gr. *polyandria* < *poly-*, many + *anēr*, a man: see ANDRO-] **1.** the state or practice of having two or more husbands at the same time **2.** [ModL. *polyandria*] *Bot.* the presence of numerous stamens in one flower **3.** *Zool.* the mating of one female animal with more than one male —**pol′y·an′-dric** *adj.* —**pol′y·an′drist** *n.*

pol·y·an·tha (päl′ē an′thə) *n.* [ModL. < Gr. *polyanthos*: see ff.] a strain of cultivated roses (*Rosa polyantha*) having numerous small flowers borne in a cluster

pol·y·an·thus (-thəs) *n.* [ModL. < Gr. *polyanthos*: see POLY- & -ANTHOUS] **1.** any of various primroses with many flowers **2.** a tender, sweet-scented narcissus (*Narcissus tazetta*) with clusters of small, star-shaped flowers

pol·y·bas·ic (päl′i bā′sik) *adj.* [POLY- + BASIC] **1.** designating an acid having more than one hydrogen atom (per molecule) replaceable by basic atoms or radicals **2.** designating a salt having more than one atom (per molecule) of a monovalent metal

pol·y·bas·ite (-bā′sīt′) *n.* [G. *polybasit* < Gr. *poly-* (see POLY-) + *basis* (see BASE[1]) + G. -*it*, -ITE[1]] an iron-black ore, Ag₉Sb₂S₁₁, with a metallic luster, a complex sulfide of silver and antimony

Po·lyb·i·us (pə lib′ē əs) 198?–117? B.C.; Gr. historian

pol·y·car·bon·ate resin (päl′i kär′bə nit) any of a class of resins that are thermoplastic, tough, transparent, and nontoxic and are used in making molded products

Pol·y·carp (päl′i kärp′), Saint 69?–155? A.D.; Gr. bishop of Smyrna: Christian martyr: his day is Jan. 26

pol·y·car·pel·lar·y (päl′i kär′pə ler′ē) *adj.* *Bot.* having numerous separate or united carpels in the gynoecium

pol·y·car·pic (-kär′pik) *adj.* [POLY- + -CARPIC] *Bot.* **1.** capable of flowering and fruiting an indefinite number of times **2.** having two or more separate carpels Also **pol′y·car′pous** —**pol′y·car′py** (-pē) *n.*

pol·y·cen·trism (-sen′triz′m) *n.* [POLY- + CENT(E)R + -ISM] the existence, or the principle advocating the existence, of independent centers of activity or power within a political system, as among Communist nations —**pol′y·cen′tric** *adj.* —**pol′y·cen′trist** *adj.*, *n.*

pol·y·chaete (päl′i kēt′) *n.* [< ModL. *Polychaeta* < Gr. *polychaitēs*, with much hair < *poly-* (< *polys*, much) + *chaitē*, hair] any of a class (Polychaeta) of mostly marine, annelid worms, having on most segments a pair of fleshy, leglike appendages covered with bristles —**pol′y·chae′tous** *adj.*

pol·y·chot·o·my (päl′i kät′ə mē) *n.*, *pl.* **-mies** [POLY- + -*chotomy* (after DICHOTOMY)] division or separation into many parts, classes, etc. —**pol′y·chot′o·mous** (-məs) *adj.*

pol·y·chro·mat·ic (-krō mat′ik) *adj.* [POLY- + CHROMATIC] having various or changing colors

pol·y·chrome (päl′i krōm′) *adj.* [Fr. < Gr. *polychrōmos*: see POLY- & -CHROME] **1.** *same as* POLYCHROMATIC **2.** done or decorated in several colors —*n.* a polychrome work of art

pol·y·chro·my (-krō′mē) *n.* [Fr. *polychromie*: see POLYCHROME] the art of combining many different colors, esp. in painting statues, vases, etc.

pol·y·clin·ic (päl′i klin′ik) *n.* [POLY- + CLINIC] a clinic or hospital for the treatment of various kinds of diseases: cf. POLICLINIC

Pol·y·cli·tus, Pol·y·clei·tus (-klīt′əs) 5th cent. B.C.; Gr. sculptor: also **Pol′y·cle′tus** (-klēt′-)

pol·y·con·ic projection (-kän′ik) a type of map projection in which the parallels are arcs of nonconcentric circles and the meridians are curves equally spaced from the central, straight meridian

pol·y·cot·y·le·don (-kät′'l ēd′'n) *n.* a plant which actually or apparently has more than two cotyledons, as in the gymnosperms —**pol′y·cot′y·le′don·ous** *adj.*

Po·lyc·ra·tes (pə lik′rə tēz′) ?–522? B.C.; Gr. tyrant of Samos

pol·y·cy·clic (päl′i sī′klik, -sik′lik) *adj.* [POLY- + CYCLIC] **1.** *Biol.* having two or more rings or whorls **2.** *Chem.* having two or more rings of atoms in the molecule

pol·y·cy·the·mi·a (-sī thē′mē ə) *n.* [POLY- + CYT(O)- + -HEMIA] an increase in the number and concentration of circulating red blood corpuscles

pol·y·dac·tyl (-dak′t'l) *adj.* [Fr. *polydactyle* < Gr. *polydaktylos*, many-toed: see POLY- & DACTYL] having more than the normal number of fingers or toes —*n.* a polydactyl person or animal —**pol′y·dac′tyl·ism, pol′y·dac′-ty·ly** *n.* —**pol′y·dac′ty·lous** *adj.*

pol·y·em·bry·o·ny (päl′ē em′brē ə nē) *n.* [< POLY- + EM-BRYO + -Y[2]] the production of two or more embryos or individuals from a single fertilized ovum

pol·y·ene (päl′ē ēn′) *n.* [POLY- + -ENE] an unsaturated compound containing more than two double bonds —**pol′y·e′nic** (-ē′nik) *adj.*

pol·y·es·ter (-es′tər) *n.* [POLY(MER) + ESTER] any of several polymeric resins formed chiefly by condensing polyhydric alcohols with dibasic acids: used in making plastics, fibers, etc.

pol·y·eth·yl·ene (päl′ē eth′ə lēn′) *n.* [POLY(MER) + ETHYLENE] any of several thermoplastic resins (C₂H₄)ₙ, made by the polymerization of ethylene: used in making translucent, lightweight, and tough plastics, films, containers, insulation, etc.

po·lyg·a·la (pə lig′ə lə) *n.* [ModL., name of the genus < L., milkwort < Gr. *polygalon* < *poly-*, much + *gala*, milk: see GALACTIC] *same as* MILKWORT

po·lyg·a·mous (pə lig′ə məs) *adj.* [Gr. *polygamos*] **1.** of, engaging in, or characterized by polygamy **2.** *Bot.* having bisexual flowers and unisexual flowers on the same plant or on different plants —**po·lyg′a·mous·ly** *adv.*

po·lyg·a·my (-mē) *n.* [Fr. *polygamie* < Gr. *polygamia*: see POLY- & -GAMY] **1.** the state or practice of having two or more wives or husbands at the same time; plural marriage **2.** *Zool.* the practice of mating with more than one of the opposite sex —**po·lyg′a·mist** *n.*

pol·y·genes (päl′i jēnz′) *n.pl.* [< POLY- + GENE] *same as* MULTIPLE FACTORS —**pol′y·gen′ic** (-jen′ik) *adj.*

pol·y·gen·e·sis (päl′i jen′ə sis) *n.* [ModL.: see POLY- & GENESIS] **1.** derivation from more than one kind of germ cell **2.** the theory that different species are descended from different ultimate ancestors —**pol′y·ge·net′ic** (-jə net′ik) *adj.* —**pol′y·ge·net′i·cal·ly** *adv.*

pol·y·glot (päl′i glät′) *adj.* [Gr. *polyglōttos* < *poly-*, many (see POLY-) + *glōtta*, the tongue: see GLOTTIS] **1.** speaking or writing several languages **2.** containing, composed of, or written in several languages —*n.* **1.** a person who speaks or writes several languages **2.** a book written in several languages **3.** a mixture or confusion of languages

Pol·yg·no·tus (päl′ig nōt′əs) 5th cent. B.C.; Gr. painter

pol·y·gon (päl′i gän′) *n.* [LL. *polygonum* < Gr. *polygōnon*, neut. of *polygōnos*: see POLY- & -GON] a closed plane figure, esp. one with more than four sides and angles —**po·lyg-o·nal** (pə lig′ə n'l) *adj.*

po·lyg·o·num (pə lig′ə nəm) *n.* [ModL. < L. *polygonon* < Gr. *polygonon*, kind of plant, knotgrass < *poly-*, many (see POLY-) + *gony*, a joint, KNEE: from the many joints] any of a genus (*Polygonum*) of annual or perennial plants of the buckwheat family, having conspicuous enlarged nodes, ocreas, and small whitish, greenish, or pink flowers in the leaf axils or in terminal clusters

pol·y·graph (päl′i graf, -gräf′) *n.* [Gr. *polygraphos*, writing much: see POLY- & -GRAPH] 1. an early device for reproducing writings or drawings 2. an instrument for recording simultaneously changes in blood pressure, respiration, pulse rate, etc.: see LIE DETECTOR 3. [Rare] an author of many works or many kinds of works —**pol′·y·graph′ic** *adj.*

po·lyg·y·ny (pə lij′ə nē) *n.* [ModL. *polygynia* < POLY- + Gr. *gynē*, a woman, wife: see GYNO-] 1. the state or practice of having two or more wives or concubines at the same time 2. *Bot.* the fact of having many styles or pistils 3. *Zool.* the mating of a male animal with more than one female —**po·lyg′y·nous** (-nəs) *adj.*

pol·y·he·dron (päl′i hē′drən) *n., pl.* -**drons**, -**dra** (-drə) [ModL. < Gr. *polyedron*, neut. of *polyedros*: see POLY- & -HEDRON] a solid figure, esp. one with more than six plane surfaces —**pol′y·he′dral** *adj.*

pol·y·hy·dric (-hi′drik) *adj.* [POLY- + HYDR(OXYL) + -IC] containing more than one hydroxyl group (OH) in the molecule: also **pol′y·hy·drox′y** (-hi dräk′sē)

Pol·y·hym·ni·a (-him′nē ə) [L. < Gr. *Polymnia* < *poly-*, many + *hymnos*, a hymn: see POLY- & HYMN] *Gr. Myth.* the Muse of sacred poetry: also **Po·lym′ni·a** (pə lim′-)

pol·y·i·so·prene (-i′sō prēn′) *n.* a polymer of isoprene, the main constituent of rubber, now made synthetically

pol·y·math (päl′i math′) *n.* [< Gr. *polymathēs*, knowing much < *poly-* (< *polys*, much) + *manthainein*, to learn] a person of great and diversified learning —**pol′y·math′ic** *adj.*

pol·y·mer (päl′i mər) *n.* [G. < Gr. *polymerēs*, of many parts: see POLY- & -MEROUS] a naturally occurring or synthetic substance consisting of giant molecules formed from smaller molecules of the same substance and often having a definite arrangement of the components of the giant molecules

pol·y·mer·ic (päl′i mer′ik) *adj.* [< G. *polymerisch*: see prec.] composed of the same chemical elements in the same proportions by weight, but differing in molecular weight —**pol′y·mer′i·cal·ly** *adv.*

po·lym·er·ism (pə lim′ər iz′m, päl′i mər-) *n.* the condition of being polymeric or polymerous

po·lym·er·i·za·tion (pə lim′ər i zā′shən, päl′i mər-) *n.* 1. the process of joining two or more like molecules to form a more complex molecule whose molecular weight is a multiple of the original and whose physical properties are different 2. the changing of a compound into a polymeric form by this process —**po·lym′er·ize** (-īz′) *vt., vi.* -**ized′, -iz′ing**

po·lym·er·ous (pə lim′ər əs) *adj.* [POLY- + -MEROUS] *Bot.* consisting of many members in each whorl

pol·y·morph (päl′i môrf′) *n.* [< Gr. *polymorphos*: see POLY- & -MORPH] 1. *Biol.* a polymorphous organism or one of its forms 2. *Chem., Mineralogy a)* a substance that can crystallize in different forms *b)* one of these forms

pol·y·mor·phism (päl′i môr′fiz′m) *n.* [POLYMORPH(OUS) + -ISM] 1. *Chem., Mineralogy* the property of certain substances of crystallizing in two or more different forms or systems 2. *Zool.* the condition in which a species has two or more very different morphological forms, as the castes of social insects

pol·y·mor·pho·nu·cle·ar (-môr′fə nōō′klē ər) *adj.* having a lobed nucleus, as the neutrophils

pol·y·mor·phous (-môr′fəs) *adj.* [Gr. *polymorphos*: see POLY- & -MORPH] of, having, or exhibiting polymorphism: also **pol′y·mor′phic** —**pol′y·mor′phous·ly** *adv.*

pol·y·myx·in (-mik′sin) *n.* [< ModL. (*Bacillus*) *polymyx(a)* (< *poly-*, POLY- + -*myxa* < Gr. *myxa*, MUCUS) + -IN¹] any of various antibiotics obtained from strains of a soil bacterium (*Bacillus polymyxa*), esp. effective against gram-negative bacteria

Pol·y·ne·sia (päl′ə nē′zhə, -shə) a major division of the Pacific islands east of the international date line, including Hawaii, Samoa, Tonga, the Society Islands, Marquesas Islands, etc.: cf. MELANESIA, MICRONESIA

Pol·y·ne·sian (-zhən, -shən) *adj.* of Polynesia, its people, their language, or culture —*n.* 1. a member of the brown people of Polynesia, including the Hawaiians, Tahitians, Samoans, and Maoris 2. the group of Malayo-Polynesian languages of Polynesia

Pol·y·ni·ces (päl′ə nī′sēz) *Gr. Legend* a son of Oedipus and brother of Eteocles: see SEVEN AGAINST THEBES

pol·y·no·mi·al (päl′i nō′mē əl) *n.* [POLY- + (BI)NOMIAL] an expression or name consisting of more than two terms; specif., *a) Algebra* a linear combination of products of integral powers of a given set of variables, with constant coefficients (Ex.: $x^3 + 3x + 2$ and $x^2 - 2xy + y^2$) *b) Biol.* a species or subspecies name consisting of more than two terms —*adj.* consisting of or characterized by polynomials

pol·y·nu·cle·ar (-nōō′klē ər, -nyōō′-) *adj.* [POLY- + NUCLEAR] having many nuclei: also **pol′y·nu′cle·ate** (-it)

po·lyn·ya (pä lin′yə, päl′in yä′) *n.* [Russ. *polyn′ya* < *polyi*, open < OSlav. **pol-no-*, level area < IE. base **plā-*, broad, flat, whence PLANE³, FLOOR] a usually oblong area of open water surrounded by sea ice

pol·yp (päl′ip) *n.* [Fr. *polype* < L. *polypus* < Gr. *polypous* < *poly-*, many (see POLY-) + *pous*, FOOT] 1. any of various coelenterates, colonial or individual, having a mouth fringed with many small, slender tentacles bearing stinging cells at the top of a tubelike body, as the sea anemone, hydra, etc. 2. a smooth projecting growth of hypertrophied mucous membrane in the nasal passages, bladder, rectum, etc.

MOUTH

HYDROTHECA

PERISARC

POLYP

pol·y·par·y (päl′i per′ē) *n., pl.* -**par′ies** [ModL. < L. *polypus*, POLYP] the common base or the connecting tissue to which each member of a colony of polyps is attached: also **pol′y·par′i·um** (-ē əm), *pl.* -**i·a** (-ə)

pol·y·pep·tide (päl′i pep′tīd) *n.* [POLY- + PEPTIDE] a substance containing two or more amino acids in the molecule joined together by peptide linkages

pol·y·pet·al·ous (-pet′'l əs) *adj.* [POLY- + PETALOUS] *Bot.* having separate petals

pol·y·pha·gi·a (-fā′jē ə, -fā′jə) *n.* [ModL. < Gr. *polyphagia* < *poly-*, many (see POLY-) + *phagein*, to eat: see -PHAGOUS] 1. excessive desire for food 2. the eating of or subsistence on many kinds of food —**po·lyph·a·gous** (pə lif′ə gəs) *adj.*

pol·y·phase (päl′i fāz′) *adj. Elec.* having, generating, or using alternating currents (usually three or a multiple of three) differing in phase [a *polyphase* system]

Pol·y·phe·mus (päl′ə fē′məs) in Homer's *Odyssey*, a Cyclops who confined Odysseus and his companions in a cave until Odysseus blinded him so that they could escape ☆**polyphemus moth** a large, yellowish-brown American silkworm moth (*Telea polyphemus*) with an eyelike spot on each hind wing

pol·y·phone (päl′i fōn′) *n. Phonet.* a polyphonic letter or other symbol

pol·y·phon·ic (päl′i fän′ik) *adj.* [Gr. *polyphōnos*, having many tones: see POLY- & -PHONE] 1. having or making many sounds 2. *Music a)* of or characterized by polyphony; having two or more harmonized melodies; contrapuntal *b)* that can produce more than one tone at a time, as a piano 3. *Phonet.* representing more than one sound, as the letter *c* (cf. *cat* and *cereal*) Also **po·lyph·o·nous** (pə lif′ə nəs) —**pol′y·phon′i·cal·ly** *adv.*

po·lyph·o·ny (pə lif′ə nē) *n.* [Gr. *polyphōnia*: see POLY- & -PHONY] 1. multiplicity of sounds, as in an echo 2. *Music* a combining of a number of individual but harmonizing melodies, as in a fugue, canon, etc.; counterpoint 3. *Phonet.* the representation of two or more sounds by the same letter or symbol

pol·y·phy·let·ic (päl′i fī let′ik) *adj.* [POLY- + PHYLETIC] *Biol.* derived from more than one ancestral type —**pol′y·phy·let′i·cal·ly** *adv.*

pol·y·pide (päl′i pīd′) *n.* [POLYP + -*ide* (var. of -ID)] 1. an individual in a colony of ectoprocts 2. same as POLYP Also **pol′yp·ite′** (-pīt′)

pol·y·ploid (päl′i ploid′) *adj.* [POLY- + -PLOID] having the number of chromosomes in the somatic cells three or more times the haploid number —*n.* a polyploid cell or organism —**pol′y·ploi′dy** *n.*

pol·y·po·dy (päl′i pō′dē) *n., pl.* -**dies** [ME. *polipodye* < L. *polypodium* < Gr. *polypodion* < *poly-* (see POLY-) + *pous* (gen. *podos*), FOOT: from its creeping rootstocks] any of a genus (*Polypodium*) of ferns with leathery pinnatifid leaves borne on creeping rootstocks

pol·y·pous (päl′i pəs) *adj.* of or like a polyp

pol·y·pro·pyl·ene (päl′i prō′pə lēn′) *n.* [POLY(MER) + PROPYLENE] polymerized propylene, a very light, highly resistant, thermoplastic resin used in packaging, coating, pipes and tubes, etc.

pol·y·ptych (päl′ip tik) *n.* [Gr. *polyptychos*, having many folds < *poly-* (see POLY-) + *ptyx*, a fold] a set of four or more panels with pictures, carvings, etc. often hinged for folding together, used as an altarpiece, etc.

pol·y·rhythm (päl′i rith′'m) *n.* [POLY- + RHYTHM] *Music* the use of strongly contrasting rhythms in simultaneous voice parts —**pol′y·rhyth′mic** *adj.*

pol·y·sac·cha·ride (päl′i sak′ə rīd′) *n.* [POLY- + SACCHARIDE] any of a group of complex carbohydrates, as starch, that decompose by hydrolysis into a large number of monosaccharide units

pol·y·sa·pro·bic (-sə prō′bik) *adj.* [POLY- + SAPROBIC] *Biol.* flourishing in a body of water carrying a heavy load of decomposed organic matter and having almost no free oxygen

pol·y·se·my (päl′i sē′mē) *n.* [ModL. *polysemia* < LL. *polysemus*, having many meanings < Gr. *polysēmos* <

poly- (< polys, much) + sēma, a sign: see SEMANTIC] the fact of having or being open to several or many meanings —pol′y·se′mous adj.

pol·y·some (-sōm′) n. [POLY- + -SOME³] a collection of ribosomes, probably connected by a single thread of ribonucleic acid (RNA), in which protein synthesis occurs

pol·y·so·mic (päl′i sō′mic) adj. [< POLY- + -SOME³ + -IC] Genetics having two complete genomes with one or more extra chromosomes that do not form a set

pol·y·sty·rene (-stī′rēn) n. a tough, clear, colorless plastic material, a polymer of styrene, used to make chemical apparatus, containers, etc.

pol·y·sul·fide (-sul′fīd) n. [POLY- + SULFIDE] a binary compound of sulfur containing more atoms of sulfur than the valence of the combining element requires

pol·y·syl·lab·ic (-si lab′ik) adj. [ML. polysyllabus < Gr. polysyllabos < poly-, many (see POLY-) + syllabē, SYLLABLE + -IC] 1. having several, esp. four or more, syllables 2. characterized by polysyllables Also pol′y·syl·lab′i·cal —pol′y·syl·lab′i·cal·ly adv.

pol·y·syl·la·ble (päl′i sil′ə b'l) n. [ML. polysyllaba < polysyllabus: see POLYSYLLABIC] a polysyllabic word

pol·y·syn·de·ton (päl′i sin′də tän′) n. [ModL. < neut. of LGr. polysyndetos, using many conjunctions < Gr. poly- (see POLY-) + syndetos, bound together < syndein, to bind together] Rhetoric the use or repetition of conjunctions in close succession

pol·y·tech·nic (-tek′nik) adj. [Fr. polytechnique < Gr. polytechnos, skilled in many arts < poly- (see POLY-) + technē: see TECHNIC] of or providing instruction in many scientific and technical subjects —n. a polytechnic school

pol·y·the·ism (päl′i thē iz′m) n. [Fr. polythéisme < Gr. polytheos, of many gods < poly-, many (see POLY-) + theos, god] belief in or worship of many gods, or more than one god: opposed to MONOTHEISM —pol′y·the·ist (-ist) adj., n. —pol′y·the·is′tic, pol′y·the·is′ti·cal adj. —pol′y·the·is′ti·cal·ly adv.

pol·y·thene (päl′i thēn′) n. Brit. var. of POLYETHYLENE

pol·y·to·nal·i·ty (päl′i tō nal′ə tē) n. [POLY- + TONALITY] Music the simultaneous use of two or more keys —pol′y·ton′al adj. —pol′y·ton′al·ly adv.

pol·y·troph·ic (-träf′ik) adj. [< Gr. polytrophos, nutritious < poly-, many (see POLY-) + trophos, feeder < trephein: see TROPHIC] obtaining nourishment from more than one kind of organic material, as many pathogenic bacteria

pol·y·typ·ic (-tip′ik) adj. [POLY- + -TYP(E) + -IC] Biol. 1. having or involving several different types, forms, or variations 2. of or pertaining to a taxonomic category having two or more immediate subdivisions

pol·y·un·sat·u·rat·ed (-un sach′ə rāt′id) adj. [POLY- + UNSATURATED] containing more than one double or triple bond in the molecule, as certain vegetable and animal fats and oils

pol·y·u·re·thane (-yoor′ə thān′) n. [POLY- + URETHANE] any of various synthetic rubber polymers produced by the polymerization of a hydroxyl (OH) radical and an NCO group from two different compounds: used in cushions, insulation, molded products, etc.

pol·y·u·ri·a (-yoor′ē ə) n. [ModL.: see POLY- & -URIA] excessive urination, as in some diseases —pol′y·u′ric adj.

pol·y·va·lent (-vā′lənt) adj. [POLY- + -VALENT] 1. Bacteriology designating a vaccine effective against two or more strains of the same species of microorganism 2. Chem. a) having a valence of more than two b) having more than one valence —pol′y·va′lence n.

pol·y·vi·nyl (-vī′n'l) adj. designating or of any of a group of polymerized vinyl compounds

pol·y·vi·nyl·i·dene (-vī nil′ə dēn′) adj. designating or of any of various polymerized vinylidene compounds

polyvinyl resin same as VINYL PLASTIC

☆pol·y·wa·ter (-wôt′ər, -wät′-) n. [POLY(MERIC) + WATER] a viscous laboratory substance, formed in minute quantities in capillary tubes, and variously identified as a hydrosol, a new form of water, contaminated water, etc.

pol·y·zo·an (päl′i zō′ən) n. [< POLY- + -ZOA + -AN] same as ECTOPROCT

pol·y·zo·ar·i·um (-zō er′ē əm) n., pl. -i·a (-ə) [ModL.: see POLY- & -ZOA & -ARY] 1. a polyzoan colony 2. its supporting skeleton

pom·ace (pum′is) n. [ML. pomacium, cider < L. pomum, fruit (in VL., apple)] 1. the crushed pulp of apples or other fruit pressed for juice 2. the crushed matter of anything pressed, as seeds for oil

po·ma·ceous (pō mā′shəs) adj. [ModL. pomaceus < L. pomum, fruit (in VL., apple)] of or like apples or other pomes

po·made (pä mād′, pō-, pə-; -mäd′) n. [Fr. pommade < It. pomata < pomo, apple < VL. pomum < L., fruit: orig. perfumed with apple pulp] a perfumed ointment, esp. for grooming the hair: also po·ma·tum (pō mät′əm) —vt. -mad′ed, -mad′ing to apply pomade to

po·man·der (pō′man der, pə man′-) n. [earlier pomamber < MFr. pome ambre, pomme d′ambre < pome (see POME) + ambre, amber] 1. a mixture of aromatic substances balled together and carried about with one, esp. formerly as a supposed safeguard against infection 2. a case for carrying this, esp. a hollow, perforated ball

pome (pōm) n. [ME. < OFr. < VL. *poma < L. pomum, fruit] Bot. a fleshy fruit derived from the inner walls of the united carpels and whose edible flesh is largely a development of the receptacle, as the apple, pear, quince, etc.

pome·gran·ate (päm′gran′it, päm′ə-; pum′-) n. [ME. pomegarnet < OFr. pome granade < pome (see prec.) + granade < L. granatum, pomegranate, lit., having seeds, neut. of granatus < granum, seed, GRAIN] 1. a round fruit with a red, leathery rind and many seeds covered with red, juicy, edible flesh 2. the bush or small tree (Punica granatum) that bears it

pom·e·lo (päm′ə lō′) n., pl. -los′ [altered (prob. after POME) < earlier pomplemous < Du. pompelmoes, shaddock] same as GRAPEFRUIT

Pom·er·a·ni·a (päm′ə rā′nē ə) region in C Europe, on the Baltic, now divided between Poland & East Germany

Pom·er·a·ni·an (-ən) adj. of Pomerania or its people —n. 1. a native or inhabitant of Pomerania 2. any of a breed of small dog with long, silky hair, pointed ears, and a bushy tail turned over the back

POMERANIAN
(5–7 in. high
at shoulder)

po·mif·er·ous (pō mif′ər əs) adj. [< L. pomum, fruit + -FEROUS] bearing fruit, esp. pomes

pom·mel (pum′'l; also, for n., päm′'l) n. [ME. pomel < OFr. dim. of pome, apple: see POME] 1. the round knob on the end of the hilt of some swords, etc. 2. the rounded, upward-projecting front part of a saddle —vt. -meled or -melled, -mel·ing or -mel·ling same as PUMMEL

Pom·mern (pôm′ərn) Ger. name of POMERANIA

Pom·my, Pom·mie (päm′ē) n., pl. -mies [said to be contr. < POMEGRANATE: ? because of rosy cheeks of English immigrants] [also p-] [Australian Slang] a British person —adj. [also p-] [Australian Slang] British

po·mol·o·gy (pō mäl′ə jē) n. [ModL. pomologia: see POME & -LOGY] the science of fruit cultivation —po′mo·log′i·cal (-mə läj′i k'l) adj. —po·mol′o·gist n.

Po·mo·na (pə mō′nə) [L. < pomum, fruit] 1. Rom. Myth. the goddess of fruits and fruit trees 2. [after prec.] city in S Calif., east of Los Angeles: pop. 87,000 3. same as MAINLAND (sense 1)

pomp (pämp) n. [ME. < MFr. pompe < L. pompa < Gr. pompē, solemn procession < pempein, to send] 1. stately or brilliant display; splendor; magnificence 2. ostentatious show or display 3. [Obs.] a pageant

pom·pa·dour (päm′pə dôr′) n. [after ff.] 1. a woman's hairdo in which the hair is swept up high from the forehead, usually over a roll ☆2. a man's hairdo in which the hair is brushed up high from the forehead

Pom·pa·dour (päm′pə dôr′, -door′; Fr. pōn pà dōōr′), marquise de (born Jeanne Antoinette Poisson le Normant d′Étioles) 1721–64; mistress of Louis XV

☆pom·pa·no (päm′pə nō′) n., pl. -no′, -nos′: see PLURAL, II, D, 2 [Sp. pámpano, a kind of fish, tendril < L. pampinus, a tendril, young shoot] any of a number of saltwater N. American and West Indian food fishes (esp. genus Trachinotus) with spiny fins and a widely forked tail

Pom·pa·no Beach (päm′pə nō′) [after prec.] city on the SE coast of Fla., near Fort Lauderdale: pop. 38,000

Pom·pei·i (päm pā′ē, -pā′) ancient city in S Italy, on the Bay of Naples: destroyed by the eruption of Mount Vesuvius (79 A.D.) —Pom·pei′an (-pā′ən) adj., n.

Pom·pey (päm′pē) (L. Gnaeus Pompeius Magnus) 106–48 B.C.; Rom. general & triumvir

pom-pom (päm′päm′) n. [echoic] 1. any of several rapid-firing automatic weapons, as an automatic cannon of the Boer war or an antiaircraft cannon of World War II 2. [altered < POMPON (sense 1)] same as pom′pon′

pom·pon (päm′pän′, -päm′; Fr. pōn pōn′) n. [Fr. < MFr. pomper, to exhibit pomp < pompe: see POMP] 1. an ornamental ball or tuft of silk, wool, feathers, etc., as worn on some hats or caps or waved in pairs by cheerleaders 2. a) any of various chrysanthemums, dahlias, etc. with small, round flower heads b) the flower head

pom·pos·i·ty (päm päs′ə tē) n. [ME. < MFr. posite < LL. pompositas: see ff. & -ITY] 1. the quality of being pompous; ostentation; self-importance 2. pl. -ties a pompous act, remark, etc.

pom·pous (päm′pəs) adj. [ME. < MFr. pompeus < LL. pomposus < L. pompa] 1. full of pomp; stately; magnificent 2. characterized by exaggerated stateliness; pretentious, as in speech or manner; self-important —pom′pous·ly adv. —pom′pous·ness n.

☆Pon·ca (päŋ′kə) n. 1. pl. -cas, -ca a member of a tribe of American Indians on reservations in Nebraska and Oklahoma 2. their Siouan dialect —adj. of this tribe

Pon·ce (pōn′se) seaport in S Puerto Rico: pop. 126,000

ponce (päns) n., vi. ponced, ponc′ing [Brit. slang < ?] [Slang] same as PIMP

Pon·ce de Le·ón (pōn′the the le ōn′; E. päns′ də lē′ən), Juan (hwän) 1460?–1521; Sp. explorer: discovered Florida while seeking the Fountain of Youth

pon·cho (pän′chō) n., pl. -chos [AmSp. < Araucan pontho] 1. a cloak like a blanket with a hole in the middle for the head, worn in Spanish America 2. any similar garment, esp. a waterproof one worn as a raincoat

pond (pänd) *n.* [ME. *ponde*, artificially enclosed body of water, form of *pounde*, POUND³] a body of standing water smaller than a lake, often artificially formed

pon·der (pän'dər) *vt.* [ME. *ponderen* < MFr. *ponderer* < L. *ponderare*, to weigh < *pondus* (gen. *ponderis*), a weight: see POUND¹] to weigh mentally; think deeply about; consider carefully —*vi.* to think deeply; deliberate; meditate —**pon'der·er** *n.*

SYN.—**ponder** implies a weighing mentally and suggests careful consideration of a matter from all sides [to *ponder* over a problem]; **meditate**, in intransitive use, suggests quiet, deep contemplation [he *meditated* on the state of the world] and, transitively, deliberate consideration of some plan [to *meditate* revenge]; **muse** implies such contemplation or reflection as seems to absorb one completely [to *muse* over the past]; **ruminate** suggests turning a matter over and over in the mind

pon·der·a·ble (-ə b'l) *adj.* [LL. *ponderabilis* < L. *ponderare*: see PONDER] **1.** that can be weighed **2.** that can be mentally weighed; appreciable —**pon'der·a·bil'i·ty** *n.*

☆**pon·der·o·sa** (pine) (pän'də rō'sə) [< ModL. *ponderosa*, lit., heavy (pine) < L. *ponderosus*, PONDEROUS] **1.** a yellow pine (*Pinus ponderosa*) of W N. America, valued for its timber **2.** its wood

pon·der·ous (pän'dər əs) *adj.* [ME. < L. *ponderosus* < *pondus*, a weight: see POUND¹] **1.** very heavy **2.** unwieldy because of weight **3.** that seems heavy; bulky; massive **4.** labored and dull [a *ponderous* joke] —**SYN.** see HEAVY —**pon'der·ous·ly** *adv.* —**pon'der·ous·ness, pon'der·os'i·ty** (-äs'ə tē) *n.*

Pon·di·cher·ry (pän'di cher'ē) **1.** territory of India, chiefly on the Coromandel Coast, formerly a part of French India: 185 sq. mi.; pop. 369,000 **2.** its capital: pop. 40,000 Fr. name **Pon·di·ché·ry** (pôn dē shā rē')

☆**pond lily** *same as* WATERLILY

pond scum a mass of filamentous algae forming a green scum on the surface of ponds, etc.

pond·weed (pänd'wēd') *n.* any of a genus (*Potamogeton*) of water plants of the pondweed family, having submerged or floating leaves and spikes of inconspicuous flowers —*adj.* designating a family (Potamogetonaceae) of water plants including pondweed and eelgrass

☆**pone¹** (pōn) *n.* [< AmInd. (Algonquian), as in Virginian *ápân*, bread] [Chiefly Southern] **1.** corn bread in the form of small, oval loaves **2.** such a loaf or cake

pone² (pōn) *n.* [< L. *pone*, imper. of *ponere*, to place: see POSITION] in various card games, the player to the right of the dealer or, in two-handed games, the player who is not the dealer

pong (päŋ) *vi., n.* [prob. < Romany *pan*, to stink] [Brit. Slang] *same as* STINK

pon·gee (pän jē') *n.* [< Chin. dial. *pen-chi*, domestic loom] **1.** a soft, thin cloth of Chinese or Indian silk, usually left in its natural light-brown color **2.** any cloth like this

pon·gid (pän'jid) *n.* [< ModL. *Pongidae*, name of the family < *Pongo*, type genus (< Kongo *mpongi*) + -IDAE] an anthropoid ape

pon·iard (pän'yərd) *n.* [Fr. *poignard*, altered < MFr. *poignal* < VL. *pugnalis* < L. *pugnus*, a fist: see PUGNACIOUS] a dagger —*vt.* to stab with a poniard

pons (pänz) *n., pl.* **pon·tes** (pän'tēz) [ModL. < L., a bridge < IE. base *pent-*, to step, go, whence FIND] *Anat., Zool.* a piece of connecting tissue; specif., the bridge of white matter at the base of the brain, containing neural connections between the cerebrum and cerebellum: full name **pons Va·ro·li·i** (və rō'li ī'), after Costanzo Varoli (1542–75), It. anatomist

pons as·i·no·rum (as'ə nôr'əm) [ModL., bridge of asses] **1.** *Geom.* the fifth proposition of the first book of Euclid (that the base angles of an isosceles triangle are equal) **2.** any problem hard for beginners

Pon·ta Del·ga·da (pôn'tə thel gä'thə; E. pän'tə del gä'də) seaport on São Miguel Island, the Azores: pop. 75,000

Pont·char·train (pän'chər trān'), **Lake** [after J. P. *Pontchartrain* (1674–1747), Fr. minister of colonies] shallow, saltwater lake in SE La.: 625 sq. mi.

Pon·ti·ac¹ (pän'tē ak') 1720?–69; Ottawa Indian chief

Pon·ti·ac² (pän'tē ak') [after prec.] city in SE Mich., just north of Detroit: pop. 85,000

Pon·ti·a·nak (pän'tē ä'näk) seaport in W Kalimantan, Indonesia, on the South China Sea: pop. 379,000

Pon·tic (pän'tik) *adj.* [L. *Ponticus* < Gr. *Pontikos* < *pontos*, sea (esp. the Black Sea), orig., path: for IE. base see PONS] **1.** of Pontus **2.** of the Black Sea

pon·ti·fex (pän'tə feks') *n., pl.* **pon·tif·i·ces** (pän tif'ə sēz') [L.: see ff.] in ancient Rome, a member of the supreme college of priests (**Pontifical College**)

pon·tiff (pän'tif) *n.* [Fr. *pontife* < LL.(Ec.) *pontifex* (gen. *pontificis*), bishop < L., high priest, orig. ? bridge maker < *pons* (gen. *pontis*), bridge (see PONS) + *facere*, to make] **1.** *same as* PONTIFEX **2.** a bishop; specif., [P-] the Pope (in full, **Supreme Pontiff**) **3.** a high priest

pon·tif·i·cal (pän tif'i k'l) *adj.* [ME. *pontificall* < L. *pontificalis* < *pontifex*: see PONTIFF] **1.** having to do with a pontifex or a high priest **2.** having to do with or celebrated by a bishop or other high-ranking prelate [a

---

pontifical Mass] **3.** having to do with the Pope; papal **4.** having the pomp, dignity, or dogmatism of a pontiff, sometimes, specif., arrogant or haughty —*n.* **1.** [*pl.*] a pontiff's vestments and insignia **2.** a book of offices for a bishop —**pon·tif'i·cal·ly** *adv.*

pon·tif·i·cate (-kit; *also, and for v. always,* -kāt') *n.* [L. *pontificatus* < *pontifex*: see PONTIFF] the office, or term of office, of a pontiff —*vi.* -**cat'ed**, -**cat'ing** [< ML. *pontificatus*, pp. of *pontificare*] **1.** to officiate as a pontiff **2.** to speak or act in a pompous or dogmatic way —**pon·tif'i·ca'tor** *n.*

pon·til (pän'til) *n.* [Fr. < It. *pontello, puntello*, dim. of *punto*, a point] *same as* PUNTY

Pon·tine Marshes (pän'tēn, -tīn) region in C Italy, southeast of Rome: formerly swampy, now reclaimed

Pontius Pilate *see* PILATE

pon·to·nier (pän'tə nir') *n.* [Fr. *pontonnier*] a military engineer or other member of the armed forces who builds, or is in charge of building, a pontoon bridge

pon·toon (pän tōōn') *n.* [Fr. *ponton* < L. *ponto* < *pons* (gen. *pontis*), a bridge (see PONS] **1.** a flat-bottomed boat **2.** any of a number of these, or of some other floating objects, as hollow cylinders, used as supports for a temporary bridge (**pontoon bridge**) **3.** a float on an aircraft Also ☆**pon'ton** (-t'n)

Pon·tus (pän'təs) [L. < Gr. *Pontos*: see PONTIC] ancient kingdom in NE Asia Minor, on the Pontus Euxinus

Pontus Eux·i·nus (yook sī'nəs) L. name of BLACK SEA

po·ny (pō'nē) *n., pl.* -**nies** [Scot. *powny*, prob. < OFr. *poulenet*, dim. of *poulain*, a colt, foal < VL. *pullamen*, young animals < L. *pullus*, young animal, FOAL] **1.** a small horse of any of a number of breeds, usually not over 58 in. high at the withers **2.** something small of its kind; specif., ☆a small liqueur glass or the amount it will hold ☆**3.** [? alteration of PONS (ASINORUM)] [Colloq.] a literal translation of a literary work in a foreign language, used in doing schoolwork, often dishonestly; crib ☆**4.** [Slang] a racehorse **5.** [Brit. Slang] the sum of twenty-five pounds —☆*vt., vi.* -**nied**, -**ny·ing** [Slang] to pay (money), as to settle an account (with *up*)

☆**pony express** a system of carrying and delivering mail by riders on swift ponies; specif., such a system in operation from April, 1860, to October, 1861, between St. Joseph, Mo., and Sacramento, Calif.

po·ny·tail (pō'nē tāl') *n.* a girl's hair style in which the hair, tied tightly as by a ribbon high at the back of the head, hangs free: also **pony tail**

☆**pooch** (pōōch) *n.* [< ? dial. form of POUCH, ? with reference to appetite] [Slang] a dog

pood (pōōd) *n.* [Russ. *pud* < LowG. *pund* < L. *pondo*, POUND¹] a Russian unit of weight, equal to 36.11 pounds avoirdupois

poo·dle (pōō'd'l) *n.* [G. *pudel* < LowG. *pudel(hund)* < *pudeln*, to splash (akin to PUDDLE) + *hund*, dog] any of a breed of dog having a solid-colored, curly coat usually clipped in any of various conventional patterns

poof (poof, pōōf) *interj.* [echoic of a sudden discharge] **1.** an exclamation used to express suddenness as of disappearance or appearance **2.** *same as* POOH¹

pooh¹ (pōō) *interj.* [prob. echoic of blowing away] an exclamation of disdain, disbelief, or impatience

pooh² (pōō) *vt.* [Slang] *same as* POOP²

pooh-bah (pōō'bä') *n.* [after *Pooh-Bah*, a character in Gilbert & Sullivan's *The Mikado* (1885)] [Colloq.] an official or leader who maintains full control as by holding several offices

pooh-pooh (pōō'pōō') *vt.* [redupl. of POOH¹] to minimize or treat disdainfully; make light of; belittle

pool¹ (pōōl) *n.* [ME. < OE. *pol*, akin to Du. *poel* & G. *pfuhl*, prob. ult. < IE. base *bhel-*, to shine, glimmer] **1.** a small pond, as in a garden **2.** a small collection of liquid, as a puddle **3.** *same as* SWIMMING POOL **4.** a deep, still spot in a river ☆**5.** a natural, isolated, underground accumulation of oil or gas —*vi.* to form, or accumulate in, a pool

pool² (pōōl) *n.* [Fr. *poule*, pool, stakes, orig. hen < LL. *pulla*, hen, fem. of L. *pullus* (see POULTRY): associated in E. with prec.] **1.** the total amount of the players' stakes played for in a single deal of a card game, etc. **2.** *a)* [Brit.] a game of billiards for such a pool *b)* any of several related games of billiards played with object balls numbered from one to fifteen and a cue ball, on a table with six pockets **3.** a combination of resources, funds, etc. for some common purpose; specif., ☆*a)* the combined wagers of bettors on a horse race, participants in a lottery, etc., the gains or losses from which are to be divided proportionately *b)* the combined investments of a group of persons or corporations undertaking, and sharing responsibility for, a joint enterprise ☆*c)* a common fund of stockholders, for speculation, manipulation of prices, etc. *d)* the persons or parties forming any such combination

POODLE
(over 15 in. high
at shoulder)

☆**4.** a combination of business firms for creating a monopoly in a particular market; trust **5.** a supply of equipment, trained personnel, etc. the use of which is shared by a group **6.** *Fencing* a contest in which each member of a team successively competes with each member of the opposing team —*vt., vi.* ☆to contribute to a pool, or common fund; make a common interest or form a pool (of)

Poole (pōōl) seaport in Dorsetshire, SE England: pop. 96,000

☆**pool·room** (-rōōm′) *n.* **1.** a room or establishment where pool is played: also **pool hall** **2.** [Now Rare] a room where bets are placed with a bookmaker

pool table a billiard table with a pocket at each corner and at the middle of both sides, for playing pool

poon (pōōn) *n.* [Singh. *pŭna*] **1.** any of several East Indian trees (genus *Calophyllum*) of the St. Johnswort family, whose seeds yield a bitter oil **2.** the wood of any of these trees, used esp. in ships, cabinetwork, etc.

Poo·na (pōō′nə) city in W India, in Maharashtra state: pop. 737,000

poop[1] (pōōp) *n.* [LME. *pouppe* < MFr. *poupe* < Pr. *popa* or It. *poppa* < L. *puppis*, stern of a ship] **1.** orig., the stern section of a ship **2.** on sailing ships, a raised deck at the stern, sometimes forming the roof of a cabin: also **poop deck** —*vt.* **1.** to break over the poop or stern of: said of waves **2.** to receive (a wave) over the poop or stern

poop[2] (pōōp) *vt.* [via dial. < ME. *poupen*, to make an abrupt sound, blow, gulp: echoic origin] [Slang] to cause to become exhausted, out of breath, etc.; tire: usually in the passive voice —☆**poop out** [Slang] **1.** to become exhausted **2.** to cease functioning

poop[3] (pōōp) *n.* [prob. < vulgar *poop*, to break wind, defecate, feces (< ME. *puopen*: see prec.)] [Slang] **1.** a foolish or contemptible person **2.** the pertinent facts: information

Po·o·pó (pô′ō pô′), Lake shallow, saltwater lake in WC Bolivia: 970 sq. mi.; altitude, c. 12,000 ft.

☆**poop sheet** a concise compilation of facts or data about a particular subject or subjects

poor (poor) *adj.* [ME. *pore* < OFr. *povre* < L. *pauper*, poor < IE. base *pōu-*, small, whence FEW, FOAL] **1.** *a)* lacking material possessions; having little or no means to support oneself; needy; impoverished *b)* indicating or characterized by poverty **2.** lacking in some quality or thing; specif., *a)* lacking abundance; scanty; inadequate [*poor* crops] *b)* lacking productivity; barren; sterile [*poor* soil] *c)* lacking nourishment; feeble; emaciated [a *poor* body] *d)* lacking excellence or worth; below average, inferior, bad, etc. or paltry, mean, insignificant, etc. *e)* lacking good moral or mental qualities; mean-spirited; contemptible *f)* lacking pleasure, comfort, or satisfaction [to have a *poor* time] *g)* lacking skill [a *poor* golfer] **3.** worthy of pity; unfortunate —**the poor** poor, or needy, people collectively —**poor′ness** *n.*

SYN.—**poor** is the simple, direct term for one who lacks the resources for reasonably comfortable living; **impoverished** is applied to one who having once had plenty is now reduced to poverty [an *impoverished* aristocrat]; **destitute** implies such great poverty that the means for mere subsistence, such as food and shelter, are lacking [left *destitute* by the war]; **impecunious** applies to one in a habitual state of poverty and suggests that this results from his own practices [an *impecunious* gambler]; **indigent** implies such relative poverty as results in a lack of luxuries and the endurance of hardships [books for *indigent* children] —**ANT.** **rich, wealthy**

poor box a box, as in a church, for alms for the poor

☆**poor-boy sandwich** (poor′boi′) *same as* HERO SANDWICH

☆**poor farm** formerly, a farm for paupers, supported by a county or other local government

poor·house (-hous′) *n.* formerly, a house or institution for paupers, supported from public funds

poor laws laws that provide for public relief and assistance for the poor

poor·ly (-lē) *adv.* **1.** in a poor manner; scantily, badly, defectively, etc. **2.** with a low opinion; disparagingly [thought *poorly* of it] —*adj.* [Colloq.] in poor health

poor-mouth (-mouth′) *vi.* [Colloq.] to complain about one's lack of money; plead poverty: also **talk** (or **cry**) **poor-mouth**

poor-spir·it·ed (-spir′it id) *adj.* having or showing a poor spirit; cowardly; timorous; abject

☆**poor white** a white person, esp. one born or living in the southern U.S., who lives in great poverty and ignorance: often an offensive term

pop[1] (päp) *n.* [ME. *poppe*: echoic] **1.** a sudden, short, light, explosive sound **2.** a shot with a revolver, rifle, etc. **3.** any carbonated, nonalcoholic beverage: from the sound produced when the cork or cap is removed from the bottle ☆**4.** *Baseball* a ball that is popped into the infield: in full **pop fly** —*vi.* **popped, pop′ping 1.** to make, or burst with, a short, light, explosive sound **2.** to move, go, come, etc. suddenly and quickly, and usually unexpectedly [to *pop* into a room] **3.** to open wide suddenly, or protrude, as with amazement: said of the eyes **4.** to shoot a pistol, etc. ☆**5.** *Baseball* to hit the ball high in the air into the infield (often with *out* or *up*) —*vt.* [ME. *poppen*] ☆**1.** to cause to pop, as corn by roasting, etc. **2.** *a)* to fire (a pistol, etc.) *b)* to shoot **3.** to put suddenly, quickly, or unexpectedly [to *pop* one's head in the door, to *pop* a question at someone] ☆**4.** *Baseball* to hit (the ball) high in the air

into the infield —*adv.* with or like a pop —**pop off** [Slang] **1.** to die suddenly ☆**2.** to speak or write carelessly, emotionally, angrily, etc. **3.** [Chiefly Brit.] to leave hastily —**pop the question** [Colloq.] to propose marriage

☆**pop**[2] (päp) *n.* [contr. < *poppa*, var. of PAPA] [Slang] father: also a familiar term of address to any elderly man

pop[3] (päp) *adj. clipped form of* POPULAR [*pop* music]

pop. 1. popular **2.** popularly **3.** population

☆**pop (art)** (päp) a realistic art style, esp. in painting and sculpture, using techniques and popular subjects adapted from commercial art and the mass communications media, such as comic strips, posters, etc.

pop concert a popular concert, chiefly of semiclassical and light classical music

☆**pop·corn** (-kôrn′) *n.* **1.** a variety of Indian corn with small ears and hard, pointed grains which pop when put into a white, puffy mass when heated **2.** the popped grains, usually salted and buttered for eating

pope (pōp) *n.* [ME. < OE. *papa* < LL.(Ec.), a bishop, Pope < Gr.(Ec.) *papas*, bishop < Gr., father < baby talk: cf. PAPA] **1.** [*usually* P-] R.C.Ch.: the bishop of Rome and head of the Church **2.** a person who is regarded as having, or acting as though he has, popelike authority **3.** *Orthodox Eastern Ch.* a parish priest —**pope′dom** (-dəm) *n.*

Pope (pōp) **1. Alexander,** 1688–1744; Eng. poet **2. John,** 1822–92; Union general in the Civil War

pop·er·y (pōp′ər ē) *n.* [POP(E) + -ERY] the doctrines, beliefs, and rituals of the Roman Catholic Church: a hostile term

☆**pop-eyed** (päp′īd′) *adj.* having wide, protruding eyes

pop·gun (-gun′) *n.* a toy gun that shoots harmless pellets or corks by air compression, with a pop

pop·in·jay (päp′in jā′) *n.* [ME. *papejai* < MFr. *papagai*, altered (after *gai*: see JAY) < Ar. *babaghā*] **1.** orig., a parrot **2.** formerly, a target consisting of a wooden parrot on a pole **3.** a talkative, conceited person

pop·ish (pōp′ish) *adj.* having to do with popery; characteristic of the Roman Catholic Church: a hostile term —**pop′ish·ly** *adv.* —**pop′ish·ness** *n.*

Pop·ish Plot (pōp′ish) *see* Titus OATES

pop·lar (päp′lər) *n.* [ME. *popler* < OFr. *poplier* < *peuple* < L. *populus*] **1.** any of a genus (*Populus*) of trees of the willow family, having soft, fibrous wood, rapid growth, alternate leaves, and flowers borne in catkins **2.** the wood of any of these trees **3.** *a) same as* TULIP TREE *b) same as* TULIPWOOD (sense 1)

Pop·lar (päp′lər) metropolitan borough of London: pop. 66,000

pop·lin (päp′lən) *n.* [Fr. *papeline*, prob. altered < (*draps de*) *Poperinghes*, (cloths from) *Poperinge*, city in Flanders, textile center in the Middle Ages] a sturdy fabric of cotton, silk, rayon, etc., in plain weave with fine cross ribbing, used for raincoats, sportswear, etc.

pop·lit·e·al (päp lit′ē əl, päp′lə tē′-) *adj.* [< ModL. *popliteus* (< L. *poples*, gen. *poplitis*, ham of the knee) + -AL] of or near the ham, or that part of the leg behind the knee

Po·po·ca·té·petl (pô pô′kä te′pet′l; E. pō′pə kat′ə pet′l) volcano in SC Mexico, in W Puebla state: 17,887 ft.

pop-off (päp′ôf′) *n.* ☆[Slang] a person who talks carelessly, angrily, etc., esp. in a sudden outburst

☆**pop·o·ver** (-ō′vər) *n.* a very light, puffy, hollow muffin that rises over the rim of the baking tin

pop·per (-ər) *n.* **1.** a person or thing that pops ☆**2.** a covered wire basket or pan for popping corn

pop·pet (päp′it) *n.* [var. of PUPPET] **1.** *same as* TAIL-STOCK **2.** a valve that moves into and from its seat, often used for regularly interrupted flow, as in a gasoline engine: in full **poppet valve** **3.** a piece of wood on the gunwale of a boat, for supporting an oarlock **4.** *a)* [Obs.] a doll *b)* [Brit. Colloq.] a little person: term of endearment, as for a child

pop·pied (päp′ēd) *adj.* **1.** covered with poppies **2.** drugging or drugged, as by opium

pop·ping crease (päp′in) *Cricket* a line beyond which the batsman may not go

pop·ple[1] (päp′l) *n. dial. var. of* POPLAR (senses 1 & 2)

pop·ple[2] (päp′l) *vi.* **-pled, -pling** [ME. *poplen*, prob. of echoic origin] to heave, toss, bubble, or ripple, as water in a choppy sea —*n.* the action of poppling

pop·py (päp′ē) *n., pl.* **-pies** [ME. *popi* < OE. *popæg* < L. *papaver*] **1.** any of a genus (*Papaver*) of annual and perennial plants of the poppy family, having a milky juice, showy pink, white, red, orange, or yellow flowers, and capsules containing many small seeds, including the **opium poppy** (*Papaver somniferum*) **2.** the flower of any of these plants **3.** any of a number of plants variously resembling the poppy **4.** an extract, as opium, made from poppy juice **5.** *same as* POPPY RED —*adj.* designating a family (Papaveraceae) of widely distributed plants including the true poppies, bloodroot, celandine, etc.

☆**pop·py·cock** (päp′ē käk′) *n.* [Du. *pappekak*, lit., soft dung] [Colloq.] foolish talk; nonsense

pop·py·head (-hed′) *n.* an ornament in the form of a small head, fleur-de-lis, finial, etc., carved at the top of pew ends or stall ends in Gothic churches

poppy red a bright yellowish red, the color of some poppies

poppy seed the small, dark seed of the poppy, used, esp.

in baking, as a flavoring or topping for bread, rolls, etc.

☆**Pop·si·cle** (päp′si k'l) [blend < POP¹ + (I)CICLE] *a trade-mark for* a flavored ice frozen around a stick —*n.* [p-] such a confection

pop·sy, pop·sie (päp′sē) *n., pl.* **-sies** [< *pop*, short for POPPET + -*s*, suffix for affectionate nicknames + -Y¹] [Chiefly Brit. Colloq.] a girl or young woman: a term of affection

pop·u·lace (päp′yə lis) *n.* [Fr. < It. *popolaccio*, mob, rabble < *popolo* < L. *populus*, PEOPLE] **1.** the common people; the masses **2.** *same as* POPULATION (sense 1 *a*)

pop·u·lar (päp′yə lər) *adj.* [L. *popularis* < *populus*, PEOPLE] **1.** of or carried on by the common people or all the people [*popular* government] **2.** suitable or intended for the general public [*popular* music] **3.** within the means of the ordinary person [*popular* prices] **4.** accepted among people in general; common; prevalent [a *popular* notion] **5.** liked by very many or most people [a *popular* actor] **6.** very well liked by one's friends and acquaintances —SYN. see COMMON —**pop′u·lar·ly** *adv.*

popular etymology *same as* FOLK ETYMOLOGY

popular front a coalition of leftist and centrist or liberal political parties and other groups, as in France (1936–39) to combat fascism

pop·u·lar·i·ty (päp′yə lar′ə tē) *n.* [Fr. *popularité* < L. *popularitas*] the state or quality of being popular

pop·u·lar·ize (päp′yə lə rīz′) *vt.* **-ized′, -iz′ing** to make popular; specif., *a*) to cause to be liked by many people *b*) to make understandable to the general public —**pop′u·lar·i·za′tion** *n.* —**pop′u·lar·iz′er** *n.*

pop·u·late (päp′yə lāt′) *vt.* **-lat′ed, -lat′ing** [< ML. *populatus*, pp. of *populare*, to populate < L. *populus*, PEOPLE] **1.** to be or become the inhabitants of; inhabit **2.** to supply with inhabitants; people

pop·u·la·tion (päp′yə lā′shən) *n.* [LL. *populatio*] **1.** *a*) all the people in a country, region, etc. *b*) the number of these *c*) a (specified) part of the people in a given area [the Japanese *population* of Hawaii] **2.** a group of persons or things used as a base in statistical measurement **3.** a populating or being populated **4.** *Biol.* all the organisms living in a given area

population explosion the very great and continuing increase in human population in modern times

☆**Pop·u·list** (päp′yə list) *n.* [< L. *populus*, PEOPLE + -IST] a member of a U.S. political party (**Populist party** or **People's party,** 1891–1904) advocating free coinage of gold and silver, public ownership of utilities, an income tax, and support of labor and agriculture —*adj.* of the Populist party: also **Pop′u·lis′tic** —**Pop′u·lism** *n.*

pop·u·lous (päp′yə ləs) *adj.* [L. *populosus* < *populus*, PEOPLE] full of people; crowded or thickly populated —**pop′u·lous·ly** *adv.* —**pop′u·lous·ness** *n.*

☆**pop-up** (päp′up′) *n. same as* POP (n. 4)

por·bea·gle (pôr′bē′g'l) *n.* [< Corn. dial. *porgh-bugel*] any of several large, fierce sharks (genus *Lamna*) of northern seas, which bring forth living young

por·ce·lain (pôr′s'l in, pôrs′lin) *n.* [Fr. *porcelaine* < It. *porcellana*, orig., a kind of shell < *porcella*, little pig, vulva (< L. *porcellus*, dim. of *porcus*, pig, vulva): shell so named from its shape] **1.** a hard, white, nonporous, translucent variety of ceramic ware, made of kaolin, feldspar, and quartz or flint **2.** porcelain dishes or ornaments, collectively —*adj.* made of porcelain —**por′ce·la′ne·ous, por′cel·la′ne·ous** (-sə lā′nē əs) *adj.*

por·ce·lain·ize (-īz′) *vt.* **-ized′, -iz′ing** to coat with porcelain or a substance resembling porcelain

porch (pôrch) *n.* [ME. *porche* < OFr. < L. *porticus* < *porta*, a gate, entrance, passage: see PORT⁶] **1.** a covered entrance to a building, usually projecting from the wall and having a separate roof **2.** an open or enclosed gallery or room on the outside of a building; veranda **3.** [Obs.] a portico —**the Porch** a portico in Athens where the Stoic philosopher Zeno taught

por·cine (pôr′sin, -sin) *adj.* [Fr. *porcin* < L. *porcinus* < *porcus*, a hog: see PORK] of or like pigs or hogs

por·cu·pine (pôr′kyə pin′) *n., pl.* **-pines′, -pine′:** see PLURAL, II, D, 1 [ME. *porkepyn* < MFr. *porc espin*, spinous hog, spine hog < OIt. *porcospino* < L. *porcus*, a pig (see PORK) + *spina*, SPINE] any of a number of large, related, Old World (family Hystricidae) or New World (family Erethizontidae) rodents, having coarse hair mixed with long, stiff, sharp spines that can be erected

porcupine fish a spiny globe-fish

Porcupine River river in N Yukon, Canada, flowing into the Yukon River in NE Alas.: 590 mi.

PORCUPINE
(2 1/2–4 ft. long, including tail)

pore¹ (pôr) *vi.* **pored, por′ing** [ME. *poren* < ?] **1.** [Now Rare] to gaze intently or steadily **2.** to read or study carefully (with *over*) [to *pore* over a book] **3.** to think deeply and thoroughly; ponder (with *over*)

pore² (pôr) *n.* [ME. < L. *porus* < Gr. *poros* < IE. *poros*, entrance < base *per-*, to bring through, whence FARE] **1.** orig., a passage; channel **2.** a tiny opening, usually microscopic, as in plant leaves, skin, etc., through which fluids may be absorbed or discharged **3.** a similar opening in rock or other substances

pore fungus a basidiomycetous fungus whose spores are produced inside microscopic tubules

☆**por·gy** (pôr′gē) *n., pl.* **-gies, -gy:** see PLURAL, II, D, 1 [prob. altered < Sp. or Port. *pargo* < L. *pagrus* < Gr. *phagros*, sea-bream] **1.** any of a number of related saltwater food fishes (family Sparidae) having spiny fins and a wide body covered with large scales, as the scup, the pinfish, and the sheepshead (sense 1) **2.** any of various other fishes, as the menhaden

po·rif·er·an (pô rif′ər ən, pə-) *n.* [< L. *porus*, PORE² + -FER + -AN] any of a phylum (Porifera) of primitive, chiefly saltwater animals constituting the sponges —*adj.* of or pertaining to the Porifera

po·rif·er·ous (-əs) *adj.* [< L. *porus*, PORE² + -FEROUS] **1.** having pores **2.** *Zool.* of the sponges, or poriferans

po·rism (pôr′iz'm) *n.* [ME. *porysme* < ML. *porisma* < Gr. *porisma*, lit., a thing brought < *porizein*, to bring < *poros*, passage: see PORE²] *Ancient Math.* a geometrical proposition variously defined, as *a*) a proposition deduced from some other demonstrated proposition; corollary *b*) a proposition that uncovers the possibility of finding such conditions as to make a specific problem capable of innumerable solutions

pork (pôrk) *n.* [ME. *porc* < OFr. < L. *porcus*, a pig < IE. base *porkos*, pig, whence OE. *fearh*, MIr. *orc*: cf. FARROW¹] **1.** orig., a pig or hog **2.** the flesh of a pig or hog, used as food, esp. when used fresh, or uncured ☆**3.** [Colloq.] money, jobs, etc. received through pork-barrel appropriations and used for political patronage

☆**pork barrel** [Colloq.] government appropriations for political patronage, as for local improvements to please legislators' constituents —**pork′-bar′rel·ing** *n.*

pork·er (pôr′kər) *n.* a hog, esp. a young one, fattened for use as food

pork pie **1.** a meat pie filled with chopped pork **2.** a man's soft hat with a round, flat crown: now often **pork′pie′** (-pī′) *n.*, **porkpie hat**

pork·y (pôr′kē) *adj.* **pork′i·er, pork′i·est** **1.** of or like pork **2.** fat, as though overfed **3.** [Slang] saucy, cocky, presumptuous, impertinent, or the like

por·nog·ra·phy (pôr näg′rə fē) *n.* [< Gr. *pornographos*, writing about prostitutes < *pornē*, a prostitute + *graphein*, to write (see GRAPHIC)] **1.** writings, pictures, etc. intended primarily to arouse sexual desire **2.** the production of such writings, pictures, etc. —**por·nog′ra·pher** *n.* —**por′no·graph′ic** (pôr′nə graf′ik) *adj.* —**por′no·graph′i·cal·ly** *adv.*

☆**por·o·mer·ic** (pôr′ə mer′ik) *n.* [arbitrary coinage, prob. < PORO(US) + (POLY)MERIC] a synthetic, leatherlike, porous material, often coated or impregnated with a polymer, used in making uppers for shoes, luggage, belts, etc.

po·ros·i·ty (pô räs′ə tē, pə-) *n., pl.* **-ties** [ME. *porositee* < ML. *porositas*: see ff. & -ITY] **1.** the quality or state of being porous **2.** the ratio, usually expressed as a percentage, of the volume of a material's pores, as in rock or soil, to its total volume **3.** anything porous **4.** *same as* PORE²

po·rous (pôr′əs) *adj.* [ME. < ML. *porosus* < L. *porus*, PORE²] full of pores, through which fluids, air, or light may pass —**por′ous·ly** *adv.* —**por′ous·ness** *n.*

por·phyr·a·tin (pôr fir′ə t'n) *n.* [PORPHYR(IN) + -AT(E)¹ + -IN¹] any of various complex compounds formed of metals and porphyrins

por·phyr·i·a (pôr fir′ē ə) *n.* [ModL. < PORPHYR(IN) + -IA] an inherited disorder of pigment metabolism with excretion of porphyrins in the urine and dangerous sensitivity to sunlight

por·phy·rin (pôr′fər in) *n.* [< Gr. *porphyra*, purple + -IN¹] any of a group of pyrrole derivatives, found in cytoplasm, that combine with iron and magnesium to form heme and chlorophyll, respectively

por·phy·rit·ic (pôr′fə rit′ik) *adj.* [ME. *porphiritike* < ML. *porphyriticus* < L. *porphyrites* < Gr. *porphyritēs*] **1.** of porphyry **2.** like porphyry; having distinct crystals embedded in a fine-grained mass

por·phy·roid (pôr′fə roid′) *n.* a metamorphic rock having large crystals embedded in a fine-grained matrix of either igneous or sedimentary origin

por·phy·rop·sin (pôr′fə räp′sin) *n.* [< Gr. *porphyra*,

FAT BACK
LOIN
HAM
BACON
SHOULDER
SPARERIBS
FOOT

CUTS OF PORK

purple + *opsis:* see RHODOPSIN] a carotenoid pigment found in the retina of freshwater fishes

por·phy·ry (pôr′fər ē) *n., pl.* **-ries** [ME. *porfirie* < OFr. *porfire* < ML. *porphyreum,* altered < L. *porphyrites* < Gr. *porphyrītēs* (*lithos*), lit., purple (stone) < *porphyros,* purple] **1.** orig., an Egyptian rock with large feldspar crystals contained in a purplish groundmass **2.** any igneous rock with large, distinct crystals, esp. of alkali feldspar, embedded in a fine-grained matrix

por·poise (pôr′pəs) *n., pl.* **-pois·es, -poise:** see PLURAL, II, D, 1 [ME. *porpoys* < OFr. *porpeis,* lit., swine fish < L. *porcus,* a pig, swine (see PORK) + *piscis,* FISH²] **1.** any of a number of small, usually gregarious toothed whales found in most seas, with a torpedo-shaped body and a blunt snout, esp. the **harbor porpoise** (*Phocaena phocaena*) **2.** a dolphin or any of several other small cetaceans

por·ridge (pôr′ij, pär′-) *n.* [altered < POTTAGE by confusion with ME. *porrey* < OFr. *poree* < VL. *porrata,* leek broth < L. *porrum,* leek, akin to Gr. *prason,* leek] **1.** orig., pottage **2.** [Chiefly Brit.] a soft food made of cereal or meal boiled in water or milk until thick

por·rin·ger (-in jər) *n.* [earlier *pottanger, pottager* < Fr. *potager,* soup dish: altered after prec.] a bowl for porridge; small, shallow bowl, orig. of pewter, etc., used for cereal or the like, esp. by children

Por·se·na (pôr′si nə), **Lars** (lärz) 6th cent. B.C.; Etruscan king who, according to legend, attacked Rome in an unsuccessful attempt to restore Tarquin to the throne: also **Por·sen·na** (pôr sen′ə)

Por·son (pôr′sən), **Richard** 1759–1808; Eng. classical scholar

port¹ (pôrt) *n.* [ME. < OFr. & OE. *port* < L. *portus,* a haven: for IE. base see FORD] **1.** a harbor **2.** a city or town with a harbor where ships can load and unload cargo **3.** *same as* PORT OF ENTRY

port² (pôrt) *n.* [< *Oporto,* city in Portugal] a sweet, fortified, usually dark-red wine

port³ (pôrt) *vt.* [MFr. *porter* < L. *portare,* to carry: see FARE] **1.** orig., to carry **2.** to carry, hold, or place (a rifle or sword) in front of one, diagonally upward from right to left, as for inspection —*n.* [ME. *porte* < MFr. < the *v.*] **1.** the manner in which one carries oneself; carriage **2.** the position of a ported weapon

port⁴ (pôrt) *n.* [prob. < PORT¹: reason for name uncertain] the left-hand side of a ship or airplane as one faces forward, toward the bow: opposed to STARBOARD —*adj.* of or on the port —*vt., vi.* to move or turn (the helm) to the port side

port⁵ (pôrt) *n.* [ME. < OFr. *porte* < L. *porta,* a door, akin to *portus:* see PORT¹] **1.** [Obs. except Scot.] a portal; gateway **2.** *a*) *same as* PORTHOLE *b*) a porthole covering **3.** an opening, as in a cylinder face or valve face, for the passage of steam, gas, water, etc.

Port. **1.** Portugal **2.** Portuguese

port·a·ble (pôr′tə b'l) *adj.* [ME. < OFr. < LL. *portabilis* < *portare,* to carry: see FARE] **1.** that can be carried **2.** *a*) easily carried or moved, esp. by hand [a *portable* TV] *b*) that can be used anywhere because operated by self-contained batteries [a *portable* radio] **3.** [Obs.] bearable; endurable —*n.* something portable —**port′a·bil′i·ty** *n.*

por·tage (pôr′tij; *for n. 2 & v.,* also, *esp. Canad.,* pôr täzh′) *n.* [ME. < MFr. < ML. *portaticum* < L. *portare,* to carry: see FARE] **1.** *a*) the act of carrying or transporting *b*) the charge for this ☆**2.** *a*) a carrying of boats and supplies overland between navigable rivers, lakes, etc., as during a canoe trip *b*) any place or route over which this is done —*vt., vi.* **-taged, -tag·ing** ☆to carry (boats, etc.) over a portage

por·tal (pôr′t'l) *n.* [ME. < MFr. < ML. *portale,* orig. neut. of *portalis,* of a door < L. *porta:* see PORT⁵] **1.** a doorway, gate, or entrance, esp. a large and imposing one **2.** any point or place of entry, as one where nerves, vessels, etc. enter an organ —*adj.* [ML. *portalis*] designating, of, or like the vein carrying blood from the intestines, stomach, etc. to the liver

☆**por·tal-to-por·tal pay** (-tə pôr′t'l) wages for workers based on the total time spent from the moment of entering the mine, factory, etc. until the moment of leaving it

por·ta·men·to (pôr′tə men′tō; *It.* pôr′tä men′tô) *n., pl.* **-men′ti** (-tē) [It. < *portare,* to carry < L. *portare:* see FARE] *Music* a continuous gliding from one note to another, sounding intervening tones; glide

port·ance (pôr′t'ns) *n.* [Early ModE. < MFr. < *porter,* to bear: see PORT³] [Archaic] one's conduct, bearing, or demeanor

Port Arthur **1.** *former name of* LÜSHUN **2.** [after *Arthur Stilwell,* local philanthropist] seaport in SE Tex., on Sabine Lake: pop. 57,000 **3.** port in W Ontario, Canada, on Lake Superior: pop. 48,000

por·ta·tive (pôr′tə tiv) *adj.* [ME. < OFr. *portatif,* lit., that is carried < L. *portatus,* pp. of *portare,* to carry (see FARE) + OFr. *-if,* -IVE] **1.** of or having the power of carrying a load, charge, etc. **2.** capable of being carried; portable

Port-au-Prince (pôrt′ō prins′; *Fr.* pôr tō prans′) capital of Haiti; seaport on the Caribbean: pop. 250,000

port authority a governmental commission in charge of the traffic, regulations, etc. of a port

port·cul·lis (pôrt kul′is) *n.* [ME. *portcoles* < MFr. *porte coleïce* < *porte,* a gate + *coleïce,* fem. of *coleis,* sliding < L. *colare,* to strain, filter] a heavy iron grating suspended by chains and lowered between grooves to bar the gateway of a castle or fortified town

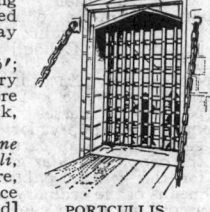
PORTCULLIS

Port du Sa·lut (pôr′ doo sa loo′; *Fr.* pôr dü sà lü′) [after monastery at *Port du Salut,* France, where orig. made] a semihard, whole-milk, yellowish cheese

Porte (pôrt) *n.* [Fr., in *la Sublime Porte,* transl. of Turk. *Babi Ali,* chief office of the Ottoman Empire, lit., High Gate: from the palace gate where justice was administered] the Ottoman Turkish government

porte-co·chere, porte-co·chère (pôrt′kō sher′) *n.* [Fr. *porte,* a gate (see PORT⁵) + *cochère,* coach, fem. adj. < *coche:* see COACH] **1.** a large entrance gateway into a courtyard **2.** a kind of porch roof projecting over a driveway at an entrance, as of a house, to protect persons entering from vehicles

Port Elizabeth seaport in S Cape Province, South Africa, on the Indian Ocean: pop. 291,000

‡**porte-mon·naie** (pôrt mō nā′; *E.* pôrt′mun′ē) *n.* [Fr., carry-money] a purse or pocketbook

por·tend (pôr tend′) *vt.* [ME. *portenden* < L. *portendere* < *por-,* akin to *per,* through + *tendere,* to stretch: see TEND] **1.** to be an omen or warning of; foreshadow; presage **2.** to be an indication of; signify

por·tent (pôr′tent) *n.* [L. *portentum* < *portendere:* see prec.] **1.** something that portends an event about to occur, esp. an unfortunate event; omen **2.** a portending; significance [a howl of dire *portent*] **3.** something regarded as portentous; marvel; prodigy

por·ten·tous (pôr ten′təs) *adj.* [L. *portentosus* < *portentum:* see prec.] **1.** that portends evil; ominous **2.** arousing awe or amazement; marvelous; prodigious **3.** ponderous or pompous; self-important —*SYN.* see OMINOUS —**por·ten′tous·ly** *adv.* —**por·ten′tous·ness** *n.*

por·ter¹ (pôr′tər) *n.* [ME. < OFr. *portier* < LL. *portarius* < L. *porta,* a gate] **1.** a doorman or gatekeeper **2.** *R.C.Ch.* a member of the lowest of the four minor orders

por·ter² (pôr′tər) *n.* [ME. *portour* < OFr. *porteour* < LL. *portator* < L. *portare,* to carry: see FARE] **1.** a person who carries things; esp., a man who carries luggage, etc. for hire or as an attendant at a railroad station, hotel, etc. ☆**2.** a man who sweeps, cleans, does errands, etc. in a bank, store, restaurant, etc. ☆**3.** a railroad employee who waits on passengers in a sleeper or parlor car **4.** [abbrev. of *porter's ale*] a dark-brown beer resembling light stout, made from charred or browned malt

Por·ter (pôr′tər) **1. Cole** (kōl), 1893–1964; U.S. composer of popular songs **2. David,** 1780–1843; U.S. naval officer & diplomat **3. David Dix·on** (dik′s'n), 1813–91; Union admiral in the Civil War: son of *prec.* **4. Katherine Anne,** 1890– ; U.S. short-story writer, essayist, & novelist **5. William Sydney,** *see* O. HENRY

por·ter·age (-ij) *n.* **1.** a porter's work **2.** the charge for this

por·ter·house (-hous′) *n.* **1.** formerly, a place where beer, porter, etc. (and sometimes steaks and chops) were served ☆**2.** [said to be so named as a specialty at a former New York porterhouse] a choice cut of beef from between the tenderloin and the sirloin: in full **porterhouse steak**

port·fo·li·o (pôrt fō′lē ō′) *n., pl.* **-li·os′** [earlier *porto folio* < It. *portafoglio* < *portare* (< L.: see FARE), to carry + *foglio* (< L. *folium:* see FOLIATE), a leaf] **1.** a flat, portable case, usually of leather, for carrying loose sheets of paper, manuscripts, drawings, etc.; briefcase **2.** such a case for state documents **3.** the office of a minister of state or member of a cabinet [a minister without *portfolio*] **4.** a list of the stocks, bonds, and commercial paper owned by a bank, an investor, etc. **5.** a selection of representative works, as of an artist

port·hole (pôrt′hōl′) *n.* **1.** an opening in a ship's side, as for admitting light and air **2.** an opening to shoot through, in the wall of a fort, etc.; embrasure **3.** an opening shaped somewhat like this, as in a furnace door

Port Huron port in E Mich., on the St. Clair River & Lake Huron: pop. 36,000

Por·tia (pôr′shə) [L. *Porcia,* fem. of *Porcius,* name of a Roman gens, prob. < *porcus* (see PORK)] **1.** a feminine name **2.** the heroine of Shakespeare's *Merchant of Venice*

por·ti·co (pôr′tə kō′) *n., pl.* **-coes′, -cos′** [It. < L. *porticus:* see PORCH] a porch or covered walk, consisting of a roof supported by columns, often at the entrance or across the front of a building; colonnade

PORTICO

por·tiere, por·tière (pôr tyer′, -tē er′) *n.* [Fr. *portière* < *porte,* a door: see PORT⁵] a curtain, usually heavy, hung in a doorway

por·tion (pôr′shən) *n.* [ME. < OFr. < L. *portio* (gen. *portionis*), a portion, akin to *pars,* PART] **1.** a part or limited quantity of any-

thing, esp. that allotted to a person; share **2.** the part of an estate received by an heir **3.** the part of a man's money or property contributed by his bride; dowry **4.** the part of experience supposedly allotted to a person by fate; one's lot; destiny **5.** the part of a meal or quantity of food served to a person; serving; helping —*vt.* [OFr. *portionner*, to divide, separate] **1.** to divide into portions **2.** to give as a portion to; apportion **3.** to give a portion to; endow; dower —*SYN.* see FATE, PART —**por′tion·er** *n.* —**por′tion-less** *adj.*

Port Jackson inlet of the Pacific, in E New South Wales, Australia: harbor of Sydney: 21 sq. mi.

Port·land (pôrt′lənd) **1.** [after ff.] city and port in NW Oreg., at the confluence of the Columbia & Willamette rivers: pop. 383,000 (met. area 1,009,000) **2.** [after *Portland*, town and island in England] seaport in SE Me., on the Atlantic: pop. 65,000

portland cement [from resemblance of the concrete made from it to stone quarried on the Isle of *Portland*, England] [*sometimes* P-] a kind of cement that hardens under water, made by burning a mixture of limestone and clay or similar materials

Port Louis capital of Mauritius; seaport on the NW coast: pop. 125,000

port·ly (pôrt′lē) *adj.* -li·er, -li·est [PORT³ + -LY¹] **1.** large and heavy in a dignified and stately way **2.** stout; corpulent —**port′li·ness** *n.*

port·man·teau (pôrt man′tō, pôrt′man tō′) *n., pl.* -teaus, -teaux [Fr. *portemanteau* < *porter*, to carry + *manteau*, a cloak: see PORT³ & MANTLE] a traveling case or bag; esp., a stiff leather suitcase that opens like a book into two compartments

portmanteau word a word that is a combination of two other words in form and meaning (Ex.: *smog*, from *smoke* and *fog*)

Port Mores·by (mōrz′bē) seaport in SE New Guinea, in the Territory of Papua; capital of the jointly administered territories of Papua & New Guinea: pop. 24,000

Pôr·to (pôr′too) *Port. name of* OPORTO

Pôrto A·le·gre (ä le′gra) seaport in S Brazil; capital of Rio Grande do Sul state: pop. 641,000

port of call a port that is a regular stopover for ships, esp. cargo ships

port of entry any place where customs officials are stationed to check the entry of people or foreign goods into a country

Port-of-Spain (pôrt′əv spän′) seaport on NW Trinidad; capital of Trinidad and Tobago: pop. 98,000: also **Port of Spain**

Por·to No·vo (pôr′tō nō′vō) capital of Dahomey; seaport on the Gulf of Guinea: pop. 70,000

Por·to Ri·co (pôr′tə rē′kō) *former name of* PUERTO RICO —**Por′to Ri′can**

Port Phillip Bay inlet of Bass Strait, in S Victoria, Australia: harbor of Melbourne: 762 sq. mi.

por·trait (pôr′trit, -trāt) *n.* [MFr., pp. of *portraire*: see PORTRAY] **1.** orig., a drawn, painted, or carved picture of something **2.** a representation of a person, esp. of his face, drawn, painted, photographed, or sculptured **3.** a description, dramatic portrayal, etc. of a person

por·trait·ist (-ist) *n.* a person who makes portraits

por·trai·ture (pôr′tri chər) *n.* [ME. *purtreiture* < MFr.: see ff.] **1.** the process, practice, or art of portraying **2.** a portrait **3.** portraits collectively

por·tray (pôr trā′) *vt.* [ME. *purtreien* < MFr. *portraire* < L. *protrahere*, to draw forth < *pro-*, forth + *trahere*, to DRAW] **1.** to make a picture or portrait of; depict; delineate **2.** to make a word picture of; describe graphically **3.** to play the part of in a play, movie, etc. —**por·tray′a·ble** *adj.* —**por·tray′er** *n.*

por·tray·al (-əl) *n.* **1.** the act of portraying **2.** a portrait; description; representation

por·tress (pôr′tris) *n.* a woman porter (doorkeeper)

Port Royal town in Jamaica, at the entrance to Kingston harbor: the original town, former capital, was destroyed by an earthquake in 1692

Port Sa·id (sä ēd′, sä′id) seaport in NE Egypt, at the Mediterranean end of the Suez Canal: pop. 244,000

Port-Sa·lut (pôr′sa lōo′; Fr. pôr sà lü′) *n. same as* PORT DU SALUT

Ports·mouth (pôrts′məth) **1.** seaport in Hampshire, S England, on the English Channel: pop. 218,000 **2.** [after prec.] seaport in SE Va., on Hampton Roads: pop. 111,000: see NORFOLK

Port Sudan seaport in NE Sudan, on the Red Sea: pop. 57,000

Por·tu·gal (pôr′chə gəl; *Port.* pôr′too gäl′) country in SW Europe, on the Atlantic: 34,308 sq. mi.; pop. 8,255,000; (with the Azores & Madeira, 35,509 sq. mi.; pop. 9,228,000); cap. Lisbon

Por·tu·guese (pôr′chə gēz′) *adj.* of Portugal, its people, their language, or culture —*n.* **1.** *pl.* -guese′ a native or inhabitant of Portugal **2.** the Romance language spoken in Portugal and Brazil

Portuguese East Africa *same as* MOZAMBIQUE

Portuguese Guinea Portuguese overseas territory in W Africa, on the coast between Senegal & Guinea: 13,948 sq. mi.; pop. 544,000; cap. Bissau

Portuguese India former Portuguese overseas territory consisting of three enclaves in India: see GOA

Portuguese man-of-war any of several large, colonial, warm-sea siphonophores (genus *Physalia*) having a large, bladderlike sac, with a saillike structure on top, which enables them to float on the water, and long, dangling tentacles that have powerful stinging cells

Portuguese Timor Portuguese overseas territory in the Malay Archipelago, consisting of the E half of Timor, an exclave of Indonesian Timor, & two offshore islands: 5,770 sq. mi.; pop. 551,000

Portuguese West Africa *same as* ANGOLA

por·tu·lac·a (pôr′chə lak′ə, -lä′kə) *n.* [ModL. < L., purslane < *portula*, dim. of *porta*, door (see PORT⁵): from the doorlike opening of the seed capsule] a fleshy annual plant (*Portulaca grandiflora*) of the purslane family with yellow, pink, or purple flowers

‡**po·sa·da** (pō sä′thä) *n.* [Sp. < fem. of *posado*, pp. of *posar*, to lodge < L. *pausare*, to stop < *pausa*, a PAUSE] in Spanish-speaking countries **1.** an inn **2.** a Christmas festival marked by a candlelight procession

pose¹ (pōz) *vt.* posed, pos′ing [ME. *posen* < OFr. *poser*, to put in position < VL. *pausare*, to place, put < LL., to stop, rest (< L. *pausa*: see PAUSE): meaning and form altered after L. *positus*, pp. of *ponere*, to place, put: see POSITION] **1.** to put forth; assert (a claim, argument, etc.) **2.** to put forward or propose (a question, problem, etc.) **3.** to put (a model, photographic subject, etc.) in a certain position or attitude —*vi.* **1.** to assume a certain position or attitude, as in modeling for an artist **2.** to strike attitudes for effect; attitudinize **3.** to pretend to be what one is not; set oneself up (*as*) [to *pose* as an officer] —*n.* [Fr. < the *v.*] **1.** a bodily attitude, esp. one held for or pictured by an artist, photographer, etc. **2.** a way of behaving or speaking that is assumed for effect; pretense *SYN.*—**pose** refers to an attitude or manner that is assumed for the effect that it will have on others [her generosity is a mere *pose*]; **affectation** is used of a specific instance of artificial behavior intended obviously to impress others [an *affectation* of speech]; a **mannerism** is a peculiarity in behavior, speech, etc. (often originally an affectation) that has become habitual and unconscious [his *mannerism* of raising one eyebrow in surprise]; **airs** is used of an affected pretense of superior manners and graces [she's always putting on *airs*] See also POSTURE

pose² (pōz) *vt.* posed, pos′ing [aphetic for APPOSE, OPPOSE] **1.** [Obs.] to question **2.** to puzzle or disconcert, as by an almost unanswerable question; baffle

Po·sei·don (pō sī′d′n, pə-) [L. < Gr. *Poseidōn*] *Gr. Myth.* god of the sea and of horses: identified with the Roman god Neptune

Po·sen (pō′zən) *Ger. name of* POZNAŃ

pos·er¹ (pō′zər) *n.* a person who poses; esp., a poseur

pos·er² (pō′zər) *n.* a baffling question or problem

po·seur (pō zur′) *n.* [Fr.] a person who assumes attitudes or manners merely for their effect upon others

posh (päsh) *adj.* [prob. < obs. Brit. slang *posh*, a dandy < ?] [Colloq.] luxurious and fashionable; elegant —**posh′ly** *adv.* —**posh′ness** *n.*

pos·it (päz′it) *vt.* [< L. *positus*: see ff.] **1.** to set in place or position; situate **2.** to set down or assume as fact; postulate

po·si·tion (pə zish′ən) *n.* [MFr. < L. *positio* < *positus*, pp. of *ponere*, to place < **posinere* < *po-*, away (< IE. base *apo-*, whence L. *ab*, from, away) + *sinere*, to put, lay: see SITE] **1.** the act of positing, or placing **2.** a positing of a proposition; affirmation **3.** the manner in which a person or thing is placed or arranged; attitude; posture; disposition **4.** one's attitude toward or opinion on a subject; stand [his *position* on foreign aid] **5.** the place where a person or thing is, esp. in relation to others; location; situation; site [the ship's *position*] **6.** the usual or proper place of a person or thing; station [the players are in *position*] **7.** a location or condition in which one has the advantage [to jockey for *position*] **8.** a strategic military site **9.** a person's relative place, as in society; rank; status **10.** a place high in society, business, etc. [a man of *position*] **11.** a post of employment; office; job [to apply for a teaching *position*] **12.** *Finance* the long or short commitment of a market trader in securities or commodities **13.** *Music a)* the arrangement of the notes of a chord with respect to their relative closeness or distance apart [open *position*] *b)* any of the fixed locations on the fingerboard of a violin, etc. that the left hand assumes for fingering a particular series of notes *c)* any of the various points to which a trombone slide may be moved to change the pitch —*vt.* **1.** to put in a particular position; place or station **2.** [Rare] to locate —**po·si′tion·al** *adj.* —**po·si′tion·er** *n.*

SYN.—**position** applies to any specific employment for salary or wages, but often connotes white-collar or professional employment; **situation** now usually refers to a position that is open or to one that is desired [situation wanted as instructor]; **office** refers to a position of authority or trust, especially in government, a corporation, etc.; a **post** is a position or office that carries heavy

responsibilities, esp. one to which a person is appointed; **job** is now the common, comprehensive equivalent for any of the preceding terms

pos·i·tive (päz′ə tiv) *adj.* [ME. *positif* < OFr. < L. *positivus* < *positus*: see POSITION] **1.** formally or arbitrarily set; conventional; artificial [a *positive* law] **2.** definitely set; explicitly laid down; admitting of no question or modification; express; precise; specific [*positive* instructions] **3.** *a)* having the mind set or settled; confident; assured [a *positive* person] *b)* overconfident or dogmatic **4.** showing resolution or agreement; affirmative; certain [a *positive* answer] **5.** tending in the direction regarded as that of increase, progress, etc. [clockwise motion is *positive*] **6.** making a definite contribution; constructive [*positive* criticism] **7.** unrelated to anything else; independent of circumstances; absolute; unqualified **8.** that has, or is considered as having, real existence in itself, not just in the absence of other attributes [a *positive* good] **9.** based, or asserted as based, on reality or facts [*positive* proof] **10.** concerned only with real things and experience; empirical; practical **11.** [Colloq.] complete; downright; out-and-out [a *positive* fool] **12.** *Biol.* directed toward the source of a stimulus [*positive* tropism] ☆**13.** *Elec. a)* of positive electricity *b)* of, generating, or charged with positive electricity *c)* having a deficiency of electrons **14.** *Gram. a)* of an adjective or adverb in its simple, uninflected or unmodified form or degree; neither comparative nor superlative *b)* of this degree **15.** *Math.* designating a quantity greater than zero, or one to be added; plus **16.** *Med.* demonstrating or proving the presence or existence of a condition, symptoms, bacteria, etc. **17.** *Photog.* with the lights and shades corresponding to those of the subject —*n.* something positive, as a degree, quality, condition, etc.; specif., *a)* the plate in a voltaic battery where the higher potential is *b)* *Gram.* the positive degree; also, a word or form in this degree *c)* *Math.* a quantity greater than zero, or one to be added; plus quantity *d)* *Photog.* a photographic print, or a film for use in a projector, on which light and shadow correspond to what they were in the original subject —*SYN.* see SURE —**pos′i·tive·ly** *adv.* —**pos′i·tive·ness** *n.*

☆**positive electricity** the kind of electricity that predominates in a glass body after it has been rubbed with silk and has a deficiency of electrons

pos·i·tiv·ism (päz′ə tiv iz′m) *n.* [Fr. *positivisme* < *positif*] **1.** the quality or state of being positive; certainty; assurance **2.** overconfidence or dogmatism **3.** a system of philosophy basing knowledge solely on data of sense experience; esp., a system of philosophy, originated by Auguste Comte, based solely on observable, scientific facts and their relations to each other: it rejects speculation about or search for ultimate origins —**pos′i·tiv·ist** *n., adj.* —**pos′i·tiv·is′tic** *adj.*

☆**pos·i·tron** (päz′ə trän′) *n.* [POSI(TIVE) + (ELEC)TRON] the positive antiparticle of an electron, having approximately the same mass and magnitude of charge

☆**pos·i·tro·ni·um** (päz′i trō′nē əm) *n.* [POSITRON + -IUM] a semistable atomic system formed of an electron and a positron before they interact to annihilate each other

po·sol·o·gy (pō säl′ə jē) *n.* [Fr. *posologie* < Gr. *posos*, how much (< IE. *kwoti* < interrogative base *kwo-*, whence WHO, WHAT) + Fr. *-logie*, -LOGY] *Med.* the scientific study of drug dosages

poss. **1.** possession **2.** possessive **3.** possibly

pos·se (päs′ē) *n.* [ML., short for *posse comitatus*, power of the county < L. *posse*, to be able (see POTENT) + *comitatus*, county < *comes*, a COUNT²] **1.** *a)* the body of men liable to be summoned by a sheriff to assist him in keeping the peace, etc. *b)* a band of men, usually armed, so summoned [in full **posse co·mi·ta·tus** (käm′ə tāt′əs)] **2.** any body of men armed with legal authority —**in posse** potentially

pos·sess (pə zes′) *vt.* [LME. < MFr. *possessier* < L. *possessus*, pp. of *possidere*, to possess < *pos-*, contr. < *potis*, able (see POTENT) + *sedere*, to SIT] **1.** to hold as property or occupy in person; have as something that belongs to one; own **2.** to have as an attribute, quality, faculty, etc. [to *possess* wisdom] **3.** to have knowledge or mastery of (a language, etc.) **4.** to gain strong influence or control over; dominate [*possessed* by an idea] **5.** to keep control over or maintain (oneself, one's mind, etc.) **6.** to manage to have sexual intercourse with (a woman) **7.** to put (someone) in possession of property, facts, etc.; cause to have something specified (usually with *of*) **8.** [Archaic] to seize; win; gain —*SYN.* see HAVE —**pos·ses′sor** *n.*

pos·sessed (pə zest′) *adj.* **1.** owned **2.** controlled by an emotion or as if by an evil spirit; crazed; mad **3.** *same as* SELF-POSSESSED —**possessed of** in possession of

pos·ses·sion (pə zesh′ən) *n.* [ME. < OFr. < L. *possessio*] **1.** a possessing or being possessed; ownership, occupancy, hold, etc. **2.** anything possessed **3.** [*pl.*] property; wealth **4.** territory ruled by an outside country **5.** control of oneself: rare except in SELF-POSSESSION **6.** *Sports* actual control of the ball or puck in play —**pos·ses′sion·al** *adj.*

pos·ses·sive (pə zes′iv) *adj.* [L. *possessivus*] **1.** of possession, or ownership **2.** showing, or characterized by a desire for, possession [a *possessive* person] '**3.** *Gram.* designating or of a case, form, or construction expressing possession or some like relationship: in English, this is expressed *a)* by a final *s* (for nouns and some pronouns) preceded or followed by an apostrophe, or sometimes by an apostrophe only, following a final *s* sound (Ex.: *John's* book, *men's* lives, *boys'* games, *conscience'* sake) *b)* by change of form of pronouns (Ex.: *my, mine, your, yours, his, her, hers, its, our, ours, their, theirs, whose*) *c)* by *of* preceding a form without the possessive ending (Ex.: lives *of men*) or preceding a form in the possessive case (Ex.: a play *of Shakespeare's*, a friend *of mine* — called a **double possessive**): cf. GENITIVE —*n. Gram.* **1.** the possessive case **2.** a possessive form or construction —**pos·ses′sive·ly** *adv.* —**pos·ses′sive·ness** *n.*

pos·ses·so·ry (-ər ē) *adj.* **1.** of, being, or characterizing a possessor **2.** of or based upon possession

pos·set (päs′it) *n.* [ME. < ?] a hot drink made of milk curdled with ale, wine, etc., usually spiced

pos·si·bil·i·ty (päs′ə bil′ə tē) *n.* [ME. *possibilite* < LL. *possibilitas*] **1.** the quality or condition of being possible **2.** *pl.* **-ties** something that is possible

pos·si·ble (päs′ə b'l) *adj.* [ME. < OFr. < L. *possibilis* < *posse*, to be able: see POTENT] **1.** that can be; capable of existing **2.** that can be in the future; that may or may not happen **3.** that can be done, known, acquired, selected, used, etc., depending on circumstances [a *possible* candidate] **4.** that may be done; permissible **5.** that may be a fact or the truth **6.** [Colloq.] that can be put up with; tolerable

SYN.—**possible** is used of anything that may exist, occur, be done, etc., depending on circumstances [a *possible* solution to a problem]; **practicable** applies to that which can readily be effected under the prevailing conditions or by the means available [a *practicable* plan]; **feasible** is used of that which is likely to be carried through to a successful conclusion and, hence, connotes the desirability of doing so [a *feasible* enterprise] See also PROBABLE

pos·si·bly (-blē) *adv.* **1.** by any possible means; in any case [it can't *possibly* work] **2.** by some possibility; perhaps; maybe [it may *possibly* be so]

☆**pos·sum** (päs′əm) *n.* [Colloq.] *same as* OPOSSUM —**play possum** to pretend to be asleep, dead, ill, unaware, etc.: opossums feign death when attacked

post¹ (pōst) *n.* [ME. < OE., akin to G. *pfosten*: WGmc. loanword < L. *postis*, a post, doorpost < *porstis*, a projection < *por-*, akin to FOR + base of *stare*, to STAND] **1.** a piece of wood, metal, etc., usually long and square or cylindrical, set upright to support a building, sign, fence, etc. **2.** anything like this in shape or purpose **3.** any place originally marked by or associated with a post, as the starting point of a horse race —*vt.* **1.** to put up (a poster, notice, etc.) on (a wall, post, etc.); placard **2.** to announce, publicize, or advertise by posting notices, signs, etc. [*post* a reward] ☆**3.** to warn persons against trespassing on (grounds, etc.) by posted notices **4.** to put (a name) on a posted or published list **5.** to denounce by a public notice **6.** to publish the name of (a ship) as lost or missing ☆**7.** *Sports* to record (a specified score)

post² (pōst) *n.* [Fr. *poste* < It. *posto* < VL. *postum*, contr. < L. *positum*, neut. pp. of *ponere*, to place: see POSITION] **1.** the place where a soldier, guard, etc. is stationed **2.** *a)* a place where a body of troops is stationed; camp *b)* the troops at such a place; garrison ☆**3.** a local unit of a veterans' organization **4.** a place where a person or group is stationed, as at a machine, a trading booth on a stock-exchange floor, etc. **5.** a position, job, or duty to which a person is assigned or appointed ☆**6.** *clipped form of* TRADING POST **7.** *Brit. Army* either of two bugle calls (**first post** and **last post**) sounded at tattoo —*vt.* **1.** to station at or assign to a post **2.** [Brit.] to appoint to a military or naval command ☆**3.** to put up or deposit (a bond, etc.) —*SYN.* see POSITION

post³ (pōst) *n.* [Fr. *poste* < It. *posta*, orig., a station, fem. of *posto*: see prec.] **1.** orig., any of a number of riders or runners posted at intervals to carry mail, etc. in relays along a route or, later, a person so posted to provide fresh horses for a courier **2.** formerly, *a)* a postrider or courier *b)* a stage of a post route *c)* a post horse or a station for one *d)* a packet (ship) **3.** [Chiefly Brit.] *a)* (the) mail *b)* a post office *c)* a mailbox *d)* [Dial.] a postman —*vi.* **1.** formerly, to travel in posts or stages **2.** to travel fast; hasten **3.** to rise and sink back in a saddle in rhythm with the horse's trot —*vt.* **1.** orig., *a)* to send by or as by post *b)* to hasten **2.** [Chiefly Brit.] to mail; put in a mailbox, etc. ☆**3.** to inform, as of events: usually in the passive voice [keep me *posted*] **4.** *Bookkeeping a)* to transfer (an item) from a daybook, etc. to the ledger *b)* to enter in the correct form and place *c)* to enter all necessary items in (a ledger, etc.) —*adv.* **1.** by post or postal courier **2.** speedily

post- (pōst) [L. < *post*, behind, after < *posti* < IE. *pos*, after (prob. < base *apo-*, away, whence L. *ab*), whence Gr. dial. *pos*, at] *a prefix meaning:* **1.** after in time, later (than), following [*postgraduate, postglacial*] **2.** after in space, behind [*postaxial*]

Post (pōst), **Emily** (Mrs. *Edwin Main Post*; born *Emily Price*) 1873–1960; U.S. writer on etiquette

post·age (pōs′tij) *n.* [POST³ + -AGE] the amount charged for mailing a letter or package, esp. as represented by stamps or indicia

☆**postage meter** a machine that prints indicia on mail, indicating that postage has been paid: it records the number of pieces processed and the cost of postage

postage stamp a government stamp to be put on a letter or package as a sign that the postage has been prepaid: it is either a small, printed, gummed label or a design imprinted on an envelope, postal card, etc.

post·al (pōs′t'l) *adj.* [Fr. < *poste*, POST³] having to do with mail or post offices —*n.* ☆[Colloq.] a postal card

☆**postal card 1.** a card with a printed postage stamp, issued by a government for sending messages at a rate lower than that for letters **2.** *popular var. of* POST CARD

post·ax·i·al (pōst ak′sē əl) *adj. Anat., Zool.* situated behind the axis of the body, as the posterior part of a limb

post-bel·lum (-bel′əm) *adj.* [L. *post bellum*, after the war] occurring after the war, ☆specif. after the American Civil War

post·box (pōst′bäks′) *n.* chiefly *Brit. var. of* MAILBOX

post·boy (-boi′) *n.* **1.** formerly, a man or boy who rode with the post **2.** *same as* POSTILION

post card 1. an unofficial card, often a picture card, that can be sent through the mail when a postage stamp is affixed **2.** *popular var. of* POSTAL CARD

post·ca·va (pōst′kā′və, -kä′-) *n., pl.* **-vae** (-vē) [POST- + (VENA) CAVA] the posterior vena cava of four-limbed vertebrates —**post′ca′val** *adj.*

post chaise a closed, four-wheeled coach or carriage drawn by fast horses, which were changed at each post, formerly used to carry mail and passengers

post·date (pōst′dāt′) *vt.* **-dat′ed, -dat′ing 1.** to assign a later date to than the actual or current date **2.** to write such a date on **3.** to be subsequent to

post·di·lu·vi·an (pōst′də loo′vē ən) *adj.* [POST- + DILUVIAN] of the time after the Biblical Flood —*n.* a postdiluvian person or thing

☆**post·doc·tor·al** (-däk′tər əl) *adj.* designating, of, or engaged in study, research, etc. following the doctorate

post·er¹ (pōs′tər) *n.* **1.** a person who posts notices, bills, etc. **2.** a relatively large printed card or sheet of paper, often illustrated, posted to advertise or publicize something; placard

post·er² (pōs′tər) *n.* **1.** orig., a person who traveled by post, or rapidly **2.** *same as* POST HORSE

poster color *same as* TEMPERA (sense 2)

poste res·tante (pōst′ res tänt′) [Fr., remaining mail] chiefly *Brit. var. of* GENERAL DELIVERY

pos·te·ri·or (päs tir′ē ər, pōs-) *adj.* [L., compar. of *posterus*, following < *post*, after: see POST-] **1.** later; following after; subsequent **2.** coming after in order; succeeding **3.** at or toward the rear; behind; specif., dorsal: opposed to ANTERIOR **4.** *Bot.* on the side next to the main stem —*n.* [*formerly pl.*] the buttocks —**pos·te′ri·or′i·ty** (-ôr′ə tē) *n.* —**pos·te′ri·or·ly** *adv.*

pos·ter·i·ty (päs ter′ə tē) *n.* [ME. *posterite* < MFr. *posterité* < L. *posteritas* < *posterus*: see POSTERIOR] **1.** all of a person's descendants: opposed to ANCESTRY **2.** all succeeding generations; future mankind

pos·tern (pōs′tərn, päs′-) *n.* [ME. < OFr. *posterne*, altered < *posterle* < LL. *posterula*, a small back door, postern, dim. < *posterus*: see POSTERIOR] formerly, a back door or gate; private entrance at the side or rear —*adj.* of or resembling a postern; rear, private, etc.

☆**post exchange** a nonprofit general store at an army post or camp, for the sale of merchandise for personal use, refreshments, etc.

post·ex·il·ic (pōst′ig zil′ik, -ik sil′-) *adj.* of that period of Jewish history following the Babylonian Exile (6th cent. B.C.): also **post′ex·il′i·an** (-ē ən)

post·fix (pōst fiks′; *for n., usually* pōst fiks′) *n., vt.* [POST- + (AF)FIX] *same as* SUFFIX

post-free (pōst′frē′) *adj.* **1.** that can be mailed free of charge **2.** [Brit.] *same as* POSTPAID

post·gan·gli·on·ic (-gaŋ′glē än′ik) *adj.* lying behind a ganglion; specif., of or pertaining to an axon leading nerve impulses away from a ganglion to some other part of the body

post·gla·cial (-glā′shəl) *adj.* existing or happening after the disappearance of glaciers from a specific area, esp. after the Pleistocene Epoch

☆**post·grad·u·ate** (-graj′oo wit, -wāt′) *adj.* of or taking a course of study after graduation —*n.* a student taking such courses

post·haste (pōst′hāst′) *n.* [Archaic] great haste, as of a postrider —*adv.* with great haste

‡**post hoc, er·go prop·ter hoc** (pōst′ häk ur′gō präp′tər häk) [L.] after this, therefore because of this: used in logic to describe the fallacy of thinking that a happening which follows another must be its result, and sometimes clipped to **post hoc**

post horse formerly, a horse kept at a post house, or inn, for couriers and post chaises or for hire to travelers

post house formerly, an inn or other place where post horses were kept

post·hu·mous (päs′choo məs, -tyoo-) *adj.* [LL. *posthumus*, for L. *postumus*, after death, orig., last, superl. of *posterus* (see POSTERIOR): altered in LL. after *humus*, ground, or *humare*, to bury (as if meaning "born after the father is buried")] **1.** born after the father's death **2.** published

after the author's death **3.** arising or continuing after one's death —**post′hu·mous·ly** *adv.*

post·hyp·not·ic (pōst′hip nät′ik) *adj.* of, having to do with, or carried out in the period following a hypnotic trance [*posthypnotic* suggestion]

‡**pos·tiche** (pōs tēsh′) *adj.* [Fr. < It. *posticcio* < VL. *appositicius* < L. *appositus:* see APPOSITE] **1.** counterfeit; artificial **2.** superfluously decorative —*n.* **1.** a substitute; counterfeit **2.** pretense **3.** a hairpiece

pos·til·ion, pos·til·lion (pōs til′yən, päs-) *n.* [Fr. *postillon* < It. *postiglione* < *posta*, POST³] **1.** a person who rides the left-hand horse of the leaders of a four-horse carriage **2.** one who rides the left-hand horse of a two-horse carriage when there is no driver

post·im·pres·sion·ism (pōst′im presh′ən iz'm) *n.* the theory, practice, or methods of a group of late 19th-cent. painters, including Cézanne, Van Gogh, and Gauguin, who revolted against the objectivity and scientific naturalism of impressionism and placed emphasis upon the subjective viewpoint of the artist or the formal structure and style of the painting —**post′im·pres′sion·ist** *adj., n.* —**post′im·pres′sion·is′tic** *adj.*

post·li·min·i·um (pōst′li min′ē əm) *n.* [L. < *post*, behind (see POST-) + *limen*, threshold: see LIMEN] in international law, the rule by which persons or things captured in war by an enemy resume their original status when restored to the jurisdiction of their own country: also **post′lim′i·ny** (-lim′ə nē)

post·lude (pōst′lood′) *n.* [POST- + (PRE)LUDE] **1.** an organ voluntary played at the end of a church service **2.** a concluding musical section or movement

post·man (-mən) *n., pl.* **-men** (-mən) *same as* MAIL CARRIER

post·mark (-märk′) *n.* a post-office mark stamped on a piece of mail, canceling the postage stamp and recording the date and place of sending or receiving —*vt.* to stamp with a postmark

post·mas·ter (-mas′tər, -mäs′-) *n.* **1.** orig., a person in charge of a station for post horses **2.** a person in charge of a post office —**post′mas′ter·ship′** *n.*

postmaster general *pl.* **postmasters general, postmaster generals** the head of a government's postal system

post·me·ri·di·an (pōst′mə rid′ē ən) *adj.* [L. *postmeridianus:* see POST- & MERIDIAN] of or in the afternoon [a *postmeridian* event]

post me·ri·di·em (-ē əm) [L.] after noon: abbrev. **P.M., p.m., PM**

post·mil·len·ni·al (pōst′mə len′ē əl) *adj.* existing or happening after the millennium —**post′mil·len′ni·al·ly** *adv.*

post·mil·len·ni·al·ism (-iz'm) *n.* the religious doctrine that the second coming of Christ will occur after, not at, the millennium: also **post′mil·le·nar′i·an·ism** (-mil ə ner′ē ə niz'm) —**post′mil·le·nar′i·an** *adj., n.* —**post′mil·len′-ni·al·ist** *n.*

post·mis·tress (pōst′mis′tris) *n.* a woman postmaster (sense 2)

post-mor·tem (pōst môr′təm) *adj.* [L., after death] **1.** happening, done, or made after death **2.** having to do with a post-mortem examination —*n.* **1.** *same as* POST-MORTEM EXAMINATION **2.** a detailed examination or evaluation of some event just ended

post-mortem examination an examination of a human body after death: see AUTOPSY

post-na·sal drip (pōst′nā′z'l) a discharge of mucus from behind the nose onto the surface of the pharynx, usually resulting from a cold or allergy

post-na·tal (pōst′nāt′'l) *adj.* [POST- + NATAL] after birth; esp., of the period immediately after birth

post·nup·tial (-nup′shəl, -chəl) *adj.* [POST- + NUPTIAL] happening or done after marriage —**post′nup′tial·ly** *adv.*

post-o·bit (-ō′bit, -äb′it) *adj.* [contr. < L. *post obitum*, after death < *post*, after + *obitus*, death: see POST- & OBIT] being, or to be, in effect after a specified person's death —*n.* a bond given by a borrower pledging to pay his debt upon the death of a specified person from whom he expects to inherit money

post office 1. the governmental department in charge of the mails **2.** an office or building where mail is sorted for distribution, postage stamps are sold, etc. ☆**3.** a children's game in which one pretending to be postman gives out kisses instead of letters

post·op·er·a·tive (pōst′äp′ər ə tiv, -äp′rə-; -ə rāt′iv) *adj.* of or occurring in the period after a surgical operation —**post′op′er·a·tive·ly** *adv.*

post·or·bit·al (-ôr′bi t'l) *adj. Anat. & Zool.* situated behind the orbit, or eye socket —*n.* a postorbital bone or scale, as in certain reptiles

post·paid (pōst′pād′) *adj.* with the postage prepaid

post·par·tum (pōst′pär′təm) *adj.* [L. < *post-*, POST- + *partum*, acc. of *partus*, a bringing forth < *parere*, to bear: see -PAROUS] of the period following childbirth

post·pone (pōst pōn′, pōs-) *vt.* **-poned′, -pon′ing** [L. *postponere* < *post-*, POST- + *ponere*, to put: see POSITION] **1.** to put off until later; defer; delay **2.** to put at or near the end of the sentence [the German verb is *postponed*]

3. [Rare] to consider less important; subordinate —*SYN.* see ADJOURN —**post·pon'a·ble** *adj.* —**post·pone'ment** *n.* —**post·pon'er** *n.*

post·po·si·tion (pōst'pə zish'ən) *n.* **1.** [< L. *postpositus,* pp. of *postponere:* see POSTPONE] a placing after or being placed after **2.** [POST- + (PRE)POSITION] *Gram.* the placing of an element after another related to it, or an element so placed, as an affix that functions as a preposition but follows its object (Ex.: *-ward* in *shoreward*) or an adjective that follows the word it modifies (Ex.: *royal* in *battle royal*)

post·pos·i·tive (pōst'päz'ə tiv) *adj.* [LL. *postpositivus* < L. *postpositus* (see prec.)] placed after or added to another word; enclitic; suffixed —*n.* a postpositive word; postposition —**post'pos'i·tive·ly** *adv.*

post·pran·di·al (-pran'dē əl) *adj.* [POST- + PRANDIAL] after a meal; esp., after-dinner —**post'pran'di·al·ly** *adv.*

post·rid·er (pōst'rīd'ər) *n.* formerly, a person who carried the post, or mail, on horseback; post

post road 1. formerly, a road provided with post houses **2.** a road over which the post, or mail, is or formerly was carried

post·script (pōst'skript', pōs'-) *n.* [ModL. *postscriptum* < L., neut. pp. of *postscribere* < *post-,* after (see POST-) + *scribere,* to write: see SCRIBE] a note, paragraph, etc. added below the signature line of a letter, or added to a book, speech, etc. as an afterthought or to give supplementary information

☆**post time** the scheduled starting time of a horse race

pos·tu·lant (päs'chə lənt) *n.* [Fr. < L. *postulans,* prp. of *postulare:* see ff.] a petitioner or candidate, esp. one for admission into a religious order

pos·tu·late (päs'chə lāt'; *for n., usually* -lit) *vt.* **-lat'ed, -lat'ing** [< L. *postulatus,* pp. of *postulare,* to demand < base of *poscere,* to demand < IE. **pṝkskā,* question < base **perk-,* to ask, whence G. *frage,* question] **1.** to claim; demand; require **2.** to assume without proof to be true, real, or necessary, esp. as a basis for argument **3.** to take as self-evident or axiomatic; assume —*n.* [ModL. *postulatum* < neut. of L. *postulatus*] **1.** something postulated; assumption or axiom **2.** a prerequisite **3.** a basic principle —*SYN.* see PRESUME —**pos'tu·la'tion** *n.*

pos·tu·la·tor (-lāt'ər) *n.* one who postulates; specif., *R.C.Ch.* an official who pleads for a candidate for beatification or canonization

pos·ture (päs'chər) *n.* [MFr. < It. *postura* < L. *positura,* a position < *ponere,* to place: see POSITION] **1.** the position or carriage of the body in standing or sitting; bearing **2.** such a position assumed as in posing for an artist **3.** the way things stand; condition with respect to circumstances [the delicate *posture* of foreign affairs] **4.** *a)* an attitude of mind; frame of mind *b)* an attitude assumed merely for effect **5.** an official stand or position, as that taken by a nation on a major issue —*vt.* **-tured, -tur·ing** to place in a posture; pose —*vi.* to assume a bodily or mental posture; esp., to assume an attitude merely for effect; pose; attitudinize —**pos'tur·al** *adj.* —**pos'tur·er** *n.*

SYN.—**posture** refers to the habitual or assumed disposition of the parts of the body in standing, sitting, etc. [erect *posture*]; **attitude** refers to a posture assumed either unconsciously, as in manifesting a mood or emotion, or intentionally for carrying out a particular purpose [an *attitude* of watchfulness]; **pose** suggests a posture assumed, usually deliberately, as for artistic effect [to hold a *pose* for a photographer]; **stance** refers to a particular way of standing, esp. with reference to the position of the feet, as in certain sports [the *stance* of a golfer]

pos·tur·ize (-chə rīz') *vt., vi.* **-ized', -iz'ing** *same as* POSTURE

post·war (pōst'wôr') *adj.* after the (or a) war

po·sy (pō'zē) *n., pl.* **-sies** [contr. < POESY] **1.** orig., a verse or motto inscribed inside a ring, etc. **2.** a flower, bouquet, or nosegay: an old-fashioned usage

pot (pät) *n.* [ME. < OE. *pott,* akin to Du. *pot* < ? IE. base **bu-,* to swell, whence POUT] **1.** a round vessel of any size, made of metal, earthenware, or glass, used for holding liquids, cooking or preserving food, etc. **2.** a pot with its contents **3.** *same as* POTFUL **4.** a pot of liquor; drink; potation **5.** *shortened form for* FLOWERPOT, LOBSTER POT, CHIMNEY POT, etc. **6.** *a) same as* CHAMBER POT *b)* a toilet: a vulgar usage **7.** [Colloq.] *a)* all the money bet at a single time; pool; kitty *b)* a large amount of money **8.** [Colloq.] a potshot **9.** [Slang] *same as:* ☆*a)* MARIJUANA *b)* POTBELLY —*vt.* **pot'ted, pot'ting 1.** to put into a pot **2.** to preserve in a pot or jar **3.** to cook in a pot **4.** to shoot (game) for food instead of for sport **5.** to hit or secure by or as by a potshot **6.** [Colloq.] to secure, win, or capture; bag —*vi.* [Colloq.] to take a potshot; shoot —**go to pot** to go to ruin; deteriorate

pot. potential

po·ta·ble (pōt'ə b'l) *adj.* [Fr. < LL. *potabilis* < L. *potare,* to drink < IE. base **pō-,* to drink, whence Sans. *pāti,* (he) drinks, L. *bibere,* to drink] fit to drink; drinkable —*n.* something drinkable; beverage —**po'ta·bil'i·ty, po'ta·ble·ness** *n.*

‡**po·tage** (pō tàzh') *n.* [Fr.] soup or broth

pot·ash (pät'ash') *n.* [earlier in pl., *potashes* < Du. *potasschen* < *pot,* pot + *asch,* ASH[1]: orig. prepared by evaporating the lixivium of wood ashes in iron pots] **1.** *same as: a)* POTASSIUM CARBONATE (esp. when obtained from wood ashes) *b)* POTASSIUM HYDROXIDE **2.** any substance con-

taining potassium; esp., salts derived from natural brines, distillery waste, flue dusts of blast furnaces, etc., whose potassium content is expressed in terms of K_2O: used in fertilizers, soaps, etc.

po·tas·si·um (pə tas'ē əm) *n.* [ModL. < *potassa* < Du. *potasch:* see POTASH] a soft, silver-white, waxlike metallic chemical element that oxidizes rapidly when exposed to air: it occurs abundantly in nature in the form of its salts, which are used in fertilizers, glass, etc.: symbol, K; at. wt., 39.102; at. no., 19; sp. gr., 0.86; melt. pt., 62.3°C; boil. pt., 760°C —**po·tas'sic** *adj.*

po·tas·si·um-ar·gon dating (-är'gän) an indirect method of dating fossils, using the known, steady rate of decay into argon of a radioactive isotope of natural potassium and estimating the amount of argon trapped within potassic minerals of the same age as the fossils

potassium bitartrate *same as* CREAM OF TARTAR

potassium bromide a white, crystalline compound, KBr, used in photography, medicine, etc.

potassium carbonate a strongly alkaline, white, crystalline compound, K_2CO_3, used in the manufacture of soap and glass, in medicine, etc.

potassium chlorate a colorless, crystalline salt, $KClO_3$, a strong oxidizing agent used in medicine and in the manufacture of explosives, matches, etc.

potassium chloride a colorless, crystalline salt, KCl, used in fertilizers, as a source of potassium salts, etc.

potassium cyanide an extremely poisonous, white, crystalline compound, KCN, used in metallurgy for extracting gold, in electroplating, as an insecticide, etc.

potassium dichromate a yellowish-red, crystalline compound, $K_2Cr_2O_7$, used as an oxidizing agent and in photography, dyeing, etc.

potassium hydroxide a white, crystalline salt or deliquescent solid, KOH, used in the manufacture of soap, glass, etc.: it is a very strong alkali and absorbs carbon dioxide from the air

potassium iodide a transparent, crystalline salt, KI, available also as a white, granular powder, used as a feed additive and in medicine, photography, etc.

potassium nitrate a colorless, crystalline compound, KNO_3, used in fertilizers, gunpowder, preservatives, etc., in medicine, and as a reagent and oxidizing agent in chemistry

potassium permanganate a dark-purple, crystalline compound, $KMnO_4$, used as an oxidizing agent, disinfectant, antiseptic, etc.

potassium sulfate a white, crystalline solid, K_2SO_4, used in fertilizers, medicine, etc.

po·ta·tion (pō tā'shən) *n.* [ME. *potacion* < MFr. < L. *potatio* < *potare,* to drink: see POTABLE] **1.** the act of drinking **2.** a drink or draft, esp. of liquor

po·ta·to (pə tāt'ō, -ə) *n., pl.* **-toes** [Sp. *patata,* var. of *batata,* sweet potato < Taino name] **1.** orig., *same as* SWEET POTATO **2.** *a)* the starchy, brown-skinned or red-skinned tuber of a widely cultivated plant (*Solanum tuberosum*) of the nightshade family, eaten as a cooked vegetable: also **Irish potato, white potato** *b)* this plant

☆**potato beetle** (or **bug**) *same as* COLORADO BEETLE

☆**potato chip** a very thin slice of potato fried crisp and then salted: also, Brit., **potato crisp**

‡**pot-au-feu** (pô tō fö') *n.* [Fr., lit., pot on the fire] a French dish made by boiling meat and vegetables, etc., with the broth customarily strained and served separately

pot·bel·lied (pät'bel'ēd) *adj.* **1.** having a potbelly **2.** having rounded, bulging sides [a *potbellied* stove]

pot·bel·ly (-bel'ē) *n., pl.* **-lies** a protruding belly

pot·boil·er (-boil'ər) *n.* a piece of writing or the like, usually inferior and uninspired, done quickly for money

pot·boy (-boi') *n.* [Brit.] a boy who serves pots of beer, ale, etc. in a public house or tavern

☆**pot cheese** a type of coarse, dry cottage cheese

po·teen (pō tēn', -tyēn') *n.* [Ir. *poitín,* dim. of *poite,* a pot] in Ireland, illicitly distilled whiskey

Po·tem·kin (pō tyôm'kin; *E.* pō tem'kin), **Gri·go·ri A·lek·san·dro·vich** (grē gō'rē ä'lyek sän'drō vich) 1739-91; Russ. field marshal & statesman; favorite of Catherine the Great

po·ten·cy (pōt''n sē) *n., pl.* **-cies** [L. *potentia*] **1.** the state or quality of being potent, or the degree of this; power; strength **2.** capacity for development; potentiality **3.** [Now Rare] something or someone influential or powerful Also, esp. for sense 1, **po'tence** —*SYN.* see STRENGTH

po·tent (pōt''nt) *adj.* [L. *potens* (gen. *potentis*), prp. of *posse,* to be able < *potis,* able (< IE. base **potis,* master, husband, whence Sans. *pāti,* master) + *esse,* to be: see ESSENCE] **1.** having authority or power; mighty; influential [a *potent* monarch] **2.** convincing; cogent [a *potent* argument] **3.** effective or powerful in action, as a drug or drink **4.** able to have an erection and hence to engage in sexual intercourse —**po'tent·ly** *adv.*

po·ten·tate (pōt''n tāt') *n.* [ME. *potentat* < LL. *potentatus* < LL.(Ec.), power, rule < L. *potens:* see prec.] a person having great power; ruler; monarch

po·ten·tial (pə ten'shəl) *adj.* [ME. *potenciall* < ML. *potentialis* < L. *potentia:* see POTENT] **1.** orig., that has power; potent **2.** that can, but has not yet, come into being; possible; latent; unrealized; undeveloped **3.** *Gram.* expressing possibility, capability, or the like [the *potential*

mood*J* —*n.* **1.** something potential; a potentiality **2.** *Elec.* the relative voltage at a point in an electric circuit or field with respect to some reference point in the same circuit or field **3.** *Gram. a)* the potential mood or aspect *b)* a potential construction or form **4.** *Physics* any scalar quantity in which energy is involved as a function of position or condition —*SYN.* see LATENT —**po·ten′tial·ly** *adv.*

potential energy energy in an inactive form that is the result of relative position or structure instead of motion, as in a coiled spring

po·ten·ti·al·i·ty (pə ten′shē al′ə tē) *n.* [ML. *potentialitas*] **1.** the state or quality of being potential; possibility or capability of becoming, developing, etc.; latency **2.** *pl.* **-ties** something potential; a possibility

po·ten·ti·ate (pə ten′shē āt′) *vt.* **-at′ed, -at′ing** [< L. *potentia*, POTENCY + -ATE[1]] to increase or multiply (the effect of a drug or toxin) by the preceding or simultaneous administration of another drug or toxin —**po·ten′ti·a′tor** *n.* —**po·ten′ti·a′tion** *n.*

po·ten·til·la (pōt′′n til′ə) *n.* [ModL., name of the genus < ML., valerian, dim. of L. *potens:* see POTENT] *same as* CINQUEFOIL (sense 1)

po·ten·ti·om·e·ter (pə ten′shē äm′ə tər) *n.* [< POTENTIAL + -METER] an instrument for measuring, comparing, or controlling electric potentials

pot·ful (pät′fool′) *n., pl.* **-fuls′** as much as a pot will hold

pot·head (pät′hed′) *n.* ☆[Slang] a user of marijuana

poth·e·car·y (päth′ə ker′ē) *n., pl.* **-car′ies** [ME. *potecarie*] [Archaic exc. Brit. Dial.] an apothecary

po·theen (pō tēn′, -tyēn′) *n. same as* POTEEN

poth·er (päth′ər) *n.* [< ?] **1.** a choking cloud of smoke, dust, etc. **2.** an uproar, commotion, fuss, fluster, or the like —*vt., vi.* to fuss or bother

pot·herb (pät′urb′, -hurb′) *n.* any herb whose leaves and stems are boiled and eaten or used as a flavoring

pot·hold·er (-hōl′dər) *n.* a small pad, or piece of thick cloth, for holding and handling hot pots, etc.

pot·hole (-hōl′) *n.* **1.** a deep hole or pit; esp., a deep, round hole formed in the rock of a river bed by gravel whirling in water **2.** *chiefly Brit. var. of* CHUCKHOLE **3.** a deep cave extending downward underground

pot·hook (-hook′) *n.* **1.** an S-shaped hook for hanging a pot or kettle over a fire **2.** a hooked rod for lifting hot pots, etc. **3.** a curved or S shaped mark in writing

pot·house (-hous′) *n.* [Brit.] a small alehouse or tavern

pot·hunt·er (-hun′tər) *n.* **1.** a hunter who kills game indiscriminately, disregarding the rules of sport **2.** a person who enters contests merely to win prizes

‡**po·tiche** (pō tēsh′) *n., pl.* **-tiches** (-tēsh′) [Fr. < *pot,* a pot < Du.] a tall vase or jar of porcelain, etc., with a rounded or polygonal body narrowing toward the top

po·tion (pō′shən) *n.* [ME. *pocion* < OFr. < L. *potio* < *potare,* to drink: see POTABLE] a drink or liquid dose, as of medicine, poison, or a supposedly magic substance

☆**pot·latch** (pät′lach′, -lash′) *n.* [< AmInd. (Chinook) *patshatl,* a gift] among some American Indians of the N Pacific coast, *a)* [often **P-**] a winter festival *b)* a distribution or exchange of gifts during such a festival, often involving the squandering of the host's belongings

pot liquor [Dial.] the liquid left after meat and vegetables have been cooked, often used for broth, gravy, etc.: also **pot′lik′ker, pot′lick′er** *n.*

pot·luck (pät′luk′) *n.* whatever the family meal happens to be [a neighbor invited in to take *potluck*]

pot·man (pät′mən) *n., pl.* **-men** (-mən) [Brit.] a serving man, or waiter, in a public house or tavern

pot marigold a cultivated calendula (*Calendula officinalis*) with showy yellow or orange flowers

Po·to·mac (pə tō′mək) [< Algonquian town name, lit., ? where tribute is brought] river in the E U.S., forming a boundary of W.Va., Md., & Va., and flowing into Chesapeake Bay: 285 mi.

Po·to·sí (pō′tō sē′) **1.** city in SW Bolivia, on the slopes of Cerro de Potosí: altitude c. 13,340 ft.; pop. 65,000 **2. Cer·ro de** (ser′rō de), mountain of the Andes, in SW Bolivia: 15,843 ft.

☆**pot·pie** (pät′pī′) *n.* **1.** a meat pie made in a pot or deep dish, usually with only a top crust **2.** a stew with dumplings

pot·pour·ri (pō′poo rē′, pät poor′ē) *n.* [Fr. < *pot,* a pot (< Du.) + *pourri,* pp. of *pourrir,* to rot, transl. of Sp. *olla podrida:* see OLLA-PODRIDA] **1.** orig., a stew **2.** a mixture of dried flower petals with spices, kept in a jar for its fragrance **3.** a medley, miscellany, or anthology

pot roast meat, usually a large cut of beef, cooked in one piece by braising

Pots·dam (päts′dam′; *G.* pōts däm′) city in East Germany, near Berlin: site of a post-World War II conference (1945): pop. 111,000

pot·sherd (pät′shurd′) *n.* [ME. *potschoord:* see POT & SHARD] a piece of broken pottery: now used esp. of archaeological finds

pot·shot (-shät′) *n.* **1.** orig., a pothunter's shot **2.** an easy shot, as at close range **3.** a random shot **4.** a haphazard try **5.** a random criticism or attack

pot·stone (-stōn′) *n.* a kind of soapstone of which cooking vessels were made in prehistoric times

☆**pot·sy** (pät′sē) *n.* [< ?] *Eastern dial. var. of* HOPSCOTCH

pot·tage (pät′ij) *n.* [ME. *potage* < MFr. < *pot,* a pot < Du.] a kind of thick soup or stew made of vegetables, or meat and vegetables

pot·ted (pät′id) *adj.* **1.** put into a pot [a *potted* plant] **2.** cooked or preserved in a pot or can ☆**3.** [Slang] intoxicated; drunk **4.** condensed or summarized, often so as to be too brief, superficial, etc. [*potted* biographies]

pot·ter[1] (-ər) *n.* [ME. < Late OE. *pottere* < *pott,* POT] a person who makes earthenware pots, dishes, etc.

pot·ter[2] (pät′ər) *vi., vt.,* [freq. formation < obs. *pote* < OE. *potian,* to push] *chiefly Brit. var. of* PUTTER[3]

Pot·ter (pät′ər) **1. Beatrix,** (Mrs. *William Heelis*) 1866?–1943; Eng. writer & illustrator of children's books **2. Paul,** 1625–54; Du. painter

potter's field [after a burial place for strangers in Jerusalem (Matt. 27:7), ? orig. a potter's field] ☆a burial ground for paupers or unknown persons

potter's wheel a rotating horizontal disk, usually operated by a treadle or motor, upon which clay is molded into bowls, etc.

☆**potter wasp** *same as* MASON WASP

pot·ter·y (pät′ər ē) *n., pl.* **-ter·ies** [LME. *poterye* < MFr. *poterie* < *potier,* a potter < *pot,* a pot] **1.** a place where earthenware is made; potter's workshop or factory **2.** the art or occupation of a potter; ceramics **3.** pots, bowls, dishes, etc. made of clay hardened by heat; earthenware

pot·tle (pät′′l) *n.* [ME. *potel* < MFr., dim. of *pot,* a pot] **1.** a former liquid measure, equal to a half gallon **2.** a pot or tankard of this capacity **3.** the contents of such a pot; esp., alcoholic liquor

POTTER'S WHEEL

pot·to (pät′ō) *n., pl.* **-tos** [< Afr. native name, as in Wolof *pata,* a kind of tailless monkey] any of a number of slow-moving, large-eyed, C African lemurs (genus *Perodictus*)

Pott's disease (pats) [after Percival *Pott* (1714–88), Eng. surgeon who described it] tuberculous caries of the vertebrae, resulting in curvature of the spine

pot·ty[1] (pät′ē) *n., pl.* **-ties** [dim. of POT] **1.** a small chamber pot for a child **2.** a child's chair used for toilet training, consisting of an open seat beneath which a pot is attached: in full **potty chair 3.** a toilet: a child's word

pot·ty[2] (pät′ē) *adj.* **-ti·er, -ti·est** [< POT (cf. sense 4) + -Y[2]] [Brit. Colloq.] **1.** trivial; petty **2.** slightly crazy —**pot′ti·ness** *n.*

pot·val·iant (pät′val′yənt) *adj.* valiant and bold from drunkenness

pot·wal·lop·er (pät′wäl′ə pər) *n.* [altered (after *wallop,* to boil) < *potwaller,* lit., a pot boiler < POT + obs. *wall,* to boil < ME. *wallen* < OE. *weallan*] *Eng. History* a person considered a householder by virtue of owning a hearth, and therefore qualified to vote

pouch (pouch) *n.* [ME. *pouche* < MFr. *poche,* var. of *poque:* see POKE[2]] **1.** a small bag or sack, as one of leather, plastic, etc., for carrying pipe tobacco in one's pocket ☆**2.** a mailbag; specif., one whose opening can be locked, as for sending diplomatic dispatches **3.** anything shaped like a pouch **4.** [Scot.] a pocket (in clothing) **5.** [Archaic] a purse **6.** *Anat.* any pouchlike cavity or part **7.** *Zool. a)* a saclike structure on the abdomen of some animals, as the kangaroo and the opossum, used to carry young; marsupium *b)* a baglike part, as of a pelican's bill or a gopher's cheeks, used to carry food —*vt.* **1.** to put in a pouch **2.** to make into a pouch; make pouchy **3.** to swallow: said of fishes and certain birds —*vi.* to form a pouch or pouchlike cavity

pouched (poucht) *adj.* having a pouch or pouches

pouch·y (pou′chē) *adj.* **pouch′i·er, pouch′i·est** resembling a pouch; baggy —**pouch′i·ness** *n.*

poud (pood) *n. same as* POOD

pouf (poof) *n.* [Fr., a puff: echoic] **1.** an elaborate headdress worn by women, esp. in the 18th cent., and characterized by high rolls or puffs of hair **2.** any part of a dress, etc. gathered into a puff, or projection **3.** a kind of ottoman or hassock Also sp. **pouff, pouffe**

Pough·keep·sie (pə kip′sē) [< Du. < Algonquian name] city in SE N.Y., on the Hudson: pop. 32,000

pou·lard, pou·larde (poo lärd′) *n.* [Fr. *poularde* < *poule,* hen: see POULTRY] **1.** a young hen spayed for fattening **2.** any fat young hen

‡**poule** (pool) *n.* [Fr., hen: see POULTRY] *Fr. slang for* PROSTITUTE

Pou·lenc (poo lank′), **Fran·cis** (frän ses′) 1899–1963; Fr. composer

poult (pōlt) *n.* [ME. *pulte,* contr. of *pulete,* PULLET] a young turkey, chicken, pheasant, or similar fowl

poul·ter·er (pōl′tər ər) *n.* [ME. *pulter* < MFr. *pouletier* < *poulet* (see POULTRY) + -ER] [Brit.] a dealer in poultry and game: also [Archaic] **poul′ter**

poul·tice (pōl′tis) *n.* [earlier *pultes* < ML. *pultes,* thick pap, orig. pl. of L. *puls:* see PULSE[2]] a hot, soft, moist

mass, as of flour, herbs, mustard, etc., sometimes spread on cloth, applied to a sore or inflamed part of the body —*vt.* **-ticed, -tic·ing** to apply a poultice to

poul·try (pōl′trē) *n.* [ME. *pultrie* < MFr. *pouleterie* < *poulet*, dim. of *poule*, hen < L. *pullus*, chicken, young animal < IE. base *pōu-*, small, small animal, whence FOAL, L. *puer*, child] domestic fowls raised for meat or eggs; chickens, turkeys, ducks, geese, etc., collectively

poul·try·man (-mən) *n., pl.* **-men** (-mən) **1.** a person who raises poultry, esp. commercially **2.** a dealer in poultry

pounce[1] (pouns) *n.* [ME. *pownce*, talon, prob. altered < MFr. *poinçon*, sharp instrument, stiletto: see PUNCHEON[1]] **1.** a claw or talon of a bird of prey **2.** the act of pouncing; swoop, spring, or leap —*vi.* **pounced, pounc′ing** to swoop down, spring, or leap (*on, upon,* or *at* a person or thing) in, or as in, attacking or seizing —**pounc′er** *n.*

pounce[2] (pouns) *n.* [Fr. *ponce* < L. *pumex,* PUMICE] **1.** a fine powder, as pulverized cuttlefish bone, formerly used to prevent ink from blotting or to prepare the writing surface of parchment **2.** a fine powder sprinkled over a stencil to make a design, as on cloth —*vt.* **pounced, pounc′ing 1.** to sprinkle, rub, finish, or prepare with pounce **2.** to stencil with pounce

poun·cet box (poun′sit) [prob. < MFr. *poncette,* box for POUNCE[2]] [Archaic] *same as* POMANDER (sense 2)

pound[1] (pound) *n., pl.* **pounds** (poundz), collectively **pound** [ME. < OE. *pund,* akin to G. *pfund:* WGmc. loanword < L. *pondo,* a pound, orig. abl. of *pondus,* a weight (in *libra pondo,* a pound in weight), akin to *pendere:* see PENDANT] **1.** a unit of weight, equal to 16 oz. (7,000 grains) avoirdupois or 12 oz. (5,760 grains) troy: abbrev. **lb. 2.** the monetary unit of the United Kingdom, equal to 20 shillings or 100 (new) pennies: in full **pound sterling:** symbol, £ (no period): see MONETARY UNITS, table **3.** the monetary unit of various other countries, as of Ireland, Israel, etc.: see MONETARY UNITS, table **4.** a former Scottish monetary unit (**pound Scots**), originally equal to the British pound **5.** in the New Testament, *same as* MINA[1]

pound[2] (pound) *vt.* [altered (with unhistoric -d) < ME. *pownen* < OE. *punian,* akin to Du. *puin,* rubbish] **1.** to beat to a pulp, powder, etc.; pulverize **2.** to strike or drive with repeated, heavy blows **3.** to make by pounding **4.** to force or impose [*pound* sense into him] —*vi.* **1.** to deliver repeated, heavy blows (*at* or *on* a door, etc.) **2.** to move with heavy steps or come down heavily while moving **3.** to beat against heavy waves: said of watercraft **4.** to beat heavily; throb —*n.* **1.** the act of pounding **2.** a hard blow **3.** the sound of this; thud; thump —*SYN.* see BEAT —**pound out 1.** to flatten, smooth, etc. by pounding **2.** to play, as on a piano, or produce, as on a typewriter, with a very heavy touch —☆**pound one's ear** [Slang] to sleep —☆**pound the pavement** [Slang] to walk the streets, as in looking for work

pound[3] (pound) *n.* [ME. *poonde* < OE. *pund-* (in compounds), akin to *pyndan,* to shut up] **1.** an enclosure, maintained by a town, etc., for confining stray animals until claimed **2.** an enclosure for keeping or sheltering animals **3.** an enclosure for trapping animals **4.** a place of confinement, as for arrested persons **5.** an enclosed area for catching or keeping fish, esp. the inner section of a pound net —*vt.* [Archaic] to confine in a pound

Pound (pound) **1. Ezra (Loomis),** 1885– ; U.S. poet, in Italy (1924–45; 1958–) **2. Louise,** 1872–1958; U.S. linguist & folklorist **3. Roscoe,** 1870–1964; U.S. educator & legal scholar: brother of *prec.*

pound·age[1] (poun′dij) *n.* **1.** a tax, rate, or commission, etc. per pound (sterling or weight) **2.** weight in pounds

pound·age[2] (poun′dij) *n.* **1.** confinement in or as in a pound, or enclosure **2.** the fee required to free animals from a pound

pound·al (poun′d'l) *n.* [POUND[1] + *-al* (as in CENTAL)] a unit of force in the fps system which will produce an acceleration of one foot per second per second on a one-pound mass

pound·cake (pound′kāk′) *n.* **1.** a rich cake made with a pound each of its principal ingredients, as flour, butter, sugar, etc. **2.** a cake resembling this

pound·er (poun′dər) *n.* a person or thing that pounds

-pound·er (poun′dər) *a combining form meaning* something weighing or worth (a specified number of) pounds: used in hyphenated compounds [*five-pounder*]

pound-fool·ish (pound′fōōl′ish) *adj.* not handling large sums of money wisely: see PENNY-WISE

☆**pound net** a fish trap consisting of staked nets arranged so as to form an enclosure with a narrow opening

pour (pôr) *vt.* [ME. *pouren < ?*] **1.** to cause to flow in a continuous stream **2.** to emit, discharge, utter, etc. profusely or steadily —*vi.* **1.** to flow freely, continuously, or copiously **2.** to rain heavily **3.** to rush in a crowd; swarm ☆**4.** to serve as a hostess at a reception or the like, by pouring tea, coffee, etc. for the guests —*n.* **1.** an act of pouring **2.** a heavy rain or downpour —☆**pour it on** [Slang] **1.** to flatter profusely **2.** to increase one's efforts greatly, work very hard, etc. **3.** to go very fast —**pour′er** *n.*

‡**pour·boire** (pōōr bwär′) *n.* [Fr. < *pour,* for + *boire,* to drink] a tip, or gratuity

‡**pour·par·ler** (pōōr pär lā′) *n.* [Fr. < *pour,* for + *parler,* to speak] a preliminary, informal discussion

pour·point (poor′point′) *n.* [ME. *purpoynt* < OFr. *porpoint,* orig., perforated: altered (after *pour,* for) < VL. **perpunctus,* pp. of **perpungere* < L. *per-,* through (see PER) + *pungere,* to prick: see POINT] a quilted doublet worn in the late Middle Ages

☆**pousse-ca·fé** (pōōs′ka fā′) *n.* [Fr., lit., coffee-chaser: see PUSH & COFFEE] **1.** a liqueur drunk with after-dinner coffee **2.** a drink made of several liqueurs, each forming its own layer in the glass

pous·sette (pōō set′) *n.* [Fr., dim. of *pousse,* a PUSH] a dance figure in which a couple or couples dance round and round with hands joined —*vi.* **-set′ted, -set′ting** to perform a poussette

Pous·sin (pōō san′), **Ni·co·las** (nē kô lä′) 1594–1665; Fr. painter

‡**pou sto** (pōō′ stō′, pou′) [Gr. *pou stō,* where I may stand: from a saying of Archimedes, *dos moi pou stō, kai kinō tēn gēn,* give me (a place) where I may stand, and I will move the earth] **1.** a place to stand on **2.** a basis of operations

pout[1] (pout) *vi.* [ME. *pouten,* ult. < IE. base **bu-,* to swell] **1.** to thrust out the lips, as in sullenness or displeasure **2.** to sulk **3.** to protrude: said of the lips —*vt.* **1.** to thrust out (the lips) **2.** to utter with a pout —*n.* **1.** the act of pouting **2.** a fit of sulking: also **the pouts**

pout[2] (pout) *n., pl.* **pout, pouts:** see PLURAL, II, D, 2 [OE. *-pute:* for IE. base see prec.] any of several fishes with a stout body, as the horned pout, the eelpout, etc.

pout·er (pout′ər) *n.* **1.** a person who pouts **2.** a breed of pigeon that can distend its crop to produce a large, puffed-up breast: in full **pouter pigeon**

pov·er·ty (päv′ər tē) *n.* [ME. *poverte* < OFr. *povreté* < L. *paupertas* < *pauper,* POOR] **1.** the condition or quality of being poor; indigence; need **2.** deficiency in necessary properties or desirable qualities, or in a specific quality, etc.; inadequacy [*poverty* of the soil, *poverty* of the imagination] ′ **3.** smallness in amount; scarcity; paucity *SYN.*—**poverty,** the broadest of these terms, implies a lack of the resources for reasonably comfortable living; **destitution** and **want** imply such great poverty that the means for mere subsistence, such as food and shelter, are lacking; **indigence,** a somewhat euphemistic term, implies a lack of luxuries to which one was formerly accustomed; **penury** suggests such severe poverty as to cause abjectness, or a loss of self-respect —*ANT.* **wealth, affluence**

pov·er·ty-strick·en (-strik′'n) *adj.* **1.** stricken with poverty; very poor **2.** characteristic of, or giving the appearance of, poverty

pow[1] (pō, pou) *n.* [Chiefly Scot.] *same as* POLL (sense 1)

pow[2] (pou) *interj.* an exclamation suggesting the sound of a shot, explosion, etc.

POW, P.O.W. prisoner of war

pow·der (pou′dər) *n.* [ME. *poudre* < OFr. < L. *pulvis* (gen. *pulveris*), dust: see POLLEN] **1.** any dry substance in the form of very fine, dustlike particles, produced by crushing, grinding, etc. **2.** a specific kind of powder [*bath powder,* face *powder*] **3.** *a)* a drug in the form of powder *b)* a dose of this **4.** *a) same as* GUNPOWDER *b)* [prob. in reference to swift explosion of powder] a sudden or impulsive rush: obs. or Brit. dial. except in phrase ☆**take a powder** [Slang] to run away; leave —*vt.* **1.** to sprinkle or cover with or as with powder **2.** to apply cosmetic powder to (the body, face, etc.) **3.** to make into powder; pulverize —*vi.* **1.** to be made into powder **2.** to use powder as a cosmetic —**keep one's powder dry** [in reference to gunpowder] [Slang] to be ready for action —**pow′der·er** *n.*

powder blue pale blue —**pow′der-blue′** *adj.*

powder burn a skin burn caused by gunpowder exploding at close range

pow·dered sugar (pou′dərd) granulated sugar ground into a powder

powder flask a small, flat case for carrying gunpowder

powder horn a container made of an animal's horn, for carrying gunpowder

☆**powder keg 1.** a small barrel used to store gunpowder **2.** a potential source of violence, war, disaster, etc

powder metallurgy the science or process of working metals and alloys by reducing them to powder and shaping this into solids under great heat and pressure

powder monkey 1. formerly, a boy who carried powder from the magazine to the guns aboard a man-of-war ☆**2.** a man who works with explosives, as in oil fields

powder puff a soft pad for applying cosmetic powder

powder room ☆a lavatory for women

pow·der·y (pou′dər ē) *adj.* **1.** of, like, or in the form of, powder **2.** easily crumbled into powder **3.** covered with or as with powder; dusty

☆**powdery mildew 1.** any of an order (Erysiphales) of ascomycetous fungi that are parasites on the surfaces of higher plants and produce closed fruiting bodies in a powdery mass **2.** a plant disease caused by a powdery mildew

pow·er (pou′ər) *n.* [ME. *pouer* < OFr. *poeir,* earlier *poter,* orig. inf. < VL. **potere,* to be able, for L. *posse,* to be able: see POTENT] **1.** ability to do, act, or produce **2.** a specific ability or faculty [the *power* of hearing] **3.** great ability to do, act, or affect strongly; vigor; force; strength **4.** *a)* the ability to control others; authority; sway; influence *b)* [*pl.*] special authority assigned to or exercised by a person or group holding office *c)* legal ability or authority; also, a document giving it **5.** a source of physical or

mechanical force or energy; force or energy that is at, or can be put to, work [electric *power*, water *power*] **6.** the capacity to exert physical force or energy, specif. in terms of the rate at which it is or can be exerted [60-watt *power*, 200 *horsepower*] **7.** a person or thing having great influence, force, or authority **8.** a nation, esp. one having influence or domination over other nations [the great *powers*] **9.** national might or political strength **10.** a spirit or divinity **11.** [Dial.] a large number or quantity (of something specified) **12.** *a)* [Archaic] an armed force; army; navy *b)* military strength [*air power*] **13.** *Math. a)* the product of the multiplication of a quantity by itself [4 is the second *power* of 2 (2²)] *b) same as* EXPONENT (sense 3) **14.** *Optics* the degree of magnification of a lens, microscope, telescope, etc., expressed as a ratio of the diameters of image and object —*vt.* to supply with power or with a source of power —*adj.* **1.** operated by electricity, a fuel engine, etc. [*power* tools, a *power* mower] **2.** served by an auxiliary, engine-powered system that reduces the effort of the operation [*power* steering] **3.** carrying electricity [*power* lines] —**in power 1.** in authority or control **2.** in office —**the powers that be** the persons in control

SYN.—**power** denotes the inherent ability or the admitted right to rule, govern, determine, etc. [the limited *power* of a president]; **authority** refers to the power, because of rank or office, to give commands, enforce obedience, make decisions, etc. [the *authority* of a teacher]; **jurisdiction** refers to the power to rule or decide within certain defined limits [the *jurisdiction* of the courts]; **dominion** implies sovereign or supreme authority [*dominion* over a dependent state]; **sway** stresses the predominance or sweeping scope of power [the Romans held *sway* over the ancient world]; **control**, in this connection, implies authority to regulate, restrain, or curb [under the *control* of a guardian]; **command** implies such authority that enforces obedience to one's orders [in *command* of a regiment] See also STRENGTH

☆**pow·er·boat** (-bōt′) *n. same as* MOTORBOAT

power dive *Aeron.* a dive speeded by engine power, as by a fighter plane —**pow′er-dive′** *vi.*, *vt.* **-dived′, -div′ing**

pow·er·ful (-fəl) *adj.* having much power; strong, mighty, influential, effective, etc. —*adv.* [Dial.] very —**pow′er·ful·ly** *adv.* —**pow′er·ful·ness** *n.*

☆**pow·er·house** (-hous′) *n.* **1.** a building where electric power is generated **2.** [Colloq.] a person, team, etc. of great strength, energy, drive, etc.

pow·er·less (-lis) *adj.* without power; weak, feeble, impotent, unable, not empowered, etc. —**pow′er·less·ly** *adv.* —**pow′er·less·ness** *n.*

power of appointment the authority granted by one person to another by deed or will to dispose of the former's property

power of attorney a written statement legally authorizing a person to act for one

power pack a unit, as of a radio or TV amplifier, that converts the power-line or battery voltage to the voltages required by the various elements

power plant 1. the entire apparatus serving as the source of power for some particular operation [the *power plant* of an automobile] ☆**2.** a building where power, esp. electric power, is generated

☆**power play** an offensive play or move, as in sports, in which force is concentrated in one spot or area

power politics international political relations in which each nation attempts to increase its own power and interests by using military or economic coercion

power series an infinite series whose terms contain successive, positive, integral powers of a variable

☆**power structure** those persons or groups in a nation, city, organization, etc. who through economic, social, and institutional position constitute the actual ruling power

power takeoff an accessory unit on a truck, tractor, etc. permitting the engine power to be used to operate other equipment, as a saw

Pow·ha·tan (pou′ə tan′) 1550?–1618; Algonquian Indian chief in E Va.: father of POCAHONTAS

☆**pow·wow** (pou′wou′) *n.* [< AmInd. (Algonquian) *powwaw*, priest, orig., prob. "he dreams"] **1.** a North American Indian medicine man or priest **2.** among North American Indians, a ceremony to conjure the cure of disease, success in war, etc., marked by feasting, dancing, etc. **3.** a conference of or with North American Indians **4.** [Colloq.] any conference or gathering —*vi.* **1.** to hold a powwow **2.** [Colloq.] to confer

Pow·ys (pō′is) name of three Eng. brothers: **1. John Cowper,** 1872–1963; novelist & critic **2. Llewelyn,** 1884–1939; author **3. T(heodore) F(rancis),** 1875–1953; novelist

pox (päks) *n.* [for *pocks* < ME. *pokkes*, pl. of *pokke:* see POCK] **1.** any of various diseases characterized by skin eruptions, as smallpox or chicken pox **2.** syphilis

Po·yang Hu (pō′yäŋ′ hōō′) lake in Kiangsi province, SE China: c. 1,000 sq. mi.

Poz·nań (pôz′nän′y′) city in W Poland, on the Warta River: pop. 436,000

poz·zuo·la·na (pät′swə lä′nə) *n.* [It. < L. *puteolana* (*pulvie*), (powder of) *Puteoli* (now It. *Pozzuoli*), site of the

quarries] **1.** a volcanic rock, powdered and used in making a hydraulic cement **2.** any of a variety of natural and artificial substances added to cement to lend particular properties Also **poz·zo·lan** (pät′sə län′), **poz′zo·la′na** (-lä′nä) —**poz′zuo·la′nic** *adj.*

Poz·zuo·li (pôt tswô′lē) seaport in S Italy: pop. 47,000

pp, pp. *Music* pianissimo

pp. 1. pages **2.** past participle **3.** privately printed

P.P., p.p. 1. parcel post **2.** parish priest **3.** past participle **4.** postpaid **5.** prepaid

ppd. 1. postpaid **2.** prepaid

pph. pamphlet

PPI plan position indicator

ppm, p.p.m., PPM parts per million

ppr., p.pr. present participle

P.P.S., p.p.s. [L. *post postscriptum*] an additional post-script

P.Q. 1. previous question **2.** Province of Quebec

Pr *Chem.* praseodymium

Pr. 1. Priest **2.** Prince **3.** Provençal

pr. 1. pair(s) **2.** power **3.** preferred (stock) **4.** present **5.** price **6.** pronoun

P.R. 1. Puerto Rico **2.** proportional representation **3.** public relations: also **PR**

prac·tic (prak′tik) *adj.* [MFr. *practique* < LL. *practicus:* see PRACTICE] *obs. var. of* PRACTICAL

prac·ti·ca·ble (prak′ti kə b′l) *adj.* [altered (after PRACTICE) < Fr. *praticable* < *pratiquer*] **1.** that can be done or put into practice; feasible [a *practicable* plan] **2.** that can be used; usable; useful [a *practicable* tool] —*SYN.* see POSSIBLE, PRACTICAL —**prac′ti·ca·bil′i·ty, prac′ti·ca·ble·ness** *n.* —**prac′ti·ca·bly** *adv.*

prac·ti·cal (prak′ti k′l) *adj.* [PRACTIC + -AL] **1.** of, exhibited in, or obtained through practice or action [*practical* knowledge] **2.** *a)* that can be used; workable; useful and sensible [*practical* proposals] *b)* designed for use; utilitarian **3.** concerned with the application of knowledge to useful ends, as distinguished from theory, speculation, etc. [*practical* science] **4.** given to, or experienced from, actual practice [a *practical* farmer] **5.** of, concerned with, or dealing realistically and sensibly with everyday activities, work, etc. **6.** that is so in practice, whether or not in theory, law, etc.; virtual **7.** matter-of-fact; prosaic —**prac′ti·cal′i·ty** (-kal′ə tē), *pl.* **-ties, prac′ti·cal·ness** *n.*

SYN.—**practical** stresses effectiveness as tested by actual experience or as measured by a completely realistic approach to life or the particular circumstances involved; **practicable** is used of something that appears to be capable of being put into effect, but has not yet been developed or tried [before the era of electronics, television did not seem *practicable*; today it is put into effect, the *practical* applications of the science] —*ANT.* **impractical, impracticable**

practical joke a trick played on someone, esp. to his discomfiture, but meant in fun —**practical joker**

prac·ti·cal·ly (prak′tik lē, -tik ′l ē) *adv.* **1.** in a practical manner **2.** from a practical viewpoint **3.** for all practical purposes; in effect; virtually [*practically* a dictator] **4.** [Colloq.] almost; nearly

☆**practical nurse** a nurse with less training than a registered nurse, often one licensed by the State (**licensed practical nurse**) for certain specified nursing duties

prac·tice (prak′tis) *vt.* **-ticed, -tic·ing** [ME. *practisen* < MFr. *practiser*, altered < *practiquer* < ML. *practicare* < LL. *practicus* < Gr. *praktikos*, concerning action, practical < *prassein*, to do] **1.** to do or engage in frequently or usually; make a habit or custom of [to *practice* thrift] **2.** to do repeatedly in order to learn or become proficient; exercise or drill oneself in [to *practice* batting] **3.** to put into practice; specif., *a)* to use one's knowledge of; work at, esp. as a profession [to *practice* law] *b)* to observe, or adhere to (beliefs, ideals, etc.) [to *practice* one's religion] **4.** to teach or train through practice; exercise —*vi.* **1.** to do something repeatedly in order to learn or acquire proficiency; exercise or drill oneself [to *practice* on the organ] **2.** to put knowledge into practice; work at or follow a profession, as medicine, law, etc. **3.** [Archaic] to scheme; intrigue —*n.* **1.** the act, result, etc. of practicing; specif., *a)* a frequent or usual action; habit; usage [to make a *practice* of being early] *b)* a usual method or custom; convention [the *practice* of tipping for services] **2.** *a)* repeated mental or physical action for the purpose of learning or acquiring proficiency *b)* the condition of being proficient or skillful as a result of this [to be out of *practice*] **3.** the doing of something as an application of knowledge [the *practice* of a theory] **4.** *a)* the exercise of a profession or occupation [the *practice* of law] *b)* a business based on this, often regarded as a legal property [to buy another's law *practice*] **5.** [Archaic] intrigue, trickery, a scheme, etc. **6.** *Law* the various procedures involved in legal work, in and out of courts —**prac′tic·er** *n.*

SYN.—**practice** implies repeated performance for the purpose of learning or acquiring proficiency [he *practiced* on the violin every day, *practice* makes perfect]; **exercise** implies a putting to or keeping at work [to *exercise* one's rights] or refers to activity, often of a systematic formal kind, that trains or develops the body or

mind [gymnastic *exercises*]; **drill** suggests disciplined group training in which something is taught by constant repetition [to *drill* a squad, an arithmetic *drill*] See also HABIT

prac·ticed (-tist) *adj.* **1.** proficient through practice; experienced; skilled **2.** learned or perfected by practice

practice teacher *same as* STUDENT TEACHER —**practice teaching**

☆**prac·ti·cum** (prak′ti kəm) *n.* [G. *praktikum* < LL. *practicum*, neut. of *practicus*, active: see PRACTICE] a course or group session emphasizing the practical application of theory, esp. one in which a student gains practical experience in a field of study

prac·tise (-tis) *vt.*, *vi.* -**tised**, -**tis·ing** *chiefly Brit. sp.* of PRACTICE

prac·ti·tion·er (prak tish′ə nər) *n.* [< earlier *practician*, one qualified by practice (< MFr. *practicien*: see PRACTICE & -IAN) + -ER] **1.** a person who practices a profession, art, etc. [a medical *practitioner*] ☆**2.** a Christian Science healer

prae- (prē) [L.: see PRE-] *same as* PRE-: the preferred form in certain words, as *praenomen*, *praetor*, etc.

prae·di·al (prē′dē əl) *adj.* [ML. *praedialis* < L. *praedium*, a farm, estate < *praes*, a surety: see PRESS²] **1.** of or relating to land or stationary property; landed **2.** associated with farming; agrarian **3.** owing service as a tenant of land

prae·fect (prē′fekt) *n. same as* PREFECT

prae·mu·ni·re (prē′myoo nī′rē) *n.* [short for ML. *praemunire* (*facias*), (*we owe to it*) that you warn, used for L. *praemonere*, to forewarn < *prae-*, before (see PRE-) + *monere*, to warn (see MONITOR)] *Eng. Law* **1.** the offense of accepting the authority of the Pope, or some other power, over that of the Crown **2.** a writ charging this offense

prae·no·men (prē nō′mən) *n.*, *pl.* -**no′mens**, -**nom′i·na** (-näm′i nə) [L.: see PRE- & NAME] the first or personal name of an ancient Roman, preceding the nomen and cognomen (Ex.: *Marcus* Tullius Cicero) —**prae·nom′i·nal** (-näm′i n'l) *adj.*

prae·tor (prēt′ər) *n.* [ME. (northern) *pretour* < L. < *praeire*, to precede < *prae-*, before (see PRE-) + *ire*, to go] a magistrate of ancient Rome, next below a consul in rank —**prae·to·ri·al** (pri tôr′ē əl) *adj.* —**prae·tor·ship′** *n.*

prae·to·ri·an (pri tôr′ē ən) *adj.* **1.** of a praetor **2.** [*often* P-] designating, of, or like the bodyguard (**Praetorian Guard**) of a Roman commander or emperor —*n.* **1.** a man with the rank of a praetor, or an ex-praetor **2.** [*often* P-] a member of the Praetorian Guard

prag·mat·ic (prag mat′ik) *adj.* [L. *pragmaticus*, skilled in business or law < Gr. *pragmatikos* < *pragma*, business, orig. a thing done < *prassein*, to do] **1.** [Rare] *a*) busy or active, esp. in a meddlesome way *b*) dogmatic; opinionated **2.** having to do with the affairs of a state or community **3.** concerned with actual practice, everyday affairs, etc., not with theory or speculation; practical **4.** dealing with historical facts, esp. in their causal relationship **5.** of or having to do with philosophical pragmatism Also, for senses 1, 3, & 5, **prag·mat′i·cal** —*n. same as* PRAGMATIC SANCTION —**prag·mat′i·cal·ly** *adv.*

prag·mat·ics (-iks) *n.pl.* [*with sing. v.*] the branch of semiotic dealing with the relationships of signs and symbols to their users

pragmatic sanction any of various royal decrees that had the force of fundamental law

prag·ma·tism (prag′mə tiz′m) *n.* **1.** the quality or condition of being pragmatic ☆**2.** a method or tendency in philosophy, started by C. S. Peirce and William James, which determines the meaning and truth of all concepts and tests their validity by their practical results —**prag′ma·tist** *n.*, *adj.* —**prag′ma·tis′tic** *adj.*

Prague (präg) capital of Czechoslovakia, on the Vltava River: pop. 1,025,000: Czech name **Pra·ha** (prä′hä)

☆**prai·rie** (prer′ē) *n.* [Fr., meadowland < OFr. *praerie* < *pré*, a meadow (< L. *pratum*, prob. < IE. base *prā-*, to bend, whence MIr. *ráith*, a fortification, W. *bedd-rod*, grave) + -*erie*, -ERY] a large area of level or slightly rolling grassland, esp. one in the Mississippi Valley

☆**prairie chicken** either of two large, brown and white, henlike grouse (genus *Tympanuchus*) with a short, rounded tail, found on the N. American prairies and along the Gulf coast: also **prairie hen**

☆**prairie dog** any of a number of related small, squirrellike, burrowing rodents (genus *Cynomys*) of N. America, having a barking cry and living in large colonies

☆**prairie oyster** [Colloq.] **1.** a drink made with a raw egg and seasoning, as Worcestershire sauce, taken as a remedy for hangover **2.** [*pl.*] the testicles of a bull calf cooked as food

Prairie Provinces Canad. provinces of Manitoba, Saskatchewan, & Alberta

☆**prairie schooner** a large covered wagon used by pioneers to cross the American prairies

☆**prairie soil** any of a zonal group of dark, heavy-textured soils, developed under tall grass

PRAIRIE DOG
(15 in. long, including tail)

cover in a temperate, relatively humid climate with moderate rainfall

☆**prairie turnip** *same as* BREADROOT

☆**prairie wolf** *same as* COYOTE

praise (prāz) *vt.* **praised**, **prais′ing** [ME. *praisen* < OFr. *preisier* < LL. *pretiare* < L. *pretium*, worth, PRICE] **1.** orig., to set a price on; appraise **2.** to commend the worth of; express approval or admiration of **3.** to laud the glory of (God, etc.), as in song; glorify; extol —*n.* **1.** a praising or being praised; commendation or glorification **2.** [Archaic] a reason or basis for praise —**sing someone's praise** (or **praises**) to praise someone highly —**prais′er** *n.*

SYN.—**praise** is the simple, basic word implying an expression of approval, esteem, or commendation [to *praise* one's performance]; **laud** implies great, sometimes extravagant praise [the critics *lauded* the actor to the skies]; **acclaim** suggests an outward show of strong approval, as by loud applause, cheering, etc. [he was *acclaimed* the victor]; **extol** implies exalting or lofty praise [the scientist was *extolled* for his work]; **eulogize** suggests formal praise in speech or writing, as on a special occasion [the minister *eulogized* the exemplary life of the deceased]

praise·wor·thy (-wur′thē) *adj.* worthy of praise; laudable; commendable —**praise′wor′thi·ly** *adv.* —**praise′wor′thi·ness** *n.*

Pra·krit (prä′krit) *n.* [< Sans. *prākṛta*, natural, simple, vulgar < *pra-* (for IE. base *per-*, before + *kṛ*, to do, make: contrast SANSKRIT] any of several vernacular, non-Sanskrit, Old Indic languages used in ancient India

☆**pra·line** (prā′lēn; *chiefly South*, prä′-) *n.* [Fr., after Marshal Duplessis-*Praslin* (1598–1675), whose cook is said to have invented it] any of various confections made of nuts, sugar, etc., as *a*) a crisp candy made of a pecan, almond, etc. browned in boiling sugar *b*) a soft or crisp candy patty made of pecans and brown sugar, maple syrup, etc.

prall·tril·ler (präl′tril′ər) *n.* [G. < *prallen*, to rebound + *triller*, a trill < It. *trillo*: see TRILL] *same as* INVERTED MORDENT: see MORDENT

pram¹ (präm) *n.* [Du. *praam* < MLowG. *prom* < Czech *prám*, ult. < IE. base *per-*, to go (see FARE), whence FERRY] a small, flat-bottomed boat with square ends

pram² (pram) *n.* [Brit. Colloq.] a perambulator

prance (prans, präns) *vi.* **pranced**, **pranc′ing** [ME. *prauncen* < ?] **1.** to rise up on the hind legs in a lively way, esp. while moving along: said of a horse **2.** to ride on a prancing horse **3.** to move about in a way suggestive of a prancing horse; caper **4.** to move or go gaily or arrogantly; swagger; strut —*vt.* to cause (a horse) to prance —*n.* **1.** an act or instance of prancing **2.** a prancing movement —**pranc′er** *n.* —**pranc′ing·ly** *adv.*

pran·di·al (pran′dē əl) *adj.* [< L. *prandium*, late breakfast, luncheon < *pram-*, early (prob. < IE. *prm-* < base *per*, beyond, whence FIRST, FROM) + *ed-*, base of *edere*, to EAT + -AL] of a meal, esp. dinner

prang (praŋ) *vt.*, *vi.* [echoic] [Chiefly Brit. Slang] **1.** to cause (an aircraft, vehicle, etc.) to crash **2.** to collide with **3.** to make by crashing **4.** to bomb heavily —*n.* [Chiefly Brit. Slang] **1.** a collision **2.** a bombing raid

prank¹ (praŋk) *n.* [Early ModE. < ? or akin ? to ff.] a mischievous trick or practical joke —**prank′ster** *n.*

prank² (praŋk) *vt.* [Early ModE., prob. < LowG. source, as in Du. *pronken*, to make a show] to dress or adorn showily —*vi.* to dress up or make a show

prank·ish (praŋ′kish) *adj.* **1.** full of pranks; mischievous or frolicsome **2.** like a prank —**prank′ish·ly** *adv.* —**prank′ish·ness** *n.*

prase (prāz) *n.* [Fr. < L. *prasius* < Gr. *prasios*, leek-green < *prason*, leek, akin to L. *porrum*, leek] a translucent, leek-green variety of chalcedony

pra·se·o·dym·i·um (prā′zē ō dim′ē əm, -sē-) *n.* [ModL. < Gr. *prasios*, green (see prec.) + (DI)DYMIUM] a silvery, malleable, metallic chemical element of the rare-earth group, whose salts are generally green in color: symbol, Pr; at. wt., 140.907; at. no., 59; sp. gr., 6.78; melt. pt., 935°C; boil. pt., 3127°C

prat (prat) *n.* [< ?] [Slang] the buttocks

prate (prāt) *vi.* **prat′ed**, **prat′ing** [ME. *praten* < MDu. *praten*, prob. of echoic origin] to talk much and foolishly; chatter —*vt.* to tell or repeat idly; blab —*n.* idle talk; chatter —**prat′er** *n.* —**prat′ing·ly** *adv.*

☆**prat·fall** (prat′fôl′) *n.* [Slang] a fall on the buttocks, esp. one for comic effect, as in burlesque

prat·in·cole (prat′in kōl′, prat′n-) *n.* [ModL. *pratincola* < L. *pratum*, meadow (see PRAIRIE) + *incola*, inhabitant < *in-*, IN-¹ + *colere*, to till: see CULT] any of a genus (*Glareola*) of small, old-world, swallowlike or ploverlike shore birds with long, pointed wings and a forked tail; esp., a common pratincole (*Glareola pratincola*) of Africa, S Europe, and SW Asia

pra·tique (pra tēk′, prat′ik) *n.* [Fr. < *pratiquer* < MFr. *practiquer*: see PRACTICE] permission to do business at a port, granted to a ship that has complied with quarantine or health regulations

Pra·to (prä′tō) commune in Tuscany, C Italy, near Florence: pop. 127,000

prat·tle (prat′'l) *vi.*, *vt.* -**tled**, -**tling** [MLowG. *pratelen*, akin to MDu. *praten*, PRATE] **1.** *same as* PRATE **2.** to speak in a childish way; babble —*n.* **1.** idle chatter **2.** childish babble —**prat′tler** *n.*

prau (prou, prä′ōō) *n. same as* PROA

prawn (prôn) *n.* [ME. *prane* < ?] any of a number of related edible, shrimplike crustaceans; esp., any of a larger variety of shrimp —*vi.* to fish for prawns —**prawn′er** *n.*

prax·is (prak′sis) *n.* [ML. < Gr. *praxis* < *prassein*, to do] 1. practice, as distinguished from theory, of an art, science, etc. 2. established practice; custom 3. a set of examples or exercises, as in grammar

Prax·it·e·les (prak sit′ə lēz′) [L. < Gr. *Praxitelēs*] 4th cent. B.C.; Athenian sculptor

pray (prā) *vt.* [ME. *preien* < OFr. *preier* < LL. *precare*, for L. *precari* < *prex* (gen. *precis*), prayer < IE. base *prek-*, var. of *perk-*, question: cf. POSTULATE] 1. orig., to implore or beseech: now seldom used except as the elliptical form of "I pray you" *[pray tell me]* 2. to ask for by prayer or supplication; beg for imploringly 3. to recite (a prayer) 4. to bring about, get, etc. by praying —*vi.* 1. to ask very earnestly; make supplication, as to a deity 2. to worship God, as by reciting certain set formulas —*SYN.* see APPEAL

prayer[1] (prer) *n.* [ME. *preiere* < OFr. < ML. *precaria* < L. *precaria*, obtained by begging < *precari*, to entreat: see prec.] 1. the act or practice of praying, as to God 2. an earnest request; entreaty; supplication 3. *a)* a humble and sincere request to God or a god *b)* an utterance to God in praise, thanksgiving, confession, etc. *c)* any set formula for praying, as to God 4. [*often pl.*] in some religions, a devotional service consisting chiefly of prayers 5. any spiritual communion with God 6. something prayed for or requested, as in a petition ☆7. [Slang] a chance to succeed *[he doesn't have a prayer]*

pray·er[2] (prā′ər) *n.* a person who prays

prayer beads *same as* ROSARY

prayer book 1. a book of formal religious prayers 2. [P- B-] *same as* BOOK OF COMMON PRAYER

prayer·ful (prer′fəl) *adj.* 1. given to frequent praying; devout 2. like or expressive of prayer —**prayer′ful·ly** *adv.* —**prayer′ful·ness** *n.*

prayer shawl *same as* TALLITH

prayer wheel a revolving drum with written prayers, used by Tibetan Buddhists, like a rosary, in counting prayers

praying mantis *same as* MANTIS

pre- (prē; also, *unstressed*, pri, prə) [ME. < OFr. & L.: L. *prae-* < *prae*, before, in front of < IE. *prai*, var. of base *per*, beyond, whence FORE, FIRST] *a prefix meaning:* 1. before in time, earlier (than), prior (to) *[presuppose, prewar]* 2. before in place, in front (of), anterior (to) *[preaxial]* 3. before in rank, superior, surpassing *[preeminent]* 4. preliminary to, in preparation for *[preschool]* Cf. PRAE-

preach (prēch) *vi.* [ME. *prechen* < OFr. *precher* < LL.(Ec.) *praedicare*, to preach the gospel < L., to proclaim, declare in public < *prae-*, PRE- + *dicare*, to proclaim, akin to *dicere*, to say: see DICTION] 1. to speak in public on religious matters; give a sermon 2. to give moral or religious advice, esp. in a tiresome manner —*vt.* 1. to expound or proclaim by preaching 2. to advocate by or as by preaching; urge strongly or persistently 3. to deliver (a sermon)

preach·er (prē′chər) *n.* [ME. *prechur*] a person who preaches; esp., a clergyman

preach·i·fy (-chə fī′) *vi.* -fied′, -fy′ing [Colloq.] to preach or moralize in a tiresome manner

preach·ment (prēch′mənt) *n.* [ME. *prechement* < OFr. < LL. *praedicamentum*: cf. PREDICAMENT] a preaching or sermon, esp. a long, tiresome one

preach·y (prē′chē) *adj.* **preach′i·er, preach′i·est** [Colloq.] given to or marked by preaching, or moralizing

pre·am·ble (prē′am′b'l, prē am′-) *n.* [ME. < MFr. *preambule* < ML. *praeambulum*, neut. of LL. *praeambulus*, going before < L. *praeambulare*, to precede < *prae-*, before + *ambulare*, to go] 1. an introduction, esp. one to a constitution, statute, etc., stating its reason and purpose 2. an introductory fact, event, etc.; preliminary —*SYN.* see INTRODUCTION

pre·am·pli·fi·er (prē am′plə fī′ər) *n.* in a radio, phonograph, etc., an auxiliary amplifier for boosting the voltage of a weak signal before it reaches the input of the main amplifier

pre·ar·range (prē′ə rānj′) *vt.* -ranged′, -rang′ing to arrange beforehand —**pre′ar·range′ment** *n.*

pre·ax·i·al (prē ak′sē əl) *adj. Anat.* situated in front of the axis of the body or a limb; esp., of the radial side of the arm or the tibial side of the leg

preb·end (preb′ənd) *n.* [ME. *prebende* < MFr. < ML. (Ec.) *prebenda* < LL. *praebenda*, state support to a private person < neut. pl. gerundive of L. *praebere*, to grant < *prae-*, before + *habere*, to have] 1. the part of the revenues of a cathedral or collegiate church paid as a clergyman's salary 2. the property or tax that yields such revenue

3. *same as* PREBENDARY —**pre·ben·dal** (pri ben′d'l) *adj.*

preb·en·dar·y (preb′ən der′ē) *n., pl.* **-dar′ies** [ME. *prebendarie* < ML. *praebendarius*] 1. a person receiving a prebend 2. in the Church of England, an honorary canon with only the title of a prebend

prec. preceding

Pre·cam·bri·an (prē kam′brē ən) *adj.* designating or of the earliest geologic era covering all the time before the Cambrian Period, often divided into a **Late Precambrian Era** and an **Early Precambrian Era** —**the Precambrian** the Precambrian Era or its rocks: see GEOLOGY, chart

pre·can·cel (-kan′s'l) *vt.* -celed or -celled, -cel·ing or -cel·ling to cancel (a postage stamp) before use in mailing: chiefly in the past participle —*n.* a precanceled stamp —**pre·can′cel·la′tion** *n.*

pre·can·cer·ous (-kan′sər əs) *adj.* that may or is likely to become cancerous *[a precancerous mole]*

pre·car·i·ous (pri ker′ē əs) *adj.* [L. *precarius*: see PRAYER[1]] 1. orig., dependent upon the will or favor of another person 2. dependent upon circumstances; uncertain; insecure *[a precarious living]* 3. dependent upon chance; risky *[a precarious foothold]* 4. dependent upon mere assumption; unwarranted *[a precarious assertion]* —**pre·car′i·ous·ly** *adv.* —**pre·car′i·ous·ness** *n.*

precast concrete concrete in the form of blocks, pillars, bridge sections, etc. that have been cast into form before being put into position

prec·a·to·ry (prek′ə tôr′ē) *adj.* [LL. *precatorius* < L. *precari*, to PRAY] of, having the nature of, or expressing entreaty: also **prec′a·tive** (-tiv)

pre·cau·tion (pri kô′shən) *n.* [Fr. *précaution* < LL. *praecautio* < L. *praecautus*, pp. of *praecavere* < *prae-*, before (see PRE-) + *cavere*, to take care: for IE. base see HEAR] 1. care taken beforehand; caution used in advance 2. a measure taken beforehand against possible danger, failure, etc. —**pre·cau′tion·ar′y** *adj.*

pre·ca·va (prē′kā′və, -kä′-) *n., pl.* **-vae** (-vē) [PRE- + (VENA) CAVA] the superior vena cava of four-limbed vertebrates —**pre·ca′val** *adj.*

pre·cede (pri sēd′) *vt.* -ced·ed, -ced·ing [ME. *preceden* < MFr. *préceder* < L. *praecedere*: see PRE- & CEDE] 1. to be, come, or go before in time, place, order, rank, or importance 2. to introduce with prefatory remarks, etc. —*vi.* to be, come, or go before

prec·e·dence (pres′ə dəns, pri sēd′'ns) *n.* [< PRECEDENT] 1. the act, right, or fact of preceding in time, place, order, or importance 2. priority as because of superiority in rank 3. an official or conventional ranking of dignitaries in order of importance Also **prec′e·den·cy**

prec·e·dent (pri sēd′'nt; *for n.*, pres′ə dənt) *adj.* [ME. < MFr. *précédent* < L. *praecedens*, prp. of *praecedere*, to PRECEDE] that precedes; preceding —*n.* 1. an act, statement, legal decision, case, etc. that may serve as an example, reason, or justification for a later one 2. existing practice resulting from earlier precedents

prec·e·den·tial (pres′ə den′shəl) *adj.* 1. of, having the nature of, or serving as a precedent 2. having precedence; preliminary

pre·ced·ing (pri sēd′in) *adj.* that precedes; going or coming before —*SYN.* see PREVIOUS

pre·cen·sor (prē′sen′sər) *vt.* to determine arbitrarily in advance what may or may not be permitted in (books, motion pictures, news releases, etc.) —**pre′cen·sor′ship** *n.*

pre·cen·tor (pri sen′tər) *n.* [LL. *praecentor* < L. *praecinere*, to sing or play before: see PRE- & CHANT] a person who directs a church choir or congregation in singing —**pre·cen·to·ri·al** (prē′sen tôr′ē əl) *adj.* —**pre·cen′tor·ship′** *n.*

pre·cept (prē′sept) *n.* [ME. < L. *praeceptum* < *praecipere*, to admonish, teach < *prae-*, before (see PRE-) + *capere*, to take] 1. a commandment or direction meant as a rule of action or conduct 2. a rule of moral conduct; maxim 3. a rule or direction, as for doing something technical 4. *Law* a written order; warrant; writ —*SYN.* see DOCTRINE

pre·cep·tive (pri sep′tiv) *adj.* [LL. *praeceptivus*] 1. of, having the nature of, or expressing a precept 2. giving precepts; instructive; didactic —**pre·cep′tive·ly** *adv.*

pre·cep·tor (-sep′tər) *n.* [L. *praeceptor* < *praecipere*: see PRECEPT] 1. a teacher 2. the head of a preceptory —**pre·cep·to·ri·al** (prē′sep tôr′ē əl) *adj.* —**pre·cep′tor·ship′** *n.* —**pre·cep′tress** *n.fem.*

pre·cep·to·ry (pri sep′tər ē) *n., pl.* **-ries** [ML. *praeceptoria*, estate of a preceptor < L. *praeceptor*: see PRECEPT] 1. a provincial community or religious house of the medieval Knights Templars, subordinate to the London Temple 2. its estates

pre·cess (pri ses′) *vi.* [back-formation < ff.] to move by precession

pre·ces·sion (pri sesh′ən) *n.* [ME. < LL. *praecessio* < L. *praecedere*, to PRECEDE] 1. the act of preceding; precedence 2. *Astron.* clipped form of PRECESSION OF THE EQUINOXES 3. *Mech.* an effect exhibited by a spinning body, as a top, when an applied torque tends to change the direction of its rotational axis, causing this axis generally to describe a cone and to turn at right angles to the direction of the torque —**pre·ces′sion·al** *adj.*

precession of the equinoxes *Astron.* the occurrence of the equinoxes earlier in each successive sidereal year, caused by the gradual westward movement of the equinoctial points along the ecliptic as the result of the change in direction of the earth's axis as it turns around the axis of the ecliptic so as to describe a complete cone approximately every 25,800 years: precession is the result of the attraction of the sun and the moon upon protuberances about the earth's equator

pre·cinct (prē'siŋkt) *n.* [ME. *precincte* < ML. *praecinctum* < L. *praecinctus*, pp. of *praecingere*, to encompass < *prae*-, before (see PRE-) + *cingere*, to surround, gird (see CINCH)] 1. [*usually pl.*] an enclosure between buildings, walls, etc.; specif., [Chiefly Brit.] the grounds immediately surrounding a religious house or church 2. [*pl.*] environs; a neighborhood ☆3. *a*) a division of a city, as for police administration *b*) a subdivision of a ward, as for voting purposes 4. any limited area, as of thought 5. a boundary

pre·ci·os·i·ty (presh'ē äs'ə tē) *n., pl.* **-ties** [ME. *preciousite* < MFr. *preciosité* < L. *pretiositas* < *pretiosus*: see ff.] great fastidiousness, overrefinement, or affectation, esp. in language

pre·cious (presh'əs) *adj.* [ME. < OFr. *precios* < L. *pretiosus* < *pretium*, a PRICE] 1. of great price or value; costly 2. of great desirability; held in high esteem [*precious rights*] 3. beloved; dear 4. very fastidious, overrefined, or affected, as in behavior, language, etc. 5. very great [a *precious* liar] —*adv.* [Colloq.] very —**pre'cious·ly** *adv.* —**pre'cious·ness** *n.*

precious stone a rare and costly gem

prec·i·pice (pres'ə pis) *n.* [Fr. *précipice* < L. *praecipitium* < *praeceps*, headlong < *prae*-, before (see PRE-) + *caput*, a head (see CHIEF)] 1. a vertical, almost vertical, or overhanging rock face; steep cliff 2. a greatly hazardous situation, verging on disaster

pre·cip·i·tan·cy (pri sip'ə tan sē) *n., pl.* **-cies** quality, fact, or instance of being precipitate; great haste; rashness: also **pre·cip'i·tance**

pre·cip·i·tant (-tənt) *adj.* [L. *praecipitans*, prp. of *praecipitare*: see ff.] *same as* PRECIPITATE —*n.* a substance which, when added to a solution, causes the formation of a precipitate —**pre·cip'i·tant·ly** *adv.*

pre·cip·i·tate (pri sip'ə tāt'; *also, for adj. & n.*, -tit) *vt.* **-tat'ed**, **-tat'ing** [< L. *praecipitatus*, pp. of *praecipitare* < *praeceps*: see PRECIPICE] 1. to throw headlong; hurl downward 2. to cause to happen before expected, warranted, needed, or desired; bring on; hasten [to *precipitate* a crisis] 3. *Chem.* to cause (a slightly soluble substance) to become insoluble, as by heat or a chemical reagent, and separate out from a solution 4. *Meteorol.* to condense (vapor, etc.) and cause to fall as rain, snow, sleet, etc. —*vi.* 1. *Chem.* to be precipitated 2. *Meteorol.* to condense and fall as rain, snow, sleet, etc. —*adj.* [L. *praecipitatus*: see the *v.*] 1. falling steeply, rushing headlong, flowing swiftly, etc. 2. acting, happening, or done very hastily or rashly; impetuous; headstrong 3. very sudden, unexpected, or abrupt —*n.* [ModL. *praecipitatum*] a substance that is precipitated out from a solution —*SYN.* see SUDDEN —**pre·cip'i·tate·ly** *adv.* —**pre·cip'i·tate·ness** *n.* —**pre·cip'i·ta'tive** *adj.* —**pre·cip'i·ta'tor** *n.*

pre·cip·i·ta·tion (pri sip'ə tā'shən) *n.* [MFr. *précipitation* < L. *praecipitatio*] 1. a precipitating or being precipitated; specif., a headlong fall or rush 2. precipitancy; rash haste; impetuosity 3. a bringing on suddenly; acceleration 4. *Chem. a*) a precipitating or being precipitated from a solution *b*) a precipitate 5. *Meteorol. a*) a depositing of rain, snow, sleet, etc. *b*) rain, snow, sleet, etc. *c*) the amount of this

pre·cip·i·tin (pri sip'ə tin) *n.* [PRECIPIT(ATE) + -IN¹] an antibody produced in the blood of an animal injected with a soluble antigen: when the antigen is added to blood serum from such an animal, a precipitate forms

pre·cip·i·tin·o·gen (pri sip'ə tin'ə jən) *n.* [prec. + -o- + -GEN] the antigen that produces a precipitin —**pre·cip'i·tin'o·gen'ic** (-jen'ik) *adj.*

pre·cip·i·tous (pri sip'ə təs) *adj.* [MFr. *precipiteux* < LL. *praecipitosus* < L. *praeceps*: see PRECIPICE] 1. steep like a precipice; sheer 2. having precipices 3. *same as* PRECIPITATE —*SYN.* see STEEP¹ —**pre·cip'i·tous·ly** *adv.* —**pre·cip'i·tous·ness** *n.*

pré·cis (prā sē', prā'sē) *n., pl.* **pré·cis** (-sēz', -sēz) [Fr.: see ff.] a concise abridgment; summary; abstract —*vt.* to make a précis of

pre·cise (pri sīs') *adj.* [MFr. *precis* < L. *praecisus*, pp. of *praecidere*, to cut off, be brief < *prae*-, before (see PRE-) + *caedere*, to cut (see -CIDE)] 1. strictly defined; accurately stated; definite 2. speaking definitely or distinctly 3. with no variation; minutely exact [the *precise* amount] 4. *a*) that strictly conforms to usage, etc.; scrupulous; fastidious *b*) too fastidious; finicky —*SYN.* see CORRECT, EXPLICIT —**pre·cise'ness** *n.*

pre·cise·ly (-lē) *adv.* in a precise manner; exactly: also an affirmative reply, equivalent to "I agree"

pre·ci·sian (pri sizh'ən) *n.* a person who is strict and precise in observing rules or customs, esp. of religion; specif., a 16th- or 17th-cent. English Puritan

pre·ci·sion (pri sizh'ən) *n.* [Fr. < L. *praecisio*, a cutting off] 1. the quality of being precise; exactness; accuracy; definiteness 2. the degree of this —*adj.* 1. characterized by precision, as in measurement, operation, etc. 2. requiring low tolerance, as in manufacturing

precision bombing the dropping of bombs on narrowly defined targets, using bombsights for maximum accuracy

pre·ci·sion·ist (-ist) *n.* a person who attaches great or too great importance to precision

pre·clin·i·cal (prē klin'i k'l) *adj. Med.* of or in the period of a disease before any of the symptoms appear

pre·clude (pri klo͞od') *vt.* **-clud'ed**, **-clud'ing** [L. *praecludere*, to shut off < *prae*-, before (see PRE-) + *claudere*, to CLOSE²] to make impossible, esp. in advance; shut out; prevent —*SYN.* see PREVENT —**pre·clu'sion** (-klo͞o'zhən) *n.* —**pre·clu'sive** (-siv) *adj.* —**pre·clu'sive·ly** *adv.*

pre·co·cial (-kō'shəl) *adj.* [< ModL. *praecoces* (< L., pl. of *praecox*), precocial birds + -AL] designating or of birds whose newly hatched young are covered with down and fully active: opposed to ALTRICIAL

pre·co·cious (-kō'shəs) [< L. *praecox* < *praecoquere*, to boil beforehand < *prae*-, before (see PRE-) + *coquere*, to mature, COOK] 1. developed or matured to a point beyond that which is normal for the age [a *precocious* child] 2. of or showing premature development —**pre·co'cious·ly** *adv.* —**pre·co'cious·ness**, **pre·coc'i·ty** (-käs'ə tē) *n.*

pre·cog·ni·tion (prē'käg nish'ən) *n.* [LL. *praecognitio* < L. *praecognitus*, pp. of *praecognoscere*, to foreknow < *prae*-, PRE- + *cognoscere*, to know: see COGNITION] the supposed perception of an event, condition, etc. before it occurs, esp. by extrasensory powers —**pre·cog'ni·tive** (-nə tiv) *adj.*

pre-Co·lum·bi·an (-kə lum'bē ən) *adj.* of any period in the Western Hemisphere before Columbus discovered America

pre·con·ceive (prē'kən sēv') *vt.* **-ceived'**, **-ceiv'ing** to form a conception or opinion of beforehand

pre·con·cep·tion (-sep'shən) *n.* [ML. *preconceptio*] 1. the act of preconceiving 2. a preconceived idea or opinion 3. bias or prejudice

pre·con·cert (-kən surt') *vt.* [PRE- + CONCERT, *v.*] to arrange or settle beforehand, as by agreement

pre·con·di·tion (-kən dish'ən) *vt.* to prepare (someone or something) to behave, react, etc. in a certain way under certain conditions —*n.* a condition required beforehand if something else is to occur, be done, etc.

pre·co·nize (prē'kə nīz') *vt.* **-nized'**, **-niz'ing** [ME. *preconisen* < ML. *praeconizare* < L. *praeco* (gen. *praeconis*), public crier < *praedicator*, a proclaimer: see PREACHER) + LL. *-izare*, -IZE] 1. to proclaim or extol in public 2. to approve and announce the name of (a new bishop) publicly: said of the Pope

pre·con·scious (prē kän'shəs) *adj. Psychoanalysis* of or pertaining to that part of a person's mental activity which is not immediately conscious, but which can be easily recalled —**the preconscious** preconscious mental activity: see also CONSCIOUS

pre·con·tract (prē kän'trakt; *for v., usually* prē'kän trakt') *n.* a previous contract, as, formerly, of marriage —*vt.* 1. formerly, to betroth beforehand 2. to agree to by advance contract

pre·cook (-kook') *vt.* to cook partially or completely, for final preparation at a later time

pre·cool (prē kool') *vt.* to cool or refrigerate before packing or shipment

pre·crit·i·cal (-krit'i k'l) *adj.* [PRE- + CRITICAL] coming before a critical period

pre·cur·sor (pri kur'sər) *n.* [L. *praecursor* < *praecurrere*, to run ahead: see PRE- & CURRENT] 1. a person or thing that goes before; forerunner; harbinger 2. a predecessor, as in office 3. a substance that precedes and is the source of another substance —*SYN.* see FORERUNNER

pre·cur·so·ry (-sə rē) *adj.* [L. *praecursorius*] 1. serving as a precursor, or harbinger; indicating something to follow 2. introductory; preliminary

pred. predicate

pre·da·cious, **pre·da·ceous** (pri dā'shəs) *adj.* [< L. *praedari*, to prey upon (< *praeda*: see PREY) + -ACEOUS] preying on other animals; predatory —**pre·dac'i·ty** (-das'ə tē), **pre·da'cious·ness**, **pre·da'ceous·ness** *n.*

pre·date (prē dāt') *vt.* **-dat'ed**, **-dat'ing** 1. to date before the actual date 2. to come before in date

pre·da·tion (pri dā'shən) *n.* [L. *praedatio* < *praedatus*, pp. of *praedari*, to plunder < *praeda*, PREY] 1. the act of plundering or preying 2. the method of existence of predatory animals

pred·a·tor (pred'ə tər) *n.* a predatory person or animal

pred·a·to·ry (pred'ə tôr'ē) *adj.* [L. *praedatorius* < *praeda*, a PREY] 1. of, living by, or characterized by plundering, robbing, or exploiting others 2. living by capturing and feeding upon other animals; predacious —**pred'a·to'ri·ly** *adv.* —**pred'a·to'ri·ness** *n.*

pre·de·cease (prē'di sēs') *vt., vi.* **-ceased'**, **-ceas'ing** to die before (someone else or, rarely, some event)

pred·e·ces·sor (pred'ə ses'ər, pred'ə ses'ər; *chiefly Brit.*, prē'di-) *n.* [ME. *predecessour* < MFr. *predecesseur* < LL. *praedecessor* < L. *prae-*, before (see PRE-) + *decessor*, retiring officer < *decessus*, pp. of *decedere*, to go away, depart < *de-*, from + *cedere*, to go: see CEDE] 1. a person who precedes or preceded another, as in office 2. a thing replaced by another thing, as in use 3. [Now Rare] an ancestor; forefather

pre·des·ig·nate (prē dez'ig nāt') *vt.* -nat'ed, -nat'ing to designate beforehand —**pre·des'ig·na'tion** *n.*

pre·des·ti·nar·i·an (prē des'tə ner'ē ən) *adj.* [PREDESTIN(ATE) + -ARIAN] of or believing in predestination —*n.* a person who believes in predestination —**pre·des'ti·nar'i·an·ism** *n.*

pre·des·ti·nate (prē des'tə nit; *for v.,* -nāt') *adj.* [ME. *predestynate* < L. *praedestinatus,* pp. of *praedestinare,* to PREDESTINE] predestinated or foreordained —*vt.* -nat'ed, -nat'ing **1.** *Theol.* to foreordain by divine decree or intent **2.** *same as* PREDESTINE —**pre·des'ti·na'tor** *n.*

pre·des·ti·na·tion (prē des'tə nā'shən) *n.* [ME. *predestinacioun* < LL.(Ec.) *praedestinatio*] **1.** *Theol.* the doctrine that *a)* God foreordained everything that would happen *b)* God predestines certain souls to salvation and others, esp. in Calvinism, others to damnation **2.** a predestinating or being predestinated; destiny; fate

pre·des·tine (prē des'tin) *vt.* -tined, -tin·ing [ME. *predestynen* < L. *praedestinare,* to predestine: see PRE- & DESTINE] to destine or decree beforehand; foreordain

pre·de·ter·mine (prē'di tur'mən) *vt.* -mined, -min·ing [LL.(Ec.) *praedeterminare:* see PRE- & DETERMINE] **1.** to determine, decide, or decree beforehand **2.** to incline, bias, or impel beforehand; prejudice —**pre'de·ter'mi·nate** (-mə nit) *adj.* —**pre'de·ter'mi·na'tion** *n.*

pre·di·al (prē'dē əl) *adj. same as* PRAEDIAL

pred·i·ca·ble (pred'i kə b'l) *adj.* [ML. *praedicabilis* < L., praiseworthy < *praedicare:* see PREACH] capable of being predicated —*n.* **1.** something predicable **2.** *Logic* any of the several sorts of predicate that can be used of a subject, as, in Aristotelian logic, genus, species, difference, property, and accident —**pred'i·ca·bil'i·ty, pred'i·ca·ble·ness** *n.* —**pred'i·ca·bly** *adv.*

pre·dic·a·ment (pri dik'ə mənt) *n.* [ME. < LL.(Ec.) *praedicamentum* < L. *praedicare:* see PREACH] **1.** a condition or situation, now specif. one that is difficult, unpleasant, embarrassing, or, sometimes, comical **2.** *same as* CATEGORY (sense 2) —**pre·dic'a·men'tal** (-men't'l) *adj.*

SYN.—**predicament** implies a complicated, perplexing situation from which it is difficult to disentangle oneself; **dilemma** implies a predicament necessitating a choice between equally disagreeable alternatives; **quandary** emphasizes a state of great perplexity and uncertainty; **plight** emphasizes a distressing or unfortunate situation; **fix** and **pickle** are both colloquial terms loosely interchangeable with any of the preceding, although more precisely **fix** is equivalent to **predicament** and **pickle,** to **plight**

pred·i·cant (pred'i kənt) *adj.* [L. *praedicans,* prp. of *praedicare:* see PREACH] preaching —*n.* a preacher; esp., formerly, a Dominican friar

pred·i·cate (pred'i kāt'; *for n. and adj.,* -kit) *vt.* -cat'ed, -cat'ing [L. *praedicatus,* pp. of *praedicare:* see PREACH] **1.** orig., to proclaim; preach; declare; affirm **2.** to affirm as a quality, attribute, or property of a person or thing [*to predicate* the honesty of another's motives]; specif., *Logic* to assert (something) about the subject of a proposition **3.** to affirm or base (something *on* or *upon* given facts, arguments, conditions, etc.) **4.** to imply or connote —*vi.* to make an affirmation or statement —*n.* [ML. *praedicatum,* neut. of *praedicatus:* see the *v.*] **1.** *Gram. a)* the verb or verbal phrase, including any complements, objects, and modifiers, that is one of the two immediate constituents of a sentence or clause *b)* in a generative grammar, the infinite set of expression that constitutes the verb phrase (**VP**) in the rule stating that a sentence consists of a noun phrase followed by a verb phrase **2.** *Logic* something that is affirmed or denied about the subject of a proposition (Ex.: *green* in "grass is green") —*adj. Gram.* of, having the nature of, or involved in a predicate [a *predicate* noun or adjective] —**pred'i·ca'tion** *n.* —**pred'i·ca'tive** *adj.* —**pred'i·ca'tive·ly** *adv.*

pred·i·ca·to·ry (-kə tôr'ē) *adj.* [LL.(Ec.) *praedicatorius,* praising, laudatory < *praedicare:* see PREACH] of or having to do with preaching

pre·dict (pri dikt') *vt., vi.* [< L. *praedictus,* pp. of *praedicere* < *prae-,* before (see PRE-) + *dicere,* to tell: see DICTION] to state (what one believes will happen); foretell (a future event or events —*SYN.* see FORETELL —**pre·dict'a·bil'i·ty** *n.* —**pre·dict'a·ble** *adj.* —**pre·dict'a·bly** *adv.* —**pre·dic'tive** *adj.* —**pre·dic'tive·ly** *adv.* —**pre·dic'tor** *n.*

pre·dic·tion (pri dik'shən) *n.* [L. *praedictio*] **1.** a predicting or being predicted **2.** the thing predicted or foretold

pre·di·gest (prē'di jest', -dī-) *vt.* to digest beforehand; specif., to treat (food) as with enzymes for easier digestion when eaten —**pre'di·ges'tion** *n.*

pre·di·lec·tion (pred''l ek'shən, prēd'-) *n.* [Fr. *prédilection* < ML. *predilectus,* pp. of *prediligere,* to prefer < L. *prae-,* before (see PRE-) + *diligere,* to prefer: for IE. base see LOGIC] a preconceived liking; partiality or preference (*for*) —*SYN.* see PREJUDICE

pre·dis·pose (prē'dis pōz') *vt.* -posed', -pos'ing to dispose, or make receptive, beforehand; make susceptible [fatigue *predisposes* one to illness]

pre·dis·po·si·tion (prē'dis pə zish'ən, prē dis'-) *n.* the condition of being predisposed; inclination or tendency; predilection; susceptibility

☆**pred·ni·sone** (pred'nə sōn') *n.* [< *pre(gnane),* a steroid hydrocarbon (< PREGNANT + -ANE: found in urine during pregnancy) + D(I)-[1] + -(E)N(E) + (CORT)ISONE] a chemical derivative, $C_{21}H_{26}O_5$, of cortisone, but with fewer side effects, used in the treatment of arthritis and certain allergic and inflammatory disorders

pre·dom·i·nant (pri däm'ə nənt) *adj.* [Fr. *prédominant* < ML. *predominans,* prp. of *predominari:* see PRE- & DOMINANT] **1.** having ascendancy, authority, or dominating influence over others; superior **2.** most frequent, noticeable, etc.; prevailing; preponderant —*SYN.* see DOMINANT —**pre·dom'i·nance, pre·dom'i·nan·cy** *n., pl.* -cies —**pre·dom'i·nant·ly** *adv.*

pre·dom·i·nate (-nāt'; *for adj.,* -nit) *vi.* -nat'ed, -nat'ing [< ML. *predominatus,* pp. of *predominari:* see PRE- & DOMINATE] **1.** to have ascendancy, authority, or dominating influence (*over* others); hold sway **2.** to be dominant in amount, number, etc.; prevail; preponderate —*adj. same as* PREDOMINANT —**pre·dom'i·nate·ly** *adv.* —**pre·dom'i·na'tion** *n.* —**pre·dom'i·na'tor** *n.*

pre·e·lec·tion (prē'i lek'shən) *adj.* occurring before an election —*n.* a choice made in advance Also **pre'e·lec'tion**

☆**pree·mie** (prē'mē) *n.* [altered < PREM(ATURE) + -IE] [Colloq.] a prematurely born infant, esp. one weighing less than 5 1/2 pounds

pre·em·i·nent, pre-em·i·nent (prē em'ə nənt) *adj.* [ME. < L. *praeeminens,* prp. of *praeeminere,* to project forward: see PRE- & EMINENCE] eminent above others; excelling others, esp. in a particular quality; prominent; surpassing: also **pre·ëm'i·nent** —*SYN.* see DOMINANT —**pre·em'i·nence, pre-em'i·nence** *n.* —**pre·em'i·nent·ly, pre-em'i·nent·ly** *adv.*

☆**pre·empt, pre-empt** (-empt') *vt.* [back-formation < ff.] **1.** to acquire (public land) by preemption **2.** to seize before anyone else can, excluding others; appropriate beforehand **3.** *Radio & TV* to replace (a regularly scheduled program) —☆*vi. Bridge* to make a preemptive bid Also **pre·ëmpt'** —**pre·emp'tor, pre-emp'tor** *n.*

☆**pre·emp·tion, pre-emp·tion** (-emp'shən) *n.* [< ML. *preemptus,* pp. of *preemere,* to buy beforehand < L. *prae-,* before (see PRE-) + *emere,* to buy: see REDEEM] **1.** the act or right of buying land, etc. before, or in preference to, others; esp., such a right granted to a settler on public land **2.** action taken to check other action beforehand Also **pre·ëmp'tion**

pre·emp·tive, pre-emp·tive (-emp'tiv) *adj.* **1.** of or having to do with preemption **2.** *Bridge* designating a high bid intended to shut out opposing bids Also **pre·ëmp'tive** —**pre·emp'tive·ly, pre-emp'tive·ly** *adv.*

preen (prēn) *vt.* [ME. *preynen,* altered (after ME. *preonen,* to prick with a pin < *preon* < OE. *preon,* a pin) < *proinen,* to PRUNE²] **1.** to clean and trim (the feathers) with the beak: said of birds **2.** to make (oneself) trim; dress up or adorn (oneself) **3.** to show satisfaction with or vanity in (oneself) —*vi.* to dress up in a fussy way; prink or primp —**preen'er** *n.*

pre·es·tab·lish, pre-es·tab·lish (prē'ə stab'lish) *vt.* to establish in advance: also **pre'es·tab'lish**

pre·ex·il·ic, pre-ex·il·ic (prē'ig zil'ik, -ik sil'-) *adj.* [< PRE- + L. *exilium,* exile + -IC] of that period of Jewish history preceding the Babylonian Exile (6th cent. B.C.): also **pre'ëx·il'ic, pre'ex·il'i·an, pre'-ex·il'i·an, pre'ëx·il'i·an**

pre·ex·ist, pre-ex·ist (-ig zist') *vt., vi.* [LL. *praeexistere*] to exist previously or before (another person or thing): also **pre'ëx·ist'** —**pre'ex·ist'ence, pre'-ex·ist'ence** *n.* —**pre'ex·ist'ent, pre'-ex·ist'ent** *adj.*

pref. 1. preface **2.** prefatory **3.** preference **4.** preferred **5.** prefix

pre·fab (prē'fab') *n.* [Colloq.] a prefabricated building

pre·fab·ri·cate (prē fab'rə kāt') *vt.* -cat'ed, -cat'ing **1.** to fabricate beforehand **2.** to construct in standardized sections for shipment and quick assembly [a *prefabricated* house] —**pre'fab·ri·ca'tion** *n.*

pref·ace (pref'is) *n.* [ME. *prefas* < MFr. < ML. *prefatia,* for L. *praefatio* < *prae-,* before (see PRE-) + *fatus,* pp. of *fari,* to speak: see FAME] **1.** [*usually* P-] *R.C.Ch.* the introduction to the Canon of the Mass, ending with the Sanctus **2.** an introductory statement to an article, book, or speech, telling its subject, purpose, plan, etc. **3.** something preliminary or introductory; prelude —*vt.* -aced, -ac·ing **1.** to furnish or introduce with a preface **2.** to be or serve as a preface to; begin —*SYN.* see INTRODUCTION

pref·a·to·ry (pref'ə tôr'ē) *adj.* [< L. *praefatus* (see PREFACE) + -ORY] of, like, serving as, or given as a preface; introductory: also **pref'a·to'ri·al** —**pref'a·to'ri·ly** *adv.*

pre·fect (prē'fekt) *n.* [ME. *prefecte* < OFr. < L. *praefectus,* pp. of *praeficere,* to set over: see PRE- & -FY] **1.** in ancient Rome, any of various high-ranking officials or chief magistrates in charge of governmental or military departments **2.** in modern times, any of various administrative officials; specif., *a)* the head of a department of France *b)* the chief of the Paris police *c)* the head of a nome in Greece **3.** in some private schools, esp. in England, a senior student with authority to discipline

---

fat, āpe, cär; ten, ēven; is, bīte; gō, hôrn, tōōl, look; oil, out; up, fur; get; joy; yet; chin; she; thin, *then*; zh, leisure; ŋ, ring; ə for *a* in *ago,* e in *agent, i* in *sanity, o* in *comply, u* in *focus;* ' as in *able* (ā'b'l); Fr. bâl; ë, Fr. coeur; ö, Fr. feu; Fr. mon; ô, Fr. coq; ü, Fr. duc; r, Fr. cri; H, G. ich; kh, G. doch. See inside front cover. ☆Americanism; ‡foreign; *hypothetical; <derived from

pre·fec·ture (prē'fek chər) *n.* [L. *praefectura*] the office, authority, territory, or residence of a prefect —**pre·fec'·tur·al** (-chər əl) *adj.*

pre·fer (pri fur') *vt.* -ferred', -fer'ring [ME. *preferren* < MFr. *preferer* < L. *praeferre*, to place before < *prae-*, PRE- + *ferre*, BEAR[1]] 1. to put before someone else in rank, office, etc.; promote; advance 2. to put before a magistrate, administrator, court, etc. for consideration, sanction, or redress [to *prefer* charges against an attacker] 3. to put before something or someone else in one's liking, opinion, etc.; like better 4. to give preference or priority to (a creditor, etc.) —*SYN.* see CHOOSE —**pre·fer'rer** *n.*

pref·er·a·ble (pref'ər ə b'l, pref'rə-) *adj.* to be preferred; more desirable —**pref'er·a·bil'i·ty, pref'er·a·ble·ness** *n.* —**pref'er·a·bly** *adv.*

pref·er·ence (-əns, -rəns) *n.* [MFr. *préférence* < ML. *praeferentia* < L. *praeferens*, prp. of *praeferre*, to PREFER] 1. a preferring or being preferred; greater liking 2. the right, power, or opportunity of prior choice or claim 3. something preferred; one's first choice 4. *a)* a giving of priority or advantage to one person, country, etc. over others, as in payment of debts or granting of credit *b)* such priority or advantage —*SYN.* see CHOICE

pref·er·en·tial (pref'ə ren'shəl) *adj.* [ML. *praeferentia* (see prec.) + -AL] 1. of, having, giving, or receiving preference 2. offering or allowing a preference [a *preferential* ballot] ☆3. designating a union shop which gives preference, as by contract, to union members in hiring, layoffs, etc. 4. receiving preferences, as in tariffs —**pref'er·en'tial·ism** *n.* —**pref'er·en'tial·ly** *adv.*

preferential voting a system of voting in which the voter indicates an order of preference for several candidates

pre·fer·ment (pri fur'mənt) *n.* 1. the act of preferring 2. an advancement in rank or office; promotion 3. an office, rank, or honor to which a person is advanced

☆**preferred stock** stock on which dividends must be paid before those of common stock: it usually also receives preference in the distribution of assets

pre·fig·u·ra·tion (prē'fig yə rā'shən, prē fig'-) *n.* 1. the act of prefiguring 2. something in which something else is prefigured; prototype

pre·fig·ure (prē fig'yər) *vt.* -ured, -ur·ing [ME. *prefiguren* < LL.(Ec.) *praefigurare* < L. *prae-*, PRE- + *figurare*, to fashion: see FIGURE] 1. to suggest beforehand; be an antecedent figure or type of; foreshadow 2. to picture to oneself, or imagine, beforehand —**pre·fig'ur·a·tive** (-yər ə tiv) *adj.* —**pre·fig'ur·a·tive·ly** *adv.* —**pre·fig'ur·a·tive·ness** *n.* —**pre·fig'ure·ment** *n.*

pre·fix (prē'fiks; *also, for v.,* prē fiks') *vt.* [ME. *prefyxen* < MFr. *prefixer* < L. *praefixus*, pp. of *praefigere* < *prae-*, before (see PRE-) + *figere*, to FIX] 1. to fix to the beginning of a word, etc.; esp., to add as a prefix 2. [Rare] to fix beforehand —*n.* [ModL. *praefixum* < neut. of L. *praefixus*: see the *v.*] 1. a syllable, group of syllables, or word united with or joined to the beginning of another word to alter its meaning or create a new word [*pre-* is a *prefix* added to *cool* to form *precool*] 2. a title before a person's name, as *Dr.* 3. an identifying letter or number placed before another number, etc. —**pre'fix·al** *adj.* —**fix'al·ly** *adv.* —**pre·fix'ion** *n.*

pre·flight (prē'flīt') *adj.* coming before a flight or the flying of aircraft [*preflight* instructions]

pre·form (prē fôrm') *vt.* to form in advance

pre·for·ma·tion (prē'fôr mā'shən) *n.* 1. previous formation 2. *Biol.* a former theory that every germ cell contains every part of the future organism in miniature, development being merely growth in size

pre·fron·tal (prē frunt'']) *adj.* of, pertaining to, or situated near the front of a structure of the brain or of the head of a vertebrate [the *prefrontal* lobe]

pre·gan·gli·on·ic (-gaŋ'glē än'ik) *adj. Zool.* of or pertaining to nerve fibers going from the spinal cord to sympathetic ganglia

preg·na·ble (preg'nə b'l) *adj.* [altered (after PREGNANT) < ME. *prenable* < MFr. *prenable* < *prendre*, to take < L. *prehendere*: see PREHENSILE] 1. that can be captured, as a fortress 2. that can be attacked or injured; assailable or vulnerable —**preg'na·bil'i·ty** *n.*

preg·nan·cy (preg'nən sē) *n., pl.* -cies the condition, quality, or period of being pregnant

preg·nant (preg'nənt) *adj.* [ME. *preignant* < L. *pregnans* (gen. *pregnantis*), heavy with young < *prae-*, PRE- (see PRE-) + base of OL. *gnasci*, to be born: see NATURE] 1. having (an) offspring developing in the uterus; that has conceived; with young or with child 2. mentally fertile; prolific of ideas; inventive 3. productive of results; fruitful [a *pregnant* cause] 4. full of or rich in meaning, significance, etc. 5. filled (*with*) or rich (*in*); abounding —**preg'nant·ly** *adv.*

pre·heat (prē hēt') *vt.* to heat beforehand

pre·hen·sile (pri hen's'l; *chiefly Brit.,* -sīl) *adj.* [Fr. *préhensile* < L. *prehensus*, pp. of *prehendere*, to take < *prae-*, PRE- + IE. base *ghend-*, *ghed-*, to grasp, whence GET, BEGET] adapted for seizing or grasping, esp. by wrapping or folding around something, as the tail of a monkey —**pre·hen·sil'i·ty** (prē'hen sil'ə tē) *n.*

pre·hen·sion (-shən) *n.* [L. *prehensio*] 1. the act of seizing or grasping 2. mental apprehension

pre·his·tor·ic (prē'his tôr'ik, -tär'-) *adj.* of the period

before recorded history: also **pre'his·tor'i·cal** —**pre'his·tor'i·cal·ly** *adv.*

pre·his·to·ry (prē his'tə rē) *n.* 1. history before recorded history, as learned from archaeology, etc. 2. the background of incidents, etc. leading to an event, crisis, etc.

pre·ig·ni·tion (prē'ig nish'ən) *n.* in an internal-combustion engine, ignition occurring before the intake valve is closed or before compression is at a maximum

pre·judge (prē juj') *vt.* -judged', -judg'ing [Fr. *préjuger* < L. *praejudicare*: see PRE- & JUDGE] to judge beforehand, prematurely, or without all the evidence —**pre·judg'er** *n.* —**pre·judg'ment, pre·judge'ment** *n.*

prej·u·dice (prej'ə dis) *n.* [ME. < MFr. < L. *praejudicium* < *prae-*, before (see PRE-) + *judicium*, judgment < *judex* (gen. *judicis*), JUDGE] 1. a judgment or opinion formed before the facts are known; preconceived idea, favorable or, more usually, unfavorable 2. *a)* a judgment or opinion held in disregard of facts that contradict it; unreasonable bias [a *prejudice* against modern art] *b)* the holding of such judgments or opinions 3. suspicion, intolerance, or irrational hatred of other races, creeds, regions, occupations, etc. 4. injury or harm resulting as from some judgment or action of another or others —*vt.* -diced, -dic·ing 1. to injure or harm, as by some judgment or action 2. to cause to have or show prejudice; bias —**without prejudice (to)** 1. without detriment or injury 2. *Law* without dismissal of or detriment to (a legal right, claim, etc.) *SYN.*—**prejudice** implies a preconceived and unreasonable judgment or opinion, usually an unfavorable one marked by suspicion, fear, intolerance, or hatred [the murder was motivated by race *prejudice*]; **bias** implies a mental leaning in favor of or against someone or something [few of us are without *bias* of any kind]; **partiality** implies an inclination to favor a person or thing because of strong fondness or attachment [the conductor has a *partiality* for the works of Brahms]; **predilection** implies a preconceived liking, formed as a result of one's background, temperament, etc., that inclines one to a particular preference [he has a *predilection* for murder mysteries]

prej·u·di·cial (prej'ə dish'əl) *adj.* causing prejudice, or harm; injurious —**prej·u·di'cial·ly** *adv.*

prel·a·cy (prel'ə sē) *n., pl.* -cies [ME. *prelacie* < ML.(Ec.) *praelatia*] 1. *a)* the office or rank of a prelate *b)* prelates collectively Also **prel'a·ture** (-chər) 2. church government by prelates: often a hostile term: also **prel'a·tism** (-it iz'm)

prel·ate (-it) *n.* [ME. *prelat* < OFr. < LL.(Ec.) *praelatus*, prelate, orig., ruler < pp. of L. *praeferre*, to place before, PREFER] a high-ranking ecclesiastic, as a bishop —**prel'ate·ship'** *n.* —**pre·lat·ic** (pri lat'ik) *adj.*

pre·lect (pri lekt') *vi.* [< L. *praelectus*, pp. of *praelegere*, to read before, lecture: see PRE- & LECTURE] to lecture in public —**pre·lec'tion** *n.* —**pre·lec'tor** *n.*

pre·li·ba·tion (prē'lī bā'shən) *n.* [LL. *praelibatio* < L. *praelibare* < *prae-*, PRE- + *libare*, to taste] [Rare] a tasting beforehand; foretaste

pre·lim (prē'lim, pri lim') *n.* [Slang] *clipped form of* PRELIMINARY

prelim. preliminary

pre·lim·i·nar·y (pri lim'ə ner'ē) *adj.* [< Fr. *préliminaire* or ModL. *praeliminaris* < L. *prae-* (see PRE-) + L. *liminaris*, of a threshold < *limen*, threshold: see LIMEN] coming before or leading up to the main action, discussion, business, etc.; introductory; prefatory; preparatory —*n., pl.* -nar·ies [Fr. *préliminaires*, pl.] [*often pl.*] 1. a preliminary step, procedure, arrangement, etc. 2. *a)* a preliminary examination *b)* a contest or match before the main one —**pre·lim'i·nar'i·ly** *adv.*

pre·lit·er·ate (prē lit'ər it) *adj.* [PRE- + LITERATE] of or belonging to a society not developed to the stage of having a written language

prel·ude (prel'yōōd, prāl'-; prā'lōōd, prē'-) *n.* [Fr. *prélude* < ML. *praeludium* < L. *praeludere*, to play beforehand < *prae-*, PRE- + *ludere*, to play < *ludus*: see LUDICROUS] 1. anything serving as the introduction to a principal event, action, performance, etc.; preliminary part; preface; opening 2. *Music a)* an introductory section or movement of a suite, fugue, etc. *b)* since the 19th cent., any short romantic composition —*vt., vi.* -ud·ed, -ud·ing [L. *praeludere*] 1. to serve as or be a prelude (*to*) 2. to introduce by or play (as) a prelude —**pre·lu·di·al** (prā lōō'dē əl, prē-) *adj.*

pre·lu·sion (pri lōō'zhən) *n.* [L. *praelusio* < *praelusus*, pp. of *praeludere*: see prec.] *rare var. of* PRELUDE (sense 1) —**pre·lu'sive, pre·lu'so·ry** (-sə rē) *adj.* —**pre·lu'sive·ly, pre·lu'so·ri·ly** *adv.*

prem. premium

pre·mar·i·tal (prē mar'ə t'l) *adj.* before marriage

pre·ma·ture (prē'mə toor', -choor', -tyoor') *adj.* [L. *praematurus*: see PRE- & MATURE] happening, done, arriving, or existing before the proper or usual time; too early; specif., born before the full term of gestation —**pre'ma·ture'ly** *adv.* —**pre'ma·tu'ri·ty, pre'ma·ture'ness** *n.*

pre·max·il·la (prē'mak sil'ə) *n., pl.* -lae (-ē) [ModL.: see PRE- & MAXILLA] either of two bones in the upper jaw of vertebrates, situated between and in front of the maxillae, and fusing with them in the adult human being —**pre·max'il·lar'y** (-mak'sə ler'ē) *adj.*

☆**pre·med** (prē'med') *adj. clipped form of* PREMEDICAL —*n.* a premedical student

pre·med·i·cal (prē med'i k'l) *adj.* designating or of the studies preparatory to the study of medicine

pre·med·i·tate (pri med'ə tāt') *vt.* **-tat'ed, -tat'ing** [< L. *praemeditatus,* pp. of *praemeditari:* see PRE- & MEDITATE] to think out, plan, or scheme beforehand [a *premeditated* murder] —*vi.* to think or meditate beforehand —**pre·med'i·ta'ted·ly** *adv.* —**pre·med'i·ta'tive** *adj.* —**pre·med'·i·ta'tor** *n.*

pre·med·i·ta·tion (pri med'ə tā'shən, prē'med-) *n.* **1.** the act of premeditating **2.** *Law* a degree of planning and forethought sufficient to show intent to commit an act

pre·mier (pri mir', -myir'; prē'mē ər; *chiefly Brit.,* prem'yər) *adj.* [ME. *primier* < MFr. *premier* < L. *primarius* < *primus,* first, PRIME] **1.** first in importance or rank; chief; foremost **2.** first in time; earliest —*n.* a chief official; specif., *the title of: a)* the prime minister of any of certain countries *b)* the governor of a Canadian province —**pre·mier'ship** *n.*

pre·mière, pre·miere (pri myer', -myir', -mir', -mē er') *n.* [Fr., fem. of *premier:* see prec.] a first performance or showing of a play, movie, etc. —*adj.* **1.** being the first or leading woman performer, as in a ballet company [*première* danseuse] **2.** same as PREMIER —*vt., vi.* **-miered'** or **-miered', -mier'ing** or **-mier'ing** to exhibit (a play, movie, etc.) for the first time

pre·mil·len·ni·al (prē'mə len'ē əl) *adj.* of or happening in the period before the millennium —**pre'mil·len'ni·al·ly** *adv.*

pre·mil·len·ni·al·ism (-iz'm) *n.* the religious doctrine that the second coming of Christ will occur before the millennium: also **pre'mil·le·nar'i·an·ism** (-mil ə ner'ē ə niz'm) —**pre'mil·le·nar'i·an** *adj., n.* —**pre'mil·len'ni·al·ist** *n.*

prem·ise (prem'is; *for v.,* also pri mīz') *n.* [ME. *premisse* < ML. *praemissa* < L. *praemissus,* pp. of *praemittere,* to send before < *prae-,* before + *mittere,* to send: see PRE- & MISSION] **1.** a previous statement or assertion that serves as the basis for an argument; specif., *Logic* either of the two propositions of a syllogism from which the conclusion is drawn: also sp. **prem'iss:** see SYLLOGISM **2.** [*pl.*] *a)* the part of a deed or lease that states the parties involved, the property in conveyance, and other pertinent facts *b)* the property so mentioned **3.** [*pl.*] a piece of real estate; house or building and its land [keep off the *premises*] —*vt.* **-ised, -is·ing 1.** to postulate beforehand; state as a premise **2.** to introduce or preface (a discourse, etc.) —*vi.* to make a premise —*SYN.* see PRESUME

pre·mi·um (prē'mē əm, prēm'yəm) *n., pl.* **-ums** [L. *praemium,* a reward, recompense < *prae-,* before + *emere,* to take: see PRE- & REDEEM] **1.** a reward or prize, as one offered free or at a special, low price as an added inducement to buy or do something; bonus **2.** an additional amount paid or charged; specif., *a)* an amount paid for a loan in addition to interest *b)* an amount paid, as for stock, above the nominal or par value *c)* additional wages paid as for overtime or dangerous work **3.** a payment; specif., *a)* the amount payable or paid, in one sum or periodically, for an insurance policy *b)* [Now Rare] a fee paid for instruction in a trade, etc. *c)* a fee paid by a borrower of stock to the lender, as in short selling **4.** very high value [to put a *premium* on punctuality] **5.** *Econ.* the amount by which one form of money exceeds another (of the same nominal value) in exchange value, or buying power —*adj.* rated as superior in quality and sold at a higher price —*SYN.* see BONUS, REWARD —**at a premium 1.** at a value or price higher than normal **2.** very valuable, usually because of scarcity

pre·mo·lar (prē mō'lər) *adj.* designating or of any of the bicuspid teeth situated in front of the molars —*n.* a premolar tooth

pre·mon·ish (pri män'ish) *vt., vi.* [PRE- + MONISH] [Rare] to advise or caution beforehand; forewarn

pre·mo·ni·tion (prē'mə nish'ən, prem'ə-) *n.* [MFr. *premonicion* < LL.(Ec.) *praemonitio* < L. *praemonere* < *prae-,* before + *monere,* to warn: see PRE & MONITOR] **1.** a warning in advance; a forewarning **2.** a feeling that something bad will happen; foreboding; presentiment —**pre·mon'i·to·ry** (pri män'ə tôr'ē) *adj.*

pre·morse (pri môrs') *adj.* [L. *praemorsus,* pp. of *praemordere,* to bite off, orig. to bite in front or at the end < *prae-,* before + *mordere,* to bite: see PRE- & MORDANT] ending abruptly and unevenly, as if bitten off: said of a leaf or root

pre·na·tal (prē nāt'l) *adj.* [PRE- + NATAL] existing or taking place before birth —**pre·na'tal·ly** *adv.*

pre·nom·i·nate (prē nam'ə nāt'; *for adj.,* -nit) *vt.* **-nat'ed, -nat'ing** [PRE- + NOMINATE, after L. *praenominare*] [Obs.] to name, or mention, beforehand —*adj.* [Obs.] previously mentioned; forenamed

pre·no·tion (prē nō'shən) *n.* [L. *praenotio* (see PRE- & NOTION), transl. of Gr. *prolēpsis,* PROLEPSIS] [Now Rare] **1.** foreknowledge **2.** a preconceived notion

pren·tice, 'pren·tice (pren'tis) *n.* [ME. *prentis,* aphetic for *aprentis,* APPRENTICE] *archaic var.* of APPRENTICE

pre·nup·tial (prē nup'shəl, -chəl) *adj.* [PRE- + NUPTIAL]

1. before a marriage or wedding **2.** *Zool.* before mating

pre·oc·cu·pan·cy (-äk'yə pən sē) *n., pl.* **-cies 1.** prior occupancy **2.** same as PREOCCUPATION

pre·oc·cu·pa·tion (-äk'yə pā'shən) *n.* [L. *praeoccupatio*] a preoccupying or being preoccupied, esp. mentally

pre·oc·cu·pied (-äk'yə pīd') *adj.* **1.** previously or already occupied **2.** wholly occupied with or absorbed in one's thoughts; engrossed **3.** *Biol.* designating or of a taxonomic name already used and hence no longer available —*SYN.* see ABSENT-MINDED

pre·oc·cu·py (-äk'yə pī') *vt.* **-pied', -py'ing** [MFr. *preoccuper* < L. *praeoccupare:* see PRE- & OCCUPY] **1.** to occupy the thoughts of to the virtual exclusion of other matters; engross; absorb **2.** to occupy or take possession of before someone else or beforehand

pre·or·dain (prē'ôr dān') *vt.* [LL. *praeordinare:* see PRE- & ORDAIN] to ordain or decree beforehand; foreordain —**pre'or·di·na'tion** *n.*

prep (prep) *adj.* ☆[Colloq.] clipped form of PREPARATORY [a *prep* school] —☆*vi.* **prepped, prep'ping** [Colloq.] **1.** to attend a preparatory school **2.** to prepare oneself by study, training, etc. —☆*vt.* to prepare (a person or thing) for something; specif., to prepare (a patient) for surgery

prep. 1. preparation **2.** preparatory **3.** preposition

☆**pre·pack·age** (prē pak'ij) *vt.* **-aged, -ag·ing** to package (foods or other merchandise) in standard weights or units before selling

pre·paid (prē pād') *pt. & pp.* of PREPAY

prep·a·ra·tion (prep'ə rā'shən) *n.* [ME. *preparacion* < MFr. *preparation* < L. *praeparatio*] **1.** the act or process of preparing **2.** the condition of being prepared; readiness **3.** something done to prepare; preparatory measure **4.** something prepared for a special purpose, as a medicine, cosmetic, condiment, etc. **5.** *Music a)* the preparing for a dissonant chord by using the dissonant tone as a consonant tone in the immediately preceding chord *b)* a tone so used —**prep'a·ra'tion·al** *adj.*

pre·par·a·tive (pri par'ə tiv) *adj.* [ME. *preparatif* < MFr. < ML. *praeparativus*] same as PREPARATORY —*n.* **1.** something preparatory **2.** a preparation —**pre·par'a·tive·ly** *adv.*

pre·par·a·to·ry (-tôr'ē) *adj.* [ME. < ML. *praeparatorius*] **1.** that prepares or serves to prepare; preliminary; introductory ☆**2.** undergoing preparation, esp. for college entrance [a *preparatory* student] —**preparatory to** in preparation for —**pre·par'a·to'ri·ly** *adv.*

preparatory school a private secondary school for preparing students to enter college

pre·pare (pri par', -per') *vt.* **-pared', -par'ing** [ME. *preparen* < MFr. *preparer* < L. *praeparare* < *prae-,* before (see PRE-) + *parare,* to set in order, get ready, akin to *parere,* to bring forth, bear: see -PAROUS] **1.** to make ready, usually for a specific purpose; make suitable; fit; adapt; train **2.** to make receptive; dispose; accustom [to *prepare* someone for bad news] **3.** to equip or furnish with necessary provisions, accessories, etc.; fit out [to *prepare* an expedition] **4.** to put together or make out of materials, ingredients, parts, etc., or according to a plan or formula; construct; compound [to *prepare* dinner, to *prepare* a medicine] **5.** *Music* to use (a dissonant tone) in preparation —*vi.* **1.** to make things ready **2.** to make oneself ready —**pre·par'ed·ly** (-id lē) *adv.*

pre·par·ed·ness (-id nis) *n.* the state of being prepared; specif., possession of sufficient armed forces, materiel, etc. for waging war

pre·pay (prē pā') *vt.* **-paid', -pay'ing** to pay or pay for in advance —**pre·pay'ment** *n.*

pre·pense (pri pens') *adj.* [altered < earlier *purpensed* < ME. < OFr. *purpensé,* pp. of *purpenser,* to meditate < *pur-,* pro- + *penser,* to think: see PENSIVE] planned beforehand; premeditated: see MALICE

pre·pon·der·ant (pri pän'dər ənt) *adj.* [L. *praeponderans,* prp.] that preponderates; greater in amount, weight, power, influence, importance, etc.; predominant —*SYN.* see DOMINANT —**pre·pon'der·ance, pre·pon'der·an·cy** *n.* —**pre·pon'der·ant·ly** *adv.*

pre·pon·der·ate (-də rāt') *vi.* **-at'ed, -at'ing** [< L. *praeponderatus,* pp. of *praeponderare* < *prae-,* before + *ponderare,* to weigh < *pondus,* a weight: see POUND[1]] **1.** [Now Rare] to weigh more; be heavier **2.** to sink or incline downward, as a scale of a balance **3.** to surpass in amount, number, power, influence, importance, etc.; predominate —**pre·pon'der·a'tion** *n.*

prep·o·si·tion (prep'ə zish'ən) *n.* [ME. *preposicioun* < L. *praepositio* (< *praepositus,* pp. of *praeponere < prae-,* before + *ponere,* to place: see PRE- & POSITION), transl. of Gr. *prothesis,* PROTHESIS] **1.** in some languages, a relation or function word, as English *in, by, for, with, to,* etc., that connects a lexical word, usually a noun or pronoun, or a syntactic construction, to another element of the sentence, as to a verb (Ex.: he went *to* the store), to a noun (Ex.: the sound *of* loud music), or to an adjective (Ex.: good *for* her) **2.** any construction of similar function (Ex.: *in back of,* equivalent to *behind*) —**prep'o·si'tion·al** *adj.* —**prep'o·si'tion·al·ly** *adv.*

prepositional phrase a phrase consisting of a preposition and its object

pre·pos·i·tive (prē päz′ə tiv) *adj.* [LL. *praepositivus* < L. *praeponere*: see PREPOSITION] *Gram.* put before; prefixed —*n.* a prepositive word —**pre·pos′i·tive·ly** *adv.*

pre·pos·i·tor (-tər) *n.* [altered < L. *praepositus*: see PROVOST] *Brit. var.* of PREFECT (sense 3)

pre·pos·sess (prē′pə zes′) *vt.* 1. orig., to take or occupy beforehand or before another 2. to preoccupy beforehand to the exclusion of later thoughts, feelings, etc. 3. to prejudice or bias, esp. favorably 4. to impress favorably at once —**pre′pos·ses′sion** *n.*

pre·pos·sess·ing (-iŋ) *adj.* that prepossesses, or impresses favorably; pleasing; attractive —**pre′pos·sess′ing·ly** *adv.* —**pre′pos·sess′ing·ness** *n.*

pre·pos·ter·ous (pri päs′tər əs) *adj.* [L. *praeposterus* < *prae-*, before (see PRE-) + *posterus*, coming after < *post*, after: see POST-] 1. orig., with the first last and the last first; inverted 2. so contrary to nature, reason, or common sense as to be laughable; absurd; ridiculous —*SYN.* see ABSURD —**pre·pos′ter·ous·ly** *adv.* —**pre·pos′ter·ous·ness** *n.*

pre·po·ten·cy (prē pōt′'n sē) *n., pl.* -cies [L. *praepotentia*] 1. superiority in power, force, or influence 2. *Biol.* the greater capacity of one parent to transmit certain characters to offspring: a concept now discredited —**pre·po′tent** *adj.*

☆ **pre·prim·er** (prē′prim′ər) *n.* a book designed to be read more easily than a primer

pre·puce (prē′pyōōs) *n.* [ME. < MFr. < L. *praeputium* < *prae-*, PRE- + IE. base **put-*, a swelling, whence Lith. *pusti*, to swell, Byelorussian *potka*, penis] 1. the fold of skin covering the end (glans) of the penis; foreskin 2. a similar fold over the end of the clitoris —**pre·pu′tial** (-pyōō′shəl) *adj.*

Pre-Raph·a·el·ite (prē raf′ē ə līt′, -rä′fē-) *n.* 1. a member of a society of artists (**Pre-Raphaelite Brotherhood**) led by Dante Gabriel Rossetti, W. Holman Hunt, and J. E. Millais, formed in England in 1848 to encourage painting with the fidelity to nature that they considered characteristic of Italian art before Raphael 2. any modern artist with similar aims 3. any Italian painter before Raphael —*adj.* of or characteristic of Pre-Raphaelites —**Pre-Raph′a·el·it′ism** *n.*

pre·re·cord (prē′ri kôrd′) *vt. Radio & TV* to record (an announcement, program, etc.) in advance, for later broadcasting

pre·req·ui·site (pri rek′wə zit) *adj.* required beforehand, esp. as a necessary condition for something following —*n.* something prerequisite

pre·rog·a·tive (pri räg′ə tiv) *n.* [ME. *prerogatif* < MFr. < L. *praerogativa*, called upon to vote first < *praerogare*, to ask before < *prae-*, before + *rogare*, to ask: see ROGATION] 1. a prior or exclusive right or privilege, esp. one peculiar to a rank, class, etc. 2. a distinctively superior advantage 3. [Obs.] priority or precedence —*adj.* of or having a prerogative

Pres. 1. Presbyterian 2. President

pres. 1. present 2. presidency

pre·sa (prā′sə; *It.* pre′sä) *n., pl.* -se (-sā; *It.* -se) [It., lit., a taking up, seizure < pp. of *prendere*, to take < L. *prehendere*: see PREHENSILE] *Music* a sign (:S:, +, ※) showing where each successive voice enters in a canon

pres·age (pres′ij; *for v., usually* pri sāj′) *n.* [ME. < MFr. < L. *praesagium*, a foreboding < *prae-*, before + *sagire*, to perceive: see PRE- & SAGACIOUS] 1. a sign or warning of a future event; omen; portent; augury 2. a foreboding; presentiment 3. [Rare] a prediction 4. foreshadowing quality [*of ominous presage*] —*vt.* -**aged′**, -**ag′ing** [Fr. *présager* < the *n.*] 1. to give a presage, or warning, of; portend 2. to have a foreboding or presentiment of 3. to predict —*vi.* 1. [Rare] to have a presentiment 2. to make a prediction —*SYN.* see FORETELL —**pres·ag′er** *n.*

Presb. Presbyterian

pres·by·cu·sis (prez′bē kyōō′sis, pres′-) *n.* [< Gr. *presbys*, old + (*a*)*kousis*, hearing < *akouein*, to hear: see ACOUSTIC] the gradual loss of acute hearing with advancing age: also **pres′by·cou′sis** (-kōō′sis)

pres·by·o·pi·a (-ō′pē ə) *n.* [ModL. < Gr. *presbys*, old (see PRIEST) + *ōps*, an EYE] a form of farsightedness occurring after middle age, caused by a diminished elasticity of the crystalline lens —**pres′by·ope′** (-ōp′) *n.* —**pres′by·op′ic** (-äp′ik) *adj.*

pres·by·ter (prez′bi tər, pres′-) *n.* [LL.(Ec.), an elder: see PRIEST] 1. in the early Christian church and in the Presbyterian Church, an elder 2. in the Episcopal Church, a priest or minister

pres·byt·er·ate (prez bit′ər it, pres-; -ə rāt′) *n.* [ML.(Ec.) *presbyteratus*] 1. the office of a presbyter 2. a body of presbyters

pres·by·te·ri·al (prez′bə tir′ē əl, pres′-) *adj.* of or having to do with a presbyter or presbytery: also **pres′byt′er·al** (-bit′ər əl) —*n.* [P-] an organization of women connected with a given presbytery of the Presbyterian Church

pres·by·te·ri·an (-ē ən) *adj.* [< LL.(Ec.) *presbyterium*, PRESBYTERY + -AN] 1. having to do with church government by presbyters 2. [P-] designating or of a church of a traditionally Calvinistic Protestant denomination governed by presbyters or elders —*n.* a member of a Presbyterian church —**Pres′by·te′ri·an·ism** *n.*

pres·by·ter·y (prez′bə ter′ē, pres′-) *n., pl.* -ter′ies [ME. *presbetory* < OFr. *presbiterie* < LL.(Ec.) *presbyterium*, council of elders < Gr.(Ec.) *presbyterion* < *presbyteros*, elder: see PRIEST] 1. a body of presbyters; specif., in Presbyterian churches, an ecclesiastical court and governing body made up of all the ministers and a number of elders from all the churches in a district 2. the district of such a court 3. the part of a church reserved for the officiating clergy 4. *R.C.Ch.* [Now Rare] a priest's house; rectory

pre·school (prē′skōōl′) *adj.* designating, of, or for a child between infancy and school age, usually between the ages of two and five (or six) —**pre·school′er** *n.*

pre·sci·ence (prē′shē əns, -shəns; presh′ē əns, presh′əns) *n.* [ME. < OFr. < LL.(Ec.) *praescientia* < L. *praescire*, to know beforehand: see PRE- & SCIENCE] apparent knowledge of things before they happen or come into being; foreknowledge —**pre′sci·ent** *adj.* —**pre′sci·ent·ly** *adv.*

pre·scind (pri sind′) *vt.* [L. *praescindere*, to cut off in front < *prae-*, before (see PRE-) + *scindere*, to cut] to detach, abstract, or isolate (a meaning, one's mind, etc.) —*vi.* to withdraw attention (*from*)

Pres·cott (pres′kət), **William Hick·ling** (hik′liŋ) 1796–1859; U.S. historian

pre·scribe (pri skrīb′) *vt.* -**scribed′**, -**scrib′ing** [L. *praescribere* < *prae-*, before + *scribere*, to write: see PRE- & SCRIBE] 1. orig., to write beforehand 2. to set down as a rule or direction; order; ordain; direct 3. to order or advise as a medicine or treatment: said of physicians, etc. 4. *Law* to invalidate or outlaw by negative prescription —*vi.* 1. to set down or impose rules; dictate 2. to give medical advice or prescriptions 3. *Law a*) to claim a right or title through long use or possession *b*) to become invalidated or outlawed by negative prescription —**pre·scrib′er** *n.*

pre·script (pri skript′; *also, and for n. always,* prē′skript) *adj.* [L. *praescriptus*, pp. of *praescribere*: see prec.] that is prescribed —*n.* [L. *praescriptum* < *praescriptus*] something prescribed; direction; rule

pre·scrip·ti·ble (pri skrip′tə b'l) *adj.* 1. that can be effectively prescribed for [*a prescriptible illness*] 2. acquired or acquirable by prescription (sense 5)

pre·scrip·tion (pri skrip′shən) *n.* [ME. *prescripcion* < L. *praescriptio*] 1. the act of prescribing 2. something prescribed; order; direction; precept 3. *a*) a doctor's written direction for the preparation and use of a medicine, the grinding of lenses for eyeglasses, etc. *b*) a medicine so prescribed 4. *a*) a long-established, authoritative custom *b*) a claim based on this 5. *Law a*) the acquirement of the title or right to something through its continued use or possession from time immemorial or over a long period *b*) a right or title so acquired —*adj.* 1. made according to a doctor's prescription [*prescription lenses*] 2. purchasable only by a prescription [*a prescription drug*]

pre·scrip·tive (-tiv) *adj.* [LL. *praescriptivus*] 1. that prescribes 2. based on legal prescription 3. prescribed by custom or long use —**pre·scrip′tive·ly** *adv.*

pres·ence (prez′'ns) *n.* [ME. < OFr. < L. *praesentia* < *praesens*: see PRESENT, *adj.*] 1. the fact or condition of being present; existence, occurrence, or attendance at some place or in some thing 2. immediate surroundings, or vicinity within close view, of a person [admitted to his *presence*] 3. a person or thing that is present, esp. a person of high station or imposing appearance 4. *a*) a person's bearing, personality, or appearance *b*) impressive bearing, personality, etc. characterized by poise, confidence, etc., often specif. that of a performer before an audience (**stage presence**) 5. an influence or a supernatural or divine spirit felt to be present 6. [Archaic] people present; an assemblage 7. [Obs.] *same as* PRESENCE CHAMBER

presence chamber the room in which a king or other person of rank or distinction formally receives guests

presence of mind ability to think clearly and act quickly and intelligently in an emergency

pres·ent (prez′'nt; *for v.,* pri zent′) *adj.* [ME. < OFr. < L. *praesens*, prp. of *praeesse*, to be present < *prae-*, before (see PRE-) + *esse*, to be (see ESSENCE)] 1. *a*) being at the specified or understood place; at hand; in attendance *b*) existing (*in a particular thing*) [*nitrogen is present in the air*] 2. of or at this time; existing or happening now; in progress 3. now being discussed, considered, written, read, etc. [*the present writer*] 4. [Archaic] readily available, effective, etc. 5. [Obs.] *a*) self-possessed; collected *b*) paying attention 6. *Gram.* indicating action as now taking place (Ex.: he *goes*) or state as now existing (Ex.: the plums *are* ripe), action that is habitual (Ex.: he *speaks* with an accent), or action that is always true (Ex.: two and two *is* four) See also HISTORICAL PRESENT —*n.* 1. the present time 2. the present occasion 3. [*pl.*] the present words or writings; esp., *Law* this very document [*know by these presents*] 4. *Gram. a*) the present tense *b*) a verb form in this tense 5. [OFr., in phr. *mettre en présent à*, to put before (someone), present, offer, hence a gift] something presented, or given; gift —*vt.* [ME. *presenten* < OFr. *presenter* < L. *praesentare*, to place before, lit., to make present < *praesens*: see the *adj.*] 1. to bring (a person) into the presence of, and introduce

formally to, another or others **2.** *a*) to offer for viewing or notice; exhibit; display; show *b*) to offer (a show, exhibit, etc.) to the public **3.** to offer for consideration [to *present* a plan, opportunity, etc.] **4.** to give or bestow (a gift, donation, award, etc.) to (a person, organization, etc.) **5.** to hand over, give, or send (a bill, credentials, etc.) to (someone) **6.** to represent, depict, or interpret in the manner indicated **7.** to point or aim (a weapon, etc.) **8.** to nominate to an ecclesiastical benefice **9.** *Law a*) to put before a legislature, court, etc. for consideration *b*) to bring a charge or indictment against —**present arms** *Mil.* **1.** to hold a rifle vertically in line with the middle of the body, with the muzzle up, at eye level, and the trigger away from the body: a position of salute **2.** *a*) this position *b*) the command to assume it —**pre·sent′er** *n.*
SYN.—**present** and **gift** both refer to something given as an expression of friendship, affection, esteem, etc., but **gift**, in current use, more often suggests formal bestowal [Christmas *presents*, the painting was a *gift* to the museum]; **donation** applies to a gift of money, etc. for a philanthropic, charitable, or religious purpose, esp. as solicited in a public drive for funds [a *donation* to the orchestra fund]; **gratuity** applies to a gift of money, etc. for services rendered, such as a tip to a waiter See also GIVE, OFFER
pre·sent·a·ble (pri zen′tə b'l) *adj.* [ML. *praesentabilis*] **1.** capable of being presented; suitable for presentation **2.** in proper or suitable attire, order, etc. for being seen, met, etc. by others —**pre·sent′a·bil′i·ty, pre·sent′a·ble·ness** *n.* —**pre·sent′a·bly** *adv.*
pres·en·ta·tion (prē′zen tā′shən, prez′'n-) *n.* [ME. < MFr. *presentacion* < LL. *praesentatio* < *praesentare:* see PRESENT, *v.*] **1.** a presenting or being presented **2.** something that is presented; specif., *a*) a performance, as of a play *b*) a gift **3.** *Commerce* same as PRESENTMENT **4.** *Eccles. a*) the naming of a clergyman to a benefice *b*) a request to the bishop to institute the clergyman named **5.** *Med.* the position of the fetus in the uterus at the time of delivery, with reference to the part presenting itself at the mouth of the uterus [an arm or breech *presentation*] **6.** *Philos., Psychol. a*) anything present in the consciousness at a single moment as an actual sensation or a mental image *b*) anything known by sense perception rather than by description; percept —**pres′en·ta′tion·al** *adj.*
pres·en·ta·tion·ism (-iz'm) *n. Philos.* the epistemological theory that in perception the mind is directly aware of an external object without any intervening medium
pres·en·ta·tive (pri zen′tə tiv) *adj.* **1.** *Eccles.* designating a benefice to or for which a patron has the right of presentation **2.** *Philos., Psychol.* known or capable of being known directly, as by sense perception
pres·ent-day (prez′'nt dā′) *adj.* of the present time
pres·en·tee (prez′'n tē′) *n.* [Anglo-Fr. < OFr., pp. of *presenter*] **1.** a person presented, as for institution to a benefice **2.** a person to whom something is presented
pre·sen·ti·ment (pri zen′tə mənt) *n.* [MFr. < *pressentir*, to have a presentiment of < L. *praesentire:* see PRE- & SENTIMENT] a feeling that something, esp. of an unfortunate or evil nature, is about to take place; premonition; foreboding —**pre·sen′ti·men′tal** *adj.*
pre·sen·tive (pri zen′tiv) *adj.* presenting an object or idea directly to the mind: said of words
pres·ent·ly (prez′'nt lē) *adv.* **1.** in a little while; soon **2.** at present; now **3.** [Archaic] at once; instantly
pre·sent·ment (pri zent′mənt) *n.* [ME. < OFr. *presentement* < *presenter:* see PRESENT, *v.*] the act of presenting; presentation; specif., *a*) an exhibition; thing presented to view *b*) *Commerce* the producing of a note, bill of exchange, etc. for acceptance or payment at the proper time and place *c*) *Law* the notice taken or report made by a grand jury of an offense on the basis of the jury's own knowledge and observations and without a bill of indictment *d*) *Philos.* same as PRESENTATION (sense 6)
present participle a participle used *a*) with auxiliaries to express present or continuing action or state of being [as *growing* in "the boy is, or was, growing"] or *b*) as an adjective [as *growing* in "a growing boy"]
present perfect 1. a tense indicating an action or state as completed at the time of speaking but not at any definite time in the past **2.** a verb form in this tense (Ex.: has gone)
pres·er·va·tion (prez′ər vā′shən) *n.* [ME. < MFr. < ML. *praeservatio*] a preserving or being preserved
pre·serv·a·tive (pri zur′və tiv) *adj.* [ME. *preseruatyve* < MFr. *preservatif* < ML. *praeservativus*] having the quality of preserving —*n.* anything that preserves; esp., a substance added to a food to keep it from spoiling
pre·serve (pri zurv′) *vt.* **-served′, -serv′ing** [ME. *preserven* < MFr. *preserver* < ML. *praeservare*, to preserve, protect < LL., to observe beforehand < L. *prae-*, PRE- + *servare:* see OBSERVE] **1.** to keep from harm, damage, danger, evil, etc.; protect; save **2.** to keep from spoiling or rotting **3.** to prepare (food), as by canning, pickling, salting, etc., for future use **4.** to keep up; carry on; maintain **5.** to maintain and protect (game, fish, etc.) in an area, esp. for regulated hunting or fishing —*vi.* **1.** to preserve fruit, etc. **2.** to maintain a game preserve —*n.* **1.** [*usually pl.*] fruit

preserved whole or in large pieces by cooking with sugar: cf. JAM[2] **2.** a place where game, fish, etc. are preserved **3.** any place or activity treated as the special domain of some person or group **4.** something that preserves or is preserved —*SYN.* see DEFEND —**pre·serv′a·ble** *adj.* —**pre·serv′er** *n.*
pre·set (prē set′) *vt.* **-set′, -set′ting** to set beforehand; esp., to set to a controlled pattern, as the guidance system of a missile before launching
pre·shrunk (prē′shrunk′) *adj.* shrunk by a special process in manufacture so as to minimize further shrinkage in laundering or dry cleaning
pre·side (pri zīd′) *vi.* **-sid′ed, -sid′ing** [Fr. *présider* < L. *praesidere*, to preside over, protect < *prae-*, PRE- + *sedere*, to SIT] **1.** to be in the position of authority in an assembly; serve as chairman **2.** to have or exercise control or authority (usually with *over*) **3.** to perform as the featured instrumentalist [*preside* at the organ] —**pre·sid′er** *n.*
pres·i·den·cy (prez′i dən sē) *n., pl.* **-cies** [ML. *praesidentia* < L. *praesidens:* see ff.] **1.** the office or function of president **2.** the term during which a president is in office ☆**3.** [*often* P-] the office of President of the U.S. ☆**4.** in the Mormon Church *a*) a council of three with local jurisdiction *b*) a council of three that is the highest administrative body: also **First Presidency 5.** [P-] *former name for* any of the three original provinces of British India
pres·i·dent (prez′i dənt) *n.* [ME. < MFr. < L. *praesidens* < prp. of *praesidere:* see PRESIDE] ☆**1.** the highest executive officer of a company, society, university, club, etc. **2.** [*often* P-] *a*) the chief executive of a republic having no prime minister *b*) in parliamentary governments, the formal head, with little or no executive power, usually the presiding member of the legislative assembly or council **3.** any presiding officer —**pres′i·den′tial** (-den′shəl) *adj.* —**pres′i·den′tial·ly** *adv.*
☆**pres·i·dent-e·lect** (-i lekt′) *n.* an elected president who has not yet taken office
pres·i·dent·ship (prez′i dənt ship′) *n.* [Brit.] the office or term of a president
☆**pre·sid·i·o** (pri sid′ē ō′) *n., pl.* **-i·os** [Sp. < L. *praesidium*, a garrison < *praeses*, a guard < *praesidere:* see PRESIDE] a fortified place or military post, esp. in the SW U.S. —**pre·sid′i·al, pre·sid′i·ar′y** *adj.*
pre·sid·i·um (-ē əm) *n., pl.* **-i·a** (-ə), **-i·ums** [Russ. *prezidium* < L. *praesidium:* see prec.] **1.** in the Soviet Union *a*) any of a number of permanent administrative committees meeting regularly and empowered to act for a larger body between its sessions *b*) [P-] the permanent administrative committee of the Supreme Soviet **2.** [P-] an administrative committee at the highest level of government in certain other countries, as Albania, Romania, etc.
pre·sig·ni·fy (prē sig′nə fī′) *vt.* **-fied′, -fy′ing** to signify or indicate beforehand; foreshadow
pres. part. present participle
press[1] (pres) *vt.* [ME. *pressen* < MFr. *presser* < L. *pressare*, freq. of *premere*, to press < IE. base *per-*, to strike, whence OBulg. *p'rati*, to strike] **1.** to act on with steady force or weight; push steadily against; squeeze **2.** *a*) to extract juice, etc. from by squeezing *b*) to squeeze (juice, etc.) out **3.** *a*) to squeeze for the purpose of making smooth, compact, etc.; compress *b*) to iron (clothes, etc.), esp. with a heavy iron or steam machine **4.** to embrace closely **5.** to force; compel; constrain **6.** to urge or request earnestly or persistently; entreat; importune **7.** to impose by persistent entreaty; try to force [to *press* a gift on a friend] **8.** to lay stress on; be insistent about; emphasize **9.** to distress or trouble; harass [to be *pressed* for time] **10.** to urge on; drive quickly **11.** to shape (a phonograph record, metal or plastic products, etc.) by use of a form or matrix **12.** [Archaic] to crowd; throng **13.** [Obs.] same as OPPRESS —*vi.* **1.** to exert pressure; specif., *a*) to weigh down; bear heavily *b*) to go forward with energetic or determined effort *c*) to force one's way *d*) to crowd; throng *e*) to be urgent or insistent **2.** to react to being pressed, or ironed **3.** to iron clothes, etc. —*n.* **1.** a pressing or being pressed; pressure, urgency, etc. **2.** a crowd; throng **3.** an instrument or machine by which something is crushed, squeezed, stamped, smoothed, etc. by pressure **4.** a viselike device in which a tennis racket, etc. can be stored to keep it from warping **5.** the condition of clothes as to smoothness, creases, etc. after pressing **6.** *a*) *clipped form of* PRINTING PRESS *b*) a printing or publishing establishment *c*) the art, business, or practice of printing *d*) newspapers, magazines, news services, etc. in general, or the persons who write for them; journalism or journalists *e*) publicity, criticism, etc. in newspapers, magazines, etc. [to receive a bad *press*] **7.** an upright closet in which clothes or other articles are kept **8.** *Weight Lifting* a lift in which the barbell is cleaned (see CLEAN, *vt.* 6) and then pushed steadily overhead until the arms are completely extended —*SYN.* see URGE —**go to press** to start to be printed
press[2] (pres) *vt.* [altered (after prec.) < obs. *prest*, to enlist for military service by advance pay < OFr. *prester* < L. *praestare*, to vouch for, warrant < *praes*, surety (< *prae-*,

PRE- + *vas*, bail, surety: for IE. base see WED) + *stare*, to STAND] 1. to force into military or naval service; impress 2. to force or urge into any kind of service 3. to use in a way different from the ordinary, esp. in an emergency —*n.* 1. an impressment, or forcing into service, esp. naval or military 2. [Obs.] an order for impressing recruits

☆**press agent** a person whose business is to advance the interests of a person, organization, etc., usually by getting publicity; publicity agent —**press′-a′gent·ry** *n.*

press·board (pres′bôrd′) *n.* 1. same as MILLBOARD 2. a smooth, stiff, heavy, often glazed, paper used in presses for finishing paper, etc.

☆**press box** a place reserved for reporters at sports events, etc.

☆**press conference** a collective interview granted to newsmen as by a celebrity or personage

press·er (-ər) *n.* a person or thing that presses; specif., a person whose work is pressing newly made or freshly cleaned clothes

press gallery a section set apart for newsmen in a chamber where an official body meets

press gang [for *prest gang*: see PRESS²] a group of men who round up other men and force them into naval or military service: also **press′gang′** *n.*

press·ing (-iŋ) *adj.* [prp. of PRESS¹] 1. calling for immediate attention; urgent 2. persistent in request or demand; insistent —*n.* 1. the process or an instance of stamping, squeezing, etc. with a press 2. the result of this, often a series or one of a series of identical articles [a *pressing* of phonograph records] —**press′ing·ly** *adv.*

press·man (-mən) *n., pl.* -**men** (-mən) 1. an operator of a printing press 2. [Brit.] a newspaperman

press·mark (-märk′) *n.* [Brit.] same as CALL NUMBER

press of sail (or **canvas**) the maximum amount of sail that a ship can safely carry under given conditions

pres·sor (pres′ər) *adj.* [PRESS(URE) + (MOT)OR] designating a nerve which, when stimulated, causes a rise in blood pressure —*n.* a substance capable of raising blood pressure

press·room (-rōōm′) *n.* a room containing the printing presses of a newspaper or printing establishment

pres·sure (presh′ər) *n.* [ME. < OFr. < L. *pressura*, a pressing, in LL.(Ec.), oppression, affliction < *pressus*, pp. of *premere*, to PRESS¹] 1. a pressing or being pressed; compression; squeezing 2. a condition of distress; oppression; affliction 3. a sense impression caused by or as by compression of a part of the body 4. a compelling influence; constraining force [social *pressure*] 5. demands requiring immediate attention; urgency 6. *clipped form of:* a) ATMOSPHERIC PRESSURE b) BLOOD PRESSURE 7. [Obs.] a mark made by pressing; impression 8. *Physics* force exerted against an opposing body; thrust distributed over a surface: expressed in units of force per unit of area —*vt.* -sured, -sur·ing ☆1. to exert pressure, or compelling influence, on 2. same as PRESSURIZE

pressure cabin *Aeron.* a pressurized cabin

☆**pres·sure-cook** (-kook′) *vt.* to cook in a pressure cooker

☆**pressure cooker** an airtight metal container for quick cooking by means of steam under pressure

pressure gauge 1. a gauge for measuring the pressure of steam, water, gas, etc. 2. a mechanism for measuring explosive pressure, as in the barrel of a gun

pressure gradient same as BAROMETRIC GRADIENT

pressure group any group that exerts pressure upon legislators and the public through lobbies, propaganda, etc. in order to affect legislation or policies

pressure point any of a number of points on the body where an artery passes close to the surface and in front of a bony structure so that pressure applied there will check bleeding from a distal injured part

pres·sur·ize (presh′ər iz′) *vt.* -ized′, -iz′ing 1. to keep nearly normal atmospheric pressure inside (an airplane, space suit, etc.), as at high altitudes 2. to place under conditions of high pressure —**pres′sur·i·za′tion** *n.* —**pres′sur·iz′er** *n.*

press·work (pres′wurk′) *n.* 1. the operation or management of a printing press 2. work done by a printing press

prest (prest) *n.* [ME. *preste* < OFr. < *prester*: see PRESS²] [Obs.] an advance of money, specif. one to men enlisting in the British army or navy: also **prest money** —*adj.* [Obs.] ready; prepared

Pres·ter John (pres′tər) [ME. *Prestre Johan* < OFr. *prestre Jehan* < ML. *presbyter Iohannes*] a legendary medieval Christian king and priest said to have ruled either in the Far East or in Ethiopia

pre·ster·num (prē stur′nəm) *n.* same as MANUBRIUM (sense b)

pres·ti·dig·i·ta·tion (pres′tə dij′i tā′shən) *n.* [Fr.: see ff.] the performance of tricks by quick, skillful use of the hands; sleight of hand; legerdemain

pres·ti·dig·i·ta·tor (-dij′ə tāt′ər) *n.* [Fr. *prestidigitateur* (after L. *prestigiator*, juggler, deceiver) < *preste*, quick < *presto* (see PRESTO) + L. *digitus*, a finger (see DIGIT)] an expert at prestidigitation

pres·tige (pres tēzh′, -tēj′) *n.* [Fr.; orig., illusion, trick < LL. *praestigium* < L. *praestigiae*, altered < *praestrigiae*, deceptions < *praestringere*, to blind, orig., to bind fast < *prae-*, PRE- + *stringere*, to bind: see STRAIN¹] 1. the power to impress or influence, as because of success, wealth, etc. 2. reputation or distinction based on brilliance of

achievement, character, etc.; renown —*SYN.* see INFLUENCE —**pres·tige′ful** *adj.*

pres·ti·gious (-tij′əs, -tē′jəs) *adj.* [L. *praestigiosus*, full of deceitful tricks < *praestigium*, delusion (see prec.)] 1. [Archaic] of or characterized by legerdemain or deception 2. [re-formed from PRESTIG(E) + -OUS] having or imparting prestige or distinction

pres·tis·si·mo (pres tis′ə mō′; *It.* pres tēs′sē mō′) *adv., adj.* [It., superl. of *presto*: see ff.] *Music* very fast; as fast as possible: a direction to the performer —*n., pl.* -mos′ a prestissimo passage or movement

pres·to (pres′tō) *adv., adj.* [It., quick, nimble < L. *praestus*, at hand, ready < *praesto*, at hand, available < *prae*, before: see PRE-] 1. fast or at once 2. *Music* in fast tempo: a direction to the performer —*n.* -tos a musical passage or movement performed in fast tempo

Pres·ton (pres′tən) port in Lancashire, NW England: pop. 107,000

☆**pre·stressed concrete** (prē′strest′) concrete containing steel cables, wires, etc. under tension to produce compressive stress and lend greater strength

pre·sum·a·ble (pri zōōm′ə b'l, -zyōōm′-) *adj.* that may be presumed, or taken for granted; probably —**pre·sum′a·bly** *adv.*

pre·sume (pri zōōm′, -zyōōm′) *vt.* -sumed′, -sum′ing [ME. *presumen* < OFr. *presumer* < L. *praesumere* < *prae-*, before (see PRE-) + *sumere*, to take: see CONSUME] 1. to take upon oneself without permission or authority; dare (to say or do something); venture 2. to take for granted; accept as true lacking proof to the contrary; assume; suppose 3. to constitute reasonable evidence for supposing [a signed invoice *presumes* receipt of the goods] —*vi.* 1. to act presumptuously; take liberties 2. to rely too much (*on* or *upon*), as in taking liberties [to *presume* on another's friendship] 3. to take something for granted; make suppositions —**pre·sum′ed·ly** (-id lē) *adv.* —**pre·sum′er** *n.* *SYN.*—**presume** implies a taking something for granted or accepting it as true, usually on the basis of probable evidence in its favor and the absence of proof to the contrary [the man is *presumed* to be of sound mind]; **presuppose** is the broadest term here, sometimes suggesting a taking something for granted unwarrantedly [this writer *presupposes* a too extensive vocabulary in children] and, in another sense, implying that something is required as a preceding condition [brilliant technique in piano playing *presupposes* years of practice]; **assume** implies the supposition of something as the basis for argument or action [let us *assume* his motives were good]; **postulate** implies the assumption of something as an underlying factor, often one that is incapable of proof [his argument *postulates* the inherent goodness of man]; **premise** implies the setting forth of a proposition on which a conclusion can be based

pre·sump·tion (pri zump′shən) *n.* [ME. < OFr. *presumpcion* < L. *praesumptio*, a taking beforehand < *praesumptus*, pp. of *praesumere*: see PRESUME] 1. the act of presuming; specif., a) an overstepping of proper bounds; forwardness; effrontery b) the taking of something for granted 2. the thing presumed; supposition 3. a ground or reason for presuming; evidence that points to the probability of something 4. *Law* the inference that a fact exists, based on the proved existence of another fact

pre·sump·tive (-tiv) *adj.* [Fr. *présomptif* < LL. *praesumptivus* < L. *praesumptus*: see prec.] 1. giving reasonable ground for belief [presumptive evidence] 2. based on probability; presumed [an heir *presumptive*] —**pre·sump′tive·ly** *adv.*

pre·sump·tu·ous (-choo wəs) *adj.* [ME. < OFr. *presuntueux* < LL. *praesumptuosus* < L. *praesumptus*: see PRESUMPTION] 1. too bold or forward; taking too much for granted; showing overconfidence, arrogance, or effrontery 2. *obs. var.* of PRESUMPTIVE —**pre·sump′tu·ous·ly** *adv.* —**pre·sump′tu·ous·ness** *n.*

pre·sup·pose (prē′sə pōz′) *vt.* -posed′, -pos′ing [ME. *presupposen* < MFr. *presupposer*, altered (after *poser*, to place) < ML. *praesupponere*, pp. *praesuppositus*: see PRE- & SUPPOSE] 1. to suppose or assume beforehand; take for granted 2. to require or imply as a preceding condition [an effect *presupposes* a cause] —*SYN.* see PRESUME —**pre′sup·po·si′tion** (-sup ə zish′ən) *n.*

pret. preterit

pre·tence (pri tens′, prē′tens) *n. Brit. sp.* of PRETENSE

pre·tend (pri tend′) *vt.* [ME. *pretenden*, to intend < MFr. *pretendre* < L. *praetendere* < *prae-*, before + *tendere*, to stretch: see TEND²] 1. to claim; profess; allege [to *pretend* ignorance of the law] 2. to claim or profess falsely; feign; simulate [to *pretend* anger] 3. to make believe, as in play [to *pretend* to be astronauts] —*vi.* 1. to lay claim [to *pretend* to a throne] 2. to make believe in play or in an attempt to deceive; feign —*adj.* [Colloq.] make-believe [*pretend* jewelry] —*SYN.* see ASSUME

pre·tend·ed (pri ten′did) *adj.* 1. not genuine; feigned 2. reputed or alleged

pre·tend·er (-dər) *n.* 1. a person who pretends 2. a claimant to a throne; specif., [P-] in English history, the son (James Edward Stuart, called **Old Pretender**) or the grandson (Charles Edward Stuart, called **Young Pretender**) of James II 3. an aspirant

pre·tense (pri tens′, prē′tens) *n.* [ME. < Anglo-Fr. *pretensse* < ML. **pretensa* < *praetensus*, alleged < pp. of L. *praetendere*: see PRETEND] 1. a claim, esp. an unsupported one, as to some distinction or accomplishment; pretension

2. a false claim or profession **3.** a false show of something **4.** a pretending, as at play; make-believe **5.** a false reason or plea; pretext **6.** [Rare] aim; intention **7.** pretentiousness; ostentation **8.** a pretentious act or remark

pre·ten·sion (pri ten'shən) *n.* [ML. *praetensio* < *praetensus:* see prec.] **1.** a pretext or allegation **2.** a claim, as to a right, title, distinction, etc. **3.** assertion of a claim **4.** pretentiousness; ostentation

pre·ten·tious (-shəs) *adj.* [Fr. *prétentieux* < *prétention,* pretension + -*eux,* -OUS] **1.** making claims, explicit or implicit, to some distinction, importance, dignity, or excellence **2.** affectedly grand, superior, etc.; ostentatious —**pre·ten'tious·ly** *adv.* —**pre·ten'tious·ness** *n.*

pre·ter- (prēt'ər) [L. *praeter-* < *praeter,* beyond, past, compar. of *prae,* before: see PRE-] *a prefix meaning* past, beyond, outside the bounds of [*preternatural*]

pre·ter·hu·man (prēt'ər hyōo'mən, -yōo'mən) *adj.* beyond that which is human; esp., superhuman

pret·er·it, pret·er·ite (pret'ər it) *adj.* [ME. *preterit* < MFr. < L. *praeteritus,* gone by, pp. of *praeterire* < *praeter-* (see PRETER-) + *ire,* to go: for IE. base see YEAR] **1.** *Gram.* expressing past action or state **2.** [Rare] past; bygone; former —*n.* **1.** the past tense **2.** a verb in the past tense

pret·er·i·tion (pret'ə rish'ən) *n.* [LL. *praeteritio* < L. *praeteritus:* see prec.] **1.** a passing over; omission **2.** *Law* an omitting of one or more legal heirs from a will **3.** *Theol.* the passing over by God of those not elect: a doctrine of Calvinism

pre·ter·mit (prēt'ər mit') *vt.* -**mit'ted,** -**mit'ting** [L. *praetermittere,* to let go by < *praeter-* (see PRETER-) + *mittere,* to send: see MISSION] **1.** to leave out or undone; neglect or omit **2.** to let pass unnoticed; overlook —**pre'ter·mis'sion** (-mish'ən) *n.*

pre·ter·nat·u·ral (-nach'ər əl) *adj.* [ML. *praeternaturalis*] **1.** differing from or beyond what is normally found in or expected from nature; abnormal [*preternatural* strength] **2.** *same as* SUPERNATURAL —**pre'ter·nat'u·ral·ism** *n.* —**pre'ter·nat'u·ral·ly** *adv.*

pre·test (prē'test'; *for v.,* prē'test') *n.* a preliminary test, as of a product —*vt.,* *vi.* to test in advance

pre·text (prē'tekst) *n.* [L. *praetextum,* neut. of *praetextus,* pp. of *praetexere,* to weave before, pretend: see PRE- & TEXTURE] **1.** a false reason or motive put forth to hide the real one; excuse **2.** a cover-up; front

pre·tor (prēt'ər) *n.* *same as* PRAETOR —**pre·to·ri·al** (pri tôr'ē əl) *adj.* —**pre·to'ri·an** *adj., n.*

Pre·to·ri·a (pri tôr'ē ə) capital of the Transvaal, in the S part: seat of the government of South Africa: pop. 423,000

pre·tri·al (prē'trī'əl) *adj.* occurring, presented, or engaged in before a court trial actually begins [a *pretrial* motion] —*n.* a pretrial proceeding for clearing up points of fact or law

pret·ti·fy (prit'ə fī') *vt.* -**fied',** -**fy'ing** to make pretty —**pret'ti·fi·ca'tion** *n.*

pret·ty (prit'ē; *by metathesis, often* pur'tē) *adj.* -**ti·er,** -**ti·est** [ME. *prati* < OE. *prættig,* crafty < *prætt,* a craft, trick] **1.** pleasing or attractive in a dainty, delicate, or graceful way rather than through striking beauty, elegance, grandeur, or stateliness **2.** *a)* fine; good; nice: often used ironically [a *pretty* fix] *b)* adroit; skillful [a *pretty* move] **3.** [Archaic] elegant **4.** [Archaic or Scot.] brave; bold; gallant **5.** [Colloq.] considerable; quite large [a *pretty* price] —*adv.* **1.** fairly; somewhat [*pretty* sure]: sometimes, by hyperbole, quite or very [*pretty* angry] **2.** [Colloq.] prettily (to talk *pretty*] —*n., pl.* -**ties** a pretty person or thing —*vt.* -**tied,** -**ty·ing** to make pretty (usually with *up*) —*SYN.* see BEAUTIFUL —☆**sitting pretty** [Slang] in a favorable position —**pret'ti·ly** *adv.* —**pret'ti·ness** *n.* —**pret'ty·ish** *adj.*

pre·typ·i·fy (prē tip'ə fī') *vt.* -**fied',** -**fy'ing** to typify beforehand; prefigure; foreshadow

☆**pret·zel** (pret's'l) *n.* [G. *brezel* < OHG. *brezitella* < ML. *brachiatellum,* dim. of *brachiatum,* biscuit baked in form of crossed arms < L. *brachium,* an arm: see BRACE[1]] a usually hard, brittle biscuit made from a slender roll of dough heavily sprinkled with salt and typically baked in the form of a loose knot or as a stick

PRETZEL

pre·vail (pri vāl') *vi.* [ME. *prevaylen* < L. *praevalere* < *prae-,* before (see PRE-) + *valere,* to be strong: see VALUE] **1.** to gain the advantage or mastery; be victorious; triumph (often with *over* or *against*) **2.** to produce or achieve the desired effect; be effective; succeed **3.** to be or become stronger or more widespread; predominate **4.** to exist widely; be in general use; be prevalent —**prevail on** (or **upon, with**) to persuade; induce —*SYN.* see PERSUADE

pre·vail·ing (-in) *adj.* **1.** superior in strength, influence, or effect **2.** most frequent, noticeable, etc.; predominant **3.** widely existing; prevalent —**pre·vail'ing·ly** *adv.*

SYN.—**prevailing** applies to that which leads all others in acceptance, usage, belief, etc. at a given time and in a given place

[a *prevailing* practice]; **current** refers to that which is commonly known or accepted or in general usage at the time specified or, if unspecified, at the present time [that pronunciation was *current* in the 18th century]; **prevalent** implies widespread occurrence or acceptance but does not now connote the predominance of **prevailing** [a *prevalent* belief]; **rife** implies rapidly increasing prevalence and often connotes excitement or commotion [rumors about the plague were *rife*]

prev·a·lent (prev'ə lənt) *adj.* [L. *praevalens,* prp. of *praevalere:* see PREVAIL] **1.** [Rare] stronger, more effective, etc.; dominant **2.** *a)* widely existing *b)* generally practiced, occurring, or accepted —*SYN.* see PREVAILING —**prev'a·lence** (-ləns) *n.* —**prev'a·lent·ly** *adv.*

pre·var·i·cate (pri var'ə kāt') *vi.* -**cat'ed,** -**cat'ing** [< L. *praevaricatus,* pp. of *praevaricari,* to prevaricate, lit., to walk crookedly < *prae-,* before + *varicare,* to straddle < *varicus,* straddling < *varus,* bent < IE. base *wā-,* apart, spread, whence L. *vacillare,* to stagger] **1.** to turn aside from, or evade, the truth; equivocate **2.** to tell an untruth; lie —*SYN.* see LIE[2] —**pre·var'i·ca'tion** *n.* —**pre·var'i·ca'tor** *n.*

pre·ven·ient (pri vēn'yənt) *adj.* [L. *praeveniens,* prp. of *praevenire:* see ff.] **1.** going before; preceding **2.** anticipating; expectant **3.** antecedent to human action [*prevenient* grace] —**pre·ven'ience** (-yəns) *n.*

pre·vent (pri vent') *vt.* [ME. *preventen* < L. *praeventus,* pp. of *praevenire,* to anticipate < *prae-,* before (see PRE-) + *venire,* to COME] **1.** formerly, *a)* to act in anticipation of (an event or a fixed time) *b)* to anticipate (a desire, need, objection, etc.) *c)* to precede **2.** to stop or keep (from doing something) **3.** to keep from happening; make impossible by prior action; hinder —*vi.* to put some obstacle in the way —**pre·vent'a·ble, pre·vent'i·ble** *adj.* —**pre·vent'er** *n.*

SYN.—**prevent** implies a stopping or keeping from happening, as by some prior action or by interposing an obstacle or impediment [to *prevent* disease]; **forestall** suggests advance action to stop something in its course and thereby make it ineffective [try to *forestall* their questions]; **preclude** implies a making impossible by shutting off every possibility of occurrence [locked doors *precluded* his escape]; **obviate** suggests the preventing of some unfavorable outcome by taking the necessary anticipatory measures [his frankness *obviated* objections]; **avert** suggests a warding off of imminent danger or misfortune [diplomacy can *avert* war] —*ANT.* permit, allow

pre·ven·tion (pri ven'shən) *n.* **1.** the act of preventing **2.** [Now Rare] a means of preventing; preventive

pre·ven·tive (-tiv) *adj.* preventing or serving to prevent; esp., preventing disease —*n.* anything that prevents; esp., anything that prevents disease; prophylactic Also **pre·vent'a·tive** (-tə tiv) —**pre·ven'tive·ly** *adv.* —**pre·ven'tive·ness** *n.*

pre·view (prē'vyōo) *vt.* to view or show beforehand; receive or give a preview of —*n.* ☆**1.** a previous or preliminary view or survey ☆**2.** *a)* a restricted showing, as of a movie, before exhibition to the public generally *b)* a showing of scenes from a movie, television show, etc. in advertising its coming appearance

pre·vi·ous (prē'vē əs) *adj.* [L. *praevius* < *prae-* (see PRE-) + *via,* a way (see VIA)] **1.** occurring before in time or order; prior ☆**2.** [Colloq.] too soon; premature —**previous to** before —**pre'vi·ous·ly** *adv.*

SYN.—**previous** generally implies a coming before in time or order [a *previous* encounter]; **prior** adds to this a connotation of greater importance or claim as a result of being first [a *prior* commitment]; **preceding,** esp. when used with the definite article, implies a coming immediately before [the *preceding* night]; **antecedent** adds to the meaning of **previous** a connotation of direct causal relationship with what follows [events *antecedent* to the war]; **foregoing** applies specif. to something previously said or written [the *foregoing* examples]; **former** always connotes comparison, stated or implied, with what follows (termed *latter*) —*ANT.* following

previous question the question, put as a motion, whether a matter under consideration by a parliamentary body should be voted on immediately: defeat of the motion permits further consideration

pre·vise (prē vīz') *vt.* -**vised',** -**vis'ing** [< L. *praevisus,* pp. of *praevidere,* to foresee < *prae-,* PRE- + *videre,* to see: see VISION] [Rare] **1.** to foresee or forecast **2.** to inform beforehand; warn

pre·vi·sion (-vizh'ən) *n.* [Fr. *prévision* < ML. *praevisio* < L. *praevisus:* see prec.] **1.** foresight or foreknowledge **2.** a prediction or prophecy —*vt.* to foresee —**pre·vi'sion·al, pre·vi'sion·ar'y** *adj.*

pre·vo·cal·ic (prē'vō kal'ik) *adj.* just before a vowel

☆**pre·vo·ca·tion·al** (-vō kā'shən 'l) *adj.* designating or of training, tests, etc. to determine suitable placement of students in a vocational school

Pré·vost d'Ex·iles (prā vō' deg zēl'), **An·toine Fran·çois** (än twän' frän swä') 1697-1763; Fr. novelist: called **Abbé Prévost**

☆**pre·vue** (prē'vyōo) *n. same as* PREVIEW (esp. sense 2)

pre·war (prē'wôr') *adj.* before a (or the) war

☆**prex·y** (prek'sē) *n., pl.* **prex'ies** [contr. of PRESIDENT] [Slang] the president, esp. of a college, etc.

prey (prā) *n.* [ME. *preye* < OFr. *preie* < L. *praeda* < base

of *prehendere*, to seize: see PREHENSILE] **1.** orig., plunder; booty **2.** an animal hunted or killed for food by another animal **3.** a person or thing that falls victim to someone or something **4.** the mode of living by preying on other animals [a bird of *prey*] —*vi.* **1.** to plunder; pillage; rob **2.** to hunt or kill other animals for food **3.** to make profit from a victim as by swindling **4.** to have a wearing or destructive influence; weigh heavily Generally used with *on* or *upon* —**prey'er** *n.*

Pri·am (prī'əm) [L. *Priamus* < Gr. *Priamos*] *Gr. Legend* the last king of Troy, who reigned during the Trojan War: he was the father of Hector and Paris

pri·ap·ic (prī ap'ik) *adj.* [PRIAP(US) + -IC] **1.** *same as* PHALLIC **2.** overly concerned with virility or masculinity

pri·a·pism (prī'ə piz'm) *n.* [LL. *priapismus* < Gr. *priapismos* < *priapizein*, to be lewd: see ff.] **1.** a pathological condition characterized by persistent erection of the penis, esp. without sexual excitement **2.** a lascivious attitude or behavior

Pri·a·pus (prī ā'pəs) [L. < Gr. *Priapos*] *Gr. & Rom. Myth.* a god, son of Dionysus and Aphrodite, personifying the male procreative power —*n.* [p-] *same as* PHALLUS

Prib·i·lof Islands (prib'ə lôf') group of four Alaskan islands in the Bering Sea, north of the Aleutian Islands: noted as a breeding place of seals: pop. 600

price (prīs) *n.* [ME. & OFr. *pris* < L. *pretium*, a price < IE. *preti-*, equivalent < base *per*, whence FAR, FIRST] **1.** the amount of money, etc. asked or paid for something; cost; charge **2.** value or worth **3.** a reward for the capture or death of a person **4.** money or other consideration sufficient to be a bribe or inducement **5.** the cost, as in life, labor, sacrifice, etc., of obtaining some benefit or advantage —*vt.* **priced, pric'ing** **1.** to put a price on; fix the price of **2.** [Colloq.] to ask or find out the price of —**at any price** no matter what the cost —**beyond (or without) price** priceless; invaluable —**price out of the market** to force (oneself or one's product) out of competition by charging prices that are too high —**pric'er** *n.*

price control the setting of ceiling prices on basic commodities by a government, as to fight inflation

price fixing the setting or maintenance of prices at a certain level, esp. by mutual agreement of competitors

price index *see* INDEX (sense 5 *b*)

price·less (prīs'lis) *adj.* **1.** of inestimable value; beyond price **2.** [Colloq.] very amusing or absurd

☆**price support** support of certain price levels at or above market values, esp. by government action, as by buying up surpluses

price war a situation in which competitors selling a certain commodity successively lower prices, as to force one or more out of business

price·y (prī'sē) *adj.* [Brit. Colloq.] expensive; dear

Prich·ard (prich'ərd) [after Cleveland *Prichard*, the founder] city in SW Ala.: suburb of Mobile: pop. 42,000

prick (prik) *n.* [ME. *prike* < OE. *prica*, a point, dot, akin to Du. *prik* < IE. base *bhrēi-*, to cut, whence L. *friare*, to rub away, *frivolus*, lit., breakable] **1.** a very small puncture or, formerly, dot, made by a sharp point **2.** [Archaic] any of various pointed objects, as a thorn, goad, etc. **3.** *same as* PRICKING **4.** a sharp pain caused by or as if by being pricked —*vt.* **1.** to make (a tiny hole) in (something) with a sharp point **2.** to cause or feel sharp pain in [remorse *pricked* his conscience] **3.** to mark or trace by dots, points, or punctures **4.** to pierce (a horse's foot) to the quick in shoeing, causing lameness **5.** to cause to point or stick up (often with *up*) **6.** [Archaic] to spur or urge on; goad; incite —*vi.* **1.** to cause or feel a slight, sharp pain **2.** to have a prickly or stinging sensation; tingle **3.** to point or stick up: said esp. of ears **4.** [Archaic] to spur a horse on; ride fast —*adj.* carried stiffly erect: said of a dog's ears —**prick out (or off)** to transplant (seedlings) as from seed pans to shallow boxes —**prick up one's (or its) ears** **1.** to raise the ears with the points upward **2.** to listen closely

prick·er (-ər) *n.* **1.** a person, animal, or thing that pricks **2.** *same as* PRICKLE (sense 1)

prick·et (-it) *n.* [ME. *pryket*, dim.: see PRICK] **1.** a small spike on which to stick a candle **2.** a candlestick having such a spike **3.** a male deer in his second year, with straight, unbranched antlers

prick·ing (-in) *n.* **1.** the act or process of one that pricks **2.** a prickly feeling

prick·le (prik'l) *n.* [ME. *prykel* < OE. *pricel*, earlier *pricels* < base of *prica* (see PRICK) + -*els*, instrumental suffix] **1.** any sharp point; specif., a small, sharply pointed, thornlike process growing from the tissue under the outer layer of a plant **2.** a prickly sensation; stinging or tingling —*vt.* **-led, -ling** **1.** to prick, as with a spine or thorn **2.** to cause to feel a tingling sensation —*vi.* to tingle

prick·ly (-lē) *adj.* **-li·er, -li·est** **1.** full of prickles **2.** stinging; smarting; tingling —**prick'li·ness** *n.*

☆**prickly ash** either of two N. American shrubs or trees (genus *Xanthoxylum*) of the rue family, with pinnately compound leaves having paired spines at the base

☆**prickly heat** *same as* MILIARIA

☆**prickly pear** **1.** *a)* any of a genus (*Opuntia*) of cactus plants having cylindrical or large, flat, oval stem joints and edible fruits: many species have barbed spines *b)* the fruit of such a plant **2.** *same as* NOPAL

☆**prickly poppy** any of a genus (*Argemone*) of plants of the poppy family, with prickly leaves, yellow juice, and large flowers of various colors

prick song **1.** [Obs.] music written down in pricks, or dots; written music **2.** *same as* DESCANT (*n.* 1 a & b)

pride (prīd) *n.* [ME. < OE. *pryte* < *prut*, PROUD] **1.** *a)* an overhigh opinion of oneself; exaggerated self-esteem; conceit *b)* haughty behavior resulting from this; arrogance **2.** proper respect for oneself; sense of one's own dignity or worth; self-respect **3.** delight or satisfaction in one's own or another's achievements, in associations, etc. **4.** a person or thing in which pride is taken **5.** the best of a class, group, society, etc.; pick; flower **6.** the best part or time; prime; flowering [in the *pride* of manhood] **7.** mettle (in a horse) **8.** *a)* a group or family (of lions) *b)* [Colloq.] any impressive group or cluster **9.** [Archaic] *a)* magnificence; splendor *b)* ornament **10.** [Obs.] sexual desire —*vt.* **prid'ed, prid'ing** [Rare] to make proud —**pride oneself on** to be proud of —**pride'ful** *adj.* —**pride'ful·ly** *adv.* —**pride'ful·ness** *n.*

SYN.—**pride** refers either to a justified or excessive belief in one's own worth, merit, superiority, etc. [he takes *pride* in his accuracy]; **conceit** always implies an exaggerated opinion of oneself, one's achievements, etc. [blinded by his overweening *conceit*]; **vanity** suggests an excessive desire to be admired by others for one's achievements, appearance, etc. [his *vanity* is wounded by criticism]; **vainglory** implies extreme conceit as manifested by boasting, swaggering, arrogance, etc. [the *vainglory* of a conquering general]; **self-esteem** implies a high opinion of oneself, sometimes a higher opinion than is held by others —**ANT. humility**

Pride (prīd), **Thomas** ?–1658; Eng. army officer: in 1648 brought about the expulsion (**Pride's Purge**) of over 100 Royalist & Presbyterian members from the House of Commons

☆**pride-of-India** *same as* CHINABERRY (sense 1)

prie-dieu (prē'dyōō') *n.* [Fr. < *prier*, to pray + *dieu*, God] a narrow, upright frame with a lower ledge for kneeling on at prayer and an upper ledge, as for a book

pri·er (prī'ər) *n.* a person who pries

priest (prēst) *n.* [ME. *prest* < OE. *preost* < LL.(Ec.) *presbyter*, an elder < Gr. *presbyteros*, elder, compar. of *presbys*, old, an old man in LGr.(Ec.), an elder) < IE. *pres-*, ahead < base *per* (cf. PER, PRE-) + *gwou-*, COW¹, ox (hence, orig., lead-ox)] **1.** a person whose function is to make sacrificial offerings and perform other religious rites as an intermediary between deity and worshipers **2.** *a)* orig., in the early Christian church, a presbyter, or elder *b)* in hierarchical Christian churches, a clergyman ranking next below a bishop and authorized to administer the sacraments **3.** any clergyman, or religious minister —**priest'hood** *n.*

priest·craft (-kraft', -kräft') *n.* the craft, methods, etc. of priests: now usually with reference to the unscrupulous use of a priestly office

priest·ess (prēs'tis) *n.* a girl or woman priest, esp. of a pagan religion

Priest·ley (prēst'lē) **1.** J(ohn) B(oynton), 1894– ; Eng. novelist, playwright, & literary critic **2.** Joseph, 1733–1804; Eng. scientist & theologian, in the U.S. after 1794: discoverer of oxygen

priest·ly (-lē) *adj.* **-li·er, -li·est** of, like, or suitable for a priest or priests —**priest'li·ness** *n.*

priest-rid·den (-rid'n) *adj.* dominated or tyrannized by priests

prig¹ (prig) *n.* [< 16th-cent. cant, prob. a merging of several words < ?] **1.** orig., any person regarded with dislike **2.** *a)* formerly, an annoyingly pedantic person *b)* a person who is excessively precise, proper, and smug in his moral behavior and attitudes, to the annoyance of others —**prig'ger·y, prig'gism** *n.* —**prig'gish** *adj.* —**prig'gish·ly** *adv.* —**prig'gish·ness** *n.*

prig² (prig) *vt.* **prigged, prig'ging** [cf. prec.] [Brit. Slang] to steal —*vi.* [Scot. or Dial.] to haggle —*n.* [Brit. Slang] a thief or pickpocket

prill (pril) *n.* [orig. colloq. term in Cornwall < ?] a small, beadlike pellet —*vt.* to make (a substance) into prills

prim (prim) *adj.* **prim'mer, prim'mest** [< ? MFr. *prim*, prime, first (also sharp, thin, slender; hence, neat) < L. *primus*, first: see PRIME] stiffly formal, precise, moral, etc.; proper; demure —*vt., vi.* **primmed, prim'ming** to assume a prim expression on (one's face or mouth) —**prim'ly** *adv.* —**prim'ness** *n.*

prim. **1.** primary **2.** primitive

pri·ma ballerina (prē'mə) [It., lit., first ballerina] the principal woman dancer in a ballet company

pri·ma·cy (prī'mə sē) *n., pl.* **-cies** [ME. *primacie* < MFr. < ML. *primatia* < LL. *primas:* see PRIMATE] **1.** the state of being first in time, order, rank, etc.; supremacy **2.** the rank, office, or authority of a primate

pri·ma don·na (prē'mə dän'ə, prim'ə) *pl.* **pri'ma don'nas** [It., lit., first lady] **1.** the principal woman singer in an opera or concert **2.** [Colloq.] a temperamental, vain, or arrogant person; esp., such a woman

pri·ma fa·ci·e (prī'mə fā'shi ē', fā'shē) [L.] at first sight; on first view, before further examination

prima facie evidence [see prec.] *Law* evidence adequate to establish a fact or raise a presumption of fact unless refuted

pri·mal (prī'm'l) *adj.* [ML. *primalis* < L. *primus*, first: see PRIME] **1.** first in time; original; primitive; primeval **2.** first in importance; chief; primary

☆**pri·ma·quine** (prī'mə kwēn') *n.* a synthetic chemical compound, $C_{15}H_{21}N_3O$, used as a cure for malaria

pri·ma·ri·ly (prī mer'ə lē, prī'mer'-) *adv.* **1.** at first; originally **2.** mainly; principally

pri·ma·ry (prī'mer'ē, -mər ē) *adj.* [ME. *prymary* < L. *primarius* < *primus*, first: see PRIME] **1.** first in time or order of development; primitive; original; earliest **2.** *a)* from which others are derived; fundamental; elemental; basic *b)* designating colors regarded as basic, or as those from which all others may be derived: classification of colors as primary varies: see COLOR (senses 2 & 3) **3.** of or in the first stage of a succession; elementary; preparatory [*primary* school] **4.** first in importance; chief; principal; main [a *primary* concern] **5.** firsthand; direct [a *primary* source of information] **6.** *Chem. a)* characterized by or resulting from the replacement of one atom or radical *b)* characterized by groups or radicals that are attached to the end carbon atom of a chain, i.e., to a $-CH_2$ group (Ex.: *primary alcohols*, $-CH_2OH$; *primary amines*, $-CH_2NH_2$; etc.) **7.** *Elec.* designating or of an inducing current, input circuit, or input coil in a tranformer, induction coil, etc. **8.** *Geol. a)* formed directly by sedimentation, solidification, or precipitation and not subsequently altered: said of rocks *b)* [Obs.] designating or of the earliest geologic periods, up through the Paleozoic Era **9.** *Linguis.* having as its fundamental form a base or other element that cannot be broken down: said of derivation **10.** *Zool.* designating or of the large, stiff feathers on the end joint of a bird's wing —*n.*, *pl.* **-ries 1.** something first in order, quality, importance, etc. ☆**2.** in the U.S., *a)* a local meeting of voters of a given political party to nominate candidates for public office, select delegates to a nominating convention, etc, *b)* same as DIRECT PRIMARY ELECTION **3.** any of the primary colors **4.** *Astron. a)* a sun, planet, etc. in relation to its satellites *b)* the brighter member of a binary star **5.** *Elec.* a primary coil **6.** *Zool.* a primary feather

primary accent (or **stress**) **1.** the heavier stress or force given to one syllable in a spoken word or to one word in an utterance **2.** a mark (in this dictionary, ') to show this

primary cell a battery cell whose energy is derived from an essentially irreversible electrochemical reaction and which is hence incapable of being efficiently recharged by an electric current

primary electron in thermionics, any of the electrons falling on a body as distinguished from electrons emitted by it

primary school same as ELEMENTARY SCHOOL

pri·mate (prī'māt; *also, for 2*, -mit) *n.* [ME. *primat* < OFr. < LL. *primas* (gen. *primatis*) of the first, chief < L. *primus*, first: see PRIME] **1.** [Rare] a person with primacy **2.** an archbishop, or the highest-ranking bishop in a province, etc. **3.** any of an order (Primata) of mammals, including man, the apes, monkeys, lemurs, etc., characterized esp. by flexible hands and feet, each with five digits —**pri'mate·ship'** ('-ship') *n.* —**pri·ma·tial** (prī mā'shəl) *adj.*

prime (prīm) *adj.* [ME. < MFr. < L. *primus*, first < OL. *pri*, before < IE. < base *per*, beyond, whence FAR, FIRST] **1.** first in time; original; primitive; primary **2.** first in rank or authority; chief [the *prime* minister] **3.** first in importance or value; principal; main [a *prime* advantage] **4.** first in quality; of the highest excellence; first-rate [*prime* beef] **5.** from which others are derived; fundamental; basic **6.** *Finance* designating the most favorable rate of interest available on loans from banks **7.** *Math. a)* of or being a prime number *b)* having no factor in common except 1 [9 and 16 are *prime* to one another] —*n.* [ME. < OE. *prim* < L. *prima* (*hora*), first (hour): see the adj.] **1.** *a) Eccles.* [*often* P-] the first daylight canonical hour or office, usually beginning at 6 A.M. or sunrise *b)* the first hour of the day, usually corresponding to this; dawn *c)* the earliest part; beginning **2.** *a)* springtime *b)* the springtime of life; youth **3.** *a)* the best, most vigorous, or most fully mature period or stage of a person or thing [a soprano in her *prime*] *b)* the best part of anything *c)* the best of several or many; pick; cream **4.** *a)* any of a number of equal parts, usually sixty, into which a unit of measure, as a degree, is divided, and which usually may in turn be subdivided in the same proportion *b)* the mark indicating this ('): it is also used to distinguish a letter, etc. from another of the same kind, as *A'* **5.** *Math.* same as PRIME NUMBER **6.** *Music* same as UNISON —*vt.* **primed, prim'ing 1.** to make ready; prepare [a team *primed* for a game] **2.** to prepare (a gun) for firing or (a charge) for exploding by providing with priming or a primer **3.** *a)* to get (a pump) into operation by pouring in water until the suction is established *b)* to get (an empty carburetor) into operation by pouring in gasoline **4.** to undercoat, size, or otherwise prepare (a surface) for painting **5.** to provide (a person) beforehand with information, answers, etc. —*vi.* **1.** to prime a person or thing

2. to let water in the form of spray mix with the steam forced into the cylinder: said of steam engines and boilers —**prime'ness** *n.*

prime cost the direct cost of labor and material in producing an article, exclusive of capital, overhead, etc.

prime·ly (-lē) *adv.* [Colloq.] very well; excellently

prime meridian the meridian from which longitude is measured both east and west; 0° longitude: it passes through Greenwich, England

prime minister in parliamentary governments, the chief executive and, usually, head of the cabinet —**prime ministry**

prime mover 1. *a)* the original force in a series of transmissions of force *b)* any initiating or principal force **2.** any natural force applied by man to produce power, as muscular energy, flowing water, etc. **3.** a machine, as a turbine, that converts a natural force into productive power **4.** in Aristotle's philosophy, the first cause of all movement, itself immovable

prime number an integer that can be evenly divided by no other whole number than itself and 1, as 2, 3, 5, or 7: distinguished from COMPOSITE NUMBER

prim·er¹ (prim'ər; *Brit.* prī'mər) *n.* [ME. *prymer* < ML. *primarius* < L. *primus*, first: see PRIME] **1.** a simple book for first teaching children to read **2.** a textbook giving the first principles of any subject **3.** see GREAT PRIMER, LONG PRIMER

prim·er² (prī'mər) *n.* a person or thing that primes; specif., *a)* a small cap, tube, etc. containing an explosive, used to set off a main charge *b)* a preliminary coat of paint, sizing, etc.

prime ribs a choice cut of beef consisting of the seven ribs immediately before the loin

pri·me·ro (pri mer'ō) *n.* [Sp. *primera*, fem. of *primero*, first: see PRIMARY] a card game popular in the 16th and 17th centuries

☆**prime time** *Radio & TV* the hours when the largest audience is regularly available; esp., the evening hours

pri·me·val (prī mē'v'l) *adj.* [< L. *primaevus* (< *primus*, first: see PRIME + *aevum*, an AGE) + -AL] of the earliest times or ages; primal; primordial [*primeval* forests]

prim·ing (prī'miŋ) *n.* **1.** the act of a person or thing that primes **2.** the gunpowder or other explosive used to set off the charge in a gun or in blasting **3.** paint, sizing, etc. used as a primer

pri·mip·a·ra (prī mip'ər ə) *n.*, *pl.* **-a·ras, -a·rae'** (-ə rē') [L. < *primus*, first (see PRIME) + *parere*, to bear: see -PAROUS] a woman who is pregnant for the first time or who has borne just one child —**pri·mi·par·i·ty** (prī'mə par'ə tē) *n.* —**pri·mip'a·rous** *adj.*

prim·i·tive (prim'ə tiv) *adj.* [ME. *primitif* < MFr. < L. *primitivus* < *primus*, first: see PRIME] **1.** of or existing in the beginning or the earliest times or ages; ancient; original **2.** *a)* characteristic or imitative of the earliest ages [*primitive* art] *b)* crude, simple, rough, uncivilized, etc. **3.** not derivative; primary; basic **4.** *Biol. a)* designating or of an organism, organ, etc. at the starting point of its evolutionary development or very little evolved from early ancestral types *b)* same as PRIMORDIAL (sense 3) —*n.* **1.** a primitive person or thing **2.** *a)* an artist or a work of art of an early, esp. preliterate, culture *b)* an artist or work of art characterized by ingenuousness and lack of formal training **3.** *Algebra, Geom.* a form from which another is derived **4.** *Gram.* the form from which a certain word or other form has been derived; root; base —**prim'i·tive·ly** *adv.* —**prim'i·tive·ness** *n.*

prim·i·tiv·ism (-tiv iz'm) *n.* **1.** belief in or practice of primitive ways, living, etc. **2.** the qualities, principles, etc. of primitive art or artists —**prim'i·tiv·ist** *n., adj.*

‡**pri·mo¹** (prē'mō) *adv.* [L. < *primus*, first: see PRIME] to begin with; first of all

‡**pri·mo²** (prē'mō) *n.* [It., lit., first < L. *primus:* see PRIME] *Music* the principal or leading part, as in a duet —*adj.* first

pri·mo·gen·i·tor (prī'mə jen'i tər) *n.* [LL. < L. *primus*, first (see PRIME) + *genitor*, a father < *genitus*, pp. of *gignere:* see ff.] **1.** an ancestor; forefather **2.** the earliest ancestor of a family, race, etc.

pri·mo·gen·i·ture (-chər) *n.* [ML. *primogenitura* < L. *primus*, first + *genitura*, a begetting < *gignere*, to beget: see GENUS] **1.** the condition or fact of being the firstborn of the same parents **2.** *Law* the exclusive right of the eldest son to inherit his father's estate

pri·mor·di·al (prī môr'dē əl) *adj.* [ME. < LL. *primordialis* < L. *primordium*, the beginning < *primus*, first (see PRIME) + *ordiri*, to begin: see ORDER] **1.** first in time; existing at or from the beginning; primitive; primeval **2.** not derivative; fundamental; original **3.** *Biol.* earliest formed in the development of an organism, organ, structure, etc.; primitive —**pri·mor'di·al·ly** *adv.*

pri·mor·di·um (-əm) *n.*, *pl.* **-di·a** (-ə) [ModL. < L.; see prec.] *Embryology* the first recognizable aggregation of cells that will form a distinct organ or part of the embryo

primp (primp) *vt., vi.* [prob. extension of PRIM] to groom or dress up in a fussy way

prim·rose (prim′rōz′) *n.* [ME. *primerose* < MFr., altered (after *rose*, ROSE) < OFr. *primerole*, primrose < ML. *primula*, a flower, daisy, primrose < L. *primus*, first (see PRIME)] **1.** any of a genus (*Primula*) of plants of the primrose family, having variously colored, tubelike corollas with five spreading lobes **2.** the flower of any of these plants **3.** the light yellow of some primroses **4.** any of various other plants, as the evening primrose —*adj.* **1.** of the primrose **2.** light-yellow **3.** designating a family (Primulaceae) of plants principally in the N Hemisphere, with flowers borne in clusters on a leafless stem and including loosestrife, primrose, and cyclamen

primrose path [popularized after Shakespeare, *Hamlet*, I, iii] **1.** the path of pleasure, self-indulgence, etc. **2.** a course of action that is deceptively easy, proper, etc. but that can lead to disaster

prim·u·la (prim′yōō lə) *n.* [ML.] *same as* PRIMROSE (*n.* 1)

‡**pri·mum mo·bi·le** (prē′moom mō′bē lā′) [ML., first movable thing: see PRIME, *adj.* & MOBILE] *Ptolemaic Astron.* the tenth and outermost concentric sphere, revolving from east to west about the earth as a center and causing all heavenly bodies to revolve with it

Pri·mus (pri′məs) [arbitrary use of L. *primus*, first: see PRIME] *a trademark for* a small, portable stove (**Primus stove**), fueled orig. with kerosene but now usually with propane or butane —*n.* [p-] such a stove

‡**pri·mus in·ter pa·res** (prē′moos in′tər pä′res) [L.] first among equals

prin. 1. principal 2. principally 3. principle

prince (prins) *n.* [ME. < OFr. < L. *princeps*, first, chief, prince < *primo-caps*, lit., first-taken < *primus* (see PRIME) + *capere*, to take] **1.** orig., any male monarch; esp., a king **2.** a ruler whose rank is below that of king; head of a principality **3.** a nonreigning male member of a royal family **4.** *a)* in Great Britain, a son of the sovereign or of a son of the sovereign *b)* any of various noblemen in other countries ✩**5.** *a)* a preeminent person in any class or group [a merchant *prince*] *b)* [Colloq.] a fine, generous, helpful fellow —**prince′dom** *n.*

Prince Albert [prob. after *Prince Albert*, later King EDWARD VII] ✩a long, double-breasted frock coat

Prince Albert National Park Canad. national park in C Saskatchewan: 1,496 sq. mi.

prince consort the husband of a queen or empress reigning in her own right

Prince Edward Island island province of SE Canada, in the S Gulf of St. Lawrence: 2,184 sq. mi.; pop. 109,000; cap. Charlottetown: abbrev. **P.E.I.**

prince·ling (prins′liŋ) *n.* a young, small, or subordinate prince: also **prince′kin** (-kin), **prince′let** (-lit)

prince·ly (-lē) *adj.* -li·er, -li·est **1.** of a prince; royal; regal; noble **2.** that is a prince **3.** characteristic of a prince; liberal; generous **4.** worthy of a prince; magnificent; lavish —**prince′li·ness** *n.*

Prince of Darkness *an epithet for* SATAN

Prince of Peace *an epithet for* JESUS CHRIST

Prince of Wales *title conferred on* the oldest son and heir apparent of a British king or queen

Prince of Wales, Cape promontory of the Seward Peninsula, NW Alas., on the Bering Strait: westernmost point of N. America

Prince of Wales Island 1. island of SE Alas., largest in the Alexander Archipelago: 2,230 sq. mi. **2.** island in the SC District of Franklin, Northwest Territories, Canada: 12,830 sq. mi.

prince royal the oldest son of a king or queen

prince's-feath·er (prin′siz feth′ər) *n.* a tropical pigweed (*Amaranthus hybridus hypochondriacus*), sometimes grown as a garden flower for its elongated spikes of bristly red flowers

⚘**prince's pine** *same as* PIPSISSEWA

prin·cess[1] (prin′sis, -ses) *n.* [ME. *princesse* < MFr.: see PRINCE & -ESS] **1.** orig., any female monarch; esp., a queen **2.** a nonreigning female member of a royal family **3.** in Great Britain, a daughter of the sovereign or of a son of the sovereign **4.** the wife of a prince **5.** any woman regarded as like a princess, as in gracefulness, aloofness, etc.

prin·cess[2] (prin′sis, prin ses′) *adj.* [< Fr. *princesse*, a princess] of or designating a woman's one-piece, close-fitting, gored garment, unbroken at the waistline and with a flared skirt: also **prin·cesse′** (-ses′)

princess royal the oldest daughter of a king or queen

Prince·ton (prins′tən) [after the *Prince* of Orange, later WILLIAM III] borough in C N.J., near Trenton: scene of a battle (1777) of the Revolutionary War in which troops led by Washington defeated the British: pop. 12,000

prin·ci·pal (prin′sə pəl) *adj.* [ME. < OFr. < L. *principalis* < *princeps*: see PRINCE] **1.** first in rank, authority, importance, degree, etc. **2.** that is or has to do with principal (*n.* 3) —*n.* **1.** a principal person or thing; specif., *a)* a chief; head *b)* a governing or presiding officer, specif. of a school *c)* a main actor or performer *d)* either of the combatants in a duel **2.** any of the main end rafters of a roof, supporting the purlins, which in turn support the ordinary rafters **3.** *Finance a)* the amount of a debt, investment, etc. minus the interest, or on which interest is computed *b)* the face value of a stock or bond *c)* the main body of an estate, etc., as distinguished from income

4. *Law a)* a person who employs another to act as his agent *b)* the person primarily responsible for an obligation *c)* a person who commits a crime or is present as an abettor to it: cf. ACCESSORY **5.** *Music a)* any of the principal open stops of an organ *b)* the soloist in a concert *c)* the first player of any section of orchestral instruments except the first violins *d)* the subject of a fugue: opposed to ANSWER —*SYN.* see CHIEF —**prin′ci·pal·ly** *adv.* —**prin′ci·pal·ship′** *n.*

prin·ci·pal·i·ty (prin′sə pal′ə tē) *n.*, *pl.* -**ties** [ME. *principalite* < OFr. < LL. *principalitas*] **1.** [Rare] the state or quality of being principal or a principal **2.** the rank, dignity, or jurisdiction of a prince **3.** the territory ruled by a prince **4.** a country with which a prince's title is identified

✩**principal meridian** a meridian line accurately laid out to serve as the reference meridian in land survey

principal parts the principal inflected forms of a verb, from which the other forms may be derived: in English, the principal parts are the present infinitive, past tense, and past participle (Ex.: *drink, drank, drunk; go, went, gone*) The present participle, derived from the present infinitive with the addition of *-ing*, is sometimes regarded as one of the principal parts

Prín·ci·pe (prin′sə pē′; *Port.* prēn′sə pə) Port. island in the Gulf of Guinea, off the W coast of Africa: 54 sq. mi.; pop. 4,500: see SÃO TOMÉ

prin·cip·i·um (prin sip′ē əm) *n.*, *pl.* -**i·a** (-ə) [L., a beginning < *princeps*: see PRINCE] **1.** a principle **2.** [*pl.*] first principles; fundamentals

prin·ci·ple (prin′sə pəl) *n.* [ME., altered < MFr. *principe* < L. *principium*: see prec.] **1.** the ultimate source, origin, or cause of something **2.** a natural or original tendency, faculty, or endowment **3.** a fundamental truth, law, doctrine, or motivating force, upon which others are based [moral *principles*] **4.** *a)* a rule of conduct, esp. of right conduct *b)* such rules collectively *c)* adherence to them; integrity; uprightness [a man of *principle*] **5.** an essential element, constituent, or quality, esp. one that produces a specific effect [the active *principle* of a medicine] **6.** *a)* the scientific law that explains a natural action [the *principle* of cell division] *b)* the method of a thing's operation [the *principle* of a gasoline engine is internal combustion] —**in principle** as far as the principle is concerned; theoretically or in essence —**on principle** because of or according to a principle

prin·ci·pled (-pəld) *adj.* having principles, as of conduct: often in hyphenated compounds [high-*principled*]

prin·cox (prin′käks) *n.* [earlier also *princocks* < ? PREEN + *cox-*, as in COXCOMB] [Obs.] a coxcomb; fop

prink (priŋk) *vt.*, *vi.* [prob. altered (? after PREEN) < PRANK[2]] *same as* PRIMP

print (print) *n.* [ME. *prente* < OFr. *preinte* < *prient*, pp. of *preindre* < L. *premere*, to PRESS[1]] **1.** a mark made in or on a surface by pressing or hitting with an object; impression; imprint [the *print* of a heel] **2.** an object for making such a mark, as a stamp, die, seal, mold, etc. **3.** an object or mass that has received such a mark [a *print* of butter] **4.** a cloth printed with a design, or a dress, blouse, etc. made of this **5.** the condition of being printed **6.** printed lettering **7.** the impression made by inked type [uneven *print*] **8.** a picture or design printed from a plate, block, roll, etc., as an etching, woodcut, lithograph, etc. **9.** printed material [*newsprint*] **10.** a printed publication **11.** an edition or printing, as of a book **12.** a photograph, esp. one made from a negative —*vt.* [ME. *prenten, printen* < the *n.*] **1.** to mark by pressing or stamping; make a print on or in **2.** to press or stamp (a mark, letter, etc.) on or in a surface **3.** to draw, trace, carve, or otherwise make (a mark, letter, etc.) on a surface **4.** to produce on the surface of (paper, etc.) the impression of inked type, plates, etc. by means of a printing press **5.** to perform or cause to be performed all processes connected with the printing of (a book, etc.), as typesetting, presswork, etc. **6.** to publish in print [to print a story] **7.** to write in letters resembling printed ones [*print* the name] **8.** to produce (a photograph, or positive picture) from (a negative) **9.** in computers, to deliver (information) by means of a printer: often with *out* **10.** to impress upon the mind, memory, etc. —*vi.* **1.** to practice the art or trade of a printer **2.** to produce an impression, print, photograph, etc. [a negative that *prints* well] **3.** to write in letters resembling printed ones **4.** to produce newspapers, books, etc. by means of a printing press —**in print** 1. in printed form; published 2. still being sold by the publisher: said of books, etc. —**out of print** no longer being sold by the publisher: said of books, etc.

print·a·ble (-ə b'l) *adj.* **1.** that can be printed or printed from **2.** fit to print —**print′a·bil′i·ty** *n.*

printed circuit an electrical circuit formed by applying conductive material in fine lines or other shapes to an insulating sheet, as by printing with electrically conductive ink, by electroplating, etc.

print·er (-ər) *n.* **1.** a person whose work or business is printing **2.** a device that prints; esp. *a)* one that makes copies by chemical or photographic means *b)* in computers, a device that produces information in printed or type-written form

printer's devil an apprentice in a printing shop

☆print·er·y (-ē) n., pl. -er·ies same as PRINT SHOP (sense 1)

print·ing (-iŋ) n. 1. the act of a person or thing that prints 2. the production of printed matter 3. the art of a printer; typography 4. something printed; printed matter 5. same as IMPRESSION (sense 7 c) 6. written letters made like printed ones; lettering

printing press a machine for printing from inked type, plates, or rolls

print·less (-lis) adj. having, making, or leaving no print or mark

print·mak·er (-mā′kər) n. a person who makes prints, etchings, etc. —print′mak′ing n.

print·out (-out′) n. the output of a computer presented in printed or typewritten form

print shop ☆1. a shop where printing is done: also printing office 2. a shop where prints, etchings, etc. are sold

pri·or (prī′ər) adj. [L., former, superior, compar. of OL. pri, before: see PRIME] 1. preceding in time; earlier; previous; former 2. preceding in order or importance; preferred [a prior choice] —n. [ME. < OE. & OFr., both < ML.(Ec.), a prior < L.: see the adj.] 1. the head of a priory or other religious house 2. in an abbey, the person in charge next below the abbot —SYN. see PREVIOUS —prior to before in time

Pri·or (prī′ər), Matthew 1664-1721; Eng. poet

pri·or·ate (prī′ər it) n. [ME. < ML.(Ec.) prioratus < LL.(Ec.), preference] 1. the rank, office, or term of a prior: also pri′or·ship′ 2. same as PRIORY

pri·or·ess (-is) n. [ME. prioresse < MFr. < ML.(Ec.) priorissa: see PRIOR & -ESS] 1. the woman head of a priory of nuns, etc. 2. in an abbey of nuns, the woman in charge next below the abbess

pri·or·i·ty (prī ôr′ə tē, -är′-) n., pl. -ties [ME. priorite < ML. prioritas] 1. the fact or condition of being prior; precedence in time, order, importance, etc. 2. a) a right to precedence over others in obtaining, buying, or doing something b) an order granting this, as in an emergency 3. something given prior attention

pri·o·ry (prī′ər ē) n., pl. -ries [ME. < Anglo-Fr. priorie < ML. prioria] a monastery governed by a prior, or a convent governed by a prioress, sometimes as a subordinate branch of an abbey —SYN. see CLOISTER

Pri·pet (prē′pet) river in the Ukrainian S.S.R. & Byelorussian S.S.R., flowing east through the Pripet (or Pinsk) Marshes into the Dnepr: c. 500 mi.: Russ. name Pri·pyat (prē′pyät′y′)

Pris·cian (prish′ən, -ē ən) (L. name Priscianus Caseriensis) fl. 500 A.D.; Latin grammarian

Pris·cil·la (pri sil′ə) [L., dim. of Prisca, fem. of Priscus, a Roman surname < priscus, ancient, primitive, akin to OL. pri: see PRIME] a feminine name

prise (prīz) vt. prised, pris′ing chiefly Brit. var. of PRIZE² (vt. 2)

prism (priz′m) n. [LL. prisma < Gr. prisma, lit., something sawed < prizein, to saw < prien, to saw, bite, akin to Alb. prish, (I) destroy, break] 1. Geom. a solid figure whose ends are parallel, polygonal, and equal in size and shape, and whose sides are parallelograms 2. a crystalline body whose lateral faces meet at edges that are parallel to each other 3. anything that refracts light, as a drop of water 4. Optics a) a transparent body, as of glass, whose ends are equal and parallel triangles, and whose three sides are parallelograms: used for refracting or dispersing light, as into the spectrum b) any similar body of three or more sides

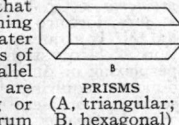

PRISMS
(A, triangular;
B, hexagonal)

pris·mat·ic (priz mat′ik) adj. [< Gr. prisma, gen. prismatos (see PRISM) + -IC] 1. of or resembling a prism 2. that refracts light as a prism 3. that forms or resembles prismatic colors 4. many-colored; brilliant; dazzling 5. same as ORTHORHOMBIC —pris·mat′i·cal·ly adv.

prismatic colors the colors of the visible spectrum produced by passing white light through a prism; red, orange, yellow, green, blue, indigo, and violet

pris·moid (priz′moid) n. [see PRISM & -OID] a prismlike solid figure whose ends are parallel but unequal polygons and whose sides are consequently trapezoids instead of parallelograms —pris·moi′dal adj.

pris·on (priz′n) n. [ME. < OFr. < L. prensio, for prehensio, a taking < prehendere, to take: see PREHENSILE] 1. a place where persons are confined 2. a building, usually with cells, where convicted criminals are confined or where accused persons are held while awaiting trial; spec., such a building maintained by a State or the Federal government: see PENITENTIARY, JAIL, & REFORMATORY 3. imprisonment —vt. archaic var. of IMPRISON

pris·on·er (priz′nər, -′n ər) n. [ME. < OFr. prisonier] 1. a person confined in prison, as for some crime 2. a person held in custody 3. a person captured or held captive: often in metaphorical usage [a prisoner of love]

prisoner of war a member of the regular or irregular armed forces of a nation at war held captive by the enemy

prisoner's base a children's game in which each side has a base to which captured opponents are brought

☆pris·sy (pris′ē) adj. -si·er, -si·est [prob. PR(IM) + (S)ISSY] [Colloq.] very prim or precise; fussy, prudish, etc. —pris′si·ly adv. —pris′si·ness n.

pris·tine (pris′tēn, -tin; pris tēn′) adj. [L. pristinus, former < OL. pri, before: see PRIME] 1. characteristic of the earliest, or an earlier, period or condition; original 2. still pure or untouched; uncorrupted; unspoiled [pristine beauty] —pris′tine·ly adv.

prith·ee (prith′ē) interj. [altered < pray thee] [Archaic] I pray thee; please

priv. 1. private 2. privative

pri·va·cy (prī′və sē; Brit. also priv′ə-) n., pl. -cies [ME. priuace: see PRIVATE & -CY] 1. the quality or condition of being private; withdrawal from public view or company; seclusion 2. secrecy [told in strict privacy] 3. one's private life or personal affairs [an invasion of one's privacy]

‡Pri·vat·do·cent (prī vät′dō tsent′) n., pl. -cent·en (-ən) [G. < privat, private + docent, dozent, teacher: see DOCENT] in German universities, an unsalaried lecturer paid only by his students' fees: also sp. Pri·vat′do·zent′, pl. -zent′en

pri·vate (prī′vit) adj. [ME. prywat < L. privatus, belonging to oneself, not to the state < privare, to separate, deprive < privus, separate, peculiar, prob. akin to OL. pri: see PRIME] 1. of, belonging to, or concerning a particular person or group; not common or general [private property, a private joke] 2. not open to, intended for, or controlled by the public [a private school] 3. for an individual person [a private room in a hospital] 4. not holding public office [a private citizen] 5. away from public view; secluded [a private dining room] 6. not publicly or generally known; secret; confidential [a private matter] 7. carried out or done on an individual basis [private medical practice] 8. engaged in work independent of institutions, organizations, agencies, etc. [private detective, private tutor] —n. 1. [pl.] the genitals: also private parts 2. an enlisted man of either of the two lowest ranks in the U.S. Army or of the lowest rank in the U.S. Marine Corps —in private privately or secretly; not publicly —pri′vate·ly adv.

private enterprise same as FREE ENTERPRISE

pri·va·teer (prī′və tir′) n. [< PRIVATE + -EER] 1. a privately owned and manned armed ship commissioned by a belligerent government to attack and capture enemy ships, esp. merchant ships 2. a commander or crew member of a privateer: also ☆pri′va·teers′man (-mən), pl. -men (-mən) —vi. to sail on or as a privateer

☆private eye [Slang] a private detective

☆private first class an enlisted man ranking just below a corporal in the U.S. Army and just below a lance corporal in the U.S. Marine Corps: abbrev. Pfc., PFC

private law that branch of the law dealing with the relationships of private individuals to one another: cf. PUBLIC LAW

pri·va·tion (prī vā′shən) n. [ME. privacion < L. privatio < privare: see PRIVATE] 1. a depriving or being deprived; deprivation; specif., the loss or absence of some quality or condition 2. lack of the ordinary necessities or comforts of life; want

pri·va·tism (prī′vit iz'm) n. concern only with one's private life and personal involvements rather than with public affairs, social values, etc. —pri′va·tist, pri′va·tis′tic adj. —pri′va·ti·za′tion n. —pri′va·tize′ (-tīz′) vt. -tized′, -tiz′ing

priv·a·tive (priv′ə tiv) adj. [L. privativus < pp. of privare: see PRIVATE] 1. depriving or tending to deprive 2. characterized by a taking away or loss of some quality 3. Gram. indicating negation, absence, or loss —n. a privative term or affix, as a-, un-, non-, or -less —priv′a·tive·ly adv.

priv·et (priv′it) n. [< ?] any of a genus (Ligustrum) of shrubs or trees of the olive family, with bluish-black berries and spikes of white flowers, often grown for hedges; esp., the common privet (Ligustrum vulgare)

priv·i·lege (priv′'l ij, priv′lij) n. [ME. < OFr. < L. privilegium, an exceptional law for or against any individual < privus, PRIVATE + lex (gen. legis), a law] 1. a right, advantage, favor, or immunity specially granted to one; esp., a right held by a certain individual, group, or class, and withheld from certain others or all others 2. a basic civil right, guaranteed by a government [the privilege of trial by jury] 3. an option, as a put, call, etc., to buy or sell a stock —vt. -leged, -leg·ing to grant a privilege or privileges to

priv·i·leged (-ijd) adj. having one or more privileges

privileged communication Law 1. a communication that one cannot legally be compelled to divulge, as that to a lawyer from his client 2. a communication made under such circumstances, as in a legislative proceeding, that it is not actionable as slander or libel

priv·i·ty (priv′ə tē) n., pl. -ties [ME. privete < OFr. < L. privus, PRIVATE] 1. a) private or secret knowledge, as shared between persons b) participation in this 2. Law a successive relationship to or mutual interest in the same property or rights, established by law or legalized by

contract, as between a testator and legatee, lessor and lessee, etc.

priv·y (priv′ē) *adj.* [ME. < OFr. *prive* < L. *privatus*, PRIVATE] **1.** orig., private; not public; personal: now only in such phrases as PRIVY COUNCIL **2.** [Archaic] hidden, secret, clandestine, surreptitious, or furtive —*n., pl.* **priv′ies 1.** a toilet; esp., an outhouse **2.** *Law* a person who is in privity with another —**privy to** secretly or privately informed about —**priv′i·ly** *adv.*

privy council a body of advisers or confidential counselors appointed by or serving a ruler or any of certain governors general —**privy councilor**

privy purse an allowance from the public revenue for the personal expenses of the British sovereign

privy seal in Great Britain, the seal placed on documents which are later to receive the great seal or which are not important enough to receive the great seal

‡prix fixe (prē fēks′) [Fr., fixed price] **1.** a set price for a complete meal **2.** such a meal

prize¹ (prīz) *vt.* **prized, priz′ing** [ME. *pris:* see PRICE] **1.** to set a value upon; appraise; price **2.** to value highly; esteem —*n.* **1.** something offered or given to the winner of a contest **2.** something won in a game of chance, lottery, etc. **3.** a reward, premium, or the like **4.** anything worth striving for; any enviable or highly valued possession **5.** [Archaic] a contest or match —*adj.* **1.** that has received a prize [a *prize* novel] **2.** worthy of a prize; first-rate **3.** given as a prize —SYN. see APPRECIATE, REWARD

prize² (prīz) *n.* [ME. *prise*, a taking hold < OFr., a taking < fem. pp. of *prendre*, to take < L. *prehendere:* see PREHENSILE] **1.** orig., the act of capturing; seizure **2.** something taken by force, as in war; esp., a captured enemy warship or its cargo **3.** [Dial.] *a*) an instrument for prying; lever *b*) leverage —*vt.* **prized, priz′ing 1.** to seize as a prize of war **2.** to pry, as with a lever —SYN. see SPOIL

prize court a court that decides how captured property, esp. that taken at sea in wartime, is to be distributed

prize·fight (prīz′fīt′) *n.* [back-formation < *prizefighter* < PRIZE¹] a professional boxing match —**prize′fight′er** *n.* —**prize′fight′ing** *n.*

prize money [< PRIZE²] money made by taking a prize; specif., profit made from a captured ship and its cargo

priz·er (prī′zər) *n.* [Archaic] a person competing for a prize, as in a contest

prize ring 1. a square platform or similar area, enclosed by ropes, for prizefights **2.** prizefighting

pro¹ (prō) *adv.* [L., for < IE. base *pro*, forward, whence Gr. *pro*, before, Goth. *fra-*, G. *ver-*] on the affirmative side; favorably —*adj.* favorable —*prep.* favorably disposed toward; for —*n., pl.* **pros 1.** a person who favors the affirmative side of some debatable question **2.** an argument in favor of something [the *pros* and cons of a matter] **3.** a vote for the affirmative

pro² (prō) *adj., n., pl.* **pros** *clipped form of* PROFESSIONAL

pro-¹ (prō) [Gr. *pro-* < *pro*, before: see PRO¹] *a prefix meaning* before in place or time [*proboscis, prolepsis*]

pro-² (prō) [L. < *pro*, before, forward, for: see PRO¹] *a prefix meaning:* **1.** moving forward or ahead of [*proclivity*] **2.** forth [*produce*] **3.** substituting for, acting for [*pronoun*] **4.** defending, supporting [*prolabor*]

PRO, P.R.O. public relations officer (or office)

pro·a (prō′ə) *n.* [Malay *prau, prao*] a swift Malayan boat having a lateen sail and one outrigger

prob. 1. probable **2.** probably **3.** problem

prob·a·bi·lism (präb′ə b'l iz'm) *n.* [Fr. *probabilisme:* see PROBABLE & -ISM] **1.** *Philos.* the doctrine that certainty in knowledge is impossible and that probability is a sufficient basis for action and belief **2.** *R.C.Ch.* the principle that in matters concerning which there is more than one probable opinion, it is lawful to follow any one of them —**prob′a·bi·list** *n., adj.*

PROA

prob·a·bil·is·tic (präb′ə bə lis′tik) *adj.* **1.** of or based on probabilism **2.** of, based on, or involving probability

prob·a·bil·i·ty (präb′ə bil′ə tē) *n., pl.* **-ties** [MFr. *probabilité* < L. *probabilitas*] **1.** the quality or state of being probable; likelihood **2.** something probable **3.** *Math.* the number of times something will probably occur over the range of possible occurrences, expressed as a ratio —**in all probability** very likely

prob·a·ble (präb′ə b'l) *adj.* [ME. < MFr. < L. *probabilis* < *probare*, to prove: see PROBE] **1.** likely to occur or be; that can reasonably but not certainly be expected [the *probable* winner] **2.** reasonably so, as on the basis of evidence, but not proved [the *probable* cause of a disease] —**prob′a·bly** *adv.*

SYN.—**probable** applies to that which appears reasonable on the basis of evidence or logic but is neither certain nor proved; **possible** applies to that which, although not probable, can conceivably exist, occur, be done, etc.; **likely** suggests greater probability than **possible**, but less credibility than **probable** —ANT. **improbable, unlikely**

probable cause *Law* reasonable grounds for presuming guilt in someone charged with a crime

pro·band (prō′band) *n.* [< L. *probandus*, gerundive of *probare*, to test: see PROVE] *same as* PROPOSITUS

pro·bang (prō′baŋ) *n.* [altered (after PROBE) < earlier *provang* < ? obs. *provet*, probe + FANG] *Med.* a flexible, slender rod tipped with a sponge, tuft, etc., used for clearing or medicating the esophagus or larynx

pro·bate (prō′bāt) *n.* [ME. *probat* < L. *probatus*, pp. of *probare*, to prove: see PROBE] **1.** the act or process of proving before a duly authorized person that a document submitted for official certification and registration, as a last will and testament, is genuine **2.** the judicial certification of a will **3.** the copy of a probated will certified as proved ☆**4.** all matters coming under the jurisdiction of probate courts —*adj.* having to do with probate or a probate court —*vt.* **-bat·ed, -bat·ing 1.** to establish officially the genuineness or validity of (a will) ☆**2.** popularly, to certify in a probate court as mentally unsound

☆**probate court** a court having jurisdiction over the probating of wills, the administration of estates, and, usually, the guardianship of minors and incompetents

pro·ba·tion (prō bā′shən) *n.* [ME. < OFr. < L. *probatio* < *probare*, to prove: see PROBE] **1.** a testing or trial, as of a person's character, ability to meet requirements, etc. **2.** the suspension of sentence of a person convicted but not yet imprisoned, on condition of continued good behavior and regular reporting to a probation officer **3.** *a*) the status of a person being tested or on trial [a student on *probation* because of low grades] *b*) the period of testing or trial **4.** [Obs.] proof —**pro·ba′tion·ar′y, pro·ba′tion·al** *adj.*

pro·ba·tion·er (-ər) *n.* a person on probation

☆**probation officer** an officer appointed by a magistrate to watch over and guide persons placed on probation

pro·ba·tive (prō′bə tiv, präb′ə-) *adj.* [ME. *probatiffe* < L. *probativus* < *probatus*, pp.: see PROBE] **1.** serving to test or try **2.** providing proof or evidence Also **pro·bato′ry** (-tôr′ē)

probe (prōb) *n.* [LL. *proba*, proof (in ML., examination) < L. *probare*, to test, prove < *probus*, good, proper < IE. *probhwos* (whence Sans. *prabhúh*, outstanding) < *pro-*, forward + base *bhu-*, to grow, whence BE] **1.** a slender, blunt surgical instrument for exploring a wound or the like **2.** the act of probing **3.** a searching examination; specif., ☆*a*) an investigation, as by a legislative committee, into corruption, etc. *b*) an exploratory advance or patrol ☆**4.** an instrumented spacecraft for exploring the upper atmosphere, space, or a celestial body in order to get information about the environment, physical properties, etc. **5.** any of various devices, as a Pitot tube, electrode, etc., inserted into an environment for measuring, testing, etc. —*vt.* **probed, prob′ing 1.** to explore (a wound, etc.) with a probe **2.** to investigate or examine with great thoroughness —*vi.* to search; investigate —SYN. see INVESTIGATION —**prob′er** *n.*

prob·i·ty (prō′bə tē, präb′ə-) *n.* [L. *probitas* < *probus*, good, proper: see prec.] uprightness in one's dealings; complete honesty; integrity —SYN. see HONESTY

prob·lem (präb′ləm) *n.* [ME. *probleme* < MFr. < L. *problema* < Gr. *problēma* < *proballein*, to throw forward < *pro-*, forward + *ballein*, to throw, drive: see PRO-¹ & BALL²] **1.** a question proposed for solution or consideration **2.** a question, matter, situation, or person that is perplexing or difficult **3.** *Math.* anything required to be done, or requiring the doing of something —*adj.* **1.** presenting a problem of human conduct or social relationships [a *problem* novel] **2.** very difficult to deal with, esp. to train or discipline [a *problem* child]

prob·lem·at·ic (präb′lə mat′ik) *adj.* [Fr. *problématique* < L. *problematicus* < Gr. *problematikos* < *problēma* (see PROBLEM) + -AL] **1.** having the nature of a problem; hard to solve or deal with **2.** not settled; yet to be determined; uncertain Also **prob′lem·at′i·cal** —SYN. see DOUBTFUL —**prob′lem·at′i·cal·ly** *adv.*

‡pro bo·no pu·bli·co (prō bō′nō pub′li kō′) [ML.] for the public good; for the commonweal

pro·bos·cid·e·an (prō′bə sid′ē ən) *n.* [see ff. & -AN] any of an order (Proboscidea) of large mammals having tusks and a long, flexible, tubelike snout, as the elephant or the extinct mastodon —*adj.* of the proboscideans Also sp. **pro′bos·cid′i·an**

pro·bos·cis (prō bäs′is) *n., pl.* **-cis·es, -ci·des′** (-ə dēz′) [L. < Gr. *proboskis* < *pro-*, before + *boskein*, to feed, graze, prob. akin to *bous*, COW¹] **1.** an elephant's trunk, or a long, flexible snout, as of a tapir **2.** any tubular organ for sucking, food-gathering, sensing, etc., as of some insects, worms, and mollusks **3.** a person's nose, esp. if large: a jocular usage

proc. 1. proceedings **2.** process

pro·caine (prō′kān) *n.* [PRO-² + (CO)CAINE] a synthetic crystalline compound, $C_{13}H_{20}O_2N_2 \cdot HCl$, used in the form of its hydrochloride as a local anesthetic

pro·cam·bi·um (prō kam′bē əm) *n.* [ModL.: see PRO-² & CAMBIUM] *Bot.* the meristem or growing layer in the tip of a stem or root which gives rise to primary phloem, primary xylem, and cambium —**pro·cam′bi·al** *adj.*

pro·carp (prō′kärp) *n.* [ModL. *procarpium:* see PRO-² & -CARP] *Bot.* a female reproductive organ in certain algae

pro·ca·the·dral (prō′kə thē′drəl) *n.* a church used as a temporary substitute for a cathedral

pro·ce·dure (prə sē′jər, prō-) *n.* [Fr. *procédure* < MFr. < *proceder:* see ff.] **1.** the act, method, or manner of proceeding in some process or course of action; esp., the sequence of steps to be followed **2.** a particular course of action or way of doing something **3.** the established way of carrying on the business of a legislature, law court, etc. —**pro·ce′dur·al** *adj.* —**pro·ce′dur·al·ly** *adv.*

pro·ceed (prə sēd′, prō-) *vi.* [ME. *proceden* < L. *procedere* < *pro-*, forward + *cedere*, to go: see PRO-² & CEDE] **1.** to advance or go on, esp. after stopping **2.** to go on speaking, esp. after an interruption **3.** to undertake and carry on some action *[to proceed to eat one's dinner]* **4.** to move along or be carried on *[a project that is proceeding well]* **5.** to take legal action (often with *against*) **6.** *a)* to come forth or issue *(from)* *b)* to arise or originate *(from)*

pro·ceed·ing (-in) *n.* **1.** an advancing or going on with what one has been doing **2.** the carrying on of an action or course of action **3.** a particular action or course of action **4.** [*pl.*] a record of the business transacted by a learned society or other organized group **5.** *a)* [*pl.*] legal action *b)* the taking of legal action

pro·ceeds (prō′sēdz) *n.pl.* that which proceeds or results, as from a transaction; esp., the sum or profit derived from a sale, venture, etc.

pro·ce·phal·ic (prō′sə fal′ik) *adj.* [PRO-² + CEPHALIC] of or relating to the fore part of the head

proc·ess¹ (präs′es; *chiefly Brit. & Canad.*, prō′ses) *n.* [ME. < OFr. *proces* < L. *processus*, pp. of *procedere:* see PROCEED] **1.** the course of being done: chiefly in **in process 2.** course (*of* time, etc.) **3.** a continuing development involving many changes *[the process of digestion]* **4.** a particular method of doing something, generally involving a number of steps or operations **5.** *Anat.* a projection or outgrowth from a larger structure, usually a bone *[the alveolar process of the jaw]* **6.** *Bot. & Zool.* an appendage or projecting part of an organism **7.** *Law a)* an action or suit *b)* a writ or summons directing a defendant to appear in court or enforcing compliance with a court's orders *c)* the total of such writs in any action or proceeding —*vt.* **1.** to prepare by or subject to a special process or method **2.** *Law a)* to prosecute *b)* to serve a process on —*adj.* **1.** prepared by a special treatment or process **2.** of, made by, used in, or using photomechanical or photoengraving methods **3.** designating a motion-picture shot, scene, etc. made by processing film, as by superimposing a foreground shot over a background shot —**in (the) process** of in or during the course of —**proc′es·sor, proc′ess·er** *n.*

proc·ess² (prə ses′) *vi.* [back-formation < PROCESSION] [Brit. Colloq.] to go in a procession

proc·ess cheese (präs′es) a cheese made by heating and blending together several natural cheeses with an emulsifying agent: also **proc′essed cheese**

pro·ces·sion (prə sesh′ən, prō-) *n.* [ME. < OFr. < L. *processio < procedere:* see PROCEED] **1.** the act of proceeding, esp. in an orderly manner **2.** a number of persons or things moving forward, as in a parade, in an orderly, formal way —*vi.* [Rare] to go in a procession

pro·ces·sion·al (-'l) *adj.* [MFr. < ML. *processionalis*] of, or used in connection with, a procession —*n.* [ME. < ML. *processionale*] **1.** a book setting forth the ritual to be observed in church processions **2.** a hymn sung at the beginning of a church service during the entrance of the clergy **3.** any musical composition to be played during a procession

proc·ess printing (präs′es) a method of reproducing color prints in almost any hue by the use of halftone plates in red, yellow, blue, and usually black

process server *Law* a policeman, sheriff, or deputy who delivers an official order, or process, to a person, commanding him to be in court at a time and place named in the order

‡**pro·cès-ver·bal** (prō se ver bȧl′) *n.*, *pl.* **-ver·baux′** (-bō′) [Fr., a verbal process] an official report of proceedings or facts; minutes (of a meeting)

pro·claim (prō klām′, prə-) *vt.* [ME. *proclamen* < MFr. *proclamer* < L. *proclamare* < *pro-*, before + *clamare*, to cry out: see PRO-¹ & CLAMOR] **1.** to announce officially; announce to be or show to be *[acts that proclaimed him a friend]* **3.** [Rare] to outlaw, ban, or otherwise restrict by a proclamation **4.** to praise or extol —*SYN.* see DECLARE

proc·la·ma·tion (präk′lə mā′shən) *n.* [ME. *proclamacion* < MFr. < L. *proclamatio*] **1.** a proclaiming or being proclaimed **2.** something that is proclaimed or announced officially

pro·clit·ic (prō klit′ik) *adj.* [ModL. *procliticus* < Gr. *proklinein*, to lean forward < *pro-*, forward (see PRO-¹) + *klinein*, to LEAN¹] *Gram.* dependent for its stress on the following word: said of a word that forms a phonetic unit with the following, stressed word (e.g., *for* in *once and for all*) —*n.* any such word or particle

pro·cliv·i·ty (prō kliv′ə tē) *n.*, *pl.* **-ties** [L. *proclivitas* < *proclivus*, downward < *pro-*, before (see PRO-²) + *clivus*, a slope (see DECLIVITY)] a natural or habitual tendency or inclination, esp. toward something discreditable —*SYN.* see INCLINATION

Pro·clus (prō′kləs, präk′ləs) 410?-485 A.D.; Gr. philosopher, born in Constantinople

Proc·ne (präk′nē) [L. < Gr. *Proknē*] *Gr. Myth.* sister of Philomela and wife of Tereus, transformed into a swallow by the gods

Pro·con·sul (prō kän′s'l) *n.* [PRO-¹ + *Consul*, name of a famous chimpanzee at the London Zoo (c. 1930)] a genus of African ape of the Miocene, a possible ancestor of the chimpanzee and gorilla

pro·con·sul (prō kän′s'l) *n.* [ME. < L. < *pro consule*, (acting) for the consul: see PRO-² & CONSUL] **1.** a Roman official invested with consular authority who commanded an army in one or more of the provinces and often acted as a provincial governor **2.** a governing official in a present-day colony, occupied territory, etc. —**pro·con′sul·ar** (-ər) *adj.* —**pro·con′sul·ate** (-it), **pro·con′sul·ship** *n.*

Pro·co·pi·us (prō kō′pē əs) 500?-565? A.D.; Byzantine historian

pro·cras·ti·nate (prō kras′tə nāt′, prə-) *vi.*, *vt.* **-nat′ed, -nat′ing** [< L. *procrastinatus*, pp. of *procrastinare* < *pro-*, forward (see PRO-²) + *crastinus*, belonging to the morrow < *cras*, tomorrow] to put off doing (something unpleasant or burdensome) until a future time; esp., to postpone (such actions) habitually —**pro·cras′ti·na′tion** *n.* —**pro·cras′ti·na′tor** *n.*

pro·cre·ant (prō′krē ənt) *adj.* [L. *procreans*, prp. of *procreare:* see ff.] **1.** producing young; fruitful **2.** of procreation

pro·cre·ate (-āt′) *vt.*, *vi.* **-at′ed, -at′ing** [< L. *procreatus*, pp. of *procreare*, to procreate < *pro-*, PRO-² + *creare*, to CREATE] **1.** to produce (young); beget (offspring) **2.** to produce or bring into existence —**pro·cre·a′tion** *n.* —**pro′cre·a′tive** *adj.* —**pro′cre·a′tor** *n.*

Pro·crus·te·an (prō krus′tē ən) *adj.* **1.** of or like Procrustes or his actions **2.** designed or acting to secure conformity at any cost; drastic or ruthless

Pro·crus·tes (-tēz) [L. < Gr. *Prokroustēs* < *prokrouein*, to beat out, stretch out] *Gr. Myth.* a giant of Attica who seized travelers, tied them to a bedstead, and either stretched them or cut off their legs to make them fit it

pro·cryp·tic (prō krip′tik) *adj.* [< PRO(TECT) + CRYPTIC] *Zool.* having protective coloration

proc·to- (präk′tō, -tə) [< Gr. *prōktos*, anus] *a combining form meaning* rectum *[proctology]*

proc·to·dae·um (präk′tə dē′əm) *n.*, *pl.* **-dae′a** (-ə), **-dae′ums** [ModL. < PROCT(O)- + Gr. *hodaios*, on the way < *hodos*, way: see -ODE¹] *Zool.* the end portion of the intestinal tract in many animals, formed in the embryo by a folding in of the body surface at the anus: also **proc′to·de′um** —**proc′to·dae′al** *adj.*

proc·tol·o·gy (präk täl′ə jē) *n.* [PROCTO- + -LOGY] the branch of medicine dealing with the rectum and anus and their diseases —**proc′to·log′ic** (-tə läj′ik), **proc′to·log′i·cal** *adj.* —**proc·tol′o·gist** *n.*

proc·tor (präk′tər) *n.* [ME. *proketour*, contr. < *procuratour:* see PROCURATOR] **1.** a person employed to manage the affairs of another; agent; attorney **2.** a college or university official who maintains order, supervises examinations, etc. —*vt.* to supervise (an academic examination) —**proc·to·ri·al** (präk tôr′ē əl) *adj.* —**proc′tor·ship′** *n.*

proc·to·scope (präk′tə skōp′) *n.* [PROCTO- + -SCOPE] an instrument used for the direct examination of the interior of the rectum —**proc′to·scop′ic** (-skäp′ik) *adj.* —**proc·tos′co·py** (-täs′kə pē) *n.*, *pl.* **-pies**

pro·cum·bent (prō kum′bənt) *adj.* [L. *procumbens*, prp. of *procumbere*, to lean forward < *pro-*, forward (see PRO-²) + *-cumbere < cubare*, to lie down (see CUBE¹)] **1.** lying face down **2.** *Bot.* trailing along the ground: said of a stem

proc·u·ra·cy (präk′yər ə sē) *n.*, *pl.* **-cies** [ME. *procuracie* < ML. *procuratia* < L. *procuratio:* see PROCURATION] the act or office of a procurator

proc·u·ra·tion (präk′yə rā′shən) *n.* [ME. *procuracion* < OFr. < L. *procuratio*] **1.** orig., management of another's affairs **2.** *a)* same as POWER OF ATTORNEY *b)* the act of granting power of attorney **3.** the act of procuring

proc·u·ra·tor (präk′yə rā′tər) *n.* [ME. *procuratour* < OFr. < L. *procurator < procurare:* see ff.] **1.** in the Roman Empire, an official who managed the financial affairs of a province or acted as governor of a territory not having the status of a province **2.** a person employed to manage another's affairs; agent —**proc′u·ra·to′ri·al** (-yər ə tôr′ē əl) *adj.*

pro·cure (prō kyoor′, prə-) *vt.* **-cured′, -cur′ing** [ME. *procuren* < MFr. *procurer*, to procure < L. *procurare*, to take care of, attend to < *pro-* (see PRO-²) + *curare*, to attend to < *cura*, a care (see CURE)] **1.** to get or bring about by some effort; obtain; secure *[to procure supplies, work, a settlement, etc.]* **2.** to obtain (women) for the purpose of prostitution —*vi.* to obtain women for the

purpose of prostitution —*SYN*. see GET —pro·cur′a·ble *adj.* —pro·cure′ment, pro·cur′ance, pro·cur′al *n.*

pro·cur·er (-ər) *n.* [ME. < Anglo-Fr. *procurour* < L. *procurator:* see PROCURATOR] a person who procures; specif., a man who obtains women for the purpose of prostitution; pimp —pro·cur′ess *n.fem.*

Pro·cy·on (prō′sē än′) [L. < Gr. *Prokyōn* < *pro-*, before + *kyōn*, dog: it rises before the Dog Star] a star of the first magnitude in the constellation Canis Minor

prod (präd) *vt.* [< ?] **prod′ded, prod′ding** 1. to jab or poke with or as with a pointed stick; goad 2. to urge or stir into action —*n.* 1. the act of prodding; jab, poke, thrust, etc. 2. something that prods; specif., a rod or pointed stick used in driving cattle —**prod′der** *n.*

prod. 1. produce 2. produced 3. product

prod·i·gal (präd′i gəl) *adj.* [MFr. < L. *prodigus*, prodigal < *prodigere*, to drive forth or away, waste < *pro-*, forth + *agere*, to drive: see PRO-² & ACT] 1. exceedingly or recklessly wasteful 2. extremely generous; lavish [*prodigal* with one's praise] 3. extremely abundant; profuse —*n.* a person who wastes his means; spendthrift —*SYN*. see PROFUSE —prod′i·gal′i·ty (-gal′ə tē) *n., pl.* -ties — prod′i·gal·ly *adv.*

prodigal son *Bible* a wastrel son who was welcomed back warmly on his homecoming in repentance: Luke 15:11–32

pro·di·gious (prə dij′əs) *adj.* [L. *prodigiosus*, marvelous < *prodigium:* see ff.] 1. wonderful; amazing 2. of great size, power, extent, etc.; enormous; huge 3. [Obs.] portentous —pro·di′gious·ly *adv.* —pro·di′gious·ness *n.*

prod·i·gy (präd′ə jē) *n., pl.* -gies [L. *prodigium* < *pro-*, before + OL. **agiom*, a thing said < *aio*, I say: see ADAGE] 1. [Rare] an extraordinary happening, thought to foretell some good or evil 2. a person, thing, or act so extraordinary as to inspire wonder; specif., a child of highly unusual talent or genius

pro·drome (prō′drōm) *n.* [Fr. < L. *prodromus* < Gr. *prodromos*, forerunner: see PRO-¹ & -DROME] *Med.* a warning symptom indicating the onset of a disease —pro·dro·mal (prō drō′m'l, präd′rə-), pro·drom′ic (-dräm′ik) *adj.*

pro·duce (prə dōōs′, -dyōōs′; *for n.*, präd′ōōs, -yōōs; prō′dōōs, -dyōōs) *vt.* **-duced′, -duc′ing** [L. *producere* < *pro-*, forward + *ducere*, to lead, draw: see PRO-² & DUCT] 1. to bring to view; offer for inspection [to *produce* identification] 2. to bring forth; bear; yield [a well that *produces* oil] 3. *a)* to make or manufacture [to *produce* steel] *b)* to bring into being; create [to *produce* a work of art] 4. to cause; give rise to [war *produces* devastation] 5. to get (a play, motion picture, etc.) ready for presentation to the public 6. *Econ.* to create (anything having exchange value) 7. *Geom.* to extend (a line or plane) —*vi.* to bear, yield, create, manufacture, etc. something —*n.* something that is produced; yield; esp., fresh fruits and vegetables —pro·duc′i·bil′i·ty *n.* —pro·duc′i·ble *adj.*

pro·duc·er (prə dōōs′ər, -dyōōs′-) *n.* 1. a person or thing that produces; specif., one who produces goods and services: opposed to CONSUMER 2. a special type of furnace for making producer gas 3. a person in charge of the financing and coordination of all activities in connection with the production of a play, motion picture, etc.

producer gas a fuel gas that is a mixture of nitrogen, carbon monoxide, and hydrogen, made by passing air or a mixture of air and steam over incandescent coal or coke

producer goods goods, such as raw materials and machines, that are used in producing consumer goods: also **producers′ goods**

prod·uct (präd′əkt) *n.* [ME. < ML. *productum* < neut. pp. of L. *producere:* see PRODUCE] 1. something produced by nature or made by human industry or art 2. result; outgrowth [a *product* of one's imagination] 3. *Chem.* any substance resulting from a chemical change 4. *Math.* the number obtained by multiplying two or more numbers together

pro·duc·tion (prə duk′shən) *n.* [LME. < MFr. < L. *productio*] 1. the act or process of producing 2. the rate of producing or amount produced 3. *a)* something produced; product *b)* a work of art, literature, etc. *c)* a work produced on the stage, as a motion picture, etc. 4. *Econ.* the creation of economic value; producing of goods and services —**make a production (out) of** [Colloq.] to dwell on, fuss over, elaborate, etc. needlessly and annoyingly

pro·duc·tive (-tiv) *adj.* [ML. *productivus* < LL., fit for prolongation < L. *productus*, pp. of *producere:* see PRODUCE] 1. producing abundantly; fertile [*productive* soil, a *productive* mind] 2. marked by abundant production or effective results [a *productive* day] 3. bringing as a result (with *of*) [war is *productive* of much misery] 4. *Econ.* of or engaged in the creating of economic value, or the producing of goods and services 5. *Linguis.* designating any prefix or suffix which can be and still is used to form new words, as *non-* —pro·duc′tive·ly *adv.* —pro·duc·tiv·i·ty (prō′dək tiv′ə tē, präd′ək-, prə duk′-), pro·duc′tive·ness *n.*

pro·em (prō′em) *n.* [ME. *proheme* < MFr. < L. *prooemium* < Gr. *prooimion* < *pro-*, before + *oimē*, song] a brief introduction or preface —pro·e·mi·al (prō ē′mē əl) *adj.*

pro·en·zyme (prō en′zīm) *n.* [PRO-¹ + ENZYME] *same as* ZYMOGEN

☆**prof** (präf) *n.* [Colloq.] *clipped form of* PROFESSOR

☆**Prof.** Professor

prof·a·na·tion (präf′ə nā′shən) *n.* [Fr. < LL.(Ec.) *profanatio* < L. *profanare:* see PROFANE] a profaning or being profaned; desecration; defilement —*SYN*. see SACRILEGE —pro·fan·a·to·ry (prə fan′ə tôr′ē, prō-) *adj.*

pro·fane (prə fān′, prō-) *adj.* [LME. *prophane* < MFr. < L. *profanus* < *pro-*, before + *fanum*, a temple; lit., before the temple, hence not sacred, common: see PRO-¹ & FANE] 1. not connected with religion or religious matters; secular [*profane* art] 2. not initiated into the inner mysteries or esoteric knowledge of something 3. not hallowed or consecrated 4. showing disrespect or contempt for sacred things; irreverent —*vt.* **-faned′, -fan′ing** 1. to treat (sacred things) with irreverence or contempt; desecrate 2. to put to a base or improper use; debase; defile —pro·fane′ly *adv.* —pro·fane′ness *n.* —pro·fan′er *n.*

pro·fan·i·ty (-fan′ə tē) *n.* [LL.(Ec.) *profanitas*] 1. the state or quality of being profane 2. *pl.* **-ties** something that is profane; esp., profane language or the use of profane language —*SYN*. see BLASPHEMY

pro·fess (prə fes′, prō-) *vt.* [< L. *professus*, pp. of *profiteri*, to avow publicly < *pro-*, before (see PRO-²) + *fateri*, to avow, akin to *fari*, to speak: see FABLE] 1. to make an open declaration of; affirm [to *profess* one's love] 2. to claim to have (some feeling, an interest, knowledge, etc.): often connoting insincerity or pretense 3. to practice as one's profession 4. to declare one's belief in [to *profess* Christianity] 5. [ME. *professen* < *profes*, professed < L. *professus*] to accept into a religious order —*vi.* 1. to make profession, or affirmation 2. to make one's profession (sense 4)

pro·fessed (-fest′) *adj.* [ME. < *profes* (see prec.) + *-ed, -ED*] 1. openly declared; avowed 2. insincerely avowed; pretended 3. having made one's profession (sense 4) 4. professing to be duly qualified [a *professed* economist] —pro·fess′ed·ly (-fes′id lē) *adv.*

pro·fes·sion (prə fesh′ən) *n.* [ME. < OFr. < L. *professio*] 1. a professing, or declaring; avowal, whether true or pretended [a *profession* of sympathy] 2. *a)* the avowal of belief in a religion *b)* a faith or religion professed 3. *a)* a vocation or occupation requiring advanced education and training, and involving intellectual skills, as medicine, law, theology, engineering, teaching, etc. *b)* the body of persons in any such calling or occupation *c)* loosely, any occupation 4. the act or ceremony of taking vows on formally entering a religious order —**the oldest profession** prostitution: a jocular usage

pro·fes·sion·al (-'l) *adj.* 1. of, engaged in, or worthy of the high standards of, a profession ☆2. designating of or a school, esp. a graduate school, offering instruction in a profession 3. earning one's living from an activity, such as a sport, not normally thought of as an occupation 4. engaged in by professional players [*professional* hockey] 5. engaged in a specified occupation for pay or as a means of livelihood [a *professional* writer] 6. being such in the manner of one practicing a profession [a *professional* hatemonger] —*n.* 1. a person practicing a profession 2. *a)* a person who engages in some art, sport, etc. for money, esp. for his livelihood, rather than as a hobby *b)* a golfer, tennis player, etc. affiliated with a particular club as a contestant, teacher, and the like: usually clipped to **pro** 3. a person who does something with great skill —pro·fes′sion·al·ly *adv.*

pro·fes·sion·al·ism (-'l iz'm) *n.* 1. professional quality, status, etc. 2. the practice or fact of using professional players in organized sports

pro·fes·sion·al·ize (-'l īz′) *vt.* **-ized′, -iz′ing** to cause to have professional qualities, status, etc. —pro·fes′sion·al·i·za′tion *n.*

pro·fes·sor (prə fes′ər) *n.* [ME. *professoure* < L., a teacher < *professus:* see PROFESS] 1. a person who professes something; esp., one who openly declares his sentiments, religious beliefs, etc. 2. a teacher; specif., a college teacher of the highest rank, usually in a specific field; full professor: see also ASSISTANT PROFESSOR, ASSOCIATE PROFESSOR ☆3. any person claiming or assumed to be especially skilled or experienced in some art, sport, etc.: a popular or humorous usage —pro·fes·so·ri·al (prō′fə sôr′ē əl) *adj.* —pro′fes·so′ri·al·ly *adv.* —pro·fes′sor·ship′, pro·fes′sor·ate (-it) *n.*

pro·fes·so·ri·ate (prō′fə sôr′ē it) *n.* [see prec. & -ATE²] 1. academic professors collectively 2. the office or position of a professor; professorship Also **pro′fes·so′ri·at** (-it, -at)

prof·fer (präf′ər) *vt.* [ME. *profren* < Anglo-Fr. & OFr. *proffrir* < *poroffrir* < *por-*, PRO-² + *offrir* < VL. **offerire*, for L. *offerre*, to OFFER] to offer (usually something intangible) [to *proffer* friendship] —*n.* [ME. & Anglo-Fr. *profre* < the *v.*] an offer or proposal —*SYN*. see OFFER

pro·fi·cient (prə fish′ənt) *adj.* [L. *proficiens*, prp. of *proficere*, to advance < *pro-*, forward + *facere*, to make: see PRO-² & FACT] highly competent; skilled; adept —*n.* an expert —pro·fi′cien·cy (-ən sē) *n., pl.* -cies —pro·fi′cient·ly *adv.*

pro·file (prō′fīl; *chiefly Brit.*, -fēl) *n.* [It. *profilo* < *profilare*, to outline < *pro-* (L. *pro-*), before + *filo*, a thread < L. *filum*, a thread: see PRO-² & FILE¹] 1. *a)* a side view of the face *b)* a drawing of such a view 2. a view of anything in contour; outline [the *profile* of a distant hill] ☆3. a short, vivid biographical and character sketch 4. a graph, diagram, writing, etc. presenting or summarizing data relevant to a particular person or thing 5. *Archit.* a side or sectional

elevation of a building, etc. —vt. -filed, -fil·ing 1. to sketch, write, or make a profile of 2. to give a specified profile to —SYN. see OUTLINE

prof·it (präf'it) n. [ME. < OFr. < L. profectus, pp. of proficere, to profit, lit., to move forward, advance: see PROFICIENT] 1. advantage; gain; benefit 2. [often pl.] a) financial or monetary gain obtained from the use of capital in a transaction or series of transactions b) the ratio of this to the amount of capital invested c) proceeds from property or investments 3. [often pl.] the sum remaining after all costs, direct and indirect, are deducted from the income of a business —vi. 1. to be of advantage or benefit 2. to reap an advantage, financial or otherwise; benefit —vt. to be of profit or advantage to —prof'it·less adj.

prof·it·a·ble (-ə b'l) adj. yielding profit, gain, or benefit —prof'it·a·bil'i·ty, prof'it·a·ble·ness n. —prof'it·a·bly adv.

profit and loss the gain and loss from business transactions, etc.: applied esp. to a bookkeeping account at the close of a fiscal period summarizing these and indicating net profit or loss

prof·i·teer (präf'ə tir') n. [PROFIT + -EER] a person who makes excessive profits, esp. by taking advantage of a shortage of supply to charge exorbitant prices —vi. to be a profiteer

profit sharing the practice of dividing a share of the profits of a business among employees, in addition to paying them stipulated wages —prof'it-shar'ing adj.

prof·li·gate (präf'lə git) adj. [L. profligatus, pp. of profligare, to strike to the ground, rout, ruin < pro-, forward (see PRO-²) + fligere, to drive, dash < IE. base *bhlĩĝ-, to strike, throw, whence W. blif, a catapult] 1. immoral and shameless; dissolute 2. extremely wasteful; recklessly extravagant —n. a profligate person —prof'li·ga·cy (-gə sē), prof'li·gate·ness n. —prof'li·gate·ly adv.

prof·lu·ent (präf'loo want) adj. [ME. < L. profluens, prp. of profluere < pro-, forth (see PRO-²) + fluere, to flow (see FLUCTUATE)] flowing smoothly or copiously

‡pro for·ma (prō fôr'mə) [L.] for (the sake of) form; as a matter of form

pro·found (prə found') adj. [ME. < OFr. profund < L. profundus < pro-, forward (see PRO-²) + fundus, BOTTOM] 1. very deep or low [a profound abyss, bow, sigh, sleep, etc.] 2. marked by intellectual depth [a profound discussion] 3. deeply or intensely felt [profound grief] 4. thoroughgoing [profound changes] 5. unbroken [a profound silence] —n. [Archaic] 1. an abyss or deep, as of the ocean or of space 2. that which is profound —pro·found'ly adv. —pro·found'ness n.

pro·fun·di·ty (-fun'də tē) n., pl. -ties [ME. profundite < MFr. < LL. profunditas] 1. depth, esp. great depth 2. intellectual depth 3. a profound idea, matter, etc.

pro·fuse (prə fyoos') adj. [ME. < L. profusus, pp. of profundere, to pour out < pro-, forth + fundere, to pour: see PRO-² & FOUND³] 1. giving or pouring forth freely; generous, often to excess (usually with in) [profuse in her apologies] 2. given, poured forth, or produced freely and abundantly —pro·fuse'ly adv. —pro·fuse'ness n. SYN.—profuse implies a pouring or giving forth freely, often to the point of excess [profuse thanks]; lavish implies an unstinted, generous, sometimes unreasonably liberal, giving [lavish attentions]; extravagant always suggests unreasonably excessive, wasteful spending or giving [extravagant living]; prodigal implies such reckless extravagance as to suggest eventual impoverishment [the prodigal heirs to a fortune]; luxuriant suggests production in great and rich abundance [luxuriant foliage]; lush implies such great luxuriance as to seem excessive [a lush jungle] See also PLENTIFUL —ANT. limited, scant, spare

pro·fu·sion (-fyoo'zhən) n. [Fr. < L. profusio < profusus: see prec.] 1. a pouring forth or expending with great liberality or wastefulness 2. great liberality or wastefulness 3. rich or lavish supply; abundance

prog (präg) vi. progged, prog'ging [via dial. < ? ME. prokken, to beg (prob. < LowG.)] [Brit. Dial.] to prowl about, as in search of food or plunder; forage —n. [Brit. Dial.] food obtained as by progging

prog. progressive

pro·gen·i·tive (prō jen'ə tiv, prə-) adj. [see ff. & -IVE] capable of begetting offspring; reproductive

pro·gen·i·tor (-tər) n. [ME. progenitour < MFr. progeniteur < L. progenitor < pp. of progenitus, to beget < pro-, forth + gignere, to beget: see PRO-² & GENUS] 1. a forefather; ancestor in direct line 2. a source from which something develops; originator or precursor

prog·e·ny (präj'ə nē) n., pl. -nies [ME. progenie < MFr. < L. progenies, descent, lineage, race, family < progignere: see prec.] children, descendants, or offspring collectively; issue

pro·ges·ta·tion·al (prō'jes tā'shən 'l) adj. [PRO-¹ + GESTATION + -AL] of or involving hormones that, in female mammals, precede, prepare for, or are active in ovulation and pregnancy

pro·ges·ter·one (prō jes'tə rōn') n. [PRO-¹ + GE(STATION) + STER(OL) + -ONE] a steroid hormone, $C_{21}H_{30}O_2$, secreted by the corpus luteum or prepared synthetically, active in preparing the uterus for the reception and development of the fertilized ovum and the mammary glands for milk secretion

pro·ges·to·gen (-tə jən) n. [PROGEST(ERONE) + -O- + -GEN] any of various substances that possess progestational activity; esp., any of a group of synthetic compounds that reproduce many of the effects of progesterone

pro·glot·tid (prō glät'id) n. [< ModL. proglottis (gen. proglottidis) < Gr. pro-, forward + glōtta, the tongue: see PRO-¹ & GLOTTIS] any of the segmentlike divisions of a tapeworm's body: each division has both male and female reproductive organs and is essentially an independent organism: also pro·glot'tis (-is), pl. -ti·des' (-ə dēz')

prog·na·thous (präg'nə thəs, präg nā'-) adj. [PRO-¹ + -GNATHOUS] having the jaws projecting beyond the upper face: also prog'nath'ic (-nath'ik) —prog'na·thism n.

prog·no·sis (präg nō'sis) n., pl. -no'ses (-sēz) [LL. < Gr. prognōsis < progignōskein < pro-, before (see PRO-¹) + gignōskein, to KNOW] a forecast or forecasting; esp., a prediction of the probable course of a disease in an individual and the chances of recovery

prog·nos·tic (-näs'tik) n. [ME. pronostike < MFr. pronostique < L. prognosticum < Gr. prognōstikon < progignōskein: see prec.] 1. a sign or indication of things to come; omen 2. a forecast; prediction —adj. [ML. prognosticus < Gr. prognōstikos] 1. foretelling; predictive 2. Med. of, or serving as a basis for, prognosis

prog·nos·ti·cate (-näs'tə kāt') vt. -cat'ed, -cat'ing [< ML. prognosticatus, pp. of prognosticare < prognosticus: see prec.] 1. to foretell or predict, esp. from signs or indications 2. to indicate beforehand —SYN. see FORETELL —prog·nos'ti·ca'tion n. —prog·nos'ti·ca'tive (-kāt'iv) adj. —prog·nos'ti·ca'tor n.

pro·gram (prō'gram, grəm) n. [< LL. & Fr.: Fr. programme < LL. programma < Gr. programma, an edict < prographein, to write in public < pro-, before + graphein, to write: see PRO-¹ & GRAPHIC] 1. orig., a) a proclamation b) a prospectus or syllabus 2. a) the acts, speeches, musical pieces, etc. that make up an entertainment, ceremony, etc. b) a printed list of these 3. a scheduled broadcast on radio or television 4. a plan or procedure for dealing with some matter 5. all the activities that can be participated in at a community center, camp, resort, etc. 6. a) a logical sequence of operations to be performed by a digital computer in solving a problem or in processing data b) the coded instructions and data for such a sequence —vt. -grammed or -gramed, -gramming or -gram·ing 1. to enter or schedule in a program ☆2. to prepare the questions and answers for (a textbook) to be used in programmed learning 3. a) to plan a computer program for (a task, problem, etc.) b) to furnish (a computer) with a program c) to incorporate in a computer program —vi. to plan or prepare a program or programs Also, Brit. sp., pro'gramme —pro'gram·mer, pro'gram·er n.

pro·gram·mat·ic (prō'grə mat'ik) adj. of, or having the nature of, a program or program music

☆**programmed learning** independent learning by a pupil, who advances, little by little, through a series of questions, the answers to which are given elsewhere in his programmed textbook

program music instrumental music that is meant to depict or suggest a particular scene, story, etc.

prog·ress (präg'res, -rəs; chiefly Brit., prō'gres; for v., prə gres') n. [ME. progresse < L. progressus, pp. of progredi < pro-, before + gradi, to step, go: see PRO-² & GRADE] 1. a moving forward or onward 2. forward course; development 3. advance toward perfection or to a higher or better state; improvement 4. [Now Rare] an official journey, as of a sovereign —vi. 1. to move forward or onward 2. to move forward toward completion, a goal, etc. 3. to advance toward perfection or to a higher or better state; improve —in progress going on; taking place; happening

pro·gres·sion (prə gresh'ən) n. [ME. < MFr. < L. progressio] 1. a moving forward or onward; progress 2. a sequence or succession, as of acts, happenings, etc. 3. Math. a series of numbers increasing or decreasing by a constant difference between terms: see ARITHMETIC PROGRESSION, GEOMETRIC PROGRESSION 4. Music a) the movement forward from one tone or chord to another b) a succession of tones or chords —pro·gres'sion·al adj.

pro·gres·sion·ist (-ist) n. a person who believes that mankind and society are progressing gradually toward desirable ends

pro·gres·sive (prə gres'iv) adj. [MFr. progressif < ML. progressivus < L. progressus: see PROGRESS] 1. moving forward or onward 2. continuing by successive steps [a progressive decline] 3. of, or concerned with, progression 4. designating a tax whose rate continues to increase as the base increases 5. favoring, working for, or characterized by progress or improvement, as through political or social reform ☆6. of an educational system stressing individuality, self-expression, etc. ☆7. designating jazz

in the later stages of bop **8.** *Gram.* indicating continuing action: said of certain verb forms, such as *am working* (as contrasted with the simple form *work*) **9.** *Med.* becoming more severe or spreading to other parts: said of a disease **10.** [P-] *Politics* of a Progressive Party —*n.* **1.** a person who is progressive, esp. one who favors political progress or reform **2.** [P-] a member of a Progressive Party —*SYN.* see LIBERAL —**pro·gres′sive·ly** *adv.* —**pro·gres′sive·ness** *n.*

Progressive Conservative 1. designating or of a major political party of Canada, characterized generally by a conservative program **2.** a member of this party

Progressive Party ☆any of several short-lived, minor American political parties; specif., *a)* one organized in 1912 by followers of Theodore Roosevelt: in full **National Progressive Party** *b)* one formed in 1924 under the leadership of Robert M. LaFollette *c)* one formed in 1948, orig. under the leadership of Henry A. Wallace

pro·gres·siv·ism (-iz′m) *n.* the doctrines, principles, and practices of progressives —**pro·gres′siv·ist** *n.*

pro·hib·it (prō hib′it, prə-) *vt.* [ME. *prohibiten* < L. *prohibitus,* pp. of *prohibere,* to prohibit < *pro-,* before (see PRO-²) + *habere,* to have (see HABIT)] **1.** to refuse to permit; forbid by law or by an order **2.** to prevent; hinder—*SYN.* see FORBID —**pro·hib′it·er, pro·hib′i·tor** *n.*

pro·hi·bi·tion (prō′ə bish′ən) *n.* [ME. *prohibicion* < MFr. *prohibition* < L. *prohibitio*] **1.** a prohibiting or being prohibited **2.** an order or law forbidding something to be done ☆**3.** the forbidding by law of the manufacture, transportation, and sale of alcoholic liquors for beverage purposes; specif., [P-] in the U.S., the period (1920–1933) of prohibition by Federal law

pro·hi·bi·tion·ist (-ist) *n.* ☆**1.** one in favor of prohibiting by law the manufacture and sale of alcoholic drinks ☆**2.** [P-] a member of an American political party (**Prohibition Party**) advocating such prohibition

pro·hib·i·tive (prō hib′ə tiv, prə-) *adj.* [Fr. *prohibitif* < LL. *prohibitivus*] **1.** prohibiting or tending to prohibit something **2.** such as to prevent purchase, use, etc. [*prohibitive* prices] Also **pro·hib′i·to·ry** (-tôr′ē) —**pro·hib′i·tive·ly** *adv.*

proj·ect (präj′ekt, -ikt; *for v.,* prə jekt′) *n.* [ME. *projecte* < L. *projectum,* neut. of *projectus,* pp. of *projicere* < *pro-,* before, forward + *jacere,* to throw: see PRO-² & JET] **1.** a proposal of something to be done; plan; scheme ☆**2.** an organized undertaking; specif., *a)* a special unit of work, research, etc., as in school, a laboratory, etc. *b)* an extensive public undertaking, as in conservation, construction, etc. ☆**3.** a complex of inexpensive apartments or houses, esp. one that is publicly owned or financed: in full **housing project** —*vt.* **1.** to propose (an act or plan of action) **2.** to throw or hurl forward **3.** *a)* to cause (one's voice) to be heard clearly and at a distance *b)* to get (ideas, feelings, one's presence, etc.) across to others effectively **4.** to send forth in one's thoughts or imagination [to *project* oneself into the future] **5.** to cause to jut out **6.** to cause (a shadow, image, etc.) to fall or appear upon a surface **7.** *same as* EXTRAPOLATE **8.** *Geom.* to transform the points of (a geometric figure) into the points of another figure, usually by means of lines of correspondence **9.** *Psychol.* to externalize (a thought or feeling) so that it appears to have objective reality —*vi.* **1.** to jut out; protrude **2.** to be effective in the projection of one's voice, ideas, etc. —*SYN.* see PLAN

pro·jec·tile (prə jek′t'l, -tīl) *n.* [Fr. < L. *projectus:* see PROJECT & -ILE] **1.** an object designed to be hurled or shot forward, as a cannon shell, bullet, or rocket **2.** anything thrown or hurled forward —*adj.* **1.** designed to be hurled forward [a javelin is a *projectile* weapon] **2.** hurling forward [*projectile* energy] **3.** *Zool.* that can be thrust out, as a tentacle

pro·jec·tion (-shən) *n.* [MFr. < L. *projectio*] **1.** a projecting or being projected **2.** something that projects, or juts out **3.** something that is projected; specif., in map making, the representation on a plane of the earth's surface (or the celestial sphere) or of a part thereof **4.** a prediction or advance estimate based on known data or observations; extrapolation **5.** *Psychiatry* the unconscious act or process of ascribing to others one's own ideas, impulses, or emotions, esp. when they are considered undesirable or cause anxiety **6.** *Photog.* the process of projecting an image, as from a transparent slide, upon a screen, etc. —**pro·jec′tion·al** *adj.*

SYN.—**projection** implies a jutting out abruptly beyond the rest of the surface [the *projection* of the eaves beyond the sides of a house]; **protrusion** suggests a thrusting or pushing out that is of an abnormal or disfiguring nature [*protrusion* of the eyeballs]; **protuberance** suggests a swelling out, usually in rounded form [the tumor on his arm formed a *protuberance*]; **bulge** suggests an outward swelling of a kind that may result from internal pressure [the *bulge* in the can resulted from the fermentation of its contents]

projection booth the small chamber in a motion-picture theater from which the pictures are projected

☆**pro·jec·tion·ist** (-ist) *n.* the operator of a motion-picture or slide projector

pro·jec·tive (-tiv) *adj.* **1.** of or made by projection **2.** designating or of a type of psychological test, as the Rorschach test, in which any response the subject makes to the test material will be indicative of personality traits and unconscious motivations

projective geometry the branch of geometry dealing with those properties of a figure (**projective properties**) that do not vary when the figure is projected

pro·jec·tor (-tər) *n.* a person or thing that projects; specif., a machine for throwing an image on a screen, as from a transparent slide or motion-picture film

Pro·kof·iev (prō kôf′yef; *E.* pra kô′fē ef′), **Ser·gei** (**Ser·geevich**) (syer gyā′) 1891–1953; Russ. composer

Pro·ko·pyevsk (prō kô′pyefsk′) city in the Kuznetsk Basin, in the S R.S.F.S.R.: pop. 291,000

pro·lac·tin (prō lak′tin) *n.* [PRO-¹ + LACT- + -IN¹] a pituitary hormone stimulating milk secretion in mammals and secretion by the crop gland in certain birds

pro·la·mine (prō′lə mēn′, -min; prō lam′in) *n.* [PROL(INE) + AMINE] any of a class of proteins found esp. in the seeds of cereals, insoluble in water and absolute alcohol, but soluble in 70% alcohol: also **pro′la·min** (-min)

pro·lan (prō′lan) *n.* [G. < L. *proles,* offspring (see PROLIFIC) + G. -an, -AN] *an earlier term:* **1.** (**prolan A**) *for* FOLLICLE-STIMULATING HORMONE **2.** (**prolan B**) *for* LUTEINIZING HORMONE

pro·lapse (prō′laps; *also, and for v. usually,* prō laps′) *n.* [ModL. *prolapsus* < LL., a falling < pp. of L. *prolabi,* to fall forward < *pro-,* forward + *labi,* to fall: see PRO-² & LAPSE] *Med.* the falling or slipping out of place of an internal organ, as the uterus or rectum: also **pro·lap′sus** (-lap′səs) —*vi.* **-lapsed′, -laps′ing** *Med.* to fall or slip out of place

pro·late (prō′lāt) *adj.* [L. *prolatus,* pp. of *proferre,* to bring forward: see PRO-¹ & BEAR¹] extended or elongated at the poles [a *prolate* spheroid]

prole (prōl) *adj., n.* [Chiefly Brit. Colloq.] *clipped form of* PROLETARIAN

pro·leg (prō′leg′) *n.* [PRO-¹ + LEG] any of the stubby, fleshy limbs attached to the abdomen of certain insect larvae, as in caterpillars

pro·le·gom·e·non (prō′li gäm′ə nän′, -nən) *n., pl.* **-e·na** (-na) [Gr. *prolegomenon,* neut. pass. prp. of *prolegein,* to say beforehand < *pro-,* before + *legein,* to speak: see PRO-¹ & LOGIC] **1.** a preliminary remark **2.** [*often pl.,* *with sing. v.*] a preliminary statement or essay; foreword —**pro′le·gom′e·nous** (-nəs) *adj.*

pro·lep·sis (prō lep′sis) *n., pl.* **-lep′ses** (-sēz) [L. < Gr. *prolēpsis,* an anticipating < *prolambanein,* to take before < *pro-,* before + *lambanein,* to take] an anticipating; esp., the describing of an event as taking place before it could have done so, the treating of a future event as if it had already happened, or the anticipating and answering of an argument before one's opponent has a chance to advance it —**pro·lep′tic** *adj.*

pro·le·tar·i·an (prō′lə ter′ē ən) *adj.* [< L. *proletarius,* citizen of the lowest class (see PROLETARY) + -AN] of the proletariat —*n.* a member of the proletariat; worker

pro·le·tar·i·an·ize (-ə nīz′) *vt.* **-ized′, -iz′ing** to make, or treat as, proletarian —**pro′le·tar′i·an·i·za′tion** *n.*

pro·le·tar·i·at (-ət) *n.* [Fr. *prolétariat* < L. *proletarius:* see ff.] **1.** the class of lowest status in ancient Roman society **2.** [Rare] the class of lowest status in any society or community **3.** the working class; esp., the industrial working class

pro·le·tar·y (prō′lə ter′ē) *n., pl.* **-tar′ies** [L. *proletarius,* a propertyless citizen of the lowest class, who served the state only by having children < *proles,* offspring: see PROLIFIC] in ancient Rome, a member of the lowest class of citizens, who had no property

pro·lif·er·ate (prō lif′ə rāt′, prə-) *vt.* **-at′ed, -at′ing** [back-formation < *proliferation* < Fr. *prolifération* < *prolifère,* PROLIFEROUS + -ATION] **1.** to reproduce (new parts) in quick succession **2.** to produce or create in profusion —*vi.* **1.** to grow by multiplying new parts, as by budding, in quick succession **2.** to multiply rapidly; increase profusely —**pro·lif′er·a′tion** *n.*

pro·lif·er·ous (-əs) *adj.* [< ML. *prolifer* < L. *proles* (see ff.) + *ferre,* to BEAR¹ + -OUS] **1.** *Bot. a)* multiplying freely by means of buds, side branches, etc. *b)* having leafy shoots growing from a flower or fruit **2.** *Zool.* reproducing by budding, as coral

pro·lif·ic (prə lif′ik, prō-) *adj.* [Fr. *prolifique* < ML. *prolificus* < L. *proles* (gen. *prolis*), offspring < *pro-,* PRO-² + base of *alere,* to nourish (see ALIMENT) + *facere,* to make, DO¹] **1.** producing many young or much fruit **2.** turning out many products of the mind [a *prolific* scholar or poet] **3.** fruitful; abounding (often with *in* or *of*) —*SYN.* see FERTILE —**pro·lif′i·ca·cy** (-i kə sē) *n.* —**pro·lif′i·cal·ly** *adv.*

pro·line (prō′lēn, -lin) *n.* [G. *prolin,* contr. < *pyrrolidin* < *pyrrol,* PYRROLE + -*id,* -IDE + -*in,* -INE¹] an amino acid, C₅H₉O₂N, formed by the decomposition of proteins

pro·lix (prō liks′, prō′liks) *adj.* [ME. *prolixe* < L. *prolixus,* extended, prolix < *pro-,* forth + base of *liquere,* to flow: see LIQUID] **1.** so wordy as to be tiresome; verbose **2.** using more words than are necessary; long-winded —*SYN.* see WORDY —**pro·lix′i·ty** *n.* —**pro·lix′ly** *adv.*

pro·loc·u·tor (prō läk′yə tər) *n.* [L., an advocate < pp. of *proloqui,* to declare < *pro,* for + *loqui,* to speak] **1.** a person who speaks for another person or for a group; spokesman **2.** a chairman

pro·logue (prō′lôg, -läg) *n.* [ME. *prologe* < MFr. < L. *prologus* < Gr. *prologos* < *pro-,* before + *logos,* a discourse: see PRO-¹ & LOGIC] **1.** an introduction to a poem, play,

etc.; esp., introductory lines spoken by a member of the cast before a dramatic performance 2. the actor speaking such lines 3. a preliminary act or course of action foreshadowing greater events —*SYN.* see INTRODUCTION

pro·logu·ize, pro·log·ize (prō′lô giz′) *vi.* -ized′, -iz′ing to compose or deliver a prologue

pro·long (prə lôn′) *vt.* [ME. *prolongen* < MFr. *prolonguer* < LL. *prolongare* < L. *pro-*, forth + *longus*, long: see PRO-[2] & LONG[1]] to lengthen or extend in time or space: also **pro·lon′gate** (-gāt) -gat·ed, -gat·ing —*SYN.* see EXTEND —**pro·lon·ga·tion** (prō′lôn gā′shən) *n.* —**pro·long′er** *n.*

pro·longe (prō länj′) *n.* [Fr. < *prolonger:* see PROLONG] *Mil. Science* a heavy rope having a hook and toggle, used to drag a gun carriage, etc.

prolonge knot a kind of knot: see KNOT, illus.

pro·lu·sion (prō lōō′zhən) *n.* [L. *prolusio*, a prelude < *prolusus*, pp. of *proludere*, to play beforehand < *pro-*, before + *ludere*, to play: see PRO-[2] & LUDICROUS] a preliminary piece, performance, essay, etc. —**pro·lu′so·ry** (-sə rē) *adj.*

☆**prom** (präm) *n.* [contr. < PROMENADE] [Colloq.] a ball or dance, as of a particular class at a school or college

prom. promontory

prom·e·nade (präm′ə nād′, -näd′) *n.* [Fr. < *promener*, to take for a walk < LL. *prominare*, to drive (animals) onward < L. *pro-*, forth (see PRO-[2]) + *minare*, to drive (animals) < *minari*, to threaten (see MENACE)] 1. a leisurely walk taken for pleasure, to display one's finery, etc. 2. a public place for such a walk, as an avenue, the deck of a ship, or the hall of a building 3. *a)* a ball, or formal dance *b)* a march of all the guests, beginning a formal ball *c)* a walking or marching figure of a square dance —*vi.* -nad′ed, -nad′ing to take a promenade; walk about for pleasure, display, etc. —*vt.* 1. to take a promenade along or through 2. to take or show on or as on a promenade; parade 3. to march (one's partner) as a figure of a square dance —**prom′e·nad′er** *n.*

Pro·me·the·an (prə mē′thē ən) *adj.* 1. of or like Prometheus 2. life-bringing, creative, or courageously original —*n.* a Promethean person in spirit or deeds

Pro·me·theus (-thyoos, -thē əs) [L. < Gr. *Promētheus*, lit., forethought < *promēthes*, forethinking < *pro-*, before (see PRO-[1]) + *mathein*, to learn (for IE. base see MATHEMATICS)] *Gr. Myth.* a Titan who stole fire from heaven for the benefit of mankind: in punishment, Zeus chained him to a rock where a vulture came each day to eat his liver, which Zeus renewed each night

☆**pro·me·thi·um** (-thē əm) *n.* [ModL. < prec.] a metallic chemical element of the rare-earth group obtained from fission of uranium or neutron bombardment of neodymium: symbol, Pm; at. wt., 145(?); at. no., 61; melt. pt., 865°C: the specific gravity and boiling point are not known at the present time

☆**pro·mine** (prō′mēn) *n.* [< PROM(OTE) + -INE[4]] a substance found in the body in minute amounts, that promotes the growth of cells: cf. RETINE

prom·i·nence (präm′ə nəns) *n.* [< MFr. < L. *prominentia* < *prominens:* see PROMINENT] 1. the state or quality of being prominent 2. something prominent 3. *Astron.* luminous clouds of gas seen at the edge of the sun, as during an eclipse, and exhibiting rapid motion, spiral whirling, etc.

prom·i·nent (-nənt) *adj.* [L. *prominens*, prp. of *prominere*, to project < *pro-*, PRO-[2] + *minere*, to project: see EMINENT] 1. sticking out; projecting [a *prominent* chin] 2. noticeable at once; conspicuous [*prominent* markings] 3. widely and favorably known [a *prominent* artist] —*SYN.* see NOTICEABLE —**prom′i·nent·ly** *adv.*

prom·is·cu·i·ty (präm′is kyōō′ə tē, prō′mis-) *n.*, *pl.* -ties state, quality, or instance of being promiscuous, esp. in sexual relations

pro·mis·cu·ous (prə mis′kyoo wəs) *adj.* [L. *promiscuus* < *pro-*, forth (see PRO-[2]) + *miscere*, to MIX] 1. consisting of different elements mixed together or mingled without sorting or discrimination 2. characterized by a lack of discrimination; specif., engaging in sexual intercourse indiscriminately or with many persons 3. without plan or purpose; casual —**pro·mis′cu·ous·ly** *adv.* —**pro·mis′cu·ous·ness** *n.*

prom·ise (präm′is) *n.* [ME. *promis* < L. *promissum* < *promittere*, to send before or forward < *pro-*, forth + *mittere*, to send: see PRO-[2] & MISSION] 1. an oral or written agreement to do or not to do something; vow 2. indication, as of a successful prospect or future; basis for expectation 3. something promised —*vi.* -ised, -is·ing 1. to make a promise 2. to give a basis for expectation (often with *well* or *fair*) —*vt.* 1. to make a promise of (something) *to* somebody 2. to engage or pledge (followed by an infinitive or a clause) [to *promise* to go] 3. to give a basis for expecting 4. [Colloq.] to declare emphatically; assure 5. [Archaic] to pledge to give in marriage —**prom′is·er** *n.*

Promised Land 1. *Bible* Canaan, promised by God to Abraham and his descendants: Gen. 17:8 2. [p- l-] any place where one expects to have a better life

prom·is·ee (präm′i sē′) *n. Law* a person to whom a promise is made

prom·is·ing (präm′i sin) *adj.* showing promise of success, excellence, etc. —**prom′is·ing·ly** *adv.*

prom·i·sor (präm′i sôr′, präm′i sôr′) *n. Law* a person who makes a promise

prom·is·so·ry (präm′i sôr′ē) *adj.* [ML. *promissorius* < L. *promissor*, one who promises] 1. containing a promise 2. stipulating conditions that must be complied with to keep an insurance contract valid [a *promissory* warranty]

promissory note a written promise to pay a certain sum of money to a certain person or bearer on demand or on a specified date

prom·on·to·ry (präm′ən tôr′ē) *n.*, *pl.* -ries [LL. *promontorium* < L. *promunturium*, prob. altered (after *mons*, MOUNT[1]) < *prominere:* see PROMINENT] 1. a peak of high land that juts out into a body of water; headland 2. *Anat.* a prominent part

pro·mote (prə mōt′) *vt.* -mot′ed, -mot′ing [ME. *promoten* < L. *promotus*, pp. of *promovere*, to move forward: see PRO-[2] & MOVE] 1. to raise or advance to a higher position or rank [*promoted* to a foremanship] 2. to help bring about or further the growth or establishment of [to *promote* the general welfare] ☆3. to further the popularity, sales, etc. of by publicizing and advertising [to *promote* a product] ☆4. [Slang] to acquire (something) by devious or cunning means ☆5. *Educ.* to move forward a grade in school —*SYN.* see ADVANCE —**pro·mot′a·ble** *adj.*

pro·mot·er (-mōt′ər) *n.* [ME. < MFr. *promoteur* < ML. *promotor*] 1. a person or thing that promotes; specif., a person who begins, secures financing for, and helps to organize an undertaking, as a business, a sports event, etc. 2. *Chem.* a substance that will accelerate the effect of a catalyst on a reaction

pro·mo·tion (-mō′shən) *n.* [ME. < MFr. < LL. *promotio*] the act or an instance of promoting; specif., *a)* advancement in rank, grade, or position *b)* furtherance of an enterprise, cause, etc. —**pro·mo′tion·al** *adj.*

pro·mo·tive (-mōt′iv) *adj.* tending to promote

prompt (prämpt) *adj.* [ME. *prompte* < MFr. < L. *promptus*, brought forth, at hand, ready, quick < pp. of *promere*, to bring forth < *pro-*, forth + *emere*, to take: see PRO-[2] & REDEEM] 1. quick to act or to do what is required; ready, punctual, etc. 2. done, spoken, etc. at once or without delay —*n.* 1. *Commerce a)* the time limit specified for the payment of an account *b)* the contract in which the due date is specified 2. any reminder or notice of payment due —*vt.* 1. to urge into action; provoke 2. to remind (a person) of something he has forgotten; specif., to help (an actor, etc. who has forgotten a line) with a cue 3. to move or inspire by suggestion —*SYN.* see QUICK —**prompt′ly** *adv.* —**prompt′ness** *n.*

prompt·book (-book′) *n.* an annotated play script, used by a stage manager or prompter, with detailed directions for action, settings, properties, etc.

prompt·er (prämpt′ər) *n.* a person who prompts; specif., one who cues performers when they forget their lines

promp·ti·tude (-tə tōōd′, -tyōōd′) *n.* [Fr. < LL.(Ec.) *promptitudo*] the quality of being prompt; promptness

prom·ul·gate (präm′əl gāt′, prō mul′gāt) *vt.* -gat′ed, -gat′ing [< L. *promulgatus*, pp. of *promulgare*, to publish, altered < ? *provulgare*, to publish < *pro-*, forth, before + *vulgus*, the people] 1. to publish or make known officially (a decree, church dogma, etc.) 2. *a)* to make known the terms of (a new or proposed law or statute) *b)* to put (a law) into effect by publishing its terms 3. to make widespread [to *promulgate* learning and culture] —**prom′ul·ga′tion** *n.* —**prom′ul·ga′tor** *n.*

pro·mulge (prō mulj′) *vt.* -mulged′, -mulg′ing *archaic var. of* PROMULGATE

pro·my·ce·li·um (prō′mī sē′lē əm) *n.*, *pl.* -li·a (-ə) [PRO-[1] + MYCELIUM] *Bot.* a short filament bearing sporidia, developed in spore germination of rusts and smuts

pron. 1. pronominal 2. pronoun 3. pronounced 4. pronunciation

pro·nate (prō′nāt) *vt.*, *vi.* -nat·ed, -nat·ing [< LL. *pronatus*, pp. of *pronare*, to bend forward < L. *pronus:* see PRONE] to rotate (the hand or forearm) so that the palm faces down or toward the body —**pro·na′tion** *n.*

pro·na·tor (prō nāt′ər, prō′nāt-) *n.* [ModL.] a muscle in the forearm by which pronation is effected

prone (prōn) *adj.* [ME. < L. *pronus* < *pro*, before: see PRO-[1]] 1. lying or leaning face downward 2. lying flat or prostrate; in a horizontal position 3. having a natural bent; disposed or inclined (*to*) [*prone* to error] 4. groveling; abject 5. [Poet.] leaning forward or sloping downward —**prone′ly** *adv.* —**prone′ness** *n.*

*SYN.—***prone**, in strict use, implies a position in which the front part of the body lies upon or faces the ground [he fell *prone* upon the ground and drank from the brook]; **supine** implies a position in which one lies on his back [he snores when he sleeps in a *supine* position]; **prostrate** implies the position of one thrown or lying flat in a prone or supine position, as in great humility or complete submission, or because laid low [the victim lay *prostrate* at the murderer's feet]; **recumbent** suggests a lying down or back in

any position one might assume for rest or sleep [she was *recumbent* on the chaise longue/ See also LIKELY —*ANT.* erect

pro·neph·ros (prō′nef′räs) *n.* [ModL. < *pro-*, PRO-¹ + Gr. *nephros*, a kidney: see NEPHRO-] *Zool.* a primitive kidney, the most anterior of three pairs of renal organs, functional only during embryonic development in most lower vertebrates, and appearing only transiently in the human embryo —**pro′neph′ric** *adj.*

prong (prôŋ) *n.* [LME. *pronge*, akin to MLowG. *prangen*, to press, pinch, G. *pranger*, pillory] **1.** any of the pointed ends of a fork; tine **2.** any pointed projecting part, as the tip of an antler —*vt.* to pierce or break up with a prong or prongs

pronged (prôŋd) *adj.* having prongs

☆**prong·horn** (prôŋ′hôrn′) *n.*, *pl.* **-horns′, -horn′:** see PLURAL, II, D, 1 an antelopelike deer (*Antilocapra americana*) of Mexico and the W U.S., having curved horns, each with one prong, that are shed annually

pro·no·grade (prō′nə grād′) *adj.* [< L. *pronus*, bent forward (see PRONE) + E. *-o-* + -GRADE] *Zool.* walking with the body parallel to the ground

pro·nom·i·nal (prō näm′i n′l) *adj.* [LL. *pronominalis* < L. *pronomen*, PRONOUN] *Gram.* of, or having the function of, a pronoun —**pro·nom′i·nal·ly** *adv.*

pro·noun (prō′noun) *n.* [altered (after NOUN) < MFr. *pronom* < L. *pronomen* < *pro*, for + *nomen*, NOUN] *Gram.* any of a small class of relationship or signal words that assume the functions of nouns within clauses while referring to other locutions within the sentence or in other sentences: *I, you, them, it, ours, who, which, myself, anybody,* etc. are pronouns

pro·nounce (prə nouns′) *vt.* **-nounced′, -nounc′ing** [ME. *pronouncen* < OFr. *pronuncier* < L. *pronuntiare* < *pro-*, before + *nuntiare*, to announce < *nuntius*, messenger: see PRO-² & NUNCIO] **1.** to say or declare officially, solemnly, or with ceremony [to *pronounce* a couple man and wife] **2.** to announce or declare (someone or something) to be as specified [to *pronounce* a man guilty] **3.** *a)* to utter or articulate (a sound or word) *b)* to utter or articulate (a word or syllable) in the accepted or standard manner [to know how to *pronounce* a name] *c)* to indicate the pronunciation of (a word) with phonetic symbols —*vi.* **1.** to state or pass a judgment; make a pronouncement (*on*) **2.** to pronounce words, syllables, etc. —**pro·nounce′-a·ble** *adj.* —**pro·nounc′er** *n.*

pro·nounced (-nounst′) *adj.* **1.** spoken or uttered **2.** clearly marked; unmistakable; decided [a *pronounced* change] —**pro·nounc′ed·ly** (-noun′sid lē) *adv.*

pro·nounce·ment (-nouns′mənt) *n.* **1.** the act of pronouncing **2.** a formal, often authoritative statement of a fact, opinion, or judgment

☆**pron·to** (prän′tō) *adv.* [Sp. < L. *promptus:* see PROMPT] [Slang] at once; quickly; immediately

pro·nu·cle·us (prō nōō′klē əs, -nyōō′-) *n., pl.* **-cle·i′** (-ī′) [ModL.: see PRO-¹ & NUCLEUS] *Zool.* the haploid nucleus of either the spermatozoon or the ovum which unite in fertilization to form the fused double (diploid) nucleus of the fertilized ovum, or zygote —**pro·nu′cle·ar** *adj.*

pro·nun·ci·a·men·to (prə nun′sē ə men′tō, prō-) *n., pl.* **-tos** [Sp. *pronunciamiento* < *pronunciar* < L. *pronuntiare:* see PRONOUNCE] **1.** a public declaration or pronouncement; proclamation **2.** *same as* MANIFESTO

pro·nun·ci·a·tion (prə nun′sē ā′shən) *n.* [ME. *pronunciacion* < MFr. *pronunciation* < L. *pronuntiatio*] **1.** the act or manner of pronouncing words with reference to the production of sounds and the placing of stress, intonation, etc. **2.** *a)* any of the accepted or standard pronunciations of a word *b)* the transcription in phonetic symbols of such a pronunciation —**pro·nun′ci·a′tion·al** *adj.*

proof (prōōf) *n.* [ME. *profe* < OFr. *prueve* < LL. *proba:* see PROBE] **1.** the act or process of proving; a testing or trying of something **2.** anything serving or tending to establish the truth of something, or to convince one of its truth; conclusive evidence **3.** the establishment of the truth of something [to work on the *proof* of a theory] **4.** a test or trial of the truth, worth, quality, etc. of something [the *proof* of the pudding is in the eating] **5.** the quality or condition of having been tested or proved **6.** tested or proved strength, as of armor **7.** *a)* the relative strength of an alcoholic liquor with reference to the arbitrary standard for proof spirit *b)* this standard, taken as 100 proof: see PROOF SPIRIT **8.** *Engraving* a trial impression taken from a plate, block, or stone **9.** *Law* all the facts, admissions, and conclusions drawn from evidence which together operate to determine a verdict or judgment **10.** *Math.* a process for checking the correctness of a computation, as by adding the result to the subtrahend to get the minuend **11.** *Numismatics* any of a limited number of coins of a new issue, struck with special care **12.** *Photog.* a trial print of a negative **13.** *Printing* an impression of composed type taken for checking errors and making changes —*adj.* **1.** of tested and proved strength **2.** impervious or invulnerable to; able to resist, withstand, etc. (with *against*) [*proof* against criticism] **3.** used in proving or testing **4.** of standard strength: said of alcoholic liquors —*vt.* **1.** to make a proof of **2.** to make resistant or impervious to something **3.** *clipped form of* PROOFREAD

SYN.—**proof,** as compared here, applies to facts, documents,

etc. that are so certain or convincing as to demonstrate the validity of a conclusion beyond reasonable doubt; **evidence** applies to something presented before a court, as a witness's statement, an object, etc. which bears on or establishes a fact; **testimony** applies to verbal evidence given by a witness under oath; **exhibit** applies to a document or object produced as evidence in a court

-proof (prōōf) [< prec.] *a combining form meaning:* **1.** impervious to [*waterproof*] **2.** protected from or against [*foolproof, rustproof*] **3.** as strong as [*armorproof*] **4.** resistant to, unaffected by [*fireproof*]

☆**proof·read** (-rēd′) *vt., vi.* to read and mark corrections on (printers' proofs, etc.) —**proof′read′er** *n.*

proof set a set of newly minted coins packaged specifically for collectors

proof spirit an alcoholic liquor, or a mixture of alcohol and water, containing 50 percent (in Great Britain, 57.10 percent) of its volume of alcohol having a specific gravity of 0.7939 at 60°F

prop¹ (präp) *n.* [ME. *proppe* < MDu. *proppe*, a prop, ? akin to G. *pfropfen*, a stopper] **1.** a rigid support, as a beam, stake, or pole, placed under or against a structure or part **2.** a person or thing that gives support or aid to a person, institution, etc. —*vt.* **propped, prop′ping 1.** to support, hold up, or hold in place with or as with a prop (often with *up*) **2.** to place or lean (something) *against* a support **3.** to sustain or bolster

prop² (präp) *n. same as* PROPERTY (sense 7)

prop³ (präp) *n. clipped form of* PROPELLER

prop. **1.** proper(ly) **2.** property **3.** proposition **4.** proprietor

pro·pae·deu·tic (prō′pi dōōt′ik, -dyōōt′-) *adj.* [< Gr. *propaideuein*, to teach beforehand < *pro-*, before + *paideuein*, to instruct < *pais* (gen. *paidos*), a child: see PEDO-¹] of, or having the nature of, elementary or introductory instruction: also **pro′pae·deu′ti·cal** —*n.* **1.** an elementary or introductory subject or study **2.** [*pl.*, *with sing. v.*] the basic principles and rules preliminary to the study of some art or science

prop·a·ga·ble (präp′ə gə b′l) *adj.* [< L. *propagare* (see PROPAGATE) + -ABLE] capable of being propagated

prop·a·gan·da (präp′ə gan′də, prō′pə-) *n.* [ModL., short for *congregatio de propaganda fide*, congregation for propagating the faith: see PROPAGATE] **1.** [P-] *R.C.Ch.* a committee of cardinals, the Congregation for the Propagation of the Faith, in charge of the foreign missions **2.** any systematic, widespread dissemination or promotion of particular ideas, doctrines, practices, etc. to further one's own cause or to damage an opposing one **3.** ideas, doctrines, or allegations so spread: now often used disparagingly to connote deception or distortion

prop·a·gan·dism (-diz′m) *n.* the art, system, or use of propaganda —**prop′a·gan′dist** *n., adj.* —**prop′a·gan·dis′tic** *adj.* —**prop′a·gan·dis′ti·cal·ly** *adv.*

prop·a·gan·dize (-dīz) *vt.* **-dized, -diz·ing 1.** to spread (a doctrine or theory) by propaganda **2.** to subject to propaganda —*vi.* to organize or spread propaganda

prop·a·gate (präp′ə gāt′) *vt.* **-gat′ed, -gat′ing** [< L. *propagatus*, pp. of *propagare*, to peg down, set < *propago*, slip for transplanting < *pro-*, before + *pag-*, base of *pangere*, to fasten: see PEACE] **1.** to cause (a plant or animal) to reproduce itself; raise or breed **2.** to reproduce (itself); multiply: said of a plant or animal **3.** to transmit (hereditary characteristics) by reproduction **4.** to spread (ideas, customs, etc.) from one person or place to another **5.** to extend or transmit (esp. sound waves or electromagnetic radiation) through air or water —*vi.* to reproduce or multiply, as plants or animals —**prop′a·ga′tive** (-gāt′iv) *adj.* —**prop′a·ga′tor** *n.*

prop·a·ga·tion (präp′ə gā′shən) *n.* a propagating or being propagated; specif., *a)* reproduction or multiplication, as of a plant or animal *b)* a spreading, as of ideas, customs, etc.

pro·pane (prō′pān) *n.* [PROP(YL) + (METH)ANE] a heavy, colorless, gaseous hydrocarbon, C_3H_8, of the methane series, occurring naturally in petroleum and used as a fuel, in aerosols, refrigerants, etc.

pro·par·ox·y·tone (prō′par äk′sə tōn′) *adj.* [Gr. *proparoxytonos:* see PRO-¹, PARA-¹, OXYTONE] having an acute accent on the antepenult, as in classical Greek —*n.* a proparoxytone word

‡**pro pa·tri·a** (prō pā′trē ə) [L.] for (one's) country

pro·pel (prə pel′) *vt.* **-pelled′, -pel′ling** [ME. *propellen* ∨ L. *propellere* < *pro-*, forward + *pellere*, to drive: see FELT¹] to push, drive, or impel onward, forward, or ahead —*SYN.* see PUSH

pro·pel·lant (-ənt) *n.* a person or thing that propels; specif., *a)* the explosive charge that propels a projectile from a gun ☆*b)* the fuel and oxidizer used to propel a rocket

pro·pel·lent (-ənt) *adj.* [L. *propellens*, prp.] propelling or tending to propel —*n. same as* PROPELLANT

pro·pel·ler (-ər) *n.* a person or thing that propels; specif., a device (in full **screw propeller**) on a ship or aircraft, consisting typically of two or more blades twisted to describe a helical path as they rotate with the hub in which they are mounted, and serving to propel the craft by the backward thrust of air or water

pro·pend (prō pend′) *vi.* [L. *propendere*, to hang forward < *pro-*, before + *pendere*, to hang: see PEND] [Obs.] to incline, or be disposed (*to* or *toward* something)

pro·pene (prō′pēn) *n.* [PROP(YL) + -ENE] *same as* PRO-PYLENE

pro·pen·si·ty (prə pen′sə tē) *n., pl.* **-ties** [< L. *propensus*, pp. of *propendere* (see PROPEND) + -ITY] 1. a natural inclination or tendency; bent 2. [Obs.] favorable inclination; bias *(for)* —*SYN.* see INCLINATION

prop·er (präp′ər) *adj.* [ME. *propre* < OFr. < L. *proprius*, one's own] 1. specially adapted or suitable to a specific purpose or specific conditions; appropriate *[the proper tool for a job]* 2. naturally belonging or peculiar *(to)* *[weather proper to April]* 3. conforming to an accepted standard or to good usage; correct *[a proper spelling]* 4. fitting; seemly; right *[proper modesty]* 5. decent; decorous; genteel: often connoting exaggerated respectability *["the proper Bostonians"]* 6. understood in its most restricted sense; strictly so called: usually following the noun modified *[the population of Chicago proper* (i.e., apart from its suburbs)*]* 7. [Chiefly Brit. Colloq.] complete; thorough *[a proper scoundrel]* 8. [Archaic or Dial.] *a)* fine; good; excellent *b)* handsome 9. *Eccles.* reserved for a particular day or festival: said of prayers, rites, etc. 10. *Gram.* designating a noun that names a specific individual, place, etc., is not used with an article, and is normally capitalized, as *Donald, Rover,* or *Boston:* opposed to COMMON 11. *Heraldry* represented in its natural colors —*adv.* [Dial.] completely; thoroughly —*n. Eccles.* [often P-] 1. the special office or prayers for a particular day or festival 2. those parts of the Mass which vary according to the particular day or festival —*SYN.* see FIT[1] —**prop′er·ly** *adv.*

☆**pro·per·din** (prō pur′d'n) *n.* [< PRO(TEIN) + L. *perdere*, to destroy + -IN[1]] a protein present in blood serum and active in the destruction of bacteria and the neutralization of viruses

proper fraction *Math.* a fraction in which the numerator is less, or of lower degree, than the denominator, as 2/5 or x/x²

proper subset a subset that does not include all the members of the set to which it belongs

prop·er·tied (präp′ər tēd) *adj.* owning property

Pro·per·tius (prō pur′shəs), **Sex·tus** (seks′təs) 50?–15? B.C.; Rom. poet

prop·er·ty (präp′ər tē) *n., pl.* **-ties** [ME. *proprete* < OFr. *propriete* < L. *proprietas* < *proprius*, one's own] 1. *a)* the right to possess, use, and dispose of something; ownership *[property in land]* *b)* something, as a piece of writing, in which copyright or other rights are held 2. a thing or things owned; possessions collectively; esp., land or real estate owned 3. a specific piece of land or real estate 4. any trait or attribute proper to a thing or, formerly, to a person; characteristic quality; peculiarity; specif., any of the principal characteristics of a substance, esp. as determined by the senses or by its effect on another substance *[the properties of a chemical compound]* 5. something regarded as being possessed by, or at the disposal of, a person or group of persons *[common property]* 6. *Logic* an essential quality common to all members of a species or class 7. *Theater, Motion Pictures & TV* any of the movable articles used as part of the setting or in a piece of stage business, except the costumes, backdrops, etc. —*SYN.* see QUALITY —**prop′er·ty·less** *adj.*

property man a man in charge of the properties in a theatrical production —**property mistress**

pro·phase (prō′fāz) *n.* [PRO-[1] + PHASE] the first stage in mitosis, during which the chromatin is formed into chromosomes which split into separate paired chromatids

proph·e·cy (präf′ə sē) *n., pl.* **-cies** [ME. *prophecie* < OFr. *prophecie* < LL.(Ec.) *prophetia* < Gr. *prophēteia* (in NT.), gift of speaking under the influence of the Holy Spirit) < *prophētēs:* see PROPHET] 1. prediction of the future under the influence of divine guidance; act or practice of a prophet 2. any prediction 3. something prophesied or predicted; specif., the divinely inspired utterance or utterances of a prophet 4. a book of prophecies

proph·e·sy (-sī′) *vt.* **-sied′, -sy′ing** [ME. *prophecien* < MFr. *prophecier* < *prophecie:* see PROPHECY] 1. to declare or predict (something) by or as by the influence of divine guidance 2. to predict (a future event) in any way 3. [Rare] to foreshadow —*vi.* 1. to speak as a prophet; utter or make prophecies 2. [Rare] to teach religious matters; preach —*SYN.* see FORETELL —**proph′e·si′er** *n.*

proph·et (präf′it) *n.* [ME. *prophete* < OFr. < LL. *propheta*, a soothsayer, in LL.(Ec.), a prophet < Gr. *prophētēs*, interpreter of a god's will (in LXX, a Hebrew prophet; in NT., an inspired preacher) < *pro-*, before + *phanai*, to speak: see BAN[1]] 1. a person who speaks for God or a god, or as though under divine guidance 2. a religious teacher or leader regarded as, or claiming to be, divinely inspired 3. a spokesman for some cause, group, movement, etc. 4. a person who predicts future events in any way —**the Prophet** 1. among Moslems, Mohammed ☆2. among Mormons, Joseph Smith —**the Prophets** 1. one of the three major divisions of the Jewish Holy Scripture, following the Pentateuch and preceding the Hagiographa 2. the authors or subjects of the prophetic books in this

division, including Amos, Hosea, Isaiah, Micah, Jeremiah, etc. —**proph′et·ess** *n.fem.*

pro·phet·ic (prə fet′ik) *adj.* [MFr. *prophetique* < LL.(Ec.) *propheticus* < Gr. *prophētikos*] 1. of, or having the powers of, a prophet 2. of, having the nature of, or containing a prophecy *[a prophetic utterance]* 3. that predicts or foreshadows Also **pro·phet′i·cal** —**pro·phet′i·cal·ly** *adv.*

pro·phy·lac·tic (prō′fə lak′tik) *adj.* [Gr. *prophylaktikos* < *prophylassein*, to be on guard < *pro-*, before (see PRO-[1]) + *phylassein*, to guard < *phylax*, a guard] preventive or protective; esp., preventing or guarding against disease —*n.* a prophylactic medicine, device, treatment, etc.; ☆esp., a condom

pro·phy·lax·is (-sis) *n., pl.* **-lax′es** (-sēz) [ModL. < *prec.*, after Gr. *phylaxis*, a watching < *phylax*, a guard] the prevention of or protection from disease; prophylactic treatment; specif., *Dentistry* a mechanical cleaning of teeth to remove plaque and tartar

pro·pine (prə pēn′, prō-) *vt.* [LME. < L. *propinare*, to give (food) to eat, orig. to drink to one's health < Gr. *propinein*, orig. to drink first < *pro-*, PRO-[1] + *pinein*, to drink < IE. *pī-*, var. of base **pō(i)-*, to drink, whence L. *potio*, POTION] [Scot. or Archaic] to offer as a gift; present —*n.* [Scot. or Archaic] a gift, or present

pro·pin·qui·ty (prō piŋ′kwə tē) *n.* [ME. *propinquite* < MFr. < L. *propinquitas* < *propinquus*, near < *prope*, near] 1. nearness in time or place 2. nearness of relationship; kinship

pro·pi·o·nate (prō′pē ə nāt′) *n.* [< ff. + -ATE[2]] a salt or ester of propionic acid

pro·pi·on·ic acid (prō′pē än′ik) [PRO(TO)- + Gr. *piōn*, fat (for IE. base see FAT) + -IC] a colorless, sharp-smelling, liquid fatty acid, $C_3H_6O_2$, found in chyme and sweat, and produced in the distillation of wood: used in making artificial flavors, perfume esters, etc.

pro·pi·ti·ate (prə pish′ē āt′) *vt.* **-at′ed, -at′ing** [< L. *propitiatus*, pp. of *propitiare*, to propitiate < *propitius:* see PROPITIOUS] to cause to become favorably inclined; win or regain the good will of; appease or conciliate *[sacrifices made to propitiate the gods]* —*SYN.* see PACIFY —**pro·pi′ti·a·ble** (-ə b'l) *adj.* —**pro·pi′ti·a′tion** *n.* —**pro·pi′ti·a′tor** *n.* —**pro·pi′ti·a·to′ry** (-ə tôr′ē), **pro·pi′ti·a′tive** (-āt′iv, -ə tiv) *adj.*

pro·pi·tious (prə pish′əs, prō-) *adj.* [ME. *propicius* < OFr. < L. *propitius*, favorable < *pro-*, before, forward + *petere*, to seek: for IE. base see -PETAL] 1. favorably inclined or disposed; gracious *[the propitious gods]* 2. boding well; favorable; auspicious *[a propitious omen]* 3. that favors or furthers; advantageous *[propitious winds]* —*SYN.* see FAVORABLE —**pro·pi′tious·ly** *adv.* —**pro·pi′tious·ness** *n.*

☆**prop·jet** (präp′jet′) *n. same as* TURBOPROP

☆**prop·man** (präp′man′) *n., pl.* **-men′** *clipped form of* PROPERTY MAN

prop·o·lis (präp′ə lis) *n.* [L. < Gr. *propolis*, suburb, also bee glue < *pro-*, before + *polis*, city: see PRO-[1] & POLICE] a brownish, waxy substance collected from the buds of certain trees by bees and used by them to cement or caulk their hives

pro·pone (prə pōn′) *vt.* **-poned′, -pon′ing** [MScot. *proponen* < L. *proponere:* see PROPOSE] [Scot.] to bring forward as a plan, excuse, etc.; propose

pro·po·nent (prə pō′nənt) *n.* [< L. *proponens*, prp. of *proponere*, to set forth: see PROPOSE] 1. a person who makes a proposal or proposition 2. a person who espouses or supports a cause, etc. 3. *Law* one who propounds something, esp. a will for probate

Pro·pon·tis (prə pän′tis) *ancient name of* the Sea of MARMARA

pro·por·tion (prə pôr′shən) *n.* [ME. *proporcioun* < MFr. *proporcion* < L. *proportio* < *pro*, FOR + *portio*, a part: see PORTION] 1. the comparative relation between parts, things, or elements with respect to size, amount, degree, etc.; ratio 2. a part, share, or portion, esp. in its relation to the whole; quota 3. relationship between parts or things; esp., harmonious, proper, or desirable relationship; balance or symmetry 4. size, degree, or extent relative to a standard 5. [*pl.*] dimensions *[a building of large proportions]* 6. *Math. a)* an equality between ratios; relationship between four quantities in which the quotient of the first divided by the second is equal to that of the third divided by the fourth (Ex.: 6 is to 2 as 9 is to 3): also called **geometrical proportion** *b) same as* RULE OF THREE —*vt.* 1. to cause to be in proper relation, harmony, or balance *[to proportion the punishment to the crime]* 2. to arrange the parts of (a whole) so as to be harmonious or properly balanced —*SYN.* see SYMMETRY —**pro·por′tion·ment** *n.*

pro·por·tion·a·ble (-ə b'l) *adj.* [ME. *proporcionable* < LL. *proportionabilis*] in proper proportion; having due correspondence; proportional

pro·por·tion·al (-'l) *adj.* [ME. *proporcional* < L. *proportionalis*] 1. of or determined by proportion; relative 2. having, or being in, proportion *[pay proportional to work done]* 3. *Math.* having the same or a constant ratio —*n.* a quantity in a mathematical proportion —*SYN.* see

PROPORTIONATE —**pro·por'tion·al'i·ty** (-al'ə tē) *n.* — **pro·por'tion·al·ly** *adv.*

proportional representation a system of voting that gives minority parties representation in a legislature in proportion to their popular vote

pro·por·tion·ate (prə pôr'shə nit; *for v.,* -nāt') *adj.* [ME. *proporcionate* < LL. *proportionatus*] in proper proportion; proportional —*vt.* **-at'ed, -at'ing** to make proportionate; proportion —**pro·por'tion·ate·ly** *adv.* **SYN.**—**proportionate** and **proportional** both imply a being in due proportion, the former usually being preferred with reference to two things that have a reciprocal relationship to each other [the output was *proportionate* to the energy expended], and the latter, with reference to a number of similar or related things [*proportional* representation]; **commensurable** applies to things measurable by the same standard or to things properly proportioned; **commensurate**, in addition, implies equality in measure or size of things that are alike or somehow related to each other [a reward *commensurate* with his heroism] —**ANT.** disproportionate

pro·pos·al (prə pōz'l) *n.* **1.** the act of proposing **2.** a plan, action, etc. proposed **3.** an offer of marriage **SYN.**—**proposal** refers to a plan, offer, etc. presented for acceptance or rejection [his *proposal* for a decrease in taxes was approved]; **proposition**, commonly used in place of **proposal** with reference to business dealings and the like, in a strict sense applies to a statement, theorem, etc. set forth for argument, demonstration, proof, etc. [the *proposition* that all men are created equal]

pro·pose (prə pōz') *vt.* **-posed', -pos'ing** [LME. < OFr. *proposer*, altered (after *poser:* see POSE[1]) < L. *proponere*, to set forth, display, propose: see PRO-[2] & POSITION] **1.** to put forth for consideration or acceptance **2.** to purpose, plan, or intend **3.** to present as a toast in drinking **4.** to nominate (someone) for membership, office, etc. —*vi.* **1.** to make a proposal; form or declare a purpose or design **2.** to offer marriage —**SYN.** see INTEND —**pro·pos'er** *n.*

prop·o·si·tion (präp'ə zish'ən) *n.* [ME. *proposicioun* < OFr. *proposition* < L. *propositio* < *proponere:* see prec.] **1.** the act of proposing **2.** *a)* something proposed; proposal; plan ☆*b)* [Colloq.] an unethical or immoral proposal, specif. one of illicit sexual relations in return for some gain ☆**3.** [Colloq.] a proposed deal, as in business ☆**4.** [Colloq.] a person, problem, undertaking, etc. being or to be dealt with **5.** [Archaic] a setting forth; offering **6.** *Logic* an expression in which the predicate affirms or denies something about the subject **7.** *Math.* a theorem to be demonstrated or a problem to be solved **8.** *Rhetoric* a subject to be discussed or a statement to be upheld —☆*vt.* to make a proposition, esp. an improper one, to —**SYN.** see PROPOSAL —**prop'o·si'tion·al** *adj.*

propositional function same as SENTENTIAL FUNCTION **pro·pos·i·tus** (prə päz'i təs) *n., pl.* **-ti'** (-tī') [ModL. < L., pp. of *proponere*, to set forth: see PROPOSE] the family member first studied who becomes the starting point of a genealogical chart

pro·pound (prə pound') *vt.* [altered < PROPONE] to put forward for consideration; set forth; propose —**pro·pound'er** *n.*

pro·prae·tor, pro·pre·tor (prō prēt'ər) *n.* [L. *propraetor*, orig. *pro praetore < pro*, for + *praetor*, PRAETOR] a magistrate who was sent to govern a Roman province after having served as praetor in Rome

pro·pri·e·tar·y (prə prī'ə ter'ē) *n., pl.* **-tar'ies** [LL. *proprietarius* < L. *proprietas:* see PROPERTY] **1.** a proprietor or owner **2.** a group of proprietors **3.** proprietorship or ownership ☆**4.** the grantee or owner of a proprietary colony in colonial America **5.** a proprietary medicine —*adj.* **1.** belonging to a proprietor **2.** holding property **3.** of property or proprietorship **4.** privately owned and operated [a *proprietary* nursing home] **5.** held under patent, trademark, or copyright by a private person or company [a *proprietary* medicine]

☆**proprietary colony** any of certain N. American colonies that were granted by the British Crown to an individual or group with full governing rights

pro·pri·e·tor (prə prī'ə tər) *n.* [irregular formation < PROPRIET(ARY) + -OR] **1.** a person who has a legal title or exclusive right to some property; owner ☆**2.** the owner of a proprietary colony **3.** one who owns and operates a business establishment —**pro·pri'e·tor·ship'** *n.* —**pro·pri'e·tress** (-tris) *n.fem.*

pro·pri·e·ty (-ə tē) *n., pl.* **-ties** [ME. *propriete* < OFr. *proprieté:* see PROPERTY] **1.** the quality of being proper, fitting, or suitable; fitness **2.** conformity with what is proper or fitting **3.** conformity with accepted standards of proper manners or behavior **4.** [Archaic] *a)* peculiar or proper nature or state *b)* a peculiarity **5.** [Obs.] private property —**SYN.** see DECORUM —**the proprieties** accepted standards of behavior in polite society

pro·pri·o·cep·tive (prō'prē ə sep'tiv) *adj.* [< L. *proprius*, one's own + (RE)CEPTIVE] designating or of stimuli produced in body tissues, as the muscles or tendons, and received there by the proprioceptors

pro·pri·o·cep·tor (-tər) *n.* [< L. *proprius*, one's own + (RE)CEPTOR] any of the sensory end organs in the muscles, tendons, etc. that are sensitive to the stimuli originating in these tissues by the movement of the body or its parts

prop root a root descending externally from the plant stem into the ground, as on the mangrove, and helping to support the stem

prop·to·sis (präp tō'sis) *n., pl.* **-ses** (-sēz) [ModL. < LL. < Gr. *proptōsis* < *propiptein*, to fall forward < *pro-*, before (see PRO-[1]) + *piptein*, to fall < IE. base *pet-*, to fall, whence L. *petere*, to seek] *Med.* a forward or downward displacement; protrusion, as of the eyeball

pro·pul·sion (prə pul'shən) *n.* [< L. *propulsus*, pp. of *propellere* (see PROPEL) + -ION] **1.** a propelling or being propelled **2.** something that propels; propelling or driving force —**pro·pul'sive, pro·pul'so·ry** *adj.*

pro·pyl (prō'pil) *n.* [PROP(IONIC) + -YL] the monovalent radical C_3H_7, occurring in two isomeric forms —**pro·pyl'ic** *adj.*

prop·y·lae·um (präp'ə lē'əm) *n., pl.* **-lae'a** (-lē'ə) [L. < Gr. *propylaion*, orig. neut. of *propylaios*, before the gate < *pro-*, before + *pylē*, gate] *Gr. & Rom. Archit.* an entrance, vestibule, or portico before a building or group of buildings; esp., [*pl.*] the architectural structure forming the entrance to the Acropolis

pro·pyl·ene (prō'pə lēn') *n.* [PROPYL + -ENE] an unsaturated, flammable hydrocarbon, $CH_3CH:CH_2$, a colorless gas obtained in the refining of petroleum, used in making polypropylene, synthetic glycerol, isopropyl alcohol, etc.

propylene glycol a colorless, viscous liquid, $C_3H_8O_2$, used as an antifreeze and solvent, and in the manufacture of polyester resins

prop·y·lite (präp'ə līt') *n.* [< Gr. *propylon*, gateway (< *pro-*, before + *pylē*, gate) + -ITE[1]] a dark-colored form of andesite altered by the action of hot springs and consisting of such minerals as calcite, chlorite, etc.

pro ra·ta (prō rāt'ə, rät'ə) [L. *pro rata (parte)*, according to the calculated (share)] in proportion; proportionate or proportionally

☆**pro·rate** (prō rāt', prō'rāt') *vt., vi.* **-rat'ed, -rat'ing** [< PRO RATA] to divide, assess, or distribute proportionally —**pro·rat'a·ble** *adj.* —**pro·ra'tion** *n.*

pro·rogue (prō rōg') *vt., vi.* **-rogued', -rogu'ing** [ME. *prorogen* < MFr. *proroguer* < L. *prorogare*, to defer, prolong < *pro-*, for + *rogare*, to ask, akin to *regere*, to direct: see RIGHT] **1.** to discontinue or end a session of (a legislative assembly, as the British Parliament) **2.** [Rare] to defer; delay; postpone —**SYN.** see ADJOURN —**pro'ro·ga'tion** (-rō gā'shən) *n.*

pros. prosody

pro·sa·ic (prō zā'ik) *adj.* [LL. *prosaicus* < L. *prosa*, PROSE] **1.** of or like prose rather than poetry **2.** matter-of-fact; commonplace; dull and ordinary —**pro·sa'i·cal·ly** *adv.* —**pro·sa'ic·ness** *n.*

pro·sa·ism (prō'zā iz'm) *n.* [Fr. *prosaïsme*] **1.** prosaic quality or style **2.** a prosaic expression Also **pro·sa'i·cism** (-ə siz'm)

pro·sce·ni·um (prō sē'nē əm) *n., pl.* **-ni·ums, -ni·a** (-ə) [L. < Gr. *proskēnion < pro-*, before + *skēnē*, a tent, stage: see SCENE] **1.** the stage of an ancient Greek or Roman theater **2.** *a)* the apron of a stage *b)* the plane separating the stage proper from the audience and including the arch (**proscenium arch**) and the curtain within it

pro·sciut·to (prō shoot'ō; *It.* prō shoot't'ō) *n.* [It. < *prosciugare*, to dry out, altered (prob. infl. by *pro-* < L., PRO-[1]) < LL. *perexsucare < per-* < L., PER-) + *exsucare*, to extract juice from < L. *exsuctus*, pp. of *exsugere*, to suck out: see EX-[1] & SUCK] a spicy Italian ham, cured by drying and served in very thin slices, often with melon

pro·scribe (prō skrīb') *vt.* **-scribed', -scrib'ing** [ME. *proscriben* < L. *proscribere < pro-*, before + *scribere*, to write: see SCRIBE] **1.** in ancient Rome, to publish the name of (a person) condemned to death, banishment, etc. **2.** to deprive of the protection of the law; outlaw **3.** to banish; exile **4.** to denounce or forbid the practice, use, etc. of; interdict —**pro·scrib'er** *n.*

pro·scrip·tion (-skrip'shən) *n.* [ME. *proscripcioun* < L. *proscriptio < proscriptus*, pp.] **1.** a proscribing or being proscribed **2.** prohibition or interdiction —**pro·scrip'tive** *adj.* —**pro·scrip'tive·ly** *adv.*

prose (prōz) *n.* [ME. < MFr. < L. *prosa*, for *prorsa (oratio)*, direct (speech) < *prorsus*, forward, straight on < *proversus*, pp. of *provertere*, to turn forward: see PRO-[2] & VERSE] **1.** the ordinary form of written or spoken language, without rhyme or meter; speech or writing that is not poetry **2.** dull, commonplace talk, expression, quality, etc. —*adj.* **1.** of prose **2.** in prose **3.** dull; unimaginative; commonplace; prosaic —*vt., vi.* **prosed, pros'ing** to speak, write, or express (one's thoughts, etc.) in prose

pro·sec·tor (prō sek'tər) *n.* [LL.(Ec.), anatomist < L. *prosectus*, pp. of *prosecare*, to cut up < *pro-*, before + *secare*, to cut: see SAW[1]] a person skilled in dissection who prepares subjects for anatomical demonstration —**pro·sect'** *vt.*

pros·e·cute (präs'ə kyoot') *vt.* **-cut'ed, -cut'ing** [ME. *prosecuten* < L. *prosecutus*, pp. of *prosequi < pro-*, before + *sequi*, to follow: see PRO-[2] & SEQUENT] **1.** to follow up or pursue (something) to a conclusion [to *prosecute* a war with vigor] **2.** to carry on; engage in **3.** *a)* to institute legal proceedings against, or conduct criminal proceedings in court against *b)* to try to get, enforce, etc. by legal process [to *prosecute* a claim] —*vi.* **1.** to institute and carry on a legal suit **2.** to act as prosecutor —**pros'e·cut'a·ble** *adj.*

☆**prosecuting attorney** a public official, as a district attorney, who conducts criminal prosecutions on behalf of the State or people

pros·e·cu·tion (präs'ə kyōō'shən) n. [ML. prosecutio < LL., a following < L. prosecutus: see PROSECUTE] 1. a prosecuting, or following up 2. a) the conducting of criminal proceedings in court against a person b) the conducting of any lawsuit 3. the State as the party that institutes and carries on criminal proceedings in court

pros·e·cu·tor (präs'ə kyōōt'ər) n. [ML. < LL., a companion, attendant] 1. a person who prosecutes 2. Law a) a person who institutes a prosecution in court b) same as PROSECUTING ATTORNEY

pros·e·lyte (präs'ə līt') n. [ME. proselite < LL.(Ec.) proselytus < Gr. prosēlytos, a stranger, sojourner (in NT., a convert) < 2d aorist stem of proserchesthai, to come < pros, toward + erchesthai, to come] a person who has been converted from one religion to another, or from one belief, sect, party, etc. to another —vt., vi. -lyt'ed, -lyt'ing 1. to try to convert (a person), esp. to one's religion 2. to persuade to do or join something, esp. by offering an inducement —pros'e·lyt'er n.

pros·e·lyt·ism (-li tiz'm, -līt iz'm) n. 1. the fact of becoming or being a proselyte 2. the act or practice of proselytizing

pros·e·lyt·ize (-li tīz') vi., vt. -ized', -iz'ing same as PROSELYTE

☆**pro·sem·i·nar** (prō sem'ə när') n. a seminar open to undergraduate students of advanced standing

pros·en·ceph·a·lon (präs'en sef'ə län', -lən) n., pl. -la (-lə) [ModL. < Gr. pros, near + encephalon: see EN-CEPHALO-] same as FOREBRAIN —pros'en·ce·phal'ic (-sə fal'ik) adj.

pros·en·chy·ma (präs eŋ'ki mə) n. [ModL. < Gr. pros, to, toward, near + enchyma, infusion] a tissue of thickwalled, elongated cells without much protoplasm, found in some plants —pros'en·chym'a·tous (-kim'ə təs) adj.

pros·er (prō'zər) n. 1. a writer of prose 2. a person who talks or writes in a prosaic or boring manner

Pro·ser·pi·na (prō sur'pi nə) [L.] Rom. Myth. the daughter of Ceres and wife of Pluto: identified with the Greek Persephone. also **Pro·ser·pi·ne** (prō sur'pi nē', präs'ər pīn')

‡**pro·sit** (prō'zit; E. prō'sit) interj. [G. < L., 3d pers. sing., subj., of prodesse, to do good < pro, for + esse, to be] to your health: a toast, esp. among Germans

☆**pro·slav·er·y** (prō slā'və rē) adj. in favor of slavery

☆**pro·so** (prō'sō) n. [Russ.] same as MILLET (sense 1 a)

pro·sod·ic (prə säd'ik) adj. of, or according to the principles of, prosody: also **pro·sod'i·cal** adj. —**pro·sod'i·cal·ly** adv.

pros·o·dist (präs'ə dist) n. a person skilled in prosody

pros·o·dy (präs'ə dē) n., pl. -dies [ME. prosodye < L. prosodia < Gr. prosoidia, tone, accent, song sung to music < pros, to + ōidē, song] 1. the science or art of versification, including the study of metrical structure, rhyme, stanza forms, etc. 2. a particular system of versification and metrical structure [Dryden's prosody]

pro·so·po·poe·ia (prə sō'pō pē'ə) n. [L. < Gr. prosōpopoiia < prosōpon, person, face, mask (< pros, near + ōps, EYE) + poiein, to make: see POET] Rhetoric 1. a figure in which an absent, dead, or imaginary person is represented as speaking 2. same as PERSONIFICATION

pros·pect (präs'pekt) n. [ME. prospecte < L. prospectus, lookout < prospicere, to look forward < pro-, forward + specere, to look: see SPY] 1. a) a looking forward; anticipation 5. a) something hoped for or expected; anticipated outcome b) [usually pl.] apparent chance for success 6. a likely or prospective customer, candidate, undertaking, etc. ☆7. Mining a) a place where a mineral deposit is sought or found b) a sample of gravel, earth, etc. tested for a particular mineral, or the resulting yield of mineral —vt., vi. ☆to explore or search (for) [to prospect for gold] —SYN. see VIEW —**in prospect** expected

pro·spec·tive (prə spek'tiv, prä-) adj. [LL. prospectivus < prospectus: see prec.] 1. looking toward the future 2. expected; likely; future —**pro·spec'tive·ly** adv.

☆**pros·pec·tor** (präs'pek tər) n. [LL., one who looks out] a person who prospects for valuable ores, oil, etc.

pro·spec·tus (prə spek'təs, prä-) n. [L.: see PROSPECT] a statement outlining the main features of a new work or business enterprise, or the attractions of an established institution such as a college, hotel, etc.

pros·per (präs'pər) vi. [ME. prosperen < MFr. prosperer < L. prosperare, to cause to prosper < prosperus, favorable < prospere, fortunately < pro spere < pro, according to (see PRO-²) + stem of spes, hope < IE. base *spēi-, to flourish, succeed, whence SPEED, SPACE] to succeed, thrive, grow, etc. in a vigorous way —vt. [Archaic] to cause to prosper —SYN. see SUCCEED

pros·per·i·ty (prä sper'ə tē) n., pl. -ties [ME. prosperite < OFr. < L. prosperitas < prosperus] prosperous condition; good fortune, wealth, success, etc.

Pros·per·o (präs'pə rō') the deposed Duke of Milan in Shakespeare's The Tempest, exiled on an island with his daughter Miranda

pros·per·ous (präs'pər əs) adj. [ME. < MFr. prospereus: see PROSPER & -OUS] 1. having continued success; prospering; flourishing 2. well-to-do; well-off 3. conducive to success; favorable —**pros'per·ous·ly** adv.

‡**prost** (prōst) interj. same as PROSIT

pros·ta·glan·din (präs'tə glan'din) n. [< PROSTA(TE) + GLAND¹ + -IN¹] any of a group of very powerful hormones or hormonelike substances, found esp. in semen and in menstrual fluid, that may be involved in control of blood pressure and other important body processes

pros·tate (präs'tāt) adj. [ML. prostata < Gr. prostatēs, one standing before < proistanai, to set before < pro-, before + histanai, to STAND] of or relating to the prostate gland: also **pros·tat'ic** (-tat'ik) —n. same as PROSTATE GLAND

pros·ta·tec·to·my (präs'tə tek'tə mē) n., pl. -mies [PROS-TAT(O)- + -ECTOMY] the surgical removal of all or part of the prostate gland

prostate gland a partly muscular gland surrounding the urethra at the base of the bladder in most male mammals: it secretes an alkaline fluid that is discharged with the sperm

pros·ta·tism (präs'tə tiz'm) n. a chronic disorder of the prostate gland, esp. enlargement of the gland resulting in obstruction of the flow of urine

pros·ta·ti·tis (präs'tə tīt'is) n. [see -ITIS] inflammation of the prostate gland

pros·ta·to- (präs'tə tō') a combining form meaning of the prostate gland: also, before a vowel, **prostat-**

pros·the·sis (präs'thə sis; for 2, often präs thē'-) n. 1. [LL. < Gr. prosthesis < prostithenai < pros, to + tithenai, to place, DO¹] same as PROTHESIS (sense 1) 2. [ModL.] pl. -**the·ses'** (-sēz') Med. a) the replacement of a missing part of the body, as a limb, eye, or tooth, by an artificial substitute b) such a substitute

pros·thet·ic (präs thet'ik) adj. 1. of a prosthesis or prosthetics 2. Chem. designating or of any of a number of nonprotein compounds when combined chemically with a protein molecule

pros·thet·ics (-iks) n.pl. [with sing. v.] [< PROSTHETIC] the branch of surgery dealing with the replacement of missing parts, esp. limbs, by artificial substitutes — **pros·the·tist** (präs'thə tist) n.

☆**pros·tho·don·tics** (präs'thə dän'tiks) n.pl. [with sing. v.] [ModL.: see PROSTHETIC, -ODONT, & -ICS] the branch of dentistry dealing with the replacement of missing teeth, as by bridges or artificial dentures: also **pros'tho·don'ti·a** (-dän'shə, -shē ə) —**pros'tho·don'tic** adj. —**pros'tho·don'tist** n.

pros·ti·tute (präs'tə tōōt', -tyōōt') vt. -tut'ed, -tut'ing [< L. prostitutus, pp. of prostituere < pro-, before + statuere, to cause to stand, akin to stare, STAND] 1. to sell the services of (oneself or another) for purposes of sexual intercourse 2. to sell (oneself, one's artistic or moral integrity, etc.) for low or unworthy purposes —adj. [Rare] given over to base purposes; debased; corrupt —n. 1. a woman who engages in promiscuous sexual intercourse for pay; whore; harlot 2. a person, as a writer, artist, etc., who sells his services for low or unworthy purposes —**pros'ti·tu'tor** n.

pros·ti·tu·tion (präs'tə tōō'shən, -tyōō'-) n. [LL.(Ec.) prostitutio] the act or practice of prostituting, or the fact of being prostituted; esp., the trade of a prostitute

pro·sto·mi·um (prō stō'mē əm) n., pl. -mi·a (-ə) [ModL.: see PRO-¹, STOMA, & -IUM] a small, noselike portion of the first body segment in many annelid worms, lying above and overhanging the mouth in earthworms

pros·trate (präs'trāt) adj. [ME. prostrat < L. prostratus, pp. of prosternere, to lay flat < pro-, before + sternere, to stretch out < IE. base *ster-, whence STREW] 1. lying with the face downward in demonstration of great humility or abject submission 2. lying flat, prone, or supine 3. thrown or fallen to the ground 4. a) laid low; completely overcome; helpless [prostrate with grief] b) in a state of physical exhaustion or weakness 5. Bot. growing on the ground; trailing —vt. -trat·ed, -trat·ing 1. to throw or put in a prostrate position; lay flat on the ground 2. to lay low; overcome; exhaust or subjugate —SYN. see PRONE

pros·tra·tion (präs trā'shən) n. [LL. prostratio] 1. a prostrating or being prostrated 2. utter physical or mental exhaustion or helplessness

pro·style (prō'stīl) adj. [L. prostylus < Gr. prostylos < pro-, before + stylos, pillar: see STYLITE] Archit. having a portico whose columns, usually four in number, extend in a line across the front only, as in a Greek temple —n. 1. such a portico 2. a prostyle building

pros·y (prō'zē) adj. pros'i·er, pros'i·est 1. like, or having the nature of, prose 2. prosaic; commonplace, dull, etc. —**pros'i·ly** adv. —**pros'i·ness** n.

Prot. Protestant

pro·tac·tin·i·um (prō'tak tin'ē əm) n. [ModL.: see PROTO- & ACTINIUM] a rare, radioactive, metallic chemical element

occurring in pitchblende: symbol, Pa; at. wt., 231.10; at. no., 91; sp. gr., 15.37

pro·tag·o·nist (prō tag′ə nist) *n.* [Gr. *prōtagōnistēs* < *prōtos*, first + *agōnistēs*, actor < *agōnizesthai*: see AGONIZE] **1.** the main character in a drama, novel, or story, around whom the action centers **2.** a person who plays a leading or active part

Pro·tag·o·ras (prō tag′ər əs) 481?–411? B.C.; Gr. philosopher; one of the principal Sophists

pro·ta·mine (prōt′ə mēn′, -min) *n.* [PROT(O)- + AMINE] any of a class of simple proteins that are soluble in ammonia, do not coagulate by heat, and yield relatively few amino acids upon hydrolysis

pro·tan·o·pi·a (prōt′n ō′pē ə) *n.* [ModL.: see PROTO-, AN-[1], & -OPIA] a defect of color vision characterized by the inability to see red —**pro′tan·op′ic** (-äp′ik) *adj.*

prot·a·sis (prät′ə sis) *n.* [LL. < Gr. *protasis* < *proteinein*, to stretch before, present < *pro-*, before + *teinein*, to stretch: see THIN] **1.** *Gr. & Rom. Drama* the opening of the play, in which the characters are introduced **2.** *Gram.* the clause that expresses the condition in a conditional sentence: cf. APODOSIS

pro·te·an[1] (prōt′ē ən, prō tē′ən) *adj.* **1.** [P-] of or like Proteus **2.** very changeable; readily taking on different shapes and forms

pro·te·an[2] (prōt′ē ən) *n.* [PROTE(IN) + -AN] any of a group of insoluble derived proteins that are the first products of the action of water, dilute acids, or enzymes on proteins

pro·te·ase (prōt′ē ās′) *n.* [PROTE(IN) + (DIAST)ASE] an enzyme that digests proteins

pro·tect (prə tekt′) *vt.* [< L. *protectus*, pp. of *protegere*, to protect < *pro-*, before + *tegere*, to cover: see THATCH] **1.** to shield from injury, danger, or loss; guard; defend **2.** *Commerce* to set aside funds toward the payment of (a note, draft, etc.) at maturity **3.** *Econ.* to guard (domestic industry) by tariffs on imported products —*SYN.* see DEFEND —**pro·tect′a·ble** *adj.*

pro·tec·tion (prə tek′shən) *n.* [ME. *proteccioun* < MFr. *protection* < LL. *protectio*] **1.** *a)* a protecting or being protected *b)* an instance of this **2.** a person or thing that protects **3.** a safe-conduct pass or passport ☆**4.** [Colloq.] *a)* money extorted by racketeers threatening violence *b)* bribes paid to officials by racketeers to avoid prosecution **5.** *Econ.* the system of protecting domestic products by taxing imported goods

pro·tec·tion·ism (-iz′m) *n. Econ.* the system, theory, or policy of protection —**pro·tec′tion·ist** *n., adj.*

pro·tec·tive (-tiv) *adj.* **1.** protecting, or serving, intended, or alleged to protect [a *protective* gesture, *protective* custody] **2.** *Econ.* serving or intended to protect domestic products, industries, etc. in competition with foreign products, industries, etc. [a *protective* tariff] —**pro·tec′tive·ly** *adv.* —**pro·tec′tive·ness** *n.*

protective coloration (or **coloring**) natural coloration of certain organisms allowing them to blend in with the normal environment and escape detection by enemies

pro·tec·tor (prə tek′tər) *n.* [ME. *protectour* < MFr. < LL. *protector*] **1.** a person or thing that protects; guardian; defender **2.** *Eng. History a)* a person ruling a kingdom during the minority, absence, or incapacity of the sovereign *b)* [P-] the title (in full **Lord Protector**) held by Oliver Cromwell (1653–1658) and his son Richard (1658–1659), during the British Protectorate —**pro·tec′tor·al** *adj.* —**pro·tec′tor·ship′** *n.* —**pro·tec′tress** (-tris) *n.fem.*

pro·tec·tor·ate (-it) *n.* **1.** government by a protector **2.** the office or term of office of a protector **3.** [P-] the government of England under Oliver Cromwell and his son Richard (1653–1659) **4.** *a)* the relation of a strong state to a weaker state under its control and protection *b)* a state or territory so controlled and protected *c)* the authority exercised by the controlling state

pro·tec·to·ry (-ē) *n., pl.* **-ries** formerly, a church-operated institution for the protection of destitute children

pro·té·gé (prōt′ə zhā′, prōt′ə zhā′) *n.* [Fr., pp. of *protéger* < L. *protegere*, PROTECT] a person guided and helped, esp. in the furtherance of his career, by another, more influential person —**pro′té·gée′** (-zhā′, -zhā′) *n.fem.*

pro·te·id (prōt′ē id, prō′tēd) *n. rare var. of* PROTEIN: also **pro′te·ide′** (-ē īd′)

pro·tein (prō′tēn, prōt′ē in) *n.* [G. < Fr. *protéine* < Gr. *prōteios*, prime, chief < *prōtos*, first: from being a chief constituent of plant and animal bodies] any of a large class of nitrogenous substances consisting of a complex union of amino acids and containing carbon, hydrogen, nitrogen, oxygen, frequently sulfur, and sometimes phosphorus, iron, iodine, or other elements: proteins occur in all animal and vegetable matter and are essential to the diet of animals

pro·tein·ase (prō′tē nās′, prōt′ē i-) *n.* any of a class of enzymes, as pepsin, trypsin, etc., that split peptide bonds in proteins to form simpler compounds: a subgroup of the proteases

pro·tein·ate (-nāt′) *n.* a protein compound

pro·tein·oid (-noid′) *n.* any of a group of synthetic, proteinlike polymers formed from amino acids subjected to great heat and other conditions such as may have prevailed on earth billions of years ago; primitive protein

pro·tein·u·ri·a (prō′tēn yoor′ē ə, prōt′ē in-) *n.* [ModL.: see -URIA] the presence of protein in the urine

pro tem·po·re (prō tem′pə rē′) [L.] for the time (being); temporary or temporarily: shortened to **pro tem**

pro·te·o- (prōt′ē ō) *a combining form meaning* protein [*proteolysis*]: also, before a vowel, **pro′te-**

pro·te·o·clas·tic (prōt′ē ō klas′tik) *adj.* [< PROTEO- + Gr. *klastos*, broken: see CLASTIC] of, related to, or initiating proteolysis

pro·te·ol·y·sis (prōt′ē äl′ə sis) *n.* [ModL.: see PROTEIN & -LYSIS] *Biochem.* the breaking down of proteins, as by gastric juices, to form simpler substances —**pro′te·o·lyt′ic** (-ə lit′ik) *adj.*

pro·te·ose (prōt′ē ōs′) *n.* [PROTE(IN) + -OSE[1]] any of a class of water-soluble products, formed in the hydrolysis of proteins, that can be broken down to peptones

Prot·er·o·zo·ic (prōt′ər ə zō′ik, prät′-) *adj.* [< Gr. *proteros*, former + ZO- + -IC] Precambrian, esp. Late Precambrian: see GEOLOGY, chart

pro·test (prə test′; *for n.*, prō′test) *vt.* [ME. *protesten* < MFr. *protester* < L. *protestari* < *pro-*, forth + *testari*, to affirm < *testis*, a witness: see TESTIFY] **1.** to state positively; affirm solemnly; assert ☆**2.** to make objection to; speak strongly against **3.** to make a written declaration of the nonpayment of (a bill of exchange or a promissory note) —*vi.* **1.** to make solemn affirmation **2.** to express disapproval; object; dissent —*n.* **1.** an objection; remonstrance **2.** a document formally objecting to something **3.** *Law a)* a written declaration by a notary on behalf of the holder of a bill or note, showing that it has not been honored by the drawer *b)* a written declaration by the master of a ship attesting to the fact that damages or losses were sustained from unavoidable natural causes, and rejecting any liability of the officers and crew *c)* a declaration by a payer, esp. of a tax, that he does not concede the legality of a claim he is paying —*SYN.* see OBJECT —**under protest** while expressing one's objections; unwillingly —**pro·test′er, pro·tes′tor** *n.*

Prot·es·tant (prät′is tənt; *for n. 3 & adj. 2, also* prə tes′tənt) *n.* [Fr. < G. < L. *protestans*, prp. of *protestari*: see prec.] **1.** orig., any of the German princes and free cities that formally protested to the Diet of Spires (1529) its decision to uphold the edict of the Diet of Worms against the Reformation **2.** *a)* a member of any of the Christian churches as a result of the Reformation; esp., a Lutheran, Calvinist, or Anglican *b)* any Christian not belonging to the Roman Catholic or Orthodox Eastern Church **3.** [p-] a person who protests —*adj.* **1.** of Protestants or Protestant beliefs, practices, etc. **2.** [p-] protesting —**Prot′es·tant·ism** *n.*

☆**Protestant Episcopal Church** the Protestant church in the U.S. that conforms to the practices and principles of the Church of England

prot·es·tant·ize (-īz′) *vt.* **-ized′, -iz′ing** [see -IZE] to introduce Protestant practices, attitudes, etc. in

prot·es·ta·tion (prät′is tā′shən, prō′tes-) *n.* [ME. *protestacion* < MFr. *protestation* < LL. *protestatio*] **1.** a strong declaration or affirmation **2.** the act of protesting **3.** a protest; objection

Pro·teus (prō′tyōōs, prōt′ē əs) [ME. *Protheus* < L. *Proteus* < Gr. *Prōteus*] *Gr. Myth.* a sea god who attended Poseidon and could change his own form or appearance at will —*n.* [*often* p-] a person who changes his appearance or principles easily

pro·tha·la·mi·on (prō′thə lā′mē ən, -än′) *n., pl.* **-mi·a** (-ə) [ModL., coined by Spenser (after EPITHALAMION) < Gr. *pro-*, before + *thalamos*, bridal chamber] a song celebrating a marriage: also **pro′tha·la′mi·um** (-əm), *pl.* **-mi·a** (-ə)

pro·thal·li·um (prō thal′ē əm) *n., pl.* **-li·a** (-ə) [ModL. < Gr. *pro-*, before + *thallos*, a shoot < IE. base *dhal-*, to bloom, whence Alb. *dal*, to sprout] *Bot.* a minute, flat, greenish disc of cells bearing sex organs on its lower side, usually attached to the ground by hairlike roots and forming the haploid, sexual generation of ferns and similar plants: also **pro·thal′lus** (-əs), *pl.* **-li** (-ī), **-lus·es** —**pro·thal′li·al** (-ē əl), **pro·thal′loid** (-oid) *adj.*

proth·e·sis (präth′ə sis) *n.* [LL. < Gr. *prothesis*, a placing before < *protithenai*, to set before < *pro-*, before + *tithenai*, to place, DO[1]] **1.** *Gram.* the addition of a letter, syllable, or phoneme to the beginning of a word **2.** *Orthodox Eastern Ch. a)* the preparation and preliminary oblation of the elements of the Eucharist *b)* the table on which, or the place where, this is done —**pro·thet′ic** (prä thet′ik) *adj.*

pro·thon·o·tar·y (prō thän′ə ter′ē, prō′thə nōt′ər ē) *n., pl.* **-tar′ies** [ME. < ML. *prothonotarius* < LL.(Ec.) *protonotarius*: see PROTO- & NOTARY] **1.** a chief clerk in any of various law courts **2.** *R.C.Ch.* any of the seven members of the College of Prothonotaries Apostolic, who record important pontifical events: also sometimes held as an honorary title by other ecclesiastics

☆**prothonotary warbler** a N. American warbler (*Protonotaria citrea*) with flaming yellow underparts and head and bluish-gray upper parts in the male

pro·tho·rax (prō thôr′aks) *n., pl.* **-rax·es, -ra·ces′** (-ə sēz′) [ModL.: see PRO-[1] & THORAX] *Zool.* that division of an insect's thorax nearest the head, and bearing the first pair of legs —**pro′tho·rac′ic** (-thô ras′ik) *adj.*

pro·throm·bin (-thräm′bin) *n.* [PRO-[1] + THROMBIN] a factor in the blood plasma that combines with calcium to form thrombin during blood clotting: it is a precursor of

thrombin and is synthesized by the liver in the presence of vitamin K

pro·tist (prōt′ist) *n.* [< Gr. *prōtistos*, first < *prōtos*, first: see PROTO-] *Biol.* any of a large group (Protista) of one-celled organisms having characters found in both plants and animals and including the algae, yeasts, bacteria, protozoans, etc. —**pro·tis·tan** (prō tis′tən) *adj., n.*

pro·ti·um (prōt′ē əm, prō′shē-) *n.* [ModL.: see ff. & -IUM] the most common isotope of hydrogen, H¹, having a mass number of 1

pro·to- (prōt′ə, -ō) [Gr. *prōto-* < *prōtos*, first < IE. *pr̥to- < base *per-, early, ahead, whence L. *pro-*, Gr. *pro-*] a combining form meaning: **1.** first in time, original, primitive [*protoplast*] **2.** first in importance, principal, chief [*protagonist*] **3.** [P-] primitive, original: said of people, their language, etc. [*Proto*-Germanic] **4.** *Chem. a)* being that member of a series of compounds having the lowest proportion of the (specified) element or radical [*protoxide*] *b)* being the parent form of a (specified) substance [*protoporphyrin*] Also, before a vowel, **prot-**

pro·to·ac·tin·i·um (prōt′ō ak tin′ē əm) *n.* earlier name for PROTACTINIUM

pro·to·col (prōt′ə kôl′, -käl′, -kōl′) *n.* [Early ModE. *prothocoll* < MFr. *prothocole* < ML. *protocollum* < LGr. *prōtokollon*, first leaf glued to a manuscript (describing the contents) < Gr. *prōto-*, PROTO- + *kolla*, glue] **1.** an original draft or record of a document, negotiation, etc. **2.** [Fr. *protocole*] *a)* a signed document containing a record of the points on which agreement has been reached by negotiating parties preliminary to a final treaty or compact *b)* the code of ceremonial forms and courtesies, of precedence, etc. accepted as proper and correct in official dealings, as between heads of states or diplomatic officials —*vt.* -**colled′** or -**coled′**, -**col′ling** or -**col′ing** to draw up or issue in a protocol —*vi.* to draw up a protocol

pro·to·his·to·ry (prōt′ō his′tə rē) *n.* the archaeological history of man in the period immediately preceding recorded history

pro·to·hu·man (-hyōō′mən, -yōō′-) *adj.* of or relating to any of the early manlike primates

pro·to·lith·ic (prōt′ə lith′ik) *adj.* [PROTO- + -LITHIC] of or relating to the earliest Stone Age; eolithic

pro·to·mar·tyr (prōt′ō mär′tər) *n.* [ME. *prothomartir* < MFr. < ML.(Ec.) *protomartyr* < LGr.(Ec.) *prōtomartyr*: see PROTO- & MARTYR] the first martyr (in some cause)

pro·ton (prō′tän) *n.* [ModL. < Gr. *prōton*, neut. of *prōtos*, first: see PROTO-] an elementary particle found in the nucleus of all atoms and comprising the atomic nucleus of the protium isotope of hydrogen: it carries a unit positive charge equal to the negative charge of an electron and has a mass of 1.672×10^{-24} gram, approximately 1836 times that of an electron: the atomic number of an atom is equal to the number of protons in its nucleus: also see NEUTRON

pro·to·ne·ma (prōt′ə nē′mə) *n.*, *pl.* -**ma·ta** (-mə tə) [ModL. < Gr. *prōto-*, PROTO- + *nēma* (gen. *nēmatos*), a thread] *Bot.* a threadlike growth in mosses, arising from a spore and developing small buds that grow into leafy moss plants —**pro′to·ne′mal** *adj.*

pro·to·ne·phrid·i·um (prōt′ō ne frid′ē əm) *n.* [PROTO- + NEPHRIDIUM] *Zool.* a pipelike excretory structure in certain worms and larvae, usually ending internally in flame cells and having an external pore

pro·ton·o·tar·y (prō tän′ə ter′ē, prōt′ə nōt′ər ē) *n.*, *pl.* -**tar′ies** same as PROTHONOTARY

☆**proton synchrotron** a synchrotron for accelerating protons and other heavy particles to very high energies

pro·to·nymph (prōt′ə nimf′) *n.* [PROTO- + NYMPH] the newly hatched form of various mites —**pro′to·nymph′al** *adj.*

pro·to·path·ic (prōt′ə path′ik) *adj.* [PROTO- + -PATHIC] *Physiol.* designating or of primary, or primitive, sensibility, which can perceive and localize only strong, gross stimuli, as pain

pro·to·plasm (prōt′ə plaz′m) *n.* [G. *protoplasma*: see PROTO- & PLASMA] a semifluid, viscous, translucent colloid, the essential living matter of all animal and plant cells: it consists largely of water, proteins, lipoids, carbohydrates, and inorganic salts and is differentiated into nucleoplasm and cytoplasm —**pro′to·plas′mic** (-plaz′mik) *adj.*

pro·to·plast (prōt′ə plast′) *n.* [Fr. *protoplaste* < LL. *protoplastus* < Gr. *protoplastos*, formed first < *protos*, first (see PROTO-) + *plastos*, formed < *plassein*, to form: see PLASTIC] **1.** a thing or being that is the first of its kind **2.** *Biol.* same as ENERGID **3.** *Bot.* a unit of protoplasm, such as makes up a single cell exclusive of the cell wall —**pro′to·plas′tic** *adj.*

pro·to·ste·le (prōt′ə stēl′, -stē′lē) *n.* [PROTO- + STELE] a simple, primitive arrangement of conducting tissues in stems and roots of certain lower plants, consisting of a solid cylinder of xylem surrounded by a layer of phloem —**pro′to·ste′lic** *adj.*

pro·to·troph·ic (prōt′ə träf′ik) *adj.* [PROTO- + TROPHIC] not requiring organic food, as the nitrogen-fixing bacteria

pro·to·type (prōt′ə tīp′) *n.* [Fr. < Gr. *prōtotypon* < *prōtotypos*, original: see PROTO- & TYPE] **1.** the first thing

or being of its kind; original; model; pattern; archetype **2.** a person or thing that serves as a model for one of a later period **3.** a perfect example of a particular type —**pro′to·typ′al** (-tī′p′l), **pro′to·typ′ic** (-tip′ik), **pro′to·typ′i·cal** *adj.*

pro·tox·ide (prō täk′sīd) *n.* that one of any series of oxides that contains the lowest proportion of oxygen

pro·to·xy·lem (prōt′ə zī′ləm, -lem) *n.* *Bot.* the first formed xylem of a root or stem, produced by the differentiation of the procambium

pro·to·zo·an (prōt′ə zō′ən) *n.* [ModL. *protozoa* (see PROTO- & -ZOA) + -AN] any of a subkingdom and phylum (Protozoa) of mostly microscopic animals made up of a single cell or a group of more or less identical cells and living chiefly in water, but including many parasitic forms: also **pro′to·zo′on** (-än), *pl.* -**zo′a** (-ə) —*adj.* of the protozoans: also **pro′to·zo′ic** (-ik)

pro·to·zo·ol·o·gy (prōt′ə zō äl′ə jē) *n.* that branch of zoology devoted to the study of the protozoans

pro·tract (prō trakt′) *vt.* [< L. *protractus*, pp. of *protrahere* < *pro-*, forward + *trahere*, to DRAW] **1.** to draw out; lengthen in duration; prolong **2.** to draw to scale, using a protractor and scale **3.** *Zool.* to thrust out; extend: opposed to RETRACT —*SYN.* see EXTEND —**pro·tract′ed·ly** *adv.* —**pro·tract′ed·ness** *n.* —**pro·tract′i·ble** *adj.* —**pro·trac′tion** *n.* —**pro·trac′tive** *adj.*

pro·trac·tile (prō trakt′l) *adj.* capable of being protracted or thrust out; extensible

pro·trac·tor (prō trak′tər) *n.* [ML.] **1.** a person or thing that protracts **2.** an instrument in the form of a graduated semicircle, used for plotting and measuring angles **3.** *Anat.* a muscle that protracts, or extends, a limb

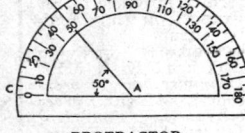
PROTRACTOR
(DAC, angle measured)

pro·trude (prō trōōd′) *vt., vi.* -**trud′ed**, -**trud′ing** [L. *protrudere* < *pro-*, forth + *trudere*, to THRUST] to thrust or jut out; project —**pro·trud′ent** *adj.*

pro·tru·sile (prō trōō′s′l) *adj.* [< L. *protrusus*, pp. of *protrudere* (see PROTRUDE) + -ILE] that can be protruded, or thrust out, as a tentacle, an elephant's trunk, etc.: also **pro·tru′si·ble** (-sə b′l)

pro·tru·sion (-zhən) *n.* [< L. *protrusus* (see prec.) + -ION] **1.** a protruding or being protruded **2.** a protruding part or thing —*SYN.* see PROJECTION

pro·tru·sive (-siv) *adj.* [< L. *protrusus*, pp. of *protrudere* (see PROTRUDE) + -IVE] **1.** protruding; jutting or bulging out **2.** same as OBTRUSIVE —**pro·tru′sive·ly** *adv.* —**pro·tru′sive·ness** *n.*

pro·tu·ber·ance (prō tōō′bər əns, -tyōō′-) *n.* **1.** the condition or fact of being protuberant **2.** a part or thing that protrudes; projection; bulge; swelling Also **pro·tu′ber·an·cy** (-ən sē), *pl.* -**cies** —*SYN.* see PROJECTION

pro·tu·ber·ant (-ənt) *adj.* [LL. *protuberans*, prp. of *protuberare*, to bulge out < L. *pro-*, forth + *tuber*, a bump, bulge: see TUBER] bulging or swelling out; protruding; prominent —**pro·tu′ber·ant·ly** *adv.*

pro·tu·ber·ate (-āt′) *vi.* -**at′ed**, -**at′ing** [< LL. *protuberatus*, pp. of *protuberare*: see prec.] to bulge or swell out

pro·tyle (prō′til) *n.* [< PROT(O)- + Gr. *hylē*, substance, stuff] in old chemistry, the hypothetical primordial substance thought to be the source of all elements

proud (proud) *adj.* [ME. < OE. *prud* < OFr. < LL. *prode*, beneficial, back-formation < L. *prodesse*, to be useful < *prod-*, var. of *pro-*, PRO-² + *esse*, to be: for IE. base see IS] **1.** having or showing a proper pride in oneself, one's position, one's family, etc. **2.** having or showing an overweening opinion of oneself, one's position, etc.; arrogant; haughty **3.** feeling or showing great pride or joy, as from being honored **4.** that is an occasion or cause of pride; highly gratifying **5.** arising from or caused by pride; presumptuous **6.** stately; splendid [a *proud* fleet] **7.** spirited; of high mettle [a *proud* stallion] **8.** [Obs.] valiant —**do oneself proud** [Colloq.] to do extremely well —**proud of** highly pleased with or exulting in —**proud′ly** *adv.* *SYN.*—**proud** is the broadest term in this comparison, ranging in implication from proper self-esteem or pride to an overweening opinion of one's importance [too *proud* to beg, *proud* as a peacock]; **arrogant** implies an aggressive, unwarranted assertion of superior importance or privileges [the *arrogant* colonel]; **haughty** implies such consciousness of high station, rank, etc. as is displayed in scorn of those one considers beneath one [a *haughty* dowager]; **insolent**, in this connection, implies both haughtiness and great contempt, esp. as manifested in behavior or speech that insults or affronts others [she has an *insolent* disregard for her servant's feelings]; **overbearing** implies extreme, domineering insolence [an *overbearing* supervisor]; **supercilious** stresses an aloof, scornful manner toward others [a *supercilious* intellectual snob]; **disdainful** implies even stronger and more overt feelings of scorn for that which is regarded as beneath one —*ANT.* humble

proud flesh [so called from the notion of swelling up] an abnormal growth of flesh around a healing wound, caused by excessive granulation

Prou·dhon (prōō dôn′), **Pierre Jo·seph** (pyer′ zhō zef′) 1809–65; Fr. socialist & writer

Proust (prōōst), **Mar·cel** (mär sel′) 1871–1922; Fr. novelist —**Proust′i·an** *adj.*

Prov. 1. Provençal 2. Proverbs 3. Province

prov. 1. province 2. provincial 3. provisional 4. provost

prove (prōōv) *vt.* **proved, proved** or **prov′en, prov′ing** [ME. *proven* < OFr. *prover* < L. *probare:* see PROBE] 1. to test by experiment, a standard, etc.; subject to a testing process; try out 2. to establish as true; demonstrate to be a fact 3. to establish the validity or authenticity of (a will, etc.) 4. to show (oneself) to be capable, dependable, etc. 5. [Archaic] to experience; learn or know by experience 6. *Math.* to test or verify the correctness of (a calculation, etc.) 7. *Printing* to take a proof of (type, etc.) —*vi.* 1. to be found or shown by experience or trial; turn out to be [a guess that *proved* right] 2. [Archaic] to make trial —**prov′a·bil′i·ty, prov′a·ble·ness** *n.* —**prov′a·ble** *adj.* —**prov′a·bly** *adv.* —**prov′er** *n.*

prov·e·nance (präv′ə nəns) *n.* [Fr. < *provenir* < L. *provenire,* to come forth < *pro-,* forth + *venire,* to COME] origin; derivation; source

Pro·ven·çal (prō′vən säl′, präv′ən-; *Fr.* prô văn säl′) *adj.* [Fr.] of Provence, its people, their language, etc. —*n.* 1. the vernacular of S France, a Romance language comprising several dialects 2. the medieval language of S France, a literary language as cultivated by the troubadours 3. a native or inhabitant of Provence

Pro·vence (prô väns′) [Fr. < L. *provincia,* PROVINCE] region & former province of SE France, on the Mediterranean

prov·en·der (präv′ən dər) *n.* [ME. < MFr. *provendre,* var. of *provende* < ML.(Ec.) *praebenda:* see PREBEND] 1. dry food for livestock, as hay, corn, oats, etc.; fodder 2. [Colloq.] provisions; food

pro·ve·ni·ence (prō vē′ nē əns, -vēn′yəns) *n.* [< L. *proveniens,* prp. of *provenire:* see PROVENANCE] origin; derivation

PROVENCE

pro·ven·tric·u·lus (prō′ven trik′yoo ləs) *n.,* *pl.* **-li′** (-lī′) [ModL.: see PRO-[1] & VENTRICULUS] *Zool.* 1. the front part of a bird's stomach, containing digestive glands 2. the thin-walled front part of the stomach of many invertebrates, as earthworms and lobsters

prov·erb (präv′ərb) *n.* [ME. < OFr. *proverbe* < L. *proverbium* < *pro-,* before + *verbum,* a word: see VERB] 1. a short saying in common use that strikingly expresses some obvious truth or familiar experience; adage; maxim 2. a person or thing that has become commonly recognized as a type of specified characteristics; byword 3. *Bible* an enigmatical saying in which a profound truth is cloaked —*vt.* [ME. *prouerben*] [Archaic] 1. to make a proverb or byword of 2. to describe in a proverb —*SYN.* see SAYING

pro·ver·bi·al (prə vur′bē əl) *adj.* [ME. < LL. *proverbialis*] 1. of, or having the nature of, a proverb 2. expressed in a proverb 3. well-known because commonly referred to [the *proverbial* glamour of Paris] —**pro·ver′bi·al·ly** *adv.*

Prov·erbs (präv′ərbz) a book of the Bible containing maxims ascribed to Solomon and others

pro·vide (prə vīd′) *vt.* **-vid′ed, -vid′ing** [ME. < L. *providere* < *pro-,* before + *videre,* to see: see VISION] 1. [Now Rare] to get ready beforehand; obtain in advance 2. to make available; supply; afford 3. to furnish with 4. to state as a condition; stipulate —*vi.* 1. to prepare (*for* or *against*) some probable or possible situation, occurrence, condition, etc. 2. to make a condition; stipulate 3. to furnish the means of support (usually with *for*) —**pro·vid′er** *n.*

pro·vid·ed (-vīd′id) *conj.* on the condition or understanding; if (often with *that*)

Prov·i·dence (präv′ə dəns) [named by Roger WILLIAMS] capital of Rhode Island, on Narragansett Bay: pop. 179,000 (met. area, with Pawtucket & Warwick, 914,000)

prov·i·dence (präv′ə dəns) *n.* [ME. < MFr. < L. *providentia,* foresight < *providens:* see ff.] 1. a looking to, or preparation for, the future; provision 2. skill or wisdom in management; prudence 3. *a)* the care or benevolent guidance of God or nature *b)* an instance of this 4. [P-] God, as the guiding power of the universe

prov·i·dent (-dənt) *adj.* [ME. < L. *providens,* prp. of *providere:* see PROVIDE] 1. providing for future needs or events; exercising or characterized by foresight 2. prudent or economical —*SYN.* see THRIFTY —**prov′i·dent·ly** *adv.*

prov·i·den·tial (präv′ə den′shəl) *adj.* [< L. *providentia* + -AL] of, by, or as if decreed by divine providence —*SYN.* see LUCKY —**prov′i·den′tial·ly** *adv.*

pro·vid·ing (prə vīd′iŋ) *conj.* on the condition or understanding (that); provided

prov·ince (präv′ins) *n.* [ME. < OFr. < L. *provincia,* province < ? IE. **prowo-* (< base **pro-*), whence Gr. *prōira,* PROW[1], OE. *frea,* lord] 1. any of the outside territories controlled and ruled by ancient Rome 2. an administrative division of a country; specif., any of the ten main administrative divisions of Canada 3. *a)* a territorial district; territory *b)* [*pl.*] the parts of a country removed from the capital and the populated, cultural centers 4. proper duties or functions; sphere 5. a department; division; branch of learning 6. a division of a country under the jurisdiction of an archbishop or metropolitan 7. a division of the world, smaller than a region, with reference to the plants or animals found there

Prov·ince·town (präv′ins toun′) [< *Province Lands,* title of public land at the end of Cape Cod] resort town in Mass., at the N tip of Cape Cod: pop. 3,000

pro·vin·cial (prə vin′shəl) *adj.* [ME. *prouyncial* < MFr. < L. *provincialis*] 1. of or belonging to a province 2. having the ways, speech, attitudes, etc. of a certain province 3. of or like that of rural provinces; countrified; rustic 4. narrow; limited; unsophisticated [a *provincial* outlook] —*n.* 1. a native of a province 2. a provincial person; esp., a narrow-minded or unsophisticated person —**pro·vin′cial·ly** *adv.*

pro·vin·cial·ism (-iz′m) *n.* 1. the condition or fact of being provincial 2. narrowness of outlook; exclusive concern with local matters 3. a provincial custom, characteristic, etc. 4. a word, phrase, or pronunciation peculiar to a province Also **pro·vin′ci·al′i·ty** (-shē al′ə tē), *pl.* **-ties** —**pro·vin′cial·ist** *n.*

proving ground a place for testing new equipment, new theories, etc.

pro·vi·sion (prə vizh′ən) *n.* [ME. *provysion* < MFr. *provision* < L. *provisio,* a foreseeing < *provisus,* pp. of *providere:* see PROVIDE] 1. a providing, preparing, or supplying of something 2. something provided, prepared, or supplied for the future; specif., [*pl.*] a stock of food and other supplies assembled for future needs 3. a preparatory arrangement or measure taken in advance for meeting some future need 4. a clause, as in a legal document, agreement, etc., stipulating or requiring some specific thing; proviso; condition 5. *Eccles.* appointment to an office; esp., advance appointment by the Pope to a see or benefice that is not yet vacant —*vt.* to supply with provisions, esp. with a stock of food —*SYN.* see FOOD —**pro·vi′sion·er** *n.*

pro·vi·sion·al (-'l) *adj.* having the nature of a temporary provision; arranged or established for the time being, pending permanent arrangement or establishment: also **pro·vi·sion·ar′y** (-er′ē) —*n.* ☆a postage stamp issued, as by a postmaster, for temporary use pending an official issue —**pro·vi′sion·al·ly** *adv.*

pro·vi·so (prə vī′zō) *n.,* *pl.* **-sos, -soes** [ML. *proviso* (*quod*), provided (that) < L., abl. of *provisus,* pp. of *providere:* see PROVIDE] 1. a clause, as in a document or statute, making some condition or stipulation 2. a condition or stipulation

pro·vi·so·ry (-zər ē) *adj.* [ML. *provisorius* < L. *provisus:* see prec.] 1. containing a proviso; conditional 2. *same as* PROVISIONAL —**pro·vi′so·ri·ly** *adv.*

pro·vi·ta·min (prō vīt′ə min) *n.* any ingested substance which can be converted to a vitamin within the organism

Pro·vo (prō′vō) [after Étienne *Provot,* early fur trader] city in NC Utah: pop. 53,000

pro·vo (prō′vō) *n.,* *pl.* **-vos** [Du., contr. < *provokateur* < Fr. *provocateur:* see AGENT PROVOCATEUR] any youth of a loosely organized anarchist movement in some European countries

prov·o·ca·tion (präv′ə kā′shən) *n.* [ME. < MFr. *provocation* < L. *provocatio*] 1. an act or instance of provoking 2. something that provokes; esp., a cause of resentment or irritation; incitement

pro·voc·a·tive (prə väk′ə tiv) *adj.* [ME. *prouocatyue,* aphrodisiac < LL. *provocativus* < L. *provocare:* see PROVOKE] provoking or tending to provoke, as to action, thought, feeling, etc.; stimulating, erotic, irritating, etc. —*n.* something that provokes —**pro·voc′a·tive·ly** *adv.* —**pro·voc′a·tive·ness** *n.*

pro·voke (prə vōk′) *vt.* **-voked′, -vok′ing** [ME. *provoken* < MFr. *provoquer* < L. *provocare,* to call forth < *pro-,* forth + *vocare,* to call < *vox,* VOICE] 1. to excite to some action or feeling 2. to anger, irritate, or annoy 3. to stir up (action or feeling) 4. to call forth; evoke [to *provoke* a smile] —**pro·vok′er** *n.*

SYN.—**provoke,** in this connection, implies rather generally an arousing to some action or feeling [*thought-provoking*]; **excite** suggests a more powerful or profound stirring or moving of the thoughts or emotions [*it excites* my imagination]; **stimulate** implies an arousing as if by goading or pricking and, hence, often connotes a bringing out of a state of inactivity or indifference [to *stimulate* one's enthusiasm]; **pique** suggests a stimulating as if by irritating [to *pique* one's curiosity] See also IRRITATE

pro·vok·ing (-vō′kiŋ) *adj.* that provokes; esp., annoying or vexing —**pro·vok′ing·ly** *adv.*

pro·vo·lo·ne (prō′və lō′nē, präv′ə-) *n.* [It.] a hard, light-colored Italian cheese, usually smoked and molded typically in a pear-shaped form

pro·vost (prō′vōst, präv′əst; *esp. military,* prō′vō) *n.* [ME. < OE. *profost* & OFr. *provost,* both < ML. *propositus,* for

L. *praepositus*, chief, prefect, orig. pp. of *praeponere*, to set before, place first < *prae-*, before + *ponere*, to place: see PRE- & POSITION] **1.** a superintendent; official in charge **2.** the chief magistrate of a Scottish burgh **3.** [Obs.] a jailer **4.** *Eccles.* the head of a cathedral chapter or principal church **5.** *Educ.* *a)* the head of any of certain colleges in England and Ireland ☆*b)* in certain American universities, an administrative official dealing chiefly with faculty, curriculum, etc. —**pro′vost·ship′** *n.*

pro·vost court (prō′vō) a military court for trying soldiers or civilians charged with minor offenses in occupied territory

☆**pro·vost guard** (prō′vō) a detail of military police under the command of an officer (**provost marshal**)

prow[1] (prou) *n.* [Fr. *proue*, earlier *proe* < It. dial. (Genoese) *prua* < L. *prora* < Gr. *prōira*, a prow: see PROVINCE] **1.** the forward part of a ship or boat; bow **2.** a part like this, as the nose of an airplane

prow[2] (prou) *adj.* [ME. < OFr. *prou*, brave, var. of *prud*: see PROUD] [Archaic] valiant; brave

prow·ess (prou′is, prō′-) *n.* [ME. < OFr. *prouesse* < *prou*, brave: see prec.] **1.** bravery; valor **2.** superior ability, skill, etc.

prowl (proul) *vi.*, *vt.* [ME. *prollen* < ?] to roam about furtively, as in search of prey or loot —*n.* the act of prowling —**SYN.** see LURK —**on the prowl** prowling about —**prowl′er** *n.*

☆**prowl car** same as SQUAD CAR

prox. proximo

prox·i·mal (präk′sə m'l) *adj.* [< L. *proximus* (see ff.) + -AL] **1.** proximate; next or nearest **2.** *Anat.* situated nearest the center of the body or nearest the point of attachment of a muscle, limb, etc. —**prox′i·mal·ly** *adv.*

prox·i·mate (-mit) *adj.* [LL. *proximatus*, pp. of *proximare*, to come near < L. *proximus*, nearest, superl. of *prope*, near] **1.** next or nearest in space, order, time, etc. **2.** nearly accurate; approximate —**prox′i·mate·ly** *adv.*

prox·im·i·ty (präk sim′ə tē) *n.* [MFr. *proximité* < L. *proximitas* < *proximus*: see prec.] the state or quality of being near; nearness in space, time, etc.

☆**proximity fuze** an electronic fuze that detonates a bomb, missile, etc. when its sensor detects the target

prox·i·mo (präk′sə mō′) *adv.* [L. *proximo* (mense), in the next (month), abl. of *proximus*: see PROXIMATE] in or of the next month [on the 9th *proximo*]

prox·y (präk′sē) *n.*, *pl.* **prox′ies** [ME. *prokecie*, contr. < *procuracie*, PROCURACY] **1.** the agency or function of a deputy **2.** the authority to act for another **3.** a document empowering a person to act for another, as in voting at a stockholders' meeting **4.** a person empowered to act for another —**SYN.** see AGENT

prs. pairs

prude (prood) *n.* [Fr., back-formation < *prudefemme*, excellent woman < OFr. *prud* (see PROUD) + *feme*, woman] a person who is overly modest or proper in behavior, dress, or speech, esp. in a way that annoys others

Pru·dence (prood′'ns) [LL., fem. of *Prudentius* < L. *prudentia*: see ff.] a feminine name: dim. **Prue**

pru·dence (prood′'ns) *n.* [ME. < MFr. < L. *prudentia*] **1.** the quality or fact of being prudent **2.** careful management; economy

pru·dent (-'nt) *adj.* [ME. < OFr. < L. *prudens*, for *providens*: see PROVIDENT] **1.** capable of exercising sound judgment in practical matters, esp. as concerns one's own interests **2.** cautious or discreet in conduct; circumspect; not rash **3.** managing carefully and with economy —**SYN.** see CAREFUL, WISE[1] —**pru′dent·ly** *adv.*

pru·den·tial (proo den′shəl) *adj.* **1.** characterized by or resulting from prudence **2.** exercising prudence, or sound judgment ☆**3.** having an advisory function [a *prudential* committee] —**pru·den′tial·ly** *adv.*

prud·er·y (prood′ər ē) *n.* [Fr. *pruderie*] the quality or condition of being prudish

prud·ish (-ish) *adj.* like or characteristic of a prude; too modest or proper —**prud′ish·ly** *adv.* —**prud′ish·ness** *n.*

pru·i·nose (proo′ə nōs′) *adj.* [L. *pruinosus*, frosty < *pruina*, hoarfrost, for earlier *pruswina* < IE. base *preus-*, to FREEZE] *Bot.* covered with a white, powdery substance or bloom

prune[1] (proon) *n.* [ME. < MFr. < VL. *pruna* < L. *prunum* < Gr. *proumnon*, plum] **1.** a plum dried for eating **2.** any of various varieties of plum that can be dried without spoiling ☆**3.** [Slang] a dull or otherwise unpleasant person

prune[2] (proon) *vt.* pruned, prun′ing [ME. *prouynen* < MFr. *prooignier*, prob. < *provaignier*, to cut < *provain* (< L. *propago*: see PROPAGATE), a slip, infl. by *rooignier*, to cut off < LL. *rotundiare* < L. *rotundus*, round: see ROTUND] **1.** to remove dead or living parts from (a plant) so as to increase fruit or flower production or improve the form **2.** to cut out or get rid of as being unnecessary **3.** to reduce or diminish by removing what is unnecessary —*vi.* to cut away or remove unnecessary parts —**prun′er** *n.*

prune[3] (proon) *vt.*, *vi.* pruned, prun′ing [ME. *proinen* < OFr. *poroindre* < *por-* (for *pro-*) + *oindre* (< L. *ungere*, to anoint) [Archaic] to preen or dress up

pru·nel·la (proo nel′ə) *n.* [Fr., lit., sloe-colored, dim. < *prune* (see PRUNE[1]): prob. because of its orig. color] a strong worsted twill, used, esp. formerly, as for clerical gowns, shoe uppers, etc.

pruning hook a long tool with a hooked blade, or a pair of shears with one hooked blade, for pruning plants

pru·ri·ent (proor′ē ənt) *adj.* [L. *pruriens* < *prurire*, to itch, long for, be lecherous < IE. base *preus-*, to burn, freeze, whence FROST, L. *pruna*, live coal] **1.** having or expressing lustful ideas or desires **2.** tending to excite lust; lascivious; lewd **3.** [Rare] itching —**pru′ri·ence, pru′ri·en·cy** *n.* —**pru′ri·ent·ly** *adv.*

pru·ri·go (proo rī′gō) *n.* [L. < *prurire*, to itch: see prec.] a chronic, inflammatory skin disease characterized by pale-red papules and intense itching —**pru·rig′i·nous** (-rij′ə nəs) *adj.*

pru·ri·tus (proo rīt′əs) *n.* [< L., pp. of *prurire*, to itch: see PRURIENT] intense itching of the skin without eruption —**pru·rit′ic** (-rit′ik) *adj.*

Prus. **1.** Prussia **2.** Prussian

Prus·sia (prush′ə) former kingdom in N Europe (1701–1871) & the dominant state of the German Empire (1871–1919): formally dissolved in 1947

PRUSSIA (c. 1812)

Prus·sian (-ən) *adj.* **1.** of Prussia, its people, their language, etc. **2.** like or characteristic of the Junkers and military caste of Prussia, regarded as harsh in discipline, militaristic, arrogant, etc. —*n.* **1.** orig., a member of a Lettish people formerly living in the coastal regions of the SE Baltic **2.** a native or inhabitant of Prussia **3.** same as OLD PRUSSIAN **4.** any of the German dialects of East or West Prussia

Prussian blue [orig. discovered in Prussia in 1704] **1.** any of a group of dark-blue powders, ferrocyanides of iron, used as dyes or pigments; esp., ferric ferrocyanide, Fe₄[Fe(CN)₆]₃ **2.** a strong, dark blue

Prus·sian·ism (-iz'm) *n.* the practices and doctrines of the Prussians; specif., the despotic militarism and harsh discipline of the Prussian ruling classes

prus·sian·ize (-īz′) *vt.* -ized′, -iz′ing [also P-] to make Prussian or subject to Prussianism

prus·si·ate (prus′ē āt′, prush′-) *n.* [Fr. < *prussique* (see ff.) + -ate, -ATE[2]] **1.** a salt of hydrocyanic acid **2.** same as: *a)* FERROCYANIDE *b)* FERRICYANIDE

prus·sic acid (prus′ik) [Fr. (*acide*) *prussique* < (*bleu de*) *Prusse*, Prussian (blue): from its chemical relationship to Prussian blue] same as HYDROCYANIC ACID

Prut (proot) river in SE Europe, flowing from the SW Ukrainian S.S.R. southeastward along the Romanian-Moldavian S.S.R. border into the Danube: c. 600 mi.

pru·ta (proo′tä, proo tot′) *n.*, *pl.* **pru·tot′** (-tōt′) [ModHeb. < Heb. *perūtāh*, small coin] in Israel, a fractional unit of currency equal to 1/1000 pound

pry[1] (prī) *n.*, *pl.* **pries** [back-formation < PRIZE[2]] **1.** a tool for raising or moving something by leverage; lever, crow-bar, etc. **2.** leverage —*vt.* **pried, pry′ing 1.** to raise, move, or force with a pry **2.** to draw forth or obtain with difficulty [to *pry* money from a miser]

pry[2] (prī) *vi.* **pried, pry′ing** [ME. *prien* < ?] to look closely and inquisitively or inquire presumptuously; peer or snoop —*n.*, *pl.* **pries 1.** the act of prying **2.** a person who is improperly curious or inquisitive

pry·er (prī′ər) *n.* same as PRIER

pry·ing (-in) *adj.* [prp. of PRY[2]] improperly curious or inquisitive —**SYN.** see CURIOUS —**pry′ing·ly** *adv.*

pryth·ee (prith′ē) *interj.* same as PRITHEE

Ps., Psa. Psalm; Psalms

ps. pieces

P.S. 1. passenger steamer **2.** permanent secretary **3.** Privy Seal **4.** Public School

P.S., p.s., PS postscript

psalm (säm) *n.* [ME. *psalme, saume* < OE. *sealm* < LL. (Ec.) *psalmus* < Gr. *psalmos*, a twanging with the fingers (in LXX & NT., a song sung to the harp) < *psallein*, to twitch, pluck] **1.** a sacred song or poem; hymn **2.** [usually P-] any of the sacred songs in praise of God constituting the Book of Psalms in the Bible —*vt.* to sing or glorify in psalms

psalm·book (-book′) *n.* a collection of psalms for use in religious worship

psalm·ist (-ist) *n.* a composer of psalms —**the Psalmist** King David, to whom all or certain of the Psalms are variously attributed

psal·mo·dy (säm′ə dē, sal′mə-) *n.* [ME. *psalmodye* <

LL.(Ec.) *psalmodia* < Gr. *psalmōdia* < *psalmos* (see PSALM) + *ōidē*, a song (see ODE)] **1.** the act, practice, or art of singing psalms **2.** psalms collectively **3.** the arrangement of psalms for singing —**psal'mo·dist** *n.*

Psalms (sämz) a book of the Bible, consisting of 150 psalms: also **Book of Psalms**

Psal·ter (sôl'tər) [altered (after L.) < ME. *sauter* < OE. *saltere* & OFr. *sautier*, both < L. *psalterium*, a stringed instrument, in LL.(Ec.), the Psalms < Gr. *psaltērion*, a harp, in LGr.(Ec.), the Psalter < *psallein*, to twitch, pluck] the Book of Psalms — *n.* [*also* p-] a version of the Psalms for use in religious services

psal·te·ri·um (sôl tir'ē əm) *n.*, *pl.* -**ri·a** (-ə) [ModL. < L. (see prec.): from the appearance of the many folds it contains] *same as* OMASUM

psal·ter·y (sôl'tər ē, sôl'trē) *n.*, *pl.* -**ter·ies** [ME. *psauterie* < OFr. *sautere*, *psalterie* < L. *psalterium*: see PSALTER] an ancient stringed instrument with a shallow sound box, played by plucking the strings with the fingers or a plectrum

PSALTERY

psam·mite (sam'it) *n.* [Fr. < Gr. *psammos*, SAND + -*ite*, -ITE[1]] *Geol. rare* name for SANDSTONE —**psam·mit'ic** (sa mit'ik) *adj.*

psam·mon (sam'än) *n.* [ModL. < Gr. *psammos*, SAND] *Ecol.* those minute organisms that live in the water held between sand grains in waterlogged sands, as on the shores of lakes, streams, etc.

pse·phite (sē'fit) *n.* [Fr. < Gr. *psēphos*, a pebble + -*ite*, -ITE[1]] conglomerate or fragmental rock —**pse·phit'ic** (-fit'ik) *adj.*

pse·phol·o·gy (sē fäl'ə jē) *n.* [< Gr. *psēphos*, pebble (used in voting) + -LOGY] the statistical evaluation of election returns or of political polls —**pse'pho·log'i·cal** (-fə läj'i k'l) *adj.* —**pse·phol'o·gist** *n.*

pseud. pseudonym

pseu·de·pig·ra·pha (sōō'də pig'rə fə, syōō'-) *n.pl.* [ModL. < Gr. *pseudepigrapha*, neut. pl. of *pseudepigraphos*, having a false title < *pseudēs*, false + *epigraphein*, to inscribe < *epi*, upon + *graphein*, to write: see GRAPHIC] [*also* P-] a group of early writings not included in the Biblical canon or the Apocrypha, some of which were falsely ascribed to Biblical characters —**pseu'de·pig'ra·phous** (-fəs) *adj.*

pseu·do (sōō'dō, syōō'-) *adj.* [ME.: see ff.] sham; false; spurious; pretended; counterfeit

pseu·do- (sōō'də, syōō'-; -dō) [ME. < LL. < Gr. *pseudo-* < *pseudēs*, false < *pseudein*, to deceive] *a combining form meaning:* **1.** fictitious, pretended, or sham [*pseudonym*] **2.** counterfeit or spurious [*pseudepigrapha*] **3.** closely or deceptively similar to (a specified thing) [*pseudomorph*] **4.** not corresponding to the reality; illusory **5.** *Chem.* an isomer or related form of (a specified compound) Also, before a vowel, **pseud-**

pseu·do·al·um (sōōd'ō al'əm, syōōd'-) *n.* [PSEUDO- + ALUM[1]] any of a class of alums in which the usual univalent metal of a true alum is replaced by a bivalent metal

pseu·do·carp (sōō'də kärp', syōō'-) *n.* [PSEUDO- + -CARP] *same as* FALSE FRUIT —**pseu'do·car'pous** *adj.*

pseu·do·clas·sic (sōō'dō klas'ik, syōō'-) *adj.* pretending, or falsely seeming, to be classic —*n.* something pseudoclassic

pseu·do·her·maph·ro·dite (-hər maf'rə dīt') *n.* [PSEUDO- + HERMAPHRODITE] a person or animal having gonads of one sex while the external genital organs and secondary sex characters resemble in whole or in part those of the opposite sex —**pseu'do·her·maph'ro·dit'ic** (-dit'ik) *adj.* —**pseu'do·her·maph'ro·dit'ism**, **pseu'do·her·maph'ro·dism** *n.*

pseu·do·morph (sōō'də môrf', syōō'-) *n.* [< Gr. *pseudomorphos*, having a false form < *pseudēs*, false + *morphē*, a form] **1.** a false or irregular form **2.** a mineral possessing the external form characteristic of another —**pseu'do·mor'phism** *n.* —**pseu'do·mor'phous**, **pseu'do·mor'phic** *adj.*

pseu·do·nym (sōō'də nim', syōō'-) *n.* [Fr. *pseudonyme* < Gr. *pseudōnymos*: see ff.] a fictitious name, esp. one assumed by an author; pen name —**pseu'do·nym'i·ty** *n.*
SYN.—a **pseudonym** is a fictitious name assumed, esp. by a writer, as for anonymity, for effect, etc.; **pen name** and **nom de plume** are applied specifically to the pseudonym of a writer; **alias** also refers to an assumed name and, in popular use, is specifically applied to one taken by a criminal to disguise his identity; **incognito** is usually applied to a fictitious name temporarily assumed by a famous person, as in traveling, to avoid being recognized

pseu·don·y·mous (sōō dän'ə məs, syōō'-) *adj.* [Fr. *pseudonyme* < Gr. *pseudōnymos*, having a false name < *pseudēs*, false + *onyma*, NAME] **1.** bearing a pseudonym **2.** written under a pseudonym —**pseu·don'y·mous·ly** *adv.*

pseu·do·po·di·um (sōō'də pō'dē əm, syōō'-) *n.*, *pl.* -**di·a**

(-ə) [ModL.: see PSEUDO- & -PODIUM] a temporary projection of the protoplasm of certain one-celled organisms or of certain cells in multicellular animals, serving as a means of moving about or for taking in food: also **pseu'do·pod'** (-päd') —**pseu·dop'o·dal** (-däp'ə dəl) *adj.*

pseu·do·preg·nan·cy (sōō'dō preg'nən sē, syōō'-) *n.*, *pl.* -**cies** changes in structure, function, etc. simulating those in pregnancy, usually caused by hysteria in nonpregnant women or by copulation without fertilization in other mammals —**pseu·do·preg'nant** *adj.*

pseu·do·salt (sōō'dō sôlt', syōō'-) *n.* [PSEUDO- + SALT] a compound whose formula is that of a salt, but that does not ionize in solution

pseu·do·sci·ence (sōō'dō sī'əns, syōō'-) *n.* any system of methods, theories, etc. that presumes without warrant to have a scientific basis or application —**pseu·do·sci'en·tif'ic** (-ən tif'ik) *adj.*

psf, p.s.f. pounds per square foot

pshaw (shô) *interj.*, *n.* an exclamation of impatience, disgust, contempt, etc.

psi (sī, psē) *n.* [LGr. < Gr. *psei*] the twenty-third letter of the Greek alphabet (Ψ, ψ)

psi, p.s.i. pounds per square inch

psi·lo·cin (sī'lə sin, sil'ə-) *n.* [contr. < ff.] a hallucinogenic drug obtained from certain species of mushrooms

psi·lo·cy·bin (sī'lə sī'bin, sil'ə-) *n.* [< Gr. *psilos*, bare < *kybē*, head) + -IN[1]] a hallucinogenic drug obtained from a Mexican fungus (*Psilocybe mexicana*) and various other mushrooms

psi·lom·e·lane (sī läm'ə lān') *n.* [< Gr. *psilos*, bare + *melan*, neut. of *melas*, black (see MELANO-)] a mineral, essentially manganese oxide, commonly occurring in rounded, grapelike, black masses

psit·ta·cine (sit'ə sīn', -sin) *adj.* [L. *psittacinus* < *psittacus*, a parrot (< Gr. *psittakos*) + -*inus*, -INE[1]] of, resembling, or pertaining to parrots —**psit'ta·cine'ly** *adv.*

psit·ta·co·sis (sit'ə kō'sis) *n.* [ModL. < L. *psittacus* < Gr. *psittakos*, a parrot + -*osis*] an acute, infectious virus disease affecting birds esp. of the parrot family: often transmitted to man, in whom it is characterized by fever and pneumonia

Pskov (pskôf) **1.** lake in the W R.S.F.S.R., connected with Chudskoye Lake by a strait: see CHUDSKOYE **2.** city near the SE end of this lake: pop. 81,000

pso·as (sō'əs) *n.*, *pl.* **pso'as** [ModL. < acc. pl. of Gr. *psoa*, muscle of the loins] either of two muscles of the loin that connect the spinal column and the thighbone

pso·cid (sō'sid) *n.* [< ModL. *Psocidae* < *Psocus*, type genus (< Gr. *psōchos*, dust < *psōchein*, to rub small < IE. base **bhes-*, to rub fine, whence SAND) + -*idae*, -IDAE] any of a family (Psocidae) of small, winged insects with biting mouthparts, related to the book lice and feeding on lichens, algae, etc.

pso·ra·le·a (sə rā'lē ə) *n.* [ModL. < Gr. *psōraleos*, scaly] any of a large genus (*Psoralea*) of legumes having scurfy leaves, white to purple flowers, and short pods with single seeds

pso·ri·a·sis (sə rī'ə sis) *n.* [ModL. < Gr. *psōriasis* < *psōra*, an itch] a chronic skin disease characterized by scaly, reddish patches —**pso·ri·at'ic** (sôr'ē at'ik) *adj.*

psst (pst) *interj.* an exclamation used to get someone's attention, usually in an unobtrusive way

PST, P.S.T. Pacific Standard Time

☆**psych** (sīk) *vt.* **psyched**, **psych'ing** [clipped < PSYCHOANALYZE] [Slang] **1.** to cause to be disturbed mentally or excited emotionally (often with *up*) **2.** to understand the motives or behavior of by intuition or psychological means, esp. so as to outwit, overcome, or control (often with *out*) —**psych out** [Slang] **1.** to lose one's courage or nerve **2.** to pretend to be mentally disturbed so as to evade a situation

psych- (sīk) *same as* PSYCHO-: used before a vowel

psych. **1.** psychological **2.** psychology

psy·chas·the·ni·a (sī'kas the'nē ə) *n.* [ModL.: see PSYCHO- & ASTHENIA] *a former classification for* a group of neuroses characterized by phobias, obsessions, undue anxiety, etc. —**psych'as·then'ic** (-then'ik) *adj.*

Psy·che (sī'kē) [L. < Gr. *Psychē* < *psychē*, the soul, akin to *psychein*, to blow, cool < IE. base **bhes-*, to blow, whence Sans. *bábhasti*, (he) blows] *Rom. Folklore* a maiden who, after undergoing many hardships due to Venus' jealousy of her beauty, is reunited with Cupid and made immortal by Jupiter

psy·che (sī'kē) *n.* [Gr.: see prec.] **1.** the human soul **2.** the mind; esp., *Psychiatry* the mind considered as a subjectively perceived, functional entity, based ultimately upon physical processes but with complex processes of its own: it governs the total organism and its interactions with the environment

☆**psy·che·de·li·a** (sī'ki dē'lē ə) *n.* [PSYCHEDEL(IC) + -IA] popularly, psychedelic drugs or anything associated with their use

☆**psy·che·del·ic** (sī'kə del'ik) *adj.* [< PSYCHE + Gr. *delein*, to make manifest] **1.** of or causing extreme changes in the conscious mind, as hallucinations, delusions, intensification of awareness and sensory perception, etc. **2.** of or associated with psychedelic drugs; specif., simulating the auditory or visual effects of the psychedelic state —*n.* a psychedelic drug —**psy'che·del'i·cal·ly** *adv.*

Psyche knot a woman's coiffure in which the hair is coiled in a knot at the back of the head

psy·chi·a·trist (sə kī′ə trist, sī-) *n.* a doctor of medicine specializing in psychiatry after postgraduate training

psy·chi·a·try (-trē) *n.* [ModL.: see PSYCHO- & -IATRY] the branch of medicine concerned with the study, treatment, and prevention of disorders of the mind, including psychoses and neuroses, emotional and social maladjustments, etc. —**psy·chi·at·ric** (sī′kē at′rik), **psy·chi·at′ri·cal** *adj.* —**psy′chi·at′ri·cal·ly** *adv.*

psy·chic (sī′kik) *adj.* [< Gr. *psychikos*, of the soul, spiritual < *psychē*, the soul: see PSYCHE] 1. of or having to do with the psyche, or mind 2. beyond natural or known physical processes 3. apparently sensitive to forces beyond the physical world Also **psy′chi·cal** —*n.* 1. a person who is supposedly sensitive to forces beyond the physical world 2. a spiritualistic medium —**psy′chi·cal·ly** *adv.*

psy·cho (sī′kō) *adj., n. colloq.* clipped form of PSYCHOTIC, PSYCHOPATHIC, PSYCHOPATH, and, earlier, PSYCHONEUROTIC

psy·cho- (sī′kō, -kə) [< Gr. *psychē*, breath, spirit, soul: see PSYCHE] *a combining form meaning* the mind or mental processes [*psychology, psychoanalysis*]

psy·cho·a·cous·tics (sī′kō ə kōōs′tiks) *n.pl.* [*with sing. v.*] [PSYCHO- + ACOUSTICS] the study of how sounds are heard subjectively and of the individual's response to sound stimuli —**psy′cho·a·cous′ti·cal** *adj.*

psy·cho·ac·tive (-ak′tiv) *adj.* [PSYCHO- + ACTIVE] designating or of a drug, chemical, etc. that has a pronounced or specific effect on the mind

psy·cho·a·nal·y·sis (-ə nal′ə sis) *n.* [ModL.: see PSYCHO- & ANALYSIS] 1. a method, developed by Freud and others, of investigating mental processes and of treating neuroses and some other disorders of the mind: it is based on the assumption that such disorders are the result of the rejection by the conscious mind of factors that then persist in the unconscious as repressed instinctual forces, causing conflicts which may be resolved or diminished by discovering and analyzing the repressions and bringing them into consciousness through the use of such techniques as free association, dream analysis, etc. 2. the theory or practice of this —**psy′cho·an′a·lyt′ic** (-an′ə lit′ik), **psy′cho·an′a·lyt′i·cal** *adj.* —**psy′cho·an′a·lyt′i·cal·ly** *adv.*

psy·cho·an·a·lyst (-an′əl ist) *n.* a specialist in psychoanalysis

psy·cho·an·a·lyze (-an′ə līz′) *vt.* -**lyzed**′, -**lyz′ing** to treat or investigate by means of psychoanalysis

psy·cho·bi·ol·o·gy (-bī äl′ə jē) *n.* 1. that branch of biology dealing with the interrelationship of the mental processes and the anatomy and physiology of the individual 2. psychology as investigated by biological methods —**psy′cho·bi′o·log′i·cal** (-bī′ə läj′i k'l) *adj.*

psy·cho·chem·i·cal (-kem′i k'l) *n.* any of various drugs or chemical compounds, as LSD, capable of affecting mental activity —*adj.* of or pertaining to psychochemicals

psy·cho·del·ic (-del′ik) *adj., n. alt. sp.* of PSYCHEDELIC

☆**psy·cho·dra·ma** (sī′kə drä′mə, -dram′ə) *n. Psychiatry* a form of cathartic therapy in which a patient acts out by spontaneous improvisation situations related to his problem, often before an audience and with the aid of others who represent persons near his problem —**psy′cho·dra·mat′ic** (-drə mat′ik) *adj.*

psy·cho·dy·nam·ics (sī′kō dī nam′iks) *n.pl.* [*with sing. v.*] the study of the mental and emotional processes underlying human behavior and its motivation, esp. as developed unconsciously in response to environmental influences —**psy′cho·dy·nam′ic** *adj.* —**psy′cho·dy·nam′i·cal·ly** *adv.*

psy·cho·gen·e·sis (sī′kə jen′ə sis) *n.* [ModL.: see PSYCHO- & -GENESIS] 1. origination and development within the psyche, or mind; specif., the development of physical disorders as a result of mental conflicts rather than from organic causes 2. the origin and development of the psyche, or mind —**psy′cho·ge·net′ic** (-jə net′ik) *adj.*

psy·cho·gen·ic (-ik) *adj.* [< PSYCHOGENESIS] of psychic origin; caused by mental conflicts —**psy′cho·gen′i·cal·ly** *adv.*

psy·cho·graph (sī′kə graf′, -gräf′) *n.* [PSYCHO- + -GRAPH] *Psychol.* a graphic chart outlining the relative strength of personality traits in an individual

psy·cho·ki·ne·sis (sī′kō kī nē′sis) *n.* [PSYCHO- + Gr. *kinēsis*, motion] the apparent ability, investigated in parapsychology, to influence physical objects or events by thought processes —**psy′cho·ki·net′ic** (-net′ik) *adj.*

psychol. 1. psychological 2. psychology

psy·cho·lin·guis·tics (-liŋ gwis′tiks) *n.pl.* [*with sing. v.*] the study of the psychological factors involved in the perception of and response to linguistic phenomena —**psy′cho·lin·guis′tic** *adj.*

psy·cho·log·i·cal (sī′kə läj′i k'l) *adj.* 1. of psychology 2. of the mind; mental 3. affecting or intended to affect the mind Also **psy′cho·log′ic** —**psy′cho·log′i·cal·ly** *adv.*

psychological moment [transl. of Fr. *moment psychologique*, a misunderstanding of G. *psychologischer moment*, psychological momentum or motive (< L. *momentum*: see MOMENT)] 1. the moment when the mind is most willing to accept a fact, suggestion, etc.; most propitious time to act 2. the critical moment

psychological warfare the use of propaganda or other psychological means to influence or confuse the thinking, undermine the morale, etc. of an enemy or opponent

psy·chol·o·gism (sī käl′ə jiz′m) *n.* any attempt to find psychological bases for historical events, philosophical concepts, etc.: usually a disparaging term

psy·chol·o·gist (-ə jist) *n.* a specialist in psychology

psy·chol·o·gize (-jīz′) *vi.* -**gized**′, -**giz′ing** 1. to study psychology 2. to reason psychologically —*vt.* to analyze psychologically

psy·chol·o·gy (-jē) *n., pl.* -**gies** [ModL. *psychologia*: see PSYCHO- & -LOGY] 1. *a)* the science dealing with the mind and with mental and emotional processes *b)* the science of human and animal behavior 2. the sum of the actions, traits, attitudes, thoughts, mental states, etc. of a person or group [*the psychology* of the adolescent] 3. a particular system of psychology

psy·cho·met·rics (sī′kə met′riks) *n.pl.* [*with sing. v.*] [PSYCHO- + METRICS] *same as* PSYCHOMETRY (sense 1) —**psy′chom·e·tri·cian** (sī käm′ə trish′ən) *n.*

psy·chom·e·try (sī käm′ə trē) *n.* [PSYCHO- + -METRY] 1. the measurement of the duration, force, interrelations, or other aspects of mental processes, as by psychological tests 2. the supposed faculty of divining knowledge about an object, or about a person connected with it, through contact with the object —**psy′cho·met′ric** (-kə met′rik), **psy′cho·met′ri·cal** *adj.* —**psy·chom′e·trist** *n.*

psy·cho·mi·met·ic (sī′kō mi met′ik) *adj.* [PSYCHO- + MIMETIC] capable of inducing a mental state that closely resembles a psychosis

psy·cho·mo·tor (sī′kə mōt′ər) *adj.* 1. of the motor effects of mental processes 2. designating or of a form of epilepsy in which the seizures are characterized by complex behavioral phenomena

psy·cho·neu·ro·sis (-noo rō′sis, -nyoo-) *n., pl.* -**ro′ses** (-sēz) [ModL.: see PSYCHO- & NEUROSIS] *same as* NEUROSIS —**psy′cho·neu·rot′ic** (-rät′ik) *adj., n.*

psy·cho·path (sī′kə path′) *n.* [back-formation: see PSYCHOPATHY] a person suffering from a mental disorder; specif., *same as* PSYCHOPATHIC PERSONALITY

psy·cho·path·ic (sī′kə path′ik) *adj.* of or characterized by psychopathy; suffering from a mental disorder

psychopathic personality 1. a person whose behavior is largely amoral and asocial and who is characterized by irresponsibility, lack of remorse or shame, perverse or impulsive (often criminal) behavior, and other serious personality defects, generally without psychotic attacks or symptoms 2. the personality of such a person

psy·cho·pa·thol·o·gy (sī′kō pa thäl′ə jē) *n.* [PSYCHO- + PATHOLOGY] 1. the science dealing with the causes and development of mental disorders 2. psychological malfunctioning, as in a mental disorder —**psy′cho·path′o·log′i·cal** (-path′ə läj′i k'l) *adj.* —**psy′cho·pa·thol′o·gist** *n.*

psy·chop·a·thy (sī käp′ə thē) *n.* [PSYCHO- + -PATHY] mental disorder

psy·cho·phar·ma·col·o·gy (sī′kō fär′mə käl′ə jē) *n.* [PSYCHO- + PHARMACOLOGY] the study of the actions of drugs on the mind —**psy′cho·phar′ma·co·log′i·cal** (-kə läj′i k'l), **psy′cho·phar′ma·co·log′ic** *adj.*

psy·cho·phys·ics (-fiz′iks) *n.pl.* [*with sing. v.*] [PSYCHO- + PHYSICS] the branch of psychology dealing with the functional relations between the mind and physical phenomena —**psy′cho·phys′i·cal** *adj.* —**psy′cho·phys′i·cist** *n.*

psy·cho·phys·i·ol·o·gy (-fiz′ē äl′ə jē) *n.* the study of the interactions between mental and physiological processes —**psy′cho·phys′i·o·log′i·cal** (-ə läj′i k'l) *adj.*

psy·cho·sex·u·al (-sek′shoo wəl) *adj.* of or having to do with the psychological aspects of sexuality in contrast to the physical aspects —**psy′cho·sex′u·al′i·ty** (-wal′ə tē) *n.*

psy·cho·sis (sī kō′sis) *n., pl.* -**cho′ses** (-sēz) [ModL.: see PSYCHO- & -OSIS] a major mental disorder in which the personality is very seriously disorganized and contact with reality is usually impaired: psychoses are of two sorts, *a)* functional (characterized by lack of apparent organic cause, and principally of the schizophrenic or manic-depressive type), and *b)* organic (characterized by a pathological organic condition such as brain damage or disease, metabolic disorders, etc.) —*SYN.* see INSANITY

psy·cho·so·cial (sī′kō sō′shəl) *adj.* of or pertaining to the psychological development of the individual in relation to his social environment

psy·cho·so·mat·ic (-sō mat′ik) *adj.* [PSYCHO- + SOMATIC] 1. designating or of a physical disorder of the body originating in or aggravated by the psychic or emotional processes of the individual 2. designating a system of medicine using a coordinated psychological and physiological approach to the study of the causes and treatment of psychosomatic disorders —*n.* an individual exhibiting a psychosomatic disorder —**psy′cho·so·mat′i·cal·ly** *adv.*

psy·cho·sur·ger·y (-sur′jər ē) *n.* brain surgery performed in treating chronic mental disorder

psy·cho·ther·a·peu·tics (-ther′ə pyōōt′iks) *n.pl.* [*with sing. v.*] *same as* PSYCHOTHERAPY —**psy′cho·ther′a·peu′tic** *adj.*

psy·cho·ther·a·py (-ther′ə pē) n. [PSYCHO- + THERAPY] treatment of mental disorder by any of various means involving communication between a trained person and the patient and including suggestion, counseling, psycho-analysis, etc. —**psy′cho·ther′a·pist** n.

psy·chot·ic (sī kät′ik) adj. **1.** of, or having the nature of, a psychosis **2.** having a psychosis —n. a person who has a psychosis

psy·chot·o·mi·met·ic (sī kät′ō mi met′ik) adj. [< PSY-CHOT(IC) + -o- + MIMETIC] designating or of certain drugs, as LSD and mescaline, that produce hallucinations, symptoms of a psychotic state, and, sometimes, chromo-somal breaks —n. a psychotomimetic drug

psy·cho·tox·ic (sī/kō täk′sik) adj. [PSYCHO- + TOXIC] of or pertaining to certain drugs or chemical compounds, as alcohol, capable of damaging the brain

psy·cho·trop·ic (-träp′ik) adj. [PSYCHO- + -TROPIC] having an altering effect on the mind, as tranquilizers, hallucino-gens, etc. —n. a psychotropic drug

psy·chro- (sī/krō, -krə) [< Gr. psychros, cold, akin to psychein, to cool: see PSYCHE] a combining form meaning cold [psychrometer]

psy·chrom·e·ter (sī kräm′ə tər) n. [prec. + -METER: orig., a thermometer] an instrument with wet- and dry-bulb thermometers, for measuring moisture in the air

psy·chro·phil·ic (sī/krō fil′ik) adj. [PSYCHRO- + -PHIL(E) + -IC] Biol. growing best at low temperatures —**psy′chro·phile′** (-fīl) n.

psyl·la (sil′ə) n. [ModL. < Gr. psylla, a flea < IE. base *blou-, var. of *blou-, whence L. pulex, FLEA] any of a family (Psyllidae) of jumping plant lice, often harmful to fruit trees

psy·war (sī/wôr′) n. acronym for PSYCHOLOGICAL WARFARE

Pt Chem. platinum

Pt. **1.** Point **2.** Port

pt. pl. **pts.** **1.** part **2.** payment **3.** pint **4.** point

p.t. **1.** past tense **2.** pro tempore

pta. pl. **ptas.** peseta

P.T.A. Parent-Teacher Association

Ptah (p′tä, p′täkh) [Egypt. Ptaḥ] the chief god of ancient Memphis, in Egypt, creator of gods and men

ptar·mi·gan (tär′mə gən) n., pl. **-gans, -gan**: see PLURAL, II, D, 1 altered (by association with PTERO-) < earlier termigan < Scot. tarmachan] any of several varieties of northern or alpine grouse (genus Lagopus), having feath-ered legs and feet and undergoing seasonal changes of color

☆**Pt boat** [p(atrol) t(orpedo) boat] same as MOTOR TORPEDO BOAT

pter·i·dol·o·gy (ter′ə däl′ə jē) n. [< Gr. pteris (gen. pteridos), a fern (akin to pteron, FEATHER: from the featherlike shape) + -LOGY] the branch of botany dealing with ferns —**pter′i·do·log′i·cal** (-də läj′i k′l) adj. —**pter′i·dol′o·gist** n.

pter·i·do·phyte (ter′ə dō fīt′, tə rid′ə-) n. [< Gr. pteris (see prec.) + -PHYTE] in some systems of plant classifica-tion, a division (Pteridophyta) of plants possessing true vascular roots, stems, and leaves and reproducing by means of spores, including the ferns, club mosses, etc. —**pter′id·o·phyt′ic** (-fit′ik), **pter′i·doph′y·tous** (-däf′i təs) adj.

pter·id·o·sperm (-spurm′) n. same as SEED FERN

pter·o- (ter′ō, -ə) [ModL. < Gr. pteron, wing, FEATHER] a combining form meaning feather, wing [pterodactyl]

pter·o·dac·tyl (ter′ə dak′t′l) n. [ModL. Pterodactylus: see prec. & DACTYL] any of an order (Pterosauria) of related flying rep-tiles, extinct at the end of the Mesozoic Era, having wings of skin stretched along the body between the hind limb and a very long fourth digit of the forelimb —**pter′o·dac′tyl·oid′** (-oid′), **pter′o·dac′tyl·ous** (-əs) adj.

pte·ro·ic acid (tə rō′ik) [ult. < Gr. pteron, wing (because found in pig-ments in butterfly wings) + -IC] a crystalline acid, $C_{14}H_{12}N_6O_3$, which can react with glutamic acid to form folic acid

pter·o·pod (ter′ə päd′) adj. [PTERO- + -POD] of or relating to a suborder (Pteropoda) of small, thin-shelled or shell-less gastropods that swim by means of winglike lobes on the foot —n. any member of this group —**pte·rop·o·dan** (tə räp′ə dən) adj., n.

pter·o·saur (ter′ə sôr′) n. [ModL. Plerosaurus: see PTERO- & -SAURUS] same as PTERODACTYL

-pter·ous (tər əs) [see PTERO- & -OUS] a combining form meaning having (a specified number or kind of) wings [homopterous]

pte·ryg·i·um (tə rij′ē əm) n., pl. **-i·ums, -i·a** (-ə) [ModL. < Gr. pterygion, dim. of pteryx, a wing, akin to pteron, FEATHER] an abnormal, triangular mass of mucous mem-brane growing over the human cornea from the inner corner of the eye —**pte·ryg′i·al** adj.

pter·y·goid (ter′ə goid′) adj. [< Gr. pteryx (gen. pterygos), a wing, fin (akin to pteron, FEATHER) + -OID] **1.** having the form of a wing; winglike **2.** designating, of, or near either of two winglike processes in the skull that descend from the sphenoid bone —n. a pterygoid bone or process

PTERODACTYL (wingspread to 20 ft.)

pter·y·la (ter′i lə) n., pl. **-lae** (-lē′) [ModL. < PTER(O)- + Gr. hylē, forest] any of the special areas on a bird's skin from which feathers grow

ptg. printing

ptis·an (tiz′ən, ti zan′) n. [ME. tysane < MFr. tisane < VL. tisana, for L. ptisana, barley groats, drink made from barley groats < Gr. ptisanē, peeled barley < ptissein, to peel] **1.** a drink made by boiling down barley with water and other ingredients; barley water **2.** any similar decoc-tion, as of herbs

P.T.O., p.t.o. please turn over (leaf)

Ptol·e·ma·ic (täl′ə mā′ik) adj. [Gr. Ptolemaïkos] **1.** of Ptolemy, the astronomer **2.** of the Ptolemies who ruled Egypt

Ptolemaic system the theory, systematized by Ptolemy, postulating the earth as the center or fixed point of the universe, around which the heavenly bodies move

Ptol·e·ma·ist (-mā′ist) n. an adherent or supporter of the Ptolemaic system of astronomy

Ptol·e·my (täl′ə mē) **1.** (L. name Claudius Ptolemaeus) 2d cent. A.D.; Alexandrian astronomer, mathematician, & geographer **2.** pl. **-mies** Macedonian family whose mem-bers formed the ruling dynasty of Egypt from 305? to 30 B.C.; esp., a) **Ptolemy I** 367?-283; general of Alexander the Great; 1st king (305?-285) of the Ptolemaic dynasty: called Ptolemy Soter ("Savior") b) **Ptolemy II** 309?-247?; king of Egypt (285-247?): called Ptolemy Philadelphus: son of prec.

pto·maine (tō′mān) n. [It. ptomaina < Gr. ptōma, a corpse < piptein, to fall < IE. base *pet-, to rush at, fall, whence L. petere, to rush at] any of a class of alkaloid substances, some of which are poisonous, formed in decaying animal or vegetable matter by bacterial action on proteins

ptomaine poisoning former term for FOOD POISONING (erroneously thought to be caused by ptomaines)

pto·sis (tō′sis) n. [ModL. < Gr. ptōsis, a fall, falling < piptein: see PTOMAINE] a prolapse, or falling of some organ or part; esp., the drooping of the upper eyelid, caused by the paralysis of its muscle —**ptot′ic** (-tik) adj.

pty·a·lin (tī′ə lin) n. [< Gr. ptyalon, spittle < ptyein, to spit (of echoic orig.) + -IN¹] an enzyme in the saliva of man (and some lower animals) that converts starch into various dextrins and maltose

pty·a·lism (-liz′m) n. [Gr. ptyalismos, a spitting < ptya-lizein, to spit often < ptyalon: see prec.] excessive secretion of saliva

pty. ltd. [Brit.] proprietary limited

Pu Chem. plutonium

pub (pub) n. [contr. < PUBLIC HOUSE] [Chiefly Brit. Colloq.] a bar or tavern

pub. **1.** public **2.** published **3.** publisher **4.** publishing

pub-crawl (pub′krôl′) vi. [Chiefly Brit. Slang] to go from one pub to another as on a drinking spree —n. the act of, or a period spent in, pub-crawling: also **pub crawl**

pu·ber·ty (pyōō′bər tē) n. [ME. puberte < L. pubertas < puber, of ripe age, adult, prob. akin to puer, boy] the state of physical development when sexual reproduction first becomes possible: the age of puberty is generally fixed in common law at fourteen for boys and twelve for girls —**pu′ber·tal** adj.

pu·ber·u·lent (pyōō ber′yoo lənt) adj. [< L. puber, adult, covered with soft down + -ULENT] covered with fine hairs or down

pu·bes¹ (pyōō′bēz) n. [L., pubic hair, groin, akin to prec.] **1.** the hair appearing on the body at puberty; esp., the hair at the lower part of the abdomen surrounding the external genitals **2.** the region of the abdomen covered by such hair

pu·bes² (pyōō′bēz) n., pl. of PUBIS

pu·bes·cence (pyōō bes′'ns) n. [Fr.] **1.** the quality or state of being pubescent **2.** the soft down that covers the surface of many plants and insects

pu·bes·cent (-'nt) adj. [Fr. < L. pubescens, prp. of pubes-cere, to reach puberty < pubes, adult: cf. PUBES¹] **1.** reaching or having reached the state of puberty **2.** covered with a soft down, as many plants and insects

pu·bic (pyōō′bik) adj. of or in the region of the pubis or the pubes

pu·bis (-bis) n., pl. **pu′bes** (-bēz) [ModL. < L.: see PUBES¹] that part of either hipbone forming, with the corresponding part of the other, the front arch of the pelvis

publ. **1.** published **2.** publisher

pub·lic (pub′lik) adj. [ME. < L. publicus: altered (prob. after pubes, adult) < poplicus, contr. of populicus, public < populus, the PEOPLE] **1.** of, belonging to, or concerning the people as a whole; or of by the community at large [the public welfare, a public outcry] **2.** for the use or benefit of all; esp., supported by government funds [a public park] **3.** as regards community, rather than private, affairs **4.** acting in an official capacity on behalf of the people as a whole [a public prosecutor] **5.** known by, or open to the knowledge of, all or most people [to make information public, a public figure] —n. **1.** the people as a whole; community at large **2.** a specific part of the people; those people considered together because of some common interest or purpose [the reading public] —**go public** Finance to issue stock in a corporation for sale to the public —**in public** openly; not in private or in secrecy

☆**pub·lic-ad·dress system** (pub′lik ə dres′) an electronic amplification system, used in auditoriums, theaters, or the

like, so that announcements, music, etc. can be easily heard by a large audience

pub·li·can (pub'li kən) *n.* [ME. < L. *publicanus* < *publicus:* see PUBLIC] **1.** in ancient Rome, a collector of public revenues, tolls, etc. **2.** [Brit.] a saloonkeeper; innkeeper

pub·li·ca·tion (pub'lə kā'shən) *n.* [ME. *publicacioun* < L. *publicatio* < *publicare:* see PUBLISH] **1.** a publishing or being published; public notification **2.** the printing and distribution, usually for sale, of books, magazines, newspapers, etc. **3.** something published, esp. a periodical

public debt 1. the total debt of all governmental units, including those of State and local governments **2.** *same as* NATIONAL DEBT

☆**public defender** an attorney employed at public expense to defend indigent persons accused of crimes

☆**public domain 1.** public lands **2.** the condition of being free from copyright or patent and, hence, open to use by anyone

public enemy 1. a government with which one's country is at war **2.** a hardened criminal or other person who is a menace to society

public house 1. an inn or tavern **2.** [Brit.] a bar or saloon

pub·li·cist (pub'lə sist) *n.* [Fr. *publiciste* < (*droit*) *public*, public (law) + *-iste*, -IST] **1.** a student of or specialist in international law **2.** a journalist who writes about politics and public affairs **3.** [PUBLIC(IZE) + -IST] a person whose business is to publicize persons, organizations, etc.

pub·lic·i·ty (pə blis'ə tē) *n.* [Fr. *publicité*] **1.** the state of being public, or commonly known or observed ☆**2.** *a*) any information, promotional material, etc. which brings a person, place, product, or cause to the notice of the public *b*) the work or business of preparing and disseminating such material **3.** notice by the public **4.** any procedure or act that seeks to gain this

pub·li·cize (pub'lə sīz') *vt.* **-cized', -ciz'ing** to give publicity to; draw public attention to

public law 1. a law or statute affecting or applicable to the public generally **2.** the branch of law concerned with the relations of individuals to the state and with the state as an entity capable of acting as if a private person

pub·lic·ly (pub'lik lē) *adv.* **1.** in a public or open manner **2.** by, or by consent or agency of, the public

public opinion the opinion of the people generally, esp. as a force in determining social and political action

☆**public relations** relations with the general public as through publicity; specif., those functions of a corporation, organization, etc. concerned with attempting to create favorable public opinion for itself

public school ☆**1.** in the U.S., an elementary or secondary school that is part of a system of free schools maintained by public taxes and supervised by local authorities **2.** in England *a*) orig., any nonprofit grammar school endowed for the general use of the public *b*) now, any of several private, expensive, endowed boarding schools for boys, preparing them for the universities or the public service

public servant an elected or appointed government official or a civil-service employee

public service 1. employment by the government, esp. through civil service **2.** some service performed for the public with no direct charge, as by a private corporation

☆**pub·lic-serv·ice corporation** (-sur'vis) a private corporation that supplies some essential commodity or service to the public, under governmental regulation

pub·lic-spir·it·ed (-spir'i tid) *adj.* having or showing zeal for the public welfare

public utility an organization supplying water, electricity, transportation, etc. to the public, operated, usually as a monopoly, by a private corporation under governmental regulation or by the government directly

public works ☆works constructed by the government for public use or service, as highways or dams

pub·lish (pub'lish) *vt.* [ME. *publisshen* < extended stem of OFr. *publier* < L. *publicare*, to make public < *publicus*, PUBLIC] **1.** to make publicly known; announce, proclaim, divulge, or promulgate **2.** *a*) to issue (a printed work, etc.) to the public, as for sale *b*) to issue the written work or works of (a particular author) **3.** *Law* to execute (a will) —*vi.* **1.** to issue books, newspapers, printed music, etc. to the public **2.** to write books, scholarly papers, etc. that are published —*SYN.* see DECLARE —**pub'lish·a·ble** *adj.*

pub·lish·er (-ər) *n.* a person or firm that publishes, esp. one whose business is the publishing of books, newspapers, magazines, printed music, etc.

Puc·ci·ni (pōōt chē'nē), **Gia·co·mo** (jä'kô mô') 1858–1924; It. operatic composer

☆**puc·coon** (pə kōōn') *n.* [see POKE³] **1.** *same as* GROMWELL **2.** [Archaic] *same as* BLOODROOT **3.** [Archaic] a dye from either of these plants

puce (pyōōs) *n.* [Fr., lit., a flea < L. *pulex*, a flea] brownish purple —*adj.* of the color puce

puck¹ (puk) *n.* [< dial. *puck*, to strike, akin to POKE¹] *Ice Hockey* the hard rubber disk which the players try to drive with their sticks into the opponents' goal

puck² (puk) *n.* [ME. *puke* < OE. *puca*, akin to ON. *puki*, a devil < IE. base **beu-*, to blow up, swell, whence POUT¹,

POKE²] a mischievous sprite or elf; specif., [P-] the mischievous sprite in Shakespeare's *A Midsummer Night's Dream;* Robin Goodfellow

puck·a (puk'ə) *adj. same as* PUKKA

puck·er (puk'ər) *vt., vi.* [freq. form of POKE²] to draw up or gather into wrinkles or small folds —*n.* a wrinkle or small fold made by puckering —**pucker up** to contract the lips as in preparing to kiss

puck·er·y (-ē) *adj.* of, causing, or characterized by puckering

puck·ish (puk'ish) *adj.* [PUCK² + -ISH] full of mischief; impish —**puck'ish·ly** *adv.* —**puck'ish·ness** *n.*

pud (pōōd) *n. same as* POOD

pud·ding (pōōd'iŋ) *n.* [ME. *puddyng*, akin ? to OE. *puduc*, a swelling, LowG. *puddig*, swollen: for IE. base see PUCK²] **1.** [Scot.] a sausage made of intestine stuffed with meat, suet. etc. and boiled **2.** a soft, mushy food, usually made with a base of flour, cereal, potato, etc. and boiled or baked **3.** a sweetened dessert of this kind, made as with rice or soaked bread, and variously containing eggs, milk, fruit, etc.

pud·ding·stone (-stōn') *n. same as* CONGLOMERATE (*n.* 2)

pud·dle (pud''l) *n.* [ME. *podel*, dim. < OE. *pudd*, a ditch: for IE. base see PUCK²] **1.** a small pool of water, esp. stagnant, spilled, or muddy water **2.** a thick mixture of clay, and sometimes sand, with water —*vt.* **-dled, -dling 1.** to make muddy **2.** to make a thick mixture of (wet clay and sand) **3.** to keep water from penetrating by the use of such a mixture **4.** to treat (iron) by puddling —*vi.* to dabble or wallow in dirty or muddy water —**pud'dler** (-lər) *n.*

pud·dling (-liŋ) *n.* [< prec.] **1.** the process of working clay or a similar substance with water so as to make a mixture which moisture cannot penetrate **2.** the process of making wrought iron from pig iron by heating and stirring it in the presence of oxidizing agents

pud·dly (-lē) *adj.* **-dli·er, -dli·est** having puddles

pu·den·cy (pyōōd''n sē) *n.* [LL. *pudentia* < L. *pudens*, prp. of *pudere*, to be ashamed] modesty or prudishness

pu·den·dum (pyōō den'dəm) *n., pl.* **-den'da** (-də) [ModL. < L., neut. of *pudendus*, (something) to be ashamed of < *pudere:* see prec.] **1.** the external genitals of the female; vulva **2.** [*pl.*] the external genitals of either sex —**pu·den'·dal** (-d'l) *adj.*

pudg·y (puj'ē) *adj.* **pudg'i·er, pudg'i·est** [< Scot. dial., prob. < Scot. *pud*, belly, akin to PUCK², PUDDLE] short and fat; dumpy —**pudg'i·ness** *n.*

Pue·bla (pwe'blä) **1.** state of SE Mexico: 13,125 sq. mi.; pop. 2,438,000 **2.** its capital: pop. 361,000

Pueb·lo (pweb'lō) [see ff.] city in SC Colo., on the Arkansas River: pop. 97,000

☆**pueb·lo** (pweb'lō; *also, for 4 & 5, Sp.* pwe'blō) *n., pl.* **-los** (-lōz; *Sp.* -blōs); *also, for 2,* **-lo** [Sp., village, people < L. *populus*, PEOPLE] **1.** a type of communal village built by certain Indians of the SW U.S. and parts of Latin America, consisting of one or more flat-roofed structures of stone or adobe, arranged in terraces and housing a number of families **2.** [P-] any Indian of the tribes inhabiting pueblos, as the Zuñi and the Hopi, characterized by a sedentary, peaceful, agricultural life **3.** any Indian village in the SW U.S. **4.** in Spanish America, a village or town **5.** in the Philippines, a municipality; town or township

pu·er·ile (pyōō'ər əl, pyōōr'əl; -il) *adj.* [< Fr. or L.: Fr. *puéril* < L. *puerilis* < *puer*, boy < IE. base **pou-*, small, infant, whence FOAL] childish; silly; immature; trivial —*SYN.* see YOUNG —**pu'er·ile·ly** *adv.*

pu·er·il·ism (-iz'm) *n.* childishness, esp. as a symptom of emotional disorder in an adult

pu·er·il·i·ty (pyōō'ə ril'ə tē, pyōō ril'-) *n.* [Fr. *puérilité* < L. *puerilitas*] **1.** the quality or condition of being puerile; childishness **2.** *pl.* **-ties** an instance of this

pu·er·per·al (pyōō ur'pər əl) *adj.* [< L. *puerpera*, woman in labor < *puer*, boy (see PUERILE) + *parere*, to bear (see -PAROUS)] of or connected with childbirth

puerperal fever sepsis sometimes occurring during childbirth: a former term no longer used

pu·er·pe·ri·um (pyōō'ər pir'ē əm) *n.* [L., childbirth: see PUERPERAL] the period or state of confinement during and just after childbirth

Puer·to Ri·co (pwer'tə rē'kō, pôr'-) island in the West Indies which, with small nearby islands, constitutes a commonwealth associated with the U.S.: 3,421 sq. mi.; pop. 2,712,000; cap. San Juan: abbrev. **P.R., PR** — **Puer'to Ri'can** (-kən)

puff (puf) *n.* [ME. *puf* < OE. *pyff* < the *v.*] **1.** *a*) a short, sudden burst or gust, as of wind, or an expulsion, as of breath *b*) the sound of this *c*) a small quantity of vapor, smoke, etc. expelled at one time **2.** a draw at a cigarette, etc. **3.** a swelling, or a protuberance caused by swelling **4.** a shell of soft, light pastry filled with whipped cream, custard, etc. **5.** a soft, bulging mass of material, full in the middle and gathered in at the edges **6.** a soft roll of hair on the head **7.** a soft pad for dabbing powder on the skin or hair **8.** a quilted bed covering with cotton, wool, or down filling **9.** *a*) [Archaic] vain show; bluff *b*) undue or exaggerated praise, as in the advertisement of a book, etc. —*vi.* [ME. *puffen* < OE. *pyffan:* for IE. base see PUCK²] **1.** to blow in puffs, as the wind **2.** *a*) to give forth puffs of

smoke, steam, etc. *b)* to breathe rapidly and hard, as from running **3.** to move, giving forth puffs (with *away, out, in,* etc.) **4.** to come in puffs, as smoke **5.** *a)* to fill (*out* or *up*), as with air *b)* to become inflated, as with pride (with *out* or *up*) *c)* to swell (*out* or *up*), as skin tissue **6.** to take a puff or puffs at a cigarette, etc. —*vt.* **1.** to blow, drive, give forth, etc. in or with a puff or puffs **2.** to swell; distend; inflate **3.** to praise unduly **4.** to write or print a puff or puffs of (a book, etc.) **5.** to smoke (a cigarette, etc.) **6.** to set (the hair) in soft, round masses or rolls

puff adder 1. a large, poisonous African snake (*Bitis arietans*) which hisses or puffs loudly when irritated ☆**2.** *same as* HOGNOSE SNAKE

puff·ball (-bôl′) *n.* any of a number of related round, white-fleshed fungi that burst at the touch, when mature, and discharge a brown powder

puff·er (puf′ər) *n.* **1.** a person or thing that puffs ☆**2.** *a)* any of various fishes (family Tetraodontidae) capable of expanding the body by swallowing water or air *b)* any of various similar fishes, as the globefish

puff·er·y (-ē) *n.* exaggerated praise, esp. in publicity, advertising, etc.

puf·fin (puf′in) *n.* [ME. *poffin* < ?: associated by folk etymology with PUFF, because of the enormous beak or blown-up appearance of the young] any of a number of related northern sea birds (genus *Fratercula*) black above and white below, with a short neck, ducklike body, and brightly colored triangular beak

puff paste a rich dough for light, flaky pastries

puff·y (puf′ē) *adj.* **puff′i·er, puff′i·est 1.** blowing or coming in puffs **2.** panting; short-winded **3.** puffed up; swollen; inflated **4.** fat; obese —**puff′i·ly** *adv.* —**puff′i·ness** *n.*

pug[1] (pug) *n.* [Early ModE.: altered < ? PUCK[2]] **1.** any of a breed of small, short-haired dog with a wrinkled face, snub nose, and curled tail **2.** *same as* PUG NOSE

pug[2] (pug) *vt.* **pugged, pug′ging** [< dial.: prob. echoic of pounding; orig. sense "to punch, strike"] **1.** to mix (wet, plastic clay) for making bricks, earthenware, etc. **2.** to fill in with clay, mortar, etc. for soundproofing —*n.* wet, plastic clay used for making bricks, earthenware, etc.

pug[3] (pug) *n. slang clipped form of* PUGILIST

pug[4] (pug) *n.* [Hind. *pag*] a footprint or trail (of an animal) —*vt.* **pugged, pug′ging** to track or trail (game) by following footprints

Pu·get Sound (pyōō′jit) [after Lt. Peter *Puget* of the Vancouver expedition (1792)] inlet of the Pacific in NW Wash.: c. 100 mi. long

pug·ging (pug′in) *n.* [PUG[2] + -ING] **1.** the mixing of pug (wet clay) **2.** clay, mortar, etc. used for soundproofing

pug·gree (pug′rē) *n.* [Hind. *pagṛī,* a turban] **1.** in India, a turban **2.** a light scarf wrapped around the crown of a sun helmet and hanging behind to protect the back of the neck Also **pug′ga·ree′, pug′a·ree′** (-ə rē′)

pugh (pyōō, pōō) *interj.* an exclamation of disgust

pu·gil·ism (pyōō′jə liz'm) *n.* [L. *pugil,* boxer, pugilist; akin to *pugnare,* to fight (see PUGNACIOUS) + -ISM] *same as* BOXING[1] —**pu′gil·ist** *n.* —**pu′gil·is′tic** *adj.*

Pu·glia (pōō′lyä) *It.* name of APULIA

pug·na·cious (pug nā′shəs) *adj.* [< L. *pugnax,* combative < *pugnare,* to fight (< IE. base *peuĝ-,* to punch, whence Gr. *pygmē,* fist, L. *pungere,* to pierce) + -OUS] eager and ready to fight; quarrelsome; combative —*SYN.* see BELLIGERENT —**pug·na′cious·ly** *adv.* —**pug·nac′i·ty** (-nas′ə tē), **pug·na′cious·ness** *n.*

pug nose a short, thick, turned-up nose —**pug′-nosed′** (-nōzd′) *adj.*

puis·ne (pyōō′nē) *adj.* [OFr., lit., born later: see PUNY] [Chiefly Brit.] *Law* of lower rank; junior, as in appointment —*n.* [Chiefly Brit.] an associate justice as distinguished from chief justice

pu·is·sant (pyōō′i sənt, pyōō is′nt, pwis′nt) *adj.* [ME. < OFr., powerful < stem of *poeir,* to be able: see POWER] [Archaic or Poet.] powerful; strong; mighty —**pu′is·sance** *n.* —**pu′is·sant·ly** *adv.*

puke (pyōōk) *n., vi., vt.* **puked, puk′ing** [akin ? to G. *spucken,* to spit] [Colloq.] *same as* VOMIT

puk·ka (puk′ə) *adj.* [Hind. *pakkā,* ripe, of full weight, cooked < Sans. *pakva* < IE. base *pekw-,* to cook, whence L. *coquere*] [Anglo-Indian] **1.** good or first-rate of its kind **2.** genuine; real

pul (pōōl) *n., pl.* **puls, pul** [Per. *pūl* < Turk. *pul* < LGr. *phollis,* a small coin < LL. *follis* < L., orig., bellows, hence bag, moneybag: cf. FOLLICLE] a coin and monetary unit of Afghanistan, equal to 1/100 of an afghani

Pu·la (pōō′lä) seaport in NW Yugoslavia, at the S end of the Istrian peninsula: pop. 37,000: also **Pulj** (pōōl′y)

Pu·las·ki (pōō las′kē; *Pol.* pōō lä′ske), **Cas·i·mir** (kaz′ə mir) 1748–79; Pol. general in the American Revolutionary army

pul·chri·tude (pul′krə tōōd′, -tyōōd′) *n.* [ME. < L. *pulchritudo* < *pulcher,* beautiful] physical beauty —☆**pul′chri·tu′di·nous** (-'n əs) *adj.*

pule (pyōōl) *vt.* **puled, pul′ing** [echoic] to whimper or whine, as a sick or fretful child

pu·li (pōō′lē) *n., pl.* **pu′lik** (-lēk), **pu′lis** [Hung.] any of a Hungarian breed of farm dog with a shaggy coat

Pul·it·zer (pool′it sər; *now often* pyōō′lit-), **Joseph** 1847–1911; U.S. newspaper owner & philanthropist, born in Hungary

☆**Pulitzer Prize** any of a number of yearly prizes established by Joseph Pulitzer, given for outstanding work in journalism, literature, and music

pull (pool) *vt.* [ME. *pullen* < OE. *pullian,* to pluck, snatch with the fingers: ? akin to MLowG. *pull,* a husk, shell] **1.** to exert force or influence on so as to cause to move toward or after the source of the force; drag, tug, draw, attract, etc. **2.** *a)* to draw out; pluck out; extract [to *pull* a tooth] *b)* to pick or uproot [to *pull* carrots] **3.** to draw apart; rip; tear [to *pull* a seam] ☆**4.** to stretch (taffy, etc.) back and forth repeatedly **5.** to stretch or strain to the point of injury [to *pull* a muscle] ☆**6.** [Colloq.] to put into effect; carry out; perform [to *pull* a raid] **7.** [Colloq.] to hold back; restrain [to *pull* one's punches] **8.** [Colloq.] ☆*a)* to take (a gun, knife, etc.) from concealment so as to threaten *b)* to take or force off or out; remove [to *pull* a wheel from a car] **9.** [Dial.] to draw the entrails from (a fowl) **10.** *Baseball, Golf* to hit (the ball) and make it curve to the left or, if left-handed, to the right **11.** *Horse Racing* to rein in or restrain (a horse) so as to keep it from winning **12.** *Printing* to take (a proof) on a hand press **13.** *Rowing a)* to work (an oar) by drawing it toward one *b)* to transport by rowing *c)* to be rowed normally by [a boat that *pulls* four oars] —*vi.* **1.** to exert force in or for dragging, tugging, or attracting something **2.** to take a deep draft of a drink or puff at a cigarette, etc. **3.** to be capable of being pulled **4.** to move or drive a vehicle (*away, ahead, around, out,* etc.) —*n.* **1.** the act, force, or result of pulling; specif., *a)* a dragging, tugging, attracting, etc. *b)* the act or an instance of rowing *c)* a drink *d)* a puff at a cigarette, etc. *e)* a difficult, continuous effort, as in climbing *f)* the force needed to move a weight, trigger, etc. as measured in pounds *g) Baseball, Golf* the act or an instance of pulling a ball **2.** something to be pulled, as the handle of a drawer, etc. ☆**3.** [Colloq.] *a)* influence or special advantage *b)* drawing power; appeal —**pull apart** to find fault with; criticize —**pull down 1.** to tear down, demolish, or overthrow **2.** to degrade; humble **3.** to reduce **4.** [Colloq.] to get (a specified wage, grade, etc.) —**pull for** [Colloq.] to cheer on, or hope for the success of —**pull in 1.** to arrive **2.** to draw in or hold back **3.** [Slang] to arrest and take to police headquarters —**pull off** [Colloq.] to bring about, accomplish, or perform —**pull oneself together** to collect one's faculties; regain one's poise, courage, etc. —**pull out** ☆**1.** to depart ☆**2.** to withdraw or retreat ☆**3.** to escape from a contract, responsibility, etc. **4.** *Aeron.* to level out from a dive or landing approach —**pull over** to drive (a vehicle) to or toward the curb —**pull through** [Colloq.] to get through or over (an illness, difficulty, etc.) —**pull up 1.** to uproot **2.** to bring or come to a stop **3.** *a)* to drive (a vehicle) to a specified place *b)* to make (an aircraft) nose up sharply **4.** to check or rebuke —**pull′er** *n.*

SYN.—**pull** is the broad, general term of this list, as defined in sense 1 of the *vt.* above; **draw** suggests a smoother, more even motion than **pull** [he *drew* his sword from its scabbard]; **drag** implies the slow pulling of something heavy, connoting great resistance in the thing pulled [he *dragged* the desk across the floor]; **tug** suggests strenuous, persistent effort in pulling but does not necessarily connote success in moving the object [he *tugged* at the rope to no avail]; **haul** implies sustained effort in transporting something heavy, often mechanically [to *haul* furniture in a truck]; **tow** implies pulling by means of a rope or cable [to *tow* a stalled automobile] —*ANT.* push, shove

pull·back (pool′bak′) *n.* **1.** a pulling back; esp., a planned military withdrawal **2.** something that retards or hinders **3.** a device for pulling something back

pul·let (pool′it) *n.* [ME. *poullet* < OFr. *poulet,* dim. of *poule,* hen: see POULTRY] a young hen, usually one not more than a year old

pul·ley (pool′ē) *n., pl.* **-leys** [ME. *poley* < OFr. *polie* < ML. *poleia* < *poledia* < MGr. *polidion,* dim. of *polos,* pivot, axis, windlass, akin to *pelein,* to turn < IE. base *kwel-,* whence WHEEL] **1.** a small wheel, sometimes turning in a block, with a grooved rim in which a rope or chain runs, as to raise a weight attached at one end by pulling on the other end **2.** a combination of such wheels, used to increase the applied power **3.** a wheel that turns or is turned by a belt, rope, chain, etc., so as to transmit power

☆**Pull·man** (pool′mən) *n.* **1.** [after George M. *Pullman* (1831–97), U.S. inventor] a railroad car with private compartments or seats that can be made up into berths for sleeping: also **Pullman car 2.** [*often* p-] a suitcase that opens flat and has a hinged divider inside: also **pullman case**

☆**Pullman kitchen** [*also* p-] a small, compact kitchen, typically built into an alcove, as in some apartments

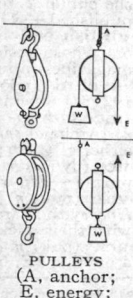

PULLEYS
(A, anchor;
E, energy;
W, weight)

pul·lor·um disease (pə lôr′əm) [< ModL. (*salmonella*) *pullorum*, the infecting bacterium < gen. pl. of L. *pullus*: see POULTRY] a highly destructive, diarrheal disease of young poultry, caused by a bacterium (*Salmonella pullorum*) and usually transmitted by the infected hen directly into the egg

pull·out (pool′out′) n. **1.** the act of pulling out; esp., removal, departure, withdrawal, etc. **2.** something meant to be pulled out, as a magazine insert

pull·o·ver (-ō′vər) adj. that is put on by being pulled over the head —n. a pullover sweater, shirt, etc.

pul·lu·late (pul′yoo lāt′) vi. **-lat·ed, -lat·ing** [< L. *pullulatus*, pp. of *pullulare*, to spread out, sprout < *pullulus*, dim. of *pullus*: see POULTRY] **1.** to sprout out; germinate; bud **2.** to breed quickly **3.** to spring up in abundance; teem or swarm —**pul′lu·la′tion** n.

pull-up (pool′up′) n. *Gym.* the act of chinning oneself

pul·mo·nar·y (pul′mə ner′ē, pool′-) adj. [L. *pulmonarius* < *pulmo* (gen. *pulmonis*), a lung < IE. *pleumon*, lung, orig., floater < base *pleu-*, to swim, float, whence FLOW: for semantic development cf. LIGHTS] **1.** of, like, or affecting the lungs **2.** having lungs or lunglike organs **3.** designating the artery conveying blood from the right ventricle of the heart to the lungs or any of the veins conveying oxygenated blood from the lungs to the left atrium of the heart

pul·mo·nate (-nit, -nāt′) adj. [ModL. *pulmonatus* < L. *pulmo*, lung: see prec.] *Zool.* **1.** having lungs or lunglike organs **2.** of or belonging to an order (Pulmonata) of gastropods having a sort of lung or air sac, as the land snails and slugs, and most freshwater snails —n. any member of this order

pul·mon·ic (pool män′ik) adj. [Fr. *pulmonique*] same as PULMONARY

☆**Pul·mo·tor** (pool′mōt′ər, pul′-) [< L. *pulmo*, a lung (see PULMONARY) + MOTOR] a trademark for an apparatus used in applying artificial respiration by forcing oxygen into the lungs —n. [p-] such an apparatus

pulp (pulp) n. [Fr. *pulpe* < L. *pulpa*, flesh, pulp of fruit] **1.** a soft, moist, formless mass that sticks together **2.** the soft, juicy part of a fruit **3.** the soft, spongy pith inside the stem of a plant **4.** the soft, sensitive substance underneath the enamel and dentine of a tooth **5.** a mixture of ground-up, moistened cellulose material, as wood, linen, rags, etc., from which paper is made **6.** ore ground to a powder and mixed with water ☆**7.** a magazine printed on rough, inferior paper stock made from wood pulp, usually containing sensational stories of love, crime, etc.: cf. SLICK —vt. **1.** to reduce to pulp **2.** to remove the pulp from —vi. to become pulp

pul·pit (pool′pit, pul′-) n. [ME. *pulpet* < L. *pulpitum*, a stage, scaffold (in LL. & ML., pulpit) < IE. base *polpo-*, structure made of boards, whence Sans. *parpam*, house] **1.** a) a raised platform or high lectern from which a clergyman preaches in a church b) preachers collectively c) the work of preaching **2.** any of several raised or enclosed areas; specif., ☆a) a harpooner's platform on a bowsprit b) an enclosed control room, as in a steel mill

pulp·wood (pulp′wood′) n. **1.** soft wood used in making paper **2.** wood ground to pulp for paper

pulp·y (pul′pē) adj. **pulp′i·er, pulp′i·est** of or like pulp: also **pulp′ous** —**pulp′i·ly** adv. —**pulp′i·ness** n.

☆**pul·que** (pool′kē; Sp. pool′ke) n. [AmSp., prob. of Mex. Ind. origin] a fermented drink, popular in Mexico, made from the juice of an agave, esp. the maguey

pul·sant (pul′s'nt) adj. pulsating

pul·sar (pul′sär, -sər) n. [PULS(E)[1] + -AR] any of several small, heavenly objects in the Milky Way that emit radio pulses at regular intervals

pul·sate (pul′sāt) vi. **-sat·ed, -sat·ing** [< L. *pulsatus*, pp. of *pulsare*, to beat < *pulsus*: see PULSE[1]] **1.** to beat or throb rhythmically, as the heart **2.** to vibrate; quiver; thrill

pul·sa·tile (pul′sə t'l, -til) adj. [ML. *pulsatilis*] **1.** pulsating **2.** played by beating, as a drum

pul·sa·tion (pul sā′shən) n. [L. *pulsatio*] **1.** the act of pulsating; rhythmical beating or throbbing **2.** a beat; throb; vibration

pul·sa·tive (pul′sə tiv) adj. that pulsates; pulsating

pul·sa·tor (pul′sāt′ər, pul sāt′-) n. [L.] a pulsometer or other device that has a throbbing action

pul·sa·to·ry (pul′sə tôr′ē) adj. characterized by pulsation; throbbing

pulse[1] (puls) n. [ME. *pous* < OFr. < L. *pulsus* (*venarum*), beating (of the veins) < *pulsus*, pp. of *pellere*, to beat: for IE. base see FELT[1]] **1.** the regular beating in the arteries, caused by the contraction of the heart **2.** any beat, signal, vibration, etc. that is regular or rhythmical **3.** the perceptible underlying feelings of the public or of a particular group **4.** a variation, characterized by a rise, limited duration, and decline, of a quantity whose value normally is constant; specif., a) *Elec.* a brief surge of voltage or current b) *Radio* a very short burst of electromagnetic waves —vi. **1.** to cause to pulsate **2.** to drive (an engine, etc.) by pulses **3.** *Elec.*

to apply pulses to **4.** *Radio* to modify (an electromagnetic wave) by means of pulses —**puls′er** n.

pulse[2] (puls) n. [ME. *pous* < OFr. *pouls* < L. *puls* (gen. *pultis*), a pottage made of meal or pulse, prob. < Gr. *poltos* < IE. base *pel-*, dust, meal, whence L. *pollen*, *pulvis*] **1.** the edible seeds of peas, beans, lentils, and similar plants having pods **2.** any member of the legume family

pulse height analyzer an instrument that records or counts an electrical pulse if its amplitude falls within specified limits: used in nuclear physics research for the determination of energy spectra nuclear radiations

pulse-jet (engine) (-jet′) a jet engine in which the high pressure developed in the burning of the fuel closes the air intake valves of the combustion chamber; when the air is expelled from the jet, the pressure is lowered enough to open the valves for fresh air

pulse modulation 1. the formation of an intermittent carrier wave by the generation and transmission of a sequence of short, periodic pulses: used in radar **2.** the modulation of the amplitude, a characteristic, etc. of a sequence of pulses in order to convey information: often used in codes

pulse radar a radar system using pulse modulation

pul·sim·e·ter (pul sim′ə tər) n. an instrument that measures the rate and force of the pulse

pul·som·e·ter (pul säm′ə tər) n. [PULS(E)[1] + -o- + -METER] **1.** a pistonless pump for raising water by the sucking effect of condensing steam **2.** same as PULSIMETER

pul·ver·iz·a·ble (pul′və rīz′ə b'l) adj. that can be pulverized: also **pul·ver·a·ble** (pul′vər ə b'l)

pul·ver·ize (pul′və rīz′) vt. **-ized′, -iz′ing** [MFr. *pulveriser* < LL. *pulverizare* < L. *pulvis*, powder: see PULSE[2]] **1.** to crush, grind, etc. into a powder or dust **2.** to break down completely; demolish —vi. to be crushed, ground, etc. into powder or dust —**pul′ver·i·za′tion** n. —**pul′ver·iz′er** n.

pul·ver·u·lent (pəl ver′yə lənt, -ver′ə-) adj. [L. *pulverulentus* < *pulvis*, dust: see PULSE[2]] **1.** consisting of or covered with a powder; powdery **2.** crumbling to powder or dust —**pul′ver′u·lence** n.

pul·vil·lus (pul vil′əs) n., pl. **-li** (-ī) [ModL. < L., small cushion, contr. < *pulvinulus*, dim. of *pulvinus*, a cushion] *Zool.* **1.** a cushionlike part between the tarsal claws of many insects **2.** a hairy pad on the tarsal segments of some insects —**pul·vil′lar** adj.

pul·vi·nate (pul′və nāt′, -nit) adj. [L. *pulvinatus* < *pulvinus*, a cushion] **1.** cushion-shaped **2.** *Bot.* having a pulvinus —**pul′vi·nate′ly** adv.

pul·vi·nus (pul vī′nəs) n., pl. **-ni** (-nī) [ModL. < L., a pillow, elevation] *Bot.* an enlarged area at the base of a petiole, at a node, or at the base of a panicle branch, producing movement by growth or swelling

pu·ma (pyōō′mə, pōō′-) n., pl. **pu′mas, pu′ma:** see PLURAL, II, D, 1 [AmSp. < Quechua] same as COUGAR

pum·ice (pum′is) n. [ME. *pomis* < OFr. < L. *pumex* < IE. base *(s)poimno-*, foam, whence FOAM] a spongy, light, porous, volcanic rock used in solid or powdered form for scouring, smoothing, and polishing: also **pumice stone** —vt. **-iced, -ic·ing** to clean, polish, etc. with pumice —**pu·mi·ceous** (pyōō mish′əs) adj.

pum·mel (pum′'l) vt. **-meled** or **-melled, -mel·ing** or **-mel·ling** [< POMMEL] to beat or hit with repeated blows, esp. with the fist

pump[1] (pump) n. [ME. *pumpe* < MDu. *pompe* < Sp. *bomba*, prob. of echoic origin] **1.** any of various machines that force a liquid or gas into or through, or draw it out of, something, as by suction or pressure **2.** [Colloq.] the heart —vt. **1.** to raise or move (fluids) with a pump **2.** to remove water, etc. from, as with a pump **3.** to drive air into with a pump or bellows **4.** to force in, draw out, drive, move up and down, pour forth, etc. by means of a pump or as a pump does **5.** to apply force to with a pumping, up-and-down motion **6.** [Colloq.] a) to question closely and persistently b) to get (information) from a person in this way **7.** *Physics* to transfer or inject energy into (particles, the electrons of a laser, etc.) —vi. **1.** to work a pump **2.** to raise or move water, etc. with a pump **3.** to move up and down or go by moving up and down like a pump handle or piston **4.** to flow in, out, or through, by or as if by being pumped

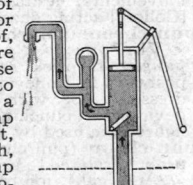

PUMP

pump[2] (pump) n. [< ? Fr. *pompe*, an ornament] a low-cut shoe without straps or ties

pump·er (pum′pər) n. **1.** a person or thing that pumps **2.** a fire truck that can pump water under great pressure

☆**pump·er·nick·el** (pum′pər nik′'l) n. [G., Westphalian rye bread, earlier a pejorative < *pumpern*, to break wind + *Nickel*, a goblin: see NICKEL] a coarse, dark, sour bread made of unsifted rye

pump·kin (pum′kin, pump′-, pun′-) n. [altered (after -KIN) < *pumpion* < MFr. *pompon* < L. *pepo* < Gr. *pepōn*, lit., cooked by the sun, ripe (hence a gourd not eaten until

ripe): for IE. base see COOK] **1.** a large, round, orange-yellow, gourdlike fruit with many seeds **2.** the vine (*Cucurbita pepo*) of the gourd family on which it grows **3.** [Brit.] any of several varieties of squash (*Cucurbita moschata* and *Cucurbita maxima*)

pump·kin·seed (-sēd′) *n.* **1.** the seed of the pumpkin ☆**2.** a small freshwater sunfish (*Lepomis gibbosus*) of N. America, greenish-yellow above and orange-yellow below

☆**pump priming** large expenditures by a government, designed to stimulate expenditures by private industry

pun (pun) *n.* [17th-c. clipped form < ? It. *puntiglio*, fine point, hence verbal quibble (cf. PUNCTILIO)] the humorous use of a word, or of words which are formed or sounded alike but have different meanings, in such a way as to play on two or more of the possible applications; a play on words —*vi.* **punned, pun′ning** to make a pun or puns

‡**pu·na** (pōō′nä) *n.* [AmSp. < Quechua] a high, cold, arid plateau, as in the Andes

Pun·a·kha, Pun·a·ka (pōōn′ə kə) city in NC Bhutan; the winter capital: pop. 8,000

Punch (punch) [contr. < *Punchinello*, earlier *Polichinello*, a character in a Neapolitan puppet play] the male character of the puppet show *Punch and Judy*, a hook-nosed, humpbacked figure —**pleased as Punch** greatly pleased or gratified

punch¹ (punch) *n.*[contr. of earlier *punchon*: see PUNCHEON¹] **1.** *a)* a tool driven or pressed against a surface that is to be shaped or stamped *b)* a tool driven against a nail, bolt, etc. that is to be worked in or out **2.** a device or machine for making holes, cuts, etc. [a paper *punch*] **3.** the hole, cut, etc. made with a punch —*vt.* **1.** to pierce, shape, stamp, cut, etc. with a punch **2.** to make (a hole, cut, etc.) with or as with a punch

punch² (punch) *vt.* [ME. *punchen*, orig. var. of *pouncen* (see POUNCE¹); infl. by PUNCH¹] **1.** to prod or poke with a stick ☆**2.** to herd (cattle) by or as by prodding **3.** to strike with the fist —*n.* **1.** a thrusting blow with the fist ☆**2.** [Colloq.] effective force; vigor —*SYN.* see STRIKE —**pull one's punches** [Colloq.] **1.** *Boxing* to deliver blows that are intentionally ineffective **2.** to attack, criticize, etc. in an intentionally ineffective manner —☆**punch a (time) clock** to insert a timecard into a time clock when coming to or going from work —☆**punch in** (or **out**) to record the time of one's arrival (or departure) by the use of a time clock

punch³ (punch) *n.* [Hind. *pāc*, five < Sans. *pañca* (cf. FIVE): it orig. consisted of five ingredients] a sweetened drink made with fruit juices, carbonated beverages, sherbet, etc., often mixed with wine or liquor, and served in cups from a large bowl

Punch-and-Ju·dy show (punch′'n jōō′dē) a puppet show in which the quarrelsome Punch constantly fights with his wife, Judy, in a comical way

☆**punch·board** (punch′bôrd′) *n.* a board or card with holes containing concealed slips or disks to be punched out, used in games of chance, raffles, etc.: the slips bear numbers, names, prize designations, or the like

punch bowl a large bowl from which punch is served

☆**punch card** a card with holes or notches positioned in it for interpretation by an automatic data-processing machine or for quick mechanical selection

punch-drunk (-druŋk′) *adj.* **1.** having or showing a condition resulting from numerous blows on the head, as from boxing, and marked by an unsteady gait, slow muscular movements, hesitant speech, mental confusion, etc. **2.** [Colloq.] acting dazed or bewildered

pun·cheon¹ (pun′chən) *n.* [ME. *punchoun* < MFr. *poinçon* < VL. *punctio* < *punctiare*, to prick < L. *punctus*, pp. of *pungere*, to prick: see POINT] **1.** a short, upright wooden post used in framework ☆**2.** a heavy, broad piece of roughly dressed timber with one side hewed flat **3.** any of various devices for punching, perforating, or stamping; esp., a figured die used by goldsmiths, etc.

pun·cheon² (pun′chən) *n.* [LME. *pwncion* < OFr. *poinçon*: prob. unrelated to prec.] **1.** a large cask of varying capacity (72–120 gal.), for beer, wine, etc. **2.** as much as such a cask will hold

punch·er (pun′chər) *n.* a person or thing that punches

pun·chi·nel·lo (pun′chə nel′ō) *n., pl.* **-los** [see PUNCH] **1.** [*also* P-] a prototype of Punch **2.** a buffoon; clown

punching bag a stuffed or inflated leather bag hung up so that it can be punched for exercise or practice

☆**punch line** the surprise line carrying the point of a joke

punch press a press in which dies are fitted for cutting, shaping, or stamping metal

punch-up (punch′up′) *n.* [Chiefly Brit. Slang] **1.** a noisy fist fight; brawl **2.** a gang fight; rumble

punch·y (pun′chē) *adj.* **punch′i·er, punch′i·est** [Colloq.] ☆**1.** forceful; vigorous ☆**2.** *same as* PUNCH-DRUNK

punc·tate (puŋk′tāt) *adj.* [ModL. *punctatus* < L. *punctum*, a POINT] marked with dots or tiny spots, as certain plants and animals: *also* **punc′tat·ed —punc·ta′tion** *n.*

punc·til·i·o (puŋk til′ē ō′) *n., pl.* **-os** [altered (after L.) < Sp. *puntillo* or It. *puntiglio*, dim. of *punto* < L. *punctum*, a POINT] **1.** a nice point of conduct, ceremony, etc. **2.** observance of petty formalities

punc·til·i·ous (-til′ē əs) *adj.* [Fr. *pointilleux* < *pointille* < It. *puntiglio*: see prec.] **1.** very careful about every detail of behavior, ceremony, etc. [a *punctilious* host] **2.** very exact; scrupulous —**punc·til′i·ous·ly** *adv.* —**punc·til′i·ous·ness** *n.*

punc·tu·al (puŋk′chōō wəl) *adj.* [ME. < ML. *punctualis* < L. *punctus*, a POINT] **1.** of, like, or drawn into a single point **2.** carefully observant of an appointed time; on time; prompt **3.** *archaic var. of* PUNCTILIOUS —**punc′tu·al′i·ty** (-wal′ə tē) *n.* —**punc′tu·al·ly** *adv.* —**punc′tu·al·ness** *n.*

punc·tu·ate (puŋk′chōō wāt′) *vt.* **-at′ed, -at′ing** [< ML. *punctuatus*, pp. of *punctuare* < L. *punctus*, a POINT] **1.** *a)* to insert a punctuation mark or marks in *b)* to function as a punctuation mark in **2.** to break in on here and there; interrupt [a speech *punctuated* with applause] **3.** to emphasize; accentuate —*vi.* to use punctuation marks —**punc′tu·a′tor** *n.*

punc·tu·a·tion (puŋk′chōō wā′shən) *n.* [ML. *punctuatio:* see prec.] **1.** the act of punctuating; specif., the act, practice, or system of using standardized marks in writing and printing to separate sentences or sentence elements or to make the meaning clearer **2.** a punctuation mark or marks —**punc′tu·a′tive** *adj.*

punctuation mark any of the marks used in punctuation, as a period or comma

punc·tu·late (puŋk′chōō lāt′, -lit) *adj.* [< L. *punctulum*, dim. of *punctum*, POINT + -ATE²] marked with very small dots or holes, as certain plants and animals —**punc′tu·la′tion** *n.*

punc·ture (puŋk′chər) *n.* [ME. < L. *punctura*, a pricking < L. *pungere*, to pierce: see POINT] **1.** the act or an instance of perforating or piercing **2.** a hole made by a sharp point, as in an automobile tire, the skin, etc. —*vt.* **-tured, -tur·ing** **1.** to perforate or pierce with a sharp point **2.** to reduce or put an end to, as if by a puncture [to *puncture* someone's pride] —*vi.* to be punctured —**punc′tur·a·ble** *adj.*

pun·dit (pun′dit) *n.* [Hind. *pandit* < Sans. *pandita*, a learned person, orig., learned] **1.** in India, a Brahman who is learned in Sanskrit and Hindu philosophy, law, and religion **2.** a person who has or professes to have great learning; actual or self-professed authority —**pun′dit·ry** *n.*

☆**pung** (puŋ) *n.* [< earlier *tom pung*, altered < *tow-pung* < AmInd. (Algonquian) name akin to TOBOGGAN] [NE U.S.] a boxlike sleigh drawn by one horse

pun·gent (pun′jənt) *adj.* [L. *pungens*, prp. of *pungere*, to prick, puncture: see POINT] **1.** producing a sharp sensation of taste and smell; acrid **2.** sharp and piercing to the mind; poignant; painful **3.** sharply penetrating; expressive; biting [*pungent* language] **4.** keenly clever; stimulating —**pun′gen·cy** *n.* —**pun′gent·ly** *adv.*

SYN.—**pungent** literally applies to taste or smell, suggesting a sharp, stinging quality [*pungent* spices], and figuratively implies a penetrating or stimulating quality [*pungent* humor]; **piquant** implies an agreeable pungency, tartness, or zest [a *piquant* salad dressing, *piquant* wit]; **racy** suggests the piquancy and tang of something in its natural and freshest condition [a *racy* flavor] and, in its now more usual figurative use, implies a spirited, vigorous quality [*racy* slang]; **spicy** suggests the pungent taste or fragrant aroma of spices [a *spicy* drink] and, figuratively, an exciting, often risqué quality [*spicy* stories] —*ANT.* bland, insipid

Pu·nic (pyōō′nik) *adj.* [L. *Punicus*, earlier *Poenicus*, Carthaginian, properly Phoenician < *Poeni*, the Carthaginians < Gr. *Phoinix*, Phoenician] **1.** of ancient Carthage or its people **2.** like or characteristic of the Carthaginians, regarded by the Romans as faithless and treacherous —*n.* the Northwest Semitic language of ancient Carthage, a dialect of Phoenician: it survived until c. 500 A.D.

Punic Wars three wars between Rome and Carthage (264–241 B.C., 218–201 B.C., and 149–146 B.C.), in which Rome was finally victorious

pu·ni·ness (pyōō′nē nis) *n.* puny quality or condition

pun·ish (pun′ish) *vt.* [ME. *punischen* < extended stem of OFr. *punir* < L. *punire*, to punish < *poena*, punishment, penalty: see PENAL] **1.** to cause to undergo pain, loss, or suffering for a crime or wrongdoing **2.** to impose a penalty on a wrongdoer for (an offense) **3.** to treat harshly or injuriously [the *punishing* rays of the sun] **4.** [Colloq.] to consume or use up —*vi.* to deal out punishment —**pun′ish·er** *n.*

SYN.—**punish** implies the infliction of some penalty on a wrongdoer and generally connotes retribution rather than correction [to *punish* a murderer by hanging him]; **discipline** suggests punishment that is intended to control or to establish habits of self-control [to *discipline* a naughty child]; **correct** suggests punishment for the purpose of overcoming faults [to *correct* unruly pupils]; **chastise** implies usually corporal punishment and connotes both retribution and correction; **castigate** now implies punishment by severe public criticism or censure [to *castigate* a corrupt official]; **chasten** implies the infliction of tribulation in order to make obedient, meek, etc. and is used especially in a theological sense ["He *chastens* and hastens His will to make known"]

pun·ish·a·ble (-ə b'l) *adj.* liable to or deserving punishment —**pun′ish·a·bil′i·ty** *n.*

pun·ish·ment (-mənt) *n.* **1.** a punishing or being punished **2.** a penalty imposed on an offender for a crime or wrongdoing **3.** harsh or injurious treatment

pu·ni·tive (pyōō′nə tiv) *adj.* [ML. *punitivus* < L. *punitus*, pp. of *punire*, to PUNISH] inflicting, concerned with, or directed toward punishment: *also* **pu′ni·to′ry —pu′ni·tive·ly** *adv.* —**pu′ni·tive·ness** *n.*

punitive damages *same as* EXEMPLARY DAMAGES

Pun·jab (pun jäb′; pun′jäb, -jab) **1.** region in NW India & NE West Pakistan, between the Indus & Jumna rivers: formerly, a state of India; divided between India & Pakistan, 1947: c. 99,000 sq. mi.; chief city, Lahore **2.** a state of India, in this region: 19,403 sq. mi.; pop. 11,147,000; cap. Chandigarh

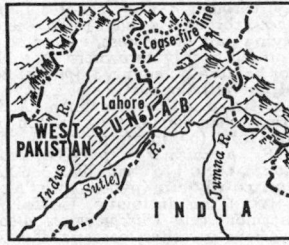

PUNJAB

Pun·ja·bi (pun jä′bē) *n.* **1.** a native of Punjab **2.** the Indic language spoken in the Punjab

pun·ji stick (or **stake, pole,** etc.) (poon′jē) [< native term in Vietnam] a bamboo stake with a needle-sharp tip, often smeared with dung or other infectious substance, concealed along the ground in jungle warfare to pierce the feet of enemy soldiers

☆**punk**[1] (puŋk) *n.* [var. of SPUNK] any substance, as decayed wood, that smolders when ignited, used as tinder; esp., a chemically treated fungous substance shaped into slender, fragile, light-brown sticks: the glowing tips are used to light fireworks, etc.

punk[2] (puŋk) *n.* [Early ModE. slang < ?] **1.** orig., a prostitute ☆**2.** [Slang] *a)* a catamite *b)* a young hoodlum *c)* any person, esp. a youngster, regarded as inexperienced, insignificant, presumptuous, etc. —☆*adj.* [Slang] poor or bad in quality, condition, etc.

pun·kah, pun·ka (puŋ′ka) *n.* [Hind. *pankā*] in India, a large fan made from the palmyra leaf, or a large, swinging fan consisting of canvas stretched over a rectangular frame and hung from the ceiling

☆**punk·ie** (puŋ′kē) *n.* [dial. Du. *punki* < AmInd. (Algonquian), as in Lenape *punk,* fine ashes: so named from their size] *same as* BITING MIDGE

pun·ster (pun′stər) *n.* a person who habitually makes, or is fond of making, puns: also **pun′ner**

punt[1] (punt) *n.* [< slang of Rugby School, England: ? form of dial. *bunt,* to strike, kick (cf. BUNT[1])] *Football* a kick in which the ball is dropped from the hands and then kicked before it strikes the ground —*vt., vi.* to kick (a football) in this way

punt[2] (punt) *n.* [OE. < L. *ponto,* a punt (in LL., PONTOON)] a flat-bottomed boat with broad, square ends, usually propelled by a single long pole —*vt.* **1.** to propel (a boat) by pushing with a pole against the bottom of a shallow river or lake **2.** to carry in a punt —*vi.* to go in a punt

punt[3] (punt) *vi.* [Fr. *ponter* < *ponte,* a point < Sp. *punto* < L. *punctum,* a POINT] **1.** in certain card games, to bet against the banker **2.** [Brit.] to gamble; bet

Pun·ta A·re·nas (poon′tä ä re′näs) seaport in S Chile, on the Strait of Magellan: southernmost city in the world: pop. 45,000

punt·er (punt′ər) *n.* a person who punts

pun·ty (pun′tē) *n., pl.* **-ties** [Fr. *pontil* < It. *pontello,* dim. of *punto* < L. *punctum,* POINT] a metal rod on which the molten glass is handled in glassmaking

pu·ny (pyoo′nē) *adj.* **-ni·er, -ni·est** [Fr. *puiné,* born later < OFr. *puisné* < *puis,* after + *né* (L. *natus*), born] **1.** of inferior size, strength, or importance; weak; slight **2.** [Obs.] *same as* PUISNE

pup (pup) *n.* [contr. < PUPPY] **1.** *a)* a young dog; puppy *b)* a young fox, wolf, etc. **2.** a young seal, whale, etc. —*vi.* **pupped, pup′ping** to give birth to pups

pu·pa (pyoo′pə) *n., pl.* **-pae** (-pē), **-pas** [ModL. < L., a girl, doll, prob. < IE. *pup-* < base *pu-,* to swell up, inflate, whence Russ. *púlja,* a ball] any insect in the non-feeding stage of development between the last larval and adult forms, characterized by many anatomical changes and, often, by enclosure in a cell or cocoon —**pu′pal** *adj.*

PUPA

pu·pate (-pāt) *vi.* **-pat·ed, -pat·ing** to become a pupa; go through the pupal stage —**pu·pa′tion** *n.*

pu·pil[1] (pyoo′p'l) *n.* [ME. *pupille* < MFr. < L. *pupillus* (dim. of *pupus,* boy), *pupilla* (dim. of *pupa,* girl: cf. PUPA), orphan, ward] **1.** a person, esp. a young person, who is being taught under the supervision of a teacher or tutor, as in school **2.** *Brit. Civil Law* a minor under the care of a guardian; ward

SYN.—**pupil** is applied either to a child in school or to a person who is under the personal supervision of a teacher [Heifetz was a *pupil* of Leopold Auer/; **student** is applied either to one attending an institution above the elementary level or to one who is making a study of a particular problem [a *student* of social problems/; **scholar,** orig. equivalent to **pupil,** is now usually applied to one who has general erudition or who is highly versed in a particular branch of learning [a linguistics *scholar/*

pu·pil[2] (pyoo′p'l) *n.* [Fr. *pupille* < L. *pupilla,* one's figure seen reflected in another's eye, hence pupil of the eye;

special use of *pupilla:* see prec.] the contractile circular opening, apparently black, in the center of the iris of the eye: see EYE, illus.

pu·pil·age, pu·pil·lage (pyoo′p'l ij) *n.* the state or period of being a pupil

pu·pil·lar·i·ty, pu·pi·lar·i·ty (pyoo′pə lar′ə tē) *n.* [Fr. *pupilarité:* see ff. & -ITY] *Scot. Law* the period before puberty

pu·pil·lar·y[1] (pyoo′pə ler′ē) *adj.* [Fr. *pupillaire* < L. *pupillaris* < *pupilla,* PUPIL[1]] of a person who is a pupil

pu·pil·lar·y[2] (pyoo′pə ler′ē) *adj.* of the pupil of the eye

Pu·pin (pyoo pēn′), **Michael Id·vor·sky** (id vôr′skē) 1858–1935; U.S. physicist & inventor, born in Hungary

pu·pip·a·rous (pyoo pip′ər əs) *adj.* [< PUPA + -PAROUS] designating or of a tribe (Pupipara) of two-winged insects bearing young already developed to the stage where they are ready to pupate, as the sheep tick

pup·pet (pup′it) *n.* [ME. *popet* < OFr. *poupette,* dim. of *poupe* < VL. *puppa* < L. *pupa,* a girl, doll: see PUPA] **1.** orig., a doll **2.** a small, usually jointed figure, as of a human being, moved, usually in a puppet show on a small stage, by manipulating with the hands, by pulling attached strings or wires, or by rods **3.** a person whose actions, ideas, etc. are controlled by another

pup·pet·eer (pup′i tir′) *n.* a person who operates, designs, or costumes puppets, or produces puppet shows

pup·pet·ry (pup′i trē) *n.* the art of making or operating puppets or producing puppet shows

puppet show a play or performance with puppets

Pup·pis (pup′is) [L., poop of a ship] a constellation in the S Milky Way, previously part of the large constellation Argo

pup·py (pup′ē) *n., pl.* **-pies** [ME. *popi* < MFr. *popee,* doll < *poupe:* see PUPPET] **1.** *a)* a young dog *b)* a young fox, seal, etc.; pup **2.** an insolent, conceited, or silly young man —**pup′py·hood′** *n.* —**pup′py·ish** *adj.*

☆**puppy love** immature love between a boy and girl

☆**pup tent** *same as* SHELTER TENT

pu·ra·na (poo rä′nə) *n.* [Sans., lit., ancient, akin to *puráh,* before < IE. base **per-:* see FORE] [*often* P-] any of a group of 18 Hindu epics dealing with creation, the gods, genealogy, etc. in fables, legends, and tales

pur·blind (pur′blīnd′) *adj.* [ME. *pur blind:* see PURE & BLIND] **1.** orig., completely blind **2.** partly blind **3.** slow in perceiving or understanding

Pur·cell (pur′s'l), **Henry** 1659?–95; Eng. composer

pur·chase (pur′chəs) *vt.* **-chased, -chas·ing** [ME. *purchacen* < OFr. *pourchacier,* to pursue < *pour,* for (< L. *pro:* see PRO[1]) + *chacier,* to CHASE[1]] **1.** to obtain for money or by paying a price; buy **2.** to obtain at a cost, as of suffering or sacrifice **3.** *a)* to move or raise by applying mechanical power *b)* to get a fast hold on so as to do this **4.** *Law* to acquire (land, buildings, etc.) by means other than inheritance or descent —*n.* **1.** anything obtained by buying **2.** the act of buying **3.** [Now Rare] income; return **4.** *a)* a fast hold applied to move something mechanically or to keep from slipping *b)* any apparatus with which such a hold is applied **5.** *Law* the acquisition of land, buildings, etc. by means other than inheritance or descent —**pur′chas·a·ble** *adj.* —**pur′chas·er** *n.*

pur·dah (pur′də) *n.* [Hind. & Per. *pardah,* a veil] **1.** a curtain or veil used by some Hindus and Moslems to seclude or hide their women from strangers **2.** the practice of secluding or hiding women in this way

pure (pyoor) *adj.* [ME. < OFr. < L. *purus,* pure < IE. base **peu-,* **pū-,* to purify, cleanse, whence Sans. *punáti,* (he) cleanses, L. *putare,* to cleanse, OHG. *fowen,* to sift] **1.** *a)* free from any adulterant; unmixed [pure maple syrup/ *b)* free from anything that taints, impairs, infects, etc.; clear [pure water or air/ **2.** simple; mere [pure luck/ **3.** utter; absolute; sheer [pure lunacy/ **4.** free from defects; perfect; faultless **5.** free from sin or guilt; blameless **6.** virgin or chaste **7.** of unmixed stock; purebred **8.** restricted to the abstract or theoretical aspects [pure physics/ **9.** *Bible* ceremonially undefiled **10.** *Phonet.* remaining unchanged in sound; monophthongal [a pure vowel/ —**SYN.** see CHASTE —**pure′ness** *n.*

pure·bred (-bred′) *adj.* belonging to a recognized breed with characters maintained through generations of unmixed descent —*n.* a purebred plant or animal

pure culture a culture medium containing only organisms of the particular species required

pu·rée (pyoo rā′; pyoor′ā, -ē) *n.* [Fr. < OFr. *purer,* to strain < L. *purare,* to purify < *purus,* PURE] **1.** a thick, moist, smooth-textured form of cooked vegetables, fruits, etc., usually made by pressing the pulp through a sieve or by whipping it in a blender **2.** a thick, smooth soup made with this —*vt.* **-réed′, -ré′ing** to make a purée of Also sp. **puree**

pure line *Genetics* a breed or strain of animals or plants that maintains a high degree of consistency in certain characters as a result of continued inbreeding for generations

pure·ly (pyoor′lē) *adv.* **1.** in a pure manner; unmixed with anything else **2.** merely **3.** innocently **4.** entirely

fat, āpe, cär; ten, ēven; is, bīte; gō, hôrn, tōōl, look; oil, out; up, fur; get; joy; yet; chin; she; thin, *th*en; zh, leisure; ŋ, ring; ə for a in ago, e in agent, i in sanity, o in comply, u in focus; ′ as in able (ā′b'l); Fr. bâl; ë, Fr. coeur; ö, Fr. feu; ô, Fr. mon; ô, Fr. coq; ü, Fr. duc; r, Fr. cri; H, G. ich; kh, G. doch. See inside front cover. ☆ Americanism; ‡foreign; *hypothetical; < derived from

pur·fle (pur′f'l) *vt.* **-fled, -fling** [ME. *purfilen* < MFr. *pourfiler* < *pour*, for (< L. *pro:* see PRO¹) + *fil*, thread: see FILE¹] **1.** to decorate the border of **2.** to adorn or edge with metallic thread, beads, lace, etc. —*n.* an ornamental border or trimming, as the inlaid border of a violin: also **pur′fling**

pur·ga·tion (pur gā′shən) *n.* [ME. *purgacion* < OFr. < L. *purgatio*] the act of purging

pur·ga·tive (pur′gə tiv) *adj.* [ME. *purgatyf* < MFr. *purgatif* < LL. *purgativus*] **1.** that purges; purging **2.** causing bowel movement —*n.* a substance that purges; specif., same as CATHARTIC —*SYN.* see PHYSIC

pur·ga·to·ri·al (pur′gə tôr′ē əl) *adj.* [< LL. *purgatorius* (see PURGATORY) + -AL] **1.** serving to atone for sins; expiatory **2.** of or like purgatory

pur·ga·to·ry (pur′gə tôr′ē) *n., pl.* **-ries** [ME. *purgatorie* < OFr. & ML.(Ec.): OFr. *purgatoire* < ML.(Ec.) *purgatorium* < LL. *purgatorius*, cleansing < L. *purgare:* see ff.] **1.** [*often* P-] *Theol.* a state or place in which, in R.C. and other Christian doctrine, those who have died in the grace of God expiate their sins by suffering **2.** any state or place of temporary punishment, expiation, or remorse

purge (purj) *vt.* **purged, purg′ing** [ME. *purgen* < OFr. *purgier* < L. *purgare*, to cleanse < *purus*, clean (see PURE) + *agere*, to do: see ACT] **1.** to cleanse or rid of impurities, foreign matter, or undesirable elements **2.** to cleanse of guilt, sin, or ceremonial defilement **3.** to remove by cleansing; clear (*away, off,* or *out*) **4.** *a)* to rid (a nation, political party, etc.) of individuals held to be disloyal or undesirable *b)* to kill or otherwise get rid of (such individuals) **5.** *Law* to free from a charge or imputation of guilt **6.** *Med. a)* to empty (the bowels) *b)* to cause (a person) to empty his bowels —*vi.* **1.** to become clean, clear, or pure **2.** to have or effect a thorough bowel movement —*n.* **1.** the act of purging **2.** that which purges; esp., a purgative, or cathartic **3.** the process of ridding a nation, political party, etc. of individuals held to be disloyal or undesirable —**purg′er** *n.*

pu·ri·fi·ca·tor (pyoor′ə fi kāt′ər) *n.* a small linen cloth used in the Eucharist to wipe the chalice and to dry the celebrant's fingers and mouth

pu·ri·fy (pyoor′ə fī′) *vt.* **-fied′, -fy′ing** [ME. *purifien* < OFr. *purifier* < L. *purificare:* see PURE & -FY] **1.** to rid of impurities or pollution **2.** to free from guilt, sin, or ceremonial uncleanness **3.** to free from incorrect or corrupting elements **4.** to purge (*of* or *from*) —*vi.* to become purified —**pu′ri·fi·ca′tion** *n.* —**pu·rif·i·ca·to·ry** (pyoo rif′i kə tôr′ē) *adj.* —**pu′ri·fi′er** *n.*

Pu·rim (poor′im, poo rēm′) *n.* [Heb. *pūrim*, pl., lit., lots] a Jewish holiday, the Feast of Lots, celebrated on the 14th day of Adar, commemorating the deliverance of the Jews by Esther from a general massacre plotted by Haman: Esth. 9:21

pu·rine (pyoor′ēn, -in) *n.* [G. *purin* < L. *purus*, pure + ModL. *uricum*, uric acid + -*in*, -INE⁴] **1.** a colorless, crystalline, organic compound, $C_5H_4N_4$, the parent substance of the uric-acid group of compounds **2.** any of several basic substances produced by the decomposition of nucleoproteins and having a purine-type molecule, as caffeine

pur·ism (pyoor′iz'm) *n.* [Fr. *purisme* < *pur*, PURE] **1.** strict observance of or insistence on precise usage or on application of formal, often pedantic rules, as in language, art, etc. **2.** an instance of this —**pur′ist** *n.* —**pu·ris′tic, pu·ris′ti·cal** *adj.* —**pu·ris′ti·cal·ly** *adv.*

Pu·ri·tan (pyoor′ə t'n) *n.* [< LL. *puritas* (see PURITY) + -AN] **1.** any member of a Protestant group in England and the American colonies who, in the 16th and 17th centuries, wanted a greater reformation of the Church of England than that established by Elizabeth I, so as to purify it further from elaborate ceremonies and forms **2.** [p-] a person regarded as extremely or excessively strict in matters of morals and religion —*adj.* **1.** of the Puritans or Puritanism **2.** [p-] *same as* PURITANICAL —**Pu′ri·tan·ism, pu′ri·tan·ism** *n.*

pu·ri·tan·i·cal (pyoor′ə tan′i k'l) *adj.* **1.** [P-] of the Puritans or Puritanism **2.** extremely or excessively strict in matters of morals and religion Also **pu′ri·tan′ic** —**pu′ri·tan′i·cal·ly** *adv.*

pu·ri·ty (pyoor′ə tē) *n.* [ME. *purete* < MFr. *pureté* < LL. *puritas* < L. *purus*, PURE] the quality or condition of being pure; specif., *a)* freedom from adulterating matter *b)* cleanness or clearness *c)* freedom from evil or sin; innocence; chastity *d)* freedom from corrupting elements: said of language, style, etc. *e)* freedom from mixture with white; color saturation

purl¹ (purl) *vi.* [< ? Scand., as in Norw. *purla*, to ripple] **1.** to move in ripples or with a murmuring sound **2.** to move in eddies; swirl —*n.* **1.** a purling stream or rill **2.** the murmuring sound of purling water

purl² (purl) *vt., vi.* [earlier *pirl*, prob. < the *n.*] **1.** *same as* PURFLE **2.** to edge (lace) with a chain of small loops **3.** to invert (a stitch or stitches) in knitting —*n.* [earlier *pyrle* < a Romance source as in It. (Venetian) *pirlo*, a joining of warp and woof by twisting together the threads < echoic base *pirl*, to twirl] **1.** twisted metal thread, as of gold or silver, used in embroidery **2.** a small loop, or a chain of loops, made on the edge of lace **3.** an inversion of stitches in knitting to produce a ribbed effect

pur·lieu (pur′loo, purl′yoo) *n.* [altered (after Fr. *lieu*, a place) < Anglo-Fr. *puralee* < OFr. *puralée* < *puraler*, to go through < *pur-, por-* (< L. *pro-*, for, but used for L. *per-*, through) + *aler*, to go: see ALLEY¹] **1.** orig., an outlying part of a forest, exempted from forest laws and returned to private owners **2.** a place that one visits often or habitually; haunt **3.** [*pl.*] *a)* bounds; limits *b)* environs **4.** an outlying part, as of a city

pur·lin, pur·line (pur′lin) *n.* [ME. *purlyn* < ?] a horizontal timber supporting the common rafters of a roof

pur·loin (pər loin′, pur′loin) *vt., vi.* [ME. *purlognen* < OFr. *purloignier* < *pur-* (L. *pro-*), for + *loin*, far < L. *longe*, LONG¹] to steal; filch —*SYN.* see STEAL

☆**pu·ro·my·cin** (pyoor′ō mīs′'n) *n.* [< PUR(INE) + -o- + -MYCIN] an antibiotic, $C_{22}H_{29}N_7O_5$, produced by a soil actinomycete (*Streptomyces alboniger*), effective against various parasites, bacteria, etc.: it interferes with protein synthesis and can inhibit long-term memory

pur·ple (pur′p'l) *n.* [ME. *purpel* < OE. (Northumbrian) *purpl(e)*, dissimilated var. of WS. *purpur(e)* < L. *purpura*, purple < Gr. *porphyra*, shellfish yielding purple dye] **1.** a dark color that is a blend of red and blue **2.** esp. formerly, *a)* deep crimson *b)* cloth or clothing of such color: an emblem of royalty or high rank —*adj.* **1.** of the color purple **2.** imperial; royal **3.** *a)* ornate or elaborate in literary style [*purple* prose] *b)* vigorous and direct, often offensively so; strong [*purple* language] —*vt., vi.* **-pled, -pling** to make or become purple —**born to** (or **in**) **the purple** being of royal or high birth —**the purple** royal or high rank

☆**pur·ple-fringed orchis** (-frinjd′) either of two N. American orchids (*Habenaria psycodes* and *Habenaria fimbriata*) with purple-fringed flowers

☆**purple gallinule** a gallinule (*Porphyrula martinica*) with purple wings and brilliant yellow legs, usually found in freshwater swamps from the southern U.S. to tropical S. America

☆**purple grackle** *see* GRACKLE

☆**Purple Heart** a decoration awarded to members of the armed forces wounded in action against an enemy: orig. established in 1782 and re-established in 1932

☆**purple martin** a large N. American swallow (*Progne subis*) with bluish-black plumage

pur·plish (pur′plish, -p'l ish) *adj.* having a purple tinge; somewhat purple: also **pur′ply** (-plē, -p'l ē)

pur·port (pər pôrt′; *also, & for n. always,* pur′pôrt) *vt.* [Anglo-Fr. *purporter* < OFr. *porporter* < *por-* (< L. *pro:* see PRO¹), forth + *porter*, to bear < L. *portare:* see PORT³] **1.** to profess or claim as its meaning **2.** to give the appearance, often falsely, of being, intending, etc. —*n.* **1.** meaning; tenor; sense; drift **2.** intention; object —*SYN.* see MEANING

pur·pose (pur′pəs) *vt., vi.* **-posed, -pos·ing** [ME. *purposen* < OFr. *porposer*, var. of *proposer:* see PROPOSE] to intend, resolve, or plan —*n.* [ME. < OFr. *porpos*] **1.** something one intends to get or do; intention; aim **2.** resolution; determination **3.** the object for which something exists or is done; end in view —*SYN.* see INTEND, INTENTION —**of set purpose 1.** with a specific end in view **2.** not accidentally; by design —**on purpose** by design; intentionally —**to good purpose** with a good result or effect; advantageously —**to little** (or **no**) **purpose** with little or no result or effect; profitlessly —**to the purpose** relevant; pertinent

pur·pose·ful (-fəl) *adj.* **1.** resolutely aiming at a specific goal **2.** directed toward a specific end; not meaningless —**pur′pose·ful·ly** *adv.* —**pur′pose·ful·ness** *n.*

pur·pose·less (-lis) *adj.* not purposeful; aimless —**pur′pose·less·ly** *adv.* —**pur′pose·less·ness** *n.*

pur·pose·ly (-lē) *adv.* with a definite purpose; intentionally; deliberately

pur·pos·ive (pur′pə siv) *adj.* **1.** serving some purpose **2.** having a purpose —**pur′pos·ive·ly** *adv.*

pur·pu·ra (pur′pyoo rə) *n.* [ModL.: see PURPLE] a disease characterized by purplish patches on the skin or mucous membranes, caused by subcutaneous hemorrhage —**pur·pu·ric** (pur pyoor′ik) *adj.*

pur·pure (-pyoor) *n.* [ME. < OE.(WS.): see PURPLE] purple as a tincture in heraldry: represented in engravings by diagonal lines downward from sinister to dexter

pur·pu·rin (pyoo rin) *n.* [< L. *purpura*, PURPLE + -IN¹] a reddish material, $C_{14}H_8O_5$, isolated from the madder root or produced synthetically: used as a dye, stain, etc.

purr (pur) *n.* [echoic] **1.** a low, vibratory sound made by a cat when it seems to be pleased **2.** any sound like this —*vi., vt.* to make or express by such a sound

purse (purs) *n.* [ME. < OE. *purs* < ML. *bursa*, a bag, purse < LL., a hide < Gr. *byrsa*] **1.** a small bag or pouch for carrying money **2.** financial resources; money **3.** a sum of money collected as a present or given as a prize ☆**4.** a woman's handbag **5.** anything like a purse in shape, use, etc. —*vt.* **pursed, purs′ing 1.** [Archaic] to put in a purse **2.** *a)* to gather into small folds *b)* to draw (the lips) tightly together, as in disapproval

purse crab *same as* PALM CRAB

purse-proud (-proud′) *adj.* proud of being wealthy

purs·er (pur′sər) *n.* [ME., a purse-bearer, treasurer] a ship's officer in charge of accounts, freight, tickets, etc., esp. on a passenger vessel

☆**purse seine** a very large net, as for catching tuna, that can be closed like a drawstring purse once it has been set

purse strings a drawstring for closing certain purses —**hold the purse strings** to be in control of the money —**tighten (or loosen) the purse strings** to make funds less (or more) readily available

purs·lane (purs′lin, -lān) *n.* [ME. *purcelane* < MFr. *porcelaine* < LL. *porcilaca,* purslane, altered < L. *portulaca* (cf. PORTULACA)] any of a number of fleshy, prostrate weeds (genus *Portulaca*) of the purslane family, with pink, fleshy stems and small, yellow, short-lived flowers; esp., an annual (*Portulaca oleracea*) sometimes used as a potherb and in salads —*adj.* designating a family (Portulacaceae) of plants including purslane, claytonia, and portulaca

pur·su·ance (pər sōō′əns, -syōō′-) *n.* [< ff.] a pursuing, or carrying out, as of a project, plan, etc.

pur·su·ant (-ənt) *adj.* [ME. *poursuiant* < OFr., prp. of *poursuir:* see PURSUE] [Now Rare] pursuing —**pursuant to** 1. following upon 2. in accordance with: also [Rare] **pursuantly to**

pur·sue (pər sōō′, -syōō′) *vt.* **-sued′, -su′ing** [ME. *pursuen* < OFr. *poursuir* < VL. *prosequere,* for L. *prosequi* < *pro-,* forth + *sequi,* to follow: see SEQUENT] 1. to follow in order to overtake, capture, or kill; chase 2. to proceed along, follow, or continue with (a specified course, action, plan, etc.) 3. to try to find, get, win, etc.; strive for; seek after [to *pursue* success] 4. to have as one's occupation, profession, or study; devote oneself to 5. to continue to annoy or distress; hound [*pursued* by bad luck] —*vi.* 1. to chase 2. to go on; continue —**pur·su′a·ble** *adj.* —**pur·su′er** *n.*

pur·suit (-sōōt′, -syōōt′) *n.* [ME. *purseute* < OFr. *poursuite*] 1. the act of pursuing 2. an occupation, career, interest, etc. to which one devotes time and energy

pursuit plane a fighter airplane: see FIGHTER (sense 3)

pur·sui·vant (pur′si vənt, -swi-) *n.* [ME. *pursevante* < OFr. *poursuivant,* prp. of *poursuivre* < *poursuir:* see PURSUE] 1. in the British College of Heralds, an officer ranking below a herald 2. a follower; attendant

pur·sy[1] (pur′sē) *adj.* **-si·er, -si·est** [ME. *purcy* < *purcyfe* < Anglo-Fr. *pursif,* for OFr. *polsif* < *polser,* to push, also breathe, pant < L. *pulsare,* to beat < *pulsus:* see PULSE[1]] 1. short-winded, esp. from being obese 2. obese; fat —**pur′si·ness** *n.*

pur·sy[2] (pur′sē) *adj.* **-si·er, -si·est** 1. drawn together like purse strings; puckered 2. proud of being wealthy

pur·te·nance (pur′t'n əns) *n.* [ME. *portenaunce,* lit., appendage, altered < OFr. *partenence* < prp. of *partenir,* to PERTAIN] [Archaic] the viscera of an animal

pu·ru·lent (pyoor′ə lənt, -yoo lənt) *adj.* [Fr. < *purulentus* < *pus* (gen. *puris*), matter, PUS] of, like, containing, or discharging pus —**pu′ru·lence, pu′ru·len·cy** *n.* —**pu′ru·lent·ly** *adv.*

Pu·rús (pōō rōōs′) river in S. America, flowing from E Peru through NW Brazil into the Amazon: c. 2,000 mi.

pur·vey (pər vā′) *vt.* [ME. *pourveien* < Anglo-Fr. *purveier* < OFr. *porveir* < L. *providere:* see PROVIDE] to furnish or supply (esp. food or provisions) —**pur·vey′or** *n.*

pur·vey·ance (-əns) *n.* [ME. *purveance* < OFr.] 1. the act of purveying 2. things purveyed; provisions

pur·view (pur′vyōō) *n.* [ME. *purveu* < Anglo-Fr. (in legal phrases *purveu est,* it is provided, *purveu que,* provided that) < OFr. *pourveü,* provided, pp. of *pourveir* (see PURVEY)] 1. the body and scope of an act or bill 2. the extent or range of control, activity, or concern; province 3. range of sight or understanding

pus (pus) *n.* [L. < IE. base *pū-, *pu-,* to rot, stink (prob. orig. echoic of cry of disgust), whence FOUL, Gr. *pyon,* pus, L. *putridus,* putrid] the usually yellowish-white liquid matter produced in certain infections, consisting of bacteria, white corpuscles, serum, etc.

Pu·san (pōō′sän) seaport in SE South Korea, on Korea Strait: pop. 1,420,000

Pu·sey·ism (pyōō′zē iz'm, -sē-) *n.* [after E. B. *Pusey* (1800–82), Eng. leader of the movement] same as TRACTARIANISM —**Pu′sey·ite** (-īt) *n.*

push (poosh) *vt.* [ME. *posshen* < MFr. *pousser* < OFr. *poulser* < L. *pulsare,* to beat < *pulsus,* pp. of *pellere,* to beat, drive: see PULSE[1]] 1. *a)* to exert pressure or force against, esp. so as to move it *b)* to move in this way *c)* to thrust, shove, or drive (*up, down, in, out,* etc.) 2. *a)* to urge on; impel; press *b)* to follow up vigorously; promote (a campaign, claim, etc.) *c)* to extend or expand (business activities, etc.) 3. to bring into a critical state; esp., to make critically needful [to be *pushed* for time] 4. to urge or promote the use, sale, success, etc. of ☆5. [Colloq.] to be near or close to [*pushing* sixty years] —*vi.* 1. to press against a thing so as to move it 2. to put forth great effort, as in seeking advancement 3. to move forward against opposition 4. to move by being pushed —*n.* 1. the act of pushing 2. a thing to be pushed so as to work a mechanism 3. a vigorous effort, campaign, etc. 4. an advance against opposition 5. pressure of affairs or of circumstances 6. an emergency 7. [Colloq.] aggressive-

ness; enterprise; drive —**push off** [Colloq.] to set out; depart —**push on** to proceed; continue advancing

SYN.—**push** implies the exertion of force or pressure by a person or thing in contact with the object to be moved ahead, aside, etc. [to *push* a baby carriage]; **shove** implies a pushing of something so as to force it to slide along a surface, or it suggests roughness in pushing [*shove* the box into the corner]; to **thrust** is to push with sudden, often violent force, sometimes so as to penetrate something [he *thrust* his hand into the water]; **propel** implies a driving forward by a force that imparts motion [the wind *propelled* the sailboat] —*ANT.* pull, draw

☆**push·ball** (-bôl′) *n.* 1. a game, played by two teams, in which a large ball about six feet in diameter is to be pushed across the opponent's goal 2. such a ball

☆**push-but·ton** (-but′'n) *adj.* controlled by a push button or push buttons: applied figuratively as to warfare making use of automated weapon systems fired over long distances

☆**push button** a small knob or button that is pushed to operate something, as by closing an electric circuit

☆**push·cart** (poosh′kärt′) *n.* a cart pushed by hand, esp. one used by street vendors

push·er (-ər) *n.* 1. a person or thing that pushes 2. an airplane with its propeller or propellers mounted behind the engine: also **pusher airplane** ☆3. [Slang] a person who sells drugs, esp. narcotics, illegally

push·ing (-in) *adj.* 1. aggressive; enterprising; energetic 2. forward; officious —*SYN.* see AGGRESSIVE

Push·kin (poosh′kin; *E.* poosh′-), **A·le·ksan·dr Ser·ge·ye·vich** (á′lyek sän′dər syer gyā′yə vich) 1799–1837; Russ. poet

☆**push·o·ver** (poosh′ō′vər) *n.* [Slang] 1. anything very easy to accomplish 2. a person, group, etc. easily persuaded, defeated, seduced, etc.

push·pin (-pin′) *n.* a tacklike pin with a large head, used as a map marker, etc.

push-pull (-pool′) *adj. Electronics* designating or of an amplifier circuit in which two tubes or transistors operate 180° out of phase with each other, usually producing a higher output of the desired wave and canceling undesired qualities, as hum

Push·tu (push′tōō) *n. same as* PASHTO

push-up, push up (poosh′up′) *n.* an exercise in which a person lying face down, with the hands under the shoulders, raises the body by pushing down with the palms: push-ups are usually done in series by alternately straightening and bending the arms

☆**push·y** (poosh′ē) *adj.* **push′i·er, push′i·est** [Colloq.] annoyingly aggressive and persistent —**push′i·ness** *n.*

pu·sil·lan·i·mous (pyōō′sil an′ə məs) *adj.* [LL.(Ec.) *pusillanimis* < L. *pusillus,* tiny (dim. of *pusus,* a little boy, akin to *puer:* see PUERILE) + *animus,* the mind (see ANIMAL) + -OUS] 1. timid, cowardly, or irresolute; fainthearted 2. proceeding from or showing a lack of courage —*SYN.* see COWARDLY —**pu·sil·la·nim′i·ty** (-ə nim′ə tē) *n.* —**pu·sil·lan′i·mous·ly** *adv.*

puss[1] (poos) *n.* [orig. ? echoic of the spitting of a cat: akin to Du. *poes,* Sw. dial. *pus,* LowG. *puus,* a cat] 1. a cat: pet name or child's term 2. a girl or young woman: term of affection

puss[2] (poos) *n.* [prob. < IrGael. *pus,* mouth] [Slang] ☆1. the face ☆2. the mouth

☆**puss·ley, puss·ly** (pus′lē) *n. same as* PURSLANE

pus·sy[1] (pus′ē) *adj.* **-si·er, -si·est** containing or like pus

puss·y[2] (poos′ē) *n., pl.* **puss′ies** [dim. of PUSS[1]] 1. *same as* PUSS[1]: also **puss′y·cat′** (-kat′) 2. [Colloq.] a catkin, as of the pussy willow

☆**puss·y·foot** (-foot′) *vi.* [Colloq.] 1. to move with stealth or caution, like a cat 2. to shy away from a definite commitment or from taking a firm stand —**puss′y·foot′er** *n.*

☆**pussy willow** any of several willows bearing velvetlike catkins before the leaves; esp., a deciduous shrub or tree (*Salix discolor*) with large silvery catkins

pus·tu·lant (pus′chə lant) *adj.* [LL. *pustulans,* prp.] causing pustules to form —*n.* a pustulant medicine, etc.

pus·tu·lar (-lər) *adj.* 1. of, or having the nature of, pustules 2. covered with pustules Also **pus′tu·lous**

pus·tu·late (-lāt′; *for adj.,* -lit) *vt., vi.* **-lat′ed, -lat′ing** [< LL. *pustulatus,* pp. of *pustulare,* to blister < *pustula,* a blister, PUSTULE] to form into pustules —*adj.* covered with pustules —**pus′tu·la′tion** *n.*

pus·tule (pus′chōōl) *n.* [L. *pustula,* a blister, pimple < IE. base *pu-,* echoic of blowing out cheeks, puffing, whence Gr. *physa,* a breath, bubble] 1. a small elevation of the skin containing pus 2. any small elevation like a blister or pimple

put (poot) *vt.* **put, put′ting** [ME. *putten* < or akin to OE. *potian,* to push: mod. senses prob. < cognate Scand., as in Dan. *putte,* Sw. dial. *putta,* to put away, push, akin to OE. *pyttan,* to sting, goad] 1. *a)* to drive or send by a blow, shot, or thrust [to *put* a bullet in a target] *b)* to propel with an overhand thrust from the shoulder [to *put* the shot] 2. *a)* to make do something [to *put* a dog through its tricks] *b)* to impel; force [*put* to flight] 3. to cause to be in a certain position or place; place; set [*put*

the box here/ **4.** *a)* to cause to be in a specified condition, situation, relation, etc. *[put* her at ease/ *b)* to make undergo; subject *[put* it to a trial/ **5.** to impose *[put* a tax on luxuries/ **6.** *a)* to bring to bear (*on*); apply (*to*) *[to put* one's mind on one's work/ *b)* to bring in or add; introduce; inject *[to put* life into a party/ *c)* to bring about; effect *[to put* a stop to cheating/ **7.** to attribute; assign; ascribe *[to put* the blame where it belongs/ **8.** to express; state *[put* it in plain language/ **9.** to translate **10.** to present for consideration, decision, etc. *[to put* the question/ **11.** *a)* to estimate as being (with *at)* *[to put* the cost at $50/ *b)* to fix or set (a price, value, etc.) *on* **12.** to adapt or fit (words) to music **13.** *a)* to bet (money) *on* *b)* to invest (money) *in* or *into* —*vi.* to take one's course; move; go (*in*, *out*, *back*, etc.) —*n.* **1.** a cast or thrust; esp., the act of putting the shot **2.** the right or option that one party buys of another to deliver to him a certain amount of a commodity or stock at a specified price, within or at a stipulated time: cf. CALL —*adj.* [Colloq.] immovable; fixed *[stay put]* —**put about 1.** to change a sailing vessel's course from one tack to another by turning into the wind **2.** to move in another direction —**put across** [Colloq.] ☆**1.** to cause to be understood or accepted **2.** to carry out with success **3.** to carry out by trickery —**put ahead** to reset the hands of (a clock) to a later time —**put aside** (or **by**) **1.** to reserve for later use **2.** to give up; discard —**put away 1.** *same as* PUT ASIDE **2.** [Colloq.] to consign to a jail or other institution **3.** [Colloq.] to consume (food or drink) **4.** [Colloq.] to kill (a pet) to prevent suffering —**put back 1.** to replace **2.** to reset the hands of (a clock) to an earlier time ☆**3.** to demote (a pupil) —**put down 1.** *a)* to crush; repress; squelch *b)* to deprive of authority, power, or position; degrade **2.** to write down; record **3.** to attribute (to) **4.** to consider as; classify **5.** to land or make a landing in an aircraft **6.** [Brit. Colloq.] *same as* PUT AWAY (sense 4) ☆**7.** [Slang] to belittle, reject, criticize, or humiliate —**put forth 1.** to grow (leaves, shoots, etc.) **2.** to bring into action; exert **3.** to propose; offer **4.** to bring out; publish; circulate **5.** to set out from port —**put forward** to advance or present (a plan, etc.) —**put in 1.** to come into a port or haven **2.** to enter (a claim, request, etc.) **3.** to interpose; insert **4.** [Colloq.] to spend (time) in a specified manner —**put in for** to request or apply for —**put it on** [Slang] to make a pretentious show; pretend or exaggerate —☆**put it** (or **something**) **over on** [Colloq.] to deceive; trick —☆**put it there!** [Slang] shake hands with me: an expression of agreement, reconciliation, etc. —**put off 1.** to leave until later; postpone; delay **2.** to discard **3.** to evade; divert **4.** to perturb; upset; distress —**put on 1.** to clothe, adorn, or cover oneself with **2.** to take on; add *[to put on* a few pounds/ **3.** to assume or pretend **4.** to apply (a brake, etc.) **5.** to stage (a play) ☆**6.** [Slang] to fool (someone) by playing on his credulity; hoax —☆**put on to** to inform (someone) about (something) —**put out 1.** to expel; dismiss **2.** to extinguish (a fire or light) ☆**3.** to spend (money) **4.** to disconcert; confuse **5.** to distress; ruffle; vex **6.** to inconvenience **7.** *a)* to publish *b)* to produce and distribute *c)* to supply, offer, or display ☆**8.** Baseball to cause (a batter or runner) to be out by a fielding play —**put over 1.** to postpone; delay ☆**2.** [Colloq.] *same as* PUT ACROSS —**put through** ☆**1.** to perform successfully; carry out **2.** to cause to do or undergo **3.** to connect (someone) by telephone with someone else —**put to it** to place in a difficult situation; press hard —**put up 1.** to offer, as for consideration, decision, auction, etc. **2.** to offer as a candidate **3.** *a)* to preserve or can (fruits, vegetables, etc.) *b)* to pack or prepare (a lunch, etc.) for carrying **4.** to erect; build **5.** to lodge, or provide lodgings for **6.** ☆*a)* to advance, provide, or stake (money) *b)* [Slang] to do or produce what is needed or wanted **7.** to arrange (the hair) with curlers, bobby pins, etc. **8.** to carry on *[to put up* a struggle/ **9.** [Colloq.] to incite (a person) *to* some action **10.** to sheathe (one's sword) —**put upon** to impose on; victimize —**put up with** to bear or suffer patiently; tolerate

pu·ta·men (pyōō tā′mən) *n., pl.* **-tam′i·na** (-tam′i nə) [ModL. < L., that which falls off in pruning, waste < *putare*, to prune, cleanse: see PURE] the hard stone, or endocarp, of certain fruits, as of the peach and the plum, or the shell of a nut

pu·ta·tive (pyōō′tə tiv) *adj.* [ME. *putative* < L. *putativus* < *putare*, to suppose, reckon (orig., to cleanse, set in order, hence compute, consider: see PURE)] generally considered or deemed such; reputed *[a putative* ancestor/ —**pu′ta·tive·ly** *adv.*

☆**put-down** (poot′doun′) *n.* [Slang] a belittling remark or crushing retort

put·log (poot′lôg′, -läg′) *n.* [altered (? after LOG¹) < earlier *putlock* < ? PUT + LOCK¹] any of the horizontal timbers which support the floor of a scaffolding

Put·nam (put′nəm), **Israel** 1718–90; Am. general in the Revolutionary War

put-on (poot′än′) *adj.* assumed or feigned *[a put-on* smile/ —*n.* [Slang] **1.** the act of fooling or hoaxing someone by playing on his credulity **2.** something, as a novel or play, intended as an elaborate hoax or practical joke on the reader or audience

☆**put·out** (-out′) *n.* Baseball a play in which the batter or runner is retired, or put out

☆**put-put** (put′put′) *n., vi.* **put′-put′ted**, **put′-put′ting** *same as* PUTT-PUTT

pu·tre·fac·tion (pyōō′trə fak′shən) *n.* [ME. *putrefaccion* < LL. *putrefactio* < L. *putrefacere:* see PUTREFY] the decomposition of organic matter by bacteria, fungi, and oxidation, resulting in the formation of foul-smelling products; a rotting —**pu′tre·fac′tive** *adj.*

pu·tre·fy (pyōō′trə fi′) *vt., vi.* **-fied′**, **-fy′ing** [ME. *putrifien* < L. *putrefacere* < *putris*, PUTRID + *facere*, to make, DO¹] to make or become putrid or rotten; decompose —*SYN.* see DECAY —**pu′tre·fi′er** *n.*

pu·tres·cent (pyōō tres′'nt) *adj.* [L. *putrescens*, prp. of *putrescere* < *putrere* < *puter*, *putris*, rotten: for IE. base see PUS] **1.** becoming putrid; putrefying; rotting **2.** of or connected with putrefaction —**pu·tres′cence** *n.*

pu·tres·ci·ble (-ə b'l) *adj.* [LL. *putrescibilis*] liable to become putrid —*n.* a putrescible substance

pu·tres·cine (-ēn, -in) *n.* [< L. *putrescere* (see PUTRESCENT) + -INE⁴] a crystalline ptomaine, $C_4H_{12}N_2$, produced by putrefaction of tissue

pu·trid (pyōō′trid) *adj.* [Fr. *putride* < L. *putridus* < *putrere:* see PUTRESCENT] **1.** decomposed; rotten and foul-smelling **2.** causing, showing, or proceeding from decay **3.** morally corrupt; depraved **4.** [Colloq.] very disagreeable or unpleasant —*SYN.* see STINKING —**pu·trid′i·ty**, **pu′trid·ness** *n.* —**pu′trid·ly** *adv.*

‡**Putsch** (pooch) *n.* [G. < Swiss dial., lit., a push, blow] a sudden political uprising or rebellion

putt (put) *n.* [< PUT, *v.*] Golf a light stroke made on the putting green in an attempt to roll the ball into the hole —*vt., vi.* to hit (the ball) with such a stroke

put·tee (pu tē′, put′ē) *n.* [Hind. *patti*, a bandage < Sans. *pattikā* < *patta*, a strip of cloth] a covering for the lower leg, in the form of a cloth or leather gaiter or a cloth strip wound spirally

put·ter¹ (poot′ər) *n.* a person or thing that puts

putt·er² (put′ər) *n.* Golf **1.** a short, straight-faced club used in putting **2.** a person who putts

put·ter³ (put′ər) *vi.* [var. of POTTER²] to busy oneself or proceed in a trifling, ineffective, or aimless way; dawdle (often with *over*, *along*, *around*, etc.) —*vt.* to dawdle or fritter (*away*)

put·ti·er (put′ē ər) *n.* a person who putties

putt·ing green (put′in) Golf the area of smooth, closely mowed turf in which the hole is sunk

PUTTEES

‡**put·to** (pōōt′tō) *n., pl.* **put′ti** (-tē) [It. < L. *putus*, var. of *pusus*, boy] a figure of a plump, young, male angel or cupid, as in baroque art

☆**putt-putt** (put′put′) *n.* [echoic] **1.** the chugging or popping sounds made by the engine of a motorboat, motorbike, etc. **2.** [Colloq.] any vehicle, engine, etc. that makes such sounds —*vi.* **putt′-putt′ed**, **putt′-putt′ing** to make, move along, or operate with such sounds

put·ty (put′ē) *n.* [Fr. *potée*, calcined tin, brass, lit., potful < *pot*, a POT] **1.** *a)* a soft, plastic mixture of finely powdered chalk and linseed oil, used in fixing glass panes, filling small cracks, etc. *b)* any substance like this in consistency, use, etc. **2.** *same as* PUTTY POWDER **3.** a cement of quicklime and water, mixed with plaster of Paris or sand for use as a finishing coat in plastering —*vt.* **-tied**, **-ty·ing** to cement, fix, cover, or fill with putty

putty knife a kind of spatula for applying putty

putty powder powdered oxide of tin, or of tin and lead, used for polishing glass or metals

☆**put·ty·root** (-rōōt′, -root′) *n.* an American orchid (*Aplectrum hyemale*) with clusters of yellowish-brown flowers, one leaf at the base of the stem, and a sticky substance in its bulbs

Pu·tu·ma·yo (pōō′tōō mä′yō) river in NW S. America, flowing from SW Colombia along the Colombia-Peru border into the Amazon in NW Brazil: c. 1,000 mi.

put-up (poot′up′) *adj.* [< phrase PUT UP] [Colloq.] planned secretly beforehand *[a put-up* job/

Pu·vis de Cha·vannes (pü vē′ də shȧ vȧn′), **Pierre** (pyer) 1824–98; Fr. painter

puz·zle (puz′'l) *vt.* **-zled**, **-zling** [ME. *poselen* (inferred < pp. *poselet*), to bewilder, confuse < ?] to perplex; confuse; bewilder; nonplus —*vi.* **1.** to be perplexed, etc. **2.** to exercise one's mind, as over the solution of a problem —*n.* **1.** the state of being puzzled; bewilderment **2.** a question, problem, etc. that puzzles **3.** a toy or problem for testing cleverness, skill, or ingenuity —**puzzle out** to solve by deep thought or study —**puzzle over** to give deep thought to; concentrate on —**puz′zle·ment** *n.* —**puz′zler** *n.*

SYN.—**puzzle** implies such a baffling quality or such intricacy, as of a problem, situation, etc., that one has great difficulty in understanding or solving it; **perplex**, in addition, implies uncertainty or even worry as to what to think, say, or do; **confuse** implies a mixing up mentally to a greater or lesser degree; **confound** implies such confusion as completely frustrates or greatly astonishes one; **bewilder** implies such utter confusion that the mind is staggered beyond the ability to think clearly; to **nonplus** is to cause such perplexity or confusion that one is utterly incapable

of speaking, acting, or thinking further; **dumbfound** specifically implies as its effect a nonplussed or confounded state in which one is momentarily struck speechless See also MYSTERY[1]

Pvt. *Mil.* Private

PW Prisoner of War

PWA, P.W.A. Public Works Administration

P wave [*p(ressure) wave*] a longitudinal wave that advances by alternate compression and expansion in a solid or fluid medium like a sound wave

PWD, P.W.D. Public Works Department

pwt. pennyweight

PX post exchange

pxt. [L. *pinxit*] he (or she) painted it

py- (pī) *same as* PYO-: used before a vowel

pya (pyä) *n., pl.* **pyas** [Burmese] a fractional monetary unit of Burma, equal to 1/100 of a kyat

pyc·nid·i·um (pik nid′ē əm) *n., pl.* **-i·a** (-ə) [ModL. < Gr. *pyknos*, thick, tight (< IE. base *puk*, to compress, whence Alb. *puth*, (I) kiss, embrace) + dim. suffix *-idion* (L. *-idium*)] a saclike spore case producing asexual spores (*conidia*) on the inside, found in certain ascomycetes and imperfect fungi —**pyc·nid′i·al** *adj.*

pyc·no- (pik′nō) [< Gr. *pyknos*: see prec.] *a combining form meaning* thick; dense [*pycnogonid*]

pyc·no·gon·id (pik′nə gän′id) *n.* [< ModL. *Pycnogonida* < *Pycnogonum*, name of a genus < PYCNO- + Gr. *gony*, KNEE] any of a class (Pycnogonida) of mostly small, saltwater arthropods with very long legs attached to a relatively tiny body

pyc·nom·e·ter (pik näm′ə tər) *n.* [PYCNO- + -METER] a vessel used to measure the specific gravity of liquids or solids

Pyd·na (pid′nə) city in ancient Macedonia, near the Gulf of Salonika: scene of a battle (168 B.C.) of the final Roman defeat of the Macedonians

pye-dog (pī′dôg′, -däg′) *n. same as* PI-DOG

py·e·li·tis (pī′ə līt′əs) *n.* [ModL. < Gr. *pyelos*, basin (akin to *plynein*, to wash: for IE. base see FLOW) + -ITIS] inflammation of a kidney pelvis —**py′e·lit′ic** (-lit′ik) *adj.*

py·e·lo·gram (pī′ə lə gram′) *n.* an X-ray picture taken by pyelography

py·e·log·ra·phy (pī′ə lag′rə fē) *n.* [< Gr. *pyelos*, basin (see PYELITIS) + -GRAPHY] the taking of X-ray pictures of the kidney and ureter after filling them with some radio-opaque solution

py·e·lo·ne·phri·tis (pī′ə lō′nc frīt′əs) *n.* [< Gr. *pyelos* (see prec.) + NEPHRITIS] infection of one or both kidneys usually involving both the pelvis and the functional tissue

py·e·mi·a (pī ē′mē ə) *n.* [ModL.: see PYO- & -EMIA] a form of blood poisoning caused by the presence in the blood of pus-producing microorganisms that are carried to various parts of the body, producing multiple abscesses, fever, chill, etc. —**py·e′mic** *adj.*

py·gid·i·um (pī jid′ē əm) *n., pl.* **-i·a** (-ə) [ModL. < Gr. *pygidion*, dim. of *pygē*, rump < IE. base *pu-*, to swell up, whence L. *pupus*, small child: cf. PUPA] *Zool.* the end division of the body of a trilobite or of certain annelids, crustaceans, or insects

pyg·mae·an, pyg·me·an (pig mē′ən) *adj.* [L. *pygmaeus* + -AN] *same as* PYGMY

Pyg·ma·li·on (pig māl′yən, -mā′lē ən) [L. < Gr. *Pygmaliōn*] Gr. Legend a king of Cyprus, and a sculptor, who fell in love with his statue of a maiden, later brought to life by Aphrodite at his prayer: cf. GALATEA

pyg·moid (pig′moid) *adj.* [PYGM(Y) + -OID] like the Pygmies, esp. in being of small stature

Pyg·my (pig′mē) *n., pl.* **-mies** [ME. *pigmey* < L. *pygmaeus* < Gr. *pygmaios*, of the length of the *pygmē*, forearm and fist] **1.** any of several races of African and Asiatic dwarfish peoples described in ancient history and legend **2.** a person belonging to any of several modern African (*Negrillo*) and Asiatic (*Negrito*) peoples of small stature **3.** [p-] any person, animal, or plant abnormally under-sized; dwarf **4.** [p-] an insignificant person or thing —*adj.* **1.** of the Pygmies **2.** [p-] *a)* very small *b)* insignificant —*SYN.* SCC DWARF

pyg·my·ism (-iz′m) *n.* the condition of being a pygmy

py·ja·mas (pə jam′əz, -jä′məz) *n.pl. Brit. sp.* of PAJAMAS

pyk·nic (pik′nik) *adj.* [< Gr. *pyknos*, compact, solid (see PYCNIDIUM) + -IC] designating or of a constitutional body type of broad, squat, fleshy physique

Pyle (pīl), **Howard** 1853–1911; U.S. illustrator & writer

py·lon (pī′län) *n.* [Gr. *pylōn*, gateway] **1.** a gateway **2.** a truncated pyramid, or two of these, serving as a gateway to an Egyptian temple **3.** any slender, towering structure flanking an entranceway, supporting electric lines, marking a course for aircraft, etc.

py·lo·rec·to·my (pī′lə rek′tə mē) *n., pl.* **-mies** [PYLOR(US) + -ECTOMY] the surgical removal of the pylorus

py·lo·rus (pī lôr′əs, pə-) *n., pl.* **-ri** (-ī) [LL. < Gr. *pylōros*, gatekeeper < *pylē*, a gate + *ouros*, watchman] the opening, surrounded by muscular tissue, from the stomach into the duodenum, the first part of the small intestine: see PANCREAS, illus. —**py·lor′ic** *adj.*

Pym (pim), **John** 1583?–1643; Eng. parliamentary leader

py·o- (pī′ō, -ə) [< Gr. *pyon*, PUS] *a combining form meaning:* **1.** pus [*pyogenesis*] **2.** suppurative [*pyosis*]

py·o·der·ma (pī′ə dur′mə) *n.* [prec. + DERMA[1]] any bacterial skin infection producing pus —**py′o·der′mic** *adj.*

py·o·gen·e·sis (-jen′ə sis) *n.* [PYO- + -GENESIS] *Med.* the formation of pus; pyosis —**py′o·gen′ic** *adj.*

py·oid (pī′oid) *adj.* [PY- + -OID] of or like pus

Pyong·yang (pyuŋ′yäŋ′) capital of North Korea, in the W part: pop. 1,225,000

py·or·rhe·a, py·or·rhoe·a (pī′ə rē′ə) *n.* [ModL.: see PYO- & -RRHEA] a discharge of pus; specif., *short for* PYORRHEA ALVEOLARIS —**py′or·rhe′al, py′or·rhoe′al** *adj.*

pyorrhea al·ve·o·la·ris (al vē′ə ler′is) an infection of the gums and tooth sockets, characterized by the formation of pus and, usually, by loosening of the teeth

py·o·sis (pī ō′sis) *n.* [ModL. < Gr. *pyōsis*: see PYO- & -OSIS] the formation or discharge of pus; suppuration

pyr- *same as* PYRO-: used before a vowel

pyr·a·can·tha (pir′ə kan′thə, pī′rə-) *n.* [ModL. < Gr. *pyrakantha* < *pyr*, FIRE + *akantha*, thorn (see ACANTHO-)] *same as* FIRETHORN

py·ral·i·did (pī ral′ə did, pə-) *adj.* [< ModL. *Pyralididae*, name of the family < L. *pyralis* (gen. *pyralidis*), kind of flying insect < Gr. *pyralis* < *pyr*, FIRE: once thought to live in fire] of a large family (Pyralididae) of small moths with narrow, triangular forewings, broader hind wings, and long legs —*n.* a moth of this family Also **pyr·a·lid** (pir′ə lid)

pyr·a·mid (pir′ə mid) *n.* [L. *pyramis* (gen. *pyramidis*) < Gr. *pyramis*, a pyramid: ME. had *piramis* < L.] **1.** any huge structure with a square base and four sloping, triangular sides meeting at the top, as those built by the ancient Egyptians for royal tombs **2.** an object, formation, or structure shaped like or suggesting a pyramid **3.** a crystal form in which the sloping faces intersect the vertical and lateral axes **4.** *Geom.* a solid figure having a polygonal base, the sides of which form the bases of triangular surfaces meeting at a common vertex —*vi., vt.* **1.** to build up, mass, or heap in the form of a pyramid ☆**2.** to engage in (a series of buying or selling operations) during an upward or downward trend in the stock market, working on margin with the profits made in the transactions —**the (Great) Pyramids** the three large pyramids at Gîza, Egypt: the largest is the Pyramid of Khufu —**py·ram·i·dal** (pi ram′ə d′l) *adj.* —**py·ram′i·dal·ly** *adv.* —**pyr′a·mid′ic, pyr′a·mid′i·cal** *adj.*

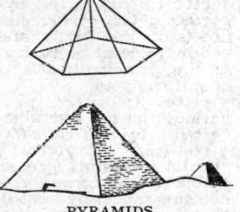

PYRAMIDS

Pyr·a·mus and This·be (pir′ə məs 'n thiz′bē) Babylonian lovers in ancient mythology: Pyramus, mistakenly thinking Thisbe has been killed by a lioness, kills himself, and Thisbe, finding his body, kills herself

py·ran (pī′ran) *n.* [PYR(ONE) + -AN] any of a group of closed-chain compounds containing a ring, C_5H_6O, of one oxygen atom and five carbon atoms

py·rar·gy·rite (pī rär′jə rīt′) *n.* [G. *pyrargyrit* < Gr. *pyr*, a FIRE + *argyros*, silver + G. *-it*, -ITE[1]] a lustrous, dark-red or black mineral, Ag_3SbS_3, a sulfide of silver and antimony

pyre (pīr) *n.* [L. *pyra* < Gr. *pyra* < *pyr*, a FIRE] a pile, esp. of wood, on which a dead body is burned in a funeral rite

py·rene[1] (pī′rēn) *n.* [ModL. *pyrena* < Gr. *pyrēn*, stone of a fruit] the stone of an apple, pear, or other drupe that contains several seeds

py·rene[2] (pī′rēn) *n.* [PYR- + -ENE] a colorless hydrocarbon, $C_{16}H_{10}$, obtained from coal tar: its structure consists of the fusion of four benzene rings

Pyr·e·nees (pir′ə nēz′) mountain range along the border between France & Spain: c. 300 mi. long: highest peak, Pico de Aneto —**Pyr′e·ne′an** (-nē′ən) *adj.*

py·re·noid (pī rē′noid) *n.* [< Gr. *pyrēn* (gen. *pyrēnos*), stone of a fruit (for IE. base see FURZE) + -OID] *Bot.* a small structure within a chloroplast, as in some algae, functioning as a center for starch production

py·re·thrin (pī rē′thrin) *n.* [< ff. + -IN[1]] either of two liquid esters, $C_{21}H_{28}O_3$ or $C_{22}H_{28}O_5$, derived from chrysanthemums: the active ingredients of pyrethrum

py·re·thrum (-thrəm) *n.* [ModL. < L. < Gr. *pyrethron*, feverfew < *pyr*, a FIRE] **1.** a perennial plant (*Chrysanthemum coccineum*) of the composite family, widely grown for the white, pink, red, or purple flower heads **2.** an insecticide made from the dried flower heads of several old-world chrysanthemums, esp. a species (*Chrysanthemum cinerariaefolium*) now grown extensively in the U.S.

py·ret·ic (pī ret′ik) *adj.* [ModL. *pyreticus* < Gr. *pyretos*, burning heat, fever < *pyr*, a FIRE] of, causing, or characterized by fever

☆**Py·rex** (pī′reks) [arbitrary coinage < PIE[1] + -*r*- + -*ex*, arbitrary suffix of manufactured products] *a trademark for* a heat-resistant glassware for cooking, etc.

---

fat, āpe, cär; ten, ēve; is, bīte; gō, hôrn, tōol, look; oil, out; up, fur; get; joy; yet; chin; she; thin, then; zh, leisure; ŋ, ring; ə for *a* in *ago*, *e* in *agent*, *i* in *sanity*, *o* in *comply*, *u* in *focus*; ' as in *able* (ā′b'l); ë, Fr. bàl; ë, Fr. coeur; ö, Fr. feu; Fr. mon; ô, Fr. coq; ü, Fr. duc; r, Fr. cri; H, G. ich; kh, G. doch. See inside front cover. ☆Americanism; ‡foreign; *hypothetical; <derived from

py·rex·i·a (pī rek′sē ə) *n*. [ModL. < Gr. *pyrexis*, feverishness < *pyressein*, to be feverish < *pyretos*: see PYRETIC] *same as* FEVER —**py·rex′i·al**, **py·rex′ic** *adj.*

pyr·he·li·om·e·ter (pir hē′lē ăm′ə tər, pir-) *n*. [PYR- + HELIO- + -METER] an instrument for measuring the amount of energy given off by the sun

pyr·i·dine (pir′ə dēn′, -din) *n*. [PYR- + -ID + -INE⁴] a flammable, colorless or pale-yellow liquid base, C_5H_5N, having a sharp, penetrating odor: it is produced in the distillation of coal tar or bone oil and is used in the synthesis of vitamins and drugs, as a solvent, etc.

pyr·i·dox·al (pir′ə däk′səl) *n*. [see PYRIDOXINE] an aldehyde, $C_8H_9O_3N$, closely related to vitamin B₆ and exhibiting vitamin activity

pyr·i·dox·a·mine (-sə mēn′) *n*. [< ff. + AMINE] a crystalline material, $C_8H_{12}O_2N_2$, exhibiting vitamin B₆ activity

pyr·i·dox·ine (-sēn, -sin) *n*. [PYRID(INE) + OX(Y)¹· + -INE⁴] a complex pyridine, $C_8H_{11}O_3N$, one of the vitamins of the B₆ group, found in various foods and prepared synthetically, usually as the hydrochloride: known to prevent nutritional dermatitis in rats

pyr·i·form (pir′ə fôrm′) *adj*. [ModL. *pyriformis* < ML. *pyrum*, for L. *pirum*, pear: see -FORM] pear-shaped

py·rim·i·dine (pi rim′ə dēn′, pī-; pir′im-) *n*. [G. *pyrimidin* < *pyridin* (cf. PYRIDINE)] 1. a colorless, liquid, crystalline organic compound, $C_4H_4N_2$, the fundamental form of a group of bases, some of which are constituents of nucleic acid 2. any of several basic substances produced by the decomposition of nucleoproteins and having a pyrimidine-type molecule

py·rite (pī′rīt) *n*., *pl*. **py·ri·tes** (pə rīt′ēz, pī-; pī′rīts) [L. *pyrites* < Gr. *pyritēs*, flint or millstone < *pyritēs* (*lithos*), fire (stone) < *pyr*, a FIRE] iron sulfide, FeS_2, a lustrous, yellow mineral occurring abundantly as a native ore and serving principally as a source of sulfur in the manufacture of sulfuric acid

py·ri·tes (pə rīt′ēz, pī-; pī′rīts) *n*. [see prec.] any of various native metallic sulfides, as pyrite —**py·rit′ic** (-rit′ik), **py·rit′i·cal** *adj.*

py·ro- (pī′rō, -rə; *occas*. pir′ə) [< Gr. *pyr* (gen. *pyros*), a FIRE] *a combining form meaning*: 1. fire, heat [*pyromania*, *pyrometer*] 2. *Chem*. *a*) a substance derived (from a specified substance) by or as if by the action of heat [*pyrogallol*] *b*) an inorganic acid derived from an ortho acid by the elimination of one molecule of water from two molecules of the acid [*pyrophosphoric* acid] 3. *Geol*. a formation due to the action of heat [*pyroxenite*]

py·ro·cat·e·chol (pī′rə kat′ə chôl′, -chōl′, -kôl′, -kōl′) *n*. [PYRO- + CATECH(U) + -OL¹] a white, crystalline phenol, $C_6H_4(OH)_2$, occurring naturally in plants and now usually produced synthetically: used as an antiseptic, as a photographic developer, etc.: also **py′ro·cat′e·chin** (-chin, -kin)

☆**Py·ro·cer·am** (pī′rō sə ram′) [PYRO- + CERAM(IC)] *a trademark for* a heavy, glasslike, ceramic material highly resistant to heat and breakage: used for cooking utensils, rocket nose cones, etc.

py·ro·chem·i·cal (pī′rə kem′i k'l) *adj*. of chemical action at high temperatures —**py′ro·chem′i·cal·ly** *adv.*

py·ro·clas·tic (-klas′tik) *adj*. [PYRO- + CLASTIC] made up of rock material broken into fragments through volcanic or igneous action

py·ro·con·den·sa·tion (-kän′dən sā′shən) *n*. a condensation of molecules induced by strong heat

py·ro·con·duc·tiv·i·ty (-kän′duk tiv′ə tē) *n*. conductivity effected in certain electric insulators when they are subjected to high temperatures

py·ro·crys·tal·line (-kris′tə lin) *adj*. crystallized from molten rock material

py·ro·e·lec·tric (-i lek′trik) *adj*. of or showing pyroelectricity —*n*. a pyroelectric substance

py·ro·e·lec·tric·i·ty (-i lek′tris′ə tē) *n*. the development of electric dipoles in certain crystalline materials as a result of temperature changes

py·ro·gal·late (-gal′āt) *n*. a salt or ether of pyrogallol

py·ro·gal·lic acid (-gal′ik) *same as* PYROGALLOL

py·ro·gal·lol (-gal′ôl, -ōl) *n*. [PYRO- + GALL(IC) + -OL¹] a poisonous, white, crystalline phenol, $C_6H_3(OH)_3$, produced by heating gallic acid: used in medicine, as a developer in photography, etc.

py·ro·gen (pī′rə jən) *n*. [PYRO- + -GEN] *Med*. a substance that produces fever

py·ro·gen·ic (pī′rə jen′ik) *adj*. [PYRO- + -GENIC] 1. producing, or produced by, heat or fever 2. *Geol*. *same as* IGNEOUS Also **py·rog·e·nous** (pī rāj′ə nəs)

py·rog·nos·tics (pī′rāg nās′tiks) *n.pl*. [< PYRO- + Gr. *gnostikos*, knowing < *gnōsis*, knowledge: see GNOSIS) + -ICS] the characteristics of a mineral, including fusibility, flame coloration, etc., as determined by a blowpipe

py·rog·ra·phy (pī rāg′rə fē) *n*. [PYRO- + -GRAPHY] 1. the art or process of burning designs on wood or leather by the use of heated tools 2. a design so made —**py·rog′ra·pher** *n*. —**py·ro·graph·ic** (pī′rə graf′ik) *adj.*

py·ro·lig·ne·ous (pī′rə lig′nē əs) *adj*. [Fr. *pyroligneux* < *pyro-* + L. *lignum*, wood) produced by the destructive distillation of wood

pyroligneous acid a reddish-brown liquid obtained by the dry distillation of wood and containing chiefly acetic acid, methanol, acetone, furfural, and various tars and oils

py·ro·lu·site (-lōō′sīt) *n*. [G. *pyrolusit* < Gr. *pyr*, FIRE +

lousis, a washing (< *louein*, to wash) + *-it*, -ITE¹: used, when heated, to remove color from glass] native manganese dioxide, MnO_2, a gray or black, lustrous mineral: used as a source of manganese, in glassmaking, etc.

py·rol·y·sis (pī räl′ə sis) *n*. [ModL.: see PYRO- & -LYSIS] chemical decomposition of a substance by heat —**py·ro·lyt·ic** (pī′rə lit′ik) *adj*. —**py·ro·lyt′i·cal·ly** *adv.*

py·ro·mag·net·ic (pī′rō mag net′ik) *adj*. *same as* THERMOMAGNETIC

py·ro·man·cy (pī′rə man′sē) *n*. [ME. *piromance* < MFr. < LL. *pyromantia*: see PYRO- & -MANCY] the practice of claiming to foretell the future by interpreting flames

py·ro·ma·ni·a (pī′rə mā′nē ə, -mān′yə) *n*. [ModL.: see PYRO- & -MANIA] a persistent compulsion to start destructive fires —**py′ro·ma′ni·ac′** (-nē ak′) *n.*, *adj*. —**py′ro·ma·ni′a·cal** (-mə nī′ə k'l) *adj.*

py·ro·met·al·lur·gy (-met′'l ur′jē) *n*. metallurgy using high temperatures, as in roasting, smelting, etc., for the extraction of metals from their ores

py·rom·e·ter (pī räm′ə tər) *n*. [PYRO- + -METER] an instrument with which unusually high temperatures, beyond the range of ordinary thermometers, are measured, as by the change of electric current —**py·ro·met·ric** (pī′rə met′rik) *adj*. —**py′ro·met′ri·cal·ly** *adv*. —**py·rom′e·try** (-trē) *n.*

py·ro·mor·phite (pī′rə môr′fīt) *n*. [G. *pyromorphit*: see PYRO- & -MORPH & -ITE¹] a lead chloride and phosphate, $Pb_5(PO_4)_3Cl$, occurring frequently in lead deposits in any of several colors

py·rone (pī′rōn) *n*. [G. *pyron*: see PYRO- & -ONE] 1. either of two isomeric, unsaturated, closed-chain compounds, $C_5H_4O_2$, from which several yellow dyes are derived 2. any of a class of compounds derived from pyrone

py·ro·nine (pī′rə nēn′, -nin) *n*. [G. *pyronin* < *pyro-*, PYRO- + *-on*, -ONE + *-in*, -INE⁴] any of a small class of dyes, used esp. as histologic stains

py·rope (pī′rōp) *n*. [ME. *pirope* < MFr. < L. *pyropus*, red bronze < Gr. *pyrōpus*, lit., fiery-eyed < *pyr*, FIRE + *ōps*, EYE] a variety of deep-red to black garnet, containing magnesium and aluminum, often used as a gem

py·ro·pho·bi·a (pī′rə fō′bē ə) *n*. [ModL.: see PYRO- & -PHOBIA] an excessive or irrational fear of fire

py·ro·phor·ic (-fôr′ik, -fär′ik) *adj*. [< ModL. *pyrophorus* (< Gr. *pyrophoros* < *pyr*, FIRE + *pherein*, to BEAR¹) + -IC] capable of igniting spontaneously when exposed to air, as certain finely divided metals

py·ro·phos·phate (-fäs′fāt) *n*. a salt or ester of pyrophosphoric acid

py·ro·phos·phor·ic acid (-fäs fôr′ik, -fär′-) [PYRO- + PHOSPHORIC] a viscous liquid acid, $H_4P_2O_7$, which crystallizes when left standing at ordinary temperatures and is easily converted to orthophosphoric acid upon dilution with water

py·ro·pho·tom·e·ter (-fō täm′ə tər) *n*. [PYRO- + PHOTOMETER] an optical instrument for measuring extremely high temperatures

py·ro·phyl·lite (-fil′īt) *n*. [G. *pyrophyllit*: see PYRO- & PHYLL- & -ITE¹] a hydrous aluminum silicate, $Al_2Si_4O_{10}$·(OH)₂, like talc in structure and color, used for polishing rice, as a filler for slate pencils, etc.

py·ro·sis (pī rō′sis) *n*. [ModL. < Gr. *pyrōsis*, a burning < *pyroun*, to burn < *pyr*, a FIRE] a condition like heartburn, accompanied by the belching of an acrid fluid

py·ro·stat (pī′rə stat′) *n*. [PYRO- + -STAT] a thermostat, esp. one for high temperatures

py·ro·sul·fate (pī′rə sul′fāt) *n*. a salt of pyrosulfuric acid

py·ro·sul·fu·ric acid (-sul fyoor′ik) [PYRO- + SULFURIC] a strong, crystalline acid, $H_2S_2O_7$, prepared commercially as a heavy, oily, fuming liquid: used in making explosives and dyes, as a sulfating agent, etc.

py·ro·tech·nic (-tek′nik) *adj*. [Fr. *pyrotechnique* < Gr. *pyr*, FIRE + *technē*, art] 1. of fireworks 2. designating or of devices or materials that activate propellants, safety systems, signals, etc. in spacecraft, by igniting or exploding on command 3. brilliant; dazzling [*pyrotechnic* wit] Also **py′ro·tech′ni·cal** —**py′ro·tech′ni·cal·ly** *adv.*

py·ro·tech·nics (-niks) *n.pl*. [see prec.] 1. [*with sing. v.*] the art of making and using fireworks: also **py′ro·tech′ny** (-nē) 2. *a*) a display of fireworks *b*) fireworks; esp., rockets, flares, smoke bombs, etc., as for signaling *c*) pyrotechnic devices in spacecraft 3. a dazzling display, as of eloquence, wit, virtuosity, etc. —**py′ro·tech′nist** *n.*

py·rox·ene (pī räk′sēn, pī′räk sēn′) *n*. [Fr. *pyroxène* < Gr. *pyr*, FIRE + *xenos*, a stranger: from its being foreign to igneous rocks] any of a group of monoclinic or orthorhombic ferromagnesian minerals that do not contain the hydroxyl radical: they are common in igneous, and some metamorphic, rocks —**py·rox·en′ic** (-sen′ik, -sē′nik) *adj.*

py·rox·e·nite (pī räk′sə nīt′) *n*. a dark-colored, granular, igneous rock composed mainly of pyroxene

py·rox·y·lin, py·rox·y·line (-sə lin) *n*. [Fr. *pyroxyline* < Gr. *pyr*, FIRE + *xylon*, wood] nitrocellulose, esp. in less highly nitrated and explosive forms than guncotton, used in the manufacture of paints, lacquers, collodion, celluloid, etc.

Pyr·rha (pir′ə) [L. < Gr. *Pyrrha*] *Gr. Myth*. a survivor of a great deluge: see DEUCALION

pyr·rhic¹ (pir′ik) *n*. [L. *pyrrhica* < Gr. *pyrrhichē*, war dance] a war dance of the ancient Greeks

pyr·rhic[2] (pir′ik) *n.* [L. *pyrrhichius* < Gr. *pyrrhichios* (*pous*), pyrrhic (foot)] a metrical foot of two short or unstressed syllables —*adj.* of or composed of pyrrhics

Pyr·rhic victory (pir′ik) [Gr. *Pyrrhikos*] a too costly victory: in reference to either of two victories of Pyrrhus, king of Epirus, over the Romans in 280 and 279 B.C., in which his losses were extremely heavy

Pyr·rho·nism (pir′ə niz'm) *n.* 1. the doctrine taught by Pyrrho (365?-275? B.C.), a Gr. skeptic, that all knowledge, including the testimony of the senses, is uncertain 2. extreme skepticism —**Pyr′rho·nist** *n.*

pyr·rho·tite (pir′ə tīt′) *n.* [< Gr. *pyrrhotēs*, redness (< *pyrrhos*, flame-colored < *pyr*, FIRE) + -ITE[1]] any of several magnetic, bronze-colored, lustrous native sulfides of iron, often containing small amounts of copper, cobalt, and nickel

☆**pyr·rhu·lox·i·a** (pir′ə läk′sē ə) *n.* [ModL. < *Pyrrhula*, name of a genus (< Gr. *pyrrhoulas*, a red-colored bird < *pyrrhos*, red < *pyr*, FIRE) + *Loxia*, the crossbill genus < Gr. *loxos*, crosswise < -IA] a brownish-gray and red bird (*Pyrrhuloxia sinuata*) having a crest and small, stubby bill, found in the SW U.S. and N Mexico, closely related to the cardinal

Pyr·rhus (pir′əs) 1. 318?-272 B.C.; king of Epirus (305?-272 B.C.) 2. *Gr. Myth.* Achilles' son

pyr·role (pir′ōl, pi rōl′) *n.* [G. *pyrrol* < Gr. *pyrros*, fiery (< *pyr*, FIRE) + -ol, -OLE] a colorless, pungent, slightly basic liquid, C₄H₅N, found in bile pigments, chlorophyll, and hematin, and obtained from coal tar, bone oil, etc. by distillation

py·ru·vate (pī rōō′vāt) *n.* a salt or ester of pyruvic acid

py·ru·vic acid (pī rōō′vik) [< PYR- + L. *uva*, grape + -IC] a colorless, liquid or crystalline organic acid, CH₃COCOOH, that is an intermediate in sugar and carbohydrate metabolism in the cell and in the generation of energy during muscle contraction

Py·thag·o·ras (pi thag′ər əs) 6th cent. B.C.; Gr. philosopher & mathematician, born on Samos —**Py·thag′o·re′an** (-ə rē′ən) *adj., n.*

Py·thag·o·re·an·ism (pi thag′ə rē′ən iz'm) *n.* the philosophy of Pythagoras, the main tenets of which were the transmigration of the soul and the belief in numbers as the ultimate elements of the universe

Pyth·i·a (pith′ē ə) the high priestess of the oracle of Apollo at Delphi in ancient Greece —**Pyth′ic** *adj.*

Pyth·i·ad (pith′ē ad′, -əd) *n.* [< Gr. *Pythios*: see ff.] the period of four years from one celebration of the Pythian games to the next

Pyth·i·an (-ən) *adj.* [< L. *Pythius* < Gr. *Pythios*, of *Pythō*, older name for Delphi and its environs] 1. of Apollo as patron of Delphi and the oracle located there 2. designating or of the games held at Delphi every four years by the ancient Greeks in honor of Apollo

Pythias *see* DAMON AND PYTHIAS

Py·thon (pī′thän, -thən) [L. < Gr. *Pythōn* < *Pythō*: see PYTHIAN] *Gr. Myth.* an enormous serpent that lurked in the cave of Mount Parnassus and was slain by Apollo —*n.* [p-] 1. any of a genus (*Python*) of very large, nonpoisonous snakes of Asia, Africa, and Australia, that crush their prey to death 2. popularly, any large snake that crushes its prey

py·tho·ness (pī′thə nis) *n.* [ME. *phitonesse* < MFr. *phitonise* < ML. *phytonissa* < LL.(Ec.) *pythonissa* < Gr. *Pythōn* < *Pythō*: see PYTHIAN] 1. a priestess of Apollo at Delphi 2. any woman soothsayer; prophetess

py·thon·ic[1] (pī thän′ik) *adj.* [LL.(Ec.) *pythonicus*, prophetic; ult. < Gr. *Pythōn*: see PYTHON] of or like an oracle; oracular; prophetic

py·thon·ic[2] (pī thän′ik) *adj.* of or like a python

py·u·ri·a (pī yoor′ē ə) *n.* [ModL.: see PY- & -URIA] the presence of pus in the urine

pyx (piks) *n.* [ME. *pixe* < L. *pyxis* < Gr. *pyxis*, a box < *pyxos*, the box tree] 1. *a)* the container in which the consecrated wafer of the Eucharist is kept *b)* a small container for carrying the Eucharist to the sick 2. a box in a mint, in which specimen coins are placed until the annual test for purity and weight

pyx·id·i·um (pik sid′ē əm) *n., pl.* -i·a (-ə) [ModL. < Gr. *pyxidion*, dim. of *pyxis*: see prec.] *same as* PYXIS

☆**pyx·ie** (pik′sē) *n.* [contr. < the genus name] a creeping evergreen plant (*Pyxidanthera barbulata*) with small, leathery leaves and white, star-shaped flowers, native to the Atlantic coastal plain of the U.S.

Pyx·is (pik′sis) [ModL., short for *Pyxis nautica*, mariner's compass < L. *pyxis*: see PYX] a S constellation, formerly part of Argo

pyx·is (pik′sis) *n., pl.* **pyx′i·des′** (-sə dēz′) [ME. < L.: see PYX] 1. a vase with a cover, used by the ancient Greeks and Romans 2. a small box or case 3. *Bot.* a dehiscent, dry fruit whose upper portion splits off as a lid

PYXIS (of hyoscyamus)

Q

Q, q (kyōō) *n., pl.* **Q's, q's** 1. the 17th letter of the English alphabet: via Latin from the early Greek *koppa*, a borrowing from the Phoenician 2. the sound of *Q* or *q*: in English words not borrowed from Arabic, *q* is always followed by *u*, and is pronounced (*kw*), as in *queen* (kwēn), or occasionally (*k*), as in *conquer* (kän′kər) 3. a type or impression for *Q* or *q* 4. *a symbol for* the 17th in a sequence or group (or the 16th if *J* is omitted) —*adj.* 1. of *Q* or *q* 2. 17th (or 16th if *J* is omitted) in a sequence or group

Q *see* Sir Arthur QUILLER-COUCH

Q 1. *Chess* queen 2. [*q*(*uality factor*)] *Electronics* the ratio of energy stored to energy lost in a coil or resonant circuit: also called **Q factor**

Q. 1. Quebec 2. Queen 3. Question

q. 1. [L. *quadrans*] farthing 2. quart 3. quarter 4. quarterly 5. quarto 6. quasi 7. queen 8. query 9. question 10. quetzal 11. quintal 12. quire

Qa·tar (kä′tär) a Persian Gulf State on a peninsula of E Arabia: 8,500 sq. mi.; pop. 75,000

QB *Chess* queen's bishop

qb. *Football* quarterback

Q.B. Queen's Bench

Q.C. Queen's Counsel

q.e. [L. *quod est*] which is

Q.E.D. [L. *quod erat demonstrandum*] which was to be proved

Q.E.F. [L. *quod erat faciendum*] which was to be done

Q.F. quick-firing

Q fever [< Q(UERY): so named because of many unanswered questions about the disease when first identified] a mild illness characterized by fever, headache, muscular pains, and pneumonia, transmitted by contact or ticks, and caused by a rickettsia (*Coxiella burnetii*)

q.i.d. [L. *quater in die*] four times a day

qin·tar (kin tär′) *n.* [Alb., ult. < L. *centenarius*, relating to a hundred: see CENTENARY] a fractional monetary unit of Albania, equal to 1/100 lek

Qishm (kish′m) island of SE Iran, in the Strait of Hormuz: 516 sq. mi.

QKt *Chess* queen's knight

ql. quintal

QM, Q.M. Quartermaster

QMC, Q.M.C. Quartermaster Corps

QMG, Q.M.G. Quartermaster General

qoph (kōf) *n. same as* KOPH

Qo·ran (kō ran′, -rän′; kō-) *n. same as* KORAN

Q.P., q.pl. [L. *quantum placet*] as much as you please

Qq quartos

qq. questions

qq.v. [L. *quae vide*] which (words, etc.) see

QR *Chess* queen's rook

qr. *pl.* **qrs.** 1. [L. *quadrans*] farthing 2. quarter 3. quire

q.s. 1. [L. *quantum sufficit*] as much as will suffice; enough 2. quarter section (of land)

qt. 1. quantity 2. quart(s)

Q.T., q.t. [Slang] quiet: usually in **on the Q.T.** (or q.t.) in secret

qto. quarto

qu. 1. quart 2. quarter 3. quarterly 4. queen 5. query 6. question

qua (kwā, kwä) *adv.* [L., abl. sing. fem. of *qui*, WHO] in the function, character, or capacity of; as [the President *qua* Commander in Chief]

quack[1] (kwak) *vi.* [echoic] to utter the characteristic sound or cry of a duck, or a sound like it —*n.* the sound made by a duck, or any sound like it

quack[2] (kwak) *n.* [short for QUACKSALVER] 1. an untrained

fat, āpe, cär; ten, ēven; is, bīte; gō, hôrn, tōōl, look; oil, out; up, fʉr; get; joy; yet; chin, she; thin, then; zh, leisure; ŋ, ring; ə for *a* in *ago*, *e* in *agent*, *i* in *sanity*, *o* in *comply*, *u* in *focus*; ' as in *able* (ā′b'l); Fr. bal; ë, Fr. coeur; ö, Fr. feu; Fr. moɲ; ô, Fr. coq; ü, Fr. duc; ɼ, Fr. cri; H, G. ich; kh, G. doch. See inside front cover. ☆ Americanism; ‡foreign; *hypothetical; <derived from

person who practices medicine fraudulently **2.** any person who pretends to have knowledge or skill that he does not have in a particular field; charlatan —*adj.* **1.** characterized by pretentious claims with little or no foundation **2.** dishonestly claiming to effect a cure —*vi.* to engage in quackery

SYN.—**quack** and **charlatan** both apply to a person who unscrupulously pretends to knowledge or skill he does not possess, but **quack** almost always is used of a fraudulent or incompetent practitioner of medicine; **mountebank**, in modern use, applies to a person who resorts to cheap and degrading methods in his work, etc.; **impostor** applies especially to a person who fraudulently impersonates another and, more generally, to anyone who pretends to be what he is not; **faker** is a colloquial term for a person who falsely represents himself as being (in character, work, etc.) what he is not

quack·er·y (-ər ē) *n.* the claims or methods of a quack

☆**quack grass** [var. of QUICK GRASS] *see* COUCH GRASS

quack·ish (-ish) *adj.* **1.** like or characteristic of a quack **2.** boastfully pretentious —**quack′ish·ly** *adv.*

quack·sal·ver (-sal′vər) *n.* [MDu. (Du. *kwaksalver*) < *quacken*, to quack, brag, boast + *zalf*, salve] [Now Rare] a quack; charlatan

quad[1] (kwäd) *n. clipped form of:* **1.** QUADRANGLE (of a college) **2.** QUADRUPLET

quad[2] (kwäd) *n.* [< QUADRAT)] *Printing* a piece of type metal lower than the face of the type, used for spacing, to fill blank lines, etc. —*vt.* **quad′ded, quad′ding** *Printing* to fill out (a line) with quads

quad[3] (kwäd) *n.* [Chiefly Brit. Slang] *same as* QUOD

quad. **1.** quadrangle **2.** quadrant **3.** quadruplicate

quadr- *same as* QUADRI-: used before a vowel

quad·ra·ge·nar·i·an (kwäd′rə ji ner′ē ən) *adj.* [L. *quadragenarius* < *quadrageni*, forty each < *quadraginta*: see ff.] forty years old, or between the ages of forty and fifty —*n.* a person of this age

Quad·ra·ges·i·ma (-jes′i mə) *n.* [LL.(Ec.) < fem. of L. *quadragesimus*, fortieth < *quadraginta*, forty < base of *quattuor*, FOUR] **1.** [Obs.] the forty days of Lent **2.** the first Sunday in Lent: also **Quadragesima Sunday**

quad·ra·ges·i·mal (-m'l) *adj.* [ML. *quadragesimalis*: see prec.] **1.** lasting forty days: said of Lent **2.** [Q-] Lenten; of or suitable for Lent

quad·ran·gle (kwäd′raŋ′g'l) *n.* [ME. < MFr. < LL. *quadrangulum* < L. *quadr-* < *quattuor*, FOUR + *angulus*, ANGLE[1]] **1.** *Geom.* a plane figure with four angles and four sides **2.** *a)* an area, as of a college campus, surrounded on its four sides by buildings *b)* the buildings surrounding a quadrangle ☆**3.** the area of land charted on each of the atlas sheets published by the U.S. Geological Survey —**quad·ran′gu·lar** (-gyə lər) *adj.*

quad·rant (kwäd′rənt) *n.* [ME. < L. *quadrans*, fourth part < *quadrare*: see QUADRATE] **1.** a fourth part of the circumference of a circle; an arc of 90° **2.** a quarter section of a circle **3.** any piece or part shaped like a quarter section of a circle **4.** an instrument for measuring altitudes or angular elevations in astronomy and navigation: it consists of a graduated arc of 90° with a movable index and a sight **5.** *Geom.* any of the four parts formed by rectangular coordinate axes on a plane surface —**quad·ran′tal** (-ran′t'l) *adj.*

quad·rat (-rat) *n.* [ME., var. of ff. (n.)] **1.** *same as* QUAD[2] **2.** *Ecol.* a sampling plot, usually one square meter, used to study and analyze plant or animal life

quad·rate (-rāt; *also, for adj. &* v., -rit) *adj.* [ME. < L. *quadratus*, pp. of *quadrare*, to make square < *quadrus*, a square < *quattuor*, FOUR] **1.** square or nearly square; rectangular **2.** *Zool.* designating a bone or cartilage of the skull in birds, bony fishes, amphibians, and reptiles, to which the lower jaw is joined —*n.* [ME. < L. *quadratum* < *quadratus*] **1.** a square or rectangle **2.** a square or rectangular space, thing, etc. **3.** *Zool.* the quadrate bone —*vi.* **-rat·ed, -rat·ing** to square; agree (*with*) —*vt.* to make square; make (something) conform

quad·rat·ic (kwäd rat′ik) *adj.* [prec. + -IC] **1.** [Rare] square **2.** *Algebra* involving a quantity or quantities that are squared but none that are raised to a higher power —*n.* *Algebra* a quadratic term, expression, or equation —**quad·rat′i·cal·ly** *adv.*

quadratic equation *Algebra* an equation in which the second power, or square, is the highest to which the unknown quantity is raised

quad·ra·ture (kwäd′rə chər) *n.* [LL. *quadratura* < L. *quadratus*: see QUADRATE] **1.** the act of squaring **2.** the determining or construction of the dimensions of a square equal in area to a given surface **3.** *Astron.* a configuration of a superior planet or the moon in which the angle between it and the sun, as seen from the earth, is 90°

quad·ren·ni·al (kwäd ren′ē əl) *adj.* [< L. *quadriennium* (see ff.) + -AL] **1.** lasting four years **2.** occurring once every four years —*n.* a quadrennial event —**quad·ren′ni·al·ly** *adv.*

quad·ren·ni·um (-ē əm) *n.*, *pl.* **-ni·ums, -ni·a** (-ə) [L. *quadriennium* < *quadri-* (see ff.) + *annus*, a year (see ANNUAL)] a period of four years

quad·ri- (kwäd′ri, -rə) [L. < base of *quattuor*, FOUR] *a combining form meaning* four times, fourfold [*quadrilingual*]

quad·ric (kwäd′rik) *adj.* [< L. *quadra*, a square (akin to *quattuor*, FOUR) + -IC] *Math.* of the second degree: used

of a function with more than two variables —*n.* a quantic of the second degree

quad·ri·cen·ten·ni·al (kwäd′ri sen ten′ē əl) *n.* [QUADRI- + CENTENNIAL] a 400th anniversary or its celebration —*adj.* of a quadricentennial

quad·ri·ceps (kwäd′ri seps′) *n.* [ModL. < QUADRI- + L. *-ceps* < *caput*, the head: see CHIEF] a muscle with four heads, or points of origin; *esp.*, the large muscle at the front of the thigh, which functions to extend the leg —**quad′ri·cip′i·tal** (-sip′ə t'l) *adj.*

quad·ri·fid (-fid) *adj.* [L. *quadrifidus*: see QUADRI- & -FID] divided into four parts, as a leaf or petal

quad·ri·ga (kwäd ri′gə) *n.*, *pl.* **-gae** (-jē) [L., sing. of *quadrigae*, team of four < *quadri-* (see QUADRI-) + *jugum*, a YOKE] in ancient Rome, a two-wheeled chariot drawn by four horses abreast

quad·ri·lat·er·al (kwäd′rə lat′ər əl) *adj.* [< L. *quadrilaterus* (see QUADRI- & LATERAL) + -AL] four-sided —*n. Geom.* **1.** a plane figure having four sides and four angles **2.** *a)* a four-sided area *b)* such an area protected by four fortresses —**quad′ri·lat′er·al·ly** *adv.*

quad·ri·lin·gual (-liŋ′gwəl) *adj.* [QUADRI- + LINGUAL] **1.** of or in four languages **2.** using or capable of using four languages

qua·drille[1] (kwə dril′, kwä-) *n.* [Fr., QUADRILATERALS orig., one of four groups of horsemen participating in certain exercises < Sp. *cuadrilla*, dim. < *cuadro*, four-sided battle square < L. *quadra*, a square: see QUADRIC] **1.** a square dance of French origin, consisting of several figures, performed by four couples **2.** music for this dance

qua·drille[2] (kwə dril′, kwä-) *n.* [Fr., altered after prec. < Sp. *cuartillo*, dim. < *cuarto*, fourth < L. *quartus*: see QUART[1]] a card game, popular in the 18th cent., played by four persons

qua·drille[3] (kwə dril′, kwä-) *adj.* [Fr. *quadrillé* < *quadrille*, a square < Sp. *cuadrillo*, a small square: see QUADRILLE[1]] marked with intersecting lines to form squares or rectangles: also **qua·drilled′** (-drild′)

quad·ril·lion (kwäd ril′yən) *n.* [Fr. < *quadri-* (see QUADRI-) + (MI)LLION] ☆**1.** in the U.S. and France, the number represented by 1 followed by 15 zeros **2.** in Great Britain and Germany, the number represented by 1 followed by 24 zeros —*adj.* amounting to one quadrillion in number —**quad·ril′lionth** *adj.*, *n.*

quad·ri·no·mi·al (kwäd′ri nō′mē əl) *n.* [QUADRI- + (BI)NOMIAL] *Algebra* an expression of four terms (Ex.: $x^2 + xy - 3y + 2y^2$) —*adj. Algebra* consisting of four terms

quad·ri·par·tite (-pär′tīt) *adj.* [ME. < L. *quadripartitus*, pp. of *quadripartire*, to divide into four parts: see QUADRI- & PART] **1.** made up of or divided into four parts **2.** shared in or formulated by four persons, nations, etc. [*a quadripartite pact*]

quad·ri·ple·gi·a (-plē′jē ə, -jə) *n.* [ModL.: see QUADRI- & -PLEGIA] total paralysis of the body from the neck down —**quad′ri·ple′gic** (-plē′jik, -plej′ik) *adj.*, *n.*

quad·ri·sect (kwäd′rə sekt′) *vt.* [< QUADRI- + L. *sectus*, pp. of *secare*, to cut: see SAW[1]] to divide into four equal parts

quad·ri·syl·la·ble (kwäd′rə sil′ə b'l) *n.* a word of four syllables —**quad′ri·syl·lab′ic** (-si lab′ik) *adj.*

quad·ri·va·lent (kwäd′rə vā′lənt, kwä driv′ə-) *adj.* **1.** having four valences **2.** *same as* TETRAVALENT (sense 1) —**quad′ri·va′lence, quad′ri·va′len·cy** *n.*

quad·riv·i·al (kwäd riv′ē əl) *adj.* [ML. *quadrivialis* < L. *quadrivium*, meeting of four roads < *quadri-* (see QUADRI-) + *via*, road (see VIA)] **1.** having or being four roads meeting in a point **2.** of the quadrivium

quad·riv·i·um (-əm) *n.* [ML. < L.: see prec.] in the Middle Ages, the higher division of the seven liberal arts, consisting of arithmetic, geometry, astronomy, and music: cf. TRIVIUM

quad·roon (kwä drōōn′) *n.* [Sp. *cuarterón* < *cuarto*, a fourth < L. *quartus*: see QUART[1]] a person who has one Negro grandparent; child of a mulatto and a white

quad·ru·ma·nous (kwä drōō′mə nəs) *adj.* [formed after QUADRUPED) < L. *quadru-* (used for *quadri-*, esp. before *p*), four + *pes*, a FOOT] an animal, *esp.* a mammal, with four feet —*adj.* having four feet —**quad·ru′pe·dal** (kwä drōō′pi d'l, kwäd′roo ped′'l) *adj.*

quad·ru·ped (kwäd′roo ped′) *n.* [L. *quadrupes* (gen. *quadrupedis*) < *quadru-* (used for *quadri-*, esp. before *p*), four + *pes*, a FOOT] an animal, *esp.* a mammal, with four feet —*adj.* having four feet —**quad·ru′pe·dal** (kwä drōō′pi d'l, kwäd′roo ped′'l) *adj.*

quad·ru·ple (kwä drōō′p'l, -drup′'l; kwäd′roo-) *adj.* [MFr. < L. *quadruplus* < *quadru-* (see prec.) + *-plus*, as in *duplus*: see DOUBLE] **1.** consisting of or including four **2.** four times as much or as many; fourfold **3.** *Music* containing four beats to the measure [*quadruple time*] —*n.* an amount four times as much or as many —*vt.*, *vi.* **-pled, -pling** to make or become four times as much or as many; multiply by four

quad·ru·plet (kwä drup′lit, -drōō′plit; kwäd′roo plit) *n.* [dim. of prec.] **1.** any of four offspring born at a single

birth **2.** a collection or group of four, usually of one kind

quad·ru·plex (kwäd′roo pleks′) *adj.* [L. < *quadru-* (see QUADRUPED) + *-plex*, -fold: see DUPLEX] **1.** fourfold ☆**2.** designating or of a former system of telegraphy in which four messages could be sent simultaneously over one wire, two in either direction

quad·ru·pli·cate (kwä droo′plə kāt′; *for adj. & n., usually* -kit) *vt.* **-cat′ed, -cat′ing** [< L. *quadruplicatus*, pp. of *quadruplicare*, to quadruple < *quadruplex*: see prec.] to quadruple; make four identical copies of —*adj.* **1.** fourfold **2.** designating the fourth of identical copies **3.** *Math.* raised to the fourth power —*n.* any of four identical copies or things —**in quadruplicate** in four identical copies —**quad·ru′pli·ca′tion** *n.*

‡**quae·re** (kwir′ē) *v. imperative* [L., imperative of *quaerere*, to ask] inquire: a note suggesting further investigation of a point —*n.* a query or question

quaes·tor (kwes′tər, kwēs′-) *n.* [L., contr. < *quaesitor* < *quaesitus*, pp. of *quaerere*, to inquire] in ancient Rome, **1.** orig., an official who judged certain criminal cases **2.** later, any of certain state treasurers —**quaes·to′ri·al** (-tôr′ē əl) *adj.* —**quaes′tor·ship′** *n.*

quaff (kwäf, kwaf) *vt., vi.* [Early ModE., prob. (by misreading of *-ss-* as *-ff-*) < LowG. *quassen*, to overindulge (in food and drink)] to drink deeply in a hearty or thirsty way —*n.* **1.** the act of quaffing **2.** a drink that is quaffed —**quaff′er** *n.*

quag (kwag, kwäg) *n.* [< ?] [Rare] a bog or marsh

quag·ga (kwag′ə) *n., pl.* **-ga, -gas:** see PLURAL, II, D, 2 [obs. Afrik. < the native (? Hottentot) name] a striped wild ass (*Equus quagga*) of South Africa, now extinct, resembling the donkey and the zebra

quag·gy (kwag′ē, kwäg′ē) *adj.* **-gi·er, -gi·est 1.** like a quagmire; boggy; soft and miry **2.** soft; flabby

quag·mire (kwag′mīr′, kwäg′-) *n.* [QUAG + MIRE] **1.** wet, boggy ground, yielding under the feet **2.** a difficult or inextricable position [*a quagmire* of debts]

☆**qua·hog, qua·haug** (kwô′hôg, kō′-; -häg) *n.* [< AmInd. (Pequot or Narraganset) name] an edible clam (*Venus mercenaria*) of the E coast of N. America, having a very hard, solid shell

quaich, quaigh (kwākh) *n.* [ScotGael. *cuach*] [Scot.] a small, shallow drinking cup, usually with two handles

Quai d'Or·say (kā′ dôr sā′; *Fr.* ke dôr se′) **1.** a quay on the Seine in Paris, toward which the French Foreign Office building faces **2.** the French Foreign Office

quail¹ (kwāl) *vi.* [ME. *quailen*, prob. < OFr. *coaillier* < L. *coagulare*, to COAGULATE] to draw back in fear; lose heart or courage; cower —*SYN.* see RECOIL

quail² (kwāl) *n., pl.* **quails, quail:** see PLURAL, II, D, 1 [ME. *quaille* < OFr. < ML. *cuacula*, prob. < Gmc. echoic name (OHG. *quahtala*)] **1.** any of various small, gallinaceous game birds of America, Europe, Asia, and Africa, resembling partridges ☆**2.** *same as* BOBWHITE

quaint (kwānt) *adj.* [ME. *cointe* < OFr. < L. *cognitus*, known: see COGNITION] **1.** orig., clever or skilled **2.** [Now Rare] wrought with skill; ingenious **3.** unusual or old-fashioned in a pleasing way **4.** singular; unusual; curious **5.** fanciful; whimsical —*SYN.* see STRANGE —**quaint′ly** *adv.* —**quaint′ness** *n.*

quake (kwāk) *vi.* **quaked, quak′ing** [ME. *quaken* < OE. *cwacian*] **1.** to tremble or shake, as the ground does in an earthquake **2.** to shudder or shiver, as from fear or cold —*n.* **1.** a shaking or tremor **2.** an earthquake —*SYN.* see SHAKE

CALIFORNIA QUAIL (11 in. long, including tail)

Quak·er (kwāk′ər) *n.* [orig. derisive: said to be so called from Fox's admonition to "quake" at the word of the Lord] *a popular name for* a member of the Society of Friends; Friend: see SOCIETY OF FRIENDS —**Quak′er·ess** [Now Rare] *n.fem.* —**Quak′er·ish** *adj.* —**Quak′er·ism** *n.* —**Quak′er·ly** *adj., adv.*

☆**Quaker gun** a dummy gun or cannon, as of wood: so called from the Quakers' opposition to war and militarism

☆**Quak·er·la·dies** (-lā′dēz) *n.pl. same as* BLUETS

Quaker meeting 1. a religious meeting of Quakers, characterized by long periods of silence **2.** [Colloq.] any meeting in which there are many silent moments

☆**quaking aspen** a N. American poplar (*Populus tremuloides*) with small, flat-stemmed leaves that tremble in the lightest breeze

quaking grass any of a genus (*Briza*) of annual or perennial grasses having delicate spikelets on very thin stalks that tremble in the lightest breeze

quak·y (kwā′kē) *adj.* **quak′i·er, quak′i·est** inclined to quake; shaky —**quak′i·ly** *adv.* —**quak′i·ness** *n.*

qua·le (kwā′lē) *n., pl.* **qua·li·a** (-lē ə) [L., neut. sing. of *qualis*, of what kind] *Philos.* a quality, as whiteness, loudness, etc., abstracted as an independent, universal essence from a thing

qual·i·fi·ca·tion (kwäl′ə fi kā′shən) *n.* [ML. *qualificatio*] **1.** a qualifying or being qualified **2.** a modification or restriction; limiting condition **3.** any quality, skill, knowledge, experience, etc. that fits a person for a position, office, profession, etc.; requisite **4.** a condition that must be met in order to exercise certain rights

qual·i·fied (kwäl′ə fid′) *adj.* **1.** having met conditions or requirements set **2.** having the necessary or desirable qualities; fit; competent **3.** limited; modified [to give *qualified* approval] —*SYN.* see ABLE —**qual′i·fied′ly** *adv.* —**qual′i·fied′ness** *n.*

qual·i·fi·er (-fi′ər) *n.* a person or thing that qualifies; specif., *a)* a person who meets set requirements *b)* a word, as an adjective or adverb, that modifies or limits the meaning of another word

qual·i·fy (-fi′) *vt.* **-fied′, -fy′ing** [Fr. *qualifier* < ML. *qualificare* < L. *qualis*, of what kind (akin to *qui*, WHO) + *facere*, to make: see FACT] **1.** to describe by giving the qualities or characteristics of **2.** to make fit for an office, occupation, exercise of a right, etc. **3.** to make legally capable; give a specific right to; license **4.** to modify; restrict; limit; make less positive [to *qualify* one's approval] **5.** to moderate; soften [to *qualify* a punishment] **6.** to change the strength of (a liquor, etc.) **7.** *Gram.* to limit or modify the meaning of (a word) —*vi.* to be or become qualified, as by meeting requirements —**qual′i·fi′a·ble** *adj.* —**qual′i·fy′ing·ly** *adv.*

qual·i·ta·tive (-tāt′iv) *adj.* [LL. *qualitativus*] having to do with quality or qualities —**qual′i·ta′tive·ly** *adv.*

qualitative analysis the branch of chemistry dealing with the determination of the elements or ingredients of which a compound or mixture is composed

qual·i·ty (kwäl′ə tē) *n., pl.* **-ties** [ME. *qualite* < OFr. < L. *qualitas* < *qualis*, of what kind (see QUALIFY)] **1.** any of the features that make something what it is; characteristic element; attribute **2.** basic nature; character; kind **3.** the degree of excellence which a thing possesses **4.** excellence; superiority **5.** [Now Rare] position, capacity, or role **6.** *a)* [Archaic] high social position *b)* [Archaic or Dial.] people of high social position **7.** *Acoustics* the property of a tone determined by its overtones; timbre **8.** *Logic* the affirmative or negative character of a proposition **9.** *Phonet.* the character of a vowel sound as determined by the resonance of the vocal cords and the shape of the passage above the larynx when the sound is produced

SYN.—**quality**, the broadest in scope of these terms, refers to a characteristic (physical or nonphysical, individual or typical) that constitutes the basic nature of a thing or is one of its distinguishing features [the *quality* of mercy]; **property** applies to any quality that belongs to a thing by reason of the essential nature of the thing [elasticity is a *property* of rubber]; **character** is the scientific or formal term for a distinctive or peculiar quality of an individual or of a class, species, etc. [a hereditary *character*]; an **attribute** is a quality assigned to a thing, esp. one that may reasonably be deduced as appropriate to it [omnipotence is an *attribute* of God]; **trait** specif. applies to a distinguishing quality of a personality [enthusiasm is one of his outstanding *traits*]

☆**quality control** a system for maintaining desired standards in production or in a product, esp. by inspecting samples of the product

qualm (kwäm) *n.* [ME. *qualme* < OE. *cwealm*, death, disaster (akin to G. *qual*, pain, Sw. *kvalm*, nausea) < base of *cwellan*, to kill (see QUELL): all extant senses show melioration of the orig. meaning] **1.** a sudden, brief feeling of sickness, faintness, or nausea **2.** a sudden feeling of uneasiness or doubt; misgiving **3.** a twinge of conscience; scruple

SYN.—**qualm** implies a painful feeling of uneasiness arising from a consciousness that one is or may be acting wrongly [he had *qualms* about having cheated on the test]; **scruple** implies doubt or hesitation arising from difficulty in deciding what is right, proper, just, etc. [to break a promise without *scruple*]; **compunction** implies a twinge of conscience for wrongdoing, now often for a slight offense [to have no *compunctions* about telling a white lie]; **misgiving** implies a disturbed state of mind resulting from a loss of confidence as to whether one is doing what is right [*misgivings* of conscience]

qualm·ish (-ish) *adj.* **1.** having qualms **2.** having the nature of a qualm **3.** of such a nature as to produce qualms —**qualm′ish·ly** *adv.* —**qualm′ish·ness** *n.*

☆**quam·ash** (kwäm′ash, kwə mash′) *n. same as* CAMASS

quan·da·ry (kwän′drē, -dər ē) *n., pl.* **-ries** [earlier *quandare*, prob. orig. jocular pseudo-L. < L. *quande*, var. of *quam*, how much (see QUANTITY) + *-are*, inf. suffix] a state of uncertainty; perplexing situation or position; dilemma —*SYN.* see PREDICAMENT

quan·dong, quan·dang (kwän′däŋ′) *n.* [native name] **1.** a small Australian tree (*Eucarya acuminata*) whose edible fruit has a single stone containing an edible kernel **2.** this fruit or stone Also **quan′tong′** (-täŋ′)

quant (kwant, kwänt) *n.* [< ?] [Brit.] a punting pole with a flat cap at the end to prevent its sinking in the mud —*vt., vi.* to propel (a boat) with a quant

quan·ta (kwän′tə) *n. pl. of* QUANTUM

quan·tic (-tik) *n.* [< L. *quantus*, how much: see QUANTITY]

Math. a rational homogeneous integral function of two or more variables

quan·ti·fi·er (kwän′tə fī′ər) *n. Logic* a word, term, prefix, symbol, etc. that quantifies

quan·ti·fy (kwän′tə fī′) *vt.* **-fied′, -fy′ing** [ML. *quantificare* < L. *quantus*, how much (see QUANTITY) + *facere*, to make (see FACT)] **1.** to determine or express the quantity of; indicate the extent of; measure **2.** *Logic* to make the quantity or extension of (a term or symbol) clear and explicit by the use of a quantifier, as *all, none,* or *some* —**quan′ti·fi′a·ble** *adj.* —**quan′ti·fi·ca′tion** *n.*

quan·tile (-til, -tīl) *n.* [< QUANT(ITY) + -ILE] *Statistics* any of the values of a random variable dividing the distribution of the individuals into a given number of groups of equal frequency

quan·ti·tate (kwän′tə tāt′) *vt.* **-tat′ed, -tat′ing** [back-formation < QUANTITATIVE] to measure or determine the quantity of —**quan′ti·ta′tion** *n.*

quan·ti·ta·tive (kwän′tə tāt′iv) *adj.* [ML. *quantitativus*] **1.** having to do with quantity **2.** capable of being measured **3.** having to do with the quantity of a speech sound **4.** having to do with a system, as in classical prosody, in which syllables are classified as long and short —**quan′ti·ta′tive·ly** *adv.* —**quan′ti·ta′tive·ness** *n.*

quantitative analysis the branch of chemistry dealing with the accurate measurement of the amounts or percentages of the various components of a substance or compound

quantitative inheritance *Genetics* the inheritance in offspring of distinctive characters, as stature in man, that are influenced by the combined activity of multiple factors and that are subject to modification by environment

quan·ti·ty (kwän′tə tē) *n., pl.* **-ties** [ME. *quantite* < OFr. < L. *quantitas* < *quantus*, how great < *quam*, how, how much < IE. interrogative base *kwo-*, whence WHO, WHAT] **1.** an amount; portion **2.** any indeterminate bulk, weight, or number **3.** the exact amount of a particular thing **4.** [also *pl.*] a great amount or number **5.** that property of anything which can be determined by measurement **6.** *Logic* that character which is determined by the extension of a proposition as universal or particular **7.** *Math. a)* a thing that has the property of being measurable in dimensions, amounts, etc. or in extensions of these which can be expressed in numbers or symbols *b)* a number or symbol expressing a mathematical quantity **8.** *Music* the relative length of a tone **9.** *Philos.* that aspect of things to which measure applies and according to which they can be compared with one another **10.** *Phonet., Prosody* the relative length, or duration, of a vowel, continuant consonant, or syllable

quan·tize (-tīz) *vt.* **-tized, -tiz·ing** [QUANT(UM) + -IZE] **1.** *Math.* to express in multiples of a basic unit **2.** *a) Physics* to limit (an observable quantity) to multiples of some small, indivisible unit, as *b)* to express in terms of the quantum theory —**quan′ti·za′tion** *n.*

quan·tum (-təm) *n., pl.* **-ta** (-tə) [L., neut. sing. of *quantus*, how much: see QUANTITY] **1.** quantity, or amount **2.** a specified quantity; portion **3.** in the quantum theory, a (or the) fixed, elemental unit, as of energy, angular momentum, etc.

quantum mechanics a mathematical theory in physics which starts with the assumption that energy is not infinitely divisible and deals with atomic structure and phenomena by the methods of quantum theory

quantum number a number indicating a quantum condition and given to each energy level in an atom

quantum theory the theory that energy is not absorbed nor radiated continuously but discontinuously, and only in multiples of definite, indivisible units (*quanta*)

qua·qua·ver·sal (kwā′kwə ver′s'l) *adj.* [< LL. *quaquaversus* (< L. *quaqua*, in all directions + *versus*, pp. of *vertere*, to turn: see VERSE) + -AL] *Geol.* directed outward from a common center toward all points of the compass; dipping uniformly in all directions

quar·an·tine (kwôr′ən tēn′, kwär′-) *n.* [It. *quarantina*, lit., space of forty days, ult. < L. *quadraginta*, forty < base of *quattuor*, FOUR] **1.** *a)* the period, orig. forty days, during which an arriving vessel suspected of carrying contagious disease is detained in port in strict isolation *b)* the place where such a vessel is stationed **2.** any isolation or restriction on travel or passage imposed to keep contagious diseases, insect pests, etc. from spreading **3.** the state of being quarantined **4.** a place where persons, animals, or plants having contagious diseases, insect pests, etc. are kept in isolation, or beyond which they may not travel **5.** any period of seclusion, social ostracism, etc. **6.** [Archaic] a period of forty days —*vt.* **-tined′, -tin′ing 1.** to place under quarantine **2.** to isolate politically, commercially, socially, etc. [to *quarantine* an aggressor nation] —**quar′an·tin′a·ble** *adj.*

quark (kwôrk) *n.* [arbitrary use (by M. Gell-Man) of a word coined by James Joyce in *Finnegan's Wake*] ☆any of three hypothetical particles postulated as forming the building blocks of baryons and mesons and accounting in theory for their properties

Quarles (kwôrlz, kwärlz), **Francis** 1592-1644; Eng. poet

quar·rel¹ (kwôr′əl, kwär′-) *n.* [ME. *quarel* < OFr. < ML. *querellus* < VL. *quadrellum*, dim. of L. *quadrus*, a square] **1.** a square-headed missile or arrow used in ancient crossbows **2.** a small diamond-shaped or square pane of glass, as in a latticed window

quar·rel² (kwôr′əl, kwär′-) *n.* [ME. *quarel* < OFr. *querele* < L. *querela*, complaint < *queri*, to complain, lament < IE. base *kwes-*, to pant, snort, whence WHEEZE] **1.** a cause for dispute **2.** a dispute or disagreement, esp. one marked by anger and deep resentment **3.** a falling out; breaking up of friendly relations —*vi.* **-reled** or **-relled, -rel·ing** or **-rel·ling 1.** to find fault; complain **2.** to dispute heatedly **3.** to have a breach in friendship —**quar′rel·er, quar′rel·ler** *n.*

SYN.—**quarrel** implies heated verbal strife marked by anger and resentment and often suggests continued hostility as a result; **wrangle** suggests a noisy dispute in which each person is vehemently insistent on his views; **altercation** implies verbal contention which may or may not be accompanied by blows; **squabble** implies undignified, childish wrangling over a small matter; **spat** is the colloquial term for a petty quarrel and suggests a brief outburst that does not have a significant effect on a relationship —*ANT.* agreement, harmony

quar·rel·some (-səm) *adj.* inclined or ready to quarrel —*SYN.* see BELLIGERENT —**quar′rel·some·ly** *adv.* —**quar′rel·some·ness** *n.*

quar·ri·er (kwôr′ē ər, kwär′-) *n.* [ME. *quaryere* < OFr. *quarrieur* < *quarrer*, to quarry < L. *quadrare*: see QUARRY³] a person who works in a stone quarry

quar·ry¹ (kwôr′ē, kwär′ē) *n., pl.* **-ries** [var. of QUARREL¹] a square or diamond-shaped piece of glass, tile, etc.

quar·ry² (kwôr′ē, kwär′ē) *n., pl.* **-ries** [ME. *querre*, orig., parts of the prey put on the hide and fed to dogs < OFr. *cuirée*, altered (after *cuir*, a hide) < *curée*, pp. of *curer*, to eviscerate < L. *curare*, to attend to] **1.** an animal that is being hunted down, esp. with dogs or hawks; prey **2.** anything being hunted or pursued

quar·ry³ (kwôr′ē, kwär′ē) *n., pl.* **-ries** [ME. *quarey* < ML. *quarreria*, contr. of *quarreria, quadraria*, lit., place where stones are squared < L. *quadrare*, to square] a place where building stone, marble, or slate is excavated, as by cutting or blasting —*vt.* **-ried, -ry·ing 1.** to excavate from a quarry **2.** to make a quarry in (land)

quar·ry·man (-mən) *n., pl.* **-men** (-mən) *same as* QUARRIER

quart¹ (kwôrt) *n.* [ME. < MFr. *quarte* < fem. of OFr. *quart*, a fourth < L. *quartus*, fourth < base of *quattuor*, FOUR] **1.** a liquid measure, equal to 1/4 gal. (57.75 cu. in. or, in Great Britain & Canada, 69.36 cu. in.) **2.** a dry measure, equal to 1/8 peck **3.** a container with a capacity of one quart

quart² (kwôrt) *n.* [Fr. *quarte*: see prec.] **1.** *same as* QUARTE **2.** a sequence of four cards of the same suit in piquet and other card games

quart. 1. quarter **2.** quarterly

quar·tan (kwôr′t'n) *adj.* [ME. *quartaine* < MFr. (*fièvre*) *quartaine* < L. (*febris*) *quartana*, (fever) occurring every fourth day, fem. of *quartanus* < *quartus*, fourth: see QUART¹] occurring every fourth day, counting both days of occurrence: said of a fever —*n.* a type of malaria in which the paroxysms occur every fourth day

quarte (kärt; Fr. kȧrt) *n.* [Fr., fem. of *quart*, fourth] *Fencing* the fourth position (of thrust or parry) in which the hand is turned nails up, and the point of the weapon is about eye level

quar·ter (kwôr′tər) *n.* [ME. *quartre* < OFr. *quartier* < L. *quartarius*, fourth part < *quartus*, fourth: see QUART¹] **1.** any of the four equal parts of something; fourth **2.** one fourth of a hundredweight: 25 pounds in the U.S., 28 pounds in England **3.** one fourth of a yard, or 9 inches; span **4.** one fourth of a pound ☆**5.** one fourth of a mile; two furlongs **6.** *a)* one fourth of a year; three months *b)* a school or college term, usually one fourth of a school year **7.** *a)* one fourth of an hour; 15 minutes *b)* the moment marking the end of each fourth of an hour ☆**8.** *a)* one fourth of a dollar; 25 cents *b)* a coin of the U.S. and Canada equal to 25 cents; the U.S. quarter is made of cupronickel **9.** any leg of a four-legged animal, with the adjoining parts **10.** *a)* any of the four main points of the compass *b)* any of the four divisions of the horizon as marked off by these points *c)* any of the regions of the earth thought of as under these divisions **11.** a particular district or section in a city [the Latin *quarter*] **12.** [*pl.*] lodgings; place of abode **13.** a particular person, group, place, etc., esp. one serving as a source or origin [news from the highest *quarters*] **14.** the part forming the side of a shoe from the heel to the vamp **15.** [Brit.] one fourth of a ton of grain, or 8 bushels **16.** *Astron. a)* the period of time in which the moon makes one fourth of its revolution around the earth *b)* the phase of the moon when it is half lighted ☆**17.** *Football, Basketball,* etc. any of the four periods into which a game is divided **18.** *Heraldry a)* any of the four equal divisions of a shield *b)* the charge occupying such a division **19.** *Mil.* mercy granted to a surrendering foe **20.** *Naut. a)* the after part of a ship's side, between the beam and the stern *b)* a direction at a 45° angle aft of the beam *c)* an assigned station or post *d)* one fourth of a fathom —*vt.* **1.** to divide into four equal parts **2.** loosely, to separate into any number of parts **3.** to defile (the body of a person put to death) by dismembering it or cutting it into quarters **4.** to provide lodgings for; specif., to assign (soldiers) to lodgings **5.** to cover (an area) by passing back and forth over it in many directions:

said of hounds searching for game **6.** *Heraldry* *a)* to place or bear (different coats of arms) on the quarters of a shield *b)* to add (a coat of arms) to a shield **7.** *Mech.* to set (a crank, etc.) at right angles to the connecting part —*vi.* **1.** to be lodged or stationed (*at* or *with*) **2.** to range over a field, etc. in search of game: said of hounds in hunting **3.** to swim, sail, etc. at an angle because of the wind, current, etc. **4.** *Naut.* to blow on the quarter of a ship: said of the wind —*adj.* constituting a quarter; equal to a quarter —**at close quarters** at close range; close together —**cry quarter** to beg for mercy

quar·ter·age (-ij) *n.* [ME. < OFr.: see prec. & -AGE] **1.** a quarterly assessment; payment, allowance, etc. **2.** [Rare] *a)* quarters for troops, etc. *b)* the provision of quarters *c)* the expense of this

☆**quar·ter·back** (-bak′) *n.* *Football* the player whose position is behind the line of scrimmage together with the fullback and halfbacks, and who calls the signals and directs the offensive plays —*vt., vi.* **1.** to act as quarterback for (a team) **2.** to direct or lead; manage

quarter crack a perpendicular fissure in some part of the wall of a horse's hoof, often causing lameness

quarter day any of the four days regarded as beginning a new quarter of the year, when quarterly payments on rents, etc. are due

quar·ter·deck, quar·ter·deck (-dek′) *n.* [so called because orig. half the length of the half deck] **1.** the after part of the upper deck of a ship, usually reserved for officers **2.** *U.S. Navy* the part of the upper deck of a ship reserved for official ceremonies

quar·tered (kwôr′tərd) *adj.* **1.** divided into quarters **2.** provided with quarters or lodgings **3.** quartersawed

quar·ter·fi·nal (kwôr′tər fī′n'l) *adj. Sports* designating or of the round of matches immediately preceding the semifinals in a tournament —*n.* a quarterfinal match —**quar′ter·fi′nal·ist** *n.*

quarter grain the grain of quartersawed lumber

☆**quarter horse** any of a breed of horse developed in America, characterized by a low, compact, muscular body and great sprinting speed for distances up to a quarter of a mile

quar·ter-hour (kwôr′tər our′) *n.* **1.** fifteen minutes **2.** the point on a clock marking the first quarter or third quarter of an hour

quar·ter·ing (-iŋ) *adj.* **1.** blowing on the after part of a ship's side: said of the wind **2.** lying at right angles —*n.* **1.** the act of dividing into quarters **2.** the act of passing back and forth over an area **3.** the providing of quarters for soldiers, etc. **4.** *Heraldry* *a)* the division of a shield into quarters *b)* any of these, or the coat of arms on it

quar·ter·ly (-lē) *adj.* **1.** occurring or appearing at regular intervals four times a year **2.** consisting of a quarter —*adv.* **1.** once every quarter of the year **2.** *Heraldry* in or by quarters, as a shield —*n., pl.* **-lies** a publication issued every three months

quar·ter·mas·ter (-mas′tər, -mäs′tər) *n.* **1.** *Mil.* an officer whose duty it is to provide troops with quarters, clothing, equipment, etc. **2.** *Naut.* a petty officer or mate who attends to the ship's compass, navigation, signals, etc.

Quartermaster Corps a former branch of the U.S. Army that supplied food, clothing, etc. to soldiers: replaced in 1962 by U.S. Army Matériel Command

quar·tern (kwôr′tərn) *n.* [ME. *quarteroun* < OFr. *quarteron* < *quart:* see QUART¹] **1.** orig., a fourth part; quarter **2.** [Brit.] one fourth of a pint, a peck, or of various other weights and measures

quarter note *Music* a note having one fourth the duration of a whole note; crotchet: see NOTE, illus.

quar·ter-phase (kwôr′tər fāz′) *adj. Elec.* generating, carrying, or run by, two alternating currents whose phases differ by a quarter cycle, or 90 degrees

quarter round a convex molding, in cross section a quarter of a circle

☆**quar·ter·saw** (-sô′) *vt.* **-sawed′, -sawed′** or **-sawn′, -saw′ing** to saw (a log) into quarters lengthwise and then into boards, in order to show the grain of the wood to advantage

☆**quarter section** one fourth of a section of land, half a mile square (i.e., 1/4 sq. mi., or 160 acres)

quarter sessions **1.** in England, a local court that sits quarterly and has limited criminal jurisdiction along with authority in ordinary civil proceedings ☆**2.** in the U.S., any of various courts that sit quarterly, usually with jurisdiction over criminal offenses less than a felony, and, sometimes, performing administrative functions

quar·ter·staff (-staf′, -stäf′) *n., pl.* **-staves′** (-stāvz′) **1.** a stout, iron-tipped wooden staff, six to eight feet long, formerly used in England as a weapon: it was held by one hand at the middle and the other between the middle and an end **2.** the use of the quarterstaff in fighting, often as a sport

quarter tone (or **step**) *Music* an interval of one half of a semitone

quar·tet, quar·tette (kwôr tet′) *n.* [Fr. *quartette* < It. *quartetto*, dim. of *quarto* < L. *quartus*, a fourth: see QUART¹] **1.** any group of four persons or things **2.** *Music* *a)* a

composition for four voices or four instruments *b)* the four performers of such a composition

quar·tic (kwôr′tik) *adj.* [< L. *quartus*, fourth (see QUART¹) + -IC] *Math.* of the fourth degree —*n.* a quantic of the fourth degree; biquadrate

quar·tile (kwôr′til, -t'l) *n.* [ML. *quartilis* < L. *quartus*, a fourth: see QUART¹] *Statistics* **1.** any of the values in a series dividing the distribution of the individuals in the series into four groups of equal frequency **2.** any of these groups

quar·to (kwôr′tō) *n., pl.* **-tos** [< L. (*in*) *quarto* < *in*, in + *quarto*, abl. of *quartus*, a fourth] **1.** the page size of a book made up of sheets each of which is folded twice to form four leaves, or eight pages, about nine by twelve inches in size **2.** a book made of pages folded in this way —*adj.* having four (quarto) leaves to the sheet

quartz (kwôrts) *n.* [G. *quarz* < ?] a brilliant, hexagonally crystalline mineral, silicon dioxide, SiO_2, occurring in abundance, most often in a colorless, transparent form, but also sometimes in colored varieties used as semiprecious stones: the principal constituent of ordinary sand —**quartz′ose** (-ōs) *adj.*

quartz crystal *Electronics* a thin plate or rod cut from quartz and accurately ground and finished so as to vibrate at a particular frequency

quartz glass same as FUSED QUARTZ

quartz·if·er·ous (kwôrt sif′ər əs) *adj.* [QUARTZ + -i- + -FEROUS] consisting of or yielding quartz

quartz·ite (kwôrt′sīt′) *n.* [QUARTZ + -ITE¹] **1.** a very hard, metamorphic sandstone so firmly cemented that breakage occurs through the grains rather than between them **2.** any sandstone tightly cemented with quartz

☆**quartz lamp** a mercury-vapor lamp with a transparent quartz envelope that emits ultraviolet rays on the passage of an electric discharge

☆**qua·sar** (kwā′sär, -zär, -sər) *n.* [< *quas(i-stell)ar* (*radio source*)] any of a number of starlike, celestial objects that emit immense quantities of light or of powerful radio waves, or both, and that appear to be extremely distant from the earth

quash¹ (kwäsh) *vt.* [altered (after ff.) < ME. *quassen* < MFr. *quasser* < LL. *cassare*, to annihilate, destroy < L. *cassus*, empty < *castus*, pp. of *carere*, to lack: for IE. base see CASTRATE] *Law* to annul or set aside (an indictment)

quash² (kwäsh) *vt.* [ME. *quashen* < MFr. *quasser* < L. *quassare*, to shake, shatter, shiver, intens. < *quassus*, pp. of *quatere*, to shake, break < IE. base *kwet-*, to shake, akin to *skut-*, whence SHUDDER] to quell or suppress (an uprising); put down —**quash′er** *n.*

qua·si (kwā′sī, -zī; kwä′sē, -zē) *adv.* [L., as if, as it were, just as < *quamsi* < *quam*, as, how + *si*, if, whether: see QUANTITY & SO¹] as if; in a sense or manner; seemingly; in part —*adj.* seeming [a *quasi* scholar] Often hyphenated as a prefix to a noun, adjective, or adverb [*quasi*-judicial]

quasi contract *Law* an obligation to do something imposed upon someone by law but bearing the force of a contract and subject to legal action as a contract: now imposed chiefly to prevent unfair gain at the expense of another

qua·si-ju·di·cial (-jōō dish′əl) *adj.* having to do with powers that are to some extent judicial, as those of certain Federal or State boards and commissions

qua·si-stel·lar radio source (-stel′ər) same as QUASAR

quass (kväs, kwäs) *n.* same as KVASS

quas·si·a (kwäsh′ē ə, kwäsh′ə) *n.* [ModL. < Graman *Quassi*, Surinam Negro who prescribed it for fever, c. 1730] **1.** any of a genus (*Quassia*) of shrubs and trees of the quassia family **2.** the wood of either of two tropical trees (*Picrasma excelsa* or *Quassia amara*) of the quassia family, used in making furniture **3.** a bitter drug extracted from this wood, used in insecticides and, formerly, in medicine —*adj.* designating a family (Simarubaceae) of tropical American shrubs and trees with alternate pinnate leaves, including ailanthus, tree of heaven, and quassia

qua·ter·na·ry (kwät′ər ner′ē, kwə tur′nər ē) *adj.* [L. *quaternarius* < *quaterni*, four together, four each < *quater*, four times < base of *quattuor*, FOUR] **1.** consisting of four; in sets of four **2.** [Q-] designating or of the geologic period following the Tertiary in the Cenozoic Era, comprising the Pleistocene and Recent epochs **3.** *Chem.* *a)* designating a compound containing four different elements [*quaternary* silver] *b)* being, of, or containing an atom linked to four carbon atoms [a *quaternary* carbon atom] —*n., pl.* **-ries** **1.** the number four **2.** a set of four —**the Quaternary** the Quaternary Period or its rocks: see GEOLOGY, chart

quaternary ammonium compound any of a class of compounds in which the four hydrogen atoms of the ammonium radical are replaced by other groups, generally organic radicals: used as solvents, disinfectants, etc.

qua·ter·ni·on (kwə tur′nē ən) *n.* [ME. < LL. *quaternio* < L. *quaterni:* see QUATERNARY] **1.** a set of four **2.** *Math.* *a)* an expression that is the sum of four terms, one of which is real and three of which contain imaginary units, and that can be written as the sum of a scalar and a three-dimensional vector *b)* [*pl.*] the form of calculus using the quaternion

quat·rain (kwä′trān) *n.* [Fr. < *quatre* < L. *quattuor*, FOUR] a stanza or poem of four lines, usually rhyming *abab*, *abba*, or *abcb*

qua·tre (kät′ər; *Fr.* kȧ′tr′) *n.* [Fr., four: see prec.] a card, domino, or die marked with four spots

quat·re·foil (kat′ər foil′, kat′rə-) *n.* [ME. *quaterfoyle* < MFr. *quatrefeuille* < *quatre* (< L. *quattuor*, FOUR) + *feuille* (< L. *folium*, leaf: see FOIL²)] 1. a flower with four petals or a leaf with four leaflets 2. *Archit.* a circular design made up of four converging arcs

quat·tro·cen·tist (kwät′trō chen′tist) *n.* an Italian artist or writer of the quattrocento

quat·tro·cen·to (-tō) *n.* [It., four hundred: short for *mille quattrocento*, one thousand four hundred] the 15th cent. as a period in Italian art and literature

qua·ver (kwā′vər) *vi.* [ME. *quaveren*, freq. of Early ME. *cwafien*, to shake, tremble, prob. < OE. *cwafian*, prob. < IE. base *gwēbh-*, wobbly, flabby, tadpole, whence G. *quappe* & Du. *kwabbe*, tadpole] 1. to shake or tremble 2. to be tremulous: said of the voice 3. *Music* to make a trill or trills in singing or playing —*vt.* 1. to utter in a tremulous voice 2. *Music* to sing or play with a trill or trills —*n.* 1. a tremulous quality in a voice or tone 2. [Chiefly Brit.] a musical eighth note; half of a crotchet —**qua′ver·er** *n.* —**qua′ver·ing·ly** *adv.* —**qua′ver·y** *adj.*

quay (kē) *n.* [ME. *kei* < MFr. *cai* < Celt. (as in W. *cae* & Bret. *kai*, enclosure) < IE. base *kagh-*, to enclose, whence HEDGE: E. sp. infl. by Fr. *quai* (OFr. *cai*)] a wharf, usually of concrete or stone, with facilities for loading and unloading ships

quay·age (-ij) *n.* [Fr.] 1. the charge made for using a quay 2. space on a quay 3. quays collectively

Que. Quebec

quean (kwēn) *n.* [ME. *queyne* < OE. *cwene*, akin to *cwen* (see QUEEN) & Goth. *qino*, woman < IE. *gwenā*, woman, whence QUEEN, Sans. *ganā*, goddess, Gr. *gynē*, a woman] 1. a bold, brazen woman; hussy 2. a prostitute 3. [Scot.] a girl or unmarried woman 4. [Slang] *same as* QUEEN (sense 7)

quea·sy (kwē′zē) *adj.* **-si·er**, **-si·est** [Late ME. *qwesye* < Scand., as in Ice. *kveisa*, stomach-ache < IE. base *gwey-*, to overpower, suppress, whence OE. *cwiesan*, to crush, beat] 1. causing nausea 2. affected with nausea 3. squeamish; qualmish; easily nauseated or disgusted 4. causing or feeling discomfort; uneasy 5. [Archaic] difficult to please; fastidious 6. [Archaic] troublous; hazardous —**quea′si·ly** *adv.* —**quea′si·ness** *n.*

Que·bec (kwi bek′) [< Algonquian (Abnaki) *kabek*, lit., the place shut in] 1. province of E Canada, between Hudson Bay & the Gulf of St. Lawrence: 594,860 sq. mi.; pop. 5,781,000: abbrev. **Que.**, **P.Q.** 2. capital of this province; seaport on the St. Lawrence River: pop. 167,000 (met. area 413,000) Fr. **Qué·bec** (kā bek′) —**Que·bec′er**, **Que·beck′er** *n.*

que·bra·cho (kā brä′chō) *n.*, *pl.* **-chos** [AmSp., contr. < *quiebrahacha*, lit., ax breaker (because of the hardness of the wood) < *quebrar*, to break + *hacha*, an ax] 1. a tropical American tree (*Schinopsis lorentzii*) of the cashew family, whose hard wood yields an extract used in tanning 2. a S. American tree (*Aspidosperma quebracho-blanco*) of the dogbane family, whose bark yields alkaloids formerly used in medicine 3. the wood or bark of either of these trees

Quech·ua (kech′wä, -wə) *n.* [Sp. < Quechua name] 1. *pl.* **-uas**, **-ua** a member of any of a group of S. American Indian tribes dominant in the former Inca Empire 2. any of these tribes 3. the language of these tribes, now spoken by Indians in Peru, Bolivia, Ecuador, Colombia, Argentina, and Chile —**Quech′uan** *adj.*, *n.*

Quech·u·ma·ran (kech′oo mə rän′) *n.* a language stock including Quechua and Aymara

queen (kwēn) *n.* [ME. *quen* < OE. *cwen* (akin to OS. *quān*, ON. *kvæn*, Goth. *qēns*, woman); for IE. base see QUEAN] 1. the wife of a king 2. a woman who rules over a monarchy in her own right; female sovereign, limited or absolute 3. a woman foremost or judged to be foremost among others in certain attributes or accomplishments, as beauty, etc. 4. a place or thing regarded as the best or most beautiful of its kind 5. the fully developed, reproductive female in a colony of bees, ants, or termites 6. a playing card with a conventionalized picture of a queen on it 7. [Slang] a male homosexual, specif. one with pronounced feminine characteristics 8. *Chess* the most powerful piece, permitted to move any number of unoccupied spaces in a straight or diagonal direction —*vt.* 1. to make (a girl or woman) a queen 2. *Chess* to make a queen of (a pawn that has been moved to the opponent's end of the board) —*vi.* to reign as queen —**queen it** to act like a queen; domineer —**queen′dom** *n.* —**queen′hood′** *n.* —**queen′like′** *adj.*

☆**Queen Anne's lace** *same as* WILD CARROT

Queen Anne style 1. a style of English architecture of the early 18th cent., characterized by construction in red brick, forms modified from classical architecture, and simple, dignified ornamentation 2. a style of furniture of the same period, characterized by simple, curved lines and the use of upholstery and veneering

Queen Charlotte Islands [after an explorer's ship, the *Queen Charlotte*] group of islands in British Columbia, Canada, off the W coast: 3,970 sq. mi.; pop. 3,000

queen consort the wife of a reigning king

queen dowager the widow of a king

queen·ly (-lē) *adj.* **-li·er**, **-li·est** of, like, or fit for a queen or queens; royal; regal —*adv.* [Archaic] in the manner of a queen —**queen′li·ness** *n.*

Queen Mab (mab) *Eng. Folklore* a fairy queen who governs people's dreams

Queen Maud Land region in Antarctica, south of Africa: it is claimed by Norway

Queen Maud Range mountain range in Antarctica, south of the Ross Ice Shelf: peaks over 13,000 ft.

queen mother a queen dowager who is mother of a reigning sovereign

☆**queen of the prairie** a perennial N. American meadow-sweet (*Filipendula rubra*), having small, peach-colored flowers

queen olive a large olive with a long, slender pit

queen post *Carpentry* either of a pair of vertical posts set between the rafters and the base, or tie beam, of a truss, at equal distances from the apex: cf. KING POST

queen regent 1. a queen reigning in behalf of another person 2. *rare var. of* QUEEN REGNANT

queen regnant a queen reigning in her own right

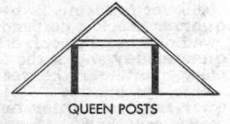

QUEEN POSTS

Queens (kwēnz) [after *Queen* Catherine, wife of CHARLES II of England] borough of New York City, on W Long Island, east of Brooklyn: pop. 1,987,000

Queen's Bench, Queen's Counsel, queen's English, etc. *see* KING'S BENCH, KING'S COUNSEL, KING'S ENGLISH, etc.

Queens·ber·ry rules (kwēnz′ber′ē) the rules for boxing formulated by the English Marquis of Queensberry (1844–1900)

☆**queen-size** (-sīz′) *adj.* [Colloq.] larger than usual, but less than king-size *[a queen-size bed is 60 by 80 in.]*

Queens·land (kwēnz′land′, -lənd) state of NE Australia: 667,000 sq. mi.; pop. 1,661,000; cap. Brisbane

queen's metal an old name for any of several alloys containing antimony and tin and resembling britannia metal

queen truss *Carpentry* a truss with queen posts

queer (kwir) *adj.* [N. Eng. & Scot. dial.: via beggars' cant < ? G. *quer*, crosswise, in the orig. sense (MHG. *twer*, crooked] 1. differing from what is usual or ordinary; odd; singular; strange 2. slightly ill; qualmish or giddy 3. [Colloq.] doubtful; suspicious 4. [Colloq.] having mental quirks; eccentric 5. [Slang] counterfeit; not genuine ☆**6.** [Slang] homosexual —*vt.* [Slang] 1. to spoil the smooth operation or success of 2. to put (oneself) into an unfavorable position —*n.* [Slang] 1. counterfeit money 2. a strange or eccentric person ☆**3.** a homosexual —*SYN.* see STRANGE —☆**be queer for (something)** [Slang] to have a strong liking for; be obsessed with —**queer′ish** *adj.* —**queer′ly** *adv.* —**queer′ness** *n.*

quell (kwel) *vt.* [ME. *quellen* < OE. *cwellan*, to kill, akin to G. *qualen*, to torture < IE. base *gwel-*, to stab, pain, death, whence Gr. *belonē*, point, needle] 1. to crush; subdue; put an end to 2. to quiet; allay —*n.* [Obs.] a killing; murder —**quell′er** *n.*

‡**quel·que chose** (kel kə shōz′) [Fr., something] a trifle

Que·moy (kē′moi′) island of a small group in Taiwan Strait, held by the Chinese Nationalist government on Taiwan: pop. 49,000

quench (kwench) *vt.* [ME. *quenchen* < OE. *cwencan*, to extinguish, caus. of *cwincan*, to go out, akin to Fris. *kwinka*, MHG. *verquinen*, to pass away < IE. base *gwey-*, to overpower, whence QUEASY] 1. to extinguish; put out *[to quench fire with water]* 2. to overcome; subdue; suppress 3. to satisfy; slake *[to quench one's thirst]* 4. to cool (hot steel, etc.) suddenly by plunging into water, oil, or the like —**quench′a·ble** *adj.* —**quench′er** *n.* —**quench′less** *adj.*

que·nelle (kə nel′) *n.* [Fr. < G. *knödel*, dumpling < MHG. *knode*, a knot, akin to KNOT¹] a seasoned dumpling of minced meat or fish poached in water

Quen·tin (kwen′t'n) [Fr. < L. *Quintinus* < *Quintus*, Roman praenomen < *quintus*, the fifth (see QUINT¹)] a masculine name: var. *Quintin*

quer·ce·tin (kwur′si tin) *n.* [< L. *quercetum*, an oak forest < *quercus*, oak (< IE. base *perkwus*, oak, whence ON. *fjorr*, tree) + -IN¹] the yellow, crystalline dyestuff, $C_{15}H_{10}O_7$, extracted from the inner bark of the black oak and also produced synthetically —**quer·cet·ic** (kwər set′ik, -sēt′-) *adj.*

quer·cine (kwur′sin, -sīn) *adj.* [LL. *quercinus* < L. *quercus*, oak: see prec.] of the oak

quer·cit·ron (kwur′si trən, kwər sit′rən) *n.* [< ModL. *quercus*, name of the oak genus < L., oak (see QUERCETIN) + CITRON] 1. the inner part of the bark of a N. American black oak (*Quercus velutina*), containing tannin and used in tanning and dyeing 2. a yellow dye made from this bark

Que·ré·ta·ro (ke re′tä rō′) 1. state of C Mexico: 4,432 sq. mi.; pop. 444,000 2. its capital: pop. 68,000

que·rist (kwir′ist) *n.* one who queries, or questions

quern (kwurn) *n.* [ME. *querne* < OE. *cweorn*, akin to ON. *kvern* < IE. base *gwer-*, heavy, whence L. *gravis*, Gr. *barys*] a primitive hand mill, esp. for grinding grain

quer·u·lous (kwer′ə ləs, -yə-) *adj.* [L. *querulus* < *queri*, to

complain: see QUARREL²] 1. inclined to find fault; complaining 2. full of complaint; peevish —**quer′u·lous·ly** *adv.* —**quer′u·lous·ness** *n.*

que·ry (kwir′ē) *n.,* *pl.* **-ries** [< L. *quaere,* 2d pers. sing., imper., of *quaerere,* to ask, inquire] 1. a question: inquiry 2. a doubt 3. a question mark (?), placed after a question or used to query written or printed matter —*vt.* **-ried, -ry·ing** 1. to call in question; ask about 2. to question (a person) 3. to question the accuracy of (some matter in a manuscript or printer's proof) by marking with a question mark —*vi.* to ask questions or express doubt —*SYN.* see ASK

ques. question

Ques·nay (ke nā′), **Fran·çois** (frän swä′) 1694-1774; Fr. economist & physician

quest (kwest) *n.* [ME. < OFr. *queste* < ML. *questa* < VL. *quaesita,* thing sought for < L. *quaesitus,* pp. of *quaerere,* to seek, ask, inquire] 1. a seeking; hunt; pursuit 2. a journey in search of adventure, as those undertaken by knights-errant in medieval times 3. the group of persons participating in a quest 4. [Rare] a jury of inquest—*vi.* 1. to follow the track of game, or to bay in pursuit of game, as hounds do 2. to go in search —*vt.* to search for; seek —**quest′er** *n.*

ques·tion (kwes′chən) *n.* [ME. < Anglo-Fr. *questiun* < OFr. *question* < L. *quaestio* < pp. of *quaerere,* to ask, inquire] 1. an asking; inquiry 2. something that is asked; interrogative sentence, as in seeking to learn or in testing another's knowledge; query 3. doubt; uncertainty [no *question* of his veracity] 4. something in controversy before a court 5. a problem; matter open to discussion or inquiry 6. a matter or case of difficulty [not a *question* of money] 7. *a)* a point being debated or a resolution brought up for approval or rejection before an assembly *b)* the procedure of putting such a matter to a vote —*vt.* [LME. *questyonen* < MFr. *questioner* < the *n.*] 1. to ask a question or questions of; interrogate; put queries to 2. to express uncertainty about; doubt 3. to dispute; challenge —*vi.* to ask a question or questions —*SYN.* see ASK —**beside the question** not related to the subject under discussion —**beyond (all) question** beyond dispute; without any doubt —**in question** being considered, debated, etc. —**out of the question** impossible; not to be considered —**ques′tion·er** *n.*

ques·tion·a·ble (-ə b'l) *adj.* 1. that can or should be questioned or doubted; open to doubt [a *questionable* story] 2. suspected with good reason of being immoral, dishonest, unsound, etc. 3. not definitely as described; uncertain [of *questionable* excellence] —*SYN.* see DOUBTFUL —**ques′tion·a·ble·ness** *n.* —**ques′tion·a·bly** *adv.*

ques·tion·less (-lis) *adj.* 1. unquestionable; indubitable 2. asking no questions; unquestioning —*adv.* [Now Rare] beyond question; unquestionably

question mark 1. a mark of punctuation (?) put after a sentence, word, etc. to indicate a direct question, and also used to express doubt, uncertainty, etc.; interrogation mark ☆2. an unknown factor

ques·tion·naire (kwes′chə ner′) *n.* [Fr.: see QUESTION, *v.*] a written or printed form used in gathering information on some subject or subjects, consisting of a set of questions to be submitted to one or more persons

ques·tor (kwes′tər, kwēs′-) *n. alt. sp.* of QUAESTOR

Quet·ta (kwet′ä) city in W West Pakistan; capital of the former province of Baluchistan: pop. 107,000

quet·zal (ket säl′) *n.* [AmSp. < Nahuatl *quetzaltototl* < *quetzalli,* tail feather + *tototl,* bird] 1. a crested bird (*Pharomachrus mocino*) of Central America, usually brilliant green above and red below, with long, streaming tail feathers in the male 2. *pl.* **-zal′es** (-sä′les) the monetary unit of Guatemala: see MONETARY UNITS, table

Quet·zal·co·atl (ket säl′kō ät′'l) the principal god of the Aztecs, symbolized by a feathered serpent

queue (kyōō) *n.* [Fr. < OFr. *coue* < L. *cauda,* tail] 1. a plait of hair worn hanging from the back of the head; pigtail 2. [Chiefly Brit.] a line or file of persons, vehicles, etc. waiting as to be served —*vi.* **queued, queu′ing** [Chiefly Brit.] to form in a line or file while waiting to be served, etc. (often with *up*)

que·zal (ke säl′) *n. same as* QUETZAL

Que·zon (**Antonio y Molina**) (ke′sōn; *E.* kā′zän), **Man·uel Lu·is** (mä nwel′ lōo ēs′) 1878-1944; Philippine statesman; 1st president of the Philippines (1935-44)

Que·zon City (ke′sōn; *E.* kā′zän) capital of the Philippines, on SW Luzon: suburb of Manila: pop. 398,000

quib·ble (kwib′'l) *n.* [dim. < obs. *quib* < L. *quibus,* abl. pl. of *qui,* which, WHO: *quibus* was common in legal documents] 1. orig., a play on words; pun 2. an evasion of the main point as by emphasizing some petty detail; cavil 3. a petty objection or criticism —*vi.* **-bled, -bling**

QUETZAL
(length, including plumes, 24 in.)

to evade the truth of a point under discussion by caviling; resort to a quibble —**quib′bler** *n.*

‡**quiche Lor·raine** (kēsh lô ren′) *pl.* **quiches Lor·raine′** (kēsh) [Fr., lit., Lorraine pastry: *quiche* < G. dial. (Lorraine) *küche,* dim. of G. *kuchen,* cake < OHG. *kuocho:* see CAKE] a kind of custard pie made with cheese, bacon, etc. and served hot

quick (kwik) *adj.* [ME. *quik,* lively, alive < OE. *cwicu,* living, akin to ON. *kvikr,* OHG. *quek* < IE. base **gwīgw-** < **gwei-,** to live, be alive, whence Gr. *bios,* life, *zōon,* animal, L. *vivus,* living, *vigere,* to be vigorous] 1. [Archaic] living; alive 2. *a)* rapid; swift [a *quick* walk] *b)* done with promptness; prompt [a *quick* reply] *c)* acting swiftly [a *quick* worker] 3. lasting only a moment [a *quick* look] 4. prompt to understand or learn; sharp in discernment [a *quick* mind] 5. sensitive; acutely perceptive [a *quick* sense of smell] 6. easily stirred; fiery [a *quick* temper] 7. sharply curved [a *quick* turn] 8. [Archaic] pregnant —*adv.* quickly; rapidly —*n.* 1. the living, esp. in **the quick and the dead** 2. the sensitive flesh under a toenail or fingernail 3. the deepest feelings or sensibilities [hurt to the *quick*] —*vt.* [Archaic] to animate; invigorate —**quick′ly** *adv.* —**quick′ness** *n.*
SYN.—**quick** implies ability to respond rapidly as an innate rather than a developed faculty [a *quick* mind]; **prompt** stresses immediate response to a demand as resulting from discipline, practice, etc. or from willingness [*prompt* to obey, a *prompt* acceptance]; **ready** also implies preparation or willingness and, in another sense, connotes fluency, expertness, etc. [a *ready* sympathy, jest, etc.]; **apt,** in this connection, implies superior intelligence or a special talent as the reason for quickness of response [an *apt* pupil] See also AGILE, FAST¹ —*ANT.* slow

quick assets *Accounting* cash on hand, current accounts receivable, and all other highly liquid assets excluding merchandise or inventory

☆**quick bread** any bread, as muffins, corn bread, etc., leavened with baking powder, soda, etc. so that it may be baked as soon as the batter is mixed

quick clay a soil substance that can promptly change from a solid to fluid state when jarred, as by an earthquake, pile driver, etc. and that can flow over land having a slope of less than one degree

quick·en (kwik′ən) *vt.* [ME. *quickenen* < ON. *kvikna,* akin to OE. *cwician* < *cwicu,* alive: see QUICK] 1. to animate; enliven; revive 2. to arouse; stimulate; stir 3. to cause to move more rapidly; hasten —*vi.* 1. to become enlivened; revive 2. *a)* to begin to show signs of life, as a fetus in the womb *b)* to enter the stage of pregnancy in which the movement of the fetus can be felt 3. to become more rapid; speed up [the pulse *quickens* with fear] —*SYN.* see ANIMATE —**quick′en·er** *n.*

quick-fire (-fīr′) *adj.* firing, or designed for firing, shots in quick succession: also **quick′-fir′ing**

☆**quick-freeze** (-frēz′) *vt.* **-froze′, -froz′en, -freez′ing** to subject (raw or freshly cooked food) to sudden freezing so that the flavor and natural juices are retained and the food can be stored at low temperatures for a long time

quick grass *same as* COUCH GRASS

☆**quick·ie** (-ē) *n.* [Slang] anything done or made quickly; specif., *a)* a motion picture made quickly and cheaply *b)* a hurriedly consumed drink of alcoholic liquor —*adj.* [Slang] done, completed, attained, etc. in less time than is usual or desirable

quick·lime (-līm′) *n.* [ME. *quykke lyme,* after L. *calx viva*] a product consisting chiefly of calcium oxide, obtained by roasting limestone, marble, shells, etc.; unslaked lime

quick·sand (-sand′) *n.* [ME. *quykkesand:* see QUICK & SAND] a loose, wet, deep sand deposit in which a person or heavy object may easily be engulfed

quick·set (-set′) *n.* [Chiefly Brit.] 1. a live slip or cutting, as of hawthorn, planted with others to grow into a hedge 2. a hedge, as of hawthorn

quick·sil·ver (kwik′sil′vər) *n.* [ME. < OE. *cwicseolfor* < *cwicu,* living (see QUICK) + *seolfor,* SILVER: transl. of L. *argentum vivum,* lit., living silver: from its liquid form] *same as* MERCURY (n. 1a) —*vt.* to cover with mercury —*adj.* of or like mercury

quick·step (-step′) *n.* 1. the step used for marching in quick time 2. *Music* a march in the rhythm of quick time 3. a spirited dance step

quick-tem·pered (-tem′pərd) *adj.* easily angered

quick time the normal rate of marching: in the U.S. Army, 120 (30-inch) paces a minute

quick-wit·ted (-wit′id) *adj.* nimble of mind; alert —**quick′-wit′ted·ly** *adv.* —**quick′-wit′ted·ness** *n.*

quid¹ (kwid) *n.* [var. of CUD] a piece, as of tobacco, to be chewed

quid² (kwid) *n., pl.* **quid** [? orig. slang use of L. *quid,* something, esp. in *quid pro quo*] [Brit. Slang] a sovereign, or one pound sterling

quid·di·ty (kwid′ə tē) *n., pl.* **-ties** [ML. *quidditas* < L. *quid,* what, neut. of *quis,* WHO] 1. the essential quality of a thing 2. a trifling distinction; quibble

quid·nunc (kwid′nunk′) *n.* [L., lit., what now?] an inquisitive, gossipy person; busybody

quid pro quo (kwid′ prō kwō′) [ModL., something for something] **1.** one thing in return for another **2.** something equivalent; substitute

qui·es·cent (kwī es′'nt) *adj.* [L. *quiescens,* prp. of *quiescere,* to become quiet: see ff.] quiet; still; inactive —*SYN.* see LATENT —**qui·es′cence** *n.* —**qui·es′cent·ly** *adv.*

qui·et (kwī′ət) *adj.* [ME. *quiete* < OFr. < L. *quietus,* pp. of *quiescere,* to keep quiet < *quies* (gen. *quietis*), rest < IE. base **kweye-,* to rest, whence WHILE] **1.** still; calm; motionless **2.** *a)* not making noise; hushed [a *quiet* motor] *b)* not speaking; silent **3.** not agitated, as in motion; gentle [a *quiet* sea] **4.** not easily excited or disturbed [a *quiet* disposition] **5.** not ostentatious or pretentious [quiet furnishings] **6.** not forward; unobtrusive [a *quiet* manner] **7.** secluded [a *quiet* den] **8.** peaceful and relaxing [a *quiet* evening at home] **9.** *Commerce* not busy [a *quiet* day on the stock exchange] —*n.* **1.** a quiet state or condition; calmness, stillness, inactivity, freedom from noise, etc. **2.** a quiet or peaceful quality; freedom from turmoil or agitation —*vt.* **1.** to make quiet; calm or pacify, bring to rest, etc. **2.** to allay (fear, doubt, etc.) **3.** *Law* to make (a title) unassailable by freeing the fact of ownership from interference, disturbance, or question —*vi.* to become quiet (usually with *down*) —*adv.* in a quiet manner —*SYN.* see STILL[1] —**qui′et·er** *n.* —**qui′et·ly** *adv.* —**qui′et·ness** *n.*

qui·et·en (-'n) *vt., vi.* [prec. + -EN, verbalizing suffix] [Brit. or Dial.] to make or become quiet

qui·et·ism (-iz′m) *n.* [It. *quietismo* < L. *quietus:* see QUIET & -ISM] **1.** a form of religious mysticism, esp. of the 17th cent., that involves extinction of the human will, withdrawal from worldly concerns, and passive contemplation of God and divine things **2.** tranquillity of the spirit or quietness of life —**qui′et·ist** *n., adj.* —**qui′et·is′tic** *adj.*

qui·e·tude (kwī′ə tōōd′, -tyōōd′) *n.* [Fr. *quiétude* < LL. *quietudo*] a state of being quiet; rest; calmness

qui·e·tus (kwī ēt′əs) *n.* [< ME. *quietus* (*est*) < ML., (he is) quit < L., QUIET] **1.** discharge or release from debt, obligation, or office **2.** discharge or release from life; death **3.** anything that kills **4.** anything that serves to quiet, curb, or end an activity

quiff[1] (kwif) *n.* [< ? It. *cuffia,* a coif < LL. *cofea:* see COIF] [Chiefly Brit.] a lock or tuft of hair; esp., a forelock

quiff[2] (kwif) *n.* [< ? obs. *quiff,* to copulate < ?] ☆[Slang] a sexually promiscuous woman

quill (kwil) *n.* [ME. *quil,* hollow stalk, weaver's quill, prob. < MLowG. or MDu., as in LowG. *quiele,* quill of a feather < IE. base **gwel-,* to stick, stab] **1.** any of the large, stiff wing or tail feathers of a bird **2.** the hollow, horny stem of a feather; calamus **3.** any of the spines of a porcupine or hedgehog **4.** any of various things made from the quill of a feather, as a pen for writing, a plectrum, as of a harpsichord, a toothpick, etc. **5.** a musical pipe made of a hollow stem, reed, or cane **6.** a weaver's spindle or bobbin **7.** a hollow shaft in certain mechanical devices **8.** *Pharmacy* a small roll of dried bark, as of cinchona, cinnamon, etc. —*vt.* **1.** to form with or into quillings **2.** to wind (thread or yarn) on a quill (sense 6) **3.** to cover or pierce with quills, as of a porcupine

quil·lai·a, quil·laj·a (ki lī′ə) *n.* [Sp. < the Chilean (Araucan) native name] *same as* SOAPBARK (sense 1): also **quil·lai′** (-lī′)

☆**quill·back** (kwil′bak′) *n., pl.* **-back′, -backs′:** see PLURAL, II, D, 2 any of a genus (*Carpiodes*) of inedible, N. American, freshwater fishes with the front margin of the dorsal fin quill-like and elongated

Quil·ler-Couch (kwil′ər kōōch′), Sir Arthur Thomas (pseud. *Q*) 1863–1944; Eng. writer

quill·ing (kwil′iŋ) *n.* a band of material fluted into small ruffles so as to resemble a row of quills

quill·wort (-wurt′) *n.* any of a genus (*Isoetes*) of water plants with short, fleshy stems and tufts of long, hollow, quill-like leaves whose bases contain spore cases

Quil·mes (kēl′mes) city in E Argentina, on the Río de la Plata: suburb of Buenos Aires: pop. 120,000

quilt (kwilt) *n.* [ME. *quilte* < OFr. < L. *culcita,* bed, mattress < IE. base **kwelek-,* whence Sans. *kūrcah,* a bundle, roll] **1.** a bedcover made of two layers of cloth filled with down, cotton, wool, etc. and stitched together in lines or patterns to keep the filling in place **2.** anything used as a quilt **3.** anything quilted or like a quilt —*vt.* **1.** to make or stitch as or like a quilt [to *quilt* a potholder] **2.** to sew up or fasten between two pieces of material **3.** to line or pad with a quiltlike material —☆*vi.* to make a quilt or quilts —**quilt′er** *n.*

quilt·ing (-iŋ) *n.* **1.** the act or process of making quilts **2.** material for making quilts, or quilted work ☆**3.** *same as* QUILTING BEE

☆**quilting bee** (or **party**) a social gathering of women at which they work together sewing quilts

quin·a·crine hydrochloride (kwin′ə krēn) [QUIN(INE) + ACR(IDINE)] *same as* ATABRINE

qui·na·ry (kwī′nə rē) *adj.* [L. *quinarius* < *quini,* five each < *quinque,* FIVE] consisting of five; in sets of five —*n., pl.* **-ries** a set of five

quince (kwins) *n.* [ME. *qwince,* orig. pl. of *quyn* < OFr. *cooin* < VL. **cotoneum,* for L. *cydonium* < Gr. *kydōnion* (*mēlon*), Cydonian (apple) < *Kydōnia,* Cydonia, town on N coast of Crete] **1.** a golden or greenish-yellow, hard, apple-shaped fruit of a small tree (*Cydonia oblonga*) of the rose family, used in preserves **2.** the tree

quin·cunx (kwin′kuŋks) *n.* [L., lit., five twelfths < *quinque,* FIVE + *uncia,* a twelfth: see OUNCE[1]] **1.** an arrangement of five objects in a square, with one at each corner and one in the middle **2.** *Bot.* an arrangement of five-petaled flowers in which two petals are interior, two are exterior, and one is partly interior and partly exterior —**quin·cun′cial** (-kun′shəl), **quin·cunx′i·al** (-kuŋk′sē əl) *adj.* —**quin·cun′cial·ly** *adv.*

Quin·cy (kwin′zē *for* 1; -sē *for* 2) **1.** [after Col. John *Quincy* (1689–1767), a local official] city in E Mass.: suburb of Boston: pop. 88,000 **2.** [after John *Quincy* ADAMS] city in W Ill., on the Mississippi: pop. 45,000

Quin·cy (kwin′zē, -sē), **Josiah** 1744–75; Am. Revolutionary patriot

quin·dec·a·gon (kwin dek′ə gän′) *n.* [< L. *quindecim,* fifteen < *quinque,* FIVE + *decem,* TEN + -agon, for -GON] *Geom.* a plane figure with fifteen angles and fifteen sides

quin·de·cen·ni·al (kwin′di sen′ē əl) *adj.* [< L. *quindecim* (see prec.) + -ennial, as in BIENNIAL] **1.** happening once every fifteen years **2.** lasting fifteen years —*n.* **1.** a fifteenth year of existence or duration; fifteenth anniversary **2.** the celebration of this

qui·nel·la (kwi nel′ə, kē-) *n.* [AmSp. *quiniela* < ?] a form of betting, esp. in horse racing, in which the bettor, to win, must pick the first two finishers, in whichever order they finish: also **qui·nie·la** (kē nye′lə)

quin·ic acid (kwin′ik) [< *quina* (see QUININE) + -IC] a colorless, crystalline acid, $C_7H_{12}O_6$, prepared from cinchona bark, coffee beans, etc.

quin·i·dine (kwin′ə dēn′, -din) *n.* [< *quina* (see QUININE) + -ID + -INE[4]] a colorless, crystalline alkaloid, $C_{20}H_{24}N_2O_2$, isomeric with and resembling quinine, extracted from cinchona bark

qui·nine (kwī′nīn; *chiefly Brit.,* kwi nēn′) *n.* [< *quina,* cinchona bark (< Sp. *quina,* contr. < *quinaquina* < Quechua name) + -INE[4]] **1.** a bitter, crystalline alkaloid, $C_{20}H_{24}N_2O_2$, extracted from cinchona bark **2.** any compound of this, as quinine sulfate, used in medicine for various purposes, esp. for treating malaria

quinine water *same as* TONIC (n. 2)

☆**quin·nat salmon** (kwin′at) [< the AmInd. (upper Chinook) name] *same as* CHINOOK SALMON

qui·no·a (ki nō′ə) *n.* [Sp. < Quechua *quinua*] an Andean goosefoot (*Chenopodium quinoa*), raised by the Indians for its edible seeds

quin·oid (kwin′oid) *n.* [QUIN(ONE) + -OID] a substance resembling quinone in structure, properties, etc.

qui·noi·dine (kwi noi′dēn, -din) *n.* [QUINOID + -INE[4]] a brownish substance containing a mixture of alkaloids formed in the process of extracting quinine from cinchona, formerly used as a substitute for quinine

quin·o·line (kwin′l ēn′, -in) *n.* [QUIN(INE) + -OL[1] + -INE[4]] **1.** a colorless, liquid compound, C_9H_7N, obtained by the destructive distillation of bones, coal tar, and various alkaloids, or by synthesis: it is used in making antiseptics, dyes, etc. and as a solvent **2.** any of various derivatives of quinoline

qui·none (kwi nōn′, kwin′ōn) *n.* [QUIN(IC ACID) + -ONE] **1.** either of two isomeric compounds, $C_6H_4O_2$, especially the yellow, crystalline isomer used in making dyes **2.** any of a series of compounds of this type

qui·non·i·mine (kwi nän′ə mēn′, -min) *n.* [< prec. + IMINE] a crystalline compound, C_6H_5NO, derived from a quinone by the replacement of an oxygen atom by an imino group

quin·o·noid (kwin′ə noid′, kwi nō′noid) *adj.* [QUINON(E) + -OID] like quinone in structure, properties, etc.

quin·qua·ge·nar·i·an (kwiŋ′kwə ji ner′ē ən) *adj.* [< L. *quinquagenarius* < *quinquageni,* fifty each < *quinquaginta,* fifty < *quinque,* FIVE + -ginta < IE. **komt-* < base **dekm,* TEN] fifty years old, or between the ages of fifty and sixty —*n.* a person of this age

Quin·qua·ges·i·ma (-jes′i mə) *n.* [LL. *quinquagesima* (*dies*), fiftieth (day), i.e., before Easter, fem. of L. *quinquagesimus,* fiftieth: cf. prec.] the Sunday before Lent: also **Quinquagesima Sunday**

quin·que- (kwin′kwə) [< L. *quinque,* FIVE] *a combining form meaning* five or a multiple of five [quinquevalent]: also, before a vowel, **quin′qu-**

quin·que·fo·li·o·late (kwin′kwə fō′lē ə līt, -lāt′) *adj.* [prec. + FOLIOLATE] *Bot.* having five leaflets

quin·quen·ni·al (kwin kwen′ē əl) *adj.* [< L. *quinquennis,* of five years < *quinque,* FIVE + *annus,* year + -AL] **1.** lasting five years **2.** taking place every five years —*n.* a quinquennial event —**quin·quen′ni·al·ly** *adv.*

quin·quen·ni·um (-ē əm) *n., pl.* **-ni·ums, -ni·a** (-ə) [L. < *quinquennis:* see prec.] a period of five years: also **quin·quen′ni·ad** (-i ad′)

quin·que·va·lent (kwin′kwə vā′lənt) *adj.* [L. *quinque,* FIVE + -VALENT] **1.** having five valences **2.** *same as* PENTAVALENT (sense 1) —**quin′que·va′lence, quin′que·va′len·cy** *n.*

quin·sy (kwin′zē) *n.* [ME. *quinaci* < ML. *quinancia* < LL. *cynanche* < Gr. *kynanchē,* inflammation of the throat, lit., dog-choking < *kyōn,* dog (see HOUND[1]) + *anchein,* to choke (see ANGER)] *an earlier term for* TONSILLITIS

quint[1] (kwint, kint) *n.* [Fr. *quinte* < L. *quinta,* fem. of

quintus, a fifth < base of *quinque*, FIVE] in piquet, a sequence of five cards in the same suit

quint² (kwint) *n. clipped form of* QUINTUPLET

quin·tain (kwin′t′n) *n.* [ME. *qwaintan* < OFr. *quintaine* < ML. *quintana* < L. *quintana (via)*, street in a Roman camp separating the fifth maniple from the sixth; later, marketplace < *quintanus*, of the fifth < *quintus*, fifth: see QUINT¹] an object supported by a crosspiece on a post, used by knights as a target in tilting

quin·tal (kwin′t′l) *n.* [ME. < MFr. < ML. *quintale* < Ar. *qințār*, ult. < L. *centenarius:* see CENTENARY] **1.** a hundredweight (100 lbs. in the U.S., 112 lbs. in Great Britain) **2.** a metric unit of weight, equal to 100 kilograms (220.46 lbs.)

quin·tan (kwin′tən) *adj.* [L. *quintanus* < *quintus*, fifth: see QUINT¹] occurring every fifth day (counting both days of occurrence) —*n.* a quintan fever

Quin·ta·na Ro·o (kēn tä′nä rô′ō) territory of SE Mexico, on E Yucatán Peninsula: 19,440 sq. mi.; pop. 72,000

quinte (kant) *n.* [Fr., fem. of *quint*, fifth: see QUINT¹] *Fencing* the fifth position (of defense or parry), similar to the fourth but with the hand lower and the point farther to the left

Quintero see ÁLVAREZ QUINTERO

quin·tes·sence (kwin tes′ns) *n.* [ME. *quyntencense* < MFr. *quinte essence* < ML. *quinta essentia*] **1.** in ancient and medieval philosophy, the fifth essence, or ultimate substance, of which the heavenly bodies were thought to be composed: distinguished from the four elements: air, fire, water, and earth **2.** the pure, concentrated essence of anything **3.** the most perfect manifestation of a quality or thing —**quin·tes·sen′tial** (-tə sen′shəl) *adj.*

quin·tet, quin·tette (kwin tet′) *n.* [< Fr. or It.: Fr. *quintette* < It. *quintetto*, dim. of *quinto*, a fifth < L. *quintus:* see QUINT¹] **1.** any group or set of five persons or things **2.** *Music a)* a composition for five voices or five instruments, as for string quartet and piano *b)* the five performers of such a composition

quin·tile (kwin′til, -til) *adj.* [< L. *quintus*, a fifth (see QUINT¹) + -ILE] *Astrol.* designating an aspect of two heavenly bodies in which they are 72 degrees, or one fifth of a circle, distant from each other —*n.* a quintile aspect

Quin·til·ian (kwin til′yən, -ē ən) (L. name *Marcus Fabius Quintilianus*) 30?-96? A.D.; Rom. rhetorician, born in Spain

quin·til·lion (kwin til′yən) *n.* [< L. *quintus*, a fifth (see QUINT¹) + (M)ILLION] **1.** in the U.S. and France, a number represented by 1 followed by 18 zeros **2.** in Great Britain and Germany, a number represented by 1 followed by 30 zeros —*adj.* amounting to one quintillion in number —**quin·til′lionth** *adj., n.*

Quin·tin (kwin′t′n) a masculine name: see QUENTIN

quin·tu·ple (kwin tōō′p′l, -tyōō′-, -tup′l; kwin′tōō p′l) *adj.* [MFr. < LL. *quintuplex* < L. *quintus*, a fifth + *-plex*, -fold: see QUINT¹ & DUPLEX] **1.** consisting of or including five **2.** five times as much or as many; fivefold —*n.* an amount five times as much or as many —*vt., vi.* -**pled**, -**pling** to make or become five times as much or as many; multiply by five

quin·tu·plet (kwin tup′lit, -tōō′plit, -tyōō′-; kwin′tōō plit) *n.* [dim. of prec.] **1.** any of five offspring born at a single birth **2.** a collection or group of five, usually of one kind

quin·tu·pli·cate (kwin tōō′plə kāt′, -tyōō′-; *for adj. & n., usually* -kit) *vt.* -**cat′ed**, -**cat′ing** [LL. *quintuplicatus*, pp. of *quintuplicare*, to quintuple < *quintuplex:* see QUINTUPLE] to quintuple; make five identical copies of —*adj.* **1.** fivefold **2.** designating the fifth of identical copies —*n.* any of five identical copies or things —**in quintuplicate** in five identical copies —**quin·tu′pli·ca′tion** *n.*

quip (kwip) *n.* [contr. < earlier *quippy* < L. *quippe*, indeed, forsooth < *quid*, what: for base see WHAT] **1.** a witty or, esp. formerly, sarcastic remark or reply; jest or gibe **2.** a quibble; cavil **3.** something curious or odd —*vt.* **quipped**, **quip′ping** [Now Rare] to direct quips, or gibes, at —*vi.* to utter quips —*SYN.* see JOKE —**quip′ster** *n.*

qui·pu (kē′pōō, kwip′ōō) *n.* [AmSp. *quipo* < Quechua *quipu*, a knot] a device consisting of an arrangement of cords variously colored and knotted, used by the ancient Peruvians to keep accounts, record events, etc.

quire¹ (kwīr) *n., vt., vi.* **quired**, **quir′ing** *archaic var. of* CHOIR

quire² (kwīr) *n.* [ME. *quair* < OFr. *quaer*, book of loose pages < VL. *quaternum*, paper packed in lots of four pages < L. *quaterni*, four each: see QUATERNARY] a set of 24 or 25 sheets of paper of the same size and stock, the twentieth part of a ream —**in quires** [Now Rare] still in sheets; unbound: said of a book

Quir·i·nal (kwir′i n′l) [L. *Quirinalis* < *Quirinus:* see ff.] one of the SEVEN HILLS OF ROME: site of a palace used (1870-1946) as a royal residence, later as the presidential residence —*n.* the Italian government —*adj.* **1.** of or situated on the Quirinal **2.** of Quirinus

Qui·ri·nus (kwi rī′nəs) [L., akin to ff.] *Rom. Myth.* an early god of war, later identified with Romulus

Qui·ri·tes (kwi rī′tēz) *n.pl.* [L., pl. of *Quiris*, orig., inhabitant of *Cures* (a Sabine town); later, Roman citizen] in ancient Rome, the people as civilians

quirk (kwurk) *n.* [< ? ON. *kverk*, a bird's crop] **1.** *a)* a sudden twist, turn, or stroke [a *quirk* of fortune] *b)* a flourish in writing **2.** an evasion, subterfuge, or quibble **3.** a peculiarity, peculiar trait, or mannerism **4.** [Now Rare] a clever turn of speech; sally; quip **5.** *Archit.* a groove running lengthwise in a molding —*vt. Archit.* to form with quirks —**quirk′i·ly** *adv.* —**quirk′i·ness** *n.* —**quirk′y** *adj.* **quirk′i·er**, **quirk′i·est**

☆**quirt** (kwurt) *n.* [AmSp. *cuarta*, a quirt, long whip < *cuarta*, guide mule, lit., fourth (of a four-mule team), fem. of Sp. *cuarto*, fourth < L. *quartus:* see QUART¹] a riding whip with a braided leather lash and a short handle —*vt.* to strike with a quirt

QUIRT

quis·ling (kwiz′liŋ) *n.* [after Vidkun *Quisling* (1887-1945), Norw. politician who betrayed his country to the Nazis and became its puppet ruler] a traitor

quit (kwit) *vt.* **quit**, **quit′ted**, **quit′ting** [ME. *quiten* < OFr. *quiter* < ML. *quittus*, *quietus*, free: see QUIET] **1.** to free (oneself) *of* **2.** to discharge (a debt or obligation); repay **3.** to stop having, using, or doing (something); give up **4.** to leave; depart from **5.** to stop, discontinue, or resign from **6.** [Archaic] to conduct (oneself) —*vi.* **1.** *a)* to stop or discontinue doing something *b)* to give up or stop trying, as in discouragement **2.** to give up one's position of employment; resign **3.** [Now Rare] to go away —*adj.* [ME. < OFr. < ML. *quietus*] clear, free, or rid, as of an obligation —*SYN.* see ABANDON, GO¹, STOP

quitch (kwich) *n.* [OE. *cwice* < base of *cwicu*, alive (cf. QUICK); apparently after the great vitality of the plant] *same as* COUCH GRASS

quit·claim (kwit′klām′) *n.* [ME. *quitclayme* < Anglo-Fr. *quiteclame* < the *v.*] **1.** the release or relinquishment of a claim, action, right, or title **2.** a deed or other legal paper in which a person relinquishes to another a claim or title to some property or right without guaranteeing or warranting such title: in full **quitclaim deed** —*vt.* [ME. *quite clamen* < Anglo-Fr. & OFr. *quiteclamer:* see QUIT & CLAIM] to give up a claim or title to, esp. by a quitclaim deed

quite (kwit) *adv.* [ME. *quite:* see QUIT, *adj.*] **1.** completely; entirely [not *quite* done] **2.** really; truly; positively [*quite* a hero] **3.** to some, or a considerable, degree or extent; very or fairly [*quite* warm outside] —☆**quite a few** (or **bit**, etc.) [Colloq.] more than a few (or bit, etc.) —**quite (so)**! certainly! I agree!

Qui·to (kē′tō) capital of Ecuador, in the NC part: pop. 355,000

quit·rent (kwit′rent′) *n.* a rent paid in lieu of required feudal services: also **quit rent**

quits (kwits) *adj.* [ME., prob. contr. < ML. *quittus*, var. of *quietus:* see QUIETUS] on even terms, as by discharge of a debt, retaliation in vengeance, etc. —**call it quits** [Colloq.] **1.** to stop working, playing, etc. **2.** to stop being friendly or intimate; end an association —**cry quits** [Chiefly Brit.] to declare oneself even with another; agree to stop competing

quit·tance (kwit′ns) *n.* [ME. *quitance* < OFr. < *quiter:* see QUIT] **1.** *a)* discharge from a debt or obligation *b)* a document certifying this; receipt **2.** recompense; repayment; reprisal

quit·ter (kwit′ər) *n.* ☆[Colloq.] a person who quits or gives up easily, without trying hard

quit·tor (kwit′ər) *n.* [ME. *quiture* < OFr. *cuiture*, cooking < L. *coctura* < pp. of *coquere*, to COOK] a foot disease, esp. of horses, characterized by a pus-forming fistula on the coronet

quiv·er¹ (kwiv′ər) *vi.* [ME. *quiveren* < IE. base *gwei-*, to live, lively: see QUICK] to shake with a tremulous motion; tremble —*n.* the act or condition of quivering; tremor; tremble —*SYN.* see SHAKE —**quiv′er·y** *adj.*

quiv·er² (kwiv′ər) *n.* [ME. *quyvere* < OFr. *coivre* < Gmc. *kukur* (whence OE. *cocer*, quiver, sheath, G. *köcher*, quiver), prob. a loan word from the Huns' language] **1.** a case for holding arrows **2.** the arrows in it

quiv·er³ (kwiv′ər) *adj.* [ME. *cwyuer* < OE. *cwifer:* for base see QUIVER¹] [Obs. or Dial.] nimble; quick

‡**qui vive?** (kē vēv′) [Fr., (long) live who? (i.e., whose side are you on?), 3d pers. sing., pres. subj., of *vivre*, to live (< L. *vivere*) + *qui*, who (< L.)] who goes there?: a sentry's challenge —**on the qui vive** on the lookout; on the alert

Quixote, Don see DON QUIXOTE

quix·ot·ic (kwik sät′ik) *adj.* **1.** [*often* Q-] of or like Don Quixote **2.** extravagantly chivalrous or romantically idealistic; visionary; impractical or impracticable: also **quix·ot′i·cal** —**quix·ot′i·cal·ly** *adv.*

quix·ot·ism (kwik′sə tiz′m) *n.* **1.** quixotic character or practice **2.** a quixotic act or idea

quiz (kwiz) *n., pl.* **quiz′zes** [prob. arbitrary use of L. *quis*, what (i.e., what sort of person or thing?)] **1.** formerly,

a) a queer or eccentric person *b)* a practical joke; hoax ☆2. a questioning; esp., a short oral or written examination to test knowledge —*vt.* **quizzed, quiz′zing** 1. formerly, to make fun of ☆2. to ask questions of, as in testing knowledge or interrogating —*SYN.* see ASK —**quiz′zer** *n.*

☆**quiz·mas·ter** (-mas′tər) *n.* the master of ceremonies on a quiz program

☆**quiz program** (or **show**) a radio or television program in which a group of people compete in answering questions

quiz·zi·cal (kwiz′i k′l) *adj.* [< QUIZ + -IC + -AL] 1. odd; comical 2. teasing; bantering 3. perplexed; questioning —**quiz′zi·cal′i·ty** (-kal′ə tē) *n.* —**quiz′zi·cal·ly** *adv.*

Qum (koom) city in NC Iran: pop. 96,000

Qum·ran (koom rän′) region in NW Jordan, near the NW shore of the Dead Sea: site of caves in which Dead Sea Scrolls have been found

quod (kwäd) *n.* [prob. var. of *quad*, contr. < QUADRANGLE (of a prison)] [Chiefly Brit. Slang] prison; jail

quod·li·bet (kwäd′lə bet′) *n.* [LME. < ML. *quodlibeta*, a disputation < L. *quod libet*, as you will < *quod*, neut. of *qui*, WHO + *libet*, 3d pers. sing., pres. of *libere*, to please] 1. an academic debate or exercise in argument, esp. on a theological question 2. a humorously incongruous musical medley

quo·hog (kwô′hôg, kō′-; -häg) *n. same as* QUAHOG

quoin (koin, kwoin) *n.* [var. of COIN] 1. the external corner of a building; esp., any of the large, squared stones by which the corner of a building is marked 2. a wedge-like piece of stone, etc., such as the keystone or one of the pieces of an arch 3. a wedge-shaped wooden or metal block used to lock up type in a galley or form, to keep casks from rolling, etc. —*vt.* 1. to secure with a quoin 2. to furnish with quoins, or corners

QUOINS

quoit (kwoit; *chiefly Brit.*, koit) *n.* [ME. *coyte* (Anglo-Fr. *jeu de coytes*), prob. < OFr. *coite*, a cushion (< L. *culcita*: see QUILT): ? orig., a cushion target] 1. a ring of rope or flattened metal, used in the game of quoits 2. [*pl.*, *with sing. v.*] a game somewhat like horseshoes, in which players throw such rings at a peg (*hob* or *tee*) in an effort to encircle it —*vt.* to throw like a quoit

‡**quo ju·re?** (kwō joor′ē) [L.] by what right?

‡**quo mo·do** (kwō mō′dō) [L.] 1. in what manner? 2. in the manner that

quon·dam (kwän′dəm) *adj.* [L.] that was at one time; former [a *quondam* companion]

☆**Quon·set hut** (kwän′sit) [after *Quonset* Point, R.I., where first manufactured] *a trademark for* a prefabricated shelter made of corrugated metal, shaped like a longitudinal half of a cylinder resting on its flat surface: it is similar to the British Nissen hut

quo·rum (kwôr′əm) *n.* [L., gen. pl. of *qui*, WHO: from use in court commissions] 1. *orig.*, the number of justices of the peace required to be present at sessions of English courts 2. the minimum number of members required to be present at an assembly or meeting before it can validly

proceed to transact business 3. a select group or company **quot.** quotation

quo·ta (kwōt′ə) *n.* [ML., short for L. *quota pars*, how large a part: fem. of *quotus*: see QUOTE] 1. a share or proportion which each of a number is called upon to contribute, or which is assigned to each; proportional share ☆2. the number or proportion that is allowed or admitted [immigration *quotas*]

quot·a·ble (kwōt′ə b'l) *adj.* worthwhile quoting or suitable for quotation —**quot′a·bil′i·ty** *n.* —**quot′a·bly** *adv.*

quo·ta·tion (kwō tā′shən) *n.* [ML. *quotatio*] 1. the act or practice of quoting 2. the words or passage quoted 3. *Commerce* the current quoted price of a stock, bond, commodity, etc.

quotation mark either of a pair of punctuation marks (". . .") used to enclose a direct quotation, or of single marks ('. . .') for enclosing within a quotation

quote (kwōt) *vt.* **quot′ed, quot′ing** [ME. *coten* < ML. *quotare*, to mark the number of, divide into chapters < L. *quotus*, of what number < IE. *kwoti-*, how many < interrogative base *kwo-*, whence WHO] 1. to reproduce or repeat a passage from or statement of [to *quote* Chaucer] 2. to reproduce or repeat (a passage from a book, a statement, etc.) 3. to refer to as authority or an example; cite 4. *Commerce* to state (a price) or state the price of (something) 5. *Printing* to enclose in quotation marks —*vi.* to make a quotation, as from a book or author —*n.* [Colloq.] *same as:* 1. QUOTATION 2. QUOTATION MARK —*tnterj.* I shall quote: used in speech to signal the beginning of a quotation —**quot′er** *n.*

quoth (kwōth) *vt.* [ME. *quath* < OE. *quæth*, pret. of *cwethan*, to speak, say, akin to Goth. *quithan*, to say] [Archaic] said: the past tense, followed by a subject in the first or third person, and taking as its object the words being repeated

quoth·a (-ə) *interj.* [altered < *quoth he*, used ironically] [Archaic] indeed! forsooth!

quo·tid·i·an (kwō tid′ē ən) *adj.* [ME. *cotidian* < OFr. < L. *quotidianus* < *quotidie*, daily < *quot*, as many as (for base see QUOTE) + *dies*, day] 1. daily; recurring every day 2. everyday; usual or ordinary —*n.* anything, esp. a fever, that recurs daily

quo·tient (kwō′shənt) *n.* [ME. *quocient* < L. *quoties, quotiens*, how often, how many times < *quot*, how many] *Arith.* 1. the result obtained when one number is divided by another 2. the fraction indicating this division

quo war·ran·to (kwō wô ran′tō, -rän′-) *pl.* **quo war·ran′tos** [ML., by what warrant < L. *quo*, abl. of *qui*, who, which + ML. *warrantus*, a warrant] 1. *orig.*, a writ ordering a person to show by what right he exercises an office, franchise, or privilege 2. a legal proceeding undertaken to recover an office, franchise, or privilege from the person in possession, initiated upon an information or petition for a writ

Qu·ran (koo rän′, -ran′) *n. same as* KORAN

qursh (koorsh) *n.* a monetary unit and coin of Saudi Arabia equal to 1/20 riyal: also **qu·rush** (koor′əsh)

q.v. [L. *quod vide*] which see

qy. query

R

R, r (är) *n.*, *pl.* **R's, r's** 1. the 18th letter of the English alphabet: from the Greek *rho*, a borrowing from the Phoenician 2. a sound of *R* or *r*: in English, it is basically a vowellike, voiced, alveolar, retroflex continuant, but it is also variously heard in British and American dialects as an alveolar flap 3. a type or impression for *R* or *r* 4. *a symbol for* the 18th in a sequence or group (or the 17th if *J* is omitted) —*adj.* 1. of *R* or *r* 2. 18th (or 17th if *J* is omitted) in a sequence or group

R (är) *n.* 1. an object shaped like *R* 2. *the symbol for: a) Chem.* radical, esp. organic radical *b) Elec.* resistance *c) Math.* ratio *d) Physics, Chem.* universal gas constant —*adj.* shaped like *R* —**the three R's** reading, writing, and arithmetic, regarded as the basic elementary studies and the fundamentals of an education: so called from the humorous spelling *reading, 'riting*, and *'rithmetic*

R Chess rook

r 1. *Math. the symbol for* radius 2. roentgen(s) 3. royal 4. ruble

R. 1. Radical 2. Reaumur 3. Republic(an) 4. *Eccles.* respond or response: also **R̸**

R., r. 1. [L. *Rex*] king 2. [L. *Regina*] queen 3. rabbi 4. radius 5. railroad 6. railway 7. rector 8. redactor 9. right 10. river 11. road 12. royal 13. ruble 14. *Baseball*

runs 15. *pl.* **Rs., Rs, R̶s̶, rs.** rupee 16. [L. *recipe*] take: used in prescriptions: also **℞**

r. 1. range 2. rare 3. received 4. residence 5. resides 6. retired 7. rises 8. rod(s) 9. rubber

Ra¹ (rä) [Egypt. *Rā, Rĕ′*, sun] the sun god and principal deity of the ancient Egyptians, usually depicted as having the head of a hawk and wearing the solar disk as a crown

Ra² *Chem.* radium

RA Regular Army

R.A. 1. Rear Admiral 2. *Astron.* right ascension 3. Royal Academician 4. Royal Academy

Ra·bat (rä bät′, rə-) capital of Morocco, in the NW part, on the Atlantic: pop. 262,000

ra·bat (rab′ē, rə bät′) *n.* [MFr., rabat, orig. (collar) turned down < *rabattre*, to turn down: see REBATE¹] a plain, black dickey worn with a clerical collar by some clergymen

ra·ba·to (rə bät′ō, -bät′-) *n.*, *pl.* **-tos** [altered < MFr., a turning down < *rabattre*: see REBATE¹] a large linen or lace collar of the 16th and 17th cent., worn up at the back or turned down so as to fall over the shoulders

Ra·baul (rä boul′) seaport on NE New Britain; chief town of the Bismarck Archipelago: pop. 6,000

Rab·bah (rab′ə) *Bible* chief city of the Ammonites: also **Rab′bath** (-əth): site now occupied by Amman, Jordan

rab·bet (rab′it) *n.* [ME. *rabet* < OFr. *rabat, rabbat,* a beating down < *rabattre:* see REBATE¹] a groove or cut made in the edge of a board, etc. in such a way that another piece may be fitted into it to form a joint (**rabbet joint**) —*vt.* 1. to cut a rabbet in 2. to join by means of a rabbet —*vi.* to be joined by a rabbet

rab·bi (rab′ī) *n., pl.* **-bis, -bies** [ME. < OE. < LL.(Ec.) < Gr.(Ec.) *rhabbi* < Heb. *rabbī,* my master, my lord < *rabh,* master, great one + -ī, my] *Judaism* a scholar and teacher of the Jewish law; now, specif., an ordained Jew, usually the spiritual head of a congregation, qualified to decide questions of law and ritual and to perform marriages, etc.

rab·bin (-in) *n.* [Fr. < ML. *rabbinus*] *archaic var. of* RABBI

rab·bin·ate (rab′ī nit, -nāt′) *n.* 1. the position or office of rabbi 2. rabbis collectively

Rab·bin·ic (rə bin′ik) *adj.* 1. designating the Hebrew language as used in the writings of rabbis of the Middle Ages 2. [r-] *same as* RABBINICAL

rab·bin·i·cal (-i k'l) *adj.* [< ML. *rabbinus* + -ICAL] 1. of the rabbis, their doctrines, learning, language, etc., esp. in the early Middle Ages 2. of or for the rabbinate —**rab·bin′i·cal·ly** *adv.*

rab·bit (rab′it) *n., pl.* **-bits, -bit:** see PLURAL, II, D, 1 [ME. *rabette,* young of the cony, prob. < MFr. dial. *rabotte,* akin to MDu. *robbe,* Fl. *robbe*] 1. *a)* a burrowing, old-world mammal (*Oryctolagus cuniculus*) of the hare family, smaller than most hares and characterized by soft fur, long ears, a stubby tail, and the production of naked young *b) same as* COTTONTAIL 2. the fur of a rabbit 3. loosely, any hare 4. *clipped form of* WELSH RABBIT —*vi.* to hunt rabbits

☆**rabbit ears** [Colloq.] an indoor television antenna, consisting of two adjustable rods that swivel apart in a V-shaped angle

☆**rabbit fever** *same as* TULAREMIA

rabbit punch *Boxing* a short, sharp blow to the back of the neck

rab·bit·ry (rab′i trē) *n., pl.* **-ries** a place where domesticated rabbits are kept; rabbit hutch

rabbit's (or **rabbit**) **foot** ☆the hind foot of a rabbit, used superstitiously as a talisman, or good-luck charm

rab·ble¹ (rab′'l) *n.* [ME. *rabel* < ? or akin to ML. *rabulus,* brawling, noisy < L. *rabula,* a pettifogger] a noisy, disorderly crowd; mob —*vt.* **-bled, -bling** to attack as or by a rabble; mob —**the rabble** the common people; the masses: a term of contempt

rab·ble² (rab′'l) *n.* [Fr. *râble* < OFr. *roable* < ML. *rotabulum,* poker < L. *rutabulum,* stirrer < *ruere,* to rake up < IE. base *reu-,* to dig up, whence RID¹, RUBBLE] an iron bar used to stir and skim molten iron in puddling —*vt.* **-bled, -bling** to stir or skim with such a bar

rab·ble·ment (-mənt) *n.* [Now Rare] 1. a noisy disturbance, as by a rabble, or mob 2. a rabble; mob

rab·ble·rous·er (-rouz′ər) *n.* a person who tries to arouse people to violent action by appeals to emotions, prejudices, etc.; demagogue —**rab′ble·rous′ing** *adj., n.*

Rab·e·lais (rà′ble′; E. rab′ə lā′), **Fran·çois** (frän swà′) 1490?-1553; Fr. satirist & humorist

Rab·e·lai·si·an (rab·ə lā′zhən, -zē ən) *adj.* of or like Rabelais or his works; broadly and coarsely humorous, satirical, etc. —*n.* a person who imitates, admires, or studies Rabelais

Ra·bi (rä′bē), **I**(sidor) **I**(saac) 1898– ; U.S. physicist, born in Austria

rab·id (rab′id; *for 3, occas.* rā′bid) *adj.* [L. *rabidus* < *rabere,* to rage, prob. < IE. base *rabh-,* to be violent, raging, whence Sans. *rábhas-,* violence, force, L. *rabies,* madness] 1. violent; raging 2. fanatical or unreasonably zealous in beliefs, opinions, or pursuits 3. of or having rabies —**ra·bid′i·ty** (rə bid′ə tē), **rab′id·ness** *n.* —**rab′id·ly** *adv.*

ra·bies (rā′bēz) *n.* [L., madness: see prec.] an infectious virus disease of the central nervous system in mammals: it can be transmitted to man through the bite of an infected dog or other animal and is characterized by choking, convulsions, inability to swallow liquids, etc.

☆**rac·coon** (ra kōōn′) *n., pl.* **-coons′, -coon′:** see PLURAL, II, D, 1 [< AmInd. (Algonquian) name, as in Virginian *ärakun,* lit., scratcher] 1. a small, tree-climbing, chiefly flesh-eating mammal (*Procyon lotor*) of N. America, active largely at night and characterized by long, yellowish gray fur, black masklike markings across the eyes, and a long, black-ringed tail 2. its fur

☆**raccoon dog** any of a genus (*Nyctereutes*) of small, raccoonlike, burrowing mammals of Asia, having long, loose fur and a short, thick tail

race¹ (rās) *n.* [ME. (North) *ras(e)* <

RACCOON
(2–3 ft. long, including tail)

ON. *rās,* a running, rush, akin to OE. *ræs,* swift movement, attack < IE. base *eras-,* to flow, move rapidly, whence L. *ros,* dew & *errare,* to ERR, Sans. *rasā,* moisture] 1. a competition of speed in running, skating, riding, etc. 2. [*pl.*] a series of such competitions for horses, cars, etc., on a regular course 3. any contest or competition likened to a race [the *race* for mayor, a *race* for power] 4. a steady onward movement or course 5. the span of life 6. *a)* a swift current of water *b)* the channel for a current of water, esp. one built to use the water industrially [a *millrace*] 7. a channel or groove for the moving parts of a machine, as the groove for the balls in a ball bearing 8. *Aeron. same as* SLIPSTREAM —*vi.* **raced, rac′ing** 1. to take part in a competition of speed; run a race 2. to go or move swiftly 3. to move or revolve so swiftly as to be out of control, because of less resistance or a lighter load: said of machinery —*vt.* 1. to compete with in a competition of speed 2. to enter or run (a horse, etc.) in a race 3. *a)* to cause to go swiftly *b)* to cause (an engine) to run at high speed with the gears disengaged

race² (rās) *n.* [Fr. < It. *razza* < ? LL. *ratio,* a sort, kind (of fruit, animal) < L., a reckoning (see RATIO)] 1. any of the different varieties of mankind, distinguished by form of hair, color of skin and eyes, stature, bodily proportions, etc.: many anthropologists now consider that there are only three primary major groups, the Caucasoid, Negroid, and Mongoloid, each with various subdivisions (sometimes also called *races*): the term has acquired so many unscientific connotations that in this sense it is often replaced in scientific usage by *ethnic stock* or *group* 2. a population that differs from others in the relative frequency of some gene or genes: a modern scientific use 3. any geographical, national, or tribal ethnic grouping 4. *a)* the state of belonging to a certain ethnic stock, group, etc. *b)* the qualities, traits, etc. belonging, or supposedly belonging, to such a category 5. any group of people having the same ancestry; family; clan; lineage 6. any group of people having the same activities, habits, ideas, etc. 7. *Biol. a)* a subspecies, or variety *b) same as* BREED (*n.* 1) 8. [Rare] distinctive flavor, taste, etc., as of wine —**the race** mankind

race·course (-kôrs′) *n. same as* RACE TRACK

race·horse (-hôrs′) *n.* a horse bred and trained for racing

ra·ce·mate (rā sē′māt′, rə-) *n.* a salt or ester of racemic acid

ra·ceme (rā sēm′, rə-) *n.* [L. *racemus,* cluster of grapes] an unbranched flower cluster, consisting of a single central stem or rachis, along which individual flowers grow on small stems at intervals from the base toward the apex, as in the lily of the valley

ra·ce·mic (-sē′mik) *adj.* [< prec. + -IC: see ff.] *Chem.* 1. consisting of an optically inactive, equimolecular mixture of the dextrorotatory and levorotatory forms of certain substances 2. designating or of a compound formed of such a mixture

racemic acid [< RACEME: orig. found in grapes] a transparent, colorless, crystalline compound occurring in nature with d-tartaric acid; it is an optically inactive isomer of tartaric acid

rac·e·mism (ras′ə miz′m, rā sē′miz′m) *n.* 1. the quality or condition of being racemic 2. *same as* RACEMIZATION

rac·e·mi·za·tion (ras′ə mi zā′shən) *n.* the conversion of an optically active substance into a racemic form

rac·e·mose (ras′ə mōs′) *adj.* [L. *racemosus*] arranged in, or bearing, a raceme or racemes

rac·er (rās′ər) *n.* 1. any person, animal, vehicle, etc. that takes part in races ☆2. any of several slim, swift, harmless snakes (genus *Coluber*), as the American blacksnake

☆**race riot** violence and fighting in a community, characterized by racist hostility

race·run·ner (-run′ər) *n.* ☆any of a genus (*Cnemidophorus*) of very active, long-tailed lizards, found chiefly in warm regions of N. and S. America

race track a course prepared for racing, esp. an oval track for horse races or dog races

☆**race·way** (-wā′) *n.* 1. a narrow channel for water 2. a tube for carrying and protecting electric wires 3. *same as* RACE¹ (sense 7) 4. a race track for harness racing 5. a race track for drag racing, stock cars, etc.

Ra·chel (rā′chəl; *for 3,* Fr. rà shel′) [LL.(Ec.) < Gr.(Ec.) *Rhachēl* < Heb. *rāhēl,* lit., ewe] 1. a feminine name: dim. **Rae** 2. *Bible* the younger of the two wives of Jacob, and mother of Joseph and Benjamin: Gen. 29–35 3. (born *Élisa Félix*) 1821?-58; Fr. actress, born in Switzerland

ra·chil·la (rə kil′ə) *n., pl.* **-lae** (-ē) [ModL., dim. of *rachis:* see RACHIS] the central stalk of a grass spikelet, to which the glumes and florets are attached

ra·chis (rā′kis) *n., pl.* **ra·chis·es, ra·chi·des** (rak′ə dēz′, rā′kə-) [ModL. < Gr. *rhachis* < IE. base *wrāgh-,* thorn, point] 1. *same as* SPINAL COLUMN 2. *Bot.* the principal axis of an inflorescence or of a compound leaf 3. *Zool.* the shaft of a feather, esp. that part bearing the barbs

ra·chi·tis (rə kīt′əs, ra-) *n.* [ModL. < Gr. *rhachitis,* inflammation of the spine: see RACHIS & -ITIS] *same as* RICKETS —**ra·chit′ic** (-kit′ik) *adj.*

Rach·ma·ni·noff (räkh mä′nü nôf′, rak-), **Ser·gei V**(assilievich) (syer gā′) 1873–1943; Russ. composer, conductor, & pianist: also sp. **Rachmaninov**

ra·cial (rā′shəl) *adj.* **1.** of or characteristic of a race, or ethnic group **2.** of or between races —**ra′cial·ly** *adv.*

ra·cial·ism (-iz′m) *n.* **1.** a doctrine or teaching, without scientific support, that claims to find racial differences in character, intelligence, etc., that asserts the superiority of one race over another or others, and that seeks to maintain the supposed purity of a race or the races **2.** *same as* RACISM (sense 2) —**ra′cial·ist** *n., adj.*

rac·i·ly (rā′sə lē) *adv.* in a racy manner

Ra·cine (rə sēn′) [Fr., root < Fr. name of the nearby Root River, translating the Ojibway name] city in SE Wis., on Lake Michigan: pop. 95,000

Ra·cine (rȧ′sēn′; *E.* rə sēn′), **Jean Bap·tiste** (zhän bȧ tēst′) 1639–99; Fr. poet & dramatist

rac·i·ness (rā′sē nis) *n.* the quality of being racy

rac·ism (rā′siz′m) *n.* **1.** *same as* RACIALISM (sense 1) **2.** any program or practice of racial discrimination, segregation, persecution, and domination, based on racialism —**rac′ist** *n., adj.*

rack[1] (rak) *n.* [ME. *racke,* prob. < MDu. *rek,* framework < *recken,* to stretch (akin to OE. *ræcan:* see REACH)] **1.** a framework, grating, case, stand, etc. for holding or displaying various things [clothes *rack,* dish *rack,* pipe *rack,* bomb *rack*]: often used in combination: see HATRACK, HAYRACK, etc. **2.** a triangular form for arranging billiard balls at the beginning of a game **3.** a device for lifting an automobile for repairs from below; lift **4.** a frame for holding cases of type **5.** a toothed bar into which a pinion, worm gear, etc. meshes for receiving or transmitting motion **6.** a pair of antlers **7.** an instrument of torture having a frame on which the victim is bound and stretched until his limbs are pulled out of place **8.** any great mental or physical torment, or its cause **9.** a wrenching or upheaval, as by a storm —*vt.* [prob. < MDu. *recken*] **1.** to arrange in or on a rack **2.** to torture on a rack (sense 7) **3.** to trouble, torment, or afflict [a body *racked* with pain] **4.** *a*) to oppress by unfair demands, esp. by exacting exorbitant rents *b*) to raise (rents) to an exorbitant degree —*SYN.* see TORMENT —**off the rack** ready-made: said of clothing —**on the rack** in a very difficult or painful situation —**rack one's brains** (or **memory,** etc.) to try very hard to remember or think of something —**rack up** [Slang] **1.** to be credited with; gain, score, or achieve [to *rack up* a victory] **2.** to be the victor over or beat decisively **3.** to knock down, as with a punch

rack[2] (rak) *n., vi.* [< ?] *same as* SINGLE-FOOT

rack[3] (rak) *n.* [var. of WRACK[1]] destruction; wreckage: now only in **go to rack and ruin** to become ruined

rack[4] (rak) *n.* [ME. *rac,* prob. < Scand., as in ON. *reka,* to drive, Norw., Sw. dial. *rak,* a wreck: for IE. base see WREAK] a broken mass of clouds blown by the wind —*vi.* to be blown by the wind: said of clouds

rack[5] (rak) *vt.* [LME. *rakken* < Pr. *arracar* < *raca,* husks and stems of grapes, thick dregs] to draw off (cider, wine, etc.) from the dregs

rack·et[1] (rak′it) *n.* [prob. echoic] **1.** a noisy confusion; loud and confused talk or activity; uproar **2.** a period of gay, exciting social life or revelry ☆**3.** *a*) an obtaining of money illegally, as by bootlegging, fraud, or, esp., threats of violence *b*) [Colloq.] any dishonest scheme or practice ☆**4.** [Slang] *a*) an easy, profitable source of livelihood *b*) any business, profession, or occupation —*vi.* **1.** to make a racket; take part in a noisy activity **2.** [Now Rare] to lead an exciting social life; revel —*SYN.* see NOISE

rack·et[2] (rak′it) *n.* [MFr. *raquette,* earlier *rachette,* palm of the hand < ML. *rasceta* (*manus*), palm (of the hand) < Ar. *rāhah* (pl. *rāhāt*), palm of the hand] **1.** a light bat for tennis, badminton, etc., with a network of catgut, silk, nylon, etc. in an oval or round frame attached to a handle **2.** a snowshoe **3.** loosely, the paddle used in table tennis **4.** [*pl., with sing. v.*] game of racquets

☆**rack·et·eer** (rak′ə tir′) *n.* [RACKET[1], *n.* 3 + -EER] a person who obtains money illegally, as by bootlegging, fraud, or, esp., extortion —*vi.* to obtain money in any of these ways —**rack′et·eer′ing** *n.*

rack·et·y (rak′ə tē) *adj.* **1.** making a racket; very noisy **2.** characterized by noise, revelry, etc.

Rack·ham (rak′əm), **Arthur** 1867–1939; Eng. illustrator

RACKETS
(A, squash; B, tennis; C, badminton; D, paddle ball)

rack·le (rak′l) *adj.* [ME. *rakel,* rash] [Scot.] **1.** headstrong; impetuous **2.** vigorous; strong

rack railway *same as* COG RAILWAY

rack-rent (rak′rent′) *n.* [RACK[1], *v.* 4 + RENT[1]] an excessively high rent; esp., a rent whose annual amount is equal, or almost equal, to the value of the property —*vt.* to exact rack-rent from

rack-rent·er (-ər) *n.* one who pays or exacts rack-rent

☆**ra·con** (rā′kän) *n.* [*ra*(*dar bea*)*con*] *same as* RADAR BEACON

rac·on·teur (rak′än tur′) *n.* [Fr. < *raconter,* to RECOUNT] a person skilled at telling stories or anecdotes

☆**ra·coon** (ra kōōn′) *n., pl.* **-coons′, -coon′:** see PLURAL, II, D, 1 *same as* RACCOON

rac·quet (rak′it) *n.* **1.** *same as* RACKET[2] **2.** [*pl., with sing. v.*] a game like court tennis, played in an enclosure with four walls

rac·y (rā′sē) *adj.* **rac′i·er, rac′i·est** [RACE[2] + -Y[2]] **1.** having the characteristic taste, flavor, or quality associated with the original or genuine type [*racy* fruit] **2.** lively; spirited; vigorous **3.** piquant; pungent ☆**4.** somewhat indecent; suggestive; risqué [a *racy* novel] —*SYN.* see PUNGENT

rad (rad) *n.* [< *rad*(*iation*)] a dosage of absorbed radiation equal to the absorption of 100 ergs of energy per gram of material

rad. 1. radical **2.** radius **3.** radix

☆**ra·dar** (rā′där) *n.* [*ra*(*dio*) *d*(*etecting*) *a*(*nd*) *r*(*anging*)] any of several systems or devices using transmitted and reflected radio waves for detecting a reflecting object, as an aircraft, and determining its direction, distance, height, or speed, or in storm detection, mapping, navigation, etc. —**ra′dar·man** (-mən) *n., pl.* **-men** (-mən)

☆**radar beacon** a beacon with its transmitter and other components that emits radar waves for reception and display, indicating its range or bearing, or both, from a receiving set: it is usually a transponder that returns coded signals only when triggered by a specific radar pulse

☆**ra·dar·scope** (-skōp′) *n.* [RADAR + -SCOPE] an oscilloscope that visually records the reflected radio beams picked up by a radar receiver

rad·dle[1] (rad′'l) *vt.* **-dled, -dling** [< dial. *raddle,* a slender rod interwoven in a fence < Anglo-Fr. *reidele,* cart rail, stout pole < OFr. *ridelle* < MHG. *reidel,* a cudgel] *same as* INTERWEAVE

rad·dle[2] (rad′'l) *n., vt.* **-dled, -dling** *var. of* RUDDLE

ra·di·al (rā′dē əl) *adj.* [< ML. *radialis:* see RADIUS] **1.** *a*) of or like a ray or rays; branching out in all directions from a common center *b*) having or characterized by parts that branch out in this way **2.** of or situated like a radius **3.** *Anat.* of or near the radius or forearm —*n.* a radial part or structure —**ra′di·al·ly** *adv.*

radial engine an internal-combustion engine with cylinders arranged radially like wheel spokes

radial (ply) tire an automobile tire in which the ply cords extending to the beads are nearly at right angles to the center line of the tread

ra·di·an (rā′dē ən) *n.* [< RADIUS] a unit of angular measurement, c.57.295°, equal to the angle formed at the center of a circle by two radii cutting off an arc whose length is equal to the radius of the circle

ra·di·ance (rā′dē əns) *n.* the quality or state of being radiant; brightness: also **ra′di·an·cy** (-ən sē)

ra·di·ant (-ənt) *adj.* [L. *radians,* prp. of *radiare:* see RADIATE] **1.** sending out rays of light; shining brightly **2.** filled with light; bright [a *radiant* morning] **3.** showing pleasure, love, well-being, etc.; beaming [a *radiant* smile] **4.** issuing (from a source) in or as in rays; radiated [*radiant* energy] —*n.* **1.** the point or object from which heat or light emanates **2.** *Astron.* the point in the heavens from which a shower of meteors appears to come —*SYN.* see BRIGHT —**ra′di·ant·ly** *adv.*

radiant energy any form of energy traveling in waves; esp., electromagnetic radiation, as heat, light, X-rays, gamma rays, etc.

radiant flux the rate of flow of radiant energy

radiant heating a method of heating a space by means of radiation, as from electric coils, hot-water or steam pipes, etc. installed in the floor or walls

ra·di·ate (rā′dē āt′) *vi.* **-at′ed, -at′ing** [< L. *radiatus,* pp. of *radiare,* to radiate < *radius,* ray: see RADIUS] **1.** to send out rays of heat, light, etc.; be radiant **2.** to come forth or spread out in rays [heat *radiating* from a stove] **3.** to branch out in lines from a center [highways *radiating* from a city] —*vt.* **1.** to send out (heat, light, etc.) in rays **2.** to give forth or spread (happiness, love, etc.) as if from a center —*adj.* **1.** having rays or raylike parts; radial **2.** *Bot.* having ray flowers or florets **3.** *Zool.* having radial symmetry or balanced arrangement around a central axis, as a jellyfish

ra·di·a·tion (rā′dē ā′shən) *n.* [L. *radiatio*] **1.** the act or process of radiating; specif., the process in which energy in the form of rays of light, heat, etc. is sent out through space from atoms and molecules as they undergo internal change **2.** the rays sent out; radiant energy **3.** radial arrangement of parts **4.** *Biol.* the dispersal and adaptation to new environments by a line of animals or plants, resulting in the evolution of divergent forms specialized to fit the new habitats **5.** *Nuclear Physics* energetic nuclear particles, as neutrons, alpha and beta particles, etc. —**ra′di·a′tion·al** *adj.* —**ra′di·a′tive** *adj.*

radiation sickness sickness produced by overexposure to radiation, as from X-rays or atomic explosions, and characterized by nausea, diarrhea, bleeding, loss of hair, and increased susceptibility to infection

ra·di·a·tor (rā′dē āt′ər) *n.* anything that radiates; specif., ☆*a)* a series of pipes or coils through which hot water or steam circulates so as to radiate heat into a room, etc. ☆*b)* a device of tubes and fins, as in an automobile, through which circulating water passes to radiate superfluous heat and thus cool the engine *c)* any radioactive material or body *d)* *Radio* a portion of any transmitting antenna capable of producing radio-frequency energy

rad·i·cal (rad′i k'l) *adj.* [ME. < LL. *radicalis* < L. *radix* (gen. *radicis*), a ROOT¹] **1.** *a)* of or from the root or roots; going to the foundation or source of something; fundamental; basic [a *radical* principle] *b)* extreme; thorough [a *radical* change in one's life] **2.** *a)* favoring fundamental or extreme change; specif., favoring basic change in the social or economic structure *b)* [R-] designating or of any of various modern political parties, esp. in Europe, ranging from moderate to conservative in program **3.** *Bot.* of or coming from the root **4.** *Math.* having to do with the root or roots of a number or quantity —*n.* **1.** *a)* a basic or root part of something *b)* a fundamental **2.** *a)* a person holding radical views, esp. one favoring fundamental social or economic change *b)* [R-] a member or adherent of a Radical party **3.** *same as* ROOT¹ (*n.* 10) **4.** *Chem.* a group of two or more atoms that acts as a single atom and goes through a reaction unchanged, or is replaced by a single atom: it is normally incapable of separate existence **5.** *Math. a)* the indicated root of a quantity or quantities, shown by an expression written under the radical sign *b) same as* RADICAL SIGN —*SYN.* see LIBERAL —**rad′i·cal·ness** *n.*

rad·i·cal·ism (-iz'm) *n.* **1.** the quality or state of being radical, esp. in politics **2.** radical principles, ideals, methods, or practices

rad·i·cal·ize (-īz′) *vt., vi.* **-ized′, -iz′ing** to make or become politically radical —**rad′i·cal·i·za′tion** *n.*

rad·i·cal·ly (rad′ik lē, -ik ′l ē) *adv.* **1.** *a)* as regards root or origin *b)* fundamentally; basically; completely **2.** in a manner characterized by radicalism

radical sign *Math.* the sign (√ or √‾) used before a quantity to indicate that its root is to be extracted: derived from the *r* in Latin *radix*, root

rad·i·cand (rad′i kand′) *n.* [< L. *radicandum*, neut. gerundive of *radicare*, to take root < *radix*, ROOT¹] the quantity under a radical sign

rad·i·ces (rad′ə sēz′, rā′də-) *n. alt. pl. of* RADIX

rad·i·cle (rad′i k'l) *n.* [L. *radicula*, dim. of *radix*, a ROOT¹] **1.** *Anat.* the rootlike beginning of a nerve, vein, etc. **2.** *Bot. a)* the lower part of the axis of an embryo seedling; strictly, the root part; often, the hypocotyl, sometimes together with the root *b)* a rudimentary root

ra·di·i (rā′dē ī′) *n. alt. pl. of* RADIUS

☆**ra·di·o** (rā′dē ō′) *n., pl.* **-os′** [contr. < RADIOTELEGRAPHY] **1.** the practice or science of communicating over a distance by converting sounds or signals into electromagnetic waves and transmitting these directly through space, without connecting wires, to a receiving set, which changes them back into sounds, signals, etc. **2.** such a receiving set, esp. one adapted for receiving the waves of the assigned frequencies of certain transmitters or broadcasting stations **3.** *a)* broadcasting by radio as an industry, entertainment, art, etc. *b)* all the facilities and related activities of such broadcasting —*adj.* **1.** of, using, used in, sent by, or operated by radio **2.** having to do with electromagnetic wave frequencies between c.10,000 hertz and c.300,000 megahertz —*vt., vi.* **-oed′, -o′ing** to send (a message, etc.) or communicate with (a person, etc.) by radio

ra·di·o- (rā′dē ō, -ə) [Fr. < L. *radius*, ray: see RADIUS] *a combining form meaning:* **1.** ray, raylike [radiolarian] **2.** by radio [radiotelegraphy] **3.** by means of radiant energy [radiotherapy] **4.** radioactive [radiothorium]

ra·di·o·ac·tive (rā′dē ō ak′tiv) *adj.* [prec. + ACTIVE] giving off, or capable of giving off, radiant energy in the form of particles or rays, as alpha, beta, and gamma rays, by the spontaneous disintegration of atomic nuclei: said of certain elements, as plutonium, radium, thorium, and uranium, and their products —**ra′di·o·ac′tive·ly** *adv.* —**ra′di·o·ac·tiv′i·ty** (-ak tiv′ə tē) *n.*

☆**radioactive dating** the determination of the age of an object or material based on the known rates of decay of radioactive isotopes of various elements

radioactive series the series of isotopes of various elements successively formed by a radioactive substance before it comes to a stable state, usually lead

radio astronomy that branch of astronomy which deals with radio waves in space in order to obtain data and information about particular regions in the universe —**radio astronomer**

☆**ra·di·o·au·to·graph** (-ôt′ə graf′, -gräf′) *n. same as* AUTORADIOGRAPH —**ra′di·o·au′to·graph′ic** *adj.* —**ra′di·o·au·tog′ra·phy** (-ô täg′rə fē) *n.*

☆**radio beacon** a radio transmitter that gives off special signals continuously to help ships or aircraft determine their positions or come in safely, as at night or in a fog

radio beam *same as* BEAM (*n.* II 3)

ra·di·o·bi·ol·o·gy (-bī äl′ə jē) *n.* [RADIO- + BIOLOGY] the branch of biology dealing with the effects of radiation on living organisms and with biological studies using radioactive tracers —**ra′di·o·bi′o·log′i·cal** (-bī′ə läj′i k'l) *adj.* —**ra′di·o·bi·ol′o·gist** *n.*

☆**ra·di·o·broad·cast** (-brôd′kast′, -käst′) *n.* a broadcast by radio —*vt., vi.* **-cast′** or **-cast′ed, -cast′ing** to broadcast by radio —**ra′di·o·broad′cast′er** *n.*

☆**ra·di·o·car·bon** (-kär′bən) *n. same as* CARBON 14: see CARBON

ra·di·o·chem·is·try (-kem′is trē) *n.* the branch of chemistry dealing with radioactive phenomena —**ra′di·o·chem′-i·cal** (-i k'l) *adj.*

radio compass a direction finder, used chiefly in navigation

radio control control as of pilotless aircraft, garage doors, etc. by means of radio signals

ra·di·o·el·e·ment (-el′ə mənt) *n.* a radioactive element that has no stable isotopes

radio frequency any frequency between normally audible sound waves and the infrared light portion of the spectrum, usually considered to lie between 10 kilohertz and 1,000,000 megahertz

ra·di·o·gen·ic (-jen′ik) *adj.* [RADIO- + -GENIC] produced by radioactivity

ra·di·o·gram (rā′dē ō gram′) *n.* **1.** a message sent by radio **2.** *same as* RADIOGRAPH **3.** [Brit.] [< *radiogram-(ophone)*] *same as* RADIO-PHONOGRAPH

ra·di·o·graph (-graf′, -gräf′) *n.* [RADIO- + -GRAPH] a picture produced on a sensitized film or plate by X-rays —**ra′di·og′ra·pher** (-äg′rə fər) *n.* —**ra′di·o·graph′ic** *adj.* —**ra′di·o·graph′i·cal·ly** *adv.* —**ra′di·og′ra·phy** *n.*

ra·di·o·i·so·tope (rā′dē ō ī′sə tōp′) *n.* a naturally occurring or artificially created radioactive isotope of a chemical element: used in medical therapy, biological research, etc.

ra·di·o·lar·i·an (-ler′ē ən) *n.* [< ModL. *Radiolaria*, name of the order < *radiolus*, dim. of L. *radius*, ray (see RADIUS): from the radiating pseudopodia] any of a large order (Radiolaria) of one-celled deep-sea animals with long, slender pseudopodia and a spiny, or solid but perforated, skeleton of silica

ra·di·o·lo·ca·tion (-lō kā′shən) *n.* the use of radar in finding the location and direction of objects

ra·di·ol·o·gy (rā′dē äl′ə jē) *n.* [RADIO- + -LOGY] the science dealing with X-rays and other forms of radiant energy, esp. as used in medicine for X-raying bones, organs, etc. and for diagnosing and treating disease —**ra′di·o·log′i·cal** (-ə läj′i k'l) *adj.* —**ra′di·o·log′i·cal·ly** *adv.* —**ra′di·ol′o·gist** *n.*

ra·di·o·lu·cent (-ō loo̅′s'nt) *adj.* [RADIO- + LUCENT] offering little or no resistance to the passage of X-rays or other forms of radiant energy —**ra′di·o·lu′cen·cy** *n.*

ra·di·ol·y·sis (-äl′ə sis) *n.* [RADIO- + -LYSIS] chemical decomposition brought about by radiation —**ra′di·o·lyt′ic** (-ə lit′ik) *adj.*

☆**ra·di·o·me·te·or·o·graph** (rā′dē ō mēt′ē ər ə graf′, -gräf′) *n. same as* RADIOSONDE

ra·di·om·e·ter (rā′dē äm′ə tər) *n.* [RADIO- + -METER] **1.** an instrument for measuring the intensity of radiant energy, as by exposing to sunlight a set of vanes blackened on one side and suspended on an axis in a vacuum, and noting their speed of rotation **2.** an instrument for measuring radiant energy in any part of the electromagnetic spectrum —**ra′di·o·met′ric** (-ō met′rik) *adj.* —**ra′di·om′e·try** *n.*

RADIOM-ETER

ra·di·o·mi·met·ic (rā′dē ō mi met′ik) *adj.* [RADIO- + MIMETIC] producing action and effects similar to radiation

☆**ra·di·on·ics** (rā′dē än′iks) *n.pl.* [RADIO + (ELECTRO)NICS] *same as* ELECTRONICS

ra·di·o·nu·clide (-ō noo̅′klīd, -nyoo̅′-) *n.* [RADIO- + NUCLIDE] a radioactive nuclide

ra·di·o·paque (rā′dē ō pāk′) *adj.* [RADIO- + (O)PAQUE] not allowing the passage of X-rays, gamma rays, or other forms of radiant energy: also **ra′di·o·o·paque′** —**ra′di·o·pac′i·ty** (-ō pas′ə tē) *n.*

ra·di·o·phar·ma·ceu·ti·cal (-ō fär′mə soo̅t′i k'l, -syoo̅t′-) *n.* a radioactive drug, compound, etc. used in the study of physiological functions or in the diagnosis and treatment of disease

☆**ra·di·o·phone** (rā′dē ō fōn′) *n. same as* RADIOTELEPHONE

☆**ra·di·o·pho·no·graph** (rā′dē ō fōn′ə graf′, -gräf′) *n.* a radio and phonograph combined in one unit and sharing some components, as the amplifier and speaker(s)

ra·di·o·pho·to (-fōt′ō) *n., pl.* **-tos** a photograph or picture transmitted by radio: also **ra′di·o·pho′to·graph′**

ra·di·os·co·py (rā′dē äs′kə pē) *n.* [RADIO- + -SCOPY] the direct examination of the inside structure of opaque objects by means of X-rays or rays from radioactive substances —**ra′di·o·scop′ic** (-ə skäp′ik) *adj.*

ra·di·o·sen·si·tive (rā′dē ō sen′sə tiv) *adj. Med.* sensitive to, or susceptible to destruction by, X-rays or other forms of radiant energy —**ra′di·o·sen′si·tiv′i·ty** *n.*

☆**ra·di·o·sonde** (rā′dē ō sänd′) *n.* [Fr. < *radio* (cf. RADIO) + *sonde*, a sounding lead < *sonder*, to SOUND⁴] a compact package of meteorological instruments and a radio transmitter, carried aloft by a small balloon to measure and transmit to ground observers temperature, pressure, and humidity data from the upper atmosphere by means of special radio signals

radio spectrum the complete range of frequencies of electromagnetic radiation useful in radio communication, commonly ranging between 10 kilohertz and 300,000 megahertz

ra·di·o·stron·ti·um (rā′dē ō strän′shē əm, -tē əm) *n.* radioactive strontium, esp. strontium 90

ra·di·o·tel·e·gram (-tel′ə gram′) *n. same as* RADIOGRAM (sense 1)

ra·di·o·tel·e·graph (-tel′ə graf′, -gräf′) *n. same as* WIRELESS TELEGRAPHY: also **ra′di·o·te·leg′ra·phy** (-tə leg′rə fē) —*vt., vi.* to send (a message or signal) by radiotelegraph —**ra′di·o·tel′e·graph′ic** *adj.*

ra·di·o·tel·e·phone (-tel′ə fōn′) *n.* the equipment needed at one station to carry on two-way voice communication by radio waves only —**ra′di·o·te·leph′o·ny** (-tə lef′ə nē) *n.*

ra·di·o·tel·e·scope (-tel′ə skōp′) *n. Astron.* a radio antenna or an array of antennae with the component parts, designed to intercept radio waves from celestial sources

ra·di·o·ther·a·py (-ther′ə pē) *n.* [RADIO- + THERAPY] the treatment of disease by the use of X-rays or rays from a radioactive substance

ra·di·o·ther·my (rā′dē ō thur′mē) *n.* [RADIO- + (DIA)THERMY] 1. the treatment of disease or alleviation of pain by radiant heat 2. short-wave diathermy

ra·di·o·tho·ri·um (rā′dē ō thôr′ē əm) *n.* [ModL.] a radioactive isotope of thorium, of mass number 228, formed from mesothorium 2

radio wave any electromagnetic wave at a radio frequency

rad·ish (rad′ish) *n.* [ME. < earlier *radiche* < OE. *rædic* < L. *radix* (gen. *radicis*), lit., a ROOT¹: form infl. by Fr. *radis*, of same origin] 1. an annual plant (*Raphanus sativus*) of the mustard family, with an edible root 2. the pungent root, eaten raw as a relish or in a salad

ra·di·um (rā′dē əm) *n.* [ModL. < L. *radius*, a ray: see RADIUS] a radioactive metallic chemical element, found in very small amounts in pitchblende and other uranium minerals, which undergoes spontaneous atomic disintegration through several stages, emitting alpha, beta, and gamma rays and finally forming an isotope of lead: it is used in the treatment of cancer and other diseases: symbol, Ra; at. wt., 226.00; at. no., 88; sp. gr., c.5; melt. pt., c.960°C; boil. pt., 1140°C

radium therapy the treatment of cancer or other diseases by the use of radium

ra·di·us (rā′dē əs) *n., pl.* **-di·i′** (-ī′), **-us·es** [L., a rod, spoke (of a wheel), hence radius, ray (of light), prob. akin to *radix*, a ROOT¹] 1. a raylike or radial part, as a spoke of a wheel 2. *a)* any straight line extending from the center to the periphery of a circle or sphere *b)* the length of such a line 3. *a)* the circular area or distance limited by the sweep of such a line [no house within a *radius* of five miles] *b)* the distance a ship or airplane can travel and still return to its point of origin without refueling 4. an extent, scope, range, etc. of a limited or specified kind [within the *radius* of one's experience] 5. *a)* the shorter and thicker of the two bones of the forearm on the same side as the thumb *b)* a corresponding bone of the forelimb of a four-legged animal 6. *Zool. a)* any of the four primary planes of division of the body of a radially symmetrical animal *b)* any of the veins of an insect wing

radius vector *pl.* **radii vectores** (vek tôr′ēz), **radius vectors** 1. a straight line joining the origin of a vector, located at the intersection of two coordinates, to a given point lying in the same plane 2. a vector whose point of origin is fixed and whose terminal point ranges over a given curve or surface, as a straight line connecting the sun with the earth at any point of the earth's orbit

ra·dix (rā′diks) *n., pl.* **ra·di·ces** (rad′ə sēz′, rā′də-), **ra′dix·es** [L., a ROOT¹] 1. the root of a plant 2. *same as* RADICLE 3. *Linguis.* a root, or base 4. *Math.* a number made the base of a system of numbers

RAdm Rear Admiral

Rad·nor·shire (rad′nər shir′) county of EC Wales: 470 sq. mi.; pop. 18,000: also called **Rad′nor**

Ra·dom (rä′dôm) city in EC Poland: pop. 143,000

ra·dome (rā′dōm) *n.* [RA(DAR) + DOME] a dome-shaped housing for protecting a radar antenna, esp. on aircraft, without modifying its electromagnetic function

ra·don (rā′dän) *n.* [RAD(IUM) + -ON] a radioactive, gaseous, chemical element formed, together with alpha rays, as a first product in the atomic disintegration of radium: symbol, Rn; at. wt., 222.00; at. no., 86; sp. gr., 973 g/l; melt. pt., −71°C; boil. pt., −68°C

rad·u·la (raj′oo lə) *n., pl.* **-lae′** (-lē′) [ModL. < L., scraper < *radere*, to scrape: for IE. base see RAT] in most mollusks, a ribbonlike oral structure, mounted on an odontophore, with rows of small teeth, used to tear up food and take it into the mouth —**rad′u·lar** *adj.*

Rae (rā) a feminine name: see RACHEL

Rae·burn (rā′bərn), Sir Henry 1756–1823; Scot. portrait painter

Rae·ti·a (rē′shē ə) *same as* RHAETIA

RAF, R.A.F. Royal Air Force

raff (raf) *n.* [ME. *raf:* see RIFFRAFF] 1. *same as* RIFFRAFF 2. [Brit. Dial.] rubbish; trash

raf·fi·a (raf′ē ə) *n.* [< Malagasy native name] 1. a palm tree (*Raphia ruffia*) of Madagascar, with large, pinnate leaves 2. fiber from its leaves, woven into baskets, hats, etc. or used for tying plants

raf·fi·nose (raf′ə nōs′) *n.* [< Fr. *raffiner*, to refine < *re-*, RE- + *affiner*, to refine < *a-* (< L. *ad*, to) + *fin*, FINE¹ + *-ose*, -OSE¹] a sweetish, crystalline trisaccharide, C₁₈H₃₂O₁₆·5H₂O, derived from sugar beets, cottonseed, etc.

raff·ish (raf′ish) *adj.* [RAFF + -ISH] 1. disreputable, rakish, or licentious 2. tawdry; vulgar; low —**raff′ish·ly** *adv.* —**raff′ish·ness** *n.*

raf·fle¹ (raf′'l) *n.* [ME. *rafle* < MFr., dice game, lit., a raking in < OHG. *raffel*, a rake, scraper, akin to OE. *hreppan*, to touch, grasp: for IE. base see HARVEST] a lottery in which each participant buys a chance or chances to win a prize —*vt.* **-fled**, **-fling** to offer as a prize in a raffle (often with *off*) —*vi.* [Now Rare] to take part in a raffle (with *for*) —**raf′fler** *n.*

raf·fle² (raf′'l) *n.* [prob. < Fr., a sweeping together < MFr., instrument for raking < MHG. *raffen*, to snatch, scrape together, akin to Du. *rafelen:* see RAFFLE¹] a jumble or tangle, esp. of ropes, canvas, etc. on a ship

raf·fle·si·a (ra flē′zhē ə, -zhə, -zē ə) *n.* [ModL., after Sir T. Stamford *Raffles* (1781–1826), Brit. governor in Sumatra] any of a genus (*Rafflesia*) of foul-smelling, parasitic Malaysian plants with large, stemless flowers and no leaves

raft¹ (raft, räft) *n.* [ME. *rafte*, a beam, rafter < ON. *raptr*, a log: see RAFTER] 1. a flat structure of logs, boards, barrels, etc. fastened together and floated on water 2. a similar structure anchored in a river or lake and used by divers, swimmers, etc. 3. an inflatable boat or pad, as of rubber, for floating on water —*vt.* 1. to transport on a raft 2. to make into a raft —*vi.* to travel, work, etc. on a raft

raft² (raft, räft) *n.* [< RAFF, 2 (with unhistoric -*t*)] [Colloq.] a large number, collection, or quantity; lot

raft·er (raf′tər, räf′-) *n.* [ME. *rafter* < OE. *ræfter;* akin to ON. *raptr*, a log] any of the beams that slope from the ridge of a roof to the eaves and serve to support the roof

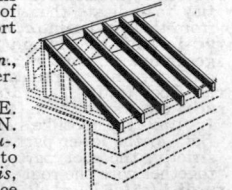

RAFTERS

rafts·man (rafts′mən, räfts′-) *n., pl.* **-men** (-mən) a man who operates, or works on, a raft

rag¹ (rag) *n.* [ME. *ragge* < OE. *ragg-* (in *raggig*, ragged) < ON. *rögg*, tuft of hair < IE. base **reu-*, to tear, tear up, whence L. *ruere*, to tumble down, rake up, *rudis*, rough: cf. RUG] 1. a waste piece of cloth, esp. one that is old or torn 2. a small piece of cloth for dusting, cleaning, washing, etc. 3. anything considered to have as little value as a rag 4. [*pl.*] old, worn clothes *b)* any clothes: used humorously: see GLAD RAGS ☆5. the axis and white, tough membrane of citrus fruits 6. [Slang] a newspaper, esp. one viewed with contempt —*adj.* made of rags [a *rag* doll] —**chew the rag** [Slang] to talk together; chat

rag² (rag) *vt.* **ragged**, **rag′ging** [< 19th-c. Brit. university slang < ?] [Slang] 1. to tease 2. to scold 3. [Brit.] to play a practical joke or jokes on —*n.* [Brit. Slang] an act or instance of ragging

rag³ (rag) *n.* [< ?] a roofing slate with one rough side

rag⁴ (rag) *n.* ☆1. *clipped form of* RAGTIME ☆2. a composition in ragtime —☆*vt.* **ragged**, **rag′ging** to play in ragtime

ra·ga (rä′gə) *n.* [Sans. *rāga*, lit., color, akin to *rajayati*, (he) dyes < IE. base **reg-*, to dye, whence Gr. *rhegma*, dyed material] any of a large number of traditional melody patterns with characteristic intervals, rhythms, and embellishments, used by Hindu musicians as source material for improvisation

rag·a·muf·fin (rag′ə muf′in) *n.* [ME. *°Ragamoffyn*, name of a demon in *Piers Plowman:* sense prob. infl. by RAG¹] a dirty, ragged person; esp., a poor, ragged child

rag·bag (rag′bag′) *n.* 1. a bag for rags 2. a collection of odds and ends; miscellaneous assortment

rage (rāj) *n.* [ME. < OFr. < LL. *rabia*, rage, madness, akin to *rabere*, to rave, be mad: see RABID] 1. [Obs.] insanity; amentia 2. a furious, uncontrolled anger; esp., a brief spell of raving fury 3. a great force, violence, or intensity, as of the wind 4. strong emotion, enthusiasm, or desire —*vi.* **raged**, **rag′ing** 1. to show violent anger in action or speech 2. to be forceful, violent, uncontrolled, etc. [a *raging* sea, a *raging* fever] 3. to spread unchecked, as a disease —SYN. see ANGER, FASHION —**(all) the rage** anything arousing widespread enthusiasm or interest; craze; fad —**rag′ing·ly** *adv.*

rag·ged (rag′id) *adj.* [< RAG¹ + -ED] 1. shabby or torn from wear; tattered [a *ragged* shirt] 2. dressed in shabby or torn clothes 3. uneven; rough; jagged [a *ragged* edge] 4. shaggy; unkempt [*ragged* hair] 5. not finished; imperfect; uneven [a *ragged* style] 6. harsh; strident [a *ragged* voice] —☆**run ragged** to cause to be exhausted, as by

constant pressure or harassment —**rag'ged·ly** *adv.* —**rag'-ged·ness** *n.*

☆**ragged edge** the extreme edge, like that of a precipice; verge *[the ragged edge of poverty]* —**on the ragged edge** precariously close to loss of self-control, mental stability, etc.

ragged robin a perennial plant (*Lychnis flos-cuculi*) of the pink family, with loose clusters of pink or red flowers

rag·ged·y (rag'ĭ dē) *adj.* somewhat ragged, or tattered

rag·gle-tag·gle (rag'l tag'l) *adj.* [extended < RAGTAG] of an odd or heterogeneous mixture; motley

rag·i, rag·gee (rag'ē) *n.* [Hind. *rāgī* < Sans. *rāgin*, red] a cereal grass (*Eleusine corocana*) of Africa and India whose grain is a staple food

rag·lan (rag'lən) *n.* [after Lord *Raglan* (1788–1855), Brit. commander in chief in the Crimean War] a loose overcoat or topcoat with sleeves that continue in one piece to the collar, so that there are no seams at the shoulder —*adj.* designating or of such a sleeve, or having such sleeves

rag·man (rag'man') *n., pl.* **-men'** (-men') a man who collects, buys, and sells rags, old paper, etc.

Rag·na·rok (rag'nə räk') [ON. *ragna rök*, judgment of the gods < *ragna*, gen. pl. of *regin*, god + *rök*, judgment, reason; confused with *ragnarøker*, twilight of the gods] *Norse Myth.* the destruction of the world in the last great conflict between the gods and the forces of evil

RAGLAN SLEEVE

ra·gout (ra gōō') *n.* [Fr. *ragoût* < *ragoûter*, to revive the appetite of < *re-*, re- + *à* (< L. *ad*), to + *goût* (< L. *gustus*), taste: see GUSTO] a highly seasoned stew of meat and vegetables —*vt.* **-gouted'** (-gōōd'), **-gout'ing** (-gōō'in) to make into a ragout

rag·pick·er (rag'pik'ər) *n.* a person who makes his living by picking up and selling rags and junk

☆**rag rug** a rug made of rag strips woven or sewn together

rag·tag (rag'tag') *n.* [RAG¹ + TAG] the lowest classes; rabble: also **ragtag and bobtail**: contemptuous term

☆**rag·time** (rag'tīm') *n.* [prob. < *ragged time*, in reference to syncopation] **1.** a type of American music, largely composed, popular from about 1890 to 1915 and characterized by strong syncopation in fast, even time: cf. JAZZ **2.** its syncopated rhythm

Ra·gu·sa (rä gōō'zä) **1.** commune in SE Sicily: pop. 55,000 **2.** *It.* name of DUBROVNIK, Yugoslavia

rag·weed (rag'wēd') *n.* [from the tattered appearance of the leaves] ☆any of a genus (*Ambrosia*) of chiefly N. American plants of the composite family, having tassellike, greenish flowers which yield large amounts of wind-borne pollen, a major cause of hay fever

rag·wort (-wûrt') *n.* [see prec.] *same as* GROUNDSEL

☆**rah** (rä) *interj.* hurrah: used in cheering for a team

☆**rah-rah** (rä'rä') *adj.* [< prec.] [Colloq.] of or like the uncritical enthusiasm exhibited at a college football game

raid (rād) *n.* [North Eng. var. of ROAD, preserving etym. sense, "a riding": used orig. of an incursion along the border] **1.** a sudden, hostile attack, esp. by troops, military aircraft, etc., or by armed, usually mounted, bandits intent on looting **2.** any sudden invasion of some place by police, for discovering and dealing with violations of the law ☆**3.** an attempt, as by a business concern, to lure employees from a competitor **4.** a deliberate attempt by one or more speculators to cause a quick, unexpected fall in stock market prices —*vt., vi.* to make a raid or raids (on) —**raid'er** *n.*

rail¹ (rāl) *n.* [ME. *raile* < OFr. *reille* < L. *regula*, RULE] **1.** a bar of wood, metal, etc. placed horizontally between upright posts to serve as a barrier or support **2.** a fence or railing; specif., the fence surrounding the infield of a race track **3.** any of a series of parallel metal bars laid upon crossties or in the ground to make a track for railroad cars, streetcars, etc. **4.** a railroad as a means of transportation *[to travel by rail]* **5.** a horizontal piece of wood separating the panels in doors or wainscoting **6.** the rim of a billiard table **7.** *Naut.* a narrow wooden piece at the top of a ship's bulwarks —*vt.* to supply with rails or a railing; fence —**go off the rails 1.** to go off the proper course **2.** to become insane —**ride on a rail** to place on a rail and carry out of the community: extralegal punishment in which the victim was usually tarred and feathered beforehand

rail² (rāl) *vi.* [ME. *raylen* < MFr. *railler* < Pr. *ralhar* < VL. *ragulare*, to bray < LL. *ragere*, to bellow] to speak bitterly or reproachfully; complain violently (with *against* or *at*) —**rail'er** *n.*

rail³ (rāl) *n., pl.* **rails, rail:** see PLURAL, II, D, 1 [ME. *rayle* < MFr. *raale* < *raaler*, to screech, rattle < VL. **rasclare*, to grate: orig. echoic] any of a number of small wading birds (family Rallidae) resembling the cranes and living in marshes, characterized by short wings and tail, long toes, and a harsh cry

rail·head (-hed') *n.* **1.** the farthest point to which

rails have been laid in a railroad **2.** *Mil.* the point on a railroad in a theater of operations at which supplies are unloaded and distributed

rail·ing (-in) *n.* **1.** material for rails **2.** rails collectively **3.** a fence or balustrade made of rails and posts

rail·ler·y (rāl'ər ē) *n., pl.* **-ler·ies** [Fr. *raillerie*: see RAIL² & -ERY] **1.** light, good-natured ridicule or satire; banter **2.** a teasing act or remark

rail·road (rāl'rōd') *n.* **1.** a road laid with parallel steel rails along which cars carrying passengers or freight are drawn by locomotives **2.** a complete system of such roads, including land, rolling stock, stations, etc. **3.** the persons or corporation owning and managing such a system —*vt.* ☆**1.** to transport by railroad ☆**2.** [Colloq.] to rush through quickly, esp. so quickly as to prevent careful consideration *[to railroad a bill through Congress]* ☆**3.** [Slang] to cause to go to prison on a trumped-up charge or with too hasty a trial —*vi.* ☆to work on a railroad —**rail'road'er** *n.*

☆**railroad flat** an apartment of rooms in a line, entered one from another, with no hallway

rail·road·ing (-in) *n.* **1.** the building or operation of railroads **2.** the act or process of one that railroads

railroad worm 1. any of several bioluminescent, wingless, female beetles (genus *Phrixothrix*) of South and Central America, with a row of green light organs along each side of the abdomen and red light organs at the front end ☆**2.** *same as* APPLE MAGGOT

☆**rail-split·ter** (-split'ər) *n.* a person who splits logs into rails, as for fences —**the Rail-Splitter** *nickname of* Abraham LINCOLN

rail·way (-wā') *n.* **1.** *a)* a railroad for light vehicles *[a street railway]* *b)* [Brit.] any railroad **2.** any track with rails for guiding wheels

rai·ment (rā'mənt) *n.* [ME. *rayment*, aphetic for *arayment*: see ARRAY & -MENT] [Archaic or Poet.] clothing; wearing apparel; attire

rain (rān) *n.* [ME. *rein* < OE. *regn*, akin to G. *regen* < IE. base **rek-*, var. of **reĝ-*, moist, wet, whence L. *rigare*, to wet, moisten (cf. IRRIGATE)] **1.** water falling to earth in drops that have been condensed from the moisture in the atmosphere **2.** the falling of such drops; shower or rainstorm **3.** *a)* rainy weather *b)* *[pl.]* seasonal rainfalls; the rainy season (preceded by *the*) **4.** a rapid falling or propulsion of many small particles or objects *[a rain of ashes]* —*vi.* **1.** to fall: said of rain, and usually in an impersonal construction *[it is raining]* **2.** to fall like rain *[bullets rained about him]* **3.** to cause rain to fall: said of the heavens, clouds, etc. —*vt.* **1.** to pour down (rain or something likened to rain) **2.** to give in large quantities *[to rain praises on someone]* —**rain cats and dogs** [Colloq.] to rain heavily —☆**rain out** to cause (an event) to be postponed or canceled because of rain —**rain'less** *adj.*

rain·band (-band') *n.* a dark band in the yellow part of the solar spectrum, due to water vapor in the atmosphere

rain·bow (-bō') *n.* [ME. *reinbowe* < OE. *regnboga*: see RAIN & BOW²] the arc containing the colors of the spectrum in consecutive bands, formed in the sky by the refraction, reflection, and dispersion of the sun's rays in falling rain or in mist —*adj.* of many colors

Rainbow Bridge natural sandstone bridge in S Utah: a national monument: 278 ft. long; 309 ft. high

rainbow fish 1. *same as* GUPPY **2.** any of a number of brightly colored ocean fishes, as the wrasses

☆**rainbow trout** a chiefly freshwater game fish (*Salmo gairdneri*), native to the mountain streams and rivers of the Pacific Coast of N. America

☆**rain check 1.** the stub of a ticket to a ball game or other outdoor event, entitling the holder to be admitted at a future date if the original event is rained out **2.** an offer to renew or defer an unaccepted invitation

☆**rain·coat** (rān'kōt') *n.* a waterproof or water-repellent coat for giving protection from rain

rain·drop (-dräp') *n.* a single drop of rain

rain·fall (-fôl') *n.* **1.** a falling of rain; shower **2.** the amount of water falling in the form of rain, snow, etc. over a given area in a given period of time: it is stated in terms of the inches in depth of water that has fallen into a rain gauge

rain forest a dense, evergreen forest occupying a tropical region having abundant rainfall throughout the year

rain gauge an instrument for measuring rainfall

Rai·nier (rā nir', rā'nir), **Mount** [after an 18th-cent. Brit. Adm. *Rainier*] mountain of the Cascade Range, in WC Wash.: 14,410 ft.: the central feature of a national park (**Mount Rainier National Park**): 378 sq. mi.

☆**rain·mak·er** (rān'mā'kər) *n.* a person who tries to make rain fall; specif., *a)* an American Indian medicine man who used certain rituals to influence the rain gods *b)* [Colloq.] a meteorologist or aircraft pilot involved in seeding clouds or the like —**rain'mak'ing** *n.*

rain·proof (-prōōf') *adj.* not letting rain through; shedding rain —*vt.* to make rainproof

rain shadow a region of little rainfall on the lee slopes of mountains whose windward slopes receive the rain

rain·storm (-stôrm') *n.* a storm with a heavy rain

rain·wa·ter (-wôt′ər, -wät′-) *n.* water that is falling or has fallen as rain, and is soft, containing relatively little soluble mineral matter

rain·wear (-wer′) *n.* rainproof clothing

rain·y (rā′nē) *adj.* **rain′i·er, rain′i·est** **1.** characterized by rain, esp. much rain [the *rainy* season] **2.** wet with rain **3.** bringing rain [*rainy* winds] —**rain′i·ness** *n.*

rainy day a possible future time of difficulty or need

raise (rāz) *vt.* **raised, rais′ing** [ME. *raisen* < ON. *reisa*, caus. of *risa*, to RISE] **1.** *a)* to cause to rise; move to a higher level; lift; elevate *b)* to bring to or place in an upright position **2.** to construct or erect (a building, etc.) **3.** *a)* to wake from sleep *b)* to stir up; arouse; incite [to *raise* a revolt] **4.** to increase in size, value, amount, etc. [to *raise* prices] **5.** to increase in degree, intensity, strength, etc. [to *raise* one's voice] **6.** to improve the position, rank, or situation of [to *raise* oneself from poverty] **7.** to advance or enhance (fame, reputation, etc.) **8.** to cause to arise, appear, come, etc.; esp., to bring back as from death; reanimate [to *raise* the dead] **9.** to cause to come about; provoke; inspire [the joke *raised* a laugh] **10.** to bring forward for consideration [to *raise* a question] **11.** to collect, gather, or procure (an army, money, etc.) **12.** to utter (a cry, shout, etc.) **13.** to bring to an end; remove [to *raise* a siege] **14.** to cause to become light; leaven (bread, etc.) **15.** *a)* to cause to grow or to breed [to *raise* corn or cattle] *b)* to bring up or rear (children) **16.** to establish radio communication with **17.** to cause (a blister) to form **18.** to make (a nap on cloth) with teasels, etc. **19.** [Scot.] to make angry or excited; madden ☆**20.** *Commerce* to increase by fraud the face value of (a check, etc.) **21.** *Naut.* to cause (land, another ship, etc.) to seem to rise over the horizon by coming nearer; come within sight of ☆**22.** *Bridge* to increase (one's partner's bid in a suit) **23.** *Phonet.* to change the sound of (a vowel) by putting the tongue in a higher position ☆**24.** *Poker* to bet more than (the highest preceding bet or bettor) —*vi.* **1.** [Dial.] to rise or arise ☆**2.** *Poker* to increase the bet —*n.* **1.** an act of raising **2.** an increase in amount; specif., ☆an increase in salary or wages, or in a bet —*SYN.* see LIFT —**raise Cain** (or **the devil, hell, a rumpus, the roof,** etc.) [Slang] to create a disturbance; cause trouble

raised (rāzd) *adj.* **1.** made in low relief; embossed **2.** having a napped surface, or having the pile cut with a design in relief: said of fabric **3.** leavened with yeast rather than baking powder or soda

rai·sin (rā′z'n) *n.* [ME. < OFr. *reisin* < VL. *racimus* < L. *racemus*, cluster of grapes] any of various kinds of sweet grapes, usually seedless, dried for eating

‡**rai·son d'é·tat** (re zōn dā tà′) [Fr., reason of state] a diplomatic or political reason

rai·son d'être (rā′zōn det′, det′rə; Fr. re zōn de′tr′) [Fr.] reason for being; justification for existence

raj (räj) *n.* [Hindi: see ff.] in India, rule; sovereignty

ra·jah, ra·ja (rä′jə) *n.* [Hindi *rājā* < Sans. *rājan* < *rāj*, to rule < IE. base *reĝ-*, to direct: cf. REGAL] **1.** a prince or chief in India **2.** a Malay or Javanese chief

Ra·ja·sthan (rä′jə stän′) state of NW India, on the border of West Pakistan: 132,152 sq. mi.; pop. 20,156,000; cap. Jaipur

Raj·kot (räj′kōt) city in Gujarat state, NW India: pop. 194,000

Raj·put (räj′pōōt) *n.* [Hindi *rājpūt*, prince < Sans. *rājaputra* < *rājan*, a king (see RAJAH) + *putra*, son < IE. base *pu-*, small, child, whence FOAL, FEW] a member of a Hindu people, the former ruling caste of northern India: also sp. **Raj′poot**

Raj·pu·ta·na (räj′pōō tä′nə) region in NW India, mostly in the state of Rajasthan

rake¹ (rāk) *n.* [ME. < OE. *raca*; akin to ON. *reka*, a spade, G. *rechen*, a rake < IE. base *reĝ-*, to direct, stretch out, whence RIGHT, L. *rex*] **1.** any of various long-handled tools with teeth or prongs at one end, used for gathering loose grass, hay, leaves, etc., or for smoothing broken ground **2.** any of various similar toothed devices [oyster *rake*] —*vt.* **raked, rak′ing** [ME. *raken* < the *n.*; also in part < ON. *raka*, to scrape, shave] **1.** *a)* to gather or scrape together with or as with a rake *b)* to make (a lawn, etc.) tidy with a rake **2.** to gather with great care **3.** to scratch or smooth with a rake, as in leveling broken ground **4.** to cover (a fire) with ashes **5.** to scratch or scrape **6.** to search through minutely; scour **7.** to direct gunfire along (a line of troops, the deck of a ship, etc.): often figurative **8.** to look over rapidly and searchingly —*vi.* **1.** to use a rake **2.** to search as if with a rake **3.** to scrape or sweep (with *over, across,* etc.) —**rake in** to gather an abundant amount of rapidly —**rake up** to uncover facts or gossip about (the past, a scandal, etc.)

rake² (rāk) *n.* [contr. of RAKEHELL] a dissolute, debauched man; roué

rake³ (rāk) *vi.* **raked, rak′ing** [? akin to Sw. *raka*, to project, G. *ragen*] to be slightly inclined; slant, as a ship's masts, etc. —*vt.* to give a slant to —*n.* **1.** a slanting or inclination from the perpendicular [the *rake* of a mast] or from the horizontal [the *rake* of a stage] **2.** the angle made by the edge of a cutting tool and a plane perpendicular to the surface that is being worked

rake⁴ (rāk) *vi.* **raked, rak′ing** [ME. *raken* < OE. *racian*, to speed forward: for IE. base see RAKE¹] **1.** to fly after

game: said of a hawk **2.** to run after game with the nose to the track instead of in the wind: said of a hunting dog

rake·hell (rāk′hel′) *n.* [prob. altered (after RAKE¹ & HELL) < ME. *rakel*, rash, wild] a dissolute, debauched man; rake —*adj.* immoral; dissolute: also **rake′hell′y**

☆**rake-off** (-ôf′) *n.* [RAKE¹ + OFF: orig. gambler's term for part of stakes raked off by the croupier as profit for the house] [Slang] a commission, rebate, or share, esp. when received in an illegitimate transaction

ra·ki, ra·kee (rä kē′, rak′ē) *n.* [Turk. *rāqi* < Ar. *'araq*: see ARRACK] an intoxicating liquor made from grape juice, grain, etc. in S Europe and the Near East

rak·ish¹ (rā′kish) *adj.* [< RAKE³ + -ISH] **1.** having a trim, neat appearance suggesting speed: said of a ship **2.** having a gay, careless look; dashing; jaunty —**rak′ish·ly** *adv.* —**rak′ish·ness** *n.*

rak·ish² (rā′kish) *adj.* like a rake; dissolute —**rak′ish·ly** *adv.* —**rak′ish·ness** *n.*

râle, rale (räl) *n.* [Fr. < *râler,* to rattle: see RAIL³] *Med.* an abnormal sound, as rattling or bubbling, accompanying the normal sound of breathing, and usually indicating a diseased condition of the lungs or bronchi

Ra·leigh (rô′lē, rä′-) [after ff.] capital of N.C., in the C part: pop. 122,000

Ra·leigh (rô′lē, rä′-), Sir Walter 1552?–1618; Eng. statesman, explorer, & poet: beheaded: also sp. **Ra′legh**

ral·len·tan·do (räl′ən tän′dō) *adj., adv.* [It., prp. of *rallentare,* to slow down < *re-* (< L. *re-*), again + *allentare,* to slacken < L. *ad-,* to + *lentus,* slow] *Music* gradually slower: a direction to the performer: abbrev. **rall.**

ral·ly¹ (ral′ē) *vt.* **-lied, -ly·ing** [Fr. *rallier* < OFr. < *re-,* again + *aleier,* to join: see ALLY] **1.** to gather together (retreating troops) so as to bring back into a state of order **2.** to summon or bring (persons) together for a common purpose **3.** to bring back to action; revive [to *rally* one's spirits] —*vi.* **1.** to come back to a state of order: said esp. of retreating troops **2.** to come together for a common purpose, esp. to assist or support a cause, person, etc. **3.** to come in order to help [to *rally* to the side of a friend] **4.** to come back to action, normal strength, etc.; revive [to *rally* from a fever] **5.** *Badminton, Tennis,* etc. to take part in a rally **6.** *Commerce* to rise in price after having fallen: said of stocks, etc. **7.** *Sports* to come from behind in scoring —*n., pl.* **-lies** **1.** a rallying or being rallied; specif., a gathering of people for a common purpose; mass meeting **2.** an organized automobile run, esp. of sports cars on public roads, designed to test driving skills: also sp. **ral′lye** **3.** *Badminton, Tennis,* etc. an exchange of several strokes before the point is won —*SYN.* see STIR¹ —**ral′li·er** *n.*

ral·ly² (ral′ē) *vt., vi.* **-lied, -ly·ing** [Fr. *rallier,* to RAIL²] to tease or mock playfully; ridicule; banter

Ralph (ralf; *Brit. usually* rāf) [ON. *Rathulfr* (akin to OE. *Rædwulf*) < *rath,* counsel (for IE. base see READ¹) + *ulfr,* WOLF] a masculine name: equiv. Fr. Raoul

ram (ram) *n.* [ME. *ramme* < OE. *ramm,* akin to MDu. & OHG. *ram* < Gmc. **ramma,* prob. < **rama-,* strong, sharp, bitter, whence ON. *rammr*] **1.** a male sheep **2.** *same as* BATTERING RAM **3.** *a)* formerly, a sharp metal beak on the prow of a ship, used to pierce enemy vessels *b)* a ship with such a beak **4.** *same as* HYDRAULIC RAM **5.** the weight, or striking part, of a pile driver **6.** the plunger of a force pump —[R-] Aries, the constellation and first sign of the zodiac —*vt.* **rammed, ram′ming** **1.** to strike against with great force; drive into **2.** to force into place; press or drive down [to *ram* a charge into a gun] **3.** to force (an idea, legislative bill, etc.) to be accepted: often with *across* or *through* **4.** to stuff or cram (*with* something) —*vi.* **1.** to strike with force; crash **2.** to move rapidly —**ram′mer** *n.*

R.A.M. **1.** Royal Academy of Music **2.** Royal Arch Mason

Ra·ma (rä′mə) [Sans. *Rāma*] any of three of the incarnations of the Hindu god Vishnu, esp. the seventh: see ff.

Ra·ma·chan·dra (rä′mə chun′drə) [Sans. *Rāmacandra*] Rama, the seventh incarnation of the Hindu god Vishnu: the hero of the Ramayana

Ram·a·dan (ram′ə dän′) *n.* [Ar. *ramaḍan,* lit., the hot month < *ramaḍa,* to be hot] **1.** the ninth month of the Moslem year, a period of daily fasting from sunrise to sunset **2.** the fasting in this period

Ra·ma·ya·na (rä mä′yə nə) [Sans. *Rāmāyaṇa*] one of the two great epics of India, written in Sanskrit some time after the Mahabharata and telling of Rama

Ram·a·zan (ram′ə zän′) *n.* [Turk. & Per. < Ar. *ramaḍān*] *same as* RAMADAN

ram·ble (ram′b'l) *vi.* **-bled, -bling** [var. of ME. *romblen,* freq. of *romen,* to ROAM] **1.** to roam about; esp., to walk or stroll about idly, without any special goal **2.** to talk or write aimlessly, without connection of ideas **3.** to grow or spread in all directions, as a vine —*vt.* to roam through —*n.* an act or instance of rambling; esp., an aimless stroll —*SYN.* see ROAM

ram·bler (ram′blər) *n.* **1.** a person or thing that rambles **2.** any of certain climbing roses, with clusters of relatively small flowers ☆**3.** *same as* RANCH HOUSE (sense 2)

Ram·bouil·let (ram′bə lā′; *Fr.* rän bōō yā′) *n.* [after *Rambouillet,* town in N France] any of a variety of merino sheep orig. bred in France and yielding fine wool and mutton

☆**ram·bunc·tious** (ram buŋk′shəs) *adj.* [earlier *rambustious*, altered (prob. after RAM) < ROBUSTIOUS] wild, disorderly, boisterous, unruly, etc. —**ram·bunc′tious·ly** *adv.* —**ram·bunc′tious·ness** *n.*

ram·bu·tan (ram bōōt′'n) *n.* [Malay < *rambut*, hair] **1.** the red, spiny, egg-shaped, edible fruit of a Malayan tree (*Nephelium lappaceum*) of the soapberry family **2.** the tree

Ra·meau (rå mō′), **Jean Phi·lippe** (zhän fē lēp′) 1683–1764; Fr. composer & organist

ram·e·kin (ram′ə kin) *n.* [Fr. *ramequin* < MDu. *rammeken*, cheese dish < dial. var. of *rom*, cream, akin to OE. *ream*, OHG. *roum*] **1.** a food mixture; specif., one made of bread crumbs, cheese, and eggs, baked in individual baking dishes **2.** such a baking dish

ra·men·tum (rə men′təm) *n., pl.* **-ta** (-tə) [ModL. < L., scrapings, shavings < *radere*, to scrape (see RAT) + *-mentum*, -MENT] *Bot.* any of the thin, brown scales found on fern leaves and stems

Ram·e·ses (ram′ə sēz) *var.* of RAMSES

ra·met (rā′met) *n.* [< L. *ramus*, a branch (for IE. base see ROOT[1]) + -ET] *Biol.* any of the members of a clone

ra·mi (rā′mī) *n. pl.* of RAMUS

ram·ie (ram′ē) *n.* [Malay *rami*] **1.** a coarse perennial plant (*Boehmeria nivea*) of the nettle family, grown in warm climates for the strong bast fiber of the stems **2.** this fiber, used in making fine cloth

ram·i·fi·ca·tion (ram′ə fi kā′shən) *n.* [MFr. < *pp.* of ML. *ramificare*] **1.** a ramifying or being ramified; specif., the arrangement of branches or offshoots, as on a plant **2.** the result of ramifying; specif., *a)* a branch or offshoot *b)* a derived effect, consequence, or result [the *ramifications* of an act]

ram·i·form (ram′ə fôrm′) *adj.* [< L. *ramus*, a branch (see ff.) + -FORM] branched or forked

ram·i·fy (-fī′) *vt., vi.* **-fied′, -fy′ing** [Fr. *ramifier* < ML. *ramificare* < L. *ramus*, a branch (see ROOT[1]) + *facere*, to make: see FACT] to divide or spread out into branches or branchlike divisions

Ra·mil·lies (rå mē yē′) village in C Belgium: site of a battle (1706) in the War of the Spanish Succession, in which the British under Marlborough defeated the French

ram·jet (**engine**) (ram′jet′) a jet engine, without moving parts, in which the air for oxidizing the fuel is continuously compressed by being rammed into the inlet by the high velocity of the aircraft

ram·mer (-ər) *n.* a person or thing that rams

ram·mish (-ish) *adj.* of or like a ram, or male sheep; specif., *a)* having a rank smell *b)* lustful

ra·mose (rā′mōs, rə mōs′) *adj.* [L. *ramosus* < *ramus*, a branch (see RAMUS)] **1.** bearing many branches **2.** branching —**ra′mose·ly** *adv.*

ra·mous (rā′məs) *adj.* **1.** same as RAMOSE **2.** branchlike

ramp[1] (ramp) *n.* [Fr. *rampe* < *ramper*: see ff.] **1.** a sloping, sometimes curved, surface, walk, road, etc. joining different levels ☆**2.** a means for boarding or leaving a plane, as a staircase on wheels rolled up to the door **3.** a concave bend or curve where a handrail or coping changes its direction, as at a staircase landing

ramp[2] (ramp) *vi.* [ME. *rampen* < OFr. *ramper*, to climb, clamber < Frank. *rampon*, to cramp together < Gmc. *rampa*, a claw] **1.** to stand upright on the hind legs; specif., *Heraldry* to be depicted rampant **2.** to assume a threatening posture **3.** to move or rush threateningly, violently, or with fury; rampage —*n.* the act of ramping

ramp[3] (ramp) *n.* [taken as sing. of *ramps*, var. of dial. *rams*, wild garlic < ME. < OE. *hramsa*, wild garlic] a wild leek (*Allium tricoccum*) of the lily family, having a pair of broad basal leaves in spring, followed by a naked flower stalk: its strongly flavored bulbs are eaten, esp. in the Appalachians

ram·page (ram pāj′; *also, and for n. always,* ram′pāj) *vi.* **-paged′, -pag′ing** [orig. Scot. & North Eng. dial., prob. < RAMP[2]] to rush violently or wildly about; rage —*n.* an outbreak of violent, raging behavior: chiefly in **on the** (or **a**) **rampage** —**ram·pa′geous** *adj.* —**ram·pa′geous·ly** *adv.* —**ram·pa′geous·ness** *n.* —**ram·pag′er** *n.*

ram·pant (ram′pənt) *adj.* [ME. < OFr., prp. of *ramper*: see RAMP[2]] **1.** growing luxuriantly; flourishing [*rampant* plants] **2.** spreading unchecked; widespread; rife **3.** violent and uncontrollable in action, manner, speech, etc. **4.** *Archit.* having one abutment higher than the other: said of an arch **5.** rearing up on the hind legs; specif., *Heraldry* depicted thus in profile, with one forepaw raised above the other [a lion *rampant*] —**ramp′an·cy** *n.* —**ramp′ant·ly** *adv.*

ram·part (ram′pärt, -pərt) *n.* [Fr. *rempart* < *remparer*, to fortify a place < *re-*, again + *emparer* < Pr. *amparer*, to fortify < L. *ante*, before + *parare*, to PREPARE] **1.** an embankment of earth surmounted by a parapet and encircling a castle, fort, etc., for defending it from attackers **2.** any defense or bulwark —*vt.* to protect with or as with a rampart

ram·pike (ram′pīk′) *n.* [< ?] [Canad.] a tall, dead tree, esp. one blackened and made branchless by fire

ram·pi·on (ram′pē ən) *n.* [altered < ? Fr. *raiponce*, It. *raponzolo* < ML. *rapunculus*, dim. < L. *rapa*: see RAPE[2]] a European bellflower (*Campanula rapunculus*) with thick, fleshy, white roots that are used with the leaves in salads or cooked, esp. formerly, as a vegetable

ramps (ramps) *n. same as* RAMP[3]

ram·rod (ram′räd) *n.* a rod used for ramming down the charge in a gun that is loaded through the muzzle

Ram·say (ram′zē) **1. Allen,** 1686–1758; Scot. poet & bookseller **2. George,** *see* DALHOUSIE **3. Sir William,** 1852–1916; Brit. chemist, born in Scotland

Ram·ses (ram′sēz) any of a number of Egyptian kings who ruled from c. 1315 to c. 1090 B.C.; esp., *a)* **Ramses I** ?–1314?; founder of the dynasty *b)* **Ramses II** ?–1225; king (1292–25): often identified as the pharaoh of Exodus *c)* **Ramses III** ?–1167; king (1198–67)

Rams·gate (ramz′gāt′; *Brit.* -git) seaport & resort in Kent, SE England, on the English Channel: pop. 38,000

ram·shack·le (ram′shak′'l) *adj.* [back-formation < *ramshackled*, for earlier *ransackled*, pp. of *ransackle*, freq. of RANSACK] loose and rickety; likely to fall to pieces; shaky [a *ramshackle* old building]

ram·til (ram′til) *n.* [Hind. *rāmtil* < Sans. *rāma*, Rama + *tila*, sesame] a weedy annual plant (*Guizotia abyssinica*) of the composite family, whose seeds yield an oil used in India for cooking, and for soaps and illumination

ram·u·lose (ram′yə lōs′) *adj.* [L. *ramulosus* < *ramulus*, dim. of *ramus*, a branch: see ROOT[1]] having many small branches

ra·mus (rā′məs) *n., pl.* **-mi** (-mī) [ModL. < L., a branch: see ROOT[1]] *Biol.* a branch or branchlike projecting part

Ran (rän) [ON. *Rān*] *Norse Myth.* a destructive sea goddess: wife of Aegir

ran (ran) *pt.* of RUN

☆**ranch** (ranch) *n.* [< RANCHO] **1.** a large farm, esp. in W States, with its buildings, lands, etc., for the raising of cattle, horses, or sheep in great numbers **2.** any large farm devoted to the raising of a particular crop or livestock [a fruit *ranch*] **3.** all the people living and working on a ranch **4.** *clipped form of* RANCH HOUSE —*vi.* to work on or manage a ranch —*vt.* to put (an animal) to graze on a ranch

☆**ranch·er** (ran′chər) *n.* **1.** a person who owns or manages a ranch **2.** a cowboy **3.** *same as* RANCH HOUSE

☆**ran·che·ro** (ran cher′ō; *Sp.* rän che′rō) *n., pl.* **-ros** (-ōz; *Sp.* -rōs) [AmSp.] in the SW U.S. and Mexico, a person who owns or works on a ranch

☆**ranch house 1.** the owner's residence on a ranch **2.** a style of house in which all the rooms are on one floor, usually with a garage attached

☆**ranch·man** (ranch′mən) *n., pl.* **-men** (-mən) a man who owns or works on a ranch

☆**ran·cho** (ran′chō, rän′-) *n., pl.* **-chos** [AmSp., small farm < Sp., small farm, group who eat together, mess < *ranchear*, to build huts < Fr. (*se*)*ranger*, to make room < *ranger*: see RANGE] in Spanish America, **1.** a hut or group of huts for ranch workers **2.** *same as* RANCH

ran·cid (ran′sid) *adj.* [L. *rancidus* < *rancere*, to be rank] having the bad smell or taste of stale fats or oils; spoiled —SYN. see STINKING —**ran·cid′i·ty** (-sid′ə tē), **ran′cid·ness** *n.* —**ran′cid·ly** *adv.*

ran·cor (raŋ′kər) *n.* [ME. *rancour* < OFr. *rancor* < LL., rankness, in LL.(Ec.), rancor < L. *rancere*, to be rank] a continuing and bitter hate or ill will; deep spite or malice: also, Brit. sp., **ran′cour** —SYN. see MALICE —**ran′cor·ous** *adj.* —**ran′cor·ous·ly** *adv.*

rand[1] (rand) *n.* [ME. *rande*, a border, strip < OE. *rand, rond*, a brink, shield, akin to ON. *rönd*, shield rim, OHG. *rant*, shield boss < IE. base *rem-*, to support, whence RIM] **1.** [Brit.] an edge, border, or margin, as the unplowed strip around a field **2.** a leather strip used to level off the back part of a shoe sole before the heel is put on

rand[2] (rand, ränd) *n., pl.* **rand** [Afrik., orig., shield < Du., akin to OE. *rand*: see prec.] the monetary unit of South Africa, Botswana, Swaziland, or Lesotho: see MONETARY UNITS, table

Rand (rand), *the same as* WITWATERSRAND

Ran·dal, Ran·dall (ran′d'l) [< OE. *Randwulf* (or cognate ON. *Ranthulfr*) < *rand*, a shield (see RAND[1]) + *wulf*, WOLF] a masculine name

R & D, R. and D. research and development

Ran·ders (rän′ərs) seaport in NE Jutland, Denmark: pop. 55,000

Ran·dolph (ran′dälf, -dôlf) [ML. *Randulfus* < OE. *Randwulf*: see RANDAL] **1.** a masculine name **2. John,** 1773–1833; U.S. statesman & orator

ran·dom (ran′dəm) *n.* [ME. *randoun* < OFr. *randon*, violence, speed (in *a random*, violently) < *randir*, to run violently < Frank. **rant*, a running, akin to OHG. *rinnan*, to RUN] impetuous and haphazard movement or course of action: now only in **at random**, without careful choice, aim, plan, etc.; haphazardly —*adj.* **1.** lacking aim or method; purposeless; haphazard **2.** not uniform; esp., of different sizes **3.** *Statistics* of, pertaining to, or characterizing a set of items every member of which has an equal

chance of occurring or of occurring with a particular frequency —**ran′dom·ly** *adv.* —**ran′dom·ness** *n.*

SYN.—**random** applies to that which occurs or is done without careful choice, aim, plan, etc. [a *random* remark]; **haphazard** applies to that which is done, made, or said without regard for its consequences, relevancy, etc. and therefore stresses the implication of accident or chance [a *haphazard* selection of books]; **casual** implies a happening or seeming to happen by chance without intention or purpose and often connotes nonchalance, indifference, etc. [a *casual* acquaintance]; **desultory** suggests a lack of method or system, as in jumping from one thing to another [his *desultory* reading in the textbook]; **chance** emphasizes accidental occurrence without prearrangement or planning [a *chance* encounter] —**ANT. deliberate**

☆**random access** the property of any digital computer memory in which the access time is independent of the address

ran·dom·ize (-īz′) *vt.* **-ized′, -iz′ing** to select or choose (items of a group) in a random order to obtain an unbiased result, often by using a table of random numbers —**ran′-dom·i·za′tion** *n.*

random variable *Statistics* a variable with more than one potential value, whose actual value is the chance result of a given experiment

random walk *Math.* a sequence of movements in which the direction of each successive move is determined entirely at random

R & R, R and R *Mil.* rest and recuperation (leave)

ran·dy (ran′dē) *adj.* [prob. < *rand*, dial. var. of RANT + -Y²] **1.** [Chiefly Scot.] coarse; crude; vulgar **2.** sexually aroused; amorous; lustful —*n.*, *pl.* **-dies** [Scot.] a coarse, vulgar, quarrelsome woman; shrew

ra·nee (rä′nē) *n. alt. sp.* of RANI

rang (raŋ) *pt.* of RING¹

range (rānj) *vt.* **ranged, rang′ing** [ME. *rangen* < OFr. *ranger*, var. of *renger* (whence ME. *rengen*) < *renc* < Frank. **hring*, akin to OE., OHG. *hring*, RING²] **1.** to arrange in a certain order; esp., to set in a row or rows **2.** to put into the proper class or classes; systematize **3.** to place with others in a cause, party, etc. [to *range* oneself with the rebels] **4.** to put (a gun, telescope, etc.) in a line with the target or object, at a proper angle of elevation; train **5.** to make level or even **6.** to travel over or through; roam about [to *range* the woods] **7.** to move along parallel to [to *range* the coastline] ☆**8.** to put out (cattle, etc.) to graze on a range **9.** to uncoil (the cable of an anchor) and arrange on deck —*vi.* **1.** to extend, reach, or lie in a given direction or in a row [hills *ranging* toward the south] **2.** to wander about; roam **3.** to roam through an area, as in hunting [dogs *ranging* through the woods] **4.** *a)* to have a specified range [a gun that *ranges* five miles] *b)* to be projected at a certain distance **5.** to vary between stated limits [children *ranging* in age from 5 to 12] **6.** *Biol., Zool.* to be native to a specified region **7.** *Gunnery* to determine the range of a target by firing alternate rounds beyond and before it —*n.* [ME. *reng* < OFr. *renc*] **1.** a row, line, or series; rank **2.** a class, kind, or order **3.** a series of connected mountains considered as a single sytem **4.** *a)* the maximum effective horizontal distance that a weapon can fire its projectile *b)* the horizontal distance from a weapon to its target *c)* the path of flight for a missile or rocket **5.** the maximum distance a plane, etc. can travel without refueling **6.** *a)* a place for shooting practice *b)* a place for testing rockets in flight **7.** the full extent over which something moves or is heard, seen, understood, effective, etc.; scope [the *range* of one's studies] **8.** full extent of pitch, from highest to lowest tones, of a voice, instrument, composition, etc. **9.** a wandering or roaming ☆**10.** a large, open area of land over which livestock can wander and graze **11.** the limits of possible variations of amount, degree, etc. [a wide *range* of price] **12.** a unit for cooking typically including an oven and surface heating units operated as by gas or electricity ☆**13.** in U.S. public surveying, a strip of land between two meridian lines six miles apart, constituting a row of townships **14.** *Biol., Zool.* the region to which a plant or animal is native **15.** *Math.* the set of all distinct values that may be taken on by a given function **16.** *Statistics* the difference between the largest and smallest values in a sample —☆*adj.* of a range, or open grazing place [*range* livestock]

SYN.—**range** refers to the full extent over which something is perceivable, effective, etc. [the *range* of his knowledge]; **reach** refers to the furthest limit of effectiveness, influence, etc. [beyond the *reach* of my understanding]; **scope** implies considerable room and freedom of range, but within prescribed limits [does it fall within the *scope* of this dictionary?]; **compass** also suggests completeness within limits regarded as a circumference [he did all within the *compass* of his power]; **gamut**, in this connection, refers to the full range of shades, tones, etc. between the limits of something [the full *gamut* of emotions] See also ROAM

range finder any of various instruments for determining the distance of a target or object from an observer, or from a gun, camera, etc.

Range·ley Lakes (rānj′lē) [after an early owner of the region] chain of lakes in W Me. & NE N.H.

rang·er (rān′jər) *n.* [ME. *raunger*, a forest officer: see RANGE] **1.** one who ranges; a wanderer **2.** *a)* any of a group of mounted troops for patrolling a region ☆*b)* [often R-] any of a group of soldiers trained for raiding and close

combat **3.** *a)* in England, the chief official of a royal park or forest ☆*b)* in the U.S., a warden who patrols government forests

Ran·goon (raŋ gōōn′) capital of Burma, a seaport in the S part: pop. 1,530,000 (met. area, 2,000,000)

rang·y (rān′jē) *adj.* **rang′i·er, rang′i·est 1.** able or inclined to range about ☆**2.** long-limbed and slender [*rangy* cattle] ☆**3.** having an open range; spacious —**rang′i·ness** *n.*

ra·ni (rä′nē) *n.* [Hindi *rānī* < Sans. *rājñī*, fem. of *rājan*: see RAJAH] in India, **1.** the wife of a rajah, king, or prince **2.** a reigning queen or princess

ran·id (ran′id, rā′nid) *n.* [< ModL. *Ranidae* < *Rana*, name of the type genus < L. *rana*, a frog] any of a large family (Ranidae) comprised of those frogs having teeth in the upper jaw and a tongue forked at the rear

rank¹ (raŋk) *n.* [MFr. *renc* < OFr. *ranc, renc*: see RANGE] **1.** a row, line, or series; specif., a set of organ pipes of the same kind **2.** an orderly arrangement **3.** a social division or class; stratum of society [men from all *ranks* of life] **4.** a high position in society; high degree; eminence [a man of *rank*] **5.** an official grade or position [the *rank* of captain] **6.** a relative position, usually in a scale classifying persons or things; grade; degree [a poet of the first *rank*] **7.** any of the horizontal rows of squares on a chessboard **8.** *Mil. a)* a row of soldiers, vehicles, etc. placed side by side, or abreast of one another: cf. FILE¹ *b)* [*pl.*] an army *c)* [*pl.*] the body of soldiers of an army, as distinguished from the officers [to rise from the *ranks*] —*vt.* **1.** to place in a rank or ranks **2.** to assign a certain rank, or position, to ☆**3.** to have a higher rank than; outrank —*vi.* **1.** to hold a certain rank, or position [to *rank* third on a list] **2.** [Archaic] to form a rank or move in ranks —☆**pull (one′s) rank on** [Mil. Slang] to take advantage of one's rank in enforcing commands to or making demands on (a subordinate) —**rank and file 1.** the body of soldiers of an army, as distinguished from the officers **2.** the ordinary people forming the large part of some group, as distinguished from its leaders or officials

rank² (raŋk) *adj.* [ME. *ranke* < OE. *ranc*, strong, proud, akin to MLowG. *rank*, slender, erect, long and thin < IE. base **reĝ-*, high, upright, whence RIGHT] **1.** growing or grown vigorously and coarsely; overly luxuriant [*rank* grass] **2.** producing or covered with a luxuriant crop, often to excess; extremely fertile **3.** strong and offensive in smell or taste; rancid **4.** in bad taste; coarse; indecent **5.** complete; extreme; utter [*rank* deceit] **6.** [Obs.] in sexual heat —**SYN.** see FLAGRANT, STINKING —**rank′ly** *adv.* —**rank′ness** *n.*

Rank (ränk), **Otto** 1884–1939; Austrian psychoanalyst

Ran·ke (räŋ′ka), **Le·o·pold von** (lā′ō pōlt′ fōn) 1795–1886; Ger. historian

rank·er (raŋ′kər) *n.* [Brit.] **1.** a soldier in the ranks **2.** a commissioned officer promoted from the ranks

Ran·kine (raŋ′kin) *adj.* [after Wm. J. M. *Rankine* (1820–72), Scot. physicist] designating or of an absolute-temperature scale in which a measurement interval equals a Fahrenheit degree and in which 0° is equal to −459.67°F, so that the freezing point of water is 491.67°R

rank·ing (raŋ′kin) *adj.* ☆**1.** of the highest rank [the *ranking* officer] ☆**2.** prominent or outstanding [a *ranking* composer]

ran·kle (raŋ′k'l) *vi., vt.* **-kled, -kling** [ME. *ranclen* < OFr. *rancler* < *raoncle, draoncle*, a fester, ulcer < ML. *dracunculus* < L., dim. of *draco*, DRAGON] **1.** orig., to fester; become or make inflamed **2.** to cause or cause to have long-lasting anger, rancor, resentment, etc.

ran·sack (ran′sak) *vt.* [ME. *ransaken* < ON. *rannsaka* < *rann*, a house (akin to OE. *ærn*, Goth. *razn* < IE. base **(e)re*, to REST¹) + *-saka* < *sœkja*, to SEEK] **1.** to search thoroughly; examine every part of in searching **2.** to search through for plunder; pillage; rob —**ran′sack·er** *n.*

ran·som (ran′səm) *n.* [ME. *raunson* < OFr. *raençon* < L. *redemptio*, REDEMPTION] **1.** the redeeming or release of a captive or of seized property by payment of money or compliance with other demands **2.** the price thus paid or demanded **3.** [Archaic] a means of freeing from sin; redemption —*vt.* **1.** to obtain the release of (a captive or property) by paying the demanded price **2.** [Now Rare] to release after such payment **3.** [Archaic] to free from sin; redeem —**SYN.** see RESCUE —**ran′som·er** *n.*

Ran·som (ran′səm), **John Crowe** (krō) 1888– ; U.S. poet & critic

rant (rant) *vi., vt.* [< obs. Du. *ranten*, to rave, akin to G. *ranzen*, to be noisy, *anragzen*, to affront] to talk or say in a loud, wild, extravagant way; declaim violently; rave —*n.* **1.** loud, wild, extravagant speech **2.** [Scot. or Brit. Dial.] a boisterous merrymaking —**rant′er** *n.* —**rant′ing·ly** *adv.*

ra·nun·cu·lus (rə nun′kyoo ləs) *n., pl.* **-lus·es, -li′** (-lī′) [ModL., name of the genus < L., tadpole, medicinal plant, dim. of *rana*, a frog] *same as* BUTTERCUP

rap¹ (rap) *vt.* **rapped, rap′ping** [ME. *rappen*, prob. of echoic orig.] **1.** to strike quickly and sharply; tap ☆**2.** [Slang] to criticize sharply —*vi.* **1.** to knock quickly and sharply ☆**2.** [Slang] to talk; chat —*n.* **1.** a quick, sharp knock; tap ☆**2.** [Slang] a talking; chat ☆**3.** [Slang] blame or punishment; specif., a judicial sentence, as to a prison term: usually in **beat** (escape) or **take** (receive) **the rap,** or **bum** (unfair) **rap** —**rap on the knuckles** a mild repri-

mand or light sentence —**rap out** to say or utter sharply [to *rap out* an order]

rap² (rap) *n*. [< ?] **1.** orig., a counterfeit Irish halfpenny **2.** [Colloq.] the least bit: now usually in **not care** (or **give**) **a rap** not care (or give) anything at all

rap³ (rap) *vt*. **rapped** or **rapt, rap'ping** [back-formation < RAPT] [Obs. or Rare] **1.** to seize; snatch **2.** to transport with rapture: now only in the pp.

ra·pa·cious (rə pā'shəs) *adj*. [< L. *rapax* (gen. *rapacis*) < *rapere*, to seize (see RAPE¹) + -OUS] **1.** taking by force; plundering **2.** greedy or grasping; voracious **3.** living on captured prey; predatory —**ra·pa'cious·ly** *adv*. —**ra·pac·i·ty** (rə pas'ə tē), **ra·pa'cious·ness** *n*.

Ra·pa Nu·i (rä'pä nōo'ē) *native name of* EASTER ISLAND

rape¹ (rāp) *n*. [ME., prob. < the *v*.] **1.** *a*) the crime of having sexual intercourse with a woman or girl forcibly and without her consent, or (**statutory rape**) with a girl below the age of consent (see AGE OF CONSENT) *b*) any sexual assault upon a person [Now Rare] the act of seizing and carrying away by force **3.** the plundering or violent destruction (*of a city, etc.*), as in warfare **4.** any outrageous assault or flagrant violation —*vt*. **raped, rap'ing** [ME. *rapen* < L. *rapere*, to seize < IE. base **rep-*, to seize, whence ON. *refsa*, to punish, OE. *repsan*, to reprove] **1.** formerly, to seize and carry away by force **2.** to commit rape on; ravish; violate **3.** to plunder or destroy —*vi*. to commit rape

rape² (rāp) *n*. [ME. < L. *rapa, rapum*, turnip < IE. base **rap-*, whence G. *rübe*, beet, Gr. *rhapys, rhaphys*] an annual old-world plant (*Brassica napus*) of the mustard family, whose seeds yield an oil and whose leaves are used for fodder

rape³ (rāp) *n*. [Fr. *râpe* < ML. *raspa*, ult. < or akin to OHG. *raspon*, to scrape together: see RASP] the crushed pulp of grapes after the juice has been extracted

rape oil a thick oil extracted from rapeseed, used as a lubricant, illuminant, etc.: also **rapeseed oil**

rape·seed (-sēd') *n*. the seed of the rape plant

Raph·a·el (rā'fē əl; *also, and for 3 usually,* raf'ē-) [LL.(Ec.) < Gr.(Ec.) *Raphaēl* < Heb. *rephā'ēl*, lit., God hath healed] **1.** a masculine name **2.** an archangel mentioned in the Apocrypha **3.** (born *Raffaello Santi* or *Sanzio*) 1483-1520; It. painter & architect

ra·phe (rā'fē) *n*. [ModL. < Gr. *rhaphē*, a seam < *rhaptein*, to stitch together < IE. base **werp-*, to turn, twist, whence WRAP] **1.** *Anat.* a seamlike joining of the two lateral halves of an organ, as of the tongue **2.** *Bot. a*) a ridge of tissue along the side of an ovule, indicating the position of the vascular bundle which supplies the developing seed *b*) the line of union of the two carpels in the fruit of members of the parsley family *c*) a line or marking along the center of a diatom shell

ra·phi·a (rā'fē ə, raf'ē ə) *n*. *same as* RAFFIA

ra·phide (rā'fid, raf'id) *n., pl.* **raph·i·des** (raf'ə dēz', rā'fidz) [ModL. < Gr. *rhaphis* (gen. *rhaphidos*), a needle: for IE. base see RAPHE] a needle-shaped crystal, usually of calcium oxalate, developed singly, or more often in bundles, in a plant cell

rap·id (rap'id) *adj*. [L. *rapidus* < *rapere*, to seize, rush: see RAPE¹] moving, progressing, or occurring with speed; swift; fast; quick —☆*n*. **1.** [*usually pl.*] a part of a river where the current is relatively swift, as because of a narrowing of the river bed **2.** a rapid transit car, train, or system —*SYN*. see FAST¹ —**ra·pid·i·ty** (rə pid'ə tē), **rap'id·ness** *n*. —**rap'id·ly** *adv*.

Rap·i·dan (rap'ə dan') [< ?] river in NC Va., flowing eastward from the Blue Ridge Mountains into the Rappahannock: c. 90 mi.

Rapid City [from its location on the *Rapid* River] city in W S.Dak., in the Black Hills: pop. 44,000

rap·id-fire (-fīr') *adj*. **1.** firing or capable of firing shots in rapid succession: said of guns **2.** done, delivered, proceeding, or carried on swiftly and sharply [*rapid-fire* talk]

☆**rapid transit** a system of rapid public transportation in an urban area, using electric trains running along an unimpeded right of way, as in a subway

ra·pi·er (rā'pē ər, rāp'yər) *n*. [Fr. *rapière*, orig. adj., in OFr. *espee* (sword) *rapiere* < *râper*, to rasp: see RAPPEE] **1.** orig., a slender, two-edged sword with a large cup hilt **2.** later, a light, sharp-pointed sword used only for thrusting

rap·ine (rap'in) *n*. [ME. < OFr. < L. *rapina* < *rapere*, to snatch, seize: see RAPE¹] the act of seizing and carrying off by force others' property; plunder; pillage

☆**rap·ist** (rāp'ist) *n*. a person who has committed rape

Rap·pa·han·nock (rap'ə han'ək) [< Algonquian, the ebb-and-flow (i.e., tidal) stream] river in NE Va., flowing southeastward into Chesapeake Bay: c. 185 mi.

rap·pa·ree (rap'ə rē') *n*. [Ir. *rapaire*, orig., pikeman < *rapaire*, short pike] **1.** formerly, an Irish freebooting soldier **2.** a plunderer or robber

rap·pee (ra pē') *n*. [Fr. (*tabac*) *râpé*, grated (tobacco), pp. of *râper*, to rasp, ult. < OHG. *raspon*, to scrape together: see RASP] a strong snuff made from coarse, dark tobacco leaves

rap·pel (ra pel', rə-) *n*. [Fr., lit., a recall < *rappeler*, to

call back < OFr. *rapeler*: see REPEAL] a descent by a mountain climber, as down a sheer face of a cliff, by means of a double rope belayed above and arranged around the climber's body so that he can control the slide downward —*vi*. **-pelled', -pel'ling** to make such a descent

rap·pen (räp'ən) *n., pl.* **-pen** [G. < *rappe*, RAVEN¹: in pejorative allusion to the eagle on an earlier Alsatian coin] *Ger. name for* the Swiss centime: see MONETARY UNITS, table

rap·per (rap'ər) *n*. a person or thing that raps; specif., a door knocker

rap·port (ra pôr', -pōrt') *n*. [Fr. < OFr. *raport*, agreement, accord, lit., a bringing back < *raporter*, to bring back < *re-* (< L. *re-*), again + *aporter*, to bring < L. *apportare* < *ad-*, to + *portare*, to carry: see PORT³] relationship; esp., a close or sympathetic relationship; agreement; harmony

rap·por·teur (rap'ôr toor'; *Fr.* rả pôr tër') *n*. [Fr. < *rapporter* (see RAPPORT) + -*eur*, -OR] a person appointed to prepare reports, studies, etc. as for a committee or conference

rap·proche·ment (ra prōsh'män; *Fr.* rả prôsh män') *n*. [Fr. < *rapprocher*, to bring together: see RE-, APPROACH, & -MENT] an establishing, or esp. a restoring, of harmony and friendly relations

ras·cal·lion (ras skal'yən) *n*. [< earlier *rascallion*, extension of RASCAL] a rascal; rogue

rapt (rapt) *adj*. [L. *raptus*, pp. of *rapere*, to snatch, seize: see RAPE¹] **1.** [Now Rare] carried away in body or spirit (*to* heaven, etc.) **2.** carried away with joy, love, etc.; enraptured **3.** completely absorbed or engrossed (*in* meditation, study, etc.) **4.** resulting from or showing rapture [a *rapt* look]

rap·to·ri·al (rap tôr'ē əl) *adj*. [L. *raptor*, plunderer < pp. of *rapere*, to snatch (see RAPE¹) + -IAL] **1.** predatory; specif., of or belonging to a group of birds of prey with a strong notched beak and sharp talons, as the eagle, hawk, owl, etc. **2.** adapted for seizing prey [*raptorial* claws]

rap·ture (rap'chər) *n*. [RAPT + -URE] **1.** the state of being carried away with joy, love, etc.; ecstasy **2.** an expression of great joy, pleasure, etc. **3.** [Now Rare] a carrying away or being carried away in body or spirit —*vt*. **-tured, -tur·ing** [Now Rare] to enrapture; fill with ecstasy —*SYN*. see ECSTASY —**rap'tur·ous** *adj*. —**rap'tur·ous·ly** *adv*.

☆**rapture of the deep** *same as* NITROGEN NARCOSIS: so called from its initial intoxicating effect

ra·ra a·vis (rer'ə ā'vis) *pl.* **ra·rae a·ves** (rer'ē ā'vēz) [L., lit., strange bird] an unusual or extraordinary person or thing; rarity

rare¹ (rer) *adj*. **rar'er, rar'est** [ME. < MFr. < L. *rarus*, loose, thin, scarce, prob. < IE. base *(*e*)*re-*, loose, whence Gr. *erēmos*, solitary] **1.** not frequently encountered; scarce; uncommon; unusual **2.** unusually good; remarkably fine; excellent [a *rare* scholar] **3.** not dense; thin; tenuous [*rare* atmosphere] **4.** [Obs.] not close together; scattered —**rare'ness** *n*.

SYN.—**rare** is applied to something of which there are not many instances or specimens and usually connotes, therefore, great value [a *rare* gem]; **infrequent** applies to that which occurs only at long intervals [his *infrequent* trips]; **uncommon** and **unusual** refer to that which does not ordinarily occur and is therefore exceptional or remarkable [her *uncommon* generosity, this *unusual* heat]; **scarce** applies to something of which there is, at the moment, an inadequate supply [potatoes are *scarce* these days] —*ANT*. frequent, common, abundant

rare² (rer) *adj*. **rar'er, rar'est** [earlier *rear* < ME. *rere* < OE. *hrere*, lightly boiled (basic sense prob. "disturbed, moved") < base of *hreran*, to move] not completely cooked; underdone; partly raw: said esp. of meat —**rare'ness** *n*.

rare³ (rer) *vi*. **rared, rar'ing** **1.** [Dial.] *same as* REAR² (esp. *vi*. 1 & 2) ☆**2.** [Colloq.] to be eager, enthusiastic, etc.: used in prp. [*raring* to go]

rare·bit (rer'bit) *n*. [altered < (WELSH) RABBIT] *same as* WELSH RABBIT

rare earth **1.** any of certain basic oxides much alike in physical and chemical properties; specif., any of the oxides of the rare-earth metals **2.** any of the rare-earth metals

rare-earth metals (rer'urth') a group of rare metallic chemical elements with consecutive atomic numbers of 57 to 71 inclusive: also **rare-earth elements**: see PERIODIC TABLE

rar·ee show (rer'ē) [< pronun. (by Savoyard showmen) of *rare show*] **1.** a portable peep show **2.** any street show

rar·e·fy (rer'ə fī') *vt., vi.* **-fied', -fy'ing** [ME. *rarefien* < MFr. *rarefier* < L. *rarefacere* < *rarus*, rare + *facere*, to make (see FACT)] **1.** to make or become thin, or less dense [the *rarefied* mountain air] **2.** to make or become more refined, subtle, or lofty [a *rarefied* sense of humor] —**rar'e·fac'tion** (-fak'shən) *n*. —**rar'e·fac'tive** *adj*.

rare·ly (rer'lē) *adv*. **1.** infrequently; seldom **2.** beautifully, skillfully, excellently, etc. **3.** uncommonly; exceptionally

rare·ripe (rer'rīp') *adj*. [*rare*, dial. var. of RATHE + RIPE] ripening early —*n*. a fruit or vegetable that ripens early

rar·i·ty (rer'ə tē) *n*. [L. *raritas*] **1.** the quality or condition

of being rare; specif., *a)* uncommonness; scarcity *b)* excellence *c)* lack of density; thinness **2.** *pl.* **-ties** something remarkable or valuable because rare

Ra·ro·ton·ga (rä′rə tôŋ′gə) largest of the Cook Islands, in the S Pacific: 26 sq. mi.; pop. 10,000

ras·bo·ra (raz bôr′ə) *n.* [ModL. < native name in E. Indies] any of a large genus (*Rasbora*) of small tropical fishes, often kept in aquariums

ras·cal (ras′k'l) *n.* [ME. *rascaile* < OFr. *rascaille*, scrapings, dregs, rabble < *rasquer*, to scrape < VL. *rasicare* < L. *rasus:* see RAZE] **1.** a scoundrel; rogue; scamp: now usually used jokingly or affectionately, as of a mischievous child **2.** [Archaic] one of the rabble —*adj.* **1.** [Rare] low; dishonest; base **2.** [Archaic] of the rabble

ras·cal·i·ty (ras kal′ə tē) *n.* **1.** the character or behavior of a rascal **2.** *pl.* **-ties** a low, mean, or dishonest act

ras·cal·ly (ras′k'l ē) *adj.* of or like a rascal; base; dishonest; mean —*adv.* in a rascally manner

rase (rāz) *vt.* **rased**, **ras′ing** *alt. Brit. sp. of* RAZE

rash[1] (rash) *adj.* [ME. *rasch*, prob. < OE. *ræsc*, akin to ON. *röskr*, G. *rasch*] **1.** too hasty or incautious in acting or speaking; reckless **2.** characterized by too great haste or recklessness [a *rash* act] **3.** [Obs.] bringing quick results —**rash′ly** *adv.* —**rash′ness** *n.*

rash[2] (rash) *n.* [MFr. *rasche* < VL. *rasica*, a scraping: see RASCAL] **1.** an eruption of red spots on the skin, usually temporary **2.** a sudden appearance of a large or excessive number; plethora [a *rash* of complaints]

rash·er (rash′ər) *n.* [< ? obs. *rash*, to cut < Fr. *raser:* see RAZE] **1.** a thin slice of bacon or, rarely, ham, for frying or broiling ☆**2.** a serving of several such slices

Rasht (rasht) city in NW Iran: pop. 119,000

Rask (räsk), **Ras·mus Chris·tian** (räs′mōōs krēs′tyän) 1787–1832; Dan. philologist

Ras·mus·sen (räs′mōō s'n), **Knud** (**Johan Victor**) (k'nōōth) 1879–1933; Dan. arctic explorer

ra·so·ri·al (ra sôr′ē əl) *adj.* [< ModL. *Rasores*, lit., scratchers < L. *rasus* (see RAZE) + -IAL] characteristically scratching the ground to find food, as a chicken; gallinaceous

rasp (rasp, räsp) *vt.* [ME. *raspen* < OFr. *rasper* < OHG. *raspon*, to scrape together, akin to OE. *hrespan*, to strip, spoil] **1.** to scrape or rub with or as with a file **2.** to utter in a rough, grating tone **3.** to grate upon; irritate [giggling that *rasped* his nerves] —*vi.* **1.** to scrape roughly; grate **2.** to make a rough, grating sound —*n.* **1.** a type of rough file with raised points instead of lines, used esp. on wood **2.** a rough, grating sound **3.** an act of rasping —**rasp′er** *n.* —**rasp′ing·ly** *adv.*

rasp·ber·ry (raz′ber′ē, -bər ē) *n., pl.* **-ries** [earlier *raspis berry* < *rasp, raspis*, raspberry (prob. same word as ME. *raspis*, kind of wine) + BERRY] **1.** the small, juicy, edible, aggregate fruit of various brambles (genus *Rubus*) of the rose family, consisting of a cluster of red, purple, or black drupelets **2.** any plant bearing this fruit **3.** [< rhyming slang *raspberry tart, fart*] [Slang] a sound of derision, contempt, etc. made by expelling air forcibly so as to vibrate the tongue between the lips

Ras·pu·tin (räs pōō′tin; *E.* ras pyōōt′'n), **Gri·go·ri E·fi·mo·vich** (gri gô′ri ye fē′mə vich) 1871?–1916; Russ. religious mystic & faith healer who exercised great control over the Czarist court: assassinated

rasp·y (ras′pē, räs′-) *adj.* **rasp′i·er, rasp′i·est** **1.** rasping; grating **2.** easily irritated —**rasp′i·ness** *n.*

ras·sle (ras′'l) *n., vi., vt.* **-sled, -sling** *dial. or colloq. var. of* WRESTLE

ras·ter (ras′tər) *n.* [G., a screen < L., a toothed hoe, rake < *rasus:* see RAZE] the pattern of illuminated horizontal scanning lines formed on a television picture tube when no signal is being received

rat (rat) *n.* [ME. *ratte* < OE. *ræt*, akin to G. *ratz, ratte* < IE. base *rōd-*, to scratch, gnaw, whence L. *radere*, to scrape, *rodere*, to gnaw] **1.** *a)* any of numerous longtailed rodents (family Muridae), resembling, but larger than, the mouse; esp., the **brown** (or **Norway**) **rat** (*Rattus norvegicus*) and the **black rat** (*Rattus rattus*): rats are very destructive pests and carriers of highly contagious diseases, as bubonic plague, typhus, etc. *b)* any of various rodents resembling rats ☆**2.** a small pad formerly used in certain styles of women's coiffures to make the hair look thicker **3.** [Slang] a sneaky, contemptible person; specif., *a)* an informer; stool pigeon *b)* a worker who is a scab *c)* a person who deserts or betrays a cause —*vi.* **rat′ted, rat′ting** **1.** to hunt for rats, esp. with dogs **2.** [Slang] *a)* to desert or betray a cause, movement, etc. as rats are reputed to desert a sinking ship *b)* to act as a stool pigeon; inform (*on*) —☆*vt.* to tease (the hair) —☆**rats!** [Slang] an exclamation of disgust, scorn, disappointment, etc. —**smell a rat** to suspect a trick, plot, etc.

rat·a·ble (rāt′ə b'l) *adj.* **1.** that can be rated, or estimated, etc. **2.** figured at a certain rate; proportional **3.** [Brit.] taxable —**rat′a·bly** *adv.*

rat·a·fi·a (rat′ə fē′ə) *n.* [Fr., prob. of Creole origin] **1.** a cordial or liqueur flavored with almond or fruit kernels **2.** [Brit.] a macaroon: in full **ratafia biscuit**

ra·tan (ra tan′) *n. alt. sp. of* RATTAN

rat·a·plan (rat′ə plan′) *n.* [Fr.: echoic of drumming] the beating of a drum, or a sound like this —*vi., vt.* **-planned′, -plan′ning** to make such a sound (*on*)

rat-a-tat (rat′ə tat′) *n.* [echoic] a series of sharp, quick rapping sounds: also **rat-a-tat′-tat′**

rat-bite fever (rat′bīt′) an infectious disease caused by a spirochete (*Spirillum minus*) and transmitted by the bite of an infected rat or other animal: it is characterized by a bluish-red rash, attacks of fever, and muscular pain

ratch·et (rach′it) *n.* [earlier *rochet* < Fr., a lance head, distaff < It. *rocchetto*, bobbin, spindle, dim. of *rocca*, distaff < Frank. *rokko*, akin to OHG. *roccho*, a spindle, distaff] **1.** a toothed wheel (in full **ratchet wheel**) or bar whose teeth slope in one direction, so as to catch and hold a pawl, which thus prevents backward movement **2.** such a pawl **3.** such a wheel (or bar) and pawl as a unit: used in certain wrenches, hand drills, etc. to allow motion in only one direction

RATCHET WHEEL

rate[1] (rāt) *n.* [ME. < OFr. < L. *rata* (*pars*), reckoned (part), fem. of *ratus*, pp. of *reri*, to reckon < IE. base *rē-*, var. of *ar-*, to fit, join: cf. ART[1], ORDER] **1.** the amount, degree, etc. of anything in relation to units of something else [the *rate* of pay per month, *rate* of speed per hour] **2.** a fixed ratio; proportion [the *rate* of exchange]: see EXCHANGE (*n.* 7) **3.** a price or value; specif., the cost per unit of some commodity, service, etc. [insurance *rate*] **4.** speed of movement or action [to read at a moderate *rate*] **5.** the amount of time gained or lost by a timepiece within a specified period of time **6.** a class or rank [of the first *rate*] **7.** [Brit.] a local property tax **8.** [Obs.] amount; quantity **9.** *U.S. Navy* the grade of an enlisted man —*vt.* **rat′ed, rat′ing** **1.** to estimate the value, worth, strength, capacity, etc. of; appraise **2.** *a)* to put into a particular class or rank *b)* *U.S. Navy* to assign a rate to **3.** to consider; esteem [to be *rated* among the best] **4.** to fix or determine the rates for **5.** [Colloq.] to deserve [to *rate* an increase] —*vi.* **1.** to be classed or ranked **2.** to have value, status, or rating —*SYN.* see ESTIMATE —**at any rate 1.** in any event; whatever happens **2.** at least; anyway

rate[2] (rāt) *vt., vi.* **rat′ed, rat′ing** [ME. *raten* < ? OFr. *reter*, to blame, accuse < L. *reputare*, to count: see REPUTE] to scold severely; chide

rate·a·ble (rāt′ə b'l) *adj. alt. sp. of* RATABLE —**rate′a·bly** *adv.*

ra·tel (rāt′'l, rät′-) *n.* [Afrik., short for *rateldas* < Du. *raat*, a honeycomb + *das*, a badger] a burrowing, flesh-eating mammal (genus *Mellivora*) of India and tropical Africa, resembling, but larger than, a badger

rate·pay·er (rāt′pā′ər) *n.* [Brit. & Canad.] a person who pays rates, or local taxes

-rat·er (rāt′ər) *a combining form used in hyphenated compounds, meaning* one of a (specified) rate, or class [second-*rater*]

☆**rat·fish** (rat′fish′) *n., pl.* **-fish′, -fish′es:** see FISH[2] same as CHIMAERA (sense 2)

rathe (rāth) *adj.* [ME. < OE. *hræth*, var. of *hræd*, quick, speedy < IE. base *kret-*, to shake, whence MIr. *crothaim*, (I) shake] [Archaic] **1.** quick; prompt; eager **2.** coming or happening early in the day, year, etc.; esp., blooming or ripening early in the season —*adv.* [Archaic] **1.** quickly; promptly **2.** early, or too early, in the day, season, etc. Also **rath** (rath, räth)

Ra·the·nau (rä′tə nou), **Wal·ther** (väl′tər) 1867–1922; Ger. industrialist & statesman: assassinated

rath·er (rath′ər, räth′-; *for interj.* rä′thur′, rä′-) *adv.* [ME. < OE. *hrathor*, compar. of *hrathe, hræthe*, quickly (see RATHE)] **1.** [Obs. or Brit. Dial.] more quickly; sooner **2.** more willingly; preferably [would you *rather* have tea?] **3.** with more justice, logic, reason, etc. [one might *rather* say] **4.** more accurately; more precisely [his sister, or *rather*, stepsister] **5.** on the contrary; quite conversely [not a help, *rather* a hindrance] **6.** somewhat; to some degree [*rather* hungry] —*interj.* [Chiefly Brit.] certainly; assuredly: in reply to a question —**had** (or **would**) **rather 1.** would choose to **2.** would prefer that —**rather than** instead of; in place of

☆**raths·kel·ler** (rät′skel′ər, rath′-) *n.* [G. < *rath* (now *rat*), council, town hall + *keller*, cellar: because frequently located in the cellar of the city hall] a restaurant of the German type, usually below the street level, where beer is served

rat·i·fy (rat′ə fī′) *vt.* **-fied′, -fy′ing** [ME. *ratifien* < MFr. *ratifier* < ML. *ratificare* < L. *rata* (see RATE[1]) + *facere*, to make, DO[1]] to approve or confirm; esp., to give official sanction to —*SYN.* see APPROVE —**rat′i·fi·ca′tion** *n.* —**rat′i·fi′er** *n.*

ra·ti·né (rat′'n ā′) *n.* [Fr., frizzed, tufted (of the nap) < pp. of OFr. *raster*, to scrape] a coarse, loosely woven fabric of cotton, wool, rayon, etc., with a nubby or knotty surface: also **ra·tine** (ra tēn′)

rat·ing[1] (rāt′iŋ) *n.* [see RATE[1]] **1.** *a)* a rank, class, or grade; specif., a classification of military or naval personnel according to specialties *b)* [Brit.] an enlisted man in the Navy **2.** a placement in a certain rank or class **3.** an expression in horsepower, British thermal units, etc. of the effectiveness of an engine, furnace, or the like **4.** an evaluation of the credit or financial standing of a businessman, firm, etc. **5.** an amount determined as a rate, or

grade ☆**6.** *Radio & TV* the relative popularity of a program, as determined by sample polls

rat·ing[2] (rāt′iŋ) *n.* [see RATE[2]] a scolding; sharp reprimand

ra·tio (rā′shō, -shē ō′) *n., pl.* **-tios** [L.: see REASON] **1.** a fixed relation in degree, number, etc. between two similar things; proportion [a *ratio* of two boys to three girls] **2.** *Finance* the relative value of gold and silver in a currency system based on both **3.** *Math.* the quotient of one quantity divided by another of the same kind, usually expressed as a fraction

ra·ti·o·ci·nate (rash′ē ō′sə nāt′, rat′ē-; -äs′ə nāt′) *vi.* **-nat·ed, -nat·ing** [< L. *ratiocinatus,* pp. of *ratiocinari,* to reckon < *ratio:* see REASON] to reason; esp., to reason using formal logic —**ra′ti·o′ci·na′tion** *n.* —**ra′ti·o′ci·na′tive** *adj.* —**ra′ti·o′ci·na′tor** *n.*

ra·tion (rash′ən, rā′shən) *n.* [MFr. < ML. *ratio,* ration < L., a reckoning: see REASON] **1.** a fixed portion; share; allowance **2.** a fixed allowance or allotment of food or provisions, esp. a fixed daily allowance, as for a soldier **3.** [pl.] food or food supply, as for soldiers, explorers, etc. —*vt.* **1.** to supply with a ration or rations **2.** to distribute (food, clothing, etc.) in rations, as in times of scarcity

ra·tion·al (rash′ən 'l) *adj.* [ME. *racional* < L. *rationalis* < *ratio:* see REASON] **1.** of, based on, or derived from reasoning [rational powers] **2.** able to reason; reasoning; in possession of one's reason **3.** showing reason; not foolish or silly; sensible [a *rational* argument] **4.** *Math. a)* designating or of a number or quantity expressible as the quotient of two integers, one of which may be unity *b)* designating a function expressible as the quotient of two polynomials —**ra′tion·al·ly** *adv.*

SYN.—**rational** implies the ability to reason logically, as by drawing conclusions from inferences, and often connotes the absence of emotionalism [man is a *rational* creature]; **reasonable** is a less technical term and suggests the use of practical reason in making decisions, choices, etc. [a *reasonable* solution to a problem]; **sensible,** also a nontechnical term, implies the use of common sense or sound judgment [you made a *sensible* decision] —**ANT.** irrational, absurd

ra·tion·a·le (rash′ə nal′, -nä′lē) *n.* [ML. < L., neut. of *rationalis,* rational] **1.** the fundamental reasons, or rational basis, for something **2.** a statement, exposition, or explanation of reasons or principles

ra·tion·al·ism (rash′ən 'l iz'm) *n.* [RATIONAL + -ISM] **1.** the principle or practice of accepting reason as the only authority in determining one's opinions or course of action **2.** *Philos.* the doctrine that knowledge comes wholly from pure reason, without aid from the senses; intellectualism **3.** *Theol.* the doctrine that rejects revelation and the supernatural, and makes reason the sole source for religious truth —**ra′tion·al·ist** *n., adj.* —**ra′tion·al·is′tic** *adj.* —**ra′tion·al·is′ti·cal·ly** *adv.*

ra·tion·al·i·ty (rash′ə nal′ə tē) *n.* [LL.(Ec.) *rationalitas*] **1.** the quality or condition of being rational; reasonableness, or the possession or use of reason **2.** *pl.* **-ties** a rational act, belief, etc.

ra·tion·al·ize (rash′ən ə līz′) *vt.* **-ized′, -iz′ing 1.** to make rational; make conform to reason **2.** to explain or interpret on rational grounds **3.** [Chiefly Brit.] to apply modern methods of efficiency to (an industry, agriculture, etc.) **4.** *Math.* to remove the radical signs from (an equation) without changing the value **5.** *Psychol.* to devise superficially rational, or plausible, explanations or excuses for (one's acts, beliefs, desires, etc.), usually without being aware that these are not the real motives —*vi.* **1.** to think in a rational or rationalistic manner **2.** to rationalize one's acts, beliefs, etc. —**ra′tion·al·i·za′tion** *n.* —**ra′tion·al·iz′er** *n.*

rat·ite (rat′īt) *adj.* [< L. *ratitus,* marked with the figure of a raft < *ratis,* a raft, prob. < IE. base *rēt-, rōt-,* a beam, whence ROOD] designating a former group (Ratitae) of large, flightless birds having a flat breastbone without the keellike ridge of flying birds —*n.* any bird with such a breastbone, as the cassowary, ostrich, etc.

rat kangaroo any of various ratlike kangaroos (genera *Bettongia, Potorous,* etc.), about the size of a rabbit

rat·line (rat′lin) *n.* [altered by folk etym. < LME. *ratling, radeling* < ?] any of the small, relatively thin pieces of tarred rope which join the shrouds of a ship and serve as a ladder for climbing the rigging: also sp. **rat′lin**

rat mite a widespread mite (*Bdellonyssus bacoti*), carried by rats, that can cause skin inflammations or transmit typhus in man by its bite

ra·toon (ra tōōn′) *n.* [Sp. *retoño* < *retoñar,* to sprout again < *re-* (< L. *re-*), again + *otoñar,* to grow in autumn < L. *autumnare* < *autumnus,* AUTUMN] a shoot growing from the root of a plant (esp. the sugar cane) that has been cut down —*vi.* to grow ratoons, or grow as a ratoon

☆**rat race** [Slang] a mad scramble or intense competitive struggle, as in the business world

rats·bane (rats′bān′) *n.* [see BANE] rat poison; esp., trioxide of arsenic

☆**rat snake** any of several large, harmless, rodent-eating snakes (genus *Elaphe*) of E and SW N. America

rat-tail (rat′tāl′) *adj.* shaped like a rat's tail; slim and tapering: also **rat′tailed′** —*n.* same as GRENADIER (sense 3)

rattail cactus a small, often cultivated cactus (*Aporocactus flagelliformis*), with weak, cylindrical, creeping or drooping stems, native to Mexico and Central America

rat·tan (ra tan′) *n.* [Malay *rotan* < *raut,* to strip, pare] **1.** a climbing palm (genera *Calamus* and *Daemonorops*) with long, slender, tough stems **2.** a stem of any of these trees, used in making wickerwork, etc. **3.** a cane or switch made from this

rat·teen (ra tēn′) *n.* [Fr. *ratine:* see RATINÉ] a coarse, heavy, twilled woolen cloth, popular in 18th-cent. Britain

rat·ter (rat′ər) *n.* **1.** a dog or cat skilled at catching rats **2.** [Slang] a betrayer or informer

rat·tish (-ish) *adj.* like or characteristic of a rat

rat·tle[1] (rat′'l) *vi.* **-tled, -tling** [ME. *ratelen,* prob. of WGmc. echoic origin, akin to G. *rasseln*] **1.** to make a series of sharp, short sounds in quick succession **2.** to go or move with such sounds [a wagon *rattling* over the stones] **3.** to talk rapidly and incessantly; chatter (often with *on*) —*vt.* **1.** to cause to rattle [to *rattle* the handle of a door] **2.** to utter or perform rapidly ☆**3.** to confuse or upset; disconcert [to *rattle* a speaker with catcalls] —*n.* **1.** a quick succession of sharp, short sounds **2.** a rattling noise made by air passing through the mucus of a partly closed throat: cf. DEATH RATTLE **3.** a noisy uproar; loud chatter ☆**4.** *a)* a series of horny rings at the end of a rattlesnake's tail, used to produce a rattling sound *b)* any of these **5.** a device, as a baby's toy or a percussion instrument, made to rattle when shaken —**SYN.** see EMBARRASS —**rattle around in** to live or work in (a house, office, etc. too big for one's needs)

rat·tle[2] (rat′'l) *vt.* **-tled, -tling** [back-formation < *rattling* (taken as prp.), var. of RATLINE] to provide with ratlines (usually with *down*)

rat·tle-box (-bäks′) *n.* ☆any of a genus (*Crotalaria*) of plants of the legume family, having small seeds that rattle in the inflated pods when ripe

rat·tle-brain (-brān′) *n.* a frivolous, talkative person: also **rat′tle·pate** (-pāt′) —**rat′tle-brained′** *adj.*

rat·tler (rat′lər) *n.* **1.** a person or thing that rattles ☆**2.** a rattlesnake ☆**3.** [Colloq.] a freight train

☆**rat·tle-snake** (rat′'l snāk′) *n.* any of various poisonous American pit vipers (genera *Crotalus* and *Sistrurus*), having an interlocking series of horny rings at the end of the tail that produce a rattling or buzzing sound when shaken

☆**rattlesnake plantain** any of a genus (*Goodyera*) of terrestrial orchids with spotted leaves and yellowish-white flower spikes

☆**rattlesnake root 1.** any of a number of perennial plants (genus *Prenanthes*) of the composite family, with small, cylindrical, drooping heads and intensely bitter roots, formerly considered a cure for snakebite **2.** any of various other plants formerly considered such a cure

RATTLESNAKE (to 5 1/2 ft. long)

☆**rattlesnake weed 1.** an American hawkweed (*Hieracium venosum*) having purple-veined basal leaves and a naked flowering stem **2.** a weedy plant (*Daucus pusillus*) with small white flowers, found in the S U.S.

rat·tle-trap (rat′'l trap′) *n.* anything worn out, rickety, or rattling; esp., a dilapidated old automobile

rat·tling (rat′liŋ) *adj.* **1.** that rattles **2.** [Colloq.] very fast, good, lively, etc. —*adv.* [Colloq.] very [a *rattling* good time]

rat·tly (-lē, -'l ē) *adj.* that rattles or tends to rattle; noisy

rat·ton (rat′'n) *n.* [ME. *raton* < OFr. < or akin to PGmc. *ratto,* whence RAT] [Scot. & Brit. Dial.] same as RAT (sense 1)

rat·toon (ra tōōn′) *vi.* same as RATOON

rat·trap (rat′trap′) *n.* **1.** a trap for catching rats **2.** a hopeless situation; desperate predicament **3.** [Colloq.] a dirty, run-down building

rat·ty (rat′ē) *adj.* **-ti·er, -ti·est 1.** of or like a rat **2.** full of rats **3.** [Slang] shabby or run-down

rau·cous (rô′kəs) *adj.* [L. *raucus* < IE. echoic base *reu-,* to give hoarse cries, mutter, whence L. *rumor,* OE. *reon,* to lament, & RUNE] **1.** hoarse; rough-sounding [a *raucous* shout] **2.** loud and rowdy [a *raucous* party] —**rau′cous·ly** *adv.* —**rau′cous·ness** *n.*

☆**raun·chy** (rôn′chē, rän′-) *adj.* **-chi·er, -chi·est** [< ?] [Slang] **1.** of poor quality, appearance, etc.; dirty, cheap, sloppy, etc. **2.** frankly sexual in content or tone; earthy, risqué, lustful, etc. —**raun′chi·ness** *n.*

rau·wol·fi·a (rô wool′fē ə, rou-) *n.* [ModL., after Leonhard *Rauwolf,* 16th-c. G. botanist] **1.** any of a genus (*Rauwolfia*) of tropical, mostly poisonous, trees and shrubs of the dog-

bane family, some of which contain substances that have been used medicinally 2. the powdered whole root of a plant (*Rauwolfia serpentina*) yielding various alkaloids, esp. reserpine

rav·age (rav′ij) *n.* [Fr. < *ravir:* see RAVISH] 1. the act or practice of violently destroying; destruction 2. ruin; havoc; devastating damage [the *ravages* of time] —*vt.* **-aged, -ag·ing** [Fr. *ravager* < the *n.*] to destroy violently; devastate; ruin —*vi.* to commit ravages —**rav′ag·er** *n.* SYN.—**ravage** implies violent destruction, usually in a series of depredations or over an extended period of time, as by an army, a plague, etc.; **devastate** stresses the total ruin and desolation resulting from a ravaging; **plunder** refers to the forcible taking of loot by an invading or conquering army; **sack** and **pillage** both specifically suggest violent destruction and plunder by an invading or conquering army, **sack** implying the total stripping of all valuables in a city or town; **despoil** is equivalent to **sack** but is usually used with reference to buildings, institutions, etc.

rave (rāv) *vi.* **raved, rav′ing** [ME. *raven*, prob. < OFr. *raver*, var. of *rever*, to rave, revel (Fr. *rêver*, to dream)] 1. to talk incoherently or wildly, as in a delirious or demented state 2. to talk with great or excessive enthusiasm (*about*) 3. to rage or roar, as a storm —*vt.* to utter incoherently —*n.* 1. an act or instance of raving 2. a raving action or speech ☆3. [Colloq.] an extremely or excessively enthusiastic commendation: often used attributively —**rav′er** *n.*

rav·el (rav′'l) *vt.* **-eled** or **-elled, -el·ing** or **-el·ling** [MDu. *ravelen* (Du. *rafelen*), akin to LowG. *rabbeln:* for IE. base see RHAPSODY] 1. orig., to make complicated or tangled; involve 2. to separate the parts, esp. threads, of; untwist; unweave; unravel 3. to make clear; disentangle —*vi.* 1. to become separated into its parts, esp. threads; become unwoven; fray (*out*) 2. [Archaic] to become complicated or tangled —*n.* 1. a raveled part in a knitted or woven fabric; raveling 2. a tangled mass or complication —**rav′el·er, rav′el·ler** *n.*

Ra·vel (rȧ vel′), **Mau·rice (Joseph)** (mô rēs′) 1875-1937; Fr. composer

rave·lin (rav′lin) *n.* [Fr. *ravelin* < It. *ravellino*, var. of *rivellino* < *riva*, slope, bank < L. *ripa*, bank] a detached fortification having two faces projecting outward from the main structure to form a salient angle

rav·el·ing, rav·el·ling (rav′'l iŋ, rav′liŋ) *n.* 1. the act of something that ravels or is raveled 2. anything raveled; esp., a thread raveled from a knitted or woven material

rav·el·ment (rav′'l mənt) *n.* a raveling or becoming raveled; esp., entanglement or complication

ra·ven[1] (rā′vən) *n.* [ME. < OE. *hræfn*, akin to ON. *hrafn*, G. *rabe* < IE. echoic base **ker-*, **kor-*, imitative of harsh sounds, whence Gr. *korax*, L. *corvus*, raven: so named from its cry] a large bird (*Corvus corax*) of the crow family, with lustrous black feathers and a straight, sharp beak, found in Europe, N Asia, and N. America —*adj.* black and lustrous

rav·en[2] (rav′'n) *vt.* [OFr. *raviner* < *ravine* < L. *rapina*, RAPINE] 1. to devour greedily 2. [Obs.] to seize forcibly —*vi.* 1. to prowl hungrily; search for prey or plunder 2. to devour food or prey greedily 3. to have a voracious appetite —*n. same as* RAVIN

rav·en·ing (-iŋ) *adj.* [prp. of prec.] greedily searching for prey —*n. same as* RAVIN

Ra·ven·na (rə ven′ə; *It.* rä ven′nä) commune in NC Italy, in Emilia-Romagna: pop. 126,000

rav·e·nous (rav′ə nəs) *adj.* [ME. *ravynous* < OFr. *ravinos* < *ravine:* see RAVEN[2]] 1. greedily or wildly hungry; voracious or famished 2. very eager for a specified gratification [*ravenous* for praise] 3. very rapacious —SYN. see HUNGRY —**rav′e·nous·ly** *adv.* —**rav′e·nous·ness** *n.*

rav·in (rav′'n) *n.* [ME. *ravine* < OFr.: see RAVEN[2]] 1. a violent preying or plundering; rapine 2. anything captured; prey or plunder —*vt., vi. same as* RAVEN[2]

ra·vine (rə vēn′) *n.* [Fr., violent rush, flood: see RAVEN[2]] a long, deep hollow in the earth's surface, esp. one worn by the action of a stream; large gully; gorge

rav·ing (rā′viŋ) *adj.* 1. raging; delirious; frenzied ☆2. [Colloq.] exciting raving admiration or praise; notable [a *raving* beauty] —*adv.* so as to cause raving [*raving* mad] —*n.* delirious, incoherent speech

ra·vi·o·li (rav′ē ō′lē) *n.pl.* [with sing. v.] [It., pl. of *raviolo* < dial. *rava*, turnip, ult. < L. *rapum*, turnip, beet: see RAPE[1]] small casings of dough, often square, containing seasoned ground meat, cheese, etc., boiled and served usually in a savory tomato sauce

rav·ish (rav′ish) *vt.* [ME. *ravishen* < inflectional stem of OFr. *ravir*, to carry away < VL. *rapire, for L. *rapere*, to seize: see RAPE[1]] 1. to seize and carry away forcibly 2. to rape (a woman) 3. to transport with joy or delight; enrapture —**rav′ish·er** *n.* —**rav′ish·ment** *n.*

rav·ish·ing (-iŋ) *adj.* causing great joy or delight; entrancing —**rav′ish·ing·ly** *adv.*

raw (rô) *adj.* [ME. *rawe* < OE. *hreaw*, akin to G. *roh* < IE. base **kreu-*, clotted blood, bloody flesh, whence L. *crusta*, lit., congealed blood: cf. CRUDE, CRUEL] 1. not cooked 2. in its natural condition; not changed by art, dilution, manufacture, aging, etc. [*raw* wool, *raw* whiskey] 3. not processed, edited, interpreted, etc. [*raw* data] 4. inexperienced; not yet developed or trained [a *raw* recruit] 5. with the skin rubbed or torn off; sore and inflamed [a

raw cut] 6. uncomfortably cold and damp; bleak [a *raw* wind] ☆7. *a)* brutal or coarse in frankness *b)* indecent; bawdy; risqué 8. [Colloq.] harsh or unfair [a *raw* deal] —*n.* [Rare] a raw or inflamed spot on the body —**in the raw** 1. in the natural or original state; without cultivation, refinement, etc. ☆2. naked; nude —**raw′ly** *adv.* —**raw′ness** *n.*

Ra·wal·pin·di (rä′wəl pin′dē) interim capital of Pakistan, in NE West Pakistan: pop. 340,000

raw·boned (rô′bōnd′) *adj.* having little flesh or fat covering the bones; lean; gaunt

raw·hide (-hīd′) *n.* 1. an untanned or only partially tanned cattle hide ☆2. a whip made of this —*vt.* **-hid′ed, -hid′ing** to beat or drive with such a whip

☆**ra·win** (rā′win) *n.* [< *ra(dio) win(d)*] 1. observation of upper-air currents by the tracking of a specially constructed balloon with radar or a radio-direction finder 2. the winds so observed

☆**ra·win·sonde** (-sänd′) *n.* [prec. + (RADIO)SONDE] observation of upper-air winds by tracking a radiosonde with radar or a radio-direction finder

Raw·lin·son (rô′lin s'n) 1. **George,** 1812-1902; Eng. historian & Orientalist 2. Sir **Henry Cres·wicke** (krez′ik), 1810-95; Eng. Orientalist, epigraphist, & diplomat: brother of *prec.*

raw material material still in its natural or original state, before processing or manufacture

raw silk 1. silk reeled from the cocoon, with the sericin, or gum, still in it 2. a silk fabric of a slub weave, used for suits, etc.

Ray (rā) a masculine name: see RAYMOND

ray[1] (rā) *n.* [ME. < OFr. *rai* < L. *radius:* see RADIUS] 1. *a)* any of the thin lines, or beams, of light that appear to come from a bright source *b)* a graphic representation of one of these, as in heraldry 2. *a)* any of several lines radiating from a center; radius *b)* any straight line that extends from a point 3. a disclosure of mental or spiritual enlightenment [a *ray* of intelligence] 4. a tiny amount; slight trace [a *ray* of hope] 5. *Bot. a) same as* RAY FLOWER *b)* any of the pedicels, or flower stalks, of an umbel *c)* a medullary ray 6. *Physics a)* a stream of particles given off by a radioactive substance *b)* any of the particles in such a stream *c)* a straight line along which any part of a wave of radiant energy is regarded as traveling from its source to any given point *d)* a beam of radiant energy of very small diameter 7. *Zool. a)* any of the bony spines supporting the fin membrane of a fish *b)* any of the sectors of a radially symmetrical animal, as a starfish —*vi.* 1. to shine forth in rays 2. to radiate —*vt.* 1. to send out in rays; emit 2. to supply with rays or radiating lines —**ray′less** *adj.* —**ray′like′** *adj.*

ray[2] (rā) *n.* [ME. < MFr. *raie* < L. *raia*] any of several cartilaginous fishes (order Rajiformes), as the sting ray, electric ray, skate, etc., with a horizontally flat body, both eyes on the upper surface, widely expanded fins at each side, and a slender or whiplike tail

ray flower any of the flowers around the margin of the flower head of certain composite plants, as the daisy: also **ray floret**

Ray·leigh (rā′lē), 3d Baron, (*John William Strutt*) 1842-1919; Eng. physicist

Ray·mond (rā′mənd) [ONormFr. *Raimund* < Frank. *Raginmund*, lit., wise protection < Gmc. **ragina-*, counsel (as in Goth. *ragin*, judgment) + **mund-*, hand, protection (as in OHG. *munt*)] a masculine name: dim. *Ray*

☆**ray·on** (rā′än) *n.* [arbitrary coinage suggested by RAY[1] as descriptive of its sheen] 1. any of various textile fibers synthetically produced by pressing cellulose acetate or some other cellulose solution through very small holes and solidifying it in the form of filaments 2. any of various woven or knitted fabrics made of such fibers

raze (rāz) *vt.* **razed, raz′ing** [ME. *rasen* < OFr. *raser* < VL. *rasare, to shave, scrape, freq. < L. *rasus*, pp. of *radere*, to scrape: see RAT] 1. orig., to scrape or graze; wound slightly 2. [Now Rare] to scrape or shave off; erase 3. to tear down completely; level to the ground; demolish —SYN. see DESTROY

ra·zee (rā zē′) *n.* [Fr. *rasé* (as in *vaisseau rasé*, leveled vessel), pp. of *raser*, to level, scrape: see prec.] a wooden ship made lower by the removal of the upper deck —*vt.* **-zeed′, -zee′ing** to remove the upper deck of (a ship)

ra·zor (rā′zər) *n.* [ME. *rasour* < OFr. < *raser:* see RAZE] 1. a sharp-edged cutting instrument for shaving off or cutting hair: cf. STRAIGHT RAZOR, SAFETY RAZOR 2. *same as* SHAVER

ra·zor·back (-bak′) *n.* 1. a wild or semiwild hog of the S U.S., with a slender body, a ridged back, and long legs 2. a finback or rorqual whale 3. a sharp, narrow ridge

ra·zor-billed auk (-bild′) an auk (*Alca torda*) of the N Atlantic coasts, with sooty black upper parts and white below, and a black, compressed bill encircled by a white band: also **ra′zor·bill′** *n.*

☆**razor clam** any of several rapidly burrowing clams (family Solenidae) of sandy beaches, having elongated, narrow shells somewhat resembling a straight razor

☆**razz** (raz) *vt., vi.* [contr. < RASPBERRY] [Slang] to tease, ridicule, deride, heckle, etc. —*n.* [Slang] *same as* RASP-BERRY (sense 3)

☆**raz·zle-daz·zle** (raz′'l daz′'l) *n.* [redupl. of DAZZLE]

[Slang] a flashy display intended to confuse, bewilder, or deceive

☆**razz·ma·tazz** (raz′mə taz′) *n.* [prob. altered < prec.] [Slang] **1.** lively spirit; vigor; excitement **2.** flashy quality or display; showiness

Rb *Chem.* rubidium

rbi, RBI, r.b.i. *Baseball* run(s) batted in

R.C. 1. Red Cross **2.** Roman Catholic

R.C.A.F., RCAF Royal Canadian Air Force

R.C.Ch. Roman Catholic Church

rcd. received

R.C.M.P., RCMP Royal Canadian Mounted Police

r-col·or (är′kul/ər) *n. Phonet.* the acoustic quality produced by retroflex articulation ending a vowel sound

R.C.P. Royal College of Physicians

rcpt. receipt

R.C.S. Royal College of Surgeons

Rct *U.S. Army* Recruit

Rd., rd. 1. road **2.** rod **3.** round

R/D, R.D. *Banking* refer to drawer

R.D. Rural Delivery

Re (rā) *same as* RA¹

re¹ (rā) *n.* [It. < L. *re*(*sonare*): see GAMUT] *Music* a syllable representing the second tone of the diatonic scale: see SOLFEGGIO

re² (rē, rā) *prep.* [L., abl. of *res*, thing: see REAL¹] in the case or matter of; as regards: short for *in re*

re- (rē, ri, rə) [< Fr. or L.: Fr. *re-, ré-* < L. *re-, red-*, back, backward] *a prefix meaning:* **1.** back [*repay, restore*] **2.** again, anew, over again [*reappear, retell*] It is used with a hyphen: 1) to distinguish between a word in which the prefix means simply *again* or *anew* and a word of similar form having a special meaning or meanings (Ex.: *re-sound, resound*) 2) to avoid ambiguity in forming nonce words [*re-urge*] 3) esp. formerly, before elements beginning with *e* [*re-edit*]: now usually written as a solid word [*reedit*] The list at the bottom of the following pages contains some of the more common words in which *re-* means simply *again* or *anew* Words with special meanings are entered in their proper alphabetical places in the vocabulary

RE *Chem.* rare-earth elements

Re *Chem.* rhenium

re. 1. *Football* right end **2.** rupee: also **Re.**

R.E. 1. Reformed Episcopal **2.** Right Excellent

REA, R.E.A. Rural Electrification Administration

reach (rēch) *vt.* [ME. *rechen* < OE. *ræcan*, akin to G. *reichen* < IE. base *reig̑-*, to stretch out, extend the hand] **1.** to thrust out or extend (the hand, etc.) **2.** to extend to, or touch, by thrusting out, throwing something, etc. **3.** to obtain and hand over [*reach* me the salt] **4.** to go as far as; attain [to *reach* town by night] **5.** to carry as far as; penetrate to [the news *reached* him late] **6.** to add up to; come to [to *reach* thousands of dollars] **7.** to have influence on; affect; impress **8.** to get in touch with, as by telephone —*vi.* **1.** to thrust out the hand, foot, etc. **2.** to stretch, or be extended, in amount, influence, space, time, etc. [power that *reaches* into other lands] **3.** to be added; amount (with *to* or *into*) **4.** to carry; penetrate, as sight, sound, etc. **5.** to try to obtain something; make an attempt **6.** to try too hard to make a point, joke, etc. **7.** *Naut.* to sail on a reach —*n.* **1.** the act of stretching or thrusting out **2.** the power of stretching, obtaining, etc. **3.** the distance or extent covered in stretching, obtaining, influencing, etc. **4.** a continuous, uninterrupted extent or stretch, esp. of water ☆**5.** a pole joining the rear axle to the forward part of a wagon **6.** *Naut.* a tack sailed with the wind coming more or less from abeam: it may be a **close reach**, with the wind forward of the beam; a **beam reach**, with the wind abeam; or a **broad reach**, with the wind abaft the beam —**reach′er** *n.*

SYN.—**reach**, the broadest of these terms, implies an arriving at some goal, destination, point in development, etc. [he's *reached* the age of 60]; **gain** suggests the exertion of considerable effort to reach some goal [they've *gained* the top of the hill]; **achieve** suggests the use of skill in reaching something [we've *achieved* a great victory]; **attain** suggests a being goaded on by great ambition to gain an end regarded as beyond the reach of most men [he has *attained* great fame in his profession]; **accomplish** implies success in completing an assigned task [to *accomplish* an end] See also RANGE

reach-me-downs (-mē dounz′) *n.pl.* [Brit. Colloq.] second-hand or ready-made clothing

re·act (rē akt′) *vi.* [RE- + ACT] **1.** to act in return or reciprocally **2.** to act in opposition **3.** to act in a reverse way; go back to a former condition, stage, etc. **4.** to respond to a stimulus; be affected by some influence, event, etc. **5.** *Chem.* to act with another substance in producing a chemical change —*vt.* to cause to react; specif., to produce a chemical change in

re·act (rē akt′) *vt.* to act or do again

re·act·ance (rē ak′təns) *n.* [REACT + -ANCE] *Elec.* opposition to the flow of alternating current in a circuit or circuit element, caused by inductance or capacitance

re·act·ant (-tənt) *n.* any of the substances participating in a chemical reaction

re·ac·tion (rē ak′shən) *n.* **1.** a return or opposing action, force, influence, etc. **2.** a response, as to a stimulus or influence **3.** a movement back to a former or less advanced condition, stage, etc.; countertendency; esp., such a movement or tendency in economics or politics; extreme conservatism **4.** *Chem. a)* the mutual action of substances undergoing chemical change *b)* a process that involves changes within the nucleus of an atom *c)* the state resulting from such changes **5.** *Med. a)* an action induced by resistance to another action *b)* the effect produced by an allergen *c)* a depression or exhaustion of energy following nervous tension, overstimulation, etc. *d)* an increased activity following depression **6.** *Physiol. & Psychol.* an organic response to a stimulus —**re·ac′tion·al** *adj.*

re·ac·tion·ar·y (-shə ner′ē) *adj.* of, characterized by, or advocating reaction, esp. in politics —*n., pl.* -ar′ies a reactionary person; advocate of reaction, esp. in politics Also [Rare] **re·ac′tion·ist**

reaction engine an engine, as a jet or rocket engine, that generates thrust by the reaction to an ejected stream of gases produced by burning fuel in the engine

reaction formation *Psychoanalysis* an unconscious reaction in which a feeling or trait finds expression as the exact opposite of a repressed feeling or impulse

reaction time *Psychol.* the lapse of time between stimulation and the beginning of the response

re·ac·ti·vate (rē ak′tə vāt′) *vt.* -vat′ed, -vat′ing to make active again; ☆specif., to place (an inactivated military unit, ship, etc.) back on an active status —*vi.* to be reactivated —**re·ac′ti·va′tion** *n.*

re·ac·tive (-tiv) *adj.* **1.** tending to react **2.** of, caused by, or showing reaction or reactance —**re·ac′tive·ly** *adv.* —**re·ac′tive·ness** *n.* —**re′ac·tiv′i·ty** *n.*

re·ac·tor (-tər) *n.* **1.** a person or thing that reacts or undergoes a reaction **2.** *same as* NUCLEAR REACTOR **3.** *Elec.* a device, as a coil, inserted in a circuit to introduce reactance **4.** *Med.* a person or animal having a positive reaction to a particular foreign substance

read¹ (rēd) *vt.* **read** (red), **read′ing** (rēd′iŋ) [ME. *reden*, to explain, hence to read < OE. *rædan*, to counsel, interpret; akin to G. *raten*, to counsel, advise < IE. *rē-dh, *rə-dh < base *(a)rē-, to join, fit, whence L. *ratio*, a reckoning, thinking] **1.** *a)* to get the meaning of (something written, printed, embossed, etc.) by using the eyes, or for Braille, the finger tips, to interpret its characters or signs *b)* clipped form of PROOFREAD **2.** to utter aloud (printed or written matter) **3.** to interpret movements of (the lips of a person speaking) **4.** to know (a language) well enough to interpret its written form **5.** to understand the nature, significance, or thinking of as if by reading [to *read* a person's character in his face, to *read* one's mind] **6.** to interpret (dreams, omens, signals, etc.) **7.** to foretell (the future) **8.** to interpret or understand (a printed passage, etc.) as having a particular meaning **9.** to interpret (a musical composition) in a particular way, as in conducting **10.** to have or give as a reading in a certain passage [this edition *reads* "show," not "shew"] **11.** to apply oneself to; study [to *read* law] **12.** to record and show; register [the thermometer *reads* 80°] **13.** to put into a (specified) state by reading [to *read* a child to sleep] **14.** to obtain (information) from (punch cards, tape, etc.): said of a computer **15.** [Slang] to hear and understand [I *read* you loud and clear] —*vi.* **1.** to read something written, printed, etc., as words, music, books, etc. **2.** to utter or repeat aloud the words of written or printed matter **3.** to learn by reading (with *about* or *of*) **4.** to study **5.** to have or give a particular meaning when read [a poem that *reads* several ways] **6.** to contain, or be drawn up in, certain words [the sentence *reads* as follows] **7.** to admit of being read as specified [a story that *reads* well] —*n.* [Brit.] something for reading, or a spell of reading —**read into** (or **in**) to attribute (a particular meaning) to —**read out** to display or record with a readout device —**read out of** to expel from (a political party, society, etc.) by public reading of dismissal —**read (someone) a lecture** (or **lesson**) to scold or reprimand (someone) —**read up** (on) to become well informed (about) by reading

read² (red) *pt. & pp.* of READ¹ —*adj.* full of knowledge got from reading; informed; learned: usually in hyphenated compounds [well-*read*]

Read (rēd), Sir **Herbert** (**Edward**) 1893-1968; Eng. poet & art critic

read·a·ble (rēd′ə b'l) *adj.* **1.** interesting or easy to read **2.** *same as* LEGIBLE —**read′a·bil′i·ty, read′a·ble·ness** *n.* —**read′a·bly** *adv.*

reabsorb	reaccommodate	reaccuse	reacquaintance
reabsorption	reaccompany	reaccustom	reacquire
reaccept	reaccredit	reacquaint	reacquisition

re·ad·dress (rē′ə dres′) *vt.* 1. to address or occupy (one-self) anew 2. to change the address on (a letter, etc.) 3. to address or speak to once more

Reade (rēd), **Charles** 1814–84; Eng. novelist

read·er (rēd′ər) *n.* 1. a person who reads 2. a reciter and interpreter of literary works in public 3. a person appointed or elected to read lessons, prayers, etc. aloud in church: cf. LECTOR 4. a person who reads and evaluates manuscripts for a publisher 5. *clipped form of* PROOF-READER 6. a person who records the readings of meters, etc., as for a public utilities company: in full **meter reader** 7. *a)* a book with selected passages for practice and instruction in reading *b)* an anthology or omnibus 8. [Chiefly Brit.] a lecturer or instructor in a university 9. an assistant who reads and marks examinations, themes, etc. for a professor ☆10. *same as* MICROREADER

read·er·ship (-ship′) *n.* 1. the people who read a particular publication, author, etc. or the estimated number of these 2. the state or position of being a reader

read·i·ly (red′'l ē) *adv.* [ME. *redili:* see READY & -LY²] 1. without hesitation; willingly 2. without delay; quickly 3. without difficulty

read·i·ness (-ē nis) *n.* a ready quality or state

Read·ing¹ (red′in), 1st Marquis of, (*Rufus Daniel Isaacs*) 1860–1935; Eng. jurist & statesman

Read·ing² (red′in) 1. city in SC England: county seat of Berkshire: pop. 125,000 2. [after prec.] city in SE Pa., on the Schuylkill River: pop. 88,000

read·ing (red′in) *adj.* 1. inclined to read or study 2. made or used for reading —*n.* 1. the act or practice of a person who reads; perusal, as of books 2. the act of reciting and interpreting a literary work or works in public 3. *a)* the study of books; academic learning *b)* the amount of material read or to be read 4. any material printed or written to be read 5. the amount measured by a barometer, thermometer, etc. 6. the form of a specified word, sentence, passage, etc. in a particular edition of a literary work 7. a particular interpretation or performance, as of something written or composed

reading desk a desk or lectern for holding the book, notes, etc. of a reader or lecturer

reading room a room (in a club, library, etc.) for reading and writing; specif., [R- R-] ☆a place for religious study maintained by Christian Scientists

re·ad·just (rē′ə just′) *vt.* to adjust again; rearrange

re·ad·just·ment (-mənt) *n.* 1. a readjusting or being readjusted 2. *Finance* rearrangement of the structure of a corporation: cf. REORGANIZATION

read·out (rēd′out′) *n.* 1. the act of retrieving information from storage in a digital computer 2. information taken out of a computer and displayed visually or recorded, as by typewriter or on tape, for immediate use 3. information immediately displayed or recorded from other sources, as from electrical instruments —*adj.* of or pertaining to any device that presents data output, as in numbers, letters, etc., for immediate use

read·y (red′ē) *adj.* **read′i·er, read′i·est** [ME. *redie* < OE. *ræde,* ready, prepared (for riding), akin to *ridan,* to ride, G. *bereit,* ready, ON. *greithr,* prepared, Goth. *garaiths,* arranged: for IE. base see RIDE] 1. prepared or equipped to act or be used immediately [*ready* to go, *ready* for occupancy] 2. unhesitant; willing [a *ready* worker] 3. *a)* likely or liable immediately [*ready* to cry] *b)* apt; inclined [always *ready* to blame others] 4. clever and skillful mentally or physically; dexterous [a *ready* wit] 5. done or made without delay; prompt [a *ready* reply] 6. convenient or handy to use; available immediately [*ready* cash] 7. [Obs.] at hand; present: a response to a roll call —*vt.* **read′ied, read′y·ing** to get or make ready; prepare (often used reflexively) —*n.* [Colloq.] ready money; cash at hand (usually with *the*) —SYN. see QUICK —**at the ready** in a position or state of being prepared for immediate use [to hold a gun *at the ready*] —**make ready** 1. to prepare; get in order 2. to dress

read·y-made (red′ē mād′) *adj.* 1. made so as to be ready for use or sale at once; not made-to-order [*ready-made* suits] 2. commonplace; stock; not original [*ready-made* opinions]

read·y-mix (-miks′) *adj.* ready to be used after the addition of liquid [*ready-mix* concrete]

☆**ready room** a room where aircraft crews gather for briefing before flights

read·y-to-wear (-tə wer′) *adj. same as* READY-MADE (as applied to clothing)

read·y-wit·ted (-wit′id) *adj. same as* QUICK-WITTED

re·a·gent (rē ā′jənt) *n.* [RE- + AGENT: cf. REACT] *Chem.* a substance used to detect or measure another substance or to convert one substance into another by means of the reaction which it causes

re·a·gin (rē ā′jin) *n.* [REAG(ENT) + -IN¹] a type of antibody in the blood associated with some allergic diseases and with syphilis

re·al¹ (rē′əl, rēl) *adj.* [ME. < OFr. < ML. *realis* < L. *res,* thing < IE. base *rei-,* property, thing, whence Sans. *rai,* wealth, property] 1. existing or happening in fact or; actual; true, objectively so, etc.; not merely seeming, pretended, imagined, fictitious, nominal, or ostensible 2. *a)* authentic; genuine *b)* not pretended; sincere 3. designating wages or income as measured by purchasing power 4. *Law* of or relating to permanent, immovable things [*real* property] 5. *Math.* designating or of the part of a complex number that is not imaginary 6. *Optics* of or relating to an image made by the actual meeting of light rays at a point 7. *Philos.* existing objectively; actual (not merely possible or ideal), or essential, absolute, ultimate (not relative, derivative, phenomenal, etc.) —*n.* anything that actually exists, or reality in general (with *the*) —*adv.* [Colloq.] very —SYN. see TRUE —**for real** [Slang] real or really

re·al² (rē′əl; *Sp.* re äl′) *n., pl.* **re′als;** *Sp.* **re·al′es** (-ä′les) [Sp. & Port., lit., royal < L. *regalis:* see REGAL] a former monetary unit and silver coin of Spain

re·al³ (re äl′) *n. sing. of* REIS

real estate 1. land, including the buildings or improvements on it and its natural assets, as minerals, water, etc. 2. ownership of or property in land, etc.

re·al·gar (rē al′gər) *n.* [ME. < ML. *realgar,* ult. < Ar. *rahj al-ghār,* lit., powder of the cave < *rahj,* powder + *al,* the + *ghār,* a cave, mine: orig. obtained by mining] an orange-red, monoclinic mineral, arsenic sulfide, with a resinous luster, used in fireworks

re·a·lign (rē′ə līn′) *vt., vi.* to align again; specif., to readjust alliances or working arrangements between or within (countries, political parties, companies, etc.) —**re·a·lign′-ment** *n.*

re·al·ism (rē′ə liz′m) *n.* [< G. *realismus* < ModL. < ML. *realis,* REAL¹ + *-ismus,* -ISM] 1. a tendency to face facts and be practical rather than imaginative or visionary 2. the picturing in art and literature of people and things as it is thought they really are, without idealizing: see also NATURALISM 3. *Philos. a)* the doctrine that universals or abstract terms are objectively actual: opposed to NOMI-NALISM *b)* the doctrine that material objects exist in themselves, apart from the mind's consciousness of them: cf. IDEALISM

re·al·ist (-list) *n.* 1. a person concerned with real things and practical matters rather than those that are imaginary or visionary 2. a believer in or advocate of realism 3. an artist or writer whose work is characterized by realism

re·al·is·tic (rē′ə lis′tik) *adj.* 1. of, having to do with, or in the style of, realism or realists 2. tending to face facts; practical rather than visionary —**re′al·is′ti·cal·ly** *adv.*

re·al·i·ty (rē al′ə tē) *n., pl.* **-ties** [ML. *realitas*] 1. the quality or fact of being real 2. a person or thing that is real; fact 3. the quality of being true to life; fidelity to nature 4. *Philos.* that which is real —**in reality** in fact; actually

reality principle *Psychoanalysis* the adjustment of the mental activity of a mature individual to meet the unavoidable demands of one's environment, as by postponing immediate pleasure

re·al·i·za·tion (rē′ə li zā′shən) *n.* 1. a realizing or being realized 2. something realized

re·al·ize (rē′ə līz′) *vt.* **-ized′, -iz′ing** [Fr. *réaliser*] 1. to make real; bring into being; achieve 2. to make appear real 3. to understand fully; apprehend [to *realize* one's danger] 4. to convert (assets, rights, etc.) into money 5. to gain; obtain [to *realize* a profit] 6. to be sold for, or bring as profit (a specified sum) —**re′al·iz′a·ble** *adj.* —**re′al·iz′er** *n.*

re·al-life (rē′əl līf′) *adj.* actual; not imaginary

re·al·ly (rē′ə lē, rēl′ē) *adv.* [ME. *rialliche:* see REAL¹ & -LY²] 1. in reality; in fact; actually 2. truly or genuinely [a *really* hot day] —*interj.* indeed: used to express surprise, irritation, doubt, etc.

realm (relm) *n.* [ME. *reame* < OFr. *reaume, realme* < L. *regimen,* rule (see REGIMEN), infl. by L. *regalis,* royal (see REGAL)] 1. a kingdom 2. a region; sphere; area [the *realm* of thought] 3. *Biol., Ecol.* any of the primary biogeographic regions of the earth

real number *Math.* any rational or irrational number

‡**Re·al·po·li·tik** (rä äl′pō li tēk′) *n.* [G.] practical politics: a euphemism for POWER POLITICS

☆**real time** 1. time in which the occurrence of an event and the reporting or recording of it are almost simultaneous 2. the actual time used by a computer in solving a problem the answer to which is immediately available to control effectively a process that is going on at the same time

☆**Re·al·tor** (rē′əl tər) *n.* [< ff. + -OR] a real estate broker, appraiser, etc. who is a member of the National Association of Real Estate Boards

re·al·ty (rē′əl tē) *n.* [REAL¹ + -TY¹] 1. *same as* REAL ESTATE 2. [Obs.] fidelity; honesty

ream¹ (rēm) *n.* [ME. *rem* < MFr. *raime* < Ar. *rizma,* a bale, packet < *razama,* to pack together] 1. a quantity of paper varying from 480 sheets (20 quires) to 516 sheets 2. [*pl.*] [Colloq.] a great amount

ream² (rēm) *vt.* [ME. dial. *remen* < OE. *reman,* akin to *ryman,* lit., to make roomy < base of *rum:* see ROOM]

readmission	readopt	reaffirm	reallocation
readmit	readorn	reaffirmation	reallot
readmittance	reaffiliate	realliance	re-ally

1. *a*) to enlarge (a hole) as with a reamer *b*) to enlarge the bore of (a gun) 2. to countersink or taper (a hole) 3. to remove (a defect) by reaming ☆4. to extract the juice from (a lemon, orange, etc.) 5. to use a reamer on (a pipe bowl) ☆6. [Slang] to cheat or deceive

ream·er (-ər) *n.* a person or thing that reams; specif., *a*) a sharp-edged tool for enlarging or tapering holes *b*) same as JUICER *c*) an implement for scraping out the caked lining of a pipe bowl

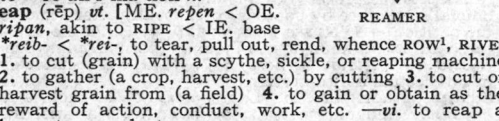

REAMER

re·an·i·mate (rē an′ə māt′) *vt.* -mat′ed, -mat′ing to give new life, power, vigor, courage, etc. to —re·an′i·ma′tion *n.*

reap (rēp) *vt.* [ME. *repen* < OE. *ripan*, akin to RIPE < IE. base **reib-* < **rei-*, to tear, pull out, rend, whence ROW¹, RIVE] 1. to cut (grain) with a scythe, sickle, or reaping machine 2. to gather (a crop, harvest, etc.) by cutting 3. to cut or harvest grain from (a field) 4. to gain or obtain as the reward of action, conduct, work, etc. —*vi.* to reap a harvest, reward, etc.

reap·er (rē′pər) *n.* [ME. *reper* < OE. *ripere*] 1. a person who reaps 2. a machine for reaping grain —**the (Grim) Reaper** death: often personified as a shrouded skeleton bearing a scythe

re·ap·por·tion (rē′ə pôr′shən) *vt.* to apportion again; specif., to change the representation pattern of (a legislature) so that each legislator represents approximately the same number of constituents —re′ap·por′tion·ment *n.*

re·ap·praise (-prāz′) *vt.* -praised′, -prais′ing to make a fresh appraisal of; reconsider —re′ap·prais′al *n.*

rear¹ (rir) *n.* [aphetic for ARREAR, prob. infl. by REAR(WARD)¹, REAR (GUARD)] 1. the back or hind part of something 2. the place or position behind or at the back [at the rear of the house] 3. the part of an army, navy, etc. farthest away from the battle front ☆4. [Slang] the buttocks: also **rear end** —*adj.* of, at, or in the rear [a rear entrance] —**bring up the rear** to come at the end, as of a procession; be last in order

rear² (rir) *vt.* [ME. *reren* < OE. *ræran*, caus. of *risan*, to RISE] 1. to put upright; elevate 2. to build; erect 3. to grow or breed (animals or plants) 4. to bring to maturity by educating, nourishing, etc. [to rear children] —*vi.* 1. to rise or stand on the hind legs, as a horse 2. to rise (*up*) in anger, etc. 3. to rise high, as a mountain peak —*SYN.* see LIFT

rear admiral a naval officer next in rank above a captain and below a vice admiral

rear guard [ME. *rier garde* < Anglo-Fr. *reregard* < OFr. < *riere*, backward (< L. *retro:* see RETRO-) + *gard*, GUARD] a military detachment to protect the rear of a main force or body

re·arm (rē ärm′) *vt., vi.* 1. to arm again 2. to arm with new or more effective weapons —re·ar′ma·ment *n.*

rear·most (rir′mōst′) *adj.* farthest in the rear; last

rear·mouse (-mous′) *n. var. of* REREMOUSE

re·ar·range (rē′ə rānj′) *vt.* -ranged′, -rang′ing 1. to arrange again 2. to arrange in a different manner

re·ar·range·ment (-mənt) *n.* 1. a rearranging or being rearranged 2. a new arrangement 3. *Chem.* a redistribution of atoms or atomic groups within a molecule, forming the molecule of a different substance

rear sight the sight on a firearm nearest the breech

rear·ward (rir′wôrd) *n.* [ME. *rerewarde* < Anglo-Fr.: see REAR GUARD & WARD] *archaic var. of* REAR¹

rear·ward² (-wərd) *adj.* [REAR¹ + -WARD] at, in, or toward the rear —*adv.* backward; toward the rear: also **rear′wards** (-wərdz)

rea·son (rē′z'n) *n.* [ME. *reisun* < OFr. < L. *ratio*, a reckoning, reason, plan < *ratus*, pp. of *reri*, to think < IE. base **rē-*, **rə-*, **ar-*, to fit, join: cf. ART¹, ARM¹] 1. an explanation or justification of an act, idea, etc. 2. a cause or motive 3. the ability to think, form judgments, draw conclusions, etc. 4. sound thought or judgment; good sense 5. normal mental powers; a sound mind; sanity 6. *Logic* any of the premises of an argument, esp. the minor —*vi.* 1. to think coherently and logically; draw inferences or conclusions from facts known or assumed 2. to argue or talk in a logical way —*vt.* 1. to think logically about; think out systematically; analyze 2. to argue, conclude, or infer: now usually with clause introduced by *that* as the object 3. to support, justify, etc. with reasons 4. to persuade or bring by reasoning (*into* or *out of*) —*SYN.* see CAUSE, THINK¹ —**by reason of** because of —**in**

(or **within**) **reason** in accord with what is reasonable —**out of all reason** unreasonable —**stand to reason** to be logical or reasonable —**with reason** justifiably; rightly

rea·son·a·ble (-ə b'l) *adj.* [ME. *raisonable* < OFr. *raisonable* < L. *rationabilis*] 1. able to reason 2. amenable to reason; just 3. using or showing reason, or sound judgment; sensible 4. *a*) not extreme, immoderate, or excessive *b*) not expensive —*SYN.* see RATIONAL —**rea′son·a·ble·ness** *n.* —**rea′son·a·bly** *adv.*

rea·son·ing (-iŋ) *n.* 1. the drawing of inferences or conclusions from known or assumed facts; use of reason 2. the proofs or reasons resulting from this

rea·son·less (-lis) *adj.* 1. not having the ability to reason 2. not reasonable; illogical or senseless

re·as·sure (rē′ə shoor′) *vt.* -sured′, -sur′ing 1. to assure again or anew 2. to restore to confidence 3. [Brit.] *same as* REINSURE —re′as·sur′ance (-əns) *n.* —re′as·sur′ing·ly *adv.*

re·a·ta (rē ät′ə) *n. var. of* RIATA

Re·au·mur, Ré·au·mur (rā′ə myoor′; Fr. rā ō mür′) *adj.* [after R. A. F. de *Réaumur* (1683–1757), Fr. physicist & naturalist] designating or of a temperature scale which registers the boiling point of water at 80° and the freezing point at 0°

reave¹ (rēv) *vt.* reaved or reft, reav′ing [ME. *reven* < OE. *reafian*, akin to G. *rauben*, to ROB] [Archaic] to take away by violence; seize; rob

reave² (rēv) *vt.* reaved or reft, reav′ing [ME. *reven*, altered (after *reven*, to BEREAVE) < ON. *rifa*, to tear < IE. **reip-*, var. of base **rei-*, whence L. *rima*, a crack] [Archaic] to break, split, tear, or the like

Reb (reb) *n.* [Yid. < Heb. *rabh:* see RABBI] a Jewish title of respect equivalent to *Mister*, used with the given name

☆**reb** (reb) *n.* [*often* R-] *clipped form of* REBEL (sense 2)

Re·ha (rē′bə) *n.* a feminine name: see REBECCA

re·bap·tize (rē′bap′tīz) *vt.* -tized, -tiz·ing [LL.(Ec.) *rebaptizare*] 1. to baptize again 2. to give a new name to —re′bap′tism *n.*

re·bar·ba·tive (ri bär′bə tiv) *adj.* [Fr. *rébarbatif* < MFr. < (*se*) *rebarbor*, to resist, earlier to face (the enemy), lit., to face beard-to-beard < *barbe*, beard < L. *barba*] repellent, unattractive, forbidding, grim, etc.

re·bate¹ (rē′bāt; *also, for v.,* ri bāt′) *vt.* -bat·ed, -bat·ing [ME. *rebaten* < OFr. *rabattre* < *re-*, re- + *abattre:* see ABATE] 1. *a*) to give back (part of an amount paid) *b*) to make a deduction from (a bill) 2. [Rare] to reduce; lessen 3. [Archaic] to make dull; blunt —*n.* [Fr. *rabat* < the *v.*] a return of part of an amount paid, as for goods or services, serving as a reduction or discount

re·bate² (rē′bāt, rab′it) *n., vt.* -bat·ed, -bat·ing *same as* RABBET

re·ba·to (rə bät′ō) *n. same as* RABATO

re·bec, re·beck (rē′bek) *n.* [Fr., altered < OFr. *rebebe* < Ar. *rabāb*] a three-stringed, pear-shaped musical instrument played with a bow, a precursor of the violin, used during the Middle Ages

Re·bec·ca (ri bek′ə) *n.* [LL.(Ec.) < Gr.(Ec.) *Rhebekka* < Heb. *ribbqāh*, lit., noose] 1. a feminine name: dim. *Becky, Reba* 2. *Bible* the wife of Isaac and mother of Jacob and Esau: usually sp. **Rebekah**

reb·el (reb′'l; *for v.* ri bel′) *n.* [ME. < OFr. *rebelle* < L. *rebellis*, rebel, rebellious < *rebellare:* see the *v.*] 1. a person who engages in armed resistance against the established government of his country 2. a person who resists any authority or controls ☆3. [*often* R-] *an epithet for* a Confederate soldier in the Civil War —*adj.* 1. rebellious 2. of rebels —*vi.* -elled′, -el′ling [ME. *rebellen* < OFr. *rebeller* < L. *rebellare* < *re-*, again + *bellare*, to wage war < *bellum*, war: for IE. base see DUEL] 1. to be a rebel against the established government of one's country 2. to resist any authority or controls 3. to feel or show strong aversion; be repelled [his mind *rebels* at the thought]

reb·el·dom (-dəm) *n.* any area held by rebels; specif., ☆the Confederate States during the Civil War

re·bel·lion (ri bel′yən) *n.* [ME. < MFr. < L. *rebellio:* see REBEL] 1. an act or state of armed resistance to one's government 2. a defiance of or opposition to any authority or control

SYN.—**rebellion** implies organized, armed, open resistance to the authority or government in power, and, when applied historically, connotes failure [Shays' *Rebellion*]; **revolution** applies to a rebellion that succeeds in overthrowing an old government and establishing a new one [the American *Revolution*] or to any movement that brings about a drastic change in society [the Industrial *Revolution*]; **insurrection** suggests a less extensive or less organized outbreak than rebellion [the Philippine *Insurrection*]; **revolt**

reanalyze	reappointment	reassertion	reattack
reannex	reargue	reassess	reattain
reanoint	rearouse	reassign	reattempt
reappear	rearrest	reassimilate	reauthenticate
reappearance	reascend	reassociate	reauthorize
reapplication	reassemble	reassume	reavail
reapply	reassembly	reassumption	reawaken
reappoint	reassert	reattach	rebeautify

stresses a casting off of allegiance or a refusal to submit to established authority [the *revolt* of the angels led by Lucifer]; **mutiny** applies to a forcible revolt of soldiers, or especially sailors, against their officers [*mutiny* on the Bounty]; **uprising** is a simple, direct term for any outbreak against a government and applies to small, limited actions or to initial indications of a general rebellion [local *uprisings* against the Stamp Act]

re·bel·lious (-yəs) *adj*. [ME. *rebellous*] 1. resisting authority; engaged in rebellion 2. of or like rebels or rebellion 3. opposing any control; defiant 4. difficult to treat or handle [a *rebellious* cowlick] —**re·bel′lious·ly** *adv*. —**re·bel′lious·ness** *n*.

re·birth (rē bʉrth′, rē′bʉrth′) *n*. 1. a new or second birth, as through reincarnation or spiritual regeneration 2. a reawakening; renaissance; revival

reb·o·ant (reb′ō ənt) *adj*. [L. *reboans*, prp. of *reboare*, to resound < *re-*, back + *boare*, to bellow, roar < Gr. *boan* < IE. echoic base *bu-*] [Poet.] loudly reechoing or reverberating

re·born (rē bôrn′) *adj*. born again; having new life, spirit, etc.; regenerated

re·bound (ri bound′; *also*, & *for n. usually*, rē′bound′) *vi*. [ME. *rebounden* < OFr. *rebondir*] 1. to bound back; spring back upon impact with something 2. to reecho or reverberate 3. to leap or spring, as in recovery [his spirits *rebounded*] —*vt*. 1. to make bound or spring back 2. to return (a sound) —*n*. 1. the act or an instance of rebounding; recoil 2. *Sports* ☆a) a basketball that bounces off the backboard or basket rim, or a hockey puck that bounds back after an attempted goal b) a play made by recovering such a rebound —**on the rebound** 1. after bouncing off the ground, a wall, etc. 2. immediately after and while reacting strongly to a rejection or frustration, as in love

☆**re·bo·zo** (ri bō′zō; *Sp*. re bô′thô, -sô) *n*., *pl*. **-zos** (-zōz; *Sp*. -thôs, -sôs) [Sp., a shawl < *rebozar*, to muffle < *re-* (< L., RE-) + *bozo*, mouth, akin to *boca*, mouth, ult. < L. *bucca* (cf. BUCCAL)] in Spain and some Spanish American countries, a long scarf worn by women around the head and shoulders

re·broad·cast (rē brôd′kast′, -käst′) *vt*., *vi*. **-cast′** or, in radio, occas. **-cast′ed**, **-cast′ing** 1. to broadcast again 2. to broadcast (a program, etc. received in a relay system from another station) —*n*. 1. the act of rebroadcasting 2. a program, etc. that is being or has been rebroadcast

re·buff (ri buf′) *n*. [MFr. *rebuffe* < It. *rabuffo* < *rabuffare*, to disarrange, altered by metathesis < *baruffare*, to scuffle < Langobardic **biraufan*, akin to OHG. *biroufan*, to tussle, pluck out] 1. an abrupt, blunt refusal of offered advice, help, etc. 2. any check or repulse —*vt*. 1. to refuse bluntly; snub 2. to check or repulse

re·build (rē bild′) *vt*. **-built′**, **-build′ing** 1. to build anew 2. to restore to a previous condition 3. to repair or remodel extensively, as by taking apart and reconstructing, often with new parts —*vi*. to build again

re·buke (ri byōōk′) *vt*. **-buked′**, **-buk′ing** [ME. *rebuken* < Anglo-Fr. *rebuker* < OFr. *rebuchier* < *re-*, back + *buchier*, to beat < *buche*, a stick, billet < Gmc. **buska*] 1. to blame or scold in a sharp way; reprimand 2. [Obs.] to force back; check —*n*. a sharp reprimand or reproof —**re·buk′er** *n*.

re·bus (rē′bəs) *n*. [L., abl. pl. of *res*, a thing (see REAL¹), lit., (meaning indicated) by things] a kind of puzzle consisting of pictures of objects, signs, letters, etc., the combination of whose names suggests words or phrases [a picture of an eye followed by an L followed by an ampersand is a *rebus* for "island"]

re·but (ri but′) *vt*. **-but′ted**, **-but′ting** [ME. *rebuten* < Anglo-Fr. *reboter* < OFr. *rebuter* < *re-*, back + *buter*, to thrust, push: see BUTT²] 1. to contradict, refute, or oppose, esp. in a formal manner by argument, proof, etc. 2. [Obs.] to force back; repel —*vi*. to provide opposing arguments —*SYN*. see DISPROVE —**re·but′ta·ble** *adj*.

re·but·tal (-'l) *n*. a rebutting, esp. in law

re·but·ter (-ər) *n*. 1. a person or thing that rebuts 2. [n. use of Anglo-Fr. *reboter*: see REBUT] *Law* a defendant's reply to a plaintiff's surrejoinder

☆**rec** (rek) *n*. *clipped form of* RECREATION: used in compounds, as **rec room, rec hall**

rec. 1. receipt 2. recipe 3. record 4. recorded 5. recorder 6. recording

re·cal·ci·trant (ri kal′si trənt) *adj*. [L. *recalcitrans*, prp. of *recalcitrare*, to kick back (in LL., to disobey) < *re-*, back + *calcitrare*, to kick < *calx*, a heel] 1. refusing to obey authority, custom, regulation, etc.; stubbornly defiant 2. hard to handle or deal with —*n*. a recalcitrant person —*SYN*. see UNRULY —**re·cal′ci·trance, re·cal′ci·tran·cy** *n*. —**re·cal′ci·trant·ly** *adv*.

re·cal·ci·trate (-trāt′) *vi*. **-trat′ed**, **-trat′ing** [L. *recalcitrare*: see prec.] [Rare] to refuse to obey; be stubborn in opposition —**re·cal′ci·tra′tion** *n*.

re·cal·cu·late (rē kal′kyə lāt′) *vt*. **-lat′ed**, **-lat′ing** to calculate again, esp. in order to detect and correct an error —**re·cal′cu·la′tion** *n*.

re·ca·les·cence (rē′kə les′'ns) *n*. [< L. *recalescens*, prp. of *recalescere*, to grow hot again < *re-*, again + *calescere*, to grow hot < *calere*, to be warm: for IE. base see CALDARIUM] a sudden and temporary increase in glow and temperature of hot iron or steel when it reaches one or more particular temperatures in the cooling process —**re′ca·les′cent** *adj*.

re·call (ri kôl′; *for n.*, *also* rē′kôl) *vt*. 1. to call back; ask or order to return 2. to bring back to mind; remember 3. to take back; cancel; annul; revoke; withdraw ☆4. to remove from office by the process of recall 5. to bring (the mind, attention, etc.) back, as to the immediate situation 6. [Poet.] to revive —*n*. 1. the act of recalling 2. the ability to remember; memory 3. *Mil*. a signal, as on a bugle, drum, etc., calling soldiers back to camp or ranks ☆4. the process of removing, or right to remove, an official from office by popular vote, usually after a successful petition —*SYN*. see REMEMBER —**re·call′a·ble** *adj*.

Ré·ca·mier (rā kà myā′), Madame (born *Jeanne Françoise Julie Adélaïde Bernard*) 1777–1849; Fr. social leader in intellectual & literary circles

re·cant (ri kant′) *vt*., *vi*. [L. *recantare* < *re-*, back, again + *cantare*, freq. of *canere*, to sing (see CHANT)] to withdraw or renounce (beliefs, statements, etc. formerly held), esp. in a formal or public manner —**re·can·ta·tion** (rē′kan tā′shən) *n*. —**re·cant′er** *n*.

re·cap¹ (rē kap′; *also*, *and for n. always*, rē′kap′) *vt*. **-capped′**, **-cap′ping** [RE- + CAP] ☆to put a new tread on (a worn pneumatic tire) by cementing a strip of crude rubber to the old casing and vulcanizing in a mold; retread —*n*. a recapped tire; retread —**re·cap′pa·ble** *adj*.

re·cap² (rē′kap′) *n*. *clipped form of* RECAPITULATION —*vt*., *vi*. **-capped′**, **-cap′ping** *clipped form of* RECAPITULATE

re·cap·i·tal·ize (rē′kap′ə t'l iz′) *vt*. **-ized′**, **-iz′ing** to capitalize again; specif., to change the capital structure of (a corporation) —**re·cap′i·tal·i·za′tion** *n*.

re·ca·pit·u·late (rē′kə pich′ə lāt′) *vi*., *vt*. **-lat′ed**, **-lat′ing** [< pp. of LL. *recapitulare*: see RE- & CAPITULATE] to repeat briefly, as in an outline; summarize —*SYN*. see REPEAT

re·ca·pit·u·la·tion (-pich′ə lā′shən) *n*. [ME. *recapitulacion* < MFr. or LL.: MFr. *recapitulation* < LL. *recapitulatio*] 1. the act of recapitulating 2. a summary, or brief restatement 3. *same as* PALINGENESIS (sense 3) 4. *Music* the section of a composition which restates themes presented earlier; esp., the final division of the sonata form —**re′ca·pit′u·la′tive, re′ca·pit′u·la·to′ry** (-lə tôr′ē) *adj*.

re·cap·ture (rē kap′chər) *vt*. **-tured**, **-tur·ing** 1. to capture again; retake; get back by capture; reacquire ☆2. to get by recapture (*n*. 2) 3. to bring back by remembering [to *recapture* a feeling] —*n*. 1. a recapturing or being recaptured ☆2. the placing in reserve or the taking by the government under law of a fixed portion of all business earnings exceeding a specified percentage of property value 3. that which is recaptured 4. *same as* POSTLIMINIUM

re·cast (rē kast′, -käst′; *for n.* rē′kast′, -käst′) *vt*. **-cast′**, **-cast′ing** 1. to cast again or anew 2. to improve the form of by redoing; reconstruct [to *recast* a sentence] 3. to calculate or count again 4. a) to provide a new cast for (a play) b) to put (an actor) in a different role —*n*. 1. the act of recasting 2. a new form produced by recasting

rec·ce (rek′ē) *n. Mil. colloq. var. of* RECONNAISSANCE

recd., rec′d. received

re·cede¹ (ri sēd′) *vi*. **-ced′ed**, **-ced′ing** [L. *recedere*: see RE- & CEDE] 1. to go or move back [the high water *receded*] 2. to withdraw (*from*) [to *recede* from a promise] 3. to slope backward 4. to become more distant, and hence indistinct [early memories *recede*] 5. to become less; diminish [*receding* prices]

☆**re·cede²** (rē′sēd′) *vt*. **-ced′ed**, **-ced′ing** to cede back

re·ceipt (ri sēt′) *n*. [altered (after L.) < ME. *receite* < Anglo-Fr., for OFr. *recete* < ML. *recepta* < L., fem. of *receptus*, pp. of *recipere*: see RECEIVE] 1. *old-fashioned var. of* RECIPE 2. a receiving or being received 3. a written acknowledgment that something, as goods, money, etc., has been received 4. a) that which is received b) [pl.] the amount received —*vt*. 1. to mark (a bill) paid ☆2. to write a receipt for (goods, etc.) —*vi*. to' write a receipt

☆**re·ceipt·or** (-ər) *n*. a person who receipts; specif., *Law* a person who receipts as bailee for attached property

re·ceiv·a·ble (ri sēv′ə b'l) *adj*. [ME. *resceyuable* < Anglo-Fr. *receivable*, for OFr. *recevable*: also < RECEIVE + -ABLE] 1. that can be received 2. due; requiring payment [accounts *receivable*] 3. suitable for acceptance —*n*. [pl.] accounts or bills receivable

re·ceive (ri sēv′) *vt*. **-ceived′**, **-ceiv′ing** [ME. *receiven* < Anglo-Fr. *receivre* < OFr. < L. *recipere* < *re-*, back + *capere*, to take] 1. to take or get (something given, offered, sent, etc.); acquire or accept 2. to encounter; experience [to *receive* acclaim] 3. to have inflicted on one; undergo; suffer [to *receive* a blow] 4. to take the effect or force of; bear [all four wheels *receive* the weight equally] 5. to react to as specified [a performance that was well *received*] 6. to apprehend mentally; get knowledge of or information about; learn [to *receive* news] 7. to accept mentally as authentic, valid, etc. 8. a) to let enter; admit b) to

rebid	rebind	rebury	recalibrate
rebiddable	reboil	rebutton	recarry
rebill	reburial	recalculate	recatalog

have room for; hold; contain [a cistern *receives* rain water] **9.** to grant admittance to or greet (visitors, guests, etc.) —*vi.* **1.** to get, accept, take, or acquire something; be a recipient **2.** to receive guests or visitors; be a host **3.** *Radio & TV* to convert incoming electromagnetic waves into sound or light, thus reproducing the sounds or images being transmitted **4.** *Sports* to catch, return, or be prepared to return a thrown or served ball, a puck, etc. —**be on the receiving end** [Colloq.] *a)* to be the recipient of a gift, or favor *b)* to be the target or victim of an attack *c) Sports* to act as the receiver

SYN.—**receive** means to get by having something given, told, absorbed, etc. and may or may not imply the consent of the recipient [to *receive* a gift, a blow, etc.]; **accept** means to receive willingly or favorably, but it sometimes connotes acquiescence rather than explicit approval [he was *accepted* as a member, to *accept* the inevitable]; **admit** stresses permission or concession on the part of the one that receives [I will not *admit* him in my home]; **take,** in this connection, means to accept something offered, presented, etc. [we can't *take* money from you] —*ANT.* **give**

Received Standard the dialect of British English spoken by the upper classes, esp. by graduates of the public schools and of Oxford and Cambridge

re·ceiv·er (ri sē'vər) *n.* **1.** a person who receives; specif., *a)* one who officially receives money for others; collector or treasurer *b)* one who knowingly receives stolen goods for gain or concealment; fence *c) Law* one appointed by a court to administer or hold in trust property in bankruptcy or in a lawsuit *d) Sports* the player or team receiving or designated to receive the ball, service, etc.; esp., a football player designated to receive a forward pass **2.** a thing that receives; specif., *a)* a receptacle; esp., *Chem.* a receptacle connected with a retort, tube, etc., into which a distilled product passes *b)* an apparatus or device that converts incoming electromagnetic waves or electrical signals into audible or visual signals, as a radio or television receiving set, or ☆that part of a telephone which is held to the ear

re·ceiv·er·ship (-ship') *n. Law* **1.** the duties or office of a receiver **2.** the state of being administered or held by a receiver

☆**receiving blanket** a small, lightweight blanket, usually of cotton, for wrapping around a baby

receiving line at formal gatherings, the host, hostess, guests of honor, etc., who stand in a row to greet guests

receiving set an apparatus for receiving radio or television signals; receiver

re·cen·sion (ri sen'shən) *n.* [L. *recensio* < *recensere,* to revise < *re-,* again + *censere,* to value: see CENSURE] **1.** a revision of a text, based on a critical examination of sources **2.** a version so produced

re·cent (rē's'nt) *adj.* [MFr. < L. *recens* < *re-,* again + base akin to Gr. *kainos,* new] **1.** done, made, etc. just before the present time; modern; new **2.** of a time just before the present **3.** [R-] designating or of the present epoch of the Quaternary Period, extending from the close of the Pleistocene —**the Recent** the Recent Epoch or its rocks: see GEOLOGY, chart —**re'cent·ly** *adv.* —**re'cent·ness, re'cen·cy** *n.*

re·cep·ta·cle (ri sep'tə k'l) *n.* [ME. < L. *receptaculum* < *receptare,* freq. of *recipere:* see RECEIVE] **1.** anything used to contain or hold something else; container; vessel **2.** an electrical wall outlet designed for use with a plug **3.** *Bot.* [ModL. *receptaculum*] *a)* the enlarged upper end of the stalk of a flowering plant on which the flower parts grow *b)* any of a number of cuplike or disklike structures supporting spores, sex organs, etc.

re·cep·tion (ri sep'shən) *n.* [ME. *recepcion* < OFr. *reception* < L. *receptio* < pp. of *recipere:* see RECEIVE] **1.** *a)* a receiving or being received *b)* the manner of this [a friendly *reception*] **2.** a social function, often formal, for the receiving of guests **3.** response or reaction, as to something presented **4.** *Radio & TV* the manner of receiving, with reference to the relative quality of reproduction [good or poor *reception*]

re·cep·tion·ist (-ist) *n.* a person employed in an office to receive callers, give information, etc.

reception room a room in a house, office, etc. for receiving visitors, clients, etc. as they arrive

re·cep·tive (ri sep'tiv) *adj.* [ML. *receptivus* < L. *receptus:* see RECEIPT] **1.** receiving or tending to receive, take in, admit, or contain **2.** inclined to the favorable reception of a request, suggestion, etc. **3.** able or ready to receive new ideas, etc. **4.** of reception or receptors —**re·cep'tive·ly** *adv.* —**re·cep·tiv'i·ty, re·cep'tive·ness** *n.*

re·cep·tor (-tər) *n.* [ME. *receptour* < OFr. < L. *receptor* < *receptus:* see RECEIPT] **1.** a receiver (in various senses) **2.** *Biochem.* a radical or group on the surface of a cell, or existing as part of an antigen, that has the power of combining with antibodies, drugs, viruses, etc. **3.** *Physiol.* a nerve ending or group of nerve endings specialized for the reception of stimuli; sense organ

re·cess (rē'ses; *also, and for v. usually,* ri ses') *n.* [L. *recessus* < pp. of *recedere:* see RECEDE] **1.** a receding or hollow place, as in a surface, wall, etc.; niche **2.** a secluded, withdrawn, or inner place [subterranean *recesses,* the *recesses* of the subconscious] **3.** a temporary withdrawal from or halting of work, business, study, etc. **4.** *Anat.* a small cavity, hollow, indentation, etc. in an organ or part —*vt.* **1.** to place or set in a recess **2.** to form a recess in —☆*vi.* to take a recess

re·ces·sion¹ (ri sesh'ən) *n.* [L. *recessio* < pp. of *recedere:* see RECEDE] **1.** a going back or receding; withdrawal **2.** a departing or withdrawing procession, as of clergy and choir after a church service **3.** a receding part, as of a wall **4.** *Econ.* a temporary falling off of business activity during a period when such activity has been generally increasing —**re·ces'sion·ar'y** *adj.*

re·ces·sion² (rē'sesh'ən) *n.* [RE- + CESSION] a ceding back, as to a former owner

re·ces·sion·al (ri sesh'ən 'l) *adj.* **1.** of a recession **2.** [Brit.] of a parliamentary recess —*n.* a hymn or other piece of music sung or played during the recession (sense 2)

re·ces·sive (ri ses'iv) *adj.* [< L. *recessus* (see RECESS) + -IVE] **1.** receding or tending to recede **2.** *Genetics* designating or relating to that one of any pair of allelic hereditary factors which, when both are present in the germ plasm, remains latent: opposed to DOMINANT: see MENDEL'S LAWS —*n. Genetics* **1.** a recessive character or factor **2.** an organism having such characters —**re·ces'sive·ly** *adv.* —**re·ces'sive·ness** *n.*

re·charge (rē chärj'; *also, & for n. always,* rē'chärj) *vt., vi.* **-charged', -charg'ing** to charge again (in various senses) —*n.* the act of recharging —**re·charge'a·ble** *adj.* —**re·charg'er** *n.*

‡**re·chauf·fé** (rā shō fā') *n., pl.* **-fés'** (-fā') [Fr., pp. of *réchauffer,* to warm over < *re-,* again + *échauffer,* to heat < LL. **excalefare,* for L. *excalefacere* < *ex-,* intens. + *calefacere,* to heat: see CHAFE] **1.** a dish of leftover food reheated **2.** any used or old literary material worked up in a new form; rehash

re·cher·ché (rə shor'shā, -sher'shā') *adj.* [Fr., pp. of *rechercher:* see RESEARCH] **1.** sought out with care; rare; choice; uncommon **2.** having refinement or studied elegance **3.** too refined; too studied

re·cid·i·vism (ri sid'ə viz'm) *n.* [< L. *recidivus* < *recidere,* to fall back < *re-,* back + *cadere,* to fall + -ISM] habitual or chronic relapse, or tendency to relapse, esp. into crime or antisocial behavior —**re·cid'i·vist** *n., adj.* —**re·cid'i·vis'tic, re·cid'i·vous** *adj.*

Re·ci·fe (re sē'fə) seaport in NE Brazil, on the Atlantic; capital of Pernambuco state: pop. 797,000

rec·i·pe (res'ə pē) *n.* [L., imperative of *recipere:* see RECEIVE] **1.** formerly, a medical prescription: symbol, ℞ **2.** a list of materials and directions for preparing a dish or drink **3.** a procedure for accomplishing or achieving something

re·cip·i·ent (ri sip'ē ənt) *n.* [< L. *recipiens,* prp. of *recipere:* see RECEIVE] a person or thing that receives —*adj.* receiving, or ready or able to receive —**re·cip'i·ence, re·cip'i·en·cy** *n.*

re·cip·ro·cal (ri sip'rə k'l) *adj.* [< L. *reciprocus,* returning, reciprocal < *re-,* back + IE. **proko-,* ahead (whence Gr. *proka,* forthwith) < base **pro-,* forward, ahead + -AL] **1.** done, felt, given, etc. in return [hoping for a *reciprocal* favor] **2.** present or existing on both sides; each to the other; mutual [to feel a *reciprocal* affection] **3.** corresponding but reversed or inverted **4.** equivalent or interchangeable; corresponding or complementary **5.** *Gram. a)* expressing mutual action or relation [each other is a *reciprocal* pronoun] *b)* [Now Rare] reflexive **6.** *Math.* of the reciprocals of quantities, or their relations —*n.* **1.** anything that has a reciprocal action on or relation to another; complement, counterpart, equivalent, etc. **2.** *Math.* the quantity resulting from the division of 1 by the given quantity; quantity which multiplied by the given quantity equals 1 (Ex.: the *reciprocal* of 7 is 1/7, of *x* is 1/*x*) —SYN. see MUTUAL —**re·cip'ro·cal'i·ty** (-kal'ə tē) *n.* —**re·cip'ro·cal·ly** *adv.*

re·cip·ro·cate (-kāt') *vt.* **-cat'ed, -cat'ing** [< L. *reciprocatus,* pp. of *reciprocare* < *reciprocus:* see RECIPROCAL] **1.** *a)* to give and get, do, feel, etc. reciprocally; interchange *b)* to give, do, feel, etc. in return; return in kind or degree **2.** to cause to move alternately back and forth —*vi.* **1.** to make some sort of return for something done, given, etc. **2.** to move alternately back and forth; interchange position **3.** [Archaic] to be correspondent or equivalent —**re·cip'ro·ca'tion** *n.* —**re·cip'ro·ca'tive, re·cip'ro·ca·to'ry** (-kə tôr'ē) *adj.* —**re·cip'ro·ca'tor** *n.*

reciprocating engine any engine in which the movement of the pistons back and forth causes the rotary motion of the crankshaft

rec·i·proc·i·ty (res'ə präs'ə tē) *n., pl.* **-ties** [Fr. *réciprocité*] **1.** reciprocal state or relationship; mutual action, depend-

recelebrate	recertify	rechart	recheck
recelebration	rechannel	recharter	rechew

ence, etc. **2.** the act of reciprocating; mutual exchange; esp., exchange of special privileges between two countries, to the advantage of both, as mutual reduction of tariffs

re·ci·sion (ri sizh′ən) *n.* [L. *recisio* < *recidere*, to cut back: see RE- + -CIDE] a rescinding or annulling

recit. *Music* recitative

re·cit·al (ri sīt′'l) *n.* [RECIT(E) + -AL] **1.** *a)* a reciting; specif., a telling of facts, events, etc. in detail *b)* what is so told; account, story, or description **2.** a detailed statement, as of facts or events **3.** a musical or dance program given by a soloist, soloists, or small ensemble —**re·cit′-al·ist** *n.*

rec·i·ta·tion (res′ə tā′shən) *n.* [L. *recitatio*] **1.** a reciting, as of facts, events, etc.; recital **2.** *a)* the speaking aloud in public of something memorized *b)* a piece of prose or verse so memorized and spoken ☆**3.** *a)* a reciting by pupils of answers to questions on a prepared lesson, etc. *b)* a class meeting or period in which this occurs

rec·i·ta·tive (res′ə tə tēv′) *n.* [It. *recitativo* < L. *recitare*, to RECITE] *Music* **1.** a type of declamatory singing, with the rhythm and tempo of speech, but uttered in musical tones, used in the prose parts and dialogue of operas and oratorios **2.** a work or passage in this style **3.** music for such passages —*adj.* having the nature, or in the style or manner, of recitative

re·cite (ri sīt′) *vt.* -**cit′ed**, -**cit′ing** [ME. *reciten* < OFr. *reciter* < L. *recitare*: see RE- & CITE] **1.** to repeat or speak aloud from or as from memory, esp. in a formal way; give a recitation on (a lesson) in class or of (a poem, speech, etc.) before an audience **2.** to tell in detail; give an account of; narrate; relate **3.** to enumerate —*vi.* **1.** to repeat or speak aloud something memorized ☆**2.** to recite a lesson or part of a lesson in a class —**re·cit′er** *n.*

reck (rek) *vi., vt.* [ME. *recken* < OE. *reccan*; akin to OHG. *ruohhen*] [Archaic] **1.** to have care or concern (*for*) or take heed (*of*) [he *recks* not of the peril] **2.** to concern or be of concern; matter (to) [it *recks* him not]

reck·less (rek′lis) *adj.* [ME. *reckeles* < OE. *recceleas:* see prec. & -LESS] **1.** careless; heedless **2.** not regarding consequences; headlong and irresponsible; rash —**reck′less·ly** *adv.* —**reck′less·ness** *n.*

Reck·ling·hau·sen (rek′liŋ hou′z'n) city in W West Germany, in North Rhine-Westphalia: pop. 128,000

reck·on (rek′ən) *vt.* [ME. *rekkenen* < OE. *-recenian*, akin to G. *rechnen*, to count < IE. base *reĝ-*, to direct, whence RIGHT, L. *regere*, to rule] **1.** to count; compute **2.** *a)* to consider as; regard as being [*reckon* them friends] *b)* to judge; consider; estimate **3.** [Colloq. or Dial.] to think; suppose —*vi.* **1.** to count up; figure **2.** [Colloq.] to depend; rely (with *on*) **3.** [Colloq.] to think; suppose —*SYN.* see CALCULATE, RELY —**reckon with 1.** to balance or settle accounts with **2.** to take into consideration —**reck′on·er** *n.*

reck·on·ing (-iŋ) *n.* **1.** the act of one who reckons; count or computation **2.** a measuring of possibilities for the future; calculated guess **3.** *a)* a bill; account *b)* the settlement of an account *c)* the settlement of rewards or penalties for any action [day of *reckoning*] **4.** *Naut.* the determination of the position of a ship; esp., short for DEAD RECKONING

re·claim (ri klām′) *vt.* [ME. *reclaimen* < OFr. *reclamer* < L. *reclamare*, to cry out against: see RE- & CLAIM] **1.** to rescue or bring back (a person or people) from error, vice, etc. to ways of living or thinking regarded as right; reform **2.** to make (wasteland, desert, etc.) capable of being cultivated or lived on, as by filling, ditching, or irrigating **3.** to recover (useful materials, etc.) from waste products **4.** [Obs.] to tame or subdue (a hawk) —*n.* reclamation [beyond *reclaim*] —*SYN.* see RECOVER —**re·claim′a·ble** *adj.* —**re·claim′ant, re·claim′er** *n.*

re-claim (rē′klām′) *vt.* to claim back; demand the return or restoration of; try to get back

rec·la·ma·tion (rek′lə mā′shən) *n.* [Fr. *réclamation* < L. *reclamatio*] **1.** a reclaiming or being reclaimed; esp., the recovery of wasteland, desert, etc. by ditching, filling, or irrigating **2.** the process or industry of obtaining useful materials from waste products

†ré·clame (rā klȧm′) *n.* [Fr. < *réclamer:* see RECLAIM] **1.** publicity or notoriety **2.** a seeking for, or skill in getting, publicity

rec·li·nate (rek′lə nāt′) *adj.* [< L. *reclinatus*, pp. of *reclinare*: bending downward, as a leaf or stem

re·cline (ri klīn′) *vt.* -**clined′**, -**clin′ing** [ME. *reclynen* < L. *reclinare* < *re-*, back + *clinare*, to lean (see INCLINE)] to cause to lean or lie back or down; lay back —*vi.* to lie or lean back or down; specif., to rest or repose lying down —**re·li·na·tion** (rek′lə nā′shən) *n.*

re·clin·er (-klī′nər) *n.* **1.** one that reclines **2.** an upholstered armchair with a movable back and seat that can be adjusted for reclining: also **reclining chair**

rec·luse (rek′lōōs, ri klōōs′) *adj.* [ME. < OFr. *reclus* < LL.(Ec.) *reclusus* < L., pp. of *recludere*, to shut off < *re-*, back + *claudere*, to close] shut away from the world; secluded; solitary —*n.* a person who lives a secluded, solitary life —**re·clu·sive** (ri klōō′siv) *adj.*

re·clu·sion (ri klōō′zhən) *n.* [ME. *reclucioun*] **1.** the condition or fact of becoming or being a recluse **2.** the condition or fact of being or being in solitary confinement

rec·og·ni·tion (rek′əg nish′ən) *n.* [L. *recognitio* < *recognitus*, pp. of *recognoscere*: see RECOGNIZANCE] **1.** *a)* a recognizing or being recognized; acknowledgment; admission, as of a fact *b)* acknowledgment and approval, gratitude, etc. [in *recognition* of his services] **2.** formal acknowledgment by a government of the independence and sovereignty of a state newly created, as by secession, or of a government newly set up, as by revolution **3.** identification of some person or thing as having been known before or as being of a certain kind **4.** notice, as in passing; greeting; salutation —**re·cog·ni·to·ry** (ri kȧg′nə tôr′ē), **re·cog′ni·tive** (-tiv) *adj.*

rec·og·niz·a·ble (rek′əg nī′zə b'l) *adj.* that can be recognized —**rec′og·niz·a·bil′i·ty** *n.* —**rec′og·niz·a·bly** *adv.*

re·cog·ni·zance (ri kȧg′ni zəns, -kȧn′i-) *n.* [ME. *reconissance* < OFr. *reconaissance* < *reconnoisant*, prp. of *reconoistre* < L. *recognoscere*, to recall to mind < *re-*, again + *cognoscere*, to know: see COGNITION] **1.** *Law a)* a bond or obligation of record entered into before a court or magistrate, binding a person to do or not do something, be in court at a certain time, etc. *b)* a sum of money pledged and subject to forfeit if this obligation is not fulfilled **2.** *archaic var. of* RECOGNITION **3.** [Obs.] a symbol, token, or badge

rec·og·nize (rek′əg nīz′) *vt.* -**nized′**, -**niz′ing** [altered (after prec.) < extended stem of OFr. *reconoistre*: see prec.] **1.** to be aware of as something or someone known before, or as the same as that known **2.** to know by some detail, as of appearance; identify [to *recognize* a butterfly by its coloring] **3.** to be aware of the significance of [to *recognize* symptoms] **4.** to acknowledge the existence, validity, authority, or genuineness of [to *recognize* a claim] **5.** to accept as a fact; admit; accept [to *recognize* defeat] **6.** to acknowledge as worthy of appreciation or approval [to *recognize* devotion] **7.** to acknowledge the legal standing of (a government, state, etc.) by formal action, as by entering into diplomatic relations **8.** to show acquaintance with (a person) by greeting ☆**9.** to acknowledge as having the right to speak, as in a meeting —**rec′og·niz′er** *n.*

re·cog·ni·zee (ri kȧg′ni zē′, -kȧn′-) *n.* *Law* a person in whose favor a recognizance is entered

re·cog·ni·zor (-zôr′) *n.* *Law* a person who enters into a recognizance

re·coil (ri koil′; *also for n., esp. of weapons,* rē′koil′) *vi.* [ME. *recoilen* < OFr. *reculer* < *re-*, back + *cul* < L. *culus*, the buttocks < IE. *(s)kulo-* < base *(s)keu-*, to cover, conceal, whence SKY, HIDE¹] **1.** *a)* to draw back, fall back, or stagger back; retreat *b)* to start or shrink back, as in fear, surprise, disgust, etc. **2.** to fly back when released, as a spring, or kick back when fired, as a gun **3.** to return to or as to the starting point or source; react (*on* or *upon*) —*n.* **1.** the act of recoiling **2.** the state of having recoiled; reaction **3.** the distance through which a gun, spring, etc. recoils

SYN.—**recoil** implies a startled reaction or movement in fear, surprise, disgust, etc. [she *recoiled* in horror]; **shrink** implies a drawing back, literally or figuratively, from that which is distressing, terrifying, etc. [she *shrank* from telling him]; **flinch** implies a show of weakness or faintheartedness in shrinking from anything difficult, dangerous, or painful [he will not *flinch* from duty]; **wince** suggests an involuntary manifestation of pain or distress, as by facial distortion [she *winced* at the blow]; **quail** suggests a cowering abjectly in the face of anything that menaces one [he *quailed* as the bully approached]

re-coil (rē′koil′) *vt., vi.* to coil anew or again

re·coil·less (ri koil′lis) *adj.* designating or of a firearm designed to minimize recoil, as by means of vents for the escape of gases

re-coin (rē koin′) *vt.* to coin anew or again —**re·coin′age** (-ij) *n.*

rec·ol·lect (rek′ə lekt′) *vt.* [< L. *recollectus*: see ff.] **1.** to call back to mind; recall; remember, esp. with some effort **2.** to recall to (oneself) something temporarily forgotten —*vi.* to have a recollection; remember —*SYN.* see REMEMBER

re-col·lect (rē′kə lekt′) *vt.* [orig. < L. *recollectus*, pp. of *recolligere* (see RE- & COLLECT¹); later felt as < RE- + COLLECT¹] **1.** to gather together again (what has been scattered) **2.** *a)* to collect or rally (one's thoughts, strength, courage, etc.) *b)* to recover or compose (oneself): in this sense sometimes written **recollect**

rec·ol·lec·tion (rek′ə lek′shən) *n.* [Fr. *recollection* < ML. *recollectio*] **1.** the act or power of recollecting, or calling back to mind; remembrance **2.** what is recollected [*recollections* of youth] **3.** [Rare] religious meditation —*SYN.* see MEMORY —**rec′ol·lec′tive** *adj.*

re·com·bi·nant (rē kȧm′bə nənt) *n. Genetics* an organism in which recombination has occurred

re·com·bi·na·tion (-kȧm′bə nā′shən) *n.* a combining again; specif., *Genetics* the appearance in offspring of new combinations of allelic genes not present in either parent,

---

recircle	reclassify	recode	recolor
recirculate	reclean	recodify	recombine
reclassification	reclothe	recolonize	recommence

produced from the mixing of genetic material, as by crossing-over

rec·om·mend (rek'ə mend') *vt.* [ME. *recomenden* < ML. *recommendare:* see RE- & COMMEND] 1. to give in charge; commit; entrust *[recommended* to his care*]* 2. to suggest favorably as suited for some use, function, position, etc. *[to recommend* a book, a doctor, etc.*]* 3. to make acceptable or pleasing *[much* on the island to *recommend* it*]* 4. to advise; counsel; suggest *[to recommend* that something be done*]* —**rec'om·mend'a·ble** *adj.* —**rec'om·mend'a·to'ry** *adj.* —**rec'om·mend'er** *n.*

rec·om·men·da·tion (-mən dā'shən) *n.* [ME. *recommendacion* < ML. *recommendatio]* 1. the act of recommending, or calling attention to, a person or thing as suited to some purpose 2. anything that recommends or makes a favorable or pleasing impression; specif., a letter recommending a person or thing 3. advice; counsel

re·com·mit (rē'kə mit') *vt.* -**mit'ted,** -**mit'ting** 1. to commit again 2. to refer (a question, bill, etc.) back to a committee —**re'com·mit'ment,** **re'com·mit'tal** *n.*

rec·om·pense (rek'əm pens') *vt.* -**pensed',** -**pens'ing** [ME. *recompensen* < MFr. *recompenser* < LL. *recompensare:* see RE- & COMPENSATE] 1. to repay (a person, etc.); reward; compensate 2. to make repayment or requital for; compensate (a loss, injury, etc.) —*n.* 1. something given or done in return for something else; repayment, remuneration, requital, or reward 2. something given or done to make up for a loss, injury, etc.; compensation —*SYN.* see PAY[1]

re·com·pose (rē'kəm pōz') *vt.* -**posed',** -**pos'ing** 1. to compose again; rearrange, recombine, or reconstitute 2. to restore to composure —**re·com·po·si·tion** (rē'käm pə zish'ən) *n.*

re·con (rē'kän, ri kän') *n.* *clipped form of* RECONNAISSANCE

rec·on·cil·a·ble (rek'ən sīl'ə b'l) *adj.* that can be reconciled —**rec'on·cil'a·bil'i·ty** *n.* —**rec'on·cil'a·bly** *adv.*

rec·on·cile (rek'ən sīl') *vt.* -**ciled',** -**cil'ing** [ME. *reconsilen* < OFr. *reconcilier* < L. *reconciliare:* see RE- & CONCILIATE] 1. to make friendly again or win over to a friendly attitude 2. to settle (a quarrel, etc.) or compose (a difference, etc.) 3. to make (arguments, ideas, texts, etc.) consistent, compatible, etc.; bring into harmony 4. to make content, submissive, or acquiescent (*to*) *[to become reconciled* to one's lot*]*

rec·on·cil·i·a·tion (rek'ən sil'ē ā'shən) *n.* [ME. *reconsiliacion* < MFr. *reconciliation* < L. *reconciliatio]* a reconciling or being reconciled: also **rec'on·cile'ment** (-sīl'mənt) —**rec'on·cil'i·a·to'ry** *adj.*

rec·on·dite (rek'ən dīt', ri kän'dīt) *adj.* [L. *reconditus,* pp. of *recondere,* to put back, hide < *re-,* back + *condere,* to put together, store up, hide < *con-,* together + *-dere* < IE. base **dhē-,* to put, whence DO[1]] 1. beyond the grasp of the ordinary mind or understanding; profound; abstruse 2. dealing with abstruse or difficult subjects 3. obscure or concealed —**rec'on·dite'ly** *adv.* —**rec'on·dite'ness** *n.*

re·con·di·tion (rē'kən dish'ən) *vt.* to put back in good condition by cleaning, patching, repairing, etc.

re·con·nais·sance (ri kän'ə səns, -zəns) *n.* [Fr., earlier *reconnoissance:* see RECOGNIZANCE] an exploratory survey or examination, as in seeking out information about enemy positions, installations, etc., or as in making a preliminary geological or engineering survey

rec·on·noi·ter (rē'kə noit'ər, rek'ə-) *vt., vi.* [Fr. *reconnoître,* old form of *reconnaître* < OFr. *reconoistre:* see RECOGNIZANCE] to make a reconnaissance (of): also, chiefly Brit. sp., **rec'on·noi'tre, -tred, -tring** —**rec'on·noi'ter·er, rec'on·noi'trer** (-noi'trər) *n.*

re·con·sid·er (rē'kən sid'ər) *vt.* 1. to consider again; think or argue over again, esp. with a view to changing a decision 2. to take up again in a meeting (a matter discussed and voted on before) —*vi.* to reconsider a matter —**re'con·sid'er·a'tion** *n.*

re·con·sign·ment (rē'kən sīn'mənt) *n.* 1. a consigning again or anew 2. *Commerce* a change (made in transit) in the route, destination, or consignee as indicated in the original bill of lading

re·con·sti·tute (rē kän'stə tōōt', -tyōōt') *vt.* -**tut'ed,** -**tut'ing** to constitute again or anew; reconstruct, reorganize, or recompose; specif., to restore (a dehydrated or condensed substance) to its full liquid form by adding water —**re·con'sti·tu'tion** *n.*

re·con·struct (rē'kən strukt') *vt.* 1. to construct again; rebuild; make over 2. to build up, from remaining parts or other evidence, a concept or reproduction of (something in its original or complete form) —**re'con·struc'tive** *adj.*

re·con·struc·tion (-struk'shən) *n.* 1. *a)* the act of recon-

structing *b)* something reconstructed ☆2. [R-] *a)* the process, after the Civil War, of reorganizing the Southern States which had seceded and reestablishing them in the Union *b)* the period of this (1867–1877)

☆**Re·con·struc·tion·ism** (-iz'm) *n.* a 20th-cent. movement in Judaism that stresses a dynamic creativity in adjusting to modern times, as by the adaptation and reinterpretation of traditional observances

re·con·vert (rē'kən vurt') *vt., vi.* to change back, as to a former status, form, religion, opinion, etc. —**re'con·ver'sion** *n.*

re·con·vey (rē'kən vā') *vt.* to convey again or back, as to a former owner or place —**re'con·vey'ance** *n.*

re·cord (ri kôrd'; *for n. & adj.,* rek'ərd) *vt.* [ME. *recorden* < OFr. *recorder* < L. *recordari,* to call to mind, remember < *re-,* again + *cor* (gen. *cordis),* mind, HEART] 1. *a)* to put in writing, print, etc. for future use; draw up an account of *[to record* the day's events*]* *b)* to make a permanent or official note of *[to record* a vote*]* 2. *a)* to indicate automatically and permanently, as on a graph or chart *[a* seismograph *records* earthquakes*]* *b)* to show, as on a dial *[a* thermometer *records* temperatures*]* 3. to remain as evidence of *[metal* tools *record* a superior civilization*]* 4. *a)* to register (sound or visual images) in some permanent form, as on a phonograph disc, magnetic tape, etc. for reproduction on a playback device *b)* to register the performance of (a musician, actor, composition, etc.) on discs, tapes, etc. in this way —*vi.* 1. to record something 2. to admit of being recorded —*n.* [ME. < OFr. < the *v.*] 1. the condition of being recorded 2. *a)* anything that is written down and preserved as evidence; account of events *b)* anything that serves as evidence of an event, etc. *c)* an official written report of public proceedings, as in a legislature or court of law, preserved for future reference 3. anything that written evidence is put on or in, as a register, monument, etc. ☆4. *a)* the known or recorded facts about anyone or anything, as about one's career *b)* the recorded offenses or crimes of a person who has been arrested one or more times ☆5. something on which sound or visual images have been recorded; esp., a thin, flat, grooved disc for playing on a phonograph 6. the best performance, highest speed, greatest amount, highest rate, etc. achieved, esp. when officially recorded —*adj.* establishing a record as the best, largest, etc. *[a record* crop*]* —☆**go on record** to state one's opinions publicly or officially —☆**off the record** not for publication or public release; confidential(ly) —**on (the) record** recorded; publicly or officially declared or known

☆**record changer** a phonograph device that automatically sets records in succession on the turntable, esp. from a stack of records on the turntable spindle

re·cord·er (ri kôr'dər) *n.* [ME. < Anglo-Fr. *recordour*] 1. a person who records; esp., an officer appointed or elected to keep records of deeds or other official papers 2. in some cities, a judge who has the same criminal jurisdiction as a police judge 3. a machine or device that records; esp., *same as* TAPE RECORDER 4. an early form of flute, with eight finger holes and a fipple, held straight up and down when played

re·cord·ing (ri kôr'din) *adj.* that records —*n.* 1. the act of one that records 2. *a)* what is recorded, as on a disc or tape *b)* the quality of this; esp., its acoustic or visual fidelity to the original *c)* the record itself

RECORDER

recording secretary an officer of an organization who keeps the minutes and other records

record player a phonograph having the pickup, turntable, amplifier, speaker, etc. operate electrically or electronically

re·count (ri kount') *vt.* [ME. *recounten* < Anglo-Fr. *reconter:* see RE- & COUNT[1]] 1. to tell in detail; give an account of; relate; narrate 2. to tell in order or one by one —*SYN.* see TELL[1]

re·count (rē'kount'; *for n.* rē'kount') *vt.* to count again —*n.* a second or additional count, as of votes: also written **recount**

re·count·al (ri kount'l) *n.* a recounting; narration

re·coup (ri kōōp') *vt.* [Fr. *recouper* < *re-,* again + *couper,* to cut] 1. *a)* to get back an equivalent for; make up for *[to recoup* a loss*]* *b)* to regain *[to recoup* one's health*]* 2. to pay back; reimburse 3. *Law* to deduct or hold back (a part of what is due), having some reasonable claim to do so —*n.* an act of recouping —*SYN.* see RECOVER —**re·coup'a·ble** *adj.* —**re·coup'ment** *n.*

re·course (rē'kôrs, ri kôrs') *n.* [ME. *recours* < OFr. < L. *recursus,* a running back: see RE- & COURSE] 1. a turning

recommission	recondense	reconquest	reconsult
recompress	reconduct	reconsecrate	recontaminate
recompute	reconfine	reconsign	reconvene
reconception	reconfirm	reconsole	recook
reconceptualize	reconquer	reconsolidate	recopy

or seeking for aid, safety, etc. [to have *recourse* to the law] **2.** that to which one turns seeking aid, safety, etc. [one's last *recourse*] **3.** *Commerce, Law* the right to demand payment from the maker or endorser of a commercial paper, as a bill of exchange: usually in **without recourse**, without obligation to pay (added by the endorser to a bill of exchange to protect himself from liability)

re·cov·er (ri kuv′ər) *vt.* [ME. *recoveren* < OFr. *recoverer* < L. *recuperare:* see RECUPERATE] **1.** *a)* to get back (something lost, stolen, etc.) *b)* to regain (health, consciousness, etc.) **2.** to compensate for; make up for [to *recover* losses] **3.** *a)* to get (oneself) back to a state of control, balance, composure, etc. *b)* to catch or save (oneself) from a slip, stumble, betrayal of feeling, etc. **4.** to reclaim (land from the sea, useful substances from waste, etc.) **5.** *Law* to get or get back by final judgment in a court [to *recover* damages] **6.** *Sports* to gain or regain control or possession of (a fumbled, muffed, wild, or free ball, puck, etc.) —*vi.* **1.** to regain health, balance, control, etc. **2.** to catch or save oneself from a slip, stumble, self-betrayal, etc. **3.** *Law* to succeed in a claim; receive judgment in one's favor **4.** *Sports* to recover a ball, puck, etc.
SYN.—**recover** implies a finding or getting back something that one has lost in any manner [to *recover* stolen property, one's self-possession, etc.]; **regain** more strongly stresses a winning back of something that has been taken from one [to *regain* a military objective]; **retrieve** suggests diligent effort in regaining something [he was determined to *retrieve* his honor]; **recoup** implies recovery of an equivalent in compensation [I tried to *recoup* my losses]; **reclaim** implies recovery or restoration to a better or useful state [to *reclaim* wasteland]

re-cov·er (rē′kuv′ər) *vt.* to cover again or anew

re·cov·er·y (ri kuv′ər ē) *n., pl.* **-er·ies** [ME. *recoverie* < Anglo-Fr.] **1.** the act or an instance of recovering; specif., *a)* a regaining of something lost or stolen *b)* a return to health, consciousness, etc. *c)* a regaining of balance, control, composure, etc. *d)* a retrieval of a capsule, nose cone, etc. after a space flight *e)* the removal of valuable substances from waste material, byproducts, etc. **2.** *Sports* a return to a position of guard, readiness, etc., as after a lunge in fencing or a stroke in rowing

☆**recovery room** a hospital room where postoperative patients are kept for close observation and care

rec·re·ant (rek′rē ənt) *adj.* [ME. < OFr. prp. of *recreire,* to surrender allegiance < ML. *recredere,* to give in or up < L. *re-,* back, again + *credere,* to believe (see CREED)] **1.** *a)* orig., crying for mercy *b)* cowardly; craven **2.** failing to keep faith; disloyal; traitorous; apostate —*n.* **1.** a coward; craven **2.** a disloyal person; traitor —**rec′re·an·cy, rec′re·ance** *n.* —**rec′re·ant·ly** *adv.*

rec·re·ate (rek′rē āt′) *vt.* **-at′ed, -at′ing** [< L. *recreatus,* pp. of *recreare,* to restore, refresh, create anew: see RE- & CREATE] to put fresh life into; refresh or restore in body or mind, esp. after work, by play, amusement, or relaxation —*vi.* to take recreation —**rec′re·a′tive** *adj.*

re-cre·ate (rē′krē āt′) *vt.* **-at′ed, -at′ing** to create anew —**re′-cre·a′tion** *n.* —**re′-cre·a′tive** *adj.*

rec·re·a·tion (rek′rē ā′shən) *n.* [ME. *recreacioun* < MFr. *recreation* < L. *recreatio:* see RECREATE] **1.** refreshment in body or mind, as after work, by some form of play, amusement, or relaxation **2.** any form of play, amusement, or relaxation used for this purpose, as games, sports, hobbies, etc. —**rec′re·a′tion·al** *adj.*

☆**recreation room** (or **hall**) a room, as in a home, (or a public hall) equipped for amusement and relaxation or for social activities

rec·re·ment (rek′rə mənt) *n.* [< Fr. or L.: Fr. *récrément* < L. *recrementum* < *re-,* back + *cernere,* to separate: see CRISIS] [Now Rare] the worthless part of anything; waste; dross —**rec′re·men′tal** *adj.*

re·crim·i·nate (ri krim′ə nāt′) *vi.* **-nat′ed, -nat′ing** [< ML. *recriminatus:* see RE- & CRIMINATE] to answer an accuser by accusing him in return; reply with a counter charge —**re·crim′i·na′tion** *n.* —**re·crim′i·na·to·ry** (-nə tôr′ē), **re·crim′i·na′tive** *adj.*

☆**rec room** (or **hall**) (rek) *clipped form of* RECREATION ROOM (or HALL)

re·cru·desce (rē′krōō des′) *vi.* **-desced′, -desc′ing** [L. *recrudescere* < *re-,* again + *crudescere,* to become harsh or raw < *crudus,* raw, CRUDE] to break out again after lying latent or relatively inactive —**re′cru·des′cence** *n.* —**re′cru·des′cent** *adj.*

re·cruit (ri krōōt′) *vt.* [Fr. *recruter* < *recrute,* a recruit, lit., new growth < *recrû,* pp. of *recroître,* to grow again < L. *re-,* again + *crescere,* to grow, increase: see CRESCENT] **1.** to raise or strengthen (an army, navy, etc.) by enlisting personnel **2.** to enlist (personnel) into an army or navy **3.** *a)* to enlist (new members) for a party, organization, etc. *b)* to hire or engage the services of **4.** [Rare] *a)* to increase or maintain by supplying anew; replenish *b)* to revive or restore (health, strength, etc.) —*vi.* **1.** to enlist new personnel, esp. for a military force **2.** [Rare] *a)* to get new supplies of something, as in replacement *b)* to regain health, strength, etc. —*n.* **1.** a recently enlisted or drafted soldier, sailor, etc. **2.** a new member of any group, body, or organization —**re·cruit′er** *n.* —**re·cruit′ment** *n.*

rec. sec. recording secretary

rect. **1.** receipt **2.** rectangle **3.** rector **4.** rectory

rec·tal (rek′t'l) *adj.* of, for, or near the rectum —**rec′tal·ly** *adv.*

rec·tan·gle (rek′taŋ′g'l) *n.* [Fr. < ML. *rectangulus,* rectangular, for L. *rectiangulus:* see RECTI- & ANGLE¹] any four-sided plane figure with four right angles

rec·tan·gu·lar (rek taŋ′gyə lər) *adj.* **1.** shaped like a rectangle; having four sides and four right angles **2.** having right-angled corners, or a base in the form of a rectangle, as a building **3.** right-angled —**rec·tan′gu·lar′i·ty** (-lar′ə tē) *n.* —**rec·tan′gu·lar·ly** *adv.*

RECTANGLES

rectangular coordinates *same as* CARTESIAN COORDINATES

rec·ti- (rek′tə, -ti) [LL. < L. *rectus,* straight < pp. of *regere,* to keep straight, direct: for IE. base see RIGHT] *a combining form meaning* straight, right [*rectilinear*]: also, before a vowel, **rect-**

rec·ti·fi·er (rek′tə fī′ər) *n.* **1.** a person or thing that rectifies, as by correction or adjustment **2.** *Elec.* a device, as a vacuum tube, that converts alternating current into direct current

rec·ti·fy (rek′tə fī′) *vt.* **-fied′, -fy′ing** [ME. *rectifien* < MFr. *rectifier* < LL. *rectificare:* see RECTI- & -FY] **1.** to put or set right; correct; amend **2.** to adjust, as in movement or balance; adjust by calculation **3.** *Chem.* to refine or purify (a liquid) by distillation, esp. by fractional or repeated distillations **4.** *Elec.* to convert (alternating current) to direct current **5.** *Math.* to find the length of (a curve) —**rec′ti·fi′a·ble** *adj.* —**rec′ti·fi·ca′tion** *n.*

rec·ti·lin·e·ar (rek′tə lin′ē ər) *adj.* [< LL. *rectilineus* < *recti-* (see RECTI-) + *linea,* LINE¹ + -AR] **1.** moving in a straight line **2.** forming a straight line **3.** bounded or formed by straight lines **4.** characterized by straight lines **5.** *Optics* corrected so as not to distort straight lines: said of a type of lens Also **rec′ti·lin′e·al** —**rec′ti·lin′e·ar·ly** *adv.*

rec·ti·tude (rek′tə tōōd′, -tyōōd′) *n.* [ME. < MFr. < LL. *rectitudo* < L. *rectus,* right (see RECTI-)] **1.** conduct according to moral principles; strict honesty; uprightness of character **2.** correctness of judgment or method **3.** [Rare] straightness

rec·to (rek′tō) *n., pl.* **-tos** [< ModL. (*folio*) *recto,* on (the page) to the right < L., abl. of *rectus:* see RECTI-] *Printing* any right-hand page of a book; front side of a leaf: opposed to VERSO

rec·to- (rek′tō, -tə) [< L. *rectum:* see RECTUM] *a combining form meaning* rectal, rectal and [*rectocele*]: also, before a vowel, **rect-**

rec·to·cele (rek′tə sēl′) *n.* [prec. + -CELE] a hernial protrusion of the rectum into the vagina

rec·tor (rek′tər) *n.* [ME. < L. *rector* < pp. of *regere,* to rule: see REGAL] **1.** a Protestant Episcopal minister in charge of a parish **2.** a clergyman in the Church of England who holds the rights and tithes of his parish **3.** *R.C.Ch.* *a)* a priest in charge of a seminary, college, etc. *b)* [Brit.] the head priest of a parish; pastor **4.** in certain schools, colleges, and universities, the head or headmaster —**rec′tor·ate** (-it) *n.* —**rec·to′ri·al** (-tôr′ē əl) *adj.*

rec·to·ry (rek′tər ē) *n., pl.* **-ries** [ML. *rectoria*] **1.** the house in which a Protestant Episcopal minister lives **2.** in the Church of England, *a)* a benefice held by a rector *b)* the house in which a rector lives **3.** *R.C.Ch.* the house in which a parish priest lives

rec·trix (rek′triks) *n., pl.* **rec·tri·ces** (rek′trə sēz′, rek trī′sēz) [ModL. < L., fem. of *rector,* a director: see RECTOR] *Zool.* any of the large tail feathers of a bird, involved in controlling the direction of flight

rec·tum (rek′təm) *n., pl.* **-tums, -ta** (-tə) [ModL. < L. *rectum* (*intestinum*), lit., straight (intestine)] the lowest, or last, segment of the large intestine, extending, in man, from the sigmoid flexure to the anus

rec·tus (rek′təs) *n., pl.* **-ti** (-tī) [ModL. < L. *rectus* (*musculus*), lit., straight (muscle)] any of various straight muscles, as of the eye, neck, or thigh

re·cum·bent (ri kum′bənt) *adj.* [L. *recumbens,* prp. of *recumbere* < *re-,* back + *cumbere,* to lie down: for IE. base see CUBE] **1.** *a)* lying down; reclining; leaning *b)* resting; idle **2.** *Biol.* designating a part that leans or lies upon some other part or surface —*SYN.* see PRONE —**re·cum′ben·cy** *n.* —**re·cum′bent·ly** *adv.*

re·cu·per·ate (ri kōō′pə rāt′, -kyōō′-) *vt.* **-at′ed, -at′ing** [< L. *recuperatus,* pp. of *recuperare,* to recover, akin to *recipere,* to bring back, recover: see RECEIVE] to get back, or recover (losses, health, etc.) —*vi.* **1.** to be restored to health, strength, etc.; get well again; recover **2.** to recover losses, etc. —**re·cu′per·a′tion** *n.* —**re·cu′per·a′tive** (-pə rāt′iv, -pər ə tiv), **re·cu′per·a·to·ry** *adj.* —**re·cu′per·a′tor** *n.*

re·cur (ri kur′) *vi.* **-curred′, -cur′ring** [L. *recurrere* < *re-,* back + *currere,* to run: see COURSE] **1.** to have recourse (*to*) **2.** to return, as in thought, talk, or memory [*recurring* to an earlier question] **3.** to occur again, as in talk or memory; come up again for consideration **4.** to happen or occur again, esp. after some lapse of time; appear at intervals —*SYN.* see RETURN

re·cur·rence (ri kur′əns) *n.* [< ff.] the act or an instance of recurring; reoccurrence, return, repetition, etc.

re·cur·rent (-ənt) *adj.* [L. *recurrens*, prp.] **1.** appearing or occurring again or periodically **2.** *Anat.* turning back in the opposite direction: said of certain arteries and nerves —*SYN.* see INTERMITTENT —**re·cur'rent·ly** *adv.*

recurring decimal *same as* REPEATING DECIMAL

re·cur·vate (ri kur'vit, -vāt) *adj.* [L. *recurvatus*, pp.] recurved; bent back

re·curve (ri kurv') *vt., vi.* **-curved', -curv'ing** [L. *recurvare* < *re-*, back + *curvare* < *curvus*: see CURVE] to curve or bend back or backward

rec·u·sant (rek'yoo zənt, ri kyoo'z'nt) *n.* [L. *recusans*, prp. of *recusare*, to reject < *re-*, against < *causari*, to dispute, pretend < *causa*, a reason, CAUSE] **1.** a person who refuses to obey an established authority; specif., in England in the 16th to 18th cent., a Roman Catholic who refused to attend the services of the Church of England or to recognize its authority **2.** any dissenter or nonconformist —*adj.* of or like a recusant —**rec'u·san·cy** *n.*

re·cuse (ri kyooz') *vt.* **-cused', -cus'ing** [ME. *recusen* < MFr. *recuser* < L. *recusare*: see prec.] [Rare] to challenge (a judge, juror, or court) as prejudiced or otherwise incompetent to act

re·cy·cle (rē sī'k'l) *vt.* **-cled, -cling 1.** to pass through a cycle or part of a cycle again, as for checking, treating, etc. **2.** to use again and again, as a single supply of water in cooling, washing, diluting, etc.

red¹ (red) *n.* [ME. < OE. *read*, akin to G. *rot*, ON. *rauthr* < IE. base *reudh-*, red, whence L. *ruber, rufus*, red, *rubere*, to be red, OIr. *ruad*, Lith. *raudas*, red] **1.** a primary color, or any of a spread of colors at the lower end of the visible spectrum, varying in hue from that of blood to pale rose or pink: see COLOR **2.** a pigment producing this color **3.** [often R-] [from the red flag symbolizing revolutionary socialism] a political radical or revolutionary; esp., a communist ☆**4.** [often R-] [pl.] N. American Indians **5.** anything colored red, as a red space on a roulette wheel, a red checker piece, red clothing, etc. —*adj.* **red'der, red'dest 1.** having or being of the color red or any of its hues **2.** having red hair **3.** *a)* having a reddish or coppery skin *b)* florid, flushed, or blushing *c)* bloodshot *d)* sore; inflamed **4.** [R-] *a)* politically radical or revolutionary; esp., communist *b)* of the Soviet Union —☆**in the red** [from the practice of entering debits in account books with red ink] in debt or losing money —☆**into the red** into debt or an unprofitable financial condition —**see red** [Colloq.] to be or become angry —**red'ly** *adv.*

red² (red) *vt., vi.* **red, red'ding** *var. of* REDD¹

re·dact (ri dakt') *vt.* [ME. *redacten* < L. *redactus*, pp. of *redigere*, to bring into a certain condition, reduce to order (see RE- & ACT): in sense 2, prob. back-formation < ff.] **1.** to write out or draw up (a proclamation, edict, etc.); frame **2.** to arrange in proper form for publication; edit —**re·dac'tor** *n.*

re·dac·tion (ri dak'shən) *n.* [Fr. *rédaction* < LL. *redactio*: see prec.] **1.** the preparation of written work for publication; editing, reediting, or revision **2.** an edited work; esp., a reissue or new edition

red admiral [cf. ADMIRAL] a purplish-black European and N. American butterfly (*Vanessa atalanta*) with white spots near the tips of the forewings and bright-orange bands across the forewings and bordering the hind wings

red algae a group (Rhodophyta) of red, brownish-red, pink, or purple algae that form masses like shrubs in the depths of the oceans

re·dan (ri dan') *n.* [Fr. < OFr. *redent* < L. *re-*, back + *dens* (gen. *dentis*), a TOOTH: from its shape] *Mil.* a fortification consisting of two walls or parapets set at an angle pointed toward the enemy

red·bait (red'bāt') *vi., vt.* [< RED¹, *adj.* 4 + BAIT, *vt.* 2] to denounce (a person or group) as being communist, esp. with little or no evidence —**red'bait'er** *n.*

☆**red·bel·ly dace** (-bel'ē) any of a genus (*Chrosomus*) of small, brightly colored dace, common in rivers and streams of E N. America

red·bird (-burd') *n.* any of several predominantly red-colored birds, as the cardinal, scarlet tanager, etc.

red blood cell *same as* ERYTHROCYTE: also called **red blood corpuscle**

red-blood·ed (red'blud'id) *adj.* high-spirited and strong-willed; vigorous, lusty, etc.

red·breast (-brest') *n.* [ME. *redbrest*, robin] **1.** any of several birds with a reddish breast; esp., the American robin, the European robin, or the knot ☆**2.** a sunfish (*Lepomis auritus*) with an orange-red belly, found in the E U.S.: also called **red-breasted bream**

red·brick, red-brick (-brik') *adj.* [from the typical building material (in contrast to the stone of Oxford and Cambridge)] designating or of a British university or college other than Oxford or Cambridge; esp., any of the newer ones in the provinces: often connoting social inferiority —*n.* a redbrick university or college

☆**red·bud** (-bud') *n. a popular name for* CERCIS

☆**red·bug** (-bug') *n.* any of various red insects; esp., *same as: a)* CHIGGER (sense 1) *b)* COTTON STAINER

red·cap (-kap') *n.* ☆**1.** a porter in a railway station, air terminal, etc. **2.** [Brit. Dial.] *same as* GOLDFINCH (sense 1) **3.** [Brit. Colloq.] a military policeman

red carpet 1. a long red carpet laid out for important guests to walk on, as at a reception ☆**2.** a very grand or impressive welcome and entertainment (with *the*) —**roll out the red carpet (for)** to welcome and entertain in a very grand and impressive style —**red'-car'pet** *adj.*

☆**red cedar 1.** any of a number of juniper trees or shrubs with bluish, berrylike fruit and red wood; esp., *a)* the **eastern red cedar** (*Juniperus virginiana*) of E N. America with fragrant wood often used to line closets and chests *b)* the **Rocky Mountain red cedar** (*Juniperus scopulorum*) valued for lumber **2.** the wood of any of these

☆**red cent** [Colloq.] a cent; penny; trifling amount: esp. in **not worth a red cent, not give a red cent**, etc.

red clay *Geol.* **1.** clayey material colored red by iron oxide **2.** a soft, reddish clay deposit, restricted to the deepest parts of the ocean bottom and containing volcanic, meteoritic, and other insoluble material

red clover a kind of clover (*Trifolium pratense*) with flowers in reddish, ball-shaped heads, grown for fodder and forage

red-coat (red'kōt') *n.* a British soldier in a uniform with a red coat, as during the American Revolution

red coral 1. a commercial coral (*Corallium nobile*) of the Mediterranean region whose smooth, hard, blood-red skeleton is used for jewelry **2.** a similar, but inferior, coral (*Corallium rubrum*) of Japanese waters

Red Crescent a Moslem organization equivalent to the Red Cross: its symbol is a red crescent

Red Cross 1. a red Greek cross on a white ground (*Geneva Cross*), emblem of neutrality in war, adapted from the Swiss flag, with colors reversed, and used since 1864 to mark hospitals, ambulances, etc. in time of war **2.** *a)* an international society (in full **International Red Cross**) for the relief of suffering in time of war or disaster: its emblem is the Geneva Cross *b)* any national branch of this

redd¹ (red) *vt., vi.* **redd** or **red'ded, red'ding** [ME. (North Eng. & Scot.) *redden* < ? or akin to OE. *hreddan*, to free] [Colloq. or Dial.] to put in order, make (a place) tidy (usually with *up*)

redd² (red) *n.* [< ?] the spawning area of trout or salmon

red deer 1. a deer (*Cervus elaphus*) native to Europe and Asia ☆**2.** the white-tailed deer in its reddish summer coat

red·den (red'n) *vt.* to make red —*vi.* to become red; esp., to blush or flush

red·dish (-ish) *adj.* somewhat red —**red'dish·ness** *n.*

red·dle (red''l) *n., vt.* **-dled, -dling** *var. of* RUDDLE

☆**red-dog** (red'dôg') *vt.* **-dogged', -dog'ging** [< RED¹ (the traditional color of shirt worn by the defense in scrimmages) + DOG (*vt.* 1)] *Football same as* BLITZ

☆**red drum** a large, edible drumfish (*Sciaenops ocellata*) of the Atlantic Coast of the U.S.

red dwarf a star that is cooler on its surface, smaller, and of fainter luminosity than the sun

rede (rēd) *n.* [ME. *rede* < OE. *ræd* (akin to G. *rat*) < base of *rædan*, to interpret (see READ¹: the *vt.* is the same word, with retained ME. sp.)] [Archaic] **1.** counsel; advice **2.** a plan; scheme **3.** a story; tale **4.** an interpretation —*vt.* **red'ed, red'ing** [Archaic] **1.** to advise; counsel **2.** to interpret (dreams, omens, etc.) **3.** to narrate; tell

☆**red·ear** (red'ir') *n.* a sunfish (*Lepomis microlophus*) of the C and SE U.S., with bright red gill covers

re·deem (ri dēm') *vt.* [LME. *redemen* < MFr. *redimer* < L. *redimere* < *re(d)-*, back + *emere*, to get, buy < IE. base **em-*, to take, whence Lith. *imu*, OBulg. *imo*, to take] **1.** to buy back **2.** to get back; recover, as by paying a fee **3.** to pay off (a mortgage or note) ☆**4.** *a)* to convert (paper money) into gold or silver coin or bullion *b)* to convert (stocks, bonds, etc.) into cash *c)* to turn in (trading stamps or coupons) for a prize, premium, etc. **5.** *a)* to set free by paying a ransom *b)* to deliver from sin and its penalties, as by a sacrifice made for the sinner **6.** to fulfill (a promise or pledge) **7.** *a)* to make amends or atone for *b)* to restore (oneself) to favor by making amends *c)* to make worthwhile; justify —*SYN.* see RESCUE —**re·deem'a·ble, re·demp'ti·ble** (-demp'tə b'l) *adj.* —**re·deem'er** *n.*

re·de·mand (rē'di mand', -mänd') *vt.* **1.** to demand again **2.** to demand back; demand the return of

re·demp·tion (ri demp'shən) *n.* [ME. *redempcion* < OFr. < L. *redemptio*, a buying back, in LL.(Ec.), release from sin < pp. of *redimere*: see REDEEM] **1.** a redeeming or being redeemed (in various senses) **2.** something that redeems —**re·demp'tion·al** *adj.*

☆**re·demp·tion·er** (-ər) *n.* [prec. + -ER] formerly, a person who paid for his passage to America by a stipulated period of service as an indentured servant

re·demp·tive (ri demp'tiv) *adj.* [ML. *redemptivus*] **1.** serving to redeem **2.** of redemption Also **re·demp'to·ry**

redamage	redecorate	redefine	redeliver
redecide	rededicate	redefinition	redemonstrate

Re·demp·tor·ist (-tər ist) *n.* [Fr. *rédemptoriste* < LL.(Ec.) *redemptor*, redeemer < L., a contractor, one who releases a debtor by paying his creditor] a member of the Congregation of the Most Holy Redeemer, a Roman Catholic order working and teaching among the poor

re·de·ploy (rē′di ploi′) *vt.*, *vi.* to move (troops, etc.) from one front or area to another —**re′de·ploy′ment** *n.*

re·de·vel·op (-di vel′əp) *vt.* 1. to develop again 2. *a)* to rebuild or restore (a run-down area) *b)* to restore or promote the economic development of (an area) 3. *Photog.* to intensify or tone (a developed negative or image) by a second developing process —*vi.* to develop again —**re′de·vel′op·ment** *n.*

red·eye (red′ī′) *n.* ☆1. any of several unrelated fishes with red eyes, as the rock bass ☆2. *same as* RED-EYED VIREO ☆3. [Slang] strong, cheap whiskey

☆**red-eyed vireo** (-īd′) a N. American vireo (*Vireo olivaceus*) with gray and olive-green coloring

red feed any of several red, surface-living, saltwater copepods, used as food by fishes

☆**red·fin** (-fin′) *n.* any of various freshwater minnows with reddish fins; esp., a small minnow (*Luxilus cornutus*) of E N. America

red fir 1. any of various firs with reddish wood, as the **California red fir** (*Abies magnifica*) 2. the wood of any of these trees ☆3. *same as* DOUGLAS FIR

red fire any of various substances, esp. one containing strontium nitrate, which burn with a bright red light and are used in fireworks, flares, etc.

red·fish (-fish′) *n.*, *pl.* **-fish′**, **-fish′es**: see FISH² any of various unrelated fishes with a reddish coloration, including the red drum, certain salmons, etc.

☆**red fox** 1. the common European fox (*Vulpes vulpes*) with reddish fur 2. the similar related fox (*Vulpes fulva*) of N. America 3. the fur of either of these

red giant a large star with a low surface temperature that is approximately twenty-five times larger and one hundred times brighter than the sun

red grouse a reddish-brown ptarmigan (*Lagopus scoticus*) of the British Isles, that does not change color in winter

red gum 1. *a)* any of several Australian eucalyptus trees *b)* the wood of any of these trees ☆2. *same as* SWEET GUM (senses 1 & 2)

red-hand·ed (red′han′did) *adv.*, *adj.* 1. with hands covered with a victim's blood 2. in the very commission of crime or wrongdoing 3. in an undeniably incriminating or compromising situation

red hat a wide-brimmed, flat, red hat presented to a new cardinal by the Pope as a symbol of the cardinal's rank

red·head (red′hed′) *n.* 1. a person with red hair ☆2. a N. American diving duck (*Aythya americana*), the male of which has a red head: it resembles the related canvasback

red·head·ed (-hed′id) *adj.* having red hair, as a person, or a red head, as a bird

☆**redheaded woodpecker** a N. American woodpecker (*Melanerpes erythrocephalus*), with a bright-red head and neck, black back, and white underparts

red heat 1. the temperature at which a substance is red-hot 2. the state of being at this temperature

red herring 1. a smoked herring 2. something used to divert attention from the basic issue: from the practice of drawing a herring across the trace in hunting, to distract the hounds

red hind a red-spotted grouper (*Epinephelus guttatus*) ranging from the West Indies to Brazil; cabrilla

red-hot (red′hät′) *adj.* 1. hot enough to glow; very hot 2. very excited, angry, eager, ardent, intense, etc. 3. very new; up-to-the-minute *[red-hot news]* —☆*n.* [Colloq.] a frankfurter; hot dog

re·di·a (rē′dē ə) *n.*, *pl.* **re′di·ae** (-dē ē) [ModL., after F. *Redi*, 17th-c. It. naturalist] a larval stage of many trematodes, usually parasitic in a host snail, produced by a sporocyst and producing daughter rediae or cercariae

red·in·gote (red′iŋ gōt′) *n.* [Fr., altered < Eng. *riding coat*] 1. formerly, a man's long, full-skirted overcoat 2. a long, unlined, lightweight coat, open down the front, worn by women

red·in·te·grate (red in′tə grāt′, ri din′-) *vt.* **-grat′ed**, **-grat′ing** [ME. *redintegraten* < L. *redintegratus*, pp. of *redintegrare*: see RE- & INTEGRATE] to make whole or perfect again; reunite; reestablish

red·in·te·gra·tion (red in′tə grā′shən, ri din′-) *n.* [ME. *redyntegracyon* < L. *redintegratio*] 1. a redintegrating or being redintegrated 2. *Psychol.* the tendency to respond to a later stimulus in the same way as to an earlier complex stimulus of which the later one was a part

re·di·rect (rē′di rekt′, -dī-) *vt.* to direct again or to a different place —*adj. Law* designating the examination of one's own witness again, after his cross-examination by the opposing lawyer —**re′di·rec′tion** *n.*

re·dis·count (rē dis′kount) *vt.* to discount (esp. commercial paper) for a second time —*n.* 1. the act or

process of rediscounting 2. rediscounted commercial paper —**re′dis·count′a·ble** *adj.*

rediscount rate ☆the rate of interest charged by a district Federal Reserve Bank for rediscounting top-grade commercial paper offered by its member banks

re·dis·trib·ute (rē′dis trib′yoot) *vt.* **-ut·ed**, **-ut·ing** to distribute again or in a different way —**re′dis·tri·bu′tion** *n.* —**re′dis·trib′u·tive** *adj.*

☆**re·dis·trict** (rē dis′trikt) *vt.* to divide anew into districts, esp. so as to reapportion electoral representatives

red·i·vi·vus (red′i vī′vəs) *adj.* [LL. < L., laid aside, used < *reduvia*, a remnant, orig. hangnail < OL. *redivia* < **reduere*, to strip away < *red-*, RE- + *-uere*, to put on (cf. EXUVIAE): sense infl. in LL. by L. *vivere*, to live] restored to life; reborn; reincarnated *[a* Napoleon *redivivus]*

Red·lands (red′ləndz) [after the reddish soil in the area] city in S Calif., near San Bernardino: pop. 36,000

red lead red oxide of lead, Pb_3O_4, derived from massicot, used in making paint, in glassmaking, etc.

red-let·ter (red′let′ər) *adj.* designating a memorable or joyous day or event: from the custom of marking holidays on the calendar in red ink

red light 1. any danger or warning signal; specif., a red lamp, flare, etc. 2. a red stoplight

☆**red-light district** (red′līt′) a district (in a town or city) containing many houses of prostitution, formerly indicated by red lights

red man ☆a North American Indian

red meat meat that is red before cooking; esp., beef or mutton as distinguished from pork, veal, poultry, etc.

☆**red·neck, red-neck** (red′nek′) *n.* [from the characteristic sunburned neck acquired in the fields by farm laborers] [Slang] a poor, white, rural resident of the South: often a somewhat derogatory term

red·ness (-nis) *n.* the state or quality of being red

re·do (rē doo′) *vt.* **-did′**, **-done′**, **-do′ing** 1. to do again or do over 2. to redecorate (a room, etc.)

☆**red oak** 1. any of several oaks having leaves with sharp-tipped lobes, dark bark, and acorns which require two years to mature 2. the reddish, hard wood of such a tree

red ocher a red, earthy hematite, used as a pigment

red·o·lence (red′'l əns) *n.* the quality or state of being redolent: also **red′o·len·cy** —*SYN.* see SCENT

red·o·lent (-ənt) *adj.* [ME. < OFr. < L. *redolens*, prp. of *redolere*, to emit a scent < *re(d)-*, intens. + *olere*, to smell (akin to *odor*, ODOR)] 1. sweet-smelling; fragrant 2. smelling (*of*) *[redolent* of the ocean*]* 3. suggestive or evocative (*of*) —**red′o·lent·ly** *adv.*

Re·don (rə dōn′), **O·di·lon** (ô dē lōn′) 1840–1916; Fr. painter & lithographer

Re·don·do Beach (rə dän′dō) [< Sp. *redondo*, circular, round + BEACH] city in SW Calif., on the Pacific: suburb of Los Angeles: pop. 56,000

☆**red osier** 1. a shrubby dogwood (*Cornus stolonifera*) with dark-red branches and white or bluish fruit 2. any of several willows with reddish or purple stems

re·dou·ble (rē dub′'l) *vt.* **-bled**, **-bling** [LME. *redoublen* < MFr. *redoubler*: see RE- & DOUBLE] 1. *a)* to double again; increase fourfold *b)* to make twice as much or twice as great *c)* to make much greater; intensify *[to redouble* one's efforts*]* 2. to make echo or reecho 3. to refold; double back 4. [Archaic] to repeat —*vi.* 1. *a)* to become twice as great or twice as much *b)* to double again; increase fourfold 2. to reecho; resound 3. to turn sharply backward, as on one's tracks 4. *Bridge* to double a bid that an opponent has already doubled —*n. Bridge* a redoubling

re·doubt (ri dout′) *n.* [Fr. *redoute* < It. *ridotta* < ML. *reductus*, a refuge, orig. pp. of L. *reducere*: see REDUCE] 1. *a)* a breastwork outside a fortification, to defend approaches, etc. *b)* a breastwork within a fortification 2. any stronghold

re·doubt·a·ble (-ə b'l) *adj.* [ME. *redowtable* < MFr. *redoutable* < *redouter*, to fear, dread < L. *re-*, intens. + *dubitare*, to DOUBT] 1. formidable; fearsome *[a redoubtable foe]* 2. not to be lightly dismissed; commanding respect *[a redoubtable* logician*]* Also [Archaic] **re·doubt′ed** —**re·doubt′a·bly** *adv.*

re·dound (ri dound′) *vi.* [ME. *redounen* < MFr. *redonder* < L. *redundare*, to overflow < *re(d)-*, intens. + *undare*, to surge, swell < *unda*, a wave: see WATER] 1. to have a result or effect (*to* the credit or discredit, etc. of someone or something) 2. to come back; react; recoil (*upon*): said of honor or disgrace 3. [Obs.] to surge up or overflow

red·out (red′out′) *n.* [RED¹ + (BLACK)OUT] a blurring of vision, as if by a red mist, caused by the forcing of blood into the head during feet-first acceleration, as in flying

re·dox (rē′däks) *n.* [< *red*(uction-)*ox*(idation)] *Chem.* same as OXIDATION-REDUCTION

red pepper 1. a plant (*Capsicum frutescens*) of the nightshade family, with a red, many-seeded fruit, cultivated in many varieties, as the sweet pepper, cayenne, etc. 2. the fruit 3. the ground fruit or seeds, used for seasoning

red pine a wide-spreading pine (*Pinus resinosa*) of the NE U.S., with glossy, green needles in groups of two

REDIN-
GOTE

redeposit	redesign	rediscover	redissolve
redescend	redetermine	rediscovery	redistill
redescribe	redifferentiate	redispose	redivide

red·poll (red′pōl′) *n.* [RED¹ + POLL] any of a number of finches (genus *Acanthis*) the males of which usually have a red patch on the head

Red Poll (pōl) any of a British breed of hornless, reddish dairy and beef cattle: also **Red Polled**

re·draft (rē′draft′, -dräft′; *for v.* rē draft′, -dräft′) *n.* **1.** a second or later draft or framing, as of a legislative bill **2.** a new draft on the original drawer or endorser of a protested bill of exchange, for the amount of the bill plus charges and costs —*vt.* to draft again or anew

re·dress (ri dres′; *for n., usually* rē′dres) *vt.* [ME. *redressen* < OFr. *redrecier:* see RE- & DRESS] **1.** to set right; rectify or remedy, often by making compensation for (a wrong, grievance, etc.) **2.** [Now Rare] to make amends to —*n.* **1.** compensation or satisfaction, as for a wrong done **2.** the act of redressing —*SYN.* see REPARATION —**redress the balance** (or **scales**) to make a fair adjustment; see that justice is done —**re·dress′a·ble** *adj.* —**re·dress′er** *n.*

re-dress (rē′dres′) *vt.* to dress again

Red River 1. river flowing southeast along the Tex.-Okla. border, through SW Ark. & C La. into the Mississippi: 1,018 mi. **2.** river flowing north along the N.Dak.-Minn. border into Lake Winnipeg in Manitoba, Canada: 545 mi.: in full **Red River of the North 3.** river in SE Asia, flowing from Yunnan province, China, southeast across North Vietnam, into the Gulf of Tonkin: c. 500 mi.: Annamese name, SONG COI; Chin. name, YUAN KIANG

☆**red·root** (red′root′, -root′) *n.* any of various plants with red roots, as *a)* a small shrub (genus *Ceanothus*) of the buckthorn family *b)* a marsh plant (*Lacnanthes tinctoria*) of the bloodwort family, with sword-shaped leaves and flat clusters of small, woolly, yellow flowers, found along the Atlantic coast of the U.S. *c)* same as PIGWEED (sense 1) *d)* same as BLOOD-ROOT

red salmon *same as* SOCKEYE

Red Sea sea between NE Africa & W Arabia, connected with the Mediterranean Sea by the Suez Canal & with the Indian Ocean by the Gulf of Aden: c. 1,400 mi. long; c. 178,000 sq. mi.

red·shank (red′shank′) *n.* a common European sandpiper (*Tringa totanus*), characterized by reddish legs

red shift *Astron.* a shift of spectral lines, as in the light from remote galaxies, toward the longer wavelengths and lower frequencies at the red end of the spectrum, explained as a Doppler effect and indicating motion away from the earth and an expanding universe

☆**red·shirt** (red′shurt′) *vt.* [from the traditional red shirts worn by the scrimmage team, with whom such players may continue to practice] [Slang] to withdraw (a player) from a varsity team for a year so that he will be eligible for an extra year later —*n.* such a player

red siskin a S. American finch (*Carduelis cucullata*) with a black head and red body, often kept as a cage bird

☆**red snapper 1.** a reddish, deep-water food fish (*Lutjanus blackfordi*), found in the Gulf of Mexico and in adjacent Atlantic waters **2.** any of several red-colored fishes, as a rockfish (*Sebastodes ruberrimus*) of the Pacific Ocean

red spider any of a number of small, red, vegetarian mites (family Tetranychidae)

red squill 1. a strain of Mediterranean squill (*Urginea maritima*), having red bulbs which yield a powder used chiefly in rat poison **2.** this powder

☆**red squirrel** a common N. American tree squirrel (*Tamiasciurus hudsonicus*) with reddish fur

red·start (-stärt′) *n.* [RED¹ + obs. *start* < ME. *stert*, tail < OE. *steort:* for IE. base see STARE] ☆**1.** an American fly-catching warbler (*Setophaga ruticilla*) the male of which is black and orange above and white below **2.** a small European warbler (*Phœnicurus phoenicurus*), with a reddish tail and darting flight

red tape [after the tape commonly used to tie official papers] **1.** official forms and routines **2.** rigid application of regulations and routine, resulting in delay in getting business done

☆**red tide** a reddish discoloration of sea waters, caused by large numbers of red protozoan flagellates (esp. genera *Gymnodinium* and *Gonyaulax*) that kill fishes and other organisms by the poisonous products released into the waters

red·top (-täp′) *n.* [from the reddish panicle of some forms] ☆a grass (*Agrostis alba*) grown in the cooler parts of N. America for hay, pasturage, and lawns

re·duce (ri dōōs′, -dyōōs′) *vt.* **-duced′, -duc′ing** [ME. *reducen* < L. *reducere*, to lead back < *re-*, back + *ducere*, to lead: see DUCT] **1.** *a)* to lessen in any way, as in size, weight, amount, value, price, etc.; diminish *b)* to put into a simpler or more concentrated form **2.** to bring into a certain order; systematize **3.** to break up into constituent elements by analysis **4.** *a)* to put into a different form [to *reduce* a talk to writing] *b)* to change to a different physical form, as by melting, crushing, grinding, etc. **5.** to lower, as in rank or position; demote; downgrade **6.** *a)* to bring to order, attention, obedience, etc., as by persuasion or force *b)* to subdue or conquer (a city or fort) by siege or attack **7.** *a)* to bring into difficult or wretched circumstances [a people *reduced* to poverty] *b)* to compel by need to do something [*reduced* to stealing] **8.** *a)* to weaken in bodily strength; make thin [*reduced* to skin and bones] *b)* to thin (paint, etc.), as with oil **9.** *Arith.* to change in denomination or form without changing in value [to *reduce* fractions to their lowest terms] **10.** *Chem. a)* to decrease the positive valence of (an element or ion) *b)* to increase the number of electrons of (an atom, element, or ion) *c)* to remove the oxygen from; deoxidize *d)* to combine with hydrogen *e)* to bring into the metallic state by removing nonmetallic elements **11.** *Phonology* to give an unstressed quality to (a vowel) **12.** *Photog.* to weaken the density of (a negative) **13.** *Surgery* to restore (a broken bone, displaced organ, etc.) to normal position or condition —*vi.* **1.** to become reduced **2.** to lose weight, as by dieting —*SYN.* see DECREASE —**re·duc′i·bil′i·ty** *n.* —**re·duc′i·ble** *adj.* —**re·duc′i·bly** *adv.*

re·duc·er (-ər) *n.* **1.** a person or thing that reduces **2.** *Mech.* a pipe fitting threaded to connect two different sizes of pipe **3.** *Photog. a)* a chemical agent in a developing solution that reduces silver halide to metallic silver *b)* an oxidizing solution for reducing negatives

reducing agent *Chem.* any substance that reduces another substance, or brings about reduction, and is itself oxidized in the process

reducing glass a double-concave lens used for reducing the visual size of something viewed through it

re·duc·tase (ri duk′tās, -tāz) *n.* [REDUCT(ION) + -ASE] any enzyme that speeds up chemical reduction

‡**re·duc·ti·o ad ab·sur·dum** (ri duk′tē ō′ ad ab sur′dəm, -shē ō′) [L., lit., reduction to absurdity] *Logic* the proof of a proposition by showing its opposite to be an obvious falsity or self-contradiction, or the disproof of a proposition by showing its consequences to be impossible or absurd when carried to a logical conclusion

re·duc·tion (ri duk′shən) *n.* [LME. *reduccion* < MFr. *reduction* < L. *reductio* < *reductus*, pp. of *reducere*] **1.** a reducing or being reduced **2.** anything made or brought about by reducing, as a smaller copy, lowered price, etc. **3.** the amount by which anything is reduced —**re·duc′tion·al** *adj.*

reduction division *same as* MEIOSIS (sense 1)

re·duc·tion·ism (-iz′m) *n.* any method or theory of reducing data, processes, or statements to seeming equivalents that are less complex or developed: usually a disparaging term —**re·duc′tion·ist** *n., adj.* —**re·duc′tion·is′tic** *adj.*

re·duc·tive (ri duk′tiv) *adj.* [ML. *reductivus*] **1.** of or characterized by reduction or reductionism **2.** reducing or tending to reduce —**re·duc′tive·ly** *adv.*

re·duc·tor (-tər) *n. Chem.* any apparatus for carrying out the reduction of metallic ions in solution for purposes of analysis; specif., a long tube filled with granular zinc for reducing a ferric solution to its ferrous salt

re·dun·dan·cy (ri dun′dən sē) *n., pl.* **-cies** [L. *redundantia*] **1.** the state or quality of being redundant; superfluity **2.** a redundant quantity; overabundance **3.** the use of redundant words **4.** the part of a redundant statement that is superfluous Also **re·dun′dance**

re·dun·dant (-dənt) *adj.* [L. *redundans*, prp. of *redundare:* see REDOUND] **1.** more than enough; overabundant; excess; superfluous **2.** using more words than are needed; wordy **3.** unnecessary to the meaning: said of words and affixes —*SYN.* see WORDY —**re·dun′dant·ly** *adv.*

re·du·pli·cate (ri dōō′plə kāt′, -dyōō′-; *for adj. & n., usually* -kit) *vt.* **-cat′ed, -cat′ing** [< ML. *reduplicatus*, pp. of *reduplicare:* see RE- & DUPLICATE] **1.** to redouble, double, or repeat **2.** *a)* to double (a root syllable or other element) so as to form an inflected or derived form of a word (as *tom-tom*), sometimes with certain changes, as of the vowel (as in *chitchat*) *b)* to form (words) by such doubling —*vi.* to be or become reduplicated —*adj.* **1.** reduplicated; doubled **2.** *same as* VALVATE (sense 2 *a*) —*n.* something reduplicated

re·du·pli·ca·tion (ri dōō′plə kā′shən, -dyōō′-) *n.* [LL. *reduplicatio*] **1.** a reduplicating or being reduplicated **2.** something produced by reduplicating, as a word containing a reduplicated element **3.** the element added in a reduplicated word form —**re·du′pli·ca′tive** *adj.*

re·du·vi·id (ri dōō′vē id, -dyōō′-) *n.* [< ModL. *Reduviidae* < *Reduvius*, name of the type genus < L. *reduvia*, hangnail: see REDIVIVUS] any of a large family (Reduviidae) of hemipterous insects with sucking beaks, including assassin bugs and kissing bugs

red·ware (red′wer′) *n.* [RED¹ + *ware*, seaweed < ME. *war* < OE.] any of several large, brown, leathery, edible kelps (genus *Laminaria*)

red·wing (-win′) *n.* **1.** a European songbird (*Turdus musicus*), the smallest of the thrushes, with an orange-red patch on the underside of the wings ☆**2.** *same as* RED-WINGED BLACKBIRD

redraw	redrill	redrive	redry

☆**red-winged blackbird** a N. American blackbird (*Agelaius phoeniceus*) with a bright-red patch on each wing near the shoulder in the male: also **redwing blackbird**

red·wood (-wood′) *n.* ☆**1.** a giant evergreen (*Sequoia sempervirens*) of the baldcypress family, having fire-resistant bark, enduring, soft wood, and needlelike leaves: found in coastal regions of California and S Oregon ☆**2.** *same as* BIG TREE **3.** any of a number of trees with reddish wood or yielding a red dye **4.** the wood of any of these trees

Redwood City city in W Calif., on San Francisco Bay: suburb of San Francisco: pop. 56,000

Redwood National Park national park in NW Calif., containing groves of redwood trees: 91 sq. mi.

red worm 1. *same as* BLOODWORM **2.** a small, reddish freshwater worm (genus *Tubifex*), often fed to aquarium fish

re·ech·o, re-ech·o (rē ek′ō) *vt., vi.* **-ech′oed, -ech′o·ing** to echo back or again; resound —*n., pl.* **-ech′oes** the echo of an echo Also **re·ech′o**

reech·y (rēch′ē) *adj.* **reech′i·er, reech′i·est** [LME. *rechy* < ME. *rech*, var. of *rek*, REEK] [Archaic or Dial.] smoky, dirty, foul, or rancid

reed (rēd) *n.* [ME. *rede* < OE. *hreod*, akin to OHG. *hriot* < IE. base *kreut-*, to shake, tremble] **1.** *a)* any of various tall, slender grasses (esp. genus *Phragmites*), with plumelike inflorescences, growing in wet or marshy land *b)* the stem of any of these grasses *c)* such plants or stems collectively, specif. as material for thatching, basketwork, etc. **2.** a rustic musical instrument made from a hollow stem or stalk and played by blowing through it **3.** an ancient Hebrew unit of length equal to 6 cubits: Ezek. 40:3 **4.** a device on a loom, by means of which threads are drawn between the separated threads of the warp **5.** [Poet.] an arrow **6.** *Archit.* a small, rounded molding; reeding **7.** *Music a)* a thin strip of some flexible substance, as cane, placed against the opening of the mouthpiece of certain wind instruments, as the clarinet, so as to leave a narrow opening: when vibrated by the breath, it produces a musical tone *b)* an instrument with a reed or reeds *c)* in some organs, a similar device that vibrates in a current of air —*vt.* to thatch or decorate with reeds

Reed (rēd) **1. John,** 1887-1920; U.S. journalist & radical **2. Walter,** 1851-1902; U.S. army surgeon & bacteriologist

☆**reed·bird** (-burd′) *n.* dial. var. of BOBOLINK

reed·buck (-buk′) *n., pl.* **-buck′,** **-bucks′:** see PLURAL, II, D, 2 [transl. of Du. *rietbok*] any of several small African antelopes (genus *Redunca*) with widely spread hooves and, in the males, backward-sloping, ringed horns turned inward and forward near the tips

reed·ing (-iŋ) *n.* **1.** a small, rounded, decorative molding **2.** a set of such moldings, as on a column

reed instrument any instrument whose sound is produced by a vibrating reed or reeds, including, specif., the oboe, clarinet, saxophone, English horn, and bassoon

reed mace *Brit. var.* of CATTAIL

reed organ an organ with a set of free metal reeds instead of pipes to produce the tones: cf. REED PIPE

reed pipe an organ pipe in which the tone is produced by a current of air striking a vibrating reed in an opening in the pipe: cf. FLUE PIPE

reed stop 1. a set of reed pipes (in an organ) operated by one knob **2.** the knob

re·ed·u·cate, re-ed·u·cate (rē ej′ə kāt′) *vt.* **-cat′ed, -cat′ing** to educate again or anew, esp. so as to rehabilitate or adapt to new situations: also **re·ëd′u·cate′** —**re·ed′u·ca′tion, re-ed′u·ca′tion** *n.* —**re·ed′u·ca′tive, re-ed′u·ca′tive** *adj.*

reed·y (rēd′ē) *adj.* **reed′i·er, reed′i·est 1.** full of reeds **2.** made of reed or reeds **3.** like a reed; slender, fragile, etc. **4.** sounding like a reed instrument; thin; piping —**reed′i·ly** *adv.* —**reed′i·ness** *n.*

reef¹ (rēf) *n.* [prob. via. Du. or MLowG. *rif* < ON. *rif*, lit., a RIB] **1.** a line or ridge of rock, coral, or sand lying at or near the surface of the water **2.** *Mining* a bed or vein of ore; lode —*SYN.* see SHOAL²

reef² (rēf) *n.* [ME. *riff* < or akin to ON. *rif* < IE. *reip-*, a strip < base *rei-*, to tear, cut, whence RIVE]: orig. used of cords for reefing] *Naut.* **1.** a part of a sail which can be folded or rolled up and tied down to reduce the area exposed to the wind **2.** the act of reefing —*vt.* **1.** to reduce the size of (a sail) by taking in and tying down part of it **2.** to lower (a spar or mast) or reduce the projection of (a bowsprit)

reef·er (rē′fər) *n.* **1.** a person who reefs: formerly a slang term for a midshipman **2.** a short, thick, double-breasted coat in the style of a seaman's jacket ☆**3.** [from the rolled appearance of a *reef* (of a sail)] [Slang] a marijuana cigarette ☆**4.** [altered contr. of REFRIGERATOR] [Slang] a refrigerator freight car, truck, ship, etc.

reef knot a square knot used for reefing

reek (rēk) *n.* [ME. < OE. *rec*, akin to ON. *reykr*, G. *rauch* < ? IE. base *reug-*, cloud, smoke] **1.** vapor; fume **2.** a strong, unpleasant smell; stench **3.** [Chiefly Scot.] smoke —*vi.* [ME. *reken* < OE. *reocan*] **1.** to give off steam or smoke **2.** to have a strong, offensive smell **3.** to be permeated with anything very unpleasant —*vt.* **1.** to expose to the action of smoke, etc. **2.** to emit or exude (vapor, fumes, etc.) —**reek′y** *adj.*

reel¹ (rēl) *vi.* [ME. *relen* < the *n.*: from the sensation of whirling] **1.** to give way or fall back; sway, waver, or stagger as from being struck **2.** to lurch or stagger about, as from drunkenness or dizziness **3.** to go around and around; whirl **4.** to feel dizzy; have a sensation of spinning or whirling —*vt.* to cause to reel —*n.* [ME. *rele* < OE. *hreol*: see REEL³] a reeling motion; whirl, stagger, etc. —*SYN.* see STAGGER

reel² (rēl) *n.* [prob. < REEL¹, *n.*] **1.** *a)* a lively Scottish dance *b)* clipped form of VIRGINIA REEL **2.** music for either of these

reel³ (rēl) *n.* [ME. < OE. *hreol* < Gmc. *hrehulaz* < IE. base *krek-*, to strike, hence to make a weaving motion, whence Gr. *krekein*, to weave, Lett. *krekls*, a shirt] **1.** a frame or spool on which thread, wire, tape, film, a net, etc. is wound **2.** such a frame set on the handle of a fishing rod, to wind up or let out the line **3.** the quantity of wire, thread, film, tape, etc. usually wound on one reel **4.** in a lawn mower, a set of spiral steel blades rotating on a horizontal bar set between wheels —*vt., vi.* to wind on a reel —**reel in 1.** to wind on a reel **2.** to pull in (a fish) by winding a line on a reel —**reel off** to tell, write, produce, etc. easily and quickly —**reel out** to unwind from a reel —☆**(right) off the reel** without hesitation or pause

re·en·force, re-en·force (rē′in fôrs′) *vt.* **-forced′, -forc′ing** *same as* REINFORCE: also **re′ën·force′**

re·en·ter, re-en·ter (rē en′tər) *vt., vi.* to enter again (in various senses): also **re·ën′ter**

re·en·trant, re-en·trant (-trənt) *adj.* that reenters; specif., pointed inward, as an angle —*n.* a reentrant angle or part Also **re·ën′trant** —**re·en′trance, re-en′trance** *n.*

reentrant angle in a polygon, an interior angle greater than 180°, with its point turning back into the figure rather than out from it

re·en·try, re-en·try (rē en′trē) *n., pl.* **-tries 1.** a reentering; specif., a coming back, as of a space vehicle, into the earth's atmosphere **2.** a second or repeated entry **3.** *Bridge, Whist* a card that will win a trick and recover the lead **4.** *Law* a coming into possession again under a right reserved in a prior transfer of property Also **re·ën′try**

reeve¹ (rēv) *n.* [ME. *reve*, earlier *irefe* < OE. *gerefa* < *ge-* + base of *rof*, a row, number] **1.** in English history, *a)* the chief officer, under the king, of a town or district *b)* the overseer of a manor; steward **2.** the elected head of a village or town council in certain Canadian provinces

reeve² (rēv) *vt.* **reeved** or **rove, rove** or **rov′en, reev′ing** [prob. < Du. *reven*, to reef, in sense "use a rope in or as in reefing"] *Naut.* **1.** to slip (a rope end, etc.) through a block, ring, or cleat **2.** *a)* to pass in, through, or around something *b)* to fasten by so doing **3.** to pass a rope through (a block or pulley)

reeve³ (rēv) *n.* [? < irreg. pl. of RUFF¹] the female of the ruff (sandpiper)

re·ex·am·i·na·tion, re-ex·am·i·na·tion (rē′ig zam′ə nā′shən) *n.* **1.** a second or repeated examination **2.** *Law* the questioning of one's own witness after, and about matters taken up in, the cross-examination Also **re′ëx·am′i·na′tion**

re·ex·am·ine, re-ex·am·ine (rē′ig zam′in) *vt.* **-ined, -in·ing 1.** to examine again **2.** *Law* to subject to reexamination Also **re′ëx·am′ine**

ref (ref) *n., vt., vi.* clipped form of REFEREE

ref. 1. referee **2.** reference **3.** referred **4.** reformation **5.** reformed **6.** reformer **7.** refund

re·face (rē fās′) *vt.* **-faced′, -fac′ing** to put a new face, facing, or surface on

Ref. Ch. Reformed Church

re·fect (ri fekt′) *vt.* [LME. *refecken* < pp. of L. *reficere*: in later use, back-formation < ff.] [Obs.] to refresh with food or drink

re·fec·tion (ri fek′shən) *n.* [ME. < OFr. < L. *refectio* < pp. of *reficere*, to remake, restore < *re-*, again + *facere*, to make, DO¹] **1.** food or drink taken after a period of hunger or fatigue; refreshment **2.** a light meal; lunch

re·fec·to·ry (rē fek′tə rē) *n., pl.* **-ries** [LME. < LL. *refectorium* < pp. of L. *reficere*: see prec.] a dining hall in a monastery, convent, college, etc.

redye	reemerge	reengage	reexhibit
reedit	reemergence	reenlist	reexperience
reelect	reemphasis	reequip	reexplain
reelection	reemphasize	reestablish	reexport
reembark	reemploy	reestablishment	refabricate
reembody	reenact	reevaluate	refashion
reembrace	reendow	reexchange	refasten

refectory table a long, narrow, rectangular table, as that used in a dining hall of a monastery or convent

re·fer (ri fur′) *vt.* **-ferred′, -fer′ring** [ME. *referren* < MFr. *referer* < L. *referre* < *re-*, back + *ferre*, to BEAR] **1.** to assign or attribute (*to*) as cause or origin **2.** to assign, or regard or name as belonging (*to* a kind, class, date, etc.) **3.** to submit (a quarrel, question, etc.) for determination or settlement **4.** to send or direct (*to* someone or something) for aid, information, etc. —*vi.* **1.** to relate or apply (*to*); be concerned or deal **2.** to direct attention, or make reference or allusion (*to*) [*to refer* to an earlier event] **3.** to turn for information, aid, authority, etc. (*to*) [*to refer* to a map] —**ref′er·a·ble** (ref′ər ə b′l, ri fur′-), **re·fer′ra·ble**, **re·fer′ri·ble** *adj.* —**re·fer′rer** *n.*
SYN.—**refer** implies deliberate, direct, and open mention of something [he *referred* in detail to their corrupt practices]; **allude** implies indirect, often casual mention, as by a hint, a figure of speech, etc. [although he used different names, he was *alluding* to his family]

ref·er·ee (ref′ə rē′) *n.* **1.** a person to whom something is referred for decision **2.** an official who enforces the rules in certain sports contests **3.** *Law* a person appointed by a court to study, take testimony in, and report his judgment on, a matter —*vt., vi.* **-eed′, -ee′ing** to act as referee (in) —**SYN.** see JUDGE

ref·er·ence (ref′ər əns, ref′rəns) *n.* **1.** a referring or being referred; *esp.*, submission of a problem, dispute, etc. to a person, committee, or authority for settlement **2.** relation; connection; regard [in *reference* to his letter] **3.** *a)* the directing of attention to a person or thing *b)* a mention or allusion **4.** *a)* an indication, as in a book or article, of some other work or passage to be consulted *b)* the work or passage so indicated *c)* the mark or sign, as a number, letter, or symbol, directing the reader to a footnote, etc.: in full **reference mark 5.** *a)* the giving of the name of another person who can offer information or recommendation *b)* the person so indicated *c)* a written statement of character, qualification, or ability, as of someone seeking a position; testimonial **6.** *a)* use or consultation to get information, as an aid in research, etc.: often attributive [*reference* books] *b)* a book, etc. used for reference —*vt.* **-enced, -enc·ing** to provide with references —**make reference to** to refer to; mention

ref·er·en·dum (ref′ə ren′dəm) *n., pl.* **-dums** or **-da** (-də) [ModL. < L., a carrying back, gerund or neut. gerundive of *referre*: see REFER] ☆**1.** *a)* the submission of a law, proposed or already in effect, to a direct vote of the people *b)* the right of the people to vote directly on such laws, superseding or overruling the legislature *c)* the vote itself **2.** a note sent by a diplomatic agent to his own government, asking for specific instructions

ref·er·ent (ref′ər ənt) *n.* [< L. *referens*, prp.] something referred to; *specif.*, *Linguis.* the object, concept, event, etc. referred to by a term or expression

ref·er·en·tial (ref′ə ren′shəl) *adj.* [< REFERENCE (as if < L. *referentia*) + -AL] **1.** containing a reference **2.** used for reference —**ref′er·en′tial·ly** *adv.*

re·fer·ral (ri fur′əl) *n.* **1.** a referring or being referred, as for professional service, etc. **2.** a person who is referred or directed to another person, an agency, etc.

re·fill (rē fil′; *for n.* rē′fil) *vt., vi.* to fill again —*n.* a new filling; *esp.*, *a)* a unit to replace the contents of a container that is not itself discarded after use [a *refill* for a ball point pen] *b)* any additional filling of a prescription for medicine —**re·fill′a·ble** *adj.*

re·fi·nance (rē′fə nans′, rē fī′nans) *vt.* **-nanced′, -nanc′ing** to finance again; *specif.*, to provide or obtain a new loan or more capital for

re·fine (ri fīn′) *vt.* **-fined′, -fin′ing** [RE- + FINE¹, *v.*, after Fr. *raffiner*, to purify] **1.** to make fine or pure; free from impurities, dross, alloy, sediment, etc.; purify; clarify **2.** to free from imperfection, coarseness, crudeness, etc.; make more elegant or cultivated; impart polish to **3.** to make more subtle or precise —*vi.* **1.** to become fine or pure; become free from impurities, etc. **2.** to become more polished or elegant **3.** to use subtleties and fine distinctions in thinking or speaking —**refine on** (or **upon**) to improve, as by adding refinements —**re·fin′er** *n.*

re·fined (ri fīnd′) *adj.* [pp. of prec.] **1.** made free from other matter, or from impurities; purified **2.** free from crudeness or coarseness; cultivated; elegant **3.** characterized by great subtlety, precision, etc.

re·fine·ment (ri fīn′mənt) *n.* **1.** *a)* a refining or being refined *b)* the result of this **2.** delicacy or elegance of language, speech, manners, etc.; polish; cultivation **3.** a development; improvement; elaboration **4.** a fine distinction; subtlety

re·fin·er·y (ri fīn′ər ē) *n., pl.* **-er·ies** [< REFINE + -ERY, after Fr. *raffinerie*] an establishment or plant for refining, or purifying, such raw materials as oil, metal, sugar, etc.

re·fin·ish (rē fin′ish) *vt.* to put a new surface on (wood, metal, etc.) —**re·fin′ish·er** *n.*

re·fit (rē fit′; *also for n.,* rē′fit′) *vt., vi.* **-fit′ted, -fit′ting** to make or be made ready or fit for use again, as by repairing, reequipping, or resupplying —*n.* an act or instance of refitting

refl. 1. reflection **2.** reflective **3.** reflex **4.** reflexive

☆**re·fla·tion** (rē flā′shən) *n.* [RE- + (IN)FLATION] a type of inflation designed to restore a former price structure, accomplished by decreasing the purchasing power of currency by the use of governmental monetary powers

re·flect (ri flekt′) *vt.* [ME. *reflecten* < MFr. *reflecter* < L. *reflectere* < *re-*, back + *flectere*, to bend] **1.** to bend or throw back (light, heat, or sound) **2.** to give back an image of; mirror or reproduce **3.** to cast or bring back as a consequence (with *on*) [deeds that *reflect* honor on him] **4.** to express or show [skills that *reflect* years of training] **5.** to recollect or realize after thought (*that*) **6.** to fold or turn back: usually used in pp. —*vi.* **1.** to be bent or thrown back [light *reflecting* from the water] **2.** to bend or throw back light, heat, sound, etc. [a *reflecting* surface] **3.** *a)* to give back an image or likeness *b)* to be mirrored **4.** to think seriously; contemplate (*on* or *upon*) **5.** to cast blame or discredit (*on* or *upon*) —**SYN.** see CONSIDER, THINK¹

re·flec·tance (-flek′t′ns) *n. Physics* the ratio of the amount of electromagnetic radiation, usually light, reflected from a surface to the amount originally striking the surface

reflecting telescope any of several telescopes having as the objective a paraboloid mirror mounted at the lower end of the tube and using various systems of mirrors for viewing the image by reflecting the incident light to an eyepiece; reflector

re·flec·tion (ri flek′shən) *n.* [ME. *reflexion* < MFr. < LL. *reflexio*] **1.** a reflecting or being reflected **2.** the throwing back by a surface of sound, light, heat, etc. **3.** anything reflected; *specif.*, an image; likeness **4.** *a)* the fixing of the mind on some subject; serious thought; contemplation *b)* the result of such thought; idea or conclusion, esp. if expressed in words **5.** *a)* blame; discredit *b)* a remark or statement imputing discredit or blame *c)* an action bringing discredit **6.** *Anat.* a turning or bending back on itself —**re·flec′tion·al** *adj.*

re·flec·tive (-tiv) *adj.* **1.** reflecting **2.** of or produced by reflection **3.** meditative; thoughtful —**SYN.** see PENSIVE —**re·flec′tive·ly** *adv.* —**re·flec′tive·ness, re′flec·tiv′i·ty** *n.*

re·flec·tor (-tər) *n.* **1.** a person or thing that reflects; *esp.*, a surface, object, etc. that reflects light, sound, heat, or the like, as a piece of glass or metal, highly polished and usually concave, which reflects and directs radiant energy, as beams of light, sound waves, etc., in a desired direction **2.** *same as* REFLECTING TELESCOPE **3.** a layer of material, as graphite, immediately surrounding the core of a nuclear reactor or bomb, that reflects back into the core a number of those neutrons that would ordinarily escape

☆**re·flec·tor·ize** (-īz′) *vt.* **-ized′, -iz′ing 1.** to process (something) for reflecting light **2.** to furnish with reflectors

‡**re·flet** (rə flā′) *n.* [Fr., reflection, earlier *reflés* < It. *riflesso* < L. *reflexus* (see ff.): sp. altered after L. *reflectere*] luster or iridescence, as a metallic glaze on pottery

re·flex (rē′fleks; *for v.* ri fleks′) *n.* [< L. *reflexus*, reflected, pp. of *reflectere*: see REFLECT] **1.** *a)* reflection, as of light *b)* light or color resulting from reflection **2.** a reflected image, likeness, or reproduction **3.** *a) Physiol.* a reflex action *b)* any quick, automatic or habitual response *c)* [*pl.*] ability to react quickly and effectively [a boxer with good *reflexes*] —*adj.* **1.** turned, bent, or reflected back **2.** coming in reaction or reflection [a *reflex* effect]; *esp.*, *Physiol.* designating or of an involuntary action, as a sneeze, resulting when a stimulus is carried by an afferent nerve to a nerve center and the response is reflected along an efferent nerve to some muscle or gland **3.** *Geom.* designating an angle greater than a straight angle (180°) **4.** *Radio* designating or of an apparatus in which some device functions in a double capacity, as a radio receiving set in which the same tube is both an audio-frequency and radio-frequency amplifier —*vt.* **1.** to bend, turn, or fold back **2.** to cause to undergo a reflex process —**re′flex·ly** *adv.*

REFLEX ANGLE

reflex arc *Physiol.* the entire nerve path involved in a reflex action

reflex camera a camera in which the image formed by the lens is reflected by a mirror onto a ground-glass plate to help in focusing the lens

re·flex·ion (ri flek′shən) *n. Brit. var. of* REFLECTION

re·flex·ive (-siv) *adj.* [ML. *reflexivus*] **1.** *rare var. of:* *a)* REFLEX *b)* REFLECTIVE **2.** *Gram. a)* designating a verb whose subject and direct object refer to the same person or thing (e.g., *wash* in "I wash myself" *b)* designating a pronoun used as the direct object of such a verb, as *myself* in the above sentence —*n.* a reflexive verb or pronoun —**re·flex′ive·ly** *adv.* —**re·flex′ive·ness, re·flex·iv·i·ty** (rē′flek siv′ə tē) *n.*

refigure	refilm	refind	refix
refile	refilter	refire	refloat

ref·lu·ent (ref'loo wənt) *adj.* [L. *refluens*, prp. of *refluere*, to flow back: see RE- & FLUENT] flowing back; ebbing, as the tide to the sea —**ref'lu·ence** *n.*

re·flux (rē'fluks') *n.* [ME. < ML. *refluxus* < pp. of L. *refluere*: see prec.] a flowing back; ebb

re·for·est (rē fôr'ist, -fär'-) *vt.*, *vi.* to plant new trees on (land once forested) —**re'for·est·a'tion** *n.*

re·form (ri fôrm') *vt.* [ME. *reformen* < OFr. *reformer* < L. *reformare*: see RE- & FORM] 1. to make better by removing faults and defects; correct [to *reform* a calendar] 2. *a*) to make better by putting a stop to abuses or malpractices or by introducing better procedures, etc. *b*) to put a stop to (abuses, etc.) 3. to cause or persuade (a person) to give up misconduct and behave better 4. *Chem.* to heat (petroleum products) under pressure, with or without catalysts, to produce cracking and a greater yield of gasoline —*vi.* to become better in behavior; give up misconduct —*n.* 1. a correction of faults or evils, as in government or society; social or political improvement 2. an improvement in character and conduct; reformation 3. a movement aimed at removing political or social abuses —*adj.* ☆[R-] designating or of a movement in Judaism that seeks to normalize rationalist thought with historical Judaism, stressing its ethical aspects and not requiring strict observance of traditional Orthodox ritual —**re·form'·a·ble** *adj.* —**re·form'a·tive** *adj.*

re·form (rē'fôrm') *vt.*, *vi.* to form again

ref·or·ma·tion (ref'ər mā'shən) *n.* [ME. *reformacion* < L. *reformatio*] 1. a reforming or being reformed 2. [R-] the 16th-cent. religious movement that aimed at reforming the Roman Catholic Church and resulted in establishing the Protestant churches —**ref'or·ma'tion·al** *adj.*

☆**re·form·a·to·ry** (ri fôr'mə tôr'ē) *adj.* reforming or aiming at reform —*n.*, *pl.* -**ries** 1. an institution to which young offenders convicted of lesser crimes are sent for training and discipline intended to reform rather than punish them 2. a penitentiary for women

re·formed (ri fôrmd') *adj.* 1. improved or corrected, as in behavior or morals, or made better by the removal of errors, abuses, etc. 2. [R-] designating or of a Protestant church or churches, esp. Calvinist as distinguished from Lutheran

reformed spelling any of various proposed systems for simplifying the spelling of English words, esp. by establishing a consistent application of phonetic values and dropping unpronounced letters

re·form·er (ri fôr'mər) *n.* 1. a person who seeks to bring about reform, esp. political or social reform 2. [R-] any of the leaders of the Reformation

re·form·ism (-miz'm) *n.* the practice or advocacy of reform, esp. political or social reform —**re·form'ist** *n.*, *adj.*

☆**reform school** *same as* REFORMATORY (sense 1)

re·fract (ri frakt') *vt.* [< L. *refractus*, pp. of *refringere*, to turn aside < *re-*, back + *frangere*, to BREAK[1]] 1. to cause (a ray or wave of light, heat, or sound) to undergo refraction 2. *Optics* to measure the degree of refraction of (an eye or lens) —**re·frac'tive** *adj.* —**re·frac'tive·ly** *adv.* —**re·frac·tiv·i·ty** (rē'frak tiv'ə tē, ri frak'-), **re·frac'tive·ness** *n.*

refracting telescope 1. a telescope in which a large double-convex lens causes light rays to converge to a focus, forming an image magnified by a double-convex eyepiece 2. a similar telescope in which the converging rays are intercepted by a double-concave eyepiece

re·frac·tion (ri frak'shən) *n.* [LL. *refractio*] 1. the bending of a ray or wave of light, heat, or sound, as it passes obliquely from one medium to another of different density, in which its speed is different, or through layers of different density in the same medium 2. *Astron.* the bending of the rays of light from a star or planet, greatest when the star or planet is lowest in the sky, so that it seems higher than it really is 3. *Optics a*) the ability of the eye to refract light entering it, so as to form an image on the retina *b*) the measuring of the degree of refraction of an eye

re·frac·tive index *same as* INDEX OF REFRACTION

re·frac·tom·e·ter (rē'frak täm'ə tər) *n.* an instrument for measuring refraction, as of the eye

ILLUSION CAUSED BY REFRACTION

re·frac·tor (ri frak'tər) *n.* 1. something that refracts 2. *same as* REFRACTING TELESCOPE

re·frac·to·ry (ri frak'tər ē) *adj.* [altered < obs. *refractary* < L. *refractarius* < *refractus*: see REFRACT] 1. hard to manage; stubborn; obstinate: said of a person or animal 2. resistant to heat; hard to melt or work: said of ores or metals 3. *a*) not yielding to treatment, as a disease *b*) able to resist disease —*n.*, *pl.* -**ries** something refractory; specif., a heat-resistant material used in lining furnaces, etc. —SYN. see UNRULY —**re·frac'to·ri·ly** *adv.* —**re·frac'to·ri·ness** *n.*

re·frain[1] (ri frān') *vi.* [ME. *refreinen* < OFr. *refrener*

< L. *refrenare* < *re-*, back + *frenare*, to curb < *frenum*, a rein] to hold back; keep oneself (*from* doing something); forbear —*vt.* [Archaic] to hold back; curb
SYN.—**refrain** usually suggests the curbing of a passing impulse in keeping oneself from saying or doing something [although provoked, he *refrained* from answering]; **abstain** implies voluntary self-denial or the deliberate giving up of something [to *abstain* from liquor]; **forbear** suggests self-restraint manifesting a patient endurance under provocation [to *forbear* venting one's wrath]

re·frain[2] (ri frān') *n.* [ME. *refreine* < MFr. *refrain* < OFr. *refraindre*, to break, repress, modulate < VL. *refrangere*, for L. *refringere*, to break off: see REFRACT] 1. a phrase or verse repeated at intervals in a song or poem, as after each stanza 2. music for this

re·fran·gi·ble (ri fran'jə b'l) *adj.* [< RE- + L. *frangere*, to break + -IBLE] that can be refracted, as light rays —**re·fran·gi·bil'i·ty**, **re·fran'gi·ble·ness** *n.*

re·fresh (ri fresh') *vt.* [ME. *refreschen* < OFr. *refrescher*: see RE- & FRESH[1]] 1. to make fresh by cooling, wetting, etc. [rains *refreshing* parched plants] 2. to make (another or oneself) feel cooler, stronger, more energetic, etc. than before, as by food, drink, or sleep 3. to replenish, as by new supplies, etc.; renew 4. to revive or stimulate (the memory, etc.) —*vi.* 1. to become fresh again; revive 2. to take refreshment, as food or drink 3. to lay in fresh supplies —SYN. see RENEW —**re·fresh'er** *n.*

refresher course a course of study reviewing material previously studied

re·fresh·ing (-iŋ) *adj.* 1. that refreshes 2. pleasingly new or different —**re·fresh'ing·ly** *adv.*

re·fresh·ment (-mənt) *n.* [ME. *refreschement* < MFr. *refreschement*] 1. a refreshing or being refreshed 2. something that refreshes, as food, drink, or rest 3. [*pl.*] food or drink or both, esp. as a light meal

re·frig·er·ant (ri frij'ər ənt) *adj.* [L. *refrigerans*, prp.] 1. that refrigerates; cooling or freezing something 2. reducing heat or fever —*n.* 1. a medicine used to reduce fever 2. a substance used in refrigeration; specif., any of various liquids that vaporize at a low temperature, used in mechanical refrigeration

re·frig·er·ate (ri frij'ər āt') *vt.* -**at'ed**, -**at'ing** [< L. *refrigeratus*, pp. of *refrigerare*, to make cool or cold < *re-*, intens. + *frigerare*, to cool < *frigus*, cold: see FRIGID] 1. to make or keep cool or cold; chill 2. to preserve (food, biologicals, etc.) by keeping cold or freezing —**re·frig'er·a'tion** *n.* —**re·frig'er·a'tive**, **re·frig'er·a·to'ry** (-ə tôr'ē) *adj.*

re·frig·er·a·tor (-rāt'ər) *n.* something that refrigerates; esp., a box, cabinet, or room in which food, drink, etc. are kept cool, as by ice or mechanical refrigeration

☆**refrigerator car** a railroad car built and equipped to keep perishable foods, etc. refrigerated in transit

re·frin·gent (ri frin'jənt) *adj.* [L. *refringens*, prp. of *refringere*: see REFRACT] refracting; refractive —**re·frin'·gen·cy**, **re·frin'gence** *n.*

reft (reft) *alt. pt. & pp. of* REAVE[1] —*adj.* robbed or bereft (*of* something)

re·fu·el (rē fyoo'əl, -fyool') *vt.* -**fu'eled** or -**fu'elled**, -**fu'el·ing** or -**fu'el·ling** to supply again with fuel —*vi.* to take on a fresh supply of fuel

ref·uge (ref'yooj) *n.* [ME. < OFr. < L. *refugium* < *refugere*, to retreat < *re-*, back + *fugere*, to flee: see FUGITIVE] 1. shelter or protection from danger, difficulty, etc. 2. a person or thing that gives shelter, help, or comfort 3. a place of safety; shelter; safe retreat 4. an expediency or shift; action taken to escape trouble or difficulty —*vt.* -**uged**, -**ug·ing** [Archaic] to give refuge to —*vi.* [Archaic] to take refuge —SYN. see SHELTER

ref·u·gee (ref'yoo jē', ref'yoo jē') *n.* [Fr. *réfugié*, pp. of *réfugier* < L. *refugere*: see prec.] a person who flees from his home or country to seek refuge elsewhere, as in a time of war, political or religious persecution, etc.

re·ful·gent (ri ful'jənt) *adj.* [L. *refulgens*, prp. of *refulgere*, to reflect light: see RE- & FULGENT] shining; radiant; glowing; resplendent —**re·ful'gence**, **re·ful'gen·cy** *n.* —**re·ful'gent·ly** *adv.*

re·fund[1] (ri fund'; *for n.* rē'fund') *vt.* [ME. *refunden* < MFr. or L. MFr. *refonder* < L. *refundere* < *re-*, back + *fundere*, to pour: see FOUND[2]] to give back or pay back (money, etc.); repay —*vi.* to make repayment —*n.* the act of refunding or the amount refunded; repayment —**re·fund'a·ble** *adj.*

re·fund[2] (rē'fund') *vt.* [RE- + FUND] to fund again or anew; specif., *Finance a*) to use borrowed money, esp. the proceeds from the sale of a bond issue, to pay back (a loan) before or at maturity *b*) to replace (an old bond issue) with a new bond issue, often at a lower rate of interest

re·fur·bish (rē fur'bish) *vt.* [RE- + FURBISH] to brighten, freshen, or polish up again; renovate —**re·fur'bish·ment** *n.*

re·fus·al (ri fyoo'z'l) *n.* 1. the act of refusing 2. the right or chance to accept or refuse something before it is offered to another; option

re·fuse[1] (ri fyooz') *vt.*, *vi.* -**fused'**, -**fus'ing** [ME. *refusen* < OFr. *refuser* < LL. *refusare* < L. *refusus*, pp. of *refundere*: see REFUND[1]] 1. to decline to accept; reject 2. *a*) to decline to do, give, or grant *b*) to decline (*to* do something) [refuse

---

reflourish	refold	refortify	refreeze
reflower	reforge	refracture	refry
refocus	reformulate	reframe	refurnish

to go/ **3.** *a)* to decline to accept or submit to (a command, etc.); decline to undergo *b)* to decline to grant the request of (a person) **4.** to stop short at (a fence, etc.), without jumping it: said of a horse **5.** [Obs.] to renounce —*vi.* to decline to accept, agree to, or do something —*SYN.* see DECLINE —**re·fus′er** *n.*

ref·use² (ref′yōōs, -yōōz) *n.* [ME. < OFr. *refus*, pp. of *refuser*: see prec.] anything thrown away or rejected as worthless or useless; waste; trash; rubbish —*adj.* thrown away or rejected as worthless or useless

ref·u·ta·tion (ref′yə tā′shən) *n.* [L. *refutatio* < *refutatus*, pp.] **1.** the act of refuting, or proving false or wrong; disproof **2.** something that refutes, as an argument Also **re·fut′al** (ri fyōōt′'l)

re·fute (ri fyōōt′) *vt.* **-fut′ed, -fut′ing** [L. *refutare*, to repel, check: see RE- & CONFUTE] **1.** to prove (a person) to be wrong; confute **2.** to prove (an argument or statement) to be false or wrong, by argument or evidence —*SYN.* see DISPROVE —**re·fut′a·ble** (-fyōōt′ə b'l, ref′yoo tə-) *adj.* —**re·fut′a·bly** *adv.* —**re·fut′er** *n.*

reg. 1. regent **2.** regiment **3.** region **4.** register **5.** registered **6.** registrar **7.** registry **8.** regular **9.** regulation **10.** regulator

re·gain (ri gān′) *vt.* [MFr. *regaigner*: see RE- & GAIN¹] **1.** to get back into one's possession; recover **2.** to succeed in reaching again; get back to —*SYN.* see RECOVER

re·gal (rē′gəl) *adj.* [ME. < MFr. or L.: MFr. *regal* < L. *regalis* < *rex* (gen. *regis*), a king < IE. base **reĝ-*, straight, lead, direct, whence L. *regere*, to rule; Sans. *rāj*, RIGHT, RICH] **1.** of a king; royal **2.** characteristic of, like, or fit for a king; splendid, stately, magnificent, etc. —**re′gal·ly** *adv.*

re·gale (ri gāl′) *vt.* **-galed′, -gal′ing** [Fr. *régaler* < the *n.*] **1.** to entertain by providing a splendid feast **2.** to delight with something pleasing or amusing —*vi.* to feast —*n.* [Fr. *régal*, earlier *régale* < *ré-* (see RE-) + OFr. *gale*, joy, pleasure (see GALLANT)] [Archaic] **1.** a feast **2.** a choice food; delicacy **3.** refreshment —**re·gale′ment** *n.* —**re·gal′er** *n.*

re·ga·li·a (ri gāl′yə, -gā′lē ə) *n.pl.* [L., neut. pl. of *regalis*: see REGAL] **1.** rights or privileges belonging to a king; prerogatives of sovereignty **2.** the emblems and insignia of kingship, as a crown, scepter, etc. **3.** the insignia or decorations of any rank or position, or of an order or society **4.** splendid clothes; finery

re·gal·i·ty (rē gal′ə tē) *n., pl.* **-ties** [ME. *regalite* < ML. *regalitas*: see REGAL & -ITY] **1.** kingship; royalty; sovereignty **2.** a country or area subject to the authority of a king; kingdom **3.** a right or privilege belonging to a king

☆**regal moth** a large moth (*Citheronia regalis*) with a heavy, hairy body and yellow-spotted green wings

Re·gan (rē′gan) in Shakespeare's *King Lear*, the younger of Lear's two cruel and disloyal daughters

re·gard (ri gärd′) *n.* [ME. < OFr. < *regarder*: see RE- & GUARD] **1.** a firm, fixed look; gaze **2.** consideration; attention; concern /to have some *regard* for one's safety/ **3.** respect and affection; esteem /to have high *regard* for one's teachers/ **4.** reference; respect; relation /in *regard* to your plan/ **5.** *[pl.]* good wishes; respects; affection /give my *regards* to your father/ **6.** [Obs.] aspect; appearance —*vt.* [ME. *regarden* < OFr. *regarder*] **1.** to observe or look at with a firm, steady gaze; look at attentively **2.** to take into account; consider **3.** [Archaic] to give attentive heed to or show concern for **4.** to hold in affection and respect /to *regard* one's friends highly/ **5.** to think of in a certain light; consider /to *regard* taxes as a burden/ **6.** to have relation to; concern; have reference to /that which *regards* our welfare/ —*vi.* **1.** to look; gaze **2.** to pay heed or attention —**as regards** concerning —**without regard to** without considering

SYN.—**regard** is the most neutral of the terms here, in itself usually implying evaluation of worth rather than recognition of it /the book is highly *regarded* by authorities/; **respect** implies high valuation of worth, as shown in deference or honor /a jurist *respected* by lawyers/; **esteem**, in addition, suggests that the person or object is highly prized or cherished /a friend *esteemed* for his loyalty/; **admire** suggests a feeling of enthusiastic delight in the appreciation of that which is superior /one must *admire* such courage/

re·gard·ant (-'nt) *adj.* [ME. < MFr., prp. of *regarder*: see REGARD] *Heraldry* looking backward, with the head in profile

re·gard·ful (-fəl) *adj.* **1.** observant; heedful; attentive; mindful (often with *of*) **2.** showing regard; respectful or considerate —**re·gard′ful·ly** *adv.*

re·gard·ing (-in) *prep.* with regard to; concerning; about

re·gard·less (-lis) *adj.* without regard; heedless; unmindful; careless —☆*adv.* [Colloq.] without regard for, or in spite of, objections, difficulties, etc.; anyway —**regardless of** in spite of; notwithstanding /*regardless* of the cost/ —**re·gard′less·ly** *adv.*

re·gat·ta (ri gät′ə, -gat′-) *n.* [It. (Venetian) *regata*, gondola race, lit., a striving for mastery < *regatar*, to compete] **1.** orig., a gondola race in Venice **2.** *a)* any boat race *b)* a series of such races

re·ge·la·tion (rē′jə lā′shən) *n.* [see RE- & GELATION¹] a freezing or refreezing together of pieces of ice after a pressure, which has caused melting at a temperature below the normal melting point, has been removed —**re′ge·late′** (-lāt′) *vi.* **-lat′ed, -lat′ing**

re·gen·cy (rē′jən sē) *n., pl.* **-cies** [ME. *regencie* < ML. *regentia*] **1.** the position, function, or authority of a regent or group of regents **2.** a group of men serving as regents **3.** a country or district governed by a regent or group of regents **4.** the time during which a regent or regency governs; specif. [R-] in England, the period between 1811 and 1820 *b)* in France, the period between 1715 and 1723 —*adj.* [R-] designating or of a style of furniture of the French or British regencies, the French style characterized by scrollwork combined with natural forms, many curves, and strict balance and proportion, the English style by a less massive adaptation of French Empire and featuring metal or ebony inlay on mahogany and rosewood

re·gen·er·ate (ri jen′ər it; *for v.* -ə rāt′) *adj.* [LME. *regenerat* < L. *regeneratus*, pp. of *regenerare*, to reproduce, in LL.(Ec.), to regenerate: see RE- & GENERATE] **1.** spiritually reborn **2.** renewed or restored, esp. after a decline to a low or abject condition —*vt.* **-at′ed, -at′ing 1.** to cause to be spiritually reborn **2.** to cause to be completely reformed or improved **3.** to form or bring into existence again; reestablish on a new basis **4.** *Biol.* to grow anew (a part to replace one hurt or lost) **5.** *Chem.* to produce (a compound, product, etc.) again chemically, as from a derivative or by modification to a physically changed, but not chemically changed, form **6.** *Electronics* *a)* to cause oscillation or to increase the amplification of (a signal) by feeding energy back from an amplifier output to its input *b)* to receive (imperfectly formed electrical signals) for retransmission in substantially perfect form **7.** *Mech.* to use (heat, energy, pressure, etc. which would otherwise be wasted) by employing special arrangements or devices **8.** *Physics* to restore (a battery, catalyst, etc.) to its original state or properties —*vi.* **1.** to form again, or be made anew **2.** to be regenerated, or spiritually reborn **3.** to have a regenerative effect —**re·gen′er·a·cy** (-ə sē), **re·gen′er·ate·ness** *n.* —**re·gen′er·ate·ly** *adv.*

re·gen·er·a·tion (ri jen′ə rā′shən) *n.* [ME. *regeneracioun* < LL.(Ec.) *regeneratio*] a regenerating or being regenerated; specif., *a)* a being renewed, reformed, or reconstituted *b)* a spiritual rebirth *c)* *Biol.* the renewal or replacement of any hurt or lost part, as the claw of a lobster *d)* *Electronics* the act or process of regenerating electrical signals

re·gen·er·a·tive (ri jen′rə rāt′iv, -ər ə tiv) *adj.* [ME. < MFr. < ML. *regenerativus*] **1.** regenerating or tending to regenerate **2.** of or characterized by regeneration —**re·gen′er·a′tive·ly** *adv.*

re·gen·er·a·tor (-ə rāt′ər) *n.* **1.** a person or thing that regenerates **2.** a device used in a furnace or engine to preheat incoming air or gas by exposing it to the heat of exhaust gases

Re·gens·burg (rā′gəns boorkh′; *E.* rā′gənz burg′) city in E Bavaria, West Germany, on the Danube: pop. 125,000

re·gent (rē′jont) *adj.* [ME. < MFr. or ML.: MFr. *regent* < ML. *regens* < L., prp. of *regere*, to rule: see REGAL] **1.** acting in place of a king or ruler /a prince *regent*/ **2.** [Now Rare] acting as ruler; ruling —*n.* [ME.] **1.** a person appointed to rule a monarchy when the sovereign is absent or too young or incapacitated to rule ☆**2.** *a)* a member of the governing board of certain institutions, as of a State university or a State system of schools *b)* any of certain other university officials **3.** [Now Rare] a ruler; governor —**re′gent·ship′** *n.*

re·ges (rē′jēz) *n. pl.* of REX

Reg·gio di Ca·la·bri·a (red′jō dē kä lä′brē ä′) seaport in Calabria, S Italy, on the Strait of Messina: pop. 159,000: also **Reggio Calabria**

Reggio nell'E·mi·lia (nel′le mē′lyä) commune in NC Italy, in Emilia-Romagna: pop. 124,000: also **Reggio Emilia**

reg·i·cide (rej′ə sid′) *n.* [ML. *regicida* < L. *rex*, gen. *regis* (see REGAL) + *-cida*: see -CIDE] **1.** a person who kills, or is responsible for the killing of, a king, esp. of his own country **2.** [ML. *regicidum*] the killing of a king —**reg′i·ci′dal** *adj.*

re·gime, ré·gime (rə zhēm′, rā-) *n.* [Fr. *régime* < L. *regimen*: see ff.] **1.** *a)* a political system *b)* a form or manner of government or rule **2.** a social system or order **3.** the period of time that a person or system is in power **4.** *same as* REGIMEN (sense 2)

reg·i·men (rej′ə mən) *n.* [ME. < L., rule, government < *regere*, to rule: see REGAL] **1.** [Rare] *a)* the act of governing; government; rule *b)* a particular system of government; regime **2.** a regulated system of diet, exercise, etc. for therapy or the maintenance or improvement of health **3.** *Gram. obs. term for* GOVERNMENT (sense 6)

reg·i·ment (rej′ə mənt; *for v.* -ment′) *n.* [ME. < MFr. < LL. *regimentum* < L. *regere*, to rule: see REGAL] **1.** a

---

regather	regear	regerminate	regild

military unit consisting of two or more battalions and forming a basic element of a division: since 1963 no longer a tactical unit in the U.S. Army **2.** a large number (of persons, etc.) **3.** [Obs.] rule; government —*vt.* **1.** to form into a regiment or regiments **2.** to assign to a regiment or group **3.** to form into an organized or uniform group or groups; organize systematically **4.** to organize in a rigid system under strict discipline and control —**reg′i·men′tal** *adj.* —**reg′i·men′tal·ly** *adv.* —**reg′i·men·ta′tion** *n.*

reg·i·men·tals (rej′ə men′t′lz) *n.pl.* **1.** the uniform and insignia worn by a particular regiment **2.** military uniform

Re·gi·na (ri jī′nə; *for 1, also* -jē′-) [L., queen, fem. of *rex:* see REGAL] **1.** a feminine name **2.** capital of Saskatchewan, Canada, in the S part: pop. 131,000 —*n.* [*also* r-] queen: the official title of a reigning queen [Victoria *Regina*]

re·gi·nal (ri jī′n′l) *adj.* [ML. *reginalis* < L. *regina:* see prec.] of, like, fit for, or characteristic of a queen; queenly; royal

Reg·i·nald (rej′i nald) [ML. *Reginaldus* < OHG. *Raganald, Raginold* < Gmc. *ragina-, *ragna-, judgment, counsel + *waldan, to rule (see WIELD)] a masculine name: dim. *Reggie;* var. *Reynold;* equiv. Fr. *Regnault, Renaud,* Ger. *Reinhold,* It. *Rinaldo,* Sp. *Reynaldos*

re·gion (rē′jən) *n.* [ME. *regioun* < Anglo-Fr. *regiun* < OFr. *region* < L. *regio* < *regere,* to rule: see REGAL] **1.** a large and indefinite part of the surface of the earth; district **2.** a division of the world characterized by a specific kind of plant or animal life **3.** an area; place; space **4.** a particular part of the world or universe **5.** an administrative division of a country, as in Italy or the U.S.S.R. **6.** a sphere or realm, as of art or science **7.** a division or part of an organism, often called after its main part or organ [the abdominal *region*] **8.** any of the levels into which the atmosphere or ocean is thought of as being divided

re·gion·al (-′l) *adj.* **1.** of a whole region, not just a locality **2.** of some particular region, district, etc.; local; sectional —**re′gion·al·ly** *adv.*

re·gion·al·ism (-′l iz′m) *n.* **1.** the division of a country into small administrative regions **2.** regional quality or character **3.** devotion to one's own geographical region **4.** a word, custom, etc. peculiar to a specific region **5.** *Literature a)* the use of a particular region of a country as the setting of stories, plays, etc., so as to depict its influence on the lives of the characters *b)* the tendency to emphasize and value the qualities of life in a particular region, esp. an agrarian region —**re′gion·al·ist** *n., adj.* —**re′gion·al·is′tic** *adj.*

†ré·gis·seur (rā zhē sër′) *n.* [Fr.] a stage director

reg·is·ter (rej′is tər) *n.* [ME. *registre* < MFr. < ML. *registrum,* altered form of *regestum* < LL. *regesta,* records, neut. pl. of L. *regestus,* pp. of *regerere,* to record, lit., to bring back < *re-,* back + *gerere,* to bear: see GESTURE] **1.** *a)* a record or list of names, events, items, etc., often kept by an official appointed to do so *b)* a book in which this is kept *c)* an entry in such a book or record **2.** [prob. altered < ME. *registrer*] a person who keeps such a record, esp. one legally appointed; registrar **3.** registration; registry; enrollment **4.** a device, as a meter or counter, for recording fares paid, money deposited, etc. [a cash *register*] **5.** *a)* a device in a stove or furnace for controlling the draft, etc. *b)* an opening into a room by which the amount of warm or cold air passing, as through a pipe leading from a furnace or ventilator, can be controlled **6.** *Music* a division of the compass of the human voice or of an instrument all the tones of which are of similar quality *b)* a set of organ pipes controlled by a given stop or the tone quality produced by such a set **7.** *Photog.* exact matching in position of the focusing screen and the sensitive film or plate which replaces it **8.** *Printing a)* exact matching in position of pages, lines, etc. on opposite sides of a single sheet *b)* exact imposition of successive colors as they are printed over each other —*vt.* ☆**1.** *a)* to enter in or as in a record or list; enroll or record officially *b)* to transcribe permanently, as if in a register **2.** to indicate on or as on a scale [a thermometer *registers* temperature] **3.** to show, as by facial expression [to *register* surprise] **4.** to safeguard (mail) by having its committal to the postal system recorded, on payment of a fee **5.** *Printing* to cause to be in register —*vi.* ☆**1.** to enter one's name in a register, as of a hotel **2.** to have one's name placed on the list of those eligible to vote in an election, by making application in the prescribed way **3.** to enroll in a school, college, etc. **4.** to make an impression **5.** *Music* to select and combine organ or harpsichord registers **6.** *Printing* to be in register —*SYN.* see LIST¹ —**reg′is·tra·ble** *adj.*

reg·is·tered (-tərd) *adj.* officially recorded or enrolled; specif., *a)* designating bonds, etc. having the owner's name listed in a register *b)* designating dogs, horses, etc. having pedigrees certified and listed by authorized breeders' associations *c)* legally certified or authenticated

registered mail 1. a postal service which, for a fee, provides a record that mail has been sent, and guarantees an indemnity if it is not received **2.** mail sent by this service

☆**registered nurse** a nurse who has completed extensive training and has passed a specific State examination qualifying her to perform complete nursing services

reg·is·trant (-trənt) *n.* [Fr. < ML. *registrans,* prp.] a person who registers

reg·is·trar (rej′i strär′, rej′i strär′) *n.* [ME. *registrer* < ML. *registrarius*] **1.** a person charged with keeping a register; ☆esp., a college or university official responsible for registering students, maintaining their records, etc. **2.** a trust company charged with keeping the records of stock transfers, etc.

reg·is·tra·tion (rej′i strā′shən) *n.* [ML. *registratio*] **1.** a registering or being registered **2.** an entry in a register **3.** the number of persons registered **4.** *Music a)* the act or technique of registering *b)* the combination of registers chosen for playing a given piece of music

reg·is·try (rej′is trē) *n., pl.* -tries **1.** *same as* REGISTRATION **2.** an office where registers are kept **3.** an official record or list; register **4.** a certificate showing the nationality of a merchant ship as recorded in an official register

re·gi·us (rē′jē əs) *adj.* [ModL. < L. < *rex,* a king: see REGAL] designating certain professors at British universities holding chairs founded by royal command

reg·let (reg′lit) *n.* [Fr. *réglet* < *règle,* a rule < L. *regula:* see RULE] **1.** *Archit.* a flat, narrow molding, used to separate panels, etc. **2.** *Printing* a flat strip of wood, lower than the type face, used to separate lines of type **3.** *a)* reglets collectively *b)* material used in making these

reg·nal (reg′nəl) *adj.* [ML. *regnalis* < L. *regnum,* REIGN] of a sovereign, sovereignty, or reign

reg·nant (-nənt) *adj.* [L. *regnans,* prp. of *regnare:* see REIGN] **1.** reigning; ruling **2.** of greatest power; predominant **3.** prevalent; widespread —**reg′nan·cy** *n.*

reg·o·lith (reg′ə lith) *n.* [< Gr. *rhēgos,* a blanket, orig. colored rug (akin to *rhezein,* to dye) + -LITH] *same as* MANTLEROCK

re·gorge (ri gôrj′) *vt.* -gorged′, -gorg′ing [Fr. *regorger:* see RE- & GORGE] to throw up or back; disgorge —*vi.* to flow or gush back, as water

reg·o·sol (reg′ə sôl′, -säl′) *n.* [< REGO(LITH) + L. *solum,* SOIL¹] a soil made up of unconsolidated material without stones and without distinct horizons

re·grant (rē grant′) *vt.* to grant again; renew the grant of —*n.* a renewed or second grant

re·gress (rē′gres; *for v.* ri gres′) *n.* [ME. *regresse* < L. *regressus,* pp. of *regredi,* to go back, return < *re-,* back + *gradi,* to go: see GRADE] **1.** a going or coming back **2.** the right or privilege of this **3.** backward movement; retrogression —*vi.* **1.** to go back; return; move backward **2.** to undergo regression —**re·gres′sor** *n.*

re·gres·sion (ri gresh′ən) *n.* [L. *regressio*] **1.** a regressing, or going back; return; movement backward **2.** *same as* RETROGRESSION **3.** *Astron.* the slow westward shifting of the nodes of the moon's orbit, caused by the attraction of the sun and completing one revolution in about 19 years **4.** *Biol.* reversion to an earlier or simpler form, or to a general or common type **5.** *Med.* a gradual subsiding of a disease or its symptoms **6.** *Psychoanalysis* reversion to earlier or more infantile behavior patterns **7.** *Statistics* a measure of the extent to which two variables increase together or of the extent to which one increases as the other decreases

re·gres·sive (ri gres′iv) *adj.* **1.** regressing or tending to regress **2.** of, like, or characteristic of regression **3.** designating a tax that becomes proportionately lower as the tax base increases —**re·gres′sive·ly** *adv.*

re·gret (ri gret′) *vt.* -gret′ted, -gret′ting [ME. *regretten* < OFr. *regreter,* to bewail the dead < *re-* + (?) Gmc. base seen in OE. *gretan,* ON. *grata,* Goth. *gretan,* to weep] **1.** to feel sorry about or mourn for (a person or thing gone, lost, etc.) **2.** to feel troubled or remorseful over (something that has happened, one's own acts, etc.) —*n.* **1.** a troubled feeling or remorse over something that has happened, esp. over something that one has done or left undone **2.** sorrow over a person or thing gone, lost, etc. —*SYN.* see PENITENCE —(one's) **regrets** a polite expression of regret, as at declining an invitation —**re·gret′ful** *adj.* —**re·gret′ful·ly** *adv.* —**re·gret′ful·ness** *n.* —**re·gret′ter** *n.*

re·gret·ta·ble (-ə b′l) *adj.* to be regretted; unfortunate —**re·gret′ta·bly** *adv.*

re·group (rē grōōp′) *vt., vi.* to group again; specif., *Mil.* to reassemble or reorganize (one's forces), as after a battle

Regt. **1.** Regent **2.** Regiment

reg·u·la·ble (reg′yə lə b′l) *adj.* that can be regulated

reg·u·lar (reg′yə lər) *adj.* [ME. *reguler* < MFr. < L. *regularis,* of a bar (in LL., regular) < *regula:* see RULE] **1.** conforming in form, build, or arrangement to a rule, principle, type, standard, etc.; orderly; symmetrical [*regular* features] **2.** characterized by conformity to a fixed principle or procedure **3.** *a)* usual; customary [his *regular* seat] ☆*b)* not a substitute; established [the *regular* quarterback] **4.** consistent or habitual in action [a *regular* customer] **5.** recurring at set times or functioning in a normal way [a *regular* pulse] **6.** conforming to a standard or to a generally accepted rule or mode of conduct; proper **7.** properly qualified [a *regular* doctor]

regive	reglorify	regrade	regrind
reglaze	reglue	regraft	regrow

8. *same as* CUBIC (sense 3) 9. [Colloq.] thorough; absolute; complete [a *regular* nuisance] ☆10. [Colloq.] pleasant, friendly, reliable, etc. [a *regular* fellow] 11. *Bot.* having all similar parts of the same shape and size; symmetrical: said of flowers 12. *Eccles.* belonging to a religious order or monastic community and adhering to its rule 13. *Gram.* conforming to the usual type in inflection, formation, etc.; specif., *same as* WEAK (adj. 15) 14. *Math.* a) having all angles and sides equal, as a polygon b) having all faces exactly the same, as a polyhedron c) governed by one law throughout, as an equation 15. *Mil.* a) designating or of the permanently constituted, or standing, army of a country b) designating soldiers recognized in international law as legitimate combatants in warfare ☆16. *Politics* designating, of, or loyal to the recognized party leadership, candidates, etc. —n. 1. a member of a religious order, as a monk, friar, etc. 2. a member of a regular army ☆3. a regular member of an athletic team, not a substitute 4. a clothing size for men of average height 5. [Colloq.] one who is regular, as in attendance ☆6. *Politics* a person who is loyal to the recognized party leadership, candidates, etc. —SYN. see NORMAL, STEADY —reg′u·lar′i·ty (-lar′ə tē) n., pl. -ties —reg′u·lar·ly adv.

Regular Army the permanent, or standing, army of the United States; the United States Army: cf. ARMY OF THE UNITED STATES

reg·u·lar·ize (reg′yə lə rīz′) vt. -ized′, -iz′ing to make regular —reg′u·lar·i·za′tion n.

reg·u·late (reg′yə lāt′) vt. -lat′ed, -lat′ing [< LL. *regulatus*, pp. of *regulare*, to rule, regulate < L. *regula*, RULE] 1. to control, direct, or govern according to a rule, principle, or system 2. to adjust to a particular standard, rate, degree, amount, etc. [*regulate* the heat] 3. to adjust (a clock, etc.) so as to make operate accurately 4. to make uniform, methodical, orderly, etc. —reg′u·la′tive, reg′·u·la·to′ry (-lə tôr′ē) adj.

reg·u·la·tion (reg′yə lā′shən) n. [ME. *regulatio*] 1. a regulating or being regulated 2. a rule, ordinance, or law by which conduct, etc. is regulated 3. *Embryology* the process by which a structure, damaged or partially changed in an early stage of an animal embryo, adjusts to the disturbance and develops normally —adj. 1. ordered or required by regulation; prescribed [a *regulation* uniform] 2. usual; normal; ordinary; regular —SYN. see LAW

reg·u·la·tor (reg′yə lāt′ər) n. [ML.] a person or thing that regulates; specif., a) a mechanism for controlling or governing the movement of machinery, the flow of liquids, gases, electricity, steam, etc.; governor b) the part of the works of a watch or clock by which its speed is adjusted c) an accurate timepiece serving as a standard by which others are regulated

Reg·u·lus (reg′yoo ləs) [ModL. < L., dim. of *rex*, king (see REGAL)] *Astron.* a first-magnitude star, the brightest in the constellation Leo —n. [r-] -lus·es, -li′ (-lī′) *Chem.*, *Metallurgy* a) [because of its ready combination with gold, the "king of metals"] metallic antimony: in full **regulus of antimony** b) impure metal produced by the smelting or reduction of various ores c) partly purified metal that sinks by its weight to the bottom of a crucible or furnace when ore is smelted

Reg·u·lus (reg′yoo ləs), (**Marcus Atilius**) ?-250? B.C.; Rom. consul & general in the 1st Punic War

re·gur·gi·tate (ri gur′jə tāt′) vi. -tat′ed, -tat′ing [< ML. *regurgitatus*, pp. of *regurgitare*, to regurgitate < *re-*, back + LL. *gurgitare*, to flood < *gurges* (gen. *gurgitis*): see GORGE] to rush, surge, or flow back —vt. to cause to surge or flow back; specif., to bring (partly digested food) from the stomach back to the mouth —re·gur′gi·tant adj.

re·gur·gi·ta·tion (ri gur′jə tā′shən) n. [ML. *regurgitatio*] a regurgitating; specif., a) the return of partly digested food from the stomach to the mouth, as in a ruminant animal b) a backward flow of blood due to the imperfect closure of a heart valve

re·ha·bil·i·tate (rē′hə bil′ə tāt′, rē′ə-) vt. -tat′ed, -tat′ing [< ML. *rehabilitatus*, pp. of *rehabilitare*, to restore: see RE- & HABILITATE] 1. to restore to rank, privileges, or property which one has lost 2. to restore the good name or reputation of; reinstate in good repute 3. to put back in good condition; reestablish on a firm, sound basis 4. a) to bring or restore to a normal or optimum state of health, constructive activity, etc. by medical treatment and physical or psychological therapy b) to prepare (the handicapped or disadvantaged) for useful employment by vocational counseling, training, etc. —re′ha·bil′i·ta′tion n. —re′ha·bil′i·ta′tive adj.

re·hash (rē hash′; *for n.* rē′hash) vt. [RE- + HASH] to work up again or go over again [to *rehash* the same old arguments] —n. the act or result of rehashing [a *rehash* of an earlier book]

re·hear (rē hir′) vt. **-heard′** (-hurd′), **-hear′ing** *Law* to hear (a case) a second time —re·hear′ing n.

re·hears·al (ri hur′s'l) n. [ME. *rehersaille*: see ff. & -AL] 1. the act of rehearsing, reciting, or recounting [a *rehearsal* of her troubles] 2. a drilling or repeating for practice before future performance 3. a practice performance of a play, concert, etc., or of part of it, in preparation for a public or formal performance —in rehearsal being rehearsed, as a play

re·hearse (ri hurs′) vt. **-hearsed′**, **-hears′ing** [ME. *rehercen* < OFr. *rehercer*, lit., to harrow again < *re-*, again + *hercer*, to harrow < *herce*, a harrow: see HEARSE] 1. to repeat aloud as heard or read; recite 2. to tell in detail; narrate or describe in sequence and at length 3. a) to perform (a play, concert, etc.) for practice, in preparation for a public or formal performance b) to repeat or practice as if rehearsing [to *rehearse* an alibi] 4. to drill or train (a person) by practice in what he is to do —vi. to rehearse a play, concert, etc.

re·heat (rē hēt′) vt. to heat again; specif., to add heat to (a fluid), as in an afterburner —re·heat′er n.

Re·ho·bo·am (rē′hə bō′əm) [Heb. *rehabh'ām*, lit., prob., enlarger of the people] *Bible* the first king of Judah: II Chr. 9:31-12:16 —n. [*often* r-] a large wine bottle, esp. for champagne, usually holding about 1.2 gal.

re·hy·drate (rē hi′drāt′) vt. -drat′ed, -drat′ing to restore water or other liquid to (something that has been dehydrated) —re′hy·dra′tion n.

Reich (rīk; *G.* rīH) n. [G. < OHG. *rihhi*, akin to OE. *rice*, Goth. *reiki* < IE. base *reĝ-*, to direct, rule: cf. REGAL, RIGHT] 1. the Holy Roman Empire, regarded as the first German empire (**First Reich**) 2. Germany or the German government; specif., a) the German Empire from 1871 to 1919 (**Second Reich**) b) the German republic from 1919 to 1933 (**Weimar Republic**) c) the German fascist state under the Nazis from 1933 to 1945 (**Third Reich**)

reichs·mark (rīks′märk′; *G.* rīHs′märk′) n., pl. -marks′, -mark′ [G.: see REICH & MARK[2]] the monetary unit of Germany from 1924 to 1948

Reichs·tag (rīks′täg′; *G.* rīHs′täkh′) n. [G. < *Reich* (see REICH) + *tag*, session, meeting, lit., day: cf. DIET[2]] formerly, the legislative assembly of Germany

re·i·fy (rē′ə fī′) vt. -fied′, -fy′ing [< L. *res*, thing (see REAL[1]) + -FY] to treat (an abstraction) as substantially existing, or as a concrete material object —re′i·fi·ca′tion n.

reign (rān) n. [ME. *regne* < OFr. < L. *regnum* < *regere*, to rule: see REGAL] 1. royal power, authority, or rule; sovereignty 2. dominance, prevalence, or sway [the *reign* of good will] 3. the period of rule, dominance, sway, etc. 4. [Archaic] a kingdom or realm —vi. [ME. *regnen* < OFr. *regner* < L. *regnare*, to rule < *regnum*] 1. a) to rule as a sovereign b) to hold the title of sovereign, as in a constitutional monarchy 2. to hold sway; prevail or predominate [when peace *reigns*]

Reign of Terror the period of the French Revolution from 1793 to 1794, during which many persons were executed as counterrevolutionaries

re·im·burse (rē′im burs′) vt. -bursed′, -burs′ing [RE- + archaic *imburse*, to pay, after Fr. *rembourser* < *re-*, again + *embourser*, to pay < *en-*, in + *bourse*, a PURSE] 1. to pay back (money spent) 2. to repay or compensate (a person) for expenses, damages, losses, etc. —SYN. see PAY[1] —re′im·burs′a·ble adj. —re′im·burse′ment n.

re·im·pres·sion (rē′im presh′ən) n. a second impression; specif., a reprint, as of a book, from the original, unchanged plates

Reims (rēmz; *Fr.* rans) city in NE France: scene of Germany's unconditional surrender to the Allies (1945): pop. 134,000

rein (rān) n. [ME. *rene* < OFr. *resne* < VL. **retina* < L. *retinere*: see RETAIN] 1. a narrow strap of leather attached to each end of the bit in the mouth of a horse, and held by the rider or driver to control the animal: *usually used in pl.*: see HARNESS, illus. 2. [pl.] a means of guiding, controlling, checking, or restraining [the *reins* of government] —vt. to guide, control, check, or restrain with or as with reins —vi. 1. to stop or slow down a horse, etc. with or as with reins (with *in* or *up*) 2. [Archaic] to submit to or be controlled by reins: said of a horse —draw rein 1. to tighten the reins 2. to slow down or stop Also draw in the reins —give (free) rein to to allow to act without restraint —keep a rein on to check, control, or restrain

re·in·car·nate (rē′in kär′nāt) vt. -nat·ed, -nat·ing to incarnate again; cause to undergo reincarnation

re·in·car·na·tion (rē′in kär nā′shən) n. [see prec.] 1. rebirth of the soul in another body, as in Hindu religious belief 2. a new incarnation or embodiment 3. the doctrine that the soul reappears after death in another and different bodily form

rehandle	rehospitalize	reimpose	reinaugurate
rehang	rehouse	reimpregnate	reincite
reharden	reignite	reimprison	reincorporate
rehire	reimplant	reimprisonment	reincur

rein·deer (rān'dir') *n.*, *pl.* **-deer'**, occas. **-deers'** [ME. *reindere* < ON. *hreindȳri* < *hreinn*, reindeer (< IE. *ʻkerei-*, horned animal < base *ʻker-*, top of the head, horn, whence HORN, L. *cerebrum*) + *dȳr*, animal, DEER] a large deer (*Rangifer tarandus*) with branching antlers in both sexes, related to the caribou and found in northern regions, where it is domesticated as a beast of burden and as a source of milk, meat, and leather

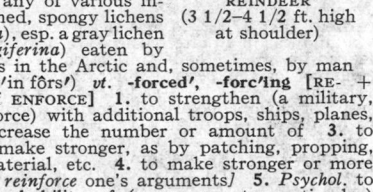

REINDEER
(3 1/2–4 1/2 ft. high at shoulder)

Reindeer Lake [transl. of AmInd. name] lake in NE Saskatchewan & NW Manitoba, Canada: 2,467 sq. mi.

reindeer moss any of various intricately branched, spongy lichens (genus *Cladonia*), esp. a gray lichen (*Cladonia rangiferina*) eaten by grazing animals in the Arctic and, sometimes, by man

re·in·force (rē'in fôrs') *vt.* **-forced', -forc'ing** [RE- + *inforce*, var. of ENFORCE] **1.** to strengthen (a military, naval, or air force) with additional troops, ships, planes, etc. **2.** to increase the number or amount of **3.** to strengthen or make stronger, as by patching, propping, adding new material, etc. **4.** to make stronger or more compelling [to *reinforce* one's arguments] **5.** *Psychol.* to increase the probability of (a response to a stimulus) by giving a reward or ending a painful stimulus —**re'in·forc'er** *n.*

reinforced concrete concrete masonry containing steel bars or mesh to increase its tensile strength

re·in·force·ment (-mənt) *n.* **1.** a reinforcing or being reinforced **2.** anything that reinforces; specif., [*pl.*] additional troops, ships, etc. **3.** *Physiol., Psychol.* any action or event that reinforces a response

Rein·hardt (rin'härt), **Max** (born *Max Goldmann*) 1873–1943; Austrian theatrical director & producer in Germany and later in the U.S.

reins (rānz) *n.pl.* [ME. *reines* < OFr. *reins* < L. *renes*, pl. of *ren*, kidney] [Archaic] **1.** the kidneys, or the region of the kidneys **2.** the loins, thought of as the seat of the emotions and affections **3.** the emotions and affections

re·in·state (rē'in stāt') *vt.* **-stat'ed, -stat'ing** to instate again; restore to a former condition, position, etc. —**re'in·state'ment** *n.*

re·in·sure (rē'in shoor') *vt.* **-sured', -sur'ing** to insure again, esp. under a contract by which the first insurer protects himself by transferring all or part of the risk to another insurer —**re'in·sur'ance** *n.* —**re'in·sur'er** *n.*

re·in·ter·pret (rē'in tur'prit) *vt.* to interpret again; specif., to give a new explanation or exposition of —**re'in·ter'pre·ta'tion** *n.*

reis (rās) *n.pl. sing.* **re·al** (re äl') [Port. *pl.* of *real*, REAL²] a former Portuguese and Brazilian money of account

re·it·er·ate (rē it'ə rāt') *vt.* **-at'ed, -at'ing** [< L. *reiteratus*, pp. of *reiterare*, to repeat: see RE- & ITERATE] to repeat (something done or said); say or do again or repeatedly —*SYN.* see REPEAT —**re·it'er·a'tion** *n.* —**re·it'er·a'tive** (-ə rāt'iv, -ər ə tiv) *adj.* —**re·it'er·a'tive·ly** *adv.*

reive (rēv) *vt.* same as REAVE¹ —**reiv'er** *n.*

re·ject (ri jekt'; *for n.* rē'jekt) *vt.* [LME. *rejecten* < L. *rejectus*, pp. of *reicere, rejicere*, to throw or fling back < *re-*, back + *jacere*, to throw: see JET¹] **1.** to refuse to take, agree to, accede to, use, believe, etc. **2.** to discard or throw out as worthless, useless, or substandard; cast off or out **3.** to pass over or skip from (a record set by a record changer) without playing **4.** to throw up (food); vomit **5.** to rebuff; esp., to deny acceptance, care, love, etc. to (someone) [a *rejected* child] **6.** *Physiol.* to be incompatible with (a part or organ grafted or transplanted into the body) —*n.* a rejected thing or person —*SYN.* see DECLINE —**re·ject'ee'** *n.* —**re·ject'er, re·jec'tor** *n.* — **re·jec'tion** *n.* —**re·jec'tive** *adj.*

rejection slip a form or note from a publisher, rejecting a work submitted for possible publication

re·joice (ri jois') *vi.* **-joiced', -joic'ing** [ME. *rejoissen* < inflectional stem of OFr. *rejoïr* < *re-* + *joïr* < VL. *gaudere*, for *gaudere*, to rejoice: see JOY] to be glad, happy, or delighted; be full of joy (often with *at* or *in*) —*vt.* to make glad; delight —**re·joic'ing·ly** *adv.*

re·joic·ing (-joi'sin) *n.* **1.** the action or feeling of one who rejoices **2.** [often *pl.*] an occasion for joy

re·join¹ (rē join') *vt.* [< MFr. *rejoindre*: see ff.] **1.** to come into the company of again **2.** to join together again; reunite **3.** to become a member of again after a lapse in membership —*vi.* to become joined together again; be reunited

re·join² (ri join') *vt.* [LME. *rejoynen* < Anglo-Fr. *rejoyner*, to reply to a charge < MFr. *rejoindre*, to join again: see RE- & JOIN] to say in answer —*vi.* **1.** to answer **2.** *Law* to answer the plaintiff's replication —*SYN.* see ANSWER

re·join·der (-dər) *n.* [LME. *rejoyner* < Anglo-Fr. substantive use of inf. *rejoindre*: see prec.] **1.** *a)* an answer to a reply *b)* a reply; answer **2.** *Law* the defendant's answer to the plaintiff's replication

re·ju·ve·nate (ri jōō'və nāt') *vt.* **-nat'ed, -nat'ing** [< RE- + L. *juvenis*, young + -ATE¹] **1.** *a)* to make feel or seem young again; bring back to youthful strength, appearance, etc. *b)* to make seem new or fresh again **2.** *Geol. a)* to increase the grade and speed of flow of (a stream), usually by uplift of the surrounding land *b)* to give youthful land forms to (a region), as steep slopes —*vi.* to restore or reacquire a youthful or new appearance —**re·ju've·na'tion** *n.* —**re·ju've·na'tor** *n.*

re·ju·ve·nes·cence (ri jōō'və nes''ns) *n.* [< L. *re-*, again <*juvenescens*, prp. of *juvenescere*, to become young < *juvenis*, YOUNG] renewal of youthfulness —**re·ju've·nes'cent** *adj.*

rel. 1. relating **2.** relative **3.** relatively **4.** religion **5.** religious

re·laid (rē lād') *pt. & pp.* of RE-LAY

re·lapse (ri laps'; *for n.* also rē'laps) *vi.* **-lapsed', -laps'ing** [< L. *relapsus*, pp. of *relabi*, to slip or slide back: see RE- & LAPSE] to slip or fall back into a former condition, esp. after improvement or seeming improvement; specif., *a)* to fall back into illness *b)* to fall back into bad habits, wrongdoing, etc.; backslide —*n.* **1.** the act or an instance of relapsing **2.** the recurrence of a disease after apparent improvement —**re·laps'er** *n.*

relapsing fever any of various acute infectious diseases caused by certain spirochetes (genus *Borrelia*) transmitted by ticks or lice, and characterized by recurrent attacks of fever and chills

re·late (ri lāt') *vt.* **-lat'ed, -lat'ing** [< L. *relatus*, pp. of *referre*, to bring back: see REFER] **1.** to tell the story of; narrate; recount **2.** to connect or associate, as in thought or meaning; show as having to do with; show a relation between [to *relate* theory and practice] —*vi.* **1.** *a)* to have some connection or relation (*to*) *b)* to show sympathetic understanding and awareness in one's personal relationships **2.** to have reference (*to*) —*SYN.* see TELL¹ —**re·lat'a·ble** *adj.* —**re·lat'er** *n.*

re·lat·ed (-lāt'id) *adj.* **1.** narrated; recounted; told **2.** connected or associated, as by origin or kind; specif., connected by kinship, marriage, etc.; of the same family **3.** *Music* closely connected melodically or harmonically: said of tones, chords, etc. —**re·lat'ed·ness** *n.*

SYN.—related, applied to persons, implies close connection through consanguinity or, less often, through marriage [we are *related* through our mothers], applied to things, close connection through common origin, interdependence, etc. [*related* subjects]; **kindred** basically suggests blood relationship but in extension connotes close connection as because of similar nature, tastes, goals, etc. [we are *kindred* souls]; **cognate** now usually applies to things and suggests connection because of a common source [*cognate* languages]; **allied**, applied to persons, suggests connection through voluntary association; applied to things, connection through inclusion in the same category [*allied* sciences]; **affiliate** usually suggests alliance of a smaller or weaker party with a larger or stronger one as a branch or dependent [several companies are *affiliated* with this corporation]

re·la·tion (ri lā'shən) *n.* [ME. *relacion* < MFr. or L.: MFr. *relation* < L. *relatio*: see RELATE] **1.** a narrating, recounting, or telling **2.** what is narrated or told; account; recital **3.** connection or manner of being connected or related, as in thought, meaning, etc. **4.** connection of persons by blood or marriage; kinship **5.** a person connected with another or others by blood or marriage; member of the same family; relative **6.** [*pl.*] *a)* the connections or dealings between or among persons in business or private affairs *b)* sexual intercourse *c)* the connections or dealings between or among groups, peoples, nations, states, etc. [foreign and trade *relations*] **7.** *Law a)* the statement of a relator at whose complaint an action is begun *b)* the referring of an act or proceeding to a time before its completion or enactment, as the time of its taking effect —**in** (or **with**) **relation to** concerning; regarding; with reference to

re·la·tion·al (-'l) *adj.* **1.** of relation or relations **2.** showing or specifying relation **3.** *Gram. a)* showing relations of syntax: said of conjunctions, prepositions, relative pronouns, etc. *b)* having to do with grammatical relations that frequently recur [the dative, genitive, etc. are *relational* cases]

re·la·tion·ship (-ship') *n.* **1.** the quality or state of being related; connection **2.** connection by blood or marriage; kinship **3.** a particular instance of being related

reinduce	reinsert	reinterrogate	reinvite
reinfect	reinspect	reintrench	reinvolve
reinflate	reinspire	reintroduce	reissue
reinform	reinstall	reintroduction	rejudge
reinfuse	reinstitute	reinvent	rekindle
reinhabit	reinstruct	reinvest	reknit
reinoculate	reinter	reinvestigate	relabel
reinscribe	reinterment	reinvigorate	relace

rel·a·tive (rel′ə tiv) *adj.* [< MFr. or L.: MFr. *relatif* < L. *relativus* < L. *relatus*: see RELATE] **1.** related each to the other; dependent upon or referring to each other [to stay in the same *relative* positions] **2.** having to do with; pertinent; relevant [documents *relative* to his life] **3.** regarded in relation to something else; comparative [living in *relative* comfort] **4.** meaningful only in relationship; not absolute ["cold" is a *relative* term] **5.** *Gram.* **a)** designating a word that introduces a subordinate clause and refers to an antecedent ["which" is a *relative* pronoun in "the hat which you bought"] **b)** introduced by such a word [a *relative* clause] —*n.* **1.** a relative word, term, or thing **2.** a person connected with another by blood or marriage; kinsman or kinswoman **3.** a plant or animal in the same taxonomic division as another —**relative to 1.** relevant to; concerning; about **2.** corresponding to; in proportion to —**rel′a·tive·ness** *n.*

relative humidity *see* HUMIDITY

rel·a·tive·ly (-lē) *adv.* in a relative manner; in relation to or compared with something else; not absolutely [a *relatively* unimportant matter]

relative major *Music* the major key whose tonic is the third degree of a specified minor key

relative minor *Music* the minor key whose tonic is the sixth degree of a specified major key

rel·a·tiv·ism (-iz′m) *n. Philos.* any theory of ethics or knowledge which maintains that the basis of judgment is relative, differing according to events, persons, etc. —**rel′a·tiv·ist** *n.* —**rel′a·tiv·is′tic** *adj.*

rel·a·tiv·i·ty (rel′ə tiv′ə tē) *n.* **1.** the condition, fact, or quality of being relative **2.** the close dependence of one occurrence, value, quality, etc. on another **3.** *Philos.* same as: **a)** RELATIVISM **b)** RELATIVITY OF KNOWLEDGE **4.** *Physics* the fact, principle, or theory of the relative, rather than absolute, character of motion, velocity, mass, etc., and the interdependence of matter, time, and space: as developed and mathematically formulated by Albert Einstein and H. A. Lorentz in the **special** (or **restricted**) **theory of relativity** and by Einstein in the **general theory of relativity** (an extension covering the phenomena of gravitation), the theory of relativity includes the statements that: 1) there is no observable absolute motion, only relative motion 2) the velocity of light is constant and not dependent on the motion of the source 3) no energy can be transmitted at a velocity greater than that of light 4) the mass of a body in motion is a function of the energy content and varies with the velocity 5) matter and energy are equivalent 6) time is relative 7) space and time are interdependent and form a four-dimensional continuum 8) the presence of matter results in a "warping" of the space-time continuum, so that a body in motion passing nearby will describe a curve, this being the effect known as gravitation, as evidenced by the deflection of light rays passing through a gravitational field

relativity of knowledge *Philos.* the theory that all knowledge is relative to the mind, or that things can be known only through their effects on the mind, and that consequently there can be no knowledge of reality as it is in itself

rel·a·tiv·ize (rel′ə tiv iz′) *vt.* **-ized′, -iz′ing** to think of or treat as relative —**rel′a·tiv·i·za′tion** *n.*

re·la·tor (ri lāt′ər) *n.* [L.] **1.** a person who relates, or tells; relater **2.** *Law* a private person at whose prompting or complaint a public action is begun to bring in question the exercise of an office, franchise, etc.

re·lax (ri laks′) *vt.* [ME. *relaxen*, to loosen < L. *relaxare* < *re-*, back + *laxare*, to loosen, widen < *laxus*, loose: cf. LAX] **1.** to make looser, or less firm or tense [to *relax* one's grip] **2.** to make less strict or severe; soften [to *relax* discipline] **3.** to abate; reduce; slacken [to *relax* one's efforts] **4.** to release from intense concentration, hard work, worry, etc.; give rest to [to *relax* the mind] —*vi.* **1.** to become looser or less firm, as the muscles **2.** to become less tense or stern, as one's features **3.** to become less strict, or milder, as discipline **4.** to become easier, or less stiff, in manner **5.** to rest from effort, worry, or work, as by lying down, engaging in recreation, etc. —**re·lax′er** *n.*

re·lax·ant (-ənt) *adj.* of, pertaining to, or causing relaxation, esp. reduction of muscular tension —*n.* a relaxant drug or agent

re·lax·a·tion (rē′lak sā′shən) *n.* [L. *relaxatio* < pp. of *relaxare*] **1.** a relaxing or being relaxed; loosening, lessening of severity, etc. **2. a)** a lessening of or rest from work, worry, or effort **b)** recreation or other activity for bringing this about

re·lax·ed·ly (ri lak′sid lē) *adv.* in a relaxed manner

☆**re·lax·in** (ri lak′sin) *n.* [RELAX + -IN¹] a polypeptide hormone associated with pregnancy, used experimentally to relax the pelvic ligaments, as in childbirth

re·lay (rē′lā; *for v.,* also ri lā′) *n.* [ME. *relai* < MFr. *relais*, pl., orig., hounds kept as reserves at points along the course of a hunt < *relaier*, to leave behind < *re-* (see RE-) + *laier*,

to leave, let: see DELAY] **1.** a fresh supply of dogs, horses, etc., kept in readiness to relieve others in a hunt, on a journey, etc. **2.** a crew of workers relieving others at work; shift **3. a)** *same as* RELAY RACE **b)** any of the legs, or laps, of a relay race **4.** an act or instance of conveying or transmitting by or as by relays **5.** *same as* SERVOMOTOR **6.** *Elec.* an electromagnetic device activated by a variation in conditions in one electric circuit and controlling a larger current or actuating other devices in the same or another electric circuit: used in telegraphy, electrical controls, etc. —*vt.* **-layed′, -lay′ing 1.** to convey by relays **2.** to convey as if by relays; receive and pass on (a message, news, etc.) **3.** to supply or replace with a relay or relays **4.** *Elec.* to control, operate, or send on by a relay

re·lay (rē′lā′) *vt.* **-laid′, -lay′ing** to lay again or anew: also written **re′lay′**

relay race a race between two or more teams, each runner going in turn only a part of the total distance

re·lease (ri lēs′) *vt.* **-leased′, -leas′ing** [ME. *relesen* < OFr. *relaisser* < L. *relaxare*: see RELAX] **1.** to set free, as from confinement duty, work, etc. **2.** to let go or let loose [to *release* an arrow] **3.** to grant freedom from a tax, penalty, obligation, etc. **4.** to set free from pain, cares, etc.; relieve ☆**5.** to permit to be issued, shown, published, broadcast, etc.; put into circulation **6.** *Law* to give up or surrender to someone else (a claim, right, etc.) —*n.* **1.** a setting free or being set free; deliverance; liberation **2.** a freeing or being freed from a tax, obligation, etc. **3. a)** a relief from pain, cares, etc. **b)** relief from emotional tension through a spontaneous, uninhibited expression of an emotion **4.** a document authorizing release, as from an obligation, from prison, etc. **5.** the act of letting loose something caught, held in position, etc. **6.** a device to release a catch, etc., as for starting or stopping a machine ☆**7. a)** the act of releasing a book, film, news story, etc. to the public **b)** the book, film, news story, etc. released **8.** *Music* **a)** the act or method of ending a tone ☆**b)** the third group of four measures in a common form of sixteen-bar chorus, as in a popular tune, which supplies a bridge between repetitions of the melody **9.** *Law* **a)** a giving up or surrender to someone else, as of a claim or right **b)** the document by which this is done; quitclaim —*SYN.* see FREE

re·lease (rē′lēs′) *vt.* **-leased′, -leas′ing** to lease again

☆**released time** regularly scheduled periods when pupils in some public school systems are excused for religious instruction off the school premises

rel·e·gate (rel′ə gāt′) *vt.* **-gat′ed, -gat′ing** [< L. *relegatus*, pp. of *relegare*, to send away < *re-*, away, back + *legare*, to send] **1.** to exile or banish (*to* a specified place) **2.** to consign or assign to an inferior position **3.** to assign to a class, sphere, realm, etc.; classify as belonging to a certain order of things **4.** to refer, commit, or hand over for decision, action, etc. —*SYN.* see COMMIT —**rel′e·ga′tion** *n.*

re·lent (ri lent′) *vi.* [ME. *relenten*, to melt, ult. < L. < *re-*, again + *lentus*, flexible, pliant, slow] **1.** to soften in temper, resolution, etc.; become less severe, stern, or stubborn **2.** [Obs.] to melt —*vt.* [Obs.] to cause to relent —*SYN.* see YIELD

re·lent·less (-lis) *adj.* **1.** not relenting; harsh; pitiless **2.** persistent; unremitting —**re·lent′less·ly** *adv.* —**re·lent′less·ness** *n.*

rel·e·vant (rel′ə vənt) *adj.* [ML. *relevans*, prp. of *relevare*, to bear upon < L., to lift up: see RELIEVE] bearing upon or relating to the matter in hand; pertinent; to the point —**rel′e·vance, rel′e·van·cy** *n.* —**rel′e·vant·ly** *adv.*

SYN.—**relevant** implies close logical relationship with, and importance to, the matter under consideration [*relevant* testimony]; **germane** implies such close natural connection as to be highly appropriate or fit [your reminiscences are not truly *germane* to this discussion]; **pertinent** implies an immediate and direct bearing on the matter in hand [a *pertinent* suggestion]; **apposite** applies to that which is both relevant and happily suitable or appropriate [an *apposite* analogy]; **applicable** refers to that which can be brought to bear upon a particular matter or problem [your description is *applicable* to several people]; **apropos** is used of that which is opportune as well as relevant [an *apropos* remark] —*ANT.* **inappropriate, extraneous**

re·li·a·ble (ri lī′ə b'l) *adj.* that can be relied on; dependable; trustworthy —**re·li′a·bil′i·ty, re·li′a·ble·ness** *n.* —**re·li′a·bly** *adv.*

SYN.—**reliable** is applied to a person or thing that can be counted upon to do what is expected or required [his *reliable* assistant]; **dependable** refers to a person or thing that can be depended on as in an emergency and often connotes levelheadedness or steadiness [she is a *dependable* friend]; **trustworthy** applies to a person, or sometimes a thing, whose truthfulness, integrity, discretion, etc. can be relied on [a *trustworthy* source of information]; **trusty** applies to a person or thing which continued experience has shown to be completely trustworthy or dependable [his *trusty* steed]

re·li·ance (-əns) *n.* **1.** the act of relying **2.** trust, dependence, or confidence **3.** a thing relied on

re·li·ant (-ənt) *adj.* having or showing trust, dependence, or confidence; dependent (*on*) —**re·li′ant·ly** *adv.*

---

relaunch	relaunder	relearn	relet

---

rel·ic (rel′ik) *n.* [ME. *relike* < OFr. *relique* < L. *reliquiae*, *pl.*, remains < *relinquere*: see RELINQUISH] **1.** *a)* an object, custom, etc. that has survived, wholly or partially, from the past *b)* something that has historic interest because of its age and associations with the past, or that serves as a keepsake, or souvenir **2.** [*pl.*] remaining fragments; surviving parts; ruins **3.** [*pl.*] *archaic var. of* REMAINS (sense 4) **4.** *same as* RELICT (*n.* 2) **5.** *Eccles.* the body or a body part of, or some object associated with, a saint, martyr, etc., kept and reverenced as a memorial, as in the Roman Catholic and Orthodox Eastern churches

rel·ict (ri likt′; *for n.* rel′ikt) *adj.* [L. *relictus*, pp. of *relinquere*: see RELINQUISH] [Archaic] a widow **2.** [< the *adj.*] *a) Biol., Ecol.* a plant or animal species living on in isolation in a small local area as a survival from an earlier period or as a remnant of an almost extinct group *b) Geol.* a physical feature, mineral, structure, etc. remaining after other components have wasted away or been altered —*n.* **1.** [LL. *relicta* < L. *relictus*]

re·lief (ri lēf′) *n.* [ME. *releef* < OFr. *relief* < *relever*: see RELIEVE] **1.** *a)* an easing, as of pain, discomfort, or anxiety *b)* a lightening of a burden, as of taxation, oppression, etc. **2.** anything that lessens tension or strain, or offers a pleasing change, as to the mind or eye **3.** aid in the form of goods or money given, as by a government agency, to persons unable to support themselves **4.** any aid given in times of need, danger, or disaster, as supplies sent into a flooded area **5.** *a)* release from work or duty *b)* the person or persons bringing such release by taking over a post **6.** a payment made by the heir of a feudal vassal to the overlord on taking over an estate **7.** [Fr. < It. *relievo* < *rilevare*, to raise: see RELIEVE] *Archit., Sculpture a)* the projection of figures and forms from a flat surface, so that they stand wholly or partly free *b)* a work of art so made **8.** *Law* the assistance or redress sought by a complainant in a court, esp. a court of equity **9.** *Literature, Drama a)* sharp contrast, as of ideas, actions, or events *b)* comic scenes in a serious drama or motion picture: in full **comic relief 10.** *a) Painting* the apparent solidity or projection of objects, obtained by modeling and gradation in color, etc. *b)* distinctness of outline; contrast **11.** *Physical Geog. a)* the differences in height, collectively, of land forms in any particular area *b)* these differences as shown by lines, colors, raised areas, etc. on a map **12.** *Printing* a method of printing in which the image is carried on raised surfaces; letterpress —☆*adj. Baseball* designating a pitcher who replaces another during a game, esp. one who is regularly used in this way —**in relief** carved or molded so as to project from a surface —**on relief** receiving government aid because of poverty, unemployment, etc.

relief map a map showing by color, raised areas, etc., the different heights of land forms, as hills and valleys

re·lieve (ri lēv′) *vt.* **-lieved′, -liev′ing** [ME. *releven* < OFr. *relever* < L. *relevare*, to lift up again < *re-*, again + *levare*, to raise: see LEVER] **1.** *a)* to ease, lighten, or reduce (pain, anxiety, etc.) *b)* to free (a person) from pain, discomfort, anxiety, etc. *c)* to restore (a part of the body, the mind, etc.) to well-being **2.** *a)* to lighten the pressure, stress, weight, etc. on (something) *b)* to lighten (pressure, stress, etc.) **3.** *a)* to give aid or assistance to [to *relieve* the poor] *b)* to bring or send help to [to *relieve* a besieged city] **4.** *a)* to set free from a burden, obligation, grievance, etc. *b)* to remove (a burden, etc.) **5.** to set free from duty or work by replacing with oneself or another [to *relieve* a nurse]; specif., ☆*Baseball* to serve as a relief pitcher for **6.** to make less tedious, monotonous, etc. by being or providing a pleasing change **7.** to set off by contrast; make distinct or prominent **8.** to ease (oneself) by urinating or defecating —**re·liev′a·ble** *adj.* —**re·liev′er** *n.*

SYN.—relieve implies the reduction of misery, discomfort, or tediousness sufficiently to make it bearable [they played a game to *relieve* the monotony of the trip]; **alleviate** implies temporary relief, suggesting that the source of the misery remains unaffected [drugs to *alleviate* the pain]; **lighten** implies a cheering or gladdening as by reducing the weight of oppression or depression [nothing can *lighten* the burden of her grief]; **assuage** suggests a softening or pacifying influence in lessening pain, calming passion, etc. [her kind words *assuaged* his resentment]; **mitigate** implies a moderating or making milder of that which is likely to cause pain [to *mitigate* a punishment]; **allay** suggests an effective, although temporary or incomplete, calming or quieting [we've *allayed* his suspicions] See also COMFORT

re·lie·vo (ri lē′vō, ril yev′ō) *n.*, *pl.* **-vos** *same as* RELIEF (sense 7).

relig. 1. religion **2.** religious

re·li·gion (ri lij′ən) *n.* [ME. *religioun* < OFr. or L.: OFr. *religion* < L. *religio*, reverence for the gods, holiness, in LL.(Ec.), a system of religious belief < *? religare*, to bind back < *re-*, back + *ligare*, to bind, bind together; or < *? re-* + IE. base *leg-*, to collect, whence Gr. *legein*, L. *legere*: cf. LOGIC] **1.** *a)* belief in a divine or superhuman power or powers to be obeyed and worshiped as the creator(s) and ruler(s) of the universe *b)* expression of such a belief in conduct and ritual **2.** *a)* any specific system of belief, worship, conduct, etc., often involving a code of ethics and a philosophy [the Christian *religion*, the Buddhist *religion*, etc.] *b)* any system of beliefs, practices, ethical values, etc. resembling, suggestive of, or likened to such a system [humanism as a *religion*] **3.** the state or way of life of a person in a monastic order or community [to enter *religion*] **4.** any object of conscientious regard and pursuit —☆**get religion** [Colloq.] **1.** to become religious **2.** to become very conscientious or earnest about something

re·li·gion·ism (-iz′m) *n.* religious zeal, esp. when excessive or affected —**re·li′gion·ist** *n.*

re·li·gi·os·i·ty (ri lij′ē äs′ə tē) *n.* [ME. *religiosite* < LL. (Ec.) *religiositas*] the quality of being religious, esp. of being excessively, ostentatiously, or mawkishly religious —**re·li′gi·ose′** (-ōs′) *adj.*

re·li·gious (ri lij′əs) *adj.* [ME. < OFr. < L. *religiosus*] **1.** characterized by adherence to religion or a religion; devout; pious; godly **2.** of, concerned with, appropriate to, or teaching religion [*religious* books] **3.** belonging to a community of monks, nuns, etc. **4.** conscientiously exact; careful; scrupulous —*n.*, *pl.* **-gious** a member of a community of monks, nuns, etc. —*SYN.* see DEVOUT — **re·li′gious·ly** *adv.* —**re·li′gious·ness** *n.*

re·line (rē līn′) *vt.* **-lined′, -lin′ing 1.** to mark with new lines **2.** to provide with a new lining

re·lin·quish (ri lin′kwish) *vt.* [LME. *relinquissen* < extended stem of OFr. *relinquir* < L. *relinquere* < *re-*, from + *linquere*, to leave: for IE. base see LOAN] **1.** to give up; abandon (a plan, policy, etc.) **2.** to renounce or surrender (something owned, a right, etc.) **3.** to let go (a grasp, hold, etc.) —**re·lin′quish·ment** *n.*

SYN.—relinquish implies a giving up of something desirable and connotes compulsion or the force of necessity [he will not *relinquish* his advantage]; **abandon**, in this connection, implies a complete and final relinquishment, as because of weariness, discouragement, etc. [do not *abandon* hope]; **waive** suggests a voluntary relinquishing by refusing to insist on one's right or claim to something [to *waive* a jury trial]; **forgo** implies the denial to oneself of something, as for reasons of expediency or altruism [I must *forgo* the pleasure of your company this evening] See also SURRENDER — *ANT.* keep, retain

rel·i·quar·y (rel′ə kwer′ē) *n.*, *pl.* **-quar′ies** [Fr. *reliquaire* < L. *reliquiae*: see RELIC] a small box, casket, or shrine in which relics are kept and shown

rel·ique (rel′ik, ri lēk′) *n. archaic var. of* RELIC

re·liq·ui·ae (ri lik′wē ē′) *n.pl.* [L.: see RELIC] remains, as of fossil organisms

rel·ish (rel′ish) *n.* [ME. *reles* < OFr. *relais*, something remaining < *relaisser*: see RELEASE] **1.** distinctive or characteristic flavor [a *relish* of garlic in the stew] **2.** a trace or touch (*of* some quality); hint or suggestion [a *relish* of malice in his action] **3.** an appetizing flavor; pleasing taste **4.** *a)* pleasure; enjoyment; zest [to listen with *relish*] *b)* liking or craving [showing little *relish* for the task] **5.** anything that gives pleasure, zest, or enjoyment; attractive quality **6.** any of a variety of foods, as pickles, olives, piccalilli, raw vegetables, etc., served with a meal to add flavor or as an appetizer —*vt.* **1.** [Now Rare] to give flavor to **2.** to enjoy; like —*vi.* **1.** to taste or have the flavor (*of* something) **2.** to have a pleasing taste

re·live (rē liv′) *vt.* **-lived′, -liv′ing** to experience again (a past event) as in the imagination

☆**re·lo·cate** (rē lō′kāt) *vt., vi.* **-cat·ed, -cat·ing 1.** to locate again **2.** to move to a new location —**re′lo·ca′tion** *n.*

re·lu·cent (ri lōō′s′nt) *adj.* [L. *relucens*, prp. of *relucere*: see RE- & LUCENT] reflecting light; bright

re·luct (ri lukt′) *vi.* [L. *reluctari* (see RELUCTANT): in later use prob. back-formation < RELUCTANCE or RELUCTANT] [Rare] **1.** to struggle (*against*); revolt (*at*) **2.** to offer opposition; show reluctance

re·luc·tance (ri luk′təns) *n.* **1.** the fact or state of being reluctant; unwillingness **2.** [Rare] opposition; revolt **3.** *Elec.* the resistance offered to magnetic flux by a magnetic circuit, equal to the magnetomotive force divided by the magnetic flux Also [Rare] **re·luc′tan·cy**

re·luc·tant (-tənt) *adj.* [L. *reluctans*, prp. of *reluctari*, to resist < *re-*, against + *luctari*, to struggle: for IE. base see LOCK[1]] **1.** opposed in mind (*to do* something); unwilling; disinclined **2.** marked by unwillingness [a *reluctant* answer] **3.** [Rare] struggling against; resisting; opposing —**re·luc′tant·ly** *adv.*

SYN.—reluctant implies an unwillingness to do something, as because of distaste, irresolution, etc. [she was *reluctant* to marry]; **disinclined** suggests a lack of desire for something, as because it fails to suit one's taste or because one disapproves of it [I feel *disinclined* to argue]; **hesitant** implies a refraining from action, as because of fear, indecision, etc. [don't be *hesitant* about asking this favor]; **loath** suggests strong disinclination or a decided unwillingness [I am *loath* to depart]; **averse** suggests a sustained, although not extreme, disinclination [she is *averse* to borrowing money] —*ANT.* inclined, disposed, eager

re·luc·tiv·i·ty (rel′ək tiv′ə tē) *n.* the reciprocal of magnetic permeability

re·lume (rē lōōm′) *vt.* **-lumed′, -lum′ing** [RE- + (IL)LUME] [Archaic] **1.** to light again; rekindle **2.** to light up again; illuminate or shine on again Also **re·lu′mine** (-lōō′mən) **-mined, -min·ing**

re·ly (ri lī′) *vi.* **-lied′, -ly′ing** [ME. *relien*, to rally < OFr.

relier < L. *religare:* see RELIGION] **1.** to have confidence; trust **2.** to look to for support or aid; depend Used with *on* or *upon*
SYN.—to **rely** (*on* or *upon*) a person or thing is to have confidence, usually on the basis of past experience, that he or it will do what is expected /he can be *relied* on to keep the secret/; to **trust** is to have complete faith or assurance that one will not be let down by another /to *trust* in God/; to **depend** (*on* or *upon*) a person or thing is to rely on him or it for support or aid /he can *depend* on his wife for sympathy/; to **count** (*on*) or, colloquially, to **reckon** (*on*) something is to consider it in one's calculations as certain /they *counted*, on or *reckoned*, on my going/; to **bank** (*on*), a colloquial term, is to have confidence like that of one who is willing to risk money on something /don't *bank* on his help/
REM (rem) *n., pl.* **REMs** [*r(apid) e(ye) m(ovement)*] *Psychol.* the periodic, rapid, jerky movement of the eyeballs under closed lids during stages of sleep associated with dreaming
rem (rem) *n., pl.* **rem** [*r(oentgen) e(quivalent), m(an)*] a dosage of any ionizing radiation that will produce a biological effect approximately equal to that produced by one roentgen of X-ray or gamma-ray radiation
re·main (ri mān′) *vi.* [ME. *remainen* < OFr. *remaindre* < L. *remanere* < *re-*, back, behind + *manere*, to stay: see MANOR] **1.** to be left or left over when the rest has been taken away, destroyed, or disposed of in some way **2.** *a)* to stay while others go *b)* to stay in the same place /remain in the house/ **3.** to continue; go on being /to *remain* a cynic/ **4.** to continue to exist; endure; persist; last /a *remaining* memory/ **5.** to be left to be dealt with, done, said, etc. —**SYN.** see STAY
re·main·der(-dər) *n.* [ME. *remaindre* < Anglo-Fr. substantive use of OFr. inf.: see REMAIN] **1.** those remaining **2.** what is left when a part is taken away; the rest **3.** a copy or number of copies of a book still held by a publisher when the sale has fallen off, usually disposed of at a greatly reduced price **4.** *Law* an estate of expectancy but not in possession, as when land is conveyed by the same deed to one person during his lifetime, and at his death to another and his heirs **5.** *Math. a)* what is left when a smaller number is subtracted from a larger *b)* what is left undivided when one number is divided by another that is not one of its factors —*adj.* [Rare] remaining; leftover —*vt.* to sell (books, etc.) as remainders
SYN.—**remainder** is the general word applied to what is left when a part is taken away /the *remainder* of a meal, one's life, etc./; **residue** and **residuum** apply to what remains at the end of a process, as after the evaporation or combustion of matter or after the settlement of claims, etc. in a testator's estate; **remnant** is applied to a fragment, trace, or any small part left after the greater part has been removed /remnants of cloth from the ends of bolts/; **balance** may be used in place of **remainder**, but in strict use it implies the amount remaining on the credit or debit side
re·mains (ri mānz′) *n.pl.* **1.** what is left after part has been used, destroyed, etc.; remainder; remnant **2.** vestiges or traces of the past **3.** a dead body; corpse **4.** writings left unpublished by an author at his death
re·make (rē māk′; *for n.* rē′māk′) *vt.* **-made′, -mak′ing** to make again or anew —*n.* **1.** the act of remaking **2.** something remade, as a motion picture
re·man (rē man′) *vt.* **-manned′, -man′ning 1.** to man (a boat, etc.) again **2.** to give new manliness or courage to
re·mand (ri mand′) *vt.* [ME. *remaunden* < OFr. *remander* < LL. *remandare*, to notify in return < L. *re-*, back + *mandare*, to order: see MANDATE] **1.** to send back; order to go back **2.** *Law a)* to send (a prisoner or accused person) back into custody, as to await trial or further investigation *b)* to send (a case) back to a lower court for additional proceedings —*n.* a remanding or being remanded
rem·a·nence (rem′ə nəns) *n.* [see ff.] *Elec.* the magnetic flux remaining in a substance after the magnetizing force has been withdrawn
rem·a·nent (-nənt) *adj.* [ME. < L. *remanens*, prp.] [Now Rare] remaining; leftover
re·mark (ri märk′) *vt.* [Fr. *remarquer* < *re-* + *marquer*, to mark < It. *marcare* < *marca*, a mark < Gmc. *marka:* see MARK[1]] **1.** to notice; observe; perceive **2.** to say or write as an observation or comment **3.** [Obs.] to mark; distinguish; indicate —*vi.* to make an observation or comment (with *on* or *upon*) —*n.* **1.** the act of noticing, perceiving, or observing /a man worthy of *remark*/ **2.** something said briefly; comment; casual observation **3.** *same as* REMARQUE
SYN.—**remark** applies to a brief, more or less casual statement of opinion, etc., as in momentarily directing one's attention to something /a *remark* about her clothes/; an **observation** is an expression of opinion on something to which one has given some degree of special attention and thought /the warden's *observations* on prison reform/; a **comment** is a remark or observation made in explaining, criticizing, or interpreting something /comments on a novel/; **commentary** is usually applied as a collective noun to a series of explanatory notes or annotations /a *commentary* on Aristotle's *Politics*/
re·mark·a·ble (-ə b'l) *adj.* **1.** worthy of remark or notice

2. unusual; extraordinary —**SYN.** see NOTICEABLE —**re·mark′a·ble·ness** *n.* —**re·mark′a·bly** *adv.*
re·marque (ri märk′) *n.* [Fr.: see REMARK] **1.** a mark, esp. a small design or sketch, made on the margin of an engraved plate and appearing only on proofs, to identify a particular stage of the plate **2.** a plate, print, or proof bearing such a mark
Re·marque (rə märk′), **E·rich Ma·ri·a** (er′ik mə rē′ə) 1897–1970; U.S. novelist, born in Germany
Rem·brandt (Harmensz) van Rijn (rem′brant van rīn′; *Du.* rem′bränt vän rīn′) 1606–69; Du. painter & etcher
re·me·di·a·ble (ri mē′dē ə b'l) *adj.* [ME., remedial < MFr. < L. *remediabilis*] that can be remedied —**re·me′di·a·ble·ness** *n.* —**re·me′di·a·bly** *adv.*
re·me·di·al (-əl) *adj.* [LL. *remedialis*] **1.** providing, or intended to provide, a remedy ☆**2.** *Educ.* designating or of any special course for helping students overcome deficiencies /remedial reading/ —**re·me′di·al·ly** *adv.*
re·me·di·a·tion (ri mē′dē ā′shən) *n.* ☆*Educ.* the act or process of remedying or overcoming learning disabilities or problems —**re·me′di·a′tion·al** *adj.*
rem·e·dy (rem′ə dē) *n., pl.* **-dies** [ME. *remedie* < Anglo-Fr. < OFr. *remede* < L. *remedium* < *re-*, again + *mederi*, to heal: see MEDICAL] **1.** any medicine or treatment that cures, heals, or relieves a disease or bodily disorder or tends to restore health **2.** something that corrects, counteracts, or removes an evil or wrong; relief; redress **3.** *Law* a means, as court action, by which violation of a right is prevented or compensated for; legal redress —*vt.* **-died, -dy·ing 1.** to cure or heal, as with medicine **2.** to put back in proper condition; put right **3.** to correct or remove (an evil, etc.) —**SYN.** see CURE —**rem′e·di·less** *adj.*
re·mem·ber (ri mem′bər) *vt.* [ME. *remembren* < OFr. *remembrer* < LL. *rememorare* < L. *re-*, back, again + *memorare*, to bring to remembrance < *memor*, mindful: see MEMORY] **1.** to have (an event, thing, person, etc.) come to mind again; think of again /suddenly *remembering* an appointment/ **2.** to bring back to mind by an effort; recollect; recall /to try to *remember* a name/ **3.** to bear in mind; keep in the memory; be careful not to forget **4.** to keep (a person) in mind with some feeling, as of pleasure, gratitude, etc. **5.** *a)* to keep (a person) in mind for a present, legacy, etc. *b)* to give a present or tip to **6.** to mention (a person) to another as sending regards or greetings /remember me to your mother/ **7.** [Archaic] to remind —*vi.* **1.** to bear something in mind or call something back to mind **2.** to have memory or the use of one's memory —**re·mem′ber·er** *n.*
SYN.—**remember** implies a putting oneself in mind of something, often suggesting that the thing is kept alive in the memory so that it can be called to conscious thought without effort /he'll *remember* this day/; **recall** and **recollect** both imply some effort or will to bring something back to mind, **recall**, in addition, often connoting an imparting of what is brought back /let me *recall* what was said, to *recollect* the days of one's childhood/; **remind** implies an agent as the cause of or stimulus for remembering /your story *reminds* me of another/; **reminisce** now usually implies the remembering and telling of past events or experiences in one's own life /they *reminisced* about school days/ —**ANT.** forget
re·mem·brance (ri mem′brəns) *n.* [ME. < OFr.: see prec. & -ANCE] **1.** a remembering or being remembered **2.** the power to remember **3.** something remembered; memory **4.** the extent of time over which one can remember **5.** an object that serves to bring to mind or keep in mind some person, event, etc.; souvenir, gift, keepsake, memento, etc. **6.** commemoration /in *remembrance* of the deceased/ **7.** [*pl.*] greetings —**SYN.** see MEMORY
Remembrance Day a British and Canadian holiday in November, equivalent to VETERANS DAY
re·mem·branc·er (-brən sər) *n.* [ME. < Anglo-Fr.: see REMEMBRANCE & -ER] **1.** a person who reminds another of something, esp. one engaged or appointed to do so **2.** [*usually* R-] in England, any of certain officials, specif. one responsible for collecting debts owed to the sovereign **3.** a reminder; memento
rem·i·ges (rem′ə jēz′) *n.pl., sing.* **re·mex** (rē′meks) [ModL., *pl.* of *remex* < L., a rower < *remus*, an oar (see ROW[2]) + *agere*, to move (see ACT)] the large quill feathers of a bird's wing —**re·mig·i·al** (ri mij′ē əl) *adj.*
re·mind (ri mīnd′) *vt., vi.* [RE- + MIND.] to put (a person) in mind (*of* something); cause (a person) to remember —**SYN.** see REMEMBER
re·mind·er (ri mīn′dər) *n.* a person or thing that reminds; thing to help one remember something else
re·mind·ful (ri mīnd′fəl) *adj.* **1.** mindful; remembering **2.** reviving memory; reminding; reminiscent
Rem·ing·ton (rem′in tən), **Frederic** 1861–1909; U.S. painter, sculptor, & illustrator
rem·i·nisce (rem′ə nis′) *vi.* **-nisced′, -nisc′ing** [backformation < ff.] to think, talk, or write about remembered events or experiences —**SYN.** see REMEMBER

remanufacture	remarry	rematch	remerge
remap	remaster	remeasure	remigrate
remarriage	remasticate	remelt	remilitarize

rem·i·nis·cence (-'ns) *n.* [Fr. *réminiscence* < LL. *remeniscentia:* see ff.] **1.** the act of remembering or recollecting; past experiences **2.** a memory or recollection **3.** [*pl.*] an account, written or spoken, of remembered experiences **4.** something that suggests or recalls something else; reminder —*SYN.* see MEMORY

rem·i·nis·cent (-'nt) *adj.* [L. *reminiscens,* prp. of *reminisci* < *re-,* again + *memini,* to remember: for IE. base see MIND] **1.** having the nature of or characterized by reminiscence **2.** given to reminiscing, or recalling past experiences **3.** bringing to mind something else; suggestive (*of*) — **rem'i·nis'cent·ly** *adv.*

re·mise (ri mīz') *vt.* -**mised', -mis'ing** [LME. *remisen* < MFr. *remis,* pp. of *remettre,* to send back < L. *remittere:* see REMIT] *Law* to give up a claim to; release by deed

re·miss (ri mis') *adj.* [L. *remissus,* pp. of *remittere:* see REMIT] **1.** careless in, or negligent about, attending to a task; lax in the performance of duty **2.** characterized by carelessness or negligence **3.** [Now Rare] not energetic; languid —**re·miss'ly** *adv.* —**re·miss'ness** *n.*
SYN.—**remiss** implies the culpable omission or the careless or indifferent performance of a task or duty [*remiss* in one's obligations]; **negligent** and **neglectful** both imply failure to attend to something sufficiently or properly, but **negligent** often stresses this as a habit or trait [*negligent* in dress] and **neglectful** carries an implication of intentional and culpable disregard [a mayor *neglectful* of his pledges to the voters]; **derelict** implies flagrant neglect of a duty or obligation; **lax** implies looseness in satisfying or enforcing requirements, observing standards or rules, etc. [*lax* discipline]; **slack,** in this connection, implies lack of necessary diligence, efficiency, etc., as because of laziness or indifference [*slack* service in a restaurant]

re·mis·si·ble (-ə b'l) [Fr. *rémissible* < LL. *remissibilis* < pp. of L. *remittere*] that can be remitted or forgiven, as sin —**re·mis'si·bil'i·ty** *n.*

re·mis·sion (ri mish'ən) *n.* [ME. < OFr. < L. *remissio,* a sending back, in LL.(Ec.), forgiveness of sin < pp. of *remittere:* see REMIT] the act or an instance of remitting; specif., *a)* forgiveness or pardon, as of sins or crimes *b)* cancellation of or release from a debt, tax, penalty, etc. *c)* a lessening or abating, as of heat or cold, pain, etc. *d)* a relatively prolonged lessening or disappearance of the symptoms of —**re·mis'sive** *adj.*

re·mit (ri mit') *vt.* -**mit'ted, -mit'ting** [ME. *remytten* < L. *remittere* (pp. *remissus*), to send back, in LL.(Ec.), to forgive sin < *re-,* back + *mittere,* to send: see MISSION] **1.** to forgive or pardon (sins, etc.) **2.** *a)* to refrain from exacting (a payment, tax, etc.) *b)* to refrain from inflicting (a punishment) or enforcing (a sentence or fine); cancel **3.** to let slacken; decrease [without *remitting* one's efforts] **4.** to submit or refer (a matter) for consideration, judgment, etc.; specif., *Law* same as REMAND (*vt.* 2) **5.** to put back, as into a state or position **6.** to put off; postpone **7.** to send (money) in payment **8.** [Obs.] to give up; surrender —*vi.* **1.** *a)* to become more moderate in force or intensity *b)* to have its symptoms lessen or disappear: said of a disease **2.** to send money, as in payment; pay —**re·mit'ment** *n.* —**re·mit'ta·ble** *adj.* —**re·mit'ter** *n.*

re·mit·tal (-'l) *n.* same as REMISSION

re·mit·tance (-'ns) *n.* [< REMIT + -ANCE] **1.** the sending of money, as by mail **2.** the money sent

remittance man [Chiefly Brit.] a man who lives abroad supported by remittances from home

re·mit·tent (-'nt) *adj.* [L. *remittens,* prp.] remitting; abating for a while or at intervals, and then returning, as a fever —*n.* a remittent fever —**re·mit'tent·ly** *adv.*

rem·nant (rem'nənt) *n.* [ME., contr. < *remenant* < OFr. *remenant,* orig. prp. of *remaindre:* see REMAIN] **1.** what is left over; remainder; residue **2.** [*often pl.*] a small remaining part, quantity, or number of persons or things **3.** a trace; last remaining indication of what has been [a *remnant* of his former pride] **4.** a piece of cloth, ribbon, etc. left over or unsold, as at the end of a bolt —*adj.* remaining —*SYN.* see REMAINDER

re·mod·el (rē mäd''l) *vt.* -**eled** or -**elled, -el·ing** or -**el·ling 1.** to model again **2.** to make over; rebuild

re·mo·lade (rā'mə läd') *n.* same as RÉMOULADE

☆**re·mon·e·tize** (rē män'ə tīz', -mun'-) *vt.* -**tized', -tiz'ing** to reinstate as legal tender [to *remonetize* silver] — **re·mon'e·ti·za'tion** *n.*

re·mon·strance (ri män'strəns) *n.* [LME. < MFr. < ML. *remonstrantia*] **1.** the act or an instance of remonstrating; protest, complaint, or expostulation **2.** a document setting forth certain points or listing complaints, grievances, etc.

re·mon·strant (-strənt) *adj.* [ML. *remonstrans,* prp.] remonstrating or objecting; expostulatory —*n.* **1.** a person who remonstrates **2.** [R-] one of the Arminians in Holland who presented a remonstrance in 1610 setting forth their differences from strict Calvinism —**re·mon'strant·ly** *adv.*

re·mon·strate (-strāt) *vt.* -**strat·ed, -strat·ing** [< ML. *remonstratus,* pp. of *remonstrare,* to demonstrate < L. *re-,* again + *monstrare,* to show: see MONSTRANCE] **1.** to say or plead in protest, objection, complaint, etc. **2.** [Obs.] to point out; demonstrate —*vi.* to present and urge reasons in opposition or complaint; protest; object; expostulate —*SYN.* see OBJECT —**re·mon·stra·tion** (rē'män

strā'shən, rem'ən-) *n.* —**re·mon'stra·tive** (-strə tiv) *adj.* —**re·mon'stra·tive·ly** *adv.* —**re·mon'stra·tor** (-strāt ər) *n.*

rem·on·toir, rem·on·toire (rem'ən twär') *n.* [Fr. *remontoir* < *remonter,* to wind up, orig. REMOUNT] a device in a clock for giving a uniform impulse to the pendulum or balance

rem·o·ra (rem'ər ə) *n.* [L., lit., hindrance < *re-,* back + *mora,* a delay: for IE. base see MOURN] **1.** any of a family (Echeneidae) of small ocean fishes with an oval sucking disc on top of the head, by which they cling to sharks and other larger fishes, turtles, passing ships, etc. **2.** anything that hinders or impedes

REMORA
(7 in. to 3 ft. long)

re·morse (ri môrs') *n.* [ME. *remors* < OFr. < LL. *remorsus* < L., pp. of *remordere* < *re-,* again + *mordere,* to bite: see MORDANT] **1.** a deep, torturing sense of guilt felt over a wrong that one has done; self-reproach **2.** pity; compassion: now only in **without remorse,** pitilessly —*SYN.* see PENITENCE

re·morse·ful (-fəl) *adj.* full of remorse; feeling, expressing, or caused by remorse —**re·morse'ful·ly** *adv.* —**re·morse'·ful·ness** *n.*

re·morse·less (-lis) *adj.* without remorse; pitiless; merciless; ruthless; cruel —**re·morse'less·ly** *adv.* —**re·morse'·less·ness** *n.*

re·mote (ri mōt') *adj.* -**mot'er, -mot'est** [ME. < L. *remotus,* pp. of *removere,* to REMOVE] **1.** distant in space; far off; far away **2.** far off and hidden away; secluded **3.** far off in (past or future) time [a *remote* ancestor] **4.** distant in connection, relation, bearing, or the like [a question *remote* from the subject] **5.** distantly related by blood or marriage [a *remote* cousin] **6.** distant in human relations; aloof [*remote* and cold in his manner] **7.** slight; faint [a *remote* chance] **8.** not immediate or primary; far removed in influence [the *remote* causes] —*SYN.* see FAR —**re·mote'ly** *adv.* —**re·mote'ness** *n.*

remote control control of aircraft, missiles, or other apparatus from a distance, as by radio waves

re·mo·tion (ri mō'shən) *n.* [ME. *remocion* < L. *remotio* < *remotus:* see REMOVE] **1.** the act of removing; removal **2.** [Obs.] the act of departing; departure

ré·mou·lade (rā'mōō läd') *n.* [Fr. < dial. *remolat,* horse-radish, ult. < L. *armoracia*] a sauce made with a mayonnaise base in which are mixed spices, herbs, chopped pickle, etc.: served with cold dishes or as a salad dressing

re·mount (rē mount'; *for n., usually* rē'mount') *vt., vi.* [ME. *remounten* < OFr. *remonter*] to mount again (in various senses) —*n.* a fresh horse, or a supply of fresh horses, to replace another or others

re·mov·a·ble (ri mōō'və b'l) *adj.* [ML. *removibilis*] that can be removed —**re·mov'a·bil'i·ty** *n.* —**re·mov'a·bly** *adv.*

re·mov·al (ri mōō'v'l) *n.* **1.** a removing or being removed; esp., *a)* a taking away or being taken away *b)* dismissal from an office or position *c)* a change of place, residence, etc. **2.** same as REMOVER (sense 2)

re·move (ri mōōv') *vt.* -**moved', -mov'ing** [ME. *remouen* < OFr. *remouvoir* < L. *removere:* see RE- & MOVE] **1.** to move (something) from where it is; lift, push, transfer, or carry away, or from one place to another **2.** to take off [to *remove* one's coat] **3.** to do away with; specif., *a)* to kill or assassinate *b)* to dismiss, as from an office or position *c)* to get rid of; eliminate [to *remove* the causes of war] **4.** to take, extract, separate, or withdraw (someone or something *from*) —*vi.* **1.** [Poet.] to go away **2.** to move away, as to another residence or place of business; move **3.** to be removable [paint that *removes* easily] —*n.* **1.** the act of removing **2.** the space or distance across which, or interval of time in which, a move is made **3.** a step; space; interval; degree [but one short *remove* from victory] **4.** [Brit.] a move to another residence or place of business —*SYN.* see MOVE

re·moved (ri mōōvd') *adj.* **1.** distant by (a specified number of degrees of relationship) [one's first cousin once *removed* is the child of one's first cousin] **2.** remote; distant; unconnected (with *from*)

re·mov·er (ri mōō'vər) *n.* **1.** a person or thing that removes something [a paint *remover*] **2.** *Law* the transfer of a suit from one court to another by a writ of error, certiorari, etc.

Rem·scheid (rem'shīt') city in W West Germany, in the Ruhr valley of North Rhine-Westphalia: pop. 134,000

☆**re·mu·da** (rə mōō'də) *n.* [AmSp. < Sp. *remuda* (de *caballos*), relay (of horses) < *remudar,* to exchange < *re-* (< L., RE-) + *mudar,* to change < L. *mutare:* see MUTATE] in the Southwest, a group of extra saddle horses kept as a supply of remounts

re·mu·ner·ate (ri myōō'nə rāt') *vt.* -**at'ed, -at'ing** [< L. *remuneratus,* pp. of *remunerari,* to reward, remunerate < *re-,* again + *munus* (gen. *muneris*), a gift: for IE. base see COMMON] to pay or compensate (a person) for (work or service done, loss incurred, etc.); reward; recompense —*SYN.* see PAY[1] —**re·mu'ner·a·ble** *adj.* —**re·mu'ner·a'tor** *n.*

re·mu·ner·a·tion (ri myōō'nə rā'shən) *n.* [L. *remuneratio*] **1.** the act of remunerating **2.** that which remunerates; reward; pay; recompense; compensation

remix	remobilize	remodify	remortgage
remixture	remodification	remold	remultiply

re·mu·ner·a·tive (ri myōō′nə rāt′iv, -nər ə tiv) *adj.* 1. remunerating 2. affording remuneration; profitable — **re·mu′ner·a′tive·ly** *adv.* —**re·mu′ner·a′tive·ness** *n.*

Re·mus (rē′məs) [L.] *Rom. Myth.* the twin brother of Romulus: see ROMULUS

ren·ais·sance (ren′ə säns′, -zäns′; ren′ə säns′, -zäns′; *chiefly Brit.*, ri nā′s'ns) *n.* [Fr. < *renaître*, to be born anew < OFr. *renestre* < *re-* + VL. **nascere*, for L. *nasci*, to be born: see NATURE] 1. a new birth; rebirth; revival; renascence 2. [R-] *a*) the great revival of art, literature, and learning in Europe in the 14th, 15th, and 16th centuries, based on classical sources: it began in Italy and spread gradually to other countries and marked the transition from the medieval world to the modern *b*) the period of this revival *c*) the style and forms of art, literature, architecture, etc. of this period *d*) any similar revival of art, literature, or learning —*adj.* [R-] 1. of, characteristic of, or in the style of, the Renaissance 2. designating or of a style of architecture developed in Italy and western Europe between 1400 and 1600, characterized by the revival and adaptation of classical orders and design

Renaissance man a highly cultivated man who is skilled and well-versed in many or, ideally, all of the arts and sciences

re·nal (rē′n'l) *adj.* [< Fr. or LL.: Fr. *rénal* < LL. *renalis* < L. *renes*, kidneys] of or near the kidneys

renal corpuscle same as MALPIGHIAN BODY (sense 2)

Re·nan (ri nan′; *Fr.* rə nän′) (*Joseph*) **Ernest** 1823–92; Fr. historian & essayist

Ren·ard (ren′ərd) same as REYNARD

re·nas·cence (ri nas′'ns, -nās′-) *n.* [< ff.] [also R-] same as RENAISSANCE

re·nas·cent (-'nt) *adj.* [L. *renascens*, prp. of *renasci*, to be born again: see RE- & NATURE] acquiring or showing new life, strength, or vigor

ren·con·tre (ren kän′tər; *Fr.* rän kōn′tr′) *n.* same as RENCOUNTER

ren·coun·ter (ren koun′tər) *vt., vi.* [Fr. *rencontrer*: see RE- & ENCOUNTER] [Rare] 1. to meet in or as in battle 2. to meet casually —*n.* 1. a hostile meeting; conflict or contest, as a battle or debate 2. a casual meeting, as with a friend

rend (rend) *vt., rent, rend′ing* [ME. *renden* < OE. *rendan*, akin to OFris. *renda* < IE. base **rendh-*, to tear apart, whence RIND, Sans. *randhram*, a fissure, split] 1. to tear, pull, or rip with violence (with *from, off, away*, etc.) 2. to tear, pull apart, rip up, or split with violence [a tree *rent* by lightning]: often used figuratively [a roar *rends* the air] 3. to tear (one's clothing) to show grief, anguish, etc. —*vi.* to tear; burst; split apart —*SYN.* see TEAR[1]

ren·der (ren′dər) *vt.* [ME. *rendren* < OFr. *rendre* < VL. **rendere*, for L. *reddere*, to restore < *re(d)-*, back + *dare*, to give] 1. to give, hand over, deliver, present, or submit, as for approval, consideration, payment, etc. [to *render* an account of one's actions, *render* a bill] 2. to give (*up*); surrender [to *render* up a city to the enemy] 3. to give in return or requital [to *render* good for evil] 4. to give (*back*); restore [to *render* back another's gift] 5. to give or pay (something due or owed) [to *render* thanks, *render* obedience] 6. to cause to be or become; make [to *render* one helpless] 7. *a*) to give or provide (aid, etc.) *b*) to do (a service, etc.) 8. to represent; depict; specif., to make a drawing in perspective 9. to perform or interpret by performance; recite (a poem, etc.), play (music), treat (a subject, as in painting), act out (a role), etc. 10. to express in other words; esp., to translate (often with *into*) 11. *a*) to melt the fat from (bacon, etc.) *b*) to melt down (fat) 12. to pronounce or declare (a judgment, verdict, etc.), as in a court 13. *Masonry* to cover (brickwork, etc.) directly with a coat of plaster —*n.* a payment, sometimes in money but usually in goods or services, as for rent in feudal times —**ren′der·a·ble** *adj.* —**ren′der·er** *n.*

ren·der·ing (-iŋ) *n.* the act of one who renders; specif., *a*) an interpretation or rendition *b*) a translation *c*) a perspective drawing depicting an architect's conception of a finished building, etc. *d*) *Masonry* a coat of plaster applied directly to brickwork, etc.: also **rendering coat**

ren·dez·vous (rän′dā vōō′, -dē-, -də-) *n., pl.* **-vous′** (-vōōz′) [Fr.: substantive use of *rendez-vous*, betake or present yourself (or yourselves)] 1. a place designated for a meeting or assembling, as of troops, ships, airplanes, space vehicles, etc. 2. a place where people are in the habit of meeting or gathering 3. *a*) an agreement or appointment between two or more persons to meet at a certain time or place *b*) the meeting itself —*vi.* **-voused′** (-vōōd′), **-vous′ing** (-vōō′iŋ) to meet or assemble at a certain time or place —*vt.* to assemble (troops, etc.) at a certain time or place

ren·di·tion (ren dish′ən) *n.* [MFr., altered (after *rendre*, to RENDER) < L. *redditio* (< pp. of *reddere*): see RENDER] a rendering or result of rendering; specif., ☆*a*) a performance or interpretation (*of* a piece of music, a role, etc.) *b*) a translation or version *c*) [Archaic] a surrender, as of a fugitive slave

ren·e·gade (ren′ə gād′) *n.* [Sp. *renegado*, pp. of *renegar*, to deny < ML. *renegare* < L. *re-*, again + *negare*, to deny (see NEGATION); the word replaces ME. *renagat* < ML. *renegatus*, of the same ult. origin] 1. a person who abandons his religion for another; apostate 2. a person who abandons a party, movement, etc. and goes over to the other side; traitor; turncoat —*adj.* of or like a renegade; disloyal; traitorous —*vi.* **-gad′ed, -gad′ing** [Rare] to turn renegade

ren·e·ga·do (ren′ə gä′dō, -gä′-) *n., pl.* **-does** [Sp., see prec.] *archaic var.* of RENEGADE

re·nege (ri nig′, -neg′, -nēg′) *vi.* **-neged′, -neg′ing** [ML. *renegare*: see RENEGADE] 1. to back out of an agreement; go back on a promise 2. *Card Games* to play a card of another suit, against the rules of the game, when holding any of the suit called for —*vt.* [Archaic] to deny; renounce —*n. Card Games* an act of reneging —**re·neg′er** *n.*

re·ne·go·ti·ate (rē′nə gō′shē āt′) *vi., vt.* **-at′ed, -at′ing** to negotiate again; specif., to review (a contract price) in order to prevent a contractor from realizing excessive profits, esp. from a government contract —**re′ne·go′ti·a·ble** *adj.* —**re′ne·go′ti·a′tion** *n.*

re·new (ri nōō′, -nyōō′) *vt.* [ME. *renewen* < *re-* + *newe* (see NEW), after L. *renovare* (see RENOVATE)] 1. to make new or as if new again; make young, fresh, or strong again; bring back into good condition 2. to give new spiritual strength to 3. to cause to exist again; reestablish; revive 4. to begin again; take up again; resume [to *renew* negotiations] 5. to go over again; say again; repeat [to *renew* one's objections] 6. *a*) to replace as by a fresh supply of [to *renew* provisions] *b*) to refill with a fresh supply 7. to give or get an extension of [to *renew* a lease] —*vi.* 1. to become new or as new again; be renewed 2. to begin again; start over —**re·new′a·bil′i·ty** *n.* —**re·new′a·ble** *adj.* —**re·new′ed·ly** *adv.* —**re·new′er** *n.*

SYN.—**renew** is the most direct but also the broadest term here, implying a making new again by replacing what is old, worn, exhausted, etc. [to *renew* a stock of goods]; to **renovate** is to clean up, replace or repair worn parts, etc. so as to bring back to good condition; to **restore** is to bring back to an original or unimpaired condition after exhaustion, illness, dilapidation, etc. [to *restore* an old castle]; **refresh** implies a restoring of depleted strength, vigor, etc. by furnishing something needed [a *refreshing* sleep]; **rejuvenate** implies a restoring of youthful appearance, vigor, etc. [she looked *rejuvenated* after the plastic surgery]

re·new·al (-əl) *n.* 1. a renewing or being renewed 2. an instance of renewing, or something renewed

Ren·frew (ren′frōō) 1. county of SW Scotland, on the Firth of Clyde: 240 sq. mi.; pop. 355,000: also **Ren′frew·shire′** (-shir′) 2. its county seat, a seaport on the Clyde River: pop. 18,000

ren·i- (ren′ə, rē′nə) [< L. *renes*, kidneys] a combining form meaning kidney, kidneys [*reniform*]

ren·i·form (ren′ə fôrm′, rē′nə-) *adj.* [ModL. *reniformis*: see RENI- & -FORM] shaped like a kidney

re·nin (rē′nin) *n.* [< L. *renes*, kidneys + -IN[1]] a proteolytic enzyme formed in the kidneys

re·ni·tent (ri nīt′'nt, ren′ə tənt) *adj.* [< Fr. or L.: Fr. *rénitent* < L. *renitens*, prp. of *reniti*, to resist < *re-*, back + *niti*, to struggle] 1. resisting pressure; resistant 2. opposing stubbornly; recalcitrant —**re·ni′ten·cy** *n.*

Rennes (ren) city in NW France: pop. 152,000

ren·net (ren′it) *n.* [ME. *rennen*, to cause to coagulate < OE. *gerennan* < *ge-*, together (see CO-) + Gmc. **rannjan*, to cause to run < base of **rinnan* (whence RUN) + **-jan*, caus. suffix] 1. *a*) the membrane lining the stomach of an unweaned animal, esp. the fourth stomach of a calf *b*) the contents of such a stomach 2. *a*) an extract of this membrane or of the stomach contents, containing rennin and used to curdle milk, as in making cheese or junket *b*) any substance used to curdle milk 3. same as RENNIN

ren·nin (ren′in) *n.* [RENN(ET) + -IN[1]] a coagulating enzyme that can curdle milk, found in rennet

Re·no (rē′nō) [after U.S. Gen. J. L. *Reno* (1823–62)] city in W Nev.: pop. 73,000

Re·noir (rə nwär′; *E.* ren′wär), **Pierre Au·guste** (pyer ō güst′) 1841–1919; Fr. painter

re·nounce (ri nouns′) *vt.* **-nounced′, -nounc′ing** [ME. *renouncen* < OFr. *renoncer* < L. *renuntiare* < *re-*, back + *nuntiare*, to tell < *nuntius*, messenger: see NUNCIO] 1. to give up (a claim, right, belief, etc.), usually by a formal public statement 2. to give up (a pursuit, practice, way of living or feeling, etc.) 3. to cast off or disown; refuse further association with; repudiate [to *renounce* a son] —*vi.* 1. *Card Games* to fail to follow suit, having no cards of the suit led 2. *Law* to give up a right, trust, etc. —*n. Card Games* failure to play the suit led —*SYN.* see ABDICATE —**re·nounce′ment** *n.* —**re·nounc′er** *n.*

ren·o·vate (ren′ə vāt′) *vt.* **-vat′ed, -vat′ing** [< L. *renovatus*, pp. of *renovare*, to renew < *re-*, again + *novare*, to make new < *novus*, NEW] 1. to make fresh or sound again, as though new; clean up, replace worn and broken parts in, repair, etc. 2. to refresh; revive —*SYN.* see RENEW —**ren′o·va′tion** *n.* —**ren′o·va′tive** *adj.* —**ren′o·va′tor** *n.*

---

re·nown (ri noun´) *n.* [ME. *renoun* < Anglo-Fr. < OFr. *renom* < *renommer*, to name again or often, make famous < *re-*, again + *nom(m)er*, to name < L. *nominare* < *nomen*, A NAME] **1.** great fame or reputation; celebrity **2.** [Obs.] report or rumor —*vt.* [Obs.] to make famous

re·nowned (ri nound´) *adj.* having renown; famous — SYN. see FAMOUS

☆**rens·se·laer·ite** (ren´sə lə rīt´, ren´sə lir´īt) *n.* [after Stephen Van *Rensselaer* (1764–1839), U.S. general and statesman] a fibrous variety of talc, used for ornamental articles

rent[1] (rent) *n.* [ME. < OFr. *rente* < LL. *rendita* (pp. of *rendere*; see RENDER), for L. *reddita (pecunia)*, paid (money)] **1.** a stated return or payment for the temporary possession or use of a house, land, or other property, made, usually at fixed intervals, by the tenant or user to the owner **2.** [Obs.] *a)* real estate or other property yielding an income *b)* income; revenue **2.** *Econ. a)* income from the use of land *b)* a return or profit realized from a differential advantage in production, as the difference in yield between relatively good land and the poorest land under cultivation in similar conditions —*vt.* **1.** *a)* to get temporary possession and use of (a house, land, etc.) by paying rent *b)* to get the temporary use of (a car, tool, furniture, etc.) by paying a fee **2.** to give temporary possession and use of in return for the payment of rent or a fee; lease or let (often with *out*) —*vi.* ☆**1.** to be leased or let for rent or a fee **2.** to lease or let a place or thing —SYN. see HIRE —☆**for rent** available to be rented —**rent´a·ble** *adj.*

rent[2] (rent) *pt.* & *pp.* of REND

rent[3] (rent) *n.* [n. use of obs. or dial. *rent*, var. of REND] **1.** a hole or gap made by rending or tearing, as a torn place in cloth, a fissure in the earth, etc. **2.** a breach of relations, as between persons or in an organized group; schism

rent·al (ren´t'l) *n.* [ME. < Anglo-Fr. < ML. *rentale*] **1.** an amount paid or received as rent **2.** an income from rents received **3.** a house, apartment, car, etc. offered for rent **4.** the act of renting —*adj.* of, in, or for rent

†**rente** (ränt) *n.*, *pl.* **rentes** (ränt) [Fr.: see RENT[1]] in France, **1.** annual income or revenue **2.** [*usually pl.*] *a)* the bonds, stocks, etc. representing the consolidated governmental debt *b)* interest paid on this

rent·er (ren´tər) *n.* **1.** a person who pays rent for the use of property **2.** an owner who rents out property

rent-free (rent´frē´) *adj., adv.* without payment of rent

†**ren·tier** (rän tyā´) *n.* [Fr. < *rente*: see RENTE] a person who has a fixed income from land, bonds, etc.

re·nun·ci·a·tion (ri nun´sē ā´shən, -shē-) *n.* [ME. < L. *renuntiatio* < *renuntiatus*, pp. of *renuntiare*: see RENOUNCE] **1.** the act or an instance of renouncing; a giving up formally or voluntarily, often at a sacrifice, of a right, claim, title, etc. **2.** a written statement or declaration of this —**re·nun´ci·a·tive** (-ə tiv), **re·nun´ci·a·to·ry** (-ə tôr´ē) *adj.*

re·o·pen (rē ō´p'n) *vt., vi.* **1.** to open again **2.** to begin again; resume [to *reopen* a debate]

re·or·der (rē ôr´dər) *n.* a second or similar order for certain goods from the same dealer —*vt.* **1.** to give a reorder for; order again **2.** to put in order again —*vi.* to order goods again

re·or·gan·i·za·tion (rē ôr´gə ni zā´shən, rē´ôr-) *n.* **1.** a reorganizing or being reorganized **2.** *Finance* a thorough reconstruction of a business corporation, comprising a considerable change in capital structure, as effected after, or in anticipation of, a failure and receivership: cf. READJUSTMENT

re·or·gan·ize (rē ôr´gə nīz´) *vt., vi.* **-ized´, -iz´ing** to organize again or anew; effect a reorganization (of) —**re·or´gan·iz´er** *n.*

rep[1] (rep) *n.* [Fr. *reps* < Eng. *ribs*: see RIB] a fabric of silk, wool, cotton, rayon, etc., with a ribbed or corded surface

rep[2] (rep) *n.* clipped form of: **1.** REPERTORY (THEATER) **2.** REPRESENTATIVE (sense 2) **3.** REPUTATION

rep[3] (rep) *n., pl.* **rep** [r(oentgen) e(quivalent), p(hysical)] a dosage of any ionizing radiation that will produce upon absorption in living tissues a rise in energy equal to that produced by one roentgen of X-ray or gamma-ray radiation

Rep. 1. Representative **2.** Republic **3.** Republican

rep. 1. repeat **2.** report(ed) **3.** reporter

re·pack·age (rē pak´ij) *vt.* **-aged, -ag·ing** to package again, esp. in or as in a better or more attractive package

re·paid (rē pād´) *pt.* & *pp.* of REPAY

re·pair[1] (ri per´) *vt.* [ME. *repairen* < OFr. *reparer* < L. *reparare* < *re-*, again + *parare*, to get ready, PREPARE] **1.** to put back in good condition after damage, decay, etc.; mend; fix **2.** to renew; restore; revive [to *repair* one's health] **3.** to amend; set right; remedy [to *repair* a mistake] **4.** to make amends for; make up or compensate for (a wrong, injury, etc.) —*n.* **1.** the act, process, or work of repairing **2.** [*usually pl.*] an instance of repairing or work done in repairing **3.** the state of being repaired, or fit for use [a car kept in *repair*] **4.** state with respect to being repaired [a house in bad *repair*] —SYN. see MEND —**re·pair´a·ble** *adj.* —**re·pair´er** *n.*

re·pair[2] (ri per´) *vi.* [ME. *repairen* < OFr. *repairer* < LL. *repatriare* < L. *re-*, back + *patria*, native country < (*terra*) *patria*, (land) of one's father, fem. of *patrius* < *pater*, FATHER] **1.** to go or betake oneself (*to* a place) **2.** to go often, customarily, or in numbers **3.** [Obs.] to return —*n.* [Archaic] a place to which one repairs; resort; haunt

re·pair·man (ri per´-man´, -mən) *n., pl.* **-men** (-mən, -men´) a man whose work is repairing things

re·pand (ri pand´) *adj.* [L. *repandus*, bent backward < *re-*, back + *pandus*, bent < IE. base *pandos*, whence ON. *fattr*, bent over, supple] *Bot.* having a wavy margin, as some leaves

rep·a·ra·ble (rep´ər ə b'l) *adj.* [Fr. *réparable* < L. *reparabilis*] that can be repaired, mended, remedied, etc. — **rep´a·ra·bly** *adv.*

rep·a·ra·tion (rep´ə rā´shən) *n.* [ME. *reparacion* < MFr. < LL. *reparatio* < pp. of L. *reparare*: see REPAIR[1]] **1.** a repairing or being repaired; restoration to good condition **2.** a making of amends; making up for a wrong or injury **3.** anything paid or done to make up for something else; compensation; specif., [*usually pl.*] compensation by a nation defeated in a war for economic losses suffered by the victor or for crimes committed against individuals, payable in money, labor, goods, etc.

SYN.—**reparation** refers to the making of amends, specif. the paying of compensation, for some wrong or injury [war *reparations*]; **restitution** implies return to the rightful owner of something that has been taken away, or of an equivalent [he made *restitution* for the libel]; **redress** suggests retaliation or resort to the courts to right a wrong [to seek *redress* for an injury]; **indemnification** refers to reimbursement, as by an insurance company, for loss, damage, etc.

re·par·a·tive (ri par´ə tiv) *adj.* **1.** repairing or tending to repair; mending, etc. **2.** of or involving reparation

rep·ar·tee (rep´ər tē´, -är-; -tā´) *n.* [Fr. *repartie*, fem. pp. of *repartir*, to return quickly a thrust or a blow, reply < *re-*, back + *partir* (L. *partire*), to PART] **1.** a quick, witty reply **2.** a series of such rejoinders **3.** skill in making witty replies —SYN. see WIT

re·par·ti·tion (rē´pär tish´ən, -pər-) *n.* **1.** the act of partitioning; distribution **2.** the act of partitioning again; redistribution —*vt.* to effect a repartition of

re·pass (rē pas´, -päs´) *vi., vt.* [Fr. *repasser*] to pass back or again —**re·pas´sage** *n.*

re·past (ri past´, -päst´) *n.* [ME. < OFr. < *re-*, RE- + *past*, food < L. *pastus* < pp. of *pascere*, to feed: see PASTOR] **1.** *a)* food and drink for a meal *b)* a meal **2.** [Archaic] *a)* the eating of food, as at a meal *b)* mealtime **3.** [Obs.] food —*vi.* [Now Rare] to eat or feast

re·pa·tri·ate (rē pā´trē āt´; *for n.*, usually -it) *vt., vi.* **-at´ed, -at´ing** [< LL. *repatriatus*, pp. of *repatriare*: see REPAIR[2]] to send back or return to the country of birth, citizenship, or allegiance [to *repatriate* prisoners of war] —*n.* a person who has been repatriated —**re·pa´tri·a´tion** *n.*

re·pay (ri pā´) *vt.* **-paid´, -pay´ing** [OFr. *repaier*] **1.** *a)* to pay back (money); refund *b)* to pay back (a person) **2.** to make some return for; compensate [*repay* a kindness] **3.** to give or make some return or recompense to (a person), as for some service **4.** to do or give (an equivalent) in return [to *repay* a visit] —*vi.* **1.** to make a repayment or return **2.** to reward or punish —SYN. see PAY[1] —**re·pay´-a·ble** *adj.* —**re·pay´ment** *n.*

re·peal (ri pēl´) *vt.* [ME. *repelen* < OFr. *rapeler*: see RE- & APPEAL] **1.** to withdraw officially or formally; revoke; cancel; annul [to *repeal* a law] **2.** [Obs.] to call back, as from exile —*n.* the act of repealing; revocation, abrogation, etc. —SYN. see ABOLISH —**re·peal´a·ble** *adj.* —**re·peal´er** *n.*

re·peat (ri pēt´) *vt.* [ME. *repeten* < OFr. *repeter* < L. *repetere* < *re-*, again + *petere*, to seek, demand, attack: see IMPETUS] **1.** to say or utter again; reiterate [to *repeat* a remark] **2.** to say over or through; recite (a poem, etc.) **3.** to say (something) as said by someone else **4.** to tell to someone else [to *repeat* a secret] **5.** *a)* to do or make again; do over again [to *repeat* a test] *b)* to make happen again or undergo again [to *repeat* an adventure] **6.** to say again what has been said before by (oneself) **7.** to present (itself or themselves) again —*vi.* **1.** to say or do again what has been said or done before **2.** to recur [experiences *repeat*] **3.** to continue to be tasted, as because of belching: often with *on* [foods that *repeat* on one] ☆**4.** to vote (illegally) more than once in the same election —*n.* **1.** the act of doing or saying again; repetition **2.** *a)* anything said, done, or occurring again *b)* a rebroadcast of a radio or television program **3.** *Music a)* a passage repeated in playing *b)* a symbol for this (:‖), placed after, and often also before, (‖:), a passage to be repeated —**re·peat´a·bil´i·ty** *n.* —**re·peat´a·ble** *adj.*

SYN.—**repeat** is the common, general word meaning to say, do, make, present, etc. over again [will you *repeat* that question, please?]; **iterate** and **reiterate** both suggest a repeating, either once or several times, but **reiterate** strongly implies insistent repetition over and over again [he keeps *reiterating* his innocence]

renumber	reoccurrence	reorient	repanel
reobserve	reoppose	reoutfit	repaper
reobtain	reorchestrate	repacify	repark
reoccupy	reordain	repack	repave
reoccur	reordination	repaint	re-pay

recapitulate suggests a repeating briefly of the main points in a discourse in summarizing [he will *recapitulate* his account of the ball game at 8:00 o'clock]

re·peat·ed (-id) *adj.* said, made, done, or happening again, or again and again —**re·peat'ed·ly** *adv.*

re·peat·er (-ər) *n.* 1. a person or thing that repeats 2. a watch or clock which, upon activation of a spring, will strike the time, sometimes to the nearest minute ☆3. *same as* REPEATING FIREARM ☆4. a person who has been convicted a number of times for violating the law ☆5. a person who fraudulently votes more than once in the same election ☆6. *Educ.* a student who repeats a course or grade that he has failed 7. *same as* REPEATING DECIMAL ☆8. *Telegraphy* a relay used to correct distortion and restore the strength of electrical signals

repeating decimal a decimal in which beyond a certain point some digit or group of digits is repeated indefinitely (Ex.: 0.47382382382 . . .)

☆**repeating firearm** a firearm that can fire a number of shots (from a magazine or clip) without reloading

re·pel (ri pel') *vt.* **-pelled', -pel'ling** [ME. *repellen* < L. *repellere*, to drive back < *re-*, back + *pellere*, to drive: see PULSE¹] 1. to drive or force back; hold or ward off [to *repel* an attack] 2. to refuse to accept, agree to, or submit to; reject [to *repel* advances] 3. to refuse to accept (a person); spurn [to *repel* a suitor] 4. *a)* to cause distaste or dislike in; disgust [the odor *repelled* him] *b)* to cause (insects, etc.) to react by staying away 5. *a)* to be resistant to, or present an opposing force to [a coating that *repels* moisture] *b)* to fail to mix with or adhere to [water *repels* oil] —*vi.* 1. to drive off, or offer an opposing force to, something 2. to cause distaste, dislike, or aversion —**re·pel'ler** *n.*

re·pel·lent (-ənt) *adj.* [L. *repellens*] 1. that repels; pushing away or driving back 2. *a)* causing distaste, dislike, or aversion; repulsive *b)* causing insects, etc. to react by staying away 3. able to resist the absorption of liquid, esp. water, to a limited extent [a water-*repellent* raincoat] —*n.* something that repels; specif., *a)* a solution applied to fabric to make it water-repellent *b)* any substance used to repel insects Also **re·pel'lant** —**re·pel'lence, re·pel'len·cy** *n.,* —**re·pel'lent·ly** *adv.*

re·pent¹ (ri pent') *vi.* [ME. *repenten* < OFr. *repentir* < VL. *repoenitere* < L. *re-*, again + *poenitere*, to repent: see PENITENT] 1. to feel sorry or self-reproachful for what one has done or failed to do; be conscience-stricken or contrite (often with *of*) 2. to feel such regret or dissatisfaction over some past action, intention, etc. as to change one's mind about (often with *of*) [to *repent* of one's generosity] 3. to feel so contrite over one's sins as to change, or decide to change, one's ways; be penitent —*vt.* 1. to feel sorry, self-reproachful, or contrite over (an error, sin, etc.) 2. to feel such regret or dissatisfaction over as to change one's mind about [to *repent* one's kindness] —**re·pent'er** *n.*

re·pent² (rē'pənt) *adj.* [L. *repens,* prp. of *repere,* to creep: see REPTILE] *Biol.* creeping or crawling

re·pent·ance (ri pent'ns) *n.* a repenting or being penitent; feeling of sorrow, etc., esp. for wrongdoing; compunction; contrition; remorse —*SYN.* see PENITENCE

re·pent·ant (-'nt) *adj.* [ME. < OFr., prp.] 1. repenting; penitent 2. characterized by or indicative of repentance —**re·pent'ant·ly** *adv.*

re·peo·ple (rē pē'p'l) *vt.* **-pled, -pling** [ME. *repeoplen* < OFr. *repeupler*] 1. to people anew; provide with new inhabitants 2. to restock with animals

re·per·cus·sion (rē'pər kush'ən, rep'ər-) *n.* [L. *repercussio* < pp. of *repercutere,* to rebound, strike back: see RE- & PERCUSSION] 1. formerly, a driving back or being driven back by something resistant; rebound; recoil 2. reflection, as of light or sound; reverberation 3. a far-reaching, often indirect effect of or reaction to some event or action: *usually used in pl.* —**re'per·cus'sive** *adj.*

rep·er·toire (rep'ər twär', rep'ə-) *n.* [Fr. *répertoire* < LL. *repertorium:* see ff.] 1. the stock of plays, operas, roles, songs, etc. that a company, actor, singer, etc. is familiar with and ready to perform 2. all the musical or theatrical works of a particular category, or of a particular writer, composer, etc., available for performance ☆3. the stock of special skills, devices, techniques, etc. of a particular person or particular field of endeavor

rep·er·to·ry (rep'ər tôr'ē, rep'ə-) *n., pl.* **-ries** [LL. *repertorium,* an inventory < L. *repertus,* pp. of *reperire,* to find out, discover < *re-,* again + *parere,* to produce, invent, bear: see -PAROUS] 1. *a)* a repository for useful things; storehouse *b)* the things stored; stock; collection 2. *same as* REPERTOIRE 3. the system of play production engaged in by repertory theaters

repertory theater a theater in which a permanent acting company prepares several productions for a season and keeps alternating them in limited runs

rep·e·tend (rep'ə tend', rep'ə tend') *n.* [L. *repetendus,* to be repeated, gerundive of *repetere,* to REPEAT] 1. a repeated sound, word, or phrase; refrain 2. *Math.* the digit or digits repeated indefinitely in a repeating decimal

rep·e·ti·tion (rep'ə tish'ən) *n.* [MFr. *repeticion* < L. *repetitio*] 1. the act of repeating; a doing or saying again, or again and again 2. *a)* something repeated *b)* something made by repeating, as a copy or imitation

rep·e·ti·tious (-əs) *adj.* full of or characterized by repetition, esp. tiresome or boring repetition —**rep'e·ti'tious·ly** *adv.* —**rep'e·ti'tious·ness** *n.*

re·pet·i·tive (ri pet'ə tiv) *adj.* of or characterized by repetition —**re·pet'i·tive·ly** *adv.*

re·phrase (rē frāz') *vt.* **-phrased', -phras'ing** to phrase again, esp. in a different way

re·pine (ri pin') *vi.* **-pined', -pin'ing** [RE- + PINE²] to feel or express unhappiness or discontent; complain; fret —**re·pin'er** *n.* —**re·pin'ing·ly** *adv.*

re·place (ri plās') *vt.* **-placed', -plac'ing** 1. to place again; put back in a former or the proper place or position 2. to take the place of; supplant [workers *replaced* by automated equipment] 3. to provide a substitute or equivalent for [to *replace* a worn tire] 4. to put back or pay back; restore; return [to *replace* embezzled funds] —**re·place'a·ble** *adj.* —**re·plac'er** *n.*

SYN.—**replace** implies a taking the place of someone or something that is now lost, gone, destroyed, worn out, etc. [we *replace* defective tubes]; **displace** suggests the ousting or dislodgment of a person or thing by another that replaces it [he had been *displaced* in her affections by another man]; **supersede** implies a replacing with something superior, more up-to-date, etc. [the steamship *superseded* the sailing ship]; **supplant** suggests a displacing that involves force, fraud, or innovation [the prince had been *supplanted* by an impostor]

re·place·ment (-mənt) *n.* 1. a replacing or being replaced 2. a person or thing that takes the place of another, esp. of one that has worn out, broken down, etc. 3. a member of the armed forces available for assignment to fill a vacancy or complete a quota; reinforcement 4. in crystallography, the replacing of an angle or edge by one face or more 5. *Geol.* the process of very gradual solution and simultaneous deposition by which one kind of mineral is substituted for another

re·plead·er (rē plēd'ər) *n.* [obs. *replead,* to plead again + -ER, sense 3] *Law* 1. a second pleading 2. the right or privilege of pleading again 3. a court order requiring the parties to plead again from that point in the pleading where an error first occurred

re·plen·ish (ri plen'ish) *vt.* [ME. *replenissen* < prp. stem of OFr. *replenir:* see RE- & PLENISH] 1. to make full or complete again, as by furnishing a new supply [to *replenish* a stock of goods] 2. to supply again with fuel or the like 3. *archaic var.* of PEOPLE —**re·plen'ish·er** *n.* —**re·plen'ish·ment** *n.*

re·plete (ri plēt') *adj.* [ME. < OFr. *replet* < L. *repletus,* pp. of *replere* < *re-,* again + *plere,* to fill: see FULL¹] 1. well-filled or plentifully supplied 2. stuffed with food and drink; gorged

re·ple·tion (ri plē'shən) *n.* 1. the state of being replete, or plentifully supplied 2. the state of having eaten and drunk to surfeit

re·plev·in (ri plev'in) *n.* [ME. < Anglo-Fr. *replevine* < OFr. *replevir,* to warrant, pledge < *re-,* again + *plevir,* to pledge < Gmc. **plegjan,* to pledge] *Law* 1. the recovery by a person of goods claimed to be his, on his promise to test the matter in court and give the goods up again if defeated 2. the writ by which he takes over the goods —*vt. same as* REPLEVY

re·plev·y (ri plev'ē) *vt.* **-plev'ied, -plev'y·ing** [OFr. *replevir:* see REPLEVIN] *Law* 1. to seize or take back (goods) under a writ of replevin 2. [Rare] to release (a man) on bail —*n. same as* REPLEVIN —**re·plev'i·a·ble** (-ē ə b'l), **re·plev'i·sa·ble** (-i sə b'l) *adj.*

rep·li·ca (rep'li kə) *n.* [It., a repetition, orig., reply < ML. an answer < L. *replicare:* see REPLY] 1. a reproduction or copy of a work of art, esp. a copy by the maker of the original 2. any very close reproduction or copy; facsimile —*SYN.* see COPY

rep·li·cate (rep'li kit; *for v.* -kāt') *adj.* [L. *replicatus,* pp. of *replicare:* see REPLY] *Bot.* folded back on itself, as a leaf —*n. Statistics* any of the individual experiments in a replication —*vt.* **-cat'ed, -cat'ing** 1. to fold; bend back 2. to repeat or duplicate 3. [Rare] to reply —**rep'li·ca·ble** *adj.*

rep·li·ca·tion (rep'lə kā'shən) *n.* [ME. *replicacioun* < MFr. *replication* < L. *replicatio* < pp. of *replicare:* see REPLY] 1. a folding back; fold 2. a reply, or answer; esp., a reply to an answer 3. repetition of a sound; echo 4. the act of copying 5. a copy; reproduction 6. *Law* the plaintiff's answer to the plea of the defendant 7. *Statistics* repetition of an experiment under controlled conditions so that a specific result may be observed

re-petition	replan	replaster	replead
rephotograph	replant	replate	repledge
repigment	replantation	replay	replunge

re·ply (ri plī′) *vi.* **-plied′, -ply′ing** [ME. *replyen* < OFr. *replier* < L. *replicare*, to fold back, make a reply < *re-*, back + *plicare*, to fold: see PLY¹] **1.** to answer, or respond, in speech or writing **2.** to respond by some action [to *reply* to the enemy's fire with a barrage] **3.** *Law* to answer a defendant's plea —*vt.* to say in answer [she *replied* that she disapproved] —*n., pl.* **-plies′ 1.** an answer, or response, in speech or writing **2.** a response by some action —*SYN.* see ANSWER —**re·pli′er** *n.*

re·port (ri pôrt′) *vt.* [ME. *reporten* < OFr. *reporter*, to carry back < L. *reportare* < *re-*, back + *portare*, to carry: see PORT³] **1.** to give an account of, often at regular intervals; give information about (something seen, done, etc.); recount **2.** to carry and repeat (a message, etc.) **3.** to write an account of for presentation to others or for publication, as in a newspaper **4.** to make known the presence, approach, etc. of [to *report* strange aircraft overhead] **5.** to give a formal statement or official account of; announce formally (the results of an investigation, etc.) **6.** to present or return (something referred for study, action, etc.) with the conclusions reached or recommendations made (often with *out*) [the committee *reported* the bill out] **7.** to make a charge about (something) or against (someone) to a person in authority [to *report* a rudeness, to *report* a thief] —*vi.* **1.** to make a report **2.** to work as a reporter **3.** to present oneself or make one's presence known [to *report* for duty] **4.** to be responsible or subordinate (*to* a superior) —*n.* [ME. < OFr. < the *v.*] **1.** rumor; gossip; common talk [*report* has it that he will resign] **2.** reputation [a man of good *report*] **3.** a statement or account brought in and presented, often for publication [a *report* of a battle] **4.** a formal or official presentation of facts or of the record of some proceedings, an investigation, etc. **5.** a loud, resounding noise, esp. one made by an explosion **6.** *Law* *a)* a formal account or record of a court case, decision, etc. *b)* [*pl.*] the official records, published periodically, of court cases, decisions, etc. —*SYN.* see TELL¹ —**re·port′a·ble** *adj.*

re·port·age (-ij) *n.* **1.** the act or process of reporting news events **2.** written reports, articles, etc. that deal with current events in a journalistic manner

☆**report card** a periodical report of a pupil's progress and behavior, sent to his parents or guardian

re·port·ed·ly (-id lē) *adv.* according to report or reports

re·port·er (-ər) *n.* [ME. *reportour* < OFr. *reporteur*] a person who reports; specif., *a)* a person authorized to report legal or legislative proceedings [a court *reporter*] *b)* a person who gathers information and writes reports for publication in a newspaper, magazine, etc. *c)* a person who reports on radio or television —**rep·or·to·ri·al** (rep′ər tôr′ē əl) *adj.* —☆**rep′or·to′ri·al·ly** *adv.*

re·pos·al (ri pō′z'l) *n.* [Obs.] the act of reposing

re·pose¹ (ri pōz′) *vt.* **-posed′, -pos′ing** [LME. *reposen* < OFr. *reposer* < LL. *repausare* < L. *re-*, again + LL. *pausare*: see POSE¹] to lay or place for rest: often reflexive [to *repose* oneself on a bed] —*vi.* **1.** to lie at rest **2.** to rest from work, travel, exercise, etc. **3.** to rest in death or a grave **4.** to lie quiet and calm **5.** to lie, rest, or be supported [shale *reposing* on a bed of limestone] **6.** [Archaic] to have trust (*in*); rely (*on* or *upon*) —*n.* **1.** a reposing, or resting **2.** *a)* rest *b)* sleep **3.** peace of mind; freedom from worry or troubles **4.** calm or ease of manner; composure **5.** calm; tranquillity; peace **6.** harmony of form or color, giving an effect of tranquillity, as in painting

re·pose² (ri pōz′) *vt.* **-posed′, -pos′ing** [ME. *reposen* < L. *repositus* (see REPOSITORY)] **1.** [Rare] to place; put **2.** to place (trust, confidence, etc.) *in* someone **3.** to place (power, management, etc.) *in* the control of some person or group

re·pose·ful (-fəl) *adj.* full of repose; tranquil —**re·pose′ful·ly** *adv.*

re·pos·it (ri päz′it) *vt.* [< L. *repositus*: see REPOSITORY] **1.** to deposit or store, as for safekeeping **2.** [Rare] to replace

re·po·si·tion¹ (rē′pə zish′ən, rep′ə-) *n.* [LL. *repositio*] a repositing or being reposited; specif., replacement, as of a part of the body by a surgical operation

re·po·si·tion² (rē′pə zish′ən) *vt.* [RE- + POSITION] to put into a new or different position

re·pos·i·to·ry (ri päz′ə tôr′ē) *n., pl.* **-ries** [LME. *repositorie* < L. *repositorium* < *repositus*, pp. of *reponere*, to put back < *re-*, back + *ponere*, to place: see POSITION] **1.** a box, chest, closet, or room in which things may be placed for safekeeping **2.** [Now Rare] a building for exhibiting objects; museum **3.** a burial vault; sepulcher **4.** any thing or person thought of as a center of accumulation or storage [a *repository* of information] **5.** a person to whom something is entrusted or confided; confidant —*adj.* acting gradually over a period of time: said of a drug

re·pos·sess (rē′pə zes′) *vt.* **1.** to get possession of again; specif., to take back from a buyer who has failed to make payments when due **2.** [Now Rare] to put in possession again —**re′pos·ses′sion** (-zesh′ən) *n.*

‡**re·pous·sé** (rə pōō sā′) *adj.* [Fr., pp. of *repousser*, to push back < *re-*, back + *pousser*: see PUSH] **1.** formed in relief, as a pattern on thin metal beaten up from the underside **2.** decorated with such patterns —*n.* **1.** a pattern or surface made in this way **2.** the art or process of hammering metal in this way

repp (rep) *n.* alt. *sp.* of REP¹

repr. 1. represented **2.** representing **3.** reprint(ed)

rep·re·hend (rep′ri hend′) *vt.* [ME. *reprehenden* < L. *reprehendere* < *re-*, back + *prehendere*: see PREHENSILE] **1.** to reprimand or rebuke (a person) **2.** to find fault with (something done); censure —*SYN.* see CRITICIZE

rep·re·hen·si·ble (-hen′sə b'l) *adj.* [ME. *reprehensyble* < LL.(Ec.) *reprehensibilis*] deserving to be reprehended —**rep′re·hen′si·bil′i·ty** *n.* —**rep′re·hen′si·bly** *adv.*

rep·re·hen·sion (-hen′shən) *n.* [ME. *reprehencion* < L. *reprehensio*] the act of reprehending; reproof or censure —**rep′re·hen′sive** (-siv) *adj.* —**rep′re·hen′sive·ly** *adv.*

rep·re·sent (rep′ri zent′) *vt.* [ME. *representen* < OFr. *representer* < L. *repraesentare* < *re-*, again + *praesentare*: see RE- & PRESENT, *v.*] **1.** to present or picture to the mind **2.** *a)* to present a likeness or image of; portray; depict *b)* to be a likeness or image of, as a picture or statue may be **3.** to present in words; describe, state, or set forth; specif., *a)* to describe as having a specified character *b)* to set forth forcibly or earnestly, so as to influence action, persuade hearers, make effective protest, etc. **4.** *a)* to be a sign or symbol for; stand for; symbolize [x *represents* the unknown] *b)* to denote by symbols, characters, etc. [to *represent* quantities by letters] **5.** to be the equivalent of; correspond to, as in a different place or time [a cave *represented* home to them] **6.** *a)* to present, produce, or perform (a play, etc.) *b)* to act the part of (a character), as in a play **7.** to act or stand in place of; be an agent, proxy, or substitute for **8.** to speak and act for by duly conferred authority, as an ambassador for his country or a legislator for his constituents **9.** to serve as a specimen, example, type, or instance of; exemplify or typify —**rep′re·sent′a·ble** *adj.*

rep·re·sen·ta·tion (rep′ri zen tā′shən) *n.* [ME. < MFr. < L. *repraesentatio*] **1.** a representing or being represented (in various senses); specif., the fact of representing or being represented in a legislative assembly **2.** legislative representatives, collectively **3.** a likeness, image, picture, etc. **4.** [*often pl.*] a description, account, or statement of facts, allegations, or arguments, esp. one intended to influence action, persuade hearers, make protest, etc. **5.** the production or performance of a play, etc. **6.** *Law* a statement or implication of fact, oral or written, as made by one party to induce another to enter into a contract

rep·re·sen·ta·tion·al (-'l) *adj.* **1.** of or characterized by representation **2.** designating or of art that represents in recognizable form objects in nature —**rep′re·sen·ta′tion·al·ly** *adv.*

rep·re·sen·ta·tion·al·ism (-iz'm) *n.* **1.** the theory or practice of representational art **2.** *Philos.* the theory that the mind apprehends external objects only through the medium of percepts or ideas —**rep′re·sen·ta′tion·al·ist** *n.*

rep·re·sent·a·tive (rep′rə zen′tə tiv) *adj.* [ME. < MFr. or ML.: MFr. *représentatif* < ML. *repraesentativus*] **1.** representing or serving to represent; specif., *a)* picturing; portraying; reproducing *b)* acting or speaking, esp. by due authority, in the place or on behalf of another or others; esp., serving as a delegate in a legislative assembly **2.** composed of persons duly authorized, as by election, to act and speak for others [a *representative* assembly] **3.** of, characterized by, or based on representation of the people by elected delegates [*representative* government] **4.** being an example or type of a certain class or kind of thing; typical [a building *representative* of modern architecture] —*n.* **1.** a person or thing enough like the others in its class or kind to serve as an example or type **2.** a person duly authorized to act or speak for another or others; specif., *a)* a member of a legislative assembly *b)* a salesman or agent for a business firm ☆**3.** [R-] a member of the lower house of Congress (*House of Representatives*) or of a State legislature —**rep′re·sent′a·tive·ly** *adv.* —**rep′re·sent′a·tive·ness** *n.*

re·press (ri pres′) *vt.* [ME. *repressen* < L. *repressus*, pp. of *reprimere*: see RE- & PRESS¹] **1.** to keep down or hold back; restrain [to *repress* a sigh] **2.** to put down; subdue **3.** to control so strictly or severely as to prevent the natural development or expression of [to *repress* a child] **4.** *Psychiatry* *a)* to force (ideas, impulses, etc. painful to the conscious mind) into the unconscious *b)* to prevent (unconscious ideas, impulses, etc.) from reaching the level of consciousness Cf. SUPPRESS —**re·press′er, re·pres′sor** *n.* —**re·press′i·ble** *adj.* —**re·pres′sive** *adj.* —**re·pres′sive·ly** *adv.* —**re·pres′sive·ness** *n.*

re-press (rē pres′) *vt.* ☆to press again; esp., to make new copies of (a recording) from the original master

re·pressed (ri prest′) *adj.* affected by, showing, or resulting from repression

re·pres·sion (ri presh′ən) *n.* [ME. *repressioun* < ML. *repressio*] **1.** a repressing or being repressed **2.** *Psychiatry* *a)* the mechanism by which ideas, impulses, etc. are repressed *b)* something repressed in this way

re·prieve (ri prēv′) *vt.* **-prieved′, -priev′ing** [earlier *repry* < Fr. *repris*, pp. of *reprendre*, to take back, prob. altered

---

repolish	repopulate	repot	re-present
repopularize	re-pose	repour	reprice

by association with ME. *repreven*, REPROVE] 1. to postpone the punishment of; esp., to postpone the execution of (a person condemned to death) 2. to give temporary relief to, as from trouble or pain —n. a reprieving or being reprieved; specif., a) postponement of a penalty, esp. that of death; also, a warrant ordering this b) a temporary relief or escape, as from trouble or pain

rep·ri·mand (rep′rə mand′, -mänd′; *also, for v.,* rep′rə mand′, -mänd′) n. [Fr. *réprimande* < L. *reprimenda*, fem. of *reprimendus*, that is to be repressed < *reprimere*, to repress: see RE- & PRESS¹] a severe or formal rebuke, esp. by a person in authority —vt. to rebuke severely or formally

re·print (rē print′; for n., usually rē′print′) vt. to print again; print an additional impression of, usually without change —n. 1. something reprinted; specif., a) an additional impression, usually without change, of something previously printed, as a book, pamphlet, etc. b) same as OFFPRINT c) Philately a stamp, not to be used for postage, printed from the original plate, often with different paper and ink, after the issue of the stamp has ceased 2. the act or an instance of reprinting —**re·print′er** n.

re·pris·al (ri prī′z'l) n. [ME. *reprisail* < MFr. *reprisaille* < It. *rappresaglia* < *riprendere*, to take back < L. *reprehendere*: see REPREHEND] 1. orig., the forcible seizure of property or subjects in retaliation for an injury inflicted by another country 2. the act or practice of using force, short of war, against another nation to obtain redress of grievances 3. injury done, or the doing of injury, in return for injury received; retaliation or an act of retaliation, specif. in war, as the killing of prisoners

re·prise (ri prīz′; for n. 2 & vt., usually -prēz′) n. [ME. < OFr., fem. of *repris*, pp. of *reprendre*, to take back < L. *reprehendere*: see REPREHEND] 1. English Law a deduction and payment, as for an annuity, out of income from lands: *usually used in pl.* 2. *Music* a) same as RECAPITULATION b) in a musical play, the repetition of all or part of a song performed earlier —vt. -prised′, -pris′ing to present a reprise of (a song)

re·pro (rē′prō) n., pl. -pros clipped form of REPRODUCTION PROOF: also **repro proof**

re·proach (ri prōch′) vt. [LME. *reprochen* < OFr. *reprochier* < VL. *repropiare* < L. *re-*, back + *prope*, near] 1. to accuse of and blame for a fault so as to make feel ashamed; rebuke; reprove 2. [Rare] to bring shame and disgrace upon; be a cause of discredit to —n. 1. shame, disgrace, discredit, or blame, or a source, cause, or occasion of this 2. a blaming or reproving; rebuke 3. an expression of blame or reproof 4. [Obs.] an object of blame, censure, scorn, etc. —**re·proach′a·ble** adj. —**re·proach′er** n. —**re·proach′ing·ly** adv.

re·proach·ful (-fəl) adj. full of or expressing reproach, or blame, censure, etc. —**re·proach′ful·ly** adv. —**re·proach′ful·ness** n.

rep·ro·bate (rep′rə bāt′) vt. -bat′ed, -bat′ing [ME. *reprobaten* < LL.(Ec.) *reprobatus*, pp. of *reprobare*: see REPROVE] 1. to disapprove of strongly; condemn 2. to reject; specif., *Theol.* to reject and abandon as beyond salvation: said of God —adj. 1. depraved; corrupt; unprincipled 2. *Theol.* rejected by God; excluded from salvation and lost in sin —n. a depraved or unprincipled person; scoundrel: often used hyperbolically of a mischievous rogue

rep·ro·ba·tion (rep′rə bā′shən) n. [ME. *reprobacioun* < LL.(Ec.) *reprobatio*] 1. the act of reprobating 2. disapproval; censure 3. rejection; specif., *Theol.* rejection by God, as beyond salvation —**rep′ro·ba′tive** adj.

re·proc·essed wool (rē präs′est) wool cloth respun and rewoven from the raveled fibers of unused cloth such as the waste or clippings from a garment factory

re·pro·duce (rē′prə dōōs′, -dyōōs′) vt. -duced′, -duc′ing to produce again; make, form, or bring into existence again or anew in some way; specif., a) to produce by generation or propagation; bring forth one or more other individuals of (the kind or species) by sexual or asexual processes b) to make (a lost part or organ) grow again c) to bring about or promote the reproduction of (plants or animals) d) to make a copy, close imitation, duplication, etc. of (a picture, sound, writing, etc.) e) to bring (a past scene, etc.) before the mind again; re-create mentally by imagination or memory f) to repeat —vi. 1. to produce offspring; bring forth others of its kind 2. to undergo reproduction, or copying, duplication, etc. —**re′pro·duc′er** n. —**re′pro·duc′i·ble** adj.

re·pro·duc·tion (rē′prə duk′shən) n. 1. a reproducing or being reproduced 2. something made by reproducing; copy, close imitation, duplication, etc. 3. the process, sexual or asexual, by which animals and plants produce new individuals —SYN. see COPY

reproduction proof an especially fine proof of type, engraving, etc., usually on glossy paper, to be photographed for making a printing plate

re·pro·duc·tive (rē′prə duk′tiv) adj. 1. reproducing or tending to reproduce 2. of or for reproduction —**re′pro·duc′tive·ly** adv. —**re′pro·duc′tive·ness** n.

re·proof (ri prōōf′) n. [ME. *reprove* < OFr. *reprouve* < *reprouver*] the act of reproving or something said in reproving; rebuke; censure Also **re·prov′al** (-prōō′v'l)

re·prove (ri prōōv′) vt. -proved′, -prov′ing [ME. *reproven* < OFr. *reprover* < LL.(Ec.) *reprobare*: see RE- & PROVE] 1. to speak to in disapproval; rebuke 2. to express disapproval of (something done or said); censure 3. [Obs.] to refute; disprove 4. [Obs.] to convince or convict —**re·prov′a·ble** adj. —**re·prov′er** n. —**re·prov′ing·ly** adv.

rept. report

rep·tant (rep′tənt) adj. [L. *reptans*, prp. of *reptare*, to crawl, creep: see ff.] *Biol.* creeping or crawling

rep·tile (rep′t'l, -tīl) n. [LL.(Ec.) < neut. of L. *reptilis*, crawling < *reptus*, pp. of *repere*, to creep < IE. base *rep-*, to creep, crawl, whence Lith. *réplioti*, to creep, OHG. *rebo*, a tendril] 1. any of a class (Reptilia) of cold-blooded vertebrates having lungs, an entirely bony skeleton, a body covered with scales or horny plates, and a heart with two atria and, usually, a single ventricle, including the snakes, lizards, turtles, crocodiles, etc. and the dinosaurs 2. a mean, sneaky, groveling person —adj. [L. *reptilis*] of, like, or characteristic of a reptile; reptilian

rep·til·i·an (rep til′ē ən, -til′yən) adj. 1. of the reptiles 2. like or characteristic of a reptile 3. sneaky, mean, groveling, etc. —n. same as REPTILE

Repub. 1. Republic 2. Republican

re·pub·lic (ri pub′lik) n. [MFr. *république* < L. *respublica* < *res*, thing, affair, interest (see REAL¹) + *publica*, fem. of *publicus*, PUBLIC] 1. a) a state or nation in which the supreme power rests in all the citizens entitled to vote (the *electorate*) and is exercised by representatives elected, directly or indirectly, by them and responsible to them b) the form of government of such a state or nation c) a specified republican regime or the government of a nation [the Fifth *Republic* of France] 2. any group whose members are regarded as having a certain equality or common aims, pursuits, etc. [the *republic* of letters] 3. a state or nation with a president as its titular head 4. any of the constituent territorial and political units of the U.S.S.R. or Yugoslavia

re·pub·li·can (ri pub′li kən) adj. 1. of, characteristic of, or having the nature of, a republic 2. favoring, or in accord with the nature of, a republic ☆3. [R-] of, belonging to, or characteristic of the Republican Party —n. 1. a person who favors a republican form of government ☆2. [R-] a member of the Republican Party —**re·pub′li·can·ize′** (-īz′) vt. -ized′, -iz′ing

re·pub·li·can·ism (-iz'm) n. 1. republican form of government 2. a) republican principles, doctrines, etc. b) adherence to these ☆3. [R-] the principles, policies, etc. of the Republican Party

☆**Republican Party** 1. one of the two major political parties in the U.S., organized in 1854 to oppose the extension of slavery 2. a former political party in the U.S., organized by Thomas Jefferson: see DEMOCRATIC PARTY

Republican River [after the "*Republican* Pawnees," so called from their form of government] river flowing from E Colo. east & southeast through Nebr. & Kans., joining the Smoky Hill River to form the Kansas River; 445 mi.

re·pub·li·ca·tion (rē′pub li kā′shən) n. 1. publication anew 2. a book, pamphlet, etc. published again

re·pub·lish (rē pub′lish) vt. 1. to publish again 2. *Law* to execute (a will once revoked) a second time

re·pu·di·ate (ri pyōō′dē āt′) vt. -at′ed, -at′ing [< L. *repudiatus*, pp. of *repudiare*, to put away, divorce < *repudium*, separation, a divorce < *re-*, away, back + base of *pudere*, to feel shame] 1. to refuse to have anything to do with; disown or cast off publicly 2. a) to refuse to accept or support; deny the validity or authority of (a belief, a treaty, etc.) b) to deny the truth of (a charge, etc.) 3. to refuse to acknowledge or pay (a debt or obligation): said esp. of a government —SYN. see DECLINE —**re·pu′di·a′tion** n. —**re·pu′di·a′tor** n.

re·pugn (ri pyōōn′) vt., vi. [ME. *repugnen* < MFr. *repugner* < L. *repugnare* < *re-*, back + *pugnare*, to fight: see PUGNACIOUS] [Rare or Obs.] to oppose or resist

re·pug·nance (ri pug′nəns) n. [ME. < MFr. < L. *repugnantia* < *repugnans*, prp.: see REPUGN] 1. inconsistency or contradiction 2. extreme dislike or distaste; aversion; antipathy Also **re·pug′nan·cy** —SYN. see AVERSION

re·pug·nant (-nənt) adj. [ME. < MFr. < L. *repugnans*, prp.: see REPUGN] 1. contradictory; inconsistent [actions *repugnant* to his words] 2. offering resistance; opposed; antagonistic [*repugnant* forces] 3. causing repugnance; distasteful; offensive; disagreeable [a *repugnant* odor] —SYN. see HATEFUL —**re·pug′nant·ly** adv.

re·pulse (ri puls′) vt. -pulsed′, -puls′ing [< L. *repulsus*, pp. of *repellere*, REPEL] 1. to drive back; repel, as an attack 2. to repel with discourtesy, coldness, indifference, etc.; refuse, reject, or rebuff 3. to be repulsive, or disgusting, to —n. [L. *repulsa* < *repulsus*] 1. a repelling or being repelled 2. a refusal, rejection, or rebuff

re·pul·sion (ri pul′shən) n. 1. a repelling or being repelled 2. strong dislike, distaste, or aversion; repugnance 3.

---

reprobe	reprocess		reprosecute	re-prove

Physics the mutual action by which bodies or particles of matter tend to repel each other: opposed to ATTRACTION

re·pul·sive (-siv) *adj.* [ML. *repulsivus*] **1.** tending to repel **2.** causing strong dislike or aversion; disgusting; offensive **3.** characterized by, or having the nature of, repulsion —**re·pul′sive·ly** *adv.* —**re·pul′sive·ness** *n.*

rep·u·ta·ble (rep′yoo tə b'l) *adj.* **1.** in good repute; having a good reputation; well-thought-of; respectable **2.** regarded as proper usage; standard [a *reputable* word] —**rep′u·ta·bil′i·ty** *n.* —**rep′u·ta·bly** *adv.*

rep·u·ta·tion (rep′yoo tā′shən) *n.* [ME. *reputacioun* < L. *reputatio* < *reputatus*, pp. of *reputare*: see REPUTE] **1.** estimation in which a person or thing is commonly held, whether favorable or not; character in the view of the public, the community, etc.; repute **2.** such estimation when favorable; good repute; good name [to lose one's *reputation*] **3.** fame; distinction **4.** the general character of being thought of as specified; name [to have the *reputation* of being a cheat]

re·pute (ri pyoot′) *vt.* -**put′ed**, -**put′ing** [ME. *reputen* < MFr. *reputer* < L. *reputare* < *re-*, again + *putare*, to think: see PUTATIVE] to consider or account (a person or thing) to be as specified; generally suppose or regard: usually in the passive [he is *reputed* to be rich] —*n.* same as REPUTATION (senses 1, 3)

re·put·ed (-id) *adj.* generally accounted or supposed to be such [the *reputed* owner] —**re·put′ed·ly** *adv.*

req. 1. request **2.** required **3.** requisition

re·quest (ri kwest′) *n.* [ME. < OFr. *requeste* < ML. *requesta* < fem. pp. of VL. **requaerere*: see REQUIRE] **1.** the act of asking, or expressing a desire, for something; solicitation or petition **2.** something asked for [to grant a *request*] **3.** the state of being asked for or wanted; demand [a song much in *request*] —*vt.* **1.** to express a wish or desire for; ask for, esp. in a polite or formal way: often followed by an infinitive or a clause beginning with *that* **2.** to ask (a person) to do something —**by request** in response to a request

Re·qui·em (rek′wē əm, rāk′-, rēk′-) *n.* [ME. < L., acc. of *requies*, rest (see RE- & QUIET): first word of the Introit in the Latin Mass for the Dead] [also r-] **1.** *R.C.Ch.* a) a Mass for the repose of the soul or souls of a dead person or persons b) a celebration of this c) a musical setting for this **2.** any musical service, hymn, or dirge for the repose of the dead **3.** a dirgelike song, chant, or poem

requiem shark any of a large family (Carcharhinidae) of voracious, chiefly tropical, sharks

†**re·qui·es·cat** (rāk′wē es′kät, rek′-; -kat) *n.* [L., for *requiescat in pace* (see ff.): subj. of *requiescere*: see RE- & QUIESCENT] a prayer for the repose of the dead

†**re·qui·es·cat in pa·ce** (in pä′chā, pä′sē) [L.] may he (or she) rest in peace: often inscribed on tombstones

re·quire (ri kwir′) *vt.* -**quired′**, -**quir′ing** [ME. *requiren* < base of OFr. *requerre* < VL. **requaerere*, for L. *requirere* < *re-*, again + *quaerere*, to ask] **1.** to ask or insist upon, as by right or authority; demand [to *require* obedience] **2.** to order; command [to *require* someone to be present] **3.** to be in need of; need [to *require* help] **4.** to call for as necessary or appropriate [work that *requires* a steady hand] **5.** to demand by virtue of a law, regulation, etc. [what is *required* by law] **6.** [Archaic] to ask for; request —*vi.* to make a demand —*SYN.* see DEMAND, LACK

re·quire·ment (-mənt) *n.* **1.** the act or an instance of requiring **2.** something required; something obligatory or demanded, as a condition [the *requirements* for college entrance] **3.** something needed; necessity; need

req·ui·site (rek′wə zit) *adj.* [L. *requisitus*, pp. of *requirere*: see REQUIRE] required, as by circumstances; necessary for some purpose; indispensable [the *requisite* supplies for a journey] —*n.* something requisite —*SYN.* see ESSENTIAL, NEED

req·ui·si·tion (rek′wə zish′ən) *n.* [L. *requisitio* < *requisitus*, pp. of *requirere*: see REQUIRE] **1.** a requiring, as by right or authority; formal demand **2.** a formal written order, request, or application, as for equipment, tools, etc. **3.** the state of being demanded for service or use **4.** [Rare] a requirement; indispensable condition **5.** *Law* a demand by one government upon another for the surrender of a fugitive criminal —*vt.* **1.** to demand or take, as by authority [to *requisition* food for troops] **2.** to demand from; make demands on [to *requisition* a town for food] **3.** to submit a written order or request for (equipment, etc.)

re·quit·al (ri kwit′'l) *n.* **1.** a requiting or being requited **2.** something given or done in return; repayment, reward, retaliation, or compensation

re·quite (ri kwit′) *vt.* -**quit′ed**, -**quit′ing** [RE- + *quite*, obs. var. of QUIT] **1.** to make return or repayment for (a benefit, service, etc., or an injury, wrong, etc.) **2.** to make return or repayment to for a benefit, injury, etc.; reward or retaliate against **3.** [Now Rare] to give or do in return —**re·quit′er** *n.*

re·ra·di·a·tion (rē′rā dē ā′shən) *n. Physics* radiation resulting from the emission of previously absorbed radiation

rere·dos (rir′däs, rer′ə-) *n.* [ME. *rerdos*, aphetic < Anglo-Fr. *areredos* < OFr. *arere* (see ARREARS) + *dos*, back (see DOSSER)] an ornamental screen or partition wall behind an altar in a church

rere·mouse (rir′mous′) *n., pl.* -**mice** (-mis′) [ME. *reremous* < OE. *hreremus* < *hreren*, to move (< IE. base **kere-*, **kra-*, to mix, whence Gr. *kerannynai*: cf. CRATER) + *mus*, MOUSE] *archaic var. of* BAT²

re·route (rē root′, -rout′) *vt.* -**rout′ed**, -**rout′ing** to send by a new or different route

re·run (rē run′; *for n.* rē′run′) *vt.* -**ran′**, -**run′ning** to run again —*n.* **1.** the act of rerunning; esp., ☆a showing of a motion picture or taped television program after the first showing ☆**2.** the picture or program so shown

res (rās, rēz) *n., pl.* **res** [L. *res*, a thing: see REAL¹] *Law* **1.** a thing; object **2.** matter; case; point; action

res. 1. research **2.** reserve **3.** residence **4.** resides **5.** residue **6.** resigned **7.** resistance **8.** resolution

re·sal·a·ble (rē sāl′ə b'l) *adj.* that can be sold again

re·sale (rē′sāl′) *n.* the act of selling again; specif., the act of selling something bought to a third party

re·scind (ri sind′) *vt.* [L. *rescindere* (pp. *rescissus*), to cut off < *re-*, back + *scindere*, to cut: see SCISSION] to revoke, repeal, or cancel (a law, order, etc.) —*SYN.* see ABOLISH —**re·scind′a·ble** *adj.* —**re·scind′er** *n.*

re·scis·sion (ri sizh′ən) *n.* [LL. *rescissio*] the act of rescinding —**re·scis·so·ry** (ri sis′ə rē, -siz′-) *adj.*

re·script (rē′skript) *n.* [L. *rescriptum* < *rescriptus*, pp. of *rescribere* < *re-*, back + *scribere*, to write: see SCRIBE] **1.** an order or decree issued by a Roman emperor or by the Pope in answer to some presented difficulty or point of law **2.** any official decree or order **3.** a) the act of rewriting b) something rewritten; copy **4.** *Law* a written order, as from a court to its clerk, or from an appellate court to a trial court, giving the disposition of a case

res·cue (res′kyoo) *vt.* -**cued**, -**cu·ing** [ME. *rescuen* < OFr. *rescourre* < *re-*, again + *escorre*, to shake, move < L. *exculere*, to shake off, drive away < *ex-*, off + *quatere*, to shake: see QUASH²] **1.** to free or save from danger, imprisonment, evil, etc. **2.** *Law* to take (a person or thing) out of legal custody by force —*n.* the act or an instance of rescuing; deliverance —**res′cu·a·ble** *adj.* —**res′cu·er** *n.* *SYN.*—**rescue** implies prompt action in freeing someone or something from imminent danger or destruction or in releasing someone from captivity [he *rescued* the drowning child]; **deliver** implies a setting free from confinement or from some restricting situation [*deliver* me from his interminable sermons]; **redeem** suggests a freeing from bondage or from the consequences of sin, or a reclaiming, as from pawn, deterioration, etc. [how can I *redeem* my good name?]; **ransom** specifically implies the payment of what is demanded in order to free one held captive; **save**, in this connection, is a general, comprehensive synonym for any of the preceding terms

re·search (ri surch′; *for n.* equally rē′surch) *n.* [MFr. *recerche* < *recercher*, to travel through, survey: see RE- & SEARCH] [sometimes *pl.*] careful, systematic, patient study and investigation in some field of knowledge, undertaken to discover or establish facts or principles —*vi.* to do research; make researches —*vt.* to do research on or in; investigate thoroughly —*SYN.* see INVESTIGATION —**re·search′a·ble** *adj.* —**re·search′er**, **re·search′ist** *n.*

re·seat (rē sēt′) *vt.* **1.** to seat again or in another seat **2.** to supply with a new seat or seats

ré·seau, re·seau (rā zō′) *n., pl.* -**seaux′** (-zōz′, -zō′) [Fr. < OFr. *resel*, dim. of *roiz* < VL. *retis*, for L. *rete*, a net, prob. < IE. base **(e)re-*, loose, whence L. *rarus* (cf. RARE¹), Lith. *rētis*, a sieve] **1.** a network; specif., a) a network of fine lines on a glass plate, forming little squares of a standard size: used in photographic telescopes to produce a similar network on photographs of stars, for aid in measurement b) a network of meteorological stations throughout the world **2.** a netted ground or meshed foundation in lace **3.** a filter screen used in color photography

re·sect (ri sekt′) *vt.* [< L. *resectus*, pp. of *resecare*, to cut off < *re-* (see RE-) + *secare*, to cut: see SAW¹] *Surgery* to perform a resection of (some part)

re·sec·tion (ri sek′shən) *n.* [L. *resectio* < *resectus*: see prec.] **1.** the surgical removal of part of an organ, bone, etc. **2.** *Surveying* a method of determining the location of a point by taking observations from it to points of known location

re·se·da (ri sē′də) *n.* [ModL. < L., a plant: said (by Pliny) to be orig. imperative of *resedare*, to allay, used in charm accompanying its medicinal use] *same as* MIGNONETTE (sense 3)

re·sem·blance (ri zem′bləns) *n.* [ME. < Anglo-Fr.] **1.** the state, fact, or quality of resembling; similarity of appearance, or, sometimes, of character; likeness **2.** a point, degree, or sort of likeness **3.** something that resembles; likeness or semblance (of someone or something) **4.** [Obs.] characteristic appearance **5.** [Obs.] likelihood; probability —*SYN.* see LIKENESS

repurchase	reread	resalute	reseed
repurify	rerecord	reschedule	resegregate
repursue	reroll	rescore	reseize
requalify	resaddle	rescreen	reseizure
reradiate	resail	reseal	resell

re·sem·ble (ri zem'b'l) *vt.* **-bled, -bling** [ME. *resemblen* < OFr. *resembler* < *re-*, again + *sembler* < L. *simulare:* see SIMULATE] **1.** to be like or similar to in appearance or nature **2.** [Archaic] to liken or compare

re·send (rē send') *vt.* **-sent', -send'ing** to send again or send back

re·sent (ri zent') *vt.* [Fr. *ressentir* < OFr. *resentir* < *re-*, again + *sentir*, to feel or perceive: see SEND[1]] to feel or show a bitter hurt or indignation at (some act, remark, etc.) or toward (a person), from a sense of being injured or offended

re·sent·ful (-fəl) *adj.* feeling or showing resentment —**re·sent'ful·ly** *adv.* —**re·sent'ful·ness** *n.*

re·sent·ment (-mənt) *n.* [Fr. *ressentiment:* see RESENT] a feeling of bitter hurt or indignation, from a sense of being injured or offended —*SYN.* see OFFENSE

re·ser·pine (ri sur'pin, -pēn; res'ər pēn') *n.* [G. *reserpin*, prob. arbitrary contr. < ModL. *Rauwolfia serpentina*] a crystalline alkaloid, $C_{33}H_{40}N_2O_9$, extracted from the root of various rauwolfias (esp. *Rauwolfia serpentina*), used in the treatment of hypertension and some forms of mental illness

res·er·va·tion (rez'ər vā'shən) *n.* [ME. < ML. *reservatio*] **1.** the act of reserving or that which is reserved; specif., *a)* a withholding of a right, interest, etc. *b)* that part of a deed or contract which provides for this ☆*c)* public land set aside for some special use [an Indian *reservation*, military *reservation*] ☆*d)* an arrangement by which a hotel room, theater or train ticket, etc. is set aside and held until called for ☆*e)* anything so reserved in advance ☆*f)* the promise of or a request for such an arrangement **2.** a limiting condition or qualification, tacit or expressed, as in an agreement [to make a promise with mental *reservations*]

re·serve (ri zurv') *vt.* **-served', -serv'ing** [ME. *reserven* < OFr. *reserver* < L. *reservare* < *re-*, back + *servare:* see OBSERVE] **1.** to keep back, store up, or set apart for later use or for some special purpose **2.** to hold over to a later time **3.** to set aside or have set aside for a special person, etc. [to *reserve* a theater seat] **4.** to keep back or retain for oneself [to *reserve* the right to refuse] —*n.* **1.** something kept back or stored up, as for later use or for a special purpose **2.** a limitation or reservation: now rare except in phrase **without reserve** (see below) **3.** the practice of keeping one's thoughts, feelings, etc. to oneself; self-restraint or aloofness in speech and manner **4.** reticence; silence **5.** restraint and control in artistic expression; freedom from exaggeration or extravagance **6.** [*pl.*] *a)* available manpower kept out of action for use in an emergency or for replacing active groups or units, as in sports or warfare *b)* men or units in the armed forces not on active duty but subject to call; militia (with *the*) **7.** cash, or assets readily turned into cash, held out of use by a bank, insurance company, or business to meet expected or unexpected demands: see also LEGAL RESERVE ☆**8.** land set apart for a special purpose [a forest *reserve*] —*adj.* being, or having the nature of, a reserve or reserves [a *reserve* supply] —*SYN.* see KEEP —**in reserve** reserved for later use or for some person —**without reserve 1.** subject to no limitation **2.** without any minimum or asking price: said of goods offered at auction

☆**reserve bank** a bank in which the reserves of other banks are deposited; specif., *same as* FEDERAL RESERVE BANK

re·served (ri zurvd') *adj.* **1.** kept in reserve; set apart for some purpose, person, etc. **2.** self-restrained and withdrawn in speech and manner; reticent —*SYN.* see SILENT —**re·serv'ed·ly** (-zur'vid lē) *adv.* —**re·serv'ed·ness** *n.*

re·serv·ist (ri zur'vist) *n.* a member of a country's military reserves

res·er·voir (rez'ər vwär', rez'ə-; -vwôr', -vôr') *n.* [Fr. *réservoir* < *réserver:* see RESERVE] **1.** a place where anything is collected and stored, generally in large quantity; esp., a natural or artificial lake or pond in which water is collected and stored for use **2.** a receptacle or part (in an apparatus) for holding a fluid, as oil, ink, etc. **3.** a large supply; esp., an extra or reserve supply **4.** *Biol. a)* a part, sac, or cavity in some animals or plants in which fluid collects or into which products are secreted *b)* a species of organism that serves as an immune host for a parasite that can cause disease in another species: in full **reservoir host**

re·set (rē set'; *for n.* rē'set') *vt.* **-set', -set'ting** to set again (a broken bone, type, a gem, bowling pins, an electrical contact switch, etc.) —*n.* **1.** the act of resetting **2.** something reset **3.** a plant that is planted again **4.** a device for resetting something

res ges·tae (jes'tē) [L., things done, deeds] *Law* facts and circumstances attendant to the act in question

resh (rāsh) *n.* [Heb. *rēsh*, lit., the head] the twentieth letter of the Hebrew alphabet (ר)

re·shape (rē shāp') *vt.* **-shaped', -shap'ing** to shape again or give new shape or form to

re·ship (rē ship') *vt.* **-shipped', -ship'ping 1.** to ship again **2.** to transfer to another ship —*vi.* **1.** to go on a ship again; embark again **2.** to sign as a member of a ship's crew for another voyage —**re·ship'ment** *n.* —**re·ship'per** *n.*

Resht (resht) *same as* RASHT

re·shuf·fle (rē shuf'l) *vt.* **-fled, -fling 1.** to shuffle again **2.** to rearrange or reorganize —*n.* a reshuffling or being reshuffled, or the result of this

re·side (ri zīd') *vi.* **-sid'ed, -sid'ing** [ME. *resyden* < MFr. *resider* < L. *residere* < *re-*, back + *sedere*, to SIT] **1.** to dwell for a long time; have one's residence; live (*in* or *at*) **2.** to be present or inherent; exist (*in*): said of qualities, etc. **3.** to be vested (*in*): said of rights, powers, etc.

res·i·dence (rez'i dəns) *n.* [ME. < MFr. < ML. *residentia*] **1.** the act or fact of residing **2.** the fact or status of living or staying in a place while working, going to school, carrying out official duties, etc., esp. long enough to qualify for certain rights, privileges, etc. **3.** the place in which a person or thing resides; dwelling place; abode; esp., a house **4.** a large or imposing house; mansion **5.** the time during which a person resides in a place

res·i·den·cy (-dən sē) *n., pl.* **-cies 1.** *same as* RESIDENCE ☆**2.** *a)* a period of advanced, specialized medical or surgical training at a hospital *b)* the position or tenure of a doctor during this period

res·i·dent (-dənt) *adj.* [ME. < L. *residens*, prp.] **1.** living in a place for some continuous period; having a residence (*in* or *at*); residing **2.** living or staying in a place while working, carrying on official duties, etc.; being in residence **3.** present, inherent, or intrinsic in something **4.** not migratory: said of birds, etc. —*n.* **1.** a person who lives in a place, as distinguished from a visitor or transient ☆**2.** a doctor who is serving a residency **3.** a bird or animal that is not migratory

☆**resident commissioner** the elected representative of Puerto Rico to the U.S. House of Representatives: he may speak in the House, but has no vote

res·i·den·tial (rez'ə den'shəl) *adj.* **1.** of or connected with residence **2.** of, characterized by, or suitable for residences, or homes [a *residential* neighborhood] ☆**3.** chiefly for residents rather than transients [a *residential* hotel] —**res'i·den'tial·ly** *adv.*

res·i·den·ti·ar·y (rez'ə den'shē er'ē, -shə rē) *adj.* [ML. *residentiarius*] **1.** living in a place; resident **2.** of, requiring, or bound to an official residence —*n., pl.* **-ar'ies 1.** a resident **2.** *Eccles.* a clergyman bound to an official residence

re·sid·u·al (ri zij'oo wəl) *adj.* [see RESIDUE & -AL] of, or having the nature of, a residue or residuum; left over after part or most is taken away; remaining —*n.* **1.** what is left at the end of a process; something remaining ☆**2.** [*pl.*] extra fees paid to performers for reruns of filmed or taped material, as on television **3.** *Geol. same as* MONADNOCK **4.** *Math.* the difference between an actual value of some variable and a mean or other estimated value —**re·sid'u·al·ly** *adv.*

re·sid·u·ar·y (-oo wer'ē) *adj.* **1.** of, or having the nature of, a residue or residuum; remaining; leftover **2.** *Law a)* receiving the residue of an estate after specific bequests [a *residuary* legatee] *b)* giving the disposition of the residue of an estate after specific bequests [the *residuary* clause in a will]

res·i·due (rez'ə dōō', -dyōō') *n.* [ME. < MFr. *residu* < L. *residuum*, neut. of *residuus*, remaining < *residere:* see RESIDE] **1.** that which is left after part is taken away; remainder; rest **2.** *Chem.* the matter remaining at the end of a process, as after evaporation, combustion, filtration, etc.; residual product **3.** *Law* that part of a testator's estate which is left after all claims, charges, and bequests have been satisfied —*SYN.* see REMAINDER

re·sid·u·um (ri zij'oo wəm) *n., pl.* **-u·a** (-wə) [L.] *same as* RESIDUE —*SYN.* see REMAINDER

re·sign (ri zīn') *vt.* [ME. *resignen* < MFr. *resigner* < L. *resignare* < *re-*, back + *signare*, to SIGN] **1.** to give up possession of, relinquish (a claim, etc.) **2.** to give up (an office, position, etc.) —*vi.* to give up an office, position of employment, etc., esp. by formal notice (often with *from*) —*SYN.* see ABDICATE, SURRENDER —**resign oneself (to)** to submit or become reconciled (to); accept (something) passively

res·ig·na·tion (rez'ig nā'shən) *n.* [ME. < MFr. *resignation* < ML. *resignatio*] **1.** *a)* the act of resigning *b)* formal notice of this, esp. in writing **2.** patient submission; passive acceptance; acquiescence

re·signed (ri zīnd') *adj.* feeling or showing resignation; submissive; yielding and uncomplaining —**re·sign'ed·ly** (-zīn'id lē) *adv.* —**re·sign'ed·ness** *n.*

re·sile (ri zīl') *vi.* **-siled', -sil'ing** [MFr. *resiler* < L. *resilire* < *re-*, back + *salire*, to jump: see SALIENT] to bounce or spring back; rebound; specif., to come back into shape or position after being pressed or stretched: said of elastic bodies

resentence	resettle	resharpen	reshow
re-serve	resew	reshine	re-sign

re·sil·ience (ri zil′yəns, -ē əns) *n.* the quality of being resilient; esp., *a*) the ability to bounce or spring back into shape, position, etc. *b*) the ability to recover strength, spirits, etc. quickly; buoyancy Also **re·sil′ien·cy**

re·sil·ient (-yənt, -ē ənt) *adj.* [L. *resiliens*, prp. of *resilire*: see RESILE] 1. bouncing or springing back into shape, position, etc. after being stretched, bent, or, esp., compressed 2. recovering strength, spirits, good humor, etc. quickly; buoyant —*SYN.* see ELASTIC —**re·sil′ient·ly** *adv.*

res·in (rez′'n) *n.* [ME. < MFr. *resine* < L. *resina* < or akin to Gr. *rhētínē*] 1. any of various solid or semisolid, viscous, usually clear or translucent, yellowish or brownish, organic substances exuded from various plants and trees: natural resins are soluble in ether, alcohol, etc., and are used in varnishes and lacquers, as modifiers in synthetic plastics, etc. 2. *same as: a*) SYNTHETIC RESIN *b*) ROSIN —*vt.* to treat or rub with resin

res·in·ate (rez′ə nāt′) *vt.* -at′ed, -at′ing to impregnate or treat with resin

resin canal *Bot.* a tubular, intercellular opening containing resin, often found in the wood and needles of gymnosperms

res·in·if·er·ous (rez′ə nif′ər əs) *adj.* [see -FEROUS] yielding resin: said of trees, etc.

res·in·oid (rez′'n oid′) *adj.* like resin —*n.* 1. a resinoid substance 2. *same as* GUM RESIN

res·in·ous (-əs) *adj.* [L. *resinosus*] 1. of or like resin 2. obtained from resin 3. containing resin Also **res′in·y**

re·sist (ri zist′) *vt.* [ME. *resisten* < MFr. *resister* < L. *resistere* < *re-*, back + *sistere*, to set, caus. of *stare*, to STAND] 1. to withstand; oppose; fend off; stand firm against; withstand the action of 2. *a*) to oppose actively; fight, argue, or work against *b*) to refuse to cooperate with, submit to, etc. [to *resist* conscription] 3. to keep from yielding to, being affected by, or enjoying [to *resist* temptation] —*vi.* to oppose or withstand something; offer resistance —*n.* a substance that resists, esp. something applied as a protective coating —*SYN.* see OPPOSE —**re·sist′er** *n.*

re·sist·ance (ri zis′təns) *n.* [ME. < MFr. *resistence* < LL. *resistentia*] 1. the act of resisting, opposing, withstanding, etc. 2. power or capacity to resist; specif., the ability of an organism to ward off disease 3. opposition of some force, thing, etc. to another or others 4. a force that retards, hinders, or opposes motion 5. [often R-] the organized underground movement in a country fighting against a foreign occupying power, a dictatorship, etc., as in France during the Nazi occupation 6. *Elec. a*) that property of a conductor by which it opposes the flow of an electric current, resulting in the generation of heat in the conducting material: the measure of the resistance of a given conductor is the electromotive force needed for a unit current, usually expressed in ohms *b*) *same as* RESISTOR 7. *Psychoanalysis* the active psychological opposition to the bringing of unconscious, usually repressed, material to consciousness

re·sist·ant (-tənt) *adj.* [L. *resistens*, prp.] offering resistance; resisting —*n.* a person or thing that resists

Re·sis·ten·cia (re′sēs ten′syä) city in N Argentina, on the Paraná River: pop. 70,000

re·sist·i·ble (ri zis′tə b'l) *adj.* that can be resisted — **re·sist′i·bil′i·ty** *n.*

re·sis·tive (-tiv) *adj.* resisting, tending to resist, or capable of resistance —**re·sis′tive·ly** *adv.*

re·sis·tiv·i·ty (rē′zis tiv′ə tē, ri zis′-) *n.* 1. property of, capacity for, or tendency toward resistance 2. *Elec.* the resistance between opposite faces of a unit cube of a substance, usually given for a one-centimeter cube

re·sist·less (ri zist′lis) *adj.* 1. that cannot be resisted; irresistible 2. without power to resist; unresisting — **re·sist′less·ly** *adv.* —**re·sist′less·ness** *n.*

re·sist·o·jet (ri zis′tə jet′) *n.* [< RESISTOR + JET[1]] a jet engine that obtains its thrust from a propellant ionized by heat from a resistance device using electrical power

re·sis·tor (ri zis′tər) *n. Elec.* a device, as a coil or length of wire, used in a circuit primarily to provide resistance

res ju·di·ca·ta (jōō′di kä′tə, -kā′-) [L., thing decided] *Law* a matter already decided by judicial authority

re·sole (rē′sōl′) *vt.* -soled′, -sol′ing to put a new sole on (a shoe, etc.) —*n.* a new sole for a shoe, etc.

re·sol·u·ble (ri zäl′yoo b'l, rez′əl yoo b'l) *adj.* [LL. *resolubilis* < L. *resolvere*] that can be resolved —**re·sol′u·bil′i·ty, re·sol′u·ble·ness** *n.*

res·o·lute (rez′ə lōōt′) *adj.* [L. *resolutus*, pp. of *resolvere*: see RE- & SOLVE] having or showing a fixed, firm purpose; determined; resolved; unwavering —*SYN.* see FAITHFUL —**res′o·lute′ly** *adv.* —**res′o·lute′ness** *n.*

res·o·lu·tion (rez′ə lōō′shən) *n.* [ME. *resolucioun*, dissolution < MFr. *resolution* < L. *resolutio* < *resolutus*: see prec.] 1. *a*) the act or process of resolving something or breaking it up into its constituent parts or elements *b*) the result of this 2. *a*) a resolving, or determining; deciding *b*) the thing determined upon; decision as to future action; resolve 3. a resolute quality of mind 4. a formal statement of opinion or determination adopted by an assembly or other formal group 5. a solving, as of a puzzle, or answering, as of a question; solution 6. that part of a drama or narrative in which the plot is unraveled 7. *Med.* the subsidence or disappearance of swelling, fever, or other manifestation of disease 8. *Music a*) the passing of a dissonant chord (or tone in a chord) to a consonant chord (or tone) *b*) a chord or tone to which such passing occurs 9. *Optics* the capability of an optical system of making clear and distinguishable the separate parts or components of an object or of differentiating between sources of light

re·solv·a·ble (ri zäl′və b'l, -zôl′-) *adj.* that can be resolved —**re·solv′a·bil′i·ty** *n.*

re·solve (ri zälv′, -zôlv′) *vt.* -solved′, -solv′ing [ME. *resolven* < L. *resolvere*: see RE- & SOLVE] 1. to break up into separate, constituent elements or parts; analyze 2. to change or transform: used reflexively [a discussion that *resolved* itself into an argument] 3. to cause (a person) to decide or make up his mind [the flood that *resolved* him to sell] 4. to reach as a decision or intention; determine [to *resolve* to go] 5. *a*) to find the solution or an answer to (a problem); solve *b*) to make a decision about [to *resolve* the points at issue] *c*) to explain or make clear; show the resolution of (a problem, a fictional plot, etc.) *d*) to remove or dispel (doubt, etc.) 6. to decide by vote; make a formal decision about; express by resolution: said of a legislative assembly, etc. 7. [Obs.] to cause to dissolve or melt 8. *Chem.* to separate (an optically inactive compound or mixture) into its optically active components 9. *Med.* to cause (a swelling, fever, etc.) to subside or disappear 10. *Music* to cause (a chord or tone) to undergo resolution 11. *Optics* to make visible the individual parts of (an image) —*vi.* 1. to be resolved, as by analysis 2. to come to a decision; make a resolution; determine 3. *Music* to undergo resolution —*n.* 1. fixed purpose or intention; firm determination 2. a formal resolution, as of an assembly —*SYN.* see DECIDE —**re·solv′er** *n.*

re·solved (ri zälvd′, -zôlvd′) *adj.* firm and fixed in purpose; determined; resolute —**re·solv′ed·ly** (-zäl′vid lē, -zôl′-) *adv.*

re·sol·vent (ri zäl′vənt, -zôl′-) *adj.* that resolves; causing solution or resolution; solvent —*n.* 1. something resolvent; specif., a medicine that can cause resolution, as of a swelling 2. something that resolves problems, etc.

resolving power 1. a measure of the smallest distance between two points in the image of an optical system when the two points can be distinguished as separate 2. the ability of a photographic emulsion to produce a picture containing fine detail

res·o·nance (rez′ə nəns) *n.* [LME. *resonnaunce* < MFr. *resonance* < L. *resonantia*, an echo] 1. the quality or state of being resonant 2. reinforcement and prolongation of a sound or musical tone by reflection or by sympathetic vibration of other bodies 3. *Chem.* the property of certain molecules of having two or more structures in which only the positions of electrons differ 4. *Elec.* a condition arising in an electric circuit in which *a*) the current or voltage flow is at maximum amplitude, produced when the frequency of the electrical source is varied, or *b*) the current or voltage is in phase respectively with the applied current or voltage, or *c*) the natural frequency of the circuit is the same as that of the incoming signal 5. *Med.* the sound produced in the percussion of some part of the body, esp. of the chest 6. *Phonet.* that quality of a vocal sound that is determined by its vibrating in a resonating cavity, as the pharynx, the mouth, or the nose 7. *Physics a*) the effect produced when the natural vibration frequency of a body is greatly amplified by reinforcing vibrations at the same or nearly the same frequency from another body *b*) a vibration caused by this phenomenon

res·o·nant (-nənt) *adj.* [L. *resonans*, prp. of *resonare*, to resound: see RE- & SOUND[1], v.] 1. resounding or reechoing [a *resonant* sound] 2. producing resonance; increasing the intensity of sounds by sympathetic vibration [*resonant* walls] 3. full of, characterized by, or intensified by, resonance [a *resonant* voice] 4. of or in resonance — **res′o·nant·ly** *adv.*

res·o·nate (-nāt′) *vi.* -nat′ed, -nat′ing [< L. *resonatus*, pp. of *resonare*: see prec.] 1. to be resonant; resound 2. to produce resonance —*vt.* to make resonant

res·o·na·tor (-nāt′ər) *n.* 1. a device for producing resonance or increasing sound by resonance 2. *Electronics* an apparatus or system, as a piezoelectric crystal or a circuit, capable of being put into oscillation by oscillations in another system

re·sorb (ri sôrb′) *vt.* [L. *resorbere* < *re-*, again + *sorbere*, to suck up < IE. base *srbh-*, to sip, slurp, whence Gr. *rhophein*, Lith. *srebiù*, to sip] to absorb again —**re·sorp′-tion** (-sôrp′shən) *n.* —**re·sorp′tive** *adj.*

res·or·cin·ol (ri zôr′si nôl′, -nōl′) *n.* [RES(IN) + ORCINOL] a colorless, crystalline compound, $C_6H_4(OH)_2$, prepared synthetically or by fusing certain resins with caustic alkalies and used in making dyes, celluloid, pharmaceuticals, etc.: also **res·or′cin** (-sin)

re·sort (ri zôrt′) *vi.* [ME. *resorten* < OFr. *resortir* < *re-*, again + *sortir*, to go out: see SORTIE] 1. to go; esp., to go often, customarily, or generally 2. to have recourse; go or turn (*to*) for use, help, support, etc. [to *resort* to harsh

---

resilver   resketch   resolder   re-solve
resituate   resmooth   resolidify   re-sort

measures/ —*n*. [ME. < OFr. < the *v*.] **1.** a place to which people go often or generally, esp. one for rest or recreation, as on a vacation **2.** a frequent, customary, or general going, gathering together, or visiting /a place of general *resort*/ **3.** a person or thing that one goes or turns to for help, support, etc. **4.** a going or turning for help, support, etc.; recourse /to have *resort* to relatives/ —*SYN*. see RESOURCE —**as a** (or **the**) **last resort** as the last available means —**re·sort′er** *n*.

re·sound (ri zound′) *vi*. [altered (after SOUND¹) < ME. *resounen* < OFr. *resoner* < L. *resonare* < *re-* + *sonare*: for base see SOUND¹] **1.** to echo or be filled with sound; reverberate **2.** to make a loud, echoing, or prolonged sound **3.** to be echoed; be repeated or prolonged: said of sounds **4.** to be celebrated; be extolled /an act that *resounded* through the ages/ —*vt*. **1.** to give back (sound); echo **2.** to give forth, utter, or repeat loudly **3.** to celebrate or extol (praises, etc.)

re·sound·ing (-iŋ) *adj*. **1.** reverberating; ringing sonorously **2.** thoroughgoing; complete /a *resounding* victory/ **3.** high-sounding —**re·sound′ing·ly** *adv*.

re·source (rē′sôrs, -zôrs; ri sôrs′, -zôrs′) *n*. [Fr. *ressource* < OFr. < *resourdre*, to arise anew < *re-*, again + *sourdre*, to spring up < L. *surgere*: see SURGE] **1.** something that lies ready for use or that can be drawn upon for aid or to take care of a need **2.** [*pl*.] available money or property; wealth; assets **3.** [*pl*.] something that a country, state, etc. has and can use to its advantage /natural *resources*, including coal and oil/ **4.** a means of accomplishing something; measure or action that can be resorted to, as in an emergency; expedient **5.** [*pl*.] a source of strength or ability within oneself: in full **inner resources 6.** ability to deal promptly and effectively with problems, difficulties, etc.; resourcefulness

SYN.—**resource** applies to any thing, person, action, etc. to which one turns for aid in time of need or emergency /what *resource* is left us?/; **resort** is usually used of a final resource, qualified as by *last* /we'll take the train as a last *resort*/; **expedient** refers to something used to effect a desired end, specifically to something used as a substitute for the usual means /the daybed was an excellent *expedient* for unexpected guests/; **makeshift** applies to a quick expedient and, as a somewhat derogatory term, connotes an inferior substitute, carelessness, etc. /she served sandwiches as a *makeshift* for dinner/; **stopgap** refers to a temporary expedient, to be replaced when the usual means is again available /he's just a *stopgap* until a new manager is appointed/

re·source·ful (ri sôrs′fəl, -zôrs′-) *adj*. full of resource; able to deal promptly and effectively with problems, difficulties, etc. —**re·source′ful·ly** *adv*. —**re·source′ful·ness** *n*.

resp. 1. respective(ly) **2.** respiration **3.** respondent

re·spect (ri spekt′) *vt*. [< L. *respectus*, pp. of *respicere*, to look at, look back on, respect < *re-*, back + *specere*, to look at: see SPY] **1.** *a*) to feel or show honor or esteem for; hold in high regard *b*) to consider or treat with deference or dutiful regard **2.** to show consideration for; avoid intruding upon or interfering with /to *respect* others' privacy/ **3.** to concern; relate to —*n*. [ME. *respecte* < L. *respectus*, a looking at, respect, regard; pp. used as n.] **1.** a feeling of high regard, honor, or esteem /to have *respect* for a great artist/ **2.** a state of being held in honor or esteem /to have the *respect* of one's sons/ **3.** deference or dutiful regard /*respect* for the law/ **4.** consideration; courteous regard /to have *respect* for the feelings of others/ **5.** [*pl*.] courteous expressions of regard: now chiefly in **pay one's respects** to show polite regard by visiting or presenting oneself **6.** a particular point or detail /right in every *respect*/ **7.** reference; relation /with *respect* to the problem/ —*SYN*. see REGARD —**in respect of** with reference to; as regards —**re·spect′er** *n*.

re·spect·a·bil·i·ty (ri spek′tə bil′ə tē) *n*., *pl*. **-ties 1.** the quality or state of being respectable **2.** respectable character, reputation, or social status **3.** respectable people as a group **4.** [*pl*.] patterns of living or behaving regarded as respectable

re·spect·a·ble (ri spek′tə b'l) *adj*. [ML. *respectabilis*] **1.** worthy of respect or esteem; estimable **2.** conforming to socially acceptable behavior, attitudes, taste, etc.; proper; correct **3.** fairly good in quality; of moderate excellence /a *respectable* meal/ **4.** fairly large in size, number, or amount /a *respectable* score/ **5.** good enough to be seen, used, etc.; presentable /a *respectable* pair of shoes/ —**re·spect′a·bly** *adv*.

re·spect·ful (-fəl) *adj*. full of or characterized by respect; showing deference or dutiful regard —**re·spect′ful·ly** *adv*. —**re·spect′ful·ness** *n*.

re·spect·ing (ri spek′tiŋ) *prep*. concerning; about

re·spec·tive (-tiv) *adj*. [ML. *respectivus* < L. *respectus*: see RESPECT] **1.** as relates individually to each of two or more persons or things; several /they went their *respective* ways/ **2.** [Obs.] worthy of respect **3.** [Obs.] heedful; attentive

re·spec·tive·ly (-tiv lē) *adv*. in regard to each of two or more, in the order named /the first and second prizes went to Mary and George, *respectively*/

re·spell (rē spel′) *vt*. to spell again; specif., to spell (a word) in a different, usually phonetic, system so as to indicate the pronunciation

Re·spi·ghi (re spē′gē), **Ot·to·ri·no** (ôt′tô rē′nô) 1879–1936; It. composer

re·spir·a·ble (ri spir′ə b'l, res′pər-) *adj*. [Fr. < LL. *respirabilis*] **1.** that is fit to be breathed **2.** that can respire; capable of breathing —**re·spir′a·bil′i·ty** *n*.

res·pi·ra·tion (res′pə rā′shən) *n*. [ME. *respiracioun* < L. *respiratio* < *respiratus*, pp.] **1.** act or process of respiring; breathing; inhaling and exhaling air **2.** the processes by which a living organism or cell takes in oxygen from the air or water, distributes and utilizes it in oxidation, and gives off products of oxidation, esp. carbon dioxide **3.** an analogous process in anaerobic organisms involving some substance other than free oxygen —**res′pi·ra′tion·al** *adj*.

res·pi·ra·tor (res′pə rāt′ər) *n*. **1.** a device, as of gauze, worn over the mouth and nose to prevent the inhaling of harmful substances, to warm the air breathed, etc. **2.** an apparatus for giving artificial respiration

res·pi·ra·to·ry (res′pər ə tôr′ē, ri spir′ə-) *adj*. [ML. *respiratorius*] of, for, or involving respiration or the respiratory system

respiratory pigment any of several colored protein substances, as hemoglobin and hemocyanin, in the circulatory system of animals and some plants, that combine reversibly with oxygen that is carried to the tissues

respiratory quotient the ratio between the volume of carbon dioxide eliminated and the volume of oxygen consumed by an animal or plant during a given period of time

respiratory system the system of organs involved in the exchange of carbon dioxide and oxygen between an organism and its environment

re·spire (ri spir′) *vi*. **-spired′, -spir′ing** [ME. *respiren* < OFr. *respirer* < L. *respirare* < *re-*, back + *spirare*, to breathe: see SPIRIT] **1.** to breathe; inhale and exhale air **2.** [Poet.] to breathe freely or easily again, as after exertion or anxiety —*vt*. to breathe

res·pite (res′pit) *n*. [ME. < OFr. *respit* < L. *respectus*: see RESPECT] **1.** a delay or postponement; esp., postponement of the carrying out of a death sentence; reprieve **2.** an interval of temporary relief or rest, as from pain, work, duty, etc.; lull —*vt*. **-pit·ed, -pit·ing** to give a respite to

re·splend·ent (ri splen′dənt) *adj*. [ME. < *resplendens*, prp. of *resplendere*: see RE- & SPLENDENT] shining brightly; full of splendor; dazzling; splendid —**re·splend′ence, re·splend′en·cy** *n*. —**re·splend′ent·ly** *adv*.

re·spond (ri spänd′) *vi*. [ME. *responden* < OFr. *respondre* < L. *respondere* < *re-*, back + *spondere*, to pledge: see SPONSOR] **1.** to answer; reply **2.** to act in return, as if in answer **3.** to have a positive or favorable reaction /an infection that *responded* to treatment/ ☆**4.** *Law* to be answerable or liable —*vt*. to say in answer; reply —*n*. **1.** *Archit*. an engaged column, pilaster, etc. supporting an arch **2.** *Eccles*. a response or responsory —*SYN*. see ANSWER

re·spond·ent (ri spän′dənt) *adj*. [L. *respondens*, prp.] responding; answering —*n*. **1.** a person who responds **2.** *Law* a defendant, esp. in equity, admiralty, appellate, and divorce proceedings —**re·spond′ence, re·spond′en·cy** *n*.

re·spond·er (-dər) *n*. **1.** a person or thing that responds **2.** *Electronics* a device that indicates reception of a signal; specif., same as TRANSPONDER

re·sponse (ri späns′) *n*. [ME. *respounse* < ML. *respons* < L. *responsum*, neut. of *responsum*, pp. of *respondere*: see RESPOND] **1.** something said or done in answer; reply or reaction **2.** *Eccles*. *a*) words, phrases, etc. sung or spoken by the congregation or choir in answer to the officiating clergyman *b*) same as RESPONSORY **3.** *Electronics* the ratio of the output to the input, as for a given frequency, of a device or system operating under specified conditions **4.** *Physiol., Psychol*. any behavior resulting from the application of a stimulus; reaction

re·spon·si·bil·i·ty (ri spän′sə bil′ə tē) *n*., *pl*. **-ties 1.** condition, quality, fact, or instance of being responsible; obligation, accountability, dependability, etc. **2.** a thing or person for whom one is responsible —*SYN*. see DUTY

re·spon·si·ble (ri spän′sə b'l) *adj*. [MFr. < L. *responsus*: see RESPONSE] **1.** expected or obliged to account (for something, to someone); answerable; accountable **2.** involving accountability, obligation, or duties /a *responsible* position/ **3.** that can be charged with being the cause, agent, or source of something /the moisture that is *responsible* for the rust/ **4.** able to distinguish between right and wrong and to think and act rationally, and hence accountable for one's behavior **5.** *a*) readily assuming obligations, duties, etc.; dependable; reliable *b*) able

| re-sound | respace | respeak | resplice |
| resow | respade | respecify | resplit |

to pay debts or meet business obligations —**re·spon'si·ble·ness** *n.* —**re·spon'si·bly** *adv.*
SYN.—**responsible** applies to one who has been delegated some duty or responsibility by one in authority and who is subject to penalty in case of default /he is *responsible* for making out the reports/; **answerable** implies a legal or moral obligation for which one must answer to someone sitting in judgment /he is not *answerable* for the crimes of his parents/; **accountable** implies liability for which one may be called to account /he will be held *accountable* for anything he may say/

re·spon·sion (-shən) *n.* [MFr. < L. *responsio*] **1.** [Rare] a responding **2.** [*pl.*] the first of three examinations for the B.A. degree at Oxford University, England

re·spon·sive (-siv) *adj.* [< Fr. or LL.: Fr. *responsif* < LL. *responsivus*] **1.** that gives or serves as an answer or response **2.** reacting easily or readily to suggestion or appeal [a *responsive* audience] **3.** containing or consisting of responses [*responsive* reading in church] —**re·spon'sive·ly** *adv.* —**re·spon'sive·ness** *n.*

re·spon·so·ry (-sə rē) *n., pl.* **-ries** [ME. *responsorye* < ML.(Ec.) *responsorium*, response (in worship)] *Eccles.* an anthem or series of responses sung in alternation by a soloist and choir after a lection

res pu·bli·ca (pōō'bli kə, pub'li-) [L., lit., public thing: see REPUBLIC] the state; commonwealth; republic

rest¹ (rest) *n.* [ME. < OE., akin to G. *rast* < IE. base *ere-, rē-*, rest, whence Gr. *erōē*, rest (from battle), OE. *row*, G. *ruhe*, rest, quiet, Goth. *razn*, house] **1.** *a)* peace, ease, and refreshment as produced by sleep *b)* sleep or repose, or a period of this **2.** refreshing ease or inactivity after work or exertion **3.** a period or occasion of inactivity, as during work or on a journey **4.** *a)* relief from anything distressing, annoying, tiring, etc. *b)* peace of mind; mental and emotional calm; tranquillity **5.** the repose of death **6.** absence of motion; state of being still; immobility **7.** a resting or stopping place; shelter or lodging place, as for travelers, sailors, etc. **8.** a thing or device for supporting something; support [a foot *rest*] **9.** *Music a)* a measured interval of silence between tones *b)* any of various symbols indicating the length of such an interval **10.** *Prosody* a short pause in a line of verse; caesura —*vi.* [ME. *restan* < OE. *ræstan* < the *n.*; infl. in some senses (esp. 5) by L. *restare* (see REST²) and the derived Fr. *rester*] **1.** *a)* to get peace, ease, and refreshment by sleeping, lying down, etc. *b)* to sleep **2.** to get ease and refreshment by ceasing from work or exertion **3.** to be at ease or at peace; be tranquil **4.** to be dead **5.** to be or become quiet, still, or inactive for a while **6.** to remain without change or further action /to let a matter *rest*/ **7.** to be, or seem to be, supported; specif., *a)* to lie, sit, or lean *b)* to be placed, based, or founded (*in, on, upon,* etc.) **8.** to be placed or imposed as a burden or responsibility **9.** to be or lie (where specified) /the fault *rests* with him/ **10.** to be directed or fixed /his eyes *rested* on the picture/ **11.** to rely; depend **12.** *Agric.* to remain unplowed or uncropped; lie fallow ☆**13.** *Law* to end voluntarily the introduction of evidence in a case —*vt.* **1.** to give rest to; refresh by rest **2.** to place, put, or lay for ease, support, etc. /to *rest* one's head on a pillow/ **3.** to base; ground /to *rest* an argument on trivialities/ **4.** to direct or fix (the eyes, etc.) **5.** to bring to rest; stop ☆**6.** *Law* to end voluntarily the introduction of evidence in (a case) —**at rest** in a state of rest; specif., *a)* asleep *b)* immobile *c)* free from distress, care, etc. *d)* dead —**lay to rest** to bury (a dead person) —**rest'er** *n.*

rest² (rest) *n.* [ME. < MFr. *reste* < OFr. *rester*, to rest, remain < L. *restare*, to stop, stand, rest, remain < *re-, back* + *stare*, to STAND] **1.** what is left after part is taken away; remainder **2.** [*with pl. v.*] the others Used with *the* —*vi.* [ME. *resten* < OFr. *rester*] to go on being; continue to be; remain (as specified) /rest assured that we will go/ —*vt.* [Obs.] to cause to remain; keep /"God *rest* ye merry, gentlemen"]

rest³ (rest) *n.* [ME. aphetic var. of *arest*, an ARREST] a support for the butt of a lance, projecting from the side of the breastplate in medieval armor

re·state (rē stāt') *vt.* **-stat'ed, -stat'ing** to state again, esp. in a different way —**re·state'ment** *n.*

☆**res·tau·rant** (res'tə rənt, -ränt') *n.* [Fr., substantive use of prp. of *restaurer*: see RESTORE] a place where meals can be bought and eaten

res·tau·ra·teur (res'tər ə tur') *n.* [Fr. < MFr., that which restores < ML. *restaurator*, one who restores] a person who owns or operates a restaurant

rest cure a treatment, as for nervous disorders, consisting of complete rest, often with special diet, etc.

rest·ful (rest'fəl) *adj.* **1.** full of or giving rest **2.** at rest; quiet; peaceful **3.** having a soothing or peaceful effect [*restful* colors] —*SYN.* see COMFORTABLE —**rest'ful·ly** *adv.* —**rest'ful·ness** *n.*

rest·har·row (rest'har'ō) *n.* [ME. *rest*, contr. < *arest* (see

ARREST) + HARROW¹: the tough roots obstruct the harrow] any of a genus (*Ononis*) of old-world plants of the legume family, with clusters of white, pink, or yellow flowers

res·ti·form (res'tə fôrm') *adj.* [ModL. *restiformis* < L. *restis*, a rope (for IE. base see RUSH²) + *-formis*, -FORM] ropelike or cordlike; specif., designating either of two cordlike bundles of nerve fibers (**restiform bodies**) connecting the medulla oblongata with each hemisphere of the cerebellum

rest·ing (res'tin) *adj.* **1.** being in a state of rest; quiescent **2.** *Biol.* remaining dormant for a period of time, as certain spores, eggs, etc. **3.** *Physiol.* not actively dividing: said of a cell, cell nucleus, etc.

res·ti·tu·tion (res'tə tōō'shən, -tyōō'-) *n.* [ME. < MFr. < L. *restitutio* < *restitutus*, pp. of *restituere*, to set up again, restore < *re-*, again + *statuere*, to set up: see STATUE] **1.** a giving back to the rightful owner of something that has been lost or taken away; restoration **2.** a making good for loss or damage; reimbursement **3.** a return to a former condition or situation **4.** *Physics* the recovery of its shape by an elastic body after pressure or strain is released —*SYN.* see REPARATION —**res'ti·tu'tive** *adj.*

res·tive (res'tiv) *adj.* [ME. *restyfe* < OFr. *restif* < *rester*: see REST²] **1.** refusing to go forward; balky, as a horse **2.** hard to control; unruly; refractory **3.** nervous or impatient under pressure or restraint; restless; unsettled —*SYN.* see CONTRARY —**res'tive·ly** *adv.* —**res'tive·ness** *n.*

rest·less (rest'lis) *adj.* **1.** characterized by inability to rest or relax; uneasy; unquiet **2.** having or giving no rest or relaxation; disturbed or disturbing [*restless* sleep] **3.** never or almost never quiet or still; always active or inclined to action **4.** seeking change; discontented —**rest'less·ly** *adv.* —**rest'less·ness** *n.*

restless cavy the wild guinea pig (*Cavia procellus*) of S. America, domesticated by the Incas

rest mass *Physics* the mass of a body at absolute rest when its velocity is zero: according to the special theory of relativity the mass increases with its rate of motion

res·to·ra·tion (res'tə rā'shən) *n.* [ME. *restauration* < MFr. < *restauration* < LL. *restauratio*] **1.** a restoring or being restored; specif., *a)* reinstatement in a former position, rank, etc. *b)* restitution for loss, damage, etc. *c)* a putting or bringing back into a former, normal, or unimpaired state or condition **2.** a representation or reconstruction of the original form or structure, as of a building, fossil animal, etc. **3.** something restored —**the Restoration 1.** the reestablishment of the monarchy in England in 1660 under Charles II **2.** the period of the reign of Charles II (1660–85): sometimes taken as including the reign of James II (1685–88)

re·stor·a·tive (ri stôr'ə tiv) *adj.* [ME. *restoratif* < MFr. < ML. *restaurativus*] **1.** of restoration **2.** tending to restore or capable of restoring; esp., capable of restoring health, strength, consciousness, etc. —*n.* something that restores; esp., something that restores to consciousness, as smelling salts

re·store (ri stôr') *vt.* **-stored', -stor'ing** [ME. *restoren* < OFr. *restorer* < L. *restaurare* (for earlier *instaurare*) < *re-*, again + *-staurare*, to place, erect: see STORE] **1.** to give back (something taken away, lost, etc.); make restitution of **2.** to bring back to a former or normal condition, as by repairing, rebuilding, altering, etc. /to *restore* a building, painting, etc./ **3.** to put (a person) back in a place, position, rank, etc. /to *restore* a king to his throne/ **4.** to bring back to health, strength, etc. **5.** to bring back into being, use, etc.; reestablish /to *restore* order, a system of government, etc./ —*SYN.* see RENEW —**re·stor'a·ble** *adj.* —**re·stor'er** *n.*

restr. restaurant

re·strain (ri strān') *vt.* [ME. *restreinen* < OFr. *restreindre* < L. *restringere* < *re-*, back + *stringere*, to draw tight: see STRICT] **1.** to hold back from action; check; suppress; curb **2.** to keep under control **3.** to deprive of physical liberty, as by shackling, arresting, etc. **4.** to limit; restrict —**re·strain'a·ble** *adj.* —**re·strain'ed·ly** *adv.*

SYN.—**restrain**, the term of broadest application in this list, suggests the use of strong force or authority either in preventing, or in suppressing and controlling, some action /try to *restrain* your zeal/; **curb, check,** and **bridle** derive their current implications from the various uses of a horse's harness, **curb** implying a sudden, sharp action to bring something under control /to *curb* one's tongue/, **check** implying a slowing up of action or progress /to *check* inflationary trends/, and **bridle** suggesting a holding in of emotion, feelings, etc. /to *bridle* one's envy/; **inhibit,** as used in psychology, implies a suppressing or repressing of some action, thought, or emotion /her natural verve had become *inhibited*/

re·strain·er (-ər) *n.* a person or thing that restrains; specif., *Photog.* a chemical, such as potassium bromide, added to a developer to retard its action

re·straint (ri strānt') *n.* [ME. *restreinte* < OFr. *restrainte* < *restreindre*, to RESTRAIN] **1.** a restraining or being restrained **2.** a restraining influence or action **3.** a means or instrument of restraining **4.** a loss or limitation of liberty; confinement **5.** control of emotions, impulses, etc.; reserve; constraint

MUSICAL RESTS
(A, whole; B, half; C, quarter; D, eighth; E, sixteenth)

---

respread	restage	resterilize	restock
restabilize	restamp	restimulate	restraighten
restaff	restart	restitch	re-strain

restraint of trade interruption of the free movement of goods in commerce; restriction or prevention of business competition, as by monopoly, price fixing, etc.

re·strict (ri strikt′) *vt.* [< L. *restrictus,* pp. of *restringere:* see RESTRAIN] to keep within certain limits; put certain limitations on; confine —*SYN.* see LIMIT

re·strict·ed (ri strik′tid) *adj.* limited; confined; specif., ☆*a*) limited to authorized personnel: said of documents, data, etc. ☆*b*) excluding a certain group or groups; esp., limited to white Christians —**re·strict′ed·ly** *adv.*

re·stric·tion (-shən) *n.* [ME. *restriccion* < MFr. *restriction* < L. *restrictio*] 1. a restricting or being restricted 2. something that restricts; limitation

re·stric·tion·ism (-shən iz′m) *n.* the policy of favoring restriction, as of trade, immigration, etc. —**re·stric′tion·ist** *n., adj.*

re·stric·tive (ri strik′tiv) *adj.* [ME. < MFr. *restrictif*] 1. restricting or tending to restrict; limiting *[restrictive regulations]* 2. *Gram.* designating a subordinate clause, phrase, or word felt as limiting the application of the word or words that it modifies and hence usually not set off by commas (Ex.: the man *who spoke to you* is my uncle) —**re·stric′tive·ly** *adv.* —**re·stric′tive·ness** *n.*

☆**restrictive covenant** a provision that restricts the action of a party to an agreement, as any covenant (unenforceable by law) seeking to prevent the sale of real estate to a member of a specified minority group

☆**rest·room** (rest′rōōm′) *n.* a room or rooms in a public building, equipped with toilets, washbowls, and sometimes couches and the like: also **rest room**

re·struc·ture (rē struk′chər) *vt.* **-tured, -tur·ing** to plan or provide a new structure or organization for

re·sult (ri zult′) *vi.* [ME. *resulten* < ML. *resultare* < L., to spring back, rebound, freq. of *resilire,* to leap back: see RESILE] 1. to happen or issue as a consequence or effect (often with *from*) *[floods resulting from heavy rains]* 2. to end as a consequence (*in* something) *[heavy rains resulting in floods]* —*n.* 1. *a*) anything that comes about as a consequence or outcome of some action, process, etc. *b*) *[pl.]* the consequence or consequences desired 2. the number, quantity, etc. obtained by mathematical calculation; answer to a problem —*SYN.* see EFFECT, FOLLOW

re·sult·ant (-′nt) *adj.* [L. *resultans,* prp.] 1. that results; following as a consequence 2. resulting from two or more forces or agents acting together —*n.* 1. something that results; result 2. *Physics* a force, velocity, etc. with an effect equal to that of two or more such forces, etc. acting together —**re·sult′ant·ly** *adv.*

re·sume (ri zōōm′, -zyōōm′) *vt.* **-sumed′, -sum′ing** [ME. *resumen,* to assume < MFr. *resumer* < L. *resumere* < *re-,* again + *sumere,* to take: see CONSUME] 1. *a*) to take, get, or occupy again *[to resume one's seat] b*) to take back or take on again *[to resume a former name]* 2. to begin again or go on with again after interruption *[to resume a conversation]* —*vi.* to begin again or go on again after interruption —**re·sum′a·ble** *adj.*

ré·su·mé (rez′ōō mā′, rā′zōō-; rā′zōō mā′) *n.* [Fr., pp. of *résumer:* see prec.] a summing up; summary; specif., ☆a statement of a job applicant's previous employment experience, education, etc.: also sp. **re′su·me′, re′su·mé′**

re·sump·tion (ri zump′shən) *n.* [ME. *resumpcioun* < L. *resumptio* < *resumptus,* pp. of *resumere*] the act of resuming

re·su·pi·nate (ri sōō′pə nāt′, -syōō′-) *adj.* [L. *resupinatus,* pp. of *resupinare,* to bend back < *re-,* back + *supinus,* SUPINE] *Bot.* having an upside-down appearance, as the flower of an orchid; inverted —**re·su′pi·na′tion** *n.*

re·su·pine (rē′soo pīn′, -syoo-) *adj.* [L. *resupinus,* back-formation < *resupinare:* see prec.] *same as* SUPINE (sense 1)

☆**re·sur·face** (rē sur′fis) *vt.* **-faced, -fac·ing** to put a new surface on —*vi.* to come to the surface again

re·surge (ri surj′) *vi.* **-surged′, -surg′ing** [L. *resurgere,* to rise again, in LL.(Ec.), to rise from the grave: see RE- & SURGE] 1. to rise again; be resurrected 2. [RE- + SURGE] to surge back again

re·sur·gent (-sur′jənt) *adj.* [L. *resurgens,* prp.] rising or tending to rise again; resurging —**re·sur′gence** *n.*

res·ur·rect (rez′ə rekt′) *vt.* [back-formation < ff.] 1. *Theol.* to raise from the dead or the grave; bring back to life 2. to bring back into notice, practice, use, etc. —*vi. Theol.* to rise from the dead

res·ur·rec·tion (rez′ə rek′shən) *n.* [ME. *resurreccion* < OFr. *resurrection* < LL.(Ec.) *resurrectio* < L. *resurrectus,* pp. of *resurgere:* see RESURGE] 1. *Theol. a*) a rising from the dead, or coming back to life *b*) the state of having risen from the dead 2. a coming back into notice, practice, use, etc.; revival, as of old customs —**the Resurrection** *Theol.* 1. the rising of Jesus from the dead after his death and burial 2. the rising of all the dead at the Last Judgment —**res′ur·rec′tion·al** *adj.*

res·ur·rec·tion·ism (-iz′m) *n.* the stealing of bodies from graves, esp. for dissection

res·ur·rec·tion·ist (-ist) *n.* 1. a person who steals bodies from graves, esp. for dissection 2. a person who brings something back into use or notice again 3. a person who believes in resurrection

☆**resurrection plant** 1. any of various small plants which curl up when dry and spread their branches or become green again when watered, including several club mosses (genus *Selaginella*) 2. *same as* ROSE OF JERICHO

re·sus·ci·tate (ri sus′ə tāt′) *vt.* **-tat′ed, -tat′ing** [< L. *resuscitatus,* pp. of *resuscitare,* to revive < *re-,* again + *suscitare,* to raise up, revive] to revive or revitalize; bring back to life; esp., to revive (someone apparently dead, in a faint, etc.), as by artificial respiration, etc. —*vi.* to revive, esp. to come back to life or consciousness again —**re·sus′ci·ta′tion** *n.* —**re·sus′ci·ta′tive** *adj.*

re·sus·ci·ta·tor (-tāt′ər) *n.* a person or thing that resuscitates; esp., an apparatus for giving artificial respiration by forcing air or oxygen into the lungs

Resz·ke (resh′ke), **Jean de** (zhän də) (born *Jan Mieczysław de Reszke*) 1850–1925; Pol. operatic tenor

ret (ret) *vt.* **re·t′ted, ret′ting** [ME. *retten, reten* < MDu. *reten, reeten*] to dampen or soak (flax, hemp, timber, etc.) in water in order to separate the fibers from woody tissue

ret. 1. retain 2. retired 3. return(ed)

re·ta·ble (ri tā′b′l) *n.* [Fr. < Sp. *retablo* < *re-,* behind (< L. *re-,* back) + *tabla,* shelf < L. *tabula:* see TABLE] a raised shelf or ledge above the back of an altar for holding altar lights, a cross, ornaments, etc.

re·tail (rē′tāl; *for vt. 2, usually* ri tāl′) *n.* [ME. *retaile* < OFr. *retaille,* lit., a cutting < *retailler,* to cut up < *re-,* again + *tailler,* to cut: see TAILOR] the sale of goods or articles individually or in small quantities directly to the consumer: cf. WHOLESALE —*adj.* of, connected with, or engaged in the sale of goods at retail —*adv.* in relatively small quantities or at a retail price —*vt.* [ME. *retaylen*] 1. to sell individually or in small quantities; sell directly to the consumer 2. to repeat or pass on (gossip, secrets, etc.) to others —*vi.* to be sold at retail *[books that retail at a dollar]* —**re′tail·er** *n.*

re·tain (ri tān′) *vt.* [ME. *reteynen* < OFr. *retenir* < LL. **retenere,* for *retinere* < *re-,* back + *tenere,* to hold: see THIN] 1. to hold or keep in possession 2. to keep in a fixed state or condition 3. to continue to have or hold in *[to retain heat]* 4. to continue to practice, use, etc. 5. to keep in mind 6. to hire, or arrange in advance for the services of, by paying a retainer —*SYN.* see KEEP —**re·tain′a·ble** *adj.* —**re·tain′ment** *n.*

retained object *Gram.* an object in passive constructions that is the same as the direct or indirect object in the corresponding active constructions (Ex.: *money* in "He was given the money by me")

re·tain·er¹ (ri tā′nər) *n.* 1. a person or thing that retains 2. a person serving another, esp. someone of rank; servant, attendant, adherent, etc. 3. any of several devices used to retain; specif., *a*) a groove, frame, etc. within which roller bearings are held *b*) a device designed to hold teeth in position after they have been adjusted by orthodontics

re·tain·er² (ri tā′nər) *n.* [ME. *reteyner:* see RETAIN & -ER, sense 3] 1. a retaining or being retained in one's service 2. *Law a*) the act of engaging the services of a lawyer, consultant, etc. *b*) a fee paid in advance to make such services available when needed

retaining wall a wall built to keep a bank of earth from sliding or water from flooding

re·take (rē tāk′; *for n.* rē′tāk′) *vt.* **-took′, -tak′en, -tak′ing** 1. to take again, take back, or recapture ☆2. to photograph again —*n.* 1. the act of retaking ☆2. a picture, motion-picture scene, etc. rephotographed or to be rephotographed

re·tal·i·ate (ri tal′ē āt′) *vi.* **-at′ed, -at′ing** [< LL. *retaliatus,* pp. of *retaliare,* to require, retaliate < L. *re-,* back + *talio,* punishment in kind] to return like for like; esp., to return evil for evil; pay back injury for injury —*vt.* to return an injury, wrong, etc. for (an injury, wrong, etc. given); requite in kind —**re·tal′i·a′tion** *n.* —**re·tal′i·a′tive, re·tal′i·a·to′ry** *adj.*

re·tard (ri tärd′) *vt.* [LME. *retarden* < OFr. *retarder* < L. *retardare* < *re-,* back + *tardare,* to make slow < *tardus,* slow: see TARDY] to hinder, delay, or slow the advance or progress of —*vi.* to be delayed or undergo retardation —*n.* a retarding; delay —*SYN.* see DELAY

re·tard·ant (-′nt) *n.* something that retards; esp., a substance that delays a chemical reaction —*adj.* tending to retard

☆**re·tar·date** (ri tär′dāt) *n.* [< L. *retardatus,* pp. of *retardare,* to RETARD] a mentally retarded person

re·tar·da·tion (rē′tär dā′shən) *n.* [ME. < L. *retardatio*]

restratify	restudy	resubmit	reswallow
restrengthen	restuff	resubscribe	resynthesize
restretch	restyle	resummon	retabulate
restrike	resubject	resupply	retack
restring	resubmerge	resurvey	retape

1. a retarding or being retarded **2.** something that retards **3.** *clipped form of* MENTAL RETARDATION **4.** a decrease in velocity **5.** the amount that something is retarded —**re·tard·a·tive** (ri tär′də tiv), **re·tard′a·to·ry** (-tôr′ē) *adj.*

re·tard·er (ri tär′did) *adj.* slowed or delayed in development or progress, esp. because of mental retardation

re·tard·er (-dər) *n.* something that retards, as a substance used to delay a chemical reaction

retch (rech) *vi.* [ME. *rechen* < OE. *hræcan*, to clear the throat, hawk < *hraca*, clearing of the throat, spittle < IE. echoic base **ker-*, whence RING[1], RAVEN[1]] to undergo the straining action of vomiting, esp. without bringing anything up

retd. **1.** retained **2.** retired **3.** returned

re·te (rēt′ē) *n.*, *pl.* **-ti·a** (-ē ə) [ME. *riet* < L. *rete*, a net: see RETINA] *Anat.* a network or plexus, as of blood vessels or nerve fibers

re·tem (rē′tem) *n.* [Ar. *ratam*, pl. of *ratamah*] a desert shrub (*Retama raetam*) of the legume family, with small, white flowers: the juniper of the Bible

re·tene (rē′tēn, ret′ēn) *n.* [< Gr. *rhētinē*, RESIN] a hydrocarbon, $C_{18}H_{18}$, obtained from resinous woods and fossil resins

re·ten·tion (ri ten′shən) *n.* [ME. *retencioun* < MFr. *retention* < L. *retentio*] **1.** a retaining or being retained **2.** power of or capacity for retaining **3.** *a)* a remembering; memory *b)* ability to remember **4.** *Med.* the retaining within the body of matter normally excreted

re·ten·tive (-tiv) *adj.* [ME. *retentif* < MFr. < LL. *retentivus*] **1.** retaining or tending to retain **2.** having the power of or capacity for retaining **3.** *a)* tenacious [a *retentive* memory] *b)* having a good memory —**re·ten′tive·ly** *adv.* —**re·ten′tive·ness** *n.*

re·ten·tiv·i·ty (rē′ten tiv′ə tē) *n.* **1.** the power of or capacity for retaining **2.** the power of remaining magnetized after the force of magnetization has stopped

re·think (rē thiŋk′) *vt.* **-thought′, -think′ing** to think over again, with a view to changing; reconsider

re·ti·a·ri·us (rē′shē er′ē əs) *n.*, *pl.* **-ri·i′** (-ī′) [L. < *rete*, a net: see RETINA] in ancient Rome, a gladiator armed with a net and a trident

re·ti·ar·y (rē′shē er′ē) *adj.* [< L. *rete*, a net (see RETINA) + -ARY] **1.** of or like nets or net-making **2.** building nets, as certain spiders **3.** armed with a net

ret·i·cence (ret′ə s′ns) *n.* [< Fr. or L.: Fr. *réticence* < L. *reticentia*] the quality or state, or an instance, of being reticent; reserve: also **ret′i·cen·cy**

ret·i·cent (-s′nt) *adj.* [L. *reticens*, prp. of *reticere*, to be silent < *re-*, again + *tacere*, to be silent: see TACIT] **1.** habitually silent or uncommunicative; disinclined to speak readily; reserved; taciturn **2.** having a restrained, quiet, or understated quality —*SYN.* see SILENT —**ret′i·cent·ly** *adv.*

ret·i·cle (ret′i k′l) *n.* [L. *reticulum*: see RETICULE] *Optics* a network of very fine lines, wires, etc. in the focus of the eyepiece of an optical instrument

re·tic·u·lar (ri tik′yə lər) *adj.* [ModL. *reticularis* < L. *reticulum*: see RETICULE] **1.** of or like a net; netlike **2.** intricate; entangled —**re·tic′u·lar·ly** *adv.*

re·tic·u·late (-lit; *also, and for v. always,* -lāt′) *adj.* [L. *reticulatus* < *reticulum*: see RETICULE] like a net or net-work; netlike; specif., *Bot.* having the veins arranged like the threads of a net: said of leaves: also **re·tic′u·lat′ed** —*vt.* **-lat′ed, -lat′ing** to divide or mark so as to look like network —*vi.* to be divided or marked like network —**re·tic′u·late·ly** *adv.*

re·tic·u·la·tion (ri tik′yə lā′shən) *n.* [ML. *reticulatio*] a reticulate arrangement, formation, or pattern; network

ret·i·cule (ret′ə kyōōl′) *n.* [Fr. *réticule* < L. *reticulum*, dim. of *rete*, a net: see RETINA] **1.** a woman's small handbag, orig. made of network and usually having a drawstring **2.** *same as* RETICLE

re·tic·u·lo·cyte (ri tik′yə lō sīt′) *n.* [< ModL. *reticulum* (see RETICULE) + -CYTE] an immature, circulating erythrocyte showing a network of fibers in the cell when stained —**re·tic′u·lo·cyt′ic** (-sit′ik) *adj.*

re·tic·u·lo·en·do·the·li·al (-en′də thē′lē əl) *adj.* [< ModL. *reticulum* (see RETICULE) + ENDOTHELIAL] designating or of the system of macrophages found in the bone marrow, liver, spleen, etc., including all the phagocytic cells except the leukocytes: they can take up certain dyes, bacteria, etc.

re·tic·u·lum (ri tik′yə ləm) *n.*, *pl.* **-la** (-lə) [L.: see RETICULE] **1.** a netlike pattern or structure; network **2.** *Biol.* any network or netlike structure, as the weblike structure found in the protoplasm of many cells **3.** *Zool.* the second division of the stomach, or second stomach, of cud-chewing animals, as cows: see RUMINANT, illus. —[R-] a S constellation between Dorado and Horologium

re·ti·form (rēt′ə fôrm′, ret′-) *adj.* [ModL. *retiformis* < L. *rete*, a net (see ff.) + *-formis*, -FORM] having crisscrossed lines; netlike in form; reticulate

ret·i·na (ret′n ə) *n.*, *pl.* **-nas** or **-nae′** (-ē′) [ML., prob. < L. *rete* (gen. *retis*), a net < IE. base **ere-*, loose, separate, whence Gr. *erēmos*, solitary, Lith. *rētis*, a sieve & (prob.)

L. *rarus*, rare] the innermost coat of the back part of the eyeball, a layer of cells sensitive to light, in part an expansion of the optic nerve fibers: the image formed by the lens on the retina is carried to the brain by the optic nerve: see EYE, illus. —**ret′i·nal** *adj.*

ret·i·nac·u·lum (ret′n ak′yə ləm) *n.*, *pl.* **-u·la** (-lə) [ModL. < L., that which holds back, tether < *retinere*, to RETAIN < *dim.* suffix] *Biol.* an often hooked structure, band, etc. serving to hold parts, seeds, eggs, etc. together or in place —**ret′i·nac′u·lar** (-lər) *adj.*

ret·ine (ret′ēn) *n.* [RET(ARD) + -INE[4]] a substance found in the body in minute amounts, that retards the growth of cells: cf. PROMINE

ret·i·nene (ret′n ēn′) *n.* [RETIN(A) + -ENE] *Biochem.* **1.** a yellowish carotenoid, $C_{20}H_{28}O$, liberated when rhodopsin or iodopsin is transformed by the action of light **2.** a similar carotenoid, $C_{20}H_{26}O$, formed by the action of light on porphyropsin

ret·i·ni·tis (ret′n īt′əs) *n.* [ModL.: see RETINA & -ITIS] inflammation of the retina

ret·in·o·scope (ret′n ə skōp′) *n.* [see RETINA & -SCOPE] *same as* SKIASCOPE

ret·i·nos·co·py (ret′n äs′kə pē) *n.* [< RETINA + -SCOPY] *same as* SKIASCOPY —**ret′i·no·scop′ic** (-ə skäp′ik) *adj.*

re·ti·nue (ret′n ōō′, -yōō′) *n.* [ME. *retenue* < OFr., fem. of *retenu*, pp. of *retenir*: see RETAIN] a body of assistants, followers, or servants attending a person of rank or importance; train of attendants or retainers

re·tire (ri tīr′) *vi.* **-tired′, -tir′ing** [Fr. *retirer* < *re-*, back + *tirer*, to draw] **1.** to go away, retreat, or withdraw to a private, sheltered, or secluded place **2.** to go to bed **3.** to give ground, as in battle; retreat; withdraw **4.** to give up one's work, business, career, etc., esp. because of advanced age **5.** to move back or away, or seem to do so —*vt.* **1.** to withdraw or move in retreat [to *retire* troops from an action] **2.** *a)* to take (money) out of circulation *b)* to take up or pay off (stocks, bonds, bills, etc.) **3.** to cause to retire from a position, job, or office **4.** to withdraw from use [to *retire* outdated machinery] ☆**5.** *Baseball*, etc. to put out (a batter, side, etc.) —*SYN.* see GO[1]

re·tired (ri tīrd′) *adj.* **1.** withdrawn or apart from the world; in seclusion; secluded **2.** *a)* that has given up one's work, business, career, etc., esp. because of advanced age *b)* of or for such retired persons

☆**re·tir·ee** (ri tīr′ē′) *n.* a person who has retired from work, business, etc.: also **re·tir′ant** (-ənt)

re·tire·ment (ri tīr′mənt) *n.* **1.** a retiring or being retired; specif., withdrawal from work, business, etc. because of age **2.** *a)* privacy; seclusion *b)* a place of privacy or seclusion

re·tir·ing (-iŋ) *adj.* **1.** that retires **2.** drawing back from contact with others, from publicity, etc.; reserved; modest; shy —**re·tir′ing·ly** *adv.*

re·took (rē took′) *pt. of* RETAKE

☆**re·tool** (rē tōōl′) *vt., vi.* **1.** to adapt the machinery of (a factory) to the manufacture of a different product by changing the tools and dies **2.** to reorganize to meet new or different needs or conditions

re·tor·sion (ri tôr′shən) *n.* [var. of RETORTION] *Law* a retaliation; reprisal; esp., in international law, mistreatment by one country of the citizens or subjects of another in retaliation for similar mistreatment received

re·tort[1] (ri tôrt′) *vt.* [< L. *retortus*, pp. of *retorquere*, to twist back < *re-*, back + *torquere*, to twist: see TORT] **1.** to turn (an insult, epithet, deed, etc.) back upon the person from whom it came **2.** to answer (an argument, etc.) in kind **3.** to say in reply or response —*vi.* to reply, esp. in a sharp, quick, or witty way, or in kind —*n.* **1.** a quick, sharp, or witty reply, esp. one that turns the words of the previous speaker back upon himself **2.** the act or practice of making such reply —*SYN.* see ANSWER

re·tort[2] (ri tôrt′) *n.* [Fr. *retorte* < ML. *retorta* < L., fem. of *retortus*, pp. of *retorquere*: see prec.] **1.** a container, generally of glass and with a long tube, in which substances are distilled, as in a laboratory **2.** a vessel in which ore is heated to extract a metal, coal is heated to produce gas, etc.

re·tor·tion (ri tôr′shən) *n.* [ML. *retortio* < L. *retortus*, pp. of *retorquere*: see RETORT[1]] **1.** a turning, bending, or twisting back or being turned, bent, or twisted back **2.** *same as* RETORSION

RETORT

re·touch (rē tuch′; *for n., also* rē′tuch′) *vt.* [Fr. *retoucher*: see RE- & TOUCH] **1.** to touch up or change details in (a painting, piece of writing, etc.) in order to improve it **2.** *Photog.* to change (a negative or print) by adding details or removing blemishes, etc. —*n.* **1.** the act or process of retouching **2.** a detail added or removed in retouching **3.** a photograph, etc. that has been retouched —**re·touch′er** *n.*

re·trace (ri trās′) *vt.* **-traced′, -trac′ing** [Fr. *retracer*: see RE- & TRACE[1]] **1.** to go back over again, esp. in the reverse direction [to *retrace* one's steps] **2.** to trace again the story of, from the beginning **3.** to go over again visually or in memory —**re·trace′a·ble** *adj.*

retax	retelevise	retest	retie
reteach	retell	retestify	retitle
retear	retemper	rethread	retold

re·trace (rē/trās′) *vt.* **-traced′, -trac′ing** to trace (a drawing, engraving, etc.) over again

re·tract (ri trakt′) *vt., vi.* [ME. *retracten:* in sense 1 < L. *retractus,* pp. of *retrahere,* to draw back < *re-,* back + *trahere,* to DRAW; in sense 2 < MFr. *retracter* < L. *retractare,* to draw back, withdraw < *re-,* back + *tractare,* to pull, draw, freq. of *trahere*] **1.** to draw back or in [to *retract* claws, to *retract* landing gear] **2.** to withdraw or disavow (a statement, promise, offer, charge, etc.); recant or revoke —**re·tract′a·bil′i·ty** *n.* —**re·tract′a·ble** *adj.* —**re·trac′tive** *adj.*

re·trac·tile (ri trak′t'l, -tīl) *adj.* [Fr. *rétractile*] **1.** that can be retracted, or drawn back or in, as the claws of a cat **2.** of retraction [*retractile* power] —**re·trac·til·i·ty** (rē/trak til′ə tē) *n.*

re·trac·tion (ri trak′shən) *n.* [ME. *retraccion* < LL. *retractio*] **1.** a retracting or being retracted; specif., *a)* withdrawal, as of a statement, promise, charge, etc. *b)* a drawing or being drawn back or in **2.** power of retracting

re·trac·tor (-tər) *n.* a person or thing that retracts; esp., *a)* a muscle that retracts an organ, protruded part, etc. *b)* a surgical instrument or device for drawing back a part or organ, as the flesh at the edge of an incision

re·tral (rē/trəl) *adj.* [< L. *retro,* backward + -AL] at, near, or toward the back; posterior —**re′tral·ly** *adv.*

re·tread (rē tred′; *for n.* rē/tred′) *vt.* same as RECAP¹ —*n.* **1.** same as RECAP¹ ☆**2.** [Slang] a person who is called back or returns to service, esp. military service

re·tread (rē/tred′) *vt.* **-trod′, -trod′den** or **-trod′, -tread′ing** to tread again

re·treat (ri trēt′) *n.* [ME. *retret* < OFr. *retraite* < pp. of *retraire,* to draw back < L. *retrahere:* see RETRACT] **1.** a going back or backward; withdrawal in the face of opposition or from a dangerous or unpleasant situation **2.** withdrawal to a safe or private place **3.** a safe, quiet, or secluded place **4.** a period of retirement or seclusion, esp. one devoted to religious contemplation away from the pressures of ordinary life, usually as a group activity **5.** an asylum for the aged, mentally ill, etc. **6.** *Mil. a)* the withdrawal of troops, ships, etc. from a position, esp. when forced by enemy attack *b)* a signal for such a withdrawal *c)* a signal given by bugle or drum at sunset for lowering the national flag *d)* the ceremony at which this is done —*vi.* [ME. *retreten*] **1.** to withdraw; go back; make a retreat; retire **2.** to slope backward —*vt.* to lead or draw back, esp., *Chess* to move (a piece) back —SYN. see SHELTER —**beat a retreat 1.** *Mil.* to signal for retreat by beating a drum **2.** to retreat; withdraw

re·trench (rē trench′) *vt.* [MFr. *retrencher:* see RE- & TRENCH] **1.** to cut down or reduce (esp. expenses); curtail **2.** to cut off or out; omit or delete (a portion of a book) —*vi.* to reduce expenses; economize

re·trench·ment (-mənt) *n.* [MFr.] **1.** a retrenching; esp., a reduction of expenses **2.** *Mil.* a rampart or breastwork within or behind the main fortifications, to which troops can retreat in case the outer line is breached

ret·ri·bu·tion (ret/rə byōō′shən) *n.* [ME. *retribucioun* < OFr. *retribution* < LL.(Ec.) *retributio* < L. *retributus,* pp. of *retribuere,* to repay < *re-,* back + *tribuere,* to pay: see TRIBUTE] **1.** deserved punishment for evil done, or, sometimes, reward for good done; merited requital **2.** *Theol.* reward or punishment in another life for things done in this —**re·trib·u·tive** (ri trib′yoo tiv), **re·trib′u·to′ry** (-tôr′ē) *adj.* —**re·trib′u·tive·ly** *adv.*

re·triev·al (ri trē′v'l) *n.* **1.** the act or process of retrieving **2.** possibility of recovery or restoration

re·trieve (ri trēv′) *vt.* **-trieved′, -triev′ing** [ME. *retreven* < inflected stem of OFr. *retrouver* < *re-,* again + *trouver,* to find: see TROVER] **1.** to get back; recover **2.** to restore; revive [to *retrieve* one's spirits] **3.** to rescue or save **4.** to set right or repair (a loss, error, etc.); make good **5.** to recall to mind ☆**6.** to recover (information) from data stored in a computer **7.** *Hunting* to find and bring back (killed or wounded game): said of dogs **8.** *Tennis,* etc. to return (a ball that is hard to reach) —*vi. Hunting* to retrieve game —*n.* a retrieval; ☆esp., a retrieving of the ball in tennis, etc. —SYN. see RECOVER —**re·triev′a·ble** *adj.*

re·triev·er (-ər) *n.* **1.** a person or thing that retrieves **2.** a dog trained to retrieve game; specif., any of several breeds of dog developed for this purpose

ret·ro (ret/rō) *n., pl.* **-ros** *clipped form of* RETROROCKET

ret·ro- (ret/rō, -rə; *occas.* rē/trō) [L. < *retro,* backward < *re-,* back + *-tro,* as in INTRO.] *a combining form meaning* backward, back, behind [*retroact, retroflex*]

ret·ro·act (ret/rō akt′) *vi.* [< L. *retroactus,* pp. of *retroagere,* to drive back, reverse < *retro-* (see prec.) + *agere,* to ACT] **1.** to act in opposition; react **2.** to have reference or application to or influence on things done in the past

ret·ro·ac·tion (-ak′shən) *n.* [RETRO- + ACTION] **1.** opposed, reverse, or reciprocal action; reaction **2.** [RETROACT + -ION] effect, as of a law, on things done prior to its enactment or effectuation

ret·ro·ac·tive (-ak′tiv) *adj.* [Fr. *rétroactif:* see RETROACT & -IVE] **1.** having application to or effect on things prior to its enactment [a *retroactive* law] **2.** going into effect as of a specified date in the past [a *retroactive* increase] —**ret′ro·ac′tive·ly** *adv.* —**ret′ro·ac·tiv′i·ty** *n.*

ret·ro·cede¹ (ret/rə sēd′) *vi.* **-ced′ed, -ced′ing** [L. *retrocedere,* to recede: see RETRO- & CEDE] to go back; recede —**ret′ro·ces′sion** (-sesh′ən) *n.*

ret·ro·cede² (ret/rə sēd′) *vt.* **-ced′ed, -ced′ing** [Fr. *rétrocéder* < ML. *retrocedere* < L.: see prec.] to cede or give back (territory) *to* —**ret′ro·ces′sion** (-sesh′ən) *n.*

ret·ro·choir (ret/rə kwir′, rē/trə-) *n.* [RETRO- + CHOIR, after ML. *retrochorus*] that part of a church which lies behind the choir or the main altar

☆**ret·ro·fire** (ret/rə fir′) *vt.* **-fired′, -fir′ing** to ignite (a retrorocket) —*vi.* to become ignited: said of a retrorocket —*n.* the igniting of a retrorocket

☆**ret·ro·fit** (-fit′) *n.* [RETRO- + FIT¹] a change in design, construction, or equipment, as of an aircraft or machine tool already in operation, in order to incorporate later improvements —*vt., vi.* **-fit′ted, -fit′ting** to modify or improve with a retrofit

ret·ro·flex (ret/rə fleks′) *adj.* [L. *retroflexus,* pp. of *retroflectere:* see RETRO- & FLEX¹] **1.** bent or turned backward; reflexed **2.** *Phonet.* pronounced with the tip of the tongue raised and bent slightly backward Also **ret′ro·flexed′** —*n. Phonet.* a retroflex sound

ret·ro·flex·ion, ret·ro·flec·tion (ret/rə flek′shən) *n.* **1.** the condition of being retroflex; specif., *Med.* the bending backward of an organ, esp. of the body of the uterus, upon itself **2.** *Phonet. a)* retroflex articulation *b)* the acoustic quality produced by this

ret·ro·grade (ret/rə grād′) *adj.* [ME. < L. *retrogradus* < *retrogradi,* to go backward: see RETRO- & GRADE] **1.** moving or directed backward; retiring or retreating **2.** inverse or reverse: said of order **3.** going back or tending to go back to an earlier, esp. worse, condition; retrogressive **4.** [Obs.] opposed; contrary **5.** *Astron. a)* moving in an orbit opposite to the usual direction of similar celestial bodies, as opposite to the direction of the earth in its journey around the sun *b)* designating motion, real or apparent, in a direction contrary to the order of the signs of the zodiac, or from east to west **6.** *Music* designating motion backward in a melody, specif. so as to begin with the last note and end with the first —*vi.* **-grad′ed, -grad′ing** [L. *retrogradi*] **1.** to go, or seem to go, backward **2.** to become worse; decline; deteriorate; degenerate **3.** *Astron.* to have a retrograde motion —**ret′ro·gra·da′tion** (-grā dā′shən) *n.* —**ret′ro·grade·ly** *adv.*

ret·ro·gress (ret/rə gres′, ret/rə gres′) *vi.* [L. *retrogressus,* pp. of *retrogradi:* see prec.] to move backward, esp. into an earlier, less complex, or worse condition; decline; degenerate —**ret′ro·gres′sive** *adj.* —**ret′ro·gres′sive·ly** *adv.*

ret·ro·gres·sion (ret/rə gresh′ən) *n.* a retrogressing; esp., *Biol.* a return to a lower, less complex stage or state; degeneration

ret·ro·len·tal (ret/rō len′t'l) *adj.* [< RETRO- + L. *lens,* gen. *lentis* (see LENS) + -AL] situated behind the lens of the eye

☆**ret·ro·rock·et, ret·ro·rock·et** (ret/rō räk′it) *n.* [RETRO- + ROCKET¹] a small rocket on a larger rocket or spacecraft, that produces thrust in a direction opposite to the direction of flight in order to reduce speed, as for landing

re·trorse (ri trôrs′) *adj.* [L. *retrorsus,* contr. of *retroversus,* bent backward < *retro,* back + *versus,* pp. of *vertere,* to turn: see VERSE] *Biol.* bent or turned backward or downward —**re·trorse′ly** *adv.*

ret·ro·spect (ret/rə spekt′) *n.* [< L. *retrospectus,* pp. of *retrospicere,* to look back < *retro-,* back + *specere,* to look: see SPY] a looking back on or thinking about things past; contemplation or survey of the past —*vi.* [Rare] to look back in thought or refer back (*to*) —*vt.* [Rare] to look or think back on —**in retrospect** in reviewing the past

ret·ro·spec·tion (ret/rə spek′shən) *n.* [see RETROSPECT & -ION] **1.** act, instance, or faculty of looking back on or reviewing past events, experiences, etc. **2.** reference to a past event **3.** a survey of past life, etc.

ret·ro·spec·tive (-tiv) *adj.* [see RETROSPECT & -IVE] **1.** looking back on or directed to the past, past events, etc. **2.** looking or directed backward **3.** applying to the past; retroactive —*n.* a representative exhibition of the lifetime work of an artist —**ret′ro·spec′tive·ly** *adv.*

ret·rous·sé (ret/rōō sā′) *adj.* [Fr., pp. of *retrousser,* to turn up: see RE- & TRUSS] turned up at the tip [a *retroussé* nose]

ret·ro·ver·sion (ret/rə vur′zhən, -shən) *n.* [< L. *retroversus* (see RETRORSE) + -ION] **1.** a looking or turning back **2.** a turning or tilting backward (*of* an organ or part), esp. of the uterus

ret·si·na (ret/sĭ nə) *n.* [ModGr., prob. < It. *resina* (< L.), RESIN] a white or red wine of Greece flavored with pine resin

re·turn (ri turn′) *vi.* [ME. *retournen* < OFr. *retourner:* see RE- & TURN] **1.** to go or come back, as to a former

retrain	retranslate	retrial	retry
retransfer	re-treat	retrim	retune

place, condition, practice, opinion, etc. **2.** to go back in thought or speech [to *return* to the subject] **3.** to revert to a former owner **4.** to answer; reply; retort —*vt.* **1.** to bring, send, carry, or put back; restore or replace **2.** to give, send, or do (something equivalent to what has been given, sent, or done); give, send, or do in requital or reciprocation [to *return* a visit, compliment, etc.] **3.** to produce (a profit, revenue, etc.); yield **4.** *a)* to report or announce officially or formally   *b)* to turn in (a writ, account, or statement) to a judge or other official **5.** to elect or reelect, as to a legislature **6.** to replace (a weapon) in its holder **7.** to turn back or in the opposite direction **8.** to reflect (sound, light, etc.) **9.** to turn away from, or cause to continue on at an angle to, the previous line of direction **10.** to render (a verdict, etc.) **11.** *Card Games* to respond to (a partner's lead) with a lead of the same suit **12.** *Sports* to hit back or throw back (a ball) —*n.* [ME. *retorn* < the *v.*] **1.** a coming or going back, as to a former place, condition, etc. **2.** a bringing, sending, carrying, or putting back; restoration or replacement **3.** something returned; specif., [*pl.*] unsold merchandise returned to the distributor by a retailer or merchandise returned to a retailer by a purchaser **4.** a coming back again; reappearance; recurrence [*many happy returns of the day*] **5.** something done or given as an equivalent for that received; repayment; requital; reciprocation **6.** *a)* profit made on an exchange of goods   *b)* [*often pl.*] yield, profit, or revenue, as from labor, investments, etc.   *c)* yield per unit as compared to cost per unit; rate of yield **7.** an answer; reply; retort **8.** a report; esp., *a)* an official or formal report, as of the financial condition of a company   *b)* [*usually pl.*] a report on a count of votes at polling places [election *returns*]   *c)* a form on which taxable income is reported and tax computed: in full **(income) tax return 9.** *Archit.*, etc. *a)* the continuation, as of a molding, colonnade, etc., in a different direction, often at a right angle   *b)* a bend or turn, as in a line, wall, etc.   *c)* the section between two such bends **10.** *Card Games* a lead in response to a partner's lead **11.** *Law a)* the bringing or sending back of a writ, subpoena, summons, etc. to the proper court or official   *b)* a certified report by an election official, assessor, etc.   *c)* a certificate or report endorsed on any such document **12.** *Sports a)* a hitting or throwing back of a ball   *b)* a ball so returned   *c)* a running back of a football received on a kick or by an interception —*adj.* **1.** of or for a return or returning [*return* postage] **2.** given, sent, done, etc. in return [a *return* match] **3.** occurring again [a *return* performance] **4.** returning or returned **5.** changing or reversing direction or formed by a change or reversal in direction, as a bend in a road —**in return** as a return; as an equivalent, response, etc. —**re·turn′er** *n.* *SYN.*—**return** is the common word meaning to go or come back, as to a former place, person, or condition [let us *return* home]; **revert** implies a return to an earlier, usually more primitive, condition, or to the original owner, to a former topic of discussion, etc. [they have *reverted* to savagery]; **recur** suggests the return of some action, occurrence, experience, etc. and often connotes its repeated return at intervals [malaria is characterized by a *recurring* fever]
re·turn·a·ble (ri tʉr′nə b'l) *adj.* **1.** that can or may be returned **2.** that must be returned, as a court writ
☆**re·turn·ee** (ri tʉr′nē′) *n.* a person who returns, as home from military service or to school after dropping out
returning officer [Brit. & Canad.] an official in charge of an election in a district
return ticket 1. a ticket for the trip back to the original starting point **2.** [Brit.] a round-trip ticket
re·tuse (ri tōōs′, -tyōōs′) *adj.* [L. *retusus*, dull, pp. of *retundere*, to beat back < *re-*, back + *tundere*, to strike: see OBTUND] *Bot.* having a blunt or rounded apex with a small notch, as some leaves
ret·zi·na (ret′si nə) *n. same as* RETSINA
Reu·ben (rōō′bin) [via LL.(Ec.) < Gr.(Ec.) < Heb. *rĕ′ūbēn*, lit., behold, a son] **1.** a masculine name; dim. *Rube, Ruby* **2.** *Bible a)* the eldest son of Jacob   *b)* the tribe of Israel descended from him
Reuch·lin (roiH′lēn, roiH lēn′), **Jo·hann** (yō′hän) 1455-1522; Ger. humanist scholar
re·u·ni·fy (rē yōō′nə fi′) *vt., vi.* -**fied′**, -**fy′ing** to unify again after being divided —**re′u·ni·fi·ca′tion** *n.*
Ré·un·ion (rā ü nyōn′; E. rē yōōn′yən) island in the Indian Ocean, east of Madagascar; overseas department of France: 969 sq. mi.; pop. 418,000; cap. St-Denis
re·un·ion (rē yōōn′yən) *n.* [Fr. *réunion* < ML. *reunio*: see RE- & UNION] **1.** a reuniting, or bringing or coming together again **2.** a gathering of persons after some separation, as of members of a college class or of a family
re·un·ion·ist (-ist) *n.* an advocate of reunion; specif., an advocate of the reunion of the Anglican Church with the Roman Catholic Church —**re·un′ion·ism** *n.*
re·u·nite (rē′yoo nīt′) *vt., vi.* -**nit′ed**, -**nit′ing** [< ML. *reunitus*, pp. of *reunire*: see RE- & UNITE¹] to unite again; bring or come together again —**re′u·nit′er** *n.*
☆**re-up** (rē′up′) *vi.* -**upped′**, -**up′ping** [RE- + (SIGN) UP] [Mil. Slang] to reenlist
Reu·ters (roit′ərz) *n.* [after Baron Paul Julius von *Reuter*

(1816-99), the founder] a private British agency for gathering and distributing news among member newspapers: also **Reuter's News Agency**
Reu·ther (rōō′thər), **Walter (Philip)** 1907-70; U.S. labor leader
rev (rev) *n.* [Colloq.] a revolution, as of an engine —*vt.* **revved, rev′ving** [Colloq.] **1.** to increase the speed of (an engine, motor, etc.) **2.** to accelerate, intensify, etc. Usually with *up* —*vi.* [Colloq.] to undergo revving
Rev. 1. *Bible* Revelation **2.** *pl.* **Revs.** Reverend
rev. 1. revenue **2.** reverse **3.** review(ed) **4.** revise(d) **5.** revision **6.** revolution **7.** revolving
re·val·u·ate (rē val′yoo wāt′) *vt.* -**at′ed**, -**at′ing** to make a new valuation or appraisal of —**re·val′u·a′tion** *n.*
☆**re·vamp** (rē vamp′) *vt.* to vamp again or anew; specif., *a)* to put a new vamp on (a shoe or boot) *b)* to renovate or revise; make over —*n.* the act or result of revamping
re·vanch·ism (rə vänsh′iz'm, -vänch′-) *n.* [< Fr. *revanche*, revenge + -ISM] the revengeful spirit moving a defeated nation to aggressively seek restoration of territories, etc. —**re·vanch′ist** *adj., n.*
re·veal¹ (ri vēl′) *vt.* [ME. *revelen* < OFr. *reveler* < L. *revelare*, lit., to draw back the veil < *re-*, back + *velum*, a VEIL] **1.** to make known (something hidden or kept secret); disclose; divulge **2.** to expose to view; show; exhibit; display **3.** *Theol.* to make known by supernatural or divine means —**re·veal′a·ble** *adj.* —**re·veal′er** *n.* —**re·veal′ment** *n.*
SYN.—**reveal** implies a making known of something hidden or secret, as if by drawing back a veil [to *reveal* one's identity]; **disclose** suggests a laying open, as to inspection, of what has previously been concealed [he refuses to *disclose* his intentions]; **divulge** suggests that what has been disclosed should properly have been kept secret or private [do not *divulge* the contents of this letter]; **tell** may also imply a breach of confidence [kiss and *tell*] but more commonly suggests the making known of necessary or requested information [*tell* me what to do]; **betray** implies either faithlessness in divulging something [*betrayed* by an informer] or inadvertence in revealing something [her blush *betrayed* embarrassment] —*ANT.* conceal, hide
re·veal² (ri vēl′) *n.* [< ME. *revalen*, to bring down < MFr. *revaler* < *re-*, back + *valer*, to lower < *val*, a VALE] **1.** that part of the side of an opening for a window or door which is between the outer edge of the opening and the frame of the window or door **2.** the entire side of such an opening; jamb
revealed religion any religion based on the belief that a deity has revealed himself and his will to his creatures
re·veil·le (rev′ə lē; *Brit.* ri val′ē, -vel′-) *n.* [< Fr. *réveillez* (-*vous*), imperative of (*se*) *réveiller*, to wake up < *ré-* (< L. *re-*) + *veiller* (< L. *vigilare*, to watch: see VIGILANT)] *Mil.* **1.** a signal on a bugle, drum, etc. at some fixed time early in the morning to waken soldiers or sailors or call them to first assembly **2.** the first assembly of the day
rev·el (rev′'l) *vi.* -**eled** or -**elled**, -**el·ing** or -**el·ling** [ME. *revelen* < MFr. *reveler*, to revel, lit., to rebel < L. *rebellare*: see REBEL] **1.** to make merry; be noisily festive **2.** to take much pleasure; delight (*in*) [to *revel* in one's freedom] —*n.* [ME. < MFr. < the *v.*] **1.** boisterous festivity; merrymaking; revelry **2.** [*often pl.*] an occasion of merrymaking or boisterous festivity; celebration —**rev′el·er**, **rev′el·ler** *n.*
rev·e·la·tion (rev′ə lā′shən) *n.* [ME. *reuelacioun* < OFr. *revelation* < LL.(Ec.) *revelatio* < pp. of L. *revelare*] **1.** a revealing, or disclosing, of something **2.** something disclosed; disclosure; esp., a striking disclosure, as of something not previously known or realized **3.** *Theol. a)* God's disclosure or manifestation to man of himself and his will *b)* an instance of this *c)* what is so disclosed or manifested *d)* something, as the Bible, containing such disclosure or manifestation —[R-] the last book of the New Testament, ascribed to John (in full **The Revelation of Saint John the Divine**); Apocalypse: also **Revelations** —**rev′e·la′tor** *n.* —**rev′e·la·to′ry** (-lə tôr′ē) *adj.*
rev·e·la·tion·ist (-ist) *n.* a person who believes in divine revelation or tells of a revelation
rev·el·ry (rev′'l rē) *n., pl.* -**ries** [ME. *revelrie*] reveling; noisy merrymaking; boisterous festivity
rev·e·nant (rev′ə nənt) *n.* [Fr. < prp. of *revenir*, to come back: see REVENUE] **1.** a person who returns, as after a long absence **2.** *same as* GHOST (sense 2)
re·venge (ri venj′) *vt.* -**venged′**, -**veng′ing** [ME. *revengen* < OFr. *revenger* < *re-*, again + *vengier*, to take vengeance < L. *vindicare*: see VINDICATE] **1.** to inflict damage, injury, or punishment in return for (an injury, insult, etc.); retaliate for **2.** to take vengeance in behalf of (a person, oneself, etc.); avenge —*vi.* [Obs.] to take vengeance —*n.* **1.** the act of revenging; vengeance **2.** what is done in revenging **3.** desire to take vengeance; vindictive spirit **4.** a chance to retaliate or get satisfaction, as by a return match after defeat in a previous one —*SYN.* see AVENGE —**be revenged** to get revenge; take vengeance —**re·veng′er** *n.* —**re·veng′ing·ly** *adv.*
re·venge·ful (-fəl) *adj.* full of revenge; feeling or showing a desire for revenge —*SYN.* see VINDICTIVE —**re·venge′ful·ly** *adv.* —**re·venge′ful·ness** *n.*

---

retwist	reusable	reutter	revaluation
retype	reuse	revaccinate	revalue
reupholster	reutilize	revalorization	revarnish

rev·e·nue (rev′ə nōō′, -nyōō′) *n.* [ME. < MFr. < fem. pp. of *revenir*, to return, come back < *re*-, back + *venir* < L. *venire*, to COME] **1.** the return from property or investment; income **2.** *a*) an item or source of income *b*) [*pl.*] items or amounts of income collectively, as of a nation **2.** the income from taxes, licenses, etc., as of a city, state, or nation **4.** the governmental service that collects certain taxes

revenue cutter *see* CUTTER (sense 3 *b*)

☆**rev·e·nu·er** (rev′ə nōō′ər, -nyōō′-) *n.* [Colloq.] a Treasury Department revenue agent, esp. one concerned with halting illegal alcohol distilling and bootlegging

revenue stamp a stamp, as on a box of cigars, that shows a tax has been paid

re·ver·ber·ant (ri vur′bər ənt) *adj.* [L. *reverberans*, prp.] reverberating; reechoing; resonant

re·ver·ber·ate (-bə rāt′; *for adj.* -bə rit) *vt.* -**at′ed**, -**at′ing** [< L. *reverberatus*, pp. of *reverberare*, to beat back, repel < *re*-, again + *verberare*, to beat < *verber*, a lash, whip, akin to VERBENA] **1.** to cause (a sound) to reecho **2.** *a*) to reflect (light, etc.) *b*) to deflect (heat, flame, etc.), as in a reverberatory furnace **3.** to subject to treatment in a reverberatory furnace or the like —*vi.* **1.** to reecho or resound **2.** *a*) to be reflected, as light or sound waves *b*) to be deflected, as heat or flame in a reverberatory furnace **3.** to recoil; rebound —*adj.* [Rare] reverberated

re·ver·ber·a·tion (ri vur′bə rā′shən) *n.* [ME. < ML. *reverberatio*] **1.** a reverberating or being reverberated; a reechoing or being reechoed, reflection of light or sound waves, deflection of heat or flame, etc. **2.** something reverberated; reechoed sound, reflected light, etc. **3.** *Physics* multiple reflection of sound waves in a confined area so that the sound persists after the source is cut off

re·ver·ber·a·tive (ri vur′bə rāt′iv, -bər ə tiv) *adj.* **1.** reverberating or tending to reverberate **2.** having the nature of reverberation —**re·ver′ber·a′tive·ly** *adv.*

re·ver·ber·a·tor (-bə rāt′ər) *n.* something that produces reverberation, as a reverberatory furnace

re·ver·ber·a·to·ry (-bər ə tôr′ē) *adj.* **1.** operating or produced by reverberation **2.** deflected, as flame or heat **3.** designating or of a furnace or kiln in which ore, metal, etc. is heated by a flame deflected downward from the roof —*n.* such a furnace or kiln

Re·vere (ri vir′) [after Paul REVERE] city in E Mass., on Massachusetts Bay: suburb of Boston: pop. 43,000

re·vere[1] (ri vir′) *vt.* -**vered′**, -**ver′ing** [< Fr. or L.: Fr. *révérer* < L. *revereri* < *re*-, again + *vereri*, to fear, feel awe: for IE. base see GUARD] to regard with deep respect, love, and awe; venerate

SYN.—**revere** implies a regarding with great respect, affection, honor, deference, etc. [*a poet revered by all*]; **reverence**, more or less equivalent to **revere**, is usually applied to a thing or abstract idea rather than to a person [*they reverence the memory of their parents*]; **venerate** implies a regarding as sacred or holy [*to venerate saints, relics, etc.*]; **worship**, in strict usage, implies the use of ritual or verbal formula in paying homage to a divine being, but broadly suggests intense love or admiration of any kind [*he worshiped his wife*]; **adore**, in strict usage, implies a personal or individual worshiping of a deity, but in broad usage, it suggests a great love for someone and, colloquially, a great liking for something [*I adore your hat*]

re·vere[2] (ri vir′) *n.* same as REVERS[1]

Re·vere (ri vir′), **Paul** 1735–1818; Am. silversmith & patriot: rode from Boston to Lexington (Apr. 18, 1775) to warn the colonists that British troops were coming

rev·er·ence (rev′ər əns, rev′rəns) *n.* [ME. < OFr. < L. *reverentia* < *reverens*: see REVERENT] **1.** a feeling or attitude of deep respect, love, and awe, as for something sacred; veneration **2.** a manifestation of this; specif., a bow, curtsy, or similar gesture of respect; obeisance **3.** the state of being revered **4.** [R-] a title used in speaking to or of a clergyman: preceded by *your* or *his* —*vt.* -**enced**, -**enc·ing** to treat or regard with reverence; venerate —SYN. see AWE, HONOR, REVERE[1]

rev·er·end (-ər ənd, -rənd) *adj.* [ME. < MFr. < L. *reverendus*, gerundive of *revereri*: see REVERE[1]] **1.** worthy of reverence; deserving to be revered: used [*usually the R-*] as a title of respect for a clergyman, often prefixed to the name **2.** of or characteristic of the clergy —*n. colloq.* term *for* CLERGYMAN

rev·er·ent (-ər ənt, -rənt) *adj.* [LME. < L. *reverens*, prp. of *revereri*: see REVERE[1]] feeling, showing, or characterized by reverence —**rev′er·ent·ly** *adv.*

rev·er·en·tial (rev′ə ren′shəl) *adj.* [ML. *reverentialis*] showing or caused by reverence —**rev′er·en′tial·ly** *adv.*

rev·er·ie (rev′ər ē) *n.* [Fr. *rêverie* < MFr., delirium < *rever*, to wander] **1.** dreamy thinking or imagining, esp. of agreeable things; fanciful musing; daydreaming **2.** a dreamy, fanciful, or visionary notion or daydream

re·vers (ri vir′, -ver′) *n., pl.* -**vers′** (-virz′, -verz′) [Fr. < L. *reversus*: see REVERSE] **1.** a part (of a garment) turned back to show the reverse side or facing, as a lapel **2.** a piece of trimming to look like this

re·ver·sal (ri vur′s'l) *n.* [LME. *reversall*: see ff. & -AL] **1.** a reversing or being reversed; esp., a change to the opposite as in one's fortune **2.** *Law* annulment, change, or revocation, as of a lower court's decision

re·verse (ri vurs′) *adj.* [ME. *revers* < OFr. < L. *reversus*, pp. of *revertere*: see REVERT] **1.** *a*) turned backward; opposite or contrary, as in position, direction, order, etc. *b*) with the back showing or in view **2.** reversing the usual effect so as to show white letters, etc. on a black background **3.** acting or moving in a way or direction opposite or contrary to the usual **4.** causing movement backward or in the opposite direction [*reverse gear*] —*n.* **1.** the opposite or contrary of something **2.** the back or rear of something; specif., the side, as of a coin or medal, that does not have the main design; verso: opposed to OBVERSE **3.** the act or an instance of reversing; change to the opposite **4.** a change from good fortune to bad; defeat, check, or misfortune **5.** a mechanism, etc. for reversing, as a gear ratio or an arrangement in an automatic transmission that causes a machine, motor vehicle, etc. to run backward or in the opposite direction **6.** a reversing movement ☆**7.** *Football* a handoff in which the backs are moving in opposite directions —*vt.* -**versed′**, -**vers′ing** **1.** to turn backward, in an opposite position or direction, upside down, or inside out **2.** to change to the opposite; alter completely **3.** to cause to go or move backward or in an opposite direction **4.** to exchange or transpose **5.** to transfer (the charges for a telephone call) to the party being called **6.** *Law* to revoke or annul (a decision, judgment, etc.) —*vi.* **1.** to move, go, or turn backward or in the opposite direction **2.** to put a motor, engine, etc. in reverse; reverse the action of a mechanism —**re·verse′ly** *adv.* —**re·vers′er** *n.*

SYN.—**reverse**, the general term, implies a changing to a contrary position, direction, order, etc. [*to reverse an automobile, a trend, etc.*]; **invert**, in strictest application, implies a turning upside down or, less commonly, inside out [*the image is inverted by the lens*]; **transpose** implies the reversing of the order of elements in a sequence [*to transpose words in a sentence*] See also OPPOSITE

reverse osmosis a method of extracting essentially pure, fresh water from polluted or salt water by forcing the water under pressure against a semipermeable membrane, which passes the pure water molecules and filters out salts and other dissolved impurities

re·vers·i·ble (ri vur′sə b'l) *adj.* **1.** that can be reversed; specif., made so that either side can be used as the outer side; finished on both sides: said of cloth, coats, etc. **2.** that can reverse; specif., that can change and then go back to the original condition by a reversal of the change: said of a chemical reaction, etc. —*n.* a reversible coat, jacket, etc. —**re·vers′i·bil′i·ty** *n.* —**re·vers′i·bly** *adv.*

re·ver·sion (ri vur′zhən, -shən) *n.* [ME. < MFr. < L. *reversio* < *reversus*: see REVERSE] **1.** a turning or being turned the opposite way; reversal **2.** a reverting, or returning, as to a former state, custom, or belief **3.** *Biol. a*) a return to a former or primitive type; atavism *b*) the return, or reappearance, of characteristics present in early ancestral generations but not in those that have intervened *c*) an individual or organism with such characteristics **4.** *Law a*) the right of succession, future possession, or enjoyment *b*) the return of an estate to the grantor and his heirs by operation of law after the period of grant is over *c*) an estate so returning —**re·ver′sion·ar′y, re·ver′sion·al** *adj.*

re·ver·sion·er (-ər) *n.* *Law* a person who has a reversion or a right to receive an estate in reversion

re·vert (ri vurt′) *vi.* [ME. *reverten* < OFr. *revertir* < VL. *revertire*, for L. *revertere* < *re*-, back + *vertere*, to turn: see VERSE] **1.** to go back in action, thought, speech, etc.; return, as to a former practice, opinion, state, or subject **2.** *Biol.* to return to a former or primitive type; show ancestral characteristics normally no longer present in the species **3.** *Law* to go back to a former owner or his heirs —*n.* a person or thing that reverts; esp., one who returns to his previous faith —SYN. see RETURN —**re·vert′i·ble** *adj.*

rev·er·y (rev′ər ē) *n., pl.* -**er·ies** same as REVERIE

re·vest (rē vest′) *vt.* [ME. *revesten* < OFr. *revestir* < LL. *revestire*, to reclothe < L. *re*-, again + *vestire*, to clothe: see VEST, v.] **1.** to vest (someone) again with possession, power, or office; reinvest; reinstate **2.** to vest (office, powers, etc.) again —*vi.* to become vested again (*in*); revert to a former owner or holder

re·vet (ri vet′) *vt.* -**vet′ted**, -**vet′ting** [Fr. *revêtir* < OFr. *revestir*: see prec.] to provide or protect with a revetment

re·vet·ment (-mənt) *n.* [see prec. & -MENT] **1.** a facing of stone, cement, sandbags, etc., as to protect a wall or a bank of earth **2.** same as RETAINING WALL **3.** an embankment or wall of sandbags, earth, etc., constructed to protect against strafing, shell fragments, etc.

re·view (ri vyōō′; *for vt.* 1, rē′-) *n.* [MFr. *reveue* < *revu*, pp. of *revoir* < L. *revidere* < *re*-, again + *videre*, to see: see VISION] **1.** a looking at or looking over again **2.** a

---

reverification   reverify   revibrate   revictual

general survey, report, or account **3.** a looking back on; retrospective view or survey, as of past events, experiences, etc. **4.** reexamination; specif., judicial reexamination, as by a higher court of the decision of a lower court **5.** a critical report and evaluation, as in a newspaper or magazine, of a recent book, play, etc., or of a performance, concert, etc. **6.** a magazine containing articles of criticism and appraisal, often in a specific field [a law *review*] **7.** the act or process of going over a lesson or subject again, as in study or recitation **8.** *same as* REVUE **9.** an examination or inspection; specif., a formal inspection, as of troops on parade, ships, etc., by a high-ranking officer or as a ceremony honoring some dignitary —*vt.* [RE- + VIEW; also < the *n.*] **1.** [Now Rare] to view, or look at, again **2.** to look back on; view in retrospect **3.** to survey in thought, speech, or writing; make or give a survey of **4.** to examine or inspect; specif., to inspect (troops, etc.) formally **5.** to give or write a critical report and evaluation of (a recent book, play, performance, etc.) **6.** to reexamine; specif., to reexamine judicially (a lower court's decision, etc.) **7.** to go over (lessons, a subject, etc.) again, as in study or recitation —*vi.* to review books, plays, etc., as for a newspaper

re·view·al (-əl) *n.* the act of reviewing; review

re·view·er (-ər) *n.* a person who reviews; esp., one who reviews books, plays, etc. as for a newspaper

re·vile (ri vīl′) *vt.* -**viled**′, -**vil**′**ing** [ME. *revilen* < OFr. *reviler*, to regard or treat as vile: see RE- & VILE] to use abusive or contemptuous language in speaking to or about; call bad names —*vi.* to use abusive language —*SYN.* see SCOLD —**re·vile**′**ment** *n.* —**re·vil**′**er** *n.*

re·vise (ri vīz′) *vt.* -**vised**′, -**vis**′**ing** [Fr. *reviser* < L. *revisere* < *re-*, back + *visere*, to survey, freq. of *videre*, to see: see VISION] **1.** to read over carefully and correct, improve, or update where necessary [to *revise* a manuscript, a *revised* edition of a book] **2.** to change or amend [to *revise* tax rates] —*n.* **1.** a revising or a revised form of something; revision **2.** *Printing* a proof taken after corrections have been made, for looking over or correcting again —**re·vis**′**al** *n.* —**re·vis**′**er, re·vi**′**sor** *n.*

Revised Standard Version a mid-20th-cent. revision of the American Standard Version of the Bible, made by a group of U.S. scholars

Revised Version a late 19th-cent. revision, or recension, of the Authorized, or King James, Version of the Bible, made by a committee of U.S. and British scholars

re·vi·sion (ri vizh′ən) *n.* [LL. *revisio*] **1.** act, process, or work of revising **2.** the result of this; revised form or version, as of a book, manuscript, etc. —**re·vi**′**sion·ar**′**y, re·vi**′**sion·al** *adj.*

re·vi·sion·ist (-ist) *n.* a person who revises, or favors the revision of, some accepted theory, doctrine, etc. —*adj.* of revisionists or their policy or practice —**re·vi**′**sion·ism** *n.*

re·vi·so·ry (ri vī′zər ē) *adj.* of, or having the nature or power of, revision [a *revisory* committee]

re·vi·tal·ize (rē vīt′'l īz′) *vt.* -**ized**′, -**iz**′**ing** to bring vitality, vigor, etc. back to after a decline —**re·vi**′**tal·i·za**′**tion** *n.*

re·viv·al (ri vī′v'l) *n.* a reviving or being revived; specif., *a)* a bringing or coming back into use, attention, or being, after a decline *b)* a new or return presentation of a play, motion picture, etc. some time after it has first been presented *c)* restoration to vigor or activity *d)* a bringing up or coming back to life or consciousness *e)* a stirring up of religious faith among those who have been indifferent, usually by fervid evangelistic preaching at public meetings ☆*f)* a series of such meetings, characterized by public confession of sins, professions of renewed faith, etc. *g)* *Law* renewal of validity, as of a judgment or contract

re·viv·al·ism (-iz'm) *n.* **1.** the fervid spirit or methods characteristic of religious revivals **2.** the tendency or desire to revive former ways, etc.

re·viv·al·ist (-ist) *n.* **1.** a person who promotes or conducts religious revivals **2.** a person who revives former ways, institutions, etc. —**re·viv**′**al·is**′**tic** *adj.*

Revival of Learning (or **Letters, Literature**) the Renaissance as related to learning and literature

re·vive (ri vīv′) *vi., vt.* -**vived**′, -**viv**′**ing** [ME. *reviven* < OFr. *revivre* < L. *revivere* < *re-*, again + *vivere*, to live: see QUICK] **1.** to come or bring back to life or consciousness; resuscitate **2.** to come or bring back to a healthy, vigorous, or flourishing condition after a decline **3.** to come or bring back into use or attention **4.** to become or make valid, effective, or operative again **5.** to come or bring to mind again **6.** to produce (a play) or exhibit (an old motion picture) again after an interval —**re·viv**′**a·bil**′**i·ty** *n.* —**re·viv**′**a·ble** *adj.* —**re·viv**′**er** *n.*

re·viv·i·fy (ri viv′ə fī′) *vt.* -**fied**′, -**fy**′**ing** [Fr. *revivifier* < LL.(Ec.) *revivificare*: see RE- & VIVIFY] to put new life or vigor into; cause to revive —*vi.* to revive —**re·viv**′**i·fi·ca**′**tion** *n.* —**re·viv**′**i·fi**′**er** *n.*

rev·i·vis·cent (rev′ə vis′'nt) *adj.* [L. *reviviscens*, prp. of *reviviscere* < *re-*, back + *viviscere*, inchoative of *vivere*, to live: see QUICK] coming or bringing back to life or vigor; reviving —**rev**′**i·vis**′**cence** *n.*

re·vo·ca·ble (rev′ə kə b'l) *adj.* [ME. < MFr. < L. *revocabilis*] that can be revoked —**rev**′**o·ca·bil**′**i·ty** *n.* —**rev**′**o·ca·bly** *adv.*

rev·o·ca·tion (rev′ə kā′shən) *n.* [ME. < MFr. < L.

revocatio < pp. of *revocare*] a revoking or being revoked; cancellation; repeal; annulment

rev·o·ca·to·ry (rev′ə kə tôr′ē) *adj.* [ME. < LL. *revocatorius*] revoking or tending to revoke; containing or expressing a revocation

re·voice (rē vois′) *vt.* -**voiced**′, -**voic**′**ing** **1.** to voice again, or in answer; echo **2.** to restore the proper tone to (an organ pipe, etc.)

re·vok·a·ble (ri vōk′ə b'l) *adj.* *same as* REVOCABLE

re·voke (ri vōk′) *vt.* -**voked**′, -**vok**′**ing** [ME. *revoken* < MFr. *revoquer* < L. *revocare* < *re-*, back + *vocare*, to call: see VOICE] **1.** to withdraw, repeal, rescind, cancel, or annul (a law, permit, etc.) **2.** [Now Rare] to recall —*vi.* *Card Games* to fail to follow suit when required and able to do so; renege —*n.* *Card Games* the act or an instance of revoking —*SYN.* see ABOLISH

re·volt (ri vōlt′) *n.* [Fr. *révolte* < *révolter*, to revolt < It. *rivoltare* < VL. **revolutare*, for L. *revolvere*: see REVOLVE] **1.** a rising up against the government; rebellion; insurrection **2.** any refusal to submit to or accept authority, custom, etc. **3.** the state of a person or persons revolting —*vi.* [Fr. *révolter*] **1.** to rise up against the government **2.** to refuse to submit to authority, custom, etc.; rebel; mutiny **3.** to turn away (*from*) in revulsion **4.** to be disgusted or shocked; feel repugnance (with *at* or *against*) —*vt.* to fill with revulsion; disgust —*SYN.* see REBELLION —**re·volt**′**er** *n.*

re·volt·ing (-vōl′tiŋ) *adj.* **1.** engaged in revolt; rebellious **2.** causing revulsion; disgusting; repulsive; offensive; loathsome —**re·volt**′**ing·ly** *adv.*

rev·o·lute (rev′ə lōōt′) *adj.* [L. *revolutus*, pp. of *revolvere*: see REVOLVE] rolled backward or downward at the tips or margins, as some leaves

rev·o·lu·tion (rev′ə lōō′shən) *n.* [ME. *revolucion* < OFr. < LL. *revolutio* < *revolutus*, pp. of *revolvere*: see REVOLVE] **1.** *a)* movement of a body, as a star or planet, in an orbit or circle: in this sense, distinguished from ROTATION *b)* apparent movement of the sun and stars around the earth *c)* the time taken for a body to go around an orbit and return to its original position **2.** *a)* a turning or spinning motion of a body around a center or axis; rotation *b)* one complete turn of such a rotating body **3.** a complete cycle of events [the *revolution* of the seasons] **4.** a complete or radical change of any kind [a *revolution* in modern physics] **5.** overthrow of a government, form of government, or social system by those governed and usually by forceful means, with another government or system taking its place [the American *Revolution* (1775), the French *Revolution* (1789), the Chinese *Revolution* (1911), the Russian *Revolution* (1917)] —*SYN.* see REBELLION

rev·o·lu·tion·ar·y (-er′ē) *adj.* **1.** of, characterized by, favoring, or causing a revolution in a government or social system **2.** bringing about or constituting a great or radical change [a *revolutionary* design] ☆**3.** [R-] of or having to do with the American Revolution **4.** revolving or rotating —*n., pl.* -**ar**′**ies** a revolutionist

Revolutionary Calendar *same as* FRENCH REVOLUTIONARY CALENDAR

☆**Revolutionary War** *see* AMERICAN REVOLUTION (sense 2)

rev·o·lu·tion·ist (-ist) *n.* a person who favors or takes part in a revolution

rev·o·lu·tion·ize (-īz′) *vt.* -**ized**′, -**iz**′**ing** **1.** to make a complete and basic change in; alter drastically or radically [automation has *revolutionized* industry] **2.** [Rare] to bring about a political revolution in

re·volve (ri välv′) *vt.* -**volved**′, -**volv**′**ing** [ME. *revolven* < L. *revolvere* < *re-*, back + *volvere*, to roll: see WALK] **1.** to turn over in the mind; reflect on **2.** to cause to travel in a circle or orbit **3.** to cause to rotate, or spin around an axis —*vi.* **1.** to move in a circle or orbit around a point **2.** to spin or turn around a center or axis; rotate **3.** to be oriented (*around* or *about* something regarded as a center) **4.** to recur at intervals; occur periodically **5.** to be pondered or reflected on —*SYN.* see TURN —**re·volv**′**a·ble** *adj.*

re·volv·er (-väl′vər) *n.* ☆**1.** a handgun with a revolving cylinder containing several cartridges so that it can be fired in quick succession without reloading **2.** a person or thing that revolves

re·volv·ing (-iŋ) *adj.* **1.** that revolves; specif., designating or of a radial engine with cylinders revolving around a stationary crankshaft ☆**2.** *Finance a)* designating a fund kept for making loans, payments, etc. and regularly replenished, as from repayments *b)* designating credit, as for a charge account, that is renewed for a stated amount as regular proportional payments are made

☆**revolving door** a door consisting of four vanes hung on a central axle, and turned around by pushing on one of the vanes: used to keep out drafts of air

re·vue (ri vyōō′) *n.* [Fr.: see REVIEW] a type of musical show consisting of loosely connected skits, songs, and dances, often parodying topical matters

re·vul·sion (ri vul′shən) *n.* [< Fr. or L.; Fr. *révulsion* < L. *revulsio* < *revulsus*, pp. of *revellere*, to pluck away < *re-*, back + *vellere*, to pull < IE. base **wel-*, to snatch, seize, injure, whence OE. *wol*, pestilence, ON. *valr*, the slain on the battlefield] **1.** [Rare] a drawing or being drawn

back or away; withdrawal **2.** a sudden, complete, and violent change of feeling; abrupt, strong reaction in sentiment **3.** extreme disgust, shock, or repugnance; feeling of great loathing —*SYN*. see AVERSION —**re·vul'sive** *adj.*

re·ward (ri wôrd') *n.* [ME. < ONormFr., for OFr. *regarde*] **1.** something given in return for good or, sometimes, evil, or for service or merit **2.** money offered, as for the capture of a criminal, the return of something lost, etc. **3.** compensation; profit; return —*vt.* [ME. *rewarden* < ONormFr. *rewarder*, for OFr. *regarder*: see REGARD] **1.** to give a reward to **2.** to give a reward for (service, etc.) —**re·ward'a·ble** *adj.* —**re·ward'er** *n.*
SYN.—**reward** usually refers to something given in recompense for a good deed, for merit, etc. [he received a *reward* for saving the child]; **prize** applies to something won in competition or, often, in a lottery, game of chance, etc. [she won first *prize* in the golf tournament]; **award** implies a decision by judges but does not connote overt competition [he received an *award* for the best news story of the year]; **premium**, in this connection, applies to a reward offered as an inducement to greater effort, production, etc. [to pay a *premium* for advance delivery]

re·ward·ing (-iŋ) *adj.* giving a sense of reward, or return [a *rewarding* experience] —**re·ward'ing·ly** *adv.*

re·wind (rē wīnd') *vt.* -**wound'**, -**wind'ing** to wind again; specif., to wind (film or tape) back on the original reel —*n.* **1.** something rewound **2.** the act of rewinding

re·wire (-wīr') *vt.*, *vi.* -**wired'**, -**wir'ing** to wire again or anew; specif., *a)* to put new wires or wiring in or on (a house, motor, etc.) *b)* to telegraph again

re·word (rē wurd') *vt.* **1.** to state or express again in other words; change the wording of **2.** [Rare] to state again in the same words; repeat

re·work (-wurk') *vt.* to work again; specif., *a)* to rewrite or revise *b)* to process (something used) for use again

re·write (rē rīt'; *for n.* rē'rīt') *vt.*, *vi.* -**wrote'**, -**writ'ten**, -**writ'ing** **1.** to write again **2.** to write over in different words or a different form; revise ☆**3.** to write (news turned in by a reporter) in a form suitable for publication —☆*n.* an article so written —**re·writ'er** *n.*

Rex (reks) [L., a king: see REGAL] a masculine name —*n.* [*also* **r-**] *pl.* **re·ges** (rē'jēz) king: the official title of a reigning king [George *Rex*]

rex·ine (rek'sēn) *n.* [REX + -INE⁴] [Brit.] a kind of imitation leather

Rey·kja·vík (rā'kyə vēk') capital of Iceland; seaport on the SW coast: pop. 78,000

Reyn·ard (ren'ərd, rā' nərd, rā'närd) [OFr. *Renard*, *Renart* < OHG. *Reginhart* < Gmc. **ragina*, counsel, judgment + *hard*, bold, brave: see HARD] the fox in the medieval beast epic *Reynard the Fox*; hence, a proper name for the fox in fable and folklore

Rey·naud (rā nō'), **Paul** (pôl) 1878–1966; Fr. statesman; premier (1940)

Reyn·old (ren'əld) a masculine name: see REGINALD

Reyn·olds (ren'əldz), Sir **Joshua** 1723–92; Eng. portrait painter

Reynolds number [after Osborne *Reynolds* (1842–1912), Eng. physicist] a nondimensional parameter used to determine the nature of fluid flow along surfaces and around objects, as in a wind tunnel

Rey·no·sa (rā nō'sä) city in N Mexico, on the Rio Grande, opposite McAllen, Tex.: pop. 74,000

RF, R.F., r.f. 1. radio frequency **2.** rapid-fire

rf., rf *Baseball* right field; right fielder

RFD, R.F.D. Rural Free Delivery

rg. *Football* right guard

Rh 1. see RH FACTOR **2.** *Chem.* rhodium

R.H. Royal Highness

r.h. relative humidity

r.h., R.H., RH right hand

rhab·do·coele (rab'də sēl') *n.* [< ModL. *Rhabdocoela* < Gr. *rhabdos*, a rod + *koilia*, body cavity] any of an order (Rhabdocoela) of small turbellarian flatworms, characterized by having an unbranched, saclike digestive cavity

rhab·do·man·cy (rab'də man'sē) *n.* [LL. *rhabdomantia* < Gr. *rhabdomanteia* < *rhabdos*, a rod < IE. base **werb-*, to twist, bend (cf. VERBENA) + *manteia*, divination (see -MANCY)] divination by a rod or wand; esp., the supposed art of finding underground water, ores, etc. by means of a divining rod; dowsing

rhab·do·my·o·ma (rab'dō mī ō'mə) *n.* [ModL. < Gr. *rhabdos*, rod (see prec.) + ModL. *myoma*, MYOMA] *Med.* a tumor composed of striated muscular fibers

rha·chis (rā'kis) *n. same as* RACHIS

Rhad·a·man·thus (rad'ə man'thəs) [L. < Gr. *Rhadamanthos*] *Gr. Myth.* a son of Zeus and Europa, rewarded for the exemplary justice that he showed by being made, after his death, a judge of the dead in the lower world: also **Rhad'a·man'thys** (-this) —**Rhad'a·man'thine** (-thin) *adj.*

Rhae·ti·a (rē'shē ə, -shə) ancient Roman province in the region of modern Bavaria, E Switzerland, & the N Tirol —**Rhae'tian** (-shən) *adj.*, *n.*

Rhaetian Alps division of the C Alps, mostly in E Switzerland: highest peak, c. 13,300 ft.

Rhae·to-Ro·man·ic (rē'tō rō man'ik) *n.* the group of closely associated Romance dialects, including Romansch, Ladin, etc., spoken in SE Switzerland, the Tirol, and N Italy —*adj.* designating or of Rhaeto-Romanic

-rhage, -rhagia, etc. *vars. of* -RRHAGE, -RRHAGIA, etc.

rham·nose (ram'nōs) *n.* [< ModL. *rhamnus*, a genus of shrubs (< Gr. *rhamnos*, buckthorn: for IE. base see VERBENA) + -OSE¹] a methyl pentose, C₆H₁₂O₅, occurring in many plants as a glycoside

rhap·sod·ic (rap säd'ik) *adj.* [Gr. *rhapsōidikos*] of, characteristic of, or having the nature of, rhapsody; extravagantly enthusiastic; ecstatic: also **rhap·sod'i·cal** —**rhap·sod'i·cal·ly** *adv.*

rhap·so·dist (rap'sə dist) *n.* **1.** in ancient Greece, a person who recited rhapsodies; esp., one who recited epic poems as a profession **2.** a person who rhapsodizes Also **rhap'sode** (-sōd)

rhap·so·dize (-dīz') *vi.* -**dized'**, -**diz'ing 1.** to speak or write in an extravagantly enthusiastic manner **2.** to recite or write rhapsodies —*vt.* to recite or utter as a rhapsody

rhap·so·dy (-dē) *n.*, *pl.* -**dies** [Fr. *r(h)apsodie* < L. *rhapsodia* < Gr. *rhapsōidia* < *rhapsōidos*, one who strings songs together, reciter of epic poetry < *rhaptein*, to stitch together (< IE. **werp-*, to twist, wind, whence WRAP, RAVEL) + *ōidē*, song (see ODE)] **1.** *a)* in ancient Greece, a part of an epic poem suitable for a single uninterrupted recitation *b)* a similar modern literary work **2.** any ecstatic or extravagantly enthusiastic utterance in speech or writing **3.** great delight; ecstasy **4.** [Obs.] a miscellany **5.** *Music* an instrumental composition of free, irregular form, suggesting improvisation

rhat·a·ny (rat''n ē) *n.*, *pl.* -**nies** [Sp. *ratania*, *rataña* < Quechua *rataña*] the root of any of several S. American plants (genus *Krameria*) containing tannins used in treating leather

Rhe·a (rē'ə) [L. < Gr. *Rhea*] *Gr. Myth.* the daughter of Uranus and Gaea, wife of Cronus, and mother of Zeus, Poseidon, Hades, Demeter, Hera, and Hestia: identified with the Roman goddess Ops and the Phrygian goddess Cybele —*n.* [**r-**] any of a group of large, S. American, nonflying birds (order Rheiformes) comprising the American ostriches, smaller than the African ostriches and having three toes and a feathered head and neck

-rhe·a (rē'ə) *var. of* -RRHEA

Rhe·a Sil·vi·a (rē'ə sil'vē ə) *Rom. Myth.* a vestal virgin who broke her vows and became by Mars the mother of Romulus and Remus

rhe·bok (rē'bäk) *n.* [Afrik. *reebok* < MDu. *reeboc*, male roe deer < *ree*, roe deer (for base see ROE²) + *boc*, buck (for base see BUCK¹)] a rare South African antelope (*Pelea capreolus*) with woolly, brownish-gray hair, found on rocky mountain sides

Rheims (rēmz; *Fr.* rans) *former sp. of* REIMS

Rhein (rīn) *Ger. name of the* RHINE

Rhein·gold (rīn'gōld'; *G.* rīn'gôlt') [G., Rhine gold] *Germanic Legend* the hoard of gold guarded by the Rhine maidens and afterward owned by the Nibelungs and Siegfried: see RING OF THE NIBELUNG

Rhein·land (rīn'länt') *Ger. name of the* RHINELAND

Rhein·land-Pfalz (-pfälts') *Ger. name of the* RHINELAND-PALATINATE

Rhen·ish (ren'ish) *adj.* [< L. *Rhenus*, Rhine + -ISH: replacing ME. *Rinische* < MHG. *rinisch* < *rin*, Rhine] of the Rhine or the regions around it —*n.* [Now Rare] *same as* RHINE WINE

rhe·ni·um (rē'nē əm) *n.* [ModL. < L. *Rhenus*, Rhine + -IUM] a rare metallic chemical element resembling manganese and used in thermocouples, electrodes, etc.: symbol, Re; at. wt., 186.2; at. no., 75; sp. gr., 20.53; melt. pt., 3167°C; boil. pt., (est.) 5900°C

rhe·o- (rē'ə, -ō) [< Gr. *rheos*, current < *rhein*, to flow: see STREAM] *a combining form meaning* a flow, current [*rheology*, *rheostat*]

rheo. rheostat; rheostats

rhe·o·base (rē'ə bās') *n.* [RHEO- + BASE¹] *Physiol.* the least amount of electric current needed to excite a tissue, esp. a nerve or muscle, given unlimited time: cf. CHRONAXIE —**rhe'o·bas'ic** (-bas'ik) *adj.*

rhe·ol·o·gy (rē äl'ə jē) *n.* [RHEO- + -LOGY] the study of the change in form and the flow of matter, embracing elasticity, viscosity, and plasticity —**rhe'o·log'i·cal** (-ə läj'i k'l) *adj.* —**rhe·ol'o·gist** *n.*

rhe·om·e·ter (rē äm'ə tər) *n.* [RHEO- + -METER] an instrument for measuring velocity of fluid flow, as of the blood in circulation —**rhe'o·met'ric** (-ə met'rik) *adj.*

rhe·o·phile (rē'ə fīl') *n.* [RHEO- + -PHILE] an animal or plant best adapted for living in flowing water —**rhe·oph'i·ly** (-äf'ə lē) *n.*

rhe·o·stat (-stat') *n.* [RHEO- + -STAT] a device for varying the resistance of an electric circuit without interrupting

rewaken	rewash	reweigh	rewin
rewarm	reweave	reweld	rezone

the circuit, used as for regulating the brightness of electric lights —**rhe′o·stat′ic** adj.

rhe·o·tax·is (rē′ə tak′sis) n. [ModL.: see RHEO- & TAXIS] the tendency of an organism to move in response to the stimulus of a current of water, either with the current or against it— **rhe′o·tac′tic** (-tak′tik) adj.

rhe·ot·ro·pism (rē ät′rə piz′m) n. [RHEO- + -TROPISM] the tendency of an organism, esp. a plant, to respond to the stimulus of a current of water by some change in the direction of growth —**rhe′o·trop′ic** (-ə träp′ik) adj.

rhe·sus (rē′səs) n. [ModL., arbitrary use of L. *Rhesus* (Gr. *Rhēsos*), proper name] a brownish-yellow macaque (*Macaca mulatta*) of India, often kept in zoos and used extensively in biological and medical research: in full **rhesus monkey**

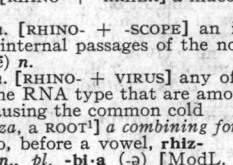

RHESUS MONKEY (head & body to 18 in.; tail to 8 in.)

rhet. 1. rhetoric 2. rhetorical

rhe·tor (rēt′ər, rē′tôr) n. [ME. *rethor* < L. *rhetor* < Gr. *rhētōr* < *eirein*, to speak: see WORD] 1. a master or teacher of rhetoric 2. an orator

rhet·o·ric (ret′ər ik) n. [ME. *rethorike* < OFr. or L.: OFr. *rethorique* < L. *rhetorica* < Gr. *rhētorikē* (*technē*), rhetorical (art) < *rhētōr*, orator: see prec.] 1. a) the art or science of using words effectively in speaking or writing; esp., now, the art or science of literary composition, particularly in prose, including the use of figures of speech b) skill in this c) a treatise or book on this 2. artificial eloquence; showiness and elaboration in language and literary style

rhe·tor·i·cal (ri tôr′i k'l, -tär′-) adj. 1. of, having the nature of, or according to rhetoric 2. using or characterized by mere rhetoric, or artificial eloquence; showy and elaborate in style —**rhe·tor′i·cal·ly** adv.

rhetorical question a question asked only for effect, as to emphasize a point, no answer being expected

rhet·o·ri·cian (ret′ə rish′ən) n. [ME. *rethoricien* < OFr.] 1. a person skilled in rhetoric 2. a teacher of rhetoric 3. a person who writes or speaks in a rhetorical, or showy, elaborate manner

rheum (rōōm) n. [ME. *reume* < OFr. < L. *rheuma* < Gr. *rheuma*, a flow, moist discharge, akin to *rhein*, to flow: see STREAM] 1. any watery discharge from the mucous membranes, as of the mouth, eyes, or nose 2. a cold; rhinitis —**rheum′y** adj. -i·er, -i·est

rheu·mat·ic (roo mat′ik) adj. [ME. *reumatike* < OFr. *reumatique* < L. *rheumaticus* < Gr. *rheumatikos*: see prec.] of, caused by, characteristic of, or having rheumatism —n. a person who has rheumatism —**the rheumatics** [Dial.] rheumatic pains —**rheu·mat′i·cal·ly** adv.

rheumatic disease any of a group of diseases of the connective tissue, of uncertain cause and including rheumatoid arthritis, gout, rheumatic fever, etc.

rheumatic fever an acute or chronic inflammatory disease usually induced by a preceding infection with certain hemolytic streptococci, characterized variously by fever, pain and swelling of the joints, inflammation of the heart, etc., and typically occurring in children and young adults

rheu·ma·tism (rōō′mə tiz′m) n. [L. *rheumatismus*, rheum < Gr. *rheumatismos* < *rheumatizein*, to suffer from a flux < *rheuma*: see RHEUM] a popular term for any of various painful conditions of the joints and muscles, characterized by inflammation, stiffness, etc., and including rheumatoid arthritis, bursitis, neuritis, etc.

rheu·ma·toid (rōō′mə toid′) adj. of or like rheumatism

rheumatoid arthritis a chronic disease whose cause is unknown, characterized by inflammation, pain, and swelling of the joints accompanied by spasms in adjacent muscles and often leading to deformity of the joints

rheu·ma·tol·o·gy (rōō′mə täl′ə jē) n. [RHEUMAT(ISM) + -OLOGY] the branch of medicine dealing with the study and treatment of rheumatic diseases —**rheu′ma·tol′o·gist** n.

☆**Rh factor** (är′āch′) [RH(ESUS): from having been discovered first in the blood of rhesus monkeys] a group of antigens, determined by heredity and usually present in human red blood cells, which may cause hemolytic reactions during pregnancy or after transfusion of blood containing this factor into someone lacking it: individuals who have this factor are **Rh positive**; those who do not have it are **Rh negative**

☆**rhig·o·lene** (rig′ə lēn′) n. [< Gr. *rhigos*, cold (see FRIGID) + -OL² + -ENE] a colorless, volatile liquid distilled from petroleum and consisting primarily of pentane and butane, formerly used as a local anesthetic

Rhin (ran) Fr. name of the RHINE

rhin- (rīn) same as RHINO-: used before a vowel

rhi·nal (rī′n'l) adj. [prec. + -AL] of the nose; nasal

Rhine (rīn) river in W Europe, flowing from E Switzerland north through Germany, then west through the Netherlands into the North Sea: c. 820 mi.: Ger. name, RHEIN, Fr. name, RHIN, Du. name, RIJN

Rhine·land (rīn′land′, -lənd) 1. that part of Germany west of the Rhine 2. same as RHINE PROVINCE

Rhine·land-Pa·lat·i·nate (-pə lat′'n āt′, -it) state of W West Germany: 7,657 sq. mi.; pop. 3,582,000; cap. Mainz

rhi·nen·ceph·a·lon (rīn′en sef′ə län′) n., pl. -la (-lə) [ModL.: see RHINO- & ENCEPHALON] the part of the brain concerned with the sense of smell —**rhi′nen·ce·phal′ic** (-sə fal′ik) adj.

Rhine Province former province of Prussia, now divided between North Rhine-Westphalia & Rhineland-Palatinate

rhine·stone (rīn′stōn′) n. [transl. of Fr. *caillou du Rhin*: so called because orig. made at Strasbourg (on the Rhine)] a colorless, bright, artificial gem made of hard glass, often cut in imitation of a diamond

Rhine wine 1. any of various wines produced in the Rhine Valley, esp. any such light, dry white wine 2. a wine of this type produced elsewhere

rhi·ni·tis (rī nīt′is) n. [ModL.: see RHINO- & -ITIS] inflammation of the nasal mucous membrane

rhi·no¹ (rī′nō) n., pl. -nos, -no clipped form of RHINOCEROS

rhi·no² (rī′nō) n. [< ?] [Brit. Slang] money; cash

rhi·no- (rī′nō, -nə) [< Gr. *rhis* (gen. *rhinos*), the nose, prob. < IE. *sreu-, to flow < base *ser-, to stream, whence L. *serum*] a combining form meaning nose [rhinology]

rhi·noc·er·os (rī näs′ər əs) n., pl. -os·es, -os: see PLURAL, II, D, 1 [ME. *rinoceros* < L. *rhinoceros* < Gr. *rhinokerōs*, lit., nose-horned < *rhis* (see prec.) + *keras*, HORN] any of various large, heavy, thick-skinned, plant-eating mammals (family Rhinocerotidae) of tropical Africa and Asia, with one or two upright horns on the snout and three toes on each foot —**rhi·noc′er·ot′ic** (-ät′ik) adj.

INDIAN RHINOCEROS (3–6 1/2 ft. high at shoulder)

rhinoceros beetle any of several medium to very large, dark-colored tropical beetles (subfamily Dyanstinae), the male of which has a large upright horn on the head

rhi·no·lar·yn·gol·o·gy (rī′nō lar′in gäl′ə jē) n. [RHINO- + LARYNGOLOGY] the branch of medicine dealing with diseases of the nose and larynx —**rhi′no·lar′yn·gol′o·gist** n.

rhi·nol·o·gy (rī näl′ə jē) n. [RHINO- + -LOGY] the branch of medicine dealing with the nose and its diseases —**rhi·nol′o·gist** n.

rhi·no·phar·yn·gi·tis (rī′nō far′in jīt′əs) n. [RHINO- + PHARYNGITIS] inflammation of the mucous membrane of the nose and pharynx, as in the common cold

rhi·no·plas·ty (rī′nə plas′tē) n. [RHINO- + -PLASTY] plastic surgery of the nose —**rhi′no·plas′tic** adj.

rhi·nor·rhe·a (rī′nə rē′ə) n. [RHINO- + -RRHEA] a mucous discharge from the nose

rhi·no·scope (rī′nə skōp′) n. [RHINO- + -SCOPE] an instrument for examining the internal passages of the nose —**rhi·nos·co·py** (rī näs′kə pē) n.

rhi·no·vi·rus (rī′nō vī′rəs) n. [RHINO- + VIRUS] any of a large subclass of viruses of the RNA type that are among the chief infectious agents causing the common cold

rhi·zo- (rī′zō, -zə) [< Gr. *rhiza*, a ROOT¹] a combining form meaning root [rhizopod]: also, before a vowel, **rhiz-**

rhi·zo·bi·um (rī zō′bē əm) n., pl. -bi·a (-ə) [ModL. < RHIZO- + Gr. *bios*, life (see QUICK)] any of a genus (*Rhizobium*) of rod-shaped, nitrogen-fixing bacteria found in nodules on the roots of certain leguminous plants, as the bean and clover

rhi·zo·car·pous (rī′zə kär′pəs) adj. [RHIZO- + -CARPOUS] having perennial roots but annual stems and leaves: said of perennial plants

rhi·zo·ceph·a·lan (-sef′ə lən) n. [RHIZO- + CEPHAL(OUS) + -AN] any of an order (Rhizocephala) of crustaceans related to the barnacles that live as parasites on crabs —**rhi′zo·ceph′a·lous** adj.

rhi·zoc·to·ni·a (rī′zäk tō′nē ə) n. [ModL. < Gr. *rhiza*, a root + *ktonos*, murder] any of various imperfect fungi (genus *Rhizoctonia*) some of which cause various diseases of many garden vegetables and ornamental plants

rhi·zo·gen·ic (rī′zə jen′ik) adj. [RHIZO- + -GENIC] Bot. producing roots: also **rhi·zog′e·nous** (-zäj′ə nəs), **rhi′zo·ge·net′ic** (-jə net′ik)

rhi·zoid (rī′zoid) adj. [RHIZ- + -OID] rootlike —n. any of the rootlike filaments in a moss, fern, etc. that attach the plant to the substratum —**rhi·zoi′dal** adj.

rhi·zome (rī′zōm) n. [ModL. *rhizoma* < Gr. *rhizōma* < *rhizousthai*, to take root < *rhiza*, a ROOT¹] a creeping stem lying, usually horizontally, at or under the surface of the soil and differing from a root in having scale leaves, bearing leaves or aerial shoots near its tips, and producing roots from its undersurface —**rhi·zom′a·tous** (-zäm′ə təs, -zō′mə-) adj.

rhi·zo·mor·phous (rī′zə môr′fəs) adj. [RHIZO- + -MORPHOUS] Bot. formed like a root; root-shaped

rhi·zo·pod (rī′zə päd′) n. [RHIZO- + -POD] any of a class (Sarcodina) of one-celled animals with pseudopodia, including the amoebas, foraminifers, etc. —**rhi·zop′o·dan** (-zäp′ə dən) adj., n. —**rhi·zop′o·dal** (-d'l), **rhi·zop′o·dous** (-dəs) adj.

RHIZOME OF GRASS

rhi·zo·pus (-pəs) *n.* [ModL. < RHIZO- + Gr. *pous*, FOOT] any of a genus (*Rhizopus*) of phycomycetous fungi, including the common bread mold and other species that cause various rots

rhi·zo·sphere (-sfir′) *n.* [RHIZO- + SPHERE] *Ecol.* the part of the soil enclosing and influenced by the roots of a plant

rhi·zot·o·my (rī zät′ə mē) *n., pl.* **-mies** [RHIZO- + -TOMY] a surgical cutting of the spinal nerve roots, esp. of the posterior nerves, as for relieving pain

☆**Rh negative** *see* RH FACTOR

rho (rō) *n.* [Gr. *rhō*] the seventeenth letter of the Greek alphabet (P, ρ)

Rho·da (rō′də) [L. *Rhode* < Gr. *Rhodē* < *rhodon*, a rose, prob. akin to L. *rosa*] a feminine name

rho·da·mine (rō′də mēn′, -min) *n.* [RHOD(O)- + -AMINE] any of a group of synthetic dyes ranging in color from red to pink, obtained by condensation of phthalic anhydride with an amino derivative of phenol

Rhode Island (rōd) [< ? Du. *Roodt Eylandt*, red island or < ? RHODES] New England State of the U.S.: one of the 13 original States; 1,214 sq. mi.; pop. 950,000; cap. Providence: abbrev. **R.I., RI** —**Rhode Islander**

☆**Rhode Island Red** any of a breed of American chickens with reddish-brown feathers and a black tail

☆**Rhode Island White** any of a breed of chickens similar to Rhode Island Reds, but with white feathers

Rhodes (rōdz) **1.** largest island of the Dodecanese, in the Aegean: 545 sq. mi. **2.** seaport on this island; capital of the Dodecanese: pop. 27,000

Rhodes (rōdz) **1. Cecil John,** 1853-1902; Brit. financier & colonial administrator in S Africa **2. James Ford,** 1848-1927; U.S. historian

Rhodes grass [after C. J. RHODES] a tender, perennial, creeping grass (*Chloris gayana*) of Africa, cultivated for forage in the S U.S.

Rho·de·sia (rō dē′zhə, -zhē ə) **1.** former region in S Africa, including **Northern Rhodesia** (now ZAMBIA) & **Southern Rhodesia** (see below) **2.** country in S Africa, north of South Africa: formerly (as *Southern Rhodesia*) a Brit. territory: 150,333 sq. mi.; pop. 5,090,000; cap. Salisbury: Bantu name, ZIMBABWE —**Rho·de′sian** *adj., n.*

Rhodesian man [skeletal remains found in Northern *Rhodesia*] a form of primitive man (*Homo sapiens rhodesiensis*) of the Upper Pleistocene, distinguished by long, sturdy limb bones, massive brow ridges, and a large face

Rhodesian Ridge·back (rij′bak′) any of a breed of strong, short-haired African hounds, having a tan or reddish-tan coat and a ridge on the back formed by hair growing forward along the spine

Rhodes scholarship any of a number of scholarships for a three-year period of study at Oxford University, England, established by the will of C. J. RHODES for selected students (**Rhodes scholars**) from the British Commonwealth and the United States

Rho·di·an (rō′dē ən) *adj.* of Rhodes, its people, or culture —*n.* a native or inhabitant of Rhodes

rho·dic (rō′dik) *adj.* of or containing rhodium, esp. tetravalent rhodium

rho·di·um (rō′dē əm) *n.* [ModL. < Gr. *rhodon*, a rose, after the color of a dilute solution of its salts] a hard, gray-white metallic chemical element of the platinum group, used in alloys with platinum and gold as an electrical contact material and in unalloyed form to electroplate optical instruments, silverware, jewelry, etc.: symbol, Rh; at. wt., 102.905; at. no., 45; sp. gr., 12.4; melt. pt., 1966°C; boil. pt., >2500°C

rho·do- (rō′dō, -də) [< Gr. *rhodon*, a rose (cf. RHODA)] *a combining form meaning* rose, rose-red [*rhodolite*]: also, before a vowel, **rhod-**

rho·do·chro·site (rō′də krō′sīt) *n.* [G. *rhodochrosit* < Gr. *rhodochrōs*, rose-colored (< *rhodon*, a rose + *chrōsis*, a coloring < *chrōs*, color, akin to *chrōma*: see CHROME) + G. *-it*, -ITE¹] a glassy, generally rose-red mineral, mainly manganese carbonate, MnCO₃, often with some calcium and iron

rho·do·den·dron (-den′drən) *n.* [L. < Gr. *rhododendron* < *rhodon*, a rose + *dendron*, a TREE] any of a genus (*Rhododendron*) of trees and shrubs of the heath family, mainly evergreen, with flowers of pink, white, or purple

rho·do·lite (rō′d′l īt′) *n.* [RHODO- + -LITE] a pink or rose-red variety of garnet, often used as a gem

rho·do·nite (rō′d′n īt′) *n.* [G. *rhodonit* < Gr. *rhodon*, a rose + G. *-it*, -ITE¹] a glassy, triclinic mineral, a native manganese silicate, MnSiO₃, generally found in rose-red masses, sometimes used as an ornamental stone

Rho·do·pe (räd′ə pē) mountain system in S Bulgaria extending into NE Greece: highest peak, 9,595 ft.

rho·do·plast (rō′də plast′) *n.* [RHODO- + -PLAST] a plastid found in red algae, containing red pigment as well as chlorophyll

rho·dop·sin (rō däp′sin) *n.* [< Gr. *rhodon*, rose + *opsis*, appearance (< *ōps*, EYE) + -IN¹] a purplish protein pigment, contained in the rods of the retina, that is transformed by the action of light and that is necessary for vision in dim light

rho·do·ra (rō dôr′ə, rə-) *n.* [ModL., earlier name of the genus < L., kind of plant: said to be of Gallic origin] a deciduous plant (*Rhododendron canadense*) of the heath family, native to NE N. America, that bears pink flowers in the spring

rhomb (rämb, räm) *n.* [Fr. *rhombe* < L.] *var. of* RHOMBUS

rhom·ben·ceph·a·lon (räm′ben sef′ə län′) *n.* [ModL.: see prec. & ENCEPHALON] *same as* HINDBRAIN

rhomb·ic (räm′bik) *adj.* **1.** of, or having the form of, a rhombus **2.** having a rhombus as the base or cross section: said of solid figures **3.** bounded by rhombuses **4.** orthorhombic, as some crystals

rhom·bo·he·dron (räm′bə hē′drən) *n., pl.* **-drons, -dra** (-drə) [ModL.: see RHOMBUS & -HEDRON] a six-sided prism each face of which is a rhombus —**rhom′bo·he′dral** *adj.*

rhom·boid (räm′boid) *n.* [Fr. *rhomboïde* < L. *rhomboides* < Gr. *rhomboeidēs*, rhomboid-shaped: see RHOMBUS & -OID] a parallelogram with oblique angles and only the opposite sides equal —*adj.* **1.** shaped like a rhomboid **2.** shaped somewhat like a rhombus —**rhom·boi′dal** *adj.*

RHOMBOIDS

rhom·boi·de·us (räm boi′dē əs) *n., pl.* **-de·i′** (-ī′) [ModL. (*musculus*) *rhomboideus*, rhomblike (muscle) < L. *rhomboides*, RHOMBOID + -eus, -ous] either of two muscles arising from the upper thoracic vertebrae and inserting into the scapula

rhom·bus (räm′bəs) *n., pl.* **-bus·es, -bi** (-bī) [L. < Gr. *rhombos*, object that can be turned, akin to *rhembein*, to turn, whirl < IE. *wremb- < base *wer-, to turn, bend, whence WORM, WARP] an equilateral parallelogram, esp. one with oblique angles

RHOMBUS

rhon·chus (räŋ′kəs) *n., pl.* **-chi** (-kī) [L., a snoring < Gr. *rhonchos*, var. of *renchos* < IE. base *srenk-, to snore, whence OIr. *srennim*, (I) snore] a rattling sound, somewhat like snoring, heard on auscultation of the chest when there is a partial bronchial obstruction; dry râle —**rhon′chal** (-k′l), **rhon′chi·al** (-kē əl) *adj.*

Rhon·dda (rän′də) city in Glamorganshire, SE Wales: pop. 98,000

Rhone, Rhône (rōn) river flowing from SW Switzerland south through France into the Gulf of Lions: 505 mi.

rho·ta·cism (rōt′ə siz′m) *n.* [ModL. *rhotacismus* < MGr. *rhōtakizein*, to make wrong use of the letter *rhō* + L. *-ismus*, -ism] the substitution of the phoneme (r) for or by some other sound

☆**Rh positive** *see* RH FACTOR

rhu·barb (rōō′bärb) *n.* [ME. *rubarbe* < OFr. *rheubarbe* < ML. *rheubarbarum*, altered < LL. *rha barbarum* < Gr. *rhēon barbaron*, foreign rhubarb < *rhēon*, rhubarb (< Per. *rēwend*) + *barbaron*, foreign, BARBAROUS] **1.** any of a genus (*Rheum*) of perennial, large-leaved plants of the buckwheat family; esp., the domestic pieplant (*Rheum rhaponticum*), having large, cordate leaf blades borne on long, thick stalks: the stalks are cooked into a sauce or baked in pies, but the blades are poisonous **2.** the roots and rhizomes of various Asiatic rhubarbs, used as a cathartic ☆**3.** [? from the practice in early radio broadcasts of repeating "rhubarb" in simulating crowd noises] [Slang] a heated discussion or argument

rhumb (rum, rumb) *n.* [< Port. & Sp. *rumbo*, prob. < L. *rhombus*: see RHOMBUS] any of the 32 points of a mariner's compass, or the sector between two consecutive points

☆**rhum·ba** (rum′bə) *n. alt. sp. of* RUMBA

rhumb line the course of a ship that keeps a constant compass direction, drawn as a line on a map, chart, or globe that cuts across all meridians at the same angle

rhyme (rīm) *n.* [ME. *rime* < OFr. < *rimer*, to rhyme, prob. < Frank. *rīm*, a row, series, akin to OE., OHG. *rim*, series, number < IE. *rei-* (whence OIr. *rim*, number) < base *are-, to join, fit (cf. ART¹, RATIO, RITE): form infl. by association with L. *rhythmus*, RHYTHM] **1.** a piece of verse, or poem, in which there is a regular recurrence of corresponding sounds, esp. at the ends of lines **2.** such verse or poetry in general **3.** correspondence of end sounds in lines of verse or in words: cf. ASSONANCE, CONSONANCE **4.** a word that corresponds with another in end sound —*vi.* **rhymed, rhym′ing 1.** to make verse, esp. rhyming verse **2.** to form a rhyme ["more" *rhymes* with "door"] **3.** to be composed in metrical form with rhymes: said of verses —*vt.* **1.** to put into rhyme **2.** to compose in metrical form with rhymes **3.** to use as a rhyme or rhymes —**rhyme or reason** order or sense: preceded by *without, no,* etc.

rhym·er (rīm′ər) *n.* a maker of rhymes, or poems; esp., a rhymester —*SYN.* see POET

rhyme royal a stanza of seven lines in iambic pentameter rhyming *ababbcc,* first used in English by Chaucer

rhyme scheme the pattern of rhymes used in a piece of verse, usually indicated by letters: cf. RHYME ROYAL

rhyme·ster (rīm′stər) *n.* a maker of trivial or inferior rhyme, or verse; poetaster —*SYN.* see POET

rhyming slang 1. a word or phrase that rhymes with, and is a slang term for, a particular word (Ex.: *trouble and strife*

---

for *wife:* see also RASPBERRY, sense 3) **2.** such words and phrases collectively, esp. as used by cockneys

rhyn·cho·ce·pha·li·an (riŋ′kō sə fā′lē ən) *adj.* [< Gr. *rhynchos*, snout + *kephalē*, head (see CEPHALIC) + -IAN] designating or of a nearly extinct order (Rhynchocephalia) of lizardlike reptiles: the only existing species is the tuatara —*n.* any member of this order

rhyn·coph·o·ran (riŋ käf′ə rən) *n.* [< ModL. *Rhyncophora* < Gr. *rhynchos*, a snout + -*phoros*, bearer (see -PHORE) + -AN] any of a suborder (Rhyncophora) of beetles, including the weevils, having the head extended to form a snout

rhy·o·lite (rī′ə līt′) *n.* [G. *rhyolit* < Gr. *rhyax*, stream (of lava) + *lithos*, stone] a kind of volcanic rock, commonly occurring as a lava flow, containing much silica, granitelike in composition but with a fine-grained texture

rhythm (ri*th*′m, ri*th*′əm) *n.* [< Fr. or L.: Fr. *rythme* < L. *rhythmus* < Gr. *rhythmos*, measure, measured motion < base of *rhein*, to flow: see STREAM] **1.** *a)* flow, movement, procedure, etc. characterized by basically regular recurrence of elements or features, as beat, or accent, in alternation with opposite or different elements or features [the *rhythm* of speech, dancing, the heartbeat, etc.] *b)* such recurrence; pattern of flow or movement **2.** flow or apparent movement in a work of art, literature, drama, etc. through patterns in the timing, spacing, repetition, accenting, etc. of the elements **3.** *Biol.* a periodic occurrence in living organisms of specific physiological changes, as the menstrual cycle, or a seasonal or daily variation in some activity, as sleep, feeding, etc., in response to geophysical factors **4.** *Music a)* basically regular recurrence of grouped strong and weak beats, or heavily and lightly accented tones, in alternation; arrangement of successive tones, usually in measures, according to their relative accentuation and duration *b)* the form or pattern of this [waltz *rhythm*] Cf. TIME, TEMPO, METER[1] **5.** *Prosody a)* basically regular recurrence of grouped, stressed and unstressed, long and short, or high-pitched and low-pitched syllables in alternation; arrangement of successive syllables, as in metrical units (*feet*) or cadences, according to their relative stress, quantity, and pitch *b)* the form or pattern of this [iambic *rhythm*] —**rhyth·mic** (ri*th*′mik), **rhyth′mi·cal** *adj.* —**rhyth′mi·cal·ly** *adv.*

☆**rhythm and blues** a form of popular American Negro music, influenced by the blues and characterized by a strong beat: rock-and-roll derives from it

rhyth·mic·i·ty (ri*th* mis′ə tē) *n.* regularity in tempo, cyclic occurrence, etc.; rhythmic quality

rhyth·mics (ri*th*′miks) *n.pl.* [*with sing. v.*] science or system of rhythm and rhythmical forms

rhyth·mist (ri*th*′mist) *n.* a person using or skilled in rhythm or one having a good sense of rhythm

rhythm method a method of seeking birth control by abstaining from sexual intercourse during the woman's probable monthly ovulation period

rhythm section those instruments in a band, as the drums, bass viol, etc., that mainly supply rhythm

rhy·ton (rī′tän) *n.* [Gr. *rhyton*, neut. of *rhytos*, flowing, akin to *rhein*, to flow: see STREAM] an ancient Greek cup shaped like a drinking horn and typically made in the form of an animal's head

R.I. 1. [L. *Rex et Imperator*] King and Emperor **2.** [L. *Regina et Imperatrix*] Queen and Empress **3.** Rhode Island

ri·a (rē′ə) *n.* [< Sp. < *río*, river < VL. *rius*, for L. *rivus*, a brook, stream] a long, narrow, wedge-shaped inlet, uniformly widening and deepening toward the sea

ri·al (rī′əl) *n.* [Per. < Ar. *riyāl* < Sp. *real*, REAL[2]] the monetary unit and a coin of Iran: see MONETARY UNITS, table

Ri·al·to (rē al′tō) *n., pl.* **-tos** [name of a bridge in Venice, Italy] **1.** a theater district, as on Broadway, in New York City **2.** [r-] a trading area or marketplace

ri·ant (rī′ənt) *adj.* [Fr., prp. of *rire* < L. *ridere*, to laugh: see RIDICULE] laughing; smiling; gay; cheerful

☆**ri·a·ta** (rē ät′ə) *n.* [AmSp. *reata* < *reatar*, to tie again < *re-* (see RE-) + *atar*, to tie. < L. *aptare*, to fit < *aptus*: see APT] Western term for LARIAT

rib (rib) *n.* [ME. *ribbe* < OE. *rib*, akin to G. *rippe* < IE. base *rebh-*, to arch over, roof over, whence Gr. *ereptein*, to crown, OSlav. *rebro*, a rib] **1.** any of the arched bones attached posteriorly to the vertebral column and enclosing the chest cavity: in man there are twelve pairs of such bones: see TRUE RIBS, FALSE RIBS, FLOATING RIBS, & SKELETON, illus. **2.** *a)* a cut of meat having one or more ribs *b)* [pl.] *clipped form of* SPARERIBS **3.** a wife: in humorous reference to the Biblical creation of Eve from Adam's rib (Gen. 2:21–22) **4.** a raised ridge in cloth, esp. in knitted material **5.** any of the curved crosspieces extending from the keel to the top of the hull in a ship, forming its framework **6.** any of the short transverse pieces placed at intervals along the length of, and giving shape to, an airplane wing **7.** any narrow riblike piece used to form, strengthen, or shape something [a *rib* of an umbrella] **8.** [< the *v.*, sense 3] [Slang] *a)* a teasing or bantering remark or action *b)* a satire or parody **9.** *Archit. a)* a long curved piece in an arch *b)* any of the transverse and intersecting arches of a vault **10.** *Bot.* any of the main veins in a leaf —*vt.* **ribbed, rib′bing 1.** to provide, form, or strengthen with a rib or ribs **2.** to put ribs in; mark with ribs **3.** [prob. < *ribtickle*] [Slang] to tease or make fun of; kid

rib·ald (rib′əld) *adj.* [ME. *ribaude* < OFr. *ribaud*, debauchee < *riber*, to be wanton < OHG. *riban*, to copulate, lit., to rub < IE. **wreip*-, to twist, whence Gr. *rhipē*, a throw, rush, storm] characterized by coarse or vulgar joking or mocking; esp., dealing with sex in a humorously earthy or direct way —*n.* a ribald person —SYN. see COARSE

rib·al·dry (-əl drē) *n.* [ME. *ribawdrye* < OFr. *ribauderie:* see prec. & -ERY] ribald language or humor

rib·and (rib′ənd, -ən) *n. archaic var. of* RIBBON

rib·band (rib′band′, -ənd, -ən) *n.* [RIB + BAND[1]] a long, flexible piece of wood or metal fastened across the ribs of a ship to hold them in place while the outside planking or plating is being put on

rib·bing (rib′iŋ) *n.* an arrangement or series of ribs, as in knitted fabric, a ship's framework, etc.

rib·bon (rib′ən) *n.* [ME. *riban* < MFr. *riban, ruban*] **1.** *a)* a narrow strip of silk, rayon, velvet, etc. finished at the edges and of various widths, used for decoration, tying things, etc. *b)* material in such strips **2.** anything suggesting such a strip [a *ribbon* of blue sky] **3.** a long, thin, flexible metal band, as for a measuring tape, band saw, etc. **4.** [pl.] torn strips or shreds; tatters [a garment torn to *ribbons*] ☆**5.** a narrow strip of inked cloth against which type characters strike for printing, as in a typewriter **6.** *a)* a small strip of colored cloth worn as a badge or awarded as a prize, symbol of honor or achievement, etc. [winner of a blue *ribbon*] *b) Mil.* a similar strip worn on the left breast of the uniform to indicate an award of a decoration or medal **7.** same as RIBBAND **8.** a strip of board attached to studding to help support the joists **9.** [pl.] [Colloq.] reins used in driving —*vt.* **1.** to decorate, trim, or mark with or as with a ribbon or ribbons **2.** to split or tear into ribbonlike strips or shreds —*vi.* to extend or form in a ribbonlike strip or strips —**rib′bon·like′** *adj.*

rib·bon·fish (-fish′) *n., pl.* **-fish′, -fish′es:** see FISH[2] any of several sea fishes (genus *Trachipterus*) having an elongated, compressed body suggestive of a ribbon

ribbon worm same as NEMERTEAN

rib cage the cagelike structure of the body formed by the ribs

Ri·bei·rão Prê·to (rē′bā roun′ prā′tōō) city in SE Brazil, in São Paulo state: pop. 104,000

Ri·be·ra (rē be′rä), **Jo·sé** (hō se′) 1588?–1656?; Sp. painter in Naples: called *Lo Spagnoletto*

rib·grass (rib′gras′, -gräs′) *n. same as* BUCKHORN (sense 2)

ri·bo·fla·vin (rī′bə flā′vin, rī′bə flā′vin) *n.* [RIBO(SE) + FLAVIN] a factor of the vitamin B complex, $C_{17}H_{20}O_6N_4$, found in milk, eggs, liver, kidney, grass, fruits, leafy vegetables, yeast, etc.: lack of riboflavin in the diet causes stunted growth, loss of hair, etc.: also **ri′bo·fla′vine** (-vin, -vēn)

ri·bo·nu·cle·ase (rī′bō nōō′klē ās′, -nyōō′-) *n.* [RIBO(SE) + NUCLEASE] any of a group of enzymes that split ribonucleic acids

ri·bo·nu·cle·ic acid (-nōō klē′ik, -nyōō-) [RIBO(SE) + NUCLEIC ACID] an essential component of all living matter, present in the cytoplasm of all cells and composed of long chains of phosphate and sugar ribose along with several bases: one form is the carrier of genetic information from the nuclear DNA and is important in the synthesis of proteins in the cell

ri·bose (rī′bōs) *n.* [< G. *rib(onsäure)*, a tetrahydroxy acid, $C_5H_{10}O_5$, arbitrarily altered < *arabinose*, ARABINOSE + *säure*, acid + -OSE[1]] a pentose sugar, $C_5H_{10}O_5$, derived from nucleic acids

ri·bo·some (rī′bə sōm′) *n.* [RIBO(SE) + -SOME[3]] a minute, spherical particle composed of RNA and proteins and present in great numbers in the cytoplasm of cells: proteins are manufactured at the ribosomal surface following genetic instructions carried there by messenger RNA —**ri′bo·so′mal** (-sō′m'l) *adj.*

rib·wort (-wurt′) *n. same as* BUCKHORN (sense 2)

-ric (rik) [ME. *-riche, -ricke*, realm, power < OE. *rice*, reign, dominion: see REICH] *a combining form meaning* jurisdiction, realm [*bishopric*]

Ri·car·do (ri kär′dō), **David** 1772–1823; Eng. economist

rice (rīs) *n.* [ME. *rys* < OFr. *ris* < It. *riso* < L. *oryza* < Gr. *oryza, oryzon:* of Oriental origin, akin to Pushtu *vriže*, Sans. *vrīhih*, rice] **1.** an aquatic cereal grass (*Oryza sativa*) grown widely in warm climates, esp. in the Orient **2.** the starchy seeds or grains of this grass, used as food —*vt.* **riced, ric′ing** to reduce (cooked potatoes, etc.) to ricelike granules, as by pressing through a ricer

Rice (rīs), **Elmer** (born *Elmer Reizenstein*) 1892–1967; U.S. playwright

rice·bird (-burd′) *n.* **1.** same as JAVA SPARROW ☆**2.** *chiefly Southern name for* BOBOLINK

rice paper 1. a thin paper made from the straw of the rice grass **2.** a fine, delicate paper made by cutting and pressing the pith of the rice-paper plant

rice-paper plant (-pā′pər) a shrubby plant (*Tetrapanax papyriferus*) of the ginseng family: see prec.

☆**ric·er** (rī′sər) *n.* a utensil for ricing cooked potatoes, etc. by forcing them through small holes

rich (rich) *adj.* [ME. *riche* < OE. & OFr.: OE. *rice*, noble, powerful < OFr. *riche*, rich < OHG. *richi*, powerful, rich: both < PGmc. **rīkja* < *rīk*, king < (prob. via Celt. **rīg-*) IE. base **reĝ-*, to direct, hence rule, whence RIGHT, L.

rex, king, Sans. *rāj*, to rule] **1.** having more than enough of material possessions; owning much money or property; wealthy **2.** having abundant natural resources [a *rich* country] **3.** well-supplied (*with*); abounding (*in*) [*rich* in minerals] **4.** worth much; valuable [a *rich* prize] **5.** of valuable materials or fine, elaborate workmanship; costly and elegant [*rich* gifts] **6.** elaborate; luxurious; sumptuous [a *rich* banquet] **7.** having an abundance of good constituents or qualities; specif., *a*) full of nutritious or choice ingredients, as butter, sugar, cream, spices, etc. [*rich* pastries] *b*) full of strength and flavor; full-bodied [*rich* wine] **8.** *a*) full, deep, and mellow: said of sounds, the voice, etc. *b*) deep; intense; vivid: said of colors *c*) very fragrant: said of odors **9.** having a high proportion of fuel to air [a *rich* fuel mixture] **10.** abundant; plentiful; ample [a *rich* fund of stories] **11.** yielding or producing in abundance, as soil, mines, etc. **12.** [Colloq.] *a*) abounding in humor; very amusing *b*) absurd; preposterous —**the rich** wealthy people collectively —**rich′ness** *n.*

SYN.—**rich** is the general word for one who has more money or income-producing property than is necessary to satisfy his normal needs; **wealthy** adds to this connotations of grand living, influence in the community, a tradition of richness, etc. [a *wealthy* banker]; **affluent** suggests a continuing increase of riches and a concomitant lavish spending [to live in *affluent* circumstances]; **opulent** suggests the possession of great wealth as displayed in luxurious or ostentatious living [an *opulent* mansion]; **well-to-do** implies sufficient prosperity for easy living —*ANT.* poor

Rich·ard (rich′ərd) [ME. *Rycharde* < OFr. *Richard* < OHG. *Richart* < Gmc. **rīk-*, king (see prec.) + **harthuz*, strong] **1.** a masculine name: dim. *Dick*; equiv. It. *Riccardo*, Sp. *Ricardo* **2. Richard I** 1157–99; king of England (1189–99): son of HENRY II: called **Richard Coeur de Li·on** (kur də lē′ən) or **Richard the Lion-Hearted 3. Richard II** 1367–1400; king of England (1377–99): last Plantagenet king: deposed: son of EDWARD, the Black Prince **4. Richard III** 1452–85; king of England (1483–85); last king of the house of York

Rich·ards (rich′ərdz) **1.** I(vor) A(rmstrong), 1893– ; Eng. literary critic in U.S. **2. Theodore William,** 1868–1928; U.S. chemist

Rich·ard·son (rich′ərd sən) [after A. S. *Richardson*, late 19th-c. railroad official] city in NE Tex.: suburb of Dallas: pop. 49,000

Rich·ard·son (rich′ərd sən) **1. Henry Handel,** (pseud. of *Ethel Florence Lindesuy Richardson Robertson*) 1880?–1946; Australian novelist **2. Henry Hobson,** 1838–86; U.S. architect **3. Sir Owen (Willans),** 1879–1959; Eng. physicist **4. Samuel,** 1689–1761; Eng. novelist

Ri·che·lieu (rish′ə lōō′; *Fr.* rēsh lyö′), duc de (born *Armand Jean du Plessis*) 1585–1642; Fr. cardinal & statesman; chief minister of Louis XIII (1624–42)

rich·en (rich′n) *vt.* to make rich or richer

rich·es (rich′iz) *n.pl.* [ME. *richess, n. sing.* < OFr. *richesse* < *riche:* see RICH] valuable possessions; much money, property, etc.; wealth

Rich·field (rich′fēld) [? in allusion to the fertile soil] village in SE Minn.: suburb of Minneapolis: pop. 47,000

rich·ly (rich′lē) *adv.* **1.** in a rich manner **2.** abundantly; amply; fully

Rich·mond (rich′mənd) **1.** [after Duke of *Richmond*, son of CHARLES II] borough of New York City, comprising Staten Island & small nearby islands: pop. 295,000 **2.** [after sense 3] *a*) capital of Va.: seaport on the James River: pop. 250,000 (met. area 518,000) *b*) seaport in W Calif., on San Francisco Bay: pop. 79,000 *c*) city in E Ind.: pop. 44,000 **3.** city in Surrey, England, on the Thames: pop. 41,000

rich rhyme *same as* PERFECT RHYME

Rich·ter (riH′tər; *E.* rik′tər), **Jean Paul Frie·drich** (zhän poul frē′driH) (pseud. *Jean Paul*) 1763–1825; Ger. writer

☆**Richter scale** [devised by Charles F. *Richter* (1900–), U.S. seismologist] a scale by which the magnitude of earthquakes is measured, having graded steps from 1 to 10, with each step approximately 60 times greater than the preceding step, and adjusted variously for different regions of the earth

ri·cin (rīs′in, ris′-) *n.* [< L. *ricinus*, castor-oil plant] an extremely toxic protein found in the castor bean and isolated as a white powder: it agglutinates red blood corpuscles

ric·in·o·le·ic acid (ris′in ō lē′ik, ris′-; -ō′lē ik) [prec. + OLEIC] an unsaturated fatty acid, $C_{18}H_{34}O_2$, found as an ester of glycerin in castor oil and used in soaps, textile finishing, etc.

ric·in·o·le·in (-ō′lē in) *n.* the glycerol ester, $C_{57}H_{104}O_9$, of ricinoleic acid: it is the main constituent of castor oil

rick¹ (rik) *n.* [ME. *rec, reek* < OE. *hreac*, akin to Du. *rook,* ON. *hruga,* a heap < IE. **(s)kreuk-:* see RIDGE] **1.** a stack of hay, straw, etc. in a field, esp. one covered or thatched for protection from rain ☆**2.** a pile of firewood like a cord, but of less width ☆**3.** a framework of shelves for storing barrels or boxes —*vt.* to pile (hay, etc.) into a rick or ricks

rick² (rik) *vt., n.* [prob. < Scand., as in Norw. *rikka, vrikka,* a wrench: for IE. base see WRY] [Brit.] sprain or wrench

Rick·en·back·er (rik′ən bak′ər), **Edward Vernon** 1890– ; U.S. aviator & aviation executive

rick·ets (rik′its) *n.* [altered < ? Gr. *rhachitis,* rachitis] a disease of the skeletal system, chiefly of children, resulting from absence of the normal effect of vitamin D in depositing calcium salts in the bone, and characterized by a softening and, often, bending of the bones: it is usually caused by a lack of vitamin D from the diet and insufficient exposure to sunlight

☆**rick·ett·si·a** (ri ket′sē ə) *n., pl.* **-si·ae′** (-ē′), **-si·as** [ModL., after Howard T. *Ricketts* (1871–1910), U.S. pathologist] any of a genus (*Rickettsia*) of Gram-negative microorganisms that are the causative agents of certain diseases, as typhus or Rocky Mountain spotted fever: they are transmitted to animals and man by the bite of certain lice, ticks, etc. in whose bodies they live as parasites —**rick·ett′si·al** *adj.*

rick·et·y (rik′it ē) *adj.* **1.** of or having rickets **2.** weak in the joints; tottering **3.** liable to fall or break down because weak; shaky —**rick′et·i·ness** *n.*

☆**rick·ey** (rik′ē) *n.* [said to be after a Col. *Rickey*] a drink made of carbonated water, lime juice, and an alcoholic liquor, esp. gin (**gin rickey**)

☆**rick·rack** (rik′rak′) *n.* [redupl. of RACK¹] flat, zigzag braid for trimming dresses, etc.

rick·shaw, rick·sha (rik′shô) *n. same as* JINRIKISHA

☆**rick·y-tick** (rik′ē tik′) *adj.* [echoic] [Slang] **1.** designating, producing, or of popular music, as of the 1920's, with a mechanical, regular beat and fast tempo **2.** old-fashioned; corny Also **rick′y-tick′y**

ric·o·chet (rik′ə shā′, rik′ə shā′; *also, chiefly Brit.,* -shet′) *n.* [Fr.; used first in *fable du ricochet* (story in which the narrator constantly evades the hearers' questions) < ?] **1.** the oblique rebound or skipping of a bullet, stone, etc. after striking a surface at an angle **2.** a bullet, etc. that ricochets —*vi.* **-cheted′** (-shād′) or **-chet′ted** (-shet′id), **-chet′ing** (-shā′in) or **-chet′ting** (-shet′in) [Fr. *ricocher* < the *n.*] to make a ricochet or skipping motion —*SYN.* see SKIP¹

ri·cot·ta (ri kät′ə; *It.* -kôt′tä) *n.* [It. < L. *recocta,* re-cooked, fem. pp. of *recoquere,* to boil again: see RE- & COOK] a soft, dry or moist Italian cheese made from whey obtained in making other cheeses

ric·tus (rik′təs) *n.* [ModL. < L., open mouth < pp. of *ringi,* to open the mouth wide] **1.** a sustained gaping, as of a bird's beak or an animal's mouth **2.** the opening so produced **3.** a fixed, gaping grin —**ric′tal** *adj.*

rid¹ (rid) *vt.* **rid** or **rid′ded, rid′ding** [ME. *ridden,* earlier *ruden* < ON. *rythja,* to clear (land), akin to OE. *ryddan,* OHG. *riuten* < IE. **reudh-* < base **reu-,* to tear up, dig out, whence RIP¹, RUG] **1.** to free, clear, relieve, or disencumber, as of something undesirable (usually *with of*) [to *rid* oneself of superstitions] **2.** [Obs.] to save or deliver, as from danger, difficulty, etc.; rescue (*from, out of,* etc.) —**be rid of** to be freed from or relieved of (something undesirable) —**get rid of 1.** to get free from or relieved of (something undesirable) **2.** to do away with; destroy; kill

rid² (rid) *archaic pt. & pp. of* RIDE

rid·a·ble, ride·a·ble (rīd′ə b'l) *adj.* **1.** that can be ridden [a *ridable* horse] **2.** that can be ridden over, through, etc. [a *ridable* path]

rid·dance (rid′'ns) *n.* a ridding or being rid; clearance or removal, as of something undesirable, or deliverance, as from something oppressive —**good riddance** welcome relief or deliverance: often used as an exclamation of satisfaction at getting rid of someone or something

rid·den (rid′'n) *pp. of* RIDE —*adj.* dominated or obsessed (by the thing specified): used in hyphenated compounds [fear-*ridden*]

rid·dle¹ (rid′'l) *n.* [ME. *ridil* < OE. *rædels,* akin to *rædan,* to guess, READ¹] **1.** a problem or puzzle in the form of a question, statement, etc. so formulated that some ingenuity is required to solve or answer it; conundrum **2.** any puzzling, perplexing, or apparently inexplicable person or thing, as a difficult problem or enigmatic saying; enigma —*vt.* **-dled, -dling** to solve or explain (a riddle) —*vi.* to propound riddles; speak enigmatically —*SYN.* see MYSTERY¹

rid·dle² (rid′'l) *n.* [ME. *ridil* < OE. *hriddel,* earlier *hridder* < base of *hridrian,* to sift, winnow, akin to G. *reiter* < IE. base **(s)ker-,* to cut, separate, whence L. *caro,* flesh, *cernere,* to sift, separate] a coarse sieve for grading gravel, separating chaff from grain, etc. —*vt.* **-dled, -dling 1.** to sift through such a sieve **2.** *a*) to make many holes in, as by a burst of buckshot; puncture throughout *b*) to find and show flaws in; criticize and disprove *c*) to affect every part of; spread throughout [*riddled* with errors]

ride (rīd) *vi.* **rode** or archaic **rid, rid′den** or archaic **rid** or **rode, rid′ing** [ME. *riden* < OE. *ridan,* akin to G. *reiten* < IE. base **reidh-,* to go, be in motion, whence L. *reda,* four-wheel carriage (< Gaul.): cf. ROAD] **1.** *a*) to sit on and be carried along by a horse or other animal, esp. one controlled by the rider *b*) to be carried along (*in* a vehicle, *on* a bicycle, etc.) *c*) to move along as if so carried *d*) to

move along or be carried or supported in motion (*on* or *upon*) [tanks *ride* on treads] **2.** to be fit for riding or admit of being ridden [a car that *rides* smoothly] **3.** *a*) to move or float on the water *b*) to lie at anchor [the ships *riding* close to shore] **4.** to seem to be floating in space **5.** to overlap, as bones in a joint **6.** to be dependent (*on*) [the change *rides* on his approval] **7.** to be placed as a bet (*on*) ☆**8.** [Colloq.] to continue undisturbed, with no action taken [let the matter *ride*] ☆**9.** *Jazz* to play well, esp. in perfect tempo —*vt.* **1.** to sit on or in and control so as to move along [to *ride* a horse, a bicycle, etc.] **2.** *a*) to move along on or be mounted, carried, or supported on [to *ride* the waves, to *ride* a merry-go-round] *b*) to rest on, as by overlapping *c*) to keep bearing down on **3.** to move over, along, or through (a road, fence, area, etc.) by horse, car, etc. **4.** to cover (a specified distance) by riding **5.** to engage in or do by riding [to *ride* a race] **6.** to cause to ride; carry; convey **7.** to mount (a female) as for copulation **8.** to keep (a ship) at anchor **9.** to control, dominate, tyrannize over, or oppress: often in the past participle [*ridden* by doubts] **10.** [Colloq.] to torment, harass, or tease by making the butt of ridicule, criticism, etc. —*n.* **1.** *a*) a riding; esp., a journey by horse, car, bicycle, etc. *b*) a way or chance to ride *c*) the way a car, etc. rides **2.** a road, track, etc. for riding, esp. on horseback **3.** a roller coaster, Ferris wheel, or other thing to ride, as at an amusement park —*SYN.* see BAIT —**ride down 1.** to hit and knock down by riding against **2.** to overtake by riding **3.** to overcome **4.** to exhaust (a horse, etc.) by riding too long or too hard —☆**ride herd** (**on**) to keep under observation and control; keep in line —**ride out 1.** to stay afloat or aloft during (a storm, etc.) without too much damage **2.** to withstand or endure successfully —**ride up** to move upward out of place, as an article of clothing —☆**take for a ride** [Slang] **1.** to take somewhere, as in an automobile, and kill, as gangsters do **2.** to cheat or swindle

ri·dent (rīd′nt) *adj.* [L. *ridens*, prp. of *ridere*: see RIDICULE] [Rare] laughing, smiling, or grinning

rid·er (rīd′ər) *n.* **1.** a person who rides **2.** *a*) an addition or amendment to a document such as a contract *b*) a clause, usually dealing with some unrelated matter, added to a legislative bill when it is being considered for passage **3.** any of various devices or pieces moving along or mounted on something else, as a sliding weight on the beam of a balance —**rid′er·less** *adj.*

ridge (rij) *n.* [ME. *rigge* < OE. *hrycg*, akin to ON. *hrygr*, backbone, G. *rücken*, back < IE. *(s)kreuk-*, a hump, mound < base *(s)ker-*, to bend, whence L. *curvus*, bent, *circus*, a ring] **1.** orig., an animal's spine or back **2.** the long, narrow top or crest of something, as of an animal's back, a wave, a mountain, etc. **3.** a long, narrow elevation of land or a similar range of hills or mountains **4.** any raised line or raised narrow strip, as in corded fabric, plowed land, etc. **5.** the horizontal line formed by the meeting of two sloping surfaces [the *ridge* of a roof] **6.** a long, narrow high-pressure area on a weather map —*vt., vi.* **ridged, ridg′ing 1.** to mark or be marked with a ridge or ridges **2.** to form into or furnish with a ridge or ridges

ridge·ling, ridg·ling (-liŋ) *n.* [prob. < RIDGE + -LING[1]: ? in reference to assumed location of the testes] a horse or domestic animal in which one or both testes have failed to pass down into the scrotal sac

ridge·pole (rij′pōl′) *n.* the horizontal timber or beam at the ridge of a roof, to which the upper ends of the rafters are attached: also **ridge′piece′** (-pēs′)

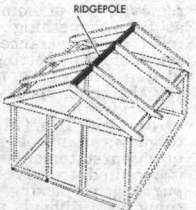

RIDGEPOLE

ridg·y (rij′ē) *adj.* **ridg′i·er, ridg′i·est** having or rising in, a ridge or ridges

rid·i·cule (rid′i kyōōl′) *n.* [Fr. < L. *ridiculum*, a jest, laughable (thing), neut. of *ridiculus*, laughable, comical < *ridere*, to laugh < IE. *wizd-*, to avert the face (whence Sans. *vrīda*, embarrassment) < base *wer-*, to turn] **1.** *a*) the act of making someone or something the object of scornful laughter by joking, mocking, etc.; derision *b*) words or actions intended to produce such láughter **2.** [Archaic] *a*) an absurdity *b*) foolishness —*vt.* **-culed′, -cul′ing** to make the object of scornful laughter; make fun of; deride; mock

SYN.—**ridicule** implies a making fun of someone or something but does not necessarily connote malice or hostility [he *ridiculed* her new hairdo]; **deride** suggests scorn or malicious contempt in ridiculing [to *deride* another's beliefs]; **mock** implies a contemptuous ridiculing, esp. by caricaturing another's peculiarities [it is cruel to *mock* his lisp]; **taunt** implies insulting ridicule, esp. by jeering and repeatedly calling attention to some humiliating fact [they *taunted* him about his failure]

ri·dic·u·lous (ri dik′yə ləs) *adj.* [L. *ridiculosus* (< *ridiculum*: see prec.) or *ridiculus*] deserving ridicule; absurd —*SYN.* see ABSURD —**ri·dic′u·lous·ly** *adv.* —**ri·dic′u·lous·ness** *n.*

rid·ing[1] (rīd′iŋ) *adj.* **1.** that rides **2.** used in or for riding or traveling [a *riding* costume, *riding* horses] ☆**3.** designed to be operated by a rider [a *riding* mower] —*n.* the act of a person or thing that rides

rid·ing[2] (rīd′iŋ) *n.* [ME. *(t)riding* < OE. *-thrithing*, a third

part (only in L. contexts) < ON. *thrithjungr* < *thrithi*, THIRD: initial *t* was lost to the preceding sound in compounds formed with *North-, East-,* and *West-*] **1.** any of the three administrative divisions (*North Riding, East Riding,* and *West Riding*) of Yorkshire, England **2.** any similar division in Great Britain or the British Commonwealth; specif., a Canadian electoral district

riding master a person who teaches horseback riding

riding school a school where horseback riding is taught

☆**rid·ley** (rid′lē) *n.* [< ? surname *Ridley*] either of two large gray or olive marine turtles (genus *Lepidochelys*) of tropical waters, with a broad, heart-shaped shell

Rid·ley (rid′lē) **, Nicholas** 1500?–55; Eng. bishop & Protestant reformer: burned at the stake for heresy

ri·dot·to (ri dät′ō) *n., pl.* **-tos** [It., a festival, REDOUBT] a public entertainment or social gathering, often in masquerade, with music and dancing, popular in 18th-cent. England

ri·el (rē el′, rēl) *n.* [? altered < Ar. *riyal* or Sp. *real*: cf. RIAL, REAL[2]] the monetary unit of Cambodia: see MONETARY UNITS, table

Rie·mann·i·an geometry (rē män′ē ən) [after G. F. B. *Riemann* (1826–66), G. mathematician] a form of non-Euclidean geometry in which there are no parallel lines, since its figures can be conceived as constructed on a curved surface where all straight lines intersect, and in which the sum of the angles of a triangle is always greater than 180°

Rien·zi (ryen′dzē; *E.* rē en′zē), **Co·la di** (kō′lä dē) 1313?–54; Rom. patriot & political reformer: also **Rien·zo** (ryen′dzō; *E.* rē en′zō)

Ries·ling (rēz′liŋ) *n.* [G. < Early ModG. *rüssling* < ?] [*also* r-] a dry, white Rhine wine

Rif (rif) mountain range along the NE coast of Morocco, extending from the Strait of Gibraltar to the Algerian border: highest peak, c. 8,000 ft.: also **Er Rif** (ər)

rife (rīf) *adj.* [ME. *rif* < OE. *ryfe*, akin to MDu. *rijf*, abundant, ON. *rīfr*, desired: for prob. IE. base see RIVE] **1.** frequently or commonly occurring; widespread; prevalent; current [gossip was *rife*] **2.** *a*) abundant; plentiful *b*) abounding; replete [*rife* with error] —*SYN.* see PREVAILING —**rife′ness** *n.*

Riff (rif) *same as* RIF —*n., pl.* **Riffs, Riff′e** (-ē) a member of a Berber people living in the Rif and nearby regions —**Rif·fi·an** (rif′ē ən) *adj., n.*

☆**riff** (rif) *n.* [prob. altered < REFRAIN?] *Jazz* a constantly repeated musical phrase used esp. as background for a soloist or as the basic theme of a final chorus —*vi. Jazz* to perform a riff

rif·fle (rif′'l) *n.* [< ? or akin to G. *riffel*, a groove, furrow < EFris., akin to OE. *rifelung*, a wrinkle < IE. base *rei-*, to slit, tear, cut, whence RIPPLE, RIVE] ☆**1.** *a*) a shoal, reef, or shallow in a stream, producing a stretch of ruffled or choppy water *b*) a stretch of such water *c*) a ripple or the ripples of such water ☆**2.** *a*) a contrivance, as of bars or slats, put across the bottom of a sluice to form grooves or open spaces for catching and holding particles of gold in mining *b*) any of the bars, slats, etc. *c*) any of the grooves or spaces **3.** the act or a method of riffling cards —*vt., vi.* **-fled, -fling** [< ? RIFF, form riffles, groove: see the *n.*] **1.** to form, become, or flow over or through, a riffle **2.** to leaf rapidly through (a book, etc.), as by letting the edges or corners of the pages slip lightly across the thumb **3.** to shuffle (playing cards) by holding part of the deck in each hand, raising the corners or edges slightly, and causing the cards to fall alternately together

riff·raff (rif′raf′) *n.* [earlier *rif and raf*, every scrap < OFr. *rif et raf, rifle et rafle:* see RIFLE[2] & RAFFLE[2]] **1.** those people or that segment of society regarded as worthless, disreputable, insignificant, etc.; rabble **2.** [Now Dial.] worthless stuff; trash

ri·fle[1] (rī′f'l) *vt.* **-fled, -fling** [Fr. *rifler*, to scrape, scratch < OFr. < MHG. *riffeln*, to scratch, heckle (flax) < OHG. *riffilon*, akin to RIPPLE[2]] **1.** to cut spiral grooves on the inside of (a gun barrel, etc.) ☆**2.** [< the *n.*] to hurl or throw with great speed —*vi.* [Rare] to use or fire a rifle —*n.* [short for *rifled gun*] **1.** ☆*a*) a shoulder gun with spiral grooves cut into the inner surface of the barrel: see RIFLING *b*) a rifled artillery piece **2.** [*pl.*] troops armed with rifles

ri·fle[2] (rī′f'l) *vt.* **-fled, -fling** [ME. *riflen* < OFr. *rifler*, to plunder, orig., to scratch: see prec.] **1.** *a*) to ransack and rob (a place, building, etc.); pillage; plunder *b*) [Now Rare] to search and rob (a person) **2.** to take as plunder; steal —**ri′fler** *n.*

☆**ri·fle·man** (-mən) *n., pl.* **-men** (-mən) **1.** a soldier, esp. an infantryman, armed with a rifle **2.** a man who uses, or is skilled in using, a rifle

rifle range a place for target practice with a rifle

☆**ri·fle·ry** (-rē) *n.* the skill or practice of shooting at targets with rifles

ri·fling (rī′fliŋ) *n.* **1.** the cutting of spiral grooves on the inside of a gun barrel to make the projectile spin when fired, thus giving it greater accuracy and distance **2.** a series or system of such grooves

rift[1] (rift) *n.* [ME. < Dan., a fissure < *rive*, to tear: see RIVE] **1.** an opening caused by or as if by splitting; cleft; fissure **2.** an open break in a previously friendly relationship **3.** *Geol.* a large fault along which movement was mainly lateral —*vt., vi.* to burst open; split; crack

☆**rift**² (rift) *n.* [? var. of obs. *riff*, altered < REEF¹] a shallow, often rocky place in a stream, forming a rapid

Rift Valley *same as* GREAT RIFT VALLEY

rig (rig) *vt.* **rigged, rig′ging** [LME. *riggen* < Scand., as in Norw. *rigga*, to bind, splice] **1.** *a)* to fit (a ship, mast, etc.) with sails, shrouds, braces, etc. *b)* to fit (a ship's sails, shrouds, etc.) to the masts, yards, etc. **2.** to assemble and adjust the wings, fuselage, etc. of (an aircraft) **3.** to fit (*out*); equip **4.** to put together, prepare for use, or arrange, esp. in a makeshift or hurried fashion (often with *up*) **5.** to arrange in a dishonest way for selfish advantage; manipulate fraudulently; fix [to *rig* an election] **6.** [Colloq.] to dress; clothe; attire (usually with *out*) —*n.* **1.** the distinctive arrangement of sails, masts, shrouds, etc. on a vessel ☆**2.** any apparatus for a special purpose; equipment; gear [a ham radio operator's *rig*] ☆**3.** equipment for drilling an oil well ☆**4.** *a)* a carriage, cart, etc. with its horse or horses *b)* a tractor-trailer or, sometimes, the tractor alone **5.** [Colloq.] dress or costume, esp. if odd or showy

Ri·ga (rē′gä) **1.** capital of the Latvian S.S.R.; seaport on the Gulf of Riga: pop. 666,000 **2. Gulf of,** inlet of the Baltic Sea, between the NW Latvian S.S.R. & SW Estonian S.S.R.: c. 100 mi. long; c. 60 mi. wide

rig·a·doon (rig′ə dōōn′) *n.* [Fr. *rigodon, rigaudon* < ?] **1.** a once popular lively dance for one couple, with a jumping step **2.** music for this

rig·a·ma·role (rig′ə mə rōl′) *n. alt. sp. of* RIGMAROLE

ri·ga·to·ni (rig′ə tō′nē; *It.* rē′gä tō′nē) *n.* [It., pl. < *rigato,* pp. of *rigare,* to mark with lines < *riga,* a line < Lombard **riga,* akin to OHG. *riga:* for base see ROW¹] small, ridged casings of pasta, typically stuffed with ground meat, tomatoes, cheese, etc. and cooked

Ri·gel (rī′j'l, -g'l) [Ar. *rijl,* foot: so called because in the left foot of Orion] a bright, bluish star, the brightest star in the constellation Orion

rig·ger (rig′ər) *n.* a person who rigs; specif., *a)* a person whose work is fitting the rigging of ships, or one who works with hoisting tackle and the like *b)* a person whose work is assembling and adjusting the fuselage, wings, etc. of aircraft

rig·ging (-iŋ) *n.* **1.** tackle; esp., the chains, ropes, etc. used for supporting and working the masts, sails, yards, etc. of a vessel ☆**2.** equipment; gear

☆**Riggs's disease** (rigz) [after John M. *Riggs* (1810–85), U.S. dentist] *same as* PYORRHEA ALVEOLARIS

right (rīt) *adj.* [ME. < OE. *riht,* straight, direct, right, akin to G. *recht* < IE. base **reĝ-,* straight, put in order, whence L. *rex,* king, *regula,* a rule & RICH, RECKON] **1.** orig., not curved; straight: now only in mathematics [a *right* line] **2.** *a)* formed by, or with reference to, a straight line or plane perpendicular to a base [a *right* angle] *b)* having the axis perpendicular to the base [a *right* cylinder] **3.** in accordance with justice, law, morality, etc.; upright; virtuous [*right* conduct] **4.** *a)* in accordance with fact, reason, some set standard, etc.; correct; true [the *right* answer] *b)* correct in thought, statement, or action [to be *right* in one's answer] **5.** *a)* fitting; appropriate; suitable *b)* most convenient or favorable **6.** designating the side, surface, etc. meant to be seen; designating the finished, principal, or upper side or surface [the *right* side of cloth] **7.** *a)* sound; normal [in one's *right* mind] *b)* mentally sound or normal; sane [not quite *right*] **8.** having sound health or good spirits **9.** in a satisfactory condition, or in good order [to make things *right* again] **10.** *a)* designating or of that side of one's body which is toward the east when one faces north, the side of the more-used hand in most people *b)* designating or of the corresponding side of anything *c)* closer to the right side of a person directly before and facing the thing mentioned or understood [the top *right* drawer of a desk] **11.** of the side or bank of a river on the right of a person facing downstream **12.** of the political right; conservative or reactionary **13.** [Archaic] not spurious or sham; genuine; real —*n.* **1.** what is right, or just, lawful, morally good, proper, correct, etc. **2.** *a)* that which a person has a just claim to; power, privilege, etc. that belongs to a person by law, nature, or tradition [the *right* of free speech] *b)* [*often pl.*] an interest in property, real or intangible: cf. COPYRIGHT **3.** the true or correct report, as of a happening (with *the*) **4.** *a)* all or part of the right side *b)* what is on the right side *c)* a direction or location on the right side (often with *the*) *d)* a turn toward the right side [take a *right* at the fork] **5.** *Boxing a)* the right hand *b)* a blow delivered with the right hand **6.** *Finance a)* the privilege given to a company's stockholders of buying additional stock or shares in a new issue of stock, usually at par or a price below the current market price *b)* the negotiable certificate indicating this privilege **7.** [*often* R-] *Politics* a conservative or reactionary position, esp. one varying from moderate capitalism to fascism, or a party or group advocating this (often with *the*): from the position of the seats occupied in some European legislatures —*adv.* [ME. < OE. *rihte*] **1.** in a straight line; straight; directly [go *right* home] **2.** *a)* properly; fittingly *b)* favorably, conveniently, or well **3.** completely; thoroughly [soaked *right* through his coat]

4. exactly; precisely [*right* here, *right* now] ☆**5.** without pause or delay; immediately [come *right* down] **6.** according to law, justice, etc.; in an upright way **7.** correctly or accurately **8.** on or toward the right hand or side **9.** very; extremely [to know something *right* well]: colloquial except in certain titles [the *right* honorable, the *right* reverend] —*interj.* agreed! I understand! OK! —*vt.* **1.** to put in or restore to an upright or proper position [to *right* a capsized boat] **2.** to correct; make conform with fact, etc. **3.** to put in order; set right [to *right* a room] **4.** to do justice to (a person); make amends to **5.** to make amends for (a wrong, etc.); redress or avenge —*vi.* to get into or resume an upright or proper position —**by right** (or **rights**) in justice; properly —**in one's own right** through one's own authority, ability, etc.; without dependence on another or others —**in the right** on the side supported by truth, justice, etc. —**right away** (or **off**) without delay or pause; at once —**to rights** [Colloq.] in or into good or proper condition or order

right·a·bout (rīt′ə bout′) *n.* **1.** *same as* RIGHTABOUT-FACE **2.** the direction directly opposite, as faced after turning completely about —*adv., adj.* with, in, or by a rightabout-face

right·a·bout-face (-fās′) *n.* **1.** a turning directly about so as to face in the opposite direction **2.** a complete reversal of belief, conduct, etc. —*interj.* a military command to perform a rightabout-face

right angle an angle of 90 degrees; angle made by the meeting of two straight lines perpendicular to each other

right-an·gled (rīt′aŋ′g'ld) *adj.* having or forming one or more right angles; rectangular: also **right′-an′gle**

right ascension *Astron.* the angular distance of the hour circle of a heavenly body from the vernal equinox, measured eastward along the celestial equator and expressed in degrees (from 0 to 360) or, more commonly, in hours (from 0 to 24), minutes, and seconds

right·eous (rī′chəs) *adj.* [altered, by analogy with adjectives in EOUS < ME. *rihtwis* < OE.: see RIGHT & -WISE] **1.** acting in a just, upright manner; doing what is right; virtuous [a *righteous* man] **2.** morally right; fair and just [a *righteous* act] **3.** morally justifiable [full of *righteous* anger] —*SYN.* see MORAL —**right′eous·ly** *adv.* —**right′eous·ness** *n.*

☆**right field** *Baseball* the right-hand part of the outfield (as viewed from home plate)

right·ful (rīt′fəl) *adj.* **1.** fair and just; right; equitable **2.** having a just, lawful claim, or right [the *rightful* owner] **3.** belonging or owned by just or lawful claim, or by right [a *rightful* rank] **4.** proper or fitting **5.** [Rare or Obs.] righteous; virtuous —**right′ful·ly** *adv.* —**right′ful·ness** *n.*

right-hand (rīt′hand′) *adj.* **1.** being on or directed toward the right **2.** of, for, or with the right hand **3.** most helpful or reliable [the president's *right-hand* man] **4.** plain-laid: said of a rope

right-hand·ed (-han′did) *adj.* **1.** using the right hand more skillfully than, and in preference to, the left **2.** done with the right hand **3.** made for use with the right hand **4.** turning left to right; worked by clockwise motion **5.** spiraling from left to right, as most shells —*adv.* with the right hand [to bat *right-handed*] —**right′-hand′ed·ly** *adv.* —**right′-hand′ed·ness** *n.* —**right′-hand′er** *n.*

right heart the half of the heart containing the right ventricle and right atrium which supply blood to the lungs

right·ist (rīt′ist) *n.* a person whose political position is conservative or reactionary; member of the right —*adj.* conservative or reactionary —**right′ism** *n.*

right·ly (rīt′lē) *adv.* [see RIGHT & -LY²] **1.** with justice; fairly **2.** properly; suitably; fitly **3.** correctly

right-mind·ed (rīt′mīn′did) *adj.* thinking or believing what is right; having correct views or sound principles —**right′-mind′ed·ly** *adv.* —**right′-mind′ed·ness** *n.*

right·ness (rīt′nis) *n.* **1.** soundness of moral principles; integrity **2.** agreement with truth or fact; correctness **3.** appropriateness; suitability

right-o (rīt′ō, rī′tō′) *interj.* [Chiefly Brit.] yes; certainly: an exclamation of affirmation or assent

right of asylum the right of a nation to extend protection, at will, to refugees, esp. political refugees

right of search the right of a nation at war to stop the merchant ships of neutral nations on the high seas and search them for contraband or the like, the finding of which makes the ship liable to seizure: also **right of visit** (or **visitation**) **and search**

right of way 1. the right, established by common or statutory law, of one ship, automobile, etc. to cross in front of another; precedence in moving, as at intersections **2.** right of passage, as over another's property **3.** a route that it is lawful to use ☆**4.** *a)* a strip of land acquired or used by a railroad for its tracks *b)* land over which a public road, an electric power line, etc. passes Also **right′-of-way′**

☆**right-to-work** (rīt′tə wurk′) *adj.* designating or of laws or legislation prohibiting the union shop (sense 1)

RIGHT ANGLE

right triangle a triangle with one right angle

right·ward (-wərd) *adv., adj.* on or toward the right: also **right'wards** *adv.*

☆**right whale** [reason for name unc.] any of several large-headed whalebone whales (genera *Balaena* and *Eubalaena*) without teeth, dorsal fin, or longitudinal wrinkles on the throat and chest

right wing [see RIGHT, *n.* 7] the more conservative or reactionary section of a political party, group, etc. — **right'-wing'** *adj.* — **right'-wing'er** *n.*

rig·id (rij'id) *adj.* [L. *rigidus* < *rigere*, to be stiff, numb < IE. *(s)rig-*, cold: cf. FRIGID] 1. not bending or flexible; unyielding; stiff and hard [a *rigid* metal girder] 2. not moving; firmly fixed; set 3. severe; strict; exacting [a *rigid* taskmaster] 4. *a)* not deviating or relaxing; rigorous [*rigid* regulations] *b)* precise; exact [*rigid* specifications] 5. *Aeron.* having a rigid framework that encloses containers for the gas: said of a dirigible or airship —*SYN.* see STIFF, STRICT — **ri·gid'i·ty** (ri jid'ə tē), **rig'id·ness** *n.* — **rig'id·ly** *adv.*

rig·id·i·fy (ri jid'ə fī') *vt., vi.* **-fied', -fy'ing** to make or become rigid — **ri·gid'i·fi·ca'tion** *n.*

rig·ma·role (rig'mə rōl') *n.* [altered < *ragman roll* < ME. *rageman rolle*, a long list or document] 1. foolish or incoherent rambling talk; nonsense 2. a foolishly involved, fussy, or time-wasting procedure

rig·or (rig'ər; *for 4 & 5, also* ri'gôr) *n.* [ME. < MFr. *rigueur* < L. *rigor* < *rigere*: see RIGID] 1. harshness or severity; specif., *a)* strictness or inflexibility [the *rigor* of martial law] *b)* extreme hardship or difficulty [the *rigors* of life] *c)* inclemency, as of weather 2. exactness in precision or accuracy; exactitude 3. a severe, harsh, or oppressive act, etc. 4. stiffness; rigidity; specif., a condition of rigidity in body tissues or organs, in which there is no response to stimuli 5. a shivering or trembling, as in the chill preceding a fever Also, Brit. sp., **rig'our** —*SYN.* see DIFFICULTY

rig·or·ism (-iz'm) *n.* [Fr. *rigorisme*] strictness or severeness, as in way of living, religious practices, moral code, artistic style, etc. — **rig'or·ist** *n.*

rig·or mor·tis (rig'ər môr'tis, ri'gôr) [ModL., stiffness of death] the progressive stiffening of the muscles that occurs several hours after death as a result of the coagulation of the muscle protein

rig·or·ous (rig'ər əs) *adj.* [ME. < OFr. < ML. *rigorosus*] 1. characterized by rigor; very strict or harsh [a *rigorous* rule, master, etc.] 2. very severe or sharp [a *rigorous* climate] 3. rigidly precise; thoroughly accurate or exact [*rigorous* scholarship] —*SYN.* see STRICT — **rig'or·ous·ly** *adv.* — **rig'or·ous·ness** *n.*

Rigs·dag (rigz'dag') *n.* [Dan. < *rige*, kingdom + *dag*, session, lit., day: cf. REICHSTAG] formerly (1849–1953), the bicameral legislature of Denmark: see FOLKETING

Rig-Ve·da (rig'vā'də, -vē'də) [Sans. *Rigveda* < *ṛic*, praise, hymn + *veda*, knowledge] the Veda of Verses (Psalms), the oldest and most important of the Hindu Vedas

Riis (rēs), **Jacob August** 1849–1914; U.S. journalist & social reformer, born in Denmark

Ri·je·ka (rē ye'kä) seaport in Croatia, NW Yugoslavia, on the Adriatic: pop. 101,000

Rijn (rīn) *Du. name of the* RHINE

rijst·ta·fel, rijs·ta·fel (rīs'tä'fəl) *n.* [Du. < *rijst*, rice (< MDu. *rijs* < OFr. *ris*, RICE) + *tafel*, a table < MDu. *tafele* < VL. **tavola* < L. *tabula*, TABLE] an Indonesian meal in which rice is served with a wide variety of foods and sauces in side dishes

Rijs·wijk (rīs'vīk) town in the W Netherlands, near The Hague: pop. 46,000

rile (rīl) *vt.* **riled, ril'ing** [var. of ROIL] [Colloq. or Dial.] 1. *same as* ROIL 2. to anger; irritate

Ri·ley (rī'lē), **James Whit·comb** (hwit'kəm, wit'-) 1849–1916; U.S. poet

‡**ri·lie·vo** (rē lye'vō) *n., pl.* **-vi** (-vē) [It.: see RELIEF] *same as* RELIEF (sense 7)

Ril·ke (ril'kə), **Rai·ner Ma·ri·a** (rī'nər mä rē'ä) 1875–1926; Austrian lyric poet, born in Prague

rill¹ (ril) *n.* [< Du. *ril* or LowG. *rille* < **ridula*, dim. of Gmc. base seen in OE. *rith*, a small stream] a little brook; rivulet — *vi.* to flow in or like a rill

rille, rill² (ril) *n.* [G. *rille*, a groove, furrow, akin to prec.] *Astron.* any of several long, narrow trenches or valleys seen on the moon's surface

rill·et (ril'it) *n.* [dim. of RILL¹] a tiny rill; brooklet

rim (rim) *n.* [ME. *rime* < OE. *rima*, an edge, border, akin to ON. *rimi*, a ridge < IE. base **rem-*, to support, rest upon, rest, whence Sans. *rámatē*, (he) stands still, rests] 1. an edge, border, or margin, esp. of something circular; often, a raised or projecting edge or border 2. *a)* the outer, circular part of a wheel *b)* the metal flange surrounding the wheel of an automobile, on which the tire is mounted 3. [pl.] *same as* FRAME (*n.* 3 e) ☆4. *Basketball* the metal hoop to which the net is attached — *vt.* **rimmed, rim'ming** 1. to put a rim or rims on or around 2. to roll around the rim of [the golf ball *rimmed* the hole] —*SYN.* see BORDER — **rim'less** *adj.*

Rim·baud (ran bō'), (**Jean Nicolas**) **Ar·thur** (är tür') 1854–91; Fr. poet

rime¹ (rīm) *n., vt., vi.* **rimed, rim'ing** [sp. preferred by many as historically correct: see RHYME] *same as* RHYME

rime² (rīm) *n.* [ME. < OE. *hrim*, akin to ON. *hrim* < IE. base **krei-*, to touch lightly, whence OE. *hrinan*, to touch] a white mass of tiny ice crystals formed on grass, leaves, etc. from atmospheric moisture; hoarfrost —*vt.* **rimed, rim'ing** to coat with rime

rime riche (rēm rēsh') *pl.* **rimes riches** (rēm rēsh') [Fr., rich rhyme] *same as* PERFECT RHYME

☆**rim·fire** (rim'fīr') *adj.* designating a cartridge with the primer set in the rim of the base: cf. CENTERFIRE

Ri·mi·ni (rim'ə nē; *It.* rē'mē nē') seaport in NC Italy, on the Adriatic: pop. 82,000

ri·mose (rī'mōs, rī mōs') *adj.* [L. *rimosus* < *rima*, a chink, fissure < IE. base **rei-*, to slit, cut, whence RIVE, REAP] full of cracks, fissures, or crevices: also **ri'mous** (-məs) — **ri'mose·ly** *adv.* — **ri·mos'i·ty** (-mäs'ə tē) *n.*

rim·ple (rim'p'l) *n., vt., vi.* **-pled, -pling** [ME. *rimpyl*, prob. < OE. **hrympel*, akin to MDu., MLowG. *rimpe*: see RUMPLE] [Now Rare] wrinkle; rumple; crease

☆**rim·rock** (rim'räk') *n.* rock forming the rim or upper part of a steep slope or precipice

Rim·sky-Kor·sa·kov (rēm'skē kôr'sä kôf'; *E.* rim'skē kôr'sə kôf'), **Ni·ko·lai An·dre·ye·vich** (nē kô lī' än dryā' ye vich) 1844–1908; Russ. composer: also sp. **Rim'ski-Kor'sa·koff**

rim·y (rīm'ē) *adj.* **rim'i·er, rim'i·est** covered with rime; frosty

rind (rīnd) *n.* [ME. *rinde* < OE. *rind, rinde* < base of *rendan*, to REND] 1. a thick, hard or tough natural outer covering, as of a watermelon, grapefruit, orange, etc. 2. any outer layer or skin suggestive of this, as of a cheese or bacon —*SYN.* see SKIN

rin·der·pest (rin'dər pest') *n.* [G. *rinder*, pl. of *rind*, horned beast + *pest*, a plague] an acute infectious disease of cattle and, often, sheep and goats, characterized by fever and inflammation of the mucous membrane of the intestines

Rine·hart (rīn'härt), **Mary Roberts** 1876–1958; U.S. mystery-story writer & playwright

ring¹ (rin) *vi.* **rang** or now chiefly dial. **rung, rung, ring'ing** [ME. *ringen* < OE. *hringan* < IE. echoic base **ker-*, whence RAVEN¹, CREAK, L. *corvus*, crow] 1. to give forth a clear, resonant sound when struck or otherwise caused to vibrate, as a bell 2. to produce, as by sounding, a specified impression on the hearer [promises that *ring* false] 3. to cause a bell or bells to sound, esp. as a summons [to ring for a maid] 4. to sound loudly or be full of sound; be resonant; resound [the room *rang* with laughter] 5. to have a sensation as of ringing, humming, etc.: said of the ears or head —*vt.* 1. to cause (a bell, etc.) to ring 2. to sound (a peal, knell, etc.) by or as by ringing a bell or bells 3. to signal, proclaim, announce, summon, etc. by or as by ringing [chimes *rang* the hours] 4. to test (coins, etc.) by the sound produced in striking on something hard 5. to call by telephone (often with *up*) 6. [Slang] to substitute (orig. a racehorse) fraudulently (often with *in*) — *n.* 1. the sound of a bell 2. *a)* any similar sound [the *ring* of laughter] *b)* any loud sound, esp. when repeated, continued, or reverberated 3. the characteristic sound or impression (*of* some feeling) [the *ring* of sincerity] 4. a set of bells 5. the act of ringing a bell, etc. 6. a telephone call: chiefly in give (someone) a ring, to telephone (someone) —**ring a bell** ☆to stir up a memory; sound familiar —**ring down the curtain** 1. to signal for a theater curtain to be lowered 2. to end something —**ring in** (or **out**) 1. to punch in (or out): see PUNCH² 2. to usher in (or out) —☆**ring the bell** [Colloq.] to achieve a success: orig. in allusion to hitting the bull's-eye and so causing a bell to ring in target shooting —**ring up** ☆to record or enter (a specified amount) on a cash register —**ring up the curtain** 1. to signal for a theater curtain to be raised 2. to begin something

ring² (rin) *n.* [ME. < OE. *hring*, akin to OHG. *hring*, ON. *hringr* < IE. **(s)krengh-* < base **(s)ker-*, to turn, bend, whence Gr. *kirkos*, a ring, L. *cortina*, a round vessel] 1. a small, circular band of metal, etc., esp. of precious metal, often set with gems, for wearing on the finger as an ornament or a symbol of betrothal, marriage, etc. 2. any similar band, as of metal, plastic, etc., used for some special purpose [a key *ring*, a napkin *ring*] 3. a circular line, mark, or figure 4. the outer edge or border of something circular; rim, as of a wheel 5. a circular cut made, or a circle of bark cut from, around the trunk or a branch of a tree 6. *same as* ANNUAL RING 7. any of the turns in a helix or spiral 8. a circular course, as in dancing 9. a number of people or things grouped in a circle ☆10. a group of people working together to advance their own interests, esp. by questionable or illegal manipulation and control, as in business, politics, etc. 11. an enclosed area, often circular, for contests, exhibitions, etc. [a circus *ring*] 12. *a)* an enclosure, now usually a square, canvas-covered area set off by stakes and ropes, in which boxing and wrestling matches are held *b)* the sport or profession of boxing; prizefighting (with *the*) 13. a contest or competition, esp. a political one, as in *throw one's hat into the ring* (see HAT) 14. *Chem.* a closed chain of atoms; number of atoms united in such a way that they can be represented graphically as a ring 15. *Geom.* the space between two concentric circles 16. *Math.* a set of elements that has two operations, addition and multiplication, and the

properties of being a commutative group under addition, of being closed and associative under multiplication and addition, and in which multiplication is distributive over addition —*vt.* **ringed, ring′ing** 1. to surround or encircle with or as with a ring 2. to form into a ring or rings 3. to furnish with a ring or rings 4. to put a ring through the nose of (an animal), as to prevent rooting or fighting 5. to circle about and so hem in (animals) 6. in some games to toss a ring, horseshoe, quoit, etc. so that it encircles (a peg) 7. to cut a circle of bark from (a tree) —*vi.* 1. to form or gather in a ring or rings 2. to move in a circular or curving course; run, fly, etc. in circles or spirals —**run rings around** [Colloq.] 1. to run much faster than 2. to excel greatly

☆**ring-a-ding** (riŋ′ə diŋ′) *adj.* [echoic] [Slang] wildly exciting; lively —*n.* [Slang] 1. wild excitement; razzledazzle 2. a wildly exciting person or thing

ring·bolt (-bōlt′) *n.* a bolt with a ring at the head

ring·bone (-bōn′) *n.* any pathological bony growth on the pastern bones of a horse, often causing lameness

ring·dove (-duv′) *n.* 1. the European wood pigeon (*Columba palumbus*) with whitish markings on each side of the neck 2. a small dove (*Streptopelia risoria*) of Europe and Asia, with a dark ring around the neck

ringed (riŋd) *adj.* 1. wearing or having a ring or rings 2. decorated or marked with a ring or rings 3. encircled by a ring or rings 4. formed like a ring or of rings

rin·gent (rin′jənt) *adj.* [L. *ringens*, prp. of *ringi*, to gape: cf. RICTUS] 1. having the mouth wide open; gaping 2. *Biol.* having the lips separated by a distinct gap, as some corollas, valves, etc.

ring·er[1] (riŋ′ər) *n.* 1. a horseshoe, quoit, etc. thrown so that it encircles the peg 2. such a throw

ring·er[2] (riŋ′ər) *n.* 1. a person or thing that rings a bell, chime, etc. ☆2. [Slang] *a)* a horse, player, etc. fraudulently entered, or substituted for another, in a competition *b)* a person or thing very closely resembling another

Ring·er's solution (or **fluid**) (riŋ′ərz) [after Sydney Ringer (1835–1910), Eng. physiologist] *Biochem., Med.* a solution of the chlorides of sodium, potassium, and calcium in purified water that has the same osmotic pressure as that found in blood or tissues, used in physiological research, to correct dehydration, etc.

ring finger the finger next to the little finger, esp. of the left hand, on which a wedding ring is usually worn

ring·hals (riŋ′hals) *n.*, *pl.* **-hals, -hals·es** [Afrik., obs. sp. of *rinkals* < Du. *ring* (for IE. base see RING[2]) + *hals*, neck: for IE. base see COLLAR] a small, rough-skinned cobra (*Haemachates haemachatus*) of S Africa that usually sprays jets of venom at the eyes of an aggressor

ring·lead·er (riŋ′lēd′ər) *n.* [RING[1] + LEADER] a person who leads others, esp. in unlawful acts, opposition to authority, etc.

ring·let (-lit) *n.* [dim. of RING[2]] 1. a little ring or circle 2. a curl of hair, esp. a long one —**ring′let·ed** *adj.*

Ring·ling (riŋ′liŋ) U.S. family of circus owners, orig. including five brothers: **Albert C.** (1852–1916), **Alfred T.** (1861–1919), **Charles** (1863–1926), **John** (1866–1936), & **Otto** (1858–1911)

ring·mas·ter (riŋ′mas′tər, -mäs′-) *n.* a man who directs the performances in a circus ring

☆**ring·neck** (-nek′) *n.* a ring-necked bird, snake, etc.

ring-necked (-nekt′) *adj. Zool.* having a distinctive colored stripe or stripes around the neck

☆**ring-necked duck** a N. American duck (*Aythya collaris*) the male of which has a black breast, neck, and back with a coppery ring around the neck

ring-necked pheasant an Asian game fowl (*Phasianus colchicus*) with a whitish collar around the neck in the male, now widely introduced and bred in N. America

☆**ring-necked snake** any of a genus (*Diadophis*) of small, nonpoisonous snakes with a yellow ring around the neck, common in moist woods throughout N. America

Ring of the Nibelung 1. *Germanic Legend* the ring made from the Rheingold by Alberich, leader of a race of dwarfs called the Nibelungs 2. the cycle of music dramas by Richard Wagner, *Das Rheingold, Die Walküre, Siegfried,* and *Götterdämmerung,* telling the story of this ring

ring ouzel a small European bird (*Turdus torquatus*) of the thrush family, with a white band on its neck and breast

ring·side (-sīd′) *n.* 1. the space or place just outside the ring, as at a boxing match or circus 2. any place that provides a close view of something

☆**ring snake** *same as* RING-NECKED SNAKE

ring-streaked (-strēkt′) *adj.* having streaks of color around the body: also [Archaic] **ring′-straked′** (-strākt′)

ring-tailed (-tāld′) *adj.* having differently colored bands or stripes around the tail

☆**ring-tailed cat** *same as* CACOMISTLE (sense 1)

☆**ring·toss** (-tôs′) *n.* a game in which rings made of rope, etc. are tossed so as to encircle a peg

ring·worm (-wurm′) *n.* any of various contagious skin diseases caused by related varieties of fungus and characterized by itching and the formation of ring-shaped, discolored patches covered with scales or vesicles

rink (riŋk) *n.* [ME.(Scot.), earlier *renk* < OFr. *renc*, RANK[1]] 1. *a)* a smooth expanse of ice marked off for the game of curling *b)* a part of a bowling green of a suitable size for a match *c)* the players on one side in a game of curling, bowls, or quoits 2. *a)* a smooth expanse of ice, often artificially prepared and enclosed, for ice skating or for playing hockey *b)* a smooth floor, usually of wood and enclosed, for roller-skating *c)* a building enclosing either of such rinks

☆**rink·y-dink** (riŋ′kē diŋk′) *adj.* [? altered < RICKY-TICK] [Slang] shoddy, cheap, worn-out, or corny —*n.* [Slang] anything that is shoddy, cheap, worn-out, or corny Also **rink′y-tink′** (-tiŋk′)

rinse (rins) *vt.* **rinsed, rins′ing** [ME. *rincen* < OFr. *rincer,* earlier *reincier* < VL. **recentiare,* to renew, rinse, purify < L. *recens,* fresh, RECENT] 1. to wash lightly, esp. by dipping into water or by letting water run over, into, or through 2. *a)* to remove soap, dirt, or impurities from in this way, esp. as a final part of washing *b)* to remove (soap, dirt, etc.) in this way 3. to flush (the mouth or teeth), as with clear water 4. *a)* to dip (fabrics, garments, etc.) into a dye solution *b)* to use a rinse on (the hair) —*n.* 1. the act of rinsing 2. the water or solution used in rinsing 3. a substance mixed with water and used to rinse or tint hair —**rins′er** *n.*

rins·ing (-iŋ) *n.* 1. [*usually pl.*] *a)* the liquid in or with which anything has been rinsed *b) same as* DREGS 2. the act of one that rinses; rinse

Río Bra·vo (rē′ō brä′vō) *Mex.* name of the RIO GRANDE: also **Rí′o Bra′vo del Nor′te** (del nôr′te)

Rio de Ja·nei·ro (rē′ō dā′ zhə ner′ō, dā′-; jə nir′ō; *Port.* rē′oo di zhə nā′roo) 1. seaport in SE Brazil, on the Atlantic; capital of Guanabara state: pop. 3,307,000 2. state of SE Brazil, adjoining Guanabara state: 16,565 sq. mi.; pop. 3,403,000; cap. Niterói

Río de la Plata *see* PLATA

Rí·o de O·ro (rē′ō de ō′rō) 1. *same as* SPANISH SAHARA 2. S region of Spanish Sahara: c.71,000 sq. mi.; pop. c.1,000

Rí·o Grande (rē′ō grand′, grand′dē, grän′dā; for 2 & 3, *Port.* rē′oo grun′di) 1. river flowing from S Colo. south through N.Mex., then southeast as the boundary between Texas and Mexico into the Gulf of Mexico: 1,885 mi. 2. river in SE Brazil in the states of Minas Gerais & São Paulo; headstream of the Paraná: c. 650 mi. 3. seaport in SE Brazil, on the Atlantic: pop. 83,000

Rí·o Gran·de do Nor·te (rē′oo grun′di doo nôr′ti) state of NE Brazil: 20,465 sq. mi.; pop. 1,157,000; cap. Natal

Rio Grande do Sul (sool) southernmost state of Brazil: 108,935 sq. mi.; pop. 5,449,000; cap. Pôrto Alegre

Rí·o Mu·ni (rē′ō mōō′nē) province of Equatorial Guinea, in C Africa, between Cameroun & Gabon: 10,000 sq. mi.; pop. 201,000

ri·ot (rī′ət) *n.* [ME. < OFr. *riote < rihoter,* to make a disturbance] 1. wild or violent disorder, confusion, or disturbance; tumult; uproar 2. a wild, violent, public disturbance of the peace, by a number of persons (specified, in law, usually as three or more) assembled together 3. an unrestrained outburst, as of laughter 4. a brilliant, vivid display [a riot of color] 5. [Now Rare] *a)* wild, loose living; debauchery *b)* unrestrained revelry *c)* a wild, noisy feast or revel ☆6. [Colloq.] an extremely amusing person, thing, or event —*vi.* [ME. *rioten* < OFr. *rihoter*] 1. to take part in a tumult or disturbance of the peace 2. [Now Rare] *a)* to live in a wild, loose manner *b)* to engage in unrestrained revelry *c)* to indulge without restraint; revel (*in* something) —*vt.* [Now Rare] to waste (money, time, etc.) in disorderly or profligate living —**run riot** [orig. of dogs barking on the wrong scent] 1. to run wild; act without restraint, control, or discipline 2. to grow in luxuriance or profusion —**ri′ot·er** *n.*

Riot Act an English law, passed in 1715, providing that if twelve or more persons are unlawfully assembled and disturbing the public peace they shall disperse on proclamation (*reading the Riot Act*) or be held guilty of felony —**read the riot act to** to command to stop doing something regarded as wrong, under threat of punishment

☆**riot gun** a short-barreled, repeating shotgun, as used to disperse rioters

ri·ot·ous (rī′ət əs) *adj.* [ME. < OFr. *rioteus*] 1. *a)* having the nature of a riot or disturbance of the peace *b)* engaging in rioting or inciting to riot 2. without restraint; disorderly or boisterous 3. dissolute; profligate [*riotous* living] 4. luxuriant or profuse —**ri′ot·ous·ly** *adv.* —**ri′ot·ous·ness** *n.*

rip[1] (rip) *vt.* **ripped, rip′ping** [LME. *rippen,* prob. < or akin to Fl. *rippen,* to tear, akin to Dan. *rippe* (*op*), tear (open): for prob. IE. base see RIVE] 1. *a)* to cut or tear apart roughly or vigorously *b)* to remove by or as by so cutting or tearing (with *off, out, away,* etc.) *c)* to make (a hole) in this way *d)* to slash with a sharp instrument *e)* to cut, tear, etc. (stitches) so as to open (a seam, hem, etc.) 2. to saw or split (wood) along the grain —*vi.* 1. to become torn or split apart 2. [Colloq.] to move with speed or violence —*n.* 1. a torn place or burst seam; tear; split 2. the act of ripping —*SYN.* see TEAR[1] —**rip into** [Colloq.] to attack violently or sharply, often with words —**rip out**

[Colloq.] to utter violently or sharply, as in angry exclamation

☆rip² (rip) n. [< ? prec.] an extent of rough, broken water caused by the meeting of cross currents or tides

rip³ (rip) n. [var. of rep, prob. abbrev. of REPROBATE] [Colloq.] 1. a dissolute, dissipated person 2. an old, worthless horse 3. a worthless thing

R.I.P. abbrev. of REQUIESCAT IN PACE

ri·par·i·an (ri per'ē ən, rī-) adj. [< L. riparius < ripa, a bank < IE. *reipa, a steep edge < base *rei-, to slit, cut, whence RIVE, REAP] 1. of, adjacent to, or living on, the bank of a river or, sometimes, of a lake, pond, etc. 2. designating any right enjoyed by the owner of riparian land

rip cord 1. a cord fastened to the gas bag of a balloon or dirigible so that pulling it will open the bag, releasing the gas and causing a rapid descent 2. a cord, etc. pulled to open a parachute during descent

ripe (rīp) adj. [ME. < OE., akin to G. reif: for IE. base see REAP, RIVE] 1. fully grown or developed; specif., ready to be harvested and used for food, as grain or fruit 2. like ripe fruit, as in being ruddy and full [ripe lips] 3. sufficiently advanced, as by being kept in storage or subjected to treatment, to be ready for use [ripe wine, ripe cheese] 4. fully or highly developed by study, experience, etc.; mature as in judgment, knowledge, etc. [ripe wisdom] 5. a) characterized by full physical or mental development [a person of ripe years] b) advanced in years [the ripe age of ninety] 6. ready to do, receive, or undergo something; fully prepared [ripe for marriage] 7. ready for some operation, treatment, or process [a boil ripe for lancing] 8. sufficiently advanced; far enough along [for some purpose]: said of time —ripe'ly adv. —ripe'ness n.

SYN.—ripe, in its basic application, implies readiness to be harvested, eaten, used, etc. [ripe apples, cheese, etc.] and, in extended use, full readiness for action, etc. [ripe for change]; mature implies full growth or development, as of living organisms, the mind, etc. [a mature tree, mature judgment]; mellow suggests the qualities typical of ripe fruit, such as softness, sweetness, etc. and therefore stresses the absence of sharpness, harshness, etc. [a mellow flavor, mood, etc.]; adult is applied to a person who has reached complete physical or mental maturity, or his legal majority, and to ideas, etc. that show mature thinking —ANT. unripe, immature

rip·en (rī'pən) vt., vi. to become or make ripe; mature, age, cure, etc. —rip'en·er n.

ri·poste, ri·post (ri pōst') n. [Fr. riposte < It. risposta < rispondere < L. respondere: see RESPOND] 1. Fencing a sharp, swift thrust made after parrying an opponent's lunge 2. a sharp, swift response or retort —vi. -post'ed, -post'ing to make a riposte

rip·per (rip'ər) n. 1. a person who rips 2. a thing that rips; device or tool for ripping

rip·ping (rip'iŋ) adj. 1. that rips or tears 2. [Chiefly Brit. Slang] excellent; fine; splendid —rip'ping·ly adv.

rip·ple¹ (rip'l) vi. -pled, -pling [prob. < RIP¹ + -LE, 3] 1. a) to form or have little waves or undulating movements on the surface, as water or grass stirred by a breeze b) to flow with such waves or movements on the surface c) to be formed or set in small folds or waves, as cloth or hair 2. to give the effect of rippling water, as by alternately rising and falling [laughter rippling through the hall] —vt. 1. to cause to ripple 2. to give a wavy or undulating form or appearance to 3. to make (a sound, tone, etc.) that ripples —n. 1. a small wave or undulation, as on the surface of water 2. a movement, appearance, or formation suggesting this 3. a sound like that of rippling water 4. a small rapid in a stream —SYN. see WAVE —rip'pler n.

rip·ple² (rip'l) vt. -pled, -pling [ME. rypelen < or akin to MLowG. or MDu. repelen, akin to OHG. riffilon, to scrape, riffila, a saw: for IE. base see REAP, RIVE] to remove the seeds from (flax, hemp, etc.) with a toothed implement resembling a comb —n. such an implement —rip'pler n.

ripple mark any of the ripply lines on the surface of sand, mud, etc. caused by waves, wind, or both

rip·plet (rip'lit) n. a little ripple

rip·ply (-lē) adj. -pli·er, -pli·est characterized by ripples; rippling

rip·rap (rip'rap') n. [echoic redupl. of RAP¹] ☆1. a foundation or wall made of broken stones thrown together irregularly or loosely, as in water or on a soft bottom ☆2. stones used for this —☆vt. -rapped', -rap'ping 1. to make a riprap in or on 2. to strengthen with riprap

☆rip-roar·ing (-rôr'iŋ) adj. [Slang] very lively and noisy; boisterous; uproarious

rip·saw (-sô') n. [RIP¹ + SAW¹] a saw with coarse teeth, for cutting wood along the grain

☆rip·snort·er (-snôrt'ər) n. [Slang] a person or thing that is strikingly active, forceful, exciting, wild, rambunctious, etc. —rip'snort'ing adj.

rip·tide (-tīd') n. [RIP² + TIDE¹] a tide opposing another tide or other tides, thus producing a violently disturbed area of water

Rip·u·ar·i·an (rip'yoo wer'ē ən) adj. [< ML. ripuarius (prob. < L. ripa, river bank) + -AN] designating or of a group of Franks who settled along the Rhine near Cologne in the 4th cent. A.D. —n. a Ripuarian Frank

Rip van Win·kle (rip' van wiŋ'k'l) the title character of a story (1819) by Washington Irving: Rip awakens after a twenty-year sleep to find everything changed

rise (rīz) vi. rose, ris'en (riz''n), ris'ing [ME. risen < OE. risan, akin to OHG. risan < IE. *ereis-, extension of base *er-, to set in motion, raise, whence L. oriri, to rise, Gr. ornynai, to arouse: cf. REAR², RUN] I. to get up 1. to stand or assume a vertical or more nearly vertical position, after sitting, kneeling, or lying 2. to get up after sleeping or resting 3. to rebel; revolt 4. to end an official assembly or meeting; adjourn 5. Theol. to return to life; become resurrected II. to go up 1. to go to a higher place or position; ascend 2. to appear above the horizon [the moon rose] 3. to attain greater height or a higher level [the river rose rapidly] 4. to advance in social status, rank, importance, etc.; become rich, famous, successful, etc. 5. to become erect or rigid 6. to form an elevation; extend upward [the tower rising above the trees] 7. to have an upward incline or slant [the Rising steeply] 8. to move upward to the surface of the water, as a fish seeking to take a fly, bait, etc. III. to increase in some way 1. to increase in amount, degree, quantity, price, etc. 2. to increase in volume of sound; become louder, shriller, etc. 3. to become stronger, more vivid, more buoyant, etc. [his spirits rose] 4. to become larger and puffier, as dough containing yeast IV. to appear by or as by rising 1. to originate, begin, or spring up 2. to have its source: said of a stream 3. to happen; occur 4. to become apparent to the senses or the mind [land rising ahead of the ship] 5. to be stirred up; become aroused [to make one's temper rise] 6. to be built [a house rising on the hill] —vt. to cause to rise, as birds from cover or a fish to the surface of the water —n. 1. the appearance of the sun, moon, etc. above the horizon 2. upward movement; ascent 3. an advance in social status, rank, importance, etc. 4. the appearance of a fish at the water's surface 5. a piece of high or rising ground; hill 6. a slope upward 7. the vertical height of something, as of a flight of stairs or a single step 8. an increase in a) height, as of water level b) volume or pitch of a sound c) degree, amount, price, value, etc. 9. a beginning, origin, springing up, etc. 10. [Brit.] a raise (in wages, etc.) —get a rise out of [Slang] to draw a desired response or retort from by teasing or provoking —give rise to to cause to appear or come into existence —rise to to prove oneself capable of coping with [to rise to the occasion]

SYN.—rise and arise both imply a coming into being, action, notice, etc., but rise carries an added implication of ascent [empires rise and fall] and arise is often used to indicate a causal relationship [accidents arise from carelessness]; spring implies sudden emergence [weeds sprang up in the garden]; originate is used in indicating a definite source, beginning, or prime cause [psychoanalysis originated with Freud]; derive implies a proceeding or developing from something else that is the source [this word derives from the Latin]; flow suggests a streaming from a source like water ["Praise God, from whom all blessings flow"]; issue suggests emergence through an outlet [not a word issued from his lips]; emanate implies the flowing forth from a source of something that is nonmaterial or intangible [rays of light emanating from the sun]; stem implies outgrowth as from a root or a main stalk [modern detective fiction stems from Poe]

ris·er (rīz'ər) n. 1. a person or thing that rises 2. any of the vertical pieces between the steps in a stairway

ris·i·bil·i·ty (riz'ə bil'ə tē) n., pl. -ties 1. the quality or state of being risible; ability or inclination to laugh ☆2. [usually pl.] a sense of the ridiculous or amusing; appreciation of what is laughable

ris·i·ble (riz'ə b'l) adj. [Fr. < LL. risibilis < L. risus, pp. of ridere, to laugh: see RIDICULE] 1. able or inclined to laugh 2. of or connected with laughter 3. causing laughter; laughable; funny; amusing

ris·ing (rī'ziŋ) adj. 1. that rises; going up, ascending, mounting, advancing, sloping upward, etc. 2. advancing to adult years; growing; maturing [the rising generation] 3. [Colloq. or Dial.] ☆fully as much as; somewhat more than; also, approaching; nearing [a man rising fifty]: in these senses sometimes construed as a preposition —n. 1. the act or process of a person or thing that rises; esp., an uprising; revolt; insurrection 2. something that rises; specif., a) a projection or prominence b) [Dial.] a boil, abscess, etc.

risk (risk) n. [Fr. risque < It. risco, risico, earlier risigo] 1. the chance of injury, damage, or loss; dangerous chance; hazard 2. Insurance a) the chance of loss b) the degree of probability of loss c) the amount of possible loss to the insuring company d) a person or thing with reference to the risk involved in insuring him or it e) the type of loss that a policy covers, as fire, storm, etc. —vt. [Fr. risquer] 1. to expose to the chance of injury, damage, or loss; hazard [to risk one's life] 2. to incur the risk of; take the chance of [to risk a fight] —SYN. see DANGER —run (or take) a risk to expose oneself to the chance of injury or loss; take a chance —risk'er n.

risk capital same as VENTURE CAPITAL

risk·y (ris'kē) adj. risk'i·er, risk'i·est involving risk; hazardous; dangerous —risk'i·ly adv. —risk'i·ness n.

†Ri·sor·gi·men·to (rē sôr'jē men'tō) n. [It., lit., resurrection] the 19th-cent. movement for the liberation and unification of Italy, or the period of this

ri·sot·to (ri sät'ō; It. rē zôt'tô) n. [It. < riso, rice] rice cooked with broth, grated cheese, etc.

ris·qué (ris kā') adj. [Fr., pp. of risquer, to RISK] very close to being improper or indecent; daring; suggestive [a risqué anecdote]

ris·sole (ris′ōl; Fr. rē sōl′) n. [Fr., ult. < LL. russeolus, reddish < L. russus, red] a small ball or roll of minced meat or fish often mixed with bread crumbs, egg, etc., enclosed in a thin pastry and fried

Ri·ta (rēt′ə) [It.] a feminine name

ri·tar·dan·do (rē′tär dän′dō) adj., adv. [It., gerund of ritardare, to delay: see RETARD] Music becoming gradually slower: a direction to the performer: abbrev. **rit., ritard.** —n., pl. **-dos** a ritardando passage: also **ri·tard** (ri tärd′)

rite (rīt) n. [ME. < L. ritus < IE. *rēi-, var. of base *ar-, to join, fit, whence READ[1]: cf. ART[1], RATE[1], ARITHMETIC] 1. a ceremonial or formal, solemn act, observance, or procedure in accordance with prescribed rule or custom, as in religious use [marriage rites] 2. any formal, customary observance, practice, or procedure [the rites of courtship] 3. a) a prescribed form or particular system of ceremonial procedure, religious or otherwise; ritual [the Scottish rite of Freemasonry] b) [often R-] liturgy; esp., any of the historical forms of the Eucharistic service [the Anglican rite] 4. [often R-] a division of (Eastern and Western) churches according to the liturgy used —SYN. see CEREMONY

rite of passage 1. a ceremony in some cultures marking the passing to another, more advanced stage, as to puberty or adulthood 2. an event in a person's life regarded as having similar ceremonial significance Also [Fr.] **rite de pas·sage** (rēt də på säzh′)

ri·tor·nel·lo (rit′ər nel′ō; It. rē′tôr nel′lō) n., pl. **-los;** It. **-li** (-lē) [It., dim. of ritorno, a return < ritornare, to return < ri- (< L. re-), RE- + tornare (< L.), to TURN] Music 1. an instrumental interlude before or after an aria, scene, etc. in early, esp. 17th-cent., operas 2. a tutti section recurring in a concerto grosso or rondo

rit·u·al (rich′ōō wəl) adj. [L. ritualis] of, having the nature of, or done as a rite or rites [ritual dances] —n. 1. a set form or system of rites, religious or otherwise 2. the observance of set forms or rites, as in public worship 3. a book containing rites or ceremonial forms 4. a practice, service, or procedure done as a rite, especially at regular intervals 5. ritual acts or procedures collectively —SYN. see CEREMONY —**rit′u·al·ly** adv.

rit·u·al·ism (-iz′m) n. 1. the observance or use of ritual 2. an excessive devotion to ritual 3. the study of religious ritual —**rit′u·al·ist** n., adj. —**rit′u·al·is′tic** adj. —**rit′u·al·is′ti·cal·ly** adv.

rit·u·al·ize (-īz′) vi. **-ized′, -iz′ing** to take part in rituals —vt. 1. to make a ritual of 2. to give the character of ritual to —**rit′u·al·i·za′tion** n.

☆**ritz·y** (rit′sē) adj. **ritz′i·er, ritz′i·est** [< the Ritz hotels founded by César Ritz (1850–1918), Swiss hotelkeeper] [Old Slang] luxurious, fashionable, elegant, etc.: often ironic —**ritz′i·ness** n.

riv·age (riv′ij) n. [ME. < OFr. < rive < L. ripa: see RIPARIAN & -AGE] [Archaic] a bank, coast, or shore

ri·val (rī′v'l) n. [Fr. < L. rivalis, orig., one living near or using the same stream as another < rivus, a brook < IE. *reie-, to flow < base *er-: see RISE] 1. a person who tries to get or do the same thing as another, or to equal or surpass another; competitor. 2. a person or thing that can equal or surpass another in some way; person or thing that can bear comparison [plastics and other rivals of many metals] 3. [Obs.] an associate or companion in some duty —adj. acting as a rival; competing —vt. **-valed** or **-valled, -val·ing** or **-val·ling** 1. to try to equal or surpass; compete with 2. to equal in some way; be a match for —vi. [Archaic] to be a rival; compete (with)

ri·val·ry (-rē) n., pl. **-ries** the act of rivaling or the fact or condition of being a rival or rivals; competition; emulation —SYN. see COMPETITION

rive (rīv) vt. **rived, rived** or **riv′en, riv′ing** [ME. riven < ON. rifa < IE. base *rei-, to tear, slit, whence RIFT[1], REAP, ROW[1]] 1. to tear apart; rend 2. to split; cleave 3. to break or dismay (the heart, spirit, etc.) —vi. to be or become rived

riv·en (riv′'n) alt. pp. of RIVE —adj. torn apart or split

riv·er[1] (riv′ər) n. [ME. rivere < OFr. riviere < VL. riparia < L. riparius: see RIPARIAN] 1. a natural stream of water larger than a creek and emptying into an ocean, a lake, or another river 2. any similar or plentiful stream or flow [a river of lava] —☆**sell down the river** to betray, deceive, abuse, etc.: from the former selling of Negro slaves into harsh servitude on the plantations of the lower Mississippi —☆**up the river** [Slang] to or confined in a penitentiary: from the sending of convicts up the Hudson River from New York to Sing Sing —**riv′er·like′** adj.

riv·er[2] (rī′vər) n. a person or thing that rives

Ri·ve·ra (ri ve′rä; E. ri ver′ə), **Die·go** (dye′gō) 1886–1957; Mex. painter, esp. of murals

river basin the area drained by a river and its tributaries

riv·er·bed (riv′ər bed′) n. the channel in which a river flows or has flowed

riv·er·head (-hed′) n. the source of a river

river horse same as HIPPOPOTAMUS

riv·er·ine (-īn′, -in) adj. 1. on or near the banks of a river; riparian 2. of, like, or produced by a river or rivers

Riv·er·side (riv′ər sīd′) [< Santa Ana River, near which it is located] city in S Calif.: pop. 140,000: see SAN BERNARDINO

riv·er·side (-sīd′) n. the bank of a river —adj. on or near the bank of a river

riv·er·weed (-wēd′) n. ☆any of a genus (Podostemon) of a family (Podostemaceae) of small, many-branched aquatic plants adhering to stones by means of suckerlike roots

riv·et (riv′it) n. [ME. ryvette < MFr. rivet < river, to clinch < ? VL. *ripare, to make firm; fasten (orig., to the shore) < L. ripa, a bank, shore] 1. a metal bolt or pin with a head on one end, used to fasten plates or beams together by being inserted through holes: the plain end is then hammered into a head or clinched, to lock it into place 2. a similar device used to fasten or strengthen seams, as on work clothes —vt. 1. to fasten with a rivet or rivets 2. to hammer or spread the end of (a bolt, etc.) into a head, for fastening something 3. to fasten or secure firmly 4. to fix or hold (the eyes, attention, etc.) firmly —**riv′et·er** n.

Riv·i·er·a (riv′ē er′ə; It. rē vye′rä) coastal strip along the Mediterranean from about La Spezia, Italy, to just west of Cannes, France: a famous resort area

RIVETS
(A, rivet holding steel beams together; B, C,D,rivets)

ri·vière (rē vyer′, riv′ē er′) n. [Fr., lit., a stream, RIVER[1]] a necklace, usually in several strands, of diamonds or other precious stones

riv·u·let (riv′yōō lit) n. [earlier rivolet < It. rivoletto, dim. of rivolo, dim. of rivo, a stream < L. rivus, a brook, stream: cf. RIVAL] a little stream; brook

rix·dol·lar (riks′däl′ər) n. [< obs. Du. rijcksdaler, lit., dollar of the realm < rijck, realm (akin to G. reich) + daler (see DOLLAR)] formerly, in the Netherlands, Germany, Denmark, etc., any of several silver coins worth about a dollar

ITALY
FRANCE
Genoa
MONACO
Nice
Cannes
La Spezia
RIVIERA
MEDITERRANEAN SEA
RIVIERA

Ri·yadh (rē yäd′) capital of the Nejd & a capital of Saudi Arabia: pop. c. 300,000

ri·yal (rē yäl′, -yôl′) n., pl. **-yals′** [Ar. riyāl < Sp. real: see REAL[2]] the monetary unit of Saudi Arabia, Qatar, and Yemen: see MONETARY UNITS, table

Ri·zal (rē säl′) same as PASAY

Ri·zal (rē säl′), **Jo·sé** (hō se′) 1861–96; Philippine patriot, novelist, & poet: shot for alleged conspiracy against Spain

Riz·zi·o (rit′sē ō; It. rēt′tsyō), **David** 1533?–66; It. musician; secretary to & favorite of Mary, Queen of Scots: murdered

RJ Mil. road junction

RM, r.m. reichsmark; reichsmarks

rm. pl. **rms.** 1. ream 2. room

R.M.A. Royal Military Academy

R.M.C. Royal Military College

rms, r.m.s. root mean square

R.M.S. 1. Royal Mail Service 2. Royal Mail Steamship

Rn Chem. radon

R.N. 1. Registered Nurse: also **RN** 2. Royal Navy

RNA ribonucleic acid

rnd round

R.N.R. Royal Naval Reserve

R.O. 1. recto 2. roan 3. rood

R.O. 1. Receiving Officer 2. Receiving Officer 3. Regimental Order 4. Royal Observatory

☆**roach[1]** (rōch) n. 1. clipped form of COCKROACH 2. [Slang] the butt of a marijuana cigarette

roach[2] (rōch) n., pl. **roach, roach′es:** see PLURAL, II, D, 2 [ME. roche < OFr., prob. < Gmc., as in MLowG. roche, OE. ruhha, roach, akin to OE. ruh, ROUGH: prob. because of the rough skin] 1. a freshwater fish (Rutilus rutilus) of the carp family, found in the rivers of N Europe 2. any of various similar American fishes, as the **California roach** (Hesperoleucus symmetricus)

roach[3] (rōch) vt. [< ?] ☆1. to brush (a person's hair) so that it arches over into a roll ☆2. to cut (a horse's mane) so that it stands up 3. to cut a roach in (a sail) —n. ☆1. hair or a mane brushed or cut by roaching 2. an upward curve cut in the bottom of a square sail

roach back an arched back, esp. of a horse

road (rōd) n. [ME. rode, a riding < OE. rad, a ride, traveling on horseback, way < riden, to RIDE] 1. a) a way made for traveling between places, esp. distant places, by automobile, horseback, etc.; highway b) same as ROADBED (sense 2) 2. a way; path; course [the road to fortune] ☆3. clipped form of RAILROAD 4. [often pl.] a

protected place near shore, not so enclosed as a harbor, where ships can ride at anchor —**on the road 1.** traveling, esp. as a salesman **2.** on tour, as a troupe of actors —**one for the road** [Slang] a last alcoholic drink before leaving —**take to the road 1.** to start traveling; set out **2.** [Archaic] to become a highwayman —**the road** all the cities and towns generally visited by touring theatrical companies

road·a·bil·i·ty (rōd′ə bil′ə tē) *n.* [ROAD + -ABILITY] the degree of operating ease and riding comfort of a vehicle on the road

☆**road agent** a highwayman, esp. as on former stagecoach routes in the western U.S.

☆**road·bed** (-bed′) *n.* **1.** *a)* the foundation laid to support the ties and rails of a railroad *b)* a layer of crushed rock, cinders, etc. immediately under the ties **2.** the foundation and surface of a road, or highway

road·block (-bläk′) *n.* **1.** an obstruction in a road; specif., *a) Mil.* a blockade of logs, wire, cement, etc., for holding up enemy vehicles at a point covered by heavy fire *b)* a blockade, often of squad cars, set up by police, as for cutting off the escape route of a fugitive from justice **2.** any hindrance or obstacle in the way of an objective

☆**road hog** a driver who keeps his car, truck, etc. in or near the middle of the road so that it is hard or impossible for others to pass

road·house (-hous′) *n.* a tavern, inn, or, esp., nightclub along a country road, as in the 1920's

road map a map for motorists, showing the roads of a given region, their route markings, condition, etc.

road metal crushed rock, cinders, etc., used for making and repairing roads and roadbeds

☆**road runner** a long-tailed crested desert bird (*Geococcyx californianus*) of the SW U.S. and N Mexico, characterized by running swiftly instead of flying: it is related to the cuckoo

☆**road·show** (-shō′) *n.* **1.** a show presented by a theatrical troupe on tour **2.** the showing of a motion picture at selected theaters with reserved seats at higher prices

road·side (-sīd′) *n.* the side of a road —*adj.* on or at the side of a road [a roadside park]

road·stead (-sted′) *n.* [ROAD + STEAD] same as ROAD (sense 4)

road·ster (-stər) *n.* ☆**1.** an earlier type of open automobile with a single seat for two or three persons and, sometimes, a rumble seat **2.** a horse for riding or driving on the road

road test a test of a vehicle, tires, etc. under actual operating conditions —**road′-test′** *vt.*

road·way (-wā′) *n.* **1.** a road **2.** that part of a road used by cars, trucks, etc.; traveled part of a road

road·work (-wurk′) *n.* a jogging or running distances as an exercise, esp. by a prizefighter in training

roam (rōm) *vi.* [ME. *romen*, akin to OE. *ǣraman*, to rise < IE. base *erei-* < *er-*, to set in motion, whence RISE, RUN] to travel from place to place, esp. with no special plan or purpose; go aimlessly; wander —*vt.* to wander over or through [to *roam* the streets] —*n.* the act of roaming; ramble —**roam′er** *n.*

SYN.—**roam** implies a traveling about without a fixed goal over a large area and carries suggestions of freedom, pleasure, etc. [to *roam* about the country]; **ramble** implies an idle moving or walking about and connotes carelessness, aimlessness, etc. [we *rambled* through the woods]; **rove** suggests extensive wandering, but it usually implies a special purpose or activity [a *roving* reporter]; **range** stresses the extent of territory covered and sometimes suggests a search for something [buffalo *ranging* the plains]; **stray** implies a wandering from a given place, fixed course, etc. [sheep *straying* from the fold]; **meander** is used of streams, paths, etc., and, in extension, of people and animals, that follow a winding, seemingly aimless course

roan¹ (rōn) *adj.* [OFr. < Sp. *roano* < L. *ravidus*, grayish < *ravus*, grayish-yellow, tawny: for IE. base see GRAY] of a solid color, as reddish-brown, brown, black, etc. with a thick sprinkling of white hairs: said chiefly of horses —*n.* **1.** a roan color **2.** a roan horse or other animal

roan² (rōn) *n.* [MScot. < ? ROUEN] a soft, flexible sheepskin used in bookbinding, often treated to look like morocco —*adj.* made of or bound in roan

Ro·a·noke (rō′ə nōk′) [< Algonquian *Roanok*, northern people] **1.** river flowing from SW Va. southeast through NE N.C. into Albemarle Sound: c. 380 mi. **2.** city in SW Va., on this river: pop. 92,000 **3.** island off the NE coast of N.C.: site of abortive English colony (1585–87)

roar (rôr) *vi.* [ME. *raren* < OE. *rarian*, akin to G. *rehren* < IE. echoic base *rei-*, to cry, whence Sans. *rāyati*, (he) bellows, ON. *rāmr*, hoarse] **1.** to utter a loud, deep, rumbling sound, as a lion or a person in excitement, pain, anger, etc. **2.** to breathe with a loud, hoarse, rasping noise, as a horse: cf. ROARING (sense 3) **3.** to talk or laugh loudly and boisterously **4.** to make a loud noise in moving, operating, etc., as a motor or gun **5.** to resound with a noisy din —*vt.* **1.** to utter in or express with a loud, deep sound **2.** to make, put, force, etc. by roaring [to *roar* oneself hoarse] —*n.* **1.** a loud, deep, rumbling sound, as of a lion, bull, person or crowd shouting, etc.; sound of roaring **2.** a loud burst of laughter **3.** a loud noise, as of waves, a storm, a motor, etc.; din —**roar′er** *n.*

roar·ing (rôr′in) *n.* **1.** the act of an animal, person, etc. that roars **2.** the loud, deep sound made by an animal,

etc. that roars **3.** a disease of horses, characterized by loud, hoarse, rasping breathing —*adj.* **1.** *a)* that roars; loud; noisy *b)* boisterous, brawling, etc. **2.** [Colloq.] very active or successful; brisk [a *roaring* business] —*adv.* to the point of being noisy, boisterous, etc. [*roaring* mad, *roaring* drunk]

roaring forties the stormy oceanic areas between 40° and 50° latitude, north or, esp., south

roast (rōst) *vt.* [ME. *rosten* < OFr. *rostir* < Frank. *raustjan*, akin to OHG. *rosten* < *rost*, gridiron, roast] **1.** to cook (something) with little or no moisture, as in an oven, over an open fire, or in hot embers [to *roast* a chicken, an ox, an ear of corn, etc.] **2.** to dry, parch, or brown (coffee, etc.) by exposure to heat **3.** to expose to great heat **4.** to heat (ore, etc.) with access of air in a furnace in order to remove impurities or cause oxidation **5.** to warm (oneself), as at a fireplace **6.** [Colloq.] to criticize severely or ridicule without mercy —*vi.* **1.** to roast meat, etc. **2.** to be cooked by being roasted **3.** to be or become very hot —*n.* **1.** something roasted; esp., roasted meat or a piece of roasted meat **2.** a cut of meat for roasting **3.** a roasting or being roasted ☆**4.** a picnic, or outdoor entertainment, at which food is roasted and eaten [a steer *roast*] **5.** [Colloq.] severe criticism or ridicule —*adj.* roasted [*roast* pork] —**roast′ing** *adj.*

roast·er (rōs′tər) *n.* **1.** a person or thing that roasts **2.** a special pan, oven, or apparatus for roasting meat, etc. **3.** a young pig, chicken, etc. suitable for roasting

rob (räb) *vt.* robbed, rob′bing [ME. *robben* < OFr. *rober* < Gmc. *raubon*, akin to OHG. *roubon*, OE. *reafian*: for IE. base see RUPTURE] **1.** *a) Law* to take personal property, money, etc. from unlawfully by using or threatening force and violence; commit robbery upon *b)* popularly, to steal something from in any way, as by embezzlement, burglary, etc. *c)* to plunder or rifle *d)* [Now Rare] to take by stealing or plundering **2.** to deprive (someone) of something belonging or due, or take or withhold something from unjustly or injuriously [the accident *robbed* him of health] —*vi.* to commit robbery; be a robber —**rob′ber** *n.*

rob·a·lo (räb′ə lō′, rō′bə-) *n.*, *pl.* -los′, -lo′: see PLURAL, II, D, 1 [Sp. *róbalo* or Port. *robalo* < Catal. *elobarro*, ult. < L. *lupus*, a wolf, also a kind of fish: see WOLF] same as SNOOK¹ (sense 1)

rob·and (räb′ənd) *n.* [earlier *raband* & *robbin* < MDu. *rabant* < *ra*, sailyard (for IE. base see ROCK²) + *bant*, BAND¹] a short piece of spun yarn or rope, used to fasten the head of a sail to a yard, spar, etc.

robber baron 1. a nobleman of feudal times who robbed people traveling through his domain ☆**2.** any of a number of U.S. capitalists of the late 19th cent. who acquired vast wealth by exploitation and ruthlessness

robber fly any of a large family (Asilidae) of two-winged, hairy flies of varying size that prey on other insects

rob·ber·y (räb′ər ē) *n.*, *pl.* -ber·ies [ME. *roberie* < OFr.: see ROB & -ERY] act or practice of robbing; specif., *Law* the felonious taking of another's property from his person or in his immediate presence by the use of violence or intimidation —SYN. see THEFT

Robbia see DELLA ROBBIA

robe (rōb) *n.* [ME. < OFr., a robe, orig. booty, spoils < Gmc. *rauba*, plunder: see ROB] **1.** a long, loose, or flowing outer garment; specif., *a)* such a garment worn on formal occasions, to show rank or office, etc., as by a judge or bishop *b)* a bathrobe or dressing gown **2.** [pl.] [Archaic] clothes; costume; dress ☆**3.** *short for* LAP ROBE —*vt.*, *vi.* robed, rob′ing to dress in or cover with a robe or robes

‡**robe-de-cham·bre** (rôb′də shän′br′) *n.*, *pl.* -cham′bres (-br′) [Fr., lit., robe of (the) chamber] a dressing gown

Rob·ert (räb′ərt) [ME. < OFr. < OHG. *Hruodperht* < *hruod-*, fame + *perht*, BRIGHT] **1.** a masculine name: dim. *Bob, Rob, Robin*; var. *Rupert*; fem. *Roberta* **2.** Robert I *a)* ?–1035; duke of Normandy (1028–35): father of WILLIAM THE CONQUEROR *b)* see BRUCE (sense 2)

Ro·ber·ta (rə bur′tə, rō-) [fem. of ROBERT] a feminine name

Robe·son (rōb′sən), **Paul** 1898– ; U.S. singer & actor

Ro·bes·pierre (rō′bes pyer′; *E.* rōbs′pyer, -pir′), **Max·i·mi·lien** (**François Marie Isidore de**) (mäk sē mē lyaṅ′) 1758–94; Fr. revolutionist & Jacobin leader: guillotined

rob·in (räb′in) *n.* [< ME. *Robin* (dim. of *Robert*) < OFr.] ☆**1.** a large N. American thrush (*Turdus migratorius*) with a dull-red breast and belly **2.** a small European warbler (*Erithacus rubecula*) with a yellowish-red breast

Robin Good·fel·low (good′fel′ō) *Eng. Folklore* a mischievous elf or fairy: identified with Puck

Robin Hood *Eng. Legend* an outlaw of the 12th cent. who lived with his followers in Sherwood Forest and robbed the rich to help the poor

☆**rob·in's-egg blue** (räb′inz eg′) a light greenish blue

Rob·in·son (räb′in s'n) **1. Edwin Arlington**, 1869–1935; U.S. poet **2. James Harvey**, 1863–1936; U.S. historian

Robinson Cru·soe (krōō′sō) the title hero of Daniel Defoe's novel (1719), a sailor who, shipwrecked on a tropical island, survives by various ingenious contrivances until rescued years later: cf. MAN FRIDAY

☆**ro·ble** (rō′blā) *n.* [AmSp. < Sp., oak < L. *robur*, hard variety of oak: see ROBUST] any of several oak trees of the Southwest; esp., a tall, white oak (*Quercus lobata*) of California

ro·bot (rō′bət, -bät) *n.* [< Czech *robota*, forced labor < OBulg. *rabota*, menial labor < *rabu*, servant < IE. base *orbho-*: see ORPHAN] **1.** *a)* any manlike mechanical being, as those in Karel Capek's play *R.U.R.* (Rossum's Universal Robots), built to do routine manual work for human beings *b)* any mechanical device operated automatically, esp. by remote control, to perform in a seemingly human way **2.** an automaton; esp., a person who acts or works mechanically and without thinking for himself —**ro′bot·ism** *n.*

robot bomb a small, jet-propelled winged bomb steered by an automatic pilot and carrying high explosives

ro·bot·ize (rō′bət tiz′) *vt.* -**ized′**, -**iz′ing 1.** to make automatic **2.** to cause (a person) to become or act like a robot —**ro′bot·i·za′tion** *n.*

Rob·son (räb′sən), **Mount** mountain in E British Columbia, surrounded by a provincial park; highest peak of the Canadian Rockies: 12,972 ft.

ro·bur·ite (rō′bə rīt′) *n.* [L. *robur*, strength (see ff.) + -ITE¹] a very powerful, flameless explosive containing dinitrobenzene or chlorinated dinitrobenzene and ammonium nitrate, used in mining operations

ro·bust (rō bust′, rō′bust) *adj.* [L. *robustus*, oaken, hard, strong < *robur*, hard variety of oak, hardness, strength, prob. akin to *ruber*, RED¹] **1.** *a)* strong and healthy; full of vigor; hardy *b)* strongly built or based; muscular or sturdy **2.** suited to or requiring physical strength or stamina [*robust* work] **3.** rough; coarse; boisterous **4.** full and rich, as in flavor [a *robust* port wine] —*SYN.* see HEALTHY —**ro·bust′ly** *adv.* —**ro·bust′ness** *n.*

ro·bus·tious (rō bus′chəs) *adj.* [prec. + -IOUS] strong and sturdy; also, rough, coarse, boisterous, etc.: now archaic except in facetious usage —**ro·bus′tious·ly** *adv.* —**ro·bus′tious·ness** *n.*

roc (räk) *n.* [Ar. *rukhkh* < Per. *rukh*] *Arabian & Persian Legend* a fabulous bird of prey, so huge and strong that it could carry off large animals

Ro·ca (rō′kə), **Cape** cape in SW Portugal, near Lisbon: westernmost point of continental Europe: Port. **Ca·bo da Ro·ca** (kä′bōō də rō′kə)

roc·am·bole (räk′əm bōl′) *n.* [Fr. < G. *rockenbolle* < *rocken*, roggen, RYE¹ + *bolle*, bulb] a European onion (*Allium scorodoprasum*) bearing a cluster of small bulbs used like garlic cloves for flavoring

Ro·cham·beau (rō shän bō′), **comte de** (*Jean Baptiste Donatien de Vimeur*) 1725-1807; Fr. general: commanded Fr. forces against Brit. in the Am. Revolutionary War

Roch·dale (räch′dāl) city in Lancashire, NW England: one of the earliest Eng. cooperative societies was founded there (1844): pop. 87,000

Ro·chelle powder (rō shel′) [see ff.] *same as* SEIDLITZ POWDER

Rochelle salt [after La *Rochelle*, France, where it was discovered] a colorless crystalline compound, potassium sodium tartrate, KNaC₄H₄O₆·4H₂O, used as a laxative and, in electronics, as a piezoelectric material

‡roche mou·ton·née (rōsh mōō tô nā′) [Fr., lit., sheep-shaped rock] *Geol.* a bare hummock of rock, usually smoothed on the upstream side and grooved on the other by glacial action

Roch·es·ter (rä′ches′tər, räch′is-) **1.** [after N. *Rochester* (1752-1831), Revolutionary officer] city & port in W N.Y., on Lake Ontario: pop. 296,000 (met. area 883,000) **2.** [after prec. city] city in SE Minn.: pop. 54,000 **3.** city in Kent, SE England: pop. 52,000

roch·et (räch′it) *n.* [ME. < OFr. < *roc*, a cloak < MHG. *roc* < OHG. *hroc, roch:* cf. FROCK] a vestment of lawn or linen, like a surplice, worn by bishops and some other church dignitaries

rock¹ (räk) *n.* [ME. *rokke* < OFr. *roche* < ML. *rocca*] **1.** a large mass of stone forming a peak or cliff **2.** *a)* a large stone detached from the mass; boulder *b)* broken pieces of any size of such stone **3.** *a)* mineral matter variously composed, formed in masses or large quantities in the earth's crust by the action of heat, water, etc. *b)* a particular kind or mass of this **4.** anything like or suggesting a rock, as in strength or stability; esp., a firm support, basis, refuge, etc. **5.** *same as: ☆a)* ROCKFISH *b)* ROCK DOVE **6.** *a)* [Chiefly Brit.] a hard candy made in sticks *b)* clipped form of ROCK CANDY **7.** [Colloq. or Dial.] any stone, large or small **8.** [Slang] a diamond or other gem —**on the rocks** [Colloq.] **1.** in or into a condition of ruin or catastrophe **2.** without money; bankrupt **3.** served undiluted over ice cubes: said of liquor, wine, etc.

rock² (räk) *vt.* [ME. *rocken* < OE. *roccian*, prob. akin to G. *rücken*, to pull, push < IE. base *orek-*, a pole, to project, totter, whence ON., MDu. *rā*, sailyard] **1.** to move or sway back and forth or from side to side (a cradle, a child in the arms, etc.), esp. in a gentle, quieting manner **2.** to bring into a specified condition by moving or swaying in this way [to *rock* a baby to sleep] **3.** *a)* to move or sway strongly; shake; cause to tremble or vibrate [the explosion *rocked* the house] *b)* to upset emotionally **4.** *Engraving* to prepare the surface of (a plate) for a mezzotint by roughening with a rocker (sense 5) **5.** *Mining* to wash (sand or gravel) in a rocker (sense 4) —*vi.* **1.** to move or sway back and forth or from side to side, as a cradle **2.** to move or sway strongly; shake; vibrate **3.** to be rocked, as ore —*n.* **1.** the act of rocking **2.** a rocking motion ☆**3.** *a) same as* ROCK-AND-ROLL *b)* popular music evolved from rock-and-roll, variously containing elements of folk music, country music, etc.

☆**rock-and-roll** (räk′n rōl′) *n.* a form of popular music, characterized by a strong and regular rhythm, which evolved from jazz and the blues

☆**rock and rye** rye whiskey bottled with pieces of rock candy and slices of fruit

☆**rock·a·way** (räk′ə wā′) *n.* [< *Rockaway*, N.J., where formerly made] a light horse-drawn carriage with four wheels, open sides, and a standing top

☆**rock bass** a freshwater game fish (*Ambloplites rupestris*) of the sunfish family, found in E N. America

☆**rock bottom** the lowest level or point; very bottom —**rock-bot·tom** (räk′bät′əm) *adj.*

rock-bound (-bound′) *adj.* surrounded or covered by rocks [a *rock-bound* inlet or coast]

rock brake any of a genus (*Cryptogramma*) of ferns that grow in rocky ground

rock candy large, hard, clear crystals of sugar formed on a string dipped in a solution of boiled sugar

☆**rock cod 1.** any of various saltwater fishes found around rocks, including a variety of the common codfish **2.** *same as* ROCKFISH (sense *b*)

Rock Cornish (hen) *same as* CORNISH (sense 2 *b*)

rock crystal a transparent, esp. colorless, quartz

rock dove the European wild pigeon (*Columba livia*) from which most domestic varieties are derived

Rock·e·fel·ler (räk′ə fel′ər) **1.** John D(avison), 1839-1937; U.S. industrialist & philanthropist **2.** John D(avison), Jr., 1874-1960; U.S. industrialist & philanthropist: son of prec.

rock·er (räk′ər) *n.* **1.** a person who rocks a cradle, etc. **2.** either of the curved pieces on the bottom of a cradle, rocking chair, etc. ☆**3.** *same as* ROCKING CHAIR ☆**4.** a cradle for washing sand or gravel in gold mining **5.** a small steel plate with a toothed and curved edge, for roughening and thus preparing the surface of a mezzotint plate —**off one's rocker** [Slang] crazy; insane

rocker arm an armlike piece attached to a rockshaft

rocker panel any of the sections of body paneling below the doors of an automobile

rock·er·y (räk′ər ē) *n., pl.* -**er·ies** rocks and soil arranged for growing a rock garden

rock·et¹ (räk′it) *n.* [OFr. *rocchetta*, a spool or bobbin, rocket, orig. dim. of *rocca*, a distaff < OHG. *roccho*, a distaff: from the resemblance in shape] **1.** any of various devices, typically cylindrical, containing a combustible substance which when ignited produces gases that escape through a rear vent and drive the container forward by the principle of reaction: simple rockets are used as fireworks, signals, or projectile weapons, and more complex rockets, containing their own source of oxygen as well as fuel, are used to propel spacecraft into and through outer space **2.** a spacecraft, missile, probe, etc. propelled by a rocket —*vi.* **1.** to go like a rocket; dart ahead swiftly **2.** to travel in a rocket **3.** to fly swiftly and almost straight up when flushed: said of game birds **4.** to soar; rise rapidly [prices *rocketed*] —*vt.* to convey in a rocket

rock·et² (räk′it) *n.* [Fr. *roquette* < It. *rochetta*, var. of *ruchetta*, dim. < *ruca*, rocket < L. *eruca*, kind of colewort] **1.** any of various plants of the mustard family, with white, yellow, pink, or purple flowers; esp., **sea rocket** (genus *Cakile*) found along seashores in Europe and N. America **2.** a European annual (*Eruca sativa*) of the mustard family, sometimes cultivated as a pungent salad herb: also called **rocket salad 3.** *same as* DAME'S VIOLET

rock·e·teer (räk′ə tir′) *n.* an expert in rocketry

rocket launcher a device for launching rockets; specif., a bazooka: also **rocket gun**

rock·et·ry (räk′ə trē) *n.* **1.** the science of designing, building, and launching rockets **2.** rockets collectively

☆**rock·et·sonde** (räk′it sänd′) *n.* [ROCKET + SONDE] *Meteorol.* a rocket designed for observations in the upper air, esp. between 100,000 and 250,000 ft.

rock·fish (räk′fish′) *n., pl.* -**fish′**, -**fish′es:** see FISH² any of a large number of unrelated fishes that stay among rocks offshore or in rocky beds; specif., ☆*a) same as* STRIPED BASS *b)* any of various fishes (genus *Sebastodes*) of the North Pacific ☆*c)* any of several groupers of the waters around Bermuda, Florida, etc.

Rock·ford (räk′fərd) [in allusion to the *rocky*-bottomed *ford* there] city in N Ill.: pop. 147,000

rock garden a garden with flowers and plants growing on rocky ground or among rocks variously arranged

rock hind a spotted food fish (*Epinephelus adscensionis*) of tropical Atlantic and Caribbean waters, related to the groupers

☆**rock·hound** (räk′hound′) *n.* [ROCK¹ + HOUND¹ (*n.* 4)] [Colloq.] a person whose hobby is hunting for and collecting rocks, esp. semiprecious stones

---

fat, āpe, cär; ten, ēven; is, bīte; gō, hôrn, tōol, look; oil, out; up, fur; get; joy; yet; chin; she; thin, then; zh, leisure; ŋ, ring; ə for a in ago, e in agent, i in sanity, o in comply, u in focus; ′ as in able (ā′b'l); Fr. bâl; ë, Fr. coeur; ö, Fr. feu; Fr. mon; ō, Fr. coq; ü, Fr. duc; r, Fr. cri; H, G. ich; kh, G. doch. See inside front cover. ☆ Americanism; ‡foreign; *hypothetical; < derived from

Rock·ies (räk′ēz) *same as* ROCKY MOUNTAINS

rock·i·ness (räk′ē nis) *n.* a rocky quality or state

☆**rocking chair** a chair mounted on rockers or springs, so as to allow a rocking movement

rocking horse a toy horse mounted on rockers or springs and big enough for a child to ride

Rock Island [< the name of the *rocky island* in the river] city in NW Ill., on the Mississippi: pop. 50,000

rock lobster *same as* SPINY LOBSTER

☆**rock maple** *same as* SUGAR MAPLE

Rock·ne (räk′nē), **Knute (Kenneth)** (nōōt) 1888–1931; U.S. football coach, born in Norway

☆**rock 'n' roll** (räk′ 'n rōl′) *same as* ROCK-AND-ROLL

rock oil *chiefly Brit. term for* PETROLEUM

☆**rock·oon** (rä kōōn′, rä′kōōn) *n.* [ROCK(ET)¹ + (BALL)OON] a rocket launched from a balloon at high altitude so as to reduce the effects of atmospheric drag

rock pigeon *same as* ROCK DOVE

☆**rock rabbit** *same as:* 1. HYRAX 2. PIKA

rock-ribbed (räk′ribd′) *adj.* 1. having rocky ridges or elevations [*rock-ribbed* coasts] ☆2. firm; rigid; unyielding [a *rock-ribbed* policy]

rock·rose (-rōz′) *n. same as* CISTUS —*adj.* designating a family (Cistaceae) of bushy plants including pinweed and cistus

rock salt common salt, natural sodium chloride, occurring in solid form, esp. in rocklike masses; halite

rock·shaft (-shaft′, -shäft′) *n.* a machine shaft designed to rock back and forth on its journals rather than to revolve

rock squirrel ☆1. a ground squirrel (*Citellus variegatus*) with a gray body and black head, living mostly in rocky areas in the W U.S. and in Mexico 2. any of a genus (*Ratufa*) of ground squirrels of SE Asia

rock tripe any of a genus (*Umbilicaria*) of large lichens, green on top and black beneath, attached to a rock surface

Rock·ville (räk′vil) [ROCK¹ + -VILLE] city in C Md.: suburb of Washington, D.C.: pop. 42,000

rock·weed (räk′wēd′) *n.* any of a number of seaweeds that grow on rocks; esp., *same as* FUCUS (sense 2)

Rock·well (räk′wel), **Norman** 1894– ; U.S. illustrator

rock wool a fibrous material that looks like spun glass, made from molten rock or slag by passing a blast of steam through the fluid; mineral wool: it is used for insulation, esp. in buildings

rock·y¹ (räk′ē) *adj.* **rock′i·er, rock′i·est** 1. full of or containing rocks 2. consisting of rock 3. like a rock; firm, hard, unfeeling, etc. 4. full of obstacles or difficulties [the *rocky* road to success]

rock·y² (räk′ē) *adj.* **rock′i·er, rock′i·est** 1. *a)* inclined to rock, or sway; unsteady; wobbly *b)* uncertain; shaky 2. [Slang] weak and dizzy; groggy

☆**Rocky Mountain goat** a white, goatlike antelope (*Oreamnos americanus*) of the mountains of NW N. America, with a thick, shaggy coat and small, slender, black horns that curve backward

Rocky Mountain National Park national park in the Front Range of the Rockies, NC Colo.: highest peak, 14,255 ft.; 400 sq. mi.

Rocky Mountains [transl. < Fr. *Montaignes Rocheuses*] mountain system in W N. America, extending from C N.Mex. to N Alas.: over 3,000 mi. long; highest peak, Mt. McKINLEY

ROCKY MOUNTAIN GOAT (2-1/2–3-1/2 ft. high at shoulder)

Rocky Mountain sheep *same as* BIGHORN

☆**Rocky Mountain spotted fever** [from being first discovered in the *Rocky Mountains*] an acute infectious disease caused by a rickettsia, transmitted to man by certain ticks (esp. genus *Dermacentor*), and characterized by fever, muscular pains, and skin eruptions

ro·co·co (rə kō′kō; *occas.* rō′kə kō′) *n.* [Fr. < *rocaille*, rock work, shell work < *roc* < OFr. *roche*, ROCK¹] 1. a style of architecture and decoration developed in France from the baroque and characterized primarily by elaborate and profuse, often delicately executed ornamentation imitating foliage, shell work, scrolls, etc.: popular esp. in the first half of the 18th cent. 2. a style of literature, music, etc. regarded, often disparagingly, as like this —*adj.* 1. of or in rococo 2. too profuse and elaborate in ornamentation; florid and tasteless

ROCKY MOUNTAINS

rod (räd) *n.* [ME. *rodde* < OE. *rodd*, akin to *rod*, a cross & ON. *rudda*, club, prob. < IE. base *rēt-, *rōt-, a bar, beam, whence L. *retae*, trees on a river bank] 1. a straight, slender shoot or stem cut from, or still part of, a bush or tree 2. *Bible* an offshoot or branch of a family or tribe; stock or race 3. any straight, or almost straight, stick, shaft, bar, staff, etc., of wood, metal, or other material [curtain *rods*, a lightning *rod*] 4. *a)* a stick or switch, or a bundle of sticks or switches, for beating as punishment *b)* punishment; chastisement 5. *a)* a staff, scepter, etc., carried as a symbol of office, rank, or power *b)* power; authority; often, tyrannical rule 6. *same as* FISHING ROD 7. a stick used to measure something 8. *a)* a measure of length equal to 16 1/2 feet, or 5 1/2 yards *b)* a square rod, equal to 30 1/4 square yards ☆9. [Slang] a pistol or revolver ☆10. [Slang] *clipped form of* HOT ROD 11. *Anat.* any of the rod-shaped cells in the retina of the vertebrate eye that are sensitive to dim light 12. *Bacteriology* any microorganism shaped like a rod —☆**ride** (or **hit**) **the rods** [Slang] to steal a ride on a freight train —**rod′like′** *adj.*

rode (rōd) *pt. & archaic pp.* of RIDE

ro·dent (rōd′'nt) *adj.* [L. *rodens*, prp. of *rodere*, to gnaw: see RAT] 1. gnawing 2. of or like a rodent or rodents —*n.* any of a very large order (Rodentia) of gnawing mammals, including rats, mice, squirrels, beavers, etc., characterized by constantly growing incisors adapted for gnawing or nibbling; esp., in popular usage, a rat or mouse

☆**ro·dent·i·cide** (rō den′tə sīd′) *n.* [RODENT + -i- + -CIDE] a poison used for killing rodents, esp. rats and mice

☆**ro·de·o** (rō′dē ō′; *also, esp. for 1*, rō dā′ō) *n., pl.* **-de·os′** [Sp., a going around, cattle ring < *rodear*, to surround < L. *rotare*: see ROTATE] 1. [Now Rare] a roundup of cattle 2. a public exhibition or competition of the skills of cowboys, as broncobusting, lassoing, etc.

Rod·er·ic, Rod·er·ick (räd′ər ik, räd′rik) [ML. *Rodericus* < OHG. *Hrodrich* < *hruod-*, fame + Gmc. *rīk-*, a king (akin to L. *rex*: see REGAL] a masculine name

Rod·gers (räj′ərz), **Richard** 1902– ; U.S. composer of musicals

Ro·din (rō dan′; E. rō dan′), **(François) Au·guste (René)** (ō güst′) 1840–1917; Fr. sculptor

rod·man (räd′mən) *n., pl.* **-men** (-mən) ☆a person who carries the leveling rod in surveying

Rod·ney (räd′nē) [< surname *Rodney* < place name *Rodney Stoke*, England] a masculine name: dim. *Rod*

rod·o·mon·tade (räd′ə män tād′, rōd′ə-; -tād′) *n.* [Fr. < *rodomont*, braggadocio < It. *Rodomonte*, boastful Saracen leader in Ariosto's *Orlando Furioso*] arrogant boasting or blustering, ranting talk —*adj.* arrogantly boastful —*vi.* **-tad′ed, -tad′ing** to boast; brag

roe¹ (rō) *n.* [ME. *rowe, rowne*, akin to (or < ?) ON. *hrogn*, akin to OHG. *rogo* < IE. base *krek-*, whence Lett. *kuřkulis*, frog's eggs] 1. fish eggs, esp. when still massed in the ovarian membrane 2. occasionally, the swollen ovaries or expelled eggs of certain crustaceans, as the coral of a lobster

roe² (rō) *n., pl.* **roe, roes**: see PLURAL, II, D, 2 [ME. *ro* < OE. *ra*, akin to OHG. *reho* < IE. *roiko-* < base *rei-, *roi*, striped, spotted, whence Lett. *ràibs*, colorful, striped, Sans. *riśya*, male antelope] a small, agile, graceful European and Asiatic deer (*Capreolus capreolus*): also called **roe deer**

Roe·bling (rō′blin), **John A(ugustus)** 1806–69; U.S. civil engineer & bridge designer, born in Germany

roe·buck (rō′buk′) *n., pl.* **-bucks′, -buck′**: see PLURAL, II, D, 1 the male of the roe deer

roent·gen (rent′gən, ren′chən) *n.* [after ff.] the international unit of quantity used in measuring ionizing radiation, as X-rays or gamma rays, equal to the quantity of radiation that will produce, in 0.001293 grams (1 cc.) of dry air at 0°C and 760 mm of mercury pressure, ions carrying one electrostatic unit of electricity of either sign

Roent·gen (rönt′gən; E. rent′gən, ren′chən), **Wil·helm Kon·rad** (vil′helm kōn′rät) 1845–1923; Ger. physicist: discoverer of X-rays: also **Rönt′gen**

roent·gen·ize (rent′gə niz′, ren′chə-) *vt.* **-ized′, -iz′ing** [Obs.] to subject to the action of X-rays

roent·gen·o- (rent′gə nə, ren′chə-) *a combining form meaning* Roentgen rays, X-rays [roentgenology]

roent·gen·o·gram (-gram′) *n.* [prec. + -GRAM] a photograph taken with X-rays

roent·gen·og·ra·phy (rent′gə näg′rə fē, ren′chə-) *n.* photography by the use of X-rays —**roent′gen·o·graph′ic** (-nə graf′ik) *adj.* —**roent′gen·o·graph′i·cal·ly** *adv.*

roent·gen·ol·o·gy (-näl′ə jē) *n.* [ROENTGENO- + -LOGY] the study and use of X-rays, esp. in connection with the diagnosis and treatment of disease —**roent′gen·o·log′ic** (-nə läj′ik) *adj.* —**roent′gen·ol′o·gist** *n.*

roent·gen·o·ther·a·py (-nə ther′ə pē) *n.* [ROENTGENO- + THERAPY] the treatment of disease by means of X-rays

Roentgen ray [*also* r-] *same as* X-RAY

Roeth·ke (ret′kə, -kē), **Theodore** 1908–63; U.S. poet

ro·ga·tion (rō gā′shən) *n.* [ME. *rogacioun* < L. *rogatio*, a question, in LL.(Ec.), a prayer, entreaty < *rogare*, to ask, orig., to stretch out the hand, akin to *regere*: see REGAL] 1. a prayer or supplication, esp. as chanted in church ceremonies during Rogation days: *usually used*

in pl. **2.** in ancient Rome, *a)* a consul's or tribune's proposal of a law to be passed or rejected by the people *b)* such a proposed law

Rogation days the three days before Ascension Day, during which supplications are chanted

Rog·er (räj′ər) [OFr. < OHG. *Ruodiger, Hrodger* (akin to OE. *Hrothgar*) < *hruod-, ruod-,* fame + *ger,* spear] a masculine name —*interj.* [< conventional name of international signal flag for *R*] [*also* r-] **1.** received: term used in radiotelephony to indicate reception of a message **2.** [Colloq.] right! OK!

Rog·ers (räj′ərz) **1. Bruce,** 1870–1957; U.S. typographer & book designer **2. Will,** (born *William Penn Adair Rogers*) 1879–1935; U.S. humorist & actor

Ro·get (rō zhā′), **Peter Mark** 1779–1869; Eng. writer & physician; compiler of a thesaurus

rogue (rōg) *n.* [< 16th-c. thieves' slang < ? L. *rogare,* to ask (see ROGATION)] **1.** formerly, a wandering beggar or tramp; vagabond **2.** a rascal; scoundrel **3.** a fun-loving, mischievous person **4.** an elephant or other animal that wanders apart from the herd and is fierce and wild **5.** *Biol.* an individual varying markedly from the standard, esp. an inferior one —*vt.* **rogued, rogu′ing 1.** to cheat **2.** to destroy (plants, etc.) as biological rogues **3.** to remove such plants, etc. from (land, ctc.) —*vi.* to live or act like a rogue

ro·guer·y (rō′gər ē) *n., pl.* **-guer·ies** the behavior or an act of a rogue; specif., *a)* trickery; cheating; fraud *b)* playful mischief

☆**rogues′ gallery** a collection of the photographs of criminals, as used by police in identification

ro·guish (rō′gish) *adj.* of, like, or characteristic of a rogue; specif., *a)* dishonest; unscrupulous *b)* playfully mischievous —**ro′guish·ly** *adv.* —**ro′guish·ness** *n.*

roil (roil) *vt.* [Fr. *rouiller* < OFr. *rouil, roille,* rust, mud, ult. < L. *robigo,* rust, akin to *ruber,* RED[1]] **1.** to make (a liquid) cloudy, muddy, unsettled, etc. by stirring up the sediment **2.** to stir up; agitate **3.** to make angry or irritable; rile —*vi.* to be agitated

roil·y (roi′lē) *adj.* **roil′i·er, roil′i·est 1.** turbid; muddy **2.** agitated; disturbed

roist·er (rois′tər) *vt.* [< earlier *roister* (*n.*), loud bully < OFr. *ruistre* < L. *rusticus:* see RUSTIC] **1.** to boast or swagger **2.** to be lively and noisy; revel boisterously —**roist′er·er** *n.* —**roist′er·ous** *adj.*

ROK Republic of (South) Korea

☆**ro·la·mite** (rō′lə mīt′) *n.* [arbitrary coinage based on ROLL] an almost frictionless bearing consisting of two or more rollers on a flexible metal band, that serves as a suspension system in various devices, as switches, valves, pumps, etc.

Ro·land (rō′lənd) [Fr. < OHG. *Hruodland* < *hruod-,* fame + *land,* LAND] **1.** a masculine name: equiv. It. *Orlando* **2.** a legendary hero of the *Chanson de Roland* and other stories of the Charlemagne cycle, famous for his strength, courage, and chivalrous spirit

role, rôle (rōl) *n.* [Fr. *rôle,* lit., a roll: from roll containing actor's part] **1.** a part, or character, that an actor plays in a performance **2.** a function or office assumed by someone [an advisory *role*]

Rolf (rälf, rôlf) a masculine name: see RUDOLPH

roll (rōl) *vi.* [ME. *rollen* < OFr. *roller* < VL. *rotulare* < L. *rotula:* see the *n.*] **1.** *a)* to move by turning on an axis or over and over *b)* to rotate about its axis lengthwise, as a spacecraft in flight **2.** *a)* to move or be moved on wheels *b)* to travel in a wheeled vehicle **3.** to travel about; wander **4.** to pass; elapse [the years *rolled* by] **5.** to move in a periodical revolution: said of stars, planets, etc. [the moon *rolling* in its course] **6.** *a)* to flow, as water, in a full swelling or sweeping motion [the waves *rolling* against the boat] *b)* to be carried in a flow **7.** to extend in gentle swells or undulations **8.** to make a loud, continuous rising and falling sound [thunder *rolls*] **9.** to rise and fall in a full, mellow cadence, as sound, speech, etc. **10.** to trill or warble **11.** to form a ball or cylinder by turning over and over on itself or something else, as yarn **12.** to turn in a circular motion or move back and forth [with eyes *rolling*] **13.** to rock from side to side [the ship pitched and *rolled*] **14.** to walk by swaying **15.** to become flattened or spread under a roller **16.** to make progress; advance [start *rolling*] **17.** to start operating [the presses *rolled*] **18.** [Colloq.] to have plenty; abound (*in*) [*rolling* in wealth] ☆**19.** *Football* to move laterally: said of the passer: in full **roll out** —*vt.* **1.** to move by turning on an axis or over and over [to *roll* a hoop] **2.** to move or send on wheels or rollers **3.** to cause to start operating **4.** to move or send in a full, sweeping motion **5.** to beat (a drum) with blows in rapid, light succession **6.** to utter with full, flowing sound [to *roll* one's words] **7.** to pronounce or say with a trill [to *roll* one's r's] **8.** to give a swaying motion to [waves *rolling* the ship along] **9.** to move gently around and around or from side to side [to *roll* one's eyes] **10.** to make into a ball or cylinder by winding over and over itself or something else [to *roll* a cigarette] **11.** to wrap or enfold, as in a covering [to *roll* a child in a blanket] **12.** to make flat, smooth, or spread out by using a roller,

rolling pin, etc. ☆**13.** to throw (the dice) as in the game of craps **14.** to iron (sleeves, etc.) without forming a crease ☆**15.** [Slang] to rob (a drunken or sleeping person) **16.** *Printing* to spread ink on (type, a form, etc.) with a roller —*n.* [ME. *rolle* < OFr. < L. *rotula,* dim. of *rota,* a wheel < IE. **roto-,* var. of **ret(h)-,* to run, roll, whence OIr. *rethim,* (I) run, OHG. *rad,* a wheel] **1.** the act or an instance of rolling **2.** *a)* a paper, parchment, etc. that is rolled up; scroll *b)* something that is, or looks as if, rolled up **3.** a register; catalog **4.** a list of names for checking attendance; muster roll **5.** a measure of something rolled into a cylinder [a *roll* of wallpaper] **6.** a cylindrical mass of something [a sausage *roll*] **7.** *a)* any of variously shaped, small cakes of bread *b)* thin cake covered with fruit, nuts, etc. and rolled [a jelly *roll*] *c)* beef, veal, etc. rolled and cooked **8.** a roller (in various senses) **9.** a swaying or rolling motion **10.** a rapid succession of light blows on a drum **11.** a loud, reverberating sound; peal, as of thunder **12.** a full, cadenced flow of words **13.** a trill or warble **14.** a slight swell or rise on the surface of something, as land ☆**15.** [Slang] money; esp., a wad of paper money **16.** *Aeron.* a maneuver in which an airplane in flight performs one complete rotation around its longitudinal axis **17.** *Bookbinding* a revolving tool used in making an impression or pattern —*SYN.* see LIST[1] —**roll back 1.** to move back ☆**2.** to reduce (prices) to a previous or standard level by government action and control —**roll in** to assemble, arrive, or appear usually in large numbers or amounts —**roll out 1.** to flatten into a sheet by rolling **2.** to spread out by unrolling **3.** [Slang] to get out of bed See also *vi.* 19 —**roll round** to recur, as in a cycle [winter *rolled* round again] —**roll up 1.** to make or put into the form of a roll **2.** to wrap up by turning over and over **3.** to acquire or increase by accumulation **4.** [Colloq.] to arrive in a vehicle —**roll with a (or the) punch** [Colloq.] **1.** to move in the same direction as a punch thrown at one so as to lessen its force **2.** to lessen the impact of a misfortune by not resisting too violently —**strike off (or from) the rolls** to expel from membership

Rol·land (rô län′), **Ro·main** (rô man′) 1866–1944; Fr. writer

☆**roll·a·way** (rōl′ə wā′) *adj.* having rollers for easy moving and storing when not in use [a *rollaway* bed]

☆**roll·back** (-bak′) *n.* a rolling back; specif., a reduction of prices to a previous level by government action and control

☆**roll bar** a heavy metal bar reinforcing the roof of an automobile to reduce injury if the car should roll over

roll call 1. the reading aloud of a roll, or list of names, as in classrooms, military formations, etc., to find out who is absent **2.** the fixed time, or a signal (as on a bugle), for such a reading

☆**rolled oats** hulled oats that have been flattened between rollers, used to make oatmeal

roll·er (rō′lər) *n.* **1.** a person or thing that rolls (in various senses) **2.** any of various rolling cylinders or wheels; specif., *a)* a cylinder of metal, wood, etc. over which something is rolled for easier movement *b)* a cylinder on which something is rolled up or wound [the *roller* of a shade, a hair *roller*] *c)* a heavy cylinder of metal, stone, etc. used to crush or smooth something *d)* a cylinder covered with a napped fabric, used for applying paint *e) Printing* a cylinder, usually of hard rubber, for spreading ink on the form just before the paper is impressed **3.** a long bandage in a roll **4.** a heavy, swelling wave that breaks on the shoreline **5.** *Ornithology a)* any of numerous old-world, tropical, bluish birds (family Coraciidae) that roll and tumble in flight and hop clumsily on the ground; esp., the **common roller** (*Coracias garrulus*) of Europe and Africa, similar to the jay *b)* a canary that rolls, or trills, its notes —*SYN.* see WAVE

☆**roller bearing** a bearing in which the shaft turns with rollers, generally of steel, arranged lengthwise in a ringlike track: used to reduce friction

☆**roller coaster** an amusement ride in which small, open cars move on tracks that dip and curve sharply

☆**roller skate** *same as* SKATE[1] (sense 2) —**roll′er-skate′** *vi.* **-skat′ed, -skat′ing** —**roller skater**

roller towel a long continuous towel suspended on a roller, or a very long towel fed through a device that rolls up the used part on a roller

roll film a strip of photographic film rolled on a spool for a series of consecutive exposures

rol·lick (räl′ik) *vi.* [< ? FROLIC] to play or behave in a gay, lively, carefree way; romp —**rol′lick·ing, rol′lick·some** (-səm) *adj.*

roll·ing (rōl′iŋ) *adj.* that rolls (in various senses); specif., rotating or revolving, recurring, swaying, surging, resounding, trilling, etc. —*n.* the action, motion, or sound of something that rolls or is rolled

rolling hitch a knot in which one or more turns are made between two hitches: see KNOT, illus.

rolling mill 1. a factory in which metal bars, sheets, etc. are rolled out **2.** a machine used for such rolling

rolling pin a heavy, smooth cylinder of wood, glass, etc.,

usually with a handle at each end, used to roll out dough

rolling stock all the locomotives, cars, etc. of a railroad, or the trucks, trailers, etc. of a trucking company

roll·mop (rōl'mäp') *n.* [G. *rollmops*, orig. Berlin dial. < *rollen*, to ROLL + *mops*, a pug dog] a fillet of fresh herring rolled up on a pickle or onion and marinated

Rol·lo (räl'ō) 1. a masculine name: see RUDOLPH 2. 860?–931? A.D.; Norse conqueror of Normandy: 1st duke of Normandy (911–927): also HROLF

☆**roll-top** (rōl'täp') *adj.* made with a flexible top of parallel slats that slides back [a *roll-top* desk]

☆**roll·way** (-wā') *n.* 1. a chute down which logs can be rolled or slid into a river, etc. for transportation 2. a pile of logs on a river bank awaiting removal

Rol·vaag (rōl'väg), **O·le Ed·vart** (ō'lə ed'värt) 1876–1931; U.S. novelist, born in Norway

ro·ly-po·ly (rō'lē pō'lē) *adj.* [redupl. of ROLL] short and plump; pudgy —*n., pl.* -**lies** 1. a roly-poly thing or person, esp. a child 2. [Chiefly Brit.] a kind of pudding made of rich pastry dough spread with fruit or jam, rolled up, and boiled, steamed, etc.

Rom, rom (rum) *n.* [see ROMANY] a Gypsy man or boy

rom, rom. roman (type)

Rom. 1. Roman 2. Romance 3. Romania 4. Romanian 5. Romanic 6. Romans (Epistle to the Romans)

Ro·ma (rō'mä) *It.* name of ROME

Ro·ma·ic (rō mä'ik) *adj.* [ModGr. *Rhōmaiikos* < Gr. *Rhōmaikos*, Roman (of the Eastern empire) < *Rhōmē*, Rome] of modern Greece or its language —*n.* the vernacular language of modern Greece

ro·maine (rō mān', rō'mān) *n.* [Fr. < fem. of *romain*: see ROMAN] a kind of lettuce (*Lactuca sativa longifolia*) with long leaves that form a cylindrical or conical head: also **romaine lettuce**

Ro·mains (rō maṅ'), **Jules** (zhül) (pseud. of *Louis Farigoule*) 1885– ; Fr. novelist, poet, & playwright

Ro·man (rō'mən) *adj.* [ME. & L.: ME. *Romain* < OFr. < L. *Romanus* < *Roma*, Rome] 1. of, characteristic of, or derived from ancient or modern Rome, its people, etc. 2. *same as* LATIN 3. of the Roman Catholic Church 4. [*usually* r-] designating or of the upright style of printing types most common in modern use; not italic —*n.* 1. a native, citizen, or inhabitant of ancient or modern Rome 2. the Italian spoken in Rome 3. [*usually* r-] roman type or characters

‡**ro·man** (rô mäṅ') *n., pl.* -**mans'** (-mäṅ') [Fr. < OFr. *romans*: see ROMANCE] 1. a type of metrical narrative developed in France in the Middle Ages 2. a novel

‡**ro·man à clef** (rô mäṅ nä klā') [Fr., lit., novel with a key] a novel in which real persons appear under fictitious names

Roman alphabet the alphabet used by the ancient Romans, from which most modern European alphabets are derived: it consisted of twenty-three letters (*J*, *U*, and *W* were added later)

Roman arch a semicircular arch

Roman architecture the style of architecture used by the ancient Romans, characterized by the rounded arch and vault, thick, massive walls, and the use of much brick and concrete

Roman calendar the calendar used by the ancient Romans before the Julian calendar: it consisted originally of ten months, later twelve

Roman candle a kind of firework consisting of a long tube that sends out balls of fire, sparks, etc.

Roman Catholic 1. of the Roman Catholic Church 2. a member of the Roman Catholic Church —**Roman Catholicism**

Roman Catholic Church the Christian church headed by the Pope (Bishop of Rome)

Ro·mance (rō mans', rō'mans) *adj.* [< obs. Fr. (*langue*) *romance*, Romance language < OFr. *romans*: see ff.] designating, of, or constituting any of the languages derived from Vulgar Latin, as Italian, Spanish, Portuguese, French, Romanian, Provençal, Rhaeto-Romanic, etc. —*n.* these languages

ro·mance (rō mans'; *also, for n.,* rō'mans) *n.* [ME. < OFr. *romanz* < *romans* (*escrire*), (to write) in Roman (i.e., the vernacular, not Latin) < VL. *Romanice* (*scribere*) < L. *Romanicus*: see ROMANTIC] 1. formerly, a long narrative in verse or prose, orig. written in one of the Romance dialects, about the adventures of knights and other chivalric heroes 2. later, a fictitious tale of wonderful and extraordinary events, characterized by much imagination and idealization 3. a type of novel in which the emphasis is on love, adventure, etc. 4. the type of literature comprising such stories 5. excitement, love, and adventure of the kind found in such literature; romantic quality or spirit 6. the tendency to derive great pleasure from romantic adventures; romantic sentiment 7. an exaggeration or fabrication that has no real substance 8. a love affair 9. *Music* a short, lyrical, usually sentimental piece, suggesting a love song —*vi.* -**manced'**, -**manc'ing** 1. to write or tell romances 2. to be fanciful or imaginative in thinking and talking 3. [Colloq.] to make love; court; woo —*vt.* [Colloq.] 1. to make love to; woo 2. to seek to gain the favor of, as by flattery, gifts, etc.; court —**ro·manc'er** *n.*

Roman Curia *R.C.Ch.* see CURIA (sense 3)

Roman Empire empire established (27 B.C.) by Augustus, succeeding the Roman Republic: at its peak it included W & S Europe, Britain, Asia Minor, N Africa, & the lands of the E Mediterranean: divided (395 A.D.) into the EASTERN ROMAN EMPIRE & the WESTERN ROMAN EMPIRE

ROMAN EMPIRE (100 A.D.)

Ro·man·esque (rō'mə nesk') *adj.* [Fr. < It. *romanesco, romanzesco* < *romanzo:* see ROMANCE & -ESQUE] 1. designating or of a style of European architecture of the 11th and 12th cents., based on the Roman and characterized by the use of the round arch and vault, thick, massive walls, interior bays, etc. 2. designating or of a style of painting, sculpture, etc. corresponding to this —*n.* the Romanesque style of architecture, painting, etc.

‡**ro·man fleuve** (rō män flöv') *pl.* **ro·mans fleuves'** (-män flöv') [Fr., lit., river novel] a long novel, usually in several volumes, dealing with a cross section of society, several generations of a family, etc.

Roman holiday [after the ancient Roman gladiatorial contests] entertainment acquired at the expense of others' suffering, or a spectacle yielding such entertainment

Ro·ma·nia, Ro·mâ·nia (rō mān'yə, -mä'nē ə; *Romanian* rō mu'nyä) country in SE Europe, on the Black Sea: 91,700 sq. mi.; pop. 19,287,000; cap. Bucharest

Ro·ma·nian (-mān'yən, -mä'nē ən) *adj.* of Romania, its people, their language, etc. —*n.* 1. a native or inhabitant of Romania 2. the Romance language of the Romanians

Ro·man·ic (-man'ik) *adj., n.* [L. *Romanicus*] *same as* ROMANCE

Ro·man·ism (rō'mən iz'm) *n.* 1. Roman Catholicism: hostile usage 2. the spirit and influence of ancient Rome

Ro·man·ist (-ist) *n.* [ModL. *Romanista*] a person who studies or is expert in Roman law, antiquities, etc.

Ro·man·ize (rō'mən īz') *vt.* -**ized'**, -**iz'ing** 1. to make Roman in character, spirit, etc. 2. to make Roman Catholic 3. to respell in the Roman alphabet —*vi.* 1. to follow or be influenced by Roman customs, law, etc. 2. to conform to Roman Catholicism —**Ro'man·i·za'tion** *n.*

Roman law the code of laws of ancient Rome: the basis for the modern legal system in many countries

Roman nose a nose with a high, prominent bridge

Roman numerals the Roman letters used as numerals until the 10th cent. A.D.: in Roman numerals I = 1, V = 5, X = 10, L = 50, C = 100, D = 500, and M = 1,000 Other numbers are formed from these by adding or subtracting: the value of a symbol following another of the same or greater value is added (e.g., III = 3, XV = 15); the value of a symbol preceding one of greater value is subtracted (e.g., IX = 9); and the value of a symbol standing between two of greater value is subtracted from that of the second, the remainder being added to that of the first (e.g., XIX = 19) Roman numerals are commonly written in capitals, though they may be written in lower-case letters, as in numbering subdivisions (e.g., Act IV, scene iii) A _bar over a letter indicates multiplication by 1,000 (e.g., V̄ = 5,000)

Ro·ma·no (rō mä'nō) *n.* [It., ROMAN] a dry, sharp, very hard Italian cheese, usually grated for use as a flavoring

Ro·ma·nov (rō mä'nôf; E. rō'mə nôf') ruling family of Russia from 1613 to 1917; esp. **Mi·kha·il Feo·do·ro·vich** (mi khä ēl' fyô'dô rô vich), 1598–1645; 1st Romanov czar & founder of the dynasty: also sp. **Romanoff**

Ro·mans (rō'mənz) the Epistle to the Romans, a book of the New Testament which was a message from the Apostle Paul to the Christians of Rome

Ro·mansch, Ro·mansh (rō mänsh') *n.* [Romansch *rumansch, rumonsh* < VL. *romanice:* see ROMANCE] the Rhaeto-Romanic dialect spoken in the Swiss canton of Grisons: sometimes used interchangeably for Ladin or for all the Rhaeto-Romanic dialects

ro·man·tic (rō man'tik) *adj.* [Fr. *romantique* < obs. *romant* (see ROMAUNT) + -*ique*, -IC] 1. of, having the nature of, characteristic of, or characterized by romance 2. without a basis in fact; fanciful, fictitious, or fabulous 3. not practical; visionary or quixotic [a *romantic* scheme] 4. full of or dominated by thoughts, feelings, and attitudes characteristic of or suitable for romance; passionate, adventurous, idealistic, etc. [a *romantic* youth] 5. a) of, characteristic of, or preoccupied with idealized lovemaking or courting b) suited for romance, or lovemaking [a *romantic* night] 6. [*often* R-] of or characteristic of romanticism and the Romantic Movement: contrasted with CLASSIC, CLASSICAL, REALISTIC, etc. —*n.* 1. a romantic person 2. [*often* R-] an adherent of romanticism, as in literature or music 3. [*pl.*] [Rare] romantic characteristics, thoughts, actions, etc. —*SYN.* see SENTIMENTAL —**ro·man'ti·cal·ly** *adv.*

ro·man·ti·cism (rō man′tə siz′m) *n.* **1.** romantic spirit, outlook, tendency, etc. **2.** *a)* *same as* ROMANTIC MOVEMENT *b)* the spirit, attitudes, style, etc. of, or adherence to, the Romantic Movement or a similar movement: contrasted with CLASSICISM, REALISM, etc.

ro·man·ti·cist (-sist) *n.* an adherent of romanticism in literature, painting, music, etc.

ro·man·ti·cize (-sīz′) *vt.* **-cized′, -ciz′ing** to treat or regard romantically; give a romantic character to or interpretation of —*vi.* **1.** to have or uphold romantic ideas, attitudes, etc. **2.** to act in a romantic way —**ro·man′ti·ci·za′tion** *n.*

Romantic Movement the revolt in the 18th and early 19th cent. against the artistic, political, and philosophical principles that had become associated with neoclassicism: characterized in literature, music, painting, etc. by freedom of form and spirit, emphasis on feeling and originality and on the personality of the artist himself, and sympathetic interest in primitive nature, medievalism, Orientalism, the common man, etc.

Rom·a·ny (räm′ə nē, rō′mə-) *n.* [Romany *romani,* fem. & pl. of *romano,* Gypsy < *rom,* a man, husband, Gypsy < Sans. *ḍomba,* low-caste musician] *1. pl.* **-ny, -nies** a Gypsy **2.** the Indic language of the Gypsies, which occurs with dialectal variations in each country where they live —*adj.* of the Gypsies, their language, etc. Also sp. **Rom′ma·ny**

Romany rye (rī) [Romany *romani* (see prec.) + *rei,* a lord < Sans. *rājan,* king: see RAJAH] a person not a Gypsy who associates with the Gypsies, speaks their language, etc.

ro·maunt (rō mänt′, -mônt′) *n.* [OFr. *romant,* var. of *romanz:* see ROMANCE] [Archaic] a romantic poem or story; romance

Rom. Cath. Roman Catholic

Rome (rōm) **1.** capital of Italy, on the Tiber River: formerly, the capital of the Roman Republic, the Roman Empire, & the Papal States: pop. 2,514,000: It. name, ROMA **2.** [after prec.] city in C N.Y., on the Mohawk River, near Utica: pop. 50,000 **3.** *same as* ROMAN CATHOLIC CHURCH

Ro·me·o (rō′mē ō′) [It. < *Romolo* < L. *Romulus*] the hero of Shakespeare's tragedy *Romeo and Juliet* (c. 1595), son of Montague and lover of Juliet, daughter of Capulet: at the death of the lovers their feuding families become reconciled —*n., pl.* **-os′** **1.** a man who is an ardent lover ☆**2.** [r-] a man's house slipper with elastic in the sides

Rom·ford (rum′fərd) city in Essex, SE England, near London: pop. 115,000

Rom·ney (rum′nē, rum′-), **George** 1734–1802; Eng. painter

romp (rämp) *n.* [< earlier *ramp,* vulgar woman, hussy, prob. < ME. *rampen* < OFr. *ramper:* see RAMP²] **1.** a person who romps, esp. a girl **2.** [< the *v.*] boisterous, lively play or frolic **3.** *a)* an easy, winning gait in a race [to win in a *romp*] *b)* an easy victory —*vi.* **1.** to play or frolic in a boisterous, lively way **2.** to win with ease in a race, contest, etc. —*SYN.* see PLAY

romp·er (räm′pər) *n.* **1.** a person who romps **2.** [pl.] a type of loose-fitting, one-piece, outer garment with bloomerlike pants, for very young children

Rom·u·lus (räm′yoo ləs) [L.] *Rom. Myth.* a son of Mars and founder and first king of Rome, deified as Quirinus: he and his twin brother Remus, left as infants to die in the Tiber, were suckled by a she-wolf

Ron·ald (rän′ld) [Scot. < ON. *Rögnvaldr,* akin to OG. *Raganald:* see REGINALD] a masculine name

ron·deau (rän′dō) *n., pl.* **-deaux** (-dōz) [Fr., earlier *rondel* < *rond,* ROUND¹] **1.** a short lyrical poem of thirteen (or sometimes ten) lines with only two rhymes, and an unrhymed refrain that consists of the opening words and is used in two places **2.** *a)* *same as* RONDO *b)* a medieval French monophonic or polyphonic song with many repetitions of two themes or phrases

ron·del (-d′l, -del) *n.* [ME. < OFr.: see prec.] **1.** a kind of rondeau, usually with fourteen lines, two rhymes, and the first two lines used as a refrain in the middle and at the end (the second line occasionally being omitted at the end) **2.** a rounded, usually circular or ring-shaped, object

ron·de·let (-et′) *n.* [ME. *roundelet* < MFr., dim. of *rondel*] a short rondel, usually of five or seven lines in one stanza and a refrain made up of the opening words

ron·do (rän′dō) *n., pl.* **-dos** [It. < Fr. *rondeau:* see RONDEAU] *Music* a composition or movement, often the last movement of a sonata, having its principal theme stated three or more times in the same key, interposed with subordinate themes

Ron·dô·nia (rôn dō′nyə) federal territory in W Brazil, on the border of Bolivia: 93,820 sq. mi.; pop. 71,000

ron·dure (rän′jər) *n.* [Fr. *rondeur* < *rond,* ROUND¹] [Rare] a circle or sphere; roundness

Ron·sard (rōn sàr′), **Pierre de** 1524–85; Fr. poet

Rönt·gen (rönt′gən; *E.* rent′gən, ren′chən) *var. sp. of* ROENTGEN

rood (rood) *n.* [ME. *rode* < OE. *rod,* a cross, measure: see ROD] **1.** orig., a cross as used in crucifixion; specif.,

the cross on which Jesus was crucified **2.** any cross representing this; crucifix, esp. a large one at the entrance to the chancel or choir of a medieval church, often supported on a rood beam or rood screen **3.** in England, *a)* a measure of length varying locally from 5 1/2 to 8 yards; sometimes, 1 rod *b)* a measure of area usually equal to 1/4 acre (40 square rods)

rood screen an ornamental screen, usually with a rood above it supported by a beam (**rood beam**), serving as a partition between the nave and the chancel or choir of a church

roof (roof, roof) *n., pl.* **roofs** [ME. *rof* < OE. *hrof,* akin to ON. *hrof,* roof, shed < IE. base **krapo-,* whence OBulg. *stropŭ,* roof] **1.** the outside top covering of a building **2.** figuratively, a house or home **3.** the top or peak of anything [the *roof* of the world] **4.** anything like a roof in position or use [the *roof* of the mouth] —*vt.* to provide or cover with or as with a roof —**raise the roof** [Slang] **1.** to be very noisy, as in applause, anger, celebration, etc. **2.** to complain loudly —**roof′less** *adj.*

roof·er (-ər) *n.* a person who builds or repairs roofs

☆**roof garden** **1.** a garden on the flat roof of a building **2.** the roof or top floor of a high building, decorated as a garden and used as a restaurant, etc.

roof·ing (-in) *n.* **1.** the act of covering with a roof **2.** material for a roof or roofs **3.** a roof

roof·top (-täp′) *n.* the roof of a building

roof·tree (-trē′) *n.* **1.** the ridgepole of a roof **2.** a roof

rook¹ (rook) *n.* [ME. *roc* < OE. *hroc,* akin to G. *ruch* < IE. echoic base **ker-,* whence CROW¹, RAVEN¹] **1.** a gregarious European bird (*Corvus frugilegus*) very similar in size and appearance to the American crow **2.** a swindler; cheat —*vt., vi.* [prob. from the bird's thievishness] to swindle; cheat

rook² (rook) *n.* [ME. *rok* < OFr. *roc* < Ar. *rukhkh* < Per. *rukh*] *Chess* either of the two corner pieces shaped like a castle tower: it can move in a vertical or horizontal direction over any number of consecutive, unoccupied squares; castle

rook·er·y (rook′ər ē) *n., pl.* **-er·ies** **1.** a breeding place or colony of rooks **2.** a breeding place or colony of other gregarious animals or birds, as seals, penguins, etc. **3.** [Now Rare] a crowded tenement house or tenement district; esp., a slum

rook·ie (rook′ē) *n.* [altered < ? RECRUIT] [Slang] **1.** an inexperienced recruit in the army ☆**2.** any novice, as on a police force or in a professional sport

rook·y (rook′ē) *adj.* full of or inhabited by rooks

room (room, room) *n.* [ME. < OE. *rum,* akin to ON., OHG. *rum* < IE. **rewe-,* to open, room, whence L. *rus,* land] **1.** space, esp. enough space, to contain something or in which to do something [room for one more, *room* to move around in] **2.** suitable scope or opportunity [room for doubt] **3.** a space within a building enclosed by walls or separated from other similar spaces by walls or partitions **4.** [pl.] living quarters; lodgings; apartment **5.** the people gathered together in a room **6.** [Obs.] a position or office —*vi.* to occupy living quarters; have lodgings; lodge —*vt.* to provide with a room or lodgings

room and board sleeping accommodations and meals

room clerk a clerk at a hotel or motel who registers guests, assigns them rooms, etc.

☆**room·er** (room′ər, room′-) *n.* a person who rents a room or rooms to live in; lodger

☆**room·ette** (room met′, roo-) *n.* a small compartment for one person in a railroad sleeping car

room·ful (room′fool′, room′-) *n., pl.* **-fuls′** **1.** as much or as many as will fill a room **2.** the people or objects in a room, collectively

☆**rooming house** a house with furnished rooms for renting; lodging house

☆**room·mate** (-māt′) *n.* the person, or any of the persons, with whom one shares a room or rooms

room·y (-ē) *adj.* **room′i·er, room′i·est** having plenty of room; spacious —**room′i·ly** *adv.* —**room′i·ness** *n.*

☆**roor·back, roor·bach** (roor′bak) *n.* [after the imaginary author of a nonexistent book, *Roorback's Tour,* etc., containing spurious charges against candidate James K. POLK] a false or slanderous story devised for political effect, esp. against a candidate for office

roose (rooz; *Scot.* röz) *n., vt., vi.* [ME. *ros, n., rosen, v.* < ON. *hros, n., hrosa, v.*] **roosed, roos′ing** [Now Scot. & Brit. Dial.] praise

Roo·se·velt (rō′zə velt′, -vəlt; rōz′velt; *by some,* roo′zə-) **1.** (**Anna**) **Eleanor,** 1884–1962; U.S. writer & delegate at UN: wife of ff. **2. Franklin Del·a·no** (del′ə nō′), 1882–1945; 32d president of the U.S. (1933–45) **3. Theodore,** 1858–1919; 26th president of the U.S. (1901–09)

roost (roost) *n.* [ME. < OE. *hrost,* akin to MDu. *roest* < IE. base **kred-,* timberwork, whence OBulg. *krada,* woodpile, Goth. *hrōt,* roof] **1.** a perch on which birds, esp. domestic fowls, can rest or sleep **2.** a place with perches for birds **3.** a place for resting, sleeping, etc. —*vi.* **1.** to rest, sit, sleep etc. on a perch **2.** to stay or settle down, as for the night —**come home to roost** to have reper-

cussions, esp. disagreeable ones; boomerang —**rule the roost** to be master

roos·ter (roos′tər) *n.* [ROOST + -ER] the male of the chicken; cock

root¹ (root, root) *n.* [ME. *rote* < Late OE. < ON. *roi*, akin to OE. *wyrt* < IE. base **wrād-*, a twig, root, whence Gr. *rhiza*, L. *radix*, root, *ramus*, branch] 1. the part of a plant, usually below the ground, that lacks nodes, shoots, and leaves, holds the plant in position, draws water and nourishment from the soil, and stores food 2. loosely, any underground part of a plant, as a rhizome 3. the attached or embedded part of a bodily structure, as of the teeth, hair, nails, tongue, etc. 4. the source, origin, or cause of an action, quality, condition, etc. 5. a person or family that has many descendants; ancestor

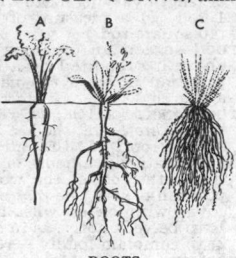

ROOTS
(A, B, tap; C, fibrous)

6. [*pl.*] the close ties one has with some place or people as through birth, upbringing, long and sympathetic association, etc. 7. a lower or supporting part; base 8. an essential or basic part; core [*the root of the matter*] 9. *Math. a*) a quantity that, multiplied by itself a specified number of times, produces a given quantity [4 is the square *root* (4 x 4) of 16 and the cube *root* (4 x 4 x 4) of 64] *b*) a number that, when substituted for the unknown quantity in an equation, will satisfy the equation 10. *Music* the basic tone of a chord, on which the chord is constructed; often, the fundamental 11. *Linguis. same as* BASE¹ (*n.* 14) —*vi.* 1. to begin to grow by putting out roots 2. to become fixed, settled, etc. —*vt.* 1. to fix the roots of in the ground 2. to establish; settle —*SYN.* see ORIGIN —**root up** (or **out, away**) to pull out by the roots; remove or destroy completely —**take root** 1. to begin growing by putting out roots 2. to become settled or established

root² (root, root) *vt.* [formerly also *wrote, rout* < ME. *wroten* < OE. *wrolan*, to root up < *wrot*, snout < IE. base **wer-*, to tear up, whence L. *rostrum*, a beak] to dig or turn (*up* or *out*) with or as with the snout —*vi.* 1. to dig in the ground, as with the snout 2. to search about; rummage [to *root* through the litter] 3. [Colloq.] to work hard; drudge [to *root* for a living] ☆4. [Colloq.] *a*) to encourage a contestant or team by applauding and cheering *b*) to lend moral support to one seeking success, recovery, etc. Usually with *for* —**root′er** *n.*

Root (root, root), **Elihu** 1845–1937; U.S. statesman; secretary of state (1905–09)

root·age (root′ij, root′-) *n.* 1. a taking root or being firmly fixed by means of roots 2. the roots of a plant, collectively

☆**root beer** a carbonated drink made of extracts from the roots and bark of certain plants, etc.

root borer any insect or insect larva that bores into the roots of plants

root canal a small, tubular channel, normally filled with pulp, in the root of a tooth

root cap the loose cells at the tip of a growing root, rubbed off by the motion of the root tip through the soil and constantly renewed from within

root climber *Bot.* a climber that adheres to its support by means of roots

root crop a crop, as turnips, beets, etc., grown for the edible roots

root hair *Bot.* any of the thin-walled, hairlike tubular outgrowths from a growing root, which serve to absorb water and minerals from the soil

root·less (-lis) *adj.* having no roots or no stabilizing ties, as to society —**root′less·ly** *adv.* —**root′less·ness** *n.*

root·let (-lit) *n.* a little root or small branch of a root; radicle

root·stock (-stäk′) *n.* 1. *Bot. a*) same as RHIZOME *b*) a plant onto which another is grafted as a new top 2. *Zool.* the rootlike, horizontal, attached portion of a hydroid colony

root·y (root′ē, root′ē) *adj.* **root′i·er, root′i·est** 1. having many roots 2. like a root or rootlike —**root′i·ness** *n.*

rope (rōp) *n.* [ME. *rop* < OE. *rap*, akin to G. *reif* (Goth. *raip*) < IE. **reip-*, rag, piece of cloth < **rei-*, to tear, whence REAP, REEF²] 1. a thick, strong cord made of intertwisted strands of fiber, thin wires, leather strips, etc. 2. [*pl.*] such cords strung between posts to enclose a boxing ring 3. *a*) such a cord, or a noose made of it, for hanging a person *b*) death by hanging: with *the* ☆4. *same as* LASSO 5. a ropelike string of things put together by or as by twisting, twining, braiding, or threading [a *rope* of pearls] 6. a ropelike, sticky formation in a liquid, as wine —*vt.* **roped, rop′ing** 1. to fasten, tie, or confine with or as with a rope 2. to connect or tie together (esp. mountain climbers) with a rope 3. to separate, mark off, or enclose with a rope (usually with *in, off,* or *out*) ☆4. to catch or throw with a lasso —*vi.* to become ropelike and sticky [to cook candy until it *ropes*] —**give someone (enough) rope** [Colloq.] to allow one freedom of action in the ex-

pectation that he will overreach himself —**know the ropes** [Colloq.] to be fully acquainted with the details or procedures of something —**on the ropes** 1. *Boxing* knocked against the ropes 2. [Slang] near collapse or ruin —☆**rope in** [Slang] to entice or trick into doing something —**the end of one's rope** the end of one's endurance, resources, etc. —**rop′er** *n.*

rop·er·y (rō′pər ē) *n., pl.* **-er·ies** 1. [Now Rare] a place for the manufacture of ropes 2. [Archaic] *same as* ROGUERY

rope·walk (rōp′wôk′) *n.* a long, low, narrow building, shed, etc. in which ropes are made

rope·walk·er (-wôk′ər) *n.* a performer who walks or does tricks on a tightrope: also **rope′danc·er** (-dan′sər, -dän′-) —**rope′walk′ing** *n.*

rop·y (rō′pē) *adj.* **rop′i·er, rop′i·est** 1. forming sticky, stringy threads, as some liquids; glutinous 2. like a rope or ropes 3. [Brit. Slang] bad, poor, inferior, etc.: also **rop′ey** —**rop′i·ness** *n.*

☆**roque** (rōk) *n.* [< CROQUET] a formalized variety of croquet played with short-handled mallets on a hard court with a raised border

Roque·fort (cheese) (rōk′fərt) [< *Roquefort*, town in S France where orig. made] a strong cheese with a bluish mold, made from goats' and ewes' milk

roq·ue·laure (räk′ə lôr′, rō′kə-; *Fr.* rôk lôr′) *n.* [Fr., after the Duc de *Roquelaure* (1656–1738)] a heavy cloak, usually knee-length, often fur-trimmed and silk-lined, worn by men in the 18th cent.

ro·quet (rō kā′) *vt., vi.* **-queted′** (-kād′), **-quet′ing** (-kā′in) [< CROQUET] *Croquet, Roque* to cause one's ball to hit (another player's ball) —*n.* the act of roqueting

ror·qual (rôr′kwəl) *n.* [Fr. < Norw. *röyrkval* < ON. *reytharhvalr* < *reythr,* rorqual (prob. akin to *rautha,* red) + *hvalr,* WHALE¹: hence lit., red whale, from the reddish streaks in the skin] any of the whalebone whales (family Balaenopteridae) with a well-developed dorsal fin, esp. a finback whale (*Balaenoptera borealis*) with longitudinal furrows on its belly and throat

Ror·schach test (rôr′shäk) [after Hermann *Rorschach* (1884–1922), Swiss psychiatrist] *Psychol.* a test for the analysis of personality, in which the person being tested tells what is suggested to him by a standard series of inkblot designs: his responses are then analyzed and interpreted

Ro·sa (rō′zä), **Mon·te** (mōn′te) mountain in the Pennine Alps, on the Swiss-Italian border; 15,217 ft.

ro·sa·ceous (rō zā′shəs) *adj.* [ModL. *rosaceus* < L., made of roses] 1. of the rose family of plants, including also the strawberry, blackberry, plum, etc. 2. like a rose 3. rose-colored; rosy

Ros·a·lie (rō′zə lē′, räz′ə-) [Fr., prob. < L. *rosalia,* annual ceremony of hanging garlands of roses on tombs < *rosa,* ROSE¹] a feminine name

Ros·a·lind (räz′ə lind) [Sp. *Rosalinda,* as if from *rosa linda,* pretty rose, but prob. ult. < OHG. *Roslindis* < Gmc. **hros,* HORSE + *lind-,* linden, shield made of linden wood] a feminine name

Ros·a·mond (räz′ə mənd, rō′zə-) [ME. *Rosamunda* < OFr. *Rosamonde* or Sp. *Rosamunda* < ML. *Rosamunda,* as if < L. *rosa munda,* clean rose, but ult. < OHG. *Hrosmund* < Gmc. **hros,* HORSE + *mund-,* hand, protection] a feminine name

ros·an·i·line (rō zan′l in, -ēn′, -īn′) *n.* [ROS(E)¹ + ANILINE] a crystalline base, $C_{20}H_{21}N_3O$, made by heating aniline and toluidine with nitrobenzene: many aniline dyes are derivatives of it

ro·sar·i·an (rō zer′ē ən) *n.* [< L. *rosarium,* a rose garden (see ROSARY) + -AN] a person who cultivates roses

Ro·sa·rio (rō sä′ryō) city & port in EC Argentina, on the Paraná River: pop. 672,000

ro·sa·ry (rō′zər ē) *n., pl.* **-ries** [ME. *rosarie* < L. *rosarium,* rose garden (in ML.), rosary, garland of roses) < neut. of *rosarius,* of roses < *rosa,* ROSE¹] 1. [Now Rare] a bed of roses or rose garden 2. *R.C.Ch. a*) a string of beads used to keep count in saying prayers: it contains sets, typically five or fifteen, of one large bead and ten small beads; each set (*decade*) is associated with a mystery of the Faith *b*) [*also* R-] the prayers said with these beads: for each set, ten Hail Marys preceded by an Our Father and followed by a Glory Be to the Father 3. a string of beads used in a similar way among other religious groups

Ros·coe (räs′kō) [< ?] a masculine name

Ros·com·mon (räs käm′ən) county in Connacht province, WC Ireland: 951 sq. mi.; pop. 56,000

Rose (rōz) [see ff.] a feminine name: dim. *Rosie;* var. *Rosita;* equiv. It. & Sp. *Rosa*

rose¹ (rōz) *n.* [ME. < OE. < L. *rosa* < or akin to Gr. *rhodon:* of Oriental origin] 1. any of a genus (*Rosa*) of shrubs of the rose family, characteristically with prickly stems, alternate compound leaves, and five-parted, usually fragrant flowers of red, pink, white, yellow, etc. having many stamens 2. the flower of any of these plants 3. any of several similar or related plants 4. pinkish red or purplish red 5. *same as* ROSETTE 6. a round, perforated nozzle for a hose, sprinkling can, etc. 7. *a*) a form in which gems, esp. diamonds, are cut with a flat, round base and a multifaceted upper surface *b*) a gem cut in this way 8. a compass card or a representation of this, as on maps —*adj.* 1. of or having to do with a rose or roses 2.

rose-colored   3. rose-scented   4. designating a large and widely distributed family (Rosaceae) of wild and cultivated flowers, shrubs, and trees, including the cinquefoils, meadowsweets, hawthorns, roses, strawberries, apples, peaches, almonds, etc. —*vt.* rosed, ros′ing to make rose-colored; specif., to flush (the cheeks, etc.) —**under the rose** same as SUB ROSA —**rose′like′** *adj.*

rose² *pt. of* RISE

ro·sé (rō zā′) *n.* [Fr., lit., pink] a light, pink wine made chiefly by removing the grape husks after partial fermentation

☆**rose acacia** a shrubby plant (*Robinia hispida*) of the legume family, with bristly stems and large, rose-colored flowers: it grows in the region of the S Alleghenies and is often cultivated

ro·se·ate (rō′zē it, -āt′) *adj.* [< L. *roseus*, rosy < *rosa*, ROSE¹ + -ATE¹] 1. rose-colored; rosy   2. bright, cheerful, or optimistic —**ro′se·ate·ly** *adv.*

rose·bay (rōz′bā′) *n.* same as: 1. RHODODENDRON   2. OLEANDER

☆**rose-breast·ed grosbeak** (-bres′tid) a N. American bird (*Pheucticus ludovicianus*) of the finch family, the male of which is black and white, with a rose-colored triangular patch on the breast, and pink wing lining

rose·bud (-bud′) *n.* the bud of a rose

rose·bush (-boosh′) *n.* a shrub that bears roses

rose campion same as MULLEIN PINK

rose chafer ☆a small N. American beetle (*Macrodactylus subspinosus*) that, as a larva, feeds on plant roots, and, as an adult, on leaves and flowers: also called **rose bug**

rose-col·ored (-kul′ərd) *adj.* 1. pinkish-red or purplish-red   2. bright, cheerful, or optimistic —**through rose-colored glasses** with optimism, esp. undue optimism

Rose·crans (rōz′krans′, rō′zi kranz′), **William Starke** (stärk) 1819–98; Union general in the Civil War

☆**rose fever** a kind of hay fever believed to be caused by the pollen of roses: also **rose cold**

☆**rose-fish** (-fish′) *n., pl.* -fish′, -fish′es: see FISH² any of several reddish food fishes, as the **ocean perch** (*Sebastes marinus*), the **red drum** (*Sciaenops ocellata*), and the **blackbelly rosefish** (*Helicolenus dactylopterus*)

rose geranium any of several pelargoniums grown for their pleasant aroma

rose mallow any of several plants (genus *Hibiscus*) of the mallow family, with showy flowers, esp., a marsh species (*Hibiscus palustris*) having large pink, red, or white flowers

Rose·mar·y (rōz′mer′ē; *chiefly Brit.*, -mə ri) [see ff.] a feminine name

rose·mar·y (-mer′ē; *chiefly Brit.*, -mə ri) *n.* [altered (after ROSE¹ & MARY) < earlier *rosmarine* < L. *ros marinus* (also *ros maris*), lit., dew of the sea: for IE. base see RACE¹ & MARINE] an evergreen plant (*Rosmarinus officinalis*) of the mint family, native to the Mediterranean region, with clusters of small, light-blue flowers and leaves that yield a fragrant essential oil, used in perfumes, in cooking, etc.

Rose·mead (rōz′mēd′) [after Leonard J. *Rose*, local horse breeder] city in SW Calif.: suburb of Los Angeles: pop. 41,000

☆**rose moss** same as PORTULACA

rose of Jericho an Asiatic plant (*Anastatica hierochuntica*) of the mustard family, with oval leaves and spikes of small, white flowers: it curls up tightly when dry and expands again when moistened

rose of Sharon [after Heb. *shārōn*, a district in Israel: cf. S. of Sol. 2:1] ☆1. a hardy plant (*Hibiscus syriacus*) of the mallow family, with white, red, pink, or purplish flowers   2. a plant mentioned in the Bible, variously identified as a tulip, crocus, etc.: S. of Sol. 2:1   3. [Chiefly Brit.] a shrubby species (*Hypericum calycinum*) of Saint Johnswort, with large, yellow flowers

rose oil same as ATTAR OF ROSES: see ATTAR

ro·se·o·la (rō zē′ə lə, rō′zē ō′lə) *n.* [ModL., dim. < L. *roseus*, rosy] any rose-colored rash; esp., German measles, or rubella: also called **rose rash**

rose quartz a variety of quartz, pink to deep rose in color, often used for gems, esp. when translucent

☆**rose slug** the sluglike larva of certain sawflies (esp. *Cladius isomerus*) that eats the leaves of roses

Ro·set·ta stone (rō zet′ə) a tablet of black basalt found in 1799 at Rosetta, a town in Egypt: because it bore parallel inscriptions in Greek and in ancient Egyptian demotic and hieroglyphic characters, it provided a key to the deciphering of ancient Egyptian writing

ro·sette (rō zet′) *n.* [Fr. < OFr., dim. of *rose*, a rose < L. *rosa*, ROSE¹] 1. an ornament made of ribbons, threads, etc. gathered or tufted in the shape of a rose   2. any formation, arrangement, etc. resembling or suggesting a rose   3. *Archit.* a painted or sculptured ornament, usually circular, having petals and leaves radiating symmetrically from the center   4. *Bot.* a circular cluster of leaves, petals, or other organs, esp. such a cluster produced at the base of a plant as a means of overwintering

ROSETTE

Rose·ville (rōz′vil) [after Wm. *Rose*, first local postmaster (1836)] city in SE Mich.: suburb of Detroit: pop. 61,000

rose water a preparation consisting of water and attar of roses, used as a perfume

rose window a decorative circular window with a symmetrical pattern of roselike tracery or mullions arranged like the spokes of a wheel

rose·wood (-wood′) *n.* [from its odor] 1. any of a number of valuable hard, reddish, black-streaked woods, sometimes with a roselike odor, obtained from certain tropical trees (esp. genus *Dalbergia*) of the legume family and used in making furniture, pianos, etc.   2. a tree yielding such wood

Rosh Ha·sha·na (rōsh′ hə shō′nə, -shä′-; *Heb.* rōsh′ hä shä nä′) [Heb. *rōsh hashānāh*, lit., head (or first) of the year] the Jewish New Year, celebrated on the 1st and 2d days of Tishri: also sp. **Rosh Hashona, Rosh Hashanah**, etc.

Ro·si·cru·cian (rō′zə kroo′shən, räz′ə-) *n.* [*Rosicruc-* < L. *rosa*, a rose + *crux*, gen. *crucis*, a cross], Latinized form of the G. pseudonym of the supposed founder, Christian *Rosenkreuz* + -IAN] 1. any of a number of persons in the 17th and 18th cent. who professed to be members of a secret society said to have various sorts of occult lore and power   2. a member of any of several later groups with doctrines and practices said to be based on those of these persons; esp., the Rosicrucian Order, or the Ancient Mystic Order Rosae Crucis (AMORC) —*adj.* of or characteristic of the Rosicrucians —**Ro′si·cru′cian·ism** *n.*

ros·i·ly (rō′zə lē) *adv.* 1. in a rosy manner; brightly; cheerfully; optimistically   2. with a rosy color

ros·in (räz′'n) *n.* [ME., altered < MFr. *resine*, RESIN] the hard, brittle resin, light-yellow to almost black in color, remaining after oil of turpentine has been distilled from crude turpentine or obtained from chemically treated pine stumps: it is rubbed on violin bows, used in making varnish, inks, soaps, insulation, etc. —*vt.* to rub with rosin; put rosin on —**ros′in·ous, ros′in·y** *adj.*

ros·i·ness (rō′zē nis) *n.* a rosy quality or state

rosin oil a viscous, odorless oil, obtained by the fractional distillation of rosin and used as a lubricant, as an adulterant in linseed oil, etc.

☆**ros·in·weed** (räz′'n wēd′) *n.* 1. any of a genus (*Silphium*) of N. American plants of the composite family that have resinous juice, sticky foliage, and strong odors; esp., same as COMPASS PLANT (sense 1)   2. any of several similar resinous plants

Ro·si·ta (rō zēt′ə) a feminine name: see ROSE

Ross (rôs) 1. **Betsy**, (*Mrs. Elizabeth Griscom Ross*) 1752–1836; Am. woman reputed to have made the first Am. flag   2. **Harold W**(allace), 1892–1951; U.S. magazine editor   3. **Sir James Clark**, 1800–62; Brit. polar explorer   4. **Sir John**, 1777–1856; Brit. arctic explorer, born in Scotland: uncle of *prec.*   5. **Sir Ronald**, 1857–1932; Eng. pathologist, born in India

Ross and Crom·ar·ty (rôs 'n kräm′ər tē, krum′-) county in N Scotland: 3,089 sq. mi.; pop. 57,000

Ross Dependency region in Antarctica, south of New Zealand, including islands & territories south of 60° latitude: claimed by Great Britain & administered by New Zealand: land area, c. 160,000 sq. mi.

Ros·set·ti (rō zet′ē, -set′ē) 1. **Christina (Georgina)**, 1830–94; Eng. poet   2. **Dante Gabriel**, 1828–82; Eng. Pre-Raphaelite painter & poet: brother of *prec.*

Ross Ice Shelf frozen S section of the Ross Sea, between Victoria Land & Marie Byrd Land: also called **Ross Shelf Ice** See LITTLE AMERICA, map

Ros·si·ni (rôs sē′nē; *E.* rō sē′nē), **Gio·ac·chi·no (Antonio)** (jō′ä kē′nō) 1792–1868; It. composer

Ross Sea arm of the Pacific, along the coast of Antarctica, east of Victoria Land

Ros·tand (rôs tän′; *E.* räs′tand), **Ed·mond** (ed mōn′) 1868–1918; Fr. dramatist & poet

ros·tel·late (räs′t'l āt′, -it) *adj.* [ModL. *rostellatus* < *rostellum*: see ff.] having a rostellum

ros·tel·lum (räs tel′əm) *n., pl.* -tel′la (-ə) [ModL. < L., dim. of *rostrum*: see ROSTRUM] a small, beaklike process or part; specif., 1. *Bot.* a modification of the stigma in certain orchids   2. *Zool.* a) a small, rounded projection bearing hooks on the head of certain tapeworms   b) a beak-shaped, sucking mouthpart in certain insects —**ros·tel′lar** (-ər), **ros·tel′lar** (-ər) *adj.*

ros·ter (räs′tər) *n.* [Du. *rooster*, orig., gridiron (< *roosten*, to roast), hence a grating, list (from the ruled paper used in making lists)] 1. a list of military or naval personnel or groups, with their regular assignments and periods of duty   2. any list; roll

Ros·tock (rôs′tôk; *E.* räs′täk) seaport in N East Germany, on the Baltic: pop. 61,000

Ros·tov (rō stôf′; *E.* räs′täv) seaport in SW R.S.F.S.R.,

at the mouth of the Don: pop. 737,000: also called **Ros′tov-on-Don′**

Ros·tov·tzeff (rə stôf′tsef), **M**(ichael) **I**(vanovich) 1870-1952; U.S. historian, born in Russia

ros·tral (räs′trəl) *adj.* [LL. *rostralis*] **1.** of, in, or on a rostrum **2.** decorated with rostrums, or beaks of ships [*rostral* pillars]

ros·trate (-trāt) *adj.* [L. *rostratus*] having a rostrum

ros·trum (räs′trəm) *n., pl.* **-trums, -tra** (-trə) [L., beak, in pl., speakers' platform (see 1 *b*) < *rosus*, pp. of *rodere*, to gnaw, peck: see RAT] **1.** in ancient Rome, *a*) a curved, beaklike projection at the prow of a ship; esp., such a projection on a war galley, used for ramming enemy vessels; beak *b*) the speakers' platform in the Forum, decorated with such beaks taken from captured ships **2.** *a*) any platform, stage, etc. for public speaking *b*) public speaking, or public speakers collectively **3.** *Biol.* a beak or beaklike process or part

ros·y (rō′zē) *adj.* **ros′i·er, ros′i·est** [ME.] **1.** like a rose, esp. in color; rose-red or pink; often, blushing or flushed with a healthy, blooming red [*rosy* cheeks] **2.** [Archaic] made or consisting of, or adorned with, roses **3.** bright, promising, cheerful, or optimistic [a *rosy* future, *rosy* expectations]
SYN.—**rosy** suggests the warm pink or red characterizing a rose in bloom [*rosy* cheeks]; **rubicund** implies a flushed, unnatural redness of the face that results from intemperance in eating, drinking, etc. [a *rubicund* nose]; **ruddy** implies such healthy redness as results from an outdoor life [the *ruddy* face of the ranger]; **florid** implies the deep, often uneven facial redness of one suffering from hypertension, strong emotional agitation, etc. [his face grew *florid* as he shouted]

rosy finch any of several finches (genus *Leucosticte*) of W N. America and E Asia, with grayish to black plumage tinted bright pink on the wings, rump, tail, etc.

rot (rät) *vi.* **rot′ted, rot′ting** [ME. *roten* < OE. *rotian,* akin to Du. *rotten*: for IE. base see ROTTEN] **1.** to decompose gradually by the action of bacteria, fungi, etc.; decay; spoil **2.** to fall or pass (*off, away,* etc.) by decaying **3.** to become unhealthy, sickly, etc. [to *rot* in prison] **4.** to become morally corrupt; degenerate —*vt.* **1.** to cause to rot, or decompose **2.** *same as* RET —*n.* [ME. < ON., akin to OE. *rotian*] **1.** a rotting or being rotten; decay, decomposition, or putrefaction **2.** a rotting or rotten thing or part **3.** any of various diseases, esp. a parasitic disease of sheep and other domestic animals, characterized by decay, emaciation, etc. **4.** any of various plant diseases caused by fungi or bacteria and characterized by decay **5.** [Slang] nonsense; rubbish; twaddle; bosh —*interj.* an exclamation expressing disgust, contempt, annoyance, etc. —*SYN.* see DECAY

rot. **1.** rotating **2.** rotation

ro·ta (rōt′ə) *n.* [L., a wheel: see ROLL] **1.** [Chiefly Brit.] a roster, esp. one listing the rotation of duties **2.** [R-] *R.C.Ch.* a high tribunal in Rome that serves esp. as a court of appeal, as from diocesan courts in matrimonial cases or from the civil and criminal courts of the Vatican City: in full, **Sacra Romana Rota,** or **Sacred Roman Rota**

ro·ta·me·ter (rōt′ə mēt′ər) *n.* [L. *rota,* a wheel (see ROLL, *n.*) + -METER] an instrument for measuring the rate of flow of a fluid by means of a movable float inserted in a vertical tube

☆**Ro·tar·i·an** (rō ter′ē ən) *n.* a member of a Rotary Club —*adj.* of Rotarians or Rotary Clubs —**Ro·tar′i·an·ism** *n.*

ro·ta·ry (rōt′ər ē) *adj.* [ML. *rotarius* < L. *rota,* a wheel: see ROLL] **1.** turning around a central point or axis, as a wheel; rotating **2.** *a*) having a rotating part or parts *b*) having blades that rotate on a hub rather than a reel [a *rotary* lawn mower] **3.** occurring around an axis [*rotary* motion] —*n., pl.* **-ries 1.** a rotary machine or engine ☆**2.** [R-] *same as* ROTARY CLUB ☆**3.** [Colloq.] *same as* TRAFFIC CIRCLE

☆**Rotary Club** any local organization of an international service club (**Rotary International**) of business and professional men, founded in Chicago in 1905

rotary engine 1. an engine in which rotary motion is produced directly, without reciprocating parts, as a steam turbine **2.** an early type of radial engine with the cylinders rotating around a stationary crankshaft

rotary press a printing press with curved plates mounted on cylinders that rotate against and print on paper fed from a roll in a continuous sheet

ro·ta·ry-wing aircraft (-wiŋ′) an aircraft, as the helicopter, which is partly or wholly sustained in the air by lifting surfaces (*rotors*) revolving around an axis

ro·tate (rō′tāt) *vi., vt.* **-tat·ed, -tat·ing** [< L. *rotatus,* pp. of *rotare,* to turn < *rota,* a wheel: see ROLL] **1.** to turn around or cause to turn around a center point or axis; revolve **2.** to go or cause to go in a regular and recurring succession of changes; take, or cause to take, turns [to *rotate* crops] —*adj.* [< L. *rota,* a wheel + -ATE¹] shaped like a wheel, with radiating parts, as the corolla of some flowers —*SYN.* see TURN —**ro′tat·a·ble** *adj.*

ro·ta·tion (rō tā′shən) *n.* [L. *rotatio*] **1.** a rotating or being rotated [the daily *rotation* of the earth]: distinguished from REVOLUTION **2.** regular and recurring succession of changes [a *rotation* of duties] ☆**3.** a form of the game of pool in which the balls must be pocketed in the order of their numbers —**ro·ta′tion·al** *adj.*

rotation of crops a system of rotating in a fixed order the kinds of crops, as grain, grass, etc., grown in the same field, to maintain soil fertility

ro·ta·tive (rō′tāt iv, rōt′ə tiv) *adj.* **1.** rotating or occurring in rotation **2.** of, causing, or caused by rotation —**ro′ta·tive·ly** *adv.*

ro·ta·tor (rō′tāt ər) *n.* [L.] a person or thing that rotates; specif., *Anat. pl.* **ro·ta·tor·es** (rō′tə tôr′ēz) a muscle that serves to rotate a part of the body

ro·ta·to·ry (rō′tə tôr′ē) *adj.* **1.** of, or having the nature of, rotation **2.** that rotates; rotary **3.** going or following in rotation **4.** causing rotation

ROTC, R.O.T.C. Reserve Officers' Training Corps

rotche, rotch (räch) *n.* [for earlier *rotge* < Du. *rotje,* petrel, brant goose] *same as* DOVEKIE (sense 1)

rote¹ (rōt) *n.* [ME. < ?] a fixed, mechanical way of doing something; routine —**by rote** by memory alone, without understanding or thought [to answer by *rote*]

rote² (rōt) *n.* [prob. via ME. dial. < Scand., as in ON. *rōt,* a commotion, akin to OHG. *rōz,* a weeping, wailing: for IE. base see RAUCOUS] the sound of the surf beating on the shore

rote³ (rōt) *n.* [ME. < OFr. < Frank. *hrōta* (akin to OHG. *hrotta*) < Celt. *chrotta,* whence W. *crwth,* CROWD²] a medieval stringed musical instrument, variously supposed to have been a kind of lyre, lute, or harp

ro·te·none (rōt′n ōn′) *n.* [Jap. *roten,* derris + -ONE] a white, odorless, crystalline substance, $C_{23}H_{22}O_6$, obtained from the roots of certain plants, as derris and cube, and used in insecticides

rot·gut (rät′gut′) *n.* [ROT + GUT] ☆[Slang] raw, low-grade whiskey or other liquor

Roth·er·ham (räth′ər əm) city in West Riding, Yorkshire, NC England: pop. 87,000

Roth·schild (rôth′chīld′, räths′-; G. rōt′shilt) family of European bankers; specif., *a*) **Mey·er An·selm** (mī′ər än′zelm) or **Am·schel** (äm′shəl), 1743-1812; Ger. founder of the banking house of Rothschild *b*) **Nathan Meyer,** 1777-1836; Eng. banker, born in Germany: son of *prec.*

ro·ti·fer (rōt′ə fər) *n.* [ModL. < L. *rota,* wheel + -FER] any of a large classification, variously phylum or class (Rotatoria or Rotifera), of microscopic, invertebrate animals found mostly in fresh waters, having one or more rings of cilia at the front end of the body that, when vibrated, resemble rotating wheels —**ro·tif′er·al, ro·tif′er·ous** *adj.* —**ro·tif′er·an** *adj., n.*

ro·ti·form (-fôrm′) *adj.* [ModL. *rotiformis* < L. *rota,* a wheel + -formis, -FORM] shaped like a wheel

☆**ro·tis·ser·ie** (rō tis′ər ē) *n.* [Fr. < MFr. *rostisserie* < *rostisseur,* one who roasts meats for sale < *rostir,* to ROAST] **1.** a shop where meats are roasted and sold **2.** a grill with an electrically turned spit

rot·l (rät′l) *n., pl.* **ar·tal** (är′täl), **rot′ls** [Ar. *ratl*] a unit of weight used in Moslem regions, varying locally from about one to about five pounds

☆**ro·to** (rōt′ō) *n., pl.* **-tos** *clipped form of* ROTOGRAVURE

☆**ro·to·gra·vure** (rōt′ə grə vyoor′) *n.* [< L. *rota,* a wheel + GRAVURE] **1.** a printing process using photogravure cylinders on a rotary press **2.** a print or newspaper pictorial section printed by this process

ro·tor (rōt′ər) *n.* [contr. of ROTATOR] **1.** the rotating part of a motor, dynamo, etc.: cf. STATOR **2.** a system of rotating, generally horizontal airfoils together with their hub, as on a helicopter

ro·tor·craft (-kraft′, -kräft′) *n. same as* ROTARY-WING AIRCRAFT: also **rotor plane**

☆**Ro·to·till·er** (rōt′ə til′ər) *a trademark for* a motorized cultivator with rotary blades, etc. —*n.* [also r-] such a cultivator —**ro′to·till′** *vt.*

rot·te (rät′ə) *n. same as* ROTE³

rot·ten (rät′n) *adj.* [ME. *roten* < ON. *rotinn* < IE. *reud-* < base *reu-,* to tear, rip open, prob. used orig. of flax left to soak and rot] **1.** in a decayed or decomposed state; spoiled, putrefied, tainted, etc. **2.** having a bad odor because of decomposition or decay; putrid; foul-smelling **3.** morally corrupt or offensive; dishonest, open to bribery, etc. **4.** unsound or weak, as if decayed within **5.** soft or easily broken as because of decomposition; friable: said of rocks, ice, etc. **6.** [Slang] very bad, unsatisfactory, nasty, etc. —**rot′ten·ly** *adv.* —**rot′ten·ness** *n.*

rotten borough 1. in England (before the Reform Act of 1832), a borough with only a few voters but with the right to send a representative to Parliament **2.** any electoral district or political unit with greater representation than its population warrants

rot·ten·stone (rät′n stōn′) *n.* a siliceous limestone decomposed to a friable state, used for polishing metals

rot·ter (rät′ər) *n.* [< ROT] [Chiefly Brit. Slang] a despicable fellow; cad, bounder, etc.

Rot·ter·dam (rät′ər dam′; Du. rôt′ər däm′) seaport in SW Netherlands, in the Rhine delta: pop. 728,000

ro·tund (rō tund′) *adj.* [L. *rotundus,* akin to *rota,* a wheel: see ROLL] **1.** round or rounded out; plump or stout **2.** full-toned; sonorous [a *rotund* voice] —**ro·tun′di·ty, ro·tund′ness** *n.* —**ro·tund′ly** *adv.*

ro·tun·da (rō tun′də) *n.* [It. *rotonda* < L. *rotunda,* fem. of *rotundus*: see *prec.*] a round building, hall, or room, esp. one with a dome

Rou·ault (rōō ō′), **Georges** (zhôrzh) 1871-1958; Fr. painter

Rou·baix (rōō bĕ′) city in N France: pop. 113,000

rou·ble (rōō′b'l) *n. same as* RUBLE

rou·é (rōō ā′) *n.* [Fr., pp. of *rouer*, to break on the wheel < L. *rota*, a wheel (see ROLL): orig. a nickname given (c. 1720) to the dissolute companions of the Duc d'Orléans] a dissipated man; debauchee; rake

Rou·en (rōō än′; *Fr.* rwän) city & port in NW France, on the Seine: pop. 121,000

rouge[1] (rōōzh) *n.* [Fr., *rouge*, red, rouge < L. *rubeus:* see RUBY] **1.** any of various red or reddish cosmetics, in powder, paste, or liquid form, for coloring the cheeks and lips **2.** a reddish powder, mainly ferric oxide, for polishing jewelry, metal, etc. —*vt.* **rouged, roug′ing** to color with rouge —*vi.* to use cosmetic rouge

rouge[2] (rōōzh) *n.* [orig. slang term at Eton, a scrimmage < ?] in Canadian football, the scoring of a point by a team that is punting when the receiving team takes the ball behind the goal line and does not run it back into the field of play —*vi., vt.* **rouged, roug′ing** to carry out or cause to carry out a rouge

rouge et noir (rōōzh′ ā nwär′) [Fr., red and black] a gambling card game in which the betting is on two groups of cards, designated red and black, that are dealt out for low score in total points (between 31 and 40)

Rou·get de Lisle (rōō zhā′ da lēl′), **Claude Jo·seph** (klôd zhô zef′) 1760–1836; Fr. army officer & composer: wrote the *Marseillaise:* also written **de l'Isle**

rough (ruf) *adj.* [ME. *ruh, rugh* < OE. *ruh*, akin to G. *rauh* < IE. **reuk* < base **reu-*, to tear, tear out (whence RUG, ROTTEN): prob. basic sense "hairy, woolly"] **1.** *a)* not smooth or level; having bumps, projections, etc.; uneven [a *rough* surface] *b)* not easily traveled over or through because rocky, overgrown, wild, etc. [*rough* country] **2.** shaggy or bristly [an animal with a *rough* coat] **3.** characterized by violent action, motion, agitation, disturbance, or irregularity; specif., *a)* stormy; tempestuous [*rough* weather] *b)* boisterous or disorderly [*rough* play] **4.** harsh, rude, brutal, etc.; not gentle or mild [a *rough* temper] **5.** sounding harsh; discordant; jarring **6.** tasting harsh or astringent [*rough* wine] **7.** coarse, as texture, cloth, food, etc. **8.** coarse in manner, tastes, etc.; lacking refinement or culture [*rough* men, *rough* language] **9.** lacking refinements, comforts, and conveniences [the *rough* life of a pioneer] **10.** not refined, polished, or prepared; natural, crude, unwrought, etc. [a *rough* diamond] **11.** not finished, elaborated, perfected, etc. [a *rough* sketch] **12.** not worked out in detail; without claim to be exact or complete; approximate [a *rough* estimate] **13.** requiring muscular energy rather than skill or intelligence [*rough* labor] **14.** [Colloq.] difficult, severe, or disagreeable [a *rough* time] **15.** *Phonet.* pronounced with an aspirate; having the sound of *h* —*n.* **1.** rough ground **2.** rough material or condition **3.** the rough part, aspect, etc. of something ☆**4.** a rough sketch or draft **5.** [Chiefly Brit.] a rough person; rowdy; tough **6.** *Golf* any part of the course where grass, weeds, etc. are allowed to grow uncut, forming a hazard or obstacle —*adv.* in a rough manner; roughly —*vt.* **1.** to make rough; roughen (often with *up*) **2.** to handle or treat roughly or brutally (usually with *up*); specif., *Football*, etc. to subject (an opponent) to intentional and unnecessary roughness **3.** to make, fashion, sketch, shape, or cut roughly (usually with *in* or *out*) [to *rough* out a scheme] **4.** to apply some preparatory or preliminary process or treatment to —*vi.* **1.** [Rare] to become rough **2.** to behave roughly [a penalty for *roughing*] —**in the rough** in a rough or crude state —**rough it** to live without customary comforts and conveniences, as in camping —**rough′ish** *adj.* —**rough′ly** *adv.* —**rough′ness** *n.*

SYN.—rough applies to any surface covered with projections, points, ridges, bumps, etc. [*rough* skin, ground, etc.]; **harsh** applies to anything disagreeably rough to the touch [a *harsh* texture]; that is **uneven** which is not uniform in height, breadth, etc. [an *uneven* floor, hem, etc.]; **rugged** implies a roughness of surface in which the sharp, irregular projections are obstacles to travel [*rugged* country] or a roughness of countenance suggestive of strength [a *rugged* jaw]; **jagged** suggests uneven, sharp-pointed projections or notches along an edge, as of broken glass, ragged cloth, etc. Most of these words have extended senses suggested by their basic meanings [*rough* weather, *harsh* sounds, an *uneven* performance, a *rugged* life] —ANT. **smooth**

☆**rough·age** (ruf′ij) *n.* [see -AGE] rough material; coarse substance; specif., coarse food or fodder, as bran, straw, vegetable peel, etc., containing a relatively high proportion of cellulose and other indigestible constituents and serving in the diet as a stimulus to peristalsis

rough-and-read·y (ruf′ 'n red′ē) *adj.* **1.** rough, or crude, rude, unpolished, etc., but effective enough [*rough-and-ready* methods] **2.** characterized by rough vigor and prompt action rather than refinement, formality, or nicety [a *rough-and-ready* fellow]

rough-and-tum·ble (-tum′b'l) *adj.* violent and disorderly, with no concern for rules [a *rough-and-tumble* fight] —*n.* a fight or struggle of this kind

rough bluegrass a cultivated bluegrass (*Poa trivialis*) often grown in shady or moist spots as a lawn grass

rough breathing [transl. of L. *spiritus asper*] in Greek, **1.** the mark (‘) placed over an initial vowel or ρ (rho) when it is pronounced with a preceding *h* sound, or aspirate **2.** the sound thus indicated

rough·cast (ruf′kast′, -käst′) *n.* **1.** a coarse plaster for covering outside surfaces, as walls **2.** a rough pattern or form, or crudely made model —*vt.* **-cast′, -cast′ing 1.** to cover (walls, etc.) with roughcast **2.** to make or shape in a rough form

rough-cut (-kut′) *adj.* cut into small, chopped, irregular pieces: said of tobacco and opposed to FINE-CUT

rough-dry (-drī′) *vt.* **-dried′, -dry′ing** to dry (washed laundry) without ironing: also **rough′dry′** —*adj.* washed and dried but not ironed

rough·en (ruf′'n) *vt., vi.* to make or become rough

rough fish any fish that is not a game fish and that has no commercial value

rough-hew (ruf′hyōō′) *vt.* **-hewed′, -hewed′** or **-hewn′, -hew′ing 1.** to hew (timber, stone, etc.) roughly, or without finishing or smoothing **2.** to form roughly; give crude shape or outline to Also **rough′hew′**

☆**rough·house** (ruf′hous′) *n.* [Slang] rough, boisterous, or rowdy play, fighting, etc., esp. indoors —*vt.* **-housed′, -hous′ing** [Slang] to treat (a person) roughly or boisterously, but usually in fun —*vi.* [Slang] to take part in roughhouse

☆**rough-leg·ged hawk** (-leg′id) either of two species of large hawks (*Buteo lagopus* and *Buteo regalis*) having legs covered with feathers to the base of the toes

☆**rough·neck** (-nek′) *n.* [Slang] a rough, crude person, esp. one who is quarrelsome and disorderly; rowdy

rough·rid·er (-rīd′ər) *n.* **1.** a person who breaks horses so that they can be ridden **2.** a person who does much hard, rough riding ☆**3.** [R-] a member of a volunteer cavalry regiment organized by Theodore Roosevelt and Leonard Wood for service in the Spanish-American War (1898): also **Rough Rider**

rough-shod (-shäd′) *adj.* shod with horseshoes that have calks, or metal points, to prevent slipping —**ride roughshod over** to treat in a harsh, arrogant, inconsiderate manner; domineer over

rou·lade (rōō läd′) *n.* [Fr. < *rouler*, to ROLL] **1.** a musical ornament consisting of a rapid succession of tones sung to one syllable **2.** a slice of meat rolled, usually with a filling of minced meat, and cooked

rou·leau (rōō lō′) *n., pl.* **-leaux′** (-lōz′) or **-leaus′** [Fr., dim. of *rôle*, a ROLL] **1.** a small roll of something; esp., a roll of coins, generally of the same denomination, stacked in a paper wrapper **2.** a roll or fold, as of ribbon for trimming hats, etc.

rou·lette (rōō let′) *n.* [Fr. < OFr. *roelette*, dim. of *roele*, small wheel < LL. *rotella*, dim. < L. *rota*, a wheel: see ROLL] **1.** a gambling game played by rolling a small ball around a shallow bowl with an inner disk (**roulette wheel**) revolving in the opposite direction: the ball finally comes to rest in one of the numbered, alternately red and black compartments into which this disk is divided, thus determining the winning and losing bets **2.** a small toothed wheel attached to a handle, for making rows of marks or dots, as in engraving, or incisions, as between postage stamps **3.** a series of small, consecutive incisions made in the paper between the stamps in a sheet of stamps, to facilitate their separation —*vt.* **-let′ted, -let′ting** to make marks, dots, or incisions in or on with a roulette

ROULETTE WHEEL

Rou·ma·ni·a (rōō mā′nē ə, -mān′yə) *same as* ROMANIA —**Rou·ma′ni·an** *adj., n.*

Rou·me·li·a (rōō mē′lē ə, -mēl′yə) *same as* RUMELIA

round[1] (round) *adj.* [ME. < OFr. *roond* < L. *rotundus:* see ROTUND] **1.** shaped like a ball; spherical; globular **2.** *a)* shaped like a circle, ring, or disk; circular *b)* shaped like a cylinder (in having a circular cross section); cylindrical **3.** curved in shape like part of a sphere or circle **4.** not angular; plump or stout **5.** involving, or done in or with, a circular motion [a *round* dance] **6.** *a)* not lacking part; full; complete [a *round* dozen] *b)* completed; perfected **7.** completed by progressing through a course which, as if circular, returns to the starting point [a *round* trip] **8.** constituting, or expressed by, a whole number, or integer; not fractional **9.** expressed in even units, as tens, hundreds, thousands, etc., rather than exactly [500 is a *round* number for 498, 503, etc.] **10.** large in amount, size, etc., considerable [a *round* sum] **11.** mellow and full in tone; sonorous [rich *round* tones] **12.** brisk; vigorous and rapid [a *round* pace] **13.** outspoken; plain and blunt; straightforward **14.** *Phonet.* pronounced with the lips forming a circular or oval opening; rounded [a *round* vowel] —*n.* **1.** something round or rounded; thing or part that is spherical, globular, circular, curved, annular, or cylindrical **2.** *a)* a rung of a ladder *b)* a crossbar connecting the legs of a chair **3.** the rounded part of the thigh of a beef animal, between the rump and the leg: see BEEF, illus. **4.** movement in a circular

course or about an axis **5.** *same as* ROUND DANCE **6.** a series or succession of actions, events, etc. that is completed at, or as if at, the point where it began [a *round* of parties] **7.** the complete extent; whole range [the *round* of human beliefs] **8.** [*often pl.*] a regular, customary course or circuit, as by a watchman of his station, a doctor of his hospital patients, a drinker of a number of bars, etc. **9.** a single serving, as of drinks, to each of a group **10.** *a)* a single shot from each of a number of rifles, artillery pieces, etc. fired together, or a shot from a single gun: cf. SALVO¹ *b)* ammunition for such a shot; cartridge, shell, etc. **11.** a single outburst, as of applause, cheering, etc.; salvo **12.** a circular slice, as of bread **13.** *Archery* a specified number of arrows shot at the target from a specified distance according to the rules **14.** *Games & Sports* a single period or division of action, usually one of a series [a *round* of poker]; specif., *a) Boxing* any of the timed periods of a fight: a round is now generally limited to three minutes, and the interval between rounds to one minute *b) Golf* a number of holes as a unit of competition, esp. eighteen **15.** *Music a)* a short song for two or more persons or groups, in which the second starts when the first reaches the second phrase, etc., as in a canon *b)* [*pl.*] the ringing in sequence of a set of bells from the smallest to the largest, in change ringing —*vt.* **1.** to make round (often with *off*) **2.** to pronounce with rounded lips **3.** to deprive of angularity or make plump (usually with *out*) **4.** to express as a round number (usually with *off*) **5.** to complete; finish; perfect (usually with *out* or *off*) **6.** to make a circuit of; pass around [we *rounded* the island] **7.** to make a turn about [to *round* a corner] **8.** [Now Rare] to encircle; surround **9.** to cause to move in a circular course —*vi.* **1.** to make a complete or partial circuit; move in a curved or circular course **2.** *a)* to turn; reverse direction *b)* to attack or oppose suddenly or unexpectedly; turn (*on*) **3.** to become round or plump (often with *out*) **4.** to develop (*into*) [the talk *rounded* into a plan] —*adv.* **1.** in a circle; along or throughout a circular course or circumference **2.** through a recurring period of time, or from beginning to end [to work the year *round*] **3.** in or through a course or circuit, as from one person or place to another **4.** for each of several; to include all in a group [not enough to go *round*] **5.** so as to encircle, surround, or envelop, or be encircled, surrounded, or enveloped **6.** in circumference **7.** on all sides; in every direction **8.** about; near **9.** by a circuitous course; in a roundabout way **10.** in various places; here and there **11.** with a rotating or revolving movement **12.** in or to the opposite direction **13.** in or to an opposite belief, viewpoint, etc. —*prep.* **1.** so as to encircle, surround, or envelop; about **2.** on the circumference, border, or outer part of **3.** on all sides of; in every direction from **4.** in the vicinity of; somewhat close to **5.** to or through every part or various parts of; in a circuit or course through **6.** from the beginning to the end of (a period of time); throughout **7.** in various places in or on; here and there in; all about **8.** *a)* so as to make a curve or partial circuit about *b)* at a point reached by making such a circuit about **9.** so as to rotate or revolve about (a center or axis) In the U.S., *round* (*adv. & prep.*) is generally superseded by *around;* in Great Britain, *round* is preferred for most senses Cf. AROUND for special senses See also phrases under BRING, COME, etc. —**go the round (or rounds) 1.** to be circulated among a number of people, as a story, rumor, etc. **2.** to walk one's regular course or circuit, as a watchman: also **make one's rounds** —**in the round 1.** with the audience or congregation seated all around a central area for a stage, altar, etc.: cf. ARENA THEATER **2.** in full and completely rounded form, not in relief: said of sculpture **3.** in full and realistic detail —**out of round** not having perfect roundness — **round about 1.** in or to the opposite direction **2.** in every direction around —**round in** *Naut.* to haul in —**round to** *Naut.* to turn so that the prow is toward the wind —**round up** ☆**1.** to drive (cattle, etc.) together; collect in a herd, group, etc. ☆**2.** [Colloq.] to gather, collect, or assemble —**round′ness** *n.*

SYN.—**round,** the most inclusive of these words, applies to anything shaped like a circle, sphere, or cylinder, or like a part of any of these; **spherical** applies to a round body or mass having the surface equally distant from the center at all points; **globular** is used of things that are ball-shaped but not necessarily perfect spheres; **circular** is applied to round lines, or round flat surfaces, in the shape of a ring or disk, and it may or may not imply correspondence in form with a perfect circle; **annular** applies to ringlike forms or structures, as the markings in a cross section of a tree

round² (round) *vt., vi.* [ME. *rounen* (+ unhistoric -d) < OE. *runian,* to whisper: see RUNE] [Obs.] to whisper (to)

round·a·bout (round′ə bout′) *adj.* **1.** not straight or straightforward; indirect; circuitous [*roundabout* answers] **2.** encircling; enclosing; surrounding —*n.* **1.** something that is indirect or circuitous ☆**2.** a short, tight jacket or coat formerly worn by men and boys **3.** *Brit. var. of: a)* MERRY-GO-ROUND *b)* TRAFFIC CIRCLE

round angle an angle of 360°

☆**round clam** *same as* QUAHOG

round dance 1. a dance with the dancers arranged or moving in a circle **2.** any of several dances, as the waltz, polka, fox trot, etc., performed by couples and characterized by revolving or circular movements

round·ed (roun′did) *adj.* **1.** made round **2.** developed or diversified, in regard to tastes, abilities, etc.: often in hyphenated compounds [a well-*rounded* person] **3.** *Phonet.* pronounced with the lips forming a circular or oval opening; labialized —**round′ed·ness** *n.*

roun·del (roun′d'l) *n.* [ME. < OFr. *rondel,* orig. dim. of *roond,* ROUND¹] **1.** orig., something round, or circular **2.** a round ornamental panel, plate, niche, etc. **3.** a small, round window or pane **4.** *a)* formerly, a rondeau *b) same as* RONDEL (sense 1) *c)* an English modification of the rondel, with three stanzas of three lines each and two refrains **5.** *same as* ROUNDELAY (sense 2)

roun·de·lay (roun′də lā′) *n.* [MFr. *rondelet,* dim. of *rondel:* see prec.] **1.** *a)* a simple song in which some phrase, line, etc. is continually repeated *b)* music for such a song **2.** a dance in a circle; roundel

round·er (roun′dər) *n.* **1.** [Obs.] a person who makes a round or rounds, as a watchman **2.** a person or thing that rounds; specif., a tool for rounding corners or edges **3.** [*pl., with sing. v.*] a British game somewhat like baseball ☆**4.** [from the idea of making the rounds of bars, etc.] [Colloq.] a dissolute person or drunkard

round hand careful handwriting in which the letters are rounded, distinct, full, and almost vertical

Round·head (round′hed′) *n.* a member or supporter of the Parliamentary, or Puritan, party in England during the English civil war (1642–52): orig. a derisive term, with reference to the Puritans' close-cropped hair in contrast to the Cavaliers' long hair

round·heel (-hēl′) *n.* [Slang] a woman who yields readily to sexual intercourse: also **round′heels′** —**round′heeled′** *adj.*

round·house (-hous′) *n.* [orig., a lockup, after Du. *rondhuis,* guardhouse] ☆**1.** a building, generally circular or semicircular, with a turntable in the center, used for storing, repairing, and switching locomotives **2.** a cabin on the after part of a ship's quarter-deck ☆**3.** *a) Baseball* a pitch with a wide curve *b) Boxing* a wide swing or hook, as to the head ☆**4.** *Pinochle* a meld of one king and queen of each of the four suits

round·ish (roun′dish) *adj.* somewhat round

round·let (round′lit) *n.* [ME. *roundelet* < MFr. *rondelet:* see ROUNDELAY] a small circle or circular thing

round·ly (-lē) *adv.* **1.** in a round form; circularly, spherically, etc. **2.** in a round manner; specif., *a)* vigorously, bluntly, severely, etc. [he was *roundly* rebuked] *b)* fully; completely and thoroughly

round of beef *see* ROUND¹ (*n.* 3)

round robin [ROUND¹ + pers. name *Robin*] **1.** a document, as a petition, protest, etc., with the signatures written in a circle to conceal the order of signing **2.** a contest or tournament, as in tennis, chess, etc., in which every entrant is matched with every other one **3.** a letter circulated among the members of a group, which is signed and forwarded by each in turn, often with additional comments, etc.

round-shoul·dered (-shōl′dərd) *adj.* stooped because the shoulders are bent forward, not held straight

rounds·man (roundz′mən) *n., pl.* **-men** (-men) a person who makes rounds, esp. of inspection

round steak a cut from a round of beef

Round Table 1. the large table around which, according to legend, King Arthur and his knights sat: it was made circular to avoid disputes about precedence **2.** King Arthur and his knights, collectively **3.** [r- t-] *a)* a group gathered together for an informal discussion or conference at, or as if at, a circular table *b)* such a discussion, conference, etc. —**round′-ta′ble** *adj.*

round-the-clock (round′thə kläk′) *adj., adv.* throughout the day and night; continuously

☆**round trip 1.** a trip to a place and back again **2.** *same as* ROUNDHOUSE (sense 4) —**round′-trip′** *adj.*

round turn a kind of knot making one complete turn around something: see KNOT, illus.

round·up (-up′) *n.* ☆**1.** *a)* the act of driving cattle, etc. together on the range and collecting in a herd, as for branding, inspection, or shipping *b)* the herd of cattle, etc. thus collected *c)* the cowboys, horses, etc. that do this work ☆**2.** any similar driving together, collecting, or gathering [a *roundup* of suspected persons] ☆**3.** a summary, as of information, news, etc.

round·worm (-wurm′) *n.* **1.** *same as* NEMATODE **2.** a species (*Ascaris lumbricoides*) of nematode worms, living as parasites, esp. in the intestines of man and other mammals

roup (rōōp) *n.* [prob. akin to or < MFr. *roupie,* snivel < ?] **1.** an infectious disease of poultry, characterized by mucous discharge from the eyes and nasal passages **2.** [Scot.] hoarseness; huskiness —**roup′y** *adj.* **roup′i·er, roup′i·est**

rouse¹ (rouz) *vt.* **roused, rous′ing** [LME. *rowsen:* orig. technical term in hawking & hunting, hence prob. < Anglo-Fr. or OFr.: cf. AROUSE] **1.** to cause (game) to rise from cover, come out of a lair, etc.; stir up to flight or attack **2.** to stir up, as to anger or action; excite **3.** to cause to come out of a state of sleep, repose, unconsciousness, etc.; wake **4.** *Naut.* to pull with force; haul —*vi.* **1.** to rise from cover, etc.: said of game **2.** to come out of a state of sleep, repose, etc.; wake **3.** to become active —*n.*

1. the act of rousing 2. a violent stir —*SYN.* see STIR[1] —**rous′er** *n.*

rouse[2] (rouz) *n.* [apheptic for CAROUSE (from mistaking *drink carouse* as *drink a rouse*)] [Archaic] 1. a drink of liquor 2. a carousal

rous·ing (rou′ziŋ) *adj.* 1. that rouses; stirring [a *rousing* speech] 2. very active or lively; vigorous; brisk [a *rousing* business] 3. extraordinary; remarkable —**rous′ing·ly** *adv.*

Rous·seau (rōō sō′) 1. **Hen·ri** (än rē′), 1844–1910; Fr. primitive painter: called *Le Douanier* (The Customs Officer) 2. **Jean Jacques** (zhän zhäk), 1712–78; Fr. political philosopher & writer, born in Switzerland 3. **(Pierre Étienne) Thé·o·dore** (tā ō dôr′), 1812–67; Fr. landscape painter

roust (roust) *vt.* [dial. form of ROUSE[1] with unhistoric -*t*] [Colloq.] 1. to rouse or stir (*up*) 2. to rout or drive (*out*)

roust·a·bout (-ə bout′) *n.* [prec. + ABOUT] ☆1. a deckhand or waterfront laborer ☆2. a laborer in a circus who helps set up the tents, etc. ☆3. an unskilled or transient laborer, as on a ranch or in an oil field

rout[1] (rout) *n.* [ME. *route* < OFr., a troop, band, lit., part broken off < L. *rupta:* see ROUTE] 1. a disorderly crowd; noisy mob; rabble 2. a disorderly flight or retreat, as of defeated troops [to be put to *rout*] 3. an overwhelming defeat 4. [Archaic or Poet.] *a)* a group of people; company; band *b)* a band of followers; retinue 5. [Archaic] a large, fashionable social gathering in the evening 6. *Law* a disturbance of the peace by two or more persons acting together with intent to create a riot —*vt.* 1. to put to disorderly flight 2. to defeat overwhelmingly —*SYN.* see CONQUER

rout[2] (rout) *vi.* [var. of ROOT[2]] 1. to dig for food with the snout, as a pig; root 2. to poke or rummage about —*vt.* 1. to dig up or turn over with the snout 2. to force out —**rout out** 1. to expose to view 2. to scoop, gouge, or hollow out; specif., to cut away (the nonprinting surface of an engraving plate) ☆3. to make (a person) get out —**rout up** 1. to find or get by turning up or poking about ☆2. to make (a person) get up

rout[3] (rout) *vi.* [ME. *routen* < ON. *rauta*, to bellow, ult. < IE. *reud-* < base *reu-*, to roar: see RUMOR] [Scot. & Brit. Dial.] to make a loud noise; roar —*n.* [Scot. & Brit. Dial.] a loud noise or shout

route (rōōt; *also, and for n. 2 & 3 usually*, rout) *n.* [ME. < OFr. *route, rote* < L. *rupta* (*via*), broken (path) < fem. of *ruptus*, pp. of *rumpere*, to break: see RUPTURE] 1. a road, way, or course for traveling; esp., a highway ☆2. *a)* a regular course traveled as in delivering mail, milk, newspapers, etc. *b)* a set of customers whom one regularly visits to make deliveries, solicit sales, etc. 3. an order for troops to march —*vt.* **rout′ed, rout′ing** ☆1. to direct, send, forward, or transport by a specified route [to *route* goods through Omaha] ☆2. to fix the order of procedure of (a series of operations, etc.) [to *route* orders through the sales department] —☆**go the route** [Colloq.] *Baseball* to pitch an entire game

rout·er (rout′ər) *n.* a person or thing that routs or a tool for routing; specif., *a)* a plane for gouging out recesses and smoothing the bottoms of grooves: in full **router plane** *b)* a machine for routing out areas on a wood or metal surface

rou·tine (rōō tēn′) *n.* [Fr. < *route:* see ROUTE] 1. a regular, more or less unvarying procedure, customary, prescribed, or habitual, as of business or daily life 2. such procedure in general [to dislike *routine*] 3. a theatrical skit or act ☆4. a series of steps for a dance 5. a set of coded instructions for a computer —*adj.* having the nature of, using, or by routine —**rou·tine′ly** *adv.*

rou·tin·ism (-tēn′iz′m) *n.* adherence to or prevalence of routine —**rou·tin′ist** *n.*

☆**rou·tin·ize** (rōō tē′nīz) *vt.* -**ized, -iz·ing** to make routine; reduce to a routine —**rou′ti·ni·za′tion** *n.*

roux (rōō) *n.* [Fr. *roux* (*beurre*), reddish-brown (butter) < L. *russus:* see RUSSET] a cooked mixture of melted butter (or other fat) and flour, used for thickening sauces, soups, gravies, etc.

rove[1] (rōv) *vi.* **roved, rov′ing** [ME. *roven*, orig. an archery term as vt. < ?: sense infl. by association with ROVER[2] (pirate)] 1. to wander about; go from place to place, esp. over an extensive area, with no particular course or destination; roam 2. to look around: said of the eyes —*vt.* to wander over; roam through [to *rove* the woods] —*n.* the act of roving; a ramble —*SYN.* see ROAM

rove[2] (rōv) *vt.* **roved, rov′ing** [< ?] to twist (fibers) together and draw out into roving before spinning —*n. Brit. var. of* ROVING

rove[3] (rōv) *alt. pt. & pp. of* REEVE[2]

rove beetle any of a large family (Staphylinidae) of swiftly moving beetles with a long, slender body and very short elytra: they feed chiefly on decomposing organic matter

rov·en (rōv′n) *alt. pp. of* REEVE[2]

rove-o·ver (rōv′ō′vər) *adj.* [term coined in connection with SPRUNG RHYTHM by G. M. HOPKINS] *Prosody* having a rhythm continued without pause from the end of one line to the beginning of the next —**n.** rove-over verse

rov·er[1] (rōv′ər) *n.* [ROVE[1] + -ER] 1. a person who roves, or wanders 2. *Archery a)* a mark, or target, chosen at random *b)* any of several set marks for distance shooting *c)* an archer who shoots for distance

rov·er[2] (rōv′ər) *n.* [ME. < MDu., a robber < *roven*, to rob (for IE. base see RUPTURE): prob. merged with prec.] [Archaic] a pirate or pirate ship

rov·er[3] (rōv′ər) *n.* 1. a person who operates a machine for roving fibers 2. such a machine

rov·ing (-viŋ) *n.* [< ?] 1. the strand of twisted and drawn-out fibers of cotton, wool, silk, etc. from which yarns are made 2. the process of preparing such a strand

row[1] (rō) *n.* [ME. *rowe* < OE. *ræw*, akin to G. *reihe* < IE. base *rei-*, to scratch, split: see RIVE, REAP] 1. a number of people or things arranged so as to form a line, esp. a straight line 2. any of a series of such horizontal lines in parallel, as of seats in a theater or airplane, corn in a field, etc. 3. a street with a line of buildings on either side, specif. one with occupants of a specified kind [fraternity *row*] —*vt.* to arrange or put in a row or rows —☆**hard** (or **long**) **row to hoe** anything difficult or wearisome to do —**in a row** in succession; consecutively

row[2] (rō) *vt.* [ME. *rowen* < OE. *rowan*, akin to ON. *rōa* < IE. base *erē-*, to row, oar, whence L. *remus*, oar, Gr. *eretēs*, a rower & RUDDER] 1. to propel (a boat, etc.) on water by or as by using oars 2. to convey in or on a boat, etc. propelled in this way 3. to require (a specified number of oars): said of a boat 4. to use (oarsmen, a stroke, etc. as specified) in rowing, esp. in a race —*vi.* 1. to use oars in propelling a boat 2. to be propelled by means of oars: said of a boat —*n.* 1. an act, instance, or period of rowing 2. *a)* a trip made by rowboat *b)* the distance of such a trip —**row′er** *n.*

row[3] (rou) *n.* [back-formation < ? ROUSE[1], with loss of *s*, as in PEA or CHERRY] a noisy quarrel, dispute, or disturbance; squabble, brawl, or commotion —*vi.* to make, or take part in, a noisy quarrel or disturbance

row·an (rō′ən, rou′-) *n.* [< Scand., as in Norw. *rogn, raun*, ON. *reynir*, akin to ON. *rauthr*, RED: from the color of the fruit] 1. the European mountain ash (*Sorbus aucuparia*), a tree with pinnately compound leaves, white flowers, and red berries 2. either of two similar American mountain ashes 3. the orange or red berry of a rowan: also **row′an·ber·ry** (-ber′ē), *pl.* -**ries**

row·boat (rō′bōt′) *n.* a small boat made to be rowed

☆**row·dy** (rou′dē) *n., pl.* -**dies** [< ? ROW[3]] a person whose behavior is rough, quarrelsome, and disorderly; hoodlum —*adj.* -**di·er, -di·est** having the nature of or characteristic of a rowdy; rough, quarrelsome, etc. —**row′di·ly** *adv.* —**row′di·ness** *n.* —**row′dy·ish** *adj.* —**row′dy·ism** *n.*

row·el (rou′əl) *n.* [ME. *rowelle* < OFr. *roele:* see ROULETTE] a small, revolving wheel with sharp projecting points, forming the end of a spur —*vt.* -**eled** or -**elled, -el·ing** or -**el·ling** to spur or prick (a horse, etc.) with or as with a rowel

ROWEL

row·en (rou′ən) *n.* [ME. *rewayn* < ONormFr. *rewain*, for OFr. *regain* < *regainer:* see RE- & GAIN[1]] the second crop of grass or hay in one season; aftermath

Ro·we·na (rə wē′nə) [< ? OE. *Hrothwina* < *hroth*, fame + *wina*, a friend] a feminine name

☆**row house** (rō) any of a line of identical houses joined along the sides by common walls

Row·land (rō′lənd) a masculine name: see ROLAND

Row·land·son (rō′lənd sən), **Thomas** 1756–1827; Eng. caricaturist & painter

row·lock (rul′ək, räl′-; rō′läk′) *n.* [altered (after ROW[2]) < earlier OARLOCK] *chiefly Brit. term for* OARLOCK

Ro·xas y A·cu·ña (rō′häs ē ä kōō′nyä), **Ma·nuel** (mä nwel′) 1892–1948; Philippine statesman; 1st president of the Republic of the Philippines (1946–48)

Rox·burgh (räks′bur′ō; *Brit.* räks′brə) county of S Scotland, on the Eng. border: 665 sq. mi.; pop. 43,000: also **Rox′burgh′shire** (-shir′)

Roy (roi) [as if < OFr. *roy* (Fr. *roi*), a king, but prob. < Gael. *rhu*, red] a masculine name

roy·al (roi′əl) *adj.* [ME. *roial* < OFr. < L. *regalis*, REGAL] 1. of, from, by, or to a king, queen, or other sovereign [the *royal* family, a *royal* edict, the *royal* allowance] 2. having the rank of a sovereign 3. of a kingdom, its government, etc. [the *royal* fleet] 4. *a)* founded, chartered, or helped by, or under the patronage of, a sovereign [the *Royal* Society] *b)* in the service of a sovereign or of the Crown 5. *a)* suitable for a sovereign; magnificent, splendid, regal, etc. [*royal* robes] *b)* like or characteristic of a sovereign; majestic, stately, noble, etc. [a *royal* bearing] 6. unusually large, great, fine, etc. —*n.* 1. a large size of paper, 20 by 25 inches (for printing) or 19 by 24 inches (for writing) 2. a small sail set on the royal mast —**roy′al·ly** *adv.*

royal blue a deep, vivid reddish or purplish blue

royal fern a bushy fern (*Osmunda regalis*) with large, tall, upright fronds, commonly found in streams and ponds

☆**royal flush** the highest poker hand, consisting of the ace, king, queen, jack, and ten of the same suit

roy·al·ism (-iz'm) *n.* **1.** the principles of royal government; monarchism **2.** adherence to monarchism

roy·al·ist (-ist) *n.* an adherent of royalism; person who supports a monarch or a monarchy, esp. in times of revolution, civil war, etc.; specif., **[R-]** *a)* a supporter of Charles I of England; Cavalier ☆*b)* a supporter of the British in the American Revolution; Tory   *c)* a supporter of the Bourbons in France —*adj.* of royalists or royalism

royal jelly a highly nutritious mixture secreted by the maxillary glands in young honeybee workers, fed to all larvae for the first few days and continued to be fed to those larvae chosen to be queens

royal mast a small mast next above the topgallant mast

Royal Oak [in allusion to an oak in which CHARLES II of England is said to have hidden] city in SE Mich.: suburb of Detroit: pop. 85,000

☆**royal palm** any of several tall, feather palms (genus *Roystonea*) native to Florida and the West Indies, extensively planted because of their rapid growth and adaptability

royal poinciana a tropical tree (*Delonix regia*) of the legume family, with a flat crown of twice pinnately compound leaves and masses of intense scarlet flowers

ROYAL PALM

royal purple 1. orig., deep crimson: cf. PURPLE (sense 2) **2.** a dark, bluish purple

royal road an easy way of reaching an objective

roy·al·ty (roi'əl tē) *n., pl.* **-ties** [ME. *roialte* < OFr.] **1.** the rank, status, or power of a king or queen; royal position, dignity, etc.; sovereignty **2.** a royal person or, collectively, royal persons **3.** a royal domain or realm; kingdom **4.** royal quality or character; regalness, nobility, magnanimity, etc. **5.** [*usually pl.*] a right, privilege, or prerogative of a monarch **6.** *a)* a royal right, as over some natural resource, granted by a monarch to a person, corporation, etc. *b)* payment for such a right **7.** *a)* a share of the proceeds or product paid to the owner of a right, as a patent, for permission to use it or operate under it *b)* such a share paid to one from whom lands rich in oil or minerals are leased *c)* a share of the proceeds from his work, usually a specified percentage, paid to an author, composer, etc.

Royce (rois), **Josiah** 1855–1916; U.S. philosopher & educator

roz·zer (räz'ər) *n.* [< ? Romany *roozlo*, strong] [Brit. Slang] a policeman

R.P. Regius Professor

rpm, r.p.m. revolutions per minute

R.P.O. Railway Post Office

rps, r.p.s. revolutions per second

rpt. report

R.Q. respiratory quotient

R.R. 1. railroad: also **RR 2.** Right Reverend **3.** Rural Route

-rrha·gi·a (rā'jē ə) [ModL. < Gr. *-rrhagia* < *rhēgnynai*, to burst < IE. base *wrēg-*, to break, whence Lith. *rēžti*, to cut, tear] *a combining form meaning* abnormal discharge, excessive flow [*menorrhagia*]: also **-rrhage** (rij), **-rrhag'y** (rā'jē)

-rrhe·a, -rrhoe·a (rē'ə) [ModL. < Gr. *-rrhoia* < *rhein*, to flow: see STREAM] *a combining form meaning* a flow, discharge [*seborrhea*]

RR Ly·rae variables (är'är' lī'rē) [*RR*, astronomical code designation of tenth variable + *Lyrae*, gen. of L. *Lyra*, LYRA] a subdivision of short-period variable stars, with periods from 1 1/2 to 29 hours: the distance of such a star can be determined from the period-luminosity relation

Rs, rs. rupees

R.S. Revised Statutes

R.S.F.S.R., RSFSR Russian Soviet Federated Socialist Republic

RSV, R.S.V. Revised Standard Version (of the Bible)

R.S.V.P., r.s.v.p. [Fr. *répondez s'il vous plaît*] please reply

rt. 1. right **2.** *Football* right tackle: also **rt**

rte. route

Rt. Hon. Right Honorable

Rt. Rev. Right Reverend

Rts. *Finance* rights

Ru *Chem.* ruthenium

Ru·an·da (roo wän'də) *n.* **1.** *pl.* **-das, -da** any member of a Bantu people living in Rwanda and the Congo (see sense 2) **2.** their Bantu language: used as one of the two trade languages in Rwanda and Burundi

Ru·an·da-U·run·di (-oo roon'dē) former Belgian-administered UN trust territory in EC Africa: divided (1962) into the independent countries of Rwanda & Burundi

rub (rub) *vt.* **rubbed, rub'bing** [ME. *rubben*, akin to Dan. *rubbe*, EFris. *rubben* < IE. *reup-*, to tear out < base *reu-*, to dig, tear out, whence RUG, RUBBLE, L. *rumpere*,

to break] **1.** to move one's hand, a cloth, etc. over (a surface or object) with pressure and friction, in a circular or back-and-forth motion **2.** to move (one's hand, a cloth, etc.) over, or spread or apply (polish, etc.) on or over, a surface or object in this way **3.** to move (a thing) against something else, or move (things) over each other with pressure and friction (often followed by *together*, etc.) **4.** to apply pressure and friction to, for cleaning, polishing, smoothing, etc. **5.** to put into a specified condition by applying pressure and friction [*to rub oneself dry*] **6.** to make sore or chafed by rubbing **7.** to force, cause to go, etc. (*in, into*, etc.) by rubbing **8.** to remove by rubbing (*out, off, away*, etc.) —*vi.* **1.** to move with pressure and friction (*on, against*, etc.) [*the tire rubbing against the fender*] **2.** to rub something; exert pressure and friction on something **3.** to admit of being rubbed or removed by rubbing (often with *off, out*, etc.) **4.** to arouse anger or irritation —*n.* **1.** the act or an instance of rubbing; specif., a massage **2.** an obstacle, hindrance, or difficulty **3.** a place or spot that has been rubbed until rough or sore **4.** something that irritates, annoys, offends, etc., as a jeer or rebuke —**rub along** (or **on** or **through**) [Chiefly Brit.] to keep going or manage in spite of difficulties —**rub down 1.** to massage **2.** to smooth, polish, wear down, etc. by rubbing —**rub it in** [Slang] to keep on mentioning to someone his failure or mistake, often with some malice —☆**rub off on** to be left on (something or someone) as a mark, as by rubbing or, figuratively, by close contact —**rub out 1.** to erase or be erased by rubbing ☆**2.** [Slang] to kill —**rub the wrong way** to be annoying, irritating, etc. to

rub-a-dub (rub'ə dub') *n.* [echoic] a sound of or as of a drum being beaten

Ru·bái·yát (roo'bi yät', -bĭ-), **The** [lit., the quatrains < Ar. *rubā'īyāt*, pl. of *rubā'īyah*, quatrain, fem. of *rubā'ī*, composed of four < *rubā*, four] a long poem in quatrains (rhyming *aaba*), written by OMAR KHAYYÁM

Rub' al Kha·li (roob' äl khä'lē) large desert of S & SE Arabia: c. 300,000 sq. mi.

ru·basse (roo bas', -bäs') *n.* [< Fr. *rubace* < *rubis*: see RUBY] a variety of crystalline quartz containing bits of iron oxide that produce a ruby-red color

ru·ba·to (roo bät'ō) *adj., adv.* [It. < (*tempo*) *rubato*, stolen (time)] *Music* with some notes arbitrarily lengthened (or shortened) in performance and, often, others correspondingly changed in length; intentionally and temporarily deviating from a strict tempo —*n., pl.* **-tos 1.** rubato modification or execution **2.** a rubato passage, phrase, etc.

rub·ba·boo, rub·a·boo (rub'ə boo') *n.* [< ?] pemmican made into a soup by boiling in water, sometimes thickened with flour

rub·ber[1] (rub'ər) *n.* **1.** a person or thing that rubs, as in polishing, scraping, massaging, etc. **2.** [from orig. use as an eraser] an elastic substance produced by coagulating and drying the milky sap (*latex*) of various tropical plants, esp. a tree (*Hevea brasiliensis*) of the spurge family: now most often produced synthetically or by chemically altering latex to obtain desired characteristics for use in making automobile tires, electrical insulation, molded objects and parts, etc.: in pure form rubber is a white, unsaturated hydrocarbon having the formula $(C_6H_8)_n$ **3.** something made of this substance; specif., *a)* an eraser ☆*b)* a low-cut overshoe *c)* [Slang] a condom ☆**4.** *Baseball* an oblong piece of whitened rubber, etc. set in the pitcher's mound —*adj.* made of rubber —*vi.* ☆[Old Slang] *clipped form of* RUBBERNECK —**rub'ber·like'** *adj.*

rub·ber[2] (rub'ər) *n.* [< ?] **1.** a series of games in bridge, whist, etc., usually three, sometimes five, the majority of which must be won to win the whole series **2.** any game played to break a tie in games won: usually **rubber game**

rubber band a narrow, continuous band of rubber as for holding small objects together

rubber cement an adhesive made of unvulcanized rubber in a solvent that quickly evaporates when exposed to air

☆**rubber check** [from the notion that it "bounces": see BOUNCE (*vi.* 3)] [Slang] a check that is worthless because of insufficient funds in the drawer's account

rub·ber·ize (-īz') *vt.* **-ized', -iz'ing** to coat or impregnate with rubber or some rubber solution

☆**rub·ber·neck** (-nek') *n.* [Old Slang] a person who stretches his neck or turns his head to gaze about in curiosity, as a sightseer —*vi.* [Old Slang] to look at things or gaze about in this way

rubber plant 1. any plant yielding a milky sap (*latex*) from which crude rubber is formed **2.** an Asian tree (*Ficus elastica*) of the mulberry family, with large, glossy, leathery leaves: often used as an ornamental house plant

rub·ber-stamp (rub'ər stamp') *vt.* **1.** to put the impression of a rubber stamp on ☆**2.** [Colloq.] to approve or endorse in a routine manner, without thought —☆*adj.* routinely approved or approving

rubber stamp 1. a stamp made of rubber, pressed on an inking pad and used for printing signatures, dates, etc. ☆**2.** [Colloq.] *a)* a person, bureau, legislature, etc. that approves or endorses something in a routine manner, without thought *b)* any routine approval

rub·ber·y (rub'ər ē) *adj.* like rubber in appearance, elasticity, toughness, etc. —**rub'ber·i·ness** *n.*

rub·bing (rub′iŋ) *n.* an impression of a design, picture, etc. taken from a raised or incised surface by placing a paper over it and rubbing with graphite, wax, etc.

rub·bish (rub′ish) *n.* [ME. *robous, robys;* ult. < base of RUB] **1.** any material rejected or thrown away as worthless; trash; refuse **2.** worthless, foolish ideas, statements, etc.; nonsense —**rub′bish·y** *adj.*

rub·ble (rub′'l) *n.* [ME. *robel,* akin to RUBBISH, RUB] **1.** rough, irregular, loose fragments of rock, broken from larger bodies either by natural processes or artificially, as by blasting **2.** masonry made of rough, broken, or waterworn fragments of stone, brick, etc.; rubblework **3.** debris from buildings, etc., resulting from earthquake, bombing, etc. —**rub·bly** (rub′lē) *adj.* **-bli·er, -bli·est**

rub·ble·work (-wʉrk′) *n.* masonry made of rubble or roughly dressed, irregular stones

rub·down (rub′doun′) *n.* a brisk rubbing of the body, as in massage

☆**rube** (rōōb) *n.* [< *Rube,* nickname of REUBEN] [Slang] a person from a rural region who lacks polish and sophistication; rustic

ru·be·fa·cient (rōō′bə fā′shənt) *adj.* [L. *rubefaciens,* prp. of *rubefacere,* to redden < *rubeus,* red + *facere,* to make: see RUBY & FACT] causing redness, as of the skin —*n. Med.* any external application, as a salve or plaster, causing redness of the skin

ru·be·fac·tion (-fak′shən) *n.* **1.** the act or process of making red, as with a rubefacient **2.** redness of the skin, esp. as caused by a rubefacient

☆**Rube Gold·berg** (rōōb′ gōld′bərg) [< *Rube* (Reuben Lucius) *Goldberg* (1883–1970), U.S. cartoonist of comically involved contrivances] designating any very complicated invention, machine, scheme, etc. laboriously contrived to perform a seemingly simple operation

ru·bel·la (rōō bel′ə) *n.* [ModL., neut. pl. of L. *rubellus,* reddish < *ruber,* RED] a mild, infectious, communicable virus disease, characterized by swollen glands, esp. of the back of the head and neck, and small red spots on the skin; German measles

ru·bel·lite (-īt) *n.* [< L. *rubellus* (see prec.) + -ITE[1]] a red variety of tourmaline, used as a gem

Ru·bens (rōō′bənz; *Fl.* rü′bəns), **Peter Paul** 1577–1640; Fl. painter

ru·be·o·la (rōō bē′ə lə, rōō′bē ō′lə) *n.* [ModL., neut. pl. dim. of L. *rubeus,* red: see RUBY] *same as* MEASLES (sense 1 *a*)

ru·bes·cent (rōō bes′'nt) *adj.* [L. *rubescens,* prp. of *rubescere,* to grow red < *rubere,* to redden < *ruber,* RED] becoming red; specif., blushing or flushing —**ru·bes′cence** *n.*

Ru·bi·con (rōō′bi kän′) [L. *Rubico* (gen. *Rubiconis*)] small river in N Italy that formed the boundary between Cisalpine Gaul & the Roman Republic: when Caesar crossed it (49 B.C.) at the head of his army to march on Rome, he began the civil war with Pompey —**cross the Rubicon** to commit oneself to a definite act or decision; take a final, irrevocable step

ru·bi·cund (rōō′bi kund′) *adj.* [Fr. *rubicond* < L. *rubicundus* < *ruber,* RED] reddish; ruddy —*SYN.* see ROSY —**ru′bi·cun′di·ty** (-kun′də tē) *n.*

ru·bid·i·um (rōō bid′ē əm) *n.* [ModL. < L. *rubidus,* red < *ruber,* RED[1] (from the red lines in its spectrum)] a soft, silvery-white metallic chemical element, resembling potassium: it ignites spontaneously in air, reacts violently in water, and is used in photocells and in filaments of vacuum tubes: symbol, Rb; at. wt., 85.47; at. no., 37; sp. gr., 1.532; melt. pt., 38.5°C; boil. pt., 700°C

ru·bied (rōō′bēd) *adj.* colored like a ruby; deep-red

ru·big·i·nous (rōō bij′ə nəs) *adj.* [LL. *rubiginosus* < L. *rubigo,* rust, akin to *rubeus,* red: see RUBY] rust-colored; reddish-brown: also **ru·big′i·nose′** (-nōs′)

Ru·bin·stein (rōō′bin stīn′; *Russ.* rōō bin shtīn′) **1. An·ton** (**Grigorevich**) (än tôn′), 1829–94; Russ. pianist & composer **2. Ar·tur** (är′toor), 1889?– ; U.S. pianist, born in Poland

ru·bi·ous (rōō′bē əs) *adj.* [Poet.] ruby colored; red

ru·ble (rōō′b'l) *n.* [Russ. *rubl′*] the monetary unit of the Soviet Union: see MONETARY UNITS, table

ru·bric (rōō′brik) *n.* [ME. *rubryke* < MFr. *rubriche* < L. *rubrica,* red ocher, hence title (esp. of a law) written in red, rubric < *ruber,* RED[1]] **1.** in early books and manuscripts, a chapter heading, initial letter, specific sentence, etc. printed or written in red, decorative lettering, etc. **2.** any heading, title, etc., as of a chapter or section **3.** a direction in a prayer book, etc. for conducting religious services **4.** an explanatory comment, or gloss **5.** the title or a heading of a law **6.** an established custom or rule of procedure —*adj.* **1.** inscribed in red **2.** [Archaic] red or reddish

ru·bri·cal (-'l) *adj.* of, prescribed by, or according to rubrics, esp. liturgical rubrics —**ru′bri·cal·ly** *adv.*

ru·bri·cate (rōō′bri kāt′) *vt.* **-cat′ed, -cat′ing** [< L. *rubricatus,* pp. of *rubricare,* to redden < *rubrica:* see RUBRIC] **1.** to mark, color, or illuminate (a book, etc.) with red; write or print in red letters **2.** to provide with, or regulate by rubrics —**ru′bri·ca′tion** *n.* —**ru′bri·ca′tor** (-kāt′ər) *n.*

ru·bri·cian (rōō brish′ən) *n.* an expert in or adherent of liturgical rubrics

Ru·by (rōō′bē) [see ff.] a feminine name

ru·by (rōō′bē) *n., pl.* **-bies** [ME. < OFr. *rubi,* ult. < L. *rubeus,* reddish, akin to *ruber,* RED[1]] **1.** a clear, deep-red variety of corundum, valued as a precious stone **2.** something made of this stone, as a watch bearing **3.** *a)* deep red *b)* something having this color, as a red wine **4.** [Brit.] *Printing* a size of type, 5-1/2 point, corresponding to agate —*adj.* deep-red

☆**ru·by-throat·ed hummingbird** (-thrōt′id) a common N. American hummingbird (*Archilochus colubris*), the male of which has a metallic green back and a red throat

ruche (rōōsh) *n.* [Fr., lit., beehive < OFr. *rusche* < Celt., as in Gaul. *rusca,* bark (used for making beehives)] a fluting or pleating of lace, ribbon, muslin, net, etc. for trimming dresses, esp. at the wrist and neck

ruch·ing (rōō′shiŋ) *n.* **1.** ruches collectively; trimming made of ruches **2.** material used to make ruches

ruck[1] (ruk) *n.* [ME. *ruke,* a heap < ON. *hroki,* a heap, pile, akin to *hruga:* see RICK[1]] **1.** orig., a heap or stack, as of fuel **2.** a large quantity, mass, or crowd **3.** the horses left behind by the leaders in a race **4.** the multitude or mass of undistinguished, ordinary people or things; common run

ruck[2] (ruk) *n., vt., vi.* [prob. via dial. < ON. *hrukka*] crease, fold, wrinkle, or pucker

ruck·le (-'l) *vt., vi.* **ruck′led, ruck′ling** *Brit. var.* of RUCK[2]

ruck·sack (ruk′sak′, rook′-) *n.* [G. < dial. form of RUCK, the back (see RIDGE) + *sack,* a SACK[1]] a kind of knapsack strapped over the shoulders

☆**ruck·us** (ruk′əs) *n.* [prob. a merging of ff. & RUMPUS] [Colloq.] noisy confusion; uproar; row; disturbance

ruc·tion (ruk′shən) *n.* [altered < INSURRECTION, orig. with reference to the Irish Insurrection of 1798] [Colloq.] a riotous outbreak or uproar; noisy disturbance or quarrel

☆**rud·beck·i·a** (rud bek′ē ə) *n.* [ModL., after Olof *Rudbeck* (1630–1702), Swed. botanist] any of a genus (*Rudbeckia*) of perennial N. American plants of the composite family, with conical disks and showy yellow, orange, or maroon ray flowers, including some of the coneflowers, the black-eyed Susan, etc.

rudd (rud) *n.* [akin to ME. *rude* < OE. *rudu,* red: for base see RED[1]] a European freshwater fish (*Scardinius erythrophthalmus*) of the carp family, now introduced in the U.S.

rud·der (rud′ər) *n.* [ME. *rother* < OE., akin to G. *ruder:* see ROW[2]] **1.** a broad, flat, movable piece of wood or metal hinged vertically at the stern of a boat or ship, used for steering **2.** a movable piece like this on an aircraft, etc., used for controlling direction to the left or right **3.** something serving to guide, direct, or control —**rud′der·less** *adj.*

RUDDER

rud·der·post (-pōst′) *n.* **1.** the sternpost, or in some ships an added sternpost, to which the rudder is fastened **2.** *same as* RUDDERSTOCK

rud·der·stock (-stäk′) *n.* the part of a ship's rudder by which it is pivoted to the sternpost or rudderpost

rud·dle (rud′'l) *n.* [< *rud,* red ocher + ME. *rude:* see RUDD] *same as* RED OCHER —*vt.* **-dled, -dling** **1.** to color or mark with red ocher, esp. to mark (sheep) thus **2.** to cause to flush; redden

rud·dle·man (-mən) *n., pl.* **-men** (-mən) a person who sells ruddle

rud·dock (rud′ək) *n.* [ME. *ruddok* < OE. *rudduc* < *rudu,* red (see RUDD) + -*uc,* -OCK] [Brit. Dial.] *same as* ROBIN (sense 2)

rud·dy (rud′ē) *adj.* **-di·er, -di·est** [ME. *rudi* < OE. *rudig* < *rudu,* red: for base see RED[1]] **1.** having a healthy red color [a *ruddy* complexion] **2.** red or reddish **3.** *Brit. slang* euphemism for BLOODY (sense 6): also used adverbially —*SYN.* see ROSY —**rud′di·ness** *n.*

☆**ruddy duck** a small, N. American duck (*Oxyura jamaicensis*) the adult male of which has a brownish-red neck and upper body, black crown, white cheeks, and blue bill

rude (rōōd) *adj.* **rud′er, rud′est** [ME. < OFr. < L. *rudis,* akin to *rudus,* debris, rubble < IE. *reud-,* to tear apart < base *reu-,* to tear out, dig up, whence RUG, ROTTEN] **1.** crude or rough in form or workmanship [a *rude* hut] **2.** barbarous or ignorant [*rude* savages] **3.** lacking refinement, culture, or elegance; uncouth, boorish, coarse, vulgar, etc. **4.** discourteous; unmannerly [a *rude* reply] **5.** rough, violent, or harsh [a *rude* awakening] **6.** harsh in sound; discordant; not musical [*rude* tones] **7.** having or showing little skill or development; primitive [*rude* drawings] **8.** not carefully worked out or finished; not precise [a *rude* appraisal] **9.** sturdy; robust; rugged [*rude* health] —**rude′ly** *adv.* —**rude′ness** *n.*

SYN.—**rude,** in this comparison, implies a deliberate lack of consideration for others' feelings and connotes, especially, insolence, impudence, etc. [it was *rude* of you to ignore your uncle]; **ill-mannered** connotes ignorance of the amenities of social behavior rather than deliberate rudeness [a well-meaning but *ill-*

mannered fellow/; **boorish** is applied to one who is rude or ill-mannered in a coarse, loud or overbearing way; **impolite** implies merely a failure to observe the forms of polite society /it would be *impolite* to leave so early/; **discourteous** suggests a lack of dignified consideration for others /a *discourteous* reply/; **uncivil** implies a disregarding of even the most elementary of good manners /her *uncivil* treatment of the waiter/ —ANT. polite, civil

ru·der·al (rōō′də rəl) *n.* [< ModL. *ruderalis*, growing in rubble < L. *rudus* (gen. *ruderis*), rubbish < *-alis*, -AL] any weedy plant growing in waste places or in rubbish, along the wayside, etc. —*adj.* weedy

rudes·by (rōōdz′bē) *n., pl.* **-bies** [orig. prob. jocular alteration (after RUDE) of personal name *Grimsby*] [Archaic] an ill-mannered, rough fellow

ru·di·ment (rōō′də mənt) *n.* [L. *rudimentum* < *rudis*: see RUDE] **1.** a first principle, element, or fundamental, as of a subject to be learned: *usually used in pl.* /the rudiments of physics/ **2.** a first slight beginning or appearance, or undeveloped form or stage, of something: *usually used in pl.* **3.** *Biol.* an incompletely developed organ or part; specif., a vestigial organ or part with no functional activity; vestige

ru·di·men·ta·ry (rōō′də men′tər ē, -men′trē) *adj.* of, or having the nature of, a rudiment or rudiments; specif., *a)* elementary *b)* incompletely or imperfectly developed *c)* vestigial Also **ru′di·men′tal** —**ru′di·men′ta·ri·ly** *adv.* —**ru′di·men′ta·ri·ness** *n.*

Ru·dolf (rōō′dälf) **Lake** lake in NW Kenya, on the border of Ethiopia: c. 3,500 sq. mi.; c. 185 mi. long

Ru·dolf I (rōō′dälf, -dôlf) 1218–91; Ger. king & emperor of the Holy Roman Empire (1273–91): founder of the Hapsburg dynasty: also called **Rudolf I of Hapsburg**

Ru·dolph (rōō′dälf, -dôlf) [G. *Rudolf* < OHG. *Rudolf*, *Hrodulf* < *hruod-*, fame + *wolf*, a WOLF] a masculine name: dim. **Rudy;** var. *Rodolph, Rolf, Rollo;* equiv. Fr. *Rodolphe*, Ger. *Rudolf*, It. & Sp. *Rodolfo*

rue¹ (rōō) *vt.* **rued, ru′ing** [ME. *reowen* < OE. *hreowan*, akin to G. *reuen*, to regret, ON. *hryggr*, sorrowful, prob. < IE. base **kreu-*, to strike, beat, whence Gr. *krouein*] **1.** to feel remorse or repentance for (a sin, fault, etc.) **2.** to wish (an act, promise, etc.) undone or unmade; regret —*vi.* to be sorrowful or regretful —*n.* [Archaic] sorrow, repentance, or regret

rue² (rōō) *n.* [ME. < OFr. < L. *ruta* < Gr. *rhytē*] any of a genus (*Ruta*) of strong-scented plants of the rue family, esp. a species (*Ruta graveolens*) with yellow flowers and bitter-tasting leaves formerly used in medicine —*adj.* designating a family (Rutaceae) of woody plants including citrus, gas plant, and rue

☆**rue anemone** a small, N. American, woodland perennial plant (*Anemonella thalictroides*) of the buttercup family, with white or pinkish flowers in early spring

rue·ful (rōō′fəl) *adj.* **1.** causing sorrow or pity; lamentable **2.** *a)* feeling or showing sorrow or pity; mournful *b)* feeling or showing regret, esp. in an abashed way —**rue′ful·ly** *adv.* —**rue′ful·ness** *n.*

ru·fes·cent (rōō fes′'nt) *adj.* [L. *rufescens*, prp. of *rufescere*, to become red < *rufus*, RED¹] having a red tinge; reddish —**ru·fes′cence** *n.*

ruff¹ (ruf) *n.* [contr. of RUFFLE¹, *n.*] **1.** a high, frilled or pleated collar of starched muslin, lace, etc., worn by men and women in the 16th and 17th cents. **2.** a band of distinctively colored or protruding feathers or fur about the neck of an animal or bird **3.** a Eurasian sandpiper (*Philomachus pugnax*), the male of which grows a large ruff during the breeding season: the female is called a *reeve* —**ruffed** (ruft) *adj.*

RUFF

ruff² (ruf) *n.* [OFr. *roffle*, altered < ? *triomphe*: see TRUMP¹] **1.** an earlier card game somewhat like whist **2.** [< the *v.*] *Card Games* the act of trumping —*vt., vi. Card Games* to trump

ruff³ (ruf) *n.* [ME. *ruffe* < ? *rugh*, ROUGH: cf. ROACH²] **1.** a small, spotted European freshwater fish (*Acerina cernua*) of the perch family: also **ruffe 2.** an Atlantic butterfish, the **black ruff** (*Centrolophus niger*)

☆**ruffed grouse** a N. American game bird (*Bonasa umbellus*) with neck feathers that can be extended into a ruff: also called *partridge* in the N U.S. and *pheasant* in the S U.S.

ruf·fi·an (ruf′ē ən, ruf′yən) *n.* [Fr. *rufian* < It. *ruffiano*, a pander < It. dial. *roffia*, filth < Gmc. **hruf-*, scurf (akin to OHG. *ruf*, OE. *hreof*) < IE. base **kreup-*, whence Lith. *kraupùs*, rough: Eng. sense infl. by ROUGH] a brutal, violent, lawless person; tough or hoodlum —*adj.* brutal, violent, and lawless: also **ruf′fi·an·ly** —**ruf′fi·an·ism** *n.*

ruf·fle¹ (ruf′'l) *vt.* **-fled, -fling** [ME. *ruffelen* < ON. or MLowG., as in LowG. *ruffelen*, ON. *hrufla*, to scratch] **1.** to take away the smoothness of; wrinkle; ripple /wind *ruffling* the water/ **2.** to gather into ruffles **3.** to put

RUFFED GROUSE
(wingspread to 25 in.)

ruffles on as trimming **4.** to make (feathers, etc.) stand up in or as in a ruff, as a bird when frightened **5.** to disturb, irritate, or annoy /*ruffled* by his questions/ **6.** *a)* to turn over (the pages of a book, etc.) rapidly *b)* to shuffle (playing cards) —*vi.* **1.** to become uneven, wrinkled, etc. **2.** to become disturbed, irritated, etc. —*n.* **1.** a strip of cloth, lace, etc. gathered in pleats and puckers and used for trimming **2.** something like this, as a bird's ruff **3.** a disturbance; irritation **4.** a break in surface smoothness; ripple —**ruf′fly** (-lē) *adj.* **-fli·er, -fli·est**

ruf·fle² (ruf′'l) *n.* [also earlier *ruff*, prob. echoic] a low, continuous beating of a drum, not so loud as a roll —*vi.*, *vt.* **-fled, -fling** to beat (a drum, etc.) with a ruffle

ruf·fle³ (ruf′'l) *vi.* **-fled, -fling** [ME. *ruffelen* < ?] [Archaic] to swagger or bluster noisily —*n.* [Now Rare] a noisy disturbance; brawl

ru·fous (rōō′fəs) *adj.* [L. *rufus*, reddish, RED¹] brownish-red; rust-colored

Ru·fus (rōō′fəs) [L., red-haired, RED¹] a masculine name

rug (rug) *n.* [< Scand., as in Norw. dial. *rugga*, coarse coverlet, Sw. *rugg*, shaggy hair, ON. *rogg*, long hair < IE. base **reu-*, to tear out, dig up: cf. RUPTURE, ROTTEN] **1.** a piece of thick, often napped fabric, woven strips of rag, an animal skin, etc. used as a floor covering: usually distinguished from CARPET in being a single piece of definite shape, not intended to cover the entire floor **2.** *chiefly Brit.* term for LAP ROBE ☆**3.** [Slang] a toupee

ru·ga (rōō′gə) *n., pl.* **-gae** (-jē) [ModL. < L., a wrinkle < ? IE. base **reu-*, to tear up, whence RUG] *Biol., Anat.*, etc. a wrinkle, fold, or ridge, as in the lining of the stomach, vagina, palate, etc.: *usually used in pl.* —**ru′gate** (-gāt, -git) *adj.*

Rug·by (rug′bē) **1.** city in Warwickshire, C England: pop. 54,000 **2.** famous school for boys located there: founded 1567 —*n.* a kind of football, a forerunner of the American game, first played at Rugby school: each team consists of 15 players, action is continuous, and the oval ball may be passed, dribbled with the feet, or carried: in full **Rugby football**

rug·ged (rug′id) *adj.* [ME., rough, shaggy, prob. < Scand., as in Sw. *rugga*, to roughen: for base see RUG] **1.** having irregular projections and depressions; uneven in surface or contour; rough; wrinkled /*rugged* ground, a *rugged* coast/ **2.** strong, irregular, and wrinkled: said of the face or facial features **3.** stormy; tempestuous /*rugged* weather/ **4.** sounding harsh /*rugged* tones/ **5.** severe; harsh; hard; stern /a *rugged* life/ **6.** not polished, cultivated, refined, or elegant; rude /*rugged* manners/ ☆**7.** strong; robust; sturdy; vigorous **8.** [Colloq.] requiring great skill, strength, endurance, etc. /a *rugged* test/ —SYN. see ROUGH —**rug′ged·ly** *adv.* —**rug′ged·ness** *n.*

rug·ger (rug′ər) *n. Brit. slang var.* of RUGBY (football)

☆**ru·go·sa rose** (rōō gō′sə) [< ModL. *Rosa rugosa*, lit., wrinkled rose < L. *rosa*, ROSE¹ + *rugosus*, wrinkled < *ruga*, a wrinkle] an upright, hardy species (*Rosa rugosa*) of rose, having very prickly stems and rough leaves with furrowed veins, often planted for hedges

ru·gose (rōō′gōs, rōō gōs′) *adj.* [L. *rugosus* < *ruga*: see RUGA] *Biol.* having or full of wrinkles; corrugated; ridged /a *rugose* leaf/: also **ru′gous** (-gəs) —**ru·gos·i·ty** (rōō gäs′ə tē) *n., pl.* **-ties**

Ruhr (roor; G. rōōr) **1.** river in C West Germany, flowing west into the Rhine: 145 mi. **2.** major coal-mining & industrial region centered in the valley of this river: also called **Ruhr Basin**

ru·in (rōō′in) *n.* [ME. *ruine* < OFr. < L. *ruina* < *ruere*, to fall, hurl to the ground < IE. **ereu-* < base **er-*, to set in motion, erect, whence RUN, RISE] **1.** orig., a falling down, as of a building, wall, etc. **2.** [pl.] the remains of a fallen building, city, etc., or of something destroyed, devastated, decayed, etc. **3.** *a)* a destroyed or dilapidated building, town, etc. *b)* a person regarded as being physically, mentally, or morally a wreck of what he was **4.** the state of being destroyed, decayed, dilapidated, etc. **5.** downfall, destruction, devastation, etc.; specif., *a)* complete loss of means, solvency, position, etc. *b)* moral downfall *c)* loss of chastity in a woman **6.** any cause of a person's downfall, destruction, etc. /gambling was his *ruin*/ —*vt.* to bring or reduce to ruin; specif., *a)* to destroy, spoil, or damage irreparably *b)* to impoverish or make bankrupt *c)* to deprive (a woman) of chastity —*vi.* to go or come to ruin —**ru′in·er** *n.* SYN.—**ruin** implies a state of decay, disintegration, etc. brought about through such natural processes as age and weather /the barn is in a state of *ruin*/; **destruction** implies annihilation or demolition, as by fire, explosion, flood, etc. /the *destruction* of the village in an air raid/; **havoc** suggests total destruction or devastation, as following an earthquake or hurricane; **dilapidation** implies a state of ruin or shabbiness resulting from neglect /the *dilapidation* of a deserted house/

RUHR BASIN

ru·in·ate (rōō′ə nāt′) *vt.*, *vi.* -at′ed, -at′ing [< ML. *ruinatus*, pp. of *ruinare*, to ruin < L. *ruina*: see RUIN] [Archaic] to ruin —*adj.* [Archaic] ruined

ru·in·a·tion (rōō′ə nā′shən) *n.* [< prec. + -ION] 1. a ruining or being ruined 2. anything that ruins or causes ruin

ru·in·ous (rōō′ə nəs) *adj.* [ME. *ruinouse* < L. *ruinosus*] 1. falling or fallen into ruin; dilapidated; decayed 2. bringing or tending to bring ruin; very destructive or harmful; disastrous [*ruinous* floods] —**ru′in·ous·ly** *adv.* —**ru′in·ous·ness** *n.*

Ruis·dael (rois′däl; *Du.* rōs′däl), **Jacob van** 1628?–82; Du. landscape painter: also sp. **Ruïsdael, Ruysdael**

rule (rōōl) *n.* [ME. *reule* < OFr. *rieule* < L. *regula*, ruler, straightedge < *regere*, to lead straight, rule: for IE. base see REGAL] 1. *a*) an authoritative regulation for action, conduct, method, procedure, arrangement, etc. [*the rules* of the school] *b*) an established practice that serves as a guide to usage [*the rules* of grammar] 2. a complete set or code of regulations in a religious order [*the Benedictine rule*] 3. a fixed principle that determines conduct; habit; custom [*to make it a* rule *never to hurry*] 4. something that usually or normally happens or obtains; customary course of events [*famine is the* rule *following war*] 5. *a*) government; reign; control *b*) the period of reigning of a particular ruler or government 6. a ruler or straightedge 7. [Obs.] way of acting; behavior 8. *Law a*) a regulation or guide established by a court governing court practice and procedure *b*) a declaration, order, etc. made by a judge or court in deciding a specific question or point of law *c*) a legal principle or maxim 9. *Math.* a method or procedure prescribed for computing or solving a problem 10. *Printing a*) a thin strip of metal, the height of type, used to print straight or decorative lines, borders, etc. *b*) a line so printed —*vt.* **ruled, rul′ing** 1. to have an influence over; guide [*to be ruled by one's friends*] 2. to lessen; restrain [*reason ruled his fear*] 3. to have authority over; govern; direct [*to rule a country*] 4. to be the most important element of; dominate [*action rules the plot*] 5. to settle by decree; determine [*the court ruled the* validity *of the point*] 6. *a*) to mark lines on with or as with a ruler *b*) to mark (a line) thus —*vi.* 1. to have supreme authority; govern 2. to be at a specified rate or level; prevail: said of prices, commodities, etc. 3. to issue a formal decree about a question —*SYN.* see GOVERN, LAW —**as a rule** usually; ordinarily —**rule out** to exclude by decision

ruled surface *Geom.* a surface that is the locus of all points on a moving straight line, as a plane, cone, etc.

rule of three *Math.* the method of finding the fourth term of a proportion when three terms are given: the product of the first and last terms is equal to the product of the second and third

rule of thumb [from the method of measuring by the thumb] 1. a rule based on experience or practice rather than on scientific knowledge 2. any method of estimating that is practical though not precise

rul·er (rōō′lər) *n.* 1. a person or thing that rules or governs 2. a thin strip of wood, metal, etc. with a straight edge and markings in inches or centimeters and their fractional parts, used in drawing straight lines, measuring length, etc.; straightedge 3. a person or device that rules lines on paper, etc. —**rul′er·ship′** *n.*

rul·ing (-liŋ) *adj.* that rules; specif., *a*) governing *b*) predominating *c*) prevalent —*n.* 1. the act of governing 2. an official decision, esp. one made by a court or judge 3. *a*) the making of ruled lines *b*) the lines so made

rum[1] (rum) *n.* [short for *rumbullion*, orig. a Devonshire dial. term, uproar, tumult < ?] 1. an alcoholic liquor distilled from fermented sugar cane, molasses, etc. ☆2. alcoholic liquor in general

rum[2] (rum) *adj.* [< obs. *rum*, good, great < ? *Rom*, a Gypsy: see ROMANY] [Chiefly Brit. Slang] 1. odd; strange; queer 2. bad, poor, etc. [*a* rum *joke*]

rum[3] (rum) *n.* ☆*same as* RUMMY[1]

Ru·ma·nia (rōō mān′yə, -mā′nē ə) *same as* ROMANIA —**Ru·ma′ni·an** *adj.*, *n.*

rum·ba (rum′bə, room′-; *Sp.* rōōm′bä) *n.* [AmSp., prob. of Afr. origin] 1. a dance of Cuban Negro origin and complex rhythm 2. a modern ballroom adaptation of this, with strong rhythmic movements of the lower part of the body 3. music for, or in the rhythm of, this dance —*vi.* to dance the rumba

rum·ble (rum′b'l) *vi.* -bled, -bling [ME. *romblen*, prob. < MDu. *rommelen* < Gmc. echoic base] 1. to make a deep, heavy, continuous, rolling sound, as thunder 2. to move or go with such a sound —*vt.* 1. to cause to make, or move with, such a sound 2. to utter or say with such a sound 3. to polish, mix, etc. in a rumble, or tumbling box —*n.* 1. a deep, heavy, continuous, rolling sound 2. a widespread expression of discontent or restiveness 3. a space for luggage or a small extra seat, as for servants, in the rear of a carriage 4. *same as* TUMBLING BOX ☆5. [Slang] a fight between gangs, esp. of teen-agers —**rum′bler** *n.* —**rum′bling·ly** *adv.* —**rum′bly** *adj.*

☆**rumble seat** in some earlier automobiles, an open seat in the rear, behind the roofed part, which could be folded shut when not in use

rum·bus·tious (rum bus′chəs) *adj.* [altered (? after RUM[1]) < ROBUSTIOUS] rambunctious, boisterous, unruly, etc.

Ru·me·li·a (rōō mē′lē ə, -mēl′yə) former Turk. possessions in the Balkan Peninsula, including Macedonia, Thrace, & an autonomous province (**Eastern Rumelia**) that was ceded to Bulgaria in 1885

ru·men (rōō′min) *n.*, *pl.* -mi·na (-mi nə) [ModL. < L., throat, gullet < IE. *reusmen*, rumination, throat, whence Sans. *rōmantha*] the first stomach of a ruminant

Rum·ford (rum′fərd), **Count** *see* Benjamin THOMPSON

ru·mi·nant (rōō′mə nənt) *adj.* [L. *ruminans*, prp. of L. *ruminare*, to ruminate < *rumen*, RUMEN] 1. chewing the cud 2. of the cud-chewing animals 3. meditative; thoughtful —*n.* any of a suborder (Ruminantia) of four-footed, hoofed, even-toed, and cud-chewing mammals, as the cattle, buffalo, goat, deer, camel, antelope, giraffe, etc., having a stomach with four chambers (the *rumen, reticulum, omasum,* and *abomasum*) —**ru′mi·nant·ly** *adv.*

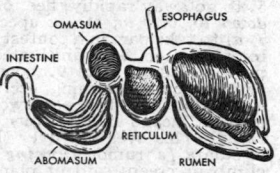
STOMACH OF A RUMINANT

ru·mi·nate (-nāt′) *vt.*, *vi.* -nat′ed, -nat′ing [< L. *ruminatus*, pp. of *ruminare*: see prec.] 1. to chew (the cud), as a cow does 2. to turn (something) over in the mind; meditate (on) —*SYN.* see PONDER —**ru′mi·na′tion** *n.* —**ru′mi·na′tive** *adj.* —**ru′mi·na′tive·ly** *adv.* —**ru′mi·na′tor** *n.*

rum·mage (rum′ij) *n.* [aphetic < MFr. *arrumage* < *arrumere*, to stow cargo in the hold < *aruner*, to arrange < *run, rum,* ship's hold < Frank. *rum*, akin to OE. *rum,* ROOM] 1. miscellaneous articles; odds and ends 2. a rummaging, or thorough search —*vt.* -maged, -mag·ing 1. to search through (a place, receptacle, etc.) diligently and thoroughly, esp. by moving the contents about, turning them over, etc.; ransack 2. to get, find, or turn up by or as by searching thoroughly (with *up* or *out*) —*vi.* to search diligently, now sometimes haphazardly, as through the contents of a receptacle —**rum′mag·er** *n.*

rummage sale a sale of contributed miscellaneous articles, used or new, to raise money for charitable purposes or for some organization

rum·mer (rum′ər) *n.* [Du. *roemer* < *roemen*, to praise: hence, orig., a glass used for drinking toasts in praise of someone] a large drinking glass or cup

rum·my[1] (rum′ē) *adj.* -mi·er, -mi·est [RUM[2] + -Y[2]] [Chiefly Brit. Colloq.] odd; strange; queer —☆*n.* [? < the *adj.*] a card game, played in many variations, in which the object is to match cards into sets of the same denomination or sequences of the same suit

rum·my[2] (rum′ē) *n.*, *pl.* -mies [RUM[1] + -Y[2]] ☆[Slang] a drunkard —*adj.* -mi·er, -mi·est of or like rum

ru·mor (rōō′mər) *n.* [ME. *rumour* < OFr. < L. *rumor*, noise < IE. echoic base *reu-*, to roar, grumble, whence RUNE, OE. *reotan*, to complain] 1. general talk not based on definite knowledge; mere gossip; hearsay 2. an unconfirmed report, story, or statement in general circulation 3. [Archaic] fame 4. [Obs.] loud protest, clamor, or uproar —*vt.* to tell, report, or spread by rumor or as a rumor Also, Brit. sp., **ru′mour**

ru·mor·mon·ger (-muŋ′gər, -mäŋ′-) *n.* a person who spreads rumors

rump (rump) *n.* [ME. *rumpe* < ON. *rumpr*, akin to G. *rumpf*, trunk (of the body) < IE. base *remb-*, *romb-*, to chop, notch, whence Czech *roubiti*, to chop] 1. the hind part of the body of an animal, where the legs and back join, or the sacral part of a bird 2. a cut of meat, usually beef, from this part, behind the loin and above the round: see BEEF, illus. 3. the buttocks 4. the last, unimportant or inferior part; mere remnant 5. a legislature, etc. having only a remnant of its former membership, as because of expulsions, and hence regarded as unrepresentative and without authority

Rum·pel·stilts·kin (rum′p'l stilt′skin) *German Folklore* a dwarf who agrees to spin flax into gold to save the life of a king's bride if she will give him her first child, unless she can guess his name, but she does

rum·ple (rum′p'l) *n.* [MDu. *rompel* < *rompe*, a wrinkle, akin to OE. *hrympel*, a wrinkle < IE. *kremb-*, to twist, shrink, wrinkle < base *(s)ker-*, to turn: cf. SHRIMP] an uneven fold or crease; wrinkle —*vt.*, *vi.* -pled, -pling 1. to make rumples (in); crumple 2. to make or become disheveled or tousled —**rum′ply** *adv.*

Rump Parliament 1. the part of the Long Parliament remaining after the purge of 1648 until disbanded by Cromwell in 1653 2. the same body recalled in 1659 and disbanded in 1660

rum·pus (rum′pəs) *n.* [< ?] [Colloq.] noisy or violent disturbance; uproar

☆**rumpus room** *earlier term for* RECREATION ROOM

☆**rum·run·ner** (rum′run′ər) *n.* a person, ship, etc. engaged in smuggling alcoholic liquor —**rum′run′ning** *n.*

run (run) *vi.* **ran** or dial. **run, run, run′ning** [altered (with vowel prob. infl. by pp.) < ME. *rinnen, rennen* < ON. & OE.: ON. *rinna,* to flow, run, *renna,* to cause to run (< Gmc. **rannjan*); OE. *rinnan, iornan:* both < Gmc. **renwo* < IE. base **er-,* to set in motion, excite, whence L. *origo,* ORIGIN & RAISE] **1.** to go by moving the legs rapidly, faster than in walking, and (in a two-legged animal) in such a way that for an instant both feet are off the ground **2.** *a)* to go rapidly; move swiftly [a ship *running* before the wind] *b)* to resort (*to*) for aid [always *running* to the police] **3.** to associate or consort (*with*) **4.** to go, move, grow, etc. easily and freely, without hindrance or restraint **5.** to go away rapidly; flee **6.** to make a quick trip (*up to, down to, over to,* etc. a specified place) for a brief stay **7.** *a)* to take part in a contest or race ☆*b)* to be a candidate in an election **8.** to finish a contest or race in the specified position [to *run* last] **9.** to swim in migration, as upstream or inshore for spawning, etc.: said of fish **10.** to go, as on a schedule; ply between two points [a bus that *runs* between Chicago and Detroit] **11.** to go or pass lightly and rapidly [his eyes *ran* over the page] **12.** to be current; circulate [a rumor *running* through the town] **13.** to climb or creep: said of plants [a vine *running* over the wall] **14.** to move continuously [his tongue *ran* on and on] **15.** to ravel lengthwise in a knitted fabric **16.** to function or operate with or as with parts that revolve, slide, etc. [a machine that is *running*] **17.** to recur or return to the mind **18.** to flow [a *running* stream] **19.** to melt and flow [the wax *ran*] **20.** *a)* to spread when put on a surface, as a liquid *b)* to spread over or be diffused through cloth, etc. when moistened, as colors *c)* to be subject to such spreading of color, as fabric **21.** to be wet or covered with a flow [eyes *running* with tears] **22.** to give passage to a fluid; specif., *a)* to discharge pus, mucus, etc. *b)* to leak, as a faucet **23.** to elapse [the days *ran* into weeks] **24.** *a)* to appear in print, as in a newspaper *b)* to appear or be presented continuously or in a continuing series [a play that *ran* for a year] **25.** *a)* to continue in effect or force [a law *running* for twenty years] *b)* to continue to occur; recur [talent *runs* in the family] **26.** to be characterized by having, producing, using, etc. (with *to*) [their taste *runs* to exotic foods] **27.** *a)* to extend in or as in a continuous line [a fence *running* through the woods] *b)* to include so as to show variety (with *from* and *to*) [a repertoire *running* from tragedy to comedy] **28.** to pass into a specified condition, situation, etc. [to *run* into trouble] **29.** to sail or float (aground, etc.): said of a ship **30.** to be written, expressed, played, etc. in a specified way [the adage *runs* like this] **31.** to be or continue at a specified size, price, amount, etc. [apples *running* four to the pound] —*vt.* **1.** to run along or follow (a specified course or route) **2.** to travel over; cover by running, driving, etc. [horses *ran* the range] **3.** to do or perform by or as by running [to *run* a race] **4.** to subject oneself to (a risk); incur ☆**5.** *a)* to get past or escape by going through [to *run* a blockade] *b)* to go past or through without making a required stop [to *run* a stop sign or a red light] **6.** to pursue or hunt (game, etc.) **7.** to compete with in or as in a race; vie with **8.** *a)* to enter (a horse, etc.) in a race ☆*b)* to put up or support as a candidate for election **9.** *a)* to make run, move, operate, etc. *b)* to cause to go between points, as on a schedule *c)* to cause (a motor or engine) to idle for a while *d)* to make (a stocking) run **10.** to bring, lead, or force into a specified condition, situation, etc. by or as by running [to *run* oneself into debt] **11.** *a)* to carry or convey, as in a ship or vehicle; transport *b)* to carry (taxable or outlawed goods) in or out illegally; smuggle **12.** to drive, force, or thrust (an object) into, through, or against (something) **13.** to make go, move, pass, flow, etc., esp. rapidly, in a specified way, direction, place, etc. [to *run* water into a glass] **14.** ☆*a)* to be in charge of; manage [to *run* a household] ☆*b)* to keep, feed, or graze (livestock) *c)* to perform the steps of (an experiment, test, etc.) *d)* to cause to undergo a test, procedure, process, etc. **15.** to cost (an amount) [boots that *run* $20] **16.** to mark, draw, or trace (lines, as on a map) **17.** to extend, pass, or trace in a specified way or direction [to *run* a story back to its source] **18.** to undergo or be affected by (a fever, etc.) **19.** to flow with, discharge, or pour forth [gutters *running* blood] **20.** to melt, fuse, or smelt (ore) **21.** to cast or mold, as from molten metal; found ☆**22.** to print; esp., to publish (an advertisement, story, etc.) in a newspaper or magazine **23.** *Billiards,* etc. to complete successfully (a specified number of strokes, shots, etc.) in uninterrupted sequence **24.** *Bridge* to lead (a suit) taking a series of tricks **25.** *Golf* to cause (a ball) to roll, esp. on a green —*n.* **1.** an act or period of running or moving rapidly **2.** *a)* a race for runners *b)* a running pace; rapid gait *c)* capacity for running **3.** the distance covered or time spent in running **4.** a trip; journey; esp., *a)* a single, customary, or regular trip, as of a train, ship, or plane *b)* a quick trip, esp. for a brief stay *c) same as* ROUTE (sense 2) **5.** *a)* movement onward, progression, or trend [the *run* of events] *b)* a continuous course or period of a specified condition, action, etc. [a *run* of good luck] **6.** direction or course, as of the grain of wood, a vein of ore, etc. **7.** a continuous course of performances,

etc. [a play that had a *run* of a year] **8.** a series of continued, sudden, or urgent requests or demands, as by customers for certain goods, or by bank depositors for payment **9.** a period of being in public demand or favor **10.** a continuous series or sequence, as of cards in one suit **11.** a continuous extent of something **12.** a flow or rush of water, etc., as of the tide **13.** a small, swift stream, as a brook, rivulet, etc. **14.** *a)* a period during which some fluid flows readily *b)* the amount of flow **15.** *a)* a period of operation of a machine *b)* the output during this period **16.** *a)* a kind, sort, or class, as of goods *b)* the ordinary, usual, or average kind or type **17.** something in, on, or along which something else runs; specif., *a)* an inclined pathway or course [a ski *run*] *b)* a track, channel, trough, pipe, etc. *c)* an enclosed area in which domestic animals or fowl can move about freely or feed [a chicken *run*] *d)* in Australia, a large grazing area or ranch *e)* a well-defined trail or path made and used by animals [a buffalo *run*] **18.** freedom to use all the facilities or move freely in any part (*of* a place) [to have the *run* of an estate] **19.** *a)* a number of animals in motion together *b)* a large number of fish migrating together, as upstream or inshore for spawning *c)* such migration of fish ☆**20.** a ravel lengthwise in something knitted, as in hosiery ☆**21.** *Baseball* a scoring point, made by a successful circuit of the bases **22.** *Billiards,* etc. an uninterrupted sequence of successful strokes, shots, etc. **23.** *Cricket* a scoring point, made by a successful running of both batsmen from one wicket to the other **24.** *Mil.* the approach to the target made by an airplane in bombing, strafing, etc. **25.** *Music* a rapid succession of tones, as a roulade **26.** *Naut.* the extreme after part of a ship's bottom, from where it starts to curve up and in toward the stern —*adj.* **1.** melted; made liquid **2.** poured or molded while in a melted state [*run* metal] **3.** drained or extracted, as honey **4.** having migrated and spawned: said of fish —**a run for one's money 1.** powerful competition **2.** some satisfaction for what one has expended, as in betting on a near winner in a race —**in the long run** in the final outcome; ultimately —**on the run 1.** running **2.** hurrying from place to place or task to task **3.** running away; in retreat —☆**run across** to encounter by chance —**run after 1.** to pursue or follow **2.** [Colloq.] to seek the company or companionship of —**run along** to leave or depart —**run away 1.** to flee **2.** to desert one's home or family **3.** to escape and run loose, as a horse —**run away with 1.** to depart and take with one; esp., to steal **2.** to carry out of control [his enthusiasm *ran away with* him] **3.** *a)* to outdo greatly all other contestants or performers in *b)* to get (a prize, honors, etc.) in this way —**run back** to carry (a football) toward the opponent's goal, as after receiving a kickoff —**run down 1.** to cease to run, or stop operating, as a mechanical device, through lack of power **2.** to run, ride, or drive against so as to knock down **3.** to pursue and capture or kill **4.** to search out the source of **5.** to speak of slightingly or injuriously; disparage **6.** to lessen or lower in worth, quality, etc.; make or become run-down **7.** to read through rapidly ☆**8.** *Baseball* to catch and tag (a base runner trapped between two bases) —**run for it** to run in order to escape or avoid something —**run in 1.** to include or insert, as something additional **2.** [Colloq.] to make a brief stop or visit at a place ☆**3.** [Slang] to take into legal custody; arrest **4.** *Printing* to make continuous without a break or paragraph —**run into 1.** to encounter by chance **2.** to run, ride, or drive against so as to hit; collide with **3.** to add up to (a large sum of money): also **run to** —**run off** ☆**1.** to print, typewrite, make copies of, etc. **2.** to cause to be run, performed, played, etc. **3.** to decide the winner of (a race, etc.) by a runoff **4.** to drive (animals, trespassers, etc.) off or away **5.** to flow off; drain **6.** *same as* RUN AWAY —**run on 1.** to continue or be continued; specif., *Printing* to continue without a break or new paragraph **2.** to add (something) at the end **3.** to talk continuously —**run out 1.** to come to an end; expire or become used up, exhausted, etc. **2.** to force to leave; drive out —**run out of** to use up a supply of (something) —**run out on** [Colloq.] to abandon or desert —☆**run out the clock** *Basketball, Football,* etc. to maintain control of the ball in the closing minutes of a game —**run over 1.** to ride or drive over as with an automobile **2.** to overflow **3.** to go beyond a limit **4.** to examine, rehearse, etc. rapidly or casually —**run scared** [Slang] to base one's actions upon the possibility or likelihood of failure —**run through 1.** to use up, spend, etc. quickly or recklessly **2.** to pierce **3.** *same as* RUN OVER (sense 4) —**run up 1.** to raise, rise, make, or build rapidly **2.** to let (bills, debts, etc.) accumulate **3.** to sew with a rapid succession of stitches

run·a·bout (run′ə bout′) *n.* **1.** a person who runs about from place to place **2.** a light, one-seated, open carriage ☆**3.** a light, one-seated, open automobile; roadster ☆**4.** a light motorboat

run·a·gate (-ə gāt′) *n.* [altered (after RUN + obs. *agate,* on the way) < ME. *renegat,* apostate, villain < OFr. *renegat* < ML. *renegatus;* see RENEGADE] [Archaic] **1.** a runaway; fugitive or deserter **2.** a person who drifts or wanders about; vagabond

run·a·round (-ə round′) *n.* ☆**1.** [Colloq.] a series of evasive excuses, deceptions, delays, etc.: usually in **get** (or **give**) **the runaround 2.** *Printing* an arrangement of

type in shorter lines than the rest of the text, as around an illustration

run·a·way (-ə wā′) *n.* **1.** a person, animal, etc. that is running away or has run away; specif., *a)* a fugitive or deserter *b)* a horse, team of horses, etc. that has broken loose from control of the rider or driver **2.** the act of running away **3.** a runaway race or victory —*adj.* **1.** running away or having run away; escaping, eloping, or breaking loose from control [*runaway* lovers, a *runaway* horse] **2.** of or done by runaways or running away [a *runaway* marriage] **3.** easily won, as a race, or decisive, as a victory **4.** *a)* rising rapidly, as prices *b)* characterized by an uncontrolled rise of prices [*runaway* inflation] ☆**5.** relocated in order to evade agreements with a local union, local taxes, etc. [a *runaway* shop]

☆**run·back** (-bak′) *n. Football* the act of running back with the ball, as after receiving the kickoff or intercepting a forward pass

run·ci·ble spoon (run′sə b'l) [coined by E. LEAR < ? ff. + -IBLE] a table utensil of indefinite form referred to by Edward Lear in his humorous poem "The Owl and the Pussycat" (1871): later applied to any of various utensils with broad tines in a spoonlike shape

run·ci·nate (run′si nit, -nāt′) *adj.* [L. *runcinatus,* pp. of *runcinare,* to plane off < *runcina,* a plane (formerly understood as "saw")] *Bot.* irregularly saw-toothed, with the teeth or lobes curved backward, as some leaves: see LEAF, illus.

Run·di (rōōn′dē) *n.* **1.** *pl.* **-dis, -di** any member of a Bantu people living in Burundi **2.** their Bantu language, used as one of the two trade languages in Burundi and Rwanda

run·dle (run′d'l) *n.* [ME. *rundel:* see ROUNDEL] **1.** a rung, or round, as of a ladder **2.** any of the bars in a lantern pinion **3.** something that rotates, as a wheel or the drum of a capstan

rund·let (rund′lit) *n.* [ME. *roundelet* < MFr. *rondelet,* dim. of *rondelle,* little tun or barrel, round shield, dim. of *rond,* ROUND¹] [Archaic] **1.** a small barrel or cask for liquor **2.** the capacity of such a cask, usually taken as equal to about 18 wine gallons

run-down (run′doun′) *adj.* **1.** not wound and therefore not running, as a spring-operated clock **2.** in poor physical condition, as from overwork; weak and exhausted; debilitated **3.** fallen into disrepair; dilapidated

run·down (run′doun′) *n.* **1.** a concise summary or outline ☆**2.** *Baseball* the act of running down a base runner

rune (rōōn) *n.* [ME. *roun* < OE. *run,* a secret, mystery, runic character; readopted in 17th c. in form of ON. *rún:* both < IE. echoic base *reu-,* hoarse sound, whence W. *rhin,* a secret, L. *raucus,* hoarse; in sense 3 *a* < Finn. *runo,* poem, canto < ON. *rún*] **1.** any of the characters of an alphabet (*futhark*) probably derived from a Greek script and used by the Scandinavians and other early Germanic peoples from about 300 A.D. **2.** something inscribed or written in such characters **3.** *a)* a Finnish or Old Norse poem or canto *b)* [Poet.] any poem, verse, or song, esp. one that is mystical or obscure

rung¹ (ruŋ) *n.* [ME. *rong* < OE. *hrung,* a staff, rod, pole, akin to G. *runge;* for prob. IE. base see RING²] **1.** any sturdy stick, bar, or rod, esp. a rounded one, used as a crossbar, support, etc.; specif., *a)* any of the crosspieces constituting the steps of a ladder *b)* a supporting crosspiece between the legs of a chair, or across the back, etc. **2.** a stage or degree in a scale, as of social acceptance **3.** [Scot.] a cudgel

rung² (ruŋ) *pp. & rare pt. of* RING¹

ru·nic (rōō′nik) *adj.* [ModL. *runicus* < ON. *rún,* a RUNE] **1.** of, consisting of, characterized by, or set down in runes **2.** like runes in decorative interlaced effect, as knots and other figures on monuments, etc. of ancient peoples of northern Europe **3.** mystical; obscure

run-in (run′in′) *adj. Printing* that is run in or inserted —*n.* **1.** run-in matter ☆**2.** [Colloq.] a quarrel, fight, etc.

run·let¹ (-lit) *n.* [RUN (*n.* 13) + -LET] a runnel, or rivulet

run·let² (-lit) *n. same as* RUNDLET

run·nel (-'l) *n.* [ME. *rinel, runel* < OE. *rynel* < base of *rinnan,* to RUN] **1.** a small stream; little brook or rivulet **2.** a small channel or watercourse

run·ner (run′ər) *n.* [ME. *renner*] **1.** a person, animal, or thing that runs; specif., *a)* a racer ☆*b)* *Baseball same as* BASE RUNNER ☆*c)* *Football* a player running with the ball **2.** a person who runs errands, carries messages, etc., as for a bank or brokerage house **3.** *a)* a smuggler *b)* a ship used in smuggling or in blockade running **4.** a person who operates or manages something, as a machine **5.** *a)* a long, narrow, decorative cloth for the top of a table, chest of drawers, etc. *b)* a long, narrow rug, as for a hall or corridor **6.** *a)* a long ravel, as in hose; run **7.** *a)* a long, slender, horizontal trailing

RUNNER
(wild strawberry)

stem that puts out roots along or just below the ground at its tip or its nodes, thus producing new plants; stolon *b)* any plant that spreads in this way, as the strawberry **8.** any of various twining plants [the scarlet *runner*] **9.** something on or in which something else moves, as a sliding part in machinery or the support along which a sliding door moves ☆**10.** either of the long, narrow pieces of metal or wood on which a sled or sleigh slides ☆**11.** the blade of a skate **12.** a ring, loop, etc. that can slide along a strap, rod, etc., often one to which another part or parts can be attached **13.** *Metallurgy* a channel through which molten metal is poured into a mold; gate **14.** *Zool.* any of a number of related edible fishes (family Carangidae) of warm seas, as the **blue runner** (*Caranx crysos*) and the **rainbow runner** (*Elagatis bipinnulatus*)

runner bean *chiefly Brit. var. of* POLE BEAN

run·ner-up (-up′) *n., pl.* **-ners-up′** **1.** a person or team that finishes second in a race, contest, tournament, etc. **2.** any of those finishing behind the winner but in positions of contention

run·ning (run′iŋ) *n.* [ME. *renning*] **1.** the act of a person or thing that runs (in various senses); racing, managing, proceeding, etc. **2.** the condition of a track with reference to its use in a race **3.** *a)* that which runs, or flows *b)* the amount or quantity that runs —*adj.* **1.** moving, passing, or advancing rapidly **2.** *a)* run at a rapid gait [a *running* race] *b)* trained to race at this gait: said of a horse **3.** flowing [*running* water] **4.** cursive: said of handwriting **5.** melting; becoming liquid or fluid **6.** discharging liquid; esp., discharging pus, etc. [a *running* sore] **7.** creeping or climbing: said of plants **8.** going, or in operation, as machinery **9.** in a straight line; linear: said of measurement [a *running* foot] **10.** going on, extending, etc. without interruption; continuous [a *running* commentary, a *running* pattern] **11.** prevalent [*running* costs] **12.** in progress; current [a *running* account] **13.** concurrent; simultaneous [a *running* translation] **14.** moving or going easily or smoothly **15.** slipping or sliding easily [a *running* knot] **16.** moving when pulled, as a rope [*running* rigging] **17.** done in a run or with a running start [a *running* jump] **18.** of the normal run (of a train, bus, etc.) [*running* time] —*adv.* in succession; consecutively [for five days *running*] —**in** (or **out of**) **the running** in (or out of) the competition; having a (or no) chance to win

☆**running board** esp. formerly, a footboard, or step, along the lower part of the side of an automobile

running bowline a kind of knot: see KNOT, illus.

running fire 1. a rapid succession of shots, as from soldiers in ranks **2.** a rapid succession, as of remarks, questions, etc.

☆**running gear** the wheels, axles, springs, and frame of a motor vehicle

running hand handwriting in which the letters are slanted and close together, formed without often lifting the pen or pencil from the paper

running head (or **title**) a descriptive heading or title printed at the top of every page or, sometimes, every other page, usually the left-hand ones

running knot *same as* SLIPKNOT

running lights the lights that a ship or aircraft traveling at night is required to display

☆**running mate 1.** a horse used in a race to set the pace for another horse from the same stable **2.** a candidate for the lesser of two closely associated offices, as for the vice-presidency, in his relationship to the candidate for the greater office

run·ny (run′ē) *adj.* **-ni·er, -ni·est** **1.** that flows, esp. too freely **2.** that keeps on discharging mucus [a *runny* nose] —**run′ni·ness** *n.*

Run·ny·mede (run′ē mēd′) meadow on the S bank of the Thames, southwest of London: see MAGNA CHARTA

run·off (run′ôf′) *n.* ☆**1.** something that runs off, as rain in excess of the amount absorbed by the ground **2.** a deciding, final race, election, etc., as in case of a tie

run-of-the-mill (run′əv thə mil′) *adj.* [see RUN, *n.,* 16 *b*] not selected or special; ordinary; average

☆**run-of-the-mine** (-mīn′) *adj.* **1.** not graded according to size or quality: said of coal **2.** not selected or special; ordinary; average Also **run′-of-mine′**

run-on (-än′) *adj.* **1.** *Printing* that is run on **2.** *Prosody* having the sense completed in the succeeding line of verse —*n.* run-on matter

run-on sentence two or more complete sentences faultily run together as one

runt (runt) *n.* [< ?] **1.** a stunted, undersized, or dwarfish animal, plant, thing, or (usually in a contemptuous sense) person **2.** the smallest animal of a litter —**runt′i·ness** *n.* —**runt′y** *adj.* **runt′i·er, runt′i·est**

run-through (run′thrōō′) *n.* a rehearsal, as of a dramatic or musical work or section, straight through from beginning to end

☆**run·way** (-wā′) *n.* a way, as a channel, track, chute, groove, trough, etc., in, on, or along which something runs, or moves; specif., *a)* the channel or bed of a stream *b)* a strip of leveled, usually paved ground, for use by airplanes in taking off and landing *c)* a track or ramp for wheeled

vehicles *d*) a beaten path made by deer or other animals *e*) a narrow extension of a stage out into the audience

Run·yon (run′yən), (Alfred) **Da·mon** (dā′mən) 1884–1946; U.S. journalist & short-story writer

ru·pee (rōō pē′, rōō′pē) *n.* [Hindi *rūpiyah* < Sans. *rūpya*, wrought silver] the monetary unit of India, Pakistan, Ceylon, etc.: see MONETARY UNITS, table

Ru·pert (rōō′pərt) [G. *Ruprecht, Rupprecht*: see ROBERT] a masculine name

ru·pes·trine (rōō pes′trin) *adj.* [< L. *rupes,* a rock (after LACUSTRINE)] *Biol.* growing on or living among rocks: also **ru·pic′o·lous** (-pik′ə ləs), **ru·pic′o·line′** (-lin′)

ru·pi·ah (rōō pē′ə) *n.* [< Hind. *rūpiyah,* RUPEE] the monetary unit of Indonesia: see MONETARY UNITS, table

rup·ture (rup′chər) *n.* [LME. *ruptur* < MFr. *rupture* < L. *ruptura* < *ruptus,* pp. of *rumpere,* to break < IE. **reup-* < base **reu-,* to tear out, tear apart, break, whence REAVE[1], RUB] **1.** the act of breaking apart or bursting, or the state of being broken apart or burst; breach **2.** a breaking off of friendly or peaceful relations, as between countries or individuals **3.** *Med.* a hernia; esp., *a*) an abdominal or inguinal hernia *b*) a forcible tearing or bursting of an organ or part, as of a blood vessel, the bladder, etc. *—vt., vi.* **-tured, -tur·ing 1.** to break apart or burst **2.** to affect with, undergo, or suffer a rupture

ru·ral (roor′əl) *adj.* [ME. < MFr. < LL. *ruralis* < L. *rus* (gen. *ruris*), the country < IE. **rewos,* space, wide, whence ROOM, Goth. *rums,* room, space] **1.** of or characteristic of the country, country life, or country people; rustic **2.** living in the country **3.** having to do with farming; agricultural *—***ru′ral·ly** *adv.*

SYN.—rural is the comprehensive, nonspecific word referring to life on the farm or in the country as distinguished from life in the city [*rural* schools]; **rustic** stresses the contrast between the supposed crudeness and unsophistication of the country and the polish and refinement of the city [*rustic* humor]; **pastoral** suggests the highly idealized primitive simplicity of rural life, originally among shepherds; **bucolic,** in contrast, suggests a down-to-earth rustic simplicity or artlessness [her *bucolic* suitor] *—ANT.* **urban**

☆**rural delivery** delivery of mail by carriers on routes in rural areas: formerly **rural free delivery**

ru·ral·ism (-iz′m) *n.* **1.** rural quality or character **2.** rural life **3.** a rural idiom, characteristic, feature, etc. Also **ru·ral·i·ty** (roo ral′ə tē), *pl.* **-ties**

ru·ral·ist (-ist) *n.* one who leads or advocates a rural life

ru·ral·ize (roor′ə līz′) *vt.* **-ized′, -iz′ing** to make rural *—vi.* to live or stay for a time in the country; rusticate *—***ru′ral·i·za′tion** *n.*

Ru·rik (roor′ik) ?–879 A.D.; Scandinavian chief regarded as the founder of the first Russian dynasty (c. 862–1598)

Rus. 1. Russia **2.** Russian

Ru·se (rōō′se) city & port in N Bulgaria, on the Danube: pop. 128,000

ruse (rōōz) *n.* [Fr. < MFr. < OFr. *reuser,* to deceive < L. *recusare,* to be reluctant, refuse: see RECUSANT] a stratagem, trick, or artifice *—SYN.* see TRICK

rush[1] (rush) *vi.* [ME. *ruschen* < Anglo-Fr. *russher* < MFr. *ruser,* to repel, avert, orig., to mislead < OFr. *reuser:* see prec.] **1.** *a*) to move or go swiftly or impetuously; dash *b*) to dash recklessly or rashly **2.** to make a swift, sudden attack or assault (*on* or *upon*); charge **3.** to pass, come, go, come into view, act, etc. swiftly, suddenly, or hastily [a thought *rushing* into the mind] ☆**4.** *Football* to advance the ball by a running play or plays *—vt.* **1.** to move, send, push, drive, etc. swiftly, violently, or hastily [we *rushed* him to the hospital] **2.** to do, make, or cause to move, go, or act, with unusual or excessive speed or haste; hurry [to *rush* an order, a person at work, etc.] **3.** *a*) to make a swift, sudden attack or assault on; charge *b*) to overcome or capture by such an attack or assault ☆**4.** [Colloq.] *a*) to lavish attentions on, as in courting *b*) to entertain with parties or the like prior to inviting to join a fraternity or sorority ☆**5.** *Football a*) to advance (the ball) by a running play or plays *b*) *same as* BLITZ *—n.* **1.** the act of rushing **2.** an eager movement of many people to get to a place, as to a region where gold has recently been found **3.** intense activity; busyness; haste; hurry [the *rush* of modern life] **4.** a sudden, swift attack or assault; onslaught ☆**5.** a kind of scrimmage contest between groups of college students, as between freshmen and sophomores **6.** a press, as of business or traffic, necessitating unusual haste or effort ☆**7.** *Football* a running play **8.** [*usually pl.*] *Motion Pictures* a first print made shortly after the filming of a scene or scenes, for inspection by the director, etc. *—adj.* **1.** necessitating haste [*rush* orders] **2.** characterized by a rush (*n.* 6) [*rush* hours] *—with a rush* suddenly and forcefully *—***rush′er** *n.*

rush[2] (rush) *n.* [ME. *rusche* < OE. *risc,* akin to MDu. *risch,* Norw. *rusk* < IE. base **rezg-,* to plait, twist, whence Sans. *rájju,* L. *restis,* a cord] **1.** any of a genus (*Juncus*) of plants of the rush family, having small, greenish flowers: rushes usually grow in wet places and the round stems and pliant leaves of some species are used in making baskets, mats, ropes, etc. **2.** any of various similar plants, as the bulrushes, horsetails, etc. *—adj.* designating a family (Juncaceae) of grasslike plants with a 6-parted perianth, tufted leaves, and the fruit in capsules

Rush (rush), **Benjamin** 1745?–1813; Am. physician: signer of the Declaration of Independence

rush candle a candle made with the pith of a rush as the wick: also **rush′light′, rush light**

☆**rush·ee** (rush ē′) *n.* a college student who is being rushed by a fraternity or sorority

☆**rush hour** a time of the day when business, traffic, etc. are especially heavy *—***rush′-hour′** *adj.*

Rush·more (rush′môr′), **Mount** [after Chas. E. *Rushmore,* N.Y. mining attorney] mountain in the Black Hills, W S.Dak., on which are carved huge heads (60 ft. high) of Washington, Jefferson, Lincoln, & Theodore Roosevelt: 6,200 ft.: it constitutes a national memorial (**Mount Rushmore National Memorial**), c. 2 sq. mi.

rush·y (-ē) *adj.* **rush′i·er, rush′i·est 1.** made of, full of, or covered with rushes (plants) **2.** like a rush

rusk (rusk) *n.* [Sp. *rosca,* twisted roll of bread, lit., a spiral, screw < VL. **rosicare,* to gnaw] **1.** sweet, raised bread or cake toasted in an oven, or baked a second time, after slicing, until browned and crisp **2.** a piece of this

Rusk (rusk), (**David**) **Dean** (dēn) 1909– ; U.S. secretary of state (1961–69)

Rus·kin (rus′kin), **John** 1819–1900; Eng. writer, art critic, & social reformer

Russ (rus) *adj., n., pl.* **Russ, Russ′es** [Russ. *Rus′*] *archaic var. of* RUSSIAN

Russ. 1. Russia **2.** Russian

Rus·sell (rus′'l) [< surname *Russell,* orig. dim. of Fr. *roux,* red < OFr. *rous:* see RUSSET] **1.** a masculine name: dim. *Russ:* also sp. **Rus′sel 2. Bertrand (Arthur William),** 3d Earl Russell, 1872–1970; Brit. philosopher, mathematician, & writer, born in Wales **3. George William,** (pseud. Æ or *A.E.*) 1867–1935; Ir. poet & essayist **4.** Lord **John,** 1st Earl Russell of Kingston Russell, 1792–1878; Eng. statesman; prime minister (1846–52; 1865–66): grandfather of *Bertrand* **5. Lillian,** (born *Helen Louise Leonard*) 1861–1922; U.S. singer & actress

Rus·sell's viper (rus′'lz) [after Patrick *Russell,* 18th-c. Brit. physician] an extremely poisonous snake (*Vipera russelli*) of SE and SC Asia, with a pale-brown body and ringlike black spots bordered with white or yellow

rus·set (rus′it) *n.* [ME. < OFr. *rousset,* dim. of *rous* < L. *russus,* reddish (akin to *ruber,* RED[1])] **1.** yellowish brown or reddish brown **2.** a coarse homespun cloth, reddish-brown or brownish, formerly used for clothing by country people **3.** a winter apple with a rough, mottled skin *—adj.* **1.** yellowish-brown or reddish-brown **2.** made of russet (cloth) **3.** [Archaic] rustic, simple, etc.

Rus·sia (rush′ə) **1.** former empire (**Russian Empire**) in E Europe & N Asia, 1547–1917, ruled by the czars: cap. St. Petersburg **2.** *a*) *popular name for* the UNION OF SOVIET SOCIALIST REPUBLICS *b*) *same as* RUSSIAN SOVIET FEDERATED SOCIALIST REPUBLIC, *esp. the European part —n.* [r-] *same as* RUSSIA LEATHER

Russia leather a fine, smooth leather, usually dyed dark red, orig. made in Russia of hides treated with oil from birch bark: used in bookbinding, etc.

Rus·sian (rush′ən) *adj.* of Russia, its people, their language, etc. *—n.* **1.** *a*) a native or inhabitant of Russia, specif. of the R.S.F.S.R. *b*) popularly, any citizen of the U.S.S.R. **2.** a member of the chief Slavic people of Russia **3.** the East Slavic language of the Russians; esp., Great Russian, the principal and official language of the U.S.S.R.

☆**Russian dressing** mayonnaise mixed with chili sauce, chopped pickles, pimentos, etc.: used on salads, etc.

Rus·sian·ize (-īz′) *vt.* **-ized′, -iz′ing** to make Russian in character *—***Rus′sian·i·za′tion** *n.*

Russian olive a small, hardy tree (*Elaeagnus angustifolia*) of the oleaster family, with silvery leaves and fragrant yellow flowers, often grown for windbreaks or ornament

Russian (Orthodox) Church an autonomous branch of the Orthodox Eastern Church: it was the national church of czarist Russia

Russian Revolution 1. the revolution of 1917 in which the government of the Czar was overthrown: it consisted of two distinct revolutions, the first (*February Revolution*) being the uprising of March (February, Old Style), in which a parliamentarian government headed by Kerensky came to power, the second (*October Revolution*) being the uprising of November (October, Old Style), in which this government was replaced by the Soviet government led by the Bolsheviks (Communists) under Lenin **2.** sometimes, the October Revolution alone

☆**Russian roulette 1.** a deadly game of chance in which a person spins the cylinder of a revolver holding only one bullet, aims the gun at his head, and pulls the trigger **2.** any activity potentially destructive to its participants

Russian Soviet Federated Socialist Republic largest republic of the U.S.S.R., stretching from the Baltic Sea to the Pacific & from the Arctic Ocean to the Chinese border: 6,592,000 sq. mi.; pop. 126,600,000; cap. Moscow

☆**Russian thistle** a spiny weed (*Salsola kali*) of the goose-foot family: it matures into a spherical tumbleweed

Russian wolfhound *same as* BORZOI

Rus·si·fy (rus′ə fī′) *vt.* **-fied′, -fy′ing** *same as* RUSSIANIZE *—***Rus′si·fi·ca′tion** *n.*

Rus·so- (rus′ō, -ə) *a combining form meaning:* **1.** Russia or Russian [*Russophobe*] **2.** Russian and [*Russo*-Japanese]

Rus·so·phile (rus′ə fīl′) *n.* [prec. + -PHILE] a person who admires or is extremely fond of Russia, its people, customs, influence, etc. *—adj.* of Russophiles

Rus·so·pho·bi·a (rus′ə fō′bē ə) *n.* [RUSSO- + -PHOBIA] hatred or fear of Russia, its people, customs, influence, etc. —**Rus′so·phobe′** *n.*, *adj.*

rust (rust) *n.* [ME. < OE., akin to G. *rost* < IE. base *reudh-*, RED[1]] **1.** the reddish-brown or reddish-yellow coating formed on iron or steel by oxidation, as during exposure to air and moisture: it consists mainly of ferric oxide, Fe_2O_3, and ferric hydroxide, $Fe(OH)_3$ **2.** any coating or film formed on any other metal by oxidation or corrosion **3.** any stain or formation resembling iron rust **4.** any habit, influence, growth, etc. injurious to usefulness, to the mind or character, etc. **5.** disuse of mental or moral powers; inactivity; idleness **6.** the color of iron rust; reddish brown or reddish yellow **7.** *Bot. a)* any of a number of plant diseases caused by parasitic, basidiomycetous fungi (order Uredinales) and characterized by a spotted reddish or brownish discoloration of stems and leaves *b)* any fungus causing such a disease: in full **rust fungus** —*vi.*, *vt.* **1.** to affect or be affected by a rust fungus **2.** to become or cause to be coated with rust, as iron **3.** to deteriorate or spoil, as through disuse, inactivity, etc. [a mind that has *rusted*] **4.** to become or make rust-colored

rust-col·ored (-kul′ərd) *adj.* having the color of iron rust; reddish-brown or reddish-yellow

rus·tic (rus′tik) *adj.* [LME. *rustyk* < MFr. *rustique* < L. *rusticus* < *rus*, the country: see RURAL] **1.** of or living in the country, as distinguished from cities or towns; rural **2.** lacking refinement, elegance, polish, or sophistication; specif., *a)* simple, plain, or artless *b)* rough, awkward, uncouth, or boorish **3.** made of rough, bark-covered branches or roots [*rustic* furniture] **4.** *Masonry* having a rough surface or irregular, deeply sunk, deliberately conspicuous joints; rusticated —*n.* a country person, esp. one regarded as unsophisticated, simple, awkward, uncouth, etc. —*SYN.* see RURAL —**rus′ti·cal·ly** *adv.* —**rus·tic′i·ty** (-tis′ə tē) *n.*

rus·ti·cal (-ti k'l) *adj.*, *n. archaic var.* of RUSTIC

rus·ti·cate (rus′ti kāt′) *vi.* -**cat′ed**, -**cat′ing** [< L. *rusticatus*, pp. of L. *rusticari*, to rusticate < *rusticus*: see RUSTIC] **1.** to go to the country **2.** to live or stay in the country, lead a rural life —*vt.* **1.** to send to, or cause to live or stay in, the country **2.** [Brit.] to suspend (a student) temporarily from a university **3.** to make (a person, etc.) rustic **4.** to make or finish (masonry) in the rustic style —**rus′ti·ca′tion** *n.* —**rus′ti·ca′tor** *n.*

rus·tle[1] (rus′'l) *vi.*, *vt.* -**tled**, -**tling** [ME. *rustelen*, freq. formation < ME. *rouslen*, akin to earlier Fl. *ruysselen* < WGmc. echoic base] to make or cause to make an irregular succession of soft sounds, as of leaves being moved by a gentle breeze or of papers being shuffled —*n.* such a succession of sounds —**rus′tling·ly** *adv.*

rus·tle[2] (rus′'l) *vi.*, *vt.* -**tled**, -**tling** [< ? RUSH[1] + HUSTLE] **1.** [Colloq.] to work or proceed with, or move, bring, or get by, energetic or vigorous action ☆**2.** *a)* orig., in the western U.S., to round up (cattle, etc.) *b)* [Colloq.] to steal (cattle, etc.) ☆**rustle up** [Colloq.] to collect or get together, as by foraging around —**rus′tler** *n.*

rust·proof (rust′proof′) *adj.* resistant to rust —*vt.* to make rustproof

rust·y (rus′tē) *adj.* **rust′i·er**, **rust′i·est** [ME. < OE. *rustig*] **1.** coated with rust, as a metal, or affected with the disease of rust, as a plant **2.** consisting of or caused by rust **3.** not working freely, easily, or quietly because of, or as if because of, rust; stiff or rasping in operation **4.** *a)* impaired by disuse, neglect, etc. [to find one's golf game *rusty*] *b)* having lost facility through lack of practice [to be a little *rusty* in chess] **5.** having the color of rust **6.** faded, old-looking, or shabby —**rust′i·ly** *adv.* —**rust′i·ness** *n.*

rut[1] (rut) *n.* [< ? MFr. *route*, ROUTE] **1.** a groove, furrow, or track, esp. one made in the ground by the passage of wheeled vehicles **2.** a fixed, routine procedure or course of action, thought, etc., esp. one regarded as dull and unrewarding —*vt.* **rut′ted**, **rut′ting** to make a rut or ruts in

rut[2] (rut) *n.* [ME. *rutte* < OFr. *ruit* < L. *rugitus*, a roaring (as of deer in rut) < *rugire*, to roar < IE. *reuk-* echoic base *reu-*, to roar, cry hoarsely, whence OE. *ryn*, OBulg. *rykati*, to roar] **1.** the periodic sexual excitement, or heat, of certain mammals: applied esp. to males, often specif. to those male ruminants in which it occurs once a year: cf. ESTRUS **2.** the period during which this occurs —*vi.* **rut′ted**, **rut′ting** to be in rut

ru·ta·ba·ga (root′ə bā′gə, root′ə bā′gə) *n.* [Sw. dial. *rotabagge*] **1.** a turnip (*Brassica napobrassica*) with a large, yellow root **2.** this root

Ruth (rooth) [LL.(Ec.) < Heb. *rūth*, prob. contr. < *rē′uth*, companion] **1.** a feminine name **2.** *Bible a)* a Moabite widow deeply devoted to her mother-in-law, Naomi, for whom she left her own people to later become the wife of Boaz of Bethlehem *b)* the book of the Bible that tells her story **3.** **George Herman**, (nicknamed "*Babe*") 1895–1948; U.S. baseball player

ruth (rooth) *n.* [ME. *reuthe* < base *reowen*: see RUE[1]] [Now Rare] **1.** pity; compassion **2.** sorrow; grief; remorse

Ru·the·ni·a (roo thē′nē ə) region in W Ukrainian S.S.R., a former province of Czechoslovakia

Ru·the·ni·an (-ən) *n.* **1.** any of a group of Ukrainians living in Ruthenia and eastern Czechoslovakia **2.** the Ukrainian dialect spoken in Ruthenia —*adj.* **1.** of Ruthenia or the Ruthenians **2.** of Ruthenian

ru·then·ic (roo then′ik, -thē′nik) *adj.* designating or of chemical compounds containing ruthenium with a higher valence than in the corresponding ruthenious compounds

ru·the·ni·ous (-thē′nē əs) *adj.* designating or of chemical compounds containing ruthenium with a lower valence than in the corresponding ruthenic compounds

ru·the·ni·um (-thē′nē əm) *n.* [ModL. < ML. *Ruthenia*, Russia: because first found in ores from the Urals] a rare metallic chemical element of the platinum group, very hard and brittle, and silvery-gray in color, used as a hardener in alloys of platinum and palladium and as a catalyst: symbol, Ru; at. wt., 101.07; at. no., 44; sp. gr., 12.30; melt. pt., 2450°C; boil pt., 4150°C

Ruth·er·ford atom (ruth′ər fərd) [after Baron Ernest *Rutherford* (1871–1937), Brit. physicist] the atom postulated as analogous to the solar system, with electrons revolving around a small, central, positive nucleus that constitutes practically the entire mass of the atom

ruth·ful (rooth′fəl) *adj.* [ME. *reuthful*] [Now Rare] full of ruth; feeling, showing, or arousing pity or sorrow —**ruth′ful·ly** *adv.* —**ruth′ful·ness** *n.*

ruth·less (-lis) *adj.* [ME. *reutheles*] without ruth; pitiless —*SYN.* see CRUEL —**ruth′less·ly** *adv.* —**ruth′less·ness** *n.*

ru·ti·lant (root′'l ənt) *adj.* [L. *rutilans*, prp. of *rutilare*, to have a reddish glow < *rutilus*: see RUTILE] [Rare] glowing, gleaming, or glittering

ru·tile (roo′tēl, -til) *n.* [< Fr. or G.: Fr. < G. *rutil* < L. *rutilus*, red, akin to *rufus*, *rubeus*, RED[1]] a lustrous, dark-red mineral, titanium dioxide, TiO_2, commonly found in prismatic crystals and usually containing some iron

Rut·land (rut′lənd) county of EC England: 152 sq. mi.; pop. 26,000: also **Rut′land·shire′** (-shir′)

Rut·ledge (rut′lij) **1. Anne,** 1813?–35; alleged fiancée of young Abraham Lincoln **2. Edward,** 1749–1800; Am. statesman: signer of the Declaration of Independence **3. John,** 1739–1800; Am. jurist & statesman: brother of *prec.*

rut·tish (rut′ish) *adj.* in or inclined to rut (sexual heat); lustful —**rut′tish·ly** *adv.* —**rut′tish·ness** *n.*

rut·ty (-ē) *adj.* -**ti·er**, -**ti·est** having or full of ruts [a *rutty* road] —**rut′ti·ness** *n.*

Ru·wen·zo·ri (roo′wen zō′rē) group of mountains in EC Africa, on the Congo-Uganda border: identified with the "Mountains of the Moon" referred to by ancient writers: highest peak, Mt. STANLEY

Ruys·dael (rois′däl) same as RUISDAEL

Ruy·ter (roi′tər), **Mi·chiel A·dri·aans·zoon de** (mi khēl′ a′drē än′sən də) 1607–76; Du. admiral

R.V. Revised Version (of the Bible)

R.W. **1.** Right Worshipful **2.** Right Worthy

Rwan·da (ur wän′dä, roo wän′də) country in EC Africa, east of Congo (sense 2): formerly part of Ruanda-Urundi: 10,169 sq. mi.; pop. 3,306,000 —**Rwan′dan** *adj.*, *n.*

Rwy. Railway

Rx [altered < ℞, conventional symbol for L. *recipe*: see RECIPE] *symbol for* PRESCRIPTION (sense 3) —*n.* a remedy, cure, or the like suggested for any disorder or problem

-ry (rē) *shortened form of* -ERY [*dentistry, jewelry*]

Ry. Railway

ry·a rug (rē′ə) [Sw. *rya* (*matta*) < ON. *ry*, coarse woolen cover, akin to OE. *ryhe*: for IE. base see ROUGH] a decorative hand-woven area rug or tapestry of Scandinavian origin, having a thick wool pile and, usually, an abstract design

Rya·zan (ryä zän′y′) city in the C European R.S.F.S.R., near the Oka River: pop. 297,000

Ry·binsk (ri′binsk) **1.** city in NC European R.S.F.S.R., on Rybinsk Reservoir: pop. 209,000 **2.** artificial lake on the upper Volga: c. 1,800 sq. mi.: in full **Rybinsk Reservoir**

Ry·der (ri′dər), **Albert Pink·ham** (piņk′əm) 1847–1917; U.S. painter

rye[1] (ri) *n.* see PLURAL, II, D, 3 [ME. < OE. *ryge*, akin to G. *roggen* < IE. base *wrughyo-*, rye, whence Lith. *rugỹs*, rye grain] **1.** a hardy cereal grass (*Secale cereale*) widely grown for its grain and straw **2.** the grain or seeds of this plant, used for making flour and whiskey, and as feed for livestock ☆**3.** *a)* whiskey distilled wholly or chiefly from this grain *b)* in the eastern U.S., a blended whiskey **4.** *clipped form of* RYE BREAD

rye[2] (ri) *n.* [see ROMANY RYE] a Gypsy gentleman

rye bread a bread made altogether or partly of rye flour, often with caraway seeds added

rye·grass (-gras′, -gräs′) *n.* any of a genus (*Lolium*) of annual or short-lived perennial grasses, often grown for quick lawns or as forage

ry·ot (ri′ət) *n.* [Hindi *raiyat* < Ar. *ra′iyah*, a flock, herd] in India, a peasant or tenant farmer

Ryu·kyu Islands (ryoo′kyoo′) chain of islands in the W Pacific, between Kyushu & Taiwan: formerly a Jap. possession, now partly under U.S. control: c. 1,800 sq. mi.; pop. 952,000: chief island, Okinawa

---

fat, āpe, cär; ten, ēven; is, bīte; gō, hôrn, tōōl, look; oil, out; up, fur; get; joy; yet; chin; she; thin, then; zh, leisure; ŋ, ring; ə for *a* in *ago, e* in *agent, i* in *sanity, o* in *comply, u* in *focus*; ' as in *able* (ā′b'l); Fr. bâl; ë, Fr. coeur; ö, Fr. feu; Fr. mon; ô, Fr. coq; ü, Fr. duc; r, Fr. cri; H, G. ich; kh, G. doch. See inside front cover. ☆ Americanism; ‡foreign; *hypothetical; <derived from

S

S, s (es) *n.*, *pl.* **S's, s's** **1.** the nineteenth letter of the English alphabet: from the Greek *sigma*, a borrowing from the Phoenician **2.** a sound of *S* or *s*, usually a voiceless palatal fricative (s) formed by the apex of the tongue, or its voiced counterpart (z), as in *rubs* (rubz) **3.** a type or impression for *S* or *s* **4.** *a symbol for* the nineteenth in a sequence or group (or the eighteenth if J is omitted) —*adj.* **1.** of *S* or *s* **2.** nineteenth (or eighteenth if J is omitted) in a sequence or group

S (es) *n.* **1.** an object shaped like *S* **2.** *Chem.* sulfur —*adj.* shaped like *S*

-s [alternate form of -ES assimilated to prec. voiceless sounds as (s) and to prec. voiced sounds as (z) when those sounds are not sibilants] **1.** the inflectional ending used to form the plural of most nouns [*hips, shoes*, etc.] **2.** the inflectional ending used to form the third person singular of verbs in the present tense, indicative mood [*gives, runs*, etc.] **3.** a suffix used to form some adverbs [*betimes, days*, etc.]

-'s[1] [assimilated contr. < ME. -*es* < OE., masc. & neut. gen. sing. inflection] the inflectional ending used to form the possessive singular of nouns (and some pronouns) and the possessive plural of nouns not ending in s [*boy's, one's, women's*]

-'s[2] *the unstressed and assimilated form of:* **1.** is [*he's here*] **2.** has [*she's eaten*] **3.** does [*what's it matter?*] **4.** us [*let's go*]

S, S., s, s. 1. south **2.** southern

S. 1. Sabbath **2.** Saturday **3.** Saxon **4.** Seaman **5.** Senate **6.** September **7.** Signor **8.** Sunday

S., s. 1. *pl.* **SS., ss.** saint **2.** school **3.** society

s. 1. second(s) **2.** section **3.** see **4.** semi **5.** series **6.** shilling(s) **7.** sign **8.** silver **9.** singular **10.** sire **11.** son **12.** soprano **13.** steamer **14.** substantive

SA Seaman Apprentice

S.A. 1. Salvation Army **2.** [Slang] sex appeal **3.** South Africa **4.** South America **5.** South Australia **6.** [G. *Sturmabteilung*] storm troops

s.a. semiannual

Saa·di (sä′dē) *same as* SADI

Saar (sär, zär) **1.** river flowing from the Vosges Mountains, NE France, north into the Moselle River, SW West Germany: c. 150 mi. **2.** rich coal-mining region (also called **Saar Basin**) in the valley of this river: administered by France (1919–35) & Germany (1935–47) until set up as an autonomous government having a customs union with France (1947–57): since 1957, the SAARLAND

Saar·brück·en (sär′brook′ən, zär′-; G. zär′brük′ən) city in SW West Germany, on the Saar; capital of the Saarland: pop. 134,000

SAAR

Saa·re·maa (sä′rə mä′) island of the Estonian S.S.R. in the Baltic Sea, at the entrance to the Gulf of Riga: 1,048 sq. mi.

Saa·ri·nen (sär′i nen′, -nən) **1. Ee·ro** (ā′rō), 1910–61; U.S. architect, born in Finland **2. (Gottlieb) E·liel** (ēl′yel), 1873–1950; Finn. architect, in the U.S. after 1923: father of *prec.*

Saar·land (sär′land, zär′-; G. zär′länt′) state of SW West Germany, in the Saar River Basin: 991 sq. mi.; pop. 1,127,000; cap. Saarbrücken

Sab. Sabbath

Sa·ba (sä′bə; *for 2,* sā′-) **1.** island of the Leeward group, in the Netherlands Antilles: 5 sq. mi.; pop. 1,000 **2.** ancient kingdom in S Arabia in the region of modern Yemen: Biblical name, *Sheba*

Sa·ba·dell (sä′bä thel′) city in NE Spain, near Barcelona: pop. 128,000

sab·a·dil·la (sab′ə dil′ə) *n.* [Sp. *cebadilla*, dim. of *cebada*, barley < L. *cibare*, to feed < *cibus*, food] **1.** a Mexican and Central American plant (*Schoenocaulon officinale*) of the lily family, with brown seeds used in insecticides and formerly in medicine **2.** the seeds, containing the alkaloids, veratrine, veratridine, etc.

Sa·bae·an (sə bē′ən) *adj.* of Saba (sense 2), its people, their language, etc. —*n.* **1.** a member of the Semitic people of Saba (sense 2) **2.** the South Arabic language of the Sabaeans, known only from inscriptions

Sa·bah (sä′bä) state of Malaysia, occupying NE Borneo & several offshore islands, including Labuan: formerly, until 1963, a Brit. colony (called *North Borneo*): 29,388 sq. mi.; pop. 588,000; cap. Jesselton

Sab·a·oth (sab′ē äth′, -ōth′; sə bā′ōth) *n.pl.* [ME. < LL.(Ec.) < Gr. (LXX & NT.) *Sabaōth* < Heb. *tsebhāōth*, pl. of *tsābhā*, host, army] *Bible* armies; hosts: in *the Lord of Sabaoth*: Rom. 9:29, James 5:4

sab·bat (sab′ət) *n.* [Fr., SABBATH] *same as* WITCHES' SABBATH

Sab·ba·tar·i·an (sab′ə ter′ē ən) *adj.* [LL.(Ec.) *sabbatarius*] **1.** of the Sabbath and its observance **2.** of the doctrines of the Sabbatarians —*n.* **1.** a person, esp. a Christian, who observes the Sabbath (sense 1) **2.** a Christian who favors rigid observance of Sunday as the Sabbath — **Sab′ba·tar′i·an·ism** *n.*

Sab·bath (sab′əth) *n.* [ME. *sabat* < OFr. & OE. *sabat*, both < L. *sabbatum* < Gr. *sabbaton* < Heb. *shabbāth*, *shābath*, to rest] **1.** the seventh day of the week (Saturday), set aside by the fourth Commandment for rest and worship and observed as such by Jews and some Christian sects **2.** Sunday as the usual Christian day of rest and worship **3.** [s-] a period of rest —*adj.* of the Sabbath

Sabbath school classes in religious instruction held on the Sabbath

Sab·bat·i·cal (sə bat′i k'l) *adj.* [< Fr. *sabbatique* < LL.(Ec.) *sabbaticus* < Gr. *sabbatikos* < *sabbaton* (see SABBATH) + -AL] **1.** of or suited to the Sabbath **2.** [s-] bringing a period of rest that recurs in regular cycles [a *sabbatical leave*] —*n.* [s-] a sabbatical year or leave Also **Sab·bat′ic** —**Sab·bat′i·cal·ly** *adv.*

sabbatical year 1. among the ancient Jews, every seventh year, in which, according to Mosaic law, the land and vineyards were to remain fallow and debtors were to be released ☆**2.** a year or shorter period of absence for study, rest, or travel, given at intervals, orig. every seven years, as to some college teachers, at full or partial salary

Sa·be·an (sə bē′ən) *adj.*, *n. same as* SABAEAN

Sa·bel·li·an (sə bel′ē ən) *n.* [< L. *Sabelli*, ancient name of the Sabines + -AN] **1.** any member of a group of pre-Roman peoples of ancient Italy including the Sabines and Samnites **2.** an extinct branch of the Italic subfamily of languages, probably related to Oscan

sa·ber (sā′bər) *n.* [Fr. *sabre* < G. *sabel* < MHG. < Pol. & Hung.: Pol. *szabla* < Hung. *szablya* < *szabni*, to cut] **1.** a heavy cavalry sword with a slightly curved blade **2.** *Fencing* a type of weapon, heavier than a foil, used with a slashing as well as thrusting movement: a touch may be scored with the edge or point —*vt.* to strike, wound, or kill with a saber

saber rattling a threatening of war, or a menacing show of armed force

sa·ber-toothed (-tootht′) *adj.* designating various animals with long, curved upper canine teeth

saber-toothed tiger any of a group of extinct animals of the cat family, closely resembling the tiger, but with a more massive body, shorter legs and tail, and long, curved upper canine teeth: found from the Oligocene to the Pleistocene, and of wide distribution

SABER

☆**sa·bin** (sā′bin) *n.* [after W. C. Sabine (1868–1919), U.S. physicist] *Acoustics* the unit for absorption of sound equal to the absorption provided by one square foot of a completely absorbing material

Sa·bin (sā′bin), **Albert B(ruce)** 1906– ; U.S. physician & bacteriologist, born in Russia: developed an oral vaccine to prevent poliomyelitis

Sa·bine[1] (sə bēn′) [in allusion to ff.] river flowing from E Tex. south along the Tex.-La. border into the Gulf of Mexico: c. 550 mi.: lower course is part of a system of channels (**Sabine-Neches Waterway**) connecting Beaumont, Tex., & Lake Charles, La., with the Gulf of Mexico

Sa·bine[2] (sā′bin) *n.* [ME. *Sabyn* < L. *Sabinus*] **1.** a member of an ancient tribe living chiefly in the Apennines of

central Italy, conquered by the Romans in the 3d century B.C. **2.** their Italic language —*adj.* of the Sabines or their language

Sabine Lake shallow lake formed by the widening of the Sabine River just above its mouth: c. 17 mi. long

sa·ble (sā′b'l) *n., pl.* **-bles, -ble:** see PLURAL, II, D, 1 [ME. < OFr. < ML. *sabelum* < MDu. *sabel* < OHG. *zobel* < Russ. *sobol′:* of Oriental origin] **1.** same as MARTEN; esp., *a*) the **European marten** (*Martes foina*), having light-colored underfur *b*) the **American marten** (*Martes americana*), with a darker pelt **2.** *a*) the costly fur or pelt of the sable *b*) [*pl.*] a coat, neckpiece, etc. made of this **3.** [*pl.*] [Now Rare] black mourning clothes **4.** *Heraldry* the color black, represented in engraving by crossing vertical and horizontal lines to produce a dark shading —*adj.* **1.** made of or with the fur of the sable **2.** black or dark brown; dark

Sa·ble (sā′b'l), **Cape** [< Fr. *sable*, sand] **1.** cape at the S tip of Fla.: southernmost point of the U.S. mainland: c. 20 mi. long **2.** cape at the S tip of Nova Scotia

sable antelope a large antelope (*Hippotragus niger*) of South Africa, with long, scimitar-shaped, ringed horns

sa·ble·fish (-fish′) *n., pl.* **-fish′, -fish′es:** see FISH[2] ☆an edible dark fish (*Anoplopoma fimbria*) of the North Pacific, superfiicially resembling the mackerel

sa·bot (sab′ō, sa bō′) *n.* [Fr. < OFr. *çabot*, altered (after *bot*, a BOOT[1]) < *savate*, a shoe, via Turk. < Ar. *sabbât*, sandal] **1.** *a*) a kind of shoe shaped and hollowed from a single piece of wood, traditionally worn by peasants in Europe *b*) a heavy leather shoe with a wooden sole **2.** bushing or similar device fitted around or in back of a projectile, as to make it fit the bore of the gun barrel or launching tube

SABOT

sab·o·tage (sab′ə täzh′) *n.* [Fr. < *saboter*, to work badly, damage < *sabot:* see prec. & -AGE: from damage done to machinery by wooden shoes] **1.** intentional destruction of machines, waste of materials, etc., as by employees during labor disputes **2.** destruction of railroads, bridges, machinery, etc. as by enemy agents or by an underground resistance **3.** the deliberate obstruction of or damage to any cause, movement, activity, effort, etc. —*vt.* **-taged′, -tag′ing** to injure or destroy by sabotage —*vi.* to engage in sabotage

sab·o·teur (sab′ə tur′) *n.* [Fr.] a person who engages in sabotage

sa·bra (sä′brə) *n.* [ModHeb. *sābrāh,* lit., prickly fruit of a native cactus] a native-born Israeli

sa·bre (sā′bər) *n., vt.* **-bred, -bring** same as SABER

☆**sabre saw** a portable electric saw with a narrow, oscillating blade

sa·bre·tache (sā′bər tash′, sab′ər-) *n.* [Fr. < G. *säbeltasche* < *säbel,* SABER + *tasche,* pocket] a square leather case hung from the saber belt of cavalrymen

sab·u·lous (sab′yoo ləs) *adj.* [L. *sabulosus* < *sabulum,* SAND] sandy or gritty

Sac (sak, sôk) *n., pl.* **Sacs, Sac** same as SAUK

sac (sak) *n.* [Fr. < L. *saccus:* see SACK[1]] a pouchlike part in a plant or animal, esp. one filled with fluid —**sac′like′** *adj.*

SAC, S.A.C. Strategic Air Command

☆**sac·a·ton** (sak′ə tōn′) *n.* [AmSp. *zacatón* < *zacate* < Nahuatl, a kind of grass] a coarse native grass (*Sporobolus wrightii*), used for hay or pasture on dry ranges in the SW U.S. and Mexico

sac·cade (sa käd′) *n.* [Fr., a jerk < obs. *saquer*, to shake, pull, dial. var. of OFr. *sachier* < VL. *saccare*, to pull from a sack < L. *saccus*, SACK[1]] any of the rapid, involuntary jumps made by the eyes from one fixed point to another, as in reading —**sac·cad′ic** *adj.*

sac·cate (sak′āt) *adj.* [ML. *saccatus* < L. *saccus:* see SAC] **1.** shaped like a sac; pouchlike **2.** having a sac

sac·char- (sak′ər) same as SACCHARO-: used before a vowel

sac·cha·rase (sak′ə rās′) *n.* [prec. + -ASE] same as INVERTASE

sac·cha·rate (-rāt′) *n.* [SACCHAR- + -ATE[2]] **1.** a salt or ester of saccharic acid **2.** a compound of sugar with the oxide of calcium, strontium, or a similar metal

sac·char·ic (sə kar′ik) *adj.* [SACCHAR- + -IC] of or derived from saccharine compounds

saccharic acid a diacid, C₆H₁₀O₈, obtained by the oxidation of glucose and other hexoses by nitric acid

sac·cha·ride (sak′ə rīd′) *n.* [SACCHAR- + -IDE] **1.** a compound of sugar with an organic base **2.** any of the carbohydrates; esp., a monosaccharide

sac·char·i·fy (sə kar′ə fī′) *vt.* **-fied′, -fy′ing** [SACCHAR- + -i- + -FY] to convert (starch or dextrin) into sugar, as by chemical means —**sac·char′i·fi·ca′tion** *n.*

sac·cha·rim·e·ter (sak′ə rim′ə tər) *n.* [Fr. *saccharimètre:* see SACCHARO- & -METER] an instrument, as a form of polarimeter used to determine the amount of sugar in a solution

sac·cha·rin (sak′ə rin) *n.* [< L. *saccharum,* sugar < Gr. *sakcharon,* ult. < Sans. *śarkarā,* grit, gravel, sugar (cf. SUGAR) + -IN[1]] ☆a white, crystalline coal-tar compound, C₇H₅O₃NS, about 500 times sweeter than cane sugar, used as a sugar substitute in diabetic diets, as a noncaloric sweetener, etc.

sac·cha·rine (-rin, -rīn) *adj.* [SACCHAR- + -INE[1]] **1.** of, having the nature of, containing, or producing sugar ☆**2.** too sweet or syrupy [*a saccharine* voice] —☆*n.* same as SACCHARIN —**sac′cha·rine·ly** *adv.* —**sac′cha·rin′i·ty** (-rin′ə tē) *n.*

sac·cha·ro- (sak′ə rō′) [< L. *saccharum,* sugar: see SACCHARIN] *a combining form meaning* sugar [*saccharometer*]

sac·cha·roi·dal (sak′ə roid′'l) *adj.* [< prec. + -OID + -AL] *Geol.* having a texture like that of loaf sugar; crystalline and granular: said esp. of some limestones and marbles: also **sac′cha·roid′**

sac·cha·rom·e·ter (-räm′ə tər) *n.* [SACCHARO- + -METER] a form of hydrometer for determining the amount of sugar in a solution

sac·cha·rose (sak′ə rōs′) *n.* [SACCHAR- + -OSE[1]] same as SUCROSE

Sac·co (sak′ō; *It.* säk′kô), **Ni·co·la** (nē kô′lä) 1891–1927; It. anarchist in the U.S.: together with B. VANZETTI, charged with murder & payroll theft in 1920; their conviction & execution aroused international protest, being regarded by many as the result of political bias

sac·cu·lar (sak′yə lər) *adj.* like a sac

sac·cu·late (-lāt′) *adj.* [< SACCULE + -ATE[1]] formed of or divided into saccules or a series of saclike expansions: also **sac′cu·lat′ed** —**sac′cu·la′tion** *n.*

sac·cule (sak′yool) *n.* [L. *sacculus,* dim. of *saccus,* a SACK[1]] a small sac; esp., the smaller of the two divisions of the membranous labyrinth of the inner ear

sac·cu·lus (sak′yoo ləs) *n., pl.* **-li′** (-lī′) [L.] same as SACCULE

sac·er·do·tal (sas′ər dōt′'l, sak′-) *adj.* [ME. *sacerdotale* < MFr. < L. *sacerdotalis* < *sacerdos,* priest < *sacer,* SACRED + -dos < IE. base *dhe-,* to do[1]] **1.** of priests or the office of priest; priestly **2.** characterized by belief in the divine authority of the priesthood —**sac′er·do′tal·ly** *adv.*

sac·er·do·tal·ism (-iz'm) *n.* [prec. + -ISM] **1.** the character, system, methods, or practices of the priesthood **2.** excessive reliance on a priesthood **sac′er·do′tal·ist** *n.*

☆**sa·chem** (sā′chəm) *n.* [< Algonquian *sâchimau,* chief] **1.** among some North American Indian tribes, the chief (of the tribe or of a confederation) **2.** any of the leading officials of the Tammany Society

sa·chet (sa shā′; *chiefly Brit.* sash′ā) *n.* [Fr. < OFr., dim. of *sac:* see SAC] **1.** a small bag, pad, etc. filled with perfumed powder and placed in dresser drawers, closets, etc. to scent clothing **2.** powder for such a bag: also **sachet powder**

Sachs (saks; *G.* zäkhs), **Hans** 1494–1576; Ger. Meistersinger, a cobbler by trade

Sach·sen (zäkh′sən) *Ger. name of* SAXONY

sack[1] (sak) *n.* [ME. *sak* < OE. *sacc,* akin to OHG. *sac,* Goth. *sakkus* < early Gmc. borrowing < L. *saccus,* a bag, in LL.(Ec.), a sackcloth garment < Gr. *sakkos* < Heb. *śaq* < Assyr. *šakku,* sackcloth] **1.** *a*) a bag, esp. a large one of coarse cloth, for holding grain, foodstuffs, etc. *b*) such a bag with its contents **2.** the quantity contained in such a bag: a measure of weight of varying amounts **3.** *a*) a short, loose-fitting jacket worn by women *b*) same as SHIFT (*n.* 7 *b*) **4.** [Slang] dismissal from a job; discharge (with *the*) ☆**5.** [Slang] a bed, bunk, etc. ☆**6.** *Baseball* same as BASE[1] (*n.* 5) —*vt.* **1.** to put into a sack or sacks **2.** [Slang] to dismiss (a person) from a job; discharge —☆**hit the sack** [Slang] to go to sleep: also **sack out** (or **in**)

sack[2] (sak) *n.* [MFr. *sac* < It. *sacco,* plunder, lit., bag < L. *saccus:* see prec.] the plundering or looting, esp. by soldiers, of a captured city or town —*vt.* to plunder or loot (a captured city, etc.) —SYN. see RAVAGE

sack[3] (sak) *n.* [earlier (*wyne*)*seck* < Fr. (*vin*)*sec,* dry (wine) < L. *siccus,* dry (see SICCATIVE)] any of various dry white wines from Spain or the Canary Islands, popular in England during the 16th and 17th cents.

sack·but (sak′but′) *n.* [MFr. *saquebute,* sackbut, earlier, hooked lance for fighting on horseback < OFr. *saquer,* to draw, pull < VL. *saccare,* to pull (from a sack) < L. *saccus,* SACK[1] + OFr. *bouter,* to push, BUTT[2]] **1.** a medieval wind instrument, forerunner of the trombone **2.** [false transl. of Aram. *sabbekha:* see SAMBUKE] *Bible* a stringed instrument resembling a lyre: Dan. 3:5

sack·cloth (-klôth′, -kläth′) *n.* [see SACK[1]] **1.** same as SACKING **2.** coarse, rough cloth, orig. made of goats' hair, worn as in Biblical times and with ashes sprinkled on the head, as a symbol of mourning or penitence —**in sackcloth and ashes** in a state of great mourning or penitence

☆**sack coat** a man's loose-fitting, straight-backed coat, usually part of a business suit

sack·er[1] (sak′ər) *n.* a person who sacks; plunderer

sack·er[2] (sak′ər) *n.* a person who makes or fills sacks

☆**sack·er[3]** (sak′ər) *n.* [Slang] *Baseball* same as BASEMAN

sack·ful (sak′fool′) *n., pl.* **-fuls′ 1.** the amount that a sack will hold **2.** a large quantity

sack·ing (-iŋ) *n.* a cheap, coarse cloth woven of flax, hemp, jute, etc., used esp. for making sacks

sack race a race in which each contestant has his legs in a sack and moves by jumping

Sack·ville (sak′vil), **Thomas**, 1st Earl of Dorset & Baron Buckhurst, 1536–1608; Eng. statesman & poet

sacque (sak) *n.* [pseudo-Fr. for SACK[1]] **1.** *same as* SACK[1] (sense 3) ☆**2.** a baby's jacket

sa·cral[1] (sā′krəl) *adj.* [< L. *sacrum*, neut. of *sacer*, SACRED + -AL] of or for religious rites or observances

sa·cral[2] (sā′krəl) *adj.* [ModL. *sacralis:* see SACRUM & -AL] of, or in the region of, the sacrum

sa·cral·ize (sā′krə līz′, sā′krə-) *vt.* **-ized′, -iz′ing** to make sacred or holy —**sa′cral·i·za′tion** *n.*

sac·ra·ment (sak′rə mənt) *n.* [ME. < OFr. *sacrement* < LL.(Ec.) *sacramentum*, the gospel, a secret, sacrament (used as transl. of Gr. *mystērion*) < L., an oath of allegiance, orig., sum deposited by the two parties to a suit < *sacrare*, to consecrate < *sacer*, SACRED] **1.** *Christianity* any of certain rites ordained by Jesus and regarded as a means of grace: baptism, confirmation, the Eucharist, penance, holy orders, matrimony, and Anointing of the Sick are the seven recognized by the Roman Catholic and Orthodox Eastern churches; Protestants generally recognize only baptism and Holy Communion **2.** [*sometimes* S-] the Eucharist, or Holy Communion; also, the consecrated bread and wine, or sometimes the bread alone, used in the Eucharist **3.** something regarded as having a sacred character or mysterious meaning **4.** [Archaic] *a)* a symbol or token *b)* a solemn oath or pledge

sac·ra·men·tal (sak′rə men′t'l) *adj.* [ME. *sacramentale* < LL. *sacramentalis*] **1.** of, having to do with, or used in a sacrament **2.** being, like, or of the nature of a sacrament —*n. R.C.Ch.* a ceremony or sacred object like a sacrament, but instituted by the Church, as the use of holy water —**sac′ra·men′tal·ly** *adv.*

sac·ra·men·tal·ism (-iz'm) *n.* belief in the efficacy of sacraments; esp., the doctrine that the sacraments are necessary to salvation —**sac′ra·men′tal·ist** *n.*

sac·ra·men·tar·i·an (sak′rə men ter′ē ən) *adj.* [ML. *sacramentarius*] **1.** of the sacraments **2.** [S-] of the Sacramentarians —*n.* **1.** [S-] a person who believes that the Eucharist is the symbolic rather than corporeal manifestation of Christ: used orig. of Zwingli, Calvin, and their followers **2.** an adherent of sacramentalism; sacramentalist —**Sac′ra·men·tar′i·an·ism** *n.*

Sac·ra·men·to (sak′rə men′tō) [Sp., sacrament] **1.** river in C Calif., flowing south into an E arm of San Francisco Bay: c. 400 mi. **2.** capital of Calif., on this river: pop. 254,000 (met. area 801,000)

sa·crar·i·um (sə krer′ē əm) *n., pl.* **-i·a** (-ə) [L. < *sacer*, SACRED] a basin with a drain, usually in a sacristy, for the disposal of baptismal water, etc.; piscina

sa·cred (sā′krid) *adj.* [ME. < pp. of *sacren*, to consecrate < OFr. *sacrer* < L. *sacrare* < *sacer*, holy < ? IE. base *sak-*, to sanctify, make a compact, whence ON. *sāttr*, reconciled, Hitt. *šakliš*, law, ritual] **1.** consecrated to or belonging to a god or deity; holy **2.** of or connected with religion or religious rites [a *sacred* song] **3.** regarded with the same respect and reverence accorded holy things; venerated; hallowed **4.** set apart for, and dedicated to, some person, place, purpose, sentiment, etc. [*sacred* to his memory] **5.** secured as by a religious feeling or sense of justice against any defamation, violation, or intrusion; inviolate —*SYN.* see HOLY —**sa′cred·ly** *adv.* —**sa′cred·ness** *n.*

sacred baboon *same as* HAMADRYAD (sense 3)

Sacred College *same as* COLLEGE OF CARDINALS

☆**sacred cow** any person or thing regarded as above criticism or attack

sac·ri·fice (sak′rə fīs′) *n.* [ME. < OFr. < L. *sacrificium* < *sacer*, SACRED + *facere*, to make: see DO[1]] **1.** *a)* the act of offering the life of a person or animal, or some object, in propitiation of or homage to a deity *b)* something so offered **2.** *a)* the act of giving up, destroying, permitting injury to, or forgoing something valued for the sake of something having a more pressing claim *b)* a thing so given up, etc. **3.** *a)* a selling or giving up of something at less than its supposed value *b)* the loss incurred ☆**4.** *Baseball same as* SACRIFICE BUNT —*vt.* **-ficed′, -fic′ing 1.** to offer as a sacrifice to God or a god **2.** to give up, destroy, permit injury to, or forgo (something valued) for the sake of something having a more pressing claim **3.** to sell at less than the supposed value ☆**4.** *Baseball* to advance (a base runner) by means of a sacrifice —*vi.* **1.** to offer or make a sacrifice ☆**2.** *Baseball* to make a sacrifice bunt —**sac′ri·fic′er** *n.*

☆**sacrifice bunt** *Baseball* a bunt by the batter so that he can be put out but a base runner will be advanced: also **sacrifice hit**

☆**sacrifice fly** *Baseball* a play in which the batter, when there are fewer than two outs, flies out and a runner scores from third base after the catch

sac·ri·fi·cial (sak′rə fish′əl) *adj.* of, having the nature of, used in, or offering a sacrifice —**sac′ri·fi′cial·ly** *adv.*

sac·ri·lege (sak′rə lij) *n.* [ME. < MFr. < L. *sacrilegium* < *sacrilegus*, temple robber < *sacer*, sacred + *legere*, to gather up, take away: see LOGIC] **1.** the act of appropriating to oneself or to secular use, or of violating, what is consecrated to God or religion **2.** the intentional desecration or disrespectful treatment of a person, place, thing, or idea held sacred

SYN.—**sacrilege** implies a violation of something sacred, as by appropriating to oneself or to a secular use something that has been dedicated to a religious purpose; **profanation** suggests a lack of reverence or a positive contempt for things regarded as sacred; **desecration** implies a removal of the sacredness of some object or place, as by defiling or polluting it

sac·ri·le·gious (sak′rə lij′əs, -lē′jəs) *adj.* **1.** that is or involves sacrilege **2.** guilty of sacrilege —**sac′ri·le′gious·ly** *adv.* —**sac′ri·le′gious·ness** *n.*

sa·cring (sā′kriŋ) *n.* [ME. < prp. of *sacren:* see SACRED] [Archaic] consecration of the bread and wine of the Eucharist

sacring bell a small bell rung during the Mass at the elevation of the bread and wine

sac·ris·tan (sak′ris tən) *n.* [ME. *sacristane* < ML.(Ec.) *sacristanus* < *sacrista* < *sacer*, SACRED] **1.** an official in charge of the sacristy of a church: also **sa′crist** (sā′krist) **2.** [Archaic] a sexton

sac·ris·ty (-tē) *n., pl.* **-ties** [Fr. *sacristie* < ML.(Ec.) *sacristia* < *sacrista*, sacristan] a room in a church, usually adjoining the sanctuary, where the sacred vessels, vestments, etc. are kept; vestry

sa·cro- (sā′krō, sak′rə) [ModL. < *sacrum*] a combining form meaning: **1.** the sacrum [*sacroiliac*] **2.** of the sacrum [*sacroiliac*]

sa·cro·il·i·ac (sā′krō il′ē ak′, sak′rō-) *adj.* [prec. + ILIAC] of the sacrum and the ilium; esp., designating the joint between them —*n.* the joint or cartilage between the sacrum and the ilium

sac·ro·sanct (sak′rō saŋkt′) *adj.* [L. *sacrosanctus* < *sacer*, SACRED + *sanctus*, holy: see SAINT] very sacred, holy, or inviolable —**sac′ro·sanc′ti·ty** *n.*

sa·cro·sci·at·ic (sā′krō sī at′ik) *adj.* [SACRO- + SCIATIC] of the sacrum and the ischium

sa·crum (sā′krəm, sak′rəm) *n., pl.* **-cra** (-krə, -rə) or **-crums** [ModL. < LL. (os) *sacrum*, lit., sacred (bone), transl. of Gr. *hieron osteon:* ? from former use in sacrifices] a thick, triangular bone situated at the lower end of the spinal column, where it joins both hipbones to form the dorsal part of the pelvis: it is formed in man of five fused sacral vertebrae

sad (sad) *adj.* **sad′der, sad′dest** [ME. < OE. *sæd*, sated, full, hence having feelings associated with satiety, akin to G. *satt*, sated < IE. base *sā-*, satisfied, sated, whence L. *satis*, enough, OIr. *sāith*, satiety] **1.** having, expressing, or showing low spirits or sorrow; unhappy; mournful; sorrowful **2.** causing or characterized by dejection, melancholy, or sorrow **3.** dark or dull in color; drab **4.** [Colloq.] very bad; deplorable: often used as an intensive **5.** [Dial.] heavy or soggy [a *sad* cake] —**sad′ly** *adv.* —**sad′ness** *n.*

SYN.—**sad** is the simple, general term, ranging in implication from a mild, momentary unhappiness to a feeling of intense grief; **sorrowful** implies a sadness caused by some specific loss, disappointment, etc. [her death left him *sorrowful*]; **melancholy** suggests a more or less chronic mournfulness or gloominess, or, often, merely a wistful pensiveness [*melancholy* thoughts about the future]; **dejected** implies discouragement or a sinking of spirits, as because of frustration; **depressed** suggests a mood of brooding despondency, as because of fatigue or a sense of futility [the novel left him feeling *depressed*]; **doleful** implies a mournful, often lugubrious, sadness [the *doleful* look on a lost child's face] —*ANT.* happy, cheerful

sad·den (sad′'n) *vt., vi.* to make or become sad

sad·dle (sad′'l) *n.* [ME. *sadel* < OE. *sadol*, akin to G. *sattel* < Gmc. *sathula*, ult. (? via Slav.) < IE. base *sed-*, to sit, whence sit, L. *sedere*] **1.** a seat for a rider on a horse, bicycle, etc., usually padded and of leather and generally straddled in riding **2.** a padded part of a harness worn over a horse's back to hold the shafts **3.** the part of an animal's back where a saddle is placed **4.** anything suggesting a saddle, as in form, placement, etc. **5.** a ridge between two peaks or summits **6.** *a)* a cut of lamb, venison, etc. including part of the backbone and the two loins *b)* the rear part of the back of a fowl —*vt.* **-dled, -dling 1.** to put a saddle upon **2.** to load or encumber, as with a burden **3.** to impose as a burden, obligation, etc. —*vi.* to put a saddle on a horse and mount it (often with *up*) —**in the saddle 1.** seated on a saddle **2.** in a position of control

sad·dle·back (-bak′) *n.* something saddle-backed

sad·dle·backed (-bakt′) *adj.* **1.** having a low, hollow back curved like a saddle, as some horses **2.** having a concave outline, as a ridge between peaks

sad·dle·bag (-bag′) *n.* **1.** a large bag, usually one of a pair, carried on either side of the back of a horse, etc., just behind the saddle ☆**2.** a similar bag carried over the back wheel of a motorcycle or bicycle

☆**saddle block (anesthesia)** a method of spinal anesthesia, often used during obstetrical delivery, that produces anesthesia in that area of the body that would be in contact with a saddle during horseback riding

sad·dle·bow (-bō′) *n.* the arched front part, or bow, of a saddle, the top of which is the pommel

sad·dle·cloth (-klôth′, -kläth′) *n.* a thick cloth placed under a saddle on an animal's back

saddle horse a horse trained or suitable for riding

sad·dler (sad′lər) *n.* [ME. *sadelere*] **1.** a person whose work is making, repairing, or selling saddles, harnesses, etc. ☆**2.** an American breed of saddle horse

saddle roof a roof with two gables and a ridge

sad·dler·y (sad′lə rē) *n.*, *pl.* **-dler·ies** [ME. *sadelarie*] **1.** the work or craft of a saddler **2.** the articles, as saddles, harnesses, bridles, etc., made by a saddler **3.** a shop where such articles are sold

☆**saddle shoes** white oxford shoes with a band of contrasting leather, usually black or brown, across the instep

☆**saddle soap** a preparation, usually of mild soap and neat's-foot oil, for cleaning and softening leather

saddle sore a sore or irritation caused by friction of a saddle on a horse or rider

sad·dle·tree (-trē′) *n.* [ME. *sadeltre*] the frame of a saddle

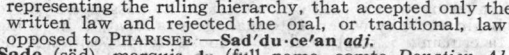
SADDLE SHOES

Sad·du·cee (saj′oo sē′, sad′yoo-) *n.* [ME. *Saducei* < OE. *Sadduce* < LL.(Ec.) *Sadducaeus* < Gr.(Ec.) *Saddoukaios* < Heb. *tsāddūqi*, prob. < *tsādhōq*, Zadok: cf. Ezek. 40:46] a member of an ancient Jewish party representing the ruling hierarchy, that accepted only the written law and rejected the oral, or traditional, law: opposed to PHARISEE —**Sad′du·ce′an** *adj.*

Sade (säd), marquis de (full name, comte *Donatien Alphonse François de Sade*) 1740–1814; Fr. soldier & novelist, whose writings describe sexual aberrations

sa·dhe (sä′dē, tsä′-) *n.* [Heb. *tsādē*] same as TSADI

sa·dhu (sä′doo) *n.* [Sans. < *sādhu*, straight, able < IE. base *sēdh-, to go straight to a goal, whence Gr. *ithyein*, to go straight] a Hindu holy man

Sa·di (sä′dē) (born *Muslih-ud-Din*) 1184?–1291?; Persian poet

Sa·die (sā′dē) a feminine name: see SARAH

sad·i·ron (sad′ī′ərn) *n.* [SAD (sense 5) + IRON] a heavy, solid flatiron, pointed at both ends

sad·ism (sad′iz′m, sā′diz′m) *n.* [Fr., after marquis de SADE] **1.** the getting of sexual pleasure from dominating, mistreating, or hurting one's partner **2.** the getting of pleasure from inflicting physical or psychological pain on another or others Cf. MASOCHISM —**sad′ist** *n.* —**sa·dis·tic** (sə dis′tik, sā-) *adj.* —**sa·dis′ti·cal·ly** *adv.*

sad·o·mas·o·chism (sad′ō mas′ə kiz′m, sad′ō-; -maz′-) *n.* [SAD(ISM) + -o- + MASOCHISM] a condition in which sadism and masochism coexist in the same individual —**sad′o·mas′o·chist** *n.* —**sad′o·mas′o·chis′tic** *adj.*

Sa·do·vá (sä′dō vä′) village in NW Czechoslovakia: see HRADEC KRÁLOVÉ

☆**sad sack** [clip of mil. slang "sad sack of dung (euphemism)"] [Slang] a person who means well but is incompetent, ineffective, etc. and is consistently in trouble

SAE, S.A.E. Society of Automotive Engineers

sa·fa·ri (sa fär′ē) *n.*, *pl.* **-ris** [Swahili < Ar. *safariy*, for a journey < Ar. *safara*, to travel] **1.** a journey or hunting expedition, esp. in E Africa **2.** the caravan of such an expedition

safe (sāf) *adj.* **saf′er, saf′est** [ME. *sauf* < OFr. < L. *salvus*, akin to *salus*, health, sound condition < IE. base *solo-, whole, well-preserved, whence Gr. *holos*, whole, Sans. *sarva*, unharmed, whole] **1.** *a)* free from damage, danger, or injury; secure *b)* having escaped danger or injury; unharmed **2.** *a)* giving protection *b)* involving no risk *c)* trustworthy **3.** no longer dangerous; unable to cause trouble or damage [*safe* in jail] **4.** taking no risks; prudent; cautious: said of persons ☆**5.** *Baseball* having reached a base without being put out —*n.* [altered (after the adj.) < earlier *save* < SAVE[1]] **1.** a container or box, capable of being locked and usually of metal, in which to store valuables **2.** any compartment, box, etc. for storing or preserving food, etc. [a meat *safe*] —**safe′ly** *adv.* —**safe′ness** *n.*
SYN.—**safe** implies freedom from damage, danger, or injury or from the risk of damage, etc. [is it *safe* to leave?]; **secure**, often interchangeable with **safe**, is now usually applied to something about which there is no need to feel apprehension [he is *secure* in his job] —ANT. **dangerous, precarious, unsure**

safe·blow·ing (-blō′iŋ) *n.* the use of explosives to open safes for robbing them —**safe′blow′er** *n.*

safe-con·duct (-kän′dukt) *n.* [ME. *saufconduit* < OFr.: see SAFE & CONDUCT] **1.** permission to travel through a dangerous area, as in time of war, with protection against arrest or harm **2.** a written pass giving such permission **3.** the act of conducting in safety

safe·crack·ing (-krak′iŋ) *n.* the breaking open and robbing of safes —**safe′crack′er** *n.*

☆**safe-de·pos·it** (-di päz′it) *adj.* designating or of a box or vault, esp. in a bank, for storing jewels and other valuables: also **safe′ty-de·pos′it**

safe·guard (-gärd′) *n.* [ME. *saufgarde* < MFr. *sauvegarde*: see SAVE[1] & GUARD] any person or thing that protects or guards against loss or injury; specif., *a)* a precaution or protective stipulation *b)* a permit or pass allowing safe passage *c)* a convoy or guard *d)* a safety device, as on machinery —*vt.* to protect or guard

safe·keep·ing (-kēp′iŋ) *n.* a keeping or being kept in safety; protection or custody

safe·light (-līt′) *n.* a dim light or lamp for a photographic darkroom shielded to filter out rays that affect film, printing paper, etc.

safe·ty (sāf′tē) *n.*, *pl.* **-ties** [ME. *sauvete* < MFr. *sauveté* < OFr. *salvetet* < ML. *salvitas*, safety < L. *salvus*: see SAFE] **1.** the quality or condition of being safe; freedom from danger, injury, or damage; security **2.** any of certain devices for preventing an accident; specif., *a)* a catch or locking device on a firearm that prevents it from firing: also **safety catch, safety lock** *b)* same as CONDOM ☆**3.** *Baseball* same as BASE HIT ☆**4.** *Football a)* a play in which the ball is grounded by a player behind his own goal line when the ball was caused to pass the goal line by his own team: it scores as two points for the opponents: cf. TOUCHBACK *b)* a player of a defensive backfield whose position is deep, behind the cornerbacks: in full **safety man** —*adj.* giving safety; reducing danger or harm

safety belt 1. same as LIFE BELT **2.** a belt attaching a telephone lineman, window washer, etc. to a telephone pole, window sill, etc. to prevent falling **3.** same as SEAT BELT

safety glass glass made to be shatterproof by fastening together two sheets of glass with a transparent, plastic substance between them

☆**safety island** same as SAFETY ZONE

safety lamp a miner's lamp designed to avoid explosion, fire, etc.; specif., same as DAVY LAMP

safety match a match that will light only when it is struck on a prepared surface

safety pin a pin bent back on itself so as to form a spring, and having the point covered and held with a guard which prevents accidental unfastening

☆**safety razor** a razor with a detachable blade fitted into a holder provided with guards and set at an angle which minimizes the danger of cutting the skin

safety valve 1. an automatic valve for a steam boiler, etc., which releases steam if the pressure becomes excessive **2.** anything which serves as an outlet for the release of strong emotion, energy, etc.

☆**safety zone** a platform or an area marked in a roadway from which vehicular traffic is diverted, for protection of pedestrians, as in boarding or leaving buses

saf·fi·an leather (saf′ē ən) *n.* [G. *saffian* < Per. *sähtijän*, goatskin < *säht*, hard, firm] leather made of sheepskin or goatskin tanned with sumac and usually dyed a bright color

saf·flow·er (saf′lou′ər) *n.* [altered (after ff. & FLOWER) < Du. or MFr.: Du. *saffloer* < MFr. *saffleur* < It. *saffiore* < Ar. *aṣ far*, a yellow plant, orig., yellow] **1.** a thistlelike, annual plant (*Carthamus tinctorius*) of the composite family, with large, orange flower heads and seeds that yield a drying oil used in paints, foods, medicine, etc. **2.** a dyestuff or drug prepared from its florets

saf·fron (saf′rən) *n.* [ME. *saffroun* < OFr. *safran* < ML. *safranum* < Ar. *za'farān*] **1.** a perennial old-world plant (*Crocus sativus*) of the iris family, with funnel-shaped purplish flowers having orange stigmas **2.** the dried, aromatic stigmas of this plant, used in flavoring and coloring foods, and formerly in medicine **3.** orange yellow: also **saffron yellow** —*adj.* orange-yellow

Sa·fi (sä fē′, saf′ē) seaport in W Morocco, on the Atlantic: pop. 100,000

S. Afr. 1. South Africa **2.** South African

saf·ra·nine (saf′rə nēn′, -nin) *n.* [Fr. *safran*, SAFFRON + -INE[4]] **1.** a yellowish-red aniline dye, $C_{18}H_{15}N_4Cl$, or any of several dyes closely related in structure to this **2.** any mixture of the various salts of the safranine dyes, used as a dye and as a stain in microscopy Also **saf′ra·nin** (-nin)

saf·role (saf′rōl) *n.* [Fr. *safran*, SAFFRON + -ole, for -OL[2]] a clear, colorless oil, $C_{10}H_{10}O_2$, found in sassafras oil, camphor wood, etc., and used in perfumes, medicines, flavors, etc.: regarded as a possible carcinogen, its use in foods and beverages is forbidden in the U.S

sag (sag) *vi* **sagged, sag′ging** [ME. *saggen*, prob. < Scand., akin to Sw. *sacka*, Norw. dial. *sakka*, *sagga* < ? IE. base *seg-, to attach, append, whence Sans. *sájati*, to attach] **1.** to sink, bend, or curve, esp. in the middle, from weight or pressure **2.** to hang down unevenly or loosely **3.** to lose firmness, strength, or intensity; weaken through weariness, age, etc.; droop [*sagging* spirits] **4.** to decline in price, value, sales, etc. **5.** *Naut.* to drift (esp. *to* leeward) —*vt.* to cause to sag —*n.* **1.** the act or an instance of sagging **2.** the degree or amount of sagging ☆**3.** a place of sagging; sunken or depressed place

sa·ga (sä′gə) *n.* [ON., thing said, tale, story, akin to OE. *sagu* (cf. SAW[2]): see SAY] **1.** a medieval Scandinavian story of battles, customs, and legends, narrated in prose and generally telling the traditional history of an important Norse family **2.** any long story of adventure or heroic deeds **3.** same as ROMAN FLEUVE: in full **saga novel**

sa·ga·cious (sa gā′shəs) *adj.* [< L. *sagax* (gen. *sagacis*), wise, foreseeing, akin to *sagire*, to perceive acutely: see SAKE[1]] **1.** having or showing keen perception or discernment and sound judgment, foresight, etc. **2.** [Obs.] having a keen sense of smell —SYN. see SHREWD —**sa·ga′cious·ly** *adv.* —**sa·ga′cious·ness** *n.*

sa·gac·i·ty (sə gas′ə tē) *n.*, *pl.* **-ties** [Fr. *sagacité* < L. *sagacitas*] the quality or an instance of being sagacious; penetrating intelligence and sound judgment

☆**sag·a·more** (sag′ə môr′) *n.* [< AmInd. (Abnaki) *sāgimau*] a chief of second rank among certain tribes of N. American Indians: sometimes equivalent to SACHEM (sense 1)

sage[1] (sāj) *adj.* **sag′er, sag′est** [ME. < OFr. < VL. *sapius* < L. *sapiens*, wise, orig. prp. of *sapere*, to know, taste < IE. base *sap-*, to taste, whence ON. *safi*, sap, *sefi*, mind] **1.** wise, discerning, judicious, etc. **2.** showing wisdom and good judgment [a *sage* comment] **3.** [Obs.] grave or solemn —*n.* a very wise man; esp., an elderly man, widely respected for his wisdom, experience, and judgment — SYN. see WISE[1] —**sage′ly** *adv.* —**sage′ness** *n.*

sage[2] (sāj) *n.* [ME. *sauge* < OFr. < L. *salvia* < *salvus*, SAFE: from its reputed healing powers] **1.** any of a genus (*Salvia*) of plants of the mint family, having a two-lipped corolla and two stamens: sages are cultivated for ornament, as the **scarlet sage** (*Salvia splendens*) with brilliant red flowers, calyx, and corolla, or for flavoring, as the **garden sage** (*Salvia officinalis*) with aromatic leaves used, when dried, for seasoning meats, cheeses, etc. **2.** any of various similar plants ☆**3.** same as SAGEBRUSH

Sage (sāj), Russell 1816-1906; U.S. financier

☆**sage·brush** (-brush′) *n.* [SAGE[2] + BRUSH[1]] any of a number of plants (genus *Artemisia*) of the composite family, common in the dry, alkaline areas of the W U.S.; esp., the **big sagebrush** (*Artemisia tridentata*), with small, aromatic leaves and minute flower heads, important as a forage plant

☆**sage grouse** a large grouse (*Centrocercus urophasianus*) living on the sagebrush plains of W N. America: also, esp. for the female, **sage hen**

sag·ger, sag·gar (sag′ər) *n.* [dial. *saggard*, contr. < ? SAFEGUARD] **1.** a protective case of fire clay for baking finer or more delicate ceramics in the kiln **2.** the clay of which it is made —*vt.* to bake in a sagger

sag·gy (sag′ē) *adj.* **-gi·er, -gi·est** inclined to sag

Sag·i·naw (sag′ə nô′) [< Ojibway village name, lit., at the mouth of a river] city in EC Mich.: pop. 92,000

Sa·git·ta (sə jit′ə) [L., lit., arrow] a small N constellation between Vulpecula and Aquila

sag·it·tal (saj′i t′l) *adj.* [ModL. *sagittalis* < L. *sagitta*, arrow] **1.** of or like an arrow or arrowhead **2.** *Anat.* *a*) designating or of the suture between the two parietal bones along the length of the skull *b*) designating, of, or in the longitudinal plane of this suture, regarded as dividing the body into right and left halves *c*) of or in any plane parallel to this —**sag′it·tal·ly** *adv.*

Sag·it·ta·ri·us (saj′i ter′ē əs) [ME. < L., archer < *sagitta*, arrow] **1.** a large S constellation in the brightest part of the Milky Way, beyond which lies the center of our galaxy **2.** the ninth sign of the zodiac (♐), which the sun enters about November 23: see ZODIAC, illus.

sag·it·tar·y (saj′ə ter′ē) *n.*, *pl.* **-tar′ies** [L. *sagittarius* < *sagitta*, arrow] same as CENTAUR

sag·it·tate (saj′ə tāt′) *adj.* [ModL. *sagittatus* < L. *sagitta*, arrow] in the shape of an arrowhead, as some leaves: see LEAF, illus.

sa·go (sā′gō) *n.*, *pl.* **-gos** [Malay *sāgū*] **1.** an edible starch prepared from the pith of the trunk of the gomuti, from the underground stems of certain cycads, as the coontie, or from some other plants, esp. palms **2.** any of the palms that yield sago: also **sago palm**

Sa·guache Range (sə wäch′) same as SAWATCH MOUNTAINS

☆**sa·gua·ro** (sə gwä′rō, -wä′-) *n.*, *pl.* **-ros** [MexSp. < the Piman native name] a giant cactus (*Carnegiea gigantea*) with a thick, spiny stem and white flowers, native to the SW U.S. and N Mexico: also **sa·hua′ro** (-wä′-)

Sag·ue·nay (sag′ə nā′) river in SC Quebec, Canada, flowing southeastward from Lake St. John into the Gulf of St. Lawrence: c. 120 mi. (incl. principal headstream north of Lake St. John, 475 mi.)

Sa·hap·tin (sä hap′tən) *n.* [< Salish name for the Nez Percé] **1.** *pl.* **-tins, -tin** any member of several N. American Indian tribes living in Washington, Oregon, and Idaho and speaking closely related dialects of one language **2.** their Penutian language **3.** a language family consisting of Sahaptin and Nez Percé Also **Sa·hap′ti·an** (-tē ən)

Sa·ha·ra (sə har′ə, -her′ə, -hä′rə) [Ar. *ṣaḥrā*, a desert] vast desert region in N Africa, extending from the Atlantic to the Nile (or to the Red Sea): c. 3,500,000 sq. mi. —**Sa·har′an** *adj.*

Sa·ha·ran·pur (sə hä′rən poor′) city in N India, in Uttar Pradesh: pop. 185,000

sa·hib (sä′ib, -hib, -ēb, -hēb) *n.* [Hind. *sāhib* < Ar. *ṣāhib*, master, lit., friend] sir; master: title formerly used in colonial India when speaking to or of a European

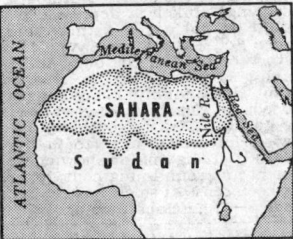

SAHARA

Sa·id[2] (sā′id) *n.* same as SAYYID

Sa·i·da (sä′ē dä′) seaport in SW Lebanon, on the site of ancient Sidon: pop. 22,000

sai·ga (sī′gə) *n.* [Russ. *saiga*] a small, stocky, sheeplike antelope (*Saiga tatarica*) with a broad, fleshy snout, native to the steppes of SE Russia and SW Siberia

Sai·gon (sī gän′) seaport & capital of South Vietnam: pop. (with Cholon) 1,431,000

sail (sāl) *n.* [ME. *seil*, sail < OE. *segl*, akin to G. *segel*, prob. ult. < IE. base *sek-*, to cut, whence L. *secare*, to cut, *segmentum*, a segment] **1.** any of the shaped sheets of canvas or other strong material spread to catch or deflect the wind, by means of which some vessels and some land vehicles are driven forward **2.** sails collectively **3.** a sailing vessel or vessels **4.** a trip in a ship or boat, esp. one moved by sails **5.** anything like a sail, as an arm of a windmill —*vi.* [ME. *seilen* < OE. *seglian* < the *n.*] **1.** to be moved forward by means of a sail or sails, or by mechanical means such as a propeller **2.** to move upon or travel by water: said of a vessel or its passengers **3.** to begin a trip by water **4.** to manage a sailboat, as in racing or cruising **5.** to glide, float, or move steadily through the air **6.** to move smoothly and with dignity, like a ship in full sail **7.** [Colloq.] to move quickly ☆**8.** [Colloq.] to begin vigorously; throw oneself (*into*) with energy ☆**9.** [Colloq.] to attack, criticize, or reprimand someone severely (with *into*) —*vt.* **1.** to move through or upon (a body of water) in a boat or ship **2.** to manage or navigate (a boat or ship) —**in sail** with sails set —**make sail 1.** to spread out a ship's sail **2.** to begin a trip by water —**sail against the wind 1.** to sail a course that slants slightly away from the true direction of the wind; sail closehauled **2.** to work under difficulties or against direct opposition Also **sail near (to) the wind** —**set sail 1.** to hoist the sails in preparation for departure **2.** to start out on a voyage by water —**take in sail** to lower sails, as in order to reduce the area of sail set —**under sail** sailing; with sails set

SAILS ON A FULL-RIGGED SHIP

1. flying jib; 2. jib; 3. fore-topmast staysail; 4. foresail; 5. lower fore-topsail; 6. upper fore-topsail; 7. fore-topgallant sail; 8. fore-royal; 9. fore-skysail; 10. lower studdingsail; 11. fore-topmast studdingsail; 12. fore-topgallant studdingsail; 13. fore-royal studdingsail; 14. main staysail; 15. maintopmast staysail; 16. main-topgallant staysail; 17. main-royal staysail; 18. mainsail; 19. lower main topsail; 20. upper main topsail; 21. main-topgallant sail; 22. main royal; 23. main skysail; 24. maintopmast studdingsail; 25. main-topgallant studdingsail; 26. main-royal studdingsail; 27. mizzen staysail; 28. mizzen-topmast staysail; 29. mizzen-topgallant staysail; 30. mizzen-royal staysail; 31. mizzen sail; 32. lower mizzen topsail; 33. upper mizzen topsail; 34. mizzen-topgallant sail; 35. mizzen royal; 36. mizzen skysail; 37. spanker

sail·boat (-bōt′) *n.* a boat having a sail or sails by means of which it is propelled

sail·cloth (-klôth′, -kläth′) *n.* **1.** long-fibered canvas or other cloth used in making sails, tents, etc. **2.** a piece of such material used as a covering, etc.

sail·er (-ər) *n.* a ship or boat, esp. one equipped with sails, specif. with reference to its sailing capability [a swift *sailer*]

sail·fish (-fish′) *n.*, *pl.* **-fish′, -fish′es;** see FISH[2] any of a genus (*Istiophorus*) of large, tropical, marine fishes related to the swordfish and the marlin, but with elongated scales and

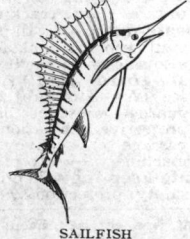

SAILFISH
(to 11 ft. long)

a large saillike dorsal fin in addition to the sword-shaped upper jaw

sail·ing (-iŋ) *n.* **1.** the act of a thing or person that sails **2.** the art of navigation **3.** the sport of managing a sailboat, as for racing **4.** the start of a trip by water —*adj.* **1.** driven forward by the action of wind on sails **2.** of ships or shipping [*sailing* orders]

sail·or (-ər) *n.* [ME. *sailer*] **1.** a person who makes his living by sailing; mariner; seaman **2.** *a)* an enlisted man in the navy *b)* any person in the navy **3.** a person sailing on a vessel, with reference to susceptibility to seasickness [a good or bad *sailor*] **4.** a straw hat with a low, flat crown and flat brim —**sail'or·ly** *adj.*

sail·or·ing (-ər iŋ) *n.* the work and life of a sailor

☆**sail·or's-choice** (-ərz chois') *n., pl.* **sail'or's-choice'** any of several food fishes of the W Atlantic and the Gulf of Mexico; specif., a small grunt (*Haemulon parrai*)

sail·plane (sāl'plān') *n.* a light glider especially designed for soaring —*vi.* -**planed'**, -**plan'ing** to fly a sailplane

sain (sān) *vt.* [ME. *sainen* < OE. *segnian* < L. *signare*: see SIGN, *v.*] [Archaic or Dial.] to make the sign of the cross over, or to bless, as a protection against evil

sain·foin (sān'foin) *n.* [Fr. < *sain*, wholesome (< L. *sanus*, healthy, confused in Fr. with *saint*) + *foin* (< L. *faenum*), hay] a Eurasian perennial plant (*Onobrychis viciaefolia*) of the legume family, cultivated as a forage or cover crop

saint (sānt) *n.* [ME. < OFr. < LL.(Ec.) *sanctus*, a saint < L., holy, consecrated, pp. of *sancire*, to consecrate, akin to *sacer*: see SACRED] **1.** a holy person **2.** a person who is exceptionally meek, charitable, patient, etc. **3.** [*pl.*] those, esp. holy persons, who have died and are believed to be with God **4.** *a)* in the New Testament, any Christian *b)* [S-] a member of any of certain religious groups calling themselves *Saints* **5.** in certain Christian churches, a person officially recognized as having lived an exceptionally holy life, and thus as being in heaven and capable of interceding for sinners; canonized person —*vt.* to make a saint of; canonize Names of saints are entered in this dictionary under the given name (see JOHN, PAUL, etc.); for some other entries, see ST. & ff.

Saint Agnes's Eve the night of January 20, when a girl was supposed to have a revelation of her future husband if she performed certain superstitious rites

Saint Andrew's cross a cross shaped like an X

Saint Anthony's cross a cross shaped like the Greek letter tau (T)

Saint Anthony's fire formerly, any of several skin conditions or inflammations, as erysipelas or ergotism

Saint Ber·nard (bər närd') a large, reddish-brown and white dog of a breed once kept by the monks of the hospice of the Great St. Bernard Pass, in the Swiss Alps, trained to rescue travelers in the snow

Sainte-Beuve (sant böv'), **Charles Au·gus·tin** (shårl ō güs tan') 1804–69; Fr. literary critic & writer

saint·ed (sān'tid) *adj.* **1.** of, like, or suitable for a saint; saintly **2.** regarded or venerated as a saint **3.** holy; sacred; hallowed

SAINT BERNARD (25-1/2–27-1/2 in. high at shoulder)

Saint Elmo's fire (or **light**) (el'mō) [after *Saint Elmo*, patron saint of sailors] a visible electric discharge (*corona*) from charged, esp. pointed, objects, as the tips of masts, spires, trees, etc.: seen sometimes during electrical storms

Saint-Ex·u·pé·ry (san teg zü pā rē'), **An·toine de** (än twän') 1900–44; Fr. aviator & writer

Saint-Gau·dens (sānt gô'd'nz), **Augustus** 1848–1907; U.S. sculptor, born in Ireland

Saint George's cross a red Greek cross on a white background

saint·hood (sānt'hood') *n.* [see -HOOD] **1.** the status or rank of a saint: also **saint'ship'** **2.** saints collectively

Saint Johns·wort (jänz'wurt') [< *Saint* JOHN + WORT²: reason for name unc.] **1.** any of a genus (*Hypericum*) of plants of the Saint Johnswort family, with usually yellow flowers, numerous stamens, and spotted leaves, sometimes cultivated for ornament **2.** designating a family (Hypericaceae) of plants including the Saint Johnsworts

Saint-Just (san zhüst'), **Louis An·toine Lé·on de** (lwē än twän' lā ōn' də) 1767–94; Fr. revolutionist

saint·ly (sānt'lē) *adj.* -**li·er**, -**li·est** like or suitable for a saint —**saint'li·ness** *n.*

Saint Patrick's Day March 17, observed by the Irish in honor of Saint Patrick, the patron saint of Ireland

Saint-Pierre *see* BERNARDIN DE SAINT-PIERRE

Saint-Saëns (san säns'), **Charles Ca·mille** (shårl kå mē'y') 1835–1921; Fr. composer

Saints·bur·y (sānts'ber'ē, -bər ē), **George (Edward Bateman)** 1845–1933; Eng. literary critic

Saint-Si·mon (san sē mōn') **1.** comte de, (*Claude Henri de Rouvroy*) 1760–1825; Fr. social philosopher **2.** duc de, (*Louis de Rouvroy*) 1675–1755; Fr. courtier & writer

Saint Valentine's Day February 14, observed in honor of a martyr of the 3d cent. and, coincidentally, as a day for sending valentines to sweethearts, etc.

Saint Vi·tus' dance (vī'təs) [after *St. Vitus*, 3d-cent. patron saint of persons having chorea] *same as* CHOREA

Sai·pan (sī pan', -pän') largest island of the Mariana Islands, in the W Pacific: 70 sq. mi.

Sa·is (sā'is) ancient city in the Nile delta; capital of Egypt (675?–525 B.C.)

Sa·i·shu (sä'ē shōō') *Jap.* name of CHEJU

saith (seth; *now also* sā'ith) *archaic 3d pers. sing., pres. indic.,* of SAY

Sa·kai (sä'kī) city in S Honshu, Japan, just south of Osaka, on Osaka Bay: pop. 466,000

sake¹ (sāk) *n.* [ME. < OE. *sacu*, cause or suit at law, contention, akin to G. *sache*, thing, affair < IE. base *sāg-*, to investigate, whence SEEK, L. *sagire*, to perceive, find, *sagax*, sharply discerning] **1.** purpose or reason; motive; cause [for the *sake* of harmony] **2.** advantage; benefit [for my *sake*] —**for heaven's** (or **gosh** or **Pete's**) **sake!** a mild exclamation of surprise, annoyance, etc.

sa·ke² (sä'kē) *n.* [Jap. *sake* < *saka-mizu*, prosperous waters] a Japanese alcoholic beverage made from fermented rice and usually warmed for serving: also sp. **sa'ki**

sa·ker (sā'kər) *n.* [ME. *sacre* < MFr. < Ar. *ṣakr*] a large, old-world falcon (*Falco sacer*), used in falconry

Sa·kha·lin (säkhä lēn'; *E.* sak'ə lēn') island of the U.S.S.R. off the E coast of Siberia: c. 29,000 sq. mi.

Sa·ki (sä'kē) (pseud. of *Hector Hugh Munro*) 1870–1916; Brit. short-story writer & novelist, born in Burma

Sak·ti (säk'tē, sak'-) *n. same as* SHAKTI —**Sak'tism** *n.*

sal (sal) *n.* [ME. < L., SALT] *Pharmacy* salt

sa·laam (sə läm') *n.* [Ar. *salām*, health, peace, akin to Heb. *shālōm*, peace] **1.** a greeting (lit., peace) used among Moslems: in full **salaam a·lei·kum** (ä lā koom'), "peace (be) to you" **2.** an Oriental greeting or ceremonial compliment, made by bowing low with the palm of the right hand placed on the forehead **3.** an obeisance or respectful greeting —*vt.* to greet with a salaam —*vi.* to make a salaam

sal·a·ble (sāl'ə b'l) *adj.* that can be sold; marketable —**sal'a·bil'i·ty** *n.*

sa·la·cious (sə lā'shəs) *adj.* [L. *salax* (gen. *salacis*) < *salire*, to leap, (of animals) cover sexually: see SALIENT] **1.** lecherous **2.** erotically stimulating; pornographic —**sa·la'cious·ly** *adv.* —**sa·la'cious·ness, sa·lac'i·ty** (-las'ə tē) *n.*

sal·ad (sal'əd) *n.* [ME. *salat* < MFr. *salade* < Pr. *salada* < L. *salata*, pp. of *salare*, to salt < *sal*, SALT] **1.** a dish, usually cold, of raw or sometimes cooked vegetables or fruits in various combinations, served with a dressing, or molded in gelatin, and sometimes with seafood, poultry, eggs, etc. added **2.** any green plant or herb used for such a dish or eaten raw; esp., [Dial.] lettuce

salad days [after Shakespeare, *Antony and Cleopatra*, I, v] time of youth and inexperience

salad dressing a preparation of olive oil or other vegetable oil, vinegar, spices, etc. served with a salad

Sal·a·din (sal'ə din) (born *Salah-ed-Din Yusuf ibn-Ayub*) 1137–93; sultan of Egypt & Syria (1174–93)

Sa·la·do (sä lä'thō) river in N Argentina, flowing from the Andes southeast into the Paraná: c. 1,100 mi.

Sal·a·man·ca (sal'ə maŋ'kə; *Sp.* säl'ä mäŋ'kä) city in León, WC Spain: pop. 101,000

sal·a·man·der (sal'ə man'dər) *n.* [ME. *salamandre* < OFr. < L. *salamandra* < Gr.] **1.** a mythological reptile resembling the lizard, that was said to live in fire **2.** a spirit supposed to live in fire: orig., one of four elemental spirits in Paracelsus' system **3.** any of various articles used in fire or able to withstand heat, as an iron poker, a plate for browning pastry, etc. **4.** any of a group of tailed amphibians (order Caudata) related to the frogs and toads, with a soft, moist skin —**sal'a·man'drine** (-drin) *adj.*

sa·la·mi (sə lä'mē) *n.* [It., pl. of *salame*, preserved meat, salt pork < VL. *salamen*, for LL. *salsamen*, salted food < L. *salsus*, pp. of *salere*, to salt < *sal*, SALT] a highly spiced, salted sausage, orig. Italian, of pork and beef, or of beef alone

Sal·a·mis (sal'ə mis; *Gr.* sä lä mēs') **1.** Gr. island in Saronic Gulf, near Athens: scene of a naval battle (480 B.C.) in which the Greeks defeated the Persians: c. 35 sq. mi. **2.** ancient ruined city on the E coast of Cyprus

sal ammoniac [ME. *sal armoniak* < L. *sal Ammoniacum*, lit., salt of Ammon: see AMMONIA] *same as* AMMONIUM CHLORIDE

sal·a·ried (sal'ə rēd) *adj.* **1.** receiving a salary **2.** yielding a salary [a *salaried* position]

sal·a·ry (sal'ə rē) *n., pl.* -**ries** [ME. *salarie* < L. *salarium*, orig., money for salt (as part of Roman soldier's pay), hence pay < *sal*, SALT] a fixed payment at regular intervals for services, esp. when clerical or professional —*SYN.* see WAGE

Sa·la·zar (sä'lə zär'), **An·to·nio de O·li·vei·ra** (än tō'nyoo dē ō'lē vā'rə) 1889–1970; prime minister & dictator of Portugal (1932–68)

sale (sāl) *n.* [ME. < OE. *sala* < ON. *sala*: for IE. base see SELL] **1.** the act of selling; exchange of property of any

kind, or of services, for an agreed sum of money or other valuable consideration **2.** opportunity to sell or be sold; market **3.** the act of offering goods to the highest bidder; auction **4.** a special offering of goods at prices lower than usual **5.** [*pl.*] receipts in business **6.** [*pl.*] the work, department, etc. of selling /a job in *sales*/ —**for** (or **on**) **sale** to be sold; offered for purchase

sale·a·ble (sāl′ə b'l) *adj. same as* SALABLE

Sa·lem (sā′ləm) **1.** [< Biblical place name: cf. Gen. 14:18, Ps. 76:2] *a*) capital of Oreg., in the NW part, on the Willamette River: pop. 68,000 *b*) city in NE Mass., on Massachusetts Bay: suburb of Boston: pop. 41,000 **2.** city in Madras state, S India: pop. 249,000

sal·ep (sal′ep) *n.* [Fr. < Sp. < Ar. *saḥlab*, altered & contr. < *khuṣa al-tha′lab*, fox's testicles: cf. ORCHID] the starchy dried tubers of various orchids (esp. genera *Orchis* and *Eulophia*), ground up and used as food

☆**sal·e·ra·tus** (sal′ə rāt′əs) *n.* [ModL. *sal aeratus*, aerated salt] sodium (or sometimes potassium) bicarbonate; baking soda, as used in cooking

Sa·ler·no (sä ler′nō; *E.* sə ler′nō) seaport in S Italy, on an inlet (**Gulf of Salerno**) of the Tyrrhenian Sea: pop. 136,000: ancient name **Sa·ler·num** (sə lur′nəm)

☆**sales·clerk** (sālz′klurk′) *n.* a person employed to sell goods in a store

sales·man (sālz′mən) *n., pl.* **-men** (-mən) **1.** a man employed as a salesclerk ☆**2.** one employed as a traveling agent or representative to sell goods or services

sales·man·ship (-ship′) *n.* [see -SHIP] the ability, skill, or technique of selling

☆**sales·per·son** (-pur′s'n) *n.* a person employed to sell goods; esp., a salesclerk —**sales′peo′ple** (-pē′p'l) *n.pl.*

☆**sales promotion** the use of publicizing methods other than paid advertising to promote a product, service, etc.

☆**sales resistance** resistance of potential customers to efforts and inducements aimed at getting them to buy

☆**sales·room** (-rōōm′) *n.* a room in which goods are shown and offered for sale

☆**sales slip** a receipt or bill of sale for a purchase from a retail store

☆**sales talk 1.** persuasion or argument used in an attempt to sell something **2.** any argument aimed at persuading one to do or believe something

☆**sales tax** a tax on sales and, sometimes, services, added to the price paid by the ultimate consumer

sales·wom·an (-woom′ən) *n., pl.* **-wom′en** (-wim′in) a woman salesclerk: also **sales′la′dy** (-lā′dē), *pl.* **-dies**, **sales′girl′** (-gurl′)

Sal·ferd (sôl′fard, sal′-) city in Lancashire, NW England, near Manchester: pop. 146,000

Sa·li·an (sā′lē ən) *adj.* [< LL. *Salii*, Salian Franks < the Gmc. name] designating or of a tribe of Franks who settled along the Ijssel River, in the Netherlands, in the 4th cent. A.D. —*n.* a Salian Frank

Sal·ic (sal′ik, sā′lik) *adj.* [ML. *Salicus*] **1.** of the Salian Franks **2.** of the Salic law

sal·i·cin (sal′ə sin) *n.* [Fr. *salicine* < L. *salix* (gen. *salicis*), willow, akin to *saliva*, saliva < IE. *salik-* < base *sal-*, gray, whence OE. *sol*, dark, dirty, *sealh*, willow] a white, crystalline glucoside, C₁₃H₁₈O₇, obtained from the bark of certain poplars and willows, and used as a reagent

Salic law 1. a code of laws of Germanic tribes, including the Salian Franks; esp., the provision of this code excluding women from inheriting land **2.** the law excluding women from succeeding to the throne in the French and Spanish monarchies

sa·lic·y·late (sə lis′ə lāt′; sal′ə sil′āt, -it) *n.* any salt or ester of salicylic acid

sal·i·cyl·ic acid (sal′ə sil′ik) [*salicyl* (radical of the acid) < Fr. *salicyle* < L. *salix* (see SALICIN) + Fr. *-yle*, -YL + -IC] a white, crystalline compound, C₇H₆O₃, prepared from salicin or phenol and used in the manufacture of aspirin, as a food preservative and mild antiseptic, and, in the form of its salts, to treat rheumatism, relieve pain, etc.

sa·lient (sāl′yənt, sā′lē ənt) *adj.* [L. *saliens*, prp. of *salire*, to leap < IE. base *sel-*, to jump, whence Gr. *halma*, a leap] **1.** *a*) leaping, jumping, or capering *b*) gushing or jetting forth **2.** pointing outward; jutting or projecting, as an angle **3.** standing out from the rest; noticeable; conspicuous; prominent —*n.* **1.** the part of a battle line, trench, fort, etc. which projects farthest toward the enemy **2.** a salient angle, part, etc. —**sa′lience, sa′lien·cy** *n., pl.* **-cies** —**sa′lient·ly** *adv.*

sa·li·en·ti·an (sā′lē en′shē ən, -shən) *n.* [ModL. *Salientia*, name of the order (< L. *saliens*: see prec.) + -AN] any of a subclass (Salientia) of tailless amphibians, with a broad body and well-developed hind legs; it includes frogs, toads, and tree toads —*adj.* of or pertaining to the salientians

sa·lif·er·ous (sə lif′ər əs) *adj.* [< L. *sal*, SALT + -FEROUS] producing or containing salt

sal·i·fy (sal′ə fi′) *vt.* **-fied′, -fy′ing** [Fr. *salifier* < L. *sal*, salt + *-ficare*, -FY] to make salty; specif., *a*) to impregnate with salt *b*) to form a salt with; convert into a salt *c*) to combine with a salt

sa·lim·e·ter (sə lim′ə tər) *n.* [SAL + -i- + -METER] a hydrometer for determining the density of salt solutions

Sa·li·na (sə lī′nə) [< L. *salina* (see ff.): for the salt deposits found there] city in C Kans.: pop. 38,000

sa·li·na (sə lī′nə) *n.* [Sp. < L. *salinae*, salt pits < *salinus*,

saline, salty: see SALINE] a salt marsh, pond, or lake

Sa·li·nas (sə lē′nəs) [after the nearby *Salinas* River < L. *salina* (see prec.): for the salt marshes at its mouth] city in WC Calif., near San Jose: pop. 59,000

sa·line (sā′līn, -lēn; *for n. 1, also* sə lēn′) *adj.* [LME. *salyne* < L. *salinus* < *sal*, SALT] **1.** of, characteristic of, or containing common salt, or sodium chloride; salty **2.** of or containing any of the salts of the alkali metals or magnesium —*n.* **1.** a salt spring, lick, marsh, mine, etc. **2.** any of the metallic salts, esp. a salt of magnesium or of an alkali metal, often used in medicine as cathartics **3.** a saline solution, esp. one that is isotonic, used in medical treatment or for biological experiments —**sa·lin·i·ty** (sə lin′ə tē) *n.*

Sal·in·ger (sal′in jər), **J(erome) D(avid)** 1919– ; U.S. novelist & short-story writer

sal·i·nom·e·ter (sal′ə näm′ə tər) *n.* [see SALINE & -METER] any device for measuring the amount of dissolved salts in a solution, esp. one that measures the electrical conductivity of a water sample

Sa·lique (sə lēk′, sal′ik, sā′lik) *adj. same as* SALIC

Salis·bur·y (sôlz′ber′ ē, -bə rē) **1.** city in Wiltshire, SC England: noted for its 13th-cent. cathedral: pop. 36,000 **2.** capital of Rhodesia, in the NE part: pop. 327,000

Salisbury, 3d Marquis of, (*Robert Arthur Talbot Gascoyne-Cecil*) 1830–1903; Eng. statesman

Salisbury Plain rolling plateau in S Wiltshire, England: site of Stonehenge

☆**Salisbury steak** *same as* HAMBURGER (sense 2)

Sa·lish (sā′lish) *n.* [Salish *sälst*, people] **1.** a family of fifteen N. American Indian languages of the NW U.S. and SW Canada, including Flathead, etc. **2.** a member of any tribe speaking a Salish language **3.** *same as* FLATHEAD (sense 1) Also **Sa′lish·an** (-ən)

sa·li·va (sə lī′və) *n.* [L.: for IE. base see SALICIN] the thin, watery, slightly viscid fluid secreted by the salivary glands: it serves as an aid to swallowing and digestion by moistening and softening food, and contains an enzyme (*ptyalin*), which converts starch to dextrin and maltose

sal·i·var·y (sal′ə ver′ē) *adj.* of or relating to saliva; specif., designating or of three pairs of glands in the mouth that secrete saliva

sal·i·vate (-vāt′) *vt.* **-vat′ed, -vat′ing** [< L. *salivatus*, pp. of *salivare*, salivate] to produce an excessive flow of saliva in —*vi.* to secrete saliva —**sal′i·va′tion** *n.*

Salk (sôlk), **Jonas E(dward)** 1914– ; U.S. physician & bacteriologist: developed a vaccine for injection to prevent poliomyelitis

‡**salle** (sal) *n.* [Fr. < Frank. or OHG. *sal*, room, house: see SALOON] a hall or room

sal·len·ders (sal′ən dərz) *n.pl.* [Fr. *solandres*, pl. of *solandre*] a dry eruption on the hock of a horse

sal·let (sal′it) *n.* [ME. < MFr. *salade* < It. *celata*, prob. < pp. *celare*, to cover < L.: see CONCEAL] a light, rounded helmet with a projecting guard for the neck and, often, a visor, worn in the 15th cent.

sal·low¹ (sal′ō) *adj.* [ME. *salou*, sallow, dark, akin to OHG. *salo* < IE. base *sal-*, dirty gray: see SALICIN] of a sickly pale-yellowish complexion —*vt.* to make sallow —**sal′low·ish** *adj.* —**sal′low·ness** *n.*

sal·low² (sal′ō) *n.* [ME. *salwe*, *sealh*: for base see prec.] **1.** a kind of willow (*Salix caprea*) with large catkins of flowers which appear before the leaves **2.** a willow twig

Sal·lust (sal′əst) (L. name *Gaius Sallustius Crispus*) 86–35? B.C.; Rom. historian

Sal·ly (sal′ē) a feminine name: see SARAH

sal·ly (sal′ē) *n., pl.* **-lies** [MFr. *saillie* < *saillir*, to come forth suddenly, rush out, leap < L. *salire*, to leap, spring: see SALIENT] **1.** a sudden rushing forth, as of troops to attack besieging forces **2.** any sudden start into activity **3.** a quick witticism; bright retort; quip **4.** an excursion or unusual side trip; jaunt —*vi.* **-lied, -ly·ing 1.** to make a sally **2.** to rush out or come out suddenly **3.** *a*) to come or go outdoors *b*) to set out on a trip Used with *forth* or *out* —*SYN.* see JOKE

Sally Lunn (lun) [said to be name of 18th-c. Eng. woman who first made these at Bath] [*also* s- l-] a variety of sweetened tea cake, usually served hot

sal·ma·gun·di (sal′mə gun′dē) *n.* [Fr. *salmigondis*, earlier *salmigondin*, altered < ? It. *salame conditi*, preserved pickled meat < *salame* < *sal*, salt + *conditi* < pp. of *condire*, to flavor < L. *condire*, to preserve, pickle] **1.** a dish of chopped meat, eggs, etc. flavored with onions, anchovies, vinegar, and oil **2.** any mixture or medley

sal·mi (sal′mē) *n.* [Fr. *salmis*, prob. contr. < *salmigondis*: see prec.] a highly seasoned dish of game or fowl, partly roasted, then stewed in wine

salm·on (sam′ən) *n., pl.* **-on, -ons**: see PLURAL, II, D, 2 [ME. *salmoun* < MFr. < OFr. *saumon* < L. *salmo* (gen. *salmonis*) < ?] **1.** any of various bony fishes (family Salmonidae); specif., any of several varieties of game and food fishes (genera *Oncorhynchus* and *Salmo*) of the N Hemisphere, with silver scales and flesh that is yellowish pink to pale red when cooked: they live in salt water and spawn in fresh water, though some varieties are landlocked in lakes **2.** yellowish pink or pale red: also **salmon pink**

☆**salm·on·ber·ry** (-ber′ē) *n., pl.* **-ries 1.** a tall, spineless raspberry (*Rubus spectabilis*) of the W coast of N. America, having salmon-colored or reddish, edible fruit **2.** its fruit

☆**sal·mo·nel·la** (sal′mə nel′ə) *n., pl.* **-nel′lae** (-ē̄), **-nel′la**, **-nel′las** [ModL.: so named after D. E. *Salmon* (d. 1914), U.S. veterinarian] any of a genus (*Salmonella*) of Gramnegative, rod-shaped bacilli that cause various diseases in man and domestic animals, including typhoid fever, food poisoning, etc.

☆**sal·mo·nel·lo·sis** (-nel ō′sis) *n.* [< prec. + -OSIS] a disease caused by various strains of salmonella and characterized by fever, malaise, and intestinal disorders

sal·mo·noid (sal′mə noid′) *adj.* **1.** like a salmon **2.** of the suborder (Salmonoidei) that includes the salmons, whitefishes, etc. —*n.* a salmonoid fish; specif., any of the salmons

Salmon River river in C Ida., flowing into the Snake River: 420 mi.

salmon trout *same as:* **1.** BROWN TROUT ☆**2.** STEELHEAD

sal·ol (sal′ōl, -ôl) *n.* [SAL(ICYLIC) + -OL¹] a colorless, crystalline compound, C₁₃H₁₀O₃, the phenyl ester of salicylic acid, formerly used in medicine and still used in suntan lotions, preservatives, etc.

Sa·lo·me (sə lō′mē; *occas.* sal′ə mā′) [LL.(Ec.) < Gr.(Ec.) *Salōmē* < Heb. *shālōm*, lit., peace] *traditional name of the* daughter of Herodias: her dancing pleased Herod so much that he granted her request for the head of John the Baptist: cf. Matt. 14:8

Sal·o·mon (sal′ə mən), **Haym** (hīm) 1740-85; Am. financier & patriot, born in Poland: helped finance the Am. Revolutionary War

sa·lon (sə län′, sal′än; *Fr.* sȧ lōn′) *n.* [Fr.: see SALOON] **1.** a large reception hall or social room, as in a hotel or on a ship; saloon **2.** a drawing room of a private home in French-speaking countries **3.** a regular gathering of distinguished guests such as might meet in a drawing room; esp., a meeting of literary or artistic people in a celebrity's home **4.** *a)* a room or gallery for the exhibition of works of art *b)* such an exhibition, esp. one held annually **5.** a shop or business establishment specially furnished for performing some personal service; parlor [beauty *salon*]

Sa·lo·ni·ka (sal′ə nē′kə, -ni′-; sə län′i kə) **1.** a seaport in Macedonia, N Greece, at the head of the Gulf of Salonika: pop. 251,000: Gr. name, THESSALONIKI **2. Gulf of,** N arm of the Aegean Sea: c. 70 mi. long: Also **sp. Sa′lo·ni′ca**

sa·loon (sə lōōn′) *n.* [Fr. *salon* < It. *salone* < *sala*, a room, hall < Langobardic **sala*, akin to OHG. *sal*, a room, dwelling < IE. base **sel-*, whence OBulg. *solo*, village] **1.** any large room or hall designed for receptions, exhibitions, entertainments, etc.; specif., the main social cabin of a passenger ship **2.** any large public room used for some specific purpose [a dining *saloon*] ☆**3.** a place where alcoholic drinks are sold to be drunk on the premises; bar: an old-fashioned term **4.** [Brit.] *a) same as* SEDAN (sense 2) *b)* a luxurious parlor car: also **saloon carriage**

☆**sa·loon·keep·er** (-kēp′ər) *n.* a person who operates a saloon (sense 3)

sa·loop (sə lōōp′) *n.* [var. of SALEP] formerly, a hot drink made from powdered salep or from sassafras

Sal·op (sal′əp) *same as* SHROPSHIRE —**Sa·lo·pi·an** (sə lō′pē ən) *adj., n.*

sal·pa (sal′pə) *n., pl.* **-pas**, **-pae** (-pē) [ModL., name of the genus < L. *salpa*, kind of stockfish < Gr. *salpē*] any of a genus (*Salpa*) of free-swimming tunicates characterized by a barrel-shaped body ringed with muscle and open at both ends: also **salp**

sal·pi·glos·sis (sal′pi gläs′is) *n.* [ModL. < Gr. *salpinx*, a trumpet + *glōssis*, tongue: see GLOSS²] a Chilean annual plant (*Salpiglossis sinuata*) of the nightshade family, cultivated for the long-stalked, trumpet-shaped flowers in various colors

sal·pin·gec·to·my (sal′pin jek′tə mē) *n., pl.* **-mies** [SALPING(O)- + -ECTOMY] the severing or excising of a Fallopian tube, as in sterilizing a woman

sal·pin·gi·tis (sal′pin jīt′əs) *n.* [< ff. + -ITIS] inflammation of a Fallopian tube or Eustachian tube

sal·pin·go- (sal pin′gō) [ModL. < Gr. *salpingos*, gen. of *salpinx*: see ff.] *a combining form meaning:* **1.** of a Fallopian tube **2.** of a Eustachian tube: Also, before a vowel, **sal·ping′-**

sal·pinx (sal′pinks) *n., pl.* **sal·pin·ges** (-pin′jēz) [ModL. < Gr. *salpinx*, a trumpet] *same as:* **1.** FALLOPIAN TUBE **2.** EUSTACHIAN TUBE —**sal·pin′gi·an** (-pin′jē ən) *adj.*

sal·si·fy (sal′sə fē′, -fī′) *n.* [Fr. *salsifis* < It. *sassefrica* < ?] a purple-flowered plant (*Tragopogon porrifolius*) of the composite family, with long, white, edible, fleshy roots having an oysterlike flavor

sal soda crystallized sodium carbonate, Na₂CO₃·10H₂O

salt (sôlt, sält) *n.* [ME. < OE. *sealt*, akin to G. *salz* < IE. base **sal-*, salt, whence L. *sal*, Gr. *hāls*, salt, Sans. *salila*, salty] **1.** sodium chloride, NaCl, a white, crystalline substance with a characteristic taste, found in natural beds, in sea water, etc., and used for seasoning and preserving food, etc. **2.** a chemical compound derived from an acid by replacing hydrogen, wholly or partly, with a metal or an electropositive radical: the salt of an *-ous* acid is usually indicated by the suffix *-ite*, the salt of an *-ic* acid by the suffix *-ate* **3.** that which lends a tang or piquancy; esp., sharp, pungent humor or wit **4.** *same as* SALTCELLAR **5.**

[*pl.*] any of various mineral salts used as a cathartic (**Epsom salts**), to soften bath water (**bath salts**), as a restorative (**smelling salts**), etc. **6.** [Colloq.] a sailor, esp. an experienced one —*adj.* **1.** containing salt **2.** preserved with salt **3.** tasting or smelling of salt **4.** [Now Rare] pungent or biting **5.** *a)* flooded with salt water *b)* growing in salt water —*vt.* **1.** to sprinkle or season with salt **2.** to preserve with salt or in a salt solution **3.** to provide with salt **4.** to treat with salt in chemical processes **5.** to season or give a tang to [to *salt* a speech with wit] **6.** to give artificial value to; specif., *a)* to alter (books, prices, etc.) in order to give false value ☆*b)* to scatter minerals or ores in (a mine), put oil in (a well), etc. in order to deceive prospective buyers —**above** (or **below**) **the salt** in a more honored (or less honored) position: from the former practice of placing guests at the upper or lower part of a table with a bowl of salt in the middle —**salt away** (or **down**) **1.** to pack and preserve with salt ☆**2.** [Colloq.] to store or save (money, etc.) —**salt of the earth** [after Matt. 5:13] any person or persons regarded as the finest, noblest, etc. —**salt out** to precipitate or separate (a substance) from its solution by the addition of a soluble salt —**with a grain** (or **pinch**) **of salt** [Latinized as *cum grano salis*] with allowance or reserve; skeptically —**worth one's salt** worth one's wages, sustenance, etc. —**salt′like′** *adj.* —**salt′ness** *n.*

salt-and-pep·per (-'n pep′ər) *adj. same as* PEPPER-AND-SALT

sal·tant (sal′tənt) *adj.* [L. *saltans*, prp. of *saltare*, to leap, freq. of *salire*: see SALIENT] [Now Rare] leaping; dancing

sal·ta·rel·lo (sal′tə rel′ō) *n.* [It. < L. *saltare*, to leap] **1.** a lively Italian dance with a hopping, skipping step **2.** music for this dance

sal·ta·tion (sal tā′shən) *n.* [L. *saltatio*, a dancing, dance < *saltatus*, pp. of *saltare*: see prec.] **1.** a leaping, jumping, or dancing **2.** sudden change, movement, or development, as if by leaping **3.** *Biol. same as* MUTATION

sal·ta·to·ri·al (sal′tə tôr′ē əl) *adj.* **1.** of saltation **2.** *Zool.* of, characterized by, or adapted for leaping

sal·ta·to·ry (sal′tə tôr′ē) *adj.* [L. *saltatorius* < pp. of *saltare*: see SALTANT] **1.** of, characterized by, or adapted for leaping or dancing **2.** proceeding by abrupt movements or changing by sudden variation

salt·box (sôlt′bäks′) *n.* **1.** a box for salt, with a sloping lid ☆**2.** a house, as in colonial New England, shaped somewhat like this, having two stories in front and one at the rear, and a gable roof with a much longer slope at the rear: Also **salt box**

salt·bush (-boosh′) *n.* any of various plants (genus *Atriplex*) of the goosefoot family, frequently growing in saline or alkaline soil, as in salt marshes or desert areas

salt cake impure sodium sulfate, used in making paper pulp, soaps, etc.

salt·cel·lar (-sel′ər) *n.* [altered (after CELLAR) < ME. *salt saler* < *salt*, SALT + MFr. *salière*, saltcellar < L. *sal*, SALT] a small dish for salt at the table; also, a saltshaker

☆**salt dome** a domelike structure produced in stratified rocks by the intrusion of a mass of salt in a plastic state and frequently containing oil, gas, etc.

salt·er (sôlt′ər) *n.* **1.** a person who makes or sells salt **2.** a person who salts meat, fish, etc.

salt·ern (-ərn) *n.* [OE. *sealtærn* < *sealt*, salt + *ærn*, a house: see RANSACK] *same as* SALTWORKS

☆**salt grass** any of various grasses growing in salt marshes or alkaline soils; esp., any of a genus (*Distichlis*) of N. American perennial grasses

sal·ti·grade (sal′ti grād′) *adj.* [< L. *saltus*, a leap (< pp. of *salire*: see SALIENT) + *gradi*, to walk: see GRADE] having legs adapted for leaping

Sal·til·lo (säl tē′yð) city in N Mexico; capital of Coahuila state: pop. 126,000

salt·i·ly (sôlt′'l ē) *adv.* in a salty manner

☆**salt·ine** (sôl tēn′) *n.* [SALT + -INE⁴] a flat, crisp cracker sprinkled with salt

salt·i·ness (sôlt′ē nis) *n.* salty quality or state

sal·tire (sal′tir) *n.* [ME. *sawtire* < MFr. *sautoir*, stirrup loop < ML. *saltatorium* < L. *saltatorius*: see SALTATORY] *Heraldry* a bearing like a Saint Andrew's cross, formed by a bend and a bend sinister crossing: also **sp. sal′tier**

salt·ish (sôlt′tish) *adj.* somewhat salty

Salt Lake City capital of Utah, near the SE end of Great Salt Lake: pop. 176,000 (met. area 558,000)

☆**salt lick 1.** an exposed natural deposit of mineral rock salt which animals come to lick **2.** a block of rock salt placed in a pasture for cattle, etc. to lick

salt marsh grassland over which salt water flows at intervals

Sal·ton Sea (sôl′t'n) [prob. coined < SALT] shallow saltwater lake, orig. a salt-covered depression (**Salton Sink**), in the Imperial Valley, S Calif., kept filled by runoff water from irrigation ditches fed by the Colorado River: c. 350 sq. mi.; c. 280 ft. below sea level

salt·pe·ter (sôlt′pēt′ər) *n.* [altered (after SALT) < ME. *salpetre* < MFr. < ML. *sal petrae*, salt of rock < L. *sal*, SALT + *petra*, a rock] **1.** *same as* POTASSIUM NITRATE **2.** *see* CHILE SALTPETER Also, Brit. sp., **salt′pe′tre**

---

fat, āpe, cär; ten, ēven; is, bīte; gō, hôrn, tōōl, look; oil, out; up, fur; get; joy; yet; chin; she; thin, then; zh, leisure; ŋ, ring; ə for *a* in *ago*, *e* in *agent*, *i* in *sanity*, *o* in *comply*, *u* in *focus*; ' as in *able* (ā′b'l); Fr. bál; ë, Fr. coeur; ö, Fr. feu; Fr. mon; ô, Fr. coq; ü, Fr. duc; r, Fr. cri; H, G. ich; kh, G. doch. See inside front cover. ☆ Americanism; ‡foreign; *hypothetical; < derived from

salt pork pork cured in salt; esp., the fatty parts from the back, side, or belly of a hog

☆**salt-ris·ing bread** (-rīz′ĭŋ) bread that is leavened by a fermented salted cornmeal batter

Salt River [because of the saltiness of the lower stream] river in SC Ariz., flowing into the Gila River: c. 200 mi.

☆**salt-shak·er** (sôlt′shā′kər) n. a container for salt, with a perforated top for shaking out the salt

salt-wa·ter (-wôt′ər, -wät′ər) adj. of, having to do with, or living in salt water or the sea

salt·works (-wurks′) n., pl. **-works′** a place where salt is made, as by evaporation of natural brines

salt·wort (-wurt′) n. [? after Du. zoutkruid] any of a genus (Salsola) of plants of the goosefoot family, growing on seashores or saline soils: one species (Salsola kali) was formerly important as a source of barilla

salt·y (sôl′tē) adj. **salt′i·er, salt′i·est** 1. of, tasting of, or containing salt 2. smelling of or suggesting the sea 3. a) sharp; piquant; witty b) coarse or earthy c) cross or caustic

sa·lu·bri·ous (sə lōō′brē əs) adj. [< L. salubris < salus, health: see SAFE] + -OUS] promoting health or welfare; healthful, wholesome, salutary, etc. —**sa·lu′bri·ous·ly** adv. —**sa·lu′bri·ty** (-brə tē), **sa·lu′bri·ous·ness** n.

‡**sa·lud** (sä lōōd′) interj. [Sp., health] to your health: a toast

Sa·lu·ki (sə lōō′kē) n. [Ar. salūqīy < Salūq, ancient Arabian city] any of an ancient breed of dog shaped like a greyhound but having long ears and silky hair

sal·u·tar·y (sal′yoo ter′ē) adj. [< Fr. or L.: Fr. salutaire < L. salutaris < salus (gen. salutis), health: see SAFE] 1. promoting or conducive to health; healthful 2. promoting or conducive to some good purpose; beneficial —**sal′u·tar′i·ly** adv. —**sal′u·tar′i·ness** n.

sal·u·ta·tion (sal′yoo tā′shən) n. [ME. salutacioun < MFr. < L. salutatio < salutatus, pp. of salutare: see SALUTE] 1. the act of greeting, addressing, or welcoming by gestures or words 2. a form of words serving as a greeting or, esp., as the opening of a letter, as "Dear Sir"

☆**sa·lu·ta·to·ri·an** (sə lōōt′ə tôr′ē ən) n. [< ff. + -AN] in some schools and colleges, the student, usually second highest in scholastic rank, who gives the salutatory

sa·lu·ta·to·ry (sə lōōt′ə tôr′ē) adj. [L. salutatorius] of or expressing a salutation —n., pl. **-ries** ☆an opening or welcoming address, esp. at a school or college commencement exercise

sa·lute (sə lōōt′) vt. **-lut′ed, -lut′ing** [ME. saluten < L. salutare, to salute, wish health to < salus (gen. salutis), health, greeting < salvus, SAFE] 1. to greet or welcome with friendly words or ceremonial gesture, such as bowing, tipping the hat, etc. 2. to honor by performing a prescribed act or gesture, such as dipping the flag, firing cannon, or raising the right hand to the forehead, as a mark of military, naval, or official respect 3. to present itself to, as if in greeting 4. to acknowledge with praise; commend —vi. to make a salute —n. [OFr. salut < L. salus] 1. an act, remark, or gesture made in saluting 2. Mil. the position of the body, or of the hand, rifle, etc., assumed in saluting —**sa·lut′er** n.

sal·va·ble (sal′və b'l) adj. [ML. salvabilis: see SAVE¹ & -ABLE] that can be saved or salvaged

Sal·va·dor (sal′və dôr′; Port. säl′və dōr′) seaport in E Brazil: capital of Bahia state: pop. 656,000

Sal·va·do·ran (sal′və dôr′ən) adj. of El Salvador, its people, or culture —n. a native or inhabitant of El Salvador Also **Sal′va·do′ri·an** (-dôr′ē ən)

sal·vage (sal′vij) n. [Fr. < MFr. < salver, to SAVE¹] 1. a) the rescue of a ship and cargo at sea from peril such as fire, shipwreck, capture, etc. b) compensation paid to those who assist in the rescue operations c) the ship or cargo so rescued d) the restoration of a sunken or wrecked ship or its cargo as by divers 2. a) the saving or rescue of any goods, property, etc. from destruction, damage, or waste b) any material, goods, etc. thus saved and sold or put to use c) the value, or proceeds from the sale, of such goods, specif. of damaged goods, as involved in insurance claim settlements —vt. **-vaged, -vag·ing** to save or rescue from shipwreck, fire, flood, etc.; engage or succeed in the salvage of (ships, goods, etc.) —**sal′vage·a·bil′i·ty** n. —**sal′vage·a·ble** adj. —**sal′vag·er** n.

Sal·var·san (sal′vər san′) [G. < L. salvar, to SAVE¹ + G. arsen, arsenic] a trademark for ARSPHENAMINE

sal·va·tion (sal vā′shən) n. [ME. salvacioun < OFr. < LL.(Ec.) salvatio < L. salvatus, pp. of salvare, to SAVE¹] 1. a saving or being saved from danger, evil, difficulty, destruction, etc.; rescue 2. a person or thing that is a means, cause, or source of preservation or rescue 3. Theol. spiritual rescue from the consequences of sin; redemption —**sal·va′tion·al** adj.

Salvation Army an international organization on semi-military lines, founded in England by William Booth in 1865 for religious and philanthropic purposes among the very poor: name adopted in 1878 —**Sal·va′tion·ist** n.

salve¹ (sav, säv) n. [ME. < OE. sealf, akin to G. salbe < IE. base *selp-, a fat, butter, whence Sans. sarpis-, melted butter] 1. any medicinal ointment applied to wounds, skin irritations, burns, etc. for purposes of soothing or healing 2. anything that soothes or heals; balm [a salve for one's conscience] —vt. **salved, salv′ing** [ME. salven < OE. sealfian < the n.] 1. [Archaic] to apply salve to (wounds, etc.) 2. to soothe; smooth over; assuage

salve² (salv) vt. **salved, salv′ing** [back-formation < SALVAGE] same as SALVAGE

sal·ver (sal′vər) n. [altered < Fr. salve < Sp. salva, the testing of food by a taster, hence tray on which food was placed, salver < salvar, to taste, save < L. salvare: see SAVE¹] a tray on which refreshments, letters, visiting cards, etc. are presented

sal·ver·form (-fôrm′) adj. [prec. + -FORM] Bot. having a slender, tubular corolla with the lobes spreading at right angles to the tube, as in phlox: also **sal′ver-shaped′**

sal·vi·a (sal′vē ə) n. [ModL., name of the genus < L.: see SAGE²] same as SAGE² (sense 1)

sal·vif·ic (sal vif′ik) adj. [LL.(Ec.) salvificus < salvificare, to save < salvus, saved from sin (< L., SAFE) + L. -ficare, -FY] offering salvation —**sal′vif′i·cal·ly** adv.

sal·vo¹ (sal′vō) n., pl. **-vos, -voes** [It. salva < L. salve, hail, imperative of salvere, to be safe < salvus, SAFE] 1. a discharge of a number of pieces of artillery or small arms, in regular succession or at the same time, either as a salute or, esp. in naval battles, as a hostile broadside 2. the release of a load of bombs or the launching of several rockets at the same time 3. a burst of cheers or applause

sal·vo² (sal′vō) n., pl. **-vos** [< ML. legal phr. salvo jure, right being reserved (< L. salvus: see SAFE)] 1. a dishonest mental reservation; excuse or quibbling evasion 2. an expedient for saving one's pride or honor 3. Law a saving clause; reservation

sal vo·la·ti·le (vō lat′'l ē′) [ModL., volatile salt] 1. a mixture of ammonium bicarbonate and ammonium carbonate, esp. in aromatic solution for use as smelling salts 2. ammonium carbonate

sal·vor (sal′vər) n. any of the persons or ships participating in the salvage of a ship or its cargo

Sal·ween (sal wēn′) river in SE Asia, flowing from E Tibet through E Burma into the Gulf of Martaban: c. 1,750 mi.

Salz·burg (zälts′boorkh; E. sôlz′bərg) city in C Austria: scene of annual music festivals: pop. 108,000

SAM (sam) surface-to-air missile

Sam. Samuel

Sa·mar (sä′mär) island of the E Philippines, southeast of Luzon: 5,181 sq. mi.

sam·a·ra (sam′ər ə, sə mer′ə) n. [ModL. < L., seed of the elm: for IE. base see SUMMER¹] a dry, one-seeded, winged fruit, as of the maple

Sa·mar·i·a (sə mer′ē ə, -mar′-) 1. region in W Jordan, west of the Jordan River 2. in ancient times, a) N kingdom of the Hebrews; Israel b) its capital c) district of Palestine between Galilee & Judaea, later a part of the Rom. province of Judaea

Sa·mar·i·tan (-ə t'n) n. [ME. < OE. < LL.(Ec.) Samaritanus < Gr. Samareitēs < Samareia, Samaria] 1. a native or inhabitant of Samaria 2. a person who comes to the aid of another: see GOOD SAMARITAN —adj. of Samaria or its people

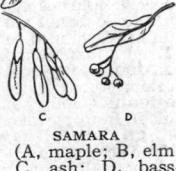

SAMARA
(A, maple; B, elm; C, ash; D, basswood)

sa·mar·i·um (sə mer′ē əm, -mar′-) n. [ModL. < Fr. samarskite < G. samarskite: see SAMARSKITE] a metallic chemical element of the rare-earth group: symbol, Sm; at. wt., 150.35; at. no., 62; sp. gr., 7.536; melt. pt., 1072°C; boil. pt., 1900°C

Sam·ar·kand (sam′ər kand′; Russ. sä mär känt′) city in E Uzbek S.S.R.; capital (as MARACANDA) of Tamerlane's empire (1370-1405): pop. 240,000

sa·mar·skite (sə mär′skīt, sam′ər skīt′) n. [Fr.: so named (1847) after Col. Samarski, Russ. mining official] a lustrous, velvet-black mineral containing oxides of iron, thorium, uranium, etc., and some of the rare-earth metals, as samarium, cerium, etc.

sam·ba (sam′bə, säm′-) n. [Port., prob. of Afr. origin] 1. a Brazilian dance of African origin, in duple time 2. music for this dance —vi. to dance the samba

sam·bar (sam′bər, säm′-), pl. **-bars, -bar:** see PLURAL, II, D, 1 [Hind. sābar < Sans. śambara] a large Asiatic deer (Cervus unicolor) with very coarse hair, a short, erectile mane, and three-pointed antlers: also sp. **sam′bur**

Sam Browne belt (sam′ broun′) [after Brit. Gen. Sir Samuel J. Browne (1824-1901)] a military officer's belt with a diagonal strap across the right shoulder, designed to carry the weight of a pistol or sword

sam·buke (sam′byook) n. [L. sambuca < Gr. sambykē < Sem., as in Aram. sabbĕkhā] an ancient, triangular stringed instrument similar to a harp

same (sām) adj. [ME. < ON. samr, akin to Goth. sama, OHG. samo, OE. same < IE. *som-, var. of base *sem-, one, together, with, whence Gr. homós, alike, L. simul, at the same time, similis, like] 1. being the very one; identical 2. alike in kind, quality, amount, or degree; corresponding 3. unchanged; not different [to look the same as ever] 4. before-mentioned; just spoken of Same is rarely used without the —pron. the same person or thing (usually with the, this, or that) —adv. in the same way; in like manner (usually with the)

SYN.—same, in one sense, agrees with selfsame and very in implying that what is referred to is one thing and not two or more distinct things [that is the same, or selfsame or very, house we once

lived in] and, in another, implies reference to things that are really distinct but without any significant difference in kind, appearance, amount, etc. [I eat the *same* food every day]; **identical**, in one sense, also expresses the first idea [this is the *identical* bed where he slept] and, in another, implies exact correspondence in all details, as of quality, appearance, etc. [the signatures are *identical*]; **equal** implies the absence of any difference in quantity, size, value, degree, etc. [*equal* weights, an *equal* advantage]; **equivalent** implies of things that they amount to the same thing in value, force, meaning, etc. [$5 or its *equivalent* in merchandise] —ANT. **different**

sa·mekh, sa·mech (sä′mekh) *n.* [Heb. *sāmekh*] the fifteenth letter of the Hebrew alphabet (ס)

same·ness (sām′nis) *n.* **1.** the state or quality of being the same; identity or uniformity **2.** lack of change or variety; monotony

☆**Sam Hill** *euphemistic slang term for* HELL

Sa·mi·an (sā′mē ən) *adj.* of Samos or its people —*n.* a native or inhabitant of Samos

sam·iel (sam′yel) *n.* [Turk. *samyel* < *sam*, poison (< Ar. *samm*) + *yel*, wind] *same as* SIMOOM

sam·i·sen (sam′ə sen′) *n.* [Jap. < Chin. *san hsien*, three strings] a Japanese musical instrument somewhat like a banjo, but with three strings

sam·ite (sam′īt, sā′mīt) *n.* [ME. *samyte* < MFr. *samit* < ML. *samitum* < MGr. *hexamiton* < *hexamitos*, woven with six threads < Gr. *hex*, SIX + *mitos*, a thread] a heavy silk fabric worn in the Middle Ages: it was sometimes interwoven with gold or silver

SAMISEN

Saml., Sam'l Samuel

sam·let (sam′lit) *n.* [< SALMON + -LET] a young salmon

Sam·nite (sam′nīt) *n.* [L. *Samnitis*] a member of a pre-Roman people, descended from the Sabines, who lived in Samnium —*adj.* of Samnium or the Samnites

Sam·ni·um (sam′nē əm) [L., contr. < *Sabinium* < *Sabinus*, Sabine] ancient country in SC Italy

Sa·mo·a (sə mō′ə) group of islands in the South Pacific, north of Tonga: see AMERICAN SAMOA & WESTERN SAMOA

Sa·mo·an (-ən) *adj.* of Samoa, its people, their language, etc. —*n.* **1.** a native or inhabitant of Samoa **2.** the Polynesian language of the Samoans

Sa·mos (sā′mäs; *Gr.* sä′môs) Gr. island in the Aegean, off the W coast of Turkey: c. 180 sq. mi.

Sam·o·thrace (sam′ə thrās′) Gr. island in the NE Aegean: c. 70 sq. mi.: Gr. name **Sa·mo·thrá·ki** (sä′mô thrä′kē) —**Sam′o·thra′cian** (-thrā′shən) *adj.*, *n.*

sam·o·var (sam′ə vär′, säm′ə vär′) *n.* [Russ., lit., self-boiler < *samo-*, self (for IE. base see SAME) + *varit′*, to boil, akin to Lith. *virti*, to boil < IE. *(a)wer-* < base *awe-*, to moisten, flow, whence WATER] a metal urn with a spigot and an internal tube for heating water in making tea: used esp. in Russia

Sam·o·yed, Sam·o·yede (sam′ə yed′) *n.* [Russ. *samoyed*, lit., self-eater < *samo-* (see prec.) + base of *jěda*, food (for IE. base see EAT)] **1.** any of a Uralic people living in N Siberia and the Taimyr Peninsula **2.** their Uralic language **3.** any of a powerful breed of Siberian dog, with a thick, white coat —*adj.* of the Samoyeds or their language: also **Sam′o·yed′ic**

☆**samp** (samp) *n.* [< AmInd. (Narragansett) *nasaump*, softened by water] **1.** coarse meal of Indian corn **2.** a porridge made from this

sam·pan (sam′pan) *n.* [Chin. *san-pan* < *san*, three + *pan*, a plank] any of various small boats used in the harbors and rivers of China and Japan, usually rowed with a scull from the stern, and often having a sail and a small cabin formed by mats

sam·phire (sam′fir′) *n.* [earlier *sampire*, *sainpere*, altered < Fr. *(herbe de) Saint Pierre*, St. Peter's (herb)] **1.** a fleshy, old-world seashore plant (*Crithmum maritimum*) of the parsley family, with cut leaves and small clusters of yellowish flowers **2.** *same as* GLASSWORT

sam·ple (sam′p'l, säm′-) *n.* [ME., aphetic for *asample* < Anglo-Fr., for OFr. *essample*: see EXAMPLE] **1.** a part, piece, or item taken or shown as representative of a whole thing, group, species, etc.; specimen; pattern **2.** an illustration; example [a *sample* of his humor] ☆**3.** *Statistics* a selected segment of a population studied to gain knowledge of the whole —*vt.* **-pled, -pling** to take a sample or samples of, as for testing quality

sam·pler (-plər) *n.* [senses 1 & 2 < prec. + -ER; sense 3 < ME. *samplere*, aphetic < OFr. *essamplaire* < LL. *exemplarium* < L. *exemplum*: see EXAMPLE] **1.** a person who prepares or selects samples for inspection **2.** a collection or assortment of representative selections **3.** a cloth embroidered with designs, mottoes, etc. in different stitches, to show a beginner's skill

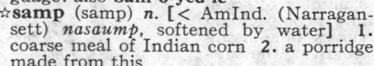

SAMOVAR

sam·pling (-pliŋ) *n.* **1.** the act or process of taking a small part or quantity of something as a sample for testing or analysis **2.** the sample so taken

sam·sa·ra (səm sä′rə) *n.* [Sans. *saṃsāra*, lit., running together < *sam-*, together (< IE. *som-*, var. of base *sem-*, whence SAME) + *sara-*, fluid (< IE. base *ser-*, to flow, whence SERUM)] *Hinduism* the continuing cycle in which the same soul is repeatedly reborn

Sam·son (sam′s'n) [LL.(Ec.) < Gr.(Ec.) *Sampsōn* < Heb. *shimshōn* < ? *shemesh*, sun: interpretation of name uncertain] **1.** a masculine name: var. *Sampson* **2.** *Bible* an Israelite judge noted for his great strength: betrayed to the Philistines by Delilah: Judges 13–16

Sam·u·el (sam′yoo wal, -yool) [LL.(Ec.) < Gr.(Ec.) *Samouēl* < Heb. *shēmū′ēl*, lit., name of God] **1.** a masculine name: dim. *Sam*, *Sammy* **2.** *Bible* a) a Hebrew judge and prophet b) either of the two books (I Samuel, II Samuel) telling of Samuel, Saul, and David

sam·u·rai (sam′ə rī′) *n.*, *pl.* **-rai′** [Jap.] **1.** a member of a military class in feudal Japan, consisting of the retainers of the daimios: a samurai wore two swords **2.** a Japanese army officer or member of the military caste

San (sän) river in SE Poland, flowing northwest into the Vistula: 276 mi.

‡**-san** (sän) [Jap.] a Japanese honorific suffix added to names, titles, etc.

Sa·na (sä nä′) capital of Yemen, in the C part: pop. 80,000: also sp. **Sana, San′a′, Sanaa**

San An·ge·lo (san an′jə lō′) [masc. of earlier name *Santa Angela*, after a Mex. nun] city in WC Tex.: pop. 64,000

San An·to·ni·o (san′ ən tō′nē ō′, an-) [Sp., St. ANTHONY (of Padua)] city in SC Tex.: site of the Alamo: pop. 654,000 (met. area 864,000)

san·a·tive (san′ə tiv) *adj.* [ME. *sanatyf* < OFr. *sanatif* < LL. *sanativus* < L. *sanatus*, pp. of *sanare*, to heal < *sanus*: see SANE] having the power to heal or cure; curative

san·a·to·ri·um (san′ə tôr′ē əm) *n.*, *pl.* **-ri·ums**, **-ri·a** (-ə) [ModL. < neut. of LL. *sanatorius*, giving health < L. *sanare*: see prec.] *chiefly Brit. var. of* SANITARIUM

san·be·ni·to (san′bə nēt′ō) *n.*, *pl.* **-tos** [Sp. *sambenito* < *San Benito*, Saint Benedict: from resembling a Benedictine scapular] under the Spanish Inquisition, **1.** a yellow garment resembling a scapular in shape, and having a red Saint Andrew's cross in front and in back, worn by a confessed, penitent heretic **2.** a similar black garment painted with flames, devils, etc., worn by a condemned heretic at an auto-da-fé

San Ber·nar·di·no (bur′nər dē′nō, -nə-) [Sp., *St. Bernardine* (of Siena)] **1.** city in S Calif.: pop. 104,000 (met. area, incl. Riverside & Ontario, 1,143,000) **2.** mountain range in S Calif., south of the Mojave Desert: highest peak, 11,502 ft.: in full **San Bernardino Mountains**

San Bru·no (broo′nō) [ult. after St. BRUNO] city in W Calif.: suburb of San Francisco: pop. 36,000

San·cho Pan·za (san′chō pan′zə; *Sp.* sän′chō pän′thä) the simple, credulous squire to Cervantes' Don Quixote: his practical, peasant common sense contrasts with the visionary idealism of his master

sanc·ti·fied (saŋk′tə fīd′) *adj.* **1.** a) dedicated; consecrated b) made holy **2.** affecting sanctity

sanc·ti·fy (saŋk′tə fī′) *vt.* **-fied′, -fy′ing** [ME. *sanctifien*, altered (after L.) < OFr. *saintifier* < LL.(Ec.) *sanctificare*: see SAINT & -FY] **1.** to make holy; specif., a) to set apart as holy; consecrate b) to make free from sin; purify **2.** to make binding or inviolable by a religious sanction **3.** to make productive of spiritual blessing —**sanc′ti·fi·ca′tion** *n.* —**sanc′ti·fi′er** *n.*

sanc·ti·mo·ni·ous (saŋk′tə mō′nē əs) *adj.* [< ff. + -OUS] pretending to be very holy or pious; affecting sanctity or righteousness —SYN. see DEVOUT —**sanc′ti·mo′ni·ous·ly** *adv.* —**sanc′ti·mo′ni·ous·ness** *n.*

sanc·ti·mo·ny (saŋk′tə mō′nē) *n.* [OFr. *sanctimonie* < L. *sanctimonia* < *sanctus*, holy: see SAINT] **1.** affected piety or righteousness; religious hypocrisy **2.** *obs. var. of* SANCTITY

sanc·tion (saŋk′shən) *n.* [< Fr. or L.: Fr. *sanction* < L. *sanctio* < *sanctus*: see SAINT] **1.** the act of a recognized authority confirming or ratifying an action; authorized approval or permission **2.** support; encouragement; approval **3.** something that gives binding force to a law, or secures obedience to it, as the penalty for breaking it, or a reward for carrying it out **4.** something, as a moral principle or influence, that makes a rule of conduct, a law, etc. binding **5.** a) [*usually pl.*] a coercive measure, as a blockade of shipping, usually taken by several nations together, for forcing a nation considered to have violated international law to end the violation b) a coercive measure, as a boycott, taken by a group to enforce demands **6.** [Obs.] a formal decree; law —*vt.* to give sanction to; specif., a) to ratify or confirm b) to authorize or permit; countenance —SYN. see APPROVE —**sanc′tion·a·ble** *adj.*

sanc·ti·ty (saŋk′tə tē) *n.*, *pl.* **-ties** [L. *sanctitas* < *sanctus* (see SAINT) + -*itas*, -ITY] **1.** saintliness or holiness **2.** the fact or being sacred or inviolable **3.** anything held sacred

sanc·tu·ar·y (saŋk′choo wer′ē) *n.*, *pl.* **-ar′ies** [ME. < MFr. *saintuaire* < LL. *sanctuarium* < L. *sanctus*, sacred: see

SAINT] **1.** a holy place, as a building set aside for worship of a god or gods; specif., *a)* the ancient Temple at Jerusalem *b)* a Christian church *c)* any church or temple *d)* a particularly holy place within a church or temple, as the part around the altar, the holy of holies in the Jewish Temple, etc. **2.** *a)* a place of refuge or protection; asylum: orig. fugitives from justice were immune from arrest in churches or other sacred places *b)* immunity from punishment or the law, as by taking refuge in a church, etc. **3.** a reservation where animals or birds are sheltered for breeding purposes and may not be hunted or trapped —*SYN.* see SHELTER

sanc·tum (saŋkʹtəm) *n., pl.* **-tums, -ta** (-tə) [L., neut. of *sanctus,* holy: see SAINT] **1.** a sacred place **2.** a study or private room where one is not to be disturbed

sanctum sanc·to·rum (saŋk tôrʹəm) [LL.(Ec.), holy of holies (cf. prec.), used in Vulgate to translate Gr.(Ec.) *to hagion tōn hagiōn* (in LXX), transl. of Heb. *qōdesh haqādōshīm*] **1.** *same as* HOLY OF HOLIES **2.** a place of utmost privacy and inviolability

Sanc·tus (saŋkʹtəs) *n.* [ME. < LL.(Ec.), holy: see SAINT] **1.** the hymn constituting the culmination of the preface of the Mass or Communion service, beginning *Sanctus, sanctus, sanctus* (Holy, holy, holy) **2.** a musical setting for this

Sanctus bell a small bell rung at various parts of the Mass, the first ringing being three times at the Sanctus

sand (sand) *n.* [ME. < AS. < akin to G. *sand,* ON. *sandr* < IE. base **bhes-,* to rub off, pulverize, whence Gr. *psammos,* L. *sabulum*] **1.** loose, gritty particles of worn or disintegrated rock, varying in size from about 1/16 mm to 2 mm in diameter, usually deposited along the shores of bodies of water, in river beds, or in deserts **2.** [*usually pl.*] a tract or area of sand; beach, etc. **3.** the sand in an hourglass **4.** [*pl.*] moments; particles of time ☆**5.** [Slang] grit; courage; determination **6.** the reddish-yellow color characteristic of sand —*vt.* **1.** to sprinkle with or as with sand **2.** to smooth or polish with sand, sandpaper, or other abrasive substance **3.** to fill or cover with sand **4.** to mix or adulterate with sand —*adj.* yellowish-red

Sand (sand; *Fr.* sänd), **George** (pseud. of *Amandine Aurore Lucie Dupin,* Baronne *Dudevant*) 1804–76; Fr. novelist

san·dal[1] (sanʹd'l) *n.* [ME. *sandalie* < L. *sandalium* < Gr. *sandalion,* dim. of *sandalon*] **1.** a kind of footwear consisting of a sole fastened in various ways to the foot by straps over the instep or toes, or around the ankle **2.** any of various low slippers or shoes —**san′daled, san′dalled** *adj.*

san·dal[2] (sanʹd'l) *n. same as* SANDALWOOD

san·dal·wood (-wood′) *n.* [*sandal,* sandalwood < ME. *sandell* < MFr. *sandal* < ML. *sandalum* < LGr. *santalon* < Ar. *çandal,* ult. < Sans. *candana* < IE. base **kand-,* to gleam, bright, whence L. *candere,* to shine] **1.** *a)* the hard, light-colored, closegrained, sweet-smelling heartwood of any of several allied trees of Asia, used for carving and cabinetmaking or burned as incense; esp., the wood of an evergreen tree (*Santalum album*) of S Asia *b)* any tree yielding such wood **2.** *a)* any of a number of similar or related trees *b)* the wood of any of these

Sandalwood Island *former name of* SUMBA

san·da·rac (sanʹdə rak′) *n.* [L. *sandaraca* < Gr. *sandarakē:* of Oriental origin, prob. akin to Sans. *candra-raga,* having the glow of the moon (for IE. base see SANDALWOOD] **1.** a brittle, slightly aromatic, somewhat transparent, yellowish resin exuded from the bark of several African and Australian trees (genera *Tetraclinus* and *Callitris*) of the pine family, used esp. in varnishes and as incense **2.** *a)* a North African tree (*Tetraclinus articulata*) yielding this resin and a mahogany-colored, durable wood used esp. in building: also **sandarac tree** *b)* this wood

sand·bag (sandʹbag′) *n.* **1.** a bag filled with sand and used for ballast, in military fortifications, for levee protection against floods, etc. ☆**2.** a small, narrow bag filled with sand and used as a bludgeon —*vt.* **-bagged′, -bag′ging 1.** to place sandbags in or around ☆**2.** to strike or stun with a sandbag ☆**3.** [Colloq.] to force into doing something ☆**4.** [Slang] to deceive (an opponent), as by deliberately playing poorly —**sand′bag′ger** *n.*

sand·bank (-baŋk′) *n.* [SAND + BANK[2]] **1.** *same as* SAND BAR **2.** a large mass of sand, as on a hillside

☆**sand bar** a ridge or narrow shoal of sand formed in a river or along a shore by the action of currents or tides

sand·blast (-blast′, -bläst′) *n.* **1.** a current of air or steam carrying sand at a high velocity, used in etching glass and in cleaning or grinding hard surfaces, as of metals, stone, etc. **2.** the machine used to apply this blast —*vt.* to engrave, clean, etc. with a sandblast —**sand′blast′er** *n.*

sand·blind (-blīnd′) *adj.* [ME., altered < OE. **samblind* < *sam,* half (akin to L. *semi-*) + *blind,* BLIND] [Archaic] weak-sighted; partially blind

sand·box (-bäks′) *n.* ☆**1.** a box or pit containing sand for children to play in **2.** a container on locomotives, etc. for holding sand and releasing it on slippery rails

sandbox tree a tropical American tree (*Hura crepitans*) of the spurge family, with small, woody fruit that bursts with a loud noise when ripe and scatters its seeds

☆**sand·bur, sand·burr** (-bʉr′) *n.* **1.** any of a genus (*Cenchrus*) of grasses, having their grains enclosed in spiny burs **2.** an annual, prickly nightshade (*Solanum rostratum*) growing as a weed in the W U.S.

Sand·burg (sandʹbʉrg, san′-), **Carl** 1878–1967; U.S. poet, writer, & ballad collector

sand-cast (sandʹkast′, -käst′) *vt.* to make (a casting) by pouring metal in a mold of sand

sand crack *same as* QUARTER CRACK

sand dab any of various small, edible flatfishes; ☆esp., any of several flounders (genus *Citharichthys*) found along the Pacific coast of N. America

☆**sand dollar** any of several flat, round, disklike echinoderms (class Echinoidea) with short spines, that live on sandy ocean beds

sand eel any of a group of small, eellike sea fishes (genus *Ammodytes*), with a pointed snout and a long, slender body, often found burrowing in coastal sands

sand·er (sanʹdər) *n.* **1.** a person who sands or sandpapers **2.** a tool or machine for sanding or sandpapering

sand·er·ling (sanʹdər liŋ) *n.* [prob. < SAND + OE. *yrthling,* farmer, kind of bird, lit., earthling] a small, gray-and-white sandpiper (*Crocethia alba*), found on sandy beaches

sand flea *same as:* **1.** CHIGOE **2.** BEACH FLEA

sand fly 1. *same as* BITING MIDGE **2.** any of various other two-winged, biting flies; esp., any of a genus (*Phlebotomus*) some species of which transmit diseases, as leishmaniasis

sand·glass (sandʹglas′, -gläs′) *n.* an hourglass used for measuring time by the flow of sand

sand grouse any of certain pigeonlike birds (family Pteroclidae) found in sandy regions of S Europe, Asia, and Africa

san·dhi (sänʹdē, san′-, sun′-) *n.* [< Sans. *saṃdhi,* a linking, lit., placing together] *Linguis.* the modification or conditioning of a speech sound by the influence of a contiguous sound or sounds (Ex.: the pronunciation of *t* as (ch) in *picture* or of *am* as ('m) in *I am glad*)

☆**sand·hog** (sandʹhôg′, -häg′) *n.* a laborer employed in underground or underwater construction projects, working under compressed air, as in a caisson or tunnel

sand hopper *same as* BEACH FLEA

Sand·hurst (sandʹhʉrst) village in Berkshire, England: nearby is the Royal Military Academy

San Di·e·go (san′ dē ā′gō) [after *San Diego* (St. Didacus), 15th-cent. Sp. friar] seaport in S Calif.: pop. 697,000 (met. area 1,358,000)

sand·i·ness (sanʹdē nis) *n.* a sandy state or quality

S & L savings and loan association

sand launce *same as* SAND EEL

☆**sand lily** a perennial spring plant (*Leucocrinum montanum*) of the lily family, native to the W U.S. and having grasslike leaves and umbels of white, star-shaped flowers

☆**sand·lot** (sandʹlät′) *adj.* of or having to do with games, esp. baseball, played by amateurs, orig. on a sandy lot or field, now usually in organized leagues —**sand′lot′ter** *n.*

sand·man (-man) *n.* [prob. < G. *sandmann*] a mythical person, as in fairy tales, supposed to make children sleepy by dusting sand in their eyes

☆**sand myrtle** a small, evergreen, white-flowered plant (*Leiophyllum buxifolium*) of the heath family, native to the sand barrens of the SE U.S.

☆**sand painting 1.** in the healing ceremonies of the Navaho Indians, the sprinkling of dry, colored sands into designs made up of conventionalized symbolic figures **2.** a design of this kind

sand·pa·per (-pā′pər) *n.* strong paper with sand or other abrasive glued on one side, used for smoothing and polishing —*vt.* to smooth or polish with sandpaper

sand·pip·er (-pī′pər) *n., pl.* **-pip′ers, -pip′er:** see PLURAL, II, D, 1 any of a number of small shore birds (family Scolopacidae) related to the snipes but distinguished by the length of the soft-tipped bill; esp., the **common sandpiper** (*Actitis hypoleucos*) of Europe and the **spotted sandpiper** (*Actitis macularia*) and **least sandpiper** (*Erolia minutilla*) of N. America

San·dra (san′drə, sän′-) a feminine name: see ALEXANDRA

sand·stone (sand′stōn′) *n.* a common bedded sedimentary rock much used for building, composed largely of sand grains, mainly quartz, cemented together by various binding materials, as silica, to produce a coherent mass

SPOTTED SANDPIPER (8 in. long, including beak)

sand·storm (-stôrm′) *n.* a windstorm in which large quantities of sand are blown about in the air

☆**sand trap** a pit or trench filled with sand, serving as a hazard on a golf course

☆**sand verbena** any of a number of chiefly trailing plants (genus *Abronia*) of the four-o'clock family, with pink, white, or yellow flowers, found in sandy areas of the W U.S.

Sand·wich (sandʹwich) town in Kent, SE England, near the Strait of Dover: one of the Cinque Ports: pop. 4,000

sand·wich (sandʹwich, san′-) *n.* [after John Montagu, 4th Earl of *Sandwich* (1718–92), said to have eaten these in order not to leave the gaming table for meals] **1.** two or more slices of bread with a filling of meat, fish, cheese, jam, etc. between them: now sometimes used of a single slice of bread covered with meat, gravy, etc. **2.** anything like a sandwich in arrangement —*vt.* to place or squeeze

between two other persons, places, things, materials, etc.

Sandwich Islands [after the 4th Earl of *Sandwich:* see prec.] *former name of the* HAWAIIAN ISLANDS (see HAWAII)

sandwich man 1. a man who walks the streets displaying two signboards (**sandwich boards**) hung from his shoulders, one in front and one behind 2. a man who makes or sells sandwiches

sand·wort (sand′wurt′) *n.* any of a genus (*Arenaria*) of low, tufted, mat-forming plants of the pink family, growing in sandy soil

sand·y (san′dē) *adj.* **sand′i·er, sand′i·est** 1. composed of, full of, or covered with sand 2. like sand; gritty, shifting, etc. 3. of the color of sand; pale reddish-yellow [*sandy* hair] **Sandy Hook** narrow, sandy peninsula in E N.J., at the S entrance to Lower New York Bay

sane (sān) *adj.* [L. *sanus,* healthy] 1. having a normal, healthy mind; able to make sound, rational judgments 2. showing good sense; sensible [*a sane* policy] 3. [Rare] not diseased; healthy —**sane′ly** *adv.* —**sane′ness** *n.*

San Fer·nan·do Valley (san′ fər nan′dō) [after a mission named for *Ferdinand III,* 13th-c. king of Castile] valley in SW Calif., partly in NW Los Angeles: c. 260 sq. mi.

San·ford, **Mount** [after the namer's family] mountain in SE Alas.: 16,208 ft.

☆**San·for·ize** (san′fə rīz′) *vt.* **-ized′, -iz′ing** [back-formation from *Sanforized,* a trademark applied to fabrics so treated: after *Sanford* L. Cluett (1874–1968), the inventor] to preshrink (cloth) permanently by a patented process before making garments

San Fran·cis·co (san′ frən sis′kō) [Sp., *St. Francis:* prob. after St. FRANCIS OF ASSISI] seaport on the coast of C Calif., separated from Oakland by an inlet (**San Francisco Bay**) of the Pacific: pop. 716,000 (met. area, incl. Oakland, 3,110,000) —**San′ Fran·cis′can** (-kən)

San Francisco Peaks three peaks of an eroded volcano in NC Ariz.: highest peak, c. 12,700 ft.

sang (saŋ) *alt. pt. of* SING

san·ga·ree (saŋ′gə rē′) *n.* [earlier *sangre* < Sp. *sangría,* SANGRÍA] a cold drink of diluted, spiced wine

Sang·er, **Margaret** (born *Margaret Higgins*) 1883–1966; U.S. nurse; leader in birth-control education

sang-froid (saŋ′frwä′; *Fr.* sän frwȧ′) *n.* [Fr., lit., cold blood] cool self-possession or composure —SYN. see EQUANIMITY

San·greal (saŋ′grāl′) [ME. *sangrayle* < MFr. *Saint Graal:* see SAINT & GRAIL] the Holy Grail: see GRAIL

San·gre de Cris·to Mountains (saŋ′grē də kris′tō) [Sp., lit., blood of Christ] range of the Rocky Mountains, in S Colo. & N N.Mex.: highest point, BLANCA PEAK

‡**san·grí·a** (sän grē′ä) *n.* [Sp., lit., bleeding < *sangre,* blood < L. *sanguis*] a Spanish fruit and wine punch

san·gui- (saŋ′gwi) [< L. *sanguis,* blood] *a combining form meaning* blood

san·gui·na·ri·a (saŋ′gwi ner′ē ə) *n.* [ModL. < L. < (*herba*) *sanguinaria,* (herb) that stanches blood < *sanguis,* blood] 1. *same as* BLOODROOT 2. the dried rootstock of bloodroot, containing several alkaloids used in medicine

san·gui·nar·y (saŋ′gwi ner′ē) *adj.* [L. *sanguinarius* < *sanguis:* see ff.] 1. accompanied by much bloodshed, murder, or carnage 2. flowing with blood; bloodstained 3. eager for bloodshed; bloodthirsty —**san′gui·nar′i·ly** *adv.* —**san′gui·nar′i·ness** *n.*

san·guine (saŋ′gwin) *adj.* [ME. *sanguin* < MFr. *sanguin* < L. *sanguineus* < *sanguis* (gen. *sanguinis*), blood < ?] 1. of the color of blood; ruddy: said esp. of complexions 2. in medieval physiology, having the warm, passionate, cheerful temperament and the healthy, ruddy complexion of one in whom the blood is the predominant humor of the four 3. cheerful and confident; optimistic; hopeful 4. *now rare var. of* SANGUINARY —**san′guine·ly** *adv.* —**san′guine·ness** *n.*

san·guin·e·ous (saŋ gwin′ē əs) *adj.* [L. *sanguineus:* see prec. & -OUS] 1. of or containing blood 2. having the color of blood; red 3. of bloodshed; sanguinary 4. sanguine; confident; hopeful

san·guin·o·lent (-ə lənt) *adj.* [MFr. < L. *sanguinolentus* < *sanguis,* blood] of, containing, or tinged with blood

San·he·drin (san hed′rin, sän-; *chiefly Brit.,* san′i drin) *n.* [Heb. *sanhedhrīn* (*gedhōlāh*), (great) council < Gr. *synedrion,* an assembly < *syn-,* together + *hedra,* seat: see SIT] the highest court and council of the ancient Jewish nation, having religious and civil functions: it was abolished with the destruction of Jerusalem in 70 A.D.: also, chiefly Brit., **San′he·drim** (-drim)

san·i·cle (san′i k'l) *n.* [ME. < OFr. < ML. *sanicula,* prob. dim. < L. *sanus,* healthy] any of a genus (*Sanicula*) of plants of the parsley family, with long-stalked leaves and clusters of small, white or yellowish flowers: formerly regarded as having healing powers

sa·ni·es (sā′nē ēz′) *n.* [L.] a thin, often greenish, discharge of pus and serum from a wound or ulcer —**sa′ni·ous** (-əs)

san·i·tar·i·an (san′ə ter′ē ən) *adj. same as* SANITARY —*n.* a person who specializes in public health and sanitation

san·i·tar·i·um (-ē əm) *n., pl.* **-i·ums, -i·a** (-ə) [ModL. <

L. *sanitas,* health] 1. a quiet resort, as in the mountains, where people go to rest and regain health 2. an institution for the care of invalids or convalescents, esp. one making use of local natural resources, as mineral springs, or one treating a specific disease, as tuberculosis

san·i·tar·y (san′ə ter′ē) *adj.* [Fr. *sanitaire* < L. *sanitas:* see SANITY & -ARY] 1. of health or the rules and conditions of health; esp., promoting health and healthful conditions by the elimination of dirt and agents of infection or disease 2. in a clean, healthy condition; hygienic —**san′i·tar′i·ly** *adv.* —**san′i·tar′i·ness** *n.*

☆**sanitary belt** a narrow elastic belt for holding a sanitary napkin in place

sanitary cordon *same as* CORDON SANITAIRE

sanitary engineering the branch of civil engineering having to do with sewage disposal, water supply, etc.

☆**sanitary napkin** an absorbent pad of cotton, cellulose, etc. worn by women during menstruation

san·i·ta·tion (san′ə tā′shən) *n.* [SANIT(ARY) + -ATION] 1. the science and practice of effecting healthful and hygienic conditions; study and use of hygienic measures such as drainage, ventilation, pure water supply, etc. 2. drainage and disposal of sewage

san·i·tize (san′ə tīz′) *vt.* **-tized′, -tiz′ing** 1. to make sanitary, as by sterilizing 2. to free from anything considered undesirable, damaging, etc. —**san′i·tiz′er** *n.*

san·i·ty (san′ə tē) *n.* [ME. *sanite* < OFr. < L. *sanitas,* health] 1. the condition of being sane; soundness of mind; mental health 2. soundness of judgment

San Ja·cin·to (san′ jə sin′tō) [Sp., *St. Hyacinth* (13th cent.)] river in SE Tex., flowing into Galveston Bay: in a battle (1836) near its mouth, troops under Sam Houston won Texas from Mexico

San Joa·quin (san′ wô kēn′, wä-) [Sp., *St. Joachim,* reputed father of the Virgin Mary] river in C Calif., flowing into the Sacramento River: c. 350 mi.

San Jo·se (san′ hō zā′, ə zā′) [Sp. *San José,* St. JOSEPH] city in WC Calif.: pop. 446,000 (met. area 1,065,000)

San Jo·sé (san′ hō se′) capital of Costa Rica, in the C part: pop. 181,000

☆**San Jo·se scale** (san′ hō zā′) [< *San Jose,* Calif., where first observed in the U.S.] a scale insect (*Quadraspidiotus perniciosus*) that is very destructive to fruit trees and ornamental shrubs

San Juan (san′ hwän′, wôn′; *Sp.* sän′ hwän′) [Sp., *St.* JOHN] capital of Puerto Rico; seaport on the Atlantic: pop. 445,000 (met. area 851,000)

San Juan Hill hill near Santiago de Cuba: captured by U.S. troops in a battle (1898) of the Spanish-American War

San Juan Islands group of islands in NW Wash., between the Strait of Georgia & Puget Sound: pop. 3,000

San Juan Mountains range of the Rocky Mountains in SW Colo. & N N.Mex.: highest peaks, over 14,000 ft.

sank (saŋk) *alt. pt. of* SINK

San·khya (sän′kya) *n.* [Sans. *sāmkhya*] a major system of Hindu philosophy, involving two ultimate, completely distinct, principles of matter and spirit

Sankt Mo·ritz (zäŋkt mō′rits) *Ger. name of* ST. MORITZ

San Le·an·dro (san′ lē an′drō) [Sp., *St. Leander,* archbishop of Seville] city in W Calif., on San Francisco Bay: suburb of Oakland: pop. 69,000

San Luis Po·to·sí (sän′ lwēs′ pō′tō sē′) 1. state of NC Mexico: 24,417 sq. mi.; pop. 1,355,000 2. its capital, in the SW part: pop. 182,000

San Ma·ri·no (sän′ mä rē′nō; *E.* san′ mə rē′nō) 1. independent country within E Italy: 23 sq. mi.; pop. 18,000 2. its capital

San Mar·tín (sän′ mär tēn′), **Jo·sé de** (hō se′ de) 1778–1850; S. American revolutionary leader, born in Argentina

San Ma·te·o (san′ mə tā′ō) [Sp., *St.* MATTHEW] city in W Calif., on San Francisco Bay: suburb of San Francisco: pop. 79,000

☆**san·nup** (san′up) *n.* [< AmInd. (Abnaki) *senanbe,* lit., man] a married male American Indian

sann·ya·si (sun yä′sē) *n.* [Hindi *sannyāsī,* < Sans. *samnyāsin,* casting away < *sam,* together (for base see SAME) + *ni,* down (for base see NETHER) + *asayati,* (he) casts] a Hindu holy man, a homeless mendicant

San Ra·fael (san′ rə fel′) [Sp., "Saint Raphael"] city in W Calif., on San Francisco Bay: suburb of San Francisco: pop. 39,000

San Re·mo (sän re′mō; *E.* san rē′mō) resort town in Liguria, NW Italy, on the Riviera: pop. 30,000

sans (sanz; *Fr.* sän) *prep.* [ME. *saun* < OFr. *sanz* (Fr. *sans*) < L. *sine,* without: form infl. by L. *absentia,* in the absence of, abl.: see ABSENCE] without; lacking

Sans. Sanskrit

San Sal·va·dor (san sal′və dôr′; *Sp.* sän säl′vä thôr′) 1. capital of El Salvador, in the C part: pop. 256,000 2. island of the E Bahamas: prob. the place of Columbus' landing (1492) in the New World: 60 sq. mi.

sans-cu·lotte (sanz′kōō lät′, -kyoo-; *Fr.* sän kü lôt′) *n.* [Fr., lit., without breeches] 1. a revolutionary: term of contempt applied by the aristocrats to the republicans of the poorly clad French Revolutionary army, who sub-

stituted pantaloons for knee breeches **2.** any radical or revolutionary —**sans'-cu·lot'tic, sans'-cu·lot'tish** *adj.* — **sans'-cu·lot'tism** *n.*

‡**sans doute** (sän dōͦt′) [Fr.] without doubt; certainly

San Se·bas·tián (sän′ se bäs tyän′; *E.* san′ si bas′chən) seaport in the Basque Provinces, N Spain: pop. 149,000

☆**san·sei** (sän′sā) *n., pl.* **-sei, -seis** [Jap. < *san*, third + *sei*, generation: cf. NISEI] [*also* **S-**] a native American citizen whose grandparents were Japanese immigrants

san·se·vi·e·ri·a (san′sə vi′rē′ə, -vi ē′rē ə) *n.* [ModL., after the Prince of *Sanseviero* (1710–71), a learned Neapolitan] any of a genus (*Sansevieria*) of succulent tropical plants of the agave family, with stiff, thick, lance-shaped leaves often yielding a strong, elastic fiber

Sansk. Sanskrit

San·skrit (san′skrit) *n.* [< Sans. *saṁskṛta*, lit., made together, well arranged < *saṁ-*, together (for base see SAME) + *-kṛta*, made < IE. base **kwer-*, to make, whence MIr. *creth*, poetry: so called in distinction to *Prākrit*, lit., the common (spoken) language] **1.** the classical Old Indic literary language, as cultivated from the 4th cent. B.C. onward and still used in the ritual of the Northern Buddhist Church: because of the antiquity of its written expression and the detailed descriptive analysis in the Sutras of the Hindu grammarian Pānini (end of the 4th cent. B.C.), Sanskrit has been very important in the origin and development of comparative Indo-European linguistics **2.** loosely, any written form of Old Indic, including Vedic —*adj.* of or written in Sanskrit Also sp. **San'scrit** —**San·skrit'ic** *adj.* —**San'skrit·ist** *n.*

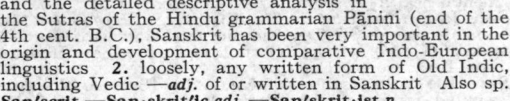

SANSEVIERIA

‡**sans peur et sans re·proche** (sän pėr′ ā sän rə prôsh′) [Fr.] without fear and without reproach

sans-ser·if (san ser′if) *n.* [see SANS & SERIF] a style of printing type with no serifs

‡**sans sou·ci** (sän sōͦ sē′) [Fr.] without care or worry; gay

San Ste·fa·no (sän ste′fä nō′) village in European Turkey, site of the signing of a peace treaty (1878) between Russia & Turkey, at the end of the Russo-Turkish War

San·ta (san′tə, -ti; *for adj., also* sän′tä) ☆*clipped form of* SANTA CLAUS —*adj.* [Sp. or It., fem. of *santo* < L. *sanctus*, holy: see SAINT] holy or saint: used in combinations [*Santa* Maria]

San·ta An·a (san′tə an′ə; *also, for 2, Sp.* sän′tä ä′nä) **1.** [Sp., *St.* ANNE] city in SW Calif.: pop. 157,000: see ANAHEIM **2.** city in W El Salvador: pop. 121,000

San·ta An·na (san′tə ä′nä), **An·to·nio Ló·pez de** (än tō′nyō lō′pes de) 1795?–1876; Mex. revolutionist & general; president (1833–35; 1841–44; 1846–47; 1853–55)

San·ta Bar·ba·ra (san′tə bär′bə rə) [Sp., *St. Barbara*, early Christian martyr] city on the coast of SW Calif.: pop. 70,000

Santa Barbara Islands group of nine islands, & many islets, off the SW coast of Calif.

Santa Catalina [Sp., *St.* CATHERINE] one of the Santa Barbara Islands, a tourist resort: c. 20 mi. long

San·ta Cat·a·ri·na (san′tə kä′tə rē′nä) state of S Brazil: 37,055 sq. mi.; pop. 2,147,000; cap. Florianópolis

San·ta Cla·ra (san′tə kler′ə; *for 1, Sp.* sän′tä klä′rä) **1.** city in C Cuba: pop. 142,000 **2.** [Sp., *St. Clare* (of Assisi)] city in W Calif., near San Jose: pop. 88,000

☆**San·ta Claus, San·ta Klaus** (san′tə klôz′, -ti) [< Du. dial. *Sinterklaas, Sante Klaas < Sant Nikolaas, St.* NICHOLAS] *Folklore* a fat, white-bearded, jolly old man in a red suit, who lives at the North Pole, makes toys for children, and distributes gifts at Christmas time: also called **Saint Nicholas, Saint Nick**

San·ta Cruz (san′tə krōͦz′; *Sp.* sän′tä krōͦs′) [Sp., holy cross] **1.** city in C Bolivia: pop. 73,000 **2.** one of the Santa Barbara Islands: c. 23 mi. long **3.** *same as* ST. CROIX

Santa Cruz de Te·ne·rife (də ten′ə rif′; *Sp.* de te′ne rē′fe) seaport on Tenerife Island, Canary Islands: pop. 151,000

San·ta Fe (san′tə fā′) [Sp., holy faith] capital of N.Mex., in the NC part: pop. 41,000

San·ta Fé (sän′tä fe′) city in E Argentina: pop. 260,000

Santa Fe Trail trade route between Santa Fe, N.Mex., & Independence, Mo.: important from 1821 to 1880

☆**San·ta Ger·tru·dis** (san′tə gər trōͦ′dis) [so named after a section of the King Ranch, in Texas] any of a hardy, red-colored, American breed of beef cattle, developed from a cross of Shorthorn and Brahman stock and able to thrive in hot climates on sparse forage

San·ta Is·a·bel (sän′tä ē sä bel′) capital of Equatorial Guinea; seaport on the island of Fernando Póo: pop. 20,000

SANTA FE TRAIL

San·ta Ma·ri·a (san′tə mə rē′ə; *Sp.* sän′tä mä rē′ä) **1.** the flagship that Columbus used in his voyage of 1492 **2.** active volcano in SW Guatemala: 12,362 ft.

San·ta Mon·i·ca (san′tə män′i kə) [Sp., *St. Monica*, mother of *St.* AUGUSTINE (of Numidia)] city in SW Calif., on the Pacific: suburb of Los Angeles: pop. 88,000

San·tan·der (sän′tän der′) seaport in N Spain, on the Bay of Biscay: pop. 128,000

San·ta Ro·sa (san′tə rō′zə) [Sp., holy rose] **1.** one of the Santa Barbara Islands: 17 mi. long **2.** city in W Calif., north of San Francisco: pop. 50,000

San·ta·ya·na (san′tē an′ə, -ä′nə; *Sp.* sän′tä yä′nä), **George** (born *Jorge Augustín Nicolás de Santayana*) 1863–1952; Sp. philosopher & writer in English, in the U.S., England, & Italy

San·tee (san tē′) [< AmInd. tribal name < ?] river in E S.C., flowing southeast into the Atlantic: 143 mi.

San·ti·a·go (sän′tē ä′gō; *E.* san′tē ä′gō) capital of Chile, in the C part: pop. 1,169,000 (met. area 2,451,000)

Santiago de Cu·ba (de kōͦ′bä) seaport in SE Cuba, on the Caribbean: pop. 166,000

San·to Do·min·go (sän′tō dō miŋ′gō; *E.* san′tō dō miŋ′gō) **1.** capital of the Dominican Republic, a seaport on the S coast: pop. 367,000 **2.** *former name of* DOMINICAN REPUBLIC **3.** *a former name of* HISPANIOLA

san·ton·i·ca (san tän′i kə) *n.* [ModL. < L. (*herba*) *santonica* < *Santoni*, a people of Aquitania] **1.** any of several European wormwoods; esp., the **Levant wormseed** (*Artemisia cina*) **2.** the unexpanded, dried flower heads of several European wormwoods, containing santonin

san·to·nin (san′tə nin) *n.* [Fr. *santonine* < ModL. *santonica*: see prec.] a colorless, poisonous, crystalline compound, $C_{15}H_{18}O_3$, obtained from certain species of wormwood and used in medicine as a vermifuge

San·tos (sän′tōͦs) seaport in S Brazil, in São Paulo state: pop. 262,000

São Fran·cis·co (souṇ′ frän sēs′kōͦ) river in E Brazil, flowing northeast into the Atlantic: c. 1,800 mi.

São Luiz (lwēs′) capital of Maranhão state, Brazil; seaport on an island off N coast: pop. 160,000

São Mi·guel (mē gel′) largest island of the Azores: 290 sq. mi.; pop. 165,000; chief city, Ponta Delgada

Saône (sōn) river in E France, flowing south into the Rhone at Lyon: c. 280 mi.

São Pau·lo (souṇ pou′lōͦ) **1.** state of SE Brazil: c. 95,750 sq. mi.; pop. 12,974,000 **2.** its capital: pop. 3,825,000

São Sal·va·dor (souṇ säl′və dôr′) *same as* SALVADOR

São To·mé (tō me′) Port. island in the Gulf of Guinea, off the W coast of Africa: 318 sq. mi.; pop. 59,000: with the nearby island of Príncipe, it constitutes an overseas province (**São Tomé e Príncipe**) of Portugal: 372 sq. mi.; pop. 65,000

sap¹ (sap) *n.* [ME. < OE. *sæp*, akin to G. *saft* < IE. base **sab-*, var. of **sap-*, to taste, perceive, whence L. *sapere*, to taste, know] **1.** the juice that circulates through a plant, esp. a woody plant, bearing water, food, etc. to the tissues **2.** any fluid considered vital to the life or health of an organism **3.** vigor; energy; vitality **4.** [< SAPHEAD] [Slang] a stupid person; fool —*vt.* **sapped, sap′ping** to drain of sap —**sap′less** *adj.*

sap² (sap) *n.* [MFr. *sappe* < the *v.*] an extended, narrow trench for approaching or undermining an enemy position or fortification —*vt.* **sapped, sap′ping** [MFr. *sapper* < *sappe*, a hoe < It. *zappe*] **1.** to undermine by digging away foundations; dig beneath **2.** to undermine in any way; weaken; exhaust —*vi.* **1.** to dig saps **2.** to approach an enemy's position by saps —SYN. see WEAKEN

sap³ (sap) *n.* [prob. orig. contr. < SAPLING] ☆[Slang] a blackjack, short club, etc. —☆*vt.* **sapped, sap′ping** [Slang] to hit on the head, or knock out, with a sap

s.ap. apothecaries' scruple

sap·a·jou (sap′ə jōͦ′; *Fr.* sȧ pȧ zhōͦ′) *n.* [Fr. < Tupi name] *same as* CAPUCHIN (sense 3)

sa·pan·wood (sə pan′wood′) *n. same as* SAPPANWOOD

sap·head (sap′hed′) *n.* [Slang] a stupid person; fool —**sap′head′ed** *adj.*

sa·phe·na (sə fē′nə) *n.* [ME. < ML. < Ar. *ṣāfin*] either of two large superficial veins of the leg —**sa·phe′nous** (-nəs) *adj.*

sap·id (sap′id) *adj.* [L. *sapidus* < *sapere*, to have a taste: see SAP¹] **1.** having a taste, esp. a pleasing taste; savory **2.** agreeable to the mind; interesting; engaging —**sa·pid′i·ty** (sə pid′ə tē) *n.*

sa·pi·ent (sā′pē ənt) *adj.* [ME. < L. *sapiens*, prp. of *sapere*, to taste, know: see SAP¹] full of knowledge; wise; sagacious; discerning —SYN. see WISE¹ —**sa′pi·ence** *n.* —**sa′pi·ent·ly** *adv.*

sa·pi·en·tial (sā′pē en′shəl) *adj.* [LL. *sapientialis* < L. *sapiens*] having, providing, or expounding wisdom

Sa·pir (sə pir′), **Edward** 1884–1939; U.S. linguist & anthropologist, born in Pomerania

sap·ling (sap′liŋ) *n.* [ME. *sappelynge:* see SAP¹ & -LING¹] **1.** a young tree **2.** a youth

sap·o·dil·la (sap′ə dil′ə) *n.* [Sp. *zapotilla*, dim. of *zapote* < Nahuatl *tzapotl*] **1.** a tropical American evergreen tree (*Achras zapota*) of the sapodilla family, yielding chicle and having a brown, rough-skinned fruit with a sweet, yellowish pulp **2.** the fruit —*adj.* designating a large family (Sapotaceae) of tropical trees and shrubs with a milky

juice and sometimes edible fruits, including the sapodilla, balata, buckthorn, marmalade tree, etc.

sap·o·na·ceous (sap'ə nā'shəs) *adj.* [ModL. *saponaceus* < L. *sapo*, soap: see SAPONIFY] soapy or soaplike

sa·pon·i·fi·ca·tion (sə pän'ə fi kā'shən) *n.* [Fr. < *saponifier*: see SAPONIFY] the conversion of an ester heated with an alkali into the corresponding alcohol and acid salt; specif., this process carried out with fats (glyceryl esters) to produce soap

sa·pon·i·fy (sə pän'ə fī') *vt.* **-fied', -fy'ing** [Fr. *saponifier* < L. *sapo* (gen. *saponis*), soap (< Gmc., as in OE. *sape*, SOAP) + Fr. -*fier*, -FY] to subject to saponification; specif., to convert (a fat) into soap by reaction with an alkali —*vi.* to undergo conversion to soap —**sa·pon'i·fi'a·ble** *adj.* —**sa·pon'i·fi'er** *n.*

sap·o·nin (sap'ə nin) *n.* [Fr. *saponine* < L. *sapo* (see prec.) + -*in*, -IN¹] any of a group of glucosides, found in soapwort, soapbark, etc., which form a soapy foam when dissolved in water: used as detergents, etc.

sap·o·nite (-nīt') *n.* [Sw. *saponit* < L. *sapo*: see SAPONIFY & -ITE¹] a complex hydrous silicate of aluminum and magnesium, occurring in soft, soapy masses in veins and cavities of rock, as in serpentine

sa·por (sā'pər) *n.* [L. < *sapere*, to taste: see SAP¹] that quality in a substance which produces taste or flavor; savor —**sa·po·rif·ic** (sā'pə rif'ik, sap'ə-), **sa·por·ous** (sā'pər əs, sap'ər-) *adj.*

sa·po·ta (sə pōt'ə) *n.* [ModL. < Sp. *zapote*: see SAPODILLA] same as SAPODILLA

sa·po·te (sə pōt'ē) *n.* [Sp. *zapote:* see SAPODILLA] **1.** any of several tropical American trees or their fruits **2.** *same as:* **a)** MARMALADE TREE **b)** SAPODILLA

sap·pan·wood (sə pan'wood') *n.* [partial transl. of Du. *sapanhout* < Malay *sapaṅ* + Du. *hout*, wood, akin to OE. *holt*: see HOLT] **1.** a wood yielding a red dye, obtained from an East Indian tree (*Caesalpinia sappan*) of the legume family **2.** the tree

sap·per (sap'ər) *n.* **1.** a soldier employed in digging saps, laying mines, etc. **2.** a person or thing that saps

Sap·phic (saf'ik) *adj.* [L. *Sapphicus* < Gr. *Sapphikos* < *Sapphō*] **1.** of Sappho **2.** designating or of certain meters or a form of stanza or strophe used by or named after Sappho, esp. a stanza of three five-stress lines followed by a short line —*n.* a Sapphic verse

Sap·phi·ra (sə fī'rə) [LL.(Ec.) *Saphira* < Gr.(Ec.) *Sappheirē* < Aram. word meaning "beautiful"] *Bible* the wife of Ananias, struck dead with her husband for lying: Acts 5:1–10

sap·phire (saf'īr) *n.* [ME. < OFr. *saphir* < L. *sapphirus* < Gr. *sappheiros* < Heb. *sappīr* < Sans. *śanipriya*, lit., dear to Saturn < *Saniḥ*, Saturn (the planet) + *priya*, beloved < IE. *prī-*, var. of base *prēi-*, to love, whence FRIEND] **1.** a hard, transparent precious stone of a clear, deep-blue corundum **2.** its color **3.** a hard, translucent or transparent variety of corundum, varying in color **4.** a gem made of this —*adj.* deep-blue

sap·phir·ine (saf'ər in, -ə rin', -ə rēn') *adj.* of or like sapphire —*n.* **1.** a rare blue or green silicate of magnesium and aluminum **2.** a blue variety of spinel

Sap·pho (saf'ō) 7th cent. B.C.; Gr. lyric poetess of Lesbos

Sap·po·ro (sä'pō rō') chief city on the island of Hokkaido, Japan, in the SW part: pop. 795,000

sap·py (sap'ē) *adj.* **-pi·er, -pi·est** [ME. *sapy* < OE. *sæpig*] **1.** full of sap; juicy **2.** [< SAP¹, *n.* 4] [Slang] foolish; silly; fatuous —**sap'pi·ness** *n.*

sa·pre·mi·a (sə prē'mē ə) *n.* [ModL.: see ff. & -EMIA] a form of blood poisoning caused by toxic products resulting from the action of putrefactive microorganisms on dead tissue: also sp. **sa·prae'mi·a** —**sa·pre'mic** *adj.*

sapro- (sap'rō, -rə) [< Gr. *sapros*, rotten] a combining *form meaning* dead, putrefying, decaying [*saprogenic*]: also, before a vowel, **sapr-**

sa·pro·bic (sa prō'bik) *adj.* [< SAPRO- + Gr. *bios*, life + -IC] *Biol.* **1.** of or pertaining to organisms living in highly polluted waters **2.** of or pertaining to saprophytes —**sa'probe** *n.* —**sa·pro'bi·cal·ly** *adv.*

sap·ro·gen·ic (sap'rə jen'ik) *adj.* [SAPRO- + -GENIC] producing, or produced by, putrefaction: also **sa·prog·e·nous** (sə präj'ə nəs)

sap·ro·lite (sap'rə līt') *n.* [SAPRO- + -LITE] *Geol.* completely decomposed rock lying in its original site —**sap'ro·lit'ic** (-lit'ik) *adj.*

sap·ro·pel (sap'rə pel') *n.* [< SAPRO- + Gr. *pelos*, mud, slime] black, decaying, organic bottom deposits in some lakes, rivers, etc. that lack oxygen and are rich in hydrogen sulfide —**sap'ro·pel'ic** *adj.*

sa·proph·a·gous (sa präf'ə gəs) *adj.* [SAPRO- + -PHAGOUS] feeding on decaying organic matter

sap·ro·phyte (sap'rə fīt') *n.* [SAPRO- + -PHYTE] any organism that lives on dead or decaying organic matter, as some fungi and bacteria —**sap'ro·phyt'ic** (-fit'ik) *adj.*

sap·ro·zo·ic (sap'rə zō'ik) *adj.* [SAPRO- + ZO- + -IC] **1.** absorbing simple organic material and dissolved salts for nourishment **2.** of a saprophyte, esp. an animal parasite lacking a functional digestive system, as the tapeworm

☆sap·sa·go (sap sä'gō, sap'sə gō') *n.* [altered < G. *schabzieger* < *schaben*, to scrape + *zieger*, whey] a variety of hard, greenish cheese made orig. in Switzerland of skim milk flavored with melilot

☆sap·suck·er (sap'suk'ər) *n.* any of several small, insect-eating American woodpeckers (genus *Sphyrapicus*) that often drill holes in maples, apple trees, etc. for the sap

sap·wood (sap'wood') *n.* the soft wood between the inner bark of a tree and the heartwood, serving to conduct water

S.A.R. Sons of the American Revolution

Sar·a (ser'ə, sar'-) a feminine name: see SARAH

sar·a·band (sar'ə band') *n.* [Fr. *sarabande* < Sp. *zarabanda*, ult. < Per. *sarband*, kind of dance and song < *sar*, head + *band*, pres. stem of *bastan*, to bind] **1.** a graceful, stately, slow Spanish dance in triple time, developed from an earlier lively dance **2.** music for, or in the tempo of, this dance, with decided emphasis on the second beat of the measure

Sar·a·cen (sar'ə s'n) *n.* [ME. *Sarasene* < OFr. & LL.: OFr. *Sarrazin* < LL. *Saracenus* < LGr. *Sarakēnos*] **1.** orig., any member of the nomadic tribes of Syria and nearby regions **2.** later, any Arab or any Moslem, esp. at the time of the Crusades —*adj.* of the Saracens —**Sar'a·cen'ic** (-sen'ik) *adj.*

Sa·ra·gos·sa (sar'ə gäs'ə) *Eng. name* of ZARAGOZA

Sar·ah (ser'ə, sar'-) [Heb. *śārāh*, lit., princess] **1.** a feminine name: dim. *Sadie, Sal, Sally;* var. *Sara* **2.** *Bible* the wife of Abraham and mother of Isaac

Sa·rai (ser'ī) *Bible* Sarah: so called before God's covenant with Abraham: Gen. 17:15

Sa·ra·je·vo (sä'rä'ye vō; E. sar'ə yā'vō) capital of Bosnia and Hercegovina, in C Yugoslavia: scene of the assassination of Archduke Francis Ferdinand (June 28, 1914), which precipitated World War I: pop. 175,000

☆sa·ran (sə ran') *n.* [arbitrary coinage] any of various thermoplastic resins obtained by the polymerization or copolymerization of vinylidene chloride usually with some other vinyl derivatives: it is used in extruded or molded form in making various fabrics, acid-resistant pipes and fittings, a transparent wrapping material, etc.

Sar·a·nac Lake (sar'ə nak') [< native name < *?*] **1.** any of three connected lakes (*Upper, Middle, & Lower*) in the Adirondacks, NE N.Y. **2.** resort village on Lower Saranac Lake: pop. 6,000

☆sa·ra·pe (sə rä'pē) *n. var.* of SERAPE

Sar·a·so·ta (sar'ə sōt'ə) [< *?*] city on the W coast of Fla., near Tampa: resort: pop. 34,000

Sar·a·to·ga (sar'ə tō'gə) [< Iroquoian place name, ? lit., beaver place] *former name of* SCHUYLERVILLE: scene of two Revolutionary War battles (1777) in which Am. forces led by Gates defeated the British under Burgoyne

Saratoga Springs [see prec.] city in E N.Y.: a resort with mineral springs: pop. 19,000

☆Saratoga trunk [after prec.] a large trunk, formerly used mainly by women when traveling

Sa·ra·tov (sä rä'tôf) city & port in SC European R.S.F.S.R., on the Volga: pop. 699,000

Sa·ra·wak (sə rä'wäk) state of Malaysia, occupying NC & NW Borneo: 48,232 sq. mi.; pop. 903,000; cap. Kuching

sar·casm (sär'kaz'm) *n.* [LL. *sarcasmos* < Gr. *sarkasmos* < *sarkazein*, to tear flesh like dogs, speak bitterly < *sarx* (gen. *sarkos*), flesh < IE. base **twerk-*, to cut, whence Avestan *thwarəs-*, to cut, whittle] **1.** a taunting, sneering, cutting, or caustic remark; gibe or jeer, generally ironical **2.** the making of such remarks **3.** their characteristic quality

sar·cas·tic (sär kas'tik) *adj.* **1.** of, having the nature of, or characterized by sarcasm; sneering, caustic, cutting, etc. **2.** using, or fond of using, sarcasm —**sar·cas'ti·cal·ly** *adv.* *SYN.*—**sarcastic** implies intent to hurt by taunting with mocking ridicule, veiled sneers, etc. [a *sarcastic* reminder that work begins at 9:00 A.M.]; **satirical** implies as its purpose the exposing or attacking of the vices, follies, stupidities, etc. of others and connotes the use of ridicule, sarcasm, etc. [Swift's *satirical* comments]; **ironical** applies to a humorous or sarcastic form of expression in which the intended meaning of what is said is directly opposite to the usual sense ["My, you're early," was his *ironical* taunt to the latecomer]; **sardonic** implies sneering or mocking bitterness in a person, or, more often, in his expression, remarks, etc. [a *sardonic* smile]; **caustic** implies a cutting, biting, or stinging wit or sarcasm [a *caustic* tongue]

sarce·net (särs'net) *n.* [ME. *sarsenet* < Anglo-Fr. *sarzinett*, dim. < OFr. *Sarrazin:* see SARACEN] a soft silk cloth, formerly used for ribbons, linings, etc.

sar·co- (sär'kō, -kə) [< Gr. *sarx*, flesh: see SARCASM] *a combining form meaning* flesh [*sarcology*]: also, before a vowel, **sarc-**

sar·co·carp (sär'kə kärp') *n.* [prec. + -CARP] *Bot.* **1.** the fleshy part of a stone fruit, as in the plum **2.** loosely, any fleshy fruit

sar·coid·o·sis (sär'koi dō'sis) *n.* [< Gr. *sarkoeidēs*, fleshy (< *sarx*, flesh: see SARCO-) + -OSIS] a chronic disease of unknown cause, characterized by the development of lesions similar to tubercles in the lungs, bones, skin, etc.

sar·col·o·gy (sär käl'ə jē) *n.* [SARCO- + -LOGY] the branch of anatomy that deals with the soft tissues of the body

sar·co·ma (sär kō′mə) *n.*, *pl.* **-mas, -ma·ta** (-mə tə) [ModL. < Gr. *sarkōma* < *sarx*, flesh: see SARCASM & -OMA] any of various malignant tumors that begin in connective tissue, or in tissue developed from the mesoblast and not epithelial —**sar·co′ma·to′sis** (-tō′sis) *n.* —**sar·co′ma·tous** (-təs, -käm′ə-) *adj.*

sar·coph·a·gus (sär käf′ə gəs) *n.*, *pl.* **-gi′** (-jī′), **-gus·es** [L. < Gr. *sarkophagos* < *sarx*, flesh (see SARCASM) + *phagein*, to eat (see -PHAGOUS): because the limestone caused rapid disintegration of the contents] **1.** among the ancient Greeks and Romans, a limestone coffin or tomb, often inscribed and elaborately ornamented **2.** any stone coffin, esp. one on display, as in a monumental tomb

sar·cous (sär′kəs) *adj.* [SARC- + -OUS] *Zool.* of or composed of flesh or muscle

sard (särd) *n.* [ME. *saarde* < L. *sarda* < or akin to Gr. *sardios*, sard, lit., ? Sardian stone < *Sardeis*, SARDIS] **1.** a very hard, deep orange-red variety of chalcedony, used in jewelry, etc. **2.** a piece of this

sar·da·na (sär dä′nə) *n.* [Sp. < Catal.] **1.** a Spanish folk dance of Catalonia, danced in a circle **2.** music for this

sar·dine[1] (sär dēn′) *n.*, *pl.* **-dines′, -dine′:** see PLURAL, II, D, 1 [ME. *sardeyne* < MFr. *sardine* < L. *sardina* < *sarda*, kind of fish, prob. < Gr. *Sardō*, Sardinia] any of a variety of small ocean fishes preserved in tightly packed tins for eating; specif., *same as* PILCHARD

sar·dine[2] (sär′din, -dīn) *n. same as* SARD

Sar·din·i·a (sär din′ē ə, -din′yə) [L.] **1.** It. island in the Mediterranean, south of Corsica: c. 9,196 sq. mi. **2.** autonomous region of Italy, comprising this island & small nearby islands: 9,300 sq. mi.; pop. 1,413,000; cap. Cagliari **3.** former kingdom (1720–1860) including this region, Piedmont, Nice, Savoy (by which the kingdom was ruled), etc.: c. 28,000 sq. mi. It. name **Sar·de·gna** (sär dā′nyä)

Sar·din·i·an (-ən, -yən) *adj.* of Sardinia or its people —*n.* **1.** a native or inhabitant of Sardinia **2.** the Romance dialects of C and S Sardinia

Sar·dis (sär′dis) capital of ancient Lydia

sar·di·us (sär′dē əs) *n.* [ME. < LL.(Ec.) < Gr. *sardios* < *Sardeis*, SARDIS] **1.** *same as* SARD **2.** *Bible* a precious stone worn in the breastplate of the Jewish high priest: Ex. 28:17

sar·don·ic (sär dän′ik) *adj.* [Fr. *sardonique* < L. *sardonius* < Gr. *sardonios*, altered after *Sardō*, Sardinia < *sardanios*, bitter, scornful (used of smiles or laughter)] disdainfully or bitterly sneering, ironical, or sarcastic [a *sardonic* smile] —SYN. see SARCASTIC —**sar·don′i·cal·ly** *adv.*

sar·do·nyx (sär′də niks) *n.* [ME. < L. < Gr. *sardonyx* < *sardios*, SARD + *onyx*, ONYX] a variety of onyx made up of alternating layers of white chalcedony and sard, used as a gem, esp. in making cameos

Sar·dou′ (sär dōō′), **Vic·to·ri·en** (vēk tô ryan′) 1831–1908; Fr. dramatist

Sa·re·ma (sä′rə mä′) *same as* SAAREMAA

Sar·gas·so Sea (sär gas′ō) region of calms in the N Atlantic, northeast of the West Indies, noted for its abundance of sargassum

sar·gas·sum (sär gas′əm) *n.* [ModL. < Port. *sargaço* < *sarga*, kind of grape] any of a genus (*Sargassum*) of floating, brown seaweeds, the gulfweeds, found in the warmer seas and having a main stem with flattened, leaflike outgrowths and special branches with berrylike air sacs: also **sar·gas′so** (-ō), *pl.* **-sos,** **sargasso weed**

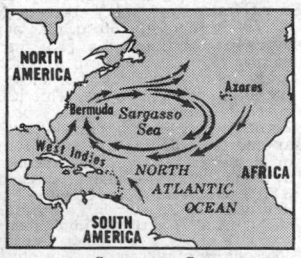

SARGASSO SEA

☆**sarge** (särj) *n. colloq. shortened form of* SERGEANT

Sar·gent (sär′jənt), **John Singer** 1856–1925; U.S. painter in Europe

Sar·gon (sär′gän) **1.** fl. c. 2300 B.C.; founder of the Akkadian kingdom **2.** Sargon II ?–705 B.C.; king of Assyria (722–705)

sa·ri (sä′rē) *n.* [Hind. *sārī* < Sans. *śāṭī*] the principal outer garment of a Hindu woman, consisting of a long piece of cloth worn wrapped around the body with one end forming an ankle-length skirt and the other end draped across the bosom, over one shoulder, and, sometimes, over the head: also sp. **sa′ree**

sark (särk) *n.* [ME. *serke* < OE. *serc* & cognate ON. *serkr*] [Scot.] a shirt or chemise

Sar·ma·ti·a (sär mā′shē ə, -shə) ancient region in E Europe, between the Vistula & Volga rivers, occupied by the Sarmatians (3d cent. B.C.–2d cent. A.D.)

Sar·ma·tian (-shən) *adj.* of Sarmatia or the Sarmatians —*n.* any of an ancient Indo-Iranian people related to the Scythians

sar·men·tose (sär men′tōs) *adj.* [L. *sarmentosus*, full of twigs < *sarmentum*, a twig <

SARI

sarpere, to trim, cut off < IE. base **ser(p)-*, a sickle, whence Gr. *harpē*, Lett. *sirpis*] producing long, slender stems which take root along the ground, as the strawberry plant

Sar·ni·a (sär′nē ə) city & port in SE Ontario, Canada, opposite Port Huron, Mich.: pop. 55,000

sa·rod, sa·rode (sə rōd′) *n.* [Hindi *sarod* < Per.] a lutelike musical instrument of India, with many strings

sa·rong (sə rôŋ′ -räŋ′) *n.* [Malay *sārung*, lit., sheath] **1.** the principal garment of men and women in the Malay Archipelago, the East Indies, etc., consisting of a long strip of cloth, often brightly colored and printed, worn around the lower part of the body like a skirt **2.** cotton cloth for such garments

Sa·ron·ic Gulf (sə rän′ik) inlet of the Aegean Sea, in SE Greece, between Attica & the Peloponnesus: c. 50 mi. long

sar·os (ser′äs) *n.* [Gr. < Bab. *shār*(*u*)] *Astron.* the eclipse cycle of the sun and moon, consisting of 223 synodic months, an interval equal to 6585.32 days, after which the eclipses in the cycle recur but are then shifted in longitude 120° farther west

Sa·roy·an (sə roi′ən), **William** 1908– ; U.S. writer

Sar·pe·don (sär pēd′'n, -pē′dän) [L. < Gr. *Sarpēdōn*] *Gr. Myth.* a son of Zeus and Europa, who became king of Lycia and was allowed to live three generations: in another version, he was killed by Patroclus in the Trojan War

☆**sar·ra·ce·ni·a** (sar′ə sē′nē ə) *n.* [ModL., name of the genus: after D. *Sarrazin*, Fr.-Canadian physician] any of a genus (*Sarracenia*) of perennial American plants of a family (Sarraceniaceae) having hollow, tubular leaves which trap insects, and single, nodding flowers

sar·sa·pa·ril·la (sas′pə ril′ə, särs′-, sär′sə-) *n.* [Sp. *zarzaparrilla* < *zarza*, bramble + *parrilla*, dim. of *parra*, vine] **1.** any of a number of tropical American, spiny, woody vines (genus *Smilax*) of the lily family, with large, fragrant roots and toothed, heart-shaped leaves **2.** the dried roots of any of these plants, formerly used in medicine **3.** an extract of this ☆**4.** a carbonated drink flavored with or as with sarsaparilla **5.** any of several N. American plants resembling sarsaparilla; esp., a woodland plant, **wild sarsaparilla** (*Aralia nudicaulis*) of the ginseng family

sarse·net (särs′net) *n. same as* SARCENET

Sar·to (sär′tō), **An·dre·a del** (än dre′ä del) (born *Andrea d'Angelo Vannucchi* or *di Francesco*) 1486–1531; Florentine painter

sar·tor (sär′tər) *n.* [LL. < L. *sartus*, pp. of *sarcire*, to patch, mend < IE. base **serk-*, woven substance, to hedge in, whence Gr. *herkos*, a hedge] a tailor: literary or humorous term

sar·to·ri·al (sär tôr′ē əl) *adj.* [LL. *sartor* (see prec.) + -IAL] **1.** of tailors or their work **2.** of clothing or dress, esp. men's —**sar·to′ri·al·ly** *adv.*

sar·to·ri·us (-əs) *n.* [ModL. < LL. *sartor*, a tailor (see SARTOR): in reference to the traditional cross-legged position of tailors at work] a narrow muscle of the thigh, the longest in the human body, that passes obliquely across the front of the thigh and helps rotate the leg to the position assumed in sitting cross-legged

Sar·tre (sär′tr'), **Jean-Paul** (zhän pôl) 1905– ; Fr. philosopher, playwright, & novelist

Sa·rum use (ser′əm) [< *Sarum*, ancient city near Salisbury, seat of the bishopric (1075–1220)] the form of the Latin rite first used in the Salisbury diocese, the prevalent form in England before the Reformation

Sa·se·bo (sä′se bō′) seaport in E Kyushu, Japan, on the East China Sea: pop. 279,000

sash[1] (sash) *n.* [Ar. *shāsh*, muslin] an ornamental band, ribbon, or scarf worn over the shoulder or around the waist, often formally as a symbol of distinction

sash[2] (sash) *n.* [taken as sing. of earlier *shashes* < Fr. *châssis*, a frame, sash: see CHASSIS] **1.** a frame for holding the glass pane or panes of a window or door, esp. a sliding frame **2.** such frames collectively —*vt.* to furnish with sashes

☆**sa·shay** (sa shā′) *vi.* [altered < CHASSÉ] **1.** to do a chassé in a square dance **2.** [Colloq.] to move, walk, or go, esp. in a casual way

sash cord a cord attached to either side of a sliding sash, having balancing weights (**sash weights**) so that the window can be raised or lowered easily

sa·shi·mi (sä shē′mē) *n.pl.* [Jap., raw fish] a Japanese appetizer consisting of thin slices of raw fish served usually with a sauce

Sas·katch·e·wan (sas kach′ə wän′, -wən) **1.** province of SC Canada: 251,700 sq. mi.; pop. 955,000; cap. Regina: abbrev. **Sask. 2.** river formed in C Saskatchewan by the junction of the North Saskatchewan & South Saskatchewan rivers, flowing east into Lake Winnipeg: 340 mi. (with principal headstream, 1,205 mi.)

Sas·ka·toon (sas′kə tōōn′) city in C Saskatchewan, Canada, on the South Saskatchewan River: pop. 116,000

sas·ka·toon (sas′kə tōōn′) *n.* [< AmInd. (Cree) *misâskwatomin* < *misâskwat*, shadbush, lit., tree with much wood + *min*, berry] [Chiefly Canad.] *same as* JUNEBERRY (sense 1); esp., a species (*Amelanchier alnifolia*) of the N and W U.S. and nearby Canada, with especially large fruit

sass (sas) *n.* [var. of SAUCE] **1.** [Dial.] *a*) garden vegetables *b*) stewed fruit or preserves **2.** [Colloq.] impudent talk —*vt.* [Colloq.] to talk impudently to

sas·sa·by (sas′ə bē) *n., pl.* **-bies** [Sechuana *tsèsèbè*] a large, reddish South African antelope (genus *Damaliscus*) with a black head and face, related to the hartebeest

☆**sas·sa·fras** (sas′ə fras′) *n.* [Sp. *sasafrás* < ? earlier Sp. *sassifragia,* saxifrage] **1.** a small E. N. American tree (*Sassafras albidum*) of the laurel family, having an aromatic bark, leaves with usually two or three finger-like lobes, and small, bluish fruits **2.** the dried root bark of this tree, used as a flavoring agent and yielding safrole: see SAFROLE

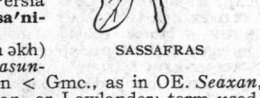

SASSAFRAS

Sas·sa·nid (sas′ə nid) *n., pl.* **Sas′-sa·nids,** **Sas·san·i·dae** (sa san′ə dē′) any member of the last dynasty of native rulers in Persia (226?-641 A.D.): also **Sas·sa′ni-an,** **Sa·sa′ni·an** (-sā′nē ən)

Sas·se·nach (sas′ə nak′, -′n əkh) *n.* [Ir. *Sasanach* or Gael. *Sasun-nach* < Gael. *Sasunn,* Saxon < Gmc., as in OE. *Seaxan,* SAXON] a Saxon, Englishman, or Lowlander: term used, often disparagingly, by Irish and Scots

Sas·soon (sa sōōn′) **Sieg·fried (Lorraine)** 1886-1967; Eng. writer & poet

sass·y (sas′ē) *adj.* **sass′i·er,** **sass′i·est** [dial. var. of SAUCY] [Colloq.] impudent; saucy

sas·sy bark (sas′ē) [prob. of Afr. origin] **1.** the bark of an African tree (*Erythrophleum guineense*) of the legume family, with poisonous bark and wood used as a poison in trial by ordeal and yielding an alkaloid used as a substitute for digitalis **2.** this tree: also called **sas′sy·wood** (-wood′) *n.* Also **sas′sy·n.**

sas·tru·gi (sas′trōō gē, zas′-; sas trōō′-) *n.pl.* [< Russ. *zastruga,* wind-formed furrow] long, wavelike ridges of hard snow, formed perpendicular to the direction of the wind and common in polar regions

sat (sat) *pt. & pp.* of SIT

SAT, S.A.T. Scholastic Aptitude Test

Sat. **1.** Saturday **2.** Saturn

Sa·tan (sāt′n) [ME. < OE. < LL.(Ec.) < Gr.(Ec.) < Heb. *sātān,* enemy < *sātan,* to be adverse, plot against] **1.** *Judaism* any of various celestial beings functioning as accuser or critic of man **2.** *Christian Theol.* the great enemy of man and of goodness; the Devil: usually identified with Lucifer, the chief of the fallen angels

sa·tang (sä taŋ′) *n., pl.* **-tang′** [Siamese *satāṅ*] a coin and unit of currency in Thailand, equal to 1/100 of a baht

sa·tan·ic (sā tan′ik, sə-) *adj.* of, characteristic of, or like Satan; devilish; wicked; infernal; diabolical: also **sa·tan′i-cal** —**sa·tan′i·cal·ly** *adv.*

Sa·tan·ism (sāt′n iz′m) *n.* [chiefly after Fr. *satanisme*] worship of Satan; esp., the principles and rites of a cult which travesties Christian ceremonies —**Sa′tan·ist** *n.*

satch·el (sach′əl) *n.* [ME. *sachel* < OFr. < L. *saccellus,* dim. of *saccus,* a bag, SACK] a small bag for carrying clothes, books, etc., sometimes having a shoulder strap

sate[1] (sāt) *vt.* **sat′ed,** **sat′ing** [prob. contr. < L. *satiare,* to fill full: see SATIATE] **1.** to satisfy (an appetite, desire, etc.) to the full; gratify completely **2.** to provide with more than enough, so as to weary or disgust; surfeit; glut —*SYN.* see SATIATE

sate[2] (sat, sāt) *archaic pt. & pp.* of SIT

sa·teen (sa tēn′, sə-) *n.* [< SATIN, after VELVETEEN] a smooth, glossy cloth, as of cotton, made to imitate satin

sat·el·lite (sat′′l īt′) *n.* [Fr. < L. *satelles* (gen. *satellitis*), an attendant, guard] **1.** *a)* a follower or attendant attached to a prince or other person of importance *b)* any obsequious or fawning follower or dependent **2.** *a)* a small planet revolving around a larger one; moon *b)* a man-made object put into orbit around the earth, the moon, or some other heavenly body **3.** something subordinate or dependent; specif., a small state that is economically dependent on, and hence adjusts its policies to, a larger, more powerful state

sa·tem (sät′əm, sät′-) *adj.* [< Av. *satəm,* hundred (for IE. base see HUNDRED): so named because the initial sound illustrates the typical development in this group of the IE. palatal stop which in the centum group is a velar stop] designating or of the group of Indo-European languages, including Indo-Iranian, Slavic, and Baltic, in which a prehistoric change of certain original stops into sibilants sets the group apart from the centum group

sa·ti (sə tē′, sut′ē) *n. var.* of SUTTEE

sa·tia·ble (sā′shə b′l, sā′shē ə-) *adj.* that can be sated or satiated —**sa′tia·bil′i·ty** *n.* —**sa′tia·bly** *adv.*

sa·ti·ate (sā′shē āt′; *for adj., usually* -it) *adj.* [L. *satiatus,* pp. of *satiare,* to fill full, satisfy < *satis,* sufficient: see SAD] having had enough or more than enough; sated —*vt.* **-at′ed, -at′ing** **1.** [Now Rare] to satisfy to the full; gratify completely **2.** to provide with more than enough, so as to weary or disgust; glut; surfeit —**sa′ti·a′tion** *n.* *SYN.*—**satiate** and **sate** in their basic sense mean to satisfy to the full, but in current use **satiate** almost always implies, as **sate**

often does, a being filled or stuffed so full that all pleasure or desire is lost [*satiated,* or *sated,* with food, success, etc.]; **surfeit** implies a being filled or supplied to nauseating or disgusting excess [*surfeited* with pleasure]; **cloy** stresses the distaste one feels for something too sweet, rich, etc. that one has indulged in to excess [*cloying,* sentimental music]; **glut** implies an overloading by filling or supplying to excess [to *glut* the market]

Sa·tie (sà tē′), **E·rik (Alfred Leslie)** (e rēk′) 1866-1925; Fr. composer

sa·ti·e·ty (sə tī′ə tē) *n.* [Fr. *satiété* < OFr. *sazieted* < L. *satietas*] the state of being satiated; surfeit

sat·in (sat′n) *n.* [ME. < MFr. < Sp. *setuni* < Ar. (*atlas*) *zaitūnī,* (satin) of *Zaitūn,* medieval name of Chuanchou, China] a fabric of silk, nylon, rayon, or the like having a smooth finish, glossy on the face and dull on the back —*adj.* made of or like satin; smooth, soft, and glossy —**sat′in·y** *adj.*

sat·i·net, sat·i·nette (sat′n et′) *n.* [Fr. < *satin*] **1.** thin or inferior satin **2.** a strong cloth of cotton and wool, made to resemble satin

sat·in·wood (sat′n wood′) *n.* **1.** any of several very smooth, hard woods used in fine furniture, marquetry, veneers, etc. **2.** any of a number of trees yielding such a wood; esp., *a)* the **East Indian satinwood** (*Chloroxylon swietenia*) of the rue family *b)* the **West Indian satinwood** (*Zanthoxylum flavum*) of the rue family

sat·ire (sa′tīr) *n.* [Fr. < L. *satira* or *satura,* a satire, poetic medley < (*lanx*) *satura,* (dish) of various fruits, prob. < Etruscan, of Thracian orig.] **1.** *a)* a literary work in which vices, follies, stupidities, abuses, etc. are held up to ridicule and contempt *b)* such literary works collectively, or the art of writing them **2.** the use of ridicule, sarcasm, irony, etc. to expose, attack, or deride vices, follies, etc. —*SYN.* see CARICATURE, WIT

sa·tir·i·cal (sə tir′i k′l) *adj.* **1.** of, having the nature of, or containing satire **2.** indulging in, or fond of indulging in, satire Also **sa·tir′ic** —*SYN.* see SARCASTIC —**sa·tir′-i·cal·ly** *adv.*

sat·i·rist (sat′ə rist) *n.* **1.** a writer of satires **2.** a person given to satirizing

sat·i·rize (-rīz′) *vt.* **-rized′, -riz′ing** [Fr. *satiriser*] to attack, ridicule, or criticize with satire —**sat′i·riz′er** *n.*

sat·is·fac·tion (sat′is fak′shən) *n.* [ME. *satisfaccioun* < OFr. *satisfaction* < L. *satisfactio*] **1.** a satisfying or being satisfied **2.** something that satisfies; specif., *a)* anything that brings gratification, pleasure, or contentment *b)* settlement of debt; payment or discharge of obligation *c)* reparation for injury or insult *d) Theol.* atonement for sin —**give satisfaction 1.** to satisfy **2.** to accept a challenge to duel or fight

sat·is·fac·to·ry (-fak′tə rē, -trē) *adj.* [Fr. *satisfactoire* < ML. *satisfactorius*] good enough to fulfill a need, wish, requirement, etc.; satisfying or adequate —**sat′is·fac′to·ri·ly** *adv.* —**sat′is·fac′to·ri·ness** *n.*

sat·is·fy (sat′is fī′) *vt.* **-fied′, -fy′ing** [ME. *satisfyen* < OFr. *satisfier* < L. *satisfacere* < *satis,* enough (see SAD) + *facere,* to make (see DO[1])] **1.** to fulfill the needs, expectations, wishes, or desires of (someone); content; gratify **2.** to fulfill or answer the requirements or conditions of (something) **3.** to comply with (rules, standards, or obligations) **4.** *a)* to free from doubt or anxiety; convince *b)* to answer (a doubt, objection, etc.) adequately or convincingly; solve **5.** *a)* to give what is due to *b)* to discharge (an obligation, debt, etc.); settle in full **6.** to make reparation to or for —*vi.* to be satisfying, adequate, sufficient, etc. —**sat′is·fi′er** *n.* *SYN.*—**satisfy** implies complete fulfillment of one's wishes, needs, expectations, etc.; **content** implies a filling of requirements to the degree that one is not disturbed by a desire for something more or different [some persons are *satisfied* only by great wealth, others are *contented* with a modest but secure income]

sa·to·ri (sä tôr′ē) *n.* [Jap.] *Zen Buddhism* spiritual enlightenment or illumination

sa·trap (sā′trap, sa′trap) *n.* [ME. < L. *satrapes* < Gr. *satrapēs* < OPer. *xšathrapāvan,* lit., protector of the land < *xšathra,* dominion (< IE. base *kthēi-,* to gain dominion, whence Gr. *ktēma,* possession) + *pā*(y)-, to protect < IE. base *pō*(i)-, to herd sheep, protect, cover, whence OE. *fothor,* a sheath] **1.** the governor of a province in ancient Persia **2.** a ruler of a dependency, esp. a despotic, subordinate official; petty tyrant

sa·trap·y (sā′trə pē, sa′trə-) *n., pl.* **-trap·ies** [Fr. *satrapie* < L. *satrapia* < Gr. *satrapeia*] the government, authority, or province of a satrap

Sat·su·ma (sat′soo mə, sät′-) *n.* [< Jap. *Satsuma* Peninsula, Kyushu, where pottery was made] **1.** a variety of Japanese pottery ☆**2.** [s-] a small, loose-skinned variety of orange, grown in Florida and Alabama

sat·u·ra·ble (sach′ər ə b′l) *adj.* [L. *saturabilis*] that can be saturated —**sat′u·ra·bil′i·ty** *n.*

sat·u·rant (-ər ənt) *adj.* [L. *saturans,* prp.] that saturates; saturating —*n.* a substance that saturates

sat·u·rate (sach′ə rāt′; *for adj., usually* -ər it) *vt.* **-rat′ed, -rat′ing** [< L. *saturatus,* pp. of *saturare,* to fill up, saturate < *satur,* full, akin to *satis:* see SAD] **1.** to cause to be

thoroughly soaked, imbued, or penetrated **2.** to cause (something) to be filled, charged, supplied, etc. with the maximum that it can absorb **3.** *Chem.* *a)* to cause (a substance) to combine to the full extent of its combining capacity with another; neutralize *b)* to dissolve the maximum amount of (a gas, liquid, or solid) in a solution at a given temperature and pressure —*adj.* same as SATURATED **SYN.** see SOAK —**sat′u·ra′tor** *n.*

sat·u·rat·ed (-rāt′id) *adj.* **1.** filled to capacity; having absorbed all that can be taken up **2.** soaked through with moisture; wet **3.** undiluted with white: said of colors **4.** *Geol.* containing as much combined silica as is possible: said of rocks and minerals

saturated compound an organic compound containing no double or triple bonds and having no free valence

saturated solution a solution in equilibrium at a definite temperature with the undissolved solute; solution containing so much dissolved substance that no more can be dissolved at the given temperature

sat·u·ra·tion (sach′ə rā′shən) *n.* [LL. *saturatio*] **1.** a saturating or being saturated **2.** the degree of purity of a color, as measured by its freedom from mixture with white; intensity of hue **3.** the condition of a magnetic substance that has been magnetized to the maximum

saturation bombing the practice of dropping an intense concentration of bombs in order to destroy virtually everything in a given target area

saturation point 1. the point at which the greatest possible amount of a substance has been absorbed **2.** the limit beyond which something cannot be continued, endured, etc.

Sat·ur·day (sat′ər dē, -dā′) *n.* [ME. *Saterdai* < OE. *Sæterdæg*, akin to MDu. *Saterdagh* < WGmc. half-transl. of L. *Saturni dies*, Saturn's day, transl. of Gr. *Kronou hēmera*, Cronus' day] the seventh and last day of the week

Sat·ur·days (-dēz, -dāz′) *adv.* on or during every Saturday

Sat·urn (sat′ərn) [ME. *Saturne* < OE. < L. *Saturnus*] **1.** *Rom. Myth.* the god of agriculture: identified with the Greek god Cronus **2.** the second largest planet in the solar system, with nine known satellites, sixth in distance from the sun and notable for the three concentric rings which revolve around it in the plane of its equator: diameter, c.72,000 mi.; period of rotation, 10 hrs., 14 min.; period of revolution, 29.65 tropical years; symbol, ♄. —*n.* [ML. use of L. *Saturnus*] alchemists' *term for* LEAD²

Sat·ur·na·li·a (sat′ər nā′lē ə, -nāl′yə) *n.pl.* [L., neut. pl. of *Saturnalis*, of Saturn] **1.** the ancient Roman festival of Saturn, held about December 17, with general feasting and revelry in celebration of the winter solstice **2.** [s-] [*often with sing. v. & with a pl.* -**li·as**] a period or occasion of unrestrained, often orgiastic, revelry

Sat·ur·na·li·an (-nā′lē ən, -nāl′yən) *adj.* **1.** of the Saturnalia **2.** [s-] riotously merry or orgiastic

Sa·tur·ni·an (sə tur′nē ən) *adj.* [< L. *Saturnius*, of Saturn + -AN] **1.** *a)* of the Roman god Saturn, whose reign was called "the golden age" *b)* prosperous, contented, happy, or peaceful: said of a period, age, etc. **2.** of the planet Saturn

sa·tur·ni·id (sə tur′nē id) *n.* [< ModL. *Saturniidae*, name of the family < *Saturnia*, type genus < L. *Juno*, daughter of Saturn] any of a family (Saturniidae) of large, brilliantly colored moths with a sunken head and hairy body

sat·ur·nine (sat′ər nīn′) *adj.* [OFr. *saturnin*, of Saturn (also, of lead, heavy < ML. *Saturnus*, lead²) < L. *Saturnus*, Saturn] **1.** *Astrol.* born under the supposed influence of the planet Saturn **2.** sluggish; gloomy; morose; grave; taciturn **3.** *a)* [Archaic] of or like lead *b)* having lead poisoning —**sat′ur·nine′ly** *adv.*

sat·ur·nism (-niz′m) *n.* [see SATURN, *n.*] chronic lead poisoning

‡**Sat·ya·gra·ha** (sut′yə gru′hə) *n.* [< Hindi, lit., a grasping for truth < Sans. *satyā*, truth + *graha*, grasping] the political doctrine of Mohandas K. Gandhi, which favored passive resistance and noncooperation in opposing British rule in India

sat·yr (sāt′ər, sat′-) *n.* [ME. *satir* < L. *satyrus* < Gr. *satyros*] **1.** *Gr. Myth.* any of a class of minor woodland deities, attendant on Bacchus, usually represented as having pointed ears, short horns, the head and body of a man, and the legs of a goat, and as being fond of riotous merriment and lechery: see also FAUN **2.** a lustful or lecherous man **3.** a man having satyriasis **4.** any of a genus (*Neonympha*) of butterflies with gray or brown wings often with eyelike spots —**sa·tyr·ic** (sə tir′ik) *adj.*

sat·y·ri·a·sis (sat′ə rī′ə sis) *n.* [LL. < Gr. *satyriasis*: see prec.] abnormal and uncontrollable desire by a man for sexual intercourse: cf. NYMPHOMANIA

satyr play a type of ancient Greek burlesque or comic play with a chorus represented as satyrs

sau (sou) *n.* [Vietnamese] a unit of currency in North Vietnam, equal to 1/100 of a dong

sauce (sôs) *n.* [ME. < OFr. *sause, saulse* < L. *salsa*, salted food < pl. of *salsus*, pp. of *salire*, to salt < *sal*, SALT] **1.** *a)* a liquid or soft dressing served with food as a relish *b)* a flavored syrup used as a topping, as on ice cream ☆**2.** stewed or preserved fruit **3.** something that adds interest, zest, or flavor **4.** [Dial.] garden vegetables eaten as a side dish **5.** [Colloq.] impertinence; impudence ☆**6.** [Slang] alcoholic liquor: usually with *the* —*vt.* **sauced, sauc′ing**

1. to flavor or season with a sauce **2.** to give flavor or relish to **3.** [Colloq.] to be impudent or saucy to

sauce·box (-bäks′) *n.* [Old Colloq.] a saucy person; esp., an impertinent child

sauce·pan (-pan′) *n.* a small pot with a projecting handle, used for cooking

sau·cer (sô′sər) *n.* [ME. *sawsere* < MFr. *saussier* < *sause*, SAUCE] **1.** a small, round, shallow dish, esp. one with an indentation designed to hold a cup **2.** anything round and shallow like a saucer

sau·cy (sô′sē) *adj.* **-ci·er, -ci·est** [SAUC(E) + -Y²] **1.** rude; impudent **2.** pert; sprightly [a *saucy smile*] **3.** stylish or smart: said esp. of a ship —**SYN.** see IMPERTINENT —**sau′ci·ly** *adv.* —**sau′ci·ness** *n.*

Sa·u·di Arabia (sä ōō′dē; *occas.* sou′dē) kingdom occupying most of Arabia: c. 617,000 sq. mi.; pop. c. 6,036,000; cap. Riyadh (Mecca is the religious cap.)

☆**sau·er·bra·ten** (sour′brät′'n, zou′ər-) *n.* [G. < *sauer*, SOUR + *braten*, roast] a dish made of beef marinated in vinegar with onion, spices, etc. before cooking

☆**sau·er·kraut** (sour′krout′) *n.* [G. *sauer*, SOUR + *kraut*, cabbage] chopped cabbage fermented in a brine of its own juice with salt

☆**sau·ger** (sô′gər) *n.* [< ?] a small American pikeperch (*Stizostedion canadense*) valued as a game or food fish

Sauk (sôk) *n.* [contr. < Algonquian tribal name *Osākiwug*, lit., ? people of the outlet] **1.** *pl.* **Sauks, Sauk** any member of a tribe of N. American Indians living orig. in Michigan, Wisconsin, and Illinois and later merging with the Fox: now settled on reservations in Oklahoma and Iowa **2.** same as FOX

Saul (sôl) [< LL.(Ec.) *Saul* (for 2 *b*, *Saulus*) < Gr.(Ec.) *Saoul* (for 2 *b*, *Saulos*) < Heb. *shā'ūl*, lit., asked (i.e., of God)] **1.** a masculine name **2.** *Bible a)* the first king of Israel: I Sam. 9 *b)* orig. *name of the Apostle* PAUL

Sault Ste. Ma·rie (sōō′ sānt′ mə rē′) [< Fr. *Sault de Sainte Marie*, lit., falls of St. Mary] **1.** city in N Mich., on the St. Marys River: pop. 15,000 **2.** city opposite it, in Ontario, Canada: pop. 75,000 Also **Sault Sainte Marie**

sau·na (sou′nə, sô′-) *n.* [Finn.] **1.** a Finnish bath, consisting basically of exposure to extremely hot, relatively dry air, accompanied by light beating of the skin with birch or cedar boughs **2.** the enclosure for such a bath

saun·ter (sôn′tər) *vi.* [LME. *santren*, to muse, meditate < ?] to walk about idly; stroll —*n.* **1.** a leisurely and aimless walk; stroll **2.** a slow, leisurely gait —**saun′ter·er** *n.*

-saur (sôr) [< Gr. *sauros*, lizard: see SAURO-] *a combining form meaning lizard* [*dinosaur*]

sau·rel (sô′rəl) *n.* [Fr. < Pr. < LL. *saurus* < Gr. *sauros*, horse mackerel] a common saltwater food fish (*Trachurus symmetricus*) of Europe and America, related to the scads

sau·ri·an (sôr′ē ən) *n.* [< ff. + -IAN] any of a large suborder (Sauria) of reptiles, consisting of the lizards —*adj.* of, or having the characteristics of, lizards

sau·ro- (sôr′ə, -ō) [< Gr. *sauros*, lizard] *a combining form meaning lizard* [*sauropod*]: also, before a vowel, **saur-**

sau·ro·pod (sôr′ə päd′) *n.* [prec. + -POD] any of a suborder (Sauropoda) of gigantic, plant-eating, four-footed dinosaurs, as the brontosaurus, with a long neck and tail, five-toed limbs, and a small head —*adj.* of the sauropods

-sau·rus (sôr′əs) [< Gr. *sauros*, a lizard] *Zool. a combining form meaning lizard*: used to form the genus names of certain reptiles [*Ichthyosaurus*]

sau·ry (sôr′ē) *n., pl.* **-ries** [prob. < ModL. *saurus*, a fish < Gr. *sauros*, horse mackerel] **1.** an edible fish (*Scomberesox saurus*) with a long, slender body and a projecting beak, found in temperate Atlantic waters **2.** a related fish (*Cololabis saira*) of Pacific waters

sau·sage (sô′sij) *n.* [ME. *sausige* < ONormFr. *saussiche*, for OFr. *saulcisse* < VL. *salsicia* < L. *salsus*: see SAUCE] pork or other meat, chopped fine, highly seasoned, and either stuffed into membranous casings of varying size, as bologna or salami, or made into patties for cooking

sau·té (sō tā′, sô-) *adj.* [Fr., pp. of *sauter*, to leap < L. *saltare*: see SALTANT] fried quickly in a little fat —*vt.* **-téed′, -té′ing** to fry quickly in a pan with a little fat —*n.* a sautéed dish

sau·terne (sō turn′, sô-) *n.* [Fr. *sauternes* < *Sauternes*, town in Gironde, France] a white, relatively sweet table wine: also **sau·ternes′** (sō turn′; *Fr.* sō tern′)

‡**sauve qui peut** (sōv kē pö′) [Fr., lit., (let him) save (himself) who can] a disorganized retreat; rout

Sa·va (sä′vä) river in N Yugoslavia, flowing east into the Danube: c. 450 mi.: see BALKAN PENINSULA, map

sav·age (sav′ij) *adj.* [ME. < OFr. *salvage* < VL. *salvaticus*, wild < L. *silvaticus*, belonging to a wood, wild < *silva*, a wood: see SYLVAN] **1.** wild, uncultivated, rugged, etc. [a *savage jungle*] **2.** fierce; ferocious; untamed [a *savage tiger*] **3.** without civilization; primitive; barbarous [a *savage tribe*] **4.** lacking polish; crude; rude **5.** cruel; pitiless **6.** furious; ill-tempered —*n.* **1.** a member of a preliterate society having a primitive way of life **2.** a fierce, brutal person **3.** a crude, boorish person —*vt.* **-aged, -ag·ing** to attack in a violent or brutal way, either physically or verbally —**sav′age·ly** *adv.* —**sav′age·ness** *n.* —**SYN.** see BARBARIAN

sav·age·ry (-rē) *n., pl.* **-ries 1.** the condition of being savage, or wild, primitive, uncultivated, etc. **2.** savage act, behavior, or disposition; barbarity

Sa·vai·i (sä vī'ē) largest & westernmost island of Western Samoa: 662 sq. mi.; pop. 32,000

sa·van·na, sa·van·nah (sə van'ə) *n.* [Sp. *sabana*, earlier *zavana* < the Taino name] a treeless plain or a grassland characterized by scattered trees, esp. in tropical or subtropical regions having seasonal rains

Sa·van·nah (sə van'ə) [< a Muskhogean var. of the native name of the Shawnees] **1.** river forming the border between Ga. & S.C., flowing southeast into the Atlantic: 314 mi. **2.** seaport in SE Ga., near the mouth of this river: pop. 118,000

sa·vant (sə vänt', sav'ənt; *Fr.* sà vän') *n.,* *pl.* **-vants'** (-vänts', -ənts; *Fr.* -vän') [*Fr.,* orig. prp. of *savoir* < L. *sapere:* see SAP¹] a learned person; eminent scholar

sa·vate (sə vät', -vat') *n.* [Fr., orig., old shoe: see SABOT] a form of boxing in which stiff-legged kicks as well as punches may be used

save¹ (sāv) *vt.* **saved, sav'ing** [ME. *saven* < OFr. *sauver, salver* < L. *salvare* < *salvus,* SAFE] **1.** to rescue or preserve from harm, danger, injury, etc.; make or keep safe **2.** to keep in health and well-being: now only in certain formulas [God *save* the king!] **3.** to preserve for future use; lay by (often with *up*) **4.** to prevent or guard against loss or waste of [to *save* time, to *save* a game] **5.** to avoid, prevent, lessen, or guard against [to *save* wear and tear] **6.** to treat or use carefully in order to preserve, lessen wear, etc. **7.** *Theol.* to deliver from sin and punishment —*vi.* **1.** to avoid expense, loss, waste, etc.; be economical **2.** to keep something or someone from danger, harm, etc. **3.** to put by money or goods (often with *up*); hoard **4.** to keep; last **5.** *Theol.* to exercise power to redeem from evil and sin —*n. Sports* an action that keeps an opponent from scoring or winning —*SYN.* see RESCUE —**sav'a·ble, save'a·ble** *adj.* —**sav'er** *n.*

save² (sāv) *prep.* [ME. *sauf* < OFr., lit., SAFE: sense developed from use in absolute constructions, e.g., *sauf le droit,* right (being) safe] except; but —*conj.* **1.** except; but **2.** [Archaic] unless

save-all (sāv'ôl') *n.* any of a number of devices which prevent waste or loss; specif., *a)* a sail placed to catch wind passing by the regular sails *b)* a net spread between a ship and pier while cargo is being loaded or unloaded

sav·e·loy (sav'ə loi') *n.* [altered < Fr. *cervelas* < MFr. *cervelat* < It. *cervellata* < *cervello,* the brains < L. *cerebellum:* see CEREBELLUM] in England, a highly seasoned, dried sausage

sav·in, sav·ine (sav'in) *n.* [ME. *savin* < OE. *safene* & OFr. *savine,* both < L. *(herba) Sabina,* lit., Sabine (herb), *savin*] **1.** a low, spreading Eurasian juniper (*Juniperus sabina*) of E N. America and Europe whose leaves and tops yield an oil (**savin oil**) used in perfumery **2.** same as RED CEDAR (sense 1 *a*)

sav·ing¹ (sā'viŋ) *adj.* that saves; specif., *a)* rescuing; preserving *b)* economizing or economical *c)* containing an exception; making a reservation [a *saving* clause] *d)* compensating; redeeming [a *saving* grace] —*n.* **1.** the act of one that saves **2.** [often *pl.,* with *sing. v.*] any reduction in expense, time, labor, etc. [a *saving(s)* of 10% is effected] **3.** *a)* anything saved *b)* [*pl.*] sums of money saved **4.** *Law* a reservation; exception

sav·ing² (sā'viŋ) *prep.* [Now Rare] **1.** with due respect for [*saving* your presence] **2.** with the exception of; except; save —*conj.* [Now Rare] except; save

savings account an account in a savings bank

☆**savings and loan association** a depositor-owned organization that solicits savings to be placed in share accounts on which dividends are paid and from which mortgage loans on homes or real estate are made

savings bank 1. a bank in which savings may be deposited; esp., a banking establishment whose business is to receive and invest depositors' savings, on which it pays interest ☆**2.** a small container with a slot for receiving coins to be saved

sav·ior, sav·iour (sāv'yər) *n.* [ME. *sauveour* < OFr. < LL. *salvator,* one who saves < *salvare,* to SAVE¹: in LL.(Ec.), Saviour, transl. of Gr.(Ec.) *sōtēr*] a person who saves —**the Saviour** (or **Savior**) **1.** God **2.** Jesus Christ

Sa·voie (sà vwá') *Fr.* name of SAVOY²

sa·voir-faire (sav'wär fer'; *Fr.* sà vwàr fer') *n.* [Fr., to know (how) to do] ready knowledge of what to do or say, and of when and how to do or say it —*SYN.* see TACT

‡**sa·voir-vi·vre** (sà vwàr vē'vr') *n.* [Fr., to know (how) to live] good breeding; good manners

Sa·vo·na·ro·la (sä'vō nä rō'lä; *E.* sav'ə nə rō'lə), **Gi·ro·la·mo** (jē rō'lä mō') 1452–98; It. monk; religious & political reformer; burned at the stake for heresy

sa·vor (sā'vər) *n.* [ME. < OFr. *savour* < L. *sapor,* akin to *sapere:* see SAP¹] **1.** *a)* that quality of a thing which acts on the sense of taste or of smell *b)* a particular taste or smell **2.** characteristic quality; distinctive property **3.** perceptible trace; tinge **4.** power to excite interest, zest, etc. **5.** [Archaic] repute —*vi.* **1.** to have the particular taste, smell, or quality; smack (*of*) **2.** to show traces or signs (*of*) [rudeness *savoring* of contempt] —*vt.* **1.** to be the source of the flavor or scent of; season **2.** to taste or

smell, esp. with relish **3.** to enjoy with appreciation; dwell on with delight Also, Brit. sp., **sa'vour** —**sa'vor·er** *n.* —**sa'vor·less** *adj.* —**sa'vor·ous** *adj.*

sa·vor·y¹ (sā'vər ē) *adj.* **-vor·i·er, -vor·i·est** [ME. *savouri* < OFr. *savouré,* pp. of *savourer,* to taste < *savour,* SAVOR] **1.** pleasing to the taste or smell; appetizing **2.** pleasant, agreeable, attractive, etc. **3.** morally acceptable; respectable **4.** salty or piquant; not sweet [a *savory* relish] —*n., pl.* **-vor·ies** in England, a small, highly seasoned portion of food served at the end of a meal or as an appetizer Also, Brit. sp., **sa'vour·y** —**sa'vor·i·ly** *adv.* —**sa'vor·i·ness** *n.*

sa·vor·y² (sā'vər ē) *n.* [ME. *saverey* < OFr. *savoreie,* altered (prob. after *savour,* SAVOR) < L. *satureia,* savory] any of a genus (*Satureia*) of aromatic mints; esp., **summer savory** (*Satureia hortensis*) and **winter savory** (*Satureia montana*), both native to Europe and used in cooking

Sa·voy¹ (sə voi') family of Europe ruling Piedmont, the duchy of Savoy, the kingdom of Sardinia, and later (1861–1946) Italy

Sa·voy² (sə voi') region in SE France, on the borders of Italy & Switzerland: a former duchy & part of the kingdom of Sardinia: annexed by France, 1860

sa·voy (sə voi') *n.* [Fr. (*chou de*) *Savoie,* (cabbage of) Savoy] a kind of cabbage with crinkled leaves and a compact head: also **savoy cabbage**

Sa·voy·ard (sə voi'ərd, sav'oi yärd'; *Fr.* sà vwà yàr') *n.* **1.** a native or inhabitant of Savoy **2.** [< the *Savoy,* London theater where the operas were first produced] an actor producer, or enthusiastic admirer, of Gilbert and Sullivan operas —*adj.* of Savoy, its people, or culture

SAVOY

☆**sav·vy** (sav'ē) *vi.* **-vied, -vy·ing** [altered < Sp. *sabe* (*usted*), do (you) know? < *saber,* to know < L. *sapere:* see SAP¹] [Slang] to understand; get the idea —*n.* [Slang] *a)* shrewdness, knowledge, or understanding *b)* skill or know-how —*adj.* [Slang] shrewd and discerning

saw¹ (sô) *n.* [ME. *sawe* < OE. *sagu,* akin to G. *säge,* Du. *zaag* < IE. base *sek-,* to cut, whence L. *secare* to cut, OE. *seax,* knife] **1.** *a)* a cutting tool, of various shapes and sizes and worked by hand or machinery, consisting essentially of a thin blade or disk of metal, usually steel, the edge of which is a series of sharp teeth *b)* any of various tools or devices somewhat like this but with a sharp edge instead of teeth **2.** a machine for operating a saw or saws —*vt.* **sawed, sawed** or chiefly Brit. **sawn, saw'ing 1.** to cut or divide with a saw **2.** to shape or form with a saw **3.** to make sawlike cutting motions through (the air, etc.) **4.** to operate or produce with a to-and-fro motion suggestive of that used in working a saw [to *saw* a knife through meat, to *saw* a tune on a fiddle] —*vi.* **1.** to cut with or as with a saw or as a saw does **2.** to be cut with a saw [wood that *saws* easily] **3.** to make sawlike cutting motions —☆**saw wood** [Slang] to snore or sleep —**saw'er** *n.*

saw² (sô) *n.* [ME. *sawe* < OE. *sagu:* see SAY] an old saying, often repeated; maxim; proverb —*SYN.* see SAYING

saw³ (sô) *pt.* of SEE¹

Sa·watch Mountains (sə wäch') [< AmInd. name < ?] range of the Rocky Mountains, in C Colo.: highest peak, Mt. ELBERT

saw·bones (sô'bōnz') *n.* [Slang] a doctor; esp., a surgeon

☆**saw·buck** (-buk') *n.* [Du. *zaagbòk* < *zaag,* SAW¹ + *bok,* BUCK²] **1.** a sawhorse, esp. one with the legs projecting above the crossbar **2.** [from the resemblance of the crossed legs of a sawbuck to an X (the Roman numeral for 10)] [Slang] a ten-dollar bill

saw·dust (-dust') *n.* minute particles of wood formed in sawing wood

sawed-off (sôd′ôf′) *adj.* ☆1. designating a shotgun with the barrel cut off short ☆2. [Colloq.] short in stature [a skinny, *sawed-off* man]

saw-fish (sô′fish′) *n., pl.* **-fish**′, **-fish**′**es**: see FISH² any of a genus (*Pristis*) of tropical, giant, sharklike rays, having the upper jaw prolonged into a flat, sawlike snout edged with teeth on both sides

saw-fly (-flī′) *n., pl.* **-flies**′ any of a group of four-winged, hymenopterous insects (esp. families Tenthredinidae and Cimbicidae): the abdomen of the female is provided with a pair of sawlike organs that cut into plants, the eggs being then deposited in the cuts

saw grass [cf. SEDGE] any of a number of related sedges with saw-edged leaves; ☆esp., the **Jamaica saw grass** (*Cladium jamaicense*) found in the SE U.S.

saw-horse (-hôrs′) *n.* a rack on which wood is placed while being sawed

☆**saw log** a log large enough for sawing into lumber

saw-mill (-mil′) *n.* 1. a factory or place where logs are sawed into boards 2. a large sawing machine

sawn (sôn) *chiefly Brit. pp.* of SAW¹

☆**saw palmetto** a dwarf palm (*Serenoa repens*) with fan-shaped leaves and spiny leafstalks, native to the SE U.S.

saw set an instrument used to set, or bend slightly outward, the teeth of a saw

saw-toothed (sô′tooth′t) *adj.* having notches along the edge like the teeth of a saw; serrate: also **saw′tooth**′

☆**saw-whet owl** (sô′hwet′, -wet′) [echoic] a very small N. American forest owl (*Aegolius acadica*) with a harsh, rasping cry and brown and white plumage

saw-yer (sô′yər) *n.* [ME. *sawier* for *sawere*, with -*ier* after OFr. suffix -*ier*: cf. CLOTHIER, LAWYER] 1. a person whose work is sawing wood, as into planks and boards ☆2. a log or tree caught in a river so that its branches saw back and forth with the water ☆3. a brown and gray beetle (*Monochamus notatus*) whose larvae burrow into wood

☆**sax** (saks) *n. colloq.* clipped form of SAXOPHONE

Sax. 1. Saxon 2. Saxony

sax-a-tile (sak′sə til) *adj.* [L. *saxatilis* < *saxum*, a rock: prob. akin to *secare*, to cut: for IE. base see SAW¹] *same as* SAXICOLOUS

Saxe (sáks; *E.* saks) *Fr. name of* SAXONY: used in the names of several former duchies of the German Empire, now mostly in Thuringia; esp., **Saxe′-Co′burg Go′tha** (kō′bərg gō′thə) a duchy of C Germany, divided (1920) between Thuringia & Bavaria: former name (1901–17) of the Brit. royal house of Windsor: cf. Prince ALBERT

sax-horn (saks′hôrn′) *n.* [after A. J. *Sax* (1814–1894), Belgian inventor] any of a group of valved brass-wind instruments, with a full, even tone and a wide range

sax-ic-o-lous (sak sik′ə ləs) *adj.* [< L. *saxum*, a rock (see SAXATILE) + *colere*, to dwell + -OUS] *Biol., Ecol.* living or growing on or among rocks: also **sax·ic′o·line′** (-lin′, -lin)

sax-i-frage (sak′sə frij) *n.* [ME. < MFr. < L. *saxifraga* < *saxum*, a rock (see SAXATILE) + base of *frangere*, to BREAK¹: prob. from growing in rock crevices] any of a genus (*Saxifraga*) of chiefly perennial plants of the saxifrage family, with white, yellow, purple, or pinkish, small flowers, and leaves massed usually at the base of the plant —*adj.* designating a family (Saxifragaceae) of plants found chiefly in the N. Temperate and Arctic zones, including the saxifrages, currants, gooseberries, etc.

Sax-o Gram-mat-i-cus (sak′sō grə mat′i kəs) 1150?–1220?; Dan. historian

Sax-on (sak′s'n) *n.* [ME. < LL. *Saxo*, pl. *Saxones* < WGmc. name, whence OE. *Seaxan* < base akin to OHG. *sahs*, sword, knife & L. *saxum*, rock, stone, *secare*, to cut: see SAW¹] 1. any member of an ancient Germanic people of northern Germany: some Saxons invaded and conquered parts of England in the 5th and 6th cent. A.D. 2. same as ANGLO-SAXON (*n.* 1 & 4) 3. a native or inhabitant of modern Saxony 4. any of the Low German dialects of the Saxon peoples, as the dialect of modern Saxony —*adj.* 1. of the Saxons, their language, etc. 2. English or Anglo-Saxon 3. of modern Saxony

Sax-on-ism (-iz′m) *n.* a word, phrase, idiom, etc. of English or Anglo-Saxon origin

Sax-on-y (sak′sə nē) [LL. *Saxonia*] 1. region in S East Germany: formerly, an electorate, kingdom, Prussian province, & state of the Weimar Republic: chief city, Dresden 2. medieval duchy at the base of the Jutland peninsula in what is now Lower Saxony —*n.* 1. [because first produced in Saxony (sense 1)] a fine wool fabric with a soft finish 2. a closely twisted yarn used for knitting

sax-o-phone (sak′sə fōn′) *n.* [Fr., after A. J. *Sax* (see SAXHORN) & -PHONE] any of a group of keyed woodwind in-

SAXONY AND LOWER SAXONY

struments having a single reed, conical bore, and metal body, usually curved —**sax′o·phon′ic** (-fŏn′ik, -fän′-) *adj.* —**sax′o·phon′ist** (-fōn′ist) *n.*

sax-tu-ba (saks′too′bə) *n.* [SAX(HORN) + TUBA] a large, bass saxhorn

say (sā) *vt.* **said, say′ing;** 3d pers. sing., pres. indic., **says** (sez), archaic **saith** [ME. *seien* (< earlier *seggen*) < OE. *secgan*, akin to *sagu*, a saying, tale, (ON. *saga*), G. *sagen*, to say < IE. base *sekw-*, to note, see, show, say, whence OE? L. *inseque* (imper.), tell!] 1. to utter, pronounce, or speak 2. to express in words; state; declare; tell 3. to state positively, with assurance, or as an opinion [who can *say* what will be?] 4. to indicate or show [the clock *says* ten] 5. to recite; repeat [to *say* one's prayers] 6. to estimate; assume; hypothesize [he is, I'd *say*, forty] 7. to allege; report [people *say* he's angry] 8. to communicate (an idea, feeling, etc.) [a painting that *says* nothing] —*vi.* to make a statement; speak; express an opinion —*n.* 1. a chance to speak [to have one's *say*] 2. power or authority, as to make or help make a final decision: often with *the* 3. [Archaic] what a person says; dictum —*adv.* 1. for example [any fish, *say* perch] 2. about; nearly [costing, *say*, 10 dollars] —*interj.* an exclamation used to express surprise, admiration, etc. —**go without saying** to be too obvious to need explanation; be self-evident —**that is to say** in other words; that means —**to say the least** to understate —**you can say that again!** [Colloq.] I agree with you! —**say′er** *n.*

Sa·yan Mountains (sä yän′) mountain system in C Asia, partially along the Mongolian-R.S.F.S.R. border: highest peak, 11,453 ft.

say-ing (sā′iŋ) *n.* 1. the act of one who says 2. something said; esp., an adage, proverb, or maxim

SYN.—**saying** is the simple, direct term for any pithy expression of wisdom or truth; a **saw** is an old, homely saying that is well worn by repetition [the preacher filled his sermon with wise *saws*]; a **maxim** is a general principle drawn from practical experience and serving as a rule of conduct (Ex.: "Keep thy shop and thy shop will keep thee"); an **adage** is a saying that has been popularly accepted over a long period of time (Ex.: "Where there's smoke, there's fire"); a **proverb** is a piece of practical wisdom expressed in homely, concrete terms (Ex.: "A penny saved is a penny earned"); a **motto** is a maxim accepted as a guiding principle or as an ideal of behavior (Ex.: "Honesty is the best policy"); an **aphorism** is a terse saying embodying a general, more or less profound truth or principle (Ex.: "He is a fool that cannot conceal his wisdom"); an **epigram** is a terse, witty, pointed statement that gains its effect by ingenious antithesis (Ex.: "The only way to get rid of a temptation is to yield to it")

‡**sa·yo·na·ra** (sä′yō nä′rä) *n., interj.* [< Jap.] farewell

says (sez) 3d pers. sing., pres. indic., of SAY

say-so (sā′sō′) *n.* [Colloq.] 1. (one's) word, opinion, assurance, etc. 2. right of decision; authority

say-yid, say-id (sä′yid) *n.* [Ar. *sayyid*] a Moslem title of respect, specif. for certain descendants of Mohammed

☆**Saz-e-rac** (saz′ə rak′) *n.* [< ?] [*often* s-] a bourbon cocktail flavored with a bitter liqueur, orig. absinthe

Sb [L. *stibium*] *Chem.* antimony

sb. substantive

S.B. [L. *Scientiae Baccalaureus*] Bachelor of Science

s.b., sb stolen base; stolen bases

SBA, S.B.A. Small Business Administration

SbE south by east

'sblood (zblud) *interj.* [Obs.] *euphemistic contraction of* God's blood, used as a swearword

SbW south by west

Sc *Chem.* scandium

SC Security Council (UN)

Sc. 1. Scotch 2. Scots 3. Scottish

sc. 1. scale 2. scene 3. science 4. scilicet 5. screw 6. scruple 7. sculpsit

S.C. 1. Sanitary Corps 2. Signal Corps 3. South Carolina 4. Supreme Court

s.c. 1. *Printing* small capitals 2. supercalendered

scab (skab) *n.* [ME. *scabbe* < ON. *skabb*, akin to OE. *sceabb* < IE. base *(s)kep-*, to cut, split, whence L. *scabies*, SCABIES, *scabere*, to SHAVE] 1. a crust that forms over a sore or wound during healing 2. a mangy skin disease, as scabies, of animals, esp. sheep 3. *a*) any of various plant diseases characterized by roughened, scablike spots on leaves, stems, or fruits *b*) any such spot 4. *a*) [Old Slang] a low, contemptible fellow; scoundrel ☆*b*) a worker who refuses to join a union, or who works for lower wages or under different conditions than those accepted by the union *c*) a worker who refuses to strike, or who takes the place of a striking worker —*vi.* **scabbed, scab′bing** 1. to become covered with a scab; form a scab ☆2. to work or act as a scab

scab-bard (skab′ərd) *n.* [ME. *scabarde*, earlier *scauberc* < Anglo-Fr. *escaubers* (pl.) < ? OHG. *scar*, sword, cutting tool (akin to SHEAR) + *bergan*, to hide, protect] a sheath or case to hold the blade of a sword, dagger, etc. —*vt.* to put into a scabbard; sheathe

scabbard fish any of several ocean fishes with an elongated,

compressed, silvery body; esp., *a*) any of a genus (*Lepidopus*) found chiefly in the South Pacific and Indian oceans ☆*b*) *same as* CUTLASS FISH

scab·ble (skab'l) *vt.* **-bled, -bling** [earlier *scapple* < ME. *scaplen*, aphetic < OFr. *escapeler*, to dress timber] to dress or shape (stone) roughly

scab·by (skab'ē) *adj.* **-bi·er, -bi·est** 1. covered with or consisting of scabs 2. diseased with scab 3. low; base; mean; scurvy —**scab'bi·ly** *adv.* —**scab'bi·ness** *n.*

sca·bies (skā'bēz, -bē ēz) *n.* [L., roughness, itch: see SCAB] a contagious skin disease caused by a parasitic mite (*Sarcoptes scabiei*) that burrows under the skin to deposit eggs, causing intense itching —**sca'bi·et'ic** (-bē et'ik) *adj.*

sca·bi·o·sa (skā'bē ō'sə) *n.* [ModL., name of the genus < ML. *scabiosa* (*herba*), lit., scabious (plant): see ff.: once considered a remedy for the itch] any of a genus (*Scabiosa*) of plants of the teasel family, having showy, variously colored flowers in flattened or dome-shaped heads, as the **sweet scabiosa** (*Scabiosa atropurpurea*), often cultivated as a garden flower

sca·bi·ous[1] (skā'bē əs) *adj.* [< Fr. or L.: Fr. *scabieux* < L. *scabiosus* < *scabies*: see SCAB] 1. covered with scabs; scabby 2. of or like scabies

sca·bi·ous[2] (skā'bē əs) *n. same as* SCABIOSA

scab·rous (skab'rəs, skā'brəs) *adj.* [LL. *scabrosus* < L. *scabere*, to scratch: see SCAB] 1. *a*) rough with small points or knobs, like a file; scaly or scabby *b*) marked with or as with scabs; blotchy, encrusted, etc. 2. full of difficulties 3. indecent, shocking, improper, scandalous, etc. —**scab'rous·ly** *adv.* —**scab'rous·ness** *n.*

scad[1] (skad) *n., pl.* **scad, scads**: see PLURAL, II, D, 2 [akin to SHAD] any of several carangid food fishes; ☆esp., the **mackerel scad** (*Decapterus macarellus*) and the **round scad** (*Decapterus punctatus*) of the W Atlantic

scad[2] (skad) *n.* [< ?] [*usually pl.*] ☆[Colloq.] a very large number or amount [*scads* of money]

Sca·fell Pike (skô'fel) peak of a mountain in Cumberland, NW England, the highest in England (3,210 ft.)

scaf·fold (skaf'ld, -ōld) *n.* [ME. < OFr. *escafalt* < *es-* (L. *ex-*, out) + VL. *catafalicum*: see CATAFALQUE] 1. a temporary wooden or metal framework for supporting workmen and materials during the erecting, repairing, or painting of a building, etc. 2. a raised platform on which criminals are executed, as by hanging 3. a temporary wooden stage or platform, as that on which medieval plays were presented 4. any raised framework —*vt.* 1. to furnish or support with, or put on, a scaffold

scaf·fold·ing (-'l diŋ) *n.* 1. the poles, planks, and other materials that form a scaffold 2. a scaffold or system of scaffolds

scagl·io·la (skal yō'lə) *n.* [It. *scagliuola*, dim. of *scaglia*, a chip, shell < Goth. *skalja*, SCALE²] an imitation marble made of gypsum and an adhesive, with colored stone dust or chips set into the surface

scal·a·ble (skāl'ə b'l) *adj.* that can be scaled

sca·lade (skə lād') *n.* [It. *scalada* < *scalare*, to scale < *scala*, ladder: see SCALE¹] *archaic var. of* ESCALADE

☆**scal·age** (skāl'ij) *n.* 1. the percentage by which a figure, as for weight, price, etc., is scaled down to allow for shrinkage, etc. 2. the estimate of lumber in a log being scaled

sca·lar (skā'lər) *adj.* [L. *scalaris*, of a ladder < *scalae*, steps, ladder: see SCALE¹] 1. in, on, or involving a scale or scales 2. *Math.* designating or of a quantity that has magnitude but no direction in space, as volume or temperature —*n.* a scalar quantity: distinguished from VECTOR (sense 3 *a*)

☆**sca·la·re** (skə ler'ē, -lär'-) *n.* [ModL. < L., neut. of *scalaris*, ladderlike (see SCALAR): from the lateral markings] any of several freshwater fishes (genus *Pterophyllum*) native to N S. America; esp., a hardy aquarium fish (*Pterophyllum scalare*) with a flattened body and transparent pectoral fins

sca·lar·i·form (skə lar'ə fôrm') *adj.* [< L. *scalaris* (see SCALAR) + -FORM] like a ladder; esp., having markings or transverse ridges like the rungs of a ladder

scalar product the product of the lengths of two vectors and the cosine of the angle between them

☆**scal·a·wag** (skal'ə wag') *n.* [< ?] 1. a scamp; rascal 2. a white Southern Republican during the Reconstruction: an opprobrious term used by Southern Democrats

scald[1] (skôld) *vt.* [ME. *scalden* < ONormFr. *escalder*, for OFr. *eschalder* < LL. *excaldare*, to wash in warm water < L. *ex-*, intens. + *calidus*, hot, akin to *calere*, to be warm: for IE. base see CALDARIUM] 1. to burn or injure with hot liquid or steam 2. to heat almost to the boiling point 3. to use boiling liquid on; specif., *a*) to sterilize by the use of boiling liquid *b*) to loosen the skin of (fruit, etc.), the feathers of (poultry), or the like, by the use of boiling water —*vi.* to be or become scalded —*n.* 1. a burn or injury caused by scalding 2. the act or an instance of scalding 3. any of various plant diseases characterized by a whitening of tissues, as if injured by scalding water; specif., *same as* SUNSCALD

scald[2] (skôld, skäld) *n. var. of* SKALD —**scald'ic** *adj.*

scale[1] (skāl) *n.* [ME. < LL. *scala* (in Vulg., Jacob's ladder) < L., usually as pl., *scalae*, flight of stairs, ladder < *scandsla* < *scandere*, to climb: cf. SCANDAL] 1. orig., *a*) a ladder or flight of stairs *b*) any means of ascent 2. *a*) a series of marks along a line, at regular or graduated intervals, used in measuring or registering something [the *scale* of a thermometer] *b*) any instrument or ruler marked in this manner 3. *a*) the proportion that a map, model, etc. bears to the thing that it represents; ratio between the dimensions of a representation and those of the object [a *scale* of one inch to a mile] *b*) a line marked off on a map to indicate this ratio or proportion 4. *a*) a system of grouping or classifying in a series of steps or degrees according to a standard of relative size, amount, rank, etc. [the social *scale*, a wage *scale*] *b*) a progressive graduated series, as of psychological or educational tests or scores *c*) any point, grade, level, or degree in such a series 5. *Math.* a system of numerical notation [the binary *scale*] 6. *Music* a series of tones arranged in a sequence of rising or falling pitches in accordance with any of various systems of intervals; esp., all of such a series contained in one octave: see also CHROMATIC, DIATONIC, MAJOR SCALE, MINOR SCALE —*vt.* **scaled, scal'ing** 1. *a*) to climb up or over; go up by or as by a ladder or by clambering *b*) to reach or surmount (specified heights) 2. to regulate, make, or set according to a scale 3. to measure by or as by a scale ☆4. to measure (logs) or estimate the board feet of (timber) —*vi.* 1. to climb; go up 2. to go up in a graduated series —**on a large** (or **small,** etc.) **scale** to a relatively large (or small, etc.) degree or extent —☆**scale down** (or **up**) to reduce (or increase) according to a fixed ratio or proportion —**scal'er** *n.*

scale[2] (skāl) *n.* [ME., aphetic < OFr. *escale*, husk, shell (< Frank. *skala*) & *escaille*, shell (< Goth. *skalja*): both < Gmc. *skalja*, something split off (whence OE. *scealu*, SHELL)] 1. any of the thin, flat, overlapping, rigid, horny plates forming the outer protective covering of the body in many fishes and reptiles and of the tails of a few mammals 2. any of the structurally similar thin plates on birds' legs or certain insects' wings 3. *a*) the single, round plate secreted by a scale insect *b*) *same as* SCALE INSECT 4. any thin, flaky or platelike layer or piece, as of dry skin, mail armor, etc. 5. a flaky film of oxide that forms on heated or rusted metals 6. a coating that forms on the inside of boilers, kettles, or other metal containers when heated 7. any greatly reduced scalelike leaf or bract; esp., such a modified leaf covering and protecting the bud of a seed plant —*vt.* **scaled, scal'ing** 1. to strip or scrape scales from 2. to remove in thin layers; pare down 3. to cause scales to form on; cover with scales 4. to throw (a thin, flat object) so that its edge cuts the air or so that it skips along the surface of water —*vi.* 1. to flake or peel off in scales 2. to become covered with scale or scales —**scale'less** *adj.*

scale[3] (skāl) *n.* [ME. < ON. *skāl*, bowl, weighing balance; akin to OHG. *scala*, OE. *scealu*, a shell, cup: see prec.] 1. either of the shallow dishes or pans of a balance 2. [*often pl.*] *a*) *same as* BALANCE (sense 1) *b*) any weighing machine —*vt.* **scaled, scal'ing** 1. to weigh in scales 2. to have a weight of —*vi.* to be weighed —**the Scales** *same as* LIBRA —**turn the scales** to determine; decide

scale insect any of a large group of small, homopterous insects (family Diaspididae) destructive to plants: the females secrete a round, wax scale under which they live and lay their eggs

sca·lene (skā lēn', skā'lēn) *adj.* [LL. *scalenus* < Gr. *skalēnos*, uneven, odd < IE. base *(s)kel-*, to bend, crooked, whence OE. *sceolh*, squinting, L. *coluber*, serpent] 1. *Anat.* designating or of any of three deeply set muscles extending from the first two ribs to the cervical vertebrae, and serving to bend the neck 2. *Geom. a*) having unequal sides and angles: said of a triangle *b*) having the axis not perpendicular to the base; oblique: said of a cone, etc.

sca·le·nus (skā lē'nəs) *n.* [LL.] a scalene muscle

scal·er (skāl'ər) *n.* 1. a person or thing that scales 2. *same as* SCALING CIRCUIT

scale·tail (skāl'tāl') *n.* any of a genus (*Anomalurus*) of African flying rodents, with scalelike structures on the lower surface of the tail

scal·i·ness (skāl'ē nis) *n.* a scaly quality or condition

scaling circuit *Electronics* a circuit designed to count large numbers of pulses by reducing a specified number of input pulses (usually a power of 2 or 10) to a single output pulse

scaling ladder a ladder used for climbing high walls

scall (skôl) *n.* [ME. < ON. *skalli*, bald head, akin to OE. *scealu*, SHELL] any scaly, or scabby, disease of the skin; scurf

☆**scal·la·wag** (skal'ə wag') *n. same as* SCALAWAG

scal·lion (skal'yən) *n.* [ME. *scalon* < ONormFr. *escalogne* (for OFr. *eschaloigne*) < VL. *escalonia* < L. (*caepa*) *Ascalonia*, (onion of) Ascalon (a city in Philistia)] any of three varieties of onion; specif., *a*) the shallot *b*) the leek *c*) a green onion with a long, thick stem and an almost bulbless root

scal·lop (skäl′əp, skal′-) *n.* [ME. *scalop* < OFr. *escalope* < *escale*; see SCALE²] 1. any of a family (Pectinidae) of bivalve mollusks; esp., any of a genus (*Pecten*) with two deeply grooved, curved shells and an earlike wing on each side of the hinge, that swims by rapidly snapping its shells together 2. the large adductor muscle of such a mollusk, used as food 3. a single shell of such a mollusk; specif., *a)* one worn formerly as a badge by pilgrims returning from the Holy Land *b)* one, or a dish shaped like one, in which fish or other food is baked and served 4. any of a series of curves, circle segments, projections, etc. forming an ornamental edge on cloth, lace, etc. —*vt.*
1. to cut the edge or border of in scallops 2. to bake until brown in a casserole, etc. with a milk sauce and bread crumbs; escallop —*vi.* to gather scallops —**scal′lop·er** *n.*
☆**scal·ly·wag** (skal′ē wag′) *n. same as* SCALAWAG

☆**sca·lo·gram** (skā′lə gram′) *n.* [SCAL(E)¹ + -o- + -GRAM] *Psychol.* a series of items, statements, etc. so arranged, as on a test, that attitudes, interests, etc. to be analyzed can be measured or defined by correlating responses

scal·op·pi·ne (skal′ə pē′nē, skäl′-) *n.* [It. *scaloppini*, pl. of *scaloppino*, dim. of *scaloppo*, thin slice, scale, prob. < OFr. *escalope*: see SCALLOP] thin slices of meat, esp. veal, sautéed slowly with herbs and, usually, wine: also sp. **scal′lo·pi′ni, scal′lop·pe′ni,** etc.

scalp (skalp) *n.* [ME. < Scand., as in Dan. dial. *skalp*, a pod, shell, ON. *skalpr*, a sheath < IE. *skelb-*, extension of *(s)kel-*: cf. SHELL] 1. the skin on the top and back of the head, usually covered with hair 2. a part of this, cut or torn from the head of an enemy for a trophy, as by certain N. American Indians, frontiersmen, etc. 3. a symbol, indication, or recognition of victory, prowess, etc. 4. the skin on the top of the head of a dog, wolf, etc. ☆5. [Colloq.] a small profit made by scalping —☆*vt.* 1. to cut or tear the scalp from 2. *a)* to cheat or rob *b)* to defeat decisively 3. [Colloq.] to buy and sell in order to make small, quick profits 4. [Colloq.] to buy (theater tickets, etc.) for later sale at higher than regular prices —☆*vi.* [Colloq.] to scalp bonds, tickets, etc. —**scalp′er** *n.*

scal·pel (skal′pəl) *n.* [L. *scalpellum*, dim. of *scalprum*, a knife < *scalpere*, to cut < IE. base *(s)kel-*: cf. SHELL] a small, light, straight knife with a very sharp blade, used by surgeons and in anatomical dissections

☆**scalp lock** a lock or tuft of hair left on the shaven crown of the head by certain N. American Indian warriors

scal·y (skā′lē) *adj.* **scal′i·er, scal′i·est** 1. having, covered with, composed of, or resembling a scale or scales 2. shedding or yielding scales or flakes 3. full of or infested with scale insects

scaly anteater *same as* PANGOLIN

☆**scam** (skam) *n.* [prob. altered < SCHEME] [Slang] *same as* CONFIDENCE GAME —*vt.* **scammed, scam′ming** [Slang] to cheat or swindle, as in a confidence game

Sca·man·der (skə man′dər) ancient name of MENDERES (sense 2)

scam·mo·ny (skam′ə nē) *n., pl.* **-nies** [ME. *skamonye* < L. *scammonia* < Gr. *skammōnia*] 1. a climbing Asian convolvulus (*Convolvulus scammonia*) with thick roots, arrowhead-shaped leaves, and white or purplish flowers 2. *a)* any of several plants whose roots yield medicinal resins; specif., **Mexican scammony** (*Ipomoea orizabensis*) *b)* the resin from the roots of any of these plants

scamp¹ (skamp) *n.* [< obs. *scamp*, to roam, aphetic < MFr. *escamper*, to flee < It. *scampare* < VL. *excampare*, to decamp < L. *ex*, out + *campus*, a field of battle: see CAMPUS] a mischievous fellow; rascal —**scamp′ish** *adj.*

scamp² (skamp) *vt.* [akin to or < ON. *skammr*, short < IE. base *(s)kem-*, stunted, whence OE. *hamola*, man with cropped hair] to make, do, or perform in a careless, inadequate way —**scamp′er** *n.*

scam·per (skam′pər) *vi.* [prob. freq. of obs. *scamp*, to roam: see SCAMP¹] to run or go hurriedly or quickly —*n.* the act of scampering —**scam′per·er** *n.*

scam·pi (skam′pē) *n., pl.* **-pi, -pies** [It., pl. of *scampo*] any of several large, greenish prawns, valued as food

scan (skan) *vt.* **scanned, scan′ning** [ME. *scannen* < L. *scandere*, to climb, mount (in LL., to scan): cf. SCANDAL] 1. to analyze (verse) into its rhythmic components, as by counting accents and syllables and marking the metrical feet 2. to look at closely or in a broad, searching way; scrutinize ☆3. to glance at quickly; consider hastily 4. in computers, *a)* to examine in sequence (written, printed, etc. data), esp. with an electronic device that then usually initiates a numerical printout, oscilloscope signal, etc. *b)* to check automatically (a state, process, etc.) with any of various devices that may then act upon the information received 5. *Radar* to traverse (a region) with a succession of transmitted radar beams, usually radiated in a systematic pattern 6. *TV* to traverse (a surface) rapidly and point by point with a beam of light or electrons in transmitting or reproducing the lights and shades of an image —*vi.* 1. to scan verse 2. to conform to metrical principles: said of verse —*n.* 1. the act or an instance of scanning 2. scope of vision —SYN. see SCRUTINIZE

Scan., Scand. 1. Scandinavia 2. Scandinavian

scan·dal (skan′d'l) *n.* [altered (after Fr. *scandale* or LL.) < ME. *scandle* < OFr. *escandele* < LL.(Ec.) *scandalum*, cause for stumbling, temptation < Gr.(Ec.) *skandalon*, a snare, prob. akin to L. *scandere*, to climb, Sans. *skandati*, (he) leaps up] 1. orig., unseemly conduct of a religious person that discredits religion or causes moral lapse in another 2. any act, person, or thing that offends or shocks moral feelings of the community and leads to disgrace 3. a reaction of shame, disgrace, outrage, etc. caused by such an act, person, or thing 4. ignominy; disgrace 5. malicious gossip; defamatory or slanderous talk —*vt.* **-daled** or **-dalled, -dal·ing** or **-dal·ling** 1. [Dial. or Archaic] to slander 2. [Obs.] to disgrace —SYN. see DISGRACE

scan·dal·ize (skan′də liz′) *vt.* **-ized′, -iz′ing** [LME. *scandalyzen* < OFr. *scandaliser* < LL.(Ec.) *scandalizare* < Gr.(Ec.) *skandalizein*, to make stumble, give offense < *skandalon*: see prec.] 1. [Now Rare] to slander; defame 2. to shock or outrage the moral feelings of; offend by some improper or unconventional conduct; shock —**scan′dal·i·za′tion** *n.* —**scan′dal·iz′er** *n.*

scan·dal·mon·ger (skan′d'l muŋ′gər, -mäŋ′-) *n.* a person who gossips maliciously and spreads scandal

scan·dal·ous (-əs) *adj.* [Fr. *scandaleux* < ML. *scandalosus*] 1. causing scandal; offensive to a sense of decency or shocking to the moral feelings of the community; shameful 2. consisting of or spreading slander; libelous; defamatory —**scan′dal·ous·ly** *adv.* —**scan′dal·ous·ness** *n.*

☆**scandal sheet** [Slang] a newspaper, magazine, etc. that features sensationalism, gossip, or the like

scan·dent (skan′dənt) *adj.* [L. *scandens*, prp. of *scandere*: see SCANDAL] climbing by attaching itself, as a vine

Scan·der·beg (skan′dər beg′) (born *George Castriota*) 1403?–68; Albanian leader & national hero

scan·di·a (skan′dē ə) *n.* [ModL.: see SCANDIUM] the oxide of scandium, Sc_2O_3, a white, amorphous powder

Scan·di·an (skan′dē ən) *adj., n. same as* SCANDINAVIAN

Scan·di·na·vi·a (skan′də nā′vē ə) 1. region in N Europe, including Norway, Sweden, & Denmark and, sometimes, Iceland & the Faeroe Islands 2. *same as* SCANDINAVIAN PENINSULA

Scan·di·na·vi·an (-ən) *adj.* of Scandinavia, its people, their languages, etc. —*n.* 1. any of the people of Scandinavia 2. the subbranch of the Germanic languages spoken by them; North Germanic

Scandinavian Peninsula large peninsula in N Europe, consisting of Norway & Sweden

scan·di·um (skan′dē əm) *n.* [ModL. < ML. *Scandia*, Scandinavia < L., N European lands] a rare metallic chemical element occurring with various elements of the rare-earth group: symbol, Sc; at. wt., 44.956; at. no., 21; sp. gr., 2.992; melt. pt., 1539°C; boil. pt., 2727°C

scan·na·ble (skan′ə b'l) *adj.* that can be scanned

scan·ner (-ər) *n.* a person or thing that scans; esp., any device used in television, computers, etc. for scanning

scan·sion (skan′shən) *n.* [Fr. < L. *scansio*] the act of scanning, or analyzing verse into its rhythmic components

scan·so·ri·al (skan sôr′ē əl) *adj.* [< L. *scansus*, pp. of *scandere*, to climb: see SCANDAL] *Zool.* 1. fitted or adapted for climbing, as a bird's feet 2. that climbs or can climb

scant (skant) *adj.* [ME. < ON. *skamt* < *skammr*, short: see SCAMP²] 1. inadequate in size or amount; not enough; meager 2. lacking a small part of the whole; not quite up to full measure [a *scant* foot] —*vt.* 1. to limit in size or amount; stint 2. to fail to give full measure of 3. to furnish with an inadequate supply, short ration, etc. 4. to treat in an inadequate manner —*adv.* [Dial.] scarcely; barely —SYN. see MEAGER —**scant′ly** *adv.* —**scant′ness** *n.*

scant·ling (skant′liŋ) *n.* [altered (as if < SCANT + -LING¹) < ME. *scantilone*, a carpenter's gauge, aphetic < ONorm.-Fr. *escantillon*, for OFr. *eschandillon*, a measure] 1. a small quantity or amount 2. dimensions of building material 3. a small beam or timber, esp. one of small cross section, as a 2 x 4 4. a small, upright timber, as in the frame of a structure

scant·y (skan′tē) *adj.* **scant′i·er, scant′i·est** [SCANT + -Y²] 1. barely sufficient; not ample; meager 2. insufficient; not enough 3. narrow; small; close —SYN. see MEAGER —**scant′i·ly** *adv.* —**scant′i·ness** *n.*

Scapa Flow (skap′ə) area of water in the Orkney Islands, off N Scotland: Brit. naval base: c.50 sq. mi.

scape¹ (skāp) *n.* [L. *scapus*: see SHAFT] 1. a leafless flower stalk growing from the crown of the root, as that of the narcissus, dandelion, etc. 2. something like a stalk, as the shaft of a feather or of an insect's antenna 3. *a)* the shaft of a column *b) same as* APOPHYGE

scape² (skāp) *n., vt., vi.* **scaped, scap′ing** [ME. *scapen*, aphetic < *escapen*] [Archaic] *same as* ESCAPE: also **'scape**

-scape (skāp) [< (LAND)SCAPE] *a combining form meaning* (a drawing, painting, etc. of) a specified kind of view or scene [*cityscape*]

scape·goat (skāp′gōt′) *n.* [coined (by Tyndale, 1530) < SCAPE² + GOAT, prob. after LL.(Vulg.) *caper emissarius*, lit., emissary goat, as transl. of Heb. *'azāzēl*, name of a desert demon, perhaps understood as *'ēz'ōzēl*, goat that leaves] 1. a goat over the head of which the high priest of the ancient Jews confessed the sins of the people on the Day of Atonement, after which it was allowed to escape: Lev. 16:7–26 2. a person, group, or thing upon whom the blame for the mistakes or crimes of others is thrust

scape·grace (-grās′) *n.* [SCAPE² + GRACE] a graceless, unprincipled fellow; scamp; rogue; rascal

scape wheel *same as* ESCAPE WHEEL: cf. ESCAPEMENT

scaph·oid (skaf′oid) *adj., n.* [ModL. *scaphoides* < Gr. *skaphoeidēs* < *skaphos*, a boat, hollow shell (< base of *skaptein*, to hollow out < IE. base *(s)kap-*, to split, hollow out, whence SHAPE) + *-eides*, -OID] *same as* NAVICULAR

scaph·o·pod (skaf′ə päd′) *n.* [< Gr. *skaphos*, a ship (see prec.) + -POD] any of a class (Scaphopoda) of mollusks that live in muddy or sandy sea bottoms and have slightly curved, tubular shells open at both ends with a long, pointed, protrusile foot at the larger end

scap·o·lite (skap′ə līt′) *n.* [< Gr. *skāpos*, rod (see SHAFT) + -LITE] any of a group of tetragonal minerals composed chiefly of silicates of aluminum, calcium, and sodium

sca·pose (skā′pōs) *adj.* [SCAPE¹ + -OSE²] *Bot.* resembling, bearing, or consisting of a scape

s. caps. *Printing* small capitals

scap·u·la (skap′yoo lə) *n., pl.* **-lae** (-lē′), **-las** [ModL. < L. (usually pl., *scapulae*), orig. prob. shovel (from use of the bone as a spade): for IE. base see SCAPHOID] either of two flat, triangular bones in the back of the shoulder in man, or a similar bone in other vertebrates; shoulder blade: see SKELETON, illus.

scap·u·lar (-lər) *adj.* [ModL. *scapularis* < L. *scapula*, scapula (in LL., shoulder)] of the shoulder, scapula, or scapulae —*n.* **1.** a sleeveless outer garment falling from the shoulders, worn as part of a monk's habit **2.** two small pieces of cloth joined by strings, worn on the chest and back, under the clothes, by some Roman Catholics as a token of religious devotion or as a badge of some order **3.** *Surgery* a bandage passed over the shoulder to support it or to keep another bandage in place **4.** *Zool.* a feather growing from a bird's scapular region

scapular medal *R.C.Ch.* a medal that has been blessed and may be substituted for a scapular (sense 2)

scar¹ (skär) *n.* [ME., aphetic < MFr. *escarre* < LL. *eschara* < Gr. *eschara*, orig., fireplace, brazier] **1.** a mark left on the skin or other tissue after a wound, burn, ulcer, pustule, lesion, etc. has healed; cicatrix **2.** a similar mark or cicatrix on a plant, as one on a stem where a leaf was attached **3.** a marring or disfiguring mark on anything **4.** the lasting mental or emotional effects of suffering or anguish —*vt.* **scarred, scar′ring** to mark with or as with a scar —*vi.* to form a scar in healing

scar² (skär) *n.* [ME. *skerre* < ON. *sker:* for IE. base see SHEAR] [Brit.] **1.** a precipitous rocky place or cliff **2.** a projecting or isolated rock, as in the sea

scar·ab (skar′əb) *n.* [Fr. *scarabée* < L. *scarabaeus*, altered < ? Gr. *karabos*, a horned beetle, crayfish] **1.** any of a large family (Scarabaeidae) of mostly stout-bodied, often brilliantly colored beetles with lamellicorn antennae, including the June bugs, cockchafers, dung beetles, etc. **2.** *a)* the black, winged dung beetle (*Scarabaeus sacer*), held sacred by the ancient Egyptians *b)* an image of this beetle, cut from a stone or gem, often engraved with religious or historical inscriptions on the flat underside and, formerly, esp. in ancient Egypt, worn as a charm or used as a seal

SCARAB
(A, top; B, bottom)

scar·a·bae·id (skar′ə bē′id) *n.* [< ModL. *Scarabaeidae*, name of the family < L. *scarabaeus:* see prec.] *same as* SCARAB (sense 1) —*adj.* of the scarab beetles

Scar·a·mouch (skar′ə mooch′, -mooch′, -mouch′) [Fr. *Scaramouche* < It. *Scaramuccia*, lit., a SKIRMISH] a stock character in old Italian comedy, depicted as a braggart and poltroon —*n.* [s-] a boastful coward or rascal

Scar·bor·ough (skär′bur′ō, -ə; -bə rə) city & seaside resort in NE England, in Yorkshire: pop. 42,000

scarce (skers) *adj.* [ME. *scars* < ONormFr. *escars* (for OFr. *eschars*) < VL. *escarpsus*, for L. *excerptus*, pp. of *excerpere*, to pick out, select (see EXCERPT); hence, that which is picked out and therefore scarce] **1.** not common; rarely seen **2.** not plentiful; not sufficient to meet the demand; hard to get —*adv. poet. or literary var. of* SCARCELY —SYN. see RARE¹ —**make oneself scarce** [Colloq.] to go or stay away —**scarce′ness** *n.*

scarce·ly (-lē) *adv.* **1.** hardly; not quite; only just **2.** probably not or certainly not [scarcely true]

scarce·ment (-mənt) *n.* [< obs. *scarce*, to make less < ME. *scarsen* < *scars:* see SCARCE & -MENT] a ledge or offset in a wall, etc.

scar·ci·ty (sker′sə tē) *n., pl.* **-ties** [ME. *scarsite* < ONormFr. *escarseté*] **1.** the condition or quality of being scarce; inadequate supply; dearth **2.** rarity; uncommonness

scare (sker) *vt.* **scared, scar′ing** [ME. *skerren* < ON. *skirra*, to scare, make timid < *skjarr*, timid, prob. < IE. base *(s)ker-*, to jump, whence L. *scurra*, buffoon] to fill with fear or terror; esp., to frighten suddenly or startle; terrify —*vi.* to become frightened, esp. suddenly [a person who *scares* easily] —*n.* [ME. *skerre* < the *v.*] **1.** a sudden

fear or panic; attack of fright, often unreasonable **2.** a state of widespread fear or panic [a war *scare*] —SYN. see FRIGHTEN —**scare away** (or **off**) to drive away (or off) by frightening —☆**scare up** [Colloq.] to produce or gather quickly

scare·crow (-krō′) *n.* **1.** anything set up in a field to scare birds away from crops, usually a figure of a man made with sticks, old clothes, etc. **2.** anything that frightens one but is actually not harmful **3.** a person who looks or is dressed like a scarecrow

scare·head (-hed′) *n.* [Colloq.] an exceptionally large newspaper headline, for sensational news

scare·mon·ger (-mun′gər, -män′gər) *n.* a person who circulates alarming rumors —**scare′mon′ger·ing** *n.*

scarf¹ (skärf) *n., pl.* **scarfs, scarves** [ONormFr. *escarpe* (OFr. *escharpe*), a purse suspended from the neck, wallet < ML. *scirpa, scrippa*, earlier *scirpea*, rush pouch or basket < L. *scirpeus*, of rushes < *scirpus*, a rush, bulrush] **1.** a long or broad piece of cloth worn about the neck, head, or shoulders for warmth or decoration; muffler, babushka, neckerchief, etc. **2.** a long, narrow covering for a table, bureau top, etc.; runner **3.** a sash worn by soldiers or officials —*vt.* to cover, wrap, or drape with or as with a scarf or scarfs

scarf² (skärf) *n., pl.* **scarfs** [prob. < Scand., as in ON. *skarfr*, obliquely cut beam-end < IE. *skerp-* < base *(s)ker-*, to cut, whence SHEAR] **1.** a joint made by notching, grooving, or otherwise cutting the ends of two pieces and fastening them so that they lap over and join firmly into one continuous piece: also **scarf joint 2.** the ends of a piece cut in this fashion ☆**3.** a groove or cut made along a whale's body —*vt.* **1.** to join by a scarf **2.** to make a scarf in the end of ☆**3.** to cut scarfs in and remove the skin and blubber of (a whale)

scarf·skin (-skin′) *n.* [SCARF¹ + SKIN] the outermost layer of skin; epidermis or cuticle

scar·i·fi·ca·tion (skar′ə fi kā′shən) *n.* [ME. *scarificacioun* < LL. *scarificatio*] **1.** the act of scarifying **2.** scratches or cuts made by scarifying

scar·i·fi·ca·tor (skar′ə fi kāt′ər) *n.* [ModL.] a surgical instrument for scarifying the skin

scar·i·fy (skar′ə fī′) *vt.* **-fied′, -fy′ing** [MFr. *scarifier* < LL. *scarificare*, altered < L. *scarifare* < Gr. *skariphasthai*, to scratch an outline, sketch < *skariphos*, a pencil, stylus, akin to L. *scribere*, to write: see SCRIBE] **1.** to make a series of small, superficial incisions or punctures in (the skin), as in surgery **2.** to criticize sharply; make cutting remarks to or about **3.** *Agric. a)* to loosen or stir (the topsoil) *b)* to make incisions in the coats of (seeds) in order to hasten germination —**scar′i·fi′er** *n.*

scar·i·ous (sker′ē əs) *adj.* [ModL. *scariosus* < L. *scaria*, thorny shrub] *Bot.* dry, thin, membranous, and not green, as some bracts

scar·la·ti·na (skär′lə tē′nə) *n.* [ModL. < ML. (*febris*) *scarlatina*, SCARLET (FEVER)] *popular term for a mild form of* SCARLET FEVER —**scar·la·ti′nal** *adj.*

Scar·lat·ti (skär lät′tē) **1.** A·les·san·dro (ä′les sän′drō), 1660?-1725; It. composer **2.** (Giuseppe) Do·me·ni·co (dō me′nē kō′), 1685-1757; It. composer: son of *prec.*

scar·let (skär′lit) *n.* [ME., aphetic < OFr. *escarlate* < ML. *scarlatum* < Per. *säqirlāt*, dress dyed crimson < Ar. *siqillāt* < Gr. *kyklas* (*esthēs*), (dress) with encircling border < *kyklas*, encircling: see CYCLE] **1.** very bright red with a slightly orange tinge **2.** cloth or clothing of this color —*adj.* **1.** of this color **2.** of sin; sinful; specif., whorish

scarlet fever an acute contagious disease, esp. of children, caused by hemolytic streptococci and characterized by sore throat, fever, and a scarlet rash

scarlet hat a cardinal's hat: see RED HAT

☆**scarlet letter** [< the novel *The Scarlet Letter* (1850) by Nathaniel Hawthorne] a scarlet letter A worn by a person convicted of adultery

scarlet runner (bean) a climbing bean plant (*Phaseolus coccineus*) of tropical America, having scarlet flowers, and pods with large, edible, red-and-black seeds: often grown in cold climates as an ornamental

scarlet sage see SAGE² (sense 1)

☆**scarlet tanager** a songbird (*Piranga olivacea*) native to the U.S., the male of which has a scarlet body and black wings and tail

scarp (skärp) *n.* [It. *scarpa*, a scarp, slope < Goth. *skrapa*, akin to OE. *scræf*, a cave, hollow < IE. *(s)cerb(h)-*, var. of base *(s)ker-*, to cut: cf. SHEAR] **1.** a steep slope; specif., an escarpment or cliff extending along the edge of a plateau, mesa, etc. **2.** the outer slope of a rampart; also, a rear slope of a ditch below the rampart —*vt.* **1.** to make or cut into a steep slope **2.** to provide with a scarp

scar·per (skär′pər) *vi.* [ult. < It. *scappare*, to run away, escape < LL. *excappare*, ESCAPE] [Brit. Slang] to run away or depart; decamp

Scar·ron (skå rōn′), Paul 1610-60; Fr. poet & dramatist

scar tissue the dense, fibrous, contracted connective tissue of which a scar is composed

scarves (skärvz) *n.* *alt. pl. of* SCARF¹

scar·y (sker′ē) *adj.* **scar′i·er, scar′i·est** [Colloq.] **1.** causing

alarm; frightening **2.** easily frightened; very timid —**scar′i·ness** *n.*

scat[1] (skat) *vi.* **scat′ted, scat′ting** [? a hiss + CAT] [Colloq.] to go away: usually in the imperative

☆**scat**[2] (skat) *adj.* [< ?] *Jazz* designating or of singing in which meaningless syllables are improvised, often in imitation of the sounds of a musical instrument —n. such singing —*vi.* **scat′ted, scat′ting** to engage in scat singing

☆**scat·back** (-bak′) *n.* [SCAT[1] + BACK[1]] [Football Slang] a fast, agile backfield player

scathe (ska*th*) *vt.* **scathed, scath′ing** [ME. *scathen* < ON. *skatha* < *skathi*, harm, akin to G. *schaden*, to harm < IE. base *skēth-, to injure, whence Gr. (*a*)*skēthēs*, (un)harmed] **1.** [Archaic or Dial.] *a)* to injure or hurt *b)* to blast; wither; sear **2.** to denounce fiercely —*n.* [Archaic or Dial.] injury or harm —**scathe′less** *adj.*

scath·ing (skā′*th*iŋ) *adj.* [prp. of prec.] searing; withering; injurious; harsh or caustic [*scathing* remarks] —**scath′-ing·ly** *adv.*

scat·o- (skat′ō, -ə) [< Gr. *skōr* (gen. *skatos*), excrement < IE. base *sker-, to defecate, whence ON. *skarn*, OE. *scearn*, dung] *a combining form meaning* feces or excrement [*scatology*]

sca·tol·o·gy (skə täl′ə jē) *n.* [SCATO- + -LOGY] **1.** the study of feces or of fossil excrement **2.** obscenity or obsession with the obscene, esp. with excrement or excretion, in literature —**scat′o·log′i·cal, scat′o·log′ic** *adj.*

scat·ter (skat′ər) *vt.* [ME. *skateren*, ult. < IE. *sked-, to split, disperse < base *sek-, to cut (cf. SECTION) **1.** *a)* to throw here and there or strew loosely; sprinkle *b)* to sprinkle over (*with*) something **2.** to separate and drive in many directions; rout; disperse **3.** [Archaic] to waste; dissipate **4.** *Physics a)* to reflect or refract in an irregular, diffuse manner *b)* to diffuse or deflect in an irregular manner —*vi.* to separate and go off in several directions [the crowd *scattered*] —*n.* **1.** the act or process of scattering **2.** that which is scattered about —**scat′ter·er** *n.*

SYN.—scatter implies a strewing around loosely [to *scatter* seeds] or a forcible driving apart in different directions [the breeze *scattered* the papers]; **disperse** implies a scattering which completely breaks up an assemblage and spreads the individuals far and wide [a people *dispersed* throughout the world]; **dissipate** implies complete dissolution, as by crumbling, wasting, etc. [to *dissipate* a fortune]; **dispel** suggests a scattering that drives away something that obscures, confuses, troubles, etc. [to *dispel* fears] See also SPRINKLE —**ANT. assemble, gather, collect**

scat·ter·a·tion (skat′ər ā′shən) *n.* a scattering or being scattered; esp., the act or result of dispersing

scat·ter·brain (-brān′) *n.* a person who is incapable of concentrated or serious thinking; giddy, frivolous, flighty person —**scat′ter·brained′** *adj.*

scat·ter·good (-good′) *n.* a person who wastes money, possessions, etc.; spendthrift

scat·ter·ing (-iŋ) *adj.* **1.** separating and going in various directions **2.** distributed over a wide area, esp. at irregular intervals **3.** distributed in small numbers among several or many candidates: said of votes —*n.* **1.** the act or process of one that scatters **2.** a small amount of something spread out or interspersed in a medium **3.** *Physics* the process by which a beam or ray is diffused in all directions when passing through a medium, caused by collisions with the constituents of the radiation with particles in the medium —**scat′ter·ing·ly** *adv.*

☆**scatter rug** a small rug for covering only a limited area

scat·ty (skat′ē) *adj.* **-ti·er, -ti·est** [contr. < ? SCATTER-BRAINED] [Brit. Slang] silly, foolish, or crazy

scaup (skôp) *n., pl.* **scaups, scaup:** see PLURAL, II, D, 1 [obs. var. of *scalp*, mussel bed: prob. so named from eating habits] any of several wild ducks (genus *Aythya*) related to the canvasback and redhead: also **scaup duck**

scav·enge (skav′inj) *vt.* **-enged, -eng·ing** [back-formation < ff.] **1.** to clean up (streets, alleys, etc.); remove rubbish, dirt, or garbage from **2.** to salvage (usable goods) by rummaging through refuse or discards **3.** to remove burned gases from (the cylinder of an internal-combustion engine) **4.** *Metallurgy* to clean (molten metal) by using a substance that will combine chemically with the impurities present —*vi.* **1.** to act as a scavenger **2.** to look for food

scav·eng·er (-in jər) *n.* [ME. *scavager* < Anglo-Fr. *scavage*, inspection < ONormFr. *escauwer*, to inspect < Fl. *scawen* or OFrank. *scouwon*, to peer at, observe: for IE. base see SHOW] **1.** a person who gathers things that have been discarded by others, as a junkman **2.** any animal that eats refuse and decaying organic matter **3.** anything that removes impurities, refuse, etc. **4.** [Chiefly Brit.] a person employed to clean the streets, collect refuse, etc.

☆**scavenger hunt** a game, as at a party, in which persons are sent out to bring back a number of prescribed, miscellaneous items without buying them

Sc.B. [L. *Scientiae Baccalaureus*] Bachelor of Science

Sc.D. [L. *Scientiae Doctor*] Doctor of Science

sce·nar·i·o (si ner′ē ō′, -när′-) *n., pl.* **-i·os′** [It. < L. *scaenarium* < *scaena*, stage, SCENE] **1.** an outline or synopsis of a play, opera, or the like, indicating scenes, characters, etc. ☆**2.** the script of a motion picture, esp. the shooting script —☆**sce·nar′ist** *n.*

scend (send) *n.* [< SEND[2], assumed to be aphetic for ASCEND] the upward heaving of a ship —*vi.* to be heaved upward, as by a wave: said of a ship

scene (sēn) *n.* [MFr. *scène* < L. *scena, scaena* < Gr. *skēnē*, covered place, tent, stage < IE. base *skai-, to gleam softly, whence SHINE] **1.** in ancient Greece or Rome, a theater stage **2.** the place in which any event, real or imagined, occurs [the *scene* of a battle] **3.** the setting or locale of the action of a play, opera, story, etc. [the *scene* of *Hamlet* is Denmark] **4.** a division of a play, usually part of an act, in which conventionally the action is continuous and in a single place **5.** a part of a play, motion picture, story, etc. that constitutes a unit of development or action, as a passage between certain characters **6.** *same as* SCENERY (sense 1) **7.** a view of people or places; picture or spectacle **8.** a display of strong or excited feeling before others [to make a painful *scene* in court] **9.** an episode, situation, or event, real or imaginary, esp. as described or represented **10.** [Colloq.] the locale or environment for a specified activity [the poetry *scene*] —**SYN.** see VIEW —**behind the scenes 1.** backstage **2.** in private or in secrecy; not for public knowledge —☆**make the scene** [Slang] **1.** to appear or be present **2.** to participate, esp. in an effective or noticeable way

scen·er·y (sē′nər ē) *n., pl.* **-ies** [< obs. *scenary*, scenic < LL. *scenarius* < L. *scena*, SCENE] **1.** painted screens, backdrops, hangings, flats, etc., used on the stage to represent places and surroundings in a play, opera, etc. **2.** the general aspect or appearance of a place; features of a landscape

scen·ic (sē′nik, sen′ik) *adj.* [MFr. *scénique* < L. *scenicus* < Gr. *skēnikos* < *skēnē*, SCENE] **1.** *a)* of the stage; dramatic; theatrical *b)* relating to stage effects or stage scenery **2.** *a)* having to do with natural scenery *b)* having beautiful scenery; affording many beautiful views **3.** representing an action, event, situation, etc. Also **sce′ni·cal** —**sce′ni·cal·ly** *adv.*

☆**scenic railway** a small railway passing through areas with a scenic view, often artificially contrived

sce·nog·ra·phy (sē näg′rə fē) *n.* [L. *scaenographia* < Gr. *skēnographia* < *skēnē*, SCENE + *graphein*, to write: see GRAPHIC] the art of drawing or painting in perspective; esp., the painting of stage scenes in ancient Greece —**sce·no·graph·ic** (sē′nə graf′ik, sen′ə-), **sce′no·graph′i·cal** *adj.*

scent (sent) *vt.* [ME. *senten* < OFr. *sentir* < L. *sentire*, to feel: see SEND[1]] **1.** to smell; perceive by the olfactory sense **2.** to get a hint or inkling of; suspect [to *scent* trouble] **3.** to fill with an odor; give fragrance to; perfume —*vi.* to hunt by the sense of smell —*n.* **1.** a smell; odor **2.** the sense of smell **3.** a manufactured fluid preparation used to give fragrance; perfume **4.** an odor left by an animal, by which it is tracked in hunting **5.** a track followed in hunting **6.** any clue by which something is followed or detected **7.** an intuitive capacity for discovering or detecting [a *scent* for news] —**scent′ed** *adj.* —**scent′less** *adj.*

SYN.—scent, in this comparison, implies a relatively faint but pervasive smell, esp. one characteristic of a particular thing [the *scent* of apple blossoms]; **perfume** suggests a relatively strong, but usually pleasant, smell, either natural or manufactured [the rich *perfume* of gardenias]; **fragrance** always implies an agreeable, sweet smell, esp. of growing things [the *fragrance* of a freshly mowed field]; **bouquet** is specifically applied to the fragrance of a wine or brandy; **redolence** implies a rich, pleasant combination of smells [the *redolence* of a grocery store] See also SMELL —**ANT. stench, stink**

scep·ter (sep′tər) *n.* [ME. *sceptre* < OFr. < L. *sceptrum* < Gr. *skēptron*, staff to lean on < base of *skēptesthai*, to prop oneself, lean on something: for IE. base see SHAFT] **1.** a rod or staff, highly ornamented, held by rulers on ceremonial occasions as a symbol of authority and sovereignty **2.** royal or imperial authority; sovereignty —*vt.* to furnish with a scepter; invest with royal or imperial authority

scep·tic (skep′tik) *n., adj. chiefly Brit. sp.* of SKEPTIC —**scep′ti·cal** *adj.* —**scep′ti·cism** *n.*

scep·tre (sep′tər) *n., vt.* **-tred, -tring** *chiefly Brit. sp.* of SCEPTER

sch. 1. school **2.** schooner

‡**Scha·den·freude** (shäd′n froi′də) *n.* [G. < *schaden*, to harm < *freude*, joy] glee at another's misfortune

Schaff·hau·sen (shäf′hou′zən) canton of Switzerland, in the northernmost part: 115 sq. mi.; pop. 71,000

schat·chen (shät′khən) *n.* [Yid. < Heb. *shadkhān*] a Jewish marriage broker or matchmaker

sched·ule (skej′ool, -əl; *Brit. & often Canad.* shed′yool, shej′ool) *n.* [altered (after LL.) < ME. *sedule* < OFr. *cedule* < LL. *schedula*, dim. of L. *scheda*, a strip of papyrus < Gr. *schidē*, splinter of wood, split piece < *schizein*, to split: see SCHIZO-] **1.** orig., a paper with writing on it **2.** a list, catalog, or inventory of details, often as an explanatory supplement to a will, bill of sale, deed, tax form, etc. ☆**3.** a list of times of recurring events, projected operations, arriving and departing trains, etc.; timetable ☆**4.** a timed plan for a procedure or project —*vt.* **-uled, -ul·ing 1.** to place or include in a schedule **2.** to make a schedule of ☆**3.** to appoint or plan for a certain time or date

Scheduled Castes the groups of people in India formerly belonging to the class of untouchables

scheel·ite (shēl′īt) *n.* [G. *scheelit*, after K. W. *Scheele*

(1742–86), Swed. chemist] a mineral, calcium tungstate, $CaWO_4$, important as an ore of tungsten

Sche·he·ra·za·de (shə her'ə zä'də, -zäd') [G. < Per. *Shīrazād*] in *The Arabian Nights*, the Sultan's bride, who saves her life by suspensefully maintaining the Sultan's interest in the tales she tells

Scheldt (skelt) river flowing from N France through Belgium and the Netherlands into the North Sea: Du. name **Schel·de** (skhel'də)

Schel·ling (shel'iŋ), **Fried·rich Wil·helm Jo·seph von** (frē'driH vil'helm yō'zef fôn) 1775–1854; Ger. philosopher

sche·ma (skē'mə) n., pl. -ma·ta (-mə tə) [Gr. *schēma*: see SCHEME] an outline, diagram, scheme, plan, or preliminary draft

sche·mat·ic (skē mat'ik, skə-) adj. [ModL. *schematicus*] of, or having the nature of, a scheme, schema, plan, diagram, etc. —n. a schematic diagram, as of electrical wiring in a circuit —**sche·mat'i·cal·ly** adv.

sche·ma·tism (skē'mə tiz'm) n. [ModL. *schematismus* < Gr. *schēmatismos* < *schēmatizein*, to form: see SCHEME] a set form for classification or exposition; arrangement of parts according to a scheme; design

sche·ma·tize (-tīz') vi., vt. -tized', -tiz'ing [Gr. *schēmatizein*] to form, form into, or arrange according to, a scheme or schemes —**sche·ma·ti·za'tion** n.

scheme (skēm) n. [L. *schema* < Gr. *schēma* (gen. *schēmatos*), a form, appearance, plan, akin to *schein*, *echein*, to hold, have < IE. base *seĝh-, to hold, hold fast, conquer, whence SCHOOL[1], Sans. *sáhas*, power, victory, Goth. *sigis*, G. *sieg*, victory] 1. a) a carefully arranged and systematic program of action for attaining some object or end b) a secret or underhanded plan; plot c) a visionary plan or project 2. an orderly combination of things on a definite plan; system [a color *scheme*] 3. an outline or diagram showing different parts or elements of an object or system 4. an analysis or summary in outline or tabular form 5. an astrological diagram —vt. schemed, schem'ing 1. to make a scheme for; plan as a scheme; devise; contrive 2. to plan in a deceitful way; plot —vi. 1. to make schemes; form plans 2. to plot; intrigue —SYN. see PLAN —schem'er n.

schem·ing (skē'miŋ) adj. given to forming schemes or plots; crafty, tricky, deceitful, etc. —**schem'ing·ly** adv.

Sche·nec·ta·dy (skə nek'tə dē) [Du. *Schaeaenhechsiede* < Iroquoian name (? lit., place of the pines) + Du. *stede*, place, town (akin to STEAD)] city in E N.Y., on the Mohawk River: pop. 78,000 (met. area, with Albany & Troy, 721,000)

scher·zan·do (sker tsän'dō, -tsan'-) adj. [It. < prp. of *scherzare*, to play < *scherzo*: see ff.] *Music* playful; sportive —adv. *Music* playfully; sportively: a direction to the performer

scher·zo (sker'tsō) n., pl. -zos, -zi (-tsē) [It., a jest, sport < Gmc., as in MHG. *scherz*, pleasure, play, ult. < IE. base *(s)ker-, to leap, jump, whence L. *cardo*, a hinge, turning point] a lively, playful movement in 3/4 time, often constituting the third section of a sonata, symphony, or quartet

Schia·pa·rel·li (skyä'pä rel'lē), **Gio·van·ni Vir·gi·nio** (jō vän'nē vir jē'nyō) 1835–1910; It. astronomer

☆**Schick test** (shik) [after Béla *Schick* (1877–1967), U.S. pediatrician, born in Hungary, who devised it] a test to determine immunity to diphtheria, made by injecting dilute diphtheria toxin into the skin: if an area of inflammation results, the patient is not immune

Schie·dam (skhē däm') city in SW Netherlands: pop. 81,000

schil·ler (shil'ər) n. [G., color play < *schillern*, to change color] a peculiar bronzelike luster in certain minerals, often iridescent, caused by the diffraction of light in embedded crystals

Schil·ler (shil'ər), **Jo·hann Chris·toph Fried·rich von** (yō'hän kris'tôf frē'driH fôn) 1759–1805; Ger. dramatist & poet

schil·ling (shil'iŋ) n. [G.: see SHILLING] the monetary unit and a coin of Austria: see MONETARY UNITS, table

schip·per·ke (skip'ər kē) n. [Fl., little skipper, dim. of *schipper* (see SKIPPER[2]): from earlier use of breed as watchdogs on boats] any of a Belgian breed of small, black, short-haired dog with a foxlike head, erect ears, and a broad chest

schism (siz'm; now occas. skiz'm) n. [ME. *scisme* < OFr. *cisme* < LL.(Ec.) *schisma* < Gr. *schisma* < *schizein*, to cleave, cut: see SCHIZO-] 1. a split or division in an organized group or society, esp. a church, as the result of difference of opinion, of doctrine, etc. 2. the offense of causing or trying to cause a split or division in a church 3. any of the sects, parties, etc. formed by such a split or division

schis·mat·ic (siz mat'ik; now occas. skiz-) adj. [ME. *scismatike* < MFr. *scismatique* < LL.(Ec.) *schismaticus* < Gr. *schismatikos*] 1. of, characteristic of, or having the nature of, schism 2. tending to, causing, or guilty of schism Also **schis·mat'i·cal** —n. a person who causes or participates in schism —**schis·mat'i·cal·ly** adv.

schist (shist) n. [Fr. *schiste* < L. *schistos* (*lapis*), split (stone) < Gr. *schistos*, easily cleft < *schizein*, to cleave: see SCHIZO-] any of a group of metamorphic rocks containing parallel layers of flaky minerals, as mica or talc, and splitting easily into thin, parallel leaves —**schist'ose** (-ōs), **schist'ous** (-əs) adj.

schis·to·some (shis'tə sōm') n. [ModL. *Schistosoma*, genus name < Gr. *schistos*, cleft (see SCHIST) + *sōma*, body: see SOMATIC] any of a genus (*Schistosoma*) of flukes that live as parasites in the blood vessels of mammals, including man, and birds

schis·to·so·mi·a·sis (shis'tə sō mī'ə sis) n. [ModL.: see prec. & -IASIS] a chronic, usually tropical, disease, caused by schistosomes and characterized in man by disorders of the liver, urinary bladder, lungs, or central nervous system

schiz·o- (skiz'ō, -ə; now also skit'sō, -sə) [ModL. < Gr. *schizein*, to cleave, cut < IE. *skeid- < base *skei-, to cut, separate, whence SHIN[1], L. *scindere*, to cut] a combining form meaning split, cleavage, division [*schizocarp*, *schizophrenia*]: also, before a vowel, **schiz-**

schiz·o·carp (skiz'ə kärp, skit'sə-) n. [prec. + -CARP] *Bot.* a dry fruit, as of the maple, that splits at maturity into two or more one-seeded carpels which remain closed —**schiz·o·car'pous**, **schiz·o·car'pic** adj.

schiz·o·gen·e·sis (skiz'ə jen'ə sis, skit'sə-) n. [ModL.: see SCHIZO- & -GENESIS] *Biol.* reproduction by fission

schiz·og·o·ny (ski zäg'ə nē, skit säg'-) n. [SCHIZO- + -GONY] asexual reproduction by multiple fission, found in many sporozoans, as the malarial parasite

schiz·oid (skit'soid, skiz'oid) adj. [SCHIZ- + -OID] 1. *Psychiatry* of, like, or having schizophrenia 2. designating a personality type characterized by quietness, seclusiveness, introversion, etc. —n. a schizoid person

schiz·o·my·cete (skiz'ō mi sēt', skit'sə-) n. [SCHIZO- + -MYCETE] any of the class (Schizomycetes) of vegetable microorganisms comprising the bacteria; bacterium —**schiz·o·my·ce'tous** (-sēt'əs) adj.

schiz·o·my·co·sis (-mi kō'sis) n. [ModL.: see SCHIZO- & MYCOSIS] any disease caused by schizomycetes

schiz·ont (skiz'änt, skit'sänt) n. [< SCHIZO- + Gr. *ōn*, gen. *ontos*: see ONTO-] a large cell in many sporozoans that multiplies by schizogony

schiz·o·phre·ni·a (skit'sə frē'nē ə, skiz'ə-) n. [ModL. < SCHIZO- + Gr. *phrēn*, the mind] a major mental disorder of unknown cause typically characterized by a separation between the thought processes and the emotions, a distortion of reality accompanied by delusions and hallucinations, a fragmentation of the personality, motor disturbances, bizarre behavior, etc., often with no loss of basic intellectual functions: this term has largely replaced *dementia praecox* since it is more inclusive and avoids the implications of age and deterioration

schiz·o·phren·ic (-fren'ik, -frē'nik) adj. of or having schizophrenia —n. a person having schizophrenia: also **schiz·o·phrene'** (-frēn')

schiz·o·phyte (skiz'ə fit', skit'sə-) n. [SCHIZO- + -PHYTE] any of a group (Schizophyta) of plants which consist of a single cell, or a chain or colony of cells, and reproduce only by simple fission or by asexual spores, including the bacteria and blue-green algae —**schiz·o·phyt'ic** (-fit'ik) adj.

schiz·o·pod (-päd') n. [< ModL. *Schizopoda*, group name < Gr. *schizopous*, having parted toes: see SCHIZO- & -POD] any of a group of crustaceans, formerly considered an order, resembling the shrimp but having thoracic appendages with two branches and including the mysids and the euphausiids —adj. of the schizopods: also **schi·zop·o·dous** (ski zäp'ə dəs)

schiz·o·thy·mi·a (skit'sə thī'mē ə, skiz'ə-) n. [ModL. < SCHIZO- + Gr. *thymos*, spirit, akin to L. *fumus*: see FUME] an emotional condition characterized by schizoid tendencies: less severe than *schizophrenia* —**schiz·o·thy'mic** (-mik) adj., n.

Schle·gel (shlā'g'l) 1. **Au·gust Wil·helm von** (ou'goost vil'helm fôn) 1767–1845; Ger. poet, critic, & translator 2. **(Karl Wilhelm) Fried·rich von** (frē'driH fôn) 1772–1829; Ger. critic & philosopher: brother of prec.

Schlei·er·ma·cher (shlī'ər mä'khər), **Frie·drich Ernst Da·ni·el** (frē'driH ernst dä'nē el) 1768–1834; Ger. theologian & philosopher

☆**schle·miel** (shlə mēl') n. [Yid. < Heb. proper name *Shelumiēl* (lit., my peace is God); current meaning prob. popularized after Peter *Schlemihl*, title character of a novel by Adelbert von Chamisso (1781–1838), G. writer] [Slang] an ineffectual, bungling person who habitually fails or is easily victimized: also sp. **schle·mihl'**

☆**schlep, schlepp** (shlep) vt. schlepped, schlep'ping [via Yid. < G. *schleppen*, to drag] [Slang] to carry, haul, drag, etc. —vi. [Slang] to go or move with effort; drag oneself —n. [Slang] an ineffectual person

Schle·si·en (shlā'zē ən) Ger. name of SILESIA

Schle·sing·er (shlā'ziŋ ər, shles'in jər) 1. **Arthur M(eier)**, 1888–1965; U.S. historian 2. **Arthur M(eier), Jr.**, 1917– ; U.S. historian: son of prec.

Schles·wig (shles′wig; *G.* shläs′viH) region in the S Jutland peninsula, divided between Denmark & West Germany: Dan. name, SLESVIG

Schles·wig-Hol·stein (-hōl′stīn; *G.* -hōl′shtīn) state of N West Germany, at the base of the Jutland peninsula: 6,046 sq. mi.; pop. 2,439,000; cap. Kiel

Schlie·mann (shlē′män), **Hein·rich** (hīn′riH) 1822–90; Ger. archaeologist

schlie·ren (shlir′ən) *n.pl., sing.* -re (-ə) [G., lit., streaks, akin to SLUR] **1.** small streaks or masses in igneous rocks, differing in composition from the main rock but blending gradually into it **2.** *Optics* regions in a translucent medium, as a fluid, that have a different density and consequently a different index of refraction than the medium and that can be photographed as shadows produced by the refraction of light passed through these regions

☆**schlock** (shläk) *n.* [via Yid. < *G. schlacke*, dregs] [Slang] anything cheap or inferior; trash —*adj.* cheap; inferior

schloss (shlôs) *n.* [G.] a castle

☆**schmaltz** (shmälts, shmôlts) *n.* [via Yid. < *G. schmalz*, lit., rendered fat, akin to *schmelzen*, to melt: see SMELT²] [Slang] **1.** highly sentimental and banal music, literature, etc. **2.** such sentimentalism Also **schmalz** —**schmaltz′y** *adj.* **schmaltz′i·er, schmaltz′i·est**

schmaltz herring herring caught just before spawning, when it has much fat

Schmidt system (shmit) [after B. *Schmidt* (1879–1935), G. astronomer] an optical system, used in certain wideangle reflecting telescopes, having a concave, spherical mirror whose aberration is neutralized by a correcting lens

☆**schmo** (shmō) *n., pl.* **schmoes, schmos** [< Yid., prob. altered < *shmok* (see SCHMUCK)] [Slang] a foolish or stupid person; dolt: also sp. **schmoe**

☆**schmooze** (shmo͞oz) *vi.* **schmoozed, schmooz′ing** [< Yid. *shmuesn* < Heb. *shĕmuoth*, items reported, gossip] [Slang] to chat or gossip —*n.* an idle talk; chat Also **schmoos** (shmo͞os)

☆**schmuck** (shmuk) *n.* [< Yid. *shmok*, penis] [Slang] a contemptible or foolish person; jerk

Schna·bel (shnä′bəl), **Ar·tur** (är′to͝or) 1882–1951; Austrian pianist & composer

schnapps (shnäps, shnaps) *n., pl.* **schnapps** [G., a dram, nip < Du. *snaps*, lit., a gulp, mouthful < *snappen*, to SNAP] **1.** *same as* HOLLANDS **2.** any strong alcoholic liquor Also sp. **schnaps**

schnau·zer (shnou′zər) *n.* [G. < *schnauzen*, to snarl, growl < *schnauze*, SNOUT] any of a breed of small active terrier with a close, wiry coat and bushy eyebrows and beard, orig. bred in Germany

☆**schnit·zel** (shnit′s′l) *n.* [G., lit., a shaving, dim. of *schnitz*, a piece cut off < MHG. *sniz*, akin to OE. *snithan*, to cut, chop < IE. base *sneit-*, whence Czech *snět*, a branch] a cutlet, esp. of veal

Schnitz·ler (shnits′lər), **Ar·thur** (är′to͝or) 1862–1931; Austrian playwright & novelist

☆**schnook** (shno͝ok) *n.* [< Yid., ? altered < SCHMUCK] [Slang] a person easily imposed upon or cheated; pitifully meek person

schnor·rer (shnôr′ər) *n.* [< Yid. < *G. schnurrer* < *schnurren*, to whir, purr (of echoic origin): from the sound made by musical instruments carried by beggars] [Slang] a person who lives by begging or by sponging on others

schnoz·zle (shnäz′′l) *n.* [via Yid. < *G. schnauze*, akin to SNOUT] [Slang] the nose: also sp. **schnoz**

Schoenberg *var. of* SCHÖNBERG

Scho·field (skō′fēld), **John Mc·Al·lis·ter** (mək al′is tər) 1831–1906; U.S. general

schol·ar (skäl′ər) *n.* [ME. *scoler* < OE. *scolere* or OFr. *escoler*, both < ML. < LL. *scholaris*, relating to a school < L. *schola*, a SCHOOL¹] **1.** *a*) a learned person *b*) a specialist in a particular branch of learning, esp. in the humanities **2.** a student given scholarship aid **3.** any student or pupil —*SYN.* see PUPIL¹

schol·ar·ly (-lē) *adj.* **1.** of or characteristic of scholars **2.** having or showing much knowledge, accuracy, and critical ability **3.** devoted to learning; studious —*adv.* [Rare] like a scholar

schol·ar·ship (-ship′) *n.* **1.** the quality of knowledge and learning shown by a student; standard of academic work **2.** *a*) the systematized knowledge of a learned man, exhibiting accuracy, critical ability, and thoroughness; erudition *b*) the knowledge attained by scholars, collec-

SCHLESWIG

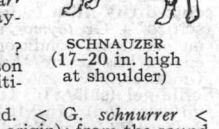

SCHNAUZER (17–20 in. high at shoulder)

tively **3.** a specific gift of money or other aid, as by a foundation, to help a student continue his studies

scho·las·tic (ska las′tik) *adj.* [L. *scholasticus* < Gr. *scholastikos* < *scholazein*, to devote one's leisure to study, be at leisure < *scholē:* see SCHOOL¹] **1.** of schools, colleges, universities, students, teachers, and studies; educational; academic **2.** [also S-] of or characteristic of scholasticism **3.** pedantic, dogmatic, formal, etc. **4.** of secondary schools [*scholastic* football games] Also **scho·las′ti·cal** —*n.* **1.** a student or scholar, esp. in a scholasticate **2.** [also S-] *same as* SCHOOLMAN (sense 1) **3.** a person who is devoted to logical subtleties and quibblings; pedant **4.** [also S-] a person who favors Scholasticism —**scho·las′ti·cal·ly** *adv.*

scho·las·ti·cate (-tə kāt′, -kit) *n.* R.C.Ch. a school for seminarians, esp. Jesuit seminaries

scho·las·ti·cism (-tə siz′m) *n.* **1.** [often S-] the system of logic, philosophy, and theology of medieval university scholars, or schoolmen, from the 10th to the 15th century, based upon Aristotelian logic, the writings of the early Christian fathers, and the authority of tradition and dogma **2.** an insistence upon traditional doctrines and methods

scho·li·ast (skō′lē ast) *n.* [ModL. *scholiasta* < MGr. *scholiastēs* < *scholiazein*, to comment < Gr. *scholion*, SCHOLIUM] one who writes marginal notes and comments; esp., an ancient interpreter and annotator of the classics —**scho′li·as′tic** *adj.*

scho·li·um (skō′lē əm) *n., pl.* -li·a (-ə), -li·ums [ML. < Gr. *scholion* < *scholē:* see SCHOOL¹] **1.** a marginal note or commentary, esp. on the text of a Greek or Latin writer **2.** a note added or following, meant to illustrate or develop a point in the text, as in mathematics

Schön·berg (shän′bərg, shōn′-; *G.* shön′berkh), **Arnold** 1874–1951; U.S. composer, born in Austria

school¹ (sko͞ol) *n.* [ME. *scole* < OE. *scol* < L. *schola*, school < Gr. *scholē*, leisure, that in which leisure is employed, discussion, philosophy, school < IE. base *seĝh-*, to hold fast, overcome: cf. SCHEME] **1.** a place or institution for teaching and learning; establishment for education; specif., *a*) an institution for teaching children *b*) a place for training and instruction in some special field, skill, etc. [a dancing *school*] ☆*c*) a college or university *d*) in the Middle Ages, a seminary of logic, metaphysics, and theology **2.** the building or buildings, classrooms, laboratories, etc. of any such establishment **3.** all the students, or pupils, and teachers at any such establishment **4.** the period of instruction at any such establishment; regular session of teaching [the date when *school* begins] **5.** *a*) attendance at a school [to miss *school* for a week] *b*) the process of formal training and instruction at a school; formal education; schooling **6.** any situation, set of circumstances, or experiences through which one gains knowledge, training, or discipline [the *school* of hard knocks] **7.** a particular division of an institution of learning, esp. of a university [the *school* of law] **8.** *a*) a group of people held together by the same teachings, beliefs, opinions, methods, etc.; followers or disciples of a particular teacher, leader, or creed [the Impressionist *school*] *b*) a group of artists associated with a specified place [the Barbizon *school*] **9.** a way of life; style of customs, manners, etc. [a gentleman of the old *school*] —*vt.* **1.** to train, as at school; teach; instruct; educate **2.** to discipline or control **3.** [Archaic] to reprimand —*adj.* **1.** of a school or schools **2.** [Obs.] of the schoolmen (sense 1) —**go to school** *Golf* to learn, from observation of another's putt, the peculiarities of a particular green —*SYN.* see GROUP, TEACH

school² (sko͞ol) *n.* [Du., a crowd, school of fish: see SHOAL¹] a large number of fish or water animals of the same kind swimming or feeding together —*vi.* to move together in a school, as fish, whales, etc.

school age 1. the age at which a child may or must be sent to school **2.** the years during which attendance at school is required or customary —**school′-age′** *adj.*

school·bag (-bag′) *n.* a bag, usually of cloth, in which a student at a school carries his books, supplies, etc.

school board a group of people, elected or appointed, who are in charge of local public schools

school·book (-sko͞ol′bo͝ok′) *n.* a book used for study in schools; textbook

school·boy (-boi′) *n.* a boy attending school

☆**school bus** a vehicle used for transporting students to or from a school or on school-related trips

☆**school·child** (-chīld′) *n., pl.* -chil·dren (-chil′drən) a child attending school

School·craft (sko͞ol′kraft′), **Henry Rowe** (rō) 1793–1864; U.S. ethnologist

school day 1. any day on which school is in session **2.** the time, during any day, when school is in session

☆**school district** an area, with specified limits, established for administering a local public school or schools

school·fel·low (-fel′ō) *n. same as* SCHOOLMATE

school·girl (-gurl′) *n.* a girl attending school

school guard a person whose duty it is to escort children across streets near schools

school·house (-hous′) *n.* a building used as a school

school·ing (-iŋ) *n.* **1.** training or education; esp., formal instruction at school; education **2.** cost of instruction and living at school **3.** [Archaic] disciplinary correction

school·man (-mən; *for 2, often* -man′) *n., pl.* -men (-mən; *for 2, often* -men′) **1.** [often S-] any of the medieval uni-

versity teachers of philosophy, logic, and theology; scholastic **2.** a teacher, educator, or scholar

☆**school·marm** (-märm′, -mäm′) *n.* [Colloq.] a woman schoolteacher, hence any person, who tends to be old-fashioned, prudish, and pedantic: also **school′ma′am′** (-mäm′, -mam′)

school·mas·ter (-mas′tər, -mäs′-) *n.* **1.** a man who teaches in a school: an old-fashioned term **2.** [Chiefly Brit.] a headmaster or master in a school **3.** a person or thing that disciplines or instructs **4.** a reddish-brown and orange snapper (*Lutjanus apodus*) with large scales, found in warm Atlantic waters

school·mate (-māt′) *n.* a person going to the same school at the same time as another

school·mis·tress (-mis′tris) *n.* a woman schoolteacher

school·room (-rōōm′) *n.* a room in which pupils are taught, as in a school

school·teach·er (-tē′chər) *n.* a person whose work is teaching in a school

school tie *same as* OLD SCHOOL TIE

school·work (-wurk′) *n.* lessons worked on in classes at school or done as homework

school·yard (-yärd′) *n.* the ground around or near a school, used as a playground, playing field, etc.

school year the part of a year when school is in session, usually from September to June

☆**schoon·er** (skōō′nər) *n.* [< ? Scot. dial. *scun,* to skip a flat stone across water] **1.** a ship with two or more masts, rigged fore and aft **2.** *clipped form of* PRAIRIE SCHOONER **3.** a large beer glass, usually holding a pint

☆**schoon·er-rigged** (-rigd′) *adj.* rigged like a schooner, fore and aft

Scho·pen·hau·er (shō′pən hou′ər), **Arthur** 1788–1860; Ger. pessimist philosopher —**Scho′pen·hau′er·ism** *n.*

schorl (shôrl) *n.* [G. *schörl*] a black variety of tourmaline —**schor·la·ceous** (shôr lā′shəs) *adj.*

schot·tische (shät′ish) *n.* [< G. (*der*) *schottische* (*tanz*), (the) Scottish (dance) < *Schotte* < OHG. *Scotto* < LL. *Scottus,* SCOT] **1.** a form of round dance in 2/4 time, similar to the polka, but with a slower tempo **2.** music for this —*vi.* -**tisched,** -**tisch·ing** to dance a schottische

Schrö·ding·er (shrō′diŋ ər), **Er·win** (er′vēn) 1887–1961; Austrian physicist

☆**schtick, schtik** (shtik) *n. same as* SHTICK

Schu·bert (shōō′bart; G. shōō′bert), **Franz (Peter)** (fränts) 1797–1828; Austrian composer

schul (shōōl) *n. same as* SHUL

Schu·man (shōō′mən), **William (Howard)** 1910– ; U.S. composer

Schu·mann (shōō′män), **Robert (Alexander)** 1810–56; Ger. composer

Schu·mann-Heink (shōō′mən hiŋk′), **Ernestine** (born *Ernestine Rössler*) 1861–1936; U.S. contralto, born in Bohemia

Schurz (shoorts), **Carl** 1829–1906; U.S. statesman, journalist, & Union general, born in Germany

schuss (shoos) *n.* [G., lit., shot, rush: see SHOT[1]] a straight run down a hill in skiing —*vi.* to ski straight down a slope at full speed —**schuss′er** *n.*

Schütz (shüts), **Hein·rich** (hīn′riH) 1585–1672; Ger. composer

Schuy·ler (skī′lər), **Philip John** 1733–1804; Am. Revolutionary general & statesman

Schuy·ler·ville (skī′lər vil′) [after prec.] resort village in E N.Y., on the Hudson: pop. 1,400: cf. SARATOGA

Schuyl·kill (skōōl′kil) [< Du. *Schuilkil,* lit., hidden channel < *schuilen,* to hide, skulk + *kil,* channel, stream] river in SE Pa., flowing southeast into the Delaware River at Philadelphia: 130 mi.

schwa (shwä; G. shvä) *n.* [G. < Heb. *sh'wā,* a diacritic marking silence instead of a vowel sound] **1.** the neutral, uncolored, central vowel sound of most unstressed syllables in English; sound of *a* in *ago, e* in *agent, i* in *sanity,* etc. **2.** the symbol (ə) used to represent this sound, as in the International Phonetic Alphabet and this dictionary

Schwa·ben (shvä′bən) Ger. *name of* SWABIA

Schwarz·wald (shvärts′vält′) Ger. *name of the* BLACK FOREST

Schweit·zer (shvīt′sər; E. shwīt′sər), **Al·bert** (äl′bert) 1875–1965; Alsatian medical missionary, theologian, & musician in Africa

Schweiz (shvīts) Ger. *name of* SWITZERLAND

Schwe·rin (shvä rēn′) city in NW East Germany: pop. 93,000

Schwyz (shvēts) canton of EC Switzerland, on Lake Lucerne: 351 sq. mi.; pop. 82,000

sci. 1. science **2.** scientific

sci·ae·nid (sī ē′nid) *n.* [< ModL. *Sciaena,* genus name (< L., a kind of fish < Gr. *skiaina*) + -ID] any of a family (Sciaenidae) of mostly saltwater fishes, including the drums and croakers, that make drumming or rumbling sounds —**sci·ae′noid** (-noid) *adj., n.*

sci·am·a·chy (sī am′ə kē) *n., pl.* -**chies** [Gr. *skiamachia* < *skia,* a shadow (see SHINE) + *machein,* to fight (see -MACHY)] a fighting with shadows or imaginary enemies

sci·at·ic (sī at′ik) *adj.* [MFr. *sciatique* < ML. *sciaticus,* altered < L. *ischiadikos* < Gr. *ischiadikos* < *ischion,* the ISCHIUM] of, in the region of, or affecting the hip or its nerves

sci·at·i·ca (sī at′i kə) *n.* [ME. < ML. < *sciaticus*] any painful condition in the region of the hip and thighs; esp., neuritis of the long nerve (**sciatic nerve**) passing down the back of the thigh

sci·ence (sī′əns) *n.* [ME. < OFr. < L. *scientia < sciens,* prp. of *scire,* to know, orig., to discern, distinguish < IE. base **sker-,* to cut, separate, whence OE. *sceadan,* to separate: cf. SCISSION] **1.** orig., the state or fact of knowing; knowledge **2.** systematized knowledge derived from observation, study, and experimentation carried on in order to determine the nature or principles of what is being studied **3.** a branch of knowledge or study, esp. one concerned with establishing and systematizing facts, principles, and methods, as by experiments and hypotheses [the *science* of mathematics] **4.** *a*) the systematized knowledge of nature and the physical world *b*) any branch of this. See NATURAL SCIENCE **5.** skill or technique based upon systematized training [the *science* of cooking] ☆**6.** [S-] *shortened form of* CHRISTIAN SCIENCE

science fiction fiction of a highly imaginative or fantastic kind typically involving some actual or projected scientific phenomenon

sci·en·tial (sī en′shəl) *adj.* **1.** of or producing science, or knowledge **2.** having knowledge

sci·en·tif·ic (sī′ən tif′ik) *adj.* [ML. *scientificus,* learned, lit., making knowledge (see SCIENCE & -FIC), orig. erroneous transl. of Gr. *epistēmonikos,* pertaining to knowledge] **1.** of or dealing with science [*scientific* study] **2.** used in or for natural science [*scientific* apparatus] **3.** *a*) based on, using, or in accordance with, the principles and methods of science; systematic and exact [*scientific* classification] *b*) designating the method of research in which a hypothesis, formulated after systematic, objective collection of data, is tested empirically **4.** *a*) done according to methods gained by systematic training [*scientific* boxing] *b*) having or showing such training —**sci·en·tif′i·cal·ly** *adv.*

sci·en·tism (sī′ən tiz′m) *n.* **1.** the techniques, beliefs, or attitudes characteristic of scientists **2.** the principle that scientific methods can and should be applied in all fields of investigation: often a disparaging usage —**sci·en·tis′tic** *adj.*

sci·en·tist (-tist) *n.* **1.** a specialist in science, as in biology, chemistry, etc. ☆**2.** [S-] a Christian Scientist

☆**sci-fi** (sī′fī′) *adj., n. clipped form of* SCIENCE FICTION

scil·i·cet (sil′i set′) *adv.* [ME. < L., contr. of *scire licet,* it is permitted to know: see SCIENCE & LICENSE] namely; to wit; that is to say

scil·la (sil′ə) *n.* [ModL. < L., SQUILL] any of a genus (*Scilla*) of low, bulbous, perennial plants of the lily family, grown for their blue or white, bell-shaped flowers; esp., **Siberian squill** (*Scilla sibirica*) blooming in early spring

Scil·ly Isles (or Islands) (sil′ē) group of about 140 islets off Cornwall, England: c.6 sq. mi.; pop. 1,800: also called **Isles of Scilly**

scim·i·tar, scim·i·ter (sim′ə tər) *n.* [It. *scimitarra* < ?] a short, curved sword with an edge on the convex side, used chiefly by Turks, Arabs, etc.

scin·coid (siŋ′koid) *adj.* [ModL. *scincoides* < L. *scincus:* see SKINK & -OID] of or like the skinks —*n.* a scincoid lizard

☆**scin·ti·gram** (sin′tə gram′) *n.* [SCINTI(LLATION) + -GRAM] a record made by scintigraphy

☆**scin·tig·ra·phy** (sin tig′rə fē) *n.* [SCINTI(LLATION) + -GRAPHY] a technique for recording with the aid of a scintiscanner the distribution of a radioactive tracer substance in body tissue

scin·til·la (sin til′ə) *n.* [L.] **1.** a spark **2.** a particle; the least trace: used only figuratively

scin·til·late (sin′t'l āt′) *vi.* -**lat′ed,** -**lat′ing** [< L. *scintillatus,* pp. of *scintillare,* to sparkle < *scintilla,* a spark] **1.** to give off sparks; flash; sparkle **2.** to sparkle intellectually; be brilliant and witty **3.** to twinkle, as a star —*vt.* to give off (sparks, flashes, etc.) —**scin′til·lant** *adj.*

scin·til·la·tion (sin′t'l ā′shən) *n.* [L. *scintillatio*] **1.** the act of scintillating; sparkling **2.** a spark; flash **3.** a brilliant display of wit **4.** *Astron.* the twinkling of the stars **5.** *Nuclear Physics* the flash of light made by ionizing radiation upon striking a crystal detector or a phosphor

scintillation counter an instrument for detecting and measuring the scintillations induced by ionizing radiation in a crystal or phosphor

scin·til·la·tor (sin′t'l āt′ər) *n.* **1.** a person or thing that scintillates **2.** *Physics* a crystal or phosphor capable of emitting scintillations

scin·til·lom·e·ter (sin′t'l äm′ə tər) *n.* [< L. *scintilla,* a spark + -METER] *same as* SCINTILLATION COUNTER

☆**scin·ti·scan·ner** (sin′tə skan′ər) *n.* [SCINTI(LLATION) + SCANNER] a type of scintillation counter used to locate and make a record (**scintiscan**) of radioactive substances

sci·o·lism (sī′ə liz′m) *n.* [< L. *sciolus,* smatterer, dim. of *scius,* knowing < *scire,* to know (see SCIENCE)] superficial knowledge or learning —**sci′o·list** *n.* —**sci′o·lis′tic** *adj.*

sci·on (sī′ən) *n.* [ME. *sioun, ciun* < OFr. *cion*, earlier *chion* < ?] **1.** a shoot or bud of a plant, esp. one for planting or grafting **2.** a descendant; offspring

Scip·i·o (sip′ē ō) **1.** (*Publius Cornelius Scipio Africanus*) 237?–183? B.C.; Rom. general: defeated Hannibal (202) in the 2d Punic War: called *Major* or *the Elder* **2.** (*Publius Cornelius Scipio Aemilianus Africanus Numantinus*) 184?–129? B.C.; Rom. general & statesman: destroyed Carthage (146): grandson (through adoption) of *prec.*: called *Minor* or *the Younger*

sci·re fa·ci·as (sī′rē fā′shē as′) [ME. < L., that you cause to know] *Law* **1.** a writ, founded on a record, requiring the person against whom it is issued to appear and show cause why the record should not be enforced or annulled **2.** a proceeding begun by issuing such a writ

scir·rhous (skir′əs, sir′-) *adj.* [ModL. *scirrhosus* < *scirrhus*] of, or having the nature of, a scirrhus; hard and fibrous

scir·rhus (skir′əs, sir′-) *n.*, *pl.* **-rhi** (-ī), **-rhus·es** [ModL. < L. *scirros* < Gr. *skirrhos*, hardened swelling, tumor < *skiros*, hard] a hard, cancerous tumor made up of much fibrous connective tissue —**scir′rhoid** (-oid) *adj.*

scis·sile (sis′il) *adj.* [L. *scissilis* < *scissus*, pp. of *scindere*, to cut: see ff.] that can be cut or split smoothly and easily, as into plates or laminae

scis·sion (sizh′ən, sish′-) *n.* [Fr. < LL. *scissio* < L. *scissus*, pp. of *scindere*, to cut < IE. base *skei-*: cf. SCIENCE] the act of cutting, dividing, or splitting, or the state of being cut, divided, or split; separation; fission

scis·sor (siz′ər) *vt.* [< ff.] to cut, cut off, or cut out with scissors —*n.* same as SCISSORS, esp. in attributive use

scis·sors (siz′ərz) *n.pl.* [ME. *sisoures* < OFr. *cisoires* < LL. *cisoria*, pl. of *cisorium*, cutting tool < L. *caedere*, to cut: Eng. sp. altered after L. *scissor*, one who cuts < *scissus*, pp. of *scindere*, to cut] **1.** [*also with sing.* v.] a cutting instrument, smaller than shears, with two opposing blades, each having a looped handle, which are pivoted together in the middle so that they work against each other as the instrument is closed on the material to be cut: also called **pair of scissors 2.** [*with sing.* v.] *a)* a gymnastic feat or exercise in which the legs are moved in a way suggestive of the opening and closing of scissors *b)* same as SCISSORS HOLD

scissors hold a wrestling hold in which one contestant clasps the other with his legs

scissors kick a swimming kick, used esp. in the sidestroke, in which one leg is bent at the knee and the other thrust backward, then both brought together with a snap

☆**scis·sor·tail** (siz′ər tāl′) *n.* a pale gray and pink variety of flycatcher (*Muscivora forficata*) found in the S U.S. and Mexico, having a forked tail

scis·sure (sizh′ər, sish′-) *n.* [ME. < L. *scissura* < *scindere*, to cut: cf. SCIENCE] [Now Rare] a cleft or opening, either natural or made by cutting

sci·u·rid (sī yoor′id) *n.* [< L. *scirus*, SQUIRREL + -ID] any of a family (Sciuridae) of rodents including the squirrels, ground squirrels, marmots, etc. —**sci·u′roid** *adj.*

sclaff (sklaf, sklåf) *vi.* [< Scot. *sclaf*, to shuffle: of echoic origin] *Golf* to strike or scrape the ground before hitting the ball —*vt. Golf* **1.** to scrape (a club) along (the ground) before hitting the ball **2.** to hit (the ball) in this way —*n.* a sclaffing stroke

SCLC, S.C.L.C. Southern Christian Leadership Conference

scle·ra (sklir′ə) *n.* [ModL. < Gr. *sklēros*, hard < IE. base *(s)kel-*, to dry out, whence SHALLOW] the outer, tough, white, fibrous membrane covering all of the eyeball except the area covered by the cornea —**scle′ral** *adj.*

scle·ren·chy·ma (skli ren′kə mə) *n.* [ModL. < Gr. *sklēros* (see prec.) + *enchyma*, infusion: see PARENCHYMA] *Bot.* plant tissue of uniformly thick-walled, dead cells, as in a stem, the shell of a nut, etc. —**scle·ren·chym·a·tous** (sklir′eŋ kim′ə təs) *adj.*

scle·rite (sklir′īt) *n.* [SCLER(O)- + -ITE[1]] any of the hard plates forming the shell-like covering of arthropods

scle·rit·is (skli rīt′əs) *n.* [SCLER(O)- + -ITIS] inflammation of the sclera

scle·ro- (sklir′ō, skler′-; -ə) [< Gr. *sklēros*, hard: see SCLERA] *a combining form meaning:* **1.** hard [*sclerometer*] **2.** of the sclera Also, before a vowel, **scler-**

scler·o·der·ma (sklir′ə dur′mə, skler′-) *n.* [ModL.: see SCLERO- & DERMA[1]] a chronic disease in which the skin becomes hard and rigid

scler·o·der·ma·tous (-dur′mə təs) *adj. Zool.* covered with a hard outer tissue, as of horny scales or plates

scler·oid (sklir′oid) *adj.* [SCLER(O)- + -OID] *Biol.* hard or hardened; indurated

scle·ro·ma (skli rō′mə) *n.*, *pl.* **-ma·ta** (-mə tə) [ModL. < Gr. *sklērōma*: see SCLERA & -OMA] a hardening of body tissues; tumorlike induration

scle·rom·e·ter (-räm′ə tər) *n.* [SCLERO- + -METER] an instrument for measuring the relative hardness of a substance by determining the pressure needed to cause a diamond point to scratch its polished surface

scle·ro·pro·tein (sklir′ə prō′tēn, skler′-; -prō′tē in) *n.* any of a class of fibrous animal proteins insoluble in water and including the keratins and collagens

scle·rosed (skli rōst′, sklir′ōzd) *adj.* hardened, or indurated, as by sclerosis

scle·ro·sis (skli rō′sis) *n.*, *pl.* **-ses** (-sēz) [ME. *sclirosis* < ML. < Gr. *sklērōsis*, a hardening < *sklēros*, hard: see

SCLERA] 1. *Bot.* a hardening of the cell wall of a plant, usually by an increase of lignin **2.** *Med. a)* an abnormal hardening of body tissues or parts, esp. of the nervous system or the walls of arteries *b)* a disease characterized by such hardening

scle·rot·ic (-rät′ik) *adj.* [ModL. *scleroticus* < Gr. *sklērotēs*, hardness: see SCLERA] **1.** hard; sclerosed **2.** of, characterized by, or having sclerosis **3.** of the sclera

scle·ro·ti·um (skli rō′shē əm) *n.*, *pl.* **-ti·a** (-ə) [ModL. < Gr. *skleros*, hard: see SCLERA] in various fungi, a hardened, black or reddish-brown mass of threads in which food material is stored and which is capable of remaining dormant for long periods —**scle·ro′tial** (-shəl) *adj.*

scle·rot·o·my (skli rät′ə mē) *n.*, *pl.* **-mies** [SCLERO- + -TOMY] surgical incision into the sclera

scle·rous (sklir′əs) *adj.* [< Gr. *sklēros*, hard (see SCLERA) + -OUS] hard; bony

Sc.M. [L. *Scientiae Magister*] Master of Science

scoff[1] (skôf, skäf) *n.* [ME. *scof*, prob. < Scand.: akin to OE. *scop*, a singer, OHG. *skof*, a poem, ridicule: for IE. base see SHOVE] **1.** an expression of mocking contempt, scorn, or derision; jeer **2.** an object of mocking contempt, scorn, etc. —*vt.* to mock at or deride —*vi.* to show mocking contempt, scorn, or derision, esp. by language; jeer (often with *at*) —**scoff′er** *n.* —**scoff′ing·ly** *adv.*
SYN.—**scoff** implies a showing of scorn or contempt as a manifestation of doubt, cynicism, irreverence, etc. [they *scoffed* at his diagnosis of the disease]; **sneer** implies a display of contempt, disparagement, etc., as by a derisive smile or scornful insinuating tone of voice ["You call this a dinner?" he *sneered*]; **jeer** suggests openly insulting, coarse remarks or mocking laughter [the crowd *jeered* at the speaker]; **gibe** implies a taunting or mocking, either in amiable teasing or in sarcastic reproach [he kept *gibing* at me for my clumsiness]; **flout** suggests a treating with contempt or disdain, esp. by ignoring or rejecting [to *flout* the law]

scoff[2] (skôf, skäf) *n.* [< dial. *scaff* < ?] [Chiefly Brit. Slang] food or rations —*vt.*, *vi.* [Slang] **1.** to eat or devour **2.** to plunder or seize

☆**scoff·law** (-lô′) *n.* [SCOFF[1] + LAW] [Colloq.] a habitual or flagrant violator of laws, esp. traffic or liquor laws

scold (skōld) *n.* [ME. *scolde* < ON. *skald*, poet (prob. because of satirical verses)] a person, esp. a woman, who habitually uses abusive language —*vt.* [ME. *scolden* < the *n.*] to find fault with angrily; rebuke or chide severely —*vi.* **1.** to find fault angrily **2.** to use abusive language habitually —**scold′er** *n.* —**scold′ing** *adj.*, *n.*
SYN.—**scold** is the common term meaning to find fault with or rebuke in angry, irritated, often nagging language [a mother *scolds* a naughty child]; **upbraid** implies bitter reproach or censure and usually connotes justification for this [she *upbraided* me for my carelessness]; **berate** suggests continuous, heated, even violent reproach, often connoting excessive abuse [the old shrew continued *berating* them]; **revile** implies the use of highly abusive and contemptuous language and often connotes deliberate defamation or slander [he *reviled* his opponent unmercifully]; **vituperate** suggests even greater violence in the attack [*vituperating* each other with foul epithets]

scol·e·cite (skäl′ə sīt′, skōl′-) *n.* [G. *scolezit* < Gr. *skōlēx*, a worm (see ff.): some forms curl when heated] a zeolite having the formula $CaAl_2Si_3O_{10} \cdot 3H_2O$

sco·lex (skō′leks) *n.*, *pl.* **sco·le·ces** (skə lē′sēz), **sco·li·ces** (skōl′ə sēz′, skäl′-) [ModL. < Gr. *skōlēx*, a grub, worm < IE. base *(s)kel-*, to bend, twist, whence L. *coluber*, serpent] the head of a tapeworm, provided with hooks or suckers and acting as a holdfast in the intestine of a host

sco·li·o·sis (skō′lē ō′sis, skäl′ē-) *n.* [ModL. < Gr. *skoliōsis*, crookedness < *skolios*, crooked, akin to prec.] lateral curvature of the spine —**sco′li·ot′ic** (-ät′ik) *adj.*

scol·lop (skäl′əp) *n.*, *vt. var. of* SCALLOP

scom·broid (skäm′broid) *adj.* [< L. *scomber*, mackerel (< Gr. *skombros*) + -OID] **1.** of a widely distributed family (Scombridae) of spiny-finned food fishes, including the mackerels, bonitos, tunas, etc. **2.** like a mackerel —*n.* a mackerel or related fish

sconce[1] (skäns) *n.* [ME. *sconse*, aphetic < OFr. *esconse*, dark lantern < pp. of *escondre*, to hide < L. *abscondere*: see ABSCOND] a bracket attached to a wall for holding a candle, candles, or the like

sconce[2] (skäns) *n.* [Du. *schans*, a fortress, orig., wickerwork, wicker basket < G. *schanze*] **1.** a small fort, bulwark, etc. **2.** [Archaic] *a)* a hut, shed, or other shelter *b)* a helmet or the like *c)* the head or skull; also, brains; good sense —*vt.* sconced, sconc′ing [Archaic] **1.** to provide with a sconce (sense 1) **2.** to shelter or protect

sconce[3] (skäns) *vt.* sconced, sconc′ing [< ?] to fine; esp., at Oxford University, to fine lightly for a breach of manners —*n.* such a fine

Scone (skōōn, skōn) village in E Perthshire, Scotland: site of an abbey that contained the stone (**Stone of Scone**) on which Scottish kings before 1296 were crowned: removed by Edward I and placed under the coronation chair at Westminster Abbey

scone (skōn) *n.* [Scot., contr. < ? MDu. *schoonbrot*, fine bread < *schoon* (akin to G. *schön*, OE. *scene*), beautiful + *brot*, BREAD] a tea cake, often quadrant-shaped and resembling a baking powder biscuit, usually baked on a griddle, and served with butter

scoop (skōōp) *n.* [ME. *scope* < MDu. *schope*, bailing vessel, *schoppe*, a shovel, akin to G. *schöpfen*, to dip out, create: see SHAPE] **1.** any of various utensils shaped like a small

shovel or a ladle; specif., *a*) a kitchen utensil used to take up sugar, flour, etc. *b*) a small utensil with a round bowl, for dishing up ice cream, mashed potatoes, etc. *c*) a small coal shovel *d*) a small, spoonlike surgical instrument 2. the deep shovel of a dredge or steam shovel, which takes up sand, dirt, etc. 3. the act or motion of taking up with or as with a scoop 4. the amount taken up at one time by a scoop 5. a hollowed-out place; bowl-shaped depression ☆6. [Colloq.] a large profit made by speculation or by a business transaction ☆7. [Colloq.] *a*) advantage gained over a competitor by being first, specif. as in the publication of a news item *b*) such a news item *c*) current, esp. confidential, information —*adj.* designating a rounded, somewhat low neckline in a dress, etc. —*vt.* 1. to take up or out with or as with a scoop 2. to empty by bailing 3. to dig (*out*); hollow (*out*) 4. to make by digging or hollowing out 5. to gather (*in* or *up*) as if with a scoop ☆6. [Colloq.] to effect a scoop (*n.* 7) in competition with —

scoop·ful (-fool′) *n.*, *pl.* **-fuls′** as much as a scoop will hold

scoot (skōōt) *vi.*, *vt.* [prob. via dial. < ON. *skjōta*, to SHOOT] [Colloq.] to go or move quickly; hurry (off); dart —*n.* [Colloq.] the act of scooting

scoot·er (-ər) *n.* [< prec.] 1. a child's toy for riding on, consisting of a low, narrow footboard with a wheel or wheels at each end, and a raised handlebar for steering: it is moved by a series of pushes made by one foot against the ground 2. a somewhat similar vehicle equipped with a seat and propelled by a small internal-combustion engine: in full **motor scooter** ☆3. a sailboat with runners, for use on water or ice

scop (skäp, skōp) *n.* [OE., poet, minstrel, lit., maker of taunting verses: for IE. base see SHOVE] an Old English poet or bard

scope (skōp) *n.* [It. *scopo* < L. *scopus*, a goal, target < Gr. *skopos*, a mark, spy, watcher < base of *skopein*, to see, altered by metathesis < IE. base *spek-*, to peer, look carefully, whence SPY, L. *specere*, to see] 1. the extent of the mind's grasp; range of perception or understanding [a problem beyond his *scope*] 2. the range or extent of action, inquiry, etc., or of an activity, concept, etc. [the *scope* of a book] 3. room or opportunity for freedom of action or thought; free play 4. [Rare] the range of a missile 5. *shortened form of* TELESCOPE, MICROSCOPE, RADARSCOPE, etc. 6. *Naut.* length, extent, or sweep, as of a cable 7. [Now Rare] end; purpose —*SYN.* see RANGE

-scope (skōp) [LL. *-scopium* < Gr. *-skopion* < *skopein*: see prec.] *a combining form meaning* an instrument, etc. for seeing or observing [*telescope*]

sco·pol·a·mine (skō päl′ə mēn′, -min) *n.* [G. *Scopolamin* < ModL. *Scopolia*, genus of plants in which the alkaloid appears (after G. A. *Scopoli* (1723–88), of Pavia, Italy) + G. *amin*, AMINE] an alkaloid, C₁₇H₂₁O₄N, obtained from various plants of the nightshade family, as belladonna, and used in medicine as a sedative, hypnotic, and sometimes with morphine to relieve pain

scop·u·la (skäp′yōō lə) *n.*, *pl.* **-las**, **-lae′** (-lē′) [ModL. < L., broom twig, dim. of *scopa*, thin branch, shoot] *Zool.* a brushlike tuft or row of hairs, as on some spiders — **scop′u·late** (-lit) *adj.*

-sco·py (skə pē) [Gr. *-skopia* < *skopein*: see SCOPE] *a combining form meaning* a seeing, observing, examination [*bioscopy*]

scor·bu·tic (skôr byōōt′ik) *adj.* [ModL. *scorbuticus* < ML. *scorbutus*, scurvy < Russ. *skorbut*, to wither, grow ill < IE. *(s)kerb(h)-*: see SHARP, SCURF] of, like, or having scurvy: also **scor·bu′ti·cal**

scorch (skôrch) *vt.* [ME. *scorchen* < ? Scand., as in ON. *scorpna*, to shrivel (< IE. *(s)kerb(h)-*: see SHARP): sp. prob. infl. by OFr. *escorcher*, to flay] 1. *a*) to char, discolor, or damage the surface of by superficial burning *b*) to parch, shrivel, or spoil by too intense heat; wither 2. to make a caustic attack on; assail scathingly; excoriate 3. to burn and destroy everything in (an area) before yielding it to the enemy [a *scorched* earth policy] —*vi.* 1. to become scorched 2. [Old Slang] to ride or drive at high speed —*n.* 1. a superficial burning or burn 2. the browning and death of plant leaves or fruits, caused by too much heat, by fungi, etc. —*SYN.* see BURN¹

scorch·er (-ər) *n.* anything that scorches; esp., [Colloq.] *a*) a very hot day *b*) a withering remark

score (skôr) *n.* [ME. < OE. *scoru* < ON. *skor*: for IE. base see SHEAR] 1. *a*) a scratch, mark, incision, etc. [*scores* made on ice by skates] *b*) a line drawn or scratched, often to mark a starting point, etc. *c*) notches made in wood, marks made as with chalk, etc., to keep tally or account 2. an amount or sum due; account; debt 3. a grievance or wrong one seeks to settle or get even for 4. anything offered as a reason or motive; ground [on the *score* of poverty] 5. the number of points made in a game or contest by a player or team, or the record of these points 6. *a*) a grade or rating, as on a test or examination *b*) a number indicative of quality, usually based on an arbitrary scale in which 100 means perfection in certain specified characteristics [92 *score* butter] 7. *a*) twenty

people or things; set of twenty *b*) [*pl.*] very many 8. [Colloq.] a successful move, stroke, remark, etc. ☆9. [Colloq.] *a*) the way that life or a certain situation really is; real facts: chiefly in **know the score** *b*) the pertinent facts; lowdown 10. [Slang] the victim of a swindle; mark 11. *Dancing* notation used to indicate dancers' movements, as in a ballet 12. *Music a*) a written or printed copy of a composition, showing all the parts for the instruments or voices *b*) the music for a stage production, motion picture, etc., esp. as distinguished from the lyrics, dialogue, etc. —*vt.* **scored, scor′ing** [ME. *scoren*] 1. to mark with notches, scratches, cuts, lines, etc. 2. to crease or partly cut (cardboard, paper, etc.) for accurate folding or tearing 3. to cancel or mark out by lines drawn (with *out*) 4. to mark with lines or notches in keeping account 5. to keep account of by or as by lines or notches; reckon; tally; mark 6. *a*) to make (runs, hits, goals, etc.) in a game and so add to one's number of points *b*) to count toward the number of points [a touchdown *scores* 6] *c*) to record or enter the score of *d*) to record or add (points) to one's score ☆*e*) *Baseball* to bring (a runner) home on one's hit 7. to get by effort or merit; gain [to *score* a resounding success] 8. to grade (an examination, etc.); rate or evaluate, as in testing 9. *a*) to raise welts on by lashing ☆*b*) to criticize severely; upbraid 10. *Cooking* to cut superficial gashes in (meat, etc.) 11. *Music, Dancing* to orchestrate, arrange, or write out in a score —*vi.* 1. to make a point or points, as in a game 2. to run up a score 3. to keep the score, as of a game 4. *a*) to gain an advantage *b*) to win or enjoy credit, popularity, success, etc. 5. to make notches, lines, gashes, etc. —**scor′er** *n.*

score·board (-bôrd′) *n.* ☆a large board for posting the score and other details of a game, as in a baseball stadium

☆**score card** 1. a card for recording the score of a game, match, etc., as in golf 2. a card printed with the names, positions, etc. of the players of competing teams Also **score′card′** (-kärd′) *n.*

☆**score·keep·er** (-kēp′ər) *n.* a person keeping score, esp. officially, at a game, competition, etc.

score·less (-lis) *adj.* having scored no points

sco·ri·a (skôr′ē ə) *n.*, *pl.* **-ri·ae′** (-ē′) [ME. < L. < Gr. *skōria*, refuse, dross < *skōr*, dung: see SCATO-] 1. the slag or refuse left after metal has been smelted from ore 2. loose, cinderlike lava —**sco′ri·a′ceous** (-ā′shəs) *adj.*

sco·ri·fy (skôr′ə fi′) *vt.* **-fied′, -fy′ing** to reduce to scoria, or slag —**sco′ri·fi·ca′tion** *n.*

scorn (skôrn) *n.* [ME. < OFr. *escharn < escharnir*, to scorn < Gmc. base akin to OHG. *skernon*, to mock, *scern*, a joke < IE. base *(s)ker-*, to leap, jump about, whence Gr. *skairein*, to jump, dance] 1. extreme, often indignant, contempt for someone or something; utter disdain 2. expression of this in words or manner 3. the object of such contempt —*vt.* 1. to regard with scorn; view or treat with contempt 2. to refuse or reject as wrong or disgraceful —*vi.* [Obs.] to scoff; mock —*SYN.* see DESPISE —**laugh to scorn** to jeer at with contempt; ridicule —**scorn′er** *n.*

scorn·ful (-fəl) *adj.* filled with or showing scorn or contempt —**scorn′ful·ly** *adv.* —**scorn′ful·ness** *n.*

scor·pae·nid (skôr pē′nid) *n.* [< L. *scorpaena*, kind of fish < Gr. *skorpaina*, fem. of *skorpios*, a spiny fish (see SCORPION) + -ID] any of a family (Scorpaenidae) of spiny-finned sea fishes, including the scorpion fishes, the rock-fishes, etc. —**scor·pae′noid** (-noid) *adj.*, *n.*

Scor·pi·o (skôr′pē ō′) [L., lit., SCORPION] 1. a S constellation north of Ophiuchus, containing Antares: also **Scor′-pi·us** (-əs) 2. *Astrol.* the eighth sign of the zodiac (♏), which the sun enters about October 24: see ZODIAC, illus.

scor·pi·oid (-oid′) *adj.* [Gr. *skorpioeidēs*] 1. like a scorpion 2. of the order consisting of the scorpions 3. with a curved end, like a scorpion's tail; circinate

scor·pi·on (-ən) *n.* [ME. < OFr. < L. *scorpio* < Gr. *skorpios*, scorpion, kind of fish < IE. base *(s)ker-*, to cut, whence SHEAR] 1. any of an order (Scorpionida) of arachnids found in warm regions, with a front pair of nipping claws and a long, slender, jointed tail ending in a curved, poisonous sting 2. *Bible* a variety of whip or scourge —[S-] same as SCORPIO

SCORPION
(to 10 in. long)

scorpion fish any of various scorpaenoid fishes; specif., any of a genus (*Scorpaena*) of chiefly tropical ocean fishes with poisonous rays on the dorsal, anal, and ventral fins

scorpion fly any of an order (Mecoptera) of insects whose abdomen, in the male, curls up at the end and resembles a scorpion's sting

Scot (skät) *n.* [< ME. *Scottes*, pl. < OE. *Scottas* < LL. *Scoti*, a people in N Britain] 1. any member of a Gaelic tribe of northern Ireland that migrated to Scotland in the 5th cent. A.D. 2. a native or inhabitant of Scotland: cf. SCOTSMAN, SCOTCHMAN

scot (skät) *n.* [ME. < ON. *skot*, tribute, SHOT¹] money

assessed or paid; tax; levy —**scot and lot 1.** an old parish tax in Great Britain, assessed according to ability to pay **2.** in full: in the phrase **pay scot and lot**

Scot. 1. Scotch **2.** Scottish **3.** Scottish

Scotch (skäch) *adj.* [contr. < SCOTTISH] of Scotland, its people, their language, etc.; Scottish: cf. SCOTTISH —*n.* **1.** *same as* SCOTTISH **2.** *same as* SCOTCH WHISKY —**the Scotch** the Scottish people

scotch[1] (skäch) *vt.* [ME. *scocchen,* prob. < Anglo-Fr. *escocher* < OFr. *coche,* a notch, nick < VL. **cocca,* knob at the end of a spindle (later, groove below this knob) < L. *coccum,* a berry < Gr. *kokkos*] **1.** to cut; scratch; score; notch **2.** [< Theobald's emendation of *scorch* in Shakespeare's *Macbeth,* III, ii, 13] to wound without killing; maim **3.** to put an end to; stifle; stamp out [to *scotch* a rumor] —*n.* a cut or scratch

scotch[2] (skäch) *vt.* [< ?] to block (a wheel, log, etc.) with a wedge, block, etc. to prevent movement —*n.* such a block, wedge, etc. used to prevent rolling, slipping, etc.

Scotch broth a broth of mutton and vegetables, thickened with barley

Scotch grain a coarse, pebble-grained finish given to heavy leather, esp. for men's shoes

☆**Scotch-I·rish** (ī'rish) *adj.* designating or of those people of northern Ireland descended from Scottish settlers, esp. those who emigrated to America —**the Scotch-Irish** Scotch-Irish persons

Scotch·man (-mən) *n., pl.* **-men** (-mən) *var. of* SCOTSMAN

Scotch pine a hardy Eurasian pine (*Pinus sylvestris*), with yellow or orange wood, much cultivated for timber, Christmas trees, etc.

☆**Scotch tape** [< *Scotch,* a trademark] a thin, transparent, cellulose adhesive tape

Scotch terrier *same as* SCOTTISH TERRIER

Scotch verdict a verdict in criminal cases of "not proved," rather than "not guilty": allowed in some jurisdictions, notably Scotland

Scotch whisky whiskey, often having a smoky flavor, distilled in Scotland from malted barley

Scotch woodcock eggs cooked and served on toast or crackers spread with anchovies or anchovy paste

sco·ter (skōt'ər) *n., pl.* **-ters, -ter:** see PLURAL, II, D, 1 [< ?] any of several large, dark-colored sea ducks (genera *Oidemia* and *Melanitta*), found chiefly along the N coasts of Europe and N. America

scot-free (skät'frē') *adj.* **1.** free from payment of scot, or tax **2.** unharmed or unpunished; clear; safe

Sco·tia (skō'shə) *n.* [LL.] *poet. term for* SCOTLAND

sco·ti·a (skō'shə, -shē ə) *n.* [L. < Gr. *skotia,* darkness (from the shadow within the cavity): see SHADE] a deep concave molding, esp. at the base of a column

Sco·tism (skōt'iz'm) *n.* the scholastic philosophy of Duns Scotus and his followers, which sharply separates philosophy from theology and makes God's reason and goodness an expression of divine will —**Sco'tist** *adj., n.*

Scot·land (skät'lənd) division of the United Kingdom, north of England, occupying the N half of Great Britain & nearby islands: 30,405 sq. mi.; pop. 5,187,000; cap. Edinburgh

Scotland Yard 1. short street in London, off Whitehall, orig. the site of police headquarters **2.** headquarters of the metropolitan London police, on the Thames embankment since 1890: officially, **New Scotland Yard 3.** the London police, esp. the detective bureau

sco·to·ma (skə tō'mə) *n., pl.* **-ma·ta** (-mə tə), **-mas** [ModL. < LL., dimness of vision < Gr. *skotōma < skotos,* darkness (see SHADE) + -OMA] a dark area or gap in the visual field —**sco·tom'a·tous** (-täm'ə təs, -tō'mə-) *adj.*

sco·to·pi·a (skə tō'pē ə) *n.* [ModL. < Gr. *skotos* (see prec.) + -OPIA] adjustment of the eye to dim light; twilight vision —**sco·top'ic** (-tō'pik, -täp'ik) *adj.*

Scots (skäts) *adj.* [ME., (northern) *Scottis,* var. of *Scottissh*] *same as* SCOTTISH —*n. same as* SCOTTISH

Scots·man (skäts'mən) *n., pl.* **-men** (-mən) a native or inhabitant of Scotland, esp. a man: *Scotsman* or *Scot* is preferred to *Scotchman* in Scotland —**Scots'wom'an** *n.fem., pl.* **-wom'en**

Scott (skät) **1. Dred** (dred), 1795?–1858; U.S. Negro slave: his claim to be free as a result of living in free territory was denied in a controversial Supreme Court decision (1857) **2. Robert Fal·con** (fôl'kən), 1868–1912; Eng. naval officer & antarctic explorer **3. Sir Walter,** 1771–1832; Scot. poet & novelist **4. Win·field** (win'fēld), 1786–1866; U.S. general

Scot·ti·cism (skät'ə siz'm) *n.* a Scottish idiom, expression, word, pronunciation, etc.

Scot·tie, Scot·ty (skät'ē) *n., pl.* **-ties** *colloq. clipped form of* SCOTTISH TERRIER

Scot·tish (skät'ish) *adj.* [ME. *Scottissh* < Late OE. *Scottisc,* for earlier *Scyttisc*] of Scotland, its people, their English dialect, etc.: *Scottish,* the original form, is preferred to *Scotch* and *Scots* in U.S. and British formal and literary usage with reference to the people, the country, etc., and in Scotland has replaced *Scotch,* the colloquial form prevailing in the U.S. and England; but with some words, *Scotch* is almost invariably used (e.g., tweed, whisky), with others, *Scots* (e.g., law, mile) —*n.* the dialect of English spoken by the people of Scotland —**the Scottish** the Scottish people

Scottish Gaelic the Celtic language of the Scottish Highlands: see GAELIC

Scottish rite a system of ceremonial procedure in Freemasonry

Scottish terrier any of a breed of terriers with short legs, a squarish muzzle, rough, wiry hair, and pointed, erect ears

Scotts·dale (skäts'dāl') [after Rev. Winfield *Scott,* a chaplain in the Civil War] city in SC Ariz.: suburb of Phoenix: pop. 68,000

Scotus see DUNS SCOTUS

scoun·drel (skoun'drəl) *n.* [prob. < a disparaging dim. < Anglo-Fr. *escoundre* (for OFr. *escondre*), to abscond < VL. **scondere,* aphetic for L. *abscondere,* ABSCOND] a mean, immoral, or wicked person; rascal; villain —*adj.* characteristic of a scoundrel; mean: also **scoun'drel·ly**

scour[1] (skour) *vt.* [ME. *scouren* < MDu. *scuren* < ? OFr. *escurer* < VL. **excurare,* to take great care of < L. *ex-,* intens. + *curare,* to take care of < *cura,* care] **1.** to clean or polish by vigorous rubbing, as with abrasives, soap and water, etc.; make clean and bright **2.** to remove dirt and grease from (wool, etc.) **3.** *a*) to wash or clear as by a swift current of water; flush *b*) to wash away, or remove in this way **4.** to clear the intestines of; purge **5.** to clean (wheat) **6.** to remove as if by cleaning; sweep away; get rid of —*vi.* **1.** to clean things by vigorous rubbing and polishing **2.** to become clean and bright by being scoured —*n.* **1.** the act of scouring **2.** a cleansing agent used in scouring **3.** a scoured place, as a part of a channel where mud has been washed away **4.** [*usually pl.,* with *sing. v.*] dysentery in cattle, etc. —**scour'er** *n.*

scour[2] (skour) *vt.* [ME. *scouren* < ? OFr. *escourre,* to run forth < VL. **excurrere* < L. *ex-,* out + *currere,* to run] to pass over quickly, or range over or through, as in search or pursuit [to *scour* a town for an escaped convict] —*vi.* to run or range about, as in search or pursuit —**scour'er** *n.*

scourge (skurj) *n.* [ME. < OFr. *escorgie* < L. *ex,* off, from + *corrigia,* a strap, whip] **1.** a whip or other instrument for flogging **2.** any means of inflicting severe punishment, suffering, or vengeance **3.** any cause of serious trouble or affliction [the *scourge* of war] —*vt.* scourged, scourg'ing **1.** to whip or flog **2.** to punish, chastise, or afflict severely —**scourg'er** *n.*

☆**scour·ing rush** (skour'in) *same as* HORSETAIL (sense 2), esp. a species (*Equisetum hyemale*) formerly used to polish metal and wood

scour·ings (-inz) *n.pl.* dirt, refuse, or remains removed by or as if by scouring

scouse (skous) *n. shortened form of* LOBSCOUSE

scout[1] (skout) *n.* [ME. *scoute* < OFr. *escoute* < *escouter, escolter,* to hear < L. *auscultare,* to listen: see AUSCULTATION] **1.** a soldier, ship, or plane sent to spy out the strength, movements, etc. of the enemy ☆**2.** a person sent out to observe the tactics of an opponent, to search out new talent, etc. [a baseball *scout*] **3.** a member of the Boy Scouts or Girl Scouts **4.** the act of reconnoitering **5.** [Slang] fellow; guy —*vt.* **1.** to follow closely so as to spy upon **2.** to look for; watch **3.** to find or get by looking around (often with *out, up*) —*vi.* **1.** to go out in search of information about the enemy; reconnoiter **2.** to go in search of something; hunt [*scout* around for some firewood] ☆**3.** to work as a scout (*n.* 2) **4.** to participate actively in the Boy Scouts or Girl Scouts —**scout'er** *n.*

scout[2] (skout) *vt.* [prob. via dial. < ON. *skuti,* a taunt, term of abuse, akin to SHOUT] to reject as absurd; flout; scoff at —*vi.* to scoff (*at*); jeer

☆**scout car** an armored military reconnaissance car

scout·craft (skout'kraft', -kräft') *n.* the art or practice of scouting; esp., active participation in the Boy Scouts or Girl Scouts: also **scout'ing**

scout·hood (-hood') *n.* **1.** the state of being a Boy Scout or Girl Scout **2.** the character or characteristics of Boy Scouts or Girl Scouts

scout·mas·ter (-mas'tər, -mäs'-) *n.* the adult leader of a troop of Boy Scouts

☆**scow** (skou) *n.* [Du. *schouw,* lit., boat which is poled along, akin to LowG. *schalde,* punt pole < IE. **skoldha-,* a pole, branch cut off < base **(s)kel-,* to cut, whence HALF, L. *scalpere,* to scratch, slit] a large, flat-bottomed boat with square ends, used for carrying coal, sand, etc. and often towed by a tug

scowl (skoul) *vi.* [ME. *scoulen,* prob. < Scand., as in Dan. *skule,* in same sense, akin to MHG. *schulen,* to be hidden, lurk < IE. **(s)kulo-,* concealment < base **(s)keu-,* to cover] **1.** to contract the eyebrows and lower the corners of the mouth in showing displeasure; look angry, irritated, or sullen **2.** to have a threatening look; lower —*vt.* to affect, influence, or express with a scowl or scowls —*n.* **1.** the act or expression of scowling; angry frown **2.** a threatening or gloomy aspect —*SYN.* see FROWN —**scowl'er** *n.* —**scowl'ing·ly** *adv.*

scr. scruple (the weight)

scrab·ble (skrab''l) *vi.* **-bled, -bling** [Du. *schrabbelen < schrabben,* to scrape: for IE. base see SCRAPE] **1.** to scratch, scrape, or paw as though looking for something **2.** to struggle **3.** to scribble; make meaningless marks —*vt.* **1.** to scrape together quickly **2.** *a*) to scribble *b*) to scribble on —*n.* **1.** a scraping with the hands or paws **2.** a scramble **3.** a scribble; scrawl **4.** a struggle —☆[S-] *a trademark for* a word game played with lettered tiles placed as in a crossword puzzle —**scrab'bler** *n.*

scrab·bly (-lē) *adj.* **-bli·er, -bli·est** [Colloq.] **1.** having a scratching sound **2.** scrubby, paltry, poor, etc.

scrag (skrag) *n.* [prob. < ON., as in Norw. *skragg*, feeble, stunted person, Dan. *skrog*, ON. *skröggr*, a fox (nickname) < IE. base *(s)ker-*, to shrivel, shrink] **1.** a lean, scrawny person or animal **2.** a thin, stunted tree or plant **3.** the neck, or back of the neck, of mutton, veal, etc. **4.** [Slang] the human neck —*vt.* **scragged, scrag′ging** [Slang] to choke or wring the neck of; hang; throttle; garrote

scrag·gly (skrag′lē) *adj.* **-gli·er, -gli·est** [see ff. & -LY²] sparse, scrubby, irregular, uneven, ragged, etc. in growth or form [*a scraggly beard*] —**scrag′gli·ness** *n.*

scrag·gy (skrag′ē) *adj.* **-gi·er, -gi·est** [< SCRAG + -Y²] **1.** rough or jagged **2.** lean; bony; skinny —**scrag′gi·ly** *adv.* —**scrag′gi·ness** *n.*

☆**scram** (skram) *vi.* **scrammed, scram′ming** [contr. of ff.] [Slang] to leave or get out, esp. in a hurry: often used in the imperative

scram·ble (skram′b'l) *vi.* **-bled, -bling** [< ? SCAMPER + SCRABBLE] **1.** to climb, crawl, or clamber hurriedly **2.** to scuffle or struggle for something, as for coins scattered on the ground **3.** to struggle or rush pell-mell, as to get something highly prized [to *scramble* for political office] **4.** to get aircraft into the air quickly to intercept enemy planes ☆**5.** *Football* to maneuver about in the backfield while seeking an open receiver to whom to pass the ball —*vt.* **1.** *a)* to throw together haphazardly; mix in a confused way; jumble *b)* *Electronics* to modify (transmitted auditory or visual signals) so as to make unintelligible without special receiving equipment **2.** to gather haphazardly; collect without method (often with *up*) ☆**3.** to cook (eggs) while stirring the mixed whites and yolks **4.** to order or get (aircraft) into the air quickly to intercept enemy planes —*n.* **1.** a hard, hurried climb or advance, as over rough, difficult ground **2.** a disorderly struggle or rush, as for something prized **3.** a disorderly heap; jumble **4.** a quick takeoff of interceptor aircraft —**scram′bler** *n.*

☆**scram·jet** (skram′jet′) *n.* [*s(upersonic) c(ombustion) ram-jet*] a ramjet that burns its fuel in an airstream moving at supersonic speed

scran·nel (skran′'l) *adj.* [< Scand., akin to Norw. *skran*, wretched < IE. base *(s)ker-*, to shrink, wrinkle: cf. SCRAG] [Archaic] **1.** thin, lean, or slight **2.** harsh and unmusical

Scran·ton (skrant′'n) [family name of the founders of a local ironworks] city in NE Pa.: pop. 104,000

scrap¹ (skrap) *n.* [ME. *scrappe* < ON. *skrap*, scraps, trifles < *skrapa*, to SCRAPE] **1.** a small piece; bit; fragment; shred **2.** a bit of something written or printed; brief extract **3.** *a)* discarded metal in the form of machinery, auto parts, etc. suitable only for reprocessing *b)* discarded articles or fragments of rubber, leather, cloth, paper, etc. **4.** [*pl.*] *a)* bits of leftover food *b)* the crisp remnants of animal fat after the oil has been removed by rendering —*adj.* **1.** in the form of fragments, pieces, odds and ends, or leftovers **2.** used and discarded —*vt.* **scrapped, scrap′ping 1.** to make into scrap; break up **2.** to get rid of or abandon as useless; discard; junk

scrap² (skrap) *n.* [prob. < *scrape*, orig., nefarious scheme: cant term] [Colloq.] a fight or quarrel —*vi.* **scrapped, scrap′ping** [Colloq.] to fight or quarrel

scrap·book (-book′) *n.* a book of blank pages for mounting newspaper clippings, pictures, souvenirs, etc.

scrape (skrāp) *vt.* **scraped, scrap′ing** [ME. *scrapen* < ON. *skrapa*, akin to Du. *schrapen*, OE. *screpan*, to scratch < IE. base *(s)ker-*, to cut: cf. SCURF, SHARP] **1.** to rub over the surface of with something rough or sharp **2.** to make smooth or clean by rubbing with a tool or abrasive **3.** to remove by rubbing with something sharp or rough (with *off, out,* etc.) **4.** to scratch or abrade by a rough, rubbing contact [to fall and *scrape* one's knee] **5.** to rub with a harsh, grating sound [chalk *scraping* a blackboard] **6.** to dig, esp. with the hands and nails **7.** to collect or gather slowly and with difficulty [to *scrape* together some money] —*vi.* **1.** to scrape something so as to remove dirt, etc. **2.** to rub against something harshly; grate **3.** to give out a harsh, grating noise **4.** to collect or gather goods or money slowly and with difficulty **5.** to manage to get by; survive (with *through, along, by*) **6.** to draw the foot back along the ground in bowing —*n.* **1.** the act of scraping **2.** a scraped place; abrasion or scratch **3.** the noise of scraping; harsh, grating sound **4.** a disagreeable or embarrassing situation; predicament, esp. when caused by one's own conduct **5.** a fight or conflict —**scrap′er** *n.*

scrap·heap (skrap′hēp′) *n.* a pile of discarded material, as of scrap iron —**throw** (or **toss, cast,** etc.) **on the scrap-heap** to discard or get rid of as useless

scrap·ing (skrā′piŋ) *n.* **1.** the act of a person or thing that scrapes **2.** the sound of this **3.** [usually *pl.*] something scraped off, together, or up

scrap iron discarded or waste pieces of iron, to be recast or reworked

scrap·per¹ (skrap′ər) *n.* a person or thing that scraps

scrap·per² (-ər) *n.* [Colloq.] a ready or effective fighter

☆**scrap·ple** (skrap′'l) *n.* [dim. of SCRAP¹] cornmeal boiled with scraps of pork, allowed to set, sliced, and fried

scrap·py¹ (skrap′ē) *adj.* **-pi·er, -pi·est** [< SCRAP¹ + -Y²] **1.** made of scraps; consisting of odds and ends **2.** disconnected; disjointed [*scrappy* memories] —**scrap′pi·ly** *adv.* —**scrap′pi·ness** *n.*

scrap·py² (skrap′ē) *adj.* **-pi·er, -pi·est** [< SCRAP² + -Y²] [Colloq.] fond of fighting, arguing, etc.; aggressive —**scrap′pi·ly** *adv.* —**scrap′pi·ness** *n.*

Scratch (skrach) [altered (after ff.) < ME. *skratte* < ON. *skratti*, monster, sorcerer, akin to OHG. *scraz*, goblin: for IE. base see SCRANNEL] [sometimes s-] the Devil: usually **Old Scratch**

scratch (skrach) *vt.* [LME. *scracchen*, prob. altered < *scratten*, to scratch, after *cracchen* < or akin to MDu. *cratsen*, to scratch < IE. base *gred-*, whence Alb. *gërüj*, (I) scratch] **1.** to mark, break, or cut the surface of slightly with something pointed or sharp **2.** to tear or dig with the nails or claws **3.** *a)* to rub or scrape lightly, as with the fingernails, to relieve itching, etc. *b)* to chafe **4.** to rub or scrape with a grating noise [to *scratch* a match on a wall] **5.** to write or draw hurriedly or carelessly **6.** to strike out or cancel (writing, etc.) **7.** to gather or collect with difficulty; scrape (*together* or *up*) ☆**8.** *Politics* to strike out the name of (a candidate) on (a party ticket or ballot) in voting other than a straight ticket **9.** *Sports* to withdraw (an entry) from a contest, specif. from a horse race —*vi.* **1.** to use nails or claws in digging or wounding **2.** to rub or scrape the skin lightly, as with the fingernails, to relieve itching, etc. **3.** to manage to get by; scrape by **4.** to make a harsh, scraping noise **5.** to withdraw from a race or contest **6.** in certain card games, to score no points **7.** *Billiards, Pool* to commit a scratch —*n.* **1.** the act of scratching **2.** a mark or tear made in a surface by something sharp or rough **3.** a wound, usually superficial, inflicted by nails, claws, or something pointed pulled across the skin, etc. **4.** a slight grating or scraping sound **5.** a hasty mark, as of a pen; scribble **6.** the starting line of a race **7.** in certain card games, a score of zero ☆**8.** [Slang] money **9.** *Billiards, Pool a)* a shot that results in a penalty *b)* a miss **10.** *Sports a)* the starting point or time of a contestant who receives no handicap *b)* such a contestant *c)* an entry withdrawn from a contest —*adj.* ☆**1.** used for hasty notes, preliminary or tentative figuring, etc. [*scratch* paper] **2.** starting from scratch; having no handicap or allowance in a contest **3.** put together in haste and without much selection [a *scratch* team] ☆**4.** *Baseball* designating a chance hit credited to a batter for a ball not hit sharply, but on which the batter reaches base safely —**from scratch 1.** from the starting line, as in a race **2.** from nothing; without advantage —**scratch the surface** to do, consider, or affect something superficially —**up to scratch 1.** toeing the mark; ready to start a race, contest, etc. **2.** [Colloq.] ready to meet difficulties, start on an enterprise, etc. **3.** [Colloq.] up to standard; acceptable; good —**scratch′er** *n.*

☆**scratch·board** (-bôrd′) *n.* chalk-covered cardboard with a glossy finish, on which line drawings in ink can be altered by scratching out parts

scratch line 1. the starting line of a race ☆**2.** a line that must not be overstepped in certain contests, as the long jump or javelin throw

scratch test a test for determining substances to which a person is allergic, made by rubbing allergens into small scratches or punctures in the skin

scratch·y (skrach′ē) *adj.* **scratch′i·er, scratch′i·est 1.** having the appearance of being drawn roughly, hurriedly, etc.; made with scratches **2.** making a scratching or scraping noise **3.** scratched together; haphazard **4.** that scratches, scrapes, chafes, itches, etc. [*scratchy* cloth] —**scratch′i·ly** *adv.* —**scratch′i·ness** *n.*

scrawl (skrôl) *vt., vi.* [< ?] to write, draw, or mark awkwardly, hastily, or carelessly; esp., to write with sprawling, poorly formed letters —*n.* **1.** sprawling, often illegible handwriting **2.** something scrawled —**scrawl′er** *n.* —**scrawl′y** *adj.* **scrawl′i·er, scrawl′i·est**

scraw·ny (skrô′nē) *adj.* **-ni·er, -ni·est** [prob. var. of dial. *scranny*, lean, thin < Scand.: see SCRANNEL] **1.** very thin; skinny and bony **2.** stunted or scrubby —SYN. see LEAN² —**scraw′ni·ness** *n.*

screak (skrēk) *vi.* [ON. *skraekja*: cf. SHRIEK, SCREECH] to screech or creak —*n.* a screech or creak

scream (skrēm) *vi.* [ME. *screamen*, akin to WFl. *schreemen*, to scream, G. *schrei*, a cry < IE. *skerei-* < echoic base *(s)ker-*, whence SHRIEK, RAVEN¹, RING¹] **1.** *a)* to utter a shrill, loud, piercing cry in fright, pain, etc. *b)* to make or move with a shrill, piercing sound **2.** to laugh loudly or hysterically **3.** to have a startling effect; leave a vivid impression **4.** to shout or yell in anger, hysteria, etc. —*vt.* **1.** to utter with or as with a scream or screams **2.** to bring into a specified state by screaming [to *scream* oneself hoarse] —*n.* **1.** *a)* a sharp, piercing cry; shriek *b)* any shrill, piercing sound **2.** [Colloq.] a person or thing considered hilariously funny

SYN.—**scream** is the general word for a loud, high, piercing cry, as in fear, pain, or anger; **shriek** suggests a sharper, more sudden cry than **scream** and connotes either extreme terror or pain or

loud, high-pitched, unrestrained laughter; **screech** suggests an unpleasantly shrill or harsh cry painful to the hearer

scream·er (-ər) *n.* **1.** a person who screams ☆**2.** [Slang] a sensational headline **3.** *Printing* [Slang] an exclamation point **4.** any of a primitive family (Anhimidae) of long-toed, gooselike S. American wading birds

scream·ing (-iŋ) *adj.* **1.** that screams **2.** startling in effect **3.** causing screams of laughter —**scream′ing·ly** *adv.*

☆**screaming mee·mies** (mē′mēz) [< SCREAMING + echoic reduplication: orig. used of German shells in World War I] [Slang] extreme nervous tension

scree (skrē) *n.* [back-formation < pl. *screes* < earlier *screethes* < ON. *skritha*, a landslide < *skritha*, to slide, creep, akin to G. *schreiten*, to step < IE. base *(s)ker-*, to turn, bend] *same as* TALUS² (sense 3)

screech (skrēch) *vi.* [ME. *scrichen* < ON. *skraekja:* for IE. base see SCREAM] to utter or make a shrill, high-pitched, harsh shriek or sound —*vt.* to utter with a screech —*n.* a shrill, high-pitched, harsh shriek or sound —*SYN.* see SCREAM —**screech′er** *n.* —**screech′y** *adj.*

screech owl ☆**1.** any of a genus (*Otus*) of small, N. American owls; esp., a small, gray or reddish-brown owl (*Otus asio*) with feathered ear tufts and an eerie, wailing cry rather than a hoot **2.** [Brit.] *same as* BARN OWL

screed (skrēd) *n.* [ME. *screde*, var. *schrede*, SHRED: sense from "long list on a strip of paper"] **1.** a long, tiresome speech or piece of writing **2.** a strip of wood or plaster put on a wall to gauge the thickness of plastering to be done **3.** [Scot.] a torn place; rent

screen (skrēn) *n.* [ME. *skrene*, a sieve, curtain < OFr. *escren* < Gmc., as in OHG. *scerm* (G. *schirm*), a guard, protection, screen < IE. base *(s)ker-*, to cut, whence SHEAR, SCORE] **1.** *a)* a light, movable, covered frame or series of frames hinged together, serving as a portable partition to separate, conceal, shelter, or protect *b)* any partition or curtain serving such a purpose **2.** anything that functions to shield, protect, or conceal like a curtain *[a smoke screen]* **3.** a coarse mesh of wire, etc., used to sift out finer from coarser parts, as of sand or coal; sieve **4.** a system for screening or separating different types of persons, etc. **5.** a frame covered with a mesh, as of wire or plastic, used to keep insects out, serve as a barrier, etc. as on a window **6.** *a)* a usually white, flat surface, as a sheet of beaded vinyl, upon which motion pictures, slides, etc. are projected *b)* the motion-picture industry or art **7.** the surface area of a television or radar receiver on which the light pattern is traced **8.** any protective formation, as of military troops sent out to protect an area or cover troop movements, or of light naval vessels, as destroyers, surrounding heavier ones, as carriers **9.** *Photoengraving* in the halftone process, a set of two glass plates cemented together so that parallel lines engraved in one plate are at right angles to the lines of the other plate **10.** *Physics* a device used as a shield to prevent interference of some sort ☆**11.** *Psychoanalysis* a form of concealment, as a person in a dream who stands for another or others with whom he has some characteristics in common —*vt.* **1.** to separate, conceal, shelter, or protect, with or as with a screen **2.** to enclose or provide with a screen or screens **3.** to sift through a coarse mesh so as to separate finer from coarser parts **4.** *a)* to interview or test so as to separate according to skills, personality, aptitudes, etc. *b)* to separate in this way (usually with *out*) **5.** *a)* to project (pictures, etc.) upon a screen, as with a motion-picture or slide projector *b)* to photograph with a motion-picture camera *c)* to adapt (a story, play, etc.) for motion pictures —*vi.* to be screened or suitable for screening, as in motion pictures —**screen′er** *n.* —**screen′less** *adj.*

screen·ing (-iŋ) *n.* **1.** the act of a person or thing that screens **2.** *a)* a screen or set of screens *b)* mesh used in a screen **3.** [pl.] material separated out by a sifting screen

screen memory *Psychoanalysis* a memory that can be tolerated and is used unconsciously as a screen against an allied memory that would be distressing if remembered

☆**screen pass** *Football* a short forward pass to a receiver preceded by blockers

☆**screen·play** (-plā′) *n.* a story written for production as a motion picture or so adapted from a novel, etc.

screen test 1. the testing of a person's suitability as a motion-picture actor or for a particular role by filming a short test sequence **2.** the test film so made

screw (skrōō) *n.* [ME. *screwe* < MFr. *escroue*, hole in which the screw turns < L. *scrofa*, sow, influenced by *scrobis*, vulva] **1.** *a)* a mechanical device for fastening things together, consisting essentially of a cylindrical or conical piece of metal threaded evenly around its outside surface with an advancing spiral ridge and commonly having a slotted head: it penetrates only by being turned, as with a screwdriver: also called **male** (or **external**) **screw** *b)* the internal thread, or helical groove, as of a nut, into which a male screw, bolt, etc. can be turned: also called **female** (or **internal**) **screw** *c)* the act or an instance of turning such a screw **2.** any of various devices operat-

ing or threaded like a screw, as a jackscrew or screw propeller **3.** *a)* anything that spirals or twists like the thread of a screw *b)* the act of spiraling, twisting, or moving like this **4.** [Slang] a prison guard **5.** [Chiefly Brit.] a bit of tobacco, etc. (in a twist of paper) **6.** [Chiefly Brit. Colloq.] *a)* a stingy person; miser *b)* a crafty bargainer *c)* a worn-out horse **7.** [Brit. Colloq.] a salary —*vt.* **1.** to twist; turn; tighten **2.** *a)* to fasten, make secure, tighten, insert, etc. with or as with a screw or screws *b)* to put together or take apart with a screwlike motion **3.** to twist out of natural shape; contort *[to screw one's face up]* **4.** to make stronger; intensify (often with up) **5.** to force or compel, as if by using screws **6.** [Slang] to practice extortion on; cheat; swindle **7.** [Slang] to have sexual intercourse with —*vi.* **1.** to go together or come apart by being turned or twisted in the manner of a screw *[a lid that screws on]* **2.** to be fitted for being put together or taken apart by a screw or screws **3.** to twist; turn; wind; have a motion like that of a screw **4.** to practice extortion —**have a screw loose** [Slang] to be eccentric, odd, etc. —**put the screws on** (or **to**) to subject to force; exert pressure on, as in exacting payment; coerce —**screw up** [Slang] to make a mess of, as by ineptness; bungle; foul up

☆**screw·ball** (skrōō′bôl′) *n.* **1.** *Baseball* a ball thrown by a right-handed pitcher that curves to the right, or one thrown by a left-handed pitcher that curves to the left **2.** [Slang] a person who seems erratic, irrational, unconventional, or unbalanced —*adj.* [Slang] peculiar; irrational

☆**screw bean 1.** the spirally twisted pod growing on a mesquite tree (*Prosopis pubescens*) of the SW U.S., often used for fodder **2.** this tree

screw·driv·er (-drī′vər) *n.* **1.** a tool used for turning screws, having an end that fits into the slot in the head of the screw ☆**2.** a cocktail made of orange juice and vodka

screwed (skrōōd) *adj.* **1.** having threads like a screw **2.** twisted **3.** [Chiefly Brit. Slang] drunk

screw eye a screw with a loop for a head

screw hook a screw with a hook for a head

screw jack *same as* JACKSCREW

screw pine any of a genus (*Pandanus*) of SE Asian, monocotyledonous trees and shrubs of a family (Pandanaceae) having daggerlike leaves and, often, prop roots

screw propeller *see* PROPELLER

screw thread the helical or spiral ridge of a screw

☆**screw·worm** (skrōō′wûrm′) *n.* a larva of any of several American flies (genus *Callitroga*) that infests wounds and the nostrils, navel, etc. of animals, often causing illness

screw·y (skrōō′ē) *adj.* **screw′i·er, screw′i·est** [Slang] ☆**1.** mentally unbalanced; crazy ☆**2.** peculiar, eccentric, or odd in a confusing way —**screw′i·ness** *n.*

Scria·bin (skryä′bēn; *E.* skrē·ä′bin), **A·lek·san·dr (Niko-layevich)** (ä′lyik sän′dr′) 1872–1915; Russ. composer & pianist

scrib·al (skrī′b'l) *adj.* **1.** of scribes, or writers **2.** arising from the process of writing *[a scribal error]*

scrib·ble (skrib′'l) *vt., vi.* **-bled, -bling** [ME. *scriblen* < ML. *scribillare* < L. *scribere*, to write: see SCRIBE] **1.** to write carelessly or illegibly **2.** to cover with or make meaningless or illegible marks **3.** to compose hastily, without regard to style —*n.* **1.** illegible or careless handwriting; scrawl **2.** meaningless marks **3.** an inferior literary work

scrib·bler (-lər) *n.* a person who scribbles; specif., *a)* a person who writes illegibly or carelessly *b)* a hack writer; inferior and unimportant author

scribe (skrīb) *n.* [ME. < L. *scriba*, public writer, scribe, in LL.(Ec.), doctor of the Jewish law < *scribere*, to write < IE. *skeribh-* < base *(s)ker-*, to cut, incise, whence SHEAR] **1.** a professional penman who copied manuscripts before the invention of printing **2.** a writer or author **3.** a person learned in the Jewish law who makes handwritten copies of the Torah **4.** a person employed by the general public to write letters, etc. **5.** a pointed instrument for scoring stone, brick, wood, etc. to show where it is to be cut: also **scrib′er** —*vt.* **scribed, scrib′ing 1.** to score (wood, bricks, etc.) with a scribe **2.** to mark (a line) with a scribe —*vi.* to work as a scribe

Scribe (skrēb), **Au·gus·tin Eu·gène** (ō güs tan′ ĕ zhen′) 1791–1861; Fr. dramatist & librettist

scrim (skrim) *n.* [< ?] **1.** a light, sheer, loosely woven cotton or linen cloth, used for curtains, upholstery linings, etc. ☆**2.** a hanging of such cloth used in theatrical productions either as an opaque backdrop or as a semitransparent curtain, depending on the lighting

scrim·mage (skrim′ij) *n.* [altered < SKIRMISH] **1.** a rough-and-tumble struggle; tussle; confused struggle ☆**2.** *Football a)* the entire play that follows the pass from center when the two teams are lined up *b)* football practice in the form of actual play between two units *c)* short for LINE OF SCRIMMAGE **3.** *Rugby same as* SCRUMMAGE —*vi.* **-maged, -mag·ing** to take part in a scrimmage —**scrim′mag·er** *n.*

scrimp (skrimp) *vt.* [prob. < Scand., as in Sw. *skrympa*, to shrink, akin to OE. *scrimman*, G. *schrumpfen* < IE. root *(s)kremb-*, to turn, twist, shrink] **1.** to make too small, short, etc.; skimp **2.** to treat stingily; stint —*vi.* to be sparing and frugal; try to make ends meet; economize —*adj.* curtailed; scanty —**scrimp′er** *n.*

scrimp·y (skrim′pē) *adj.* **scrimp′i·er, scrimp′i·est 1.**

MACHINE SCREW

MACHINE SCREW

WOOD SCREW

LAG SCREW

SET SCREW

SCREWS

skimpy; scanty; meager 2. frugal or economical —**scrimp′-i·ly** adv. —**scrimp′i·ness** n.

☆**scrim·shaw** (skrim′shô′) n. [earlier also *scrimshander* < ?] 1. careful decoration and carving of shells, bone, ivory, etc., done esp. by sailors on long voyages 2. an article so made, or such articles collectively —vt., vi. to carve (shells, bone, etc.) in making scrimshaw

scrip[1] (skrip) n. [ME. *scrippe* < ML. *scrippa*: see SCARF[1]] [Archaic] a small bag, wallet, or satchel

scrip[2] (skrip) n. [contr. < SCRIPT] 1. a brief writing, as a note, list, receipt, etc. 2. a small piece or scrap, esp. of paper 3. a certificate of a right to receive something; specif., a) a certificate representing a fraction of a share of stock b) a temporary paper to be exchanged for money, goods, land, etc. ☆c) a certificate of indebtedness, issued as currency, as by a local government during a financial depression ☆4. paper money in amounts of less than a dollar, formerly issued in the U.S.; fractional currency

Scripps (skrips), **Edward Wyl·lis** (wil′is) 1854–1926; U.S. newspaper publisher

‡**scrip·sit** (skrip′sit) [L.] he (or she) wrote (it): placed after the author's name on a manuscript, etc.

script (skript) n. [ME. < MFr. *escript* < L. *scriptum* < neut. of *scriptus*, pp. of *scribere*, to write: see SCRIBE] 1. a) handwriting; written words, letters, or figures b) a style of handwriting; manner or method of forming letters or figures c) *Printing* a typeface that looks like handwriting, with the letters connected: cf. CURSIVE 2. a written document; original manuscript 3. the manuscript, or a copy of the text, of a stage, film, radio, or television show —vt. [Colloq.] to write the script for (a film, etc.)

Script. 1. Scriptural 2. Scripture

scrip·to·ri·um (skrip tôr′ē əm) n., pl. -**ri·a** (-ə) [ML. < L. *scriptorius*: see SCRIPT] a writing room; esp., a room in a monastery for copying manuscripts, writing, and studying

scrip·ture (skrip′chər) n. [ME. < L. *scriptura*, a writing, in LL.(Ec.), a Scripture, passage of Scripture < *scriptus*: see SCRIPT] 1. orig., anything written 2. [S-] [often pl.] a) the sacred writings of the Jews, identical with the Old Testament of the Christians b) the Christian Bible; Old and New Testaments 3. [S-] [Rare] a Bible passage 4. a) any sacred writing or books b) any writing regarded as authoritative and inviolable —**scrip′tur·al** adj.

script·writ·er (skript′rīt′ər) n. a person who writes scripts for motion pictures, television, etc.

scriv·e·ner (skriv′nər, -′n ər) n. [ME. *scriveyner*, extended < *scrivein* < OFr. *escrivain* < VL. *scribanus* < L. *scriba*, a SCRIBE] [Archaic] 1. a scribe, copyist, or clerk 2. a notary

scro·bic·u·late (skrō bik′yə lit) adj. [< L. *scrobiculus*, dim. of *scrobis*, a ditch (for IE. base see SHARP) + -ATE[1]] *Biol.* pitted or furrowed

☆**scrod** (skräd) n. [prob. < MDu. *schrode*, piece cut off, strip: for base see SHRED] a young codfish or haddock, esp. one split and prepared for cooking

scrof·u·la (skräf′yə lə) n. [ML. < L. *scrofulae*, pl., swellings of the neck glands < dim. of *scrofa*, a sow: prob. from the swollen condition of the glands] tuberculosis of the lymphatic glands, esp. of the neck, characterized by the enlargement of the glands, suppuration, and scar formation

scrof·u·lous (-ləs) adj. 1. of, like, or having scrofula 2. morally corrupt; degenerate —**scrof′u·lous·ly** adv.

scroll (skrōl) n. [ME. *scrowle*, altered (? after *rowle*, var. of *rolle*, ROLL) < *scrowe* < OFr. *escroue*: see ESCROW] 1. a roll of parchment, paper, etc. usually with writing or pictures on it 2. an ancient book in the form of a rolled manuscript 3. a list of names; roll; roster [the *scroll* of Fame] 4. anything having the form of a partly

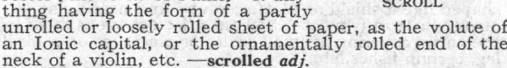

SCROLL

unrolled or loosely rolled sheet of paper, as the volute of an Ionic capital, or the ornamentally rolled end of the neck of a violin, etc. —**scrolled** adj.

scroll saw a thin, ribbonlike saw for cutting thin wood into spiral or ornamental designs

scroll·work (-wurk′) n. 1. ornamental work marked by scrolls 2. ornamental work done with a scroll saw

scrooch, scrootch (skrooch) vt., vi. [prob. alt. < SCROUGE] [Colloq.] to crouch, hunch, huddle, squeeze, etc.

Scrooge (skrooj) n. [after Ebenezer *Scrooge*, such a character in Dickens' *A Christmas Carol*] [also s-] a hard, miserly misanthrope

scroop (skroop) vi. [echoic, after SCRAPE] [Dial.] to creak or grate —n. [Dial.] a creaking or grating sound

scro·tum (skrōt′əm) n., pl. -**ta** (-tə), -**tums** [L.: for IE. base see SHRED] in most male mammals, the pouch of skin holding the testicles and related structures —**scro′tal** adj.

scrouge (skrouj, skrooj) vt. **scrouged**, **scroug′ing** [earlier *scruze*: prob. echoic, suggested by SCREW, SQUEEZE] [Dial.] to crowd, squeeze, press, etc.

scrounge (skrounj) vt. **scrounged**, **scroung′ing** [prob. altered < prec.] [Colloq.] 1. to manage to get or find by hunting around 2. to get by begging or sponging; mooch 3. to take without permission; pilfer —vi. [Colloq.] to seek (around) for something; forage —**scroung′er** n.

scrub[1] (skrub) n. [ME., var. of *shrubbe*, SHRUB[1], infl. ? by ON. *skroppa*, a lean creature] 1. a) a scraggly, stunted tree or shrub b) short, stunted trees, bushes, or shrubs growing thickly together c) land covered with such growth 2. a) any animal or thing smaller than the usual, or inferior in quality, breed, etc. b) any small or insignificant person ☆3. *Sports* a) a player not on the varsity squad or regular team b) [pl.] a secondary or practice team made up of such players —adj. 1. mean; poor; inferior 2. undersized, undernourished, or stunted ☆3. *Sports* of or for the scrubs

scrub[2] (skrub) vt. **scrubbed**, **scrub′bing** [ME. *scrobben*, prob. < Scand., as in Dan. *skrubbe*, Norw. dial. *skrubba*, to rub hard, akin to MLowG. *schrubben*: for IE. base see SCRAPE] 1. to clean or wash by rubbing or brushing hard 2. to remove (dirt, etc.) by brushing or rubbing 3. to rub hard 4. to cleanse (a gas) of impurities 5. [Colloq.] a) to cancel or call off (esp. a rocket launch just before or during the countdown) b) to get rid of; eliminate —vi. to clean something by rubbing, as with a brush —n. 1. the act of scrubbing 2. a person who scrubs —**scrub′ber** n.

scrub·by (skrub′ē) adj. -**bi·er**, -**bi·est** 1. stunted in growth; undersized or inferior 2. covered with or consisting of scrub, or brushwood 3. paltry, shabby, etc. —**scrub′bi·ly** adv. —**scrub′bi·ness** n.

scrub typhus same as TSUTSUGAMUSHI DISEASE

scrub·wom·an (-woom′ən) n., pl. -**wom′en** same as CHAR-WOMAN

scruff (skruf) n. [< ON. *skrufr*, a tuft of hair, forelock, var. of *skruf*, altered by metathesis < *skufr*, a tuft < IE. base *(s)keup-*, whence OE. *scyfel*, woman's headdress] the back of the neck; nape

scruff·y (skruf′ē) adj. **scruff′i·er**, **scruff′i·est** [< dial. *scruff*, var. of SCURF + -Y[2]] shabby, unkempt, or untidy; grubby —**scruff′i·ly** adv. —**scruff′i·ness** n.

scrum·mage (skrum′ij) n. [dial. var. of SCRIMMAGE] *Rugby* a play in which the two sets of forwards, lined up facing each other in a compact formation, try to kick the ball between them back to their teammates —vi. -**maged**, -**mag·ing** to take part in a scrummage Also **scrum**

scrump·tious (skrump′shəs) adj. [altered < SUMPTUOUS] [Colloq.] very pleasing, attractive, etc., esp. to the taste; delicious —**scrump′tious·ly** adv. —**scrump′tious·ness** n.

scrunch (skrunch) vt., vi. [< CRUNCH, with emphatic initial s-] 1. to crunch, crush, or crumple 2. to hunch, huddle, or squeeze —n. a crunching or crumpling sound

scru·ple (skroo′p'l) n. [MFr. *scrupule* < L. *scrupulus*, small sharp stone (hence small weight, difficulty, doubt), dim. of *scrupus*, a sharp stone < IE. *skreup-* < base *(s)ker-*, to cut] 1. a very small quantity, amount, or part 2. a) an ancient Roman weight equal to 1/24 ounce b) an apothecaries' weight equal to 1/3 dram (20 grains, or 1/24 ounce) 3. a feeling of hesitancy, doubt, or uneasiness arising from difficulty in deciding what is right, proper, ethical, etc.; qualm or misgiving about something one thinks is wrong —vt., vi. -**pled**, -**pling** to hesitate (at) from doubt or uneasiness; be unwilling because of one's conscience; have scruples (about) —SYN. see QUALM

scru·pu·lous (skroo′pyə ləs) adj. [< MFr. or L.: MFr. *scrupuleux* < L. *scrupulosus*] 1. having or showing scruples; characterized by careful attention to what is right or proper; conscientiously honest 2. demanding, or characterized by, precision, care, and exactness —SYN. see CAREFUL, UPRIGHT —**scru′pu·los′i·ty** (-läs′ə tē), pl. -**ties**, **scru′pu·lous·ness** n. —**scru′pu·lous·ly** adv.

scru·ta·ble (skroot′ə b'l) adj. [LL. *scrutabilis*: see INSCRUTABLE] not inscrutable; open to being understood

scru·ti·nize (skroot′'n īz′) vt. -**nized′**, -**niz′ing** [< ff. + -IZE] to look at very carefully; examine closely; inspect minutely —**scru′ti·niz′er** n.

SYN.—**scrutinize** implies a looking over carefully and searchingly in order to observe the minutest details [he slowly *scrutinized* the bank note]; **inspect** implies a close, critical observation, esp. for detecting errors, flaws, etc. [to *inspect* a building for fire hazards]; **examine** suggests a close observation or investigation to determine the condition, quality, validity, etc. of something [examined thoroughly by a doctor]; **scan**, in its earlier, stricter sense, implies a close scrutiny, but in current, popular usage, it more frequently connotes a quick, rather superficial survey [to *scan* the headlines]

scru·ti·ny (-′n ē) n., pl. -**nies** [L. *scrutinium* < L. *scrutari*, to search into carefully < *scruta*, trash, prob. altered < Gr. *grutē*: for prob. IE. base see CRUMB] 1. a close examination; minute inspection 2. a careful, continuous watch; surveillance 3. a lengthy, searching look

☆**scu·ba** (skoo′bə) n.[*s(elf-) c(ontained) u(nderwater) b(reathing) a(pparatus)*] equipment worn by divers for breathing under water, consisting typically of one or two compressed-air tanks strapped to the back and connected by a hose to a mouthpiece

scud (skud) vi. **scud′ded**, **scud′ding** [prob. < ON. form akin to OE. *scudan*, to hurry: see SHUDDER] 1. to run or move swiftly; glide or skim along easily 2. to be driven or run before the wind —n. 1. the act of scudding 2. spray, rain, or snow driven by the wind 3. a sudden gust of wind 4. *Meteorol.* very low, dark, patchy clouds moving swiftly, generally characteristic of bad weather

scu·do (skōō′dō) *n.*, *pl.* **-di** (-dē) [It., orig., a shield < L. *scutum*, a shield: it bore a shield] a former monetary unit and gold or silver coin of Italy and Sicily

scuff (skuf) *vt.* [prob. < or akin to ON. *skufa*, to SHOVE] **1.** to scrape (the ground, floor, etc.) with the feet **2.** to wear a rough place or places on the surface of (a shoe, etc.) **3.** to move (the feet) with a dragging motion —*vi.* **1.** to walk without lifting the feet; shuffle **2.** to become scraped or worn in patches on the surface —*n.* **1.** a noise or act of scuffing **2.** a worn or rough spot **3.** a loose-fitting house slipper, esp. one without a heel or counter

scuf·fle (skuf′'l) *vi.* **-fled**, **-fling** [freq. of prec.] **1.** to struggle or fight in rough confusion **2.** to move in a confused hurry or bustle **3.** to drag the feet; shuffle —*n.* **1.** a rough, confused fight; close, haphazard struggle **2.** the act or sound of feet shuffling

scuffle hoe a hoe with a flat blade held parallel to the ground and pushed back and forth through the surface soil, as to destroy weeds

scull (skul) *n.* [ME. *skulle*, prob. < Scand. form akin to obs. Sw. *skolle*, thin plate < IE. base *(s)kel-*, to cut, whence HELM²] **1.** an oar mounted at the stern of a boat and worked from side to side to move the boat forward **2.** either of a pair of light oars used, one on each side of a boat, by a single rower **3.** a light, narrow racing boat for one, two, or four rowers —*vt.*, *vi.* to propel with a scull or sculls — **scull′er** *n.*

SCULL

scul·ler·y (skul′ər ē) *n.*, *pl.* **-ler·ies** [ME., room for care of plates, pans, and kitchen utensils < OFr. *escuelerie* < *escuelle*, a dish < L. *scutella*, salver, tray, dim. of *scutra*, platter] a room adjoining the kitchen, where pots and pans are cleaned and stored or where the rough, dirty kitchen work is done

scul·lion (skul′yən) *n.* [LME. *sculyon* < OFr. *escouillon*, a mop, cloth < *escouve*, a broom < L. *scopa*, a broom; lit., twig, akin to *scapus*: see SHAFT] [Archaic] a servant doing the rough, dirty work in a kitchen

sculp., sculpt. **1.** sculpsit: also **sculps.** **2.** sculptor **3.** sculptural **4.** sculpture

scul·pin (skul′pin) *n.*, *pl.* **-pin**, **-pins**: see PLURAL, II, D, 2 [prob. altered < Fr. *scorpene* < L. *scorpaena*: see SCORPION] **1.** any of a family (Cottidae) of spiny, mostly scaleless, mostly sea fishes with a big head and wide mouth ☆**2.** a scorpion fish (*Scorpaena guttata*) of the S California coast

‡**sculp·sit** (skulp′sit) [L.] he (or she) carved (it): placed after the artist's name on a sculpture, etc.

sculpt (skulpt) *vt.*, *vi.* [Fr. *sculpter*, altered (after *sculpture*) < *sculper* < L. *sculpere*: see SCULPTURE] **1.** to carve or model as a sculptor **2.** to give sculpturelike form to (hair, fabric, etc.) Also **sculp**

sculp·tor (skulp′tər) *n.* [L. < *sculpere*, to carve in stone, akin to *scalpere*: see SCALPEL] a person who models, carves, or otherwise fashions figures or forms of clay, stone, metal, wood, etc.; artist who creates three-dimensional representations —**sculp′tress** *n.fem.* [Now Rare]

sculp·ture (skulp′chər) *n.* [ME. < L. *sculptura* < *sculptus*, pp. of *sculpere*: see prec.] **1.** the art of carving wood, chiseling stone, casting or welding metal, modeling clay or wax, etc. into three-dimensional representations, as statues, figures, forms, etc. **2.** any work of sculpture, or such works collectively —*vt.* **-tured**, **-tur·ing** **1.** to cut, carve, chisel, cast, weld, mold, etc. into statues, figures, etc. **2.** to represent or portray by means of sculpture **3.** to make or form as or like sculpture **4.** to decorate with sculpture **5.** to change in form by erosion [rock *sculptured* by a river] —*vi.* to work as a sculptor —**sculp′tur·al** *adj.* —**sculp′tur·al·ly** *adv.*

sculp·tur·esque (skulp′chə resk′) *adj.* like or suggesting sculpture; shapely, statuelike, etc.

scum (skum) *n.* [ME. < MDu. *schum*, akin to G. *schaum*, foam, scum, prob. < IE. base *(s)keu-*, to cover, whence SKY] **1.** a thin layer of impurities which forms on the top of liquids or bodies of water, often as the result of boiling or fermentation **2.** the dross or refuse on top of molten metals **3.** worthless parts or things; refuse **4.** a mean, despicable person, or such people collectively —*vt.* **scummed**, **scum′ming** [Archaic] to remove scum from; skim —*vi.* to form scum; become covered with scum

scum·ble (skum′b'l) *vt.* **-bled**, **-bling** [freq. of prec.] **1.** *a)* to soften the outlines or color of (a painting) by applying a thin coat of opaque color *b)* to apply (color) in this manner **2.** to soften the outlines of (a drawing) by rubbing or blurring **3.** to make by either of these processes —*n.* **1.** a coat of color added in scumbling **2.** the softening of outline produced by scumbling

scum·my (skum′ē) *adj.* **-mi·er**, **-mi·est** **1.** of, like, or covered with scum **2.** [Colloq.] despicable; low; mean

scun·ner (skun′ər) *vi.* [LME. (Northern dial.) < ?] to feel disgust or strong aversion —*n.* strong dislike or disgust

Scun·thorpe (skun′thôrp) city in Lincolnshire, E England: pop. 69,000

☆**scup** (skup) *n.*, *pl.* **scup**, **scups**: see PLURAL, II, D, 2 [short for *scuppaug* < AmInd. (Narragansett) *mishcùppaûog*, lit., close (scaled)] a brown and white porgy (*Stenotomus chrysops*), found along the N Atlantic coast of the U.S.

scup·per (skup′ər) *n.* [LME. < ?] **1.** an opening in a ship's side to allow water to run off the deck **2.** a similar outlet in a building, as for water to run off from a floor or roof —*vt.* [Brit. Colloq.] to annihilate or disable, as by a surprise attack

☆**scup·per·nong** (skup′ər nŏŋ′, -näŋ′) *n.* [< the *Scuppernong* River in N. Carolina < AmInd. (Algonquian) name, lit., place of the magnolia] **1.** a golden-green grape of the S U.S. **2.** a sweet, light-colored wine made from this grape

scurf (skurf) *n.* [ME. < ON. *skurfr*, akin to OE. *sceorf*, G. *schorf* < IE. base *(s)ker-*, to cut, whence SHEAR] **1.** little, dry scales shed by the skin, as dandruff **2.** any scaly coating, as on some plants, sometimes indicating a diseased condition —**scurf′y** *adj.* **scurf′i·er, scurf′i·est**

scur·rile, scur·ril (skur′əl) *adj.* [MFr. *scurrile* < L. *scurrilis* < *scurra*, buffoon, prob. < IE. base *(s)ker-*, to jump, whence G. *scherz*, a joke] archaic var. of SCURRILOUS

scur·ril·i·ty (skə ril′ə tē) *n.* [L. *scurrilitas*] **1.** the quality of being scurrilous; coarseness or indecency of language, esp. in invective or joking **2.** *pl.* **-ties** a scurrilous act or remark

scur·ril·ous (skur′ə ləs) *adj.* [SCURRIL(E) + -OUS] **1.** using indecent or abusive language; coarse; vulgar; foulmouthed **2.** containing coarse vulgarisms or indecent abuse —**scur′ril·ous·ly** *adv.* —**scur′ril·ous·ness** *n.*

scur·ry (skur′ē) *vi.* **-ried**, **-ry·ing** [< *hurry-scurry*, reduplication of HURRY, prob. suggested by SCOUR²] to run hastily; scamper —*vt.* to cause to scurry —*n.* **1.** the act or sound of scurrying **2.** a short run or race

scur·vy (skur′vē) *adj.* **-vi·er, -vi·est** [< SCURF] **1.** *earlier var. of* SCURFY **2.** low; mean; vile; contemptible —*n.* [< the *adj.*] a disease resulting from a deficiency of vitamin C in the body, characterized by weakness, anemia, spongy gums, bleeding from the mucous membranes, etc. —**scur′vi·ly** *adv.* —**scur′vi·ness** *n.*

scurvy grass an arctic plant (*Cochlearia officinalis*) of the mustard family, with white flowers and a tarlike flavor, formerly used in treating scurvy: also **scurvy weed**

scut (skut) *n.* [ME., a hare < ?] **1.** a short, stumpy tail, esp. of a hare, rabbit, or deer **2.** a contemptible person

scu·ta (skyōōt′ə) *n. pl.* of SCUTUM

scu·tage (-ij) *n.* [ML. *scutagium* < L. *scutum*, a shield: see SCUTUM] a tax paid by the holder of a knight's fee, usually in lieu of feudal military service

Scu·ta·ri (skōō′tä rē) **1.** *It. name for:* a) SHKODËR b) ÜSKÜDAR **2.** Lake, lake on border of S Yugoslavia & NW Albania: 140-200 sq. mi.

scu·tate (skyōō′tāt) *adj.* [ModL. *scutatus* < L. *scutum*, a shield: see SCUTUM] **1.** *Bot.* same as PELTATE **2.** *Zool.* covered or protected by bony or horny plates or scales

scutch (skuch) *vt.* [prob. < OFr. *escoucher* < VL. *excuticare*, to remove skin or rind < L. *ex-* + *quatere*, to shake: see QUASH²] to free the fibers of (flax, cotton, etc.) from woody parts by beating —*n.* an instrument for doing this: also **scutch′er**

scutch·eon (skuch′ən) *n.* [ME. *scochoun*, aphetic for *escutcheon*] same as ESCUTCHEON

scute (skyōōt) *n.* [L. *scutum*, a shield: see SCUTUM] *Zool.* **1.** any external bony or horny plate, as on some fishes and many reptiles **2.** any scalelike structure

scu·tel·late¹ (skyōōt′'l āt′, -it) *adj.* [ModL. *scutellatus* < *scutellum*: see SCUTELLUM] covered or protected with scutella, or small scales or plates

scu·tel·late² (skyōōt′'l āt′, -it; skyōō tel′it) *adj.* [ModL. *scutellatus* (see prec.), mistaken for L. *scutulatus* < *scutulum*, dim. of *scutum*, a shield: see SCUTUM] *Biol.* shaped like a shield or platter; round and nearly flat

scu·tel·la·tion (skyōōt′'l ā′shən) *n.* [< SCUTELLATE¹] *Zool.* the entire covering of small scales or plates, as on a bird's leg, certain fishes, etc.

scu·tel·lum (skyōō tel′əm) *n.*, *pl.* **-tel′la** (-ə) **1.** [ModL., mistaken for L. *scutulum*: see SCUTELLATE²] *Bot.* any of various parts shaped like a shield **2.** [ModL. < L. *scutella*, a salver: see SCUTTLE¹] *Zool.* a small, horny scale or plate

scu·ti·form (skyōōt′ə fôrm′) *adj.* [ModL. *scutiformis* < L. *scutum*, a shield (see SCUTUM) + *-formis*, -FORM] shaped like a shield; scutate

scut·ter (skut′ər) *vi.* [var. of SCUTTLE²] [Brit.] to scurry about; bustle —*n.* [Brit.] a scurrying or bustling about

scut·tle¹ (skut′'l) *n.* [ME. *scutel*, a dish < OE. < L. *scutella*, a salver, dim. of *scutra*, a flat dish] **1.** a broad, open basket for carrying grain, vegetables, etc. **2.** a kind of bucket, usually with a wide lip, used for pouring coal on a fire: in full **coal scuttle**

scut·tle² (skut′'l) *vi.* **-tled**, **-tling** [ME. *scutlen*, prob. akin to SCUD] to run or move quickly; scurry, esp. away from danger, trouble, etc. —*n.* a scurry or scamper; hasty flight

scut·tle³ (skut′'l) *n.* [LME. *skottele* < MFr. *escoutille*, trapdoor < Sp. *escotilla*, an indentation, hollowing < *escote*, a notch, tuck, prob. < Goth. *skauts*, a seam, border] **1.** an opening in a wall or roof, fitted with a lid or cover **2.** a small, covered opening or hatchway in the outer hull or deck of a ship **3.** the lid or cover for any such opening —*vt.* **-tled**, **-tling** **1.** to make or open holes in the hull of (a ship or boat) below the waterline; esp., to sink in this way **2.** to scrap or abandon (a plan, undertaking, etc.)

scut·tle·butt (skut′'l but′) *n.* [orig. < *scuttled butt,* a cask or butt with an opening for a dipper] **1.** *Naut.* a drinking fountain on shipboard ☆**2.** [Colloq.] rumor or gossip, such as might be passed at a scuttlebutt

scu·tum (skyōōt′əm) *n., pl.* **scu′ta** (-ə) [L., prob. < IE. base *(s)keut-, to cover, skin, whence L. *cutis,* skin, Gr. *skutos,* a hide, leather] **1.** the long, leather-covered, wooden shield carried by infantrymen in the Roman legions **2.** *Zool.* a heavy, horny scale or plate, as on the body of certain reptiles and insects; scute —[S-] a small S constellation between Aquila and Sagittarius

Scyl·la (sil′ə) [L. < Gr. *Skylla*] a dangerous rock on the Italian side of the Straits of Messina, opposite the whirlpool Charybdis: in classical mythology both Scylla and Charybdis were personified as female monsters —**between Scylla and Charybdis** between two perils or evils, neither of which can be evaded without risking the other

scy·phi- (si′fə) [< L. *scyphus:* see SCYPHUS] *a combining form meaning* scyphus or cup [scyphiform]

scy·phi·form (si′fə fôrm′) *adj.* [prec. + -FORM] shaped like a cup or bowl

scy·phis·to·ma (si fis′tə mə) *n., pl.* **-mae** (-mē′), **-mas** [ModL. < L. *scyphus,* cup (see SCYPHUS) + Gr. *stoma,* mouth (see STOMA)] the small, attached polyp stage of the scyphozoan jellyfishes, preceding the strobila stage

scy·pho·zo·an (si′fə zō′ən) *n.* [< ModL. *Scyphozoa,* name of the class < Gr. *skyphos,* a cup + *zōion,* an animal] any of a class (Scyphozoa) of sea coelenterates, consisting of jellyfishes lacking a velum and their attached polyp stages

scy·phus (si′fəs) *n., pl.* **scy′phi** (-fi) [L. < Gr. *skyphos*] **1.** a form of ancient Greek cup with two handles and a flat bottom **2.** *Bot.* a cup-shaped part, as in some flowers

Scy·ros (si′rəs) *Latin name of* SKÍROS

scythe (si*th*) *n.* [altered (after L. *scindere,* to cut) < ME. *sithe* < OE. *sithe, sigthe,* a scythe, akin to LowG. *seged* < IE. base *sek-, to cut, whence SAW[1], L. *secure,* to cut] a tool with a long, single-edged blade set at an angle on a long, curved handle, used in cutting long grass, grain, etc. by hand —*vt.* **scythed, scyth′ing** to cut with a scythe

Scyth·i·a (sith′ē ə) ancient region in SE Europe, centered about the N coast of the Black Sea

Scyth·i·an (-ən) *adj.* of ancient Scythia, its people, their language, etc. —*n.* **1.** any of a nomadic and warlike people who lived in ancient Scythia **2.** their extinct Iranian language

SCYTHE

S/D sight draft

S.D., s.d. *Statistics* standard deviation

s.d. [L. *sine die*] without date

S.Dak. South Dakota: also **S.D.**

'sdeath (zdeth) *interj.* [Obs.] *euphemistic contraction of* God's death, used as a swearword

SDS Students for a Democratic Society

Se *Chem.* selenium

SE, S.E., s.e. 1. southeast **2.** southeastern

sea (sē) *n.* [ME. *see* < OE. *sæ,* akin to Du. *zee,* G. *see*] **1.** the continuous body of salt water covering the greater part of the earth's surface; ocean **2.** a large body of salt water wholly or partly enclosed by land [the Red Sea, Irish Sea] **3.** a large body of fresh water [Sea of Galilee] **4.** the state of the surface of the ocean with regard to waves or swells [a calm sea] **5.** a heavy swell or wave **6.** something like or suggesting the sea in extent or vastness; very great amount or number [lost in a sea of debt] **7.** *Astron.* same as MARE[2] (sense 2) —*adj.* of, connected with, or for use at sea —**at sea 1.** on the open sea **2.** uncertain; bewildered —**follow the sea** to make one's living by serving on oceangoing ships —**go to sea 1.** to become a sailor **2.** to embark on a voyage —**put (out) to sea** to sail away from land

sea anchor a large, canvas-covered frame, usually conical, let out from a ship as a drag or float to reduce drifting or to keep the ship heading into the wind

sea anemone any of various flowerlike, anthozoan sea polyps having a firm, gelatinous, often large, body without a skeleton, topped with petallike tentacles: they are often brightly colored and live attached to rocks, pilings, etc.

sea bag a large, cylindrical canvas bag in which a sailor carries his clothing and personal belongings

☆**sea bass 1.** any of numerous sea fishes (family Serranidae); esp., *a)* the **black sea bass** (*Centropristes striatus*), a dark-brown or black marine food fish with large scales and a wide mouth, found along the Atlantic coast of the U.S. *b)* the **giant sea bass** (*Stereolepis gigas*) found along the California coast and southward **2.** any of various similar fishes, as the **white sea bass** (*Cynoscion nobilis*), a drum found in warm waters, esp. along the California coast

Sea·bee (sē′bē′) *n.* [< *C B,* short for *Construction Battalion*] a member of any of the construction battalions of the Civil Engineer Corps of the United States Navy, that build harbor facilities, airfields, etc.

sea bird a bird living on or near the sea, as a gull or tern

sea biscuit *same as* HARDTACK: also **sea bread**

sea·board (-bôrd′) *n.* [SEA + BOARD] land or coastal region bordering on the sea —*adj.* bordering on the sea

Sea·borg (sē′bôrg), **Glenn T**(heodore) 1912– ; U.S. nuclear chemist

sea·borne (-bôrn′) *adj.* **1.** carried on or by the sea **2.** afloat: said of ships

sea bream *same as* BREAM[1] (sense 2); ☆esp., a porgy (*Archosargus rhomboidalis*) of the Atlantic coast of the U.S.

sea breeze a breeze blowing inland from the sea

sea calf *same as* SEAL[1] (sense 1)

sea captain the commander of a merchant ship

sea·coast (-kōst′) *n.* land bordering on the sea; seashore

sea·cock (-käk′) *n.* a valve below the waterline in the hull of a ship, used to control the intake of sea water

sea cow 1. any of several sea mammals (order Sirenia), as the dugong and manatee **2.** *earlier name for:* *a)* HIPPOPOTAMUS *b)* WALRUS

sea crawfish *same as* SPINY LOBSTER: also **sea crayfish**

sea cucumber *same as* HOLOTHURIAN, esp. one with a cucumber-shaped body, used as food in the Orient

sea devil *same as* DEVILFISH

sea dog 1. an experienced sailor **2.** [transl. of G. *seehund* (or cognate Du. *zeehond*), altered (as if < *see,* SEA) < earlier *seelhund* < *seel,* akin to SEAL[2] + *hund,* dog: from its bark] any of various seals **3.** [Obs.] *same as* DOGFISH (sense 1)

sea duck any of various ducks found chiefly on the seas

sea eagle 1. any of several fish-eating eagles related to the bald eagle, as the erne **2.** *same as* OSPREY

sea elephant either of two very large seals (genus *Mirounga*) that are hunted for oil: the male has a long proboscis

sea fan any of several gorgonians with the axial skeleton formed into a fanlike structure; esp., a horny coral (*Gorgonia flabellum*) of the West Indies and Florida Keys

sea·far·er (-fer′ər) *n.* a traveler by sea; esp., a sailor

sea·far·ing (-fer′iŋ) *adj.* of or engaged in life at sea —*n.* **1.** the business or profession of a sailor **2.** travel by sea

sea feather any of several anthozoans with the skeleton branched into a featherlike form; esp., *same as* SEA PEN

sea fight a battle fought between ships at sea

☆**sea·food** (-fōōd′) *n.* food prepared from or consisting of saltwater fish or shellfish

sea·fowl (-foul′) *n.* any bird living on or near the sea

sea·front (-frunt′) *n.* the part of a town or other built-up area facing on the sea

sea·girt (-gurt′) *adj.* surrounded by the sea

sea·go·ing (-gō′iŋ) *adj.* **1.** made for use on the open sea [a seagoing schooner] **2.** same as SEAFARING

sea green a pale bluish green —**sea′-green′** *adj.*

sea gull *same as* GULL[1]; esp., any gull living along a seacoast

sea hare any of a number of large, sluglike, gastropod sea mollusks (genus *Aplysia*), with a rudimentary internal shell and a prominent front pair of tentacles

sea holly a European plant (*Eryngium maritimum*) of the parsley family, with leathery, bluish, spiny leaves and globular heads of small, bluish flowers

sea horse 1. any of various small, semitropical, marine fishes (family Syngnathidae), with a slender prehensile tail, plated body, and a head and foreparts somewhat like those of a horse: it normally swims in an upright position **2.** *same as* WALRUS **3.** a mythical sea creature, half fish and half horse

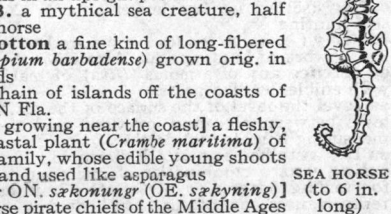

SEA HORSE (to 6 in. long)

☆**sea-island cotton** a fine kind of long-fibered cotton (*Gossypium barbadense*) grown orig. in the Sea Islands

Sea Islands chain of islands off the coasts of S.C., Ga., & N Fla.

sea kale [from growing near the coast] a fleshy, European, coastal plant (*Crambe maritima*) of the mustard family, whose edible young shoots are blanched and used like asparagus

sea king [after ON. *sækonungr* (OE. *sækyning*)] any of the Norse pirate chiefs of the Middle Ages

seal[1] (sēl) *n.* [ME. *seel* < OFr. < L. *sigillum,* a seal, mark, dim. of *signum:* see SIGN] **1.** a design, initial, or other device placed on a letter, document, etc., as a mark of genuineness or authenticity: letters were formerly closed with a wafer of molten wax into which was pressed the distinctive seal of the sender **2.** a stamp, signet ring, etc. used for making such an impression **3.** a wax wafer, piece of paper, etc. bearing the impression of some official design and used to authenticate a signature or document **4.** *a)* something that seals, closes, or fastens tightly or securely; specif., a piece of metal, paper, etc. so placed over a lid, cap, etc. that it must be broken before the container can be opened *b)* a tight closure, as against the passage of air or water **5.** anything that confirms, authenticates, or guarantees; pledge **6.** an indication; sign; token [a handshake as a seal of friendship] **7.** any device, as a looped trap filled with water, preventing the passage of gas through a pipe ☆**8.** an ornamental stamp placed on envelopes, packages, etc. [a Christmas seal] —*vt.* [ME.

selen < OFr. *seeler* < the *n.*] **1.** to mark with a seal; fix a seal to **2.** to secure the contents of (a letter, envelope, etc.), orig. by closing with a sealed wax wafer, now usually with mucilage, tape, or a gummed flap **3.** to confirm or authenticate (a document, etc.) by marking with a seal **4.** to attest to or confirm the truth or genuineness of (a promise, bargain, etc.) **5.** to certify as being accurate, exact, of a given size, quality, capacity, etc. by fixing a stamp or seal to **6.** to grant, assign, or designate with a seal, pledge, etc. **7.** to settle, determine, or decide finally or irrevocably *[to seal one's fate]* **8.** *a)* to close, shut, or fasten with or as with a seal *[to seal one's lips].* *b)* to close completely so as to make airtight or watertight *c)* to apply a nonpermeable coating to (a porous surface, as of wood) as before painting **9.** *Elec.* to bring (a plug and jack) into full, interlocking contact ☆**10.** *Mormonism a)* to make formal and binding; solemnize (a marriage, adoption, etc.) *b)* to give (a woman) in marriage —**seal off 1.** to close completely **2.** to enclose or surround (an area, etc.) with barriers, a cordon, etc. —**set one's seal to 1.** to mark with one's seal **2.** to endorse; approve —**the seals** [Brit.] symbols or marks of office, esp. of public office —**under (one's) seal** in a document authenticated by one's seal

seal² (sēl) *n.*, *pl.* **seals, seal:** see PLURAL, II, D, 1 [ME. *sele* < OE. *seolh,* akin to OHG. *selah,* prob. < IE. base **selk-,* to pull, draw (with reference to the seal's labored movements on land)] **1.** any of various sea mammals (suborder Pinnipedia) with a torpedo-shaped body, a doglike head, and four webbed feet or flippers: they live in cold or temperate waters and eat chiefly fish: see EARED SEAL, EARLESS SEAL **2.** *a)* the fur of a fur seal *b)* a similar fur used as a substitute for this **3.** leather made from sealskin —*vi.* to hunt seals

FUR SEAL
(5–7 ft. long)

☆**Sea·lab** (sē'lab') *n.* [SEA + LAB(ORATORY)] any of a series of experimental underwater laboratories developed by the U.S. Navy for undersea explorations and for research in oceanography, marine biology, etc.

sea lamprey a parasitic lamprey (*Petromyzon marinus*) of the N. Atlantic that ascends streams to spawn: now landlocked in the Great Lakes, where it is highly destructive to lake trout

sea lane a commonly used route for travel by sea

seal·ant (sēl'ənt) *n.* [SEAL¹ + -ANT] a substance, as a wax, plastic, silicone, etc., used for sealing

sea lavender any of a genus (*Limonium*) of stiff plants with white, pink, lavender, or yellow flowers and many branches: often dried for winter bouquets

sea lawyer [Colloq.] a contentious sailor, who habitually argues, questions orders and regulations, etc.

seal brown a rich, dark brown

sealed orders written orders or instructions, as to the captain of a ship informing him of his destination, mission, etc., given in a sealed envelope not to be opened until a specified time or place is reached

sea legs the ability to walk without loss of balance on board ship, esp. in a rough sea

seal·er¹ (sēl'ər) *n.* **1.** a person or thing that seals; specif., a substance used to seal a porous surface, as before painting **2.** an inspector who tests and certifies weights and measures

seal·er² (sēl'ər) *n.* **1.** a hunter of seals **2.** a ship used in seal hunting

seal·er·y (-ē) *n., pl.* **-er·ies 1.** a place where seals are hunted **2.** the work of hunting seals Also **seal fishery**

sea lettuce any of a genus (*Ulva*) of marine green algae with edible, leaflike parts

sea level the level of the surface of the sea, esp. at a mean level between high and low tide: used as a standard in measuring heights and depths

sea lily a stalked and attached crinoid

sealing wax a combination of resin and turpentine used for sealing letters, dry cells, etc.: it is hard at normal temperatures but softens when heated

sea lion any of several large, eared seals (genera *Zalophus, Eumetopias,* and *Otaria*) of the N Pacific, lacking underfur

seal ring *same as* SIGNET RING

seal·skin (sēl'skin') *n.* **1.** the skin or pelt of the fur seal, esp. with the coarse outer hair removed and the soft undercoat dyed dark-brown or black **2.** a garment made of this —*adj.* made of sealskin

Sea·ly·ham terrier (sē'lē ham'; *also, chiefly Brit.,* -lē əm) [from being bred at *Sealyham,* an estate in Pembrokeshire, Wales] any of a breed of small, long-bodied terrier, with short legs, a white coat, a long head and square jaws

seam (sēm) *n.* [ME. *seme* < OE. *seam,* akin to G. *saum* < IE. base **siw-, sū-,* whence SEW] **1.** the line formed by sewing together two pieces of material **2.** a line formed by the joining together of any separate pieces; line marking adjoining edges, as of boards **3.** a mark, line, ridge, etc. like this, as a scar, wrinkle, mold line on glass, etc. **4.** a thin layer or stratum of ore, coal, etc. —*vt.* **1.** to join together so as to form a seam **2.** to mark with a seamlike line, crack, wrinkle, etc. **3.** *Knitting same as* PURL.² —*vi.* [Rare] to develop cracks or fissures

sea-maid (sē'mād') *n.* [Obs. or Poet.] **1.** a mermaid **2.** a sea nymph or goddess Also **sea'-maid'en**

sea·man (sē'mən) *n., pl.* **-men** (-mən) [ME. *seeman* < OE. *sæman:* see SEA & MAN] **1.** a sailor; mariner **2.** an enlisted man ranking below a petty officer in the navy

☆**seaman apprentice** an enlisted man ranking below a seaman in the navy

sea·man·like (-līk') *adj.* like or characteristic of a good seaman; showing seamanship: also **sea'man·ly**

☆**seaman recruit** an enlisted man holding the lowest rank in the navy, below seaman apprentice

sea·man·ship (-ship') *n.* skill in sailing, navigating, or working a ship

sea·mark (sē'märk') *n.* **1.** a line marking the limit of the tide **2.** any prominent object on shore, as a lighthouse, serving as a guide for ships

sea mew [ME. *semewe:* see MEW³] *Brit. var. of* SEA GULL

seam·less (sēm'lis) *adj.* made without a seam or seams

sea·mount (sē'mount') *n.* a mountain rising from the sea floor but not reaching the surface

sea mouse any of a genus (*Aphrodite*) of large, segmented sea worms, with a flat, oval body covered with bristles

seam·ster (sēm'stər; *Brit. usually* sem'-) *n.* [Brit. or Archaic] *same as* TAILOR

seam·stress (-stris) *n.* [ME. *seamestre,* man or woman who sews < OE. *seamestre* < *seam,* a seam + additional fem. suffix -ESS] a woman who is expert at sewing, esp. one who makes her living by sewing

seam·y (sē'mē) *adj.* **seam'i·er, seam'i·est 1.** having or showing seams, esp. with rough, unfinished edges, as the underside of a garment **2.** unpleasant, squalid, or sordid *[the seamy side of life]* —**seam'i·ness** *n.*

Sean·ad Éir·eann (shan'äd er'ən) [Ir.] the upper house of the legislature of Ireland

sé·ance (sā'äns) *n.* [Fr., lit., a sitting < *seoir* < L. *sedere,* to SIT] a meeting or session; now specif., a meeting at which spiritualists seek or profess to communicate with the spirits of the dead

sea nettle any of several large stinging jellyfishes, esp. a reddish species (*Dactylometra quinquecirrha*) found along the Atlantic coast of N. America

sea onion 1. *same as* SQUILL (senses 1 & 2) **2.** a European scilla (*Scilla verna*) with blue flowers

sea otter a web-footed sea mammal (*Enhydra lutris*) of the otter family, found along the N Pacific coast: its dark-brown fur is very valuable

sea pen any of several marine, mud-dwelling coelenterates (genus *Pennatula*) that form feather-shaped colonies

sea·plane (sē'plān') *n.* any airplane designed to land on and take off from water

sea·port (-pôrt') *n.* **1.** a port or harbor used by ocean ships **2.** a town or city having such a port or harbor

sea power 1. naval strength **2.** a nation having great naval strength

sea purse a horny egg case or egg capsule produced by certain skates, rays, and sharks

sea·quake (-kwāk') *n.* an earthquake on the ocean floor

sear¹ (sir) *adj.* [ME. *seer* < OE. *sear,* dry < IE. base **saus-,* whence Sans. *śúṣyati,* (he) dries, withers, L. *sudus,* dry] *var. of* SERE² —*vt.* [ME. *seeren* < OE. *searian* < the adj.] **1.** to dry up; wither **2.** to scorch or burn the surface of **3.** to brand or cauterize with a hot iron **4.** to make callous or unfeeling; harden —*vi.* [Archaic] to dry up; wither —*n.* a mark or condition caused by searing —*SYN.* see BURN¹

sear² (sir) *n.* [< MFr. *serre,* a bolt < OFr. *serrer,* to close, press < VL. **serrare,* altered (after L. *serrare,* to saw) < LL. *serare,* to bolt, bar < L. *sera,* a bar, bolt] the catch in a gunlock that holds the hammer cocked or half-cocked

sea raven ☆a kind of sculpin (*Hemitripterus americanus*) found in the North Atlantic

search (surch) *vt.* [ME. *searchen* < OFr. *cercher* < LL. *circare,* to go round, go about, explore < *circus,* a ring: see CIRCUS] **1.** to go over or look through for the purpose of finding something; explore; rummage; examine *[to search a house for a lost article]* **2.** to examine (a person) for something concealed, as by running one's hands over the clothing, through the pockets, etc. **3.** to examine closely and carefully; test and try; probe *[to search one's conscience]* **4.** to look through (writings, records, etc.) to establish certain facts **5.** to find out or uncover by investigation (usually with *out*) —*vi.* to try to find something; make a search —*n.* **1.** an act of searching; scrutiny, inquiry, or examination in an attempt to find something, gain knowledge, establish facts, etc. **2.** the act of a belligerent in stopping and searching a neutral ship for contraband; see RIGHT OF SEARCH —**in search of** making a search for; trying to find, learn, etc. by searching —☆**search me** [Slang] I do not know the answer to your query —**search'a·ble** *adj.* —**search'er** *n.*

search·ing (-in) *adj.* **1.** examining or exploring thoroughly; scrutinizing; thorough **2.** sharp; piercing; penetrating *[the searching wind]* —**search'ing·ly** *adv.*

search·light (-līt') *n.* **1.** an apparatus containing a light and reflector on a swivel for projecting a strong, far-reaching beam in any direction **2.** such a beam

search party a group of people taking part in a search, as for a lost or missing person

search warrant a legal document authorizing or directing a peace officer to search a specified person, premises, dwelling, etc., as for stolen or contraband articles, items to be used in evidence, etc.

☆**sea robin** any of a number of spiny-finned sea fishes (family Triglidae) having a broad head covered with plates of bone, and large, winglike pectoral fins; esp., any of a genus (*Prionotus*) with reddish coloring

sea room enough open space for maneuvering a ship

sea rover a pirate or a pirate ship

sea·scape (sē′skāp′) *n.* [SEA + -SCAPE] **1.** a view of the sea **2.** a drawing, painting, etc. of such a scene

sea scorpion any of an extinct order (Eurypterida) of large arachnidlike arthropods

sea serpent 1. any large, unidentified or imaginary serpent-like animal reported to have been seen in the sea **2.** *same as: a)* OARFISH *b)* SEA SNAKE

sea·shell (-shel′) *n.* the shell of any saltwater mollusk

sea·shore (-shôr′) *n.* land along the sea; seacoast; specif., *Law* the ground lying between the usual high-water and low-water marks

sea·sick (-sik′) *adj.* suffering from seasickness

sea·sick·ness (-sik′nis) *n.* nausea, dizziness, etc. caused by the rolling and pitching of a ship at sea

Sea·side (sē′sīd′) city in W Calif., on an inlet of the Pacific: pop. 36,000

sea·side (sē′sīd′) *n.* land along the sea; seashore —*adj.* at or of the seaside

sea slug *same as* NUDIBRANCH

sea snake any of a large family (Hydrophidae) of poisonous snakes with a flattened, oarlike tail, living in tropical seas

sea·son (sē′z'n) *n.* [ME. *sesoun* < OFr. *seson* < VL. *satio*, season for sowing < L., a sowing, planting < base of *serere*, to sow: for IE. base see SEED] **1.** any of the four arbitrary divisions of the year, characterized chiefly by differences in temperature, precipitation, amount of daylight, and plant growth; spring, summer, fall (or autumn), or winter **2.** a time or part of the year during which a specified kind of agricultural work is done or a specified kind of weather prevails [the harvest *season*, the rainy *season]* **3.** the time when something specified flourishes, develops, takes place, is popular, permitted, or at its best [the opera *season*, the hunting *season]* **4.** a period of time [a slack *season* in business] **5.** the suitable, fitting, or convenient time **6.** the time of a specified festival or holiday [the Christmas *season]* **7.** [< the v.] [Obs.] something that seasons —*vt.* [ME. *sesonen*, aphetic < MFr. *assaisonner*, to season, orig., to ripen < a- (< L. *ad-*), to + *saison]* **1.** to make (food) more tasty by adding salt, spices, etc. **2.** to add zest or interest to [to *season* a lecture with humor] **3.** *a)* to make more suitable for use; improve the quality of, as by aging, drying, etc.; cure; mature [to *season* lumber] *b)* to give (an athlete, actor, etc.) experience to improve his performance **4.** to make used to; accustom; inure; acclimate [*seasoned* to a hard life] **5.** to make less harsh or severe; temper; soften [discipline *seasoned* with kindness] —*vi.* to become seasoned, as wood by drying —**for a season** for a while —**in good season** early enough —**in season 1.** available fresh for use as food: said of fruits, vegetables, seafood, etc. **2.** at the legally established time for being hunted or caught: said of game, etc. **3.** in or at the suitable or proper time **4.** in good season; early enough **5.** in heat: said of animals —**out of season** not in season —**sea′son·er** *n.*

sea·son·a·ble (-ə b'l) *adj.* [ME. *sesonable]* **1.** suitable to or usual for the time of year **2.** coming or done at the right time; opportune; timely —*SYN.* see TIMELY —**sea′son·a·ble·ness** *n.* —**sea′son·a·bly** *adv.*

sea·son·al (-əl) *adj.* of, characteristic of, or depending on the season or seasons —**sea′son·al·ly** *adv.*

sea·son·ing (-in) *n.* anything that adds zest; esp., salt, spices, etc. added to food to make it more tasty

season ticket a ticket or set of tickets as for a series of concerts, baseball games, etc. or for transportation between fixed points for a limited period of time

sea spider *same as* PYCNOGONID

sea squirt *same as* ASCIDIAN

sea swallow 1. any of several terns; esp., the **common tern** (*Sterna hirundo*) **2.** [Brit.] *same as* STORMY PETREL

seat (sēt) *n.* [ME. *sete* < ON. *sæti*: for IE. base see SIT] **1.** the manner of sitting, as on horseback **2.** *a)* a place or space to sit, or the right to such a place, esp. as evidenced by a ticket [to buy two *seats* to the opera] *b)* a thing to sit on; chair, bench, stool, etc. **3.** *a)* the buttocks *b)* the part of a garment covering the buttocks *c)* the part of a chair, bench, etc. that supports the buttocks **4.** the right to sit as a member; position of a member; membership [a *seat* on the stock exchange] **5.** *a)* a part forming the base of something *b)* a part or surface on which another part rests or fits snugly **6.** the place where something is carried on, settled, established, etc.; center; location; site [the *seat* of government, a *seat* of learning] **7.** a part of the body in which some power, function, quality, etc. is or is thought to be centered **8.** a home or residence; esp., a large house that is part of a country estate —*vt.* **1.** to put or set in or on a seat **2.** to lead to a seat or help to settle into a seat **3.** to have seats for; accommodate with seats [a hall that *seats* 500] **4.** to put a seat in or on; patch or renew the seat of; reseat **5.** to put, fix, or establish in a particular place,

position of authority, etc. —**be seated 1.** to assume a seated position; sit down: also **take a seat 2.** to be sitting **3.** to be located, settled, or established

sea tangle any of various seaweeds

seat belt a restraining device, usually consisting of anchored straps that buckle across the hips, to protect a seated passenger from abrupt jolts, as in a collision

-seat·er (sēt′ər) *a combining form meaning* a thing, as an automobile or airplane, having (a specified number of) seats [a two-*seater]*

seat·ing (-in) *n.* **1.** the act of providing with or directing to a seat or seats **2.** material for covering chair seats, etc. **3.** the arrangement of seats or of persons seated **4.** *same as* SEAT (*n.* 5 *b*)

☆**seat·mate** (-māt′) *n.* a person in an adjoining seat in an airplane, bus, etc.

SEATO (sē′tō) Southeast Asia Treaty Organization

sea trout any of various saltwater fishes (genus *Cynoscion*) related to the drums and including several weakfishes

Se·at·tle (sē at′'l) [after *Seathl*, an Indian chief] seaport in WC Wash., on Puget Sound: pop. 531,000 (met. area, incl. Everett, 1,422,000)

☆**seat·work** (sēt′wurk′) *n.* lessons done by students reading or writing at their desks

sea urchin any echinoderm (class Echinoidea) having a somewhat globular body of fused skeletal plates studded with long, calcareous, movable spines

sea wall a wall or embankment made to break the force of the waves and to protect the shore from erosion

sea walnut *same as* CTENOPHORE

sea·ward (sē′wərd) *n.* a direction or position away from the land and toward the sea —*adj.* **1.** directed, going, or situated toward the sea **2.** from the sea: said of a wind —*adv.* toward, or in the direction of, the sea: also **sea′wards**

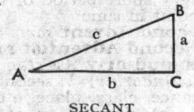
SEA URCHIN
(1 1/2–10 in. in diameter)

sea·ware (-wer′) *n.* [via dial. < OE. *sæware*, seaweed < *sæ*, sea + *war*, alga] seaweed; cap., large, coarse seaweed tossed up on shore, used as fertilizer

sea·way (-wā′) *n.* **1.** a way or route by sea; sea as a means of travel **2.** a ship's headway **3.** a rough sea **4.** an inland waterway to the sea for ocean ships [St. Lawrence *Seaway]*

sea·weed (-wēd′) *n.* **1.** any sea plant or plants; esp., any marine alga, as kelp: in full **marine seaweed 2.** any similar freshwater plant: in full **freshwater seaweed**

sea whip any of several gorgonians with the axial skeleton branched, forming long, whiplike colonies

sea·wor·thy (-wur′thē) *adj.* fit to travel in on the open sea; sturdy: said of a ship —**sea′wor′thi·ness** *n.*

sea wrack seaweed, esp. any of the kinds cast ashore

se·ba·ceous (si bā′shəs) *adj.* [L. *sebaceus* < *sebum*, tallow: see SOAP] of or like fat, tallow, or sebum; esp., designating certain skin glands that secrete sebum

se·bac·ic acid (si bas′ik, -bā′sik) [< L. *sebaceus* (see prec.) + -IC] a white, crystalline acid, $C_{10}H_{18}O_4$, obtained by the distillation of oleic acid or castor oil: used in making plasticizers, alkyd resins, etc.

Se·bas·tian (si bas′chən) [L. *Sebastianus* < Gr. *Sebastianos*, lit., a man of *Sebastia*, ancient name of Sivas, or a man of *Sebaste*, name of Samaria after the time of Herod the Great] **1.** a masculine name **2.** Saint, ?–288? A.D.; Christian martyr of Rome: his day is Jan. 20

Se·bas·to·pol (si bas′tə pōl′) *same as* SEVASTOPOL

SEbE southeast by east

se·bif·er·ous (si bif′ər əs) *adj.* [< L. *sebum*, tallow (see SOAP) + -FEROUS] *Biol.* secreting a fatty or waxlike substance; sebaceous: also **se·bip′a·rous** (-bip′ər əs)

seb·or·rhe·a, seb·or·rhoe·a (seb′ə rē′ə) *n.* [ModL.: SEBUM & -RRHEA] an excessive discharge from the sebaceous glands resulting in an abnormally oily skin —**seb′or·rhe′ic, seb′or·rhoe′ic** *adj.*

SEbS southeast by south

se·bum (sē′bəm) *n.* [L., tallow: see SOAP] the semiliquid, greasy secretion of the sebaceous glands

‡**sec** (sek) *adj.* [Fr., (see SACK³)] dry; not sweet: said of wine

SEC, S.E.C. Securities and Exchange Commission

sec secant

sec. 1. second(s) **2.** secondary **3.** secretary **4.** section(s) **5.** sector **6.** security

se·cant (sē′kənt, -kant) *adj.* [L. *secans*, prp. of *secare*, to cut: see SAW¹] cutting; intersecting —*n.* **1.** *Geom.* any straight line intersecting a curve at two or more points **2.** *Trigonometry a)* a straight line extending from the center of a circle through the end of an arc of its circumference to another straight line that is tangent to the radius at the other end of the arc *b)* the length of this *c)* the ratio of the length of this line to the length of the radius of the circle *d)* the ratio of the length of the hypotenuse of any right triangle

SECANT
($\frac{c}{b}$, secant of angle A; $\frac{c}{a}$, secant of angle B)

to the length of either of the other two sides with reference to the enclosed angle; reciprocal of the cosine of an angle

sec·a·teurs (sek′ə tərz) *n.pl.* [< Fr. *secateur* < L. *secare*, to cut (see SAW¹) + Fr. *-ateur* < L. *-ator*, -ATOR] [Chiefly Brit.] shears used for pruning

‡**sec·co** (sek′kō) *adj.* [It. < L. *siccus* (see SICCATIVE)] dry —*n.* painting done on dry plaster

se·cede (si sēd′) *vi.* -ced′ed, -ced′ing [L. *secedere* < *se-*, apart (< IE. base *swe-, *swe-*, apart, lone, whence OE. *swās*, special, dear) + *cedere*, to go: see CEDE] to withdraw formally from membership in, or association with, a group, federation, organization, etc., esp. a political or religious group —**se·ced′er** *n.*

se·cern (si surn′) *vt.* [L. *secernere*, to sunder, separate < *se-* (see prec.) + *cernere*, to separate: see CRISIS] to discriminate, or distinguish

se·ces·sion (si sesh′ən) *n.* [L. *secessio*] 1. an act of seceding; formal withdrawal or separation ☆2. [*often* S-] the withdrawal of the Southern States from the Federal Union at the start of the Civil War —**se·ces′sion·al** *adj.*

☆**se·ces·sion·ist** (-ist) *n.* a person who favors or takes part in secession, or upholds the right to secede; specif., [*often* S-] one who favored the secession of the Southern States —**se·ces′sion·ism** *n.*

☆**Seck·el** (**pear**) (sek′'l) [after the Pa. fruit grower who originated it] a small, sweet, juicy, reddish-brown pear

sec. leg. [L. *secundum legum*] according to law

se·clude (si klōōd′) *vt.* -clud′ed, -clud′ing [ME. *secluden* < L. *secludere* < *se-*, apart + *claudere*, to CLOSE²] 1. to keep away or apart from others; bar or shut off from the view of or relations with others; isolate 2. to make private or hidden; screen

se·clud·ed (-klōōd′id) *adj.* 1. shut off or kept apart from others; isolated; withdrawn 2. cut off from public view; hidden [a *secluded* garden]

se·clu·sion (si klōō′zhən) *n.* [ML. *seclusio*] 1. a secluding or being secluded; retirement; isolation; privacy 2. a secluded spot —*SYN.* see SOLITUDE

se·clu·sive (-siv) *adj.* [< L. *seclusus*, pp. of *secludere* (see SECLUDE) + -IVE] tending to seclude 2. fond of or seeking seclusion —**se·clu′sive·ly** *adv.* —**se·clu′sive·ness** *n.*

Sec·o·nal (sek′ə nôl′, -nal) [< arbitrary base + -AL] *a trademark for* a white, odorless, bitter powder, C₁₂H₁₈N₂O₃, used chiefly in the form of its water-soluble sodium salt as a sedative and hypnotic —*n.* [*also* s-] a capsule of this

sec·ond¹ (sek′ənd) *adj.* [ME. *secunde* < OFr. < L. *secundus*, following, second < *sequi*, to follow: cf. SEQUENT] 1. coming next after the first in order of place or time; 2d or 2nd 2. another; other; additional; supplementary [to take a *second* helping] 3. being of the same kind as another; resembling a given original [a *second* Shakespeare] 4. alternate; other [every *second* day] 5. next below the first in rank, power, value, merit, excellence, etc. 6. inferior; subordinate; secondary 7. designating the forward gear ratio of a motor vehicle next after low gear 8. *Music* a) lower in pitch b) playing or singing a part that is lower in pitch —*n.* 1. any person, thing, class, place, etc. that is second 2. the next after the first 3. an article of merchandise that falls below the standard set for first quality 4. [*pl.*] a) a kind of coarse flour b) bread made from this 5. an aid or official assistant, esp. to one of the principals in a duel or boxing match 6. second gear of a motor vehicle 7. the act or an instance of seconding 8. [Slang] [*pl.*] a second helping of something to eat 9. *Music* a) the second tone of an ascending diatonic scale, or a tone one degree above or below any given tone in such a scale; supertonic b) the interval between two such tones, or a combination of them c) the second part in a harmonized composition, esp. the alto d) an instrument or voice taking this part —*vt.* 1. to act as an aid or second to; aid; assist 2. to give support or encouragement to; further; reinforce 3. to indicate formally one's approval or support of (a motion, nomination, etc.) as a necessary preliminary to discussion of or vote on it 4. [Brit.] to transfer (a military officer) from his regular service to special service, civil or military —*adv.* in the second place, rank, group, etc. —**sec′ond·er** *n.*

sec·ond² (sek′ənd) *n.* [ME. *seconde* < ML. (*pars minuta*) *secunda*, second (small part): from being a further division (i.e., beyond the minute) < L. *secundus*: see prec.] 1. 1/60 of a minute of time 2. 1/60 of a minute of angular measurement; 1/3600 of a degree of arc: symbol (″) 3. a very short period of time; moment; instant 4. a specific point in time

Second Advent *same as* SECOND COMING
☆**Second Adventist** *same as* ADVENTIST

sec·ond·ar·y (sek′ən der′ē) *adj.* [ME. *secundary* < L. *secundarius*] 1. second, or below the first, in rank, importance, class, place, etc.; subordinate; minor; not primary 2. a) derived or resulting from something considered primary or original; dependent; derivative b) second-hand; not original [a *secondary* source of information] c) designating colors produced by mixing two primary colors: see COLOR (sense 3) 3. coming after that which is first in a series of processes, events, stages, etc., as of growth or development 4. coming next in sequence after the primary or elementary level [*secondary* education] 5. *Chem.* a) formed by the replacement of two atoms or radicals in the molecule [*secondary* sodium phosphate, Na₂HPO₄] b)

characterized by or designating a carbon atom that is directly attached to two other carbon atoms in a closed or open chain 6. *Elec.* designating or of an induced current or its circuit in a transformer, induction coil, etc. 7. *Geol.* formed as a result of the alteration, disintegration, or erosion of preexisting rocks or minerals 8. *Linguis.* a) derived from a word that is itself a derivative b) derived from a base that is itself a word, by the addition of a prefix or derivational suffix 9. *Zool.* designating or of the long flight feathers attached to the second joint or segment of a bird's wing —*n., pl.* -ar′ies 1. a person or thing that is secondary, subordinate, or inferior 2. any of the secondary colors 3. *Elec.* an output winding of a transformer from which the power is taken ☆4. *Football* the defensive backfield 5. *Zool.* a secondary feather —**sec′ond·ar′i·ly** *adv.*

secondary accent (or **stress**) 1. any accent, or stress, that is weaker than the full, or primary, accent 2. a mark (in this dictionary, ′), to show this

secondary cell a battery cell in which the electrochemical reaction is reversible so that it can be economically recharged by an electric current

secondary emission 1. the emission of electrons (**secondary electrons**) from a material, following impact by high-speed electrons 2. the emission of electrons or electromagnetic radiation from a liquid, solid, or gas, following impact by a charged particle or higher energy electromagnetic radiation

☆**secondary school** a school, as a high school, coming after elementary school

secondary sex characteristic any of the physical characteristics that differentiate male and female individuals, as distribution of hair or fat on the body, breast formation, etc., that are not directly related to reproduction and usually appear at puberty

☆**second banana** [Slang] 1. a performer in show business, esp. burlesque, who plays a subordinate role, as straight man, to the top banana, or star comedian 2. any person in a subordinate, often servile, position

☆**second base** *Baseball* the base between first base and third base, located behind the pitcher

second best something of quality next below the first; something next to the best —**sec′ond-best′** *adj.*

second childhood senility; dotage

sec·ond-class (sek′ənd klas′, -kläs′) *adj.* 1. of the class, rank, excellence, etc. next below the highest; of secondary quality 2. designating or of accommodations next below the best [a *second-class* railway carriage] ☆3. designating or of a class of mail consisting of newspapers, periodicals, etc.: such mail carries lower postage rates than first-class mail 4. inferior, inadequate, etc. —*adv.* 1. with accommodations next below the best [to travel *second-class*] 2. as or by second-class mail

Second Coming in the theology of some Christian sects, the expected return of Christ, at the Last Judgment

second cousin the child of one's parent's first cousin

se·conde (si känd′; Fr. zgōnd) *n.* [Fr., fem. of *second*: see SECOND¹] a parrying position in fencing, the second of the eight positions

Second Empire the government of France under Louis Napoleon, 1852-1870

second estate *see* ESTATE (sense 2)

second fiddle the part played by the second violin section of an orchestra or by the second violin of a quartet, etc. —**play** (or **be**) **second fiddle** to have secondary status, as in the affection or attention of another

second floor ☆1. the floor above the ground floor of a building 2. in Europe and Great Britain, the floor two stories above the ground floor: sometimes used in this sense in hotels, etc. in the U.S.

second growth ☆tree growth on land stripped of virgin forest

sec·ond-guess (sek′ənd ges′) *vt., vi.* [Colloq.] to use hindsight in criticizing or advising (someone), re-solving (a past problem), remaking (a decision), etc. —**sec′ond-guess′er** *n.*

sec·ond·hand (-hand′) *adj.* 1. not direct from the original source; not original 2. used or worn previously by another; not new 3. of or dealing in merchandise that is not new —*adv.* not firsthand; not directly

second hand 1. the hand (of a clock or watch) that indicates the seconds and moves around the dial once every minute 2. one who or that which is intermediate: now only in **at second hand**, indirectly

second lieutenant a commissioned officer of the lowest rank in the U.S. Army, Air Force, or Marine Corps

sec·ond·ly (sek′ənd lē) *adv.* in the second place; second: used chiefly in enumerating topics

second mate a merchant ship's officer next in rank below the first mate: also **second officer**

second mortgage an additional mortgage placed on property already mortgaged: it ranks below the first mortgage in priority of claim

second nature habits, characteristics, etc. acquired and fixed so deeply as to seem part of a person's nature

‡**se·con·do** (se kôn′dō) *n., pl.* -di (-dē) [It. < L. *secundus*, SECOND¹] the second, usually the lower, part in a concerted piece, esp. in a piano duet

☆**second papers** *popular name for* the documents by which an alien formerly made application for U.S. citizenship after having earlier filed a declaration of intention

second person that form of a pronoun (as *you*) or verb (as *are*) which refers to the person or persons spoken to

sec·ond-rate (sek'ənd rāt') *adj.* **1.** second in quality, rank, etc.; second-class **2.** inferior; mediocre —**sec'ond-rate'ness** *n.* —**sec'ond-rat'er** *n.*

Second Republic the republic established in France in 1848, when Louis Philippe was deposed, lasting until 1852, when the Second Empire was established

second self a person so intimately associated with another as to have taken on many of his personality traits, attitudes, beliefs, etc.

second sight the supposed ability to see things not physically present, to foresee the future, etc.

☆**sec·ond-sto·ry man** (-stôr'ē) [Colloq.] a burglar who enters a building through an upstairs window

sec·ond-string (-striŋ') *adj.* [Colloq.] **1.** *Sports* that is the second or a substitute choice for play at the specified position **2.** subordinate or inferior in rank, importance, etc. —**sec'ond-string'er** *n.*

second thought a change in thought about a matter after reconsidering it —**on second thought** after reconsideration

second wind 1. the return of relatively normal ease in breathing following the initial exhaustion that occurs during severe exertion or exercise, as while running **2.** recovered capacity for continuing any sort of effort

se·cre·cy (sē'krə sē) *n., pl.* -**cies** [altered < ME. *secretee* < *secre*, secret < OFr. *secré* < L. *secretus*: see ff.] **1.** the condition of being secret or concealed **2.** a tendency to keep things secret; practice or habit of being secretive

se·cret (sē'krit) *adj.* [ME. < OFr. < L. *secretus*, pp. of *secernere*, to set apart < *se-*, apart (see SECEDE) + *cernere*, to sift, distinguish: see CRISIS] **1.** kept from public knowledge or from the knowledge of a certain person or persons **2.** withdrawn, remote, or secluded [a *secret* hideaway] **3.** keeping one's affairs to oneself; secretive **4.** beyond general knowledge or understanding; mysterious or esoteric **5.** concealed from sight or notice; hidden [a *secret* drawer] **6.** acting in secret [a *secret* society] —*n.* **1.** something known only to a certain person or persons and purposely kept from the knowledge of others **2.** something not revealed, understood, or explained; mystery [the *secret* of Stonehenge] **3.** the true cause or explanation, regarded as not obvious [the *secret* of one's success] **4.** [S-] a prayer said just before the Preface of the Mass —**in secret** without the knowledge of others; secretly —**se'cret·ly** *adv.* **SYN.**—**secret,** the general term, implies a concealing or keeping from the knowledge of others, for whatever reason [my *secret* opinion of him]; **covert** implies a concealing as by disguising or veiling [a *covert* threat]; **clandestine** suggests that what is being kept secret is of an illicit, immoral, or proscribed nature [their *clandestine* meetings in the park]; **stealthy** implies a slow, quiet secrecy of action in an attempt to elude notice and often connotes deceit [the *stealthy* advance of the panther]; **furtive** adds to this connotations of slyness or watchfulness and suggests a reprehensible objective [the *furtive* movement of his hand toward my pocket]; **surreptitious** connotes a feeling of guilt in the one who is acting in a furtive or stealthy manner [she stole a *surreptitious* glance at him]; **underhanded** implies a stealthiness characterized by fraudulence or deceit [*underhanded* business dealings] —**ANT.** open, obvious

secret agent a person who carries on espionage or similar work of a secret nature, as for a government

sec·re·tar·i·at (sek'rə ter'ē ət) *n.* [Fr. *secrétariat* < ML. *secretariatus*] **1.** the office, position, or quarters of a secretary, esp. of an administrative secretary in a government or organization **2.** a secretarial staff; specif., an administrative staff or department, headed by a secretary-general

sec·re·tar·y (sek'rə ter'ē) *n., pl.* -**tar'ies** [ML. *secretarius*, one entrusted with secrets < L. *secretum*: see SECRET] **1.** *a)* a person whose work is keeping records, taking care of correspondence and other writing tasks, etc. as for an individual in a business office *b)* an officer of a company, club, etc. having somewhat similar functions ☆**2.** an official in charge of a department of government **3.** a writing desk, esp. one topped with a small bookcase —**sec're·tar'i·al** *adj.* —**sec're·tar'y·ship'** *n.*

secretary bird [from the penlike feathers of its crest] a large, grayish-blue and black African bird of prey (*Sagittarius serpentarius*) with a long neck, long legs, and tufts of penlike feathers sticking out from the back of its head: it feeds on insects, snakes, etc.

sec·re·tar·y-gen·er·al (-jen'ər əl) *n., pl.* -**tar'ies-gen'er·al** the chief administrative officer of an organization, in charge of a secretariat

se·crete (si krēt') *vt.* -**cret'ed,** -**cret'ing** [< earlier *secret*, to hide < L. *secretus*, pp. of *secernere:* see SECRET] **1.** to put or keep in a secret place; hide; conceal **2.** [back-formation < SECRETION] to form and release (a specified secretion) as a gland, etc. does —**SYN.** see HIDE[1]

se·cre·tin (si krēt'n) *n.* [SECRET(ION) + -IN[1]] a hormone produced in the

SECRETARY BIRD
(4 ft. high)

small intestine: it stimulates secretion of pancreatic juice

se·cre·tion (si krē'shən) *n.* [MFr. < L. *secretio,* a separation < *secretus,* pp. of *secernere:* see SECRET] **1.** the act of hiding or concealing something **2.** *a)* the separation and elaboration of a substance from materials in the blood or sap, and its release for special use by the organism or for excretion as waste *b)* the substance thus released

se·cre·tive (sē'krə tiv; *also, & for 2 always,* si krēt'iv) *adj.* [SECRET + -IVE] **1.** tending to conceal one's thoughts, feelings, affairs, etc. from others; reticent; not frank or open **2.** *same as* SECRETORY —**SYN.** see SILENT —**se'cre·tive·ly** *adv.* —**se'cre·tive·ness** *n.*

se·cre·to·ry (si krēt'ər ē) *adj.* of, or having the function of, secretion; secreting —*n.* a secretory gland, etc.

secret police a police force that operates secretly, esp. for suppressing opposition to the government

secret service a government service organized to carry on secret investigation; specif., ☆[S- S-] a division of the U.S. Treasury Department concerned with the discovery and arrest of counterfeiters, protection of the President, etc.

secret society any organized group that conceals some of its rituals and other activities from nonmembers

sect (sekt) *n.* [ME. *secte* < MFr. < L. *secta,* a path, way, method, party, faction, in LL.(Ec.), doctrine, sect < *sequi,* to follow: see SEQUENT] **1.** a religious denomination, esp. a small group that has broken away from an established church **2.** any group of people having a common leadership, set of opinions, philosophical doctrine, political principles, etc.; specif., a faction of a larger group

-sect (sekt) [< L. *sectus,* pp. of *secare,* to cut: see SAW[1]] *a combining form meaning* cut, separated [*pinnatisect*]

sect. section

sec·tar·i·an (sek ter'ē ən) *adj.* [< ff. + -AN] **1.** of or characteristic of a sect **2.** devoted to, or prejudiced in favor of, some sect **3.** narrow-minded; limited; parochial —*n.* **1.** orig., an apostate from an established church **2.** a member of any religious sect **3.** a person who is blindly and narrow-mindedly devoted to a sect —**sec·tar'i·an·ism** *n.* —**sec·tar'i·an·ize'** (-īz') *vt., vi.* -**ized',** -**iz'ing**

sec·ta·ry (sek'tər ē) *n., pl.* -**ries** [ML. *sectarius* < L. *secta:* see SECT] **1.** a member of a sect **2.** [*often* S-] a dissenter from an established church; esp., a Nonconformist

sec·tile (sek't'l, -tīl) *adj.* [Fr. < L. *sectilis < secare,* to cut: see SAW[1]] **1.** capable of being cut smoothly with a knife **2.** *Bot.* cut into small divisions —**sec·til'i·ty** (-til'ə tē) *n.*

sec·tion (sek'shən) *n.* [L. *sectio < sectus,* pp. of *secare,* to cut: see SAW[1]] **1.** the act or process of cutting or separating by cutting; specif., an incision in surgery **2.** *a)* a part separated or removed by cutting; slice; division *b)* a very thin slice, as of tissue, used for microscopic study **3.** *a)* a part or division of a book, newspaper, etc. *b)* a numbered paragraph of a writing, a law, etc. **4.** any distinct, constituent part [a bookcase in five *sections,* various *sections* of society] **5.** a segment of an orange, grapefruit, etc. ☆**6.** a division of public lands constituting 640 acres, or 1/36 of a township **7.** a loose subdivision of a biological genus, group, family, etc. **8.** a view or drawing of a thing as it would appear if cut straight through in a given plane **9.** any of the distinct groups of instruments or voices in an orchestra or chorus [the woodwind *section*] **10.** any of several tactical subdivisions of military or naval forces ☆**11.** *a)* part of a sleeping car containing an upper and lower berth *b)* the smallest administrative division of a railroad right of way, usually several miles of track under the care of a single maintenance crew ☆**12.** any of two or more buses, trains, or airplanes put into service for a particular route and schedule to accommodate extra passengers **13.** *Printing* a mark (§) used to indicate a section in a book, etc., or as a reference mark: also **section mark** —*vt.* **1.** to cut or divide into sections **2.** to represent in sections, as in mechanical drawing —**SYN.** see PART

sec·tion·al (sek'shən 'l) *adj.* **1.** of a section **2.** of, characteristic of, or devoted to a given section or district; regional **3.** made up of or divided into sections or parts that may be used as separate units —☆*n.* a sectional sofa, bookcase, etc. —**sec'tion·al·ly** *adv.*

☆**sec·tion·al·ism** (-iz'm) *n.* narrow-minded concern for or devotion to the interests of one section of a country; sectional spirit, bias, etc. —**sec'tion·al·ist** *adj., n.*

sec·tion·al·ize (-īz') *vt.* -**ized',** -**iz'ing 1.** to make sectional **2.** to divide into sections, esp. geographical sections —**sec'tion·al·i·za'tion** *n.*

☆**Section Eight** (or 8) [former section number of the U.S. Army regulation governing this] **1.** discharge from the U.S. Armed Forces because of military unsuitability, esp. psychological unfitness **2.** a soldier given such a discharge

☆**section gang** a crew of men (**section hands**) who do the maintenance work on a railroad section

sec·tor (sek'tər) *n.* [LL. < L., cutter < *sectus,* pp. of *secare,* to cut: see SAW[1]] **1.** part of a circle bounded by any two radii and the arc included between them **2.** a mathematical instrument consisting of two rulers marked with various scales and jointed together at one end, used in solving problems, measuring angles, etc. **3.** any of the districts into which an area is divided for military

operations **4.** a distinct part of society or of an economy, group, area, etc.; section; segment —*vt.* to divide into sectors —**sec′tor·al** *adj.*

sec·to·ri·al (sek tôr′ē əl) *adj.* [prec. + -IAL] **1.** of a sector **2.** *Bot.* designating or of a chimera having two or more distinct types of tissue set apart as sectors in the stem **3.** *Zool.* specialized for slicing or shearing; carnassial —*n.* a sectorial tooth

sec·u·lar (sek′yə lər) *adj.* [ME. *seculer* < OFr. < LL.(Ec.) *saecularis*, worldly, profane, heathen < L., of an age < *saeculum*, an age, generation < IE. *seitlo-* < base *sei-*, to scatter, SOW²] **1.** *a)* of or relating to worldly things as distinguished from things relating to church and religion; not sacred or religious; temporal; worldly [*secular* music, *secular* schools] *b)* of or marked by secularism; secularistic **2.** living in the outside world and not bound by a monastic vow or rule [the *secular* clergy] **3.** *a)* coming or happening only once in an age or century *b)* lasting for an age or ages; continuing for a long time or from age to age —*n.* **1.** a member of the secular clergy **2.** a layman —**sec′u·lar·ly** *adv.*

sec·u·lar·ism (-iz′m) *n.* [prec. + -ISM] **1.** worldly spirit, views, or the like; esp., a system of doctrines and practices that disregards or rejects any form of religious faith and worship **2.** the belief that religion and ecclesiastical affairs should not enter into the functions of the state, esp. into public education —**sec′u·lar·ist** *n., adj.* —**sec′u·lar·is′tic** *adj.*

sec·u·lar·i·ty (sek′yə ler′ə tē) *n.* [ME. *seculerte* < ML. *saecularitas*] **1.** the state or quality of being secular **2.** *same as* SECULARISM **3.** *pl.* -**ties** a secular concern, matter, etc.

sec·u·lar·ize (sek′yə lə rīz′) *vt.* -**ized′**, -**iz′ing** [Fr. *séculariser* < LL.(Ec.) *saecularis*: see SECULAR] **1.** *a)* to change from religious to civil ownership or use *b)* to deprive of religious character, influence, or significance *c)* to convert to secularism **2.** to change (a regular clergyman) to the status of secular clergyman —**sec′u·lar·i·za′tion** *n.*

se·cund (sē′kənd, sek′ənd) *adj.* [L. *secundus*, following: see SECOND¹] *Bot.* growing on one side only, as the flowers in the lily of the valley

Se·cun·der·a·bad (si kun′dər ə bäd′, -bad′) former city in SC India: now part of the city of Hyderabad

sec·un·dines (sek′ən dīnz′) *n.pl.* [ME. < LL. *secundinae*, pl., the afterbirth < L. *secundus*, following: see SECOND¹] *same as* AFTERBIRTH

se·cure (si kyoor′) *adj.* [L. *securus* < *se-*, free from, apart (see SECEDE) + *cura*, care: see CURE] **1.** free from fear, care, doubt, or anxiety; not worried, troubled, or apprehensive **2.** free from danger; not exposed to damage, attack, etc.; safe **3.** in safekeeping or custody **4.** not likely to fail or give way; firm; strong; stable [to make a knot *secure*] **5.** reliable; dependable [a *secure* investment] **6.** [Archaic] overconfident and careless —*vt.* -**cured′**, -**cur′ing 1.** to make secure, or safe; guard; protect [to *secure* a position against attack] **2.** to make sure or certain; guarantee; ensure, as with a pledge [to *secure* a loan with collateral] **3.** *a)* to make firm, fast, tight, etc. [*secure* the bolt] *b)* to put under restraint; tie up **4.** to get hold or possession of; obtain; acquire [to *secure* aid] **5.** to take into custody; capture **6.** to bring about; cause [to *secure* a laugh] **7.** *Naut. a)* to relieve from duty *b)* to bring to a halt; cease; stop —*vi.* **1.** to give security [a policy that *secures* against loss] **2.** *Naut. a)* to stop working *b)* to moor: said of a ship —*SYN.* see GET, SAFE —**se·cur′a·ble** *adj.* —**se·cur′ance** *n.* —**se·cure′ly** *adv.* —**se·cure′ness** *n.* —**se·cur′er** *n.*

se·cu·ri·ty (si kyoor′ə tē) *n., pl.* -**ties** [ME. *securite* < L. *securitas* < *securus*: see SECURE] **1.** the state of being or feeling secure; freedom from fear, anxiety, danger, doubt, etc.; state or sense of safety or certainty **2.** something that gives or assures safety, tranquillity, certainty, etc.; protection; safeguard **3.** *a)* protection or defense against attack, interference, espionage, etc. [funds for national *security*] *b)* protection or defense against escape [a maximum *security* prison] *c)* procedures to provide such protection or defense **4.** *a)* something given as a pledge of repayment, fulfillment of a promise, etc.; guarantee *b)* a person who agrees to make good the failure of another to pay, perform a duty, etc.; surety **5.** any evidence of debt or ownership, esp. a stock certificate or bond: *usually used in pl.*

security blanket a small blanket or other soft cloth, as clutched or stroked by a child for the feeling of comfort and security it affords

Security Council the United Nations council responsible for maintaining international peace and security

secy., sec′y. secretary

sed. 1. sediment **2.** sedimentation

Se·dan (si dan′; *Fr.* sə dän′) city in N France, on the Meuse River: scene of a decisive Fr. defeat (1870) in the Franco-Prussian War: pop. 20,000

se·dan (si dan′) *n.* [? coined by Sir S. Duncombe (1634), Eng. holder of the patent < ? L. *sedere*, to SIT, after the It. name *seggietta*, dim. of *seggia*, a chair < L. *sedere*] **1.** *same as* SEDAN CHAIR ☆**2.** an enclosed automobile with two or four doors, and two wide seats, front and rear

sedan chair an enclosed chair for one person, carried on poles by two men

se·date¹ (si dāt′) *adj.* [L. *sedatus*, pp. of *sedare*, to settle, caus. of *sedere*, to SIT] calm, quiet, or composed; esp., serious and unemotional; staid; decorous —*SYN.* see SERIOUS — **se·date′ly** *adv.* —**se·date′ness** *n.*

☆**se·date²** (si dāt′) *vt.* -**dat′ed**, -**dat′ing** [back-formation < SEDATIVE] to dose with a sedative

SEDAN CHAIR

se·da·tion (si dā′shən) *n.* [L. *sedatio*, a calming < *sedare*: see SEDATE¹] *Med.* **1.** the act or process of reducing excitement, nervousness, or irritation. esp. by means of sedatives **2.** the state so induced

sed·a·tive (sed′ə tiv) *adj.* [MFr. *sédatif* < ML. *sedativus* < L. *sedatus*: see SEDATE¹] tending to soothe or quiet; specif., *Med.* having the property of lessening excitement, nervousness, or irritation —*n.* a sedative medicine

sed·en·tar·y (sed′'n ter′ē) *adj.* [Fr. *sédentaire* < L. *sedentarius* < *sedens*, prp. of *sedere*, to SIT] **1.** *a)* of or marked by much sitting about and little travel *b)* keeping one seated much of the time [a *sedentary* job] **2.** *a)* remaining in one locality; not migratory: said of birds, etc. *b)* fixed to one spot, as a barnacle —**sed′en·tar′i·ly** *adv.* —**sed′en·tar′i·ness** *n.*

Se·der (sā′dər) *n., pl.* **Se·dars′, Se′ders** [Heb. *sēdher*, arrangement, service] *Judaism* the feast commemorating the exodus of the Jews from Egypt, observed in the home by the reading of the Haggada on the eve of the first day of Passover (and by Orthodox Jews outside Israel also the eve of the second day)

sedge (sej) *n.* [ME. *segge* < OE. *secg*, akin to *sagu*, SAW¹: from the shape of the leaves] any of a family (Cyperaceae) of grasslike plants often found on wet ground or in water, having usually triangular, solid stems, three rows of narrow, pointed leaves, and minute flowers borne in spikelets —*adj.* designating this family of plants including papyrus —**sedg′y** *adj.* **sedg′i·er, sedg′i·est**

se·dil·i·a (si dil′ē ə) *n.pl., sing.* **se·dil′e** (-dī′lē) [L., pl. of *sedile*, a seat < *sedere*, to SIT] a set of seats, usually three, traditionally along the south side of a church, for the use of officiating clergy

sed·i·ment (sed′ə mənt) *n.* [Fr. *sédiment* < L. *sedimentum* < *sedere*, to SIT] **1.** matter that settles to the bottom of a liquid **2.** *Geol.* matter deposited by water or wind — **sed′i·men′tal** (-men′t′l) *adj.*

sed·i·men·ta·ry (sed′ə men′tər ē) *adj.* **1.** of, having the nature of, or containing sediment **2.** formed by the deposit of sediment, as certain rocks —**sed′i·men′ta·ri·ly** *adv.*

sed·i·men·ta·tion (sed′ə men tā′shən, -mən-) *n.* the depositing or formation of sediment

se·di·tion (si dish′ən) *n.* [ME. *sedicion* < OFr. < L. *seditio* < *sed-*, apart (see SECEDE) + *itio*, a going < *ire*, to go: see YEAR] **1.** the stirring up of discontent, resistance, or rebellion against the government in power **2.** [Rare] revolt or rebellion —**se·di′tion·ist** *n.*

SYN.—**sedition** applies to anything regarded by a government as stirring up resistance or rebellion against it and implies that the evidence is not overt or absolute; **treason** implies an overt act in violation of the allegiance owed to one's state, specif. a levying war against it or giving aid or comfort to its enemies

se·di·tion·ar·y (-er′ē) *adj. same as* SEDITIOUS —*n., pl.* -**ar′ies** a person engaging in sedition

se·di·tious (si dish′əs) *adj.* [ME. *cedicious* < MFr. *seditieux* < L. *seditiosus*] **1.** of, like, or constituting sedition **2.** inclined toward or engaging in sedition —**se·di′tious·ly** *adv.* —**se·di′tious·ness** *n.*

se·duce (si doos′, -dyoos′) *vt.* -**duced′**, -**duc′ing** [ME. *seduisen* < LL.(Ec.) *seducere*, to mislead, seduce < L., to lead aside < *se-*, apart (see SECEDE) + *ducere*, to lead: see DUKE] **1.** *a)* to persuade to do something disloyal, disobedient, etc. *b)* to persuade or tempt to evil or wrongdoing; lead astray *c)* to persuade to engage in unlawful sexual intercourse, esp. for the first time **2.** to entice —*SYN.* see LURE —**se·duce′ment** *n.* —**se·duc′i·ble** *adj.*

se·duc·er (-ər) *n.* a person or thing that seduces; esp., a man who seduces a woman

se·duc·tion (si duk′shən) *n.* [MFr. < LL.(Ec.) *seductio* < L., a leading away] **1.** the act of seducing or the state of being seduced **2.** something that seduces

se·duc·tive (-tiv) *adj.* [< L. *seductus*, pp. of *seducere* (see SEDUCE) + -IVE] tending to seduce, or lead astray; tempting; enticing —**se·duc′tive·ly** *adv.* —**se·duc′tive·ness** *n.*

se·duc·tress (-tris) *n.* a woman who seduces, esp. one who seduces a man sexually

se·du·li·ty (si dyool′ə tē, -dool′-) *n.* [L. *sedulitas*] the quality or fact of being sedulous

sed·u·lous (sej′oo ləs) *adj.* [L. *sedulus* < *sedulo*, diligently, orig., without guile < *se-*, apart (see SECEDE) + *dolus*, trickery: for IE. base see TALE] **1.** working hard and steadily; diligent **2.** constant; persistent —*SYN.* see BUSY —**sed′u·lous·ly** *adv.* —**sed′u·lous·ness** *n.*

se·dum (sē′dəm) *n.* [ModL., name of the genus < L., houseleek] any of a genus (*Sedum*) of mainly perennial plants of the orpine family, found on rocks and walls, with fleshy stalks and leaves and white, yellow, or pink flowers

see[1] (sē) *vt.* **saw, seen, see'ing** [ME. *seen* < OE. *seon* (< *sehwan*), akin to G. *sehen*, Goth. *saihwan* < IE. base *sekw-*, to observe, show, see, tell, whence L. *inseque*, tell!: cf. SAY] **1.** *a)* to get knowledge or an awareness of through the eyes; perceive visually; look at; view *b)* to visualize as though present; picture **2.** *a)* to get a clear mental impression of; grasp by thinking; understand /to *see* the point of a joke/ *b)* to accept as right, proper, or suitable /I can't *see* him as president/ *c)* to consider to be; judge /*saw* it as his duty/ **3.** *a)* to learn; discover; find out /*see* what they want/ *b)* to learn by reading, as in a newspaper **4.** to have personal knowledge of; experience; witness /to have *seen* better days/ **5.** to look over; inspect; examine /let me *see* that burn/ **6.** to take care; make sure /*see* that he does it right/ **7.** *a)* to escort; accompany; attend /to *see* someone home/ *b)* to keep company with; be dating regularly **8.** *a)* to encounter; meet; come in contact with /have you *seen* John?/ *b)* to recognize by sight **9.** *a)* to call on; visit *b)* to have an interview with; consult /*see* a lawyer/ **10.** to admit to one's presence; receive /too ill to *see* anyone/ **11.** to be a spectator at; view or attend /to *see* a show/ **12.** *Card Games* *a)* to meet (a bet) by staking an equal sum *b)* to meet the bet of (another) in this way —*vi.* **1.** to have the power of sight **2.** to discern objects, colors, etc. by using the eyes /to be able to *see* far/ **3.** *a)* to take a look /go and *see*/ *b)* to investigate or inquire /*see* if he wants anything/ **4.** to comprehend; understand **5.** to think over a given matter; reflect /let me *see*, where did I put it?/ —*interj.* behold! look! —**see about 1.** to investigate or inquire into **2.** to attend to —**see after** to take care of; look after —**see double** to see two of every object through inability to focus the eyes, as from drunkenness —**see fit (to)** to consider that it is desirable, proper, etc. (to do something) —**see into 1.** to investigate; look into **2.** to perceive the true meaning, character, or nature of —**see off** to go with (another) to the place from which he is to leave, as on a journey —**see out 1.** to carry out; finish; go through with **2.** to wait till the end of —**see through 1.** to perceive the true meaning, character, or nature of **2.** to carry out to the end; finish **3.** to help out or carry through a time of difficulty —**see to** to attend to —**see'a·ble** *adj.*
SYN.—**see**, the most simple and direct of these terms, is the basic term for the use of the organs of sight; **behold** implies a directing of the eyes on something and holding it in view, usually stressing the strong impression made /he never *beheld* a sight more beautiful/; **espy** and **descry** both imply a catching sight of with some effort, **espy** suggesting the detection of that which is small, partly hidden, etc. /he *espied* the snake crawling through the grass/ and **descry** the making out of something from a distance or through darkness, mist, etc. /he *descried* the distant steeple/; **view** implies a seeing or looking at what lies before one, as in inspection or examination /the jury *viewed* the evidence/

see[2] (sē) *n.* [ME. *se* < OFr. *sie*, *sied* < L. *sedes*, a seat, in ML.(Ec.), a see of a bishop] **1.** the official seat, or center of authority, of a bishop **2.** the position, authority, or jurisdiction of a bishop **3.** [Obs.] a seat of authority, esp. a throne

See·beck effect (zā'bek, sē'-) [after T. J. *Seebeck* (1770–1831), G. physicist] *Elec.* **1.** the production of a current in a circuit when junctions composed of unlike metals have different temperatures **2.** the current so produced

☆**see·catch** (sē'kach') *n.* [Russ. *sekach*, *sekachi* < G. *seekatze*, lit., sea cat, transl. of Russ. (*morskoy*) *kot*, (sea) cat, term used in Kamchatka] the adult male fur seal of Alaskan waters: also **see'catch'ie** (-ē-)

seed (sēd) *n.*, *pl.* **seeds, seed:** see PLURAL, II, D, 4 [ME. *sede* < OE. *sæd*, akin to G. *saat* < IE. base *sei-*, to cast, let fall, whence L. *serere*, to sow, plant, *sator*, sower, *semen*, seed] **1.** the part of a flowering plant that typically contains the embryo with its protective coat and stored food and that will develop into a new plant if sown; fertilized and mature ovule **2.** loosely, *a)* any part, as a bulb, tuber, etc., from which a new plant will grow /a potato *seed*/ *b)* a small, usually hard, seedlike fruit **3.** seeds collectively **4.** the source, origin, or beginning of anything /the *seeds* of revolt/ **5.** family stock; ancestry **6.** descendants; posterity **7.** *a)* in the development of certain lower animals, a form suitable for transplanting; specif., *same as* SPAT[4] *b)* the seed-bearing stage or condition /in *seed*/ **8.** *same as* SPORE (*n.* 2) **9.** sperm or semen **10.** something tiny, like a seed; esp., ☆*a)* a tiny crystal or other particle, as one added to a solution or liquid to start crystallization *b)* a tiny bubble, as a flaw in glassware ☆**11.** *Sports* a seeded player —*vt.* **1.** to plant with seed **2.** to sow (seeds) **3.** to remove the seeds from ☆**4.** to inject, fill, or scatter with seeds (sense 10 *a*); esp., to sprinkle particles of dry ice, silver iodide, etc. into (clouds) as in an attempt to induce rainfall **5.** to provide with the means or stimulus for growing or developing ☆**6.** *Sports* *a)* to distribute the names of the ranking contestants in (the draw for position in a tournament) so that those with the greatest skill are not matched together in the early rounds *b)* to treat (a player) as a ranking contestant in this way —*vi.* **1.** to form seeds; specif., to become ripe and produce seed **2.**

to go to seed; shed seed **3.** to sow seed —**go** (or **run**) **to seed 1.** to shed seeds after the time of flowering or bearing has passed **2.** to become weak, useless, unprofitable, etc.; deteriorate —**seed'ed** *adj.* —**seed'less** *adj.*

seed·bed (-bed') *n.* a bed of soil, usually covered with glass, in which seedlings are grown for transplanting

seed·cake (-kāk') *n.* any cake or cookie containing spicy seeds, as of caraway

seed·case (-kās') *n. same as* SEED VESSEL

seed coat the outer layer or coating of a seed

seed coral fragments of coral used in ornaments

seed corn corn set aside for planting a new crop

seed·er (-ər) *n.* a person or thing that seeds; specif., *a)* one that sows or plants seeds *b)* a device for removing seeds, as from raisins

seed fern any of an extinct order (Cycadofilicales) of Paleozoic, fernlike plants, that bore naked seeds upon their leaves

seed leaf *same as* COTYLEDON

seed·ling (-lin) *n.* **1.** a plant grown from a seed, rather than from a cutting, etc. **2.** any young plant; esp., a young tree less than three feet high

☆**seed money** money made available to begin the financing of, or to attract additional funds for, a long-term project

seed oysters oyster spat; very young oysters, esp. at the stage suitable for transplanting

seed pearl a very small pearl, often imperfect

seed plant *same as* SPERMATOPHYTE

seed·pod (-päd') *n.* a carpel or pistil, enclosing ovules or seeds in angiosperms

seed shrimp *same as* OSTRACOD

seeds·man (sēdz'mən) *n., pl.* **-men** (-mən) **1.** a sower of seeds **2.** a dealer in seeds Also **seed'man**

seed·time (sēd'tīm') *n.* the season for sowing seeds

seed vessel any dry, hollow fruit, as a pod, containing seed

seed·y (sēd'ē) *adj.* **seed'i·er, seed'i·est 1.** containing many seeds **2.** gone to seed **3.** having tiny bubbles: said of glass **4.** shabby, run-down, etc. **5.** feeling or looking physically bad or low in spirits —**seed'i·ly** *adv.* —**seed'i·ness** *n.*

See·ger (sē'gər), **Pete(r)** 1919– ; U.S. folk singer

see·ing (sē'in) *n.* **1.** the sense or power of sight; vision **2.** the act of using the eyes to see —*adj.* having the sense of sight —*conj.* in view of the fact; considering; inasmuch as

☆**Seeing Eye dog** [also ☆ **s- e-**] a guide dog, specif. one trained by Seeing Eye, Inc., near Morristown, N.J.

seek (sēk) *vt.* **sought, seek'ing** [ME. *seken* < OE. *secan*, akin to OS. *sōkian*, G. *suchen* < IE. base *sag-*, to track down, trace, whence L. *sagire*, to scent out, perceive] **1.** to try to find; search for; look for **2.** to go to; resort to /to *seek* the woods for peace/ **3.** *a)* to try to get or find out by asking or searching /to *seek* the answer to a question/ *b)* to request; ask for **4.** to bend one's efforts toward; aim at; pursue /*seeking* perfection/ **5.** to try; attempt: used with an infinitive /to *seek* to please someone/ **6.** [Obs.] to explore —*vi.* **1.** to look for someone or something **2.** [Obs.] to resort (*to*) —**seek'er** *n.*

seel (sēl) *vt.* [LME. *silen* < OFr. *ciller* < *cil* < L. *cilium*, lower eyelid, orig. eyelash] **1.** *Falconry* to sew together the eyelids of (a young hawk) **2.** [Obs.] *a)* to close (the eyes) *b)* to blind

seem (sēm) *vi.* [ME. *semen*, prob. < ON. *sœma*, to conform to (akin to OE. *seman*, to bring to agreement): for IE. base see SAME] **1.** *a)* to appear to be; have the look of being /to *seem* happy/ *b)* to appear; give the impression (usually followed by an infinitive) /he *seems* to know the facts/ *c)* to have the impression; think (followed by an infinitive) /I *seem* to have lost it/ **2.** to appear to exist /there *seems* no point in going/ **3.** to be apparently true /it *seems* he was here/

seem·ing (sēm'in) *adj.* that seems real, true, etc. without necessarily being so; apparent /her *seeming* anger/ —*n.* outward appearance; semblance —**seem'ing·ly** *adv.*

seem·ly (sēm'lē) *adj.* **-li·er, -li·est** [ME. *semlich* < ON. *sœmiligr* < *sœmr*, fitting: cf. SEEM] **1.** pleasing in appearance; fair; handsome **2.** suitable, proper, fitting, or becoming, esp. as regards conventional standards of conduct or good taste; decorous —*adv.* in a seemly manner; properly, fittingly, etc. —**seem'li·ness** *n.*

seen (sēn) *pp.* of SEE[1]

seep (sēp) *vi.* [ME. *sipen* < OE. *sipian*, to soak, akin to MLowG. *sipen*, to drip < IE. base *seib-*, to run out, drip, whence SOAP] to leak, drip, or flow out slowly through small openings or pores; ooze —*n.* **1.** a place where water, oil, etc. oozes from the ground to form a pool **2.** *same as* SEEPAGE —**seep'y** *adj.*

seep·age (-ij) *n.* **1.** the act or process of seeping; leakage; oozing **2.** liquid that seeps

seer[1] (sē'ər for 1; sir for 2) *n.* **1.** a person who sees **2.** a person with the supposed power to foretell the future; prophet —**seer'ess** (sir'is) *n.fem.*

seer[2] (sir) *n.* [Hind. *sēr*] a unit of weight, usually equal to 2.06 pounds, used in Nepal, Pakistan, Aden, and certain other Middle East countries

seer·suck·er (sir'suk'ər) *n.* [Hind. *shirshaker* < Per. *shir u shakar*, lit., milk and sugar, also a kind of striped linen

cloth] a light, crinkled fabric of linen, cotton, etc., usually with a striped pattern

see·saw (sē′sô′) *n.* [redupl. of SAW¹: from the action of sawing] **1.** a plank balanced on a support at the middle, used by children at play, who ride the ends so that when one goes up, the other comes down **2.** the act of riding a plank in this way **3.** any up-and-down or back-and-forth movement or change, as in the lead in a competition —*adj.* moving up and down or back and forth —*vt., vi.* to move up and down or back and forth on or as on a seesaw

seethe (sēth) *vt.* **seethed, seeth′ing** [ME. *sethen* < OE. *sēothan,* akin to G. *sieden* < IE. base *sew-,* to cook, boil, whence Sans. *hāvayən,* (they) stew] **1.** to cook by boiling **2.** to soak, steep, or saturate in liquid —*vi.* **1.** to boil or to surge, bubble, or foam as if boiling **2.** to be violently agitated or disturbed —*n.* the act or condition of seething —*SYN.* see BOIL¹

seg·ment (seg′mənt; *for v.* -ment) *n.* [L. *segmentum* < *secare,* to cut: see SAW¹] **1.** any of the parts into which a body is separated or separable; division; section **2.** *Geom.* a) a part of a figure, esp. of a circle or sphere, marked off or made separate by a line or plane, as a part of a circular area bounded by an arc and its chord b) any of the finite sections of a line **3.** *Linguis.* a phone, or single sound, or a lack of sound in the stream of speech **4.** *Zool.* a) *same as* METAMERE b) the part of an arthropod appendage between joints —*vt., vi.* to divide into segments —*SYN.* see PART —seg′men·tar′y *adj.*

seg·men·tal (seg men′t'l) *adj.* **1.** having the form of a segment of a circle **2.** of, like, or made up of a segment or segments —seg·men′tal·ly *adv.*

segmental phonemes the vowel, consonant, and semi-vowel sounds of a language: cf. SUPRASEGMENTAL PHONEMES

seg·men·ta·tion (seg′mən tā′shən, -men-) *n.* **1.** a dividing or being divided into segments **2.** *Biol.* the progressive growth and cleavage of a single cell into many others to form a new organism

segmentation cavity the central cavity of a blastula

se·gno (sān′yō; *It.* se′nyô) *n., pl.* se′gni (-yē; *It.* -nyē) [It. < L. *signum,* a sign] *Music* a sign; esp., the sign (𝄊 or :𝄊:) used at the beginning or end of a repeat

☆**se·go** (sē′gō) *n., pl.* -gos [< AmInd. (Shoshonean), as in Ute *sigo*] **1.** a perennial bulb plant (*Calochortus nuttallii*) of the lily family, with trumpet-shaped flowers, found in W. N. America: in full sego lily **2.** its edible bulb

Se·go·via (se gō′vyä) city in C Spain: pop. 34,000

Se·go·via (se gō′vyä; *E.* sə gō′vē ə), **An·drés** (än dres′) 1894–   ; Sp. guitarist & composer

seg·re·gate (seg′rə gāt′; *for adj., usually* -git) *adj.* [ME. *segregat* < L. *segregatus,* pp. of *segregare,* to set apart, lit., to set apart from the flock (< *se-,* apart (see SECEDE) + *grex* (gen. *gregis*), a flock (see GREGARIOUS)] separate; set apart; segregated —*vt.* -gat′ed, -gat′ing to set apart from others or from the main mass or group; isolate; specif., to impose a system of segregation on (racial groups, social facilities, etc.) —*vi.* **1.** to separate from the main mass and collect together in a new body: said of crystals **2.** to separate from others; be segregated **3.** *Genetics* to undergo segregation —*n.* a segregated person, thing, group, etc. —seg′re·gat′ive *adj.*

seg·re·gat·ed (seg′rə gāt′id) *adj.* ☆conforming to a system that segregates racial groups

seg·re·ga·tion (seg′rə gā′shən) *n.* [LL. *segregatio*] **1.** a segregating or being segregated; specif., the policy or practice of compelling racial groups to live apart from each other, go to separate schools, use separate social facilities, etc. **2.** *Genetics* the separation of allelic genes into different gametes during meiosis so that a particular gamete receives only one member of a pair of characters: see MENDEL'S LAWS

seg·re·ga·tion·ist (-ist) *n.* a person who favors or practices segregation, esp. racial segregation —*adj.* of, like, or favoring segregation or segregationists

se·gue (seg′wä, sā′gwä) *vi.* -gued, -gu·ing [It., 3d pers. sing., pres. indic., of *seguire,* to follow < VL. *sequere,* for L. *sequi:* see SEQUENT] to continue without break (*to* or *into* the next part) —*n.* an immediate transition from one part to another, as in music

se·gui·dil·la (seg′ə dēl′yə, sā′gə-; -dē′yə) *n.* [Sp. < *seguida,* a following < *seguir,* to follow < VL. *sequere* (see prec.)] **1.** a fast Spanish dance, to the accompaniment of castanets **2.** the music for this dance, in 3/4 time **3.** a stanza of four to seven short lines, partly assonant, with a distinctive rhythm, sung to this music

†**sei·cen·to** (se chen′tô) *n.* [It., short for *mille seicento,* one thousand six hundred] the 17th century, as a period in Italian art and literature

seiche (sāsh) *n.* [< Swiss-Fr.] an oscillation of the water in a lake, bay, etc., caused by changes in atmospheric pressure, seismic disturbances, winds or waves, etc.

sei·del (zī′d'l, sī-) *n., pl.* -dels, -del [G. < MHG. *sidelin* < L. *situla,* a bucket] a large beer mug, sometimes with a hinged lid

Seid·litz powders (sed′lits) [their properties are said to resemble those of natural waters from the spring at Sedlčany (G. *Seidlitz*), Czechoslovakia] a laxative composed of two powders, one of sodium bicarbonate and Rochelle salt, the other of tartaric acid: the two are

separately dissolved in water, combined, and drunk while effervescing: also **Seidlitz powder**

sei·gneur (sen yur′, sān-, sēn-) *n.* [Fr. < MFr.: see SEIGNIOR] **1.** *same as* SEIGNIOR (sense 1) **2.** in French Canada, the owner of an estate granted by royal decree to 17th-cent. French settlers —sei·gneur′i·al (-ē əl) *adj.*

sei·gneur·y (sen′yər ē, sān′-, sēn′-) *n., pl.* -gneur·ies **1.** *same as* SEIGNIORY (sense 1) **2.** in French Canada, the estate or manor of a seigneur

sei·gnior (sēn′yər) *n.* [ME. *segnour* < Anglo-Fr. *segnour* < OFr. *seignor* < L. *senior:* see SENIOR] **1.** a lord or noble; specif., the lord of a fee or manor **2.** *same as* SEIGNEUR (sense 2)

sei·gnior·age (-ij) *n.* [ME. *seignorage* < OFr. < *signor:* see prec.] **1.** something claimed or taken by a sovereign or other superior as his just right or due **2.** any profits or charges arising from the minting of gold and silver coins from bullion, usually the difference between face value and intrinsic value

sei·gnio·ri·al, sei·gno·ri·al (sēn yôr′ē əl) *adj.* of or characteristic of a seignior: also **sei·gnior·al, sei·gnor·al** (sēn′yər əl)

sei·gnior·y (sēn′yər ē) *n., pl.* -gnior·ies [ME. *seignorie* < OFr.] **1.** the dominion or estate of a seignior **2.** the rights or authority of a feudal lord **3.** a body of lords, esp. those of a medieval Italian republic **4.** *same as* SEIGNEURY (sense 2)

Seine (sān; *Fr.* sen) river in N France, flowing northwest through Paris into the English Channel: 482 mi.

seine (sān) *n.* [ME. *seyne* < OE. *segne* < early WGmc. borrowing < L. *sagena* < Gr. *sagēnē* < IE. base *twak-,* to enclose tightly] a large fishing net with floats along the top edge and weights along the bottom —*vt., vi.* seined, sein′ing to fish with a seine —sein′er *n.*

seise (sēz) *vt.* seised, seis′ing *alt. sp.* of SEIZE (sense 1)

sei·sin (sē′zin) *n. same as* SEIZIN

seis·mic (sīz′mik, sīs′-) *adj.* [< Gr. *seismos,* an earthquake < *seiein,* to shake < IE. base *twei-,* to excite, shake, shock, whence Sans. *tvis-,* to be excited, sparkle] **1.** of, having to do with, or caused by an earthquake or earthquakes or by man-made earth tremors **2.** subject to earthquakes —seis′mi·cal·ly *adv.*

seis·mic·i·ty (sīz mis′ə tē, sīs-) *n.* **1.** the property or state of being seismic **2.** the degree to which a region of the earth is subject to earthquakes

seis·mism (sīz′miz'm, sīs′-) *n.* [see SEISMIC & -ISM] the phenomena of earthquakes, collectively

seis·mo- (sīz′mə, sīs′-) [< Gr. *seismos:* see SEISMIC] *a combining form meaning* earthquake [*seismogram*]

seis·mo·gram (sīz′mə gram′, sīs′-) *n.* [prec. + -GRAM] the chart of an earthquake as recorded by a seismograph

seis·mo·graph (-graf′, -gräf′) *n.* [SEISMO- + -GRAPH] an instrument that records the intensity and duration of earthquakes and other earth tremors —seis·mog·ra·pher (sīz mäg′rə fər, sīs-) *n.* —seis′mo·graph′ic *adj.* —seis·mog′ra·phy *n.*

seis·mol·o·gy (sīz mäl′ə jē, sīs-) *n.* [SEISMO- + -LOGY] a geophysical science dealing with earthquakes and related phenomena —seis′mo·log′ic (-mə läj′ik), seis′mo·log′i·cal *adj.* —seis′mo·log′i·cal·ly *adv.* —seis·mol′o·gist *n.*

seis·mom·e·ter (-mäm′ə tər) *n.* [SEISMO- + -METER] a seismograph, esp. one that records actual earth movements —seis′mo·met′ric (-mə met′rik), seis′mo·met′ri·cal *adj.*

seis·mo·scope (sīz′mə skōp′, sīs′-) *n.* [SEISMO- + -SCOPE] an instrument indicating only the occurrence and time of earthquakes —seis′mo·scop′ic (-skäp′ik) *adj.*

seize (sēz) *vt.* seized, seiz′ing [ME. *saisen* < OFr. *saisir* < ML. *sacire,* prob. < Frank. *sakjan,* to lay claim to one's rights < *saka,* legal case: see SAKE¹] **1.** a) orig., to put in legal possession of a feudal holding b) to put in legal possession of a particular thing; assign ownership to: in the passive voice [*seized* of the lands] **2.** a) to take forcible legal possession of; confiscate [to *seize* contraband] b) to capture and put into custody; arrest; apprehend [to *seize* a criminal suspect] **3.** to take forcibly and quickly; grab [to *seize* power] **4.** to take hold of suddenly or forcibly, with or as with the hand; clutch **5.** a) to suddenly penetrate, illumine, or fill the mind of [an idea *seized* him] b) to grasp with the mind, esp. in a sudden or intuitive way [*seized* their intent] **6.** to take quick advantage of (an opportunity, etc.) **7.** to attack or afflict suddenly or severely [*seized* with a fit of sneezing] **8.** *Naut.* to fasten together (ropes, etc.), as by lashings; bind; lash —*SYN.* see TAKE —**seize on** (or **upon**) **1.** to take hold of suddenly and forcibly **2.** to take possession of **3.** to turn eagerly to (an idea, etc.) —seiz′a·ble *adj.* —seiz′er *n.*

sei·zin (sē′zin) *n.* [ME. *seisine* < OFr. *saisine* < *saisir:* see SEIZE] *Law* legal possession, esp. of a freehold estate

seiz·ing (sēz′in) *n.* **1.** *same as* SEIZURE (sense 1) **2.** *Naut.* a) the act of binding or fastening together, as with lashings b) lashings or cordage used for this c) a fastening made in this way

sei·zor (sē′zər, -zôr) *n.* [SEIZ(E) + -OR] *Law* a person who takes possession of a freehold estate

sei·zure (sē′zhər) *n.* **1.** a seizing or being seized **2.** a sudden attack, as of disease

se·jant, se·jeant (sē′jənt) *adj.* [Anglo-Fr. *seiant,* prp. of *seier* (OFr. *seoir*), to sit < L. *sedere,* to SIT] *Heraldry* sitting with the forelegs upright

Sejm (sām) *n.* [Pol., assembly] the Polish Parliament

sel. 1. selected **2.** selection(s)

se·la·chi·an (si lā′kē ən) *n.* [< ModL. *Selachii*, name of the order (< Gr. *selachos*, cartilaginous fish, akin to *selas*, light, gleam: from its phosphorescent appearance, prob. < IE. base **swel-*, to burn, smolder, whence SWELTER] + -AN] any of an order (Selachii) of cartilaginous fishes including the sharks and rays —*adj.* of the selachians

sel·a·gi·nel·la (sel′ə ji nel′ə) *n.* [ModL., dim. < L. *selago* (gen. *selaginis*), kind of plant] any of a genus (*Selaginella*) of small-leaved, mosslike, vascular plants, having two kinds of spores borne in cones at the tips of the branches

se·lah (sē′lə, se lä′) *n.* [Heb. *selāh*] a Hebrew word of unknown meaning at the end of verses in the Psalms: perhaps a musical direction, but traditionally interpreted as a blessing meaning "forever"

Se·lan·gor (se läŋ′gôr) W state of the Federation of Malaya: 3,167 sq. mi.; pop. 1,317,000

Selassie *see* HAILE SELASSIE

Sel·den (sel′dən), **John** 1584–1654; Eng. politician & legal historian

sel·dom (sel′dəm) *adv.* [ME. *selden* < OE. *seldan*, strange, rare, akin to G. *selten* < Gmc. base **selda-* < ? IE. **selo-*: see SELF] not often; rarely; infrequently —*adj.* rare; infrequent —**sel′dom·ness** *n.*

se·lect (sə lekt′) *adj.* [L. *selectus*, pp. of *seligere*, to choose, pick out < *se-*, apart + *legere*, to choose: see LOGIC] **1.** chosen in preference to another or others; picked out, esp. for excellence or some special quality; picked **2.** choice; excellent; outstanding **3.** careful in choosing or selecting; fastidious **4.** limited to certain people or groups; exclusive —*vt.* to choose or pick out from among others, as for excellence, desirability, etc. —*vi.* to make a selection; choose —*SYN.* see CHOOSE —**se·lect′ness** *n.*

☆**se·lect·ee** (sə lek′tē′) *n.* a person inducted into the armed forces under selective service

se·lec·tion (sə lek′shən) *n.* [L. *selectio*] **1.** a selecting or being selected **2.** *a*) a person or thing chosen *b*) a group or collection of these *c*) a variety from which to choose [*a selection* of colors] **3.** *Biol.* any process, natural or artificial, by which certain organisms or characters are favored or perpetuated in, or as if in, preference to others: cf. NATURAL SELECTION —*SYN.* see CHOICE

se·lec·tive (-tiv) *adj.* **1.** of or characterized by selection **2.** having the power of selecting; tending to select **3.** *Radio* excluding oscillations on all frequencies except the one desired —**se·lec′tive·ly** *adv.* —**se·lec′tive·ness** *n.*

☆**selective service** compulsory military training and service according to age, physical fitness, etc.

se·lec·tiv·i·ty (sə lek′tiv′ə tē) *n.* **1.** the state or quality of being selective **2.** the degree to which a radio receiver will reproduce the signals of a given transmitter while rejecting the signals of the others

☆**se·lect·man** (sə lekt′mən; *locally, also* sē′lekt man′) *n., pl.* **-men** (-mən, -men′) [SELECT + MAN] any of a board of officers elected in most New England towns to manage municipal affairs

se·lec·tor (sə lek′tər) *n.* [LL.] a person or thing that selects

sel·e·nate (sel′ə nāt′) *n.* [Sw. *selenat* < *selen*, selenic + -*at*, -ATE²] a salt or ester of selenic acid

Se·le·ne (si lē′nē) [Gr. *Selēnē* < *selēnē*, the moon] the Greek goddess of the moon: cf. LUNA, ARTEMIS, HECATE

se·le·nic (sə lē′nik, -len′ik) *adj.* [cf. SELENIUM & -IC] designating or of compounds in which selenium has a higher valence than in corresponding selenious compounds

selenic acid a colorless, crystalline acid, H₂SeO₄, resembling sulfuric acid in its action

se·le·ni·ous (sə lē′nē əs) *adj.* designating or of compounds in which selenium has a lower valence than in corresponding selenic compounds

selenious acid a colorless, transparent, crystalline powder, H₂SeO₃, soluble in water and used as a reagent

sel·e·nite (sel′ə nīt′) *n.* [L. *selenites* < Gr. *selēnitēs* (*lithos*), lit., moon (stone) < *selēnē*, the moon: once thought to wax and wane with the moon] **1.** a kind of gypsum found in transparent crystals **2.** a salt of selenious acid

se·le·ni·um (sə lē′nē əm) *n.* [ModL. < Gr. *selēnē*, the moon (akin to *selas*, light: see SELACHIAN) : so named by its discoverer, Berzelius, by analogy with tellurium < L. *tellus*, the earth] a gray, nonmetallic chemical element of the sulfur group, existing in many allotropic forms: used in photoelectric devices because its electrical conductivity varies with the intensity of light: also used in making red glass, in certain electrostatic copying processes, etc.: symbol, Se; at. wt., 78.96; at. no., 34; sp. gr., 4.81; melt. pt., 217°C; boil. pt., 684.8°C

selenium cell a photoelectric cell using selenium as the photoconductive element

sel·e·no- (sel′ə nō) [< Gr. *selēnē*, the moon (see SELENIUM)] *a combining form meaning* moon [*selenography*]

sel·e·nod·e·sy (sel′ə näd′ə sē) *n.* [< SELENO- + -*desy*, after GEODESY] the branch of astronomy concerned with measuring, or determining the shape of, the moon or its surface features, locating exactly points on its surface, etc. —**sel′e·nod′e·sist** *n.*

sel·e·nog·ra·phy (-näg′rə fē) *n.* [ModL. *selenographia*: see SELENO- & -GRAPHY] the study of the surface and physical features of the moon —**sel′e·nog′ra·pher** *n.* —**se·le·no·graph·ic** (sə lē′nə graf′ik) *adj.*

sel·e·nol·o·gy (-näl′ə jē) *n.* [SELENO- + -LOGY] the branch of astronomy dealing with the moon —**se·le·no·log·i·cal** (sə lē′nə läj′i k'l) *adj.* —**sel′e·nol′o·gist** *n.*

Se·leu·ci·a (sə loō′shē ə, -shə) any of several ancient cities of SW Asia, founded by Seleucus I; esp., the chief city of the Seleucid Empire, on the Tigris

Se·leu·cid (sə loō′sid) *n., pl.* **-cids, -ci·dae′** (-si dē′) [< L. *Seleucides* < Gr. *Seleukidēs*] a member of a dynasty founded by Seleucus I and ruling (312–64? B.C.) over S Asia Minor & the region between the Mediterranean Sea & the Indus River —*adj.* of the Seleucids: also **Se·leu′ci·dan**

Se·leu·cus I (sə loō′kəs) (*Seleucus Nicator*) ?–280 B.C.; Macedonian general & founder of the Seleucid dynasty

self (self) *n., pl.* **selves** [ME. < OE., prob. < IE. **selo-* < base **se-*, reflexive pronoun, orig. separate, apart (whence L. *sibi, se*) + **(o)lo-*, pron. suffix: basic sense "itself, by itself"] **1.** the identity, character, or essential qualities of any person or thing **2.** one's own person as distinct from all others **3.** one's own welfare, interest, or advantage; selfishness [obsessed with *self*] —*pron.* [Colloq.] myself, himself, herself, or yourself [tickets for *self* and *wife*] —*adj.* **1.** being uniform or the same throughout **2.** of the same kind, nature, color, material, etc. as the rest [a *self* lining, *self* trim]

self- (self) [ME. < OE. < *self*: see prec.] *a prefix used in hyphenated compounds, meaning:* **1.** of oneself or itself: the object of the action [*self-*appraisal, *self-*restraint] **2.** by oneself or itself: the subject of the action [*self-*appointed, *self-*starting] **3.** in oneself or itself [*self-*centered] **4.** to or with oneself or itself [*self-*addressed]

self-a·base·ment (self′ə bās′mənt) *n.* abasement or humiliation of oneself

self-ab·ne·ga·tion (-ab′nə gā′shən) *n.* lack of consideration for oneself or one's own interest; self-denial

self-ab·sorp·tion (-ab zôrp′shən, -sôrp′) *n.* **1.** absorption in one's own interests, affairs, etc. **2.** *Physics* the absorption of radiation by the substance emitting the radiation —**self′-ab·sorbed′** *adj.*

self-a·buse (-ə byoōs′) *n.* **1.** misuse of one's own abilities, talents, etc. **2.** accusation, blame, or revilement of oneself **3.** *a euphemism for* MASTURBATION

self-act·ing (-ak′tiŋ) *adj.* acting without outside influence or stimulus; working by itself; automatic

self-ac·tu·al·i·za·tion (-ak′choo wə li zā′shən) *n.* full development of one's abilities, ambitions, etc.

self-ad·dressed (-ə drest′) *adj.* addressed to oneself [a *self-addressed* envelope]

self-ad·vance·ment (-əd vans′mənt, -väns′-) *n.* the act of advancing or promoting one's own interests

self-ag·gran·dize·ment (-ə gran′diz mənt) *n.* the act of making oneself more powerful, wealthy, etc., esp. in a ruthless way —**self′-ag·gran′diz′ing** (-dīz′iŋ) *adj.*

self-a·nal·y·sis (-ə nal′ə sis) *n.* analysis of one's own personality without the help of another

self-an·ni·hi·la·tion (-ə nī′ə lā′shən) *n.* **1.** *same as* SELF-DESTRUCTION **2.** loss of awareness of self, as in a mystical union with God

self-ap·point·ed (-ə poin′tid) *adj.* declared to be so by oneself, but not so appointed by others [a *self-appointed* censor]

self-as·ser·tion (-ə sur′shən) *n.* the act of demanding recognition for oneself or of insisting upon one's rights, claims, etc. —**self′-as·ser′tive, self′-as·sert′ing** *adj.*

self-as·sur·ance (-ə shoor′əns) *n.* confidence in oneself, or in one's own ability, talent, etc. —**self′-as·sured′** *adj.*

self-cen·tered (-sen′tərd) *adj.* occupied or concerned only with one's own affairs; egocentric; selfish

self-clos·ing (-klōz′iŋ) *adj.* closing automatically

self-col·lect·ed (-kə lek′tid) *adj. same as* SELF-POSSESSED

self-col·ored (-kul′ərd) *adj.* **1.** of only one color **2.** of the natural or original color, as a fabric

self-com·mand (-kə mand′) *n. same as* SELF-CONTROL

self-com·pla·cent (-kəm plā′s'nt) *adj.* self-satisfied, esp. in a smug way —**self′-com·pla′cen·cy** *n.*

self-com·posed (-kəm pōzd′) *adj.* having or showing composure; calm; cool

self-con·ceit (-kən sēt′) *n.* too high an opinion of oneself; conceit; vanity —**self′-con·ceit′ed** *adj.*

self-con·cept (-kän′sept) *n. same as* SELF-IMAGE

self-con·fessed (-kən fest′) *adj.* being such by one's own admission [a *self-confessed* thief]

self-con·fi·dence (-kän′fə dəns) *n.* confidence in oneself, one's own abilities, etc. —*SYN.* see CONFIDENCE —**self′-con′fi·dent** *adj.* —**self′-con′fi·dent·ly** *adv.*

self-con·scious (-kän′shəs) *adj.* **1.** *a*) unduly conscious of oneself as an object of notice; awkward or embarrassed in the presence of others; ill at ease *b*) showing embarrassment, etc. [a *self-conscious* cough] **2.** *Philos., Psychol.* having or showing awareness of one's own existence, actions, etc.; conscious of oneself or one's ego —**self′-con′scious·ly** *adv.* —**self′-con′scious·ness** *n.*

self-con·sis·tent (-kən sis/t'nt) *adj.* having all parts, ideas, actions, etc. consistent with one another

self-con·sti·tut·ed (-kän/stə tōōt/id) *adj.* constituted as such by oneself or itself [a *self-constituted* arbiter]

self-con·tained (-kən tānd/) *adj.* 1. keeping one's affairs to oneself; reserved 2. showing self-command or self-control 3. having all working parts, complete with motive power, in an enclosed unit: said of machinery 4. having within oneself or itself all that is necessary; self-sufficient, as a community —**self/-con·tain/ment** *n.*

self-con·tent·ed (-kən ten/tid) *adj.* contented with what one is or has —**self/-con·tent/, self/-con·tent/ment** *n.*

self-con·tra·dic·tion (-kän/trə dik/shən) *n.* 1. contradiction of oneself or itself 2. any statement or idea containing elements that contradict each other —**self/-con/tra·dic/to·ry** *adj.*

self-con·trol (-kən trōl/) *n.* control of oneself, or of one's own emotions, desires, actions, etc.

self-de·cep·tion (-di sep/shən) *n.* the deceiving of oneself as to one's true feelings, motives, circumstances, etc.: also **self-de·ceit** —**self/-de·ceiv/ing** *adj.*

self-de·feat·ing (-di fēt/iŋ) *adj.* that defeats its own purpose or unwittingly works against itself

self-de·fense (-di fens/) *n.* 1. defense of oneself or of one's rights, beliefs, actions, etc. 2. the skill of boxing: usually in the phrase **manly art of self-defense** 3. *Law* the right to defend oneself with whatever force is reasonably necessary against actual or threatened violence —**self/-de·fen/sive** *adj.*

self-de·lu·sion (-di lōō/zhən) *n.* same as SELF-DECEPTION

self-de·ni·al (-di nī/əl) *n.* denial or sacrifice of one's own desires or pleasures, often for the sake of others —**self/-de·ny/ing** *adj.* —**self/-de·ny/ing·ly** *adv.*

☆**self-de·struct** (-di strukt/) *vi.* same as SELF-DESTRUCT

self-de·struc·tion (-di struk/shən) *n.* destruction of oneself or itself; specif., suicide —**self/-de·struc/tive** *adj.*

self-de·ter·mi·na·tion (-di tur/mə nā/shən) *n.* 1. determination or decision according to one's own mind or will, without outside influence 2. the right of a people to decide upon its own political status or form of government, without outside influence —**self/-de·ter/mined** *adj.* —**self/-de·ter/min·ing** *adj.*

self-de·vo·tion (-di vō/shən) *n.* devotion of oneself to a cause or to others' interests

self-dis·ci·pline (-dis/ə plin) *n.* the act or power of disciplining or controlling oneself, one's desires, actions, habits, etc. —**self/-dis/ci·plined** *adj.*

self-doubt (-dout/) *n.* lack of confidence in oneself

self-driv·en (-driv/'n) *adj.* containing its own drive or motive power

self-ed·u·cat·ed (-ej/ə kāt/id) *adj.* educated or trained by oneself, with little or no formal schooling

self-ef·face·ment (-i fās/mənt) *n.* the practice of keeping oneself in the background and minimizing one's own actions; modest, retiring behavior —**self/-ef·fac/ing** *adj.*

self-em·ployed (-im ploid/) *adj.* working for oneself, with direct control over work, services, etc. undertaken and fees, charges, etc. set —**self/-em·ploy/ment** *n.*

self-es·teem (-ə stēm/) *n.* 1. belief in oneself; self-respect 2. undue pride in oneself; conceit —*SYN.* see PRIDE

self-ev·i·dent (-ev/i dənt) *adj.* evident without need of proof or explanation —**self/-ev/i·dent·ly** *adv.*

self-ex·am·i·na·tion (-ig zam/ə nā/shən) *n.* examination or study of one's own qualities, thoughts, conduct, motives, etc.; analysis of oneself; introspection

self-ex·cit·ed (-ik sīt/id) *adj. Elec.* excited by field current supplied from its own armature: said of a generator

self-ex·e·cut·ing (-ek/sə kyōōt/iŋ) *adj.* coming into effect automatically when specified, without further provision being made, as a death clause in a contract

self-ex·ist·ent (-ig zis/tənt) *adj.* having independent existence; existing of or by itself without external cause or agency —**self/-ex·ist/ence** *n.*

self-ex·plan·a·to·ry (-ik splan/ə tôr/ē) *adj.* explaining itself; obvious without explanation: also **self/-ex·plain/ing**

self-ex·pres·sion (-ik spresh/ən) *n.* expression of one's own personality or emotions, esp. in the arts

self-feed·ing (-fēd/iŋ) *adj.* 1. automatically supplying itself with what is needed, as a machine ☆2. designating or of a system of supplying feed to animals so that they can eat the kind and amount they want when they want it

self-fer·til·i·za·tion (-fur/t'l i zā/shən) *n.* fertilization of a plant or animal by its own pollen or sperm

self-for·get·ful (-fər get/f'l) *adj.* ignoring one's own interests; selfless; unselfish

self-ful·fill·ment (-fəl fil/mənt) *n.* fulfillment of one's aspirations, hopes, etc. through one's own efforts

self-gov·ern·ment (-guv/ər mənt, -ərn-) *n.* 1. [Rare] self-control 2. government of a group by the action of its own members, as in electing representatives to make its laws —**self/-gov/erned** *adj.* —**self/-gov/ern·ing** *adj.*

self-hard·en·ing (-här/d'n in) *adj.* designating or of any steel that will harden if air-cooled after being heated above red heat

self-hate (-hāt/) *n.* hatred directed against oneself or one's own people, often in despair: also **self/-ha/tred**

self-heal (-hēl/) *n.* any of various plants supposed to have healing properties; esp., a common, old-world, lawn and pasture weed (*Prunella vulgaris*) of the mint family

self-help (-help/) *n.* care or betterment of oneself by one's own efforts, as through study

self-hood (-hood/) *n.* 1. all the things that make a person what he is; personality or individuality 2. the condition of being self-centered; selfishness

self-hyp·no·sis (-hip nō/sis) *n.* same as AUTOHYPNOSIS

self-i·den·ti·ty (-ī den/tə tē) *n.* the identity of a thing with itself, or the awareness of this identity in the self

self-im·age (-im/ij) *n.* an individual's conception of himself and his own identity, abilities, worth, etc.

self-im·por·tant (-im pôr/t'nt) *adj.* having or showing an exaggerated opinion of one's own importance; pompous or officious —**self/-im·por/tance** *n.*

self-im·posed (-im pōzd/) *adj.* imposed or inflicted on oneself by oneself

self-im·prove·ment (-im prōōv/mənt) *n.* improvement of one's status, mind, abilities, etc. by one's own efforts

self-in·clu·sive (-in klōō/siv) *adj.* including oneself or itself

self-in·crim·i·na·tion (-in krim/ə nā/shən) *n.* incrimination of oneself by one's own statements or answers —**self/-in·crim/i·nat/ing** *adj.*

self-in·duced (-in dōōst/) *adj.* 1. induced by oneself or itself 2. produced by self-induction

self-in·duc·tance (-in duk/təns) *n.* same as INDUCTANCE (sense 2)

self-in·duc·tion (-in duk/shən) *n.* the induction of a counter electromotive force in a circuit by the variation of current in that circuit

self-in·dul·gence (-in dul/jəns) *n.* indulgence of one's own desires, impulses, etc. —**self/-in·dul/gent** *adj.*

self-in·flict·ed (-in flik/tid) *adj.* inflicted on oneself by oneself, as an injury

self-in·i·ti·at·ed (-i nish/ē āt/id) *adj.* initiated by oneself or itself

self-in·sur·ance (-in shoor/əns) *n.* insurance of oneself or one's property by setting apart one's own funds rather than by paying for an insurance policy

self-in·ter·est (-in/trist, -in/tər ist) *n.* 1. one's own interest or advantage 2. an exaggerated regard for this, esp. when at the expense of others

self·ish (sel/fish) *adj.* 1. too much concerned with one's own welfare or interests and having little or no concern for others; self-centered 2. showing or prompted by self-interest —**self/ish·ly** *adv.* —**self/ish·ness** *n.*

self-jus·ti·fi·ca·tion (-jus/tə fi kā/shən) *n.* the act of justifying or rationalizing one's actions or motives —**self/-jus/ti·fy/ing** *adj.*

self-knowl·edge (-self/näl/ij) *n.* knowledge of one's own qualities, character, abilities, etc.

self·less (self/lis) *adj.* 1. devoted to others' welfare or interests and not one's own; unselfish; altruistic 2. showing or prompted by unselfishness or altruism; self-sacrificing —**self/less·ly** *adv.* —**self/less·ness** *n.*

self-liq·ui·dat·ing (-lik/wə dāt/iŋ) *adj.* having within itself the means of quickly or eventually making up for, or yielding a profit on, the initial outlay [a *self-liquidating* investment]

self-load·ing (-lōd/iŋ) *adj.* loading again by its own action [a *self-loading* gun]

self-love (-luv/) *n.* love of self or regard for oneself and one's own interests

self-made (-mād/) *adj.* 1. made by oneself or itself 2. successful, rich, etc. through one's own efforts

self-mov·ing (-mōō/viŋ) *adj.* moving or able to move under its own power, or of itself

self-o·pin·ion·at·ed (-ə pin/yə nāt/id) *adj.* 1. without regard for others' opinions; stubbornly holding to one's own opinions 2. conceited

self-per·pet·u·at·ing (-pər pech/oo wāt/iŋ) *adj.* of a kind that causes or promotes indefinite continuation or renewal of itself or oneself [a *self-perpetuating* caste system] —**self/-per·pet/u·a/tion** *n.*

self-pit·y (-pit/ē) *n.* pity for oneself

self-pol·li·na·tion (-päl/ə nā/shən) *n.* the transfer of pollen from anthers to stigmas in the same flower, or to stigmas of another flower on the same plant or of a flower on a plant of the same clone —**self/-pol/li·nat/ed** *adj.*

self-por·trait (-pôr/trit, -trāt) *n.* a painting, drawing, etc. of oneself, done by oneself

self-pos·ses·sion (-pə zesh/ən) *n.* full possession or control of one's feelings, actions, etc.; self-command; composure —*SYN.* see CONFIDENCE —**self/-pos·sessed/** *adj.*

self-pres·er·va·tion (-prez/ər vā/shən) *n.* 1. preservation of oneself from danger, injury, or death 2. the urge to preserve oneself, regarded as an instinct

self-pro·claimed (-prō klāmd/) *adj.* so proclaimed or announced by oneself [a *self-proclaimed* ruler]

self-pro·duced (-prə dōōst/, -dyōōst/) *adj.* produced by oneself or itself

self-pro·nounc·ing (-prə noun/siŋ) *adj.* showing pronunciation by means of accent marks or diacritical marks added directly to the original spelling instead of in a separate phonetic transcription

self-pro·pelled (-prə peld/) *adj.* propelled by its own motor or power: also **self/-pro·pel/ling**

self-pro·tec·tion (-prə tek/shən) *n.* protection of oneself; self-defense

self-ques·tion·ing (-kwes/chən iŋ) *n.* a querying or doubting of one's own beliefs, motives, etc.

self-re·al·i·za·tion (-rē′ə li zā′shən) *n.* complete fulfillment of the self or full development of one's own talents, capabilities, etc.

self-re·cord·ing (-ri kôr′diŋ) *adj.* recording its own operations or reactions automatically, as a seismograph

self-re·gard (-ri gärd′) *n.* **1.** regard or concern for oneself and one's own interests **2.** *same as* SELF-RESPECT —**self′-re·gard′ing** *adj.*

self-reg·u·lat·ing (-reg′yə lāt′iŋ) *adj.* regulating itself or itself, so as to function automatically or without outside control —**self′-reg′u·la′tion** *n.*

self-re·li·ance (-ri lī′əns) *n.* reliance on one's own judgment, abilities, etc. —**self′-re·li′ant** *adj.*

self-re·nun·ci·a·tion (-ri nun′sē ā′shən) *n.* renunciation of one's own interests or desires, esp. when directed toward the benefit of others

self-re·proach (-ri prōch′) *n.* accusation or blame of oneself; guilt feeling —**self′-re·proach′ful** *adj.*

self-re·spect (-ri spekt′) *n.* proper respect for oneself and one's worth as a person —**self′-re·spect′ing** *adj.*

self-re·straint (-ri strānt′) *n.* restraint imposed on oneself by oneself; self-control —**self′-re·strained′** *adj.*

self-re·veal·ing (-ri vēl′iŋ) *adj.* revealing or expressing one's innermost thoughts, emotions, etc.: also **self′-rev′e·la·to·ry** (-rev′ə lə tôr′ē) —**self′-rev′e·la′tion** *n.*

self-right·eous (-rī′chəs) *adj.* filled with or showing one's own conviction of being morally superior, or more righteous than others; smugly virtuous —**self′-right′eous·ly** *adv.* —**self′-right′eous·ness** *n.*

☆**self-ris·ing** (-rī′ziŋ) *adj.* rising by itself; specif., rising without the addition of a ferment, as certain flour

self-rule (-rool′) *n. same as* SELF-GOVERNMENT

self-sac·ri·fice (-sak′rə fis′) *n.* sacrifice of oneself or one's own interests for the benefit, or the supposed benefit, of others —**self′-sac′ri·fic′ing** *adj.*

self·same (-sām′) *adj.* exactly the same; identical; (the) very same —*SYN.* see SAME —**self′same′ness** *n.*

self·sat·is·fied (-sat′is fid′) *adj.* feeling or showing satisfaction with oneself or one's accomplishments —**self′·sat′is·fac′tion** *n.*

self·sat·is·fy·ing (-sat′is fi′iŋ) *adj.* satisfying to oneself

self-seal·ing (-sēl′iŋ) *adj.* **1.** containing a substance that automatically seals punctures, etc. [a *self-sealing* tire] **2.** that can be sealed by pressure alone [a *self-sealing* envelope]

self-seek·er (-sē′kər) *n.* a person who seeks only or mainly to further his own interests —**self′-seek′ing** *n., adj.*

☆**self-serv·ice** (-sur′vis) *n.* the practice of serving oneself from a display of articles in a store, cafeteria, etc. and paying a cashier on the way out —*adj.* operating with such self-service

self-serv·ing (-sur′viŋ) *adj.* serving one's own selfish interests, esp. at the expense of others

self-sown (-sōn′) *adj.* sown by wind, water, or other natural means, as some weeds, instead of by man or an animal

self-start·er (-stärt′ər) *n.* **1.** an electric motor connected to, and used for automatically starting, an internal-combustion engine ☆**2.** [Colloq.] a person who works on his own initiative and without prodding

self-ster·ile (-ster′'l) *adj. Biol.* incapable of self-fertilization —**self′-ste·ril′i·ty** (-stə ril′ə tē) *n.*

self-stud·y (-stud′ē) *n.* study by oneself, as through correspondence courses, without classroom instruction

self-styled (-stīld′) *adj.* so named by oneself [a *self-styled* guardian of democracy]

self-suf·fi·cient (-sə fish′ənt) *adj.* having the necessary resources to get along without help; independent: also **self′-suf·fic′ing** (-fis′iŋ) —**self′-suf·fi′cien·cy** *n.*

self-sug·ges·tion (-səg jes′chən) *n. same as* AUTOSUGGESTION

self-sup·port (-sə pôrt′) *n.* support of oneself or itself without aid or reinforcement —**self′-sup·port′ed** *adj.* —**self′-sup·port′ing** *adj.*

self-sur·ren·der (-sə ren′dər) *n.* surrender of oneself or one's will to an influence, emotion, etc.

self-sus·tain·ing (-sə stān′iŋ) *adj.* **1.** supporting or able to support oneself or itself **2.** able to continue once begun —**self′-sus·tained′** *adj.*

self-taught (-tôt′) *adj.* **1.** having taught oneself through one's own efforts without help from others; self-educated **2.** learned by oneself without instruction

self-tor·ture (-tôr′chər) *n.* any mental or physical distress inflicted by oneself upon oneself

self-ward (-wərd) *adv.* toward oneself: also **self′wards** — *adj.* directed toward oneself

self-will (-wil′) *n.* persistent carrying out of one's own will or wishes, esp. when in conflict with others; stubbornness; obstinacy —**self′-willed′** *adj.*

self-wind·ing (-wīn′diŋ) *adj.* wound automatically, as certain wristwatches with internal winding mechanisms activated by external motion, as by normal arm movements

Sel·juk (sel jook′) *n.* [Turk. *Seljuq,* legendary ancestor of the dynasties] a member of any of the several dynasties of the Seljuk Turks —*adj.* of these dynasties or the Seljuk Turks Also **Sel·juk′i·an** (-joo′kē ən)

Seljuk Turks a branch of Turkic peoples that expanded westward from Turkestan in the 11th cent.

Sel·kirk (sel′kurk) inland county of S Scotland: 267 sq. mi.; pop. 21,000: also **Sel′kirk·shire′** (-shir′)

Selkirk Mountains range of the Rocky Mountain system, in SE British Columbia: highest peak, 11,590 ft.

sell (sel) *vt.* **sold, sell′ing** [ME. *sellen* < OE. *sellan,* to give, offer, akin to Goth. *saljan,* to offer (sacrifice): caus. formation in sense "to cause to take" < IE. base *sel-,* to take, grasp, whence Gr. *helein,* to take] **1.** to give up, deliver, or exchange (property, goods, services, etc.) for money or its equivalent **2.** *a)* to have or offer regularly for sale; deal in [a store that *sells* hardware, to *sell* real estate] *b)* to make or try to make sales in or to [to *sell* chain stores] **3.** *a)* to give up or deliver (a person) to his enemies or into slavery, bondage, etc. *b)* to be a traitor to; betray (a country, cause, etc.) **4.** to give up or dispose of (one's honor, one's vote, etc.) for profit or a dishonorable purpose **5.** to bring about, help in, or promote the sale of [television *sells* many products] ☆**6.** [Colloq.] *a)* to establish faith, confidence, or belief in [to *sell* oneself to the public] *b)* to persuade (someone) of the value of something; convince (with on) [*sell* him on the idea] **7.** [Slang] to cheat or dupe —*vi.* **1.** to exchange property, goods, or services for money, etc. **2.** to work or act as a salesman or salesperson **3.** to be a popular item on the market; attract buyers **4.** to be sold (*for* or *at*) [belts *selling* for two dollars] **5.** [Colloq.] to be accepted, approved, etc. [a scheme that won't *sell*] —*n.* [Slang] **1.** a trick or hoax ☆**2.** selling or salesmanship: cf. HARD SELL, SOFT SELL —**sell off** to get rid of by selling, esp. at low prices —**sell oneself 1.** to exchange one's services for a price, esp. for a dishonorable purpose, as for prostitution ☆**2.** [Colloq.] to convince another of one's worth —**sell out 1.** to get rid of completely by selling ☆**2.** [Colloq.] to sell or betray (someone, one's trust, etc.) —**sell short 1.** to sell securities, etc. not yet owned: see SHORT SALE **2.** to value at less than its worth; underestimate —**sell up** [Brit.] to sell all of (the land or household goods) of (a debtor) so as to satisfy his debts —*SYN.*—**sell** implies a transferring of the ownership of something to another for money [to *sell* books, a house, etc.]; **barter** implies an exchange of goods or services without using money [to *barter* food for clothes]; **trade,** in transitive use, also implies the exchange of articles [let's *trade* neckties], and, intransitively, implies the carrying on of a business in which one buys and sells a specified commodity [to *trade* in wheat]; **auction** implies the public sale of items one by one, each going to the highest of the competing bidders [to *auction* off unclaimed property]; **vend** applies especially to the selling of small articles, as by peddling, slot machine, etc. [*vending* machines] —*ANT.* buy

sell·er (sel′ər) *n.* **1.** a person who sells; vendor **2.** something that sells, usually with reference to its rate of sale [a good *seller*]

selling race a horse race immediately after which the winning horse is offered for sale at auction, and the losers may be claimed for prices previously set

sell-off (-ôf′) *n.* a decline in the prices of all or certain stocks and bonds due to pressure to sell

☆**sell-out** (-out′) *n.* [Colloq.] **1.** the act of selling out something or someone **2.** an entertainment for which all the seats have been sold

Sel·ma (sel′mə) [< ? Gr. *selma,* a ship] a feminine name

Selt·zer (selt′sər) *n.* [altered < G. *Selterser (wasser)* < *Niederselters,* village near Wiesbaden, Germany] **1.** natural mineral water that is effervescent **2.** [*often* **s-**] any similar water prepared artificially Also **Seltzer water**

sel·va (sel′və) *n.* [Sp. & Port., forest < L. *silva*] a tropical rain forest, esp. in S. America

sel·vage, sel·vedge (sel′vij) *n.* [< SELF + EDGE, after MDu. *selfegge*] **1.** a specially woven edge that prevents cloth from raveling **2.** any specially defined edge of fabric or paper, esp. such an edge that is to be trimmed off or covered **3.** [Rare] the edge plate of a lock through which the bolt passes

selves (selvz) *n. pl. of* SELF

Sem. 1. Seminary **2.** Semitic

sem. 1. semester **2.** semicolon

se·man·tic (sə man′tik) *adj.* [Gr. *sēmantikos,* significant < *sēmainein,* to show, explain by a sign < *sēma,* a sign, symbol < IE. *dhyāmn* (whence Sans. *dhyāman,* a thought) < base *dhyā-,* to see, behold] **1.** of or pertaining to meaning, esp. meaning in language **2.** of or according to semantics as a branch of philosophy Also **se·man′ti·cal** —**se·man′ti·cal·ly** *adv.*

se·man·ti·cist (-tə sist) *n.* a specialist in semantics

se·man·tics (-tiks) *n.pl.* [*with sing. v.*] [< SEMANTIC, after cognate Fr. *sémantique*] **1.** the branch of linguistics concerned with the nature, structure, and, esp., the development and changes, of the meanings of speech forms, or with contextual meaning **2.** *a) same as* SEMIOTIC *b)* the branch of semiotic dealing with relationships of signs and symbols to the things to which they refer, or with referential meaning **3.** the relationships between signs and symbols and the concepts, feelings, etc. associated with them in the minds of their interpreters; notional meaning **4.**

loosely, deliberate distortion or twisting of meaning, as in some types of advertising, propaganda, etc. **5.** *see* GENERAL SEMANTICS

sem·a·phore (sem′ə fôr′) *n.* [Fr. *sémaphore* < Gr. *sēma*, a sign (see SEMANTIC) + *-phoros:* see -PHOROUS] **1.** any apparatus for signaling, as by an arrangement of lights, flags, and mechanical arms on railroads **2.** a system of signaling by the use of two flags, one held in each hand: the letters of the alphabet are represented by the various positions of the arms **3.** any system of signaling by semaphore —*vt.*, *vi.* **-phored′**, **-phor′ing** to signal by semaphore —**sem′a·phor′ic** *adj.* —**sem′a·phor′ist** *n.*

SEMAPHORE
(signals for letters A, B, C, D)

Se·ma·rang (sə mä′räŋ) seaport in N Java, Indonesia, on the Java Sea: pop. 503,000

se·ma·si·ol·o·gy (si mä′sē äl′ə jē, -zē-) *n.* [< Gr. *sēmasia*, signification of a word (< *sēmainein:* see SEMANTIC) + -LOGY] *same as* SEMANTICS (senses 1, 2, 3) —**se·ma′si·o·log′i·cal** (-ə läj′i k′l) *adj.* —**se·ma′si·ol′o·gist** *n.*

se·mat·ic (si mat′ik) *adj.* [< Gr. *sēma* (gen. *sēmatos*), a sign (see SEMANTIC) + -IC] *Zool.* serving as a sign of danger, as the coloration of some poisonous snakes

sem·bla·ble (sem′blə b′l) *adj.* [ME. < MFr. < *sembler:* see ff.] [Archaic] **1.** similar **2.** suitable **3.** apparent —*n.* [Archaic] **1.** something similar **2.** likeness

sem·blance (sem′bləns) *n.* [ME. < OFr. < *sembler*, to seem, appear < L. *similare*, to make like < *similis*, like: see SAME] **1.** outward form or appearance; aspect **2.** the look or appearance of something else; resemblance **3.** a likeness, image, representation, or copy **4.** false, assumed, or deceiving form or appearance **5.** mere empty show; pretense —*SYN.* see APPEARANCE

se·mé (sə mā′) *adj.* [Fr., orig. pp. of *semer*, to sow < L. *seminare* < *semen*, a SEED] *Heraldry* having a design of many small figures; dotted, as with stars

Sem·e·le (sem′ə lē′) [L. < Gr. *Semelē*] *Gr. Myth.* the daughter of Cadmus, and mother of Dionysus: seeing Zeus in all his glory, she was consumed in his lightning

☆**sem·eme** (sem′ēm) *n.* [coined (1933) by L. BLOOMFIELD < Gr. *sēma*, a sign (see SEMANTIC) + (MORPH)EME] *Linguis.* the meaning of a morpheme

se·men (sē′mən) *n.*, *pl.* **sem·i·na** (sem′ə nə) [ModL. < L., a SEED] the thick, whitish fluid secreted by the male reproductive organs and containing the spermatozoa

se·mes·ter (sə mes′tər) *n.* [G. < L. (*cursus*) *semestris*, half-yearly (period) < *sex*, SIX + *mensis*, MONTH] **1.** a six-month period; half year **2.** either of the two terms, of about eighteen weeks each, which usually make up a school or college year —**se·mes′tral** (-trəl) *adj.*

sem·i- (sem′i; *also variously* -ē, -i, -ə) [L. < IE. **semi-*, whence Gr. *hēmi-*, Sans. *sāmi-*, OE. *sām-*] *a prefix meaning:* **1.** half [*semicircle*] **2.** partly, not fully, imperfectly [*semicivilized*] **3.** twice in a (specified period) [*semiannually*]

sem·i·ab·stract (sem′ē ab strakt′) *adj.* designating or of a style of art in which an identifiable object is dealt with as an abstraction, as in some cubist works —**sem′i·ab·strac′tion·ism** *n.*

sem·i·an·nu·al (-an′yoo wəl) *adj.* **1.** happening, prepared, presented, etc. every half year **2.** lasting only half a year, as some plants —**sem′i·an′nu·al·ly** *adv.*

sem·i·a·quat·ic (-ə kwät′ik, -kwat′-) *adj. Biol.* **1.** growing in or near water, as certain plants **2.** spending some time in water, as muskrats

sem·i·ar·id (-ar′id) *adj.* characterized by little yearly rainfall and by the growth of short grasses and shrubs: said of a climate or region

sem·i·au·to·mat·ic (-ôt′ə mat′ik) *adj.* **1.** partly automatic and partly hand-controlled: said of machinery **2.** having an automatic chambering mechanism but requiring a trigger pull for each round fired: said of some firearms —*n.* a semiautomatic firearm —**sem′i·au′to·mat′i·cal·ly** *adv.*

sem·i·breve (sem′i brēv′) *n.* [It.] [Brit.] *Music* a whole note (○), equal to four crotchets

sem·i·cen·ten·ni·al (sem′i sen ten′ē əl) *adj.* [SEMI- + CENTENNIAL] happening once every 50 years —*n.* a 50th anniversary or its celebration

sem·i·cir·cle (sem′i sur′k′l) *n.* [L. *semicirculus:* see SEMI- & CIRCLE] **1.** a half circle **2.** anything in the form of a half circle —**sem′i·cir′cu·lar** (-kyə lər) *adj.*

semicircular canal any of the three loop-shaped, tubular structures of the inner ear that serve to maintain balance in the organism: see EAR[1], illus.

sem·i·civ·i·lized (sem′i siv′ə līzd) *adj.* partly civilized

sem·i·clas·si·cal (-klas′i k′l) *adj.* somewhat classical in form, quality, etc.; specif., designating or of music that is like classical music but is less complex in nature and has a more immediate appeal

sem·i·co·lon (sem′i kō′lən) *n.* a mark of punctuation (;) indicating a degree of separation greater than that marked by the comma and less than that marked by the period,

etc.: used chiefly to separate units that contain elements separated by commas, and to separate closely related coordinate clauses

sem·i·con·duc·tor (sem′i kən duk′tər) *n.* a substance, as germanium or silicon, whose conductivity is poor at low temperatures but is improved by minute additions of certain substances or by the application of heat, light, or voltage: used in transistors, rectifiers, etc.

sem·i·con·scious (sem′i kän′shəs) *adj.* not fully conscious or awake; half-conscious —**sem′i·con′scious·ness** *n.*

sem·i·dai·ly (-dā′lē) *adj.*, *adv.* twice daily

sem·i·de·tached (-di tacht′) *adj.* partly separate or detached, as a pair of houses joined by a common wall

sem·i·di·am·e·ter (-dī am′ət ər) *n.* **1.** half a diameter; radius **2.** *Astron.* half the angular diameter of a heavenly body with a visible disk, as the moon

sem·i·di·ur·nal (-dī ur′n′l) *adj.* **1.** of, lasting, or performed in half a day **2.** coming twice a day, or about every twelve hours, as the tides

sem·i·dome (sem′i dōm′) *n.* a curved ceiling or roof covering a semicircular room, bay, etc.; half dome

sem·i·dou·ble (sem′i dub′′l) *adj.* having more than the normal numbers of petals, ray flowers, etc., but not enough to completely conceal the stamens and pistils

sem·i·el·lip·ti·cal (sem′ē i lip′ti k′l) *adj.* having the form of a half ellipse —**sem′i·el·lipse′** (-lips′) *n.*

sem·i·fi·nal (sem′i fī′n′l; *for n., usually* sem′i fī′n′l) *adj.* coming just before the final match, as of a tournament —*n.* **1.** a semifinal match **2.** [*pl.*] a semifinal round

sem·i·fi·nal·ist (sem′i fī′n′l ist) *n.* a person taking part in a semifinal round, match, etc.

sem·i·flu·id (-floo′id) *adj.* heavy or thick but capable of flowing; viscous —*n.* a semifluid substance

sem·i·for·mal (-fôr′məl) *adj.* designating or requiring attire that is less than strictly formal but not informal

sem·i·hard (-härd′) *adj.* somewhat hard, but easily cut

sem·i·liq·uid (-lik′wid) *adj.*, *n. same as* SEMIFLUID

sem·i·lit·er·ate (-lit′ər it) *adj.* **1.** knowing how to read and write a little **2.** knowing how to read but not how to write

sem·i·lu·nar (-loo′nər) *adj.* [ModL. *semilunaris:* see SEMI- & LUNAR] shaped like a half-moon; crescent-shaped

semilunar valve either of two crescent-shaped valves, one at the junction of the right ventricle and pulmonary artery (**pulmonary valve**), the other at the junction of the left ventricle and aorta (**aortic valve**), which keep blood from flowing back into the ventricles

☆**sem·i·month·ly** (-munth′lē) *adj.* coming, happening, done, etc. twice a month —*n.* something coming, appearing, etc. twice a month, esp. a magazine issued twice a month —*adv.* twice monthly; every half month

sem·i·nal (sem′ə n′l) *adj.* [ME. < MFr. < L. *seminalis* < *semen* (gen. *seminis*), a SEED] **1.** of or containing seed or semen **2.** of reproduction [*seminal power*] **3.** like seed in being a source or in having a potential for development; germinal; originative —**sem′i·nal·ly** *adv.*

sem·i·nar (sem′ə när′) *n.* [G. < L. *seminarium:* see SEMINARY] **1.** a group of supervised students doing research or advanced study, as at a university **2.** a) a course for such a group, or any of its sessions   b) the room where the group meets **3.** any similar group discussion

sem·i·nar·i·an (sem′ə ner′ē ən) *n.* a student at a theological seminary: also [Chiefly Brit.] **sem′i·nar′ist**

sem·i·nar·y (sem′ə ner′ē) *n.*, *pl.* **-nar′ies** [ME., seed plot < L. *seminarium*, seed plot, nursery, neut. of *seminarius*, of seed < *semen*, a SEED] **1.** a place where something develops, grows, or is bred [slums are *seminaries* of crime] **2.** a school, esp. a private school for young women: an old-fashioned term **3.** a school or college where priests, ministers, or rabbis are trained

sem·i·na·tion (sem′ə nā′shən) *n.* [L. *seminatio* < *seminare*, to sow < *semen*, a SEED] **1.** propagation or dissemination **2.** *Bot.* the act or process of sowing seed

sem·i·nif·er·ous (-nif′ər əs) *adj.* [< L. *semen* (gen. *seminis*, a seed + -FEROUS] **1.** seed-bearing **2.** containing or conveying semen [*seminiferous* tubules]

sem·i·niv·o·rous (sem′ə niv′ər əs) *adj.* [< L. *semen* (gen. *seminis*), a SEED + -VOROUS] feeding on seeds

Sem·i·nole (sem′ə nōl′) *n.* [Creek *Simanóle*, lit., separatist, runaway] **1.** *pl.* **-noles**, **-nole** any of an American Indian people who separated from the Creeks and settled in Florida in the 18th cent. after migrating from S Alabama and S Georgia: they now live in S Florida and Oklahoma **2.** their Muskogean language

sem·i·of·fi·cial (sem′ē ə fish′′l) *adj.* having some, but not full, official authority —**sem′i·of·fi′cial·ly** *adv.*

se·mi·ol·o·gy (sē′mē äl′ə jē) *n.* [< Gr. *sēmeion* (see ff.) + -LOGY] the science of signs in general —**se′mi·o·log′ic** (-ə läj′ik), **se′mi·o·log′i·cal** *adj.* —**se′mi·ol′o·gist** *n.*

se·mi·ot·ic (sē′mē ät′ik) *n.* [Gr. *sēmeiōtikos* < *sēmeion*, a sign, akin to *sēma:* see SEMANTIC] [*often pl., with sing. v.*] *Philos.* a general theory of signs and symbols; esp., the analysis of the nature and relationships of signs in language, usually including three branches, syntactics, semantics, and pragmatics —*adj.* of or pertaining to semiotic: also **se′mi·ot′i·cal** —**se′mi·o·ti′cian** (-ə tish′ən) *n.*

sem·i·o·vip·a·rous (sem′ē ō vip′ər əs) *adj.* [SEMI- + OVIPAROUS] *Zool.* producing living young whose natal development is incomplete, as marsupials

Se·mi·pa·la·tinsk (sye′mē pə lä′tinsk) city in NE Kazakh S.S.R., on the Irtysh River: pop. 197,000

sem·i·pal·mate (sem′i pal′māt) *adj.* with only a partial webbing of the anterior toes, as in some shore birds: also **sem′i·pal′mat·ed** —**sem′i·pal·ma′tion** *n.*

sem·i·par·a·site (-par′ə sit′) *n. same as* HEMIPARASITE —**sem′i·par′a·sit′ic** (-sit′ik) *adj.*

sem·i·per·me·a·ble (-pur′mē ə b′l) *adj.* allowing some substances to pass; permeable to smaller molecules but not to larger ones, as a membrane in osmosis

sem·i·po·lit·i·cal (-pə lit′i k′l) *adj.* political in some respects only; partly political

sem·i·por·ce·lain (-pôr′sə lin) *n.* a type of glazed earthenware that looks like porcelain but is opaque

sem·i·post·al (-pōs′t′l) *adj.* designating or of a postage stamp part of the indicated value of which is used for some nonpostal public service —*n.* such a stamp

sem·i·pre·cious (-presh′əs) *adj.* designating gems of lower value than those classified as precious: said of the garnet, turquoise, opal, etc.

sem·i·pri·vate (-pri′vit) *adj.* partly but not completely private; *specif.,* designating of a hospital room with two, three, or sometimes four, beds

☆**sem·i·pro** (sem′i prō′) *adj., n.* clipped form of SEMIPROFESSIONAL

sem·i·pro·fes·sion·al (sem′i prə fesh′ən ′l) *adj.* not fully professional; *specif., a)* engaging in a sport or other activity for pay but not as a regular occupation *b)* engaged in by semiprofessional players —*n.* a semiprofessional player, etc. —**sem′i·pro·fes′sion·al·ly** *adv.*

sem·i·pub·lic (-pub′lik) *adj.* partly public; public in some respects, as a private institution offering some public services or facilities

sem·i·qua·ver (sem′i kwā′vər) *n.* [Chiefly Brit.] a musical sixteenth note

Se·mir·a·mis (si mir′ə mis) legendary queen of Assyria (based on an historical queen of the 9th cent. B.C.), who reputedly founded Babylon and was noted for her beauty, wisdom, & sexual excesses

sem·i·re·li·gious (sem′i ri lij′əs) *adj.* religious in some respects only; partly religious

sem·i·rig·id (sem′ē rij′id) *adj.* somewhat or partly rigid; *specif.,* designating an airship having a rigid internal keel but no other supporting framework

sem·i·skilled (-skild′) *adj.* **1.** partly skilled **2.** of or doing manual work that requires only limited training

sem·i·soft (-sôft′) *adj.* soft but firm and easily cut, as brick cheese, Edam cheese, etc.

sem·i·sol·id (-säl′id) *adj.* viscous and slowly flowing, as asphalt —*n.* a semisolid substance

sem·i·sweet (-swēt′) *adj.* only slightly sweetened

Sem·ite (sem′it; *chiefly Brit.,* sē′mit) *n.* [prob. < Fr. *Sémite* < ModL. *Semita,* back-formation < *Semiticus:* see ff.] **1.** a person regarded as descended from Shem **2.** a member of any of the peoples speaking a Semitic language, including the Hebrews, Arabs, Assyrians, Phoenicians, etc. **3.** *same as* JEW: a loose usage

Se·mit·ic (sə mit′ik) *adj.* [G. *semitisch* < ModL. *Semiticus,* assumed form < LL.(Ec.) *Sēm, Shem* < Gr.(Ec.) *Sem* < Heb. *Shēm*] **1.** of, like, or relating to a Semite or the Semites **2.** designating or of a major subfamily of the Afro-Asiatic family of languages, usually divided into eastern (Akkadian), northwestern (Phoenician, Aramaic, Hebrew, etc.), and southwestern (Arabic, Ethiopic, etc.) branches —*n.* this subfamily, or any member of it

Se·mit·ics (-iks) *n.pl.* [with sing. v.] ☆the study of Semitic culture, languages, literature, etc.

Sem·i·tism (sem′ə tiz′m) *n.* **1.** a Semitic word or idiom **2.** characteristics of the Semites; esp., the ideas, cultural qualities, etc. originating with the Jews

Sem·i·to-Ha·mit·ic (sem′ə tō′ha mit′ik) *adj. same as* AFRO-ASIATIC

sem·i·tone (sem′i tōn′) *n. Music* a tone at an interval of a half step from another; half of a whole tone —**sem′i·ton′ic** (-tän′ik), **sem′i·ton′al** (-tō′n′l) *adj.* —**sem′i·ton′al·ly** *adv.*

☆**sem·i·trail·er** (-trā′lər) *n.* a detachable trailer designed to be attached to a coupling at the rear of a tractor (sense 2), by which it is partly supported

sem·i·trans·par·ent (sem′i trans per′ənt) *adj.* not perfectly or completely transparent

sem·i·trop·i·cal (-träp′i k′l) *adj.* having some of the characteristics of the tropics: also **sem′i·trop′ic**

sem·i·vow·el (sem′i vou′əl) *n.* a vowellike sound occurring in consonantal positions in the same syllable with a true vowel, characterized by brief duration and rapid change from one position of articulation to another: the English glides *w* and *y,* as in *wall* and *yoke,* are semivowels

☆**sem·i·week·ly** (sem′i wēk′lē) *adj.* appearing, happening, done, etc. twice a week —*n., pl.* **-lies** a semiweekly publication —*adv.* twice weekly

sem·i·year·ly (-yir′lē) *adj.* coming, happening, done, etc. twice a year —*adv.* twice yearly

sem·o·li·na (sem′ə lē′nə) *n.* [It. *semolino,* dim. of *semola,* bran < L. *simila,* finest wheat flour: of Oriental orig., as in Assyr. *samidu,* fine meal] meal consisting of particles of

coarsely ground durum, a byproduct in the manufacture of fine flour: used in making macaroni, puddings, etc.

‡**sem·per** (sem′pər) *adv.* [L.] always

‡**semper fi·de·lis** (fi dā′lis) [L.] always faithful: motto of the U.S. Marine Corps

‡**semper par·a·tus** (pə rāt′əs, -rāt′əs) [L.] always prepared: motto of the U.S. Coast Guard

sem·per·vi·vum (sem′pər vī′vəm) *n.* [ModL. < L., neut. of *sempervivus,* ever living < *semper,* ever, always + *vivus,* living: see QUICK] any of a genus (*Sempervivum*) of plants of the orpine family, with yellow, pink, or red flowers and compact rosettes of thick, fleshy leaves

sem·pi·ter·nal (sem′pi tur′n′l) *adj.* [ME. < ML. *sempiternalis* < L. *sempiternus* < *semper,* always (< IE. base *sem-,* one, together, whence SAME + L. *per,* through: see PER) + *aeternus,* ETERNAL] everlasting; perpetual; eternal —**sem′pi·ter′nal·ly** *adv.* —**sem′pi·ter′ni·ty** *n.*

sem·pli·ce (sem′pli chā′) *adv.* [It., simply < L. *simplex,* SIMPLE] with simplicity: a direction to the performer in music

sem·pre (sem′prā) *adv.* [It., always < L. *semper*] without varying: a direction to the performer in music

semp·stress (sem′stris, scmp′-) *n. var.* of SEAMSTRESS

sen (sen) *n., pl.* **sen** [Jap., adopted in Cambodia to replace earlier *centime* (< Fr.) and in Indonesia to replace earlier *cent* (< Du.)] **1.** a unit of currency equal in Japan to 1/100 yen, in Cambodia to 1/100 riel, and in Indonesia to 1/100 rupiah **2.** a coin representing such a unit

sen. 1. senate **2.** senator **3.** senior

sen·a·ry (sen′ər ē) *adj.* [L. *senarius* < *seni,* six each < base of *sex,* SIX] of six; on the basis of six

sen·ate (sen′it) *n.* [ME. *senat* < OFr. < L. *senatus* < *senex,* old, aged < IE. base *sen(o)-,* old, whence Sans. *sána-,* Gr. *henos,* OIr. *sen,* old] **1.** lit., a council of elders **2.** the supreme council of the ancient Roman state, orig. only of patricians but later including the plebeians **3.** a lawmaking assembly; state council **4.** [S-] ☆*a)* the upper branch of the legislature of the U.S., or of most of the States of the U.S. *b)* a similar body in other countries **5.** a governing or advisory council in a college or university **6.** the building where a senate meets

sen·a·tor (sen′ə tər) *n.* [ME. *senatour* < OFr. *senateur* < L. *senator*] a member of a senate

sen·a·to·ri·al (sen′ə tôr′ē əl) *adj.* [< L. *senatorius* (< *senator*) + -IAL] **1.** of or suitable for a senator or a senate **2.** composed of senators

☆**senatorial courtesy** a custom of the U.S. Senate whereby nominations to official positions (except in the cabinet) made by the President may be refused if the Senators of the State in which the nominee resides, who belong to the majority party, have not approved the nomination

☆**senatorial district** any of the districts into which a State is divided for electing members to the State senate

send[1] (send) *vt.* **sent, send′ing** [ME. *senden* < OE. *sendan,* akin to G. *senden,* Goth. *sandjan,* caus. formation in sense "to cause to go" < IE. base *sent-,* to go, find out, discover, whence L. *sentire,* to feel, sense, OIr. *sēt,* way] **1.** *a)* to cause to go or be carried; dispatch, convey, or transmit *b)* to dispatch, convey, or transmit (a letter, message, etc.) by mail, radio, etc. **2.** to ask, direct, or command to go [send the boy home] **3.** to arrange for the going of; enable to go or attend [to send one's son to college] **4.** to cause or force to move, as by releasing, hitting, discharging, throwing, etc. [he sent the ball over the fence] **5.** to bring or drive into some state or condition [sent him to his ruin] **6.** to cause to happen, come, etc.; give [a misfortune sent by the gods] ☆**7.** [Slang] to make very excited or exhilarated; thrill —*vi.* **1.** to send a message, messenger, emissary, etc. [to send for help] **2.** to transmit, as by radio —**send away** to dispatch or banish —**send down** [Brit.] to suspend or expel from a university —**send flying 1.** to dismiss or cause to depart hurriedly **2.** to stagger or repel, as with a blow **3.** to put to flight; rout **4.** to scatter abruptly in all directions —**send for 1.** to ask for the arrival of; summon **2.** to place an order for; make a request for delivery of —**send forth** to be a source of; cause to appear; give out or forth; produce, emit, utter, etc. —**send in 1.** to dispatch, hand in, or send to a central point or to one receiving **2.** to put (a player) into a game or contest —**send off 1.** to mail or dispatch (a letter, gift, etc.) **2.** to dismiss **3.** to give a send-off to —**send out 1.** to dispatch, distribute, issue, mail, etc. from a central point **2.** to send forth **3.** to send someone on an errand (for something) —**send round** to put into circulation —**send up 1.** to cause to rise, climb, or go up ☆**2.** [Colloq.] to sentence to prison **3.** [Brit. Slang] to make seem ridiculous, esp. by parody —**send′er** *n.*

send[2] (send) *n.* [prob. < prec., but infl. by ASCEND] **1.** the driving motion of a wave or the sea **2.** *same as* SCEND —*vi.* **1.** to be plunged forward, as by a wave **2.** *same as* SCEND

Sen·dai (sen′dī′) seaport in NE Honshu, Japan: pop. 481,000

sen·dal (sen′d′l) *n.* [ME. *cendal* < OFr. < ML. *cendallum,* prob. ult. < Gr. *sindōn,* fine linen] a light silk fabric used in the Middle Ages for costumes, flags, etc.

☆**send-off** (send′ôf′) *n.* [Colloq.] **1.** an expression or demon-

stration of friendly feeling toward someone starting out on a trip, career, etc. **2.** a start given to someone or something

send·up (send′up′) *n.* [Brit. Slang] a mocking parody, esp. when done with seeming gravity; takeoff; spoof

Sen·e·ca (sen′i kə) *n.* [< Du. *Sennacaas*, the Five Nations < Mohegan *a'sinnika*, transl. of Iroquois *onĕñiute'*, short for *onĕñiute' roñ non*, Oneida, lit., people of the standing rock] **1.** *pl.* **-cas, -ca** any of a N. American Indian people who formerly lived in the area of the Genesee River, N.Y., and now live chiefly in New York and Ontario: see FIVE NATIONS **2.** their Iroquoian language —**Sen′e·can** *adj.*

Sen·e·ca (sen′i kə) (*Lucius Annaeus Seneca*) 4? B.C.– 65 A.D.; Rom. philosopher, dramatist, & statesman

☆**sen·e·ga** (sen′i gə) *n.* [< *Senega* (root), var. of SENECA: from use by the Seneca against snake bites] **1.** an E. N. American milkwort (*Polygala senega*) with single racemes of white flowers **2.** its dried root, formerly used as an expectorant Also **senega (snake) root**

Sen·e·gal (sen′i gôl′) **1.** country in W Africa, on the Atlantic: a member state of the French Community: 76,124 sq. mi.; pop. 3,490,000; cap. Dakar **2.** river flowing from W Mali northwest into the Atlantic: c. 1,000 mi. Also, Fr. **Sé·né·gal** (sā nā gàl′)

Sen·e·ga·lese (sen′i gə lēz′) *n., pl.* **-lese′** a native or inhabitant of Senegal —*adj.* of Senegal or its people

Sen·e·gam·bi·a (sen′ə gam′bē ə) *former name of* a region in W Africa between the Senegal & Gambia rivers

se·nes·cent (sə nes′'nt) *adj.* [L. *senescens*, prp. of *senescere*, to grow old < *senex*, old: see SENATE] growing old; aging —**se·nes′cence** (-'ns) *n.*

sen·es·chal (sen′ə shəl) *n.* [ME. < OFr. < Frank. *siniskalk*, oldest servant < **sini*, old (for IE. base see SENATE) + *skalk*, servant (for IE. base see MARSHAL)] a steward or major-domo in the household of a medieval noble

‡**se·nhor** (si nyôr′) *n., pl.* **se·nhor′es** (-nyôr′əsh, -əs) [Port. < L. *senior* (see SENIOR)] a man; gentleman: Portuguese title equivalent to *Mr.* or *Sir:* abbrev. **Sr.**

‡**se·nho·ra** (si nyôr′ə) *n., pl.* **se·nho′ras** (-nyôr′əsh, -əs) [Port., fem. of prec.] a married woman: Portuguese title equivalent to *Mrs.* or *Madam:* abbrev. **Sra.**

‡**se·nho·ri·ta** (si′nyô rē′tə) *n., pl.* **se′nho·ri′tas** (-təsh, -təs) [Port., dim. of prec.] an unmarried woman or girl: Portuguese title equivalent to *Miss:* abbrev. **Srta.**

se·nile (sē′nīl, sen′īl) *adj.* [L. *senilis* < *senex*, old: see SENATE] **1.** *a)* of, typical of, or resulting from old age *b)* showing the marked deterioration often accompanying old age, esp. the mental impairment characterized by confusion, memory loss, etc. **2.** *Geol.* nearing the end of an erosion cycle —**se′nile·ly** *adv.* —**se·nil·i·ty** (si nil′ə tē) *n.*

sen·ior (sēn′yər) *adj.* [ME. < L. *senior*, compar. of *senex*, old: see SENATE] **1.** of the greater age; older: written *Sr.* after the name of a father whose son has been given the same name: opposed to JUNIOR **2.** of higher rank or standing, or longer in service ☆**3.** of or for seniors in a high school or college —*n.* **1.** a person older than another or others **2.** a person of greater rank, standing, or length of service ☆**3.** a student in the last year of a high school or college —**one's senior** a person older than oneself

senior citizen an elderly person, esp. one who is retired

☆**senior high school** high school (usually grades 10, 11, & 12) following junior high school

sen·ior·i·ty (sēn yôr′ə tē, -yär′-) *n., pl.* **-ties** [ML. *senioritas*] **1.** the state or quality of being senior; precedence in birth, rank, etc. **2.** status, priority, or precedence achieved by length of service in a given job

Sen·lac (Hill) (sen′lak) hill in Sussex, SE England: site of the Battle of HASTINGS

sen·na (sen′ə) *n.* [ML. *sene* < Ar. *sanā*] **1.** any of a genus (*Cassia*) of plants of the legume family, with finely divided leaves and yellow flowers **2.** the dried leaflets of various sennas, used, esp. formerly, as a laxative **3.** any of various similar plants, as **bladder senna** (*Colutea arborescens*) with dull green leaves and yellow flowers

Sen·nach·er·ib (sə nak′ər ib) ?–681 B.C.; king of Assyria (705–681): son of SARGON II

sen·net (sen′it) *n.* [prob. via Anglo-Fr. < OFr. *senet*, var. of *signet:* see SIGNET] a trumpet call used as a signal for ceremonial entrances and exits: a stage direction in Elizabethan drama

Sen·nett (sen′it), **Mack** (mak) (born *Michael Sinnott*) 1884–1960; U.S. motion-picture producer & director, esp. of slapstick comedies, born in Canada

sen·night, se′n·night (sen′īt, -it) *n.* [ME. < OE. *seofon nihta:* see SEVEN & NIGHT] [Archaic] a week

sen·nit (sen′it) *n.* [< ?] a flat braided material made by plaiting strands of rope yarn **2.** plaited straw, grass, etc. used for making hats

‡**se·ñor** (se nyôr′) *n., pl.* **se·ñor′es** (-nyôr′res) [Sp. < L. *senior:* see SENIOR] a man; gentleman: Spanish title equivalent to *Mr.* or *Sir:* abbrev. **Sr.**

‡**se·ño·ra** (se nyôr′rä) *n., pl.* **se·ño′ras** (-räs) [Sp., fem. of prec.] a married woman: Spanish title equivalent to *Mrs.* or *Madam:* abbrev. **Sra.**

‡**se·ño·ri·ta** (se′nyô rē′tä) *n., pl.* **se′ño·ri′tas** (-täs) [Sp., dim. of prec.] an unmarried woman or girl: Spanish title corresponding to *Miss:* abbrev. **Srta.**

sen·sate (sen′sāt) *adj.* [LL. *sensatus*, intelligent < L. *sensus*, SENSE] **1.** having the power of physical sensation **2.** perceived by the senses —**sen′sate·ly** *adv.*

sen·sa·tion (sen sā′shən) *n.* [LL. *sensatio* < *sensatus:* see prec.] **1.** the power or process of receiving conscious sense impressions through direct stimulation of the bodily organism [*the sensations* of hearing, seeing, touching, etc.] **2.** an immediate reaction to external stimulation of a sense organ; conscious feeling or sense impression [a *sensation* of cold] **3.** a generalized feeling or reaction, often vague and without reference to immediate stimulus [a *sensation* of happiness] **4.** *a)* a state or feeling of general excitement and interest [the play caused a *sensation*] *b)* the action, event, person, etc. causing such a feeling

sen·sa·tion·al (-'l) *adj.* **1.** of the senses or sensation **2.** of, or in accordance with, philosophical sensationalism **3.** *a)* arousing intense interest and excitement; startling; exciting *b)* using or having effects intended to startle, shock, thrill, etc. **4.** [Colloq.] exceptionally good, fine, etc. —**sen·sa′tion·al·ly** *adv.*

sen·sa·tion·al·ism (-'l iz'm) *n.* **1.** *a)* the use of strongly emotional subject matter, or wildly dramatic style, language, or artistic expression, that is intended to shock, startle, thrill, excite, etc. *b)* preoccupation with or exploitation of what is sensational in literature, art, etc. **2.** same as SENSUALISM (sense 3 *a*) **3.** *Philos.* the belief that all knowledge is acquired through the senses —**sen·sa′tion·al·ist** *n.* —**sen·sa′tion·al·is′tic** *adj.*

sen·sa·tion·al·ize (-'l īz′) *vt.* **-ized′, -iz′ing** to make sensational; treat in a sensational way

sense (sens) *n.* [Fr. *sens* < L. *sensus* < *sentire*, to feel, perceive: for IE. base see SEND[1]] **1.** the ability of the nerves and the brain to receive and react to stimuli, as light, sound, impact, constriction, etc.; specif., any of five faculties of receiving impressions through specific bodily organs and the nerves associated with them (sight, touch, taste, smell, and hearing): see also SIXTH SENSE **2.** the senses considered as a total function of the bodily organism, as distinguished from intellect, movement, etc. **3.** *a)* feeling, impression, or perception through the senses [a *sense* of warmth, pain, etc.] *b)* a generalized feeling, awareness, or realization [a *sense* of longing] **4.** an ability to judge, discriminate, or estimate external conditions, sounds, etc. [a *sense* of direction, pitch, etc.] **5.** an ability to feel, appreciate, or understand some quality [a *sense* of humor, honor, etc.] **6.** *a)* the ability to think or reason soundly; normal intelligence and judgment, often as reflected in behavior *b)* soundness of judgment or reasoning [some *sense* in what he says] *c)* something wise, sound, or reasonable [to talk *sense*] **7.** *a)* meaning; esp., any of several meanings conveyed by or attributed to the same word or phrase *b)* essential signification; gist [to grasp the *sense* of a remark] **8.** the general opinion, sentiment, or attitude of a group **9.** *Math.* either of two contrary directions that may be specified, as clockwise or counterclockwise for the circumference of a circle, positive or negative for a line segment, etc. —*vt.* **sensed, sens′ing 1.** to be or become aware of; perceive [to *sense* another's hostility] **2.** to comprehend; understand **3.** to detect automatically, as by sensors —*SYN.* see MEANING —**in a sense** from one aspect; to a limited extent or degree —**make sense** to be intelligible or logical —**senses** normal ability to think or reason soundly [to come to one's *senses*]

sense datum that which is immediately perceived as the direct effect of stimulus on a sense organ

sense·less (-lis) *adj.* **1.** unconscious **2.** not having or showing good sense; stupid; foolish **3.** having no real point or purpose; nonsensical; meaningless —**sense′less·ly** *adv.* —**sense′less·ness** *n.*

sense organ any organ or structure, as an eye or taste bud, specialized to receive specific stimuli and transmit them as sensations to the brain; receptor

sense perception perception by sight, touch, etc.

sen·si·bil·i·ty (sen′sə bil′ə tē) *n., pl.* **-ties** [ME. < MFr. < LL. *sensibilitas* < LL. *sensibilis:* see ff.] **1.** the capacity for physical sensation; power of responding to stimuli; ability to feel **2.** [often *pl.*] *a)* the capacity for being affected emotionally or intellectually, whether pleasantly or unpleasantly; receptiveness to impression *b)* the capacity to respond perceptively to intellectual, moral, or aesthetic values; delicate, sensitive awareness or responsiveness *c)* liability to be offended, repelled, etc. **3.** [Rare] responsiveness, as of a plant, to changing conditions

sen·si·ble (sen′sə b'l) *adj.* [ME. < MFr. < L. *sensibilis* < *sensus*, pp. of *sentire*, to feel, SENSE] **1.** that can cause physical sensation; perceptible to the senses **2.** perceptible to the intellect **3.** easily perceived or noticed; marked; striking; appreciable **4.** having senses; capable of receiving sensation; sensitive **5.** having appreciation or understanding; emotionally or intellectually aware [*sensible* of another's grief] **6.** having or showing good sense or sound judgment; intelligent; reasonable; wise —*SYN.* see AWARE, MATERIAL, PERCEPTIBLE, RATIONAL —**sen′si·bly** *adv.*

sen·si·tive (sen′sə tiv) *adj.* [ME. *sensitife* < MFr. *sensitif* < ML. *sensitivus* < L. *sensus:* see SENSE] **1.** of the senses or sensation; esp., connected with the reception or transmission of sense impressions; sensory **2.** receiving and responding to stimuli from outside objects or agencies; having sensation **3.** responding or feeling readily and acutely; very keenly susceptible to stimuli [a *sensitive* ear] **4.** easily hurt; tender; raw **5.** having or showing keen sensibilities; highly perceptive or responsive intellectually,

aesthetically, etc. **6.** easily offended, disturbed, shocked, irritated, etc., as by the actions of others; touchy **7.** changing readily in the presence of some external force or condition; specif., *a)* readily affected by light: said of photographic film *b)* readily receiving very weak radio signals *c)* operating readily in weak light, as certain television camera tubes **8.** designed to indicate or measure small changes or differences **9.** showing, or liable to show, unusual variation; fluctuating *[a sensitive stock market]* ☆**10.** designating, of, or dealing with highly secret or delicate government matters —*n.* same as MEDIUM (*n.* 7) —**sen′si·tive·ly** *adv.* —**sen′si·tive·ness** *n.*

sensitive plant a tropical American plant (*Mimosa pudica*) of the legume family, with a spiny stem, minute, purplish flowers in spherical clusters, and leaflets that fold and leafstalks that droop at the slightest touch

sen·si·tiv·i·ty (sen′sə tiv′ə tē) *n.* the condition or quality of being sensitive; specif., *a)* the responsiveness of an organ or organism to external stimuli *b) Radio & TV* the capacity of a receiver to respond to incoming signals

sen·si·tize (sen′sə tīz′) *vt.* **-tized′**, **-tiz′ing** [SENSIT(IVE) + -IZE] to make sensitive or susceptible; specif., *a) Photog.* to make (a film or plate) sensitive to light, etc. *b) Immunology* to make (an individual) sensitive or hypersensitive to an antigen —**sen′si·ti·za′tion** *n.* —**sen′si·tiz′er** *n.*

sen·si·tom·e·ter (sen′sə täm′ə tər) *n.* [SENSIT(IVITY) + -o- + -METER] an instrument used for measuring sensitivity, as of photographic film —**sen′si·to·met′ric** (-tə met′rik) *adj.* —**sen′si·tom′e·try** (-trē) *n.*

sen·sor (sen′sər, -sôr) *n.* [< L. *sensus*, pp. of *sentire*, SENSE + -OR] any of various devices designed to detect, measure, or record physical phenomena, as radiation, heat, blood pressure, etc., and to respond, as by transmitting information, initiating changes, or operating controls

sen·so·ri·mo·tor (sen′sə rē mōt′ər) *adj.* [< SENSORY + MOTOR] **1.** *Physiol.* of, pertaining to, or concerned with both the sensory and motor impulses of an organism **2.** *Psychol.* of or pertaining to motor responses initiated by sensory stimulation

sen·so·ri·um (sen sôr′ē əm) *n.*, *pl.* **-ri·ums**, **-ri·a** (-ə) [LL. < L. *sensus*, SENSE] **1.** the supposed seat of physical sensation in the gray matter of the brain **2.** the whole sensory apparatus of the body

sen·so·ry (sen′sər ē) *adj.* [SENS(E) + -ORY] **1.** of the senses or sensation **2.** connected with the reception and transmission of sense impressions Also **sen·so′ri·al** (-sôr′ē əl)

sen·su·al (sen′shoo wəl) *adj.* [L. *sensualis* < *sensus*, feeling, SENSE] **1.** of the body and the senses as distinguished from the intellect or spirit; bodily *[sensual pleasures]* **2.** *a)* connected or preoccupied with bodily or sexual pleasures; voluptuous *b)* full of lust; licentious; lewd **3.** resulting from, or showing preoccupation with, bodily or sexual pleasure *[a sensual expression]* **4.** [Now Rare] sensory or sensuous —SYN. see CARNAL, SENSUOUS —**sen′su·al·ly** *adv.*

sen·su·al·ism (-iz′m) *n.* **1.** frequent or excessive indulgence in sensual pleasures **2.** same as SENSATIONALISM (sense 3) **3.** *a)* the system of ethics which holds that the pleasures of the senses constitute the greatest good *b)* the aesthetic expression of this belief, esp. in art —**sen′su·al·ist** *n.* —**sen′su·al·is′tic** *adj.*

sen·su·al·i·ty (sen′shoo wal′ə tē) *n.* [ME. *sensualite* < OFr. < LL. *sensualitas*] **1.** the state or quality of being sensual; fondness for or indulgence in sensual pleasures **2.** lasciviousness; lewdness

sen·su·al·ize (sen′shoo wə līz′) *vt.* **-ized′**, **-iz′ing** to make sensual —**sen′su·al·i·za′tion** *n.*

sen·su·ous (sen′shoo wəs) *adj.* [< L. *sensus*, SENSE + -OUS] **1.** of, derived from, based on, affecting, appealing to, or perceived by the senses **2.** readily susceptible through the senses; enjoying the pleasures of sensation —**sen′su·ous·ly** *adv.* —**sen′su·ous·ness** *n.*
SYN.—**sensuous** suggests the strong appeal of that which is pleasing to the eye, ear, touch, etc. and, of a person, implies susceptibility to the pleasures of sensation *[soft, sensuous music]*; **sensual** refers to the gratification of the grosser bodily senses or appetite *[sensual excesses]*; **voluptuous** implies a tending to excite, or giving oneself up to the gratification of, sensuous or sensual desires *[her voluptuous charms]*; **luxurious** implies a reveling in that which luxuriously provides a high degree of physical comfort or satisfaction *[a luxurious feeling of drowsiness]*; **epicurean** implies delight in luxury and sensuous pleasure, esp. that of eating and drinking

sent (sent) *pt. & pp.* of SEND¹
sen·tence (sen′t'ns) *n.* [ME. < OFr. < L. *sententia*, way of thinking, opinion, sentiment, prob. for *sentientia* < *sentiens*, prp. of *sentire*, to feel, SENSE] **1.** *a)* a decision or judgment, as of a court; esp., the determination by a court of the punishment of a convicted person *b)* the punishment itself **2.** *Gram. a)* a word or group of words stating, asking, commanding, or exclaiming something; conventional unit of connected speech or writing, usually containing a subject and predicate: in writing, a sentence is begun with a capital letter and concluded with an end mark (period, question mark, etc.); in speaking, a sentence begins following a silence and concludes with any of

various final pitches followed by a terminal juncture ☆*b)* in a generative grammar, a noun phrase followed by a verb phrase to which a degree of grammaticalness may be assigned: see PREDICATE, SUBJECT **3.** [Archaic] a short moral saying; maxim **4.** *Music* same as PERIOD —*vt.* **-tenced**, **-tenc·ing** to pronounce judgment or punishment upon (a convicted person); condemn (*to* a specified punishment) —**sen·ten′tial** (sen ten′shəl) *adj.*

sentence stress 1. the sequence of voice stresses normally given to words in a sentence **2.** voice stress given to certain words or syllables in a sentence for emphasis, contrast, irony, etc.

sentential function *Logic* an expression with free variables that becomes a declarative sentence when constants replace these variables (Ex.: *x* is a man; *x* is heavier than *y*)

sen·ten·tious (sen ten′shəs) *adj.* [L. *sententiosus* < *sententia:* see SENTENCE] **1.** expressing much in few words; short and pithy; pointed **2.** full of, or fond of using, maxims, proverbs, and axioms; aphoristic, esp. in a way that is ponderously trite and moralizing —**sen·ten′tious·ly** *adv.* —**sen·ten′tious·ness** *n.*

sen·tience (sen′shəns, -shē əns) *n.* **1.** a sentient state or quality; capacity for feeling or perceiving; consciousness **2.** mere awareness or sensation that does not involve thought or perception Also **sen′tien·cy**

sen·tient (-shənt, -shē ənt) *adj.* [L. *sentiens*, prp. of *sentire*, to perceive by the senses: see SENSE] of, having, or capable of feeling or perception; conscious —*n.* [Now Rare] a sentient person or thing —**sen′tient·ly** *adv.*

sen·ti·ment (sen′tə mənt) *n.* [ME. *sentement* < OFr. < ML. *sentimentum* + L. *sentire*, to feel, SENSE] **1.** a complex combination of feelings and opinions as a basis for action or judgment; general emotionalized attitude *[the sentiment of romantic love]* **2.** a thought, opinion, judgment, or attitude, usually the result of careful consideration, but often colored with emotion: *often used in the pl.* **3.** susceptibility to feeling or to emotional appeal; sensibility **4.** appeal to the emotions in literature or art; expression of delicate, sensitive feeling **5.** sentimentality; maudlin emotion **6.** a short sentence or aphorism expressing some thought or wish, as in a toast **7.** the thought or meaning behind something said, done, or given, as distinct from the literal statement, act, etc. SYN. see FEELING, OPINION

sen·ti·men·tal (sen′tə men′t'l) *adj.* **1.** having or showing tender, gentle, or delicate feelings, as in aesthetic expression **2.** having or showing such feelings in an excessive, superficial, or maudlin way; mawkish **3.** influenced more by emotion than reason; acting from feeling rather than from practical motives **4.** of or resulting from sentiment *[a sentimental reason]* —**sen′ti·men′tal·ly** *adv.*
SYN.—**sentimental** suggests emotion of a kind that is felt in a nostalgic or tender mood *[sentimental music]* or emotion that is exaggerated, affected, foolish, etc. *[a trashy, sentimental novel]*; **romantic** suggests emotion aroused by that which appeals to the imagination as it is influenced by the idealization of life in literature, art, etc. *[a romantic girl waiting for her Prince Charming]*; that is **mawkish** which is sentimental in a disgustingly weak, insincere, or exaggerated way *[a mawkish soap opera]*; that is **maudlin** which is tearfully or weakly sentimental in a foolish way *[an intoxicated, maudlin guest]*; **gushy**, an informal word, implies an effusive display of sentiment or enthusiasm *[gushy congratulations]*

sen·ti·men·tal·ism (-iz′m) *n.* **1.** the habit, quality, or condition of being sentimental **2.** any expression of this —**sen′ti·men′tal·ist** *n.*

sen·ti·men·tal·i·ty (sen′tə men tal′ə tē) *n.* **1.** the quality or condition of being sentimental, esp. in a superficial or maudlin way **2.** *pl.* **-ties** any expression of this

sen·ti·men·tal·ize (-men′tə līz′) *vi.* **-ized′**, **-iz′ing** to be sentimental; think or behave in a sentimental way —*vt.* to regard or treat in a sentimental way *[to sentimentalize war]* —**sen′ti·men′tal·i·za′tion** *n.*

sen·ti·nel (sen′ti n'l) *n.* [Fr. *sentinelle* < It. *sentinella*, ult. < L. *sentire*, to feel, SENSE] a person or animal set to guard a group; specif., a sentry —*vt.* **-neled** or **-nelled**, **-nel·ing** or **-nel·ling** **1.** to guard or watch over as a sentinel **2.** to furnish or protect with a sentinel **3.** to post as a sentinel

sen·try (sen′trē) *n.*, *pl.* **-tries** [< ? obs. *centery*, sanctuary, guardhouse] **1.** a sentinel; esp., any of the men of a military guard posted to guard against, and warn of, danger **2.** [Now Rare] guard or watch *[to keep sentry]*

sentry box a small, boxlike structure serving as a shelter for a sentry on duty during bad weather

Se·nus·si, **Se·nu·si** (se noo′sē) *n.*, *pl.* **-si** any member of a militant brotherhood of North African Moslems —**Se·nus′si·an**, **Se·nu′si·an** *adj.*

Se·oul (sōl; *Kor.* syô′ool′) capital of South Korea, in the NW part: pop. 3,471,000

Sep. 1. September **2.** Septuagint

sep. 1. sepal **2.** separate

se·pal (sē′p'l; *chiefly Brit.*, sep′'l) *n.* [Fr. *sépale* < ModL. *sepalum*, arbitrary blend < Gr. *skepē*, a covering + L. *petalum*, petal] *Bot.* any of the usually green, leaflike parts of the calyx —**se′paled**, **se′palled** *adj.*

se·pal·oid (-oid′) *adj.* like or having the nature of a sepal: also **se′pal·ine** (-in)

-sep·al·ous (sep′l əs) [< SEPAL + -OUS] *a combining form meaning* having (a specified number or kind of) sepals [*trisepalous*]

sep·a·ra·ble (sep′ər ə b'l, sep′rə-) *adj.* [ME. < L. *separabilis*] that can be separated —**sep′a·ra·bil′i·ty** *n.* —**sep′a·ra·bly** *adv.*

sep·a·rate (sep′ə rāt′; *for adj. & n.*, sep′ər it, sep′rit) *vt.* **-rat′ed, -rat′ing** [ME. *separaten* < L. *separatus*, pp. of *separare*, to separate < *se-*, apart (see SECEDE) + *parare*, to arrange, PREPARE] **1.** to set or put apart into sections, groups, sets, units, etc.; cause to part; divide; disunite; sever **2.** to see the differences between; distinguish or discriminate between **3.** to keep apart by being between; divide [a hedge that *separates* the yards] **4.** to bring about a separation between (a man and wife) **5.** to single out or set apart from others for a special purpose; sort; segregate **6.** to take away (a part or ingredient) from a combination or mixture **7.** to discharge; specif., *a)* to release from military service ☆*b)* to dismiss from employment —*vi.* **1.** to withdraw or secede [to *separate* from a party] **2.** to part, come or draw apart, or become disconnected **3.** to part company; go in different directions; cease to associate **4.** to stop living together as man and wife without a divorce **5.** to become distinct or disengaged, as from a mixture —*adj.* **1.** set apart or divided from the rest or others; not joined, united, or connected; severed **2.** not associated or connected with others; having existence as an entity; distinct; individual **3.** thought of or regarded as having individual form or function [the *separate* parts of the body] **4.** of or for one only; not shared or held in common [*separate* beds] **5.** [Archaic] withdrawn from others; solitary —*n.* **1.** *same as* OFFPRINT **2.** [*pl.*] coordinated articles of dress worn as a set or separately in various combinations —**sep′a·rate·ly** *adv.* —**sep′a·rate·ness** *n.*
SYN.—**separate** implies the putting apart of things previously united, joined, or assembled [to *separate* machine parts, a family, etc.]; **divide** implies a separation into parts, pieces, groups, etc. by or as by cutting, splitting, branching, etc., often for purposes of apportionment [to *divide* the profits into equal shares]; **part** is now usually applied to the separation of persons or things that have been closely connected or associated ["till death us do *part*"]; **sever** implies a forcible and complete separation, as by cutting off a part from a whole [to *sever* a branch from a tree]; **sunder**, now a literary term, implies a violent splitting, tearing, or wrenching apart —**ANT. unite, combine**

sep·a·ra·tion (sep′ər ə rā′shən) *n.* [ME. *separacion* < MFr. < L. *separatio*] **1.** a separating or being separated **2.** the place where a separating occurs; break; division; gap **3.** something that separates **4.** an arrangement by which a man and wife live apart by agreement or by court decree
☆**separation center** a center where persons in the armed forces are discharged or released from active duty

sep·a·ra·tism (sep′ər ə tiz′m) *n.* a condition or the advocacy of political, religious, or racial separation

sep·a·ra·tist (sep′ər ə tist, -ə rāt′ist) *n.* **1.** a person who withdraws or secedes, esp. a member of a group that has seceded from a larger group; dissenter **2.** a person who advocates political, religious, or racial separation —*adj.* of separatists or separatism

sep·a·ra·tive (sep′ə rāt′iv, -ər ə tiv) *adj.* [< Fr. or LL.: Fr. *séparatif* < LL. *separativus*] tending to separate or cause separation: also **sep′a·ra·to′ry** (-ər ə tôr′ē)

sep·a·ra·tor (sep′ə rāt′ər) *n.* [LL.] **1.** a person or thing that separates **2.** any of several devices for separating one substance from another, as cream from milk

Se·phar·dim (sə fär′dim, -fär dēm′) *n.pl., sing.* **Se·phard** (sə färd′), **Se·phar′di** (-fär′dē, -fär dē′) [Heb. *sephārādhīm* < *Sēphāradh*, a region mentioned in Ob. 20, often identified with Spain, but prob. orig. an area in Asia Minor] the Jews of Spain and Portugal before the Inquisition, or their descendants: cf. ASHKENAZIM —**Se·phar′dic** *adj.*

se·pi·a (sē′pē ə) *n.* [ModL., name of a genus of cuttlefishes < L., the cuttlefish < Gr. *sēpia* < *sēpein*, to cause to rot (from the inky fluid emitted), akin to *sapros*, rotten: see SAPRO-] **1.** a dark-brown pigment prepared from the inky fluid secreted by cuttlefish **2.** a dark reddish-brown color **3.** a photographic print in this color —*adj.* **1.** of sepia **2.** dark reddish-brown

se·pi·o·lite (sē′pē ə līt′) *n.* [G. *sepiolith* < Gr. *sēpion*, cuttlebone < *sēpia* (see prec.) + *-lith* (see -LITH)] *same as* MEERSCHAUM (sense l)

se·poy (sē′poi) *n.* [Port. *sipae* < Hind. & Per. *sipāhī* < *sipāh*, army] formerly, a native of India serving in a European army, esp. the British army

sep·pu·ku (se pōō′kōō) *n.* [Jap.] *same as* HARA-KIRI

sep·sis (sep′sis) *n.* [ModL. < Gr. *sēpsis*, putrefaction < *sēpein*, to make putrid: see SEPIA] a poisoned state caused by the absorption of pathogenic microorganisms and their products into the bloodstream

sept (sept) *n.* [var. of SECT (prob. by confusion with L. *septum*: see SEPTUM)] **1.** a clan or subdivision of a clan, as in ancient Ireland and Scotland **2.** any similar group based on supposed descent from a common ancestor

sept- *same as* SEPTI-: used before a vowel

Sept. **1.** September **2.** Septuagint

sep·ta (sep′tə) *n. pl. of* SEPTUM

sep·tal (-t'l) *adj.* of or forming a septum or septa

sep·tar·i·um (sep ter′ē əm) *n., pl.* **-i·a** (-ə) [ModL. < L. *septum*: see SEPTUM] a cementlike mass, as of limestone, shot through with fissures filled with some other material, as calcite —**sep·tar′i·an** *adj.*

sep·tate (sep′tāt) *adj.* [ModL. *septatus*] having or divided by a septum or septums

Sep·tem·ber (sep tem′bər, səp-) *n.* [ME. & OFr. *Septembre* < L. *September* < *septem*, seven (+ *-ber* < ?): so named as the seventh month of the ancient Roman year, which began with March] the ninth month of the year, having 30 days: abbrev. **Sept., Sep., S.**

September massacre the massacre of the Royalists in Paris, Sept. 2 to 6, 1792, during the French Revolution

Sep·tem·brist (sep tem′brist, səp-) *n.* a person who took part in the September massacre

sep·te·nar·y (sep′tə ner′e) *adj.* [L. *septenarius* < *septem*, SEVEN] **1.** of the number seven **2.** consisting of or forming a group of seven **3.** *same as* SEPTENNIAL —*n., pl.* **-nar′ies** **1.** a group or set of seven, esp. seven years **2.** a line of verse of seven feet

sep·ten·ni·al (sep ten′ē əl) *adj.* [< L. *septennium*, a period of seven years < *septem*, SEVEN + *annus*, year (see ANNUAL) + -AL] **1.** lasting seven years **2.** coming, happening, etc. every seven years —**sep·ten′ni·al·ly** *adv.*

sep·ten·tri·o·nal (sep ten′trē ə n'l) *adj.* [ME. < L. *septentrionalis* < *septentriones*, the seven stars of Ursa Major, lit., seven plowing oxen < *septem*, SEVEN + *trio*, a plow ox] [Archaic] northern; boreal

sep·tet, sep·tette (sep tet′) *n.* [G. < L. *septem*, SEVEN + G. (*du*)*ett*] **1.** a group of seven persons or things **2.** *Music a)* a composition for seven voices or seven instruments *b)* the seven performers of this

sep·ti-¹ (sep′tə, -ti) [< L. *septem*, SEVEN] *a combining form meaning* seven or seventh [*septilateral*]

sep·ti-² (sep′tə, -ti) [< SEPTUM] *a combining form meaning* divider, partition [*septifragal*]

sep·tic (sep′tik) *adj.* [L. *septicus* < Gr. *sēptikos* < *sēpein*, to make putrid: see SEPIA] causing, or resulting from, sepsis or putrefaction —**sep′ti·cal·ly** *adv.* —**sep·tic′i·ty** (-tis′ə tē) *n.*

sep·ti·ce·mi·a (sep′tə sē′mē ə) *n.* [ModL. *septicemia*: see prec. & -EMIA] a systemic disease caused by the presence of pathogenic microorganisms and their toxic products in the blood —**sep′ti·ce′mic** (-mik) *adj.*

sep·ti·ci·dal (-sī′d'l) *adj.* [< SEPTI-² + L. *caedere*, to cut + -AL] *Bot.* splitting open, or dehiscent, down the middle of the partitions uniting carpels —**sep·ti·ci′dal·ly** *adv.*

septic tank an underground tank in which waste matter is putrefied and decomposed through bacterial action

sep·tif·ra·gal (sep tif′rə gəl) *adj.* [SEPTI-² + base of L. *frangere*, to BREAK¹ + -AL] *Bot.* opening, or dehiscing, by the breaking away of the outer walls of the carpels from the partitions —**sep·tif′ra·gal·ly** *adv.*

sep·ti·lat·er·al (sep′tə lat′ər əl) *adj.* [SEPTI-¹ + LATERAL] having seven sides

sep·til·lion (sep til′yən) *n.* [Fr. < L. *septem*, SEVEN + Fr. (*m*)*illion*] **1.** in the U.S. and France, the number represented by 1 followed by 24 zeros. **2.** in Great Britain and Germany, the number represented by 1 followed by 42 zeros —*adj.* amounting to one septillion in number

sep·time (sep′tēm) *n.* [< L. *septimus*, seventh (< *septem*, SEVEN)] a parrying position in fencing, the seventh of the eight positions

sep·tu·a·ge·nar·i·an (sep′tōō wə ji ner′ē ən, -tyōō-, -choo-) *adj.* [< LL. (*homo*) *septuagenarius*, (man) of seventy (< *septuageni*, seventy each < *septuaginta*, seventy) + -AN] seventy years old, or between the ages of seventy and eighty —*n.* a person of this age

Sep·tu·a·ges·i·ma (-jes′i mə) *n.* [ME. *Septuagesme* < L., fem. of *septuagesimus*, seventieth] the third Sunday before Lent: also **Septuagesima Sunday**

Sep·tu·a·gint (sep′too wə jint, -tyoo-, -choo-) [< L. *septuaginta*, seventy: because of the ancient tradition that it was completed in 70 (or 72) days by 72 Palestinian Jews for Ptolemy II, king of Egypt] a translation into Greek of the Old Testament made several centuries B.C.

sep·tum (sep′təm) *n., pl.* **-tums, -ta** (-tə) [ModL. < L., enclosure, hedge < *sepire*, to enclose, fence < *saepes*, a hedge < IE. base *saip-*, hedge fence, whence Gr. *haimos*, a thicket] *Biol.* a part that separates two cavities or two masses of tissue, as in the nose, a fruit, etc.; partition

sep·tu·ple (sep tōō′p'l, -tyōō′-, -tup′l; sep′too p'l) *adj.* [LL. *septuplus* < L. *septem*, seven] **1.** consisting of or including seven **2.** seven times as much or as many; sevenfold —*n.* an amount seven times as much or as many —*vt., vi.* **-pled, -pling** to make or become seven times as much or as many; multiply by seven

sep·tu·plet (sep tup′lit, -tōō′plit, -tyōō′-; sep′too plit) *n.* [dim. of prec.] **1.** any of seven offspring born at a single birth **2.** a collection or group of seven, usually of one kind

sep·ul·cher (sep′l kər) *n.* [ME. < OFr. *sepulcre* < L. *sepulcrum* < *sepelire*, to bury < IE. *sepel-*, veneration < base *sep-*, to honor, whence Sans. *sápati*, (he) cultivates, cherishes] **1.** a vault for burial; grave; tomb **2.** a place for the safekeeping of relics, as in an altar —*vt.* to place in a sepulcher; bury

se·pul·chral (sə pul′krəl) *adj.* [L. *sepulcralis*] **1.** of sepulchers, burial, etc. **2.** suggestive of the grave or burial; dismal; gloomy **3.** deep and melancholy: said of sound —**se·pul′chral·ly** *adv.*

sep·ul·chre (sep′l kər) *n., vt.* **-chred, -chring** *Brit. sp. of* SEPULCHER

sep·ul·ture (sep′'l chər) *n.* [ME. < OFr. < L. *sepultura* < *sepelire*, to bury: see SEPULCHER] **1.** burial; interment **2.** [Archaic] a burial place; sepulcher

seq. 1. sequel **2.** [L. *sequentes* or *sequentia*] the following: also **seqq.**

se·qua·cious (si kwā′shəs) *adj.* [L. *sequax* < *sequi*, to follow (see SEQUENT) + -OUS] **1.** tending to follow any leader; lacking individuality, as in thought; dependent; servile; compliant **2.** [Rare] showing or following logical or smooth sequence —**se·qua′cious·ly** *adv.* —**se·quac′i·ty** (-kwas′ə tē) *n.*

se·quel (sē′kwəl) *n.* [ME. *sequele* < MFr. *sequelle* < L. *sequela*: see ff.] **1.** something that follows; anything subsequent or succeeding; continuation **2.** something that comes as a result of something else; aftermath; effect; consequence **3.** any literary work complete in itself but continuing a story begun in an earlier work

se·que·la (si kwē′lə, -kwel′ə) *n., pl.* **-lae** (-lē, -ē) [L. < *sequi*, to follow: see SEQUENT] a thing that follows; consequence; specif., *Med.* a diseased condition following, and usually resulting from, a previous disease

se·quence (sē′kwəns) *n.* [MFr. < LL., a following < L. *sequens*: see ff.] **1.** *a*) the following of one thing after another in chronological, causal, or logical order; succession or continuity *b*) the order in which this occurs **2.** a continuous or related series, often of uniform things [a sonnet *sequence*] **3.** three or more playing cards in unbroken order in the same suit; run **4.** a resulting event; consequence; sequel **5.** *Math.* an ordered set of quantities or elements **6.** *Motion Pictures* a succession of shots constituting a single, uninterrupted episode **7.** *Music* a succession of phrases based on the same melodic pattern but repeated at different pitches, sometimes in different keys **8.** [ME. < ML. *sequentia* < LL.(Ec.), used as transl. of Gr.(Ec.) *akolouthia*, a succession of notes on the last syllable of the alleluia: cf. ACOLYTE] *R.C.Ch.* a hymn coming immediately before the Gospel in certain Masses —*vt.* **-quenced, -quenc·ing** to arrange in a sequence; put in order —*SYN.* see SERIES

se·quent (-kwənt) *adj.* [L. *sequens*, prp. of *sequi*, to follow < IE. base *sekw-*, to follow, whence OE. *secg*, a warrior] **1.** following in time or order; subsequent **2.** following as a result or effect; consequent —*n.* something that follows, esp. as a result; consequence

se·quen·tial (si kwen′shəl) *adj.* **1.** *same as* SEQUENT **2.** characterized by or forming a regular sequence of parts —**se·quen′tial·ly** *adv.*

se·ques·ter (si kwes′tər) *vt.* [ME. *sequestren* < MFr. *sequestrer* < LL. *sequestrare*, to remove, lay aside, separate < L. *sequester*, trustee, akin to *sequi*: see SEQUENT] **1.** to set off or apart; separate; segregate **2.** to take possession of (property) as security for a debt, claim, etc. **3.** to take over; confiscate; seize, esp. by authority **4.** to withdraw; seclude: often used reflexively

se·ques·tered (-tərd) *adj.* removed from others; secluded

se·ques·trant (-trənt) *n. Chem.* an agent producing sequestration

se·ques·trate (-trāt) *vt.* **-trat·ed, -trat·ing** [< LL. *sequestratus*, pp.: see SEQUESTER] *same as* SEQUESTER —**se′ques·tra′tor** *n.*

se·ques·tra·tion (sē′kwes trā′shən, si kwes′-) *n.* [ME. *sequestracion* < MFr. < LL. *sequestratio*] **1.** a sequestering or being sequestered; seclusion; separation **2.** *a*) the legal seizure of property for security *b*) confiscation of property, as by court or government action **3.** the process by which a sequestrum forms **4.** *Chem.* the close union of ions in solution with an added material so that a stable, soluble complex is produced

se·ques·trum (si kwes′trəm) *n., pl.* **-trums, -tra** (-trə) [ModL.: see SEQUESTER] *Med.* a piece of dead bone which has become separated from the surrounding healthy bone

se·quin (sē′kwin) *n.* [Fr. < It. *zecchino* < *zecca*, a mint < Ar. *sikkah*, a stamp, die] **1.** an obsolete Italian gold coin **2.** a small, shiny ornament or spangle, as a metal disk, esp. one of many sewn on fabric for decoration —*vt.* **se′quined** or **se′quinned, se′quin·ing** or **se′quin·ning** to adorn with sequins

☆**se·quoi·a** (si kwoi′ə) *n.* [ModL., name of the genus: after *Sequoya* (Cherokee *Sikwâyi*), Am. Indian (c. 1760–1843) who devised the Cherokee syllabary] either of two giant evergreen, coniferous trees of the W U.S.; specif., *same as: a*) BIG TREE *b*) REDWOOD (sense 1)

Sequoia National Park national park in EC Calif., containing giant sequoias: 602 sq. mi.

ser (sir) *n.* [Hind. *sēr*] *same as* SEER²

ser- (sir) *same as* SERO-: used before a vowel

ser. 1. series **2.** sermon

se·ra (sir′ə) *n. alt. pl. of* SERUM

sé·rac (sə rak′, sā-) *n.* [Swiss-Fr., orig., a type of white cheese < VL. *seraceum*, soft cheese, whey < L. *serum*: see SERUM] a pointed mass or pinnacle of ice left standing among the crevasses of a glacier

se·rag·lio (si ral′yō, -räl′-) *n., pl.* **-lios** [It. *serraglio*, enclosure, padlock, also (infl. by Turk. *serai*, palace: see ff.), place, seraglio < ML. *serraculum*, a bolt, bar <

LL. *serare*, to lock, bar < L. *sera*, a bolt, lock] **1.** the part of a Moslem's household where his wives or concubines live; harem **2.** the palace of a Turkish sultan Also **se·rail** (sə rīl′, -rīl′, -rāl′)

se·ra·i (si rä′ē) *n.* [Turk., palace, inn < Per. *sarāi*] **1.** in the Orient, an inn; caravansary **2.** a Turkish palace

Se·ra·je·vo (ser′ə yä′vō) *same as* SARAJEVO

ser·al (sir′əl) *adj. Ecol.* of or pertaining to a sere

Se·ram (si ram′) *same as* CERAM

☆**se·ra·pe** (sə rä′pē) *n.* [MexSp.] a woolen blanket, often brightly colored, used as an outer garment by men in Spanish-American countries

ser·aph (ser′əf) *n., pl.* **-aphs, -a·phim'** (-ə fim′) [back-formation < LL.(Ec.) *seraphim*, pl. < Heb. *šĕrāphīm*, pl., prob. < *sāraph*, to burn] **1.** *Bible* one of the heavenly beings surrounding the throne of God, represented as having three pairs of wings: Isa. 6:2 **2.** *Christian Theol.* any of the highest order of angels, above the cherubim —**se·raph′ic** (sə raf′ik) *adj.* —**se·raph′i·cal·ly** *adv.*

Se·ra·pis (sə rā′pis) [L. < Gr. *Sarapis*] an Egyptian god of the lower world whose cult spread to Greece and Rome

Serb (surb) *n.* [Serb. *Srb*] **1.** a native or inhabitant of Serbia; esp., any of a Slavic people of Serbia and adjacent areas **2.** *same as* SERBIAN (*n.* 1) —*adj. same as* SERBIAN

Serb. 1. Serbia **2.** Serbian

Ser·bi·a (sur′bē ə) republic of Yugoslavia, in the E part, formerly a kingdom: 21,580 sq. mi.; pop. 4,823,000; cap. Belgrade

Ser·bi·an (-ən) *adj.* of Serbia, the Serbs, or their language —*n.* **1.** Serbo-Croatian as spoken in Serbia **2.** *same as* SERB (*n.* 1)

Ser·bo- (sur′bō) *a combining form meaning* Serbian

Ser·bo-Cro·a·tian (sur′bō krō ā′shən) *n.* the major South Slavic language spoken in Yugoslavia: it is generally written in the Roman alphabet in Croatia and in the Cyrillic alphabet in Serbia —*adj.* of this language or the people who speak it

sere¹ (sir) *n.* [back-formation < SERIES] *Ecol.* the complete series of stages occurring in succession in communities of plants and animals until the climax is reached

sere² (sir) *adj.* [var. of SEAR¹] [Poet.] dried up; withered

Ser·em·ban (sur′əm bän′) city in SW Malaya; capital of Negri Sembilan state: pop. 52,000

ser·e·nade (ser′ə nād′) *n.* [Fr. *sérénade* < It. *serenata* < *sereno*, serene, open air < L. *serenus*, clear, SERENE; meaning infl. by asso. with L. *sera*, evening < *serus*, late] **1.** a vocal or instrumental performance of music outdoors at night, esp. by a lover under the window of his sweetheart **2.** a piece of music suitable for this (cf. AUBADE); formally, an instrumental composition somewhat like a suite —*vt., vi.* **-nad′ed, -nad′ing** to play or sing a serenade (to) —**ser′a·nad′er** *n.*

ser·e·na·ta (ser′ə nät′ə) *n., pl.* **-tas, -te** (-ā) [It.: see prec.] **1.** a type of 18th-cent. dramatic cantata for a special occasion, as a royal birthday **2.** *same as* SERENADE

ser·en·dip·i·ty (ser′ən dip′ə tē) *n.* [coined by Horace Walpole (c. 1754) after *The Three Princes of Serendip* (i.e., Ceylon), a Per. fairy tale in which the princes make such discoveries] an apparent aptitude for making fortunate discoveries accidentally —**ser′en·dip′i·tous** *adj.*

se·rene (sə rēn′) *adj.* [L. *serenus* < IE. base *-ksero-*, dry, whence Gr. *xēros*, dry, OHG. *serawēn*, to dry out] **1.** clear; bright; unclouded [a *serene* sky] **2.** not disturbed or troubled; calm, peaceful, tranquil, quiet, etc. **3.** [S-] exalted; high-ranking: used in certain royal titles [His *Serene* Highness] —*n.* [Poet.] a serene expanse, as of sky or water —*SYN.* see CALM —**se·rene′ly** *adv.* —**se·rene′ness** *n.*

se·ren·i·ty (sə ren′ə tē) *n., pl.* **-ties** [Fr. *sérénité* < L. *serenitas*] **1.** the quality or state of being serene; calmness; tranquillity **2.** [S-] a royal title of honor: preceded by *His, Her,* or *Your* —*SYN.* see EQUANIMITY

serf (surf) *n.* [ME. < OFr. < L. *servus*, a slave, prob. of Etruscan orig.] **1.** orig., a slave **2.** a person in feudal servitude, bound to his master's land and transferred with it to a new owner **3.** any person who is oppressed or without freedom —**serf′dom, serf′hood'** *n.*

Serg., serg. sergeant

serge (surj) *n.* [ME. *sarge* < OFr. < VL. *sarica* < L. *serica*, silken garments < *sericus*, silken, lit., of the *Seres*, an Oriental people, prob. the Chinese < Gr. *Sēres*, prob. ult. < Chin. *se*, silk] a strong twilled fabric with a diagonal rib, made of wool or silk, rayon, etc. and used for suits, coats, etc. —*vt.* **serged, serg′ing** to finish off (a cut or raveling edge, as on a carpet) with overcast stitches

ser·gean·cy (sär′jən sē) *n., pl.* **-cies** the position or rank of a sergeant: also **ser′geant·ship'**

ser·geant (sär′jənt) *n.* [ME. *serjaunt* < OFr. *sergant* < L. *serviens*, serving < *servire*, to SERVE] **1.** formerly, a feudal servant who attended his master in battle **2.** *same as* SERGEANT-AT-ARMS ☆**3.** *a*) a noncommissioned officer of the fifth grade, ranking above a corporal and below a staff sergeant in the U.S. Army and Marine Corps *b*) generally, any of the noncommissioned officers in the U.S. armed forces with *sergeant* as part of the title of their rank **4.** a police officer ranking next below a captain or a lieutenant

ser·geant-at-arms (-ət ärmz′) *n., pl.* **ser′geants-at-arms′** an officer appointed to keep order in a legislature, court, social club, etc.

☆**sergeant first class** *U.S. Army* the seventh grade of enlisted man, ranking just below master sergeant

☆**sergeant fish** *same as:* **1.** COBIA **2.** SNOOK¹ (sense 1)

sergeant major *pl.* **sergeants major 1.** the chief administrative noncommissioned officer in a military headquarters: an occupational title and not a rank ☆**2.** *U.S. Army & Marine Corps* the highest ranking noncommissioned officer **3.** *same as* PINTANO

Ser·gi·pe (sər zhē′pə) state of E Brazil: 8,490 sq. mi.; pop. 760,000

Sergt., sergt. sergeant

se·ri·al (sir′ē əl) *adj.* [ModL. *serialis* < L. *series*, a row, order, SERIES] **1.** of, arranged in, or forming a series *[serial* numbers] **2.** appearing, published, issued, etc. in a series or succession of continuous parts at regular intervals **3.** of a serial or serials *[serial* rights to a novel] **4.** *same as* TWELVE-TONE —*n.* **1.** *a)* a novel, story, motion picture, etc. published or presented in serial form *b)* any of the separate parts or episodes **2.** a periodical publication —**se′ri·al·ly** *adv.*

se·ri·al·ism (-iz′m) *n. Music* the twelve-tone system or technique of composition —**se′ri·al·ist** *n.*

se·ri·al·ize (-īz′) *vt.* **-ized′, -iz′ing** to put or publish (a story, etc.) in serial form —**se′ri·al·i·za′tion** *n.*

serial number a number, usually one of a series, given for identification, as to soldiers at enlistment or to engines at the time of manufacture

se·ri·ate (sir′ē it, -āt′) *adj.* [ML. *seriatus*, pp. of *seriare*, to arrange in a series] arranged or occurring in a series —**se′ri·ate·ly** *adv.* —**se′ri·a′tion** *n.*

se·ri·a·tim (sir′ē āt′im) *adv., adj.* [ML. < L. *series*, after *gradatim*, step by step] one after another in order; point by point; serial(ly)

se·ri·ceous (si rish′əs) *adj.* [LL. *sericeus* < L. *sericum*, silken garment < *sericus:* see SERGE] **1.** of or like silk; silky **2.** *Bot.* covered with fine, silky hairs

ser·i·cin (ser′ə sin) *n.* [< L. *sericus*, silk (see SERGE) + -IN¹] a resinous, amorphous substance that bonds the two gossamer filaments in a raw silk fiber

ser·i·cul·ture (ser′i kul′chər) *n.* [Fr. *sériculture*, contr. < *séciculture* < L. *sericus* (see SERGE) + Fr. *culture*] the raising and keeping of silkworms for the production of raw silk —**ser′i·cul′tur·al** *adj.* —**ser′i·cul′tur·ist** *n.*

se·ri·e·ma (ser′i ē′mə, -ā′mə) *n.* [ModL. < Tupi *seriema*, lit., crested] **1.** a crested Brazilian bird (*Cariama cristata*) of the crane family, with long legs and neck **2.** a similar but smaller Argentinian bird (*Chunga burmeisteri*)

se·ries (sir′ēz) *n., pl.* **-ries** [L. < *serere*, to join or weave together < IE. base *ser-*, to line up, join, whence Gr. *eirein*, to join together, OE. *searu*, a snare, armor, ON. *sǫrvi*, a necklace] **1.** a group or number of similar or related things arranged in a row *[a series* of arches] **2.** a group or number of related or similar persons, things, or events coming one after another; sequence; succession **3.** a number of things produced as a related group; set, as of books or television programs, related in subject, format, etc., or dealing with the same characters **4.** *Bowling* a set of three consecutive games **5.** *Elec.* a method of circuit interconnection in which the components are joined end to end so that the same current passes through each component: usually in the phrase **in series 6.** *Geol.* a subdivision of a system of stratified rocks comprising the rocks laid down during an epoch **7.** *Math.* a sequence, often infinite, of terms to be added or subtracted **8.** *Rhetoric* a group of successive coordinate elements of a sentence —*adj. Elec.* designating or of a circuit in series **SYN.—series** applies to a number of similar, more or less related things following one another in time or place *[a series* of concerts]; **sequence** emphasizes a closer relationship between the things, such as logical connection, numerical order, etc. *[the sequence* of events]; **succession** merely implies a following of one thing after another, without any necessary connection between them *[a succession* of errors]; **chain** refers to a series in which there is a definite relationship of cause and effect or some other logical connection *[a chain* of ideas]

series winding the winding of an electric motor or generator in such a way that the field and armature circuits are connected in series —**se′ries-wound′** (-wound′) *adj.*

ser·if (ser′if) *n.* [Du. *schreef*, a stroke, line < *schrijven*, to write < L. *scribere:* see SCRIBE] *Printing* a fine line projecting from a main stroke of a letter in the usual fonts of type: see TYPE, illus.

ser·i·graph (ser′ə graf′, -gräf′) *n.* [< L. *sericum* (see SERICEOUS) + -GRAPH] a color print made by the silkscreen process and printed by the artist himself —**se·rig·ra·pher** (sə rig′rə fər) *n.* —**se·rig′ra·phy** *n.*

ser·in (ser′in) *n.* [Fr., prob. < OProv. *serena*, bee-eater, a green bird < LL. *sirena*, for L. *siren*, SIREN] a small, domesticated, yellow or yellowish-green European finch (*Serinus canarius*), related to the canary

ser·ine (ser′ēn, sir′-; -in) *n.* [< L. *sericum*, silk (see SERICEOUS) + -INE⁴] a nonessential amino acid, C₃H₇NO₃, present in small quantities in many proteins

se·rin·ga (sə riŋ′gə) *n.* [Port. < ModL. *syringa:* see SYRINGA] any of several Brazilian trees (genus *Hevea*) of the spurge family, yielding rubber

se·ri·o·com·ic (sir′ē ō käm′ik) *adj.* partly serious and partly comic —**se·ri·o·com′i·cal·ly** *adv.*

se·ri·ous (sir′ē əs) *adj.* [ME. *seryows* < ML. *seriosus* < L. *serius*, grave, orig., prob. weighty, heavy < ? IE. base **swer-*, whence OE. *swær*, heavy, sad, Goth. *swers*, important, orig., heavy] **1.** of, showing, having, or caused by earnestness or deep thought; earnest, grave, sober, or solemn *[a serious* man] **2.** *a)* meaning what one says or does; not joking or trifling; sincere *b)* meant in earnestness; not said or done in play **3.** concerned with grave, important, or complex matters, problems, etc.; weighty *[a serious* novel] **4.** requiring careful consideration or thought; involving difficulty, effort, or considered action *[a serious* problem] **5.** giving cause for concern; dangerous *[a serious* wound] —**se′ri·ous·ly** *adv.* —**se′ri·ous·ness** *n.*

SYN.—serious implies absorption in deep thought or involvement in something really important as distinguished from something frivolous or merely amusing *[he takes a serious* interest in the theater]; **grave** implies the dignified weightiness of heavy responsibilities or cares *[a grave* expression on his face]; **solemn** suggests an impressive or awe-inspiring seriousness *[a solemn* ceremony]; **sedate** implies a dignified, proper, sometimes even prim seriousness *[a sedate* clergyman]; **earnest** suggests a seriousness of purpose marked by sincerity and enthusiasm *[an earnest* desire to help]; **sober** implies a seriousness marked by temperance, self-control, emotional balance, etc. *[a sober* criticism] —*ANT.* frivolous, flippant

se·ri·ous-mind·ed (-mīn′did) *adj.* of, having, or showing earnestness or seriousness of purpose, method, etc.; not frivolous, jocular, etc.

ser·jeant (sär′jənt) *n. Brit. var. of* SERGEANT

ser·jeant-at-law (-ət lô′) *n., pl.* **ser′jeants-at-law′** any of a former group of high-ranking British barristers

Ser·kin (sur′kin), **Rudolf** 1903– ; U.S. pianist, born in Bohemia

ser·mon (sur′mən) *n.* [ME. < OFr. < L. *sermo* < LL.(Ec.) *sermo* < L., a talk, discourse ? < IE. base **swer-* (also ? **ser-*), to speak, whence SWEAR] **1.** a speech given as instruction in religion or morals, esp. by a clergyman during services, using a text from Scripture **2.** any serious talk on behavior, responsibility, etc., esp. a long, tedious one —*SYN.* see SPEECH —**ser·mon′ic** (-män′ik) *adj.*

ser·mon·ize (sur′mə nīz′) *vi.* **-ized′, -iz′ing 1.** to deliver a sermon or sermons **2.** to preach, esp. in a dogmatic, moralizing fashion; lecture —*vt.* to preach to; exhort; lecture —**ser′mon·iz′er** *n.*

Sermon on the Mount the sermon delivered by Jesus to his disciples: Matt. 5–7, Luke 6:20–49: it contains basic teachings of Christianity

se·ro- (sir′ə, -ō) [< L. *serum*] *a combining form meaning* serum *[serology]*

se·rol·o·gy (si räl′ə jē) *n.* [prec. + -LOGY] the science dealing with the properties and actions of serums —**se·ro·log′ic** (sir′ə läj′ik), **se′ro·log′i·cal** *adj.* —**se·rol′o·gist** *n.*

se·ro·pu·ru·lent (sir′ō pyoor′ə lənt, -yoo lənt) *adj.* [SERO- + PURULENT] composed of pus and serum

se·ro·sa (si rō′sə, -zə) *n., pl.* **-sas, -sae** (-sē) [ModL. < L. *serosus*, SEROUS] **1.** *same as: a)* SEROUS MEMBRANE *b)* CHORION **2.** *Zool.* the outermost membrane around the embryo in many insects —**se·ro′sal** *adj.*

se·rot·i·nal (sə rät′'n əl) *adj.* [< L. *serotinus* < *serus*, late (see SEREIN) + -AL] **1.** of or pertaining to the latter part of the summer **2.** *Bot.* late or delayed in development: said esp. of late-flowering plants Also **se·rot′i·nous** (-əs)

se·ro·to·nin (sir′ə tō′nin, ser′-) *n.* [SERO- + TON(IC) + -IN¹] a complex amine, C₁₀H₁₂N₂O, found in blood, the brain, etc. or produced synthetically: it constricts the blood vessels and contracts smooth muscle tissue, and is important in mental activity

se·rous (sir′əs) *adj.* [MFr. *séreux* < *serum* < L.: see SERUM] **1.** of or containing serum **2.** like serum; thin and watery

serous fluid any of several serumlike fluids in the body cavities, esp. in those lined with serous membrane

serous membrane the thin membrane lining most of the closed cavities of the body and folded back over the enclosed organs, as the peritoneum or pericardium

ser·ow (ser′ō) *n.* [< *sŭ-ro*, native name in Sikkim] any of a genus (*Capricornis*) of dark-colored, sometimes maned, goat antelopes of E Asia

ser·pent (sur′pənt) *n.* [ME. < OFr. < L. *serpens* (gen. *serpentis*) < *serpens*, prp. of *serpere*, to creep < IE. base **serp-*, to creep, whence Sans. *sárpati*, (he) creeps] **1.** a snake, esp. a large or poisonous one **2.** a sly, sneaking, treacherous person **3.** *Bible* Satan, in the form he assumed to tempt Eve: Gen. 3:1–5 **4.** *Music* an obsolete, coiled, bass wind instrument of wood covered with leather

☆**ser·pen·tar·i·um** (sur′pən ter′ē əm) *n.* [SERPENT + (AQU)ARIUM] a place where snakes are kept, as for exhibition

ser·pen·tine (sur′pən tēn′, -tin′) *adj.* [ME. *serpentyn* < OFr. *serpentin* < LL.(Ec.) *serpentinus*] of or like a serpent; esp., *a)* evilly cunning or subtle; treacherous *b)* coiled or twisted; winding —*n.* **1.** something that twists or coils like a snake, as a coil of thin paper thrown out to unwind as a streamer **2.** [from resemblance to a serpent's skin] a mineral or rock composed primarily of a hydrated magnesium silicate,

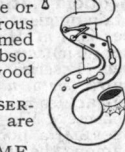

SERPENT (sense 4)

$Mg_8Si_2O_7·2H_2O$, green, yellow, or brown in color and often mottled with red

ser·pi·go (sər pī'gō) *n.* [ME. < ML. < L. *serpere*, to creep: see SERPENT] any spreading skin disease, as ringworm

Ser·ra (ser'ä), **Ju·ní·pe·ro** (hōō nē'pe rō') (born *Miguel José Serra*) 1713–84; Sp. missionary in W N. America

ser·ra·nid (ser'ə nid) *n.* [< ModL. *Serranidae*, the family name < L. *serra*, a saw] any of a large family (Serranidae) of predatory percoid fishes, including the sea basses —*adj.* designating or of this family Also **ser'ra·noid'** (-noid')

ser·rate (ser'āt, -it; *for v., usually* sə rāt') *adj.* [L. *serratus* < *serra*, a saw] having sawlike notches along the edge, as some leaves: also **ser·rat'ed** —*vt.* -**rat'ed**, -**rat'ing** to make serrate

ser·ra·tion (sə rā'shən) *n.* **1.** the condition of being serrate **2.** a single tooth or notch in a serrate edge **3.** a formation of these Also **ser'ra·ture** (ser'ə chər)

ser·ried (ser'ēd) *adj.* [pp. of obs. *serry* < Fr. *serrer*, to crowd < LL. *serare*, to lock: see SERAGLIO] placed close together; crowded; compact, as soldiers in ranks

ser·ru·late (ser'yoo lit, ser'ə-; -lāt') *adj.* [ModL. *serrulatus* < L. *serrula*, dim. of *serra*, a saw] having small, fine teeth or notches along the edge; finely serrate: also **ser'ru·lat'ed**

ser·ru·la·tion (ser'yoo lā'shən, ser'ə-) *n.* **1.** the condition of being serrulate **2.** a single tooth or notch in a serrulate edge **3.** a formation of these

ser·tu·lar·i·an (sur'choo ler'ē ən) *n.* [< ModL. *Sertularia*, name of the genus < L. *sertula*, dim. of *serta*, a garland < fem. pp. of *serere*, to join together (see SERIES) + -AN] any of a family (Sertulariidae) of hydroids growing in colonies made up of double-rowed branches of cupped polyps

se·rum (sir'əm) *n., pl.* -**rums**, -**ra** (-ə) [L., whey < IE. *serom*, a fluid < base *ser-*, to flow, whence Sans. *sara-*, fluid, Gr. *hormē*, an attack] **1.** *a)* any watery animal fluid; specif., *same as* SEROUS FLUID *b)* the clear yellowish fluid which separates from a blood clot after coagulation and shrinkage: in full **blood serum** **2.** blood serum containing agents of immunity, taken from an animal made immune to a specific disease by inoculation: it is used as an antitoxin and for diagnosis **3.** the whey of milk **4.** the thin, watery part of a plant fluid

serum albumin the most abundant protein of blood serum: it is synthesized by the liver and serves to regulate osmotic pressure and to carry certain metabolic products

serum globulin a component of blood serum consisting of proteins with larger molecular weights than serum albumin, and including antibodies, transport proteins, etc.

serv. **1.** servant **2.** service

ser·val (sur'v'l) *n., pl.* -**vals**, -**val**: see PLURAL, II, D, 1 [Fr. < Port. (*lobo*) *cerval* < *lobo* (< L. *lupus*), WOLF + *cerval* (< L. *cervus*: see CERVINE), a stag] an African wildcat (*Felis capensis*) with a black-spotted tawny coat, long legs, and no ear tufts

ser·vant (sur'vənt) *n.* [ME. < OFr. < prp. of *servir* < L. *servire*, to SERVE] **1.** a person employed to perform services, esp. household duties, for another **2.** a person employed by a government: cf. PUBLIC SERVANT, CIVIL SERVANT **3.** a person ardently devoted to another or to a cause, creed, etc. —**serv'ant·less** *adj.*

serve (surv) *vt.* served, serv'ing [ME. *serven* < OFr. *servir* < L. *servire*, to serve < *servus*, a servant, slave: see SERF] **1.** to work for as a servant **2.** *a)* to do services or duties for; give service to; aid; assist; help *b)* to give obedience and reverent honor to (God, one's lord, etc.) *c)* [Archaic] to pay court to (a lady) **3.** to do military or naval service for **4.** to pass or spend (a term of imprisonment, military service, etc.) [to *serve* a year in prison] **5.** *a)* to carry out the duties connected with (a position, office, etc.) *b)* to act as server during (Mass) **6.** *a)* to wait on (customers), as in a store *b)* to provide (customers, clients, or users) with goods or services, esp. professional services *c)* to provide (goods) for customers; supply **7.** *a)* to prepare and offer (food, etc.) in a certain way [*serve* the beef with rice] *b)* to offer or set food, etc. before (a person) **8.** *a)* to meet the needs or satisfy the requirements of [a tool to *serve* many purposes] *b)* to promote or further [to *serve* the national interest] **9.** to be used by [a hospital that *serves* the entire city] **10.** to function or perform for [if memory *serves* me well] **11.** to behave toward; treat [to be cruelly *served*] **12.** *a)* to deliver (a legal instrument, as a summons) *b)* to deliver a legal instrument to; esp., to present with a writ **13.** to hit (a tennis ball, etc.) to one's opponent in order to start play **14.** to operate or tend (a large gun) **15.** to copulate with (a female): said of an animal **16.** *Naut.* to put a binding around in order to protect or strengthen (rope, etc.) —*vi.* **1.** to work as a servant **2.** to be in service; do service [to *serve* in the navy] **3.** to carry out the duties connected with an office or position **4.** to be used or usable; be of service; function **5.** to meet needs or satisfy requirements **6.** to provide guests with something to eat or drink, as by waiting on table **7.** to be suitable or favorable: said of weather, wind, etc. **8.** to start play by hitting the ball, etc. to one's opponent, as in tennis **9.** to act as server at Mass —*n.* the act or manner of serving the ball in tennis, etc., or one's

turn to serve —**serve (someone) right** to be what (someone) deserves, for doing something wrong or foolish

serv·er (sur'vər) *n.* **1.** a person who serves, as an assistant to the celebrant at Mass, a waiter, a player who serves the ball, etc. **2.** a thing used in serving, as a tray, cart, etc.

Ser·ve·tus (sər vē'təs), **Michael** (Sp. name *Miguel Serveto*) 1511–53; Sp. physician & theologian: burned at the stake on the charge of heresy

Ser·vi·a (sur'vē ə) *former name of* SERBIA

serv·ice¹ (sur'vis) *n.* [ME. *servise* < OFr. < L. *servitium* < *servus*, a slave: see SERF] **1.** the occupation or condition of a servant **2.** *a)* employment, esp. public employment [diplomatic *service*] *b)* a branch or department of this, including the people working in it; specif., the armed forces; army, navy, etc. **3.** *a)* formerly, work done for a master or feudal lord *b)* work done or duty performed for another or others [repair *service*, public *service*] **4.** the serving of God, as through good works, prayer, etc. **5.** *a)* public worship *b)* any religious ceremony [the marriage *service*] *c)* a musical setting for a religious service **6.** *a)* an act giving assistance or advantage to another *b)* the result of this; benefit; advantage *c)* [pl.] friendly help; also, professional aid or attention [the fee for his *services*] **7.** the act or manner of serving food [a restaurant noted for its fine *service*] **8.** a set of utensils or articles used in serving [silver tea *service*] **9.** a system or method of providing people with the use of something, as electric power, water, transportation, mail delivery, etc. **10.** installation, maintenance, repairs, etc., provided by a dealer or manufacturer to purchasers of equipment **11.** the act or manner of serving the ball in tennis, etc., or one's turn to serve **12.** [Archaic] devotion, as of a lover to his lady **13.** *Animal Husbandry* the act of bringing a male animal to copulate with a female **14.** *Law* notification of legal action, esp. through the serving of a writ, etc. **15.** *Naut.* any material, as wire, used in serving (ropes, etc.) —*adj.* **1.** of, for, or in service; specif., *a)* of or relating to the armed forces *b)* providing repair, maintenance, supplies, etc. *c)* providing services, rather than goods **2.** of, for, or used by servants, tradespeople, etc. [a *service* entrance] **3.** *a)* for use during active service [a *service* uniform] *b)* serviceable; durable [service weight stockings] —*vt.* -**iced**, -**ic·ing** **1.** to furnish with a service **2.** to copulate with (a female): said of a male animal ☆**3.** to make or keep fit for service, as by inspecting, adjusting, repairing, refueling, etc. —**at one's service** **1.** ready to serve or cooperate with one **2.** ready for one's use —**in service** **1.** in use; functioning: said esp. of an appliance, vehicle, etc. **2.** in the armed forces **3.** working as a domestic servant —**of service** giving aid or assistance; helpful; useful

serv·ice² (sur'vis) *n. same as* SERVICE TREE

Ser·vice (sur'vis), **Robert (William)** 1874?–1958; Canad. writer, born in England

serv·ice·a·ble (sur'vis ə b'l) *adj.* [ME. *servisable* < OFr.] **1.** that can be of service; ready for use; useful; usable **2.** that will give good service, esp. in long, hard use; durable [a *serviceable* fabric] **3.** [Archaic] willing to serve; attentive and obliging —**serv'ice·a·bil'i·ty**, **serv'ice·a·ble·ness** *n.* —**serv'ice·a·bly** *adv.*

serv·ice·ber·ry (-ber'ē) *n., pl.* -**ries** ☆**1.** *same as* JUNEBERRY **2.** the fruit of any service tree

service cap a military cap with a round, flat top and a visor

service ceiling the altitude at which a specified kind of aircraft cannot, because of reduced atmospheric pressure, climb faster than a specified rate

☆**service club** **1.** any of various clubs, as Rotary, Kiwanis, etc., organized to provide certain services for its own members and to promote the community welfare **2.** an armed-services recreation center

☆**service elevator** an elevator used by servants and tradespeople and for carrying goods, baggage, etc.

☆**service entrance** an entrance used by tradespeople, employees, etc. rather than by the general public

serv·ice·man (sur'vis man', -mən) *n., pl.* -**men'** (-men', -mən) **1.** a member of the armed forces **2.** a person whose work is servicing or repairing something [a radio *serviceman*]: also **service man**

☆**service mark** a symbol, word, etc. used by a supplier of services, as transportation, laundry, etc., to distinguish his services from those of competitors: usually registered and protected by law: cf. TRADEMARK

☆**service station** **1.** a place providing maintenance service, parts, supplies, etc. for mechanical or electrical equipment **2.** a place providing such service, and selling gasoline and oil, for motor vehicles; gas station

☆**service stripe** a stripe, or any of the parallel diagonal stripes, worn on the left sleeve of a uniform to indicate years spent in the service

service tree [ME. *serves*, pl. of obs. *serve* < OE. *syrfe* < VL. *sorbea* < L. *sorbus*] **1.** a European tree (*Sorbus domestica*) of the rose family, resembling the mountain ash and having small, edible fruit **2.** a European tree, the **wild service tree** (*Sorbus torminalis*), similar to this

ser·vi·ette (sur'vē et') *n.* [Fr. < MFr. < *servir*, to serve] a table napkin

ser·vile (sur′v'l, -vīl) *adj.* [ME. < L. *servilis* < *servus*, a slave] **1.** of a slave or slaves **2.** like that of slaves or servants [*servile* employment] **3.** like or characteristic of a slave; humbly yielding or submissive; cringing; abject **4.** [Archaic] held in slavery; not free —**ser′vile·ly** *adv.* —**ser·vil·i·ty** (sər vil′ə tē) *pl.* -**ties, ser′vile·ness** *n.*
SYN.—**servile** suggests the cringing, submissive behavior characteristic of a slave [*servile* flattery]; **subservient** applies to one who occupies an inferior or subordinate position that furthers another's ends, and may or may not connote servility [a faculty *subservient* to the board of trustees]; **slavish** implies utter abjectness and submissiveness in obeying, depending on, or following another [*slavish* adherence to the rules]; **menial** applies to work or a position of a kind regarded as low or degrading [restricted to the *menial* job of a porter]; **obsequious** implies a servile, fawning attitude toward someone regarded as one's superior [an *obsequious* courtier] —*ANT.* **domineering, imperious**

serv·ing (sur′viŋ) *n.* **1.** the act of one who serves **2.** a helping, or single portion, of food —*adj.* used for serving food [a *serving* spoon]

ser·vi·tor (sur′və tər) *n.* [ME. *servitour* < OFr. < LL. *servitor* < pp. of L. *servire*, to SERVE] a person who serves another; servant, attendant, or, formerly, soldier

ser·vi·tude (sur′və tōōd′, -tyōōd′) *n.* [ME. < MFr. < L. *servitudo* < *servus*, a slave] **1.** the condition of a slave, serf, or the like; subjection to a master; slavery or bondage **2.** work imposed as punishment for crime **3.** *Law* the burden placed upon the property of a person by a specified right another has in its use
SYN.—**servitude** refers to compulsory labor or service for another, often, specif., such labor imposed as punishment for crime; **slavery** implies absolute subjection to another person who owns and completely controls one; **bondage** originally referred to the condition of a serf bound to his master's land, but now implies any condition of subjugation or captivity —*ANT.* **freedom, liberty**

ser·vo (sur′vō) *n., pl.* -**vos** *clipped form of:* **1.** SERVO-MECHANISM **2.** SERVOMOTOR —*adj.* of, pertaining to, incorporating, or controlled by a servomechanism

ser·vo·mech·a·nism (sur′vō mek′ə niz′m) *n.* [SERVO-(MOTOR) + MECHANISM] an automatic control system in which the output is constantly or intermittently compared with the input through feedback so that the error or difference between the two quantities can be used to bring about the desired amount of control

ser·vo·mo·tor (sur′vō mōt′ər) *n.* [< Fr. *servo-moteur* < L. *servus*, a slave + *moteur*, MOTOR] a device, as an electric motor, hydraulic piston, etc., that is controlled by an amplified signal from a command device of low power, as in a servomechanism

ses·a·me (ses′ə mē′) *n.* [altered (after Gr.) < earlier *sesama* < L. *sesamum, sesama* < Gr. *sēsamon, sēsamē*, of Sem. orig., as in Aram. *šumšemā*, Assyr. *šamaššamu*] **1.** an East Indian plant (*Sesamum indicum*) whose flat seeds yield an edible oil and are used for flavoring bread, rolls, etc. **2.** its seeds See also OPEN SESAME

ses·a·moid (-moid′) *adj.* [Gr. *sēsamoeidēs* < *sēsamon* (see prec.) + *eidos*, a form] shaped like a sesame seed; specif., designating or of any of certain small bones developing in tendons, as at a joint, or any of certain small cartilaginous nodules in the nose —*n.* such a bone or cartilage

ses·qui- (ses′kwi) [L., more by a half < *semis*, half (< *semi-*: see SEMI-) + *-que*, and < IE. *kwe* (enclitic), whence Sans. *ca*, Gr. *te*, OIr. *-ch*, Goth. *-h*] *a combining form meaning:* **1.** one and a half [*sesquicentennial*] **2.** *Chem.* containing two atoms of one radical or element combined with three of another [iron *sesquioxide*, Fe₂O₃]

ses·qui·car·bon·ate (ses′kwi kär′bə nit, -nāt′) *n.* [prec. + CARBONATE] a carbonate in which there are three carbonate radicals for each two metal atoms

☆**ses·qui·cen·ten·ni·al** (-sen ten′ē əl) *adj.* of or ending a period of 150 years —*n.* a 150th anniversary or its celebration

ses·qui·ox·ide (-äk′sīd) *n.* [SESQUI- + OXIDE] an oxide in which three atoms or equivalents of oxygen are combined with two of some other element or radical

ses·qui·pe·da·li·an (-pə dā′lē ən, -pə dāl′yən) *adj.* [< L. *sesquipedalis*, of a foot and a half < *sesqui-* (see SESQUI-) + *pedalis* < *pes* (gen. *pedis*), a FOOT] **1.** measuring a foot and a half **2.** very long: said of words **3.** using, or characterized by the use of, long words Also **ses·quip′e·dal** (-kwip′ə dəl) —*n.* a long word —**ses′qui·pe·da′li·an·ism** *n.*

ses·sile (ses′il, -īl) *adj.* [L. *sessilis* < *sessus*, pp. of *sedere*, to SIT] **1.** *Anat., Zool.* a) attached directly by its base b) permanently fixed; immobile **2.** *Bot.* having no pedicel or peduncle; attached directly to the main stem, as some flowers and leaves

ses·sion (sesh′ən) *n.* [ME. < L. *sessio* < *sedere*, to SIT] **1.** a) the sitting together or meeting of a group; assembly, as of a court, legislature, council, etc. b) a continuous, day-to-day series of such meetings c) the term or period of such a meeting or meetings **2.** a school term or period of study, classes, etc. **3.** the governing body of a Presbyterian church, consisting of the minister and elders **4.** a period of activity of any kind [a *session* with

SESSILE LEAVES
(A, trillium; B, Solomon's seal)

the dentist] —**in session** meeting; assembled —**ses′sion·al** *adj.*

Ses·sions (sesh′ənz), **Roger (Huntington)** 1896–   ; U.S. composer

ses·terce (ses′tərs) *n.* [L. *sestertius (nummus)*, for *semis tertius*, two and a half, because equal in value to two and a half asses] an old Roman coin, orig. of silver, later of brass or copper, equal to 1/4 denarius

ses·ter·ti·um (ses tur′shē əm, -shəm) *n., pl.* -**ti·a** (-shē ə, -shə) [L. < *mille sestertium*, a thousand sesterces] an old Roman monetary unit, equal to 1,000 sesterces

ses·tet (ses tet′, ses′tet) *n.* [It. *sestetto*, dim of *sesto*, sixth < L. *sextus*, sixth < *sex*, SIX] **1.** *Music* same as SEXTET **2.** a) the final six lines of a sonnet b) a poem or stanza of six lines

ses·ti·na (ses tē′nə) *n., pl.* -**nas, -ne** (-nē) [It. < *sesto*, sixth (see prec.)] a form of poem having six six-line stanzas and a tercet: the end words of the first stanza are repeated with progressively changed order in the other five stanzas and are included, medially and finally, in the tercet

Ses·tos (ses′täs) town in ancient Thrace, on the Hellespont opposite Abydos

Set (set) [Gr. *Sēth* < Egypt. *Setesh*] an Egyptian god of evil, represented with an animal's head

set (set) *vt.* **set, set′ting** [ME. *setten* < OE. *settan* (akin to G. *setzen* & Goth. *satian*), causative formation "to cause to sit" < base of SIT] **1.** to place in a sitting position; cause to sit; seat **2.** a) to cause (a fowl) to sit on eggs in order to hatch them b) to put (eggs) under a fowl or in an incubator to hatch them **3.** to put in a certain place or position; cause to be, lie, stand, etc. in a place [*set* the book on the table] **4.** to put in the proper or designated place [to *set* a wheel on an axle] **5.** to put or move (a part of the body) into or on a specified place [to *set* foot on land] **6.** to bring (something) into contact with something else [to burn a paper by *setting* a match to it] **7.** a) [Archaic] to put in writing; record b) to put or affix (one's signature, seal, etc.) to a document **8.** to cause to be in some condition or relation; specif., a) to cause to be or become [to *set* a house on fire] b) to put in a certain physical position [to *set* a book on end] **9.** to cause to be in working or proper condition; put in order; arrange; fix; adjust; specif., a) to fix (a net, trap, etc.) in a position to catch animals b) to fix (a sail) in a position to catch the wind c) to put (a part of a device) in position to work [to *set* a chuck on a lathe] d) to adjust so as to be in a desired position for use; regulate [to *set* a radio dial, a clock, a thermostat, etc.] e) to place (oneself) in readiness for action f) to put an edge on (a knife, razor, etc.) g) to adjust (a saw) by slightly deflecting alternate teeth in opposite directions h) to sink (the head of a nail, screw, etc.) below a surface i) to arrange (a table) with knives, forks, plates, etc. for a meal j) to put (a dislocated joint or fractured bone) into normal position for healing, mending, etc. **10.** to cause to be in a settled or firm position; specif., a) to put or press into a fixed or rigid position [to *set* one's jaw] b) to cause (one's mind, purpose, etc.) to be fixed, unyielding, determined, etc. c) to cause to become firm or hard in consistency [pectin *sets* jelly] d) to make (a color) fast in dyeing e) to mount, embed, or fix (gems) in rings, bracelets, etc. f) to cover, encrust, or decorate (gold, watches, etc.) with gems g) to fix firmly in a frame [*set* the glass in the window] h) to arrange (hair) in the desired style with lotions, hairpins, etc. and let it dry i) to transplant (a shoot, etc.) **11.** to cause to take a particular direction; specif., a) to cause to move as specified; propel [the current *set* them eastward] b) to point, direct, or face as specified [to *set* one's face toward home] c) to direct (one's desires, hopes, heart, etc.) with serious attention (*in* or *on* someone or something) **12.** to appoint, establish, ordain, etc.; specif., a) to post or station for certain duties [to *set* sentries at a gate] b) to place in a position of authority c) to fix (limits or boundaries) d) to fix or appoint (a time) for something to happen [to *set* Friday as the deadline] e) to fix a time for (an event) f) to establish (a regulation, law, record, etc.) or prescribe (a form, order, etc.) g) to give or furnish (an example, pattern, etc.) for others h) to introduce (a fashion, style, etc.) i) to allot or assign (a task, lesson, etc.) for work or study j) to fix (a quota, as of work) for a given period k) to begin to apply (oneself) to a task, etc. **13.** to estimate or fix; place mentally; specif., a) to fix (the amount of a price, fine, etc.) b) to fix (a price, fine, etc.) at a specified amount c) to estimate or value [to *set* at naught all that one has won] d) to fix or put as an estimate [to *set* little store by someone] **14.** *Baking* to put aside (leavened dough) to rise **15.** *Bridge* to prevent (one's opponents) from making their bid **16.** *Hunting* to point toward the position of (game): said of a dog **17.** *Music* to write or fit (words to music or music to words) **18.** *Printing* a) to arrange (type) for printing b) to put (manuscript) into type **19.** *Theater* a) to place (a scene) in a given locale b) to make up or arrange (scenery) on the stage c) to arrange the scenery and properties on the (stage) —*vi.* **1.** to sit on eggs: said of a fowl **2.** to become firm or hard in consistency [cement *sets* after several hours] **3.** to become fast: said of a dye, color, etc. **4.** a) to begin to move, travel, etc. (with *out, forth, on, off*, or *forward*) b) to begin or get started [to *set* to work] **5.** to

have a certain direction; tend **6.** *a)* to make an apparent descent toward and below the horizon; go down [the *setting* sun] *b)* to wane; decline **7.** to hang, fit, or suit in a certain way [a jacket that *sets* well] **8.** to grow together; mend: said of a broken bone **9.** [Now Dial.] to sit **10.** *Bot.* to begin to develop into a fruit after pollination **11.** *Hunting* to point toward the position of game: said of a dog —*adj.* **1.** fixed or appointed in advance [a *set* time] **2.** established; prescribed, as by authority **3.** deliberate; intentional; purposeful **4.** conventional; stereotyped; not spontaneous [a *set* speech] **5.** fixed; motionless; rigid; immovable **6.** *a)* resolute; determined *b)* obstinate; unyielding **7.** firm or hard in consistency **8.** ready to begin some action or activity [get *set* to run] **9.** formed; put together; built —*n.* **1.** a setting or being set; specif., *a)* the act of a dog in setting game *b)* a becoming hard or firm in consistency **2.** the way or position in which a thing is set; specif., *a)* direction; course, as of a current *b)* tendency; inclination *c)* change of form resulting from pressure, twisting, strain, etc.; warp; bend *d)* sidewise deflection in opposite directions of the alternate teeth of a saw *e)* the way in which an article of clothing fits or hangs *f)* the position or attitude of a limb or part of the body [the *set* of her head] *g) Psychol.* an adjustment of an organism in preparation for a certain definite kind of activity **3.** something which is set; specif., *a)* a twig or slip for planting or grafting *b)* a young plant; esp., a dwarfed bulb, as of an onion, dried and kept over winter for early spring planting *c)* a number of backdrops, flats, properties, etc. constructed and arranged for a scene in a play, motion picture, etc. **4.** *a)* the act or a style of setting hair *b)* the lotion, etc. used for this purpose: in full **hair set 5.** a group of persons; specif., *a)* a company or group with common habits, occupation, interests, etc. [a *set* of smugglers] *b)* an exclusive or select group; clique; coterie *c)* the number of couples needed for a country or square dance **6.** a collection of things belonging, issued, used, or growing together; specif., *a)* a number of tools or instruments used together [a carpentry *set*] *b)* the collection of objects necessary for playing a game, esp. a parlor game *c)* a number of books, magazines, etc., often in a similar format, by one author, on one subject, etc. *d)* a matching collection of china, silverware, etc. *e)* the complement of natural or artificial teeth of a person or animal *f)* a clutch of eggs *g)* the figures that make up a country or square dance *h)* several pieces of dance music played, or danced to, in quick succession *i)* receiving equipment for radio or television assembled, as in a cabinet, for use *j) Tennis* a group of six or more games won before the other side wins five, or by a margin of two if the score is tied at more than four games each **7.** *Math.* a prescribed collection of points, numbers, or other objects that satisfy a given condition **8.** *Printing* the width of the body of a piece of type —*SYN.* see COTERIE —☆all set [Colloq.] prepared; ready —**set about** to begin; start doing —**set against 1.** to balance **2.** to compare **3.** to make hostile toward; make an enemy of —**set apart 1.** to separate and keep for a purpose; reserve —**set aside 1.** to set apart **2.** to discard; dismiss; reject **3.** to annul; declare void —**set back 1.** to put (a clock or its hands) to an earlier time, esp. to standard time **2.** to reverse or hinder the progress of ☆**3.** [Slang] to cost (a person) a specified sum of money —**set down 1.** to place so as to rest upon a surface; put down; let alight **2.** to land (an airplane) **3.** to put in writing or print; record **4.** to establish (rules, principles, etc.) **5.** to consider, ascribe, attribute, etc. —**set forth 1.** to publish **2.** to express in words; state —**set in 1.** to begin **2.** *a)* to blow or flow toward the shore: said of wind, current, etc. *b)* to direct (a ship) toward shore **3.** to insert —**set off 1.** *a)* to start (a person) doing something *b)* to make begin; start going **2.** to set in relief; make prominent by contrast **3.** to show to advantage; enhance **4.** to cause to explode —**set on 1.** to incite or urge on, as to attack [to *set* dogs *on* intruders] **2.** to attack —**set out 1.** to limit; define; mark out **2.** to plan; lay out (a town, garden, etc.) **3.** to display, as for sale; exhibit **4.** to plant **5.** to take upon oneself; undertake [to *set out* to prove a theory] —**set straight** to give the correct facts to; inform properly —**set to 1.** to make a beginning; get to work; begin **2.** to begin fighting —**set up 1.** *a)* to place in an upright position *b)* to place in a high position *c)* to raise to power *d)* to raise *e)* to present (oneself) as being something specified *f)* to present (something) as exemplary **2.** to put together or erect (a tent, machine, etc.) **3.** to establish; found **4.** to make detailed plans for **5.** to begin **6.** to provide with money, etc., as for a business; fit out **7.** to cause to feel stimulated, exhilarated, etc. **8.** to make successful, well-to-do, etc. **9.** to advance or propose (a theory, etc.) **10.** to cause **11.** *a)* to put (drinks, etc.) before customers ☆*b)* to pay for (food, drinks, etc.) for (another or others) —**set upon** to attack, esp. with violence

se·ta (sēt′ə) *n., pl.* **-tae** (-ē) [ModL. < L., a stiff hair < IE. base *sei-*, a cord, whence SINEW, OE. *sal*, rope] *Bot., Zool.* a bristle or bristlelike part or organ

se·ta·ceous (si tā′shəs) *adj.* [ModL. *setaceus* < *seta:* see prec.] **1.** having bristles **2.** like a bristle or bristles; bristlelike —**se·ta′ceous·ly** *adv.*

set·back (set′bak′) *n.* **1.** a reversal, check, or interruption in progress; relapse; upset **2.** an upper part of a wall or building set back to form a steplike section **3.** *same as* PITCH² (*n.* 8)

set chisel a broad-pointed chisel used in cutting the heads from rivets, bolts, etc.

Seth¹ (seth) [LL.(Ec.) < Gr.(Ec.) *Sēth* < Heb. *shēth,* lit., appointed] **1.** a masculine name **2.** *Bible* the third son of Adam: Gen. 4:25

Seth² (sāt) *same as* SET

se·ti- (sēt′i, -ə) [< L. *saeta,* a bristle: see SETA] *a combining form meaning* bristle [*setiform*]

se·ti·form (sēt′ə fôrm′) *adj.* [SETI- + -FORM] resembling a seta, or bristle, in shape

set-in (set′in′) *adj.* made as a separate unit to fit within another part [a *set-in* sleeve]

set-off (set′ôf′) *n.* **1.** a thing that makes up for or sets off something else; counterbalance; compensation **2.** *a)* a counterbalancing debt claimed by a debtor against his creditor *b)* a claim for this **2.** *same as* OFFSET (*n.* 4 & 8)

Se·ton (sēt′n), **Ernest Thompson** (born *Ernest Seton Thompson*) 1860–1946; U.S. naturalist, writer, & illustrator, born in England

se·tose (sēt′ōs) *adj.* [L. *saetosus*] *same as* SETACEOUS

set piece 1. an artistic composition, in literature, music, sculpture, etc., designed to give an impressive effect, often in a conventional style **2.** a scenic display of fireworks **3.** a piece of stage scenery **4.** any situation carefully planned beforehand, as in a military or diplomatic maneuver

set·screw (set′skroo′) *n.* **1.** a machine screw passing through one part and against or into another to prevent movement, as of a ring around a shaft **2.** a screw used in regulating or adjusting the tension of a spring, etc.

‡set·te·cen·to (set′te chen′tō) *n.* [It., short for *mille settecento,* one thousand seven hundred] the 18th cent. as a period in Italian art and literature

set·tee (se tē′) *n.* [prob. altered < SETTLE¹] **1.** a seat or bench with a back, usually for two or three people **2.** a small or medium-sized sofa

set·ter (set′ər) *n.* **1.** a person who sets or a thing used in setting: often used in compounds [*pinsetter*] **2.** any of several breeds of long-haired bird dog trained to find game and point out its position by standing rigid (formerly by crouching): see ENGLISH SETTER, GORDON SETTER, IRISH SETTER

set theory the branch of mathematics that deals with the properties and relations of sets (cf. SET, *n.* 7)

set·ting (set′in) *n.* **1.** the act of one that sets **2.** the position or adjustment of something, as a dial, that has been set **3.** a thing in or upon which something, esp. a gem, is set **4.** the time, place, environment, and surrounding circumstances of an event, story, play, etc. **5.** actual physical surroundings or scenery whether real or, as on a stage, artificial **6.** the music or the composing of music for a set of words, as a poem **7.** the eggs in the nest of a setting hen **8.** *same as* PLACE SETTING

set·ting-up exercises (set′in up′) *same as* CALISTHENICS

set·tle¹ (set′l) *n.* [ME. *settel* < OE. *setl* (akin to G. *sessel*) < base of SIT] a long wooden bench with a back, armrests, and sometimes a chest beneath the seat

set·tle² (set′l) *vt.* **-tled, -tling** [ME. *setlen* < OE. *setlan* < *setl,* a seat: see prec.] **1.** to put in order; arrange or adjust as desired [to *settle* one's affairs] **2.** to set in place firmly or comfortably [to *settle* oneself in a chair] **3.** to establish as a resident or residents [he *settled* his family in London] **4.** to migrate to and set up a community in; colonize [New York was *settled* by the Dutch] **5.** to cause to sink and become more dense and compact [the rain *settled* the dust] **6.** to clarify (a liquid) by causing the sediment to sink to the bottom **7.** to free (the mind, nerves, stomach, etc.) from disturbance; calm or quiet **8.** to prevent from creating a disturbance or interfering, or from continuing in such action, as by a reprimand or a blow **9.** to make stable or permanent; establish **10.** to establish in business, office, work, marriage, etc. **11.** to fix definitely; determine or decide (something in doubt) **12.** to end (a dispute) **13.** to pay (a bill, debt, account, etc.) **14.** to make over (property, etc.) to someone by legal action (with *on* or *upon*) **15.** to decide (a legal dispute) by agreement without court action **16.** to impregnate (a female): said of an animal —*vi.* **1.** to stop moving and stay in one place; come to rest **2.** to cast itself, as darkness, fog, etc. over a landscape, or gloom or silence over a person or group; descend **3.** to become localized in a given part of the body: said of pain or disease **4.** to take up permanent residence; make one's home **5.** to move downward; sink, esp. gradually [the car *settled* in the mud] **6.** to become more dense or compact by sinking, as sediment or loose soil when shaken **7.** to become clearer by the settling of sediment or dregs **8.** to become more stable or composed; stop fluctuating or changing **9.** *a)* to reach an agreement or

decision (usually with *with*, *on*, or *upon*) ☆b) to accept something in place of what is hoped for, demanded, etc. (with *for*) [he'll *settle* for any kind of work] 10. to pay a bill or debt —*SYN.* see DECIDE —**settle down** 1. to take up permanent residence, a regular job, etc.; lead a more routine, stable life, as after marriage 2. to become less nervous, restless, or erratic 3. to apply oneself steadily or attentively —**settle up** to determine what is owed and make the necessary adjustments

set·tle·ment (-mənt) *n.* 1. a settling or being settled (in various senses) 2. a new colony, or a place newly colonized 3. *a)* a small or isolated community; village *b)* a community established by the members of a particular religious or social group 4. an agreement, arrangement, or adjustment 5. *a)* the conveyance or disposition of property for the benefit of a person *b)* the property thus conveyed 6. an institution in a depressed and congested neighborhood offering social services and educational and recreational activities: also **settlement house**

set·tler (set′lər) *n.* 1. a person or thing that settles ☆2. a person who settles in a new country or colony

set·tlings (set′linz) *n.pl.* the solid matter that settles to the bottom of a liquid; sediment; dregs

set·tlor (set′lər) *n. Law* a person who makes a settlement of property

set-to (set′tōō′) *n., pl.* **-tos′** (-tōōz′) [< phr. SET TO] [Colloq.] 1. a fight or struggle, esp. a fist fight 2. any brisk or vigorous contest or argument; bout

set·up (set′up) *n.* 1. the way in which something is set up; specif., *a)* plan, makeup, or arrangement, as of equipment, an organization, etc. *b)* the details of a situation, plan of action, etc. ☆2. bodily posture; carriage ☆3. the glass, ice, soda water, etc. provided for preparing an alcoholic drink ☆4. [Colloq.] *a)* a contest deliberately arranged as an uneven match to result in an easy victory *b)* the contestant marked for defeat in such a contest *c)* an undertaking that is, or is purposely made, very easy, or a goal or result that is easy to achieve *d)* a person who is easily tricked

Seu·rat (sö rä′), **Georges (Pierre)** (zhôrzh) 1859–91; Fr. painter: noted for his use of pointillism

Se·vas·to·pol (sə vas′tə pōl; *Russ.* se′väs tô′pəl y′) seaport in SW Crimea, on the Black Sea: pop. 200,000

sev·en (sev′'n) *adj.* [ME. *seoven* < OE. *seofon*, akin to G. *sieben* < IE. base *septm̥*, whence L. *septem*, Gr. *heptā*] totaling one more than six —*n.* 1. the cardinal number between six and eight; 7; VII 2. any group of seven people or things 3. something numbered seven, or having seven units, as a playing card, throw of dice, etc.

Seven against Thebes *Gr. Myth.* the expedition of seven heroes to help one of their number, Polynices, recover his share of the throne of Thebes from his brother Eteocles: subject of a tragedy by Aeschylus

seven deadly sins *same as* DEADLY SINS

sev·en·fold (sev′'n fōld′) *adj.* [ME. -FOLD] 1. having seven parts 2. having seven times as much or as many —*adv.* seven times as much or as many

Seven Hills of Rome seven low hills on the E bank of the Tiber, on & about which Rome was originally built; Aventine, Caelian, Capitoline, Esquiline, Palatine (approximately in the center), Quirinal, & Viminal

seven seas all the oceans of the world

sev·en·teen (sev′'n tēn′) *adj.* [ME. *seventene* < OE. *seofentyne*: see SEVEN & -TEEN] seven more than ten —*n.* the cardinal number between sixteen and eighteen; 17; XVII

sev·en·teenth (-tēnth′) *adj.* [ME. *sevententhe*: see prec. & -TH²] 1. preceded by sixteen others in a series; 17th 2. designating any of the seventeen equal parts of something —*n.* 1. the one following the sixteenth 2. any of the seventeen equal parts of something; 1/17

☆**sev·en·teen-year locust** (sev′'n tēn′yir′) a cicada (*Magicicada septendecim*) which lives underground as a larva for from thirteen to seventeen years before emerging as an adult to live in the open for a brief period

sev·enth (sev′nth) *adj.* [ME. *seventhe*, a new formation < *seoven* + -*th*, replacing OE. *seofande* (akin to G. *siebente*) & *seofotha*] 1. preceded by six others in a series; 7th 2. designating any of the seven equal parts of something —*n.* 1. the one following the sixth 2. any of the seven equal parts of something· 1/7 3. *Music a)* the seventh tone of an ascending diatonic scale, or a tone six degrees above or below any given tone in such a scale; leading tone; subtonic *b)* the interval between two such tones, or a combination of them *c)* the chord formed by any tone and the third, fifth, and seventh of which it is the fundamental: in full **seventh chord**

sev·enth-day (-dā′) *adj.* 1. of the seventh day (Saturday) 2. [often S- D-] observing the Sabbath on Saturday [*Seventh-Day* Adventists]

seventh heaven 1. in certain ancient cosmologies, the outermost of the concentric spheres enclosing the earth, in which God and his angels are 2. a condition of perfect happiness

sev·en·ti·eth (sev′'n tē ith) *adj.* [ME. *seventithe*: see ff. & -TH²] 1. preceded by sixty-nine others in a series; 70th 2. designating any of the seventy equal parts of something —*n.* 1. the one following the sixty-ninth 2. any of the seventy equal parts of something; 1/70

sev·en·ty (-tē) *adj.* [ME. *seofentig* < OE. (*hund*)*seofontig*: see SEVEN & -TY²] seven times ten —*n., pl.* **-ties** the cardinal number between sixty-nine and seventy-one; 70; LXX —**the seventies** the numbers or years, as of a century, from seventy through seventy-nine

☆**sev·en-up** (sev′'n up′) *n.* a card game for two, three, or four persons in which seven points constitute a game

Seven Wonders of the World seven remarkable objects of ancient times: the Egyptian pyramids, the walls and hanging gardens of Babylon, the Mausoleum at Halicarnassus, the temple of Artemis at Ephesus, the Colossus of Rhodes, the statue of Zeus by Phidias at Olympia, and the Pharos (or lighthouse) at Alexandria

Seven Years' War a war (1756–63) in which England and Prussia defeated Austria, France, Russia, Sweden, and Saxony

sev·er (sev′ər) *vt., vi.* [ME. *severen* < OFr. *sevrer, severer* < VL. **seperare* < L. *separare*, to SEPARATE] 1. to separate; make or become distinct; divide [*severed* from his family by the war] 2. to part or break off, as by cutting or with force; cut in two [to *sever* a cable, to *sever* all relationship] —*SYN.* see SEPARATE

sev·er·a·ble (-ə b'l) *adj.* that can be severed or divided; specif., *Law* separable into distinct, independent obligations: said of a contract —**sev′er·a·bil′i·ty** *n.*

sev·er·al (sev′ər əl, sev′rəl) *adj.* [ME. < Anglo-Fr. < ML. *separalis* < L. *separ*, separate, back-formation < *separare*: see SEPARATE] 1. existing apart; separate; distinct; individual 2. different; respective [parted and went their *several* ways] 3. more than two but not many; of an indefinite but small number; few 4. *Law* of or having to do with an individual person; not shared or joint —*n.* [with *pl. v.*] an indefinite but small number (*of* persons or things) —*pron.* [with *pl. v.*] several persons or things; a few

sev·er·al·ly (-ē) *adv.* 1. separately; distinctly 2. respectively; individually

sev·er·al·ty (-tē) *n., pl.* **-ties** [ME. *severalte* < Anglo-Fr. *severauté*: see SEVERAL + -TY¹] 1. the condition or character of being several or distinct 2. property owned by individual right, not shared with any other 3. the condition of property so owned

sev·er·ance (sev′ər əns, sev′rəns) *n.* [ME. < Anglo-Fr. < OFr. *sevrance*] a severing or being severed

☆**severance pay** extra pay given to an employee who is dismissed through no fault of his own

se·vere (sə vir′) *adj.* **-ver′er, -ver′est** [< MFr. < OFr. < L. *severus*, prob. < *se-*, apart (see SECEDE) + IE. base **wer-*, (to be) friendly, whence OE. *wær*, faith, pledge, bond (of friendship)] 1. harsh, strict, or highly critical, as in treatment; unsparing; stern 2. serious or grave; forbidding, as in expression or manner 3. serious or grievous [a *severe* wound] 4. conforming strictly to a rule, method, standard, etc.; rigidly accurate or demanding [a *severe* philosophy] 5. extremely plain or simple; unornamented; restrained [a dress with *severe* lines] 6. keen; extreme; intense [*severe* pain] 7. difficult; rigorous; trying [a *severe* test] —**se·vere′ly** *adv.* —**se·vere′ness** *n.* *SYN.*—**severe** applies to a person or thing that is strict and uncompromising and connotes a total absence of softness, laxity, frivolity, etc. [a *severe* critic, hairdo, etc.]; **stern** implies an unyielding firmness, esp. as manifested in a grim or forbidding aspect or manner [a *stern* guardian]; **austere** suggests harsh restraint, self-denial, stark simplicity [the *austere* diet of wartime], or an absence of warmth, passion, ornamentation, etc. [an *austere* bedroom]; **ascetic** implies extreme self-denial and self-discipline or even, sometimes, the deliberate self-infliction of pain and discomfort, as by religious fanatics [an *ascetic* hermit] —*ANT.* mild, lax, indulgent

se·ver·i·ty (sə ver′ə tē) *n.* [Fr. *sévérité* < L. *severitas*] 1. the quality or condition of being severe; specif., *a)* strictness; harshness *b)* gravity, as of expression *c)* rigid accuracy *d)* extreme plainness or restraint, as in style *e)* keenness, as of pain; intensity *f)* rigorous or trying character 2. *pl.* **-ties** something severe, as a punishment

Sev·ern (sev′ərn) river flowing from C Wales through England & into the Bristol Channel: c. 200 mi.

Se·ver·na·ya Zem·lya (sev′ər nə yä′ zem lyä′) group of Russ. islands north of the Taimyr Peninsula, between the Kara & Laptev seas: c. 14,500 sq. mi.

Seversky *see* DE SEVERSKY

Se·ver·us (sə vir′əs), **(Lucius Septimius)** 146–211 A.D.; Rom. emperor (193–211)

Sé·vi·gné (sā vē nyā′), **marquise de** (born *Marie de Rabutin-Chantal*) 1626–96; Fr. writer

Se·ville (sə vil′; *Brit.* sev′il) city & port in SW Spain, on the Guadalquivir River: pop. 532,000 Sp. name **Se·vil·la** (sā vē′lyä)

SEVEN HILLS OF ROME
(350 A.D.)

Sè·vres (sev′rə) n. [< Sèvres, SW suburb of Paris, where made] a type of fine French porcelain

sew (sō) vt. sewed, sewn or sewed, sew′ing [ME. sewen < OE. siwian, akin to Goth. siujan < IE. base *siw-, to sew, whence SEAM, L. suere (pp. sutus), to sew, sew together] 1. to join or fasten with stitches made with needle and thread 2. to make, mend, enclose, etc. by such means —vi. to work with needle and thread or at a sewing machine —sew up 1. to close or bring together the edges of with stitches 2. to enclose in something by sewing ☆3. [Colloq.] a) to get or have absolute control of or right to; monopolize b) to bring to a successful conclusion c) to make certain of success in [to sew up an election]

sew·age (sōō′ij) n. [SEW(ER)¹ + -AGE] the waste matter carried off by sewers or drains

Sew·all (sōō′əl), **Samuel** 1652–1730; Am. jurist, born in England; presided over witchcraft trials at Salem

☆**se·wan** (sē′wən) n. [Du. < AmInd. (Algonquian), as in Narragansett siwân, unstrung shell beads] shells used as money by the Algonquian Indians

Sew·ard (sōō′ərd), **William Henry** 1801–72; U.S. statesman; secretary of state (1861–69)

Sew·ard Peninsula (sōō′ərd) [after prec.] peninsula of W Alas. on the Bering Strait: c. 200 mi. long

sew·er¹ (sōō′ər, syōō′-) n. [ME. < MFr. esseweur < essever, to drain off < VL. *exaquare < L. ex, out + aqua, water] a pipe or drain, usually underground, used to carry off water and waste matter —vi. to clean or maintain sewers

sew·er² (sō′ər) n. a person or thing that sews

sew·er³ (sōō′ər, syōō′-) n. [ME., aphetic < Anglo-Fr. asseour < OFr. asseoir, to seat, cause to sit < L. assidere, to sit by < ad-, to + sedere, to SIT] a medieval servant of high rank in charge of serving meals and seating guests

sew·er·age (-ij) n. 1. removal of surface water and waste matter by sewers 2. a system of sewers 3. same as SEWAGE

sew·ing (sō′iŋ) n. 1. the act or occupation of a person who sews 2. material for sewing; needlework

☆**sewing circle** a group of women who meet regularly to sew, as for some charitable purpose

☆**sewing machine** a machine with a mechanically driven needle used for sewing and stitching

scwn (sōn) alt. pp. of SEW

sex (seks) n. [ME. < L. sexus < ? secare, to cut, divide: see SAW¹] 1. either of the two divisions, male or female, into which persons, animals, or plants are divided, with reference to their reproductive functions 2. the character of being male or female; all the attributes by which males and females are distinguished 3. anything connected with sexual gratification or reproduction or the urge for these; esp., the attraction of individuals of one sex for those of the other 4. sexual intercourse —adj. [Colloq.] same as SEXUAL —vt. to ascertain the sex of (chickens, etc.)

sex- (seks) [< L. sex, SIX] a combining form meaning six

sex·a·ge·nar·i·an (sek′sə jə ner′ē ən) adj. [< L. sexagenarius, of sixty < sexageni, sixty each + -AN] sixty years old, or between the ages of sixty and seventy —n. a person of this age

Sex·a·ges·i·ma (sek′sə jes′i mə) n. [ME. sexagesime < LL.(Ec.) sexagesima (dies) < fem. of L. sexagesimus, sixtieth (+ dies, day)] the second Sunday before Lent: also **Sexagesima Sunday**

sex·a·ges·i·mal (-m′l) adj. [ML. sexagesimalis < L. sexagesimus, sixtieth < sexaginta, sixty] of or based on the number sixty —n. a fraction whose denominator is sixty or a power of sixty

☆**sex appeal** the physical attractiveness and erotic charm that attract members of the opposite sex

sex·cen·te·nar·y (seks′sen′tə ner′ē, -sen ten′ə rē) adj. [SEX- + CENTENARY] of six hundred, especially six hundred years —n., pl. -nar′ies a six-hundredth anniversary

sex chromosome a sex-determining chromosome in the germ cells of most animals and a few plants: in most animals, including man, all the eggs carry an X chromosome and the spermatozoa either an X or Y chromosome, and an egg receiving an X chromosome at fertilization will develop into a female (XX) while one receiving a Y will develop into a male (XY)

sexed (sekst) adj. 1. of or having sex or sexual differentiation 2. having (a specified degree of) sexuality

sex·en·ni·al (sek sen′ē əl) adj. [< L. sexennium, six years < sex, SIX + annus, year (see ANNUAL) + -AL] 1. lasting six years 2. occurring once every six years —n. a sexennial event —sex·en′ni·al·ly adv.

sex hormone any hormone, as testosterone, estrogen, etc., influencing the development of, or having an effect upon, the reproductive organs, secondary sex characteristics, etc.

☆**sex hygiene** the branch of hygiene dealing with sex and sexual behavior: an earlier term for sexual instruction

sex·i- (seks′sə) same as SEX-

sex·i·ly (sek′sə lē) adv. [Colloq.] in a sexy manner

sex·i·ness (-sē nis) n. [Colloq.] a sexy state or quality

☆**sex·ism** (sek′siz'm) n. [SEX + (RAC)ISM] the economic exploitation and social domination of members of one sex by the other, specif. of women by men —**sex′ist** adj.

sex·i·va·lent (sek′sə vā′lənt) adj. 1. having six valences 2. same as HEXAVALENT (sense 1)

sex·less (seks′lis) adj. 1. lacking the characteristics of sex; asexual; neuter 2. lacking in normal sexual appetite or appeal; sexually cold —**sex′less·ly** adv. —**sex′less·ness** n.

sex linkage Genetics the phenomenon by which inherited characters are determined by genes carried on one of the sex chromosomes and are consequently linked with the sex of an individual —**sex′-linked′** (-liŋkt) adj.

sex·ol·o·gy (sek säl′ə jē) n. the science dealing with human sexual behavior —**sex·ol′o·gist** n.

sex·par·tite (seks pär′tīt) adj. [SEX- + PARTITE] of or divided into six parts

☆**sex·pot** (seks′pät′) n. [SEX + POT] [Slang] a woman or girl who has much sex appeal

sext (sekst) n. [ME. sexte < ML.(Ec.) sexta < L. sexta (hora), sixth (hour), fem. of sextus, SIXTH] [often S-] the fourth of the canonical hours, orig. set for the sixth hour of the day (counting from 6 A.M.), or noon

Sex·tans (seks′tanz) n. [ModL., lit., SEXTANT] a small equatorial constellation directly south of Leo

sex·tant (seks′tənt) n. [ModL. sextans (gen. sextantis), arc of a sixth part of a circle < L. a sixth part < sextus, SIXTH] an instrument used by navigators for measuring the angular distance of the sun, a star, etc. from the horizon, as in finding the position of a ship

sex·tet, sex·tette (seks tet′) n. [altered, after L. sex, SIX < SESTET] 1. any group of six 2. Music a) a composition for six voices or six instruments b) the six performers of such a composition

sex·tile (seks′t'l) n. [L. sextilis < sextus, SIXTH] Astrol. the position or aspect of two heavenly bodies sixty degrees apart —adj. Astrol. designating such an aspect

SEXTANT

sex·til·lion (seks til′yən) n. [Fr. < L. sextus, sixth (< sex, SIX) + Fr. (m)illion] 1. in the U.S. and France, the number represented by 1 followed by 21 zeros 2. in Great Britain and Germany, the number represented by 1 followed by 36 zeros —adj. amounting to one sextillion in number

sex·to·dec·i·mo (seks′tə des′ə mō′) n., pl. -mos′ [< L. (in) sextodecimo, (in) sixteen, abl. of sextusdecimus, sixteenth] same as SIXTEENMO

sex·ton (seks′tən) n. [ME. sextein, altered < segerstane < OFr. segrestain < ML. sacristanus: see SACRISTAN] 1. a church official in charge of the maintenance of church property: he sometimes rings the church bells and formerly dug the graves in the churchyard ☆2. an official in a synagogue who manages its day-to-day affairs

sex·tu·ple (seks tōō′p'l, -tyōō′-, -tup′'l; seks′too p'l) adj. [< L. sextus, SIXTH, after QUADRUPLE] 1. consisting of or including six 2. six times as much or as many; sixfold 3. Music having six beats to the measure —n. an amount six times as much or as many —vt., vi. -pled, -pling to make or become six times as much or as many

sex·tu·plet (seks tup′lit, -tōō′plit, -tyōō′-; seks′too plit) n. [dim. of prec.] 1. any of six offspring born at a single birth 2. a collection or group of six, usually of one kind

sex·u·al (sek′shoo wal) adj. [LL. sexualis] 1. of, characteristic of, or involving sex, the sexes, the organs of sex and their functions, or the instincts, drives, behavior, etc. associated with sex 2. Biol. a) having sex b) designating or of reproduction by the union of male and female germ cells —**sex′u·al·ly** adv.

sex·u·al·i·ty (sek′shoo wal′ə tē) n. 1. the state or quality of being sexual 2. a) interest in or concern with sex b) sexual drive or activity

sex·u·al·ize (sek′shoo wə līz′) vt. -ized′, -iz′ing to make sexual; endow with sexual significance, feeling, etc.

sex·y (sek′sē) adj. **sex′i·er, sex′i·est** [Colloq.] 1. exciting or intended to excite sexual desire; erotic 2. concerned to a large extent with sex [a sexy movie]

Sey·chelles (sā shel′, -shelz′) group of islands in the Indian Ocean, northeast of Madagascar, constituting a Brit. crown colony: 156 sq. mi.; pop. 46,000

Sey·mour (sē′môr) [orig. Eng. family name, prob. < OE. sæ, sea + mor, a hill] 1. a masculine name 2. **Jane**, 1509?–37; 3d wife of HENRY VIII: mother of EDWARD VI

s.f., sf, SF science fiction

sfz., sfz. sforzando

Sfax (sfäks) seaport on the E coast of Tunisia: pop. 250,000

SFC Sergeant First Class

☆**sfer·ics** (sfir′iks, sfer′-) n.pl. [with sing. v.] [altered & shortened < ATMOSPHERICS] 1. same as ATMOSPHERICS 2. the study of atmospherics; esp., the locating, tracking, and evaluating of natural electrical discharges

Sfor·za (sfôr′tsä) 1. **Count Car·lo** (kär′lō), 1873–1952; It. statesman & anti-Fascist leader 2. **Fran·ces·co** (frän ches′kō), 1401–66; It. condottiere & duke of Milan 3. **Lu·do·vi·co** (lōō′dō vē′kō) or **Lo·do·vi·co** (lō′-), 1451–1508; duke of Milan & patron of Leonardo da Vinci: son of prec.

---

fat, āpe, cär; ten, ēven; is, bīte; gō, hôrn, tōōl, look; oil, out; up, fur; get; joy; yet; chin; she; thin, then; zh, leisure; ŋ, ring; ə for a in ago, e in agent, i in sanity, o in comply, u in focus; ' as in able (ā′b'l); Fr. bāl; ë, Fr. coeur; ö, Fr. feu; Fr. mon; ô, Fr. coq; ü, Fr. duc; r, Fr. cri; H, G. ich; kh, G. doch. See inside front cover. ☆ Americanism; ‡foreign; *hypothetical; < derived from

sfor·zan·do (sfôr tsän′dō) *adj.*, *adv.* [It. < *sforzare*, to force] *Music* with sudden force or emphasis; accented: a direction to the performer —*n.*, *pl.* **-dos** a sforzando note or chord Also **sfor·za′to** (-tsä′tō)

sg, s.g. 1. senior grade 2. specific gravity

sgd. signed

sgraf·fi·to (skra fē′tō; *It.* zgräf fē′tō) *n.*, *pl.* **-fi′ti** (-tē) [It. < *sgraffiare*, to scratch < *s-*, intens. (< L. *ex-*) + *graffiare*, to scratch < L. *graphium*, a writing style < Gr. *graphion* < *graphein*: see GRAPHIC] 1. a method of producing a design on ceramics, murals, etc. by incising the outer coating of slip or glaze to reveal a ground of a different color 2. such a design 3. an object bearing such a design

's Gra·ven·ha·ge (skhrä′vən hä′khə) *Du.* name of The HAGUE

Sgt., Sgt. Sergeant

Sgt. Maj. Sergeant Major

sh (sh: *a prolonged sound*) *interj.* an exclamation used to urge or request silence

sh. 1. share(s) 2. *Bookbinding* sheep 3. sheet 4. shilling(s)

SHA *Navigation* sidereal hour angle

‡Shab·bat (shä bät′) *n.*, *pl.* **Shab·bat·im′** (-bä tēm′) [Heb., SABBATH] *Judaism* the Sabbath: also [Yid.] **Shab′bos** (shä′bəs)

shab·by (shab′ē) *adj.* **-bi·er**, **-bi·est** [< dial. *shab*, scab, scoundrel < OE. *sceabb*, a scab, scale: see SCAB] 1. run down; dilapidated; deteriorated *[shabby surroundings]* 2. *a)* showing much wear; ragged; threadbare: said of clothing *b)* wearing such clothing; seedy 3. beggarly; unworthy *[a shabby offering]* 4. disgraceful; shameful *[shabby treatment of guests]* —**shab′bi·ly** *adv.* —**shab′bi·ness** *n.*

shab·by-gen·teel (-jen tēl′) *adj.* shabby but genteel in trying to keep up appearances

Sha·bu·oth (shä vōō′ōt, -ōs) *n. var. of* SHAVUOT

☆shack (shak) *n.* [prob. < Scot. dial. *shachle*, a shanty] a small house or cabin that is crudely built and furnished; shanty —**☆shack up** [Slang] 1. to live or room (*in a certain place*) 2. to live (*with* one's mistress or paramour)

shack·le (shak′'l) *n.* [ME. *schakel* < OE. *sceacel*, akin to MDu. *schakel*, chain link < *?* IE. base *(s)kenk-*, to gird, bind] 1. a metal fastening, usually one of a linked pair, for the wrists or ankles of a person kept prisoner; fetter; manacle 2. anything that restrains freedom of expression or action 3. any of several devices used in fastening or coupling —*vt.* **-led**, **-ling** 1. to put shackles on; fetter 2. to fasten or connect with a shackle or shackles 3. to restrain in freedom of expression or action —*SYN.* see HAMPER[1] —**shack′ler** *n.*

SHACKLES

Shack·le·ton (shak′'l tən), Sir Ernest Henry 1874–1922; Brit. antarctic explorer, born in Ireland

shad (shad) *n.*, *pl.* **shad, shads**: see PLURAL, II, D, 2 [OE. *sceadd*, akin to Norw. dial. *skadd*, prob. < IE. base *skēt-*, to leap, spring up] 1. any of several saltwater fishes (genus *Alosa*) related to the herring but having a deeper body and spawning in rivers: the **American shad** (*Alosa sapidissima*) of the N Atlantic coast is a valuable food fish and has been introduced along the Pacific coast ☆2. any of various similar fishes; esp., the **gizzard** or **hickory shad** (*Dorosoma cepedianum*), widely introduced into fresh waters of the U.S. as food for other fish

☆shad·ber·ry (-ber′ē, -bər ē) *n.*, *pl.* **-ries** *same as* JUNEBERRY

☆shad·bush (-boosh′) *n.* [it flowers when shad appear in U.S. rivers] *same as* JUNEBERRY (sense 1): also called **shad′blow′** (-blō′)

shad·chan, shad·chen (shät′khən) *n. same as* SCHATCHEN

shad·dock (shad′ək) *n.* [after a Capt. *Shaddock*, who first carried this fruit from the East to the West Indies (late 17th c.)] 1. a large, yellow, coarsegrained, pear-shaped citrus fruit resembling a grapefruit 2. the tree (*Citrus grandis*) it grows on

shade (shād) *n.* [ME. *schade* < OE. *sceadu* (gen. & dat. *sceadwe*), akin to Goth. *skadus* < IE. base *skot-*, darkness, shadow, whence Gr. *skotos*, darkness] 1. comparative darkness caused by a more or less opaque object cutting off rays of light, as from the sun 2. *a)* a place giving protection from the heat and light of the sun, as under a tree *b)* an area less brightly lighted than its surroundings 3. [Archaic] *a)* a shadow *b)* [*often pl.*] a retired or secluded place 4. an indication or representation of darkness in painting, drawing, photography, etc. 5. degree of darkness of a color; gradation of a color with reference to its mixture with black *[various shades of blue]*: cf. TINT 6. *a)* a small difference or variation *[shades of opinion]* *b)* a slight amount or degree; trace; touch; suggestion *[a shade of humor in his voice]* 7. [Chiefly Literary] *a)* a ghost; specter *b)* anything lacking substance or reality; phantom 8. any of various devices used to protect or screen from light; specif., *a)* a partial cover for an electric lamp, etc. designed to diffuse or direct light: in full **lamp shade** ☆*b)* same as WINDOW SHADE ☆9. [*pl.*] [Slang] sunglasses —*vt.* **shad′ed**, **shad′ing** 1. to protect or screen from light or heat 2. to provide with a shade 3. to hide or screen with or as with a shadow 4. to make dark, as with a shade or a shadow; darken; dim; obscure 5. *a)* to represent the effects of shade in (a painting, photograph, etc.) *b)* to depict in, or mark with, gradations of light or color 6. to change by very slight degrees or gradations ☆7. to lessen or reduce (a price) slightly —*vi.* to change, move, or vary slightly or by degrees —*SYN.* see COLOR —**in** (or **into**) **the shade** 1. in or into darkness or shadow 2. in or into comparative obscurity, or a position of minor importance —**shades of** (**something**)! an exclamation used to refer to something reminding one of something past *[shades of* Prohibition!*]* —**the shades** 1. the increasing darkness, as of evening 2. *a)* the world of the dead; nether world; Hades *b)* the disembodied spirits of the dead, collectively —**shade′less** *adj.* —**shad′er** *n.*

shad·i·ly (shād′'l ē) *adv.* in a shady manner

shad·i·ness (-ē nis) *n.* a shady state or quality

shad·ing (-in) 1. protection or shielding against light or heat 2. the representation of light or shade in a picture 3. any small difference or variation, as in quality, kind, etc.

sha·doof (shä dōōf′) *n.* [Ar. *shādūf*] a device consisting of a long, pivoted pole with a bucket on one end and a weight on the other, used in the Near East for raising water, esp. in irrigating land

shad·ow (shad′ō) *n.* [ME. *schadwe* < inflected forms (gen. & dat. *sceadwe*) of OE. *sceadu*, SHADE] 1. a definite area of shade cast upon a surface by a body intercepting the light rays 2. the dark image made by such a body 3. [*pl.*] the growing darkness after sunset 4. *a)* a feeling of gloom or depression, a suggestion of doubt, etc. *b)* anything causing gloom, doubt, etc. 5. a shaded area in a picture 6. a dark area, as of a very short growth of beard 7. a mirrored image; reflection 8. *a)* something without reality or substance; imaginary vision *b)* a ghost; apparition 9. a vague indication or omen; prefiguration *[coming events cast their shadows before]* 10. *a)* a faint suggestion or appearance; trace *[not a shadow of hope]* *b)* remnant; vestige *[a mere shadow of his former self]* 11. a close or constant companion ☆12. a person who trails another closely, as a detective or spy 13. [Rare] protection or shelter —*vt.* 1. [Archaic] *a)* to shelter from light or heat *b)* to shelter; protect 2. to throw a shadow upon 3. to make dark or gloomy; cloud 4. to represent vaguely, mystically, or prophetically; prefigure (often with *forth*) 5. to stay close to or follow, esp. in secret so as to observe the movements and activities of 6. [Rare] to shade (a painting, drawing, etc.) —*vi.* 1. to change gradually 2. to become shadowy or clouded (*with* doubt, sorrow, etc.): said of the features —**in** (or **under**) **the shadow of** 1. very close to; verging upon 2. under the influence or domination of —**under the shadow of** 1. *see prec. phrase* 2. in danger of; apparently fated for —**shad′ow·er** *n.* —**shad′ow·less** *adj.*

shad·ow·box (-bäks′) *vi.* to spar with an imaginary opponent, esp. in training as a boxer —**shad′ow·box′ing** *n.*

☆shadow box a small, shallow open box, usually framed and hung on a wall, for displaying small objects

shadow cabinet [Chiefly Brit.] members of the opposition party selected to form a cabinet that is a counterpart of the one in power

shad·ow·graph (-graf′, -gräf′) *n.* an image or silhouette produced by throwing a shadow upon a lighted surface

shadow play a play produced by showing to the audience only the shadows of actors or puppets on a screen

shad·ow·y (shad′ə wē) *adj.* 1. that is or is like a shadow; specif., *a)* without reality or substance; illusory *b)* dim; indistinct 2. shaded or full of shadow —**shad′ow·i·ness** *n.*

Sha·drach (shad′rak) [Heb. *shadhrakh*, of Bab. origin] *Bible* one of the three captives who came out of the blazing furnace miraculously unharmed: Dan. 3

Shad·well (shad′wel, -wəl), **Thomas** 1642?–92; Eng. playwright & poet: poet laureate (1688–92)

shad·y (shād′ē) *adj.* **shad′i·er**, **shad′i·est** 1. giving shade 2. shaded, as from the sun; full of shade 3. of darkness, secrecy, or concealment 4. [Colloq.] of questionable character or honesty —**on the shady side of** beyond (a given age); older than

shaft (shaft, shäft) *n.* [ME. *schaft* < OE. *sceaft*, akin to G. *schaft* < IE. base *(s)kap-*, to cut with a sharp tool, whence SHAVE, L. *scapus*, shaft, stalk] 1. *a)* the long stem or body of an arrow or spear *b)* an arrow or spear 2. a missile or something that seems to be hurled like a missile; bolt *[shafts* of lightning, derision, etc.*]* 3. a cone or column of light; ray; beam 4. a long, slender part or object; specif., *a)* [Rare] the trunk of a tree or stem of a plant *b)* the stem or rib of a feather *c)* the midsection of a long bone *d)* the supporting stem of a branched candlestick *e)* a column or obelisk; also, the main, usually cylindrical, part between the ends of a column or pillar; verge: see COLUMN, illus. *f)* a flagpole *g)* a tall, slender building or part of a building; spire *h)* a handle, as on some tools or implements *i)* either of the two poles between which an animal is harnessed to a vehicle; thill *j)* a bar supporting, or transmitting motion to, a mechanical part *[the drive shaft* of an engine*]* 5. a long, narrow, vertical or slanting passage sunk into the earth *[a mine shaft]* 6. a vertical opening passing through the floors of a building, as for an elevator 7. a conduit for air, as used in heating and ventilating —*vt.* [Slang] to cheat, trick, exploit, etc. —**get**

the shaft [Slang] to be cheated, tricked, etc. —**give (someone) the shaft** [Slang] to cheat or trick (someone)

Shaftes·bur·y (shafts'bēr'ē, shäfts'-; -bər ē), 1st Earl of, (*Anthony Ashley Cooper*) 1621–83; Eng. statesman; lord chancellor (1672–73)

shaft·ing (shaf'tiŋ, shäf'-) *n.* **1.** a system or group of shafts, as for transmitting motion, conveying air, etc. **2.** material for making shafts

shag[1] (shag) *n.* [ME. *shagge* < OE. *sceaga*, akin to ON. *skegg*, a beard < IE. base *skek-*, to spring forth, whence G. *schicken*, to send: cf. SHAKE] **1.** [Rare] heavily matted wool or hair **2.** *a)* a heavy, rough nap, as on some woolen cloth *b)* cloth with such a nap **3.** any disordered or tangled mass **4.** coarse, shredded tobacco —*vt.* **shagged**, **shag'ging** to make shaggy or rough

shag[2] (shag) *n.* [specialized use of prec. with reference to the rough crest] any of several cormorants, esp. the **American cormorant** (*Phalacrocorax auritus*) and the **European cormorant** (*Phalacrocorax carbo*)

shag[3] (shag) *vt.* **shagged**, **shag'ging** [< ?] ☆to chase after and retrieve (baseballs hit in batting practice)

shag·a·nap·pi (shag'ə nap'ē) *n.* [altered < AmInd. (Cree) *pishaganābii* < *pishagan*, a hide + *āhii*, a cord] rawhide thongs or lacings, collectively

☆**shag·bark** (shag'bärk') *n.* **1.** a hickory tree (*Carya ovata*) with gray, loose, rough bark **2.** its wood **3.** its edible nut

shagged (shagd) *adj.* [Brit. Colloq.] exhausted; tired (often with *out*)

shag·gy (shag'ē) *adj.* **-gi·er**, **-gi·est** **1.** covered with or having long, coarse hair or wool **2.** carelessly groomed; unkempt **3.** of tangled, coarse growth; straggly; scrubby **4.** having a rough nap or surface —**shag'gi·ly** *adv.* — **shag'gi·ness** *n.*

shaggy dog (story) [from such an anecdote involving a shaggy dog] a long, rambling joke, typically involving ludicrously unreal or irrational behavior and usually having an irrelevant conclusion

☆**shag·gy·mane** (-mān') *n.* an edible inky cap mushroom (*Coprinus comatus*) with yellowish scales: also called **shaggy cap**

sha·green (shə grēn') *n.* [altered (after SHAG[1] & GREEN) < Fr. *chagrin* < Turk. *saghri*, horse's back, hide] **1.** rawhide with a rough, granular surface, made from the skin of the horse, seal, etc. **2.** the hard, rough skin of the shark or dogfish, used as a polisher

shah (shä) *n.* [Per. *shāh*, akin to Sans. *kṣáyati*, (he) rules < IE. base *kthē(i)-*, to acquire, gain power over, whence Gr. *kteanon*, possessions] a title of the ruler of Iran

Sha·hap·ti·an (shä hap'tē ən) *n. same as* SAHAPTIN

Shah Ja·han (shä' jə hän') 1592?–1666; Mogul emperor of Delhi (1628–58): builder of the Taj Mahal

Shahn (shän), **Ben(jamin)** 1898–1969; U.S. painter, born in Lithuania

shai·tan (shī tän') *n.* [Ar. *šaitān*, akin to Heb. *sātān*: see SATAN] an evil being or fiend; specif., [*often* S-] Satan, or the Devil, in Moslem usage

Shak. Shakespeare

shake (shāk) *vt.* **shook**, **shak'en**, **shak'ing** [ME. *schaken* < OE. *sceacan*, akin to LowG. *schaken* < IE. *skeg-*, var. of base *skek-*, whence SHAG[1]] **1.** to cause to move up and down, back and forth, or from side to side with short, quick movements **2.** to bring, force, mix, stir up, dislodge, rearrange, etc. by or as by abrupt, brisk movements [to *shake* a medicine before taking it] **3.** to scatter by short, quick movements of the container [to *shake* pepper on a steak] **4.** to cause to quiver or tremble [chills that *shook* his body] **5.** *a)* to cause to totter or become unsteady *b)* to unnerve; disturb; upset [*shaken* by the news] **6.** to brandish; flourish; wave **7.** to clasp (another's hand), as in greeting ☆**8.** [Colloq.] to get away from or rid of [to *shake* one's pursuers] **9.** *Music same as* TRILL —*vi.* **1.** to move or be moved quickly and irregularly up and down, back and forth, or from side to side; vibrate **2.** to tremble, quake, or quiver, as from cold or fear **3.** to become unsteady; totter; reel **4.** to clasp each other's hand, as in greeting **5.** *Music same as* TRILL —*n.* **1.** an act of shaking; back-and-forth movement **2.** an unsteady or trembling movement; tremor **3.** a natural split or fissure in rock or timber **4.** a long shingle split from a log **5.** [Colloq.] an earthquake ☆**6.** *short for* MILKSHAKE **7.** [*pl.*] [Colloq.] a convulsive trembling, as from disease, fear, alcoholism, etc. (usually with *the*) **8.** [Colloq.] a very short time; moment [be back in a *shake*] **9.** [Colloq.] a particular kind of treatment; deal [to get a fair *shake*] **10.** *Music same as* TRILL —☆**give (a person or thing) the shake** [Slang] to avoid or get rid of (an undesirable person or thing) —**no great shakes** [Colloq.] not of outstanding ability, importance, etc.; ordinary —**shake down 1.** to bring down or cause to fall by shaking **2.** to cause to settle by shaking **3.** to test or condition (new equipment, etc.) ☆**4.** [Slang] to extort money from, as by blackmail —**shake hands** to clasp each other's hand as a token of agreement or friendship, or in parting or greeting —**shake off 1.** to get away from or rid of (an undesirable person or thing) **2.** to get rid of (a suggestion, request, etc.) —**shake out 1.** to

cause to fall out by shaking **2.** to empty or clear by shaking **3.** to straighten out by shaking —**shake up 1.** to shake, esp. so as to mix, blend, or loosen **2.** to disturb or rouse by or as by shaking **3.** to jar or shock **4.** to redistribute or reorganize by or as by shaking —**shak'a·ble, shake'a·ble** *adj.*

SYN.—**shake** is the general word for a moving up and down or back and forth with quick, short motions; **tremble** implies such an involuntary shaking of the body as to suggest a loss of coordination or control, as from fear, fatigue, etc. [she *trembled* at the lion's roar]; **quake** usually suggests a relatively violent trembling, as in great agitation [to *quake* in one's boots with dread]; **quiver** suggests a slight, tremulous vibration, as of a taut string that has been plucked [the leaves *quivered* in the breeze]; **shiver** implies a slight, momentary quivering of the body, as from cold or in fear [he *shivered* at the thought of facing them]; **shudder** implies a sudden, convulsive quivering, as in horror or revulsion [she *shuddered* at the grisly sight]; **wobble** suggests a shaking or tottering that connotes instability [the chair *wobbled* on its unsteady legs]

shake·down (shāk'doun') *n.* **1.** a crude, makeshift bed, as a pallet of straw **2.** [Slang] an extortion of money, as by blackmail ☆**3.** a thorough search of a person or place —☆*adj.* for testing the performance or operational characteristics or acclimating the personnel [a *shakedown* cruise]

shak·en (-'n) *pp. of* SHAKE

shake·out (-out') *n.* ☆**1.** any movement in the market prices of securities that forces speculators to sell their holdings ☆**2.** any drop in economic activity that eliminates marginal or unprofitable businesses, products, etc.

shak·er (shā'kər) *n.* **1.** a person or thing that shakes **2.** a device used in shaking [a cocktail *shaker*] ☆**3.** [S-] [short for earlier *Shaking Quaker*: so named because of trembling caused by emotional stress of devotions: cf. QUAKER] a member of a former religious sect observing a doctrine of celibacy, common property, and community living —**Shak'er·ism** *n.*

Shaker Heights [orig. settled by a SHAKER group] city in NE Ohio: suburb of Cleveland: pop. 36,000

Shake·speare (shāk'spir), **William** 1564–1616; Eng. poet & dramatist: also sp. **Shakespere, Shakspere,** etc.

Shake·spear·e·an, Shake·spear·i·an (shāk spir'ē ən) *adj.* of or like Shakespeare, his works, or style —*n.* a scholar specializing in Shakespeare and his works

Shakespearean sonnet a sonnet composed of three quatrains, typically with the rhyme scheme *abab cdcd efef*, and a final couplet with the rhyme *gg*

shake·up (shāk'up') *n.* the act or an instance of shaking up; specif., ☆a reorganization of a drastic or extensive nature, as in policy or personnel

Shakh·ty (shäkh'tē) city in SW R.S.F.S.R., in the Donets Basin: pop. 208,000

shaking palsy *same as* PARKINSON'S DISEASE

shak·o (shak'ō) *n., pl.* **shak'os** [Fr. *schako* < Hung. *csákó* < ? G. *zacke*, a peak, point] a stiff, cylindrical military dress hat, usually with a flat top and a plume

Shak·ti (shuk'tē) *n.* [Sans. *śakti*] Hinduism divine power or energy worshiped in the person of the female consort of the particular god —**Shak'tism** *n.*

shak·y (shā'kē) *adj.* **shak'i·er**, **shak'i·est** **1.** not firm, substantial, or secure; weak, unsound, or unsteady, as a structure, belief, etc. **2.** *a)* trembling or tremulous *b)* nervous or jittery **3.** not dependable or reliable; questionable [*shaky* evidence] —**shak'i·ly** *adv.* —**shak'i·ness** *n.*

SHAKO

shale (shāl) *n.* [< ME., lit., shell < OE. *scealu*, SHELL] a kind of fine-grained, thinly bedded rock formed largely by the hardening of clay: it splits easily into thin layers

shale oil a dark mineral oil produced by the destructive distillation of bituminous shale or brown coal

shall (shal; *unstressed* shəl) *v., pt.* **should** [ME. *schal*, pl. *schullen* < OE. *sceal*, inf. *sceolan*, akin to G. *sollen* < IE. base *(s)kel-*, to be indebted, whence Lith. *skeliù*, to owe] an auxiliary used in formal speech: **1.** to express simple futurity in the first person [I *shall* tell him] and determination, compulsion, obligation, or necessity in the second and third persons [you *shall* obey] **2.** in a question expecting *shall* in the answer [*shall* we leave?] **3.** in laws and resolutions [the fine *shall* not exceed $100] **4.** in subordinate clauses introduced by *if, when,* etc. These formal conventions, however, do not reflect prevailing usage in which *shall* and *will* are used interchangeably, with *will* predominating in all persons See also WILL[2], SHOULD, WOULD[1]

shal·loon (sha loon', shə-) *n.* [Fr. *chalon* < *Châlons-sur-Marne*, town in N France] a twilled woolen fabric used largely for linings

shal·lop (shal'əp) *n.* [Fr. *chaloupe*, prob. orig. fig. use of *chaloupe*, nutshell, aphetic < MFr. *eschalope*, var. of *escalope*, SCALLOP] any of various earlier small open boats fitted with oars or sails or both

shal·lot (shə lät′) *n*. [obs. Fr. *eschalotte*, altered < OFr. *eschaloigne:* see SCALLION] 1. a small onion (*Allium ascalonicum*) whose clustered bulbs, like garlic but milder, are used for flavoring 2. *same as* GREEN ONION

shal·low (shal′ō) *adj*. [ME. *shalow* < OE. **scealw* < IE. base **(s)kel-*, to dry out, whence Gr. *skellein*] 1. not deep [a *shallow* lake] 2. lacking depth of character, intellect, or meaning; superficial —*n*. [*usually pl., often with sing. v.*] a shallow place in a body of water; shoal —*vt., vi*. to make or become shallow —*SYN*. see SUPERFICIAL —**shal′low·ly** *adv*. —**shal′low·ness** *n*.

sha·lom (shä lōm′) *n., interj*. [Heb. *shālōm*, lit., peace] a word used as the traditional Jewish greeting or farewell

shalt (shalt; *unstressed* shəlt) *archaic 2d pers. sing., pres. indic., of* SHALL: *used with* thou

shal·y (shā′lē) *adj*. **shal′i·er, shal′i·est** of, like, or containing shale

sham (sham) *n*. [prob. < a N.Eng. dial. var. of SHAME] 1. formerly, a trick or fraud 2. *a)* an imitation that is meant to deceive; counterfeit *b)* any hypocritical action, deceptive appearance, etc. 3. a person who falsely affects a certain character ☆4. *shortened form of* PILLOW SHAM —*adj*. not genuine or real; false, counterfeit, pretended, etc. —*vt*. **shammed, sham′ming** 1. formerly, to cheat or trick 2. to be or make an imitation or false show of; counterfeit —*vi*. to pretend to be what one is not —*SYN*. see FALSE

sha·man (shä′mən, shā′-; sham′ən) *n., pl*. **sha′mans** [Russ. < Tungusic *šaman* < Prakrit *šamana*, Buddhist monk < Sans. *śramana*, orig., ascetic, akin to *śram*, to fatigue] a priest or medicine man of shamanism —**sha·man·ic** (shə man′ik) *adj*.

sha·man·ism (-iz′m) *n*. 1. the religion of certain peoples of NE Asia, based on a belief in good and evil spirits who can be influenced only by the shamans 2. any similar religion, as of some American Indians and Eskimos —**sha′man·ist** *n*. —**sha′man·is′tic** *adj*.

sha·mas (shä′məs) *n., pl*. **sha·mo′sim** (-môs′im) [Yid. < Heb. *shamāsh*, servant, sexton] 1. *same as* SEXTON (sense 2) 2. the candle used to light the other candles in a Hanuka menorah Also **sha′mos, sha′mes**

Sha·mash (shä′mäsh) [Assyr.] the Assyro-Babylonian sun god, responsible for summer warmth and the success of crops, and a symbol for justice

sham·ble (sham′b'l) *vi*. **-bled, -bling** [< obs. *shamble, adj., in shamble legs*, prob. < ff., in obs. sense of stool, bench] to walk in a lazy or clumsy manner, barely lifting the feet; shuffle —*n*. a shambling walk

sham·bles (-b'lz) *n.pl*. [*with sing. v.*] [ME. *schamel*, a bench, as for displaying meat for sale < OE. *scamol*, a bench or stool, akin to G. *schemel* < early WGmc. borrowing, ult. < L. *scamellum*, dim. < *scamnum*, a bench] 1. [Archaic exc. Brit. Dial.] a place where meat is sold; butcher's stall or shop 2. a slaughterhouse 3. a scene of great slaughter, bloodshed, or carnage 4. any scene or condition of great destruction or disorder [rooms left a *shambles* by conventioneers]

shame (shām) *n*. [ME. < OE. *scamu*, akin to G. *scham*] 1. a painful feeling of having lost the respect of others because of the improper behavior, incompetence, etc. of oneself or another 2. a tendency to have feelings of this kind, or a capacity for such feeling 3. dishonor or disgrace [to bring *shame* to one's family] 4. a person or thing that brings shame, dishonor, or disgrace 5. something regrettable, unfortunate, or outrageous [it's a *shame* that he wasn't told] —*vt*. **shamed, sham′ing** 1. to cause to feel shame; make ashamed 2. to dishonor or disgrace 3. to drive, force, or impel by a sense of shame [*shamed* into apologizing] —*SYN*. see DISGRACE —**for shame!** you ought to be ashamed!; here is cause for shame! —**put to shame** 1. to cause to feel shame 2. to do much better than; surpass; outdo —**shame on** shame should be felt by; this is shameful of

shame·faced (-fāst′) *adj*. [altered, by folk etym. < ME. *schamfast* < OE. *scamfæst* < *scamu*, shame + *fæst*, firm, FAST[1]] 1. very modest, bashful, or shy 2. showing a feeling of shame; ashamed Also [Archaic] **shame′fast′** (-fäst′) —**shame·fac·ed·ly** (shām′fās′id lē, shām′fāst′lē) *adv*. —**shame′fac′ed·ness** *n*.

shame·ful (-fəl) *adj*. 1. bringing or causing shame or disgrace; disgraceful 2. not just, moral, or decent; offensive —**shame′ful·ly** *adv*. —**shame′ful·ness** *n*.

shame·less (-lis) *adj*. having or showing no feeling of shame, modesty, or decency; brazen; impudent —**shame′less·ly** *adv*. —**shame′less·ness** *n*.

sham·mer (sham′ər) *n*. a person who shams

sham·mes, sham·mas (shä′məs) *n. same as* SHAMAS

sham·my (sham′ē) *n., pl*. **-mies**; *adj., vt*. **-mied, -my·ing** *same as* CHAMOIS (*n*. 2, *adj*. 1, *vt*.)

Sha·mo (shä′mō′) *Chin. name for the* GOBI

sham·poo (sham pōō′) *vt*. **-pooed′, -poo′ing** [Hind. *chāmpo*, imper. of *chāmpnā*, to press, knead, shampoo] 1. formerly, to massage 2. to wash (the hair and scalp), esp. with a shampoo 3. to wash the hair and scalp of 4. to clean or wash (a rug, upholstery, etc.) with a shampoo —*n*. 1. the act of washing hair, a rug, etc. 2. a special soap, or soaplike preparation, that produces suds —**sham·poo′er** *n*.

sham·rock (sham′räk′) *n*. [Ir. *seamrog*, dim. of *seamar*, clover] any of certain clovers or cloverlike plants with leaflets in groups of three, used as the emblem of Ireland; specif., *a) same as* RED CLOVER or WHITE CLOVER *b)* a wood sorrel (*Oxalis acetosella*) *c) same as* BLACK MEDIC

☆**sha·mus** (shā′məs, shä′-) *n*. [prob. blend of SHAMAS & Ir. *Séamas*, James] [Slang] 1. a policeman 2. a private detective

Shan (shän, shan) *n*. 1. *pl*. **Shans, Shan** any member of a group of Mongoloid peoples who live in SE Asia 2. their Sino-Tibetan language related to the Thai languages

shan·dry·dan (shan′dri dan′) *n*. [< ?] [Dial.] 1. a two-wheeled chaise or cart 2. any decrepit, old-fashioned vehicle

shan·dy·gaff (shan′dē gaf′) *n*. [< ?] a beverage of ale or beer mixed with ginger ale, ginger beer, or lemonade: also **shan′dy**

Shang·hai[1] (shaŋ′hī′, shäŋ′-) seaport in Kiangsu province, E China, near the mouth of the Yangtze: pop. c. 10,000,000

Shang·hai[2] (shaŋ′hī; *also for v.*, shaŋ hī′) *n*. [< prec.] a kind of chicken with long, feathered legs: ancestor of the Cochin and Brahma —☆*vt*. **-haied, -hai·ing** [s-] 1. [orig. said of sailors thus kidnapped for crew duty on the China run] to kidnap, usually by drugging, for service aboard ship 2. [Slang] to induce (another) to do something through force or underhanded methods —**shang′hai·er** *n*.

Shan·gri-La (shaŋ′grə lä′) *n*. [< the scene of James Hilton's novel, *Lost Horizon* (1933)] any imaginary, idyllic utopia or hidden paradise

shank (shaŋk) *n*. [ME. *shanke* < OE. *scanca*, akin to G. *schenkel*, thigh < IE. base **(s)keng-*, to limp, whence Gr. *skazein*, G. *hinken*] 1. the lower part of the leg; part between the knee and the ankle in man or a corresponding part in animals 2. the whole leg 3. a cut of meat from the leg of an animal 4. a straight, narrow part between other parts, as *a)* the part of a tool or instrument between the handle and the working part; shaft *b)* the part of a tobacco pipe between the bowl and the bit *c)* the part of an anchor between the crown and the ring *d)* the narrow part of a shoe sole in front of the heel and beneath the instep 5. a projection or wire loop on some buttons by which they are sewn to fabric 6. the whole of a piece of type exclusive of the printing surface; body 7. *Bot. same as* FOOTSTALK —*vi*. *Bot*. to decay and fall off a diseased footstalk, as a flower —*vt*. *Golf* to hit (the ball) with the heel of the club —**ride** (or **go**) **on shank's mare** to walk —**shank of the evening** orig., the latter part of the afternoon (see EVENING, sense 2); hence, a relatively early part of the evening

Shan·non (shan′ən) river in WC Ireland, flowing southwestward to the Atlantic: c.220 mi.

shan·ny (shan′ē) *n., pl*. **-nies, -ny:** see PLURAL, II, D, 1 [< Brit. dial. *shan*] any of several ocean fishes (family Stichaeidae) resembling the blennies, esp. a yellowish arctic species (*Lumpenus maculatus*) with dark spots

Shan·si (shän′sē′) province of NE China, on the Hwang Ho: 60,656 sq. mi.; pop. 15,960,000; cap. Taiyüan

Shan State administrative division of EC Burma, occupying a plateau region (**Shan Plateau**), inhabited by Shans

shan't (shant, shänt) shall not

shan·tey (shan′tē, shän′-) *n., pl*. **shan′teys** *var. of* CHANTEY

Shan·tung (shan′tuŋ′, shän′dooŋ′) province of NE China, including a peninsula (**Shantung Peninsula**) which projects between the Yellow Sea & Po Hai: 59,189 sq. mi.; pop. 54,030,000; cap. Tsinan —*n*. [*sometimes* s-] 1. a fabric with a slub filling, made from the silk of wild silkworms 2. a similar fabric of rayon, acetate, cotton, etc.

☆**shan·ty**[1] (shan′tē) *n., pl*. **-ties** [< CanadFr. *chantier*, workshop, applied to lumberers' living quarters < OFr., lit., GANTRY] a small, shabby dwelling; shack; hut

shan·ty[2] (shan′tē) *n., pl*. **-ties** *var. of* CHANTEY

☆**shan·ty·town** (-toun′) *n*. the section of a city where there are many shanties or ramshackle houses

shape (shāp) *n*. [ME. *schap* < OE. (*ge*)*sceap*, form, created thing, akin to *scieppan*, to create, form < IE. **skeb-*, var. of base **(s)kep-*, to cut with a sharp tool, whence SHAFT, SHAVE] 1. that quality of a thing which depends on the relative position of all points composing its outline or external surface; physical or spatial form 2. the form characteristic of a particular person or thing, or class of things 3. the contour of the body, exclusive of the face; figure 4. assumed or feigned appearance; guise [a foe in the *shape* of a friend] 5. an imaginary or spectral form; phantom 6. something having a particular shape, used as a mold or basis for shaping or fashioning 7. any of the forms, structures, etc. in which a thing may exist [dangers of every *shape*] 8. definite, regular, or suitable form; orderly arrangement [to begin to take *shape*] ☆9. [Colloq.] *a)* condition; state, esp. of health [a patient in poor *shape*] *b)* good physical condition [exercises that keep one in *shape*] —*vt*. **shaped, shap′ing** 1. to give definite shape to; make, as by cutting or molding material 2. to arrange, fashion, express, or devise (a plan, answer, etc.) in definite form 3. to adapt or adjust [to *shape* one's plans to one's abilities] 4. to direct or conduct (one's life, the course of events, etc.) 5. [Obs.] to appoint or decree —*vi*. 1. formerly, to become suited; conform 2. [Rare] to come about; happen 3. [Colloq.] to take shape or form (often with *into* or *up*) —*SYN*. see FORM, MAKE[1] —**out of shape** [Colloq.] 1. not in good condition, esp. good physical health 2. damaged, bent, etc. so as not to have its usual form —☆**shape up** [Colloq.] 1. to develop

to a definite form, condition, etc. **2.** to develop satisfactorily or favorably **3.** to do what is expected of one; behave as required —**take shape** to begin to have definite form, condition, etc. —**shap′er** *n.*

SHAPE (shāp) Supreme Headquarters Allied Powers, Europe

☆**shaped charge** a charge arranged in an armor-piercing projectile, in such a way as to concentrate its explosive force in a desired direction

shape·less (shāp′lis) *adj.* **1.** without distinct or regular shape or form **2.** without a pleasing or symmetrical shape; unshapely —**shape′less·ly** *adv.* —**shape′less·ness** *n.*

shape·ly (-lē) *adj.* **-li·er, -li·est** having a pleasing or graceful shape or form; well-proportioned: used esp. of a woman with a full, rounded figure —**shape′li·ness** *n.*

☆**shape-up** (-up′) *n.* a method of selecting a daily work crew, as, esp. formerly, of longshoremen, from an assembled group of those available

Shap·ley (shap′lē), **Har·low** (här′lō) 1885– ; U.S. astronomer

shard (shärd) *n.* [ME. < OE. *sceard*, akin to *scieran*, to SHEAR] **1.** a fragment or broken piece, esp. of pottery; potsherd **2.** *Zool.* *a)* a hard covering, as a shell, plate, or scale *b)* *same as* ELYTRON

share[1] (sher) *n.* [ME. < OE. *scearu*, akin to *scieran*, to SHEAR] **1.** a part or portion that belongs or is allotted to an individual, or the part contributed by one **2.** a just, due, reasonable, or full share [*to do one's share of work*] **3.** any of the parts or portions into which the ownership of a piece of property is divided; esp., any one of the equal parts into which the capital stock of a corporation is divided —*vt.* **shared, shar′ing 1.** to distribute in shares; give out a portion or portions of; divide; apportion **2.** to receive, use, experience, enjoy, endure, etc. in common with another or others —*vi.* **1.** to have or take a share or part; participate (often with *in*) **2.** to share or divide something equally (often with *out* or *with*) —**go shares** to take part jointly, as in an enterprise —☆**on shares** with each person concerned taking a (usually equal) share of the profit or loss —**share and share alike** with each having an equal share —**shar′er** *n.*

SYN.—**share** means to use, enjoy, possess, etc. in common with others and generally connotes a giving or receiving a part of something [*to share expenses, glory, etc.*]; **participate** implies a taking part with others in some activity, enterprise, etc. [*to participate in the talks*]; **partake** implies a taking one's share, as of a meal, responsibility, etc. [*to partake of a friend's hospitality*]

share[2] (sher) *n.* [ME. *schar* < OE. *scear*, akin to *scieran*, to SHEAR] the part of a plow or other agricultural tool that cuts the soil; plowshare

☆**share·crop** (sher′kräp′) *vi., vt.* **-cropped′, -crop′ping** to work (land) for a share of the crop, esp. as a tenant farmer —**share′crop′per** *n.*

☆**shared time** an arrangement whereby pupils from parochial or other private schools attend some classes in public schools

share·hold·er (sher′hōl′dər) *n.* a person who holds or owns a share or shares, esp. in a corporation

Sha·ri (shä′rē) river in C Africa, flowing northwest through the Central African Republic & Chad into Lake Chad: c.500 mi.

shark[1] (shärk) *n.* [prob. < G. *schurke*, scoundrel, rogue, sharper] **1.** a person who victimizes others, as by swindling or cheating ☆**2.** [Slang] a person with great ability in a given activity; adept; expert —*vt., vi.* [Archaic] to get or live by fraud or stratagems

shark[2] (shärk) *n.* [? akin to prec.] any of numerous, usually large, mostly marine, selachian fishes, with a tough, spiny, usually slate-gray skin, separate lateral gill openings, and a slender, rounded body with the mouth on the underside: most sharks are fish-eaters and some will attack man

SHARK
(45 ft. maximum length)

shark·skin (-skin′) *n.* **1.** leather made from the skin of a shark ☆**2.** a cloth of cotton, wool, rayon, etc. with a smooth, silky surface, used for suits, etc. **3.** a fabric woven with a pebbly pattern

shark·suck·er (-suk′ər) *n.* *same as* REMORA

Shar·on (sher′ən) **1.** [? contr. < ROSE OF SHARON] a feminine name **2. Plain of,** coastal plain in W Israel, extending from Tel Aviv to Mount Carmel

sharp (shärp) *adj.* [ME. < OE. *scearp*, akin to G. *scharf*, ON. *skarpr* < IE. *(*s*)*kerb*(*h*)- < base *(*s*)*ker-*, to cut, whence SHEAR, HARVEST, L. *caro*, flesh] **1.** suitable for use in cutting or piercing; having a very thin edge or fine point; keen **2.** having a point or edge; not rounded or blunt; peaked [*a sharp ridge, features, etc.*] **3.** not gradual; abrupt; acute [*a sharp turn*] **4.** clearly defined; distinct; clear [*a sharp contrast*] **5.** made up of hard, angular particles, as sand **6.** quick, acute, or penetrating in perception or intellect; specif., *a)* acutely sensitive in seeing, hearing, etc. *b)* clever; shrewd **7.** showing or having a keen awareness; attentive; vigilant [*a sharp lookout*] **8.** crafty; designing; underhanded **9.** harsh, biting, or severe [*a sharp temper, criticism, etc.*] **10.** violent or impetuous; sudden and forceful [*a sharp attack*] **11.** brisk; active; vigorous [*a sharp run*] **12.** having a keen effect on the senses or feelings; specif., *a)* severe; intense; acute; keen [*a sharp pain, grief, appetite, etc.*] *b)* strong; biting; pungent, as in taste or smell *c)* high-pitched; shrill [*a sharp sound*] *d)* brilliant; intense [*a sharp flash of light*] *e)* cold and cutting [*a sharp wind*] **13.** [Slang] attractively or stylishly dressed or groomed **14.** *Music* *a)* higher in pitch by a half step [*C sharp (C♯)*] *b)* out of tune by being above true pitch —*n.* **1.** a sewing needle with an extremely fine point **2.** [Colloq.] an expert or adept **3.** [Colloq.] *same as* SHARK[1], SHARPER **4.** *Music* *a)* a note or tone one half step above another *b)* the symbol (♯) indicating such a note —*vt.* *Music* to make sharp; raise a half step or semitone —*vi.* *Music* to sing or play above true pitch —*adv.* **1.** in a sharp manner; specif., *a)* abruptly or briskly *b)* attentively or alertly *c)* so as to have a sharp point or edge *d)* keenly; piercingly *e)* *Music* above the true pitch **2.** precisely; exactly [*one o'clock sharp*] —**sharp′ly** *adv.* —**sharp′ness** *n.*

SYN.—**sharp** and **keen** both apply to that which is cutting, biting, incisive, or piercing, as because of a fine edge, but **sharp** more often implies a harsh cutting quality [*a sharp pain, tongue, flavor, etc.*] and **keen,** a pleasantly biting or stimulating quality [*keen wit, delight, etc.*]; **acute** literally implies sharp-pointedness and figuratively suggests a penetrating or poignant quality [*acute hearing, distress, etc.*] —*ANT.* **dull**

sharp-eared (-ird′) *adj.* having keenly sensitive hearing

sharp·en (shär′p′n) *vt., vi.* to make or become sharp or sharper —**sharp′en·er** *n.*

sharp·er (-pər) *n.* a person, esp. a gambler, who is dishonest in dealing with others; cheat; swindler

sharp-eyed (shärp′īd′) *adj.* having keen sight or perception

☆**sharp·ie** (shär′pē) *n.* [< SHARP: in sense 1, referring to its sharp lines] **1.** a long, narrow, flat-bottomed, New England fishing boat with a centerboard and one or two masts, each rigged with a triangular sail **2.** [Colloq.] a shrewd, cunning person, esp. a sharper or cheat

sharp-nosed (shärp′nōzd′) *adj.* **1.** having a thin, pointed nose **2.** having a keen sense of smell

sharp-set (-set′) *adj.* **1.** having a keen desire or appetite, as for food **2.** set so as to be sharp or at an acute angle

☆**sharp-shinned hawk** (-shind′) a small, N. American hawk (*Accipiter velox*) with a dark-blue back and a barred, reddish and white breast, feeding mainly on small birds

sharp·shoot·er (-shōōt′ər) *n.* a person who shoots with great accuracy; good marksman —**sharp′shoot′ing** *n.*

sharp-sight·ed (-sīt′id) *adj.* **1.** having keen sight; sharp-eyed **2.** keenly observant or perceptive; sharp-witted —**sharp′-sight′ed·ly** *adv.* —**sharp′-sight′ed·ness** *n.*

sharp-tongued (-tuŋd′) *adj.* using or characterized by severe, sharp, or harshly critical language

sharp-wit·ted (-wit′id) *adj.* having or showing keen intelligence or discernment; thinking quickly and effectively —**sharp′-wit′ted·ly** *adv.* —**sharp′-wit′ted·ness** *n.*

shash·lik (shäsh′lik) *n.* [Russ. *shashlyk*, ult. of Turk. orig.] kebabs of meat, esp. lamb, skewered and broiled

Shas·ta (shas′tə), **Mount** [< a tribal name < ?] volcanic mountain in the Cascade Range, N Calif.: 14,162 ft.

☆**Shasta daisy** [after prec.] any of several varieties of a daisylike chrysanthemum (*Chrysanthemum maximum*), having large flowers

SHASTA DAISY

Shatt-al-A·rab (shat′əl ä′räb) river in SE Iraq, formed by the confluence of the Tigris & Euphrates rivers, & flowing southeast into the Persian Gulf: 120 mi.

shat·ter (shat′ər) *vt.* [ME. *schateren*, var. of *scateren*, to scatter] **1.** orig., to scatter; strew **2.** to break or burst into pieces suddenly, as with a blow **3.** to damage severely; destroy, wreck, or disable [*to shatter one's health*] —*vi.* to break or burst into pieces; be damaged; smash —*n.* [*pl.*] broken pieces; fragments: chiefly in **in** (or **into**) **shatters**—*SYN.* see BREAK[1]

☆**shatter cones** cone-shaped flaws in certain solid rocks, probably formed by violent shock waves, as from meteoritic impact, atomic explosions, etc.

shat·ter·proof (-prōōf′) *adj.* that will resist shattering [*shatterproof glass*]

shave (shāv) *vt.* **shaved, shaved** or **shav′en, shav′ing** [ME. *schaven* < OE. *sceafan*, akin to G. *schaben* < IE. base *(*s*)*kab-*, to cut, whence L. *scabere*, to shave] **1.** to cut or scrape away a thin slice or slices from [*to shave the edge of a door*] **2.** to cut or scrape into thin sections or slices [*shaved ham*] **3.** *a)* to cut off (hair, esp. the beard) at the surface of the skin (often with *off* or *away*) *b)* to cut the hair to the surface of [*to shave the chin, the legs, etc.*] *c)* to cut the beard of (a person) **4.** to barely touch or just miss touching in passing; graze **5.** to cut short or trim (grass, etc.) closely **6.** [Colloq.] to lower (a price, etc.) by a slight margin ☆**7.** [Colloq.] *Commerce* to purchase (a note, draft, etc.) at a discount greater than the legal or customary rate of interest —*vi.* to cut off hair or beard with a razor

or shaver; shave oneself —*n.* **1.** a tool used for cutting thin slices, as of wood, from a surface **2.** something shaved or sliced off; shaving **3.** the act or an instance of shaving the beard See also CLOSE SHAVE

shave·ling (-liŋ) *n.* **1.** [Now Rare] a person whose head is entirely or partly shaved, esp. a priest or monk: used contemptuously **2.** a youth; stripling

shav·en (shā′v'n) *alt. pp.* of SHAVE —*adj.* **1.** shaved or tonsured **2.** closely trimmed

shav·er (-vər) *n.* **1.** a person who shaves **2.** an instrument used in shaving, esp. a device with a small electric motor that operates a set of vibrating or rotating cutters **3.** [Colloq.] a boy; lad **4.** [Archaic] a person who is hard or grasping in bargaining

☆**shave·tail** (shāv′tāl′) *n.* [orig. an unbroken mule; ? in allusion to the untrained mules, with closely cropped tails formerly sent to the Quartermaster Corps] [Slang] a second lieutenant, esp. one recently appointed

Sha·vi·an (shā′vē ən) *adj.* [< ModL. *Shavius*, Latinized < SHAW] of or characteristic of George Bernard Shaw or his work —*n.* an admirer of Shaw or his work

shav·ing (shā′viŋ) *n.* **1.** the action of a person or thing that shaves **2.** something shaved off, esp. a thin slice of wood or metal

shaving cream a soap, cream, etc. used to moisten and soften the beard for shaving

Sha·vu·ot (shä vōō′ōt, shə vōō′ōs) *n.* [Heb. *shābhū′oth*, lit., weeks] a Jewish holiday, the Feast of Weeks, or Pentecost, orig. celebrating the spring harvest, now chiefly commemorating the revelation of the Law at Mount Sinai: celebrated on the 6th & 7th days of Sivan

shaw (shô) *n.* [ME. *shawe* < OE. *sceaga*, akin to ON. *skagi*: for IE. base see SHAG¹] [Dial.] a thicket; copse

Shaw (shô) **1. George Bernard,** 1856–1950; Brit. dramatist & critic, born in Ireland **2. Henry Wheeler,** see Josh BILLINGS **3. Thomas Edward,** see T. E. LAWRENCE

shawl (shôl) *n.* [prob. via Urdu < Per. *shāl*] an oblong or square cloth worn, esp. by women, as a covering for the head or shoulders

shawm (shôm) *n.* [ME. *schalme* < MFr. *chalemie,* altered < OFr. *chalamel* < LL. *calamellus,* dim. of L. *calamus,* a reed: see CALAMUS] an early double-reed wind instrument resembling the oboe

Shawn (shôn), **Ted** (born *Edwin Myers Shawn*) 1891– ; U.S. dancer & choreographer: husband of Ruth ST. DENIS

Shaw·nee (shô nē′, shô′nē) *n.* [< Algonquian *Shawunogi,* souther!ern < *shawun,* south + *ogi,* people] **1.** *pl.* -nees′, -nee′ any member of a tribe of N. American Indians living at various times in the East and Midwest, and now chiefly in Oklahoma **2.** their Algonquian language

shay (shā) *n.* [back-formation < CHAISE, assumed as pl.] [Dial.] a light carriage; chaise

Shays (shāz), **Daniel** 1747?–1825; Am. Revolutionary soldier: leader of an insurrection (**Shays' Rebellion**) in W Mass. (1786–87), protesting high land taxes

☆**sha·zam** (shə zam′) *interj.* [from its use (c. 1940) by Captain Marvel, comic book character] an exclamation used in mock incantations to accompany the sudden appearance or disappearance of something

she (shē; *unstressed* shi) *pron. for pl. see* THEY [ME. *sche, scho,* prob. formed after OE. *seo,* fem. def. article, replacing OE. *heo,* she: but Brit. Western dialects still have (*h*)*u* < OE. *heo* as the regular fem. pron.] the woman, girl, or female animal (or, sometimes, the object regarded as female) previously mentioned: *she* is the nominative case form, *her* the objective, *her* or *hers* the possessive, and *herself* the intensive and reflexive, of the feminine third personal pronoun —*n., pl.* **shes** a woman, girl, or female animal

she- (shē) *a combining form meaning* female: used in hyphenated compounds *[she-bear]*

shea (shē) *n.* [Mandingo *si, se*] an African tree (*Butyrospermum parkii*) of the sapodilla family, whose seeds yield a thick, white fat (**shea butter**) used as a food, in soap, etc.

sheaf (shēf) *n., pl.* **sheaves** [ME. *schefe* < OE. *sceaf,* akin to G. *schaub* < IE. base **skeup-, *skeubh-,* a bundle, clump, whence (prob.) SHOP] **1.** a bunch of cut stalks of grain, etc. bound up in a bundle **2.** a quiverful of arrows, usually 24 in number **3.** a collection of things gathered together; bundle, as of papers —*vt. same as* SHEAVE²

shear (shir) *vt.* **sheared, sheared** or **shorn, shear′ing** [ME. *scheren* < OE. *scieran,* akin to G. *scheren* < IE. base **(s)ker-,* to cut: cf. SHARE², HARVEST, CORTEX] **1.** to cut with shears or a similar sharp-edged instrument **2.** *a)* to remove (the hair, wool, etc.) by cutting or clipping *b)* to cut or clip the hair, wool, etc. from **3.** to tear or wrench (*off*) by shearing stress **4.** to move through as if cutting **5.** to strip or divest (*of* a power, right, etc.) **6.** [Dial.] to reap with a sickle —*vi.* **1.** *a)* to use a cutting tool, as shears, in trimming or cutting wool, shrubbery, metal, etc. *b)* [Dial.] to use a sickle in reaping **2.** to come apart or break under the action of shearing stress **3.** to move by or as if by cutting —*n.* [ME. *schere* < OE. *scear*] **1.** *a)* rare *var.* of SHEARS *b)* a single blade of a pair of shears **2.** a machine used in cutting metal, esp. sheet metal **3.** the action, process, or result of shearing; specif., the shearing of wool from an animal: used in designating a sheep's age *[a sheep of three shears]* **4.** *a) same as* SHEARING STRESS *b)* any strain or distortion in shape resulting from the action of shearing stress —**shear′er** *n.*

sheared (shird) *adj.* subjected to shearing; esp., designating fur trimmed to give it an even surface *[sheared beaver]*

shear·ing (shir′iŋ) *n.* **1.** the action or process of cutting with or as with shears **2.** something cut off with shears, as the amount of wool cut from sheep

shearing stress the action or force causing two contacting parts or layers to slide upon each other, moving apart in opposite directions parallel to the plane of their contact

shear·ling (-liŋ) *n.* [see SHEAR & -LING¹] **1.** a sheep that has been sheared once, usually a yearling **2.** tanned sheepskin or lambskin from an animal killed not long after being sheared

shears (shirz) *n.pl.* [*also with sing. v.*] **1.** large scissors: also called **pair of shears 2.** any of several large tools or machines used to cut metal, etc. by the scissors action of two opposed cutting edges **3.** a device used in hoisting, consisting of two or more guyed poles or legs spread at the base and joined at the top to hold hoisting tackle: also **shear′legs′**

shear·wa·ter (shir′wôt′ər, -wät′-) *n.* [SHEAR + WATER] any of a genus (*Puffinus*) of black-and-white sea birds, related to the albatrosses, that skim the water in flight

sheat·fish (shēt′fish′) *n., pl.* **-fish′, -fish′es:** see FISH² [earlier *sheath-fish,* prob. < ff. + FISH²] an extremely large freshwater catfish (*Silurus glanis*) of E and C Europe

sheath (shēth) *n., pl.* **sheaths** (shēthz, shēths) [ME. *schethe* < OE. *sceath,* akin to G. *scheide* < IE. base **skei-,* to cut, split, divide (whence L. *scire,* to know: cf. SCIENCE: the earliest form of sheath was prob. a split stick] **1.** a case for the blade of a knife, sword, etc. **2.** a covering or receptacle resembling this, as the membrane around a muscle, a leaf base enveloping a stem of grass, etc. **3.** a woman's closefitting dress —*vt. same as* SHEATHE

sheath·bill (-bil′) *n.* either of two white-plumed antarctic sea birds (genus *Chionis*) distinguished by a horny, saddlelike sheath at the base of the upper bill

sheathe (shēth) *vt.* **sheathed, sheath′ing** [ME. *schethen* < *schethe*] **1.** to put into a sheath or scabbard **2.** to enclose in or protect with a case or covering *[wood sheathed with tin]* **3.** to thrust (a sword, knife, etc.) into flesh **4.** to retract (claws)

sheath·ing (shē′thiŋ) *n.* **1.** the act of one that sheathes **2.** something that sheathes or encases; casing; specif., *a)* the inner covering of boards or waterproof material on the roof or outside wall of a frame house *b)* the protective covering of a ship's bottom or hull *c)* material for any such covering

SHEATHBILL
(16 in. long)

sheath knife a knife carried in a sheath

sheave¹ (shēv, shiv) *n.* [ME. *scheve,* var. of *schive* < OE. **scife,* akin to G. *scheibe,* a disk < IE. **skeip-* < base **skei-,* to cut, whence SHEATH] a wheel with a grooved rim, such as is mounted in a pulley block to guide the rope or cable; pulley wheel or the like

sheave² (shēv) *vt.* **sheaved, sheav′ing** [< SHEAF] to gather and fix (grain, papers, etc.) in a sheaf or sheaves

sheaves¹ (shēvz) *n. pl.* of SHEAF

sheaves² (shēvz, shivz) *n. pl.* of SHEAVE¹

She·ba (shē′bə) *Biblical name of* SABA (sense 2)

Sheba, Queen of *Bible* the queen who visited King Solomon to investigate his reputed wisdom: I Kings 10:1–13

☆**she·bang** (shə baŋ′) *n.* [prob. var. of SHEBEEN] **1.** [Old Slang] a shack or hut **2.** [Colloq.] an affair, business, contrivance, thing, etc.: chiefly in the **whole shebang**

She·bat (shə vät′) *n.* [Heb. *shebhāt*] the fifth month of the Jewish year: see JEWISH CALENDAR

she·been (shi bēn′) *n.* [Anglo-Ir. < Ir. *síbín,* little mug] [Chiefly Irish & Scot.] a house or establishment where liquor is sold without a license

She·boy·gan (shi boi′gən) [< ? Ojibwa *jibaigan,* perforated object] city & port in E Wis., on Lake Michigan: pop. 48,000

shed¹ (shed) *n.* [< ME. *shadde,* var. of *shade* < OE. *scead,* shelter, protection, SHADE] **1.** a small, rough building or lean-to, used for shelter or storage, as a workshop, etc. **2.** a large, strongly built, barnlike or hangarlike structure, often with open front or sides

shed² (shed) *vt.* **shed, shed′ding** [ME. *scheden* < OE. *sceadan,* to separate, distinguish, akin to G. *scheiden,* to cut, separate: for IE. base see SHEATH] **1.** to pour out; give off; emit **2.** to cause to flow in a stream or fall in drops *[to shed tears]* **3.** to send forth or spread about; radiate; diffuse; impart *[to shed confidence]* **4.** to cause to flow off without penetrating; repel *[oilskin sheds water]* **5.** to cast off or lose (a natural growth or covering, as leaves, skin, hair, etc.) —*vi.* **1.** to shed a natural growth or covering, as hair **2.** to drop off or fall out: said of leaves, seeds, etc. —*n.* [ME. *schede,* division] **1.** a ridge of high ground; specif., *same as* WATERSHED **2.** an opening in the warp threads of a loom for the shuttle to pass through —**shed blood** to kill in a violent way

she'd (shēd) **1.** she had **2.** she would

shed·der (shed′ər) *n.* **1.** a person or thing that sheds ☆**2.** a lobster, crab, etc. that is shedding or has just shed its shell

sheen (shēn) *n.* [< the adj.] **1.** brightness; shininess; luster

2. bright or shining attire —*adj.* [ME. *schene* < OE. *sciene*, beautiful, splendid, akin to G. *schön* (< IE. base *(s)keu-*, to observe, heed, whence HEAR): sense infl. by association with SHINE] [Archaic] of shining beauty; bright —*vi.* [Dial.] to shine; gleam —**sheen′y** *adj.* **sheen′i·er, sheen′i·est**

sheep (shēp) *n., pl.* **sheep** [ME. *schep* < OE. *sceap, scæp*, akin to G. *schaf:* known only in WGmc.] **1.** any of a wide variety of cud-chewing, bovid mammals (genus *Ovis*) related to the goats, with heavy wool, edible flesh called mutton, and skin used in making leather, parchment, etc.; esp., the domesticated sheep (*Ovis aries*) **2.** leather made from the skin of the sheep, as for bookbinding **3.** a person who is meek, stupid, timid, defenseless, etc. —**make** (or **cast**) **sheep's eyes at** to look shyly but amorously at

☆**sheep·ber·ry** (-ber′ē) *n., pl.* **-ries 1.** a tall, N. American shrub or small tree (*Viburnum lentago*) with white flowers and juicy blue-black berries **2.** this berry

sheep·cote (-kōt′) *n.* [cf. COTE[1]] *chiefly Brit. var. of* SHEEP- FOLD: also **sheep′cot′** (-kät′)

sheep-dip (-dip′) *n.* any chemical preparation used as a bath to free sheep from vermin and sheep scab or to clean the fleece and skin before shearing

sheep dog any dog trained to herd and protect sheep

sheep fescue a widespread perennial grass (*Festuca ovina*) of temperate climates, growing in small, grayish-green tufts

sheep·fold (-fōld′) *n.* [ME. < OE. *sceapa fald:* cf. FOLD[2]] a pen or enclosure for sheep

☆**sheep·herd·er** (-hur′dər) *n.* a person who herds or takes care of a large flock of sheep grazing in open pasture —**sheep′herd′ing** *n.*

sheep·ish (-ish) *adj.* [ME. *shepisse*, like a sheep] **1.** *a)* embarrassed as because of feeling chagrin *b)* awkwardly shy or bashful **2.** resembling sheep in meekness, timidity, etc. —**sheep′ish·ly** *adv.* —**sheep′ish·ness** *n.*

sheep ked (ked) [*ked* < ?] *same as* SHEEP TICK

☆**sheep laurel** a small E N. American plant (*Kalmia angustifolia*) of the heath family, with pinkish flowers and evergreen leaves poisonous to sheep and other animals

sheep·man (-man′, -mən) *n., pl.* **-men** (-men′, -mən) ☆a person who raises sheep for the market

sheep·shank (-shaŋk′) *n.* a knot used for shortening a rope: see KNOT, illus.

sheeps·head (shēps′hed′) *n.,* ☆*1., pl.* **-head′, -heads′:** see PLURAL, II, D, 2 *a)* a large, saltwater food fish (*Archosargus probatocephalus*) with a massive head, a striped, deep body, and sheeplike incisor and molar teeth: found along the Atlantic and Gulf coasts of the U.S. *b)* the freshwater drum (*Aplodinotus grunniens*) common in the Great Lakes and Mississippi watershed *c)* a red wrasse (*Pimelometopon pulchrum*) of the California coast **2.** [Archaic] a foolish or stupid person

sheep·shear·ing (shēp′shir′iŋ) *n.* **1.** the act of shearing sheep **2.** the time when sheep are sheared **3.** a traditional feast held at this time —**sheep′shear′er** *n.*

sheep·skin (-skin′) *n.* **1.** the skin of a sheep, esp. one dressed with the fleece on it, as for a coat **2.** parchment or leather made from the skin of a sheep: the parchment is often used for documents, as diplomas ☆**3.** [Colloq.] *same as* DIPLOMA

sheep sorrel a low-growing dock (*Rumex acetosella*) with reddish or yellowish flowers, often found on dry soils

sheep tick a wingless, flattened, leathery fly (*Melophagus ovinus*) that is an external parasite on sheep

sheep·walk (-wôk′) *n.* [Chiefly Brit.] a range for sheep

sheer[1] (shir) *vi.* [var. of SHEAR, prob. infl. by cognate Du. or LowG. *scheren*, to cut, deviate, warp away] to turn aside from a course; swerve; deviate —*vt.* to cause to sheer —*n.* **1.** deviation from a course; abrupt turn; swerve **2.** the oblique heading or position of a ship riding at a single bow anchor **3.** the upward curve of a ship's hull or deck lines as seen from the side

sheer[2] (shir) *adj.* [ME. *schere*, prob. var. of *scere*, free, exempt < ON. *skærr*, bright, clear, akin to G. *schier:* for IE. base see SHINE] **1.** very thin; transparent; diaphanous: said of textiles **2.** not mixed or mingled with anything else; pure [*sheer ice*] **3.** absolute; downright; unqualified; utter [*sheer* persistence] **4.** perpendicular or extremely steep, as the face of a cliff —*adv.* **1.** completely; utterly; outright **2.** perpendicularly or very steeply —*n.* thin, fine material, or a garment made of it —SYN. see STEEP[1] —**sheer′ly** *adv.* —**sheer′ness** *n.*

sheer·legs (shir′legz′) *n.pl. same as* SHEARS (sense 3)

sheet[1] (shēt) *n.* [ME. *schete* < OE. *sceat*, piece of cloth, lappet, region, akin to G. *schoss*, lap, ON. *skaut*, lappet: for prob. IE. base see SHOOT] **1.** a large, rectangular piece of cotton, linen, etc., used on a bed, usually in pairs, one under and one over the body **2.** *a)* a rectangular piece of paper, esp. one of a number of pieces cut to a definite, uniform size, as for use in writing, printing, etc. *b)* a large piece of such paper with a number of pages printed on it, to be folded into a signature for binding into a book: *usually used in pl. c)* [Colloq.] a newspaper [a scandal *sheet*] **3.** a broad, continuous surface, layer, or expanse, as of flame, water, ice, etc. **4.** a broad, thin, usually rectangular piece of any material, as glass, plywood, metal, etc.

5. a flat baking pan [a cookie *sheet*] **6.** [Chiefly Poet.] a sail **7.** *Geol.* any layer or deposit of rock, gravel, soil, ice, etc. that is broad in extent and comparatively thin **8.** *Philately* the unseparated block of stamps printed by a single impression of a plate —*vt.* to cover or provide with, or form into, a sheet or sheets —*adj.* in the form of a sheet [*sheet iron*] —**sheet′like′** *adj.*

sheet[2] (shēt) *n.* [ME. *shete*, as if < OE. *sceata*, lower corner of a sail (akin to prec.) but actually short for *sceatline*, line attached to that part of a sail] **1.** a rope or chain attached to a lower corner of a sail: it is shortened or slackened to control the set of the sail **2.** [*pl.*] the spaces not occupied by thwarts, or cross seats, at the bow and stern of an open boat —**sheet home** to tighten the sheets of (a square sail) so as to extend it against the wind —**three sheets in** (or **to**) **the wind** [Slang] very drunk

sheet anchor [ME. *shute anker* < *schuten*, to SHOOT + *anker*, ANCHOR: hence, orig., one that can be shot out rapidly] **1.** a large anchor carried amidships and used only in emergencies **2.** a person or thing to be relied upon in danger or emergency

sheet bend *Naut.* a knot used in fastening a rope to the bight of another rope or to an eye: see KNOT, illus.

sheet·ing (shēt′iŋ) *n.* **1.** cotton or linen material used for making sheets **2.** material used in covering or lining a surface [*copper sheeting*] **3.** the action or process of covering with or forming into sheets

sheet lightning a sheetlike illumination caused by lightning reflected and diffused by clouds, etc.

sheet metal metal rolled thin in the form of a sheet

sheet music music printed on unbound sheets of paper

Shef·field (shef′ēld) city in NC England, in West Riding, Yorkshire: pop. 486,000

sheik, sheikh (shēk; *Brit. usually* shāk) *n.* [Ar. *shaikh*, lit., old man < *shakha*, to grow old] **1.** the chief of an Arab family, tribe, or village **2.** an official in the Moslem religious organization **3.** [< E. M. Hull's novel, *The Sheik*] [Old Slang] a masterful man to whom women are supposed to be irresistibly attracted —**sheik′dom, sheikh′dom** *n.*

Shei·la (shē′lə) [Ir.] a feminine name: see CECILIA **n.** [s-] [Austral. Slang] a girl or young woman

shek·el (shek′'l) *n.* [Heb. *shegel* < *shāqal*, to weigh] **1.** an ancient unit of weight used by Hebrews, Babylonians, etc., equal to about half an ounce **2.** a half-ounce gold or silver coin of the ancient Hebrews **3.** [*pl.*] [Slang] money

She·ki·nah (shə kē′nə, -kī′-; *Heb.* shə khē nä′) *n.* [Heb. *shekhinah* < *shakhan*, to dwell] *Hebrew Theol.* the manifestation of the presence of God; Divine Presence

shel·drake (shel′drāk′) *n., pl.* **-drakes′, -drake′:** see PLURAL, II, D, 2 [ME. *sheldedrake*, prob. < a ME. cognate of MDu. *schillede*, variegated < *schillen*, to make different + *drake*, DRAKE[1]] **1.** any of several large, old-world wild ducks (genera *Tadorna* and *Casarca*) that feed on fish, shellfish, etc. and nest in burrows: the plumage is variegated and often brightly colored **2.** any of several other ducks; esp., *same as* MERGANSER

shelf (shelf) *n., pl.* **shelves** [ME., prob. < MLowG. *schelf*, akin to OE. *scylf*, shelf, ledge < IE. **skelp* < base *(s)kel-*, to cut, divide, whence SHIELD, HALF] **1.** a thin, flat length of wood or other material fixed horizontally at right angles to a wall and used for holding things **2.** a similar support, usually one of a set, built into a frame, as in a bookcase or cupboard **3.** the contents or capacity of a shelf **4.** something like a shelf; specif., *a)* a flat ledge jutting out from a cliff *b)* a sand bar or reef **5.** a layer of bedrock, as under deposits of soil, gravel, etc. —**on the shelf** out of use, activity, or circulation —**shelf′like′** *adj.*

shelf ice *same as* ICE SHELF

shelf life the length of time a packaged food, chemical preparation, etc. can be stored without deteriorating

shell (shel) *n.* [ME. *schelle* < OE. *sciel*, akin to MDu. *schelle* < IE. base *(s)kel-*: see prec.] **1.** a hard outer covering, as of a turtle, mollusk, insect, egg, fruit, seed, etc. **2.** something like or suggestive of a shell in being hollow, empty, or simply a covering or framework, as the hull of a boat, a hollow pastry or unfilled pie crust, the framework of a building, a structure with an arched or hemispherical roof or back, a tapered beer glass, etc. **3.** a shy, reserved, or uncommunicative attitude or manner [to come out of one's *shell*] ☆**4.** a woman's pullover, sleeveless, loose-fitting knit blouse ☆**5.** a long, narrow, thin-hulled racing boat rowed usually by a team of oarsmen **6.** an explosive artillery projectile containing high explosives and sometimes shrapnel, chemicals, etc. ☆**7.** a small-arms cartridge consisting of a metal, paper, or plastic case holding the primer, powder charge, and shot or bullet **8.** a pyrotechnic cartridge which explodes high in the air **9.** a mollusk, esp. [*pl.*] shellfish **10.** *Chem., Physics a)* any of the spherical or elliptical orbits of electrons around the nucleus of an atom, all with the same principal quantum number and approximately the same energy *b)* a like configuration for nucleons in a nucleus *c)* the space taken up by such an orbit —*vt.* **1.** to remove the shell or covering from; take out of the shell [to *shell* peas, oysters, etc.] **2.** to separate (kernels of corn,

wheat, etc.) from the cob or ear **3.** to fire shells at from a large gun or guns; bombard —*vi.* **1.** to separate or become freed from the shell or covering /peanuts *shell* easily/ **2.** to fall, slough, or peel off, as a shell —**shell out** [Colloq.] to pay out (money) —**shell′-like′** *adj.* —**shell′y** *adj.*

she'll (shēl; *unstressed* shil) **1.** she shall **2.** she will

shel·lac, shel·lack (shə lak′) *n.* [SHEL(L) + LAC, used as transl. of Fr. *laque en écailles*, lac in fine sheets] **1.** refined lac, a resin usually produced in thin, flaky layers or shells and used in making varnish, phonograph records, insulating materials, etc. **2.** a thin, usually clear kind of varnish containing this resin and alcohol —*vt.* **-lacked′, -lack′ing 1.** to apply shellac to; cover or varnish with shellac ☆**2.** [Slang] *a)* to beat *b)* to defeat decisively

shel·lack·ing (-iɳ) *n.* ☆[Slang] **1.** a whipping; flogging; beating **2.** a thorough defeat

shell·back (shel′bak′) *n.* [SHELL + BACK[1], prob. referring to the shell of the sea turtle] **1.** an old, experienced sailor **2.** anyone who has crossed the equator by ship

☆**shell·bark** (-bärk′) *n. same as* SHAGBARK

☆**shell bean** any bean, as the lima, whose seeds but not pods are used as food

-shelled (sheld) *a combining form meaning* having a (specified kind of) shell /soft-*shelled* crab/

Shel·ley (shel′ē) **1. Mary Woll·stone·craft** (wool′stən kraft′, ˌkräft′), 1797–1851; Eng. novelist: daughter of Mary & William GODWIN: 2d wife of *ff.* **2. Percy Bysshe** (bish), 1792–1822; Eng. poet

shell·fire (shel′fīr′) *n.* the firing of large shells

shell·fish (-fish′) *n., pl.* **-fish′, -fish′es:** see FISH[2] [ME. *shellfyssche* < OE. *scilfisc*] any aquatic animal with a shell, as a shelled mollusk or crustacean, esp. an edible one, as the clam, lobster, etc.

☆**shell game 1.** a swindling game in which spectators are challenged to bet on the location of a small object ostensibly concealed under one of three cups or nutshells manipulated by a sleight-of-hand operator; thimblerig **2.** any game or scheme in which the customers are victimized

shell jacket a closefitting semiformal jacket; mess jacket

shell·proof (-prööf′) *adj.* proof against damage from shells or bombs

shell shock *an earlier term for* COMBAT FATIGUE — **shell′shocked′** *adj.*

shel·ta (shel′tə) *n.* [earlier *sheldru,* shelter: ? a repatterning of OIr. *bēlre,* speech] an esoteric jargon based on Irish and Gaelic and still spoken by tinkers, vagrants, etc. in some parts of Ireland and England

shel·ter (shel′tər) *n.* [< ? ME. *scheltroun,* earlier *scheltrum* < OE. *sceldtruma,* lit., shield troop, body of men protected by interlocked shields < *scield* (cf. SHIELD) + *truma,* an array, troop (cf. TRIM)] **1.** something that covers, protects, or defends; protection, or place affording protection, as from the elements, danger, etc. **2.** the state of being covered, protected, or defended; protection; refuge —*vt.* to provide shelter or refuge for; protect —*vi.* to find protection or refuge —**shel′ter·er** *n.* —**shel′ter·less** *adj.* **SYN.—shelter** implies the protection of something that shields, as a roof or other structure that shields one from the elements, danger, etc. /to find *shelter* from the rain/; **refuge** suggests a place of safety that one flees to in escaping danger, difficulties, etc. /he sought political *refuge* in France/; **retreat** implies retirement from that which threatens one's peace, etc. and withdrawal to a safe, quiet, or secluded place /a country *retreat*/; **asylum** is applied to a refuge where one is immune from seizure or harm, as because it is beyond a particular legal jurisdiction /the convict sought *asylum* abroad/; a **sanctuary** is an asylum that has a sacred or inviolable character /the former right of *sanctuary* in churches/

☆**shel·ter·belt** (-belt′) *n* a moderately dense barrier zone of trees or shrubs planted to protect crops, soil, etc. against strong winds and storms

☆**shelter tent** a small, portable tent large enough to shelter two men: it is made by fastening together two sections (**shelter halves**), each of which is carried by a soldier as part of his field equipment

shel·tie, shel·ty (shel′tē) *n., pl.* **-ties** [prob. < Orkney pronun. of ON. *hjalti,* Shetlander] *same as:* **1.** SHETLAND PONY **2.** SHETLAND SHEEPDOG

shelve (shelv) *vi.* **shelved, shelv′ing** [< SHELF] to incline or slope gradually —*vt.* [< *pl.* of SHELF] **1.** to furnish or equip with shelves **2.** to put on a shelf or shelves **3.** *a)* to put away as if on a shelf; lay aside; defer /to *shelve* a discussion/ *b)* to dismiss or retire from active service

shelves (shelvz) *n. pl. of* SHELF

shelv·ing (shel′viɳ) *n.* **1.** material for shelves **2.** shelves collectively **3.** the condition or degree of sloping

Shem (shem) [Heb. *shēm*] *Bible* the eldest of Noah's three sons: Gen. 5:32

She·ma (shə mä′) *n.* [< Heb. *shemá yisrōēl* (Hear, O Israel), the opening words: cf. Deut. 6:4-9] a declaration of the basic principle of Jewish belief, proclaiming the absolute unity of God

Shem·ite (shem′īt) *n. rare var. of* SEMITE

Shen·an·do·ah (shen′ən dō′ə) *n* [< AmInd. (? Iroquois), lit., ? spruce stream] river in N Va., flowing through a valley (**Shenandoah Valley**) between the Blue Ridge & Allegheny mountains, into the Potomac: c.200 mi.

Shenandoah National Park national park in the Blue Ridge Mountains of N Virginia: 302 sq. mi.

☆**she·nan·i·gan** (shi nan′i g'n) *n.* [altered < ? Ir. *sion-*

nachuighim, I play the fox] [*usually pl.*] [Colloq.] nonsense; trickery; mischief; often, a treacherous or deceitful trick

Shen·si (shen′sē′; *Chin.* shun′shē′) province of NC China: 75,598 sq. mi.; pop. 18,130,000; cap. Sian

shent (shent) *adj.* [ME. *schent* < *pp. of schenden,* to put to shame, akin to G. *schänden,* shame] [Archaic or Dial.] **1.** disgraced **2.** lost, ruined, or defeated, as a cause **3.** injured; damaged **4.** reproached

Shen·yang (shun′yäɳ′) city in NE China; capital of Liaoning province: pop. 2,423,000

She·ol (shē′ōl, shē ōl′) [Heb. *shě′ōl* < *shā·al,* to dig] *Bible* a place in the depths of the earth conceived of as the dwelling of the dead

shep·herd (shep′ərd) *n.* [ME. *shephirde* < OE. *sceaphyrde:* see SHEEP & HERD[2]] **1.** a person who herds and takes care of sheep **2.** a leader of a group; esp., a clergyman —*vt.* to tend, herd, guard, lead, etc. as or like a shepherd

shepherd dog *same as* SHEEP DOG

shep·herd·ess (-is) *n.* a girl or woman shepherd, esp. as a stock character in pastoral poetry

shepherd's check (or **plaid**) **1.** a pattern of small checks formed by stripes of black and white **2.** fabric woven in this pattern Also **shepherd check**

shepherd's pie a meat pie baked with a top crust of mashed potatoes

shepherd's purse a small weed (*Capsella bursa-pastoris*) of the mustard family, with triangular, pouchlike pods

Sher·a·ton (sher′ə tən) *adj.* [after Thomas *Sheraton* (1751–1806), Eng. cabinetmaker] designating or of a style of furniture characterized by simplicity of form, straight lines, and classically chaste decoration

sher·bet (shur′bət) *n.* [Turk. *sharbat* < Ar. *sharbah,* a drink, var. of *sharāb:* see SYRUP] **1.** [Brit.] a beverage, orig. from the Orient, made of watered fruit juice and sugar, and served cold **2.** a frozen dessert like an ice but with gelatin and, often, milk added

Sher·brooke (shur′brook) city in S Quebec, Canada: pop. 76,000

sherd (shurd) *n. same as* SHARD

Sher·i·dan (sher′i d'n) **1. Philip Henry,** 1831–88; Union general in the Civil War **2. Richard Brins·ley** (brinz′lē), 1751–1816; Brit. dramatist & politician, born in Ireland

she·rif (shə rēf′) *n.* [Ar. *sharīf,* noble] **1.** a descendant of Mohammed through his daughter Fatima **2.** an Arab prince or chief **3.** the chief magistrate of Mecca

sher·iff (sher′if) *n.* [ME. *schirreve* < OE. *scirgerefa* < *scir,* SHIRE + *gerefa,* REEVE[1]] **1.** in England, esp. formerly, any of various officers of a shire, or county ☆**2.** in the U.S., the chief law-enforcement officer of a county, charged in general with the keeping of the peace and the execution of court orders —**sher′iff·dom** *n.*

Sher·lock Holmes (shur′läk hōmz′, hōlmz′) a fictitious British detective with great powers of deduction, the main character in many stories by A. Conan Doyle

Sher·man (shur′mən) **1. John,** 1823–1900; U.S. statesman: brother of *William* **2. Roger,** 1721–93; Am. statesman; signer of the Declaration of Independence **3. William Tecumseh,** 1820–91; Union general in the Civil War

Sher·pa (shur′pə, sher′-) *n., pl.* **-pas, -pa** a member of a Tibetan people living on the southern slopes of the Himalayas in Nepal, famous as mountain climbers

sher·ris (sher′is) *n. archaic var. of* SHERRY

sher·ry (sher′ē) *n., pl.* **-ries** [taken as sing. of earlier *sherris* < *Xeres* (now *Jerez*), Spain, where first made] **1.** a strong, fortified Spanish wine varying in color from light yellow to dark brown **2.** any similar wine made elsewhere

's Her·to·gen·bosch (ser′tō khən bôs′) city in SC Netherlands; capital of North Brabant province: pop. 78,000

Sher·wood (shur′wood), **Robert Emmet** 1896–1955; U.S. playwright

Sher·wood Forest (shur′wood) forest in Nottinghamshire, England, made famous in the Robin Hood legends

she's (shēz) **1.** she is **2.** she has

Shet·land (shet′lənd) [ON. *Hjaltland*] county of NE Scotland, consisting of a group of islands (**Shetland Islands**) in the Atlantic, northeast of the Orkneys: 550 sq. mi.; pop. 17,000 —*n.* **1.** *same as: a)* SHETLAND PONY *b)* SHETLAND SHEEPDOG **2.** [*also* **s-**] *a) same as* SHETLAND WOOL *b)* a fabric made from Shetland wool

Shetland pony any of a breed of sturdy ponies with a rough coat and long tail and mane, orig. from the Shetland Islands

Shetland sheep·dog (shep′dôg′, -däg′) any of a breed of dogs closely resembling collies but smaller: orig. from the Shetland Islands

Shetland wool 1. fine wool from the undercoat of sheep from Shetland **2.** a soft, fine, loosely twisted wool yarn made from this wool

She·vu·oth (shə voo′ōt) *n.* [Heb.] *same as* SHAVUOT

SHERATON CHAIR

WILD SHETLAND PONY
(40 in. high at
shoulder)

shew (shō) n., vt., vi. **shewed**, **shewn** or **shewed**, **shew′ing** archaic sp. of SHOW

shew·bread (shō′bred′) n. [prec. + BREAD, after G. schaubrot, Luther's transl. for Heb. lehem pānim, lit., bread of faces, presence bread] Ancient Judaism the twelve loaves of unleavened bread placed at the altar in the Temple as a token offering every Sabbath by the priests

SHF, S.H.F., shf, s.h.f. superhigh frequency

Shi·ah (shē′ə) n., pl. **Shi′ah** same as SHIITE

shib·bo·leth (shib′ə ləth) n. [ME. sebolech, after LL.(Ec.) sciboleth < Heb. shibbōleth, a stream: present meaning from the use of the word as a test word] 1. Bible the test word used by the men of Gilead to distinguish the escaping Ephraimites, who pronounced the initial (sh) as (s): Judg. 12:4–6 2. any test word or password 3. any phrase, practice, custom, etc. that is distinctive of a particular party, class, faction, etc.

Shi·be·li (shə bel′ē) river in E Africa, flowing from SE Ethiopia through Somalia into a swamp near the Juba River: c. 1,200 mi.

shick·er (shik′ər) adj. [< Yid. < Heb. shikōr] same as DRUNK (sense 1) —n. same as DRUNKARD Also **shik′ker**

shied (shīd) pt. & pp. of SHY¹

shield (shēld) n. [ME. schelde < OE. scield, akin to G. schild: for IE. base see SHELF] 1. a broad piece of protective armor carried in the hand or worn on the forearm to ward off blows or missiles 2. any person or thing that guards, protects, or defends 3. a heraldic escutcheon 4. anything shaped like a shield, as a plaque, trophy, badge, or emblem 5. a movable canopy protecting workers from cave-ins in mines, tunnels, etc. 6. a heavy metal screen attached to an artillery piece for the protection of the gunners 7. a) a guard or safety screen, as over the moving parts of machinery b) an insulating covering on electric wires, etc. c) any material or structure used for protection against radiation 8. same as DRESS SHIELD 9. Zool. a hard surface covering or shell; protective plate, as on a turtle —vt. 1. to be or provide a shield for; defend; protect; guard 2. to hide from view; screen 3. [Obs.] to prevent or forbid —vi. to serve as a shield, or protection —SYN. see DEFEND —**shield′er** n.

shiel·ing (shēl′iŋ) n. [< Scot. shiel, shieling (< ME. schele, a shelter, akin to ON. skjol, ult. < IE. base *(s)keu-, to cover, whence HOUSE, HIDE¹) + -ING] [Scot.] 1. a grazing ground; pasture 2. a rude hut or cottage

shi·er¹ (shī′ər) n. a horse that tends to shy

shi·er² (shī′ər) adj. alt. compar. of SHY¹

shi·est (-əst) adj. alt. superl. of SHY¹

shift (shift) vt. [ME. schiften < OE. sciftan, to divide, separate, akin to G. schichten: for IE. base see SHIP] 1. to move or transfer from one person, place, or position to another [to shift the blame] 2. to replace by another or others; change or exchange 3. to change (gears) from one arrangement to another in driving a motor vehicle 4. to change phonetically, as by Grimm's law 5. [Archaic or Dial.] to change (clothes) —vi. 1. a) to change position, direction, form, character, etc. b) to undergo phonetic change 2. to get along; manage [to shift for oneself] 3. to use tricky, evasive, or expedient methods ☆4. to change from one gear arrangement to another 5. in typing, to change from small letters, etc. to capitals, etc. by depressing a key (**shift key**) 6. [Archaic or Dial.] to change one's clothing —n. 1. the act of shifting from one person, place, position, etc. to another; change; transfer; substitution 2. a means or plan of conduct, esp. one followed in an emergency or difficulty; expedient; stratagem 3. a deceitful scheme or method; evasion; trick ☆4. shortened form of GEARSHIFT 5. a) a group of people working in relay with another or other groups [the night shift] b) the regular work period of such a group 6. a change in direction, as of the wind 7. a) [Now Rare] a chemise, or woman's slip b) a loose dress that hangs straight with no waistline 8. [Archaic or Dial.] a change of clothing ☆9. Football a regrouping of the offensive backfield shortly before the ball is put in play 10. Linguis. a phonetic change or series of changes that alters the system of sounds in a language: see GREAT VOWEL SHIFT 11. Mining a fault or displacement, as in a vein 12. Music a change in the position of the hand, as on the fingerboard of a violin 13. Physics a change in the observed frequency of a wave, as of light, sound, etc., caused by an increase or decrease in the distance between the source and the observer: see DOPPLER EFFECT —SYN. see MOVE —**make shift** to manage or do the best one can (with whatever means are at hand) —**shift′a·ble** adj. —**shift′er** n.

shift·less (-lis) adj. 1. lacking the will or ability to do or accomplish; incapable, inefficient, lazy, etc. 2. showing such lack or incapacity —**shift′less·ly** adv. —**shift′less·ness** n.

shift·y (shif′tē) adj. **shift′i·er**, **shift′i·est** 1. full of shifts or expedients; resourceful 2. having or showing a tricky or deceitful nature; evasive [a shifty look] —**shift′i·ly** adv. —**shift′i·ness** n.

shi·gel·la (shi gel′ə) n., pl. **-gel′lae** (-ē), **-gel′las** [ModL.: after Kiyoshi Shiga (1870–1957), Jap. bacteriologist]

any of a genus (Shigella) of Gram-negative, rod-shaped bacilli, certain species of which cause dysentery

shi·gel·lo·sis (shi′gə lō′sis) n. [< prec. + -OSIS] dysentery caused by various strains of shigella

Shih-chia-chuang (shu′jyä′jwän′) city in Hopei province, NE China: pop. 1,118,000

Shi·ite (shē′īt) n. [Ar. shī'i, follower, partisan + -ITE¹] a member of one of the two great sects of Moslems: Shiites consider Ali, Mohammed's son-in-law and the fourth of the caliphs, as the first Imam and the rightful successor of Mohammed and do not accept the Sunna as authoritative: cf. SUNNITE —**Shi·ism** n. —**Shi·it′ic** (-it′ik) adj.

shi·kar (shi kär′) n. [Per. shikār] in India, hunting as a sport —vt., vi. in India, to hunt

shi·ka·ri, shi·ka·ree (shi kä′rē) n. [Hind. shikāri < Per. shikār, a hunt] in India, a hunter, esp. a native hunter who serves as a guide

Shi·ko·ku (shē′kō kōō′) island of Japan, south of Honshu: c. 6,860 sq. mi.: pop. 4,022,000

shill (shil) n. [prob. contr. < shillaber < shillaber < ?] [Slang] the confederate of a gambler, pitchman, auctioneer, etc. who pretends to buy, bet, or bid so as to lure onlookers into participating

shil·le·lagh, shil·la·lah (shi lā′lē, -lə) n. [< Shillelagh, village in County Wicklow, Ireland, famous for its oaks and blackthorns] a club or cudgel: also sp. **shil·le′lah**

shil·ling (shil′iŋ) n. [ME. schilling < OE. scylling, akin to G. schilling < Gmc. *skildling: for bases see SHIELD & -LING¹] 1. a) a British money of account and silver coin, equal to 5 (new) pennies or 1/20 of a pound: symbol, / b) any of several coins or moneys of account used in other countries: see MONETARY UNITS, table 2. a coin of colonial America, varying from about 12 to 16 cents

Shil·long (shi lôŋ′) city in NE India; capital of Assam state: pop. 102,000

Shil·luk (shi lōōk′) n. 1. pl. **-luks′**, **-luk′** any of a Nilotic people of Sudan living principally on the west bank of the White Nile 2. their Eastern Sudanic language

shil·ly-shal·ly (shil′ē shal′ē) adv. [a redupl. of shall I? meaning "shall I or shall I not?"] in a vacillating manner; hesitantly; irresolutely —adj. vacillating; hesitant; irresolute —n. indecision, vacillation, or irresolution, esp. over a trivial matter —vi. **-lied**, **-ly·ing** to be irresolute; vacillate, esp. over trifles

Shi·loh (shī′lō) [after an ancient town in Israel: Josh. 18:1] national military park in SW Tenn., on the Tennessee River; scene of a Civil War battle (1862)

shim (shim) n. [< ?] ☆a thin, usually wedge-shaped piece of wood, metal, etc. used for filling space, leveling, etc., as in masonry —☆vt. **shimmed**, **shim′ming** to fit with a shim or shims

shim·mer (shim′ər) vi. [ME. schimeren < OE. scymrian, freq. formation on base of scima, a ray, light: for IE. base see SHINE] 1. to shine with an unsteady light; glimmer 2. to form a wavering image, as by reflection from waves of water or heat —n. a shimmering light; glimmer —SYN. see FLASH —**shim′mer·y** adj.

shim·my (shim′ē) n. 1. [< CHEMISE, misapprehended as a pl.] [Old Slang] a chemise ☆2. [< phr. to shake a shimmy] a) a jazz dance, popular in the 1920's, characterized by much shaking of the body b) a marked shaking, vibration, or wobble, as in the front wheels of an automobile —☆vi. **-mied**, **-my·ing** 1. to dance the shimmy 2. to shake, vibrate, or wobble

Shi·mo·no·se·ki (shē′mō nō sä′kē) seaport at the SW tip of Honshu, Japan: pop. 254,000

shin¹ (shin) n. [ME. schine < OE. scinu, akin to G. schiene, thin plate, schien-, shin: for IE. base see SHEATH] 1. the front part of the leg between the knee and the ankle 2. the lower foreleg in beef —vt., vi. **shinned**, **shin′ning** to climb (a rope, pole, etc.) by using both hands and legs for gripping: often with up

shin² (shēn) n. [Heb. sīn, shin, lit., tooth] the twenty-first letter of the Hebrew alphabet (ש)

Shi·nar (shī′när) region mentioned in the Bible, prob. corresponding to Sumer, in Babylonia

shin·bone (shin′bōn′) n. same as TIBIA (sense 1)

☆shin·dig (shin′dig′) n. [folk-etym. form of ff., as if shin-dig, jovial kick in the shin] [Colloq.] a dance, party, entertainment, or other gathering, esp. of an informal kind

shin·dy (-dē) n., pl. **-dies** [< ?] [Colloq.] 1. a noisy disturbance; commotion; row 2. same as SHINDIG

shine (shin) vi. **shone**, or, esp. for vt. 2, **shined**, **shin′ing** [ME. schinen < OE. scinan, akin to G. scheinen < IE. base *skai-, to glimmer, whence Gr. skia, shadow & SHIMMER] 1. to emit or reflect light; be radiant or bright with light; gleam; glow 2. to be eminent, conspicuous, or brilliant; stand out; excel 3. to exhibit itself clearly or conspicuously [love shining from her face] —vt. 1. to direct the light of [to shine a flashlight] 2. to make shiny or bright by polishing [to shine shoes] —n. 1. brightness; radiance 2. luster; polish; gloss ☆3. shortened form of SHOESHINE 4. splendor; brilliance; show 5. sunshine; fair weather ☆6. [Slang] a trick or prank: usually used in pl. —SYN. see POLISH —**shine up to** [Slang] to try to

ingratiate oneself with; curry favor with —☆**take a shine to** [Slang] to take a liking to (someone)

shin·er (-ər) *n.* **1.** a person or thing that shines ☆**2.** *pl.* **-ers, -er:** see PLURAL, II, D, 1 any of a number of fresh-water minnows (genus *Notropis*) with silvery scales: often used as fish bait ☆**3.** [Slang] *same as* BLACK EYE (sense 2)

shin·gle¹ (shiŋ′g'l) *n.* [prob. < Scand., as in Norw. *singel*, akin to MDu. *singele*, coastal detritus < OFr. *sengle*, lit., belt < L. *cingula:* see CINCH] [Chiefly Brit.] **1.** large, coarse, waterworn gravel, as found on a beach **2.** an area, as a beach, covered with such gravel —**shin′gly** *adv.* **-gli·er, -gli·est**

shin·gle² (shiŋ′g'l) *n.* [ME. *schingel*, prob. altered < OE. *scindel*, akin to OS. *scindula* < WGmc. borrowing < L. *scindula*, later form of *scandula*, a shingle < IE. base *(s)k(h)end-*, to split, whence SCATTER] **1.** a thin, wedge-shaped piece of wood, slate, etc. laid with others in a series of overlapping rows as a covering for roofs and the sides of houses ☆**2.** a woman's short haircut in which the hair over the nape is shaped close to the head ☆**3.** [Colloq.] a small signboard, esp. that which a physician or lawyer hangs outside his office —*vt.* **-gled, -gling 1.** to cover (a roof, etc.) with shingles ☆**2.** to cut (hair) in shingle style

shin·gle³ (shiŋ′g'l) *vt.* **-gled, -gling** [< Fr. dial. (Picardy) *chingler*, var. of Fr. *cingler*, to strike with a flexible rod, ult. < L. *cingula:* see CINGULUM] to work on (puddled iron) by hammering and squeezing it to remove impurities

shin·gles (shiŋ′g'lz) *n.* [ME. *schingles*, altered < ML. *cingulus* < L. *cingulum*, a belt < *cingere*, to gird (see CINCH): used in ML. as transl. of Gr. *zōnē*, a girdle, shingles] *same as* HERPES ZOSTER

shin·guard (shin′gärd′) *n.* a padded guard worn to protect the shins, as by a baseball catcher or hockey goalie

shin·i·ness (shin′ē nis) *n.* the state or quality of being shiny; luster; polish

shin·ing (shin′iŋ) *adj.* **1.** giving off or reflecting light; radiant; bright **2.** brilliant; remarkable; splendid [a *shining* example of generosity] —SYN. see BRIGHT

☆**shin·leaf** (shin′lēf′) *n.* [? because once used as shin-plasters] any of a genus (*Pyrola*) of plants of the heath family, with slender stalks having small, rounded ever-green leaves at the base and racemes of globular flowers

shin·ny¹ (shin′ē) *n., pl.* **-nies** [prob. < SHIN¹] **1.** a simple form of hockey, esp. as played by children **2.** the curved stick or club used in this game —*vi.* **-nied, -ny·ing** to play shinny Also sp. **shin′ney**

☆**shin·ny²** (shin′ē) *vi.* **-nied, -ny·ing** *same as* SHIN¹

☆**shin·plas·ter** (shin′plas′tər, -pläs′-) *n.* **1.** a plaster or poultice for use on sore shins **2.** a piece of paper money made almost worthless, as by inflation or inadequate security **3.** formerly, a piece of paper money of small face value, usually less than a dollar, esp. one issued by some private banks or the U.S. government, as between 1862 and 1878

Shin·to (shin′tō) *n.* [Jap. < Chin. *shin*, god, spirit + *tao*, way, law] a principal religion of Japan, with emphasis upon the worship of nature and of ancestors and ancient heroes and upon the divinity of the emperor: prior to 1945, the state religion —**Shin′to·ism** *n.* —**Shin′to·ist** *n., adj.* —**Shin′to·is′tic** *adj.*

shin·y (shin′ē) *adj.* **shin′i·er, shin′i·est 1.** full of, or re-flecting, light; bright; shining **2.** highly polished; glossy **3.** worn or rubbed smooth, and having a glossy finish

ship (ship) *n.* [ME. < OE. *scip*, akin to G. *schiff*, ON. *skip* < IE. *skeib-* < base *skei-*, to cut, separate (whence L. *scindere*, to cut): basic sense "hollowed-out tree trunk"] **1.** any vessel of considerable size navigating deep water; esp., one powered by an engine and larger than a boat **2.** a sailing vessel with a bowsprit and at least three square-rigged masts, each composed of lower, top, and topgallant members **3.** a ship's officers and crew **4.** an aircraft —*vt.* **shipped, ship′ping 1.** to put or take on board a ship ☆**2.** to send or transport by any carrier [to *ship* cattle by rail] **3.** to take in (water) over the gunwale or side, as in a heavy sea **4.** to put or fix (an object) in its proper place on a ship or boat [*ship* the oars] **5.** to engage (a person or persons) for work on a ship **6.** [Colloq.] to send (*away, out,* etc.); get rid of —*vi.* **1.** to go aboard ship; embark **2.** to engage to serve on a ship **3.** to travel by ship —**ship over** to enlist or reenlist in the U.S. Navy —**when** (or **if,** etc.) **one's ship comes in** (or **home**) when (or if, etc.) one's fortune is made, or one becomes rich

-ship (ship) [ME. < OE. *-scipe* (akin to *-schaft*, Du. *-scap*) < base of *scieppan*, to create: see SHAPE] a *n.-forming suffix meaning:* **1.** the quality, condition, or state of [*fellowship, friendship*] **2.** a) the rank or office of [*kingship, governorship*] b) a person having the rank or status of [*lordship*] **3.** ability or skill as [*penmanship, leadership*] **4.** all individuals (of the specified class) collectively [*readership*]

ship biscuit *same as* HARDTACK

ship·board (ship′bôrd′) *n.* **1.** a ship: chiefly in **on ship-board,** aboard a ship **2.** [Obs.] the side of a ship —*adj.* done, happening, used, etc. on a ship [a *shipboard* romance]

ship·build·er (-bil′dər) *n.* a person whose business is the designing and building of ships —**ship′build′ing** *n.*

☆**ship canal** a canal large enough for seagoing ships

ship chandler a person who deals in ship supplies

ship·fit·ter (-fit′ər) *n.* **1.** a person whose work is to lay out,

fabricate, and position plates, bulkheads, etc. inside the hull of a ship in readiness for riveting or welding ☆**2.** *U.S. Navy* a petty officer who maintains metal fittings

ship·lap (-lap′) *n.* **1.** a kind of boarding or siding in which adjoining boards are rabbeted along the edge so as to make a flush joint **2.** such a joint

ship·load (-lōd′) *n.,* a full load for a ship; cargo

ship·man (-mən) *n., pl.* **-men** *archaic var. of:* **1.** SEAMAN (sense 1) **2.** SHIPMASTER

ship·mas·ter (-mas′tər, -mäs′-) *n.* the officer in command of a merchant ship; captain

ship·mate (-māt′) *n.* a fellow sailor on the same ship

ship·ment (-mənt) *n.* **1.** the shipping or transporting of goods **2.** goods shipped or consigned

ship money a former tax levied on English ports, maritime counties, etc. to provide money for warships

ship of the line formerly, a warship of the largest class, having a position in the line of battle

ship·own·er (-ō′nər) *n.* an owner of a ship or ships

ship·pa·ble (-ə b'l) *adj.* that can be shipped

ship·per (-ər) *n.* a person or agent who ships goods

ship·ping (-iŋ) *n.* **1.** the act or business of sending or transporting goods **2.** ships collectively, as of a nation, port, etc., esp. with reference to tonnage

shipping clerk an employee who supervises workers in packing and shipping merchandise and keeps records of shipments

shipping room a room or department, as in a factory, from which goods are taken by a carrier for shipment

ship-rigged (-rigd′) *adj.* rigged as a ship, with three or more masts and square sails; full-rigged

ship's boy *same as* CABIN BOY

ship·shape (-shāp′) *adj.* having everything neatly in place, as on board ship; trim —*adv.* in a neat and orderly manner

ship·side (-sīd′) *n.* the area on a dock or pier alongside a ship

ship's papers all the documents that a merchant ship must carry to meet the requirements of port authorities, international law, etc.

ship·way (ship′wā′) *n.* **1.** the supporting structure or track on which a ship is built and from which it is launched **2.** *same as* SHIP CANAL

ship·worm (-wurm′) *n.* any of a number of small, marine, bivalve mollusks (esp. genera *Teredo* and *Bankia*), with wormlike bodies: they burrow into and damage sub-merged wood, as of ships, pilings, etc.

ship·wreck (-rek′) *n.* **1.** the remains of a wrecked ship; wreckage **2.** the loss or destruction of a ship through storm, collision, going aground, etc. **3.** any ruin, failure, or destruction —*vt.* **1.** to cause to undergo shipwreck **2.** to destroy, ruin, or wreck

ship·wright (-rīt′) *n.* a man, esp. a carpenter, whose work is the construction and repair of ships

ship·yard (-yärd′) *n.* a place where ships are built and repaired

Shi·raz (shē räz′) city in SC Iran: pop. 230,000

Shi·re (shē′rē) river in SE Africa, flowing from Lake Nyasa south into the Zambezi: c. 250 mi.

shire (shīr) *n.* [ME. < OE. *scir*, office, charge, akin to OHG. *scīra*, official charge] **1.** any of the former districts or regions in Great Britain coinciding generally with the modern county **2.** any of the counties of Great Britain with a name ending in *-shire* —**the Shires** the Midland counties of England

shire horse any of a breed of large, powerful draft horses, orig. raised in the Shires

shirk (shurk) *vt.* [? akin to G. *schurke*, scoundrel, rascal] to neglect or evade doing (something that should be done) —*vi.* to neglect or evade work, duty, an obligation, etc. —**shirk′er** *n.*

Shir·ley (shur′lē) [orig. a surname < the place name *Shirley* (England) < OE. *scire*, SHIRE + *leah*, meadow, LEA¹: hence lea where the shire moot was held] **1.** a feminine name: dim. *Shirl* **2.** James, 1596–1666; Eng. dramatist

☆**shirr** (shur) *n.* [< ?] *same as* SHIRRING —*vt.* **1.** to make shirring in (cloth or a garment) **2.** to bake (eggs) with crumbs in small buttered dishes

☆**shirr·ing** (-iŋ) *n.* **1.** a gathering made in cloth by drawing the material up on parallel rows of short, running stitches **2.** any trim made by shirring

shirt (shurt) *n.* [ME. < OE. *scyrte* (akin to G. *schürze*, apron, ON. *skyrta*, shirt) < base of *scort*, SHORT] **1.** *a)* the usual sleeved garment worn by men on the upper part of the body, often under a coat or jacket, typically having a collar and a buttoned opening down the front *b)* a similar garment for women **2.** *same as* UNDERSHIRT —**in one's shirt sleeves** not wearing a coat or jacket over one's shirt —☆**keep one's shirt on** [Slang] to remain patient or calm —**lose one's shirt** [Slang] to lose all that one has

shirt·ing (-iŋ) *n.* material used in making shirts

shirt-sleeve (-slēv′) ☆*adj.* **1.** in, or suitable for being in, one's shirt sleeves **2.** simple, plain, or direct **3.** homespun; unpolished [*shirt-sleeve* philosophy]

☆**shirt·tail** (shurt′tāl′) *n.* the part of a shirt extending below the waist —☆*adj.* [Colloq.] being only distantly related [a *shirttail* cousin]

☆**shirt·waist** (-wāst′) *n.* **1.** a woman's blouse tailored more or less like a shirt **2.** a dress with a bodice like a shirtwaist: also **shirtwaist dress, shirt′dress′** *n.*

shirt·y (shur'tē) *adj.* **shirt'i·er, shirt'i·est** [< SHIRT (in phr. *to have one's shirt out,* to make or become angry) + -Y³] [Chiefly Brit. Slang] ill-tempered, cross, angry, etc.

shish ke·bab (shish' kə bäb') [Arm. *shish kabab,* ult. < Ar. *shīsh,* skewer + *kabāb,* kebab] a dish consisting of small chunks of meat, esp. lamb, placed on skewers alternately with tomatoes, onions, green peppers, etc., and broiled: also **shish' ka·bob'**

shit·tah (shit'ə) *n., pl.* **shit'tahs, shit'tim** (-im) [Heb. *shiṭṭāh,* pl. *shiṭṭīm*] a tree mentioned in the Bible, now generally identified as an Asiatic acacia (*Acacia seyal* or *Acacia iortils*), with closegrained, yellowish-brown wood

shit·tim (wood) (shit'im) [Heb., see prec.] **1.** the wood of the shittah, used in making the ark of the covenant and parts of the Jewish tabernacle: Ex. 25:10, 13, 23, etc. ☆**2.** a small tree or shrub (*Bumelia lanuginosa*) of the sapote family, growing in the S U.S.

shiv (shiv) *n.* [earlier *chiv,* prob. < Romany *chiv,* a blade] [Slang] a knife, esp. one with a narrow blade used as a weapon

Shi·va (shē'və) *var.* of SIVA

shiv·a·ree (shiv'ə rē', shiv'ə rē') *n.* [altered < CHARIVARI] a noisy demonstration or celebration; esp., a mock serenade with kettles, horns, etc. to a couple on their wedding night; charivari —*vt.* **-reed', -ree'ing** to serenade with a shivaree

shive (shīv) *n.* [ME. *schive* < OE. *scife,* akin to G. *scheibe,* a disk, slice < IE. *skeip-* < base *skei-,* to cut: cf. SHIP] **1.** a splinter or fragment, as of flax husk **2.** a broad, shallow cork, as for a wide-mouthed bottle

shiv·er¹ (shiv'ər) *n.* [ME. *schivere,* freq. formation < base of prec.] a fragment or splinter of something broken, as glass —*vt., vi.* [ME. *schiveren*] to break into many fragments or splinters; shatter

shiv·er² (shiv'ər) *vi.* [ME. *sheveren,* altered < *cheveren,* altered < ? *chivelen* in same sense < OE. *ceafl,* a jaw (cf. JOWL¹): prob. basic sense "to have chattering teeth"] to shake, quiver, or tremble, as from fear or cold —*vt.* to cause (a sail) to flutter by turning the edge to the wind —*n.* a shaking, quivering, or trembling, as from fear or cold —SYN. see SHAKE —**the shivers** a fit of shivering

shiv·er·y¹ (shiv'ər ē) *adj.* easily broken into shivers, or fragments; brittle

shiv·er·y² (shiv'ər ē) *adj.* **1.** shivering or inclined to shiver; suffering from cold, fear, etc. **2.** causing or likely to cause shivering; chilling; terrifying

Shi·zu·o·ka (shē'zo͞o ō'kä) city on the S coast of Honshu, Japan: pop. 368,000

Shko·dër (shko͝o'dər) city in N Albania: pop. 46,000

☆**shlep, shlepp** (shlep) *n., vt., vi.* **shlepped, shlep'ping** [Slang] *var.* of SCHLEP

☆**shmaltz** (shmälts) *n.* [Slang] *var.* of SCHMALTZ —**shmaltz'y** *adj.* **shmaltz'i·er, shmaltz'i·est**

☆**shmuck** (shmuk) *n.* [Slang] *var.* of SCHMUCK

☆**shnook** (shno͝ok) *n.* [Slang] *var.* of SCHNOOK

shoal¹ (shōl) *n.* [via dial. < OE. *scolu,* a multitude, school of fish, akin to Du. *school* < IE. base *skēl-* < base *(s)kel,* to cut: cf. SHIELD] **1.** a large group; mass; crowd **2.** a large school of fish —*vi.* to come together in or move about as a shoal or school

shoal² (shōl) *n.* [< earlier *shoal, adj.,* shallow < ME. *scholde* < OE. *sceald,* shallow: for IE. base see SHALLOW] **1.** a shallow place in a river, sea, etc.; a shallow **2.** a sand bar or piece of rising ground forming a shallow place that is a danger to navigation, esp. one visible at low water —*vi.* to become shallow —*vt.* **1.** to make shallow **2.** to sail into a shallow or shallower part of (water) —**shoal'y** *adj.* **shoal'i·er, shoal'i·est**

SYN.—**shoal** applies to any place in a sea, river, etc. where the water is shallow and difficult to navigate; **bank,** in this connection, applies to a shallow place, formed by an elevated shelf of ground, that is deep enough to be safely navigated by lighter vessels; a **reef** is a ridge of rock, coral, etc. lying at or very close to the surface of the sea, just offshore; **bar** applies to a ridge of sand, etc. silted up across the mouth of a river or harbor and hindering navigation

shoat (shōt) *n.* [ME. *schote,* akin to WFl. *schote* < ?] a young hog of between about 100 and 180 lbs.

shock¹ (shäk) *n.* [Fr. *choc* < *choquer:* see the *v.*] **1.** the impact of persons, forces, etc. in combat or collision **2.** *a)* a sudden, powerful concussion; violent blow, shake, or jar [the *shock* of an earthquake] *b)* the result or effect of such concussion **3.** *a)* any sudden disturbance or agitation of the mind or emotions, as through great loss or surprise *b)* something causing this **4.** an extreme stimulation of the nerves, muscles, etc. accompanying the passage of electric current through the body **5.** [Colloq.] *clipped form of* SHOCK ABSORBER: used in pl. **6.** Med. a disorder resulting from ineffective circulation of the blood, produced by hemorrhage, severe infection, disturbance of heart function, etc., and characterized by a marked decrease in blood pressure, rapid pulse, decreased kidney function, etc. —*vt.* [MFr. *choquer,* prob. < MDu. *schokken,* to collide < IE. base *skeug,* to push, shoot, var. of *skeub-,* SHOVE] **1.** to disturb the mind or emotions of; affect with great surprise, distress, disgust, etc. **2.** to affect with physical shock **3.** to produce electrical shock in (a body) —*vi.* **1.** [Archaic or Poet.] to come together violently; collide **2.** to be shocked, distressed, disgusted, etc. [one who does not *shock* easily]

SYN.—**shock** suggests the violent impact on the mind or emotions of an unexpected, overwhelming event that comes as a blow [*shocked* by her sudden death]; **startle** implies a shock of surprise or fright of a kind that often causes one to literally jump or shrink [*startled* by the clap of thunder]; **paralyze** implies such extreme shock as to make one temporarily unable to move, escape, etc. [*paralyzed* with fear]; to **stun** is to shock with such impact as to stupefy or daze [*stunned* by the disaster]

shock² (shäk) *n.* [ME. *schokke,* prob. via MDu. or MLowG. *schok* < IE. *(s)keug-* < base *keu-,* to bend, arch, whence Russ. *kúča,* a pile, HEAP: basic sense "rounded heap"] a number of grain sheaves, as of corn or wheat, stacked together on end to cure and dry —*vt., vi.* to gather and pile in shocks

shock³ (shäk) *n.* [< ? prec.] a thick, bushy or tangled mass, as of hair —*adj.* bushy or shaggy, as hair

SHOCKS OF CORN

shock absorber a device, as on the springs of a car, that lessens the effect or absorbs the force of shocks and jarring

shock·er (shäk'ər) *n.* **1.** a person or thing that shocks **2.** a sensational story, play, etc.

shock·head·ed (-hed'id) *adj.* having a thick, bushy head of hair: also **shock'head'**

shock·ing (-in) *adj.* **1.** having an effect like that of a heavy blow or shock; staggering [the *shocking* news of his death] **2.** *a)* highly offensive to good taste, propriety, etc.; extremely revolting *b)* very bad —**shock'ing·ly** *adv.*

☆**shock·proof** (-pro͞of') *adj.* able to absorb shock without being damaged [a *shockproof* watch]

shock therapy a method of treating certain psychotic conditions by injecting such drugs as insulin or Metrazol or by applying electric current to the brain, which results in convulsion or coma: also **shock treatment**

shock troops troops especially chosen, trained, and equipped to lead an attack

shock wave *Physics* **1.** a surface of discontinuity in a flow of air, sound, etc. set up when the flow suddenly changes from subsonic to supersonic, characterized by marked increases in temperature, pressure, and density of the flow, as in a supersonic flow about an airplane wing **2.** same as BLAST (*n.* 6 c)

shod (shäd) *pt. & pp.* of SHOE

shod·den (shäd'n) *alt. pp.* of SHOE

shod·dy (shäd'ē) *n., pl.* **shod'dies** [19th c. < ?] **1.** *a)* an inferior woolen yarn made from fibers taken from used fabrics and reprocessed *b)* cheap woolen cloth made from this **2.** anything of less worth or quality than it seems to have; esp., an inferior imitation —*adj.* **shod'di·er, shod'di·est 1.** *a)* made of shoddy *b)* made of any cheap, inferior material *c)* poorly done or made **2.** pretentious, but cheap, vulgar, or counterfeit; sham [*shoddy* gentility] **3.** contemptible; mean; low [a *shoddy* trick] —**shod'di·ly** *adv.* —**shod'di·ness** *n.*

shoe (sho͞o) *n.* [ME. *sho* < OE. *sceoh,* akin to G. *schuh* < IE. base *(s)keu-,* to cover, whence SKY, HIDE¹] **1.** an outer covering for the human foot, made of leather, canvas, etc. and usually having a stiff or thick sole and a heel: sometimes restricted to footwear that does not cover the ankle, as distinguished from a BOOT¹ **2.** *shortened form of* HORSE-SHOE **3.** something like a shoe in shape or use; specif., *a)* a metal cap or ferrule fitted over the end of a cane, pole, staff, etc. *b) shortened form of* BRAKE SHOE *c)* a part forming a base for the supports of a superstructure, as a roof, bridge, etc. *d)* the metal strip along the bottom of a sled runner *e)* the casing of a pneumatic tire *f)* the sliding contact plate by which an electric train picks up current from the third rail *g)* a metal protecting plate upon which a mechanical part moves —*vt.* **shod or shoed, shod or shoed or shod'den, shoe'ing 1.** to furnish or fit with a shoe or shoes **2.** to cover, tip, or sheathe (a stick, wearing surface, etc.) with a metal plate, ferrule, etc. —**fill one's shoes** to take one's place —**in another's shoes** in another's position —☆**the shoe is on the other foot** the situation is reversed for the persons involved —**where the shoe pinches** the source of trouble, grief, difficulty, etc.

shoe·bill (-bil') *n.* a large wading bird (*Balaeniceps rex*) of the heron family, with long legs and a heavy shoelike bill: found along the White Nile in C Africa

shoe·black (-blak') *n.* same as BOOTBLACK

shoe·horn (-hôrn') *n.* an implement of metal, horn, plastic, etc. with a troughlike blade, inserted at the back of a shoe to aid in slipping the heel in —*vt.* to force or squeeze into a narrow space

shoe·lace (-lās') *n.* a length of cord, leather, etc. used for lacing and fastening a shoe

shoe·mak·er (-māk'ər) *n.* a person whose business is making or repairing shoes —**shoe'mak'ing** *n.*

☆**shoe·pac** (-pak') *n.* [altered by folk etym. (after SHOE &

PAC] < AmInd. (Delaware) *shipak*, contr. < *machtshipak* < *machtschi*, bad + *paku*, shoe] *same as* PAC (sense 2)

sho·er (shōō′ər) *n.* a person who shoes horses

shoe·shine (-shīn′) *n.* **1.** the cleaning and polishing of a pair of shoes **2.** the shiny surface of polished shoes

shoe·string (-striŋ′) *n.* **1.** *same as* SHOELACE ☆**2.** a small or barely adequate amount of capital [a business started on a *shoestring*] —☆*adj.* at, near, or around the ankles [a *shoestring* catch of a ball, a *shoestring* tackle]

☆**shoestring potatoes** potatoes cut into long, narrow strips and fried crisp in deep fat

shoe tree a form, as of wood or metal, inserted in a shoe to stretch it or preserve its shape

sho·far (shō′fər; *Heb.* shô fär′) *n., pl.* **-fars**; *Heb.* **-frot′** (-frōt′) [Heb. *shōphār*] a ram's horn used in ancient times as a signaling trumpet, and still blown in synagogues on Rosh Hashana and at the end of Yom Kippur

sho·gun (shō′gun′, -gōōn′) *n.* [Jap. < Chin. *chiang-chun*, leader of an army] any of the military governors of Japan who, until 1868, constituted a quasi-dynasty exercising absolute rule and relegating the emperors to a nominal position —**sho′gun·ate** (-it, -ga nāt′) *n.*

SHOFAR

sho·ji (shō′jē) *n., pl.* **sho′ji, -jis** [Jap. *shōji*] **1.** a translucent sliding panel of rice paper on a wooden frame, used in Japanese homes as a partition or door **2.** any panel, screen, etc. like this Also **shoji screen**

Sho·la·pur (shō′lə poor′) city in Maharashtra state, W India: pop. 338,000

Sho·lo·khov (shô′lô khôf′), **Mi·kha·il** (Aleksandrovich) (mi khä ēl′) 1905- ; Russ. novelist

sho·lom (shä lōm′) *n., interj. var. of* SHALOM

Sho·lom A·leich·em (shô′ləm ä läkh′em) (pseud. of *Solomon Rabinowitz*) 1859-1916; Russ. writer (also in the U.S.) of humorous stories, dramas, etc. in Yiddish

Sho·na (shō′nä) *n.* **1.** *pl.* **Sho′nas, Sho′na** any member of an agricultural people living in Rhodesia and adjacent Mozambique **2.** their Bantu language

shone (shōn) *alt. pt. & pp. of* SHINE

shoo (shōō) *interj.* [echoic] **1.** an exclamation used in driving away chickens and other animals **2.** go away! get out! —*vi.* **shooed, shoo′ing** to cry "shoo" —*vt.* to drive away abruptly, by or as by crying "shoo"

☆**shoo·fly** (shōō′flī′) *n.* **1.** [< phr. *shoo, fly, don't bother me*, in a Civil War nonsense song] orig., a kind of shuffling dance **2.** a child's rocker with a seat mounted between supports typically designed in the form of horses, swans, etc. **3.** [said to be so named from attracting flies which must be shooed away] an open pie with a filling of molasses and brown sugar: in full **shoofly pie**

☆**shoo-in** (shōō′in′) *n.* [SHOO + -IN¹] [Colloq.] someone or something expected to win easily in an election, a race, etc.

shook¹ (shook) *n.* [prob. var. of SHOCK²] ☆**1.** a set of the pieces used in assembling a single box, barrel, cask, etc. **2.** a shock of grain sheaves

shook² (shook) *pt. and dial. pp. of* SHAKE —☆**shook up** [Slang] upset; disturbed; agitated

shoon (shōōn) *n. archaic or dial. pl. of* SHOE

shoot (shōōt) *vt.* **shot, shoot′ing** [ME. *shoten* < OE. *sceotan*, akin to ON. *skjōta*, G. *schiessen* < IE. base *(s)keud-*, to throw, shoot, whence OBulg. *is-kydati*, to throw out: cf. SHUT] **1.** *a)* to move swiftly over, by, across, etc. [to *shoot* the rapids in a canoe] *b)* to make move with great speed or sudden force [to *shoot* an elevator upward] **2.** to pour, empty out, or dump, as down a chute **3.** *a)* to throw or hurl out or forth [volcanoes *shooting* molten rock into the air] *b)* to cast (an anchor, fish net, etc.) ☆*c)* to throw away or spoil (an opportunity, chance, etc.) *d)* [Colloq.] to use up or waste (time, money, etc.) **4.** to slide (a door bolt) into or out of its fastening **5.** *a)* to variegate, streak, fleck, etc. (with another color or substance) [a blue sky *shot* with white clouds] *b)* to vary (with something different) [a story *shot* with humor] **6.** *a)* to thrust out suddenly [snakes *shooting* out their tongues] *b)* to put forth (a branch, leaves, etc.) **7.** *a)* to send forth (a missile or projectile); discharge or fire (a bullet, arrow, etc.) *b)* to discharge or emit (rays) with force **8.** to send forth (a question, reply, glance, fist, etc.) swiftly, dartingly, or with force or feeling **9.** *a)* to discharge or fire (a gun, bow, charge of explosive, etc.) *b)* to hit, wound, kill, or destroy with a bullet, arrow, etc. **10.** to hunt game in or on (a tract of land) **11.** to take the altitude of (a star) with a transit, sextant, etc. **12.** *a)* to take a picture of with a camera; photograph; film *b)* to photograph (a motion picture) **13.** to inject, as with drugs **14.** to plane (the edge of a board) straight ☆**15.** [Slang] to send, hand, or give in a swift or hasty way **16.** *Games, Sports a)* to throw, drive, or propel (a ball, marble, etc.) toward the objective ☆*b)* to roll (dice) *c)* to make or score (a goal, points, total strokes, etc.) *d)* to play (golf, pool, craps, etc.) *e)* to play a round of golf on (a particular course) *f)* to make (a specified bet), as in craps —*vi.* **1.** *a)* to move swiftly, as an arrow from a bow; rush; dart *b)* to spurt or gush, as water from a hose 2. to be felt suddenly and keenly, as heat, pain, etc. **3.** to grow or sprout, esp. rapidly **4.** to jut out; project **5.** to send forth a missile or pro-

jectile; discharge bullets, arrows, etc.; go off; fire **6.** *a)* to use guns, bows and arrows, etc., as in hunting *b)* to have skill in using a gun, etc. ☆**7.** *a)* to photograph a scene or subject *b)* to start the cameras working in photographing a scene or movie **8.** *Sports a)* to propel a ball, etc. toward the objective *b)* to roll dice —*n.* **1.** *a)* the act of shooting *b)* a shooting trip, party, or contest [a turkey *shoot*] *c)* a round of shots in a shooting contest **2.** the action of growing or sprouting **3.** a new growth; sprout or twig **4.** action or motion like that of something shot, as of water from a hose **5.** the launching of a rocket, guided missile, etc. ☆**6.** a sloping trough or channel; chute **7.** a body of ore in a vein, usually elongated and vertical or steeply inclined **8.** a twinge or spasm of pain **9.** *Rowing* the interval between strokes —*interj.* **1.** an exclamation expressing disgust, disappointment, etc. **2.** begin talking! start telling me! —**shoot at** (or **for**) [Colloq.] to try to reach, gain, or accomplish; strive for —**shoot down** to bring down by hitting with a shot or shots —**shoot from the hip** to act or talk in a rash, impetuous way —☆**shoot off one's** (or **at the**) **mouth** [Slang] **1.** to speak without caution or discretion; blab **2.** to boast; brag —**shoot up 1.** to grow or rise rapidly **2.** to hit with several or many shots ☆**3.** [Colloq.] to spread terror and destruction throughout by lawless and wanton shooting —**shoot′er** *n.*

shooting box (or **lodge**) [Chiefly Brit.] a small house or lodge used by hunters during the shooting season

shooting gallery a place, as at an amusement park, for practice shooting at enclosed targets

☆**shooting iron** [Slang] any firearm

☆**shooting script** the final version of a movie or television script as it is to be filmed or taped

shooting star 1. *same as* METEOR ☆**2.** any of a genus (*Dodecatheon*) of N. American plants of the primrose family, with clusters of flowers whose petals are turned back

shooting stick a canelike stick with a spike at one end and a narrow, folding seat at the top for resting on

☆**shoot-the-chute** (shōōt′thə shōōt′) *n. same as* CHUTE-THE-CHUTE

shop (shäp) *n.* [ME. *schoppe* < OE. *sceoppa*, booth, stall, akin to G. *schopf*, porch < IE. base *(s)keup-*, a bundle, sheaf of straw: prob. basic meaning "roof made of straw thatch"] **1.** *a)* a place where certain goods or services are offered for sale; esp., a small store *b)* a specialized department in a large store [the gourmet *shop*] **2.** a place where a particular kind of work is done [a printing *shop*] ☆**3.** in some schools, a manual-training course, class, or department —*vi.* **shopped, shop′ping** to visit a shop or shops so as to look at and buy or price things for sale —*vt.* ☆**1.** [Colloq.] to shop at (a specified store) or for (a specified article or service) **2.** [Brit. Slang] *a)* to inform on, esp. to the police *b)* to arrest or imprison —**set up shop** to open or start a business —☆**shop around 1.** to go from shop to shop, looking for bargains or special items **2.** to search about for a good or better job, idea, etc. —**shut up shop 1.** to close a place of business, as for the night **2.** to go out of business —**talk shop** to discuss one's work or things related to one's work

shop·girl (-gurl′) *n.* [Brit.] *same as* SALESWOMAN

sho·phar (shō′fər; *Heb.* shô fär′) *n. var. of* SHOFAR

shop·keep·er (shäp′kē′pər) *n.* a person who owns or operates a shop, or small store —**shop′keep′ing** *n.*

shop·lift·er (-lif′tər) *n.* a person who steals articles from a store during shopping hours —**shop′lift′** *vt., vi.*

shop·man (-mən) *n., pl.* **-men** (-mən) [Brit.] *same as* SALESCLERK

shoppe (shäp) *n. var. of* SHOP (sense 1): early sp. used faddishly esp. in the names of such shops

shop·per (-ər) *n.* **1.** a person who shops **2.** a person hired by a store to shop for others **3.** a person hired by a store to compare competitors' merchandise and prices ☆**4.** a handbill containing advertisements of local stores

shopping center a complex of stores, restaurants, etc. grouped together and having a common parking area

shop steward a person elected by his fellow workers in a union shop to represent them in dealing with the employer

shop·talk (shäp′tôk′) *n.* **1.** the specialized or technical vocabulary and idioms of those in the same work, profession, etc.: see SLANG¹ **2.** conversation about one's work or business, esp. after hours

shop·walk·er (-wôk′ər) *n.* [Brit.] *same as* FLOORWALKER

shop·worn (-wôrn′) *adj.* **1.** soiled, faded, etc. from having been displayed in a shop **2.** no longer fresh, interesting, or attractive; drab, dull, trite, etc.

☆**Shor·an** (shôr′an) *n.* [*Sho(rt) Ra(nge) N(avigation)*] [also **s-**] a radar system for fixing the position of a plane or guided missile by the answering signals sent from a pair of precisely located transponders on the ground

shore¹ (shôr) *n.* [ME. *schore* < OE. *score* (akin to MLowG. *schore*) < or akin to *scorian*, to jut out < IE. base *(s)ker-*, to cut: cf. SHEAR] **1.** land at or near the edge of a body of water, esp. along an ocean, large lake, etc. **2.** land as opposed to water **3.** *Law same as* SEASHORE
SYN.—shore is the general word applied to an edge of land directly bordering on the sea, a lake, a river, etc.; **coast** applies only to land along the sea; **beach** applies to a level stretch of sandy or pebbly seashore or lake shore, usually one that is washed by high water; **strand** is a poetic word for **shore** or **beach**; **bank** applies to the rising or steep land at the edge of a stream

shore[2] (shôr) *n.* [ME. *schore,* akin to MDu. *schore,* OIce. *skortha,* a prop, stay: for IE. base see prec.] a prop, as a beam, placed under or against something for support or stability; specif., any of the timbers used to support a boat or ship that is out of water —*vt.* **shored, shor·ing** to support or make stable with or as if with a shore or shores; prop (usually with *up*)

shore[3] (shôr) *archaic or dial. pt. & pp.* of SHEAR

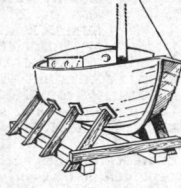

SHORES

shore bird any of a number of birds that feed or nest on the shores of the oceans, rivers, etc., as the curlews, snipes, sandpipers, ruffs, etc.

☆**shore dinner** a meal with a variety of seafood dishes

shore leave leave granted to a ship's crew for going ashore

shore·less (-lis) *adj.* having no shore; boundless

shore·line (-līn′) *n.* the edge of a body of water

☆**shore patrol** a detail of the U.S. Navy, Coast Guard, or Marine Corps acting as military police on shore

shore·ward (shôr′wərd) *adv.* toward the shore: also **shore′wards** —*adj.* moving toward the shore

shor·ing (shôr′iŋ) *n.* **1.** the act of supporting with or as with shores **2.** a system of shores used for support

shorn (shôrn) *alt. pp.* of SHEAR

short (shôrt) *adj.* [ME. < OE. *scort,* akin to ON. *skort,* short piece of clothing, OHG. *scurz,* short < IE. *(s)kerd- < base *(s)ker-,* to cut, SHEAR] **1.** not extending far from end to end; not long or not long enough **2.** not great in span, range, or scope [a *short* distance, journey, throw, view, etc.] **3.** low or relatively low in height; not tall **4.** *a)* lasting but a little time; brief *b)* passing quickly [a few *short* weeks] **5.** not retentive for long [a *short* memory] **6.** condensed or concise, as a literary style, story, speech, etc. **7.** brief or abrupt to the point of rudeness; curt **8.** quickly angered or irked **9.** less than or lacking a sufficient or correct amount, amount of time, etc. [a *short* measure, *short* on money, *short* notice] **10.** not far enough to reach the mark, objective, etc. [the shot fell *short*] **11.** having a tendency to break or crumble; friable; specif., *a)* crisp or flaky, as pastry made from dough rich in shortening *b)* brittle and inductile when cold (**cold short**) or hot (**hot short**): said of metal ☆**12.** *a)* not having in possession at the time of sale the commodity or security one is selling in anticipation of a decline in price *b)* designating or of a sale of commodities or securities not in the possession of the seller See also SHORT SALE **13.** *a)* requiring a relatively short time to pronounce: said of syllables in quantitative verse *b)* unstressed: said of syllables in accentual verse **14.** *Phonet. a)* held for a relatively short time: said of a speech sound *b)* popularly, having the quality determined by its relative front position as compared with other vowel variants —*n.* **1.** something that is short; specif., *a)* a short sound or syllable contrasted with one that is long *b)* *same as* SHORT SUBJECT *c)* a fish or lobster below the size that may be legally taken *d)* a shot that falls short of the target or objective **2.** a variation of clothing size shorter than the average for that size **3.** [*pl.*] *a)* formerly, knee breeches *b)* short, loose trousers reaching part way to the knee, worn in sports, etc. ☆*c)* a man's undergarment of similar form **4.** [*pl.*] items needed to make up a shortage or deficiency **5.** [*pl.*] a byproduct of wheat milling that consists of bran, germ, and coarse meal **6.** [*pl.*] trimmings, clippings, etc. left over in the manufacture of various products **7.** *clipped form of:* ☆*a)* SHORTSTOP *b)* SHORT CIRCUIT —*adv.* **1.** abruptly; suddenly **2.** rudely; curtly **3.** briefly; concisely **4.** so as to be short in length **5.** by surprise; unawares [caught *short*] **6.** by a short sale —*vt., vi.* **1.** to give less than what is needed, wanted, or usual **2.** *clipped form of:* *a)* SHORT-CHANGE *b)* SHORT-CIRCUIT —*SYN.* see BRIEF —**fall** (or **come**) **short 1.** to be lacking or insufficient **2.** to fail to reach a given mark, objective, etc. —**for short** by way of abbreviation or contraction —**in short 1.** in summing up; to summarize **2.** in a few words; briefly —**run short** to have or be less than enough —**short and sweet** agreeably or expeditiously brief —**short for** being a shortened form of, or an abbreviation or nickname for —**short of 1.** not equaling; less than **2.** without a sufficient or correct amount of; lacking **3.** not far enough to reach (the mark, objective, etc.) **4.** without actually resorting to —**the short end of the stick** the worst of a deal —**short′ness** *n.*

☆**short·age** (-ij) *n.* a deficiency in the quantity or amount needed or expected, or the extent of this; deficit

short·bread (-bred′) *n.* a rich, crumbly cake or cookie made with much shortening

short·cake (-kāk′) *n.* **1.** a crisp, light biscuit served with fruit, whipped cream, etc. as a dessert **2.** any sweet cake, as spongecake, served in this way **3.** a dessert made with either of these [strawberry *shortcake*]

☆**short·change** (-chānj′) *vt., vi.* **-changed′, -chang′ing** [Colloq.] **1.** to give less money than is due in change **2.** to cheat by depriving of something due —**short′chang′er** *n.*

short-cir·cuit (-sur′kit) *vt.* **1.** *Elec.* to make a short circuit in **2.** to bypass (an obstruction, custom, etc.) **3.** to cause a sudden break in; impede; thwart —*vi.* to develop a short circuit

short circuit 1. a usually accidental low-resistance connection between two points in an electric circuit resulting in a side circuit that deflects most of the circuit current from desired paths or in excessive current flow that often causes damage **2.** popularly, a disrupted electric circuit resulting from this

short·com·ing (-kum′iŋ) *n.* a falling short of what is expected or required; defect or deficiency

☆**short covering** the buying of securities or commodities to close out a short sale

short·cut (-kut′) *n.* **1.** a shorter way to get to the same place **2.** any way of saving time, effort, expense, etc.

short-day (-dā′) *adj. Bot.* maturing and blooming under short periods of light and long periods of darkness

short division the process of dividing a number by another, ordinarily a single digit, without putting down the steps of the process in full

short·en (shôrt′'n) *vt.* **1.** to make short or shorter; reduce in length, amount, or extent **2.** to furl or reef (a sail) so that less canvas is exposed to the breeze **3.** to add shortening in making (pastry, etc.) for crispness or flakiness —*vi.* to become short or shorter

SYN.—**shorten** implies reduction in length, extent, or duration [to *shorten* a rope, a visit, one's life, etc.]; **curtail** implies a making shorter than was originally intended, as because of necessity or expediency [expenditures *curtailed* because of a reduced income]; **abridge** implies reduction in compass by condensing, omitting parts, etc. but usually connotes that what is essential is kept [to *abridge* a dictionary]; **abbreviate** usually refers to the shortening of a word or phrase by contraction or by substitution of a symbol, but also has extended, sometimes jocular applications [an *abbreviated* costume]—*ANT.* **lengthen, extend**

short·en·ing (shôrt′'n iŋ, shôrt′niŋ) *n.* **1.** the act of making or becoming short or shorter **2.** edible fat, esp. as used to make pastry, etc. crisp or flaky

short·fall (-fôl′) *n.* the act or an instance of falling short, or the amount of the shortage

short·hand (-hand′) *n.* any system of speed writing using quickly made symbols to represent letters, words, and phrases —*adj.* using or written in shorthand

short-hand·ed (-han′did) *adj.* short of workers or helpers —**short′-hand′ed·ness** *n.*

short·head (shôrt′hed′) *n.* a brachycephalic person —**short′head′ed** *adj.* —**short′head′ed·ness** *n.*

short·horn (-hôrn′) *n.* any of a breed of cattle with short, curved horns, orig. from England: they are raised for both beef and milk and vary widely in color

☆**short-horned grasshopper** (-hôrnd′) any of a family (Acrididae) of grasshoppers with antennae much shorter than the body, including most common grasshoppers

☆**shor·ti·a** (shôr′tē ə) *n.* [ModL. *Shortia,* after C. W. Short (1794–1863), U.S. horticulturist] any of a genus (*Shortia*) of evergreen plants with nodding, bell-shaped, white flowers on long stalks; esp., an American species (*Shortia galacifolia*) native to the mountains of the Carolinas

short·ie (shôrt′ē) *n.* [Colloq.] *var.* of SHORTY

short·ish (-ish) *adj.* rather short

short-lived (-līvd′, -livd′) *adj.* [SHORT + -LIVED] having or tending to have a short life span or existence

short·ly (-lē) *adv.* **1.** in a few words; briefly **2.** in a short time; soon **3.** abruptly and rudely; curtly

short order any food that can be cooked or served quickly when ordered, as at a lunch counter —**short′-or′der** *adj.*

☆**short position 1.** the position of a person who sells securities or commodities short **2.** the total short sales in a particular commodity or in the market as a whole

short-range (shôrt′rānj′) *adj.* **1.** designating or of a gun, aircraft, missile, etc. that has only a relatively short range **2.** not looking far into the future [*short-range* plans]

short ribs the rib ends of beef from the forequarter

☆**short sale** a sale of securities or commodities which the seller does not yet have but expects to cover later at a lower price

short short story a story so short that it can usually be printed complete on one page of a magazine: characteristically it conveys a single mood, is concise, fast-moving, and has a surprise ending

short shrift 1. orig., a brief time granted a condemned person for religious confession and absolution before his execution **2.** very little care or attention, as from lack of patience or sympathy —**make short shrift of** to make short work of; dispose of quickly and impatiently

short-sight·ed (-sīt′id) *adj.* **1.** *same as* NEARSIGHTED **2.** having or showing a lack of foresight —**short′sight′ed·ly** *adv.* —**short′sight′ed·ness** *n.*

☆**short snort** [Slang] a quick drink of liquor

short-spo·ken (-spō′k'n) *adj.* **1.** using only a few words to express one's thoughts; laconic **2.** brief to the point of rudeness; curt

☆**short·stop** (-stäp′) *n. Baseball* the infielder stationed between second and third base

short story a kind of story varying widely in length but shorter than the novel or novelette: characteristically it develops a single central theme or impression and is limited in scope and number of characters

short subject any short presentation, as an animated cartoon or travelogue, shown along with the featured picture in a motion-picture program

short·tem·pered (-tem′pərd) *adj.* having a tendency to lose one's temper; easily or quickly angered

short-term (-turm′) *adj.* **1.** for or extending over a short time **2.** designating or of a capital gain, loan, etc. that involves a relatively short period

short ton a unit of weight, equal to 2,000 pounds avoirdupois: see TON

short-waist·ed (-wās′tid) *adj.* unusually short between shoulders and waistline; with a high waistline

short·wave (-wāv′) *n.* **1.** an electromagnetic wave that is shorter than those used in commercial broadcasting, usually a radio wave sixty meters or less in length **2.** a radio or radio band for broadcasting or receiving shortwaves: in full **shortwave radio**

short-wind·ed (-win′did) *adj.* **1.** easily put out of breath by exertion **2.** breathing with quick, labored breaths **3.** brief or concise; terse; succinct: said of speech or writing —**short′-wind′ed·ness** *n.*

short·y (-ē) *n., pl.* **short′ies** [Colloq.] a person or thing of less than average height or size

Sho·sho·ne¹ (shō shō′nē) *n.* [< ? Shoshonean *tsosoni*, curly head, in allusion to their hairdo] **1.** *pl.* **-sho′nes, -sho′ne** any member of a group of N. American Indians scattered over Idaho, Nevada, Utah, Wyoming, and California **2.** their Shoshonean language Also sp. **Sho·sho′ni**

Sho·sho·ne² (shō shō′nē) river in NW Wyo., flowing northeast into the Bighorn River: c. 100 mi.

Sho·sho·ne·an (shō shō′nē ən, shō′shə nē′ən) *adj.* designating or of a branch of the Uto-Aztecan language family, including Shoshone, Comanche, Ute, Paiute, Hopi, etc. —*n.* this branch of the Uto-Aztecan language family

Shoshone Falls waterfall on the Snake River, in S Ida.: c. 200 ft.

Sho·sta·ko·vich (shō′stä kō′vich; *E.* shäs′tə kō′vich), **Dmi·tri** (d′mē′trē) 1906– ; Russ. composer

shot¹ (shät) *n.* [ME. < OE. *sceot* < *sceotan* (akin to ON. *skol,* G. *schuss*): see SHOOT] **1.** the act of shooting; discharge of a missile, esp. from a gun **2.** *a)* the distance over which a missile travels *b)* range; reach; scope **3.** an attempt to hit with a missile **4.** *a)* any attempt or try *b)* a guess or conjecture **5.** a pointed, critical remark **6.** the flight or path of an object thrown, struck, driven, etc., as in any of several games **7.** *a)* a solid projectile designed for discharge from a firearm or cannon, as distinguished from an explosive shell *b)* such projectiles collectively **8.** *a)* lead in small pellets, of which a quantity is used for a single charge of a shotgun *b)* a single pellet of this kind **9.** the heavy metal ball used in the shot put: cf. SHOT PUT **10.** a blast, or the amount of explosive used for a blast, as in mining **11.** a marksman [a fair *shot*] ☆**12.** *a)* the act of taking a single photograph *b)* a single photograph *c)* a sequence or view in a motion picture or television program taken by a single continuous run of a camera **13.** [cf. SCOT] an amount due, esp. for drinks or entertainment ☆**14.** a hypodermic injection, as of vaccine ☆**15.** a drink of liquor; specif., *same as* JIGGER **16.** [Colloq.] something to bet on, considered from the standpoint of odds or chances of winning [a horse that is a ten-to-one *shot*] **17.** *Naut.* a 90-foot length of chain, esp. for an anchor —*vt.* **shot′ted, shot′ting** to load or weight with shot —**a shot in the arm** something that bolsters up, reinvigorates, encourages, etc., esp. in a difficult situation —**call the shots 1.** to give orders **2.** to control what is done or what happens —**have** (or **take**) **a shot at** [Colloq.] to make a try at —**like a shot 1.** quickly; rapidly **2.** suddenly

shot² (shät) *pt. & pp.* of SHOOT —*adj.* **1.** variegated, streaked, flecked, etc. with another color or substance **2.** woven with threads of different colors so as to appear iridescent **3.** varied with something different [a novel *shot* through with pathos/ ☆**4.** [Colloq.] ruined or worn out

shote (shōt) *n. var.* of SHOAT

shot effect random fluctuations in the number of electrons emitted by a heated cathode, producing a popping sound (**shot noise**) upon amplification

☆**shot·gun** (shät′gun′) *n.* a smoothbore gun used for firing a charge of small shot at short range, as in hunting small game —*vt., vi.* to shoot, force, or threaten with a shotgun —*adj.* done or made under duress —**ride shotgun** [West] formerly, in the W U.S., to go along as an armed guard, esp. with the driver of a stagecoach

☆**shotgun wedding** a wedding into which a man is forced, as because of previous sexual intimacy with the woman

shot hole 1. a drilled hole in which an explosive charge is put for blasting **2.** a hole bored in timber by an insect

shot put (poot′) **1.** a contest in which a heavy metal ball is propelled for distance with an overhand thrust from the shoulder **2.** a single put of the shot —**shot′-put′ter** *n.* —**shot′-put′ting** *n.*

shott (shät) *n.* [Fr. *chott* < Ar. *shatt*, orig., river bank] in N Africa, a closed basin, often containing a temporary, shallow, salt lake

shot·ten (shät′'n) *obs. pp.* of SHOOT —*adj.* [in specialized sense (esp. applied to herrings), prob. influenced by Du.

schoten] **1.** that has recently spawned and so become of inferior food value: said of fish **2.** [Archaic] undesirable

should (shood; *unstressed, often* shəd) *v.* [ME. *scholde* < OE. *sceolde*, pt. of *sceal, scal,* I am obliged: see SHALL] **1.** *pt.* of SHALL **2.** an auxiliary used to express: *a)* obligation, duty, propriety, necessity, etc. [children *should* be loved/ *b)* expectation or probability [he *should* be here soon/: equivalent to *ought to* and not replaceable by *would* *c)* futurity from the standpoint of the past in indirect quotations where *shall* and *will* were used in the direct quotations: replaceable by *would* [I said I *should* (or *would*) be home by ten/ *d)* futurity in polite or unemphatic requests or in statements with implications of uncertainty or doubt: replaceable by *would* [I *should* (or *would*) think he'd like it/ *e)* a future condition [if I *should* die tomorrow/: in this use *would* is considered colloquial or, by some, substandard *f)* a past condition, real or unreal: replaceable by *would* [I *should* (or *would*) have gone, but you never asked me/ **N.B.** In formal speech the distinctions between *should* and *would* are the same as those between *shall* and *will*

shoul·der (shōl′dər) *n.* [ME. *schuldere* < OE. *sculdor,* akin to G. *schulter* < IE. **skĺdhrā,* shoulder blade used as a spade < base **(s)kel-,* to cut, whence SHELL, SHILLING, SKULL] **1.** *a)* the joint connecting the arm or forelimb with the body *b)* the part of the body including this joint and extending to the base of the neck **2.** [*pl.*] the two shoulders and the part of the back between them: often used figuratively with reference to this region as a place where burdens are often carried **3.** a cut of meat consisting of the upper foreleg and attached parts: see PORK, illus. **4.** the part of a garment that covers the shoulder **5.** something like a shoulder in shape or position; shoulderlike projection **6.** the angle between the face and flank of a bastion in a fortification **7.** that part of the top of a piece of type which extends beyond the base of the raised character ☆**8.** the strip of land along the edge of a paved road; berm —*vt.* **1.** to push or thrust along or through, with or as with the shoulder [to *shoulder* one's way through a crowd/ **2.** to take or carry upon the shoulder **3.** to assume the burden of —*vi.* to push with the shoulder or shoulders —**cry on someone's shoulder** to tell one's troubles to someone in seeking comfort or sympathy —**put one's shoulder to the wheel** to set to work vigorously; put forth vigorous effort —**rub shoulders with** to associate or mingle with (famous or prominent people, etc.) —**shoulder arms** *Mil.* **1.** to rest a rifle against the (right or left) shoulder, supporting the butt with the hand on the same side **2.** *a)* this position *b)* the command to assume it —**shoulder to shoulder 1.** side by side and close together **2.** working together; with common effort —**straight from the shoulder 1.** moving straight forward from the shoulder: said of a blow **2.** without reserve or evasion; frankly —**turn** (or **give**) **a cold shoulder to 1.** to treat with disdain; snub **2.** to avoid or shun

shoulder blade either of the two flat bones in the upper back: see SCAPULA

shoulder girdle *same as* PECTORAL GIRDLE

☆**shoulder harness** a restraining device consisting of an anchored strap passing diagonally across the body, from the shoulder to hip, and used in conjunction with a seat belt, as in an automobile

shoulder knot 1. a knot of ribbon or lace formerly worn as an ornament on the shoulder **2.** a detachable ornament of braided cord worn on the shoulders of full-dress uniforms

☆**shoulder mark** (or **board**) either of a pair of oblong pieces of stiffened cloth worn on the shoulders of certain uniforms and showing insignia of rank

☆**shoulder patch** a cloth insignia identifying the wearer's unit, branch of service, etc., worn on the sleeve of a uniform, just below the shoulder

shoulder strap 1. a strap, usually one of a pair on a garment, worn over the shoulder to support the garment **2.** a strap worn over the shoulder for carrying an attached purse, camera, etc. **3.** a piece of cloth fixed to the shoulder of a uniform to hold insignia

should·n't (shood′'nt) should not

shouldst (shoodst) *archaic 2d pers. sing. pt.* of SHALL: used with thou: also **should·est** (shood′ist)

shout (shout) *n.* [ME. *schoute,* prob. < an OE. cognate of ON. *skúta,* a taunt, prob. < IE. **(s)kud-,* to cry out] **1.** a loud cry or call **2.** any sudden, loud outburst or uproar —*vt.* to utter or express in a shout —*vi.* to utter a shout; cry out loudly —**shout down** to silence or overwhelm by loud shouting —**shout louder than** —**shout′er** *n.*

shove (shuv) *vt., vi.* **shoved, shov′ing** [ME. < OE. *scufan,* akin to ON. *skufa,* G. *schieben* < IE. base **skeubh-,* to throw, shove, whence SCOFF¹] **1.** to push or thrust, as along a surface **2.** to push roughly or hastily —*n.* the act or an instance of shoving; a push or thrust —*SYN.* see PUSH —**shove off 1.** to push (a boat) away from shore, as in departing ☆**2.** [Colloq.] to start off; leave —**shov′er** *n.*

shov·el (shuv′'l) *n.* [ME. *schovele* < OE. *sceofl* < base of *scufan:* see prec.] **1.** *a)* a tool with a broad, deep scoop or blade and a long handle: used in lifting and moving loose material, as earth, snow, gravel, etc. *b)* any machine equipped with a shovellike device [a steam *shovel*]. **2.** *same as* SHOVELFUL —*vt.* **-eled** or **-elled, -el·ing** or **-el·ling 1.** to lift and move with a shovel **2.** to clean or dig out (a path, etc.) with a shovel **3.** to put or throw in large quantities [to *shovel* food into one's mouth] —*vi.* to use a shovel

shov·el·er, shov·el·ler (shuv'l ər, shuv'lər) *n.* **1.** a person or thing that shovels **2.** a freshwater duck (*Spatula clypeata*) with a very long, broad, flattened bill, living in the N Hemisphere mainly in marshes: also **shov'el·bill'**
shov·el·ful (shuv'l fool') *n., pl.* **-fuls'** as much as a shovel will hold
shovel hat a stiff, low-crowned hat with a broad brim turned up at the sides, worn by some Anglican clergymen
☆**shov·el·head** (-hed') *n.* a small shark (*Sphyrna tiburo*) related to the hammerhead, but with a narrower head resembling the blade of a shovel
shov·el-nosed (-nōzd') *adj.* having a broad, flattened nose, head, or bill
shovel-nosed shark ☆any of several flat-headed sharks, as the shovelhead: also **shov'el·nose' shark**
☆**shovel-nosed sturgeon** a freshwater sturgeon (*Scaphirhynchus platorhynchus*) of the Mississippi Valley, with a broad, shovellike snout
show (shō) *vt.* **showed, shown** or **showed, show'ing** [ME. *schewen* < OE. *sceawian*, akin to G. *schauen*, to look at < IE. base *(s)keu-*, to notice, heed, whence L. *cavere*, to beware, OE. *hieran*, to HEAR] **1.** to bring or put in sight or view; cause or allow to appear or be seen; make visible; exhibit; display **2.** *a)* to enter (animals, flowers, etc.) in a competitive show *b)* to exhibit (paintings, sculpture, etc.), as in a gallery **3.** to guide; conduct [to *show* a guest to his room] **4.** to direct to another's attention; point out [to *show* the sights to visitors] **5.** to reveal, manifest, or make evident (an emotion, condition, quality, etc.) by behavior or outward sign **6.** to exhibit or manifest (oneself or itself) in a given character, condition, etc. [to *show* oneself to be reliable] **7.** to open (a house, apartment, etc.) to prospective buyers or renters **8.** to make evident by logical procedure; explain or prove [to *show* that something is right] **9.** to make clear by going through a procedure; demonstrate [to *show* how to tie a bowknot] **10.** to register; indicate [a clock *shows* the time] **11.** to grant or bestow (favor, kindness, mercy, etc.) **12.** *Law* to allege; plead [to *show* cause] —*vi.* **1.** to be or become seen or visible; appear **2.** to be apparent or noticeable [a scratch that hardly *shows*] **3.** to have a given appearance; appear [to *show* to good effect] ☆**4.** to finish third or better in a horse race or dog race **5.** [Colloq.] to come or arrive as expected; make an appearance **6.** *Theater* to give a performance; appear —*n.* **1.** a showing, demonstration, or manifestation [a *show* of passion] **2.** a display or appearance, specif. a colorful or striking one **3.** spectacular, pompous display; ostentation **4.** an indication of the presence of metal, coal, oil, etc. in the earth; trace **5.** something false or superficial; semblance; pretense [sorrow that was mere *show*] **6.** a person or thing looked upon as peculiar, ridiculous, laughable, etc.; spectacle; sight **7.** a public display or exhibition, as of art, animals, flowers, automobiles, etc. **8.** a presentation of entertainment, as a theatrical production, television or radio program, motion picture, etc. ☆**9.** third position at the finish of a horse race or dog race **10.** [Colloq.] any undertaking, matter, or affair —**for show** in order to attract notice or attention —**good show!** [Chiefly Brit.] an exclamation of appreciation and congratulations on another's accomplishment —☆**put** (or **get**) **the show on the road** [Slang] to set things in operation; start an activity, venture, etc. —**show in** (or **out**) to usher into (or out of) a given place —**show off** **1.** to make a display of; exhibit in a showy manner **2.** to behave in a manner intended to attract attention; make a vain display —**show up** **1.** to bring or come to light; expose or be exposed, as faults **2.** to be clearly seen; be prominent or apparent **3.** to come; arrive; make an appearance **4.** [Colloq.] to surpass in intelligence, performance, etc. —☆**stand** (or **have**) **a show** [Colloq.] to have a chance, esp. a remote one —**steal the show** to become the main focus of attention, plaudits, etc., esp. if in a subordinate role or position
SYN.—**show** implies a putting or bringing something into view so that it can be seen or looked at [*show* us the garden]; to **display** something is to spread it out before one so that it is shown to advantage [jewelry *displayed* on a sales counter]; **exhibit** implies prominent display, often for the purpose of attracting public attention or inspection [to *exhibit* products at an exposition]; **expose** implies the laying open and displaying of something that has been covered or concealed [this bathing suit *exposes* her scar]; **flaunt** implies an ostentatious, impudent, or defiant display [to *flaunt* one's riches, vices, etc.]
show bill a sheet or poster containing a notice or advertisement: also **show card**
☆**show·boat** (-bōt') *n.* **1.** a boat containing a theater and carrying a troupe of actors who play river towns **2.** [Slang] a showoff; exhibitionist —*vi.* [Slang] to show off
show·bread (-bred') *n.* same as SHEWBREAD
☆**show business** the theater, motion pictures, television, etc. as a business or industry: also [Colloq.] **show biz**
☆**show·case** (-kās') *n.* **1.** a glass-enclosed case for protecting things on display, as in a store or exhibition **2.** anything displaying someone or something to good advantage [the revue was a *showcase* for new talent] —☆*vt.* **-cased', -cas'ing** to display to good advantage

☆**show·down** (-doun') *n.* [Colloq.] **1.** *Poker* the laying down of the cards face up to see who wins **2.** any action or confrontation that brings matters to a climax or settles them
show·er¹ (shō'ər) *n.* a person who shows, exhibits, etc.
show·er² (shou'ər) *n.* [ME. *schoure* < OE. *scur*, akin to G. *schauer*, shower, squall < IE. base *(s)keu-*, to cover: cf. SHOE, HIDE¹] **1.** a brief fall of rain, or sometimes of hail, sleet, or snow **2.** a sudden, abundant fall or discharge, as of tears, meteors, rays, sparks, etc. **3.** an abundant flow; rush [a *shower* of compliments] ☆**4.** a party at which a number of gifts are presented to the guest of honor [a bridal *shower*] ☆**5.** *a)* a bath in which the body is sprayed with fine streams of water from a perforated nozzle, usually fixed overhead: in full **shower bath** *b)* an apparatus, as in a bathtub, or a room or enclosure used for this —*vt.* **1.** to make wet as with a spray of water; sprinkle; spray **2.** to pour forth or scatter in or as in a shower [*showered* with praise] —*vi.* **1.** to fall or come as a shower **2.** to bathe under a shower —**show'er·y** *adj.*
☆**show·girl** (shō'gurl') *n. same as* CHORUS GIRL
show·i·ly (shō'ə lē) *adv.* in a showy manner
show·i·ness (-ē nis) *n.* the quality or condition of being showy
show·ing (-iŋ) *n.* **1.** the act of presenting or bringing to view or notice **2.** an exhibition; formal display ☆**3.** a performance, appearance, etc. [a good *showing* in the contest]
show·man (shō'mən) *n., pl.* **-men** (-mən) **1.** a person whose business is producing or presenting shows **2.** a person skilled at this or at presenting anything in an interesting or dramatic manner —**show'man·ship'** *n.*
shown (shōn) *alt. pp. of* SHOW
show·off (shō'ôf') *n.* **1.** the act of showing off; vain or showy display **2.** a person who shows off
show of hands a display or raising of hands, as in voting, volunteering, etc.
show·piece (shō'pēs') *n.* **1.** something displayed or exhibited **2.** something that is a fine example of its kind
show·place (-plās') *n.* **1.** a place that is displayed or exhibited to the public for its beauty, etc. **2.** any place that is beautiful, lavishly furnished, etc.
show·room (-room') *n.* a room where merchandise is displayed, as for advertising or sale
☆**show window** a store window in which merchandise is displayed
show·y (-ē) *adj.* **show'i·er, show'i·est** **1.** of striking or attractive appearance **2.** attracting attention in a gaudy or flashy way; ostentatious — *SYN.* see GAUDY
shp, s.hp. shaft horsepower
shpt. shipment
shr. share; shares
shrank (shraŋk) *alt. pt. of* SHRINK
shrap·nel (shrap'n'l) *n.* [after H. *Shrapnel* (1761–1842), Brit. general who invented it] **1.** an artillery shell filled with an explosive charge and many small metal balls, designed to explode in the air over the objective **2.** the balls scattered by such an explosion, or any fragments scattered by an exploding shell
shred (shred) *n.* [ME. *schrede* < OE. *screade*, akin to G. *schrot* < IE. *(s)kreu(t)* (whence L. *scrotum*, SCROTUM) < base *(s)ker-*, to cut, whence SHEAR, SHARP] **1.** a long, narrow strip or piece cut or torn off **2.** a very small piece or amount; fragment; particle [not a *shred* of evidence] —*vt.* **shred'ded** or **shred, shred'ding** to cut or tear into shreds —**shred'da·ble** *adj.* —**shred'der** *n.*
Shreve·port (shrēv'pôrt) [after H. M. *Shreve* (1785–1854), U.S. inventor] city in NW La.: pop. 182,000
shrew (shrōō) *n.* [ME. *schrewe*, a malicious person < OE. *screawa*, shrewmouse, akin to OHG. *scrawaz*, dwarf, goblin, MHG. *schröuwel*, devil < IE. *(s)keru-*: see SHRED] **1.** any of a number of small, slender, mouselike mammals (family Soricidae) with soft, brown fur and a long, pointed snout: one species is the smallest of all mammals **2.** a scolding, nagging, evil-tempered woman
shrewd (shrōōd) *adj.* [ME. *schrewed*, pp. of *schrewen*, to curse < *schrewe*: see prec.] **1.** orig., *a)* evil, bad, wicked, mischievous, shrewish, etc. *b)* artful, cunning, wily, etc. in one's dealings with others **2.** keen-witted, clever, or sharp in practical affairs; astute: the usual current sense **3.** [Archaic] keen; piercing; sharp —**shrewd'ly** *adv.* —**shrewd'ness** *n.*
SYN.—**shrewd** implies keenness of mind, sharp insight, and a cleverness or sharpness in practical matters [a *shrewd* comment, businessman, etc.]; **sagacious** implies keenness of discernment and farsightedness in judgment [a *sagacious* counselor]; **perspicacious** suggests the penetrating mental vision or discernment that enables one clearly to see and understand what is obscure, hidden, etc. [a *perspicacious* judge of character]; **astute** implies shrewdness combined with sagacity and sometimes connotes, in addition, artfulness or cunning [an *astute* politician] See also CLEVER
shrew·ish (shrōō'ish) *adj.* like a shrew in disposition; evil-tempered —**shrew'ish·ly** *adv.* —**shrew'ish·ness** *n.*
shrew·mouse (-mous') *n., pl.* **-mice'** (-mīs') *same as* SHREW (sense 1)
Shrews·bur·y (shrōōz'ber'ē, shrōz'-; -bə rē) city in W England; county seat of Shropshire: pop. 51,000

shriek (shrēk) *vi.* [ME. *schriken,* var. of *scriken,* prob. < ON. **skrīka,* to cry, akin to *skrīkja,* cry of birds: for IE. base see SCREAM] to make a loud, sharp, piercing cry or sound, as certain animals, or a person in terror, pain, or laughter; screech —*vt.* to utter with a shriek —*n.* a loud, piercing cry or sound —*SYN.* see SCREAM —**shriek'er** *n.*

shriev·al·ty (shrēv'l tē) *n., pl.* **-ties** [Brit.] **1.** a sheriff's office or term of office **2.** the district served by a sheriff —**shriev'al** *adj.*

shrieve (shrēv) *n. obs. form of* SHERIFF

shrift (shrift) *n.* [ME. *schrift* < OE. *scrift* < *scrifan,* to SHRIVE] [Archaic] **1.** confession to and absolution by a priest **2.** the act of shriving See also SHORT SHRIFT

shrike (shrīk) *n.* [via dial. < OE. *scric,* thrush, shrike, akin to ME. *schriken,* SHRIEK] any of several predatory, shrill-voiced birds (family Laniidae) with hooked beaks, gray, black, and white plumage, and long tails: most types feed on insects, some on small birds, frogs, etc. which are sometimes impaled on thorns

shrill (shril) *adj.* [ME. *shrille,* akin to LowG. *schrell,* G. *schrill:* echoic, prob. akin to SHRIEK] **1.** having or producing a high, thin, piercing tone; high-pitched **2.** characterized or accompanied by shrill sounds **3.** unrestrained and irritatingly insistent **4.** [Archaic or Poet.] keen; sharp; biting; poignant —*adv.* [Rare] in a shrill manner —*vi.* to make a shrill noise or sound —*vt.* to utter shrilly —**shrill'ly** *adv.* —**shrill'ness** *n.*

shrimp (shrimp) *n., pl.* **shrimps, shrimp:** see PLURAL, II, D, 1 [ME. *schrimpe,* shrimp, puny person < base of OE. *scrimman* (akin to G. *schrimpfen*), to shrink, dry up < IE. base **(s)kemb-,* to turn, twist, shrink] **1.** any of a large number of small, slender, long-tailed, decapod, mostly marine crustaceans: many are highly valued as food **2.** [Colloq.] a small or insignificant person —*vi.* to fish for shrimp —**shrimp'er** *n.*

shrimp plant [from the fancied resemblance of the spike to the tail of a shrimp] a widely grown tropical American plant (*Beloperone guttata*) of the acanthus family, with small, white flowers borne in long curving spikes of overlapping reddish-brown bracts

SHRIMP
(to 9 in. long)

shrine (shrīn) *n.* [ME. *schrin* < OE. *scrin* < L. *scrinium,* chest, box, orig., a round container < IE. **(s)krei-* < base **(s)ker-,* to turn: see ff.] **1.** a case or other container holding sacred relics, as the bones of a saint **2.** the tomb of a saint or other person held sacred **3.** a place of worship, usually one centered around some sacred scene or object, as a religious image in a niche, etc. **4.** a place or thing hallowed or honored because of its history or associations —*vt.* **shrined, shrin'ing** *rare var. of* ENSHRINE

shrink (shriŋk) *vi.* **shrank** or **shrunk, shrunk** or **shrunk'en, shrink'ing** [ME. *schrynken* < OE. *scrincan,* akin to Sw. *skrynka,* to wrinkle < IE. **(s)ker-,* to bend, turn, whence Gr. *kirkos,* a ring, L. *curvus,* curved] **1.** to become or seem to become smaller, more compact, etc.; contract, as from heat, cold, moisture, etc. **2.** to lessen, as in amount, worth, etc. **3.** to draw back; turn away; cower, as from fear **4.** to avoid or wish to avoid taking action; be reluctant [to *shrink* from doing one's duty] —*vt.* to cause to shrink or contract; specif., to cause (fabric) to shrink by a special process in manufacturing so as to minimize later shrinkage —*n.* **1.** a shrinking; shrinkage ☆**2.** [< (HEAD)SHRINK(ER)] [Slang] a psychiatrist: also **shrink'er** —*SYN.* see CONTRACT, RECOIL —**shrink'a·ble** *adj.*

shrink·age (shriŋ'kij) *n.* **1.** the act or process of shrinking; contraction in size, as of a fabric in washing **2.** decrease in value; depreciation **3.** the total loss in weight of livestock from the time of shipment to the final processing as meat **4.** the amount of such shrinking, decrease, etc.

shrinking violet a very shy or unassuming person

shrive (shrīv) *vt.* **shrived** or **shrove, shriv'en** (shriv''n) or **shrived, shriv'ing** [ME. *shriven* < OE. *scrifan,* akin to G. *schreiben,* to write < early WGmc. borrowing < L. *scribere,* to write (see SCRIBE)] **1.** [Archaic] to hear the confession of and, usually after penance, give absolution to **2.** [Archaic or Rare] to get absolution for (oneself) by confessing and doing penance —*vi.* [Archaic] **1.** to make one's confession; go to confession **2.** to hear confessions

shriv·el (shriv'l) *vt., vi.* **-eled** or **-elled, -el·ing** or **-el·ling** [Early ModE., prob. < Scand., as in Sw. dial. *skryola,* to wrinkle] **1.** to shrink and make or become wrinkled or withered **2.** to make or become helpless, useless, or inefficient —*SYN.* see WITHER

shroff (shräf) *n.* [Anglo-Ind. *sharaf* < Hind. *ṣarrāf* < Ar., ult. < Assyr. *ṣarpu,* silver] in the Orient, **1.** a banker or moneychanger **2.** an expert in testing coins —*vt.* to examine (coins) to separate the genuine from the counterfeit

Shrop·shire (shräp'shir) county of W England, on the border of Wales: 1,347 sq. mi.; pop. 307,000; county seat, Shrewsbury —*n.* a breed of large, black-faced, hornless sheep orig. developed in Shropshire

shroud (shroud) *n.* [ME. *schroude* < OE. *scrud,* akin to ON. *skrud,* accouterments, cloth, OE. *screade,* SHRED] **1.** a cloth sometimes used to wrap a corpse for burial; winding sheet **2.** something that covers, protects, or screens; veil; shelter **3.** any of a set of ropes or wires stretched from a ship's side to a masthead to offset lateral strain on the mast **4.** any of the set of lines from the canopy of a parachute to the harness: in full **shroud line** —*vt.* **1.** to wrap (a corpse) in a shroud **2.** to hide from view; cover; screen **3.** [Archaic] to shelter and protect —*vi.* [Archaic] to take shelter

shroud-laid (-lād') *adj.* made of four strands laid together with a right-handed twist: said of a rope

shrove (shrōv) *alt. pt. of* SHRIVE

Shrove·tide (shrōv'tīd') *n.* [ME. *schroffetide,* prob. (as also with *Shrove Monday,* etc.) a 15th-c. formation in which the 1st element (< *shriven,* to SHRIVE) replaces earlier *fast-, fasten-*] the three days before Ash Wednesday (**Shrove Sunday, Monday,** and **Tuesday**), formerly set aside as a special period for going to confession and a season of festivity just before Lent

shrub[1] (shrub) *n.* [Early ME. *schrubbe* < OE. *scrybb,* brushwood, akin to Dan. *skrubbe* & SCRUB[1]] a low, woody plant with several permanent stems instead of a single trunk; bush —**shrub'like'** *adj.*

shrub[2] (shrub) *n.* [< Ar. *sharāb,* drink: see SYRUP] a drink made of fruit juice, esp. of a citrus fruit, sugar and, usually, rum or brandy

shrub·ber·y (shrub'ər ē) *n., pl.* **-ber·ies** **1.** shrubs collectively **2.** a place where many shrubs are grown

shrub·by (-ē) *adj.* **-bi·er, -bi·est** **1.** covered with shrubs **2.** like a shrub —**shrub'bi·ness** *n.*

shrug (shrug) *vt., vi.* **shrugged, shrug'ging** [ME. *schruggen,* orig., to shiver (as with cold)] to draw up (the shoulders), as in expressing indifference, doubt, disdain, contempt, etc. —*n.* **1.** the gesture so made **2.** a woman's short jacket or sweater with wide, loose sleeves —**shrug off** to dismiss or disregard in a carefree way

shrunk (shruŋk) *alt. pt. & pp. of* SHRINK

shrunk·en (-'n) *alt. pp. of* SHRINK —*adj.* contracted in size; shriveled

‡**shtet·l** (shtet'l) *n., pl.* **shtet'lach** (-läkh); *E.* **shtet'ls** (-'lz) [Yid., dim. of *shtat,* city < G. *stadt*] any of the former Jewish village communities of E Europe, esp. in Russia

shtg. shortage

☆**shtick** (shtik) *n.* [Yid., prank, caprice] [Slang] **1.** a comic scene or piece of business, as in a vaudeville act **2.** an attention-getting device **3.** a special trait, talent, etc.

shuck (shuk) *n.* [< ?] **1.** a shell, pod, or husk; esp., the husk of an ear of corn ☆**2.** the shell of an oyster or clam ☆**3.** [*pl.*] [Colloq.] something valueless [not worth *shucks*] —*vt.* **1.** to remove shucks from (corn, clams, etc.) **2.** to remove like a shuck [to *shuck* one's clothes] —**shuck'er** *n.*

☆**shucks** (shuks) *interj.* [prob. < prec.] an exclamation of mild disappointment, disgust, etc.

shud·der (shud'ər) *vi.* [ME. *schoderen,* akin to G. *schaudern,* to feel dread, OFris. *skedda,* to shake < IE. base **(s)kut-,* to shake, whence Lith. *kutù,* to shake up] to shake or tremble suddenly and violently, as in horror or extreme disgust —*n.* the act of shuddering; convulsive tremor of the body, as in horror, etc. —*SYN.* see SHAKE —**the shudders** a feeling of horror, repugnance, etc. —**shud'der·ing·ly** *adv.* —**shud'der·y** *adj.*

shuf·fle (shuf'l) *vt.* **-fled, -fling** [Early ModE., prob. < or akin to LowG. *schuffeln,* to walk clumsily, shuffle cards < base of SHOVE] **1.** *a)* to move (the feet) with a dragging or shoving gait *b)* to perform (a dance) with such steps **2.** to mix (playing cards) so as to change their order or arrangement **3.** to push or mix together in a jumbled or disordered mass **4.** to shift (things) about from one place to another **5.** to bring, put, or thrust (*into* or *out of*) clumsily or trickily —*vi.* **1.** to move by dragging or scraping the feet, as in walking or dancing **2.** to get (*into* or *out of* a situation or condition) by trickery, evasion, lies, etc. **3.** to act in a shifty, dishonest manner; practice deceit, trickery, evasion, etc. **4.** to change or shift repeatedly from one position or place to another **5.** to shuffle playing cards **6.** to move clumsily (*into* or *out of* clothing) —*n.* **1.** the act of shuffling **2.** a tricky or deceptive action; evasion or inconsistency; trick **3.** *a)* a shuffling of the feet *b)* a gait, dance, motion, etc. characterized by this **4.** *a)* the act of shuffling playing cards *b)* the right of, or one's turn at, shuffling the cards —☆**lose in the shuffle** to leave out or disregard in the confusion of things —**shuffle off** to get rid of —**shuf'fler** *n.*

shuf·fle·board (shuf'l bôrd') *n.* [< earlier *shovel board:* so named because of the shape of the cues] **1.** a game in which large disks are pushed with a cue to slide along a smooth lane and land in numbered squares of a diagram **2.** the marked surface on which it is played

shul (shōōl) *n.* [Yid. < MHG. *schuol,* school] same as SYNAGOGUE

Shu·lam·ite (shōō'lə mīt') *the name or an epithet of the* maiden in the Song of Solomon, 6:13

shun (shun) *vt.* **shunned, shun'ning** [ME. *schunien* < OE. *scunian*] to keep away from; avoid scrupulously or consistently —**shun'ner** *n.*

☆**shun·pike** (-pīk') *adj.* avoiding turnpikes and expressways [a *shunpike* tour] —**shun'pik·er** *n.* —**shun'pik·ing** *n.*

shunt (shunt) *vt., vi.* [ME. *schunten* < ? or akin to SHUN] **1.** to move or turn to one side; turn aside or out of the way

2. to shift or switch, as a train, car, etc. from one track to another **3.** *Elec.* to divert or be diverted by a shunt: said of a current **4.** to provide or connect with a shunt —*n.* **1.** the act of shunting **2.** a railroad switch **3.** *Elec.* a conductor connecting two points in a circuit in parallel and serving to divert part of the current from the main circuit —**shunt'er** *n.*

shunt winding the winding of an electric motor or generator in such a way that the field and armature circuits are connected in parallel —**shunt'-wound'** *adj.*

shush (shush) *interj.* [echoic] hush! be quiet! —*vt.* to say "shush" to; tell (another) to be quiet; hush

Shu·shan (shōō'shän) *Biblical name for* SUSA

shut (shut) *vt.* **shut, shut'ting** [ME. (West Midland) *schutten* < OE. *scyttan* < base of *sceotan*, to cast (see SHOOT)] **1.** *a)* to move (a door, window, lid, etc.) into a position that closes the opening to which it is fitted *b)* to fasten (a door, etc.) securely, as with a bolt or catch **2.** to close (an opening, passage, container, etc.) **3.** *a)* to prevent or forbid entrance to or exit from; close or bar *b)* to confine or enclose (*in* a room, cage, building, etc.) **4.** to fold up or bring together the parts of (an umbrella, book, etc. or the mouth, eyes, etc.) **5.** to stop or suspend the operation of (a business, school, etc.) —*vi.* to move to a closed position; be or become shut —*adj.* closed, fastened, or secured —*n.* **1.** the act or time of shutting or closing; close **2.** the connecting line between two pieces of welded metal —**shut down 1.** to close by lowering **2.** to settle (*over* a place) darkly or obscuringly, as night, fog, etc. **3.** to cease or cause to cease operating; close (a factory, etc.), usually temporarily ☆**4.** [Colloq.] to bring to an end or restrict severely (with *on* or *upon*) —**shut in** to surround or enclose; hem in —**shut of** [Dial.] rid of; free from —**shut off 1.** to prevent the passage of (water, steam, etc.) **2.** to prevent passage through (a road, faucet, etc.) **3.** to separate; isolate —**shut out 1.** to deny entrance or admission to; exclude (sound, a view, etc.) ☆**2.** to prevent (an opposing side or team) from scoring in a game —**shut up 1.** to enclose, confine, or imprison **2.** to close all the entrances to **3.** [Colloq.] *a)* to stop or cause to stop talking *b)* to prevent from speaking or writing freely; silence or censor

☆**shut·down** (-doun') *n.* a stoppage or suspension of work or activity, as in a factory

shut-eye (-ī') *n.* [Slang] sleep

shut-in (-in') *adj.* **1.** confined to one's home, an institution, etc. by illness or infirmity **2.** inclined to shun others; withdrawn —*n.* an invalid who is shut-in

shut-off (-ôf') *n.* **1.** something that shuts off a flow or movement, as a valve **2.** a stoppage or interruption

shut·out (-out') *n.* ☆**1.** the act of preventing the opposing team from scoring in a game ☆**2.** a game in which one team is shut out

shut·ter (shut'ər) *n.* **1.** a person or thing that shuts **2.** a movable screen or cover for a window, usually hinged and often fitted with louvers **3.** anything used to cover an opening, as a slide or door on a lantern **4.** a device for opening and closing the aperture of a lens in a camera to expose the film or plate —*vt.* to close or furnish with a shutter or shutters

☆**shut·ter·bug** (-bug') *n.* [< (CAMERA) SHUTTER + BUG¹] [Slang] a person whose hobby is photography

shut·tle (shut'l) *n.* [ME. *schutylle* < OE. *scytel*, missile < base of *sceotan*, to SHOOT: so called because shot to and fro with the thread in weaving] **1.** *a)* an instrument containing a reel or spool of the woof thread, used in weaving to carry the thread back and forth between the warp threads *b)* a smaller but similar thread holder used in tatting, etc. *c)* a device that carries the lower thread back and forth in making a lock stitch on a sewing machine *d)* any of several devices having a similar to-and-fro action ☆**2.** a bus, train, helicopter, etc. making frequent trips back and forth over a short route **3.** *clipped form of* SHUTTLECOCK —*vt., vi.* **-tled, -tling 1.** to move or go back and forth rapidly or frequently ☆**2.** to move or go by or as by means of a shuttle

shut·tle·cock (-käk') *n.* a rounded piece of cork having a flat end stuck with feathers: it is struck back and forth across a net with rackets in playing badminton or with paddles in battledore and shuttlecock **2.** the game of battledore and shuttlecock: cf. BATTLEDORE —*vt., vi.* to go, send, or bandy back and forth

shy¹ (shī) *adj.* **shy'er** or **shi'er, shy'est** or **shi'est** [ME. *schei*, dial. development < OE. *sceoh*, akin to G. *scheu*, shy, prob. < IE. *skeuk-*, harassed (whence OBulg. *ščuti*, to pursue), akin to *skeub-*, whence SCOFF¹] **1.** easily frightened or startled; timid **2.** not at ease with other people; extremely self-conscious; bashful **3.** showing distrust or caution; wary **4.** not bearing or breeding well, as some plants or animals; unproductive ☆**5.** [Slang]

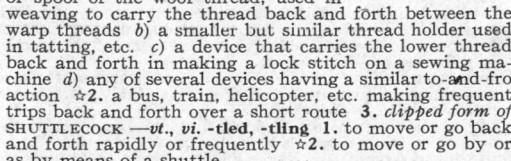

SHUTTERS

a) not having paid money due, as one's poker ante *b)* lacking; short (*on* or *of*) —*vi.* **shied, shy'ing 1.** to move suddenly as when startled; jump; start; recoil [the horse *shied* at the gunshot] **2.** to react negatively; be or become cautious or unwilling; draw back (often with *at* or *from*) —*n., pl.* **shies** an act of shying; start, as of a horse —**fight shy of** to keep from; avoid; evade —**shy'er** *n.* —**shy'ly** *adv.* —**shy'ness** *n.*

SYN.—**shy** implies a shrinking from the notice of others and a reticence in approaching them, either as an inherent trait or as resulting from inexperience; **bashful** implies such shyness as is displayed in awkward behavior and embarrassed timidity; **diffident** implies a self-distrust and lack of self-confidence that makes one reluctant to assert oneself; **modest** implies an unassuming manner in one who, because of his ability, achievements, etc., might be expected to assert himself strongly; **demure**, in current usage, suggests a decorously modest manner, often one that is affectedly so.—*ANT.* **bold, confident**

shy² (shī) *vt., vi.* **shied, shy'ing** [< ? or akin to prec.] to throw or fling, esp. sidewise with a jerk (*shying* stones at a target) —*n., pl.* **shies 1.** the act of shying; fling **2.** [Colloq.] a try or attempt **3.** [Colloq.] a verbal fling; gibe

Shy·lock (shī'läk') the relentless moneylender in Shakespeare's *Merchant of Venice* —*n.* a person without sentiment in business matters; exacting creditor

☆**shy·ster** (shī'stər) *n.* [earlier *shuyster*, prob. altered < G. *scheisser*, defecator] [Slang] a person, esp. a lawyer, who uses unethical or tricky methods; pettifogger

si (sē) *n.* [< ML. *S(ancte) I(ohannes)*: see GAMUT] *Music* same as TI: see also SOLFEGGIO

‡**sí** (sē) *adv.* [Sp.] yes: also [It.] **sì**

Si *Chem.* silicon

si·al (sī'al) *n.* [SI(LICON) + AL(UMINUM)] *Geol.* the light, granitic rock material near the surface of the earth's crust, underlying the continents —**si·al'ic** *adj.*

si·al·a·gogue (sī al'ə gäg') *n.* [ModL. *sialagogus* < Gr. *sialon*, saliva (< IE. echoic base whence SPEW) + ModL. *-agogus, -AGOGUE*] any substance that stimulates the flow of saliva —**si·al·a·gog'ic** (-gäj'ik) *adj.*

si·a·lid (sī'ə lid) *adj.* [< ModL. *Sialidae*, name of the family < Gr. *sialis*, a kind of bird] of a family (Sialidae) of neuropterous insects including the dobsonflies —*n.* a sialid insect Also **si·al·i·dan** (sī al'i dən)

Si·al·kot (sē äl'kōt) city in the Punjab region of NE West Pakistan: pop. 165,000

si·a·loid (sī'ə loid') *adj.* [< Gr. *sialon*, saliva (see SIALAGOGUE) + -OID] resembling saliva

Si·am (sī am') **1.** *former name of* THAILAND **2.** Gulf of, arm of the South China Sea, between the Malay & Indochinese peninsulas

si·a·mang (sē'ə man') *n.* [Malay *siāmaṅ* < *āmaṅ*, black] a very agile, black gibbon (*Symphalangus syndactylus*) of the Malay Peninsula and Sumatra

Si·a·mese (sī'ə mēz', -mēs') *n., pl.* **Si'a·mese'** same as THAI —*adj.* **1.** same as THAI **2.** [*also* s-] [< SIAMESE TWINS] designating or of a pipe coupling or joint in the form of a Y, for joining two pipes or hoses to one pipe

Siamese cat a breed of short-haired cat characterized by usually slanting, blue eyes and a fawn-colored coat shading to a darker color at the face, ears, paws, and tail

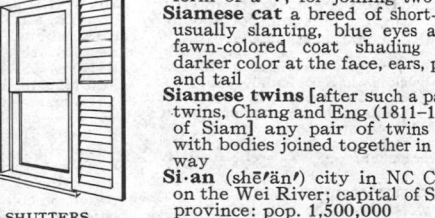

SIAMESE CAT

Siamese twins [after such a pair of twins, Chang and Eng (1811-1874), of Siam] any pair of twins born with bodies joined together in some way

Si·an (shē'än') city in NC China, on the Wei River; capital of Shensi province: pop. 1,500,000

Siang (shyän) river in SE China, flowing from Kwangtung province north into Tungting Lake: c. 715 mi.

sib (sib) *n.* [ME. *sibb* < OE., kinsman, kinship, akin to G. *sippe*, kinship < IE. *s(w)ebh-*, of the same kind (whence OHG. *Swaba*, Swabian) < base *se-*, apart, whence L. *se*] **1.** blood relatives; kin **2.** a blood relative; kinsman or kinswoman; esp., a brother or sister **3.** *Anthropology* a group of persons in a community tracing their descent unilaterally from a traditional or actual common ancestor **4.** *Zool.* any of the offspring of the same parents in relation to one another —*adj.* **1.** related by blood **2.** [Rare] closely related; akin

Si·be·li·us (si bā'lē əs; *E.* sə bāl'yəs) **Jean** (zhän) (born *Johan Julius Christian Sibelius*) 1865-1957, Finn. composer

Si·ber·i·a (sī bir'ē ə) region in N Asia, between the Urals & the Pacific; Asiatic section of the R.S.F.S.R.: c. 5,000,000 sq. mi. —**Si·ber'i·an** *adj., n.*

Siberian husky *full name of* HUSKY¹

sib·i·lant (sib'ī lənt) *adj.* [L. *sibilans* < *sibilare*, to hiss] having or making a hissing sound —*n. Phonet.* a consonant characterized by a hissing sound, as (s), (z), (sh), (zh), (ch), and (j) —**sib'i·lance, sib'i·lan·cy** *n., pl.* **-cies** —**sib'i·lant·ly** *adv.*

sib·i·late (-āt′) *vt., vi.* -**lat′ed**, -**lat′ing** [< L. *sibilatus*, pp.: see prec.] to hiss, or pronounce with a hissing sound —**sib′i·la′tion** *n.*

Si·biu (sē byōō′) city in C Romania: pop. 103,000

sib·ling (sib′liŋ) *n.* [20th-c. readoption of OE. *sibling*, a relative (see SIB & -LING¹)] one of two or more persons born of the same parents or, sometimes, having one parent in common; brother or sister

Sib·yl (sib′l) [L. *Sibylla*: see ff.] a feminine name

sib·yl (sib′l) *n.* [ME. *sibille* < L. *sibylla* < Gr. *sibylla*] 1. any of certain women consulted as prophetesses or oracles by the ancient Greeks and Romans 2. a witch; sorceress; fortuneteller

sib·yl·line (sib′l īn′, -ēn′, -in) *adj.* [L. *sibyllinus*] 1. of or like the sibyls in their prophecies 2. prophetic; oracular; mysterious Also **si·byl·ic, si·byl·lic** (si bil′ik)

Sibylline Books a number of oracular manuscripts consulted regularly by the ancient Romans and thought to have been written by the sibyl of Cumae

‡**sic¹** (sik) *adj.* [L.] thus; so: used within brackets, [*sic*], to show that a quoted passage, esp. one containing some error or something questionable, is precisely reproduced

sic² (sik) *adj. Scot. var. of* SUCH

sic³ (sik) *vt.* [var. of SEEK] **sicked**, **sick′ing** 1. to set upon; pursue and attack: said esp. of or to a dog 2. to urge or incite to attack [to *sic* a dog on someone]

Si·ca·ni·an (si kā′nē ən) *adj. same as* SICILIAN

sic·ca·tive (sik′ə tiv) *adj.* [LL. *siccativus* < L. *siccatus*, pp. of *siccare*, to dry < *siccus*, dry: see DESICCATE] causing to dry; drying —*n.* a substance that promotes drying, esp. one added to paints; drier

Si·ci·lia (sē chē′l′yä) *It. name of* SICILY

Si·cil·ian (si sil′yən, -ē ən) *adj.* of Sicily, its people, their dialect, etc. —*n.* 1. a native or inhabitant of Sicily 2. the Italian dialect of the Sicilians

Sicilies, Two *see* TWO SICILIES

Sic·i·ly (sis′l ē) 1. island of Italy, off its S tip 2. autonomous region of Italy, comprising this island & small nearby islands: 9,926 sq. mi.; pop. 4,712,000; cap. Palermo

sick¹ (sik) *adj.* [ME. *sik, seke* < OE. *seoc*, akin to G. *siech* < IE. base *seug-*, to be troubled or grieved, whence Arm. *hiucanim*, (I) am weakening] 1. suffering from disease or illness; unwell; ill: in this sense, now rare or literary in England 2. having nausea; vomiting or about to vomit: the predominant sense in England 3. characteristic of or accompanying sickness [a *sick* expression] 4. of or for sick people [*sick* leave] 5. deeply disturbed or distressed; extremely upset, as by grief, disappointment, disgust, failure, etc. 6. disgusted by reason of excess; annoyed or exasperated (usually with *of*) [*sick* of such excuses]: often **sick and tired** 7. in poor condition; impaired; unsound 8. having a great longing or nostalgia (*for*) [*sick* for the hills] 9. of sickly color; pale 10. having a discharge of the menses; menstruating 11. mentally ill or emotionally disturbed 12. [Colloq.] sadistic, morbid, or abnormally unwholesome [a *sick* joke] ☆13. *Agric. a*) incapable of producing an adequate yield of a certain crop [*wheatsick* soil] *b*) infested with harmful microorganisms [a *sick* field] —**the sick** sick or ill people collectively

SYN.—**sick** and **ill** both express the idea of being in bad health, affected with disease, etc. (for differences in American and British usage, see definition above), but **sick** is more commonly used than **ill**, which is somewhat formal [he's a *sick* person; he is *sick*, or *ill*, with the flu/; **ailing** usually suggests prolonged or even chronic poor health [she has been *ailing* ever since her operation/; **indisposed** suggests a slight, temporary illness or feeling of physical discomfort [*indisposed* with a headache/ —**ANT.** well, healthy

sick² (sik) *vt. same as* SIC³

sick bay a hospital and dispensary, esp. on board ship

sick·bed (sik′bed′) *n.* [ME. *seke bed*] the bed to which a sick person is confined

sick call *Mil.* 1. a daily formation made up of those men who wish to receive medical attention 2. a signal for or the time of such a formation

sick·en (sik′n) *vt., vi.* [ME. *sekenen*] to make or become sick, ill, disgusted, distressed, etc. —**sick′en·er** *n.*

sick·en·ing (-iŋ) *adj.* 1. causing sickness or nausea 2. disgusting or revolting —**sick′en·ing·ly** *adv.*

sick headache 1. any headache accompanied by or resulting from nausea 2. *same as* MIGRAINE

sick·ish (sik′ish) *adj.* 1. somewhat sick or nauseated 2. somewhat sickening or nauseating —**sick′ish·ly** *adv.* —**sick′ish·ness** *n.*

sick·le (sik′l) *n.* [ME. *sikel* < OE. *sicol* (akin to G. *sichel*) < early WGmc. borrowing < L. *secula* < *secare*, to cut: see SAW¹] a cutting tool consisting of a crescent-shaped blade with a short handle: used for cutting down tall grasses and weeds

sick leave leave from work granted for illness, often with pay (**sick pay**) for a limited number of days

☆**sickle bar** a mowing device, as in a harvesting machine, consisting of a heavy bar which supports and protects the cutting blade or blades

☆**sick·le·bill** (-bil′) *n.* any bird with a sharply curved bill resembling a sickle, as a curlew or thrasher

SICKLE

☆**sickle cell anemia** an inherited chronic anemia found chiefly among Negroes, characterized by an abnormal red blood cell (**sickle cell**) containing a defective form of hemoglobin that causes the cell to become sickle-shaped when deprived of oxygen: also **sickle cell disease**

sickle feather any long, curving feather, as in the tail of a rooster

☆**sick·le·mi·a** (sik lē′mē ə, sik′l ē′-) *n.* [SICKLE (CELL) + -(E)MIA] the presence of sickle cells in the blood, with or without accompanying anemia

sick·ly (sik′lē) *adj.* -**li·er**, -**li·est** [ME. *sekly*] 1. in poor health; chronically sick or prone to sickness; not strong or robust 2. of or produced by sickness [a *sickly* pallor] 3. characterized by the prevalence of disease or sickness; unhealthful 4. sickening; nauseating [a *sickly* odor] 5. faint; feeble; pale [a *sickly* light] 6. weak; mawkish; insipid [a *sickly* smile] —*adv.* in a sick manner: also **sick′li·ly** —*vt.* -**lied**, -**ly·ing** to make sickly, as in color, vigor, etc. —**sick′li·ness** *n.*

sick·ness (-nis) *n.* 1. the condition of being sick or diseased; illness 2. a malady or disease 3. nausea

sick·room (-rōōm′) *n.* the room to which a sick person is confined

‡**sic pas·sim** (sik pas′im) [L., lit., so everywhere] thus throughout (the book, etc.): said of a word, phrase, etc.

‡**sic trans·it glo·ri·a mun·di** (sik tran′sit glôr′ē ə mun′dē) [L.] thus passes away worldly glory

Si·cy·on (sish′ē än′, sis′-) city of ancient Greece, in the NE Peloponnesus

Sid·dhar·tha (sid där′tə) *see* BUDDHA

Sid·dons (sid′nz), **Sarah** (born *Sarah Kemble*) 1755–1831; Eng. actress

sid·dur (si door′, sid′oor) *n., pl.* -**dur·im′** (-ēm′); E. -**durs′** [Heb. *siddūr*, arrangement, order] the Jewish prayer book that contains the daily and Sabbath liturgy: cf. MAHZOR

side (sīd) *n.* [ME. < OE., akin to G. *seite*, sides, OE. *sīd*, ample, broad < IE. base *sēi-*, to stretch out the hand, orig., to throw, whence SOW²] 1. the right or left half of a human or animal body, esp. either half of the trunk 2. a position or space beside one 3. *a*) any of the lines or surfaces that bound or limit something [a square has four *sides*, a cube six] *b*) any bounding line or surface of an object other than the ends or top and bottom *c*) either of the two bounding surfaces of an object that are distinguished from the front, back, top, and bottom 4. either of the two surfaces of a thing having no appreciable thickness, as paper, cloth, etc. 5. a surface or part of a surface having a specified aspect [the visible *side* of the moon] 6. any aspect or phase as contrasted with another or others [his cruel *side*] 7. either of the two lateral surfaces of a ship from stem to stern above the waterline 8. a slope of a hill, bank, etc. 9. the shore of a river or other body of water 10. any location, area, space, direction, etc. with reference to its position in relation to an observer or to a central part, point, or line 11. the action, position, or attitude of one person or faction opposing another [his *side* of the argument] 12. one of the parties in a contest, conflict, etc.; faction 13. either of the longitudinal halves of an animal carcass processed for use as meat 14. line of descent through either parent; maternal or paternal lineage 15. any of the pages containing an actor's lines and cues for his role in a play 16. [Brit. Slang] superior or patronizing manner 17. [Brit.] *Billiards same as* ENGLISH (*n.* 6) —*adj.* 1. of, at, or on a side or sides [a *side* door] 2. to or from one side [a *side* glance] 3. made, done, happening, etc. on the side, or incidentally [a *side* effect] 4. not of primary importance; secondary [a *side* issue] ☆5. ordered separately, along with the main dish [a *side* order of cole slaw] —*vt.* **sid′ed**, **sid′ing** to furnish with sides or siding —☆**on the side** in addition to the main thing, part, course, etc. —**side by side** 1. beside each other 2. in close companionship; together —**side with** to sympathize with or support (one of opposing parties, factions, etc.) —**take sides** to support one of the parties in a discussion, dispute, etc.

☆**side·arm** (-ärm′) *adj., adv.* with a sweeping forward motion of the arm from the side of the body at or below shoulder level [a *sidearm* pitch]

side arms weapons of the kind that may be worn at the side or at the waist, as sword, bayonet, pistol, etc.

side·band (-band′) *n. Radio* the frequency or frequencies on either side of a carrier frequency that are generated by the process of modulation of the carrier

side·board (-bôrd′) *n.* 1. a piece of dining room furniture for holding linen, silver, china, etc. 2. a board that forms or is part of a side [the *sideboards* of a wagon] 3. [*pl.*] *Hockey* the solid wooden fence surrounding the rink

☆**side·burns** (-burnz′) *n.pl.* [reversed < BURNSIDES] 1. *same as* BURNSIDES 2. the hair growing on the sides of a man's face, just in front of the ears, esp. when the rest of the beard is cut off

side·car (-kär′) *n.* 1. a small car attached to the side of a motorcycle, for carrying a passenger, parcels, etc. ☆2. a cocktail of brandy, an orange-flavored liqueur, and lemon juice

side chain *Chem.* a chain of similar atoms attached to either a ring of atoms or another and longer chain

☆**side check** a checkrein passing back to the saddle from the side of a horse's head

sid·ed (sīd′id) *adj.* having (a specified number or kind of) sides [six-*sided*]

side dish any food served along with the main course, usually in a separate dish

☆**side·kick** (-kik′) *n.* [Slang] **1.** a companion; close friend **2.** a partner; confederate

side·light (-līt′) *n.* **1.** a light coming from the side **2.** a bit of incidental knowledge or information on a subject **3.** a window or opening in or at the side of a wall, door, etc. **4.** a lamp or light carried on the side of a ship or boat, a red one on the port side and a green one on the starboard

side·line (-līn′) *n.* a line at or along the side; specif., *a)* either of two lines marking the side limits of a playing field, court, etc., as in hockey or tennis *b)* [*pl.*] the areas just outside these lines *c)* a small line branching off the main line, as of a railroad, pipeline, etc. *d)* a hobble attached to an animal's foreleg and hind leg on the same side ☆*e)* a line, as of merchandise or work, in addition to one's main line —*vt.* **-lined′, -lin′ing** ☆to remove from active participation [*sidelined* by an injury] —☆**on the sidelines 1.** in the area along the sidelines **2.** outside the main sphere of action **3.** not actively participating —**side′lin′er** *n.*

side·ling (-liŋ) *adv.* [ME. *sydelinge:* see SIDE & -LING²] sidelong; sideways; obliquely —*adj.* **1.** directed or moving to the side [a stealthy, *sideling* approach] **2.** inclined; sloping

side·long (-lôŋ′) *adv.* [altered (after ALONG) < prec.] **1.** toward the side; laterally; obliquely **2.** on the side; side downward —*adj.* **1.** inclined; slanting; sloping **2.** directed to the side, as a glance **3.** indirect; subtle or devious [a *sidelong* remark]

☆**side·man** (-man′) *n.*, *pl.* **-men′** (-men′) [as distinguished from the *front man*, or leader] a member of a jazz or dance band other than the leader or a featured soloist

☆**side meat** [Dial.] meat from the side of a pig; specif., bacon or salt pork

side·piece (-pēs′) *n.* a piece forming or attached to the side of something

si·de·re·al (sī dir′ē əl) *adj.* [< L. *sidereus* < *sidus* (gen. *sideris*), a star < IE. base *sweid-*, to gleam, whence Lith. *svidù*, to gleam] **1.** of or pertaining to the stars or constellations; stellar; astral **2.** expressed in reference to the stars —**si·de′re·al·ly** *adv.*

sidereal day the time elapsed between two successive passages of the vernal equinox over the upper meridian: it measures one rotation of the earth; its length is 23 hours, 56 minutes, 4.091 seconds of mean solar time

sidereal month the time required for the moon to complete one revolution from a given star to the same star, as seen from the center of the earth: its average value is 27 days, 7 hours, 43 minutes, and 11.5 seconds of mean solar time

sidereal time 1. time measured by the sidereal day which is divided into the **sidereal hour** (1/24 of a sidereal day), the **sidereal minute** (1/60 of a sidereal hour), and the **sidereal second** (1/60 of a sidereal minute) **2.** the hour angle of the vernal equinox

sidereal year see YEAR (sense 3)

sid·er·ite (sid′ə rīt′) *n.* [G. *siderit* < L. *siderites*, lodestone < Gr. *sideritēs* < *sideros*, iron: Early ModE. *siderite*, lodestone, is < L.] **1.** a valuable ore of iron, FeCO₃, iron carbonate, usually yellowish to light-brown **2.** a meteorite consisting chiefly of iron —**sid′er·it′ic** (-rit′ik) *adj.*

sid·er·o-¹ (sid′ər ō, -ə) [< Gr. *sideros*] a combining form meaning iron [*siderolite*]: also, before a vowel, **sider-**

sid·er·o-² (sid′ər ō, -ə) [< L. *sidus:* see SIDEREAL] a combining form meaning star: also, before a vowel, **sider-**

sid·er·o·lite (sid′ər ə līt′) *n.* [SIDERO-¹ + -LITE] any meteorite containing large proportions of both iron and silicates

sid·er·o·sis (sid′ə rō′sis) *n.* [ModL.: see SIDERO-¹ & -OSIS] any disease of the lungs caused by the inhaling of particles of iron or other metal —**sid′er·ot′ic** (-rät′ik) *adj.*

side·sad·dle (sīd′sad′'l) *n.* a saddle, designed esp. for women riders in skirts, upon which the rider sits with both legs on the same side of the animal —*adv.* on or as if on a sidesaddle

☆**side·show** (-shō′) *n.* **1.** a small, separate show in connection with a main show, as of a circus **2.** something of minor importance; subordinate event

side·slip (-slip′) *vi.* **1.** to slip or skid sideways, as on skis **2.** *Aeron.* to move in a sideslip —*vt.* to cause to sideslip —*n.* **1.** a slip or skid to the side **2.** *Aeron.* a sidewise and downward movement in reaction to gravity and toward the inside of the turn by an airplane in a sharp bank

side·split·ting (-split′iŋ) *adj.* **1.** very hearty: said of laughter **2.** causing hearty laughter [a *sidesplitting* comedy]

☆**side·step** (-step′) *vt.* **-stepped′, -step′ping** to avoid by or as by stepping aside; dodge [to *sidestep* a difficulty] —*vi.* to step to one side; take a side step or side steps

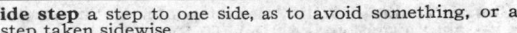

SIDESADDLE

side step a step to one side, as to avoid something, or a step taken sidewise

side·stroke (-strōk′) *n.* a swimming stroke performed, while lying sideways in the water, by working the arms alternately backward and forward while executing a scissors kick with the legs

☆**side·swipe** (-swīp′) *vt., vi.* **-swiped′, -swip′ing** to hit along the side in passing —*n.* a glancing blow of this kind

☆**side·track** (-trak′) *vt., vi.* **1.** to switch, as a train, from a main line to a siding **2.** to turn away from the main issue or course; divert or be diverted —*n.* a railroad siding

☆**side·walk** (-wôk′) *n.* a path for pedestrians, usually paved, along the side of a street

☆**sidewalk superintendent** [Colloq.] an onlooker at a construction or demolition site

☆**side·wall** (-wôl′) *n.* the side of an automobile tire between the tread and the rim of the wheel

side·ward (-wərd) *adv., adj.* directed or moving toward one side: also **side′wards** *adv.*

side·ways (-wāz′) *adv.* **1.** from the side **2.** so as to present a side; with one side forward **3.** toward one side; laterally; obliquely —*adj.* turned or moving toward or from one side Also **side′way′, side′wise′** (-wīz′)

☆**side·wheel** (sīd′hwēl′, -wēl′) *adj.* designating a steamboat having a paddle wheel on each side

☆**side-wheel·er** (-ər) *n.* a side-wheel steamboat

side whiskers whiskers growing at the side of the face

side·wind·er (sīd′wīn′dər) *n.* ☆**1.** a small desert rattlesnake (*Crotalus cerastes*) of the SW U.S. that moves over shifting sand by looping its body sideways **2.** [Colloq.] a hard, swinging blow of the fist, delivered from the side ☆**3.** [S-] an air-to-air missile that homes in on a target by a heat-seeking device

Si·di-bel-Ab·bès (sē′dē bel′ ă bes′) city in NW Algeria, near Oran: pop. 105,000

sid·ing (sīd′iŋ) *n.* ☆**1.** a covering for an outside wall, as of a frame building, consisting generally of overlapping shingles, boards, aluminum panels, etc. **2.** a short railway track connected with a main track by a switch and used for unloading, bypassing, etc.; sidetrack

si·dle (sī′d'l) *vi.* **-dled, -dling** [back-formation < SIDELING] to move sideways, esp. in a shy or stealthy manner —*vt.* to make go sideways —*n.* a sidling movement

Sid·ney (sid′nē) [< the surname *Sidney*, prob. reduced < *St. Denis*] **1.** a masculine or feminine name: dim. *Sid* **2.** Sir **Philip**, 1554–86; Eng. poet, soldier, & statesman

Si·don (sī′d'n) [L. < Gr. *Sidōn* < Heb. & Phoen. *Tsīdōn*] chief city of ancient Phoenicia: site of modern SAIDA —**Si·do′ni·an** (-dō′nē ən) *adj., n.*

‡**siè·cle** (sye′k'l) *n., pl.* **-cles** (-k'l) [Fr.] a century; era

siege (sēj) *n.* [ME. *sege* < OFr. *siege*, aphetic < *assiege* < VL. *absedium*, for L. *obsidium*, a siege, blockade, ambush < *obsidere*, to besiege < *ob-*, against + *sedere*, to SIT] **1.** the encirclement of a fortified place by an opposing armed force intending to take it, usually by blockade and bombardment **2.** any persistent attempt to gain control, overcome opposition, etc. ☆**3.** a long, distressing or wearying period [a *siege* of illness] **4.** [ME. *sege* < OFr. < VL. *sedicum* < *sedicare*, to set < L. *sedere*, to SIT] [Obs.] a seat; throne **5.** [Obs.] rank; position —*vt.* **sieged, sieg′ing** *same as* BESIEGE —**lay siege to** to subject to a siege; attempt to win, gain, overcome, etc.

Siege Perilous a seat at King Arthur's Round Table, fatal to any occupant except the knight destined to find the Holy Grail

Sieg·fried (sēg′frēd, sig′-; *G.* zēk′frēt′) [G. < Gmc. *segu-*, power, victory + *frith-*, peace, protection] a hero of Germanic legend who wins the treasure of the Nibelungs, kills a dragon, and helps Gunther win Brunhild for a wife

Siegfried line a system of heavy fortifications built before World War II on the W frontier of Germany

‡**Sieg Heil** (zēk′ hīl′) [G.] hail to victory: a Nazi salute

Sie·mens (sē′mənz; *G.* zē′mans), Sir **William** (born *Karl Wilhelm von Siemens*) 1823–83; Brit. engineer & inventor, born in Germany

Si·en·a (sē en′ə; *It.* sye′nä) commune in Tuscany, C Italy: pop. 62,000 —**Si′en·ese′** (-ə nēz′, -nēs′) *adj., n.*

Sien·kie·wicz (shen kye′vich), **Hen·ryk** (hen′rik) 1846–1916; Pol. novelist

si·en·na (sē en′ə) *n.* [It. *terra di Siena*, lit., earth of SIENA, where first obtained] **1.** an earth pigment containing iron and manganese oxides, yellowish-brown in the natural state and reddish-brown when burnt (cf. BURNT SIENNA) **2.** either of these colors

si·er·ra (sē er′ə) *n.* [Sp. < L. *serra*, a saw] **1.** a range of hills or mountains having a saw-toothed appearance from a distance **2.** any of several saltwater game and food fishes (genus *Scomberomorus*) resembling the mackerel

Si·er·ra Le·one (sē er′ə lē ōn′) country in W Africa, on the Atlantic, between Guinea & Liberia: a member of the Brit. Commonwealth: 27,925 sq. mi.; pop. 2,439,000; cap. Freetown

Si·er·ra Ma·dre (sē er′ə mä′drä; *Sp.* sye′rä mä′dre) mountain system of Mexico, consisting of three ranges bordering the central plateau: highest peak, Orizaba

Sierra Nevada [Sp., lit., snowy range] mountain range in E Calif.: highest peak, Mt. WHITNEY

si·es·ta (sē es′tə) *n.* [Sp. < L. *sexta* (*hora*), sixth (hour), noon] a brief nap or rest taken after the noon meal, esp. in Spain and some Latin American countries

‡sieur (syër) *n.* [OFr., inflected form of *sire,* SIRE] *archaic French title of respect meaning* SIR

sieve (siv) *n.* [ME. *sive* < OE. *sife,* akin to G. *sieb* < IE. base *seip-,* to drip, whence SEEP] a utensil having many small meshed or perforated openings, used to strain solids from liquids, to separate fine particles of loose matter from coarser ones, etc.; sifter; strainer —*vt., vi.* **sieved, siev′ing** to put or pass through a sieve; sift

sieve tube *Bot.* a longitudinal tube in the phloem of flowering plants, consisting of a connected series of individual cells (**sieve cells**) and serving to conduct organic food materials through the plant

sift (sift) *vt.* [ME. *siften* < OE. *siftan* < *sife,* a SIEVE] **1.** to pass through a sieve so as to separate the coarse from the fine particles, or to break up lumps, as of flour **2.** to scatter (a pulverized substance) by or as by the use of a sieve **3.** to inspect or examine with care, as by testing or questioning; weigh (evidence, etc.) **4.** to separate; screen; distinguish [to *sift* fact from fable] —*vi.* **1.** to sift something **2.** to pass through or as through a sieve —**sift′er** *n.*

sift·ings (-iŋz) *n.pl.* **1.** something sifted or having fallen as if sifted [*siftings* of snow beside the door] **2.** something removed by sifting; residue

Sig., sig. **1.** [L. *signa* or *signetur*] label it or let it be labeled **2.** signal **3.** signature **4.** signor, signore, or signori

sigh (sī) *vi.* [ME. *sighen,* back-formation < *sihten,* pt. of *siken* < OE. *sican,* to sigh: prob. echoic] **1.** to take in and let out a long, deep, audible breath, esp. in expressing sorrow, relief, fatigue, longing, etc. **2.** to make a sound like that of a sigh [trees *sighing* in the wind] **3.** to feel longing or grief; yearn or lament (*for*) —*vt.* **1.** to express with a sigh **2.** to spend (time) in sighing [to *sigh* one's youth away] **3.** [Rare] to lament with sighing —*n.* the act or sound of sighing —**sigh′er** *n.*

sight (sīt) *n.* [ME. *siht* < OE. (*ge*)*siht* < base of *seon,* to SEE[1]] **1.** *a*) something seen; view *b*) a remarkable or spectacular view; spectacle *c*) [Chiefly *pl.*] a thing worth seeing [the *sights* of the city] **2.** the act of seeing; perception by the eyes **3.** a view; look; glimpse **4.** any of various devices used to aid the eyes in lining up a gun, optical instrument, etc. on its objective **5.** aim or an observation taken with mechanical aid, as on a sextant, gun, etc. **6.** the faculty or power of seeing; vision; eyesight **7.** mental vision or perception **8.** range or field of vision **9.** mental view; opinion; judgment [a hero in her *sight*] **10.** [Colloq.] any person or thing of a strikingly unpleasant or unusual appearance **11.** [Dial.] a large amount; great deal [a *sight* better than fighting] **12.** *obs. var. of* INSIGHT —*vt.* **1.** to observe or examine by taking a sight **2.** to catch sight of; see ☆**3.** to bring into the sights of a rifle, etc.; aim at **4.** *a*) to furnish with sights or a sighting device *b*) to adjust the sights of **5.** to aim (a gun, etc.) using the sights —*vi.* **1.** to take aim or an observation with a sight **2.** to look carefully in a specified direction [*sight* along the line] —*adj.* **1.** read, done, understood, etc. quickly and easily as soon as seen ☆**2.** due or payable when presented [*sight* draft] —**a sight for sore eyes** [Colloq.] a person or thing that is pleasant to see; welcome sight —**at first sight** when seen or considered for the first time —**at** (or **on**) **sight** **1.** when or as soon as seen **2.** *Commerce* upon demand or presentation —**by sight** by appearance; by recognizing but not through being acquainted —**catch sight of 1.** to make out by means of the eyes; discern; see **2.** to see briefly; glimpse —**lose sight of 1.** to fail to keep in sight; see no longer **2.** to fail to keep in mind; forget —**not by a long sight 1.** not nearly **2.** not at all —**out of sight 1.** not in sight **2.** far off; remote **3.** [Colloq.] beyond reach; unattainable; extremely high, as in standards, price, etc. —**out of sight of 1.** not in sight of **2.** not close or near to; remote from —**out of sight, out of mind** persons or things not seen or present are forgotten or neglected —**sight unseen** without seeing (the thing mentioned) beforehand

sight·ed (-id) *adj.* **1.** having sight; not blind **2.** having a (specified kind of) sight: used in combination [farsighted]

☆**sight gag** a bit of comic business, as on the stage, whose effect depends on action rather than speech

sight·less (-lis) *adj.* **1.** blind **2.** unseen; invisible —**sight′less·ly** *adv.* —**sight′less·ness** *n.*

sight·line (-līn′) *n.* any of the straight lines of unimpeded vision from various points in a theater to the stage

sight·ly (-lē) *adj.* **-li·er, -li·est** **1.** pleasant to the sight; comely **2.** providing a fine view —**sight′li·ness** *n.*

sight reading the act or skill of performing unfamiliar written music, or of translating something written in a foreign language, readily on sight, without previous study —**sight′-read′** *vt., vi.* —**sight reader**

sight·see·ing (-sē′iŋ) *n.* the act of visiting places and things of interest, for pleasure, education, etc. —*adj.* for or engaged in seeing sights —**sight′se′er** *n.*

sig·il (sij′əl; *occas.* sīg′-) *n.* [L. *sigillum,* dim. of *signum,* a SIGN] **1.** a seal; signet **2.** an image or sign supposedly having some mysterious power in magic or astrology

sigill. [L. *sigillum*] signet; seal

Sig·is·mund (sij′is mənd, sig′-; *G.* zē′gis moont′) 1368–1437; Holy Roman emperor (1411–37)

sig·ma (sig′mə) *n.* [G.] the eighteenth letter of the Greek alphabet (Σ, σ, ς)

sig·mate (sig′māt) *adj.* shaped like a sigma or an S

sig·moid (-moid) *adj.* [Gr. *sigmoeidēs:* see SIGMA & -OID] **1.** *a*) having a double curve like the letter S *b*) curved like the letter C (uncial form of sigma) **2.** of the sigmoid flexure of the colon Also **sig·moi′dal** —**sig·moi′dal·ly** *adv.*

sigmoid flexure 1. *Anat.* the last curving part of the colon, ending in the rectum **2.** *Zool.* an S-shaped curve

sig·moid·o·scope (sig moid′ə skōp′) *n.* [SIGMOID + -O- + -SCOPE] an illuminated, tubular instrument for the direct examination of the rectum, colon, and sigmoid flexure —**sig·moid′o·scop′ic** (-skäp′ik) *adj.* —**sig·moid·os′co·py** (-äs′kə pē) *n., pl.* **-pies**

Sig·mund (sig′mənd) [< G. *Siegmund* & ON. *Sigmundr* < Gmc. **sig-,** victory + *mund-,* hand, protection] a masculine name

sign (sīn) *n.* [ME. *signe* < OFr. < L. *signum,* a mark, token, prob. < base of *secare,* to cut (see SAW[1]): orig. sense prob. "incised mark"] **1.** something that indicates a fact, quality, etc.; indication; token [black as a *sign* of mourning] **2.** *a*) a gesture or motion that conveys information, gives a command, etc. [a nod as a *sign* of approval] *b*) any of the gestures used in sign language **3.** a mark or symbol having an accepted and specific meaning [the *sign* ¢ for cent(s)] **4.** any linguistic unit, as a word, letter, etc., that is the symbol of an idea, function, etc. **5.** a publicly displayed board, placard, etc. bearing information, warning, advertising, etc. ☆**6.** anything marking the trail of an animal, as footprints **7.** any visible trace or indication [the *signs* of spring] **8.** *a*) an act or happening regarded as a miraculous demonstration of divine will or power *b*) an omen; portent **9.** *same as* SIGN OF THE ZODIAC **10.** *Med.* an objective indication or symptom of a disease —*vt.* **1.** to mark with a sign, esp. with the sign of the cross, as in blessing **2.** to write one's name on, as in acknowledging authorship, authorizing action, etc. **3.** to write (one's name) as a signature **4.** to engage by written contract; sign on **5.** [Now Rare] to indicate or express by a sign; signal —*vi.* **1.** to write one's signature, as in attesting or confirming something **2.** to make a sign; signal —**sign away** (or **over**) to abandon or transfer title to (something) by or as by signing a document; convey —**sign in** (or **out**) to sign a register on arrival (or departure) —**sign off 1.** to announce the end of broadcasting, as for the day, and stop transmitting **2.** [Slang] to stop talking —**sign on** to engage (oneself or others) for employment; hire or be hired, esp. by a signed agreement —**sign up 1.** *same as* SIGN ON **2.** to enlist in military service —**sign′er** *n.*

SYN.—**sign,** the broadest in scope of these terms, applies to an action, condition, quality, occurrence, or visible object that points to a fact or conveys a meaning [a *sign* of spring, decay, the zodiac, etc.]; **mark** suggests that which is imprinted on, or is intrinsically characteristic of, something [suffering left its *mark* on his face]; **token** suggests something given or serving as a symbol or sign of some quality, feeling, value, etc. [a *token* of good will]; a **symptom** is an outward, recognizable sign of the existence of a disease, disorder, etc. [prejudice is a *symptom* of social maladjustment]; **indication** is interchangeable with any of the preceding words

sig·nal (sig′n'l) *n.* [ME. < OFr. < VL. *signale* < neut. of LL. *signalis* < L. *signum,* a SIGN] **1.** [Now Rare] a token or indication **2.** a sign or event fixed or understood as the occasion for prearranged combined action [a bugle *signal* to attack] **3.** anything which occasions a certain action or response **4.** *a*) a sign given by gesture, flashing light, etc. to convey a command, direction, warning, etc. *b*) an object or device, as a red flag, flashing light, etc., providing such a sign **5.** in some card games, a bid or play designed to guide one's partner **6.** in telegraphy, radio, television, etc., the electrical impulses, sound or picture elements, etc. transmitted or received —*adj.* **1.** not average or ordinary; remarkable; notable **2.** used as a signal or in signaling —*vt.* **-naled** or **-nalled, -nal·ing** or **-nal·ling 1.** to make a signal or signals to **2.** to make known or communicate (information) by signals —*vi.* to make a signal or signals —**sig′nal·er, sig′nal·ler** *n.*

☆**Signal Corps** *U.S. Army* the combat arm in charge of most forms of communication and many meteorological, photographic, and range-finding services

sig·nal·ize (-īz′) *vt.* **-ized′, -iz′ing 1.** to make remarkable or noteworthy [a career *signalized* by great achievement] **2.** to make clearly known; draw attention to [the cheers which *signalized* his arrival] —**sig′nal·i·za′tion** *n.*

sig·nal·ly (-ē) *adv.* in a signal manner; remarkably

sig·nal·man (-mən, -man′) *n., pl.* **-men** (-mən, -men′) a man responsible for signaling or receiving signals

sig·nal·ment (-mənt) *n.* [Fr. *signalement* < *signaler,* to signal] a description giving distinguishing or identifying marks, as of someone wanted by the police

signal word *Linguis.* a word of a particular form occupying a clearly marked position in an utterance and indicating the character of a subsequent structure: conjunctions, pronouns, articles, and prepositions all function variously as signal words

sig·na·to·ry (sig′nə tôr′ē) *adj.* [L. *signatorius,* of sealing, of a signer < *signator,* one who seals or signs < *signare,* to set a seal upon, sign: see SIGN] that has joined in the

signing of something —*n.*, *pl.* **-ries** any of the persons, states, etc. whose signature is attached to a document

sig·na·ture (sig′nə chər) *n.* [LL. *signatura* < L. *signare*: see prec.] **1.** a person's name written by himself; also, a representation of this in a mark, stamp, deputy's handwriting, etc. **2.** the act of signing one's name **3.** an identifying characteristic or mark **4.** that part of a doctor's prescription telling the patient how to use the medicine prescribed: usually marked *S* or *Sig.* **5.** a theme song, sound effect, picture, etc. used to identify a program or performer on radio or television **6.** *Music* a sign or signs placed at the beginning of a staff to show key or time **7.** *Printing* *a)* a large sheet upon which are printed a number of pages in some multiple of four, and which, when folded to page size, forms one section of a book *b)* a letter or number at the bottom of the first page in such a sheet showing in what order that section is to be gathered for binding

sign·board (sīn′bôrd′) *n.* a board bearing a sign or notice, esp. one advertising a business, product, etc.

sig·net (sig′nit) *n.* [ME. < MFr., dim. of *signe*, a SIGN] **1.** a seal, esp. one used as a signature in marking documents as official, etc. **2.** a mark or impression made by or as by a signet —*vt.* to stamp or make official with a signet

signet ring a finger ring containing a signet, often in the form of an initial or monogram

sig·nif·i·cance (sig nif′ə kəns) *n.* [LME. < L. *significantia* < *significans*: see SIGNIFICANT] **1.** that which is signified; meaning **2.** the quality of being significant; suggestiveness; expressiveness **3.** importance; consequence; moment Also **sig·nif′i·can·cy** —SYN. see IMPORTANCE, MEANING

sig·nif·i·cant (-kənt) *adj.* [L. *significans*, prp. of *significare*, to SIGNIFY] **1.** *a)* having or expressing a meaning *b)* full of meaning **2.** important; momentous **3.** having or conveying a special or hidden meaning; suggestive **4.** of or pertaining to an observed departure from a hypothesis too large to be reasonably attributed to chance *[a significant statistical difference]* —*n.* [Archaic] something that has significance; sign —**sig·nif′i·cant·ly** *adv.*

sig·ni·fi·ca·tion (sig′nə fi kā′shən) *n.* [ME. *significacion* < OFr. < L. *significatio*] **1.** significance; meaning **2.** the act of signifying; indication —SYN. see MEANING

sig·nif·i·ca·tive (sig nif′ə kāt′iv) *adj.* same as SIGNIFICANT (esp. sense 3)

sig·ni·fy (sig′nə fī′) *vt.* **-fied′, -fy′ing** [ME. *signifien* < OFr. *signifier* < L. *significare* < *signum*, a SIGN + *facere*, to make: see DO¹] **1.** to be a sign or indication of; mean *[the rags that signify their poverty]* **2.** to show or make known, as by a sign, words, etc. *[to signify approval by saying "aye"]* —*vi.* to have meaning or importance; be significant; matter —**sig′ni·fi′a·ble** *adj.*

si·gnior (sēn′yôr) *n.* an Eng. *sp.* of SIGNOR

sign language communication of thoughts or ideas by means of manual signs and gestures

sign manual a personal signature, esp. that of a monarch on an official document

sign of the cross an outline of a cross (sense 5 *a*) made symbolically by a movement of the hand or fingers

sign of the zodiac any of the twelve divisions or houses of the zodiac, each represented by a symbol: see ZODIAC

‡**si·gnor** (sē nyôr′; *E.* sēn′yôr) *n.*, *pl.* **si·gno′ri** (-nyô′rē); *E.* **si′gnors** [It., reduced form of *signore*: see SIGNORE] **1.** [S-] Mr.: Italian title of respect, used before the name **2.** a gentleman; man

‡**si·gno·ra** (sē nyô′rä; *E.* sēn yôr′ə) *n.*, *pl.* **si·gno′re** (-re); *E.* **si·gno′ras** [It., fem. of prec.] **1.** [S-] Mrs., Madam: Italian title of respect **2.** a married woman

‡**si·gno·re** (sē nyô′re) *n.*, *pl.* **si·gno′ri** (-rē) [It. < ML. *senior*, lord < L.: see SENIOR] **1.** [S-] sir: Italian title of respect, used in direct address without the name **2.** a gentleman; man

‡**si·gno·ri·na** (sē′nyô rē′nä; *E.* sēn′yə rē′nə) *n.*, *pl.* **-ri′ne** (-ne); *E.* **-ri′nas** [It., dim. of *signora*] **1.** [S-] Miss: Italian title of respect **2.** an unmarried woman or girl

‡**si·gno·ri·no** (sē′nyô rē′nô; *E.* sēn′yə rē′nō) *n.*, *pl.* **-ri′ni** (-nē); *E.* **-ri′nos** [It., dim. of *signore*] **1.** [S-] Master: Italian title of courtesy for a young man or youth **2.** a young man or youth

si·gno·ry (sēn′yər ē) *n.*, *pl.* **-ries** same as SEIGNIORY

sign·post (sīn′pōst′) *n.* **1.** a post bearing a sign; guidepost **2.** a clear indication; obvious clue, symptom, etc.

Si·gurd (sig′ərd) *Norse Legend* the hero of the Volsunga Saga: identified with the German SIEGFRIED

Sikh (sēk) *n.* [Hindi, a disciple] a member of a Hindu religious sect founded in northern India about 1500 and based on belief in one God and on rejection of the caste system and of idolatry —*adj.* of or like Sikhs —**Sikh′ism** *n.*

Si Kiang (sē′ kyän′; *Chin.* shē′ jyän′) river in S China, flowing from Yunnan province east through Kwangsi & Kwantung into the South China Sea: 1,250 mi.

Sik·kim (sik′im) protectorate of India, in the E Himalayas: 2,818 sq. mi.; pop. 183,000; cap. Gangtok See INDIA, map —**Sik′kim·ese′** (-ēz′, -ēs′) *n. sing. & pl., adj.*

Si·kor·sky (si kôr′skē), **I·gor (Ivanovich)** (ē′gôr) 1889– ; U.S. aeronautical engineer, born in Russia

si·lage (sī′lij) *n.* [contr. (after SILO) < ENSILAGE] green fodder preserved in a silo; ensilage

Si·las (sī′ləs) [LL.(Ec.) < Gr.(Ec.) < Aram. *sh'îlâ*, lit., asked for] a masculine name: dim. *Si*

Si·las·tic (si las′tik) [SIL(ICONE RUBBER) + (EL)ASTIC] *a trademark for* a soft, flexible, inert silicone rubber, used esp. in prosthetic medicine —*n.* [s-] this material

sild (sild) *n.*, *pl.* **sild, silds**: see PLURAL, II, D, 2 [Norw., herring] any of several small or young herrings that are not brislings and are canned as Norwegian sardines

si·lence (sī′ləns) *n.* [ME. < OFr. < L. *silentium* < *silens*: see SILENT] **1.** the state or fact of keeping silent; a refraining from speech or from making noise **2.** absence of any sound or noise; stillness **3.** a withholding of knowledge or omission of mention *[to note an author's silence on a point]* **4.** failure to communicate, write, keep in touch, etc. **5.** oblivion or obscurity —*vt.* **-lenced, -lenc·ing** **1.** to cause to be silent; still; quiet **2.** to put down; repress **3.** to put (enemy guns) out of action —*interj.* be silent!

si·lenc·er (sī′lən sər) *n.* **1.** a person or thing that silences ☆**2.** a device attached to the muzzle of a firearm to muffle the report **3.** [Chiefly Brit.] *same as* MUFFLER (sense 2)

si·lent (sī′lənt) *adj.* [L. *silens* < prp. of *silere*, to be silent, still, prob. < IE. base *sei-, *sī-, to rest, to let the hand fall, whence SEED, SIDE, Goth. (*ana*)*silan*, to cease (of the wind)] **1.** making no vocal sound; not speaking; speechless; mute **2.** seldom speaking; saying little; not talkative **3.** free from, or not making, sound or noise; quiet; still; noiseless **4.** *a)* not spoken, uttered, or expressed *[silent longing]* *b)* written but not pronounced *["debt" has a silent "b"]* **5.** withholding knowledge or omitting mention; uncommunicative **6.** not active *[factories silent for months]* **7.** designating or of motion pictures without a synchronized sound recording —**si′lent·ly** *adv.*

SYN.—**silent** is the simple, direct word for one who is temporarily not speaking or one who seldom speaks; **taciturn** applies to a person who is habitually uncommunicative; **reserved** implies a habitual disposition to be withdrawn in speech and self-restrained or aloof in manner; **reticent** implies a disinclination, sometimes temporary as from embarrassment, to express one's feelings or impart information; **secretive** suggests the furtive or evasive reticence of one who conceals things unnecessarily See also STILL —ANT. **talkative, voluble**

☆**silent butler** a dish with a hinged cover and handle, in which to empty ashtrays, brush crumbs, etc.

☆**silent partner** a partner who shares in financing but not in managing a business, firm, etc.

Si·le·nus (sī lē′nəs) [L. < Gr. *Seilēnos*] *Gr. Myth.* the foster father and tutor of Dionysus and leader of the satyrs, traditionally pictured as a fat, drunken, jovial old man with pointed ears —*n.* [s-] *pl.* **-ni** (-nī) any of a group of woodland deities resembling the satyrs

Si·le·sia (sī lē′shə, si-; -zhə) region in E Europe, on both sides of the upper Oder, mainly in what is now SW Poland —**Si·le′si·an** *adj., n.*

si·le·sia (sī lē′shə, si-; -zhə) *n.* **1.** orig., a linen cloth made in Silesia **2.** a strong, lightweight, twilled cotton cloth used for linings and pockets

si·lex (sī′leks) *n.* [L. (gen. *silicis*), dissimulated < *scilec-* > *scelic-* < IE. base *(s)kel-*, to cut: see SHELF, SHIELD] **1.** silica, esp. in the form of flint or quartz **2.** heat-resistant glass made of fused quartz

SILESIA

sil·hou·ette (sil′oo wet′) *n.* [Fr., after Étienne de *Silhouette* (1709–67), Fr. minister of finance, in derogatory reference to his fiscal policies and to such amateur portraits by him, both regarded as inept] **1.** *a)* an outline drawing, esp. a profile portrait, filled in with a solid color: silhouettes are usually cut from black paper and fixed on a light background *b)* any dark shape or figure seen against a light background **2.** the outline of a figure, garment, etc.; contour —*vt.* **-et′ted, -et′ting** to show or project in silhouette —SYN. see OUTLINE

sil·i·ca (sil′i kə) *n.* [ModL. < L. *silex*, flint: see SILEX] the dioxide of silicon, SiO₂, a hard, glassy mineral found in a variety of forms, as in quartz, sand, opal, etc.

silica gel an amorphous, highly adsorbent form of silica used as a drying agent in air-conditioning equipment, as a carrier of catalysts in chemical reactions, etc.

SILHOUETTE

sil·i·cate (sil′i kit, -kāt′) *n.* a salt or ester derived from silica or a silicic acid

si·li·ceous (sə lish′əs) *adj.* [L. *siliceus*] 1. of, containing, or like silica 2. growing in soil that has a large proportion of silica in it Also **si·li′cious**

si·lic·ic (sə lis′ik) *adj.* [SILIC(A) or SILIC(ON) + -IC] of, like, or derived from silica or silicon

silicic acid 1. any of several jellylike masses, $SiO_2 \cdot nH_2O$, precipitated by acidifying sodium silicate solution 2. any of several hypothetical acids of which the different mineral silicates may be regarded as salts

sil·i·cide (sil′i sīd′) *n.* a binary compound of silicon and another element, usually a metal

sil·i·cif·er·ous (sil′ə sif′ər əs) *adj.* [< L. *silex* (see SILEX) + -FEROUS] containing or producing silica

si·lic·i·fy (sə lis′ə fī′) *vt.* **-fied′, -fy′ing** [< L. *silex* (see SILEX) + -FY] to convert into or impregnate with silica; specif., *same as* PETRIFY (*vt.* 1) —*vi.* to become silicified, as wood —**si·lic′i·fi·ca′tion** *n.*

si·li·ci·um (si lish′ē əm, -lis′-) *n.* [ModL.: so named (1808) by Sir H. DAVY < L. *silex*, flint (see SILEX)] *earlier name for* SILICON

sil·i·cle (sil′i k'l) *n.* [< Fr. or L.: Fr. *silicule* < L. *silicula*, dim. of *siliqua*, a pod: for IE. base see SILEX] *Bot.* a short, broad silique: also **si·lic·u·la** (sə lik′yoo lə), *pl.* **-lae′** (-lē′) —**si·lic′u·lar** (-lər) *adj.*

sil·i·co- (sil′i kō′, -kə) [< ff.] *a combining form meaning* silicon, silica [*silicosis*]: also, before a vowel, **silic-**

sil·i·con (sil′i kən, -kän′) *n.* [ModL.: altered (after BORON, CARBON, because of chemical resemblances) < SILICIUM] a nonmetallic chemical element occurring in several forms, found always in combination, and more abundant in nature than any other element except oxygen, with which it combines to form silica: used in the manufacture of transistors, solar cells, rectifiers, silicones, ceramics, etc.: symbol, Si; at. wt., 28.086; at. no., 14; sp. gr., 232; melt. pt., 1410°C; boil. pt., 2355°C

silicon carbide a bluish-black crystalline substance, SiC, produced in an electric furnace: see CARBORUNDUM

sil·i·cone (-kōn′) *n.* [SILIC(O)- + -ONE] any of a group of polymerized, organic silicon compounds containing a basic structure of alternate oxygen and silicon atoms usually with various organic groups attached to the chain: characterized by relatively high resistance to temperature changes, to water, etc. and used in lubricants, synthetic rubber, resins, polishes, and the like

silicone rubber a rubberlike polymer prepared from certain silicones: it maintains its elasticity and electrical properties over a wide range of temperatures and is used in gaskets, insulation, tapes, prosthetics, etc.

sil·i·co·sis (sil′ə kō′sis) *n.* [ModL.: see SILICO- & -OSIS] a chronic disease of the lungs marked by diffuse fibrosis and caused by the continued inhalation of silica dust

si·lic·u·lose (sə lik′yoo lōs′) *adj.* [ModL. *siliculosus*] 1. having silicles 2. having the form of a silicle

si·lique (si lēk′, sil′ik) *n.* [Fr. < L. *siliqua*: cf. SILICLE] the pod of plants of the mustard family, with two valves that fall away from a thin membrane bearing the seeds — **sil·i·quose** (sil′ə kwōs′), **sil′i·quous** (-kwəs) *adj.*

silk (silk) *n.* see PLURAL, II, D, 3 [ME. *silke* < OE. *seoluc*, prob. via Slavic (as in OPrus. *silkas*) < ? L. *sericus* (or Gr. *sērikos*), silken: see SERGE] 1. the fine, soft, shiny fiber produced by silkworms to form their cocoons 2. thread or fabric made from this fiber 3. *a*) a garment or other article made of this fabric *b*) [*pl.*] a distinctive silk uniform, as of a jockey *c*) the silk gown worn by a king's (or queen's) counsel in British law courts 4. any silklike filament or substance, as that produced by spiders, or that within a milkweed pod, on the end of an ear of corn, etc. —*adj.* of or like silk; silken —☆*vi.* to develop silk: said of Indian corn —**hit the silk** [Slang] to parachute from an aircraft

silk cotton *same as* KAPOK

silk-cot·ton tree (silk′kät′'n) any of several large tropical trees of the bombax family that have capsular fruits with silky hairs around the seeds; esp., *same as* CEIBA (sense 1)

silk·en (sil′k'n) *adj.* [ME. < OE. *seolcen*: see SILK & -EN] 1. made of silk 2. dressed in silk 3. like silk in appearance, texture, quality, etc.; specif., *a*) soft, smooth, or glossy *b*) smooth and ingratiating [*silken* flattery] *c*) elegant; luxurious [*silken* ease] *d*) soft; gentle [a *silken* caress]

silk hat a tall, cylindrical hat covered with silk or satin, worn by men in formal dress

silk-screen print (silk′skrēn′) a print made by the silk-screen process: cf. SERIGRAPH

silk-screen process a stencil method of printing a flat color design through a piece of silk or other fine cloth on which all parts of the design not to be printed have been stopped out by an impermeable film —**silk′-screen′** *vt.*

silk-stock·ing (-stäk′iŋ) *adj.* 1. fashionably or richly dressed; elegant 2. wealthy, aristocratic, or upper-class —*n.* ☆a member of the wealthy or aristocratic class

☆**silk·weed** (-wēd′) *n. same as* MILKWEED (*n.* 1)

silk·worm (-wurm′) *n.* any of certain moth caterpillars that produce cocoons of silk fiber: they feed chiefly on mulberry leaves and some species (esp. *Bombyx mori*) are cultivated as the source of commercial silk

silk·y (sil′kē) *adj.* **silk′i·er, silk′i·est** 1. of or like silk; soft, smooth, lustrous, etc. 2. having fine, soft, silklike hairs, as some leaves —**silk′i·ly** *adv.* —**silk′i·ness** *n.*

sill (sil) *n.* [ME. *sille* < OE. *syll*, akin to Dan. *sville*, G. *schwelle* < IE. base *sel-, *swel-, a beam, plank, whence Gr. *selma*, a beam] 1. a heavy, horizontal timber or line of masonry supporting a house wall, etc. 2. a horizontal piece forming the bottom frame of the opening into which a window or door is set 3. *Geol.* an intrusive body of igneous rock that has solidified in horizontal, flattened sheets between and parallel to the bedding planes in stratified rocks

sil·la·bub (sil′ə bub′) *n. var. of* SYLLABUB

☆**sil·li·man·ite** (sil′ə mə nīt′) *n.* [after B. *Silliman* (1779–1864), U.S. chemist and geologist] a native aluminum silicate, Al_2SiO_5, occurring in orthorhombic crystals in certain metamorphic rocks

sil·ly (sil′ē) *adj.* **-li·er, -li·est** [ME. *seli, sili* (with shortened vowel), good, blessed, innocent < OE. *sælig*, happy, prosperous, blessed (akin to G. *selig*, blessed) < *sæl*, happiness (sense development: happy → blissful → unaware of reality → foolish) < IE. base *sel-, favorable, in good spirits, whence Gr. *hilasia*, propitiation, *hilaros*, gay, L. *solari*, to comfort] 1. orig., *a*) simple; plain; innocent *b*) feeble; infirm; helpless 2. [Now Rare] feebleminded; imbecile 3. having or showing little sense, judgment, or sobriety; foolish, stupid, absurd, ludicrous, irrational, etc. 4. trivial 5. [Colloq.] dazed or senseless, as from a blow —*n., pl.* **-lies** a silly person —**sill′li·ly** (or **sil′ly**) *adv.* —**sill′li·ness** *n.* SYN.—**silly** implies ridiculous or irrational behavior that seems to demonstrate a lack of common sense, good judgment, or sobriety [it was *silly* of you to dress so lightly]; **stupid** implies a dull-wittedness or lack of normal intelligence or understanding [he is *stupid* to believe that]; **fatuous** suggests stupidity, inanity, or obtuseness coupled with a smug complacency [a *fatuous* smile]; **asinine** implies the extreme stupidity conventionally attributed to an ass [an *asinine* argument] See also ABSURD —ANT. wise, intelligent

si·lo (sī′lō) *n., pl.* **-los** [Fr. < Sp. < L. *sirus* < Gr. *siros*, an underground granary, pit, prob. < IE. base *swe(i)-, to bend] 1. an airtight pit or tower in which green fodder is preserved ☆2. a large, underground structure for the storage and launching of a long-range ballistic missile —*vt.* **-loed, -lo·ing** to store in a silo

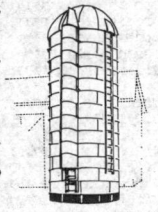

SILO

Si·lo·am (si lō′əm, sī-) [LL. (Ec.) < Gr.(Ec.) *Silōam* < Heb. *shilōah*, lit., sending forth] *Bible* a spring and pool outside Jerusalem: John 9:7

Si·lo·ne (sē lō′ne; *E.* sə lō′nē) **Ig·na·zio** (ē nyä′tsyō) (born *Secondo Tranquilli*) 1900– ; It. writer

si·lox·ane (si läk′sān) *n.* [SIL(ICON) + OX(YGEN) + -ANE] any of a class of compounds, varying from liquids to hard resins, whose molecules are composed of chains of alternate silicon and oxygen atoms, usually with hydrogen or hydrocarbon groups attached to the free valences of the silicon atoms

silt (silt) *n.* [ME. *cylte*, prob. < Scand., as in Norw. & Dan. dial. *sylt*, salt marsh, akin to OHG. *sulza*, brine: for IE. base see SALT] 1. a fine-grained, unconsolidated sediment, with particles intermediate in size between those of sand and clay, carried or laid down as sediment by moving water 2. soil composed of 80 percent or more silt and less than 12 percent clay —*vt., vi.* to fill or choke up with silt —**sil·ta·tion** (sil tā′shən) *n.* —SYN. see WASH

silt·y (sil′tē) *adj.* **silt′i·er, silt′i·est** 1. of or like silt 2. full of or clouded with silt

Sil·u·res (sil′yoo rēz′) *n.pl.* [L.] an ancient tribe of SE Wales, conquered (c.80 A.D.) by the Romans

Si·lu·ri·an (si loor′ē ən, sī-) *adj.* 1. of the Silures 2. [because the rocks were first found in an area in SE Wales: see prec.] designating or of the geological period after the Ordovician and before the Devonian in the Paleozoic Era, characterized in some regions by extensive coral reefs and by an abundance of invertebrate marine animals —**the Silurian** the Silurian Period or its rocks: see GEOLOGY, chart

si·lu·rid (si loor′id, sī-) *n.* [< ModL. *Siluridae*, name of the family < L. *silurus*, a kind of river fish < Gr. *silouros*] any of a family (Siluridae) of freshwater catfishes found in Europe and Asia, with anal and caudal fins fused —*adj.* of or pertaining to this family

sil·va (sil′və) *n.* [ModL. < L., a forest] 1. the forest trees of a certain area 2. *pl.* **-vas, -vae** (-vē) a book or treatise describing the trees of a certain area

sil·van (sil′vən) *adj., n. same as* SYLVAN

Sil·va·nus (sil vā′nəs) a Roman god of woods and fields

sil·ver (sil′vər) *n.* [ME. *selver* < OE. *seolfer*, akin to G. *silber*, Goth. *silubr*, prob. a loanword < a non-IE. source] 1. a white, metallic chemical element that is extremely ductile and malleable, capable of a high polish, and the best metal conductor of heat and electricity: it is a precious metal and is used in the manufacture of coins, jewelry, alloys, etc.: symbol, Ag; at. wt., 107.868; at. no., 47; sp. gr., 10.5; melt. pt., 960.8°C; boil. pt., 1950°C 2. *a*) silver coin *b*) money; riches; wealth 3. something, esp. tableware, made of or plated with silver; silverware 4. the lustrous, grayish-white color of silver 5. something having this color, as the material used in coating the back of a mirror 6. a salt of silver as used in photography, etc. —*adj.* 1. made of, containing, or plated with silver [*silver* thread] 2. of, based on, or having to do with silver [the *silver* standard] ☆3. of

or advocating the adoption of silver as a standard of currency [the *silver* bloc] **4.** having the color or luster of silver; silvery **5.** having a silvery tone or sound **6.** eloquent [a *silver* tongue] **7.** marking or celebrating the twenty-fifth year [a *silver* wedding anniversary] —*vt.* **1.** to cover or coat with silver or something like silver **2.** to cause to resemble silver in color or luster [hair *silvered* with age] —*vi.* to become silvery in color

Sil·ver (sil′vər), **Ab·ba Hil·lel** (ab′ə hil′el) 1893–1963; U.S. rabbi, born in Lithuania

Silver Age 1. *Gr. & Rom. Myth.* the second age of the world, inferior to the earlier Golden Age **2.** [s- a-] any period of progress, prosperity, etc. of a lesser degree than that of a corresponding golden age

☆**silver bell** any of a genus (*Halesia*) of small trees of the storax family, with drooping, bell-shaped, white flowers, native to the E U.S. and to China: also **sil′ver-bell′ tree**

☆**sil·ver·ber·ry** (-ber′ē) *n., pl.* **-ries** a shrub (*Elaeagnus commutata*) of the oleaster family, with silvery leaves and fruit, native to the N U.S. and to Canada

☆**silver birch** *same as* PAPER BIRCH

silver bromide a yellow-white crystalline compound, AgBr, which becomes dark when exposed to light: used as an emulsion coating in photography

☆**silver certificate** formerly, a type of U.S. paper currency redeemable in silver

silver chloride a white crystalline compound, AgCl, which becomes dark when exposed to light: used in photography and as lenses and cell walls in infrared spectroscopy

sil·ver·fish (-fish′) *n.* **1.** *pl.* **-fish′, -fish′es:** see FISH² any of various unrelated fishes of silvery color, as the tarpon, silverside, etc. **2.** *pl.* **-fish′** a primitive, wingless insect (*Lepisma saccharina*) with silvery scales, long feelers, and a bristly tail: it thrives in dampness and darkness and is injurious to books and other paper products

silver foil silver beaten into thin sheets

silver fox 1. a color phase of the N. American red fox in which the fur is black and the individual hairs are banded with white near the tips: foxes of this color phase are bred for their pelts **2.** the fur

silver gilt 1. gilded silver, or an imitation of this **2.** silver leaf, used for decoration

sil·ver-gray (-grā′) *adj., n.* gray with a silvery luster

☆**silver hake** a hake (*Merluccius bilinearis*) of the Atlantic coast of the U.S.

sil·ver·ing (-iŋ) *n.* **1.** the act of covering with silver or a silvery substance **2.** a coating of silver or a silvery substance **3.** a silvery sheen or appearance

silver iodide a yellow powder, AgI, which becomes dark when exposed to light: used in photography, medicine, and in seeding clouds to make rain

silver leaf very thin sheets of silver foil

silver lining some basis for hope or some comforting aspect in the midst of despair, misfortune, etc.

sil·ver·ly (-lē) *adv.* with a silvery appearance or sound

sil·vern (sil′vərn) *adj.* [ME. *silveren* < OE. *seolfren:* see SILVER & -EN] [Archaic] of or like silver

silver nitrate a colorless, crystalline salt, AgNO₃, prepared by dissolving silver in dilute nitric acid and used in silver plating, photography, etc. as an antiseptic, etc.

☆**silver perch 1.** a common drumfish (*Bairdiella chrysura*) of the Atlantic coast of the U.S., with a silvery body and yellow fins **2.** any of various silvery, perchlike fishes

sil·ver-plate (-plāt′) *vt.* **-plat′ed, -plat′ing** to coat with silver, esp. by electroplating

silver plate tableware made of, or plated with, silver

sil·ver-point (-point′) *n.* a method of drawing on specially prepared paper with an instrument tipped with silver

silver protein any of several colloidal silver solutions containing silver and a protein, as albumin: formerly used in treating inflammation of mucous membranes

☆**silver salmon** *same as* COHO

silver screen 1. a screen on which motion pictures are projected in theaters ☆**2.** motion pictures collectively

☆**sil·ver·side** (sil′vər sīd′) *n.* any of a number of small, mostly saltwater fishes (family Atherinidae) with silver stripes along the sides: also **sil′ver·sides′**

sil·ver·smith (-smith′) *n.* a craftsman whose work is making and repairing silver articles

Silver Spring [from the silvery mica flakes on the bottom of a nearby spring] town in C Md.: suburb of Washington, D.C.: pop. 77,000

silver standard a monetary standard solely in terms of silver, in which the basic currency unit is made equal to and redeemable by a specified quantity of silver

☆**Silver Star Medal** a U.S. military decoration in the form of a bronze star with a small silver star at the center, awarded for gallantry in action

silver thaw *same as* GLITTER ICE: also **silver frost**

sil·ver-tongued (-tuŋd′) *adj.* eloquent; persuasive

☆**sil·ver·ware** (sil′vər wer′) *n.* **1.** articles, esp. tableware, made of or plated with silver **2.** any metal tableware

silver wedding the 25th anniversary of a wedding

sil·ver·weed (sil′vər wēd′) *n.* **1.** a trailing perennial cinquefoil (*Potentilla anserina*) with pinnately compound

leaves which are silvery beneath **2.** any of a genus (*Argyreia*) of tropical, shrubby, climbing plants of the morning-glory family, with silvery leaves

sil·ver·y (sil′vər ē) *adj.* **1.** *a*) resembling silver, as in color or luster *b*) covered with or containing silver **2.** soft and clear, like the sound of a silver bell —**sil′ver·i·ness** *n.*

Sil·ves·ter (sil ves′tər) a masculine name: see SYLVESTER

Sil·vi·a (sil′vē ə) a feminine name: see SYLVIA

sil·vi·cal (sil′vi k′l) *adj.* [SILVIC(S) + -AL] of or pertaining to forests or forestry

sil·vic·o·lous (sil vik′ə ləs) *adj.* [< L. *silvicola*, inhabiting woods (< *silva*, a forest + *colere*, to cultivate, inhabit) + -OUS] living or growing in woodlands

sil·vics (sil′viks) *n.pl.* [with *sing. v.*] [SILV(A) + -ICS] the study of forests and their ecology including the application of soil science, botany, zoology, etc. to forestry

sil·vi·cul·ture (sil′vi kul′chər) *n.* [Fr. *sylviculture* < L. *silva*, forest (see SYLVAN) + *cultura*, CULTURE] the art of cultivating a forest; forestry —**sil′vi·cul′tur·al** *adj.* — **sil′vi·cul′tur·ist** *n.*

‡**s'il vous plaît** (sē voo ple′, sēl) [Fr., lit., if it pleases you] if you please; please

si·ma (sī′mə) *n.* [G. < si(*licium*), SILICIUM + *ma*(*gnesium*), MAGNESIUM] *Geol.* the heavy igneous rock material of the earth's inner crust, forming a continuous shell and underlying the sial and also the ocean floors

si·mar (si mär′) *n.* [Fr. *simarre* < It. *cimarra* < Ar. *sammūr*, sable] a flowing robe or long loose jacket formerly worn by women, orig. in the late medieval period

Sim·e·on (sim′ē ən) [Gr.(Ec.) *Symeon* < Gr.(Ec.) *Symeōn* < Heb. *shim'ōn*, lit., heard] **1.** a masculine name **2.** *Bible a*) the second son of Jacob and Leah, or the tribe of Israel descended from him *b*) a pious man who, on seeing the infant Jesus in the Temple, spoke the words later set to the canticle "Nunc Dimittis": Luke 2:25–32

Simeon Styl·i·tes (stī lī′tēz), Saint 390?–459? A.D.; Syrian monk who lived & preached on the top of a pillar near Antioch for over 30 years: his day is Jan. 5

Sim·fe·ro·pol (sim′fe rô′pôl y′) capital of the Crimea, Ukrainian S.S.R.: pop. 217,000

Sim·hat To·rah (sim khät′ tō rä′, sim′khäs tō′rə) [Heb. *śimḥath tōrāh*, lit., rejoicing in the Torah] a Jewish festival, celebrated on the 23d day of Tishri, that marks the end of the annual cycle of Torah readings and the beginning of the next cycle: also sp. **Simchath Torah**

sim·i·an (sim′ē ən) *adj.* [< L. *simia*, an ape, prob. < *simus*, flat-nosed < Gr. *simos* < IE. base *swei-*, to bend: cf. SWEEP, SWIFT] of or like an ape or monkey —*n.* an ape or monkey, esp. an anthropoid ape

sim·i·lar (sim′ə lər) *adj.* [Fr. *similaire* < L. *similis:* for IE. base see SAME] **1.** nearly but not exactly the same or alike; having a resemblance **2.** *Geom.* having the same shape, but not the same size or position —**sim′i·lar·ly** *adv.*

sim·i·lar·i·ty (sim′ə lar′ə tē) *n.* [prec. + -ITY] **1.** the state or quality of being similar; resemblance or likeness **2.** *pl.* **-ties** a point, feature, or instance in which things are similar —SYN. see LIKENESS

sim·i·le (sim′ə lē′) *n.* [ME. < L., a likeness < neut. of *similis*, SIMILAR] a figure of speech in which one thing is likened to another, dissimilar thing by the use of *like, as,* etc. (Ex.: a heart as big as a whale, her tears flowed like wine): distinguished from METAPHOR

si·mil·i·tude (sə mil′ə tōōd′, -tyōōd′) *n.* [ME. < MFr. < L. *similitudo*] **1.** a person or thing resembling another; counterpart; facsimile **2.** the form or likeness (*of* some person or thing) **3.** *a*) [Rare] a simile *b*) a parable or allegory **4.** similarity; likeness; resemblance

sim·i·ous (sim′ē əs) *adj. same as* SIMIAN

sim·i·tar (sim′ə tər) *n. var. of* SCIMITAR

Si·mi Valley (sə mē′; *popularly,* sē′mē) [prob. < AmInd. *shimiji*, little white clouds] city n SW Calif., northwest of Los Angeles: pop. 56,000

Sim·la (sim′lə) capital of Himachal Pradesh, in an exclave of Punjab, N India: pop. 43,000

sim·mer (sim′ər) *vi.* [earlier *simper* < LME. *simperen:* orig. echoic] **1.** to remain at or just below the boiling point, usually forming tiny bubbles with a low, murmuring sound **2.** to be about to break out, as in anger, revolt, etc. —*vt.* **1.** to keep (a liquid) at or just below the boiling point **2.** to cook in such a liquid —*n.* the state of simmering —SYN. see BOIL¹ —**simmer down 1.** to simmer, as a liquid, until the volume is reduced or condensed ☆**2.** to become calm; cool off

sim·nel (sim′n′l) *n.* [ME. *simenel* < OFr. < L. *simila*, fine wheat flour: see SEMOLINA] in England, **1.** formerly, a kind of bread or roll prepared by boiling, or boiling and baking **2.** a rich fruitcake traditionally eaten in mid-Lent or at Easter or Christmas

☆**si·mo·le·on** (sə mō′lē ən) *n.* [prob. < obs. *simon*, a dollar, after NAPOLEON] [Old Slang] a dollar

Si·mon (sī′mən) [ME. < LL.(Ec.) < Gr.(Ec.) *Simōn, Seimōn* < Heb. *shim'ōn*, lit., heard] **1.** a masculine name: dim. **Si 2.** *Bible a*) one of the twelve apostles, called *Peter* or *Simon Peter:* see PETER *b*) one of the twelve apostles, called *Simon the Canaanite:* Mark 3:18: also

called *Saint Simon:* his day is Oct. 28 *c)* a brother or relative of Jesus: Mark 6:3

si·mo·ni·ac (si mō′nē ak′) *n.* [ME. *symoniak* < ML. *simoniacus*] a person who practices simony —**si·mo·ni·a·cal** (sī′mə nī′ə k′l, sim′ə-) *adj.*

Si·mon·i·des (sī män′ə dēz′) 556?–468? B.C.; Gr. lyric poet: also **Simonides of Keos**

Simon Le·gree (lə grē′) **1.** the villainous slave overseer in H. B. Stowe's *Uncle Tom's Cabin* **2.** any cruel taskmaster

Simon Ma·gus (mā′gəs) *Bible* a Samaritan magician who offered money for instruction in the rite of imparting the Holy Ghost by the laying on of hands: Acts 8:9–24

si·mon-pure (sī′mən pyoor′) *adj.* [after *Simon Pure,* a Quaker in Susanna Centlivre's play *A Bold Stroke for a Wife* (1718), who must prove his identity against an impostor's claims] genuine; real; authentic

si·mo·ny (sī′mə nē, sim′ə-) *n.* [ME. *simonie* < OFr. < ML.(Ec.) *simonia* < Simon Magus] the buying or selling of sacred or spiritual things, as sacraments or benefices

si·moom (si mōōm′) *n.* [Ar. *samūm* < *samma,* to poison] a hot, violent, sand-laden wind of the African and Asiatic deserts: also **si·moon′** (-mōōn′)

☆**simp** (simp) *n. slang clipped form of* SIMPLETON

sim·pa·ti·co (sim pät′i kō, -pat′-) *adj.* [< It. *simpatico* or Sp. *simpático,* both ult. < L. *sympathia,* SYMPATHY + -*icus,* -IC] that gets along well with or goes well with another or others; compatible or congenial

sim·per (sim′pər) *vi.* [Early ModE., akin to Dan. dial. *semper,* MDu. *simperlijc,* dainty, affected] to smile in a silly, affected, or self-conscious way —*vt.* to say or express with a simper —*n.* a silly, affected, or self-conscious smile —*SYN.* see SMILE —**sim′per·er** *n.* —**sim′per·ing·ly** *adv.*

sim·ple (sim′p'l) *adj.* **-pler, -plest** [ME. < OFr. < L. *simplex,* akin to Gr. *haplos* < IE. **sem-,* one, together (whence SAME) + **plak-,* surface (cf. DUPLEX)] **1.** having or consisting of only one part, feature, substance, etc.; not compounded or complex; single **2.** having few parts or features; not complicated or involved [a *simple* pattern] **3.** easy to do, solve, or understand, as a task, question, etc. **4.** without additions or qualifications; mere; bare [the *simple* facts] **5.** *a)* not ornate; unembellished; unadorned [*simple* clothes] *b)* not luxurious or elegant; plain [*simple* tastes] **6.** pure; unadulterated **7.** without guile or deceit; innocent; artless **8.** *a)* without ostentation or affectation; natural *b)* lacking sophistication; naive **9.** of low rank or position; specif., *a)* humble; lowly *b)* common; ordinary **10.** lacking significance; unimportant **11.** *a)* having or showing little sense or reasoning ability; easily misled or deceived; stupid or foolish *b)* uneducated or ignorant **12.** *Bot. a)* consisting of one piece; whole *b)* not branched *c)* developing from a single pistil or carpel [a *simple* fruit] **13.** *Chem. a)* elementary *b)* unmixed **14.** *Law* unconditional; absolute [in fee *simple*] **15.** *Music a)* not compound: said of time or measure *b)* not having overtones [a *simple* tone] *c)* not elaborated [*simple* harmony] **16.** *Zool.* not divided into or made up of parts; not compounded [a *simple* eye] —*n.* **1.** a person who is ignorant or easily misled **2.** something having only one part, substance, etc. **3.** [Archaic] *a)* a medicinal plant or herb *b)* a medicine made from such a plant **4.** [Archaic] a person of humble parentage or position —*SYN.* see EASY —**sim′ple·ness** *n.*

simple equation *same as* LINEAR EQUATION

simple fraction a fraction in which both the numerator and denominator are whole numbers, as 1/2

simple fracture a bone fracture in which the broken ends of bone do not pierce the skin

sim·ple-heart·ed (-härt′id) *adj.* artless or unsophisticated in nature; sincere

simple interest interest computed on principal alone, and not on principal plus interest

simple machine any of the basic mechanical devices, including the lever, wheel and axle, pulley, wedge, screw, and inclined plane, one or more of which are essential to any more complex machine

sim·ple-mind·ed (-mīn′did) *adj.* **1.** artless; unsophisticated; simple-hearted **2.** foolish; stupid **3.** mentally retarded —**sim′ple-mind′ed·ly** *adv.* —**sim′ple-mind′ed·ness** *n.*

simple protein a protein composed only of amino acids

simple sentence a sentence having one main clause and no subordinate clauses (Ex.: The boy ran home quickly.)

Simple Simon 1. a foolish character in a nursery rhyme **2.** a simpleton

sim·ple·ton (-tən) *n.* [< SIMPLE, after names ending in -*ton*] a person who is stupid or easily deceived; fool

sim·plex (sim′pleks) *adj.* [L., SIMPLE] **1.** having only one part; not complex or compounded **2.** designating or of a system of telegraphy, telephony, etc. in which a signal can be transmitted in only one direction at a time —*n., pl.* **-plex·es, -pli·ces′** (-plə sēz′) *Math.* an element or figure contained within a Euclidean space of a specified number of dimensions and having one more boundary point than the number of dimensions

sim·plic·i·ty (sim plis′ə tē) *n., pl.* **-ties** [ME. *simplicite* < OFr. *simplicité* < L. *simplicitas*] **1.** a simple state or quality, as of form or composition; freedom from intricacy or complexity **2.** absence of elegance, embellishment, luxury, or the like; plainness **3.** freedom from affectation, subtlety, etc.; artlessness **4.** lack of sense; foolishness

sim·pli·fy (sim′plə fī′) *vt.* **-fied′, -fy′ing** [Fr. *simplifier* < ML. *simplificare*] to make simpler; make less complex, involved, abstruse, etc.; make plainer or easier —**sim′-pli·fi·ca′tion** *n.* —**sim′pli·fi′er** *n.*

sim·plist (sim′plist) *n.* a person given to simplistic explanations, theories, etc. —*adj. same as* SIMPLISTIC — **sim′plism** *n.*

sim·plis·tic (sim plis′tik) *adj.* making complex problems unrealistically simple; oversimplifying or oversimplified —**sim·plis′ti·cal·ly** *adv.*

Sim·plon (sim′plän; *Fr.* saN plôN′) **1.** mountain pass in the Alps of S Switzerland: 6,589 ft. **2.** railway tunnel near this pass: 12.4 mi. long

sim·ply (sim′plē) *adv.* **1.** in a simple manner; with simplicity **2.** merely; only; just [*simply* trying to help] **3.** absolutely; completely [*simply* overwhelmed]

sim·u·la·crum (sim′yoo lā′krəm) *n., pl.* **-cra** (-krə) [L. < *simulare:* see SIMULATE] **1.** an image; likeness **2.** a vague representation; semblance **3.** a mere pretense; sham

sim·u·lant (sim′yoo lənt) *adj.* [L. *simulans,* prp.: see SIMULATE] that simulates; simulating —*n.* a person or thing that simulates; simulator

sim·u·lar (sim′yoo lər) *adj., n. archaic var. of* SIMULANT

sim·u·late (sim′yoo lāt′) *vt.* **-lat′ed, -lat′ing** [< L. *simulatus,* pp. of *simulare,* to feign < *simul,* together with, likewise: for IE. base see SAME] **1.** to give a false indication or appearance of; pretend; feign [to *simulate* an interest] **2.** to have or take on the external appearance of; look or act like [an insect *simulating* a twig] —*adj.* [Archaic] pretended; mock —*SYN.* see ASSUME —**sim′u·la′tor** *n.*

sim·u·la·tion (sim′yoo lā′shən) *n.* [ME. *simulacion* < MFr. < L. *simulatio*] **1.** the act of simulating; pretense; feigning **2.** *a)* a simulated resemblance *b)* an imitation or counterfeit —**sim′u·la′tive** *adj.*

☆**si·mul·cast** (sī′m'l kast′, -käst′) *vt.* **-cast′** or **-cast′ed, -cast′ing** [SIMUL(TANEOUS) + (BROAD)CAST] to broadcast (a program, event, etc.) simultaneously by radio and television —*n.* a program, etc. so broadcast

si·mul·ta·ne·ous (sī′m'l tā′nē əs, -tän′yəs; *chiefly Brit.,* sim′'l-) *adj.* [ML. *simultaneus* < *simultas,* simultaneity < L., competition, rivalry < *simul:* see SIMULATE] occurring, done, existing, etc. together or at the same time —*SYN.* see CONTEMPORARY —**si′mul·ta·ne′i·ty** (-tə nē′ə-tē), **si′mul·ta′ne·ous·ness** *n.* —**si′mul·ta′ne·ous·ly** *adv.*

simultaneous equations two or more equations used together in the same problem and having unknowns of the same value

sin[1] (sēn) *n.* [Heb.] a variant of the twenty-first letter (SHIN[2]) of the Hebrew alphabet (ש)

sin[2] (sin) *n.* [ME. (East Midland) *sinne* < OE. *synne* (for **sunjo*), akin to G. *sünde*] **1.** *a)* the breaking of religious law or a moral principle, esp. through a willful act *b)* a state of habitual violation of such principles **2.** any offense, misdemeanor, or fault —*vi.* **sinned, sin′ning 1.** to break a religious law or moral principle; commit a sin **2.** to commit an offense or fault of any kind; do wrong —*vt.* [Archaic] to commit (a sinful offense)

sin[3] *var. of* SINE

Si·nai (sī′nī; *occas.* sī′ni ī′), **Mount** *Bible* the mountain (probably in the S Sinai Peninsula but not identified) where Moses received the law from God: Ex. 19

Sinai Peninsula broad peninsula in NE Egypt, between the Gulf of Suez & the Gulf of Aqaba: see EGYPT, map: occupied by Israel, 1967

Si·na·it·ic (sī′ni it′ik) *adj.* of or from Mount Sinai or the Sinai Peninsula: also **Si·na·ic** (sī nā′ik)

Si·na·lo·a (sē′nä lō′ä) state of NW Mexico, on the Gulf of California: 22,582 sq. mi.; pop. 1,106,000; cap. Culiacán

Sin·an·thro·pus (sī nan′thrə pəs, si-) *n.* [ModL.: see SINO- & ANTHROPO] *earlier name for* PEKING MAN

sin·a·pism (sin′ə piz′m) *n.* [L. *sinapismus* < Gr. *sinapismos* < *sinapi,* mustard] *same as* MUSTARD PLASTER

Sin·bad the Sailor (sin′bad) a merchant in *The Arabian Nights* who makes seven adventurous voyages

since (sins) *adv.* [ME. *syns,* contr. < *sithens,* adv. gen. of *sithen* < OE. *siththan,* for earlier **siththon < sith,* after, since (for IE. base see SIDE) + *thon,* instrumental form of *thæt,* THAT] **1.** from then until now [he arrived Tuesday and remained ever *since*] **2.** at some or any time between then and now; subsequently [he was ill last week but has *since* recovered] **3.** before the present time; before now; ago [they are long *since* gone] —*prep.* **1.** continuously from (the time given) until now [out walking *since* one o'clock] **2.** during the period between (the time given) and now; subsequently to [many achievements *since* his election] —*conj.* **1.** after the time that [two years *since* she was last here] **2.** continuously from the time when [lonely ever *since* he left] **3.** inasmuch as; because [*since* you are finished, let's go]

sin·cere (sin sir′) *adj.* **-cer′er, -cer′est** [MFr. *sincère* < L. *sincerus,* clean, pure, sincere] **1.** without deceit, pretense, or hypocrisy; truthful; straightforward; honest [*sincere* in his desire to help] **2.** being the same in actual character as in outward appearance; genuine; real [*sincere* grief] **3.** [Archaic] not adulterated [*sincere* wine] **4.** [Obs.] uninjured; whole —**sin·cere′ly** *adv.* —**sin·cere′ness** *n.*

SYN.—**sincere** implies an absence of deceit, pretense, or hypocrisy and an adherence to the simple, unembellished truth [a *sincere* desire to help]; **unaffected** implies a natural, genuine simplicity

and a freedom from artificial behavior [an *unaffected* prose style]; **unfeigned** suggests behavior that is honestly spontaneous [she looked at him with *unfeigned* admiration]; **heartfelt** stresses depth as well as sincerity of feeling, esp. as expressed in warm words, acts, etc. [he extended his *heartfelt* sympathy]; **hearty** adds to this connotations of exuberance and geniality [my *hearty* congratulations] —*ANT.* **false**

sin·cer·i·ty (sin ser′ə tē) *n., pl.* **-ties** [MFr. *sincérité* < L. *sinceritas*] the quality or state of being sincere; honesty, genuineness, good faith, etc.

sin·ci·put (sin′sə put′) *n.* [L., half a head < *semi*, half (see SEMI-) + *caput*, HEAD] the upper part of the skull or head; esp., the forehead —**sin·cip·i·tal** (-sip′ə t'l) *adj.*

Sin·clair (sin kler′), **Up·ton** (**Beall, Jr.**) (up′t'n) 1878–1968; U.S. novelist & socialist

Sind (sind) region (a former province) of West Pakistan, in the lower Indus River valley: chief city, Karachi

Sind·bad (sin′bad, sind′-) *same as* SINBAD (THE SAILOR)

Sin·dhi (sin′dē) *n.* [Ar. *Sindi* < *Sind*, Sind < Hindi < Sans. *sindhu*, river] the Indic language of the Sind

sine (sin) *n.* [ML. *sinus* < L., a bending, curve, hanging fold of a toga, used as transl. of Ar. *jaib*, bosom of a garment, sine] *Trigonometry* the ratio between the side opposite a given acute angle in a right triangle and the hypotenuse; reciprocal of the cosecant of an angle or arc

‡si·ne (sī′nē, sē′nā) *prep.* [L.] without

si·ne·cure (sī′nə kyoor′, sin′ə-) *n.* [< ML.(Ec.) (*beneficium*) *sine cura*, (benefice) without a cure < L. *sine*, without + *cura*, care: see CURE] **1.** a church office that pays a salary without involving cure (care) of souls **2.** any office or position that brings profit or advantage without involving much work, responsibility, etc.

($\frac{a}{c}$, sine of angle A; $\frac{b}{c}$, sine of angle B)

SINE

sine curve a graphic representation of the sine ratio; specif., the graph of $y = \sin x$

si·ne di·e (sī′nē dī′ē, sin′ā dē′ā) [LL.] without (a) day (being set for meeting again); for an indefinite period [to adjourn an assembly *sine die*]

‡si·ne pro·le (sī′nē prō′lē, sin′ā) [L.] *Law* without offspring; childless

si·ne qua non (sī′nē kwä nän′, sin′ā kwä nōn′) [L., without which not] an essential condition, qualification, etc.; indispensable thing; absolute prerequisite

sin·ew (sin′yōō) *n.* [ME. < OE. *seonwe*, oblique form < nom. *seonu*, akin to OHG. *senawa*, ON. *sin* < IE. base *sēi-*, to bind, a band, whence Sans. *sināti*, (he) ties] **1.** a tendon **2.** muscular power; strength; force **3.** [often *pl.*] any source of power or strength; means of supplying strength —*vt.* to strengthen with or as with sinews

sine wave a wave form corresponding to a single-frequency, periodic oscillation which can be shown as a function of amplitude against angle and in which the value of the curve at any point is a function of the sine of that angle

sin·ew·y (sin′yoo wē) *adj.* **1.** of or like sinew; tough; strong **2.** having many or large sinews, as a cut of meat **3.** having good muscular development [*sinewy* shoulders] **4.** vigorous; powerful; robust [a *sinewy* style of writing]

sin·fo·ni·a (sin′fə nē′ə) *n.* [It. < L. *symphonia*, SYMPHONY] any of various early Italian instrumental works; esp., a type of overture, as to an opera

sin·fo·niet·ta (sin′fən yet′ə) *n.* [It., dim. of *sinfonia*: see prec.] a small or brief symphony, usually for a small orchestra

sin·ful (sin′fəl) *adj.* full of or characterized by sin; wicked; immoral —**sin′ful·ly** *adv.* —**sin′ful·ness** *n.*

sing (siŋ) *vi.* **sang** or now rarely **sung, sung, sing′ing** [ME. *singen* < OE. *singan*, akin to G. *singen* < IE. base *sengwh-*, whence Gr. *omphē*, a voice, oracle] **1.** *a)* to produce musical sounds or notes with the voice, esp. in a connected series, as in giving voice to a song *b)* to perform musical selections vocally, esp. as a professional **2.** to use song or verse in description, praise, etc. [of thee I *sing*] **3.** *a)* to make musical sounds like those made by the human voice, as a violin or songbird *b)* to make a sound of whistling, buzzing, humming, etc., as a steaming teakettle, a bee, a strong wind, etc. **4.** to have a sensation of ringing, humming, buzzing, etc., as the ears **5.** to admit of being sung **6.** to be exultant; rejoice [a sight to make one's heart *sing*] **7.** [Slang] to confess to a crime, esp. so as to implicate others —*vt.* **1.** to render or deliver (a song, musical role, etc.) by singing; utter with musical inflections **2.** to chant or intone (part of a church service, etc.) **3.** to describe, proclaim, extol, celebrate, etc. in or as in song or verse [to *sing* someone's praises] **4.** to bring to a given state or place by or with singing [to *sing* a baby to sleep] —*n.* **1.** a sound of whistling, humming, buzzing, etc. [the *sing* of arrows overhead] **2.** [Colloq.] *a)* singing by a group gathered for the purpose *b)* such a gathering of people —**sing out** [Colloq.] to speak or call out loudly; shout —**sing′a·ble** *adj.*

sing. singular

sing-a·long (siŋ′ə lôŋ′) *n.* [Colloq.] an informal gathering of people to join in the singing of songs

Sin·ga·pore (siŋ′gə pôr′, siŋ′ə-) **1.** island off the S tip of the Malay Peninsula **2.** country comprising this island & nearby islets: a member of the Brit. Commonwealth: 225 sq. mi.; pop. 1,956,000 **3.** its capital, a seaport on the S coast: pop. c. 1,000,000 **4.** **Strait of**, channel between Singapore & a group of Indonesian islands to the south: 65 mi. long: also **Singapore Strait**

singe (sinj) *vt.* **singed, singe′ing** [ME. *sengen* < OE. *sengan*, akin to G. *sengen* < IE. base *senk-*, to burn, dry out, whence OBulg. *isǫčii*, to dry, *sǫcilo*, oven] **1.** to burn superficially or slightly **2.** to expose (the carcass of an animal or fowl) to flame in removing bristles or feathers **3.** to burn the nap from (cloth) as a process of manufacture **4.** to burn the tips of (hair), as after a haircut —*n.* **1.** the act of singeing **2.** a superficial burn —*SYN.* see BURN[1]

sing·er[1] (siŋ′ər) *n.* **1.** a person who sings, esp. professionally **2.** a bird that sings; a poet

sing·er[2] (sin′jər) *n.* a person or thing that singes

Sing·er (siŋ′ər) **1.** **Isaac Ba·shev·is** (bä shev′is), 1904– ; Pol. writer in Yiddish, in the U.S. **2.** **Isaac Mer·ritt** (mer′it), 1811–75; U.S. inventor: improved the sewing machine

Sin·gha·lese (siŋ′gə lēz′, -lēs′) *adj., n., pl.* **-lese′** [< Sans. *Sinhala*, Ceylon + -ESE] *same as* SINHALESE

sin·gle (siŋ′g'l) *adj.* [ME. < OFr. *sengle* < L. *singulus*, single: for base see SIMPLE] **1.** *a)* one only; one and no more; individual *b)* separate and distinct from others of the same kind [every *single* time] **2.** without another or others; alone; solitary **3.** of or for one person, as a bed or room, or one family, as a house **4.** between two persons only; with only one on each side [*single* combat] **5.** *a)* unmarried *b)* of or characteristic of the unmarried state **6.** having only one part; not double, compound, multiple, etc. **7.** the same for all; uniform [a *single* scale of pay] **8.** being a whole, or unbroken [forming a *single* front] **9.** having only one row or set of petals: said of flowers and plants **10.** honest; sincere **11.** seeing justly [to judge with a *single* eye] **12.** [Rare] unique; singular **13.** [Archaic] weak; inferior: said of beer, ale, etc. —*vt.* **-gled, -gling 1.** to select or distinguish from others (now usually with out) ☆**2.** *Baseball* to advance (a runner) by hitting a single —*vi.* ☆*Baseball* to hit a single —*n.* **1.** a single person or thing; specif., *a)* a hotel room, travel space, etc. for one person *b)* [*pl.*] unmarried persons collectively ☆*c)* [Colloq.] a one-dollar bill ☆**2.** *Baseball* a hit by which the batter reaches first base **3.** *Cricket* a hit by which one run is scored **4.** *Golf* a match between two players **5.** [*pl.*] *Tennis*, etc. a match with only one player on each side

SYN.—**single** simply refers to one that is not united with or accompanied by another [a *single* chair in the room, a *single* man]; **sole** applies to the only one of its kind under consideration or in a particular situation [my *sole* dependent, his *sole* contribution]; **unique** strictly applies to the only one of its kind in existence [a *unique* bronze statue], but in popular usage often implies mere rareness or unusualness [a *unique* experience]; **solitary** adds to the sense of singleness connotations of isolation or separation [a *solitary* tree in the meadow]; **individual** refers to every one of a group or class as distinguished from all the others [an *individual* listing of members]; **particular** applies to a single, distinct instance, example, etc. of a group or class [must you have this *particular* seat?]

sin·gle-act·ing (-ak′tiŋ) *adj.* acting in or impelled from one direction only, as an engine; not reciprocating

sin·gle-ac·tion (-ak′shən) *adj.* ☆designating a firearm whose hammer must be cocked by hand before each shot

single bond *Chem.* the sharing of two electrons between two atoms, represented in formulas as C:C or C–C

sin·gle-breast·ed (-bres′tid) *adj.* overlapping the front of the body just enough to fasten with a single row of buttons or a single button, as a coat

single entry a system of bookkeeping in which the only account kept is a single one consisting usually of a record of cash and of debts owed to and by the concern in question —**sin′gle-en′try** *adj.*

single file 1. a single column of persons or things placed or moving one directly behind another **2.** in such a column [to march *single file*]

☆**sin·gle-foot** (-foot′) *n.* the gait of a horse in which the legs move in lateral pairs, each foot falling separately —☆*vi.* to move with this gait

sin·gle-hand·ed (-han′did) *adj.* **1.** having only one hand **2.** using or requiring the use of only one hand [a *single-handed* sword] **3.** without help; done or working alone; unaided —*adv.* **1.** by means of only one hand **2.** without help —**sin′gle-hand′ed·ly** *adv.* —**sin′gle-hand′ed·ness** *n.*

sin·gle-heart·ed (-härt′id) *adj.* honest; faithful; sincere —**sin′gle-heart′ed·ly** *adv.* —**sin′gle-heart′ed·ness** *n.*

sin·gle-mind·ed (-mīn′did) *adj.* **1.** same as SINGLE-HEARTED **2.** with only one aim or purpose —**sin′gle-mind′ed·ly** *adv.* —**sin′gle-mind′ed·ness** *n.*

sin·gle-phase (-fāz′) *adj.* designating or of a circuit or device energized by a single alternating voltage, either in phase or 180° out of phase

☆**sin·gle-side·band** (-sīd′band′) *adj.* of or pertaining to a system of radio transmission in which one of the two sidebands produced during modulation is suppressed

sin·gle-space (-spās′) *vt.* **-spaced′, -spac′ing** to type (copy) so as to leave no blank space between lines

☆**single standard** **1.** a moral code with the same standard of behavior for men and women alike, esp. in matters of sex **2.** *same as* MONOMETALLISM

sin·gle·stick (-stik′) *n.* **1.** a swordlike stick fitted with a guard and formerly used for fencing **2.** the sport of fencing with such sticks

☆**sin·gle-stick·er** (-stik′ər) *n.* [Old Colloq.] a sailboat, esp. a sloop, having only one mast

sin·glet (siŋ′glit) *n.* [Brit.] a man's undershirt or jersey

☆**single tax** **1.** a system of taxation in which all revenue is to be derived from a tax on a single object, specif. on the value of land **2.** such a tax —**sin′gle-tax′** *adj.*

sin·gle·ton (-tən) *n.* [< SINGLE, after proper names ending in *-ton*] **1.** a playing card that is the only one of its suit held by a given player **2.** something occurring or existing singly and not as one of a pair or of a group

☆**sin·gle-track** (-trak′) *adj. same as* ONE-TRACK

☆**sin·gle·tree** (-trē′) *n.* [altered (as if < SINGLE) < *swingletree* < ME. *swingle*, a rod, whip + *tre*, TREE] a wooden bar swung at the center from a hitch on a plow, wagon, etc. and hooked at either end to the traces of a horse's harness

sin·gly (siŋ′glē) *adv.* **1.** as a single, separate person or thing; alone **2.** individually and in sequence; one by one **3.** single-handed; unaided; alone

Sing Sing [< Du. *Sintsing* < same source as OSSINING] a N.Y. State penitentiary at Ossining

sing·song (siŋ′sôŋ′, -säŋ′) *n.* **1.** *a)* an unvarying rise and fall of tone, as in speaking *b)* speech, tones, etc. marked by this **2.** *a)* monotonous, stereotyped rhyme or rhythm in verse *b)* verse marked by this **3.** [Brit.] *same as* SING (*n.* 2) —*adj.* unvaryingly rising and falling, as in tone

‡**sing·spiel** (ziŋ′shpēl′) *n., pl.* **-spiel′en** (-ən) [G., lit., sing-play] an 18th-cent. German musical play of a popular type

sin·gu·lar (siŋ′gyə lər) *adj.* [ME. *singuler* < OFr. < L. *singularis* < *singulus*, SINGLE] **1.** being the only one of its kind; single; unique [a *singular* specimen] **2.** exceptional; extraordinary; remarkable [*singular* beauty] **3.** peculiar; strange; odd [what a *singular* remark!] **4.** [Archaic] existing apart from others; separate; individual **5.** Gram. designating or of that category of number referring to only one **6.** *Logic* of an individual or particular thing considered by itself —*n.* **1.** *Gram. a)* the singular number *b)* the singular form of a word *c)* a word in singular form **2.** *Logic* a thing considered apart from all others —**sin′gu·lar·ly** *adv.*

sin·gu·lar·i·ty (siŋ′gyə lar′ə tē) *n., pl.* **-ties** [ME. *singularite* < OFr. < LL. *singularitas*] **1.** the condition or quality of being singular **2.** a unique, distinct, or peculiar feature or thing

sin·gu·lar·ize (siŋ′gyə lə rīz′) *vt.* **-ized′, -iz′ing** to make singular

Sin·ha·lese (sin′hə lēz′, sin′ə-; -lēs′) *adj.* [< Sans. *Siṅhala*, Ceylon + -ESE] of Ceylon, its principal people, their language, etc. —*n.* **1.** *pl.* **-lese′** any member of the Sinhalese people **2.** their Indic language

Sin·i·cism (sin′i siz′m, sī′ni-) *n.* [< ML. *Sinicus*, Chinese (< LL. *Sinae*, an Oriental people < Gr. *Sinai*) + -ISM] a custom, language trait, etc. peculiar to the Chinese

Si·ning (shē′niŋ′) city in NW China; capital of Tsinghai province: pop. 320,000

sin·is·ter (sin′is tər) *adj.* [ME. *sinistre* < L. *sinister*, left-hand, or unlucky (side), orig. lucky (side) < IE. base *sene-*, to prepare, achieve, whence Sans. *sániyān*, more favorable: early Roman augurs faced south, with the east (lucky side) to the left, but the Greeks (followed by later Romans) faced north] **1.** *a)* orig., on, to, or toward the left-hand side; left *b)* forming, or placed on, the left half of a coat of arms (the right, from the observer's point of view) **2.** threatening harm, evil, or misfortune; ominous; portentous [*sinister* storm clouds] **3.** wicked, evil, or dishonest, esp. in some dark, mysterious way [a *sinister* plot] **4.** most unfavorable or unfortunate; disastrous [met a *sinister* fate] —**sin′is·ter·ly** *adv.* —**sin′is·ter·ness** *n.* SYN.—**sinister**, in this connection, applies to that which can be interpreted as presaging imminent danger or evil [a *sinister* smile]; **baleful** refers to that which is inevitably deadly, destructive, pernicious, etc. [a *baleful* influence]; **malign** is applied to that which is regarded as having an inherent tendency toward evil or destruction [a *malign* doctrine]

sin·is·tral (sin′is trəl) *adj.* [OFr. < L. *sinistra*, left hand: see prec.] **1.** on the left-hand side; left **2.** left-handed **3.** having whorls that rise to the apex in clockwise spirals: said of the shells of certain mollusks with the apex toward the viewer Opposed to DEXTRAL —**sin′is·tral′i·ty** (-i stral′ə tē) *n.* —**sin′is·tral·ly** *adv.*

sin·is·tro- (sin′is trō, -trə) [< L. *sinister*: see SINISTER] a combining form meaning of, at, or toward the left [*sinistrodextral*]: also, before a vowel, **sinistr-**

sin·is·tro·dex·tral (sin′is trō deks′trəl) *adj.* [prec. + DEXTRAL] going or directed from left to right

sin·is·trorse (sin′is trôrs′, sin′is trôrs′) *adj.* [ModL. *sinistrorsus* < L., contr. of *sinistrovorsus* < *sinister*, to the left (see SINISTER) + *versus, vorsus*, pp. of *vertere*, to turn: see VERSE] *Bot.* twining upward to the left, as the stems of some vines: opposed to DEXTRORSE —**sin′is·trorse′ly** *adv.*

sin·is·trous (sin′is trəs) *adj. same as* SINISTER

Si·nit·ic (si nit′ik) *n.* [see SINO-, -ITE[1], & -IC] a branch of the Sino-Tibetan family of languages, including Chinese and its dialects —*adj.* of China, the Chinese, their language, culture, etc.

sink (siŋk) *vi.* **sank** or **sunk, sunk** or obs. **sunk′en, sink′ing** [ME. *sinken* < OE. *sincan*, akin to G. *sinken* < IE. base **sengw-*, to fall, sink, whence Gr. *heaphthē*, (he) sank] **1.** to go beneath the surface of water, deep snow, soft ground, etc. so as to be partly or completely covered **2.** to go down slowly; fall or descend gradually **3.** to appear to fall or descend [the sun *sinking* in the west] **4.** *a)* to become lower in level; diminish in height or depth [a lake that has *sunk* three inches] *b)* to slope downward (*from, to,* etc.) **5.** to diminish or decrease in degree, volume, or strength; subside, as wind, flames, a sound, spirits, etc. **6.** to become lower in value or amount; lessen, as prices, funds, etc. **7.** to seem or become hollow or shrunken; recede, as the cheeks or eyes **8.** to pass gradually (*into* sleep, despair, lethargy, etc.) **9.** to become increasingly and dangerously ill; approach death; fail **10.** *a)* to lose position, wealth, prestige, dignity, etc. *b)* to lose or abandon one's moral values and stoop (*to* some unworthy action) **11.** to become absorbed; penetrate —*vt.* **1.** to cause to submerge or go beneath the surface [to *sink* a boat, to *sink* a spade into the ground] **2.** to cause or allow to fall or go down; lower **3.** to make (a well, mine, engraved design, etc.) by digging, drilling, or cutting **4.** to cause to penetrate or become absorbed **5.** to reduce in volume, amount, degree, or intensity **6.** *a)* to invest (money, capital, etc.) *b)* to lose by investing **7.** to hold back, suppress, or conceal (evidence, identity, personal interests, etc.) **8.** to pay up (a debt) **9.** *a)* to cause to lose courage, strength, etc. or position, dignity, etc. *b)* to debase (character, dignity, etc.) **10.** to defeat; undo; ruin ☆**11.** *Sports* to put (a basketball, golf ball, etc.) through the net, into the cup, etc. so as to score —*n.* [ME. *sinke* < the *v.*] **1.** a cesspool or sewer **2.** any place or thing considered morally filthy or corrupted **3.** any of various basins, as in a kitchen or laundry, connected with a drainpipe and, usually, a water supply ☆**4.** *Geol. a)* an area of slightly sunken land, esp. one in which water collects, often forming a salt lake, or disappears by evaporation or percolation into the ground ☆*b) same as* SINKHOLE (sense 2) —**sink in** [Colloq.] to be grasped by the mind, esp. with difficulty; be recognized or understood in full —**sink′a·ble** *adj.*

sink·age (siŋ′kij) *n.* **1.** the act of sinking **2.** the degree to which something has sunk or been sunk **3.** an area or part sunk below the surrounding level; depression

sink·er (-kər) *n.* **1.** a person or thing that sinks **2.** a lead weight used in fishing ☆**3.** [Colloq.] a doughnut

sink·hole (siŋk′hōl′) *n.* **1.** *same as* CESSPOOL ☆**2.** a hollow into which surface water flows to join an underground drainage system, produced by the solution of underlying material, as limestone, salt, etc.

Sin·kiang (sin′kyaŋ′; *Chin.* shin′jyäŋ′) autonomous region of NW China, between Tibet & the U.S.S.R.: 635,830 sq. mi.; pop. 5,640,000; cap. Urumchi: also **Sinkiang-Uigur**

sinking fund a fund made up of sums of money set aside at intervals, usually invested at interest, to pay a debt, meet depreciation expenses, etc.

sin·less (sin′lis) *adj.* without sin; innocent —**sin′less·ly** *adv.* —**sin′less·ness** *n.*

sin·ner (-ər) *n.* a person who sins; wrongdoer

Sinn Fein (shin′ fān′) [Ir., we ourselves] an Irish revolutionary movement of the early part of the 20th cent., working to establish political and economic independence and to revive Irish culture —**Sinn′ Fein′er**

Si·no- (sī′nō, sin′ō) [Fr. < LL. *Sinae* < Gr. *Sinai*, an Oriental people] *a combining form meaning:* **1.** of the Chinese people or language [*Sinology*] **2.** Chinese and [*Sino*-Japanese]

Si·nol·o·gist (sī näl′ə jist, si-) *n.* a student of or specialist in Sinology: also **Si·no·logue** (sī′nə lôg′, sin′ə-; -läg′)

Si·nol·o·gy (-jē) *n.* [SINO- + -LOGY] the study of Chinese language, literature, art, customs, etc. —**Si·no·log·i·cal** (sī′nə läj′i k′l, sin′ə-) *adj.*

Si·no-Ti·bet·an (sī′nō ti bet′′n) *adj.* designating or of a family of languages spoken in C and SE Asia, including Sinitic and Tibeto-Burman —*n.* this family of languages

sin·ter (sin′tər) *n.* [G., akin to CINDER] **1.** *Geol.* a concretionary sediment of silica or calcium carbonate deposited near the mouth of a mineral spring, geyser, etc. **2.** *Metallurgy* a bonded mass of metal particles shaped and partially fused by pressure and heating below the melting point —*vi., vt.* to become or make into a sinter (*n.* 2)

sin·u·ate (sin′yoo wit; *also, and for v. always,* -wāt′) *adj.* [L. *sinuatus*, pp. of *sinuare*, to bend < *sinus*, a bend] **1.** *same as* SINUOUS **2.** *Bot.* having an indented wavy margin, as some leaves —*vi.* **-at′ed, -at′ing** to bend or wind in and out; be sinuous or wavy —**sin′u·ate·ly** *adv.* —**sin′u·a′tion** *n.*

sin·u·os·i·ty (sin′yoo wäs′ə tē) *n.* [Fr. *sinuosité*] **1.** the state or quality of being sinuous **2.** *pl.* **-ties** a sinuous turn or movement; undulation

sin·u·ous (sin′yoo wəs) *adj.* [L. *sinuosus* < *sinus*, a bend] **1.** bending, winding, or curving in and out; wavy; serpen-

tine **2.** not straightforward; devious; crooked **3.** *same as* SINUATE (*adj.* 2) —**sin′u·ous·ly** *adv.*

si·nus (sī′nəs) *n.* [L., a bent surface, curve, fold] **1.** a bend or curve **2.** any cavity or hollow formed by a bending or curving **3.** *Anat., Zool.* any of various cavities, hollows, or passages; esp., *a*) any of the air cavities in the skull opening into the nasal cavities *b*) a large channel for venous blood *c*) a dilated part in a blood vessel, etc. **4.** *Bot.* a rounded depression between two consecutive lobes, as of a leaf **5.** *Med.* a channel leading from a pus-filled cavity

si·nus·i·tis (sī′nə sīt′əs) *n.* [ModL.: see prec. & -ITIS] inflammation of a sinus or sinuses, esp. of the skull

si·nu·soid (sī′nə soid′) *n. same as* SINE CURVE —**si′nu·soi′dal** *adj.*

sinusoidal projection a map projection showing the entire surface of the earth with all lines of latitude as straight lines and all lines of longitude as curved lines

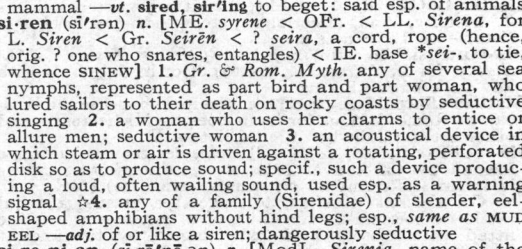

SINUSES
(A, frontal;
B, maxillary)

Si·on (sī′ən) *rare var. of* ZION

-sion (shən; *sometimes* zhən) [L. -*sio* (gen. -*sionis*)] *a n.-forming suffix meaning* act, quality, condition, or result of [*discussion, confusion*]

Siou·an (sōō′ən) *adj.* designating or of a language family of N. American Indians formerly inhabiting the WC U.S., C Canada, and parts of Virginia and the Carolinas: it includes Iowa, Mandan, Dakota, Crow, Omaha, Hidatsa, Osage, etc. —*n.* this family of languages

Sioux (sōō) *n., pl.* **Sioux** (sōō, sōōz) [Fr., contr. < *Nadowessioux* < Ojibway *nadowe-is-iw*, dim. of *nadowe*, an adder, hence, an enemy] *same as* DAKOTA (*n.* 1 & 2) —*adj. same as* DAKOTA (*adj.* 1)

Sioux City city in W Iowa, on the Missouri River: pop. 86,000

Sioux Falls city in SE S.Dak.: pop. 72,000

sip (sip) *vt., vi.* **sipped, sip′ping** [ME. *sippen;* akin to LowG. *sippen:* for IE. base see SUP[1]] to drink a little at a time; drink by bits —*n.* **1.** the act of sipping **2.** a small quantity sipped —**sip′per** *n.*

si·phon (sī′fən) *n.* [Fr. < L. *sipho* (gen. *siphonis*) < Gr. *siphon,* a tube, siphon < IE. base *twibh-,* tubelike, hollow, whence L. *tibia*] **1.** a bent tube used for carrying liquid out over the top edge of a container through the force of atmospheric pressure upon the surface of the liquid; one end of the tube is placed in the liquid, the other, the longer end, outside the container at a point below the surface level of the liquid: the tube must be filled, as by suction, before flow will start **2.** *same as* SIPHON BOTTLE **3.** a tubelike organ in some animals, as cuttlefishes, used for drawing in or ejecting liquids —*vt.* to draw off or carry through or as through a siphon —*vi.* to pass through a siphon —**si′phon·al** (-′l), **si·phon·ic** (sī fän′ik) *adj.*

SIPHON

si·phon·age (-ij) *n.* the act of siphoning

siphon bottle a heavy, sealed bottle with a tube on the inside connected at the top with a nozzle and valve which, when opened, allows the flow of pressurized, carbonated water contained within

si·pho·no·phore (sī fän′ə fôr′, sī′fə nə-) *n.* [< Gr. *siphon,* a tube (see SIPHON) + -PHORE] any of an order (Siphonophora) of small, transparent, often colored, swimming or floating sea hydrozoans composed of several kinds of polyps and including the Portuguese man-of-war

si·pho·no·stele (sī fän′ə stēl′, sī′fə nə-; sī fän′ə stē′lē) *n.* [< Gr. *siphon,* a tube (see SIPHON) + STELE] *Bot.* a type of vascular system consisting of a ring of vascular bundles surrounding a central pith —**si′pho·no·ste′lic** (-stē′lik) *adj.*

sip·pet (sip′it) *n.* [prob. dim. of SOP] **1.** a small piece of toasted or fried bread used as a garnish, dipped in gravy, etc. **2.** any small piece; fragment

Si·quei·ros (sē ke′rōs), (José) **Da·vid Al·fa·ro** (dä vēd′ äl fä′rō) 1896– ; Mex. painter, esp. of murals

sir (sur) *n.* [ME. < *sire:* see SIRE] **1.** orig., a man of rank; lord **2.** [*sometimes* S-] a respectful term of address used to a man: not followed by the given name or surname and often used in the salutation of a letter [*Dear Sir*] **3.** [S-] the title used before the given name or full name of a knight or baronet [*Sir Walter (Raleigh)*] **4.** [Archaic] a term of address used with the title of a man's office, rank, or profession [*sir priest, sir judge, sir knight*]

Si·ra·cu·sa (sē′rä kōō′zä) *It. name of* SYRACUSE (sense 2)

sir·dar (sər där′, sur′där) *n.* [Hind. *sardār* < Per., leader < *sar,* the head + *dār,* holding] **1.** in India, Pakistan, and Afghanistan, *a*) a chief or noble *b*) a high military officer **2.** in India, a person holding an important position

sire (sīr) *n.* [ME. < OFr., a master < L. *senior:* see SENIOR] **1.** orig., a person of authority; man of high rank: now used only as a title of respect in addressing a king, equivalent to "your majesty" **2.** [Poet.] a father or forefather **3.** the male parent of an animal, esp. of a four-legged

mammal —*vt.* **sired, sir′ing** to beget: said esp. of animals

si·ren (sī′rən) *n.* [ME. *syrene* < OFr. < LL. *Sirena,* for L. *Siren* < Gr. *Seirēn* < ? *seira,* a cord, rope (hence, orig. ? one who snares, entangles) < IE. base **sei-,* to tie, whence SINEW] **1.** *Gr. & Rom. Myth.* any of several sea nymphs, represented as part bird and part woman, who lured sailors to their death on rocky coasts by seductive singing **2.** a woman who uses her charms to entice or allure men; seductive woman **3.** an acoustical device in which steam or air is driven against a rotating, perforated disk so as to produce sound; specif., such a device producing a loud, often wailing sound, used esp. as a warning signal ☆**4.** any of a family (Sirenidae) of slender, eel-shaped amphibians without hind legs; esp., *same as* MUD EEL —*adj.* of or like a siren; dangerously seductive

si·re·ni·an (sī rē′nē ən) *n.* [ModL. *Sirenia,* name of the order (< L. *siren:* see prec.) + -AN] any of several large, vegetarian sea mammals (order Sirenia), as the dugong, manatee, etc., with a cigar-shaped body, a blunt snout, large, mobile lips, flipperlike forelimbs, and a large tail fluke

Si·ret (si ret′) river in SE Europe, flowing from the Carpathian mountains southeast through E Romania into the Danube: 450 mi.

Sir·i·us (sir′ē əs) *n.* [ME. < L. < Gr. *Seirios,* lit., scorcher] *same as* DOG STAR (sense 1)

sir·loin (sur′loin) *n.* [Early ModE. *surloyn* < MFr. *surlonge* < OFr. *sur,* over + *loigne,* LOIN] a choice cut of meat, esp. of beef, from the loin end just in front of the rump

si·roc·co (sə räk′ō) *n., pl.* **-cos** [It. < Ar. *sharq,* the east < *sharaqa,* to rise (of the sun)] **1.** a hot, steady, oppressive wind blowing from the Libyan deserts across the Mediterranean into S Europe, often bringing dust, and sometimes accompanied by rain **2.** any hot, oppressive wind, esp. one blowing toward a center of low barometric pressure

sir·rah, sir·ra (sir′ə) *n.* [< SIR] [Archaic] a contemptuous term of address used, as in anger, to a man

☆**sir·ree, sir·ee** (sə rē′) *interj.* [< SIR] an interjection used for emphasis after *yes* or *no*

sir·rev·er·ence (sur′rev′ər əns) *interj.* [confused form for *sa'reverence,* contr. < *save reverence,* saving (your) reverence, transl. of ML. *salva reverentia*] [Obs.] begging your pardon: an expression of apology formerly used before a word or remark that might be regarded as indelicate

sir·up (sir′əp, sur′-) *n. same as* SYRUP —**sir′up·y** *adj.*

sir·ventes (sir vent′; *Fr.* sir vänt′) *n., pl.* **-ventes** (-vents′; *Fr.* -vänt′) [Pr. < *sirvent,* servant (< L. *servient-,* root of *serviens,* prp. of *servire,* to SERVE) + -*es,* -*esc* < It. -*esco:* see -ESQUE] a Provençal form of verse or troubadour song, usually satirical —**sir·vent′** (-vent′)

☆**sis** (sis) *n. colloq. clipped form of* SISTER

si·sal (sī′s'l) *n.* [after *Sisal,* Yucatán, a former seaport (< Maya *Sisal,* lit., cold waters)] **1.** a strong fiber obtained from the leaves of an agave (*Agave sisalana*) native to S Mexico and now cultivated throughout the tropics, used for making rope, sacking, insulation, etc. **2.** the plant yielding this fiber, related to henequen   Also **sisal hemp**

Sis·e·ra (sis′ər ə) [Heb. *shīsherā′;* prob. of Hittite origin] *Bible* a military leader of the Canaanites against the Israelites, murdered by Jael: Judg. 4:17–22

sis·kin (sis′kin) *n.* [via Fl. or Du. < G. *zeischen,* dim. of *zeizig* < Czech *čižek,* dim. of *čiž* (akin to Pol. *czyz,* Russ. *čiž*), of echoic origin] **1.** a European and Asiatic finch (*Carduelis spinus*) with green plumage and black and yellow markings **2.** *same as* PINE SISKIN

Sis·ley (sēs lā′; *E.* sis′lē), **Al·fred** (äl fred′) 1839–99; Fr. painter

Sis·mon·di (sēs môn dē′; *E.* sis män′dē), **Jean Charles Lé·o·nard Si·monde de** (zhän shärl lē ô när′ sē mônd′ də) 1773–1842; Swiss historian & economist

☆**sis·si·fied** (sis′ə fīd′) *adj. colloq. var. of* SISSY

☆**sis·sy** (sis′ē) *n., pl.* **-sies** [dim. of SIS] **1.** [Colloq.] *a*) an effeminate boy or man *b*) a timid person or coward **2.** [Slang] a homosexual —*adj.* [Colloq.] of or like a sissy —**sis′sy·ish** *adj.*

sis·ter (sis′tər) *n.* [ME. < ON. *systir* (akin to OE. *sweoster,* whence dial. *suster*), akin to G. *schwester* < IE. base **swesor-,* sister, whence Sans. *svasar,* L. *soror,* OIr. *siur*] **1.** a woman or girl as she is related to the other children of her parents: sometimes also used of animals **2.** a woman or girl related to one by having a parent in common; half sister **3.** a stepsister **4.** a foster sister **5.** a close friend who is like a sister **6.** a female fellow member of the same race, creed, profession, organization, etc. **7.** a member of a female religious order; nun **8.** a thing thought of as feminine and associated with some kindred thing; one of the same kind, model, etc. **9.** [Brit.] a nurse, esp. a head nurse **10.** [Colloq.] any woman: often used as a familiar term of address —*adj.* related or seeming to be related as sisters

sis·ter·hood (-hood′) *n.* **1.** the state of being a sister or sisters; bond between sisters **2.** an association of women united in a common interest, work, creed, etc., as a sorority or religious group

sis·ter-in-law (-in lô′) *n., pl.* **sis′ters-in-law′ 1.** the sister of one's husband or wife **2.** the wife of one's brother **3.** the wife of the brother of one's husband or wife

sis·ter·ly (-lē) *adj.* **1.** of, like, or befitting a sister or sisters **2.** friendly, kind, affectionate, etc. —*adv.* [Archaic] as a sister —**sis′ter·li·ness** *n.*

Sis·tine (sis′tēn, -tin) *adj.* [It. *Sistino* < *Sisto* (< ML. *Sixtus*, for L. *Sextus*, lit., SIXTH)] of or having to do with any pope named Sixtus

Sistine Chapel [see prec.] the principal chapel in the Vatican at Rome, famous for its frescoes by Michelangelo and other artists: built by order of Sixtus IV

sis·troid (sis′troid) *adj.* [< ?] *Math.* designating the angle formed by the convex sides of two intersecting curves

sis·trum (sis′trəm) *n.,* *pl.* **-trums, -tra** (-trə) [ME. < L. < Gr. *seistron* < *seiein,* to shake: see SIRIUS] a metal rattle or noisemaker consisting of a handle and a frame fitted with loosely held rods, jingled by the ancient Egyptians in the worship of Isis

Sis·y·phe·an (sis′ə fē′ən) *adj.* [< L. *Sisypheius* < Gr. *Sisypheios* < *Sisyphos* + -AN] **1.** of or like Sisyphus **2.** endless and toilsome, useless, etc. [a Sisyphean task]

Sis·y·phus (sis′ə fəs) [L. < Gr. *Sisyphos*] *Gr. Myth.* a greedy king of Corinth doomed forever in Hades to roll uphill a heavy stone which always rolled down again

sit (sit) *vi.* **sat, sit′ting** [ME. *sitten* < OE. *sittan,* akin to ON. *sitja,* G. *sitzen* < IE. base *sed-*, to sit, whence L. *sedere,* Gr. *hizein,* W. *seddu,* to sit] **1.** *a)* to rest the weight of the body upon the buttocks and the back of the thighs, as on a chair; be seated *b)* to rest on the haunches with the forelegs braced: said of quadrupeds *c)* to perch or roost: said of birds **2.** to cover and warm eggs for hatching; set; brood **3.** *a)* to occupy a seat in the capacity of judge, legislator, etc. *b)* to be in session, as a court or legislature **4.** to pose for one's portrait or as a model **5.** [Chiefly Brit.] to take an examination (*for* a degree, scholarship, etc.) **6.** to be or remain inactive **7.** to be located or have a place [a house *sitting* up on the hill] **8.** to fit or hang on the wearer [a coat that *sits* loosely] **9.** to rest or lie as specified [cares *sit* lightly upon him] ☆**10.** *same as* BABYSIT **11.** to have a certain direction; set: said of the wind —*vt.* **1.** to place in a seat; cause to sit; seat (often used reflexively) [to *sit* oneself down] **2.** to keep one's seat on (a horse, etc.) **3.** to have seats or seating space for —*n.* [Colloq.] **1.** the time spent in a seated position, esp. while waiting **2.** the way a coat, dress, etc. hangs when put on —**sit back 1.** to relax **2.** to remain passive —**sit down 1.** to lower oneself to a sitting position; take a seat **2.** to settle down for or as for a siege —**sit in** to take part; participate; attend (often with *on*) —**sit on** (or **upon**) **1.** to serve as a member of (a jury, committee, etc.) **2.** to confer on or investigate **3.** [Colloq.] to suppress, repress, or squelch **4.** [Colloq.] to hold (something) back from being considered or acted on —☆**sit on one's hands 1.** to fail to applaud **2.** to fail to do what is needed or expected —**sit out 1.** to stay until the end of **2.** to stay longer than (another); outsit **3.** to remain seated during or take no part in (a dance, game, etc.) —**sit up 1.** to rise to a sitting position **2.** to sit erect **3.** to sit on the haunches with the forelegs drawn up before the chest: said of animals **4.** to postpone going to bed **5.** [Colloq.] to become suddenly alert —**sit well with** to be suitable or agreeable to

si·tar (si tär′) *n.* [Hindi *sitār*] a lutelike instrument of India with a long, fretted neck, a resonating gourd or gourds, and usually six playing strings and a number of strings that vibrate sympathetically —**si·tar′ist** *n.*

☆**sit-down** (sit′doun′) *n.* **1.** a strike in which the strikers stay inside a factory, etc. refusing to work or leave until agreement is reached: in full **sit-down strike 2.** a form of civil disobedience in which demonstrators sit down, as in public streets or places, in resistance to being moved away —**sit′-down′er** *n.*

site (sīt) *n.* [ME. < L. *situs,* position, situation < pp. of *sinere,* to put down, permit, allow < IE. base *sei-*, to cast out, let fall: cf. SEED, SIDE] **1.** a piece of land considered from the standpoint of its use for some specified purpose [a good *site* for a town] **2.** the place where something is, was, or is to be; location or scene [the *site* of a battle] —*vt.* **sit′ed, sit′ing** to locate or position on a site

sith (sith) *adv., conj., prep.* [ME. < OE. *siththa,* contr. form of *siththan* (cf. SINCE)] *archaic form of* SINCE

sit-in (sit′in′) *n.* a sit-down inside a public place by a group demonstrating for civil rights, against war, etc.

Sit·ka (sit′kə) [< Tlingit tribal name < ? *Shi,* native name of Baranof Island + -*ka,* locative ending] city in SE Alas., on Baranof Island: pop. 3,400

si·to- (sī′tō, -tə) [< Gr. *sitos,* food, grain] *a combining form meaning:* **1.** food [*sitology*] **2.** grain [*sitosterol*]

si·tol·o·gy (sī täl′ə jē) *n.* [prec. + -LOGY] the study of foods, food values, nutrition, diet, etc.; dietetics

si·tos·ter·ol (sī täs′tə rōl′, -rôl′) *n.* [SITO- + (CHOLE)STEROL] any of a group of crystalline alcoholic sterols resembling cholesterol in their properties

Si·tsang (sē′tsäŋ′) *Chin. name of* TIBET

sit·ten (sit′'n) *obs. pp. of* SIT

sit·ter (sit′ər) *n.* a person or thing that sits; specif., ☆*a) short for* BABY SITTER *b)* a brooding hen

Sit·ter (sit′ər), **Wil·lem de** (vil′əm də) 1872–1934; Du. astronomer

sit·ting (sit′iŋ) *n.* **1.** the act or position of one that sits, as for a portrait **2.** a session or meeting, as of a court **3.** a period of being seated at some activity [to read a book in two *sittings*] **4.** *a)* a brooding upon eggs, as by a hen *b)* the number of eggs upon which a hen sits for a single hatching **5.** a space in which to be seated **6.** one of two or more spells at which a meal is served, as aboard a ship [assigned to the second *sitting*] —*adj.* that sits; seated

Sitting Bull 1834?–90; Sioux Indian chief in the Battle of the LITTLE BIGHORN

sitting duck [Colloq.] ☆a person or thing especially vulnerable to attack; easy target

sitting room 1. *same as* LIVING ROOM **2.** any room, esp. a small one next to a bedroom, used as a living room

sit·u·ate (sich′oo wit; *also, and for v. always,* -wāt′) *adj.* [ML. *situatus,* pp. of *situare,* to place < L. *situs:* see SITE] *rare or archaic var. of* SITUATED —*vt.* **-at′ed, -at′ing** to put in a certain place or position; place; locate

sit·u·at·ed (-wāt′id) *adj.* [pp. of prec.] **1.** placed as to site or position; located **2.** placed as to circumstances, esp. financial circumstances [securely *situated*]

sit·u·a·tion (sich′oo wā′shən) *n.* [LME. *setuacyon* < ML. *situatio:* see SITUATE] **1.** manner in which a thing is situated in relation to its surroundings; location; position **2.** a place; locality **3.** position or condition with regard to circumstances **4.** *a)* the combination of circumstances at any given time *b)* a difficult or critical state of affairs *c)* any significant combination of circumstances developing in the course of a novel, play, etc. *d) Psychol.* the objective conditions, environment, stimuli, etc. immediately affecting an individual **5.** a position of employment —*SYN.* see POSITION, STATE

sit·u·a·tion·al (-'l) *adj.* **1.** of or resulting from a situation **2.** altered to fit a specific situation [*situational* ethics] —**sit′u·a′tion·al·ly** *adv.*

situation comedy a comedy, esp. a comic television series, with a story line made up of contrived episodes involving stock characters

☆**sit-up, sit·up** (sit′up′) *n.* an exercise in which a person lying flat on the back rises to a sitting position without using the hands and keeping the legs straight

si·tus (sīt′əs) *n.* [L.: see SITE] position or location; esp., the normal position, as of an organ of the body or a plant part

Sit·well (sit′wəl, -wel) **1.** Dame **Edith,** 1887–1964; Eng. poet & critic: sister of *Osbert & Sacheverell* **2.** Sir **Os·bert** (äz′bərt), 1892–1969; Eng. poet & essayist **3.** Sa·**chev·er·ell** (sə shev′ər əl), 1897– ; Eng. poet & art critic

sitz bath (sits, zits) [partial transl. of G. *sitzbad* < *sitz,* a seat, sitting (< *sitzen,* to SIT) + *bad,* BATH¹] **1.** a bath in which only the hips and buttocks are immersed, usually for therapy **2.** a tub or basin used for such a bath

sitz·mark (sits′märk′, zits′-) *n.* [< G. *sitzmarke < sitz,* seat (< *sitzen,* SIT) + *marke,* MARK¹] the depression made in snow by a skier who has fallen backward

Si·va (sē′və, shē′-) [Hind. < Sans., auspicious] Hindu god of destruction and reproduction, a member of the supreme Hindu trinity: see BRAHMA¹, VISHNU

Si·va·ism (-iz′m) *n.* worship of Siva —**Si′va·is′tic** *adj.*

Si·van (sē vän′, siv′ən) *n.* [Heb. *sīwān* < Akkadian name] the ninth month of the Jewish year

Si·vas (sē väs′) city in C Turkey: pop. 93,000

six (siks) *adj.* [ME. < OE. *sex,* akin to G. *sechs,* ON. *sex,* Goth. *saihs* < IE. base *seks, sweks,* whence L. *sex,* Gr. *hex,* Sans. *ṣáṭ*] totaling one more than five —*n.* **1.** the cardinal number between five and seven; 6; VI **2.** any group of six people or things; half a dozen **3.** something numbered six or having six units, as a playing card, domino, face of a die, etc. —**at sixes and sevens** [Colloq.] **1.** in confusion or disorder **2.** at variance; disagreeing

six·fold (-fōld′) *adj.* [see -FOLD] **1.** having six parts **2.** having six times as much or as many —*adv.* six times as much or as many

Six Nations the Indian confederation of the Five Nations and the Tuscarora tribe

☆**six-pack** (-pak′) *n.* a package containing six units of a product, esp. one with six cans of beer

six·pence (-pəns) *n.* **1.** the sum of six pence (pennies) **2.** a small British silver coin of this value

six·pen·ny (-pen′ē, -pə nē) *adj.* **1.** worth or costing sixpence **2.** of small worth; cheap **3.** designating a size of nails, usually two inches long

☆**six-shoot·er** (-shoot′ər) *n.* [Colloq.] a revolver that fires six shots without reloading: also **six′-gun′**

six·teen (siks′tēn′) *adj.* [ME. *sixtene* < OE. *syxtene:* see SIX & -TEEN] six more than ten —*n.* the cardinal number between fifteen and seventeen; 16; XVI

six·teen·mo (-mō′) *n., pl.* **-mos′** [prec. + -mo, as in SEXTODECIMO] **1.** the page size of a book made up of printer's sheets folded into sixteen leaves, each leaf being approximately 4 1/2 by 6 3/4 inches **2.** a book consisting of pages of this size Usually written *16mo* or *16°* —*adj.* consisting of pages of this size

six·teenth (siks′tēnth′) *adj.* [ME. *sixtenthe,* replacing OE. *syxteotha:* see SIXTEEN & -TH²] **1.** preceded by fifteen others in a series; 16th **2.** designating any of the sixteen equal

SITAR

parts of something —*n.* **1.** the one following the fifteenth **2.** any of the sixteen equal parts of something; 1/16 **3.** *Music* a sixteenth note

sixteenth note *Music* a note having one sixteenth the duration of a whole note; semiquaver: see NOTE, illus.

sixth (siksth) *adj.* [ME. *sixte* < OE. *sixta*, akin to G. *sechste*, L. *sextus*: see SIX & -TH²] **1.** preceded by five others in a series; 6th **2.** designating any of the six equal parts of something —*n.* **1.** the one following the fifth **2.** any of the six equal parts of something; 1/6 **3.** *Music a)* the sixth tone of an ascending diatonic scale, or a tone five degrees above or below any given tone in such a scale; submediant; superdominant *b)* the interval between two such tones, or a combination of them *c)* the chord formed by a triad in which the fundamental tone is moved above the fifth, as e-g-c: in full **sixth chord** —**sixth′ly** *adv.*

sixth sense a power of perception in addition to the commonly accepted five senses; intuitive power

six·ti·eth (siks′tē ith) *adj.* [ME. *sixtithe* < OE. *sixteogotha* < *sixtig*: see SIXTY & -TH²] **1.** preceded by fifty-nine others in a series; 60th **2.** designating any of the sixty equal parts of something —*n.* **1.** the one following the fifty-ninth **2.** any of the sixty equal parts of something; 1/60

Six·tine (siks′tēn, -tin) *adj.* same as SISTINE

Six·tus (siks′təs) the name of five popes; esp., *a)* Sixtus IV (born *Francesco della Rovere*) 1414–84; Pope (1471–84) *b)* Sixtus V (born *Felice Peretti*) 1521–90; Pope (1585–90)

six·ty (siks′tē) *adj.* [ME. *sixti* < OE. *sixtig*: see SIX & -TY²] ten times six —*n., pl.* **-ties** the cardinal number between fifty-nine and sixty-one; 60; LX —**the sixties** the numbers or years, as of a century, from sixty through sixty-nine

six·ty-fourth note (-fôrth′) *Music* a note having one sixty-fourth the duration of a whole note: see NOTE, illus.

siz·a·ble (sī′zə b'l) *adj.* quite large or bulky: also **size′a·ble** —**siz′a·ble·ness** *n.* —**siz′a·bly** *adv.*

siz·ar (sī′zər) *n.* [< ff. (sense 6) + -AR] a student receiving a scholarship allowance at Cambridge University or Trinity College, Dublin: also, earlier, **siz′er**

size¹ (sīz) *n.* [ME. < OFr. *sise*, aphetic for *assise*: see ASSIZE] **1.** that quality of a thing which determines how much space it occupies; dimensions or magnitude of a thing **2.** any of a series of graded classifications of measure into which merchandise is divided *[jumbo size* peanuts, *size* nine shoes*]* **3.** *a)* extent, magnitude, amount, etc. *[an undertaking of great size] b)* sizable amount, dimensions, etc. **4.** character of a person with regard to ability to meet requirements **5.** [Colloq.] actual condition; true state of affairs *[that's the size of it]* **6.** [Obs.] standard ration or allowance, as of food —*vt.* **sized, siz′ing** **1.** to make or shape in accordance with a given size **2.** to arrange or grade according to size —**of a size** of one or the same size —**size up** [Colloq.] **1.** to make an estimate or judgment of **2.** to meet requirements or specifications —**siz′er** *n.*

size² (sīz) *n.* [ME. *syse*] any thin, pasty or gluey substance used as a glaze or filler on porous materials, as on plaster, paper, or cloth —*vt.* **sized, siz′ing** to apply size to; fill, stiffen, or glaze with size

-sized (sīzd) *a combining form, usually in hyphenated compounds, meaning* having a (specified) size *[small-sized]*: also **-size** *[life-size]*

siz·ing (sī′zin) *n.* **1.** same as SIZE² **2.** the act or process of applying such size

siz·zle (siz′'l) *vi.* **-zled, -zling** [echoic] **1.** to make a hissing sound when in contact with heat, as a drop of water on hot metal **2.** to be extremely hot **3.** to be in a state of suppressed emotion or passion; esp., to simmer with rage —*vt.* to make sizzle —*n.* a sizzling sound

☆siz·zler (-lər) *n.* [Colloq.] something hot (in various senses), as a very hot day

S.J. Society of Jesus

Sjæl·land (shel′län) *Dan. name of* ZEALAND

sjam·bok (sham′bäk) *n.* [Afrik. < Malay *cambok*, a large whip < Hindi *cābuk*] in South Africa, a whip made of rhinoceros or hippopotamus hide

S.J.D. [L. *Scientiæ Juridicæ Doctor*] Doctor of Juridical Science

sk. sack

Ska·gen (skä′yən), **Cape** same as The SKAW

Skag·er·rak (skag′ə rak′) arm of the North Sea, between Norway & Denmark: 150 mi. long; 70–90 mi. wide

skald (skôld, skäld) *n.* [ON. *skāld*: see SCOLD] any of the ancient Scandinavian poets, specif. of the Viking period —**skald′ic** *adj.*

Skan·der·beg (skan′dər beg′) *var. of* SCANDERBEG

skat (skat, skät) *n.* [G. < It. *scarto*, discard < *scartare*: to discard < *s-* (< L. *ex-*, out) + *carta*, card (< L. *charta*: see CARD¹)] a card game for three people, played with thirty-two cards

skate¹ (skāt) *n.* [taken as sing. of earlier *skates* < Du. *schaats*, a skate, stilt < ONormFr. *escache* < OFr. *eschace*, stilt, crutch < Frank. *skatja*, stilt] **1.** *a)* a bladelike metal runner mounted in a frame having clamps and straps for fastening it to the sole of a shoe and used for gliding on ice *b)* a shoe with such a runner permanently attached Also **ice skate** **2.** a similar frame or shoe with a pair of small wheels near the toe and another pair at the heel, for gliding on a hardwood floor, sidewalk, etc.: also **roller skate** **3.** the act or a spell of skating —*vi.* **skat′ed, skat′ing** to move along or glide on or as on skates —**skat′er** *n.*

skate² (skāt) *n., pl.* **skates, skate:** see PLURAL, II, D, 1 [ME. *scate* < ON. *skata* < ? L. *squatus*, flat fish] any of a family (Rajidae) of rays, with a broad, flat body and a short, spineless tail with two dorsal fins

skate³ (skāt) *n.* [< ?] [Old Slang] ☆**1.** a broken-down horse; nag **2.** a person: now only in **good skate**, a congenial, likable person

☆skate·board (skāt′bôrd′) *n.* a toy consisting of a short, oblong board with a pair of small wheels at each end, ridden, as down an incline, usually in a standing position —*vi.* **-board′ed, -board′ing** to ride or coast on a skateboard —**skate′board′er** *n.*

skat·ole (skat′ōl) *n.* [< Gr. *skōr* (gen. *skatos*), dung (see SCATO-) + -OL²] a foul-smelling, colorless, crystalline compound, C_9H_9N, formed by the decomposition of proteins, as in the intestine

Skaw (skô), **The** cape at the N tip of the Jutland peninsula, Denmark

skean (skēn) *n.* [ScotGael. *sgian*, akin to MIr. *scian*, a knife < IE. base *skei-*, to cut, whence L. *scire*: cf. SCIENCE, SCISSION] a kind of dagger or short sword formerly used in Scotland and Ireland

Skeat (skēt), **Walter William** 1835–1912; Eng. philologist & lexicographer

ske·dad·dle (ski dad′'l) *vi.* **-dled, -dling** [popularized in military slang of Civil War period: prob. a fanciful formation] [Colloq.] to run off or away; leave in a hurry —*n.* [Colloq.] a running or scurrying away

skee (skē) *n., vi.* **skeed, skee′ing** *rare var. of* SKI

☆skeet (skēt) *n.* [20th-c. adoption and alteration of ON. *skeyti*, a projectile, akin to *skjóta*, to SHOOT] trapshooting in which the shooter fires from different angles, usually eight, at clay disks thrown from traps to simulate birds in flight

skeg (skeg) *n.* [Du. *schogge* < ON. *skegg*, a beard (basic sense "a projection"): see SHAG¹] *Naut.* the after part of the keel, or an extension of this upon which the rudderpost is mounted

skein (skān) *n.* [ME. *skeyn* < MFr. *escaigne*] **1.** *a)* a quantity of thread or yarn wound in a coil *b)* something like this, as a coil of hair **2.** a flock of wild fowl

skel·e·ton (skel′ə t'n) *n.* [ModL. < Gr. < *skeleton* (*sōma*), dried (body), mummy < *skel-etos*, dried up, akin to *sklēros*, dry, hard: for IE. base see SHALLOW] **1.** The hard framework of an animal body for supporting the tissues and protecting the organs; specif., all the bones collectively, or the bony framework, of a human being or other vertebrate animal **2.** anything like a skeleton in any of various ways; specif., *a)* a very lean or emaciated person or animal *b)* a supporting framework, as of a ship *c)* an outline or preliminary sketch, as of a novel *d)* the meager or devitalized remains of something —*adj.* of or like a skeleton; specif., of, or having the nature of, the main or essential outline, framework, etc. *[a skeleton force]* —**skeleton at the feast** a person or event that brings gloom or sadness to an occasion of joy or celebration —**skeleton in the closet** some fact, as about one's family, kept secret because of shame or fear of disgrace —**skel′e·tal** (-t'l) *adj.*

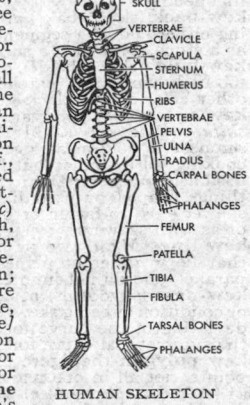

SKULL
VERTEBRAE
CLAVICLE
SCAPULA
STERNUM
HUMERUS
RIBS
VERTEBRAE
PELVIS
ULNA
RADIUS
CARPAL BONES
PHALANGES
FEMUR
PATELLA
TIBIA
FIBULA
TARSAL BONES
PHALANGES

HUMAN SKELETON

skel·e·ton·ize (-īz′) *vt.* **-ized′, -iz′ing** **1.** to reduce to a skeleton or a bare framework **2.** to outline or sketch (a story, report, etc.) briefly **3.** to reduce (a work force, etc.) greatly in number or size

skeleton key a key having a large part of the bit filed away so that it can be used to open any of various simple locks as a master key

skel·lum (skel′əm) *n.* [Early ModE. < Du. *schelm*, akin to OHG. *skelmo*, one deserving to die < IE. base *(s)kel-*, to cut: cf. SHELL, HELM²] [Archaic or Brit. Dial.] a rascal; rogue; scamp

skelp (skelp) *vt.* [ME. *skelpen*, to beat, flog] [Brit. Dial.] to slap or spank —*vi.* to hurry along; hustle —*n.* [Brit. Dial.] a slap; blow

Skel·ton (skel′t'n), **John** 1460?–1529; Eng. poet

skene (skēn) *n.* same as SKEAN

skep (skep) *n.* [ME. *skeppe* < OE. *sceppe* < ON. *skeppa*, a measure, bushel: for IE. base see SHAPE] **1.** a round, wooden or wicker basket **2.** a beehive, esp. one of straw

skep·tic (skep′tik) *adj.* [L. *scepticus* < Gr. *skeptikos*,

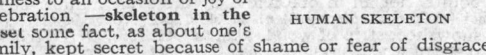

thoughtful, inquiring < *skeptesthai*, to consider: altered by metathesis < IE. base **spek-*, to peer: cf. SPY] *var. of* SKEPTICAL: used esp. in philosophy —*n.* 1. [S-] a member of any of the ancient Greek philosophical schools that denied the possibility of real knowledge of any kind 2. a person who believes in or practices philosophical skepticism 3. a person who habitually doubts, questions, or suspends judgment upon matters generally accepted 4. a person who doubts religious doctrines

skep·ti·cal (skep′ti k'l) *adj.* 1. of or characteristic of skeptics or skepticism 2. not easily persuaded or convinced; doubting; questioning 3. doubting the fundamental doctrines of religion —**skep′ti·cal·ly** *adv.*

skep·ti·cism (-siz'm) *n.* 1. [S-] the doctrines of the ancient Greek Skeptics 2. the philosophical doctrine that the truth of all knowledge must always be in question and that inquiry must be a process of doubting 3. skeptical or doubting attitude or state of mind 4. doubt about fundamental religious doctrines —*SYN.* see UNCERTAINTY

sker·ry (sker′ē) *n., pl.* **-ries** [via Orkney dial. < ON. *sker* (< IE. base **sker-*, to cut, whence SHEAR) + *ey*, ISLAND] [Scot.] an isolated rock or reef in the sea

sketch (skech) *n.* [earlier *schitz* < Du. *schets* < It. *schizzo* < L. *schedium*, extempore poem < Gr. *schedios*, extempore, sudden] 1. a simple, rough drawing or design, done rapidly and without much detail 2. a brief plan or description of major parts or points; outline 3. a short, light, informal story, description, play, skit, or piece of music —*vt.* to draw or describe quickly or in outline; make a sketch of —*vi.* to make a sketch or sketches —**sketch′er** *n.*

sketch·book (-book′) *n.* 1. a book of drawing paper for making sketches 2. a book of literary sketches Also **sketch book**

sketch·y (-ē) *adj.* **sketch′i·er, sketch′i·est** 1. having the form of a sketch; presenting only major parts or points; not detailed 2. lacking completeness; rough; inadequate —**sketch′i·ly** *adv.* —**sketch′i·ness** *n.*

skew (skyōō) *vi.* [ME. *skewen* < ONormFr. *eskiuer*, altered < OFr. *eschiver*: see ESCHEW] 1. to take a slanting or oblique course or direction; swerve or twist 2. to squint or glance sideways (*at*) —*vt.* 1. to make slanting or oblique; set at a slant 2. to bias, distort, or pervert —*adj.* 1. turned aside or to one side; slanting; oblique 2. having such a part, as gearing 3. not symmetrical —*n.* 1. a slant or twist 2. a slanting part or movement

skew arch an arch with jambs not at right angles with the face, as in a vault or tunnel which narrows or widens from its opening

skew·back (skyōō′bak′) *n.* 1. the slanting surface supporting either end of a segmental arch 2. a supporting piece, as a stone, with such a surface

skew·bald (skyōō′bôld′) *adj.* [< ME. *skewed*, piebald + BALD] having large patches of white and brown or any other color except black —*n.* a skewbald horse

skew·er (skyōō′ər) *n.* [var. of *skiver* < ON. *skifa*, a slice < *skifa*, to slice: see SKIVE] 1. *a*) a long pin used to hold meat together while cooking *b*) a similar but longer pin used as a brochette 2. any of several things shaped or used like a meat skewer —*vt.* to fasten or pierce with or as with skewers

skew lines *Math.* two or more lines that lie in different planes, are not parallel, and do not intersect

SKEWERS

skew·ness (skyōō′nis) *n.* 1. the fact or condition of being skew, esp. unsymmetrical 2. *Statistics* deviation of the curve for a frequency distribution from the symmetrical curve for such a distribution

skew polygon the figure formed by joining four or more points, not all in one plane, by the same number of lines

ski (skē; *Brit. also* shē) *n., pl.* **skis, ski** [Norw. < ON. *skith*, snowshoe, strip of wood, akin to OE. *scid*, OHG. *scit*, thin piece of wood, shingle: for IE. base see SHEATH] 1. either of a pair of long, thin runners of wood, metal, etc., fastened to the shoes for gliding over snow 2. *short for* WATER SKI —*vi.* **skied** (skēd), **ski′ing** 1. to travel on skis by gliding over the snow 2. to engage in the sport of gliding down snow-covered inclines on skis 3. *short for* WATER-SKI

ski·a·graph (skī′ə graf′, -gräf′) *n.* [Gr. *skia*, a shadow (for IE. base see SHINE) + -GRAPH] *same as* RADIOGRAPH: also **ski′a·gram** (-gram′) —**ski·ag·ra·phy** (skī ag′rə fē) *n.*

ski·a·scope (-skōp′) *n.* the instrument used in skiascopy

ski·as·co·py (skī as′kə pē) *n.* [Gr. *skia*, a shadow (see SKIAGRAPH) + -SCOPY] a method for refracting an eye by illuminating the retina with a skiascope and observing the movements of light and shadow on the pupil

skid (skid) *n.* [Early ModE., prob. < ON. *skith*: see SKI] ☆1. a plank, log, etc., often one of a pair or set, used as a support or as a track upon which to slide or roll a heavy object 2. a low, movable wooden platform for holding loads or stacks 3. [*pl.*] a wooden fender placed against the side of a ship to protect it from damage, as when unloading 4. a runner used in place of a wheel on an aircraft landing gear 5. a sliding wedge or drag used to check the motion of a vehicle by pressure against a wheel 6. the act of skidding —*vt.* **skid′ded, skid′ding** 1. to brake or lock (a wheel) with a skid 2. to support with or slide on a skid or skids ☆3. to haul, roll, or drag (logs) along a special track or

trail, as through a forest 4. to cause (a wheel, vehicle, etc.) to slide or slip —*vi.* 1. to slide without turning, as a wheel when skids or brakes are applied on a slippery surface 2. to slide or slip sideways, as a vehicle when not gripping the road on ice 3. to slide sharply downward 4. *Aeron.* to move sideways and outward while turning, as a result of failing to bank sufficiently —*SYN.* see SLIDE —☆**be on** (or **hit**) **the skids** [Slang] to be on the decline or downgrade; meet with failure —☆**put the skids on** (or **under**) [Slang] to thwart or cause to fail —**skid′der** *n.*

☆**skid·doo** (ski dōō′) *vi.* [prob. < SKEDADDLE] [Old Slang] to go away; leave: usually in the imperative

skid·dy (skid′ē) *adj.* **-di·er, -di·est** having a slippery surface on which vehicles are liable to skid

skid·proof (skid′prōōf′) *adj.* that resists or prevents skidding, as some automobile tires, road surfaces, etc.

☆**skid road** 1. in lumbering, a trail along which newly cut logs are skidded 2. *a*) [Western] a section of town where loggers gathered in taverns, inns, etc. *b*) *same as* SKID ROW

☆**skid row** [altered < prec.] a section of a city frequented by hobos, vagrants, derelicts, etc.

Ski·en (shā′ən, shē′-) city in S Norway: pop. 45,000

ski·er (skē′ər; *Brit. also* shē′-) *n.* a person who skis

skiff (skif) *n.* [MFr. *esquif* < It. *schifo* < Langobardic **skif*, akin to SHIP] 1. any light rowboat 2. a long, narrow rowboat, esp. one with a centerboard, outrigger, and a small sail

☆**ski·jor·ing** (skē′jôr′iŋ, skē jôr′-) *n.* [Norw. *skikjøring* < *ski*, SKI + *kjøre*, to ride, drive] a sport in which skiers are drawn over snow or ice by a horse, tractor, etc.

☆**ski jump** 1. a jump made by a skier after gaining momentum by a glide down a long incline or track 2. such an incline or track

skil·ful (skil′fəl) *adj. alt. sp. of* SKILLFUL —**skil′ful·ly** *adv.* —**skil′ful·ness** *n.*

☆**ski lift** a motor-driven, endless cable, typically with seats attached, for carrying skiers up a ski slope

skill (skil) *n.* [ME., discernment, reason < ON. *skil*, distinction, akin to *skilja*, to cut apart, separate < IE. base **(s)kel-*, to cut (whence SHIELD, SHELL): basic sense "ability to separate," hence "discernment"] 1. great ability or proficiency; expertness that comes from training, practice, etc. 2. *a*) an art, craft, or science, esp. one involving the use of the hands or body *b*) ability in such an art, craft, or science 3. [Obs.] knowledge, understanding, or judgment —*vi.* [Archaic] to matter, avail, or make a difference —*SYN.* see ART[1]

skilled (skild) *adj.* 1. having skill; skillful 2. having or requiring an ability, as in a particular industrial occupation, gained by special experience or training

skil·let (skil′it) *n.* [ME. *skelett* < ? OFr. *escuellette*, dim. of *escuelle*, porringer, basin < L. *scutella*, dim. of *scutra*, dish] 1. [Chiefly Brit.] a pot or kettle with a long handle and, sometimes, legs 2. *same as* FRYING PAN

skill·ful (skil′fəl) *adj.* having or showing skill; accomplished; expert —**skill′ful·ly** *adv.* —**skill′ful·ness** *n.*

skil·ling (skil′iŋ) *n.* [Norw., Dan., Sw., akin to SHILLING] a former Scandinavian copper coin and money of account, equal to less than a cent

skim (skim) *vt.* **skimmed, skim′ming** [ME. *skimen*, prob. akin to SCUM] 1. *a*) to clear (a liquid) of floating matter *b*) to remove (floating matter) from a liquid 2. to coat or cover with a thin layer [a pond *skimmed* with ice] 3. to look at hastily or carelessly; glance through (a book, etc.) without reading word for word 4. *a*) to glide or pass swiftly and lightly over *b*) to throw so as to cause to bounce or ricochet swiftly and lightly [to *skim* a flat stone across a creek] 5. [Slang] to refrain from reporting for tax purposes (a percentage of income, gambling gains, etc.) —*vi.* 1. to move along swiftly and lightly over a surface, through space, etc.; glide; sail 2. to make a rapid or careless examination, as of a book (usually with *over* or *through*) 3. to become thinly coated, as with scum —*n.* 1. something that has been skimmed 2. the act of skimming 3. a thin coating or film —*adj.* 1. that has been skimmed 2. designating or of a finishing coat of plaster [*skim* coat]

skim·ble-scam·ble (skim′b'l skam′b'l, skim′'l skam′'l) *adj.* rambling, incoherent, nonsensical, etc.

skim·mer (skim′ər) *n.* 1. a person or thing that skims 2. any utensil used in skimming liquids 3. any of several long-winged sea birds (family Rhynchopidae) that use their elongated lower bill to scoop up food while skimming over water 4. any of a family (Libellulidae) of large dragonflies that hover low over ponds, ditches, etc. ☆5. a hat, usually of straw, with a flat crown and a wide, straight brim

skim milk milk from which cream has been removed: also **skimmed milk**

skim·ming (skim′iŋ) *n.* [*usually pl.*] anything that has been skimmed from a liquid

skimp (skimp) *adj.* [prob. altered < SCRIMP] [Colloq.] *same as* SCANTY —*vi.* [Colloq.] 1. to give or allow too little; be stingy; scrimp 2. to keep expenses very low —*vt.* [Colloq.] 1. to do poorly or carelessly 2. to be stingy in or toward; specif., to make too small, too short, etc.

skimp·y (skim′pē) *adj.* **skimp′i·er, skimp′i·est** [Colloq.] barely or not quite enough; somewhat less in size, fullness, etc. than is needed; scanty —**skimp′i·ly** *adv.* —**skimp′i·ness** *n.*

skin (skin) *n.* [ME. *skinn* < ON., akin to G. *schinden*, to flay, peel < IE. *(s)ken(d)-*, to split off (< base *sek-*, to cut: cf. SAW¹), whence OIr. *ceinn*, a scale, scurf] **1.** the outer covering or integument of the animal body **2.** such a covering, esp. that of a small animal, when removed from the body and prepared for use; pelt **3.** something like skin in appearance or function; any outer layer, as fruit rind, the shell or plating of a ship, a film or scum, the outermost nacreous layer in a pearl, etc. **4.** a container made of animal skin, used for holding liquids ☆**5.** [Slang] [*pl.*] a set of drums, esp. in a jazz band ☆**6.** [Slang] a dollar —*vt.* **skinned, skin′-ning 1.** to cover with or as with skin; grow skin on **2.** to remove skin from **3.** to strip or peel off, as or like skin **4.** to injure by scraping or abrading (one's knee, elbow, etc.) **5.** [Colloq.] *a)* to defraud or cheat; swindle ☆*b)* to criticize or scold severely ☆**6.** [Colloq.] to drive or urge on (a mule, ox, etc.), esp. by whipping —*vi.* **1.** to become covered with skin **2.** [Colloq.] to climb (*up* or *down*) **3.** [Colloq.] to move (*through*), pass (*by*), succeed, etc. by a very narrow margin —☆**be no skin off one's nose** (or **back**) [Colloq.] to affect one not at all; be of no direct concern to one —**by the skin of one's teeth** by the smallest possible margin; barely —☆**get under one's skin** [Colloq.] to anger or irritate one —**have a thick** (or **thin**) **skin** to be insensitive (or acutely sensitive) to blame, criticism, insults, etc. —**in** (or **with**) **a whole skin** [Colloq.] without injury —**save one's skin** [Colloq.] to avoid death or injury —**skin alive 1.** to remove the skin from (a living person or animal) ☆**2.** [Colloq.] to scold or punish severely **3.** [Colloq.] to defeat decisively

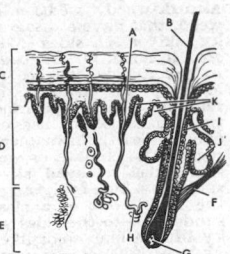

CROSS SECTION OF SKIN
(A, duct of a sweat gland; B, hair; C, epidermis; D, dermis; E, subcutaneous tissue; F, erector muscle of a hair; G, papilla of a hair; H, body of a sweat gland; I, hair follicle; J, sebaceous gland; K, papillae of dermis)

SYN.—skin is the general term for the outer covering of the animal body and for the covering, especially if thin and tight, of certain fruits and vegetables [human *skin*, the *skin* of a peach]; **hide** is used of the tough skins of certain large animals, as of a horse, cow, elephant, etc.; **pelt** refers to the skin, esp. the untanned skin, of a fur-bearing animal, as of a mink, fox, sheep, etc.; **rind** applies to the thick, tough covering of certain fruits, as of a watermelon, or of cheeses, bacon, etc.; **peel** is used of the skin or rind of fruit that has been removed, as by stripping [potato *peel*, lemon *peel*]; **bark** applies to the hard covering of trees and woody plants

skin-deep (-dēp′) *adj.* **1.** penetrating no deeper than the skin **2.** without real depth or significance; superficial; shallow —*adv.* so as to be only skin-deep

skin diving underwater swimming in which the swimmer, without lines to the surface, is variously equipped with a transparent face mask, flipperlike foot attachments, a skintight rubber garment, a snorkel or scuba equipment, etc. —**skin′-dive′** *vi.* **-dived′, -div′ing** —**skin diver**

skin effect the phenomenon, esp. noticeable at radio frequencies, in which an alternating current tends to concentrate at or near the surface of a conductor

skin-flint (-flint′) *n.* [< thieves' slang: lit., one who would skin a flint for gain or economy] a niggardly person; miser

skin-ful (skin′fool′) *n., pl.* **-fuls′ 1.** as much liquid as a skin container can hold **2.** [Colloq.] *a)* as much as the stomach can hold; bellyful *b)* enough alcoholic liquor to make one drunk

☆**skin game** [Colloq.] **1.** a crooked or fraudulent game of chance **2.** any cheating, swindling trick

skin grafting the surgical transplanting of skin (**skin graft**) from another part of the body or from another person to replace skin destroyed, as by burning

skink (skiŋk) *n.* [L. *scincus* < Gr. *skinkos*] any of a number of widely distributed lizards (family Scincidae) having an elongated, shiny body, smooth scales, and short legs

skin-less (skin′lis) *adj.* without a skin, casing, etc.

skinned (skind) *adj.* having skin (of a specified kind): used in hyphenated compounds [dark-*skinned*]

skin-ner (skin′ər) *n.* **1.** a person who strips skins or processes them for market ☆**2.** [Colloq.] a (mule) driver

skin-ny (skin′ē) *adj.* **-ni-er, -ni-est 1.** of or like skin **2.** without much flesh; emaciated; thin **3.** of less than normal or usual size, growth, etc.; inferior or inadequate —*SYN.* see LEAN² —**skin′ni-ness** *n.*

☆**skin-ny-dip** (-dip′) *vi.* **-dipped′, -dip′ping** [Colloq.] to swim in the nude —*n.* [Colloq.] a swim in the nude

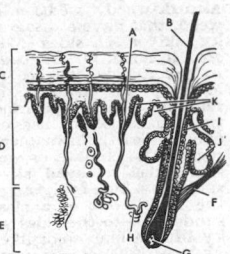

SKINK
(to 10 in. long)

skin test any test for detecting the presence of a disease or allergy from the reaction of the skin to a test substance

skin-tight (-tīt′) *adj.* clinging closely to the skin; tight-fitting [a *skintight* dress]

skip¹ (skip) *vi.* **skipped, skip′ping** [ME. *skippen*, prob. < Scand. form akin to ON. *skopa*, to jump, run < IE. *skeub-*, to shoot, throw: cf. SCOP] **1.** to leap, jump, or spring lightly; specif., to move along by hopping lightly on first one foot and then the other **2.** to be deflected from a surface; ricochet **3.** to pass, or direct the attention, from one point to another, omitting what lies between ☆**4.** to be promoted in school beyond the next regular grade **5.** [Colloq.] to leave hurriedly, esp. under questionable circumstances; abscond —*vt.* **1.** to jump or leap lightly over **2.** to pass over or omit, either deliberately or inadvertently **3.** to omit attending a session or sessions of (school, church, etc.) **4.** to cause to skip or ricochet ☆**5.** to promote to the grade beyond the next regular one in school ☆**6.** [Colloq.] to leave (a town, country, etc.) hurriedly —*n.* **1.** *a)* an act of skipping; leap; spring *b)* a skipping gait alternating light hops on each foot **2.** a passing over or omitting —☆**skip it!** never mind! it doesn't matter!

SYN.—skip suggests a springing forward lightly and quickly, leaping on alternate feet, and, of inanimate things, deflection from a surface in a series of jumps; **bound** implies longer, more vigorous leaps, as in running, or by an elastic object thrown along the ground; **hop** suggests a single short jump, as on one leg, or a series of short, relatively jerky jumps; **ricochet** is used of an inanimate object that has been thrown or shot and that bounds or skips in glancing deflection from a surface

skip² (skip) *n.* **1.** *clipped form of* SKIPPER² **2.** the captain of a lawn bowling team or of a curling team —*vt.* **skipped, skip′ping** to act as a skip for

ski pants pants that fit snugly at the ankles, worn for skiing and other winter sports

skip-bomb (skip′bäm′) *vt., vi.* to fly low and drop bombs so that they glance off the water or ground and explode against the side of (a ship or other target)

skip-jack (-jak′) *n., pl.* **-jacks′, -jack′:** see PLURAL, II, D, 1 any of several unrelated fishes, as the bluefish, saury, etc., that leap out of, or play at the surface of, the water

ski-plane (skē′plān′) *n.* an airplane with skis instead of wheels for landing on, and taking off from, snow

ski pole either of a pair of light poles with a sharp metal tip surmounted by a projecting ring: they are secured to the hands with straps and are used by skiers to gain speed and as a help in climbing and keeping balance

skip-per¹ (skip′ər) *n.* **1.** a person or thing that skips **2.** *same as* SAURY **3.** any of a superfamily (Hesperioidea) of mostly small, heavy-bodied butterflies, having threadlike antennae usually ending in a hook, and characterized by short, erratic bursts of flight **4.** any skipping insect

skip-per² (skip′ər) *n.* [ME. < MDu. *schipper* < *schip*, a SHIP] **1.** the captain of a ship, esp. of a small ship or boat **2.** any leader, director, or captain —*vt.* to act as skipper of

skip-pet (skip′it) *n.* [dim. of SKEP] a small box or envelope used to protect a seal tied to a document

skirl (skurl) *vt., vi.* [ME. (northern) *skrille, skyrle*, prob. < Scand., as in Norw. dial. *skrylla*, to scream: for IE. base see SHRILL] [Scot. & Dial.] to sound out in shrill, piercing tones, as a bagpipe —*n.* a shrill sound, as of a bagpipe

skir-mish (skur′mish) *n.* [ME. *scarmoch* < MFr. *escharmuche* < It. *scaramuccia* < *schermire*, to fight < Gmc., as in OHG. *skirmjan*, to protect < *skirm*, a guard: see SCREEN] **1.** a brief fight or encounter between small groups, usually an incident of a battle **2.** any slight, unimportant conflict; brush —*vi.* [ME. *scarmishen*] to take part in a skirmish —*SYN.* see BATTLE¹ —**skir′mish-er** *n.*

Skí-ros (skē′rôs) Gr. island of the N Sporades, in the Aegean Sea: c. 80 sq. mi.

skirr (skur) *vi.* [of echoic origin] to move, run, fly, etc. swiftly and, esp., with a whirring sound —*vt.* **1.** to cover in searching; scour **2.** to throw and cause to skim —*n.* a whirring sound

skirt (skurt) *n.* [ME. < ON. *skyrt*, shirt, kirtle, akin to OE. *scyrte*, SHIRT] **1.** that part of a dress, coat, robe, etc. that hangs below the waist **2.** a woman's garment of varying length that hangs down from the waist **3.** something like a skirt, as a flap hanging from the side of a saddle or one covering the legs of a sofa, chair, etc. **4.** [*pl.*] the outer or bordering parts; outskirts, as of a city **5.** [Old Slang] a girl or woman —*vt.* **1.** to lie along or form the border or edge of **2.** *a)* to move along the edge of or pass around rather than through *b)* to miss narrowly **3.** to avoid (something controversial, difficult, etc.) **4.** to border or edge with something —*vi.* to be on, or move along, the edge or border [a path *skirting* along the pond] —**skirt′ed** (-id) *adj.* having a (specified kind of) skirt: often in hyphenated compounds [short-*skirted*]

ski run a slope or course used for skiing

skit (skit) *n.* [< dial. v., to be skittish, taunt, prob. < Scand. var. of ON. *skjóta*, to SHOOT] **1.** [Now Rare] a taunting remark; gibe **2.** a short piece of satirical or humorous writing **3.** a short, usually comic theatrical sketch, as in a revue

☆**ski tow** a kind of ski lift enabling skiers to glide up the slope on their skis, towed by the endless cable

skit·ter (skit′ər) vi. [freq. of dial. *skite*, to dart about < Scand., akin to SHOOT] 1. to skip or move along quickly and lightly, esp. over water ☆2. to draw a fish bait or lure over the surface of the water with a skipping motion —vt. to cause to skitter

skit·tish (skit′ish) adj. [ME.: see SKIT & -ISH] 1. lively or playful, esp. in a coy manner 2. easily frightened; jumpy [a *skittish* horse] 3. fickle or undependable —skit′tish·ly adv. —skit′tish·ness n.

skit·tle (skit′l) n. [prob. < Scand. cognate of SHUTTLE (as in Dan. *skyttel*, a shuttle, marble) 1. [pl., with sing. v.] a British form of ninepins in which a wooden disk or ball is used to knock down the pins 2. any of these pins —(not) **all beer and skittles** (not) pure pleasure and enjoyment

skive (skīv) vt. skived, skiv′ing [ON. *skifa*, akin to SHIVE] to slice off (leather, rubber, etc.) in thin layers; shave

skiv·er (skī′vər) n. 1. a soft, thin leather made from the outer half of split sheepskin and used for bookbindings, hat linings, etc. 2. a person who skives leather 3. a tool used in skiving leather

skiv·vy[1] (skiv′ē) n., pl. -vies [< ?] [Slang] 1. a man's, esp. a sailor's, short-sleeved undershirt: usually **skivvy shirt** 2. [pl.] men's underwear

skiv·vy[2] (skiv′ē) n., pl. -vies [< ?] [Brit. Slang] same as HOUSEMAID

skoal (skōl) interj. [Dan. & Norw. *skaal*, a cup < ON. *skāl*, a bowl: for base see SCALE[3]] to your health!: a toast

Sko·kie (skō′kē) [prob. < AmInd. term for swampland] village in NE Ill.: suburb of Chicago: pop. 69,000

☆**skoo·kum** (skōō′kəm) adj. [Chinook jargon, evil spirit] [Northwest & Canad.] strong, big, excellent, etc.

Sko·pje (skô′pye) city in SE Yugoslavia; capital of Macedonia: pop. 172,000: also **Skop·lje** (skôp′lye)

Skr., Skrt., Skt. Sanskrit

sku·a (skyōō′ə) n. [ModL., adapted (c. 1604) < Faroese *skūgver* < ON. *skūfr*, a tuft, sheaf (akin to SHOP)] 1. any of several varieties of a large, brown and white, predatory sea gull (*Catharacta skua*), found in cold seas 2. [Brit.] same as JAEGER (sense 2)

☆**skul·dug·ger·y, skull·dug·ger·y** (skul dug′ər ē) n. [Early ModScot. *sculduddrie* < ?] [Colloq.] sneaky, dishonest behavior; trickery

skulk (skulk) vi. [ME. *sculken*, prob. < LowG. *schulken*, to play truant, or cognate Dan. *skulke*, to skulk] 1. to move or lurk about in a stealthy, craven, or sinister manner; slink 2. [Chiefly Brit.] to avoid work or responsibility; shirk; malinger —n. 1. a person who skulks 2. [Obs.] a group or pack (of foxes) —SYN. see LURK —skulk′er n. —skulk′ing·ly adv.

skull (skul) n. [ME. *scolle* < Scand., as in Sw. *skulle*, skull, akin to SCALE[3], SHELL] 1. the entire bony or cartilaginous framework of the head of a vertebrate, enclosing and protecting the brain and sense organs and composed of the cranium and the bones of the face and jaws 2. the human head regarded as the seat of thought or intelligence: usually with derogatory allusion [a thick *skull*, an empty *skull*]

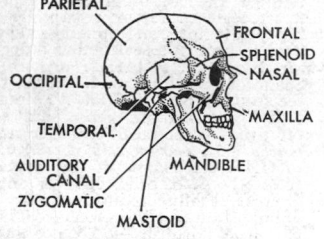

HUMAN SKULL

PARIETAL
FRONTAL
SPHENOID
NASAL
OCCIPITAL
MAXILLA
TEMPORAL
MANDIBLE
AUDITORY CANAL
ZYGOMATIC
MASTOID

skull and crossbones a human skull facing forward with two long bones crossed beneath it, as formerly pictured on pirates' flags: now used as a warning sign, as on poisons

skull·cap (-kap′) n. 1. a light, closefitting, brimless cap, usually worn indoors; specif., a zucchetto or a yarmulke 2. any of a genus (*Scutellaria*) of mints with a closed, helmet-shaped calyx

☆**skull practice** (or **session**) [Slang] a class session, as of a football team, at which plays are studied and discussed

☆**skunk** (skuŋk) n. [< AmInd. name (as in Abnaki *segonku*)] 1. a) pl. **skunks, skunk:** see PLURAL, II, D, 1 any of several bushy-tailed mammals (family Mustelidae) of the New World, about the size of a house cat: it has glossy black fur, usually with white stripes or spots down the back, and ejects a foul-smelling, musky liquid when molested b) its fur 2. [Colloq.] a despicable, offensive person —vt. [Slang] to defeat overwhelmingly in a game or contest; often, specif., to keep from scoring any points

SKUNK
(head & body to 15 in. long; tail 8–12 in. long)

☆**skunk cabbage** 1. a perennial E. N. American plant (*Symplocarpus foetidus*) of the arum family, growing in wet soil and having large, cabbagelike leaves, a spadix of small flowers concealed in a

purple, hooded spathe, and a disagreeable smell 2. a related plant (*Lysichitum americanum*) of W. N. America

☆**skunk·weed** (-wēd′) n. any of several plants, as joe-pye weed, that have a disagreeable smell

sky (skī) n., pl. **skies** [ME. < ON., a cloud, akin to OE. *sceo*, a cloud, OHG. *scuwo*, shadow < IE. base *(s)keu-, to cover, hide, whence HIDE[1], L. *cutis*, skin, Gr. *skytos*, leather] 1. [often pl.] the upper atmosphere, esp. with reference to its appearance [blue *skies*, a cloudy *sky*] 2. the expanse of the heavens that forms an apparent arch over the earth; firmament 3. a) heaven, or the celestial regions b) climate or weather [the balmy southern *sky*] —vt. skied or skyed, sky′ing [Colloq.] 1. to hit, throw, shoot, etc. high in the air 2. to hang (a picture) high up on the wall —out of a clear (blue) sky without warning; suddenly —to the skies without reserve; extravagantly

sky blue a blue color like that of the sky on a clear day

☆**sky·cap** (-kap′) n. a porter, or redcap, at an air terminal

☆**sky diving** the sport of jumping from an airplane and executing free-fall maneuvers before opening the parachute, often at the last possible moment —sky′-dive′ (-dīv′) vi. -dived′, -div′ing —sky diver

Skye (skī), **Isle of** island off the W coast of Scotland; largest of the Inner Hebrides: 643 sq. mi.

Skye terrier [after prec.] any of a breed of small terrier, with long hair, a long body, and short legs

sky·ey (skī′ē) adj. 1. of or like the sky, as a shade of blue 2. of great height; lofty

sky-high (skī′hī′) adj., adv. 1. of or to a great height, amount, degree, etc.; very high 2. so as to be completely blasted; to pieces

☆**sky·jack** (-jak′) vt. [Colloq.] to hijack (an aircraft) —**sky′jack′er** n.

sky·lark (-lärk′) n. a Eurasian lark (*Alauda arvensis*), famous for the song it utters as it soars toward the sky —vi. [< SKY + LARK[2]: orig. naut., of playing in the rigging] to play about boisterously; frolic

sky·light (-līt′) n. a window in a roof or ceiling

sky·line (-līn′) n. 1. the line along which the sky seems to touch the earth; visible horizon 2. the outline, as of a city, seen against the sky

sky pilot [Slang] a clergyman; esp., a chaplain (sense 2)

sky·rock·et (-räk′it) n. a firework rocket that explodes in midair, giving off a display of colored flame, sparks, etc. —☆vi., vt. to rise or cause to rise rapidly to a great height, success, etc.

Ský·ros (skē′rôs) same as SKÍROS

sky·sail (skī′sāl′, -s'l) n. the small sail set above the royal at the top of a square-rigged mast: see SAIL, illus.

sky·scrap·er (-skrā′pər) n. ☆a very tall building

sky·ward (-wərd) adv., adj. toward the sky: also **sky′wards** adv.

sky wave a radio wave that is reflected back to earth from one of the layers of the ionosphere

sky·ways (-wāz′) n.pl. routes of air travel; air lanes

sky·writ·ing (-rīt′iŋ) n. the act or result of tracing words, figures, etc. in the sky by trailing smoke from an airplane in flight —sky′write′ vi., vt. —sky′writ′er n.

s.l. [L. *sine loco*] without place (of publication)

slab[1] (slab) n. [ME. *sclabbe*] 1. a piece that is flat, broad, and fairly thick [a *slab* of concrete, a *slab* of bread] 2. any of the rough, outer pieces removed from a log in sawing it into lumber —vt. slabbed, slab′bing 1. to make into a slab or slabs 2. to cut the slabs from (a log) 3. to pave or cover with slabs

slab[2] (slab) adj. [< Scand., as in Sw. dial. *slabb*, muddy water, Dan. *slab*, slippery] [Archaic] thick and heavy; viscid [*slab* porridge]

slab·ber (slab′ər) vi., vt., n. same as SLOBBER

slab-sid·ed (slab′sīd′id) adj. [Colloq.] 1. flat-sided 2. tall and slender; lank

slack[1] (slak) adj. [ME. *slakke* < OE. *slæc*, akin to Du. *slak* < IE. base *(s)lēg-, loose, slack, whence L. *laxus*, lax] 1. slow; idle; sluggish 2. barely moving: said of a current, as of air or water 3. characterized by little work, trade, or business; not busy or active; dull [a *slack* period] 4. loose; relaxed; not tight, taut, or firm 5. easily changed or influenced; weak; lax 6. careless or negligent [a *slack* workman] —vt. 1. to make slack; slacken 2. to slake —vi. 1. to be or become slack; slacken 2. to be idle, careless, or negligent —adv. in a slack manner; so as to be slack —n. 1. a part that is slack or hangs loose 2. a lack of tension or tautness; looseness 3. a stoppage of movement in a current 4. a time of little activity; dull period; lull 5. *Prosody* the unstressed syllable or syllables within a foot, esp. in sprung rhythm —SYN. see REMISS —**slack off** to slacken —**slack up** to go more slowly —**slack′ly** adv. —**slack′ness** n.

slack[2] (slak) n. [ME. *sleck*, akin to Fl. *slecke*, dross, Du. *slak*: for base see SLAG] a mixture of small pieces of coal, coal dust, and dirt left from the screening of coal

slack[3] (slak) n. [ME. *slak* < ON. *slakki* < IE. base *sk̑lēk̑-, wet, sprinkle: cf. SLOUGH[2]] [Scot. & Brit. Dial.] 1. a small valley; dell 2. a boggy hollow; morass

slack-baked (-bākt′) adj. not fully or properly baked, made, etc.

slack·en (slak′n) vi. [< SLACK[1]] 1. to become less active, intense, brisk, etc. [*slackening* trade] 2. to become less tense; loosen, as rope —vt. 1. to reduce the intensity or

severity of; retard; abate; moderate **2.** to reduce the tension of; relax; loosen /to *slacken* one's grip/ —*SYN.* see DELAY —**slack'en·er** *n.*

slack·er (-ər) *n.* **1.** a person who shirks his work or duty **2.** a person who evades military service in wartime

slacks (slaks) *n.pl.* trousers for men or women; esp., trousers that are not part of a suit

slack water 1. the period between tides when the water is neither in ebb nor flood **2.** any stretch of water having little or no current

slag (slag) *n.* [< MLowG. *slagge*, akin to G. *schlacke* < base of *schlagen*, to strike: for IE. base see SLAY] **1.** the fused refuse or dross separated from a metal in the process of smelting **2.** lava resembling this —*vt., vi.* **slagged, slag'ging** to form into slag —**slag'gy** *adj.* **-gi·er, -gi·est**

slain (slān) *pp.* of SLAY

slain·te (slän'chə) *interj.* [Ir. *slāinte*, health] to your health!: a toast

slake (slāk) *vt.* **slaked, slak'ing** [ME. *slakien* < OE. *slacian* < *slæc*, SLACK[1]] **1.** to allay or make (thirst, desire, etc.) less active or intense by satisfying; assuage; satisfy **2.** to cause (a fire) to die down or go out **3.** to produce a chemical change in (lime) by combination with water [*slaked* lime is calcium hydroxide] **4.** [Obs.] to lessen, reduce, or relieve **5.** [Obs.] to lessen the tension of —*vi.* **1.** to become slaked or undergo slaking, as lime, thirst, etc. **2.** [Archaic] to become less active or intense; slacken

sla·lom (slä'ləm) *n.* [Norw., ski track with an even slope < dial. *slad*, sloping gently + *lom*, trail] a downhill skiing race over a zigzag course marked by flag-topped poles or gates (see GATE[1] *n.* 8) —*vi.* to ski in or as in a slalom

slam[1] (slam) *vt.* **slammed, slam'ming** [prob. < Scand., as in Norw. dial. *slamra, slemma*] **1.** to shut or allow to shut with force and noise /to *slam* a door/ **2.** to hit, throw, or put in place or action with force and noise /to *slam* a baseball over the fence/ ☆**3.** [Colloq.] to criticize or depreciate severely —*vi.* to shut, go into place, etc. with force and noise —*n.* **1.** *a)* a heavy, noisy impact, shutting, etc. *b)* the noise made by this ☆**2.** [Colloq.] severe criticism

slam[2] (slam) *n.* [< ?] **1.** an old card game resembling ruff **2.** *Bridge* shortened form of GRAND SLAM or LITTLE SLAM

slam-bang (slam'baŋ') *adv.* [Colloq.] **1.** swiftly or abruptly and recklessly **2.** with loud noise —*adj.* characterized by liveliness, noise, etc.

slan·der (slan'dər) *n.* [ME. *sclaunder* < Anglo-Fr. *esclaundre* (OFr. *esclandre, escandle*) < LL.(Ec.) *scandalum*: see SCANDAL] **1.** the utterance in the presence of another person of a false statement or statements, damaging to a third person's character or reputation: usually distinguished from *libel*, which is written **2.** such a spoken statement —*vt.* to utter a slanderous statement about —**slan'der·er** *n.*

slan·der·ous (-əs) *adj.* [ME. *sclaunderous*] **1.** characterized by or constituting slander **2.** uttering slander

slang[1] (slaŋ) *n.* [18th-c. cant < ?] **1.** orig., the specialized vocabulary and idioms of criminals, tramps, etc., the purpose of which was to disguise from outsiders the meaning of what was said: now usually called CANT[1] **2.** the specialized vocabulary and idioms of those in the same work, way of life, etc.: now usually called SHOPTALK, ARGOT, JARGON **3.** highly informal language that is outside of conventional or standard usage and consists of both coined words and phrases and of new or extended meanings attached to established terms: slang develops from the attempt to find fresh and vigorous, colorful, pungent, or humorous expression, and generally either passes into disuse or comes to have a more formal status —*vi.* to use slang or abusive talk —*vt.* [Chiefly Brit.] to address with abusive talk

slang[2] (slaŋ) *dial. or archaic pt.* of SLING[1]

slang·y (slaŋ'ē) *adj.* **slang'i·er, slang'i·est 1.** of, having the nature of, or containing slang **2.** given to using slang —**slang'i·ly** *adv.* —**slang'i·ness** *n.*

slank (slaŋk) *archaic pt.* of SLINK[1]

slant (slant) *vt., vi.* [ME. *slenten*, to glide, slope < Scand., as in ODan. *slente*, to slip < IE. *(s)lend(h)-* < base *(s)leidh-*, slippery, to glide, whence SLIDE] **1.** to incline or turn from a direct line or course, esp. one that is perpendicular or level; slope ☆**2.** *a)* to write or tell so as to appeal to a particular interest *b)* to distort in writing or telling so as to express a particular bias —*n.* **1.** *a)* an oblique or inclined surface, line, direction, etc.; slope; incline *b)* same as VIRGULE ☆**2.** *a)* a point of view, attitude, or opinion *b)* a distortion or bias in narration **3.** [Colloq.] a quick, oblique look; glance —*adj.* [prob. aphetic < ME. *aslonte, aslant*] oblique; sloping; inclined

slant rhyme rhyme in which there is close but not exact correspondence of sounds (Ex.: *lid, lad; wait, made*); imperfect rhyme

slant·wise (-wīz') *adv.* so as to slant or slope; obliquely: also **slant'ways'** —*adj.* slanting; oblique

slap (slap) *n.* [LowG. *slappp*: of echoic origin] **1.** *a)* a blow or smack, esp. with something flat, specif. the palm of the hand *b)* the sound of this, or a sound like it **2.** an injury to pride, self-respect, etc., as an insult or rebuff —*vt.* **slapped, slap'ping 1.** to strike with something flat, specif. the palm of the hand **2.** to put, throw, hit, etc. carelessly or with force /to *slap* a hat on one's head/ —*vi.* to make a dull, sharp noise, as upon impact —*adv.* **1.** [Colloq.] straight; directly /he ran *slap* into the wall/ **2.** [Brit. Colloq.] suddenly —*SYN.* see STRIKE —**slap down** [Colloq.] to rebuke, suppress, or rebuff harshly —**slap'per** *n.*

slap-bang (-baŋ') *adv.* [Chiefly Brit. Colloq.] suddenly; violently —*adj. colloq. var.* of SLAPDASH

slap·dash (-dash') *n.* something done carelessly and hastily —*adv.* in a hasty, careless manner; haphazardly —*adj.* hasty, careless, impetuous, etc.

☆**slap-hap·py** (-hap'ē) *adj.* [Slang] **1.** dazed or mentally impaired by or as by blows to the head; punch-drunk **2.** silly or giddy

☆**slap·jack** (-jak') *n.* same as FLAPJACK

☆**slap·stick** (-stik') *n.* **1.** an implement made of two flat pieces of wood that slap together loudly when hit against something: formerly used by stage comedians to strike others with loud, harmless slaps **2.** crude comedy in which the humor depends upon violent activity, horseplay, etc. —*adj.* characterized by such comedy

slap-up (-up') *adj.* [Brit. Colloq.] stylish; lavish; elegant

slash[1] (slash) *vt.* [ME. *slaschen* < ? OFr. *esclachier*, to break] **1.** to cut or wound with a sweeping stroke or strokes, as of a knife **2.** to whip viciously; lash; scourge **3.** to cut slits in (a fabric, dress, etc.), esp. so as to expose underlying material, usually of another color **4.** to reduce drastically /to *slash* prices/ **5.** to criticize severely —*vi.* to make a sweeping stroke or strokes with or as with something sharp; cut or criticize violently —*n.* **1.** a sweeping stroke made as with a knife **2.** a cut made by or as by such a stroke; gash; slit **3.** same as VIRGULE **4.** an ornamental slit in a fabric, dress, etc. ☆**5.** *a)* an open place in a forest, cluttered with branches, chips, or other debris, as from the cutting of timber *b)* such debris —**slash'er** *n.*

☆**slash[2]** (slash) *n.* [< dial. *slash*, boggy hollow, *slashy*, swampy, prob. < Scand., as in Norw. dial. *slask*, mud, slush] a low, swampy area, usually covered with brush

slash·ing (-iŋ) *adj.* **1.** severe; merciless; violent **2.** dashing; spirited **3.** [Colloq.] immense; tremendous /a *slashing* success/ —*n.* **1.** the act of one that slashes **2.** same as SLASH[1] (*n.* 4 & 5) —**slash'ing·ly** *adv.*

☆**slash pine 1.** a common pine (*Pinus caribaea*) growing in slashes, or swamps, in the SE U.S., the West Indies, and Central America **2.** the hard wood of this tree

slash pocket a pocket (in a garment) the opening of which is a finished, usually diagonal slit

Śląsk (shlônsk) *Pol. name of* SILESIA

slat[1] (slat) *n.* [ME. *sclat* < OFr. *esclat*, a fragment < *esclater*, to splinter < Langobardic *slaitan*, to tear apart, split, akin to OHG. *slizzan*, OE. *slitan* < IE. **skleid-* < base **(s)kel-*, to cut] **1.** a thin, narrow strip of wood, metal, etc. /*slats* of a Venetian blind/ ☆**2.** [*pl.*] [Slang] *a)* the ribs *b)* the buttocks —*vt.* **slat'ted, slat'ting** to provide or make with slats

slat[2] (slat) *vi.* **slat'ted, slat'ting** [ME. *sclatten*, prob. < ON. *sletta*, to throw: intr. by prec.] to flap or beat vigorously, as sails in a strong wind —*vt.* [Brit. Dial.] **1.** to throw forcefully **2.** to beat; strike —*n.* [Brit. Dial.] a sharp blow

S. Lat., S. lat. south latitude

slate[1] (slāt) *n.* [ME. *sclate* < OFr. *esclate*, fem. of *esclat*: see SLAT[1]] **1.** a hard, fine-grained, metamorphic rock that cleaves naturally into thin, smooth-surfaced layers **2.** a thin piece of slate or slatelike material, esp. one used as a roofing tile or as a tablet for writing on with chalk **3.** the bluish-gray color of most slate: also **slate blue** ☆**4.** a list of candidates proposed for nomination or election —*vt.* **slat'ed, slat'ing 1.** to cover with slate ☆**2.** to put on a list or designate, as for candidacy, appointment, engagement, etc.; choose or schedule —**a clean slate** a record showing no marks of discredit, dishonor, etc.

slate[2] (slāt) *vt.* **slat'ed, slat'ing** [prob. < ON. **sleita* (akin to OE. *slætan*, to bait, torment)] [Chiefly Brit. Colloq.] **1.** to punish severely, as by thrashing **2.** to scold or criticize harshly

slat·er (slāt'ər) *n.* **1.** a person who slates **2.** any of various isopod crustaceans; esp., same as WOOD LOUSE

slath·er (sla*th*'ər) *n.* [< ?] [*usually pl.*] [Dial. or Colloq.] a large amount; a lot —*vt.* [Dial. or Colloq.] **1.** to cover or spread thickly **2.** to use or use up in a lavish or wasteful way

slat·ing (slāt'iŋ) *n.* **1.** the act of one who slates **2.** slates collectively, as a material for roofing

slat·tern (slat'ərn) *n.* [< dial. *slatter*, to spill, slop < or akin to ON. *slattari*, idler] **1.** a woman who is careless and sloppy in her habits, appearance, work, etc. **2.** a sexually promiscuous woman; slut

slat·tern·ly (-lē) *adj.* **1.** having the habits of a slattern; dirty; slovenly; untidy **2.** characteristic of or fit for a slattern —*adv.* in a slatternly manner —**slat'tern·li·ness** *n.*

slat·ting (slat'iŋ) *n.* **1.** slats collectively **2.** material for making slats

slat·y (slāt′ē) *adj.* **slat′i·er**, **slat′i·est** **1.** of or like slate **2.** having the bluish-gray color of slate

slaugh·ter (slôt′ər) *n.* [ME. *slahter* < ON. *slātr*, lit., slain flesh, contr. < *slattr*, akin to OE. *sleaht*, slaughter, death: for IE. base see SLAY] **1.** the killing of an animal or animals for food; butchering **2.** the killing of a human being, esp. in a brutal manner **3.** the killing of people in large numbers, as in battle —*vt.* **1.** to kill (an animal or animals) for food; butcher **2.** to kill (people), esp. brutally or in large numbers —**slaugh′ter·er** *n.*
SYN.—**slaughter**, as applied to people, suggests extensive and brutal killing, as in battle or by deliberate acts of wanton cruelty; **massacre** implies the indiscriminate and wholesale slaughter of those who are defenseless or helpless to resist; **butchery** adds implications of extreme cruelty and of such coldblooded heartlessness as one might display in the slaughtering of animals; **carnage** stresses the result of bloody slaughter and suggests the accumulation of the bodies of the slain; **pogrom** refers to an organized, often officially inspired, massacre of a minority group, specifically of the Jews in czarist Russia

slaugh·ter·house (-hous′) *n.* a place where animals are butchered for food; abattoir

slaugh·ter·ous (-əs) *adj.* brutally destructive or murderous —**slaugh′ter·ous·ly** *adv.*

Slav (släv, slav) *n.* [ME. *Sclave* < ML. *Slavus*: see SLAVE] a member of any of a group of Slavic-speaking peoples of E, SE, and C Europe, generally divided into **Eastern Slavs** (Russians, Ukrainians, and Byelorussians), **Southern Slavs** (Serbs, Croats, Bulgars, etc.), and **Western Slavs** (Czechs, Poles, Slovaks, etc.) —*adj.* same as SLAVIC

Slav. Slavic

slave (slāv) *n.* [ME. *sclave* < OFr. or ML.: OFr. *esclave* < ML. *sclavus*, slave, orig., Slav < LGr. *Sklabos*, ult. < OBulg. *Slověne*, native name of a Slavic people: first used of captives of Slavic origin in SE Europe] **1.** a human being who is owned as property by another and is absolutely subject to his will; bondservant divested of all freedom and personal rights **2.** a person who is completely dominated by some influence, habit, person, etc. [a *slave* to fashion] **3.** same as SLAVE ANT **5.** a device actuated or controlled by another, similar device —*vi.* **slaved, slav′ing 1.** to work like a slave; drudge **2.** to deal in slaves; be a slaver —*vt.* [Archaic] to enslave

slave ant any ant enslaved by slave-making ants

Slave Coast W African coast between the Volta & Niger rivers, on the Bight of Benin: its ports were the former centers of the African slave trade

☆**slave driver 1.** a person who directs or oversees the work of slaves **2.** any merciless taskmaster

slave·hold·er (slāv′hōl′dər) *n.* a person who owns slaves —**slave′hold′ing** *adj., n.*

slave-mak·ing ant (-māk′iŋ) an ant of any of several species that enslave ants of other species, as by raiding their nests to carry off pupae that are raised to be workers

SLAVE COAST

slav·er[1] (slav′ər, slāv′-) *vi.* [ME. *slaveren* < Scand., as in Ice. *slafra*, to slobber < IE. *slep-* < base *(s)lāp-*, whence LIP, SLEEP] to let saliva run or dribble from the mouth; drool —*vt.* [Archaic] to slobber on or cover with saliva —*n.* saliva drooling from the mouth

slav·er[2] (slā′vər) *n.* **1.** same as SLAVE SHIP **2.** a person who deals in slaves; slave hunter or trader

Slave River river in NE Alberta & S Mackenzie District, Canada, flowing from Lake Athabasca northwest into Great Slave Lake: 258 mi.

slav·er·y (slā′vər ē, slāv′rē) *n.* **1.** the owning or keeping of slaves as a practice or institution; slaveholding **2.** the condition of being a slave; bondage; servitude **3.** a condition of submission to or domination by some influence, habit, etc. **4.** hard work or toil like that done by slaves; drudgery —*SYN.* see SERVITUDE

slave ship a ship for transporting slaves, esp. one used in the African slave trade

Slave State any of the States in which slavery was legal before the Civil War: Ala., Ark., Del., Fla., Ga., Ky., La., Md., Miss., Mo., N.C., S.C., Tenn., Tex., & Va.

slave trade traffic in slaves; specif., the former transportation of African Negroes to America for sale as slaves

slav·ey (slā′vē, slav′ē) *n., pl.* **-eys** [Brit. Colloq.] a woman or girl who is a domestic servant, esp. one who does hard, menial work

Slav·ic (släv′ik, slav′-) *adj.* [ML. *Sclavicus*, Baltic] of the Slavs, their languages, etc. —*n.* a principal branch of the Indo-European family of languages, generally divided into **East Slavic** (Russian, Ukrainian, Byelorussian), **South Slavic** (Old Church Slavic, Bulgarian, Serbo-Croatian, Slovenian), and **West Slavic** (Polish, Sorbian, Czech, Slovak)

Slav·i·cist (-ə sist) *n.* a student of or specialist in Slavic languages, cultures, etc.: also **Slav′ist**

slav·ish (slā′vish) *adj.* **1.** of or characteristic of a slave or slaves; specif., *a)* hopelessly submissive; servile *b)* involving drudgery; laborious **2.** blindly dependent or imitative [*slavish* adherence to a model] —*SYN.* see SERVILE —**slav′ish·ly** *adv.* —**slav′ish·ness** *n.*

Slav·ism (släv′iz'm, slav′-) *n.* characteristics, interests, culture, etc. of Slavs collectively

Slav·kov (släf′kôf) Czech name of AUSTERLITZ

Sla·vo- (släv′ō, slav′-; -ə) a combining form meaning Slav [*Slavophile*]

☆**slav·oc·ra·cy** (slā väk′rə sē) *n.* [SLAV(E) + -o- + -CRACY] slaveholders and pro-slavery forces as a dominant or powerful class in the U.S. before 1865

Sla·vo·ni·a (slə vō′nē ə) region in Croatia, N Yugoslavia —**Sla·vo′ni·an** *adj., n.*

Sla·von·ic (slə vän′ik) *adj., n.* same as SLAVIC

Slav·o·phile (släv′ə fil′, slav′ə-) *n.* [SLAVO- + -PHILE] a person who admires or is very fond of the Slavs, their customs, culture, etc.: also **Slav′o·phil** (-fil) —**Sla·voph·i·lism** (slə väf′ə liz'm) *n.*

Slav·o·phobe (-fōb′) *n.* [SLAVO- + -PHOBE] a person who hates or fears the Slavs, their culture, influence, etc. —**Sla·vo′pho·bi·a** (-fō′bē ə) *n.*

☆**slaw** (slô) *n.* short for COLESLAW

slay (slā) *vt.* **slew** or for **2 slayed, slain, slay′ing** [ME. *slean* < OE. < *slahan*, akin to G. *schlagen* < IE. base *slak-*, to hit, whence MIr. *slacc*, sword] **1.** to kill or destroy in a violent way **2.** [Slang] to impress, delight, amuse, etc. with overwhelming force —*SYN.* see KILL[1] —**slay′er** *n.*

sld. 1. sailed **2.** sealed

sleave (slēv) *n.* [< OE. -*slæfan*, to separate < IE. base *(s)kel-*, to cut, whence SLIT, SHIELD] **1.** [Obs.] *a)* a fine silk thread separated from a large thread *b)* untwisted silk that tends to mat or tangle; floss **2.** [Rare] any tangle, as of ravelings —*vt.* **sleaved, sleav′ing** [Obs.] to separate or pull apart (twisted or tangled threads)

slea·zy (slē′zē) *adj.* **-zi·er, -zi·est** [< *Slesia*, var. of SILESIA] **1.** flimsy or thin in texture or substance; lacking firmness [a *sleazy* rayon fabric] **2.** shoddy, shabby, cheap, mean, etc. —**slea′zi·ly** *adv.* —**slea′zi·ness** *n.*

sled (sled) *n.* [ME. *sledde* < MLowG. or MDu., akin to G. *schlitten*: for IE. base see SLIDE] any of several types of vehicle mounted on runners for use on snow, ice, etc.: small sleds are used in the sport of coasting, large ones (also called *sledges*), for carrying loads —☆*vt.* **sled′ded, sled′ding** to carry on a sled —☆*vi.* to ride or coast on a sled

sled·der (sled′ər) *n.* **1.** a person who rides or drives a sled **2.** an animal used for drawing a sled

☆**sled·ding** (-iŋ) *n.* **1.** a riding or carrying on a sled **2.** the condition of the ground with reference to the use of sleds: often used figuratively [the work was hard *sledding*]

sledge[1] (slej) *n., vt., vi.* **sledged, sledg′ing** [ME. *slegge* < OE. *slecge* < base of *slean*, to strike, SLAY] same as SLEDGE-HAMMER

sledge[2] (slej) *n.* [MDu. *sleedse*, akin to *sledde*, but of Fris. origin] a sled or sleigh for carrying passengers or loads over ice, snow, etc. —*vi., vt.* **sledged, sledg′ing** to go or take by sledge

sledge·ham·mer (-ham′ər) *n.* [see SLEDGE[1]] a long, heavy hammer, usually held with both hands —*vt., vi.* to strike with or as with a sledgehammer —*adj.* crushingly powerful

sleek (slēk) *adj.* [var. of SLICK, with Early ModE. lengthening of vowel] **1.** smooth and shiny; glossy, as a highly polished surface, well-kept hair or fur, etc. **2.** of well-fed or well-groomed appearance [fat, *sleek* pigeons] **3.** polished in speech and behavior, esp. in a specious way; unctuous; oily **4.** highly fashionable, or stylish; luxurious, elegant, etc. —*vt.* to make sleek; smooth; polish: also **sleek′en** —**sleek′ly** *adv.* —**sleek′ness** *n.*

sleek·it (slē′kit) *adj.* [Scot. var. of pp. of SLEEK] [Scot.] **1.** sleek, or smooth and shiny **2.** sly, crafty, or sneaky

sleep (slēp) *n.* [ME. *slep* < OE. *slæp*, akin to G. *schlaf*, sleep, *schlaff*, loose, lax < IE. *slab* < base *(s)leb-*, *(s)lab-*, loose, slack, whence L. *labor*, to slip, sink & LIP, LIMP[1]] **1.** *a)* a natural, regularly recurring condition of rest for the body and mind, during which the eyes are usually closed and there is little or no conscious thought or voluntary movement, but there is intermittent dreaming *b)* a spell of sleeping **2.** any state of inactivity thought of as like sleep, as death, unconsciousness, hibernation, etc. **3.** *Bot.* same as NYCTITROPISM —*vi.* **slept, sleep′ing 1.** to be in the state of sleep; slumber **2.** to be in a state of inactivity like sleep, as that of death, quiescence, hibernation, inattention, etc. **3.** [Colloq.] to have sexual intercourse (*with*) **4.** [Colloq.] to postpone a decision (*on*) to allow time for deliberation **5.** *Bot.* to assume a nyctitropic position at night, as petals or leaves —*vt.* **1.** to slumber in (a specified kind of sleep) [to *sleep* the sleep of the just] **2.** to provide sleeping accommodations for [a boat that *sleeps* four] —**last sleep** death —**sleep around** [Slang] to have promiscuous sexual relations —**sleep away 1.** to spend in sleeping; sleep during **2.** to get rid of by sleeping —**sleep in 1.** to sleep at the place where one is employed as a household servant **2.** to sleep later in the morning than one usually does —**sleep off** to rid oneself of by sleeping —**sleep out 1.** to spend in sleeping; sleep

throughout 2. to sleep outdoors —**sleep over** [Colloq.] to spend the night at another's home

sleep·er (slē'pər) *n.* [ME. *slepere* < OE. *slæpere*] 1. a person or animal that sleeps, esp. as specified [a sound *sleeper*] 2. a timber or beam laid horizontally, as on the ground, to support something above it 3. [Chiefly Brit.] a tie supporting a railroad track ☆4. same as SLEEPING CAR ☆5. a previously disregarded person or thing that unexpectedly achieves success, assumes importance, etc. ☆6. a) [*usually pl.*] a kind of pajamas for infants and young children, that enclose the feet b) same as BUNTING¹ (sense 3) ☆7. *Bowling* a pin concealed by one before it, in bowling for a spare

sleep·i·ly (-pə lē) *adv.* in a sleepy or drowsy manner
sleep·i·ness (-pē nis) *n.* a sleepy quality or state
☆**sleeping bag** a large, warmly lined, zippered bag, often waterproof, for sleeping in, esp. outdoors
☆**sleeping car** a railway car equipped with berths, compartments, etc. for passengers to sleep in
sleeping partner *Brit. term for* SILENT PARTNER
☆**sleeping pill** a pill or capsule containing a drug, esp. a barbiturate, that induces sleep
sleeping sickness 1. an infectious disease, esp. common in tropical Africa, caused by either of two trypanosomes (*Trypanosoma gambiense* or *Trypanosoma rhodesiense*) that are transmitted by the bite of a tsetse fly: it is characterized by fever, weakness, tremors, and lethargy, usually ending in prolonged coma and death 2. inflammation of the brain, caused by a virus and characterized by apathy, drowsiness, and lethargy

sleep·less (slēp'lis) *adj.* 1. unable to sleep; wakeful; restless 2. marked by absence of sleep [a *sleepless* night] 3. constantly moving, active, or alert —**sleep'less·ly** *adv.* —**sleep'less·ness** *n.*

sleep·walk·ing (slēp'wôk'iŋ) *n.* the act or practice of walking while asleep; somnambulism —**sleep'walk'** *vi.* —**sleep'walk'er** *n.*

sleep·wear (-wer') *n.* same as NIGHTCLOTHES

sleep·y (slē'pē) *adj.* **sleep'i·er, sleep'i·est** 1. ready or inclined to sleep; needing sleep; drowsy 2. characterized by an absence of activity; dull; idle; lethargic [a *sleepy* little town] 3. causing drowsiness; inducing sleep 4. of or exhibiting drowsiness
SYN.—**sleepy** applies to a person who is nearly overcome by a desire to sleep and, figuratively, suggests either the power to induce sleepiness or a resemblance to this state [a *sleepy* town, song, etc.]; **drowsy** stresses the sluggishness or lethargic heaviness accompanying sleepiness [the *drowsy* sentry fought off sleep through his watch]; **somnolent** is a formal equivalent of either of the preceding [the *somnolent* voice of the speaker]; **slumberous**, a poetic equivalent, in addition sometimes suggests latent powers in repose [a *slumberous* city]

sleep·y·head (-hed') *n.* a sleepy person
sleet (slēt) *n.* [ME. *slete* < OE. *sliete, akin to G. *schlosse*, hail < IE. base *(*s*)*leu*-, loose, lax, whence SLUR, SLUG¹] 1. partly frozen rain, or rain that freezes as it falls 2. a mixture of rain with snow or hail 3. the icy coating formed when rain freezes on trees, streets, etc. —*vi.* to shower in the form of sleet —**sleet'y** *adj.* **sleet'i·er, sleet'i·est**

sleeve (slēv) *n.* [ME. *sleve* < OE. *sliefe*, akin to Du. *sloof*, apron: for IE. base see SLIP²] 1. that part of a garment that covers an arm or part of an arm 2. a tube or tubelike part fitting over or around another part 3. a thin paper or plastic cover for protecting a phonograph record 4. a drogue towed by an airplane for target practice —*vt.* **sleeved, sleev'ing** to provide or fit with a sleeve or sleeves —**up one's sleeve** hidden or secret but ready at hand
sleeved (slēvd) *adj.* fitted with sleeves: often in hyphenated compounds [short-*sleeved*]
sleeve·less (slēv'lis) *adj.* having no sleeve or sleeves [a *sleeveless* sweater]
sleeve·let (-lit) *n.* a covering fitted over the lower part of a garment sleeve, as to protect it from soiling
☆**sleigh** (slā) *n.* [Du. *slee*, contr. of *slede*, a SLED] a light vehicle on runners, usually horse-drawn, for carrying persons over snow and ice —*vi.* to ride in or drive a sleigh
☆**sleigh bells** a number of small, spherical bells fixed to the harness straps of an animal drawing a sleigh
sleight (slīt) *n.* [ME. < ON. *slægth* < *slægr*, crafty, clever (cf. SLY)] 1. cunning or craft used in deceiving 2. skill or dexterity
sleight of hand 1. skill with the hands, esp. in confusing or deceiving onlookers, as in doing magic tricks; legerdemain 2. a trick or tricks thus performed
slen·der (slen'dər) *adj.* [ME. *slendre, sclendre* < ?] 1. small in width as compared with the length or height; long and thin 2. having a slim, trim figure [a *slender* girl] 3. small or limited in amount, size, extent, etc.; meager [*slender* earnings] 4. of little force or validity; having slight foundation; feeble [*slender* hope] —SYN. see THIN —**slen'der·ly** *adv.* —**slen'der·ness** *n.*
slen·der·ize (-īz') *vt.* **-ized', -iz'ing** to make or cause to seem slender —*vi.* to become slender
slept (slept) *pt. & pp. of* SLEEP
Sles·vig (sles'vikh) *Dan. name of* SCHLESWIG

sleuth (slooth) *n.* 1. clipped form of SLEUTHHOUND ☆2. [Colloq.] a detective —☆*vi.* to act as a detective
sleuth·hound (-hound') *n.* [ME. *sleuthhund* < *sleuth*, trail, spoor < ON. *sloth*, akin to *slothra*, to drag (oneself) ahead (for IE. base see SLUR) + ME. *hund*, dog, HOUND¹] a dog, esp. a bloodhound, that can follow a trail by scent
☆**slew¹** (sloo) *n.* same as SLOUGH² (sense 4)
slew² (sloo) *n., vt., vi.* same as SLUE¹
☆**slew³** (sloo) *n.* [Ir. *sluagh*, a host] [Colloq.] a large number, group, or amount; a lot
slew⁴ (sloo) *pt. of* SLAY
Slez·sko (sles'kŏ) *Czech name of* SILESIA
slice (slīs) *n.* [ME. < OFr. *esclice* < *esclicier*, to slice < Frank. *slizzan*, akin to SLIT] 1. a relatively thin, broad piece cut from an object having some bulk or volume [a *slice* of apple] 2. a part, portion, or share [a *slice* of one's earnings] 3. any of various implements with a flat, broad blade, as a spatula 4. a) the path of a hit ball that curves away to the right from a right-handed player or to the left from a left-handed player b) a ball that follows such a path —*vt.* **sliced, slic'ing** 1. to cut into slices 2. a) to cut off as in a slice or slices (often with *off, from, away,* etc.) b) to cut across or through like a knife 3. to separate into parts or shares 4. to use a slice (*n.* 3) or slice bar to work at, spread, remove, etc. 5. to hit (a ball) in a slice (*n.* 4 a) —*vi.* 1. to cut (*through*) like a knife [a plow *slicing* through the earth] 2. to be hit in a slice (*n.* 4 a) —**slic'er** *n.*
slice bar an iron bar with a broad, thin end, used in a coal furnace to loosen coals, clear out ashes, etc.
slick (slik) *vt.* [ME. *slikien* < OE. *slician*, to make smooth, akin to ON. *slikr*, smooth < IE. *(*s*)*leig*-, slimy, to smooth, glide < base *lei-, whence LIME¹, LOAM] 1. to make sleek, glossy, or smooth 2. [Colloq.] to make smart, neat, or tidy (usually with *up*) —*adj.* [ME. *slike* < the *v*] 1. sleek; glossy; smooth 2. slippery; oily, as a surface 3. accomplished; adept; clever; ingenious 4. [Colloq.] clever in deception or trickery; deceptively plausible; smooth [a *slick* alibi] 5. [Colloq.] having or showing skill in composition or technique but little depth or literary significance [a *slick* style of writing] 6. [Old Slang] excellent, fine, enjoyable, attractive, etc. —*n.* ☆1. a) a smooth area on the surface of water, as resulting from a film of oil b) an oily film on the surface of water 2. something used for smoothing and polishing, as a kind of broad, flat chisel ☆3. [Colloq.] a magazine printed on paper with a glossy finish: distinguished from PULP —*adv.* smoothly, cleverly, deftly, easily, etc. —**slick'ly** *adv.* —**slick'ness** *n.*
slick·en·side (slik'n sīd') *n.* [dial. *slicken*, var. of SLICK + SIDE] [*usually pl.*] *Geol.* a smooth, polished rock surface produced by friction, pressure, or cleavage
slick·er (-ər) *n.* [SLICK, *adj.* + -ER] ☆1. a loose, waterproof coat made of oil-treated cloth ☆2. [Colloq.] a tricky, cleverly deceptive person
slid·den (slid'n) *archaic or dial. pp. of* SLIDE
slide (slīd) *vi.* **slid** (slid), **slid'ing** [ME. *sliden* < OE. *slidan* < IE. *(*s*)*leidh*-, slippery < base *(*s*)*lei*-, slimy, whence SLICK, SLIME] 1. to move along in constant frictional contact with some surface or substance [windows that *slide* open] 2. to move in this manner on a sled, the feet, etc. in contact with a smooth surface, esp. snow or ice 3. to move quietly and smoothly; glide 4. to move stealthily or unobtrusively 5. to shift from a position; slip [the wet cup *slid* from his hand] 6. to pass gradually (*into* or *out of* some condition) [to *slide* into bad habits] ☆7. *Baseball* to drop down and slide along the ground toward a base to avoid being tagged out by the baseman —*vt.* 1. to cause to slide; make move with a smooth, gliding motion 2. to move, place, or slip quietly, deftly, or stealthily (*in* or *into*) —*n.* 1. an act of sliding 2. a smooth, usually inclined track, surface, or chute down which to slide, as on a playground 3. something that works by sliding; part that slides or is slid on 4. a photographic transparency mounted for use with a viewer or projector 5. a small glass plate used as a mounting for objects to be examined under a microscope 6. a) the fall of a mass of rock, snow, earth, etc. down a slope ☆b) the mass that falls 7. *Music* a) same as PORTAMENTO b) an ornament made up of two or more notes ascending or descending to a principal note c) a U-shaped section of tubing which is moved to change the pitch of certain brass-wind instruments, esp. the trombone —**let slide** to fail to take some expected or required action on; allow to drift along
SYN.—**slide** implies easy movement, as over a smooth surface, and usually suggests continuous contact with it [to *slide* on ice, to *slide* back into old habits]; **slip** more often implies that the surface is frictionless and the contact not continuous, therefore suggesting an involuntary movement or an accident [to *slip* and fall on the ice, her name *slipped* from his mind]; **glide** suggests a flowing, smooth, easy, usually silent movement and continuous or intermittent contact with a surface [*gliding* dancers]; **skid** means to slide or slip sideways and out of control, as a vehicle when not gripping an icy road
☆**slide fastener** a zipper or a zipperlike device having two grooved plastic edges joined or separated by a slide
slide knot a kind of slipknot: see KNOT, illus.

slid·er (slīd′ər) *n.* **1.** a person or thing that slides ☆**2.** *Baseball* a curve ball that breaks only slightly

slide rule an instrument consisting of a ruler with a central sliding piece, both being marked with logarithmic scales: used in making rapid mathematical calculations by adding and subtracting logarithms

slide trombone *see* TROMBONE

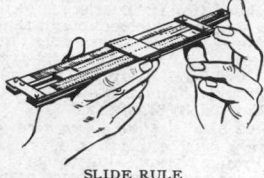

SLIDE RULE

slide valve a valve which opens and closes a passageway, as the cylinder port of a steam engine, by sliding back and forth across it

slid·ing (-iŋ) *adj.* **1.** varying in accordance with given conditions **2.** operating or moving on a track or groove, as a door or panel

sliding scale a standard or schedule, as of costs, wages, tariff rates, etc., that varies in accordance with given conditions or standards

slight (slīt) *adj.* [ME. (northern dial.) *sliht* < OE., akin to OHG. *sleht*, straight, smooth: for IE. base see SLICK] **1.** *a)* light in form or build; not stout or heavy; slender *b)* frail; fragile **2.** having little weight, strength, substance, or significance [a *slight* criticism] **3.** small in amount or extent; not great or intense [a *slight* fever] —*vt.* **1.** to do carelessly or poorly; neglect **2.** to treat with disrespect or indifference; be discourteous toward **3.** to treat as unimportant —*n.* a slighting or being slighted by pointedly indifferent, disrespectful, or supercilious treatment —SYN. see NEGLECT, THIN —**slight′ly** *adv.* —**slight′ness** *n.*

slight·ing (-iŋ) *adj.* constituting a slight; disdainful; disparaging [a *slighting* remark] —**slight′ing·ly** *adv.*

Sli·go (slī′gō) **1.** county in Connacht province, NW Ireland: 694 sq. mi.; pop. 51,000 **2.** its county seat; a seaport: pop. 13,000

sli·ly (slī′lē) *adv. var.* of SLYLY

slim (slim) *adj.* **slim′mer, slim′mest** [orig., useless, bad, weak < Du., crafty, bad, akin to G. *schlimm*, bad] **1.** small in girth in proportion to height or length; slender **2.** small in amount, degree, or extent; slight; scant; meager [*slim* pickings, a *slim* hope] **3.** [Brit. Colloq.] sly; crafty —*vt., vi.* **slimmed, slim′ming** to make or become slim [dieting to *slim* down] —SYN. see THIN —**slim′ly** *adv.* —**slim′ness** *n.*

slime (slim) *n.* [ME. < OE. *slim*, akin to G. *schleim* < IE. base *(s)lei-*, slimy, whence SLIDE, LIME¹, SLICK] any soft, moist, slippery, sometimes sticky matter, as thin mud, the mucous coating on fish, etc.; specif., moist or sticky matter considered filthy or disgusting —*vt.* **slimed, slim′ing** **1.** to cover with slime **2.** to clean slime from —*vi.* to become slimy

slime mold (or **fungus**) same as MYXOMYCETE

slim·sy (slim′zē) *adj.* **-si·er, -si·est** [SL(IM) + (FL)IMSY] [Colloq.] slight; flimsy: also **slimp·sy** (slimp′sē)

slim·y (slī′mē) *adj.* **slim′i·er, slim′i·est** **1.** of or like slime **2.** covered with or full of slime **3.** disgusting; repulsive —**slim′i·ly** *adv.* —**slim′i·ness** *n.*

sling¹ (sliŋ) *n.* [ME. *slinge* < the v.] **1.** *a)* a primitive instrument for throwing stones, etc., consisting of a piece of leather tied to cords that are whirled by hand for releasing the missile ☆*b)* same as SLINGSHOT **2.** the act of throwing with or as with a sling; cast; throw; fling **3.** *a)* a looped or hanging band, strap, etc. used in raising and lowering a heavy object or for carrying or supporting something [a rifle *sling*] *b)* a wide piece of cloth suspended from the neck and looped under an injured arm for support **4.** a rope or chain for supporting a yard **5.** a woman's open-heeled slipper having a strap across the top of the heel: also **sling-back** —*vt.* **slung, sling′ing** [ME. *slingen*, prob. < ON. *slyngva*, to throw, akin to OE. & OHG. *slingan*, to twist oneself, worm along < IE. base *slenk-*, to twist, turn, creep, whence Lith. *slenkù*, to creep: cf. SLINK¹] **1.** to throw (stones, etc.) with a sling **2.** to throw, cast, fling, or hurl **3.** to place, carry, raise, lower, etc. in a sling **4.** to hang loosely or in a sling; suspend (a hammock, etc.), esp. by several attachments

sling² (sliŋ) *n.* [< ?] a drink made with alcoholic liquor, water, sugar, and, usually, lemon juice

sling·er (sliŋ′ər) *n.* **1.** a man using a sling for throwing missiles, as in ancient warfare **2.** a person who throws or slings **3.** a person operating, or supervising the use of, a sling, as in loading

slinger ring a ring-shaped tube, fitted around the hub of an airplane propeller, through which alcohol or some other de-icing fluid is applied to the blades by centrifugal force

☆**sling·shot** (sliŋ′shät′) *n.* a Y-shaped piece of wood, metal, etc. with an elastic band or bands attached to the upper tips for shooting stones, etc.

slink¹ (sliŋk) *vi.* **slunk, slink′ing** [ME. *slinken* < OE. *slincan*, to creep, crawl along, akin to LowG. *slinken* < IE. base *sleng-*, to wind, twist, turn, var. of *slenk-*: cf. SLING¹] to move in a quiet, furtive, or sneaking manner, as from fear, guilt, etc.; sneak —SYN. see LURK —**slink′ing·ly** *adv.*

slink² (sliŋk) *vt.* **slinked** or **slunk, slink′ing** [prob. < SLING¹] to expel (a fetus) prematurely: said of animals —*n.* an

animal, esp. a calf, born prematurely —*adj.* born prematurely

slink·y (sliŋ′kē) *adj.* **slink′i·er, slink′i·est** [SLINK¹ + -Y²] **1.** sneaking; stealthy; furtive **2.** [Slang] sinuous and graceful in movement, line, etc.

slip¹ (slip) *vi.* **slipped, slip′ping** [ME. *slippen* < MLowG., akin to OHG. *slifan* < IE. *(s)leib-*, to glide, slip < base *(s)lei-*, slimy, sliding: cf. LIME¹, SLIDE] **1.** to go quietly or secretly; move without attracting notice [to *slip* out of a room] **2.** *a)* to go, move, pass, etc. smoothly, quickly, or easily *b)* to get (*into* or *out of* clothes) quickly *c)* to go imperceptibly; pass unmarked [time *slipped* by] **3.** to pass gradually into or out of some condition, activity, habit, opinion, etc. [to *slip* off to sleep] **4.** to escape or pass from a person's memory, mind, power, grasp, etc. [to let a chance *slip* by] **5.** to move out of place by sliding; shift or slide from position [a napkin *slipping* from one's lap] **6.** to slide accidentally on a slippery surface, lose footing, etc. **7.** to make a mistake; fall into error; err **8.** to become worse; lose strength, ability, mental keenness, etc. **9.** to decline slightly; fall off [a *slipping* market] **10.** *Aeron.* same as SIDESLIP —*vt.* **1.** to cause to slip or move with a smooth, sliding motion **2.** to put (*on*) or take (*off*) quickly or easily, as an article of clothing **3.** to put, pass, insert, etc. quickly, deftly, or stealthily [to *slip* a pill into one's mouth, to *slip* in a cutting remark] **4.** *a)* to escape or pass from (the mind or memory) *b)* [Now Rare] to let pass unheeded; overlook; miss **5.** to get loose or away from (a restraint, pursuer, etc.); become free of [the dog *slipped* its leash] **6.** to let loose (hounds) to pursue game **7.** to transfer (a stitch) from one needle to another without knitting it, as in forming patterns in, or decreasing the width of, a knitted piece **8.** to slink (a fetus) **9.** to put out of joint; dislocate **10.** *Naut.* to free an anchored ship from (the anchor) by parting or unshackling the cable —*n.* **1.** *a)* a pier or platform sloping into the water to serve as a landing place *b)* an inclined plane leading down to water, on which ships are built or repaired ☆*c)* a water channel between piers or wharves, used for the docking of ships **2.** the difference between the distance moved by a vessel and the distance it would move if the propeller were advancing through a soft solid instead of mobile water; lost motion of a propeller **3.** a leash for a dog made to be quickly releasable **4.** *a)* a woman's sleeveless undergarment, suspended from shoulder straps to the hemline of the skirt *b)* a petticoat or half slip **5.** a cloth cover for a pillow **6.** an act of slipping, sliding, or falling down **7.** a deviation or turning aside, esp. from a practice, course of conduct, etc. considered right **8.** an error or mistake, esp. one made inadvertently in speaking, writing, etc. **9.** an accident or mishap **10.** the amount or degree of operative inefficiency of a mechanical device, expressed in terms of the difference between theoretical and actual output **11.** movement of one part upon another, usually where no movement is meant to exist; play **12.** *Aeron.* same as SIDESLIP **13.** *Cricket* a fielder placed behind the wickets on the offside of the batter **14.** *Geol. a)* any movement displacing parts of rock or soil masses in relation to one another; small fault or landslide *b)* a smooth surface or joint where such movement has taken place **15.** *Metallurgy* the process by which plastic deformation is produced in metal crystals by one part of a crystal moving in relation to another, usually in a particular crystallographic plane —SYN. see ERROR, SLIDE —**give someone the slip** to evade or escape from someone —**let slip** to say or tell without intending to —☆**slip one over on** [Colloq.] to trick; hoodwink; cheat —**slip over** to pass over (a matter, etc.) superficially or without adequate attention —☆**slip up 1.** to make a mistake; be in error **2.** to undergo a mishap; miscarry

slip² (slip) *n.* [ME. *slippe* < MDu. *slippe* < *slippen*, to cut] **1.** a stem, root, twig, etc. cut or broken off a plant and used for planting or grafting; cutting; scion **2.** a young, slim person [a mere *slip* of a girl] **3.** a long, thin piece or strip, as of cloth **4.** a small piece of paper, esp. one prepared for a specific use [an order *slip*] ☆**5.** a narrow church pew —*vt.* **slipped, slip′ping** to take a slip from (a plant) for planting or grafting

slip³ (slip) *n.* [ME. < OE. *slypa*, a paste, slime < IE. base *sleub-*, to glide, slip, whence SLEEVE, L. *lubricus*, slippery] *Ceramics* clay thinned to the consistency of cream for use in decorating or casting, or as a cement or coating

slip·case (-kās′) *n.* a boxlike container for a book or set of books, open at one end to expose the spine or spines

slip·cov·er (-kuv′ər) *n.* a removable, fitted cloth cover for an armchair, sofa, etc. —*vt.* **-cov′ered, -cov′er·ing** to cover (a chair, etc.) with a slipcover

slip·knot (-nät′) *n.* a knot made so that it will slip along the rope, etc. around which it is tied: see KNOT, illus.

slip noose a noose made with a slipknot

slip-on (-än′) *adj.* easily put on or taken off, as shoes without laces, or a garment to be slipped on or off over the head —*n.* a slip-on shoe or garment

slip·o·ver (-ō′vər) *adj., n.* same as PULLOVER

slip·page (slip′ij) *n.* **1.** the act or an instance of slipping, as of one gear past another **2.** the amount of this **3.** the resulting loss of motion or power, as in a chain drive

slipped disk a herniated intervertebral disk, esp. of the lumbar spine, often causing sciatica

slip·per (slip′ər) *n.* a light, low shoe easily slipped on the foot, esp. one for indoor wear —**slip′pered** *adj.*

slip·per·y (slip′ə rē, slip′rē) *adj.* -**per·i·er**, -**per·i·est** [altered < ME. *sliper*, slippery < OE. *slipur*, akin to MHG. *slupferic*: for IE. base see SLIP[1]] 1. causing or liable to cause sliding or slipping, as a wet, waxed, or greasy surface 2. tending to slip away, as from a grasp 3. not reliable or trustworthy; deceitful 4. subject to change [a *slippery* situation] 5. [Obs.] immoral —**slip′per·i·ness** *n.*

☆**slippery elm** 1. a wide-branching N. American elm (*Ulmus rubra*) with fragrant, mucilaginous, inner bark and hard wood 2. the wood or bark

slip·py (slip′ē) *adj.* 1. [Colloq. or Dial.] *same as* SLIPPERY 2. [Brit. Colloq.] alert; sharp; quick

slip rings *Elec.* metal rings mounted on, and insulated from, the rotor shaft of an alternating-current machine to lead current into or away from the rotor winding through stationary brushes pressing on the rings

slip·sheet (slip′shēt′) *n.* a blank sheet of paper inserted between freshly printed sheets to prevent offset —*vt.*, *vi.* to insert slipsheets between (printed sheets)

slip·shod (-shäd′) *adj.* [SLIP[1] + SHOD, after dial. or obs. *slip-shoe*, a slipper] 1. wearing shoes with worn-down heels 2. careless, as in appearance or workmanship [a *slipshod* job] —*SYN.* see SLOVENLY

slip·slop (-släp′) *n.* [redupl. of SLOP] [Colloq.] 1. cheap, weak liquor 2. shallow, pointless talk or writing

slip·sole (-sōl′) *n.* 1. a half sole between the bottom sole and the insole 2. *same as* INSOLE (sense 2)

☆**slip·stick** (-stik′) *n. slang term for* SLIDE RULE

slip stitch a continuous stitch, especially for a hem, in which the needle is put through the folded part of the hem, picking up a few threads of the fabric on the inside, so as to be invisible on the outside

slip·stream (-strēm′) *n.* the current of air thrust backward by the spinning propeller of an aircraft; propeller wash

slipt (slipt) *archaic or poetic pt.* of SLIP[1]

☆**slip-up** (slip′up′) *n.* [Colloq.] 1. an error or oversight 2. an unlucky happening; mishap

slip·way (-wā′) *n. same as* SLIP[1] (*n.* 1 b)

slit (slit) *vt.* **slit**, **slit′ting** [ME. *slitten* < OE. **slittan*, akin to MHG. *slitzen* < WGmc. **slitjan* < base of Gmc. **slitan* (whence OE. *slitan*) < IE. base **(s)kel-*, to cut: cf. SHIELD, SHELL] 1. to cut or split open, esp. by a straight, lengthwise incision 2. to cut lengthwise into strips 3. to cut (off); sever —*n.* 1. a cut or tear, esp. one that is long and straight 2. a long, narrow opening or crack —**slit′ter** *n.*

slith·er (slith′ər) *vi.* [ME. *slitheren*, var. of *slideren* < OE. *sliderian*, freq. < base of *slidan*, to SLIDE] 1. to slip or slide on or as on a slope with a loose or broken surface 2. *a)* to move along by sliding or gliding, as a snake *b)* to walk with a sliding motion —*vt.* to cause to slither or slide —*n.* a sliding, slithering motion

slith·er·y (-ē) *adj.* 1. slippery 2. like or characterized by a slither [a *slithery* walk]

slit trench a narrow, relatively shallow trench for protecting a soldier from shellfire, bombs, etc.

sliv·er (sliv′ər) *n.* [ME. *slivere* < *sliven*, to cut, cleave < OE. *slifan*: for IE. base see SLIT, SLEAVE] 1. a thin, sharp piece that has been cut, split, or broken off; splinter 2. a loose, thin, continuous fiber, as of wool or flax, ready to be drawn and twisted —*vt.*, *vi.* to cut or break into slivers

sli·vo·vitz (sliv′ə vits′) *n.* [Serb. *sljivovica* < *sliva*, plum < OBulg.: for IE. base see SLOE] a usually colorless plum brandy drunk esp. in E Europe

Sloan (slōn), **John** 1871-1951; U.S. painter & etcher

slob (släb) *n.* [Ir. *slab*, mud < Scand.: see SLAB[2]] [Colloq.] a sloppy, coarse, or gross person

slob·ber (släb′ər) *vi.* [ME. *sloberen*, prob. < or akin to LowG. *slubberen*, to swig, lap: for IE. base see SLOVEN] 1. to let saliva, food, etc. run from the mouth; slaver 2. to speak, write, etc. in a mawkish or maudlin way —*vt.* to wet, smear, or dribble on with saliva —*n.* 1. saliva, etc. running from the mouth 2. mawkish talk or writing —**slob′ber·er** *n.* —**slob′ber·y** *adj.*

slob ice a dense mass of sludge or floating ice

sloe (slō) *n.* [ME. *slo* < OE. *sla*, akin to G. *schlehe*, Russ. & OBulg. *sliva*, plum (cf. SLIVOVITZ): for IE. base see LIVID] 1. *same as* BLACKTHORN (sense 1) 2. the small, blue-black, plumlike fruit of the blackthorn 3. any of various wild plums

sloe-eyed (-īd′) *adj.* 1. having large, dark eyes 2. having almond-shaped eyes

☆**sloe gin** a red liqueur made of dry gin flavored with sloes

slog[1] (släg) *vt.*, *vi.* **slogged**, **slog′ging** [var. of SLUG[4]] to hit hard; slug —**slog′ger** *n.*

slog[2] (släg) *vt.*, *vi.* **slogged**, **slog′ging** [ME. *sluggen*: see SLUGGARD] 1. to make (one's way) with great effort; plod 2. to work hard (*at* something); toil

slo·gan (slō′gən) *n.* [Gael. *sluagh-ghairm < sluagh*, a host + *gairm*, a call] 1. orig., a cry used by Scottish Highland and Irish clans in battle or as an assembly signal 2. a catchword or rallying motto distinctly associated with a political party or other group 3. a catch phrase used to advertise a product

☆**slo·gan·eer** (slō′gə nir′) *vi.* to coin or make use of slogans —*n.* a person who coins or uses slogans

☆**slo·gan·ize** (slō′gə nīz′) *vt.* -**ized**, -**iz′ing** to express or generalize in the form of a slogan —**slo·gan·is′tic** *adj.*

sloid, **slojd** (sloid) *n. same as* SLOYD

sloop (slōōp) *n.* [Du. *sloep* < LowG. *sluup* < *slupen* (akin to OE. *slupan*), to glide: for IE. base see SLIP[3]] a fore-and-aft rigged, single-masted sailing vessel with a mainsail and a jib, and, sometimes, a spinnaker for racing

sloop of war 1. orig., a sailing vessel mounting from 10 to 32 guns 2. later, a small war vessel, having guns mounted on one deck only

SLOOP

sloop-rigged (-rigd′) *adj.* having rigging like that of a sloop

slop (släp) *n.* [ME. *sloppe* < OE. *sloppe* (only in comp.) < base of *slypa* (cf. SLIP[3])] 1. watery snow or mud; slush 2. a splash or puddle of spilled liquid 3. any liquid or semiliquid food that is unappetizing or of poor quality 4. [*often pl.*] *a)* liquid waste of any kind ☆*b)* kitchen waste or swill, used for feeding pigs, etc. 5. [*pl.*] distillery mash after the liquor has been removed 6. [Slang] a sloppy, careless, or slovenly person See also SLOPS —*vi.* **slopped**, **slop′ping** 1. to spill or splash 2. to walk or splash through slush or mud —*vt.* 1. to spill liquid on 2. to feed swill or slops to (pigs, etc.) ☆3. to splash or spatter with liquid —**slop over** 1. to overflow or spill, as a liquid when its container is tilted ☆2. [Colloq.] to make a display of sentimentality; gush

slop bowl (or **basin**) [Chiefly Brit.] a bowl into which the dregs from tea cups are emptied at table

slope (slōp) *n.* [ME. < *aslope*, sloping (read as *a slope*) < OE. *aslopen*, pp. of *aslupan*, to slip away < *slupan*, to glide (cf. SLOOP)] 1. a piece of ground that is not flat or level; rising or falling ground 2. any inclined line, surface, position, etc.; slant 3. *a)* deviation from the horizontal or vertical *b)* the amount or degree of this ☆4. the land area that drains into a given ocean 5. *Math. a)* the trigonometric tangent of the positive angle formed between a given straight line and the x-axis of a pair of Cartesian coordinates *b)* the slope of the tangent line to a given curve at a designated point —*vi.* **sloped**, **slop′ing** 1. to have an upward or downward inclination; take an oblique direction; incline; slant 2. [Colloq.] *a)* to run away; decamp *b)* to go or come —*vt.* to cause to slope —*adj.* [Poet.] that slopes; slanting; inclined —**slop′er** *n.*

slop·py (släp′ē) *adj.* -**pi·er**, -**pi·est** 1. consisting of or covered with slop; wet and splashy; muddy; slushy 2. splashed or spotted with liquids 3. *a)* very untidy; showing lack of care; slovenly or messy *b)* careless; slipshod 4. [Colloq.] gushingly sentimental —*SYN.* see SLOVENLY —**slop′pi·ly** *adv.* —**slop′pi·ness** *n.*

☆**sloppy Joe** ground meat cooked with tomato sauce, spices, etc. and served on a bun

slops (släps) *n.pl.* [ME. *sloppes*, pl. of *slop*, *sloppe* < OE. *-slop* (as in *oferslop*, loose outer garment), akin to *sliefe*, SLEEVE: for IE. base see SLIP[3]] 1. loose-fitting outer garments; specif., *a)* a smock, coveralls, or the like *b)* formerly, baggy trousers or breeches 2. clothing, bedding, etc. issued or sold to sailors 3. cheap, ready-made clothing

☆**slop sink** a deep sink for filling and emptying scrub pails, washing out mops, etc.

slop·work (-wurk′) *n.* 1. the manufacture of cheap clothing 2. work that is carelessly done —**slop′work′er** *n.*

slosh (släsh) *vt.* [var. of SLUSH] 1. to shake or agitate (a liquid or something in a liquid) 2. to apply (a liquid) lavishly or carelessly —*vi.* 1. to splash or move clumsily through water, mud, etc. 2. to splash about: said of a liquid —*n.* 1. *same as* SLUSH 2. the sound of liquid splashing about —**slosh′y** *adj.*

sloshed (släsht) *adj.* [Chiefly Brit. Slang] drunk

slot[1] (slät) *n.* [ME., the hollow between the breasts < OFr. *esclot*] 1. a narrow notch, groove, or opening, as a keyway in a piece of machinery, a slit for a coin in a vending machine, etc. 2. any of various openings in the wing or tail surface of an airplane used in connection with a high-lift or control device; specif., an air gap between the wing and an auxiliary airfoil, as an aileron or flap, providing for a smooth flow of air on the upper surface ☆3. [Colloq.] a position in a group, series, sequence, etc. —*vt.* **slot′ted**, **slot′ting** 1. to make a slot or slots in ☆2. [Colloq.] to place in a series or sequence

slot[2] (slät) *n.* [OFr. *esclot* < ? ON. *sloth*: cf. SLEUTH] a track or trail of an animal, esp. a deer —*vt.* **slot′ted**, **slot′-ting** to follow the trail of

☆**slot car** a plastic, electrically driven, miniature car, built to exact scale and raced as a game against other such cars over a slotted track: each car is remotely controlled by a hand-held rheostat

sloth (slôth, slōth, släth) *n.* [ME. *slouthe* < *slou*, slow, used for older *slewthe, sleuthe* < OE. *slæwth*, sloth < *slaw*, slow: see SLOW & -TH¹] **1.** disinclination to work or exert oneself; indolence; laziness **2.** [Now Rare] slowness; delay **3.** any of several slow-moving, tree-dwelling mammals (family Bradypodidae) of tropical Central and South America that hang, back down, from branches and feed on fruits and vegetation: the **three-toed sloth** (genus *Bradypus*) has three toes on each front foot, and the **two-toed sloth** (genus *Choloepus*) has two

SLOTH
(22–27 in. long, including tail)

sloth bear a bear (*Melursus ursinus*) with shaggy black fur, a flexible snout, and long white claws: it is found in India and Ceylon and feeds chiefly on fruits and insects

sloth·ful (slôth′fəl, slōth′-, släth′-) *adj.* characterized by sloth; indolent; lazy —**sloth′ful·ly** *adv.* —**sloth′ful·ness** *n.*

slot machine a machine, as a vending machine, worked by inserting a coin in a slot; specif., a gambling device operated in this way

slouch (slouch) *n.* [< ? dial. *slouk*, a lazy fellow < ON. *slōkr* < *slōka*, to hang down, droop < IE. *(s)leug-*, var. of base *(s)leu-*, to hang limply, whence SLUG¹, SLEET] ☆**1.** a person who is awkward, lazy, or (in colloquial usage, usually with a negative) incompetent [he's no *slouch* at golf] **2.** *a)* a drooping or bending forward of the head and shoulders *b)* slovenly posture in general **3.** a hanging down or drooping, as of a hat brim —*vi.* **1.** to sit, stand, walk, etc. in a slouch **2.** to droop, as a hat brim —*vt.* to cause to slouch

slouch hat a soft hat with a broad, drooping brim

slouch·y (-ē) *adj.* **slouch′i·er, slouch′i·est** slouching, esp. in posture —**slouch′i·ly** *adv.* —**slouch′i·ness** *n.*

slough¹ (sluf) *n.* [ME. *slough*, akin to G. *schlauch*, a skin, bag < IE. base *sleug̑-*, to glide, slip, whence Lett. *sl′užât*, to slide] **1.** the skin of a snake, esp. the outer layer that is periodically cast off **2.** any castoff layer, covering, etc.: often used figuratively **3.** *Med.* a mass of dead tissue in, or separating from, living tissue or an ulceration —*vi.* [< the *n.*] **1.** *a)* to be shed, cast off, or discarded; come off *b)* to drop off; become fewer or less **2.** to shed skin or other covering **3.** *Med.* to separate from the surrounding tissue: said of dead tissue Often with *off* —*vt.* **1.** to shed or throw (*off*) as or like slough; get rid of **2.** *Bridge* to get rid of (a card considered valueless) —**slough over** to gloss over; minimize —**slough′y** *adj.*

slough² (slou; *for 4* slōō) *n.* [ME. *slowe* < OE. *sloh*, akin to MLowG. *slōch*, a swamp < IE. base *(s)leug-*, to swallow, whence Gr. *lynx*, a hiccup, Ir. *sloigim*, (I) swallow] **1.** a place, as a hollow, full of soft, deep mud **2.** [< *Slough of Despond*, a deep swamp in Bunyan's *Pilgrim's Progress*] deep, hopeless dejection or discouragement **3.** moral degradation ☆**4.** a swamp, bog, or marsh, esp. one that is part of an inlet or backwater —**slough′y** *adj.*

Slo·vak (slō′väk, -vak) *n.* **1.** any of a Slavic people living chiefly in Slovakia **2.** the West Slavic language of the Slovaks, closely related to Czech —*adj.* of Slovakia, the Slovaks, or their language

Slo·va·ki·a (slō vä′kē ə, -vak′ē ə) region comprising E Czechoslovakia: c. 18,900 sq. mi.; pop. 4,392,000; chief city, Bratislava —**Slo·va′-ki·an** *adj., n.*

SLOVAKIA

slov·en (sluv′ən) *n.* [ME. *slovein*, prob. < MDu. *slof*, lax, limp (< IE. base *(s)leubh-*, to hang loosely, whence Lith. *slûbnas*, limp) + Anglo-Fr. *-ain, -ein*, -AN] a person who is careless in his appearance, habits, work, etc.; dirty or untidy person

Slo·ve·ni·a (slō vē′nē ə, -vēn′yə) republic of Yugoslavia, in the NW part: 7,896 sq. mi.; pop. 1,619,000; cap. Ljubljana

Slo·ve·ni·an (slō vē′nē ən, -vēn′yən) *n.* **1.** any of a Slavic people living chiefly in Slovenia **2.** their South Slavic language —*adj.* of Slovenia, the Slovenians, or their language Also **Slo·vene** (slō′vēn, slō vēn′)

slov·en·ly (sluv′ən lē) *adj.* **-li·er, -li·est 1.** characteristic of a sloven **2.** careless in appearance, habits, work, etc.; untidy; slipshod —*adv.* in a slovenly manner —**slov′en·li·ness** *n.*

SYN.—**slovenly** implies a general carelessness or shiftlessness as characterized by a want of attention to cleanliness, orderliness, etc. [a *slovenly* housewife]; **slipshod** suggests a carelessness about details and a resulting lack of precision, accuracy, thoroughness, etc. [*slipshod* work]; **untidy** implies a lack of neatness in appearance or arrangement [an *untidy* room]; **unkempt**, basically meaning uncombed, stresses untidiness as resulting from neglect [an *unkempt* ragamuffin, lawn, etc.]; **sloppy** suggests a careless spilling over of something loose and therefore implies messiness, lack of restraint, etc. [a *sloppy* eater, *sloppy* thinking, etc.] —*ANT.* **neat, tidy, fastidious**

Slo·ven·sko (slô′ven skô′) *Czech name of* SLOVAKIA

slow (slō) *adj.* [ME. *slowe* < OE. *slaw*, akin to Du. *sleeuw*, ON. *slær*, dull < ?] **1.** not quick or clever in understanding; dull; obtuse **2.** *a)* taking a longer time than is expected or usual to act, move, go, happen, etc. *b)* not hasty, quick, ready, or prompt [a *slow* retort, *slow* to anger] **3.** making relatively little progress for the time spent; marked by low speed, rate of rhythm, etc.; not fast or rapid **4.** holding back fast progress, development, etc.; making speed or progress difficult [a *slow* growing season, a *slow* track] **5.** showing a time that is behind the correct time: said of a timepiece **6.** *a)* passing slowly or tediously; dull [a *slow* afternoon] *b)* not lively or interesting; dull or boring [a *slow* town] **7.** characterized by little activity; slack [*slow* trading] **8.** lacking in energy; sluggish **9.** behind the times; out of fashion **10.** burning so as to give off a low or moderate heat [a *slow* fire] **11.** gradual, as growth **12.** *Photog.* adapted to a relatively long exposure time —*vt.* **1.** to make slow or slower **2.** to retard; delay Often with *up* or *down* —*vi.* to go or become slow or slower (often with *up* or *down*) —*adv.* in a slow manner or at a slow speed; slowly —*SYN.* see STUPID —**slow′ly** *adv.* —**slow′ness** *n.*

slow burn ☆[Slang] a gradual working up or show of anger: often in the phrase **do a slow burn**

slow·down (-doun′) *n.* a slowing down, as of production

slow match a match, or fuse, that burns slowly, used for setting off blasting charges

slow-mo·tion (-mō′shən) *adj.* **1.** moving or operating below usual or normal speed **2.** designating a motion-picture or taped television sequence in which the action is made to appear slower than the actual action by exposing more frames per minute than is usual and projecting the film at normal speed or by filming or taping at normal speed and projecting or replaying at a lower than usual speed

slow-mov·ing (-mōōv′iŋ) *adj.* **1.** moving slowly; showing little progress or activity **2.** selling in a relatively small quantity, as merchandise, stocks, etc.

slow·poke (-pōk′) *n.* [Slang] a person who acts or moves slowly

slow time [Colloq.] standard time, as distinguished from daylight-saving time

slow-wit·ted (-wit′id) *adj.* having a mind that works slowly and ineffectively; not bright or alert; dull —**slow′-wit′ted·ly** *adv.* —**slow′-wit′ted·ness** *n.*

slow·worm (-wurm′) *n.* [altered (after SLOW) < ME. *slaworme* < OE. *slawyrm* < *sla-*, akin to Norw. *slo*, slowworm, ult. < IE. base *(s)lei-*, slimy, whence LIME¹, Gr. *leimax*, a snail + OE. *wyrm*, WORM] *same as* BLINDWORM

sloyd (sloid) *n.* [Sw. *slöjd*, skill < or akin to ON. *slægth*, cunning: see SLEIGHT] a system of manual training originating in Sweden, based upon the use of hand tools in wood carving and joining

slub (slub) *n.* [< ?] **1.** a roll of fiber, as of wool or cotton, twisted slightly for use in spinning **2.** a soft lump or thick irregular place in yarn —*vt.* **slubbed, slub′bing** to draw out (fibers of wool, cotton, etc.) and twist slightly for use in spinning

sludge (sluj) *n.* [var. of *slutch*, sludge, mud: akin to ME. *sluchched*, muddy, prob. ult. < IE. base *(s)leu-*, to hang limply, whence MHG. *slote*, mud, ooze & SLEET] **1.** mud, mire, or ooze covering the ground or forming a deposit at the bottom of bodies of water **2.** spongy lumps of drift ice **3.** any heavy, slimy deposit, sediment, or mass, as the waste resulting from oil refining, the mud brought up by a mining drill, the precipitate in a sewage tank, the sediment in a steam boiler or crankcase, etc. —**sludg′y** *adj.* **sludg′i·er, sludg′i·est**

sludge·worm (-wurm′) *n.* a small, freshwater worm (*Tubifex tubifex*) able to live in very low oxygen concentrations, as in sewage sludges and other bottom muds rich in organic matter

slue¹ (slōō) *vt., vi.* **slued, slu′ing** [< ?] to turn or swing around, as on a pivot or fixed point —*n.* **1.** the act of sluing **2.** the position to which a thing has been slued

slue² (slōō) *n. same as* SLOUGH² (sense 4)

slue³ (slōō) *n. same as* SLEW³

slug¹ (slug) *n.* [ME. *slugge*, slow, clumsy person or thing < Scand., as in Sw. dial. *slugga*, to be sluggish < IE. base *(s)leu-*, to hang loosely, lax, whence SLUMBER: cf. SLUDGE] **1.** any of a large number of small, gastropod, land mollusks (as genus *Limax*), resembling a land snail, but usually having only a rudimentary internal shell buried in the mantle **2.** rarely, a smooth, soft moth or sawfly larva, resembling a slug **3.** a person, vehicle, etc. that moves sluggishly

slug² (slug) *n.* [prob. < prec.] **1.** a small piece or lump of metal; specif., a bullet ☆**2.** a piece of metal shaped like and used in place of a coin in automatic coin machines; esp., such a substitute coin when used illegally ☆**3.**

Printing a) a strip of nonprinting metal used to space between lines or as a temporary marker b) a line of type made in one piece or strip, as by a linotype machine **4.** *Physics* a unit of mass, equal to c.32.2 pounds, to which a force of one pound imparts an acceleration of one foot per second per second —*vt.* **slugged, slug′ging** *Printing* to insert (a slug) between lines

slug³ (slug) *n.* [prob. < akin to Dan. *sluge*, to gulp] [Slang] a single drink, esp. of straight alcoholic liquor

slug⁴ (slug) *vt.* **slugged, slug′ging** [< dial. (Shetland) *slog*, *slag*, a blow < ON. *slag*, akin to OE. *slean*, to strike: see SLAY] [Colloq.] to hit hard, esp. with the fist or a bat —*n.* [Colloq.] a hard blow or hit

slug·a·bed (slug′ə bed′) *n.* [< ME. *sluggen* (see SLUGGARD) + BED] a lazy person who stays in bed when he should be up

☆**slug·fest** (-fest′) *n.* [SLUG⁴ + -FEST] [Colloq.] **1.** a fight or boxing match with much heavy punching **2.** a baseball game in which many hits are made

slug·gard (slug′ərd) *n.* [ME. *slogarde* < *sluggen*, to be lazy, go slowly, prob. < Scand., as in Sw. *slogga*, to be slow: see SLUG¹ & -ARD] a habitually lazy or idle person —*adj.* lazy or idle: also **slug′gard·ly**

☆**slug·ger** (-ər) *n.* [Colloq.] a person who slugs; specif., a) a prizefighter who punches hard b) a baseball player with a high percentage of extra-base hits

☆**slugging average** a number expressing a baseball player's average effectiveness in making extra-base hits, figured by dividing the total number of bases his hitting has enabled him to reach by the number of times at bat

slug·gish (-ish) *adj.* [< SLUG¹ + -ISH] **1.** lacking energy, alertness, or vigor; indisposed to exertion; slothful **2.** slow or slow-moving; not active; dull **3.** not functioning with normal vigor —**slug′gish·ly** *adv.* —**slug′gish·ness** *n.*

sluice (slōōs) *n.* [ME. *scluse* < OFr. *escluse*; LL. *exclusa* < fem. pp. of L. *excludere*, to shut out, EXCLUDE] **1.** an artificial channel or passage for water, having a gate or valve at its head to regulate the flow, as in a canal or millstream **2.** the water held back by or passing through such a gate **3.** a gate or valve used in opening or closing a sluice; floodgate: also **sluice gate 4.** any channel, esp. one for excess water ☆**5.** a sloping trough or flume through which water is run, as in washing gold ore, carrying logs, etc. —*vt.* **sluiced, sluic′ing 1.** to draw off by or as by means of a sluice **2.** a) to wash with water flowing in or from a sluice b) to wash off with a rush of water [to *sluice* a deck with hoses] ☆**3.** to carry (logs, etc.) in a sluice —*vi.* to run or flow in or as in a sluice

☆**sluice·way** (-wā′) *n.* an artificial channel for water, with or without a floodgate; sluice

slum (slum) *n.* [c. 1800 < cant: orig. sense, a room < ?] a heavily populated area of a city characterized by poverty, poor housing, etc. —*vi.* **slummed, slum′ming** to visit or tour slums, esp. in a manner or for reasons held to be condescending —**slum′mer** *n.* —**slum′my** *adj.* **-mi·er, -mi·est**

slum·ber (slum′bər) *vi.* [ME. *slumeren* < *sluma*, slumber: for IE. base see SLUG¹] **1.** to sleep **2.** to be dormant, negligent, or inactive —*vt.* to spend in sleeping —*n.* **1.** sleep **2.** an inactive or quiescent state —**slum′ber·er** *n.*

slum·ber·ous (-əs) *adj.* **1.** inclined to slumber; sleepy; drowsy **2.** suggestive of or characterized by slumber **3.** causing sleep or drowsiness; soporific **4.** tranquil; calm; quiet [a *slumberous* little town] Also **slum′brous** (-brəs) —*SYN.* see SLEEPY

☆**slumber party** a house party at which young teen-age girls, dressed in night clothes, spend much of the night in talk, eating, games, etc.

☆**slum·gul·lion** (slum′gul′yən) *n.* [< ?] [Colloq.] any inexpensive stew or hash

☆**slum·lord** (slum′lôrd′) *n.* [SLUM + (LAND)LORD] [Slang] an absentee landlord of slum dwellings, esp. one who charges inflated rents and neglects upkeep

slump (slump) *vi.* [prob. < or akin to MLowG. *slumpen*, to come about by accident: for IE. base see LIMP¹] **1.** to fall, sink, or collapse, esp. suddenly or heavily **2.** to decline suddenly, as in value, activity, etc. **3.** to have a drooping posture or gait —*n.* **1.** a sudden or sharp fall **2.** a decline in business activity, prices, etc. **3.** a drooping posture or gait ☆**4.** an extended period during which a player, team, worker, etc. is below normal in performance

slung (slun) *pt. & pp.* of SLING¹

☆**slung shot** a small, heavy weight attached to a strap or thong, used like a blackjack

slunk¹ (slunk) *pt. & pp.* of SLINK¹

slunk² (slunk) *alt. pt. & pp.* of SLINK²

slur (slur) *vt.* **slurred, slur′ring** [prob. < MDu. *sleuren*, to drag, move slowly, trail in mud: for IE. base see SLUG¹] **1.** to pass over quickly and carelessly; make little of (often with *over*) **2.** to pronounce rapidly and indistinctly, as by combining or dropping sounds **3.** [Dial.] to stain, smirch, or sully **4.** to blur or smear, as in printing **5.** to disparage or discredit; cast aspersions on **6.** *Music* a) to sing or play (different and successive notes) by gliding from one to another without a break b) to mark (notes)

with a slur —*n.* **1.** the act or process of slurring **2.** something slurred, as a pronunciation **3.** a blot, stain, or smear **4.** any remark or action that harms or is meant to harm someone's reputation; aspersion, reproach, stigma, etc. **5.** *Music* a curved symbol (⌣) or (⌢) grouping! together musical notes that are to be played or sung without a break, or, on a stringed instrument, in one bow

slurb (slurb) *n.* [SL(UM) + (SUB)URB] [Slang] a suburb with poorly planned, cheaply built housing developments

slurp (slurp) *vt., vi.* [Du. *slurpen*, to sip, lap, akin to G. *schlürfen*; prob. ult. < IE. echoic base **serbh-*, to slurp, whence L. *sorbere*, to suck in] [Slang] to drink or eat noisily —*n.* [Slang] a loud sipping or sucking sound

slur·ry (slur′ē) *n., pl.* **-ries** [ME. *slory* < *slore*, thin mud < MDu., akin to SLUR] a thin, watery mixture of a fine, insoluble material, as clay, cement, soil, etc.

slush (slush) *n.* [prob. < Scand., as in obs. Dan. *slus*] **1.** partly melted snow or ice **2.** soft mud; mire **3.** refuse fat or grease from cooking, esp. on board ship **4.** any of several greasy compounds used as lubricants or rust preventives for machinery ☆**5.** overly sentimental talk or writing; drivel —*vt.* **1.** to splash or cover with slush, esp. in lubricating or protecting **2.** to patch with mortar or cement —*vi.* to walk or move through slushy snow, ice, or mud —**slush′i·ness** *n.* —**slush′y** *adj.* **slush′i·er, slush′i·est**

☆**slush fund 1.** orig., a fund established aboard ship from the sale of refuse fat, etc. and used to buy small luxuries **2.** money used for bribery, political pressure, or other corrupt purposes

slut (slut) *n.* [ME. *slutte*, prob. < Scand. or LowG. form akin to MLowG. *slote*, ditch, mud puddle, Ice. *sluta*, to dangle: for IE. base see SLUG¹] **1.** a careless, dirty, slovenly woman; slattern **2.** a sexually immoral woman ☆**3.** a female dog; bitch —**slut′tish** *adj.* —**slut′tish·ly** *adv.* —**slut′tish·ness** *n.*

sly (slī) *adj.* **sli′er** or **sly′er, sli′est** or **sly′est** [ME. *sley* < ON. *slægr*, clever, cunning, lit., able to strike < base of *slā* & OE. *slean*, to strike (see SLAY)] **1.** [Dial.] skillful or clever **2.** skillful at trickery or deceit; crafty; wily **3.** showing a secretive, crafty, or wily nature; cunningly underhanded **4.** mischievous in a playful way; roguish —**on the sly** secretly; stealthily —**sly′ly** *adv.* —**sly′ness** *n.* *SYN.*—**sly** implies a working to achieve one's ends by evasiveness, insinuation, furtiveness, duplicity, etc. [a *sly* bargain]; **cunning** implies a cleverness or shrewd skillfulness at deception and circumvention [a *cunning* plot]; **crafty** implies an artful cunning in contriving stratagems and subtle deceptions [a *crafty* diplomat]; **tricky** suggests a shifty, unreliable quality rather than cleverness at deception [tricky subterfuges]; **foxy** suggests slyness and craftiness that have been sharpened by experience [a *foxy* old trader]; **wily** implies the deceiving or ensnarement of others by subtle stratagems and ruses [wily blandishments]

sly·boots (-bōōts′) *n.* [SLY + BOOTS] a person who is clever or crafty in an appealing or engaging way

Sm *Chem.* samarium

S.M. 1. [L. *Scientiae Magister*] Master of Science **2.** Soldier's Medal **3.** State Militia

smack¹ (smak) *n.* [ME. *smac* < OE. *smæc*, akin to G. (ge)*schmack* < IE. base **smeg(h)-*, to taste, whence Lith. *smaguriáuti*, to nibble] **1.** a distinctive taste or flavor, esp. one that is faint or slight **2.** a) a small amount; bit b) a touch, trace, or suggestion —*vi.* to have a smack (of) [diction that *smacks* of the stage]

smack² (smak) *n.* [< ? or akin to MDu. *smack*, LowG. *smacke*, of echoic orig.] **1.** a sharp noise made by pressing the lips together and parting them suddenly, as in showing enjoyment of a taste **2.** a loud kiss **3.** a) a sharp blow with the hand or any flat object; slap b) the sound of such a blow —*vt.* **1.** to press (the lips) together and part them suddenly so as to make a smack **2.** to kiss or slap loudly —*vi.* to make a loud, sharp noise, as on impact —*adv.* **1.** with or as with a smack; violently; sharply **2.** directly; precisely; squarely: also [Colloq.] **smack′-dab′** —**smack down** [Slang] ☆to humble or reprimand (someone who is overstepping bounds)

smack³ (smak) *n.* [prob. < Du. *smak* (whence also Dan. *smakke*, Sp. *esmaque*)] **1.** a small sailboat, usually rigged as a sloop ☆**2.** a fishing boat with a well for keeping fish alive

smack·er (-ər) *n.* **1.** a person or thing that smacks ☆**2.** [Slang] a dollar

smack·ing (smak′iŋ) *adj.* [prp. of SMACK², *vi.*] brisk; sharp; lively; vigorous

small (smôl) *adj.* [ME. *smal*, narrow, slender < OE. *smæl*, akin to G. *schmal*, narrow < IE. base **(s)mēlo-*, smaller animal; cf. MAL-] **1.** little in size, esp. when compared with others of the same kind; not large or big; limited in size **2.** a) little in quantity, extent, numbers, duration, etc. [a *small* income] b) of slight intensity; of limited degree or scope c) consisting of relatively few units; numerically low **3.** of little importance or significance; trivial **4.** young [a book for *small* children] **5.** having relatively little investment, capital, etc. [a *small* business] **6.** small-minded; mean; petty **7.** a) of low or inferior rank; ordinary; not notable b) modest or humble **8.**

gentle and low; soft: said of sound or the voice 9. diluted; light; weak [*small ale*] 10. *same as* LOWER-CASE —*adv.* 1. in small pieces 2. in a low, faint tone; softly 3. in a small manner —*n.* 1. the small or narrow part [*the small of the back*] 2. [*pl.*] small things or articles collectively 3. [*pl.*] [Brit.] underclothes, or, formerly, smallclothes —**feel small** to feel shame or humiliation —**small′ness** *n.* SYN.—**small** and **little** are often used interchangeably, but **small** is preferred with reference to something concrete of less than the usual quantity, size, amount, value, importance, etc. [*a small man, tax, audience, matter,* etc.] and **little** more often applies to absolute concepts [*he has his little faults*], in expressing tenderness, indulgence, etc. [*the little woman*], and in connoting insignificance, meanness, pettiness, etc. [*of little importance*]; **diminutive** implies extreme, sometimes delicate, smallness or littleness [*the diminutive Lilliputians*]; **minute** and the more informal **tiny** suggest that which is extremely diminutive, often to the degree that it can be discerned only by close scrutiny [*a minute,* or *tiny,* difference]; **miniature** applies to a copy, model, representation, etc. on a very small scale [*miniature painting*]; **petite** has specific application to a girl or woman who is small and trim in figure —*ANT.* large, big, great

small·age (smôl′ij) *n.* [ME. *smalache* < *smal* (see SMALL) + *ache,* smallage < OFr. < L. *apium,* parsley] [Rare] a variety of wild celery (*Apium graveolens*)

small arms firearms of small caliber, held in the hand or hands when fired, as pistols, rifles, etc.

small beer 1. [Brit.] weak or inferior beer 2. [Colloq.] a person or thing of little importance

small calorie *see* CALORIE (sense 1)

small capital a capital letter of smaller size than the regular capital letter used: the regular capitals used in this dictionary are A, B, C, D, etc.; the small capitals are A, B, C, D, etc.

small change 1. coins, esp. those of low denomination 2. something of little value or importance

small·clothes (smôl′klōz′, -klō*th*z′) *n.pl.* [Archaic] close-fitting knee breeches worn during the 18th cent.

small game small wild animals, and sometimes birds, hunted as game

small hours the first few hours after midnight

small intestine the narrow, convoluted upper part of the intestines, extending from the pyloric end of the stomach to the large intestine

small·ish (-ish) *adj.* somewhat small; not large

small-mind·ed (-min′did) *adj.* blindly selfish, prejudiced, vindictive, etc.; petty; mean; narrow —**small′-mind′ed·ly** *adv.* —**small′-mind′ed·ness** *n.*

☆**small·mouth (black) bass** (-mouth′) a black bass (*Micropterus dolomieu*) found in cool, clear waters

☆**small potatoes** [Colloq.] a petty or insignificant person (or people) or thing (or things)

small·pox (-päks′) *n.* [SMALL + POX] an acute, highly contagious virus disease characterized by prolonged fever, vomiting, and pustular eruptions that often leave pitted scars, or pockmarks, when healed

small-scale (-skāl′) *adj.* 1. drawn to a small scale: said of a map, etc. 2. of limited scope; not extensive [*small-scale business operations*]

small stores small miscellaneous articles stocked by a ship's store, along with extra articles of standard issue, for sale to the crew

small·sword (-sôrd′) *n.* a light, tapering, straight sword, used esp. in fencing

small talk light conversation about common, everyday things; chitchat

☆**small-time** (-tīm′) *adj.* [Colloq.] of little importance or significance; minor or petty

☆**small-town** (-toun′) *adj.* of or characteristic of a small town; provincial, unsophisticated, etc.

smalt (smôlt) *n.* [Fr. < It. *smalto* < Frank. **smalt* < Gmc. base of OHG. *smelzan,* to melt: cf. SMELT²] 1. deep-blue glass prepared from silica, potash, and oxide of cobalt: used, when pulverized, as a pigment 2. pigment made in this way 3. the deep-blue color of this pigment

smalt·ite (smôl′tīt) *n.* [SMALT + -ITE¹] a white to gray, natural, isometric, cobalt-nickel arsenide, (Co,Ni)As₂

smal·to (smäl′tō; *It.* zmäl′tō) *n., pl.* **-tos, -ti** (-tē) [It.: see SMALT] 1. a kind of colored glass or enamel used in mosaics 2. a piece of this

smar·agd (smar′agd) *n.* [ME. *smaragde* < OFr. < L. *smaragdus:* see EMERALD] *now rare var.* of EMERALD (sense 1) —**sma·rag·dine** (smə rag′din) *adj.*

sma·rag·dite (smə rag′dīt) *n.* [Fr.: see prec. & -ITE¹] a bright-green kind of amphibole

smarm·y (smär′mē) *adj.* **smarm′i·er, smarm′i·est** [< ?] [Chiefly Brit. Colloq.] flattering in an oily, insincere manner; unctuous

smart (smärt) *vi.* [ME. *smerten* < OE. *smeortan,* akin to G. *schmerzen* < IE. **mer-d* < base **mer-,* to rub away, fret, whence L. *mordere,* to bite, sting, Gr. *smerdnos,* frightful] 1. *a)* to cause sharp, stinging pain, as a slap *b)* to be the source of such pain, as a wound *c)* to feel such pain 2. to feel mental distress or irritation, as in resentment, remorse, etc. —*vt.* to cause to smart —*n.* [ME. *smerte* < base of *v.*] a smarting sensation, pain, or distress —*adj.* [ME. *smerte* < OE. *smeart* < base of *v.*] 1. causing sharp or stinging pain [*a smart slap*] 2. sharp or stinging, as pain 3. brisk; vigorous; lively [*walking a smart pace*] 4. *a)* intelligent, alert, clever, capable, witty, etc. *b)*

shrewd or sharp, as in one's dealings 5. neat; trim; spruce 6. *a)* in keeping with the current fashion; stylish *b)* characteristic of or used by those who follow the current fashions 7. [Colloq.] impertinent, flippant, or saucy 8. [Dial.] quite strong, intense, numerous, etc.; considerable [*a right smart rain*] —*adv.* in a smart way —SYN. see INTELLIGENT —**smart′ly** *adv.* —**smart′ness** *n.*

☆**smart al·eck, smart al·ec** (al′ik) [SMART + *Aleck,* dim. of ALEXANDER] [Colloq.] a person who is offensively conceited and self-assertive; cocky, bumptious person —**smart′-al′eck, smart′-al′eck·y** *adj.*

smart·en (smärt′'n) *vt.* to make smart or smarter; specif., *a)* to improve in appearance or style *b)* to make more alert, knowing, aware, etc. Usually with *up*

smart money ☆1. [< SMART, *adj.* 4] money bet or invested by those in the best position to know what might be advantageous ☆2. [< SMART, *n.*] *Law same as* EXEMPLARY DAMAGES

☆**smart set** sophisticated, fashionable people, collectively

smart·weed (-wēd′) *n.* any of various knotgrasses (sense 1) whose acrid juice is thought to cause skin irritation

☆**smart·y** (smär′tē) *n., pl.* **smart′ies** [Colloq.] *same as* SMART ALECK: also **smart′y-pants′**

smash (smash) *vt.* [prob. < *s-,* intens. + MASH] 1. to break or shatter into pieces with noise or violence 2. to hit (a tennis ball, badminton bird, etc.) with a hard overhand stroke 3. to hit with a hard, heavy blow or impact 4. to ruin completely; defeat utterly; wreck —*vi.* 1. to break into pieces 2. to be destroyed; come to ruin 3. to collide with crushing force 4. to move by smashing or with force —*n.* 1. a hard, heavy hit or blow; specif., a hard overhand stroke, as in tennis, that is difficult to return 2. *a)* a violent, noisy breaking or shattering *b)* the sound of this 3. *a)* a violent collision *b)* a wreck 4. complete ruin or defeat; total failure, esp. in business 5. a drink made of bruised mint leaves, sugar, water, and an alcoholic liquor ☆6. an overwhelming popular success —☆*adj.* that is a smash (*n.* 6) —SYN. see BREAK¹ —**go to smash** [Colloq.] 1. to become smashed, broken, or ruined 2. to fail completely

smashed (smasht) *adj.* [Slang] drunk; intoxicated

smash·er (smash′ər) *n.* 1. a person or thing that smashes 2. [Chiefly Brit. Colloq.] a handsome, attractive, or beautiful person or thing

smash·ing (-in) *adj.* 1. that smashes 2. [Colloq.] outstandingly good; extraordinary —**smash′ing·ly** *adv.*

smash·up (-up′) *n.* 1. a wreck or collision, esp. one that does great damage 2. complete defeat or failure; ruin 3. any disaster or catastrophe

smat·ter (smat′ər) *vt.* [ME. *smateren,* to chatter, prob. akin to MHG. *smetern,* to chatter, gossip] [Now Rare] 1. to speak or utter with only slight or superficial knowledge 2. to dabble in; study or learn superficially —*n. same as* SMATTERING

smat·ter·ing (-in) *n.* [prec. + -ING] 1. slight or superficial knowledge 2. a small number

☆**smaze** (smāz) *n.* [SM(OKE) + (H)AZE¹] a mixture of smoke and haze

sm. c., sm. caps small capitals

smear (smir) *vt.* [ME. *smerien* < OE. *smerian,* to anoint, akin to G. *schmieren* < IE. base **smeru-,* grease, whence OIr. *smir,* marrow & (prob.) L. *medulla,* marrow] 1. to cover, daub, or soil with something greasy, sticky, or dirty 2. to apply or daub (something greasy, sticky, or dirty) so as to leave a coating, mark, etc. 3. to make an unwanted mark or streak on, or to obscure, by rubbing [*to smear a wet signature*] 4. to make a smear with [*to smear one's hand across a surface*] 5. to harm the reputation of; malign; slander 6. [Slang] to overwhelm or defeat decisively —*vi.* to be or become smeared —*n.* [ME. *smere* < OE. *smeoru,* grease] 1. a spot or mark made by smearing 2. a small quantity of some substance, as blood, smeared on a slide for microscopic study, etc. 3. the act of smearing or slandering a reputation 4. *a)* [Obs.] ointment *b)* a substance to be smeared on something

☆**smear·case** (-kās′) *n.* [G. *schmierkäse* < *schmieren,* to spread (see prec.) + *käse,* CHEESE¹] *same as* COTTAGE CHEESE

smear·y (smir′ē) *adj.* **smear′i·er, smear′i·est** 1. covered with or having smears; smeared 2. tending to smear, as wet ink —**smear′i·ness** *n.*

smec·tic (smek′tik) *adj.* [< L. *smecticus,* cleansing < Gr. *smēktikos* < *smēktos,* smeared (< *smēchein,* to wipe off: for IE. base see SMITE) + -*ikos,* -IC] designating or of a phase of the mesomorphic state in which the liquid does not flow in a normal way but moves by one layer gliding over another, showing an X-ray pattern in one direction

smeg·ma (smeg′mə) *n.* [ModL. < L., a detergent < Gr. *smēgma* < *smēchein,* to wipe off: see prec.] a cheeselike, foul-smelling, sebaceous secretion that accumulates under the foreskin or around the clitoris

smell (smel) *vt.* **smelled** or **smelt, smell′ing** [ME. *smellen* < OE. **smyllan* < IE. base **smel-,* to burn slowly, whence SMOLDER: basic sense "to give off smoke"] 1. to be or become aware of by means of the nose and the olfactory nerves; detect the scent or odor of 2. to sense the presence or existence of [*to smell trouble*] 3. to test by the scent or odor; sniff [*smell the milk to tell if it's sour*] —*vi.* 1. to use the sense of smell; sniff (often with *at* or *of*) 2. *a)* to have or emit a scent or odor [*flowers that do not smell*] *b)* to

have or emit an unpleasant odor; stink **3.** to have the odor or a suggestion (of) [breath that *smells* of garlic] **4.** [Colloq.] *a*) to lack ability, worth, etc.; be of poor quality *b*) to be foul, corrupt, mean, etc. —*n.* [ME. *smel*] **1.** that one of the five senses of the body by which a substance is perceived through the chemical stimulation of nerves (*olfactory nerves*) in the nasal cavity by particles given off by that substance **2.** the characteristic stimulation of any specific substance upon the olfactory nerves; odor; scent **3.** an act of smelling **4.** that which suggests the presence or existence of something; trace; suggestion —**smell out** to look for or find by or as by smelling —**smell up** to fill with a bad odor; cause to stink —**smell′er** *n.*
SYN.—**smell** is the most general word for any quality perceived through the olfactory sense [foul and fresh *smells*]; **scent** refers to the emanation from the thing smelled, often implying that it can be discriminated only by a sensitive sense of smell [the *scent* of a hunted animal]; **odor** suggests a heavier emanation and, therefore, one that is more generally perceptible and more clearly recognizable [chemical *odors*]; **aroma** suggests a pervasive, pleasant, often spicy odor [the *aroma* of fine tobacco]
smelling salts an aromatic mixture of carbonate of ammonium with some fragrant scent, used as an inhalant in relieving faintness, headaches, etc.
smell·y (smel′ē) *adj.* **smell′i·er**, **smell′i·est** having an unpleasant smell —**smell′i·ness** *n.*
smelt¹ (smelt) *n.*, *pl.* **smelts**, **smelt:** see PLURAL, II, D, 1 [ME. < OE., akin to Norw. *smelt*, whiting, Du. *smelt*, G. *schmelte*, sand eel] any of a number of small, silvery, salmonlike food fishes (family Osmeridae) found in northern seas: most run up rivers to spawn, and the **American smelt** (*Osmerus mordax*) has been introduced into inland fresh waters where it has become landlocked
smelt² (smelt) *vt.* [MDu. or MLowG. *smelten*, akin to G. *schmelzen* < IE. **(s)mel-*, to crush, grind fine, whence MELT, MALT] **1.** to melt or fuse (ore, etc.) so as to separate impurities from pure metal **2.** to refine or extract (metal) in this way —*vi.* to undergo fusing or smelting
smelt³ (smelt) *alt. pt. & pp.* of SMELL
smelt·er (smel′tər) *n.* **1.** a person engaged in the work or business of smelting **2.** a place where smelting is done: also **smelt′er·y**, *pl.* **-er·ies**
Sme·ta·na (sme′tä nä; *E.* smet′n ə), **Be·dřich** (bed′rzhikh) 1824–84; Czech composer
Smeth·wick (smeth′ik) city in Staffordshire, C England, near Birmingham: pop. 69,000
smew (smyōō) *n.* [var. of *smee*, akin to obs. Du. *smeente*, MHG. *smiche*, kind of small duck] a small merganser (*Mergus albellus*) of N Europe and Asia, the male of which has a white crest
☆**smidg·en** (smij′ən) *n.* [prob. < dial. *smidge*, var. of *smitch*, a particle] [Colloq.] a small amount; a bit: also **smidg′in**, **smidg′eon**
smi·lax (smī′laks) *n.* [L. < Gr. *smilax*, bindweed] **1.** *same as* CAT BRIER **2.** a twining greenhouse vine (*Asparagus asparagoides*) of the lily family, with bright green foliage
smile (smīl) *vi.* **smiled**, **smil′ing** [ME. *smilen*, akin to Norw. *smile*, Sw. *smila*, prob. via MLowG. **smilen* < IE. base **smei-*, to smile, be astonished, whence L. *mirus*, wonderful, OE. *smearcian*, to smile] **1.** to have or take on a facial expression showing usually pleasure, amusement, affection, friendliness, etc., or, sometimes, irony, derision, etc. and characterized by an upward curving of the corners of the mouth and a sparkling of the eyes **2.** to look (*at*, *on*, or *upon* someone) with a pleasant expression of this kind **3.** to regard with favor or approval (with *on* or *upon*) **4.** to have a favorable, pleasing, or agreeable appearance —*vt.* **1.** to express with a smile **2.** to change or affect by smiling —*n.* **1.** the act of smiling **2.** the facial expression made in smiling **3.** a favorable, pleasing, or agreeable appearance —**smile away** to drive away or get rid of by a smile or smiling —**smil′er** *n.* —**smil′ing·ly** *adv.*
SYN.—**smile** is the general term for a facial expression somewhat resembling that in a laugh but not accompanied by vocal sound; **grin**, applied to a broad smile showing the teeth, implies mischievous amusement, unaffected cheerfulness, foolishness, etc. [an impish *grin*, the *grin* of an idiot]; **simper** is applied to a silly, affected, or coy smile [a coquette with a *simper* on her face]; a **smirk** is a simpering smile that is conceited, knowing, or annoyingly complacent [a self-satisfied *smirk*] —ANT. **frown**
smirch (smurch) *vt.* [ME. *smorchen*, prob. < OFr. *esmorcher*, to hurt] **1.** to make dirty or discolor, as by smearing or staining with grime **2.** to sully or dishonor (a reputation, good name, etc.) —*n.* **1.** a smudge; smear; stain **2.** a stain on reputation, etc.
smirk (smurk) *vi.* [ME. *smirken* < OE. *smearcian*, to SMILE] to smile in a conceited, knowing, or annoyingly complacent way —*n.* a smile of this kind —*SYN.* see SMILE —**smirk′er** *n.* —**smirk′ing·ly** *adv.*
smite (smīt) *vt.* **smote**, **smit′ten** or **smote**, **smit′ing** [ME. *smiten* < OE. *smitan*, akin to G. *schmeissen*, to throw < IE. base **sme-*, to smear, smear on, stroke on] **1.** [Now Rare or Literary] *a*) to hit or strike hard *b*) to bring into a specified condition by or as by a blow [to *smite* someone dead] *c*) to defeat, punish, destroy, or kill **2.** to strike or

attack with powerful or disastrous effect **3.** to affect strongly and suddenly (*with* some feeling) [*smitten* with dread] **4.** to disquiet mentally; distress [*smitten* by conscience] **5.** to strike or impress favorably; inspire with love [*smitten* with her charms] —*vi.* [Now Rare or Literary] to hit or strike hard —*SYN.* see STRIKE —**smit′er** *n.*
smith (smith) *n.* [ME. < OE., akin to G. *schmied* (older *schmid*) < IE. base **smēi-*, to work with a sharp tool, whence Gr. *smilē*, a knife] **1.** a person who makes or repairs metal objects, esp. by shaping the metal while it is hot and soft; metalworker: usually in combination [*silversmith*] **2.** *shortened form of* BLACKSMITH
Smith (smith) **1.** Adam, 1723–90; Scot. economist **2.** **Alfred E(manuel)**, 1873–1944; U.S. politician **3.** **Bes·sie** (bes′ē), 1898?–1937; U.S. jazz singer **4.** Captain **John**, 1580–1631; Eng. colonist in America: cf. POCAHONTAS **5.** **Joseph**, 1805–44; U.S. founder of the Mormon Church **6.** **Sydney**, 1771–1845; Eng. clergyman & essayist **7.** **William**, 1769–1839; Eng. geologist
smith·er·eens (smith′ə rēnz′) *n.pl.* [Ir. *smidirīn*] [Colloq.] small fragments or broken pieces; bits
smith·er·y (smith′ər ē) *n.*, *pl.* **-er·ies 1.** the work or craft of a smith **2.** *same as* SMITHY
Smith·so·ni·an Institution (smith sō′nē ən) institution & museum founded in 1846 in Washington, D.C., by a bequest of James Smithson (1765?–1829), Eng. scientist: branches of the Institution cover a wide range of fields in the arts and sciences: also, unofficially, **Smithsonian Institute**
smith·son·ite (smith′sə nīt′) *n.* [after James *Smithson* (see prec.) + -ITE¹] ☆native zinc carbonate, ZnCO₃, an important ore of zinc
smith·y (smith′ē; *chiefly Brit.*, smith′-) *n.*, *pl.* **smith′ies** [ME. *smithi* < OE. *smithhe* (< *smith*) or ON. *smithja* (< *smithr*, smith)] **1.** the workshop of a smith, esp. a blacksmith ☆**2.** *same as* BLACKSMITH
smit·ten (smit′'n) *alt. pp.* of SMITE
smock (smäk) *n.* [ME. *smoc* < OE. *smoc* or cognate ON. *smokkr* < IE. **(s)meugh* < base **meug-*, slippery, to slip, slip on, whence SMUGGLE, MEEK, L. *mucus*] **1.** a loose, shirtlike, outer garment worn to protect the clothes **2.** [Archaic] a chemise, or sliplike undergarment —*vt.* **1.** to dress in a smock **2.** to decorate with smocking
smock frock a heavy smock, esp. of the kind worn by European farm laborers
smock·ing (smäk′iŋ) *n.* shirred, decorative stitching used in gathering cloth, as to make it hang in even folds
smog (smôg, smäg) *n.* [SM(OKE) + (F)OG¹] a noxious mixture of fog and smoke —*SYN.* see MIST —**smog′gy** *adj.* **-gi·er**, **-gi·est**
smoke (smōk) *n.* [ME. < OE. *smoca*, akin to G. *schmauch* < IE. base **smeukh-*, to smoke, whence Gr. *smychein*, to smolder, Ir. *múch*, smoke] **1.** *a*) the vaporous matter arising from something burning and made visible by minute particles of carbon suspended in it *b*) a mass or cloud of this **2.** any vapor, fume, mist, etc. resembling smoke **3.** ☆*a*) an act or period of smoking tobacco, etc. [time out for a *smoke*] *b*) something to smoke, as a cigarette or pipeful of tobacco **4.** something without substance, significance, or lasting reality **5.** something that beclouds or obscures **6.** a dusky gray **7.** *Physical Chem.* a suspension of solid particles in a gas —*vi.* **smoked**, **smok′ing 1.** to give off smoke or a smokelike substance **2.** to discharge smoke in the wrong place, esp. into a room, as a furnace, fireplace, etc. **3.** to give off too much smoke, as a lamp, type of fuel, etc. **4.** [Now Rare] to move very rapidly, esp. so as to raise dust **5.** *a*) to draw the smoke of tobacco, etc. into the mouth, and often lungs, and blow it out again *b*) to be a habitual smoker —*vt.* **1.** to stain or color with smoke **2.** to treat (meat, fish, etc.) with smoke, as in flavoring or curing **3.** to fumigate as with smoke **4.** to drive or force out with or as with smoke [to *smoke* an animal from its lair] **5.** to stupefy or stun (bees, etc.) with smoke **6.** to draw the smoke of or from (tobacco, a pipe, etc.) into the mouth, and often lungs, and blow it out again **7.** [Archaic] to detect or be suspicious of **8.** [Obs.] to tease or mock —**smoke out** to drive or force into the open with or as with smoke; force out of hiding, secrecy, etc. —**smok′a·ble**, **smoke′a·ble** *adj.*
smoke bomb a kind of bomb containing chemicals which when ignited give off dense clouds of smoke
smoke·house (-hous′) *n.* ☆a building, esp. an outbuilding on a farm, where meats, fish, etc. are smoked in order to cure and flavor them
smoke·jack (-jak′) *n.* [SMOKE + JACK¹] a device which turns a fireplace roasting spit, taking its power from a wheel rotated by the heated air rising in the chimney
☆**smoke jumper** an employee of the forest service parachuted to strategic spots in fighting forest fires
smoke·less (-lis) *adj.* having or making little or no smoke
smokeless powder a propellant or explosive that consists mainly of nitrocellulose and makes little or no smoke when it is fired
smok·er (smō′kər) *n.* **1.** a person or thing that smokes; specif., a person who habitually smokes tobacco ☆**2.** a

railroad car or compartment reserved esp. for smoking: also **smoking car** ☆3. an informal social gathering for men only: an old-fashioned term

smoke screen 1. a cloud of smoke spread to screen the movements of troops, ships, etc. 2. anything said or done to conceal or mislead

☆**smoke·stack** (smōk′stak′) *n.* a pipe for the discharge of smoke from a steamship, locomotive, factory, etc.

smoke tree 1. a small, bushy, old-world tree (*Cotinus coggygria*) of the cashew family, with filmy, feathery flower clusters resembling smoke. 2. a related tree (*Cotinus americanus*), growing in the SW U.S. and having brilliant orange and scarlet coloring in the fall

☆**Smok·ey** (smō′kē) a cartoon figure of a bear dressed as a forest ranger, used as the symbol of the need for preventing forest fires

Smok·ies (smō′kēz) *same as* GREAT SMOKY MOUNTAINS

smoking jacket a man's lounging jacket for wear at home

smoking lamp *Naut.* formerly, a lamp lit aboard a ship to indicate when the crew might smoke

smoking room a room or lounge set apart for smoking

smok·y (smō′kē) *adj.* smok′i·er, smok′i·est 1. giving off smoke, esp. excessive smoke 2. like, of, or as of smoke [a *smoky* haze] 3. filled with smoke 4. having the color of smoke 5. flavored by smoking 6. darkened or soiled by smoke —**smok′i·ly** *adv.* —**smok′i·ness** *n.*

Smoky Hill river flowing from E Colo. eastward through Kans., joining the Republican River to form the Kansas River: 540 mi.

Smoky Mountains *same as* GREAT SMOKY MOUNTAINS

smoky quartz *same as* CAIRNGORM

smol·der (smōl′dər) *vi.* [ME. smoldren < Gmc. *smul-: for IE. base see SMELL] 1. to burn and smoke without flame; be consumed by slow combustion 2. to exist in a suppressed state or with activity stifled 3. to have or show feelings of suppressed anger or hate —*n.* the act or condition of smoldering

Smo·lensk (smō lensk′, smä-; *Russ.* smô lyensk′) city in W European R.S.F.S.R., on the Dnepr: pop. 189,000

Smol·lett (smäl′it), **Tobias George** 1721–71; Brit. novelist, born in Scotland

smolt (smōlt) *n.* [LME. (Scot.)] a young salmon when it first leaves fresh water and descends to the sea

smooch[1] (smōōch) *vt., n. same as* SMUTCH

smooch[2] (smōōch) *n.* [var. of dial. smouch, akin to G. dial. (Westphalian) smuck: ult. akin to SMACK²] [Slang] a kiss —*vi., vt.* [Slang] 1. to kiss 2. to hug, kiss, and caress in making love —**smooch′y** *adj.*

smooth (smōōth) *adj.* [ME. smothe < OE. smoth < IE. *somo-s, fitting together, even < base *sem-, together, SAME] 1. *a)* having an even or level surface; having no roughness or projections that can be seen or felt *b)* having its projections leveled by wear [a *smooth* tire] 2. having an even consistency; without lumps [a *smooth* paste] 3. even, calm, or gentle in flow or movement [a *smooth* voyage] 4. free from interruptions, obstacles, difficulties, etc. [*smooth* progress] 5. not easily agitated or ruffled; calm; serene [a *smooth* temper] 6. free from hair, beard, etc. 7. pleasing to the taste; not sharp or harsh; bland 8. having an easy, gentle, flowing rhythm or sound ☆9. suave, polished, or ingratiating, esp. in a flattering insincere way ☆10. [Colloq.] polished; competent [a *smooth* dancer] 11. [Slang] very pleasant, attractive, or enjoyable 12. *Mech.* frictionless 13. *Phonet.* not aspirated —*vt.* 1. to make level or even 2. to remove the lumps from 3. to remove wrinkles from by pressing 4. to free from interruptions, difficulties, etc.; make easy 5. to make calm or serene; soothe 6. to make less crude; polish or refine —*vi.* to become smooth —*adv.* in a smooth manner —*n.* 1. something smooth; smooth part 2. an act of smoothing —*SYN.* see EASY, LEVEL —**smooth away** to remove (difficulties, obstacles, etc.) —**smooth down** to make or become smooth, or even, level, calm, etc. —**smooth over** to gloss over or make light of (a fault, unpleasant situation, etc.) —**smooth′er** *n.* —**smooth′ly** *adv.* —**smooth′ness** *n.*

☆**smooth·bore** (-bôr′) *adj.* having no grooves or ridges on the inner surface of the barrel; not rifled: said of guns —*n.* a smoothbore gun

smooth breathing [transl. of L. *spiritus lenis*] in Greek, 1. the mark (ʼ) placed over an initial vowel when it is pronounced without a preceding *h* sound, or aspirate 2. the sound thus indicated

☆**smooth dogfish** a requiem shark (*Mustelus canis*) without spines in front of the dorsal fin, common in the Atlantic

smooth·en (-′n) *vt., vi.* to make or become smooth

smooth-faced (smōōth′fāst′) *adj.* 1. having no beard or mustache; smooth-shaven 2. having a smooth face, or surface [a *smooth-faced* tile] 3. having a false semblance of sincerity; plausibly ingratiating

smooth·hound (-hound′) *n.* any of several requiem sharks (esp. genus *Mustelus*), common in the Atlantic and Pacific

☆**smooth·ie** (smōōth′ē) *n.* [Slang] a suave, glib, attractive person, esp. a man: also sp. **smooth′y**

smooth muscle a contractile type of muscle tissue controlled by the involuntary nervous system, occurring in the walls of the uterus, intestines, blood vessels, etc., and characterized by nonstriated, spindle-shaped cells

smooth-shav·en (smōōth′shā′v'n) *adj.* wearing no beard or mustache

smooth-spo·ken (-spō′k'n) *adj.* speaking in a pleasing, persuasive, or polished manner

smooth-tongued (-tuņd′) *adj.* smooth-spoken, esp. in a plausible or flattering way

☆**smor·gas·bord, smör·gås·bord** (smôr′gəs bôrd′, smur′-) *n.* [Sw. *smörgåsbord* < *smörgås*, buttered bread < *smör*, butter (akin to SMEAR) + dial. *gås*, a clump of butter + *bord*, table (akin to BOARD)] 1. a wide variety of appetizers and other tasty foods, as cheeses, fishes, meats, salads, etc., served buffet style 2. a meal composed of these 3. a restaurant serving smorgasbord

‡**smor·zan·do** (smôr tsän′dô) *adj.* [It.] *Music* dying away

smote (smōt) *pt. & alt. pp.* of SMITE

smoth·er (smuth′ər) *vt.* [ME. smorthren < smorther, dense smoke < base of OE. smorian, to suffocate, akin to MLowG. smoren, to smoke < var. of IE. base *smel-, whence SMELL] 1. *a)* to keep from getting enough air to breathe; stifle *b)* to kill in this way; suffocate 2. to cover (a fire), excluding air from it and causing it to smolder or die down 3. to cover over thickly [liver *smothered* in onions] 4. to hide or suppress by or as by covering; stifle [to *smother* a yawn] —*vi.* 1. *a)* to be kept from getting enough air to breathe *b)* to die in this way; be suffocated 2. to be hidden, stifled, or suppressed —*n.* 1. dense, suffocating smoke or any thick cloud of dust, steam, fog, etc. 2. a confused turmoil; welter 3. [Archaic] a smoldering fire 4. [Archaic] a smoldering state or condition —**smoth′er·y** *adj.*

smoul·der (smōl′dər) *vi., n. Brit. sp.* of SMOLDER

smudge (smuj) *n.* [Early ModE., prob. < the *v.*] 1. a stain, blur, or smear; dirty spot 2. *a)* a fire made to produce dense smoke *b)* such smoke produced by burning a material in containers (**smudge pots**), esp. for driving away insects or protecting plants from frost —*vt.* **smudged, smudg′ing** [ME. smogen, akin to Du. smotsen, to besmirch: for IE. base see SMUT] 1. to protect (an orchard, etc.) with smudge 2. to make dirty; soil; smutch —*vi.* 1. to blur or smear 2. to become smudged

smudg·y (smuj′ē) *adj.* **smudg′i·er, smudg′i·est** covered with smudges; stained, blurred, etc. —**smudg′i·ly** *adv.* —**smudg′i·ness** *n.*

smug (smug) *adj.* **smug′ger, smug′gest** [prob. < LowG. smuk, trim, neat, akin to G. schmuck, neat: for IE. base see SMOCK] 1. orig., neat, spruce, trim, etc. 2. narrowly contented with one's own accomplishments, beliefs, morality, etc.; self-satisfied to an annoying degree; complacent —**smug′ly** *adv.* —**smug′ness** *n.*

smug·gle (smug′'l) *vt.* **-gled, -gling** [< LowG. smuggeln, akin to OE. smugan, to creep: for IE. base see SMOCK] 1. to bring into or take out of a country secretly, under illegal conditions or without paying the required import or export duties 2. to bring, take, carry, etc. secretly or stealthily —*vi.* to practice smuggling; be a smuggler

smug·gler (-lər) *n.* [< LowG. smuggeler] 1. a person engaged in smuggling 2. a ship used in smuggling

smut (smut) *n.* [< or akin to LowG. smutt, akin to G. schmutz, dirt < IE. *(s)meud- < base *meu-, wet, musty, whence, MUD, MOSS] 1. *a)* sooty matter *b)* a particle of this 2. a mark made by something dirty; soiled spot 3. pornographic or indecent talk or writing 4. *Bot. a)* any of various plant diseases, esp. of cereal grasses, characterized by the appearance of masses of black spores which usually break up into a fine powder *b)* any of a number of basidiomycetous fungi (order Ustilaginales) causing smut —*vt.* **smut′ted, smut′ting** [later var. of ME. smoten, besmirch] to mark or affect with smut —*vi.* to be marked or affected by smut

smutch (smuch) *vt.* [akin to prec.] to make dirty; smudge —*n.* 1. a dirty spot or mark; smudge 2. soot, smut, grime, or dirt —**smutch′y** *adj.* **smutch′i·er, smutch′i·est**

Smuts (smuts), **Jan Chris·ti·aan** (yän′ kris′tē än) 1870–1950; South African general; prime minister (1919–24; 1939–48)

smut·ty (smut′ē) *adj.* **-ti·er, -ti·est** 1. soiled with smut 2. affected with plant smut 3. pornographic or indecent —**smut′ti·ly** *adv.* —**smut′ti·ness** *n.*

Smyr·na (smur′nə) *former name of* IZMIR

Sn [L. *stannum*] *Chem.* tin

SN *U.S. Navy* Seaman

snack (snak) *n.* [ME. snake, a bite < snaken, to bite, snap, prob. < MDu. snacken, to snap] 1. formerly, a share or part 2. a small quantity of food; light meal or refreshment taken between regular meals —*vi.* to eat a snack or snacks

snack bar a lunch counter, cafeteria, etc. serving snacks

snaf·fle (snaf′'l) *n.* [short for snaffle piece, prob. < Du. snavel, horse's muzzle < ODu. snabel, dim. of snabbe, bill of a bird, akin to G. schnabel: cf. SNAP] a bit, usually light and jointed, attached to a bridle and having no curb —*vt.* **-fled, -fling** 1. to fit with or control by a snaffle 2. [Brit. Slang] to purloin or snitch

☆**sna·fu** (sna fōō′, snaf′ōō) *adj.* [orig. military slang for s(*ituation*) n(ormal), a(ll) f(ouled)–a euphemism–u(p)] [Slang] in characteristic disorder or confusion; mixed up as usual —*vt.* **-fued′, -fu′ing** [Slang] to throw into confusion; mix up

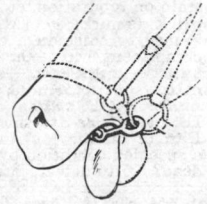

SNAFFLE

snag (snag) *n.* [< Scand., as in ON. *snagi*, a wooden peg, Norw. *snage*, sharp point, projection, akin to G. *schnake*] **1.** a piece, part, or point that sticks out, esp. one that is sharp or rough, as the broken end of a tree limb ☆**2.** an underwater tree stump or branch dangerous to navigation **3.** a broken or irregular tooth; snaggletooth **4.** a small branch of an antler **5.** *a)* a break or tear, as in cloth, made by a splinter, snag, etc. *b)* a pulled thread in knitted material, causing a loop at the point where it is caught ☆**6.** an unexpected or hidden obstacle, difficulty, etc. —*vt.* **snagged, snag′ging 1.** to catch, tear, etc. on a snag **2.** to impede with or as with a snag ☆**3.** to clear (a body of water) of snags **4.** to catch or grab quickly —*vi.* ☆**1.** to strike or become caught on a snag in water **2.** to form or develop a snag

snag·gle·tooth (snag′'l tooth′) *n.*, *pl.* **-teeth′** [< prec.] **1.** a tooth that sticks out beyond the others **2.** a crooked or broken tooth —**snag′gle-toothed′** *adj.*

snag·gy (snag′ē) *adj.* **-gi·er, -gi·est 1.** of, or having the nature of, a snag **2.** full of snags, as a body of water **3.** having snags

snail (snāl) *n.* [ME. *snaile* < OE. *snægl*, akin to G. dial. *schnägel*, ON. *snigill* < IE. base **sneg-*, to creep, whence SNAKE, SNEAK] **1.** any of a large number of slow-moving gastropod mollusks living on land or in water and having a spiral protective shell: some kinds are used as food **2.** any lazy, slow-moving person or animal —**snail′like′** *adj.*

snail-paced (-pāst′) *adj.* very slow-moving

snake (snāk) *n.* [ME. < OE. *snaca*, akin to ON. *snakr*, MLowG. *snake*: for IE. base see SNAIL] **1.** any of a wide variety of limbless reptiles (suborder Serpentes), with an elongated, scaly body, lidless eyes, and a tapering tail: some species have a poisonous bite **2.** a treacherous or deceitful person **3.** a plumber's tool consisting of a long, flexible rod of spiraled wire for removing obstructions from pipes, etc. —*vi.* **snaked, snak′ing** to move, curve, twist, or turn like a snake —*vt.* [Colloq.] ☆**1.** to drag or pull, esp. lengthwise and with force **2.** to pull quickly; jerk **snake′like′** *adj.*

☆**snake·bird** (-burd′) *n.* same as DARTER (sense 2)

snake·bite (-bīt′) *n.* a bite by a snake, esp. a poisonous one, or the condition caused by it

snake charmer a person who, as an entertainer, seems to hypnotize snakes by means of movements or, supposedly, music

☆**snake dance 1.** a ceremonial dance by American Indians involving the handling, imitation, etc. of snakes; esp., a ceremony performed every two years by the Hopi Indians, in which live rattlesnakes are handled **2.** an informal parade in which the celebrants join hands in a long line, winding back and forth as they progress

snake doctor same as: ☆**1.** DRAGONFLY ☆**2.** HELLGRAMMITE

☆**snake eyes** [Slang] a throw of two ones (two) at dice

☆**snake fence** a zigzag fence of rails that cross each other at an angle

☆**snake·head** (-hed′) *n.* same as TURTLEHEAD

snake in the grass a treacherous person or harmful thing that is hidden or seemingly harmless

☆**snake·mouth** (-mouth′) *n.* same as POGONIA

☆**snake oil** a liquid substance with no real medicinal value sold as a cure-all or nostrum, esp. in a medicine show

snake pit 1. a pit where snakes are kept ☆**2.** a place of horror and confusion, as a crowded mental hospital where patients are improperly cared for

Snake River [transl. (prob. erroneous) of earlier *Shoshone River*] river in NW U.S., flowing from Yellowstone National Park into the Columbia River in Wash.; 1,038 mi.

☆**snake·root** (-root′, -root′) *n.* **1.** any of a number of plants reputed to be remedies for snake bites, as **black snakeroot** (*Cimicifuga racemosa*) and **white snakeroot** (*Eupatorium rugosum*) **2.** the roots of any of these plants

snake·skin (-skin′) *n.* a snake's skin or leather from it

snake·weed (-wēd′) *n.* any of several plants supposedly resembling snakes or reputedly a cure for snake bites; specif., *a)* any of various plants (genus *Gutierrezia*) of the composite family, with small, yellow flower heads *b)* same as BISTORT ☆*c)* same as SNAKEROOT

snak·y (snā′kē) *adj.* **snak′i·er, snak′i·est 1.** of or like a snake or snakes **2.** having a snakelike form; serpentine; winding; twisting **3.** cunningly treacherous or evil **4.** full of or infested with snakes **5.** formed of or entwined with snakes, as a caduceus —**snak′i·ly** *adv.* —**snak′i·ness** *n.*

snap (snap) *vi.* **snapped, snap′ping** [< MDu. or MLowG. *snappen*, akin to G. *schnappen* < Gmc. base **snab-*] **1.** to bring the jaws together sharply; bite suddenly (often with *at*) [a fish snaps at bait] **2.** to snatch or grasp quickly or eagerly (with *at*) [to snap at a chance] **3.** to speak sharply, abruptly, or irritably (often with *at*) **4.** to break, part, or be released suddenly, esp. with a sharp, cracking sound **5.** to give way suddenly under strain, as nerves, resistance, etc. **6.** to make a sudden, sharp cracking or clicking sound, as a whip **7.** to close, fasten, go into place, etc. with a snapping sound [the lock snapped shut] **8.** to move or act suddenly and smartly [to snap to attention] **9.** to appear to flash or sparkle, as in anger: said of the eyes —*vt.* **1.** to grasp or get suddenly with or as with a bite; snatch (often with *up*) **2.** to break or sever suddenly or with a snapping sound **3.** to speak or utter sharply or harshly, as in anger (often with *out*) **4.** to cause to make a snapping sound [to snap one's fingers] **5.** to close, fasten, put into place, etc. with a snapping sound [to snap a lid shut] **6.** to strike sharply by releasing one end of something held under tension [to snap someone with a rubber band] **7.** to cause to move suddenly and smartly [snap the ball to first base] ☆**8.** to take a snapshot of ☆**9.** *Football* to put (the ball) into play by sending it back from the line of scrimmage to a member of the offensive backfield —*n.* [MDu. *snap*] **1.** a sudden bite, grasp, snatch, catch, etc. **2.** a sudden breaking or parting **3.** a sudden, sharp cracking or clicking sound [the snap of a whip] **4.** a short, angry utterance or manner of speaking **5.** a brief period or spell of cold weather **6.** any clasp or fastening that closes with a click or snap **7.** a hard, thin cookie [gingersnaps] ☆**8.** *clipped form of* SNAPSHOT ☆**9.** [Colloq.] alertness, vigor, or energy ☆**10.** [Slang] an easy task, job, problem, etc. **11.** [Slang] a person who is easy to influence, persuade, control, etc.; tractable person ☆**12.** *Football* the act of snapping the ball —*adj.* ☆**1.** made or done quickly or on the spur of the moment without deliberation; impulsive [a snap decision] **2.** that fastens with a snap ☆**3.** [Slang] simple; easy [a snap assignment] —*adv.* with, or as with, a snap —**not a snap** not a bit; not at all —**snap back** to recover quickly from an illness, disappointment, etc. —**snap one's fingers at** to show lack of concern for; be careless of or indifferent toward —☆**snap out of it** to change suddenly from a bad condition to a better one; recover quickly or regain one's senses —**snap someone's head off** to speak sharply or harshly to someone

SNAP systems for nuclear auxiliary power

☆**snap·back** (-bak′) *n.* same as SNAP (*n.* 12)

snap bean any of various green beans or wax beans

snap-brim hat (snap′brim′) a man's hat with the crown creased lengthwise and the brim turned down in front

snap·drag·on (-drag′ən) *n.* [SNAP + DRAGON: from the mouth-shaped flowers] **1.** any of a genus (*Antirrhinum*) of perennial plants of the figwort family; esp., a common garden species (*Antirrhinum majus*) with white, purple, crimson, etc., saclike, two-lipped, closed flowers **2.** *a)* a game in which raisins or the like are snatched from a bowl of burning brandy *b)* that which is so snatched

snap·per (-ər) *n.* **1.** a person or thing that snaps **2.** *pl.* **-pers, -per:** see PLURAL, II, D, 1 ☆*a)* same as SNAPPING TURTLE *b)* any of a family (Lutjanidae) of percoid fishes inhabiting most warm seas; esp., the red snapper

☆**snapping beetle** same as CLICK BEETLE

☆**snapping turtle** any of several large, freshwater turtles (family Chelydridae) of N. America, with a small shell and powerful jaws which snap with great force; esp., a common species (*Chelydra serpentina*)

snap·pish (snap′ish) *adj.* **1.** likely to snap or bite **2.** cross or irritable; uncivil; sharp-tongued —**snap′pish·ly** *adv.* —**snap′pish·ness** *n.*

snap·py (snap′ē) *adj.* **-pi·er, -pi·est 1.** snappish; cross **2.** that snaps; snapping **3.** [Colloq.] *a)* brisk, vigorous, or lively [a snappy reply, pace, etc.] *b)* sharply chilly [snappy weather] **4.** [Colloq.] stylish; smart —☆**make it snappy** [Slang] be quick; hurry —**snap′pi·ly** *adv.* —**snap′pi·ness** *n.*

snap roll a maneuver in which an airplane makes one complete fast roll about its longitudinal axis while keeping its general horizontal direction

snap·shot (-shät′) *n.* **1.** a hurried shot fired with little or no aim **2.** an informal photograph taken with brief exposure by snapping the shutter of a hand camera

snare (sner) *n.* [ME. < OE. *sneare* < ON. *snara*, akin to OHG. *snarha* < IE. **(s)nerk-* < base **(s)ner-*, to twist, wind, whence NARROW, G. *schnur*] **1.** a kind of trap for small animals, usually consisting of a noose which jerks tight upon the release of a spring trigger **2.** anything dangerous, risky, etc. that tempts or attracts; thing by which a person is entangled; trap **3.** *a)* a length of spiraled wire or of gut strung across the bottom of a snare drum for added vibration *b)* [*pl.*] a set of snare drums **4.** *Surgery* a wire noose for removing tumors, polyps, etc. —*vt.* **snared, snar′ing** [< Du. *snaar*, akin to G. *schnur*] **1.** to catch in a trap or snare **2.** to tempt or attract into a situation, esp. one that is dangerous, risky, etc. —*SYN.* see CATCH, TRAP[1] —**snar′er** *n.*

snare drum a small, double-headed drum with snares

snark (snärk) *n.* [prob. < SN(AKE) + (SH)ARK[2]] an imaginary animal created by Lewis Carroll in his poem *The Hunting of the Snark*

snarl[1] (snärl) *vi.* [extended from earlier *snar*, to growl, akin to Sw. *snarra*, MHG., MDu., MLowG. *snarren*, to growl < IE. echoic base **(s)ner-*, **(s)nur-*, whence SNEER, SNORE, OIce. *norn*, NORN] **1.** to

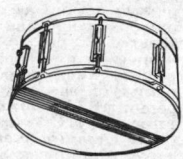

SNARE DRUM

growl fiercely, baring the teeth, as a threatening dog 2. to speak harshly and sharply, as in anger, impatience, etc. —vt. to utter or give vent to with a snarl [to snarl one's contempt] —n. 1. a fierce, harsh growl 2. a harsh utterance expressing anger, impatience, etc. —snarl′er n. —snarl′ing·ly adv.

snarl² (snärl) vt. [ME. snarlen < snare: see SNARE] 1. to make (thread, hair, etc.) knotted or tangled 2. to make disordered or confused; complicate [to snarl traffic] 3. to ornament (metalwork) with a raised design, as by hammering —vi. to become knotted or tangled —n. [ME. snarle] 1. a knotted or tangled mass or tuft; tangle [hair full of snarls] 2. a confused, disordered state or situation; complication; confusion

snarl·y¹ (snär′lē) adj. snarl′i·er, snarl′i·est snarling; cross; bad-tempered

snarl·y² (snär′lē) adj. snarl′i·er, snarl′i·est snarled; tangled; confused

snatch (snach) vt. [ME. snacchen, prob. var. of snakken, to seize (cf. SNACK)] 1. to grasp or seize suddenly, eagerly, or without right, warning, etc.; grab 2. to remove abruptly or hastily 3. to take, get, or avail oneself of hastily or while there is a chance [to snatch some rest] ☆4. [Slang] to kidnap —vi. 1. to try to grasp or seize a thing suddenly; grab (at) 2. to accept or take advantage of a chance, etc. eagerly (with at) —n. [ME. snacche] 1. the act of snatching; a grab 2. a brief period; short time or spell [to sleep in snatches] 3. a small portion, esp. one that is incomplete or disconnected; fragment; bit [snatches of gossip] ☆4. [Slang] an act of kidnapping 5. Weight Lifting a lift in which the barbell is raised in one continuous motion from the floor to a position directly overhead with the arms completely extended —SYN. see TAKE —snatch′er n.

snatch block Naut. a block with a hinged hook that can be opened for the insertion of the bight of a rope

snatch·y (-ē) adj. snatch′i·er, snatch′i·est done in snatches; not complete or continuous; disconnected

snath (snath) n. [altered (after dial. snathe, to lop, prune < ON. sneitha, to cut: cf. SCHNITZEL) < OE. snæd] the curved shaft or handle of a scythe: also **snathe** (snāth)

☆**snaz·zy** (snaz′ē) adj. -zi·er, -zi·est [< ? SN(APPY) + (J)AZZY [Slang] stylishly or showily attractive; flashy

sneak (snēk) vi. sneaked or colloq. snuck, sneak′ing [prob. < OE. *snecan, akin to snican: for IE. base see SNAIL] 1. to move quietly and stealthily so as to avoid being seen or heard; go furtively 2. to be a sneak; behave in a stealthy, underhanded, or cowardly manner —vt. to give, put, carry, take, etc. secretly or in a stealthy, sneaking manner —n. 1. a person who sneaks; stealthy, underhanded, contemptible person 2. an act of sneaking ☆3. clipped form of SNEAKER —adj. without warning; stealthy [a sneak attack] —SYN. see LURK —sneak out of to avoid (duty, a task, etc.) by sneaking or stealth

sneak·er (snē′kər) n. 1. a person or animal that sneaks ☆2. [so named from the noiseless tread] a shoe or slipper with a cloth upper and a continuous sole and heel as of one piece of soft rubber, used for play and sports

sneak·ing (-kiŋ) adj. 1. cowardly, stealthy, underhanded, or furtive [a sneaking manner] 2. not admitted or made known to others; secret [a sneaking fondness for candy] —sneaking suspicion a slight or increasing suspicion —sneak′ing·ly adv.

☆**sneak preview** an advance, single showing of a motion picture, as for evaluating audience reaction prior to the regular showing

☆**sneak thief** a person who commits thefts in a sneaking way, without the use of force or violence

sneak·y (snē′kē) adj. sneak′i·er, sneak′i·est of or like a sneak; underhanded —sneak′i·ly adv. —sneak′i·ness n.

☆**sneaky Pete** [Slang] very cheap wine, often the dregs

sneer (snir) vi. [ME. sneren, akin to Fris. sneere, to scorn, Dan. snaere, to grin like a dog: for IE. base see SNARL¹] 1. to smile derisively; show scorn or contempt as by curling the upper lip 2. to express derision, scorn, or contempt in speech or writing —vt. 1. to utter with a sneer or in a sneering manner 2. to affect in a particular way by sneering [to sneer down a proposal] —n. 1. an act of sneering 2. a sneering expression, insinuation, etc. —SYN. see SCOFF —sneer′er n. —sneer′ing·ly adv.

sneeze (snēz) vi. sneezed, sneez′ing [ME. snesen, altered (prob. by confusion of initial f with ʃ, long s) < fnesen < OE. fneosan: for IE. base see PNEUMA] to exhale breath from the nose and mouth in a sudden, involuntary, explosive action, as a result of an irritation of the nasal mucous membrane —n. an act of sneezing —not to be sneezed at not to be considered lightly or disregarded —sneez′er n. —sneez′y adj.

☆**sneeze·weed** (-wēd′) n. any of a genus (Helenium) of plants of the composite family; esp., a N. American perennial (Helenium autumnale) said to cause sneezing

☆**sneeze·wort** (-wurt′) n. a strong-smelling, white-flowered plant (Achillea ptarmica) of the composite family, with leaves and flowers formerly used in medicine

snell¹ (snel) adj. [ME. < OE., akin to G. schnell] [Dial.] 1. quick; active 2. clever; smart; acute 3. severe; extreme; harsh 4. keen; sharp

☆**snell²** (snel) n. [U.S. dial. < ?] a short length of gut, nylon, etc. used to attach a fishhook to a fish line —vt. to attach (a fishhook) to a snell

snick¹ (snik) n. [prob. a back-formation < snick or snee: see SNICKERSNEE] 1. a small cut or notch; nick 2. Cricket a glancing blow —vt. 1. to cut slightly; nick 2. Cricket to hit (the ball) a glancing blow

snick² (snik) n., vt., vi. [echoic] same as CLICK

snick·er (snik′ər) vi. [echoic] 1. to laugh in a sly or derisive, partly stifled manner 2. to neigh; nicker —vt. to utter with a snicker —n. a sly or derisive, partly stifled laugh —SYN. see LAUGH —snick′er·ing·ly adv.

snick·er·snee (snik′ər snē′) n. [< snick or snee, earlier stick or snee, combat with knives < Du. steken, to thrust, stab + snijden, to cut] a large knife designed for use as a thrusting and cutting weapon

snide (snīd) adj. [orig., counterfeit, bogus < thieves' slang, prob. of Du. dial. or G. origin < base of G. schneiden, to cut, with reference to coin clipping and, later, to cutting remarks] slyly malicious or derisive [a snide remark] —snide′ly adv. —snide′ness n.

sniff (snif) vi. [ME. sniffen, akin to Dan. snive, of echoic orig.] 1. to draw in air through the nose with enough force to be heard, as in clearing the nose or smelling something 2. to express disdain, skepticism, etc. by sniffing —vt. 1. to breathe in forcibly through the nose; draw in or inhale nasally 2. to smell (a substance) by sniffing 3. to detect, perceive, or get a suspicion of by or as by sniffing (often with out) —n. 1. an act or sound of sniffing 2. something sniffed —sniff′er n.

snif·fle (snif′'l) vi. -fled, -fling to sniff repeatedly, as in checking mucus running from the nose —n. an act or sound of sniffling —the sniffles [Colloq.] 1. a head cold 2. the sniffling that accompanies a crying spell —snif′fler n.

sniff·y (-ē) adj. sniff′i·er, sniff′i·est [Colloq.] characterized by or having a tendency to sniff, esp. as a sign of contempt; scornful: also **sniff′ish** —sniff′i·ly adv. —sniff′i·ness n.

snif·ter (snif′tər) n. [< snift, var. of SNIFF] ☆1. a footed goblet that tapers to a small opening to concentrate the aroma, as of brandy ☆2. [Slang] a small drink of liquor

snig·ger (snig′ər) vi., vt., n. [echoic] same as SNICKER

snig·gle (snig′'l) vi. -gled, -gling [< dial. snig, an eel < ME. snygge, a young eel, prob. akin to snegge, a snail, akin to G. schnecke: for base see SNAIL] to fish for eels by putting a baited hook into their hiding holes —vt. to catch (eels) by this method

snip (snip) vt. snipped, snip′ping [Du. snippen, akin to SNAP] 1. to cut with scissors or shears in a short, quick stroke or strokes 2. to remove by or as by such cutting —vi. to make a short, quick cut or cuts —n. 1. a small cut made with scissors, etc. 2. the sound of this 3. a) a small piece cut off b) any small piece; bit 4. [pl.] heavy hand shears used for cutting sheet metal, etc. 5. [Colloq.] a young, small, or insignificant person, esp. one regarded as impudent or insolent —snip′per n.

snipe (snīp) n. [ME. snype < ON. snipa (akin to G. schnepfe) < base seen in SNIP, SNAP] 1. pl. snipes, snipe: see PLURAL, II, D, 1 a) any of several wading birds (esp. genus Capella) related to the woodcock, living chiefly in marshy places and characterized by a long, flexible bill used in digging b) loosely, any of various slender-billed birds, as the dowitcher 2. a shot from a hidden position ☆3. [Slang] a cigar butt or cigarette butt —vi. sniped, snip′ing 1. to hunt or shoot snipe 2. to shoot from a hidden position at individuals of an enemy force 3. to direct an attack (at someone) in a sly or underhanded way —snip·er (snī′pər) n. a person, esp. a soldier, who snipes

☆**snip·er·scope** (-skōp′) n. a snooperscope for mounting on a rifle or carbine: used chiefly in World War II

snip·pet (snip′it) n. [dim. of SNIP] 1. a small, snipped piece; small scrap or fragment, specif. of information, a writing, etc. 2. [Colloq.] same as SNIP (n. 5)

snip·pet·y (-ē) adj. 1. made up of scraps or snippets 2. [Colloq.] same as SNIPPY

snip·py (snip′ē) adj. -pi·er, -pi·est 1. made up of small scraps or snips; fragmentary 2. [Colloq.] curt, sharp, or snappish, esp. in an insolent manner —snip′pi·ly adv. —snip′pi·ness n.

snit (snit) n. [< ? SN(IPPY) + (F)IT²] a fit of anger, pique, etc.: usually in (or into) a snit

snitch (snich) vt. [< 18th-c. thieves' slang: orig. sense "a nose"] [Slang] to steal (usually something of little value); pilfer —vi. [Slang] to be an informer; tattle (on) —n. [Slang] an informer: also **snitch′er**

sniv·el (sniv′'l) vi. -eled or -elled, -el·ing or -el·ling [ME. snivelen < OE. *snyflan, < base seen in snofl, mucus prob. ult. < IE. base *sneu-, to flow] 1. to have mucus running from the nose 2. to sniff repeatedly, as from a head cold, crying, etc.; sniffle 3. to cry and sniffle 4. to fret or complain in a whining, tearful manner 5. to make a whining, tearful, often false display of grief, sympathy, disappointment, etc. —n. 1. nasal mucus 2. the act of sniveling 3. a sniveling display of grief, etc. —sniv′el·er n.

snob (snäb) n. [orig. dial. "boy, cobbler's boy" < ? ON. snāpr; other senses via cant < ?] 1. formerly, a person having no wealth or social rank; one of the common people 2. a person who attaches great importance to wealth, social position, etc., having contempt for those whom he considers his inferiors, and admiring and seeking to associate with those whom he considers his superiors 3. a person who feels and acts smugly superior about his particular tastes or interests [an intellectual snob] —

snob′bish adj. —**snob′bish·ly** adv. —**snob′bish·ness** n. —**snob′bism** n.
snob·ber·y (-ər ē) n., pl. **-ber·ies** snobbish behavior or character, or an instance of this
snood (snōōd) n. [via ME. dial. < OE. snod, ult. < IE. base *snē-, to twist threads, spin, whence NEEDLE] 1. a tie or ribbon for the hair, esp. as formerly worn by young unmarried women in Scotland 2. a baglike net worn at the back of a woman's head to hold the hair 3. a hat or part of a hat resembling this 4. same as SNELL² —vt. to bind or hold up (the hair) with a snood
snook¹ (snook) n., pl. **snook, snooks**: see PLURAL, II, D, 2 [Du. snoek, pike < MDu. snoec, akin to ON. snokr, small shark & OE. snacc, a small vessel] 1. any of a family (Centropomidae) of pikelike fishes of warm seas; esp., a large game and food fish (Centropomus undecimalis) of the tropical Atlantic 2. any of several similar sea fishes
snook² (snook) n. [< ?] [Chiefly Brit.] the gesture of thumbing one's nose in defiance or derision: used chiefly in the phrase **cock a snook at**, to indicate contempt for by this gesture
snook·er (snook′ər) n. [< ?] a variety of the game of pool played with fifteen red balls and six other balls
☆**snoop** (snōōp) vi. [Du. snoepen, to eat snacks on the sly] [Colloq.] to look about in a sneaking, prying way —n. [Colloq.] a person who snoops: also **snoop′er** 2. the act of snooping —**snoop′y** adj. **snoop′i·er, snoop′i·est** —**snoop′i·ness** n.
☆**snoop·er·scope** (snōōp′ər skōp′) n. [see SNOOP & -SCOPE] an electronic viewing device using infrared radiation that allows an observer to see objects, areas, etc. in the dark
snoot (snōōt) n. [ME. snute: see SNOUT] [Colloq.] 1. the nose 2. the face 3. a grimace —vt. to snub
☆**snoot·y** (-ē) adj. **snoot′i·er, snoot′i·est** [prec. + -Y²: from the elevation of the nose of haughty people] [Colloq.] haughty; snobbish —**snoot′i·ly** adv. —**snoot′i·ness** n.
snooze (snōōz) n. [< 18th-c. cant < ? or akin to LowG. snūsen (Dan. snuse), to sniff, snore] [Colloq.] a brief sleep; nap; doze —vi. **snoozed, snooz′ing** [Colloq.] to take a brief sleep; nap; doze —**snooz′er** n.
Sno·qual·mie Falls (snō kwäl′mē) [< Salish tribal name < ?] waterfall (270 ft.) in WC Wash., on a river (**Snoqual·mie River**) that flows west out of the Cascades
snore (snôr) vi. **snored, snor′ing** [ME. snoren: see SNARL¹] to breathe, while asleep, with harsh sounds caused by vibration of the soft palate, usually with the mouth open —n. the act or sound of snoring —**snor′er** n.
☆**snor·kel** (snôr′k'l) n. [G. schnörkel, spiral] 1. a device for submarines, consisting of air intake and exhaust tubes: it permits submergence for long periods 2. a breathing tube extending above the surface of the water, used in swimming just below the surface 3. a hydraulic crane with a bucketlike aerial platform, mounted on a truck for firefighting, etc. —vi. **-keled, -kel·ing** to move or swim underwater using a snorkel —**snor′kel·er** n.

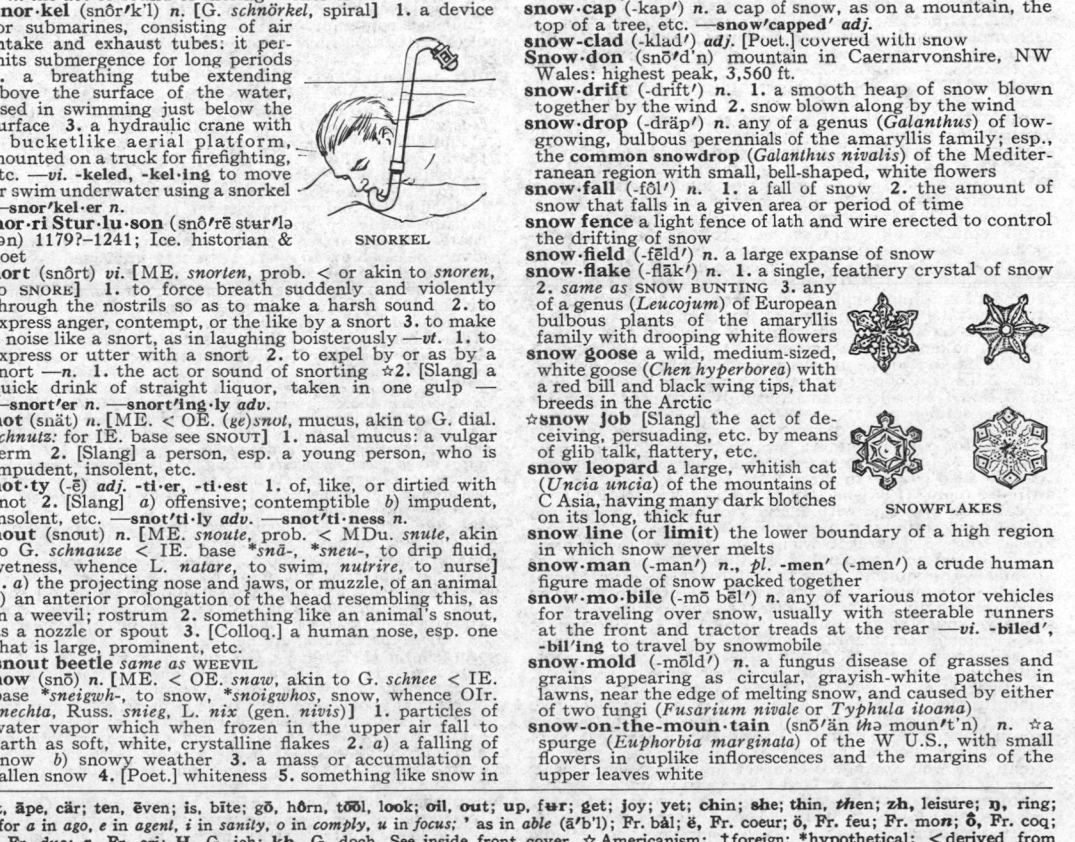

SNORKEL

Snor·ri Stur·lu·son (snô′rē stur′lə sən) 1179?-1241; Ice. historian & poet
snort (snôrt) vi. [ME. snorten, prob. < or akin to snoren, to SNORE] 1. to force breath suddenly and violently through the nostrils so as to make a harsh sound 2. to express anger, contempt, or the like by a snort 3. to make a noise like a snort, as in laughing boisterously —vt. 1. to express or utter with a snort 2. to expel by or as by a snort —n. 1. the act or sound of snorting ☆2. [Slang] a quick drink of straight liquor, taken in one gulp —**snort′er** n. —**snort′ing·ly** adv.
snot (snät) n. [ME. < OE. (ge)snot, mucus, akin to G. dial. schnutz: for IE. base see SNOUT] 1. nasal mucus: a vulgar term 2. [Slang] a person, esp. a young person, who is impudent, insolent, etc.
snot·ty (-ē) adj. **-ti·er, -ti·est** 1. of, like, or dirtied with snot 2. [Slang] a) offensive; contemptible b) impudent, insolent, etc. —**snot′ti·ly** adv. —**snot′ti·ness** n.
snout (snout) n. [ME. snoute, prob. < MDu. snute, akin to G. schnauze < IE. base *snā-, *sneu-, to drip fluid, wetness, whence L. natare, to swim, nutrire, to nurse] 1. a) the projecting nose and jaws, or muzzle, of an animal b) an anterior prolongation of the head resembling this, as in a weevil; rostrum 2. something like an animal's snout, as a nozzle or spout 3. [Colloq.] a human nose, esp. one that is large, prominent, etc.
☆**snout beetle** same as WEEVIL
snow (snō) n. [ME. < OE. snaw, akin to G. schnee < IE. base *sneigwh-, to snow, *snoigwhos, snow, whence OIr. snechta, Russ. snieg, L. nix (gen. nivis)] 1. particles of water vapor which when frozen in the upper air fall to earth as soft, white, crystalline flakes 2. a) a falling of snow b) snowy weather 3. a mass or accumulation of fallen snow 4. [Poet.] whiteness 5. something like snow in

whiteness, texture, etc. ☆6. fluctuating spots appearing on a television screen as a result of a weak signal ☆7. [Slang] cocaine or heroin —vi. [ME. snowen < OE. sniwian] to fall as or like snow —vt. 1. to shower or let fall as or like snow ☆2. to cover, obstruct, etc. with or as with snow (usually with in, up, under, etc.) ☆3. [Slang] to deceive, mislead, or win over by glib talk, flattery, etc. —☆**snow under** 1. to weigh down or overwhelm with work, etc. 2. to defeat decisively
Snow (snō), (Sir) **C(harles) P(ercy)** 1905- ; Eng. novelist & physicist
snow·ball (-bôl′) n. 1. a mass of snow packed together into a ball ☆2. a cultivated European cranberry bush (Viburnum opulus) of the honeysuckle family, with spherical clusters of sterile white or pinkish flowers —vi. 1. to increase or accumulate rapidly and out of control like a ball of snow rolling downhill 2. to throw snowballs —vt. 1. to throw snowballs at 2. to cause to increase or accumulate rapidly
snow·bank (-baŋk′) n. a large mass of snow, esp. a drift on a hillside, in a gully, etc.
☆**snow·bell** (-bel′) n. any of several shrubby, white-flowered plants (genus Styrax) of the storax family, native to the E U.S. and the Orient
snow·ber·ry (-ber′ē) n., pl. **-ries** 1. a hardy, N. American, shrubby plant (Symphoricarpos albus) of the honeysuckle family, with tubular, small, pink flowers and soft, white berries 2. any of various other plants having white berries 3. any of these berries
snow·bird (-burd′) n. 1. a widely distributed N. American junco (Junco hyemalis) 2. same as SNOW BUNTING ☆3. [cf. SNOW, 7 & BIRD, 5] [Slang] a person addicted to the use of cocaine or heroin
snow-blind (-blind′) adj. blinded temporarily by ultra-violet rays reflected from snow —**snow blindness**
snow·blink (-bliŋk′) n. a bright glare on the underside of clouds reflected from a snowy surface
☆**snow blower** a motorized, hand-guided machine on wheels, for removing snow as from walks. also **snow thrower**
snow·bound (-bound′) adj. shut in or blocked off by snow
snow·broth (-brôth′) n. a mixture of snow and water, or melted snow
snow bunting a small finch (Plectrophenax nivalis) inhabiting cold regions in the Northern Hemisphere: the male is white in winter with black streaks on the back
☆**snow·bush** (-boosh′) n. a California plant (Ceanothus cordulatus) of the buckthorn family, with white flowers
snow·cap (-kap′) n. a cap of snow, as on a mountain, the top of a tree, etc. —**snow′capped′** adj.
snow-clad (-klad′) adj. [Poet.] covered with snow
Snow·don (snō′d'n) mountain in Caernarvonshire, NW Wales: highest peak, 3,560 ft.
snow·drift (-drift′) n. 1. a smooth heap of snow blown together by the wind 2. snow blown along by the wind
snow·drop (-dräp′) n. any of a genus (Galanthus) of low-growing, bulbous perennials of the amaryllis family; esp., the **common snowdrop** (Galanthus nivalis) of the Mediterranean region with small, bell-shaped, white flowers
snow·fall (-fôl′) n. 1. a fall of snow 2. the amount of snow that falls in a given area or period of time
snow fence a light fence of lath and wire erected to control the drifting of snow
snow·field (-fēld′) n. a large expanse of snow
snow·flake (-flāk′) n. 1. a single, feathery crystal of snow 2. same as SNOW BUNTING 3. any of a genus (Leucojum) of European bulbous plants of the amaryllis family with drooping white flowers
snow goose a wild, medium-sized, white goose (Chen hyperborea) with a red bill and black wing tips, that breeds in the Arctic
☆**snow job** [Slang] the act of deceiving, persuading, etc. by means of glib talk, flattery, etc.
snow leopard a large, whitish cat (Uncia uncia) of the mountains of C Asia, having many dark blotches on its long, thick fur

SNOWFLAKES

snow line (or **limit**) the lower boundary of a high region in which snow never melts
snow·man (-man′) n., pl. **-men′** (-men′) a crude human figure made of snow packed together
snow·mo·bile (-mō bēl′) n. any of various motor vehicles for traveling over snow, usually with steerable runners at the front and tractor treads at the rear —vi. **-biled′, -bil·ing** to travel by snowmobile
snow·mold (-mōld′) n. a fungus disease of grasses and grains appearing as circular, grayish-white patches in lawns, near the edge of melting snow, and caused by either of two fungi (Fusarium nivale or Typhula itoana)
snow-on-the-moun·tain (snō′än thə moun′t'n) n. ☆a spurge (Euphorbia marginata) of the W U.S., with small flowers in cuplike inflorescences and the margins of the upper leaves white

snow plant ☆a red, fleshy, saprophytic plant (*Sarcodes sanguinea*) of the heath family, with hanging red flowers and no leaves, growing in the pine forests of the Sierra Nevada: often found in spring before the snow has melted

☆**snow·plow** (snō′plou′) *n.* **1.** any plowlike device or machine used to clear snow off a road, railroad, etc. **2.** *Skiing* a stemming of both skis, as for stopping, with the inside ski edges dug into the snow, and the tips of the skis pointed at each other —*vi.* to stem with both skis

snow pudding a kind of fluffy pudding made with beaten egg whites, sugar, and gelatin or cornstarch

☆**snow·shed** (-shed′) *n.* a long shed to protect a section of railroad track against snow

☆**snow·shoe** (-shōō′) *n.* a racket-shaped frame of wood fitted with crosspieces and criss-crossed with strips of leather, etc., worn on the feet to prevent sinking in deep snow —*vi.* -shoed′, -shoe′ing to use snowshoes in walking —**snow′sho′er** *n.*

snowshoe hare [from its broad feet, heavily furred in winter] a large, nonburrowing hare (*Lepus americanus*) of N N. America whose coloration changes from brown in summer to white in winter: also **snowshoe rabbit**

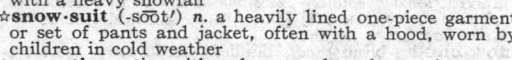
SNOWSHOES

☆**snow·slide** (-slīd′) *n.* an avalanche of mainly snow

☆**snow·storm** (-stôrm′) *n.* a storm with a heavy snowfall

☆**snow·suit** (-sōōt′) *n.* a heavily lined one-piece garment or set of pants and jacket, often with a hood, worn by children in cold weather

☆**snow tire** a tire with a deep tread, and sometimes protruding studs, for added traction on snow or ice

snow-white (-hwīt′, -wīt′) *adj.* white as snow

snow·y (snō′ē) *adj.* **snow′i·er, snow′i·est** [ME. *snawi* < OE. *snawig*] **1.** characterized by snow **2.** covered or filled with snow [a *snowy* valley] **3.** like or suggestive of snow; specif., *a)* pure; unsoiled; spotless *b)* white **4.** of or consisting of snow —**snow′i·ly** *adv.* —**snow′i·ness** *n.*

snub (snub) *vt.* **snubbed, snub′bing** [ME. *snubben* < ON. *snubba,* to chide, snub] **1.** orig., to check or interrupt with sharp or slighting words **2.** to treat with scorn, contempt, disdain, etc.; behave coldly toward; slight or ignore **3.** *a)* to check suddenly the movement of (a rope, cable, etc.) by turning it around a post *b)* to make (a boat, etc.) fast by such a movement ☆**4.** to put out (a cigarette) —*n.* **1.** scornful, slighting action or treatment; affront **2.** a snubbing, or checking —*adj.* short and turned up; pug: said of the nose —**snub′ber** *n.*

snub·by (-ē) *adj.* **-bi·er, -bi·est 1.** turned up; snub **2.** tending to snub or slight

snub-nosed (-nōzd′) *adj.* having a snub nose

☆**snuck** (snuk) *colloq. pt. of* SNEAK

snuff[1] (snuf) *n.* [ME. < ?] the charred end of a candlewick —*vt.* [ME. *snuffen* < the *n.*] **1.** to trim off the charred end of (a candlewick) **2.** to put out (a candle) with snuffers or by pinching —**snuff out 1.** to put out (a candle, etc.); extinguish **2.** to bring to an end suddenly; destroy

snuff[2] (snuf) *vt.* [< MDu. *snuffen*: prob. ult. < IE. *sneub-* < base *sneu-*: see SNOUT] **1.** to draw in through the nose; inhale strongly; sniff **2.** to smell, sniff, or sniff at —*vi.* **1.** to sniff or snort **2.** [Rare] to use snuff —*n.* **1.** the act or sound of snuffing; sniff **2.** *a)* a preparation of powdered tobacco taken up into the nose by sniffing or applied to the gums as with a snuff stick *b)* a pinch of this **3.** any powder taken by inhaling **4.** smell; scent —**up to snuff 1.** [Colloq.] up to the usual standard, as in health, quality, etc. **2.** [Brit. Colloq.] not easily cheated or deceived; alert

snuff·box (-bäks′) *n.* a small, usually ornamental box for holding snuff

snuff·er (-ər) *n.* **1.** a device with a cone on the end of a handle, for extinguishing a burning candle: in full **candle snuffer 2.** [*pl.*] an instrument like shears, for snuffing a candle: also **pair of snuffers**

snuf·fle (snuf′'l) *vi.* **-fled, -fling** [freq. of SNUFF[2], *v.*] **1.** to breathe audibly and with difficulty or by constant sniffing, as a dog in trailing; sniff or sniffle **2.** to speak or sing in a nasal tone **3.** [Rare] to whine —*vt.* to utter by snuffling —*n.* **1.** the act or sound of snuffling **2.** a nasal tone or twang —**the snuffles** *same as* the SNIFFLES —**snuf′fler** *n.*

☆**snuff stick** a soft twig chewed at one end until frayed and used to dip snuff and bring it to the mouth

snuff·y (snuf′ē) *adj.* **snuff′i·er, snuff′i·est 1.** like snuff, as in color or texture **2.** having the habit of taking snuff **3.** soiled with snuff **4.** disagreeable; unattractive

snug (snug) *adj.* **snug′ger, snug′gest** [Early ModE. < nautical lang., prob. via EFris. *snugge,* Du. *snugger,* smooth, neat < Scand., as in ON. *snøggr,* short-haired, short (hence, tight, taut) < IE. *ksneu-* < base *kes-,* to comb, shear (hair), whence Gr. *xainein,* to comb] **1.** protected from the weather or the cold; warm and cozy **2.** small but well arranged; compact and convenient; neat; trim [a *snug* cottage] **3.** large enough to provide ease and comfort: said of an income **4.** tight or close in fit [a *snug* coat, a *snug* joint] **5.** trim and well-built; seaworthy **6.** hidden or concealed [to lie *snug*] —*adv.* so as to be snug

—*vi.* **snugged, snug′ging** [Dial.] *same as* SNUGGLE —*vt.* to make snug or secure —*n.* [Brit. Slang] *same as* SNUGGERY —**SYN.** see COMFORTABLE —**snug down** *Naut.* to make ready for a storm by reducing sail, lashing movable gear, etc. —**snug′ly** *adv.* —**snug′ness** *n.*

snug·ger·y (-ər ē) *n., pl.* **-ger·ies** [Chiefly Brit.] a snug or comfortable place, room, etc.; esp., a small private room or booth in a public house

☆**snug·gies** (-ēz) *n.pl.* women's long, warm underwear

snug·gle (-'l) *vi.* **-gled, -gling** [freq. of SNUG] to lie closely and comfortably; nestle; cuddle, as for warmth, in affection, etc. —*vt.* to hold or draw close or in a comfortable position; cuddle; nestle

so[1] (sō) *adv.* [ME. *so, swo* < OE. *swa,* so, as, akin to Goth. *swa,* OHG. *so* < IE. base **se-, *swe-,* reflexive particle] **1.** in the way or manner shown, expressed, indicated, understood, etc.; as stated or described; in such a manner [hold the bat just *so*] **2.** *a)* to the degree expressed or understood; to such an extent [why are you *so* late?] *b)* to an unspecified but limited degree, amount, number, etc. [to go *so* far and no further] *c)* to a very high degree; very [they are *so* happy] *d)* [Colloq.] very much [she *so* wants to go] **3.** for the reason specified; therefore [they were tired, and *so* left] **4.** more or less; approximately that number, amount, etc. [fifty dollars or *so*]: in this sense, *so* is often regarded as a pronoun **5.** also; likewise [she enjoys music, and *so* does he]: also used colloquially in contradicting a negative statement [I did *so* tell the truth!] **6.** then [and *so* to bed] —*conj.* **1.** in order that; with the purpose that: usually followed by *that* [talk louder *so* (that) all may hear] **2.** [Colloq.] with the result that; therefore [he smiled, *so* I did too] **3.** if only; as long as; provided (*that*) As a conjunction, *so* is sometimes used colloquially as a superfluous element connecting clauses or to preface or resume one's remarks —*pron.* **1.** that which has been specified or named [he is a friend and will remain *so*] **2.** *see adv.* (sense 4) —*interj.* an exclamation expressing surprise, approval or disapproval, triumph, etc., or a command to stop —*adj.* **1.** true; in reality [that's *so*] **2.** in proper order [everything must be just *so*] —**and so on** (or **forth**) and others; and the rest; and in like manner; et cetera (etc.) —**so as 1.** with the purpose or result (followed by an infinitive) **2.** provided that —**so much** to an unspecified but limited degree, amount, etc. [paid *so much* per day]: often used as an intensive [*so much* the worse for him!] —**so much for** no more need be said about [*so much for* my problems] —☆**so what?** [Colloq.] even if so, what then?: used to express disregard, challenge, contempt, etc.

so[2] (sō) *n. Music same as* SOL[2]

So. 1. south **2.** southern

S.O. 1. Signal Officer **2.** Special Order

soak (sōk) *vt.* [ME. *soken* < OE. *socian* < base of *sucan:* see SUCK] **1.** to make thoroughly wet; drench or saturate [*soaked* to the skin by the rain] **2.** to submerge or keep in a liquid, as for thorough wetting, softening, for hydrotherapy, etc. **3.** *a)* to take in (liquid) by sucking or absorbing (usually with *up*) *b)* to absorb by exposure to it [to *soak* up sunshine] *c)* to take in mentally, esp. with little effort [to *soak* up knowledge] *b)* to immerse (oneself) in some study or branch of learning ☆**5.** [Colloq.] to charge heavily or too dearly; overcharge ☆**6.** [Slang] to give a heavy blow to —*vi.* **1.** to stay immersed in water or other liquid for wetting, softening, etc. **2.** to pass or penetrate as a liquid does; permeate [rain *soaking* through his coat] **3.** to become absorbed mentally [the fact *soaked* into his head] —*n.* **1.** the act or process of soaking **2.** the state of being soaked **3.** liquid used for soaking or steeping **4.** [Slang] a drunkard —**soak out** to draw out (dirt, etc.) by or as by soaking

SYN.—soak implies immersion in a liquid, etc. as for the purpose of absorption, thorough wetting, softening, etc. [to *soak* bread in milk]; **saturate** implies absorption to a point where no more can be taken up [air *saturated* with moisture]; **drench** implies a thorough wetting as by a downpour [a garden *drenched* by the rain]; **steep** usually suggests soaking for the purpose of extracting the essence of something [to *steep* tea]; **impregnate** implies the penetration and permeation of one thing by another [wood *impregnated* with creosote]

soak·age (-ij) *n.* **1.** a soaking or being soaked **2.** liquid that has seeped out or been absorbed

soak·ers (-ərz) *n.pl.* short knitted pants of absorbent material, esp. wool, put on over a baby's diaper

☆**so-and-so** (sō′an sō′) *n., pl.* **so′-and-sos′** [Colloq.] some person or thing whose name is either not specified or not known: often used euphemistically in place of a strong or vulgar, disparaging epithet

soap (sōp) *n.* [ME. *sope* < OE. *sape,* akin to G. *seife* < IE. base **seib-,* to trickle, run out, whence L. *sebum,* tallow] **1.** a substance used with water to produce suds for washing or cleaning: soaps are usually sodium or potassium salts of fatty acids, produced by the action of an alkali, as caustic soda or potash, on fats or oils **2.** any metallic salt of a fatty acid —*vt.* to lather, scrub, etc. with soap —☆**no soap** [Slang] **1.** the offer, suggestion, etc. is not acceptable **2.** to no avail

soap·bark (-bärk′) *n.* **1.** *a)* a S. American tree (*Quillaja saponaria*) of the rose family, with leathery leaves and white flower clusters *b)* its inner bark, used in cleansing

preparations for its saponin content **2.** any of several tropical American trees (genus *Pithecolobium*) of the legume family, whose bark contains saponin

soap·ber·ry (-ber′ē) *n., pl.* -**ries 1.** any of a genus (*Sapindus*) of trees of the soapberry family, with fruits containing saponin **2.** the globular fruit, with yellowish flesh and a large round seed —*adj.* designating a family (Sapindaceae) of chiefly tropical trees and shrubs, including the soapberries, the litchi, the longan, etc.

soap·box (-bäks′) *n.* **1.** a box or crate for soap ☆**2.** any improvised platform used by a person (**soapbox orator**) making an informal, often impassioned speech to a street audience, as on a current, controversial issue

soap bubble 1. a filmy bubble of soapy water, specif. one blown up, as from a pipe **2.** something short-lived, insubstantial, or ephemeral

☆**soap opera** [Colloq.] a daytime radio or television serial drama of a highly melodramatic, sentimental nature: so called since many original sponsors were soap companies

☆**soap plant** any of various plants some parts of which can be used as soap; esp., a tall W N. American plant (*Chlorogalum pomeridianum*) of the lily family

soap·stone (-stōn′) *n. same as* STEATITE

soap·suds (-sudz′) *n.pl.* **1.** soapy water, esp. when stirred into a foam **2.** the foam on soapy water

soap·wort (-wurt′) *n. same as* BOUNCING BET

soap·y (sō′pē) *adj.* **soap′i·er, soap′i·est 1.** covered with or containing soap; lathery **2.** of, like, or characteristic of soap **3.** [Slang] suave; unctuous; oily —**soap′i·ly** *adv.* —**soap′i·ness** *n.*

soar (sôr) *vi.* [ME. *soren* < OFr. *essorer*, to expose (wings) to the air, hence soar, as a falcon < VL. *exaurare* < L. *ex-*, out + *aura*, air (cf. AURA)] **1.** to rise or fly high into the air **2.** to fly, sail, or glide along high in the air **3.** to glide along without engine power, keeping or gaining altitude on currents of air: said of an aircraft, esp. a glider **4.** to rise above the usual or ordinary level or bounds; be elevated [*soaring* prices, *soaring* spirits] —*vt.* [Poet.] to reach by soaring —*n.* **1.** soaring range or height **2.** the act of soaring —*SYN.* see FLY[1] —**soar′er** *n.*

sob (säb) *vi.* **sobbed, sob′bing** [ME. *sobben*] **1.** to weep aloud with a catch or break in the voice and short, gasping breaths **2.** to make a sound like that of sobbing, as the wind —*vt.* **1.** to bring (oneself) into a given state, esp. sleep, by sobbing **2.** to utter with sobs —*n.* the act or sound of one that sobs —*SYN.* see CRY —**sob′bing·ly** *adv.*

S.O.B., s.o.b., SOB son of a bitch

so·be·it (sō bē′it) *conj.* [Archaic] provided; if it should be that

so·ber (sō′bər) *adj.* [ME. *sobre* < OFr. < L. *sobrius*, akin to *ebrius*, drunk] **1.** temperate or sparing in the use of alcoholic liquor **2.** not drunk **3.** temperate in any way; not extreme or extravagant **4.** serious, solemn, grave, or sedate **5.** not bright, garish, or flashy; quiet; plain: said of color, clothes, etc. **6.** not exaggerated or distorted [the *sober* truth] **7.** characterized by reason, sanity, or self-control; showing mental and emotional balance —*vt., vi.* to make or become sober (often with *up* or *down*) —*SYN.* see SERIOUS —**so′ber·ly** *adv.* —**so′ber·ness** *n.*

so·ber-mind·ed (-mīn′did) *adj.* sensible and serious —**so′ber-mind′ed·ly** *adv.* —**so′ber-mind′ed·ness** *n.*

so·ber·sides (-sīdz′) *n., pl.* -**sides′** a sedate, serious-minded person —**so′ber·sid′ed** *adj.*

So·bies·ki (sō byes′kē), **John** *see* JOHN III

so·bri·e·ty (sō brī′ə tē, sō-) *n.* [ME. *sobrete* < OFr. *sobriete* < L. *sobrietas* < *sobrius*, SOBER] the state or quality of being sober; specif., *a)* temperance or moderation, esp. in the use of alcoholic liquor *b)* seriousness; sedateness

so·bri·quet (sō′brə kā′, sō′brə kā′) *n.* [Fr.] **1.** a nickname **2.** an assumed name

☆**sob sister** [Old Slang] a journalist, esp. a woman, who writes sentimental human-interest stories

☆**sob story** [Colloq.] a very sad story, esp. an account of personal troubles meant to arouse sympathy

Soc., soc. 1. social **2.** socialist **3.** society

soc·age (säk′ij) *n.* [ME.: see SOKE & -AGE] a medieval English system of land tenure in which a tenant held land in return for a fixed payment or for certain stated nonmilitary services to his lord

so-called (sō′kôld′) *adj.* **1.** popularly known or called by this term [the *so-called* nuclear powers] **2.** inaccurately or questionably designated as such [a *so-called* liberal]

soc·cer (säk′ər) *n.* [altered < (AS)SOC(IATION FOOTBALL)] a game played with a round ball by two teams of eleven men on a field with a goal at either end: the ball is moved chiefly by kicking or by using any part of the body except the hands and arms

So·che (sō′che′) city in W Sinkiang province, China: a trading center; pop. 80,000

So·chi (sō′chē) seaport & resort in Krasnodar territory, R.S.F.S.R., on the Black Sea: pop. 182,000

so·cia·bil·i·ty (sō′shə bil′ə tē) *n., pl.* -**ties** the quality or an instance of being sociable

so·cia·ble (sō′shə b'l) *adj.* [Fr. < L. *sociabilis* < *sociare*, to associate < *socius*: see ff.] **1.** enjoying or requiring the

company of others; fond of companionship; gregarious **2.** friendly or agreeable, esp. in an easy, informal way; affable **3.** characterized by pleasant, informal conversation and companionship [a *sociable* evening] —*n.* ☆a social, esp. a church social —**so′cia·ble·ness** *n.* —**so′cia·bly** *adv.*

so·cial (sō′shəl) *adj.* [< Fr. or L.: Fr. *social* < L. *socialis* < *socius*, companion, akin to *sequi*, to follow < IE. base **sekw-*, to follow, whence OE. *secg*, a man, warrior] **1.** of or having to do with human beings living together as a group in a situation in which their dealings with one another affect their common welfare [*social* consciousness, *social* problems] **2.** living in this way; gregarious [man as a *social* being] **3.** of or having to do with the ranks or activities of society, specif. the more exclusive or fashionable of these [a *social* event] **4.** getting along well with others; sociable [a *social* nature] **5.** of, for, or involving friends, companionship, or sociability [a *social* club] **6.** offering material aid, counseling services, group recreational activities, etc. to those who need it; of or engaged in welfare work [a *social* worker or agency] **7.** living or associating in groups or communities [the ant is a *social* insect] **8.** [Now Rare] of or between allies or confederates [a *social* war] **9.** *Bot.* growing in clumps or masses —*n.* an informal gathering of people for recreation or amusement; party —**so′cial·ly** *adv.*

☆**social climber** a person who tries to improve his social status by seeking acquaintanceship with distinguished or wealthy people

social contract (or **compact**) in the theories of certain political philosophers, as Locke, Rousseau, etc., the agreement among individuals uniting for various reasons, by which organized society was begun and sets of regulations were instituted to govern interrelations of members

social dancing *same as* BALLROOM DANCING

Social Democrat a member or adherent of a Social Democratic Party —**Social Democracy** —**Social Democratic**

Social Democratic Party 1. a German Marxist political party formed in 1875 **2.** any of various similar political parties in other countries, advocating a gradual transition from capitalism to socialism

social disease any venereal disease: see VENEREAL

social insurance any insurance program undertaken by a government to provide income or payments to persons who are unemployed, disabled, elderly, etc.

so·cial·ism (sō′shəl iz′m) *n.* **1.** any of various theories or systems of the ownership and operation of the means of production and distribution by society or the community rather than by private individuals, with all members of society or the community sharing in the work and the products **2.** [*often* S-] *a)* political movement for establishing such a system *b)* the doctrines, methods, etc. of the Socialist parties **3.** the stage of society, in Marxist doctrine, coming between the capitalist stage and the communist stage (see COMMUNISM, sense 2), in which private ownership of the means of production and distribution has been eliminated

so·cial·ist (-ist) *n.* **1.** an advocate or supporter of socialism **2.** [S-] a member of a Socialist Party —*adj.* **1.** of, characteristic of, or like socialism or socialists **2.** advocating or supporting socialism **3.** [S-] of or having to do with a Socialist Party Also **so′cial·is′tic** —**so′cial·is′ti·cal·ly** *adv.*

Socialist Party a political party based on the principles of socialism advocated by Marx and Engels; specif., the U.S. political party formed in 1901 from earlier parties, under the leadership of Eugene V. DEBS

☆**so·cial·ite** (sō′shə līt′) *n.* a person who is prominent in fashionable society

so·ci·al·i·ty (sō′shē al′ə tē) *n.* [L. *socialitas*] **1.** the quality or state of being social or sociable; sociability **2.** *pl.* -**ties** the trait or tendency in individuals to join together in groups and associate with one another

so·cial·ize (sō′shə līz′) *vt.* -**ized′, -iz′ing 1.** to make social; adjust to or make fit for cooperative group living **2.** to adapt or make conform to the common needs of a social group **3.** to subject to governmental ownership and control; nationalize **4.** to cause to become socialist —☆*vi.* to take part in social activity —**so′cial·i·za′tion** *n.* —**so′cial·iz′er** *n.*

socialized medicine any system supplying complete medical and hospital care, through public funds, for all the people in a community, district, or nation

social science 1. the study of people living together in groups, as families, tribes, communities, etc. **2.** any of several studies, as history, economics, civics, etc., dealing with the structure of society and the activity of its members —**social scientist**

social secretary a secretary employed by an individual to handle his social appointments and correspondence

☆**social security** any system by which a group provides for those of its members who may be in need; specif. in the U.S., a Federal system of old age, unemployment, or disability insurance for various categories of employed and dependent persons, financed by a fund maintained jointly by employees, employers, and the government

social service *same as* SOCIAL WORK —**so′cial-serv′ice** *adj.*

social settlement *same as* SETTLEMENT (sense 6)

☆**social studies** a course of study, esp. in elementary and secondary schools, including history, civics, geography, etc.

social welfare 1. the welfare of society, esp. of those segments of society that are underprivileged or disadvantaged because of poverty, poor education, unemployment, etc. **2.** *same as* SOCIAL WORK

social work any service or activity designed to promote the welfare of the community and the individual, as through counseling services, health clinics, recreation halls and playgrounds, aid for the needy, the aged, the physically handicapped, etc. —**social worker**

so·ci·e·tal (sə sī′ə t′l) *adj.* of or pertaining to society; social —**so·ci′e·tal·ly** *adv.*

so·ci·e·ty (sə sī′ə tē) *n., pl.* **-ties** [MFr. *société* < L. *societas* < *socius*, companion: see SOCIAL] **1.** a group of persons regarded as forming a single community, esp. as forming a distinct social or economic class **2.** the system or condition of living together as a community in such a group [an agrarian *society*] **3.** all people, collectively, regarded as constituting a community of related, interdependent individuals [a law for the good of *society*] **4.** company or companionship [to seek another's *society*] **5.** one's friends or associates **6.** any organized group of people joined together because of work, interests, etc. in common [a medical *society*] **7.** *a)* a group of persons regarded or regarding itself as a dominant class, usually because of wealth, birth, education, etc. [her debut into *society*] *b)* the conduct, standards, activities, etc. of this class **8.** a group of animals or plants living together in a single environment and regarded as constituting a homogeneous unit or entity —*adj.* of or characteristic of society (*n. 7 a*) [the *society* page of a newspaper]

Society Islands group of islands in the South Pacific, constituting a division of French Polynesia: c.650 sq. mi.; pop. 75,000; chief town, Papeete

Society of Friends a Christian religious sect founded in England c.1650 by George Fox: the Friends have no formal creed, rites, liturgy, or priesthood, and reject violence in human relations, including war: see QUAKER

Society of Jesus *see* JESUIT

society verse [transl. of Fr. *vers de société*] light, witty, polished poetry

So·cin·i·an·ism (sō sin′ē ən iz'm) *n.* the theological doctrines of Faustus Socinus, denying the divinity of Jesus, the Trinity, etc., and explaining sin and salvation rationalistically —**So·cin′i·an** *n., adj.*

So·ci·nus (sō sī′nəs), **Faus·tus** (fôs′təs) (L. name of *Fausto Sozzini*) 1539–1604; It. religious reformer, in Poland after 1579

so·ci·o- (sō′sē ō′, -shē-; -ə) [Fr. < L. *socius*, companion: see SOCIAL] *a combining form meaning* social, society, sociological [*socioeconomic*]

so·ci·o·cul·tu·ral (sō′sē ō kul′chər əl, -shē-) *adj.* of or involving both social and cultural factors

☆**so·ci·o·e·co·nom·ic** (-ē′kə näm′ik, -ek′ə-) *adj.* of or involving both social and economic factors

so·ci·o·gram (sō′sē ə gram′, sō′shē-) *n.* [SOCIO- + -GRAM] *Sociology* a diagram designed to indicate from answers to sociometric questions how individuals in a group feel toward each other

sociol. 1. sociological **2.** sociology

so·ci·o·log·i·cal (sō′sē ə läj′i k′l, -shē-) *adj.* **1.** of or having to do with human society, its organization, needs, development, etc. **2.** of sociology Also **so′ci·o·log′ic** —**so′ci·o·log′i·cal·ly** *adv.*

so·ci·ol·o·gy (sō′sē äl′ə jē, -shē-) *n.* [Fr. *sociologie* (coined by COMTE): see SOCIO- & -LOGY] **1.** the science of human society and of social relations, organization, and change; specif., the study of the beliefs, values, interrelationships, etc. of societal groups and of the principles or processes governing social phenomena **2.** *same as* SYNECOLOGY —**so′ci·ol′o·gist** *n.*

so·ci·om·e·try (-äm′ə trē) *n.* [SOCIO- + -METRY] **1.** the quantitative study of group relationships ☆**2.** a technique for measuring what members of a group perceive, think, and feel about other members of the group —**so′ci·o·met′ric** (-ə met′rik) *adj.*

so·ci·o·path (sō′sē ə path′, -shē-) *n.* [SOCIO- + (PSYCHO)-PATH] a psychopathic personality whose behavior is aggressively antisocial —**so′ci·o·path′ic** *adj.*

so·ci·o·po·lit·i·cal (sō′sē ō pə lit′i k′l, -shē-) *adj.* of or involving both social and political factors

sock¹ (säk) *n.* [ME. *socke* < OE. *socc* < L. *soccus*, type of light, low-heeled shoe] **1.** a light shoe worn by comic characters in ancient Greek and Roman drama **2.** comedy or the muse of comedy **3.** *pl.* **socks, sox** a short stocking reaching only part way to the knee **4.** *shortened form of* WINDSOCK —☆**sock in** to ground (an aircraft) or close (an airfield) as because of fog: usually in the passive voice

sock² (säk) *vt.* [Early ModE. < cant] [Slang] to hit or strike with force, esp. with the fist —*n.* [Slang] a blow —*adv.* [Slang] directly; squarely —☆**sock away** to set aside (money), esp. as savings

☆**sock·dol·a·ger, sock·dol·o·ger** (säk däl′ə jər) *n.* [metathetic alteration (after prec.) < DOXOLOGY (in sense of "conclusion") + -ER] [Old Slang] **1.** something so effective or forceful as to be final or decisive, as a heavy blow; finisher **2.** something outstanding or very large

sock·et (säk′it) *n.* [ME. *soket*, spearhead shaped like a plowshare < Anglo-Fr., dim. < OFr. *soc*, plowshare < Gaul. *soccus, plowshare, orig., pig's snout (hence, that which roots out) < IE. *suk-, var. of *su-, SOW¹] a hollow piece or part into which something fits [the *socket* for a light bulb, of the eye, of the hipbone, etc.] —*vt.* to furnish with or fit into a socket

socket wrench a wrench with a socket that fits over a nut or bolt of a specific size and shape

sock·eye (säk′ī′) *n.* [altered < Salish *suk-kegh*] a red salmon (*Oncorhynchus nerka*) of the N Pacific, often canned

☆**sock·o** (säk′ō) *adj.* [< SOCK²] [Slang] very popular, impressive, or successful

so·cle (säk′'l, sōk′-) *n.* [Fr. < It. *zoccolo*, pedestal, wooden shoe < L. *socculus*, dim. of *soccus*, SOCK¹] *Archit.* a projecting foundation piece, as for a column, wall, statue, etc.

So·co·tra (sō kō′trə) island of Southern Yemen, in the Indian Ocean, off the E tip of Africa: 1,400 sq. mi.; pop. c.12,000

Soc·ra·tes (säk′rə tēz′) 470?–399 B.C.; Athenian philosopher & teacher —**So·crat·ic** (sə krat′ik, sō-) *adj., n.*

Socratic irony pretense of ignorance in a discussion to expose the fallacies in the opponent's logic

Socratic method the dialectical method of teaching or discussion used by Socrates, involving the asking of a series of easily answered questions that inevitably lead the answerer to a logical conclusion foreseen by the questioner

sod¹ (säd) *obs. pt. of* SEETHE

sod² (säd) *n.* [ME., prob. < MDu. or MLowG. *sode*, akin to OFris. *sada, satha*] **1.** a surface layer of earth containing grass plants with their matted roots; turf; sward **2.** a piece of this layer —*vt.* **sod′ded, sod′ding** to cover with sod or sods —**the old sod** one's native land: used esp. by the Irish —**under the sod** dead and buried

sod³ (säd) *n.* [clip of SODOMITE] [Brit. Slang] *same as* BUGGER

so·da (sō′də) *n.* [ML. (or It. or Sp.) < Ar. *suwwād*, a plant burned to produce soda] **1.** *a)* sodium oxide, Na₂O *b) same as:* (1) SODIUM BICARBONATE (2) SODIUM CARBONATE (3) SODIUM HYDROXIDE **2.** *a) same as* SODA WATER (sense 1) *b)* [Chiefly East] a drink of soda water flavored with syrup ☆*c)* a confection of soda water flavored with syrup, fruit, etc. and served with ice cream in it ☆**3.** in faro, the card turned up in the dealing box before play starts

soda ash crude sodium carbonate (sense 1)

☆**soda biscuit 1.** a biscuit made with baking soda and sour milk or buttermilk **2.** [Chiefly Brit.] *same as* SODA CRACKER

☆**soda cracker** a light, crisp cracker, usually salted, prepared from dough made of flour, water, and leavening, orig. baking soda and cream of tartar

☆**soda fountain 1.** a counter fitted with equipment for making and serving soft drinks, sodas, milkshakes, sundaes, etc. **2.** an apparatus for making soda water, with faucets for drawing it off

☆**soda jerk** [Slang] a person who works at a soda fountain: also **soda jerk·er** (jur′kər)

soda lime a white, powdery mixture of sodium hydroxide and calcium oxide, used as a chemical reagent and as an absorbent for moisture and acid gases

so·da·lite (sōd′'l it′) *n.* [SODA + -LITE] a silicate of sodium and aluminum with some chlorine, Na₄Al₃Si₃O₁₂Cl, that somewhat resembles the feldspars

so·dal·i·ty (sō dal′ə tē) *n., pl.* **-ties** [L. *sodalitas* < *sodalis*, companion: for IE. base see ETHICAL] **1.** fellowship; companionship **2.** an association or brotherhood **3.** *R.C.Ch.* a lay society for devotional or charitable activity

☆**soda pop** a flavored, carbonated soft drink, esp. as sold in tightly capped bottles or in cans

soda water **1.** *a)* water charged under pressure with carbon dioxide gas, used in ice-cream sodas, as a chaser, etc. *b) same as* SODA POP **2.** formerly, an effervescent solution of water, acid, and sodium bicarbonate

sod·den (säd′'n) *obs. pp. of* SEETHE —*adj.* **1.** formerly, boiled or steeped **2.** filled with moisture; soaked through **3.** heavy or soggy as a result of improper baking or cooking, as bread **4.** dull or stupefied, as from overindulgence in liquor —*vt., vi.* to make or become sodden —**sod′den·ly** *adv.* —**sod′den·ness** *n.*

so·di·um (sō′dē əm) *n.* [ModL.: so named (1807) by Sir H. DAVY < SODA] a soft, silver-white, alkaline metallic chemical element having a waxlike consistency: it is found in nature only in combined form and is extremely active chemically: symbol, Na; at. wt., 22.9898; at. no., 11; sp. gr., 0.971; melt. pt., 97.5°C; boil. pt., 883°C

sodium benzoate a sweet, odorless, white powder, C₆H₅COONa, the sodium salt of benzoic acid, used as a food preservative, antiseptic, etc.

sodium bicarbonate a white, crystalline compound, NaHCO₃, used in baking powder, as an antacid, etc.

sodium bromide a white, crystalline compound, NaBr, used in medicine as a sedative and in photography to produce silver bromide

sodium carbonate 1. the anhydrous sodium salt of carbonic acid, Na₂CO₃ **2.** any of the hydrated carbonates of sodium; esp., *same as* SAL SODA

sodium chlorate a colorless, crystalline salt, NaClO₃, used as an oxidizing agent in matches, explosives, etc.

sodium chloride common salt, NaCl

sodium cyanide a white, highly poisonous salt, NaCN, used in electroplating, as an insecticide, etc.

sodium dichromate a red, crystalline salt, Na₂Cr₂O₇, used as an oxidizing agent, corrosion inhibitor, antiseptic, etc.

sodium fluo·ro·ac·e·tate (floor'ō as'ə tāt', flôr'-, floo'ər ō-) a powder, CH₂FCOONa, used as a rodent poison

sodium hydroxide a white deliquescent substance, NaOH, in the form of powder, flakes, sticks, etc.: it is a strong caustic base, widely used in chemistry, oil refining, etc.

sodium hyposulfite same as: 1. HYDROSULFITE (sense 2) 2. SODIUM THIOSULFATE

sodium nitrate a clear, odorless, crystalline salt, NaNO₃, used in manufacturing nitric acid, sodium nitrite, explosives, fertilizers, etc., and as an oxidizing agent

sodium pentothal same as THIOPENTAL SODIUM

sodium perborate a white, odorless crystalline compound, NaBO₃·4H₂O, used chiefly as a bleaching and oxidizing agent and in germicides, deodorants, etc.

sodium peroxide a yellowish-white powder, Na₂O₂, used as an antiseptic, bleaching and oxidizing agent, etc.

sodium phosphate any of three clear, crystalline sodium salts of phosphoric acid, widely used in industry

sodium propionate a transparent, almost odorless, deliquescent, crystalline compound, C₃H₅O₂Na, used as a mold preventive, esp. in foods

sodium sulfate a white, crystalline salt, Na₂SO₄, used in medicine and in the making of dyes, glass, etc.

sodium thiosulfate a white, crystalline salt, Na₂S₂O₃, used as an antichlor, as a fixing agent in photography, etc.: popularly but wrongly called (sodium) hyposulfite or hypo

so·di·um-va·por lamp (sō'dē əm vā'pər) an electric lamp used for street lighting, fitted with two electrodes and filled with sodium vapor which gives off a soft yellow light

Sod·om (säd'əm) [LL.(Ec.) Sodoma < Gr.(Ec.) Sodoma < Heb. s'dhom] Bible a city destroyed by fire together with a neighboring city, Gomorrah, because of the sinfulness of the people: Gen. 18-19

Sod·om·ite (-īt') n. [ME. < OFr. < LL.(Ec.) Sodomita < Gr.(Ec.) Sodomita] 1. an inhabitant of Sodom 2. [s-] a person who practices sodomy

sod·om·y (-ē) n. [ME. sodomie < Sodome, SODOM] any sexual intercourse held to be abnormal, as bestiality; specif., anal intercourse between two male persons

Soekarno, Soemba, Soembawa, Soenda Islands, Soerabaja, Soerakarta former sp. of SUKARNO, SUMBA, SUMBAWA, SUNDA ISLANDS, SURABAJA, SURAKARTA

so·ev·er (sō ev'ər) adv. [see SO¹ & EVER] 1. in any way; to any extent or degree (usually following how and an adjective) [how dark soever the night may be] 2. of any kind; at all; whatever [no rest soever]

-so·ev·er (sō ev'ər) a combining form added for emphasis or generalization to who, what, when, where, how, etc., and meaning any (person, thing, time, place, or manner) of all those possible

so·fa (sō'fə) n. [Fr. < Ar. ṣuffah, a bench, cushion] an upholstered couch, usually of spring construction, with fixed back and arms

sofa bed a sofa that can be opened into a double bed

☆**so·far** (sō'fär) n. [< so(und) f(ixing) a(nd) r(anging)] a system for locating an underwater explosion, specif. one set off as a distress signal, by calculations of the time the sound vibrations take to reach several shore stations

sof·fit (säf'it) n. [Fr. soffite < It. soffitta < VL. *suffictus, for L. suffixus: see SUFFIX] 1. the horizontal underside of an eave, cornice, etc. 2. the intrados of an arch or vault

So·fi·a (sō'fē ə, sō fē'ə; Bulg. sô'fē yä') capital of Bulgaria, in the W part: pop. 801,000: also Bulg. **So'fi·ya'**

S. of Sol. Song of Solomon

soft (sôft, säft) adj. [ME. < OE. softe, gentle, quiet < sefte, akin to G. sanft < IE. base *sem-, together, together with, whence SAME: basic sense "fitting, friendly, suited to"] 1. giving way easily under pressure, as a feather pillow or moist clay 2. easily cut, marked, shaped, or worn away, as pine wood or pure gold 3. not hard for its kind; not as hard as is normal, desirable, etc. [soft butter] 4. smooth or fine to the touch; not rough, harsh, or coarse 5. a) bland; not acid, sour, or sharp b) easy to digest because free from roughage: said of a diet 6. nonalcoholic: said of drinks 7. having in solution few or none of the mineral salts that interfere with the lathering and cleansing properties of soap: said of water 8. mild, gentle, or temperate, as a breeze, the weather, climate, etc. 9. a) weak or delicate; not strong or vigorous; esp., not able to endure hardship, as because of easy living b) having flabby muscles 10. requiring little effort; not difficult; easy [a soft job] 11. a) kind or gentle, esp. to the point of weakness; not severe; lenient or compassionate b) easily impressed, influenced, or imposed upon 12. not bright, intense, or glaring; subdued: said of color or light 13. showing little contrast or distinctness; not sharp in lines, tones, focus, etc., as a photograph 14. gentle; low; not loud or harsh: said of sound 15. Finance a) unstable and declining: said of a market, prices, etc. b) long-term at low interest: said of a loan 16. Mil. above ground and vulnerable: said of military targets or bases 17. Phonet. a) sibilant: said of c and g, as in citrus and germ b) lenis, or lenis and voiced c) palatalized, as certain consonants in

Slavic languages 18. Radiology of low penetrating power: said of X-rays —adv. softly; gently; quietly —n. something soft; soft part —interj. [Archaic] 1. be quiet! hush! 2. slow up! stop! —**be soft on** 1. to treat gently and without harshness 2. to feel affectionate or amorous toward —**soft in the head** stupid or foolish

SYN.—**soft**, in this connotation, implies an absence or reduction of all that is harsh, rough, too intense, etc., so as to be pleasing to the senses [soft colors, a soft voice]; **bland** implies such an absence of irritation, stimulation, pungency, etc. as to be soothing, unexciting, and hence, sometimes, uninteresting [bland foods, climate, etc.]; **mild** applies to that which is not as rough, harsh, irritating, etc. as it might be [a mild cigarette, criticism, etc.]; **gentle**, often equivalent to **mild**, carries a more positive connotation of being pleasantly soothing or tranquil [a gentle breeze, voice, etc.] —ANT. harsh, rough

☆**soft·ball** (sôft'bôl', säft'-) n. 1. a game like baseball played on a smaller diamond and with a larger and softer ball, for seven innings 2. the ball used

soft-boiled (-boild') adj. boiled only a short time so that the yolk is still soft: said of an egg

soft chancre same as CHANCROID

soft coal same as BITUMINOUS COAL

soft-cov·er (-kuv'ər) n. same as PAPERBACK —adj. bound as a paperback

soft drink a nonalcoholic, esp. carbonated drink

sof·ten (sôf'n, säf'-) vt., vi. [ME. softnen: see SOFT & -EN] 1. to make or become soft or softer 2. to weaken the resistance or opposition of

sof·ten·er (-ər) n. something that softens, as a) a positively charged compound added to water in treating fabrics to make them softer and fluffier: in full **fabric softener** b) shortened form of WATER SOFTENER

softening of the brain 1. degeneration of the brain tissues into a soft, fatty substance 2. [Colloq.] loss of mind

soft-finned (sôft'find') adj. Zool. having fins with soft rods or rays instead of hard spines

soft-goods (-goodz') n.pl. goods that last a relatively short time, esp. textile products: also **soft goods**

soft-head·ed (-hed'id) adj. stupid or foolish —**soft'head'ed·ly** adv. —**soft'head'ed·ness** n.

soft-heart·ed (-härt'id) adj. 1. full of compassion or tenderness 2. not strict or severe, as in discipline or authority —**soft'heart'ed·ly** adv. —**soft'heart'ed·ness** n.

soft·ie (sôf'tē) n. [Colloq.] var. of SOFTY

☆**soft landing** a safe landing, as of a spacecraft on the moon, in which the craft and its contents remain unharmed —**soft'-land'** vi., vt.

soft palate the soft, fleshy part at the rear of the roof of the mouth; velum

soft-ped·al (-ped'l) vt. -aled or -alled, -al·ing or -al·ling 1. to soften or dampen the tone of (a musical instrument) by use of a special pedal 2. [Colloq.] to make less emphatic, less obtrusive, less conspicuous, etc.; tone down; play down

soft pedal a pedal used to soften or dampen the tone of a musical instrument, as a piano or harp

soft rot any of various plant diseases, characterized by watery decay of rhizomes, roots, fruits, etc. and caused by any of numerous fungi or bacteria

☆**soft sell** selling that relies on subtle inducement or suggestion rather than high-pressure salesmanship —**soft'-sell'** adj.

☆**soft-shell** (-shel') adj. 1. having a soft shell 2. having an unhardened shell as the result of recent molting Also **soft'-shelled'** —n. a soft-shell animal; esp., a crab that has recently molted

☆**soft-shell clam** an edible clam (Mya arenaria) of the E coast of N. America, having elongated siphons and a chalky, white shell

☆**soft-shelled turtle** any of various aquatic turtles (family Trionychidae) of N. America, Asia, and Africa, with a soft, oval, leathery shell; esp., a N. American genus (Trionyx) common in the Mississippi drainage

soft-shoe (-shoo') adj. designating a kind of tap dancing done without metal taps on the shoes

☆**soft shoulder** soft ground along the edge of a highway

soft-soap (-sōp') vt. 1. to apply soft soap to 2. [Colloq.] to flatter —**soft'-soap'er** n.

soft soap 1. soap in liquid or semifluid form 2. [Colloq.] flattery or smooth talk

soft-spo·ken (-spō'k'n) adj. 1. speaking or spoken with a soft, low voice 2. smooth; ingratiating; suave

☆**soft touch** [Slang] a person who is easily persuaded, esp. to give or lend money

soft·ware (-wer') n. ☆the programs, data, routines, etc. for use in a digital computer, as distinguished from the physical components: cf. HARDWARE (sense 3 b)

soft wheat a kind of wheat with low protein content and soft kernels, yielding a flour used in pastries, etc.

soft·wood (-wood') n. 1. a) any light, easily cut wood b) any tree yielding such wood 2. Forestry the wood of any gymnospermous tree, as a pine, spruce, fir, etc.

soft·y (sôf'tē, säf'-) n., pl. soft'ies [Colloq.] 1. a person who is overly sentimental or trusting 2. a person who lacks physical stamina or vigor

Sog·di·an (säg′dē ən) *n.* **1.** any of an Iranian people who lived in Sogdiana **2.** their extinct Iranian language

Sog·di·a·na (säg′dē an′ə) ancient region in C Asia, between the Oxus & Jaxartes rivers

sog·gy (säg′ē, sôg′ē) *adj.* **-gi·er, -gi·est** [< obs. *sog*, damp, boggy place, prob. < or akin to ON. *sog*, lit., a sucking < base of SUCK] **1.** saturated with moisture or liquid; soaked **2.** moist and heavy; sodden [*soggy cake*] **3.** dull, heavy, and boring —**sog′gi·ly** *adv.* —**sog′gi·ness** *n.*

So·ho (sō′hō, sō hō′) district in Westminster, C London: noted for its foreign restaurants, night life, etc.

‡**soi-di·sant** (swà dē zän′) *adj.* [Fr., lit., self-saying] so-called by oneself; self-styled

‡**soi·gné** (swà nyā′) *adj.* [Fr., pp. of *soigner*, to care for < ML. (Gallic) *soniare* < *sonium*, care < Frank. *sunnja*] **1.** well-cared for or attended to **2.** neat; tidy; well-groomed —**soi·gnée′** (-nyā′) *fem.*

soil¹ (soil) *n.* [ME. *soile* < Anglo-Fr. *soil*, for OFr. *suel* < L. *solum*, floor, ground, soil] **1.** the surface layer of earth, supporting plant life **2.** any place for growth or development **3.** land; country; territory [*native soil*] **4.** ground or earth [*barren soil*] —**the soil** life and work on a farm —**soil′less** *adj.*

soil² (soil) *vt.* [ME. *soilen* < OFr. *soillier* < VL. *suculare* < L. *suculus*, dim. of *sus*, pig: see SOW¹] **1.** to make dirty, esp. on the surface **2.** to smirch or stain **3.** to bring disgrace upon **4.** to corrupt or defile; sully —*vi.* to become soiled or dirty —*n.* [ME. *soile* < OFr. *soile*, pig sty < L. *suile* < *sus*] **1.** a soiled spot; stain; smirch **2.** manure used for fertilizing **3.** excrement, sewage, refuse, etc. **4.** a soiling or being soiled

soil³ (soil) *vt.* [altered < ? OFr. *saoler* < L. *satullare*, to satiate < *satullus*, filled (with food), dim. of *satur*: see SATURATE] **1.** to feed (livestock) on soilage **2.** to purge (livestock) by means of green food

soil·age (-ij) *n.* [prec. + -AGE] green crops cultivated for fodder

☆**soil bank** a Federal program under which subsidies are paid to farmers to stop growing certain surplus crops and to enrich the idle land by various methods

soil conservation the protection of fertile topsoil from erosion by wind and water and the replacement of nutrients in the soil, as by means of cover crops, terracing, contour farming, crop rotation, etc.

soil pipe a pipe for carrying off liquid waste from toilets

soil·ure (soil′yoor) *n.* [ME. *soylure* < MFr. *soilleure* < *soillier*: see SOIL²] [Archaic] **1.** a soiling, dirtying, or sullying **2.** the result of this; stain; blot

soi·ree, soi·rée (swä rā′) *n.* [Fr. *soirée* < *soir*, evening < L. *sero*, at a late hour < *serus*, late: see SEREIN] a party or gathering in the evening

so·journ (sō′jurn; *also, for v.*, sō jurn′) *vi.* [ME. *sojournen* < OFr. *sojorner* < VL. *subdiurnare* < L. *sub-*, under + *diurnus*, of a day: see JOURNEY] to live somewhere temporarily, as on a visit; stay for a while —*n.* a brief or temporary stay; visit —**so′journ·er** *n.*

soke (sōk) *n.* [ME. < ML. *soca* < OE. *socn*, jurisdiction, prosecution < base of *secan* (< *sokjan*), to SEEK] *Eng. History* **1.** the right to hold court and dispense justice within a given territory **2.** the territory under the jurisdiction of a court

so·kol (sō′kôl) *n.* [Czech, lit., falcon] an organization promoting physical health, esp. in gymnastics

So·ko·to (sō′ko to′) former kingdom in WC Africa, now in N Nigeria: c.40,000 sq. mi.; pop. 3,193,000

Sokotra *var. of* SOCOTRA

Sol (säl) [ME. < L. < **sawol*, **saol* < IE. base **sāwel*, whence Gr. *hēlios*, Goth. *sauil*, sun] **1.** *Rom. Myth.* the sun god: identified with the Greek god Helios **2.** the sun personified

sol¹ (sōl; *Sp.* sôl) *n., pl.* **sols**; *Sp.* **so′les** (sô′les) [Sp., lit., sun: from the radiant sun used as a device on one side] the monetary unit of Peru: see MONETARY UNITS, table

sol² (sōl) *n.* [< ML. *sol(ve)*: see GAMUT] *Music* a syllable representing the fifth tone of the diatonic scale: see SOLFEGGIO

sol³ (säl, sōl) *n.* [< (HYDRO)SOL] a colloidal dispersion in a liquid

Sol. **1.** Solicitor **2.** Solomon

sol. **1.** soluble **2.** solution

‡**so·la** (sō′lä) *adj.* [L.] *fem. of* SOLUS

so·la (sō′lə) *n. alt. pl. of* SOLUM

sol·ace (säl′is) *n.* [ME. < OFr. *solaz* < L. *solacium* < *solari*, to comfort < IE. base **sel-*, favorable, in good spirits, whence OE. *sæl:* cf. SILLY] **1.** an easing of grief, loneliness, discomfort, etc. **2.** something that eases or relieves; comfort; consolation; relief Also **sol′ace·ment** (-mənt) —*vt.* **-aced, -ac·ing 1.** to give solace to; comfort; console **2.** to lessen or allay (grief, sorrow, etc.) —SYN. see COMFORT —**sol′ac·er** *n.*

so·lan (goose) (sō′lən) [Scot. < ME. *soland* < ON. *sūla*, gannet + -*and*, *ǫnd*, a duck, akin to OE. *ænid*, G. *ente* < IE. **anet-*, whence L. *anas*] *same as* GANNET

so·la·nine (sō′lə nēn′, -nin) *n.* [Fr. < L. *solanum*, nightshade + Fr. -*ine*, -INE⁴] a complex glycosidic alkaloid, C₄₅H₇₃NO₁₅, found in potato sprouts and various plants of the nightshade family: also **so′la·nin** (-nin)

so·la·num (sō lā′nəm) *n.* [L., nightshade] any of a large genus (*Solanum*) of trees, vines, shrubs, and plants of the

nightshade family: most are poisonous, but a few are cultivated for food, as the potato, eggplant, etc.

so·lar (sō′lər) *adj.* [L. *solaris* < *sol*, the sun: see SOL] **1.** of or having to do with the sun **2.** produced by or coming from the sun [*solar energy*] **3.** depending upon the sun's light or energy [*solar heating*] **4.** fixed or measured by the earth's motion with relation to the sun [*mean solar time*] **5.** *Astrol.* under the influence of the sun

☆**solar battery** an assembly of one or more photovoltaic cells (**solar cells**) used to convert the radiant energy of sunlight into electric power

solar constant the mean amount of solar radiation received normally by a unit area just outside the earth's atmosphere, equal to c.1.94 gram calories per square centimeter per minute

solar cycle a period of time, averaging c.11 years, during which certain phenomena, as maximum sunspot activity, recur on the sun

solar day *Law* the period from sunrise to sunset

solar flare a sudden, short-lived increase of intensity in the light of the sun, usually near sunspots, often accompanied by a large increase in cosmic rays, X-rays, etc. and by resultant magnetic storms

solar furnace a furnace for heating, smelting, etc. that uses concave mirrors to concentrate the sun's rays

so·lar·i·um (sō ler′ē əm, sə-) *n., pl.* **-i·a** (-ə) [L., sundial, place exposed to the sun < *sol*, the sun: see SOL] a glassed-in porch, room, etc. where people sun themselves, as in treating illness

so·lar·ize (sō′lə rīz′) *vt.* **-ized′, -iz′ing 1.** to affect by exposing to the light and heat of the sun **2.** to overexpose (a photographic film or plate) —*vi.* to become injured by such overexposure —**so′lar·i·za′tion** *n.*

solar plexus 1. a network of nerves in the abdominal cavity behind the stomach and in front of the uppermost part of the aorta, containing ganglia that send nerve impulses to the abdominal viscera **2.** [Colloq.] the area of the belly just below the sternum

solar prominences nearly vertical sheets of luminous gases, as hydrogen, sodium, etc., extending beyond the solar chromosphere

solar sail a thin, lightweight surface designed to use the pressure of sunlight to stabilize, propel, etc. an artificial satellite in space

solar system the sun and all the heavenly bodies that revolve around it

solar wind streams of ionized gas particles constantly emitted by the sun in all directions at speeds of up to two million miles an hour

solar year *see* YEAR (sense 2)

sol·ate (säl′āt) *vi.* **-at·ed, -at·ing** [SOL³ + -ATE¹] to convert into a sol —**sol·a′tion** *n.*

so·la·ti·um (sō lā′shē əm) *n., pl.* **-ti·a** (-shē ə) [LL. < L., SOLACE] compensation or damages, esp. for injury to the feelings

sold (sōld) *pt. & pp. of* SELL

sol·der (säd′ər) *n.* [ME. *soudre* < OFr. *souldure* < *soulder*, to make solid < L. *solidare* < *solidus*, SOLID] **1.** a metal alloy used when melted for joining or patching metal parts or surfaces: **soft solders** of tin-lead alloys melt easily; **hard** (or **brazing**) **solders** of copper-zinc alloys melt only at red heat **2.** anything that joins or fuses; bond —*vt.* **1.** to join, patch, etc. with solder **2.** to act as a bond between; unite —*vi.* **1.** to become joined or united as by solder **2.** to join things with solder —**sol′der·er** *n.*

sol·der·ing iron (säd′ər in) a pointed metal tool heated, as in a flame or electrically, and used for melting and applying solder

sol·dier (sōl′jər) *n.* [ME. *soldiour* < OFr. *soldier* < *solde*, a coin, pay < LL. *solidus:* see SOLIDUS] **1.** a man serving in an army; member of an army **2.** an enlisted man, as distinguished from one holding a warrant or commission **3.** a man of much military experience or military skill **4.** a person who works zealously for a specified cause **5.** an ant or termite of a caste having an enlarged head and jaws and serving as fighters in defense of the colony —*vi.* **1.** to serve as a soldier **2.** to shirk one's duty, as by making a pretense of working, feigning illness, etc.

sol·dier·ly (-lē) *adj.* of, like, or characteristic of a good soldier —**sol′dier·li·ness** *n.*

soldier of fortune 1. a mercenary soldier, esp. one seeking adventure or excitement **2.** any adventurer

☆**Soldier's Medal** a U.S. military decoration given for deeds of heroism outside of combat

sol·dier·y (-ē) *n., pl.* **-dier·ies 1.** soldiers collectively **2.** a group of soldiers **3.** military science: also **sol′dier·ship′**

sol·do (säl′dō; *It.* sôl′dô) *n., pl.* **-di** (-dē) [It. < LL. *solidus*, SOLIDUS] a former Italian copper coin and unit of money, equal to 1/20 of a lira

sole¹ (sōl) *n.* [ME. < OFr. < VL. **sola*, for L. *solea*, a sandal, sole, kind of fish < *solum*, a sole, base, ground, bottom] **1.** the bottom surface of the foot **2.** the part of a shoe, boot, sock, etc. corresponding to this **3.** the bottom or resting surface of any of several objects, as a golf club, plow, etc. —*vt.* **soled, sol′ing** to furnish (a shoe, etc.) with a sole, esp. a new one

sole² (sōl) *adj.* [ME. < OE. *sol* < L. *solus* < ? IE. **sōlo-* < base **se-*, **s(e)wo-*, apart, whence L. *suus*, one's own] **1.** *a)* without another or others; single; one and only

b) acting, working, etc. alone without help **2.** of or having to do with only one (specified) person or group **3.** given or belonging to no other; not shared or divided; exclusive *[the sole rights to a patent]* **4.** [Archaic] alone; solitary **5.** *Law* unmarried: cf. FEME SOLE —**SYN.** see SINGLE

sole² (sōl) *n.* [ME. < OFr. < VL. *sola,* for L. *solea* (see SOLE¹): so named from its shape] **1.** any of certain sea flatfishes (order Pleuronectiformes) related to the flounders, esp. any of a family (Soleidae) most species of which are highly valued as food **2.** loosely, any of several species of plaice or halibut

sol·e·cism (säl′ə siz′m) *n.* [L. *soloecismus* < Gr. *soloikismos* < *soloikos,* speaking incorrectly < *Soloi,* city in Cilicia, whose dialect was a corrupt form of Attic] **1.** a violation of the conventional usage, grammar, etc. of a language; substandard use of words (Ex.: "We done it" for "We did it"): see also BARBARISM, IMPROPRIETY **2.** a violation of good manners; breach of etiquette **3.** a mistake or impropriety —**sol′e·cist** *n.* —**sol′e·cis′tic** *adj.* —**sol′e·cis′ti·cal·ly** *adv.*

sole·ly (sōl′lē) *adv.* **1.** without another or others; alone *[to be solely to blame]* **2.** only, exclusively, merely, or altogether *[to read solely for pleasure]*

sol·emn (säl′əm) *adj.* [ME. *solemne* < OFr. < L. *sollemnis, sollennis,* yearly, annual, hence religious, solemn (from association with annual religious festivals) < *sollus,* all, entire (for IE. base see SAFE) + *annus,* year] **1.** *a)* observed or done according to ritual or tradition: said esp. of religious holidays, rites, etc. *b)* sacred in character **2.** according to strict form; formal *[a solemn ceremony]* **3.** serious; grave; deeply earnest **4.** arousing feelings of awe; very impressive *[a solemn occasion]* **5.** somber because dark in color —**SYN.** see SERIOUS —**sol′emn·ly** *adv.* —**sol′emn·ness** *n.*

so·lem·ni·fy (sə lem′nə fī′) *vt.* **-fied′, -fy′ing** to make solemn

so·lem·ni·ty (sə lem′nə tē) *n., pl.* **-ties** [ME. *solempnete* < OFr. *solempneté* < L. *sollemnitas*] **1.** solemn ceremony, ritual, observance, etc. **2.** solemn feeling, character, or appearance; serious or awesome quality; gravity **3.** *Law* the formality needed to validate an act, contract, etc.

sol·em·nize (säl′əm nīz′) *vt.* **-nized′, -niz′ing** [ME. *solempnisen* < OFr. *solemniser* < ML. (R.c.) *solemnizare* < L. *sollemnis,* SOLEMN] **1.** to celebrate with formal ceremony or according to ritual **2.** to perform the ceremony of (marriage, etc.) **3.** to make solemn, or serious, grave, etc. —**SYN.** see CELEBRATE —**sol′em·ni·za′tion** *n.* —**sol′em·niz′er** *n.*

Solemn Mass *see* HIGH MASS

so·le·no·cyte (sə lē′nə sit′) *n.* [< Gr. *sōlēn,* a channel + -CYTE] an elongated, tubular flame cell with one or more long flagella, occurring in certain annelids, lancelets, etc.

so·le·no·glyph (-glif′) *n.* [< ModL. Solenoglypha, name of the classification < Gr. *sōlēn,* a channel (in reference to the tubular fangs) + *glyphein,* to carve: for IE. base see CLEAVE¹] any poisonous snake with paired, erectile fangs, a member of the viper family or pit viper family

so·le·noid (sō′lə noid′, säl′ə-) *n.* [Fr. *solénoïde* < Gr. *sōlēn,* a tube, channel (< IE. *tul-* < base *twō-,* whence Sans. *tūṇa,* a quiver) + *eidos,* a form] a coil of wire, usually wound in the form of a helix, that acts like a bar magnet when carrying a current: used in brakes, switches, relays, etc. —**so′le·noi′dal** *adj.*

So·lent (sō′lənt), **The** W part of the channel between the Isle of Wight & the mainland of Hampshire, England: c.15 mi. long: the E part is called *Spithead*

sole·plate (sōl′plāt′) *n.* [SOLE¹ + PLATE] the ironing surface of a flatiron

so·les (sō′les) *n. Sp. pl. of* SOL¹

So·leure (sō lēr′) *Fr. name of* SOLOTHURN

sol-fa (sōl′fä′) *n.* [It. *solfa* < *sol* + *fa:* see GAMUT] **1.** the syllables *do* (formerly *ut*), *re, mi, fa, sol, la, ti* (or *si*), *do* (or *ut*), used to represent the tones of a scale, regardless of its key **2.** the use of these syllables, as in vocal exercises; solfeggio —*vt., vi.* **-faed′** (-fäd′), **-fa′ing** to sing (a scale, phrase or song) to the sol-fa syllables —**sol′-fa′ist** *n.*

sol·fa·ta·ra (sōl′fə tä′rə) *n.* [It. < *solfo,* sulfur < L. *sulfur*] a volcanic vent or fissure giving off only vapors, esp. sulfurous gases

sol·fège (säl fezh′) *n.* [Fr. < It. *solfeggio:* see ff.] **1.** orig. *same as* SOLFEGGIO **2.** the teaching of the essentials of music theory, including tonality, tempo, rhythm, etc.

sol·feg·gio (säl fej′ō, -fej′ē ō′) *n., pl.* **-feg′gios, -feg′gi** (-fej′ē) [It. < *solfa:* see SOL-FA] **1.** voice practice in which scales are sung to the sol-fa syllables; solmization **2.** the use of these syllables in singing, esp. in reading a song, etc. at sight

so·lic·it (sə lis′it) *vt.* [ME. *soliciten* < MFr. *solliciter* < *sollicitare* < *sollicitus:* see SOLICITOUS] **1.** to ask or seek earnestly or pleadingly; appeal to or for *[to solicit aid, to solicit members for donations]* **2.** to tempt or entice (someone) to do wrong **3.** to approach for some immoral purpose, as a prostitute does —*vi.* to solicit someone or something —**SYN.** see BEG —**so·lic′i·tant** (-i tənt) *n., adj.* —**so·lic′i·ta′tion** *n.*

so·lic·i·tor (-ər) *n.* [ME. *solycitour* < MFr. *solliciteur*] **1.** a person who solicits; esp., one who seeks trade, asks for contributions, etc. **2.** in England, a member of the legal profession who is not a barrister: solicitors are not members of the bar and may not plead cases in superior courts ☆**3.** in the U.S., a lawyer serving as official law officer for a city, department, etc. —**SYN.** see LAWYER

☆**solicitor general** *pl.* **solicitors general, solicitor generals 1.** a law officer (in the Department of Justice in the U.S.) serving the national government and ranking next below the attorney general **2.** the chief law officer in some States having no attorney general

so·lic·i·tous (sə lis′ə təs) *adj.* [L. *sollicitus* < *sollus,* whole (for IE. base see SAFE) + *citus,* pp. of *ciere,* to set in motion: see CITE] **1.** showing care, attention, or concern *[solicitous for her welfare]* **2.** showing anxious desire; eager *[solicitous to make friends]* **3.** full of anxiety or apprehension; troubled —**so·lic′i·tous·ly** *adv.* —**so·lic′i·tous·ness** *n.*

so·lic·i·tude (-tōōd′, -tyōōd′) *n.* [ME. < L. *sollicitudo*] **1.** the state of being solicitous; care, concern, etc.; sometimes, excessive care or concern **2.** [*pl.*] causes of care or concern —**SYN.** see CARE

sol·id (säl′id) *adj.* [ME. *solide* < MFr. < L. *solidus*] **1.** tending to keep its form rather than to flow or spread out like a liquid or gas; relatively firm or compact **2.** filled with matter throughout; not hollow **3.** *a)* having the three dimensions of length, breadth, and thickness *[prisms and other solid figures]* *b)* dealing with bodies or figures in three dimensions **4.** *a)* firm, strong, and dependable *[a solid structure]* *b)* substantial, sound, and reliable *[solid reasoning]* *c)* sturdy or vigorous *[a solid build, a solid punch]* **5.** serious; not superficial or trivial *[solid scholarship]* **6.** complete, thoroughgoing, or genuine *[solid satisfaction]* **7.** *a)* having no breaks or divisions *[a solid line of fortifications]* *b)* written or printed without a hyphen *[a solid compound]* **8.** characterized by no pauses or interruptions *[to talk for a solid hour]* **9.** *a)* of one or the same color, material, or consistency throughout *[a solid walnut table]* *b)* consisting of one unalloyed metal throughout; also, containing no more alloy than is necessary to insure hardness: said of gold, etc. ☆**10.** characterized by or showing complete unity; unanimous *[a solid vote]* **11.** thick or dense in appearance or texture *[a solid fog]* **12.** firm or dependable *[a solid friendship]* ☆**13.** [Colloq.] having a firmly favorable or good relationship *[to be in solid with someone]* **14.** [Colloq.] healthful and filling *[a solid meal]* ☆**15.** [Slang] very good; excellent *[a solid dance band]* **16.** *Printing* set without leads between the lines of type —*n.* **1.** a substance that is solid, not a liquid or gas **2.** an object or figure having or represented as having length, breadth, and thickness —**SYN.** see FIRM¹ —**sol′id·ly** *adv.* —**sol′id·ness** *n.*

sol·i·da·go (säl′i dā′gō) *n., pl.* **-gos** [ModL., name of the genus < ML., goldenrod < L. *solidare,* to strengthen (see SOLDER) in reference to its supposed healing powers] *same as* GOLDENROD

solid angle the angle formed by three or more planes meeting in a common point or formed at the vertex of a cone

sol·i·dar·i·ty (säl′ə dar′ə tē) *n., pl.* **-ties** [Fr. *solidarité* < *solidaire:* see SOLID & -ARY] combination or agreement of all elements or individuals, as of a group; complete unity, as of opinion, purpose, interest, feeling, etc. —**SYN.** see UNITY

solid fuel any of various rocket fuels, neither liquid nor gaseous, consisting of a homogeneous base that acts as both fuel and oxidizer or of a composite mixture of fuel and oxidizer: also called **solid propellant**

solid geometry the branch of geometry dealing with solid, or three-dimensional, figures

so·lid·i·fy (sə lid′ə fī′) *vt., vi.* **-fied′, -fy′ing** [Fr. *solidifier:* see SOLID & -FY] **1.** to make or become solid, firm, hard, compact, etc. **2.** to crystallize **3.** to make or become solid, strong, or united —**so·lid′i·fi·ca′tion** *n.*

so·lid·i·ty (-tē) *n.* [L. *soliditas*] the quality or condition of being solid; firmness, soundness, hardness, etc.

solid motor any of various motors using solid fuel

☆**Solid South** those Southern States traditionally regarded as solidly supporting the Democratic Party

sol·id-state (säl′id stāt′) *adj.* **1.** designating or of the branch of physics dealing with the fundamental properties of solids, as structure, binding forces, electrical, magnetic, and optical properties, etc., and with their effects **2.** designating, of, or equipped with electronic devices, as semiconductors, that can control current without heated filaments, moving parts, etc.

sol·i·dus (säl′i dəs) *n., pl.* **sol′i·di** (-dī′) [ME. < LL. < L. *solidus (nummus),* lit., SOLID (coin)] **1.** a gold coin of the Late Roman Empire, valued at about three dollars **2.** a medieval money of account worth twelve denarii: abbreviated **s** in £ s.d. **3.** *a)* a slant line (/), orig. the old long **s** (ſ), used to separate shillings from pence (Ex.: 7/6) *b) same as* VIRGULE

so·lil·o·quize (sə lil′ə kwīz′) *vi.* **-quized′, -quiz′ing** to deliver a soliloquy; talk to oneself —*vt.* to utter in or as a soliloquy —**so·lil′o·quist** (-kwist) *n.*

so·lil·o·quy (-kwē) *n., pl.* **-quies** [LL. *soliloquium* < L.

solus, alone, SOLE[2] + *loqui*, to speak] **1.** an act or instance of talking to oneself **2.** lines in a drama in which a character reveals his thoughts to the audience, but not to the other characters, by speaking as if to himself

So·li·mões (sō'li moins') the upper Amazon, between the Peruvian border & the Negro River: Brazilian name

So·ling·en (zō'liŋ ən) city in W West Germany, in the Ruhr valley of North Rhine-Westphalia: pop. 175,000

sol·ip·sism (säl'ip siz'm) n. [< L. *solus*, alone, SOLE[2] + *ipse*, self + -ISM] **1.** the theory that the self can be aware of nothing but its own experiences and states **2.** the theory that nothing exists or is real but the self —**sol'ip·sis'tic** *adj.* —**sol'ip·sist** n.

sol·i·taire (säl'ə ter') n. [Fr. *solitaire* < L. *solitarius*: see ff.] **1.** orig., a hermit or recluse **2.** a diamond or other gem set by itself, as in a ring **3.** any of many games, esp. card games, played by one person

sol·i·tar·y (säl'ə ter'ē) adj. [ME. < OFr. *solitaire* < L. *solitarius* < *solus*, alone, SOLE[2]] **1.** living or being alone **2.** without others; single; only [a *solitary* example] **3.** characterized by loneliness or lack of companions **4.** lonely; remote; unfrequented [a *solitary* place] **5.** done in solitude **6.** *Bot.* occurring singly, as a flower **7.** *Zool.* living alone or in pairs; not colonial, social, etc. —n., pl. **-tar'ies 1.** a person who lives by himself; esp., a hermit **2.** [Colloq.] same as SOLITARY CONFINEMENT —SYN. see ALONE, SINGLE —**sol'i·tar'i·ly** adv. —**sol'i·tar'i·ness** n.

solitary confinement confinement of a prisoner in isolation from all other prisoners, often in a dungeonlike cell: a form of extra punishment for misconduct

sol·i·tude (säl'ə tōōd', -tyōōd') n. [ME. < MFr. < L. *solitudo* < *solus*, alone, SOLE[2]] **1.** the state of being solitary, or alone; seclusion, isolation, or remoteness **2.** a lonely or secluded place —**sol'i·tu'di·nous** adj.

SYN.—**solitude** refers to the state of one who is completely alone, cut off from all human contact, and sometimes stresses the loneliness of such a condition [the *solitude* of a hermit]; **isolation** suggests physical separation from others, often an involuntary detachment resulting from the force of circumstances [the *isolation* of a forest ranger]; **seclusion** suggests retirement from intercourse with the outside world, as by confining oneself to one's home, a remote place, etc.

sol·ler·et (säl'ə ret', säl'ə ret') n. [MFr. *soleret*, dim. of *soler*, a shoe < *sole*: see SOLE[1]] a kind of shoe worn with a suit of armor, made of hinged steel plates: see ARMOR, illus.

sol·mi·za·tion (säl'mi zā'shən) n. [Fr. *solmisation* < *solmiser*, to sol-fa < *sol* + *mi*: see GAMUT] solfeggio, or any similar use of a system of syllables in singing

so·lo (sō'lō) n., pl. **-los;** for n. 1 & 3, sometimes **-li** (-lē) [It. < L. *solus*, alone, SOLE[2]] **1.** a) a musical piece or passage to be played or sung by one person, with or without accompaniment b) a dance, pantomime, etc., for performance by one person **2.** an airplane flight made by a pilot alone, without an assistant, instructor, etc. **3.** any performance by one person alone **4.** any card game in which each person plays for himself, without a partner —adj. **1.** designed for or performed by a single voice, person, or instrument **2.** performing a solo —adv. without another or others; alone —vi. to perform a solo; esp., to make a solo flight

so·lo·ist (-ist) n. a person who performs a solo

So·lo man (sō'lō) [< *Solo* River in C Java] a type of primitive man (*Homo sapiens soloensis*) known from fossil remains found in Upper Pleistocene deposits in C Java

Sol·o·mon (säl'ə mən) [LL.(Ec.) *Solomon, Salomon* < Gr.(Ec.) *Solomōn, Salomōn* < Heb. *shĕlōmōh*, lit., peaceful < *shālōm*, peace] **1.** a masculine name: dim. *Sol* **2.** *Bible* king of Israel; son & successor of DAVID: he built the 1st Temple and was noted for his wisdom —n. a very wise man; sage —**Sol'o·mon'ic** adj.

Solomon Islands group of islands in the SW Pacific, east of New Guinea: 15,820 sq. mi.; pop. 298,000: Bougainville, Buka, & nearby islands are in the Territory of New Guinea; other islands, including Guadalcanal, constitute a Brit. protectorate (**British Solomon Islands Protectorate**)

Solomon's seal 1. a mystic symbol in the form of a six-pointed star: cf. STAR OF DAVID **2.** [transl. of ModL. *sigillum Salomonis:* so called prob. from starlike markings on the rootstock] any of a genus (*Polygonatum*) of perennial plants of the lily family, with broad, waxy leaves, drooping, greenish flowers, and blue or black berries

So·lon (sō'lən, -län) c.640–559? B.C.; Athenian statesman & lawgiver: framed the democratic laws of Athens —n. [sometimes s-] a wise lawmaker

so long colloq. term for GOODBYE

So·lo·thurn (zō'lō toorn') **1.** canton of NW Switzerland: 305 sq. mi.; pop. 214,000 **2.** its capital: pop. 19,000

sol·stice (säl'stis, sōl'-) n. [ME. < MFr. < L. *solstitium* < *sol*, the sun (see SOL) + *sistere*, to cause to stand still < *stare*, to STAND] **1.** either of two points on the sun's ecliptic at which it is farthest north or farthest south of the equator **2.** the time at which the sun reaches either of these two points: see SUMMER SOLSTICE, WINTER SOLSTICE **3.** a furthest point, turning point, or point of culmination —**sol·sti'tial** (-stish'əl) adj.

sol·u·bil·i·ty (säl'yoo bil'ə tē) n., pl. **-ties 1.** the quality, condition, or extent of being soluble; capability of being dissolved **2.** the amount of a substance that can be dissolved in a given solvent under specified conditions

sol·u·ble (säl'yoo b'l) adj. [ME. < MFr. < L. *solubilis* < *solvere*, to loosen: see SOLVE] **1.** that can be dissolved **2.** capable of being solved or explained —**sol'u·bly** adv.

soluble glass same as WATER GLASS (sense 4)

so·lum (sō'ləm) n., pl. **-lums, -la** (-lə) [ModL. < L., base, soil] the altered soil or material overlying the parent material, often including the A-horizon and the B-horizon

‡so·lus (sō'ləs) adj. [L., SOLE[2]] alone: a stage direction

sol·ute (säl'yōōt, sō'lōōt) n. [< L. *solutus*, pp. of *solvere*, to loosen: see SOLVE] the substance dissolved in a solution —adj. dissolved; in solution

so·lu·tion (sə lōō'shən) n. [ME. *solucion* < OFr. < L. *solutio* < *solutus*: see prec.] **1.** a) the act, method, or process of solving a problem b) the answer to a problem c) an explanation, clarification, etc. [the *solution* of a mystery] **2.** a) the act or process of dispersing one or more liquid, gaseous, or solid substances in another, usually a liquid, so as to form a homogeneous mixture; a dissolving b) the state or fact of being dissolved c) a homogeneous molecular mixture, usually a liquid, so produced **3.** a breaking up or coming to an end; dissolution; break; breach **4.** *Med.* a) the termination of a disease b) the crisis of a disease c) a drug in solution; liquid medicine

So·lu·tre·an, So·lu·tri·an (sə lōō'trē ən) adj. [after *Solutre*, village in France where artifacts were found] designating or of an upper paleolithic culture of Europe, characterized by delicate, laurel-leaf flint points

solv·a·ble (säl'və b'l) adj. **1.** that can be solved **2.** [Now Rare] that can be dissolved —**solv'a·bil'i·ty** n.

sol·vate (säl'vāt) n. [SOLV(ENT) + -ATE[1]] *Chem.* a complex formed by the combining of molecules or ions of a solvent and solute —vt. **-vat·ed, -vat·ing** to convert (molecules or ions) into a solvate —**sol·va'tion** n.

Sol·vay process (säl'vā) [developed by Ernest *Solvay* (1838–1922), Belg. chemist] a process for making soda (sodium carbonate) by treating common salt (sodium chloride) with ammonia and carbon dioxide

solve (sälv) vt. **solved, solv'ing** [ME. *solven* < L. *solvere* (for *se-luere*), to loosen, release, free < *se-*, apart + *luere*, to let go, set free: see SECEDE & LOOSE] **1.** to find or provide a satisfactory answer or explanation for; make clear; explain **2.** to find or provide the correct or a satisfactory solution to (a problem) —**solv'er** n.

sol·ven·cy (säl'vən sē) n. a solvent state or quality

sol·vent (-vənt) adj. [L. *solvens*, prp. of *solvere*, to loosen: see SOLVE] **1.** able to pay all one's debts or meet all financial responsibilities **2.** that dissolves or can dissolve another substance —n. **1.** a substance, usually liquid, that dissolves or can dissolve another substance **2.** something that solves or explains; solution

sol·vol·y·sis (säl väl'ə sis) n. [SOLV(ENT) + -o- + -LYSIS] a chemical interaction, as hydrolysis, between a solute and solvent with the production of new compounds

Sol·way Firth (säl'wā) arm of the Irish Sea, between England & Scotland: c.40 mi. long

Sol·y·man (säl'i mən) same as SULEIMAN

so·ma[1] (sō'mə) n., pl. **so'ma·ta** (-mə tə) [ModL. < Gr. *sōma*, body < IE. *twōmṇ*, something compact, sturdy < base *tĕu-*, to swell, thick, whence THUMB, L. *tumor*, Gr. *sōros*, a heap] the entire body of an animal or plant, with the exception of the germ cells

so·ma[2] (sō'mə) n. [Sans. < IE. base *seu-*, juice, whence OE. *seaw*, sap, L. *sucus*, juice: cf. SUCK] **1.** an intoxicating plant juice referred to in the literature of Vedic ritual **2.** [so called as a supposed source of this juice] an E Indian plant (*Sarcostemma acidum*) of the milkweed family

So·ma·li (sō mä'lē, sə-) n. **1.** pl. **-lis, -li** any member of an Islamic, pastoral people of Somalia and nearby regions **2.** their Eastern Cushitic language

So·ma·li·a (sō mä'lē ə, sə-; -mäl'yə) country of E Africa, on the Indian Ocean & the Gulf of Aden: formed (1960) by the merger of It. Somaliland & Brit. Somaliland: 246,201 sq. mi.; pop. 2,500,000; cap. Mogadishu Also called **Somali Republic**

So·ma·li·land (-land') region in E Africa, including Somalia, French Somaliland, & E Ethiopia

so·mat·ic (sō mat'ik) adj. [Gr. *sōmatikos* < *sōma* (gen. *sōmatos*), body: see SOMA[1]] **1.** of the body, as distinguished from the soul, mind, or psyche; corporeal; physical **2.** *Biol.* of the soma **3.** *Anat., Zool.* of the framework or outer walls of the body, as distinguished from the viscera; parietal —SYN. see BODILY —**so·mat'i·cal·ly** adv.

somatic cell any of the cells of an organism that become differentiated into the tissues, organs, etc. of the body: opposed to GERM CELL

ARABIA

FRENCH SOMALILAND   Gulf of Aden
Djibouti

ETHIOPIA   Somaliland

KENYA   Mogadishu   INDIAN OCEAN

SOMALILAND

so·ma·to- (sō′mə tō, -tə; sō mat′ə-) [< Gr. *sōma* (gen. *sōmatos*), body: see SOMA[1]] *a combining form meaning* body [*somatoplasm*]: also, before a vowel, **somat-**

so·ma·tol·o·gy (sō′mə täl′ə jē) *n.* [SOMATO- + -LOGY] **1.** the science concerned with the properties of organic bodies **2.** the branch of anthropology that deals with the physical nature and characteristics of man —**so′ma·to·log′ic** (-tə läj′ik), **so′ma·to·log′i·cal** *adj.* —**so′ma·to·log′i·cal·ly** *adv.* —**so′ma·tol′o·gist** *n.*

so·ma·to·plasm (sō′mə tə plaz′m′, sō mat′ə-) *n.* [SOMATO- + -PLASM] the body cells collectively as distinguished from germ cells —**so′ma·to·plas′tic** *adj.*

so·ma·to·pleure (-ploor′) *n.* [SOMATO- + Gr. *pleura*, a side] *Embryology* a mass of tissue formed from the fusion of the ectoderm and the outer of the two layers of the mesoderm of the primary mesoblast, forming much of the body wall and the amnion and chorion —**so′ma·to·pleu′ral** *adj.*

so·ma·to·type (-tīp′) *n.* [SOMATO- + -TYPE] body type or physique

som·ber (säm′bər) *adj.* [Fr. *sombre* < LL. *subumbrare*, to shade < L. *sub*, under + *umbra*, shade] **1.** dark and gloomy or dull **2.** mentally depressed or depressing; melancholy **3.** earnest and solemn; grave Also, chiefly Brit. sp., **som′bre** —**som′ber·ly** *adv.* —**som′ber·ness** *n.*

☆**som·bre·ro** (säm brer′ō, səm-) *n., pl.* **-ros** [Sp. < *sombra*, shade: see prec.] a broad-brimmed, tall-crowned felt or straw hat of a kind worn in Mexico, the Southwest, etc.

some (sum; *unstressed* səm) *adj.* [ME. *som* < OE. *sum*, a certain one, akin to Goth. *sums*: for IE. base see SAME] **1.** being a certain one or ones not specified or known [*open some evenings*] **2.** being of a certain unspecified (but often considerable) number, quantity, degree, etc. [*to have some fear, married for some years*] **3.** about [*some ten of them*] ☆**4.** [Colloq.] remarkable, striking, etc. [*it was some fight*] —*pron.* **1.** a certain one or ones not specified or known; some one or ones [*some agree*] **2.** a certain indefinite or unspecified number, quantity, etc. as distinguished from the rest [*take some*] —*adv.* **1.** approximately; about [*some ten men*] **2.** [Colloq.] to some extent; somewhat [*slept some*] ☆**3.** [Colloq.] to a great extent or at a great rate [*must run some to catch up*] —☆**and then some** [Colloq.] and more than that

SOMBRERO

-some[1] (səm) [ME. *-som* < OE. *-sum*, akin to prec.] *a suffix meaning* like, tending to, tending to be [*toilsome, tiresome, lonesome*]

-some[2] (səm) [ME. *-sum* < *sum, som,* SOME] *a suffix meaning* in a (specified) number [*threesome*]

-some[3] (sōm) [< Gr. *sōma*, body: see SOMA[1]] *a combining form meaning:* **1.** body [*chromosome*] **2.** chromosome [*monosome*]

some·bod·y (sum′bud′ē, -bäd′ē, -bəd ē) *pron.* a person unknown or not named; some person; someone —*n., pl.* **-bod′ies** a person of importance

some·day (-dā′) *adv.* at some future day or time

some·how (-hou′) *adv.* in a way or by a method not known, stated, or understood [*was somehow completed*]: often in the phrase **somehow or other**

some·one (-wun′, -wən) *pron. same as* SOMEBODY

som·er·sault (sum′ər sôlt′) *n.* [altered < MFr. *sombresault, soubresault* < L. *supra,* over + *saltus,* a leap < pp. of *saltare:* for IE. base see SALIENT] an acrobatic stunt performed by turning the body one full revolution forward or backward, heels over head: often used figuratively, as of a complete reversal of opinion, sympathies, etc. —*vi.* to perform a somersault Also **som′er·set′** (-set′)

Som·er·set (sum′ər set′) county of SW England, on Bristol Channel: 1,612 sq. mi.; pop. 616,000; county seat, Taunton: also **Som′er·set·shire′** (-shir′)

Som·er·ville (sum′ər vil′) [? after Capt. R. *Somers* (1778–1804)] city in E Mass.: suburb of Boston: pop. 89,000

some·thing (sum′thiŋ) *n.* **1.** a thing that is not definitely known, understood, or identified; some undetermined thing [*something went wrong*] **2.** some thing or things, definite but unspecified [*have something to eat*] **3.** a bit; a little [*something over an hour*] **4.** [Colloq.] an important or remarkable person or thing —*adv.* **1.** a little; somewhat [*looks something like me*] **2.** [Colloq.] really; quite [*sounds something awful*] Also used after a figure to indicate a fraction beyond [*the bus leaves at six something*] —**make something of 1.** to find a use for; turn to good account **2.** to treat as of great importance ☆**3.** [Colloq.] to treat as a point of dispute; make an issue of —☆**something else** [Slang] someone or something quite remarkable

some·time (sum′tīm′) *adv.* **1.** at some time not known or specified **2.** at some unspecified time in the future **3.** [Archaic] *a)* sometimes *b)* formerly —*adj.* **1.** former; erstwhile [*his sometime friend*] **2.** merely occasional; sporadic [*his wit is a sometime thing*]

some·times (-tīmz′) *adv.* **1.** at times; on various occasions; occasionally **2.** [Obs.] formerly

some·way (-wā′) *adv.* in some way or manner; somehow or other: also **some′ways′**

some·what (-hwut′, -hwät′, -wut′, -wət) *n.* some degree, amount, portion, or part; a bit; often followed by *of* [*somewhat of a surprise*] —*adv.* to some extent or degree; a little; rather [*somewhat late*]

some·where (-hwer′, -wer′) *adv.* **1.** in, to, or at some place not known or specified [*lives somewhere nearby*] **2.** at some time, degree, age, figure, etc. (with *about, around, near, in, between,* etc.) [*somewhere about ten o'clock*] —*n.* an unspecified or undetermined place Also [Chiefly Dial.] **some′wheres′**

some·whith·er (-hwith′ər) *adv.* [Archaic] to some place; somewhere

some·wise (-wīz′) *adv.* [Archaic] in some way or to some degree (usually preceded by *in*)

so·mite (sō′mīt) *n.* [< Gr. *sōma,* body (see SOMA[1]) + -ITE[1]] **1.** *same as* METAMERE **2.** a blocklike segment of mesodermal tissue in the vertebrate embryo, giving rise to muscle, bone, etc. —**so·mit′ic** (-mit′ik), **so′mi·tal** (-mit ′l) *adj.*

Somme (sum; *Fr.* sôm) river in N France flowing west into the English Channel: c.150 mi.

som·me·lier (sum′əl yā′; *Fr.* sô mə lyā′) *n., pl.* **-liers** (-yāz′; *Fr.* -lyā′) [Fr. < MFr., orig., person in charge of pack animals (hence, steward) < OFr. *sommerier* < *sommier* < LL. *sagmarius:* see SUMMER[2]] a wine steward

som·nam·bu·late (säm nam′byoo lāt′, səm-) *vt.* **-lat′ed, -lat′ing** [< L. *somnus,* sleep (see SOMNUS) + *ambulatus,* pp. of *ambulare,* to walk] to get up and move about in a trancelike state while asleep —**som·nam′bu·lant** *adj.* —**som·nam′bu·la′tion** *n.* —**som·nam′bu·la′tor** *n.*

som·nam·bu·lism (-liz′m) *n.* **1.** the act or practice of somnambulating; sleepwalking **2.** the trancelike state of one who somnambulates —**som·nam′bu·list** *n.* —**som·nam′bu·lis′tic** *adj.* —**som·nam′bu·lis′ti·cal·ly** *adv.*

som·nif·er·ous (säm nif′ər əs, səm-) *adj.* [L. *somnifer* < *somnus,* sleep (see SOMNUS) + *ferre,* to bring, BEAR[1] + -OUS] inducing sleep; soporific: also **som·nif′ic** —**som·nif′er·ous·ly** *adv.*

som·nil·o·quy (-nil′ə kwē) *n.* [< L. *somnus,* sleep (see SOMNUS) + *loqui,* to speak] **1.** the act or habit of talking while asleep **2.** the words so spoken —**som·nil′o·quist** *n.*

som·no·lent (säm′nə lənt) *adj.* [LME. *sompnolent* < MFr. < L. *somnolentus* < *somnus,* sleep: see ff.] **1.** sleepy; drowsy **2.** inducing drowsiness —*SYN.* see SLEEPY —**som′no·lence, som′no·len·cy** *n.* —**som′no·lent·ly** *adv.*

Som·nus (säm′nəs) [L., sleep < IE. *swopnos* < base **swep-,* to sleep, whence Sans. *svapiti,* (he) sleeps, OE. *swefan,* to sleep] *Rom. Myth.* the god of sleep: identified with the Greek god Hypnos

son (sun) *n.* [ME. *sone* < OE. *sunu,* akin to G. *sohn,* Goth. *sunus* < IE. **sūnus* < base **seu-,* to give birth to, whence Sans. *sūyáte,* (she) bears, OIr. *suth,* birth] **1.** a boy or man as he is related to either or both parents: sometimes also used of animals **2.** a male descendant **3.** *a)* a son-in-law *b)* a stepson **4.** a male thought of as if in the relation of child to parent or to a formative influence [*a son of revolution*] **5.** an affectionate or familiar form of address to a boy or man, as used by an older person —**the Son** Jesus Christ, as the second person of the Trinity

so·nance (sō′nəns) *n.* **1.** sonant quality or state **2.** [Obs.] *a)* a sound *b)* a tune —*SYN.* see SOUND[1]

so·nant (sō′nənt) *adj.* [L. *sonans,* sounding, prp. of *sonare,* to SOUND[1]] **1.** of sound **2.** having sound; sounding —*n. Linguis.* a speech sound in a language that may occur in both syllabic and nonsyllabic positions

so·nar (sō′när) *n.* [*so(und) n(avigation) a(nd) r(anging)*] an apparatus that transmits high-frequency sound waves through water and registers the vibrations reflected back from an object, used in locating submarines, finding depths, etc.

so·na·ta (sə nät′ə) *n.* [It., lit., a sounding < L. *sonare,* to SOUND[1]: orig., an instrumental composition as opposed to CANTATA, lit., something sung] an extended composition for one or two instruments, consisting of from two to five movements related either by congruity or contrast of tempo, key, mood, or style, and, sometimes, by theme: some modern sonatas have single movements

sonata form a pattern of musical composition typically, though not always, used for the first movement of a sonata, symphony, concerto, etc., and consisting basically of an exposition of two distinct themes, a development, and a recapitulation of both themes: the second theme is always at first stated in a key different from that of the first theme but becomes transposed in the recapitulation: in full **sonata-allegro form**

so·na·ti·na (sän′ə tē′nə, sō′nə-) *n.* [It., dim. of *sonata*] a short or simplified sonata

☆**sonde** (sänd) *n.* [Fr., a sounding line < *sonder:* see SOUND[4]] any of various devices for measuring and usually telemetering meteorological and other physical conditions at high altitudes

sone (sōn) *n.* [< L. *sonus,* SOUND[1]] a unit of loudness,

subjectively determined, equal to the loudness of a sound of one kilohertz at 40 decibels above the threshold of hearing of a given listener

‡**son et lu·mière** (sôn nä lü myer′) [Fr., lit., sound and light] 1. a technique of presenting a historical spectacle, esp. at night before a monument, etc., using special lighting effects and live or recorded narration, music, etc. 2. such a spectacle

song (sôŋ) *n.* [ME. < OE. *sang:* for IE. base see SING] 1. the act or art of singing [to break into *song*] 2. a piece of music sung or as if for singing 3. *a)* poetry; verse *b)* a relatively short metrical composition for, or suitable for, singing, as a ballad or simple lyric 4. a musical sound like singing [the *song* of the lark] —**for a song** for very little money; cheap —☆**song and dance** 1. singing and dancing, esp. in vaudeville 2. [Colloq.] talk, esp. an explanation, that is pointless or evasive —**song′ful** *adj.* —**song′less** *adj.*

song·bird (-burd′) *n.* 1. a bird that makes vocal sounds that are like music 2. a woman singer

Song Coi (säŋ′ koi′) *Annamese name of the* RED RIVER (sense 3)

☆**song·fest** (sôŋ′fest′) *n.* [SONG + -FEST] an informal gathering of people for singing, esp. folk songs

Song of Solomon a book of the Bible consisting of a love poem, dramatic and lyrical in character, traditionally ascribed to Solomon: also called *Song of Songs* or (in the Douay Bible) *Canticle of Canticles*

☆**song sparrow** a common N. American sparrow (*Melospiza melodia*) with a striped breast, noted for its sweet song

song·ster (sôŋ′stər) *n.* [ME. < OE. *sangestre:* cf. SONG & -STER] 1. a singer 2. a writer of songs or poems 3. *same as* SONGBIRD —**song′stress** (-stris) *n.fem.*

song thrush a European songbird (*Turdus ericetorum*) with brown wings and a white breast

song·writ·er (-rit′ər) *n.* a person who writes the words or music or both for songs, esp. popular songs

son·ic (sän′ik) *adj.* [< L. *sonus,* SOUND¹ + -IC] 1. of or having to do with sound 2. designating or of a speed equal to the speed of sound (about 1088 feet per second through air at sea level at 32°F)

son·i·cate (sän′ə kāt′) *vt.* -cat′ed, -cat′ing [SONIC + -ATE] to subject (a cell, virus, etc.) to the energy produced by sound waves —**son′i·ca′tion** *n.* —**son′i·ca′tor** *n.*

sonic barrier the large increase of aerodynamic resistance encountered by some aircraft when flying near the speed of sound

sonic boom an explosive sound generated by the accumulation of pressure in a wave preceding an aircraft or other object traveling at or above the speed of sound: where this wave touches the ground, the variation in pressure is experienced as a loud report

sonic depth finder *same as* FATHOMETER

so·nif·er·ous (sō nif′ər əs) *adj.* [< L. *sonus,* a SOUND¹ + -FEROUS] carrying or producing sound

son-in-law (sun′in lô′) *n., pl.* **sons′-in-law′** the husband of one's daughter

son·net (sän′it) *n.* [Fr. < It. *sonnetto* < Pr. *sonet,* dim. of *son,* a sound, song < L. *sonus,* a SOUND¹] a poem normally of fourteen lines in any of several fixed verse and rhyme schemes, typically in rhymed iambic pentameter: sonnets characteristically express a single theme or idea: see PETRARCHAN SONNET, SHAKESPEAREAN SONNET —*vt., vi. same as* SONNETIZE

son·net·eer (sän′ə tir′) *n.* [prec. + -EER] 1. a person who writes sonnets 2. any minor or inferior poet: used contemptuously —*vi.* to write sonnets

son·net·ize (sän′ə tīz′) *vt., vi.* -ized′, -iz′ing to write sonnets (about)

son·ny (sun′ē) *n., pl.* -nies little son: used in addressing any young boy in a familiar way

son·o·buoy (sän′ō boo′ē, sō′nō-; -boi′) *n.* [< L. *sonus,* SOUND¹ + BUOY] a buoy that amplifies sound signals picked up under water and transmits them by radio

son of a bitch [Slang] 1. a person or thing regarded with anger, contempt, etc. 2. an interjection expressing surprise, annoyance, etc. A vulgar term

son of Adam any man or boy

son of a gun [Slang] a euphemistic alteration of SON OF A BITCH: often with overtones of indulgence, familiarity, etc.

Son of God (or **Man**) Jesus Christ

So·no·ra (sō nō′rä) state of NW Mexico, on the Gulf of California & the S Ariz. border: 70,484 sq. mi.; pop. 1,136,000; cap. Hermosillo

so·no·rant (sə nôr′ənt, sō-) *n.* [SONOR(OUS) + (CONSON)ANT] *Phonet.* a voiced consonant that is less sonorous than a vowel but more sonorous than an unvoiced plosive and that may occur as a syllabic [l, m, n, r, y, and w are English *sonorants*]

so·nor·i·ty (-ə tē) *n., pl.* -ties [< Fr. or LL.: Fr. *sonorité* < LL. *sonoritas*] quality, state, or instance of being sonorous; resonance

so·no·rous (sə nôr′əs, sän′ər əs) *adj.* [L. *sonorus* < *sonor,* a sound, din, akin to *sonus,* a SOUND¹] 1. producing or capable of producing sound, esp. sound of full, deep, or rich quality; resonant 2. full, deep, or rich: said of sound 3. having a powerful, impressive sound; high-sounding [*sonorous* prose] 4. *Phonetics* having a degree of resonant tonality: said esp. of vowels, semivowels, nasals, etc. —**so·no′rous·ly** *adv.* —**so·no′rous·ness** *n.*

son·ship (sun′ship) *n.* the fact or state of being a son

son·sy, son·sie (sän′sē) *adj.* [< dial. *sonse,* prosperity, plenty < ScotGael. *sonas,* good fortune + -Y²] [Brit. Dial.] 1. buxom; handsome 2. good-natured

Soo (soo) [alteration of *Sault*] region in N Mich. & S Ontario, Canada, at the St. Marys Falls Canal & the cities of Sault Ste. Marie —**Soo Locks** locks of this canal

Soo

Soo·chow (soo′chou′, Chin. soo′jō′) city in S Kiangsu province, E China, on the Grand Canal: pop. 500,000

sook (sook) *n. var. of* SOUK

soon (soon) *adv.* [ME. *sone* < OE. *sona,* at once, akin to OHG. *sān,* Goth. *suns*] 1. in a short time (after a time specified or understood); shortly; before long [will *soon* be there] 2. promptly; quickly [as *soon* as possible] 3. ahead of time; early [he left too *soon*] 4. readily; willingly [I would as *soon* go as stay] 5. [Obs.] at once; immediately —**had sooner** would rather; would prefer to —**sooner or later** inevitably; eventually

☆**soon·er** (soon′nər) *n.* [< compar. of prec.] 1. a person occupying homestead land, as formerly in the western U.S., before the authorized time for doing so, thus gaining an unfair advantage in choice of location 2. [S-] a native or inhabitant of Oklahoma: a nickname

Soong (soon) a prominent Chin. family whose members include **Ching-ling** (1890–), widow of SUN YAT-SEN, and **Mei-ling** (1898–), wife of CHIANG KAI-SHEK

soot (soot, soot) *n.* [ME. < OE. *sot,* akin to MDu. *soet* < IE. base *sed-,* to SIT: basic sense "what settles"] a black substance consisting chiefly of carbon particles formed by the incomplete combustion of burning matter —*vt.* to cover, soil, or treat with soot

sooth (sooth) *adj.* [ME. *soth* < OE., akin to Goth. *sunja,* truth, ON. *sannr,* true < IE. base **es-,* to be (cf. AM, IS): basic sense "that is"] 1. [Archaic] true or real 2. [Poet.] soothing; smooth —*n.* [Archaic] truth; fact —**in sooth** [Archaic] in truth; truly —**sooth′ly** *adv.*

soothe (soo͞th) *vt.* **soothed, sooth′ing** [ME. *sothen* < OE. *sothian,* to bear witness to, prove true < *soth:* see prec.] 1. to make calm or composed, as by gentle treatment, flattery, etc.; appease; mollify 2. to allay or relieve (pain, an ache, etc.); assuage —*vi.* to have a soothing effect —SYN. see COMFORT —**sooth′er** *n.* —**sooth′ing** *adj.* —**sooth′ing·ly** *adv.*

sooth·fast (sooth′fast′, -fäst′) *adj.* [ME. *sothfast* < OE. *sothfæst*] [Archaic] 1. truthful or loyal 2. true or real

sooth·say (sooth′sā′) *vi.* -said′, -say′ing to make predictions; foretell —**sooth′say′ing** *n.*

sooth·say·er (-ər) *n.* [ME. *sothseyere,* one who speaks the truth] 1. a person who predicts or pretends to predict the future 2. *same as* MANTIS

soot·y (soot′ē, soot′ē) *adj.* **soot′i·er, soot′i·est** [ME. < OE. *sotig:* acc SOOT & Y²] 1. of, like, or covered with, soot 2. dark or black like soot —**soot′i·ness** *n.*

sooty mold 1. a black fungal coating on plant parts, caused by fungi living on the honeydew secretions of aphids 2. a fungus producing such a coating

sop (säp) *n.* [ME. *soppe* < *sopp* < base of *supan:* see SUP¹] 1. a piece of food, as bread, soaked in milk, gravy, etc. 2. *a)* something given by way of concession or appeasement *b)* a bribe *same as* MILKSOP —*vt.* **sopped, sop′ping** [OE. *soppian* < the *n.*] 1. to soak, steep, or saturate in or with liquid 2. to take up (liquid) by absorption (usually with *up*) —*vi.* 1. to soak (*in, into,* or *through* something) 2. to be or become thoroughly wet

SOP, S.O.P. 1. *Mil.* standing operating procedure 2. popularly, standard operating procedure

sop. soprano

☆**soph** (säf) *n. clipped form of* SOPHOMORE

So·phi·a (sō fē′ə) [< Gr. *sophia,* skill, wisdom < *sophos,* wise] a feminine name: var. *Sophy, Sophie*

soph·ism (säf′iz′m) *n.* [altered (after L.) < ME. *sophim* < OFr. *soffime* < L. *sophisma* < Gr. *sophisma* < *sophizesthai,* to play the sophist < *sophos,* clever, skillful, wise] a clever and plausible but fallacious argument or form of reasoning, whether or not intended to deceive; fallacy or sophistry

soph·ist (-ist) *n.* [L. *sophista* < Gr. *sophistēs,* wise man: see prec.] 1. [*often* S-] in ancient Greece, any of a group of teachers of rhetoric, politics, philosophy, etc., some of whom were notorious for their clever, specious arguments 2. a learned person 3. any person practicing clever, specious reasoning

soph·ist·er (säf′is tər) *n.* 1. *same as* SOPHIST (sense 3) 2. a student in his second year (junior sophister) or third year (**senior sophister**) at certain British universities

so·phis·ti·cal (sə fis′ti k′l) *adj.* [ML. *sophisticalis* < L.

sophisticus < Gr. *sophistikos* < *sophistēs*, wise man, sophist] **1.** of or characteristic of sophists or sophistry **2.** clever and plausible, but unsound and tending to mislead *[a sophistical argument]* **3.** using sophistry Also **so·phis'tic** —**so·phis'ti·cal·ly** *adv.*

so·phis·ti·cate (sə fis'tə kāt'; *for n., usually* -kit) *vt.* **-cat'ed, -cat'ing** [ME. *sophisticaten* < ML. *sophisticatus*, pp. of *sophisticare* < L. *sophisticus*, SOPHISTICAL] **1.** to change from being natural, simple, artless, etc. to being artificial, worldly-wise, urbane, etc. **2.** to bring to a more developed, complex, or refined form, technique, level, etc. **3.** [Now Rare] *a)* to make impure by mixture or adulteration *b)* to alter (a text, etc.) without authority; falsify **4.** [Archaic] to corrupt or mislead —*vi.* [Rare] to use sophistical reasoning —*n.* a sophisticated person

so·phis·ti·cat·ed (-kāt'id) *adj.* **1.** not simple, artless, naive, etc.; urbane, worldly-wise, etc. or knowledgeable, perceptive, subtle, etc. **2.** designed for or appealing to sophisticated people **3.** highly complex, refined, or developed; characterized by advanced form, technique, etc. *[sophisticated equipment]* —**so·phis'ti·cat'ed·ly** *adv.*

so·phis·ti·ca·tion (sə fis'tə kā'shən) *n.* [ME. *sophisticacioun* < ML. *sophisticatio*] **1.** [Now Rare] the use of sophistry **2.** *a)* the act or process of sophisticating *b)* the state, quality, or character of being sophisticated

soph·is·try (säf'is trē) *n., pl.* **-tries** [ME. *sophistrie* < ML. *sophistria*] **1.** unsound or misleading but clever, plausible, and subtle argument or reasoning; sophism **2.** the methods or practices of the Sophists

Soph·o·cles (säf'ə klēz') 496?–406 B.C.; Gr. writer of tragic dramas

soph·o·more (säf'ə môr') *n.* [altered (after Gr. *sophos*, wise + *mōros*, foolish) < older *sophumer* < *sophum*, sophism, prob. < ME. *sophime*, SOPHISM] **1.** a student in the second year of college or in the tenth grade at high school ☆**2.** a person in his second year of some enterprise —*adj.* of sophomores

☆**soph·o·mor·ic** (säf'ə môr'ik) *adj.* of, like, or characteristic of a sophomore or sophomores, often regarded as self-assured, opinionated, etc. though immature: also **soph·o·mor'i·cal** —**soph'o·mor'i·cal·ly** *adv.*

Soph·o·ni·as (säf'ə nī'əs) *Douay Bible name for* ZEPHANIAH

-so·phy (sə fē) [< Gr. *sophia*, skill, wisdom] *a combining form meaning* knowledge or thought *[philosophy]*

so·por (sō'pər) *n.* [L.: for IE. base see SOMNUS] an unnaturally deep sleep; stupor

sop·o·rif·ic (säp'ə rif'ik, sō'pə-) *adj.* [Fr. *soporifique*: see SOPOR & -FIC] **1.** causing or tending to cause sleep: also **sop'o·rif'er·ous** (-rif'ər əs) **2.** of or characterized by sleep or sleepiness —*n.* something, as a drug, that causes sleep

sop·ping (säp'iŋ) *adj.* thoroughly wet; drenched

sop·py (säp'ē) *adj.* **-pi·er, -pi·est** **1.** very wet; sopping **2.** rainy **3.** [Colloq.] sentimental

so·pra·ni·no (sō'prə nē'nō) *adj.* [It., dim. of *soprano*] designating or of any musical instrument smaller than and of a higher pitch than the soprano of that family —*n.* a sopranino instrument, esp. a recorder

so·pra·no (sə pran'ō, -prä'nō) *n., pl.* **-nos, -ni** (-prä'nē) [It. < *sopra*, above < L. *supra*] **1.** the highest singing voice of women or boys, usually ranging two octaves or more up from middle C **2.** *a)* a voice or singer with such a range *b)* a musical instrument with a similar range *c)* a part for such a voice or instrument —*adj.* of, for, or having the range of, a soprano

☆**so·ra** (sôr'ə) *n.* [< ? AmInd. name] a small, short-billed wading bird (*Porzana carolina*) of the rail family, common in marshes of N. America: also **sora rail**

Sorb (sôrb) *n.* [G. *Sorbe*, of Slav. origin: cf. SERB] any member of an old Slavic people living in an enclave in East Germany, south of Berlin; Wend

sorb (sôrb) *n.* [Fr. *sorbe* < L. *sorbum*, serviceberry, *sorbus*, service tree < IE. base *ser-, *sor-, red, reddish, whence Russ. *sorobalina*, haw] **1.** any of a number of European trees of the rose family, as the rowan and the service tree **2.** the fruit of any of these trees

Sor·bi·an (sôr'bē ən) *adj.* of the Sorbs or their language —*n.* **1.** the West Slavic language of the Sorbs **2.** *same as* SORB

sor·bic acid (sôr'bik) [SORB + -IC] a white, crystalline solid, C₆H₈O₂, isolated from the berries of mountain ash or made synthetically: used in drying oils, and as a food preservative, fungicide, etc.

sor·bi·tol (sôr'bi tôl', -tōl') *n.* [SORB + -IT(E)¹ + -OL¹] a white, sweet, odorless, crystalline alcohol, C₆H₈(OH)₆, found in certain berries and fruits, used as a moistening agent in lotions, creams, etc., as a sugar substitute, etc.

Sor·bonne (sôr bän'; *Fr.* sôr bôn') [Fr., after the founder, Robert de *Sorbon* (1201–74), chaplain of Louis IX] **1.** a former theological college in Paris, established about the middle of the 13th cent. **2.** the University of Paris; specif., the seat of the faculties of letters and science

sor·bose (sôr'bōs) *n.* [SORB(ITOL) + -OSE¹] a white crystalline carbohydrate, C₆H₁₂O₆, obtained by fermenting sorbitol: it is used in the manufacture of vitamin C

sor·cer·er (sôr'sər ər) *n.* [extended < ME. *sorcer* < OFr. *sorcier*, sorcerer < *sorz*, a lot, chance < L. *sors* (gen. *sortis*), a lot, share: see SORT] a person who practices sorcery; wizard —**sor'cer·ess** *n.fem.*

sor·cer·y (-ē) *n., pl.* **-cer·ies** [ME. < OFr. *sorcerie* < *sorcier*: see prec.] **1.** the supposed use of an evil supernatural power over people and their affairs; witchcraft; black magic **2.** seemingly magical power, influence, or charm —*SYN.* see MAGIC —**sor'cer·ous** *adj.* —**sor'cer·ous·ly** *adv.*

sor·did (sôr'did) *adj.* [Fr. *sordide* < L. *sordidus* < *sordes*, filth < IE. base *swordo(s)-*, black, dirty, whence SWARTHY] **1.** *a)* dirty; filthy *b)* squalid; depressingly wretched **2.** *a)* base; ignoble; mean *b)* mercenary, avaricious, grasping, or meanly selfish —*SYN.* see BASE² —**sor'did·ly** *adv.* —**sor'did·ness** *n.*

sor·di·no (sôr dē'nō) *n., pl.* **-ni** (-nē) [It. < *sordo*, deaf, silent < L. *surdus*: see SURD] *same as* MUTE (*n.* 5)

sor·dor (sôr'dər) *n.* [ModL. < L. *sordes*, filth: see SORDID] wretchedness or squalor; sordidness

sore (sôr) *adj.* **sor'er, sor'est** [ME. *sor* < OE. *sar*, akin to G. *sehr*, very, lit., sore < IE. base *sai-*, pain, sickness, whence L. *saevus*, raging, terrible, OIr. *sáeth*, illness] **1.** *a)* giving physical pain; painful; tender *[a sore throat]* *b)* feeling physical pain, as from wounds, bruises, etc. *[to be sore all over]* **2.** *a)* filled with sadness, grief, or sorrow; distressed *[with a sore heart]* *b)* causing sadness, grief, misery, or distress *[a sore hardship]* *c)* distressingly intense or bitter; extreme *[a sore lack]* **3.** provocative of irritation or disagreeable feelings *[a sore point]* **4.** [Now Rare] irritable; touchy ☆**5.** [Colloq.] angry; offended; feeling hurt or resentful —*n.* [OE. *sar*, pain] **1.** a sore, usually infected spot on the body, as an ulcer, boil, or blister **2.** a source of pain, irritation, grief, distress, etc. —*adv.* [Archaic] sorely; greatly —**sore'ness** *n.*

sore·head (-hed') *n.* ☆[Colloq.] a person who is angry, resentful, disgruntled, vindictive, etc., or one easily made so, as by defeat

sore·ly (-lē) *adv.* [ME. *sorelie* < OE. *sarlice*: see SORE & -LY²] **1.** grievously; painfully *[sorely vexed]* **2.** urgently; greatly; extremely *[sorely needed]*

sor·ghum (sôr'gəm) *n.* [ModL., name of the genus < It. *sorgo* < dial. *soreg* < L. *syricus*, Syrian: hence, orig., Syrian grass] **1.** any of a genus (*Sorghum*) of tropical, old-world grasses that have solid stems bearing large, compact panicles of flowers followed by numerous small glossy seeds: grown for grain, syrup, fodder and pasture, etc. ☆**2.** syrup made from the sweet juices of a sorgo

sor·go (sôr'gō) *n., pl.* **-gos** [It.: see prec.] any of several varieties of sorghum with sweet, watery juice, grown for syrup, fodder, or silage: also **sor'gho**, *pl.* **-ghos**

so·ri (sō'rī) *n. pl. of* SORUS

so·ri·cine (sôr'ə sin', -sin; sär'-) *adj.* [L. *soricinus* < *sorex* (gen. *soricis*), a shrew: for IE. base see SWARM¹] of or like the shrews; shrewlike

so·ri·tes (sō rīt'ēz) *n., pl.* **so·ri'tes** [L. < Gr. *sōreitēs* (*syllogismos*), heaped up (syllogism) < *sōros*, a heap: for IE. base see SOMA¹] *Logic* a series of premises followed by a conclusion, arranged so that the predicate of the first premise is the subject of the next, and so forth, the conclusion uniting the subject of the first with the predicate of the last in an elliptical series of syllogisms —**so·rit'i·cal** (-rit'i k'l) *adj.*

so·ror·al (sə rôr'l) *adj.* of or characteristic of a sister or sisters; sisterly —**so·ror'al·ly** *adv.*

so·ro·rate (-it, -āt) *n.* [ModL. < L. *soror*, SISTER + -ATE²] the custom in some cultures of marrying the younger sister of one's deceased wife

so·ror·i·cide (-ə sīd') *n.* [LL. *sororicidium* < L. *soror*, SISTER + *caedere*, to strike, kill] **1.** the act of killing one's own sister **2.** [L. *sororicida*] a person who kills his sister —**so·ror'i·ci'dal** *adj.*

so·ror·i·ty (-ə tē) *n., pl.* **-ties** [ML. *sororitas*, a sisterhood < L. *soror*, SISTER] a group of women or girls joined together by common interests, for fellowship, etc.; ☆specif., a Greek-letter college organization

so·ro·sis (sə rō'sis) *n., pl.* **-ses** (-sēz) [ModL. < Gr. *sōros*, a heap: see SOMA¹] a multiple fruit formed by the merging of many flowers into a fleshy mass, as in the mulberry

sorp·tion (sôrp'shən) *n.* [back-formation < ABSORPTION & ADSORPTION] absorption or adsorption

sor·rel¹ (sôr'əl, sär'-) *n.* [ME. < OFr. *surele* < Frank. *sur*, akin to OHG. *sur*, SOUR] *same as:* **1.** DOCK³ **2.** WOOD SORREL

sor·rel² (sôr'əl, sär'-) *n.* [LME. < OFr. *sorel* < *sor*, *sore*, light brown < ML. *saurus* < Gmc. *saur*, light brown, color of dry leaves, orig., dry, akin to SEAR¹] **1.** light reddish brown **2.** a horse or other animal of this color —*adj.* light reddish-brown

☆**sorrel tree** *same as* SOURWOOD

Sor·ren·to (sə ren'tō; *It.* sôr ren'tô) resort town in S Italy, on the Bay of Naples: pop. 8,000

sor·row (sär'ō, sôr'ō) *n.* [ME. *sorwe* < OE. *sorg*, akin to G. *sorge* < IE. base *swergh-*, to worry, be ill, whence Sans. *sūrkṣati*, he worries about, Lith. *sergù*, to be sick] **1.** mental suffering caused by loss, disappointment, etc.;

sadness, grief, or regret 2. that which produces such suffering; trouble, loss, affliction, etc. 3. the outward expression of such suffering; mourning; lamentation 4. earnest repentance; contrition [*sorrow* for sin] —*vi.* to feel or show sorrow; grieve —**sor′row·er** *n.*
SYN.—**sorrow** refers to the deep, often long-continued mental anguish caused by a sense of loss, disappointment, etc. [her secret, life-long *sorrow*]; **grief** suggests a more painfully intense anguish, usually of relatively shorter duration, for some specific misfortune, disaster, etc. [his *grief* over the stricken child]; **sadness** refers to a condition of low spirits or mournfulness, resulting either from a specific cause or from a general feeling of depression, hopelessness, etc.; **woe** refers to intense unhappiness or sharp grief that cannot be consoled —**ANT. joy, happiness**
sor·row·ful (-ə fəl) *adj.* [ME. *soruful* < OE. *sorgful*] full of sorrow; feeling, causing, or expressing sorrow —**SYN.** see SAD —**sor′row·ful·ly** *adv.* —**sor′row·ful·ness** *n.*
sor·ry (sär′ē, sôr′ē) *adj.* -**ri·er**, -**ri·est** [ME. *sorie* < OE. *sarig* < *sar*, SORE] **1.** full of sorrow, pity, or sympathy: also used as an expression of apology or mild regret **2.** *a)* inferior in worth or quality; poor [a *sorry* exhibit] *b)* wretched; miserable [a *sorry* tenement] —**sor′ri·ly** *adv.* —**sor′ri·ness** *n.*
sort (sôrt) *n.* [ME. < MFr. < VL. *sorta* < L. *sors* (gen. *sortis*), a lot, chance, fate, akin to *serere*, to join together, arrange: see SERIES] **1.** any group of persons or things related by having something in common; kind; class **2.** quality or type; nature [remarks of that *sort*] **3.** [Archaic] manner or way **4.** [*usually pl.*] *Printing* any of the kinds of characters in a font of type —*vt.* to place, separate, or arrange according to class or kind (often with *out*) —*vi.* [Archaic] **1.** to associate; consort **2.** to harmonize or agree; suit —**SYN.** see TYPE —**after a sort** in some way but not very well —**of sorts 1.** of various kinds **2.** of a poor or inferior kind: also **of a sort** —**out of sorts 1.** *Printing* lacking certain sorts of type **2.** [Colloq.] *a)* not in a good humor; cross *b)* not feeling well; slightly ill —**sort of** [Colloq.] somewhat —**sort′a·ble** *adj.* —**sort′er** *n.*
sor·tie (sôr′tē) *n.* [Fr. < *sortir*, to issue, go out] **1.** *a)* a sudden rushing forth; sally; specif., a quick raid on besiegers by those besieged *b)* the forces making such a raid **2.** one mission by a single military plane
sor·ti·lege (sôr′ti lij) *n.* [ME. < ML. *sortilegium* < LL. *sortilegus*, fortuneteller < L. *sors*, a lot (see SORT) + *legere*, to read: see LOGIC] **1.** divination or prophecy by casting lots **2.** sorcery; black magic
so·rus (sō′rəs) *n.*, *pl.* -**ri** (-rī) [ModL. < Gr. *sōros*, a heap: see SOMA¹] a cluster of spore cases on the undersurface of a fern frond, or a similar cluster or spot, as of fungus spores
SOS (es′ō′es′) **1.** a signal of distress in code (. . . — — — . . .) used internationally in wireless telegraphy, as by ships **2.** [Colloq.] any call for help
Sos·no·wiec (sôs nô′vyets) city in S Poland: pop. 140,000
so-so (sō′sō′) *adv.* indifferently; just tolerably or passably —*adj.* neither very good nor very bad; just fair Also **so so**
sos·te·nu·to (säs′tə nōōt′ō; *It.* sôs′te nōō′tô) *adj., adv.* [It., pp. of *sostenere* < L. *sustinere*, to SUSTAIN] *Music* played at a slower but sustained tempo, with each note held for its full value —*n.*, *pl.* -**tos**, -**ti** (-tē) a sostenuto passage
sot (sät) *n.* [ME. < Late OE. *sott*, a fool, or OFr. *sot*, a fool < VL. *sottus*] a drunkard
so·te·ri·ol·o·gy (sō tir′ē äl′ə jē) *n.* [< Gr. *sōtēria*, deliverance (in LXX & NT., salvation) < *sōtēr*, a deliverer (in NT., Saviour) + -LOGY] **1.** spiritual salvation, esp. that believed in Christian theology to have been accomplished through Jesus **2.** the study of this —**so·te′ri·o·log′i·cal** (-ə läj′i k'l) *adj.*
Soth·ern (suth′ərn), **E(dward) H(ugh)** 1859–1933; U.S. actor: husband of Julia MARLOWE
So·thic (sō′thik, säth′ik) *adj.* [Gr. *Sōthiakos* < *Sōthis*, the Dog Star < ? Egypt.] **1.** of or having to do with Sirius, the Dog Star **2.** designating or of an ancient Egyptian cycle or period of time based on a fixed year of 365 1/4 days (**Sothic year**) and equal to 1,460 such years
So·tho (sō′thō) *n.* **1.** *pl.* **So′thos**, **So′tho** any member of a people living in S Africa **2.** their Bantu language
☆**so·tol** (sō tōl′, sō′tōl) *n.* [AmSp. < Nahuatl *tzotolli*] any of a genus (*Dasylirion*) of yuccalike desert plants of the agave family, with dense clusters of whitish, lilylike flowers, growing in the SW U.S. and N Mexico
sot·ted (sät′id) *adj.* besotted; stupefied
sot·tish (-ish) *adj.* **1.** of or like a sot **2.** stupid or foolish from or as from too much drinking —**sot′tish·ly** *adv.*
sot·to vo·ce (sät′ō vō′chē; *It.* sôt′tô vô′che) [It., under the voice] in an undertone, so as not to be overheard
sou (sōō) *n.*, *pl.* **sous** (sōōz; *Fr.* sōō) [Fr. < OFr. *sol* < LL. *solidus*: see SOLIDUS] any of several former French coins, esp. one equal to five centimes
sou·a·ri (sōō wär′ē) *n.* [Fr. *saouari* < the native name in Guiana] any of a genus (*Caryocar*) of trees of N S. America having durable timber (**souari wood**) and large, edible nuts (**souari nuts**) that yield an oil used in cooking, etc.
sou·bise (sōō bēz′) *n.* [Fr., after Charles de Rohan, Prince de Soubise (1715–87), Marshal of France] a sauce containing onions and melted butter, or purée of onions
sou·brette (sōō bret′) *n.* [Fr. < Pr. *soubreto* < *soubret*, affected, sly < *soubra*, to put aside, exceed < L. *superare*, to be above: see SUPER-] **1.** in a play, light opera, etc., the role of a lady's maid, esp. one involved in intrigue, or

of any pretty, flirtatious, or frivolous young woman **2.** an actress who plays such roles
sou·bri·quet (sōō′brə kā′) *n. var. of* SOBRIQUET
sou·chong (sōō′shŏn′) *n.* [Chin. *hsiao*, small or young + *chung*, kind] a black tea with large leaves
Sou·dan (sōō dän′) *Fr. sp. of* SUDAN
souf·fle (sōō′f'l) *n.* [Fr. < *souffler*, to blow: see ff.] *Med.* a soft, blowing sound heard on auscultation
souf·flé (sōō flā′, sōō′flā) *adj.* [Fr. < pp. of *souffler*, to blow < L. *sufflare*, to inflate, blow up, puff out < *sub-* (see SUB-) + *flare*, to BLOW¹] made light and puffy in cooking: also **souf·fléed′** (-flād′) —*n.* any of several baked foods, as a dish prepared with white sauce and egg yolks and some additional ingredient, as cheese, made light and puffy by adding beaten egg whites before baking
sough (sou, suf) *n.* [19th c. < Northern dial. < ME. *swough* < OE. *swogan*, to sound < ? IE. base *(s)uagh-*, to cry, sound, whence Gr. *ēchē*, noise] a soft, low, murmuring, sighing, or rustling sound —*vi.* [ME. *swowen*, *soghen* < OE. *swogan*, to sound] to make a sough
sought (sôt) *pt. & pp. of* SEEK
souk (sōōk) *n.* [Ar. *sūq*] an open-air marketplace in North Africa and the Middle East
soul (sōl) *n.* [ME. *soule* < OE. *sawol*, akin to G. *seele*, Goth. *saiwala*: only in Gmc. languages] **1.** an entity which is regarded as being the immortal or spiritual part of the person and, though having no physical or material reality, is credited with the functions of thinking and willing, and hence determining all behavior **2.** the moral or emotional nature of man **3.** spiritual or emotional warmth, force, etc., or evidence of this [a cold painting, without *soul*] **4.** vital or essential part, quality, or principle ["brevity is the *soul* of wit"] **5.** the person who leads or dominates; central figure [Daniel Boone, *soul* of the frontier] **6.** embodiment; personification [the very *soul* of kindness] **7.** a person [a town of 1,000 *souls*] **8.** the spirit of a dead person, thought of as separate from the body and leading an existence of its own ☆**9.** [Colloq.] *a)* among U.S. Negroes, a sense of racial pride and social and cultural solidarity, often with opposition to white, middle-class practices and values *b)* clipped form of SOUL FOOD or SOUL MUSIC —☆*adj.* [Colloq.] of, for, like, or characteristic of Negroes, esp. U.S. Negroes —**upon my soul!** an exclamation of surprise
☆**soul food** [Colloq.] items of inexpensive food popular orig. in the South esp. among Negroes, as chitterlings, ham hocks, yams, cornbread, turnip greens, etc.
soul·ful (sōl′fəl) *adj.* full of or showing deep feeling —**soul′ful·ly** *adv.* —**soul′ful·ness** *n.*
soul·less (-lis) *adj.* lacking soul, sensitivity, or deepness of feeling; without spirit or inspiration
soul mate [Colloq.] a person, esp. of the opposite sex, with whom one has a deeply personal relationship
☆**soul music** [Colloq.] a form of RHYTHM AND BLUES (with added elements of U.S. Negro gospel singing)
soul-search·ing (-sur′chin) *n.* close, honest examination of one's true feelings, motives, etc.
sound¹ (sound) *n.* [< ME. *soun* (+ unhistoric -*d*) < OFr. *son* < L. *sonus* < IE. *swonos*, a sound, noise < base *swen-*, to sound, whence OE. *swinsian*, to sing, make music] **1.** *a)* vibrations in air, water, etc. that stimulate the auditory nerves and produce the sensation of hearing *b)* the auditory sensation produced by such vibrations **2.** *a)* any auditory effect that is distinctive or characteristic of its source; identifiable noise, tone, vocal utterance, etc. [the *sound* of a violin, a speech *sound*] *b)* such effects as transmitted by or recorded for radio, television, or motion pictures **3.** the distance within which a given sound may be heard; earshot [within *sound* of the bells] **4.** the mental impression produced by the way something is worded; tenor; drift [the *sound* of his report] **5.** meaningless noise; racket **6.** [Archaic] *a)* report; rumor *b)* meaning; significance —*vi.* [ME. *sounen* < OFr. *soner* < L. *sonare*] **1.** to make a sound or sounds **2.** to seem, from the manner of wording or utterance [to *sound* troubled] —*vt.* **1.** *a)* to cause to sound [to *sound* a gong] *b)* to produce the sound of [to *sound* a *C* on a piano] *c)* to utter distinctly; articulate [to *sound* one's *r's*] **2.** to express, signal, indicate, or announce [the clock *sounds* the hour] **3.** to make widely known; proclaim [to *sound* someone's praises] **4.** to examine (the chest) by auscultation or percussion —**sound off** ☆**1.** *a)* to speak in turn, as in counting off for a military formation *b)* to count cadence in marching ☆**2.** [Slang] *a)* to give voice freely to opinions, complaints, etc. *b)* to speak in a loud or offensive way, as in boasting
SYN.—**sound** is the general term for anything that is or may be heard [the *sound* of footsteps]; **noise** usually refers to a sound that is unpleasant or disagreeable because it is too loud, harsh, discordant, etc. [the *noise* of a boiler factory]; **tone** is generally applied to a sound regarded as pleasant or musical because it has regularity of vibration resulting in a constant pitch [the range of *tones* in a violin]; **sonance**, in its general use, is an obsolete synonym for **sound**, but in its restricted use in phonetics, applies to the quality of a sound that is voiced [all vowels have *sonance*] —**ANT. silence**
sound² (sound) *adj.* [ME. < OE. (ge)*sund*, akin to Dan. *sund*, G. *gesund*: only in Gmc. languages] **1.** free from defect, damage, or decay; whole and in good condition [*sound* timber] **2.** normal and healthy; not weak, diseased,

or impaired [a *sound* body and mind] **3.** *a*) firm and safe; stable; secure [a *sound* alliance] *b*) safe and secure financially [a *sound* bank] **4.** based on truth or valid reasoning; accurate, reliable, judicious, sensible, etc. [*sound* advice] **5.** agreeing with established views or beliefs; not heterodox [*sound* doctrine] **6.** thorough, solid, substantial, forceful, etc. [a *sound* defeat] **7.** deep and undisturbed: said of sleep **8.** morally strong; honest, honorable, loyal, etc. **9.** legally valid [a *sound* title to a property] —*adv.* completely; deeply [*sound* asleep] —*SYN.* see VALID, HEALTHY —**sound′ly** *adv.* —**sound′ness** *n.*

sound³ (sound) *n.* [ME. < OE. *sund*, a swimming, water, strait & ON. *sund* (its cognate and synonym): for IE. base see SWIM¹] **1.** a wide channel or strait linking two large bodies of water or separating an island from the mainland **2.** a long inlet or arm of the sea **3.** the air sac, or swimming bladder, of certain fishes

sound⁴ (sound) *vt.* [ME. *sounden* < MFr. *sonder* < VL. *subundare*, to submerge < L. *sub*, under + *unda*, a wave] **1.** *a*) to measure the depth or various depths of (water or a body of water), esp. with a weighted line *b*) to measure (depth) in this way *c*) to investigate or examine (the bottom of the sea, etc.) with a weighted line that brings up adhering particles *d*) to probe (the atmosphere or space) so as to gain data **2.** *a*) to investigate, examine, or try to find out (a person's opinions) *b*) to try to find out the opinions or feelings of (a person), as by roundabout questioning (often with *out*) **3.** *Med.* to examine with a sound, or probe —*vi.* **1.** to sound water or a body of water **2.** to dive suddenly downward through the water: said esp. of whales or large fish **3.** to try to find out something, as by roundabout questioning —*n. Med.* a long probe used in examining body cavities

Sound (sound), **The** *same as* ÖRESUND

sound barrier *same as* SONIC BARRIER

sound·board (sound′bôrd′) *n. same as* SOUNDING BOARD

sound effects sounds, as of thunder, blows, animals, traffic, etc., produced artificially or by recording to supply sounds called for in the script of a radio, stage, motion-picture, or television production

sound·er¹ (soun′dər) *n.* **1.** a person or thing that makes a sound or sounds **2.** a telegraphic device that converts electric code impulses into sound

sound·er² (soun′dər) *n.* a person or thing that sounds the depth of water, etc.

sound·ing¹ (-diŋ) *adj.* **1.** making or giving forth sound **2.** resonant; sonorous **3.** high-sounding; bombastic

sound·ing² (-diŋ) *n.* **1.** *a*) the act of measuring the depth or examining the bottom of a body of water, etc. with or as with a weighted line *b*) depth so measured *c*) [*pl.*] a place, usually less than 600 feet in depth, where a sounding line will touch bottom **2.** *a*) an examination of the atmosphere at or to a given height, as with a radiosonde *b*) a probe of space, as with a rocket **3.** [*pl.*] measurements learned or data acquired by sounding **4.** [*often pl.*] an exploratory sampling, as of public opinion

sounding board 1. *a*) a thin plate, as of wood, built into a musical instrument to increase its resonance *b*) a structure over or behind a rostrum, stage, etc. designed to reflect sound toward the audience **2.** *a*) a person or thing used for spreading ideas around, esp. other people's ideas *b*) a person on whom one tests one's ideas, opinions, etc.

sounding line *same as* LEAD LINE

sound·less¹ (sound′lis) *adj.* without sound; quiet; noiseless —**sound′less·ly** *adv.* —**sound′less·ness** *n.*

sound·less² (-lis) *adj.* so deep as to be incapable of being sounded; unfathomable

sound·man (-man′) *n., pl.* -**men′** (-men′) a man in charge of sound effects

sound·proof (-prōōf′) *adj.* that keeps sound from coming through —*vt.* to make soundproof

sound track the area along one side of a motion-picture film, carrying the sound record of the film

☆**sound truck** a motor truck with amplifiers, loudspeakers, etc., for broadcasting campaign speeches, advertising, etc. on the streets

sound wave *Physics* a longitudinal pressure wave stimulated by a mechanical disturbance of an elastic medium, as air, at some source and propagated by the action of disturbed particles on adjacent particles; esp., any of such waves within the range of those audible to the human ear (c.15 cycles to 20,000 cycles per second)

soup (sōōp) *n.* [Fr. *soupe* < OFr., soup, orig., sop: of Gmc. origin: cf. SUP¹] **1.** a liquid food, with or without solid particles, made by cooking meat, vegetables, fish, etc. in water, milk, or the like **2.** [Slang] a heavy fog ☆**3.** [Slang] nitroglycerin —**in the soup** [Slang] in trouble —**soup up** [Slang] to increase the power, capacity for speed, etc. of (an engine, etc.)

soup·çon (sōōp sôn′, sōōp′sôn′) *n.* [Fr. < OFr. *sospeçon* < VL. *suspectio*, for L. *suspicio*: see SUSPICION] **1.** lit., a suspicion **2.** a slight trace, as of a flavor; hint; suggestion **3.** a tiny amount; bit

‡**soupe du jour** (sōōp dü zhōōr′; *Eng.* sōōp′ doo zhoor′) [Fr., lit., soup of the day] the special, sometimes the only,

soup served in a restaurant on any particular day: also, Eng. sp., **soup du jour**

soup kitchen a place where hot soup or the like is given to people in dire need

soup·spoon (sōōp′spōōn′) *n.* a large-bowled spoon for eating soup

soup·y (sōō′pē) *adj.* **soup′i·er, soup′i·est 1.** watery like soup **2.** [Colloq.] *a*) thick and dank [a *soupy* fog] *b*) disagreeably wet [*soupy* weather] ☆**3.** [Slang] sloppily sentimental; mawkish

sour (sour) *adj.* [ME. *soure* < OE. *sur*, akin to G. *sauer*, ON. *surr* < IE. *suro*, sour, salty, whence Lett. *sūrs*, salty, bitter] **1.** having the sharp, acid taste of lemon juice, vinegar, green fruit, etc. **2.** made acid or rank by or as by fermentation [*sour* milk] **3.** *a*) cross, bad-tempered, peevish, morose, etc. [a *sour* mood] *b*) ill-disposed and bitter [*sour* toward former associates] **4.** below what is usual or normal; poor; bad [his game has gone *sour*] **5.** distasteful or unpleasant **6.** gratingly wrong or off pitch [a *sour* note] **7.** excessively acid: said of soil **8.** tainted with sulfur compounds: said of gasoline, etc. —*n.* **1.** that which is sour; something sour ☆**2.** a cocktail made with lemon or lime juice [a whiskey *sour*] —*vt., vi.* to make or become sour —**sour′ly** *adv.* —**sour′ness** *n.* —*SYN.* —**sour** usually implies an unpleasant sharpness of taste and often connotes fermentation or rancidness [*sour* milk]; **acid** suggests a sourness that is normal or natural [a lemon is an *acid* fruit]; **acidulous** suggests a slightly sour or acid quality [*acidulous* spring water]; **tart** suggests a slightly stinging sharpness or sourness and usually connotes that this is pleasant to the taste [a *tart* cherry pie] —*ANT.* sweet

sour·ball (-bôl′) *n.* a small ball of tart, hard candy

source (sôrs) *n.* [ME. *sours* < OFr. *sourse* < pp. of *sourdre*, to rise < L. *surgere*: see SURGE] **1.** a spring, fountain, etc. that is the starting point of a stream **2.** that from which something comes into existence, develops, or derives [the sun is our *source* of energy, the *source* of a difficulty] **3.** *a*) any person, place, or thing by which something is supplied [a *source* of pleasure] *b*) a person, book, document, etc. that provides information [to consult various *sources*] **4.** the point or thing from which light rays, sound waves, etc. emanate —*SYN.* see ORIGIN

☆**source·book** (-book′) *n.* a collection of documents or a diary, journal, etc. used as basic information in studying, evaluating, and writing about a person, period, etc.

sour cherry 1. an old-world cherry tree (*Prunus cerasus*) bearing acid fruits, usually used in cooking, preserves, etc. **2.** this fruit

sour cream cream soured and thickened naturally or by processing for use in cooking, dressings, dips, etc.

sour·dine (soor dēn′) *n.* [Fr. < It. *sordina* < *sordo*, deaf: see SORDINO] *Music* **1.** any of several obsolete instruments having a low or soft tone **2.** a mute, esp. one for a trumpet

sour·dough (sour′dō′) *n.* **1.** [Dial.] leaven; esp., fermented dough saved from one baking so that it can be used in the next, thus avoiding the need for fresh yeast **2.** a prospector or settler in the western U.S. or Canada, esp. one living alone: so called because their staple was sourdough bread

sour gourd 1. an Australian tree (*Adansonia gregorii*) of the bombax family with a gourdlike fruit **2.** its woody fruit, with acid pulp and large seeds **3.** *same as* BAOBAB

sour grapes [from Aesop's fable in which the fox, after futile efforts to reach some grapes, scorns them as being sour] a scorning or belittling of something only because it cannot be had or done

☆**sour gum** *same as* BLACK GUM

☆**sour mash** a grain mash made with some mash from an earlier run, used in distilling some whiskeys

sour orange 1. an orange tree (*Citrus aurantium*) widely grown as a rootstock for grafting other citrus trees **2.** its fruit, used in making marmalade

☆**sour·puss** (sour′poos′) *n.* [Slang] a person who has a gloomy or disagreeable expression or nature

sour salt crystals of citric acid or tartaric acid, used in flavoring foods, in pharmaceuticals, etc.

sour·sop (-säp′) *n.* **1.** a tropical American tree (*Annona muricata*) of the custard-apple family, with large, pulpy, acid fruit **2.** this fruit

☆**sour·wood** (-wood′) *n.* a N. American tree (*Oxydendrum arboreum*) of the heath family, with thick, fissured bark, small white flowers, grayish fruit, and sour leaves

Sou·sa (sōō′zə, -sə), **John Philip** 1854–1932; U.S. bandmaster & composer of marches

☆**sou·sa·phone** (sōō′zə fōn′, sōō′sə-) *n.* [after prec., who suggested its form] a brass-wind instrument of the tuba class: it was developed from the helicon and is used esp. in military bands

souse¹ (sous) *n.* [ME. *sows* < OFr. *souz* < OHG. *sulza*, brine, akin to *salz*, SALT] **1.** a pickled food, esp. the feet, ears, and head of a pig **2.** liquid used for pickling; brine **3.** the act of plunging into a liquid, esp. into brine for pickling ☆**4.** [Slang] a drunkard —*vt., vi.* **soused, sous′ing 1.** to pickle **2.** to plunge or steep in a liquid **3.** to make or become soaking wet ☆**4.** [Slang] to make or become intoxicated

souse[2] (sous) *n.* [altered < ME. *source* < OFr. *sors, source*, in the same sense: cf. SOURCE] [Obs.] *Falconry* the act of rising in flight by a hunted bird or of swooping down on prey by a hawk, falcon, etc. —*vt., vi.* **soused, sous'ing** [Obs.] *Falconry* to swoop down (on)

sou·tache (sōō tȧsh′) *n.* [Fr. < Hung. *sujtás*, a pendant] a narrow, flat braid used for trimming, decoration, etc.

sou·tane (sōō tän′, -tän′) *n.* [Fr. < It. *sottana* < *sotto*, under < L. *subtus*, under, beneath < *sub*, under] *same as* CASSOCK

south (south) *n.* [ME. < OE. *suth*, akin to OHG. *sund*-, ON. *suthr* < IE. **sun*, SUN¹] **1.** the direction to the left of a person facing the sunset; direction of the South Pole from any other point on the earth's surface **2.** the point on a compass at 180°, directly opposite north **3.** a region or district in or toward this direction **4.** [*often* S-] the southern part of the earth, esp. the antarctic regions —*adj.* **1.** in, of, to, toward, or facing the south **2.** from the south [*a south* wind] **3.** [S-] designating the southern part of a continent, country, etc. [*South* Asia] —*adv.* in or toward the south; in a southerly direction —☆**the South** that part of the U.S. which is bounded on the north by the southern border of Pennsylvania, the Ohio River, and the eastern and northern borders of Missouri; specif., in the Civil War, the Confederacy

South Africa country in southernmost Africa: until 1961, as the **Union of South Africa**, a member of the Brit. Commonwealth: 472,358 sq. mi.; pop. 19,618,000; caps. Cape Town, Pretoria

South African 1. of southern Africa **2.** of South Africa **3.** a native or inhabitant of South Africa; esp., *same as* AFRIKANER

South African Dutch 1. the Boers **2.** *same as* AFRIKAANS

South African Republic *former name of* TRANSVAAL

South America S continent in the Western Hemisphere: c.6,864,000 sq. mi.; pop. 186,000,000 —**South American**

South·amp·ton (sou thamp′tən, south amp′-) **1.** seaport in S England, on an inlet (**Southampton Water**) of The Solent: pop. 209,000 **2.** *official name of* HAMPSHIRE (sense 1)

Southampton Island island in N Hudson Bay, Canada: 15,700 sq. mi.

South Australia state of SC Australia: 380,070 sq. mi.; pop. 1,091,000; cap. Adelaide

South Bend [from its being at a southernmost bend in the St. Joseph River] city in N Ind.: pop. 126,000

south·bound (south′bound′) *adj.* going southward

south by east the direction, or the point on a mariner's compass, halfway between due south and south-southeast; 11°15′ east of due south

south by west the direction, or the point on a mariner's compass, halfway between due south and south-southwest; 11°15′ west of due south

South Carolina [see CAROLINA] Southern State of the SE U.S., on the Atlantic: one of the 13 original states; 31,055 sq. mi.; pop. 2,591,000; cap. Columbia: abbrev. **S.C., SC** —**South Carolinian**

South China Sea arm of the W Pacific, touching Taiwan, the Philippines, Borneo, the Malay Peninsula, Indochina, & China: c.895,000 sq. mi.

South Dakota [see DAKOTA] Middle Western State of the NC U.S.: admitted, 1889; 77,047 sq. mi.; pop. 666,000; cap. Pierre: abbrev. **S. Dak., SD** —**South Dakotan**

South·down (south′doun′) *n.* [after ff.] any of a breed of English sheep having short wool and bred chiefly for food

South Downs *see* THE DOWNS (at entry DOWN³)

south·east (south′ēst′; *in nautical usage*, sou-) *n.* **1.** the direction, or the point on a mariner's compass, halfway between south and east; 45° east of due south **2.** a region or district in or toward this direction —*adj.* **1.** in, of, to, toward, or facing the southeast **2.** from the southeast, as a wind —*adv.* in, toward, or from the southeast —**the Southeast** the southeastern part of the U.S.

southeast by east the direction, or the point on a mariner's compass, halfway between southeast and east-southeast; 11°15′ east of southeast

southeast by south the direction, or the point on a mariner's compass, halfway between southeast and south-southeast; 11°15′ south of southeast

south·east·er (south′ēs′tər; *in nautical usage*, sou-) *n.* a storm or strong wind from the southeast

south·east·er·ly (-tər lē) *adj., adv.* **1.** in or toward the southeast **2.** from the southeast [*a southeasterly* wind]

south·east·ern (-tərn) *adj.* **1.** in, of, or toward the southeast **2.** from the southeast [*a southeastern* wind] ☆**3.** [S-] of or characteristic of the Southeast —**South′east′ern·er** *n.*

south·east·ward (-ēst′wərd) *adv., adj.* toward the southeast —*n.* a southeastward direction, point, or region

south·east·ward·ly (-wərd lē) *adj., adv.* **1.** toward the southeast **2.** from the southeast, as a wind

south·east·wards (-wərdz) *adv. same as* SOUTHEASTWARD

South·end-on-Sea (south′end′än sē′) seaport in Essex, SE England, on the Thames estuary: pop. 166,000

south·er (sou′thər) *n.* a storm or wind from the south

south·er·ly (suth′ər lē) *adj.* **1.** in, of, or toward the south **2.** from the south [*a southerly* wind] —*adv.* **1.** toward the south **2.** from the south

south·ern (suth′ərn) *adj.* [ME. < OE. *suthern*] **1.** in, of, toward, or facing the south **2.** from the south [*a southern*

wind] ☆**3.** [S-] of or characteristic of the South ☆**4.** [S-] designating a dialect area of American English spoken in the Delmarva Peninsula, the Virginia Piedmont, eastern North Carolina and South Carolina, Georgia, Florida, and the States along the Gulf of Mexico —*n.* ☆[*also* S-] *dial. var. of* SOUTHERNER (sense 2)

Southern Alps mountain range on South Island, New Zealand: highest peak, Mt. COOK

Southern Cross a small S constellation whose four brightest stars appear as if at the tips of a cross

Southern Crown *same as* CORONA AUSTRALIS

south·ern·er (suth′ər nər, -ə nər) *n.* **1.** a native or inhabitant of the south ☆**2.** [S-] a native or inhabitant of the Southern part of the U.S.

Southern Hemisphere that half of the earth south of the equator

southern lights *same as* AURORA AUSTRALIS

south·ern·most (suth′ərn mōst′) *adj.* farthest south

Southern Ocean that part of the Indian Ocean south of Australia: name used by Australians

Southern Rhodesia *former name of* RHODESIA

Southern Sporades *same as the* SPORADES (sense 2)

Southern Up·lands (up′ləndz) hilly moorland region in S Scotland, between the English border & the Lowlands

south·ern·wood (suth′ərn wood′) *n.* [ME. *suthernewode* < OE. *sutherne wudu*: as it is native to southern Europe] a shrubby, European wormwood (*Artemisia abrotanum*) with yellowish flowers and fragrant leaves

Southern Yemen country in S Arabia including Aden & a group of Arab states formerly under Brit. protection: c.110,000 sq. mi.; pop. 1,146,000

Sou·they (suth′ē, sou′thē), **Robert** 1774–1843; Eng. poet & writer: poet laureate (1813–43)

South·field (south′fēld′) city in SE Mich.: suburb of Detroit: pop. 69,000

South·gate (south′git, -gāt) city in Middlesex, SE England: suburb of London: pop. 71,000

South Gate [< *South Gate Gardens* south of Los Angeles] city in SW Calif.: suburb of Los Angeles: pop. 57,000

South Georgia island dependency of the Falkland Islands in the South Atlantic: 1,600 sq. mi.; pop. 400

South Holland province of the W Netherlands, on the North Sea: 1,101 sq. mi.; pop. 2,876,000; cap. The Hague

south·ing (sou′thiŋ, -thiŋ) *n.* **1.** southerly movement **2.** the distance covered sailing or traveling southward

South Island S island of the two main islands of New Zealand: 59,439 sq. mi.; pop. 783,000

south·land (south′lənd′, -land) *n.* [*also* S-] **1.** the southern region of a country **2.** land in the south —**south′land′er** *n.*

South Orkney Islands group of Brit. islands in the South Atlantic, southeast of S. America: 240 sq. mi.

☆**south·paw** (-pô′) *n.* [SOUTH + PAW¹: the ballpark in Chicago (c.1885) was so located that the pitcher's left arm was toward the south] [Slang] a person who is left-handed; esp., a left-handed baseball pitcher —*adj.* [Slang] left-handed

South Platte river flowing from C Colo. through N Nebr., joining the North Platte to form the Platte: 424 mi.

South Pole 1. the southern end of the earth's axis: its zenith (called the **south pole of the heavens**) is the point at which this axis extended intersects the celestial sphere **2.** [s- p-] that end of a straight magnet that points to the south when the magnet hangs free

South·port (south′pôrt′) city in Lancashire, NW England, on the Irish Sea: pop. 80,000

south·ron (suth′rən) *n.* [LME. *sothron*, altered (prob. after BRITON, SAXON) < *southren*, dial. var. of *southern*] a southerner: applied in Scottish dialect to an Englishman and, formerly, in the U.S. to a Southerner

South San Francisco city in W Calif., on San Francisco Bay: suburb of San Francisco: pop. 47,000

South Saskatchewan river flowing from SW Alberta east & northeast through Saskatchewan, joining the North Saskatchewan to form the Saskatchewan: 865 mi.

South Sea Islands islands in temperate or tropical parts of the South Pacific —**South Sea Islander**

South Seas 1. the South Pacific **2.** all the seas located south of the equator

South Shetland Islands group of Brit. islands in the South Atlantic, south of S. America: 1,800 sq. mi.

South Shields seaport in Durham, N England, on the Tyne estuary: pop. 108,000

south-south·east (south′south′ēst′; *in nautical usage*, sou′sou-) *n.* the direction, or the point on a mariner's compass, halfway between due south and southeast; 22°30′ east of due south —*adj., adv.* **1.** in or toward this direction **2.** from this direction, as a wind

south-south·west (-west′) *n.* the direction, or the point on a mariner's compass, halfway between due south and southwest; 22°30′ west of due south —*adj., adv.* **1.** in or toward this direction **2.** from this direction, as a wind

south·ward (south′wərd; *in nautical usage*, suth′ərd) *adv., adj.* toward the south —*n.* a southward direction, point, or region

south·ward·ly (-lē) *adj., adv.* **1.** toward the south **2.** from the south [*a southwardly* wind]

south·wards (-wərdz) *adv. same as* SOUTHWARD

South·wark (suth′ərk) metropolitan borough of London: pop. 86,000

south·west (south'west'; *in nautical usage*, sou-) *n.* **1.** the direction, or the point on a mariner's compass, halfway between south and west; 45° west of due south **2.** a district or region in or toward this direction —*adj.* **1.** in, of, toward, or facing the southwest **2.** from the southwest [a *southwest* wind] —*adv.* in, toward, or from the southwest —☆**the Southwest** the southwestern part of the U.S., esp. Okla., Tex., N.Mex., Ariz., and S Calif.

South West (or **South-West**) **Africa** territory in S Africa, on the Atlantic, a former mandate of South Africa: revocation of mandate (1966) by UN not recognized by South Africa: 318,261 sq. mi.; pop. 574,000; cap. Windhoek See NAMIBIA

southwest by south the direction, or the point on a mariner's compass, halfway between southwest and south-southwest; 11°15' south of southwest

southwest by west the direction, or the point on a mariner's compass, halfway between southwest and west-southwest; 11°15' west of southwest

south·west·er (south'wes'tər; *in nautical usage*, sou-) *n.* **1.** a storm or strong wind from the southwest **2.** a sailor's waterproof coat or hat of oilskin, canvas, etc., for wearing in stormy weather: the hat has a brim that broadens in the back to protect the neck

south·west·er·ly (-tər lē) *adj., adv.* **1.** in or toward the southwest **2.** from the southwest, as a wind

south·west·ern (-tərn) *adj.* **1.** in, of, or toward the southwest **2.** from the southwest [a *southwestern* wind] ☆**3.** [S-] of or characteristic of the Southwest —**South'·west'ern·er** *n.*

south·west·ward (-west'wərd) *adv., adj.* toward the southwest —*n.* a southwestward direction, point, or region

south·west·ward·ly (-wərd lē) *adj., adv.* **1.** toward the southwest **2.** from the southwest, as a wind

south·west·wards (-wərdz) *adv. same as* SOUTHWESTWARD

South Whittier suburb of Los Angeles, south of Whittier, in SW Calif.: pop. 47,000

Sou·tine (soo tēn'), **Cha·im** (khī'im) 1894-1943; Lithuanian painter in France

sou·ve·nir (soo'və nir', soo'və nir') *n.* [Fr., orig. inf., to remember < L. *subvenire*, to come to mind: see SUBVENE] something kept or serving as a reminder of a place, person, or occasion; keepsake; memento

sou'·west·er (sou wes'tər) *n. same as* SOUTHWESTER

sov·er·eign (säv'rən, -ər in; *occas.* suv'-) *adj.* [ME. *soveraine* < OFr. < VL. **superanus* < L. *super*, above, OVER] **1.** above or superior to all others; chief; greatest; supreme **2.** supreme in power, rank, or authority **3.** of or holding the position of ruler; royal; reigning **4.** independent of all others [a *sovereign* state] **5.** excellent; outstanding **6.** very effectual, as a cure or remedy —*n.* **1.** a person who possesses sovereign authority or power; specif., a monarch or ruler **2.** a group of persons or a state that possesses sovereign authority **3.** esp. formerly, a British gold coin valued at 20 shillings or one pound sterling —**sov'er·eign·ly** *adv.*

sov·er·eign·ty (-tē) *n., pl.* **-ties** [ME. *soverainete* < Anglo-Fr. *sovereyneté*, OFr. *soveraineté*] **1.** the state or quality of being sovereign **2.** the status, dominion, rule, or power of a sovereign **3.** supreme and independent political authority **4.** a sovereign state or governmental unit

so·vi·et (sō've it, -et'; sō've et') *n.* [Russ., lit., council] **1.** *a)* in the Soviet Union, any of the various governing councils, local, intermediate, and national, elected by and representing the people: they constitute a pyramidal governmental structure, with the village and town soviets as its base and the Supreme Soviet as its apex *b)* any similar council in a socialist governing system **2.** [S-] [pl.] the government officials or the people of the Soviet Union —*adj.* **1.** of a soviet or soviets **2.** of or connected with government by soviets **3.** [S-] of or connected with the Soviet Union

Soviet Central Asia that part of the U.S.S.R. in C Asia; the Kazakh, Kirghiz, Tadzhik, Turkmen, & Uzbek S.S.R.

so·vi·et·ism (sō've it iz'm) *n.* [*often* S-] **1.** government by soviets or the Soviets **2.** the system, principles, practices, etc. of such government

so·vi·et·ize (sō've ə tīz') *vt.* **-ized', -iz'ing** [*often* S-] **1.** to change to a soviet form of government **2.** to make conform with the system, principles, practices, etc. of the Soviets —**so'vi·et·i·za'tion** *n.*

Soviet Russia *same as:* **1.** SOVIET UNION **2.** RUSSIAN SOVIET FEDERATED SOCIALIST REPUBLIC

Soviet Union *same as* UNION OF SOVIET SOCIALIST REPUBLICS

sov·ran (säv'rən; *occas.* suv'-) *adj., n.* [old sp., infl. by It. *sovrano* (< OFr.)] *now rare var. of* SOVEREIGN

sow¹ (sou) *n.* [ME. *sowe* < OE. *sugu*, akin to G. *sau* (OHG. *su*) < IE. base **sū-*, pig, whence L. *sus*: cf. SWINE] **1.** *a)* an adult female pig or hog *b)* an adult female of certain other mammals, as the bear **2.** *a)* a channel or sluice carrying molten metal from a blast furnace to the molds in which pig bars are cast *b)* metal solidified in this channel

sow² (sō) *vt.* **sowed, sown** (sōn) *or* **sowed, sow'ing** [ME. *sowen* < OE. *sawan*, akin to G. *säen*: for IE. base see

SEED] **1.** to scatter or plant (seed) for growing **2.** to plant seed in or on (a field, ground, earth, etc.) **3.** to spread or scatter; broadcast, disseminate, or propagate [to *sow* hate] **4.** to implant; inculcate [to *sow* suspicion] —*vi.* to sow seed for growing —**sow'er** *n.*

☆**sow·bel·ly** (sou'bel'ē) *n.* [Colloq.] *same as* SALT PORK

sow bug (sou) any of several small terrestrial isopods (suborder Oniscoidea) living in damp places, as under rocks

sow·ens (sō'ənz, soo'-) *n.pl.* [Gael. *sughan* < *sugh*, sap] [Scot.] a porridge made from fermented oat husks

sow thistle (sou) [ME. *sowethistle* (parallel with G. *saudistel*): see SOW¹ & THISTLE] any of several old-world weeds (genus *Sonchus*) of the composite family, with yellow flower heads and spiny leaves

sox (säks) *n. alt. pl. of* SOCK¹ (sense 3)

soy (soi) *n.* [Jap., colloq. for *shōyu* < Chin. *chiang-yu* < *chiang*, salted bean + *yu*, oil] **1.** a dark, salty sauce made from soybeans fermented and steeped in brine, used esp. as a flavoring in Chinese and Japanese dishes: also **soy sauce 2.** the soybean plant or its seeds Also, chiefly Brit., **soy'a** (soi'ə)

soy·bean (soi'bēn') *n.* [prec. + BEAN] **1.** an annual crop plant (*Soja* or *Glycine max*) of the legume family, native to China and Japan but widely grown for its seeds, which contain much protein and oil, and as a forage and cover crop **2.** its seed

Soy·er (soi'ər), **Moses** (1899-) & **Raphael** (1899-); twin brothers; U.S. painters, born in Russia

soz·zled (säz'ld) *adj.* [pp. of dial. *sozzle*, *sossle*, to mix in a sloppy manner, splash] [Colloq.] drunk; intoxicated

SP, S.P. 1. Shore Patrol **2.** Submarine Patrol

Sp. 1. Spain **2.** Spaniard **3.** Spanish

sp. 1. special **2.** specialist **3.** *pl.* **spp.** species **4.** specific **5.** spelling

s.p. [L. *sine prole*] without issue; childless

spa (spä) *n.* [< *Spa*, celebrated watering place in Belgium] **1.** a mineral spring **2.** any place, esp. a health resort, having a mineral spring

space (spās) *n.* [ME. < OFr. *espace* < L. *spatium* < IE. base **spōi-*, to flourish, expand, succeed, whence SPEED, L. *spes*, hope, ON. *sparr*, OE. *spær*, thrifty] **1.** *a)* distance extending in all directions; the continuous expanse extending in all directions or in three dimensions, within which all things exist, variously thought of as boundless or indeterminately finite *b) same as* OUTER SPACE **2.** *a)* the distance, expanse, or area between, over, within, etc. things *b)* area or room sufficient for or allotted to something [a parking *space*] *c)* the area available or used on a page [*space* for an ad] **3.** an interval or period of time, often one of specified length ☆**4.** reserved accommodations [to buy *space* on a ship] **5.** *Math.* a set of points or elements assumed to satisfy a given set of postulates [four-dimensional *space*] **6.** *Music* the open area between any two lines of a staff **7.** *Printing a)* a blank piece of type metal used to separate characters, etc. *b)* the area, or its equivalent, left vacant by this on a printed or typed line **8.** *Telegraphy* an interval when the key is open, or not in contact, during the sending of a message —*adj.* of or pertaining to space, esp. to outer space —*vt.* **spaced, spac'ing** to arrange with space or spaces between; divide into or by spaces —**space out** to insert more space between letters, words, or lines so as to extend to the required length

Space Age [*also* s- a-] the period characterized by the launching of artificial satellites and manned space vehicles: regarded as beginning with the launching of the first sputnik on October 4, 1957 —**space'-age'** *adj.*

space bar a bar, as at the bottom of a typewriter keyboard, pressed to leave a blank space or spaces rather than to produce a character

space charge *Thermionics* a gathering of electrons existing in one of the spaces between electrodes, usually the cathode and first grid, in a vacuum tube

space·craft (spās'kraft', -kräft') *n., pl.* **-craft'** any spaceship or satellite designed for travel, exploration, etc. in outer space

space fiction fiction about adventures in space travel

☆**space·flight** (-flīt') *n.* a flight through outer space

space heater a small heating unit for warming the air of a single confined area, as a room

space lattice an array of points formed by the exact repetition in three dimensions of the structural units of a crystal

space·less (-lis) *adj.* **1.** having no spatial limits **2.** occupying no space

space·man (-man', -mən) *n., pl.* **-men'** (-men', -mən) an astronaut or, as in space fiction, any of the crew of a spaceship

☆**space medicine** a branch of medicine concerned with diseases and disorders incident to flight in outer space: cf. AEROMEDICINE

space·port (-pôrt') *n.* a center where spacecraft are assembled, tested, and launched

SOYBEAN PLANT

spac·er (spā'sər) *n.* **1.** *same as* SPACE BAR **2.** any person or thing that spaces

space·ship (spās'ship') *n.* a rocket-propelled vehicle for travel in outer space

Space Shoes 1. *a trademark for* custom shoes molded to the contours of the wearer's feet **2.** [s- s-] such shoes

space station (or **platform**) a structure designed to orbit in space as a satellite from which to launch other spacecraft, or as an experimentation or observation center

☆**space·suit** (-sōōt') *n. same as* G-SUIT, esp. one modified for use in spaceflights

space-time (-tīm') *n.* **1.** a four-dimensional continuum with four coordinates, the three dimensions of space and that of time, in which any event can be located: also called **space-time continuum 2.** the physical reality inherent in such a continuum

☆**space·walk** (-wôk') *n.* the act of an astronaut in moving about in space outside of his spacecraft —*vi.* to engage in a spacewalk —**space'walk'er** *n.*

space writer a journalist or other writer paid according to the amount of space occupied by his copy

spa·cial (spā'shəl) *adj. alt. sp.* of SPATIAL

spac·ing (spā'sin) *n.* **1.** the arrangement of spaces **2.** space or spaces, as between printed words **3.** the act of a person or thing that spaces

spa·cious (spā'shəs) *adj.* [ME. < OFr. *spacieux* < L. *spatiosus*] **1.** having or giving more than enough space or room; vast; extensive **2.** great; large; not confined or limited —**spa'cious·ly** *adv.* —**spa'cious·ness** *n.*

☆**Spack·le** (spak'']) [prob. adapted < G. *spachtel*, a spatula, *spachteln*, to fill or smooth (a surface), ult. < L. *spatula*: see SPATULA] *a trademark for* a powdery substance (**spackling compound**) mixed with water and applied to wallboard, etc. to dry very hard and cover seams, nail holes, etc. —**[s-]** this substance —*vt.* -**led**, -**ling** [s-] to put spackle on

spade[1] (spād) *n.* [ME. < OE. *spadu*, akin to G. *spaten* < IE. base *spē-*, long flat piece of wood, whence SPOON, Gr. *spathē* (cf. SPATULA)] **1.** a heavy, flat-bladed, long-handled tool used for digging by pressing the metal blade into the ground with the foot **2.** any of several tools resembling a spade **3.** a part of the trail of a gun carriage which digs into the ground to take up recoil —*vt.*, *vi.* **spad'ed, spad'ing** to dig or cut with or as with a spade —**call a spade a spade** to call something by its right name; use plain, blunt words —**spade'ful** *n.* —**spad'er** *n.*

spade[2] (spād) *n.* [Sp. *espada*, sword (the sign used on Spanish cards) < L. *spatha*, SPATULA] **1.** the black figure (♠) marking one of the four suits of playing cards **2.** [*pl.*] the suit of cards so marked **3.** a card of this suit —☆**in spades** [from the fact that spades are the highest suit in bridge, etc.] [Colloq.] in an extreme or emphatic way

spade[3] (spād) *n. spad'ed, spad'ing dial. var.* of SPAY

spade·fish (spād'fish') *n.*, *pl.* -**fish'**, -**fish'es**: see FISH[2] **1.** *a)* a disk-shaped food fish (*Chaetodipterus faber*) with sharp-spined fins, found along the Atlantic coast of N. America *b)* a related fish (*Chaetodipterus zonatus*) of the Pacific coast **2.** *same as* PADDLEFISH

spade·foot toad (-foot') any of several toads (family Pelobatidae) with a hornlike projection on the hind foot, used in digging burrows

spade·work (-wurk') *n.* preparatory work for some main project, esp. when tiresome or difficult

spa·di·ceous (spā dish'əs) *adj.* [ModL. *spadiceus* < L. *spadix*, date-brown color: see ff.] **1.** bright brown in color **2.** bearing or like a spadix

spa·dix (spā'diks) *n.*, *pl.* -**dix·es**, -**di·ces** (spā'də sēz', spā dī'sēz) [ModL. < L., a palm branch broken off together with the fruit, date-brown color < Gr. *spadix* < IE. base *spē-*, to pull, whence SPAN[1]] a fleshy spike of tiny flowers, usually enclosed in a spathe

spa·ghet·ti (spə get'ē) *n.* [It., *pl.* of *spaghetto*, dim. of *spago*, small cord] **1.** pasta in the form of long, thin strings, cooked by boiling or steaming and served with a sauce **2.** *Elec.* an insulating tubing somewhat resembling macaroni, used for sheathing bare wire

spa·hi, spa·hee (spä'hē) *n.* [Fr. < Turk. *sipāhī* < Per.: see SEPOY] formerly **1.** a member of a corps of Turkish irregular cavalry **2.** a member of a corps of native Algerian cavalry in the French armed forces

Spain (spān) [ME. *Spaine*, aphetic < Anglo-Fr. *Espaigne* < OFr. < LL. *Spania*, for L. *Hispania* (prob. infl. by Gr. *Spania*)] country in SW Europe, on the Iberian peninsula: 194,346 sq. mi.; pop. 32,411,000; cap. Madrid: Sp. name, ESPAÑA

spake (spāk) *archaic pt.* of SPEAK

Spa·la·to (spä'lä tō') It. *name* of SPLIT

spall (spôl) *n.* [ME. *spalle*, prob. < or akin to *spalden* > to chip, split, akin to G. *spalten*, to split: for IE. base see SPOOL] a flake or chip, esp. of stone —*vt.*, *vi.* **1.** to break up or split **2.** to break off in layers parallel to a surface

spall·a·tion (spô lā'shən) *n.* [< prec.] a nuclear reaction produced by high-energy projectiles in which two or more fragments or particles, as neutrons or protons, are ejected from the target nucleus

spal·peen (spal pēn', spal'pēn) *n.* [Ir. *spailpín*] [Irish] a scamp or rascal

Sp. Am. 1. Spanish America **2.** Spanish-American

span[1] (span) *n.* [ME. *spanne* < OE. *sponn*, akin to G. *spanne* < IE. base *spē-*, to extend, whence Gr. *span*, to

pull] **1.** a measure of length, equal to nine inches, based on the distance between the tips of the extended thumb and little finger **2.** *a)* the full amount or extent between any two limits *b)* the distance between ends or supports [the *span* of an arch] *c)* the full duration of [*span* of attention, the *span* of a man's life] **3.** a part between two supports [a bridge of four *spans*] **4.** *shortened form of* WINGSPAN ☆**5.** [borrowed in U.S. < Du. *span*, in same sense] a team of two animals used together —*vt.* **spanned, span'ning** [ME. *spannen* < OE. *spannan*, join: see *n.*] **1.** to measure, esp. by the hand with the thumb and little finger extended **2.** to encircle with the hand or hands, in or as in measuring **3.** to extend, stretch, reach, or pass over or across [the bridge that *spans* the river] **4.** to furnish with something that extends or stretches over [to *span* an aisle with an arch] —*SYN.* see PAIR

span[2] (span) *archaic pt.* of SPIN

Span. 1. Spaniard **2.** Spanish

span·cel (span's'l) *n.* [LowG. *spansel* < *spannen*, to stretch, tie: see SPAN[1]] a rope for fettering or hobbling cattle, horses, etc. —*vt.* -**celed** or -**celled**, -**cel·ing** or -**cel·ling** to fetter or hobble as with a spancel

☆**span·dex** (span'deks) *n.* [arbitrary metathesis of EXPAND] an elastic fiber, chiefly a synthetic polymer of polyurethane, used in girdles, swimsuits, etc.

span·drel (span'drəl) *n.* [ME. *spaundrell*, dim. of Anglo-Fr. *spaundre* < OFr. *espandre*, to expand < L. *expandere*] **1.** the triangular space between the exterior curve of an arch and a rectangular frame or mold enclosing it **2.** any of the spaces between a series of arches and a straight cornice running above them

SPANDRELS

spang (span) *adv.* [< dial. *spang*, with a leap < dial. *spang*, to leap] ☆[Colloq.] abruptly, directly, or exactly

span·gle (span'g'l) *n.* [ME. *spangel*, dim. of *spang*, a buckle, clasp < OE., akin to G. *spange*: for IE. base see SPAN[1]] **1.** a small piece of bright metal, esp. any of a number of these sewn on fabric for decoration **2.** any small, bright object that glitters —*vt.* -**gled**, -**gling** to cover or decorate with spangles or other bright objects —*vi.* to glitter with or as with spangles —**span'gly** *adj.* -**gli·er**, -**gli·est**

Span·iard (span'yərd) *n.* [ME. *Spaignard* < OFr. *Espaignart* < *Espaigne*, SPAIN] a native or inhabitant of Spain

span·iel (span'yəl) *n.* [ME. *spainel* < MFr. *espagnol*, lit., Spanish < Sp. *español* < *España*, Spain < L. *Hispania*] **1.** any of several breeds of dog characterized by a silky coat, large drooping ears, a small tail, and short legs **2.** a servile, fawning person

Span·ish (span'ish) *adj.* of Spain, its people, their language, etc. —*n.* the Romance language of Spain and of Spanish America: cf. CASTILIAN —**the Spanish** the people of Spain

Spanish America Mexico and those countries in Central and South America and islands in the Caribbean in which Spanish is the chief language

Span·ish-A·mer·i·can (-ə mer'ə kən) *adj.* **1.** of both Spain and America **2.** of Spanish America or its people —*n.* a native or inhabitant of Spanish America, esp. one of Spanish descent

Spanish-American War the war between the U.S. and Spain (1898)

Spanish Armada *see* ARMADA (sense 2)

☆**Spanish bayonet** any of a number of yuccas, esp. any of two species (*Yucca aloifolia* or *Yucca gloriosa*) with stiff, sword-shaped leaves: also called **Spanish dagger**

Spanish cedar 1. a West Indian tree (*Cedrela odorata*) of the mahogany family, yielding a light, aromatic wood used in making cigar boxes, etc. **2.** its wood

Spanish Civil War the civil war in Spain (1936–39)

Spanish fly 1. a bright green blister beetle (*Lytta vesicatoria*) of S Europe **2.** *same as* CANTHARIDES (sense 2)

Spanish Guinea *former name of* EQUATORIAL GUINEA

Spanish Inquisition the Inquisition as reorganized in Spain in 1478: notorious for its cruel and extreme practices against those accused of heresy and against Marranos

Spanish mackerel any of several edible sea fishes (genus *Scomberomorus*), as the pintado, related to the mackerel

Spanish Main 1. orig., the coastal region of the Americas along the Caribbean Sea; esp., the N coast of S. America between the Isthmus of Panama & the mouth of the Orinoco **2.** later, the Caribbean Sea itself, or that part of it adjacent to the N coast of S. America, traveled in the 16th–18th cent. by Sp. merchant ships, which were often harassed by pirates

Spanish Morocco the former Sp. zone of Morocco, constituting a coastal strip along the Mediterranean

☆**Spanish moss** a rootless epiphytic plant (*Tillandsia usneoides*) of the pineapple family, made up of slender, grayish, scaly stems and leaves and often found growing in long, graceful strands from the branches of trees in the SE U.S. and tropical America

☆**Spanish needles 1.** a bur marigold (*Bidens bipinnata*) of the E U.S. **2.** its barbed fruit

☆**Spanish omelet** an omelet folded around a sauce of chopped onion, green pepper, and tomato

Spanish onion any of several large, globe-shaped, mild-flavored onions, often eaten raw

Spanish paprika paprika made from a variety of mild red pepper grown in Spain

☆**Spanish rice** boiled rice cooked with tomatoes and chopped onions, green peppers, etc.

Spanish Sahara Sp. province at the W end of the Sahara, on the Atlantic: 109,000 sq. mi.; pop. 48,000

Spanish Succession, War of the a war (1701–14) between European powers disputing the succession to the Spanish throne

spank (spaŋk) *vt.* [echoic] to strike with something flat, as the open hand, esp. on the buttocks, as in punishment —*vi.* [< SPANKING, *adj.*] to move along swiftly or smartly —*n.* a smack given in spanking

spank·er (spaŋ′kər) *n.* **1.** a person or thing that spanks **2.** [Colloq.] an exceptionally fine, large, etc. person or thing **3.** *Naut. a)* a fore-and-aft sail, usually hoisted on a gaff, on the after mast of a square-rigged vessel: see SAIL, illus. ☆*b)* the after mast and its sail on a schooner-rigged vessel of more than three masts

spank·ing (-kiŋ) *adj.* [< intens. use of prp. of SPANK] **1.** swiftly moving; rapid **2.** brisk: said of a breeze **3.** [Colloq.] exceptionally fine, large, vigorous, etc. —*adv.* [Colloq.] altogether; completely [*spanking* new] —*n.* a series of smacks, esp. on the buttocks, in punishment

span·ner (span′ər) *n.* **1.** a person or thing that spans **2.** [G. < *spannen,* to stretch: see SPAN¹] [Chiefly Brit.] *same as* WRENCH

span-new (span′nōō′, -nyōō′) *adj.* [ME. *span-newe* < ON. *span-nȳr* < *spānn,* a chip (akin to SPOON) + *nȳr,* NEW] [Now Rare] perfectly new

☆**Span·sule** (span′sool, -syool) [SPAN¹ + (CAP)SULE] *a trademark for* a medicinal capsule containing many tiny beads of medicine that dissolve at spaced intervals for long-acting medication —*n.* [s-] such a capsule

☆**span·worm** (span′wurm′) *n. same as* MEASURING WORM

☆**Spar, SPAR** (spär) *n.* [< *s(emper) par(atus),* always prepared, L. motto of the U.S. Coast Guard] a woman member of the U.S. Coast Guard

spar¹ (spär) *n.* [< MDu. or MLowG. *spar,* akin to OE. *spær(stan),* gypsum, chalk] any shiny, crystalline, nonmetallic mineral that cleaves easily into chips or flakes

spar² (spär) *n.* [ME. *sparre* < ON. *sparri* or MDu. *sparre* < IE. base *sper-,* a pole, rod, whence SPEAR, L. *sparus,* short spear] **1.** any pole, as a mast, yard, boom, or gaff, supporting or extending a sail of a ship **2.** a structural member running along, and supporting the ribs of, an airplane wing —*vt.* **sparred, spar′ring** to equip with spars

spar³ (spär) *vi.* **sparred, spar′ring** [ME. *sparren,* prob. < MFr. *esparer* < It. *sparare,* to fling out the hind legs, kick < *parare,* to PARRY] **1.** to fight with the feet and spurs: said of a fighting cock **2.** to box with jabbing or feinting movements, landing few heavy blows, as in exhibition or practice matches **3.** to wrangle or dispute —*n.* **1.** a sparring match or movement **2.** a dispute

spar·a·ble (spar′ə b′l) *n.* [altered < *sparrow bill:* from its shape] a small, headless nail used by shoemakers

spar buoy a sparlike buoy anchored at one end so as to float perpendicularly or obliquely: see BUOY, illus.

spar deck the upper deck running a ship's full length

spare (sper) *vt.* **spared, spar′ing** [ME. *sparien* < OE. *sparian* (akin to G. *sparen,* to save), akin to *spær,* thrifty: see SPACE] **1.** to treat with mercy or leniency; refrain from killing, injuring, troubling, or distressing; save **2.** to save or free a person from (something) [to *spare* someone trouble] **3.** to refrain from, omit, avoid using, or use frugally [to *spare* no effort] **4.** to give up the use or possession of; part with or give up conveniently [able to *spare* a cup of sugar] —*vi.* **1.** to practice close economy; be frugal or sparing **2.** to be merciful or restrained, as in punishing —*adj.* **1.** not in regular use or immediately needed; extra [a *spare* room, a *spare* tire] **2.** not taken up by regular work or duties; free [*spare* time] **3.** frugal; meager; scanty [to live on *spare* rations] **4.** not fleshy; lean; thin —*n.* **1.** a spare, or extra, part, thing, etc. ☆**2.** *Bowling a)* the act of knocking down all the pins with two consecutive rolls of the ball *b)* a score so made —*SYN.* see LEAN², MEAGER —**(something) to spare** a surplus of (something) —**spare′ly** *adv.* —**spare′ness** *n.* —**spar′er** *n.*

spare·ribs (sper′ribz′) *n.pl.* [altered (after SPARE, *adj.*) < MLowG. *ribbesper,* cured pork ribs roasted on a spit < *ribbe,* RIB + *sper,* a spit, SPEAR] a cut of meat, esp. pork, consisting of the thin end of the ribs with most of the meat cut away: see PORK, illus.

sparge (spärj) *vt., vi.* **sparged, sparg′ing** [MFr. *espargier* < L. *spargere:* see SPARK¹] to splash or sprinkle —**sparg′er** *n.*

spar·id (spar′id) *n.* [< ModL. *Sparidae* < *Sparus,* name of the type genus (< L., gilthead) + *-idae,* -IDAE] any of a family (Sparidae) of bony fishes with an elongated, elevated body, large head, and small mouth, including the porgies, sheepshead, sea bream, etc.

spar·ing (sper′iŋ) *adj.* **1.** that spares **2.** careful in spending or using; frugal **3.** scanty or meager —*SYN.* see THRIFTY —**spar′ing·ly** *adv.* —**spar′ing·ness** *n.*

spark¹ (spärk) *n.* [ME. *sperke* < OE. *spearca,* akin to MDu. *sparke* < IE. base *sp(h)er(e)-g-,* to strew, sprinkle, whence L. *spargere,* to SPRINKLE] **1.** a glowing bit of matter, esp. one thrown off by a fire **2.** any flash or sparkle of light like this **3.** a tiny beginning or vestige, as of life, interest, excitement, etc.; particle or trace **4.** liveliness; vivacity **5.** *Elec. a)* a very brief flash of light accompanying an electric discharge through air or some other insulating material, as between the electrodes of a spark plug *b)* such a discharge ☆**6.** [Slang] [*pl.,* *with sing. v.*] *an epithet for* a ship's radio operator —*vi.* **1.** to make or throw off sparks **2.** to come forth as or like sparks **3.** to produce the sparks properly: said of the ignition in an internal-combustion engine —*vt.* to serve as the activating or animating influence of or in; stir up; activate [to *spark* interest] —**spark′er** *n.*

spark² (spärk) *n.* [ON. *sparkr,* lively: for IE. base see prec.] **1.** a gay, dashing, gallant young man **2.** a beau or lover —*vt., vi.* ☆[Colloq.] to court, woo, pet, etc. An old-fashioned term —**spark′er** *n.*

☆**spark arrester** any device used to prevent sparks from escaping, as from a chimney

spark chamber any of several devices for detecting charged subatomic particles, decay products, rays, etc., consisting usually of a large group of closely spaced, oppositely charged metal plates between which sparks will jump through an inert gas, as neon, along the ionized path created by the passage of radiation

spark coil an electric induction coil for producing a spark, as in the ignition of an internal-combustion engine

spark gap a space between two electrodes through which a spark discharge may take place

spar·kle (spär′k′l) *vi.* **-kled, -kling** [ME. *sparklen,* freq. of *sparken,* to SPARK¹] **1.** to throw off sparks **2.** to gleam or shine in flashes; glitter or glisten, as jewels, sunlit water, etc. **3.** to be brilliant and lively [*sparkling* wit] **4.** to effervesce or bubble, as soda water and some wines —*vt.* to cause to sparkle —*n.* **1.** a spark, or glowing particle **2.** a sparkling, or glittering **3.** brilliance; liveliness; vivacity —*SYN.* see FLASH

spar·kler (-klər) *n.* a person or thing that sparkles; specif., *a)* a thin, light stick of pyrotechnic material that burns with bright sparks *b)* [*pl.*] [Colloq.] clear, brilliant eyes *c)* [Colloq.] a diamond or similar gem

☆**spark plug** **1.** a piece fitted into the cylinder of an internal-combustion engine to ignite the fuel mixture within: it carries an electric current into the cylinder, which sparks between two terminals in the presence of the mixture **2.** [Colloq.] a person or thing that inspires, activates, or advances something —**spark′plug′** *vt.* **-plugged′, -plug′ging**

spark transmitter an early type of radio transmitter that uses the oscillatory discharge of a capacitor through an inductor in series with a spark gap to generate its high-frequency power

SPARK PLUG (in cross section)

spar·ling (spär′liŋ) *n., pl.* **-ling, -lings:** see PLURAL, II, D, 2 [ME. *sperlynge* < MFr. *esperlinge* < MDu. *spirlinc,* orig. dim. of *spīr,* a small point, grass shoot: see SPIRE²] a European smelt (*Osmerus eperlanus*)

spar·oid (sper′oid, spar′-) *adj.* [< ModL. *sparoides* < *sparus,* gilthead < L. < Gr. *sparos:* for IE. base see SPEAR] of or pertaining to the sparids —*n. same as* SPARID

sparring partner any person with whom a prizefighter boxes for practice

spar·row (spar′ō) *n.* [ME. *sparwe* < OE. *spearwa,* akin to MHG. *sparwe* < IE. base *sper-,* bird name, esp. for sparrow, whence Gr. *sporgilos,* sparrow, *psar,* starling] **1.** any of several old-world weaverbirds; esp., any of a genus (*Passer*) including the ENGLISH SPARROW **2.** any of numerous finches native to both the Old and New Worlds; ☆esp., any of various American species, as the SONG-SPARROW **3.** any of several other sparrowlike birds

spar·row·grass (spar′ō gras′, -gräs′) *n.* [altered by folk etym. < ASPARAGUS] *dial. var. of* ASPARAGUS

sparrow hawk [ME. *sparowhawke:* so named from preying on sparrows] **1.** a small European hawk (*Accipiter nisus*) with short, rounded wings ☆**2.** a small American falcon (*Falco sparverius*) with a reddish-brown back and tail

spar·ry (spär′ē) *adj.* **-ri·er, -ri·est** of, like, or rich in mineral spar

sparse (spärs) *adj.* [L. *sparsus,* pp. of *spargere,* to scatter: see SPARK¹] thinly spread or distributed; not dense or crowded —*SYN.* see MEAGER —**sparse′ly** *adv.* —**sparse′ness, spar′si·ty** (-sə tē) *n.*

Spar·ta (spär′tə) city in the S Peloponnesus, Greece, a powerful military city in ancient Laconia

Spar·ta·cus (spär′tə kəs) ?-71 B.C.; Thracian slave & gladiator in Rome: leader of a slave revolt

Spar·tan (spär′t′n) *adj.* [L. *Spartanus*] **1.** of ancient Sparta, its people, or their culture **2.** like or characteristic of the Spartans; warlike, brave, hardy, stoical, severe, frugal, highly disciplined, etc. —*n.* **1.** a native or citizen of Sparta **2.** a person with Spartan traits —**Spar′tan·ism** *n.*

---

fat, āpe, cär; ten, ēven; is, bīte; gō, hôrn, tōōl, look; oil, out; up, fur; get; joy; yet; chin; she; thin, then; zh, leisure; ŋ, ring; ə for *a* in *ago, e* in *agent, i* in *sanity, o* in *comply, u* in *focus;* ' as in *able* (ā′b'l); Fr. bal; ë, Fr. coeur; ö, Fr. feu; Fr. mon; ô, Fr. coq; ü, Fr. duc; r, Fr. cri; H, G. ich; kh, G. doch. See inside front cover. ☆ Americanism; ‡foreign; *hypothetical; < derived from

Spar·tan·burg (-burg′) [after the "Spartan Regiment" raised there in the Am. Revolution] city in NW S.C.: pop. 45,000

spar·te·ine (spär′ti ēn′, -tē in) *n.* [< ModL. *Spartium*, name of the broom genus (< L. *spartum*, broom (see ESPARTO) + -INE¹] a clear, oily, poisonous, liquid alkaloid, C₁₅H₂₆N₂, obtained from a broom (*Spartium scoparium*)

spar varnish a varnish that forms a hard, durable, protective finish, used esp. on outdoor surfaces

spasm (spaz′m) *n.* [ME. *spasme* < MFr. < L. *spasmus* < Gr. *spasmos* < *span*, to draw, pull, wrench: see SPAN¹] 1. a sudden, convulsive, involuntary muscular contraction: a **tonic spasm** is persistent and sustained, and a **clonic spasm** is one of a series of relatively brief contractions alternating with relaxations 2. any sudden, violent, temporary activity, feeling, etc.

spas·mod·ic (spaz mäd′ik) *adj.* [ModL. *spasmodicus* < Gr. *spasmōdēs* < *spasmos*: see prec. & -OID] 1. of, having the nature of, like, or characterized by a spasm or spasms; sudden, violent, and temporary; fitful; intermittent 2. [Rare] highly emotional or excitable Also **spas·mod′i·cal** —**spas·mod′i·cal·ly** *adv.*

spas·tic (spas′tik) *adj.* [L. *spasticus* < Gr. *spastikos*, drawing, pulling < *span* (see SPASM)] 1. of, characterized by, affected with, or produced by spasm [*spastic* colon] 2. afflicted with or involving spastic paralysis —*n.* a person with spastic paralysis —**spas′ti·cal·ly** *adv.*

spastic paralysis a condition, as in cerebral palsy, in which certain muscles are in a state of continuous contraction, causing rigidity of a normally movable part, accompanied by exaggerated tendon reflexes

spat¹ (spat) *n.* [prob. echoic] 1. [Rare] a slap 2. a quick, slapping sound 3. [Colloq.] a brief, petty quarrel or dispute —*vi.* **spat′ted, spat′ting** 1. [Rare] to slap 2. to strike with a quick, slapping sound ☆3. [Colloq.] to engage in a spat, or quarrel —*vt.* [Rare] to slap —**SYN.** see QUARREL²

spat² (spat) *n.* [contr. < SPATTERDASH] a gaiterlike covering for the instep and ankle, usually of heavy cloth

spat³ (spat) *alt. pt. & pp. of* SPIT²

spat⁴ (spat) *n.* [Anglo-Fr. < ?] 1. the spawn of the oyster or other bivalve shellfish 2. *a*) young oysters collectively *b*) a young oyster —*vi.* **spat′ted, spat′ting** to spawn: said of oysters

spate (spāt) *n.* [ME. (northern dial.) < ?] 1. [Chiefly Brit.] *a*) a flash flood *b*) a sudden, heavy rain 2. an unusually large outpouring, as of words

spa·tha·ceous (spə thā′shəs) *adj.* [ModL. *spathaceus*: see ff. & -ACEOUS] 1. having a spathe 2. of, or having the nature of, a spathe

spathe (spāth) *n.* [ModL. *spatha* < L., a flat blade, spathe (of a palm tree) < Gr. *spathē*, flat blade: for IE. base see SPADE¹] a large, leaflike part or pair of such parts enclosing a flower cluster (esp. a spadix) —**spathed** (spāthd) *adj.*

spath·ic (spath′ik) *adj.* [G. *spath*, obs. sp. for *spat*, SPAR¹ < MHG. *spat* (for IE. base see SPADE¹) + -IC] *Mineralogy* of or like spar

spa·those¹ (spā′thōs, spath′ōs) *adj. same as* SPATHACEOUS

spath·ose² (spath′ōs) *adj. same as* SPATHIC

spath·u·late (spath′yoo lit) *adj. same as* SPATULATE (sense 1)

spa·tial (spā′shəl) *adj.* [< L. *spatium*, SPACE] 1. of space 2. happening or existing in space —**spa·ti·al′i·ty** (-shē al′ə tē) *n.* —**spa′tial·ly** *adv.*

spa·ti·o·tem·po·ral (spā′shē ō tem′pər əl) *adj.* 1. existing in both space and time 2. of space-time —**spa′ti·o·tem′po·ral·ly** *adv.*

spat·ter (spat′ər) *vt.* [akin to Fris. *spateren*, freq. of *spatten*, to splash, spurt] 1. to scatter in drops or small blobs [to *spatter* red paint over blue] 2. to splash, spot, or soil with such drops or blobs 3. to defame or slander —*vi.* 1. to emit or spurt out in drops or small blobs, as fat in frying 2. to fall or strike in or as in a shower, as raindrops or pellets —*n.* 1. *a*) the act or an instance of spattering *b*) the sound of this 2. a mark or wet spot caused by spattering 3. a small amount or number

spat·ter·dash (-dash′) *n.* [prec. + DASH] a long legging formerly worn to protect the stocking or trouser leg, as in wet weather

☆**spat·ter·dock** (-däk′) *n.* any of several waterlilies; esp., a N. American pond lily (*Nuphar advena*) with thick roots, heart-shaped leaves, and yellow flowers

spat·u·la (spach′ə lə) *n.* [L., dim. of *spatha*, flat blade, SPATHE] any of various knifelike implements with a flat, flexible blade, used for spreading or blending foods, paints, etc., for scraping, etc. —**spat′u·lar** *adj.*

spat·u·late (-lit, -lāt′) *adj.* [ModL. *spatulatus*] 1. *Bot.* spoon-shaped in outline and attached at the narrow end, as some leaves 2. *Zool.* spoon-shaped or spatula-shaped

spav·in (spav′in) *n.* [ME. *spavine* < MFr. *esparvain* < ?] a disease of horses in which a deposit of bone (**bone spavin**) or an infusion of lymph (**bog spavin**) develops in the hock joint, usually causing lameness

spav·ined (-ind) *adj.* afflicted with spavin; lame

spawn (spôn) *vt., vi.* [ME. *spaunnen* (for *spaunden*) < Anglo-Fr. *espaundre* < OFr. *espandre*, to shed < L. *expandere*: see EXPAND] 1. to produce or deposit (eggs,

sperm, or young) 2. to bring forth or be the source of (esp. something regarded with contempt and produced in great numbers) 3. *Hort.* to plant with spawn, or mycelium —*n.* 1. the mass of eggs or young produced by fish, mollusks, crustaceans, amphibians, etc. 2. something produced, esp. in great quantity; specif., numerous offspring or progeny: usually contemptuous 3. the mycelium of fungi, esp. of mushrooms grown to be eaten

spay (spā) *vt.* [ME. *spayen*, aphetic < Anglo-Fr. *espeier* < OFr. *espeer*, to cut with a sword < *espee*, sword < L. *spatha*: see SPATHE] to sterilize (a female animal) by removing the ovaries

S.P.C.A. Society for the Prevention of Cruelty to Animals

S.P.C.C. Society for the Prevention of Cruelty to Children

speak (spēk) *vi.* **spoke** or archaic **spake**, **spok′en** or archaic **spoke**, **speak′ing** [ME. *speken* < OE. *specan*, earlier *sprecan*, akin to G. *sprechen* < IE. base *sp(h)er(e)-g-*, to strew, sprinkle, whence SPARK¹, L. *spargere*, to sprinkle: basic sense "to scatter (words)"] 1. to utter words with the ordinary voice; talk 2. to express or communicate opinions, feelings, ideas, etc. by or as by talking [*speak* in our behalf, actions *speak* louder than words] 3. to make a request or reservation (*for*): usually in the passive voice [a seat not yet *spoken* for] 4. to make a speech; deliver an address or lecture; discourse 5. to be a spokesman (*for*) 6. to talk with another or others; converse 7. to make or give out sound, as a gun firing or a dog barking —*vt.* 1. to express or make known by or as by speaking 2. to use or be able to use (a given language) in speaking 3. to utter (words) orally 4. [Archaic] to speak to; address 5. [Archaic] to declare or show to be; reveal 6. *Naut.* to hail (a ship) —**so to speak** in a manner of speaking; that is to say —**speak for itself** to be self-evident —**speak out** (or **up**) 1. to speak audibly or clearly 2. to speak freely or forcefully —**speak well for** to say or indicate something favorable about —**to speak of** worthy of mention [no gains *to speak of*] —**speak′a·ble** *adj.*

SYN.—**speak** and **talk** are generally synonymous, but **speak** often connotes formal address to an auditor or audience [who will *speak* at the dinner?] and **talk** often suggests informal colloquial conversation [we were *talking* at dinner]; **converse** suggests a talking together by two or more people so as to exchange ideas, information, etc. [they are *conversing* in the parlor]; **discourse** suggests a somewhat formal, detailed, extensive talking to another or others [he was *discoursing* to us on Keats]

☆**speak·eas·y** (-ē′zē) *n., pl.* **-eas′ies** [SPEAK + EASY: so named from the secretive atmosphere] [Slang] a place where alcoholic drinks are sold illegally, esp. such a place in the U.S. during Prohibition

speak·er (spē′kər) *n.* 1. a person who speaks; esp., *a*) a person who makes a speech or speeches in public *b*) the officer presiding over any of various lawmaking bodies; specif., ☆[S-] the presiding officer of the U.S. House of Representatives: in full **Speaker of the House** ☆2. a book of selections for use as exercises in declamation 3. *shortened form of* LOUDSPEAKER —**speak′er·ship′** *n.*

speak·ing (-kiŋ) *adj.* 1. that speaks or seems to speak; expressive; eloquent; vivid [a *speaking* likeness] 2. used in or for speech 3. allowing or admitting of speech [within *speaking* range] —*n.* 1. the act or art of a person who speaks 2. that which is spoken; utterance; discourse —**on speaking terms** friendly enough to exchange greetings or carry on conversation

speaking in tongues *same as* GLOSSOLALIA

speaking tube a tube or pipe made to carry the voice, as from one part of a building or ship to another

spear (spir) *n.* [ME. *spere* < OE. (akin to G. *speer*): for IE. base see SPAR³] 1. *a*) a weapon consisting of a long wooden shaft with a sharp point, usually of metal or stone, for thrusting or throwing *b*) its point 2. any spearlike, often forked, implement used for thrusting, as in one kind of fishing 3. *clipped form of* SPEARMAN 4. [var. of SPIRE²; ? infl. by *n.* 1 above] a long blade or shoot, as of grass —*vt.* 1. to pierce or stab with something pointed, as a spear 2. to catch (fish, etc.) with a spear 3. [Colloq.] to extend the arm so as to make a one-handed catch of (a baseball, etc.) —*vi.* 1. to pierce or shoot like a spear 2. [cf. *n.* 4] to sprout into a long stem —**spear′er** *n.*

☆**spear·fish** (-fish′) *n., pl.* **-fish′, -fish′es**: see FISH² 1. any of a genus (*Tetrapturus*) of large billfishes of the open seas, related to the marlin and sailfish 2. any of several large marine fishes with a long, spearlike growth on the upper jaw, as the swordfish, sailfish, etc. —*vi.* to fish with a spear or a spear-thrusting device (**spear gun**)

spear grass any of several perennial grasses (genus *Stipa*) having hard, sharp-pointed, bearded fruits

spear·head (-hed′) *n.* 1. the pointed head of a spear 2. the leading person, part, or group in an endeavor, esp. in a military attack —*vt.* to take the lead in (an attack, etc.)

spear·man (-mən) *n., pl.* **-men** (-mən) a fighting man armed with a spear

spear·mint (-mint′) *n.* [prob. after the appearance of the flowers on the stem] a fragrant perennial plant (*Mentha spicata*) of the mint family, used for flavoring

spec. 1. special 2. specification 3. speculation

spe·cial (spesh′əl) *adj.* [ME. < OFr. *especial* < L. *specialis* < *species*, kind, sort: see SPECIES] 1. of a kind different from others; distinctive, peculiar, or unique 2. exceptional; extraordinary [a *special* treat] 3. highly regarded or valued

SPATHE

SPADIX

[a *special* friend] **4.** of or for a particular person, occasion, purpose, etc. [by *special* permission, a *special* edition] **5.** not general or regular; specific or limited [*special* legislation] —*n.* **1.** a special person or thing; specialty, a special train, edition, sale offer or item, etc. ☆**2.** a relatively elaborate television program not part of a regular series **SYN.—special** and **especial** both imply that the thing so described has qualities, aspects, uses, etc. which differentiate it from others of its class, and the choice of word generally depends on euphony, but **especial** is usually preferred where pre-eminence is implied [a matter of *especial* interest to you]; **specific** and **particular** are both applied to something that is singled out for attention, but **specific** suggests the explicit statement of an example, illustration, etc. [he cited *specific* cases], and **particular** emphasizes the distinctness or individuality of the thing so described [in this *particular* case] —**ANT. general**

special assessment a special tax levied on a property to pay for a local public improvement, as a sewer, that will presumably benefit that property

special court-martial a military court for judging offenses less grave than those judged by a general court-martial

☆**special delivery** a postal service through which, for an extra fee, mail is delivered by a special messenger

special effects devices used to create illusions in motion pictures, television, etc.

☆**special handling** a postal service through which, for an extra fee, fourth-class or parcel-post mail is handled as expeditiously as is practicable

spe·cial·ism (-iz'm) *n.* the act of specializing in a branch or field of a study, profession, etc.

spe·cial·ist (-ist) *n.* **1.** a person who specializes in a particular field of study, professional work, etc. ☆**2.** *U.S. Army* any of six grades for enlisted personnel with technical training and duties, corresponding to the grades of corporal through sergeant major —*adj.* of a specialist or specialism: also **spe'cial·is'tic**

spe·ci·al·i·ty (spesh'ē al'ə tē) *n., pl.* **-ties** [ME. *specialite* < OFr. *spécialité*] *chiefly Brit. var. of* SPECIALTY

spe·cial·ize (spesh'ə līz') *vt.* **-ized'**, **-iz'ing** [Fr. *spécialiser*] **1.** to make special, specific, or particular; specify **2.** to direct toward or concentrate on a specific end **3.** *Biol.* to adapt (parts or organs) to a special condition, use, or requirement —*vi.* **1.** to follow a special or limited line of endeavor; concentrate on only one part or branch of a subject, profession, etc. **2.** *Biol.* to become adapted to meet a special condition, use, etc. —**spe'cial·i·za'tion** *n.*

special jury *Law* **1.** a blue-ribbon jury **2.** *same as* STRUCK JURY

spe·cial·ly (spesh'əl ē) *adv.* **1.** in a special manner; particularly **2.** for a special purpose

special pleading 1. *Law* the allegation that special or new matter exists which will offset matter presented by the opposite side **2.** an argument or presentation that leaves out what is unfavorable and develops only what is favorable to the case

spe·cial·ty (spesh'əl tē) *n., pl.* **-ties** [ME. *specialte* < OFr. *especialté*] **1.** a special quality, feature, point, characteristic, etc. **2.** a thing specialized in; special interest, field of study or professional work, etc. **3.** the state of being special **4.** an article or class of article characterized by special features, superior quality, novelty, etc. [a bakery whose *specialty* is pie] **5.** *Law* a special contract, obligation, agreement, etc. under seal, or a contract by deed

☆**spe·ci·a·tion** (spē'shē ā'shən, -sē-) *n.* [< SPECI(ES) + -ATION] *Biol.* the process of developing new species through evolution —**spe'ci·ate'** (-āt'ed, -at'ing

spe·cie (spē'shē, -sē) *n.* [abl. of L. *species*: used as Eng. word from occurrence in the phrase (*paid*) *in specie*] coin, as distinguished from paper money —**in specie 1.** in kind **2.** in coin

spe·cies (-shēz, -sēz) *n., pl.* **-cies** [L., a seeing, appearance, shape, kind, or quality < base of *specere*, to see: see SPY] **1.** a distinct kind; sort; variety; class [a *species* of bravery] **2.** [Obs.] outward form, appearance, or mental image **3.** *obs. var. of* SPECIE **4.** *Biol.* the fundamental biological classification, comprising a subdivision of a genus and consisting of a number of plants or animals all of which have a high degree of similarity, can generally interbreed as among themselves, and show persistent differences from members of allied species: a species is the uncapitalized, second name in a binomial: cf. GENUS (sense 2) **5.** *Logic* a class of individuals or objects having certain distinguishing attributes in common, given a common name, and comprised with other similar classes in a more comprehensive grouping called a GENUS **6.** *Physics* a) a specific kind of atomic nucleus b) *same as* NUCLIDE **7.** *R.C.Ch.* a) the outward form, or appearance of bread or wine, of the transubstantiated elements of the Eucharist b) either of these elements —**the species** the human race

specif. specifically

spe·ci·fi·a·ble (spes'ə fī'ə b'l) *adj.* that can be specified

spe·cif·ic (spi sif'ik) *adj.* [LL. *specificus* < L. *species* (see SPECIES) + *-ficus*, -FIC] **1.** limiting or limited; specifying or specified; precise; definite; explicit [no *specific* plans] **2.** of or constituting a species **3.** peculiar to or character-

istic of something [*specific* traits] **4.** of a special, or particular, sort or kind **5.** *Med.* a) specially indicated as a cure for a particular disease [a *specific* remedy] b) produced by a particular microorganism [a *specific* disease] **6.** *Physics* designating a certain constant characteristic of a substance or phenomenon measured against some arbitrary, fixed standard of reference or expressed as an amount per unit area, volume, etc. Also [Rare] **spe·cif'i·cal** —*n.* **1.** something specially suited for a given use or purpose **2.** a specific cure or remedy **3.** a distinct item or detail; particular —**SYN.** see EXPLICIT, SPECIAL —**spe·cif'i·cal·ly** *adv.* —**spe·cif'i·cic·i·ty** (spes'ə fis'ə tē) *n.*

spec·i·fi·ca·tion (spes'ə fi kā'shən) *n.* [ML. *specificatio*] **1.** the act of specifying; detailed mention or definition **2.** [*usually pl.*] a detailed description of the parts of a whole; statement or enumeration of particulars, as to actual or required size, quality, performance, terms, etc. [*specifications* for a new building] **3.** something specified; specified item, particular, etc.

specific characters the persistent features that distinguish one species from all others

specific gravity the ratio of the weight or mass of a given volume of a substance to that of an equal volume of another substance (water for liquids and solids, air or hydrogen for gases) used as a standard

specific heat 1. the number of calories needed to raise the temperature of one gram of a given substance 1°C **2.** the ratio of the amount of heat required to raise the temperature of a given mass of a substance one degree to the amount of heat required to raise the temperature of an equal mass of water one degree

specific performance *Law* the exact performance of a contract or an order enjoining it

spec·i·fy (spes'ə fī') *vt.* **-fied'**, **-fy'ing** [ME. *specifien* < OFr. *specifier* < LL. *specificare* < *specificus*, SPECIFIC] **1.** to mention, describe, or define in detail; state definitely [to *specify* the time and place] **2.** to include as an item in a set of specifications **3.** to state explicitly as a condition —**spec'i·fi'er** *n.*

spec·i·men (spes'ə mən) *n.* [L., a mark, token, example < *specere*, to see: see SPY] **1.** a part of a whole, or one individual of a class or group, used as a sample or example of the whole, class, or group; typical part, individual, etc. **2.** [Colloq.] a (specified kind of) individual or person [an unsavory *specimen*] **3.** *Med.* a sample, as of urine, sputum, blood, etc., for analysis

spe·cious (spē'shəs) *adj.* [ME., fair, beautiful < L. *speciosus*, showy, beautiful, plausible < *species*, look, show, appearance: see SPECIES] **1.** seeming to be good, sound, correct, logical, etc. without really being so; plausible but not genuine [*specious* logic] **2.** [Obs.] pleasing to the sight —**SYN.** see PLAUSIBLE —**spe'cious·ly** *adv.* —**spe'cious·ness, spe'ci·os'i·ty** (-shē äs'ə tē) *n.*

speck (spek) *n.* [ME. *specke* < OE. *specca*: for IE. base see SPARK[1], SPEAK] **1.** a small spot, mark, or stain **2.** a very small bit; particle —*vt.* to mark with specks

speck·le (spek'l) *n.* [ME. *spakle*, dim. of *specke*, SPECK] a small mark of contrasting color; speck —*vt.* **-led, -ling** to mark with speckles

☆**speckled trout** *local name for* any of various fishes, as the sea trout, brook trout, etc.

specs (speks) *n.pl.* [Colloq.] **1.** spectacles; eyeglasses ☆**2.** specifications: see SPECIFICATION (sense 2)

spec·ta·cle (spek'tə k'l) *n.* [ME. < OFr. < L. *spectaculum* < *spectare*, to behold, freq. of *specere*, to see: see SPY] **1.** something to look at, esp. some strange or remarkable sight; unusual display **2.** a public show or exhibition on a grand scale **3.** [*pl.*] a pair of eyeglasses: old-fashioned term **4.** [*usually pl.*] something making like a pair of eyeglasses in shape, use, etc. —**make a spectacle of oneself** to behave foolishly or improperly in public

spec·ta·cled (-k'ld) *adj.* **1.** wearing spectacles **2.** having markings that resemble spectacles

spec·tac·u·lar (spek tak'ə lər) *adj.* [< L. *spectaculum* (see SPECTACLE) + -AR] **1.** of or like a spectacle, or show **2.** unusual to a striking degree; characterized by a great display, as of daring —*n.* an elaborate show or display —**spec·tac'u·lar·ly** *adv.*

spec·ta·tor (spek'tāt ər, spek tāt'-) *n.* [L. < pp. of *spectare*, to behold: see SPECTACLE] a person who sees or watches something without taking an active part; onlooker

spec·ter (spek'tər) *n.* [Fr. *spectre* < L. *spectrum*, an appearance, apparition < *spectare*, to behold: see SPECTACLE] **1.** a ghost; apparition **2.** any object of fear or dread Also, Brit. sp., **spec'tre**

spec·tra (-trə) *n. alt. pl. of* SPECTRUM

spec·tral (-trəl) *adj.* [< SPECTER + -AL] **1.** of, having the nature of, or like a specter; phantom; ghostly **2.** of or caused by a spectrum or spectra —**spec·tral'i·ty** (-tral'ə tē), **spec'tral·ness** *n.* —**spec'tral·ly** *adv.*

spectral line any of a number of lines in an atomic spectrum produced by the emission of electromagnetic radiation from an excited atom: a spectral line represents the energy difference between two energy levels

spec·tro- (spek'trō, -trə) [< SPECTRUM] *a combining form*

meaning: **1.** of radiant energy as exhibited in a spectrum [*spectrogram*] **2.** of or by a spectroscope [*spectroheliogram*]

spec·tro·chem·is·try (spek′trə kem′is trē) *n.* the branch of chemistry dealing with the analysis of the spectra of substances —**spec′tro·chem′i·cal** *adj.*

spec·tro·gram (spek′trə gram′) *n.* [SPECTRO- + -GRAM] a photograph of a spectrum

spec·tro·graph (-graf′, -gräf′) *n.* [SPECTRO- + -GRAPH] an instrument for dispersing light radiation into a spectrum and recording the spectrum photographically —**spec′tro·graph′ic** *adj.* —**spec′tro·graph′i·cal·ly** *adv.*

☆**spec·tro·he·li·o·gram** (spek′trə hē′lē ə gram′) *n.* [SPECTRO- + HELIO- + -GRAM] a photograph of the sun made by monochromatic light, usually showing streaks or prominences on the sun's surface

☆**spec·tro·he·li·o·graph** (-graf′, -gräf′) *n.* an instrument used for making spectroheliograms

☆**spec·tro·he·li·o·scope** (-skōp′) *n.* a spectroheliograph adapted for visual use

spec·trom·e·ter (spek träm′ə tər) *n.* [G. *spektrometer*: see SPECTRO- & -METER] **1.** an instrument used for measuring spectral wavelengths **2.** an instrument used for determining the index of refraction —**spec′tro·met′ric** (-trə met′rik) *adj.* —**spec′trom·e·try** (-ə trē) *n.*

spec·tro·pho·tom·e·ter (spek′trō fə täm′ə tər) *n.* [SPECTRO- + PHOTOMETER] an instrument used for comparing the color intensities of different spectra —**spec′tro·pho′to·met′ric** (-fōt′ō met′rik) *adj.* —**spec′tro·pho·tom′e·try** *n.*

spec·tro·scope (spek′trə skōp′) *n.* [G. *spektroskop:* see SPECTRO- & -SCOPE] an optical instrument used for forming spectra for study —**spec′tro·scop′ic** (-skäp′ik) *adj.* —**spec′tro·scop′i·cal·ly** *adv.*

spec·tros·co·py (spek träs′kə pē) *n.* the study of spectra by use of the spectroscope —**spec·tros′co·pist** (-pist) *n.*

spec·trum (spek′trəm) *n.,* *pl.* **-tra** (-trə), **-trums** [ModL., special use (by NEWTON, 1671) of L. *spectrum:* see SPECTER] **1.** the series of colored bands diffracted and arranged in the order of their respective wavelengths by the passage of white light through a prism or other diffracting medium and shading continuously from red (produced by the longest wave visible) to violet (produced by the shortest) **2.** any of various arrangements of colored bands or lines, together with invisible components at both ends of the spectrum (cf. INFRARED, ULTRAVIOLET), similarly formed by light from incandescent gases or other sources of radiant energy, which can be studied by a spectrograph **3.** an afterimage **4.** a continuous range or entire extent [a wide *spectrum* of opinion] **5.** *same as: a)* RADIO SPECTRUM *b)* ELECTROMAGNETIC SPECTRUM

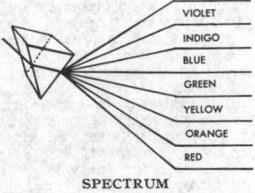

VIOLET
INDIGO
BLUE
GREEN
YELLOW
ORANGE
RED

SPECTRUM

spectrum analysis analysis of substances or bodies through study of their spectra

spec·u·lar (spek′yə lər) *adj.* [L. *specularis*] of, like, or by means of, a speculum —**spec′u·lar·ly** *adv.*

spec·u·late (-lāt′) *vi.* **-lat′ed, -lat′ing** [< L. *speculatus,* pp. of *speculari,* to view < *specula,* watchtower < *specere,* to see: see SPY] **1.** to think about the various aspects of a given subject; meditate; ponder; esp., to conjecture **2.** to buy or sell stocks, commodities, land, etc., hoping to take advantage of an expected rise or fall in price; also, to take part in any risky venture on the chance of making huge profits —*SYN.* see THINK[1] —**spec′u·la′tor** *n.*

spec·u·la·tion (spek′yə lā′shən) *n.* **1.** *a)* the act of speculating, or meditating *b)* a thought or conjecture **2.** *a)* the act of speculating in stocks, land, etc. *b)* a speculative business venture

spec·u·la·tive (spek′yə lāt′iv, -lə tiv) *adj.* [ME. *speculatif* < LL. *speculativus*] **1.** of, characterized by, or having the nature of, speculation, or meditation, conjecture, etc. **2.** theoretical, not practical **3.** of or characterized by financial speculation **4.** uncertain; risky **5.** indulging in or fond of speculation —**spec′u·la′tive·ly** *adv.*

spec·u·lum (spek′yə ləm) *n.,* *pl.* **-la** (-lə), **-lums** [L., a mirror < *specere,* to look: see SPY] **1.** a mirror, esp. one of polished metal used as a reflector in a telescope, etc. **2.** *Med.* an instrument for dilating a passage or cavity to facilitate its examination **3.** *Zool.* a distinctive patch of color on the wings of certain birds, esp. ducks

speculum metal an alloy of copper and tin that will take a mirrorlike polish, used for making mirrors and ruled gratings for spectrographs

sped (sped) *alt. pt. & pp.* of SPEED

speech (spēch) *n.* [ME. *speche* < OE. *spæc, spræc* < base of *sprecan,* to speak (see SPEAK)] **1.** the act of speaking; expression or communication of thoughts and feelings by spoken words **2.** the power or ability to speak **3.** the manner of speaking [her lisping *speech*] **4.** that which is spoken; utterance, remark, statement, talk, conversation, etc. **5.** a talk or address given to an audience **6.** the language used by a certain group of people; dialect or tongue **7.** the study of the theory and practice of oral expression and communication **8.** [Archaic] rumor; report

SYN.—**speech** is the general word for a discourse delivered to an audience, whether prepared or impromptu; **address** implies a formal, carefully prepared speech and usually attributes importance to the speaker or the speech [an *address* to a legislature/; **oration** suggests an eloquent, rhetorical, sometimes merely bombastic speech, esp. one delivered on some special occasion [political *orations* at the picnic/; a **lecture** is a carefully prepared speech intended to inform or instruct the audience [a *lecture* to a college class/; **talk** suggests informality and is applied either to an impromptu speech or to an address or lecture in which the speaker deliberately uses a simple, conversational approach; a **sermon** is a speech by a clergyman intended to give religious or moral instruction and usually based on Scriptural text

speech clinic a clinic for correcting speech disorders

speech community all the people speaking a particular language or dialect, whether in a single geographical area or dispersed throughout various regions

speech disorder any conspicuous speech imperfection, or variation from the accepted speech standards, caused either by a physical defect in the speech organs or by a mental disorder, as aphasia, stuttering, etc.

speech form *same as* LINGUISTIC FORM

speech·i·fy (spē′chə fī′) *vi.* **-fied′, -fy′ing** to make a speech: used humorously or contemptuously —**speech′i·fi′er** *n.*

speech·less (spēch′lis) *adj.* **1.** incapable of speech; lacking the ability to speak **2.** temporarily unable to speak; silent, as from shock **3.** not expressed or expressible in words [*speechless* terror] —*SYN.* see VOICELESS —**speech′less·ly** *adv.* —**speech′less·ness** *n.*

speech·mak·er (-māk′ər) *n.* a person who makes a speech or speeches; orator —**speech′mak′ing** *n.*

speed (spēd) *n.* [ME. *sped* < OE. *spæd,* wealth, power, success, akin to *spowan,* to prosper, succeed < IE. base **spēi-,* to flourish, expand: cf. SPACE, SPARE] **1.** the act or state of moving rapidly; swiftness; quick motion **2.** *a)* the rate of movement or motion; velocity [the *speed* of sound] *b)* the rate or rapidity of any action [reading *speed*] **3.** a gear or arrangement of gears for the drive of an engine [a truck with five forward *speeds*] **4.** [Colloq.] one's kind or level of taste, capability, etc. ☆**5.** [Slang] any of various amphetamine compounds, esp. Methedrine **6.** [Archaic] luck; success; prosperity [to wish someone good *speed*] **7.** *Photog. a)* the sensitivity to light of film as measured by the rate of exposure it requires *b)* the widest effective aperture of a camera lens: see also F-NUMBER *c)* the length of time the shutter is opened for an exposure —*adj.* of or having to do with speed —*vi.* **sped** or **speed′ed, speed′ing 1.** to move rapidly, ☆esp. more rapidly than is safe or allowed by law **2.** [Archaic] *a)* to get along; fare *b)* to have fortune, good or bad *c)* to have good fortune; prosper; succeed —*vt.* **1.** to help (a project) to succeed; aid; promote **2.** to wish Godspeed to [to *speed* the parting guest] **3.** to send, convey, or cause to move, go, etc. swiftly [to *speed* a letter on its way] **4.** to cause or design (a machine, etc.) to operate at a certain speed or speeds **5.** [Archaic] to cause to succeed or prosper —*SYN.* see HASTE —**speed up** to increase in speed; go or make go faster; accelerate

speed·boat (-bōt′) *n.* a motorboat built for speed

speed brake an airplane flap designed to decrease speed while in flight

speed·er (-ər) *n.* ☆a person or thing that speeds; esp., a motorist who drives faster than is safe or legal

speed·ing (-in) *n.* ☆the act of driving a motor vehicle at a higher speed than is safe or legal

speed·om·e·ter (spi däm′ə tər) *n.* [< SPEED + -METER] a device attached to a motor vehicle, etc. to indicate speed, as in miles per hour, often combined with another (ODOMETER) registering the distance traveled

☆**speed·ster** (spēd′stər) *n.* **1.** a very fast driver, runner, vehicle, etc. **2.** *same as* SPEEDER

☆**speed trap** a strip of road where conditions are rigged for the frequent apprehension of speed violators, and where even minor violations are dealt with severely

speed·up (-up′) *n.* an increase in speed; esp., an increase in the rate of output, etc., as required by an employer without any increase in pay

☆**speed·way** (-wā′) *n.* **1.** a track for racing automobiles or motorcycles **2.** a road for high-speed traffic

speed·well (-wel′) *n.* [< SPEED, *v.* + WELL[2]: orig. sense prob. "prosper well"] any of a genus (*Veronica*) of plants of the figwort family, with white or bluish flower spikes

speed·y (spēd′ē) *adj.* **speed′i·er, speed′i·est 1.** characterized by speed of motion; rapid; swift **2.** without delay; quick; prompt [a *speedy* reply] —*SYN.* see FAST[1] —**speed′i·ly** *adv.* —**speed′i·ness** *n.*

speiss (spīs) *n.* [G. *speise,* amalgam, lit., food < ML. *spesa,* cost, expense < L. *expendere,* to EXPEND] a mixture of metallic arsenides produced during the smelting of copper, iron, and certain other ores

spe·lae·an, spe·le·an (spi lē′ən) *adj.* [< L. *spelaeum* < Gr. *spēlaion,* a cave + -AN] **1.** of or like a cave **2.** dwelling in caves

spe·le·ol·o·gy (spē′lē äl′ə jē) *n.* [< L. *spelaeum* (see prec.) + -LOGY] the scientific study and exploration of caves —**spe′le·ol′o·gist** *n.*

spell[1] (spel) *n.* [ME. < OE., a saying, tale, charm, akin to Goth. *spill,* tale < IE. base **(s)pel-,* to speak loudly, whence Gr. *apeilein,* to threaten, vow] **1.** a word, formula, or form of words supposed to have some magic power;

incantation **2.** seemingly magical power or irresistible influence; charm; fascination —**cast a spell on 1.** to enchant **2.** to win the complete affection of —**under a spell** held in a spell or trance; enchanted

spell² (spel) *vt.* **spelled** or **spelt, spell′ing** [ME. *spellen* < OFr. *espeller*, to explain, relate < Frank. *spellōn*, akin to prec.] **1.** to name, write, or signal the letters which make up (a word, syllable, etc.), esp. the right letters in the right order **2.** to make up, cr form (a word, etc.): said of specified letters **3.** to signify; mean *[hard work spelled success]* —*vi.* to spell a word, words, etc.; esp., to do so correctly —**spell out 1.** to read letter by letter or with difficulty **2.** to make out, or discern, as if by close reading ☆**3.** to explain exactly and in detail

spell³ (spel) *vt.* **spelled, spell′ing** [ME. *spelien* < OE. *spelian*, to substitute for, akin to *spala*, a substitute] **1.** [Colloq.] to serve or work in place of (another), esp. so as to give a period of rest to; relieve **2.** [Chiefly Australian] to give a period of rest to —*vi.* [Chiefly Australian] to take a period of rest or relief —*n.* **1.** a turn of serving or working in place of another **2.** a period or turn of work, duty, etc. *[a two-year spell as reporter]* **3.** a turn, period, or fit of something *[a spell of brooding]* **4.** a period of a specified sort of weather *[a cold spell]* **5.** [Colloq.] a period of time that is indefinite, short, or of a specified character ☆**6.** [Dial.] a short distance **7.** [Colloq.] a period or fit of some illness, indisposition, etc. **8.** [Chiefly Australian] a period of rest or relief from activity

spell·bind (spel′bīnd′) *vt.* **-bound′, -bind′ing** [backformation < SPELLBOUND] to hold by or as by a spell; fascinate; enchant

☆**spell·bind·er** (-bīn′dər) *n.* a speaker, esp. a politician, who can sway an audience with his eloquence

spell·bound (-bound′) *adj.* [SPELL¹ + BOUND²] held or affected by or as by a spell; fascinated; enchanted

☆**spell·down** (-doun′) *n.* a spelling match, esp. one in which a contestant is eliminated when he misspells a word or a specified number of words

spell·er (-ər) *n.* **1.** a person who spells words *[a poor speller]* ☆**2.** an exercise book for teaching spelling

spell·ing (-in) *n.* **1.** the act of one who spells words **2.** the way in which a word is spelled; orthography

☆**spelling bee** same as SPELLDOWN

spelling pronunciation the pronunciation of a word in conformity with its spelling rather than with established usage *((fôr′kas/'l)* is a *spelling pronunciation of* forecastle*)*

spelt¹ (spelt) *alt. pt. & pp. of* SPELL²

spelt² (spelt) *n.* [ME. < OE. < LL. *spelta* < Gmc. *speltö* < IE. base *(s)p(h)el-*, to split off, whence SPILL¹] **1.** a primitive species (*Triticum spelta*) of wheat with grains that do not thresh free of the chaff: now seldom cultivated **2.** *local name for* EMMER

spel·ter (spel′tər) *n.* [< or akin to MDu. *speauter*, LowG. *spialter*: akin to PEWTER] crude zinc from the smelter, esp. as used in galvanizing

☆**spe·lunk·er** (spi lun′kər) *n.* [< obs. *spelunk*, a cave (< ME. *spelunke* < L. *spelunca* < Gr. *spēlynx*, akin to *spēlaion*, a cave) + -ER] a person who explores caves as a hobby —**spe·lunk′ing** *n.*

spence (spens) *n.* [ME. < ML. *spensa*, aphetic for *dispensa* < L., fem. pp. of *dispendere*, to weigh out: see DISPENSE] [Archaic or Dial.] a larder or pantry: also sp. **spense**

Spen·cer (spen′sər) [< the surname *Spencer* < ME. *spenser*, butler, steward < OFr. *despencier* < *despense*, a larder, buttery < ML. *dispensa*: see prec.] **1.** a masculine name: sometimes sp. **Spenser 2.** **Herbert,** 1820–1903; Eng. philosopher

spen·cer¹ (spen′sər) *n.* [after the 2d Earl *Spencer* (1758–1834)] a short jacket of an early 19th-cent. style

spen·cer² (spen′sər) *n.* [< pers. name SPENCER] a trysail on a gaff

Spen·ce·ri·an (spen sir′ē ən) *adj.* **1.** of or having to do with Herbert Spencer or his system of philosophy, which attempted to systematize all the sciences into a coherent whole ☆**2.** of or characteristic of the style of penmanship taught by Platt Rogers Spencer (1800–64), U.S. teacher, characterized by rounded, well-formed letters —*n.* a follower of Herbert Spencer

spend (spend) *vt.* **spent, spend′ing** [ME. *spenden* < OE. *spendan* (in comp.) < ML. *spendere* < L. *expendere:* see EXPEND] **1.** to use up, exhaust, consume, or wear out *[his fury was spent]* **2.** to pay out (money); disburse **3.** to give or devote (time, labor, thought, or effort) to some enterprise or for some purpose **4.** to pass (a period of time) *[spending hours together]* **5.** to waste; squander —*vi.* **1.** to pay out or use up money, etc. **2.** [Obs.] to be or become consumed, wasted, etc. —**spend′a·ble** *adj.*

spend·er (-ər) *n.* a person who spends, esp. lavishly

Spen·der (spen′dər), **Stephen** 1909– ; Eng. poet & critic

spending money money for small personal expenses

spend·thrift (spend′thrift′) *n.* a person who spends money carelessly or wastefully; squanderer —*adj.* wasteful; extravagant; prodigal

Speng·ler (speŋ′lər; *G.* shpeŋ′lər), **Oswald** 1880–1936; Ger. philosopher

Spen·ser (spen′sər), **Edmund** 1552?–99; Eng. poet

Spen·se·ri·an (spen sir′ē ən) *adj.* of or characteristic of Edmund Spenser or his writing —*n.* **1.** a follower or imitator of Spenser **2.** a Spenserian stanza, or a poem in such stanzas

Spenserian stanza a stanza consisting of eight lines of iambic pentameter and a final line of iambic hexameter (an alexandrine), with a rhyme scheme *ababbcbcc*, used by Spenser in *The Fairie Queene*

spent (spent) *pt. & pp. of* SPEND —*adj.* **1.** tired out; physically exhausted; without energy **2.** used up; worn out; without power **3.** exhausted of sperm or spawn

sperm¹ (spurm) *n.* [ME. *sperme* < MFr. *esperme* < LL. *sperma* < Gr. *sperma*, seed, germ < *speirein*, to sow, scatter: for IE. base *see* SPARK¹] **1.** the male generative fluid; semen **2.** *same as* SPERMATOZOON

sperm² (spurm) *n. clipped form of:* **1.** SPERMACETI **2.** SPERM OIL **3.** SPERM WHALE

-sperm (spurm) [see SPERM¹] *a combining form meaning* seed *[gymnosperm]*

sper·ma·ce·ti (spur′mə set′ē, -sēt′ē) *n.* [ML. *sperma ceti,* lit., whale sperm < LL. *sperma,* SPERM¹ + L. *ceti,* gen. of *cetus,* a whale < Gr. *kētos]* a white, waxlike substance taken from the oil in the head of a sperm whale or dolphin, used in making cosmetics, ointments, candles, etc.

sper·ma·go·ni·um (-gō′nē əm) *n., pl.* **-ni·a** (-ə) [ModL. < LL. *sperma,* SPERM¹ + ModL. *-gonium,* -GONIUM] *Bot.* a flasklike structure found in certain fungi and lichens, which produces small, nonmotile sperm cells (*spermatia*)

-sper·mal (spur′m'l) *same as* -SPERMOUS

sper·ma·ry (spur′mə rē) *n., pl.* **-ries** [ModL. *spermarium* < LL. *sperma,* SPERM¹] an organ in which male germ cells are formed; male gonad; testis

sper·ma·the·ca (spur′mə thē′kə) *n.* [ModL.: see SPERM¹ & THECA] a small, saclike structure in the female reproductive tract in many invertebrates, esp. insects, for receiving and storing sperm

sper·mat·ic (spər mat′ik) *adj.* [MFr. *spermatique* < LL. *spermaticus* < Gr. *spermatikos*] **1.** of, like, or having to do with sperm or sperm cells; generative or seminal **2.** of or having to do with a spermary

spermatic cord the cord suspending a testicle within the scrotum and containing the vas deferens, blood vessels, and nerves supplying the testicle, etc.

sper·ma·tid (spur′mə tid) *n.* [SPERMAT(O)- + -ID] *Zool.* any of the four haploid cells formed by the two consecutive meiotic divisions of a primary spermatocyte, each of which develops into a spermatozoon

sper·ma·ti·um (spər mā′shē əm) *n., pl.* **-ti·a** (-ə) [ModL. < Gr. *spermation,* dim. of *sperma,* a seed] *Bot.* **1.** a nonmotile male sex cell in red algae **2.** a very small, nonmotile male gamete, found in some lichens and fungi

sper·ma·to- (spər mat′ō-; spər mā′tō; *also*; spur′mə tə-) [< Gr. *sperma* (gen. *spermatos*), a seed, SPERM¹] *a combining form meaning* seed or sperm *[spermatogenesis]*: also, before a vowel, **spermat-**

sper·ma·to·cyte (spər mat′ə sīt′, spur′mə tə-) *n.* [prec. + -CYTE] **1.** *Bot.* a cell that develops into a spermatozoid **2.** *Zool.* a stage in the development of the male sex cell, originating by growth from a spermatogonium

sper·ma·to·gen·e·sis (spər mat′ə jen′ə sis, spur′mə tō-) *n.* [ModL.: see SPERMATO- & -GENESIS] the production and development of spermatozoa —**sper·ma·to·ge·net′ic** (-jə net′ik) *adj.*

sper·ma·to·go·ni·um (-gō′nē əm) *n., pl.* **-ni·a** (-ə) [ModL. < SPERMATO- + Gr. *gonē,* offspring: see GONAD] *Zool.* a primitive male germ cell before becoming a spermatocyte —**sper·ma·to·go′ni·al** *adj.*

sper·ma·to·phore (spər mat′ə fôr′, spur′mə tə-) *n.* [SPERMATO- + -PHORE] *Zool.* a case or capsule containing a number of spermatozoa, expelled whole by the male of certain animals, as in many copepods, leeches, etc. —**sper·ma·toph·o·ral** (spur′mə täf′ər əl) *adj.*

sper·ma·to·phyte (-fīt′) *n.* [SPERMATO- + -PHYTE] **1.** any seed-bearing plant **2.** any of the largest group (Spermatophyta) of plants living today, comprising the seed-bearing plants and including the angiosperms and the gymnosperms —**sper·ma·to·phyt′ic** (-fit′ik) *adj.*

sper·ma·tor·rhe·a (spər mat′ə rē′ə, spur′mə tə-) *n.* [SPERMATO- + -RRHEA] the too frequent involuntary discharge of semen without an orgasm

sper·ma·to·zo·id (-zō′id) *n.* [< ff. + -ID] *Bot.* in certain mosses, ferns, etc., a male gamete that moves by means of flagella: it is usually produced in an antheridium

sper·ma·to·zo·on (-zō′än, -ən) *n., pl.* **-zo′a** (-ə) [ModL. < SPERMATO- + Gr. *zōion,* animal, living being] the male germ cell, found in semen, which penetrates the ovum, or egg, of the female to fertilize it: typically it consists of a head containing a large nucleus, a small midsection, and a whiplike tail used for locomotion —**sper·mat′o·zo′al, sper·mat′o·zo′an, sper·mat′o·zo′ic** *adj.*

sperm·i·cide (spur′mə sīd′) *n.* [SPERM¹ + -i- + -CIDE] an agent that kills spermatozoa —**sperm′i·ci′dal** *adj.*

sperm·ine (spur′mēn, -min) *n.* [SPERM¹ + -INE⁴] a basic substance, $C_{10}H_{26}N_4$, found in semen, yeast, etc.

sper·mi·o·gen·e·sis (spur′mē ō jen′ə sis) *n.* [ModL. < *spermium* (< Gr. *spermeion*, sperm < *sperma*: see SPERM[1]) + -GENESIS] *Zool.* 1. the changing of a spermatid into a spermatozoon 2. *same as* SPERMATOGENESIS

sper·mo- (spur′mə) *same as* SPERMATO-

sper·mo·go·ni·um (spur′mə gō′nē əm) *n., pl.* -**ni·a** (-ə) [ModL.: see SPERM[1] & GONAD] *var. sp.* of SPERMAGONIUM

sperm oil a valuable lubricating oil from the sperm whale

sper·mo·phile (spur′mə fil′, -fil) *n.* [< Gr. *sperma*, a seed (see SPERM[1]) + -PHILE] any of several squirrellike rodents, as the ground squirrels, that live in burrows, feed on vegetation, and sometimes damage crops

sper·mous (spur′məs) *adj.* or of like sperm

-sper·mous (spur′məs) *a combining form meaning* having (a specified number or kind of) seed [*monospermous*]

sperm whale a large, toothed whale (*Physeter catodon*) inhabiting the warm seas: a closed cavity in its roughly square head contains sperm oil

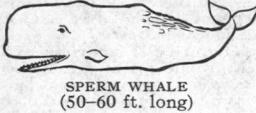

SPERM WHALE
(50–60 ft. long)

Sper·ry (sper′ē), **Elmer Ambrose** 1860–1930; U.S. inventor, electrical engineer, & manufacturer

sper·ry·lite (sper′ē līt′) *n.* [after its Canad. discoverer, F. L. *Sperry* + -LITE] a silvery-white, granular or crystalline, native compound of platinum and arsenic, PtAs₂

spes·sar·tite (spes′ər tit′) *n.* [Fr. < *Spessart*, mountain range in Bavaria + -*ite*, -ITE[1]] a usually dark-red variety of garnet containing manganese and aluminum, often with some iron: also called **spes′sar·tine′** (-tēn′)

spew (spyoo) *vt., vi.* [ME. *spewen* < OE. *spiwan*, akin to G. *speien*, Goth. *speiwan* < IE. base *(s)p(h)yēu-*, whence L. *spuere*, to vomit, Gr. *ptyein*, to spit] 1. to throw up from or as from the stomach; vomit; eject 2. to flow or gush forth —*n.* something spewed; vomit —**spew′er** *n.*

Spezia *see* LA SPEZIA

sp. gr. specific gravity

sphac·e·late (sfas′ə lāt′) *vt., vi.* -**lat′ed**, -**lat′ing** [< ModL. *sphacelatus*, pp. of *sphacelare*, to mortify < *sphacelus*, gangrene < Gr. *sphakelos*] to make or become gangrenous; mortify —**sphac′e·la′tion** *n.*

sphag·num (sfag′nəm) *n.* [ModL. < Gr. *sphagnos*, kind of moss] 1. any of a genus (*Sphagnum*) of highly absorbent, spongelike, grayish mosses found in bogs; peat moss 2. a mass of such mosses, used to improve soil, to pack and pot plants, etc. —**sphag′nous** (-nəs) *adj.*

sphal·er·ite (sfal′ə rit′) *n.* [G. *sphalerit* < Gr. *sphaleros*, deceptive (< *sphallein*, to trip, deceive: for IE. base see SPOIL) + -*it*, -ITE[1]: so named from being mistaken for other ores] native zinc sulfide, ZnS, the principal ore of zinc, usually brownish with a resinous luster

sphene (sfēn) *n.* [Fr. *sphène* < Gr. *sphēn*, a wedge (for IE. base see SPOON): so named because of its crystal form] a mineral, CaTiSiO₅, a silicate of calcium and titanium with varying amounts of other elements

sphe·no- (sfē′nō, -nə) [< Gr. *sphēn* (see SPHENE)] *a combining form meaning:* 1. shaped like a wedge [*sphenogram*] 2. of the sphenoid bone Also, before a vowel, **sphen-**

sphe·no·don (sfē′nə dän′) *n.* [< prec. + Gr. *odōn*, TOOTH] *same as* TUATARA

sphe·no·gram (sfē′nə gram′) *n.* [SPHENO- + -GRAM] a cuneiform, or wedge-shaped, character

sphe·noid (sfē′noid) *adj.* [ModL. *sphenoides* < Gr. *sphēnoeides*: see SPHENE & -OID] 1. wedge-shaped 2. *Anat.* designating or of the wedge-shaped compound bone at the base of the skull: see SKULL, illus. Also **sphe·noi′dal** —*n.* 1. the sphenoid bone 2. *Mineralogy* a wedge-shaped crystal form having four triangular faces

spher·al (sfir′əl) *adj.* [LL. *sphaeralis*] 1. of or like a sphere 2. rounded in form; spherical 3. symmetrical

sphere (sfir) *n.* [ME. *spere* < OFr. *espere* < L. *sphaera* < Gr. *sphaira*] 1. any round body or figure having the surface equally distant from the center at all points; globe; ball 2. a star or planet 3. the visible heavens; sky 4. *shortened form of* CELESTIAL SPHERE 5. any of a series of hypothetical spherical shells, transparent, concentric, and postulated as revolving one within another, in which the stars, planets, sun, moon, etc. were supposedly set: a concept of ancient astronomy 6. the place, range, or extent of action, existence, knowledge, experience, influence, etc.; province; compass 7. social stratum; place in society; walk of life —*vt.* **sphered**, **spher′ing** [Chiefly Poet.] 1. to put in or as in a sphere 2. to put among the heavenly spheres 3. to form into a sphere

-sphere (sfir) *a combining form meaning:* 1. of or like a sphere [*planisphere*] 2. of any of the layers of gas surrounding the earth [*ionosphere*]

sphere of influence 1. political and economic influence or control exerted by one nation over another nation or other nations 2. the nation or nations so dominated

spher·i·cal (sfer′i k'l, sfir′-) *adj.* [< LL. *sphaericus* < Gr. *sphairikos* < *sphaira*] 1. shaped like a sphere; globular 2. of a sphere or spheres 3. of the heavenly spheres (sometimes with astrological reference) Also **spher′ic** —SYN. see ROUND[1] —**spher′i·cal·ly** *adv.*

spherical aberration optical distortion resulting from the spherical shape of a lens or mirror

spherical angle an angle formed by the intersecting arcs of two great circles on a sphere

spherical coordinate *Math.* either of the coordinates in a system for locating a point in space by reference to the length of its radius vector and the two polar angles that determine the position of this vector

spherical geometry the study of the geometry of figures drawn on a sphere

spherical polygon a closed figure on the surface of a sphere bounded by the arcs of three or more great circles

spherical triangle a closed figure on the surface of a sphere bounded by the arcs of three great circles

spherical trigonometry the application of trigonometry to spherical triangles

sphe·ric·i·ty (sfi ris′ə tē) *n.* [ML. *sphaericitas*] the state of being spherical; round form; roundness

spher·ics[1] (sfer′iks, sfir′-) *n.pl.* [*with sing. v.*] *same as:* 1. SPHERICAL GEOMETRY 2. SPHERICAL TRIGONOMETRY

spher·ics[2] (sfer′iks, sfir′-) *n.pl.* [*with sing. v.*] *var. sp.* of SFERICS

sphe·roid (sfir′oid) *n.* [L. *sphaeroides* < Gr. *sphairoeidēs*] a body that is almost but not quite a sphere, esp. one generated by the rotation of an ellipse about one of its axes —*adj.* of this shape: also **sphe·roid′al**

sphe·rom·e·ter (sfi räm′ə tər) *n.* [Fr. *sphéromètre*: see SPHERE & -METER] an instrument used for measuring the curvature of a surface, as of a lens

spher·ule (sfer′ool, sfir′-; -yool) *n.* [L. *sphaerula*, dim. of *sphaera*: see SPHERE] a small sphere or spherical body; globule —**spher′u·lar** *adj.*

spher·u·lite (-oo lit′, -yoo lit′) *n.* [prec. + -ITE[1]] a rounded or spherical crystalline body found in some glassy volcanic rocks —**spher′u·lit′ic** (-lit′ik) *adj.*

spher·y (sfir′ē) *adj.* **spher′i·er**, **spher′i·est** [Poet.] 1. of or like a sphere 2. of the heavenly spheres

sphinc·ter (sfiŋk′tər) *n.* [LL. < Gr. *sphinktēr* < *sphingein*, to draw close < IE. *spheig-* < base *spēi-*, to flourish, grow thick, whence SPEED, SPARE] *Anat.* a ring-shaped muscle that surrounds a natural opening in the body and can open or close it by expanding or contracting —**sphinc′ter·al** *adj.*

sphin·gid (sfin′jid) *n.* [< ModL. *Sphingidae*, name of the family < *sphinx* (gen. *sphingis*), type genus (< L.: see SPHINX): see -IDAE] *same as* HAWKMOTH

sphinx (sfiŋks) *n., pl.* **sphinx′es**, **sphin·ges** (sfin′jēz) [ME. *spynx* < L. *sphinx* < Gr., lit., the strangler: for base see SPHINCTER]
1. any ancient Egyptian statue or figure having, typically, the body of a lion and the head of a man, ram, or hawk; specif., [S-] a huge statue of this kind with the head of a man, at Gîza, near Cairo, Egypt 2. *Gr. Myth. a)* a winged monster with a lion's body and the head and breasts of a woman; specif., [S-] a monster like this at Thebes who strangled passers-by unable to guess its riddle *b)* a person who is difficult to know or understand 3. *Zool. same as* HAWKMOTH

SPHINX

sphra·gis·tics (sfrə jis′tiks) *n.pl.* [*with sing. v.*] [< LGr. *sphragistikos*, of seals < Gr. *sphragis*, a seal] the study of engraved seals and signets —**sphra·gis′tic** *adj.*

sp. ht. specific heat

sphyg·mic (sfig′mik) *adj.* [ModL. *sphygmicus* < Gr. *sphygmikos* < *sphygmos*, the pulse] *Physiol.* of the pulse

sphyg·mo- (sfig′mō, -mə) [< Gr. *sphygmos*, the pulse] *a combining form meaning* the pulse [*sphygmograph*]

sphyg·mo·gram (sfig′mə gram′) *n.* [prec. + -GRAM] the record or tracing made by a sphygmograph

sphyg·mo·graph (-graf′, -gräf′) *n.* [SPHYGMO- + -GRAPH] an instrument for recording the rate, force, and variations of the pulse —**sphyg′mo·graph′ic** *adj.* —**sphyg·mog′ra·phy** (-mäg′rə fē) *n.*

sphyg·mo·ma·nom·e·ter (sfig′mō mə näm′ə tər) *n.* [SPHYGMO- + MANOMETER] an instrument for measuring arterial blood pressure, consisting of an inflatable band wrapped around the upper arm to compress the artery, and an attached manometer

sphyg·mom·e·ter (sfig mäm′ə tər) *n.* [SPHYGMO- + -METER] an instrument for measuring the force and rate of the pulse

spi·ca (spi′kə) *n.* [L., ear of grain, orig., a point: see SPIKE[2]] 1. *pl.* -**cae** (-sē) *Bot.* a spike, as of a flower 2. *Med.* a kind of bandage wrapped back and forth with spiral overlapping around parts a a joint —[S-] a first-magnitude star in the constellation Virgo

spi·cate (spi′kāt) *adj.* [L. *spicatus*, pp. of *spicare*, to provide with spikes < *spica*, a point, SPIKE[2]] *Bot., Zool.* 1. spikelike in form 2. arranged in a spike or spikes

spic·ca·to (spi kät′ō) *adj.* [It., pp. of *spiccare*, to detach] *Music* played with the bow wrist relaxed so that the bow rebounds rapidly between notes: a direction to the violinist, etc.

spice (spis) *n.* [ME. < OFr. *espice* < L. *species:* see SPECIES): in LL., wares, assorted goods, esp. spices and drugs] 1. *a)* any of several vegetable substances, as clove, cinnamon, nutmeg, pepper, etc., used to season food: spices are

usually dried for use and have distinctive flavors and aromas *b*) such substances collectively or as a material **2**. a spicy fragrance or aroma **3**. that which adds zest, piquancy, or interest **4**. [Archaic] a small bit; trace —*vt.* **spiced, spic′ing 1**. to season or flavor with spice **2**. to add zest, piquancy, or interest

☆**spice·ber·ry** (-ber′ē) *n., pl.* **-ries 1**. *a*) a Caribbean tree (*Eugenia rhombea*) of the myrtle family, having orange or black fruit *b*) this fruit **2**. any of several aromatic plants, esp. wintergreen (sense 1)

☆**spice·bush** (-boosh′) *n.* **1**. an aromatic E N. American plant (*Lindera benzoin*) of the laurel family, with leathery leaves, small yellowish flowers, and red fruit formerly dried for use as a spice **2**. *same as* CAROLINA ALLSPICE

Spice Islands *former name of the* MOLUCCAS

spic·er·y (spis′ə rē) *n., pl.* **-er·ies** [ME. *spicerie* < MFr. *espicerie* < *espice* (see SPICE)] **1**. spices **2**. spicy quality, flavor, or aroma **3**. [Obs.] a place to keep spices

spick-and-span (spik′n span′) *adj.* [short for *spick-and-span-new* < *spick*, var. of SPIKE¹ + SPAN-NEW < ME. *spon-neowe* < ON. *spān-nȳr* < *spānn*, a chip, shaving + *nȳr*, NEW] **1**. new or fresh **2**. neat and clean

spic·u·late (spik′yə lāt′) *adj.* [L. *spiculatus*] **1**. shaped like a spicule; needlelike **2**. covered with or consisting of spicules Also **spic′u·lar** (-lər)

spic·ule (spik′yōol) *n.* [< ModL. & L.: ModL. *spicula* < ML., head of a lance or arrow < L. *spiculum*, dim. of *spica*, a point, ear, SPIKE²] **1**. *Astron.* a long, fingerlike jet of hot gases spurting upward from the surface of the sun's chromosphere **2**. *Bot.* a small spike; spikelet **3**. *Zool.* a small, hard, needlelike piece or process, esp. of bony or calcareous material, as in the skeleton of the sponge

spic·u·lum (spik′yə ləm) *n., pl.* **-la** (-lə) [L.] *same as* SPICULE; esp., any of several spinelike organs found in lower animals, as the starfish

spic·y (spi′sē) *adj.* **spic′i·er, spic′i·est 1**. containing or abounding in spices **2**. having the flavor or aroma of spice; fragrant, aromatic, or pungent **3**. piquant or zestful; lively, interesting, etc. **4**. risqué; racy —SYN. see PUNGENT —**spic′i·ly** *adv.* —**spic′i·ness** *n.*

spi·der (spi′dər) *n.* [ME. *spithre* < OE. *spithra*, for *spinthra* < *spinnan*, to SPIN] **1**. any of an order (*Araneae*) of small, chiefly land arachnids having a body composed of two unsegmented divisions, a cephalothorax bearing the legs and an abdomen bearing two or more pairs of spinnerets, whose function is to spin the silk threads from which are made nests, cocoons for the eggs, or webs for trapping insects ☆**2**. a cast-iron frying pan, orig. one with legs for use on a hearth **3**. something resembling a spider; esp., any of various devices or frameworks with several leglike extensions

spider crab any of a number of sea crabs (suborder Brachyura) with a pear-shaped body and long, slender legs: they are often overgrown with algae, hydroids, etc.

spider mite *same as* RED SPIDER

spider monkey any of a group (genus *Ateles*) of monkeys of South and Central America with long, spidery limbs, a long, prehensile tail, and the thumb rudimentary or absent

spi·der·wort (-wurt′) *n.* any of a genus (*Tradescantia*) of fleshy perennial plants of the spiderwort family, having grasslike leaves and showy purplish, white, or pink flowers —*adj.* designating a family (Commelinaceae) of plants, including the dayflower, wandering Jew, etc.

spi·der·y (-ē) *adj.* **1**. like a spider **2**. long and thin like a spider's legs **3**. infested with spiders

spie·gel·ei·sen (spē′g'l ī′z'n) *n.* [G. < *spiegel*, mirror (< OHG. *spiagal* < L. *speculum*: see SPECULUM) + *eisen*, IRON] a hard, white pig iron containing 15 to 32% manganese: also **spie′gel, spiegel iron**

☆**spiel** (spēl) *n.* [G., play, game] [Slang] a talk, speech, or harangue, as in persuading or selling —*vi.* [G. *spielen*, to play] [Slang] to give a spiel —**spiel off** [Slang] to recite by or as if by rote —**spiel′er** *n.*

spi·er (spi′ər) *n.* a person who spies

spiff (spif) *vt.* [see ff.] [Slang] to make spiffy; spruce (*up*)

spiff·y (spif′ē) *adj.* **spiff′i·er, spiff′i·est** [< dial. *spiff*, well-dressed person: prob. orig. a cant term] [Slang] spruce, smart, or dapper —**spiff′i·ness** *n.*

spig·ot (spig′ət, spik′-) *n.* [ME. *spigote*, prob. akin (? via OFr.) to OIt. dial. *spigorare*, to tap (a cask) < L. *spicaum*: see SPICULE] **1**. a plug or peg used to stop the vent in a barrel, etc. **2**. *a*) a faucet *b*) the valve or plug in a faucet **3**. the end of a pipe that is inserted into an enlarged end of another pipe to form a joint

spike¹ (spik) *n.* [ME. < ON. *spīkr*, a nail, spike, or < MDu. & MLowG. *spiker*, both ult. < IE. base *(s)p(h)ei-*, sharp, pointed splinter, whence L. *spica*, ear of grain, SPIT¹, SPINE] **1**. a long, heavy nail **2**. a sharp-pointed part or projection, usually slender and of metal, as along the top of an iron fence, etc. **3**. any long, slender, pointed object, as the unbranched antler of a young deer **4**. *a*) any of a number of sharp or pointed metal projections on the soles, and often on the heels, of shoes used for baseball, golf, track, etc., to prevent slipping *b*) [*pl.*] a pair of such shoes *c*) a high, very thin heel on a woman's shoe:

also **spike heel** ☆**5**. a young mackerel not more than six inches long **6**. *a*) a sporadic, rapid, short-lived variation in potential difference, as a self-propagating electrical variation (**spike** or **action potential**) along a nerve axon *b*) a graphic recording or tracing of this, as any of the jagged peaks in an electroencephalogram —*vt.* **spiked, spik′ing 1**. to fasten or fit with or as with a spike or spikes **2**. to mark, pierce, cut, etc. with a spike or spikes, or impale on a spike **3**. to make (a cannon) unusable by driving a spike into the touchhole **4**. to thwart, frustrate, or block (a scheme, etc.) ☆**5**. [Slang] to add alcoholic liquor to (a drink) **6**. *Baseball*, etc. to injure with the spikes on one's shoes ☆**7**. *Volleyball* to leap at the net and smash (the ball) into the opponents' court —**hang up one's spikes** [Colloq.] to retire, as from a professional sport

spike² (spik) *n.* [ME. *spik* < L. *spica*: see prec.] **1**. an ear of grain **2**. a long flower cluster with flowers attached directly to the stalk —**spiked** *adj.*

spike lavender a European lavender-like mint (*Lavandula latifolia*) that yields an oil used in art

spike·let (-lit) *n.* a small spike, as in a flower cluster of grass

spike·nard (-nərd, -närd) *n.* [ME. < LL.(Ec.) *spica nardi* < L. *spica*, an ear of grain (see SPIKE²) + *nardus*, NARD] **1**. a fragrant ointment used in ancient times **2**. an Asiatic plant (*Nardostachys jatamansi*) of the valerian family that yielded this ointment ☆**3**. a perennial N. American plant (*Aralia racemosa*) of the ginseng family, with whitish flowers, purplish berries, and fragrant roots

SPIKES
(left, plantain; right, common mullein)

spike-tooth harrow (-tooth′) a harrow with sharp teeth

spik·y (spi′kē) *adj.* **spik′i·er, spik′i·est 1**. shaped like a spike; long and pointed **2**. having spikes —**spik′i·ness** *n.*

spile (spil) *n.* [MDu., a splinter, skewer, bar, spindle: for IE. base see SPIKE¹] **1**. a plug or spigot, as for a barrel ☆**2**. a tap or spout driven into a maple tree to draw off sap **3**. a heavy stake or timber driven into the ground as a foundation or support —*vt.* **spiled, spil′ing 1**. to furnish or support with spiles, or stakes **2**. to set a spile into (a tree, barrel, etc.) **3**. to draw off (liquid) through a spile **4**. to stop up (a hole) with a spile, or plug

spil·ing (spil′in) *n.* [< SPILE + -ING] spiles or timbers collectively; piling

spill¹ (spil) *vt.* **spilled** or **spilt, spill′ing** [ME. *spillen* < OE. *spillan*, to destroy, squander, akin to MHG. *spillen*, to split < IE. base *sp(h)el-*, to split, split off, whence SPALL, L. *spolium*: cf. SPOIL] **1**. to allow or cause, esp. unintentionally or accidentally, to run, fall, or flow over from a receptacle or container, usually so as to result in loss or waste [*didn't spill a drop of the milk*] **2**. to shed (blood) **3**. *a*) to empty the wind from (a sail) *b*) to lessen the pressure of (wind) on a sail **4**. to scatter at random from a receptacle or container **5**. [Colloq.] to let (something secret) become known; divulge **6**. [Colloq.] to cause or allow (a rider, load, etc.) to fall off; throw off **7**. [Obs.] *a*) to kill *b*) to destroy or ruin *c*) to squander; waste —*vi.* to be spilled from a receptacle or container; overflow; run out —*n.* **1**. the act of spilling **2**. the amount spilled **3**. *same as* SPILLWAY **4**. [Colloq.] a fall or tumble, as from a horse or from a vertical position —**spill over** to overflow in superabundance or excess

spill² (spil) *n.* [ME. *spille*, prob. via dial. *spil* < ON. *spila*, a splinter, akin to SPILE] **1**. a splinter **2**. a splinter, thin roll of paper, etc., set on fire and used to light a pipe, candle, etc. **3**. a paper cone or roll used as a container **4**. a small plug for stopping up a hole; spile **5**. a small metal peg, pin, or rod

spill·age (-ij) *n.* the act of spilling or the amount spilled

spil·li·kin (spil′i k'n) *n.* [< MDu. *spilleken*, dim. of *spille*: see SPILE] [Chiefly Brit.] **1**. any of the strips used in playing jackstraws **2**. [*pl.*, with *sing. v.*] the game of jackstraws Also sp. **spilikin**

spill·o·ver (spil′ō′vər) *n.* **1**. the act of spilling over **2**. that which spills over; excess or overabundance

☆**spill·way** (-wā′) *n.* [SPILL¹ + WAY] a passageway or channel to carry off excess water, as around a dam

spilt (spilt) *alt. pt. & pp. of* SPILL¹

spilth (spilth) *n.* [SPIL(L) + -TH¹] [Archaic] **1**. the act of spilling **2**. that which is spilled, esp. profusely

spin (spin) *vt.* **spun** or archaic **span, spun, spin′ning** [ME. *spinnen* < OE. *spinnan*, akin to G. *spinnen* < IE. base *(s)pen(d)-*, to pull, draw, spin, whence Lith. *spéndžiu*, to lay a snare & (prob.) L. *pendere*, to hang] **1**. *a*) to draw out and twist fibers of (wool, cotton, etc.) into thread *b*) to make (thread, yarn, etc.) by this process **2**. to make (a web, cocoon, etc.) from a filament of a viscous fluid that is extruded from the body and hardens on exposure to the air: said of spiders, silkworms, etc. **3**. to make or produce in a way suggestive of spinning [*to spin a tale*]

4. to draw *out* (a story, etc.) to a great length; prolong; protract **5.** to cause to whirl or rotate swiftly [to *spin* a top] **6.** to cause (wheels of a vehicle) to rotate freely without traction, as on ice or in sand **7.** to extract water from (clothes) in a washer by the centrifugal force of swift rotation —*vi.* **1.** to spin thread or yarn **2.** to form a thread, web, etc.: said of spiders, etc. **3.** to fish with a spinning reel **4.** to whirl or rotate swiftly **5.** to go into or descend in a spin: said of an aircraft **6.** to seem to be spinning from dizziness **7.** to move along swiftly and smoothly **8.** to rotate freely without traction [wheels *spinning* on ice] —*n.* **1.** the act of spinning or rotating something **2.** a spinning or rotating movement **3.** a moving along swiftly and smoothly **4.** a ride or pleasure trip in a motor vehicle **5.** any descent in which an airplane comes down nose first along a spiral path of large pitch and small radius **6.** any sudden, steep downward movement **7.** *Physics a)* the intrinsic angular momentum of an elementary particle or photon, produced by rotation about its own axis *b)* the total angular momentum of a nuclide —*SYN.* see TURN —**spin off 1.** to produce as an outgrowth or secondary benefit, development, etc. **2.** to get rid of

spin·ach (spin'ich, -ij) *n.* [< MFr. *espinach* < (? via ML. *spinachia*) OSp. *espinaca* < Ar. *ispānakh* < Per. *aspanākh*] **1.** *a)* a plant (*Spinacia oleracea*) of the goosefoot family, with large, dark-green, juicy, edible leaves, usually eaten cooked *b)* the leaves ☆**2.** [Slang] a beard

spi·nal (spī'n'l) *adj.* [LL. *spinalis*] **1.** of or having to do with the spine or spinal cord **2.** of a spine or needle-shaped process —*n.* clipped form of SPINAL ANESTHETIC —**spi'nal·ly** *adv.*

spinal anesthesia *Surgery* anesthesia of the lower part of the body by the injection of an anesthetic into the spinal cord, usually in the lumbar region —**spinal anesthetic**

spinal canal the canal, or tube, formed by the vertebral arches, containing the spinal cord

spinal column the series of joined vertebrae forming the axial support for the skeleton; spine; backbone

spinal cord the thick cord of nerve tissue of the central nervous system, extending down the spinal canal from the medulla oblongata

spin casting same as SPINNING (*n.*, 2) —**spin'·cast'** *vi.*

spin·dle (spin'd'l) *n.* [ME. (with intrusive -*d*-) < OE. *spinel* < *spinnan*, to SPIN] **1.** a slender rod or pin used in spinning; specif., *a)* in hand spinning, a rounded rod, usually wooden, tapering toward each end, for twisting into thread the fibers pulled from the material on the distaff, and notched at one end so as to hold the thread *b)* on a spinning wheel, the rod by which the thread is twisted and on which it is then wound *c)* in a spinning machine, any of the rods holding the bobbins on which the spun thread is wound **2.** a measure for yarn, equal to 14,400 yards in linen or 15,120 yards in cotton **3.** the spindle-shaped bundle of nuclear fibers formed during one stage of mitosis **4.** a short turned piece or decorative rod, as in a baluster, the back of some chairs, etc. **5.** any rod, pin, or shaft that revolves or serves as an axis for a revolving part, as an axle, arbor, or mandrel **6.** in a lathe, a shaftlike part (**live spindle**) that rotates while holding the thing to be turned, or a similar part (**dead spindle**) that does not rotate **7.** the small, square shaft passing through a door lock, to which the doorknobs are attached ☆**8.** a metal spike on a base, on which papers are impaled for temporary filing: also **spindle file 9.** same as HYDROMETER ☆**10.** *Naut.* a metal rod or pipe with a lantern, ball, etc. at its top, fastened to a rock, shoal, or the like as a warning to vessels —*adj.* of or like a spindle or spindles —*vi.* **-dled, -dling 1.** to grow in a long, slender shape **2.** to grow into a long, slender stalk or stem —*vt.* **1.** to form into a spindle **2.** to fit or equip with a spindle ☆**3.** to impale (papers, etc.) on a spindle (sense 8)

spin·dle·ged (-leg'id, -legd') *adj.* having thin legs: also **spin'dle-shanked'** (-shaŋkt')

spin·dle·legs (-legz') *n.pl.* **1.** thin legs **2.** [with sing. *v.*] [Colloq.] a person with thin legs

spindle tree same as EUONYMUS

spin·dling (spin'dliŋ) *adj.* same as SPINDLY —*n.* a spindly person or thing

spin·dly (spin'dlē) *adj.* **-dli·er, -dli·est** long or tall and very thin or slender, often so as to be or seem frail or weak

spin·drift (spin'drift') *n.* [earlier *spenedrift*, Scot. var. of *spoondrift* < *spoon*, to scud (< ?) + DRIFT] spray blown from a rough sea or surf

spine (spin) *n.* [ME. < OFr. *espine* < L. *spina*, a thorn, prickle, backbone < IE. base *(s)p(h)ei-, sharp, pointed splinter, whence SPIT[1], SPIRE[2]] **1.** any of the short, sharp, woody processes projecting from certain plants, as the cactus **2.** *a)* a sharp process of bone *b)* any of the sharp, stiff projections on the bodies of certain animals, as the quill of a porcupine or a ray of a fish's fin *c)* anything resembling either of these projections **3.** the spinal column; backbone **4.** anything regarded as resembling a backbone, as *a)* a ridge of ground, crest of a hill, etc. *b)* the part of a bound book covering the backbone, and usually bearing the title and author's name ☆**5.** courage, willpower, etc.

spi·nel (spi nel', spin'l) *n.* [Early ModE. *spynel* < MFr. *spinelle* < It. *spinella*, dim. of *spina*, a thorn, spine < L. (see prec.)] a hard, crystalline isometric mineral, (Mg,Fe) Al₂O₄, composed chiefly of oxide of aluminum, magnesium,

and iron, and found in various colors: a red variety (**ruby spinel**) is used as a gem

spine·less (spin'lis) *adj.* **1.** having no backbone; invertebrate **2.** having a weak or flexible backbone **3.** lacking courage, resistance, willpower, etc. **4.** without spines, or thorny processes —**spine'less·ly** *adv.* —**spine'less·ness** *n.*

spi·nes·cent (spī nes''nt) *adj.* [LL. *spinescens*, prp. of *spinescere*, to grow spiny < L. *spina*, SPINE] **1.** spiny; having spines **2.** becoming spiny or spinelike

spin·et (spin'it) *n.* [MFr. *espinette* < It. *spinetta*, prob. < *spina*, a thorn (< L., SPINE): so named from the pointed quills used to strike the strings] **1.** an obsolete, small variety of harpsichord with a single keyboard **2.** *a)* a small upright piano of relatively low height *b)* a small electronic organ of similar design

spi·nif·er·ous (spī nif'ər əs) *adj.* [L. *spinifer* < *spina*, SPINE + -FEROUS] bearing spines

spin·i·fex (spin'i feks') *n.* [ModL. < L. *spina*, SPINE + *facere*, to make, DO[1]] any of a genus (*Spinifex*) of Australian grasses with pointed leaves and bristly seed heads

spin·i·ness (spī'nē nis) *n.* a spiny quality or condition

spin·na·ker (spin'ə kər) *n.* [said to be < *spinx*, altered < *Sphinx*, name of a yacht which carried the sail] a large, triangular, baggy headsail used on some racing yachts when running before the wind

spin·ner (spin'ər) *n.* a person or thing that spins; specif., *a)* a fishing lure with attached blades that revolve or flutter when drawn through the water; also, any of these blades *b)* a domelike cap that fits over the hub of an airplane propeller and rotates with it *c)* a pitched baseball, etc. that is made to spin ☆*d)* a football play in which the back who receives the ball from the center spins around to hand it off or to fake handing it off

spin·ner·et (spin'ə ret') *n.* [dim. of *spinner*] **1.** the organ in spiders, caterpillars, etc. with which they spin silky threads **2.** a thimblelike device or metal plate with tiny holes through which a solution is forced in the making of synthetic fibers

spin·ney, spin·ny (spin'ē) *n., pl.* **-neys, -nies** [ME. *spenne*, a thorn hedge < OFr. *espinei* < VL. *spinēta*, for L. *spinetum* < *spina*, thorn, SPINE] [Brit.] a thicket or grove

spin·ning (spin'iŋ) *n.* **1.** the act of making thread or yarn from fibers or filaments **2.** the act of fishing with a rod that has a fixed spool, a light line, and light lures —*adj.* that spins or is used in spinning

spinning frame any of various spinning machines with many spindles

spinning jenny an early spinning machine with several spindles, for spinning more than one thread at a time

spinning mule same as MULE[1] (sense 3)

spinning wheel a simple spinning machine fitted with a single spindle driven by the rotation of a large wheel spun by a foot treadle or by hand

SPINNING WHEEL

spin·off (spin'ôf') *n.* **1.** the distribution to its shareholders by a parent corporation of the stock it holds in a subsidiary corporation **2.** a secondary benefit, product, development, etc., as a television series built around a character in an earlier series

spi·nose (spī'nōs) *adj.* [L. *spinosus* < *spina*, SPINE] full of or covered with spines —**spi'nose·ly** *adv.*

spi·nos·i·ty (spī näs'ə tē) *n., pl.* **-ties** [LL. *spinositas*] **1.** the condition of being spinose **2.** something spinose, or thorny, nettling, etc.

spi·nous (spī'nəs) *adj.* [L. *spinosus*] **1.** same as SPINOSE **2.** like a spine or thorn in form **3.** thorny; nettling

Spi·no·za (spi nō'zə), **Ba·ruch** (bə rook') or (in Latin) **Benedict** 1632-77; Du. philosopher

Spi·no·zism (-ziz'm) *n.* the philosophy of Spinoza, who taught that there is but one infinite substance, God (or Nature), having infinite attributes of which only thought and extension are knowable —**Spi·no'zist** *n.*

spin·ster (spin'stər) *n.* [ME. < *spinnen*, to SPIN + -STER] **1.** a woman who spins thread or yarn **2.** an unmarried woman; esp., an elderly woman who has never married; old maid —**spin'ster·hood'** *n.* —**spin'ster·ish** *adj.*

spin·thar·i·scope (spin thar'ə skōp') *n.* [< Gr. *spintharis*, a spark + -SCOPE] a small device with a fluorescent screen, for visually observing the scintillations produced by the impact of alpha rays given off by a radioactive substance

☆**spin the bottle** a kissing game played by young people, in which a bottle is spun to point to the one to be kissed

‡**spin·to** (spēn'tô) *adj.* [It., pp. of *spingere*, to push, spur on < VL. *expingere* < L. *ex-*, intens. + *pangere*, to fasten, drive in: see FANG] *Music* essentially lyric in quality, but with a strong dramatic element [a *spinto* soprano] —*n.* a spinto voice or singer

spi·nule (spī'nyool, spin'yool) *n.* [L. *spinula*, dim. of *spina*, SPINE] a small spine —**spi·nu·lose** (spī'nyoo lōs', spin'yoo-) *adj.*

spin·y (spī'nē) *adj.* **spin'i·er, spin'i·est 1.** covered with or having spines, thorns, or prickles **2.** full of difficulties; troublesome; thorny **3.** spine-shaped

spiny anteater same as ECHIDNA

spiny dogfish a small dogfish shark (*Squalus acanthias*)

spin·y-finned (spǐ′nē find′) *adj.* having fins in which the membrane is supported by pointed, stiff rays

spin·y-head·ed worm (-hed′id) *same as* ACANTHO-CEPHALAN

spiny lobster any of a family (Palinuridae) of sea crustaceans, similar to the common lobster, but lacking the large pincers and having a spiny shell

spin·y-rayed (-rād′) *adj.* 1. having pointed, stiff rays: said of a fin 2. *same as* SPINY-FINNED

spi·ra·cle (spǐ′rə k'l, spir′ə-) *n.* [ME. < L. *spiraculum* < *spirare*, to breathe: see SPIRIT] 1. a small opening allowing the outer air to come through into a confined space; air hole 2. *Geol.* a small vent formed on the surface of a thick lava flow 3. *Zool.* an aperture for breathing, as *a*) any of the small external openings of the tracheal respiratory system in most terrestrial arthropods, ordinarily along the sides of certain thoracic and abdominal segments; stigma *b*) any of various similar openings for the passage of air or respiratory water, as in tadpoles, etc. *c*) *same as* BLOW-HOLE (sense 1) —**spi·rac·u·lar** (spī rak′yoo lər, spi-) *adj.*

spi·rae·a (spī rē′ə) *n. var. sp. of* SPIREA

spi·ral (spī′rəl) *adj.* [ML. *spiralis* < L. *spira*, a coil < Gr. *speira* < IE. base **sper-*, to turn, wrap, whence Gr. *spargein*, to swathe, Lett. *sprangât*, to lace up] 1. circling around a central point in a flat curve that constantly increases (or decreases) in size; coiled or coiling in one plane 2. circling around a central axis in a curve of conical or cylindrical form; coiled or coiling as a screw thread or bolt thread; helical —*n.* 1. a spiral curve occurring in a single plane

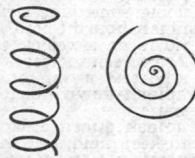

SPIRALS

2. a spiral curve occurring in a series of planes; helix 3. something having a spiral form, as a wire for holding sheets in some notebooks 4. a spiral path or flight [the descending *spiral* of a falling leaf] 5. a section or segment of a spiral 6. a continuous, widening decrease or increase [an inflationary *spiral* ending in financial collapse] ☆7. *Football* a kick or pass in which the ball rotates on its longer axis as its moves through the air —*vi.* -raled or -ralled, -ral·ing or -ral·ling to move in or form a spiral —*vt.* to cause to move in or form a spiral —**spi′ral·ly** *adv.*

spiral galaxy a galaxy having the visible form of a spiral: *also* **spiral nebula**

spi·rant (spī′rənt) *n.* [< L. *spirans*, prp. of *spirare*, to breathe: see SPIRIT] a consonantal sound, as (sh) or (v), produced by the passage of breath through the partially closed oral cavity; fricative —*adj.* having the nature of a spirant; fricative

spire[1] (spīr) *n.* [Fr. < L. *spira* < Gr. *speira*] 1. a spiral or coil 2. any of the convolutions of a spiral or coil 3. *Zool.* the upper part of a spiral shell

spire[2] (spīr) *n.* [ME. < OE. *spir*, akin to ON. *spīra*: for IE. base see SPINE] 1. a sprout, spike, or stalk of a plant, as a blade of grass, etc. 2. the top part of a pointed, tapering object or structure, as a mountain peak 3. anything that tapers to a point, as a pointed structure capping a tower or steeple —*vi.* spired, spir′ing to extend upward, tapering to a point; shoot up or rise in, or put forth, a spire or spires —**spired** *adj.*

spi·re·a (spī rē′ə) *n.* [ModL. *Spiraea*, name of the genus < L. *spiraea*, meadowsweet < Gr. *speiraia* < *speira*, SPIRAL] any of a genus (*Spiraea*) of plants of the rose family, with dense clusters of small, pink or white flowers

spi·reme (spī′rēm) *n.* [Gr. *speirēma*, a coil < *speira*, SPIRAL] *Biol.* a thin, threadlike tangle of chromatin at the beginning of the prophase in mitosis

spi·rif·er·ous (spī rif′ər əs) *adj.* [< ModL. *spirifer*: see SPIRAL & -FEROUS] *Zool.* characterized by a spire, or spiral structure, as some shells, or by spiral appendages, as a brachiopod

spi·ril·lum (spī ril′əm) *n., pl.* -la (-ə) [ModL., dim. of L. *spira* (see SPIRAL)] 1. any of a genus (*Spirillum*) of bacteria having the form of a spiral thread and characterized by flagella 2. any of various similar microorganisms

spir·it (spir′it) *n.* [ME. < OFr. *espirit* < L. *spiritus*, breath, courage, vigor, the soul, life, in L.(Ec.), a spirit < *spirare*, to blow, breathe < IE. base **(s)peis-*, to blow, whence (prob.) Norw. *fisa*, to puff, blow, OSlav. *piskati*, to pipe, whistle] 1. *a*) the life principle, esp. in man, orig. regarded as inherent in the breath or as infused by a deity *b*) *same as* SOUL (sense 1) 2. the thinking, motivating, feeling part of man, often as distinguished from the body; mind; intelligence 3. [*also* S-] life, will, consciousness, thought, etc., regarded as separate from matter 4. a supernatural being, esp. one thought of as haunting or possessing a person, house, etc., as a ghost, or as inhabiting a certain region, being of a certain (good or evil) character, etc., as an angel, demon, fairy, or elf 5. an individual person or personality thought of as showing or having some specific quality [the brave *spirits* who pioneered] 6. [*usually pl.*] frame of mind; disposition; mood; temper [in high *spirits*] 7. vivacity, courage, vigor, enthusiasm, etc. [to answer with *spirit*] 8. enthusiasm and loyalty [school *spirit*] 9. real meaning; true intention [to follow the *spirit* if not the letter of the law] 10. a pervading animating principle, essential or characteristic quality, or prevailing tendency or attitude [the *spirit* of the Renaissance] 11. a divine animating influence or inspiration 12. [*usually pl.*] strong alcoholic liquor produced by distillation 13. [Obs.] *a*) any of certain substances or fluids thought of as permeating organs of the body *b*) *Alchemy* sulfur, sal ammoniac, mercury, or orpiment 14. [*often pl.*] *Chem. a*) any liquid produced by distillation, as from wood, shale, etc. [*spirits* of turpentine] *b*) *same as* ALCOHOL (sense 1) 15. *Dyeing* a solution of a tin salt, etc., used as a mordant 16. *Pharmacy* an alcoholic solution of a volatile or essential substance [*spirits* of camphor] —*vt.* 1. to inspirit, animate, encourage, cheer, etc. (often with *up*) 2. to carry (*away, off*, etc.) secretly and swiftly, or in some mysterious way —*adj.* 1. *a*) of spirits or spiritualism ☆*b*) supposedly manifested by spirits [*spirit* rapping] 2. operating by the burning of alcohol [a *spirit* lamp] —**out of spirits** sad; depressed —**the Spirit** *same as* HOLY GHOST

spir·it·ed (-id) *adj.* 1. full of spirit; lively; vigorous; energetic; animated 2. having a (specified) character, mood, or disposition [public-*spirited*, low-*spirited*] —**spir′it·ed·ly** *adv.* —**spir′it·ed·ness** *n.*

☆**spirit gum** a solution of gum arabic in ether, etc. used as in the theater to attach false hair, whiskers, etc. to the face

spir·it·ism (-iz'm) *n. same as* SPIRITUALISM —**spir′it·ist** *n., adj.* —**spir′it·is′tic** *adj.*

spir·it·less (-lis) *adj.* lacking spirit, energy, or vigor; listless; depressed —**spir′it·less·ly** *adv.* —**spir′it·less·ness** *n.*

spirit level an instrument for determining a horizontal plane: see LEVEL (*n.* 1)

spi·ri·to·so (spir′i tō′sō; *It.* spē′rē tô′sô) *adj., adv.* [It.] lively; with spirit: a direction to the performer in music

spir·it·ous (spir′i təs) *adj.* 1. *same as* SPIRITUOUS 2. [Obs.] lively; high-spirited

spirits of ammonia a 10% solution of ammonia in alcohol: *also* **spirit of ammonia**

spirits of hartshorn *old-fashioned name for* AMMONIUM HYDROXIDE: *also* **spirit of hartshorn**

spirits of turpentine *same as* TURPENTINE (sense 3): *also* **spirit of turpentine**

spirits of wine *same as* ALCOHOL (sense 1): *also* **spirit of wine**

spir·it·u·al (spir′i choo wəl, -chool) *adj.* [ME. *spirituel* < OFr. < L. *spiritualis* < LL.(Ec.) < L., of breathing or air] 1. of the spirit or the soul as distinguished from the body or material matters 2. of, from, or concerned with the intellect; intellectual 3. of, or consisting of spirit; not corporeal 4. characterized by the ascendancy of the spirit; showing much refinement of thought and feeling 5. of religion or the church; sacred, devotional, or ecclesiastical; not lay or temporal 6. spiritualistic or supernatural —*n.* ☆1. any of a class of U.S. Negro religious folk songs, often dealing with Biblical themes and characterized by fervor and vigorous rhythm 2. [*pl.*] religious or church matters —**spir′it·u·al·ly** *adv.* —**spir′it·u·al·ness** *n.*

spiritual bouquet *R.C.Ch.* the doing of specific good works or acts of devotion, for the spiritual benefit of another, living or dead

spir·it·u·al·ism (-iz'm) *n.* ☆1. *a*) the belief that the dead survive as spirits which can communicate with the living, esp. with the help of a third party (medium) *b*) any practice arising from this belief 2. the philosophical doctrine that all reality is in essence spiritual; idealism 3. spirituality; spiritual quality —**spir′it·u·al·ist** *n.* —**spir′it·u·al·is′tic** *adj.* —**spir′it·u·al·is′ti·cal·ly** *adv.*

spir·it·u·al·i·ty (spir′i choo wal·ə tē) *n., pl.* -ties 1. spiritual character, quality, or nature 2. [*often pl.*] the rights, jurisdiction, tithes, etc. belonging to the church or to an ecclesiastic 3. the fact or state of being incorporeal

spir·it·u·al·ize (spir′i choo wə liz′, -choo liz′) *vt.* -ized′, -iz′ing 1. to make spiritual; deprive of materiality or worldliness 2. to give a spiritual sense or meaning to —**spir′it·u·al·i·za′tion** *n.*

spir·it·u·al·ty (spir′i choo wəl tē, -chool tē) *n., pl.* -ties 1. the clergy 2. [*often pl.*] *same as* SPIRITUALITY (sense 2)

‡**spi·ri·tu·el** (spē rē tü el′; *E.* spir′i choo wel′) *adj.* [Fr.: see SPIRITUAL] having or showing a refined nature or, esp., a quick, graceful wit or mind —**spi·ri·tu·elle** (-el′; *E.* -wel′) *adj. fem.*

spir·it·u·ous (spir′i choo wəs) *adj.* [< L. *spiritus*, SPIRIT + -OUS] of, like, or containing alcohol: said esp. of distilled as opposed to fermented beverages —**spir′it·u·os′i·ty** (-wäs′ə tē) *n.*

spir·i·tus as·per (spir′i təs as′pər) [L.] *same as* ROUGH BREATHING

spiritus fru·men·ti (froo men′tī) [L., lit., spirit of grain] *same as* WHISKEY

spiritus le·nis (lē′nis) [L.] *same as* SMOOTH BREATHING

spi·ro-[1] (spī′rō, -rə) [< L. *spirare*, to breathe: see SPIRIT] a combining form meaning respiration [*spirograph*]

spi·ro-² (spī'rō, -rə) [< Gr. *speira*, a coil: see SPIRAL] *a combining form meaning* spiral or coil [*spirochete*]

spi·ro·chete (spī'rə kēt') *n.* [ModL. *spirochaeta* < Gr. *speira*, a SPIRAL + *chaitē*, hair] any of a group of slender, flexible, nonflagellated, spiral-shaped bacteria (order Spirochaetales), including some species that cause disease, some that are parasitic, and some that are free-living: also sp. **spi'ro·chaete'** —**spi'ro·chet'al** (-kēt'l) *adj.*

spi·ro·che·to·sis (spī'rə kē tō'sis) *n.* any disease, as syphilis, relapsing fever, etc., caused by spirochetes

spi·ro·graph (spī'rə graf', -gräf') *n.* [SPIRO-¹ + -GRAPH] an instrument for recording the movements of breathing —**spi'ro·graph'ic** *adj.*

spi·ro·gy·ra (spī'rə jī'rə) *n.* [ModL., name of the genus < Gr. *speira*, a SPIRAL + *gyros*, a ring: see GYRATE] any of a genus (*Spirogyra*) of freshwater green algae containing spiral chlorophyll bands in their cylindrical cells

spi·roid (spī'roid) *adj.* [ModL. *spiroides*: see SPIRE] like a spiral; having a spiral form

spi·rom·e·ter (spī räm'ə tər) *n.* [SPIRO-¹ + -METER] an instrument for measuring the breathing capacity of the lungs —**spi'ro·met'ric** (-rə met'rik) *adj.* —**spi·rom'e·try** (-räm'ə trē) *n.*

spirt (spurt) *n., vt., vi. same as* SPURT

spir·u·la (spir'yoo lə, -oo lə) *n., pl.* **-lae'** (-lē') [ModL., name of the genus, dim. of L. *spira*: see SPIRAL] any of a genus (*Spirula*) of two-gilled, deep-water, cephalopod mollusks, having a flat spiral shell with a series of chambers

spir·y¹ (spīr'ē) *adj.* **spir'i·er, spir'i·est** [Poet.] spiral; coiled; curled

spir·y² (spīr'ē) *adj.* **spir'i·er, spir'i·est** 1. of, or having the form of, a spire, steeple, etc. 2. having many spires

spit¹ (spit) *n.* [ME. *spite* < OE. *spitu*, akin to OHG. *spizzi*, sharp: for IE. base see SPIKE¹] 1. a thin, pointed rod or bar on which meat is impaled for broiling or roasting over a fire or before other direct heat 2. a narrow point of land, or a narrow reef or shoal, extending into a body of water —*vt.* **spit'ted, spit'ting** to fix or impale on or as on a spit —**spit'ter** *n.*

spit² (spit) *vt.* spit or, esp. Brit., spat, spit'ting [ME. *spitten* < OE. *spittan*, akin to Dan. *spytte*: for IE. base see SPEW] 1. to eject from within the mouth 2. to eject, throw (*out*), emit, or utter explosively [to *spit* out an oath] 3. to light (a fuse) —*vi.* 1. to eject saliva from the mouth; expectorate 2. to rain or snow lightly or briefly 3. to make an explosive hissing noise, as an angry cat 4. to express contempt or hatred by or as if by spitting saliva (*on* or *at*) 5. to sputter, as frying fat —*n.* 1. the act of spitting 2. saliva; spittle 3. something like saliva, as the frothy secretion of certain insects 4. a light, brief shower of rain or fall of snow 5. [Colloq.] the perfect likeness or exact image, as of a person: usually in the phrase **spit and image** (spit'n im'ij) —**spit up** to regurgitate or cough up

spit·al (spit'l) *n.* [respelling (after HOSPITAL) of earlier *spittle* < ME. *spitel* < ML. *hospitale:* see HOSPITAL] [Obs.] 1. a hospital, esp. one for the poor or for lepers, etc. 2. a travelers' wayside shelter

spit and polish formal or ceremonial, sometimes superficial, orderliness, neatness, or preciseness, as in the military

☆**spit·ball** (-bôl') *n.* 1. a piece of paper chewed up into a wad for throwing 2. *Baseball* a pitch, now illegal, made to curve by moistening one side of the ball as with saliva

☆**spit curl** a curled lock of hair dampened, as with spit, and pressed flat against the forehead or temple

spite (spīt) *n.* [ME., aphetic < *despite*: see DESPITE] 1. *a)* a mean or evil feeling toward another, characterized by the inclination to hurt, humiliate, annoy, frustrate, etc.; ill will; malice *b)* an instance of this; a grudge 2. [Archaic] something annoying or irritating —*vt.* **spit'ed, spit'ing** to behave in a spiteful manner toward; vent one's spite upon by hurting, annoying, frustrating, etc. —SYN. see MALICE —**in spite of** in defiance of; regardless of; notwithstanding

spite·ful (-fəl) *adj.* full of or showing spite; purposefully annoying; malicious —SYN. see VINDICTIVE —**spite'ful·ly** *adv.* —**spite'ful·ness** *n.*

spit·fire (spit'fīr') *n.* a person, esp. a woman or girl, who is easily aroused to violent outbursts of anger

Spit·head (spit'hed') *see* The SOLENT

Spits·ber·gen (spits'bur'gən) 1. group of Norw. islands in the Arctic Ocean, constituting the major part of Svalbard: 23,658 sq. mi. 2. *same as* SVALBARD

spit·ter (spit'ər) *n.* 1. a person or animal that spits saliva, etc. ☆2. [Colloq.] *same as* SPITBALL (sense 2)

spitting image (spit'n im'ij) alteration of SPIT AND IMAGE: see SPIT²

spit·tle (spit'l) *n.* [earlier *spettle* < ME. *spetil* < OE. *spætl*, var. of *spatl:* for IE. base see SPEW] 1. saliva; spit 2. the frothy secretion of larval spittlebugs

☆**spit·tle·bug** (-bug') *n. same as* FROGHOPPER: also called **spittle insect**

☆**spit·toon** (spi toon') *n.* [< SPIT²] a jarlike container to spit into; cuspidor

spitz (spits) *n.* [G. < *spitz*, pointed < OHG. *spizzi:* see SPIT¹] a variety of small Pomeranian dog, usually white, with sharp-pointed muzzle and ears and a long, silky coat

spiv (spiv) *n.* [prob. dial. var. of 19th-c. slang *spiff*, person who dresses flashily] [Brit. Colloq.] a man who lives by his wits, without doing any regular or honest work, esp. one engaged in petty, shady dealings

splanch·nic (splaŋk'nik) *adj.* [ModL. *splanchnicus* < Gr. *splanchnikos* < *splanchnon*, an entrail: for IE. base see SPLEEN] of the viscera; visceral

splanch·no- (splaŋk'nō) [< Gr. *splanchnon:* see prec.] *a combining form meaning* the viscera [*splanchnology*]

splanch·nol·o·gy (splaŋk näl'ə jē) *n.* [prec. + -LOGY] the branch of medical study dealing with the structure, functions, and diseases of the viscera

splash (splash) *vt.* [intens. extension of PLASH²] 1. to cause (a liquid substance) to scatter and fall in drops or blobs 2. to dash or scatter a liquid substance, mud, etc. on, so as to wet or soil 3. to cause to splash a liquid [to *splash* one's feet in puddles] 4. to make (one's way) by splashing 5. to mark or spot by or as by splashing [a glade *splashed* with sunlight] 6. to display conspicuously [scandal *splashed* all over the front page] —*vi.* 1. to dash or scatter a liquid substance about 2. to fall, strike, or scatter with a splash or splashes [rain *splashing* against the window] 3. to move with splashes —*n.* 1. the act or sound of splashing 2. a mass of splashed water, mud, etc. 3. a spot or mark made by or as by splashing 4. a patch of color, light, etc. 5. a small amount (*of* soda water, etc.) 6. [Colloq.] a conspicuous or ostentatious display —**make a splash** [Colloq.] to attract great, often brief attention by doing something striking or ostentatious —**splash'er** *n.*

splash·board (-bôrd') *n.* 1. any screen or board protecting riders on a vehicle from being splashed in wet weather 2. a screen to keep water from splashing onto the deck of a boat 3. a trap for closing a sluice or spillway

☆**splash·down** (-doun') *n.* the landing of a spacecraft on water

☆**splash guard** a flap behind a rear wheel, as of a truck, to keep mud, etc. from splashing on a following vehicle

splash·y (-ē) *adj.* **splash'i·er, splash'i·est** 1. splashing; making splashes 2. liable to splash; wet, muddy, etc. 3. covered or marked with splashes 4. [Colloq.] attracting much notice or attention; spectacular; striking —**splash'i·ly** *adv.* —**splash'i·ness** *n.*

splat¹ (splat) *n.* [via dial. < base of SPLIT] a thin, flat piece of wood, esp. as used in the back of a chair

splat² (splat) *n., interj.* a splattering or wet, slapping sound

splat·ter (-ər) *n., vt., vi.* [altered (after SPLASH) < SPATTER] spatter or splash

splay (splā) *vt., vi.* [ME. *splaien*, aphetic < *displaien*, to DISPLAY] 1. to spread out or apart; expand; extend (often with *out*) 2. to make or be beveled or sloping —*n.* [< the *v.*] 1. a sloping or beveled surface or angle, as of the side of a doorway 2. a spreading; expansion; enlargement —*adj.* 1. sloping, spreading, or turning outward 2. broad and flat 3. awkwardly awry

splay·foot (-foot') *n., pl.* **-feet'** 1. a foot that is flat and turned outward 2. the condition of having feet of this kind —*adj.* of or having splayfoot: also **splay'foot'ed**

spleen (splēn) *n.* [ME. *splen* < OFr. *esplen* < L. *splen* < Gr. *splēn*, spleen < IE. *sp(h)elgh-*, whence Sans. *plīhan*, OSlav. *slĕzena*, spleen] 1. a large, vascular, lymphatic organ in the upper left part of the abdominal cavity of vertebrates, near the stomach: it has various functions in modifying the structure of the blood, and was formerly regarded as the seat of certain emotions 2. *a)* malice; spite; bad temper *b)* [Archaic] melancholy; low spirits *c)* [Obs.] a whim or caprice

spleen·ful (-fəl) *adj.* full of spleen; irritable, peevish, spiteful, etc.: also **spleen'ish, spleen'y** —**spleen'ful·ly** *adv.*

spleen·wort (-wurt') *n.* any of a genus (*Asplenium*) of ferns with simple or compound fronds and linear or oblique sori on the upper surface of an oblique veinlet

splen- (splēn) *same as* SPLENO-: used before a vowel

splen·dent (splen'dənt) *adj.* [LME. < L. *splendens*, prp. of *splendere:* see ff.] [Poet.] 1. shining; lustrous 2. brilliant, splendid, or illustrious

splen·did (splen'did) *adj.* [L. *splendidus* < *splendere*, to shine < IE. *splend-* < base *sp(h)el-*, to gleam, shine, whence Sans. *sphulinga*, a spark, G. *flink*, lively] 1. having or showing splendor; specif., *a)* shining; lustrous; brilliant *b)* magnificent; gorgeous 2. worthy of high praise; grand; glorious; illustrious [a *splendid* accomplishment] 3. [Colloq.] very good; excellent; fine [*splendid* weather] —**splen'did·ly** *adv.* —**splen'did·ness** *n.*

SYN.—**splendid** applies to that which literally or figuratively dazzles or impresses with its brilliance, luster, etc. [a *splendid* uniform, hero, etc.]; **gorgeous** applies to that which is striking for its brilliance and variety of color [a *gorgeous* floral display]; **glorious** refers to that which is radiantly beautiful or distinctive [a *glorious* sunset]; **sublime** implies such an exalted beauty or grandeur as to inspire awe or admiration [the *sublime* Grand Canyon]; **superb** is applied to that which exceeds all others in grandeur, splendor, etc. [a *superb* performance of an opera] All of these words are now used hyperbolically, in informal speech, with weakened effect

splen·dif·er·ous (splen dif'ər əs) *adj.* [< SPLENDOR + -FEROUS, a recoinage of obs. *splendiferous* < ME. < ML. *splendiferus*, for LL. *splendorifer* < L. *splendor* + *-fer*, -FER] [Colloq.] gorgeous; splendid: a jocularly pretentious usage —**splen·dif'er·ous·ly** *adv.* —**splen·dif'er·ous·ness** *n.*

splen·dor (splen'dər) *n.* [ME. *splendure* < OFr. *splendour* < L. *splendor* < *splendere*, to shine: see SPLENDID] 1. great luster or brightness; brilliance 2. magnificent richness or glory; pomp; grandeur —**splen'dor·ous, splen'drous** *adj.*

splen·dour (splen′dər) *n. Brit. sp.* of SPLENDOR

sple·nec·to·my (spli nek′tə mē) *n., pl.* **-mies** [SPLEN- + -ECTOMY] the surgical removal of the spleen

sple·net·ic (spli net′ik) *adj.* [LL. *spleneticus*] **1.** of the spleen; splenic **2.** bad-tempered, irritable, peevish, spiteful, etc.; spleenful **3.** [Obs.] melancholy Also **sple·net′i·cal** —*n.* a spleenful person —*SYN.* see IRRITABLE —**sple·net′i·cal·ly** *adv.*

splen·ic (splen′ik, splēn′-) *adj.* [L. *splenicus* < Gr. *splēnikos*] **1.** of or having to do with the spleen **2.** in or near the spleen

sple·ni·us (splē′nē əs) *n., pl.* **-ni·i′** (-nē ī′) [ModL. < L. *splenium*, a patch, plaster < Gr. *splēnion*, dim. of *splēn*, SPLEEN] either of two large, flat muscles at the back of the neck, serving to rotate and extend the head and rotate and flex the neck —**sple′ni·al** *adj.*

sple·no- (splē′nō, splen′ə) [< Gr. *splēn* (gen. *splēnos*), SPLEEN] *a combining form meaning* the spleen

sple·no·meg·a·ly (splē′nə meg′ə lē) *n.* [ModL.: see prec. & MEGALO-] enlargement of the spleen

spleu·chan (splōō′khən) *n.* [< IrGael. *spliúchān*] [Scot. & Irish] a pouch, as for money or tobacco

splice (splīs) *vt.* **spliced, splic′ing** [MDu. *splissen*, akin to *splitten*, to SPLIT] **1.** to join or unite (ropes or rope ends) by weaving together the end strands **2.** to join the ends of (timbers) by overlapping and binding or bolting together **3.** to fasten the ends of (wire, motion-picture film, sound tape, etc.) together, as by twisting, soldering, cementing, etc. **4.** [Slang] to join in marriage —*n.* a joint or joining made by splicing —**splic′er** *n.*

SPLICE
(A, short splice; B, eye splice)

spline (splīn) *n.* [< E. Anglian dial., prob. akin to Norw. dial. *splindra*, a large, flat splinter: for IE. base see SPLIT] **1.** a long, flat, pliable strip, as of wood or metal, esp. one used in drawing curves **2.** *a)* a flat key or strip that fits into a groove or slot between parts *b)* the groove or slot into which it fits —*vt.* **splined, splin′ing 1.** to fit with a spline **2.** to cut a groove or slot in for a spline

splint (splint) *n.* [ME. *splente* < MDu. or MLowG. *splinte*: for IE. base see SPLIT] **1.** a thin strip of wood or cane woven together with others to make baskets, chair seats, etc. **2.** a thin strip of metal used in overlapping construction with others to make medieval armor **3.** a thin, rigid strip of wood, metal, etc. set along a broken bone to keep the pieces in place or used to keep a part of the body in a fixed position **4.** a bony growth or tumor on the cannon bone of a horse, mule, etc. —*vt.* to fit, support, or hold in place with or as with a splint or splints

splint bone in horses and related animals, either of two small bones, one on each side of the cannon bone

splin·ter (splin′tər) *vt., vi.* [ME. < MDu., akin to *splinte*, SPLINT] **1.** to break or split into thin, sharp pieces **2.** to break into small parts or into groups with divergent views; fragment —*n.* **1.** a thin, sharp piece of wood, bone, etc., made by splitting or breaking; sliver **2.** a splinter group —*adj.* designating a group that separates from a main party, church, etc. because of divergent views —*SYN.* see BREAK[1]

splin·ter·y (-ē) *adj.* **1.** easily splintered **2.** of or like a splinter **3.** resulting in splinters, as a fracture **4.** full of splinters; splintered; jagged; rough

Split (splēt) seaport in Croatia, W Yugoslavia, on the Adriatic: pop. 93,000

split (split) *vt.* **split, split′ting** [MDu. *splitten*, akin to MHG. *splizen* < IE. base *(s)plei-*, to split, crack, whence FLINT] **1.** to separate, cut, or divide into two or more parts; cause to separate along the grain or length; break into layers **2.** to break or tear apart by force; burst; rend **3.** to divide into parts or shares; portion out [to split the cost] ☆**4.** to cast (one's vote) or mark (one's ballot) for candidates of more than one party **5.** to cause (a group, political party, etc.) to separate into divisions or factions; disunite **6.** *Chem., Physics a)* to break (a molecule) into atoms or into smaller molecules *b)* to produce nuclear fission in (an atom) **7.** *Finance* to divide (stock) by substituting some multiple of the original shares that will usually have the same aggregate par value as the old, but a proportionately lower value per share —*vi.* **1.** to separate lengthwise into two or more parts; separate along the grain or length **2.** to break or tear apart; burst; rend **3.** to separate or break up through failure to agree, etc. (often with *up*) **4.** [Colloq.] to divide something with another or others, each taking a share [winners *split*] ☆**5.** [Slang] to leave a place; depart **6.** [Brit. Slang] to inform (*on* an accomplice); peach —*n.* **1.** the act or process of splitting **2.** the result of splitting; specif., *a)* a break; fissure; crack; tear *b)* a breach or division in a group, between persons, etc. **3.** a splinter; sliver **4.** a single thickness of hide split horizontally **5.** a flexible strip of wood, as osier,

used in basketmaking ☆**6.** a confection made of a split banana or other fruit with ice cream, nuts, sauces, whipped cream, etc. **7.** *[often pl.]* the feat of spreading the legs apart until they lie flat on the floor, the body remaining upright **8.** [Colloq.] *a)* a small bottle of carbonated water, wine, etc., usually about six ounces *b)* a drink or portion half the usual size **9.** [Colloq.] a share, as of loot or booty **10.** *Bowling* an arrangement of pins after the first bowl, so widely separated as to make a spare extremely difficult —*adj.* **1.** divided or separated along the length or grain; broken into parts **2.** divided, separated, or disunited —*SYN.* see BREAK[1] —**split off** to break off or separate as by splitting —**split′ter** *n.*

☆**split decision** a decision in a boxing match that is not a unanimous one of the judges and referee

☆**split end** *Football* an end separated by a varying distance from the rest of the offensive line

split infinitive *Gram.* an infinitive with the verbal and the *to* separated as by an adverb (Ex.: he decided *to gradually change* his procedures): despite the objections of some people to this construction, many writers use split infinitives where ambiguity or wrong emphasis would otherwise result

split-lev·el (-lev′'l) *adj.* designating or of a type of house with floor levels so staggered that each level is about a half story above or below the adjacent one

☆**split pea** a green or yellow pea that has been shelled, dried, and split: used esp. for making soup

split personality 1. *a popular name for* SCHIZOPHRENIA **2.** a condition in which a person assumes intermittently two or more distinct, unrelated personalities

split second a fraction of a second —**split′-sec′ond** *adj.*

☆**split shift** a shift, or work period, divided into two parts that are separated by an interval longer than that of the usual meal or rest period

☆**split ticket** a ballot cast for candidates of more than one party

split·ting (split′iŋ) *adj.* **1.** that splits **2.** *a)* aching severely: said of the head *b)* severe, as a headache

☆**split-up** (-up′) *n.* a breaking up or separating into two or more parts, units, groups, etc.

splodge (släj) *n., vt.* **splodged, splodg′ing** *Brit. var.* of SPLOTCH

splotch (släch) *n.* [prob. a fusion of SPOT + BLOTCH] a spot, splash, or stain, esp. one that is irregular —*vt., vi.* to mark or soil, or be marked or soiled, with a splotch or splotches —**splotch′y** *adj.* **splotch′i·er, splotch′i·est**

☆**splurge** (splurj) *n.* [echoic blend of SPL(ASH) + (S)URGE] [Colloq.] **1.** any very showy display or effort **2.** a spell of extravagant spending —*vi.* **splurged, splurg′ing** [Colloq.] **1.** to make a splurge; show off **2.** to spend money extravagantly —**splurg′er** *n.*

splut·ter (splut′ər) *vi.* [var. of SPUTTER] **1.** to make hissing or spitting sounds, or to throw off particles in an explosive way, as something frying; sputter **2.** to speak hurriedly and confusedly, as when excited or embarrassed —*vt.* **1.** to utter hurriedly and confusedly; sputter **2.** to spatter —*n.* **1.** a spluttering sound or utterance **2.** a loud sputtering or splash —**splut′ter·er** *n.* —**splut′ter·y** *adj.*

Spock (späk), **Benjamin (McLane)** 1903– ; U.S. pediatrician, educator, & writer of books on child care

Spode (spōd) *n.* a fine porcelain or chinaware produced by Josiah Spode (1754–1827), Eng. potter

spod·u·mene (späj′ōō mēn′) *n.* [< Gr. *spodumenos*, prp. of *spodousthai*, to be burned to ashes < *spodos*, ashes: from being reduced to an ashlike form before the blowpipe] a monoclinic mineral, lithium aluminum silicate, $LiAl(SiO_3)_2$, usually light-green or yellow

spoil (spoil) *vt.* **spoiled** or **spoilt, spoil′ing** [ME. *spoilen* < MFr. *espoillier* < L. *spoliare*, to plunder < *spolium*, arms taken from a defeated foe, plunder, orig., hide stripped from an animal < IE. base *(s)p(h)el-*, to split, tear off, whence SPALL, SPILL[1]] **1.** to damage or injure in such a way as to make useless, valueless, etc.; destroy **2.** to mar or impair the enjoyment, quality, or functioning of [rain *spoiled* the picnic] **3.** to overindulge so as to cause to demand or expect too much **4.** [Archaic] *a)* to strip (a person) of goods, money, etc. by force *b)* to rob; pillage; plunder *c)* to seize (goods) by force —*vi.* **1.** to be damaged or injured in such a way as to become useless, valueless, etc.; specif., to decay, as food **2.** [Archaic] to pillage; plunder —*n.* [ME. *spoile* < MFr. *espoille* < L. *spolia*, pl.] **1.** *[usually pl.]* *a)* goods, territory, etc. taken by force in war; plunder; loot; booty ☆*b)* public offices to which the successful political party has the power of appointment **2.** an object of plunder; prey **3.** waste material removed in making excavations, etc. **4.** [Archaic] the act of plundering; spoliation **5.** [Obs.] damage; impairment —☆**be spoiling for a fight,** etc. to be aggressively eager for a fight, etc. —**spoil′a·ble** *adj.*

SYN.—**spoil** (now, more commonly, **spoils**) refers to any property, territory, etc. taken in war by the conqueror; **pillage** suggests violence and destructiveness in the taking of spoils; **plunder** is equivalent to **pillage** but also applies to property taken by bandits, highwaymen, etc.; **booty** suggests plunder taken by a

band or gang, to be divided among the members; **prize** refers specifically to spoils taken at sea, esp. an enemy warship or its cargo; **loot,** a more derogatory equivalent for any of the preceding, emphasizes the immorality or predatory nature of the act See also DECAY, INDULGE, INJURE

spoil·age (spoil′ij) *n.* **1.** a spoiling or being spoiled **2.** something spoiled or the amount spoiled

spoil·er (-ər) *n.* **1.** a person or thing that spoils **2.** any projecting device serving to break up airflow around a body; specif., a movable flap on an airplane wing for increasing drag and decreasing lift

☆**spoils·man** (spoilz′mən) *n., pl.* **-men** (-mən) a person who aids a political party in order to share in the spoils, or one who advocates the spoils system

spoil·sport (spoil′spôrt′) *n.* a person who behaves in such a way as to ruin the pleasure of others

☆**spoils system** the system or practice of regarding and treating appointive public offices as the booty of the successful party in an election, to be distributed, with their opportunities for profit, among party workers

spoilt (spoilt) *alt. pt. & pp. of* SPOIL

Spo·kane (spō kan′) [< ? Salish *spokanee,* sun] city in E Wash.: pop. 171,000

spoke[1] (spōk) *n.* [ME. < OE. *spaca,* akin to G. *speiche* < IE. base *spei-,* a point, pointed wood, whence SPIKE[1], SPINE] **1.** any of the braces or bars extending between the hub and the rim of a wheel **2.** a ladder rung **3.** any of the grips or handholds fixed along the rim of a ship's steering wheel —*vt.* spoked, spok′ing to equip with spokes

spoke[2] (spōk) *pt. & archaic pp. of* SPEAK

spo·ken (spō′k'n) *pp. of* SPEAK —*adj.* **1.** uttered; oral **2.** characterized by or uttered in a (specified) kind of voice [fair-*spoken*]

spoke·shave (spōk′shāv′) *n.* a cutting or planing tool consisting of a blade with a curved handle at either end: orig. used to shape spokes, but now used for trimming and smoothing rounded surfaces

spokes·man (spōks′mən) *n., pl.* **-men** (-mən) [irregularly formed < SPOKE[2]] a person who speaks or gives information for another or for a group

spo·li·ate (spō′lē āt′) *vt.* **-at′ed, -at′ing** [< L. *spoliatus,* pp. of *spoliare:* see SPOIL] to rob, plunder, or despoil

spo·li·a·tion (spō′lē ā′shən) *n.* [ME. *spoliacioun* < L. *spoliatio*] **1.** a spoliating or being spoliated; robbery; plundering: said esp. of the authorized seizure of neutral ships in wartime **2.** the act of spoiling or damaging **3.** *Law* the destruction or alteration of a document by an unauthorized person

spon·dee (spän′dē) *n.* [ME. *sponde* < L. *spondeum* < *spondeus,* of a libation < Gr. *spondeios* < *spondē,* solemn libation (such libations were accompanied by a solemn melody) < *spendein,* to present a libation: see SPONSOR] a metrical foot consisting, in English poetry, of two heavily accented syllables or, in Greek and Latin poetry, of two long syllables —**spon·da·ic** (spän dā′ik) *adj.*

spon·dy·li·tis (spän′də līt′is) *n.* [SPONDYL(O)- + -ITIS] inflammation of the vertebrae

spon·dy·lo- (spän′də lō, -lə) [< Gr. *spondylos,* vertebra < IE. base *sp(h)e(u)d-,* to jerk, dangle, whence Sans. *spandatē,* (he) jerks] *a combining form meaning* vertebra [*spondylitis*]: also, before a vowel, **spon′dyl-**

sponge (spunj) *n.* [ME. < OE. < L. *spongia* < Gr. *spongia*] **1.** a plantlike animal (phylum Porifera) having a porous structure and a tough, fibrous skeleton, and growing exclusively under water, esp. in the sea, attached to the bottom or to other solid objects **2.** the skeleton, or a piece of the skeleton, of such an animal, which is light in weight, remains somewhat tough while becoming soft when wet, has a characteristic elastic compressibility, and can absorb many times its own weight in water: it is used for washing surfaces, in bathing, etc. **3.** any substance like this; specif., *a)* a piece of spongy plastic, cellulose, rubber, etc., used like a natural sponge *b)* a pad of gauze or cotton, as used in surgery *c)* any of several light, porous puddings *d)* raised dough, as for bread *e)* any of several metals, as platinum, found in a porous mass **4.** *a)* a person having a spongelike capacity, as for drink, knowledge, etc. *b)* [Colloq.] *same as* SPONGER (sense 3) —*vt.* sponged, spong′ing [ME. *spongen* < the *n.*] **1.** to use a sponge on so as to dampen, wipe clean, etc. **2.** to remove or obliterate with or as with a damp sponge (usually with *out, off, away,* etc.) **3.** to absorb with, as with, or like a sponge (often with *up*) **4.** [Colloq.] to get without cost, as by begging, imposition, etc. —*vi.* **1.** to gather sponges from the sea **2.** to take up liquid like a sponge **3.** [Colloq.] to be a sponger (sense 3): often with *off* or *on* —SYN. see PARASITE —**throw** (or **toss,** etc.) **in the sponge** [Colloq.] to admit defeat; give up: from the practice of a boxer's second of throwing a sponge into the ring to concede defeat

sponge bath a bath taken by using a wet sponge or cloth without getting into water or under a shower

sponge·cake (-kāk′) *n.* a light cake of spongy texture,

SPONGES

made of flour, beaten eggs, sugar, etc., but no shortening: also **sponge cake**

spong·er (spun′jər) *n.* **1.** a person or vessel that gathers sponges **2.** a person who cleans, etc. with a sponge **3.** [Colloq.] a person who, though able to work, depends on others for food, money, etc.; parasite

sponge rubber rubber processed so that it has a spongelike texture that is firmer and denser than foam rubber: used for gaskets, rubber balls, etc.

spon·gin (spun′jin) *n.* [G. < L. *spongia,* SPONGE + G. *-in,* -INE[4]] a sulfur-containing protein making up the resilient fibrous network that forms the skeleton in many sponges

spon·gy (-jē) *adj.* **-gi·er, -gi·est** **1.** of or like a sponge; specif., *a)* light, soft, and elastic *b)* full of holes; porous *c)* absorbent **2.** soft and thoroughly soaked with moisture [*spongy* ground] —**spon′gi·ness** *n.*

spon·sion (spän′shən) *n.* [L. *sponsio* < *spondere,* to promise solemnly: see SPONSOR] **1.** a formal promise, or pledge, esp. one made on behalf of another person, as by a godparent **2.** in international law, an act done or engagement made for a state by an unauthorized agent

spon·son (spän′sən) *n.* [altered < ? EXPANSION: orig. applied to the platforms on each side of a steamer's paddle wheels] **1.** a structure that projects over the side of a ship or boat; specif., *a)* a projecting gun platform *b)* an air chamber built into the gunwale of a canoe **2.** a short, winglike piece attached to the hull of a seaplane just above water level to give stability in the water

spon·sor (spän′sər) *n.* [L., surety < *spondere,* to promise solemnly < IE. base *spend-,* to bring a libation, vow, whence Gr. *spendein,* to promise, *spondē,* libation] **1.** a person or agency that undertakes certain responsibilities in connection with some other person or some group or activity, as in being a proponent, endorser, adviser, underwriter, surety, etc. **2.** a godfather or godmother; person who answers for a child, as at baptism, making the profession of faith and the promises prescribed ☆**3.** a business firm or other agency that alone or with others pays the costs of a radio or television program on which it advertises or promotes something —*vt.* to act as sponsor for — **spon·so′ri·al** (-sôr′ē əl) *adj.* —**spon′sor·ship′** *n.*
SYN.—a **sponsor** is one who assumes a certain degree of responsibility for another in any of various ways [the **sponsors** of a television program assume the costs of production]; a **patron** is one who assumes the role of protector or benefactor, now usually in a financial capacity, as of an artist, an institution, etc.; a **backer** is one who lends support, esp. financial support, to someone or something but does not necessarily assume any responsibilities [the magazine failed when it lost its *backers*]; **angel** is a colloquial term for the backer of a theatrical enterprise

spon·ta·ne·i·ty (spän′tə nē′ə tē; *now also* -nā′-) *n.* **1.** the state or quality of being spontaneous **2.** *pl.* **-ties** spontaneous behavior, movement, action, etc.

spon·ta·ne·ous (spän tā′nē əs) *adj.* [LL. *spontaneus* < L. *sponte,* of free will < IE. base *(s)pen(d)-,* to pull, whence SPIN] **1.** acting in accordance with or resulting from a natural feeling, impulse, or tendency, without any constraint, effort, or premeditation **2.** having no apparent external cause or influence; occurring or produced by its own energy, force, etc. or through internal causes; self-acting **3.** growing naturally without being planted or tended; indigenous; wild —**spon·ta′ne·ous·ly** *adv.* — **spon·ta′ne·ous·ness** *n.*
SYN.—**spontaneous** applies to that which is done so naturally that it seems to come without prompting or premeditation [a *spontaneous* demonstration]; **impulsive** applies to that which is prompted by some external incitement or sudden inner inclination rather than by conscious, rational volition [an *impulsive* retort]; **instinctive** suggests an instantaneous, unwilled response to a stimulus, as if prompted by some natural, inborn tendency [he took an *instinctive* liking to her]; **involuntary** refers to that which is done without thought or volition, as a reflex action [an *involuntary* flicker of the eyelid]; **automatic** suggests an unvarying, machinelike reaction to a given stimulus or situation [an *automatic* response] —ANT. deliberate, voluntary

spontaneous combustion the process of catching fire as a result of heat generated by internal chemical action

spontaneous generation the theory, now discredited, that living organisms can originate in nonliving matter independently of other living matter; abiogenesis

spon·toon (spän tōōn′) *n.* [Fr. *sponton* < It. *spuntone* < *punto* < L. *punctum,* a POINT] a short pike or halberd carried by 18th-cent. infantry officers

spoof (spōōf) *n.* [orig. a game involving hoaxing and nonsense, invented (c.1889) by Arthur Roberts, Brit. comedian (1852-1933)] [Slang] **1.** a hoax, joke, or deception **2.** a light parody or satire —*vt., vi.* [Slang] **1.** to fool; deceive **2.** to satirize in a playful, amiable manner —**spoof′er** *n.*

☆**spook** (spōōk) *n.* [Du., akin to G. *spuk*] [Colloq.] **1.** a specter; ghost **2.** any person suggestive of a specter or ghost, as an eccentric, a secret agent, etc. —*vt.* [Colloq.] **1.** to haunt (a person or place) **2.** to startle, frighten, make nervous, annoy, etc. —*vi.* [Colloq.] to become frightened or startled

☆**spook·y** (spōō′kē) *adj.* **spook′i·er, spook′i·est** [Colloq.] **1.** of, like, or suggesting a spook or spooks; weird; eerie **2.** easily spooked; nervous, apprehensive, fearful, jumpy, etc. —**spook′i·ly** *adv.* —**spook′i·ness** *n.*

spool (spōōl) *n.* [ME. *spole* < MFr. *espole* < MDu. *spoele,* akin to G. *spule* < IE. base *sp(h)el-,* to split, split off,

whence SPILL[1], SPOIL] **1.** a cylinder or roller, usually with a hole for a spindle from end to end and a rim at either end, upon which thread, wire, etc. is wound **2.** something like a spool, as a bobbin, reel, etc. **3.** the material wound on a spool —*vt.* to wind on a spool

spool (spōōn) *n.* [ME. *spon* < OE. *spon* a chip: sense infl. by cognate ON. *spōnn*, a spoon < IE. base *spē-*, a flat piece of wood, whence SPADE[1], SPATHE] **1.** a utensil consisting of a small, shallow, usually oval-shaped bowl and a handle, used for picking up or stirring food, etc., as in eating or cooking **2.** something shaped like a spoon; specif., a shiny, curved fishing lure, usually made of metal, set above a hook or hooks so as to wobble when drawn through the water **3.** a golf club with a wooden head and more loft than a brassie: also called *number 3 wood* —*vt.* **1.** to take up with or as with a spoon **2.** to push, lift, or hit (a ball) with a scooping motion instead of a direct blow —*vi.* **1.** to spoon or scoop a ball, etc. **2.** [Colloq.] to make love, as by kissing and caressing: an old-fashioned term —**born with a silver spoon in one's mouth** born rich

spoon·bill (-bil′) *n.* **1.** any of several wading birds (family Threskiornithidae) with a broad, flat bill that is spoon-shaped at the tip; esp., the **roseate spoonbill** (*Ajaia ajaja*) of N. and S. America **2.** any of a number of other birds with a bill like this; esp., *same as* SHOVELER (sense 2) ☆**3.** *same as* PADDLEFISH

☆**spoon bread** a soft, light, moist bread of cornmeal, that is served with a spoon

spoon·drift (-drift′) *n. early form of* SPINDRIFT

spoon·er·ism (spōōn′ər iz′m) *n.* [after Rev. W. A. *Spooner* (1844–1930), of New College, Oxford, famous for such slips] an unintentional interchange of sounds, usually initial sounds, in two or more words (Ex.: "a well-boiled icicle" for "a well-oiled bicycle")

SPOONBILL
(to 40 in. long,
including bill)

spoon-feed (spōōn′fēd′) *vt.* **-fed′**, **-feed′ing 1.** to feed with a spoon **2.** to pamper; coddle **3.** to treat, instruct, or inform in a manner that destroys initiative or curbs independent thought and action

spoon·ful (-fool′) *n., pl.* **-fuls′** as much as a spoon will hold

spoon·y, spoon·ey (spōō′nē) *adj.* **spoon′i·er, spoon′i·est** [Colloq.] silly or foolish; esp., foolishly sentimental, or amorous in a mawkish way —*n., pl.* **spoon′ies** [Colloq.] a spoony person An old-fashioned term

spoor (spoor, spôr) *n.* [Afrik. < MDu., akin to OE. *spor*, G. *spur*: for IE. base see SPUR] the track or trail of an animal, esp. of a wild animal hunted as game —*vt., vi.* to trace or track by a spoor

Spo·ra·des (spôr′ə dēz′; Gr. spô räʹthes) **1.** formerly, all the Gr. islands in the Aegean Sea except the Cyclades **2.** sometimes, the Gr. islands along the W coast of Turkey, esp. the Dodecanese See also NORTHERN SPORADES

spo·rad·ic (spô rad′ik, spə-) *adj.* [ML. *sporadicus* < Gr. *sporadikos* < *sporas*, scattered: for base see SPORE] **1.** happening from time to time; not constant or regular; occasional **2.** widely separated from others, scattered, or isolated in occurrence; appearing singly, apart, or in isolated instances —**spo·rad′i·cal·ly** *adv.*

spo·ran·gi·um (spô ran′jē əm, spə-) *n., pl.* **-gi·a** (-ə) [ModL. < *spora* (see ff.) + Gr. *angeion*, vessel] *Bot.* an organ or single cell producing spores —**spo·ran′gi·al** *adj.*

spore (spôr) *n.* [ModL. *spora* < Gr. *spora*, a sowing, seed, akin to *speirein*, to sow < IE. base *sp(h)er-*, to strew, sow, whence SPREAD, SPROUT] **1.** *Biol.* any of various small reproductive bodies, usually consisting of a single cell, produced by bacteria, algae, mosses, ferns, certain protozoans, etc., either asexually (**asexual spore**) or by the union of gametes (**sexual spore**): they are capable of giving rise to a new adult individual, either immediately or after an interval of dormancy **2.** any small organism or cell that can develop into a new individual; seed, germ, etc. —*vi.* **spored, spor′ing** to bear or develop spores

spore case *same as* SPORANGIUM

spore fruit any specialized structure, as an ascocarp, in which spores are formed

spo·rif·er·ous (spô rif′ər əs) *adj.* bearing spores

spo·ro- (spôr′ə, -ō) *a combining form meaning* spore [*sporocarp*]: also, before a vowel, **spor-**

spo·ro·carp (spôr′ə kärp′) *n.* [prec. + -CARP] *Bot.* a many-celled body produced from a fertilized archicarp, serving for the development of spores in red algae, lichens, etc.

spo·ro·cyst (-sist′) *n.* [SPORO- + -CYST] **1.** *Bot.* a resting cell giving rise to asexual spores **2.** *Zool. a)* a saclike larval stage in the development of many trematodes which produces rediae by asexual internal division *b)* a protective cyst produced by some protozoans before sporulation, or a protozoan in such a cyst

spo·ro·gen·e·sis (spôr′ə jen′ə sis) *n.* [ModL.: see SPORO- & -GENESIS] *Biol.* **1.** reproduction by means of spores **2.** the formation of spores —**spo′ro·gen′ic** *adj.* —**spo·rog·e·nous** (spô räj′ə nəs) *adj.*

spo·ro·go·ni·um (spôr′ə gō′nē əm) *n., pl.* **-ni·a** (-ə) [ModL.: see SPORO- & -GONY] the sporophyte in mosses and liverworts, usually a spore-bearing capsule on a stalk that never separates from the mother plant

spo·rog·o·ny (spô räg′ə nē) *n.* [SPORO- + -GONY] the process by which a large number of sporozoites are produced by cell divisions from a single zygote

spo·ro·phore (spôr′ə fôr′) *n.* [SPORO- + -PHORE] *Bot.* an organ or structure in various fungi that bears spores —**spo·roph·o·rous** (spô räf′ər əs) *adj.*

spo·ro·phyll (-fil) *n.* [SPORO- + -PHYLL] a leaf, modified leaf, or leaflike part producing one or more sporangia —**spo′ro·phyl′la·ry** (-fil′ə rē) *adj.*

spo·ro·phyte (-fīt′) *n.* [SPORO- + -PHYTE] in plants, the spore-bearing generation that is diploid and reproduces by spores: the sporophyte generation begins with the fertilized egg and ends with meiosis: distinguished from GAMETOPHYTE —**spo′ro·phyt′ic** (-fit′ik) *adj.*

-spor·ous (spôr′əs, spər əs) [SPORO(- + -OUS] *a combining form meaning* having (a specified number or kind of) spores [*homosporous*]

spo·ro·zo·an (spôr′ə zō′ən) *n.* [< ModL. *Sporozoa*, name of the group (see SPORO- & -ZOA) + -AN] any of a class (Sporozoa) of always parasitic protozoans that usually pass through phases of both sexual and asexual generation, frequently in different hosts, during which sporogenesis takes place: the organisms of malaria and Texas fever belong to this group: also **spo′ro·zo′on** (-än), *pl.* **-zo′a** (-ə) —*adj.* of the sporozoans: also **spo′ro·zo′ic, spo′ro·zo′al** *adj.*

spo·ro·zo·ite (-īt) *n.* [< ModL. *Sporozoa* (see prec.) + -ITE[2]] an infective body or group of cells released from spores in many sporozoans and formed by the division of a zygote: it is the infective stage of the malaria parasite

spor·ran (spär′ən, spôr′-) *n.* [ScotGael. *sporan*] a leather pouch or purse, usually covered with fur or hair, worn hanging from the front of the belt in the dress costume of Scottish Highlanders

sport (spôrt) *n.* [ME. *sporte*, aphetic for DISPORT] **1.** any activity or experience that gives enjoyment or recreation; pastime; diversion **2.** such an activity requiring more or less vigorous bodily exertion and carried on, sometimes as a profession, according to some traditional form or set of rules, whether outdoors, as football, golf, etc., or indoors, as basketball, bowling, etc. **3.** fun or play **4.** *a)* an object of ridicule; laughingstock *b)* a thing or person buffeted about, as though a plaything ☆**5.** [Colloq.] a gambler **6.** [Colloq.] *a)* a person who is sportsmanlike, easygoing, or companionable [be a *sport!*] *b)* a person judged according to his ability to take loss, defeat, teasing, etc. [a good (or poor) *sport*] ☆**7.** [Colloq.] a pleasure-loving, showy person; flashy fellow **8.** [Obs.] amorous trifling or sexual play **9.** *Biol.* a plant or animal showing some marked variation from the normal type, usually as a result of mutation —*vt.* **1.** [Colloq.] to wear or display, esp. with unnecessary show [to *sport* a loud tie] **2.** [Obs.] to amuse (oneself, etc.) —*vi.* **1.** to play or frolic **2.** to engage in a sport or sports **3.** *a)* to joke or jest *b)* to dally, or play (*with*) *c)* to mock or ridicule someone or something **4.** [Obs.] to engage in amorous trifling or sexual play **5.** *Biol.* to vary markedly from the normal type; mutate —*adj.* **1.** *same as* SPORTING (sense 1) **2.** suitable for informal, casual wear; not dressy [a *sport* coat] —*SYN.* see PLAY —**in** (or **for**) **sport** in joke or jest; not in earnest —**make sport of** to mock or ridicule; poke fun at —**sport′er** *n.* —**sport′ful** *adj.* —**sport′ful·ly** *adv.*

sport·ing (-iŋ) *adj.* **1.** of, having to do with, or for sports, or athletic games, etc. **2.** interested in or taking part in sports, or athletic games, etc. **3.** sportsmanlike; fair ☆**4.** interested in or having to do with games, races, etc. characterized by gambling or betting **5.** *Biol.* inclined to mutate —**sport′ing·ly** *adv.*

sporting chance [Colloq.] a fair or even chance

sporting house [Colloq.] ☆**1.** formerly, a gambling house ☆**2.** a house of prostitution; brothel

spor·tive (-iv) *adj.* **1.** *a)* fond of or full of sport or merriment; playful *b)* done in fun or play, not in earnest **2.** of, or having the nature of, sport, esp. outdoor sport **3.** [Obs.] amorous or erotic —**spor′tive·ly** *adv.* —**spor′tive·ness** *n.*

sports (spôrts) *adj. same as* SPORT [*sports* clothes]

sports (or **sport**) **car** a low, small automobile, typically with seats for two and a high-compression engine

☆**sports·cast** (spôrts′kast′, -käst′) *n.* a sports broadcast, esp. of sports news, on radio or television —**sports′cast′er** *n.*

sports·man (-mən) *n., pl.* **-men** (-mən) **1.** a man who is interested in or takes part in sports, esp. in hunting, fishing, etc. **2.** a person who can take loss or defeat without complaint, or victory without gloating, and who treats his opponents with fairness, generosity, courtesy, etc. —**sports′man·like′, sports′man·ly** *adj.*

sports·man·ship (-mən ship′) *n.* **1.** skill in or fondness for sports **2.** qualities and behavior befitting a sportsman

sports·wear (-wer′) *n.* clothes worn while engaging in sports or for informal, casual wear

sports·wom·an (-woom′ən) *n.*, *pl.* **-wom′en** (-wim′ən) a woman who is interested in or takes part in sports

sports·writ·er (-rīt′ər) *n.* a reporter who writes about sports or sports events

sport·y (spôr′tē) *adj.* **sport′i·er**, **sport′i·est** [Colloq.] 1. sporting or sportsmanlike 2. characteristic of a sport or sporting man 3. loud, flashy, or showy, as clothes — **sport′i·ly** *adv.* **—sport′i·ness** *n.*

spor·u·late (spôr′yoo lāt′) *vi.* **-lat′ed**, **-lat′ing** [SPORUL(E) + -ATE¹] to undergo sporulation

spor·u·la·tion (spôr′yoo lā′shən) *n.* [< ff. + -ATION] 1. *Bot.* the formation of spores 2. *Zool.* a type of multiple fission in certain protozoans by which a parent spore becomes almost completely broken up into buds

spor·ule (spôr′yool) *n.* [ModL. *sporula*, dim. of *spora*] a small spore or, sometimes, any spore

spot (spät) *n.* [ME. < or akin to MDu. *spotte*, akin to ON. *spotti*, small piece (of ground)] 1. a small area of different color or texture from the main area of which it is a part; often, a mark made by some foreign matter; stain, blot, speck, patch, etc. 2. *a)* any of the pips used on playing cards, dice, etc. *b)* a playing card having (a specified number of) pips [the ten *spot* of spades] 3. a flaw or defect, as in character or reputation; something blameworthy; fault 4. *a)* a locality; place [a good fishing *spot*] *b)* any small area or space 5. *clipped form of* SPOTLIGHT ☆6. a saltwater food fish (*Leiostomus xanthurus*), having a black spot behind the gill edge 7. [Chiefly Brit. Colloq.] a small quantity; bit [a *spot* of tea] 8. [Colloq.] position; situation; job 9. [Colloq.] position or place in a schedule or listing 10. [Colloq.] a spot advertisement or announcement ☆11. [Slang] a nightclub ☆12. [Slang] a piece of paper money of a specified value [a ten *spot*] *—vt.* **spot′ted**, **spot′ting** 1. to mark with spots; to sully; stain; blemish 3. to mark for future consideration 4. *a)* to place in or on a given spot or spots; locate [to *spot* men at strategic points] *b)* [Colloq.] to put in a spot in a schedule or listing 5. to be located at various places in or on 6. to shine a spotlight on 7. to remove (individual spots, marks, etc.), as in dry cleaning 8. *a)* to pick up; detect; see; recognize [to *spot* someone in a crowd] *b)* to determine the location of (a target, the enemy, etc.) *c)* to correct the accuracy of (gunfire) for a gun crew 9. to observe and report on (plays) as a spotter in sports ☆10. [Colloq.] to allow as an advantage or handicap [to *spot* an opponent points] *—vi.* 1. to become marked with spots 2. to cause a spot or spots; make a stain, as ink, water, etc. 3. to act as a spotter, esp. for a gun crew or in sports *—adj.* 1. *a)* that can be paid out or delivered immediately; ready [*spot* cash] *b)* involving immediate payment of cash *c)* involving cash transactions only 2. made at random or according to an arbitrary sampling procedure [a *spot* survey] 3. *a)* broadcast from the place of occurrence [*spot* news] *b)* inserted between regular radio or television programs [a *spot* advertisement or announcement] *—*☆**hit the high spots** [Colloq.] to treat only the main points of a topic, as in a cursory discussion **—hit the spot** [Colloq.] to satisfy a craving or need **—**☆**in a (bad) spot** [Slang] in a bad situation; in trouble **—on the spot** 1. on or at the place mentioned 2. at once; immediately ☆3. [Slang] in trouble or difficulty 4. [Slang] in a position where something, as a reply, is expected of one ☆5. [Slang] in danger, esp. in danger or death by murder

spot-check (-chek′) *vt.* to check or examine at random or according to an arbitrary sampling procedure *—n.* an act or instance of such checking

spot·less (-lis) *adj.* 1. having no spots; perfectly clean 2. having no faults or defects, as in character; irreproachable **—spot′less·ly** *adv.* **—spot′less·ness** *n.*

☆**spot·light** (-līt′) *n.* 1. *a)* a strong beam of light used to illuminate prominently a particular person, thing, or group, as on a stage, in a window display, etc. *b)* a lamp used to project such a beam of light 2. a lamp with a strong, focused beam, as on an automobile, that can be directed on a small area 3. public notice or prominence *—vt.* to light up or draw attention to by, or as by, a spotlight

spot·ted (-id) *adj.* 1. marked with spots 2. stained; blemished; sullied

☆**spotted adder** *same as:* 1. MILK SNAKE 2. FOX SNAKE

spotted fever any of various febrile diseases accompanied by skin eruptions; esp., typhus, cerebrospinal meningitis, ☆ or Rocky Mountain spotted fever

spot·ter (spät′ər) *n.* a person or thing that spots; specif., *a)* a person whose work is removing spots, etc. in dry cleaning ☆*b)* a person hired to watch for dishonesty, etc. among employees, as in a store *c)* a person who watches for, and reports, enemy aircraft *d)* a person who determines, as for a gun crew, the position of a target and the closeness to it of the projectiles fired ☆*e)* a football coach's assistant in the stands who reports on the plays to the bench by phone; also, an assistant to a sports announcer who helps identify the players for him

spot·ty (-ē) *adj.* **-ti·er**, **-ti·est** 1. having, occurring in, or marked with spots 2. not uniform or consistent; irregular, as in quality; uneven **—spot′ti·ly** *adv.* **—spot′ti·ness** *n.*

spot welding a welding process in which overlapping metal pieces are held under great pressure between two elec-

trodes, between which a brief, powerful current is passed, effecting the weld **—spot′-weld′** *vt.*, *vi.* **—spot′-weld′er** *n.*

spous·al (spou′z′l) *n.* [ME. *spousaile* < OFr. *espousaille*: see ESPOUSAL] 1. [Obs.] wedlock 2. [*often pl.*] [Now Rare] a marriage ceremony *—adj.* [Now Rare] of marriage

spouse (spous; *also, esp. for vt.,* spouz) *n.* [ME. *spus* < OFr. *espous* < L. *sponsus*, betrothed, pp. of *spondere*: see SPONSOR] a partner in marriage; (one's) husband or wife *—vt.* **spoused**, **spous′ing** [Archaic] to marry; wed

spout (spout) *n.* [ME. *spute*, *spoute* < the *v.*] 1. a lip, orifice, or projecting tube, as on a teapot, in a drinking fountain, etc., by which a liquid is poured or discharged 2. *a)* a stream, jet, or discharge or or as of liquid from a spout *b)* the stream of air and water rising from the blowhole of a whale 3. *same as:* *a)* DOWNSPOUT *b)* WATER-SPOUT 4. a chute for conveying substances, as grain or flour, or articles 5. [Brit. Slang] [from chute formerly used as a conveyance in shop] a pawnshop *—vt.* [ME. *spouten*, to spout, vomit, akin to MDu. *spuiten*, to spout: prob. < base of SPEW] 1. to shoot out (liquid, etc.) from or as from a spout 2. to speak or utter in a loud, pompous manner or in a ready, rapid flow of words *—vi.* 1. to flow or shoot out with force in a jet: said of liquid, etc. 2. to discharge liquid, etc. from or as from a spout 3. to spout words, esp. (usually **spout off**) in a way that is hasty, irresponsible, etc. **—up the spout** [Brit. Slang] 1. in pawn 2. in straits; lost; ruined **—spout′er** *n.* **—spout′less** *adj.*

spp. species (*pl. of* SPECIES)

SPQR [L. *Senatus Populusque Romanus*] the Senate and the Roman people

sprad·dle (sprad′′l) *vt.*, *vi.* **-dled**, **-dling** [< a merging of SPREAD & STRADDLE] [Dial. or Colloq.] to spread (the legs) in a sprawling or straddling way

sprag (sprag) *n.* [prob. < Scand., as in Dan. *sprag*, a twig < base of *sprage*, to crack, crackle: for IE. base see SPARK¹] 1. a roof prop used in a coal mine ☆2. a device for preventing a vehicle from rolling backward on a grade

sprain (sprān) *vt.* [< ? OFr. *espreindre*, to force out, strain < VL. **expremere*, for L. *exprimere*: see EXPRESS] to wrench or twist a ligament or muscle of (a joint, as the ankle) without dislocating the bones *—n.* 1. an act of spraining 2. the resulting condition, characterized by swelling, pain, and disablement of the joint

sprang (spraŋ) *alt. pt. of* SPRING

sprat (sprat) *n.* [< ME. *sprotte* < OE. *sprott*: for IE. base see SPROUT] 1. a small, sardinelike, European fish (*Clupea sprattus*) of the herring family, often canned 2. any of several other small herrings

sprawl (sprôl) *vi.* [ME. *spraulen* < OE. *spreawlian*, to move convulsively, akin to Norw. dial. *sprala*: for IE. base see SPROUT] 1. *a)* to spread the limbs in a relaxed, awkward, or unnatural position *b)* to sit or lie in such a position [to *sprawl* in a chair] 2. to crawl in an awkward, ungainly way 3. to spread out in an awkward or uneven way, esp. so as to take up more space than is necessary, as handwriting, a line of men, etc. *—vt.* to cause to sprawl *—n.* a sprawling movement or position **—sprawl′er** *n.* **—sprawl′y** *adj.* **sprawl′i·er**, **sprawl′i·est**

spray¹ (sprā) *n.* [< or akin to MDu. *spraeien*, to spray, akin to G. *sprühen*: for IE. base see SPREAD] 1. a cloud or mist of fine liquid particles, as of water from breaking waves 2. *a)* a jet of fine liquid particles, or mist, as from an atomizer or spray gun *b)* a device for shooting out such a jet *c)* any liquid for spraying from such a device 3. something likened to a spray of liquid particles [a *spray* of gunfire] *—vt.* 1. to direct a spray on; treat with a spray 2. to direct a spray of on some surface, etc. *—vi.* 1. to shoot out a spray 2. to be shot out as a spray **—spray′er** *n.*

spray² (sprā) *n.* [ME.: for IE. base see SPARK¹] 1. a small branch or sprig of a tree or plant, with leaves, berries, flowers, etc. 2. a design or ornament like this

spray can a can in which gas under pressure is used to disperse the contents in the form of a spray

☆**spray gun** a device that shoots out a spray of liquid, as paint or insecticide, by air pressure

spread (spred) *vt.* **spread**, **spread′ing** [ME. *spreden* < OE. *sprædan*, akin to G. *spreiten* < IE. **sprei-d-*, to sprinkle, strew < base **sp(h)er-*, whence SPRAWL, SPROUT] 1. to draw out so as to display more fully; open or stretch out so as to cover more space; unfold or unfurl 2. to lay out in display; exhibit 3. to move apart (the fingers, arms, legs, wings, etc.) 4. *a)* to distribute over a surface or area; scatter; disperse *b)* to distribute among a group [to *spread* the wealth] 5. *a)* to distribute in a thin layer; smear [to *spread* butter on toast] *b)* to cover by smearing (with something) [to *spread* bread with jelly] 6. to extend or prolong in time [to *spread* payments over a two-year period] 7. to cause to be widely or more widely known, felt, existent, etc.; disseminate; propagate; diffuse [to *spread* news, a disease, etc.] 8. to cover, overlay, or deck (with something) 9. *a)* to set (a table) for a meal *b)* to set (food) on a table 10. to push apart or farther apart ☆11. to record in full; enter (*on a record*) 12. to flatten out (a rivet, etc.) by hammering *—vi.* 1. to extend itself; be extended or expanded 2. to become distributed or dispersed 3. to be made widely or more widely known, felt, existent, etc.; be disseminated, propagated, or diffused 4. to be pushed apart or farther apart 5. to be of such consistency that it can be distributed in a thin

layer, as butter; admit of being smeared —*n.* **1.** the act of spreading; extension; expansion; diffusion **2.** *a)* the extent to which something is spread or can be spread *b)* the interval or difference between the highest and lowest figures of a set, as of the scores of a test or of the prices bid and asked on the market **3.** an expanse; extent; stretch; compass ☆**4.** *a)* two facing pages of a newspaper, magazine, etc., treated as a single continuous sheet, as in advertising *b)* printed matter set across a page, or across several columns, of a newspaper, magazine, etc. ☆**5.** a cloth cover for a table, bed, etc. ☆**6.** any soft substance, as jam, butter, etc., used for spreading on bread **7.** in rummy, etc. a set of three or four cards of the same denomination, or three or more cards of the same suit and consecutive denominations **8.** [Colloq.] a meal, esp. one with a wide variety of food **9.** [Colloq.] a pretentious display ☆**10.** [Western] a ranch —☆**spread oneself** [Colloq.] **1.** to exert oneself in order to make a good impression, etc. **2.** to show off; brag —☆**spread oneself thin** to try to do too many things at once

spread-ea·gle (spred′ē′g'l) *adj.* **1.** having the figure of an eagle with wings and legs spread ☆**2.** [Colloq.] boastful or jingoistic about the U.S. —*vt.* **-gled, -gling** to stretch out in the form of a spread eagle, as for a flogging —*vi.* to perform a spread eagle: see SPREAD EAGLE (sense 2)

spread eagle 1. the figure of an eagle with wings and legs spread, used as an emblem of the U.S. **2.** something resembling or suggesting such a figure, as an acrobatic figure in fancy skating

spread·er (-ər) *n.* a person or thing that spreads; specif., *a)* a small, dull knife for spreading butter, etc. *b)* a contrivance for scattering something *[a fertilizer spreader] c)* a device, as a bar, for keeping apart wires, stays, etc.

spreading factor a substance, as hyaluronidase, that promotes the diffusion of a material through body tissues

‡**sprech·stim·me** (shpreH′shtim′ma) *n.* [G.] a form of vocal expression partly like speech and partly like song

Spree (shprā) river in E East Germany, flowing northwest through Berlin into the Havel: c.250 mi.

spree (sprē) *n.* [late 18th-c. slang, for earlier *spray* < ?] **1.** a lively, noisy frolic **2.** a period of drunkenness **3.** a period of uninhibited activity *[a shopping spree]*

sprig (sprig) *n.* [ME. *sprigge*, prob. akin to MDu. *sprik*, a dry twig: for IE. base see SPARK¹] **1.** *a)* a little twig or spray *b)* a design or ornament like this **2.** a small, headless brad **3.** a young fellow; stripling **4.** a person as the offspring or scion of a family, institution, class, etc.: used humorously —*vt.* **sprigged, sprig′ging 1.** to remove sprigs from (a bush, tree, etc.) **2.** to decorate with a design of sprigs **3.** to fasten with small, headless brads

sprig·gy (sprig′ē) *adj.* **-gi·er, -gi·est 1.** having many sprigs, as a plant **2.** suggestive of a sprig or sprigs

spright·ly (sprīt′lē) *adj.* **-li·er, -li·est** [< *spright*, var. of SPRITE + -LY¹] full of energy and spirit; gay, lively, brisk, etc. —*adv.* in a sprightly manner —SYN. see AGILE, LIVELY —**spright′li·ness** *n.*

spring (sprin) *vi.* **sprang** or **sprung, sprung, spring′ing** [ME. *springen* < OE. *springan,* akin to G. *springen* < IE. *spreng̑h-,* to move quickly (< base *sper-,* to jerk), whence Sans. *sprhayati,* (he) strives for] **1.** to move suddenly and rapidly; specif., *a)* to move upward or forward from the ground by suddenly contracting the muscles; leap; bound; also, to make a series of such leaps *b)* to rise suddenly and quickly from or as from a sitting or lying position *[to spring to one's feet] c)* to come, appear, etc. suddenly and quickly *[curses springing to his lips] d)* to move as a result of resilience; bounce **2.** to come or arise as from some source; specif., *a)* to grow or develop *[the plant springs from a seed] b)* to come into existence, usually quickly *[towns sprang up] c)* to be descended *d)* [Archaic] to begin to appear, as day; dawn **3.** to become warped, bent, split, loose, etc. *[the door has sprung]* **4.** to rise up above surrounding objects; tower *[a steeple springing high above the town]* **5.** *Archit.* to rise from the impost with an outward curve In many senses of the *vi., spring* is often followed by *up* —*vt.* **1.** to cause to leap or come forth suddenly *[to spring a covey of quail]* **2.** [Rare] to leap over; vault **3.** to cause to close or snap shut, as by a spring *[to spring a trap]* **4.** *a)* to cause to warp, bend, strain, split, etc., as by force *b)* to stretch (a spring, etc.) beyond the point where it will spring back fully **5.** to explode (a military mine) **6.** to make known or cause to appear suddenly or unexpectedly *[to spring a surprise]* **7.** [< the *n.,* sense 3] to equip with springs ☆**8.** [Slang] to get (someone) released from jail or custody, as by paying bail —*n.* [ME. & OE. *springe*] **1.** the act or an instance of springing; specif., *a)* a jump or leap forward or upward, or the distance covered by this *b)* a sudden darting or

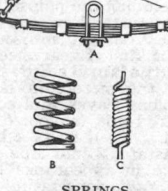

SPRINGS
(A, leaf; B, helical;
C, expansion)

flying back **2.** *a)* the quality of elasticity; resilience *b)* energy or vigor, as in one's walk **3.** a device, as a coil of wire, that returns to its original form after being forced out of shape: springs are used to absorb shock, and as the motive power in clocks and similar mechanisms **4.** *a)* a flow of water from the ground, often a source of a stream, pond, etc. *b)* any source, origin, or motive **5.** *a)* that season of the year in which plants begin to grow after lying dormant all winter: in the North Temperate Zone, generally regarded as including the months of March, April, and May: in the astronomical year, that period between the vernal equinox and the summer solstice *b)* any period of beginning or newness **6.** [Scot.] a gay, lively song or dance **7.** [Archaic] the dawn or dawning, as of day or light **8.** *Archit.* the line or plane in which an arch rises from its impost **9.** *Naut.* a split or break in a mast or spar —*adj.* **1.** of, for, appearing in, or planted in the spring **2.** of or acting like a spring; elastic; resilient **3.** having, or supported on, a spring or springs *[a spring mattress]* **4.** coming from a spring *[spring water]* —SYN. see RISE —**spring a leak** to begin to leak suddenly

spring·al (sprin′əl) *n.* [Scot. *springel, springald* < ME. *sprynhold,* prob. < *springen:* see prec.] [Archaic] an active young man; youth: also **spring′ald** (-əld)

☆**spring beauty** popular name for CLAYTONIA

spring·board (sprin′bôrd′) *n.* **1.** a flexible, springy board used by acrobats, gymnasts, etc. as a takeoff in performing various feats of leaping **2.** *same as* DIVING BOARD **3.** anything serving as the starting point or providing the impetus for something else

spring·bok (-bäk′) *n., pl.* **-bok′, -boks′:** see PLURAL, II, D, 2 [Afrik. < Du. *springen,* to SPRING + *bok,* a BUCK¹] a graceful gazelle (*Antidorcas euchore*) of S Africa, noted for its tendency to leap high in the air, as when startled: also **spring′buck′** (-buk′)

☆**spring chicken 1.** a young chicken, esp. one only a few months old, used for broiling or frying **2.** [Slang] a young or inexperienced person, esp. such a woman

spring-clean·ing (-klēn′in) *n.* a thorough cleaning of the interior of a house, etc. as conventionally done in the spring

springe (sprinj) *n.* [ME. *sprenge < sprongen < OE. sprengan,* to cause to spring, caus. of *springan,* to SPRING] [Now Rare] a snare consisting of a noose attached to something under tension, as a bent tree branch —*vt.* **springed, springe′ing** to snare in a springe

spring·er (sprin′ər) *n.* **1.** a person or thing that springs **2.** *clipped form of* SPRINGER SPANIEL ☆**3.** *same as* SPRING CHICKEN **4.** *Archit. a)* the support upon which an arch rests; impost *b)* the lowest stone or lowest part of an arch

springer spaniel a breed of field spaniel used for flushing, or springing, game

☆**spring fever** the laziness and listlessness that many people feel during the first warm, sunny days of spring

Spring·field (sprin′fēld′) [sense 1 after *Springfield,* village in Essex, England; others perh. after sense 1] **1.** city in SW Mass., on the Connecticut River: pop. 164,000 (met. area, incl. Chicopee & Holyoke, 530,000) **2.** city in SW Mo.: pop. 120,000 **3.** capital of Ill., in the C part: pop. 92,000 **4.** city in WC Ohio: pop. 82,000

☆**Springfield rifle** [< SPRINGFIELD, Mass., location of a U.S. armory] a .30-caliber, breech-loading, magazine-fed rifle, operated by a bolt, adopted for use by the U.S. Army in 1903 and replaced as the standard infantry weapon by the Garand rifle in World War II

spring·halt (sprin′hôlt′) *n. same as* STRINGHALT

spring·head (-hed′) *n.* a source or fountainhead

☆**spring·house** (-hous′) *n.* a small structure built over a spring or brook, used for cooling milk, etc.

spring·let (-lit) *n.* a small spring of water

spring lock a lock in which the bolt is shot automatically by a spring

☆**spring peeper** a small tree frog (*Hyla crucifer*) of the E U.S., that makes shrill, peeping sounds in early spring

Springs (sprinz) city in NE South Africa: pop. 142,000

spring·tail (-tāl′) *n.* any of an order (Collembola) of small, primitive, wingless insects, able to leap great distances by the sudden release of a forklike, abdominal appendage

spring·tide (-tīd′) *n. same as* SPRINGTIME

spring tide 1. a tide occurring at or shortly after the new and the full moon: it is normally the highest tide of the month **2.** any great flow, rush, or flood

spring·time (-tīm′) *n.* **1.** the season of spring **2.** a period or time resembling or suggesting spring; earliest period

spring·wood (-wood′) *n.* the first-formed woody portion of the annual growth ring of a shrub or tree

spring·y (-ē) *adj.* **spring′i·er, spring′i·est 1.** having spring; elastic, resilient, etc. **2.** having many springs of water —**spring′i·ly** *adv.* —**spring′i·ness** *n.*

sprin·kle (sprin′k'l) *vt.* **-kled, -kling** [ME. *sprinklen,* akin to G. *sprenkeln:* for IE. base see SPARK¹] **1.** to scatter (water, sand, etc.) in drops or particles **2.** *a)* to scatter drops or particles upon; cover or strew with a sprinkling *b)* to dampen before ironing **3.** to distribute at random or in a pattern —*vi.* **1.** to scatter something in drops or particles **2.** to fall in drops or particles **3.** to rain lightly

or infrequently —**n.** **1.** the act of sprinkling **2.** a small quantity of something that has been sprinkled **3.** a light rain —**sprin′kler** n.
SYN.—to **sprinkle** is to cause to fall in small drops or particles [to *sprinkle* water, to *sprinkle* sugar over berries]; to **scatter** is to disperse the units of a group in different directions, usually in an irregular distribution [the wind *scattered* the papers on the desk/]; to **strew** is to scatter, either regularly or irregularly, esp. so as to more or less cover a surface [to *strew* sawdust on a floor]

☆**sprinkler system** **1.** a system of pipes and attached nozzles carrying water or other extinguishing fluid throughout a building for protection against fire: it usually operates automatically when exposed to abnormal heat **2.** a system of pipes and nozzles, often underground, for watering a lawn, golf course, etc.: also **sprinkling system**

sprin·kling (-kliŋ) n. **1.** a small number, quantity, or amount, esp. one that is sprinkled, scattered, or thinly distributed **2.** the act of one that sprinkles

sprint (sprint) vi. [ME. *sprenten*, to leap, run < Scand., as in Sw. dial. *sprinta*, ON. *spretta*, to run] to run or race at full speed, esp. for a short distance —n. **1.** the act of sprinting **2.** a short run or race at full speed; dash **3.** a brief period of intense activity —**sprint′er** n.

sprit (sprit) n. [ME. *spret* < OE. *sprēot*, a sprout or a pole, akin to Du. *spriet*: for IE. base see SPREAD] a pole or spar extended diagonally upward from a mast to the topmost corner of a fore-and-aft sail, serving to extend the sail

sprite (sprīt) n. [ME. *sprit* < OFr. *esprit* < L. *spiritus*, SPIRIT] **1.** an elf, pixie, fairy, or goblin **2.** an elflike person **3.** [Archaic] a ghost

sprit·sail (sprit′sāl′, -s′l) n. a sail extended by a sprit

spritz (sprits; G. shprits) vt., vi., n. [via Pennsylvania Dutch & Yid. < G. *spritze* < MHG. *sprütze* < *sprützen*, to spray: for IE. base see SPROUT] squirt or spray

sprock·et (spräk′it) n. [Early ModE. < ?] **1.** any of a number of teeth or points, as on the rim of a wheel, arranged to fit into the links of a chain **2.** a wheel fitted with sprockets on its outer rim, used in a chain drive: in full **sprocket wheel**

SPROCKET WHEELS

sprout (sprout) vi. [ME. *sprouten* < OE. *sprutan*, akin to G. *spriessen* < IE. *spreud-* < base *(s)p(h)er-*, to strew, sow, whence SPREAD] **1.** to begin to grow or germinate; give off shoots or buds **2.** to grow or develop rapidly —vt. to cause to sprout or grow —n. [ME. *sprute* < the v.] **1.** a young growth on a plant, as a stem or branch; shoot **2.** a new growth from a bud, rootstock, germinating seed, etc. **3.** something like or suggestive of a sprout, as an offshoot or young person **4.** [pl.] shortened form of BRUSSELS SPROUTS

spruce[1] (sprōōs) n. [ME. *Spruce*, for *Pruce*, Prussia < OFr. < ML. *Prussia*: prob. because the tree was first known as a native of Prussia] **1.** any of a genus (*Picea*) of evergreen trees of the pine family, having slender needles that are rhombic in cross section **2.** the soft, light wood of any of these trees **3.** any of several evergreen trees, as the Douglas fir, resembling the spruces

spruce[2] (sprōōs) adj. **spruc′er, spruc′est** [< ME. *Spruce* (see prec.), esp. in the phr. *Spruce leather*, fine leather imported from Prussia] neat and trim in a smart, dapper way —vt. **spruced, spruc′ing** to make spruce (usually with *up*) —vi. to make oneself spruce (usually with *up*) —**spruce′ly** adv. —**spruce′ness** n.

spruce beer a fermented beverage made with an extract of spruce leaves and twigs

☆**spruce grouse** a gray, black, and brown grouse (*Canachites canadensis*) of the spruce forests of N N. America

☆**spruce pine** **1.** a large pine (*Pinus glabra*) of the SE U.S. **2.** any of several similar pines, spruces, or hemlocks

sprue[1] (sprōō) n. [Du. *spruw*] a chronic, chiefly tropical disease characterized by defective absorption of food, anemia, gastrointestinal disorders, etc.

sprue[2] (sprōō) n. [< ?] **1.** an opening through which molten metal is poured into a foundry mold **2.** the waste piece of metal cast in such an opening

sprung (spruŋ) pp. & alt. pt. of SPRING —adj. **1.** having the springs broken, overstretched, or loose **2.** provided with or mounted on springs

sprung rhythm [term coined by G. M. HOPKINS] a kind of rhythm in English poetry based on the normal rhythms of speech and made up of a mixture of feet, each foot consisting of either a single stressed syllable or a stressed syllable followed by one or more unstressed syllables

spry (sprī) adj. **spri′er** or **spry′er, spri′est** or **spry′est** [< Brit. dial. *sprey* < Scand., as in Sw. dial. *sprygg*, lively] full of life; active, nimble, brisk, etc., esp. though elderly —**SYN.** see AGILE —**spry′ly** adv. —**spry′ness** n.

spt. seaport.

spud (spud) n. [ME. *spudde*, prob. < Scand., as in ON. *spjöt*, a spear (for base see SPIT[1]): sense 2 from the use of the implement in potato digging] **1.** any of various sharp, spadelike or chisellike tools used for rooting out weeds, stripping off bark, etc. **2.** [Colloq.] a potato —vt., vi. **spud′ded, spud′ding** to dig, strip, drill, etc. with or as with a spud —**spud′der** n.

spue (spyōō) vt., vi. **spued, spu′ing** same as SPEW

spume (spyōōm) n. [ME. < MFr. *espume* < L. *spuma* <

IE. *(s)poimno-*, whence FOAM] foam, froth, or scum —vt., vi. **spumed, spum′ing** to foam or froth —**spu′mous, spum′y, -i·er, -i·est** adj.

spu·mes·cent (spyoo mes′'nt) adj. [L. *spumescens*, prp. of *spumescere*, to grow frothy < *spuma*: see prec.] **1.** like froth or foam **2.** frothing; foaming —**spu·mes′cence** n.

spu·mo·ni (spə mō′nē) n. [It., pl. of *spumone*, aug. of *spuma*, foam (< L.: see SPUME)] an Italian frozen dessert made of variously flavored and colored layers of smooth ice cream, often containing candied fruits and pistachio nuts: also sp. **spu·mo′ne**

spun (spun) pt. & pp. of SPIN —adj. formed by or as if by spinning

spun glass fine glass fiber, made by forming liquid glass into a thread

spunk (spuŋk) n. [IrGael. *sponc*, tinder, touchwood, sponge < L. *spongia*, a SPONGE] **1.** a kind of wood or fungus that smolders when ignited; punk **2.** [Colloq.] courage; spirit

spunk·y (spuŋ′kē) adj. **spunk′i·er, spunk′i·est** [Colloq.] having spunk; courageous; spirited —**spunk′i·ly** adv. —**spunk′i·ness** n.

spun silk a kind of yarn made from silk floss or waste

spun sugar same as COTTON CANDY

spun yarn **1.** yarn spun from staple fibers **2.** Naut. a line made of several rope yarns twisted together

spur (spur) n. [ME. *spure* < OE. *spura*, akin to G. *sporn* < IE. base *spÄ(h)er-*, to jerk, whence Sans. *sphurāti*, (he) kicks away, L. *spernere*, lit., to push away] **1.** any of various pointed devices worn on the heel by horsemen and used to urge the horse forward **2.** anything that urges, impels, or incites; stimulus to action **3.** something like a spur; specif., a) a spinelike process, as on the wings or legs of certain birds b) a spinelike outgrowth of bone, as on the human heel, resulting from injury, disease, etc. c) a climbing iron, as used by lumberjacks d) a sharp metal device attached as a weapon to the leg of a gamecock in a cockfight e) a short, stunted, or projecting branch or shoot of a tree, etc. **4.** a range or ridge projecting in a lateral direction from the main mass of a mountain or mountain range **5.** a) same as GRIFFE b) a buttress, as of masonry, or any similar structure c) a short wooden reinforcing piece; brace; strut **6.** same as SPUR TRACK **7.** Bot. a slender, tubelike structure formed by a basal extension of one or more petals or sepals, often serving as a nectar receptacle; calcar —vt. **spurred, spur′ring 1.** to strike or prick with a spur or spurs **2.** to urge, incite, or stimulate to action, greater effort, etc. **3.** to provide with a spur or spurs **4.** to strike or injure as with a spur (sense 3 d) —vi. **1.** to spur one's horse **2.** to hurry; hasten —**SYN.** see MOTIVE —**on the spur of the moment** hastily and abruptly; without forethought or preparation —**win one's spurs** to attain distinction or honor, esp. for the first time; establish one's reputation —**spur′rer** n.

spurge (spurj) n. [ME. < MFr. *espurge* < *espurger*, to purge < L. *expurgare*: see EXPURGATE] any of a genus (*Euphorbia*) of plants of the spurge family, with milky juice and minute, simplified flowers borne in cuplike inflorescences —adj. designating a family (Euphorbiaceae) of plants, usually with milky juice and diclinous flowers, including the poinsettia, cassava, rubber tree, etc.

spur gear **1.** a gearwheel having radial teeth parallel to the axle: also **spur wheel** **2.** a system of gearing having this kind of gearwheel: also **spur gearing**

spurge laurel a Eurasian evergreen shrub (*Daphne laureola*) of the mezereum family, with yellowish-green flowers, oblong leaves, and poisonous berries

spu·ri·ous (spyoor′ē əs) adj. [L. *spurius*, illegitimate (in LL., false), orig., a bastard] **1.** [Now Rare] illegitimate; bastard **2.** not true or genuine; false; counterfeit **3.** Bot. like in appearance but unlike in structure or function **4.** Radio designating or of an unwanted signal transmitted or received at other than the desired frequency —**SYN.** see ARTIFICIAL —**spu′ri·ous·ly** adv. —**spu′ri·ous·ness** n.

spurn (spurn) vt. [ME. *spurnen* < OE. *spurnan*, to spurn, kick: for IE. base see SPUR] **1.** to push or drive away contemptuously with or as with the foot **2.** to refuse or reject with contempt or disdain; scorn —vi. to show contempt or disdain in refusing or rejecting —n. **1.** a kick **2.** scornful treatment or rejection —**SYN.** see DECLINE —**spurn′er** n.

spurred (spurd) adj. having, wearing, or fitted with spurs or spurlike parts

spur·ri·er (spur′ē ər) n. a person who makes spurs

spur·ry, spur·rey (spur′ē) n. [Du. *spurrie* < ML. *spergula*] any of a genus (*Spergula*) of European plants of the pink family; esp., the **common corn spurry** (*Spergula arvensis*) with small white flowers, now a weed in N. America

spurt (spurt) vt. [prob. altered by metathesis < ME. *sprutten*, to sprout, spring forth < OE. *spryttan* < base of *sprutan*: see SPROUT] to expel suddenly in a stream or gushing flow; squirt; jet —vi. **1.** to gush forth in a stream or jet **2.** to show a sudden, brief burst of energy, increased activity, etc., as near the end of a race —n. **1.** a sudden gushing or shooting forth; jet **2.** a sudden, brief burst of energy, increased activity, etc.

spur track a short side track connected with the main track of a railroad

sput·nik (spoot′nik, sput′-) n. [< Russ., lit., co-traveler < *s(o)*, with (< IE. base *sem-*: see SAME) + *put′*, a way

< OBulg. *pǫt'* < IE. base **pent-**, to go, whence FIND + *-nik*, -NIK] an artificial satellite of the earth; specif., [*often* S-] any of those put into orbit by the U.S.S.R. beginning in October, 1957

sput·ter (sput′ər) *vi.* [Du. *sputteren*, freq. < MDu. *spotten*, to spit: for base see SPEW] **1.** to spit out drops of saliva, bits of food, etc. in an explosive manner, as when talking excitedly; splutter **2.** to speak hastily in a confused, explosive manner **3.** to make sharp, sizzling or spitting sounds, as burning wood, frying fat, etc. —*vt.* **1.** to spit or throw out (bits or drops) in an explosive manner **2.** to utter by sputtering —*n.* **1.** the act or noise of sputtering **2.** matter thrown out in sputtering **3.** hasty, confused, explosive utterance

spu·tum (spyoot′əm) *n.*, *pl.* **spu′ta** (-ə) [L., that which is spit out < *sputus*, pp. of *spuere*, to SPIT²] saliva, usually mixed with mucus from the respiratory tract, ejected from the mouth

Spuy·ten Duy·vil (spīt′'n dī′v'l) [Du., lit., spouting devil, nickname for a dangerous ford] ship canal between N Manhattan Island & the mainland, connecting the Hudson & Harlem rivers

spy (spī) *vt.* **spied, spy′ing** [ME. *spien* < OFr. *espier* < OHG. *spehōn*, to search out, examine < IE. base *spek-*, to spy, watch closely, whence L. *specere*, to see, Sans. *spaśati*, (he) sees, Gr. *skopein*, to observe] **1.** to watch or observe closely and secretly, usually with unfriendly purpose (often *with* out) **2.** to catch sight of; make out; perceive; see —*vi.* **1.** to watch or observe closely and secretly; specif., to act as a spy **2.** to make a close examination or careful inspection —*n.*, *pl.* **spies 1.** a person who keeps close and secret watch on another or others **2.** *a)* a person employed by a government to get secret information about the affairs, plans, armed forces, etc. of another government *b)* a person who, in time of war, acts clandestinely and while not in military uniform to get information for the enemy **3.** [Now Rare] an act of spying —**spy out** to discover or seek to discover by close observation, inspection, etc.

spy·glass (-glas′, -gläs′) *n.* a small telescope

sq. 1. sequence **2.** squadron **3.** square **4.** [L. *sequens*] the following one

sq. ft., sq. in., etc. square foot, square inch, etc.

sqq. [L. *sequentes; sequentia*] the following ones

squab (skwäb, skwôb) *n.* [prob. < Scand., as in Sw. *sqvabb*, loose flesh] **1.** a nestling pigeon, still unfledged **2.** a short, stout person **3.** [Brit.] *a)* a cushion *b)* a sofa or couch —*adj.* **1.** newly hatched or not fully fledged **2.** short and stout

squab·ble (skwäb′'l, skwôb′-) *vi.* **-bled, -bling** [< Scand. as in Sw. *skvabbel*, a dispute] to quarrel noisily over a small matter; wrangle —*vt. Printing* to disarrange (type that has been set) so that letters or lines become mixed —*n.* a noisy, petty quarrel or dispute; wrangle —*SYN.* see QUARREL² —**squab′bler** *n.*

squab·by (-ē) *adj.* **-bi·er, -bi·est** short and stout

squad (skwäd, skwôd) *n.* [Fr. *escouade* < Sp. *escuadra* or It. *squadra*, a square, both < VL. *exquadrare*, to form into a square: see SQUARE] **1.** *a)* a small group of soldiers assembled for inspection, duty, etc. *b)* the smallest military tactical unit, often a subdivision of a platoon ☆**2.** *a)* any small group of people working together [a police *squad*] *b)* an athletic team [a football *squad*] —*vt.* **squad′ded, squad′ding 1.** to form into squads **2.** to assign to a squad ☆**squad car** a police patrol car, usually communicating with headquarters by radiotelephone

squad·ron (-rən) *n.* [It. *squadrone* < *squadra*, a square: see SQUAD] **1.** a group of warships, usually of the same type, assigned to some special duty; specif., a naval unit consisting of two or more divisions **2.** a unit of cavalry consisting of from two to four troops, a headquarters troop, and certain auxiliary units **3.** *a) U.S. Air Force* a unit, usually a subdivision of an air group, consisting of two or more flights *b)* a formation of usually six or more aircraft **4.** any organized body or group

squa·lene (skwā′lēn) *n.* [< ModL. *Squalus*, a genus of sharks (< L., a kind of sea-fish: see WHALE¹) + -ENE] an unsaturated hydrocarbon, C₃₀H₅₀, found in shark livers, etc. that is a precursor of cholesterol in biosynthesis

squal·id (skwäl′id, skwôl′-) *adj.* [L. *squalidus* < *squalere*, to be foul or filthy] **1.** foul or unclean, esp. as the result of neglect or unsanitary conditions **2.** wretched; miserable; sordid —**squa·lid·i·ty** (skwä lid′ə tē, skwô-), **squal′id·ness** *n.* —**squal′id·ly** *adv.*

squall¹ (skwôl) *n.* [< Scand., as in Sw. *sqval*, a sudden shower, downpour: for prob. base see ff.] **1.** a brief, violent windstorm, usually with rain or snow **2.** [Colloq.] trouble or disturbance —*vi.* to storm briefly; blow a squall —**squall′y** *adj.* **squall′i·er, squall′i·est**

squall² (skwôl) *vi.*, *vt.* [< ON. *skvala*, to cry out, yell: see SQUEAL] to cry or scream loudly and harshly —*n.* a harsh, shrill cry or loud scream —**squall′er** *n.*

squal·or (skwäl′ər, skwôl′-) *n.* [L., foulness, akin to *squalere*, to be filthy] the quality or condition of being squalid; filth and wretchedness

squa·ma (skwā′mə) *n.*, *pl.* **-mae** (-mē) [L., a scale, husk] a scale or scalelike part of an animal or plant

squa·mate (skwā′māt) *adj.* [LL. *squamatus* < L. *squama*, a scale] having or covered with scales; scaly

squa·ma·tion (skwə mā′shən, skwā-) *n.* **1.** the condition of being squamate **2.** epidermal scale arrangement

squa·mo- (skwā′mō, -mə) [< L. *squama*, a scale] *a combining form meaning* squama: also, before a vowel, **squam-**

squa·mo·sal (skwə mō′s'l) *adj.* **1.** *same as* SQUAMOUS **2.** *Zool.* designating or of a bone in the skull of lower vertebrates analogous to the squamosal portion of the temporal bone in man —*n.* a squamosal bone

squa·mous (skwā′məs) *adj.* [L. *squamosus* < *squama*, a scale] **1.** like, formed of, or covered with scales **2.** *Anat.* designating or of the thin, scalelike, upper anterior portion of the temporal bone Also **squa′mose** (skwā′mōs)

squam·u·lose (skwam′yə lōs′, skwā′myə-) *adj.* [ModL. *squamulosus* < L. *squamula*, dim. of *squama*, a scale] having, covered with, or consisting of small scales

squan·der (skwän′dər, skwôn′-) *vt.* [prob. a specialized use of dial. *squander*, to scatter, popularized after Shakespeare's *Merchant of Venice*, I, iii, 22] to spend or use wastefully or extravagantly —*vi.* to be wasteful or extravagant —*n.* [Rare] a squandering; extravagant expenditure

square (skwer) *n.* [ME. < OFr. *esquarre* < VL. *exquadra* < *exquadrare*, to make square < L. *ex*, out + *quadrare*, to square < *quadrus*, a square < *quattuor*, FOUR] **1.** *a)* a plane figure having four equal sides and four right angles **2.** *a)* anything having or approximating this shape [a *square* of cloth] *b)* any of the spaces on a board for chess, checkers, etc. ☆**3.** an area bounded by streets or buildings on four sides; also, the distance along one side of such an area; block **4.** *a)* an open area bounded by, or at the intersection of, several streets, usually used as a park, plaza, etc. *b)* buildings surrounding such an area **5.** an instrument having two sides that form an angle of 90 degrees, used for drawing or testing right angles

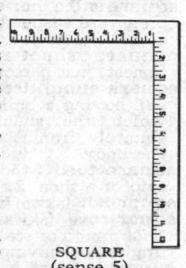

SQUARE
(sense 5)

6. a solid piece with at least one face that is a square [to cut a cake into *squares*] **7.** the product of a number or quantity multiplied by itself [9 is the *square* of 3] ☆**8.** [Slang] a person who is square (*adj.* 12) —*vt.* **squared, squar′ing** [ME. *squaren* < OFr. *esquarrer* < VL. *exquadrare*] **1.** *a)* to make into a square; make square *b)* to make into any rectangle **2.** to test or adjust with regard to straightness or evenness [to *square* a surface with a straightedge] **3.** to bring to or near to the form of a right angle [to *square* one's shoulders] **4.** *a)* to settle; adjust; make right or even [to *square* accounts] *b)* to adjust or settle the accounts of [to *square* oneself with another] **5.** to make equal [to *square* the score of a game] **6.** to bring into agreement; make conform [to *square* a statement with the facts] **7.** to mark off (a surface) in a series of connected squares **8.** to bring into the correct position, as with reference to a line, course, etc. **9.** to multiply (a number or quantity) by itself **10.** to determine the square that is equal in area to (a figure) **11.** [Old Slang] to bribe —*vi.* to fit; agree; accord (*with*) —*adj.* [ME. < OFr. *esquarre*, pp. of *esquarrer*] **1.** *a)* having four equal sides and four right angles *b)* more or less cubical; rectangular and three-dimensional, as a box **2.** forming a right angle, or having a rectangular part or parts **3.** correctly adjusted or positioned; straight, level, even, etc. **4.** *a)* leaving no balance; balanced; even *b)* even in score; tied **5.** just; fair; honest **6.** clear; direct; straightforward; unequivocal [a *square* refusal] **7.** *a)* designating or of a unit of surface measure in the form of a square having sides of a specified length *b)* given or stated in terms of such surface measure **8.** having a shape broad for its length or height, with a solid, sturdy appearance, and somewhat rectangular or rectilinear [a *square* joint] **9.** square or rectangular in cross section, as some files **10.** designating a number that is the product of another number multiplied by itself ☆**11.** [Colloq.] satisfying; solid; substantial [a *square* meal] ☆**12.** [Slang] not conversant with the current fads, styles, slang, etc.; old-fashioned, unsophisticated, conservative, etc. **13.** *Naut.* at right angles to the keel and mast, as the yards of a square-rigged ship —*adv.* **1.** honestly; fairly; justly **2.** so as to be or form a square; at right angles **3.** directly; exactly **4.** so as to face —**on the square 1.** at right angles (to something specified) **2.** [Colloq.] honest(ly), fair(ly), genuine(ly), etc. —**out of square 1.** not at right angles (with something specified) **2.** [Colloq.] not in harmony, order, or agreement —**square away 1.** to bring a ship's yards around so as to sail directly before the wind **2.** *same as* SQUARE OFF **3.** [Colloq.] to get ready; put in order —☆**square off** to assume a posture of attack or self-defense, as in boxing —☆**square oneself** [Colloq.] to make amends for a wrong, damage, hurt, etc. done by oneself

to another —**square the circle 1.** to construct or find a square equal in area to a circle: an insoluble problem **2.** to do or attempt something that seems impossible —**square up 1.** to make a settlement, as by paying, balancing accounts, etc. **2.** to assume a posture of opposition (*to* an adversary) —**square′ly** *adv.* —**square′ness** *n.*

square dance a lively dance with various steps, figures, etc., in which the couples are grouped in a given form, as a square —**square′-dance′** *vi.* **-danced′, -danc′ing**

☆**squared circle** [Old Colloq.] the boxing ring

☆**square deal** [Colloq.] any dealing that is honest and fair

square knot a double knot in which the free ends run parallel to the standing parts: see KNOT, illus.

square measure a system of measuring area, esp. the system in which 144 square inches = 1 square foot or that in which 10,000 square centimeters = 1 square meter: see TABLE OF WEIGHTS AND MEASURES in Supplement

square-rigged (-rigd′) *adj.* rigged with square sails as the principal sails

square-rig·ger (-rig′ər) *n.* a square-rigged ship

square root the number or quantity which when squared will produce a given number or quantity *[3* is the *square root of 9]*

square sail a four-sided sail rigged on a yard suspended horizontally across the mast

☆**square shooter** [Colloq.] an honest, just person

square-shoul·dered (-shōl′dərd) *adj.* having a build or posture in which the shoulders jut out squarely from the main axis of the body

SQUARE-RIGGED SHIP

square-toed (-tōd′) *adj.* **1.** having a broad, square toe: said of a shoe **2.** [Now Rare] old-fashioned; conservative

squar·ish (skwer′ish) *adj.* more nearly square than round

squar·rose (skwar′rōs, skwär′-) *adj.* [L. *squarrosus*] **1.** *Biol.* rough or scaly **2.** *Bot.* having tips projecting at right angles, or having spreading bracts —**squar′rose·ly** *adv.*

squash[1] (skwäsh, skwôsh) *vt.* [OFr. *esquasser* < VL. *exquassare* < L. *ex-*, intens. + *quassus*, pp. of *quatere*, to shake, shatter: see QUASH[2]] **1.** *a)* to squeeze or crush into a soft, flat mass or pulp *b)* to press or squeeze tightly or too tightly **2.** to suppress or bring to an abrupt end; quash *[to squash* a rebellion] **3.** [Colloq.] to silence or disconcert (another) in a crushing manner —*vi.* **1.** to be squashed, as by a heavy fall, pressure, etc. **2.** to make a sound of squashing or splashing **3.** to force one's way; crowd; squeeze —*n.* **1.** something squashed; soft, pulpy mass **2.** a squashing or being squashed **3.** the sound of squashing **4.** either of two similar games combining elements of both tennis and handball; specif., *a)* one played in a four-walled court with a small, long-handled racket and a small rubber ball: in full **squash racquets** *b)* one played in a similar court, but with a larger racket and a larger, livelier ball: in full **squash tennis 5.** [Brit.] a drink made of sweetened fruit juice or fruit-flavored syrup and soda water *[lemon squash]* —*adv.* **1.** so as to squash **2.** with a squashing sound

☆**squash**[2] (skwäsh, skwôsh) *n.* [< AmInd. (Algonquian), as in Massachusett *askootasquash*] **1.** the fleshy fruit of any of various plants (genus *Cucurbita*) of the gourd family, eaten as a vegetable **2.** a plant, usually a vine, bearing this fruit

☆**squash bug** a large, dark-colored insect (*Anasa tristis*) that attacks squash vines and similar plants

squash·y (-ē) *adj.* **squash′i·er, squash′i·est 1.** soft and wet; mushy **2.** easily squashed or crushed, as overripe fruit — **squash′i·ly** *adv.* —**squash′i·ness** *n.*

squat (skwät, skwôt) *vi.* **squat′ted** or rare **squat, squat′ting** [ME. *squatten* < MFr. *esquatir* < *es-* (L. *ex-*), intens. + *quatir*, to press flat < VL. **coactire* < L. *coactus*, pp. of *cogere*, to force, compress: see COGENT] **1.** to crouch so as to sit on the heels with the knees bent and the weight resting on the balls of the feet **2.** to crouch or cower close to the ground, as an animal ☆**3.** to settle on land, esp. public or unoccupied land, without right or title ☆**4.** to settle on public land under regulation by the government, in order to get title to it —*vt.* to cause to squat: usually reflexive —*adj.* **1.** crouched in a squatting position **2.** short and heavy or thick —*n.* **1.** the act of squatting **2.** the position taken in squatting; crouching posture —**squat′ly** *adv.* —**squat′ness** *n.*

squat·ter (-ər) *n.* **1.** a person or animal that squats, or crouches ☆**2.** a person who settles on public or unoccupied land: see SQUAT (*vi.* 3, 4)

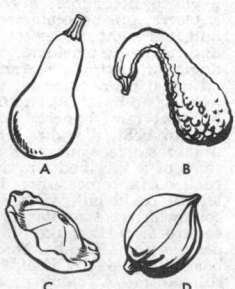

SQUASH
(A, butternut; B, crookneck; C, white bush; D, acorn)

squat·ty (-ē) *adj.* **-ti·er, -ti·est** squat; thickset

☆**squaw** (skwô) *n.* [< AmInd. (Algonquian), as in Massachusett *squas*] **1.** a N. American Indian woman, esp. a wife **2.** one's wife: a jocular usage

☆**squaw·fish** (-fish′) *n., pl.* **-fish′, -fish′es:** see FISH[2] **1.** any of several long, slender, cyprinoid fishes (genus *Ptychocheilus*), found in rivers of the W U.S. and Canada and reaching five feet in length **2.** a surfperch (*Embiotoca lateralis*) found off the Pacific coast of N. America

squawk (skwôk) *vi.* [echoic] **1.** to utter a loud, harsh cry, as a parrot or chicken ☆**2.** [Colloq.] to complain or protest, esp. in a loud or raucous voice —*vt.* to utter in a squawk —*n.* **1.** a loud, harsh cry ☆**2.** [Slang] a loud, raucous complaint or protest ☆**3.** the black-crowned night heron —**squawk′er** *n.*

☆**squawk box** [Slang] an intercom speaker

☆**squaw man** a white man married to a N. American Indian woman, esp. one living with her tribe

☆**squaw·root** (skwô′rōōt′) *n.* **1.** an E N. American yellowish-brown, scaly, leafless plant (*Conopholis americana*) of the broomrape family, parasitic on the roots of some trees, esp. oaks **2.** a purple trillium (*Trillium erectum*)

Squaw Valley [SQUAW (popular in names) + VALLEY] valley in the Sierra Nevada Mountains, E Calif., near Lake Tahoe: a ski resort

squeak (skwēk) *vi.* [ME. *squeken*, prob. akin to ON. *skvakka*, to gurgle] **1.** to make or utter a thin, sharp, high-pitched sound or cry **2.** [Chiefly Brit. Slang] to act as an informer; squeal —*vt.* **1.** to utter or produce in a squeak **2.** to cause (a door, etc.) to squeak —*n.* a thin, sharp, usually short sound or cry —**narrow** (or **close, near**) **squeak** [Colloq.] a narrow escape —**squeak through** (or **by,** etc.) [Colloq.] to succeed, get through, survive, etc. by a narrow margin or with difficulty —**squeak′y** *adj.* **squeak′i·er, squeak′i·est** —**squeak′i·ly** *adv.*

squeak·er (-ər) *n.* **1.** a person, animal, or thing that squeaks ☆**2.** [Colloq.] a narrow escape, victory, etc.

squeal (skwēl) *vi.* [ME. *squelen*, prob. akin to ON. *skvala*, to cry out, yell < IE. **skwel-*, var. of base **kel-*, whence L. *calare*, to cry out, *clamor*, a cry] **1.** to utter or make a long, high, shrill cry or sound **2.** [Slang] to act as an informer; betray a secret (often with *on*) —*vt.* to utter in a squeal —*n.* a high-pitched, shrill cry or sound, somewhat prolonged —**squeal′er** *n.*

squeam·ish (skwēm′ish) *adj.* [ME. *squaymysch*, earlier *squaimous* < Anglo-Fr. *escoimous*, orig., disdainful, shy] **1.** having a digestive system that is easily upset; easily nauseated; queasy **2.** easily shocked or offended; prudish **3.** excessively fastidious; oversensitive —SYN. see DAINTY —**squeam′ish·ly** *adv.* —**squeam′ish·ness** *n.*

squee·gee (skwē′jē) *n.* [prob. < *squeege*, intens. form of SQUEEZE] **1.** a T-shaped tool with a blade of rubber, etc. set across the handle, used to scrape water from a flat surface, as in washing windows **2.** a tool with a rubber blade, roller, etc. used to remove surface liquid, apply ink, etc., as in photographic development or lithography —*vt.* **-geed, -gee·ing** to scrape or treat with a squeegee

squeeze (skwēz) *vt.* **squeezed, squeez′ing** [intens. of ME. *queisen* < OE. *cwysan*, to squeeze, dash against, bruise, akin to Goth. *quistjan*, to destroy < IE. base **gweye-*, to overpower, whence Sans. *jināti*, (he) conquers] **1.** to press hard or closely; exert pressure on, esp. from two or more sides; compress **2.** *a)* to press in order to extract liquid, juice, etc. *[to squeeze oranges] b)* to get, bring forth, or extract by pressure *[to squeeze* water from a sponge] **3.** to force (*into, out, through,* etc.) by or as by pressing **4.** to get, extract, or extort by force or unfair means **5.** to oppress with exactions, burdensome taxes, etc. **6.** to put pressure or bring influence to bear upon (someone) to do a certain thing, as to pay money, etc. **7.** to embrace closely; hug ☆**8.** *Baseball* to score (a run) or cause (a runner) to score by a squeeze play ☆**9.** *Bridge* to force (an opponent) to discard a potentially winning card —*vi.* **1.** to yield or give way to pressure **2.** to exert pressure **3.** to force one's way by pushing or pressing (*in, out, through,* etc.) —*n.* **1.** a squeezing or being squeezed; hard or close pressure **2.** *a)* a close embrace; hug *b)* a firm pressing or grasping of another's hand in one's own **3.** the state of being closely pressed or packed; crush **4.** a period or situation marked by scarcity, hardship, insecurity, etc. **5.** a facsimile impression made by pressing a soft substance onto something, as a coin or inscription **6.** a quantity of something extracted by squeezing **7.** [Colloq.] pressure or influence brought to bear, as in extortion: used esp. in the phrase ☆**put the squeeze on** ☆**8.** *clipped form of* SQUEEZE PLAY —**squeeze through** (or **by,** etc.) [Colloq.] to succeed, survive, get through, etc. by a narrow margin or with difficulty

☆**squeeze bottle** a flexible plastic container which is squeezed to eject its contents through a tiny hole or holes

☆**squeeze play 1.** *Baseball* a play in which the batter tries to bunt so that a runner on third base, starting to run at the pitcher's first pitching motion, may have a chance to score **2.** *Bridge* any play that forces an opponent to discard a potentially winning card **3.** pressure or coercion exerted to achieve some goal

squelch (skwelch) *n.* [prob. echoic] **1.** the sound of liquid, mud, slush, etc. moving under pressure or suction, as in wet shoes **2.** a crushed mass of something **3.** [Colloq.] the

act of suppressing or silencing; esp., a crushing retort, answer, rebuke, etc. —*vt.* 1. to crush or smash by or as by falling or stamping upon; squash 2. [Colloq.] to suppress, subdue, or silence completely and with a crushing effect —*vi.* 1. to walk heavily, as through mud or slush, making a splashing sound 2. to make such a sound —**squelch′er** *n.*

squelch circuit *Radio* a circuit which disconnects a receiver in order to eliminate output noise when no signal or an extremely weak signal is received

☆**sque·teague** (skwē tēg′) *n., pl.* **sque·teague′** [< AmInd. (Narragansett) name] *same as* WEAKFISH

squib (skwib) *n.* [prob. echoic] 1. a type of firecracker that burns with a hissing, spurting noise before exploding 2. a short, sharp, usually witty attack in words; lampoon 3. a short news item; filler —*vt., vi.* **squibbed, squib′bing** 1. to shoot off (a squib) 2. to write or utter a squib or squibs (against) 3. to explode with the sound of a squib

squid (skwid) *n., pl.* **squids, squid:** see PLURAL, II, D, 1 [prob. < *squit*, dial. for SQUIRT] any of a number of long, slender, fish-eating, cephalopod sea mollusks (esp. genera *Loligo, Illex,* and *Omma-strephes*) having ten arms, two being much longer than the others: small squid are used as food and for fish bait —☆*vi.* **squid′ded, squid′ding** 1. to take on an elongated squidlike shape due to strong air pressure: said of a parachute 2. to fish for squid or with squid as bait

SQUID
(small species to 8 in. long)

squif·fy (skwif′ē) *adj.* **-fi·er, -fi·est** [< dial. *skew-whiff*, askew, tipsy + -Y³] [Chiefly Brit. Slang] drunk; intoxicated: also **squiffed** (skwift)

squig·gle (skwig′'l) *n.* [SQU(IRM) + (W)IGGLE] 1. a short curved or wavy line; curlicue 2. an illegible or meaningless scribble or scrawl —*vt.* **-gled, -gling** 1. to form into squiggles 2. to write as a squiggle or scrawl —*vi.* 1. to make squiggles 2. to move with a squirming motion; wriggle —**squig′gly** *adj.*

squil·gee (skwē′jē) *n., vt.* **-geed, -gee·ing** *naut. var. of* SQUEEGEE (sense 1)

squill (skwil) *n.* [ME. < L. *squilla, scilla* < Gr. *skilla*] 1. the dried bulb of white varieties of a plant (*Urginea maritima*) of the lily family, formerly used in medicine 2. *same as:* a) RED SQUILL b) SCILLA

squil·la (skwil′ə) *n., pl.* **-las, -lae** (-ē) [L. *squilla, scilla,* prawn, shrimp, sea onion: see SQUILL] any of a genus (*Squilla*) of large stomatopods that burrow along the seashore and grasp their prey with strong, spiny claws

squinch¹ (skwinch) *n.* [var. of *scunch,* contr. < LME. *scuncheon* < MFr. *escoinson,* altered (after *coin,* corner) < *escoisson* < LL. *excussio,* a striking out] an interior corner support, as a small arch, corbeling, or lintel, supporting a weight, as of a spire, resting above

☆**squinch²** (skwinch) *vt.* [SQU(INT) + (P)INCH] 1. *a*) to squint (the eyes) *b*) to pucker or screw up (the face, nose, brow, etc.) 2. to squeeze or compress —☆*vi.* 1. to squint or pucker 2. to crouch down or draw oneself together so as to seem smaller 3. to flinch Often with *up, down, away*

squin·ny (skwin′ē) *n., vi., vt.* **-nied, -ny·ing** [altered < ff. + -Y²] *rare var. of* SQUINT

squint (skwint) *vi.* [contr. of ASQUINT] 1. to look or peer with the eyes partly closed, as when the light is too strong 2. to look with the eyes turned to the side; look obliquely or askance 3. to be cross-eyed 4. to incline or have a tendency (*toward* a given direction, belief, etc.) 5. to deviate from a given line, tendency, etc. —*vt.* 1. to cause to squint 2. to keep (the eyes) partly closed in peering at something —*n.* 1. the act of squinting 2. an inclination or tendency 3. an oblique or perverse tendency or bent 4. the condition of being cross-eyed; strabismus 5. [Colloq.] a look or glance, often sidelong, quick, or casual —*adj.* 1. squinting; looking obliquely, askance, or sidelong 2. characterized by strabismus [*squint* eyes] —**squint′er** *n.* —**squint′ing·ly** *adv.* —**squint′y** *adj.*

squint-eyed (-īd′) *adj.* squinting; specif., *a*) cross-eyed *b*) looking askance; malicious; prejudiced; spiteful

☆**squinting modifier** *Gram.* a misplaced adverb, etc. that can be interpreted as modifying either of two words (Ex.: *often* in "those who lie often are found out")

squire (skwīr) *n.* [ME. *squier* < OFr. *esquier:* see ESQUIRE] 1. a young man of high birth who served a knight as an attendant or armor-bearer 2. in England, a country gentleman or landed proprietor, esp. the main landowner in a district ☆3. a title of respect applied commonly to a justice of the peace or similar local dignitary, as in a rural district 4. an attendant; esp., a man escorting a woman; gallant —*vt., vi.* squired, squir′ing to act as a squire (to)

squire·ar·chy (skwīr′är kē) *n.* [prec. + -ARCHY, after HIERARCHY] 1. country gentry or large landowners collectively 2. government by country gentry or large landowners Also sp. **squir′ar·chy** —**squire·ar′chal** *adj.*

squir·een (skwīr ēn′) *n.* [SQUIRE + Ir. dim. suffix -*een* < Gael. *in*] [Irish] a small landowner; petty squire

squirm (skwurm) *vi.* [prob. echoic, infl. by WORM] 1. to twist and turn the body in a snakelike movement; wriggle; writhe 2. to show or feel distress, as from painful embarrassment, humiliation, etc. —*n.* 1. the act of squirming 2. a squirming motion —**squirm′y** *adj.* **squirm′i·er, squirm′i·est**

squir·rel (skwur′əl; *chiefly Brit.,* skwir′-) *n., pl.* **-rels, -rel:** see PLURAL, II, D, 1 [ME. *squirel* < OFr. *escuriuel* < VL. **scuriolus,* dim. of **scurius,* for L. *sciurus* < Gr. *skiouros,* squirrel < *skia,* a shadow (see SHINE) + *oura,* tail: for IE. base see URO-²] 1. *a*) any of a group of small, tree-dwelling rodents (family Sciuridae) with heavy fur and a long, bushy tail: common U.S. species are the GRAY SQUIRREL, the RED SQUIRREL, and the FOX SQUIRREL *b*) any of various other rodents of this family, as the chipmunks, ground squirrels, etc. 2. the fur of some of these animals —*vt.* **-reled** or **-relled, -rel·ing** or **-rel·ling** to store, hide, or hoard (usually with *away*)

squirrel cage a cage for a squirrel, hamster, etc. containing a drum that revolves when the animal runs inside it: often used figuratively of an existence, repetitive task, etc. that seems endless and without purpose

☆**squirrel corn** a delicate, E N. American, woodland, spring wildflower (*Dicentra canadensis*) of the fumitory family, having finely divided leaves and racemes of whitish, spurred flowers

☆**squir·rel·ly, squir·rel·y** (-ē) *adj.* [in allusion to a squirrel's diet of nuts: see NUT, *n.* 8 *a*] [Slang] odd, crazy, etc.

squirt (skwurt) *vt.* [LME. *squyrten,* prob. altered < or akin to LowG. & Du. *swirtjen,* to squirt] 1. to shoot out (a liquid) in a jet or narrow stream 2. to wet with liquid so shot out —*vi.* to be squirted out; spurt —*n.* 1. something used to squirt liquid, as a syringe 2. the act of squirting 3. a small amount of squirted liquid; jet or narrow stream 4. [Colloq.] a small or young person, esp. one who is impudent; whippersnapper —**squirt′er** *n.*

☆**squirt gun** a toy gun that shoots a stream of water

squirting cucumber a sprawling vine (*Ecballium elaterium*) of the gourd family, with a small, fleshy fruit that separates from its stalk and squirts out its seeds when ripe

squish (skwish) *vi.* to make a soft, splashing sound when walked on, squeezed, etc. —*vt.* [Colloq.] to squeeze into a soft mass; squash —*n.* 1. a squishing sound 2. [Colloq.] the act of squashing; squash

squish·y (-ē) *adj.* **squish′i·er, squish′i·est** 1. soft and pliable; yielding to pressure 2. making a squishing sound

Sr *Chem.* strontium

Sr. 1. [Port.] *Senhor* 2. Senior 3. [Sp.] *Señor* 4. Sister

Sra. 1. [Port.] *Senhora* 2. [Sp.] *Señora*

‡**sri** (shrē) *n.* [Hind., lit., glorious < Sans. *śrī* < IE. base **krei-,* to shine forth, whence Gr. *kreiōn,* noble] a Hindu title of address, equivalent to English *Mr.*

Sri·nag·ar (srē nug′ər) city in W Kashmir, on the Jhelum River; summer capital of Jammu & Kashmir: pop. 285,000

S.R.O. standing room only

Srta. 1. [Port.] *Senhorita* 2. [Sp.] *Señorita*

SS. 1. [L. *scilicet*] namely 2. [L. *Sancti*] Saints

ss., ss *Baseball* shortstop

S.S. 1. Sunday School 2. [L. *supra scriptum*] written above

S.S., SS [G. *Schutzstaffel,* lit., protective rank] a quasi military unit of the Nazi party, used as special police

S.S., SS, S/S steamship

S.S.A. Social Security Administration

SSB single sideband

SSE, S.S.E., s.s.e. south-southeast

SSgt Staff Sergeant

S.S.R., SSR Soviet Socialist Republic

SSS Selective Service System

SST supersonic transport

SSW, S.S.W., s.s.w. south-southwest

-st *same as* -EST

St. 1. Saint: terms beginning with *St.* are entered in this dictionary as if spelled *St-* 2. Strait 3. Street

St., st. 1. statute(s) 2. stratus

st. 1. stanza 2. stet 3. stitch 4. stone (unit of weight)

s.t. short ton

Sta. 1. Santa 2. Station

sta. 1. stationary 2. stator

stab (stab) *n.* [ME. *stabbe,* prob. < *stobbe,* var. of *stubbe,* STUB] 1. a wound made by piercing with a knife, dagger, or other pointed weapon 2. a thrust, as with a knife or dagger 3. a sudden sensation of anguish or pain —*vt.* **stabbed, stab′bing** 1. to pierce or wound with or as with a knife, etc. 2. to thrust or plunge (a knife, etc.) into something 3. to go into in a sharp, thrusting way —*vi.* 1. to make a thrust or cause a wound with or as with a knife, etc. 2. to give the sensation of a knife wound: said of pain —☆**make** (or **take**) **a stab at** to make an attempt at —**stab in the back** 1. to harm (someone) by treachery 2. an act of betrayal —**stab′ber** *n.*

‡**Sta·bat Ma·ter** (stä′bät mät′ər, stä′bat mät′ər) [ML., lit., the mother was standing (the opening words of the text)] 1. a Latin hymn about the sorrows of the Virgin

Mary at the crucifixion of Jesus **2.** any musical setting of this hymn

sta·bile (stā′b'l, -bil; *also, and for n. usually,* -bēl) *adj.* [L. *stabilis:* see STABLE¹, *adj.*] **1.** stable; stationary; fixed in position **2.** *Med.* resistant to moderate heat —*n.* a large piece of stationary abstract sculpture, usually a construction of metal, wire, wood, etc.: the analogue of MOBILE

sta·bil·i·ty (stə bil′ə tē) *n., pl.* -**ties** [ME. *stablete* < OFr. *stableté* < L. *stabilitas*] **1.** the state or quality of being stable, or fixed; steadiness **2.** firmness of character, purpose, or resolution **3.** *a*) resistance to change; permanence *b*) resistance to chemical decomposition **4.** the capacity of an object to return to equilibrium or to its original position after having been displaced **5.** *R.C.Ch.* a vow taken by some monks to remain for life in the same monastery

sta·bi·lize (stā′bə līz′) *vt.* -**lized**′, -**liz**′**ing** [Fr. *stabiliser* < L. *stabilis:* see STABLE¹ & -IZE] **1.** to make stable, or firm **2.** to keep from changing or fluctuating, as in price **3.** to give stability to (an airplane, ship, etc.) with a stabilizer —*vi.* to become stabilized —**sta′bi·li·za′tion** *n.*

sta·bi·liz·er (-lī′zər) *n.* a person or thing that stabilizes; specif., *a*) any of the airfoils or vanes that keep an airplane steady in flight, specif. the horizontal component of the tail section *b*) a device used to steady a ship in rough waters, esp. a gyrostabilizer; also, a gyroscope used to keep instruments on a ship, aircraft, etc. in a steady position *c*) any additive used in substances and compounds to keep them in a stable state, retard deterioration, act as an antioxidant, etc.

sta·ble¹ (stā′b'l) *adj.* -**bler,** -**blest** [ME. < OFr. *estable* < L. *stabilis* < *stare,* to STAND] **1.** *a*) not easily moved or thrown off balance; firm; steady *b*) not likely to break down, fall apart, or give way; fixed **2.** firm in character, purpose, or resolution; steadfast **3.** not likely to change or be affected adversely; lasting; enduring **4.** capable of returning to equilibrium or original position after having been displaced **5.** *Chem., Physics a*) not readily decomposing or changing from one state of matter to another *b*) not undergoing spontaneous physical, chemical, or nuclear change **6.** *Nuclear Physics* incapable of radioactive decay —**sta′bly** *adv.*

sta·ble² (stā′b'l) *n.* [ME. < OFr. *estable* < L. *stabulum* < *stare,* to STAND] **1.** *a*) a building in which horses or cattle are sheltered and fed *b*) a group of animals kept or belonging in such a building **2.** *a*) all the racehorses belonging to one owner *b*) the people employed to take care of and train such a group of racehorses **3.** [Colloq.] all the athletes, writers, performers, etc. under one management, with one agent, etc. —*vt., vi.* -**bled,** -**bling** to lodge, keep, or be kept in or as in a stable

sta·ble·boy (-boi′) *n.* a boy who works in a stable

sta·ble·man (-mən, -man′) *n., pl.* -**men** (-mən, -men′) a man who works in a stable

sta·bling (stā′blin) *n.* **1.** a stable or stables **2.** accommodations in a stable or stables, for horses, etc.

stab·lish (stab′lish) *vt. archaic var.* of ESTABLISH

stac·ca·to (stə kät′ō) *adj.* [It., pp. of *staccare,* short for *distaccare,* to detach] **1.** *Music* with distinct breaks between successive tones: usually indicated by a dot (**staccato mark**) placed over or under each note to be so produced: cf. LEGATO: abbrev. **stacc. 2.** made up of abrupt, distinct elements or sounds [a *staccato* outburst of gunfire] —*adv.* so as to be staccato —*n., pl.* -**tos** something, as a speech pattern, that is staccato

stack (stak) *n.* [ME. *stac* < ON. *stakkr* < IE. **stāk-,* to stand, be placed < **stā-,* to stand (cf. STAND)] **1.** a large pile of straw, hay, etc., esp. one neatly arranged, as in a conical form, for outdoor storage **2.** any somewhat orderly pile or heap, as of boxes, books, poker chips, etc. **3.** a number of arms, esp. three rifles, leaning against one another on end so as to form a cone **4.** in Great Britain, a unit of measure for wood, equal to 108 cubic feet **5.** *a*) a number of chimney flues or pipes arranged together *b*) *same as* SMOKESTACK ☆**6.** [*pl.*] an extensive series of bookshelves, or the main area for shelving books in a library **7.** [Colloq.] a large number or amount —*vt.* **1.** to pile or arrange in a stack **2.** to load with stacks of something **3.** to assign (aircraft) to various altitudes for circling while awaiting a turn to land **4.** to arrange in advance underhandedly so as to predetermine the outcome [to *stack* a jury] —☆**stack the cards** (or **deck**) **1.** to arrange the order of playing cards secretly so that certain cards are dealt to certain players **2.** to prearrange circumstances, usually secretly and unfairly —**stack up** ☆**1.** to amount (*to* a specified sum) ☆**2.** to stand in comparison (*with* or *against*); measure up —**stack′a·ble** *adj.* —**stack′er** *n.*

stacked (stakt) *adj.* ☆[Slang] having a full, shapely figure; curvaceous: said of a woman

☆**stacked** (or **stack**) **heel** a heel on a woman's shoe composed of several layers, as of leather, of alternating shades

stack·up (stak′up′) *n.* an arrangement of circling aircraft at various altitudes awaiting their turn to land

stac·te (stak′tē) *n.* [ME. *stacten* < acc. of L. *stacte,* oil of myrrh < Gr. *staktē* < *stazein,* to drip: for IE. base see STAGNATE] a spice used by the ancient Hebrews in preparing incense: Ex. 30:34

stad·dle (stad′'l) *n.* [ME. *stadel* < OE. *stathol,* akin to G. *stadel,* barn: for IE. base see STAND] [Archaic or Dial.]

a lower part or support; specif., the base or supporting framework of a stack, as of hay

stade (stād) *n.* [Fr. < L. *stadium,* STADIUM] *same as* STADIUM (sense 1 b)

stad·hold·er (stad′hōl′dər) *n.* [< Du. *stadhouder* < *stad,* a place (akin to STEAD) + *houder,* a holder < *houden,* to HOLD¹] **1.** orig., the governor or viceroy of a province of the Netherlands **2.** the chief magistrate of the 16th–17th-cent. Netherlands republic Also **stadt′hold′er** (stat′-)

sta·di·a¹ (stā′dē ə) *n.* [It., prob. < L., pl. of *stadium* (see STADIUM)] a method of surveying in which distances and elevations are obtained by observing the interval on a graduated, upright rod (**stadia rod**) intercepted by two parallel horizontal lines (**stadia hairs** or **wires**) in a surveyor's transit set up at a distance from the rod

sta·di·a² (stā′dē ə) *n. alt. pl.* of STADIUM

sta·di·um (stā′dē əm) *n., pl.* -**di·a** (-ə); *also, and for* sense 2 usually, -**di·ums** [ME. < L. < Gr. *stadion,* fixed standard of length, altered (after *stadios,* standing) < earlier *spadion* < *span,* to draw, pull (for IE. base see SPAN¹)] **1.** in ancient Greece and Rome, *a*) a unit of linear measure, orig. equal to 600 Greek feet, or about 607 English feet *b*) a track for footraces, typically one stadium in length, with tiers of seats for spectators **2.** a large oval, round, or U-shaped open structure, as for football, baseball, track events, etc., surrounded by tiers of seats, usually for thousands of spectators **3.** *Zool.* a period or stage in the life history of an animal

Staël (stäl), **Madame de,** baronne de Staël-Holstein, (born *Anne Louise Germaine Necker*) 1766–1817; Fr. writer & mistress of a popular salon

staff¹ (staf, stäf) *n., pl.* **staffs;** also, for senses 1 & 5 **staves** [ME. *staf* < OE. *stæf,* akin to G. *stab* < IE. base **stebh-,* post, pole, whence STAMP, STEM¹, Sans. *stabh-nāti,* (he) supports] **1.** a stick, rod, or pole; specif., *a*) a stick used as a support in walking *b*) a pole or club used as a weapon *c*) a pole for supporting a banner or flag *d*) a rod, wand, crosier, etc. used as a symbol of authority *e*) [Archaic] a shaft, as of a lance *f*) any of several graduated sticks or rules used for measuring, as in surveying **2.** a group of people assisting a chief, manager, president, or other leader **3.** a group of officers serving a military or naval commanding officer in an advisory and administrative capacity without combat duties or command **4.** a specific group of workers or employees [a teaching *staff,* newspaper *staff,* maintenance *staff*] **5.** *Music* the five horizontal lines and four intermediate spaces on which music is written or printed —*adj.* of, by, for, or on a staff; specif., employed full-time on a magazine staff, etc. rather than as a freelance writer —*vt.* to provide with a staff, as of workers

☆**staff²** (staf, stäf) *n.* [< G. *staffieren,* to fill out, decorate; via Du. < OFr. *estoffe,* STUFF] a building material of plaster and fiber, used for temporary decorative work

staff·er (-ər) *n.* a member of a staff, as of a newspaper

staff officer 1. an officer serving on a staff ☆**2.** *U.S. Navy* a commissioned officer with nonmilitary duties, as a surgeon, chaplain, etc.

staff of life bread, regarded as the basic food

Staf·ford (staf′ərd) **1.** county seat of Staffordshire, in the C part: pop. 49,000 **2.** *same as* STAFFORDSHIRE

Staf·ford·shire (-shir′) county of WC England: 1,154 sq. mi.; pop. 1,787,000; county seat, Stafford

staff sergeant ☆**1.** *U.S. Army & Marine Corps* an enlisted man ranking above sergeant ☆**2.** *U.S. Air Force* an enlisted man ranking above airman first class

staff-tree (-trē′) *n.* any of a genus (*Celastrus*) of shrubby, usually climbing, plants of the staff-tree family, growing in Asia, Australia, and N. America and including BITTERSWEET (sense 1) —*adj.* designating a family (Celastraceae) of widely distributed trees and twining shrubs bearing red seeds in pods and including khat, euonymus, etc.

stag (stag) *n., pl.* **stags, stag:** see PLURAL, II, D, 1 [ME. < OE. *stagga,* akin to ON. (*andar*)*steggi,* drake; IE. base **stegh-,* to stick] **1.** *a*) a full-grown male deer; hart: said specif. of the European red deer *b*) the male of various other animals, as the caribou **2.** a male animal, esp. a hog, castrated in maturity ☆**3.** *a*) a man who attends a social gathering unaccompanied by a woman *b*) a social gathering attended by men only —*adj.* ☆for men only [a *stag* dinner] —*vt.* **stagged, stag′ging** [Brit. Slang] to observe or follow secretly or furtively; spy on —*vi.* ☆to go to a party, etc. as a stag (sense 3 *a*) —☆**go stag** [Colloq.] **1.** to go as a stag (sense 3 *a*) **2.** to go unescorted by a man

stag beetle any of a family (Lucanidae) of large beetles: the male has long, branched, antlerlike mandibles

stage (stāj) *n.* [ME. < OFr. *estage* < VL. **staticum* < L. *status,* pp. of *stare,* to STAND] **1.** a platform or dock **2.** a scaffold for workmen **3.** a level, floor, or story **4.** *a*) a platform on which plays, speeches, etc. are presented *b*) any area, as in an arena theater, in which actors perform *c*) the whole working section of a theater, including the acting area, the backstage area, etc. *d*) the theater, drama, or acting as a profession (with *the*) **5.** *a*) the scene of an event or series of events *b*) the center of attention **6.** a place where a stop is made on a journey, esp., formerly, a regular stopping point for a stagecoach **7.** the distance or a part of a route between stopping places; leg of a journey **8.** *clipped form of* STAGECOACH **9.** a shelf

attached to a microscope for holding the object to be viewed **10.** a period, level, or degree in a process of development, growth, or change *[the larval* stage *of an insect]* **11.** any of two or more propulsion units used in sequence as the rocket of a missile, spacecraft, etc.: when no longer operational or useful, it usually separates from the adjacent unit **12.** *Geol.* a subdivision of a series of stratified rocks comprising the rocks laid down during an age in the geologic time scale **13.** *Radio* an element or part in some complex arrangement of parts; specif., any of several tubes with its accessory components in an amplifier —*vt.* **staged, stag′ing 1.** to present, represent, or exhibit on or as on a stage ☆**2.** to plan, arrange, and carry out *[to* stage *a counteroffensive]* —*vi.* **1.** to be suitable for presentation on the stage *[a play that* stages well*]* **2.** to travel by stagecoach —**by easy stages 1.** traveling only a short distance at a time **2.** working or acting unhurriedly, with stops for rest

stage·coach (-kōch′) *n.* a horse-drawn coach that formerly carried passengers, parcels, and mail on scheduled trips over a regular route

stage·craft (-kraft′, -kräft′) *n.* skill in, or the art of, writing or staging plays

stage direction 1. an instruction in the script of a play, directing the movements of the actors, the arrangement of scenery, etc. **2.** the art or practice of directing the production of a play

stage door an outside door leading to the backstage part of a theater, used by actors, production staff, etc.

stage effect an effect or impression created on the stage by lighting, scenery, sound, etc.

stage fright nervousness felt when appearing as a speaker or performer before an audience

stage·hand (-hand′) *n.* a person who helps to set and remove scenery and furniture, operate the curtain, etc. for a performance, as of a stage play

stage-man·age (-man′ij) *vt.* **-aged, -ag·ing** [back-formation < ff.] **1.** to serve as stage manager for **2.** to arrange or display with dramatic effect, esp. as if from behind the scenes

stage manager an assistant to the director of a play, in overall charge backstage during the actual performances

stag·er (-ər) *n.* [STAG(E) + -ER] **1.** a person or animal of much experience; old hand; veteran (usually with *old*) **2.** [Archaic] an actor

stage-struck (-struk′) *adj.* having an intense desire to be associated with the theater, esp. to be an actor or actress

stage whisper 1. a loud whisper by an actor on the stage, heard by the audience but supposed not to be heard by other actors on stage **2.** any similar loud whisper meant to be overheard

stag·y (-ē) *adj.* **stag′i·er, stag′i·est** *same as* STAGY

stag·gard (stag′ərd) *n.* [ME. *stagard:* see STAG & -ARD] a stag, or male red deer, in its fourth year

stag·ger (stag′ər) *vi.* [ME. *stakeren* < ON. *stakra*, to totter, intens. of *staka*, to push (for IE. base see STAKE): akin to & prob. infl. in form by MDu. *staggeren*] **1.** to move unsteadily, as though about to collapse; totter, sway, or reel, as from a blow, fatigue, drunkenness, etc. **2.** to lose determination, strength of purpose, etc.; hesitate; waver —*vt.* **1.** to cause to stagger, as with a blow **2.** to affect strongly with astonishment, horror, grief, etc.; overwhelm **3.** to set, arrange, or incline alternately, as on either side of a line; make zigzag or alternating *[to* stagger *the teeth of a saw]* **4.** to arrange (periods of activity, duties, etc.) so as to eliminate crowding or overconcentration *[to* stagger *employees' vacations]* **5.** *Aeron.* to set in a stagger —*n.* **1.** the act of staggering, or reeling, tottering, etc. **2.** a staggered or zigzag arrangement **3.** *[pl., with sing. v.]* any of several diseases or toxic conditions of horses, cattle, etc., characterized by a loss of coordination, staggering, falling, etc. —**stag′ger·er** *n.*

SYN.—**stagger** implies unsteady movement characterized by a loss of equilibrium and failure to maintain a fixed course *[to* stagger *under a heavy load]*; **reel** suggests a swaying or lurching so as to appear on the verge of falling *[the drunken man* reeled *down the hall]*; **totter** suggests the uncertain, faltering steps of a feeble old person or of an infant learning to walk

☆**stag·ger·bush** (-boosh′) *n.* an E. N. American shrub (*Lyonia mariana*) of the heath family, with white or pinkish flowers, poisonous to livestock

stag·ger·ing (-in) *adj.* **1.** that staggers **2.** that causes one to stagger; astonishing; overwhelming; specif., astonishingly great *[a* staggering *sum]* —**stag′ger·ing·ly** *adv.*

stag·hound (stag′hound′) *n.* any large hound formerly used in hunting stags, boars, etc.

stag·ing (stā′jin) *n.* **1.** a temporary structure used for support; scaffolding **2.** the business of operating stagecoaches **3.** travel by stagecoach **4.** the act or process of presenting a play on the stage

staging area *Mil.* an area where troops are assembled and processed, as for regrouping, transportation, etc.

Stag·i·rite (staj′ə rīt′) *n.* a native or inhabitant of **Sta·gi·ra** (stə jī′ra), city in ancient Macedonia; specif., [the S-] *epithet for* ARISTOTLE

stag·nant (stag′nənt) *adj.* [L. *stagnans,* prp. of *stagnare,* to STAGNATE] **1.** without motion or current; not flowing or moving **2.** foul from lack of movement: said of water, etc. **3.** lacking in activity, interest, etc.; sluggish *[a* stagnant *mind]* —**stag′nan·cy** (-nən sē) *n.* —**stag′nant·ly** *adv.*

stag·nate (-nāt) *vi.* **-nat·ed, -nat·ing** [< L. *stagnatus,* pp. of *stagnare,* to stagnate < *stagnum,* a pool, swamp, standing water < IE. base **stag-,* to trickle, seep, whence Gr. *stazein,* to drip] to be or become stagnant —*vt.* to make stagnant —**stag·na′tion** *n.*

stag·y (stā′jē) *adj.* **stag′i·er, stag′i·est 1.** of or characteristic of the stage; theatrical (usually in an unfavorable sense) **2.** affected; not real *[stagy diction]* —**stag′i·ly** *adv.*

staid (stād) *archaic pt. & pp. of* STAY³ —*adj.* **1.** [Rare] resisting change; fixed; settled **2.** sober; sedate; settled and steady —**staid′ly** *adv.* —**staid′ness** *n.*

stain (stān) *vt.* [ME. *stainen,* aphetic < *desteignen* < OFr. *desteindre,* to discolor, lose color < L. *dis-,* from + *tingere,* to color (see TINGE): sense and form infl. by ON. *steinn,* color, lit., STONE (hence, mineral pigment)] **1.** to spoil the appearance of by patches or streaks of color or dirt; discolor; spot **2.** to bring shame upon (one's character, reputation, etc.); taint; disgrace; dishonor **3.** to change the appearance of (wood, glass, etc.) by applying a stain or pigment **4.** to treat (material for microscopic study) with a coloring matter that facilitates study, as by making transparent parts visible or by producing a different effect upon different structures or tissues —*vi.* to impart or take a color or stain —*n.* **1.** a color, discoloration, streak, or spot resulting from or as from staining **2.** a moral blemish; dishonor; guilt; taint **3.** a substance used to impart color in staining; specif., *a)* a dye or pigment in solution, esp. one that penetrates a wood surface *b)* a dye used to stain material for microscopic study —**stain′a·ble** *adj.* —**stain′er** *n.*

stained glass glass colored in any of various ways, as by fusing metallic oxides into it, by enameling, by burning pigments into its surface, etc., and used as for church windows —**stained′-glass′** *adj.*

stain·less (-lis) *adj.* **1.** without a mark or stain **2.** that resists staining, rusting, etc. **3.** made of stainless steel —*n.* flatware made of stainless steel —**stain′less·ly** *adv.*

stainless steel steel alloyed with chromium, etc., virtually immune to rust and corrosion

stair (ster) *n.* [ME. *steire* < OE. *stæger* < base of *stigan,* to climb: see STILE¹] **1.** [*usually pl.*] a flight of steps; staircase **2.** a single step, usually one of a series leading from one level or floor to another

stair·case (-kās′) *n.* a flight or series of flights of stairs, including a supporting structure and, usually, a handrail or balustrade: also **stair′way′** (-wā′)

stair·head (-hed′) *n.* the head, or top, of a staircase

stair·well (-wel′) *n.* a vertical shaft (in a building) containing a staircase: also **stair well**

staith, staithe (stāth) *n.* [ME. *stathe* < OE. *stæth,* shore, infl. by cognate ON. *stoth,* landing place: for IE. base see STAND] [Brit. Dial.] a stage or wharf equipped to load and unload (coal, etc.) from railroad cars into vessels

stake (stāk) *n.* [ME. < OE. *staca,* akin to Du. *staak:* for IE. base see STICK] **1.** a length of wood or metal pointed at one end for driving into the ground, as for marking a boundary, supporting a plant, etc. **2.** *a)* the post to which a person was tied for execution by burning *b)* execution by burning **3.** a pole or post fitted upright into a socket, as at the edge of a railway flatcar, truck bed, etc., to help hold a load *b) clipped form of* STAKE TRUCK **4.** [*often pl.*] something, esp. money, risked or hazarded, as in a wager, game, or contest **5.** [*often pl.*] a reward given a winner, as in a race; prize **6.** [*pl., with sing. v.*] a race in which a prize is offered **7.** a share or interest, as in property, a person, or a business venture ☆**8.** in the Mormon Church, a district made up of a number of wards ☆**9.** [Colloq.] a grubstake —*vt.* **staked, stak′ing** ☆**1.** *a)* to mark the location or boundaries of with or as with stakes *b)* to establish (a claim) in this way Often with *out* **2.** to support (a plant, etc.) by tying to a stake **3.** to hitch or tether to a stake **4.** [infl. by MDu. *staken,* to fix, place] to risk or hazard; gamble; bet **5.** [Colloq.] to furnish with money or resources ☆**6.** [Colloq.] to grubstake —**at stake** being risked or hazarded; in danger of being lost, injured, etc. —☆**pull up stakes** [Colloq.] to change one's place of residence, business, etc. —**stake out 1.** to station (policemen, detectives, etc.) for surveillance of a suspected criminal **2.** to put (a suspected criminal, a place, etc.) under such surveillance —**stake up** (or **in**) to close up or in with a fence or stakes

☆**stake body** a flat truck body having sockets into which stakes may be fitted, as to support railings

Staked Plain *same as* LLANO ESTACADO

stake·hold·er (-hōl′dər) *n.* one who holds money, etc. bet by others and pays it to the winner

☆**stake·out** (-out′) *n.* **1.** the staking out of policemen, etc. in a surveillance of a suspected criminal **2.** an area staked out with policemen

☆**stake truck** a truck having a stake body

Sta·kha·no·vism (stə khä′nə viz′m) *n.* [after Aleksei *Stakhanov*, Soviet miner whose efforts inspired it in 1935] in the Soviet Union, a system whereby teams of workers seek to increase their production by improving efficiency and, if successful, are rewarded with bonuses and privileges —**Sta·kha′no·vite′** (-vīt′) *adj., n.*

sta·lac·ti·form (stə lak′tə fôrm′) *adj.* having the form of a stalactite

sta·lac·tite (stə lak′tīt; *chiefly Brit.,* stal′ək tīt′) *n.* [ModL. *stalactites* < Gr. *stalaktos,* trickling or dropping < *stalassein,* to let fall drop by drop: see STALE²] an icicle-shaped deposit of carbonate of lime hanging from the roof of a cave, formed by the evaporation of dripping water full of lime —**stal·ac·tit·ic** (stal′ək tit′ik) *adj.*

‡**sta·lag** (shtä′läk; *E.* stal′ag) *n.* [G. < *sta(mm)lag(er)* < *stamm,* a base, lit., stem + *lager,* a camp (cf. STEM¹ & LAIR)] a German prisoner-of-war camp

sta·lag·mite (stə lag′mīt; *chiefly Brit.,* stal′əg mīt′) *n.* [ModL. *stalagmites* < Gr. *stalagmos,* a dropping < *stalassein,* to drop or drip: see STALE²] a cone-shaped deposit of carbonate of lime built up on the floor of a cave by drip, often from a stalactite above: see STALACTITE, illus. —**stal·ag·mit·ic** (stal′əg mit′ik) *adj.*

St. Al·bans (ôl′bənz) city in Hertfordshire, SE England: pop. 51,000

stale¹ (stāl) *adj.* **stal′er, stal′est** [ME., prob. < a LowG. source; akin to WFl. *stel-* in same sense] **1.** having lost freshness; made musty, dry, bad, etc. by having been kept too long; specif., *a)* flat; vapid; tasteless [*stale* beer] *b)* hard and dry: said of bread, etc. *c)* low in oxygen content; stagnant [*stale* air] *d)* in an early stage of decay, as meat or eggs **2.** having lost originality or newness; lacking in interest through familiarity or overuse; hackneyed; trite [a *stale* joke, *stale* gossip] **3.** out of condition, ineffective, enervated, bored, etc. from either too much or too little activity **4.** *Law* having lost legal force or effect through lack of use or action, as a claim or lien —*vt., vi.* **staled, stal′ing** to make or become stale —**stale′ly** *adv.* —**stale′ness** *n.*

stale² (stāl) *vi.* **staled, stal′ing** [ME., akin to MLowG. *stal,* urine < IE. base *(s)tel-,* to let flow, urinate, whence Gr. *stalassein,* to drip, *telma,* a puddle] to urinate: said as of horses and cattle —*n.* urine, as of horses or cattle

stale·mate (stāl′māt′) *n.* [obs. *stale,* stalemate < ME. < OFr. *estal,* a fixed location, safe place < Gmc., as in OHG. *stal* (see STALL¹) + MATE²] **1.** *Chess* any situation in which it is impossible for one of the players to move without placing his king in check: it results in a draw **2.** any unresolved situation in which further action is impossible or useless; deadlock; draw —*vt.* **-mat′ed, -mat′ing** to bring into a stalemate

Sta·lin (stä′lin), **Joseph** (born *Iosif Vissarionovich Dzhugashvili*) 1879–1953; Soviet premier (1941–53); general secretary of the Communist party of the U.S.S.R. (1922–53) —**Sta′lin·ism** *n.* —**Sta′lin·ist** *adj., n.*

Sta·lin·a·bad (stä′li nä bät′) *former name of* DUSHANBE

Sta·lin·grad (stä′lin grät′; *E.* stä′lin grad′) *former name of* VOLGOGRAD

Sta·li·no (stä′li nô′) *former name of* DONETSK

Sta·linsk (stä′linsk) *former name of* NOVOKUZNETSK

stalk¹ (stôk) *vi.* [ME. *stalken* < OE. *stealcian* (in comp.) < *stealc,* high, steep < IE. *stelg-* < base *stel-,* to place, set up, stiff, whence L. *stolidus, locus:* cf. ff. & STALL¹] **1.** *a)* to walk in a stiff, haughty, or grim manner *b)* to advance or spread grimly [plague *stalks* across the land] **2.** to pursue or approach game, an enemy, etc. stealthily, as from cover **3.** [Obs.] to walk or move along stealthily or furtively —*vt.* **1.** to pursue or approach (game, etc.) stealthily **2.** to stalk through [terror *stalked* the streets] —*n.* **1.** a slow, stiff, haughty, or grim stride **2.** the act of stalking game, an enemy, etc. —**stalk′er** *n.*

stalk² (stôk) *n.* [ME. *stalke,* akin to OE. *stela,* a stalk, stem of a plant, akin to G. *stiele,* Gr. *stēlē,* a post: for IE. base see prec.] **1.** any stem or stemlike part, as a slender rod, shaft, or support **2.** *Bot. a)* the main stem or axis of a plant *b)* a lengthened part of a plant on which an organ grows or is supported, as the petiole of a leaf, the peduncle of a flower, etc. **3.** *Zool. a)* a lengthened support for an animal organ *b)* a similar structure supporting a whole animal body, as the peduncle of a goose barnacle —**stalked** *adj.* —**stalk′less** *adj.*

stalk-eyed (-īd′) *adj.* having eyes on short, movable stalks, as crayfish, crabs, etc.

stalk·ing-horse (stôk′iŋ hôrs′) *n.* **1.** a horse, or a figure of a horse, used as cover by a hunter stalking game **2.** anything used to disguise or conceal intentions, schemes, or activities; blind **3.** *Politics* a person whose candidacy is advanced temporarily to conceal the actual choice or to divide the opposition

stalk·y (stôk′ē) *adj.* **stalk′i·er, stalk′i·est 1.** like a stalk; long and slender **2.** having, or consisting mainly of, stalks —**stalk′i·ness** *n.*

stall¹ (stôl) *n.* [ME. *stal* < OE. *steall,* a place, station, stall,

stable, akin to OHG. *stal:* for base see STALK¹] **1.** *a)* formerly, a stable or livestock shed *b)* a compartment for one animal in a stable **2.** any of various compartments, booths, separate sections, etc.; specif., *a)* a booth, table, or counter, as at a market or fair, at which goods are sold *b)* a pew or enclosed seat in the main part of a church or in the choir *c)* [Brit.] a seat near the stage in a theater, esp. one in the front part of the orchestra, separated from adjacent seats by railings or the like *d)* a small, enclosed space, as a compartment in which one showers ☆*e)* any of the spaces marked off, as in a garage, for parking individual automobiles **3.** a protective sheath, as of rubber, for a finger or thumb; cot **4.** the condition of being brought to a stop or standstill, as through some malfunction **5.** *Aeron.* any condition in which there is such a loss of lift and increase in drag that the aircraft tends to drop or go out of control —*vt., vi.* [ME. *stallen* < the *n.* & < OFr. *estaler* < Gmc., as in OHG. *stal*] **1.** to put, keep, or be kept in a stall **2.** to cause to stick fast or to be stuck fast, as in mud **3.** to bring or be brought to a stop or standstill, esp. unintentionally **4.** to stop or cause to stop through some malfunction: said of a motor or engine **5.** *Aeron.* to put or go into a stall

stall² (stôl) *vi.* [< *stall,* a decoy, var. of obs. *stale,* one who lures < Anglo-Fr. *estale* < OFr. *estaler:* see prec., *v.*] to act or speak evasively or hesitantly so as to deceive or delay [to *stall* for time] —*vt.* to put off or delay by stalling (usually *with off*) [to *stall* off creditors] —*n.* [Colloq.] any action, device, etc. used to deceive or delay; evasive trick

stall-feed (-fēd′) *vt.* **-fed′** (-fed′), **-feed′ing** to feed (an animal kept inactive in a stall) for fattening

stal·lion (stal′yən) *n.* [ME. *stalon* < OFr. *estalon* < Gmc. *stal:* see STALL¹] an uncastrated male horse, esp. one used as a stud

stal·wart (stôl′wərt) *adj.* [ME. *stalworthe* < OE. *stælwyrthe,* short for *statholwyrthe,* firm < *stathol,* foundation (see STADDLE) + *wyrthe,* worth: hence, lit., having a firm foundation] **1.** strong and well-built; sturdy; robust **2.** brave; valiant **3.** resolute; firm; unyielding —*n.* **1.** a stalwart person **2.** a person supporting a cause, esp. that of a political party, with firm partisanship —*SYN.* see STRONG —**stal′wart·ly** *adv.* —**stal′wart·ness** *n.*

Stam·boul, Stam·bul (stäm bool′) **1.** *earlier name for* ISTANBUL **2.** the old section of Istanbul

sta·men (stā′mən) *n., pl.* **-mens, stam′i·na** [ModL. < L., a thread, orig., warp (in an upright loom), akin to Gr. *stēmōn* < IE. *stamen-,* a standing < base *sta-,* whence STAND] a pollen-bearing organ in a flower, made up of a slender stalk (*filament*) and a pollen sac (*anther*); microsporophyll of a flowering plant

Stam·ford (stam′fərd) [after *Stamford,* town in Lincolnshire, England] city in SW Conn.: pop. 109,000

stam·i·na¹ (stam′ə nə) *n.* [L., pl. of *stamen:* see STAMEN] resistance to fatigue, illness, hardship, etc.; endurance

stam·i·na² (stam′ə nə) *n. alt. pl.* OF STAMEN

stam·i·nal¹ (stam′ə n′l) *adj.* of or having to do with stamina

stam·i·nal² (stam′ə n′l, stā′ma-) *adj.* of or having to do with a stamen or stamens

stam·i·nate (-nit, -nāt′) *adj.* [ModL. *staminatus* < L., consisting of threads] **1.** bearing stamens but no pistils, as male flowers **2.** having or bearing a stamen or stamens

stam·i·ni- (stam′ə ni) [< L. *stamen* (gen. *staminis*)] a combining form meaning stamen [staminiferous]: also, before a vowel, **stamin-**

stam·i·nif·er·ous (stam′ə nif′ər əs) *adj.* [prec. + -FEROUS] having or bearing a stamen or stamens

stam·i·node (stam′ə nōd′) *n.* [ModL. *staminodium* < *stamen* + -*odium* (see -ODE²)] an abortive or sterile stamen: also **stam′i·no′di·um** (-nō′dē əm), *pl.* **-di·a** (-ə)

stam·i·no·dy (-nō′dē) *n.* [< STAMIN(I)- + Gr. -*ōdia,* a becoming like < -*ōdēs* (see -ODE²)] the change of other organs of a flower into stamens

stam·mel (stam′'l) *n.* [prob. < MFr. *estamel* < OFr. *estame,* woolen thread < L. *stamen:* see STAMEN] **1.** a type of rough woolen cloth used by some medieval ascetics for undergarments **2.** a red color like that usually used in dyeing such cloth

stam·mer (stam′ər) *vt., vi.* [ME. *stameren* < OE. *stamerian,* akin to Du. *stameren,* freq. formation < IE. base *stem-,* to stumble in speech, halt, whence STEM², STUMBLE, G. *stumm,* dumb] to speak or say with involuntary pauses or blocks, often with rapid repetitions of syllables or initial sounds, as temporarily from excitement, embarrassment, etc. or chronically as a result of muscle spasms believed to result from mental conflicts; stutter —*n.* act, instance, or habit of stammering —**stam′mer·er** *n.* —**stam′mer·ing·ly** *adv.*

stamp (stamp) *vt.* [ME. *stampen,* akin to OHG. *stampfon,* OE. *stempan,* to press to pieces < IE. *stembh-,* to crush < base *stebh-,* a post, pole, whence STAFF¹, STEP, STUMP] **1.** to bring (the foot) down forcibly on the ground, a floor, etc. **2.** *a)* to strike down on forcibly with the foot [to *stamp* the floor in anger] *b)* to beat, crush, etc. in a specified way by treading on heavily [to *stamp* the grass down to the earth] *c)* to remove by stamping the foot or feet [to *stamp* the snow from one's boots] *d)* to pulverize (ore, etc.) by grinding or crushing **3.** *a)* to imprint or cut out (a mark, design, lettering, etc.) by bringing a form forcibly against a material [to *stamp* initials in leather] *b)* to cut out, form, or make as by applying a die

to metal (often with *out*) [to *stamp* auto bodies] **4.** to impress, mark, or imprint with some design, characters, etc., as to decorate or to show authenticity, ownership, sanction, or the like **5.** to impress or mark distinctly or indelibly [the incident was *stamped* in her memory] **6.** to put an official seal or a stamp on (a document, letter, etc.) **7.** to characterize or reveal distinctly, as if by imprinting [the courage that *stamped* him as a hero] —*vi.* **1.** to bring the foot down forcibly on the ground **2.** to walk with loud, heavy steps, as in anger, etc. —*n.* **1.** the act of stamping **2.** a machine, tool, etc. used for stamping or crushing ore, etc. **3.** *a)* any tool or implement, as a die, used by being brought forcibly against something to mark or shape it *b)* a mark or form made by such a tool or implement **4.** a mark, seal, impression, etc. used to show officially that a tax has been paid, authority given, etc. **5.** *a)* a small piece of paper, distinctively imprinted on the face and usually gummed on the back, issued by a government for a specified price and required to be affixed to a letter, parcel, document, commodity subject to duty, etc., as evidence that the prescribed fee, as for carrying mail, has been paid *b)* any somewhat similar piece of paper, issued by an organization, business firm, etc. [trading *stamps*] **6.** any characteristic sign or impression; indication [the *stamp* of truth] **7.** character; kind; class; type —**stamp out 1.** to beat, crush, or put out by treading on forcibly [to *stamp out* a fire, a cigarette, etc.] **2.** to crush, suppress, or put down (a revolt, rebellion, etc.)

Stamp Act a law passed by the British Parliament in 1765 to raise revenue, requiring that stamps be used for all legal and commercial documents, newspapers, etc. in the American colonies: it was repealed in March, 1766, because of strong colonial opposition

☆**stam·pede** (stam pēd′) *n.* [AmSp. *estampida* < Sp., a crash, uproar < *estampar*, to stamp < Gmc., as in OHG. *stampfon*: see STAMP] **1.** a sudden, headlong running away of a group of frightened animals, esp. horses or cattle **2.** a confused, headlong rush or flight of a large group of people **3.** any sudden, impulsive, spontaneous mass movement [a *stampede* to support a candidate] —*vi.* **-ped′ed, -ped′ing** to move, or take part, in a stampede —*vt.* to cause to stampede —**stam·ped′er** *n.*

stamp·er (stam′pər) *n.* a person or thing that stamps; specif., *a)* a person who cancels stamps, etc. in a post office *b)* a worker who stamps (something specified) *c)* any of various machines or tools for stamping, as for pulverizing ore

☆**stamp·ing ground** (stam′piŋ) [Colloq.] a regular or favorite gathering place, resort, or haunt

stamp mill a mill or machine for pulverizing ore

stance (stans) *n.* [OFr. *estance* < VL. *stantia* < L. *stans* (gen. *stantis*), prp. of *stare*, to STAND] **1.** the way a person or animal stands; standing posture, with special reference to placement of the feet, as the posture of a golfer, baseball batter, etc. ☆**2.** the attitude adopted in confronting or dealing with a particular situation [a belligerent political *stance*] —*SYN.* see POSTURE

stanch (stônch, stanch, stänch) *vt., vi., adj.* see STAUNCH

stan·chion (stan′chən, -shən) *n.* [ME. *stanchon* < OFr. *estanson, estancon* < *estance*: see STANCE] **1.** an upright bar, beam, or post used as a support ☆**2.** a restraining device fitted loosely around the neck of a cow to confine it to its stall —*vt.* **-chioned, -chion·ing 1.** to provide or support with stanchions ☆**2.** to confine (a cow) with a stanchion

stand (stand) *vi.* **stood, stand′ing** [ME. *standen* < OE. *standan*; akin to MDu. *standen*, Goth. *standan* < IE. base *stā-*, to stand, be placed, whence L. *stare*, to stand, Gr. *histanai*, to set, cause to stand] **1.** *a)* to be or remain in a generally upright position, supported on the feet (or foot) *b)* to be or remain in an upright position, supported on its base, bottom, pedestal, etc.: said of physical objects *c)* to grow upright or erect: said of plants **2.** to rise to an upright position, as from a sitting, lying, or crouching position **3.** *a)* to take, move into, or be in a (specified) upright position [*stand* straight!] *b)* to take, maintain, or be in a (specified) position, attitude, or course, as of support, antagonism, responsibility, sponsorship, etc. [to *stand* opposed to an act] **4.** to have a (specified) height when standing [he *stands* six feet] **5.** to point: said of a dog. *a)* to be placed; be situated *b)* to remain where situated, built, etc. **7.** to gather and remain: said of a liquid [sweat *stood* on his brow] **8.** *a)* to remain unchanged, intact, effective, or valid [the law still *stands*] *b)* to be or remain in a printed or written form **9.** to be in a (specified) condition, relation, or circumstance: used with a phrase, infinitive, or adverb [they *stood* in awe, he *stands* to lose ten dollars] **10.** to be of a (specified) rank, degree, or the like [to *stand* first in one's class] **11.** to maintain one's opinion, viewpoint, adherence, etc.; remain resolute or firm **12.** to make resistance, as to hostile action **13.** *a)* to come to a stop; halt *b)* to be or remain stationary **14.** to show the (specified) relative position of those involved [the score *stands* at 28 to 20] ☆**15.** to be available for breeding: said of a stallion **16.** [Chiefly Brit.] to be a

candidate, as for an office; run **17.** *Naut.* to take or hold a certain course at sea, or go in a certain direction [the ship *stood* to sea] **18.** *Printing* to remain set: said of type —*vt.* **1.** to make stand; set or place upright **2.** to go on enduring; put up with; bear; tolerate [to *stand* pain] **3.** to remain uninjured or unaffected by; withstand [*stood* the trip quite well] **4.** to be subjected to; undergo [to *stand* trial] **5.** to do the duty of [to *stand* watch] **6.** [Colloq.] *a)* to bear the cost of (a dinner, etc.), as when treating *b)* to treat (a person) to food, drink, etc. **7.** *Mil.* to stand in formation at (reveille, retreat, etc.) —*n.* [OE. *stand* < *standan*, to stand] **1.** the act or position of standing (in various senses); esp., a stopping; halt or stop; specif., *a)* a stopping to counterattack, resist, etc., as in a retreat ☆*b)* a halt made by a touring theatrical company to give a performance; also, the place stopped at **2.** the place where a person stands or is supposed to stand; position; station [to take one's *stand* at the rear] **3.** a view, opinion, or position, as on an issue [to make one's *stand* clear] **4.** a structure for a person or persons to stand or sit on; specif., *a)* a raised platform, as for a band or for spectators along a parade route *b)* [often *pl.*] a set of steplike tiers of benches, as for the spectators at a ball game ☆*c)* the place where a witness testifies in a courtroom ☆**5.** a place of business; specif., *a)* a booth, stall, etc. where goods are sold *b)* a parking space along the side of a street, reserved for taxicabs, etc. *c)* a business site or location **6.** a rack, small table, etc. for holding something [a music *stand*] ☆**7.** a standing growth of trees or plants **8.** [Obs. or Dial.] a group, set, etc. —*SYN.* see BEAR[1] —**make a stand 1.** to take a position for defense or opposition **2.** to support a definite position, opinion, etc. **3.** to come to a stop —**stand a chance** to have a chance (of winning, surviving, etc.) —**stand by 1.** to be near and ready to act if or when needed **2.** to aid or support **3.** *a)* to make good (a promise, etc.) *b)* to maintain (a policy) **4.** to be near or present, esp. in a passive manner or as a mere onlooker **5.** *Radio & TV* to remain tuned in, as for continuance of a program, or to remain ready to transmit without actually doing so —**stand down** *Law* to leave the witness stand, as after testifying —**stand for 1.** to be a symbol for or sign of; represent; mean ☆**2.** [Colloq.] to put up with; endure; tolerate —**stand in 1.** [Colloq.] to be on good terms; be friendly (usually followed by *with*) **2.** to take a share or part in —**stand in for** to substitute for —**stand off 1.** to keep at a distance **2.** to fail or refuse to agree or comply ☆**3.** to put off, stave off, or evade (a creditor or assailant) **4.** *Naut.* to take or hold a course away from shore —**stand on 1.** to be based or founded upon; depend on **2.** to insist upon; demand due observance of (ceremony, one's dignity or rights, etc.) **3.** *Naut.* to hold the same course or tack —**stand one's ground** to maintain one's position, as against attack —**stand out 1.** to stick out; project **2.** to show up clearly; be distinct in appearance **3.** to be prominent, notable, or outstanding; have distinction **4.** to refuse to give in; be firm in resistance **5.** *Naut.* to take or hold a course away from shore —**stand over 1.** to hover over (someone) **2.** to postpone or be postponed; hold over —**stand up 1.** to rise to or be in a standing position **2.** to prove valid, satisfactory, durable, etc. ☆**3.** [Slang] to fail to keep an engagement with —**stand up for** to take the side of; defend; support —**stand up to** to confront fearlessly; refuse to be cowed or intimidated by —**stand up with** to act as a wedding attendant to —☆**take the stand** to sit (or stand) in the designated place in a courtroom and give testimony —**stand′er** *n.*

stand·ard (stan′dərd) *n.* [ME. < OFr. *estendard* < Frank. *standord*, place of formation < Gmc. *standan*, to STAND + *ort*, a place, orig., a point, akin to OE. *ord* (see ODD): hence, orig., a standing place] **1.** any figure or object, esp. a flag or banner, used as an emblem or symbol of a leader, people, military unit, etc.; specif., *a)* *Heraldry* a long, tapering flag used as an ensign, as by a king *b)* *Mil.* the colors of a cavalry unit **2.** something established for use as a rule or basis of comparison in measuring or judging capacity, quantity, content, extent, value, quality, etc. [*standards* of weight and measure] **3.** *a)* the proportion of pure gold or silver and base metal prescribed for use in coinage *b)* the basis for the measure of value in a given monetary system: see GOLD STANDARD, SILVER STANDARD **4.** the type, model, or example commonly or generally accepted or adhered to; criterion set for usages or practices [moral *standards*] **5.** a level of excellence, attainment, etc. regarded as a measure of adequacy **6.** any upright object used as a support, often a part of the thing it supports; supporting piece; base; stand **7.** a grade of classification, as in elementary schools in England **8.** a piece of popular music that continues to be included in the repertoire of many singers, bands, etc. through the years **9.** *Bot. a)* the large, upper petal of a butterfly-shaped flower; vexillum *b)* any of the three erect petals in the flower of an iris **10.** *Horticulture a)* a tree or shrub with a tall, erect stem, that stands alone without support *b)* a plant grafted on a single erect stem to grow in tree form —*adj.* **1.** used as, or meeting the requirements of,

a standard, rule, model, etc. **2.** generally accepted as reliable or authoritative [*standard* reference books] **3.** conforming to what is usual; regular or typical; not special or extra; ordinary [*standard* procedure] **4.** of or in accord with a level of linguistic usage that excludes locutions, constructions, pronunciations, etc. considered too informal, vulgar, provincial, mistaken, or otherwise likely to detract from the dignity or prestige of the user
SYN.—**standard** applies to some measure, principle, model, etc. with which things of the same class are compared in order to determine their quantity, value, quality, etc. [*standards* of purity for drugs]; **criterion** applies to a test or rule for measuring the excellence, fitness, or correctness of something [mere memory is no accurate *criterion* of intelligence]; **gauge** literally applies to a standard of measurement [a wire *gauge*], but figuratively it is equivalent to **criterion** [sales are an accurate *gauge* of a book's popularity]; **yardstick** refers to a test or criterion for measuring genuineness or value [time is the only true *yardstick* of a book's merit] See also MODEL

stand·ard-bear·er (-ber′ər) *n.* **1.** the man assigned to carry the standard, or flag, of a group, esp. of a military organization **2.** the leader or chief representative of a movement, political party, etc.

☆**stand·ard·bred** (-bred′) *n.* [*often* S-] any horse of an American breed developed for trotting or pacing, esp. in harness racing

standard deviation *Statistics* the square root of the arithmetic average of the squares of the deviations from the mean in a frequency distribution

standard error *Statistics* a measure of the variance to be expected in making statistical estimates of an unknown parameter, normal in form and having its own mean and standard deviation: it is equal to the standard deviation of the original frequency distribution divided by the square root of the sample size

standard gauge 1. a width of 4 feet, 8 1/2 inches between the rails of a railroad track, established as standard **2.** a railroad having such a gauge **3.** a locomotive or car for tracks of such a gauge —**stand′ard-gauge′** *adj.*

stand·ard·ize (stan′dər dīz′) *vt.* **-ized′, -iz′ing 1.** to make standard or uniform; cause to be without variations or irregularities **2.** to compare with or test by a standard —**stand′ard·i·za′tion** *n.* —**stand′ard·iz′er** *n.*

standard of living a level of subsistence, as of a nation, social class, or person, with reference to the adequacy of necessities and comforts in daily life

☆**standard time** the official civil time for any given region; mean solar time, determined by distance east or west of Greenwich, England: the earth is divided into twenty-four time zones extending from pole to pole, four of them (*Eastern, Central, Mountain,* and *Pacific*) falling within the conterminous U.S. and using the civil times of the 75th, 90th, 105th, and 120th meridians, respectively; throughout the world, adjacent time zones are one hour (15°) apart, but some slight variations occur in legal time, as when a country extending across more than one time zone keeps a uniform legal time nationally: see TIME, chart

stand·by (stand′bī′) *n., pl.* **-bys′ 1.** a person or thing that can always be depended on, is always effective, etc. **2.** a person or thing ready to serve or be put into service on an emergency basis or as a substitute **3.** a person waiting to board an airplane, etc. if space becomes available, as through a cancellation —*adj.* of, for, or functioning as a standby —**on standby** ready or waiting as a standby

☆**stand·ee** (stan dē′) *n.* [Colloq.] a person who stands, usually because there are no vacant seats, as on a bus

stand·fast (stand′fast′, -fäst′) *n.* a firm, fixed position

☆**stand-in** (stand′in′) *n.* **1.** a person who serves as a substitute for a motion-picture or television actor or actress as while lights and cameras are being adjusted **2.** any substitute for another **3.** [Slang] a position of favor and influence, as with an important person

stand·ing (stan′diŋ) *n.* **1.** the act, state, or position of a person or thing that stands **2.** a place to stand; standing room **3.** *a)* status, position, rank, or reputation [in good *standing*] *b)* [*pl.*] a list showing rank or order, as in achievement, resources, etc. [team *standings* in a league] **4.** duration or length of service, existence, membership, etc. [a record of long *standing*] —*adj.* **1.** that stands; upright or erect [a *standing* position] **2.** done or made in or from a standing position [a *standing* jump] **3.** not flowing; stagnant, as water **4.** going on regularly without change; lasting; permanent [a *standing* order] **5.** stationary; not movable **6.** not in use; idle, as a machine

standing army an army maintained on a permanent basis, in peacetime as well as in time of war

standing order 1. an order remaining in effect indefinitely until canceled or modified **2.** [*pl.*] *Parliamentary Procedure* the rules for procedure which continue in force through all sessions until changed or repealed

standing rigging the heavy ropes and stays that support the masts and spars of a ship

standing room room in which to stand, esp. when there are no vacant seats, as in a theater

standing wave an oscillatory motion with a definite wavelength, frequency, and amplitude and having stationary, regularly spaced points where there is no motion: all the movement of the wave is contained between these nodes, thus providing for no net transport of energy

stand·ish (stan′dish) *n.* [? < STAND + DISH] [Archaic] a stand for writing materials; inkstand

Stan·dish (stan′dish), **Miles** (or **Myles**) 1584?–1656; Eng. colonist; military leader of Plymouth Colony

stand·off (stand′ôf′) *n.* **1.** a standing off or being stood off **2.** a counterbalancing or equalizing effect **3.** a tie or draw in a game or contest —*adj.* **1.** that stands off **2.** *same as* STANDOFFISH

stand·off·ish (stand′ôf′ish) *adj.* reserved and cool; aloof —**stand′off′ish·ly** *adv.* —**stand′off′ish·ness** *n.*

stand oil linseed oil thickened by heat treatment, as for use in paint

☆**stand·out** (stand′out′) *n.* [Colloq.] a person or thing conspicuously superior or notable in performance, quality, etc. —*adj.* [Colloq.] outstanding

☆**stand·pat** (-pat′) *adj.* [Colloq.] of or characterized by a tendency to stand pat, or resist change; conservative —**stand′pat′ter** *n.* —**stand′pat′tism** *n.*

stand·pipe (-pīp′) *n.* a large vertical pipe or cylindrical tank for storing water; esp., such a pipe or tank used in a water-supply system for a town, etc.

stand·point (-point′) *n.* [after G. *standpunkt*] **1.** a position from which something is or may be viewed **2.** the mental position from which things are judged; point of view

stand·still (-stil′) *n.* a stop, halt, or cessation

stand-up (-up′) *adj.* **1.** standing upright or erect **2.** done, taken, etc. in a standing position [a *stand-up* lunch] **3.** high, stiff, and without folds: said of a collar ☆**4.** designating or of a comedian who delivers monologues, as in nightclubs

stane (stān) *n., adj., vt. Scot. & Brit. dial. var.* of STONE

☆**Stan·ford-Bi·net test** (stan′fərd bi nā′) a revision of the Binet-Simon test: developed at Stanford University, it covers a wider range and offers more tests than the original scale: also called **Stanford revision**

stang¹ (staŋ) *archaic pt. & pp.* of STING

stang² (staŋ) *n., vi., vt.* [< ME. *stangen* < ON. *stanga*, to prick, goad: for IE. base see STING] *Scot. & Brit. dial. var.* of STING

stan·hope (stan′hōp, -əp) *n.* [after Fitzroy *Stanhope* (1787–1864), Eng. clergyman for whom the first was built] a light, open, horse-drawn carriage with two or four wheels and usually one seat

Stan·hope (stan′əp), **Philip Dor·mer** (dôr′mər) *see* 4th Earl of CHESTERFIELD

Stan·i·slav·sky (stan′i släf′skē, stän′-), **Kon·stan·tin** (kän′stən tēn′) (born *Konstantin Sergeyevich Alekseyev*) 1863–1938; Russ. actor, director, & teacher of acting

stank (staŋk) *alt. pt.* of STINK

Stan·ley (stan′lē) [< the surname *Stanley* < the place name *Stanley* < OE. *stan leah*, stone lea] **1.** a masculine name **2.** Sir **Henry Morton,** (born *John Rowlands*) 1841–1904; Brit. journalist & explorer in Africa

Stanley, Mount mountain in EC Africa, highest peak of the Ruwenzori group: 16,795 ft.

Stanley Falls series of seven cataracts of the upper Congo River, just south of Kisangani

Stanley Pool broad, lakelike expansion of the Congo River between the two Congo republics: c.320 sq. mi.

Stan·ley·ville (stan′lē vil′) *former name of* KISANGANI

stan·na·ry (stan′ər ē) *n., pl.* **-ries** [ML. *stannaria* < LL. *stannum,* tin] a region of tin mines and tinworks; specif., [*usually pl.*] such a region in Devon and Cornwall, England

stan·nic (-ik) *adj.* [< LL. *stannum,* tin + -IC] of or containing tin, specif. with a valence of four

stan·nite (-īt) *n.* [< LL. *stannum,* tin + -ITE¹] a gray or black tetragonal mineral, Cu₂FeSnS₄, with metallic luster, a native sulfide of tin, copper, and iron

stan·nous (-əs) *adj.* [< LL. *stannum,* tin + -OUS] of or containing tin, specif. with a valence of two

Stan·ton (stan′t'n) **1. Edwin McMas·ters** (mək mas′tərz), 1814–69; U.S. statesman; secretary of war (1862–68) **2. Elizabeth Ca·dy** (kā′dē), 1815–1902; U.S. reformer & suffragist leader

stan·za (stan′zə) *n.* [It., lit., stopping place, room < VL. *stantia:* see STANCE] a group of lines of verse forming one of the divisions of a poem or song: it is usually made up of four or more lines and typically has a regular pattern in the number of lines and the arrangement of meter and rhyme —**stan·za·ic** (-zā′ik) *adj.*

sta·pe·di·al (stə pē′dē əl) *adj.* of the stapes

sta·pe·li·a (stə pē′lē ə, -pēl′yə) *n.* [ModL., name of the genus, after Jan Bode van *Stapel* (died 1636), Du. botanist and physician] any of a genus (*Stapelia*) of cactuslike, African plants of the milkweed family, with large, star-shaped, bad-smelling, yellowish or purple flowers

sta·pes (stā′pēz) *n., pl.* **sta′pes, sta·pe·des** (stə pē′dēz, stā′pə dēz′) [ModL. < ML., a stirrup, prob. < Gmc., as in MDu. *stap,* a STEP, Langobardic *staffa,* a step, stirrup] *Anat.* a small, stirrup-shaped bone, the innermost of a chain of three bones in the middle ear of mammals; stirrup

staph (staf) *n. clipped form of* STAPHYLOCOCCUS

staph·y·lo- (staf′ə lō, -lə) [< Gr. *staphylē,* bunch of grapes: for IE. base see STAMP] *a combining form meaning:* **1.** uvula [*staphylorrhaphy*] **2.** grapelike [*staphylococcus*] Also, before a vowel, **staphyl-**

staph·y·lo·coc·cus (staf′ə lō käk′əs) *n., pl.* **-coc′ci** (-käk′sī) [ModL.: see prec. & -COCCUS] any of a genus (*Staphylococcus*) of spherical, Gram-positive bacteria that generally

occur in irregular clusters or short chains: the pathogenic species (esp. *Staphylococcus aureus*) are the cause of pus formation in boils, abscesses, etc. —**staph′y·lo·coc′cal** (-kăk′ʒl), **staph′y·lo·coc′cic** (-kăk′sik) *adj.*

staph·y·lo·plas·ty (staf′ʒ lō plas′tē) *n.* [STAPHYLO- + -PLASTY] the use of plastic surgery to repair defects of the soft palate —**staph′y·lo·plas′tic** *adj.*

staph·y·lor·rha·phy (staf′ʒ lôr′ʒ fē) *n.*, *pl.* **-phies** [< STAPHYLO- + Gr. *rhaphē*, a sewing, suture] the operation of uniting a cleft palate by plastic surgery

sta·ple¹ (stā′p'l) *n.* [ME. *stapel* < OFr. *estaple* < MDu. *stapel*, mart, emporium, post, orig. support, akin to ff.] **1.** the chief commodity, or any of the most important commodities, made, grown, or sold in a particular place, region, country, etc. **2.** a chief item, part, material, or element in anything **3.** raw material **4.** any chief item of trade, regularly stocked and in constant demand [flour, sugar, and salt are *staples*] **5.** the fiber of cotton, wool, flax, etc., with reference to length and fineness **6.** [Now Rare] a principal market, trading center, etc. —*adj.* **1.** regularly found on the market or in stock as a result of a constant demand **2.** produced, consumed, or exported regularly and in quantity **3.** most important; leading; principal [*staple* industries] —*vt.* **-pled, -pling** to sort (wool, cotton, etc.) according to the nature of its staple

sta·ple² (stā′p'l) *n.* [ME. *stapel* < OE. *stapol*, a post, pillar, akin to G. *stapel*, stake, beam: for IE. base see STEP] **1.** a U-shaped piece of metal with sharp-pointed ends, driven into a surface to keep a hook, hasp, wire, etc. firmly in place **2.** a similar piece of thin wire driven through papers and clinched over as a binding —*vt.* **-pled, -pling** to fasten or bind with a staple or staples

sta·pler¹ (stā′plər) *n.* **1.** a person who deals in staple goods **2.** a person who staples (wool, etc.)

sta·pler² (stā′plər) *n.* any of various devices or machines for driving staples through paper, etc., as for binding pamphlets; also, a heavier device (also called **staple gun**) for stapling insulation, upholstery fabric, etc. in place

star (stär) *n.* [ME. *sterre* < OE. *steorra*, akin to Du. *ster* < IE. base **ster-*, a star, whence Gr. *astēr*, L. *stella* (dim. < **ster-ela*), star] **1.** any of the luminous or self-luminous heavenly bodies seen as points of light in the night sky; specif., *Astron.* any self-luminous, gaseous, spheroidal heavenly body, as the sun, seen (except for the sun) as a fixed point of light **2.** a conventionalized flat figure having (usually five or six) symmetrical projecting points, regarded as a representation of a star of the sky **3.** any mark, shape, emblem, or the like resembling such a figure, often used as an award, symbol of rank or authority, etc. **4.** *same as* ASTERISK **5.** *a*) *Astrol.* a planet, zodiacal constellation, etc. regarded as influencing human fate or destiny *b*) [*often pl.*] fate; destiny; fortune **6.** a person who excels or performs brilliantly in a given activity, esp. a sport **7.** a prominent actor or actress, esp. one playing a leading role and having special billing in a given production —*vt.* **starred, star′ring 1.** to mark or set with stars as a decoration **2.** to mark with one or more stars as a grade of quality **3.** to mark with an asterisk **4.** to present or feature (an actor or actress) in a leading role —*vi.* **1.** to perform brilliantly; excel **2.** to perform as a star, as in a theatrical production —*adj.* **1.** having exceptional skill and talent; outstanding; excelling others; leading [a *star* performer] **2.** of a star or stars —**see stars** [Colloq.] to experience the sensation of lights brightly flashing before the eyes, as from a blow on the head —**thank one's (lucky) stars** to be thankful for what appears to be good luck

star apple 1. a tropical American evergreen tree (*Chrysophyllum cainito*) of the sapodilla family, with shiny leaves, whitish flowers, and applelike fruit showing a starlike figure inside when cut across **2.** its fruit

Sta·ra Za·go·ra (stä′rä zä gô′rä) city in C Bulgaria: pop. 89,000

star·board (stär′bərd, -bôrd′) *n.* [ME. *sterbord* < OE. *steorbord* < *steoran*, to STEER¹ (the old rudder being a large oar used on the right side of the ship) + *bord*: see BOARD] the right-hand side of a ship or airplane as one faces forward, toward the bow: opposed to PORT⁴, LARBOARD —*adj.* of or on the starboard —*vt.*, *vi.* to move or turn (the helm) to the right

starch (stärch) *n.* [ME. *starche* < *sterchen*, to stiffen < OE. **stercan* < *stearc*, rigid, stiff, akin to G. *stark*, strong: see STARK] **1.** a white, tasteless, odorless food substance found in potatoes, rice, corn, wheat, cassava, and many other vegetable foods: it is a granular solid, chemically a complex carbohydrate, ($C_6H_{10}O_5$)n, and is used in adhesives, sizes, foods, cosmetics, medicine, etc. **2.** a powdered form of this, used in laundering for stiffening cloth fabrics, etc. **3.** [*pl.*] starchy foods **4.** formal, unbending manner or behavior; stiffness **5.** [Colloq.] energy; vigor —*vt.* to stiffen with or as if with starch —**starch′less** *adj.*

Star Chamber [ME., earlier *Sterred Chambre*: said to be so called because the roof was ornamented with stars] **1.** a royal English court or tribunal abolished in 1641, notorious for its secret sessions without jury, and for its harsh and arbitrary judgments and its use of torture to

force confessions **2.** [*also* **s- c-**] any similar tribunal or inquisitorial body

starch·y (stär′chē) *adj.* **starch′i·er, starch′i·est 1.** of, containing, or like starch **2.** stiffened with starch **3.** stiff; formal; unbending —**starch′i·ly** *adv.* —**starch′i·ness** *n.*

star-crossed (stär′krôst′) *adj.* [see STAR (sense 5)] destined to an unhappy fate; sure to end up in misfortune; unlucky

star·dom (-dəm) *n.* **1.** the status of a star (senses 6 & 7) **2.** stars of motion pictures, etc., collectively

star·dust (-dust′) *n.* **1.** a cluster of stars too distant to be seen separately with the naked eye **2.** [Colloq.] an enchanting, dreamlike state or mood; starry-eyed quality

stare (ster) *vi.* **stared, star′ing** [ME. *staren* < OE. *starian*, akin to ON. *stara* < Gmc. **stara-*, having fixed eyes, rigid < IE. base **(s)ter-*, rigid, stiff, whence STARK, Gr. *strēnēs*, hard] **1.** to gaze or look steadily and intently with eyes wide open, as in fear, admiration, wonder, etc. **2.** [Now Rare] *a*) to stand out conspicuously [*staring* bones] *b*) to stand on end, as hair —*vt.* **1.** to look fixedly at [to *stare* a person up and down] **2.** to affect in a given way by staring [to *stare* someone into confusion] —*n.* the act of staring; steady, intent look or gaze —*SYN.* see LOOK —**stare down** to stare back at (another) until he turns his gaze away —**stare one in the face 1.** to look at one steadily and intently **2.** to be imminent, pressing, or inescapable —**stare out of countenance** to stare at (another) until he becomes annoyed, embarrassed, etc. —**star′er** *n.*

‡**sta·re de·ci·sis** (stā′rē di sī′sis) [L., lit., to stand by things decided] a policy of law that requires courts to abide by laws and precedents previously laid down as applicable to a similar set of facts

star·fish (stär′fish′) *n.*, *pl.* **-fish′, -fish′es:** see FISH² any of a class (Asteroidea) of echinoderms with a hard, spiny skeleton and five or more arms or rays arranged like the points of a star; sea star; asteroid

star·flow·er (-flou′ər) *n.* **1.** any of a genus (*Trientalis*) of small woodland plants of the primrose family, with white or pink, five-petaled, star-shaped flowers **2.** any of various other plants with star-shaped flowers, as the star-of-Bethlehem

star·gaze (-gāz′) *vi.* **-gazed′, -gaz′ing** [back-formation < ff.] **1.** to gaze at the stars **2.** to indulge in dreamy, fanciful or visionary musing; daydream

star·gaz·er (-gā′zər) *n.* **1.** a person who stargazes, as an astrologer or astronomer **2.** any of several tropical marine fishes (family Uranoscopidae) having eyes at the top of the head

star grass any of a number of grasslike plants with star-shaped flowers, including a genus (*Hypoxis*) of the amaryllis family and a genus (*Aletris*) of the lily family

STARFISH
(A, disc; B, madreporite; C, spines; D, anus)

stark (stärk) *adj.* [ME. *starc* < OE. *stearc:* for base see STARE] **1.** *a*) stiff or rigid, as a corpse *b*) rigorous; harsh; severe [*stark* discipline] **2.** sharply outlined or prominent [one *stark* tree] **3.** bleak; desolate; barren [*stark* wasteland] **4.** *a*) emptied; stripped [*stark* shelves] *b*) totally naked; bare **5.** grimly blunt; unsoftened, unembellished, etc. [*stark* realism] **6.** sheer; utter; downright; unrelieved [*stark* terror] **7.** [Archaic] strong; powerful —*adv.* in a stark manner; esp., utterly; wholly [*stark* mad] —**stark′ly** *adv.* —**stark′ness** *n.*

stark-nak·ed (stärk′nā′kid) *adj.* [altered (after STARK) < ME. *stertnaked*, lit., tail-naked < *stert-* < OE. *steort*, tail, rump < IE. base **(s)ter-*, stiff, rigid, whence STARE] absolutely naked

star·less (stär′lis) *adj.* **1.** without stars **2.** with no stars visible [a *starless* sky]

star·let (-lit) *n.* **1.** a small star ☆**2.** a young actress being promoted as a possible future star

star·light (-līt′) *n.* light given by the stars —*adj.* **1.** of starlight **2.** lighted by the stars; starlit

star·like (-līk′) *adj.* **1.** like a star in brilliance **2.** star-shaped; having radial points

star·ling (stär′liŋ) *n.* [ME. < OE. *stærlinc*, dim. of *stær*, starling < IE. **stor(n)os*, starling, bird with similar cry, whence L. *sturnus*] any of a family (Sturnidae) of dark-colored, old-world, passerine birds with a short tail, long wings, and a sharp, pointed bill; esp., the **common starling** (*Sturnus vulgaris*) with iridescent plumage, introduced into the U.S. where it is now often a pest

star·lit (stär′lit′) *adj.* lighted by the stars

☆**star-nosed mole** (-nōzd′) a brownish-black, long-tailed, N. American mole (*Condylura cristata*) having a ring of fleshy tentacles around its nose

star-of-Beth·le·hem (-əv beth′lə hem′, -lē əm) *n.*, *pl.* **stars′-of-Beth′le·hem′** a bulbous plant (*Ornithogalum umbellatum*) of the lily family, with white, star-shaped flowers and long, narrow leaves

star of Bethlehem *Bible* the bright star over Bethlehem at the birth of Jesus, guiding the Magi: Matt. 2:1–10

Star of David [transl. < Heb. *māgēn dāvīd*, lit., shield of David] a six-pointed star formed of two, often interlaced, equilateral triangles: a symbol of Judaism and now of the Republic of Israel: as a mystic symbol in the Middle Ages, called *Solomon's Seal*

starred (stärd) *adj.* **1.** marked or decorated with or as with a star or stars **2.** thought, as in astrology, to be influenced by the stars [ill-*starred*] **3.** presented as a star, or leading performer

☆**star route** [such routes are marked with a star, or asterisk, in postal records] a route between postal stations, specif. between one city or town and another over which mail is transported in bulk by a private carrier under contract

STAR OF DAVID

star·ry (stär′ē) *adj.* **-ri·er, -ri·est 1.** set or marked with stars **2.** shining like stars; bright **3.** shaped like a star **4.** lighted by or full of stars **5.** of or coming from the stars **6.** consisting of, or having the nature of, stars —**star′ri·ness** *n.*

☆**star·ry-eyed** (-īd′) *adj.* with the eyes sparkling in a glow of wonder, romance, visionary dreams, etc.

☆**Stars and Bars** the original flag (1861) of the American Confederacy, with a white horizontal bar between two parallel red ones and at the upper left, on a blue field, a circle of seven white stars, one for each seceded State

☆**Stars and Stripes** the flag of the United States, with seven horizontal red stripes and six white ones, the colors alternating, and in the upper left corner a blue field with white stars (now 50), one for each State

star sapphire a sapphire cut with a convex surface that produces a star-shaped reflection of light in it

star shell *Mil.* a shell timed to burst in midair in a shower of bright particles that light up the surrounding terrain

star-span·gled (stär′spaŋ′g'ld) *adj.* studded or spangled with stars

☆**Star-Spangled Banner 1.** the United States flag **2.** the United States national anthem: the words were written by Francis Scott Key during the War of 1812

start (stärt) *vi.* [ME. *sterten* < OE. *styrtan* & cognate ON. *sterta*, akin to G. *stürzen*, to overthrow < IE. **sterd-* < base **(s)ter-*, stiff, walk stiffly, whence L. *torpere*, to be stiff: cf. STARE, STARVE] **1.** to make a sudden, involuntary or unexpected movement, as when surprised; jump, leap, jerk, etc. in a startled way **2.** to be displaced; become loose, warped, etc. **3.** to stick out or seem to stick out [eyes *starting* in fear] **4.** *a)* to begin to do something or go somewhere; go into action or motion *b)* to make or have a beginning; commence **5.** to be among the beginning entrants, as in a race; be a starter **6.** to spring into being, activity, view, or the like —*vt.* **1.** to cause to jump or move suddenly; rouse or flush (game) **2.** to displace, loosen, warp, etc. [the collision *started* a seam] **3.** *a)* to enter upon; begin to perform, play, do, etc. *b)* to cause or enable to begin; set into motion, action, or operation **4.** to introduce (a subject, topic, or discussion) **5.** to open and make the contents flow from (a receptacle); tap **6.** *a)* to give the starting signal for (a race) or to (the contestants in a race) *b)* to cause to be an entrant in a race, etc. **7.** [Archaic or Dial.] to cause to start, or move involuntarily; startle —*n.* **1.** a sudden, brief shock or fright; startled reaction **2.** a sudden, startled movement; jump, leap, jerk, etc. **3.** [*pl.*] sudden, usually brief bursts of activity: usually in the phrase *by fits and starts* **4.** *a)* a part that is loosened, warped, etc. *b)* a break or gap resulting from this **5.** a starting, or beginning; a getting into action or motion; commencement; specif., the fact of being part of the team that starts a game [a pitcher with 30 *starts* for the season] **6.** *a)* a place where, or a time when, a beginning is made, as in a race; starting point *b)* a lead or other advantage, as at the beginning of a race or contest *c)* a signal to begin, as in a race **7.** an opportunity of beginning or entering upon a career, etc. **8.** [Archaic] an outburst or fit, as of emotion, or a sally, as of wit —*SYN.* see BEGIN —☆**start in** to begin a task, activity, etc. —**start out** (or **off**) **1.** to start a journey **2.** to make a start on some course of action or procedure —**start up 1.** to rise up or stand suddenly, as in fright **2.** to come into being suddenly; spring up **3.** to cause (a motor, etc.) to begin running

start·er (-ər) *n.* a person or thing that starts; specif., *a)* the first in a series *b)* a person or animal that starts in a race or game *c)* a person who gives the signal to start, as in a race *d)* a person who supervises the departure of commercial trucks, buses, etc. *e)* any of various devices for starting an internal-combustion engine; specif., *same as* SELF-STARTER *f)* a device within a fluorescent lamp for initiating high voltage across the electrodes *g)* a pure culture used to start fermentation of cream, etc.

star thistle any of several European plants (genus *Centaurea*) of the composite family; esp., an annual weed (*Centaurea calcitrapa*) with spiny involucres and purple, rayless flower heads; also, a yellow-flowered species (*Centaurea solstitialis*) of this plant

starting gate a movable set of stalls with gates that open simultaneously at the start of a horse race

star·tle (stärt′'l) *vt.* **-tled, -tling** [ME. *stertlen*, to rush, stumble along, freq. of *sterten*: see START] to surprise,

frighten, or alarm suddenly or unexpectedly; esp., to cause to start, or move involuntarily, as from sudden fright —*vi.* to be startled —*n.* a start, or shock, as of surprise or fright —*SYN.* see SHOCK[1] —**star′tler** *n.*

star·tling (stärt′liŋ) *adj.* causing a shock of fright or surprise —**star′tling·ly** *adv.*

star·va·tion (stär vā′shən) *n.* **1.** the act of starving **2.** the state of being starved —*adj.* likely to cause starving [a *starvation* diet]

starve (stärv) *vi.* **starved, starv′ing** [ME. *sterven* < OE. *steorfan*, to die, perish, akin to G. *sterben*: for IE. base see START] **1.** *a)* to die from lack of food *b)* to suffer or become weak from hunger *c)* [Colloq.] to be ravenously hungry **2.** to suffer great need (with *for*) [*starving* for affection] **3.** [Obs. or Dial.] to suffer and die slowly from any cause, esp. from extreme cold —*vt.* **1.** to cause to starve by depriving of food **2.** to force by starvation [to *starve* an enemy into submission] **3.** to cause to suffer from a lack or need of something specified **4.** [Obs. or Dial.] to cause to die from extreme cold —*SYN.* see HUNGRY

starve·ling (-liŋ) *n.* [STARVE + -LING[1]] a person or animal that is thin or weak from lack of food —*adj.* **1.** starving; weak and hungry **2.** suffering, showing, or caused by extreme deprivation; impoverished

☆**stash** (stash) *vt., vi.* [prob. a blend of STORE & CACHE] [Colloq.] to put or hide away (money, valuables, etc.) in a secret or safe place, as for future use —*n.* [Slang] **1.** a place for hiding things **2.** something hidden away

sta·sis (stā′sis, stas′is) *n., pl.* **-ses** (-sēz) [ModL. < Gr. *stasis*, a standing < *histanai*, to STAND] **1.** *a)* a stoppage of the flow of some fluid in the body, as of blood *b)* reduced peristalsis of the intestines resulting in the retention of feces **2.** a state of equilibrium, balance, or stagnancy

-stat (stat) [ModL. *-stata* < Gr. *-statēs*, akin to prec.] a combining form meaning stationary, making stationary [gyrostat, thermostat]

stat. 1. [L. *statim*] *Pharmacy* at once **2.** statuary **3.** statue **4.** statute(s)

state (stāt) *n.* [ME. < OFr. & L.: OFr. *estat* < L. *status*, state, position, standing < pp. of *stare*, to STAND] **1.** a set of circumstances or attributes characterizing a person or thing at a given time; way or form of being; condition [a *state* of poverty] **2.** a particular mental or emotional condition [a *state* of bliss] **3.** condition as regards physical structure, constitution, internal form, stage or phase of existence, etc. [liquid *state*] **4.** [Now Rare] *a)* condition or position in life; social status, rank, or degree *b)* high rank or position *c)* the style of living characteristic of people having high rank and wealth; rich, imposing, ceremonious display [drove up in *state*] **5.** [*sometimes* S-] [*pl.*] legislative bodies in any of several countries; estates **6.** [*sometimes* S-] *a)* the power or authority represented by a body of people politically organized under one government, esp. an independent government, within a territory or territories having definite boundaries *b)* such a body of people; body politic ☆**7.** [*usually* S-] any of the territorial and political units that together constitute a federal government, as in the U.S. ☆**8.** the territory of a state (senses 6b & 7) **9.** the political organization constituting the basis of civil government [church and *state*] **10.** the sphere of highest governmental authority and administration [matters of *state*] —*adj.* **1.** of, for, or characteristic of occasions of great ceremony; formal; ceremonial **2.** [*sometimes* S-] of or controlled, maintained, etc. by the government or a state —*vt.* **stat′ed, stat′ing 1.** to fix or establish by specifying [at the *stated* hour] **2.** *a)* to set forth in words, esp. in a specific, definite, or formal way [to *state* one's objectives] *b)* to express or present in a nonverbal way [to *state* a musical theme in the first three measures] —**in** (or **into**) **a state** [Colloq.] in (or into) a condition of agitation or excitement —**lie in state** to be displayed formally to the public before burial: said of a corpse in an open or closed casket —**the States** the United States —**stat′a·ble** *adj.*

SYN.—**state** and **condition** both refer to the set of circumstances surrounding or characterizing a person or thing at a given time [what is his mental *state*, or *condition*?], but **condition** more strongly implies some relationship to causes or circumstances [his *condition* will not permit him to travel]; **situation** implies a significant interrelationship of the circumstances, and connection between these and the person involved [to be in a difficult *situation*]; **status**, basically a legal term, refers to one's state as determined by such arbitrary factors as age, sex, training, mentality, service, etc. [his *status* as a veteran exempts him]

☆**State bank** a bank controlled or chartered by a State

state capitalism a form of capitalism in which much of the capital, industry, etc. is state-owned: a loose term sometimes equivalent to STATE SOCIALISM

state church *same as* ESTABLISHED CHURCH

state·craft (-kraft′, -kräft′) *n. same as* STATESMANSHIP

stat·ed (stāt′id) *adj.* **1.** fixed or set, as by agreement **2.** declared, esp. in specific terms; expressed —**stat′ed·ly** *adv.*

stated clerk an elected officer in the Presbyterian Church, serving as clerk or secretary for a session, synod, etc.

☆**State Department** the department of the executive branch of the U.S. government in charge of relations with foreign countries

☆**State flower** the floral emblem selected for or adopted by a State, often by action of the legislature

☆**State·hood** (stāt′hood) *n.* the condition of being a State of the U.S. rather than a Territory

State·house (-hous′) *n.* ☆the official meeting place of the legislature of a State of the U.S.: also **State House** or **State Capitol**

state·less (-lis) *adj.* having no state or nationality

state·ly (-lē) *adj.* **-li·er, -li·est** **1.** imposing; dignified; majestic **2.** slow, dignified, and deliberate *[a stately pace]* —*adv.* [Now Rare] in a stately manner —*SYN.* see GRAND —**state′li·ness** *n.*

state·ment (-mənt) *n.* **1.** *a)* an act of stating *b)* the thing stated; account, declaration, assertion, etc. **2.** *a)* an abstract, usually itemized, of a financial account *[a bank statement] b)* a listing of charges for goods or services; bill

Stat·en Island (stat′n) [< Du. *Staaten Eylandt,* States Island, referring to the States-General of the Dutch Republic] island in New York Bay, forming the borough of Richmond in New York City: 60 sq. mi.

state of the art the current level of sophistication of a developing technology, as of computer science

state of war a condition or period of armed conflict between nations, either undeclared or officially declared

☆**State prison** a prison maintained by a State for adult criminals, usually those convicted of serious crimes

stat·er (stāt′ər) *n.* [ME. < LL.(Ec.) < Gr. *statēr,* orig., a weight < IE. base *stā-,* to STAND] any of various gold and silver coins of ancient Greece and Persia

state·room (stāt′rōōm′) *n.* **1.** a private cabin on a ship ☆**2.** a private sleeping room in a railroad car

☆**State's attorney** a lawyer appointed or elected to prepare cases for the State and represent it in court

☆**state's evidence** *Law* evidence given by or for the prosecution in a criminal case, usually evidence given by a criminal against his associates —**turn state's evidence** to give evidence for the prosecution in a criminal case

States-Gen·er·al (stāts′jen′ər əl) *n.* [transl. of Fr. *états généraux,* Du. *staaten generaal*] **1.** the legislative body in France before the Revolution of 1789, made up of representatives of the clergy, the nobility, and the third estate **2.** the legislative assembly of the Netherlands

☆**state·side** (stāt′sīd′) *adj.* [Colloq.] of or characteristic of the U.S. (as viewed from abroad) *[stateside newspapers]* —*adv.* [Colloq.] in, to, or toward the U.S.

states·man (stāts′mən) *n., pl.* **-men** (-mən) *[state's,* gen. of STATE + MAN, after Fr. *homme d'état]* a person who shows wisdom, skill, and vision in conducting state affairs and treating public issues, or one engaged in the business of government —**states′man·like′, states′man·ly** *adj.*

states·man·ship (-ship′) *n.* [see -SHIP] the ability, character, or methods of a statesman; skill and vision in managing public affairs

state socialism the theory, doctrine, or practice of an economy planned and controlled by the state, based on state ownership of public utilities, basic industries, etc.

States of the Church *same as* PAPAL STATES

☆**State's rights** all the rights and powers which the Constitution neither grants to the Federal government nor denies to the various State governments: also **State rights**

☆**State university** a university supported and controlled by a State as part of its public educational system

☆**state-wide** (stāt′wīd′) *adj.* extending throughout a state

stat·ic (stat′ik) *adj.* [ModL. *staticus* < Gr. *statikos,* causing to stand < *histanai,* to cause to stand: see STAND] **1.** acting through weight only: said of the pressure exerted by a motionless body or mass **2.** of bodies, masses, or forces at rest or in equilibrium: opposed to DYNAMIC **3.** not moving or progressing; at rest; inactive; stationary **4.** *Elec.* designating, of, or producing stationary electrical charges, as those resulting from friction **5.** *Radio* of or having to do with static Also **stat′i·cal** —*n.* ☆**1.** *a)* electrical discharges in the atmosphere that interfere with radio or television reception, etc. *b)* interference or noises produced by such discharges **2.** [Slang] adversely critical remarks —**stat′i·cal·ly** *adv.*

stat·i·ce (stat′ə sē′) *n.* [ModL. < L., an astringent herb < Gr. *statikē* < fem. of *statikos,* causing to stand, astringent: see STATIC] *same as:* **1.** SEA LAVENDER **2.** THRIFT (sense 4)

stat·ics (stat′iks) *n.pl.* [with sing. v.] [see STATIC & -ICS] the branch of mechanics dealing with bodies, masses, or forces at rest or in equilibrium

static tube a tube with openings in its walls, inserted in a fluid in motion so that the flow is across the openings and used to measure the static pressure of the fluid; specif., such a tube in a Pitot-static tube

sta·tion (stā′shən) *n.* [ME. *stacioun* < OFr. *station* < L. *statio,* a standing, post, station < *status,* pp. of *stare,* to STAND] **1.** the place where a person or thing stands or is located, esp. an assigned post, position, or location; specif., *a)* the place where a person, as a guard, stands while on duty *b)* the post, building, base, or headquarters assigned to a group of people working together, as in providing a service, making scientific observations, etc. *[a police station,* service *station] c)* in Australia, a sheep or cattle ranch *d)* a place or region to which a naval fleet, ship, etc. is assigned for duty *e)* a branch post office in a community with a main post office **2.** *a)* a regular stopping place, as on a bus line or railroad *b)* the building or buildings at such a place, for passengers, etc. **3.** social standing, position, or rank **4.** *a)* a place equipped to transmit or receive radio waves; esp., the studios, offices, and technical installations collectively of an establishment for radio or television transmission *b)* such an establishment *c)* a broadcasting frequency or channel assigned to such an establishment **5.** a fixed point from which measurements are made in surveying **6.** [Archaic] the fact or condition of being stationary **7.** *Biol.* a habitat, esp. the exact location of a given plant or animal —*vt.* to assign to a station; place; post

☆**station agent** an official in charge of a small railroad station, or of a department in a larger station

sta·tion·ar·y (stā′shə ner′ē) *adj.* [ME. *stacionarye* < L. *stationarius* < *statio:* see STATION] **1.** not moving or not movable; fixed or still **2.** unchanging in condition, value, etc.; not increasing or decreasing **3.** not migratory or itinerant —*n., pl.* **-ar′ies** a person or thing that is stationary

stationary engine a large engine fixed in place, as a steam engine or boiler, a turbine, etc.

stationary engineer a person who operates and maintains stationary engines and mechanical equipment

stationary wave *same as* STANDING WAVE: also called **stationary vibration**

☆**station break** a pause in radio and television programs for station identification and, usually, commercials

sta·tion·er (stā′shə nər) *n.* [ME. *stacionere* < ML. *stationarius,* tradesman with a fixed station or shop (by contrast with a peddler) < L. *stationarius,* STATIONARY] **1.** orig., a bookseller or publisher **2.** a person who sells office supplies, greeting cards, some books, etc.

sta·tion·er·y (stā′shə ner′ē) *n.* [see prec. & -ERY] writing materials; specif., paper and envelopes used for letters

station house a building used as a station, esp. by a company of police or firemen

☆**sta·tion·mas·ter** (stā′shən mas′tər, -mäs′tər) *n.* an official in charge of a large railroad station

Stations of the Cross [also s- c-] a series of fourteen images or pictures, as along the walls of a church, representing the stages of Jesus' sufferings, visited in succession as a devotional exercise

☆**station wagon** an automobile with folding or removable rear seats and a tailgate that can be opened for loading luggage, packages, etc.

stat·ism (stāt′iz′m) *n.* **1.** the doctrine or advocacy of the sovereignty of a state **2.** the doctrine or practice of vesting economic control, economic planning, etc. in a centralized state government: the current sense

stat·ist (-ist) *n.* **1.** a person who believes in or advocates statism **2.** [Archaic] a politician or statesman —*adj.* of, characteristic of, or advocating statism

sta·tis·tic (stə tis′tik) *adj. rare var. of* STATISTICAL —*n.* a statistical item or element

sta·tis·ti·cal (-ti k'l) *adj.* [< ModL. *statisticus,* of politics < L. *status:* see STATE] of, having to do with, consisting of, or based on statistics —**sta·tis′ti·cal·ly** *adv.*

stat·is·ti·cian (stat′is tish′ən) *n.* an expert or specialist in statistics

sta·tis·tics (stə tis′tiks) *n.pl.* [< G. *statistik* < ModL. *statisticus:* see STATISTICAL] **1.** facts or data of a numerical kind, assembled, classified, and tabulated so as to present significant information about a given subject **2.** [with sing. v.] the science of assembling, classifying, tabulating, and analyzing such facts or data

Sta·ti·us (stā′shē əs, stā′shəs), **Pub·li·us Pa·pin·i·us** (pub′lē əs pə pin′ē əs) 45?-96? A.D.; Rom. poet

stat·o·blast (stat′ə blast′) *n.* [< Gr. *statos,* standing (see ff.) + -BLAST] *Zool.* a bud, enclosed in a hard covering, produced by most freshwater ectoprocts and able to survive freezing, drying, etc. to germinate and form a new colony

stat·o·cyst (-sist′) *n.* [< Gr. *statos,* standing < *histasthai,* to STAND + -CYST] **1.** *Bot.* a plant cell containing plastids, starch grains, or other statoliths **2.** *Zool.* a sense organ found in many invertebrate animals, consisting typically of a sac filled with fluid and containing small sensory hairs, particles of lime, etc.: it functions as an organ of balance or equilibrium —**stat′o·cys′tic** (-sis′tik) *adj.*

stat·o·lith (-lith′) *n.* [< Gr. *statos,* standing (see prec.) + -LITH] **1.** *Bot.* any of the small, freely moving concretions, often a starch grain, found in statocysts **2.** *Zool. same as* OTOLITH (sense 2) —**stat′o·lith′ic** *adj.*

sta·tor (stāt′ər) *n.* [ModL. < L., one who stands < pp. of *stare,* to STAND] a fixed part forming the pivot or housing for a revolving part (*rotor*), as in a motor, dynamo, etc.

stat·o·scope (stat′ə skōp′) *n.* [< Gr. *statos,* standing (see STATOCYST) + -SCOPE] **1.** a highly sensitive aneroid barometer **2.** such a barometer adapted for use as an altimeter to indicate slight variations in the altitude of an aircraft

stat·u·ar·y (stach′ōō wer′ē) *n., pl.* **-ar′ies** [L. *statuaria < statuarius,* of statues < *statua,* STATUE] **1.** statues collec-

tively; group of statues **2.** the art of making statues **3.** *now rare var. of* SCULPTOR —*adj.* of or suitable for statues

stat·ue (stach′ōō) *n.* [ME. < OFr. < L. *statua* < *statuere*, to set, place < base of *stare*, to STAND] the form of a person or animal carved in stone, wood, etc., modeled in a plastic substance or cast in plaster, bronze, etc., esp. when done in the round rather than in relief

stat·ued (-ōōd) *adj.* ornamented with or represented in a statue or statues

☆**Statue of Liberty** a colossal copper statue personifying Liberty in the form of a crowned woman holding a torch in her upraised hand: it was given to the U.S. by France and is located on Liberty Island in New York harbor: official name *Liberty Enlightening the World*

stat·u·esque (stach′ōō wesk′) *adj.* [STATU(E) + -ESQUE] of or like a statue; specif., *a*) tall and well-proportioned *b*) having a stately grace and dignity —**stat′u·esque′ly** *adv.* —**stat′u·esque′ness** *n.*

stat·u·ette (-wet′) *n.* [Fr., dim. of *statue*] a small statue

stat·ure (stach′ər) *n.* [ME. < OFr. *estature* < L. *statura*, height or size of body < *statuere*: see STATUE] **1.** the height of a person, or sometimes an animal, in a natural standing position **2.** [Rare] the height of any object **3.** development, growth, or level of attainment, esp. as worthy of esteem [moral *stature*] —SYN. see HEIGHT

sta·tus (stāt′əs, stat′-) *n., pl.* **-tus·es** [L.: see STATE] **1.** condition or position with regard to law [the *status* of a minor] **2.** *a*) position; rank; standing [high *status*] *b*) high position; prestige [seeking *status*] **3.** state or condition, as of affairs [economic *status*] —SYN. see STATE

status quo (kwō′) [L., lit., the state in which] the existing state of affairs (at a particular time): also **status in quo**

status symbol a possession, practice, etc. regarded as a mark of social status, esp. high social status

stat·u·ta·ble (stach′ōō tə b'l) *adj.* same as STATUTORY

stat·ute (stach′ōōt, -oot) *n.* [ME. < OFr. *statut* < LL. *statutum*, neut. of L. *statutus*, pp. of *statuere*: see STATUE] **1.** an established rule; formal regulation **2.** *a*) a law passed by a legislative body and set forth in a formal document *b*) such a document —SYN. see LAW

statute book a book or other record of the body of statutes of a particular jurisdiction

statute law law established by a legislative body

statute mile a unit of measure (5,280 feet): see MILE

statute of limitations a statute limiting the period within which a specific legal action may be taken

stat·u·to·ry (stach′ōō tôr′ē) *adj.* **1.** of, or having the nature of, a statute or statutes **2.** fixed, authorized, or established by statute **3.** declared by statute to be such, and hence legally punishable: said of an offense, as **statutory rape** (see RAPE[1])

St. Augustine (after St. AUGUSTINE, sense 2 *a*] seaport in NE Fla.: oldest city (founded 1565) in the U.S.: pop. 12,000

staunch (stônch, stänch) *vt.* [ME. *stanchen* < OFr. *estanchier* < VL. *stanticare*, to bring to a stop < L. *stans*: see STANCE] **1.** to stop or check (the flow of blood or of tears, etc.) from (a wound, opening, etc.) **2.** *a*) to stop or lessen (the flow or drain of funds, resources, etc.) *b*) to stop up or close off (a source of draining or leakage) **3.** [Archaic or Dial.] *a*) to quench; quell *b*) to allay; appease —*vi.* to cease flowing or draining out or away —*adj.* [OFr. *estanche*, fem. of *estanc*, akin to *stare*] **1.** watertight; seaworthy [a *staunch* ship] **2.** firm; steadfast; loyal [a *staunch* supporter] **3.** strong; solidly made; substantial Also **stanch** For the *adj.*, **staunch** is now the prevailing form in the U.S.; for the *v.*, usage is about evenly divided between **staunch** and **stanch** —SYN. see FAITHFUL —**staunch′ly** *adv.* —**staunch′ness** *n.*

stau·ro·lite (stôr′ə līt′) *n.* [Fr. < Gr. *stauros*, a cross, post < IE. *steu-*, whence ON. *staurr*, a post (for base, cf. STORE) + -*lite*, -LITE] a dark-colored mineral, a silicate of iron and aluminum: the crystals are often found twinned in the form of a cross —**stau′ro·lit′ic** (-lit′ik) *adj.*

Sta·vang·er (stä van′ər) seaport in SW Norway, on the North Sea: pop. 78,000

stave (stāv) *n.* [ME., taken as sing. of *staves*, pl. of *staf*, STAFF[1]] **1.** *a*) any of the thin, shaped strips of wood, metal, etc. set edge to edge to form or strengthen the walls, floor, or top of a barrel, bucket, etc. *b*) any similar slat, bar, rung, stay, etc. **2.** a stick or staff **3.** a set of verses, or lines, of a poem or song; stanza **4.** *Music* same as STAFF[1] —*vt.* **staved** or **stove**, **stav′ing** **1.** *a*) to puncture or smash, esp. by breaking in a stave or staves *b*) to beat as with a staff **2.** to furnish with staves —*vi.* to be or become stove in, as a boat; break up or in —**stave off** to break or crush inward —**stave off** to ward off, hold off, or put off, as by force, guile, etc.

STAVE

staves (stāvz) *n.* **1.** alt. pl. of STAFF[1] **2.** pl. of STAVE

staves·a·cre (stāvz′ā′kər) *n.* [ME. *staphisagre* < ML. *staphisagria* < Gr. *staphis*, raisin + *agrios*, wild: for IE. base see ACRE] **1.** a tall, purple-flowered larkspur (*Delphinium staphisagria*) of Europe and Asia, with poisonous seeds having strongly emetic and cathartic properties **2.** its seeds

---

Stav·ro·pol (stäv′rȯ pȯl′y′) city in SW R.S.F.S.R., in the N Caucasus: pop. 171,000

stay[1] (stā) *n.* [ME. *staie* < OE. *stæg*, akin to Du. *stag* < IE. **stāk-*, to stand, place < base **sta-*: see STAND] a heavy rope or cable, usually of wire, used as a brace or support, as for a mast of a ship; guy —*vt.* **1.** to brace or support with a stay or stays **2.** to change the angle of (a mast) by shifting the stays **3.** to put (a ship) on the other tack —*vi.* to tack: said of a ship —**in stays** in the process of tacking: said of a ship

stay[2] (stā) *n.* [MFr. *estaie* < Frank. *staka, akin to OE. *staca*, a STAKE] **1.** anything used as a support, or prop **2.** a strip of stiffening material used in a corset, the collar of a shirt, etc. **3.** [*pl.*] [Chiefly Brit.] a corset stiffened as with whalebone —*vt.* **1.** to support, or prop up **2.** to strengthen, comfort, or sustain in mind or spirit **3.** to cause to rest *on*, *upon*, or *in* for support

stay[3] (stā) *vi.* **stayed** or *archaic* **staid**, **stay′ing** [ME. *staien* < Anglo-Fr. *estaier* < OFr. *ester* < L. *stare*, to STAND] **1.** to continue in the place or condition specified; remain; keep [to *stay* at home, to *stay* healthy] **2.** to live, dwell, or reside, esp. temporarily (*for* the time specified) **3.** to stand still; stop; halt **4.** to pause; tarry; wait; delay **5.** [Colloq.] to continue or endure; last [to *stay* with a project] **6.** [Colloq.] to keep up (*with* another contestant in a race, etc.) **7.** [Archaic] to cease doing something; stop **8.** [Archaic] to make a stand; stand one's ground ☆**9.** *Poker* to remain in a hand by meeting the bet or raise —*vt.* **1.** to stop, halt, or check **2.** to hinder, impede, restrain, or detain **3.** to postpone or delay (legal action or proceedings) **4.** [Rare] to quell or allay (strife, etc.) **5.** to satisfy or appease for a time the pangs or cravings of (thirst, appetite, etc.) **6.** *a*) to remain through or during (often with *out*) [to *stay* the week (out)] *b*) to be able to last through [to *stay* the distance in a long race] **7.** [Archaic] to await; wait for —*n.* **1.** *a*) a stopping or being stopped *b*) a stop, halt, check, or pause **2.** a postponement or delay in legal action or proceedings [a *stay* of execution] **3.** *a*) the action of remaining or continuing in a place for a time *b*) time spent in a place [a long *stay* in the hospital] **4.** [Colloq.] ability to continue or endure **5.** [Archaic] a standstill **6.** [Obs.] *a*) a hindrance *b*) restraint or control *c*) delay —☆**stay put** [Colloq.] to remain in place or unchanged

SYN.—**stay**, the general term, implies a continuing in a specified place [*stay* there until you hear from me]; **remain** specifically suggests a staying behind while others go [he alone *remained* at home]; **wait** suggests a staying in anticipation of something [*wait* for me at the library]; **abide**, now somewhat archaic, implies a staying fixed for a relatively long period, as in settled residence [he came for a visit and has been *abiding* here since]; **tarry** and **linger** imply a staying on after the required or expected time for departure, **linger** esp. implying that this is deliberate, as from reluctance to leave [we *tarried* in town two days, he *lingered* at his sweetheart's door] —ANT. go, leave, depart

staying power ability to last or endure; endurance

stay·sail (-sāl′; *in nautical usage*, -s'l) *n.* a sail, esp. a triangular sail, fastened on a stay

S.T.B. [L. *Sacrae Theologiae Baccalaureus*] Bachelor of Sacred Theology

St. Ber·nard (bər närd′) **1.** see GREAT and LITTLE ST. BERNARD PASS **2.** same as SAINT BERNARD

St. Boniface city in S Manitoba, Canada: pop. 43,000

St. Catharines city in SE Ontario, Canada, on the Welland Canal: pop. 97,000

St. Christopher island in the Leeward group of the West Indies: 65 sq. mi.; pop. 38,000; chief town, Basseterre: see ANGUILLA

St. Clair (kler) [after Fr. *Sainte Claire* (St. Clare of Assisi, 1194–1253)] **1. Lake**, lake between SE Mich. & Ontario, Canada: 460 sq. mi. **2.** river between Mich. & Ontario, connecting this lake & Lake Huron: 40 mi.

St. Clair Shores city in SE Mich., on Lake St. Clair: suburb of Detroit: pop. 88,000

St-Cloud (san klōō′) city in NC France: suburb of Paris: pop. 26,000

St. Cloud (kloud) [after prec.] city in C Minn., on the Mississippi: pop. 40,000

St. Croix (kroi) [Fr., holy cross] **1.** largest island of the Virgin Islands of the U.S.: 80 sq. mi.; pop. 32,000 **2.** river flowing from NW Wis. south along the Wis.-Minn. border into the Mississippi: c.165 mi.

std. standard

S.T.D. [L. *Sacrae Theologiae Doctor*] Doctor of Sacred Theology

St-De·nis (san nē′) **1.** city in NC France: suburb of Paris: pop. 94,000 **2.** capital of Réunion Island: pop. 78,000

St. Den·is (sānt′ den′is), **Ruth** (born *Ruth Dennis*) 1877?–1968; U.S. dancer & choreographer: wife of Ted SHAWN

Ste. [Fr. *Sainte*] Saint (female)

stead (sted) *n.* [ME. *stede* < OE., akin to G. *statt*, a place, *stadt*, town < IE. base **stā-*, to STAND] **1.** the place or position of a person or thing as filled by a replacement, substitute, or successor [to send another in one's *stead*] **2.** advantage, service, or avail: now only in **stand (one) in good stead** to give (one) good use, service, or advantage **3.** [Obs.] a place, site, or locality —*vt.* [Archaic] to be of advantage, service, or avail to

stead·fast (sted'fast', -fäst', -fəst) *adj.* [ME. < OE. *stedefæste*: see STEAD & FAST¹] 1. firm, fixed, settled, or established 2. not changing, fickle, or wavering; constant —**stead'fast'ly** *adv.* —**stead'fast'ness** *n.*

stead·ing (-iŋ) *n.* [ME. *steding*: see STEAD & -ING] *Brit. var.* of FARMSTEAD

stead·y (sted'ē) *adj.* **stead'i·er, stead'i·est** [see STEAD & -Y³] 1. that does not shake, tremble, totter, etc.; firm; fixed; stable 2. constant, regular, uniform, or continuous; not changing, wavering, faltering, etc. [a *steady* gaze, a *steady* diet, a *steady* rhythm] 3. not given to sudden changes in behavior, loyalty, disposition, etc. 4. habitual or regular; by habit [a *steady* customer] 5. not easily agitated, excited, or upset; calm and controlled [*steady* nerves] 6. grave; sober; staid; reliable; not frivolous or dissipated 7. keeping almost upright, as in a rough sea, or staying headed in the same direction: said of a ship —*interj.* 1. remain calm and controlled! 2. keep the ship headed in the same direction! —*vt., vi.* **stead'ied, stead'y·ing** to make or become steady —*n.* ☆[Colloq.] a person whom one dates regularly and exclusively; sweetheart —*adv.* in a steady manner —☆**go steady** [Colloq.] to date someone of the opposite sex regularly and exclusively; be sweethearts —**stead'i·ly** *adv.* —**stead'i·ness** *n.*
SYN.—**steady** implies a fixed regularity or constancy, esp. of movement, and an absence of deviation, fluctuation, faltering, etc. [a *steady* breeze]; **even**, often interchangeable with **steady**, emphasizes the absence of irregularity or inequality [an *even* heartbeat]; **uniform** implies a sameness or likeness of things, parts, events, etc., usually as the result of conformity with a fixed standard [a *uniform* wage rate]; **regular** emphasizes the orderliness or symmetry resulting from evenness or uniformity [*regular* features, attendance, etc.]; **equable** implies that the quality of evenness or regularity is inherent [an *equable* temper] —**ANT.** changeable, jerky

stead·y-state (-stāt') *adj.* designating of or that a system, operation, mixture, rate, etc. that does not change with time or that maintains a state of relative equilibrium even after undergoing fluctuations or transformations

steady-state theory a theory of cosmology holding that as the universe expands and galaxies separate, new matter is continuously created

steak (stāk) *n.* [ME. *steike* < ON. *steik* < base of *steikja*, to roast on a spit: for IE. base see STICK] 1. a slice of meat, esp. beef, or of a large fish, cut thick for broiling or frying 2. ground beef or other meat cooked in this way

☆**steak·house** (-hous') *n.* a restaurant that specializes in steaks, esp. of beef

☆**steak knife** a table knife with a very sharp, often serrated, steel blade

☆**steak tar·tare** (tär tär') [*tartare*, pseudo-Fr. for TARTAR: hence, steak in Tartar style] raw sirloin or tenderloin steak ground up and mixed with chopped onion, raw egg, salt, and pepper, and garnished with capers, parsley, etc., and eaten uncooked

steal (stēl) *vt.* **stole, stol'en, steal'ing** [ME. *stelen* < OE. *stælan*, akin to G. *stehlen*, prob. altered < IE. base *ster-*, to rob, whence Gr. *sterein*, to rob] 1. to take or appropriate (another's property, ideas, etc.) without permission, dishonestly, or unlawfully, esp. in a secret or surreptitious manner 2. to get, take, or give slyly, surreptitiously, or without permission [to *steal* a look, to *steal* a kiss] 3. to take or gain insidiously or artfully [to *steal* someone's heart, to *steal* the puck in hockey] 4. to be the outstanding performer in (a scene, act, etc.) esp. in a subordinate role 5. to move, put, carry, or convey surreptitiously or stealthily (*in, into, from, away*, etc.) ☆6. *Baseball* to gain (a base) safely without the help of a hit, walk, or error, as by running to it from another base while the pitch is being delivered —*vi.* 1. to be a thief; practice theft 2. to move, pass, etc. stealthily, quietly, gradually, or without being noticed ☆3. *Baseball* to steal a base —*n.* [Colloq.] 1. an act of stealing 2. something stolen 3. something obtained at a ludicrously low cost —**steal'er** *n.*
SYN.—**steal** is the general term implying the taking of another's money, possessions, etc. dishonestly or in a secret or surreptitious manner [to *steal* jewelry, a time, etc.]; **pilfer** implies the stealing of small sums or petty objects [a *pilfering* house guest]; **filch** also implies petty theft, but connotes that it is done by surreptitiously snatching [to *filch* candy in a store]; **purloin**, a literary word interchangeable with any of the preceding, stresses the removal of that which one means to appropriate for his own use [letters *purloined* by a blackmailer]; **lift, swipe**, and **pinch** are slang terms meaning to steal, pilfer, or filch, **lift**, in addition, having specific colloquial application to plagiarism

stealth (stelth) *n.* [ME. *stelthe* < base of *stelen*, to STEAL] 1. secret, furtive, or artfully sly action or behavior 2. [Obs.] theft

stealth·y (stel'thē) *adj.* **stealth'i·er, stealth'i·est** characterized by stealth; secret, furtive, or sly —SYN. see SECRET —**stealth'i·ly** *adv.* —**stealth'i·ness** *n.*

steam (stēm) *n.* [ME. *steme* < OE. *steam*, akin to Du. *stoom*, WFris. *steam*] 1. orig., a vapor, fume, or exhalation 2. *a)* water as converted into an invisible vapor or gas by being heated to the boiling point; vaporized water: it is used for heating, cooking, cleaning, and, under pressure,

as a source of power *b)* the power supplied by steam under pressure *c)* [Colloq.] driving force; vigor; energy 3. condensed water vapor, seen as the mist condensed on windows or in the air above boiling water —*adj.* 1. using steam; heated, operated, propelled, etc. by steam 2. containing or conducting steam [a *steam* pipe] 3. treated with, or exposed to the action of, steam —*vi.* 1. to give off steam or a steamlike vapor, esp. condensed water vapor 2. to rise or be given off as steam 3. to become covered with condensed steam, as a window (usually with *up*) 4. to generate steam 5. to move or travel by or as if by steam power ☆6. [Colloq.] to seethe with anger, vexation, etc.; fume —*vt.* 1. to treat with, or expose to the action of, steam; cook, soften, open, etc. by using steam 2. to give off (vapor) or emit as steam —**let (or blow) off steam** [Colloq.] to express strong feeling; release pent-up emotion

steam bath 1. the act of bathing by exposing oneself to steam, as to induce sweating 2. a room or establishment for so exposing oneself to steam

☆**steam·boat** (-bōt') *n.* a steamship, esp. a relatively small one for use on inland waterways

steam boiler a tank in which water is heated to produce steam and hold it under pressure

steam chest a compartment in a steam engine through which steam passes from the boiler to the cylinder

steam engine 1. an engine using steam under pressure to supply mechanical energy, usually through the action of a piston sliding in a cylinder 2. a locomotive powered by steam

steam·er (stē'mər) *n.* 1. something operated by steam power, as a steamship or, formerly, a steam-powered automobile 2. a container in which things are cooked, cleaned, etc. with steam 3. a person or thing that steams 4. *same as* SOFT-SHELL CLAM

☆**steamer chair** *same as* DECK CHAIR

☆**steamer rug** a heavy woolen blanket used by passengers in deck chairs on shipboard to cover the lap and legs

☆**steamer trunk** a broad, low, rectangular trunk, orig. designed to fit under a bunk on shipboard

steam fitter a mechanic whose work (**steam fitting**) is installing and maintaining boilers, pipes, etc. in steam-pressure systems

steam heat heat given off by steam in a closed system of pipes and radiators

☆**steam iron** an electric iron that forms steam from water and releases it through the soleplate onto the material being pressed

steam·roll·er (stēm'rōl'ər) *n.* 1. a heavy, steam-driven roller used in building and repairing roads 2. an overwhelming power or influence, esp. when used relentlessly to force acceptance of a policy, override opposition, etc. —*vt.* 1. to bring overwhelming force to bear upon; crush or override as if with a steamroller 2. to cause the passage or defeat of (a legislative bill, etc.), or make (one's way, etc.), by crushing opposition or overriding obstacles —*vi.* to move with overwhelming force, or use steam-roller tactics Also **steam'roll'** —*adj.* relentlessly overpowering

steam room a room for taking a steam bath

steam·ship (- ship') *n.* a ship driven by steam power

☆**steam shovel** a large, mechanically operated digger, powered by steam

steam table a serving table or counter, as in restaurants, having a metal top with compartments heated by steam or hot water to keep foods warm

steam·tight (-tīt') *adj.* preventing leakage of steam

steam turbine a turbine turned by steam moving under great pressure

steam·y (stē'mē) *adj.* **steam'i·er, steam'i·est** 1. of or like steam 2. covered or filled with steam 3. giving off steam or steamlike vapor —**steam'i·ly** *adv.* —**steam'i·ness** *n.*

Ste-Anne-de-Beau·pré (sānt an'də bō prā'; *Fr.* san tän də bō prā') village in S Quebec, Canada, on the St. Lawrence: site of a Roman Catholic shrine: pop. 1,500

ste·ap·sin (stē ap'sin) *n.* [< Gr. *stea(r)*, fat (see STONE) + (PE)PSIN] *Biochem.* the lipase present in pancreatic juice

ste·a·rate (stē'ə rāt', stir'āt) *n.* a salt or ester of stearic acid

ste·ar·ic (stē ar'ik, stir'ik) *adj.* [Fr. *stéarique* < Gr. *stear*, tallow: for IE. base see STONE] 1. of, derived from, or like stearin or fat 2. of or pertaining to stearic acid

stearic acid 1. a colorless, odorless, waxlike fatty acid, $C_{18}H_{36}O_2$, found in many animal and vegetable fats, and used in making candles, stearates, soaps, etc. 2. a commercial mixture of palmitic and stearic acids

ste·a·rin (stē'ə rin) *n.* [Fr. *stéarine*: see STEARIC & -INE⁴] a white, crystalline substance, glyceryl stearate, $(C_{18}H_{35})_2C_3H_5$, found in the solid portion of most animal and vegetable fats and used in soaps, adhesives, textile sizes, etc.: also **ste'a·rine** (-rin, -rēn'; -in, -ēn)

ste·a·rop·tene (stē'ə räp'tēn) *n.* [STEAR(IC) + (ELE)OPTENE] the oxygenated, chiefly solid part of an essential oil

ste·a·tite (stē'ə tīt') *n.* [L. *steatitis* < Gr. *stear*, tallow (see STONE)] a compact, usually impure, massive variety of talc, used to make electrical insulators, etc.; soapstone —**ste'a·tit'ic** (-tit'ik) *adj.*

fat, āpe, cär; ten, ēven; is, bīte; gō, hôrn, tōōl, look; oil, out; up, fur; get; joy; yet; chin; she; thin, then; zh, leisure; ŋ, ring; ə for *a* in *ago, e* in *agent, i* in *sanity, o* in *comply, u* in *focus*; ' as in *able* (ā'b'l); Fr. bâl; ë, Fr. coeur; ö, Fr. feu; Fr. mon; ö, Fr. coq; ü, Fr. duc; r, Fr. cri; H, G. ich; kh, G. doch. See inside front cover. ☆ Americanism; ‡foreign; *hypothetical; < derived from

ste·a·tol·y·sis (stē′ə tăl′ə sis) *n.* [ModL. < Gr. *stear* (gen. *steatos*), fat + ModL. *-lysis*, -LYSIS] the hydrolysis of a fat into glycerol and fatty acids

ste·a·to·pyg·i·a (stē′ə tō pij′ē ə, -pī′jē ə) *n.* [ModL. < Gr. *stear* (gen. *steatos*), fat (see STONE) + *pygē* < IE. base *pu-, to swell, whence L. *pustula:* see PUSTULE] a marked protuberance of the buttocks, formed by fatty deposits, esp. in women, as among Hottentots —**ste′a·to·pyg′ic**, **ste′a·to·py′gous** (-pī′gəs) *adj.*

ste·at·or·rhe·a (stē′ə tə rē′ə) *n.* [ModL. < Gr. *stear* (gen. *steatos*), fat (see STONE) + -RRHEA] an excessive amount of fat in the feces

sted·fast (sted′fast′, -fäst′, -fəst) *adj. earlier var. of* STEADFAST —**sted′fast′ly** *adv.* —**sted′fast′ness** *n.*

steed (stēd) *n.* [ME. *stede* < OE. *steda*, stud horse, stallion < base of *stod*, STUD²] a horse, esp. a high-spirited riding horse: literary term

steel (stēl) *n.* see PLURAL, II, D, 3 [ME. *stel* < OE. *stiele*, *stæli*, akin to G. *stahl* < IE. *stak-*, to stand (whence Av. *staxta-*, strong, firm) < base *stā-*, to STAND] 1. a hard, tough metal composed of iron alloyed with various small percentages of carbon and often variously with other metals, as nickel, chromium, manganese, etc., to produce hardness, resistance to rusting, etc. 2. something made of steel; specif., *a)* [Poet.] a sword or dagger *b)* a piece of steel used with flint for making sparks *c)* a steel strip used for stiffening, as in a corset *d)* a roughened steel rod on which to sharpen knives 3. great strength, hardness, or toughness 4. [*often pl.*] stock in steel-making companies as traded on the market —*adj.* of or like steel —*vt.* 1. to cover, point, or edge with steel 2. to make hard, tough, relentless, unfeeling, etc.

steel band a percussion band, of a kind originated in Trinidad, beating on steel oil drums modified to produce varying pitches

steel blue a metallic blue color like that of tempered steel —**steel′-blue′** *adj.*

Steele (stēl), Sir **Richard** 1672-1729; Brit. essayist & dramatist, born in Ireland

steel engraving 1. an engraving made on a steel plate 2. a print from this 3. the process used for this

steel gray a bluish gray color —**steel′-gray′** *adj.*

☆**steel·head** (stēl′hed′) *n., pl.* **-head′**, **-heads′**: see PLURAL, II, D, 2 any of a variety of large rainbow trout found along the Pacific coast, that go up rivers to spawn

steel mill a mill where steel is made, processed, and shaped

steel wool long, hairlike shavings of steel in a pad or ball, used for scouring, smoothing, and polishing

steel·work (-wurk′) *n.* 1. articles or parts made of steel 2. a frame or structure made of steel 3. [*pl.*, *often with sing. v.*] *same as* STEEL MILL

steel·work·er (-wur′kər) *n.* a worker in a steel mill

steel·y (stē′lē) *adj.* **steel′i·er**, **steel′i·est** of or like steel, as in hardness —**steel′i·ness** *n.*

steel·yard (stēl′yärd′, stil′yərd) *n.* [STEEL + YARD¹ (in obs. sense of "rod, bar")] a balance or scale consisting of a metal arm suspended off center from above: the object to be weighed is hung from the shorter end, and a sliding weight is moved along the graduated longer end until the whole arm balances

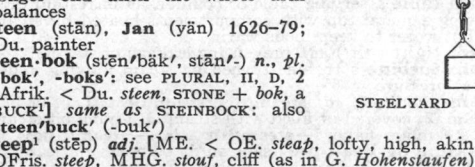
STEELYARD

Steen (stān), **Jan** (yän) 1626-79; Du. painter

steen·bok (stēn′bäk′, stän′-) *n., pl.* **-bok′**, **-boks′**: see PLURAL, II, D, 2 [Afrik. < Du. *steen*, STONE + *bok*, a BUCK¹] *same as* STEINBOCK: also **steen′buck′** (-buk′)

steep¹ (stēp) *adj.* [ME. < OE. *steap*, lofty, high, akin to OFris. *steep*, MHG. *stouf*, cliff (as in G. *Hohenstaufen*) < IE. *steu-p* < base *s)teu-*, to strike, butt, whence L. *tundere*, to strike & STOCK, STUB] 1. having a sharp rise or highly inclined slope; precipitous [a *steep* incline] 2. [Colloq.] *a)* unreasonably high or great; exorbitant; excessive [*steep* demands, a *steep* price] *b)* extreme; exaggerated [a rather *steep* statement] 3. [Obs.] high; lofty —*n.* a steep slope or incline —**steep′ly** *adv.* —**steep′ness** *n.*

SYN.—**steep** suggests such sharpness of rise or slope as to make ascent or descent very difficult [a *steep* hill]; **abrupt** implies a sharper degree of inclination in a surface breaking off suddenly from the level [an *abrupt* bank at the river's edge]; **precipitous** suggests the abrupt and headlong drop of a precipice [a *precipitous* height]; **sheer** applies to that which is perpendicular, or almost so, and unbroken throughout its length [cliffs falling *sheer* to the sea]

steep² (stēp) *vt.* [ME. *stepen*, akin to ON. *steypa*, to overturn, cast (metals), plunge into: for prob. IE. base see prec.] 1. to soak in liquid, so as to soften, clean, extract the essence of, etc. 2. to immerse, saturate, absorb, or imbue [*steeped* in folklore] —*n.* 1. a steeping or being steeped 2. liquid in which something is steeped —*vi.* to undergo the process of being soaked in liquid, as tea leaves —SYN. see SOAK

steep·en (-'n) *vt., vi.* to make or become steep or steeper

stee·ple (stē′p'l) *n.* [ME. *stepel* < OE. < base of *steap*, lofty: see STEEP¹] 1. a tower rising above the main structure of a building, esp. of a church, usually capped with a spire 2. a church tower with a spire 3. *same as* SPIRE²

☆**stee·ple·bush** (-boosh′) *n.* [from the steeplelike shape of the flower clusters] a shrub (*Spiraea tomentosa*) of the rose family, with clusters of pink, purple, or sometimes white flowers and hairy leaves, native to the E U.S.

stee·ple·chase (-chās′) *n.* [the race orig. had as its goal a distant, visible steeple] 1. orig., a horse race run across country 2. a horse race run over a prepared course with artificial obstructions, such as ditches, hedges, and walls 3. a footrace run across country or over a prepared course with ditches and other obstacles —*vi.* **-chased′**, **-chas′ing** —**stee′ple·chas′er** *n.*

stee·ple·jack (-jak′) *n.* a man whose work is building, painting, or repairing steeples, smokestacks, etc.

steer¹ (stir) *vt.* [ME. *steren* < OE. *stieran*, akin to G. *steuern*, ON. *styra* < IE. *steur-*, a support, post (whence Gr. *stauros*, ON. *staurr*, a post) < base *stā-*, to STAND] 1. to guide (a ship or boat) by means of a rudder 2. to direct the course or movement of [to *steer* an automobile] 3. to oversee, direct, or guide [to *steer* a team to victory] 4. to set and follow (a course) —*vi.* 1. to steer a ship, automobile, etc. 2. to be steered or guided [a car that *steers* easily] 3. to set and follow a course or way —*n.* ☆[Colloq.] a suggestion on how to proceed; tip —SYN. see GUIDE —**steer clear of** to keep clear of or away from; avoid —**steer′a·ble** *adj.* —**steer′er** *n.*

steer² (stir) *n.* [ME. *ster* < OE. *steor*, akin to G. *stier* < IE. *steu-ro* (whence MPer. *stor*, horse, draft animal) < base *stā-*, to STAND] 1. a castrated male of the cattle family 2. loosely, any male of cattle raised for beef

steer·age (stir′ij) *n.* 1. *a)* the act of steering (a ship, etc.) *b)* the response of a ship to the helmsman's guidance 2. [because orig. located near the steering mechanism] formerly, a section in some passenger ships, with the poorest accommodations, occupied by the passengers paying the lowest fare

steer·age·way (-wā′) *n.* the minimum forward speed needed to make a ship respond to the helmsman's guidance

☆**steering committee** a committee, as of a legislative body, appointed to arrange the order of business

steering gear any mechanism used for steering, as in a ship, automobile, airplane, etc.

steering wheel a wheel that is turned by hand to operate a steering gear

steers·man (stirz′mən) *n., pl.* **-men** (-mən) a person who steers a ship or boat; helmsman

steeve¹ (stēv) *vt.* **steeved**, **steev′ing** [Fr. *estiver* < Sp. or Port. *estivar* < L. *stipare*, to compress, cram: see STONE] to stow (cargo), as in the hold of a ship, by means of a spar or derrick —*n.* such a spar or derrick

steeve² (stēv) *vi., vt.* **steeved**, **steev′ing** [< ? or akin to OFr. *estive*, tail of a plow < L. *stiva*, plow handle] to set or be set at an angle above the line of the horizon or of the keel: said of a bowsprit —*n.* the angle so formed

Ste·fans·son (stef′ən sən), **Vil·hjal·mur** (vil′hyoul′mər) 1879-1962; U.S. arctic explorer, born in Canada

Stef·fens (stef′ənz), (**Joseph**) **Lincoln** 1866-1936; U.S. journalist & author

☆**steg·o·sau·rus** (steg′ə sôr′əs) *n., pl.* **-ri** (-ī) [ModL. < Gr. *stegos*, a roof (see THATCH) + -SAURUS] any of a genus (*Stegosaurus*) of large dinosaurs having a small head and heavy bony plates with sharp spikes down the backbone: found in the Upper Jurassic rocks of N. America

Stei·chen (stī′kən), **Edward** 1879- ; U.S. photographer, born in Luxembourg

Stei·er·mark (shtī′ər märk′) *Ger. name of* STYRIA

stein (stīn) *n.* [G. < *steingut*, stoneware < *stein*, STONE + *gut*, goods] 1. an earthenware beer mug, or a similar mug of pewter, glass, etc. 2. the amount that a stein will hold

Stein (stīn), **Gertrude** 1874-1946; U.S. writer in France

Stein·beck (stīn′bek′), **John** (**Ernst**) 1902-68; U.S. novelist & short-story writer

stein·bok (stīn′bäk′) *n., pl.* **-bok′**, **-boks′**: see PLURAL, II, D, 2 [G. *steinbock*] a small, reddish antelope (*Raphicerus campestris*) found in grassy areas of S and E Africa

Stein·metz (stīn′mets), **Charles Proteus** 1865-1923; U.S. electrical engineer & inventor, born in Germany

ste·la (stē′lə) *n., pl.* **-lae** (-lē) *var. sp. of* STELE (senses 1 & 2)

ste·le (stē′lē; *also*, & *for 2 & 3 usually*, stēl) *n.* [L. *stela* < Gr. *stēlē*, a post or slab: see STALK²] 1. an upright stone slab or pillar engraved with an inscription or design and used as a monument, grave marker, etc. 2. *Archit.* a prepared surface, as on a façade, having an inscription, carved design, etc. 3. *Bot.* a central cylinder of vascular tissues in the stems and roots of plants

St. Elias 1. range of the Coast Ranges, in SW Yukon & SE Alas.: highest peak, Mt. LOGAN: in full **St. Elias Mountains** 2. **Mount**, mountain in this range, on the Canada-Alaska border: 18,008 ft.

Stel·la (stel′ə) [L. *stella*, a STAR] a feminine name: see ESTELLA

stel·lar (stel′ər) *adj.* [LL. *stellaris* < L. *stella*, a STAR] 1. of the stars or a star 2. like a star, as in shape 3. by or as by a star performer; excellent; outstanding 4. leading; chief [a *stellar* role]

☆**stel·lar·a·tor** (stel′ə rāt′ər) *n.* [STELLAR + -ATOR] *Physics* a magnetic bottle in the shape of a toroid, that uses changeable magnetic fields to confine a plasma

stel·late (stel′āt, -it) *adj.* [L. *stellatus*, pp. of *stellare*, to cover with stars < *stella*, a STAR] shaped like a star;

coming out in rays or points from a center: also **stel′lat·ed** —**stel′late·ly** *adv.*

stel·lif·er·ous (ste lif′ər əs) *adj.* [L. *stellifer* (< *stella*, a STAR + *ferre*, to BEAR¹) + -OUS] [Rare] having or full of stars

stel·li·form (stel′ə fôrm′) *adj.* [ModL. *stelliformis* < L. *stella*, a STAR + -*formis*, -FORM] shaped like a star

stel·lu·lar (-yoo lər) *adj.* [< LL. *stellula*, dim. of L. *stella*, a STAR + -AR] 1. shaped like a small star or stars 2. covered with small stars or starlike spots

stem¹ (stem) *n.* [ME. < OE. *stemn, stefn*, akin to G. *stamm*, tree trunk < IE. base **stebh-*, post, pole, stub, trunk, whence STEP, STAFF¹] 1. the main upward-growing axis of a plant, having nodes and bearing leaves, usually extending in a direction opposite to that of the root and above the ground, and serving to support the plant and to transport and store food materials; specif., the main stalk or trunk of a tree, shrub, or other plant, from which leaves, flowers, and fruit develop 2. *a)* any stalk or part supporting leaves, flowers, or fruit, as a pedicel, petiole, or peduncle *b)* a stalk of bananas 3. a piece or part like a stem; specif., *a)* the slender part of a tobacco pipe between the bowl and the bit; pipestem *b)* a narrow supporting part between the foot and the bowl, as of a wineglass *c)* the cylindrical shaft projecting from a watch, with a knurled knob at its end for winding the spring *d)* the rounded rod in some locks, about which the key fits and is turned *e)* the main or thick stroke of a letter, as in printing *f)* the vertical line forming part of a musical note (other than a whole note) *g)* the shaft of a feather or hair 4. *a)* the upright piece to which the side timbers or plates are attached to form the prow of a ship *b)* the forward part of a ship; prow; bow 5. *a)* a branch of a family *b)* lineage; ancestry; stock 6. *Linguis.* the part of a word, consisting of a base or a base with an affix, to which inflectional endings are added or in which inflectional phonetic changes are made —*vt.* **stemmed, stem′ming** 1. to remove the stem or stems from (a fruit, etc.) 2. to provide (artificial flowers, etc.) with stems 3. [< *n.* 4] to make headway or progress against [*to row upstream, stemming the current*] —*vi.* to originate, derive, or be descended —SYN. see RISE —**from stem to stern** 1. from one end of a ship to the other 2. through the entire length of anything —**stem′less** *adj.* —**stem′like** *adj.*

stem² (stem) *vt.* **stemmed, stem′ming** [ME. < ON. *stemma* (akin to G. *stemmen*), to stop: for base see STAMMER] 1. to stop or check; esp., to dam up (a river, etc.), or to stop or check as if by damming up 2. to stop up, plug, or tamp (a hole, etc.) 3. to turn (a ski) in stemming —*vi.* to stop or slow down in skiing by turning one ski (**single stemming**) or both skis (**double stemming**) with the heel thrust outward and the tip of the ski(s) turned in —*n.* an act or manner of stemming on skis

stemmed (stemd) *adj.* 1. having a stem, usually of a specified kind [*a thin-stemmed goblet*] 2. with the stem or stems removed

stem·mer (stem′ər) *n.* a person or thing that stems; ☆specif., one that removes stems as from fruit or tobacco

stem·son (stem′s'n) *n.* [STEM¹ + (KEEL)SON] a timber connecting stem and keelson in the frame of a wooden ship

stem turn a turn made in skiing by stemming with one of the skis and bringing the other parallel

☆**stem·ware** (stem′wer′) *n.* goblets, wineglasses, etc. having stems

☆**stem-wind·er** (-wīn′dər) *n.* a stem-winding watch

☆**stem-wind·ing** (-wīn′diŋ) *adj.* wound by turning a knurled knob at the outer end of the stem

stench (stench) *n.* [ME. < OE. *stenc* < base of *stincan*, to STINK] an offensive smell or odor; stink

sten·cil (sten′s'l) *vt.* **-ciled** or **-cilled**, **-cil·ing** or **-cil·ling** [< ME. *stansilen*, to ornament with spangles < OFr. *estenceler* < *estencele*, a spangle, spark < VL. **stincilla*, for L. *scintilla*, a spark: see SCINTILLATE] to make, mark, or paint with a stencil —*n.* 1. a thin sheet, as of paper or metal, perforated or cut through in such a way that when ink, paint, etc. is applied to the sheet, the patterns, designs, letters, etc. are marked on the surface beneath 2. a pattern, design, letter, etc. made by stenciling —**sten′cil·er, sten′cil·ler** *n.*

Sten·dhal (sten′däl; *Fr.* stän däl′) (pseud. of *Marie Henri Beyle*) 1783–1842; Fr. novelist and essayist

☆**sten·o** (sten′ō) *n.*, *pl.* **sten′os** *clipped form of:* 1. STENOGRAPHER 2. STENOGRAPHY

sten·o- (sten′ō, -ə) [< Gr. *stenos*, narrow < IE. base **sten-*, whence OE. *stith*, hard, austere] *a combining form meaning* narrow, thin, small, etc. [*stenography*]

sten·o·bath (sten′ə bath′) *n.* [prec. + Gr. *bathos*, depth] *Biol.* an organism that can live only in a narrow range of water depths: opposed to EURYBATH —**sten′o·bath′ic** *adj.*

sten·o·graph (sten′ə graf′, -gräf′) *vt.* [back-formation < ff.] to write in shorthand —*n.* ☆a keyboard machine that prints shorthand symbols

☆**ste·nog·ra·pher** (stə näg′rə fər) *n.* a person skilled in stenography

ste·nog·ra·phy (-fē) *n.* [STENO- + -GRAPHY] shorthand writing; specif., the skill or work of writing down dictation, testimony, etc. in shorthand and later transcribing it, as on a typewriter —**sten·o·graph·ic** (sten′ə graf′ik), **sten′o·graph′i·cal** *adj.* —**sten′o·graph′i·cal·ly** *adv.*

sten·o·ha·line (sten′ə hā′lin, -hal′in) *adj.* [STENO- + HAL(O)- + -INE⁴] *Biol.* able to exist only in waters with a very narrow range in their salt content: opposed to EURYHALINE

sten·o·hy·gric (-hī′grik) *adj.* [STENO- + HYGR- + -IC] *Biol.* able to withstand only a narrow range of humidity: opposed to EURYHYGRIC

ste·no·ky (stə nō′kē) *n.* [< STEN(O)- + -oky: see EUROKY] *Biol.* the ability of an organism to live only under a very narrow range of environmental conditions: opposed to EUROKY —**ste·no′kous** *adj.*

ste·noph·a·gous (stə näf′ə gəs) *adj.* [STENO- + -PHAGOUS] *Biol.* eating only a limited variety of foods: opposed to EURYPHAGOUS

ste·nosed (-nōst′, -nōzd′) *adj.* that has undergone stenosis; narrowed; constricted

ste·no·sis (stə nō′sis) *n.* [ModL. < Gr. *stenōsis*: see STENO- & -OSIS] *Med.* a narrowing, or constriction, of a passage, duct, opening, etc. —**ste·not′ic** (-nät′ik) *adj.*

sten·o·therm (sten′ə therm′) *n.* [STENO- + -THERM] an organism that can live only in a narrow range of temperatures: opposed to EURYTHERM —**sten′o·ther′mal** (-thur′m'l), **sten′o·ther′mous** (-məs), **sten′o·ther′mic** (-mik) *adj.*

sten·o·top·ic (sten′ə täp′ik) *adj.* [< G. *stenotop*, stenotopic (< *steno-*, STENO- + *-top* < Gr. *topos*, place: see TOPIC) + -IC] *Biol.* able to withstand only a limited range of variations in environmental conditions: opposed to EURYTOPIC

☆**sten·o·type** (sten′ə tīp′) *n.* [STENO- + -TYPE] 1. a symbol or symbols representing a sound, word, or phrase in stenotypy 2. a keyboard machine that prints such symbols —*vt.* **-typed′, -typ′ing** to record by stenotype

sten·o·typ·y (-tī′pē) *n.* shorthand in which symbols representing sounds, words, or phrases are typed on a keyboard machine —**sten′o·typ′ist** *n.*

Sten·tor (sten′tôr) [L. < Gr. *Stentōr*, akin to *stenein*, to rumble, roar < IE. base **(s)ten-*, whence L. *tonare*, to THUNDER] a Greek herald in the *Iliad* as having the voice of fifty men —*n.* 1. [*usually* s-] a person having a very loud voice 2. [s-] any of a genus (*Stentor*) of large, trumpet-shaped, ciliate protozoans, found in stagnant fresh waters

sten·to·ri·an (sten tôr′ē ən) *adj.* [prec. + -IAN] very loud

step (step) *n.* [ME. *steppe* < OE. *stepe*, akin to G. *stapf* < IE. base **steb-*, post, pole: basic sense "to stamp feet": cf. STAMP] 1. the act of moving and placing the foot forward, backward, sideways, up, or down, as in walking, dancing, or climbing 2. the distance covered by such a movement 3. a short distance 4. *a)* a manner of stepping; gait *b)* any of various paces or strides in marching [*the goose step*] *c)* a sequence of movements in dancing, usually repeated in a set pattern 5. the sound of stepping; tread; footfall 6. a mark or impression made by stepping; footprint 7. a rest for the foot in climbing, as a stair or the rung of a ladder 8. [*pl.*] *a)* a flight of stairs *b)* [Brit.] a stepladder 9. something resembling a stair step; specif., *a)* a bend or angle, as in a supply pipe, for passing around an obstruction *b)* a shelf or ledge cut in mining or quarrying *c)* a raised frame or platform supporting the butt end of a mast *d)* any of a series of angled surfaces on the underside of the hull of a hydroplane or seaplane 10. a degree; rank; level; stage [*one step nearer victory*] 11. any of a series of acts, processes, etc. [*explain the next step*] 12. *Music a)* a degree of the staff or scale *b)* the interval between two consecutive degrees —*vi.* **stepped, step′ping** [ME. *steppen* < OE. *steppan*] 1. to move by executing a step or steps 2. to walk, esp. a short distance [*step outside*] 3. to move with measured steps, as in dancing 4. to move quickly or briskly: often with *along* 5. to come or enter (into a situation, condition, etc.) [*to step into a fortune*] 6. *a)* to put the foot down (*on* or *in* something) *b)* to press down with the foot (*on* something) [*to step on the brake*] —*vt.* 1. to take (one or more strides or paces) 2. *a)* to set (the foot) down *b)* to move across or over on foot 3. to execute the steps of (a dance) 4. to measure by taking steps: usually with *off* [*step off ten paces*] 5. to provide with steps; specif., *a)* to cut steps in (a slope, etc.) *b)* to arrange in a series of degrees or grades [*to step tests*] 6. *Naut.* to set and fix (a mast) in its step —**break step** to stop marching in cadence —**in step** 1. conforming to a rhythm or cadence in marching, dancing, etc.; esp., conforming to the cadence of another marcher or other marchers 2. in conformity or agreement —**keep step** to stay in step —**out of step** not in step —**step by step** carefully or slowly; by degrees; gradually —**step down** ☆1. to resign or abdicate (*from* an office, position, etc.) ☆2. to decrease or reduce, as in rate, by or as by one or more steps, or degrees —**step in** to start to participate; intervene —**step it** to dance —**step on it** [Colloq.] to go faster;

hurry; hasten —**step out 1.** to leave a room, building, etc., esp. for a short time **2.** to start to walk briskly, esp. with long strides ☆**3.** [Colloq.] to go out for a good time; go on a date —**step up 1.** to go or come near; approach **2.** to advance or progress ☆**3.** to increase or raise, as in rate, by or as by one or more steps, or degrees —**take steps** to adopt certain means or measures —☆**watch one's step 1.** to exercise care in walking or stepping **2.** [Colloq.] to be careful or cautious

step- (step) [ME. < OE. *steop-*, orphaned (akin to G. *stief-*, ON. *stjup-*) < base of *stiepan*, to bereave, prob. < IE. *(s)teub-*, to strike (hence "cut off"), whence STUMP, STEEP¹: orig. used of orphaned children] *a combining form meaning* related through the remarriage of a parent [*stepchild, stepparent*]

step·broth·er (step′bruth′ər) *n.* [prec. + BROTHER] one's stepparent's son by a former marriage

step·child (-chīld′) *n., pl.* **-chil′dren** (-chil′drən) [ME. < OE. *steopcild:* see STEP- & CHILD] a child of one's husband or wife by a former marriage

step·dame (-dām′) *n.* [Archaic] *same as* STEPMOTHER

step·daugh·ter (-dôt′ər) *n.* a female stepchild

step-down (-doun′) *adj.* that steps down, or decreases; specif., *a*) designating a transformer that converts electric power or signals from a higher to a lower voltage *b*) designating a gear that reduces the ratio —*n.* a decrease, as in amount, intensity, etc.

step·fa·ther (-fä′thər) *n.* a male stepparent

Steph·a·nie (stef′ə nē) [var. of *Stephana*, fem. of *Stephanus:* see STEPHEN] a feminine name

steph·a·no·tis (stef′ə nōt′is) *n.* [ModL. < Gr. *stephanōtis*, fit for a crown < *stephanos*, that which surrounds, a crown < *stephein*, to encircle, crown, akin to Per. *tāj*, a crown] any of a genus (*Stephanotis*) of climbing plants of the milkweed family; esp., a woody vine (*Stephanotis floribunda*) grown for its white, waxy, sweet-scented flowers

Ste·phen (stē′vən) [L. *Stephanus* < Gr. *Stephanas* < *stephanos*, a crown: see prec.] **1.** a masculine name: dim. *Steve;* equiv. L. *Stephanus,* Fr. *Étienne,* Ger. *Stephan,* It. *Stefano,* Sp. *Esteban,* Russ. *Stepan;* fem. *Stephanie* **2.** *Bible* one of the seven chosen to assist the Apostles (Acts 6 & 7); the 1st Christian martyr (called **Saint Stephen**): his day is Dec. 26 **3.** (*Stephen of Blois*) 1100?–54; king of England (1135–54): grandson of WILLIAM THE CONQUEROR **4. Stephen I** 975?–1038; king of Hungary (1001?–38): also **Saint Stephen:** his day is Sept. 2 (in Hungary, Aug. 20) **5. Sir Leslie,** 1832–1904; Eng. critic & philosopher: father of Virginia WOOLF

Ste·phens (stē′vənz) **1. Alexander Hamilton,** 1812–83; U.S. statesman; vice president of the Confederacy (1861–65) **2. James,** 1882–1950; Ir. poet & novelist

Ste·phen·son (stē′vən sən) **1. George,** 1781–1848; Eng. engineer: developed the steam locomotive **2. Robert,** 1803–59; Eng. engineer & bridge builder: son of *prec.*

step-in (step′in′) *adj.* put on by being stepped into [a *step-in* dress] —*n.* a step-in garment or [*pl.*], esp. formerly, undergarment

step·lad·der (-lad′ər) *n.* a ladder with broad, flat steps, typically consisting of two frames joined at the top, usually with a hinge, so that it stands on four legs

step·moth·er (-muth′ər) *n.* a female stepparent

Step·ney (step′nē) metropolitan borough of London: pop. 92,000

step·par·ent (-per′ənt, -par′-) *n.* [STEP- + PARENT] the person who has married one's parent after the death or divorce of the other parent; stepfather or stepmother

steppe (step) *n.* [Russ. *step'*] **1.** any of the great plains of SE Europe and Asia, having few trees **2.** any similar plain

☆**stepped-up** (stept′up′) *adj.* increased, as in tempo; accelerated

step·per (step′ər) *n.* a person or animal that steps, usually in a specified manner, as a dancer or a horse

step·ping-stone (step′iŋ stōn′) *n.* **1.** a stone, usually one of a series, used to step on, as in crossing a stream, soft turf, etc. **2.** something used to better one's position or situation; means of advancement Also **stepping stone**

step·sis·ter (step′sis′tər) *n.* [STEP- + SISTER] one's stepparent's daughter by a former marriage

step·son (-sun′) *n.* a male stepchild

step-up (-up′) *adj.* that steps up, or increases; specif., *a*) designating a transformer that converts electric power or signals from a lower to a higher voltage *b*) designating a gear that increases the ratio —*n.* an increase, as in amount, intensity, etc.

step·wise (-wīz′) *adv.* like a series of steps

-ster (stər) [ME. < OE. *-estre*, orig. a fem. agent suffix] *a suffix meaning:* **1.** a person who is, does, or creates (something specified) [*oldster, punster*]: often derogatory [*rhymester, trickster*] **2.** a person associated with (something specified) [*gangster*]

ster. sterling

ste·ra·di·an (stə rā′dē ən) *n.* [STE(REO)- + RADIAN] the unit of measure of solid angles, equal to the angle subtended at the center of a sphere of unit radius by unit area on its surface

ster·co·ra·ceous (stur′kə rā′shəs) *adj.* [< L. *stercus* (gen. *stercoris*), dung < IE. base *(s)ter-*, whence ON. *threkkr*, G. *dreck*, dirt, filth + -ACEOUS] of, containing, like, or having the nature of feces, or dung

ster·co·ric·o·lous (-rik′ə ləs) *adj.* [< L. *stercus* (gen. *stercoris*), dung + -COLOUS] *Biol.* living in dung, as some insects

ster·cu·li·a (stur kyōō′lē ə) *adj.* [< L. *Sterculius*, the deity presiding over manuring < *stercus:* see STERCORACEOUS] designating a family (Sterculiaceae) of tropical plants, mostly shrubs and trees, including the cacao, cola, etc.

stere (stir) *n.* [Fr. *stère* < Gr. *stereos*, solid, cubic: see STEREO-] a cubic meter

ster·e·o- (ster′ē ō′, stir′-) *n., pl.* **-os'** ☆**1.** *a*) a stereophonic record player, radio, etc. *b*) a stereophonic system or effect [to record in *stereo*] *c*) a stereophonic record, tape, etc. **2.** *a*) a stereoscope or similar device *b*) a stereoscopic system or effect *c*) a stereoscopic picture, film, etc. **3.** *clipped form of: a*) STEREOTYPE *b*) STEREOTYPY —*adj. clipped form of:* **1.** STEREOPHONIC **2.** STEREOTYPIC

ster·e·o- (ster′ē ō′; *also*, -ə) [< Gr. *stereos*, hard, firm, solid < IE. base *ster-*, stiff, whence STARE] *a combining form meaning* solid, firm, three-dimensional [*stereoscope, stereography*]: also *stereo-*, before some vowels, *ster-*

ster·e·o·bate (ster′ē ə bāt′, stir′-) *n.* [L. *stereobata* < Gr. *stereobatēs* < *stereos*, solid (see STEREO-) + *batēs*, that which steps or treads < *bainein*, to COME] a foundation, as of a building, or a solid substructure or platform of masonry

ster·e·o·chem·is·try (ster′ē ō kem′is trē, stir′-) *n.* [STEREO- + CHEMISTRY] the branch of chemistry dealing with the spatial arrangement of atoms or groups of atoms that make up molecules

ster·e·o·chrome (ster′ē ə krōm′, stir′-) *n.* a picture produced by stereochromy

ster·e·o·chro·my (-krō′mē) *n.* [G. *stereochromie* < Gr. *stereos*, solid (see STEREO-) + *chrōma*, color: see CHROME] a process of mural painting using water glass as a fixative, either mixed with the pigment or laid over the finished painting —**ster′e·o·chro′mic** *adj.*

ster·e·o·gram (-gram′) *n.* **1.** a stereographic diagram or picture **2.** *same as* STEREOGRAPH

ster·e·o·graph (-graf′, -gräf′) *n.* [STEREO- + -GRAPH] a picture or a pair of pictures prepared for use with a stereoscope

ster·e·og·ra·phy (ster′ē äg′rə fē, stir′-) *n.* [STEREO- + -GRAPHY] the art of representing the forms of solids on a plane surface; specif., the branch of solid geometry that deals with the construction of regularly defined solids —**ster′e·o·graph′ic** (-ə graf′ik), **ster′e·o·graph′i·cal** *adj.* —**ster′e·o·graph′i·cal·ly** *adv.*

ster·e·o·i·so·mer (ster′ē ō ī′sə mər, stir′-) *n.* [STEREO- + ISOMER] any of two or more isomers containing the same number and kind of atoms linked in an identical manner in the molecule and differing from each other only in the spatial arrangement of the atoms or groups of atoms —**ster′e·o·i′so·mer′ic** (-mer′ik) *adj.* —**ster′e·o′i·som′er·ism** (-ī säm′ər iz′m) *n.*

ster·e·om·e·try (ster′ē äm′ə trē, stir′-) *n.* [STEREO- + -METRY] the art of determining the dimensions and volume of solids —**ster′e·o·met′ric** (-ə met′rik), **ster′e·o·met′ri·cal** *adj.* —**ster′e·o·met′ri·cal·ly** *adv.*

ster·e·o·phon·ic (ster′ē ə fän′ik) *adj.* [STEREO- + PHONIC] designating of sound reproduction, as in motion pictures, records, tapes, or broadcasting, using two or more channels to carry and reproduce the sounds from the directions in which they were originally picked up by corresponding microphones —**ster′e·o·phon′i·cal·ly** *adv.* —**ster′e·oph′o·ny** (-äf′ə nē, ster′ē ə fō′nē, stir′-) *n.*

ster·e·op·sis (-äp′sis) *n.* [ModL.: see STEREO- & -OPSIS] stereoscopic vision

☆**ster·e·op·ti·con** (-äp′ti kən, -kän′) *n.* [< Gr. *stereos*, solid (see STEREO-) + *optikon*, neut. of *optikos*, of sight, OPTIC] a kind of slide projector designed to allow one view to fade out while the next is fading in

ster·e·o·scope (ster′ē ə skōp′, stir′-) *n.* [STEREO- + -SCOPE] an instrument with two eyepieces through which a pair of photographs of the same scene or subject, taken at slightly different angles, are viewed side by side: the two photographs are seen as a single picture apparently having depth, or three dimensions — **ster′e·o·scop′ic** (-skäp′ik) *adj.* — **ster′e·o·scop′i·cal·ly** *adv.*

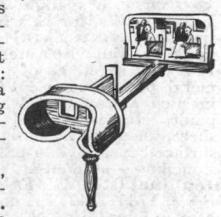

STEREOSCOPE

ster·e·os·co·py (ster′ē äs′kə pē, stir′-) *n.* **1.** the science of stereoscopic effects and techniques **2.** the viewing of things as in three dimensions

ster·e·o·tax·is (-ə tak′sis) *n.* [see STEREO- & TAXIS] *Biol.* a taxis for which the stimulus is contact with a solid body —**ster′e·o·tac′tic** (-tak′tik) *adj.*

ster·e·ot·o·my (-ät′ə mē) *n.* [Fr. *stéréotomie* < *stéréo-*, STEREO- + *-tomie*, -TOMY] the art or science of cutting solid bodies, esp. stone, into desired shapes

ster·e·ot·ro·pism (-ät′rə piz′m) *n.* *Biol.* a tropism in which the directing stimulus is contact with a solid body —**ster′e·o·trop′ic** (-ə träp′ik) *adj.*

ster·e·o·type (ster′ē ə tīp′, stir′-) *n.* [Fr. *stéréotype, adj.:* see STEREO- & -TYPE] **1.** a one-piece printing plate cast in type metal from a mold (*matrix*) taken of a printing surface, as a page of set type **2.** *same as* STEREOTYPY **3.**

an unvarying form or pattern; specif., a fixed or conventional notion or conception, as of a person, group, idea, etc., held by a number of people, and allowing for no individuality, critical judgment, etc. —*vt.* **-typed′, -typ′ing 1.** to make a stereotype of **2.** to print from stereotype plates —**ster′e·o·typ′er, ster′e·o·typ′ist** *n.*

ster·e·o·typed (-tīpt′) *adj.* **1.** having the nature of a stereotype; esp., hackneyed; trite; not original or individualized **2.** printed from stereotype plates —*SYN.* see TRITE

ster·e·o·typ·ic (ster′ē ə tip′ik, stir′-) *adj.* **1.** of or produced by stereotypy **2.** stereotyped; hackneyed Also **ster′e·o·typ′i·cal**

ster·e·o·typ·y (ster′ē ə tī′pē, stir′-) *n.* [Fr. *stéréotypie*] **1.** the process of making or printing from stereotype plates **2.** abnormal repetition of an action, speech phrase, etc., or abnormal sustained maintenance of a single position or posture, as seen in some phases of schizophrenia

ster·ic (ster′ik, stir′-) *adj.* [STER(EO-) + -IC] *Chem.* having to do with the spatial arrangement of the atoms in a molecule —**ster′i·cal·ly** *adv.*

steric hindrance the prevention or retardation of a chemical reaction, caused by the steric arrangement of atoms

ster·i·lant (ster′ə lənt) *n.* a sterilizing agent, as a chemical, hormone, heat, etc.

ster·ile (ster′l; *Brit. & Canad., usually* -īl) *adj.* [L. *sterilis* < IE. **ster-*, barren (whence Gr. *steira*, barren, OE. *stierc*, calf), special use of base **ster-*, stiff, rigid, whence STARE] **1.** incapable of producing others of its kind; barren **2.** producing little or nothing; unfruitful [*sterile* soil, a *sterile* policy] **3.** lacking in interest or vitality; not stimulating or effective [a *sterile* style] **4.** free from living microorganisms; esp., aseptic **5.** *Bot. a)* unable or failing to bear fruit or spores, as a plant, or to germinate, as a seed *b)* having stamens only, as a male flower, or having neither pistils nor stamens —**ste·ril·i·ty** (stə ril′ə tē) *n.*

SYN.—**sterile** and **infertile** imply incapability of producing offspring or fruit, as because of some disorder of the reproductive system; **barren** and **unfruitful** are specifically applied to a sterile woman or to plants, soil, etc.; **impotent** is specif. applied to a man who cannot engage in sexual intercourse because of an inability to have an erection All of these words have figurative uses [*sterile* thinking, an *infertile* mind, a *barren* victory, *unfruitful* efforts, *impotent* rage] —*ANT.* **fertile**

ster·i·lize (ster′ə līz′) *vt.* **-lized′, -liz′ing** to make sterile; specif., *a)* to make incapable of producing others of its kind, as by removing the organs of reproduction or preventing them from functioning effectively *b)* to make (land) unproductive *c)* to free from living microorganisms, as by subjecting to great heat or chemical action Also [Chiefly Brit.] **ster′i·lise′** —**ster·i·li·za·tion** (ster′ə li zā′shən) *n.* —**ster′i·liz′er** *n.*

ster·let (stur′lit) *n.* [Russ. *sterlyad′*] a small sturgeon (*Acipenser ruthenus*) found in the Caspian Sea and used as food and as a source of caviar

ster·ling (stur′liŋ) *n.* [ME. *sterlinge*, Norman silver penny < ?] **1.** orig., an early English silver penny: a pound weight of these pennies was later standardized as a money of account **2.** English money having the fineness of quality of the standard silver penny **3.** sterling silver or articles made of it **4.** the standard of fineness of legal British coinage: for silver, 0.500; for gold, 0.91666 **5.** British money —*adj.* **1.** of standard quality; specif., designating a silver alloy that is at least 92.5 percent pure silver **2.** of or payable in British money **3.** made of sterling silver **4.** of genuinely high quality; excellent [*sterling* principles]

sterling area an association of countries, including the British Commonwealth (except Canada), that informally peg the value of their currencies to that of the British pound sterling: former name **sterling bloc**

Ster·ling Heights (stur′liŋ) [? ult. after Lord *Sterling*, general in the Am. Revolutionary Army, or STIRLING, Scotland] city in SE Mich.: suburb of Detroit: pop. 61,000

stern¹ (sturn) *adj.* [ME. *sterne* < OE. *styrne* < IE. base **ster-*, stiff, rigid (cf. STARE, STARVE)] **1.** hard; severe; unyielding; strict [*stern* measures] **2.** grim; forbidding [a *stern* face] **3.** relentless; inexorable [*stern* reality] **4.** unshakable; firm [*stern* determination] —*SYN.* see SEVERE —**stern′ly** *adv.* —**stern′ness** *n.*

stern² (sturn) *n.* [ME. *steorne*, stern, rudder < ON. *stjorn*, steering < *styra*, to STEER¹] **1.** the rear end of a ship, boat, etc. **2.** the rear end of anything

ster·na (stur′nə) *n.* alt. *pl.* of STERNUM

ster·nal (stur′n'l) *adj.* of or near the sternum

stern chaser a gun mounted on the stern of a ship, used for firing to the rear

Sterne (sturn), **Laurence** 1713-68; Brit. novelist & clergyman, born in Ireland

stern·fore·most (sturn′fôr′mōst) *adv.* **1.** with the stern foremost; backward **2.** awkwardly; clumsily

stern·most (sturn′mōst) *adj.* **1.** nearest the stern **2.** farthest astern; rearmost

☆**Ster·no** (stur′nō) *a trademark for* gelatinized methyl alcohol with nitrocellulose, sold in cans as a fuel for small stoves or chafing dishes

ster·no- (stur′nō, -nə) [< STERNUM] *a combining form meaning* of the sternum and

stern·post (sturn′pōst′) *n.* the main, upright piece at the stern of a vessel, usually supporting the rudder

stern sheets the space at the stern of an open boat

stern·son (sturn′s'n) *n.* [STERN² + (KEEL)SON] a heavy curved piece connecting a ship's keelson to the sternpost: also **sternson knee, stern knee**

ster·num (stur′nəm) *n., pl.* **ster′nums, ster′na** (-nə) [ModL. < Gr. *sternon*, the breastbone < IE. base **ster-*, to spread out] a thin, flat structure of bone and cartilage to which most of the ribs are attached in the front of the chest in most vertebrates; breastbone: see SKELETON, illus.

ster·nu·ta·tion (stur′nyoo tā′shən) *n.* [L. *sternutatio* < *sternutare*, freq. of *sternuere*, to sneeze < IE. echoic base **pster-*, to sneeze, whence Gr. *ptarnysthai*] a sneeze or the act of sneezing

ster·nu·ta·tor (stur′nyoo tāt′ər) *n.* a gas designed to incapacitate by severely irritating the respiratory passages

ster·nu·ta·to·ry (stər nyōōt′ə tôr′ē) *adj.* **1.** of or causing sternutation **2.** being, or having the effect of, a sternutator Also **ster·nu·ta·tive** (stur′nyoo tāt′iv) —*n., pl.* **-ries** a sternutatory substance

stern·ward (sturn′wərd) *adv., adj.* toward the stern; astern: also **stern′wards** (-wərdz) *adv.*

stern·way (-wā′) *n.* backward movement of a ship

☆**stern-wheel·er** (-hwēl′ər, -wēl′ər) *n.* a steamer propelled by a paddle wheel at the stern

ster·oid (stir′oid, ster′-) *n.* [STER(OL) + -OID] any of a group of compounds including the sterols, bile acids, sex hormones, etc., characteristically having the carbon-atom ring structure of the sterols —**ste·roi′dal** *adj.*

ster·ol (stir′ōl, ster′-; -ōl) *n.* [< (CHOLE)STEROL] any of a group of solid cyclic unsaturated alcohols, as cholesterol, found in plant and animal tissues

ster·tor (stur′tər) *n.* [ModL. < L. *stertere*, to snore] loud, raspy, labored breathing, or snoring, caused by obstructed respiratory passages —**ster′to·rous** *adj.* —**ster′to·rous·ly** *adv.* —**ster′to·rous·ness** *n.*

stet (stet) [L., 3d pers. sing., pres. subj., of *stare*, to STAND] let it stand: a printer's term used to indicate that matter previously marked for deletion is to remain —*vt.* **stet′ted, stet′ting** to cancel a change in or a marked deletion of (a word, character, passage, etc., as in a proof or manuscript), as by writing "stet" in the margin

steth·o- (steth′ō, -ə) [Gr. *stētho-* < *stēthos*, the chest, breast] *a combining form meaning* chest, breast [*stethoscope*]: also, before a vowel, **steth-**

steth·o·scope (steth′ə skōp′) *n.* [Fr. *stéthoscope:* see STETHO- & -SCOPE] *Med.* a hearing instrument used in auscultation, for examining the heart, lungs, etc. by listening to the sounds they make —**steth′o·scop′ic** (-skäp′ik), **steth′o·scop′i·cal** *adj.* —**steth′o·scop′i·cal·ly** *adv.* —**ste·thos·co·py** (ste thäs′kə pē) *n.*

St-É·tienne (san tā tyen′) city in SE France: pop. 201,000

☆**Stet·son** (stet′s'n) *a trademark for* hats of various kinds —*n.* [*often* s-] a man's hat, worn esp. by Western cowboys, usually of felt, with a broad brim and a high, soft crown

Stet·tin (shte tēn′) *Ger. name of* SZCZECIN

Steu·ben (stōō′b'n; *G.* shtoi′bən), Baron **Frederick William Augustus von** 1730-94; Prussian military officer: served as Am. general in the American Revolution

☆**ste·ve·dore** (stē′və dôr′) *n.* [Sp. *estivador* < *estivar*, to stow, ram tight: see STEEVE¹] a person employed at loading and unloading ships; longshoreman —*vt., vi.* **-dored′, -dor′ing** to load or unload the cargo of (a ship)

stevedore's knot a kind of knot: see KNOT, illus.

Ste·ven (stē′vən) *a masculine name:* see STEPHEN

Ste·vens (stē′vənz) **1. Thaddeus,** 1792-1868; U.S. statesman & abolitionist **2. Wallace,** 1879-1955; U.S. poet

Ste·ven·son (stē′vən s'n), **Robert Louis (Balfour)** 1850-94; Scot. novelist, poet, & essayist

stew (stōō, styōō) *vt.* [ME. *stuen* < MFr. *estuver*, to stew, bathe < VL. **extufare* < L. *ex*, out + Gr. *typhos*, steam, smoke < IE. **dheubh-* < base **dheu-*, to drizzle, be stormy, whence DEAF, DUMB, L. *fumus*, smoke] to cook by simmering or boiling slowly for a long time —*vi.* **1.** to undergo cooking in this way **2.** to be oppressed with heat, crowded conditions, etc. **3.** to fret, fume, or worry; be vexed or troubled —*n.* [ME. *stewe* < MFr. *estue*] **1.** [< obs. sense, a public room for hot baths] *earlier term for* BROTHEL: *usually used in pl.* **2.** a dish, esp. a mixture of meat and vegetables, cooked by stewing **3.** a state of vexation or worry —*SYN.* see BOIL¹ —**stew in one's own juice** to suffer from one's own actions

stew·ard (stōō′ərd, styōō′-) *n.* [ME. *stiward* < OE. *stiweard* < *stig*, enclosure, hall, STY¹ + *weard*, a keeper, WARD] **1.** a person put in charge of the affairs of a large household or estate, whose duties include supervision of the kitchen and the servants, management of household accounts, etc. **2.** one who acts as a supervisor or administrator, as of finances and property, for another or others **3.** a person variously responsible for the food and drink, the service personnel, etc. in a club, restaurant, etc. **4.** a person, usually one of a group, in charge of arrangements

for a ball, race, meeting, etc. **5.** an attendant, as on a ship, airplane, etc., employed to look after the passengers' comfort **6.** an officer on a ship who is in charge of stores and culinary arrangements **7.** *short for* SHOP STEWARD —*vi.* to act as a steward —**stew′ard·ship′** *n.*

stew·ard·ess (-ər dis) *n.* a woman steward (esp. sense 5)

Stew·art (stōo′ərt, styōo′-) **1.** a masculine name: see STUART **2. Potter,** 1915– ; U.S. jurist; associate justice, U.S. Supreme Court (1958–)

Stewart Island island of New Zealand, just south of South Island: 670 sq. mi.; pop. 540

stewed (stōod) *adj.* **1.** cooked by stewing, as food **2.** [Slang] drunk; intoxicated

stew·pan (stōo′pan′, styōo′-) *n.* a pan used for stewing

stg. sterling

St. Gal·len (gäl′ən) **1.** canton of NE Switzerland, on the Rhine: 775 sq. mi.; pop. 353,000 **2.** its capital, in the N part: pop. 77,000 Fr. name **St-Gall** (san gàl′)

stge. storage

St. George's Channel strait between Ireland & Wales, connecting the Irish Sea with the Atlantic: c.100 mi. long

St. Gott·hard (gät′ərd, gäth′-) **1.** mountain group in the Lepontine Alps, SC Switzerland: highest peak, 10,490 ft. **2.** pass through these mountains: c.6,935 ft. high **3.** railway tunnel below this pass: 9 1/4 mi. long Fr. name **St-Got·hard** (san gô tàr′)

St. He·le·na (hə lē′nə, hel′i nə) **1.** Brit. island in the South Atlantic, c.1,200 mi. from Africa: site of Napoleon's exile (1815–21): 47 sq. mi.; pop. 4,600 **2.** Brit. colony including this island, Ascension, & the Tristan da Cunha group: c.120 sq. mi.; pop. 5,200

St. Hel·ens (hel′ənz) city in Lancashire, NW England, near Liverpool: pop. 107,000

sthen·ic (sthen′ik) *adj.* [< Gr. *sthenos*, strength + -IC] **1.** designating or of a constitutional body type of athletic physique **2.** designating or of feelings marked by excessive excitement or heightened nervous energy

stib·ine (stib′ēn, -in) *n.* [< L. *stibium*, antimony + -INE⁴] antimonous hydride, SbH₃, a colorless, poisonous gas

stib·nite (-nīt) *n.* [< STIBINE + -ITE¹] native trisulfide of antimony, Sb₂S₃, a lead-gray, usually crystalline mineral

stich (stik) *n.* [Gr. *stichos* < base of *steichein*, to go, walk < IE. base *steigh-*, whence STAIR] *Prosody* a line, or verse

sti·chom·e·try (sti käm′ə trē) *n.* [< Gr. *stichos*, a line (see prec.) + -METRY] the practice of expressing the successive ideas in a prose composition in single lines of lengths corresponding to natural cadences or sense divisions —**stich·o·met·ric** (stik′ə met′rik), **stich′o·met′ri·cal** *adj.*

stich·o·myth·i·a (stik′ə mith′ē ə) *n.* [Gr. *stichomythia* < *stichos*, a line (see STICH) + *mythos*, speech, MYTH] dialogue in brief, alternate lines, as in ancient Greek drama: also **sti·chom·y·thy** (sti käm′ə thē) —**stich′o·myth′ic** *adj.*

-stich·ous (stik′əs) [< Gr. *stichos*, a line (see STICH) + -OUS] *a combining form meaning* having (a specified number or kind of) rows [tristichous]

stick (stik) *n.* [ME. *stikke* < OE. *sticca*, akin to Du. *stek*, ON. *stik* < IE. base *steig-*, a point, whence Gr. *stigma*, L. *instigare* (cf. INSTIGATE)] **1.** a long, usually slender piece of wood; specif., *a)* a twig or small branch broken off or cut off, esp. a dead and dry one *b)* a tree branch of any size, used for fuel, etc. *c)* a long, slender, and usually tapering piece of wood shaped for a specific purpose, as a wand, staff, club, baton, cane, rod, etc. **2.** a stalk, as of celery **3.** something shaped like a stick; sticklike piece [a *stick* of chewing gum] **4.** a separate item; article [every *stick* of furniture] **5.** an implement used for striking a ball, puck, etc. [a hockey *stick*] **6.** something made of sticks, as a racing hurdle **7.** a sticking, as with a pointed weapon; stab **8.** anything, as a threat, used in compelling another **9.** the power of adhering or making adhere **10.** *clipped form of* STICK SHIFT **11.** a number of bombs dropped from the air in such a way as to fall in a line across a target **12.** [Archaic] a stoppage, delay, or obstacle **13.** [Colloq.] a dull, stupid, or spiritless person **14.** [Slang] a marijuana cigarette **15.** *Aeron. short for* CONTROL STICK **16.** *Naut.* a mast or a part of a mast **17.** *Printing* a composing stick or its contents —*vt.* **stuck** or for *vt.* 9 **sticked, stick′ing** [combination of ME. *steken*, to prick, fasten (< OE. *stecan*) & ME. *stikien* < OE. *stician*, to stick, stab, prick: both akin to the *n.*] **1.** to pierce or puncture, as with a pointed instrument **2.** to kill by piercing; stab **3.** to pierce something with (a knife, pin, etc.) **4.** to thrust or push (*in, into, out,* etc.) [to *stick* one's finger into a hole] **5.** to set with piercing objects [a cushion *stuck* with pins] **6.** *a)* to fasten or attach as by gluing, pinning, etc. [to *stick* a poster on a wall] *b)* to decorate with things fastened in this way **7.** *a)* to transfix or impale *b)* to impale (insect specimens, etc.), as on a pin, and mount for exhibit **8.** to obstruct, entangle, bog down, etc.; also, to detain, delay, etc.: usually used in the passive [the wheels were *stuck*, he was *stuck* in town] **9.** [< the *n.*] *a)* to prop (a vine, etc.) with a stick or sticks *b) Printing* to set in a composing stick **10.** [Colloq.] to place; put; set **11.** [Colloq.] to make sticky by smearing **12.** [Colloq.] to puzzle; baffle [to be *stuck* by a question] **13.** [Slang] *a)* to make pay, often exorbitantly *b)* to impose a disagreeable task, burden, expense, etc. upon *c)* to cheat or defraud **14.** [Chiefly Brit. Slang] to endure

or tolerate —*vi.* **1.** to be or remain fixed or embedded by a pointed end, as a nail, etc. **2.** to be or remain attached by adhesion; adhere; cleave **3.** *a)* to remain in the same place; stay; abide [they *stick* at home] *b)* to remain fixed in the memory *c)* to remain in effect [to make the charges *stick*] **4.** to remain in close association; be fixed; cling [friends *stick* together, the nickname *stuck*] **5.** to keep close [to *stick* to a trail] **6.** to persevere; persist [to *stick* at a job] **7.** to remain firm and resolute; endure [she *stuck* through thick and thin] **8.** to become fixed, blocked, lodged, etc., as by an obstacle; specif., *a)* to become embedded and immovable [a shoe *stuck* in the mud] *b)* to become unworkable; jam [the gears *stuck*] *c)* to become stopped or delayed; come to a standstill [a bill *stuck* in committee] **9.** to be puzzled **10.** to be reluctant; hesitate; scruple [a person who will *stick* at nothing] **11.** to protrude, project, or extend (*out, up, through,* etc.) —☆**be on the stick** [Slang] to be alert, efficient, etc. —**stick around** [Slang] to stay near at hand; not go away —**stick by** (or **to**) to remain faithful or loyal to —**stick it out** [Slang] to carry on or endure something until it is ended —☆**stick to one's ribs** to be nourishing and satisfying: said of food —**stick up** [Slang] to commit armed robbery upon —**stick up for** [Colloq.] to support; uphold; defend —☆**the sticks** [Colloq.] the rural districts; hinterland

SYN.—stick is the simple, general term here, implying attachment by gluing or fastening together in any way, by close association, etc. [to *stick* a stamp on a letter, to *stick* to a subject]; **adhere** implies firm attachment and, of persons, denotes voluntary allegiance or devotion to an idea, cause, leader, etc. [to *adhere* to a policy]; **cohere** implies such close sticking together of parts as to form a single mass [glue made the particles of sawdust *cohere*]; **cling** implies attachment by embracing, entwining, or grasping with the arms, tendrils, etc. [a vine *clinging* to the trellis]; **cleave** is a poetic or lofty term implying a very close, firm attachment [his tongue *cleaved* to the roof of his mouth, Ruth *cleaved* to Naomi] —*ANT.* part, detach, separate

stick·a·bil·i·ty (stik′ə bil′ə tē) *n.* [prec. + ABILITY] the ability to endure something or persevere in something

☆**stick·ball** (stik′bôl′) *n.* a game like baseball played by children, as on city streets, with improvised equipment such as a broom handle and a soft rubber ball

stick·er (-ər) *n.* a person or thing that sticks; specif., ☆*a)* a bur, barb, or thorn ☆*b)* a gummed patch or label *c)* a tenacious or persistent person *d)* [Colloq.] *same as* STICK-LER *e)* [Slang] a knife used as a weapon

stick·ful (-fool′) *n. Printing* the contents or capacity of a composing stick

stick·i·ly (-′l ē) *adv.* in a sticky manner

stick·i·ness (-ē nis) *n.* a sticky quality or condition

sticking plaster adhesive material for covering a slight wound, usually a thin cloth gummed on one side

stick insect *same as* PHASMID

stick-in-the-mud (stik′′n thə mud′) *n.* [Colloq.] a person who resists change or progress, new ideas, etc.

stick·le (stik′′l) *vi.* **-led, -ling** [prob. < ME. *stightlen*, to rule, order, dispose, freq. of *stighten*, to dispose, destine < OE. *stihtan*, prob. akin to G. *stiften*, to arrange, establish: for prob. IE. base see STAIR] **1.** to raise objections, haggle, or make difficulties, esp. in a stubborn, narrow manner and usually about trifles **2.** to have objections; scruple (*at*)

stick·le·back (stik′′l bak′) *n.* [ME. *stykylbak* < OE. *sticel*, a prick, sting < base of *sticca* (see STICK) + ME. *bak*, BACK¹] any of several small, scaleless, saltwater and freshwater fishes (family Gasterosteidae) with two to eleven sharp spines in front of the dorsal fin: the male builds a nest for the female's eggs

STICKLEBACK
(2-3 in. long)

stick·ler (stik′lər) *n.* [cf. STICKLE] **1.** a person who insists uncompromisingly on the observance of something specified (usually with *for*) [a *stickler* for discipline] **2.** [Colloq.] something puzzling or difficult to solve

stick·man (stik′man′) *n., pl.* **-men′** (-men′) [Slang] ☆**1.** an employee of a gambling house who oversees the play, esp. at a dice table, raking in the dice and chips, as with a stick **2.** a player, as in hockey, with reference to his skill with the stick [a good *stickman*]

☆**stick·pin** (-pin′) *n.* a pin, esp. one set with a gem, worn as an ornament in a cravat or necktie

☆**stick·seed** (-sēd′) *n.* any of several plants with barbs or prickles on the seeds or fruit; esp., any of a genus (*Lappula*) of weedy plants of the borage family with small blue or whitish flowers

☆**stick shift** a gearshift for an automotive vehicle operated manually, rather than automatically, by moving a lever, esp. one on the floor of the vehicle

☆**stick·tight** (stik′tīt′) *n.* **1.** *same as:* a) BUR MARIGOLD b) STICKSEED **2.** the barbed achene of any of these plants

☆**stick-to-it·ive·ness** (stik tōo′it iv nis) *n.* [Colloq.] pertinacity; persistence; perseverance

☆**stick·um** (stik′əm) *n.* [STICK + 'em, short for THEM] [Colloq.] any sticky, or adhesive, substance

☆**stick up** (- up) *n. slang term for* HOLDUP (sense 2)

☆**stick·weed** (-wēd′) *n.* any of various N. American plants with barbed seeds, as the ragweed, stickseed, etc.

stick·work (-wurk′) *n.* skill in using a stick, as a hockey stick, a drumstick, a baseball bat, etc.

stick·y (-ē) *adj.* **stick′i·er, stick′i·est** **1.** that sticks; adhesive; tending to cling to anything touched **2.** covered with an adhesive substance [*sticky* fingers] **3.** [Colloq.] hot and humid [a *sticky* climate] ☆**4.** [Colloq.] difficult to deal with; troublesome [a *sticky* problem] ☆**5.** [Colloq.] overly sentimental; maudlin

☆**sticky fingers** [Slang] an inclination to steal or pilfer —**stick′y-fin′gered** *adj.*

sticky wicket **1.** *Cricket* the playing area between the wickets when it is damp and hence strong and slow **2.** [Chiefly Brit.] a difficult or awkward situation

Stieg·litz (stēg′lits), **Alfred** 1864–1946; U.S. photographer: husband of Georgia O'KEEFFE

stiff (stif) *adj.* [ME. *stif* < OE., akin to G. *steif* < IE. base *stip-*, a pole, sticking, whence L. *stipes*, a stem, stake, *stipare*, to crowd, cram: cf. STIFLE¹] **1.** hard to bend or stretch; rigid; firm; not flexible or pliant **2.** hard to move or operate; not free or limber **3.** stretched tight; taut; tense **4.** *a)* sore or limited in movement: said of joints and muscles *b)* having such joints or muscles, as from exertion, cold, etc. **5.** not fluid or loose; viscous; thick; dense; firm [to beat egg whites until *stiff*] **6.** strong; specif., *a)* moving swiftly, as a breeze or current *b)* containing much alcohol: said of a drink *c)* of high potency [a *stiff* dose of medicine] *d)* done or delivered with great force; powerful **7.** harsh [*stiff* punishment] **8.** difficult to do or deal with [a *stiff* climb, *stiff* competition] **9.** excessively formal, constrained, or awkward; not easy, natural, or graceful **10.** resolute, stubborn, or uncompromising, as a person, a fight, etc. **11.** [Colloq.] high or excessive [a *stiff* price] **12.** [Slang] drunk; intoxicated **13.** *Naut.* not careening or heeling over much despite the amount of sail carried or the strength of the wind —*adv.* **1.** to a stiff condition **2.** [Colloq.] completely; thoroughly [scared *stiff*] —*n.* [Slang] ☆**1.** a corpse ☆**2.** a drunken person **3.** an excessively formal or constrained person ☆**4.** an awkward or rough person ☆**5.** a hobo ☆**6.** a man [a working *stiff*] **7.** a person who gives a small tip or no gratuity at all —☆*vt.* **stiffed, stiff′ing** [Slang] to leave empty-handed, esp. with no tip, or gratuity —**stiff′ish** *adj.* —**stiff′ly** *adv.* —**stiff′ness** *n.*

SYN.—**stiff** implies a firmness of texture which makes a substance resist a bending force to a greater or lesser degree and figuratively connotes formality or constraint [a *stiff* collar, manner, etc.]; **rigid** implies such stiffness in a thing that it resists a bending force to the breaking point and figuratively connotes strictness or severity [a *rigid* framework, disciplinarian, etc.]; **inflexible** is applied to that which cannot be bent or, figuratively, diverted [an *inflexible* rod, will, etc.]; **inelastic** implies a lack of resilience and, figuratively, of adaptability [the brittle, *inelastic* bones of the aged, *inelastic* regulations] See also FIRM¹ —**ANT.** limp, pliant

stiff-arm (-ärm′) *vt.* to push away (an opponent, etc.) with one's arm out straight —☆*n.* the act of stiff-arming

stiff·en (stif′'n) *vt., vi.* to make or become stiff or stiffer —**stiff′en·er** *n.*

stiff-necked (stif′nekt′) *adj.* stubborn; obstinate

sti·fle¹ (stī′f'l) *vt.* **-fled, -fling** [altered (prob. after ON. *stīfla*, to stop up: for IE. base see STIFF) < ME. *stuflen*, a freq. formation < MFr. *estouffer*, to smother] **1.** to kill by cutting off the supply of air from; suffocate; smother; choke **2.** to suppress or repress; hold back; check, stop, inhibit, etc. [to *stifle* a sob, to *stifle* protests] —*vi.* **1.** to die from lack of air **2.** to suffer from lack of fresh, cool air —**sti′fler** *n.*

sti·fle² (stī′f'l) *n.* [ME.] the kneelike joint above the hock in the hind leg of a horse, dog, etc.: also **stifle joint**

sti·fling (stī′fliŋ) *adj.* so close as to be oppressive; suffocating —**sti′fling·ly** *adv.*

stig·ma (stig′mə) *n., pl.* **-mas**; also, and for 4, 5, 7, & 8 usually, **stig·ma·ta** (stig mät′ə, stig′mə tə) [L. < Gr., lit., a prick with a pointed instrument < *stizein*, to prick: for IE. base see STICK] **1.** formerly, a distinguishing mark burned or cut into the flesh, as of a slave or criminal **2.** something that detracts from the character or reputation of a person, group, etc.; mark of disgrace or reproach **3.** a mark, sign, etc. indicating that something is not considered normal or standard **4.** a small mark, scar, opening, etc. on the surface of a plant or animal, as a pore, eyespot, etc. **5.** *a)* a spot on the skin, esp. one that bleeds as the result of certain nervous tensions *b)* [*pl.*] marks resembling the crucifixion wounds of Jesus, appearing on some devout persons in a state of intense religious fervor **6.** *Bot.* the free upper tip of the style of a flower on which pollen falls and develops **7.** *Med.* any sign characteristic of a specific disease **8.** *Zool.* same as SPIRACLE (sense 3 a) —**stig′mal** *adj.*

stig·mas·ter·ol (stig mas′tə rôl′, -rōl′) *n.* [contr. < ModL. *Physostigma* (see PHYSOSTIGMINE) + STEROL] a sterol, C₂₉H₄₈O, isolated from soy or Calabar beans

stig·mat·ic (stig mat′ik) *adj.* **1.** of, like, or having a stigma, stigmas, or stigmata: also **stig·mat′i·cal** **2.** of or having stigmatism (sense 2) —*n.* a person marked with stigmata: also **stig′ma·tist** —**stig·mat′i·cal·ly** *adv.*

stig·ma·tism (stig′mə tiz'm) *n.* **1.** the condition characterized by the presence of stigmas or stigmata **2.** the condition of a lens, and the normal condition of the eye, in which rays of light from a single point are focused upon a single point

stig·ma·tize (stig′mə tīz′) *vt.* **-tized′, -tiz′ing** [ML. *stigmatizare*: see STIGMA & -IZE] **1.** to mark with a stigma, stigmas, or stigmata **2.** to characterize or mark as disgraceful —**stig′ma·ti·za′tion** *n.*

stil·bene (stil′bēn) *n.* [< Gr. *stilbein*, to glitter + -ENE] a crystalline hydrocarbon, C₁₄H₁₂, used in the manufacture of dyes and as a crystal scintillation detector

stil·bes·trol (stil bes′trōl, -trōl) *n.* [STILB(ENE) + ES-TR(ONE) + -OL²] same as DIETHYLSTILBESTROL

stil·bite (stil′bīt) *n.* [Fr. < Gr. *stilbein*, to glitter: see -ITE¹] a native hydrous silicate of sodium, calcium, and aluminum, one of the zeolite group, often found in the form of sheaflike crystalline aggregates

stile¹ (stīl) *n.* [ME. < OE. *stigel* < *stigan*, to climb < IE. base *steigh-*, to step, climb, whence Sans. *stighnoti*, (he) climbs, Gr. *stichos*, a row, line] **1.** a step or set of steps used in climbing over a fence or wall **2.** shortened form of TURNSTILE

stile² (stīl) *n.* [Du. *stijl*, doorpost] a vertical piece in a panel or frame, as of a door or window

sti·let·to (sti let′ō) *n., pl.* **-tos, -toes** [It., dim. of *stilo*, dagger < L. *stilus*: see STYLE] **1.** a small dagger having a slender, tapering blade **2.** a small, sharp-pointed instrument used for making eyelet holes in cloth, etc. **3.** *chiefly Brit.* term for SPIKE HEEL (see SPIKE¹, *n.* 4 *c*): in full **stiletto heel** —*vt.* **-toed, -to·ing** to stab, or kill by stabbing, with a stiletto

still¹ (stil) *adj.* [ME. < OE. *stille*, akin to G. *still* < IE. *stelnu-* < base *stel-*, to place, set up, standing, immobile, whence STALK¹, STALL¹, L. *locus*, place] **1.** without sound; quiet; silent **2.** hushed, soft, or low in sound **3.** not moving; stationary; at rest; motionless: following *stand, sit, lie*, etc., sometimes regarded as an adverb **4.** characterized by little or no commotion or agitation; tranquil; calm; serene [the *still* water of the lake] **5.** not effervescent or bubbling: said of wine **6.** *Motion Pictures* designating or of a single posed photograph or a photograph made from a single frame of motion-picture film, for use as in publicity —*n.* **1.** silence; quiet [in the *still* of the night] **2.** *Motion Pictures* a still photograph —*adv.* **1.** at or up to the time indicated, whether past, present, or future **2.** even; yet: used as an intensifier with a comparative form, etc. [cold yesterday, but *still* colder today] **3.** nevertheless; even then; yet [rich but *still* unhappy] **4.** [Archaic] ever; constantly —*conj.* nevertheless; yet —*vt.* to make still; quiet; specif., *a)* to make silent *b)* to make motionless *c)* to calm; relieve —*vi.* to become still —**still′ness** *n.*

SYN.—**still** implies the absence of sound and, usually, of movement [the *still* hours before dawn, a *still* pool]; **quiet** also implies the absence of sound but usually stresses freedom from excitement, commotion, agitation, etc. [a *quiet* town, motor, etc.]; **noiseless** stresses the absence of noise or sound and often suggests movement unaccompanied by sound [a *noiseless* typewriter]; **hushed** suggests the suppression of sound [the *hushed* corridors of a hospital] —**ANT.** noisy, stirring

still² (stil) *n.* [< obs. *still*, to distill < L. *stillare*, to drop, drip, trickle < *stilla*, a drop: see DISTILL] **1.** an apparatus used for distilling liquids, esp. alcoholic liquors **2.** same as DISTILLERY —*vt., vi.* to distill, esp. [Dial.] to distill (alcoholic liquor) illegally

☆**still alarm** a fire alarm given by telephone or by any means other than the regular signal device

still-birth (stil′burth′) *n.* **1.** the birth of a stillborn fetus **2.** a stillborn fetus

still·born (-bôrn′) *adj.* **1.** dead when delivered from the womb **2.** unsuccessful from the beginning; abortive

☆**still hunt** a stealthy hunt for game, as by stalking or using cover —**still′-hunt′** *vt., vi.*

still life **1.** small inanimate objects, as fruit, bottles, flowers, books, etc., used as subjects for a picture **2.** *pl.* **still lifes** a picture having such a subject —**still′-life′** *adj.*

☆**Still·son wrench** (stil′s'n) [after its U.S. inventor (in 1869), Daniel *Stillson*] a trademark for a wrench having a jaw that moves through a collar pivoted loosely to the shaft, used for turning pipes, etc.: the jaw tightens as pressure is applied to the handle

still·y (stil′ē; for adv., stil′lē) *adj.* **still′i·er, still′i·est** [ME. *stillich* < OE. *stillic*] [Literary] still; silent; quiet; calm —*adv.* [ME. *stilleli* < OE. *stillice*] in a still manner; silently; quietly; calmly

stilt (stilt) *n.* [ME. *stilte*, prob. < MLowG. or MDu. *stelte*, akin to G. *stelze*: for base see STALL¹] **1.** either of a

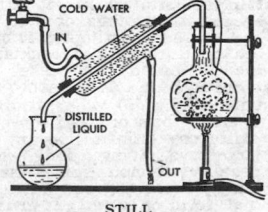

COLD WATER
IN
BOILING IMPURE LIQUID
DISTILLED LIQUID
OUT
STILL

pair of poles fitted with a footrest somewhere along its length and used for walking with the feet above the ground, as by children at play, by acrobats, etc. **2.** any of a number of long posts used to hold a building, etc. above the ground or out of the water **3.** *pl.* **stilts, stilt:** see PLURAL, II, D, **1** any of several wading birds (genus *Himantopus*) of the avocet family, with a long, slender bill, long legs, and three-toed feet; esp., the **black-necked stilt** (*Himantopus mexicanus*) living chiefly in marshes and ponds of temperate N. America and N S. America

stilt·ed (stil′tid) *adj.* **1.** raised or elevated on or as on stilts **2.** artificially formal or dignified; pompous —**stilt′-ed·ly** *adv.* —**stilt′ed·ness** *n.*

Stil·ton (**cheese**) (stil′t'n) [orig. sold at *Stilton*, village in EC England] a rich, crumbly cheese with veins of blue-green mold

Stim·son (stim′sən), **Henry L(ewis)** 1867–1950; U.S. statesman; secretary of state (1929–33); secretary of war (1911–13; 1940–45)

stim·u·lant (stim′yə lənt) *adj.* [L. *stimulans*, prp.] that stimulates; stimulating —*n.* anything that stimulates; specif., *a)* any drug, etc. that temporarily increases the activity of some vital process or of some organ *b)* popularly, an alcoholic drink: alcohol is physiologically a depressant

stim·u·late (-lāt′) *vt.* **-lat′ed, -lat′ing** [< L. *stimulatus*, pp. of *stimulare*, to prick, goad, excite < *stimulus*, a goad: see STYLE] **1.** to rouse or excite to action or increased action; animate; spur on **2.** to invigorate or seem to invigorate, as by an alcoholic drink **3.** *Med., Physiol.* to excite (an organ, part, etc.) to activity or increased activity —*vi.* to act as a stimulant or stimulus —*SYN.* see ANIMATE, PROVOKE —**stim′u·lat′er** *n.* —**stim′u·la′tor** *n.* —**stim′u·la′tion** *n.* —**stim′u·la′tive** *adj., n.*

stim·u·lus (-ləs) *n., pl.* **-u·li′** (-lī′) [L., a goad, sting, torment, pang, spur, incentive: see STYLE] **1.** something that rouses or incites to action or increased action; incentive **2.** *Physiol., Psychol.* any action or agent that causes or changes an activity in an organism, organ, or part, as something that excites an end organ, starts a nerve impulse, activates a muscle, etc.

sti·my (stī′mē) *n., pl.* **-mies** & *vt.* **-mied, -my·ing** same as STYMIE

sting (stiŋ) *vt.* **stung** or archaic **stang, sting′ing** [ME. *stingen* < OE. *stingan*, akin to ON. *stinga* < IE. base *stegh-*, to pierce, sharp, whence STAG] **1.** to prick or wound with a sting: said of plants and insects **2.** to cause sharp, sudden, smarting pain to, by or as by pricking with a sharp point [the cold wind *stinging* their cheeks] **3.** to cause to suffer mentally; make unhappy [to be *stung* by one's conscience] **4.** to stir up or stimulate suddenly and sharply [*stung* into action by her words] **5.** [Slang] to cheat; esp., to overcharge —*vi.* **1.** to use a sting; prick or wound with a sting **2.** to cause or feel sharp, smarting pain, either physical or mental [his arm *stinging* from the blow] —*n.* [OE. *sting*] **1.** the act of stinging **2.** a pain or wound resulting from or as from stinging **3.** a thing that urges or stimulates; goad **4.** the ability or power to sting or wound [criticism with much *sting* in it] **5.** a sharp-pointed organ in insects and certain other animals, used to prick, wound, or inject poison **6.** any of the stinging, hollow hairs on some plants, as nettles —**sting′less** *adj.*

☆**sting·a·ree** (stiŋ′ə rē′, stiŋ′ə rē′) *n. var.* of STINGRAY

sting·er (stiŋ′ər) *n.* **1.** a person or thing that stings; specif., *a)* an animal or plant that stings *b)* a sharp-pointed organ used for stinging; sting *c)* [Colloq.] a blow, reply, etc. that stings **2.** a cocktail made with white crème de menthe, brandy, and ice

stinging hair same as STING (*n.* 6)

stin·go (stiŋ′gō) *n.* [< sting: from the taste] [Brit. Slang] **1.** strong beer or ale **2.** energy; vim; zest

☆**sting·ray** (stiŋ′rā′) *n.* any of a family (Dasyatidae) of large rays having a long, whiplike tail with one or more usually poisonous spines that can inflict painful wounds

stin·gy¹ (stin′jē) *adj.* **stin′gi·er, stin′gi·est** [< *stinge*, dial. form of STING] **1.** giving or spending grudgingly or only through necessity; mean; miserly **2.** less than needed or expected; scanty —**stin′gi·ly** *adv.* —**stin′gi·ness** *n.*

SYN.—**stingy** implies a grudging, mean reluctance to part with anything belonging to one; **close** suggests the keeping of a tight hold on what one has accumulated; **niggardly** implies such close-fistedness that one grudgingly spends or gives the least amount possible; **parsimonious** implies unreasonable economy or frugality, often to the point of niggardliness; **penurious** implies such extreme parsimony and niggardliness as to make one seem poverty-stricken or destitute; **miserly** implies the penuriousness of one who is meanly avaricious and hoarding —*ANT.* generous, bountiful

sting·y² (stin′ē) *adj.* stinging or capable of stinging

stink (stiŋk) *vi.* **stank** or **stunk, stunk, stink′ing** [ME. *stinken* < OE. *stincan*, akin to G. *stinken*] **1.** to give off a strong, unpleasant smell **2.** to be very offensive; be hateful or abhorrent **3.** [Slang] to be of low standard or quality; be no good **4.** [Slang] to have much or an excess (with *of* or *with*) —*n.* **1.** a strong, unpleasant smell; stench **2.** [Slang] a strong public reaction, as one of outrage, censure, protest, etc. —**stink out** to drive or force out by a strong, unpleasant smell —**stink up** to cause to stink

stink·ard (-ərd) *n. rare var.* of STINKER

stink bomb a device made to burn or explode and give off an offensive smell

☆**stink·bug** (-bug′) *n.* any of various foul-smelling insects; esp., any of a large number of hemipterous bugs (family Pentatomidae) with a broad, shield-shaped body

stink·er (-ər) *n.* **1.** a person or thing that stinks **2.** [Slang] *a)* a person regarded with disgust *b)* a very difficult task, problem, etc. *c)* something of very low standard or quality

stink·horn (-hôrn′) *n.* any of several foul-smelling basidiomycetous fungi (order Phallales)

stink·ing (-iŋ) *adj.* **1.** that stinks; bad-smelling **2.** [Slang] *a)* very bad, unsatisfactory, etc. *b)* offensive, disgusting, etc. —*adv.* [Slang] to an excessive or offensive degree —**stink′ing·ly** *adv.*

SYN.—**stinking** and the more formal **fetid** both imply foulness of odor [a *stinking* cesspool, a *fetid* gum resin]; **malodorous** is the broadest term here, ranging in application from an unpleasant smell to one that is strongly offensive [*malodorous* cheeses]; **noisome** stresses the unwholesomeness or harmfulness of that which gives off a foul odor [the *noisome* stench of open sewers]; **putrid** suggests the disgusting foul smell of decomposed or rotting organic matter [buzzards feeding on *putrid* corpses]; **rank** implies a disagreeably strong odor that offends to a greater or lesser degree [the *rank* smell of a goat]; **rancid** specifically suggests the bad smell or taste of stale fats or oils [*rancid* butter]; **musty** suggests the stale, moldy smell of a long-closed room, food kept in a damp place, etc.

☆**stinking smut** same as BUNT²

stink·o (stiŋk′ō) *adj.* [Slang] drunk; intoxicated

stink·pot (-pät′) *n.* **1.** a kind of stink bomb formerly used in naval warfare ☆**2.** a small musk turtle (*Stenotherus odoratus*) of the E and S U.S. ☆**3.** [Slang] a motorboat

stink·stone (-stōn′) *n.* any stone, as some limestones, which gives off a foul smell when rubbed or struck, as from decayed organic matter contained in it

stink·weed (-wēd′) *n.* any of various plants, as the jimson weed, dog fennel, etc., having a foul or strong smell

stink·wood (-wood′) *n.* **1.** any of several trees whose wood has an offensive odor; esp., a South African tree (*Ocotea bullata*) of the laurel family, yielding a hard, durable wood **2.** the wood of any such tree

stint¹ (stint) *vt.* [ME. *stinten*, to stint, cease, stop < OE. *styntan*, to blunt or dull, akin to *stunt*, blunt, dull: see STUNT¹] **1.** to restrict or limit to a certain quantity, number, share, or allotment, often small or scanty **2.** [Archaic] to stop —*vi.* **1.** to be sparing or grudging in giving or using **2.** [Archaic] to stop —*n.* **1.** restriction; limit; limitation **2.** [Now Rare] a limited or fixed quantity, allotment, share, etc. **3.** an assigned task, period, or quantity of work **4.** [Obs.] cessation or pause —*SYN.* see TASK —**stint′er** *n.*

stint² (stint) *n.* [LME. *stynte* < ?] any of various small sandpipers

stipe (stīp) *n.* [Fr. < L. *stipes*, a log, stock, trunk of a tree: for IE. base see STIFF] **1.** *Bot.* a usually short, thick stem, as *a)* the stalk of a mushroom *b)* the petiole of a fern frond *c)* a stalklike extension of the receptacle of a spermatophyte *d)* the stemlike part supporting the thallus in certain algae **2.** *Zool.* same as STIPES

sti·pel (stī′p'l) *n.* [ModL., dim. of *stipula*, STIPULE] a small or secondary stipule at the base of a leaflet —**sti·pel·late** (stī pel′it, -āt) *adj.*

sti·pend (stī′pend, -pənd) *n.* [ME. *stipende* < L. *stipendium*, a tax, impost, tribute, contr. < *stipipendum* < *stips*, small coin or a contribution in small coin (prob. < IE. *steip-*: see STIFF) + *pendere*, to hang, weigh out, pay: see PENDANT] **1.** a regular or fixed payment for services, as a salary **2.** any periodic payment, as a pension or allowance —*SYN.* see WAGE

sti·pen·di·ar·y (stī pen′dē er′ē) *adj.* [L. *stipendiarius*] **1.** receiving or performing services for, a stipend **2.** paid for by a stipend [*stipendiary* services] **3.** of, or having the nature of, a stipend —*n., pl.* **-ar′ies** a person who receives a stipend

sti·pes (stī′pēz) *n., pl.* **stip·i·tes** (stip′ə tēz′) [L.: see STIPE] *Zool.* a stalklike part or peduncle, as *a)* the second subbasal segment of the typical maxilla in insects *b)* same as EYESTALK —**stip·i·tate** (stip′ə tāt′) *adj.*

stip·ple (stip′'l) *vt.* **-pled, -pling** [Du. *stippelen* < *stippel*, a speckle, dim. of *stip*, a point, akin to *stippen*, to prick: for IE. base see STIFF] **1.** to paint, draw, engrave, or apply in small points or dots rather than in lines or solid areas **2.** to cover or mark with dots; fleck —*n.* **1.** *a)* the art or method of painting, drawing, or engraving in dots *b)* the effect produced by this, or an effect, as in nature, resembling it **2.** stippled work —**stip′pler** *n.*

stip·u·lar (stip′yoo lər) *adj.* **1.** of or like a stipule or stipules **2.** growing on or near a stipule

stip·u·late¹ (stip′yə lāt′) *vt.* **-lat′ed, -lat′ing** [< L. *stipulatus*, pp. of *stipulari*, to bargain < or akin to Umbrian *stiplo*, to stipulate: for prob. IE. base see STIFF] **1.** to include specifically in the terms of an agreement, contract, etc.; arrange definitely **2.** to specify as an essential condition of or requisite in an agreement —*vi.* to make a specific demand or arrangement (*for* something) as a condition of or requisite in an agreement —**stip′u·la′tor** *n.* —**stip′u·la·to·ry** (-lə tôr′ē) *adj.*

stip·u·late² (stip′yoo lit, -lāt′) *adj.* [ModL. *stipulatus*] having stipules: also **stip′u·lat′ed**

stip·u·la·tion (stip′yə lā′shən) *n.* [L. *stipulatio*] **1.** the act of stipulating **2.** something stipulated; point or condition agreed upon, as in a contract

stip·ule (stip′yōōl) *n.* [ModL. *stipula* < L., a stalk, straw, dim. of *stipes*, trunk: see STIPE] either of a pair of small, leaflike parts at the base of some leaf petioles

stir[1] (stur) *vt.* **stirred, stir′ring** [ME. *stirien* < OE. *styrian*: for IE. base see STORM] **1.** to move, shake, agitate, etc., esp. slightly **2.** to change the position of slightly; displace [to stir a log] **3.** to rouse from sleep, lethargy, indifference, etc. **4.** to put (oneself, one's limbs, etc.) into motion or activity, esp. briskly **5.** *a)* to move an implement, the hand, etc. through (a liquid or loose substance) with an agitated motion so that the particles change position with relation to one another *b)* to mix by or as by imparting such a motion to **6.** to excite the feelings of; move strongly **7.** to incite or provoke (often with *up*) [to stir up trouble] **8.** to evoke, or call up [to stir memories] —*vi.* **1.** to move or change position, esp. only slightly [not a leaf *stirred*] **2.** to be up and about; be busy and active **3.** to be taking place, going on, happening, etc. **4.** to begin to show signs of activity; begin to come to life **5.** to impart an agitated motion to a liquid, mixture, etc. as with a spoon **6.** to be stirred [a mixture that *stirs* easily] —*n.* **1.** the act, an instance, or sound of stirring **2.** movement; activity; agitation **3.** a state of excitement; commotion; tumult —**stir′rer** *n.*

SYN.—**stir** (in this sense, often **stir up**) implies a bringing into action or activity by exciting or provoking [the colonies were *stirred* to rebellion]; **arouse** and **rouse** are often used interchangeably, but **arouse** usually implies merely a bringing into consciousness, as from a state of sleep [she was *aroused* by the bell] and **rouse** suggests an additional incitement to vigorous action [the rifle shot *roused* the sleeping guard]; **awaken** and **waken** literally mean to arouse from sleep, but figuratively they suggest the elicitation of latent faculties, emotions, etc. [it *awakened*, or *wakened*, her maternal feelings]; **rally** implies a gathering of the component elements or individuals so as to stir to effective action [to *rally* troops, one's energy, etc.]

stir[2] (stur) *n.* [19th-c. thieves' slang, prob. altered < or akin to 18th-c. slang *start*, prison < Romany, as in *stardo*, imprisoned] [Slang] a prison

stir·a·bout (stur′ə bout′) *n.* [Brit.] porridge made by stirring oatmeal or cornmeal in boiling water or milk

☆**stir-cra·zy** (-krā′zē) *adj.* [Slang] neurotically affected by long, close confinement, specif. in prison

stirk (sturk) *n.* [ME. < OE. *stierc*, akin to Goth. *stairo*, barren: for IE. base see STERILE] [Brit. Dial.] a bullock or heifer, esp. one between one and two years old

Stir·ling (stur′liŋ) county of C Scotland: 451 sq. mi.; pop. 199,000: also **Stir′ling·shire′** (-shir′)

stirps (sturps) *n., pl.* **stir·pes** (stur′pēz) [L., lit., a stalk, trunk, root < IE. base **ster-*, rigid, stiff, whence STARE] **1.** stock, race, or lineage; family or branch of a family **2.** *Law* the person from whom a family or branch of a family is descended

stir·ring (stur′iŋ) *adj.* **1.** active; busy **2.** that stirs one's feelings; rousing [*stirring* music] —**stir′ring·ly** *adv.*

stir·rup (stur′əp, stir′-) *n.* [ME. *stirop* < OE. *stigrap*, akin to *stegreif*: for bases of components see STILE[1] & ROPE] **1.** a ring with a flat bottom hung by a strap from a saddle and used as a footrest in mounting and riding **2.** any of various supports, clamps, etc. resembling or suggesting such a ring **3.** *Naut.* a rope hung from a yard and having an eye at the end for supporting a footrope passed through it

stirrup (bone) *same as* STAPES

stirrup cup 1. a farewell drink taken by a rider mounted to depart **2.** any farewell drink

stirrup leather (or **strap**) a strap connecting a stirrup with the saddle

stirrup pump a hand pump for putting out fires, set in a bucket and held firm by a stirrup, or bracket, for one foot

stish·ov·ite (stish′ə vit′) *n.* [after S. *Stishov*, Soviet mineralogist who discovered it + -ITE[1]] a very dense, crystalline form of silica similar to coesite

stitch (stich) *n.* [ME. *stiche* < OE. *stice*, a puncture, stab: for IE. base see STICK] **1.** *a)* a single complete in-and-out movement of the threaded needle in sewing *b)* *same as* SUTURE (sense 4 *c*) **2.** a single loop of yarn worked off a needle in knitting, crocheting, etc. **3.** the piece of thread worked in, or a loop, knot, etc. made, by stitching **4.** a particular kind of stitch or style of stitching **5.** a sudden, sharp pain in the side or back **6.** a bit or piece; specif., an article of clothing [wearing not a *stitch*] —*vi.* to make stitches; sew —*vt.* **1.** to fasten, join, repair, adorn, or operate upon with or as with stitches; sew **2.** to fasten or unite (cartons, booklets, etc.) with staples —**in stitches** in a state of uproarious laughter —**stitch′er** *n.*

stitch·er·y (-ər ē) *n.* **1.** the art of ornamental needlework, as embroidery, crewelwork, etc. **2.** *pl.* **-er·ies** something made or decorated in this way

stitch·wort (-wurt′) *n.* [ME. *stichwurt*: see STITCH & WORT[2]] any of several chickweeds; esp., an old-world perennial (*Stellaria holostea*) with grasslike leaves

stith·y (stith′ē, stith′-) *n., pl.* **stith′ies** [ME. *stethie* < ON. *stethi*, anvil: for base see STEAD] [Archaic or Dial.] an anvil or smithy —*vt.* **stith′ied, stith′y·ing** [Archaic] to forge

sti·ver (sti′vər) *n.* [Du. *stuiver* < MDu. *stüver* < *stüf*, stumpy, cut short: for base see STEEP[1]] **1.** a former Dutch coin equal to 1/20 of a guilder **2.** a trifling sum

St. James city in SE Manitoba, Canada: suburb of Winnipeg: pop. 36,000

St. James's Palace palace in Westminster, London: the royal residence from 1697 to 1837

St. John 1. seaport in S New Brunswick, Canada, at the mouth of the St. John River: pop. 52,000 **2.** island of the Virgin Islands of the U.S.: 20 sq. mi.; pop. 1,700 **3.** river flowing from N Maine through New Brunswick, Canada, into the Bay of Fundy: 418 mi. **4. Lake**, lake in SC Quebec, Canada: 321 sq. mi.: Fr. name **Lac St-Jean** (läk san zhän′)

St. John, Henry *see* BOLINGBROKE

St. Johns river in E & NE Fla., flowing into the Atlantic near Jacksonville: 276 mi.

St. John's 1. capital of Newfoundland; seaport on the SE coast: pop. 80,000 **2.** seaport & chief town of Antigua, on the N coast: pop. 13,000

St. Joseph city in NW Mo., on the Missouri River: pop. 73,000

stk. stock

St. Kitts (kits) *popular name of* ST. CHRISTOPHER

St-Lau·rent (san lō rän′) city in SW Quebec, Canada, on Montreal Island: suburb of Montreal: pop. 59,000

St. Lau·rent (san lō rän′), **Louis Stephen** 1882– ; Canad. statesman; prime minister (1948–57)

St. Lawrence [< Fr. *St. Laurent*, Rom. martyr (?–285)] **1.** river flowing from Lake Ontario northeast into the Gulf of St. Lawrence: c.750 mi. **2. Gulf of,** large inlet of the Atlantic in E Canada: c.100,000 sq. mi.

St. Lawrence Seaway inland waterway for oceangoing ships, connecting the Great Lakes with the Atlantic: operated jointly by the U.S. & Canada, it consists of the Welland Canal, the St. Lawrence River, & several locks & canals between Montreal & Lake Ontario

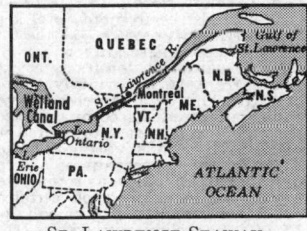

ST. LAWRENCE SEAWAY

stlg. sterling

St. Lou·is (loo′is, loo′ē) city & port in E Mo., on the Mississippi: pop. 622,000 (met. area 2,363,000)

St. Louis Park city in SE Minn.: suburb of Minneapolis: pop. 49,000

St. Lu·ci·a (loo′shē ə, -shə; loo sē′ə) self-governing island of the Windward group, West Indies, south of Martinique: it is under Brit. protection: 238 sq. mi.; pop. 110,000

S.T.M. [L. *Sacrae Theologiae Magister*] Master of Sacred Theology

St-Ma·lo (san má lō′) **1.** seaport & resort town on an island in the Gulf of St-Malo, NW France: pop. 17,000 **2. Gulf of,** inlet of the English Channel, on the N coast of Brittany, NW France, c.60 mi. wide

St. Martin island of the Leeward group, West Indies, south of Anguilla: the N part belongs to Guadeloupe, the S part to the Netherlands Antilles: 13 sq. mi.; pop. 8,000 Fr. name **St-Mar·tin** (san mår tan′); Du. name **St. Maar·ten** (sint mär′t'n)

St. Mar·y·le·bone (mer′i lə bōn′) metropolitan borough of London: pop. 69,000

St. Marys 1. river flowing from the Okefenokee Swamp along the Ga.-Fla. border into the Atlantic: c.180 mi. **2.** river flowing from Lake Superior into Lake Huron, between NE Mich. & Ontario, Canada: 63 mi.

St. Marys Falls Canals three ship canals (two U.S., one Canad.) bypassing a rapids of the St. Marys River at Sault Ste. Marie: see Soo

St-Mi·chel (san mē shel′) city in SW Quebec, Canada, on Montreal Island: suburb of Montreal: pop. 71,000

St. Mo·ritz (sānt′ mō rits′; Fr. san mō rēts′) mountain resort town in SE Switzerland: pop. 3,700

sto·a (stō′ə) *n., pl.* **sto′ae** (-ē), **sto′as** [Gr. *stoa* < IE. **stōu-* < base **stā-*, whence STAND] a portico, as in ancient Greece, having a wall on one side and pillars on the other

stoat (stōt) *n., pl.* **stoats, stoat:** see PLURAL, II, D, 1 [ME. *stote*] a large European weasel, esp. in its brown summer coat: see ERMINE (sense 1)

stoc·ca·do (stə kä′dō) *n.* [OIt. *stoccata* < *stocca*, a dagger, sword point < MFr. *estoc* < OFr. *estoquier*, to strike with the edge or point < Low G. *stoken*, to stick, prick: for IE. base see STOCK] [Archaic] a stab or thrust with a pointed weapon: also **stoc·ca′ta** (-kät′ə)

sto·chas·tic (stō kas′tik) *adj.* [< Gr. *stochastikos*, proceeding by guesswork, lit., skillful in aiming < *stochazesthai*, to aim at < *stochos*, a target: for IE. base see STING] 1. of, pertaining to, or arising from chance; involving probability; random 2. *Math.* designating a process having an infinite progression of jointly distributed random variables

stock (stäk) *n.* [ME. *stocke* < OE. *stocc*, akin to G. *stock*, Du. *stok*, a stick < IE. base **steu-*, to push, hit, chop, whence STUMP, STUB] 1. the trunk of a tree 2. [Archaic] *a)* a tree stump *b)* a wooden block or log 3. *a)* a blockhead *b)* anything lacking life, motion, or feeling 4. *a)* a plant stem into which a graft is inserted *b)* a plant from which cuttings are taken 5. an underground plant stem; rhizome or rootstock 6. any of a number of plants of the mustard family, as **evening stock** (*Mathiola bicornis*), or **Virginian stock** (*Malcomia maritima*) 7. *a)* the first of a line of descent; original progenitor, as of a human line, or type, as of a group of animals or plants *b)* a line of descent; lineage *c)* a strain, race, or other related group of animals or plants *d)* any of the major subdivisions of the human race *e)* a group of related languages or families of languages 8. a supporting or main part, as the handle of an implement, weapon, etc., to which the working parts are attached; specif., *a)* a bitstock or brace *b)* the butt or handle of a whip, fishing rod, etc. *c)* the block of a plane, in which the cutting blade is inserted *d)* the frame of a plow, to which the share, handles, etc. are attached *e)* the part of a rifle, shotgun, etc., usually wooden, held by the user and containing the barrel, etc. *f)* the long beam forming the basic part of the body of a field-gun carriage 9. a kind of wrench for holding thread-cutting dies 10. [*pl.*] a framework; specif., *a)* a former instrument of punishment consisting of a heavy wooden frame with holes for confining an offender's ankles and, sometimes, his wrists *b)* a frame of timbers supporting a ship during construction ☆*c)* a frame in which an animal is held, as for shoeing 11. something out of which other things are made; specif., *a)* raw material *b)* water in which meat, fish, etc. has been boiled, used as a base for soup or gravy 12. a specified kind of paper [heavy *stock*] 13. a store or supply; specif., *a)* all the animals, equipment, etc. kept and used on a farm *b)* *short for* LIVESTOCK *c)* the total amount of goods on hand in a store, etc.; inventory *d)* the portion of a pack of playing cards or dominoes not dealt out but left to be drawn from 14. *a)* formerly, the part of a tally given to the creditor *b)* a debt represented by a tally or tallies *c)* the capital invested in a company or corporation by the owners through the purchase of shares, usually entitling them to interest, dividends, voting rights, etc. *d)* the proportionate share in the ownership of a corporation held by an individual stockholder, as represented by shares of this capital in the form of stock certificates *e)* *clipped form of* STOCK CERTIFICATE *f)* [Colloq.] a part interest in something 15. a stock company (sense 2), or its repertoire 16. a former type of large, wide, stiff cravat 17. [Obs.] a stocking —*vt.* 1. to provide with or attach to a stock [to *stock* a firearm, plow, etc.] 2. *a)* to furnish (a farm) with stock or (a shop, etc.) with a stock *b)* to supply with [to *stock* a pond with fish] 3. to keep or put in a supply of, as for sale or for future use ☆4. to sow (land) with grass, clover, etc. 5. [Obs.] to punish by putting into the stocks —*vi.* 1. to put forth new shoots: said of a plant 2. to put in a stock, or supply (often with *up*) —*adj.* 1. continually kept in stock [*stock* sizes] 2. of the nature of something kept in stock; common, ordinary, hackneyed, or trite [a *stock* excuse] 3. that deals with stock [a *stock* boy] 4. relating to stock or a stock company 5. for breeding [a *stock* mare] 6. of, or for the raising of, livestock [*stock* farming] —**in stock** available for sale or use; on hand —**on the stocks** being built: said of a ship, etc. —**out of stock** not immediately available for sale or use; not on hand —**take stock** 1. to inventory the amount of stock on hand 2. to make an estimate or appraisal, as of available resources, probabilities, etc. —☆**take stock in** 1. to buy a share or shares of stock in (a company, etc.) 2. to have faith in, give credence to, or attribute real significance to: also **put stock in**

stock·ade (stä kād′) *n.* [Fr. *estacade* (also *estocade*, by association with OFr. *estoc*, a trunk, log < Frank. **stock*, akin to G. *stock*: see prec.) < Pr. *estacado* < *estaca*, a post, stake < Gmc. base akin to STAKE] 1. a barrier of stakes driven into the ground side by side, for defense against attack ☆2. an enclosure, as a fort, made with such stakes ☆3. an enclosure for military prisoners —*vt.* -**ad′ed**, -**ad′ing** to surround, protect, or fortify with a stockade

stock·breed·er (stäk′brēd′ər) *n.* a breeder and raiser of livestock —**stock′breed′ing** *n.*

stock·bro·ker (-brō′kər) *n.* a person who acts as an agent in buying and selling stocks and bonds

stock·bro·ker·age (-brō′kər ij) *n.* a stockbroker's work or business: also **stock′bro′king** (-kin)

☆**stock car** a railway car built to carry livestock 2. a passenger automobile of standard make, modified in various ways for use in racing

stock certificate *same as* CERTIFICATE OF STOCK

stock company 1. a company or corporation whose capital is divided into shares 2. a commercial theatrical company that presents a repertoire of plays, usually at one theater

stock dividend 1. a dividend in the form of additional shares of the same stock 2. the payment of such a dividend

stock dove [ME. *stockdowe*: see STOCK, *n.* 1 & DOVE[1]: it nests in hollow trees] a European pigeon (*Columba oenas*)

stock exchange 1. a place where stocks and bonds are regularly bought and sold 2. an association of stockbrokers who meet together for the business of buying and selling stocks and bonds according to regulations

stock farm a farm for raising livestock —**stock farming**

stock·fish (stäk′fish′) *n., pl.* -**fish′**, -**fish′es**: see FISH[2] [ME. *stokfysshe* < MDu. *stokvisch* < *stok*, stick (see STOCK) + *visch*, FISH[2]] any fish cured by being split and hung in the open air to dry without salt, as cod, haddock, etc.

stock·hold·er (-hōl′dər) *n.* 1. a person owning stock in a given company 2. in Australia, one who raises cattle

Stock·holm (stäk′hōm′, -hōlm′; *Sw.* stȯk′hȯlm′) capital of Sweden; seaport on the Baltic Sea: pop. 792,000 (met. area 1,215,000)

stock·i·ness (-ē nis) *n.* the quality of being stocky

stock·i·nette, stock·i·net (stäk′ə net′) *n.* [prob. for earlier *stocking net*] 1. an elastic, machine-knitted cloth used for making stockings, underwear, etc. 2. a knitting stitch fashioned by alternating rows of knitting and purling

stock·ing (stäk′in) *n.* [< STOCK, in obs. sense of leg covering + -ING] 1. a closefitting covering, usually knitted, for the foot and, usually, most of the leg 2. something resembling this, as a patch of color on the leg of an animal —**in one's stocking feet** wearing stockings or socks but no shoes —**stock′inged** (-ind) *adj.*

stocking cap a long, tapered knitted cap, often with a tassel or pompon at the end of the taper

stock in trade 1. goods kept available for sale at a store or shop 2. tools, materials, etc. used in carrying on a trade or a business 3. any resources, practices, or devices characteristically employed by a given person or group

stock·ish (stäk′ish) *adj.* like a stock, or block of wood; stupid; dull; thickheaded —**stock′ish·ly** *adv.*

stock·job·ber (-jäb′ər) *n.* ☆1. a stockbroker, esp. one engaged in irregular trading: often used contemptuously 2. [Brit.] an operator in the stock exchange who deals only with brokers, not with the public —**stock′job′ber·y** (-ē), **stock′job′bing** (-in) *n.*

stock·man (-mən; *also, esp. for 3,* -man′) *n., pl.* -**men** (-mən, -men′) 1. a man who owns or raises livestock 2. [Chiefly Austral.] a man who has charge of livestock 3. a man who works in a stockroom or warehouse

stock market 1. *same as* STOCK EXCHANGE 2. the business carried on at a stock exchange 3. the prices quoted on stocks and bonds

☆**stock option** an option granting its holder the privilege of buying a specified number of shares of stock from a corporation before a specified date at a specified price

stock·pile (-pīl′) *n.* a reserve supply of goods, raw material, etc., accumulated esp. in anticipation of future shortage or emergency —*vt., vi.* -**piled′**, -**pil′ing** to accumulate a stockpile (of) —**stock′pil′er** *n.*

Stock·port (stäk′pȯrt′) city in Cheshire, NW England, near Manchester: pop. 141,000

stock·pot (-pät′) *n.* 1. a pot used for preparing soup stock 2. a pot, etc. containing any mixture 3. a soup containing various kinds of meat and vegetables

☆**stock raising** the raising of livestock —**stock raiser**

stock·room (-rōōm′) *n.* a room in which a store of goods, materials, etc. is kept: also **stock room**

stock split the act or result of splitting stock: see SPLIT (*vt.* 7)

stock-still (stäk′stil′) *adj.* as still as a stock, or log; perfectly motionless

Stock·ton (stäk′tən) [after R. F. *Stockton* (1795–1866), U.S. naval officer] city in C Calif.: pop. 108,000

Stock·ton-on-Tees (-än tēz′) seaport in Durham, N England, on the Tees River: pop. 83,000

stock·y (stäk′ē) *adj.* **stock′i·er**, **stock′i·est** [STOCK, *n.* 2 + -Y[2]] 1. heavily built; sturdy; short and thickset 2. having a strong, often thick, stem: said of a plant

stock·yard (-yärd′) *n.* 1. an enclosure for stock on a farm ☆2. an enclosure with pens, sheds, etc. where cattle, hogs, sheep, or horses are kept temporarily before slaughtering or shipment: *usually used in pl.*

stodge (stäj) *n.* [< ?] [Chiefly Brit. Colloq.] 1. heavy, filling food, often unpalatable 2. anything boring or hard to learn —*vi., vt.* **stodged**, **stodg′ing** [Brit. Slang] to cram (oneself) with food

stodg·y (stäj′ē) *adj.* **stodg′i·er**, **stodg′i·est** [< prec. + -Y[2]] 1. heavy and unpalatable: said of food 2. heavily built; bulky and slow in movement 3. crammed full; packed 4. dull; tedious; uninteresting 5. drab, unfashionable, or unattractive 6. stubbornly old-fashioned; narrow and conventional —**stodg′i·ly** *adv.* —**stodg′i·ness** *n.*

☆**sto·gie, sto·gy** (stō′gē) *n., pl.* -**gies** [contr. < *Conestoga*, town in Pa.: said to be so named because favored by drivers of Conestoga wagons] 1. a long, thin, inexpensive cigar 2. a heavy, roughly made shoe or boot

Sto·ic (stō′ik) *n.* [ME. *Stoycis* (pl.) < L. *stoicus* < Gr. *stōikos* < *stoa*, porch, colonnade (see STOA): because Zeno taught under a colonnade at Athens] 1. a member of a Greek school of philosophy founded by Zeno about 308 B.C., holding that all things, properties, relations, etc. are governed by unvarying natural laws, and that the wise man should follow virtue alone, obtained through reason, remaining indifferent to the external world and

to passion or emotion 2. [s-] a stoical person —*adj.* 1. of the Stoics or their philosophy 2. [s-] *same as* STOICAL —*SYN.* see IMPASSIVE

sto·i·cal (-i k'l) *adj.* [ME.: see prec. & -AL] 1. showing austere indifference to joy, grief, pleasure, or pain; calm and unflinching under suffering, bad fortune, etc. 2. [S-] *same as* STOIC —**sto'i·cal·ly** *adv.*

stoi·chi·om·e·try (stoi'kē äm'ə trē) *n.* [< Gr. *stoicheion*, a first principle, element, base, akin to *steichein*, to step, go (for IE. base see STAIR) + -METRY] 1. the determination of the proportions in which chemical elements combine and the weight relations in any chemical reaction 2. the branch of chemistry dealing with the relationships of elements entering into and resulting from combination, esp. with quantitative relationships Brit. sp. **stoi'chei·om'e·try** —**stoi'chi·o·met'ric** (-ə met'rik) *adj.*

Sto·i·cism (stō'i siz'm) *n.* 1. the philosophical system of the Stoics 2. [s-] indifference to pleasure or pain; stoical behavior; impassivity —*SYN.* see PATIENCE

stoke (stōk) *vt., vi.* **stoked, stok'ing** [back-formation < STOKER] 1. to stir up and feed fuel to (a fire, furnace, etc.) 2. to tend (a furnace, boiler, etc.) 3. to feed or eat large quantities of food; fill (*up*)

stoke·hold (-hōld') *n.* 1. a room in which the boilers are stoked on a ship 2. *same as* STOKEHOLE (sense 2)

stoke·hole (-hōl') *n.* [STOKE + HOLE: in part transl. of Du. *stookgat* < *stoken*, to stoke + *gat*, a hole] 1. the opening in a furnace or boiler through which the fuel is put 2. a space in front of a furnace or boiler from which the fire is tended, as on a ship 3. *same as* STOKEHOLD (sense 1)

Stoke New·ing·ton (stōk nōō'in tən) metropolitan borough of London: pop. 52,000

Stoke-on-Trent (stōk'än trent') city in Staffordshire, WC England, on the Trent River: pop. 276,000

stok·er (stō'kər) *n.* [Du. < *stoken*, to poke, stir up < *stok*, a stick: see STOCK] 1. a man who tends a furnace, specif. of a steam boiler, as, esp. formerly, on a ship, locomotive, etc. 2. a mechanical device that stokes a furnace

☆**sto·ke·si·a** (stō kē'zhē ə, stōk'sē ə) *n.* [after Jonathan Stokes (1755–1831), Eng. botanist] a perennial plant (*Stokesia luevis*) of the composite family, native to the SE U.S.: cultivated for its large blue or purple flowers

Sto·kow·ski (stə kôf'skē, -kou'-), **Leopold (Boleslawowicz Stanislaw Antoni)** 1887?– ; U.S. orchestra conductor, born in England

☆**STOL** (stōl) *adj.* [s(hort) t(ake)o(ff and l(anding)] designating, of, or for an aircraft that can take off and land on a relatively short airstrip —*n.* a STOL aircraft, airstrip, etc.

stole[1] (stōl) *n.* [ME. < OE. < L. *stola* < Gr. *stolē*, a garment, orig., array, equipment < base of *stellein*, to place, array: for IE. base see STALK[1]] 1. a long, robelike outer garment worn by matrons in ancient Rome 2. a long, decorated strip of cloth worn like a scarf by officiating clergymen of various churches 3. a woman's long scarf of cloth or fur worn around the shoulders, with the ends hanging in front

stole[2] (stōl) *pt.* of STEAL

stol·en (stō'lən) *pp.* of STEAL

stol·id (stäl'id) *adj.* [L. *stolidus*, firm, slow, stupid: for IE. base see STALK[1]] having or showing little or no emotion or sensitivity; unexcitable; impassive —*SYN.* see IMPASSIVE —**sto·lid·i·ty** (stə lid'ə tē), **stol'id·ness** *n.* —**stol'id·ly** *adv.*

☆**stol·len** (stō'lən) *n.; G.* **shtô'lən**) *n., pl.* **-len, -lens** [G., lit., post (in reference to shape) < OHG. *stollo* < IE. base *stel-*, to place, whence STALK[2]] a sweet, yeast-raised, German bread containing fruit and nuts

sto·lon (stō'län) *n.* [ModL. *stolo* (gen. *stolonis*) < L., a shoot, twig, scion: for IE. base see STALK[1]] 1. *Bot.* a runner; esp., a stem running underground 2. *Zool.* a stemlike, cylindrical structure, as in certain hydroids and tunicates, giving rise to buds from which new individuals grow —**sto·lon'ic** (-län'ik) *adj.*

sto·ma (stō'mə) *n., pl.* **-ma·ta** (-mə tə), **-mas** [ModL. < Gr. *stoma*, mouth < IE. *stomen*, mouth, whence Av. *staman-*, (dog's) mouth] 1. *Bot.* a microscopic opening in the epidermis of plants, surrounded by guard cells and serving for gaseous exchange 2. *Zool.* a mouth or mouthlike opening; esp., an ingestive opening in lower invertebrates

stom·ach (stum'ək) *n.* [ME. *stomak* < OFr. *estomac* < L. *stomachus*, gullet, esophagus, stomach < Gr. *stomachos*, throat, gullet < *stoma*, a mouth: see prec.] 1. *a*) the large, saclike organ of vertebrates into which food passes from the esophagus or gullet for storage while undergoing the early processes of digestion *b*) any of the separate sections of such a digestive organ, as in ruminants, or all these sections collectively 2. any digestive cavity, as in invertebrates 3. the abdomen, or belly 4. appetite for food 5. desire or inclination of any kind 6. [Archaic] character or disposition 7. [Obs.] *a*) spirit *b*) pride *c*) resentment —*vt.* 1. to be able to eat or digest 2. to tolerate; bear; endure 3. [Obs.] to resent

stom·ach·ache (-āk') *n.* pain in the stomach or abdomen

stom·ach·er (-ər) *n.* [ME. *stomachere*: see STOMACH & -ER] an ornamented, triangular piece of cloth formerly worn, esp. by women, as a covering for the chest and abdomen

sto·mach·ic (stə mak'ik) *adj.* [L. *stomachicus* < Gr. *stomachikos*] 1. of or having to do with the stomach 2. acting as a digestive tonic Also **sto·mach'i·cal** —*n.* a digestive tonic —**sto·mach'i·cal·ly** *adv.*

stomach pump a suction pump with a flexible tube led into the stomach through the mouth and esophagus to remove its contents, as in cases of poisoning

☆**stomach tooth** [so called because its appearance is sometimes accompanied by gastric disorders] either of the canine teeth in the lower jaw of an infant

sto·ma·ta (stō'mə tə, stäm'ə-) *n. alt. pl.* of STOMA

sto·ma·tal (-t'l) *adj.* of or having a stoma or stomata

sto·mat·ic (stō mat'ik) *adj.* [ModL. *stomaticus* < Gr. *stomatikos* < *stomata*, pl. of *stoma*, a mouth: see STOMA] 1. of the mouth 2. of, or having the nature of, a stoma

sto·ma·ti·tis (stō'mə tīt'əs, stäm'ə-) *n.* [ModL.: see ff. & -ITIS] inflammation of the mouth

sto·ma·to- (stō'mə tə, stäm'ə-) [< Gr. *stoma* (gen. *stomatos*), a mouth: see STOMA] *a combining form meaning* of, like, or relating to a mouth [*stomatology*]: also, before a vowel, **stomat-**

sto·ma·tol·o·gy (stō'mə täl'ə jē) *n.* [prec. + -LOGY] the branch of medicine dealing with the mouth and its diseases —**sto'ma·to·log'i·cal** (-tə läj'i k'l) *adj.*

sto·ma·to·pod (stō'mə tə päd', stäm'ə tə-) *n.* [< ModL. *Stomatopoda*, name of the order: see STOMATO- & -POD] any of an order (Stomatopoda) of crustaceans, as the squillas, having strong, clasping claws on the second pair of legs and gills on the abdominal appendages

sto·ma·tous (stō'mə təs, stäm'ə-) *adj.* having a stoma or stomata

-stome (stōm) [< Gr. *stoma*, a mouth: see STOMA] *a combining form meaning* mouth [*cyclostome*]

sto·mo·dae·um, sto·mo·de·um (stō'mə dē'əm, stäm'ə-) *n., pl.* **-dae'a, -de'a** (-dē'ə) [ModL. < Gr. *stoma*, mouth (see STOMA) + *hodios*, on the way < *hodos*, way, road: see CEDE] the oral cavity in the digestive tract of an embryo, lined with ectoderm and developing into the mouth area

-sto·mous (stə məs) [< Gr. *stoma* (see STOMA) + -OUS] *a combining form meaning* having a (specified kind of) mouth

stomp (stämp) *vt., vi. var.* of STAMP; esp., to injure or kill by stamping (on) —*n.* formerly, 1. a jazz tune with a lively rhythm and a strong beat 2. a dance to this music

-sto·my (stə mē) [Gr. *-stomia* < *stoma*, mouth: see STOMA] *a combining form meaning* a surgical opening into (a specified part or organ) [*colostomy*]

stone (stōn) *n.* [ME. < OE. *stan*, akin to G. *stein* < IE. base *stāi-*, to become thick, compress, stiffen, whence Gr. *stear*, fat, L. *stipare*, to compress, *stilla*, a drop] 1. the hard, solid, nonmetallic mineral matter of which rock is composed 2. a piece of rock of relatively small size 3. a piece of rock shaped or finished for some purpose; specif., *a*) a building block *b*) a paving block *c*) a gravestone or memorial *d*) a boundary mark or milestone *e*) a grindstone or whetstone 4. something that resembles a small stone; specif., *a*) a hailstone *b*) the stonelike seed of certain fruits, as of a date *c*) the hard endocarp and the enclosed seed of a drupe, as of a peach *d*) [Archaic] a testicle 5. *short for* PRECIOUS STONE 6. *pl.* **stone** in Great Britain, a unit of weight equal to 14 pounds 7. *Med. same as* CALCULUS (sense 1) 8. *a*) *Printing* a table with a smooth top, orig. of stone, on which page forms are composed *b*) a surface incised or engraved with a design or text to be lithographed —*vt.* **stoned, ston'ing** 1. to throw stones at; esp., to kill by pelting with stones 2. to furnish, pave, line, etc. with stones 3. to polish, sharpen, etc. with a stone 4. to remove the stone from (a peach, cherry, etc.) 5. [Obs.] to make stony, or hard, unfeeling, etc. —*adj.* of stone or stoneware —**cast the first stone** to be the first to censure, criticize, or attack —**leave no stone unturned** to do everything possible —**ston'er** *n.*

stone- (stōn) [< prec., with the sense of "like, or as is, a stone"] *a combining form used in hyphenated compounds, meaning* very, completely [*stone*-blind]

Stone (stōn) 1. **Edward Du·rell** (də rel'), 1902– ; U.S. architect 2. **Harlan Fiske**, 1872–1946; U.S. jurist: chief justice of the U.S. (1941–46) 3. **Lucy**, (Mrs. **Henry Brown Blackwell**) 1818–93; U.S. reformer & suffragist

Stone Age the period in human culture during which stone implements were used: it is usually divided into the paleolithic, mesolithic, and neolithic periods

stone-blind (-blind') *adj.* [cf. STONE-] completely blind

stone-broke (-brōk') *adj.* [STONE- + BROKE] [Slang] having no money at all; penniless

stone·chat (-chat') *n.* [from its cry, like the sound of pebbles knocked together] any of a genus (*Saxicola*) of small, insect-eating birds; esp., a European bird (*Saxicola torquata*) with a black head and back and a white rump

stone·crop (-kräp') *n.* [ME. *stoncroppe* < OE. *stancrop* < *stan*, STONE + *crop*, a sprout] *popular name for* SEDUM

stone·cut·ter (-kut'ər) *n.* a person or machine that cuts and dresses stone —**stone'cut'ting** *n.*

stoned (stōnd) *adj.* 1. having the stones removed [*stoned* prunes] ☆2. [Slang] drunk; intoxicated

stone-deaf (-def') *adj.* [cf. STONE-] completely deaf

stone·fly (-flī′) *n.*, *pl.* **-flies′** any of various soft-bodied, winged insects (order Plecoptera) whose nymphs live under stones in swift streams: often used as bait in fishing

stone fruit any fruit, as a plum, having a stone; drupe

Stone·henge (stōn′henj′) [ME. *stonheng < ston*, STONE + OE. *henge*, (something) hanging: for base see HANG] a circular arrangement of prehistoric monoliths on Salisbury Plain, England, probably set up in the neolithic period

stone lily a fossil crinoid

stone martin *same as* SABLE (*n.* 1 a & 2)

stone·ma·son (-mā′s′n) *n.* a person who cuts stone to shape and uses it in making walls, buildings, etc. — **stone′ma′son·ry** (-rē) *n.*

Stone Mountain mountain near Atlanta, Ga., on which a huge Confederate memorial is carved: c.2,000 ft. high

☆**stone roller** 1. a small, N. American minnow (*Campostoma anomalum*) that hollows out its nest in gravelly stream beds 2. any of several suckers; esp., the **northern hog sucker** (*Hypentelium nigricans*) found in rocky streams

Stones River [after Uriah *Stone*, the discoverer, 1766] river in C Tenn., flowing into the Cumberland: c.60 mi.

stone's throw 1. the distance that a stone can be thrown 2. a relatively short distance

stone·wall (stōn′wôl′) *vi.* 1. *Cricket* to play only a defensive game in order to gain a draw: said of a batsman 2. [Chiefly Brit. Colloq.] to obstruct a debate, negotiation, etc.; esp., to filibuster

stone·ware (stōn′wer′) *n.* a coarse, dense, glazed or unglazed pottery containing much silica or sand and flint

stone·work (-wurk′) *n.* 1. the art or process of working in stone, as in masonry or jewelry 2. something made or built in stone; specif., masonry 3. [*pl.*] a place where masonry stone is cut and dressed

stone·wort (-wurt′) *n.* any of a group (Charophyta) of green algae with jointed axes and whorled branches, usually covered with lime

ston·y (stō′nē) *adj.* **ston′i·er**, **ston′i·est** [ME. < OE. *stanig*] 1. covered with or having many stones 2. of or like stone; specif., *a*) hard *b*) relentless; unfeeling; pitiless *c*) cold; fixed; rigid 3. petrifying Also **ston′ey** —**ston′i·ly** *adv.* —**ston′i·ness** *n.*

stony coral a true coral having a dense, calcareous, external skeleton: see MADREPORE

ston·y·heart·ed (-härt′id) *adj.* unfeeling; pitiless; cruel —**ston′y·heart′ed·ness** *n.*

Stony Point village in SE N.Y., on the Hudson: site of a Brit. fort in the Revolutionary War: pop. 8,300

stood (stood) *pt.* & *pp.* of STAND

☆**stooge** (stōōj) *n.* [< ?] [Colloq.] 1. an actor who assists a comedian by feeding him lines, being the victim of pranks, etc. 2. any person who acts as a foil, underling, etc. to another: term of contempt —*vi.* **stooged**, **stoog′ing** [Colloq.] to be a stooge (*for* someone)

stook (stook, stook) *n.*, *vt.*, *vi.* [ME. *stouke*, prob. < or akin to MLowG. *stūke*, a shock, *stūken*, to set up stooks] *Brit. var.* of SHOCK[2]

stool (stōōl) *n.* [ME. < OE. *stol*, akin to G. *stuhl* < IE. *stal-*, (whence OSlav. *stolŭ*, throne, seat) < base *sta-*, to STAND] 1. *a*) a single seat having three or four legs and no back or arms *b*) *same as* FOOTSTOOL 2. the inside ledge at the bottom of a window 3. a toilet, or water closet 4. the fecal matter eliminated in a single bowel movement 5. *a*) a root or tree stump sending out shoots *b*) a cluster of such shoots ☆6. *a*) a perch to which a bird is fastened as a decoy for others *b*) a bird or other object used as a decoy —*vi.* 1. to put out shoots in the form of a stool ☆2. [Colloq.] to act as a stool pigeon, or informer

☆**stool pigeon** 1. a pigeon or other bird used as a decoy 2. a person serving as a decoy 3. [Colloq.] a spy or informer, esp. for the police: also **stool·ie** (stōōl′ē) *n.*

stoop[1] (stōōp) *vi.* [ME. *stupen* < OE. *stupian*, akin to ON. *stūpa* < IE. *steup-* < base *steu-*, to push, strike, whence STEEP[1], STUMP, L. *stupere*, to be struck senseless] 1. to bend the body forward or in a crouch 2. to carry the head and shoulders or the upper part of the body habitually bent forward 3. *a*) to condescend, or deign *b*) to demean or degrade oneself 4. to pounce or swoop down, as a bird of prey 5. [Archaic] to yield or submit —*vt.* 1. to bend (the head, etc.) forward 2. [Archaic] to humble or debase —*n.* 1. the act or position of stooping the body, esp. habitually 2. the act of condescending 3. a swoop, as by a hawk at prey —**stoop′er** *n.* —**stoop′ing·ly** *adv.*

SYN.—**stoop**, in this connection, implies a descending in dignity, as by committing some shameful or immoral act [*to stoop to cheating*]; **condescend** implies a voluntary descent by one high in rank, power, etc. to act graciously or affably toward one regarded as his inferior [the general *condescended* to talk with the private]; **deign** is usually used in negative constructions or with such qualifications as *hardly*, *barely*, etc. and, hence, connotes unwilling or arrogant condescension [she scarcely *deigned* to answer me]

☆**stoop**[2] (stōōp) *n.* [Du. *stoep*, akin to G. *stufe*: for base see STEP[1]] a small porch or platform with steps and, orig., seats, at the door of a house

stoop[3] (stōōp) *n. same as* STOUP

☆**stoop labor** work done by stooping, as in picking fruit from low-growing plants

stop (stäp) *vt.* **stopped**, **stop′ping** [ME. *stoppen* < OE. *-stoppian* (in comp.) < WGmc. *stoppōn* < VL. **stuppare*, to stop up, stuff < L. *stuppa* < Gr. *styppē*, tow < IE.

*stewe-, to thicken, contract, whence Sans. *stuka*, a tuft] **I.** *to close by filling, shutting off, covering, etc.* 1. to staunch (a cut, wound, etc.) 2. to block up (a passage, road, pipe, etc.) so as to make impassable; obstruct: often with *up* 3. to fill in, plug up, or cover (a hole, cavity, opening, mouth, etc.): often with *up* 4. to close (a bottle, jug, etc.) as with a cork or cap 5. *a*) to close (a finger hole of a wind instrument) so as to produce a desired tone *b*) to produce (a tone) in this way **II.** *to cause to cease motion, activity, etc.* 1. to prevent the passage or further passage of (water, light, etc.); block; intercept 2. to prevent the movement or further movement of; specif., *a*) to halt the progress of (a person, animal, vehicle, etc.) *b*) to check (a blow, stroke, or thrust); parry; counter *c*) to defeat (an opponent) *d*) to intercept (a letter, etc.) in transit *e*) to baffle; perplex; nonplus 3. to cease; desist from (with a gerund) **III.** 4. *a*) to cause to cease or end [*stop* that racket] *b*) to bring to an end; discontinue [to *stop* a subscription] *c*) to kill *d*) to defeat, as by knocking out 5. to cause (an engine, machine, etc.) to cease operation 6. to press down (a violin string, etc.) against the fingerboard to produce a desired tone 7. to place a stop order on (a stock or other security) 8. *Bridge* to hold key cards that will prevent an opponent from running (a suit) 9. *Rhetoric* to punctuate **III.** *to keep from beginning, acting, happening, etc.; prevent* 1. to keep (a person) from doing something contemplated 2. to prevent the starting, advent, etc. of; preclude 3. to notify one's bank to withhold payment on (one's check) —*vi.* 1. to cease moving, walking, proceeding, etc.; halt 2. to leave off doing something; desist from continuing 3. to cease operating or functioning 4. to be able to go no further; come to an end 5. to become clogged or choked 6. to tarry or stay for a while, esp. as a transient or guest (often with *at* or *in*) —*n.* 1. a stopping or being stopped; check; arrest; cessation; halt; specif., a pause in speech or at the end of a sense unit in verse 2. a coming to an end; finish; end 3. a stay or sojourn 4. a place stopped at, as on a bus route 5. an indentation in the face of an animal, esp. a dog, between the forehead and the nose or muzzle 6. something that stops; obstruction; obstacle; specif., *a*) a plug or stopper *b*) *same as* STOP ORDER *c*) an order to withhold payment on a check *d*) a mechanical part that stops, limits, or regulates motion, as a pawl *e*) [Chiefly Brit.] a punctuation mark, esp. a period 7. *a*) pressure, as of a finger, on a string of a violin, etc. to produce a desired tone *b*) a fret on a guitar, etc. 8. *a*) the closing of a finger hole of a wind instrument to produce a desired tone *b*) such a hole 9. *a*) a tuned set of organ pipes, reeds, or electronic devices of the same specific type and tone quality *b*) a pull, lever, or key for putting such a set or sets into or out of operation 10. *Naut.* a piece of line used to secure something 11. *Phonet.* *a*) the act of completely stopping the outgoing breath, as with the lips, tongue, or velum *b*) a consonant formed in this way, as *p*, *b*, *k*, *g*, *t*, and *d* 12. *Photog.* *a*) the aperture, usually adjustable, of a lens *b*) the f-number —*adj.* ☆that stops or is meant to stop [a *stop* signal] —**pull out all (the) stops** 1. to play an organ with all the stops in operation 2. to apply maximum effort; use everything possible —**put a stop to** to cause to cease; stop; end —**stop down** to reduce the lens aperture by adjustment of the diaphragm —☆**stop off** to stop for a short stay en route to a place —☆**stop over** 1. to visit for a while: also **stop in** (or **by**) 2. to break a journey, as for rest

SYN.—**stop** implies a suspension or ending of some motion, action, or progress [my watch *stopped*]; **cease** implies a suspension or ending of some state or condition or of an existence [the war had *ceased*]; **quit** is equivalent to either **stop** or **cease** [to *quit* working means either to stop working, as for the day, or to cease working, i.e., to retire]; **discontinue** suggests the suspension of some action that is a habitual practice, an occupation, etc. [he has *discontinued* the practice of law]; **desist** implies a ceasing of some action that is annoying, harmful, futile, etc. [*desist* from further bickering] —*ANT.* begin, start, commence

stop bath *Photog.* a weak solution of acetic acid used to stop development of photographic prints before fixing

stop·cock (-käk′) *n.* a cock or valve for stopping or regulating the flow of a fluid, as through a pipe

stope (stōp) *n.* [prob. < MLowG. *stōpe*, akin to STEP] a steplike excavation formed by the removal of ore from around a mine shaft —*vt.*, *vi.* **stoped**, **stop′ing** to mine in stopes

stop·gap (stäp′gap′) *n.* a person or thing serving as a temporary substitute for another; makeshift —*adj.* used as a stopgap —*SYN.* see RESOURCE

☆**stop·light** (-līt′) *n.* 1. a traffic light, esp. when red and signaling vehicles to stop 2. a light at the rear of a vehicle, that lights up when the brakes are applied

stop order an order to a broker to buy or sell a certain stock when a specified price is reached

☆**stop·o·ver** (-ō′vər) *n.* 1. a brief stop or stay at a place in the course of a journey 2. a place for such a stop Also **stop′-off′**

stop·page (-ij) *n.* [see -AGE] 1. a stopping or being stopped 2. an obstructed condition; block

stop·per (-ər) *n.* 1. a person or thing that stops or causes a stoppage 2. something inserted to close an opening; plug —*vt.* to close with a plug or stopper

stop·ple (-'l) *n.* [ME. *stoppel*, dim. < *stoppen*, to STOP] a stopper, or plug —*vt.* **-pled, -pling** to close with a stopple

☆**stop street** a street intersection at which vehicles must come to a complete stop before continuing

stopt (stäpt) *poet. pt. & pp.* of STOP

stop·watch (stäp'wäch) *n.* a watch with a hand that can be started and stopped instantly so as to indicate fractions of seconds, as for timing races, etc.

stor·age (stôr'ij) *n.* **1.** a storing or being stored **2.** *a)* a place or space for storing goods *b)* the cost of keeping goods stored **3.** the charging of a storage battery so as to make possible the subsequent generation of electricity **4.** *same as* MEMORY (sense 8)

storage battery a battery of electrochemical cells (*secondary cells*) for generating electric current: the cells can be recharged by passing a current through them in the direction opposite to the discharging flow of current

sto·rax (stôr'aks) *n.* [ME. < L. *storax, styrax* < Gr. *styrax*] **1.** the aromatic balsam exuded by liquidambar trees, used in medicine and perfumery **2.** a fragrant, solid resin obtained from a small eastern Mediterranean tree (*Styrax officinalis*) of the storax family, formerly used as incense **3.** any of a genus (*Styrax*) of chiefly tropical trees and shrubs of the storax family, with drooping clusters of showy white flowers —*adj.* designating a family (Styracaceae) of widely distributed trees or shrubs including storax and snowball

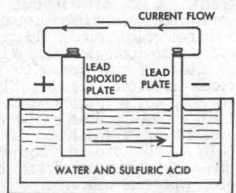

CURRENT FLOW

LEAD DIOXIDE PLATE

LEAD PLATE

WATER AND SULFURIC ACID

STORAGE BATTERY CELL
(current flow
when charging)

store (stôr) *vt.* **stored, stor'ing** [ME. *storen* < OFr. *estorer*, to erect, furnish, store < L. *instaurare*, to repair, restore, erect < *in-*, IN-[1] + *-staurare* < IE. base *stā-*, to STAND, whence ON. *staurr*, Gr. *stauros*, a post] **1.** to put aside, or accumulate, for use when needed **2.** to fill or furnish with a supply or stock [a mind *stored* with trivia] **3.** to put in a warehouse, etc. for safekeeping **4.** to be a place for the storage of **5.** to put or keep (information) in a computer memory unit —*vi.* to undergo storage in a specified manner —*n.* [ME. < OFr. *estor* < the *v.*] **1.** a supply (*of* something) for use when needed; reserve; stock **2.** [*pl.*] supplies, esp. of food, clothing, arms, etc. ☆**3.** a retail establishment where goods are regularly offered for sale **4.** a place where supplies are kept; storehouse; warehouse **5.** a great amount or number; abundance —*adj.* of a kind sold in stores; being a commercial or mass-produced article —**in store** set aside for, or awaiting one in, the future; in reserve or in prospect —☆**mind the store** to tend to business —**set** (or **put** or **lay**) **store by** to have regard or esteem for; value —**stor'a·ble** *adj.*

☆**store·front** (-frunt') *n.* **1.** the front of a store **2.** a room at the ground front of a building, usually with display windows, designed for use as a retail store —*adj.* housed in or as in a storefront [a storefront church]

store·house (-hous') *n.* a place where things are stored; esp., a warehouse

store·keep·er (-kē'pər) *n.* **1.** a person in charge of stores, esp. military or naval stores ☆**2.** a retail merchant

store·room (-rōōm') *n.* a room where things are stored

☆**store·wide** (-wīd') *adj.* throughout a store, including many or all departments [a storewide sale]

sto·rey (stôr'ē) *n., pl.* **-reys** *Brit. sp.* of STORY[2]

sto·ried[1] (stôr'ēd) *adj.* **1.** ornamented with designs showing scenes from history, a story, etc. **2.** famous in story or history

sto·ried[2] (stôr'ēd) *adj.* having stories, or floors: usually in hyphenated compounds [many-*storied*]

stork (stôrk) *n., pl.* **storks, stork:** see PLURAL, II, D, 1 [ME. < OE. *storc*, akin to G. *storch* < IE. *sterg-* < base *ster-*, to be rigid, stiff, whence STARK, STRETCH: so named from its stiff-legged walk] any of a family (Ciconiidae) of large, long-legged, mostly old-world wading birds, having a long neck and bill, and related to the herons: esp., the common European stork (*Ciconia ciconia*) that nests on chimneys and in trees: a symbol of childbirth from the notion perpetrated in euphemistic tales to children that it brings newborn babies

stork's-bill (stôrks'bil') *n.* **1.** any of a number of related geraniums with beak-shaped fruit; esp., *same as* PELARGONIUM **2.** *same as* HERONSBILL

storm (stôrm) *n.* [ME. < OE., akin to G. *sturm* < IE. base *(s)twer-*, to whirl, move or turn quickly, whence STIR[1], L. *turbare*, to agitate] **1.** an atmospheric disturbance characterized by a strong wind, usually accompanied by rain, snow, sleet, or hail, and, often, thunder and lightning **2.** any heavy fall of snow, rain, or hail **3.** anything resembling a storm; specif., *a)* a heavy shower or volley of things [a *storm* of bullets] *b)* a strong outburst of emotion, passion, excitement, etc. *c)* a strong disturbance or upheaval of a political or social nature *d) Mil.* a sudden, strong attack on a fortified place **4.** *Meteorol.* a wind whose speed is 64 to 72 miles per hour: see BEAUFORT SCALE —*vi.* **1.** to be stormy; blow violently, rain, snow, etc. **2.** to be violently angry; rage; rant **3.** to rush or move violently and tumultuously [to *storm* into a room] —*vt.* **1.** to attack or direct something at (someone) in a vigorous or angry outburst [to *storm* a speaker with questions] **2.** *Mil.* to capture or attempt to capture (a fortified place) with a sudden, strong attack —SYN. see ATTACK

storm·bound (stôrm'bound') *adj.* halted, delayed, or cut off by storms

☆**storm cellar** *same as* CYCLONE CELLAR

storm center 1. the shifting center of a cyclone, an area of lowest barometric pressure and comparative calm **2.** a center or focus of trouble, turmoil, or disturbance

☆**storm door** a door placed outside the regular entrance door as added protection against winter weather

storm petrel *same as* STORMY PETREL (sense 1)

storm·proof (-prōōf') *adj.* **1.** that can withstand a storm **2.** giving protection against storms

storm trooper a member of Hitler's Nazi party militia, notorious for their brutal and terroristic methods

☆**storm window** a window placed outside a regular window as protection against winter weather: also **storm sash**

storm·y (stôr'mē) *adj.* **storm'i·er, storm'i·est** [ME. *stormi* < OE. *stormig*] **1.** of, characteristic of, or affected by storms **2.** having or characterized by storms **3.** violent, raging, turbulent, etc. —**storm'i·ly** *adv.* —**storm'i·ness** *n.*

stormy petrel 1. any of several small petrels thought to presage storms; esp., a small black-and-white petrel (*Hydrobates pelagicus*) of the N Atlantic and the Mediterranean **2.** a person thought to presage or bring trouble

Stor·ting, Stor·thing (stôr'tin') *n.* [Norw. *storting* (earlier *storthing*) < *stor*, great + *ting*, assembly: see THING[2]] the parliament of Norway

sto·ry[1] (stôr'ē) *n., pl.* **-ries** [ME. *storie* < OFr. *estoire* < L. *historia:* see HISTORY] **1.** the telling of a happening or connected series of happenings, whether true or fictitious; account; narration **2.** an anecdote or joke **3.** *a)* a fictitious literary composition in prose or poetry, shorter than a novel; narrative; tale; specif., *same as* SHORT STORY *b)* such tales, collectively, as a form of literature **4.** the plot of a novel, play, etc. **5.** *a)* a report or rumor *b)* [Colloq.] a falsehood or fib **6.** romantic legend or history ☆**7.** *Journalism* a news event or a report of it —*vt.* **-ried, -ry·ing 1.** [Archaic] to tell the story of **2.** to decorate with paintings, etc. representing scenes from history or legend

SYN.—**story**, the broadest in scope of these words, refers to a series of connected events, true or fictitious, that is written or told with the intention of entertaining or informing; **narrative** is a more formal word, referring to the kind of prose that recounts happenings; **tale**, a somewhat elevated or poetical term, usually suggests a simple, leisurely story, more or less loosely organized, especially a fictitious or legendary one; **anecdote** applies to a short, entertaining account of a single incident, usually personal or biographical

sto·ry[2] (stôr'ē) *n., pl.* **-ries** [ME. < ML. *historia*, a picture (< L.: see HISTORY): prob. from use of "storied" windows or friezes marking the outside of different floors] **1.** a section or horizontal division of a building, extending from the floor to the ceiling or roof lying directly above it; floor [a hotel ten *stories* high] **2.** all the rooms on the same level of a building **3.** any horizontal section or division

Sto·ry (stôr'ē), **Joseph** 1779-1845; U.S. jurist; associate justice, U.S. Supreme Court (1811-45)

sto·ry·book (stôr'ē book') *n.* a book of stories, esp. one for children —*adj.* typical of romantic tales in storybooks [*storybook* ending]

sto·ry·tell·er (-tel'ər) *n.* **1.** a person who narrates stories **2.** [Colloq.] a fibber or liar —**sto'ry·tell'ing** *n.*

☆**stoss** (stäs, stôs; *G.* shtôs) *adj.* [G. < *stossen*, to push < OHG. *stozan* < IE. base *(s)teu-*, to push, beat, whence L. *tundere*, to strike: cf. STUDY] facing or located in the direction from which a glacier moves: opposed to LEE

sto·tin·ka (stô tin'kə) *n., pl.* **-tin'ki** (-kē) [Bulg.] a unit of currency in Bulgaria, equal to 1/100 lev

St-Ouen (san twän') city in NC France, on the Seine: suburb of Paris; pop. 52,000

stound (stound) *n.* [ME. *stunde* < OE. *stund*, akin to G. *stunde*, ON. *stund*, hour, while: for IE. base see STAND] **1.** [Archaic or Dial.] a short time **2.** [Obs. or Dial.] a pain or pang; shock —*vi.* [Scot. or Brit. Dial.] to ache or pain

stoup (stōōp) *n.* [ME. *stowpe*, bucket < ON. *staup:* for IE. base see STEEP[1]] **1.** [Archaic or Brit. Dial.] a drinking cup; tankard **2.** [Scot.] a pail, or bucket **3.** a basin for holy water in a church

stour (stoor) *n.* [ME. *stoure* < OFr. *estour* < OHG. *sturm*, STORM] [Archaic or Dial.] **1.** combat or conflict **2.** turmoil **3.** a storm **4.** wind-blown dust

stout (stout) *adj.* [ME. < OFr. *estout*, bold, prob. < Frank. *stolt*, proud, bold, akin to MDu. *stelte*, STILT] **1.** courageous; brave; undaunted **2.** *a)* strong in body; sturdy *b)* strong in construction; firm; substantial [a *stout* wall] **3.** powerful; forceful **4.** fat; thickset; corpulent —*n.* **1.** a fat person **2.** a garment in a size for a fat man **3.** a heavy dark-brown brew like porter, but with a higher

percentage of hops —*SYN.* see STRONG —**stout′ish** *adj.* —**stout′ly** *adv.* —**stout′ness** *n.*

stout·heart·ed (-härt′id) *adj.* courageous; brave; undaunted —**stout′heart′ed·ly** *adv.* —**stout′heart′ed·ness** *n.*

stove[1] (stōv) *n.* [ME. < MDu., a heated room, akin to G. *stube*, sitting room, OE. *stofa*, hot air bath < early borrowing < VL. *extufa*, back-formation < *extufare*, to give off steam < L. *ex-* + VL. *tufus*, steam < Gr. *typhos:* see TYPHUS] 1. an apparatus using fuel or electricity for heating a room, for cooking, etc. 2. any heated chamber or room, as a kiln for drying manufactured articles

stove[2] (stōv) *alt. pt. & pp.* of STAVE

stove·pipe (stōv′pīp′) *n.* 1. a metal pipe used to carry off smoke or fumes from a stove, as into a chimney flue ☆2. [Colloq.] a man's tall silk hat: in full **stovepipe hat**

sto·ver (stō′vər) *n.* [ME., aphetic < OFr. *estover:* see ESTOVERS] ☆1. cured stalks of grain, without the ears, used as fodder for animals 2. [Brit. Dial.] any fodder

stow (stō) *vt.* [ME. *stowen* < *stowe*, a place < OE. < IE. base *stā-*, to STAND] 1. to pack or store away; esp., to pack in an orderly, compact way 2. to fill by packing in an orderly way 3. to hold or receive: said of a room, container, etc. 4. [Obs.] to provide lodging for 5. [Slang] to stop; cease [*stow* the chatter!] —**stow away** 1. to put or hide away, as in a safe place 2. to be a stowaway 3. to consume (food or drink), esp. in large amounts

stow·age (-ij) *n.* 1. a stowing or being stowed 2. place or room for stowing 3. something stowed; amount stowed 4. charges for stowing

stow·a·way (-ə wā′) *n.* a person who hides aboard a ship, airplane, etc. to get free passage, evade port officials, etc.

Stowe (stō), **Harriet (Elizabeth) Beecher** 1811–96; U.S. novelist: sister of Henry Ward BEECHER

☆**STP** [prob. arbitrary use of *STP*, a commercial motor oil additive (< *S*(*cientifically*) *T*(*reated*) *P*(*etroleum*)), said to "make your motor run better"] a hallucinogenic drug similar to mescaline and amphetamine

St. Paul capital of Minn., on the Mississippi: pop. 310,000: see MINNEAPOLIS

St. Pe·ters·burg (pē′tərz burg′) 1. *former name* (1703–1914) *of* LENINGRAD 2. city in WC Fla., on Tampa Bay: pop. 216,000: see TAMPA

St-Pierre (san pyer′) town in NW Martinique, West Indies, on the site of a city completely destroyed (1902) by eruption of Mont Pelée: pop. 6,000

St. Pierre and Miquelon Fr. territory in the Atlantic, south of Newfoundland, consisting of the islands of St. Pierre (c.10 sq. mi.) & MIQUELON & six islets: 93 sq. mi.; pop. 5,000

St-Quen·tin (san kän tan′) city in N France, on the Somme: pop. 61,000

str. 1. steamer 2. *Music* string(s)

stra·bis·mus (strə biz′məs) *n.* [ModL. < Gr. *strabismos* < *strabizein*, to squint < *strabos*, twisted < IE. *streb-* < base *ster-*, stiff, taut, whence START, STARE] a disorder of the muscles of the eyes, as cross-eye, in which both eyes cannot be focused on the same point at the same time; squint —**stra·bis′mal, stra·bis′mic** *adj.* —**stra·bis′mal·ly** *adv.*

Stra·bo (strā′bō) 63? B.C.–19? A.D.; Gr. geographer

Stra·chey (strā′chē), **(Giles) Lyt·ton** (lit′ʼn) 1880–1932; Eng. biographer

Strad (strad) *n. clipped form of* STRADIVARIUS

strad·dle (strad′ʼl) *vt.* **-dled, -dling** [freq. of STRIDE] 1. to place oneself with a leg on either side of; stand or sit astride of 2. to spread (the legs) wide apart ☆3. to take or appear to take both sides of (an issue); avoid committing oneself on 4. *same as* BRACKET (*vt.* 4) —*vi.* 1. to sit, stand, or walk with the legs wide apart 2. to be spread apart: said of the legs ☆3. to straddle an issue, argument, etc.; refuse to commit oneself; hedge —*n.* 1. the act or position of straddling 2. the distance straddled ☆3. a refusal to commit oneself definitely to either side of an issue, etc. ☆4. in the securities trade, a combination of two separate options, a put and a call, giving the holder the right to buy from the seller, or sell to him, a specified number of shares at a specified option price within a stated time —**strad′dler** *n.*

Stra·di·va·ri (strä′dē vä′rē), **An·to·nio** (än tô′nyō) (L. name *Antonius Stradivarius*) 1644–1737; It. violin maker

Strad·i·var·i·us (strad′ə var′ē əs) *n.* a string instrument, esp. a violin, made by A. Stradivari or his sons

strafe (strāf; *chiefly Brit.*, sträf) *vt.* **strafed, straf′ing** [< G. phr. *Gott strafe England* (God punish England) used in World War I] to attack with gunfire; esp., to attack (ground positions, troops, etc.) with machine-gun fire from low-flying aircraft —**straf′er** *n.*

Straf·ford (straf′ərd), **1st Earl of,** *(Thomas Wentworth)* 1593–1641; Eng. statesman: adviser of Charles I: beheaded

strag·gle (strag′ʼl) *vi.* **-gled, -gling** [ME. *straglen*, prob. for *straklen*, freq. of *straken*, to go about, wander, roam] 1. to stray from the path or course or wander from the main group 2. to wander or be scattered over a wide area; ramble 3. to leave, arrive, or occur at scattered, irregular intervals 4. to hang in an unkempt or disheveled manner, as hair, clothes, etc. —*n.* a straggly arrangement or group —**strag′gler** *n.*

strag·gly (-lē) *adj.* **-gli·er, -gli·est** spread out in a straggling, irregular way

straight (strāt) *adj.* [ME. *streght*, pp. of *strecchen*, to STRETCH] 1. having the same direction throughout its length; having no curvature or angularity [a *straight* line] 2. not crooked, bent, bowed, wavy, curly, etc. [*straight* hair] 3. upright; erect [*straight* posture] 4. level; even [a *straight* hemline] 5. with all cylinders in a direct line: said of some internal-combustion engines 6. direct; undeviating, uninterrupted, etc. [to hold a *straight* course] ☆7. following strictly the principles, slate of candidates, etc. of a political party [to vote a *straight* ticket] 8. following a direct or systematic course of reasoning, etc.; methodical; accurate 9. in order; properly arranged, etc. [to put a room *straight*] 10. *a)* honest; sincere; upright *b)* reliable; factual [*straight* information] 11. outspoken; frank ☆12. *a)* without anything added or mixed in; undiluted [a *straight* shot of whiskey] *b)* not blended with neutral grain spirits 13. not qualified, modified, slanted, etc. [a *straight* denial] ☆14. at a fixed price per unit regardless of the quantity bought or sold [apples at ten cents *straight*] ☆15. [Slang] normal or conventional; specif., not a homosexual, not a drug addict, etc. —*adv.* 1. in a straight line or direction; unswervingly 2. upright; erectly 3. *a)* without detour, delay, etc. [go *straight* to bed] *b)* without equivocation, circumlocution, etc.; directly [tell it *straight*] *c)* without alteration, addition, etc. [play the role *straight*] —*n.* 1. the quality or condition of being straight 2. something straight; specif., *a)* the straight part of a race track between the last turn and the winning post ☆*b)* *Poker* a hand consisting of any five cards in sequence: it ranks just above three of a kind and below a flush —**straight away** (or **off**) at once; without delay —**the straight and narrow (path)** a morally strict code of behavior —**straight′ly** *adv.* —**straight′ness** *n.*

straight angle an angle of 180 degrees

☆**straight-arm** (-ärm′) *vt.* to push away (an opponent, as a would-be tackler in football) with the arm outstretched —*n.* the act of straight-arming

straight·a·way (-ə wā′) *adj.* extending in a straight line —*n.* 1. a race track, or part of a track, that extends in a straight line 2. a straight and level stretch of highway

straight chain *Chem.* a linear chain of atoms without any branches, as the carbon atoms in hydrocarbons

straight chair a chair with a back that is straight, or almost vertical, and not upholstered

straight-edge (-ej′) *n.* a piece or strip of wood, etc. having a perfectly straight edge used in drawing straight lines, testing plane surfaces, etc.

straight·en (-'n) *vt., vi.* to make or become straight —**straighten out** 1. to make or become less confused, easier to deal with, etc. ☆2. to make or become more correct or moral in behavior; reform —**straight′en·er** *n.*

straight face a facial expression showing no amusement or other emotion —**straight′-faced′** *adj.*

straight flush *Poker* a flush in which all five cards are in sequence: it is the highest ranking hand

straight·for·ward (strāt′fôr′wərd) *adj.* 1. moving or leading straight ahead; direct 2. honest; frank; open —*adv.* in a straightforward manner; directly; openly: also **straight′for′wards** —**straight′for′ward·ly** *adv.* —**straight′for′ward·ness** *n.*

straight·jack·et (strāt′jak′it) *n. same as* STRAITJACKET

straight·laced (-lāst′) *adj. same as* STRAIT-LACED (sense 2)

straight-line (-līn′) *adj.* 1. composed of straight lines 2. *Finance* designating or of a method of allocating costs to given time periods at a fixed rate [*straight-line* depreciation] 3. *Mech. a)* designating or of a device, mechanism, etc. whose main parts are positioned or move in a straight line *b)* designating a device designed to transmit or cause motion in a straight line

☆**straight man** an actor who serves as a foil for a comedian, feeding him lines

straight-out (-out′) *adj.* [Colloq.] 1. straightforward; direct 2. unrestrained ☆3. thoroughgoing; unqualified

☆**straight razor** a razor with a long, unguarded blade that can be folded into the handle

☆**straight time** 1. the number of working hours fixed as a standard for a given work period 2. the rate of pay for work during these hours

straight·way (-wā′) *adv.* at once; without delay

strain[1] (strān) *vt.* [ME. *streinen* < OFr. *estraindre*, to strain, wring hard < L. *stringere*, to draw tight: see STRICT] 1. to draw or stretch tight 2. to exert, use, or tax to the utmost [to *strain* every nerve] 3. to overtax; injure by overexertion; wrench [to *strain* a muscle] 4. to injure or weaken by force, pressure, etc. [the wind *strained* the roof] 5. to stretch or force beyond the normal, customary, or legitimate limits [to *strain* a rule to one's own advantage] 6. to change the form or size of, by applying external force 7. *a)* to pass through a screen, sieve, filter, etc.; filter *b)* to remove or free by filtration, etc. 8. to hug or embrace: now only in **to strain to one's bosom** (or **heart**, etc.) 9. [Obs.] to force; constrain —*vi.* 1. to make violent or continual efforts; strive hard 2. to be or become strained 3. to be subjected to great stress or pressure 4. to pull or push with force 5. to filter, ooze, or trickle 6. [from a misunderstanding of "strain at a gnat" (Matt. 23:24)] to hesitate or be unwilling; balk (*at*) —*n.* 1. a straining or being strained 2. great effort, exertion, or tension 3. an injury to a part of the body as a result of

great effort or overexertion [heart *strain*] **4.** *a*) change in form or size, or both, resulting from stress or force *b*) stress or force **5.** a great or excessive demand on one's emotions, resources, etc. [a *strain* on the imagination]

strain[2] (strān) *n.* [ME. *stren* < OE. *streon*, gain, procreation, stock, race < base of *strynan*, *streonan*, to produce: for IE. base see STREW] **1.** orig., *a*) a begetting *b*) offspring **2.** ancestry; lineage; descent **3.** the descendants of a common ancestor; race; stock; line; breed; variety **4.** a line of individuals of a certain species or race, differentiated from the main group by certain, generally superior qualities, esp. as the result of artificial breeding **5.** an inherited or natural character or tendency **6.** a trace; streak **7.** the manner, style, or tone of a speech, book, action, etc. [to write in an angry *strain*] **8.** [*often pl.*] a passage of music; tune; air **9.** a passage of poetry, esp. of a lyric sort **10.** a flight or outburst of eloquence, profanity, etc.

strained (strānd) *adj.* not natural or relaxed; forced

strain·er (strān′ər) *n.* a person or thing that strains; specif., a device for straining, sifting, or filtering; sieve, filter, colander, etc.

strain·ing piece (strān′iŋ) a horizontal brace or beam connected at either end to opposite rafters in a roof truss: also **straining beam**

strait (strāt) *adj.* [ME. *streit* < OFr. *estreit* < L. *strictus*: see STRICT] **1.** [Archaic] restricted or constricted; narrow; tight; confined **2.** [Archaic] strict; rigid; exacting **3.** [Now Rare] straitened; difficult; distressing —*n.* **1.** [Rare] a narrow passage **2.** [*often pl.*] a narrow waterway connecting two large bodies of water **3.** [*often pl.*] difficulty; distress **4.** [Rare] an isthmus —*SYN.* see EMERGENCY

strait·en (strāt′'n) *vt.* **1.** esp. formerly, *a*) to make strait or narrow *b*) to hem in closely *c*) to restrict or confine in scope, range, etc.; hamper **2.** to bring into difficulties; cause to be in distress or want: usually in the phrase **in straitened circumstances**, lacking sufficient money

strait-jack·et (-jak′it) *n.* a coatlike device that binds the arms tight against the body: used to restrain persons in a violent state

strait-laced (-lāst′) *adj.* **1.** formerly, *a*) tightly laced, as a corset *b*) wearing tightly laced garments **2.** narrowly strict or severe in behavior or moral views

Straits Settlements former Brit. crown colony in SE Asia, comprising Singapore, Malacca, Penang, Labuan, Christmas Island, & the Cocos Islands

strake (strāk) *n.* [ME., akin to *strecchen*, to STRETCH] a single line of planking or metal plating extending along the hull of a ship or boat from stem to stern

Stral·sund (shtrāl′zoont) seaport in N East Germany, on the Baltic Sea: pop. 66,000

stra·mo·ni·um (strə mō′nē əm) *n.* [ModL.] **1.** *same as* JIMSON WEED **2.** the dried leaves and flowering top of this plant, formerly used in medicine as an antispasmodic

strand[1] (strand) *n.* [ME. < OE., akin to ON. *strǫnd*, G. *strand*, prob. < IE. base *ster-*, to extend, stretch out, whence STREW] land at the edge of a body of water; shore, esp. ocean shore —*vt.*, *vi.* **1.** to run or drive aground [a ship *stranded* by the storm, grunion *stranding* to spawn] **2.** to leave in, or be put into, a difficult, helpless position [*stranded* penniless in a strange city] —*SYN.* see SHORE[1]

strand[2] (strand) *n.* [ME. *stronde* < ?] **1.** any of the bundles of thread, fiber, wire, etc. that are twisted together to form a length of string, rope, or cable **2.** a ropelike length of anything [a *strand* of pearls, a *strand* of hair] **3.** any of the parts that are bound together to form a whole [the *strands* of one's life] —*vt.* **1.** to form (rope, etc.) by twisting together strands **2.** to break a strand or strands of (a rope, etc.) —**strand′er** *n.*

strand line a shoreline, esp. a former one from which the water has receded

strange (strānj) *adj.* **stran′ger, strang′est** [ME. < OFr. *estrange* < L. *extraneus*, that is without < *extra*, on the outside] **1.** of another place or locality; foreign; alien **2.** not previously known, seen, heard, or experienced; unfamiliar **3.** quite unusual or uncommon; extraordinary **4.** queer; peculiar; odd **5.** reserved, distant, or cold in manner **6.** lacking experience; unaccustomed [*strange* to the job] —*adv.* in a strange manner —**strange′ly** *adv.*
SYN.—**strange**, the term of broadest application here, refers to that which is unfamiliar, as because of being uncommon, unknown, new, etc. [a *strange* voice, idea, device, etc.]; **peculiar** applies either to that which puzzles or to that which has unique qualities [a *peculiar* smell, pattern, etc.]; **odd** suggests that which differs from the ordinary or conventional, sometimes to the point of being bizarre [*odd* behavior]; **queer** emphasizes an element of eccentricity, abnormality, or suspicion [a *queer* facial expression]; **quaint** suggests an oddness, esp. an antique quality, that is pleasing or appealing [a *quaint* costume, etc.]; **outlandish** suggests an oddness that is decidedly, often outrageously, fantastic or bizarre [*outlandish* customs] —*ANT.* **familiar, ordinary**

strange·ness (-nis) *n.* **1.** the state or quality of being strange **2.** a not yet identified property of elementary particles, described by a quantum number and introduced to explain the absence of certain types of radioactive decay among these particles

stran·ger (strān′jər) *n.* [ME. < MFr. *estranger* < OFr. *estrange*: see prec.] **1.** an outsider, newcomer, or foreigner **2.** a guest or visitor **3.** a person not known or familiar to one; person who is not an acquaintance **4.** a person unaccustomed (to something specified); novice [a *stranger* to hate] **5.** *Law* a person who is not party (to an act, agreement, title, etc.) —*SYN.* see ALIEN

stran·gle (straŋ′g'l) *vt.* **-gled, -gling** [ME. *stranglen* < OFr. *estrangler* < L. *strangulare* < Gr. *strangalan* < *strangalē*, halter < *strangos*, twisted: for IE. base see STRONG] **1.** to kill by squeezing the throat as with the hands, a noose, etc., so as to shut off the breath; throttle; choke **2.** to suffocate or choke in any manner **3.** to suppress, stifle, or repress [free speech *strangled* by tyranny] —*vi.* to be strangled —**stran′gler** *n.*

stran·gle·hold (-hōld′) *n.* **1.** an illegal wrestling hold that chokes off an opponent's breath **2.** any force or action that restricts or suppresses freedom

stran·gles (-g'lz) *n.* an infectious disease of horses, characterized by inflammation of the mucous membrane of the respiratory tract

stran·gu·late (straŋ′gyə lāt′) *vt.* **-lat′ed, -lat′ing** [< L. *strangulatus*, pp. of *strangulare*] **1.** *same as* STRANGLE **2.** *Med.* to constrict (a tube, herniated organ, etc.) so as to cut off a flow, esp. so as to cut off circulation of the blood—*vi. Med.* to become constricted—**stran′gu·la′tion** *n.*

stran·gu·ry (straŋ′gyə rē) *n.* [ME. < L. *stranguria* < Gr. *strangouria* < *stranx* (gen. *strangos*), a drop, akin to *strangos*, twisted (see STRONG) + *ouron*, URINE] slow and painful urination, drop by drop

strap (strap) *n.* [dial. form of STROP] **1.** a narrow strip or band of leather or other flexible material, often with a buckle or similar fastener at one end, for binding or securing things **2.** any flat, narrow piece, as of metal, used as a fastening **3.** any of several straplike parts or things, as a shoulder strap, a loop for pulling on boots, a razor strop, etc. —*vt.* **strapped, strap′ping 1.** to fasten with a strap **2.** to beat with a strap **3.** to strop (a razor)

strap·hang·er (-haŋ′ər) *n.* [Colloq.] a standing passenger, as on a crowded bus or subway car, who supports himself by holding onto a hanging strap, etc.

strap hinge a hinge with long, usually triangular, parts by which it is fastened: see HINGE, illus.

strap·less (-lis) *adj.* having no strap or straps; specif., having no shoulder straps [a *strapless* bra]

strap·pa·do (stra pā′dō, -pä′-) *n., pl.* **-does** [It. *strappata* < *strappare*, to pull < Gmc., as in G. dial. (Swiss) *strapfen*, to pull tight (akin to G. *strafen*, to punish) < IE. *strep-* < base *ster-*, taut, stiff: cf. STARK] **1.** a former kind of torture in which the victim's wrists were tied to a long rope behind his back, and he was lifted in the air, then suddenly dropped part way to the ground **2.** the instrument used in this torture

☆**strapped** (strapt) *adj.* [pp. of STRAP] [Colloq.] in utter need; penniless

strap·per (strap′ər) *n.* **1.** a person or thing that straps **2.** [Colloq.] a strapping person

strap·ping (-iŋ) *adj.* [prp. of STRAP, used (like *thumping*, *whopping*, expressing violent action) to denote large size] [Colloq.] tall and well-built; robust

Stras·bourg (stras′burg; Fr. strȧz bōōr′) city & port in NE France, on the Rhine: pop. 229,000

strass (stras) *n.* [Fr. & G. < ?: said to be after a J. *Strass* (or *Strasser*), G. jeweler] a lustrous lead glass used in making artificial jewels; paste

stra·ta (strāt′ə, strat′-) *n. alt. pl.* of STRATUM

strat·a·gem (strat′ə jəm) *n.* [LME. *stratageme* < L. *strategema* < Gr. *stratēgēma*, device or act of a general < *stratēgos*, a general < *stratos*, army (for IE. base see STREW) + *agein*, to lead (see ACT)] **1.** a trick, scheme, or plan for deceiving an enemy in war **2.** any trick or scheme for achieving some purpose —*SYN.* see TRICK

stra·tal (strāt′'l) *adj.* of a stratum or strata

stra·te·gic (strə tē′jik) *adj.* **1.** of or having to do with strategy **2.** characterized by sound strategy; favorable; advantageous **3.** *a*) essential to effective military strategy [*strategic* materials] ☆*b*) operating or designed to operate directly against the military, industrial, etc. installations of the enemy or a potential enemy [the *Strategic* Air Command] Also **stra·te′gi·cal** —**stra·te′gi·cal·ly** *adv.*

strat·e·gist (strat′ə jist) *n.* one skilled in strategy

strat·e·gy (-jē) *n., pl.* **-gies** [Fr. *stratégie* < Gr. *stratēgia*, generalship < *stratēgos*: see STRATAGEM] **1.** *a*) the science of planning and directing large-scale military operations, specif. (as distinguished from TACTICS) of maneuvering forces into the most advantageous position prior to actual engagement with the enemy *b*) a plan or action based on this **2.** *a*) skill in managing or planning, esp. by using stratagem *b*) a stratagem or artful means to some end Also, esp. for sense 1, **stra·te·gics** (strə tē′jiks) *n.pl.*

Strat·ford (strat′fərd) [after ff.] town in SW Conn., on Long Island Sound: suburb of Bridgeport: pop. 50,000

Strat·ford-on-A·von (-än ā′vän) town in S Warwickshire, England, on the Avon River: birthplace & burial place of Shakespeare: pop. 25,000 Also **Strat′ford-up·on-A′von**

strath (strath) *n.* [< ScotGael. *srath*] a wide river valley
strath·spey (-spā′) *n.* [< *Strathspey*, valley of Spey River, N Scotland (see prec.)] **1.** a Scottish dance resembling, but slower than, the reel **2.** the music for this
strat·i·fi·ca·tion (strat′ə fi kā′shən) *n.* **1.** the process of stratifying or the state of being stratified **2.** *Geol.* a stratified arrangement or appearance **3.** *Geol.* a structure characterized by a succession of tabular layers, beds, strata, etc.
strat·i·form (strat′ə fôrm′) *adj.* [< STRATUM + -FORM] having the form of a stratum; showing stratification; specif., designating or of clouds arranged in extensive horizontal patterns
strat·i·fy (-fī′) *vt.* **-fied′, -fy′ing** [Fr. *stratifier* < ModL. *stratificare* < L. *stratum*, layer + *facere*, to make: see STRATUM & DO¹] **1.** to form or arrange in layers or strata **2.** to preserve (seeds) by placing them between layers of moisture-retaining soil, peat moss, etc. **3.** to classify or separate (people) into groups graded according to status as variously determined by birth, income, education, etc. —*vi.* to become stratified
stra·tig·ra·phy (strə tig′rə fē) *n.* [< STRATUM + -GRAPHY] **1.** the arrangement of rocks in layers or strata **2.** the branch of geology dealing with the study of the nature, distribution, and relations of the stratified rocks of the earth's crust —**stra·tig′ra·pher** *n.* —**strat·i·graph·ic** (strat′ə graf′ik) *adj.* —**strat′i·graph′i·cal·ly** *adv.*
stra·toc·ra·cy (strə täk′rə sē) *n., pl.* **-cies** [< Gr. *stratos* (see STRATAGEM) + -CRACY] government by the military
stra·to·cu·mu·lus (strāt′ō kyōōm′yə ləs, strat′-) *n., pl.* **-li′** (-lī′) [ModL.: see STRATUS & CUMULUS] a stratiform cloud type occurring in a continuous gray or whitish layer or in patches, usually with dark areas and with rounded masses in orderly lines or waves
strat·o·sphere (strat′ə sfir′) *n.* [Fr. *stratosphère* < ModL. *stratum*, STRATUM + Fr. *sphère*, SPHERE] the atmospheric zone above the troposphere, extending variously from six to fifteen miles above the earth's surface, in which the temperature is fairly constant, ranging from about −45°C to −75°C —**strat′o·spher′ic** (-sfer′ik, -sfir′-) *adj.*
stra·tum (strāt′əm, strat′-) *n., pl.* **stra′ta** (-ə), **-tums** [ModL. < L., a covering, blanket < *stratus*, pp. of *sternere*, to spread, stretch out, cover: for IE. base see STREW] **1.** a horizontal layer or section of material, esp. any of several lying one upon another; specif., *a) Biol.* a layer of tissue *b) Geol.* a single layer of sedimentary rock **2.** a section, level, or division, as of the atmosphere or ocean, regarded as like a stratum **3.** any of the socioeconomic groups of a society as determined by birth, income, education, etc.
stra·tus (-əs) *n., pl.* **stra′ti** (-ī) [L., a strewing: see prec.] a cloud type extending in a long, low, gray layer with an almost uniform base
Straus (strous; *G.* shtrous) **Oscar** (or **Oskar**) 1870–1954; Austrian composer, later in France & the U.S.
Strauss (shtrous; *E.* strous) **1. Jo·hann** (yō′hän), 1825–99; Austrian composer, esp. of waltzes **2. Rich·ard** (riH′ärt), 1864–1949; Ger. composer & conductor
stra·vage (strə väg′) *vi.* **-vaged′, -vag′ing** [aphetic contr. < ML. *extravagari*, to stray: see EXTRAVAGANT] [Scot.] to wander about; roam: also sp. **stra·vaig′**
Stra·vin·sky (strə vin′skē; *Russ.* strä vēn′ski), **I·gor** (**Fe·dorovich**) (ē′gôr) 1882–1971; U.S. composer & conductor, born in Russia
straw (strô) *n.* [ME. *stra* < OE. *streaw*, akin to *streawian*: see STREW] **1.** hollow stalks or stems of grain after threshing, collectively; used for fodder, for bedding, for making hats, etc. **2.** a single one of such stalks **3.** such a stalk or, now esp., a tube of waxed paper, plastic, glass, etc. used for sucking beverages **4.** something, as a hat, made of straw **5.** something of little or no value; worthless trifle **6.** *clipped form of* STRAW MAN (sense 4) —*adj.* **1.** straw-colored; yellowish **2.** made of straw **3.** of little or no value or significance; worthless; meaningless —**a straw in the wind** an indication of what may happen —**grasp** (or **clutch, catch**) **at a straw** (or **straws**) to try any measure, however unlikely, that offers even the least hope
straw·ber·ry (-ber′ē, -bər ē) *n., pl.* **-ries** [ME. *strawberi* < OE. *streawberie* < *streaw*, straw + *berige*; berry: prob. from the small achenes on the fruit] **1.** the small, red, fleshy accessory fruit of a stolon-bearing plant (genus *Fragaria*) of the rose family **2.** this plant
☆**strawberry bass** the black crappie: see CRAPPIE
☆**strawberry blonde** reddish blonde
☆**strawberry bush** an E American euonymus (*Euonymus americana*) with red pods, and seeds with a red covering
strawberry mark a small, red birthmark
strawberry roan reddish roan
☆**strawberry shrub** *same as* CAROLINA ALLSPICE
☆**strawberry tomato** *same as* GROUND-CHERRY, esp. an E American species (*Physalis pruinosa*) with a small, edible, yellow fruit
strawberry tree **1.** a European evergreen tree (*Arbutus unedo*) of the heath family, with small, white flowers and red, berrylike fruit ☆**2.** *same as* STRAWBERRY BUSH
straw·board (strô′bôrd′) *n.* a coarse cardboard made of straw and used in making boxes, etc.
☆**straw boss** [Colloq.] **1.** a person having subordinate authority, as a foreman's assistant **2.** a supervisor who has little or no authority to support his orders
straw color a pale-yellow color —**straw′-col′ored** *adj.*

straw·flow·er (-flou′ər) *n.* **1.** an annual Australian plant (*Helichrysum bracteatum*) of the composite family, whose brightly colored flower heads are dried for winter bouquets **2.** any of several bellworts (sense 1)
☆**straw-hat** (-hat′) *adj.* [from the practice, esp. formerly, of wearing straw hats in summer] designating, of, or having to do with a summer theater or summer theaters
straw man **1.** *same as* SCARECROW **2.** a person of little importance; nonentity **3.** a weak argument or opposing view set up by a politician, debater, etc. so that he may attack it and gain an easy, showy victory **4.** a person used to disguise another's intentions, activities, etc.; blind
☆**straw vote** an unofficial vote or poll taken to determine general group opinion on a given issue
straw wine a sweet, rich wine made from grapes that have been dried in the sun, as on a bed of straw
straw·worm (-wurm′) *n.* any of several insect larvae (family Eurytomidae) which damage the stalks of wheat, etc.; esp., *same as* JOINTWORM
straw·y (-ē) *adj.* **straw′i·er, straw′i·est 1.** of or like straw **2.** covered or thatched with straw
stray (strā) *vi.* [ME. *straien* < OFr. *estraier*, prob. < VL. **estragare* < L. *extra vagari*, to wander outside: see EXTRAVAGANT] **1.** to wander from a given place, limited area, direct course, etc., esp. aimlessly; roam; rove **2.** to go wrong; be in error; deviate (*from* what is right) **3.** to fail to concentrate; be inattentive or digress —*n.* **1.** a person or thing that strays; esp., a domestic animal wandering at large **2.** [*usually pl.*] static interfering with radio reception —*adj.* **1.** having strayed or wandered; lost **2.** occurring alone or infrequently; isolated; incidental [a few *stray* words] —SYN. see ROAM —**stray′er** *n.*
streak (strēk) *n.* [ME. *streke* < OE. *strica*: for IE. base see STRIKE] **1.** a line or long, thin mark; stripe or smear, generally differing in color or texture from the surrounding area **2.** a ray of light or a flash, as of lightning **3.** a vein or stratum of a mineral **4.** a layer, as of fat in meat **5.** a strain, element, or tendency in behavior, temperament, etc.; trait [a jealous *streak*] ☆**6.** a period, spell, or series [a *streak* of bad luck, a *streak* of losses] **7.** *Bacteriology* an inoculum placed, as in a line, on a solid culture medium **8.** *Mineralogy* a colored line of powder produced by rubbing a mineral over a hard, white surface (**streak plate**): it serves as a distinguishing character —*vt.* **1.** to make streaks on or in; mark with streaks —*vi.* **1.** to form streaks; become streaked **2.** to move at high speed; go fast; hurry —☆**like a streak** [Colloq.] at high speed; swiftly
streak·y (strē′kē) *adj.* **streak′i·er, streak′i·est 1.** marked with or showing streaks **2.** occurring in streaks **3.** uneven or variable, as in quality —**streak′i·ly** *adv.* —**streak′i·ness** *n.*
stream (strēm) *n.* [ME. *strem* < OE. *stream*, akin to G. *strom* < IE. base **sreu-*, to flow, whence Gr. *rheein*, to flow] **1.** a current or flow of water or other liquid, esp. one running along the surface of the earth; specif., a small river **2.** a steady movement or flow of any fluid [a *stream* of cold air] or of rays of energy [a *stream* of light] **3.** a continuous series or succession [a *stream* of cars] **4.** a trend or course [the *stream* of events] **5.** [Brit.] *Educ.* any of the sections formed when students within a grade level are grouped according to their supposed intellectual capacity —*vi.* **1.** to flow in or as in a stream **2.** to give off a stream; flow (*with*) [eyes *streaming* with tears] **3.** to move steadily or continuously **4.** to move swiftly; rush [fire *streamed* up the wall] **5.** to extend or stretch out; float; fly, as a flag in the breeze —*vt.* **1.** to cause to flow **2.** to extend (a flag, etc.) out to its length **3.** [Brit.] *Educ.* to group (students) into streams
stream·er (strē′mər) *n.* **1.** something that streams **2.** a long, narrow, ribbonlike flag or banner **3.** any long, narrow strip of cloth, colored paper, ribbon, etc., hanging loose at one end **4.** a ray or stream of light extending up from the horizon **5.** a newspaper headline across the full page
stream·let (strēm′lit) *n.* a small stream; rivulet
stream·line (-līn′) *n.* **1.** the path, or a section of the path, of a fluid moving past a solid object **2.** a shape or contour with reference to its resistance to air, etc. —*vt.* **-lined′, -lin′ing 1.** to design or construct with a contour that offers the least resistance in moving through air, water, etc. ☆**2.** to arrange or organize so as to gain simplicity and efficiency —*adj. same as* STREAMLINED
stream·lined (-līnd′) *adj.* **1.** having a contour designed to offer the least resistance in moving through air, water, etc. ☆**2.** so arranged or organized as to gain simplicity and efficiency **3.** with no excess, as of fat, decoration, etc.; trim, simplified, etc. [a *streamlined* figure or design]
streamline flow *same as* LAMINAR FLOW
☆**stream-of-con·scious·ness** (-əv kän′shəs nis) *adj.* designating, of, or using a narrative technique whereby the thoughts, percepts, etc. of one or more of the characters of a novel, short story, etc. are recorded
☆**stream of consciousness** [term originated by William James] *Psych.* individual conscious experience regarded as a continuous series of occurrences rather than as separate, disconnected events
stream·y (strē′mē) *adj.* **stream′i·er, stream′i·est 1.** full of streams or currents **2.** like a stream; streaming; flowing; running
street (strēt) *n.* [ME. < OE. *strǣt*, akin to G. *strasse* < early WGmc. loanword < LL. *strata* < L. *strata* (*via*),

paved (road), fem. of *stratus*: see STRATUM] **1.** a public road in a town or city; esp., a paved thoroughfare with sidewalks and buildings along one or both sides **2.** such a road apart from its sidewalks [children playing in the *street*] **3.** the people living, working, etc. in the buildings along a given street —*adj.* **1.** of, in, on, or near the street [the *street* floor] **2.** suitable for everyday wear in public [*street* clothes]

street Arab a homeless or neglected child left to roam the streets; gamin: also **street urchin**

☆**street·car** (-kär′) *n.* a large coach or car on rails that provides public transportation along certain streets

street·walk·er (-wôk′ər) *n.* a prostitute who solicits customers along the streets —**street′walk′ing** *n.*

strength (strenkth, strenth) *n.* [ME. *strengthe* < OE. *strengthu* < **strang-ithu*: see STRONG & -TH[1]] **1.** the state or quality of being strong; force; power; vigor **2.** the power to resist strain, stress, etc.; toughness; durability **3.** the power to resist attack; impregnability **4.** legal, moral, or intellectual force or effectiveness **5.** *a)* capacity for producing a reaction or effect *b)* potency or concentration, as of drugs, liquors, etc. *c)* great effectiveness or high potency **6.** intensity, as of sound, color, odor, etc. **7.** force as measured in numbers [a battalion at full *strength*] **8.** vigor or force of feeling or expression **9.** a source of strength or support **10.** a tendency to rise or remain firm in prices —**on the strength of** based or relying on *SYN.*—**strength** refers to the inherent capacity to act upon or affect something, to endure, to resist, etc. [the *strength* to lift something, tensile *strength*]; **power**, somewhat more general, applies to the ability, latent or exerted, physical or mental, to do something [the *power* of the press, of a machine, etc.]; **force** usually suggests the actual exertion of power, esp. in producing motion or overcoming opposition [the *force* of gravity]; **might** suggests great or overwhelming strength or power [with all one's *might*]; **energy** specifically implies latent power for doing work or affecting something [the *energy* in an atom]; **potency** refers to the inherent capacity or power to accomplish something [the *potency* of a drug] —*ANT.* **weakness, impotence**

strength·en (-'n) *vt., vi.* to increase in strength; make or become stronger —**strength′en·er** *n.*

stren·u·ous (stren′yoo wəs) *adj.* [L. *strenuus*, vigorous, active < IE. base **ster-*, stiff, taut, whence Gr. *strēnēs*, strong: cf. STARE] **1.** requiring or characterized by great effort or energy [a *strenuous* game of handball] **2.** vigorous, arduous, zealous, etc. [*strenuous* efforts] —*SYN.* see ACTIVE —**stren′u·ous·ly** *adv.* —**stren′u·ous·ness** *n.*

strep (strep) *n. clipped form of* STREPTOCOCCUS

strep·to·coc·cus (strep′tə käk′əs) *n., pl.* **-coc′ci** (-käk′sī) [ModL., name of the genus < Gr. *streptos*, twisted (see STREPTOMYCES) + COCCUS] any of a genus (*Streptococcus*) of spherical, Gram-positive bacteria that divide in only one plane and occur generally in chains: some species cause various serious diseases —**strep′to·coc′cal** (-käk′əl), **strep′to·coc′cic** (-käk′sik) *adj.*

strep·to·ki·nase (-kī′nās, -kin′ās) *n.* [< prec. + KINASE] a proteolytic enzyme derived from certain hemolytic streptococci, used in dissolving blood clots

strep·to·my·ces (-mī′sēz) *n., pl.* **-ces** [< Gr. *streptos*, twisted < *strephein*, to turn (see STROPHE) + *mykēs*, fungus (see MYCO-)] any of a genus (*Streptomyces*) of funguslike, chiefly soil bacteria, including several species that yield antibiotics

☆**strep·to·my·cin** (-mī′sin) *n.* [< prec. + -IN[1]] an antibiotic drug, $C_{21}H_{39}N_7O_{12}$, obtained from the actinomycete (*Streptomyces grisens*) and used in the treatment of various bacterial diseases, including tuberculosis

strep·to·thri·cin (-thrī′sin) *n.* [< ModL. *Streptothrix*, name of the fungus < Gr. *streptos*, twisted (see STREPTOMYCES) + *thrix*, hair + -IN[1]] an antibiotic drug derived from the actinomycete (*Streptomyces lavendulae*) and used for the topical treatment of various bacterial infections

stress (stres) *n.* [ME. *stresse* < OFr. *estresse* < VL. **strictia* < L. *strictus*, STRICT; also, in some senses, aphetic < DISTRESS] **1.** strain or straining force; specif., *a)* force exerted upon a body, that tends to strain or deform its shape *b)* the intensity of such force, usually measured in pounds per square inch *c)* the opposing reaction or cohesiveness of a body resisting such force **2.** emphasis; importance; significance **3.** *a)* mental or physical tension or strain *b)* urgency, pressure, etc. causing this **4.** *Music* same as ACCENT (senses 13 & 14) **5.** *Phonet. a)* the relative force with which a syllable is uttered *b)* an accented syllable: for stress marks, see PRIMARY ACCENT, SECONDARY ACCENT **6.** *Prosody a)* the relative force of utterance given a syllable or word according to the meter *b)* an accented syllable —*vt.* [OFr. *estrecer*, prob. < the *n.*] **1.** to put stress, pressure, or strain on **2.** to give stress or accent to **3.** to emphasize —**stress′ful** *adj.* —**stress′ful·ly** *adv.*

-stress (stris) [< -STER + -ESS] *a feminine suffix corresponding to* -STER [*songstress*]

stretch (strech) *vt.* [ME. *strecchen* < OE. *streccan*, akin to G. *strecken* < IE. **sterg-* < base **ster-*, to be stiff, rigid, whence STARE] **1.** to hold out or reach out; extend [to *stretch* out a helping hand] **2.** to cause (the body or limbs)

to reach out to full length, as in yawning, relaxing, reclining, etc. **3.** to pull or spread out to full extent or to greater size [to *stretch* sheets out to dry] **4.** to cause to reach or extend over a given space, distance, or time [to *stretch* pipelines across a continent] **5.** *a)* to cause to reach or extend farther or too far; force or strain *b)* to strain in interpretation, application, scope, etc. to questionable or unreasonable limits [to *stretch* a rule, to *stretch* the truth] **6.** to make tense or tight with effort; strain (a muscle, etc.) **7.** [Slang] to knock down, esp. so as to cause to lie at full length **8.** [Archaic or Dial.] to execute by hanging —*vi.* **1.** *a)* to spread or be spread out to full extent or beyond normal limits *b)* to extend or continue over a given space, distance, or time **2.** *a)* to extend the body or limbs to full length, as in yawning or reaching for something *b)* to lie down at full length (usually with *out*) **3.** to become stretched or be capable of being stretched to greater size, as any elastic substance **4.** [Slang] to be executed by hanging —*n.* **1.** a stretching or being stretched **2.** *a)* an unbroken period; continuous space (*of* time) [over a *stretch* of ten days] *b)* [Slang] a term served in prison under a sentence **3.** the extent to which something can be stretched **4.** an unbroken length, tract, or space; continuous extent or distance [a long *stretch* of beach] **5.** any of the sections of a course or track for racing; esp., *short for* HOMESTRETCH **6.** a course or direction —*adj.* made of elasticized fabric so as to stretch easily and fit closely [*stretch* pants] —**stretch′a·bil′i·ty** *n.* —**stretch′a·ble** *adj.*

stretch·er (strech′ər) *n.* **1.** a person or thing that stretches; specif., *a)* a brace or tie used to extend or support a framework; crosspiece *b)* a brick or stone laid lengthwise in a wall *c)* any of several framelike devices used for stretching and shaping cloth, garments, curtains, etc. **2.** *a)* a light frame covered with canvas, etc. and used for carrying the sick, injured, or dead; litter *b)* any similar device, as a wheeled cot used in ambulances

stretch·er-bear·er (-ber′ər) *n.* a person who helps carry a stretcher, esp. in military combat

☆**stretch·out** (strech′out′) *n.* a system of industrial operation in which workers are required to do more work with little or no increase in pay

stretch·y (-ē) *adj.* **stretch′i·er, stretch′i·est 1.** that can be stretched; elastic **2.** tending to stretch too far —**stretch′i·ness** *n.*

stret·to (stret′ō) *n., pl.* **-tos, -ti** (-ē) [It. < L. *strictus*, tight, narrow: see STRICT] **1.** in a fugue, the following of the voices in close succession, esp. in the closing section **2.** any concluding passage performed with a climactic increase in speed: also **stret′ta,** *pl.* **-tas, -te** (-ā)

streu·sel (stroo′z'l, stroi′-; G. shtroi′zəl) *n.* [G., lit., something strewn < MHG. *ströusel* < *ströuwen*, to strew < OHG. *strewen*: see ff.] a crumbly topping, as for coffeecake, made with flour, butter, sugar, and cinnamon

strew (stroo) *vt.* **strewed, strewed** or **strewn, strew′ing** [ME. *strewen* < OE. *streawian*, akin to G. *streuen* < IE. **streu-* < base **ster-*, to extend, stretch out, strew, whence STRAW, L. *struere*, to pile up] **1.** to spread about here and there by or as by sprinkling; scatter **2.** to cover by or as by scattering or sprinkling **3.** to be scattered or dispersed over (a surface) —*SYN.* see SPRINKLE

stri·a (strī′ə) *n., pl.* **stri′ae** (-ē) [L.: for IE. base see STRIKE] **1.** a narrow groove or channel **2.** any of a number of parallel lines, stripes, bands, furrows, etc.; specif., *a)* any of the cylindrical fibers in voluntary muscles *b)* any of the parallel lines on glaciated surfaces or crystal faces *c)* any of the luminous bands in an electric discharge through a gas at low pressure, etc.

stri·ate (strī′āt; *for adj., usually* -it) *vt.* **-at·ed, -at·ing** [< L. *striatus*, grooved, furrowed, pp. of *striare*, to groove, channel < *stria*: see prec.] to mark with striae; stripe, band, furrow, etc. —*adj.* marked with striae: also **stri′at·ed**

stri·a·tion (strī ā′shən) *n.* **1.** the condition of having striae; striated pattern, appearance, etc. **2.** the arrangement of striae **3.** *same as* STRIA

strick (strik) *n.* [ME. strik, prob. < MDu. or LowG.: MDu. *stric* (or MLowG. *strik*), rope, akin to OHG. *stric*, rope & OE. *strician*, to knit together] any of the bast fibers, as of flax or hemp, made ready to be drawn into sliver form

strick·en (strik′'n) *alt. pp.* of STRIKE —*adj.* **1.** struck or wounded, as by a missile **2.** afflicted or affected, as by something disagreeable, painful, or very distressing [the *stricken* man, a *stricken* conscience] **3.** having the contents level with the top of a container

strick·le (strik′'l) *n.* [ME. *strikile* < OE. *stricel* < base in *strican*, to STRIKE] **1.** a stick used to level the top of a measure of grain **2.** a tool used for sharpening a scythe, etc. **3.** *Metallurgy* a bevel-edged finishing tool used in shaping molds in sand, etc. —*vt.* **-led, -ling** to use a strickle on

strict (strikt) *adj.* [L. *strictus*, pp. of *stringere*, to draw tight, compress < IE. **streig-*, stiff, taut, a rope < base **ster-*, rigid: cf. STARE] **1.** exact or precise; not loose, vague, or broad [a *strict* translation] **2.** perfect; absolute; entire [the *strict* truth] **3.** *a)* following or enforcing a rule or rules with great care; punctilious *b)* closely enforced or

rigidly maintained *c*) disciplining rigorously or severely **4.** [Obs.] *a*) close; tight *b*) narrow **5.** *Bot.* stiff and upright; erect —**strict′ly** *adv.* —**strict′ness** *n.*
SYN.—**strict,** in this connection, implies exact, undeviating conformity to standards, rules, conditions, etc. [the *strict* interpretation of a law]; **rigid** implies an unyielding inflexibility, often connoting excessive firmness [*rigid* rules]; **rigorous** implies such uncompromising strictness as to impose hardships or difficulties [*rigorous* discipline]; **stringent** implies such strictness as to limit, bind, curb, or confine [a *stringent* censorship code] —*ANT.* **lax, flexible**

stric·tion (strik′shən) *n.* [L. *strictio:* see prec.] the act of drawing tight; constriction

stric·ture (strik′chər) *n.* [ME. *strictture* < L. *strictura* < *strictus:* see STRICT] **1.** sharp adverse criticism; censure **2.** a limiting or restricting condition; restriction **3.** [Obs.] strictness **4.** *Med.* an abnormal narrowing of a passage in the body; stenosis —**stric′tured** *adj.*

stride (strīd) *vi.* **strode, strid′den, strid′ing** [ME. *striden* < OE. *stridan,* akin to G. *streiten,* to quarrel < IE. **streidh-* < base **ster-,* to be stiff, rigid, whence STARE, STARVE] **1.** to walk with long steps, esp. in a vigorous or swaggering manner **2.** to take a single, long step (esp. *over* something) **3.** [Rare] to sit or stand astride —*vt.* **1.** to take a single, long step in passing over (an obstacle, etc.) **2.** to walk with long steps along or through [to *stride* the street] **3.** to sit or stand astride of; straddle; bestride —*n.* **1.** the act of striding **2.** a long step **3.** *a*) any single forward movement by a four-legged animal, completed when the legs return to their original relative positions *b*) the distance covered in such a movement **4.** [*usually pl.*] progress; advancement [to make rapid *strides*] —*adj.* ☆*Jazz* designating or of a style of piano playing in which the left hand alternates rhythmically between a strong bass note and middle range chords —☆**hit one's stride** to reach one's normal speed or level of efficiency —**take in one's stride** to cope with easily and without undue effort or hesitation —**strid′er** *n.*

stri·dent (strīd′'nt) *adj.* [L. *stridens,* prp. of *stridere,* to make a grating noise, rasp < IE. echoic base **(s)trei-,* whence Gr. *trizein,* to chirp, screech, L. *strix,* screech owl] harsh-sounding; shrill; grating —*SYN.* see VOCIFEROUS —**stri′dence, stri′den·cy** *n.* —**stri′dent·ly** *adv.*

stri·dor (strī′dər) *n.* [L. < *stridere:* see prec.] **1.** a strident sound **2.** *Med.* a harsh, high-pitched whistling sound, produced in breathing by an obstruction in the bronchi, trachea, or larynx

strid·u·late (strij′oo lāt′) *vi.* **-lat′ed, -lat′ing** [< ModL. *stridulatus,* pp. of *stridulare* < L. *stridulus* (see STRIDULOUS)] to make a shrill grating or chirping sound by rubbing certain body parts together, as certain insects do —**strid′u·la′tion** *n.* —**strid′u·la·to′ry** (-lə tôr′ē) *adj.*

strid·u·lous (-ləs) *adj.* [L. *stridulus* < *stridere:* see STRIDENT] making a shrill grating or chirping sound: also **strid′u·lant** (-lənt)

strife (strīf) *n.* [ME. *strif* < OFr. *estrif:* see STRIVE] **1.** the act of striving or vying with another; contention or competition **2.** the act or state of fighting or quarreling, esp. bitterly; struggle; conflict **3.** [Archaic] strong endeavor —*SYN.* see DISCORD

strig·il (strij′əl) *n.* [L. *strigilis:* see STRIKE] an instrument of bone, metal, etc. used by the ancient Greeks and Romans for scraping the skin during a bath

stri·gose (strī′gōs, stri gōs′) *adj.* [ModL. *strigosus* < *striga,* a stiff bristle < L. *striga,* a furrow: for base see ff.] **1.** *Bot.* having stiff hairs or bristles, as some leaves **2.** *Zool.* having fine, close-set grooves or streaks

strike (strīk) *vt.* **struck, struck** or occas. (but for *vt.* 11 commonly and for *vt.* 8 & 15 usually) **strick′en, strik′ing** [ME. *striken,* to proceed, flow, strike with rod or sword < OE. *strican,* to go, proceed, advance, akin to G. *streichen* < IE. **streig-* < base **ster-,* a streak, strip, to stroke, whence L. *stringere,* to touch, *strigilis,* a scraper, G. *strahl,* a ray] **1.** to hit with the hand or a tool, weapon, etc.; smite; specif., *a*) to give a blow to; hit with force [to *strike* a nail with a hammer] *b*) to give (a blow, etc.) *c*) to remove, knock off, etc. by or as by a blow [to *strike* a gun from someone's hand] *d*) to make or impress by stamping, punching, printing, etc. [to *strike* coins in a mint] *e*) to pierce or penetrate [*struck* in the head by a bullet] *f*) to harpoon or shoot (a whale) *g*) to hook (a fish that has risen to the bait) by a pull on the line *h*) to seize (the bait): said of a fish **2.** *a*) to produce (a tone or chord) by hitting a key or keys or touching a string or strings on a musical instrument *b*) to touch the strings of (a musical instrument) **3.** to announce (time), as by causing a hammer to hit a bell: said of clocks, etc. **4.** to cause to come into violent or forceful contact; specif., *a*) to cause to hit something [to *strike* one's head on a beam] *b*) to thrust (a weapon, implement, etc.) in or into something *c*) to bring forcefully into contact [to *strike* cymbals together] *d*) to cause to ignite by friction [to *strike* a match] **5.** *a*) to produce (a light, etc.) by friction *b*) to make (an arc) in an arc lamp **6.** to come into violent or forceful contact with; crash into; hit [the stone *struck* his head] **7.** *a*) to wound with the fangs: said of snakes *b*) to attack **8.** to afflict, as with disease, pain, or death **9.** to come into contact with; specif., *a*) to fall on; shine on [light *striking* the wall] *b*) to catch or reach (the ear): said of a sound ☆*c*) to come upon; arrive at [the bus *struck* the main road] *d*) to make (a path, trail, etc.) as one goes along *e*) to notice, find, or hit upon suddenly or unexpectedly ☆*f*) to discover, as after drilling or prospecting [to *strike* oil] *g*) to appear to [the sight that *struck* his eyes] **10.** to affect as if by contact, a blow, etc.; specif., *a*) to come into the mind of; occur to [*struck* by an idea] *b*) to be attractive to or impress (one's fancy, sense of humor, etc.) *c*) to seem to [an idea that *strikes* one as silly] *d*) to cause to become suddenly [to be *struck* dumb] *e*) to influence, inspire, or overcome suddenly with strong feeling [to be *struck* with amazement] *f*) to cause (a feeling, emotion, etc.) to come suddenly; arouse [to *strike* terror to the heart] **11.** to remove or expunge *from* a list, minutes, record, etc. **12.** *a*) to make and ratify (a bargain, agreement, truce, etc.) *b*) to arrive at by figuring, estimating, etc. [to *strike* a balance] **13.** *a*) to lower or haul down (a sail, flag, etc.), as in surrendering: sailors formerly *struck* sails in protest of grievances, to prevent a ship from sailing *b*) to take down (a tent, etc.) *c*) to abandon (a camp) as by taking down tents **14.** [from *vt.* 13 *a* via obs. sense "to put (tools) out of use" in protest of grievances] to refuse to continue to work at (a factory, company, etc.) until certain demands have been met **15.** *a*) orig., to stroke or smooth *b*) to level (a measure of grain, sand mold, etc.) by stroking the top with a straight instrument; strickle **16.** to assume (an attitude, pose, etc.) **17.** *a*) to send down or put forth (roots): said of plants, etc. *b*) to cause (cuttings, etc.) to take root **18.** [Obs.] to wage (battle) **19.** [cf. *vt.* 13] *Theater* *a*) to dismantle and remove (scenery or a set) *b*) to remove the scenery of (a play) *c*) to turn (a light) down or off —*vi.* **1.** to deliver a blow or blows **2.** to aim a blow or blows [to *strike* in vain at a ball] **3.** *a*) to attack [the enemy *struck* at dawn] *b*) to take part in a fight or struggle (*for* some objective) **4.** *a*) to make a sound or sounds as by being struck: said of a bell, clock, etc. *b*) to be announced by the striking of a bell, chime, etc.: said of the time **5.** *a*) to make sudden and violent contact; hit; collide (*against, on,* or *upon*) *b*) to be noticed; have an effect **6.** to ignite or be capable of igniting, as a match **7.** to seize or snatch at a bait: said of a fish **8.** to make a darting movement in an attempt to inflict a wound: said of a snake, tiger, etc. **9.** to penetrate or pierce (*to, through,* etc.) **10.** to come suddenly or unexpectedly; fall, light, etc. (*on* or *upon*) [to *strike* on the right combination] **11.** to run upon a reef, rock, etc.: said of a ship **12.** *a*) to lower sail *b*) to haul down one's flag in token of surrender **13.** to refuse to continue to work until certain demands are met; go on strike **14.** to send out roots; take root: said of a plant **15.** to begin, advance, or proceed, esp. in a new way or direction; turn **16.** to move or pass quickly; dart ☆**17.** *U.S. Navy* to try hard to qualify (*for* a rating) —*n.* **1.** the act of striking; blow; specif., a military attack [an air *strike*] **2.** *same as* STRICKLE **3.** *a*) a concerted refusal by employees to go on working in an attempt to force an employer to grant certain demands, as for higher wages, better working conditions, etc. *b*) any similar refusal by a person or group of people to do something, undertaken as a form of protest [a hunger *strike,* a buyers' *strike*] **4.** the discovery of a rich deposit of oil, coal, minerals, etc. ☆**5.** any sudden success, esp. one bringing large financial return **6.** ☆*a*) the pull on the line by a fish seizing or snatching at bait *b*) the pull that a fisherman gives the line to engage a baited hook in a fish's mouth **7.** the number of coins, medals, etc. struck at one time **8.** the part of a timepiece that strikes **9.** the metal piece on a door jamb into which the latch fits when the door is shut: also **strike plate** ☆**10.** *Baseball* a pitched ball which is *a*) struck at but missed *b*) delivered through the strike zone but not struck at *c*) hit foul but not caught (unless there are already two strikes) *d*) on a third strike, hit as a foul tip caught by the catcher Three strikes put the batter out ☆**11.** *Bowling* *a*) the act of knocking down all the pins on the first bowl *b*) the score made in this way **12.** *Geol., Mining* the trace of a rock bed, fault, or vein on the horizontal, at right angles to the direction of dip —**be struck with** to be attracted to or impressed by —☆**have two strikes against one** [Colloq.] to be at a decided disadvantage: from the three strikes permitted a batter in baseball —**(out) on strike** striking (*vi.* 13) —**strike down** **1.** to cause to fall by a blow, etc.; knock down **2.** to do away with; undo, cancel, etc. **3.** to have a disastrous or disabling effect upon: said of illness, etc. —**strike dumb** to amaze; astound; astonish —**strike hands** **1.** to show agreement by clasping hands **2.** to make a bargain, contract, etc. —**strike home** **1.** to deliver an effective or crippling blow **2.** to achieve a desired or significant effect —☆**strike it rich** **1.** to discover a rich deposit of ore, oil, etc. **2.** to become rich or successful suddenly —**strike off** **1.** to separate, or remove, by or as by a blow or cut **2.** to remove from a record, list, etc.; erase; expunge **3.** to print —**strike out** **1.** to make by hitting or striking **2.** to originate; produce; devise **3.** to aim or strike a blow; hit out **4.** to remove from a record, etc.; erase; expunge **5.** to begin moving or acting; start out ☆**6.** *Baseball* *a*) to be put out as the result of three strikes *b*) to put (a batter) out by pitching three strikes ☆**7.** to be a failure —**strike up** **1.** to begin playing, singing,

sounding, etc. **2.** to begin (a friendship, etc.) **3.** to emboss (metal, decorative figures, etc.)

SYN.—**strike** and **hit** are more or less interchangeable in meaning to deliver a blow to or toward someone or something [he *struck*, or *hit*, the boy], but each is more frequently used in certain connections than the other [lightning *struck* the barn, he *hit* the bull's-eye]; **punch** implies a hitting with or as with the closed fist [to *punch* one on the jaw]; **slap** implies a hitting with or as with the palm of the hand [to *slap* one's face]; **smite**, a literary or rhetorical word, emphasizes the force used in striking or hitting [he will *smite* you dead]; **knock** implies either a hitting so as to displace [he *knocked* the vase from the table] or a repeated striking [he *knocked* at the window]

strike·bound (-bound') *adj.* closed or hampered because of striking employees [a *strikebound* plant]

strike·break·er (-brā'kər) *n.* a person who is active in trying to break up a strike, as by working as a scab, supplying scabs for the employer, intimidating strikers, etc. —**strike'break'ing** *n.*

strike fault *Geol.* a fault running parallel to the strike of the strata that it cuts

☆**strike·out** (-out') *n. Baseball* an out made by a batter charged with three strikes

strik·er (strī'kər) *n.* **1.** a person who strikes; specif., *a)* a worker who is on strike *b)* an assistant who wields the heavy sledgehammer for a blacksmith **2.** a thing that strikes, as the clapper in a bell, the striking device in a clock, etc. ☆**3.** *a) U.S. Army* an enlisted man doing extra-duty work for an officer for extra pay *b) U.S. Navy* an enlisted man who is working to qualify for a rating

☆**strike zone** *Baseball* the area over home plate, between the batter's knees and armpits, through which the ball must be pitched for a strike to be called by the umpire

strik·ing (strī'kiŋ) *adj.* **1.** that strikes or is on strike **2.** very noticeable or impressive; unusual, outstanding, remarkable, etc. —*SYN.* see NOTICEABLE —**strik'ing·ly** *adv.*

Stri·mon (strē'môn') *Gr. name of* STRUMA

Strind·berg (strind'burg, strin'-; *Swed.* strin'bär'y'), (**Johan**) **August** 1849-1912; Swed. dramatist & novelist

string (striŋ) *n.* [ME. *streng* < OE., akin to G. *strang*; for IE. base see STRONG] **1.** *a)* a thin line of twisted fiber used for tying, pulling, fastening, etc.; slender cord or thick thread *b)* a narrow strip of leather or cloth for tastening shoes, clothing, etc.; lace [apron *strings*] **2.** a length or loop of like things threaded, strung, or hung on a string [a *string* of pearls] **3.** *a)* a number of things arranged in a line or row [a *string* of houses] *b)* any series of things in close or uninterrupted succession [a *string* of victories] **4.** *a)* a number of racehorses belonging to one owner *b)* a number of business enterprises under one ownership or management [a *string* of gift shops] ☆**5.** any of the groupings of players on a team according to ability: the **first string** is more skilled than the **second string**, etc. **6.** *a)* a slender cord of wire, gut, nylon, etc. stretched on a musical instrument, as a violin, guitar, piano, etc., and bowed, plucked, or struck to make a musical sound *b)* [*pl.*] all the stringed instruments of an orchestra played with a bow *c)* [*pl.*] the players of such instruments **7.** a strong, slender organ, structure, etc. resembling a string; specif., *a)* [Archaic] an animal nerve or tendon *b)* a fiber of a plant, esp. one connecting the two halves of a bean pod, etc. ☆**8.** [Colloq.] a condition, limitation, or proviso attached to a plan, offer, donation, etc.: *usually used in pl.* **9.** *Archit. a)* an inclined board at either end of stairs, notched to support the treads and risers *b)* same as STRINGCOURSE ☆**10.** *Billiards a)* a line indicated but unmarked across the table at one end, from behind which the cue ball must be played after being out of play: in full **string line** *b)* the act of stroking the cue ball so that it rebounds from the far cushion to stop as close as possible to the string line, for determining the order of play —*vt.* **strung, strung** or *rare* **stringed, string'ing 1.** to fit or provide with a string or strings [to *string* a longbow, a violin, etc.] **2.** to thread or bead on a string **3.** to tie, pull, fasten, hang, lace, etc. with a string or strings **4.** to adjust or tune the strings of (a musical instrument) by tightening, etc. **5.** to make tense, nervous, or keyed (*up*) **6.** to remove the strings from (beans, etc.) **7.** to arrange or set forth in a row or successive series **8.** to stretch or extend like a string [to *string* a cable] —*vi.* **1.** to form into a string or strings **2.** to stretch out in a line; extend; stretch; move or progress in a string **3.** *Billiards* same as LAG[1] (*vi.* 4) —**on a** (or **the) string** completely under one's control or subject to one's whims —**pull strings 1.** to get someone to use influence in one's behalf, often secretly **2.** to direct action of others, often secretly —☆**string along** [Colloq.] **1.** to follow faithfully or accept trustingly **2.** to go along or agree **3.** to fool, hoax, or deceive —**string up** [Colloq.] to kill by hanging —**string'less** *adj.*

string band a band of stringed instruments, as guitar, banjo, violin, etc., playing folk or country music —**string'-band'** *adj.*

string bass same as DOUBLE BASS

☆**string bean 1.** same as SNAP BEAN **2.** [Colloq.] a tall, skinny person

string·board (-bôrd') *n.* a board placed along the side of a staircase to cover the ends of the steps

string·course (-kôrs') *n.* a decorative, horizontal course of brick or stone set in the wall of a building

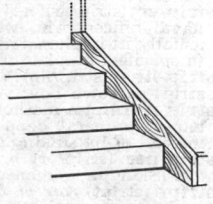

STRINGBOARD

stringed (striŋd) *rare pp. of* STRING —*adj.* having strings, as certain musical instruments

strin·gen·cy (strin'jən sē) *n., pl.* **-cies** the quality or state of being stringent; strictness; severity

strin·gen·do (strin jen'dō) *adv.* [It. < *stringere*, to tighten, bind < L.: see STRICT] *Music* with accelerated tempo, as toward a climax: a direction to the performer

strin·gent (strin'jənt) *adj.* [L. *stringens*, prp. of *stringere*, to draw tight: see STRICT] **1.** rigidly controlled, enforced, etc.; strict; severe ☆**2.** tight in loan or investment money [a *stringent* money market] **3.** compelling; convincing [*stringent* reasons] —*SYN.* see STRICT —**strin'gent·ly** *adv.* —**strin'gent·ness** *n.*

string·er (striŋ'ər) *n.* **1.** a person or thing that strings **2.** a long piece of timber used as a support; specif., *a)* a horizontal timber connecting upright posts in a frame *b)* same as STRINGPIECE **3.** a long, lightweight structural member of an airplane fuselage, wing, etc. ☆**4.** a string or metal line with clips on which caught fish are strung ☆**5.** a person serving as a part-time, local correspondent for a newspaper, magazine, etc. published elsewhere ☆**6.** a person ranked according to ability [second-*stringer*]

string·halt (striŋ'hôlt') *n.* a condition in horses causing one or both hind legs to jerk spasmodically in walking —**string'halt'ed, string'halt'y** *adj.*

string·piece (-pēs') *n.* a long, horizontal timber for supporting a framework, as at the edge of a floor

string quartet 1. a quartet of players on stringed instruments, usually first and second violins, a viola, and a violoncello **2.** a composition for such a group

☆**string tie** a narrow necktie, usually tied in a bow

string·y (striŋ'ē) *adj.* **string'i·er, string'i·est 1.** like a string or strings; long, thin, wiry, sinewy, etc. **2.** consisting of strings or fibers **3.** having tough fibers [*stringy* meat, celery, etc.] **4.** forming strings; viscous; ropy [*stringy* molasses] —**string'i·ness** *n.*

strip[1] (strip) *vt.* **stripped, strip'ping** [ME. *strepen* < OE. *strypan* (in comp.), akin to G. *streifen*, to strip off < IE. *streub-* < base *ster-*, to touch lightly, whence STRIKE] **1.** to remove the clothing or covering) of or from (a person); make naked; undress **2.** to deprive or dispossess (a person or thing) of (honors, titles, attributes, etc.) **3.** to despoil of wealth, property, etc.; plunder; rob **4.** to pull, tear, or take off (a covering, skin, etc.) from (a person or thing) **5.** to make bare or clear by removing fruit, growth, removable parts, etc. [to *strip* a room of furniture] **6.** to take apart (a firearm, etc.) piece by piece, as for cleaning; dismantle **7.** to break or damage the thread of (a nut, bolt, or screw) or the teeth of (a gear) **8.** to remove the last milk from (a cow) with a stroking movement of the thumb and forefinger **9.** to remove the large central rib from (tobacco leaves) or the leaf from (the stalk) —*vi.* **1.** to take off all clothing; undress ☆**2.** to perform a striptease —*n. clipped form of* STRIPTEASE *SYN.*—**strip** implies the pulling or tearing off of clothing, outer covering, etc. and often connotes forcible or even violent action and total deprivation [to *strip* paper off a wall, *stripped* of sham]; **denude** implies that the thing stripped is left exposed or naked [land *denuded* of vegetation]; **divest** implies the taking away of something with which one has been clothed or invested [an official *divested* of authority]; **bare** simply implies an uncovering or laying open to view [to *bare* one's head in reverence]; **dismantle** implies the act of stripping a house, ship, etc. of all of its furniture or equipment [a *dismantled* room]

strip[2] (strip) *n.* [altered (after prec.) < STRIPE] **1.** a long, narrow piece, as of land, ribbon, wood, etc. ☆**2.** short for COMIC STRIP **3.** a runway for the takeoff and landing of airplanes; landing strip **4.** *Philately* a vertical or horizontal row of three or more attached stamps —*vt.* to cut or tear into strips

strip cropping crop planting in which strips of heavy-rooted plants are alternated with loose-rooted plants so as to lessen erosion, as on a hillside

stripe (strip) *n.* [< MLowG. & MDu. *stripe* < IE. *streib-* < base *ster-*: cf. STRIP[2]] **1.** a long, narrow band, mark, or streak, differing in color, texture, or material from the surrounding area **2.** [*often pl.*] a fabric or garment with a pattern of parallel stripes **3.** any of various strips of cloth or braid worn on the sleeve of a military uniform or the like to indicate rank, length of service, etc. **4.** a distinctive type, kind, or sort [a man of his *stripe*] **5.** [Archaic] *a)* a stroke with a whip, etc. *b)* a long welt on the skin —*vt.* **striped, strip'ing** to mark with a stripe or stripes **striped** (stript, strī'pid) *adj.* having a stripe or stripes

☆**striped bass** (bas) a silvery game and food fish (*Roccus saxatilis*) with dark stripes along the sides, found along the coasts of N. America: it goes up rivers to spawn

strip·er (strip′ər) *n.* [Mil. Slang] any enlisted man, or a naval officer, who wears a stripe or stripes (sense 3): usually in hyphenated compounds meaning "one wearing (a specified number of) stripes" *[a four-striper]*

strip·ling (strip′liŋ) *n.* [ME. *strypling*, lit., one slim as a strip] a grown boy; youth passing into manhood

strip mining a method of mining, esp. for coal, by laying bare a mineral deposit near the surface of the earth, instead of by sinking a shaft

strip·per (strip′ər) *n.* 1. a person or thing that strips ☆2. [Slang] a woman who does a striptease

stript (stript) *rare pt. & pp. of* STRIP[1]

☆**strip·tease** (strip′tēz′) *n.* a performance, as in burlesque shows, in which a woman takes off her clothes slowly, usually to the accompaniment of music —**strip′tease′** *vi.* -**teased′**, -**teas′ing** —**strip′teas′er** *n.*

strip·y (stri′pē) *adj.* **strip′i·er**, **strip′i·est** characterized by, like, or marked with stripes

strive (strīv) *vi.* **strove** or **strived**, **striv·en** (striv′n) or **strived**, **striv′ing** [ME. *striven* < OFr. *estriver*, to quarrel, contend < *estrif*, effort < Gmc., as in MHG. *striben*, obs. Du. *strijven*, to strive, struggle < IE. *streibh-* (whence Gr. *striphnos*, hard, solid) < base *ster-*, stiff, whence STARE, STARK] 1. to make great efforts; try very hard *[to strive to win]* 2. to be in conflict; struggle; contend; fight *[to strive against oppression]* 3. [Obs.] to compete; vie —*SYN.* see TRY —**striv′er** *n.*

strobe (strōb) *n.* 1. *clipped form of* STROBOSCOPE 2. an electronically regulated discharge tube that can emit extremely rapid, brief, and brilliant flashes of light: used in photography, the theater, etc.: also **strobe light** —*adj. same as* STROBOSCOPIC

stro·bi·la (strō bi′lə) *n., pl.* -**lae** (-lē) [ModL. < Gr. *strobilē*, plug of lint twisted into oval shape < *strobilos*: see ff.] *Zool.* 1. the main, jointed body of a tapeworm 2. the late stage of the scyphozoan jellyfishes during which the immature jellyfishes are released by transverse budding —**stro·bi′lar** *adj.* —**stro′bi·la′tion** (-bə lā′shən) *n.*

stro·bile (strō′bil, -bil; străb′il) *n.* [< Fr. or LL.: Fr. *strobile* < LL. *strobilus* < Gr. *strobilos*, anything twisted, pine cone < base of *strephein*, to twist: see STROPHE] *Bot. same as* CONE (*n.* 3)

stro·bi·lus (strō bī′ləs) *n., pl.* -**li** (-lī) [ModL. < LL.: see prec.] *same as:* 1. CONE (*n.* 3) 2. STROBILA (sense 1)

stro·bo·scope (strō′bə skōp′, străb′ə-) *n.* [< Gr. *strobos*, a twisting around (akin to *strabos*: see STRABISMUS) + -SCOPE] 1. an instrument for studying periodic or varying motion; specif., a device using a rapidly flickering flash tube that illuminates a moving body, machine, etc. very briefly at frequent intervals 2. *same as* STROBE (sense 2) —**stro′bo·scop′ic** (-skăp′ik), **stro′bo·scop′i·cal** *adj.* —**stro′bo·scop′i·cal·ly** *adv.*

strode (strōd) *pt. of* STRIDE

stro·ga·noff (strō′gə nôf′, străf′-) *adj.* [prob. after Count Sergei *Stroganoff* (1794–1882), Russ. official and gourmet] cooked with sour cream, bouillon, mushrooms, etc.: used as a postpositive *[beef stroganoff]*

stroke (strōk) *n.* [ME., akin to G. *streich*, a stroke, OE. *strican*: see STRIKE] 1. a striking of one thing against another; blow or impact of an ax, whip, etc. 2. *a)* a sudden action resulting in a powerful or destructive effect, as if from a blow *[a stroke of lightning]* *b)* a sudden occurrence, often a pleasant one *[a stroke of luck]* 3. any sudden attack of disease or illness, esp. of apoplexy or paralysis 4. *a)* a single effort to do, produce, or accomplish something, esp. a successful effort *b)* something accomplished by such an effort; feat *c)* a distinctive effect or touch in an artistic, esp. literary, work 5. the sound of striking, as of a clock 6. *a)* a single movement, as with some tool, club, etc. *[a stroke of the pen, a backhand stroke in tennis]* *b)* any of a series of repeated rhythmic motions made against water, air, etc. *[the stroke of a swimmer, rower, etc.]* *c)* a type, manner, or rate of such movement *[a slow stroke]* 7. a mark made by or as by a pen or similar marking tool 8. a beat of the heart 9. a gentle, caressing motion with the hand 10. *Mech.* any of a series of continuous, often reciprocating, movements; specif., a single movement of a piston from one end of its range to the other, constituting a half revolution of the engine 11. *Rowing a)* the rower who sits nearest the stern and sets the rate of rowing for the others *b)* the position occupied by this rower —*vt.* **stroked**, **strok′ing** [ME. *stroken* < OE. *stracian*, akin to *strican* (cf. STRIKE)] 1. to draw one's hand, a tool, etc. gently over the surface of, as in caressing or smoothing 2. to mark with strokes or draw a line through (often with *out*) 3. to hit; esp., to hit (a ball) in playing tennis, golf, pool, etc. 4. to set the rate of rowing for (a crew) or for the crew of (a boat) —*vi.* 1. to hit a ball in playing tennis, golf, etc. 2. to act as stroke (*for*) in rowing —**keep stroke** to make strokes in rhythm

stroke oar 1. the oar set nearest the stern of a boat 2. *same as* STROKE (*n.* 11)

stroll (strōl) *vi.* [Early ModE. *strowl*, prob. < SwissG. dial. *strolen*, var. of *strolchen*, to stroll < G. *strolch*, a vagabond, rascal, altered < It. *astrologo*, astrologer] 1. to walk in an idle, leisurely manner; saunter 2. to go from place to place; wander —*vt.* to stroll along or through (a street, the countryside, etc.) —*n.* the act of strolling; leisurely walk

stroll·er (-ər) *n.* 1. a person who saunters 2. *a)* a wanderer; esp., an itinerant actor *b)* a vagrant ☆3. a light, chairlike baby carriage with openings for the legs at the front

stro·ma (strō′mə) *n., pl.* -**ma·ta** (-tə) [ModL. < L., coverlet, bed covering < Gr. *strōma*, mattress, bed: for IE. base see STREW] 1. *Anat. a)* the connective tissue forming the framework or matrix of an organ or part *b)* the colorless framework of a red blood corpuscle or other cell 2. *Bot.* in some fungi, a cushionlike mass of hyphae, frequently having fruiting bodies embedded in it —**stro′mal**, **stro·mat′ic** (-mat′ik) *adj.*

Strom·bo·li (strōm′bō lē′) northernmost of the Lipari Islands, north of Sicily: site of an active volcano (3,040 ft. high): c.5 sq. mi.

strong (strôŋ) *adj.* [ME. < OE. *strang*, akin to ON. *strangr*, strong, severe, G. *streng*, severe < IE. base *strenk-*, *streng-*, tense, taut, whence Gr. *strangos*, twisted, L. *stringere*, to draw taut] 1. *a)* physically powerful; having great muscular strength; robust *b)* in a healthy and sound condition; hale; hearty 2. *a)* performing well or in a normal manner *[a strong heart]* *b)* not easily affected or upset *[a strong stomach]* 3. morally powerful; having strength of character or will 4. *a)* intellectually powerful; able to think vigorously and clearly *b)* having special competency or ability (*in a specified area*) *[to be strong in botany]* 5. governing or leading with firm authority; authoritarian 6. *a)* powerfully made, built, or constituted; tough; firm; durable *[a strong wall, a strong fabric]* *b)* holding firmly; tenacious *[a strong grip]* *c)* binding tightly *[strong glue]* 7. *a)* hard to capture; able to resist and endure attack *[a strong fort]* *b)* not easily defeated; formidable *[a strong opponent]* *c)* not easily dislodged; deep-rooted *[strong prejudice]* 8. having many resources; powerful in wealth, numbers, supplies, etc. *[a strong nation]* 9. of a specified number; reaching a certain degree in number or strength *[a task force 6,000 strong]* 10. having a powerful effect; drastic *[strong measures]* 11. having a large amount of its essential quality; not weak or diluted *[strong coffee]* 12. affecting the senses powerfully; intense *[a strong light, strong smell, etc.]* 13. having an offensive taste or smell; rank *[strong butter]* 14. firm and loud *[a strong voice]* 15. intense in degree or quality; not mild; specif., *a)* ardent; passionate; warm *[strong affection]* *b)* forceful; persuasive; cogent *[strong reasons]* *c)* felt deeply; pronounced; decided *[a strong opinion]* *d)* vigorously active; zealous *[a strong socialist]* *e)* vigorous, forthright, and unambiguous, often offensively so *[strong language]* *f)* clear; distinct; marked *[a strong resemblance]* *g)* receiving or showing emphasis or stress *[a strong accent or beat]* 16. moving rapidly and with force *[a strong wind]* 17. having high powers of magnification *[strong lenses]* 18. tending toward higher prices: said of a stock or stock market 19. *Chem.* having a high ion concentration, as certain acids and bases 20. *Gram.* in English and other Germanic languages, designating or of those verbs that express variation in tense by internal change of a syllabic vowel rather than by the addition of inflectional endings; irregular (Ex.: *swim, swam, swum*) —*adv.* in a strong manner; greatly; severely; with force —☆**come on strong** [Slang] to make a strong impression, often in an aggressive way —**strong′ish** *adj.* —**strong′ly** *adv.*

SYN. —**strong** is the broadest in scope of these terms, implying power that can be exerted actively as well as power that resists destruction *[a strong body, fortress, etc.]*; **stout** implies ability to stand strain, pressure, wear, etc. without breaking down or giving way *[a stout rope, heart, etc.]*; **sturdy** suggests the strength of that which is solidly developed or built and hence difficult to shake, weaken, etc. *[sturdy oaks, faith, etc.]*; **tough** suggests the strength of that which is firm and resistant in consistency or character *[tough leather, opposition, etc.]*; **stalwart** stresses staunchness or reliability *[a stalwart supporter]* —*ANT.* weak

☆**strong-arm** (strôŋ′ärm′) *adj.* [Colloq.] using physical force or violence —*vt.* [Colloq.] to use physical force or violence upon, esp. in robbing

strong·box (-bäks′) *n.* a heavily made box or safe for storing valuables

strong breeze a wind whose speed is 25 to 31 miles per hour: see BEAUFORT SCALE

strong drink drink containing much alcohol

strong gale a wind whose speed is 47 to 54 miles per hour: see BEAUFORT SCALE

strong·hold (-hōld′) *n.* 1. a place having strong defenses; fortified place 2. a place where a group having certain views, attitudes, etc. is concentrated

strong-mind·ed (-mīn′did) *adj.* having a strong, unyielding mind or will; determined —**strong′-mind′ed·ly** *adv.* —**strong′-mind′ed·ness** *n.*

strong·room (-rōōm′) *n.* a strongly built room used for the safekeeping of valuables

strong-willed (-wild′) *adj.* having a strong, resolute, or obstinate will

stron·gyle (strän′jil, -jīl) *n.* [ModL. *Strongylus*, type genus < Gr. *strongylos*, round, turned: for IE. base see STRONG] any of various roundworms (suborder Strongylina), as hookworms, living as parasites esp. in domestic animals

stron·gy·lo·sis (strän′jə lō′sis) *n.* [ModL.: see prec. & -OSIS] the condition of being infested by strongyles

stron·ti·a (strän′shē ə, -shə, -tē ə) n. [ModL. < ff.] **1.** the oxide of strontium, SrO, a white powder somewhat like lime **2.** loosely, strontium hydroxide, Sr(OH)$_2$

stron·ti·an (strän′shē ən, -shən, -tē ən) n. [< *Strontian*, Argyllshire, Scotland, in whose lead mines it was first found] strontium, esp. in the form of a compound

stron·ti·an·ite (-ə nit′) n. [prec. + -ITE^1] native strontium carbonate, SrCO$_3$, a white, greenish, or yellowish mineral

stron·tic (strän′tik) adj. of strontium

stron·ti·um (-shē əm, -shəm, -tē əm) n. [ModL.: so named (1808) by Sir H. DAVY < STRONTIA] a pale-yellow, metallic chemical element resembling calcium in properties and found only in combination: strontium compounds burn with a red flame and are used in fireworks: symbol, Sr; at. wt., 87.62; at. no., 38; sp. gr., 2.6; melt. pt., 774°C; boil. pt., 1366°C: a deadly radioactive isotope of strontium (**strontium 90**) is present in the fallout of nuclear explosions

strook (strook) obs. pp. of STRIKE

strop (sträp) n. [ME., a band, thong, noose < OE., akin to MHG. *strupfe* < early WGmc. loanword < L. *struppus* < Gr. *strophos*, a twisted band: for IE. base see STROPHE] **1.** var. of STRAP **2.** a device, esp. a thick leather band, used for putting a fine edge on razors —vt. **stropped, strop′ping** to sharpen on a strop —**strop′per** n.

stro·phan·thin (strō fan′thin) n. [ModL. *Strophanthus*, type genus < Gr. *strophos* (see prec.) + *anthos*, flower + -IN^1] a glycoside or mixture of glycosides obtained from a tropical plant (*Strophanthus kombé*) of the dogbane family, used as a heart stimulant

stro·phe (strō′fē) n. [Gr. *strophē*, lit., a turning, twist < *strephein*, to turn < IE. *strebh-* < base *ster-*, stiff, taut, whence STARE, STARVE] **1.** in the ancient Greek theater, *a)* the movement of the chorus in turning from right to left of the stage: cf. ANTISTROPHE *b)* the part of the choric song performed during this **2.** in a Pindaric ode, the stanza which is answered by the antistrophe, in the same metrical pattern **3.** a stanza; esp., any of the irregular divisions of an ode —**stroph·ic** (sträf′ik, strō′fik), **stroph′i·cal** adj.

strove (strōv) alt. pt. of STRIVE

strow (strō) vt. strowed, strown (strōn) or strowed, strow′ing archaic form of STREW

stroy (stroi) vt. obs. form of DESTROY

struck (struk) pt. & pp. of STRIKE —adj. closed or affected in some other way by a labor strike

struck·en (struk′n) obs. pp. of STRIKE

struck jury a jury of 12 drawn from the panel of names remaining after each side has been permitted to strike out a certain number of the original list of names

struc·tur·al (struk′chər əl) adj. **1.** of, having, associated with, or characterized by structure [*structural* complexity] **2.** used in or suitable for constructing buildings, etc. [*structural* steel] **3.** of, or in accordance with, structural linguistics **4.** Geol. of or related to the structure of the earth's crust and to changes produced in it by movement; geotectonic —**struc′tur·al·ly** adv.

structural formula a formula which illustrates the arrangement of the atoms and bonds in a molecule: see BENZENE RING, illus.

struc·tur·al·ist (-ist) n. a follower or advocate of structural principles, as in the analysis or application of social, economic, or linguistic theory —adj. of or relating to structuralists or their theories —**struc′tur·al·ism** n.

structural linguistics language study based on the assumptions that a language is a coherent system of formal signs and that the task of linguistic study is to inquire into the nature of those signs and their peculiar systematic arrangement, without reference to historical antecedents or comparison with other languages —**structural linguist**

struc·ture (struk′chər) n. [ME. < L. *structura* < *structus*, pp. of *struere*, to heap together, arrange: see STREW] **1.** manner of building, constructing, or organizing **2.** something built or constructed, as a building or dam **3.** the arrangement or interrelation of all the parts of a whole; manner of organization or construction [the *structure* of the atom, the *structure* of society] **4.** something composed of interrelated parts forming an organism or an organization —vt. **-tured, -tur·ing** to put together systematically; construct; organize —SYN. see BUILDING —**struc′ture·less** adj.

stru·del (strood′'l; G. shtroo′dəl) n. [G., lit., whirlpool (ult. akin to STREAM): from its spiral cross section] a kind of pastry made of a very thin sheet of dough filled with apple slices, cherries, cheese, etc., rolled up, and baked

strug·gle (strug′'l) vi. -gled, -gling [ME. *strogelen* < ?] **1.** to contend or fight violently with an opponent **2.** to make great efforts or attempts; strive; labor **3.** to make one's way with difficulty [to *struggle* through a thicket] —vt. [Rare] **1.** to bring, put, do, etc. by struggling **2.** to make (one's way) with difficulty —n. **1.** great effort or a series of efforts; violent exertion **2.** conflict; strife; contention —SYN. see CONFLICT, TRY —**strug′gler** (-lər) n.

strum (strum) vt.,vi. strummed, strum′ming [echoic] **1.** to play (a guitar, banjo, etc.) esp. with long strokes across the strings and often in a casual or aimless way, or without much skill **2.** to play (a tune) in this way —n. the act or sound of this —**strum′mer** n.

Stru·ma (stroo′mä) river in the Balkan Peninsula, flowing from W Bulgaria south across NE Greece into the Aegean Sea: c.220 mi.

stru·ma (stroo′mə) n., pl. -mae (-mē) [L., a scrofulous tumor < IE. *streu-*: see STRUT] **1.** Bot. a cushionlike swelling on a plant organ, esp. on one side at the base of the capsule of a moss **2.** Med. same as: *a)* GOITER *b)* [Archaic] SCROFULA —**stru′mose** (-mōs′), **stru′mous** (-məs) adj.

strum·pet (strum′pit) n. [ME. < ?] a prostitute; harlot

strung (strun) pt. & alt. pp. of STRING

strut (strut) vi. strut′ted, strut′ting [ME. *strouten*, to spread out, swell out < OE. *strutian*, to stand rigid < IE. *streu-* < base *ster-*, stiff, rigid, whence STARK] to walk in a vain, stiff, swaggering manner —vt. **1.** to provide with a strut or brace **2.** to make a display of; show off —n. **1.** the act of strutting; vain, swaggering walk or gait **2.** a brace fitted into a framework to resist pressure in the direction of its length —**strut′ter** n.

stru·thi·ous (stroo′thē əs) adj. [< L. *struthio* (< Gr. *strouthion*, sparrow, ostrich) + -OUS] designating or of any of an order (Struthioniformes) of large, flightless birds, including the ostriches, rheas, emus, etc.

strych·nine (strik′nin, -nīn, -nēn) n. [Fr. < ModL. *Strychnos*, name of the genus < L. < Gr. *strychnos*, nightshade] a highly poisonous, colorless, crystalline alkaloid, C$_{21}$H$_{22}$N$_2$O$_2$, obtained from nux vomica and related plants (genus *Strychnos*): it is used in small doses as a stimulant to the nervous system

strych·nin·ism (-iz'm) n. a diseased condition resulting from an overdose or improper use of strychnine

St. Thomas 1. second largest island of the Virgin Islands of the U.S.: 32 sq. mi.; pop. 30,000 **2.** former name of CHARLOTTE AMALIE **3.** Eng. name of SÃO TOMÉ

Stu·art (stoo′ərt) [< the surname *Stuart* < ? OE. *stigweard*, chamberlain (cf. STEWARD)] **1.** a masculine name **2.** ruling family of Scotland (1371–1603) & of England & Scotland (1603-1714) except during the Commonwealth (1649–60) **3.** Charles Edward, 1720–88; Eng. prince: grandson of JAMES II: called *The Young Pretender, Bonnie Prince Charlie* **4.** Gilbert (Charles), 1755–1828; U.S. portrait painter **5.** James Francis Edward, 1688–1766; Eng. prince: son of JAMES II: called *The Old Pretender* **6.** J(ames) E(well) B(rown), (nicknamed *Jeb*) 1833–64; Confederate general

stub (stub) n. [ME. < OE. *stybb*, akin to ON. *stubbr*: for IE. base see STEEP^1] **1.** the stump of a tree or plant **2.** a short piece or length remaining after the main part has been removed or used up [the *stub* of a tail, cigar, pencil, etc.] **3.** any short projection [a mere *stub* of a horn] **4.** a pen having a short, blunt point **5.** same as STUB NAIL ☆**6.** the part of a ticket, bank check, etc. kept as a record after the rest has been torn off —vt. stubbed, stub′bing **1.** to dig or pull (weeds, etc.) out by the roots **2.** to cut down, leaving only a stump **3.** to clear (land) of stubs, or stumps **4.** to strike (one's foot, toe, etc.) accidentally against something **5.** to put out (a cigarette, cigar, etc.) by pressing the end against a surface: often with out

stubbed (stubd) adj. **1.** like a stub; short; stubby **2.** covered with stubs or stumps

stub·ble (stub′'l) n. [ME. *stobil* < OFr. *estouble, stuble* < VL. *stupula*, for L. *stipula*, a stalk, stem: see STIPULE] **1.** the short stumps of grain, corn, etc., collectively, left standing after harvesting **2.** any short, bristly growth suggestive of this [a *stubble* of beard] —**stub′bled** adj. —**stub′bly** adj. -bli·er, -bli·est

stub·born (stub′ərn) adj. [ME. *stoburn*, prob. < OE. *stubb*, var. of *stybb*, STUB] **1.** refusing to yield, obey, or comply; resisting doggedly or unreasonably; resolute or obstinate **2.** done or carried on in an obstinate or doggedly persistent manner [a *stubborn* campaign] **3.** hard to handle, treat, or deal with; intractable [a *stubborn* cold] —**stub′born·ly** adv. —**stub′born·ness** n.
SYN. —**stubborn** implies an innate fixedness of purpose, course, condition, etc. that is strongly resistant to change, manipulation, etc. [a *stubborn* child, belief, etc.]; **obstinate** applies to one who adheres persistently, and often unreasonably, to his purpose, course, etc., against argument or persuasion [a panel hung by an *obstinate* juror]; **dogged** implies thoroughgoing determination or, sometimes, sullen obstinacy [the *dogged* pursuit of a goal]; **pertinacious** implies a strong tenacity of purpose that is regarded unfavorably by others [a *pertinacious* critic] —ANT. compliant, tractable

stub·by (stub′ē) adj. -bi·er, -bi·est **1.** covered with stubs or stubble **2.** short and heavy or dense [*stubby* bristles] **3.** short and thickset —**stub′bi·ly** adv. —**stub′bi·ness** n.

stub nail 1. a short, thick nail **2.** an old horseshoe nail, esp. one broken off or worn down

stuc·co (stuk′ō) n., pl. -coes, -cos [It., prob. < Langobardic *stukki*, akin to OHG. *stucki*, a rind, crust, orig., piece: for IE. base see STOCK] **1.** plaster or cement, either fine or coarse, used for surfacing inside or outside walls or for molding relief ornaments, cornices, etc. **2.** the work done in this: also **stuc′co·work** —vt. **-coed, -co·ing** to cover or decorate with stucco

stuck (stuk) pt. & pp. of STICK

stuck-up (stuk′up′) adj. [Colloq.] snobbish; conceited

stud¹ (stud) *n.* [ME. *stode* < OE. *studu*, column, pillar, post, akin to ON. *stoth*, G. *stützen*, to prop < IE. **stŭt-* < base **stā-*, to STAND] **1.** any of a series of small knobs or rounded nailheads used to ornament a surface, as of leather **2.** a small, buttonlike device with a smaller button or shank on the back, inserted in a shirt front as an ornament or fastener **3.** any of a number of upright pieces in the outer or inner walls of a building, to which panels, siding, laths, etc. are nailed **4.** a metal crossbar bracing a link, as in a chain cable **5.** a projecting pin or peg used as a support, pivot, stop, etc. or, as in an automobile tire, to increase traction on ice **6.** a screw threaded at each end, used in fastening metal to metal or concrete —*vt.* **stud′ded, stud′ding** **1.** to set or decorate with studs or studlike objects **2.** to be set thickly on; be scattered over [rocks *stud* the hillside] **3.** to scatter or cluster (something) thickly [a crown *studded* with jewels] **4.** to provide (a building) with studs or upright members

stud² (stud) *n.* [ME. *stod* < OE., akin to G. *stute*, mare (OHG. *stuot*, stud of horses): for IE. base see prec.] **1.** *a)* a number of horses, or sometimes other animals, esp. as kept for breeding *b)* the place where these are kept ☆**2.** *a)* same as STUDHORSE *b)* any male animal used esp. for breeding **3.** [Slang] a virile, sexually promiscuous man —*adj.* **1.** of or having to do with a stud [a *stud* farm] **2.** kept for breeding —**at stud** available for breeding: said of male animals

stud·book (-book′) *n.* a register of purebred animals, esp. racehorses: also **stud book**

stud·ding (stud′iŋ) *n.* **1.** studs collectively, esp. for walls **2.** material used for or as studs

stud·ding·sail (stud′iŋ sāl′, stun′s'l) *n.* [< ?] an auxiliary sail, usually of light canvas, set outside the edge of a working sail in light weather by means of an extensible boom: also **studding sail**: see SAIL, illus.

stu·dent (stōōd′'nt, styōōd′-) *n.* [ME. *studiante, studente* < OFr. & L.: OFr. *estudiant* < L. *studens*, prp. of *studere*, to STUDY] **1.** a person who studies, or investigates [a *student* of human behavior] **2.** a person who is enrolled for study at a school, college, etc. —*SYN.* see PUPIL¹

☆**student lamp** any of various lamps for use on a desk, as one with a gooseneck

stu·dent·ship (-ship′) *n.* **1.** the state of being a student **2.** [Brit.] a grant for study; scholarship

☆**student teacher** a student in a college or university who teaches school under the supervision of an experienced teacher as a requirement for a degree in education

stud·horse (stud′hôrs′) *n.* a stallion kept for breeding

stud·ied (stud′ēd) *adj.* **1.** prepared or planned by careful study [a *studied* reply] **2.** deliberate; premeditated [in *studied* disarray] **3.** [Now Rare] learned; well-informed —**stud′ied·ly** *adv.* —**stud′ied·ness** *n.*

stu·di·o (stōō′dē ō′, styōō′-) *n., pl.* **-di·os′** [It. < L. *studium*, a STUDY] **1.** a room or rooms where an artist or photographer does his work ☆**2.** a room or rooms where dancing lessons, music lessons, etc. are given **3.** an establishment where motion pictures are made **4.** a room or rooms where radio or television programs are produced or where recordings are made

☆**studio couch** a kind of couch that can be made into a full-sized bed, as by sliding out the spring frame fitted beneath it

stu·di·ous (stōō′dē əs, styōō′-) *adj.* [ME. < L. *studiosus*] **1.** of, given to, or engaged in study **2.** characterized by close attention; thoughtful [a *studious* inspection] **3.** zealous; wholehearted [*studious* efforts] **4.** [Now Rare] studied; deliberate **5.** [Poet.] conducive to study —**stu′di·ous·ly** *adv.* —**stu′di·ous·ness** *n.*

☆**stud poker** [< STUD²] a variety of poker in which each player is dealt five cards, the first face down and the others face up, the betting being done on each round of open cards dealt: sometimes seven cards are dealt, the first two, and usually the last, face down

stud·y (stud′ē) *n., pl.* **stud′ies** [ME. *studie* < OFr. *estudie* < L. *studium*, zeal, study < *studere*, to busy oneself about, apply oneself to, study, orig., prob., to aim toward, strike at, akin to *tundere*, to strike, beat < IE. **(s)teud-* < base **(s)teu-*, to beat: cf. STOCK, STEEP¹] **1.** the act or process of applying the mind so as to acquire knowledge or understanding, as by reading, investigating, etc. **2.** careful attention to, and critical examination and investigation of, any subject, event, etc. **3.** *a)* a branch of learning or knowledge *b)* any subject of study **4.** [*pl.*] formal education; schooling **5.** a product of studying; specif., *a)* an essay or thesis embodying the results of a particular investigation *b)* a work of literature or art treating a subject in careful detail and typically done as an exercise in technique, experimentation, or exploration *c)* a first sketch for a story, picture, etc. *d)* same as ÉTUDE **6.** an earnest effort or intention **7.** a state of mental absorption; reverie **8.** a room, as in a house, designed for study, writing, reading, etc. **9.** a person, esp. an actor, with reference to his ability to memorize [a quick *study*] —*vt.* **stud′ied, stud′y·ing** **1.** to apply one's mind to attentively; try to learn or understand by reading, thinking, etc. [to *study* history] **2.** *a)* to examine or investigate carefully [to *study* the problem of air pollution] *b)* to look at carefully; scrutinize [to *study* a map] **3.** *a)* to read (a book, lesson, etc.) so as to know and understand it *b)* to con-

centrate on so as to memorize **4.** to take a course in, as at a school or college **5.** to give attention, thought, or consideration to [*studying* possible changes] —*vi.* **1.** to study something **2.** to be a student; take a regular course (at a school or college) **3.** to make earnest efforts; try hard **4.** to meditate; ponder —☆**study up on** [Colloq.] to make a careful study of —*SYN.* see CONSIDER

☆**study hall** **1.** a room in a school for studying and doing homework **2.** an assigned period there

stuff (stuf) *n.* [ME. < OFr. *estoffe* < *estoffer*, prob. < Frank. **stopfon*, to stop up: for base see STOP] **1.** the material or substance out of which anything is or can be made; raw material **2.** constituent elements or basic nature; essence; character [a man made of stern *stuff*] **3.** matter or substance of an unspecified or generalized kind **4.** cloth, esp. woolen cloth **5.** *a)* household goods *b)* personal belongings *c)* things in general; objects *d)* things grouped together or viewed in a certain way **6.** something to be drunk, swallowed, etc.; specif., a medicine or ☆[Slang] a drug, as heroin **7.** worthless objects; refuse; junk **8.** *a)* anything said, done, written, composed, etc.; talk or action of a specified kind *b)* foolish or worthless ideas, words, actions, etc. [*stuff* and nonsense!] **9.** [Colloq.] *a)* basic ability; capability *b)* superior ability; exceptional capability ☆*c)* special skill or knowledge; specialty [to do or know one's *stuff*] ☆**10.** [Colloq.] *a)* ability of a baseball pitcher, billiards player, etc. to control the ball, esp. to make it curve or spin *b)* such control, or speed, a curve, spin, etc. given to a ball —*vt.* [ME. *stoffen* < OFr. *estoffer*] **1.** to fill the inside of (something); pack; specif., *a)* to fill (a cushion, chair, toy, etc.) with padding or stuffing *b)* to fill the skin of (a dead animal, bird, etc.) in taxidermy *c)* to fill (a chicken, turkey, etc.) with seasoning, bread crumbs, etc. before cooking **2.** *a)* to fill too full; cram; overload *b)* to fill to excess with food **3.** to pack, cram, or crowd (something) into a container, etc. **4.** to fill with information, ideas, etc. [to *stuff* one's head with facts] ☆**5.** to put fraudulent votes into (a ballot box) **6.** *a)* to plug; block *b)* to choke up or stop up, as with phlegm **7.** to force or push [to *stuff* money into a wallet] **8.** to treat (leather) with a preparation designed to soften and preserve —*vi.* to eat too much or too quickly —**stuff′er** *n.*

☆**stuffed shirt** [Slang] a pompous, pretentious person

stuff·er (stuf′ər) *n.* **1.** a person or thing that stuffs ☆**2.** something, as a piece of advertising, inserted in an envelope along with a bill, statement, paycheck, etc.

stuff·ing (-iŋ) *n.* **1.** the action of filling, packing, or gorging **2.** something used to fill or stuff; specif., *a)* soft, springy material used as padding in cushions, upholstered furniture, etc. *b)* a seasoned mixture for stuffing fowl, roasts, etc.

stuffing box a chamber that holds packing tightly around a moving part, as a piston rod, boat propeller shaft, etc., to prevent leakage of fluid along the part

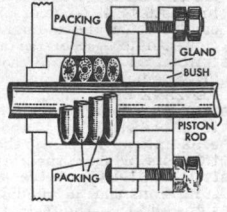

STUFFING BOX

stuff·y (stuf′ē) *adj.* **stuff′i·er, stuff′i·est** [STUFF + -Y²] **1.** *a)* poorly ventilated; having little fresh air; close *b)* stale or oppressive [the *stuffy* air] **2.** having the nasal passages stopped up, as from a cold **3.** [Colloq.] *a)* dull or stodgy; not interesting or stimulating *b)* conservative, conventional, old-fashioned, etc. *c)* prim; strait-laced *d)* pompous; pretentious —**stuff′i·ly** *adv.* —**stuff′i·ness** *n.*

stull (stul) *n.* [prob. < G. *stolle*, a post, orig., short, thick prop: for IE. base see STALK¹] any of several kinds of supports or frameworks used in mines to prevent cave-ins, support a platform, etc.

stul·ti·fy (stul′tə fī′) *vt.* **-fied′, -fy′ing** [LL. *stultificare* < L. *stultus*, foolish, akin to *stolidus*, STOLID + *facere*, to make: see DO¹] **1.** *a)* to make seem foolish, stupid, inconsistent, etc.; make absurd or ridiculous *b)* to make dull or torpid **2.** to render worthless, useless, or futile **3.** *Law* to allege to be of unsound mind and therefore not legally responsible —**stul′ti·fi·ca′tion** *n.* —**stul′ti·fi′er** *n.*

stum (stum) *n.* [Du. *stom*, must, new wine < *stom*, dumb: see IT.] **1.** grape juice that is unfermented or only partly fermented **2.** wine revived by adding stum to it so as to produce new fermentation —*vt.* **stummed, stum′ming** to revive (wine) by adding stum

stum·ble (stum′b'l) *vi.* **-bled, -bling** [ME. *stumblen* < Scand., as in Norw. dial. *stumla*, ON. *stumra* < IE. base **stem-*, to bump against, hamper, whence STAMMER, G. *stumm*, mute] **1.** to trip or miss one's step in walking, running, etc. **2.** to walk or go in an unsteady or awkward manner, as from age, weakness, etc. **3.** to speak, act, or proceed in a confused, blundering manner [to *stumble* through a speech] **4.** to fall into sin or error; do wrong **5.** to come by chance; happen [to *stumble* across a clue] —*vt.* **1.** to cause to stumble **2.** to puzzle or perplex; confound —*n.* **1.** the act of stumbling **2.** a blunder, error, or sin —**stum′bler** *n.* —**stum′bling·ly** *adv.*

☆**stum·ble·bum** (-bum′) *n.* [Slang] same as BUM¹ (senses 1, 2, & 4)

stumbling block an obstacle, hindrance, or difficulty standing in the way of progress or understanding

stump (stump) *n.* [ME. *stumpe*, prob. < or akin to MLowG. *stump* < IE. *stomb-* < base *steb-*, whence STAMP, STAFF[1]] **1.** the lower end of a tree or plant remaining in the ground after most of the stem or trunk has been cut off **2.** anything like a stump; specif., *a)* the part of a limb or tooth left after the rest has been cut off, broken off, etc. *b)* the part of anything left after the main part is gone; butt; stub [the *stump* of a pencil] ☆**3.** [from earlier use of tree stumps as speakers' platforms] the place where a political speech is made; political rostrum: a figurative usage **4.** *a)* the sound of a heavy, clumsy, tramping step *b)* such a step **5.** a pointed roll of leather or paper used for shading charcoal or pencil drawings **6.** [*pl.*] [Slang] the legs **7.** *Cricket* any of the three upright sticks of a wicket —*vt.* **1.** to reduce to a stump; lop **2.** to remove stumps from (land) ☆**3.** to travel over (a district), making political speeches; canvass **4.** to tone down or soften with a stump (sense 5) **5.** [Colloq.] to stub (one's toes, etc.) ☆**6.** [Colloq.] to puzzle, perplex, or baffle **7.** *Cricket* to put (a batsman) out by striking a bail from the wicket with the ball while the batsman is out of his ground: said of the wicketkeeper —*vi.* **1.** to walk with a heavy, clumsy, thumping step, as with a wooden leg ☆**2.** to travel about making political speeches —☆**up a stump** [Colloq.] unable to act, think, answer, etc.; in a dilemma; perplexed —**stump'er** *n.*

stump·age (stum'pij) *n.* **1.** standing timber or its value **2.** the right to cut such timber

stump·y (-pē) *adj.* **stump'i·er, stump'i·est** ☆**1.** covered with stumps **2.** like a stump; short and thickset; stubby

stun (stun) *vt.* **stunned, stun'ning** [ME. *stonien* < OFr. *estoner*, to stun: see ASTONISH] **1.** to make senseless or unconscious, as by a blow **2.** to daze or stupefy; shock deeply; astound; overwhelm [*stunned* by the news] **3.** to overpower or bewilder as by a loud noise or explosion —*n.* the effect or condition of being stunned —*SYN.* see SHOCK[1]

stung (stun) *pt. & pp.* of STING

stunk (stunk) *pp. & alt. pt.* of STINK

stun·ner (stun'ər) *n.* one that stuns; specif., [Colloq.] a remarkably attractive, excellent, etc. person or thing

stun·ning (-in) *adj.* **1.** that stuns **2.** [Colloq.] remarkably attractive, excellent, etc. —**stun'ning·ly** *adv.*

stun·sail, stun·s'le (stun's'l) *n.* studdingsail: phonetic spellings

stunt[1] (stunt) *vt.* [< dial. *stunt*, short and thick, stunted < ME., dull, stupid (with sense infl. by cognate ON. *stuttr*, short) < OE. < IE. *(ʰ)teud-* < base *(s)teu-*, to strike, whence STUB] **1.** to check the growth or development of; dwarf **2.** to hinder (growth or development) —*n.* **1.** the act or process of stunting or dwarfing **2.** a stunted creature or thing **3.** any of various plant diseases causing stunting

☆**stunt**[2] (stunt) *n.* [< ?] **1.** a display of skill or daring; feat; trick **2.** something done for a thrill, to attract attention, etc. —*vi.* to perform a stunt or stunts

☆**stunt man** *Motion Pictures* a person, as a professional acrobat, who takes the place of an actor in scenes involving dangerous or acrobatic falls, leaps, etc.

Stu·pa (stōō'pə) *n.* [Sans.] a towerlike Buddhist shrine

stupe[1] (stōōp) *n.* [< L. *stupa, stuppa*, tow: see STOP] *Med.* a soft cloth dipped in hot water, wrung dry, often medicated, and applied to the body as a compress

stupe[2] (stōōp, styōōp) *n.* [Slang] a stupid person

stu·pe·fa·cient (stōō'pə fā'shənt, styōō'-) *adj.* [L. *stupefaciens*, prp. of *stupefacere*, to STUPEFY] having a stupefying or narcotic effect: also **stu'pe·fac'tive** (-fak'tiv) —*n.* a stupefacient drug; narcotic

stu·pe·fac·tion (-fak'shən) *n.* [Fr. *stupéfaction*] **1.** a stupefying or being stupefied **2.** stunned amazement or utter bewilderment

stu·pe·fy (stōō'pə fī', styōō'-) *vt.* **-fied', -fy'ing** [Fr. *stupéfier* < L. *stupefacere* < *stupere*, to be stunned (see STUPID) + *facere*, to make: see DO[1]] **1.** to bring into a state of stupor; stun; make dull or lethargic **2.** to astound, amaze, or bewilder —**stu'pe·fi'er** *n.*

stu·pen·dous (stoo pen'dəs, styoo-) *adj.* [L. *stupendus*, gerundive of *stupere*, to be stunned (see ff.)] **1.** astonishing; overwhelming [a *stupendous* development] **2.** astonishingly great or large [a *stupendous* success] —**stu·pen'dous·ly** *adv.*

stu·pid (stōō'pid, styōō'-) *adj.* [L. *stupidus* < *stupere*, to be stunned or amazed < IE. *steup-*, to strike, whence STEEP[1], STUB] **1.** in a state of stupor; dazed; stunned; stupefied **2.** lacking normal intelligence or understanding; slow-witted; dull **3.** showing or resulting from a lack of normal intelligence; foolish; irrational [a *stupid* idea] **4.** dull and boring; tiresome [a *stupid* party]: also used colloquially as a generalized term of disapproval [a *stupid* hat] —*n.* a stupid person —**stu'pid·ly** *adv.* —**stu'pid·ness** *n.*

SYN.—stupid implies such lack of intelligence or incapacity for perceiving, learning, etc. as might be shown by one in a mental stupor [a *stupid* idea]; **dull** implies a mental sluggishness that may be constitutional or may result from overfatigue, disease, etc. [the fever left him *dull* and listless]; **dense** suggests obtuseness, or an irritating failure to understand quickly or to react intelligently [too *dense* to take a hint]; **slow** suggests that the quickness to learn, but not necessarily the capacity for learning, is below average [a pupil *slow* in his studies]; **retarded** is applied to those

behind others of the same age or class because of mental deficiency [a *retarded* pupil] See also SILLY —*ANT.* intelligent, bright

stu·pid·i·ty (stoo pid'ə tē, styoo-) *n.* [L. *stupiditas*] **1.** the quality or condition of being stupid **2.** *pl.* **-ties** something stupid; foolish remark, irrational act, etc.

stu·por (stōō'pər, styōō'-) *n.* [ME. < L. < *stupere*: see STUPID] **1.** a state in which the mind and senses are dulled; partial or complete loss of sensibility, as from the use of a narcotic or from shock **2.** mental or moral dullness or apathy —*SYN.* see LETHARGY —**stu'por·ous** *adj.*

stur·dy[1] (stur'dē) *adj.* **-di·er, -di·est** [ME., defiant, refractory, hardy < OFr. *estourdi*, stunned, reckless (basic sense "hard to influence or control") < VL. *exturdire*, to be dizzy (? from too much chattering) < L. *ex-*, intens. + *turdus*, a thrush] **1.** that will not yield or compromise; firm; resolute [*sturdy* defiance] **2.** physically strong; vigorous; hardy **3.** strongly built or constructed —*SYN.* see STRONG —**stur'di·ly** *adv.* —**stur'di·ness** *n.*

stur·dy[2] (stur'dē) *n.* [OFr. *estourdi*, giddiness: see prec.] same as GID —**stur'died** *adj.*

stur·geon (stur'jən) *n., pl.* **stur'geons, stur'geon:** see PLURAL, II, D, 1 [ME. *sturgiun* < OFr. *esturjon* < Frank. *sturjo*, akin to OE. *styria*, G. *stör*] any of several large, primitive food fishes (family Acipenseridae), having rows of spiny plates along the body and a projecting snout: valuable as a source of caviar and isinglass

STURGEON
(to 7 ft. long)

‡**Sturm und Drang** (shtoorm' oont dräŋ') [G. < *Wirrwarr, oder Sturm und Drang*, lit., Confusion, or Storm and Stress, play by F. M. v. Klinger (1752–1831), G. dramatist] a movement in 18th-century German literature away from the influence of French neoclassicism: it is the early phase of German romanticism

stut·ter (stut'ər) *vt., vi.* [freq. of dial. *stut*, to stutter < ME. *stutten*, akin to G. *stossen*, to knock, push: for base see STUDY] **1.** *same as* STAMMER **2.** to make (a series of repeated sounds) [stuttering machine guns] —*n.* the act or an instance of stuttering —**stut'ter·er** *n.*

Stutt·gart (stoot'gärt; G. shtoot'gärt) city in S West Germany; capital of Baden-Württemberg: pop. 629,000

Stuy·ve·sant (stī'və s'nt), Peter 1592–1672; last Du. governor of New Netherland (1646–64)

St. Vincent **1.** island of the Windward group in the West Indies: 133 sq. mi. **2.** Brit. colony consisting of this island & the N Grenadines: 150 sq. mi.; pop. 80,000

sty[1] (stī) *n., pl.* **sties** [ME. *stie* < OE. *sti, stig*, hall, enclosure, prob. < IE. base *stāi-*, to stop up, thicken, whence STONE] **1.** a pen for pigs **2.** any foul or depraved place —*vt., vi.* **stied, sty'ing** to lodge in or as in a sty

sty[2], **stye** (stī) *n., pl.* **sties** [< obs. dial. *styany* (taken as *sty on eye*) < dial. *styan*, rising < OE. *stigend*, prp. of *stigan*, to climb, rise: see STILE[1]] a small, inflamed swelling of a sebaceous gland on the rim of an eyelid

Styg·i·an (stij'ē ən) *adj.* [< L. *Stygius* (<Gr. *Stygios* < *Styx*) + -AN] **1.** of or characteristic of the river Styx and the infernal regions **2.** [*also* s-] *a)* infernal or hellish *b)* dark or gloomy *c)* inviolable; completely binding, as an oath sworn by the river Styx

sty·lar (stī'lər) *adj.* of or like a style, stylus, etc.

style (stīl) *n.* [ME. < L. *stilus* (sp. infl. by unrelated Gr. *stylos*, pillar) < IE. base *(s)tei-*, pointed, whence L. *stimulus*] **1.** a sharp, slender, pointed instrument used by the ancients in writing on wax tablets **2.** any of several devices, etc. similar in shape or use; specif., *a)* [Obs.] a pen *b)* an etching needle *c)* a phonograph needle; stylus *d)* an engraving tool *e)* the pointer on a dial, chart, etc. *f)* the gnomon of a sundial *g)* *Bot.* the slender, stalklike part of a carpel between the stigma and the ovary *h)* *Zool.* a small, pointed projection or bristlelike process, as on some insects **3.** *a)* manner or mode of expression in language, as distinct from the ideas expressed; way of using words to express thoughts *b)* specific or characteristic manner of expression, execution, construction, or design, in any art, period, work, employment, etc. [the Byzantine *style*, modern *style*] **4.** distinction, excellence, originality, and character in any form of artistic or literary expression [an author who lacks *style*] **5.** the way in which anything is made or done; manner **6.** *a)* the current, fashionable way of dressing, speaking, acting, etc. *b)* something stylish; esp., a garment of current, smart design *c)* a fashionable, luxurious existence [to live in *style*] **7.** distinction and elegance of manner and bearing **8.** form of address; title [entitled to the *style* of Mayor] **9.** sort; kind; variety; type **10.** a way of reckoning time, dates, etc.: see OLD STYLE (sense 2), NEW STYLE **11.** *Printing* a particular manner of dealing with spelling, punctuation, word division, etc., as by a specific publisher, newspaper, etc. —*vt.* **styled, styl'ing** **1.** to name; call [Abraham Lincoln, *styled* the Great Emancipator] ☆**2.** to design the style of **3.** to bring into accord with an accepted style, as

of a publisher; normalize spelling, punctuation, etc. of —*SYN*. see FASHION —**style′less** *adj.* —**styl′er** *n.*

style·book (-book′) *n.* a book consisting of examples or rules of style (esp. sense 11)

sty·let (stī′lit) *n.* [Fr. < It. *stiletto*: see STILETTO] **1.** a slender, pointed weapon; esp., a stiletto **2.** *Surgery a)* a slender probe *b)* a wire inserted into a soft catheter to keep it rigid **3.** *Zool.* same as STYLE (*n.* 2 *h*)

sty·li·form (stī′lə fôrm′) *adj.* [ModL. *stiliformis*: see STYLE & -FORM] shaped like a style or stylus

styl·ish (stī′lish) *adj.* conforming to current style in dress, decoration, behavior, etc.; smart; fashionable —**styl′ish·ly** *adv.* —**styl′ish·ness** *n.*

styl·ist (-list) *n.* **1.** a writer, etc. whose work has style and distinction or is characterized by a particular style **2.** a person who designs, creates, or advises on, current styles, as in dress

sty·lis·tic (stī lis′tik) *adj.* [< STYLE, after G. *stilistisch*] of or having to do with style, esp. literary style: also **sty·lis′ti·cal** —**sty·lis′ti·cal·ly** *adv.*

sty·lite (stī′līt) *n.* [LGr.(Ec.) *stylitēs* < Gr., dwelling on a pillar < *stylos*, a pillar: for IE. base see STEER¹] any of a class of Christian ascetics of the early Middle Ages who lived on the tops of pillars —**sty·lit′ic** (-lit′ik) *adj.* —**styl′-lit·ism** (-līt iz′m) *n.*

styl·ize (stī′līz) *vt.* **-ized, -iz·ing** [< STYLE + -IZE, after G. *stilisieren*] to make conform to a given style; specif., to design or represent according to the rules of a style rather than according to nature; conventionalize —**styl′i·za′tion** *n.* —**styl′iz·er** *n.*

sty·lo- (stī′lō, -lə) [< L. *stylus*, for *stilus*, pointed instrument: see STYLE] *a combining form meaning* pointed, sharp [*stylograph*]: also, before a vowel, **styl-**

sty·lo·bate (stī′lə bāt′) *n.* [L. *stylobates* < Gr. *stylobatēs* < *stylos* (see STYLITE) + *bainein*, to GO¹] *Archit.* a continuous base or coping for a row of columns

sty·lo·graph (-graf′, -gräf′) *n.* [STYLO- + -GRAPH] a fountain pen having a pierced conical point, rather than a nib, through which the ink flows

sty·lo·graph·ic (stī′lə graf′ik) *adj.* **1.** of or like a stylograph **2.** of or used in stylography —**sty′lo·graph′i·cal·ly** *adv.*

sty·log·ra·phy (stī läg′rə fē) *n.* [STYLO- + -GRAPHY] drawing, writing, or engraving done with a style or stylus

sty·loid (stī′loid) *adj.* resembling a style; styliform; specif., *Anat.* designating or of any of various long, slender processes, esp. that at the base of the temporal bone

sty·lo·lite (stī′lə līt′) *n.* [STYLO- + -LITE] a small, columnlike formation in a rock deposit, usually composed of limestone with grooved or scratched sides

sty·lo·po·di·um (stī′lə pō′dē əm) *n., pl.* **-di·a** (-ə) [ModL.: see STYLO- & -PODIUM] a disk or swelling at the base of the style in plants of the parsley family

sty·lus (stī′ləs) *n., pl.* **-lus·es, -li** (-lī) [L., for *stilus*, pointed instrument: see STYLE] **1.** a style or other needlelike marking device **2.** any of various pointed tools, as one used for marking mimeograph stencils or one used in Braille embossing **3.** *a)* a sharp, pointed device for cutting the grooves of a phonograph record *b)* the needle for reproducing the sound of such a record

sty·mie (stī′mē) *n.* [prob. a use of earlier Scot. *stymie*, a person partially blind < *styme* < ME. *stime* (sense obscure): the reference is to the blind shot caused by a stymie] **1.** *Golf* the condition that exists on a putting green when an opponent's ball lies in a direct line between the player's ball and the hole **2.** any situation in which one is obstructed or frustrated —*vt.* **-mied, -mie·ing 1.** to hinder or obstruct as with a stymie **2.** to block; impede

sty·my (stī′mē) *n., pl.* **-mies,** *vt.* **-mied, -my·ing** same as STYMIE

styp·sis (stip′sis) *n.* [LL. < Gr. *stypsis*: see ff.] the action or use of a styptic

styp·tic (-tik) *adj.* [LME. *stiptik* < L. *stypticus* < Gr. *styptikos*, astringent < *styphein*, to contract: for IE. base see STOP] tending to halt bleeding by contracting the tissues or blood vessels; astringent —*n.* any styptic substance —**styp·tic′i·ty** (-tis′ə tē) *n.*

styptic pencil a small stick of a styptic substance, as alum, used to stop bleeding, as from razor nicks

Styr (stir) river in W Ukrainian S.S.R., flowing north into the Pripyat River in the Pinsk Marshes: c.290 mi.

sty·rene (stī′rēn, stir′ēn) *n.* [< L. *styrax* (see STORAX) + -ENE] a colorless or yellowish, easily polymerized, aromatic liquid, $C_6H_5CH:CH_2$, used in organic synthesis, esp. in manufacturing synthetic rubber and plastics

Styr·i·a (stir′ē ə) province of SE Austria: 6,326 sq. mi.; pop. 1,138,000; cap. Graz: Ger. name, STEIERMARK

☆**Sty·ro·foam** (stī′rə fōm′) [(POLY)STYR(ENE) + -o- + FOAM] *a trademark for* rigid, lightweight, cellular polystyrene, used in boat construction, insulation, commercial displays, etc. —*n.* [s-] this substance

Styx (stiks) *n.* [L. < Gr. *Styx*, lit., the Hateful < *stygein*, to hate] *Gr. Myth.* the river encircling Hades over which Charon ferried the souls of the dead

su·a·ble (sōō′ə b'l, syōō′-) *adj.* liable to suit in a court that may be sued —**su′a·bil′i·ty** *n.*

sua·sion (swā′zhən) *n.* [ME. < L. *suasio* < *suasus*, pp. of *suadere*, to persuade: see SWEET] same as PERSUASION: now chiefly in **moral suasion**, the act of persuading by appeal-

ing to one's sense of morality —**sua′sive** (-siv) *adj.* —**sua′-sive·ly** *adv.* —**sua′sive·ness** *n.*

suave (swäv; *Brit.* also swāv) *adj.* [MFr. < L. *suavis*, SWEET] smoothly gracious or polite; polished; blandly ingratiating; urbane —**suave′ly** *adv.* —**suave′ness** *n.*
SYN.—**suave** suggests the smoothly gracious social manner of one who deals with people easily and tactfully [a *suave* sophisticate]; **urbane** suggests the social poise of one who is highly cultivated and has had much worldly experience [an *urbane* cosmopolite]; **diplomatic** implies adroitness and tactfulness in dealing with people and handling delicate situations, sometimes in such a way as to gain one's own ends [a *diplomatic* answer]; **politic** also expresses this idea, often stressing the expediency or opportunism of a particular policy pursued [a *politic* move]; **bland** is the least complex of these terms, simply implying a gentle or ingratiating pleasantness [a *bland* disposition]

suav·i·ty (swä′və tē, swav′ə-) *n.* [ME. *suavitee* < OFr. *suavité* < L. *suavitas*] **1.** the quality of being suave; graceful politeness **2.** *pl.* **-ties** a suave action, speech, etc.

sub (sub) *n. clipped form of:* **1.** SUBMARINE **2.** SUBSCRIPTION **3.** SUBSTITUTE —*vi.* **subbed, sub′bing** [Colloq.] to be a substitute (*for* someone)

sub- (sub, səb) [< L. *sub*, under, below: see UP¹] *a prefix meaning:* **1.** under, beneath, below [*submarine, subsoil*] **2.** lower in rank, position, or importance than; inferior or subordinate to [*subaltern, subagent, subhead*] **3.** to a lesser degree than, somewhat, slightly [*subhuman, subtropical, subconscious*] **4.** *a)* so as to form a division into smaller or less important parts [*sublet, subdivide*] *b)* forming such a division [*subsection, subdivision*] **5.** *Chem. a)* with less than the normal amount of (the specified substance) [*subchloride*] *b)* basic [*subcarbonate*] In words of Latin origin, *sub-* is assimilated to *suc-* before *c*, *suf-* before *f*, *sug-* before *g*, *sum-* before *m*, *sup-* before *p*, and *sur-* before *r*: *sub-* often changes to *sus-* before *c, p,* and *t*

sub. 1. subaltern **2.** substitute(s) **3.** suburb(an)

sub·ac·e·tate (sub as′ə tāt′) *n.* a basic acetate

sub·ac·id (-as′id) *adj.* [L. *subacidus*] **1.** slightly acid or sour, as certain fruits **2.** slightly sharp or biting, as a remark —**sub′a·cid′i·ty** (-ə sid′ə tē) *n.* —**sub·ac′id·ly** *adv.*

sub·a·cute (sub′ə kyōōt′) *adj.* **1.** somewhat acute [*subacute* angle] **2.** between acute and chronic [a *subacute* disease] —**sub′a·cute′ly** *adv.*

sub·a·gent (sub ā′jənt) *n.* a person representing an agent; agent of an agent

sub·al·pine (-al′pīn) *adj.* [L. *subalpinus*, lit., lying near the Alps: see SUB- & ALPINE] **1.** designating or of regions at the foot of the Alps **2.** designating, of, or growing in mountain regions at an altitude of between four and six thousand feet, below the timberline; alpestrine

sub·al·tern (səb ôl′tərn; *chiefly Brit.*, sub′əl tərn) *adj.* [Fr. *subalterne* < LL. *subalternus* < L. *sub-*, SUB- + *alternus*, ALTERNATE] **1.** subordinate; of lower rank **2.** [Brit.] holding an army commission below that of captain **3.** in traditional logic, particular, with reference to a universal proposition of which it is part —*n.* **1.** a subordinate **2.** [Brit.] a subaltern officer **3.** a subaltern proposition in logic

sub·al·ter·nate (səb ôl′tər nit) *adj.* [ME. < LL. *subalternatus*, pp. of *subalternare* < *subalternus*: see prec.] **1.** following in order; successive **2.** *Bot.* in an alternate arrangement, but tending to become opposite: said of leaves —*n.* same as SUBALTERN (*n.* 3) —**sub·al′ter·nate·ly** *adv.* —**sub·al′ter·na′tion** *n.*

sub·ant·arc·tic (sub′ant ärk′tik, -är′-) *adj.* designating or of the area surrounding the Antarctic Circle

sub·a·quat·ic (-ə kwät′ik, -kwat′-) *adj.* partly aquatic

sub·a·que·ous (sub ā′kwē əs, -ak′wē-) *adj.* [SUB- + AQUEOUS] **1.** adapted for underwater use or existence; underwater **2.** formed, living, or occurring under water

sub·arc·tic (-ärk′tik, -är′-) *adj.* designating or of the area immediately surrounding the Arctic Circle

sub·ar·id (-ar′id) *adj.* slightly arid; moderately dry

☆**sub·as·sem·bly** (sub′ə sem′blē) *n., pl.* **-blies** an assembled unit designed to be fitted to a larger unit of which it is a component [a *subassembly* of an electronic circuit]

sub·at·om (sub at′əm) *n.* a constituent part of an atom

sub·a·tom·ic (sub′ə täm′ik) *adj.* of or pertaining to the inner part of an atom or to a particle smaller than an atom

sub·au·di·tion (-ô dish′ən) *n.* [LL. *subauditio* < *subaudire*, to understand or supply a word omitted < L. *sub-*, under + *audire*, to hear (see AUDIENCE)] **1.** the act or process of understanding or mentally filling in a word or thought implied but not expressed **2.** something thus understood or filled in

sub·au·ric·u·lar (-ô rik′yōō lər) *adj.* situated below the auricle of the ear

sub·base (sub′bās′) *n.* the lowest section of a base or pedestal that is divided horizontally

sub·base·ment (-bās′mənt) *n.* any floor or room below the principal basement

sub·bass (-bās′) *n.* a pedal stop of 16 or 32 feet, producing the lowest tones in an organ

sub·branch (-branch′) *n.* a division of a branch

sub·cal·i·ber (sub kal′ə bər) *adj.* **1.** smaller than the caliber of the gun from which it is fired: said of a projectile fired, as in practice, through a tube of proper caliber inserted in or slipped on the barrel **2.** of or having to do with a subcaliber projectile

sub·car·ti·lag·i·nous (-kär'tə laj'ə nəs) *adj.* **1.** situated beneath cartilage **2.** partly cartilaginous

sub·ce·les·tial (sub'sə les'chəl) *adj.* [< ML. *subcaelestis* (see SUB- & CELESTIAL) + -AL] beneath the heavens; terrestrial or mundane

sub·cel·lar (sub'sel'ər) *n.* a cellar beneath the principal cellar

sub·cen·tral (sub'sen'trəl) *adj.* close to or beneath the center —sub'cen'tral·ly *adv.*

sub·chas·er (sub'chā'sər) *n. contracted form of* SUBMARINE CHASER

sub·chlo·ride (sub klôr'īd) *n.* a chloride containing a relatively small proportion of chlorine

sub·class (sub'klas', -kläs') *n.* **1.** a subdivision of a class; specif., *Biol.* any main natural subdivision of a class of plants or animals **2.** *Math.* same as SUBSET

sub·cla·vi·an (sub klā'vē ən) *adj.* situated under the clavicle —*n.* a subclavian vein, artery, etc.

subclavian groove either of two grooves in the first rib, one for the main artery (**subclavian artery**) and the other for the main vein (**subclavian vein**) of the arm

sub·cli·max (-klī'maks) *n. Ecol.* the successional stage just preceding a climax formation

sub·clin·i·cal (-klin'i k'l) *adj.* without obvious clinical symptoms, as a disease in its early stages

sub·com·mit·tee (sub'kə mit'ē) *n.* any of the small committees chosen from among the members of a main committee to carry out special assignments

sub·con·scious (sub kän'shəs) *adj.* **1.** occurring without conscious perception, or with only slight perception, on the part of the individual: said of mental processes and reactions **2.** not fully conscious; imperfectly aware —the **subconscious** subconscious mental activity: term now seldom used in psychiatry —sub·con'scious·ly *adv.* —sub·con'scious·ness *n.*

sub·con·ti·nent (-kän'tə nənt) *n.* a large land mass, smaller than that usually called a continent; often, a subdivision of a continent, regarded as a geographic or political entity

sub·con·tract (-kän'trakt; *also, for v.,* sub'kən trakt') *n.* a secondary contract undertaking some or all of the obligations of a primary or previous contract: construction companies often let *subcontracts* for the electrical work, plumbing, etc. —*vt., vi.* to make a subcontract (for)

sub·con·trac·tor (-kän'trak tər, -kən trak'-) *n.* a person or company that assumes by secondary contract some or all of the obligations of an original contractor

sub·con·tra·ry (-kän'trer ē) *n.* -ries *Logic* either of two propositions so related that both can be true but both cannot be false

sub·cos·tal (-käs't'l) *adj.* [SUB- + COSTAL] lying beneath the ribs —*n.* a subcostal muscle, etc.

sub·crit·i·cal (-krit'i k'l) *adj.* **1.** less than critical **2.** unable to sustain a fission chain reaction: said of a nuclear reactor, device, etc.

sub·cul·ture (sub'kul'chər) *n.* **1.** *a)* a group (within a society) of persons of the same age, social or economic status, ethnic background, etc. and having its own interests, goals, etc. *b)* the distinct cultural patterns of such a group **2.** a culture, as of bacteria, grown on a fresh medium from a previous culture —sub·cul'tur·al *adj.*

sub·cu·ta·ne·ous (sub'kyoo tā'nē əs) *adj.* [LL. *subcutaneus:* see SUB- & CUTANEOUS] being, used, or introduced beneath the skin —sub'cu·ta'ne·ous·ly *adv.*

sub·dea·con (sub dē'k'n) *n.* [ME. *subdecon* < LL.(Ec.) *subdiaconus:* see SUB- & DEACON] a cleric ranking below a deacon

☆**sub·deb** (sub'deb') *n.* [SUB- + DEB(UTANTE)] **1.** a girl in the years just preceding her debut into society **2.** any girl of such age —*adj.* of or suitable for a subdeb

sub·di·ac·o·nate (sub'dī ak'ə nit) *n.* [SUB- + DIACONATE] the office or position of a subdeacon

sub·dis·trict (sub'dis'trikt) *n.* a subdivision of a district

sub·di·vide (sub'di vīd', sub'di vīd') *vt., vi.* -vid'ed, -vid'ing [ME. *subdividen* < LL. *subdividere:* see SUB- & DIVIDE] **1.** to divide further after previous division has been made **2.** to divide (land) into small parcels for sale, as by a real-estate firm —sub'di·vid'er *n.*

sub·di·vi·sion (sub'di vizh'ən, sub'di vizh'ən) *n.* [LL. *subdivisio*] **1.** a subdividing or being subdivided **2.** a piece of land resulting from this; esp., a large tract subdivided into small parcels for sale

sub·dom·i·nant (sub däm'ə nənt) *adj.* less than or only partly dominant —*n.* **1.** something that is subdominant **2.** *Ecol.* a species having considerable importance in a community but much less influence than the dominant species **3.** *Music* the fourth tone of a diatonic scale; tone next below the dominant

sub·duce (səb dōōs', -dyōōs') *vt.* -duced', -duc'ing [L. *subducere* < sub-, from + *ducere,* to lead (see DUCT)] [Obs.] to withdraw; take away

sub·duct (-dukt') *vt., vi.* [< L. *subductus,* pp.: see prec.] **1.** [Now Rare] to withdraw; subtract; remove **2.** *Med.* to draw downward —sub·duc'tion *n.*

sub·due (-dōō', -dyōō') *vt.* -dued', -du'ing [ME. *subdewen* (altered in sense and form after L. *subdere,* to put under,

subject) < OFr. *soduire,* to withdraw, seduce < L. *subducere:* see SUBDUCE] **1.** to bring into subjection; conquer; vanquish **2.** to overcome, as by persuasion or training; control **3.** to make less intense; reduce; diminish; soften; allay **4.** to repress (emotions, passions, etc.) **5.** to bring (land) under cultivation —*SYN.* see CONQUER —sub·du'a·ble *adj.* —sub·du'al *n.* —sub·du'er *n.*

sub·en·try (sub'en'trē) *n.* -tries an entry listed under a main entry

su·be·re·ous (soo bir'ē əs, syoo-) *adj.* [LL. *subereus* < *suber,* cork, cork tree < or akin to Gr. *syphar,* wrinkled skin] *Bot.* of or like cork: also **su'ber·ose'** (-bə rōs')

su·ber·ic acid (-ber'ik) [Fr. *suberique* < L. *suber,* cork tree: see prec.] a dibasic acid, $C_8H_{14}O_4$, obtained by the oxidation of cork and from other sources

su·ber·in (soo'bər in, svoo'-) *n.* [Fr. *subérine* < L. *suber,* cork + Fr. *-ine,* -INE[4]] a waxy or fatty substance contained in cork

su·ber·ize (-bə rīz') *vt.* -ized', -iz'ing [L. *suber,* cork + -IZE] *Bot.* to make impermeable by the formation of suberin in the cell walls, changing them into cork —su'ber·i·za'tion *n.*

sub·fam·i·ly (sub'fam'ə lē) *n.* -lies any main natural subdivision of a family of plants or animals

sub·floor (sub'flôr') *n.* a rough floor upon which a finished floor is laid

sub·freez·ing (sub'frē'zin) *adj.* below freezing

sub·fusc (sub fusk') *adj.* [L. *subfuscus,* brownish, dusky < *sub-,* below (see SUB-) + *fuscus,* FUSCOUS] [Chiefly Brit.] having a dull or dark, often drab, color —*n.* [Chiefly Brit.] subfusc clothing

sub·ge·nus (sub'jē'nəs) *n., pl.* -gen'er·a (-jen'ər ə), -ge'nus·es any main natural subdivision of a genus of plants or animals

sub·gla·cial (sub glā'shəl) *adj.* presently or formerly at the bottom of, or deposited beneath, a glacier [a *subglacial* stream, a *subglacial* deposit] —sub·gla'cial·ly *adv.*

sub·grade (sub'grād') *n.* a layer of rock or earth leveled and graded for a foundation, as of a road

sub·group (-grōōp') *n.* **1.** a subdivision of a group; subordinate group **2.** *Chem.* a vertical subdivision of a group in the periodic table of chemical elements: see PERIODIC TABLE, chart **3.** *Math.* a subset of a group

☆**sub·gum** (sub'gum') *n.* [Cantonese, lit., mixed vegetables] designating any of various Chinese-American dishes, as chow mein, prepared with water chestnuts, mushrooms, almonds, etc.

sub·head (sub'hed') *n.* **1.** the title of a subdivision of a chapter, article, etc. **2.** a subordinate heading or title, as of a newspaper article Also **sub'head'ing**

sub·hu·man (sub'hyōō'mən) *adj.* **1.** below the human race in development; less than human **2.** nearly human

sub·in·dex (-in'deks) *n., pl.* -di·ces' (-də sēz') **1.** an index to a subdivision of a main category **2.** *Math.* a figure or character added below and to the side of a symbol to distinguish it from others [in Y_a and X_a, 3 and a are *subindices*]

sub·in·feu·da·tion (sub'in fyoo dā'shən) *n.* **1.** the transfer of feudal lands by a vassal lord to a subtenant with all the privileges and responsibilities falling to the new holder **2.** tenure so established **3.** the lands or fief so held

☆**sub·ir·ri·gate** (sub ir'ə gāt') *vt.* -gat'ed, -gat'ing to irrigate (land) by a system of underground pipes —sub'ir·ri·ga'tion *n.*

su·bi·to (sōō'bi tō') *adv.* [It. < L., suddenly < pp. of *subire,* to approach, spring up: see SUDDEN] *Music* quickly; abruptly: a direction to the performer

subj. 1. subject **2.** subjective **3.** subjunctive

sub·ja·cent (sub jā's'nt) *adj.* [L. *subjacens,* prp. of *subjacere,* to lie under < *sub-,* under + *jacere,* to lie] **1.** situated directly under or below; underlying **2.** being lower but not directly beneath —sub·ja'cen·cy *n.*

sub·ject (sub'jikt; *for v.* səb·jekt') *adj.* [ME. *suget* < OFr. < L. *subjectus,* pp. of *subjicere,* to place under, put under, subject < *sub-,* under + *jacere,* to throw: see JET[1]] **1.** under the authority or control of, or owing allegiance to, another [*subject* peoples] **2.** having a disposition or tendency; liable (to) [*subject* to fits of anger] **3.** liable to receive; exposed (to) [*subject* to censure] **4.** contingent or conditional upon (with to) [*subject* to his approval] —*n.* [ME. *suget* < OFr. < L. *subjectus:* see the *adj.*] **1.** a person under the authority or control of another; esp., a person in his relationship to a ruler, government, etc. to which he owes allegiance **2.** someone or something made to undergo a treatment, experiment, analysis, dissection, etc. **3.** [L. *subjectum,* foundation, subject (transl. of Gr. *to hypokeimenon*) < neut. of *subjectus:* see the *adj.*] something dealt with in discussion, study, writing, painting, etc.; theme **4.** the main theme of a musical composition or movement **5.** originating cause, reason, or motive **6.** any of the various courses of study in a school or college; branch of learning **7.** *Gram. a)* the noun, noun phrase, or noun substitute in a sentence about which something is said in the predicate *b)* in a generative grammar, the infinite set of expression that constitutes the noun phrase (NP) in the rule stating

that a sentence consists of a noun phrase followed by a verb phrase **8.** *Logic* that part of a proposition about which something is said; that which is affirmed or denied **9.** *Philos. a)* the actual substance of anything as distinguished from its qualities and attributes *b)* the mind, or ego, that thinks and feels, as distinguished from everything outside the mind —*vt.* **1.** [Obs.] to place under or below **2.** to bring under the authority or control of; cause to owe allegiance **3.** to make liable or vulnerable [*to subject* oneself to the contempt of others] **4.** to cause to undergo or experience some action or treatment [*to subject* someone to a thorough questioning] **5.** [Rare] to place before; submit [a plan *subjected* for approval] —**sub·jec′tion** *n.* **SYN.—subject** is the general word for whatever is dealt with in discussion, study, writing, art, etc. [*the subject* of a talk, painting, etc.]; a **theme** is a subject developed or elaborated upon in a literary or artistic work, or one that constitutes the underlying motif of the work [a novel with a social *theme*]; a **topic** is a subject of common interest selected for individual treatment, as in an essay, or for discussion by a group of persons [baseball is their favorite *topic* of conversation]; **text** is specifically applied to a Biblical passage chosen as the subject of a sermon

sub·jec·tive (səb jek′tiv) *adj.* [ME. < LL. *subjectivus*, of the subject < *subjectus*: see SUBJECT] **1.** of, affected by, or produced by the mind or a particular state of mind; of or resulting from the feelings or temperament of the subject, or person thinking; not objective; personal [a *subjective* judgment] **2.** determined by and emphasizing the ideas, thoughts, feelings, etc. of the artist or writer, not just rigidly transcribing or reflecting reality **3.** *Gram.* same as NOMINATIVE **4.** *Philos.* of or having to do with the perception or conception of a thing by the mind as opposed to its reality independent of the mind **5.** *Med.* designating or of a symptom or condition perceptible only to the patient **6.** *Psychol. a)* existing or originating within the observer's mind or sense organs and, hence, incapable of being checked externally or verified by other persons *b)* introspective —**sub·jec′tive·ly** *adv.* —**sub·jec·tiv·i·ty** (sub′jek tiv′ə tē), **sub·jec′tive·ness** *n.*

sub·jec·tiv·ism (-iz′m) *n.* **1.** the philosophic theory that all knowledge is subjective and relative, never objective **2.** any philosophic theory that restricts knowledge in some way to the subjective elements, as by limiting external reality to only what can be known or inferred by subjective standards of truth **3.** an ethical theory holding that personal attitudes and feelings are the sole determinants of moral and aesthetic values —**sub·jec′ti·vist** *adj., n.* —**sub·jec′ti·vis′tic** *adj.*

subject matter the thing or things considered in a book, course of instruction, discussion, etc.

sub·join (səb join′) *vt.* [MFr. *subjoindre* < L. *subjungere*: see SUB- & JOIN] to add (something) at the end of what has been stated; append —**sub·join′der** [Rare] *n.*

sub ju·di·ce (sub joo′də sē) [L., lit., under judgment] before the court; under judicial consideration

sub·ju·gate (sub′jə gāt′) *vt.* **-gat′ed, -gat′ing** [ME. *subiugaten* < L. *subjugatus*, pp. of *subjugare*, to bring under the yoke < *sub-*, under + *jugum*, a YOKE] **1.** to bring under control or subjection; conquer **2.** to cause to become subservient; subdue —*SYN.* see CONQUER —**sub′ju·ga′tion** *n.* —**sub′ju·ga′tor** *n.*

sub·junc·tive (səb juŋk′tiv) *adj.* [LL. *subjunctivus* < L. *subjunctus*, pp. of *subjungere*, to SUBJOIN] designating or of that mood of a verb used to express supposition, desire, hypothesis, possibility, etc., rather than to state an actual fact, as the mood of *were* in "if I *were* you": cf. INDICATIVE, IMPERATIVE —*n.* **1.** the subjunctive mood **2.** a verb in this mood

sub·king·dom (sub′kiŋ′dəm) *n.* any main natural subdivision of the plant or animal kingdom

sub·lap·sar·i·an (sub′lap ser′i ən, -sar′-) *n., adj.* [ModL. *sublapsarius* < L. *sub-*, below + *lapsus*, a LAPSE, fall] same as INFRALAPSARIAN —**sub′lap·sar′i·an·ism** *n.*

sub·late (səb lāt′) *vt.* **-lat′ed, -lat′ing** [< L. *sublatus* (suppletive pp. of *tollere*, to lift up, take away, annul) < *sub-*, up (see SUB-) + *latus*, suppletive pp. of *ferre*, to BEAR] *Logic* to deny, contradict, or negate

sub·lease (sub′lēs′; *for v.* sub lēs′) *n.* a lease granted by a lessee to another person of all or part of the property —*vt.* **-leased′, -leas′ing** to grant, obtain, or hold a sublease of —**sub′les·see′** (-les ē′) *n.* —**sub′les·sor** (sub les′ôr, sub′les ôr′) *n.*

sub·let (sub let′, sub′let′) *vt.* **-let′, -let′ting** **1.** to let to another (property which one is renting) **2.** to let out (work) to a subcontractor

sub·le·thal (sub lē′thəl) *adj.* not quite lethal; insufficient to cause death [a *sublethal* dose of poison]

sub·lieu·ten·ant (sub′loo ten′ənt; *Brit. & Canad.* -lef ten′-) *n.* [Brit. & Canad.] a naval officer ranking below a lieutenant

sub·li·mate (sub′lə māt′; *for adj. & n., also* -mit) *vt.* **-mat′ed, -mat′ing** [< L. *sublimatus*, pp. of *sublimare*: see SUBLIME] **1.** to purify or refine (a substance) by subliming **2.** to have a purifying or ennobling influence or effect on **3.** to express (socially or personally unacceptable impulses, specif. sexual impulses) in constructive, acceptable forms, often unconsciously —*vi.* to undergo sublimation —*adj.* sublimated —*n.* a substance that is the product of sublimation —**sub′li·ma′tion** *n.*

sub·lime (sə blīm′) *adj.* [L. *sublimis* < *sub-*, up to + *limen*, lintel (hence, orig., up to the lintel): see LIMEN] **1.** noble; exalted; majestic **2.** inspiring awe or admiration through grandeur, beauty, etc. **3.** [Colloq.] outstandingly or supremely such [a man of *sublime* taste] **4.** [Archaic] *a)* elated; joyful *b)* proud; lofty; haughty *c)* upraised; aloft —*vt.* **-limed′, -lim′ing** [ME. *sublimen* < MFr. *sublimer* < ML. *sublimare* < L., to lift high < the *adj.*] **1.** to make sublime **2.** to purify (a solid) by heating directly to a gaseous state and condensing the vapor back into solid form —*vi.* to go through this process —*SYN.* see SPLENDID —**sub·lime′ly** *adv.* —**sub·lime′ness** *n.*

sub·lim·i·nal (sub lim′ə n'l) *adj.* [see SUB- & LIMEN & -AL] below the threshold of consciousness or apprehension; specif., involving or using stimuli that become effective subconsciously by repetition —**sub·lim′i·nal·ly** *adv.*

sub·lim·i·ty (sə blim′ə tē) *n.* [L. *sublimitas*] **1.** the state or quality of being sublime, majestic, noble, etc. **2.** *pl.* **-ties** something sublime

sub·lin·gual (sub liŋ′gwəl) *adj.* [ML. *sublingualis*: see SUB- & LINGUAL] situated under the tongue

sub·lu·nar·y (sub′loo ner′ē, sub loo′nər ē) *adj.* [ML. *sublunaris* < L. *sub-*, under + *luna*, the moon] **1.** situated beneath the moon; terrestrial **2.** earthly; mundane Also **sub·lu′nar**

☆**sub·ma·chine gun** (sub′mə shēn′) a portable, automatic or semiautomatic firearm with a short barrel and a stock, fired from the shoulder or hip

sub·mar·gin·al (sub mär′ji n'l) *adj.* **1.** below minimum requirements or standards [*submarginal* housing] **2.** not yielding a satisfactory return; unproductive [*submarginal* land] **3.** *Biol.* near the margin of an organ or part —**sub·mar′gin·al·ly** *adv.*

sub·ma·rine (sub′mə rēn′; *for n. & v., usually* sub′mə rēn′) *adj.* [SUB- + MARINE] being, living, used, or carried on beneath the surface of the water, esp. of the sea —*n.* **1.** a submarine plant or animal **2.** a kind of warship, armed with torpedoes, guided missiles, etc., that can operate under water —*vt.* **-rined′, -rin′ing** to attack, esp. to torpedo, with a submarine

submarine chaser a small, fast naval patrol vessel equipped for use against submarines

sub·ma·rin·er (sub′mə rēn′ər, sub′mə rēn′ər) *n.* a member of a submarine crew

☆**submarine sandwich** same as HERO SANDWICH

sub·max·il·la (sub′mak sil′ə) *n., pl.* **-lae** (-ē), **-las** [ModL.: see SUB- & MAXILLA] the lower jaw or jawbone

sub·max·il·lar·y (-mak′sə ler′ē) *adj.* designating, of, or below the lower jaw; esp., designating or of either of two salivary glands, one on each side, below the inside edge of the lower jaw

sub·me·di·ant (-mē′dē ənt) *n.* [SUB- + MEDIANT] the sixth tone of a diatonic scale; tone just above the dominant and below the subtonic; superdominant

sub·merge (səb murj′) *vt.* **-merged′, -merg′ing** [L. *submergere* < *sub-*, under + *mergere*, to plunge: see MERGE] **1.** to place under or cover with water or the like; plunge into water, inundate, etc. **2.** to cover over; suppress; hide **3.** to sink below a decent level of life [the *submerged* people of the slums] —*vi.* to sink or plunge beneath the surface of water, etc. —**sub·mer′gence** (-mur′jəns) *n.* —**sub·mer′gi·ble** (-jə b'l) *adj.*

sub·merse (-murs′) *vt.* **-mersed′, -mers′ing** [< L. *submersus*, pp. of *submergere*] same as SUBMERGE —**sub·mer′sion** (-mur′zhən, -shən) *n.*

sub·mersed (-murst′) *adj.* submerged; specif., *Bot.* growing under water

sub·mers·i·ble (səb mur′sə b'l) *adj.* that can be submersed, esp. so as to continue functioning —*n.* any of various ships that can operate under water and are used for exploration, research, etc.

sub·mi·cro·scop·ic (sub′mī krə skäp′ik) *adj.* too small to be seen through a microscope

sub·min·i·a·ture (sub min′ē ə chər) *adj.* designating or of a very small camera, electronic component, etc., smaller than one described as "miniature"

sub·min·i·a·tur·ize (-īz′) *vt., vi.* **-ized′, -iz′ing** to construct (something) on a subminiature scale —**sub·min′i·a·tur′i·za′tion** *n.*

sub·miss (səb mis′) *adj.* [Archaic] submissive; humble

sub·mis·sion (-mish′ən) *n.* [ME. < OFr. < L. *submissio* < *submissus*, pp. of *submittere*] **1.** the act of submitting, yielding, or surrendering **2.** the quality or condition of being submissive; resignation; obedience; meekness **3.** the act of submitting something to another for decision, consideration, etc. **4.** *Law* an agreement whereby parties to a dispute submit the matter to arbitration and agree to be bound by the decision

sub·mis·sive (-mis′iv) *adj.* [< L. *submissus*, pp. of *submittere* (see ff.) + -IVE] having or showing a tendency to submit without resistance; docile; yielding —**sub·mis′sive·ly** *adv.* —**sub·mis′sive·ness** *n.*

sub·mit (-mit′) *vt.* **-mit′ted, -mit′ting** [ME. *submitten* < L. *submittere* < *sub-*, under, down + *mittere*, to send: see MISSION] **1.** to present or refer to others for decision, consideration, etc. **2.** to yield to the action, control, power, etc. of another or others; also, to subject or allow to be subjected to treatment, analysis, etc. of some sort: often used reflexively **3.** to offer as an opinion;

suggest; propose —*vi.* 1. *a)* to yield to the power, control, etc. of another or others; give in *b)* to allow oneself to be subjected (*to* treatment, analysis, etc.). 2. to defer to another's judgment or decision 3. to be submissive, obedient, humble, etc. —*SYN.* see SURRENDER —**sub·mit'ta·ble** *adj.* —**sub·mit'tal** *n.* —**sub·mit'ter** *n.*

sub·mon·tane (sub'män'tān) *adj.* [< SUB- + L. *montanus,* of a mountain: see MOUNTAIN] 1. located at the foot of a mountain or mountain range 2. of or characteristic of foothills 3. beneath a mountain or mountains

sub·mul·ti·ple (sub mul'ti p'l) *n.* [SUB- + MULTIPLE] a number that will divide another with no remainder; exact divisor (of a specified number) [3 is a *submultiple* of 12]

sub·nor·mal (-nôr'm'l) *adj.* below the normal; less than normal, esp. in intelligence —*n.* a subnormal person —**sub'nor·mal'i·ty** (-mal'ə tē) *n.* —**sub·nor'mal·ly** *adv.*

sub·o·ce·an·ic (sub'ō shē an'ik) *adj.* situated or occurring on or beneath the ocean floor

sub·or·bit·al (sub ôr'bit 'l) *adj.* 1. designating or of a space flight in which the spacecraft follows a steep, short-range trajectory instead of going into orbit 2. beneath the orbit of the eye

sub·or·der (sub'ôr'dər) *n.* any natural subdivision of an order of plants or animals —**sub·or'di·nal** (-di n'l) *adj.*

sub·or·di·nate (sə bôr'də nit; *for v.* -nāt') *adj.* [ME. < ML. *subordinatus,* pp. of *subordinare* < L. *sub-,* under + *ordinare,* to order: see ORDAIN] 1. inferior to or placed below another in rank, power, importance, etc.; secondary 2. under the power or authority of another 3. subservient or submissive 4. *Gram.* functioning as a noun, adjective, or adverb within a sentence [a *subordinate* phrase]: cf. SUBORDINATE CLAUSE —*n.* a subordinate person or thing —*vt.* -nat'ed, -nat'ing 1. to place in a subordinate position; treat as less important or inferior (*to*) 2. to make obedient or subservient (*to*); control; subdue —**sub·or'di·nate·ly** *adv.* —**sub·or'di·na·tive** (-nāt'iv) *adj.*

subordinate clause in a complex sentence, a clause that cannot function syntactically as a complete sentence by itself; dependent clause: distinguished from MAIN CLAUSE (Ex.: She will visit us *if she can*)

subordinating conjunction a conjunction that connects subordinate words, phrases, or clauses to some other sentence element (Ex.: *if, as, so, unless, although, when*): also **subordinate conjunction**

sub·or·di·na·tion (sə bôr'də nā'shən) *n.* 1. a subordinating or being subordinated 2. [Now Rare] subjection or submission to rank, power, or authority; obedience

sub·or·di·na·tion·ism (-iz'm) *n. Theol.* any doctrine that the second and third persons of the Trinity are subordinate to the first person

sub·orn (sə bôrn') *vt.* [MFr. *suborner* < L. *subornare,* to furnish or supply, instigate, incite secretly < *sub-,* under + *ornare,* to furnish, adorn: see ORNAMENT] 1. to get or bring about through bribery or other illegal methods 2. to induce or instigate (another) to do something illegal, esp. to commit perjury —**sub·or'na·tive** (-bôr'nə tiv) *adj.* —**sub·orn'er** *n.*

sub·or·na·tion (sub'ôr nā'shən) *n.* [MFr.] a suborning or being suborned; esp., the crime of inducing another to commit perjury (**subornation of perjury**)

Su·bo·ti·ca (sōō'bô'tē tsä) city in NE Yugoslavia, near the Hungarian border: pop. 75,000

sub·ox·ide (sub äk'sīd) *n.* an oxide containing a relatively small proportion of oxygen

sub·phy·lum (sub'fī'ləm) *n., pl.* -la (-lə) any main natural subdivision of a phylum

sub·plot (-plät') *n.* a secondary or subordinate plot in a play, novel, etc.

sub·poe·na (sə pē'nə) *n.* [ME. *suppena* < ML. < L. *sub poena,* lit., under penalty: see SUB- & PAIN] a written legal order directing a person to appear in court to give testimony, show specified records, etc. —*vt.* -naed, -na·ing to summon with such an order Also sp. **sub·pe'na**

sub·prin·ci·pal (sub prin'sə p'l) *n.* 1. an assistant principal in a school, etc. 2. a secondary brace or rafter 3. *Music* an open diapason subbass in an organ

sub·re·gion (sub'rē'jən) *n.* any of the divisions of a region, esp. with reference to the distribution of plants and animals —**sub·re'gion·al** *adj.*

sub·rep·tion (səb rep'shən) *n.* [L. *subreptio* < *subreptus,* pp. of *subripere, surripere,* to take away secretly: see SURREPTITIOUS] 1. the fraudulent concealment or misrepresentation of facts so as to gain a favor, esp. an ecclesiastical dispensation 2. a false inference drawn from such deception —**sub·rep·ti·tious** (sub'rep tish'əs) *adj.*

sub·ro·gate (sub'rə gāt') *vt.* -gat'ed, -gat'ing [< L. *subrogatus, surrogatus:* see SURROGATE] to substitute (one person) for another

sub·ro·ga·tion (sub'rə gā'shən) *n.* [ME. *subrogacioun* < ML. *subrogatio* < L. *subrogatus*] a subrogating; esp., the substitution of one creditor for another, along with a transference of the claims and rights of the old creditor

sub ro·sa (sub rō'zə) [L., lit., under the rose: the rose in ancient times was a symbol of silence or secrecy] secretly; privately; confidentially

sub·rou·tine (sub'rōō tēn') *n.* 1. a short set of instructions, often used repeatedly, that directs a digital computer in the solution of part of a problem 2. the set of instructions needed to direct a digital computer in completing a strictly defined mathematical or logical operation

sub·scap·u·lar (sub skap'yoo lər) *adj.* situated beneath the scapula

sub·scribe (səb skrīb') *vt.* -scribed', -scrib'ing [ME. *subscriben* < L. *subscribere:* see SUB- & SCRIBE] 1. to sign (one's name) at the end of a document, etc. 2. to write one's signature on (a document, etc.) as an indication of consent, approval, attestation, etc. 3. to support; consent to; favor; sanction 4. to promise to contribute (a sum of money), esp. by signing a pledge —*vi.* 1. to sign one's name at the end of a document, etc. 2. to give support, sanction, or approval; consent or agree (*to*) [to *subscribe* to certain measures] 3. to promise to contribute, or to give, a sum of money 4. to agree to receive and pay for a periodical, service, theater tickets, etc. for a specified period of time (with *to*) —**sub·scrib'er** *n.*

sub·script (sub'skript) *adj.* [L. *subscriptus,* pp. of *subscribere,* to SUBSCRIBE] written below; esp., *same as* INFERIOR (*adj.* 8) —*n.* a figure, letter, or symbol written below and to the side of another [in Y₃ and Xₐ, 3 and *a* are *subscripts*]

sub·scrip·tion (səb skrip'shən) *n.* [L. *subscriptio*] 1. the act of subscribing 2. something subscribed; specif., *a)* a written signature *b)* a signed document, etc. *c)* consent or sanction, esp. in writing *d)* an amount of money subscribed *e)* a formal agreement to receive and pay for a periodical, books, theater tickets, etc. for a specified period of time *f)* the right to receive a periodical, etc., as by payment of a fixed sum 3. that part of a doctor's prescription giving directions to the pharmacist: cf. SIGNATURE (*n.* 4) 4. *Eccles.* assent to certain doctrines for promoting uniformity; specif., in the Anglican Church, acceptance of the Thirty-nine Articles of Faith and the Book of Common Prayer

sub·se·quence (sub'si kwens', -kwəns) *n.* 1. the fact or condition of being subsequent 2. a subsequent happening

sub·se·quent (-kwənt, -kwent') *adj.* [ME. < L. *subsequens,* prp. of *subsequi,* to follow close after: see SUB- & SEQUENT] coming after; following in time, place, or order —**subse·quent** *to* after; following —**sub'se·quent·ly** *adv.*

sub·sere (sub'sir') *n.* [SUB- + SERE¹] *Ecol.* a secondary succession occurring after all or part of the vegetation in an area has been destroyed, as by man, fire, etc.

sub·serve (səb surv') *vt.* -served', serv'ing [L. *subservire* < *sub-,* under + *servire,* to SERVE] to be useful or helpful to (a purpose, cause, etc.); serve; promote; aid

sub·ser·vi·ence (-sur've əns) *n.* 1. the state or quality of being subservient 2. subservient behavior or manner; obsequiousness; servility Also **sub·ser'vi·en·cy**

sub·ser·vi·ent (-ənt) *adj.* [L. *subserviens,* prp. of *subservire,* to SUBSERVE] 1. that is useful, helpful, or of service, esp. in an inferior or subordinate capacity 2. submissive; obsequious *SYN.* see SERVILE —**sub·ser'vi·ent·ly** *adv.*

sub·set (sub'set') *n.* a mathematical set containing some or all of the elements of a given set

sub·shrub (-shrub') *n.* a partly shrubby plant that has woody stems growing new shoots annually at the tips

sub·side (səb sīd') *vi.* -sid'ed, -sid'ing [L. *subsidere* < *sub-,* under + *sidere,* to settle < *sedere,* to SIT] 1. to sink or fall to the bottom; settle, as sediment 2. to sink to a lower level 3. to become less active, violent, intense, etc.; become quiet; abate —*SYN.* see WANE —**sub·sid'ence** (-sīd'·ns, sub'si dəns) *n.*

sub·sid·i·ar·y (səb sid'ē er'ē) *adj.* [L. *subsidiarius* < *subsidium:* see SUBSIDY] 1. giving aid, support, service, etc.; serving to supplement; auxiliary 2. being in a secondary or subordinate relationship 3. of, constituting, or maintained by a subsidy or subsidies —*n., pl.* -ar'ies a person or thing that is subsidiary; specif., *a)* a company controlled by another company which owns all or a majority of its shares: in full **subsidiary company** *b) Music* a subordinate theme —**sub·sid'i·ar'i·ly** *adv.*

sub·si·dize (sub'sə dīz') *vt.* -dized', -diz'ing [SUBSID(Y) + -IZE] 1. to support with a subsidy 2. to buy the aid or support of with a subsidy, often as a kind of bribe —**sub'·si·di·za'tion** *n.* —**sub'si·diz'er** *n.*

sub·si·dy (sub'sə dē) *n., pl.* -dies [ME. < Anglo-Fr. *subsidie* < L. *subsidium,* auxiliary forces, reserve troops, aid, support < *subsidere,* to sit down, remain: see SUBSIDE] a grant of money; specif., *a)* a grant of money from one government to another, as for military aid *b)* a government grant to a private enterprise considered of benefit to the public *c)* in England, formerly, money granted by Parliament to the king

sub·sist (səb sist') *vi.* [L. *subsistere,* to stand still, stay, abide < *sub-,* under + *sistere,* to place, stand, redupl. of base of *stare,* to STAND] 1. *a)* to continue to be or exist; have existence as a reality, entity, etc. *b)* to continue to be in use, force, etc. 2. to continue to live; remain alive (*on* sustenance, *by* specific means, etc.); be sustained 3. to consist or inhere (*in*) 4. *Philos.* to be logically con-

ceivable and have being as a nonactual, conceptual entity that may be the subject of true statements —*vt.* to maintain with sustenance; support

sub·sist·ence (-sis'təns) *n.* [ME. < LL. *subsistentia* < L. *subsister:* see prec.] **1.** existence; being; continuance **2.** the act of providing sustenance **3.** means of support or livelihood; often, specif., the barest means in terms of food, clothing, and shelter needed to sustain life **4.** the quality of being inherent **5.** *Philos.* a) the status of something that exists in itself as an individual whole b) the status of something whose very act of existing is its essence, as God —**sub·sist'ent** *adj.*

sub·soil (sub'soil') *n.* the layer of soil beneath the surface soil —*vt.* to stir or turn up the subsoil of —**sub·soil'er** *n.*

sub·so·lar (sub sō'lər) *adj.* [SUB- + SOLAR] **1.** located under the sun **2.** having the sun in the zenith **3.** being between the tropics; equatorial

sub·son·ic (-sän'ik) *adj.* [SUB- + SONIC] **1.** designating, of, or moving at a speed in a surrounding fluid less than that of sound in the same fluid **2.** *same as* INFRASONIC

sub·space (sub'spās') *n.* *Math.* a space which forms a proper subset of some larger space

‡**sub spe·ci·e** (sub spē'shi ē') [L.] under the aspect (of)

‡**sub specie ae·ter·ni·ta·tis** (ē tur'ni tā'tis) [L., lit., under the aspect of eternity] with reference to eternity or to universal implications

sub·spe·cies (sub'spē'shēz) *n.* [ModL.: see SUB- & SPECIES] any natural subdivision of a species that exhibits small, but persistent, morphological variations from other subdivisions of the same species living in different geographical regions: the subspecies name is usually a third, uncapitalized term in a trinomial (Ex.: the scientific name for the *eastern robin* is *Turdus migratorius migratorius*, for the *western robin*, *Turdus migratorius propinquus*) —**sub'·spe·cif'ic** (-spə sif'ik) *adj.*

subst. **1.** substantival **2.** substantive **3.** substitute

sub·stance (sub'stəns) *n.* [ME. < OFr. < L. *substantia* < *substare*, to be present < *sub-*, under + *stare*, to STAND] **1.** the real or essential part or element of anything; essence, reality, or basic matter **2.** a) the physical matter of which a thing consists; material b) matter of a particular kind or chemical composition **3.** a) solid quality; substantial character b) consistency; body **4.** the real content, meaning, or gist of something said or written **5.** material possessions; property; resources; wealth **6.** *Philos.* something that has independent existence and is acted upon by causes or events —**in substance 1.** with regard to essential elements **2.** actually; really

sub·stand·ard (sub stan'dərd) *adj.* below standard; specif., a) below a standard established as by law b) *Linguis.* *same as* NONSTANDARD; specif., designating or of any language dialect regarded as below the standards of the dialect of educated speakers [*substandard* speech is often marked by disagreement between the subject and verb]

sub·stan·tial (səb stan'shəl) *adj.* [ME. *substancial* < LL. *substantialis*] **1.** of or having substance **2.** real; actual; true; not imaginary **3.** strong; solid; firm; stout **4.** considerable; ample; large **5.** of considerable worth or value; important **6.** having property or possessions; wealthy **7.** with regard to essential elements; in substance **8.** *Philos.* of, or having the nature of, substance —*n.* a substantial thing: *usually used in pl.* —**sub·stan'ti·al'i·ty** (-shē al'ə tē), **sub·stan'tial·ness** *n.* —**sub·stan'tial·ly** *adv.*

sub·stan·tial·ism (-iz'm) *n.* *Philos.* the doctrine that there are entities or beings underlying all phenomena as the subjects in which various properties inhere

sub·stan·ti·ate (səb stan'shē āt') *vt.* -at'ed, -at'ing [< ModL. *substantiatus*, pp. of *substantiare* < L. *substantia*, SUBSTANCE] **1.** to give substance or true existence to **2.** to give concrete form or body to; convert into substance; embody **3.** to show to be true or real by giving evidence; prove; confirm —SYN. see CONFIRM —**sub·stan'ti·a'tion** *n.* —**sub·stan'ti·a'tive** *adj.* —**sub·stan'ti·a'tor** *n.*

sub·stan·tive (sub'stən tiv) *adj.* [LME. < LL. *substantivus* < L. *substantia:* see SUBSTANCE] **1.** existing independently; not dependent upon or subordinate to another **2.** of considerable amount or quantity; substantial **3.** having a real existence; actual **4.** a) of, containing, or dealing with the essential elements; essential b) having direct bearing on a matter **5.** of or relating to legal rights and principles as distinguished from legal procedures **6.** becoming fixed without the use of a mordant: said of a dye **7.** *Gram.* a) showing or expressing existence [the *substantive* verb "to be"] b) of or used as a substantive —*n.* **1.** something substantive **2.** *Gram.* a noun or any word or group of words functioning as a noun —**sub'stan·ti'val** (-tī'v'l) *adj.* —**sub'stan·ti'val·ly**, **sub·stan'tive·ly** *adv.* —**sub'stan·tive·ness** *n.*

substantive right a basic right of man, as life, liberty, etc., which exists independently from all man-made laws

sub·sta·tion (sub'stā'shən) *n.* a branch station, as of a post office

sub·stit·u·ent (sub stich'oo wənt) *n.* [< L. *substituens*, prp. of *substituere*, to SUBSTITUTE] *Chem.* an atom or group of atoms replacing another atom or group in a compound

sub·sti·tute (sub'stə tōōt', -tyōōt') *n.* [ME. < L. *substitutus*, pp. of *substituere*, to put instead of < *sub-*, under + *statuere*, to put, place: see STATUE] **1.** a person or thing serving or used in place of another **2.** *Gram.* any word,

as a pronoun, the verb *to do*, etc., used in place of another word or words (Ex.: *did* for *shouted* in "she shouted and he did, too") —*vt.* -tut'ed, -tut'ing **1.** to put or use in place of another **2.** [Now Rare] to take the place of **3.** *Chem.* to replace as a substituent —☆*vi.* to act or serve in place of another (often with *for*) —*adj.* being a substitute or substitutes —**sub'sti·tut'a·ble** *adj.*

sub·sti·tu·tion (sub'stə tōō'shən, -tyōō'-) *n.* the substituting of one person or thing for another —**sub'sti·tu'tion·al**, **sub'sti·tu'tion·ar'y** *adj.* —**sub'sti·tu'tion·al·ly** *adv.*

sub·sti·tu·tive (sub'stə tōōt'iv, -tyōōt'-) *adj.* [LL. *substitutivus*] **1.** of or having to do with substitution **2.** being or capable of being a substitute —**sub'sti·tu'tive·ly** *adv.*

sub·strate (sub'strāt) *n.* **1.** *same as* SUBSTRATUM **2.** *Biochem.* a substance acted upon, as by an enzyme **3.** *Biol.*, *Bacteriology same as* MEDIUM (*n.* 6)

sub·strat·o·sphere (sub strat'ə sfir') *n.* loosely, the highest part of the troposphere

sub·stra·tum (sub'strāt'əm, -strat'-) *n.*, *pl.* -ta (-ə), -tums [L., neut. of *substratus*, pp. of *substernere*, to strew beneath < *sub-*, under + *sternere*, to spread out < IE. base *ster-*, whence STREW] **1.** a) a part, substance, element, etc. which lies beneath and supports another; foundation b) any basis or foundation **2.** *same as* SUBSTRATE (senses 2 & 3) **3.** loosely, *same as* SUBSOIL **4.** *Bot.* the base or material to which a plant is attached and from which it gets nutriment **5.** *Metaphysics* substance, with reference to the events or causes which act upon it, the changes occurring in it, the attributes that inhere in it, etc. **6.** *Photog.* a thin layer of material on a photographic film or plate serving as a base for the sensitive emulsion **7.** *Zool.* the ground or other solid material on which an animal moves or is fastened

sub·struc·ture (-struk'chər) *n.* a part or structure acting as a support, base, or foundation: also **sub'struc'tion** —**sub·struc'tur·al** *adj.*

sub·sume (səb sōōm', -syōōm') *vt.* -sumed', -sum'ing [ModL. *subsumere* < L. *sub-*, under + *sumere*, to take: see CONSUME] **1.** to include within a larger class, group, order, etc. **2.** to show (an idea, instance, etc.) to be covered by a rule, principle, etc.

sub·sump·tion (səb sump'shən) *n.* [ModL. *subsumptio* < *subsumptus*, pp. of *subsumere*] **1.** a subsuming or being subsumed **2.** something subsumed; esp., a minor concept or premise —**sub·sump'tive** *adj.*

sub·sur·face (sub'sur'fis) *adj.* lying below the surface, esp. of the earth, the oceans, etc. —*n.* a subsurface part

sub·sys·tem (-sis'təm) *n.* any system that is part of a larger system; component system

sub·tan·gent (sub tan'jənt) *n.* *Geom.* the segment of the x-axis included between the ordinate of a given point on a curve and the tangent at that point

☆**sub·teen** (sub'tēn') *n.* a child nearly a teen-ager

sub·tem·per·ate (sub tem'pər it) *adj.* of or occurring in the colder areas of the temperate zones

sub·ten·ant (-ten'ənt) *n.* a person who rents from a tenant; tenant of a tenant —**sub·ten'an·cy** *n.*

sub·tend (səb tend') *vt.* [L. *subtendere* < *sub-*, under + *tendere*, to stretch: see TEND²] **1.** to extend under or be opposite to in position [each side of a triangle *subtends* the opposite angle] **2.** *Bot.* to enclose in an angle, as between a leaf and its stem

sub·ter- (sub'tər) [L. < *subter*, below, beneath] *a prefix meaning* below, under, less than, secretly

sub·ter·fuge (sub'tər fyōōj') *n.* [LL. *subterfugium* < L. *subterfugere*, to flee secretly, escape < *subter-*, below + *fugere*, to flee] any plan, action, or device used to hide one's true objective, evade a difficult or unpleasant situation, etc.; stratagem; artifice —SYN. see DECEPTION

sub·ter·nat·u·ral (sub'tər nach'ər əl) *adj.* falling short of what is natural; not quite natural

sub·ter·ra·ne·an (sub'tə rā'nē ən) *adj.* [L. *subterraneus* < *sub-*, under + *terra*, earth: see TERRAIN] **1.** lying beneath the earth's surface; underground **2.** secret; hidden Also **sub'ter·ra'ne·ous** —*n.* one who lives underground —**sub'ter·ra'ne·an·ly** *adv.*

sub·tile (sut''l, sub'til) *adj.* [ME. < MFr. *subtil*, altered (after L.) < OFr. *soutil:* see SUBTLE] *now rare var.* of SUBTLE —**sub'tile·ly** *adv.* —**sub'tile·ness** *n.* —**sub'til·ty**, **sub·til·i·ty** (səb til'ə tē) *n.*, *pl.* -ties

sub·til·ize (sut''l īz', -sub'tl'l-) *vt.*, *vi.* -ized', -iz'ing [ML. *subtilizare* < L. *subtilis*, SUBTLE] to make or become subtle; esp., to discuss or argue with subtle distinctions —**sub'til·i·za'tion** *n.*

sub·ti·tle (sub'tīt''l) *n.* **1.** a secondary or explanatory title, as of a book or play **2.** a book title repeated at the top of the first page of text **3.** lines of dialogue or of descriptive material shown on a movie screen or television tube either by interrupting a scene or by superimposing on the scene —*vt.* -ti'tled, -ti'tling to add a subtitle or subtitles to

sub·tle (sut''l) *adj.* **sub'tler** (-lər, -'l ər), **sub'tlest** (-list, -'l ist) [ME. *sotil* < OFr. *soutil* < L. *subtilis*, fine, thin, precise, orig., closely woven < *sub-*, under + *tela*, web < *texla* < *texere*, to weave: see TEXT] **1.** thin; rare; tenuous; not dense or heavy [a *subtle* gas] **2.** a) capable of making or noticing fine distinctions in meaning, etc. [a *subtle* thinker] b) marked by or requiring mental keenness

[subtle reasoning] **3.** delicately skillful or clever; deft or ingenious [a *subtle* filigree] **4.** not open or direct; crafty; sly **5.** delicately suggestive; not grossly obvious [a *subtle* hint] **6.** working insidiously; not easily detected [a *subtle* poison] —**sub′tle·ness** *n.* —**sub′tly** *adv.*

sub·tle·ty (-tē) *n.* [ME. *sutelte* < OFr. *sotillete* < L. *subtilitas*] **1.** the quality or condition of being subtle; esp., the ability or tendency to make fine distinctions **2.** *pl.* **-ties** something subtle; esp., a fine distinction

sub·ton·ic (sub tän′ik) *n. Music* the seventh tone of a diatonic scale; tone next below the upper tonic

sub·top·ic (sub′täp′ik) *n.* a topic that is a division of a main topic

sub·to·tal (sub′tōt′′l) *n.* a total that forms part of a final, complete total —*vt., vi.* **-taled** or **-talled, -tal·ing** or **-tal·ling** to add up so as to form a subtotal

sub·tract (səb trakt′) *vt., vi.* [< L. *subtractus*, pp. of *subtrahere*, to draw away underneath, subtract < *sub-*, under + *trahere*, to DRAW] **1.** to take away (a part from a whole) **2.** to take away or deduct (one number or quantity from another) —**sub·tract′er** *n.*

sub·trac·tion (səb trak′shən) *n.* a subtracting or being subtracted; esp., the mathematical process of finding the difference between two numbers or quantities

sub·trac·tive (-tiv) *adj.* [ML. *subtractivus*] **1.** tending to subtract **2.** capable of or involving subtraction **3.** that is to be subtracted; marked with the minus sign (−)

sub·tra·hend (sub′trə hend′) *n.* [L. *subtrahendus*, gerundive of *subtrahere:* see SUBTRACT] a number or quantity to be subtracted from another (the *minuend*)

☆**sub·treas·ur·y** (sub′trezh′ər ē, sub trezh′-) *n., pl.* **-ur·ies** a branch treasury

sub·trop·i·cal (sub träp′i k′l) *adj.* **1.** designating of or regions bordering on the tropical zone **2.** characteristic of such regions; nearly tropical Also **sub·trop′ic**

sub·trop·ics (-iks) *n.pl.* subtropical regions

su·bu·late (soo′byoo lit, -lāt′) *adj.* [ModL. *subulatus* < L. *subula*, an awl < *sudhla:* for IE. base see SEW] *Biol.* slender and tapering to a point; awl-shaped

sub·um·brel·la (sub′um brel′ə) *n.* [SUB- + UMBRELLA] *Zool.* the concave lower, or oral, surface of a jellyfish

sub·urb (sub′ərb) *n.* [ME. < L. *suburbium* < *sub-*, under, near + *urbs* (gen. *urbis*), town] a district, esp. a residential district, on or near the outskirts of a city and often a separately incorporated city or town **2.** [*pl.*] a region made up of such districts (with *the*)

sub·ur·ban (sə bur′bən) *adj.* **1.** of, in, or residing in a suburb or the suburbs **2.** characteristic of the suburbs or suburbanites

sub·ur·ban·ite (-īt′) *n.* a person living in a suburb

sub·ur·ban·ize (-īz′) *vt., vi.* **-ized′, -iz′ing** to make or become suburban —**sub·ur′ban·i·za′tion** *n.*

sub·ur·bi·a (sə bur′bē ə) *n.* the suburbs or suburbanites collectively: usually used to connote the values, attitudes, and activities regarded as characteristic of suburban life

sub·ur·bi·car·i·an (sə bur′bi ker′ē ən) *adj.* [< LL. *suburbicarius* < L. *suburbanus* (see SUBURB) + -AN] being in the suburbs of Rome; specif., *R.C.Ch.*, designating or of the seven dioceses adjoining Rome

sub·vene (səb vēn′) *vi.* -**vened′, -ven′ing** [L. *subvenire*, to come to one's assistance, lit., to come up < *sub-*, under + *venire*, to COME] [Rare] to happen or come so as to help

sub·ven·tion (-ven′shən) *n.* [ME. < *subvencioun* < OFr. *subvencion* < LL. *subventio*] **1.** orig., the act of subvening **2.** money granted, as by a government, in support of a study, institution, etc.; subsidy —**sub·ven′tion·ar′y** *adj.*

‡**sub ver·bo** (sub vur′bō) [L.] under the word (specified): with reference to an entry in a dictionary, index, etc.

sub·ver·sion (səb vur′zhən, -shən) *n.* [ME. < OFr. < L. *subversio*] a subverting or being subverted; ruin; overthrow

sub·ver·sive (-siv) *adj.* [ML. *subversivus* < L. *subversus*, pp. of *subvertere:* see ff.] tending or seeking to subvert, overthrow, or destroy (an established government, institution, belief, etc.) —*n.* a person regarded as subversive —**sub·ver′sive·ly** *adv.* —**sub·ver′sive·ness** *n.*

sub·vert (səb vurt′) *vt.* [ME. *subverten* < MFr. *subvertir* < L. *subvertere* < *sub-*, under + *vertere*, to turn: see VERSE] **1.** to overthrow or destroy (something established) **2.** to undermine or corrupt, as in morals —**sub·vert′er** *n.*

‡**sub vo·ce** (sub vō′sē) [L.], under the voice, i.e., utterance or term] *same as* SUB VERBO

sub·way (sub′wā′) *n.* **1.** an underground way or passage; specif., [Chiefly Brit.] *same as* UNDERPASS ☆**2.** an underground, metropolitan electric railway or the tunnel through which it runs

suc- (suk, sək) *same as* SUB-: used before *c*

suc·ce·da·ne·um (suk′si dā′nē əm) *n., pl.* **-ne·a** (-ə) [ModL. < neut. sing. of L. *succedaneus*, substituted < *succedere:* see ff.] *rare var. of* SUBSTITUTE

suc·ceed (sək sēd′) *vi.* [ME. *succeden* < L. *succedere*, to go beneath or under, follow after < *sub-*, under + *cedere*, to go: see CEDE] **1.** *a)* to come next after another; follow; ensue *b)* to follow another into office, possession, etc., as by election, appointment, or inheritance (often with *to*) *c)* [Obs.] to devolve, as an estate **2.** to happen or turn out

as planned or attempted [a plan that *succeeded*] **3.** to achieve or accomplish something planned or attempted [to *succeed* in convincing someone] **4.** to have or enjoy success; realize a goal or goals, esp. in becoming wealthy, winning fame or approval, etc. [to *succeed* in business] —*vt.* **1.** to take the place left by; follow into office, etc. **2.** to come or occur after; follow —**suc·ceed′er** *n.* **SYN.**—**succeed** implies the favorable outcome of an undertaking, career, etc. or the attainment of a desired goal [to *succeed* as a businessman]; **prosper** implies continued, often increasing, good fortune or success [the nation *prospered* under his administration]; **flourish** more specifically suggests a figurative state of flowering, when a person or thing is at the peak of development, influence, etc. [militarism *flourishes* in a fascist state]; **thrive** implies vigorous growth or development, as because of favorable conditions [industry *thrived* in the North] See also FOLLOW —**ANT. fail**

‡**suc·cès de scan·dale** (sük set skän däl′) [Fr., lit., success of scandal] **1.** notoriety gained by something scandalous, as a shocking play, movie, novel, etc. **2.** something that causes such notoriety

‡**suc·cès d'es·time** (sük se de stēm′) [Fr., lit., success of esteem] **1.** the gaining of acclaim from professional critics; critical success **2.** an artistic work receiving such acclaim, often without being a financial success

‡**suc·cès fou** (sük se foo′) [Fr., lit., mad success] an extraordinary success, esp. financially

suc·cess (sək ses′) *n.* [L. *successus* < pp. of *succedere:* see SUCCEED] **1.** orig., result; outcome **2.** *a)* a favorable or satisfactory outcome or result *b)* something having such an outcome **3.** the gaining of wealth, fame, rank, etc. **4.** a successful person

suc·cess·ful (-fəl) *adj.* **1.** coming about, taking place, or turning out to be as was hoped for [a *successful* mission] **2.** having achieved success; specif., having gained wealth, fame, etc. —**suc·cess′ful·ly** *adv.* —**suc·cess′ful·ness** *n.*

suc·ces·sion (sək sesh′ən) *n.* [ME. < OFr. < L. *successio* < *succedere:* see SUCCEED] **1.** the act of succeeding or coming after another in order or sequence or to an office, estate, throne, etc. **2.** the right to succeed to an office, estate, etc. **3.** a number of persons or things coming one after another in time or space; series; sequence [a *succession* of delays] **4.** *a)* a series of heirs or rightful successors of any kind *b)* the order or line of such a series **5.** *Ecol.* the slow, regular sequence of changes in the regional development of communities of plants and associated animals, culminating in a climax characteristic of a specific geographical environment —**SYN.** see SERIES —**in succession** one after another in a regular series or sequence; successively —**suc·ces′sion·al** *adj.* —**suc·ces′sio·nal·ly** *adv.*

suc·ces·sive (sək ses′iv) *adj.* [ME. < LL. *successivus*] **1.** coming in succession; following one after another in sequence; consecutive **2.** of or involving succession —**suc·ces′sive·ly** *adv.* —**suc·ces′sive·ness** *n.*

suc·ces·sor (-ər) *n.* [ME. < OFr. *successour* < L. *successor* < *successus*, pp. of *succedere:* see SUCCEED] a person or thing that succeeds, or follows, another; esp., one who succeeds to an office, title, etc.

suc·ci·nate (suk′sə nāt′) *n.* a salt or ester of succinic acid

suc·cinct (sək siŋkt′) *adj.* [ME., girdled, girded < L. *succinctus*, prepared, short, contracted, pp. of *succingere*, to gird, tuck up, prepare < *sub-*, under + *cingere*, to gird: see CINCH] **1.** clearly and briefly stated; terse **2.** characterized by brevity and conciseness of speech **3.** [Archaic] *a)* enclosed as by a girdle *b)* closefitting —**SYN.** see CONCISE —**suc·cinct′ly** *adv.* —**suc·cinct′ness** *n.*

suc·cin·ic acid (sək sin′ik) [Fr. *succinique* < L. *succinum*, amber] a colorless, crystalline dibasic acid, $(CH_2CO_2H)_2$, found in amber, lignite, and many plants, and produced synthetically or during alcoholic fermentation: it is used in medicine and organic synthesis

suc·cor (suk′ər) *vt.* [ME. *socouren* < OFr. *sucurre, socorre* < L. *succurrere* < *sub-*, under + *currere*, to run: see COURSE] to give assistance to in time of need or distress; help; aid; relieve —*n.* [ME. *socur*, assumed sing. of *socours* < OFr. *sucurs* < ML. *succursus* < L., pp.: see the v.] **1.** aid; help; relief **2.** a person or thing that succors —**SYN.** see HELP Also, Brit. sp., **suc′cour**

suc·cor·y (suk′ər ē) *n.* [altered, after MLowG. *suckerie* < older *sycory*, early form of CHICORY] *same as* CHICORY

☆**suc·co·tash** (suk′ə tash′) *n.* [< AmInd. (Narragansett) *misickquatash*, ear of corn] a dish consisting of lima beans and kernels of corn cooked together

Suc·coth (soo kōt′, sook′ōs) *n. same as* SUKKOT

suc·cu·bus (suk′yoo bəs) *n., pl.* **-bi** (-bī′) [ME. < ML. (altered after INCUBUS) < *succuba*, strumpet < *succubare*, to lie under < *sub-*, under + *cubare*, to lie: see CUBE] a female demon thought in medieval times to have sexual intercourse with sleeping men: also **suc′cu·ba** (-bə), *pl.* **-bae′** (-bē′): cf. INCUBUS

suc·cu·lent (suk′yoo lənt) *adj.* [L. *succulentus* < *sucus*, juice: see SUCK] **1.** full of juice; juicy **2.** full of interest, vigor, etc.; not dry or dull **3.** *Bot.* having thick, fleshy tissues for storing water, as a cactus —*n.* a succulent plant —**suc′cu·lence, suc′cu·len·cy** *n.* —**suc′cu·lent·ly** *adv.*

suc·cumb (sə kum′) *vi.* [L. *succumbere* < *sub-*, under +

cumbere, nasalized form of *cubare,* to lie: see CUBE[1]] 1. to give way (*to*); yield; submit [*to* succumb *to persuasion*] 2. to die [*to* succumb *to a plague*] —SYN. see YIELD

suc·cuss (sə kus*ʹ*) *vt.* [< L. *succussus,* pp. of *succutere,* to toss up < *sub-,* under + *quatere,* to shake: see QUASH[2]] to shake forcibly; esp. formerly, to shake (a patient) from side to side in order to detect the presence of a liquid in some body cavity, esp. in the thorax —**suc·cus'sion** (-kush*ʹ*ən) *n.* —**suc·cus'sive** (-kus*ʹ*iv) *adj.*

such (such) *adj.* [ME. *suche* < OE. *swilc, swelc,* akin to G. *solch,* Goth. *swaleiks* < PGmc. *swalika-:* for components see SO[1] & LIKE[1]] 1. *a*) of the kind mentioned or implied [*a* man *such as his father*] *b*) of the same or a similar kind; like [*pens, pencils, crayons, and* such *supplies*] 2. certain but not specified; whatever [*at* such *time as you go*] 3. so extreme, so much, so great, etc.: used, according to the context, for emphasis [*embarrassed by* such *praise*] *Such* is a term of comparison, although that with which comparison is made is not always expressed; when it is expressed, *as* or *that* is used as a correlative with *such* (Ex.: *such love as his is seldom experienced*) *Such* is not preceded by an article, although the article may occur between it and the noun it modifies (Ex.: *such a fool*!) —*adv.* to so great a degree; so [*such good news*] —*pron.* 1. such a person (or persons) or thing (or things) [*such* as live by the sword*] 2. the person or thing mentioned or implied [*such* was his nature*] —**as such** 1. as being what is indicated or suggested 2. in itself [*a* name, *as* such, means nothing*] —**such as** 1. for example 2. like or similar to (something specified) —**such as it is** (or **was,** etc.) being the kind it is (or was, etc.): used in referring to something in either an apologetic or a derogatory way **such and such** (being) something particular but not named or specified [*he went to* such and such *a place*] **such·like** (such*ʹ*līk*ʹ*) *adj.* of such a kind; of like or similar kind —*pron.* persons or things of such a kind

Sü·chow (shōō*ʹ*jō*ʹ*) city in NW Kiangsu province, E China: pop. 710,000

suck (suk) *vt.* [ME. *suken* < OE. *sucan,* akin to G. *saugen* < IE. *seuk-, seug-* < base **seu-,* damp, juice, whence SUP[1], L. *sucus,* juice, *sugere,* to suck] 1. *a*) to draw (liquid) into the mouth by creating a vacuum or partial vacuum with the lips, cheeks, and tongue *b*) to draw up (water, oil, etc.) by the action of a pump 2. to take up or in by or as by sucking; absorb, inhale, etc. [*to* suck *air into the lungs*] 3. to suck liquid from (a breast, fruit, etc.) 4. to hold (candy, ice, etc.) in the mouth and lick so as to dissolve and consume 5. to place (the thumb, a pencil, etc.) in the mouth and draw on as if sucking 6. to bring into a specified state by sucking [*to* suck *an orange dry*] —*vi.* 1. to draw in water, air, etc. by creating a partial vacuum 2. to suck milk from the breast or udder 3. to make a sound or movement of sucking 4. to draw in air instead of liquid: said of a faulty pump —*n.* 1. the act of sucking; sucking action or force; suction 2. a sound or movement of sucking 3. *a*) something drawn in by sucking *b*) [Colloq.] the amount sucked at one time; sip —**suck in** 1. to compress and pull inward [*to* suck in *one's belly*] 2. [Slang] to take advantage of; swindle, etc. —**suck up to** [Slang] to flatter or fawn upon ingratiatingly

suck·er (suk*ʹ*ər) *n.* 1. a person or thing that sucks ☆2. a soft-rayed, freshwater, bony fish (genus *Catostomus*) with a mouth adapted for sucking 3. a part or device used for sucking; specif., *a*) a pipe or conduit through which something is sucked *b*) the piston or piston valve of a suction pump *c*) an organ used by the leech, fluke, remora, etc. for sucking or holding fast to a surface by suction ☆4. *same as* LOLLIPOP ☆5. [Slang] *a*) a person easily cheated or taken in; dupe *b*) a person highly susceptible to the attractions of something specified 6. *Bot. a*) *same as* HAUSTORIUM *b*) a subordinate shoot springing from a bud on the root or stem of a plant —*vt.* 1. to remove suckers, or shoots, from ☆2. [Slang] to make a sucker or dupe of; trick —*vi.* to bear suckers, or shoots

suck·er·fish (-fish*ʹ*) *n., pl.* **-fish'**, **-fish'es:** see FISH[2] *same as* REMORA

suck·fish (-fish*ʹ*) *n., pl.* **-fish'**, **-fish'es:** see FISH[2] ☆a small clingfish (*Gobiesox maeandricus*) of the Pacific coast

sucking louse *same as* LOUSE (*n.* 1 *a*)

suck·le (suk*ʹ*'l) *vt.* **-led, -ling** [ME. *sokelen,* prob. backformation < *sokelynge,* SUCKLING] 1. to cause to suck at the breast or udder; nurse 2. to bring up; rear; foster —*vi.* to suck at the breast

suck·ler (-lər) *n.* 1. an animal that suckles its young; mammal 2. *same as* SUCKLING

suck·ling (-liŋ) *n.* [ME. *sokelynge:* see SUCK & -LING[1]] an unweaned child or young animal

Suck·ling (suk*ʹ*liŋ), **Sir John** 1609–42; Eng. poet

su·crase (sōō*ʹ*krās) *n.* [< Fr. *sucre,* SUGAR + -ASE] *same as* INVERTASE

Su·cre (sōō*ʹ*kre) city in SC Bolivia; legal capital & seat of the judiciary (cf. LA PAZ): pop. 58,000

su·cre (sōō*ʹ*kre) *n.* [AmSp., after ff.] the monetary unit of Ecuador: see MONETARY UNITS, table

Su·cre (sōō*ʹ*kre), **An·to·nio Jo·sé de** (än tō*ʹ*nyō hō se*ʹ* de) 1795–1830; S. American liberator; 1st president of Bolivia (1826–28)

su·crose (sōō*ʹ*krōs) *n.* [< Fr. *sucre,* SUGAR + -OSE[1]] *Chem.* pure, crystalline sugar, $C_{12}H_{22}O_{11}$, extracted from sugar cane or sugar beets and consisting of glucose and fructose joined together in the molecule

suc·tion (suk*ʹ*shən) *n.* [L. *suctio* < *suctus,* pp. of *sugere,* to SUCK] 1. the act or process of sucking 2. the production of a vacuum or partial vacuum in a cavity or over a surface so that the external atmospheric pressure forces the surrounding fluid into the cavity or causes something to adhere to the surface 3. the sucking force created in this way —*adj.* 1. causing suction 2. operating by suction

suction pump a pump that draws liquid up by suction created by pistons fitted with valves

suc·to·ri·al (suk tôr*ʹ*ē əl) *adj.* [< ModL. *suctorius* < L. *suctus* (see SUCTION) + -AL] 1. of or adapted for sucking or suction 2. having organs used for sucking 3. feeding by sucking fluids

Su·dan (sōō dan*ʹ*) 1. vast semiarid region in NC Africa, south of the Sahara, extending from the Atlantic to the Red Sea: see SAHARA, map 2. country in the E part of this region, south of Egypt: formerly, a Brit. & Egyptian condominium called *Anglo-Egyptian Sudan:* 967,500 sq. mi.; pop. 14,770,000; cap. Khartoum —**Su'da·nese'** (-də nēz*ʹ*) *adj., n., pl.* **-nese'**

☆**Sudan grass** [after prec., where it is cultivated] a tall annual grass (*Sorghum sudanense*) grown for summer pasture and hay

Su·dan·ic (sōō dan*ʹ*ik) *adj.* 1. of or pertaining to Sudan 2. designating or of either of two branches (**Eastern Sudanic** and **Central Sudanic**) of the Chari-Nile subfamily of languages, including various languages spoken in Sudan —*n.* any Sudanic language

su·dar·i·um (sōō der*ʹ*ē əm, syōō-) *n., pl.* **-i·a** (-ə) [L. < *sudor,* SWEAT] in ancient Rome, a cloth for wiping sweat from the face: also **su·da·ry** (sōō*ʹ*də rē), *pl.* **-ries**

su·da·to·ri·um (sōō*ʹ*də tôr*ʹ*ē əm, syōō*ʹ*-) *n., pl.* **-ri·a** (-ə) [L., neut. of *sudatorius:* see ff.] a heated room, as in a bath, for inducing sweating

su·da·to·ry (sōō*ʹ*də tôr*ʹ*ē, syōō*ʹ*-) *adj.* [L. *sudatorius* < *sudor,* SWEAT] 1. of a sudatorium 2. *same as* SUDORIFIC —*n., pl.* **-ries** *same as* SUDATORIUM

Sud·bur·y (sud*ʹ*ber*ʹ*ē, -bər ē) city in SE Ontario, Canada: pop. 85,000

sudd (sud) *n.* [Ar.] floating masses of weeds, reeds, etc. that often obstruct navigation on the White Nile

sud·den (sud*ʹ*'n) *adj.* [ME. *sodain* < OFr. < VL. **subitanus,* for L. *subitaneus,* sudden, extended < *subitus,* pp. of *subire,* to go stealthily < *sub-,* under + *ire,* to go or come (see YEAR)] 1. *a*) happening or coming unexpectedly; not foreseen or prepared for *b*) sharp or abrupt [*a* sudden *turn in the road*] 2. done, coming, or taking place quickly or abruptly; hasty —**all of a sudden** suddenly; unexpectedly —**sud'den·ly** *adv.* —**sud'den·ness** *n.* SYN.—**sudden** implies extreme quickness or hastiness and, usually, unexpectedness [*a* sudden *outburst of temper*]; **precipitate** adds the implication of rashness or lack of due deliberation [*a* precipitate *decision*]; **abrupt** implies a breaking in or off suddenly and, hence, suggests the lack of any warning or a curtness, lack of ceremony, etc. [*an* abrupt *dismissal*]; **impetuous** implies vehement impulsiveness or extreme eagerness [*an* impetuous *suitor*] —ANT. **deliberate**

sudden death *Sports* an extra period added to a tied game, the game ending as soon as one side scores: usually **sudden-death overtime**

Su·der·mann (zōō*ʹ*dər män*ʹ*; *E.* sōō*ʹ*dər mən), **Her·mann** (her*ʹ*män*ʹ*) 1857–1928; Ger. playwright & novelist

Su·de·ten (sōō dāt*ʹ*'n; *G.* zōō dā*ʹ*tən) 1. *same as* SUDETES MOUNTAINS 2. *same as* SUDETENLAND —*n., pl.* **-tens, -ten** a native or inhabitant of the Sudetenland —*adj.* 1. of the Sudetenland or its people 2. of the Sudetes Mountains

Su·de·ten·land (-land*ʹ*; *G.* -länt*ʹ*) region in the Sudetes Mountains, N Czechoslovakia: annexed by Germany, 1938; returned to Czechoslovakia, 1945: c. 8,900 sq. mi.

Su·de·tes Mountains (sōō dēt*ʹ*ēz) mountain range along the borders of N Czechoslovakia & SW Poland: highest peak, 5,259 ft.: see SILESIA, map

su·dor·if·er·ous (sōō*ʹ*də rif*ʹ*ər əs, syōō*ʹ*-) *adj.* [ModL. *sudoriferus* < L. *sudor* (gen. *sudoris*), SWEAT: see -FEROUS] secreting sweat

su·dor·if·ic (-rif*ʹ*ik) *adj.* [ModL. *sudorificus* < L. *sudor,* SWEAT + *facere,* to make, DO[1]] causing or increasing sweating —*n.* a sudorific drug

Su·dra (sōō*ʹ*dra) *n.* [Sans. *śūdra*] a member of the fourth and lowest Hindu caste, that of menial laborers

suds (sudz) *n.pl.* [prob. (via East Anglian dial.) < MDu. *sudse,* marsh, marsh water: for IE. base see SEETHE] 1. soapy water with a froth or foam on the surface 2. froth or foam ☆3. [Slang] beer or ale —☆*vi.* to produce suds —☆*vt.* [Colloq.] to wash in suds

☆**suds·y** (sud*ʹ*zē) *adj.* **suds'i·er, suds'i·est** full of or like suds or froth; foamy

sue (sōō) *vt.* **sued, su'ing** [ME. *suen* < OFr. *sivre, suir* < VL. **sequere* < L, *sequi,* to follow: see SEQUENT] 1. to appeal to; petition; beseech 2. [Archaic] to be a suitor of; woo 3. *Law a*) to petition (a court) for legal redress *b*) to bring civil action against or prosecute in a court of law in seeking justice or redress of wrongs *c*) to carry (an action) through to its final decision —*vi.* 1. to make an appeal; petition; plead (*for* or *to*) 2. [Archaic] to pay suit; woo 3. to institute legal proceedings in court; bring suit

—*SYN.* see APPEAL —**sue out** to apply for and receive from a court (a writ or other legal process) —**su′er** *n.*

Sue (sü; *E.* sōō), **Eu·gene** (ō zhen′) (born *Marie Joseph Sue*) 1804–57; Fr. novelist

suede, suède (swād) *n.* [Fr. *Suède*, Sweden, in *gants de Suède*, Swedish gloves] 1. tanned leather of calf, kid, cowhide, etc., with the flesh side buffed into a nap 2. a kind of cloth made to resemble this: also **suede cloth**

sued·ed, suèd·ed (-id) *adj.* made to resemble suede

su·et (sōō′it, syōō′-) *n.* [ME. dim. < Anglo-Fr. *sue* < OFr. *sieu, seu* < L. *sebum,* fat: see SOAP] the hard fat deposited around the kidneys and loins of cattle and sheep: used in cooking and as a source of tallow —**su′et·y** *adj.*

Sue·to·ni·us (swi tō′nē əs) (*Gaius Suetonius Tranquillus*) 69?–140? A.D.; Rom. biographer & historian

Su·ez (sōō ez′, sōō′ez) 1. seaport in NE Egypt, on the Suez Canal: pop. 203,000 2. **Gulf of,** N arm of the Red Sea: c. 180 mi. long 3. **Isthmus of,** strip of land connecting Asia & Africa, between the Mediterranean & the Gulf of Suez: narrowest point, 72 mi.

Suez Canal ship canal across the Isthmus of Suez, joining the Mediterranean & the Gulf of Suez: c.107 mi. long

suf- (suf) *same as* SUB-: used before *f*

suf., suff. suffix

suf·fer (suf′ər) *vt.* [ME. *suffren* < Anglo-Fr. *suffrir* < OFr. *sofrir* < VL. *sufferire,* for L. *sufferre,* to undergo, endure < *sub-,* under + *ferre,* to BEAR[1] 1. to undergo (something painful or unpleasant, as injury, grief, a loss, etc.); endure; bear; be afflicted with 2. to undergo or experience (any process, esp. change) 3. to allow; permit; tolerate 4. to bear up under; endure:

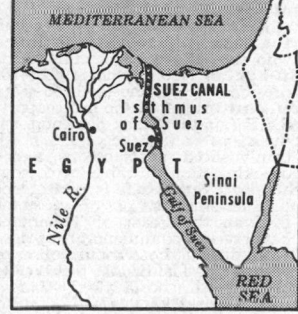

MEDITERRANEAN SEA

SUEZ CANAL

Isthmus of Suez

Cairo

Suez

EGYPT

Sinai Peninsula

Nile R.

Gulf of Suez

RED SEA

SUEZ CANAL

now chiefly in negative constructions [he could not *suffer* opposition] —*vi.* 1. to experience pain, harm, injury, loss, etc. 2. to be punished; receive a penalty, esp. death 3. [Archaic] to tolerate or endure evil, injury, etc. —*SYN.* see BEAR[1], LET[1] —**suf′fer·er** *n.*

suf·fer·a·ble (-ə b'l) *adj.* that can be suffered, endured, or allowed —**suf′fer·a·bly** *adv.*

suf·fer·ance (suf′ər əns, suf′rəns) *n.* [ME. < Anglo-Fr. *souffrance* < OFr. < LL.(Ec.) *sufferentia* < L. *sufferens,* prp.: see SUFFER] 1. the power or capacity to endure or tolerate pain, distress, etc. 2. consent, permission, or sanction implied by failure to interfere or prohibit; toleration 3. [Archaic] suffering —**on sufferance** allowed or tolerated but not supported or encouraged

suf·fer·ing (suf′ər in, suf′rin) *n.* 1. the bearing or undergoing of pain, distress, or injury 2. something suffered; pain, distress, or injury —*SYN.* see DISTRESS

suf·fice (sə fis′, -fiz′) *vi.* **-ficed′, -fic′ing** [ME. *suffice* < stem of OFr. *soufire* < L. *sufficere,* to provide, suffice < *sub-,* under + *facere,* to make, DO[1] 1. to be enough; be sufficient or adequate 2. [Obs.] to be competent or able —*vt.* [Archaic] to be enough for; meet the needs of; satisfy

suf·fi·cien·cy (sə fish′ən sē) *n.* 1. sufficient means, ability, or resources; specif., *a*) an ample amount or quantity (*of* what is needed) *b*) enough wealth or income 2. the state or quality of being sufficient or adequate; adequacy

suf·fi·cient (-'nt) *adj.* [ME. < L. *sufficiens,* prp. of *sufficere:* see SUFFICE] 1. as much as is needed; equal to what is specified or required; enough 2. [Archaic] competent; well-qualified; able —**suf·fi′cient·ly** *adv.*

SYN.—**sufficient** and **enough** agree in describing that which satisfies a requirement exactly and is neither more nor less in amount than is needed [a word to the wise is *sufficient, enough* food for a week]; **adequate** suggests the meeting of an acceptable (sometimes barely so) standard of fitness or suitability [the supporting players were *adequate*] —ANT. **deficient, inadequate**

sufficient condition 1. *Logic* a consequent whose validity implies the validity of the antecedent 2. *Philos.* an antecedent of an event or proposition that is always present but is not the only or indispensable antecedent

suf·fix (suf′iks; *also, for v.,* sə fiks′) *n.* [ModL. *suffixum* < neut. of L. *suffixus,* pp. of *suffigere,* to fasten on beneath < *sub-,* under + *figere,* to FIX] 1. a syllable, group of syllables, or word added at the end of a word or word base to change its meaning, give it grammatical function, or form a new word (Ex.: *-ish* in *smallish, -ed* in *walked, -ness* in *darkness*) 2. anything added to the end of something else —*vt.* to add as a suffix —**suf′fix·al** *adj.* —**suf·fix′ion** *n.*

suf·flate (sə flāt′) *vt.* **-flat′ed, -flat′ing** [< L. *sufflatus,* pp. of *sufflare* < *sub-,* under + *-flare,* to BLOW[1] *obs. var. of* INFLATE —**suf·fla′tion** *n.*

suf·fo·cate (suf′ə kāt′) *vt.* **-cat′ed, -cat′ing** [< L. *suffocatus,* pp. of *suffocare,* to choke < *sub-,* under + *fauces,* gullet, throat: see FAUCES] 1. to kill by cutting off the supply of oxygen to the lungs, gills, etc. 2. to hinder the free breathing of; deprive of fresh air; stifle; choke 3. to smother, suppress, extinguish, etc. by or as by cutting off the supply of air —*vi.* 1. to die by being suffocated 2. to be unable to breathe freely; choke; stifle; smother 3. to be unable to develop properly as because of a repressive or dulling environment —**suf′fo·cat′ing·ly** *adv.* —**suf′fo·ca′tion** *n.* —**suf′fo·ca′tive** *adj.*

Suf·folk (suf′ək) county in E England: divided into *a*) **East Suffolk** 872 sq. mi.; pop. 357,000 *b*) **West Suffolk** 611 sq. mi.; pop. 138,000 —**n.** 1. any of a breed of hornless mutton sheep having a black face and feet: also **Suffolk Down** 2. any of a breed of English draft horses having a small, heavy body and chestnut-colored coat

suf·fra·gan (suf′rə gən) *n.* [ME. < MFr. < ML.(Ec.) *suffraganus* < L. *suffragari,* to vote for, support, favor < *suffragium,* a ballot: see ff.] 1. a bishop appointed to assist the bishop of a diocese 2. any bishop in his capacity as a subordinate to his archbishop —*adj.* 1. designating or of such a bishop 2. subordinate to a larger see

suf·frage (suf′rij) *n.* [ME. < MFr. < ML.(Ec.) < L. *suffragium,* a decision, vote, suffrage < *sub-* (see SUB-) + *fragor,* loud applause, orig., din, a crashing < IE. base **bhreĝ-,* to crash, BREAK[1] 1. a short prayer of intercession or supplication 2. a vote or voting; esp., a vote in favor of some candidate or issue ☆3. the right to vote, esp. in political elections; franchise

suf·fra·gette (suf′rə jet′) *n.* [< prec. + -ETTE] a woman who militantly advocates the right of women to vote —**suf′fra·get′tism** *n.*

suf·fra·gist (suf′rə jist) *n.* a person who believes in extending political suffrage, esp. to women

suf·fru·ti·cose (sə frōōt′i kōs′) *adj.* [ModL. *suffruticosus* < L. *sub-* (see SUB-) + *fruticosus,* FRUTICOSE] *Bot.* having a woody base that persists but branches that die after flowering: also **suf·fru·tes·cent** (suf′rōō tes′'nt)

suf·fu·mi·gate (sə fyōō′mə gāt′) *vt.* **-gat′ed, -gat′ing** [< pp. of L. *suffumigare:* see SUB- & FUMIGATE] to fumigate from below —**suf·fu′mi·ga′tion** *n.*

suf·fuse (sə fyōōz′) *vt.* **-fused′, -fus′ing** [< L. *suffusus,* pp. of *suffundere,* to pour beneath, diffuse beneath or upon < *sub-,* under + *fundere,* to pour: see FOUND[2] to overspread so as to fill with a glow, color, fluid, etc.: said of light, a blush, air, etc. —**suf·fu′sion** (-fyōō′zhən) *n.* —**suf·fu′sive** (-siv) *adj.*

Su·fi (sōō′fē) *n.* [Ar. *ṣūfī,* ascetic, lit., (a man) of wool < *ṣūf,* wool] a member of an Islamic group practicing a form of mysticism originated in Persia —**Su′fism** (-fiz′m) *n.*

sug- (sug) *same as* SUB-: used before *g*

sug·ar (shoog′ər) *n.* [ME. *sucre* < OFr. < OSp. *azúcar* or OIt. *zucchero,* both < Ar. *sukkar* < Per. *šakar* < Sans. *śarkarā,* akin to *śarkarah,* a pebble] 1. any of a class of sweet, soluble, crystalline carbohydrates, as the disaccharides (sucrose, lactose, and maltose) and the monosaccharides (glucose and fructose) 2. sucrose, esp. when prepared as a crystalline or powdered substance from sugar cane and sugar beets and used as a food and sweetening agent 3. a sugar bowl, specif. as forming a set with a creamer 4. flattery; honeyed words 5. *clipped form of* SUGAR DIABETES 6. [Colloq.] darling; sweetheart 7. [Slang] money —*vt.* 1. to mix, cover, sprinkle, or sweeten with sugar 2. *clipped form of* SUGARCOAT —*vi.* ☆1. to form sugar ☆2. to boil down maple syrup to form maple sugar (usually with *off*) —**sug′ar·like′** *adj.*

sugar apple *same as* SWEETSOP

sugar beet a variety or cultivar of the common beet (*Beta vulgaris*) having a root with white flesh and a high sugar content, grown commercially as a source of sugar

☆**sug·ar·ber·ry** (-ber′ē) *n., pl.* **-ries** *same as* HACKBERRY

sug·ar·bush (-boosh′) *n.* a grove of sugar maples

sugar cane a very tall, perennial, tropical grass (*Saccharum officinarum*) cultivated as the main source of sugar

sug·ar·coat (-kōt′) *vt.* 1. to cover or coat with sugar 2. to make (something disagreeable) seem more acceptable or less unpleasant, as by using flattery, euphemism, etc.

☆**sug·ar·cured** (-kyoord′) *adj.* treated with a pickling preparation of sugar, salt, and nitrate or nitrite, as ham, bacon, etc.

☆**sugar daddy** [Slang] a rich, esp. older, man who lavishes gifts on young women in return for their favors

sugar diabetes *popular term for* DIABETES MELLITUS

sug·ar·house (-hous′) *n.* a place where sugar is processed; esp., a building where maple sap is boiled for producing maple syrup and sugar

SUGAR CANE

sug·ar·less (-lis) *adj.* having no sugar; specif., prepared with synthetic sweeteners

sugar loaf **1.** a conical mass of crystallized sugar **2.** a similarly shaped hill, mountain, etc.

Sugar Loaf Mountain granite mountain at the entrance to the harbor of Rio de Janeiro: 1,296 ft.

☆**sugar maple** an E. N. American maple (*Acer saccharum*), valued for its hard wood and for its sap, which yields maple syrup and maple sugar

sugar of lead *same as* LEAD ACETATE

sugar of milk *same as* LACTOSE

☆**sugar pine** a giant pine (*Pinus lambertiana*) of the Pacific coast, with soft, reddish-brown wood, large cones, sugarlike resin, and needles in groups of five

sug·ar·plum (-plum′) *n.* **1.** a round or oval piece of sugary candy; bonbon ☆**2.** *same as* JUNEBERRY

sug·ar·tit (-tit′) *n.* cloth tied around a bit of sugar to form a nipplelike pacifier for a baby

sugar tongs small tongs for serving lumps of sugar

sug·ar·y (shoog′ər ē, shoog′rē) *adj.* **1.** of, like, or containing sugar; sweet, granular, etc. **2.** cloyingly or mawkishly sweet or sentimental —**sug′ar·i·ness** *n.*

sug·gest (səg jest′; *also, & Brit. usually,* sə jest′) *vt.* [< L. *suggestus,* pp. of *suggerere,* to carry or lay under, furnish < *sub-,* under + *gerere,* to carry] **1.** to mention as something to think over, act on, etc.; bring to the mind for consideration **2.** to bring or call to mind through association of ideas [*objects suggested* by the shapes of clouds] **3.** to propose as a possibility [to *suggest* a course of study] **4.** to show indirectly; imply; intimate [a silence that *suggested* agreement] **5.** to serve as a motive for; prompt [a success that *suggested* further attempts] —**sug·gest′er** *n.* **SYN.**—**suggest** implies a putting of something into the mind either intentionally, as by way of a proposal [I *suggest* you leave now], or unintentionally, as through association of ideas [the smell of ether *suggests* a hospital]; **imply** stresses the putting into the mind of something involved, but not openly expressed, in a word, a remark, etc. and suggests the need for inference [his answer *implied* a refusal]; **hint** connotes faint or indirect suggestion that is, however, intended to be understood [he *hinted* that he would come]; **intimate** suggests a making known obliquely by a very slight hint [he only dared to *intimate* his feelings]; **insinuate** implies the subtle hinting of something disagreeable or of that which one lacks the courage to say outright [are you *insinuating* that she is dishonest?]

sug·gest·i·ble (-jes′tə b'l) *adj.* **1.** readily influenced by suggestion; often, specif., susceptible to suggestion through hypnosis **2.** that can be suggested —**sug·gest′i·bil′i·ty** *n.*

sug·ges·tion (-jes′chən) *n.* [ME. < OFr. *suggestioun* < L. *suggestio*] **1.** a suggesting or being suggested **2.** something suggested **3.** the process by which an idea is brought to the mind through its connection or association with an idea already in the mind **4.** a faint hint or indication; small amount; trace [a *suggestion* of boredom in her tone] **5.** *Psychol. a)* the inducing of an idea that is accepted or acted on readily and uncritically, as in hypnosis *b)* the idea induced or the stimulus used to induce it

sug·ges·tive (-jes′tiv) *adj.* **1.** that suggests or tends to suggest thoughts or ideas **2.** tending to suggest something considered improper or indecent; risqué —**sug·ges′tive·ly** *adv.* —**sug·ges′tive·ness** *n.*

su·i·ci·dal (soo′ə sīd′'l, syoo′-) *adj.* **1.** of, involving, or leading to suicide **2.** having an urge to commit suicide **3.** rash to the point of being very dangerous —**su′i·ci′dal·ly** *adv.*

su·i·cide (soo′ə sīd′, syoo′-) *n.* [L. *sui,* of oneself (< IE. **sewe-,* reflexive pronoun < **se-,* apart, whence OE. *swæs,* own) + -CIDE] **1.** the act of killing oneself intentionally **2.** ruin of one's interests or prospects through one's own actions, policies, etc. **3.** a person who commits or tries to commit suicide —*vi.* **-cid′ed, -cid′ing** [Rare] to commit suicide

su·i ge·ne·ris (soo′ē jen′ər is, soo′ī) [L., lit., of his (or her or its) own kind] altogether unique; unduplicated

‡**su·i ju·ris** (joor′is) [L., of one's own right] *Law* legally competent to manage one's own affairs, because of legal age and sound mind

su·int (soo′int, syoo′-; swint) *n.* [Fr. < *suer,* to sweat < L. *sudare:* see SWEAT] the natural grease found in sheep's wool: a source of potash

Suisse (swēs) *Fr. name of* SWITZERLAND

suit (soot, syoot) *n.* [ME. *sute,* a pursuit, action of suing, garb, set of garments, sequence < OFr. *suite* < VL. **sequita,* fem. pp. of *sequere,* to follow < L. *sequi,* to follow: see SEQUENT] **1.** *a)* a set of clothes to be worn together; now, esp., a coat and trousers (or skirt), and sometimes a vest, usually all of the same material *b)* any complete outfit [a *suit* of armor] **2.** a group of similar things forming a set or series; specif., any of the four sets of thirteen playing cards each (*spades, clubs, hearts,* and *diamonds*) that together make up a pack **3.** formerly, the act or obligation of following or attending a feudal court **4.** action to secure justice in a court of law; attempt to recover a right or claim through legal action **5.** *a)* an act of suing, pleading, or requesting *b)* a petition **6.** the act of wooing; courtship —*vt.* **1.** to meet the requirements of; be right for or appropriate to; befit **2.** to make right or appropriate; fit; adapt **3.** to please; satisfy [anything that *suits* his fancy] **4.** to furnish with clothes, esp.

with a suit —*vi.* **1.** [Archaic] to correspond or harmonize (usually with *to* or *with*) **2.** to be fit, suitable, convenient, or satisfactory —**bring suit** to institute legal action; sue —**follow suit 1.** to play a card of the same suit as the card led **2.** to follow the example set —**suit oneself** to act according to one's own wishes

suit·a·ble (soot′ə b'l, syoot′-) *adj.* that suits a given purpose, occasion, condition, propriety, etc.; fitting; appropriate; apt —**SYN.** see FIT[1] —**suit′a·bil′i·ty, suit′a·ble·ness** *n.* —**suit′a·bly** *adv.*

suit·case (-kās′) *n.* a case for carrying clothes, etc. when traveling, esp. one that is more or less rigid and rectangular and that opens into two hinged compartments

suite (swēt; *for 2 b, occas.* soot, syoot) *n.* [Fr.: see SUIT] **1.** a group of attendants or servants; train; retinue; staff **2.** a set or series of related things; specif., *a)* a group of connected rooms used as a unit, such as an apartment *b)* a set of pieces of matched furniture for a given room [a bedroom *suite*] **3.** *Music a)* an early form of instrumental composition consisting of a series of dances in the same related keys *b)* a modern instrumental composition in a number of movements

suit·ing (soot′iŋ, syoot′-) *n.* cloth used for making suits

suit·or (soot′ər, syoot′-) *n.* [ME. *sutere* < Anglo-Fr. *seutor* < L. *secutor* < *secutus,* pp. of *sequi,* to follow: see SEQUENT] **1.** a person who requests, petitions, or entreats **2.** a person who sues at law **3.** a man courting or wooing a woman

Su·kar·no (soo kär′nō) 1902?–70; Indonesian statesman; president of Indonesia (1945–67)

Su·khu·mi (sookh′oo mi) seaport & resort in the Georgian S.S.R., on the Black Sea: pop. 64,000

☆**su·ki·ya·ki** (soo′kē yä′kē) *n.* [Jap.] a Japanese dish of thinly sliced meat, onions, and other vegetables cooked quickly, often at table, with soy sauce, sake, sugar, etc.

Suk·kot, Suk·koth (soo kōt′, sook′ōs) *n.* [Heb. *sukkōth,* lit., tabernacles, pl. of *sukkāh,* orig., booth] a Jewish festival, the Feast of Tabernacles, celebrating the fall harvest and commemorating the desert wandering of the Jews during the Exodus: observed from the 15th to the 22d day of Tishri: also **Suk·kos** (sook′ōs)

Su·la·we·si (soo′lä wä′sē) *Indonesian name of* CELEBES

sul·cate (sul′kāt) *adj.* [L. *sulcatus,* pp. of *sulcare,* to furrow < *sulcus,* a furrow < IE. base **swelk-,* to pull, whence OE. *sulh,* a furrow] *Biol.* having deep, parallel furrows or grooves; grooved; fluted: also **sul′cat·ed** —**sul·ca′tion** *n.*

sul·cus (sul′kəs) *n., pl.* **-ci** (-sī) [L.: see prec.] a groove or furrow; esp., *Anat.* any of the shallow grooves separating the convolutions of the brain

Su·lei·man (I) (soo′lä män′) 1494?–1566; sultan of the Ottoman Empire (1520–66): called *the Magnificent*

sulf- (sulf) *a combining form meaning* of or containing sulfur

sul·fa (sul′fa) *adj.* [contr. < SULFANILAMIDE] designating or of a family of drugs of the sulfanilamide type, used in combating certain bacterial infections

sul·fa·di·a·zine (sul′fə dī′ə zēn′, -zin) *n.* [prec. + DIAZINE] a sulfa drug, $C_{10}H_{10}N_4O_2S$, used in treating certain pneumococcal, streptococcal, and staphylococcal infections

sul·fa·gua·ni·dine (-gwä′nə dēn′, -din) *n.* [SULFA + GUANIDINE] a sulfa drug, $C_7H_{10}N_4O_2S·H_2O$, formerly used in the treatment of various intestinal infections

sul·fa·mer·a·zine (-mer′ə zēn′) *n.* [SULFA + -*mer* (as in ISOMER) + AZINE] a sulfa drug, $C_{11}H_{12}N_4O_2S$, a methyl derivative of sulfadiazine that is more rapidly absorbed

sul·fa·nil·a·mide (-nil′ə mīd′, -mid) *n.* [< ff. + AMIDE] a white crystalline compound, $C_6H_8N_2O_2S$, formerly used in treating gonorrhea, streptococcal infections, etc.: a synthetic coal-tar product

sul·fa·nil·ic acid (-ik) [SULF- + ANIL(INE) + -IC] a colorless crystalline acid, $C_6H_7O_3NS$, prepared by heating aniline with sulfuric acid: used in dyes and medicines

sulf·ar·se·nide (sul fär′sə nīd′) *n.* a double salt of sulfide and arsenide

sul·fate (sul′fāt) *n.* [Fr. < L. *sulphur,* sulfur + Fr. -*ate,* -ATE[2]] a salt or ester of sulfuric acid —*vt.* **-fat·ed, -fat·ing 1.** to treat with sulfuric acid or a sulfate **2.** to convert into a sulfate **3.** to cause a deposit of lead sulfate to form on (the negative plates of a storage battery) —*vi.* to become sulfated —**sul·fa′tion** *n.*

sul·fa·thi·a·zole (sul′fə thī′ə zōl′) *n.* [SULFA + THIAZOLE] a sulfa drug, $C_9H_9N_3O_2S_2$, formerly used to treat certain infections

sul·fide (sul′fīd) *n.* a compound of sulfur with another element or a radical

sul·fi·nyl (sul′fə nil) *n.* [SULF- + -IN[1] + -YL] the bivalent sulfur radical SO, present in certain organic compounds

sul·fite (sul′fīt) *n.* a salt or ester of sulfurous acid

sul·fo- (sul′fō, -fə) *a combining form meaning:* **1.** containing sulfur, esp. bivalent sulfur **2.** replacing oxygen with sulfur **3.** having the sulfonic or sulfonyl group

sul·fon·a·mide (sul fän′ə mīd′, -mid) *n.* [SULFON(YL) + AMIDE] any of the sulfa drugs, as sulfadiazine, containing the monovalent radical -SO₂NH₂

sul·fo·nate (sul′fə nāt′) *n.* a salt or ester of a sulfonic acid —*vt.* **-nat′ed, -nat′ing** to introduce the sulfonic group into (an aromatic hydrocarbon) by treating with sulfuric acid

sul·fone (sul′fōn) *n.* [G. *sulfon* < *sulfur,* sulfur] any of a group of organic compounds containing the radical SO₂

the sulfur atom of which is linked chemically with a carbon atom of each of two alkyl groups

sul·fon·ic (sul fän′ik) *adj.* [< prec. + -IC] designating or of the univalent acid group SO₃H

sulfonic acid any of numerous organic acids containing the sulfonic group SO₃H, and derived from sulfuric acid by the replacement of an OH group: used in the manufacture of dyes, drugs, phenols, etc.

sul·fo·ni·um (sul fō′nē əm) *n.* [ModL. < SULF(O)- + (AMM)ONIUM] a univalent electropositive radical made up of three alkyl radicals and one atom of sulfur, as the triethyl sulfonium radical (C₂H₅)₃S—

sul·fon·meth·ane (sul′fōn meth′ān) *n.* [SULFON(E) + METHANE] a colorless, crystalline compound, C₇H₁₆O₄S₂, used in medicine as a soporific and hypnotic

sul·fo·nyl (sul′fə nil) *n.* [SULFON(E) + -YL] the bivalent radical SO₂

sulf·ox·ide (sul fäk′sīd) *n.* [SULF(O)- + OXIDE] the bivalent radical SO

sul·fur (sul′fər) *n.* [ME. *sulphur* < L.] 1. a pale-yellow, nonmetallic chemical element found in crystalline or amorphous form: it burns with a blue flame and a stifling odor and is used in vulcanizing rubber, making matches, paper, gunpowder, insecticides, sulfuric acid, etc.: symbol, S; at. no., 16; sp. gr., 2.07; melt. pt., 118.7°C; boil. pt., 444.6°C 2. any of numerous small to medium-sized butterflies (family Pieridae) having yellow or orange wings with dark borders 3. a greenish-yellow color —*vt. same as* SULFURIZE

sul·fu·rate (sul′fyoo rāt′, -fə-) *vt.* -rat′ed, -rat′ing [L. *sulphuratus*] *same as* SULFURIZE —**sul′fu·ra′tion** *n.*

sul·fur-bot·tom (-bät′əm) *n. same as* BLUE WHALE

sulfur dioxide a heavy, colorless, suffocating gas, SO₂, easily liquefied and used as a bleach, disinfectant, refrigerant, preservative, etc.

sul·fu·re·ous (sul fyoor′ē əs) *adj.* [L. *sulfureus*] 1. of, like, or containing sulfur 2. greenish-yellow

sul·fu·ret (sul′fyoo rit; *for v.* -ret′) *n.* [ModL. *sulphuretum*] *same as* SULFIDE —*vt.* -ret′ed *or* -ret′ted, -ret′ing *or* -ret′ting *same as* SULFURIZE

sul·fu·ric (sul fyoor′ik) *adj.* [Fr. *sulfurique*] 1. of or containing sulfur, esp. sulfur with a valence of six 2. of or derived from sulfuric acid

sulfuric acid an oily, colorless, corrosive liquid, H₂SO₄, used in making dyes, paints, explosives, fertilizers, etc.

sul·fu·rize (sul′fyoo rīz′, -fə-) *vt.* -rized′, -riz′ing [Fr. *sulfuriser*: see SULFUR & -IZE] to combine, treat, or impregnate with sulfur or a compound of sulfur, esp. with sulfur dioxide fumes in bleaching or disinfecting — **sul′fu·ri·za′tion** *n.*

sul·fu·rous (sul′fər əs; *for 1, usually* sul fyoor′əs) *adj.* [L. *sulphurosus*] 1. of or containing sulfur, esp. sulfur with a valence of four 2. like burning sulfur in odor, color, etc. 3. of or suggesting the fires of hell; infernal; hellish 4. violently emotional; heated; fiery —**sul′fu·rous·ly** *adv.* —**sul′fu·rous·ness** *n.*

sulfurous acid a colorless acid, H₂SO₃, known only in the form of its salts or in aqueous solution and used as a chemical reagent, a bleach, in medicine, etc.

sul·fur·y (sul′fər ē) *adj.* of or like sulfur

sul·fur·yl (sul′fər il, -fyoor il) *n. same as* SULFONYL

sulk (sulk) *vi.* [back-formation < ff.] to be sulky —*n.* 1. [*often pl.*] a sulky mood or state (with *the*) 2. a sulky person —**in a sulk** sulky

sulk·y (sul′kē) *adj.* sulk′i·er, sulk′i·est [prob. < OE. *solcen* (in comp.), idle, sluggish, pp. of *-seolcan*, to become slack < IE. base **selǵ-*, to let go, let loose, whence Sans. *sarjati*, (he) releases] 1. showing resentment and ill humor by sullen, withdrawn behavior 2. gloomy; dismal; sullen [a *sulky* day] —*n., pl.* sulk′ies [prob. < the *adj.*, in the sense of keeping aloof, because the vehicle seats only one person] a light, two-wheeled, one-horse carriage having a seat for only one person, esp., now, one used in harness races —*SYN.* see SULLEN —**sulk′i·ly** *adv.* —**sulk′i·ness** *n.*

Sul·la (sul′ə) (*Lucius Cornelius Sulla Felix*) 138?-78 B.C.; Rom. general; dictator of Rome (82-79)

sul·lage (sul′ij) *n.* [prob. < Fr. *souiller*, to SULLY + -AGE] 1. filth or refuse; sewage 2. silt or sediment deposited by running water 3. *Metallurgy* scoria on the surface of molten metal in a ladle

sul·len (sul′ən) *adj.* [ME. *solein*, alone, solitary < VL. **solanus*, alone < L. *solus*, alone, SOLE²] 1. showing resentment and ill humor by morose, unsociable withdrawal; sulky; glum 2. gloomy; dismal; sad; depressing 3. somber; dull [*sullen* colors] 4. slow-moving; sluggish 5. [Obs.] baleful; threatening —**sul′len·ly** *adv.* —**sul′len·ness** *n.* *SYN.*—**sullen** suggests a gloomy, withdrawn silence, usually connoting anger, resentment, or bitterness [the *sullen* prisoners marched along]; **glum** implies a dejected silence resulting from low spirits or a feeling of depression [he listened with a *glum* expression]; **morose** suggests a sour, unsociable glumness [he took a *morose* view of the future]; **surly** suggests a brusque, ill-tempered gruffness [a *surly* answer]; **sulky** suggests a sullenness characterized by petulance and discontent [a *sulky* child] —*ANT.* genial, amiable, good-natured

Sul·li·van (sul′ə vən) 1. Sir **Arthur Seymour,** 1842-1900; Eng. composer: see Sir William GILBERT 2. **John L(aw- rence),** 1858-1918; U.S. prizefighter 3. **Louis Hen·ri** (hen′rē), 1856-1924; U.S. architect

sul·ly (sul′ē) *vt.* -lied, -ly·ing [prob. < OFr. *souiller*: see SOIL¹] to soil, stain, tarnish, or besmirch, now esp. by disgracing —*vi.* [Obs.] to become sullied —*n., pl.* -lies [Archaic] a stain or tarnish; defilement

Sul·ly (sul′ē; *also, for 1,* sü lē′) 1. **duc de,** (*Maximilien de Béthune*) 1560-1641; Fr. statesman 2. **Thomas,** 1783-1872; U.S. painter, born in England

Sul·ly-Pru·dhomme (sü lē prü dôm′), **Re·né Fran·çois Ar·mand** (rə nā′ frän swä′ àr män′) 1839-1907; Fr. poet & critic

sulph- (sulf) *var.,* now *esp. Brit., sp.* of SULF-: for words beginning **sulph-,** see forms under **sulf-**

sul·phur (sul′fər) *n. var.,* now *esp. Brit., sp.* of SULFUR

sul·tan (sul′t'n) *n.* [Fr. < Ar. *sultān,* ruler, prince, orig., dominion] a Moslem ruler; esp. [S-], formerly, the ruler of Turkey

sul·tan·a (sul tan′ə, -tä′nə) *n.* [It., fem. of *sultano* < Ar. *sultān:* see prec.] 1. the wife of a sultan, or the mother, sister, or daughter of a sultan: also **sul·tan·ess** (sul′tən is) 2. a mistress, esp. of a king, prince, etc. 3. *a)* a small, white, seedless grape used for raisins and in wine making *b)* such a raisin

sul·tan·ate (sul′t'n it, -āt′) *n.* 1. the authority, office, or reign of a sultan 2. the land ruled by a sultan

sul·try (sul′trē) *adj.* -tri·er, -tri·est [var. of SWELTRY] 1. oppressively hot and moist; close; sweltering 2. extremely hot; fiery 3. *a)* hot or inflamed, as with passion or lust *b)* suggesting or expressing smoldering passion —**sul′tri·ly** *adv.* —**sul′tri·ness** *n.*

Su·lu (soo′loo) *n.* a member of a Moro tribe of the Sulu Archipelago —**Su·lu′an** *adj.*

su·lu (soo′loo) *n.* [Fijian] a garment similar to a sarong, worn by Melanesians, as in the Fiji Islands

Sulu Archipelago group of islands in the Philippines, southwest of Mindanao: 1,038 sq. mi.; pop. 390,000

Sulu Sea arm of the W Pacific, between the SW Philippines & NE Borneo

sum (sum) *n.* [ME. *somme* < MFr. < L. *summa,* fem. of *summus,* highest, superl. < base of *super:* see SUPER] 1. an amount of money [a *sum* paid in reparation] 2. the whole amount; totality; aggregate [the *sum* of our experience] 3. the gist or a summary of something said, done, etc.: usually in **sum and substance** 4. *a)* the result obtained by adding numbers or quantities; total *b)* a series of numbers to be added together, or any problem in arithmetic *c)* the limit of the sum of the first *n* terms of an infinite series as *n* grows indefinitely *d)* the set containing every element belonging to one or both of two original sets and no other elements *e)* in Boolean algebra, *same as* DISJUNCTION (sense 2) 5. [Archaic] the highest degree; height; summit —*vt.* **summed, sum′ming** 1. to determine the sum of by adding 2. to summarize or review briefly; sum up —*vi.* to get, or come to, a total —**in sum** to put it briefly; in short —**sum up** 1. to add up or collect into a whole or total 2. to review briefly; summarize *SYN.*—**sum** refers to the number or amount obtained by adding individual units [the *sum* of 3 and 5 is 8]; **amount** applies to the result obtained by combining all the sums, quantities, measures, etc. that are involved [he paid the full *amount* of the damages]; **aggregate** refers to the whole group or mass of individual items gathered together [the *aggregate* of his experiences]; **total** stresses the wholeness or inclusiveness of a sum or amount [the collection reached a *total* of $200]

sum- (sum) *same as* SUB-: used before *m*

su·mac, su·mach (shoo′mak, soo′-) *n.* [ME. *sumac* < MFr. < Ar. *summāq*] 1. *a)* any of numerous nonpoisonous plants (genus *Rhus*) of the cashew family, with pinnately compound leaves and large, cone-shaped clusters of hairy, red fruit *b)* the powdered leaves of some of these plants, used in tanning and dyeing *c)* the wood of any of these plants 2. any of several poisonous plants (genus *Toxicodendron*) of the cashew family, as poison ivy, poison sumac, certain Asiatic sumacs yielding Japan wax, etc.

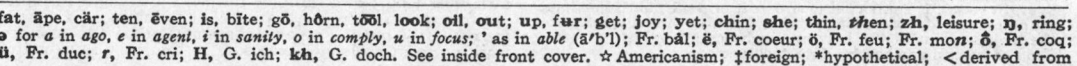

SUMAC

Su·ma·tra (soo mä′trə) large island of Indonesia, just south of the Malay Peninsula: c.165,000 sq. mi.; pop. (with small near-by islands) 15,739,000; chief cities, Medan & Palembang —**Su·ma′tran** *adj., n.*

Sum·ba (soom′bə) island of Indonesia, west of Timor & south of Flores: c.4,300 sq. mi.

Sum·ba·wa (soom bä′wä) island of Indonesia, between Lombok & Flores: c.5,500 sq. mi.

Su·mer (soo′mər) ancient region in the lower valley of the Euphrates River

Su·mer·i·an (soo mir′ē ən, -mer′-) *adj.* 1. of Sumer 2. designating or of the inhabitants of Sumer, an ancient,

non-Semitic people —*n.* **1.** any of the Sumerian people **2.** the language of the Sumerians, of undetermined relationship, extinct since the 3d cent. B.C.: its tablets and inscriptions date back to 4000 B.C.

‡**su·mi** (sōō'mē) *n.* [Jap.] black sticks of carbon mixed with glue, dipped in water and used in a Japanese style of writing and painting

‡**sum·ma** (soom'ə) *n., pl.* **-mae** (-ē) [ML. < L.: see SUM] **1.** a comprehensive treatise, as by a medieval scholastic **2.** anything comprehensive

‡**sum·ma cum lau·de** (soom'ə koom lou'de, sum'ə kum lô'dē) [L.] with the greatest praise: phrase used to signify graduation with the highest honors from a college or university: cf. CUM LAUDE, MAGNA CUM LAUDE

sum·ma·rist (sum'ə rist) *n.* a person who summarizes

sum·ma·rize (sum'ə rīz') *vt.* **-rized', -riz'ing 1.** to make a summary of; state briefly **2.** to be a summary of — **sum'ma·ri·za'tion** *n.* —**sum'ma·riz'er** *n.*

sum·ma·ry (sum'ə rē) *adj.* [ME. < ML. *summarius* < L. *summa,* a SUM] **1.** that presents the substance or general idea in brief form; summarizing; concise; condensed **2.** *a)* prompt and without formality; expeditious *[summary punishment] b)* hasty and arbitrary *[a summary dismissal]* —*n., pl.* **-ries** [L. *summarium:* see the *adj.*] a brief statement or account covering the substance or main points; digest; abridgment; compendium —*SYN.* see ABRIDGMENT —**sum·mar·i·ly** (sə mer'ə lē, sum'ə rə lē) *adv.* —**sum'ma·ri·ness** *n.*

summary court-martial the least formal military court, consisting of one officer, for judging minor offenses

sum·ma·tion (sə mā'shən) *n.* [ModL. *summatio*] **1.** the act or process of summing up, or of finding a total **2.** a total or aggregate **3.** the final summing up of arguments, as in a court trial or debate, before the decision is given —**sum·ma'tion·al** *adj.*

sum·mer¹ (sum'ər) *n.* [ME. *sumer* < OE. *sumor,* akin to G. *sommer* < IE. base **sem-,* summertime, whence Sans. *sáma,* half year, season] **1.** the warmest season of the year, in the North Temperate Zone generally regarded as including the months of June, July, and August: in the astronomical year, that period between the summer solstice and the autumnal equinox **2.** a year as reckoned by this season *[a youth of sixteen summers]* **3.** any period or condition regarded, like summer, as a time of growth, development, fulfillment, perfection, etc. —*adj.* **1.** of or typical of summer **2.** designed for or taking place during the summer *[summer activities]* —*vi.* to pass the summer —*vt.* to keep, feed, or maintain during the summer

sum·mer² (sum'ər) *n.* [ME. < OFr. *somier,* pack horse < LL. *sagmarius,* a pack horse < *sagma,* pack saddle < Gr. *sagma* < base of *sattein,* to stuff] **1.** a large, horizontal, supporting beam or girder **2.** *same as* LINTEL **3.** the capstone of a column supporting an arch or lintel

summer cypress an annual plant (*Kochia scoparia*) of the goosefoot family, cultivated for its brilliant red or purplish foliage in the fall

sum·mer·house (sum'ər hous') *n.* a small, open structure in a garden, park, etc., for providing a shady rest

summer house a house or cottage, as in the country, used during the summer

sum·mer·sault (sum'ər sôlt') *n., vi. var. of* SOMERSAULT

☆**summer sausage** a type of hard, dried and smoked sausage that does not spoil easily

☆**summer school** a session at a school or college during the regular summer vacation

summer solstice the time during the summer when the sun is farthest from the equator: June 21 or 22 in the Northern Hemisphere

☆**summer squash** any of a variety (*Cucurbita pepo melopepo*) of small garden squashes grown in summer and eaten before fully ripe

sum·mer·time (sum'ər tīm') *n.* the season of summer

☆**sum·mer·wood** (-wood') *n.* the last-formed woody portion of the annual growth ring of a shrub or tree, usually containing more fibers and fewer vessels than springwood

sum·mer·y (-ē) *adj.* of, like, or typical of summer

sum·mit (sum'it) *n.* [ME. *sommete* < OFr., dim. of *som,* summit < L. *summum,* highest part < *summus,* highest: see SUM] **1.** the highest point, part, or elevation; top or apex **2.** the highest degree or state; acme ☆**3.** *a)* the highest level of officialdom; specif., in connection with diplomatic negotiations, the level restricted to heads of government *[a meeting at the summit] b)* a conference at the summit —*adj.* ☆of the heads of government *[a summit parley]*

SYN.—**summit** literally refers to the topmost point of a hill or similar elevation and, figuratively, to the highest attainable level, as of achievement; **peak** refers to the highest of a number of high points, as in a mountain range or, figuratively, in a graph; **climax** applies to the highest point, as in interest, force, excitement, etc., in a scale of ascending values; **acme** refers to the highest possible point of perfection in the development or progress of something; **apex** suggests the highest point (literally, of a geometric figure such as a cone; figuratively, of a career, process, etc.) where all ascending lines, courses, etc. ultimately meet; **pinnacle,** in its figurative uses, is equivalent to **summit** or **peak,** but sometimes connotes a giddy or unsteady height; **zenith** literally refers to the highest point in the heavens and hence figuratively suggests fame or success reached by a spectacular rise

sum·mit·ry (sum'i trē) *n., pl.* **-ries** the use of, or reliance upon, summit conferences to resolve problems of international diplomacy

sum·mon (sum'ən) *vt.* [ME. *somonen* < OFr. *somondre* < VL. **submonere,* for L. *summonere,* to remind privily < *sub-,* under, secretly + *monere,* to advise, warn: see MONITOR] **1.** to call together; order to meet or convene **2.** to order to come or appear; call for or send for with authority or urgency **3.** to order, as by a summons, to appear in court **4.** to call upon to do something **5.** to call forth; rouse; gather; collect (often with *up*) *[to summon (up) one's strength]* —*SYN.* see CALL —**sum'mon·er** *n.*

sum·mons (-ənz) *n., pl.* **-mons·es** [ME. *somounce* < Anglo-Fr. *somonse* < OFr. *sumunse* < pp. of *somondre:* see prec.] **1.** an order or command to come, attend, appear, or perform some action; specif., *Law* an official order to appear in court, specif. to respond as a defendant to a charge; also, the writ containing such an order **2.** a call, command, knock, or other signal that summons —*vt.* [Colloq.] to serve a court summons upon

‡**sum·mum bo·num** (soom'əm bō'nəm) [L.] the highest, or supreme, good

Sum·ner (sum'nər) **1. Charles,** 1811–74; U.S. statesman & abolitionist **2. William Gra·ham** (grā'əm), 1840–1910; U.S. sociologist & economist

su·mo (wrestling) (sōō'mō) [Jap. *sumō*] [*sometimes* S-] a highly stylized Japanese form of wrestling engaged in by a hereditary class of large, extremely heavy men

sump (sump) *n.* [ME. *sompe,* a SWAMP] **1.** *a)* a pit for draining, collecting, or storing liquids; cistern, reservoir, cesspool, etc. *b)* [Brit.] an oil trap or reservoir at the bottom of the lubricating system of an internal-combustion engine **2.** *Mining a)* a pit or pool at the bottom of a shaft or mine, in which water collects and from which it is pumped *b)* an excavation at the head of a tunnel or shaft

sump pump a pump used for removing collected liquid from a sump, or pit

sump·ter (sump'tər) *n.* [ME. *sompter,* pack horse, orig., driver of a pack horse < OFr. *sometier* < LL. **sagmatarius* < LL. *sagma* (gen. *sagmatis*), pack saddle: see SUMMER²] a pack horse, mule, or other pack animal

sump·tu·ar·y (sump'choo wer'ē) *adj.* [L. *sumptuarius* < *sumptus,* expense < pp. of *sumere,* to take] of or regulating expenses or expenditures; specif., seeking to regulate extravagance on religious or moral grounds

sump·tu·ous (sump'choo wəs) *adj.* [L. < OFr. *sumptueux* < L. *sumptuosus* < *sumptus:* see prec.] **1.** involving great expense; costly; lavish **2.** magnificent or splendid, as in furnishings, etc. —**sump'tu·ous·ly** *adv.* —**sump'tu·ous·ness** *n.*

Sumter, Fort *see* FORT SUMTER

sum total 1. the total arrived at by adding up a sum or sums **2.** everything involved or included

sum-up (-up') *n.* [Colloq.] the act or result of summarizing

sun¹ (sun) *n.* [ME. *sunne* < OE., akin to G. *sonne,* Goth. *sunnō* < IE. **sun-* < base **sāu-,* whence L. *sol,* Gr. *hēlios*] **1.** *a)* the self-luminous, gaseous sphere about which the earth and other planets revolve and which furnishes light, heat, and energy for the solar system: it is the star nearest the earth, whose mean distance from it is nearly 93,000,000 miles: its diameter is about 864,400 miles; its mass is about 333,400 times, and its volume more than 1,300,000 times, that of the earth, and its mean density, about one fourth that of the earth *b)* the heat or light of the sun *[to lie in the sun]* **2.** any star that is the center of a planetary system **3.** something like the sun, as in warmth, brilliance, splendor, etc. **4.** [Poet.] *a)* a day *b)* a year **5.** [Poet.] a clime; climate **6.** [Archaic] sunrise or sunset —*vt.* **sunned, sun'ning** to expose to the sun's rays; warm, dry, bleach, tan, etc. in or as in the sunlight —*vi.* to sun oneself —**from sun to sun** [Archaic] from sunrise to sunset —**place in the sun** a prominent or favorable position —**under the sun** on earth; in the world

sun² (sun) *n.* [Hind. *san* < Sans. *śaṇa,* hempen] **1.** an East Indian annual plant (*Crotalaria juncea*) of the legume family, grown for its bast fiber used in making rope, bagging, cigarette papers, etc. **2.** its fiber Also **sun hemp**

Sun. Sunday

sun·baked (-bākt') *adj.* **1.** baked by the heat of the sun, as bricks **2.** made very dry, parched, cracked, etc. by the heat of the sun

sun bath exposure of the body to direct sunlight or to a sunlamp

sun·bathe (-bāth') *vi.* **-bathed', -bath'ing** to take a sun bath —**sun'bath'er** *n.*

sun·beam (-bēm') *n.* a ray or beam of sunlight

sun·bird (-burd') *n.* **1.** any of several small, brightly colored tropical songbirds (family Nectariniidae), resembling the hummingbird **2.** *same as* SUN-GREBE

sun bittern either of two wading birds (genus *Eurypyga*) of tropical America, with a slim body and long neck: related to the cranes and herons **2.** *same as* SUN-GREBE

sun·bon·net (-bän'it) *n.* a bonnet with a large brim and back flap for shading the face and neck from the sun, worn, esp. formerly, by women and girls

sun·bow (-bō') *n.* a rainbow formed by sunlight refracted in fine spray, as from a waterfall or fountain

sun·burn (-burn') *n.* an inflammation of the skin resulting from prolonged exposure to the sun's rays or to a

sunlamp —*vi.*, *vt.* -**burned'** or -**burnt'**, -**burn'ing** to get or cause to get a sunburn

sun·burst (-burst') *n.* **1.** the sudden appearance of sunlight, as through a break in clouds ☆**2.** a decorative device representing the sun with spreading rays

☆**sun-cured** (-kyoord') *adj.* cured, as meat or fruit, by drying in the sun

☆**sun·dae** (sun'dē, -dā) *n.* [prob. < SUNDAY, from being orig. sold only on this day] a serving of ice cream covered with a syrup, fruit, nuts, whipped cream, etc.

Sun·da Islands (sun'də; *Du.* soon'dä) group of islands in the Malay Archipelago, consisting of two smaller groups: *a*) **Greater Sunda Islands** Sumatra, Java, Borneo, Celebes, & small nearby islands *b*) **Lesser Sunda Islands** Bali & islands stretching east through Timor

☆**sun dance** a religious dance in worship of the sun performed at the summer solstice by certain Plains Indians

Sunda Strait narrow strait between Java & Sumatra, connecting the Java Sea with the Indian Ocean

Sun·day (sun'dē, -dā) *n.* [ME. < OE. *sunnandæg*, lit., sun day, akin to ON. *sunnudagr*, G. *Sonntag* < 3d-cent. transl. of LL. *dies solis*, day of the sun, transl. of Gr. *hēmera hēlion*] the first day of the week: it is observed by most Christian denominations as a day of worship (*Lord's Day*) or as the Sabbath —*adj.* **1.** of, having to do with, or characteristic of Sunday **2.** done, worn, taking place, performing, etc. usually or only on Sunday [*Sunday* suit, *Sunday* golfer]

Sun·day (sun'dē, -dā), **Bil·ly** (bil'ē) (nickname of *William Ashley Sunday*) 1863–1935; U.S. evangelist

Sunday best [Colloq.] one's best clothes

☆**Sun·day-go-to-meet·ing** (-gō'tə mēt'iŋ) *adj.* [Colloq.] appropriate to Sunday church services; i.e., best or most presentable, as clothes, manners, etc.

☆**Sunday punch** [Slang] **1.** a boxer's hardest punch **2.** any measure most effective against an opponent

Sun·days (-dēz, -dāz) *adv.* on or during every Sunday

Sunday school 1. a school, usually affiliated with some church or synagogue, giving religious instruction on Sunday **2.** the teachers and pupils of such a school

sun deck any open porch, deck, etc. for taking sun baths

sun·der (sun'dər) *vt.*, *vi.* [ME. *sundren* < OE. *sundrian* < *sunder*, asunder, akin to G. *sonder* < IE. **sṇter-* < base **seni-*, away from, separate, whence L. *sine*, without] to break apart; separate; part; split —*SYN.* see SEPARATE —**in sunder** into parts or pieces; apart —**sun'der·a·ble** *adj.* —**sun'der·ance** *n.*

Sun·der·land (sun'dər lənd) seaport in Durham, N England, on the North Sea: pop. 188,000

sun·dew (sun'dōō', -dyōō') *n.* [transl. of ML. *ros solis* < L. *ros*, dew (for IE. base see RACE[1]) + *solis*, gen. of *sol*, SUN[1]] *same as* DROSERA —*adj.* designating a family (Droseraceae) of plants including drosera and the Venus' flytrap

sun·di·al (-dī'əl, -dīl') *n.* an instrument that indicates time by the position of the shadow of a gnomon cast by the sun on the face of a dial marked in hours

sun disk a disk flanked by two serpents and set in a pair of outspread wings, a symbol of the Egyptian sun god, Ra

sun·dog (-dôg') *n. same as* PARHELION

sun·down (-doun') *n.* [contr. < ? *sun go(ing) down*] *same as* SUNSET (esp. sense 1 *b*)

sun·down·er (-ər) *n.* **1.** [prec. + -ER: from habitually arriving at a stock farm too late for work but early enough to receive a night's lodging and food] [Austral. Colloq.] a tramp or vagrant **2.** [Brit. Colloq.] an alcoholic drink taken at sunset ☆**3.** [from requiring return from shore leave by sundown] [Naut. Slang] an officer who is a strict disciplinarian

sun-dried (-drīd') *adj.* dried by the sun

sun·dries (sun'drēz) *n.pl.* sundry, esp. minor, items; miscellaneous things of various sorts

☆**sun-drops** (sun'dräps') *n.pl.* any of a number of plants (genus *Oenothera*) of the evening-primrose family, with large, usually yellow flowers

sun·dry (sun'drē) *adj.* [ME. *sundri* < OE. *syndrig*, separate < *sunder*, apart: see SUNDER & -Y[2]] various; miscellaneous; divers [*sundry* items of clothing] —*pron.* [with *pl.* v.] sundry persons or things: chiefly in **all and sundry** everybody; one and all

sun·fast (sun'fast', -fäst') *adj.* not fading in sunlight

sun·fish (-fish') *n., pl.* -**fish'**, -**fish'es**: see FISH[2] ☆**1.** any of a large family (Centrarchidae) of N. American, freshwater fishes, closely related to the perches and including the bluegill, crappie, pumpkinseed, black bass, etc. **2.** *same as* OCEAN SUNFISH

sun·flow·er (-flou'ər) *n.* any of a genus (*Helianthus*) of tall plants of the composite family, having large, yellow, daisylike flowers with yellow, brown, purple, or almost black disks that contain edible seeds from which an oil is extracted

Sunflower State *nickname of* KANSAS

Sung (soon) Chin. dynasty (960–1279 A.D.), noted for achievement in art & literature

sung (suŋ) *pp. & rare pt. of* SING

Sun·ga·ri (soon'gä rē') river in Manchuria, NE China, flowing into the Amur River: c.1,150 mi.

sun·glass (sun'glas', -gläs') *n.* **1.** *same as* BURNING GLASS **2.** [*pl.*] eyeglasses with special lenses, usually tinted, to protect the eyes from the sun's glare

sun·glow (-glō') *n.* a colored glow seen in the sky at sunrise or sunset as a result of the diffraction of the sun's rays by particles in the air

Sung Mass *R.C.Ch.* a Mass, ceremonially between a Low Mass and High Mass, in which certain parts are sung, but at which neither a deacon nor subdeacon assists

sun god 1. the sun personified and worshiped as a god **2.** any god associated or identified with the sun

sun-grebe (sun'grēb') *n.* any of several marsh birds (family Heliornithidae) of tropical America and Africa

sunk (suŋk) *pp. & alt. pt. of* SINK —*adj.* **1.** *same as* SUNKEN **2.** [Colloq.] utterly ruined; undone

sunk·en (-ən) *obs. pp. of* SINK —*adj.* **1.** submerged [a *sunken* ship] **2.** below the level of the surrounding or adjoining area [a *sunken* patio] **3.** fallen in; hollow [*sunken* cheeks] **4.** depressed; dejected [*sunken* spirits]

sunk fence *same as* HA-HA[2]

☆**sun·lamp** (sun'lamp') *n.* an electric lamp that radiates ultraviolet rays, used therapeutically as a substitute for sunlight

sun·less (sun'lis) *adj.* without sun or sunlight; dark

sun·light (-līt') *n.* the light of the sun

sun·lit (-lit') *adj.* lighted by the sun

sunn (sun) *n. same as* SUN[2]: also **sunn hemp**

Sun·na, Sun·nah (soon'ə) *n.* [Ar. *sunnah*, lit., a form, course, tradition] Moslem law based, according to tradition, on the teachings and practices of Mohammed and observed by orthodox Moslems: a supplement to the Koran

Sun·ni (soon'ē) *n., pl.* **Sun'ni** *same as* SUNNITE

Sun·nite (soon'īt) *n.* [< Ar. *sunnah* (see SUNNA) + -ITE[1]] any member of one of the two great sects of Moslems: Sunnites approve the historical order of the first four caliphs as the rightful line of succession to Mohammed and accept the Sunna as an authoritative supplement to the Koran: cf. SHIITE —**Sun'nism** *n.*

sun·ny (sun'ē) *adj.* -**ni·er**, -**ni·est 1.** shining or bright with sunlight; full of sunshine **2.** bright and cheerful [a *sunny* smile] **3.** of or suggestive of the sun [a *sunny* radiance] —**sun'ni·ly** *adv.* —**sun'ni·ness** *n.*

sunny side 1. the side exposed to sunlight **2.** the more pleasant or cheerful aspect —☆**on the sunny side of** somewhat younger than (a specified age) —☆**sunny side up** fried with the yolk unbroken and without being turned over [two eggs *sunny side up*]

Sun·ny·vale (sun'ē vāl') city in W Calif.: suburb of San Jose: pop. 95,000

☆**sun parlor** (or **porch**, or **room**) a sitting room (or a porch) with large windows to let sunlight in freely

sun·proof (sun'proof') *adj.* impervious to or unaffected by sunlight

sun·rise (-rīz') *n.* [SUN[1] + RISE, *v.*, prob. in such phrases as *before the sun rise*] **1.** the daily appearance of the sun above the eastern horizon **2.** the varying time of this **3.** the atmospheric phenomena at this time

sun·scald (-skôld') *n.* a plant injury caused by exposure to bright sunlight or to excessive heat and manifested by whitening or browning of the leaves, fruits, or flowers

sun·set (-set') *n.* [ME. *sunne set, sonsette*: see SUNRISE] **1.** *a*) the daily disappearance of the sun below the western horizon *b*) the varying time of this *c*) the atmospheric phenomena at this time; esp., the color of the western sky at sunset **2.** the final phase or decline (*of a period*)

sun·shade (-shād') *n.* a parasol, awning, broad hat, etc. used for protection against the sun's rays

sun·shine (-shīn') *n.* **1.** *a*) the shining of the sun *b*) the light and heat from the sun *c*) a sunny place or part **2.** *a*) cheerfulness, happiness, etc. *b*) a source of this —**sun'shin'y** (-shī'nē) *adj.*

sun·spot (-spät') *n.* any of the temporarily cooler regions appearing cyclically as dark spots on the surface of the sun and associated with geomagnetic disturbances

sun·stroke (-strōk') *n.* a form of heatstroke caused by excessive exposure to the sun and characterized by high body temperature and collapse —**sun'struck'** (-struk') *adj.*

sun·suit (-soot') *n.* short pants with a bib and shoulder straps, worn by babies and young children

sun·tan (-tan') *n.* **1.** a darkened condition of the skin resulting from exposure to the sun or a sunlamp **2.** a reddish-brown color —**sun'-tanned'** *adj.*

sun·up (-up') *n. same as* SUNRISE

Sun Valley resort city in SC Ida.: pop. 180

SUNDIAL

SUN DISK

sun·ward (-wərd) *adv.* toward the sun: also **sun′wards** —*adj.* facing the sun

sun·wise (-wīz′) *adv., adj.* in the direction of the sun's apparent motion across the sky; clockwise

Sun Yat-sen (soon′ yät′sen′) 1866–1925; Chin. political & revolutionary leader: see CHINESE REVOLUTION

‡**su·o ju·re** (soō′ō joor′ē) [L.] in or by one's own right

‡**su·o lo·co** (lō′kō) [L.] in its own (i.e., proper) place

Su·o·mi (soo wō′mē) *Finn.* name of FINLAND

sup[1] (sup) *vt., vi.* **supped, sup′ping** [ME. *soupen* < OE. *supan*, to sup, drink, akin to G. *saufen*: for IE. base see SUCK] to take (liquid food) into the mouth in small amounts; sip —*n.* a small mouthful, as of soup

sup[2] (sup) *vi.* **supped, sup′ping** [ME. *soupen* < OFr. *souper* < *soupe*, soup, orig., a sop < VL. *suppa* < WGmc. **suppa* (whence SOP) < IE. **seub-*: for base see SUCK] to eat the evening meal; have supper —*vt.* [Rare] to provide with supper

sup- (sup) *same as* SUB-: used before *p*

sup. 1. [L. *supra*] above 2. superior 3. superlative 4. supine 5. supplement 6. supplementary 7. supply

su·per (soō′pər) *n.* [< ff. as used in numerous Eng. compounds] 1. *clipped form of: a)* SUPERNUMERARY (esp. sense 2) *b)* SUPERINTENDENT (esp. sense 2) 2. [Colloq.] a product of superior grade, extra-large size, etc.: a trade term 3. *Bookbinding* a kind of starched cotton gauze used as reinforcing material in the spine of a book —*adj.* 1. outstanding; exceptionally fine 2. great, extreme, or excessive —*vt. Bookbinding* to reinforce with super

su·per- (soō′pər) [L. < *super*, above < IE. **eksuper* (whence Gr. *hyper*) < **eghs* (cf. EX-[1]) + **uper*, OVER] a *prefix meaning:* 1. over, above, on top of [*superstructure*] 2. higher in rank or position than, superior to [*superintendent*] 3. *a)* greater in quality, amount, or degree than, surpassing [*superfine, superabundance*] *b)* greater or better than others of its kind [*supermarket*] 4. to a degree greater than normal [*supersaturate*] 5. extra, additional [*supertax*] 6. to a secondary degree [*superparasite*] 7. *Chem.* with a large or unusually large amount of (the specified substance) [*superphosphate*]: an earlier prefix now largely replaced by *bi-, di-, per-*, etc.

super. 1. superfine 2. superior

su·per·a·ble (soō′pər ə b'l) *adj.* [L. *superabilis* < *superare*, to overcome < *super:* see SUPER-] that can be overcome or conquered; surmountable —**su′per·a·bly** *adv.*

su·per·a·bound (soō′pər ə bound′) *vi.* [ME. *superhabounden* < LL. *superabundare:* see SUPER- & ABOUND] to be greatly or excessively abundant

su·per·a·bun·dant (-ə bun′dənt) *adj.* [ME. *superhabundaunt* < LL. *superabundans*, prp. of *superabundare:* see SUPER- & ABOUND] being more than is usual or needed; surplus; excess; overly abundant —**su′per·a·bun′dance** *n.* —**su′per·a·bun′dant·ly** *adv.*

su·per·add (-ad′) *vt.* [L. *superaddere:* see SUPER- & ADD] to put in as extra; add to what has already been added —**su′per·ad·di′tion** (-ə dish′ən) *n.*

su·per·al·loy (-al′oi) *n.* an alloy that resists oxidation and can withstand high temperatures and stresses

su·per·al·tern (-ôl′tərn) *n.* [SUPER- + (SUB)ALTERN] in traditional logic, a universal proposition that is the basis for immediate inference to a corresponding subaltern

su·per·an·nu·ate (-an′yoo wāt′) *vt., vi.* **-at·ed, -at′ing** [back-formation < ff.] 1. to set aside as, or become, old-fashioned or obsolete 2. to retire from service, esp. with a pension, because of old age or infirmity

su·per·an·nu·at·ed (-an′yoo wāt′id) *adj.* [< ML. *superannuatus*, pp. of *superannuari*, to be too old < L. *super* (see SUPER-) + *annus*, year (see ANNUAL)] 1. *a)* too old or worn for further work, service, etc. *b)* discharged from service, esp. with a pension, because of old age or infirmity 2. obsolete; old-fashioned; outdated

su·per·an·nu·a·tion (-an′yoo wā′shən) *n.* 1. a superannuating or being superannuated 2. a pension received by a superannuated person

su·perb (soo purb′, soō-) *adj.* [L. *superbus*, proud, haughty, delicate < *super* (see SUPER-) + *-bus* < IE. **bhwos* < base **bhū-*, var. of **bheu-*, to grow, whence BE] 1. noble, grand, or majestic 2. rich, splendid, or magnificent 3. extremely fine; excellent —*SYN.* see SPLENDID —**su·perb′ly** *adv.* —**su·perb′ness** *n.*

su·per·cal·en·der (soō′pər kal′ən dər) *n.* [SUPER- + CALENDER] a series of polished rollers used in papermaking to give an extra-high gloss to the paper —*vt.* to process with a supercalender

su·per·car·go (soō′pər kär′gō) *n., pl.* **-goes, -gos** [earlier *supracargo* < Sp. *sobrecargo* < *sobre*, over (< L. *super:* see SUPER-) + *cargo*, CARGO] an officer on a merchant ship who has charge of the cargo, representing the shipowner in all transactions

su·per·charge (-chärj′) *vt.* **-charged′, -charg′ing** 1. to increase the power of (an engine), as by the use of a supercharger 2. *same as* PRESSURIZE (sense 1)

su·per·charg·er (-chär′jər) *n.* a blower or compressor used to increase the power of an internal-combustion engine by increasing the supply of air or combustible mixture to the cylinders beyond that normally pumped in by the pistons at the prevailing atmospheric pressure

su·per·cil·i·ar·y (soō′pər sil′ē er′ē) *adj.* [ModL. *superciliarius* < L. *supercilium:* see ff.] of or near the eyebrow

su·per·cil·i·ous (-sil′ē əs) *adj.* [L. *superciliosus* < L. *supercilium*, eyebrow, hence (with reference to facial expression with raised brows) pride, haughtiness < *super-*, above + *cilium*, eyelid] disdainful or contemptuous; full of or characterized by pride or scorn; haughty; arrogant —*SYN.* see PROUD —**su′per·cil′i·ous·ly** *adv.* —**su′per·cil′i·ous·ness** *n.*

su·per·class (soō′pər klas′, -kläs′) *n.* a natural subdivision that includes a group of related classes within a zoological phylum or a botanical division

☆**su·per·co·los·sal** (soō′pər kə läs′əl) *adj.* extremely great, large, impressive, etc.: a term of hyperbolic description

su·per·co·lum·ni·a·tion (-kə lum′nē ā′shən) *n.* an architectural plan characterized by one order of columns above another —**su′per·co·lum′nar** (-nər) *adj.*

su·per·con·duc·tiv·i·ty (-kän′dək tiv′ə tē) *n. Physics* the phenomenon, exhibited by certain metals and alloys, as cadmium, aluminum, mercury, etc., of continuously conducting electrical current without resistance when cooled to temperatures near absolute zero: also **su′per·con·duc′tion** (-kən duk′shən) —**su′per·con·duct′ing, su′per·con·duc′tive** *adj.* —**su′per·con·duc′tor** *n.*

su·per·cool (-kool′) *vt.* to cool (a liquid) below its freezing point without causing solidification —*vi.* to become supercooled

su·per·dom·i·nant (-däm′ə nənt) *n. same as* SUBMEDIANT

☆**su·per·du·per** (soō′pər doo′pər) *adj.* [reduplication of SUPER] [Slang] extremely great, large, impressive, etc.: a term of hyperbolic description

su·per·e·go (soō′pər ē′gō) *n., pl.* **-gos** *Psychoanalysis* that part of the psyche which is critical of the self or ego and enforces moral standards: at an unconscious level it blocks unacceptable impulses of the id

su·per·em·i·nent (soō′pər em′ə nənt) *adj.* [LL. *supereminens* < prp. of L. *supereminere*, to rise above: see SUPER- & EMINENT] eminent beyond others in rank, dignity, etc.; supremely remarkable, distinguished, etc. —**su′per·em′i·nence** *n.* —**su′per·em′i·nent·ly** *adv.*

su·per·e·rog·ate (-er′ə gāt′) *vi.* **-gat′ed, -gat′ing** [< LL. *supererogatus*, pp. of *supererogare*, to pay out beyond what is expected < *super-* (see SUPER-) + *erogare*, to pay out (after consent by the people) < *e-* (for *ex-*), out + *rogare*, to ask] [Obs.] to do more than is required or expected

su·per·e·rog·a·tion (-er′ə gā′shən) *n.* [LL. *supererogatio* < *supererogatus:* see prec.] the act of doing more than what is required or expected

su·per·e·rog·a·to·ry (-i räg′ə tôr′ē) *adj.* [ML. *supererogatorius:* see SUPEREROGATE & -ORY] 1. done or observed beyond the degree required or expected 2. superfluous

☆**su·per·ette** (soō′pər et′, soō′pər et′) *n.* [SUPER(MARKET) + -ETTE] a small self-service grocery store

su·per·fam·i·ly (soō′pər fam′ə lē) *n., pl.* **-lies** a natural subdivision ranking above a family and below an order, usually less extensive than a suborder

su·per·fe·cun·da·tion (soō′pər fē′kən dā′shən, -fek′ən-) *n.* [SUPER- + FECUNDATION] the fertilization of two ova at separate times during the same ovulation period

su·per·fe·ta·tion (-fē tā′shən) *n.* [ML. *superfetatio* < L. *superfetatus*, pp. of *superfetare* < *super-* (see SUPER-) + *fetare*, to bring forth, impregnate < *fetus*, FETUS] the fertilization of an ovum during a pregnancy already in existence

su·per·fi·cial (-fish′əl) *adj.* [ME. *superficyall* < L. *superficialis* < *superficies:* see ff.] 1. *a)* of or being on the surface [a *superficial* burn] *b)* of or limited to surface area; plane [*superficial* measurements] 2. concerned with and understanding only the easily apparent and obvious; not profound; shallow 3. quick and cursory [a *superficial* reading] 4. seeming such only at first glance; merely apparent [a *superficial* resemblance] —**su′per·fi′ci·al′i·ty** (-ē al′ə tē) *n., pl.* **-ties** —**su′per·fi′cial·ly** *adv.* —**su′per·fi′cial·ness** *n.* *SYN.*—**superficial** implies concern with the obvious or surface aspects of a thing [*superficial* characteristics] and, in a derogatory sense, lack of thoroughness, profoundness, significance, etc. [*superficial* judgments]; **shallow**, in this connection always derogatory, implies a lack of depth of character, intellect, meaning, etc. [*shallow* writing]; **cursory**, which may or may not be derogatory, suggests a hasty consideration of something without pausing to note details [a *cursory* inspection] —*ANT.* deep, profound

su·per·fi·ci·es (-fish′i ēz′, -fish′ēz) *n., pl.* **-ci·es** [L. < *super-* (see SUPER-) + *facies*, FACE] 1. a surface; outer area 2. the outward form or aspect

su·per·fine (soō′pər fīn′, soō′pər fīn′) *adj.* [ME. *superfyne*: see SUPER- & FINE[1]] 1. too subtle, delicate, or refined; overnice [a *superfine* distinction] 2. of exceptionally fine quality [*superfine* glassware] 3. extremely fine-grained [*superfine* sugar]

su·per·fix (soō′pər fiks′) *n.* [SUPER- + (AF)FIX] *Linguis.* stress pattern superposed on the segmental phonemes, as for indicating grammatical function: Ex., *in′sert* (for the *n.*) and *in·sert′* (for the *v.*)

su·per·flu·id·i·ty (soō′pər floo wid′ə tē) *n.* the phenomenon, exhibited by liquid helium at temperatures below 2.18°K, of flowing without friction and having very high thermal conductivity —**su′per·flu′id** (-floo′id) *n., adj.*

su·per·flu·i·ty (-floo′ə tē) *n., pl.* **-ties** [ME. *superfluite* < OFr. *superfluité* < L. *superfluitas*] 1. the state or quality of being superfluous 2. a quantity or number beyond what is needed; excess; superabundance 3. something superfluous; thing not needed

su·per·flu·ous (soo pur′floo wəs) *adj.* [L. *superfluus* < *superfluere*, to overflow: see SUPER- & FLUCTUATE] 1. being more than is needed, useful, or wanted; surplus; excessive 2. not needed; unnecessary; irrelevant [a *superfluous* remark] 3. [Obs.] extravagant; prodigal —**su·per′flu·ous·ly** *adv.* —**su·per′flu·ous·ness** *n.*

su·per·fuse (soo′pər fyooz′) *vt., vi.* -**fused**′, -**fus′ing** [< L. *superfusus*, pp. of *superfundere*: see SUPER- & FOUND[3]] 1. [Rare] to pour or be poured over or on something 2. same as SUPERCOOL —**su′per·fu′sion** (-fyoo′zhən) *n.*

su·per·gi·ant (soo′pər jī′ənt) *n.* an immense and extremely luminous star, as Betelgeuse or Antares, that has a diameter at least 100 times that of the sun and that is 100 to 10,000 times as bright

su·per·heat (soo′pər hēt′; *for n.*, soo′pər hēt′) *vt.* 1. same *as* OVERHEAT 2. to heat (a liquid) above its boiling point without vaporization 3. to heat (steam not in contact with water) beyond its saturation point, so that a drop in temperature will not cause reconversion to water —*n.* the number of degrees by which the temperature of superheated steam exceeds the temperature of the steam at its saturation point —**su′per·heat′er** *n.*

su·per·het·er·o·dyne (soo′pər het′ər ə dīn′) *adj.* [SUPER- (SONIC) + HETERODYNE] designating or of a form of radio reception in which part of the amplification prior to demodulation is carried out at an intermediate supersonic frequency produced by beating the frequency of the received carrier waves with that of locally generated oscillations —*n.* a radio set for this method of reception

su·per·high frequency (soo′pər hī′) *Radio* any frequency between 3,000 and 30,000 megahertz

☆**su·per·high·way** (-hi′wā′) *n.* same as EXPRESSWAY

su·per·hu·man (soo′pər hyoo′mən) *adj.* 1. having powers or a nature above that of man; divine; supernatural 2. greater than that of a normal human being —**su′per·hu′man·ly** *adv.* —**su′per·hu′man·ness** *n.*

su·per·im·pose (-im pōz′) *vt.* -**posed**′, -**pos′ing** 1. to put, lay, or stack on top of something else 2. to add as a dominant or unassimilated feature —**su′per·im′po·si′tion** (-im′pə zish′ən) *n.*

su·per·in·cum·bent (-in kum′bənt) *adj.* [L. *superincumbens*, prp. of *superincumbere*: see SUPER- & INCUMBENT] 1. *a*) lying or resting on something else *b*) brought to bear from above: said of pressure 2. arching over or overhanging —**su′per·in·cum′bence, su′per·in·cum′ben·cy** *n.* —**su′per·in·cum′bent·ly** *adv.*

su·per·in·duce (-in doos′, -dyoos′) *vt.* -**duced**′, -**duc′ing** [L. *superinducere*: see SUPER- & INDUCE] to introduce or bring in as an addition to an existent condition, effect, etc. —**su′per·in·duc′tion** (-duk′shən) *n.*

su·per·in·tend (-in tend′) *vt.* [LL.(Ec.) *superintendere*: see SUPER- & INTEND] to act as superintendent of; direct; supervise; manage —**su′per·in·tend′ence, su′per·in·tend′en·cy** *n.*

su·per·in·tend·ent (-in ten′dənt) *n.* [< LL.(Ec.) *superintendens*, prp. of *superintendere*, to superintend] 1. a person in charge of a department, institution, etc.; director; supervisor 2. a person responsible for the maintenance of a building; custodian —*adj.* that superintends

Su·pe·ri·or (sə pir′ē ər, soo-), **Lake** [orig. so called in Fr. (*Supérieur*), from its position above Lake Huron] largest & westernmost of the Great Lakes, between Mich. & Ontario, Canada: 32,483 sq. mi.

su·pe·ri·or (sə pir′ē ər, soo-) *adj.* [ME. < OFr. < L. compar. of *superus*, that is above < *super:* see SUPER-] 1. higher in space; placed higher up; upper 2. high or higher in order, status, rank, etc. 3. greater in quality or value than (with *to*) 4. good or excellent in quality; above average 5. unaffected by or indifferent to (something painful, unpleasant, etc.): with *to* 6. showing a feeling of being better than others; haughty 7. more comprehensive or inclusive; generic: said of words, terms, concepts, etc. 8. *Astron. a*) farther from the sun than the earth is: said of six planets *b*) designating that conjunction which occurs when the sun is directly between the earth and an inferior planet 9. *Bot. a*) situated over some other organ *b*) growing free from the calyx: said of an ovary *c*) embedded in the expansion end of the stem with the ovary under it: said of a calyx 10. *Printing* placed above the type line, as 2 in x[2] —*n.* 1. a superior person or thing 2. the head of a religious community —**su·pe′ri·or·ly** *adv.*

☆**superior court** in some States, a court of general jurisdiction, specif. one between the trial courts and the appellate courts

su·pe·ri·or·i·ty (sə pir′ē ôr′ə tē, soo-) *n.* the state or quality of being superior, or higher, greater, better, etc.

superiority complex popularly, a feeling of superiority or exaggerated self-importance, often accompanied by excessive aggressiveness, arrogance, etc. which are compensation for feelings of inferiority: cf. INFERIORITY COMPLEX

su·per·ja·cent (soo′pər jā′s′nt) *adj.* [LL. *superjacens*, prp. of *superjacere* < *super-*, over (see SUPER-) + *jacere*, to lie] lying or resting above or upon

superl. superlative

su·per·la·tive (sə pur′lə tiv, soo-) *adj.* [ME. < MFr. *superlatif* < LL. *superlativus* < L. *superlatus*, excessive < *super-*, above, beyond + *latus*, pp. of *ferre*, to BEAR[1]] 1. superior to or excelling all other or others; of the highest kind, quality, degree, etc.; supreme 2. excessive or exaggerated 3. *Gram.* designating or of the extreme degree of comparison of adjectives and adverbs; expressing the greatest degree of the quality or attribute expressed by the positive degree: usually indicated by the suffix -*est* (*hardest*) or by the use of *most* with the positive form (*most beautiful*) —*n.* 1. the highest or utmost degree; acme; height; peak 2. something superlative 3. *Gram. a*) the superlative degree *b*) a word or form in this degree —**su·per′la·tive·ly** *adv.* —**su·per′la·tive·ness** *n.*

su·per·lu·na·ry (soo′pər loo′nər ē) *adj.* [< SUPER- + L. *luna*, moon (see LUNAR) + -ARY] located above or beyond the moon Also **su′per·lu′nar**

su·per·man (soo′pər man′) *n., pl.* -**men**′ (-men′) [a calque < G. *übermensch* (< *über*, over + *mensch*, person), Nietzsche's term] 1. in the philosophy of Nietzsche, an idealized, superior, dominating man, regarded as the goal of the evolutionary struggle for survival 2. a man having apparently superhuman powers

☆**su·per·mar·ket** (-mär′kit) *n.* a large, self-service, retail food store or market, often one of a chain

su·per·nal (soo pur′n′l) *adj.* [LME. < MFr. < L. *supernus*, upper < *super*, above: see SUPER-] of, from, or as though from the heavens or the sky; celestial, heavenly, or divine —**su·per′nal·ly** *adv.*

su·per·na·tant (soo′pər nāt′′nt) *adj.* [L. *supernatans*, prp. of *supernatare*, to swim above < *super-* (see SUPER-) + *natare*, to swim (see NATANT)] 1. floating on the surface or over something 2. *Chem.* designating or of a liquid standing above a precipitate

su·per·nat·u·ral (soo′pər nach′ər əl) *adj.* [ML. *supernaturalis*: see SUPER- & NATURAL] 1. existing or occurring outside the normal experience or knowledge of man; not explainable by the known forces or laws of nature; specif., of, involving, or attributed to God or a god 2. of, involving, or attributed to ghosts, spirits, the occult, etc. 3. exceeding normal bounds; extreme [skating with *supernatural* grace] —**the supernatural** supernatural beings, forces, happenings, etc., esp. ghosts, spirits, and the like —**su′per·nat′u·ral·ly** *adv.*

su·per·nat·u·ral·ism (-iz′m) *n.* 1. the quality or state of being supernatural 2. belief in the supernatural, esp. a belief that some supernatural, or divine, force controls nature and the universe —**su′per·nat′u·ral·ist** *n., adj.* —**su′per·nat′u·ral·is′tic** *adj.*

su·per·nat·u·ral·ize (-īz′) *vt.* -**ized**′, -**iz′ing** 1. to make supernatural 2. to think of or treat as supernatural

su·per·nor·mal (-nôr′m′l) *adj.* 1. above normal 2. same *as* PARANORMAL —**su′per·nor′mal·ly** *adv.*

su·per·no·va (-nō′və) *n., pl.* -**vae** (-vē), -**vas** [ModL.: see SUPER- & NOVA] an extremely bright nova, occurring in a stellar system about once in 600 years, that suddenly increases 10 million to 100 million times in brightness

su·per·nu·mer·a·ry (-noo′mə rer′ē, -nyoo′-) *adj.* [LL. *supernumerarius* < L. *super*, above (see SUPER-) + *numerus*, NUMBER] 1. that exceeds or is beyond the regular or prescribed number; extra 2. that is beyond the number or quantity needed or desired; superfluous —*n., pl.* -**ar′ies** 1. a supernumerary person or thing 2. *Theater* a person with a small, nonspeaking part, as in a mob scene

su·per·or·der (soo′pər ôr′dər) *n.* a natural subdivision between an order and a class or subclass of plants or animals

su·per·or·di·nate (soo′pər ôr′d′n it, -āt′) *adj.* [SUPER- + (SUB)ORDINATE] of a superior kind, rank, status, etc.

su·per·or·gan·ism (-ôr′gə niz′m) *n.* a colony of interdependent organisms, as in the social insects, whose castes, individuals, etc. act as a unit

su·per·par·a·site (-par′ə sīt′) *n.* an organism that lives as a parasite upon another parasite

su·per·pa·tri·ot (-pā′trē ət) *n.* a person who is or professes to be a devout patriot, often to the point of fanaticism —**su′per·pa′tri·ot′ic** (-pā′trē ät′ik) *adj.* —**su′per·pa′tri·ot·ism** *n.*

su·per·phos·phate (-fäs′fāt) *n.* an acid phosphate, esp. a mixture mainly of monobasic calcium phosphate and gypsum, made by treating bone, phosphate rock, etc. with sulfuric acid and used as fertilizer

su·per·phys·i·cal (-fiz′i k′l) *adj.* beyond the physical or the known laws of physics; hyperphysical

su·per·plas·tic·i·ty (-plas tis′ə tē) *n.* the phenomenon, exhibited by certain metals and alloys usually at high temperatures, of stretching to extreme lengths without breaking —**su′per·plas′tic** (-tik) *adj., n.*

su·per·pose (-pōz′) *vt.* -**posed**′, -**pos′ing** [Fr. *superposer* < L. *superpositus*, pp. of *superponere*, to place over: see SUPER- & POSE[1]] 1. to lay or place on, over, or above something else 2. *Geom.* to make (one figure) coincide with another in all parts, by or as if by placing one on top of the other —**su′per·pos′a·ble** *adj.* —**su′per·po·si′tion** (-pə zish′ən) *n.*

su·per·posed (-pōzd′) *adj.* [pp. of prec.] *Bot.* growing or lying directly above another part or organ

su·per·pow·er (sōō′pər pou′ər) *n.* 1. power that is superior or very great 2. any of the few top world powers competing with one another for influence over states

su·per·sat·u·rate (sōō′pər sach′ə rāt′) *vt.* -rat·ed, -rat·ing [SUPER- + SATURATE, after Fr. *sursaturer*] to make more highly concentrated than in normal saturation at a given temperature —su′per·sat′u·ra′tion *n.*

su·per·scribe (-skrīb′) *vt.* -scribed′, -scrib′ing [L. *superscribere*: see SUPER- & SCRIBE] to write, mark, or engrave (an inscription, name, etc.) at the top or on an outer surface of (something); specif., to write (a name, address, etc.) on (an envelope, parcel, etc.)

su·per·script (sōō′pər skript′) *adj.* [L. *superscriptus*, pp.: see prec.] written above; esp., *same as* SUPERIOR (adj. 10) —*n.* a figure, letter, or symbol written above and to the side of another [in y² and xⁿ, *2* and *n* are *superscripts*]

su·per·scrip·tion (sōō′pər skrip′shən) *n.* [ME. *superscripcioun* < L. *superscriptio*] 1. the act of superscribing 2. something superscribed; esp., an address on a letter, etc. 3. *Pharmacy* the Latin word *recipe* (meaning "take") or its symbol, ℞, on a prescription

su·per·sede (-sēd′) *vt.* -sed′ed, -sed′ing [MFr. *superseder*, to leave off, give over < L. *supersedere*, lit., to sit over, preside over, forbear: see SUPER- & SIT] 1. to cause to be set aside or dropped from use as inferior or obsolete and replaced by something else 2. to take the place of in office, function, etc.; succeed 3. to remove or cause to be removed so as to make way for another; supplant —*SYN.* see REPLACE —su′per·sed′er *n.* —☆su′per·se′dure (-sē′jər), su′per·sed′ence *n.*

su·per·se·de·as (-sē′dē as, -əs) *n.* [ME. < L., you shall desist < *supersedere*: see prec.] a legal document issued to halt or delay the action of some process of law

su·per·sen·si·ble (-sen′sə b'l) *adj.* outside or beyond the range of perception by the senses —su′per·sen′si·bly *adv.*

su·per·sen·si·tive (-sen′sə tiv) *adj.* extremely sensitive —su′per·sen′si·tiv′i·ty *n.*

su·per·sen·so·ry (-sen′sə rē) *adj. same as* SUPERSENSIBLE

su·per·sen·su·al (-sen′shōō wəl) *adj. same as:* 1. SUPERSENSIBLE 2. SPIRITUAL

su·per·ses·sion (-sesh′ən) *n.* [ML. *supersessio* < L. *supersessus*, pp. of *supersedere*] a superseding or being superseded —su′per·ses′sive (-ses′iv) *adj.*

su·per·son·ic (-sän′ik) *adj.* [SUPER- + SONIC] 1. designating, of, or moving at a speed in a surrounding fluid greater than that of sound in the same fluid 2. *same as* ULTRASONIC —su′per·son′i·cal·ly *adv.*

su·per·son·ics (-sän′iks) *n.pl.* [with sing. v.] [see prec. & -ICS] the science dealing with supersonic phenomena; specif., the study of the aerodynamics of supersonic speeds

su·per·state (sōō′pər stāt′) *n.* a state or government having power over other subordinated states

su·per·sti·tion (sōō′pər stish′ən) *n.* [ME. *supersticion* < MFr. < L. *superstitio*, excessive fear of the gods, superstition, orig., a standing still over < *superstare*, to stand over < *super-*, SUPER- + *stare*, to STAND] 1. any belief or attitude, based on fear or ignorance, that is inconsistent with the known laws of science or with what is generally considered in the particular society as true and rational; esp., such a belief in charms, omens, the supernatural, etc. 2. any action or practice based on such a belief or attitude 3. such beliefs or attitudes collectively

su·per·sti·tious (-əs) *adj.* 1. of, characterized by, or resulting from superstition 2. having or manifesting superstitions —su′per·sti′tious·ly *adv.* —su′per·sti′tious·ness *n.*

su·per·stra·tum (sōō′pər strāt′əm, -strat′-) *n., pl.* -stra·ta (-ə), -stra′tums a stratum lying over another

su·per·struc·ture (-struk′chər) *n.* 1. a structure built on top of another: sometimes used figuratively 2. that part of a building above the foundation 3. that part of a ship, esp. of a warship, above the main deck ☆4. the rails and ties of a railroad as distinguished from the roadbed

su·per·sub·tle (sōō′pər sut′'l) *adj.* extremely subtle or too subtle —su′per·sub′tle·ty (-tē) *n.*

su·per·tax (sōō′pər taks′) *n.* an additional tax; specif., a) *same as* SURTAX b) [Brit.] an additional income tax on large incomes

su·per·ton·ic (sōō′pər tän′ik) *n. same as* SECOND¹ (n. 9 a)

su·per·vene (sōō′pər vēn′) *vi.* -vened′, -ven′ing [L. *supervenire*, to come over or upon, follow < *super-* (see SUPER-) + *venire*, to COME] 1. to come or happen as something additional, unexpected, or foreign to the normal course of events 2. to take place; ensue —su′per·ven′ient (-vēn′yənt) *adj.* —su′per·ven′tion (-ven′shən), su′per·ven′ience (-vēn′yəns) *n.*

su·per·vise (sōō′pər vīz′) *vt., vi.* -vised′, -vis′ing [< ML. *supervisus*, pp. of *supervidere* < L. *super-* (see SUPER-) + *videre*, to see: see VISION] to oversee, direct, or manage (work, workers, a project, etc.); superintend —su′per·vi′sion (-vizh′ən) *n.*

su·per·vi·sor (sōō′pər vī′zər) *n.* [ML.] 1. a person who supervises; superintendent; manager; director ☆2. in certain school systems, an official in charge of the courses of study for a particular subject and of all teachers of that subject —su′per·vi′so·ry *adj.*

su·pi·nate (sōō′pə nāt′) *vt., vi.* -nat′ed, -nat′ing [< L.

supinatus, pp. of *supinare*, to lay backward < *supinus*, SUPINE] to rotate (the hand or forearm) so that the palm faces upward or away from the body —su′pi·na′tion *n.*

su·pi·na·tor (sōō′pə nāt′ər) *n.* the muscle in the forearm by which supination is effected

su·pine (soo pīn′; *for n.* sōō′pīn) *adj.* [L. *supinus*, prob. akin to *sub-*: see SUB-] 1. lying on the back, face upward 2. with the palm upward or away from the body: said of the hand 3. [Poet.] leaning or sloping backward 4. mentally or morally inactive; sluggish; listless; passive —*n.* 1. a Latin verbal noun formed from the stem of the past participle and having only an accusative and an ablative form 2. an infinitive in English preceded by *to* —*SYN.* see PRONE —su·pine′ly *adv.* —su·pine′ness *n.*

supp., suppl. 1. supplement 2. supplementary

sup·per (sup′ər) *n.* [ME. *souper* < OFr., orig. inf., to SUP²] 1. an evening meal; specif., a) dinner, when eaten in the evening b) a late, usually light, evening meal, as one eaten after attending the theater ☆2. an evening social affair at which a meal is served [church *supper*]

supper club an expensive nightclub, esp. one featuring fine food and liquors

sup·plant (sə plant′, -plänt′) *vt.* [ME. *supplanten* < OFr. *supplanter* < L. *supplantare*, to put under the sole of the foot, trip up < *sub-*, under (see SUB-) + *planta*, sole of the foot: see PLANT] 1. to take the place of; supersede, esp. through force or plotting 2. to remove or uproot in order to replace with something else —*SYN.* see REPLACE —sup·plan·ta·tion (sup′lan tā′shən) *n.* —sup·plant′er *n.*

sup·ple (sup′'l) *adj.* [ME. *souple* < OFr. < L. *supplex*, humble, submissive, akin to *supplicare*: see SUPPLICATE] 1. easily bent or twisted; flexible; pliant 2. able to bend and move easily and nimbly; lithe; limber [a *supple* body] 3. easily changed or influenced; yielding; compliant 4. yielding too easily; obsequious; servile 5. adaptable, as to changes; resilient; elastic: said of the mind, etc. —*vt., vi.* -pled, -pling to make or become supple —*SYN.* see ELASTIC —sup′ple·ly *adv.* —sup′ple·ness *n.*

sup·ple·jack (-jak′) *n.* ☆1. a twining, woody, N. American vine (*Berchemia scandens*) of the buckthorn family, with tough stems, greenish-white flowers, and dark-purple fruit 2. *a)* a tropical American woody vine (*Paullinia curassavica*) of the soapberry family, the wood of which is used for walking sticks *b)* such a walking stick

sup·ple·ment (sup′lə mənt; *for v.* -ment′) *n.* [ME. < L. *supplementum* < *supplere*: see SUPPLY¹] 1. something added, esp. to make up for a lack or deficiency 2. a section added to a book or the like to give additional information, correct errors in the body of the work, etc. ☆3. a separate section containing feature stories, comic strips, or the like, issued with a newspaper 4. the amount to be added to a given angle or arc to make 180° or a semicircle —*vt.* to provide a supplement to; add to, esp. so as to make up for a lack or deficiency —sup′ple·men′tal *adj.* —sup′ple·men·ta′tion (-mən tā′shən) *n.*

sup·ple·men·ta·ry (sup′lə men′tər ē) *adj.* supplying what is lacking; serving as a supplement; additional —*n., pl.* -ries a supplementary person or thing

supplementary angle either of two angles that together form 180°

sup·ple·tion (sə plē′shən) *n.* [ME. *suplecioun* < ML. *suppletio* < L. *suppletus*: see ff.] *Linguis.* the supplying of a deficient form of a word by a completely different form (**suppletive form**) drawn from another basic word (Ex.: *went*, orig. the past tense of *wend*, is a suppletive form expressing the past tense of *go*) —sup′ple′tive (-plēt′iv, sup′lə tiv) *adj.*

SUPPLEMENTARY ANGLES
(angle BCA and angle DCB are supplementary)

sup·ple·to·ry (sup′lə tôr′e, sə plēt′ə rē) *adj.* [LL. *suppletorius* < L. *suppletus*, pp. of *supplere*, to SUPPLY¹] *same as* SUPPLEMENTARY

sup·pli·ance (sup′lē əns) *n.* [< ff.] *same as* SUPPLICATION

sup·pli·ant (sup′lē ənt) *n.* [ME. *suppliaunt*: see the adj.] a person who supplicates; petitioner —*adj.* [MFr., prp. of *supplier* < L. *supplicare*, to SUPPLICATE] 1. asking humbly; supplicating; entreating 2. expressing supplication [*suppliant* words] —sup′pli·ant·ly *adv.*

sup·pli·cant (sup′lə kənt) *adj.* [L. *supplicans*, prp. of *supplicare*: see ff.] that supplicates; supplicating —*n.* a person who supplicates; suppliant

sup·pli·cate (sup′lə kāt′) *vt.* -cat′ed, -cat′ing [ME. *supplicaten* < L. *supplicatus*, pp. of *supplicare*, to kneel down, pray < *sub-*, under + *plicare*, to fold, double up: see PLY¹] 1. to ask for humbly and earnestly, as by prayer 2. to make a humble request of; petition earnestly —*vi.* to make a humble request or supplication, esp. in prayer —*SYN.* see APPEAL —sup′pli·ca·to′ry (-kə tôr′ē) *adj.*

sup·pli·ca·tion (sup′lə kā′shən) *n.* 1. the act of supplicating 2. a humble request, prayer, petition, etc.

sup·ply¹ (sə plī′) *vt.* -plied′, -ply′ing [ME. *supplyen* < MFr. *supplier* < L. *supplere*, to fill up < *sub-*, under + *plere*, to fill: for IE. base see FULL¹] 1. to give, furnish, or provide (what is needed or wanted) [to *supply* tools to workers] 2. to meet the needs or requirements of; furnish, provide, or equip with what is needed or wanted [to

supply workers with tools*]* **3.** to compensate for; make good *[to supply* a deficiency*]* **4.** to act as a substitute in; fill or serve in temporarily *[to supply* another's pulpit*]* —*vi.* to serve as a temporary substitute —*n., pl.* **-plies'** **1.** the act of supplying **2.** an amount or quantity available for use; stock; store **3.** *[pl.]* materials, provisions, etc. for supplying an army, expedition, a business, etc.; sometimes, specif., provisions for an army other than materiel, vehicles, etc. **4.** *[pl.]* an amount of money granted for government expenses; appropriation **5.** a temporary substitute, as for a minister **6.** [Obs.] *a)* assistance *b)* reinforcements **7.** *Econ.* the amount of a commodity available for purchase at a given price: opposed to DEMAND —*adj.* **1.** having to do with a supply or supplies **2.** serving as a substitute —**sup·pli'er** *n.*

sup·ply² (sup'lē) *adv.* in a supple manner; supplely

sup·port (sə pôrt') *vt.* [ME. *supporten* < MFr. *supporter* < LL.(Ec.) *supportare*, to endure, bear < L., to carry, bring to a place < *sub-*, under + *portare*, to carry: see PORT³] **1.** *a)* to carry or bear the weight of; keep from falling, slipping, or sinking; hold up *b)* to carry or bear (a specified weight, strain, pressure, etc.) **2.** to give courage, faith, or confidence to; help or comfort **3.** to give approval to or be in favor of; subscribe to; uphold **4.** to maintain or provide for (a person, institution, etc.) with money, or subsistence **5.** to show or tend to show to be true; help prove, vindicate, or corroborate *[evidence to support* a claim*]* **6.** to bear; endure; submit to; tolerate **7.** to keep up; maintain; sustain; specif., to maintain (the price of a specified commodity) as by purchases or by making loans **8.** *Theater* to act a subordinate role in the same play with (a specified star) —*n.* **1.** a supporting or being supported **2.** a person or thing that supports; specif., *a)* a prop, base, brace, etc. *b)* a means of subsistence *c)* an elastic, girdlelike device to support or bind a part of the body —**sup·port'a·ble** *adj.* —**sup·port'a·bly** *adv.*

SYN.—**support**, the broadest of these terms, suggests a favoring of someone or something, either by giving active aid or merely by approving or sanctioning *[to support* a candidate for office*]*; **uphold** suggests that what is being supported is under attack *[to uphold* civil rights for all*]*; **sustain** implies full active support so as to strengthen or keep from failing *[sustained* by his hope for the future*]*; **maintain** suggests a supporting so as to keep intact or unimpaired *[to maintain* the law, a family, etc.*]*; **advocate** implies support in speech or writing and sometimes connotes persuasion or argument *[to advocate* a change in policy*]*; **back** (often **back up**) suggests support, as financial aid, moral encouragement, etc., given to prevent failure *[I'll back* you *up* in your demands*]*

sup·port·er (-ər) *n.* **1.** a person who supports; advocate; adherent; partisan **2.** a thing that supports; esp., *a)* an elastic, girdlelike device worn to support the back, abdomen, etc. ☆*b) same as* JOCKSTRAP: in full **athletic supporter** ☆*c) same as* GARTER **3.** *Heraldry* either of a pair of figures, as of animals or men, standing one on either side of an escutcheon —*SYN.* see FOLLOWER

sup·port·ive (-iv) *adj.* that gives support, help, or approval

sup·pose (sə pōz') *vt.* **-posed', -pos'ing** [ME. *supposen* < MFr. *supposer*, to suppose, imagine, altered (after *poser:* see POSE¹) < ML. *supponere*, to suppose, assume < L., to put under, substitute < *sub-* + *ponere:* see POSITION] **1.** to assume to be true, as for the sake of argument or to illustrate a proof *[suppose* A equals B*]* **2.** to believe, imagine, think, guess, or presume **3.** to involve the assumption of; presuppose **4.** to consider as a proposed or suggested possibility: used in the imperative *[suppose* he doesn't come*]* **5.** to expect or obligate: always in the passive *[she's supposed* to telephone*]* —*vi.* to make a supposition; conjecture —**sup·pos'a·ble** *adj.* —**sup·pos'a·bly** *adv.* —**sup·pos'er** *n.*

sup·posed (sə pōzd') *adj.* **1.** regarded as true, genuine, etc., without actual knowledge **2.** merely imagined

sup·pos·ed·ly (sə pōz'id lē) *adv.* according to what is, was, or may be supposed

sup·po·si·tion (sup'ə zish'ən) *n.* [ME. < OFr. < L. *suppositio* < *suppositus*, pp. of *supponere:* see SUPPOSE] **1.** the act of supposing **2.** something supposed; assumption; hypothesis Also **sup·pos·al** (sə pōz'l) —**sup'po·si'tion·al** *adj.* —**sup'po·si'tion·al·ly** *adv.*

sup·po·si·tious (-əs) *adj. same as* SUPPOSITITIOUS

sup·po·si·ti·tious (sə päz'ə tish'əs) *adj.* [L. *suppositicius* < *suppositus:* see SUPPOSITION] **1.** substituted with intent to deceive or defraud; spurious; counterfeit **2.** suppositional; hypothetical —**sup·pos'i·ti'tious·ly** *adv.* —**sup·pos'i·ti'tious·ness** *n.*

sup·pos·i·tive (sə päz'ə tiv) *adj.* [LL. *suppositivus*] having the nature of, based on, or involving supposition —*n. Gram.* a conjunction introducing a supposition, as *if, assuming, provided*, etc.

sup·pos·i·to·ry (sə päz'ə tôr'ē) *n., pl.* **-ries** [ModL. *suppositorium* < neut. of L. *suppositorius:* see SUPPOSITION] a small piece of medicated substance, usually conical, ovoid, or cylindrical, introduced into a body passage, as the rectum or vagina, where it is melted and diffused by the body temperature

sup·press (sə pres') *vt.* [ME. *suppressen* < L. *suppressus*, pp. of *supprimere*, to press under, suppress < *sub-*, under + *premere*, to PRESS¹] **1.** *a)* to put down by force; subdue; quell; crush *b)* to abolish by authority **2.** to keep from appearing or being known, published, etc. *[to suppress* a news story, a book, etc.*]* **3.** to keep back; restrain; check *[to suppress* a laugh, a cough, etc.*]* **4.** to check or stop (a natural flow, secretion, or excretion) **5.** *Electronics, Radio,* etc. to eliminate or weaken (an unwanted oscillation, echo, etc.) in a circuit **6.** *Psychiatry* to consciously dismiss from the mind (unacceptable ideas, impulses, etc.): cf. REPRESS —**sup·press'i·ble** *adj.* —**sup·pres'sive** *adj.* —**sup·pres'sive·ly** *adv.* —**sup·pres'sor** *n.*

sup·pres·sion (sə presh'ən) *n.* [L. *suppressio*] **1.** a suppressing or being suppressed **2.** *Psychiatry a)* the mechanism by which unacceptable ideas, impulses, etc. are suppressed *b)* something suppressed in this way

sup·pu·rate (sup'yoo rāt') *vi.* **-rat'ed, -rat'ing** [< L. *suppuratus*, pp. of *suppurare*, to form pus underneath < *sup-* (see SUB-) + *pus* (gen. *puris*), PUS] to form or discharge pus; fester —**sup'pu·ra'tion** *n.* —**sup'pu·ra'tive** *adj.*

supr. supreme

su·pra- (soo'prə) [< L. *supra*, above, over, akin to *super:* see SUPER-] *a prefix meaning* above, over, beyond *[supra-renal]*

su·pra·lap·sar·i·an (soo'prə lap ser'ē ən, -sar'-) *n.* [< prec. + L. *lapsus*, a fall + -ARIAN] any of a group of Calvinists who held that God's plan of salvation for some people preceded the fall of man from grace, which had been predestined: opposed to INFRALAPSARIAN —*adj.* of this doctrine —**su'pra·lap·sar'i·an·ism** *n.*

su·pra·lim·i·nal (-lim'i n'l) *adj.* [SUPRA- + LIMINAL] above the threshold of consciousness; at a conscious level —**su'pra·lim'i·nal·ly** *adv.*

su·pra·mo·lec·u·lar (-mə lek'yoo lar) *adj.* composed of more than one molecule

su·pra·na·tion·al (-nash'ə n'l) *adj.* of, for, involving, or over all or a number of nations *[supranational* authority*]* —**su'pra·na'tion·al·ism** *n.*

su·pra·or·bit·al (-ôr'bi t'l) *adj. Anat.* situated above the orbit of the eye

su·pra·pro·test (-prō'test) *n.* [< It. *sopra protesto*, upon protest: cf. SUPRA- & PROTEST] *Law* an acceptance or payment of a bill of exchange by someone other than the drawer, after protest for nonacceptance or nonpayment by the drawee

su·pra·re·nal (-rē'n'l) *adj.* [ModL. *suprarenalis:* see SUPRA- & RENAL] situated on or above the kidney; specif., designating or of an adrenal gland —*n.* an adrenal gland

su·pra·seg·men·tal phonemes (-seg men't'l) phonemes or features of speech, as pitch, stress, and juncture, that may extend over and modify series of segmental phonemes

su·prem·a·cist (sə prem'ə sist, soo-) *n.* a person who believes in or promotes the supremacy of a particular group *[a white supremacist]*

su·prem·a·cy (sə prem'ə sē, soo-) *n., pl.* **-cies** [SUPREM(E) + -ACY] **1.** the quality or state of being supreme **2.** supreme power or authority

su·preme (sə prēm', soo-) *adj.* [L. *supremus*, superl. of *superus*, that is above, higher: see SUPER-] **1.** highest in rank, power, authority, etc.; dominant **2.** highest in quality, achievement, performance, etc.; most excellent **3.** highest in degree; utmost *[a supreme* fool*]* **4.** final; ultimate —**su·preme'ly** *adv.* —**su·preme'ness** *n.*

Supreme Being God

Supreme Court ☆**1.** the highest Federal court, consisting of nine judges: its decisions are final and take precedence over those of all other judicial bodies in the country ☆**2.** the highest court in most States

supreme sacrifice the sacrifice of one's life

Supreme Soviet the parliament of the Soviet Union: it consists of two equal chambers, the Council of the Union (whose members are elected on the basis of population) and the Council of the Nationalities (whose members are elected by the various nationality groups)

Supt., supt. Superintendent

Sur (soor) *Arabic name of* TYRE

sur-¹ (sur) [ME. < OFr. *sur-, sour-* < L. *super, supra*, over, above] *a prefix meaning* over, upon, above, beyond *[surcoat, surface]*

sur-² (sur) *same as* SUB-: used before *r*

su·ra (soor'ə) *n.* [Ar. *sūrah*, lit., step, degree] any of the main divisions, or chapters, of the Koran

Su·ra·ba·ja (soo'rä bä'yä) seaport in NE Java, Indonesia, opposite Madura: pop. 1,008,000

su·rah (soor'ə) *n.* [< SURAT: orig. used of coarse cotton goods made there] a soft, twilled fabric of silk or rayon

Su·ra·kar·ta (soo'rä kär'tä) city in C Java, Indonesia: pop. 368,000

su·ral (soor'əl) *adj.* [ModL. *suralis* < L. *sura*, calf of the leg] *Anat.* of the calf of the leg

Su·rat (soo rat', soor'ət) seaport in Gujarat state, W India, on the Arabian Sea: pop. 288,000

sur·base (sur'bās') *n.* a molding along the top of a base, as of a pedestal, baseboard, etc.

fat, āpe, cär; ten, ēven; is, bīte; gō, hôrn, tōōl, look; oil, out; up, fur; get; joy; yet; chin; she; thin, *th*en; zh, leisure; ŋ, ring; ə for *a* in ago, *e* in agent, *i* in sanity, *o* in comply, *u* in focus; ' as in able (ā'b'l); Fr. bàl; ë, Fr. coeur; ö, Fr. feu; ô, Fr. mon; ô, Fr. coq; ü, Fr. duc; ʀ, Fr. cri; H, G. ich; kh, G. doch. See inside front cover. ☆ Americanism; ‡foreign; *hypothetical; <derived from

sur·based (-bāst′) *adj.* 1. [< *prec.* + -ED] having a surbase 2. [< Fr. *surbaissé* < *sur-* (see SUR-¹) + *baissé*, pp. of *baisser*, to lower < VL. **bassiare* < *bassus* (see BASE²)] designating an arch whose rise is less than half its span

sur·cease (sur sēs′; *for n., usually* sur′sēs) *vt., vi.* -ceased′, -ceas′ing [ME. *sursessen* < OFr. *sursis*, pp. of *surseoir*, to pause, delay < L. *supersedere*, to refrain from: see SUPERSEDE] [Archaic] to stop; end —*n.* an end, or cessation

sur·charge (sur′chärj; *also, for v.*, sur chärj′) *vt.* -charged′, -charg′ing [ME. *surchargen* < OFr. *surcharger*: see SUR-¹ & CHARGE] 1. to overcharge 2. to overload; overburden 3. to fill to excess or beyond normal capacity 4. to mark (a postage stamp) with a surcharge 5. *Law* to show an omission, as of a credit, in (an account) —*n.* 1. *a)* an additional amount added to the usual charge *b)* an overcharge 2. an extra or excessive load, burden, etc. 3. a new valuation overprinted on a postage stamp, etc., to change its denomination 4. *Law* the act of surcharging

sur·cin·gle (sur′siŋ′g'l) *n.* [ME. *surcengle* < MFr. < *sur-*, over + L. *cingulum*, a belt: see CINGULUM] 1. a strap passed around a horse's body to bind on a saddle, blanket, pack, etc. 2. a girdle, esp. of a cassock

sur·coat (-kōt′) *n.* [ME. *surcote* < MFr.: see SUR-¹ & COAT] an outer coat or gown; esp., in the Middle Ages, a loose, short cloak worn over armor

sur·cu·lose (sur′kyoo lōs′) *adj.* [ModL. *surculosus* < L., woody < *surculus*, a twig, graft, sucker, dim. of *surus*, a twig, branch] *Bot.* having suckers

surd (surd) *adj.* [L. *surdus*, deaf, dull, mute: used to transl. Gr. *alogos*, irrational, lit., without reason] 1. *Math.* same as IRRATIONAL 2. *Phonet.* same as VOICELESS —*n.* 1. *Math.* an irrational number or quantity; specif., a root which can be expressed only approximately [√5 is a surd] 2. *Phonet.* a voiceless sound

sure (shoor) *adj.* sur′er, sur′est [ME. < OFr. < L. *securus*: see SECURE] 1. orig., secure or safe 2. that will not fail; always effective [a *sure* method] 3. that can be relied or depended upon; trustworthy [a *sure* friend] 4. that cannot be doubted, questioned, or disputed; absolutely true; certain 5. having or showing no doubt or hesitancy; assured; positive; confident [to be *sure* of one's facts] 6. that can be counted on to be or happen [a *sure* defeat] 7. bound or destined to do, experience, or be something specified [*sure* to be elected] 8. never missing or faltering; unerring; steady [a *sure* aim] —*adv.* [Colloq.] 1. surely; inevitably 2. certainly; indeed: an intensive, often used as an affirmative answer to questions —**for sure** certain(ly); without doubt —**make sure** to be or cause to be certain —**sure enough** [Colloq.] certainly; without doubt —**to be sure** surely; certainly —**sure′ness** *n.*

SYN.—**sure**, the simple word, suggests merely an absence of doubt or hesitancy [I'm *sure* you don't mean it]; **certain** usually suggests conviction based on specific grounds or evidence [this letter makes me *certain* of his innocence]; **confident** stresses the firmness of one's certainty or assurance, esp. in some expectation [he's *confident* he'll win]; **positive** suggests unshakable confidence, esp. in the correctness of one's opinions or conclusions, sometimes to the point of dogmatism [he's too *positive* in his beliefs] —ANT. doubtful

☆**sure-e·nough** (shoor′i nuf′) *adj.* [Colloq.] real; actual

☆**sure-fire** (-fīr′) *adj.* [Colloq.] sure to be successful or as expected; that will not fail

sure-foot·ed (-foot′id) *adj.* not likely to stumble, slip, fall, or err —**sure′-foot′ed·ly** *adv.* —**sure′-foot′ed·ness** *n.*

sure·ly (-lē) *adv.* 1. with assurance or confidence; in a sure, unhesitating manner 2. without a doubt; assuredly; unquestionably; certainly: often used as an intensive emphasizing a supposition [*surely* you don't believe that!] 3. without risk of failing: chiefly in **slowly but surely**

☆**sure thing** 1. [Colloq.] something considered certain to win, succeed, etc. 2. all right; OK: used interjectionally

sur·e·ty (shoor′ə tē, shoor′tē) *n., pl.* -ties [ME. *seurte* < OFr. < L. *securitas* < *securus*, sure, SECURE] 1. the state of being sure; sureness; assurance 2. something sure; certainty 3. something that makes sure or gives assurance, as against loss, damage, or default; security; guarantee 4. a person who makes himself responsible for another; specif., *Law* one who makes himself liable for another's debts, defaults of obligations, etc. —**sur′e·ty·ship′** *n.*

surf (surf) *n.* [earlier *suffe*, prob. var. of SOUGH] 1. the waves or swell of the sea breaking on the shore or a reef 2. the foam or spray caused by this —*vi.* to engage in the sport of surfing —**surf′er** *n.*

sur·face (sur′fis) *n.* [Fr. < *sur-* (see SUR-¹) + *face*, FACE, after L. *superficies*] 1. *a)* the outer face, or exterior, of an object *b)* any of the faces of a solid *c)* the area or extent of such a face 2. superficial features, as of a personality; outward appearance 3. *same as* AIRFOIL 4. *Geom.* an extent or magnitude having length and breadth, but no thickness —*adj.* 1. of, on, or at the surface 2. intended to function or be carried on land or sea, rather than in the air or under water [*surface* forces, *surface* mail] 3. merely apparent; external; superficial —*vt.* -faced, -fac·ing 1. to treat the surface of, esp. so as to make smooth or level 2. to give a surface to, as in paving 3. to bring to the surface; esp., to bring (a submarine) to the surface of the water —*vi.* 1. to work at or near the surface, as in mining 2. to rise to the surface of the water 3. to become known, esp. after being concealed —**sur′fac·er** *n.*

sur·face-ac·tive (-ak′tiv) *adj. Chem.* designating or of a substance, such as a detergent, wetting agent, etc., that lowers the surface tension of the solvent in which it is dissolved or the tension at the interface between two immiscible liquids

surface noise noise produced by the friction of a phonograph needle moving in the grooves of a record

surface plate a steel plate having a tooled flat surface used as a standard of flatness, as in manufacturing

surface tension a property of liquids in which the exposed surface tends to contract to the smallest possible area, as in the formation of a meniscus: it is caused by unequal molecular cohesive forces near the surface

☆**sur·face-to-air** (-tə er′) *adj.* launched from the surface of the earth and directed at a target in the air [*surface-to-air* missile]

☆**sur·face-to-sur·face** (-tə sur′fis) *adj.* launched from the surface of the earth and directed at a target elsewhere on the surface [*surface-to-surface* missile]

sur·fac·tant (sur fak′tənt) *n.* [surf(ace)-act(ive) a(ge)nt] a surface-active agent

☆**surf·bird** (surf′burd′) *n.* a shore bird (*Aphriza virgata*) of the sandpiper family, found on the Pacific coast of the Americas: it has a short, square tail, white at the base and black at the tip

surf·board (-bôrd′) *n.* a long, narrow board used in the sport of surfing —*vi.* to engage in this sport —**surf′board′er** *n.* —**surf′board′ing** *n.*

surf·boat (-bōt′) *n.* a sturdy, light boat used in heavy surf

☆**surf-cast** (-kast′, -käst′) *vi.* to fish by casting into the ocean surf from or near the shore —**surf′-cast′er** *n.*

☆**surf clam** any of several large, mostly tropical clams (genera *Mactra* and *Spisula*) living in the region of the surf

☆**surf duck** any of various scoters; esp., *same as* SURF SCOTER

SURFBOARD

sur·feit (sur′fit) *n.* [ME. *surfet* < OFr. *sorfait* < *sorfaire*, to overdo < *sur-* (< L. *super*), over + *faire* (< L. *facere*), to make: see DO¹] 1. too great an amount or supply; excess (*of*) [a *surfeit* of compliments] 2. overindulgence, esp. in food or drink 3. discomfort, disgust, nausea, etc. resulting from any kind of excess; satiety —*vt.* [ME. *sorfeten*] to feed or supply to satiety or excess —*vi.* [Now Rare] to indulge or be supplied to satiety or excess; overindulge —SYN. see SATIATE —**sur′feit·er** *n.*

☆**surf fish** 1. any of a number of unrelated fishes, esp. the surfperches, living in shallow water along the Pacific coast of N. America 2. any of several croakers of this region

surf·ing (sur′fiŋ) *n.* the sport of riding in toward shore on the crest of a wave, esp. on a surfboard

☆**surf·perch** (surf′purch′) *n., pl.* -perch′, -perch′es: see PLURAL, II, D, 2 any of a family (Embiotocidae) of sea fishes that bear living young and live in shallow water along the Pacific coast of N. America

surf·rid·ing (-rīd′iŋ) *n. same as* SURFING

surf scoter an American sea duck (*Melanitta perspicillata*) living in northern waters: the males are black with white-marked faces and necks, the females are grayish-brown

surf·y (sur′fē) *adj.* surf′i·er, surf′i·est 1. of, like, or forming surf 2. having surf, esp. heavy surf

surg. 1. surgeon 2. surgery 3. surgical

surge (surj) *n.* [LME. *sourge*, a fountain, stream, prob. < OFr. *sourgeon* < stem of *sourdre*, to rise < L. *surgere*, to rise, spring up < **subsregere* < *subs-*, var. of *sub-* (see SUB-) + *regere*, to direct (see RIGHT)] 1. *a)* a large mass of or as of moving water; wave; swell; billow *b)* such waves or billows collectively or in a series 2. a movement of or like that of a mass of water; violent rolling, sweeping, or swelling motion [the *surge* of the sea] 3. a sudden, sharp increase of electric current or voltage in a circuit 4. any sudden, strong increase, as of energy, enthusiasm, etc. 5. *Naut. a)* the concave part of a capstan or windlass, upon which the rope surges, or slips *b)* such a surging, or slipping —*vi.* surged, surg′ing [< OFr. *sourg-*, stem of *sourdre*: see the *n.*] 1. to have a heavy, violent swelling motion; move in or as in a surge or surges 2. to rise and fall or be tossed about on waves, as a ship 3. to increase suddenly or abnormally: said of electric current or voltage 4. to slip, as a rope or cable on a capstan or windlass —*vt.* to slacken or release (a rope or cable) suddenly

sur·geon (sur′jən) *n.* [ME. *surgien* < OFr. *cirurgien* < *cirurgie*, SURGERY] a doctor who specializes in surgery, as distinguished from a physician

☆**sur·geon·fish** (-fish′) *n., pl.* -fish′, -fish′es: see FISH² any of a family (Acanthuridae) of edible, usually brightly colored, tropical sea fishes with one or more movable, lancelike spines on either side of the base of the tail

☆**Surgeon General** *pl.* **Surgeons General, Surgeon Generals** 1. the chief general officer or admiral in charge of the medical department of the U.S. Army, Air Force, or Navy 2. the chief medical officer in the U.S. Public Health Service or in some State health services Abbrev. **Surg. Gen.**

surgeon's knot any of several knots used as by surgeons in tying ligatures: see KNOT, illus.

sur·ger·y (sur′jər ē) *n., pl.* **-ger·ies** [ME. < OFr. *cirurgie* < L. *chirurgia* < Gr. *cheirourgia*, a working with the hands, handicraft, skill < *cheir* (gen. *cheiros*), the hand + *ergein*, to WORK] **1.** *a)* the treatment of disease, injury, or deformity by manual or instrumental operations, as the removal of diseased parts or tissue by cutting *b)* the branch of medicine dealing with this **2.** the operating room of a surgeon or hospital **3.** [Brit.] a doctor's office   See also TREE SURGERY

sur·gi·cal (-ji k'l) *adj.* **1.** of surgeons or surgery **2.** used in or connected with surgery **3.** resulting from or after surgery —**sur′gi·cal·ly** *adv.*

su·ri·cate (soor′ə kāt′) *n.* [Fr. *surikate*] any of a genus (*Suricata*) of small, four-toed, burrowing mammals of S Africa, related to the civet and mongoose

Su·ri·nam (soor′i näm′, soor′i nam′) state of the kingdom of the Netherlands, on the NE coast of S. America: 55,144 sq. mi.; pop. 363,000; cap. Paramaribo: see GUIANA, map

sur·ly (sur′lē) *adj.* **-li·er, -li·est** [earlier *sirly*, masterful, imperious < *sir*, SIR] **1.** bad-tempered; sullenly rude; hostile and uncivil **2.** gloomy and threatening: said of weather **3.** [Obs.] haughty; arrogant —*SYN.* see SULLEN —**sur′li·ly** *adv.* —**sur′li·ness** *n.*

sur·mise (sər mīz′; *for n., also* sur′mīz) *n.* [ME. *surmyse* < OFr. *surmise*, accusation, fem. of *surmis*, pp. of *sur-mettre*, to put upon, hence to accuse < *sur-* (see SUR-¹) + *mettre*, to put < L. *mittere*, to send (see MISSION)] **1.** an idea or opinion formed from evidence that is neither positive nor conclusive; conjecture; guess **2.** the act or process of surmising; conjecture in general —*vt.,* *vi.* **-mised′, -mis′ing** to imagine or infer (something) without conclusive evidence; conjecture; guess —*SYN.* see GUESS

sur·mount (sər mount′) *vt.* [ME. *surmounten* < OFr. *surmonter:* see SUR-¹ & MOUNT²] **1.** orig., to surpass or exceed; go beyond **2.** to get the better of; conquer; overcome **3.** to be or lie at the top of; be or rise above **4.** to climb up and across; get over (a height, obstacle, etc.) **5.** to place something above or on top of —**sur·mount′-a·ble** *adj.*

sur·mul·let (sər mul′it) *n., pl.* **-lets, -let:** see PLURAL, II, D, 1 [Fr. *surmulet* < OFr. *sormulet* < *sor*, red (see SORREL²) + *mulet*, MULLET] same as MULLET (sense 2)

sur·name (sur′nām′; *for v., also* sur′nām′) *n.* [ME. < *sur-* (see SUR-¹) + *name*, after earlier *surnoun* < OFr. *surnom* < *sur-* + *nom* < L. *nomen*, NAME] **1.** the family name, or last name, as distinguished from a given name **2.** a name or epithet added to a person's given name (Ex.: Ivan *the Terrible*) —*vt.* **-named′, -nam′ing** to give a surname to

sur·pass (sər pas′, -päs′) *vt.* [MFr. *surpasser* < *sur-* (see SUR-¹) + *passer*, to PASS²] **1.** to excel or be superior to **2.** to exceed in quantity, degree, amount, etc. **3.** to go beyond the limit, capacity, range, etc. of (*riches surpassing belief*) —*SYN.* see EXCEL

sur·pass·ing (-iŋ) *adj.* that surpasses the average or usual; exceeding or excelling; unusually excellent —*adv.* [Archaic] exceedingly —**sur·pass′ing·ly** *adv.*

sur·plice (sur′plis) *n.* [ME. *surplis* < Anglo-Fr. *surpliz* < OFr. *surpliz* < ML. *superpelliceum* < L. *super-*, above (see SUPER-) + *pelliceum*, fur robe, neut. of L. *pelliceus*, made of skins < *pellis*, skin (see FELL⁴)] a loose, white, wide-sleeved outer vestment worn by the clergy and choir in some churches —**sur′-pliced** *adj.*

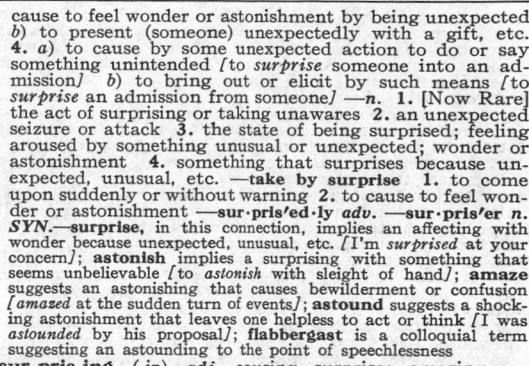

SURPLICE

sur·plus (sur′plus, -pləs) *n.* [ME. < OFr. < *sur-*, above (see SUR-¹) + L. *plus*, more (see PLUS)] **1.** a quantity or amount over and above what is needed or used; something left over; excess **2.** *a)* the excess of the assets of a business over its liabilities for a given period *b)* the excess of the total accumulated assets of a business over its liabilities and capital stock outstanding —*adj.* **1.** forming a surplus; excess; extra ☆**2.** designating or of commodities (specif., certain excess farm products) bought, stored, distributed, etc. by the government under the Federal price-support program: cf. PRICE SUPPORT

sur·plus·age (-ij) *n.* [ME.: see prec. & -AGE] **1.** surplus; excess **2.** irrelevant or superfluous words or matter; specif., *Law* such matter in the pleading of a case

surplus value in Marxist economics, the amount by which the value of the worker's product exceeds that of his pay, viewed as the source of capitalist profit

sur·print (sur′print′) *vt., n. same as* OVERPRINT

sur·pris·al (sər prī′z'l) *n.* [Now Rare] *same as* SURPRISE

sur·prise (sər prīz′) *vt.* **-prised′, -pris′ing** [ME. *surprysen* < OFr. *surpris*, pp. of *sorprendre*, to surprise, take napping < *sur-* (see SUR-¹) + *prendre*, to take (see PRIZE²)] **1.** to come upon suddenly or unexpectedly; take unawares **2.** to attack or capture suddenly and without warning **3.** *a)* to

cause to feel wonder or astonishment by being unexpected *b)* to present (someone) unexpectedly with a gift, etc. **4.** *a)* to cause by some unexpected action to do or say something unintended (*to surprise* someone into an admission) *b)* to bring out or elicit by such means (*to surprise* an admission from someone) —*n.* **1.** [Now Rare] the act of surprising or taking unawares **2.** an unexpected seizure or attack **3.** the state of being surprised; feeling aroused by something unusual or unexpected; wonder or astonishment **4.** something that surprises because unexpected, unusual, etc. —**take by surprise 1.** to come upon suddenly or without warning **2.** to cause to feel wonder or astonishment —**sur·pris′ed·ly** *adv.* —**sur·pris′er** *n.* *SYN.*—**surprise,** in this connection, implies an affecting with wonder because unexpected, unusual, etc. (I'm *surprised* at your concern); **astonish** implies a surprising with something that seems unbelievable (to *astonish* with sleight of hand); **amaze** suggests an astonishing that causes bewilderment or confusion (*amazed* at the sudden turn of events); **astound** suggests a shocking astonishment that leaves one helpless to act or think (I was *astounded* by his proposal); **flabbergast** is a colloquial term suggesting an astounding to the point of speechlessness

sur·pris·ing (-iŋ) *adj.* causing surprise; amazing —**sur·pris′ing·ly** *adv.*

sur·re·al·ism (sə rē′ə liz'm) *n.* [Fr. *surréalisme:* see SUR-¹ & REALISM] a modern movement in art and literature, in which an attempt is made to portray or interpret the workings of the unconscious mind as manifested in dreams: it is characterized by an irrational, noncontextual arrangement of material —**sur·re′al, sur·re′al·is′tic** *adj.* —**sur·re′al·ist** *adj., n.* —**sur·re′al·is′ti·cal·ly** *adv.*

sur·re·but·tal (sur′ri but′l) *n. Law* the act of presenting evidence in support of a surrebutter

sur·re·but·ter (-ri but′ər) *n. Law* a plaintiff's reply to a defendant's rebutter

sur·re·join·der (-ri join′dər) *n. Law* a plaintiff's reply to a defendant's rejoinder

sur·ren·der (sə ren′dər) *vt.* [ME. *surrendren* < MFr. *surrendre* < *sur-*, up (see SUR-¹) + *rendre*, to RENDER] **1.** to give up possession of or power over; yield to another on demand or compulsion **2.** to give up claim to; give over or yield, esp. voluntarily, as in favor of another **3.** to give up or abandon (*surrendering* all hope) **4.** to yield or resign (oneself) to an emotion, influence, etc. —*vi.* **1.** to give oneself up to another's power or control, esp. as a prisoner **2.** to give in (*to* something); yield (*to surrender* to temptation, a whim, etc.) —*n.* [LME. < MFr. *surrendre*, inf. used as *n.*] **1.** the act of surrendering, yielding, or giving up, over, or in **2.** *Insurance* the voluntary abandonment of a policy or by an insured person in return for a cash payment (**surrender value**), thus freeing the company of liability *SYN.*—**surrender** commonly implies the giving up of something completely after striving to keep it (to *surrender* a fort, one's freedom, etc.); **relinquish** is the general word implying an abandoning, giving up, or letting go of something held (to *relinquish* one's grasp, a claim, etc.); to **yield** is to concede or give way under pressure (to *yield* one's consent); to **submit** is to give in to authority or superior force (to *submit* to a conqueror); **resign** implies a voluntary, formal relinquishment and, used reflexively, connotes submission or passive acceptance (to *resign* an office, to *resign* oneself to failure)

sur·rep·ti·tious (sur′əp tish′əs) *adj.* [ME. *surreptitious* < L. *surrepticius* < *surreptus*, pp. of *surripere*, to take away secretly < *sub-* (see SUB-) + *rapere*, to seize (see RAPE¹)] **1.** done, got, made, etc. in a secret, stealthy way; clandestine **2.** acting in a secret, stealthy way —*SYN.* see SECRET —**sur′rep·ti′tious·ly** *adv.* —**sur′rep·ti′tious·ness** *n.*

Sur·rey (sur′ē) county of SE England: 722 sq. mi.; pop. 1,756,000

sur·rey (sur′ē) *n., pl.* **-reys** [so named as modification of the *Surrey cart*, a light pleasure cart first built in SURREY] ☆a light pleasure carriage having four wheels, two seats, and usually a flat top

SURREY

Sur·rey (sur′ē), **Earl of,** (*Henry Howard*) 1517?-47; Eng. poet & courtier: executed for treason

sur·ro·gate (sur′ə gāt′, sur′-; *for n., also* -git) *n.* [L. *surrogatus*, pp. of *surrogare*, to elect in place of another, substitute < *sub-* (see SUB-) + *rogare*, to ask, propose (for election)] **1.** a deputy or substitute ☆**2.** in some States, probate court, or a judge of this court **3.** *Psychiatry* a substitute figure, esp. a person of some authority, who replaces a father or mother in one's feelings —*vt.* **-gat′ed, -gat′ing** to put in another's place as a substitute or deputy

sur·round (sə round′) *vt.* [ME. *surrounden*, altered (as if < *sur-*, SUR-¹ + *round*) < *surunden*, to overflow < OFr. *suronder* < LL. *superundare* < L. *super-* (see SUPER-) + *undare*, to move in waves, rise < *unda*, a wave (see WATER)] **1.** to cause to be encircled on all or nearly all

sides [to *surround* a house with police] 2. to form an enclosure around; encircle; encompass [a wall *surrounds* the city] 3. to enclose (a fort, military unit, etc.) with troops so as to cut off communication or retreat; invest —*n.* [Chiefly Brit.] something serving as a border, etc.

sur·round·ing (-roun′diŋ) *n.* that which surrounds; esp., [*pl.*] the things, conditions, influences, etc. that surround a given place or person; environment —*adj.* that surrounds

‡**sur·sum cor·da** (sur′səm kôr′də) [L., lit., lift up (your) hearts: opening words of the Preface of the Mass] an incitement to courage, fervor, etc.

sur·tax (sur′taks′; *for v., also* sur′taks′) *n.* [SUR-[1] + TAX, after Fr. *surtaxe*] an extra tax on something already taxed; esp., a graduated tax on the amount by which an income exceeds a given figure —*vt.* to levy a surtax on

sur·tout (sər tōō′, -tōōt′; *Fr.* sür tōō′) *n.* [Fr., lit., overall < *sur-* (see SUR-[1]) + *tout* < L. *totus*, all (see TOTAL)] a man's long, closefitting overcoat of the late 19th cent.

surv. 1. survey 2. surveying 3. surveyor

sur·veil·lance (sər vā′ləns, -vāl′yəns) *n.* [Fr. < *surveiller*, to watch over < *sur-* (see SUR-[1]) + *veiller* < L. *vigilare*, to watch, WAKE[1]] 1. watch kept over a person, esp. one who is a suspect or a prisoner 2. supervision or inspection

sur·veil·lant (-lənt, -vāl′yənt) *n.* a person who watches, observes, or supervises

sur·vey (sər vā′; *also, and for n. usually,* sur′vā) *vt.* [ME. *surveien* < Anglo-Fr. *surveier* < OFr. *surveoir* < *sur-* (see SUR-[1]) + *veoir* < L. *videre*, to see (see VISION)] 1. to examine for some specific purpose; inspect or consider carefully; review in detail 2. to look at or consider, esp. in a general or comprehensive way; view 3. to determine the location, form, or boundaries of (a tract of land) by measuring the lines and angles in accordance with the principles of geometry and trigonometry 4. to make a survey of —*vi.* to survey land —*n., pl.* **-veys** 1. a detailed study or inspection, as by gathering information through observations, questionnaires, etc. and analyzing it 2. a general view; comprehensive study or examination [a *survey* of Italian art] 3. *a*) the process of surveying a tract of land *b*) a tract surveyed *c*) a plan or written description of this

sur·vey·ing (sər vā′iŋ) *n.* 1. the act of one who surveys 2. the science or work of making land surveys

sur·vey·or (-ər) *n.* [ME. *surveior* < OFr. *surveour*] a person who surveys, esp. one whose work is surveying land

surveyor's level an instrument consisting of a revolving telescope mounted on a tripod and fitted with cross hairs and a spirit level, used by surveyors in finding points of identical elevation

surveyor's measure a system of measurement used in surveying, based on the chain (**surveyor's chain**) as a unit: see CHAIN (*n.* 5 *a*)

sur·viv·al (sər vī′v'l) *n.* 1. the act, state, or fact of surviving 2. someone or something that survives, esp. an ancient belief, custom, usage, etc.

survival of the fittest *popular term for* NATURAL SELECTION

sur·vive (sər vīv′) *vt.* **-vived′, -viv′ing** [ME. *surviven* < OFr. *survivre* < L. *supervivere* < *super-*, above (see SUPER-) + *vivere*, to live (see QUICK)] 1. to live or exist longer than or beyond the life or existence of; outlive 2. to continue to live after or in spite of [to *survive* a wreck] —*vi.* to continue living or existing, as after an event or after another's death —*SYN.* see OUTLIVE —**sur·viv′a·bil′i·ty** *n.* —**sur·viv′a·ble** *adj.* —**sur·viv′al** *adv.*

sur·vi·vor·ship (-vī′vər ship′) *n.* 1. the state of being a survivor 2. *Law* the right of a surviving joint owner or owners to the share of an owner who dies

Su·sa (sōō′sä) capital of ancient Elam, now a ruined city in W Iran

Su·san (sōō′z'n) [Fr. *Susanne* < LL.(Ec.) *Susanna* < Gr.(Ec.) *Sousanna* < Heb. *shōshannāh*, lily] a feminine name: dim. *Sue, Susie, Suzy;* var. *Susanna, Susannah;* equiv. Fr. *Susanne, Suzanne*

Su·san·na, Su·san·nah (sōō zan′ə) a feminine name: see SUSAN

sus·cep·tance (sə sep′təns) *n.* [SUSCEPT(IBILITY) + -ANCE] *Elec.* the reactance divided by the square of the impedance: loosely, the reciprocal of reactance

sus·cep·ti·bil·i·ty (sə sep′tə bil′ə tē) *n., pl.* **-ties** [ML. *susceptibilitas*] 1. the quality or state of being susceptible 2. [*pl.*] sensitivities; feelings 3. a susceptible temperament or disposition; capacity for receiving impressions 4. *Physics a*) the amount of attraction exerted on a given substance by a magnet, expressed as the ratio of the intensity of magnetization to the magnetic field strength *b*) in a medium subjected to an electric field, the polarization per unit electric intensity

sus·cep·ti·ble (sə sep′tə b'l) *adj.* [ML. *susceptibilis* < L. *susceptus*, pp. of *suscipere*, to receive, undertake < *sus-* (see SUB-), under + *capere*, to take (see HAVE)] easily affected emotionally; having a sensitive nature or feelings —**susceptible** of that can be affected with; admitting, allowing [testimony *susceptible* of error] —**susceptible to** easily influenced by or affected with [*susceptible to* tuberculosis] —**sus·cep′ti·ble·ness** *n.* —**sus·cep′ti·bly** *adv.*

sus·cep·tive (sə sep′tiv) *adj.* [ML. *susceptivus*] *same as:* 1. SUSCEPTIBLE 2. RECEPTIVE —**sus·cep·tiv·i·ty** (sus′ep tiv′ə tē), **sus·cep′tive·ness** *n.*

su·shi (sōō′shē) *n.* [Jap.] a Japanese dish consisting of thin strips of raw fish wrapped about cakes of cold cooked rice

sus·lik (sus′lik) *n.* [Russ., akin to OBulg. *sysati*, to whistle, buzz < IE. echoic base *sūs-*, whence G. *sausen*, to whistle] 1. a small spermophile or ground squirrel (*Citellus citellus*) of NC Eurasia. its fur

sus·pect (sə spekt′; *for adj. usually, & for n. always,* sus′pekt) *vt.* [LME. *suspecten* < L. *suspectus*, pp. of *suspicere*, to look under, look up to, admire, also to mistrust < *sus-* (see SUB-), under + *spicere*, to look (see SPY)] 1. to believe (someone) to be guilty of something specified, on little or no evidence 2. to believe to be bad, wrong, harmful, questionable, etc.; distrust 3. to think it probable or likely; guess; surmise; suppose —*vi.* to be suspicious; have suspicion —*adj.* viewed with suspicion; suspected —*n.* a person who is suspected, esp. one suspected of a crime, etc.

sus·pend (sə spend′) *vt.* [ME. *suspenden* < OFr. *suspendre* < L. *suspendere*, to hang up < *sus-* (see SUB-), under + *pendere*, to hang (see PEND)] 1. to bar or exclude as a penalty from an office, school, position, etc., usually for a specified time; debar 2. to cause to cease or become inoperative for a time; stop temporarily [to *suspend* train service, to *suspend* a rule] 3. *a*) to defer or hold back (judgment), as until more is known *b*) to hold in abeyance or defer action on (a sentence, etc.) 4. to hang by a support from above so as to allow free movement 5. to hold or keep (dust in the air, particles in a liquid, etc.) in suspension 6. to keep in suspense, wonder, etc. 7. to continue (a musical note) into the following chord —*vi.* 1. to stop temporarily 2. to withhold payment of debts or obligations, as through inability to pay 3. to be suspended; hang —*SYN.* see ADJOURN, EXCLUDE

sus·pend·ed animation (sə spen′did) a temporary cessation of the vital functions resembling death

sus·pend·ers (-dərz) *n.pl.* 1. a pair of straps or bands passed over the shoulders to hold up the trousers or a skirt 2. [Brit.] garters for holding up stockings

sus·pense (sə spens′) *n.* [ME. < MFr. *suspens, suspense,* delay, deferring < ML. *suspensum* < L. *suspensus,* suspended, uncertain, lit., hung up, pp. of *suspendere,* to SUSPEND] 1. the state of being undecided or undetermined 2. a state of usually anxious uncertainty, as in awaiting a decision 3. the growing interest and excitement felt while awaiting a climax or resolution, as of a novel, play, series of events, etc. 4. [Rare] suspension or interruption, as of a legal right —**sus·pense′ful** *adj.*

suspense account *Bookkeeping* an account in which items are temporarily entered until their disposition can be determined

sus·pen·sion (sə spen′shən) *n.* [ML. *suspensio* < LL., an arching < L. *suspensus:* see SUSPENSE] 1. a suspending or being suspended; specif., *a*) a temporary barring from an office, school, etc. *b*) a temporary stoppage of payment, service, etc. *c*) a temporary canceling, as of rules *d*) a deferring of action on a sentence *e*) a holding back of a judgment, etc. 2. a supporting device or framework upon or from which something is suspended 3. the system of springs, etc. supporting a vehicle upon its undercarriage or axles 4. the act or means of suspending the balance or pendulum in a timepiece 5. *Chem. a*) the condition of a substance whose particles are dispersed through a fluid but not dissolved in it *b*) a substance in this condition *c*) a mixture of tiny, solid particles suspended in a liquid in such a way that the particles will separate out on standing: cf. COLLOID 6. *Music a*) the continuing of one or more tones of one chord into a following chord while the others are changed, so that a temporary dissonance is created *b*) the tone or tones so continued

suspension bridge a bridge suspended from chains or cables which are anchored at either end and supported by towers at regular intervals

suspension point any of a series of dots, properly three, indicating the omission of a word, phrase, sentence, etc., as from something quoted

sus·pen·sive (sə spen′siv) *adj.* [ML. *suspensivus*] 1. that suspends, defers, or temporarily stops something 2. tending to suspend judgment; undecided 3. of, characterized by, expressing, or in suspense 4. [Rare] of or characterized by physical suspension —**sus·pen′sive·ly** *adv.*

SUSPENSION BRIDGE

sus·pen·soid (-soid) *n.* [SUSPENS(ION) + (COLL)OID] a system of solid, colloidal particles suspended in a liquid

sus·pen·sor (-sər) *n.* [ML.] 1. *same as* SUSPENSORY 2. *Bot.* a cell or group of cells that forces the embryo of a higher plant into its food supply, the endosperm

sus·pen·so·ry (-sə rē) *adj.* [< L. *suspensus* (see SUSPENSE) + -ORY] 1. suspending, supporting, or sustaining [a *suspensory* muscle or bandage] 2. suspending or delaying, esp. so as to leave something undecided —*n., pl.* **-ries** 1. a suspensory muscle or bandage 2. a mesh fabric pouch for supporting the scrotum, held by a band around the hips

suspensory ligament any of various ligaments supporting body organs; esp., a ligament supporting the lens of the eye

sus·pi·cion (sə spish′ən) *n.* [ME. *suspecion* < Anglo-Fr. *suspecioun* < OFr. *sospeçon* < LL. *suspectio,* orig., a looking up to, esteeming, later with sense and sp. of L. *suspicio,* suspicion < L. *suspectus,* pp. of *suspicere,* to look up at, admire, look secretly at, mistrust, suspect] **1.** the act or an instance of suspecting guilt, a wrong, harmfulness, etc. with little or no supporting evidence **2.** the feeling or state of mind of a person who suspects **3.** a very small amount or degree; suggestion; inkling; trace —*vt.* [Dial.] to suspect —**above suspicion** not to be suspected; honorable —**on suspicion** on the basis of suspicion; because suspected —**under suspicion** suspected

sus·pi·cious (-əs) *adj.* [ME. *suspecious* < OFr. < L. *suspiciosus*] **1.** arousing or likely to arouse suspicion in others **2.** showing or expressing suspicion **3.** *a)* feeling suspicion *b)* tending habitually to suspect, esp. to suspect evil —**sus·pi′cious·ly** *adv.* —**sus·pi′cious·ness** *n.*

sus·pi·ra·tion (sus′pi rā′shən) *n.* [L. *suspiratio* < *suspirare:* see ff.] [Rare] a prolonged, deep sigh

sus·pire (sə spīr′) *vi.* **-pired′, -pir′ing** [ME. *suspiren* < L. *suspirare,* to breathe out < *sub-,* under + *spirare:* see SPIRIT] [Rare] to take a long, deep breath; esp., to sigh

Sus·que·han·na (sus′kwi han′ə) [< a Iroquoian tribal or stream name < ?] river flowing from C N.Y. through Pa. & Md. into Chesapeake Bay: 444 mi.

Sus·sex (sus′iks) **1.** county in SE England, on the English Channel: divided into *a)* **East Sussex** 824 sq. mi.; pop. 680,000 *b)* **West Sussex** 663 sq. mi.; pop. 426,000 **2.** *see* HEPTARCHY (sense 2)

sus·tain (sə stān′) *vt.* [ME. *sustemen* < OFr. *sustenir* < L. *sustinere* < *sus-* (see SUB-), under + *tenere,* to hold (see TENSE[1])] **1.** to keep in existence; keep up; maintain or prolong [to *sustain* a mood] **2.** to provide for the support of; specif., to provide sustenance or nourishment for **3.** to support from or as from below; carry the weight or burden of **4.** to strengthen the spirits, courage, etc. of; comfort; buoy up; encourage **5.** to bear up against; endure; withstand **6.** to undergo or suffer (an injury, loss, etc.) **7.** to uphold the validity or justice of [to *sustain* a verdict] **8.** to confirm; corroborate —SYN. see SUPPORT —**sus·tain′a·ble** *adj.* —**sus·tain′er** *n.* —**sus·tain′ment** *n.*

☆**sus·tain·ing program** (-iŋ) any radio or television program presented and paid for by a station or network rather than by a commercial sponsor

sus·te·nance (sus′ti nəns) *n.* [ME. < OFr. *soustenance* < LL. *sustinentia,* patience, endurance < L. *sustinere:* see SUSTAIN] **1.** a sustaining or being sustained **2.** one's means of livelihood; maintenance; support **3.** that which sustains life; nourishment; food

sus·ten·tac·u·lum (sus′ten tak′yoo ləm) *n., pl.* **-la** (-lə) [ModL., a support < L. < *sustentare,* to hold up, support, intens. of *sustinere* (see SUSTAIN)] *Anat.* a supporting structure —**sus′ten·tac′u·lar** (-lər) *adj.*

sus·ten·ta·tion (-tā′shən) *n.* [ME. < MFr. < L. *sustentatio* < *sustentare,* freq. of *sustinere,* to SUSTAIN] **1.** a sustaining or being sustained; maintenance, support, or preservation **2.** something that sustains or supports; sustenance —**sus·ten′ta·tive** (-tāt′iv, sə sten′tə tiv) *adj.*

sus·ten·tion (sə sten′shən) *n.* [< SUSTAIN by analogy with RETENTION] a sustaining or being sustained

Su·su (soo soo′) *n.* **1.** *pl.* **Su·sus′, Su·su′** any member of an agricultural people living chiefly in the countries of Guinea and Sierra Leone **2.** their Mande language

su·sur·rant (soo sur′ənt) *adj.* [L. *susurrans,* prp. of *susurrare,* to whisper < IE. base **swer-,* to hum, whence SWARM[1], L. *surdus,* deaf] whispering; murmuring; rustling: also **su·sur′rous** (-əs)

su·sur·rate (-āt) *vi.* **-rat·ed, -rat·ing** [L. *susurratus,* pp.: see prec.] to whisper; murmur; rustle —**su·sur·ra·tion** (soo′sə rā′shən) *n.*

su·sur·rus (-əs) *n.* [L.: see SUSURRANT] a whispering, murmuring, or rustling sound

Suth·er·land (suth′ər lənd) county of Scotland, on the N coast: 2,028 sq. mi.; pop. 13,000: also **Suth′er·land·shire′** (-shir′)

Sutherland Falls waterfall of SW South Island, New Zealand: 1,904 ft.

Sut·lej (sut′lej) river flowing from SW Tibet across the Punjab, into the Indus River in West Pakistan: c.900 mi.

sut·ler (sut′lər) *n.* [Early ModDu. *soeteler* < *soetelen,* to do dirty work, akin to G. *sudeln,* to do in a slovenly way < L. base **seu-,* juice, sap, rain, whence Gr. *hyein,* to rain, L. *sugere,* to suck] formerly, a person following an army to sell food, liquor, etc. to its soldiers

su·tra (soo′trə) *n.* [Sans. *sūtra,* a thread, string < IE. base **syu-,* to SEW] **1.** *Brahmanism a)* a precept or maxim *b)* a collection of these **2.** *Buddhism* a scriptural narrative; esp., an account of a dialogue or sermon of the Buddha Also **sut·ta** (soot′ə)

sut·tee (su tē′, sut′ē) *n.* [Hind. *satī* < Sans. *satī,* chaste and virtuous wife < *sat,* good, pure, prp. of *as,* to be: for base see IS] **1.** a Hindu widow who threw herself alive, and was cremated, on the funeral pyre of her husband's body **2.** the former Hindu custom of such self-immolation: also **sut·tee′ism**

Sut·ter's Mill (sut′ərz) a mill, owned by John Sutter (1803–80), northeast of Sacramento, Calif.: discovery of gold near there led to the gold rush of 1849

su·ture (soo′chər) *n.* [L. *sutura* < *sutus,* pp. of *suere,* to SEW] **1.** *a)* the act of joining together by or as by sewing *b)* the line along which such a joining is made **2.** *Anat.* the joining together, or the irregular line of junction, of certain vertebrate bones, esp. of the skull **3.** *Bot. a)* a seam formed when two parts unite *b)* a line of dehiscence along which a fruit, as a pod or capsule, splits **4.** *Surgery a)* the act or method of joining together the two edges of a wound or incision by stitching or similar means *b)* any material, as gut, thread, wire, etc., so used *c)* a single loop or knot of such material made in suturing —*vt.* **-tured, -tur·ing** to join together with or as with sutures —**su′tur·al** *adj.*

Su·va (soo′vä) capital of the Fiji Islands; seaport on Viti Levu Island: pop. 37,000

Su·vo·rov (soo vô′rôf), Count **A·lek·san·dr** (**Vasilievich**) (ä′lyik sän′dr′) 1729–1800; Russ. field marshal

Su·wan·nee (sə wôn′ē, -wän′-; swô′nē, swä′-) [< AmInd. (? Creek) name < ?] river flowing from the Okefenokee Swamp across N Fla. into the Gulf of Mexico: c.250 mi.

su·ze·rain (soo′zə rin, -rān′) *n.* [Fr. < *sus,* above < L. *susum, sursum,* upward, above (contr. of *subversum* < *sub-,* under + *versum,* a turning < pp. of *vertere:* see VERSE) + ending of *souverain,* SOVEREIGN] **1.** a feudal lord **2.** a state in its relation to a semiautonomous state over which it exercises political control

su·ze·rain·ty (-tē) *n., pl.* **-ties** [Fr. *suzeraineté* < MFr. *suserenete*] the position or power of a suzerain

s.v. sub verbo (or sub voce)

Sval·bard (sväl′bär) group of Norw. islands, including Spitsbergen, in the Arctic Ocean, between Greenland & Franz Josef Land: 23,979 sq. mi.

svelte (svelt, sfelt) *adj.* [Fr. < It. *svelto,* pp. of *svegliere,* to pull out, hence, to free < L. *evellere,* to pluck out < *e-,* out + *vellere,* to pluck: see VELLICATE] **1.** slender and graceful; lithe: used chiefly of women **2.** suave, polished, etc.

Sverd·lovsk (sferd lôfsk′) city in W R.S.F.S.R., in the Ural Mountains: pop. 940,000

Sve·ri·ge (sver′ye) *Swed.* name of SWEDEN

SW, S.W., s.w. 1. southwest **2.** southwestern

Sw. 1. Sweden **2.** Swedish

swab (swäb) *n.* [contr. < ff.] **1.** a mop for cleaning decks, floors, etc. **2.** *a)* a small piece of cotton, cloth, sponge, etc. used to apply medicine to, or clean discharged matter from, the throat, mouth, etc. *b)* matter collected in this way **3.** a long-handled brush for cleaning the barrel of a gun, etc. **4.** [Slang] *a)* a clumsy, loutish person *b)* a sailor, ☆esp. an enlisted man in the U.S. Navy: also **swab′bie, swab′by** (-ē) —*vt.* **swabbed, swab′bing** to use a swab on; clean, medicate, etc. with a swab

swab·ber (-ər) *n.* [< or akin to Early ModDu. *zwabber* < *zwabben,* to do dirty work, splash, akin to G. *schwappen* < IE. base **swep-,* to throw, pour out, whence L. *supare,* to throw around] **1.** a person who uses a swab **2.** a device for swabbing

Swa·bi·a (swä′bē ə) region in SW West Germany, formerly a duchy: Ger. name, SCHWABEN —**Swa′bi·an** *adj., n.*

swacked (swakt) *adj.* [< ? or akin to MLowG. *swaken,* to totter] [Slang] drunk; intoxicated

swad·dle (swäd′l) *vt.* **-dled, -dling** [ME. *swathlen,* prob. altered (after *swathen,* to SWATHE[1]) < *swethlen* < *swethel,* swaddling band, akin to *swathian,* to SWATHE[1]] **1.** to wrap (a newborn baby) in long, narrow bands of cloth, as was formerly the custom **2.** to bind in or as in bandages; swathe —*n.* [ME. *swathil* < OE. *swethel:* see the *v.*] a cloth or bandage used for swaddling

swaddling clothes 1. the long, narrow bands of cloth wrapped around a newborn baby in former times **2.** rigid controls or restrictions, such as those imposed on infants, the immature, etc. Also **swaddling bands**

swag (swag) *vi.* **swagged, swag′ging** [< or akin to Norw. *svagga,* to sway (in walking), SWAGGER] **1.** to sway or lurch **2.** to sink down; sag —*vt.* **1.** to decorate with swags **2.** to hang in a swag —*n.* **1.** a swaying or lurching **2.** a valance, wreath, garland, chain, etc. hanging decoratively in a loop or curve; festoon **3.** [Slang] stolen money or property; loot; plunder **4.** [Austral.] a bundle containing personal belongings, as of an itinerant worker

swage (swāj) *n.* [ME. < OFr. *souage*] **1.** a kind of tool for bending or shaping metal **2.** a die or stamp for shaping or marking metal by hammering —*vt.* **swaged, swag′ing** to use a swage on; shape, bend, etc. with a swage

swage block a block of metal made with grooves and perforations, used as a form in hammering out bolt heads, etc.

swag·ger (swag′ər) *vi.* [prob. < Norw. dial. *svagra,* to sway in walking, freq. of *svagga,* to sway < IE. base **swek-,* to bend, turn: cf. SWING] **1.** to walk with a bold, arrogant, or

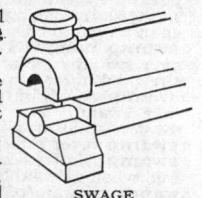

SWAGE

lordly stride; strut **2.** to boast, brag, or show off in a loud, superior manner —*vt.* [Rare] to influence, force, etc. by blustering —*n.* swaggering walk, manner, or behavior —*adj.* [Brit. Colloq.] stylish, esp. in an elegant way —*SYN.* see BOAST[1] —**swag′ger·er** *n.* —**swag′ger·ing·ly** *adv.*

swagger stick a short stick or cane as carried by some army officers, etc.: also [Brit.] **swagger cane**

Swa·hi·li (swä hē′lē) *n.* [< Ar. *sawāhil,* pl. of *sāhil,* coast + -*i,* belonging to] **1.** *pl.* **-lis, -li** any of a Bantu people inhabiting Zanzibar and the nearby mainland **2.** their Northern Bantu language, characterized by a vocabulary with many Arabic roots and used as a lingua franca in EC Africa and parts of Congo (sense 2)

swain (swān) *n.* [ME. *swein* < ON. *sveinn,* boy, servant, akin to OE. *swan,* shepherd, peasant, youth < IE. **swe-,* one's own, apart: cf. SECEDE] [Poet. or Archaic] **1.** a country youth **2.** a young rustic lover or gallant **3.** a lover —**swain′ish** *adj.* —**swain′ish·ness** *n.*

S.W.A.K. sealed with a kiss: written on a letter, as from a lover or a child: also **SWAK, swak** (swak)

swale (swāl) *n.* [ME., shade, prob. < ON. *svalr,* cool, akin to OE. *swelan,* to burn, ignite: for base see SWELTER] a hollow, depression, or low area of land; ☆specif., such a place in a wet, marshy area

swal·low[1] (swäl′ō) *n.* [ME. *swalwe* < OE. *swealwe,* akin to G. *schwalbe,* ON. *svala,* swallow, & prob. Russ. *solovej,* Czech *slavík,* nightingale] **1.** any of a family (Hirundinidae) of small, swift-flying, insect-eating birds, including the barn swallow, purple martin, etc., with long, pointed wings and a forked tail, known for their regular migrations **2.** any of certain swifts resembling swallows

swal·low[2] (swäl′ō) *vt.* [ME. *swolwen* < OE. *swelgan,* akin to G. *schwelgen* < IE. base **swel-,* to devour, whence SWILL] **1.** to pass (food, drink, etc.) from the mouth through the gullet or esophagus into the stomach, usually by a series of muscular actions in the throat **2.** to take in; absorb; engulf; envelop (often with *up*) **3.** to take back (words said); retract; withdraw **4.** to put up with; tolerate; bear humbly [to *swallow* an insult] **5.** to refrain from expressing; hold back; suppress [to *swallow* one's pride] **6.** to utter (words) indistinctly **7.** [Colloq.] to accept as true without question; receive gullibly —*vi.* to move the muscles of the throat as in swallowing something; specif., to do so under stress of emotion —*n.* **1.** the act of swallowing **2.** the amount swallowed at one time **3.** [Now Chiefly Brit.] the throat or gullet **4.** *Naut.* the opening in a block or pulley through which the rope runs —**swal′low·er** *n.*

swallow dive [Brit.] *same as* SWAN DIVE

swal·low·tail (-tāl′) *n.* **1.** something having a forked shape like that of a swallow's tail **2.** any of a large family (Papilionidae) of brightly colored butterflies found worldwide, having the hind wings extended in taillike points

swal·low-tailed (-tāld′) *adj.* having a tail or end extended in forked points like that of a swallow

swallow-tailed coat a man's full-dress coat, with long, tapering tails at the back

swal·low·wort (-wurt′) *n.* **1.** *same as* CELANDINE (sense 1) **2.** any of several plants of the milkweed family, as **black swallowwort** (*Cynanchum nigrum*), a twining European vine with purplish-brown flowers, now wild in the E U.S.

swam (swam) *pt.* of SWIM[1] & SWIM[2]

swa·mi (swä′mē) *n., pl.* **-mis** [Hindi *svāmī* < Sans. *svāmin,* a lord] **1.** lord; master: a Hindu title of respect, esp. for a Hindu religious teacher **2.** a learned man; pundit Also sp. **swa′my,** *pl.* **-mies**

swamp (swämp, swômp) *n.* [< dial. var. (or LowG. cognate) of ME. *sompe,* SUMP, akin to MLowG. *swamp,* Goth. & OE. *swamm,* fungus, mushroom < IE. base **swomb(h)os,* spongy, porous, whence Gr. *somphos,* spongy] a piece of wet, spongy land; marsh; bog —*adj.* of or native to a swamp —*vt.* **1.** to plunge or sink in a swamp, deep water, etc. **2.** to flood or submerge with or as with water **3.** to overcome or overwhelm; ruin [*swamped* by debts] **4.** to sink (a boat) by filling with water ☆**5.** to make (a path) or clear (an area) by removing underbrush and slash, as in logging —*vi.* to become swamped; sink in or as in a swamp or water —**swamp′ish** *adj.*

☆**swamp buggy** **1.** an automotive vehicle for traveling over swampy or muddy terrain, esp. one with very large tires and often amphibious **2.** *same as* AIRBOAT

☆**swamp·er** (swäm′pər, swôm′-) *n.* **1.** a person who lives in a swamp **2.** a person who works at swamping (see SWAMP, *vt.* 5) **3.** a handyman or helper

☆**swamp fever** *same as* MALARIA

☆**swamp·land** (-land′) *n.* a swamp, or land in a swamp, esp. when cultivable

swamp·y (swäm′pē, swôm′-) *adj.* **swamp′i·er, swamp′i·est** **1.** of or consisting of a swamp or swamps **2.** like a swamp; wet and spongy; marshy —**swamp′i·ness** *n.*

swan[1] (swän, swôn) *n.* [ME. < OE., akin to G. *schwan* < IE. base **swen-,* to sound, sing, whence L. *sonus,* SOUND[1]] **1.** *pl.* **swans, swan:** see PLURAL, II, D, 1 any of several

large-bodied, web-footed water birds (genus *Cygnus*) with a long, graceful neck and, usually, pure white feathers: swans are graceful swimmers and strong fliers **2.** a poet or singer of great ability: from the myth that swans sing sweetly just before dying **3.** [S-] the constellation Cygnus

☆**swan[2]** (swän, swôn) *vi.* [< ? Brit. dial. *Is′ wan,* I'll warrant] [Dial.] to swear: usually in the phrase **I swan!,** an exclamation of surprise, impatience, etc.

☆**swan dive** a forward dive in which the legs are held straight and together, the back is arched, and the arms are stretched out to the sides: the arms are brought forward and together just before entering the water

Swa·nee (swô′nē) *same as* SUWANNEE

swang (swan) *archaic or dial. pt.* of SWING

swan·herd (swän′hurd′, swôn′-) *n.* a person who tends swans

swank[1] (swank) *n.* [orig. slang < dial. *vi.,* akin to OE. *swancor,* pliant, supple, with notion of swinging the body: for IE. base see SWING] [Colloq.] **1.** stylish display or ostentation in dress, etc. **2.** swaggering, ostentatious behavior, speech, etc. —*adj.* [Colloq.] ostentatiously stylish —*vi.* [Slang] to act in a showy, pretentious manner; swagger

swank[2] (swank) *alt. pt.* of SWINK

swank·y (swan′kē) *adj.* **swank′i·er, swank′i·est** [SWANK + -Y[2]] [Colloq.] ostentatiously stylish; expensive and showy —**swank′i·ly** *adv.* —**swank′i·ness** *n.*

swan·ner·y (swän′ər ē, swôn′-) *n., pl.* **-ner·ies** a place where swans are kept or bred

Swans·combe man (swänz′kəm) [after *Swanscombe,* town in Kent, England, where the remains were found] a type of primitive man (*Homo sapiens steinheimensis*) known from fossil remains

swan's-down (swänz′doun′, swônz′-) *n.* **1.** the soft, fine underfeathers, or down, of the swan, used for trimming clothes, making powder puffs, etc. **2.** a soft, thick fabric of wool and silk, rayon, or cotton, used for making baby clothes, etc. **3.** a cotton fabric with a satin weave and a heavy napped finish **4.** a very soft cotton flannel Also **swans′down′**

Swan·sea (swän′sē, -zē) seaport in Glamorganshire, S Wales, on Bristol Channel: pop. 170,000

swan·skin (swän′skin′, swôn′-) *n.* **1.** the skin of a swan with feathers on it **2.** a closely woven flannel with a twill weave, used for work clothes

swan song **1.** the sweet song supposed in ancient fable to be sung by a dying swan **2.** the last act, final creative work, etc. of a person, as before his death

swan-up·ping (-up′in) *n.* [< SWAN[1] + UP[1], *v.*] the practice in England of marking young swans with a notch in the upper beak as a sign of ownership

swap (swäp, swôp) *vt., vi.* **swapped, swap′ping** [ME. *swappen,* to strike (prob. echoic): from the striking of hands on concluding a bargain] [Colloq.] to exchange, trade, or barter —*n.* [Colloq.] an exchange, trade, or barter —**swap′per** *n.*

‡**swa·raj** (swä räj′) *n.* [Hindi < Sans. *svarāj,* self-ruling < *sva-,* own (for IE. base see SECEDE) + *rāj,* rule: see RAJAH] in India, home rule; self-government: during the period of British rule, [S-] the name of the political party seeking Indian independence —**swa·raj′ism** *n.* —**swa·raj′ist** *n.*

sward (swôrd) *n.* [ME. *swarde* < OE. *sweard,* a skin, hide, akin to G. *schwarte,* rind, hard skin, ON. *svorthr,* skin] grass-covered soil; turf —*vt.* to cover with sward

sware (swer) *archaic pt.* of SWEAR

swarm[1] (swôrm) *n.* [ME. < OE. *swearm,* akin to G. *schwarm,* prob. < IE. base **swer-,* to buzz, hum, whence L. *susurrare,* to hiss] **1.** a large number of bees, led by a queen, leaving one hive for another to start a new colony **2.** a colony of bees in a hive **3.** a moving mass, crowd, or throng —*vi.* **1.** to gather and fly off in a swarm: said of bees **2.** to move, collect, be present, etc. in large numbers; throng; abound **3.** to be filled or crowded; teem —*vt.* to fill with a swarm; crowd; throng —*SYN.* see CROWD[1], GROUP —**swarm′er** *n.*

swarm[2] (swôrm) *vi., vt.* [orig. nautical word < ?] to climb (a tree, mast, pole, etc.) using the hands and feet; shin (*up*)

swarm spore *Biol. same as* ZOOSPORE

swart (swôrt) *adj.* [ME. < OE. *sweart,* akin to G. *schwarz,* black < IE. **swordos,* dirty, black, whence L. *sordidus,* SORDID] *dial. or poet. var. of* SWARTHY

swarth (swôrth) *n. dial. var. of* SWARD —*adj. var. of* SWARTHY

swarth·y (swôr′thē, -thē) *adj.* **swarth′i·er, swarth′i·est** [< dial. *swarth,* var. of SWART + -Y[2]] having a dark complexion; dusky —*SYN.* see DUSKY —**swarth′i·ly** *adv.* —**swarth′-i·ness** *n.*

Swart·krans ape-man (sfärt′kränz) [after *Swartkrans,* near Johannesburg, South Africa, where the remains were found] an extinct apelike man (*Australopithecus robustus crassidens*) known from fossil remains

swash (swäsh, swôsh) *vi.* [echoic] **1.** to dash, strike, wash, etc. with a splashing sound; splash **2.** to swagger or bluster —*vt.* to splash (a liquid), as in a container —*n.* **1.** a body of swift, dashing water; specif., a channel cutting through or behind a sandbank **2.** a bar washed over by the sea **3.** the splashing of water or the sound of this **4.** a swaggering or blustering action

swash·buck·ler (-buk′lər) *n.* [prec. + BUCKLER] a blustering, swaggering fighting man

swash·buck·ling (-buk′liŋ) *n.* the characteristic behavior of a swashbuckler; loud boasting or bullying —*adj.* of or typical of a swashbuckler Also **swash′buck′ler·ing**

swash·ing (-iŋ) *adj.* **1.** *same as* SWASHBUCKLING **2.** splashing or dashing —**swash′ing·ly** *adv.*

swash letters italic capital letters formed with long tails and flourishes

swas·ti·ka (swäs′ti kə) *n.* [Sans. *svastika* < *svasti*, well-being, benediction < *su*, well (< IE. base *su-*, var. of *swe-*, *se*, separate, one's own: cf. SWABIAN) + *asti*, he is: for IE. base see IS] **1.** a design or ornament of ancient origin in the form of a cross with four equal arms, each bent in a right-angle extension: a mystic symbol found in both the Old World and New World **2.** this design with the arms bent back clockwise, used in Nazi Germany and by other Nazi fascists as a party emblem and symbol of anti-Semitism

SWASTIKAS (left, Indian; right, Nazi)

Swat (swät) region in NE West Pakistan, on the Indus River: formerly, a princely state of India —*n., pl.* **Swa·ti** (swä′tē) any of a people of Moslem faith who live in Swat

swat (swät) *vt.* **swat′ted, swat′ting** [echoic] [Colloq.] to hit with a quick, sharp blow —*n.* [Colloq.] a quick, sharp blow, as with a bat or swatter

swatch (swäch) *n.* [orig., a cloth tally < ?] **1.** a sample piece of cloth or other material **2.** a small amount or number in a cluster, bunch, or patch

swath (swäth, swôth) *n.* [ME. *swathe* < OE. *swathu*, a track, akin to G. *schwade*, space covered by a scythe swing: for base see ff.] **1.** the space or width covered with one cut of a scythe or other mowing device **2.** [Rare] a stroke with a scythe **3.** a line or row of grass, wheat, etc. cut in one course by a scythe, mower, etc. **4.** a long strip, track, or belt of any particular kind —☆**cut a wide swath** to make an ostentatious display or forceful impression

swathe[1] (swāth) *vt.* **swathed, swath′ing** [ME. *swathen* < OE. *swathian*, akin to ON. *svatha*, to glide, prob. < IE. base *swei-*, to turn, bend, whence SWAY, SWEEP] **1.** to wrap or bind up in a long strip or bandage **2.** to wrap (a bandage, etc.) around something **3.** to surround or envelop; enclose —*n.* a bandage or wrapping —**swath′er** *n.*

swathe[2] (swāth) *n. same as* SWATH

Swa·ti (swä′tē) *n., pl.* **-ti, -tis** *same as* SWAT

Swa·tow (swä′tou′) seaport in Kwangtung province, SE China, on the South China Sea: pop. 250,000

swat·ter (swät′ər) *n.* **1.** a person who swats **2.** a device, as of fine wire mesh at the end of a handle, for swatting flies, etc.: in full **fly swatter**

S wave [< *s*(*econdary*) *wave*] a transverse wave that travels from side to side through a solid medium but that cannot be transmitted through a fluid

sway (swā) *vi.* [ME. *sweyen* < ON. *sveigja*, to turn, bend: for base see SWATHE[1]] **1.** *a)* to swing or move from side to side or to and fro *b)* to vacillate or alternate between one position, opinion, etc. and another **2.** *a)* to lean or incline to one side; veer *b)* to incline or tend in judgment or opinion **3.** [Chiefly Poet.] to rule; reign; hold sway —*vt.* **1.** *a)* to cause to swing or move from side to side *b)* to cause to vacillate **2.** *a)* to cause to lean or incline to one side *b)* to cause (a person or his opinion, actions, etc.) to be inclined a certain way or be turned from a given course; influence or divert [*swayed* by promises] **3.** [Archaic] *a)* to wield (a scepter, etc.) *b)* to rule over or control; dominate **4.** *Naut.* to hoist (a mast, etc.) into place (usually with *up*) —*n.* **1.** a swaying or being swayed; movement to the side; a swinging, leaning, fluctuation, etc. **2.** influence, force, or control [*moved by the sway* of passion] **3.** sovereign power or authority; rule; dominion —**hold sway** to reign or prevail —*SYN.* see AFFECT[1], POWER, SWING —**sway′er** *n.*

sway·backed (-bakt′) *adj.* [prob. < (or transl. of) Dan. *sveibaget* or *sveirygget* < ON. *sveigja*, to bend, SWAY + *bak*, BACK[1] or *rygg*, back, RIDGE] having an abnormal sagging of the spine, usually as a result of strain or overwork, as some horses, etc. —**sway′back′** *n.*

Swa·zi (swä′zē) *n.* **1.** *pl.* **Swa′zis, Swa′zi** any member of a farming people of Swaziland **2.** their Bantu language

Swa·zi·land (-land′) country in SE Africa, surrounded on three sides by South Africa: a member of the Brit. Commonwealth: 6,705 sq. mi.; pop. 375,000; cap. Mbabane

SWbS southwest by south

SWbW southwest by west

swear (swer) *vi.* **swore, sworn, swear′ing** [ME. *swerien* < OE. *swerian*, akin to G. *schwören* < IE. base *swer-*, to speak, whence OBulg. *svariti*, to revile: cf. ANSWER] **1.** to make a solemn declaration with an appeal to God or to something held sacred for confirmation [to *swear* on one's honor] **2.** to make a solemn promise; vow **3.** to use profane or obscene language; curse **4.** *Law* to give evidence under oath —*vt.* **1.** to declare solemnly in the name of God or of something held sacred **2.** to pledge or vow on oath **3.** to assert or promise with great conviction or emphasis **4.** to take (an oath) by swearing **5.** to administer a legal oath to —**swear by 1.** to name (something held sacred) in taking an oath **2.** to have great faith or confidence in —**swear for** to give assurance for; guarantee —**swear in** to administer an oath to (a person taking office, a witness, etc.) —**swear off** to promise to give up, leave off, or renounce —☆**swear out** to obtain (a warrant for someone's arrest) by making a charge under oath —**swear′er** *n.*

☆**swear·word** (-wurd′) *n.* a word or phrase used in swearing or cursing; profane or obscene word or phrase

sweat (swet) *vi.* **sweat** or **sweat′ed, sweat′ing** [ME. *sweten* < OE. *swætan* < *swat*, sweat, akin to G. *schweissen* < IE. base *sweid-*, to sweat, whence Gr. *idos*, L. *sudor*, sweat] **1.** to give forth a characteristic salty moisture through the pores of the skin; perspire **2.** *a)* to give forth moisture in droplets on its surface, as a ripening cheese *b)* to collect and condense water in droplets on its surface, as a glass of ice water in a warm room **3.** to ferment: said of tobacco leaves, etc. **4.** to come forth in drops through pores or a porous surface; ooze **5.** to work hard enough to cause sweating **6.** [Colloq.] to suffer distress, anxiety, etc. —*vt.* **1.** *a)* to give forth (moisture) through pores or a porous surface *b)* to collect and condense (moisture) on the surface **2.** to cause to sweat, or perspire, as by drugs, exercise, heat, etc. **3.** to cause to give forth moisture; esp., to ferment [to *sweat* tobacco leaves] **4.** to make wet with sweat, or perspiration **5.** to heat (a metal) in order to extract an easily fusible constituent **6.** *a)* to heat (solder) until it melts *b)* to unite (metal parts) by heating at the point of contact **7.** to remove particles of metal from (a coin) illegally, as by abrading **8.** *a)* to cause to work so hard as to sweat; overwork *b)* to cause (employees) to work long hours at low wages under poor working conditions; exploit (workers) ☆**9.** [Colloq.] to get information from by torture or by long, grueling questioning; subject to the third degree **10.** [Slang] to try hard or too hard to get or achieve —*n.* [altered, after the *v.* < ME. *swat* < OE.] **1.** the clear, alkaline, salty liquid given forth in drops through the pores of the skin; perspiration **2.** moisture given forth or collected in droplets on the surface of something **3.** *a)* the act or condition of sweating or being sweated *b)* an artificially induced sweating **4.** a condition of eagerness, anxiety, impatience, etc. **5.** hard work; drudgery **6.** exercise, as a run, given a horse before a race —☆**no sweat** [Slang] no trouble or difficulty at all; easily done: often used interjectionally —**sweat blood** [Slang] **1.** to work very hard; overwork **2.** to be impatient, apprehensive, anxious, etc. —**sweat it** [Slang] to be annoyed by something —**sweat off** to get rid of (weight) by sweating —**sweat out** [Slang] **1.** to wait or suffer through (some ordeal, nuisance, etc.) **2.** to anticipate or wait anxiously or impatiently for

☆**sweat·band** (-band′) *n.* a band of leather, etc. inside a hat to protect it against sweat from the brow

sweat·box (-bäks′) *n.* **1.** a box in which hides, dried fruits, etc. are sweated **2.** a place in which one sweats profusely, as because of close confinement, heat, etc.

sweat·er (swet′ər) *n.* **1.** a person or thing that sweats, esp. to excess **2.** a knitted or crocheted outer garment for the upper part of the body, with or without sleeves, styled either as a pullover or a jacket

sweat gland any of the many, very small, coiled, tubular glands in the subcutaneous tissue that secrete sweat

sweating sickness an acute, infectious, rapidly fatal disease, epidemic in Europe in the 15th and 16th cent., characterized by high fever and profuse sweating

☆**sweat shirt** a heavy, long-sleeved cotton jersey, worn as by athletes to absorb sweat during or after exercise, sometimes with loose trousers (**sweat pants**) of the same material, forming an ensemble (**sweat suit**)

☆**sweat·shop** (-shäp′) *n.* a shop where employees work long hours at low wages under poor working conditions

sweat·y (-ē) *adj.* **sweat′i·er, sweat′i·est 1.** sweating; covered with sweat **2.** of or like that of sweat [a *sweaty* odor] **3.** causing sweat [a hot, *sweaty* day] **4.** laborious or labored —**sweat′i·ly** *adv.* —**sweat′i·ness** *n.*

Swed. **1.** Sweden **2.** Swedish

Swede (swēd) *n.* **1.** a native or inhabitant of Sweden **2.** [s-] *same as* SWEDISH TURNIP

Swe·den (swē′d'n) country in N Europe, in the E part of the Scandinavian Peninsula: 173,620 sq. mi.; pop. 7,869,000; cap. Stockholm: Swed. name, SVERIGE

Swe·den·borg (swēd′'n bôrg′; *Swed.* svåd′'n bôr′y′), **Emanuel** (born *Emanuel Swedberg*) 1688–1772; Swed. scientist, mystic, & religious philosopher

Swe·den·bor·gi·an (swēd′'n bôr′jē ən, -gē-) *n.* any of the followers of Swedenborg; specif., any member of the Church of the New Jerusalem —*adj.* of Swedenborg, his doctrines, or his followers —**Swe′den·bor′gi·an·ism, Swe′den·borg′ism** (-bôrg′-) *n.*

Swed·ish (swē′dish) *adj.* of Sweden, its people, their language, etc. —*n.* the North Germanic language of the Swedes —**the Swedish** the people of Sweden

Swedish massage massage combined with a set of exercises (**Swedish movements**), used in treating certain diseases

Swedish turnip *same as* RUTABAGA

☆**swee·ny** (swē′nē) *n.* [altered (prob. via PennDu. *schwinne*) < G. dial. *schweine*, atrophy < *schweinen*, to atrophy, shrink < OHG. *suinan*, to decrease, akin to ON. *svina*, to disappear < IE. base *swi-*, to disappear, decrease] atrophy of the shoulder muscles of horses

sweep (swēp) *vt.* **swept, sweep′ing** [ME. *swepen*, akin to (or ? altered <) OE. *swapan*: see SWOOP] **1.** to clear or clean (a surface, room, etc.) as by brushing with a broom **2.** to remove or clear away (dirt, debris, etc.) with or as a brush or broom or with a brushing movement **3.** to clear (a space, path, etc.) with or as with a broom **4.** to strip, clear, carry away, remove, or destroy with a forceful movement or movements **5.** to move or carry along with a sweeping movement [to sweep one's hand through one's hair] **6.** to touch or brush in moving across [hands *sweeping* the keyboard] **7.** to pass swiftly over or across; traverse, as in search [searchlights *sweeping* the sky] **8.** to direct (the eyes, a glance, etc.) over something swiftly **9.** *a)* to drag (a river, pond, etc.) with a net, grapple, etc. *b)* to clear (the sea, etc.) with a mine sweeper **10.** to direct gunfire along; rake **11.** *a)* to win all the games or events of (a series, set, or match) *b)* to win overwhelmingly [to *sweep* an election] —*vi.* **1.** to clean a surface, room, etc. with or as a broom or the like **2.** to move, pass, or progress steadily or smoothly, esp. with speed, force, or gracefulness [planes *sweeping* across the sky, music *sweeping* to a climax] **3.** to trail, as skirts or the train of a gown **4.** to reach or extend in a long, graceful curve or line [a road *sweeping* up the hill] —*n.* **1.** the act of sweeping, as with a broom **2.** *a)* a steady sweeping or driving movement [the *sweep* of a scythe] *b)* a stroke or blow resulting from this **3.** a trailing, as of skirts **4.** range or scope [within the *sweep* of their guns] **5.** extent or range; stretch; reach [a long *sweep* of meadow] **6.** a line, contour, curve, etc. that gives an impression of flow or movement **7.** a person whose work is sweeping; specif., short for CHIMNEY SWEEP **8.** [*usually pl.*] things swept up; sweepings **9.** *a)* the taking or winning of all; complete victory or success, as in a series of contests *b)* in casino, the taking of all the cards on the board, by pairing or combining *c)* in whist, the winning of all the tricks in one deal **10.** a long oar **11.** a long pole mounted on a pivot, with a bucket at one end, used for raising water, as from a well ☆**12.** a blade or plow-point of various widths, used in the shallow cultivation of row crops **13.** a sail of a windmill **14.** *clipped form of* SWEEP-STAKES **15.** *Electronics a)* a single horizontal traverse of the fluorescent screen by an electron beam in a cathode-ray tube or kinescope *b)* the deflection voltage or current that causes the visible dot to move across the screen, as in an oscilloscope **16.** *Physics* the irreversible process by which a substance tends to settle into thermal equilibrium

sweep·back (-bak′) *n.* **1.** the backward slant of an airfoil surface, its leading edge, etc. **2.** the angle formed by some reference line along the incline span of an airplane wing and the lateral axis of the airplane

sweep·er (-ər) *n.* **1.** a person who sweeps **2.** a device for sweeping; specif., ☆short for CARPET SWEEPER

sweep hand a second hand on a timepiece, mounted on the same spindle as the hour and minute hands: also **sweep second hand**

sweep·ing (-iŋ) *adj.* **1.** that sweeps; cleansing or carrying away with or as with a broom **2.** reaching in a long curve or line **3.** extending over the whole range or a great space **4.** *a)* extensive; comprehensive; thoroughgoing *b)* complete; decisive *c)* indiscriminate [a *sweeping* generalization] —*n.* **1.** [*pl.*] things swept up, as dirt, particles, etc. swept from a floor **2.** the act, work, etc. of a person or thing that sweeps —**sweep′ing·ly** *adv.*

sweep·stakes (-stāks′) *n., pl.* **-stakes** [because the winner "sweeps in" all of the stakes] **1.** a lottery in which each participant puts up money in a common fund which is given as the prize to the winner or in shares to several winners **2.** *a)* a contest, esp. a horse race, the result of which determines the winner or winners of such a lottery *b)* the prize or prizes won in such a lottery **3.** any of various other lotteries Also **sweep′stake′, sweeps**

sweet (swēt) *adj.* [ME. *swete* < OE., akin to *swot*, sweetness, G. *süss*, sweet < IE. base *swad-*, pleasing to taste, whence Gr. *hēdys*, sweet, L. *suadere*, to persuade & *suavis*, sweet] **1.** *a)* having a taste of, or like that of, sugar *b)* containing sugar in some form [*sweet* wines] **2.** *a)* having a generally agreeable taste, smell, sound, appearance, etc.; pleasant *b)* agreeable to the mind; gratifying [*sweet* praise] *c)* having a friendly, pleasing disposition; characterized by kindliness and gentleness [a *sweet* girl]: formerly a polite form of address [*sweet* sir] *d)* sentimental, saccharine, or cloying *e)* [Slang] good, delightful, etc.: a generalized epithet of approval **3.** *a)* not rancid, spoiled, sour, or fermented [*sweet* milk, *sweet* cider] *b)* not salty or salted: said of water or butter *c)* free from sourness or acidity: said of soil **4.** *Chem. a)* free from unpleasant odors and gases *b)* purified and free from acid, corrosive elements, etc. **5.** *Jazz* designating or of music or playing characterized by more or less strict adherence to melody, sentimentality or blandness in tone and rhythm, and a moderate tempo —*n.* **1.** the quality of being sweet; sweetness **2.** something sweet, as a sweet food; specif., *a)* [Chiefly Brit.] a candy; sweetmeat *b)* [Brit.] a sweet dish served as dessert *c)* [*usually pl.*] pleasure or a pleasurable experience ☆*d)*

clipped form of SWEET POTATO **3.** a sweet, or beloved, person; darling —*adv.* in a sweet manner —**be sweet on** [Colloq.] to be in love with —**sweet′ly** *adv.* —**sweet′ness** *n.*

Sweet (swēt), **Henry** 1845-1912; Eng. linguist

sweet alyssum a short garden plant (*Lobularia maritima*) of the mustard family, with small spikes of tiny flowers

sweet-and-sour (swēt′'n sour′) *adj.* cooked with both sugar and a sour substance, as vinegar or lemon juice

sweet basil a basil (*Ocimum basilicum*): see BASIL

sweet bay 1. *same as* LAUREL (*n.* 1) ☆**2.** a N. American magnolia (*Magnolia virginiana*) with fragrant white flowers, common along the coast from Maine to Texas

sweet·bread (swēt′bred′) *n.* [Early ModE. < SWEET + BREAD, in OE. sense "morsel"] the thymus (**heart**, or **throat, sweetbread**) or sometimes the pancreas (**stomach sweetbread**) of a calf, lamb, etc., when used as food

sweet·bri·er, sweet·bri·ar (-brī′ər) *n. same as* EGLANTINE

sweet cherry 1. an old-world cherry (*Prunus avium*) whose fruits have a sweet pulp and juice: many varieties have been derived from this tree **2.** its fruit

sweet cicely ☆**1.** any of several perennial N. American herbs (genus *Osmorhiza*) of the parsley family, with compound leaves and clusters of small white flowers **2.** a European perennial herb (*Myrrhis odorata*) of the parsley family, with anise-scented leaves formerly used in flavoring

sweet clover any of a genus (*Melilotus*) of annual or biennial plants of the legume family, with small white or yellow flowers, leaflets in groups of three, and single-seeded pods: grown for hay, forage, or green manure

☆**sweet corn** any of various strains of Indian corn with kernels rich in sugar, eaten as a table vegetable in the unripe, or milky, stage **2.** an ear of such corn

sweet·en (swēt′'n) *vt.* **1.** to make sweet with or as with sugar **2.** to make pleasant or agreeable, as to the sense of smell **3.** to counteract the acidic condition of (the soil, the stomach, etc.) **4.** to mollify; alleviate; appease **5.** [Colloq.] *Finance* to increase the value of (collateral for a loan) by adding additional securities **6.** [Slang] *Poker* to add further stakes to (a pot) before opening —*vi.* to become sweet

sweet·en·er (-ər) *n.* a sweetening agent, esp. a synthetic substance, such as saccharin, calcium cyclamate, etc.

sweet·en·ing (-iŋ) *n.* **1.** the process of making sweet **2.** something that sweetens

☆**sweet fern** a flowering plant (*Comptonia peregrina*) of the wax-myrtle family, with fragrant, fernlike leaves

sweet flag a perennial marsh plant (*Acorus calamus*) of the arum family, with sword-shaped leaves, small, green flowers, and a sweet-scented rhizome

sweet gale a fragrant marsh plant (*Myrica gale*) of the wax-myrtle family, with bitter leaves and yellowish flowers

☆**sweet gum 1.** a large N. American tree (*Liquidambar styraciflua*) of the witch hazel family, with alternate maple-like leaves, spiny fruit balls, and fragrant juice **2.** the wood of this tree **3.** *same as* STORAX (*n.* 1)

sweet·heart (-härt′) *n.* **1.** *a)* someone with whom one is in love and by whom one is loved; lover *b)* darling: a term of endearment **2.** [Slang] a very agreeable person or an excellent thing

☆**sweetheart contract** a contract arranged by collusion between union officials and an employer with terms disadvantageous to union members: also **sweetheart deal**

☆**sweet·ie** (swēt′ē) *n. colloq. var. of* SWEETHEART: also **sweetie pie**

sweet·ing (-iŋ) *n.* **1.** a variety of sweet apple **2.** *archaic var. of* SWEETHEART

sweet·ish (-ish) *adj.* rather sweet

sweet marjoram *see* MARJORAM

sweet·meat (-mēt′) *n.* [LME. *sweit meit* < OE. *swetmete*: see SWEET & MEAT] any sweet food or delicacy prepared with sugar or honey, as a cake, confection, preserve, etc.: specif., a candy, candied fruit, etc.

sweet oil a mild, edible oil, as olive oil

sweet pea a climbing annual plant (*Lathyrus odoratus*) of the legume family, with butterfly-shaped flowers

sweet pepper 1. a variety of the red pepper producing a large, mild fruit: see RED PEPPER (sense 1) **2.** the fruit

☆**sweet potato 1.** a tropical, trailing plant (*Ipomoea batatas*) of the morning-glory family, with purplish flowers and a fleshy, orange or yellow, tuberlike root used as a vegetable **2.** its root **3.** [Colloq.] *same as* OCARINA

sweet·sop (-säp′) *n.* **1.** a tropical American tree (*Annona squamosa*) of the custard-apple family, having green fruit with a sweet pulp and black seeds **2.** its edible fruit

☆**sweet-talk** (-tôk′) *vt., vi.* [Colloq.] to talk in a flattering or blandishing way (to)

sweet tooth [Colloq.] a fondness or craving for sweets

sweet william, sweet William a perennial pink (*Dianthus barbatus*) with dense, flat clusters of small flowers

swell (swel) *vi.* **swelled, swelled** or **swol′len, swell′ing** [ME. *swellen* < OE. *swellan*, akin to G. *schwellen*, ON. *svella*] **1.** to increase in volume or become larger as a result of pressure from within; expand; dilate **2.** to become larger at a particular point; curve out; bulge; protrude **3.** to extend beyond or above the normal or surrounding level **4.** to form swells, or large waves: said of the sea **5.** to be or become filled (*with* pride, indignation, self-importance, etc.) **6.** to increase within one [the anger *swelling* in him] **7.** to increase in size, force, intensity, degree, etc. [member-

ship *swelled* to a thousand/ 8. to increase in volume or loudness —*vt.* to cause to swell; specif., *a)* to cause to increase in size, volume, extent, degree, etc. *b)* to cause to bulge or protrude *c)* to fill with pride, indignation, etc.; inflate; puff *d)* to cause (a tone, chord, etc.) to increase in loudness —*n.* 1. a part that swells; bulge; curve; protuberance; specif., *a)* a large wave that moves steadily without breaking *b)* a piece of rising ground; rounded hill or slope 2. a swelling or being swollen 3. an increase in size, amount, extent, degree, etc. 4. [Colloq.] *a)* a person who is strikingly stylish, esp. in dress *b)* a person of social prominence 5. an increase in loudness of sound; specif., *Music a)* a gradual increase in volume (*crescendo*), usually followed by a gradual decrease (*diminuendo*) *b)* a sign (<>) indicating this *c)* a device for controlling the loudness of tones, as in an organ [ME. *swelle*, tumid, proud] 1. [Colloq.] stylish; very fashionable 2. [Slang] first-rate; excellent: a generalized epithet of approval —*SYN.* see EXPAND

swell box a chamber enclosing one or more sets of organ pipes or reeds and fitted with movable shutters that regulate the loudness of tone

swelled head [Colloq.] undue self-esteem; conceit

☆**swell·fish** (swel'fish′) *n., pl.* **-fish′, -fish′es:** see FISH² *same as* PUFFER (sense 2 *a*)

swell·head (-hed′) *n.* a vain or conceited person; egotist —**swell′head′ed** *adj.* —**swell′head′ed·ness** *n.*

swell·ing (-iŋ) *n.* 1. an increasing or being increased in size, volume, etc. 2. something swollen; esp., an abnormally swollen part of the body

swel·ter (swel'tər) *vi.* [freq. of ME. *swelten*, to die, swoon away, faint < OE. *sweltan*, to die < IE. base *swel-*, to burn, whence SULTRY] to be or feel oppressively hot; sweat and wilt from great heat —*vt.* 1. to cause to swelter 2. [Archaic] to exude (venom or poison) —*n.* 1. the condition of sweltering 2. oppressive heat

swel·ter·ing (-iŋ) *adj.* 1. that swelters or suffers from the heat 2. very hot; sultry Also **swel′try** (-trē), **-tri·er, -tri·est** —**swel′ter·ing·ly** *adv.*

swept (swept) *pt. & pp. of* SWEEP

swept·back (swept'bak′) *adj.* 1. having a sweepback: said of a wing of an aircraft 2. having sweptback wings: said of an aircraft

swept·wing (-wiŋ′) *adj. Aeron.* having sweptback wings

swerve (swurv) *vi., vt.* **swerved, swerv′ing** [ME. *swerven* < OE. *sweorfan*, to file away, scour < IE. base *swerbh-*, to turn, wipe, sweep, whence Gr. *syrphetos*, sweepings, litter] to turn aside or cause to turn aside from a straight line, course, etc. —*n.* the act or degree of swerving —*SYN.* see DEVIATE —**swerv′er** *n.*

swev·en (swev′'n) *n.* [ME. < OE. *swefn*, a dream, sleep < IE. *swepnos* < base *swep-*, whence L. *somnus*, Gr. *hypnos*, sleep] [Archaic] a dream or vision

S.W.G. standard wire gauge

swift (swift) *adj.* [ME. < OE. < IE. *sweip-* < base *swei-*, to bend, turn, whence SWATHE¹, SWOOP] 1. moving or capable of moving with great speed; rapid; fast 2. coming, happening, or done quickly or suddenly; undelayed 3. acting or responding quickly; prompt; ready —*adv.* in a swift manner —*n.* 1. a cylinder in a carding machine 2. an expanding reel used to hold skeins of silk, etc. that are being wound off 3. any of a large family (Micropodidae) of insect-eating, swift-flying birds resembling the swallow, as the chimney swift, with long, stiff wings and a small, weak bill 4. any of several swift-moving, N. American lizards (genera *Sceloporus* and *Uta*) living esp. in arid or desert regions 5. a small fox (*Vulpes velox*) of the plains of W U.S. and S Canada: in full **swift fox** —*SYN.* see FAST¹ —**swift′ly** *adv.* —**swift′ness** *n.*

Swift (swift), **Jonathan** 1667–1745; Eng. satirist, born in Ireland

swift·er (swif'tər) *n.* [< obs. *swift*, to tighten, fasten with a taut rope] *Naut.* any of various ropes used for tightening or securing some part or thing

swift-foot·ed (swift'foot'id) *adj.* that can run swiftly

swig (swig) *vt., vi.* **swigged, swig′ging** [< ?] [Colloq.] to drink, esp. in great gulps or quantities —*n.* [Colloq.] an instance of swigging; deep draft, esp. of liquor —**swig′ger** *n.*

swill (swil) *vt.* [ME. *swilen* < OE. *swilian* < IE. base *swel-*, to devour, whence SWALLOW²] 1. to flood with water so as to wash or rinse 2. to drink greedily or in large quantity 3. to feed swill to (pigs, etc.) —*vi.* to drink, esp. liquor, in large quantities —*n.* 1. garbage, table scraps, etc. mixed with liquid and used for feeding pigs, etc.; wash 2. garbage or slop 3. the act of swilling 4. a deep draft of liquor; swig

swim¹ (swim) *vi.* **swam, swum, swim′ming** [ME. *swimmen* < OE. *swimman*, akin to G. *schwimmen* < IE. base *swem-*, to move vigorously, be in motion, as also in W. *chwyfio*, to move] 1. to move through water by movements of the arms and legs, or of flippers, fins, tail, etc. 2. to move with a smooth, gliding motion, as though swimming 3. to float on the surface of a liquid 4. to be covered or saturated with or as with a liquid 5. to overflow; be flooded /eyes *swimming* with tears/ —*vt.* 1. to move in or across (a body of water) by swimming 2. to cause to swim or float 3. to

perform (a specified stroke) in swimming —*n.* 1. the act or motion of swimming 2. a period of swimming for sport /a short *swim* before lunch/ 3. a distance swum or to be swum 4. *clipped form of* SWIM BLADDER —**In the swim** conforming to the current fashions, or active in the main current of affairs —**swim′ma·ble** *adj.* —**swim′mer** *n.*

swim² (swim) *n.* [ME. *swime* < OE. *swima*, akin to Du. *zwijmen*, to faint < IE. base *swei-*, to bend, turn, whence SWIFT] the condition of being dizzy; dizzy spell —*vi.* **swam, swum, swim′ming** 1. to be dizzy 2. to have a hazy, reeling, or whirling appearance /the room *swam* before him/

swim bladder a gas-filled sac in the dorsal portion of the body cavity of most bony fishes, giving buoyancy to the body and used as an accessory, lunglike organ in lungfishes

☆**swim fin** *same as* FLIPPER (sense 2)

swim·mer·et (swim'ə ret′) *n.* any of the small, abdominal appendages, or pleopods, in certain crustaceans, used primarily in swimming and for carrying eggs

swim·ming¹ (swim'iŋ) *n.* the act, practice, sport, etc. of a person or animal that swims —*adj.* 1. that swims 2. of, for, or used in swimming 3. flooded or overflowing with or as with water /*swimming* eyes/

swim·ming² (swim'iŋ) *n.* [cf. SWIM²] dizziness —*adj.* affected with a dizzy, whirling sensation

☆**swimming hole** a pool or a deep place in a river, creek, etc. used for swimming

swim·ming·ly (-lē) *adv.* easily and with success

☆**swimming pool** a pool of water used for swimming; esp., an artificially created pool, or tank, either indoors or outdoors and usually with water-filtering equipment

swim·suit (swim'soot′) *n.* a garment worn for swimming

Swin·burne (swin'bərn), **Algernon Charles** 1837–1909; Eng. poet & critic

swin·dle (swin'd'l) *vt.* **-dled, -dling** [back-formation < ff.] 1. to get money or property from (another) under false pretenses; cheat; defraud 2. to get by false pretenses or fraud —*vi.* to engage in swindling others —*n.* an act of swindling; trick; cheat; fraud —*SYN.* see CHEAT

swin·dler (-dlər) *n.* [G. *schwindler* < *schwindeln*, to be dizzy, defraud, cheat < OHG. *swintilom*, freq. of *swintan*, to disappear, wither, prob. < IE. base *swendh-*, to disappear, whence OBulg. *uvędati*, to wither] a person who swindles; cheat

☆**swindle sheet** *slang term for* EXPENSE ACCOUNT

swine (swin) *n., pl.* **swine** [ME. *swin* < OE., akin to G. *schwein* < IE. base *su-*, pig, sow, whence Gr. *hys*, sow¹, L. *sus*] 1. *a)* the domesticated pig or hog *b)* any of several omnivorous mammals (family Suidae) with a bristly coat and elongated, flexible snout Usually used collectively 2. a vicious, contemptible, or disgusting person

swine·herd (-hurd′) *n.* a person who tends swine

swing (swiŋ) *vi.* **swung, swing′ing** [ME. *swingen* < OE. *swingan*, akin to G. *schwingen*, to brandish < IE. base *sweng-*, to curve, swing: cf. SWANK¹] 1. to sway or move backward and forward with regular movement, as a freely hanging object or a ship at anchor; oscillate 2. to walk, trot, etc. with freely swaying, relaxed movements of the limbs 3. to deliver or aim a blow; strike (*at*) 4. to turn or pivot, as on a hinge or swivel /the door *swung* open/ 5. *a)* to hang; be suspended *b)* [Colloq.] to be hanged in execution 6. to move backward and forward on a swing (*n.* 10) 7. to have an exciting rhythmic quality /music that really *swings*/ ☆8. [Slang] to be ultra-fashionable, sophisticated, active, etc., esp. in the pursuit of pleasure —*vt.* 1. *a)* to move or wave (a weapon, tool, bat, etc.) with a sweeping motion; flourish; brandish *b)* to lift or hoist with a sweeping motion 2. to cause (a hanging object) to sway backward and forward; specif., to cause (a person on a swing) to move backward and forward by pushing or pulling 3. to cause to turn or pivot, as on a hinge or swivel /to *swing* a door open/ 4. to cause to hang freely, so as to be capable of easy movement /to *swing* a hammock/ 5. to cause to move in a curve /to *swing* a car around a corner/ 6. to move (a ship or aircraft) through the points of the compass in order to check compass error ☆7. [Colloq.] to cause to come about successfully; manage with the desired results /to *swing* an election/ ☆8. to play (music) in the style of swing —*n.* 1. the act or process of swinging 2. the arc, or the length of the arc, through which something swings /the *swing* of a pendulum/ 3. the manner of swinging; specif., the manner of striking with a golf club, baseball bat, the arm, etc. 4. freedom to do as one wishes or is naturally inclined /given full *swing* in the matter/ 5. a free, relaxed motion, as in walking 6. a sweeping blow or stroke 7. the course, development, or movement of some activity, business, etc. 8. the power, or force, behind something swung or thrown; impetus 9. rhythm, as of poetry or music 10. a device, as a seat hanging from ropes or chains, on which one can sit and swing backward and forward as a form of amusement 11. a trip or tour /a *swing* around the country/ ☆12. jazz music, esp. in its development from about 1935 to 1945, characterized by the use of large bands, strong, driving rhythms, improvised counterpoint, etc. ☆13. [Colloq.] *Commerce* regular upward and downward change in the price of stocks or in some other business

activity —☆*adj.* of, in, or playing swing (music) —**in full swing** **1.** in complete and active operation **2.** going on without reserve or restraint —☆**swing round the circle** a political campaign tour
SYN.—**swing** suggests the to-and-fro motion of something that is suspended, hinged, pivoted, etc. so that it is free to turn or swivel at the point or points of attachment [a *swinging* door]; **sway** describes the swinging motion of something flexible or self-balancing, whether attached or unattached, in yielding to pressure, weight, etc. [branches *swaying* in the wind]; to **oscillate** is to swing back and forth, within certain limits, in the manner of a pendulum; **vibrate** suggests the rapid, regular, back-and-forth motion of a plucked, taut string and is applied in physics to a similar movement of the particles of a fluid or elastic medium [sound *vibrations*]; **fluctuate** implies continual, irregular alternating movements and is now most common in its extended sense [*fluctuating* prices]; **undulate** implies a gentle wavelike motion or form [*undulating* land]

swing bridge a bridge that can be swung back in a horizontal plane to allow tall vessels, etc. to pass
☆**swing·by** (-bī′) *n.* a flight path of a spacecraft using the gravitational field of an intermediate planet or the destination planet to achieve a desired change in course or orbit
swinge (swinj) *vt.* **swinged, swinge′ing** [ME. *swengen* < OE. *swengan*, caus. of *swingan*, to SWING] [Archaic] to punish with blows; beat; whip
swinge·ing (-iŋ) *adj.* [prp. of prec.: cf. STRAPPING] [Brit. Colloq.] **1.** huge; very large **2.** extremely good; first-rate
swing·er¹ (swiŋ′ər) *n.* **1.** one that swings ☆**2.** [Slang] a person who is sophisticated, ultra-fashionable, active, uninhibited, etc., esp. in the pursuit of pleasure
swing·er² (swiŋ′jər) *n.* **1.** [Obs.] a powerful fellow **2.** [Brit. Colloq.] something huge
swing·ing (swiŋ′iŋ) *adj.* **1.** that swings **2.** done with a swing ☆**3.** [Slang] lively, sophisticated, ultra-fashionable, etc. —**swing′ing·ly** *adv.*
swinging door a door hung so that it can be opened in either direction and swings shut by itself
swin·gle (swiŋ′g'l) *vt.* **-gled, -gling** [ME. *swinglen* < MDu. *swinghelen* < *swinghel*, a swingle: see the *n.*] to clean (flax or hemp) by beating or scraping with a swingle —*n.* [ME. < OE. *swingle* & MDu. *swinghel*: for IE. base see SWING] **1.** a wooden, swordlike tool used to clean flax or hemp by beating or scraping **2.** the swiple of a flail
swin·gle·tree (-trē′) *n.* same as SINGLETREE
☆**swing shift** [Colloq.] the evening work shift in some factories, from about midafternoon to about midnight
swin·ish (swīn′ish) *adj.* [ME. *swinisch*] of, like, fit for, or characteristic of swine; beastly, piggish, coarse, etc.: —**swin′ish·ly** *adv.* —**swin′ish·ness** *n.*
swink (swiŋk) *vi.* **swank, swink′ing** [ME. *swinken* < OE. *swincan*: for IE. base see SWING] [Archaic] to labor; toil; drudge —*n.* [Archaic] labor; toil; drudgery
swipe (swīp) *n.* [prob. var. of SWEEP] **1.** a lever or handle **2.** [Colloq.] a hard, sweeping blow ☆**3.** [Colloq.] a groom for horses, esp. at a race track —*vt.* **swiped, swip′ing** **1.** [< ? ON. *svipa*, to whip, make a swift motion, akin to SWOOP] [Colloq.] to hit with a hard, sweeping blow ☆**2.** [Slang] to steal; pilfer —*vi.* to make a sweeping blow or stroke —**SYN.** see STEAL
swipes (swīps) *n.pl.* [< SWIPE, in obs. sense of "gulp down"] [Brit. Colloq.] beer, esp. weak or inferior beer
swi·ple, swip·ple (swip′'l) *n.* [ME. *swepyl* < *swepen*, to SWEEP] the part of a flail that strikes the grain in threshing
swirl (swûrl) *vi.* [ME. (Scot.) *swyrl*, prob. < Norw. dial. *svirla*, freq. of *sverra*, to whirl: for IE. base see SWARM¹] **1.** to move with a twisting, whirling motion; eddy **2.** to swim, or be dizzy, as the head —*vt.* to cause to swirl; whirl —*n.* **1.** a swirling motion; whirl; eddy **2.** something having a twisting, curving form; twist; curl; whirl; whorl **3.** dizzy confusion —**swirl′ing·ly** *adv.*
swirl·y (swûr′lē) *adj.* **1.** full of swirls **2.** [Scot.] tangled
swish (swish) *vi.* [echoic] **1.** to move with a sharp, hissing sound, as a cane swung through the air **2.** to rustle, as skirts in walking —*vt.* **1.** to cause to swish **2.** to whip or flog —*n.* **1.** a hissing or rustling sound **2.** a movement, etc. that makes this sound ☆**3.** [Slang] an effeminate male homosexual —*adj.* **1.** [Chiefly Brit. Colloq.] fashionable ☆**2.** [Slang] of, like, or for effeminate male homosexuals
swish·y (-ē) *adj.* **swish′i·er, swish′i·est** **1.** making a hissing or rustling sound ☆**2.** [Slang] designating, of, like, or for effeminate male homosexuals
Swiss (swis) *adj.* [Fr. *Suisse* < MHG. *Swiz*] of Switzerland, its people, or its culture —*n.* **1.** *pl.* **Swiss** a native or inhabitant of Switzerland **2.** [s-] a type of sheer fabric: see DOTTED SWISS —**the Swiss** the people of Switzerland
Swiss chard same as CHARD
Swiss (cheese) [orig. made in Switzerland] a white or pale-yellow hard cheese with many large holes
Swiss Guards a corps of Swiss mercenary soldiers, esp. those hired as Vatican bodyguards to the Pope
☆**Swiss steak** a thick cut of steak, esp. round steak, pounded with flour, browned, and cooked slowly, usually with a sauce of tomatoes, onions, etc.
Swit. Switzerland
switch (swich) *n.* [Early ModE. *swits*, prob. < MDu. or LowG., as in MDu. *swick*, akin to ON. *sveigr*, a flexible stalk: for IE. base see SWOOP] **1.** a thin, flexible twig, rod, stick, etc., esp. one used for whipping **2.** the bushy part of the tail in some animals, as the cow **3.** a

tress of detached, sometimes false, hair bound at one end and used by women as part of a coiffure **4.** an abrupt, sharp, lashing movement, as with a switch **5.** a device used to open, close, or divert an electric circuit **6.** *a)* a movable section of railroad track used in transferring a train from one set of tracks to another *b)* the act or process of changing the position of such a switch ☆*c)* same as SIDING (sense 2) **7.** a shift or transference, esp. if sudden or unexpected —*vt.* **1.** to whip or beat with or as with a switch **2.** to jerk or swing sharply; lash [a cow *switching* its tail] **3.** to shift; transfer; change; turn aside; divert **4.** *a)* to operate the switch of (an electric circuit) so as to connect, disconnect, or divert *b)* to turn (an electric light or appliance) *on* or *off* in this way ☆**5.** to transfer (a railroad train or car) from one set of tracks to another by use of a switch; shunt **6.** [Colloq.] to change or exchange [to *switch* places] —*vi.* ☆**1.** to move from or as from one set of tracks to another **2.** to shift; transfer; change **3.** to swing sharply; lash —**switch′er** *n.*
☆**switch·back** (-bak′) *n.* **1.** a road or railroad following a zigzag course up a steep grade **2.** [Brit.] same as ROLLER COASTER
☆**switch-blade knife** (-blād′) a large jackknife that snaps open when a release button on the handle is pressed
☆**switch·board** (-bôrd′) *n.* a board or panel equipped with apparatus for controlling the operation of a system of electric circuits, as in a telephone exchange
☆**switch cane** a small bamboo (*Arundinaria tecta*) native to the SE U.S.
☆**switch-hit·ter** (-hit′ər) *n.* a baseball player who bats sometimes right-handed and sometimes left-handed
switch·man (-mən) *n., pl.* **-men** (-mən) a railroad employee who operates switches
☆**switch·yard** (-yärd′) *n.* a railroad yard where cars are shifted from one track to another by means of a system of switches, as in making up trains
Swith·in, Swith·un (swith′ən, swith′-), Saint 800?–862? A.D.; Eng. prelate: his day is July 15
Switz. Switzerland
Switz·er (swit′sər) *n.* [MHG. < *Switz, Swiz*, Switzerland] **1.** a Swiss **2.** a Swiss mercenary soldier
Switz·er·land (swit′sər lənd) country in WC Europe, in the Alps: 15,941 sq. mi.; pop. 6,036,000; cap. Bern: Ger. name, SCHWEIZ, Fr. name, SUISSE
swiv·el (swiv′'l) *n.* [ME. *swiuel* < base of OE. *swifan*, to revolve, turn: for IE. base see SWIFT] a coupling device that allows free turning of the parts attached to it; specif., a chain link made in two parts, one piece fitting like a collar below the bolt head of the other and turning freely about it —*vt.* **-eled** or **-elled, -el·ing** or **-el·ling** **1.** to cause to turn or rotate on or as if on a swivel **2.** to fit, fasten, or support with a swivel —*vi.* to turn on or as if on a swivel
☆**swivel chair** a chair whose seat turns horizontally on a pivot in the base
swiv·et (swiv′ət) *n.* [< ?] [Dial. or Colloq.] a condition of irritation, exasperation, annoyance, etc.
swiz·zle (swiz′'l) *n.* [< ?] any of several alcoholic drinks containing liquor, ice, sugar, lime juice, etc.

SWIVEL CHAIR

swizzle stick a small rod for stirring mixed drinks
swob (swäb) *n., vt.* **swobbed, swob′bing** *var. sp.* of SWAB
swol·len (swō′lən) *alt. pp.* of SWELL —*adj.* increased in volume or size, as from inner pressure; blown up; distended; bulging
swoon (swōōn) *vi.* [ME. *swounen*, prob. back-formation < *swoweninge*, swooning < OE. *geswogen*, unconscious, pp. of *swogan* < ?] **1.** to faint **2.** to feel strong, esp. rapturous emotion —*n.* an act or instance of swooning —**swoon′er** *n.* —**swoon′ing·ly** *adv.*
swoop (swōōp) *vt.* [ME. *swopen* < OE. *swapan*, to sweep along, rush, akin to G. *schweifen*, ON. *sveipa*: for IE. base see SWIFT] to snatch (*up*) or seize suddenly, with a sweeping movement —*vi.* to descend suddenly and swiftly, as a bird in hunting; pounce or sweep (*down* or *upon*) —*n.* the act of swooping or pouncing; sudden, violent descent
swoosh (swoosh, swōōsh) *vi., vt.* [echoic intens. of SWISH] to move, pour, etc. with, or as with, a sharp, rustling or whistling sound —*n.* such a sound
swop (swäp) *n., vt., vi.* **swopped, swop′ping** *var. sp.* of SWAP
sword (sôrd) *n.* [ME. < OE. *sweord*, akin to G. *schwert*, prob. < IE. base *swer-*, to cut, pierce] **1.** a hand weapon having a long, sharp-pointed blade, usually with a sharp edge on one or both sides, set in a hilt; broadsword, rapier, saber, scimitar, etc. **2.** *a)* the sword regarded as an instrument of death, destruction, etc. *b)* power; esp., military power *c)* the military class or profession *d)* war; warfare —**at swords' points** ready to quarrel or fight —**cross swords** **1.** to fight **2.** to argue violently —**put to the sword** **1.** to kill with a sword or swords **2.** to slaughter, esp. in war —**sword′like′** *adj.*
sword bayonet a short sword that can be mounted on a rifle for use as a bayonet
sword belt a belt from which a sword is hung
sword cane a weapon consisting of a sword or dagger concealed in a walking stick: also **sword stick**

sword·craft (-kraft′, -kräft′) *n.* **1.** the skill or art of a swordsman; swordsmanship **2.** [Now Rare] military force or skill

sword dance any dance, esp. by men, involving the use of swords, esp. one performed around bare swords laid on the ground —**sword dancer**

☆**sword fern** any of various ferns with sword-shaped leaves; esp., a giant fern (*Nephrolepis biserrata*) of S Florida, with simply pinnate leaves

sword·fish (-fish′) *n.*, *pl.* **-fish′**, **-fish′es**: see FISH² a large marine food and game fish (*Xiphias gladius*) having a saillike dorsal fin, and with the upper jawbone extending in a long, flat, swordlike projection

SWORDFISH (to 15 ft. long)

sword grass any of a number of sedges or grasses with toothed or sword-shaped leaves

sword knot a loop of leather, ribbon, etc. attached to a sword hilt as an ornament or, orig., as a wrist support

sword·play (-plā′) *n.* the act or skill of using a sword in fencing or fighting

swords·man (sôrdz′mən) *n.*, *pl.* **-men** (-mən) **1.** a person who uses a sword in fencing or fighting **2.** a person skilled in using a sword Also [Archaic] **sword·man** (sôrd′mən), *pl.* **-men** (-mən) —**swords′man·ship′** *n.*

sword·tail (sôrd′tāl′) *n.* a small, vividly colored, live-bearing, freshwater fish (*Xiphophorus helleri*) of Mexico and Central America, often used in genetic research

swore (swôr) *pt.* of SWEAR

sworn (swôrn) *pp.* of SWEAR —*adj.* bound, pledged, promised, etc. by or as by an oath

swot¹ (swät) *n.*, *vt.* **swot′ted**, **swot′ting** *var. sp.* of SWAT

swot² (swät) *vi.*, *vt.* **swot′ted**, **swot′ting** [dial. var. of SWEAT] [Brit. Colloq.] to study hard; cram —*n.* [Brit. Colloq.] a person who studies hard; grind —**swot′ter** *n.*

swound (swound, swoond) *n.*, *vi.* [ME. *swounde, swounden* < *swounen* (cf. SWOON) with unhistoric -*d*] [Archaic] swoon; faint

swum (swum) *pp.* of SWIM¹ & SWIM²

swung (swuŋ) *pp.* & *pt.* of SWING

Syb·a·ris (sib′ə ris) ancient Gr. city in S Italy, famed as a center of luxury: destroyed 510 B.C.

Syb·a·rite (-rīt′) *n.* [L. *Sybarita* < Gr. *Sybaritēs*] **1.** any of the people of ancient Sybaris **2.** [s-] anyone very fond of luxury and self-indulgence; voluptuary —**Syb′a·rit′ic**, **syb′a·rit′i·cal** (-rit′ik) *adj.* —**syb′a·rit′i·cal·ly** *adv.* —**syb′a·rit′ism** (-rīt′iz′m) *n.*

Syb·il (sib′l) a feminine name: see SIBYL

syc·a·mine (sik′ə min, -mīn′) *n.* [L. *sycaminus* < Gr. *sykaminos* < Sem., as in Heb. *shiqmāh*, mulberry] a tree mentioned in the Bible (Luke 17:6), believed to be the black mulberry (*Morus nigra*)

syc·a·more (sik′ə môr′) *n.* [ME. *sicomore* < OFr. *sicamor* < L. *sycomorus* < Gr. *sykomoros*, prob. altered (after *sykon*, fig + *moron*, black mulberry) < Heb. *shiqmāh*, mulberry] **1.** a shade tree (*Ficus sycamorus*) of the mulberry family, native to Egypt and Asia Minor, with edible figlike fruit: the sycamore of the Bible **2.** a maple shade tree (*Acer pseudoplatanus*) with yellow flowers, found in Europe and Asia ☆**3.** *same as* PLANE¹

syce (sīs) *n.* [Ar. *sa′is* < *sus*, to tend a horse] in India, a groom (for horses)

sy·cee (sī′sē′) *n.* [Cantonese dial. < Chin. *hsi ssŭ*, fine silk: so called because it may, when heated, be spun into fine threads] silver in the form of ingots, usually stamped, formerly used in China as money

sy·co·ni·um (sī kō′nē əm) *n.*, *pl.* **-ni·a** (-ə) [ModL. < Gr. *sykon*, fig] *Bot.* a pear-shaped, fleshy, hollow, false fruit, as of the fig, containing many flowers

syc·o·phan·cy (sik′ə fən sē) *n.*, *pl.* **-cies** [L. *sycophantia* < Gr. *sykophantia*] the behavior or character, or an act, of a sycophant; servile flattery

syc·o·phant (sik′ə fənt) *n.* [L. *sycophanta* < Gr. *sykophantēs*, informer, lit., maker of the sign of the fig < *sykon*, a fig + *phainein*, to show] a person who seeks favor by flattering people of wealth or influence; parasite; toady —SYN. see PARASITE —**syc′o·phan′tic** (-fan′tik), **syc′o·phant′ish** *adj.* —**syc′o·phan′ti·cal·ly**, **syc′o·phant′ish·ly** *adv.* —**syc′o·phant·ism** *n.*

sy·co·sis (sī kō′sis) *n.* [ModL. < Gr. *sykōsis* < *sykon*, fig] a chronic disease of the hair follicles, esp. of the beard, caused by certain staphylococci and characterized by the formation of papules and pustules

Syd·ney (sid′nē) **1.** a masculine name: see SIDNEY **2.** seaport in SE Australia; capital of New South Wales: pop. (with suburbs) 2,431,000

Sy·e·ne (sī ē′nē) ancient name of ASWAN

sy·e·nite (sī′ə nīt′) *n.* [Fr. *syénite* < L. *Syenites* (*lapis*), Syenite (stone) < *Syene* < Gr. *Syēnē*, Syene] a gray, igneous rock typically containing feldspar, hornblende, and some silicates —**sy′e·nit′ic** (-nit′ik) *adj.*

syl- (sil) *same as* SYN-: used before *l*

syl·la·bar·y (sil′ə ber′ē) *n.*, *pl.* **-bar′ies** [ModL. *syllabarium* < L. *syllaba*; see SYLLABLE] **1.** a set or table of syllables **2.** a set of the written signs or characters of a language representing syllables

syl·lab·ic (si lab′ik) *adj.* [LL. *syllabicus* < Gr. *syllabikos*] **1.** of a syllable or syllables **2.** forming a syllable or the nucleus of a syllable; specif., *a)* being the most prominent sound in a phonemic syllable: said of a vowel *b)* constituting the more heavily stressed part of a diphthong, as the *o* in *loud c)* standing by itself as the nucleus of a syllable without an accompanying vowel: said of a consonant, as the *l* in *tattle* (tat′′l) **3.** designating or of a form of verse whose structure is based on the number of syllables in a line rather than on rhythm, stress, or quantity **4.** pronounced with the syllables distinct —*n.* **1.** a syllabic sound **2.** [*pl.*] syllabic verse —**syl·lab′i·cal·ly** *adv.*

syl·lab·i·cate (si lab′ə kāt′) *vt.* **-cat′ed**, **-cat′ing** *same as* SYLLABIFY —**syl·lab′i·ca′tion** *n.*

syl·lab·i·fy (si lab′ə fī′) *vt.* **-fied′**, **-fy′ing** [back-formation < *syllabification* < L. *syllaba*, SYLLABLE + -FICATION] to form or divide into syllables —**syl·lab′i·fi·ca′tion** *n.*

syl·la·bism (sil′ə biz′m) *n.* [< L. *syllaba*, SYLLABLE + -ISM] **1.** the use of syllabic characters, rather than letters, in writing **2.** division into syllables

syl·la·ble (sil′ə b′l) *n.* [ME. *sillable* < L. *syllaba* < Gr. *syllabē*, a syllable, lit., that which holds together < *syllambanein*, to join < *syn-*, together + *lambanein*, to hold: for IE. base see LATCH] **1.** a word or part of a word pronounced with a single, uninterrupted sounding of the voice; unit of pronunciation, consisting of a single sound of great sonority (usually a vowel) and generally one or more sounds of lesser sonority (usually consonants) **2.** any of the parts into which a written word is divided in approximate representation of its spoken syllables to show where the word can be broken at the end of a line: in this dictionary, the syllables of entry words are separated by centered dots **3.** the least bit of expression; slightest detail, as of something said —*vt.*, *vi.* **-bled**, **-bling** to pronounce in or as in syllables

syl·la·bub (sil′ə bub′) *n.* [Early ModE. *solybubbe* < ?] a dessert or beverage made of sweetened milk or cream mixed with wine or cider and beaten to a froth

syl·la·bus (sil′ə bəs) *n.*, *pl.* **-bus·es**, **-bi′** (-bī′) [LL.(Ec.), a list, altered < L. *sillybus* < Gr. *sillybos*, a parchment strip used as a label] **1.** a summary or outline containing the main points, esp. of a course of study **2.** *Law* brief notes preceding and explaining the decision or points of law in the written report of an adjudged case

syl·lep·sis (si lep′sis) *n.*, *pl.* **-lep′ses** (-sēz) [L. < Gr. *syllēpsis*, a putting together < *syllambanein*: see SYLLABLE] a grammatical construction in which a single word is used to modify or govern syntactically two or more words in the same sentence, though it can grammatically agree with only one of them (Ex.: either they or I am wrong) —**syl·lep′tic** *adj.*

syl·lo·gism (sil′ə jiz′m) *n.* [ME. *silogisme* < MFr. < L. *syllogismus* < Gr. *syllogismos*, a reckoning together < *syllogizesthai*, to reckon together, sum up < *syn-*, together + *logizesthai*, to reason < *logos*, a word: see LOGIC] **1.** an argument or form of reasoning in which two statements or premises are made and a logical conclusion drawn from them Ex.: All mammals are warm-blooded (*major premise*); whales are mammals (*minor premise*); therefore, whales are warm-blooded (*conclusion*) **2.** reasoning from the general to the particular; deductive logic **3.** an instance of subtle, tricky, or specious reasoning —**syl′lo·gis′tic**, **syl′lo·gis′ti·cal** *adj.* —**syl′lo·gis′ti·cal·ly** *adv.*

syl·lo·gize (sil′ə jīz′) *vi.*, *vt.* **-gized′**, **-giz′ing** [ME. *sylogysen* < ML. *syllogizare*] to reason or infer by the use of syllogisms

sylph (silf) *n.* [ModL. *sylphus*, special use (by Paracelsus) of L., a spirit < ?] **1.** in Paracelsus' system, any of a class of mortal, soulless, beings supposed to inhabit the air **2.** a slender, graceful woman or girl —**sylph′like′** *adj.*

sylph·id (sil′fid) *n.* [Fr. *sylphide*: see SYLPH & -ID] a small or young sylph —**sylph′id·ine** (-fi din, -dīn′) *adj.*

syl·va (sil′və) *n.*, *pl.* **-vas**, **-vae** (-vē) *same as* SILVA

Syl·van (sil′vən) a masculine name: see SYLVANUS

syl·van (sil′vən) *adj.* [ML. *silvanus* < L. *silva*, a wood, prob. < IE. *(k)selwa-*, whence Gr. *xylon*, wood] **1.** of or characteristic of the woods or forest **2.** living, found, or carried on in the woods or forest **3.** wooded —*n.* [L. *silvanus*] one who lives in the woods

syl·van·ite (sil′və nīt′) *n.* [(TRAN)SYLVAN(IA), where first found + -ITE¹] a gray or silvery telluride of gold and silver (Ag,Au)Te₂, crystallizing in the monoclinic system

Syl·va·nus (sil vā′nəs) [L. *Silvanus*: see SYLVAN] a masculine name: var. *Sylvan*; fem. *Sylvia*

syl·vat·ic (-vat′ik) *adj.* of or in the woods, or affecting the animals in the woods [*sylvatic plague*]

Syl·ves·ter (sil ves′tər) [L. *Silvester* < *silvester*, of a wood or forest < *silva*, a wood] a masculine name

Syl·vi·a (sil′vē ə) [L. *Silvia* < *silva*, a wood] a feminine name: dim. *Syl, Sylvie*

syl·vite (sil′vīt) *n.* [earlier *sylvine* < Fr. < ModL. *sal digestivus sylvii*, lit., digestive salt of Sylvius (after Franz de la Boë *Sylvius*, 1614–1672, physician at Leyden)] native potassium chloride, KCl, occurring in isometric crystalline masses and used as a source of potash for fertilizers

sym- (sim) *same as* SYN-: used before *m*, *p*, and *b*

sym. 1. symbol 2. *Chem.* symmetrical 3. symphony

sym·bi·ont (sim′bī änt′, -bē-) *n.* [G. < Gr. *symbiountos*, prp. of *symbioun*: see ff.] an organism living in a state of symbiosis —**sym′bi·on′tic** *adj.*

sym·bi·o·sis (sim′bī ō′sis, -bē-) *n.* [ModL. < Gr. *symbiōsis* < *symbioun*, to live together < *syn-*, together + *bios*, life: see BIO-] 1. *Biol.* the intimate living together of two kinds of organisms, esp. where such association is of mutual advantage: see COMMENSALISM, MUTUALISM, PARASITISM 2. a similar relationship of mutual interdependence between persons or groups —**sym′bi·ot′ic** (-ät′ik) *adj.*

sym·bol (sim′b'l) *n.* [< Fr. & L.: Fr. *symbole* < L. *symbolus, symbolum* < Gr. *symbolon*, token, pledge, sign by which one infers a thing < *symballein*, to throw together, compare < *syn-*, together + *ballein*, to throw] 1. something that stands for or represents another thing; esp., an object used to represent something abstract; emblem [the dove is a *symbol* of peace] 2. a written or printed mark, letter, abbreviation, etc. standing for an object, quality, process, quantity, etc., as in music, mathematics, or chemistry 3. *Psychoanalysis* an act or object representing an unconscious desire that has been repressed —*vt.* **-boled** or **-bolled, -bol·ing** or **-bol·ling** *same as* SYMBOLIZE

sym·bol·ic (sim bäl′ik) *adj.* [LL. *symbolicus* < Gr. *symbolikos*] 1. of or expressed in a symbol or symbols 2. that serves as a symbol (*of* something) 3. characterized by symbolism Also **sym·bol′i·cal** —**sym·bol′i·cal·ly** *adv.*

symbolic logic a modern type of formal logic using special mathematical symbols for propositions, quantifiers, and relationships among propositions and concerned with the elucidation of permissible operations upon such symbols

sym·bol·ism (sim′b'l iz'm) *n.* 1. the representation of things by use of symbols, esp. in art or literature 2. a system of symbols 3. symbolic meaning 4. the theories or practices of a group of symbolists, as in art or literature

sym·bol·ist (-ist) *n.* 1. a person who uses symbols 2. a person who practices symbolism in representing ideas, etc., esp. in art or literature; specif., any of a group of French and Belgian writers and artists of the late 19th cent. who rejected realism and tried to express ideas, emotions, and attitudes by the use of symbolic words, figures, objects, etc. 3. a person who studies or is expert in interpreting symbols or symbolism —**sym′bol·is′tic** *adj.* —**sym′bol·is′ti·cal·ly** *adv.*

sym·bol·ize (-īz′) *vt.* **-ized′, -iz′ing** [Fr. *symboliser* < ML. *symbolizare*] 1. to be a symbol of; typify; stand for 2. to represent by a symbol or symbols —*vi.* to use symbols —**sym′bol·i·za′tion** *n.* —**sym′bol·iz′er** *n.*

sym·bol·o·gy (sim bäl′ə jē) *n.* [SYMBO(L) + -LOGY] 1. the study or interpretation of symbols 2. representation or expression by means of symbols; symbolism

sym·met·al·lism (sim met′'l iz'm) *n.* [< SYM- + METAL + -ISM] a system of coinage based on a unit of currency made up of two or more metals in combination, each of a specified minimum weight

sym·met·ri·cal (si met′ri k'l) *adj.* [SYMMETR(Y) + -ICAL] having or showing symmetry; specif., *a*) *Bot.* that can be divided into similar halves by a plane passing through the center; also, having the same number of parts in each whorl of leaves: said of a flower *b*) *Chem.* exhibiting a regular repeated pattern of atoms in the structural formula; specif., designating a compound (benzene derivative) in which substitution takes place at the alternate carbon atoms *c*) *Math., Logic* designating an equation, relation, etc. whose terms can be interchanged without affecting its validity *d*) *Med.* affecting corresponding parts of the body simultaneously in the same way: said of a disease, infection, etc. Also **sym·met′ric** —**sym·met′ri·cal·ly** *adv.*

sym·me·trize (sim′ə trīz′) *vt.* **-trized′, -triz′ing** to make symmetrical —**sym′me·tri·za′tion** *n.*

sym·me·try (sim′ə trē) *n., pl.* **-tries** [< MFr. or L.: MFr. *symmetrie* (now *symétrie*) < L. *symmetria* < Gr. *symmetria* < *symmetros*, measured together < *syn-*, together + *metron*, a MEASURE] 1. similarity of form or arrangement on either side of a dividing line or plane; correspondence of opposite parts in size, shape, and position; condition of being symmetrical: the whole or the corresponding parts are said to have symmetry 2. balance or beauty of form or proportion resulting from such correspondence

SYN.—symmetry, with reference to the interrelation of parts to form an aesthetically pleasing whole, strictly implies correspondence in the form, size, arrangement, etc. of parts on either side of a median line or plane; **proportion** implies a gracefulness that results from the measured fitness in size or arrangement of parts to each other or to the whole; **harmony** implies such agreement or proportionate arrangement of parts in size, color, form, etc. as to make a pleasing impression; **balance** suggests the offsetting or contrasting of parts so as to produce an aesthetic equilibrium in the whole

Sym·onds (sim′ənz, -əndz), **John Ad·ding·ton** (ad′iŋ tən) 1840–93; Eng. poet, writer, & scholar

sym·pa·thec·to·my (sim′pə thek′tə mē) *n., pl.* **-mies** [< ff. + -ECTOMY] the interruption by surgical means of part of the sympathetic nervous system

sym·pa·thet·ic (sim′pə thet′ik) *adj.* [ModL. *sympatheticus* < Gr. *sympatheia*, SYMPATHY, after Gr. *pathētikos*, PATHETIC] 1. of, expressing, resulting from, feeling, or showing sympathy; sympathizing 2. in agreement with one's tastes, mood, feelings, disposition, etc.; congenial 3. showing favor, approval, or agreement [to be *sympathetic* to a plan] 4. *Anat., Physiol.* designating or of that part of the autonomic nervous system whose nerves originate in the lumbar and thoracic regions of the spinal cord and that is esp. concerned with mediating the involuntary response to alarm, as by speeding the heart rate, raising the blood pressure, and dilating the pupils of the eyes: cf. PARASYMPATHETIC 5. *Physics, Acoustics* designating of vibrations, sounds, etc. caused by other vibrations of the same period transmitted from a neighboring vibrating body —SYN. see TENDER[1] —**sym′pa·thet′i·cal·ly** *adv.*

sympathetic ink *same as* INVISIBLE INK

sym·pa·thize (sim′pə thīz′) *vi.* **-thized′, -thiz′ing** [Fr. *sympathiser*] 1. to share or understand the feelings or ideas of another; be in sympathy 2. to feel or express sympathy, esp. in pity or compassion; commiserate 3. to be in harmony or accord —**sym′pa·thiz′er** *n.* —**sym′pa·thiz′ing·ly** *adv.*

sym·pa·tho·lyt·ic (sim′pə thō lit′ik) *adj.* [< SYMPATH(ETIC) + -o- + -LYTIC] having the effect of decreasing the activity of the sympathetic nervous system: said of certain drugs, chemicals, etc.

sym·pa·tho·mi·met·ic (-mi met′ik) *adj.* [< SYMPATH(ETIC) + -o- + MIMETIC] having an effect similar to that produced when the sympathetic nervous system is stimulated: said of certain drugs, chemicals, etc.

sym·pa·thy (sim′pə thē) *n., pl.* **-thies** [L. *sympathia* < Gr. *sympatheia* < *syn-*, together + *pathos*, feeling: see PATHOS] 1. sameness of feeling; affinity between persons or of one person for another 2. agreement in qualities; harmony; accord 3. a mutual liking or understanding arising from sameness of feeling 4. an entering into, or the ability to enter into, another person's mental state, feelings, emotions, etc.; esp., [often *pl.*] pity or compassion felt for another's trouble, suffering, etc. 5. a feeling of approval of or agreement with an idea, cause, etc. 6. *Physics* a relation or harmony between bodies of such a nature that vibrations in one cause sympathetic vibrations in the other or others 7. *Physiol.* a relation between body parts of such a nature that a disorder, pain, etc. in one induces a similar effect in another —SYN. see PITY

sympathy (or **sympathetic**) **strike** a strike by a group of workers in support of another group on strike

sym·pat·ric (sim pat′rik) *adj.* [SYM- + PATR(I)- + -IC] *Biol., Ecol.* of or pertaining to closely related species of organisms occurring in the same geographic area —**sym·pat′ri·cal·ly** *adv.* —**sym·pat·ry** (sim′pə trē) *n.*

sym·pet·al·ous (sim pet′'l əs) *adj.* [SYM- + PETALOUS] *Bot. same as* GAMOPETALOUS

sym·phon·ic (sim fän′ik) *adj.* 1. of, like, or for a symphony or symphony orchestra 2. of or having to do with harmony of sound —**sym·phon′i·cal·ly** *adv.*

symphonic poem a musical composition for full symphony orchestra that is programmatic in nature, musically interpreting particular poetic or descriptive ideas, and free in form, usually with no division into parts

sym·pho·ni·ous (sim fō′nē əs) *adj.* [< L. *symphonia*, harmony (see SYMPHONY) + -OUS] [Now Rare] harmonious, esp. in sound —**sym·pho′ni·ous·ly** *adv.*

sym·pho·nist (sim′fə nist) *n.* a composer of symphonies

sym·pho·ny (sim′fə nē) *n., pl.* **-nies** [ME. *symfonye* < OFr. *simphonie* < L. *symphonia* < Gr. *symphōnia* < *syn-*, together + *phōnē*, a sound: see PHONO-] 1. harmony of sounds, esp. of instruments 2. harmony of any kind, esp. of color 3. anything, as a picture, characterized by harmonious composition 4. *Music a*) an extended composition for full orchestra, having several (usually four) movements related in subject, but varying in form and execution *b*) an instrumental passage in a composition that is largely vocal or choral *c*) *clipped form of* SYMPHONY ORCHESTRA *d*) [Colloq.] a concert by a symphony orchestra

symphony orchestra a large orchestra of string, wind, and percussion sections for playing symphonic works

sym·phy·sis (sim′fə sis) *n., pl.* **-phy·ses′** (-sēz′) [ModL. < Gr. *symphysis*, a growing together < *syn-*, with + *phyein*, to grow: see BONDAGE] a growing together or fusing; specif., *a*) *Anat., Zool.* the growing together of bones originally separate, as of the two halves of the lower jaw or the two pubic bones; also, the line of junction and fusion of such bones *b*) *Bot.* the growing together of similar parts of a plant; coalescence —**sym·phys′i·al** (-fiz′ē əl), **sym·phys′e·al** *adj.*

sym·po·di·um (sim pō′dē əm) *n., pl.* **-di·a** (-ə) [ModL.: see SYM- & -PODIUM] *Bot.* an apparent stem actually made up of a series of axillary branches growing one from another, giving the effect of a simple stem, as in the grape —**sym·po′di·al** *adj.*

sym·po·si·ac (sim pō′zē ak′) *adj.* [L. *symposiacus*, belonging to a banquet, convivial < Gr. *symposiakos*] of, having the nature of, or appropriate to a symposium

sym·po·si·arch (-ärk′) *n.* [Gr. *symposiarchos*, master of a feast: see SYMPOSIUM & -ARCH] the master or director of a symposium, esp. in ancient Greece

sym·po·si·ast (-ast′) *n.* [SYMPOSI(UM) + -*ast*, as in ENTHUSIAST] a person participating in a symposium

sym·po·si·um (-əm) *n., pl.* **-si·ums, -si·a** (-ə) [L. < Gr. *symposion* < *syn-*, together + *posis*, a drinking < IE. base *pō-*, to drink, whence L. *potio*: cf. POTION] **1.** in ancient Greece, a drinking party at which there was intellectual discussion **2.** any meeting or social gathering at which ideas are freely exchanged **3.** a conference organized for the discussion of some particular subject **4.** a collection of opinions, esp. a published group of essays, on a given subject

symp·tom (simp′təm) *n.* [altered (after LL. or Gr.) < ME. *symthoma* < ML. *sinthoma* < LL. *symptōma* < Gr. *symptōma*, anything that has befallen one, casualty < *sympiptein*, to fall together, happen < *syn-*, together + *piptein*, to fall (for IE. base see FEATHER] any circumstance, event, or condition that accompanies something and indicates its existence or occurrence; sign; indication; specif., *Med.* any condition accompanying or resulting from a disease or a physical disorder and serving as an aid in diagnosis —*SYN.* see SIGN

symp·to·mat·ic (simp′tə mat′ik) *adj.* [Fr. *symptomatique* < Gr. *symptōmatikos*, accidental] **1.** of or having to do with symptoms **2.** that constitutes a symptom, as of a disease; indicative (*of*) **3.** in accordance with symptoms [a *symptomatic* treatment] —**symp′to·mat′i·cal·ly** *adv.*

symp·tom·a·tize (simp′tə mə tīz′) *vt.* -**tized′, -tiz′ing** to be a symptom or sign of; indicate: also **symp′tom·ize′**

symp·tom·a·tol·o·gy (simp′tə mə täl′ə jē) *n.* [ModL. *symptomatologia* < Gr. *symptōma* (gen. *symptomatos*), SYMPTOM + -*logia*, -LOGY] **1.** symptoms of disease, collectively **2.** all the symptoms of a given disease

syn- (sin) [Gr. < *syn*, with, with, earlier *xyn*] a *prefix meaning* with, together with, at the same time, by means of [*synagogue, synapse*]: syn- is assimilated to *syl-* before *l*; *sym-* before *m, p, b*; and *sys-* before *s* and aspirate *h*

syn. 1. synonym **2.** synonymous **3.** synonymy

syn·aer·e·sis (si ner′ə sis) *n. var. sp. of* SYNERESIS

syn·aes·the·si·a (sin′is thē′zhə, -zhē ə, -zē ə) *n. var. sp. of* SYNESTHESIA —**syn′aes·thet′ic** (-thet′ik) *adj.*

syn·a·gogue (sin′ə gäg′, -gôg′) *n.* [ME. *sinagoge* < OFr. < LL.(Ec.) *synagoga* < Gr.(Ec.) *synagōgē* < Gr., a bringing together, assembly < *synagein*, to bring together < *syn-*, together + *ugein*, to bring: see ACT] **1.** an assembly of Jews for worship and religious study **2.** a building or place used by Jews for worship and religious study **3.** the Jewish religion as organized in such local congregations Also **syn′a·gog′** —**syn′a·gog′al** (-gäg′′l, -gôg′-), **syn′a·gog′i·cal** (-gäj′i k′l) *adj.*

syn·a·loe·pha, syn·a·le·pha (sin′ə lē′fə) *n.* [L. *synaloephe* < Gr. *synaloiphē*, lit., a melting together < *syn-*, together + *aleiphein*, to smear, anoint, akin to *lipos*, fat: see LIPO-] the contraction into one syllable of two adjacent vowels, usually by elision (Ex.: *th′ eagle* for *the eagle*)

syn·apse (si naps′) *n.* [ModL. *synapsis*: see ff.] the point of contact between adjacent neurons, where nerve impulses are transmitted from one to the other

syn·ap·sis (si nap′sis) *n., pl.* **-ses** (-sēz) [ModL. < Gr. *synapsis*, a junction, connection < *syn-*, together + *apsis*, a joining < *haptein*, to join] **1.** *Genetics* the association side by side of homologous maternal and paternal paired chromosomes in the early stages of meiosis **2.** *Physiol.* same as SYNAPSE —**syn·ap′tic** (-tik) *adj.*

syn·ar·thro·sis (sin′är thrō′sis) *n., pl.* **-ses** (-sēz) [ModL. < Gr. *synarthrōsis*, a being jointed together < *synarthroun*, to link together < *syn-*, with + *arthron*, a joint: see ART¹] *Anat.* any of various immovable articulations, or joints —**syn′ar·thro′di·al** *adj.*

sync, synch (sink) *vt., vi. clipped form of* SYNCHRONIZE —*n. clipped form of* SYNCHRONIZATION

syn·carp (sin′kärp) *n.* [ModL. *syncarpium*: see SYN- & -CARP] **1.** same as MULTIPLE FRUIT **2.** an aggregate fruit

syn·car·pous (sin kär′pəs) *adj. Bot.* **1.** composed of carpels growing together **2.** of a syncarp —**syn′car·py** *n.*

syn·chro (sin′krō) *n., pl.* **-chros** [< ff.] a system consisting of a generator and one or more motorlike devices connected electrically so that, upon receipt of a signal from the generator, the rotors of the synchronous motors always assume positions identical with that of the generator rotor

syn·chro- (sin′krō) *a combining form meaning* synchronized, synchronous [*synchromesh*]

☆**syn·chro·cy·clo·tron** (sin′krō sī′klə trän′) *n.* a modified cyclotron in which the frequency of the accelerating voltage is modulated to take into account the increase in the relativistic mass of the particle as it reaches high energies

syn·chro·mesh (sin′krə mesh′) *adj.* [SYNCHRO- + MESH] designating or employing a device by which gears to be meshed are automatically brought to the same speed of rotation before the shift is completed —*n.* **1.** a synchromesh gear system **2.** any gear in such a system

syn·chro·nal (sin′krə n′l) *adj.* [< LL. *synchronus* (see SYNCHRONOUS) + -AL] *same as* SYNCHRONOUS

syn·chron·ic (sin krän′ik, sin-) *adj.* **1.** same as SYNCHRONOUS **2.** of or concerned with language, mores, etc. at a given time, without reference to historical antecedents —**syn·chron′i·cal·ly** *adv.*

synchronic linguistics *same as* DESCRIPTIVE LINGUISTICS

syn·chro·nism (sin′krə niz′m) *n.* [ModL. *synchronismus* < Gr. *synchronismos* < *synchronos*: see ff.] **1.** the fact or state of being synchronous; simultaneous occurrence **2.** a chronological, usually tabular, listing of persons or events in history, showing synchronous existence or occurrence —**syn′chro·nis′tic** *adj.* —**syn′chro·nis′ti·cal·ly** *adv.*

syn·chro·nize (sin′krə nīz′) *vi.* **-nized′, -niz′ing** [Gr. *synchronizein*, to be contemporary with < *synchronos*, contemporary < *syn-*, together + *chronos*, time] to move or occur at the same time or rate; be synchronous —*vt.* **1.** to cause to agree in rate or speed; regulate (clocks, a flash gun and camera shutter, etc.) so as to make synchronous **2.** to assign (events, etc.) to the same date or period; represent as or show to be coincident or simultaneous **3.** *Motion Pictures* to adjust (the picture and sound effects or dialogue of a film) so as to coincide perfectly —**syn′chro·ni·za′tion** *n.* —**syn′chro·niz′er** *n.*

syn·chro·nous (-nəs) *adj.* [LL. *synchronus* < Gr. *synchronos*: see prec.] **1.** happening at the same time; occurring together; simultaneous **2.** having the same period between movements, occurrences, etc.; having the same rate and phase, as vibrations see CONTEMPORARY —*SYN.* see CONTEMPORARY —**syn′chro·nous·ly** *adv.* —**syn′chro·nous·ness** *n.*

synchronous machine an alternating-current motor, generator, or converter whose normal operating speed is exactly proportional to the frequency of the current in the circuit to which it is connected

synchronous speed a speed associated with any alternating-current machine, fixed by the alternating-current frequency and the number of poles for which the machine is wound or connected

syn·chro·ny (sin′krə nē) *n. same as* SYNCHRONISM (sense 1)

syn·chro·scope (sin′krə skōp′) *n.* [SYNCHRO(NISM) + -SCOPE] a device for indicating the degree of synchronism, as between two or more airplane engines

☆**syn·chro·tron** (-trän′) *n.* [SYNCHRO- + (ELEC)TRON] a circular machine for accelerating charged particles, esp. electrons, to very high energies through the use of a low-frequency magnetic field in combination with a high-frequency electrostatic field

syn·cli·nal (sin kli′n′l, sin′kli n′l) *adj.* [< Gr. *synklinein*, to incline together < *syn-*, together + *klinein*, to INCLINE] **1.** sloping downward in opposite directions so as to meet **2.** of, formed by, or forming a syncline

syn·cline (sin′klīn) *n.* [back-formation < prec.] *Geol.* a down fold in stratified rocks from whose central axis the beds rise upward and outward in opposite directions: opposed to ANTICLINE

syn·cli·no·ri·um (sin′klə nôr′ē əm) *n., pl.* **-ri·a** (-ə) [ModL. < prec. + Gr. *oros*, mountain] *Geol.* a large, generally synclinal structure consisting of a succession of subordinate synclines and anticlines: opposed to ANTICLINORIUM

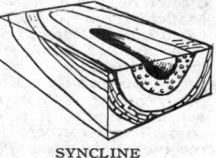

SYNCLINE

syn·co·pate (sin′kə pāt′) *vt.* **-pat′ed, -pat′ing** [< ML. *syncopatus*, pp. of *syncopare*, to cut short < LL., to swoon < *syncope*: see SYNCOPE] **1.** to shorten (a word) by syncope **2.** *Music* *a)* to shift (the regular accent) as by beginning a tone on an unaccented beat and continuing it through the next accented beat, or on the last half of a beat and continuing it through the first half of the following beat *b)* to use such shifted accents in (a musical composition, passage, rhythmic pattern, etc.) —**syn′co·pa′tor** *n.*

syn·co·pa·tion (sin′kə pā′shən) *n.* **1.** a syncopating or being syncopated **2.** syncopated music, a syncopated rhythm, etc. **3.** *Gram.* same as SYNCOPE

syn·co·pe (sin′kə pē) *n.* [LL. < Gr. *synkopē* < *syn-*, together + *koptein*, to cut: see CAPON] **1.** the dropping of sounds or letters from the middle of a word, as in *Gloster* for *Gloucester* **2.** a fainting, or loss of consciousness, caused by a temporary deficiency of blood supply to the brain —**syn′co·pal** *adj.*

syn·cre·tism (sin′krə tiz′m) *n.* [Fr. *syncrétisme* < ModL. *syncretismus* < Gr. *synkrētismos*, union of two parties against a third < *synkrētizein*, to combine] **1.** the combination or reconciliation of differing beliefs or practices in religion, philosophy, etc., or an attempt to effect such compromise **2.** *Linguis.* the merging into one of two or more differently inflected forms —**syn·cret·ic** (sin kret′ik), **syn·cre·tis·tic** (sin′krə tis′tik) *adj.* —**syn′cre·tist** *n.*

syn·cre·tize (sin′krə tīz′) *vt., vi.* **-tized′, -tiz′ing** [ModL. *syncretizare* < Gr. *synkrētizein*, to combine] to combine, unite, or reconcile

syn·cy·ti·um (sin sish′ē əm) *n., pl.* **-ti-a** (-ə) [SYN- + CYT(O) + -IUM] *Zool.* a mass of protoplasm containing scattered nuclei that are not separated into distinct cells, as in striated muscle fibers —**syn·cy′ti·al** (-əl) *adj.*

syn·dac·tyl, syn·dac·tyle (sin dak′t′l) *adj.* [Fr. *syndactyle* < Gr. *syn-*, together + *daktylos*, finger, toe: see DACTYL] having two or more digits united, as by webbing —*n.* a syndactyl mammal or bird —**syn·dac′tyl·ism** *n.*

syn·de·sis (sin′də sis) *n., pl.* **-ses** (-sēz′) [ModL. < Gr. *syndesis*, a binding together < *syndein*, to tie up: see SYNDETIC] 1. the state of being bound, linked, or connected together 2. *same as* SYNAPSIS (sense 1)

syn·des·mo·sis (sin′des mō′sis) *n., pl.* **-ses** (-sēz) [ModL. < Gr. *syndesmos*, ligament < *syndein*, to bind together: see SYNDETIC] the joining of adjacent bones as by ligaments —**syn′des·mot′ic** (-mät′ik) *adj.*

syn·det·ic (sin det′ik) *adj.* [Gr. *syndetikos* < *syndein*, to tie up < *syn-*, together + *dein*, to bind < IE. base *dēi-*, whence Sans. *dyati*, (he) binds] connecting or connected by means of conjunctions; connective

syn·dic (sin′dik) *n.* [Fr. < LL. *syndicus*, representative of a corporation < Gr. *syndikos*, helping in a court of justice, hence, defendant's advocate, judge < *syn-*, together + *dikē*, justice: see DICTION] 1. [Brit.] a business agent or manager, esp. of a university 2. any of various government officials; esp., a civil magistrate or the like

syn·di·cal (sin′di k′l) *adj.* of a syndic or syndicalism

syn·di·cal·ism (-iz′m) *n.* [Fr. *syndicalisme* < *syndical*, of a syndic or labor union (*chambre syndicale*) < *syndic*: see SYNDIC] a theory and movement of trade unionism in which all means of production and distribution would be brought under the control of federations of labor unions by the use of direct action, such as general strikes — **syn′di·cal·ist** *adj., n.* —**syn′di·cal·is′tic** *adj.*

syn·di·cate (sin′də kit; *for v.* -kāt′) *n.* [Fr. *syndicat* < *syndic*, SYNDIC] 1. a group or council of syndics 2. *a)* an association of individuals or corporations formed to carry out some financial project requiring much capital *b)* any group organized to further some undertaking; ☆*specif.*, an association of criminals set up to control vice, gambling, etc. *c)* a group of similar organizations, ☆as of newspapers, owned as a chain ☆3. an organization that sells special articles or features for publication by many newspapers or periodicals —*vt.* **-cat′ed, -cat′ing** 1. to manage as or form into a syndicate ☆2. to sell (an article, feature, etc.) through a syndicate for publication in many newspapers or periodicals —*vi.* to form a syndicate —SYN. see MONOPOLY —**syn′di·ca′tion** *n.* —**syn′di·ca′tor** *n.*

syn·drome (sin′drōm) *n.* [ModL. < Gr. *syndromē* < *syn-*, with + *dramein*, to run: see DROMEDARY] 1. a number of symptoms occurring together and characterizing a specific disease or condition 2. any set of characteristics regarded as identifying a certain type, condition, etc. —**syn·drom′ic** (-drō′mik, -dräm′ik) *adj.*

syne (sin) *adv., conj., prep.* [Scot. < ME. *sithen*: see SINCE] [Scot.] since; ago

syn·ec·do·che (si nek′də kē) *n.* [LME., altered (after L.) < *synodoche* < ML. *sinodoche*, for L. *synecdoche* < Gr. *synekdochē*, lit., a receiving together < *synekdechesthai*, to receive together < *syn-*, together + *ekdechesthai*, to receive < *ek-*, from + *dechesthai*, to receive: for IE. base see DECENT] a figure of speech in which a part is used for a whole, an individual for a class, a material for a thing, or the reverse of any of these (Ex.: *bread* for *food*, *the army* for *a soldier*, or *copper* for *a penny*) —**syn·ec·doch′ic** (sin′ek däk′ik), **syn′ec·doch′i·cal** *adj.* —**syn′ec·doch′i·cal·ly** *adv.*

syn·e·col·o·gy (sin′i käl′ə jē) *n.* [G. *synökologie* < *syn-*, SYN- + *ökologie*, ECOLOGY] the ecological study of different natural communities or ecosystems: cf. AUTECOLOGY

syn·er·e·sis (si ner′ə sis) *n.* [ModL. < Gr. *synairesis*, a taking or drawing together < *syn-*, together + *hairein*, to take] 1. the contraction of two consecutive vowels or syllables into one syllable, esp. so as to form a diphthong 2. *same as* SYNIZESIS 3. *Chem.* contraction of a gel so that liquid is exuded at the surface, as in the separation of serum from a blood clot

syn·er·get·ic (sin′ər jet′ik) *adj.* [Gr. *synergētikos* < *synergein*, to work together: see SYNERGY] working together; cooperating; synergic —**syn′er·get′i·cal·ly** *adv.*

syn·er·gid (si nur′jid, sin′ər-) *n.* [ModL. *synergida* < Gr. *synergein*, to work together (see SYNERGY) + ModL. *-ida*, sing. of *-idae*, -IDAE] either of the two cells that lie alongside of the egg cell in the embryo sac of flowering plants

syn·er·gism (sin′ər jiz′m) *n.* [ModL. *synergismus* < Gr. *synergos*, working together: see SYNERGY] 1. the simultaneous action of separate agencies which, together, have greater total effect than the sum of their individual effects: said esp. of drugs 2. the combined or correlated action of different organs or parts of the body, as of muscles working together —**syn′er·gis′tic** *adj.* —**syn′er·gis′ti·cal·ly** *adv.*

syn·er·gist (sin′ər jist) *n.* a synergistic organ, drug, etc.

syn·er·gy (sin′ər jē) *n.* [ModL. *synergia* < Gr. *synergia*, joint work < *synergein*, to work together < *syn-*, together + *ergon*, WORK] combined or cooperative action or force; *specif.*, *same as* SYNERGISM —**syn·er·gic** (si nur′jik) *adj.*

syn·e·sis (sin′ə sis) *n.* [ModL. < Gr. *synesis*, sagacity, quick perception < *synienai*, to perceive, lit., to bring together < *syn-*, together + *hienai*, to go: see JET[1]] grammatical construction which conforms to the meaning rather than to strict syntactical agreement or reference (Ex.: Has *everyone* washed *their* hands?)

syn·es·the·si·a (sin′əs thē′zhə, -zhē ə, -zē ə) *n.* [ModL. *synaesthesia*: see SYN- & ESTHESIA] 1. *Physiol.* sensation felt in one part of the body when another part is stimulated 2. *Psychol.* a process in which one type of stimulus produces a secondary, subjective sensation, as when a specific color evokes a specific smell sensation —**syn′es·thet′ic** (-thet′ik) *adj.*

syn·ga·my (sin′gə mē) *n.* [SYN- + -GAMY] sexual reproduction; union of gametes to form a fertilized ovum —**syn·gam·ic** (sin gam′ik), **syn·ga·mous** (sin′gə məs) *adj.*

Synge (sin), (Edmund) John Mil·ling·ton (mil′iŋ tən) 1871–1909; Ir. dramatist

syn·gen·e·sis (sin jen′ə sis) *n.* [ModL.: see SYN- & -GENESIS] sexual reproduction —**syn·ge·net·ic** (sin′jə net′ik) *adj.*

syn·i·ze·sis (sin′ə zē′sis) *n.* [LL. < Gr. *synizēsis* < *synizanein*, to sink in, collapse < *syn-*, with + *hizein*, to SIT] 1. the contraction of two adjacent vowels into a single syllable, without forming a diphthong 2. *Biol.* the massing of the chromatin in meiosis during synapsis

syn·kar·y·on (sin kar′ē än′, -ən) *n.* [ModL. < *syn-*, SYN- + Gr. *karyon*, a nut] the nucleus resulting from the fusion of male and female nuclei during fertilization

syn·od (sin′əd) *n.* [ME., altered (after LL.) < OE. *sinoth* < LL.(Ec.) *synodus* < LGr.(Ec.) *synodos*, a church synod < Gr., a meeting, lit., a coming together < *syn-*, together + *hodos*, way: see -ODE[1]] 1. a council of churches or church officials; ecclesiastical council; specif., a high governing body in any of certain Christian churches 2. any assembly or council —**syn′od·al** (-′l) *adj.*

syn·od·i·cal (si näd′i k′l) *adj.* [LL. *synodicus* < Gr. *synodikos* < *synodos*: see prec.] 1. of a synod; synodal 2. *Astron.* of or having to do with conjunction, esp. with the interval between two successive conjunctions of the same celestial bodies Also **syn·od′ic** —**syn·od′i·cal·ly** *adv.*

syn·oe·cious (si nē′shəs) *adj.* [< SYN- + Gr. *oikos*, house (see WICK[2]) + -OUS] *Bot.* 1. having male and female flowers in the same inflorescence 2. having both antheridia and archegonia in the same cluster —**syn·oe′cious·ly** *adv.*

syn·oi·cous (si noi′kəs) *adj.* same as SYNOECIOUS (sense 2)

syn·o·nym (sin′ə nim) *n.* [ME. *sinonime* < L. *synonymum* < Gr. *synōnymon*, of like meaning or like name < *syn-*, together + *onyma*, a NAME] 1. a word having the same or nearly the same meaning in one or more senses as another in the same language: opposed to ANTONYM 2. *same as* METONYM 3. *Biol.* an incorrect taxonomic name —**syn′o·nym′ic, syn′o·nym′i·cal** *adj.* —**syn′o·nym′i·ty** (-ə tē) *n.*

syn·on·y·mize (si nän′ə miz′) *vt.* **-mized′, -miz′ing** to furnish a synonym or synonyms for (a word)

syn·on·y·mous (-məs) *adj.* [ML. *synonymus* < Gr. *synōnymos*: see SYNONYM] being a synonym or synonyms; equivalent or similar in meaning —**syn·on′y·mous·ly** *adv.*

syn·on·y·my (-mē) *n., pl.* **-mies** [LL. *synonymia* < Gr. *synōnymia*] 1. the study of synonyms 2. a list or listing of synonyms, esp. one in which the terms are discriminated from one another 3. *a)* the scientific names used in different nomenclature systems to designate the same species, genus, etc. *b)* a list of such names 4. the quality of being synonymous; identity or near identity of meaning

syn·op·sis (si näp′sis) *n., pl.* **-ses** (-sēz) [LL. < Gr. *synopsis* < *syn-*, together + *opsis*, a seeing, visual image: for ult. base see EYE] a statement giving a brief, general review or condensation; summary —SYN. see ABRIDGMENT

☆**syn·op·size** (-siz) *vt.* **-sized, -siz·ing** to make a synopsis of; summarize or epitomize

syn·op·tic (-tik) *adj.* [ModL. *synopticus* < Gr. *synoptikos*] 1. of or constituting a synopsis; presenting a general view or summary 2. giving an account from the same point of view: said esp. [*often* S-] of the first three Gospels 3. *Meteorol.* presenting or involving data on weather and atmospheric conditions over a wide area at a given time [a synoptic chart] Also **syn·op′ti·cal** —**syn·op′ti·cal·ly** *adv.*

syn·o·vi·a (si nō′vē ə) *n.* [ModL.: coined by Paracelsus < ?] the clear, albuminous lubricating fluid secreted by the membranes of joint cavities, tendon sheaths, etc. — **syn·o′vi·al** *adj.*

syn·o·vi·tis (sin′ə vīt′əs) *n.* [see -ITIS] inflammation of a synovial membrane

syn·sep·al·ous (sin sep′′l əs) *adj.* [SYN- + SEPAL + -OUS] same as GAMOSEPALOUS

syn·tac·tic (sin tak′tik) *adj.* [< ModL. *syntacticus* < Gr. *syntaktikos* < *syntaxis*: see SYNTAX] of or in accordance with the rules of syntax: also **syn·tac′ti·cal** —**syn·tac′ti·cal·ly** *adv.*

syntactic foam any of several buoyant materials consisting of tiny glass bubbles embedded in a surrounding plastic: used in submersibles, spacecraft, etc.

syn·tac·tics (-tiks) *n.pl.* [with sing. v.] the branch of semiotic dealing with the formal relationships of signs and symbols to one another apart from their users or external reference

syn·tax (sin′taks) *n.* [Fr. *syntaxe* < LL. *syntaxis* < Gr. *syntaxis* < *syntassein*, to join, put together < *syn-*, together + *tassein*, to arrange: see TAXIS] 1. orig., orderly or systematic arrangement 2. *Gram. a)* the arrangement of

words as elements in a sentence to show their relationship to one another b) the organization and relationship of word groups, phrases, clauses, and sentences; sentence structure c) the branch of grammar dealing with this 3. *Logic* syntactics as applied to language in the abstract with no meaning attached to either the symbols or to the expressions constructed from these symbols

syn·the·sis (sin′thə sis) *n., pl.* **-ses′** (-sēz′) [Gr. *synthesis* < *syn-*, together + *tithenai*, to place: see DO¹] 1. the putting together of parts or elements so as to form a whole 2. a whole made up of parts or elements put together 3. *Chem.* the formation of a complex compound by the combining of two or more simpler compounds, elements, or radicals 4. *Philos.* a) [Obs.] deductive reasoning b) in Hegelian philosophy, the unified whole in which opposites (thesis and antithesis) are reconciled —**syn′the·sist** *n.*

syn·the·size (-sīz′) *vt.* **-sized′, -siz′ing** 1. to bring together into a whole by synthesis 2. to form by bringing together separate parts; specif., *Chem.* to produce by synthesis rather than by extraction, refinement, etc.

syn·the·siz·er (-sī′zər) *n.* a person or thing that synthesizes; ☆specif., an electronic device containing filters, oscillators, and voltage-control amplifiers, used to produce sounds unobtainable from ordinary musical instruments

syn·thet·ic (sin thet′ik) *adj.* [Fr. *synthétique* < Gr. *synthetikos*] 1. of, involving, or using synthesis 2. produced by synthesis; specif., produced by chemical synthesis, rather than of natural origin 3. not real or genuine; artificial [*synthetic* enthusiasm] 4. *Linguis.* characterized by the use of inflection to express grammatical relationships 5. *Logic* not true by the meaning of component terms alone but by virtue of observation and not resulting in self-contradiction with denial Also **syn·thet′i·cal** —*n.* something synthetic; specif., a substance produced by chemical synthesis —*SYN.* see ARTIFICIAL —**syn·thet′i·cal·ly** *adv.*

synthetic resin 1. any of a large class of complex organic liquids or solids formed from simpler molecules by condensation or polymerization, used esp. in making plastics 2. any of various chemically modified natural resins

synthetic rubber any of several elastic substances resembling natural rubber, prepared by polymerization of butadiene, isoprene, and other unsaturated hydrocarbons

syn·ton·ic (sin tän′ik) *adj.* [< Gr. *syntonos*, in harmony < *syn-*, with + *tonos*, voice, TONE] *Psychol.* in emotional equilibrium and responsive to the environment

syph·i·lis (sif′ə lis) *n.* [ModL. < *Syphilis sive Morbus Gallicus*, lit., Syphilis or the French disease, title of a poem (1530) by Girolamo Fracastoro: after the hero *Syphilus*, a shepherd] an infectious venereal disease, caused by a spirochete (*Treponema pallidum*) and usually transmitted by sexual intercourse or acquired congenitally: if untreated, it can ultimately lead to the degeneration of bones, heart, nerve tissue, etc. —**syph′i·lit′ic** *adj., n.*

syph·i·loid (-loid′) *adj.* resembling syphilis

syph·i·lol·o·gy (sif′ə läl′ə jē) *n.* the study and treatment of syphilis —**syph′i·lol′o·gist** (-jist) *n.*

sy·phon (sī′fən) *n., vi., vt. var. sp.* of SIPHON

Syr. 1. Syria 2. Syriac 3. Syrian

Syr·a·cuse (sir′ə kyoos′, -kyooz′) 1. [after ff.] city in C N.Y.: pop. 197,000 (met. area 636,000) 2. seaport on the SE coast of Sicily (in ancient times, a Gr. city-state): pop. 90,000: It. name, SIRACUSA: see CARTHAGE, map

Syr Dar·ya (sir där′yä) river in C U.S.S.R., flowing from Uzbek S.S.R. into the Aral Sea: c.1,700 mi.

☆Syr·ette (si ret′) [SYR(INGE) + -ETTE] *a trademark for* a small, collapsible tube fitted with a hypodermic needle and filled with a single dose of medication

Syr·i·a (sir′ē ə) 1. region of ancient times at the E end of the Mediterranean 2. country in the NW part of this region, south of Turkey: 71,227 sq. mi.; pop. 5,866,000; cap. Damascus

Syr·i·ac (sir′ē ak′) *n.* the ancient Aramaic language of Syria, used from the 3d cent. A.D. to the 13th

Syr·i·an (-ən) *adj.* of Syria, its people, their language, culture, etc. —*n.* 1. a member of the Semitic people of Syria 2. the modern Arabic dialect of the Syrians

sy·rin·ga (sə rin′gə) *n.* [ModL., name of the genus < Gr. *syrinx* (gen. *syringos*), a pipe, tube (see ff.): from the use of the plants for making pipes] 1. *same as* LILAC (senses 1 & 2) 2. *earlier name for* MOCK ORANGE

sy·ringe (sə rinj′, sir′inj) *n.* [ME. *siringe* < ML. *syringa* < Gr. *syrinx* (gen. *syringos*), a reed, pipe, prob. < IE. base *two-*, a tube, whence Sans. *tūṇa*, a quiver] 1. a device consisting of a narrow tube fitted at one end with a rubber bulb or piston by means of which a liquid can be drawn in and then ejected in a stream: used to inject fluids into, or extract fluids from, body cavities, to cleanse wounds, etc. 2. *short for* HYPODERMIC SYRINGE —*vt.* **-ringed′, -ring′ing** to cleanse, inject, etc. by using a syringe

sy·rin·ge·al (sə rin′jē əl) *adj.* of the syrinx

SYRINGE

sy·rin·go·my·e·li·a (sə rin′gō mī ē′lē ə) *n.* [ModL. < Gr. *syrinx* (see SYRINGE) + *myelos*, marrow] a chronic, progressive disease of the spinal cord, characterized by the formation of cavities filled with liquid within the spinal cord

syr·inx (sir′iŋks) *n., pl.* **sy·rin·ges** (sə rin′jēz), **syr′inx·es** [ModL. < Gr. *syrinx*, a pipe: see SYRINGE] 1. the vocal organ of songbirds, located at the base of the trachea, the branching of the bronchi, or both 2. *same as* PANPIPE

syr·phus fly (sur′fəs) [ModL. *Syrphus*, name of the genus < Gr. *syrphos*, a gnat] any of a family (Syrphidae) of two-winged flies, many of which mimic bees or wasps: the adults feed on nectar and pollen, and the larvae of various species feed on plant lice, plants, etc.: also **syr′phid** (-fid) *n.*

syr·up (sir′əp, sur′-) *n.* [ME. *sirupe* < OFr. *sirop* < ML. *sirupus* < Ar. *sharāb*, a drink: cf. SHERBET] any sweet, thick liquid; specif., a) a solution made by boiling sugar with water and, often, flavored b) any solution of sugar used in pharmacy as a vehicle for medicines c) the sweet, thick liquid obtained in the process of manufacturing cane sugar or glucose d) *short for* MAPLE SYRUP, CORN SYRUP, etc. —**syr′up·y** *adj.*

sys·sar·co·sis (sis′är kō′sis) *n.* [ModL. < Gr. *syssarkōsis*, a being overgrown with flesh < *syssarkousthai*, to cover over with flesh < *syn-*, with + *sarx* (gen. *sarkos*), flesh: see SARCASM] the connection of two or more bones by muscle

syst. system

sys·tal·tic (sis tôl′tik, -tal′-) *adj.* [LL. *systalticus* < Gr. *systaltikos*, drawing together < *systellein*, to draw together < *syn-*, together + *stellein*, to send: for IE. base see STALK¹] characterized by alternate contraction and dilatation, as the action of the heart

sys·tem (sis′təm) *n.* [LL. *systema* < Gr. *systēma* (gen. *systēmatos*) < *synistanai*, to place together < *syn-*, together + *histanai*, to set: see STAND] 1. a set or arrangement of things so related or connected as to form a unity or organic whole [a solar *system*, school *system*, *system* of highways] 2. a set of facts, principles, rules, etc. classified or arranged in a regular, orderly form so as to show a logical plan linking the various parts 3. a method or plan of classification or arrangement 4. a) an established way of doing something; method; procedure b) orderliness or methodical planning in one's way of proceeding 5. a) the body considered as a functioning organism b) a number of bodily organs acting together to perform one of the main bodily functions [the digestive *system*] 6. a related series of natural objects or elements, as cave passages, rivers, etc. 7. *Chem.* a group of substances in or approaching equilibrium: a system with two components, phases, or variables is called binary, one with three, ternary, etc. 8. *Crystallography* any of the seven divisions (cubic, tetragonal, hexagonal, trigonal, orthorhombic, monoclinic, and triclinic) in which all crystal forms can be placed, based on the degree of symmetry of the crystals 9. *Geol.* a major division of stratified rocks comprising the rocks laid down during a period —see METHOD

sys·tem·at·ic (sis′tə mat′ik) *adj.* [Gr. *systēmatikos*] 1. forming or constituting a system 2. based on or involving a system 3. made or arranged according to a system, method, or plan; regular; orderly 4. characterized by the use of method or orderly planning; methodical 5. of or having to do with classification; taxonomic Also **sys′tem·at′i·cal** —*SYN.* see ORDERLY —**sys′tem·at′i·cal·ly** *adv.*

sys·tem·at·ics (-iks) *n.pl.* [with sing. v.] the science or a method of classification; esp., *same as* TAXONOMY

sys·tem·a·tism (sis′təm ə tiz′m) *n.* the practice or process of systematizing

sys·tem·a·tist (-tist) *n.* 1. a person who works according to a system 2. a taxonomist

sys·tem·a·tize (sis′təm ə tīz′) *vt.* **-tized′, -tiz′ing** to form into a system; arrange according to a system; make systematic —**sys′tem·a·ti·za′tion** *n.* —**sys′tem·a·tiz′er** *n.*

sys·tem·ic (sis tem′ik) *adj.* of a system; specif., *Physiol.* of or affecting the entire organism or bodily system —☆*n.* any of a group of pesticides that are absorbed into the tissues of plants, which in consequence become poisonous to insects, etc. that feed on them —**sys·tem′i·cal·ly** *adv.*

sys·tem·ize (sis′tə mīz′) *vt.* **-ized′, -iz′ing** *same as* SYSTEMATIZE —**sys′tem·i·za′tion** *n.*

☆systems analysis an engineering technique that breaks down complex technical, social, biological, etc. problems into basic elements and subsystems whose interrelations are evaluated and programmed, with the aid of mathematics, computers, etc., into a complete and integrated system —**systems analyst**

☆systems engineering a branch of engineering using esp. information theory, computer science, and facts from systems-analysis studies to design integrated operational systems for specific complexes —**systems engineer**

sys·to·le (sis′tə lē′) *n.* [ModL. < Gr. *systolē* < *systellein*, to contract, shorten: see SYSTALTIC] 1. the usual rhythmic contraction of the heart, esp. of the ventricles, following each dilatation (*diastole*), during which the blood is driven onward from the chambers 2. *Gr. & Lat. Prosody* the shortening of a naturally long syllable: opposed to DIASTOLE —**sys·tol·ic** (sis täl′ik) *adj.*

Syz·ran (siz'rän) city in SW R.S.F.S.R., on the Volga, near Kuibyshev: pop. 167,000
syz·y·gy (siz'ə jē) n., pl. **-gies** [LL. *syzygia* < Gr. *syzygia* < *syn-*, together + *zygon*, a YOKE] 1. a pair of things, esp. a pair of opposites 2. *Astron.* [Rare] either of two opposing points in the orbit of a heavenly body, specif. of the moon, at which it is in conjunction with or in opposition to the sun 3. *Gr. & Lat. Prosody* a group of two feet, as a dipody —**syz·y·gi·al** (si zij'ē əl) *adj.*
Szcze·cin (shche tsēn') river port in NW Poland, on the Oder: pop. 310,000

Sze·chwan (se'chwän'; *Chin.* su'-) province of SC China: 219,691 sq. mi.; pop. 72,160,000; cap. Chengtu
Sze·ged (se'ged) city in SE Hungary, at the junction of the Mureş & Tisza rivers: pop. 116,000
Szell (sel), **George** 1897–1970; U.S. orchestra conductor & pianist, born in Hungary
Szi·lard (zē'lärd, si'-; zi lärd'), **Leo** 1898–1964; U.S. nuclear physicist, born in Hungary
Szold (zōld), **Henrietta** 1860–1945; U.S. Zionist leader
Szom·bat·hely (sôm'bät hā') city in W Hungary, near the Austrian border: pop. 57,000

T

T, t (tē) n., pl. **T's, t's** 1. the twentieth letter of the English alphabet: from the Greek *tau*, derived from the Hebrew *taw* 2. the sound of *T* or *t*, usually a voiceless alveolar stop 3. a type or impression for *T* or *t* 4. *a symbol for* the 20th in a sequence or group (or the 19th if J is omitted) —*adj.* 1. of *T* or *t* 2. 20th (or 19th if J is omitted) in a sequence or group
T (tē) n. 1. an object shaped like *T* 2. *a symbol for: a)* absolute (Kelvin) temperature *b*) *Chem.* triple bond *c*) *Physics* half-life —*adj.* shaped like *T* —**to a T** to perfection; exactly
't it: a contraction used with a verb initially, as in *'twas*, or finally, as in *do't*
-t a suffix used to form past participles and adjectives derived from participles: var. of -ED [*slept, gilt*]
T 1. Technician 2. temperature 3. tension 4. time (of firing or launching)
T. 1. tablespoon(s) 2. Territory 3. Testament 4. Tuesday
t. 1. [L. *tempore*] in the time (of) 2. tare 3. target 4. teaspoon(s) 5. telephone 6. temperature 7. tempo 8. tenor 9. tense 10. time 11. ton(s) 12. town 13. township 14. transit 15. transitive 16. troy 17. [L. *tomus*] volume
ta (tä) *interj.* [Brit.] thank you: orig. a child's term
Ta *Chem.* tantalum
tab¹ (tab) n. [< ?] 1. a small, flat loop or strap fastened to something for pulling it, hanging it up, etc. 2. a small, often ornamental, flap or piece fastened to the edge or surface as of a dress, coat, etc. 3. an attached or projecting piece of a card or paper, useful in filing 4. *Aeron.* an auxiliary airfoil set into the trailing edge of a larger control surface, such as an aileron —*vt.* **tabbed, tab'bing** 1. to provide with tabs 2. to choose or select
tab² (tab) ✩n. [prob. short for TABULATION] [Colloq.] 1. a bill or check, as for expenses 2. total cost or expenses —✩**keep tabs** (or **a tab**) **on** [Colloq.] to keep a check on; follow or watch every move of —✩**pick up the tab** [Colloq.] to pay the bill or total cost
tab³ (tab) n. *clipped form of:* 1. TABLET 2. TABLOID 3. TABULATOR —*vt.* **tabbed, tab'bing** *clipped form of* TABULATE
tab. 1. table(s) 2. *Pharmacy* tablet
tab·a·nid (tab'ə nid) n. [< L. *tabanus*, horsefly + -ID] any of a family (Tabanidae) of large, bloodsucking flies, comprising the horseflies and deerflies
tab·ard (tab'ərd) n. [ME. < OFr. *tabart*] 1. a loose jacket of heavy material, sleeved or sleeveless, worn outdoors as by peasants in the Middle Ages 2. a short-sleeved, blazoned cloak worn by a knight over his armor 3. a herald's official coat, blazoned with his king's or lord's arms
tab·a·ret (tab'ər it) n. [trade name < ? TABBY] a strong silk cloth with stripes of satin or moiré, used as an upholstery and drapery fabric
Ta·bas·co (tə bas'kō; *Sp.* tä bäs'kō) 1. state of SE Mexico, on the Gulf of Campeche: 9,783 sq. mi.; pop. 644,000; cap. Villahermosa ✩2. *a trademark for* a very hot sauce made from a kind of red pepper
tab·by (tab'ē) n., pl. **-bies** [Fr. *tabis*, earlier *atabis* < ML. *attabi* < Ar. *'attābi* < *al-'attābīya*, quarter of Baghdad where it was manufactured: after a prince *'Attāb*, of the Omayyad dynasty] 1. a silk taffeta with stripes or wavy markings; watered silk 2. a gray or brown cat with dark stripes 3. any domestic cat, esp. a female 4. [Chiefly Brit.] *a*) an old maid *b*) a malicious woman gossip —*adj.* 1. made of, or like, tabby 2. having dark stripes over gray or brown; brindled —*vt.* **-bied, -by·ing** to make wavy markings in (silk, etc.)
tab·er·nac·le (tab'ər nak'l) n. [ME. < LL.(Ec.) *tabernaculum*, the Jewish tabernacle (transl. of Heb. *'ohēl*

mō'ēdh, tent of meeting) < L., a tent, dim. of *taberna*, a hut, shed, TAVERN] 1. formerly, *a*) a temporary shelter, as a tent *b*) a dwelling place 2. the human body considered as the dwelling place of the soul 3. [T-] *a*) the portable sanctuary carried by the Jews in their wanderings from Egypt to Palestine: Ex. 25, 26, 27 *b*) later, the Jewish Temple 4. a shrine, niche, etc. with a canopy 5. a place of worship; esp., one with a large seating capacity 6. *Eccles.* a cabinetlike enclosure for consecrated Hosts, usually in the center of the altar at the back —*vi.* **-led, -ling** to dwell temporarily —*vt.* to place in or as in a tabernacle —**tab'er·nac'u·lar** (-yə lər) *adj.*
ta·bes (tā'bēz) n. [L., a wasting away < *tabere*, to waste away < IE. base *ta-*, to melt, whence THAW] *Med.* 1. any wasting or atrophy due to disease 2. *clipped form of* TABES DORSALIS —**ta·bet·ic** (tə bet'ik) *adj., n.*
ta·bes·cent (tə bes''nt) *adj.* [L. *tabescens*, prp. of *tabescere*, to dwindle away < *tabere*, to waste away: see prec.] wasting or withering away —**ta·bes'cence** n.
tabes dor·sa·lis (dôr sā'lis, -sal'is) [ModL., tabes of the back: see TABES & DORSAL¹] a chronic disease of the nervous system, usually caused by syphilis and characterized by disturbances of sensations, loss of reflexes and of muscular coordination, functional disorders of organs, etc.
Tab·i·tha (tab'ə thə) n. [L.(Ec.) < Gr.(Ec.) *Tabeitha* < Aram. *ṭabhīthā*, lit., roe, gazelle] a feminine name
tab·la (täb'lä) n. [< or akin to Ar. *ṭabl*, drum (cf. ATABAL)] a set of two small drums whose pitch can be varied, used esp. in India and played with the hands
tab·la·ture (tab'lə chər) n. [Fr. < ML. *tabulatura* < *tabulatus*, a tablet < L. *tabula*: see ff.] 1. a form of musical notation; specif., a form used for the lute, guitar, and other stringed instruments, in which the lines of the staff represent the strings, and the letters or figures on them indicate the finger stops 2. [Archaic] a flat surface or tablet with an inscription, painting, or design on it
ta·ble (tā'b'l) n. [ME. < OFr. < L. *tabula*, a board, painting, tablet < ? IE. *tel-*, flat, a board, whence OE. *thille*, thin board, flooring] 1. orig., a thin, flat tablet or slab of metal, stone, or wood, used for inscriptions 2. *a*) a piece of furniture consisting of a flat, horizontal top usually set on legs *b*) such a table set with food for a meal *c*) food served at table; feasting as entertainment *d*) the people seated at a table to eat, talk, etc. 3. any of various large, flat-topped pieces of furniture or equipment used for games, as a working surface, etc. [*pool table, examining table*] 4. *a*) a compact, systematic list of details, contents, etc. *b*) a compact arrangement of related facts, figures, values, etc. in orderly sequence, and usually in rows and columns, for convenience of reference [*the multiplication table*] 5. same as TABLELAND 6. the upper, flat surface cut in a precious stone 7. *Anat.* the hard inner or outer layer of the bony tissue of the skull 8. *Archit. a*) any horizontal, projecting piece, as a molding or cornice; stringcourse *b*) a plain or decorated rectangular piece set into or raised on a wall; panel 9. *Backgammon* either of the two folding leaves of a backgammon board —*adj.* 1. of, for, or on a table 2. fit for serving at table [*table salt*] —*vt.* **-bled, -bling** 1. orig., to make a list or compact arrangement of; tabulate 2. to put on a table ✩3. to postpone indefinitely the discussion or consideration of (a legislative bill, motion, etc.) 4. [Brit.] to submit for discussion or consideration —**at table** at a meal —**on the table** ✩postponed or shelved: said of a bill, etc. —**the tables** laws, as the Ten Commandments or ancient Roman codes, inscribed on flat stone slabs —**turn the tables** to reverse completely a situation as it affects two opposing persons or groups —**under the table** [Colloq.] 1. covertly, as a bribe 2. drunk to the point of unconsciousness
tab·leau (tab'lō, ta blō²) n., pl. **-leaux** (-lōz, -blōz²), **-leaus** [Fr. < OFr. *tablel*, dim. of *table*: see prec.] 1. a striking, dramatic scene or picture 2. *same as* TABLEAU VIVANT

TABARD

‡**tab·leau vi·vant** (tá blō vē vän′) *pl.* **tab·leaux vi·vants′** (-blō vē vän′) [Fr., lit., living tableau] a representation of a scene, picture, etc. by a person or group in costume, posing silently without moving

ta·ble·cloth (tā′b'l klôth′, -kläth′) *n.* a cloth for covering a table, esp. at meals

ta·ble d'hôte (tä′b'l dōt′, tab′'l; *Fr.* tá bl′ dôt′) *pl.* **ta′bles d'hôte** (-b'lz, -'lz; *Fr.* -bl′) [Fr., lit., table of the host] a complete meal with courses as specified on the menu, served at a restaurant or hotel for a set price: distinguished from À LA CARTE

☆**ta·ble-hop** (tā′b'l häp′) *vi.* **-hopped′**, **-hop′ping** to leave one's table in a restaurant, nightclub, etc. and visit about at other tables —**ta′ble-hop′per** *n.*

ta·ble·land (-land′) *n.* a high, broad, level region; plateau

table linen tablecloths, napkins, etc.

ta·ble·mount (-mount′) *n. same as* GUYOT

Table Mountain flat-topped mountain in SE Cape Province, South Africa: 3,549 ft.

ta·ble·spoon (-spōōn′) *n.* **1.** *a)* a large spoon used for serving at table *b) same as* SOUPSPOON **2.** a spoon used as a measuring unit in cookery, equal to 3 teaspoonfuls or 1/2 fluid ounce **3.** *same as* TABLESPOONFUL

ta·ble·spoon·ful (-spōōn′fool) *n., pl.* **-fuls** as much as a tablespoon will hold

tab·let (tab′lit) *n.* [ME. *tablette* < MFr. *tablete*, dim. of *table*: see TABLE] **1.** a flat, thin piece of stone, wood, metal, etc. shaped for a specific purpose **2.** such a piece with an inscription, used as a memorial wall panel; plaque **3.** *a)* a smooth, flat leaf made of wood, ivory, metal, etc. and used to write on *b)* a set of such leaves fastened together **4.** a writing pad consisting of sheets of paper glued together at one edge **5.** a small, flat piece of solid or compressed material, as of medicine, soap, etc.

table talk informal conversation, as that at meals

table tennis a game somewhat like tennis in miniature, played on a large, rectangular table, with a small, hollow celluloid or plastic ball and short-handled, wooden paddles

ta·ble·ware (tā′b'l wer′) *n.* dishes, glassware, silverware, etc. for use at table

table wine a wine for serving with meals, with from 8 to 13 percent alcohol

Tab·loid (tab′loid) [TABL(ET) + -OID] *a trademark for* a small tablet of medicine —*n.* [t-] a newspaper, usually half the ordinary size, with many pictures and short, often sensational, news stories —*adj.* condensed; short

ta·boo (ta bōō′, ta-) *n.* [Tongan *tabu*] **1.** *a)* among some Polynesian peoples, a sacred prohibition put upon certain people, things, or acts which makes them untouchable, unmentionable, etc. *b)* the highly developed system or practice of such prohibitions **2.** *a)* any social prohibition or restriction that results from convention or tradition *b) Linguis.* the substitution of one term for another because of such restriction —*adj.* **1.** sacred and prohibited by taboo **2.** restricted by taboo: said of people **3.** prohibited or forbidden by tradition, convention, etc. —*vt.* **1.** to put under taboo **2.** to prohibit or forbid because of tradition, convention, etc.

ta·bor (tā′bər) *n.* [ME. < OFr. *tabur* < Per. *tabīrah*, a drum: cf. TAMBOUR] a small drum, formerly used by a fife player to beat out his own rhythmic accompaniment —*vi.* to beat on or as on a tabor. Also sp. **ta′bour**

Ta·bor (tā′bər), **Mount** mountain in N Israel, east of Nazareth: c.1,900 ft.

tab·o·ret (tab′ər it, tab′ə ret′) *n.* [OFr., a stool, lit., little drum, dim. of *tabur*: see prec.] **1.** a small tabor **2.** a stool Also sp. **tab′ou·ret**

tab·o·rin (tab′ər in) *n.* [MFr. *tabourin*, dim. of *tabur*: see TABOR] a small tabor played with only one stick: also **tab′o·rine′** (-ə rēn′)

Ta·briz (tá brēz′) city in NW Iran: pop. 388,000

ta·bu (ta bōō′, ta-) *n., adj., vt. var. sp. of* TABOO

tab·u·lar (tab′yə lər) *adj.* [L. *tabularis* < *tabula*, a board, tablet: see TABLE] **1.** having a tablelike surface; flat *[tabular* rock*]* **2.** *a)* of or arranged in a table or tabulated scheme *b)* computed from or calculated by such a table or tables —**tab′u·lar·ly** *adv.*

ta·bu·la ra·sa (tab′yə lə rä′sə, rā′sə) [ML. < L. *tabula* (see TABLE) + *rasa*, fem. pp. of *radere*, to scrape, ERASE] **1.** a blank tablet; clean slate **2.** the mind before impressions are recorded upon it by experience

tab·u·late (tab′yə lāt′; *for adj.* -lit) *vt.* **-lat′ed**, **-lat′ing** [< L. *tabula* (see TABLE) + -ATE¹] to put (facts, statistics, etc.) in a table or columns; arrange systematically —*adj.* **1.** having a flat surface **2.** having or made of thin, horizontal plates, as some corals —**tab′u·la′tion** *n.*

tab·u·la·tor (-lāt′ər) *n.* a person or thing that tabulates; specif., *a)* a device on a typewriter used to facilitate the typing of matter in columns *b)* a machine for automatically compiling lists, tabulations, etc. from information encoded on punch cards

TAC Tactical Air Command

tac·a·ma·hac (tak′ə mə hak′) *n.* [Sp. *tacamahaca*, earlier *tecomahaca* < Nahuatl *tecomahca*, lit., stinking copal] **1.** a strong-smelling gum resin used in ointments and incenses

2. any of several trees, as the balsam poplar, yielding this resin Also **tac′a·ma·hac′a** (-ə), **tac′ma·hack′**

ta·cet (tā′set, tä′ket) [L., 3d pers. sing., pres. indic., of *tacere*, to be silent: see TACIT] *Music* it is silent: a direction to be silent for the indicated time

tache, tach (tach) *n.* [ME. < MFr., a nail < Gmc.: see TACK (*n.* 1)] [Archaic] a device, as a buckle, hook and eye, etc., for fastening two parts together

tach·i·na fly (tak′i nə) [ModL. *tachina* < Gr. *tachinos* < *tachys*, swift: see TACHY-] any of a large family (Tachinidae) of bristly, gray and black, two-winged flies, whose larvae are parasitic on caterpillars, etc.: also **tach′i·nid** (-nid) *n.*

tach·isme (tash′iz′m; *Fr.* tá shēz′m′) *n.* [< *tache*, a spot (< OFr. *teche, teiche*, a mark < Gmc. base akin to Goth. *taikns*, a sign: for IE. base see TOKEN) + -*isme*, -ISM] a method of action painting in which the paint is splashed, dribbled, etc. upon the canvas in apparently random patterns —**tach′iste** (-ist; *Fr.* -shēst′) *adj.*

ta·chis·to·scope (tə kis′tə skōp′) *n.* [< Gr. *tachistos*, superl. of *tachys*, swift (see TACHY-) + -SCOPE] an apparatus that exposes words, pictures, etc. for a measured fraction of a second, used to increase reading speed, test memory, etc. —**ta·chis′to·scop′ic** (-skäp′ik) *adj.*

ta·chom·e·ter (ta käm′ə tər, tə-) *n.* [< Gr. *tachos*, speed + -METER] a device that indicates or measures the revolutions per minute of a revolving shaft

ta·chom·e·try (-trē) *n.* the use of a tachometer

tach·y- (tak′i) [Gr. < *tachys*, swift < IE. base *dhengh-*, to reach, strong, fast, whence Sans. *daghnōti*, (he) reaches] *a combining form meaning* rapid, swift, fast *[tachymeter]*

tach·y·car·di·a (tak′i kär′dē ə) *n.* [ModL. < Gr. *tachys* (see prec.) + *kardia*, HEART] an abnormally fast heartbeat

tach·y·graph (tak′i graf′, -gräf′) *n.* [Fr. *tachygraphe* < Gr. *tachygraphos*, swift writer: see TACHY- & -GRAPH] **1.** something written in tachygraphy **2.** a person skilled in tachygraphy: also **ta·chyg·ra·pher** (ta kig′rə fər, tə-)

ta·chyg·ra·phy (ta kig′rə fē, tə-) *n.* [TACHY- + -GRAPHY] the art or use of rapid writing; esp., ancient Greek and Roman shorthand or the medieval cursive writing, with abbreviations, etc., in these languages —**tach·y·graph·ic** (tak′ə graf′ik), **tach′y·graph′i·cal** *adj.*

tach·y·lyte, tach·y·lite (tak′ə lit′) *n.* [G. *tachylyt* < Gr. *tachys*, swift + *lytos*, soluble < *lyein*, to dissolve: (see LYSIS): from its rapid decomposition in acids] a kind of basaltic volcanic glass —**tach′y·lyt′ic** (-lit′ik) *adj.*

ta·chym·e·ter (ta kim′ə tər, tə-) *n.* [TACHY- + -METER] a surveying instrument for rapid determination of distances, elevations, etc. —**ta·chym′e·try** *n.*

ta·chys·ter·ol (ta kis′tə rōl′, tə-) *n.* [TACHY- + STEROL] an isomer of ergosterol, $C_{28}H_4O$, formed during the production of calciferol by the irradiation of ergosterol

tac·it (tas′it) *adj.* [< Fr. or L.: Fr. *tacite* < L. *tacitus*, pp. of *tacere*, to be silent < IE. base *takē-*, to be silent, whence Goth. *thahan*, ON. *thegja*] **1.** making no sound; saying nothing; still **2.** unspoken; silent **3.** not expressed or declared openly, but implied or understood *[tacit* approval*]* **4.** *Law* happening without contract but by operation of law —**tac′it·ly** *adv.* —**tac′it·ness** *n.*

tac·i·turn (tas′ə turn′) *adj.* [< Fr. or L.: Fr. *taciturne*; L. *taciturnus < tacere*: see prec.] almost always silent; not liking to talk; uncommunicative —*SYN.* see SILENT —**tac′i·tur′ni·ty** (-tur′nə tē) *n.* —**tac′i·turn′ly** *adv.*

Tac·i·tus (tas′ə təs), (**Publius Cornelius**) 55?-117? A.D., Rom. historian

tack (tak) *n.* [ME. *takke* < MDu. *tacke*, a twig, point, akin to G. *zacke*: for prob. IE. base see TAIL¹] **1.** a short nail or pin with a sharp point and a relatively large, flat head **2.** *a)* a fastening, esp. in a slight or temporary way *b) Sewing* a stitch for marking darts, etc. from a pattern, clipped and later removed: in full **tailor's tack** *c)* stickiness; adhesiveness **3.** a zigzag course, or movement in such a course **4.** a course of action or policy, esp. one differing from another or preceding course **5.** [< ?] food; foodstuff *[hardtack]* **6.** *Naut. a)* a rope for holding securely the forward lower corner of some sails *b)* the corner thus held *c)* the rope that secures the studdingsail to the end of the boom *d)* the direction in which a ship is moving in relation to the position of the sails *e)* a change of direction made by changing the position of the sails *f)* a course against the wind *g)* any of a series of zigzag movements in such a course **7.** a horse's equipment, as saddles, bridles, etc.; saddlery —*vt.* **1.** to fasten or attach with tacks **2.** to attach temporarily, as by sewing with long stitches **3.** to attach as a supplement; add *[to tack* an amendment onto a bill*]* **4.** *Naut. a)* to change the course of (a ship) by turning its head to the wind *b)* to maneuver (a ship) against the wind by a series of tacks —*vi.* **1.** *a)* to tack a ship *b)* to change its course by being tacked, or sail against the wind by a series of tacks: said of a ship **2.** to go in a zigzag course **3.** to change suddenly one's policy or course of action —**tack′er** *n.*

WIND

TACKING

tack·le (tak′'l; *in nautical usage, often* tā′k'l) *n.* [ME. *takel* < MDu. *takel*, pulley, rope, equipment in general, prob. akin to MLowG. *taken*, to TAKE] 1. apparatus; equipment; gear *[fishing tackle]* 2. a rope and pulley block, or a system of ropes and pulleys, used to lower, raise, or move weights 3. the act or an instance of tackling, as in football ☆4. *Football* either of the two players (**right tackle** and **left tackle**) between each guard and end on either the offensive or defensive line 5. *Naut. a)* orig., a ship's rigging *b)* later, the running rigging and pulleys to operate the sails —*vt.* **tack′led, tack′ling** 1. to fasten by means of tackle 2. to harness (a horse) 3. to take hold of; seize 4. *a)* to undertake to do or solve (something difficult); begin dealing with *[to tackle a job] b)* to deal with (a difficult person) 5. *Football* to stop or throw (an opponent carrying the ball) —*vi. Football* to stop or throw an opponent —**tack′ler** *n.*

tack·ling (-liŋ) *n.* [Rare] gear; tackle

tack room a room near a stable in which tack is kept

tack·y¹ (tak′ē) *adj.* **tack′i·er, tack′i·est** [TACK (*n.* 2) + -Y²] sticky, as varnish, glue, etc. before completely dry —**tack′i·ness** *n.*

☆**tack·y²** (tak′ē) *adj.* **tack′i·er, tack′i·est** [< *tacky*, a hillbilly < ?] [Colloq.] dowdy or shabby, as in dress or appearance —**tack′i·ness** *n.*

Tac·na (täk′nə, tak′-) 1. city in S Peru: pop. 34,000 2. region in S Peru which, with an adjacent region (ARICA) in Chile, was under dispute until divided between the two countries in 1929: c.12,000 sq. mi.

☆**ta·co** (tä′kō) *n., pl.* **-cos** [AmSp. < Sp., a plug, wadding, light lunch] a Mexican dish consisting of a fried, folded tortilla filled with chopped meat, shredded lettuce, etc.

Ta·co·ma (tə kō′mə) [AmInd., lit., snowy peak] seaport in W Wash., on Puget Sound: pop. 155,000

☆**tac·on·ite** (tak′ə nīt′) *n.* [< *Taconic*, old name for rock formations first identified in the Taconic Range (in Vt. and Mass.) + -ITE¹] an iron-bearing chert containing from 25 to 35 percent hematite and magnetite: it is a low-grade iron ore that is pelletized for blast-furnace reduction

tact (takt) *n.* [Fr. < L. *tactus*, pp. of *tangere*, to touch < IE. base *tag-*, to touch, grasp, whence OE. *thaccian*, to stroke] 1. orig., the sense of touch 2. delicate perception of the right thing to say or do without offending; skill in dealing with people 3. delicate sensitivity, esp. in aesthetics **SYN**—**tact** implies the skill in dealing with persons or difficult situations of one who has a quick and delicate sense of what is fitting and thus avoids giving offense *[it will require tact to keep him calm]*; **poise** implies composure in the face of disturbing or embarrassing situations *[despite the social blunder, she maintained her poise]*; **diplomacy** implies a smoothness and adroitness in dealing with others, sometimes in such a way as to gain one's own ends *[his lack of diplomacy lost him the contract]*; **savoir-faire** implies a ready knowledge of the right thing to do or say in any situation

tact·ful (takt′fəl) *adj.* having or showing tact —**tact′ful·ly** *adv.* —**tact′ful·ness** *n.*

tac·tic¹ (tak′tik) *adj.* [ModL. *tacticus* < Gr. *taktikos:* see TACTICS] *Biol.* of, showing, or characteristic of taxis

tac·tic² (tak′tik) *n.* [ModL. *tactica* < Gr. *taktikē (technē)*, (art) of arranging: see TACTICS] 1. *same as* TACTICS 2. a detail or branch of tactics —*adj.* of arrangement or system

tac·ti·cal (tak′ti k'l) *adj.* 1. of or having to do with tactics, esp. in military or naval maneuvers 2. characterized by or showing cleverness and skill in tactics —**tac′ti·cal·ly** *adv.*

tac·ti·cian (tak tish′ən) *n.* an expert in tactics

tac·tics (tak′tiks) *n.pl.* [Gr. (*ta*) *taktika*, lit., (the) matters of arrangement < *taktikos*, fit for arranging < *tassein*, to arrange, put in order < IE. base *tāg-*, to set aright, whence Gr. *taxis*, order] 1. *a)* [*with sing. v.*] the science of arranging and maneuvering military and naval forces in action or before the enemy, esp. (as distinguished from STRATEGY) with reference to short-range objectives *b)* actions in accord with this science 2. any methods used to gain an end; esp., skillful methods or procedure

tac·tile (tak′t'l; *chiefly Brit.*, -til) *adj.* [Fr. < L. *tactilis* < *tangere*, to touch: see TACT] 1. that can be perceived by the touch; tangible 2. of, having, or related to the sense of touch —**tac·til′i·ty** (-til′ə tē) *n.*

tactile corpuscle any of various small, epidermal structures with nerve endings sensitive to touch or pressure

tac·tion (tak′shən) *n.* [L. *tactio* < *tactus:* see TACT] [Rare] a touching or being touched; contact

tact·less (takt′lis) *adj.* not having or showing tact —**tact′less·ly** *adv.* —**tact′less·ness** *n.*

tac·tu·al (tak′choo wəl) *adj.* [< L. *tactus* (see TACT) + -AL] 1. of the sense or organs of touch 2. causing a sensation of touch; caused by touch —**tac′tu·al·ly** *adv.*

☆**tad** (tad) *n.* [prob. < TAD(POLE)] a little child, esp. a boy

Tad·mor (tad′môr) *Biblical name of* PALMYRA

tad·pole (tad′pōl′) *n.* [ME. *taddepol* < *tadde*, toad + *poll*, head, hence, toad that seems all head] 1. the larva of certain amphibians, as frogs and toads, having gills and a tail and living in water: as it matures, the gills are lost and legs develop 2. the free-swimming larval stage of tunicates, having gill slits and a notochord that are lost during metamorphosis

Ta·dzhik (tä′jik) *n. var. sp. of* TAJIK

Tadzhik Soviet Socialist Republic republic of the U.S.S.R., in C Asia, north of Afghanistan: 55,250 sq. mi.; pop. 2,600,000; cap. Dushanbe Also **Ta·dzhik·i·stan** (tä jēk′i stän′, -stan′)

‡**tae·di·um vi·tae** (tē′dē əm vī′tē) [L., weariness of life] the view that life is intolerably dreary and boring

Tae·gu (tī′gōō′) city in SE South Korea: pop. 779,000

Tae·jon (tī′jän′) city in EC South Korea: pop. 229,000

tael (tāl) *n.* [Port. < Malay *tahil*, a weight] 1. any of various units of weight of eastern Asia 2. formerly, a Chinese unit of money equal in value to a tael of silver

ta'en (tān) [Archaic or Poet.] taken

tae·ni·a (tē′nē ə) *n., pl.* **-ni·ae** (-ē′) [L. < Gr. *tainia*, ribbon, tape, akin to *teinein*, to stretch: see TENSE¹] 1. an ancient Greek headband or fillet 2. *Anat.* a ribbonlike part or structure, as of muscle or nerve tissue 3. *Archit.* a band between the frieze and the architrave of a Doric entablature 4. *Zool.* a tapeworm

tae·ni·a·cide (tē′nē ə sīd′) *n.* [prec. + -CIDE] a drug, etc. that destroys tapeworms —**tae′ni·a·ci′dal** *adj.*

tae·ni·a·sis (tē ni′ə sis) *n.* [ModL.: see TAENIA & -IASIS] infestation with tapeworms

taf·fer·el (taf′ər əl, -ə rel′) *n.* [Du. *tafereel*, a panel, picture, dim. of *tafel*, table < L. *tabula*, a tablet: see TABLE] 1. formerly, the upper, flat part of a ship's stern: so called from its carved panels 2. *same as* TAFFRAIL

taf·fe·ta (taf′i tə) *n.* [ME. *taffata* < OFr. *taffetas* < It. *taffetà* < Per. *tāftah*, woven < *tāftan*, to weave, spin, twist] a fine, rather stiff fabric of silk, nylon, acetate, etc., with a sheen —*adj.* like or made of taffeta

taff·rail (taf′rāl′) *n.* [altered (after RAIL¹) < TAFFEREL] the rail around the stern of a ship

taf·fy (taf′ē) *n.* [< ?] 1. a chewy candy made of sugar or molasses boiled down and pulled: cf. TOFFEE ☆2. [Old Colloq.] flattery or cajolery

taffy pull esp. formerly, a party at which taffy is made

☆**taf·i·a, taf·fi·a** (taf′ē ə) *n.* [Fr. < WInd. Creole < ?] a low-grade rum made in the West Indies

Taft (taft) 1. **Lo·ra·do** (lə rä′dō), 1860–1936; U.S. sculptor 2. **William Howard**, 1857–1930; 27th president of the U.S. (1909–13); chief justice of the U.S. (1921–30)

tag (tag) *n.* [ME. *tagge*, prob. < Scand., as in Sw. *tagg*, a point, spike, Norw. *tagg*, a point, akin to G. *zacke*, a point, jag: for IE. base see TAIL¹] 1. orig., a hanging end or rag, as on a torn skirt 2. any small part or piece hanging from or loosely attached to the main piece 3. a hard-tipped end, as of metal, on a cord or lace, to give stiffness for drawing through holes; aglet 4. a piece of bright material tied next to the fly on a fishhook ☆5. a card, paper, metal marker, etc. tied or attached to something as a label or worn as identification, etc. *[a price tag, a name tag]* 6. an epithet or sobriquet 7. *a)* an ornamental, instructive, or strikingly effective ending for a speech, story, etc. *b)* a short, familiar quotation, esp. when used as such an ending 8. the last line or lines of an actor's speech, as at his exit or at a curtain: also **tag line** 9. the last part of any proceeding 10. a loop on a garment for hanging it up, or on a boot for pulling it on 11. a flourish or decorative stroke in writing 12. *a)* a lock of hair *b)* a matted lock of wool 13. a children's game in which one player, called "it," chases the others with the object of touching, or tagging, one of them and making him "it" in turn 14. a tiny amount of radioactive isotope incorporated into a compound so that it can be readily traced through a chemical reaction, physiological cycle, etc. 15. [Obs.] the rabble: cf. RAGTAG ☆16. *Baseball* the act of tagging —*vt.* **tagged, tag′ging** 1. to provide with a tag; fasten a tag to; label 2. to identify by an epithet 3. to choose or select 4. to end (a speech, story, etc.) with a tag ☆5. to overtake and touch in or as in the game of tag 6. *Baseball* to touch (a base runner) with the ball, thus putting him out 7. [Colloq.] to strike or hit hard 8. [Colloq.] to follow close behind ☆9. [Colloq.] *a)* to put a parking ticket on (a vehicle) *b)* to give a ticket to (a driver) for a traffic violation —*vi.* [Colloq.] to follow close behind a person or thing (usually with *along, after,* etc.) —☆**tag up** *Baseball* to return to the base and touch it before taking another lead or running: said of a base runner

Ta·ga·log (tä gä′läg, -lôg) *n.* 1. *pl.* **-logs, -log** any member of a Malayan people of the Philippine Islands 2. their Indonesian language, the chief native language of the Philippine Islands: cf. PILIPINO

Ta·gan·rog (tä′gän rôk′) seaport in the SW R.S.F.S.R., on the Sea of Asov, near Rostov: pop. 238,000

☆**tag·board** (tag′bôrd′) *n.* sturdy cardboard used for tags, posters, mountings, etc.

☆**tag day** a day on which money is publicly solicited as for some charity, each contributor being given a tag

tag end 1. any loosely attached or hanging end 2. the last part of something; remnant

tag·ger (tag′ər) *n.* 1. a person or thing that tags 2. [*pl.*] thin sheets of metal, usually coated with tin

☆**tag·meme** (tag′mēm) *n.* [< Gr. *tagma*, a rank, arrangement (< *tassein*, to arrange: see TACTICS) + E. *-eme* as in PHONEME] *Linguis.* the smallest meaningful unit of grammatical form —**tag·me′mic** (-mē′mik) *adj.*

☆**tag·me·mics** (tag mē′miks) *n.pl.* [*with sing. v.*] a theory of language viewing it as a structured collection of particles, of which the tagmeme is the basic unit

Ta·gore (tä′gôr, tə gôr′), **Sir Ra·bin·dra·nath** (rə bēn′drə nät′) 1861–1941; Hindu poet

Ta·gus (tā′gəs) river flowing west across C Spain & Portugal into the Atlantic through a broad estuary: c.600 mi. Sp. name, TAJO; Port. name, TEJO

Ta·hi·ti (tə hēt′ē, tä-) one of the Society Islands of French Polynesia, in the South Pacific: c.600 sq. mi.; chief town, Papeete

Ta·hi·ti·an (tə hēsh′ən, tä-; -hēt′ē ən) adj. of Tahiti, its people, their language, etc. —n. 1. a native or inhabitant of Tahiti; esp., a member of the native Polynesian people of Tahiti 2. the Polynesian language of the Tahitians

Ta·hoe (tä′hō), **Lake** [< native (AmInd.) tah-oo, lake] lake between Calif. & Nev.: a summer resort: 193 sq. mi.

tah·sil·dar (tə sēl′där′) n. [Hindi tahṣīldār < Per. tahṣīl, collection + dār, holder] in India, a revenue officer

Tai (tī) n., adj. same as THAI

Tai·chung (tī′choon′; Chin. tī′joon′) city in WC Taiwan: pop. 207,000

tai·ga (tī′gə) n. [Russ.] the coniferous forests in the far northern regions of Eurasia and North America

tail[1] (tāl) n. [ME. < OE. tægel, akin to OHG. zagel < IE. base *dek-, to tear, tear off, whence Sans. daśā, fringe] 1. the rear end of an animal's body, esp. when forming a distinct, flexible appendage to the trunk 2. anything like an animal's tail in form or position [the tail of a shirt] 3. a luminous train behind a comet or meteor 4. the hind, bottom, last, or inferior part of anything 5. [often pl.] the reverse side of a coin 6. a long braid or tress of hair 7. a train of followers or attendants; retinue 8. the lower end of a pool or stream 9. a) the rear or back section of an aircraft b) a set of stabilizing planes at the rear of an airplane c) the rear part of a rocket or missile ☆10. [pl.] [Colloq.] a) a swallow-tailed coat b) full-dress attire for men 11. [Colloq.] a person or vehicle that follows another, esp. in surveillance 12. [Slang] the buttocks 13. Printing the bottom of a page 14. Prosody the short line or lines ending certain stanzas or verse forms —adj. 1. at the rear or rear end 2. from the rear [a tail wind] —vt. 1. to provide with a tail 2. to cut or detach the tail or taillike part from 3. to form the tail or end of, as a group or procession; be at the rear or end of 4. to fasten or connect at or by the tail 5. to fasten one end of (a brick, board, etc.) into a wall, etc. (with in or on) ☆6. [Slang] to follow stealthily; shadow —vi. 1. to become scattered in a line; straggle 2. to become gradually smaller or fainter (with off or away) 3. to form, or become part of, a line or tail 4. to be fastened into a wall, etc. by one end: said of a brick or board ☆5. [Colloq.] to follow close behind, as in surveillance 6. Naut. to go aground or be anchored stern foremost —☆on one's tail following or shadowing one closely —turn tail to run from danger, difficulty, hardship, etc. —with one's tail between one's legs in defeat or in escape from expected defeat; esp., with fear or dejection —tail′less adj. —tail′like′ adj.

tail[2] (tāl) n. [ME. taile < OFr. taille, a cutting < taillier: see TAILOR] same as ENTAIL (n. 2 & 3) —adj. limited in a specific way, as to certain heirs, order of succession, etc.

☆**tail·back** (tāl′bak′) n. Football the offensive back farthest from the line of scrimmage

tail coat same as SWALLOW-TAILED COAT

tail covert any of the small feathers covering the basal parts of the large tail feathers of a bird

tailed (tāld) adj. having a (specified kind of) tail: usually in combination [bobtailed]

tail end 1. the rear or bottom end of anything 2. the concluding part of anything 3. [Colloq.] the buttocks

tail·fan (tāl′fan′) n. the fanlike structure at the rear of a crayfish or lobster, used for swimming backward

☆**tail·gate** (-gāt′) n. a board or gate at the back of a wagon, truck, station wagon, etc., designed to be removed or swung down on hinges for loading or unloading: also **tail′board′** —vi., vt. -gat′ed, -gat′ing to drive closely, esp. too closely, behind (another vehicle) —tail′gat′er n.

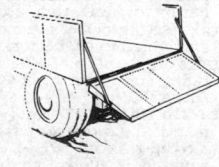

TAILGATE

tail·ing (-iŋ) n. [TAIL[1], v. + -ING] 1. [pl.] waste or refuse left in various processes of milling, mining, distilling, etc. 2. the part of a projecting brick, stone, etc. fastened into a wall

tail lamp chiefly Brit. var. of TAILLIGHT

taille (tä′y') n. [OFr. < taillier, to cut: see TAILOR] 1. a French feudal tax imposed by the king or a lord 2. [Rare] the shape of the bust or cut of a bodice

tail·light (tāl′līt′) n. a light, usually red, at the rear of a vehicle to warn vehicles coming from behind

tai·lor (tā′lər) n. [ME. < OFr. tailleor < taillier, to cut, decide, fix < LL. taliare, to split, cut, orig. prob. to prune < L. talea, a stick, twig, scion < IE. base *tal-, to grow, sprout, whence ON. thöll, a young fir] a person who makes, repairs, or alters clothes, esp. suits, coats, etc. —vi. to work as a tailor —vt. 1. a) to make (clothes) by tailor's work b) to fit or provide (a person) with clothes made by a tailor 2. a) to make by cutting and sewing to fit a particular thing [to tailor slipcovers] b) to cut, form, alter, etc. so

as to meet requirements or particular conditions [a novel tailored to popular taste] 3. to fashion (women's garments) with trim, simple lines like those of men's clothes

tai·lor·bird (-burd′) n. any of several small Asiatic and African birds that stitch leaves together to make a camouflaged holder for their nests

tai·lored (tā′lərd) adj. having trim, simple lines, as some women's garments, or specially fitted, as slipcovers

tai·lor·ing (-lər iŋ) n. 1. the occupation of a tailor 2. the workmanship or skill of a tailor

tai·lor·made (-mād′) adj. made by or as by a tailor or according to his methods; specif., a) having trim, simple lines; tailored b) made to order or to meet particular conditions [a sofa tailor-made for a small room] ☆c) designating cigarettes made in a factory rather than rolled by hand

tail·piece (tāl′pēs′) n. 1. a piece or part added to, or forming the end of, something 2. the small triangular piece of wood at the lower end of a violin, cello, etc., to which the strings are attached: see VIOLIN, illus. 3. a short beam or rafter with one end tailed in a wall and the other supported by a header 4. Printing an ornamental design put at the end of a chapter or at the bottom of a page

☆**tail·pipe** (-pīp′) n. 1. an exhaust pipe at the rear of an automotive vehicle 2. the exhaust duct of a jet engine

tail·race (-rās′) n. 1. the lower part of a millrace, through which water flows after going over a water wheel 2. a water channel to carry away tailings from a mine

tail·spin (-spin′) n. 1. same as SPIN (n. 5): also **tail spin** 2. a state of rapidly increasing mental depression or confusion

tail·stock (-stäk′) n. Mech. the adjustable part of a lathe, containing the dead center which holds the work

tail wind a wind blowing in the same direction as the course of a ship or aircraft

Tai·myr Peninsula (tī mir′) large peninsula in N R.S.F.S.R., between the Kara & Laptev seas: c.700 mi. wide at its base: also sp. **Tai·mir′, Tay·myr′**

Tai·nan (tī′nän′) city in SW Taiwan: pop. 230,000

Taine (ten; E. tān), **Hip·po·lyte A·dolphe** (ē pô lēt′ á dôlf′) 1828–93; Fr. literary critic & historian

Tai·no (tī′nō) n. 1. pl. **-nos, -no** any member of an extinct, aboriginal Indian people of the West Indies 2. their Arawakan language

taint (tānt) vt. [prob. a merging of ME. taynten, to touch (aphetic < ataynten, ATTAINT) + Anglo-Fr. teinter, to color < teint, pp. of OFr. teindre < L. tingere, to wet, moisten: see TINGE] 1. a) to affect with something physically injurious, unpleasant, etc.; infect, poison, etc. b) to affect with putrefaction or decay; spoil 2. to make morally corrupt or depraved 3. [Obs.] to dye; color 4. [Obs.] to sully or stain (a person's honor) —vi. to become tainted —n. 1. a trace of corruption, disgrace, evil, etc. 2. infectious or contaminating trace; infection, decay, contamination, etc. 3. [Obs.] a tinge or tint —SYN. see CONTAMINATE —taint′less adj.

Tai·pei, Tai·peh (tī′pā′) capital of Taiwan, in the N part: pop. 964,000

Tai·ping (tī′piŋ′) n. [Chin. t'ai-p'ing, great peace: designation of the dynasty that was to be established] any participant in the unsuccessful rebellion (c.1850–64) against the Manchu dynasty

Tai·wan (tī′wän′) island province of China, off the SE coast: the seat of the Kuomintang (Nationalist) government since 1949: 13,885 sq. mi.; pop. 13,466,000; cap. Taipei —**Tai′wan′l·an** (-lē ən), **Tai′wan·ese′** (-ēz′) adj., n.

Taiwan Strait strait between Taiwan & Fukien province, China, joining the East & South China seas: c.100 mi. wide

Tai·yü·an (tī′yü än′) city in N China; capital of Shansi province: pop. 1,500,000

Ta·jik (tä′jik) n. 1. pl. **-jiks, -jik** any member of an ethnic group of Iranian stock living in Afghanistan, the Tadzhik S.S.R., and parts of the Uzbek S.S.R. 2. same as TAJIKI

Ta·jik·i (tä′jik ē, tä′kē) n. the Persian dialect of the Tajik poeple

Taj Ma·hal (täzh′ mə häl′, täj′) [Per., best of buildings] famous mausoleum at Agra, India, built (1630?–48?) by Shah Jahan for his favorite wife

Ta·jo (tä′hō) Sp. name of the TAGUS

Tak·a·mat·su (täk′ə mät′sōō) seaport in N Shikoku, Japan, on the Inland Sea: pop. 243,000

take (tāk) vt. **took, tak′en, tak′ing** [ME. taken < OE. tacan < ON. taka < IE. base *dēg-, to lay hold of] **I.** to get possession of by force or skill; seize, grasp, catch, capture, win, etc. 1. to get by conquering; capture; seize 2. to trap, snare, or catch (a bird, animal, or fish) 3. a) to win (a game, a trick at cards, etc.) b) to capture (an opponent's piece in chess or checkers) 4. to get hold of; grasp or catch 5. to hit (a person) in or on some part 6. to affect; attack [taken with a fit] 7. to catch in some act, esp. a moral fault [taken in adultery] 8. to capture the fancy of; charm **II.** to get by action not involving force or skill; obtain, acquire, assume, etc. 1. to get into one's hand or hold; transfer to oneself 2. to eat, drink, swallow, etc. for nourishment or as medicine 3. to admit; let in [the bus takes 20 riders] 4. to get benefit from by exposure to (the air, sun, etc.)

5. to enter into a special relationship with /to *take* a wife/ 6. to have sexual intercourse with 7. to buy /he *took* the first suit he tried on/ 8. to rent, lease, or pay for so as to occupy or use /to *take* a cottage/ 9. to get regularly by paying for /to *take* a daily newspaper/ 10. to assume as a responsibility, task, etc. /to *take* a job/ 11. to assume or adopt (a symbol of duty or office) /the president *took* the chair/ 12. to obligate oneself by /to *take* a vow/ 13. to join or associate oneself with (one party or side in a contest, disagreement, etc.) 14. to assume as if granted or due one /to *take* the blame, to *take* deductions/ 15. [Slang] to cheat; trick 16. *Gram.* to have or admit of according to usage, nature, etc.; be used with in construction /a transitive verb *takes* an object/ III. *to get, adopt, use, etc. by selection or choice* 1. to choose; select 2. to use or employ; resort to /to *take* a mop to the floor/ 3. *a)* to travel by /to *take* a bus/ *b)* to set out on; follow /to *take* the old path/ 4. to go to (a place) for shelter, safety, etc. /to *take* cover/ 5. to deal with; consider /to *take* a matter seriously/ 6. *a)* to occupy /*take* a chair/ *b)* to use up; consume /to *take* all day/ 7. to require; demand; need: often used impersonally /it *takes* money, to *take* a size ten/ ☆8. *Baseball* to allow (a pitched ball) to pass without swinging one's bat IV. *to get from a source* 1. to derive, inherit, or draw (a name, quality, etc.) from something or someone specified 2. to extract, as for quotation; excerpt /to *take* a verse from the Bible/ 3. to obtain or ascertain by observation, query, experiment, etc. /to *take* a poll, to *take* one's temperature/ 4. to study; specif., to be enrolled as a student in /to *take* an art course/ 5. to write down; copy /*take* notes/ 6. *a)* to make (a photograph, picture, etc.) *b)* to draw, photograph, etc. a likeness of /*take* the scene in color/ 7. to make an impression of /*take* his fingerprints/ V. *to get as offered or due; receive, accept, suffer, etc.* 1. to win (a prize, reward, etc.) 2. to be the object of; undergo or endure /to *take* punishment/ 3. to occupy oneself in; enjoy /*take* a nap/ 4. to accept (something offered) /to *take* a bet, to *take* advice/ 5. to have a specified reaction to /to *take* a joke in earnest/ 6. to confront and get over, through, etc. /the horse *took* the jump/ 7. to be affected by (a disease, etc.) /to *take* cold/ 8. to absorb; become impregnated or treated with (a dye, polish, etc.) VI. *to receive mentally* 1. *a)* to understand the remarks of (a person) *b)* to comprehend the meaning of (words, remarks, etc.) *c)* to understand or interpret in a specified way 2. to suppose; presume /he *took* her to be a teacher/ 3. to have or feel (an emotion, mental state, etc.) /*take* pity, *take* notice/ 4. to hold and act upon (an idea, point of view, etc.) VII. *to make or complete by action* 1. to do; perform (an act) /to *take* a walk/ 2. to make or put forth (a resolution or objection) as the result of thought 3. [Colloq.] to aim and execute (a specified action) at an object /to *take* a jab at someone/ VIII. *to move, remove, etc.* 1. to be the way, means, etc. of going to a place, condition, etc.; conduct; lead /the path *takes* you to the river/ 2. to escort or accompany /to *take* a friend to dinner/ 3. to carry or transport /to *take* a book with one/ 4. to remove from a person, thing, or place; specif., to steal 5. to remove by death; bring to an end /cancer *takes* many lives/ 6. to subtract /to *take* two from ten/ 7. to direct or move (oneself) —*vi.* 1. to get possession 2. to hook or engage with another part: said of a mechanical device 3. to take root; begin growing: said of a plant 4. to lay hold; catch /the fire *took* rapidly/ 5. to gain public favor; be popular 6. to be effective in action, operation, desired result, etc. /the vaccination *took*, the dye *takes* well/ 7. to remove a part; detract (*from*) /nothing *took* from the scene's beauty/ 8. to be made or adapted to be taken (*up, down, apart,* etc.) 9. to go; proceed /to *take* to the road/ 10. [Colloq. or Dial.] to become (ill or sick) 11. [Colloq.] to be photographed in a specified way /she *takes* well in profile/ 12. *Law* to take possession of property —*n.* 1. the act or process of taking 2. something that has been taken 3. *a)* the amount or quantity of something taken /the day's *take* of fish/ *b)* [Slang] money received; receipts or profit 4. a vaccination that takes 5. *a)* a movie scene photographed or to be photographed with an uninterrupted run of the camera *b)* the process of photographing such a scene 6. *a)* any of a series of recordings or tapes of a performance, from which one will be made for release to the public *b)* the process of so recording 7. *Printing* the amount of copy sent to the compositor at one time —☆**on the take** [Slang] willing or seeking to take bribes or illicit income —**take after** 1. to be, act, or look like 2. to run after or pursue: also **take out** (or **off**) **after** —**take amiss** 1. orig., to be wrong concerning; mistake 2. to misunderstand the reason behind (an act), esp. so as to become offended —**take back** 1. to regain use or possession of 2. to retract (something said, promised, etc.) 3. to return (something), as to be exchanged —**take down** 1. to remove from a higher place and put in a lower one; pull down 2. to unfasten; take apart 3. to make less conceited; humble 4. to put in writing; record —☆**take five** (or **ten**, etc.) take a five (or ten, etc.) minute break, as from working —**take for** 1. to consider to be; regard as 2. to mistake for —**take in** 1. to admit; receive 2. to shorten (a sail) by reefing or furling 3. to make smaller or more compact 4. to include; comprise 5. to understand; comprehend 6. to cheat; trick; deceive ☆7. to visit /to *take in* all the sights/ 8. to

receive into one's home for pay /to *take in* boarders/ —**take it** 1. to suppose; believe ☆2. [Slang] to withstand difficulty, criticism, hardship, ridicule, etc. —**take it or leave it** accept it or not —**take it out of** [Colloq.] 1. to exhaust; tire 2. to obtain payment or satisfaction from —☆**take it out on** [Colloq.] to make (another) suffer for one's own anger, irritation, bad temper, etc. —**take off** 1. to remove (a garment, etc.) 2. to draw or conduct away 3. *a)* to go away; depart *b)* to absent oneself, as from work 4. to deduct; subtract 5. to kill 6. to make a copy or likeness of 7. to leave the ground or water in flight: said of an airplane 8. [Colloq.] to start 9. [Colloq.] to imitate in a burlesque manner; mimic —**take on** 1. to acquire; assume (form, quality, etc.) 2. to employ; hire 3. to begin to do (a task, etc.); undertake 4. to play against; oppose 5. [Colloq.] to show violent emotion, especially anger or sorrow —**take one's time** to be slow or unhurried; delay —**take out** 1. to remove; extract 2. to obtain by application to the proper authority 3. [Colloq.] to escort 4. *Bridge* to bid higher than (one's partner) but in a different suit —**take over** to begin controlling, managing, etc. —**take to** 1. to develop a habit or practice of doing, using, etc. 2. to go to, as for hiding, rest, etc. 3. to apply oneself to (one's studies, work, etc.) 4. to become fond of; care for; be attracted to —**take up** 1. to raise; lift 2. to make tighter or shorter 3. to pay off; recover by buying (a mortgage, note, etc.) 4. to absorb (a liquid) 5. to accept (a challenge, bet, etc.) 6. to assume protection, custody, etc. of 7. to interrupt in disapproval, rebuke, etc. 8. to resume (something interrupted) 9. *a)* to become interested in or devoted to (an occupation, study, hobby, belief, etc.) *b)* to adopt (an idea) 10. to occupy or fill (place or time) —**take upon** (or **on**) **oneself** 1. to take the responsibility for; accept as a charge 2. to begin (to do anything) Also **take upon** (or **on**) **one** —**take up with** [Colloq.] to become a friend or companion of —**tak′a·ble, take′a·ble** *adj.*

SYN.—**take** is the general word meaning to get hold of by or as by the hands /to *take* a book, the opportunity, etc./; to **seize** is to take suddenly and forcibly /he *seized* the gun from the robber, to *seize* power/; **grasp** implies a seizing and holding firmly /to *grasp* a rope, an idea, etc./; **clutch** implies a tight or convulsive grasping of that which one is eager to take or keep hold of /she *clutched* his hand in terror/; **grab** implies a roughness or unscrupulousness in seizing /the child *grabbed* all the candy, to *grab* credit/; **snatch** stresses an abrupt quickness and, sometimes, a surreptitiousness in seizing /she *snatched* the letter from my hand, to *snatch* a purse/ See also BRING, RECEIVE

take·down (tāk′doun′) *n.* 1. the act or process of taking down, esp. of disassembling mechanically 2. [Colloq.] humiliation or mortification —*adj.* made to be easily taken apart /a *takedown* firearm/

☆**take-home pay** (-hōm′) wages or salary after deductions for income tax, social security, etc. have been made

take-in (tāk′in′) *n.* [Colloq.] a taking in; specif., cheating, trickery, etc. or a deception, trick, etc.

tak·en (tāk′'n) *pp. of* TAKE

take·off (-ôf′) *n.* 1. the act of leaving the ground, as in jumping or flight 2. the place from which one leaves the ground ☆3. the starting point or launching stage; specif., *Econ.* the early stages of rapid, self-sustained growth and development 4. [Colloq.] an amusing or mocking imitation; caricature; burlesque Also **take′-off**

take·out (-out′) *n.* the act of taking out —*adj.* ☆1. designating or of prepared food sold as by a restaurant to be eaten away from the premises 2. *Bridge* designating a double intended to give one's partner information rather than to penalize one's opponents Also **take′-out′**

take·o·ver (-ō′vər) *n.* the act or an instance of assuming control or possession; esp., the usurpation of power in a nation, organization, etc.: also **take′-o′ver**

tak·er (tāk′ər) *n.* a person who takes something; esp., an available buyer, bettor, etc.

take·up (-up′) *n.* 1. the act or process of taking up, making tight, etc. 2. a mechanical device to tighten something Also **take′-up′**

ta·kin (tä′kin, tä′-) *n.* [< native name in Tibet] a goatlike mammal (*Budorcas taxicolor*) of the Himalayan forests

tak·ing (tāk′in) *adj.* 1. that captures interest; attractive; winning 2. [Obs.] contagious; infectious: said of disease —*n.* 1. the act of one that takes 2. something taken; catch 3. [*pl.*] earnings; profits; receipts 4. [Brit. Colloq.] a state of agitation or excitement —**tak′ing·ly** *adv.*

ta·la (tä′lə) *n.* [< ?] any of the various repeating rhythmic patterns of stressed and unstressed units, played on a percussion instrument in the music of India

tal·a·poin (tal′ə poin′) *n.* [Port. *talapões*, pl. of *talapão* < Burmese *tala pôi,* my lord] 1. a Buddhist monk 2. a small, long-tailed monkey (*Miopithecus talapoin*) of West Africa, with a naked face and yellowish side whiskers

ta·la·ri·a (tə ler′ē ə, -lar′-) *n.pl.* [L. < *talaris,* of the ankles < *talus,* an ankle] winged sandals or wings on the ankles, represented in mythology as an attribute, esp. of Hermes, or Mercury

talc (talk) *n.* [Fr. < Ar. *ṭalq*] 1. a very soft, usually massive and foliated mineral, magnesium silicate, $Mg_3Si_4O_{10}(OH)_2$, with a greasy feel, used to make talcum powder, lubricants, etc. 2. *clipped form of* TALCUM POWDER —*vt.* **talcked** or **talced, talck′ing** or **talc′ing** to use talc on

Tal·ca (täl′kə) city in C Chile: pop. 72,000

Tal·ca·hua·no (täl′kä hwä′nō) seaport in SC Chile, near Concepción: pop. 75,000

talc·ose (tal′kōs) *adj.* of or containing talc: also **talc′ous**

tal·cum (**powder**) (tal′kəm) a powder for the body and face made of powdered, purified talc, usually perfumed

tale (tāl) *n.* [ME. < OE. *talu*, speech, number, akin to G. *zahl*, number, Du. *taal*, speech < IE. base **del-*, to aim, reckon, figure on, whence Gr. *dolos*, L. *dolus*, guile, artifice] **1.** something told or related; relation or recital of happenings **2.** *a*) a story or account of true, legendary, or fictitious events; narrative *b*) a literary composition in narrative form **3.** a piece of idle or malicious gossip **4.** a fiction; falsehood; lie **5.** [Archaic] a tally; count; enumeration **6.** [Obs.] the act of telling; talk —*SYN.* see STORY[1]

tale·bear·er (-ber′ər) *n.* a person who spreads scandal, tells secrets, etc.; gossip —**tale′bear′ing** *adj., n.*

tal·ent (tal′ənt) *n.* [ME. < OE. *talente* < L. *talentum*, a coin, orig., unit of weight < Gr. *talanton*, a unit of money, weight, orig., a balance < IE. base **tel-*, to lift up, weigh, bear, whence L. *tollere*, to raise: senses 2-4 from the parable of the talents (Matt. 25:14–30)] **1.** any of various large units of weight or of money (the value of a talent weight in gold, silver, etc.) used in ancient Greece, Rome, the Middle East, etc. **2.** any natural ability or power; natural endowment **3.** a superior, apparently natural ability in the arts or sciences or in the learning or doing of anything **4.** people collectively, or a person, with talent [to encourage young *talent*] —**tal′ent·ed** *adj.*

SYN.—**talent** implies an apparently native ability for a specific pursuit and connotes either that it is or can be cultivated by the one possessing it [a *talent* for drawing]; **gift** suggests of a special ability that it is bestowed upon one, as by nature, and not acquired through effort [a *gift* for making plants grow]; **aptitude** implies a natural inclination for a particular work, specif. as pointing to special fitness for, or probable success in, it [*aptitude* tests]; **faculty** implies a special ability that is either inherent or acquired, as well as a ready ease in its exercise [the *faculty* of judgment]; **knack** implies an acquired faculty for doing something cleverly and skillfully [the *knack* of rhyming]; **genius** implies an inborn mental endowment, specif. of a creative or inventive kind in the arts or sciences, that is exceptional or phenomenal [the *genius* of Edison].

☆**talent scout** a person whose work is seeking out and recruiting persons of superior ability in a certain field, as in the theater or professional sports

ta·ler (tä′lər) *n., pl.* **ta′ler** [G.: see DOLLAR] a former German silver coin

ta·les (tā′lēz) *n.pl.* [ME., *talesmen* < ML. *tales* (*de circumstantibus*), such (of those standing about), phr. in writ summoning them < L., pl. of *talis*, such: see THAT] *Law* **1.** people summoned to fill jury vacancies when the regular panel has become deficient in number by challenge, etc. **2.** [*with sing. v.*] the writ that summons them

ta·les·man (tālz′mən, tā′lēz-) *n., pl.* **ta′les·men** (-mən) a person summoned as one of the tales

tale·tell·er (tāl′tel′ər) *n. same as:* **1.** STORYTELLER **2.** TALEBEARER

ta·li (tā′lī) *n. alt. pl. of* TALUS[1]

Ta·lien (dä′lyen′) seaport in Liaoning province, NE China: pop. 544,000: see LÜTA: also **Ta′lien′wan′** (-wän′)

tal·i·on (tal′ē ən) *n.* [ME. *talioun* < MFr. *talion* < L. *talio* (gen. *talionis*) < *talis*, such: see THAT] punishment that exacts a penalty corresponding in kind to the crime; retaliation, as the principle of an eye for an eye

tal·i·ped (tal′ə ped′) *adj.* having talipes; clubfooted

tal·i·pes (tal′ə pēz′) *n.* [ModL. < L. *talus*, an ankle + *pes* (gen. *pedis*), a FOOT] *same as* CLUBFOOT

tal·i·pot (tal′ə pät′) *n.* [Beng. *tālipāt*, palm leaf < Sans. *tālī*, fan palm + *pattra*, leaf: for IE. bases see TAILOR & FEATHER] a fan palm (*Corypha umbraculifera*) of the East Indies, with gigantic leaves used for fans, umbrellas, etc., and seeds used for buttons: also **talipot palm**

tal·is·man (tal′is mən, -iz-) *n., pl.* **-mans** [Fr. < Ar. *tilasm*, colloq. *tilsam*, magic figure, horoscope < MGr. *telesma*, a consecrated object (hence, one with power to avert evil) < LGr., a religious rite < Gr. *telein*, to initiate, orig., to complete < *telos*, an end: see TELEOLOGY] **1.** something, as a ring or stone, bearing engraved figures or symbols supposed to bring good luck, keep away evil, etc.; amulet **2.** anything supposed to have magic power; a charm —**tal′is·man′ic, tal′is·man′i·cal** *adj.*

talk (tôk) *vi.* [ME. *talken* (akin to Fris. *talken*, to chatter), prob. freq. based on OE. *talian*, to reckon, akin to *talu*, TALE] **1.** *a*) to put ideas into, or exchange ideas by, spoken words; speak; converse *b*) to express something in words; make a statement (*of, on, about*, etc. something) **2.** to express ideas by speech substitutes [to *talk* by signs] **3.** to speak emptily or trivially; chatter **4.** to gossip **5.** to confer; consult **6.** to make noises suggestive of speech **7.** to reveal secret information; esp., to confess or inform on someone **8.** to make a speech, esp. a somewhat informal one —*vt.* **1.** to put into spoken words; utter **2.** to use in speaking [to *talk* Spanish, to *talk* slang] **3.** to speak about; discuss [to *talk* sports] **4.** to put into a specified condition, state of mind, etc. by talking [to *talk* oneself hoarse] —*n.* **1.** *a*) the act of talking; speech *b*) conversation, esp. of an informal nature **2.** a speech, esp. a somewhat informal one **3.** a formal discussion; conference **4.** rumor; gossip **5.** the subject of conversation, gossip, etc. **6.** empty or frivolous remarks, discussion, or conversation **7.** a particular kind of speech; dialect; lingo **8.** sounds, as by an animal, suggestive of speech —*SYN.* see SPEAK, SPEECH —**big talk** [Slang] a bragging, or boasting —**make talk 1.** to talk idly, as in an effort to pass time **2.** to cause gossip —**talk around** to talk (a person) over; persuade —**talk at** to speak to in a way that indicates a response is not really desired —**talk away 1.** to pass (a period of time) by talking **2.** to talk continuously; chatter —☆**talk back** to answer impertinently or rudely —**talk big** [Slang] to boast; brag —**talk down 1.** to silence by talking louder, longer, or more effectively than **2.** to aid (a pilot) in landing by giving spoken instructions —**talk down to** to talk in a patronizing way to, as by pointedly simple speech —**talk out** to discuss (a problem, etc.) at length in an effort to reach an understanding —**talk over 1.** to have a conversation about; discuss **2.** to win (a person) over to one's view by talking; persuade —**talk someone's arm** (or **ear, leg,** etc.) **off** [Slang] to talk to someone at great length or without pause —**talk up** ☆**1.** to promote or praise in discussion **2.** to speak loudly and clearly —☆**3.** to speak boldly, frankly, etc. —**talk′er** *n.*

☆**talk·a·thon** (tôk′ə thän′) *n.* [TALK + (MAR)ATHON] any prolonged period of talking; extended speech, debate, etc.

talk·a·tive (-tiv) *adj.* talking, or fond of talking, a great deal; loquacious —**talk′a·tive·ly** *adv.* —**talk′a·tive·ness** *n.*

SYN.—**talkative**, implying a fondness for talking frequently or at length, is perhaps the least derogatory of these words [a gay, *talkative* girl]; **loquacious** usually implies a disposition to talk incessantly or to keep up a constant flow of chatter [a *loquacious* mood]; **garrulous** implies a wearisome loquacity about trivial matters [a *garrulous* old man]; **voluble** suggests a continuous flow of glib talk [a *voluble* oration]

talk·ing (tôk′iŋ) *n.* the act of a person who talks; discussion; conversation —*adj.* that talks; talkative

☆**talking book** a recording of a reading of a book, etc. for use esp. by the blind

talking picture *earlier name for* a motion picture with a synchronized sound track: also [Colloq.] ☆**talk′ie** (-ē) *n.*

☆**talking point** a persuasive point to be emphasized, as in presenting an argument

talk·ing-to (tôk′iŋ tōō′) *n.* [Colloq.] a rebuke; scolding

talk·y (tôk′ē) *adj.* **1.** talkative **2.** containing too much talk, or dialogue [a *talky* novel] —**talk′i·ness** *n.*

tall (tôl) *adj.* [ME. *tal*, dexterous, seemly < OE. (ge)*tæl*, swift, prompt, akin to OHG. *gizal*, swift < IE. base **del-*, to aim, reckon, count, whence TALE, TELL[1]] **1.** of more than normal height or stature [a *tall* man, a *tall* building] **2.** having a specified height [five feet *tall*] ☆**3.** [Colloq.] hard to believe because exaggerated or untrue [a *tall* tale] ☆**4.** [Colloq.] large; of considerable size [a *tall* drink] ☆**5.** [Colloq.] high-flown; pompously eloquent [*tall* talk] **6.** [Obs.] *a*) handsome *b*) brave —*SYN.* see HIGH —**tall′ness** *n.*

tal·lage (tal′ij) *n.* [ME. *taillage* < OFr.: see TAIL[2] & -AGE] in feudalism, **1.** a tax levied by kings upon towns and crown lands **2.** a tax levied by a feudal lord upon his tenants —*vt.* **-laged, -lag·ing** to levy a tallage upon; tax

Tal·la·has·see (tal′ə has′ē) [< Muskhogean (Creek) town name < ?] capital of Fla., in the N part: pop. 72,000

tall·boy (tôl′boi′) *n. Brit. term for* HIGHBOY

Tal·ley·rand (tal′ē rand′; *Fr.* tá lā rän′) (born *Charles Maurice de Talleyrand-Périgord*), Prince of Benevento, 1754–1838; Fr. statesman & diplomat

Tal·linn (tä′lin) capital of the Estonian S.S.R., on the Gulf of Finland: pop. 335,000: also sp. **Tal′lin**

Tal·lis (tal′is), **Thomas** 1505?–85; Eng. composer

tall·ish (tôl′ish) *adj.* somewhat tall

tal·lit, tal·lith (tä lēt′, täl′is) *n.* [LHeb. *tallīth*, a sheet, cover, cloak < *tālal*, to cover] *Judaism* the prayer shawl with fringes (*zizith*) on each corner, worn over the shoulders or head by men during morning prayer: cf. Deut. 22:12

TALLIT

☆**tall oil** (tal) *n.* [half-transl. of G. *tallöl*, half-transl. of Sw. *tallolja*, lit., pine oil < *tall*, pine < ON. *thöll*, a young fir (for IE. base see TAILOR) + Sw. *olja*, oil < MLowG. *olie* < VL. *olium*, for L. *oleum*, OIL] a resinous liquid obtained as a by-product in the manufacture of chemical wood pulp: it is used in the manufacture of soap, varnishes, etc.

tal·low (tal′ō) *n.* [ME. *talgh*, prob. < MLowG. *talg*, akin to OE. *talg*, a color, *telgan*, to color, prob. < IE base **del-*, to drip, whence MIr. *delt*, dew] the nearly colorless and tasteless solid fat extracted from the natural fat of cattle, sheep, etc., used in making candles, soaps, lubricants, etc.: see VEGETABLE TALLOW —*vt.* to cover or smear with tallow

tal·low·y (tal′ə wē) *adj.* **1.** like tallow in consistency; oily; greasy **2.** like tallow in color; pale yellow

tal·ly (tal′ē) n., pl. **-lies** [ME. talye < Anglo-L. talia < L. talea, a stick, cutting: see TAILOR] **1.** a) orig., a stick with cross notches representing the amount of a debt owing or paid: usually the stick was split lengthwise, half for the debtor and half for the creditor b) anything used as a record for an account, reckoning, or score **2.** an account, reckoning, score, etc. **3.** a) either of two corresponding parts of something; counterpart b) agreement; correspondence **4.** any number of objects used as a unit in counting **5.** an identifying tag or label —vt. **-lied, -ly·ing 1.** to put on or as on a tally; record **2.** to count; add (usually with up) **3.** to put a label or tag on **4.** [Archaic] to make (two things) agree or correspond —vi. **1.** to tally something **2.** to score a point or points in a game **3.** to agree; correspond —SYN. see AGREE

tal·ly·ho (tal′ē hō′; for n. & v., tal′ē hō′) interj. [altered < Fr. taiaut] the cry of a hunter on sighting the fox —n., pl. **-hos′ 1.** a cry of "tallyho" **2.** a coach drawn by four horses —vi. to cry "tallyho"

tal·ly·man (tal′ē mən) n., pl. **-men** (-mən) **1.** a person who tallies something **2.** [Brit.] a person who sells goods to be paid for in installments

Tal·mud (täl′mood, tal′-; -məd) n. [LHeb. talmūdh, lit., learning < lāmadh, to learn] the collection of writings constituting the Jewish civil and religious law: it consists of two parts, the Mishnah (text) and the Gemara (commentary), but the term is sometimes restricted to the Gemara: cf. HALAKHA and HAGGADA —**Tal·mud′ic, Tal·mud′i·cal** adj. —**Tal′mud·ism** n.

Tal·mud·ist (-ist) n. **1.** any of the compilers of the Talmud **2.** a student of or expert in the Talmud **3.** a person who accepts the authority of the Talmud

tal·on (tal′ən) n. [ME., a talon, claw < OFr., a heel, spur < VL. *talo < L. talus, an ankle] **1.** the claw of a bird of prey or, sometimes, of an animal **2.** a human finger or hand when like a claw in appearance or grasp **3.** the part of the bolt of a lock upon which the key presses as it is turned **4.** in card games, the stock remaining after the cards are dealt or, as in solitaire, laid out **5.** Archit. an ogee molding —**tal′oned** adj.

Ta·los (tā′läs) Gr. Myth. **1.** an inventor killed because of jealousy by Daedalus, his uncle **2.** a man of brass given by Zeus to Minos, King of Crete, as a watch

ta·lus¹ (tā′ləs) n., pl. **-lus·es, -li** (-lī) [ModL. < L., an ankle] **1.** the bone of the ankle that joins with the ends of the fibula, tibia, and calcaneus to form the ankle joint; anklebone **2.** the entire ankle

ta·lus² (tā′ləs) n. [Fr. < OFr. talu < L. talutium, surface indications of the presence of subterranean gold, prob. of Iberian orig.] **1.** a slope **2.** the sloping face of a wall, narrow at the top and wide at the base, in a fortification **3.** Geol. a) a pile of rock debris at the foot of a cliff b) a mantle of rock fragments on a slope below a rock face

tam (tam) n. clipped form of TAM-O'-SHANTER

tam·a·ble (tām′ə b'l) adj. that can be tamed

☆**ta·ma·le** (tə mä′lē) n. [MexSp. tamal, pl. tamales < Nahuatl tamalli] a native Mexican food of minced meat and red peppers rolled in cornmeal, wrapped in corn husks, and cooked by baking, steaming, etc.

ta·man·dua (tä′män dwä′) n. [Port. tamanduá < Braz. (Tupi) tamanduá < taixi, ant + mondê, to catch] a small, tree-dwelling anteater (Tamandua tetradactyla) of tropical America, with a naked tail and large ears

☆**tam·a·rack** (tam′ə rak′) n. [< AmInd. (Algonquian)] **1.** an American larch tree (Larix laricina), usually found in swamps **2.** the wood of this tree

ta·ma·rau (tä′mə rou′) n. [Tag.] a small, black, wild buffalo (Anoa mindorensis), native to Mindoro in the Philippines and now rare: also sp. **ta′ma·rao′**

tam·a·rin (tam′ə rin) n. [Fr. < the native (Carib) name in Guiana] any of several S. American marmosets (family Callithricidae), having long, silky fur; specif., a species (Saguinus tamarin) having black hands and feet

tam·a·rind (tam′ə rind) n. [Sp. tamarindo < Ar. tamr hindī, date of India] **1.** a tropical leguminous tree (Tamarindus indica) with red-streaked, yellow flowers and brown pods with an acid pulp **2.** its fruit, used in foods, beverages, medicine, etc.

tam·a·risk (tam′ə risk) n. [ME. tamarisc < LL. tamariscus, for L. tamarix] any of a genus (Tamarix) of trees or shrubs with slender branches and feathery flower clusters, common near salt water and often grown for a windbreak

ta·ma·sha (tə mä′shə) n. [Ar. tamāsha, a walking around] in India, a spectacle; show; entertainment

Ta·ma·tave (tä′mä täv′) seaport on the E coast of the Malagasy Republic: pop. 51,000

Ta·ma·u·li·pas (tä′mä oo lē′päs) state of NE Mexico, on the Gulf of Mexico: 30,734 sq. mi.; pop. 1,379,000

Ta·ma·yo (tä mä′yô), **Ru·fi·no** (roo fē′nô) 1899– ; Mex. painter

tam·bour (tam′boor) n. [ME. < MFr. < OFr. tambor, a drum < Ar. ṭanbūr, altered (prob. after at-ṭambūr, a stringed instrument) < Per. tabīrah, a drum] **1.** a drum **2.** a) an embroidery frame of two closely fitting, concentric hoops that hold the cloth stretched between them b) embroidery worked on such a frame **3.** a door, panel, etc., as in a cabinet, consisting of narrow, wooden slats glued to a flexible base, as canvas, that slides in grooves, as around curves —vt., vi. to embroider on a tambour

tam·bour·a, tam·bur·a (täm boor′ə) n. [Per. ṭambūra] a lutelike instrument of India, etc., usually with four strings, used to give a drone or ostinato accompaniment

tam·bou·rin (tam′bər in; Fr. tän bōō ran′) n. [Fr., dim. of tambour: see TAMBOUR] **1.** a type of long drum used in Provence **2.** a quick, sprightly dance of Provence, or music for it

tam·bou·rine (tam′bə rēn′) n. [Fr. tambourin: see prec.] a shallow, single-headed hand drum having jingling metal disks in the rim: it is played by shaking, hitting with the knuckles, etc. —**tam′bou·rin′ist** n.

TAMBOURINE

Tam·bov (täm bôf′) city in SW R.S.F.-S.R., southeast of Moscow: pop. 206,000

tam·bu·rit·za (tam boor′it sə) n. [Serb., ult. < Ar. at-tambūr, a stringed instrument: see TAMBOUR] any of a family of plucked stringed instruments of South Slavic regions, somewhat resembling the mandolin

tame (tām) adj. **tam′er, tam′est** [ME. < OE. tam < IE. base *dom-, to tame, subdue, whence L. domare, Gr. daman, to tame] **1.** changed from a wild to a domesticated state, as animals trained for use by man or as pets **2.** like a domesticated animal in nature; gentle and easy to control; docile **3.** crushed by or as by domestication; submissive; servile **4.** without spirit or force; dull [a tame boxing match] **5.** cultivated: said of plants or land —vt. **tamed, tam′ing 1.** to make tame, or domestic **2.** to overcome the wildness or fierceness of; make gentle, docile, obedient, or spiritless; subdue **3.** to make less intense; soften; dull —vi. to become tame —**tame′ly** adv. —**tame′ness** n. —**tam′er** n.

tame·a·ble (tām′ə b'l) adj. same as TAMABLE

tame·less (-lis) adj. **1.** not tamed **2.** not tamable

Tam·er·lane (tam′ər lān′) [< Timur lenk, Timur the lame] 1336?–1405; Mongol warrior whose conquests extended from the Black Sea to the upper Ganges

Tam·il (tam′'l, täm′-, tum′-) n. **1.** pl. **-ils, -il** any of a Tamil-speaking people living chiefly in S India and N Ceylon **2.** the Dravidian language of the Tamils, ancient or modern: official language of the state of Tamil Nad

Tamil Na·du (nä′doo) state of S India: 50,331 sq. mi pop. 33,687,000; cap. Madras

Tamm (täm), **I·gor (Evgenyevich)** (ē′gôr) 1895–1971; Soviet physicist

☆**Tam·ma·ny** (tam′ə nē) n. [altered < Tamanend, lit., the affable, name of a 17th-c. Delaware Indian chief known for his friendliness toward white men, and hence, as St. Tammany, humorously regarded as patron saint of the U.S.] a powerful Democratic political organization of New York City, incorporated in 1789 and historically often associated with bossism and other political abuses: also **Tammany Society** —adj. of Tammany's theories, practices, members, etc.

☆**Tammany Hall 1.** same as TAMMANY **2.** any of the buildings which have served as headquarters of Tammany

Tam·muz (tä′mooz) n. [Heb. tammūz] the tenth month of the Jewish year: see JEWISH CALENDAR

tam-o'-shan·ter (tam′ə shan′tər) n. [< the name of the main character of Robert Burns's poem "Tam o' Shanter"] a Scottish cap with a wide, round, flat top and, often, a center tassel

tamp (tamp) vt. [? back-formation < tampin, var. of TAMPION] **1.** in blasting, to pack clay, sand, etc. around the charge in (the drill hole) **2.** to pack firmly or pound (down) by a series of blows or taps

TAM-O'-SHANTER

Tam·pa (tam′pə) n. [< AmInd. village name < ?] seaport in WC Fla., on an arm (**Tampa Bay**) of the Gulf of Mexico: pop. 278,000 (met. area, with St. Petersburg, 1,013,000)

tam·pal·a (tam pal′ə) n. [< native name in India] a cultivated strain of pigweed (Amaranthus gangeticus)

tamp·er¹ (tam′pər) n. a person or thing that tamps; specif., any of various instruments or tools for tamping

tam·per² (tam′pər) vi. [var. of TEMPER] [Archaic] to contrive something secretly; plot; scheme —**tamper with 1.** to make secret, illegal arrangements with, as by bribing **2.** to interfere or meddle with, esp. so as to damage, corrupt, etc. —**tam′per·er** n.

Tam·pe·re (täm′pe re) city in SW Finland: pop. 147,000

Tam·pi·co (tam pē′kō; Sp. täm pē′kô) seaport in E Mexico, in Tamaulipas state: pop. 148,000

tam·pi·on (tam′pē ən) n. [Fr. tampon, nasalized form of tapon < Frank. *tappo, akin to TAP²] a plug or stopper put in the muzzle of a gun not in use

tam·pon (tam′pän) n. [Fr.: see prec.] a plug of cotton or other absorbent material put into a body cavity, wound, etc. to stop bleeding or absorb secretions —vt. to put a tampon into

tam-tam (tum′tum′, tam′tam′) n. [Hindi ṭamṭam] **1.** a large, slightly convex, dish-shaped gong, struck with a felt-covered drumstick **2.** var. of TOM-TOM

tan (tan) n. [MFr. < ML. tanum, prob. < Gaul.] **1.** same as TANBARK **2.** tannin or a solution made from it, used to

tan leather **3.** *a)* a yellowish-brown color *b)* such a color given to fair skin as by exposure to the sun or a sunlamp —*adj.* **tan'ner, tan'nest** **1.** of or for tanning **2.** yellowish-brown; tawny —*vt.* **tanned, tan'ning** [ME. *tannen* < Late OE. *tannian* < ML. *tannare* < the n.] **1.** to change (hide) into leather by soaking in tannin **2.** to produce a tan color in, as by exposure to the sun **3.** [Colloq.] to whip severely; flog —*vi.* to become tanned —**tan someone's hide** [Colloq.] to flog someone severely

tan tangent

Ta·na (tä'nä) **1.** lake in N Ethiopia: source of the Blue Nile: c.1,400 sq. mi. **2.** river in E Kenya, flowing southeast into the Indian Ocean: c.500 mi. **3.** river in Lapland, flowing north into the Arctic Ocean and forming part of the Finnish-Norwegian border: c.200 mi.

Ta·nach (tä näkh') *n.* [acronym formed from Heb. *torāh* (the Pentateuch), *nebi'im* (the Prophets), and *ketūbim* (the Hagiographa)] the Holy Scriptures of Judaism

tan·a·ger (tan'ə jər) *n.* [ModL. *tanagra* < Port. *tángara* < Braz. (Tupi) *tangara*] any of a large family (Thraupidae) of small, perching, sparrowlike, new-world songbirds: the males usually are brilliantly colored

Tan·a·gra (tan'ə grə, tə nag'rə) ancient Gr. town in Boeotia, known for the terra cotta figurines found there

Ta·na·na (tan'ə nä') river in E Alas., flowing northwest into the Yukon River: 800 mi.

Ta·na·na·rive (tä nä nä rēv'; *E.* tə nan'ə rēv') capital of the Malagasy Republic, in the C part: pop. 322,000

tan·bark (tan'bärk') *n.* any bark containing tannin, used to tan hides and, after the tannin has been extracted, to cover race tracks, circus rings, etc.

Tan·cred (taŋ'krid) 1078?-1112; Norman leader of the 1st Crusade

tan·dem (tan'dəm) *adv.* [orig. punning use of L. *tandem*, at length (of time)] one behind another; in single file —*n.* **1.** a two-wheeled carriage drawn by horses harnessed tandem **2.** a team, as of horses, harnessed tandem **3.** a bicycle with two seats and sets of pedals placed tandem **4.** a relationship between two persons or things involving cooperative action, mutual dependence, etc. [to work in *tandem*] —*adj.* having two parts or things placed tandem

Ta·ney (tô'nē), **Roger B(rooke)** 1777-1864; U.S. jurist; chief justice of the U.S (1836-64)

Tang (täŋ) 618-906 A.D.; Chin. dynasty under which literature & art flourished & printing was developed

tang[1] (taŋ) *n.* [ME. *tange* < ON. *tangi*, a sting, point, dagger, nasalized form of base seen in TAG] **1.** a projecting point or prong on a chisel, file, knife, etc. that fits into a handle, shaft, etc. **2.** a strong and penetrating taste or odor **3.** a touch or trace (*of* some quality) **4.** a special or characteristic flavor, quality, etc. ☆**5.** same as SURGEON-FISH —*vt.* to provide (a knife, etc.) with a tang

tang[2] (taŋ) *n.* [echoic] a loud, ringing sound; twang —*vt., vi.* to sound with a loud ringing

Tan·gan·yi·ka (taŋ'gən yē'kə) **1.** mainland region of Tanzania, on the E coast of Africa, a former Brit. trust territory: 361,800 sq. mi. **2. Lake,** lake in EC Africa, between Tanganyika & the Congo: 12,700 sq. mi.

☆**tan·ge·lo** (tan'jə lō') *n., pl.* **-los'** [TANG(ERINE) + (POM)ELO] a fruit produced by crossing a tangerine with a grapefruit

tan·gent (tan'jənt) *adj.* [L. *tangens*, prp. of *tangere*, to touch: see TACT] **1.** that touches; touching **2.** *Geom.* touching and not intersecting a curve or curved surface at one and only one point: said of a line or plane —*n.* [< ModL. (*linea*) *tangens*, tangent (line)] **1.** *Geom. a)* a tangent line, curve, or surface *b)* the length of a straight line tangent to a curve, measured from the point of tangency to the intersection of the tangent line with the x-axis **2.** *Trigonometry* the ratio between the side opposite a given acute angle in a right triangle to the adjacent side; reciprocal of the cotangent of an angle or arc —*SYN.* see ADJACENT —**go** (or **fly**) **off at** (or **on**) **a tangent** to break off suddenly from a line of action or train of thought and pursue another course —**tan'gen·cy** *n.*

tan·gen·tial (tan jen'shəl) *adj.* **1.** of, like, or in the direction of, a tangent **2.** drawn as a tangent **3.** going off at a tangent; diverging or digressing **4.** merely touching a subject, not dealing with it at length —**tan·gen'tial·ly** *adv.*

Tan·ger (tăn zhä') Fr. name of TANGIER

tan·ge·rine (tan'jə rēn', tan'jə rēn') *n.* [< prec. + -INE[1]] **1.** a variety of mandarin orange with a deep, reddish-yellow color and segments that are easily separated **2.** a deep, reddish-yellow color

tan·gi·ble (tan'jə b'l) *adj.* [LL. *tangibilis* < L. *tangere*, to touch: see TACT] **1.** that can be touched or felt by touch; having material form and substance **2.** corporeal and able to be appraised for value [*tangible* assets] **3.** that can be understood; definite; objective —*n.pl.* property that can be appraised for value; assets having real substance; material things —*SYN.* see PERCEPTIBLE —**tan'gi·bil'i·ty, tan'gi·ble·ness** *n.* —**tan'gi·bly** *adv.*

Tan·gier (tan jir') seaport in N Morocco, on the Strait of Gibraltar: pop. 170,000: formerly capital of an internationalized zone (**Tangier Zone**)

tan·gle (taŋ'g'l) *vt.* **-gled, -gling** [ME. *tanglen*, prob. nasalized var. of *taglen*, to entangle, akin to Sw. dial. *taggla*, to disarrange] **1.** to hinder, obstruct, or confuse by or as by covering, circling, entwining, etc. **2.** to catch in or as in a net or snare; trap **3.** to make a knot or snarl of; intertwist —*vi.* **1.** to become tangled **2.** [Colloq.] to fight, quarrel, or argue —*n.* **1.** an intertwisted, confused mass of things, as string, branches, etc.; snarl **2.** a jumbled, confused condition; muddle **3.** a perplexed or bewildered state —**tan'gler** *n.*

☆**tan·gle·foot** (-foot') *n.* [Western Slang] cheap whiskey

tan·gly (taŋ'glē) *adj.* **-gli·er, -gli·est** full of tangles; snarled

tan·go (taŋ'gō) *n., pl.* **-gos** [AmSp.] **1.** a S. American dance with long gliding steps and dips **2.** music for this dance in 2/4 or 4/4 time —*vi.* to dance the tango

tan·gram (taŋ'grəm) *n.* [prob. arbitrary coinage on analogy of ANAGRAM] a Chinese puzzle made by cutting a square into five triangles, a square, and a rhomboid, and using these pieces to form various figures and designs

TANGRAM

Tang·shan (täŋ'shän') city in Hopei province, NE China, near Tientsin: pop. 812,000

Tan·guy (tän gē'), **Yves** (ēv) 1900-55; Fr. painter in the U.S.

tang·y (taŋ'ē) *adj.* **tang'i·er, tang'i·est** having a tang, or flavor —**tang'i·ness** *n.*

Ta·nis (tā'nis) city in ancient Egypt, in the Nile delta: probable capital of the Hyksos kings

tan·ist (tan'ist, thôn'-) *n.* [Ir. & Gael. *tānaiste*, next heir, hence lord of a country, lit., second, parallel < OIr. *tān*, estate] in ancient Ireland, the elected heir of a living Celtic chief in a system (**tanistry**) limiting the choice to the chief's kin

tank (taŋk) *n.* [in sense 1 prob. < Gujarati *tānkh*; in other senses < or infl. by Sp. & Port. *tanque*, aphetic < *estanque*, a pool, stoppage of flow < *estancar*, to stop the flow of < VL. *stantcare*, to STAUNCH] **1.** orig., in India, a natural or artificial pool or pond used for water storage **2.** any large container for liquid or gas [a gasoline *tank*, a swimming *tank*] **3.** [name orig. used for purpose of secrecy during manufacture] a heavily armored, self-propelled combat vehicle armed with guns and moving on full tractor treads ☆**4.** [Slang] a jail cell, esp. one for new prisoners charged with misdemeanors —*vt.* to put, store, or process in a tank —**tank up** [Colloq.] **1.** to supply with or get a full tank of gasoline ☆**2.** to drink much liquor

tan·ka (täŋ'kə) *n.* [Jap.] **1.** a Japanese verse form of 31 syllables in five unrhymed lines, the first and third having five syllables each and the others seven **2.** a poem in this form

tank·age (taŋ'kij) *n.* **1.** the capacity of a tank or a number of tanks collectively **2.** *a)* the storage of fluids, gases, etc. in tanks *b)* the charge for such storage ☆**3.** slaughter-house waste from which the fat has been rendered in tanks, dried and ground for use as fertilizer or feed

tank·ard (taŋ'kərd) *n.* [ME., akin to OFr. *tanquart*, Du. *tanckaert*, ML. *tancardus*] a large drinking cup with a handle and, often, a hinged lid

☆**tank car** a large tank on wheels, for carrying liquids and gases by rail

tank destroyer a highly mobile, armored halftrack on which antitank guns are mounted

☆**tanked** (taŋkt) *adj.* [Colloq.] drunk: also **tanked up**

tank·er (taŋ'kər) *n.* **1.** a ship with large tanks in the hull for carrying a cargo of oil or other liquids ☆**2.** same as: *a)* TANK CAR *b)* TANK TRUCK ☆**3.** a plane equipped to carry a cargo of gasoline and to refuel another plane in flight

tank farming same as HYDROPONICS

tank·ful (taŋk'fool') *n.* as much as a tank will hold

☆**tank town** **1.** a railroad stop for locomotives to fill their boilers with water: it usually became the site of a small town **2.** any small or unimportant town

☆**tank truck** a motor truck built to transport gasoline, oil, or other liquids

tan·nage (tan'ij) *n.* **1.** the act or process of tanning **2.** something that has been tanned

tan·nate (tan'āt) *n.* a salt of tannic acid

tan·ner[1] (tan'ər) *n.* a person whose work is tanning hides

tan·ner[2] (tan'ər) *n.* [< ?] [Brit. Colloq.] a sixpence

tan·ner·y (-ē) *n., pl.* **-ner·ies** a place where hides are tanned

Tann·häu·ser (tän'hoi zər; *E.* tän'hoi zər, -hou-) [G.] a German knight and minnesinger of the 13th century, dealt with in legend as a knight who seeks absolution after giving himself up to revelry in the Venusberg

tan·nic (tan'ik) *adj.* [Fr. *tannique* < *tanin*, TANNIN + -*ique*, -IC] of, like, or obtained from tanbark or tannin

tannic acid **1.** a yellowish, astringent substance, $C_{14}H_{10}O_9$, derived from oak bark, gallnuts, etc. and used in tanning, medicine, etc. **2.** any of a number of similar substances

tan·nin (tan'in) *n.* [Fr. *tanin* < *tan*, TAN + -*in*, -IN[1]] *same as* TANNIC ACID

tan·ning (-iŋ) *n.* **1.** the art or process of making leather

from hides 2. the act of making fair skin brown, as by exposure to the sun 3. [Colloq.] a severe whipping; flogging

Ta·no·an (tä′nō ən) *n.* [< *Tano*, name of a group of Indian pueblos + -AN] a family of four N. American Indian languages including Kiowa and three now spoken in a group of pueblo villages of New Mexico

tan·sy (tan′zē) *n., pl.* -**sies** [ME. < OFr. *tanesie* < VL. *tanaceta < LL. *tanacetum* < ?] any of a genus (*Tanacetum*) of plants of the composite family; esp., a poisonous, old-world plant (*Tanacetum vulgare*) with strong-smelling foliage and flat-topped clusters of small, yellow, rayless flower heads: now a common weed in the U.S.

Tan·ta (tän′tä) city in N Egypt, in the center of the Nile delta: pop. 184,000

tan·ta·late (tan′tə lāt′) *n.* a salt of tantalic acid

tan·tal·ic (tan tal′ik) *adj.* 1. of, derived from, or containing tantalum, esp. with a valence of five 2. designating any of several colorless, crystalline, acidic, hydrated tantalum pentoxides, $Ta_2O_5 \cdot xH_2O$, that form salts with bases

tantalic acid a colorless, crystalline acid, $HTaO_3$, that forms complex salts

tan·ta·lite (tan′tə līt′) *n.* [G. *tantalit*: see TANTALUM & -ITE[1]] a heavy, black, crystalline, orthorhombic mineral, (Fe,Mn)(Ta,Nb)₂O₆, the principal ore of tantalum

tan·ta·lize (tan′tə līz′) *vt.* -**lized′**, -**liz′ing** [< TANTALUS + -IZE] to tease or disappoint by promising or showing something desirable and then withholding it —**tan′ta·li·za′tion** *n.* —**tan′ta·liz′er** *n.* —**tan′ta·liz′ing·ly** *adv.*

tan·ta·lous (tan′tə ləs) *adj.* of, derived from, or containing tantalum, esp. with a valence of three

tan·ta·lum (-ləm) *n.* [ModL. < *Tantalus*: its insolubility in most acids made extraction from the mineral difficult] a rare, steel-blue, corrosion-resisting, metallic chemical element found in various minerals and used to make nuclear reactors, aircraft and missile parts, grids and plates in radio tubes, surgical instruments, etc.: symbol, Ta; at. wt., 180.948; at. no., 73; sp. gr., 16.6; melt. pt., 2996°C; boil. pt., c.5425°C

Tan·ta·lus (tan′tə ləs) [L. < Gr. *Tantalos*] *Gr. Myth.* a king, son of Zeus, doomed in the lower world to stand in water that always receded when he tried to drink it and under branches of fruit he could never reach

tan·ta·mount (tan′tə mount′) *adj.* [< Anglo-Fr. *tant amunter*, to amount to as much < OFr. *tant* (< L. *tantus*, so much) + *amonter* (see AMOUNT)] having equal force, value, effect, etc.; equal or equivalent (*to*)

tan·ta·ra (tan′tə rə; tan tar′ə, -tär′ə) *n.* [echoic] 1. a trumpet blast or fanfare 2. a sound like this

tan·tiv·y (tan tiv′ē) *adv.* [prob. echoic of sound of a horse galloping] at full gallop; headlong —*n., pl.* -**tiv′ies** a gallop; rapid movement

‡**tant mieux** (tän myö′) [Fr.] so much the better

‡**tan·to** (tän′tō) *adv.* [It. < L. *tantum*, so much] too much; so much: used in musical directions [*allegro non tanto*]

‡**tant pis** (tän pē′) [Fr.] so much the worse

tan·tra (tun′trə, tän′-) *n.* [Sans., a doctrine, lit., warp, akin to *tanti*, a cord, string < IE. base *ten-, to stretch, whence THIN] [*often* T-] any of a class of Hindu or Buddhist religious writings that are mystical in nature —**tan′tric** *adj.*

tan·trum (tan′trəm) *n.* [< ?] a violent, willful outburst of annoyance, rage, etc.; childish fit of bad temper

Tan·za·ni·a (tan′zə nē′ə, tän′-) country in E Africa, formed by the merger of Tanganyika & Zanzibar: it is a member of the Brit. Commonwealth: 362,820 sq. mi.; pop. 12,231,000; cap. Dar es Salaam —**Tan′za·ni′an** *adj., n.*

Tao·ism (dou′iz′m, tou′-) *n.* [Chinese *tao*, the way + -ISM] a Chinese religion and philosophy based on the doctrines of Lao-tse (6th cent. B.C.) and advocating simplicity, selflessness, etc. —**Tao′ist** *n., adj.* —**Tao·is′tic** *adj.*

Taos (tous) [Sp. pl. < AmInd. name of a pueblo, lit., ? willow people] resort town in N N.Mex.: pop. 2,000

tap[1] (tap) *vt.* **tapped**, **tap′ping** [ME. *tappen* < OFr. *taper*, prob. of echoic origin] 1. to strike lightly and rapidly 2. to strike something lightly, and often repeatedly, with 3. to make or do by tapping [to *tap* a message with the fingers] ☆4. to choose or designate, as for membership in a club 5. to repair (a shoe) by adding a thickness of leather, etc. to the heel or sole —*vi.* 1. to strike a light, rapid blow or a series of such blows 2. to perform a tap dance 3. to move with a tapping sound —*n.* 1. a light, rapid blow, or the sound made by it 2. the leather, etc. added in tapping a shoe 3. a small metal plate attached to the heel or toe of a shoe, as for tap dancing —**tap′per** *n.*

tap[2] (tap) *n.* [ME. *tappe* < OE. *tæppa*, akin to G. *zapfen*, ON. *tappi* < IE. *dāp- < base *da-, to divide, cut, tear up] 1. a device for starting or stopping the flow of liquid in a pipe, barrel, etc.; faucet 2. a plug, cork, etc. for stopping a hole in a container holding a liquid 3. liquor of a certain kind or quality, as drawn from a certain tap 4. *clipped form of* TAPROOM 5. the act or an instance of draining liquid, as from a body cavity 6. a tool used to cut threads in a female screw ☆7. the act or an instance of wiretapping ☆8. *Elec.* a place in a circuit where a connection can be made —*vt.* **tapped**, **tap′ping** [ME. *tappen* < OE. *tæppian* < the *n.*] 1. to put a tap or spigot on 2. to make a hole in for drawing off liquid [to *tap* a sugar maple] 3. to pull out the tap or plug from 4. to draw (liquid) from a container, cavity, etc. 5. to draw upon; make use of [to *tap* new resources] 6. to make a connection with (a water

main, electrical circuit, etc.); specif., ☆to make a secret connection with (a telephone line) in order to overhear or record private conversations 7. to cut threads on the inner surface of (a nut, pipe, etc.) 8. [Slang] to borrow or get money from —**on tap** 1. in a tapped or open cask (of liquor) and ready to be drawn; on draft 2. [Colloq.] ready for consideration or action —**tap′per** *n.*

ta·pa (tä′pä) *n.* [< native Polynesian name] an unwoven cloth made by people in the Pacific islands from the treated inner bark of the paper mulberry tree

Ta·pa·jós, Ta·pa·joz (tä′pə zhôs′) river in N Brazil, flowing northeast into the Amazon: c.500 mi. (with principal headstream, c.1,200 mi.)

tap dance a dance performed with sharp, loud taps of the foot, toe, or heel at each step —**tap′-dance′** *vi.* -**danced′**, -**danc′ing** —**tap′-danc′er** *n.*

tape (tāp) *n.* [ME. < OE. *tæppe*, a fillet, akin to *tæppa*: see TAP[2]] 1. a strong, narrow, woven strip of cotton, linen, etc. used to bind seams in garments, tie bundles, etc. 2. a narrow strip or band of steel, paper, etc. 3. a strip of cloth stretched between posts above the finishing line of a race 4. *clipped form of* TAPE MEASURE 5. *shortened form of* ADHESIVE TAPE, FRICTION TAPE, MAGNETIC TAPE, TICKER TAPE, etc. —*vt.* **taped**, **tap′ing** 1. to put tape on or around, as for binding, tying, etc. 2. to measure by using a tape measure 3. to record (sound, video material, digital computer data, etc.) on magnetic tape —**tap′er** *n.*

☆**tape deck** a simplified, magnetic-tape assembly, without an amplifier or speaker but having tape reels, drive, and recording and playback heads

☆**tape grass** any of several submerged, freshwater, flowering plants (genus *Vallisneria*) of a family (Hydrocharitaceae) with elongated, ribbonlike leaves

tape measure a tape with marks in inches, feet, etc. for measuring: also **tape′line′** (-lin′) *n.*

ta·per (tā′pər) *n.* [ME. < OE. *tapur*, prob. by dissimilation < L. *papyrus* (see PAPER): from use of papyrus pith as wick] 1. a wax candle, esp. a long, slender one 2. a long wick coated with wax, used for lighting candles, lamps, etc. 3. any feeble light 4. *a)* a gradual decrease in width or thickness [the *taper* of a pyramid] *b)* a gradual decrease in action, power, etc. 5. something that tapers —*adj.* gradually decreased in breadth or thickness toward one end —*vt., vi.* 1. to decrease gradually in width or thickness 2. to lessen; diminish —**taper off** 1. to become smaller gradually toward one end 2. to diminish or stop gradually

tape-re·cord (tāp′ri kôrd′) *vt.* to record on magnetic tape

tape recorder a device for recording on magnetic tape: see MAGNETIC RECORDING

tap·es·try (tap′is trē) *n., pl.* -**tries** [LME. *tapsterie*, earlier *tapicerie* < MFr. *tapisserie* < OFr. *tapis*, a carpet < MGr. *tapētion* < Gr., dim. of *tapēs* (gen. *tapētos*), a carpet, prob. < Iran.] a heavy cloth woven by hand or machinery with decorative designs and pictures and used as a wall hanging, furniture covering, etc. —*vt.* -**tried**, -**try·ing** to decorate as with a tapestry: usually in the pp.

tape transport the mechanism in a tape-recording and playback system that moves the tape past the various heads from reel to reel

ta·pe·tum (tə pēt′əm) *n., pl.* -**pe′ta** (-ə) [ModL. < L. *tapete*, a carpet < Gr. *tapēs*: see prec.] 1. *Anat., Zool.* any of various membranous layers; esp., *a)* the iridescent choroid membrane in the eye of certain animals, as the cat *b)* a layer of fibers from the corpus callosum forming a portion of the roof of each lateral ventricle of the brain 2. *Bot.* a nutritive layer of cells lining the inner wall of a fern sporangium or of an anther —**ta·pe′tal** *adj.*

tape·worm (tāp′wurm′) *n.* any of various cestode flatworms that live in the adult stage as parasites in the intestines of man and other vertebrates and in the larval stage usually in various intermediate hosts

tap·house (tap′hous′) *n.* [TAP[2] + HOUSE] a tavern or inn

tap·i·o·ca (tap′ē ō′kə) *n.* [Port. & Sp. < Braz. (Tupi) *typyoca* < *ty*, juice + *pýa*, heart + *oc*, to squeeze out] a starchy granular substance prepared from the root of the cassava plant, used to make puddings, thicken soups, etc.

ta·pir (tā′pər) *n., pl.* **ta′pirs, ta′pir**: see PLURAL, II, D, 1 [Sp. < Braz. (Tupi) *tapyra*, large mammal, tapir] any of several large, hoofed, hoglike mammals (family Tapiridae) of tropical America and the Malayan peninsula, related to the rhinoceros: tapirs have flexible snouts, feed on plants, and are active at night

tap·is (tap′ē, -is; ta pē′) *n.* [MFr.: see TAPESTRY] tapestry used as a curtain, tablecloth, carpet, etc.: now only in **on** (or **upon**) **the tapis** under consideration

TAPIR
(2 1/2–3 1/2 ft. high at shoulder)

tap·pet (tap′it) *n.* [TAP[1] + -ET] a projection or lever that moves or is moved by intermittent contact, as with a cam, in an engine or machine

tap·ping (tap′iŋ) *n.* 1. the act of a person or thing that taps 2. [*pl.*] that which is drawn by tapping

tap·room (tap′rōōm′) *n. same as* BARROOM

tap·root (-rōōt′, -root′) *n.* [TAP[2] + ROOT[1]] a main root, growing almost vertically downward, from which small branch roots spread out: see ROOT, illus.

taps (taps) *n.* [< TAP¹, because orig. a drum signal] ☆a bugle call to put out lights in retiring for the night, as in an army camp: also sounded at a military funeral

tap·ster (tap′stər) *n.* [ME. < OE. *tæppestre,* barmaid < *tæppa*: see TAP²] [Now Rare] a barmaid or bartender

tar¹ (tär) *n.* [ME. *terre* < OE. *teru,* prob. < base of *treow,* TREE, in sense "product of trees"] **1.** a thick, sticky, brown to black liquid with a pungent odor, obtained by the destructive distillation of wood, coal, peat, shale, etc.: tars are composed of hydrocarbons and their derivatives, and are used for protecting and preserving surfaces, in making various organic compounds, etc. **2.** loosely, any of the solids in smoke, as from tobacco —*vt.* **tarred, tar′ring** to cover or smear with or as with tar —*adj.* **1.** of or like tar **2.** covered with tar; tarred —☆**tar and feather** to cover (a person) with tar and feathers as in punishment by mob action —**tarred with the same brush** (or **stick**) having similar faults or obnoxious traits

tar² (tär) *n.* [< TAR(PAULIN)] [Colloq.] a sailor

tar·a·did·dle (tar′ə did′'l) *n.* [fanciful elaboration of DIDDLE²] [Chiefly Brit. Colloq.] a petty lie; fib

ta·ran·tass (tä′rän täs′) *n.* [Russ. *tarantas*] a large, low, four-wheeled Russian carriage without springs

tar·an·tel·la (tar′ən tel′ə) *n.* [It., dim. of TARANTO: popularly associated with ff., because of its lively character] **1.** a fast, whirling southern Italian dance for couples, in 6/8 time **2.** music for this

tar·ant·ism (tar′ən tiz′m) *n.* [It. *tarantismo*: because formerly epidemic in the vicinity of TARANTO; popularly associated with the *tarantula,* by whose bite it was erroneously said to be caused] a nervous disease characterized by hysteria and popularly believed to be curable by dancing or manifested by a mania for dancing: prevalent in S Italy during the 16th and 17th cent.

Ta·ran·to (tə ran′tō; *It.* tä′rän tō′) **1.** seaport in SE Italy, on the Gulf of Taranto: pop. 210,000 **2.** Gulf of, arm of the Ionian Sea, in SE Italy: c.85 mi. long

ta·ran·tu·la (tə ran′choo lə) *n., pl.* **-las, -lae** (-lē) [ML. < It. *tarantola* < prec., near which the wolf spider was found] **1.** any of numerous large, hairy spiders (suborder Mygalomorphae) with a poisonous bite that has little effect on warmblooded animals; specif., ☆any of a family (Theraphosidae) found in the SW U.S. and tropical America **2.** a wolf spider (*Lycosa narbonensis*) of S Europe, whose bite was popularly but wrongly supposed to cause tarantism

Ta·ra·wa (tä′rä wä, tä′rä wä) coral atoll in the WC Pacific: headquarters of the Brit. colony of Gilbert and Ellice Islands: 7 1/2 sq. mi.; pop. 7,000

TARANTULA (body to 3 1/2 in.; legs to 5 in.)

Tar·bell (tär′bel), **Ida M(inerva)** 1857–1944; U.S. journalist & author

tar·boosh (tär boosh′) *n.* [Ar. *ṭarbūsh*] a brimless cap of cloth or felt shaped like a truncated cone, worn by Moslem men, sometimes as the inner part of a turban

Tar·de·noi·si·an (tär′də noi′zē ən) *adj.* [after *Fère-en-Tardenois,* town in NE France, where implements were found] designating or of a mesolithic culture characterized by small flint implements of geometric form

tar·di·grade (tär′də grād′) *n.* [Fr. < L. *tardigradus*: see TARDY & GRADE] any of a phylum (Tardigrada) of minute water animals with segmented bodies and four pairs of unsegmented legs, often regarded as primitive arthropods

tar·do (tär′dō) *adj., adv.* [It. < L. *tardus*: see ff.] *Music* slow: a direction to the performer

tar·dy (tär′dē) *adj.* **-di·er, -di·est** [LME. *tardyve* < OFr. *tardif* < VL. *tardivus* < L. *tardus,* slow, prob. < IE. base *ter-,* delicate, weak, whence Gr. *terēn,* tender] **1.** slow in moving, acting, etc. **2.** behind time; late, delayed, or dilatory —**tar′di·ly** *adv.* —**tar′di·ness** *n.*

SYN.—**tardy** applies to that which comes or occurs after the proper or appointed time, either from a lack of punctuality or because of inadvertent delay [two of the pupils were *tardy* this morning]; **late** applies to that which fails to occur at the usual or proper time, as because of slowness of movement, development, etc. [summer came *late* that year]; **overdue** is applied to something delayed, unpaid, etc. beyond the scheduled time, as because of someone's tardiness, procrastination, etc. [an *overdue* ship, rent, etc.] —**ANT. prompt**

tare¹ (ter) *n.* [ME., small seed, vetch < or akin to MDu. *tarwe,* wheat < IE. base *derwā-,* kind of grain, whence Sans. *dūrvā,* millet grass: used in ME. and Early ModE. versions of NT. to transl. LL.(Ec.) *zizania,* darnel] **1.** any of several vetches, esp. the common vetch (*Vicia sativa*) **2.** the seed of any of these plants **3.** *Bible* a noxious weed thought to be darnel: Matt. 13:25-40

tare² (ter) *n.* [LME. < MFr. < It. *tara* < Ar. *ṭarḥah* < *ṭaraḥa,* to reject] **1.** the weight of a container, wrapper, vehicle, etc. deducted from the total weight to determine the weight of the contents or load **2.** the deduction of this —*vt.* **tared, tar′ing** to find out, allow for, or mark the tare of

tare³ (ter) *archaic or dial. pt. & pp.* of TEAR¹

Ta·ren·tum (tə ren′təm) *ancient name of* TARANTO

targe (tärj) *n.* [ME. < OE. < ON. *targa,* akin to OHG. *zarga,* a rim, frame < IE. base *dergh-,* to grip, whence Gr. *drakhmē* (see DRACHMA)] [Archaic] a shield or buckler

tar·get (tär′git) *n.* [ME. < MFr. *targette,* dim. of *targe,* a shield < Frank. *targa,* akin to prec.] **1.** orig., a small shield, esp. a round one **2.** *a)* a round, flat board, straw coil, etc., often one marked with concentric circles, set up to be aimed at, as in archery or rifle practice *b)* any object that is shot at, thrown at, etc. **3.** an objective; goal **4.** a ship, building, site, etc. that is the object of a military attack **5.** an object of verbal attack, criticism, or ridicule **6.** something resembling a target in shape or use; specif., ☆a) the sliding sight on a surveyor's leveling rod ☆b) a disk-shaped signal on a railroad switch *c)* a metallic insert, usually of tungsten or molybdenum, in the anode of an X-ray tube, upon which the stream of cathode rays impinge and from which X-rays emanate *d)* a surface, object, etc. subjected to irradiation or to bombardment as by nuclear particles —*vt.* to establish a target, or goal, for ☆**target date** a date aimed at, as for the start or completion of something

Tar·gum (tär′goom; *Heb.* tär gōōm′) *n., pl.* **Tar′gums;** *Heb.* **Tar·gu·mim** (tär gōōm′im) [LHeb. < Aram. *targūm,* lit., interpretation] any of several translations or paraphrases of parts of the Hebrew Scriptures, written in the vernacular (Aramaic) of Judea

☆**Tar·heel** (tär′hēl′) *n.* [Colloq.] a native or inhabitant of North Carolina, called the **Tarheel State**

tar·iff (tar′if) *n.* [It. *tariffa* < Ar. *ta′rif,* information, explanation < *′arafa,* to know, inform] **1.** a list or system of taxes placed by a government upon exports or, esp., imports **2.** a tax of this kind, or its rate **3.** any list or scale of prices, charges, etc. ☆**4.** [Colloq.] any bill, charge, fare, etc. —*vt.* **1.** to make a schedule of tariffs on; set a tariff on **2.** to fix the price of according to a tariff

Ta·rim River (tä′rēm′, dä′-) river in NW China, flowing from the Tien Shan into E Sinkiang region: c.1,300 mi.

Tar·king·ton (tär′kiŋ tən), **(Newton) Booth** 1869-1946; U.S. novelist

tar·la·tan, tar·le·tan (tär′lə tən) *n.* [Fr. *tarlatane,* earlier *tarnatane* < ?] a thin, stiff, open-weave muslin

Tar·mac (tär′mak) [< *tarmacadam* < TAR¹ + MACADAM] a trademark for a coal-tar material used in paving —*n.* [t-] [Chiefly Brit.] a road, airport runway or apron, etc. paved with a mixture of crushed stone and tar

tarn (tärn) *n.* [ME. *terne* < or akin to ON. *tjörn,* a tarn, lit., hole filled with water: for IE. base see TEAR¹] a small mountain lake

'tar·nal (tär′n′l) *adj. shortened dial. form of* ETERNAL: used chiefly as an intensive [a '*tarnal* fool]

tar·na·tion (tär nä′shən) *interj., n.* [prob. < 'TAR(NAL) + (DAM)NATION] *dial. var. of* DAMNATION: used as an intensive [what in *tarnation* is that?]

tar·nish (tär′nish) *vt.* [< Fr. *terniss-,* inflectional stem of *ternir,* to make dim < MFr., prob. < OHG. *tarnjan,* to conceal] **1.** to dull the luster of or discolor the surface of (a metal) by exposure to air **2.** *a)* to besmirch or sully (a reputation, honor, etc.) *b)* to spoil, mar, or debase [to *tarnish* a memory] —*vi.* **1.** to lose luster; grow dull; discolor, as from oxidation **2.** to become sullied, soiled, spoiled, marred, etc. —*n.* **1.** the condition of being tarnished; dullness **2.** the film of discoloration on the surface of tarnished metal **3.** a stain; blemish —**tar′nish·a·ble** *adj.*

ta·ro (tä′rō) *n., pl.* **-ros** [Tahitian] **1.** a large, tropical Asiatic plant (*Colocasia esculenta*) of the arum family, with shield-shaped leaves: it is cultivated for its edible corms that are the source of poi **2.** the tuber of this plant

tar·ot (tar′ō, -ət; ta rō′) *n.* [Fr. < MFr. < OIt. *tarocco* < Ar. *taraha,* to remove, reject (cf. TARE²)] [often T-] any of a set of playing cards bearing pictures of certain traditional allegorical figures, used in fortunetelling

☆**tarp** (tärp) *n.* [Colloq.] *clipped form of* TARPAULIN

☆**tar paper** a heavy paper impregnated with tar, used as a base for roofing, etc.

tar·pau·lin (tär pô′lin, tär′pə lin) *n.* [TAR¹ + -*paulin,* prob. < *palling* < PALL², a covering] **1.** *a)* waterproof material; specif., canvas coated with a waterproofing compound *b)* a sheet of this spread over something to protect it from getting wet **2.** [Archaic] a sailor; tar

Tar·pe·ia (tär pē′ə) *Rom. Myth.* a girl who treacherously opened the Capitoline citadel to the invading Sabines, who then crushed her to death with their shields

Tar·pe·ian (-ən) *adj.* [L. *Tarpeianus* < *Tarpeia*: see prec.] designating or of a cliff on the Capitoline Hill in Rome from which traitors to the state were hurled to their death

tar·pon (tär′pən, -pän) *n., pl.* **-pons, -pon:** see PLURAL, II, D, I [< ?] a large, silvery game fish (*Megalops atlanticus*) with very large scales, found in the warmer parts of the western Atlantic: tarpons belong to the herring group, measure up to seven feet in length, and weigh up to two hundred pounds

Tar·quin (tär′kwin) (*Lucius Tarquinius Superbus*) semilegendary Etruscan king of Rome (534?–510? B.C.)

tar·ra·did·dle (tar′ə did′'l) *n. alt. sp.* of TARADIDDLE

tar·ra·gon (tar′ə gän′) *n.* [Sp. *taragona* < Ar. *tarkhun* < Gr. *drakōn*, dragon] 1. an old-world wormwood (*Artemisia dracunculus*) whose fragrant leaves are used for seasoning, esp. in vinegar 2. the leaves of this plant

tar·ri·ance (tar′ē əns) *n.* [Archaic] 1. the act of tarrying; delay 2. a sojourn; stay

tar·ry¹ (tar′ē) *vi.* **-ried, -ry·ing** [ME. *tarien*, to delay, vex, hinder, prob. < OE. *tergan*, to vex, provoke, merged with OFr. *targer*, to delay < VL. *tardicare* < L. *tardare*, to delay < *tardus*, slow (cf. TARDY)] 1. to delay, linger, be tardy, etc. 2. to stay for a time, esp. longer than originally intended; remain temporarily 3. to wait —*vt.* [Archaic] to wait for —*n.* [Now Rare] a sojourn; stay —SYN. see STAY³ —**tar′ri·er** *n.*

tar·ry² (tär′ē) *adj.* **-ri·er, -ri·est** 1. of or like tar 2. covered or smeared with tar —**tar′ri·ness** *n.*

tar·sal (tär′s'l) *adj.* [< ModL. *tarsus* (see TARSUS) + -AL] of the tarsus of the foot or the tarsi of the eyelids —*n.* a tarsal bone or plate See SKELETON, illus.

tar sands *Geol.* sands or sandstone deposits containing tarry, viscous, bituminous oil

Tar·shish (tär′shish) seaport or maritime region of uncertain location, mentioned in the Bible: cf. I Kings 10:22

tar·si·er (tär′sē ər) *n.* [Fr., so named by BUFFON < *tarse*, TARSUS, from the foot structure] any of several small primates (family Tarsiidae) of the East Indies and the Philippines, with very large, gogglelike eyes, and a long, tufted, nonprehensile tail: tarsiers are related to the lemurs, live in trees, are active at night, and feed esp. on lizards and insects

tar·so- (tär′sō) [< ModL. *tarsus*] a combining form meaning tarsus or tarsal: also, before a vowel, **tars-**

tar·so·met·a·tar·sus (tär′sō met′ə tär′səs) *n.* [prec. + METATARSUS] the large bone in the lower part of a bird's leg, connecting with the tibia and the toes

Tar·sus (tär′səs) city in S Turkey, near the Mediterranean: in ancient times, the capital of Cilicia & birthplace of the Apostle Paul: pop. 51,000

TARSIER
(head & body
3-7 in. long;
tail 5-10 in.
long)

tar·sus (tär′səs) *n., pl.* **tar′si** (-sī) [ModL. < Gr. *tarsos*, flat of the foot, any flat surface, orig., a wickerwork frame for drying fruits or cheeses < IE. base *ters-*, to dry, whence THIRST, L. *torridus*] 1. *Anat.* a) the human ankle, consisting of seven bones between the tibia and metatarsus b) the small plate of connective tissue stiffening the eyelid 2. *Zool.* a) a group of bones in the ankle region of the hind limbs of tetrapods b) *same as* TARSOMETATARSUS c) the fifth segment from the base of an insect leg

tart¹ (tärt) *adj.* [ME. < OE. *teart* < Gmc. *trat-*: for IE. base see TEAR¹] 1. sharp in taste; sour; acid; acidulous 2. sharp in meaning or implication; cutting [a *tart* answer] —SYN. see SOUR —**tart′ly** *adv.* —**tart′ness** *n.*

tart² (tärt) *n.* [ME. *tarte* < MFr.] 1. a small shell of pastry filled with jam, jelly, etc. 2. in England, a small pie filled with fruit or jam and often having a top crust

tart³ (tärt) *n.* [< prec., orig., slang term of endearment] a prostitute or any woman of loose morals —**tart up** [Chiefly Brit. Slang] to clothe, furnish, or decorate, often, specif., in a cheap and showy way

tar·tan¹ (tär′t'n) *n.* [prob. < MFr. *tiretaine*, a cloth of mixed fibers < OFr. *tiret*, a kind of cloth < *tire*, oriental cloth (of silk) < ML. *tyrius*, material from Tyre < L. *Tyrus*, TYRE; sp. infl. by ME. *tartarin*, a rich material < MFr. (*drap*) *tartarin*, Tartar (cloth)] 1. woolen cloth with a woven pattern of straight lines of different colors and widths crossing at right angles, as worn in the Scottish Highlands, where each clan has its own pattern 2. any plaid cloth like this 3. any tartan pattern 4. a garment made of tartan —*adj.* of, like, or made of tartan

tar·tan² (tär′t'n) *n.* [Fr. *tartane* < It. *tartana*, prob. ult. < Ar. *tarīdah*, freighter, cattle boat] a small, single-masted Mediterranean ship with a large lateen sail and a jib

Tar·tar (tär′tər) *n.* [ME. *Tartre* < ML. *Tartarus*, a Tatar, altered (after TARTARUS) < Per. *Tātār*] 1. *same as* TATAR 2. [*usually* t-] an irritable, violent, intractable person —*adj.* of Tatary or the Tatars —**catch a Tartar** to attack or oppose someone too strong for one; get more than one bargained for

tar·tar (tär′tər) *n.* [ME. < ML. *tartarum* < MedGr. *tartaron* < ? Ar.] 1. potassium bitartrate, KHC₄H₄O₆, present in grape juice, and forming a reddish or whitish, crustlike deposit (*argol*) in wine casks: in its purified form, called CREAM OF TARTAR 2. a hard deposit on the teeth, consisting of saliva proteins, food deposits, and various salts, as calcium phosphate; dental calculus

Tar·tar·e·an (tär ter′ē ən, -tar′-) *adj.* of Tartarus; infernal

tartar emetic antimony potassium tartrate, K(SbO)C₄H₄O₆·1/2H₂O, a poisonous, odorless, white salt used in medicine to cause expectoration, vomiting, and perspiring, and in dyeing as a mordant

Tar·tar·i·an (tär ter′ē ən) *adj.* of Tatary or the Tatars

tar·tar·ic (tär tar′ik, -tär′-) *adj.* of, containing, or derived from tartar or tartaric acid

tartaric acid a clear, colorless, crystalline acid, C₄H₆O₆, found in vegetable tissues and fruit juices and obtained commercially from tartar: it is used in dyeing, photography, medicine, etc.

tar·tar·ous (tär′tar əs) *adj.* of, like, or containing tartar

tar·tar sauce (tär′tər) [Fr. *sauce tartare*] a sauce, as for seafood, consisting of mayonnaise with chopped pickles, olives, capers, etc.: also sp. **tartare sauce**

tartar steak *same as* STEAK TARTARE

Tar·ta·rus (tär′tər əs) *Gr. Myth.* 1. an infernal abyss below Hades, where Zeus hurled the rebel Titans, later a place of punishment for the wicked after death 2. *same as* HADES (sense 1 a)

Tar·ta·ry (tär′tər ē) *same as* TATARY

Tar·ti·ni (tär tē′nē), **Giu·sep·pe** (jōō zep′pe) 1692–1770; It. violinist, composer, & musical theorist

tart·let (tärt′lit) *n.* [see -LET] a small pastry tart

tar·trate (tär′trāt) *n.* [Fr. < *tartre*, TARTAR + -ate, -ATE²] a salt or ester of tartaric acid

tar·trat·ed (-trāt id) *adj.* 1. derived from or containing tartar 2. combined with tartaric acid

Tar·tu (tär′tōō) city in the E Estonian S.S.R.: pop. 85,000

Tar·tuffe (tär toof′; *Fr.* tär tüf′) [Fr. < It. *Tartufo*, lit., a truffle] the title hero, a religious hypocrite, of a satirical comedy (1664–69) by Molière —*n.* [t-] a hypocrite

☆**Tar·zan** (tär′zən, -zan) *n.* [after *Tarzan*, jungle-raised hero of stories by E. R. BURROUGHS] [*also* t-] any very strong, virile, and agile man: often used ironically or humorously

Tash·kent (täsh kent′) capital of the Uzbek S.S.R., on a branch of the Syr Darya: pop. 1,127,000

Ta·si·an (tä′sē ən) *adj.* [< *Deir Tasa*, village in upper Egypt, where artifacts were found] designating or of the earliest known neolithic farming culture of upper Egypt, preceding the Badarian

☆**ta·sim·e·ter** (tə sim′ə tər) *n.* [< Gr. *tasis*, a stretching < *teinein*, to stretch (see TENANT) + -METER] an electric instrument for measuring minute expansions or motions of solids and the variations in temperature that cause these —**tas·i·met·ric** (tas′ə met′rik) *adj.* —**ta·sim′e·try** *n.*

task (task, täsk) *n.* [ME. *taske* < ONormFr. *tasque* (OFr. *tasche*) < ML. *tasca*, for *taxa*, a tax < L. *taxare*, to rate, value, TAX] 1. orig., a tax 2. a piece of work assigned to or demanded of a person 3. any piece of work 4. an undertaking involving labor or difficulty —*vt.* 1. orig., to tax 2. to assign a task to; require or demand a piece of work of 3. to put a burden on; strain; overtax —**take to task** to reprimand or scold; reprove

SYN.—**task** refers to a piece of work assigned to or demanded of someone, as by another person, by duty, etc., and usually implies that this is difficult or arduous work [he has the *task* of answering letters]; **chore** applies to any of the routine domestic activities for which one is responsible [his *chore* is washing the dishes]; **stint** refers to a task that is one's share of the work done by a group and usually connotes a minimum to be completed in the allotted time [we've all done our daily *stint*]; **assignment** applies to a specific, prescribed task allotted by someone in authority [classroom *assignments*]; **job**, in this connection, refers to a specific piece of work, as in one's trade or as voluntarily undertaken for pay [the *job* of painting our house]

☆**task force** 1. a specially trained, self-contained military unit assigned a specific mission or task, as the raiding of enemy installations 2. any group assigned to a specific project

task·mas·ter (-mas′tər, -mäs′tər) *n.* a person who assigns tasks to others, esp. when exacting or severe; overseer

task·work (-wurk′) *n.* 1. hard, distasteful work 2. *rare var. of* PIECEWORK

Tas·man (täs′mən; *E.* taz′mən), **A·bel Jans·zoon** (ä′bəl yän′sōn) 1603?–59; Du. navigator who discovered Tasmania & New Zealand

Tas·ma·ni·a (taz mā′nē ə, -mān′yə) 1. island south of Victoria, Australia: c.24,450 sq. mi. 2. state of Australia comprising this island & smaller nearby islands: 26,383 sq. mi.; pop. 371,000; cap. Hobart —**Tas·ma′ni·an** *adj., n.*

Tasmanian devil a stout, badgerlike, extremely voracious, flesh-eating marsupial (*Sarcophilus harrisii*) of Tasmania, having black fur with white patches and a large head

Tasmanian wolf (or tiger) a fierce, flesh-eating marsupial (*Thylacinus cynocephalus*) of Tasmania, somewhat like a dog but with dark stripes on the back: it is almost extinct

Tas·man Sea (taz′mən) section of the South Pacific, between SE Australia & New Zealand

Tass (täs) *n.* [Russ. < *T*(*elegrafnoye*) *A*(*genstvo*) *S*(*ovyet-skovo*) *S*(*oyuza*), Telegraph Agency of the Soviet Union] a Soviet agency for gathering and distributing news

tass (tas, täs) *n.* [LME. *tasse* < MFr. < Ar. *tassa* < Per. *tast*, a cup] [Obs. or Scot.] 1. a small drinking cup or goblet 2. its contents; a small draft

tasse (tas) *n.* [MFr., purse, pouch] any of a series of jointed metal plates forming a skirtlike protection of armor for the lower trunk and thighs: see ARMOR, illus.

tas·sel¹ (tas′'l) *n.* [ME. < OFr., a knob, knot, button < VL. *tassellus*, altered < L. *taxillus*, a small die (akin to *talus*, ankle), after L. *tessella*, small cube, piece of mosaic] 1. orig., a clasp or fibula 2. an ornamental tuft of threads, cords, etc. of equal length, hanging loosely from a knob or from the knot by which they are tied together 3. something resembling this; specif., the tassellike infores-

cence of some plants, as corn —*vt.* **-seled** or **-selled, -sel·ing** or **-sel·ling** to ornament with tassels —☆*vi.* to grow tassels, as corn

tas·sel² (tas/'l) *n.* [Obs.] same as TIERCEL

Tas·so (täs/sō; *E.* tas/ō), **Tor·qua·to** (tôr kwä/tō) 1544-95; It. epic poet

taste (tāst) *vt.* **tast'ed, tast'ing** [ME. *tasten* < OFr. *taster*, to handle, touch, taste < VL. **tastare,* prob. < **taxitare,* freq. of L. *taxare,* to feel, touch sharply, judge of, freq. of *tangere:* see TACT] **1.** orig., to test by touching **2.** to test the flavor of by putting a little in one's mouth **3.** to detect or distinguish the flavor of by the sense of taste [*to taste* sage in a dressing] **4.** to eat or drink, esp. a small amount of **5.** to receive the sensation of, as for the first time; experience; have [*to have* tasted *freedom at last*] **6.** [Archaic] to like the taste of; like —*vi.* **1.** to discern or recognize flavors by the sense of taste; have the sense of taste **2.** to eat or drink a small amount (*of*) **3.** to have the specific flavor (*of*) [*a salad that* tastes *of garlic*] **4.** to have a sensation, limited experience, or anticipating sense (*of* something) —*n.* [ME. < OFr. *tast* < the *v.*] **1.** orig., *a)* a test; trial *b)* the act of tasting **2.** that one of the five senses that is stimulated by contact of a substance with the taste buds on the surface of the tongue and is capable of distinguishing between sweet, sour, salt, and bitter: the flavor of any specific substance is usually recognized by its combined taste, smell, and texture **3.** the quality of a thing that is perceived through the sense of taste; flavor; savor **4.** a small amount put into the mouth to test the flavor **5.** the distinguishing flavor of a substance [*a chocolate* taste] **6.** a slight experience of something; sample [*to get a* taste *of another's anger*] **7.** a small amount; bit; trace; suggestion; touch **8.** *a)* the ability to notice, appreciate, and judge what is beautiful, appropriate, or harmonious, or what is excellent in art, music, decoration, clothing, etc. *b)* a specific preference; partiality; predilection [*a* taste *for red ties*] *c)* an attitude or a style reflecting such ability or preferences on the part of a group of people of a particular time and place **9.** a liking; inclination; fondness; bent [*to have no* taste *for business*] —**in bad** (*poor,* etc.) **taste** in a form, style, or manner showing lack or impairment of a sense of beauty, excellence, fitness, propriety, etc. —**in good** (**excellent,** etc.) **taste** in a form or manner showing a sense of beauty, excellence, fitness, etc. —**in taste** in good taste —**to one's taste** 1. pleasing to one 2. so as to please one

taste bud any of the cells embedded principally in the epithelium of the tongue and functioning as the sense organs of taste

taste·ful (tāst/fəl) *adj.* having or showing good taste [*tasteful* décor] —**taste'ful·ly** *adv.* —**taste'ful·ness** *n.*

taste·less (-lis) *adj.* **1.** *a)* without taste or flavor; flat; insipid *b)* dull; uninteresting **2.** lacking good taste or showing poor taste **3.** [Archaic] unable to taste —**taste'less·ly** *adv.* —**taste'less·ness** *n.*

tast·er (tās/tər) *n.* [ME. *tastour* < Anglo-Fr.] **1.** a person who tastes; specif., *a)* a person employed to test the quality of wines, teas, etc. by tasting *b)* a servant, as of a royal house, who tastes his master's food and drink to detect poisoning **2.** any of several devices used for tasting, sampling, or testing

tast·y (-tē) *adj.* **tast'i·er, tast'i·est** **1.** that tastes good; flavorful; savory **2.** [Now Rare] same as TASTEFUL — **tast'i·ly** *adv.* —**tast'i·ness** *n.*

tat¹ (tat) *vt.* **tat'ted, tat'ting** [prob. back-formation < TATTING] to make by tatting —*vi.* to do tatting

tat² (tat) *n.* [< ? TAP¹] *see* TIT FOR TAT

TAT thematic apperception test

ta-ta (tä tä/) *interj.* [Brit.] goodbye: orig. a child's term

ta·ta·mi (tä tä/mē) *n., pl.* **-mi, -mis** [Jap.] a floor mat woven of rice straw, used traditionally in Japanese homes for sitting on, as when eating

Ta·tar (tät/ər) *n.* [Per.] **1.** a member of any of the Mongolian and Turkic tribes that took part in the invasion of C and W Asia and E Europe in the Middle Ages **2.** any of a Turkic people living in a region of EC European Russia, the Crimea, and parts of Asia **3.** any of their Turkic languages; specif., a language (**Kazan Turkic**) spoken around Kazan —*adj.* of the Tatars or their languages: also **Ta·tar·i·an** (tä ter/ē ən), **Ta·tar'ic** *adj.*

Tatar Strait strait between Sakhalin Island & the Asia mainland: c.350 mi. long

Ta·ta·ry (tät/ə rē) vast region in Europe & Asia under the control of Tatar tribes in the late Middle Ages: its greatest extent was from SW Russia to the Pacific

Tate (tāt) **1.** (John Orley) **Allen,** 1899- ; U.S. poet & critic **2. Nahum,** 1652-1715; Brit. poet & dramatist, born in Ireland: poet laureate (1692-1715)

'ta·ter, ta·ter (tāt/ər) *n.* altered dial. form of POTATO

Ta·tra Mountains (tä/trə) range of the Carpathian Mountains in N Czechoslovakia & S Poland: highest peak, 8,737 ft.

tat·ter (tat/ər) *n.* [ME., prob. < ON. *töturr,* rags, tatters, akin to G. *zotte,* a tuft < IE. base **dā(i)-,* to cut out, tear out: cf. TEASE] **1.** a torn and hanging shred or piece,

as of a garment **2.** a separate shred or scrap; rag **3.** [*pl.*] torn, ragged clothes —*vt.* to reduce to tatters; make ragged —*vi.* to become ragged

tat·ter·de·mal·ion (tat/ər di māl/yən, -mal/-; -ē ən) *n.* [< prec. + ?] a person in torn, ragged clothes; ragamuffin

tat·tered (tat/ərd) *adj.* [ME. *tatered*] **1.** in tatters; torn and ragged **2.** wearing torn and ragged clothes

tat·ter·sall (tat/ər sôl/) *n.* [< *Tattersall's,* a London horse market and gamblers' rendezvous, founded by Richard Tattersall in 1766] a checkered pattern of dark lines on a light background —*adj.* having such a pattern

tat·ting (tat/in) *n.* [prob. < Brit. dial. *tat,* to tangle] **1.** a fine lace made by looping and knotting thread that is wound on a hand shuttle: used for edging, trimming, etc. **2.** the act or process of making this

tat·tle (tat/'l) *vi.* **-tled, -tling** [LME. *tattlen,* prob. < MDu. *tatelen,* of echoic origin] **1.** to talk idly; chatter; gossip **2.** to reveal other people's secrets; tell tales —*vt.* to reveal (a secret) through gossiping —*n.* idle talk; chatter; tattling

TATTING

tat·tler (tat/lər) *n.* **1.** a person who tattles; gossip ☆**2.** a grayish-brown sandpiper (*Heteroscelus incanus*) of the Pacific coastal region, known for its loud cry

☆**tat·tle·tale** (tat/'l tāl/) *n.* an informer or talebearer: now chiefly a child's term

tat·too¹ (ta tōō/) *vt.* **-tooed', -too'ing** [Tahitian *tatau*] **1.** to puncture (the skin) with a needle and insert indelible colors so as to leave permanent marks or designs **2.** to make (marks or designs) on the skin in this way —*n., pl.* **-toos'** a tattooed mark or design —**tat·too'er, tat·too'ist** *n.*

tat·too² (ta tōō/) *n., pl.* **-toos'** [earlier *taptoo* < Du. *taptoe* < *tap toe,* shut the tap: a signal for closing barrooms] **1.** *a)* a signal on a drum, bugle, etc. summoning soldiers, etc. to their quarters at night *b)* in England, a military spectacle featuring music, marching, military exercises, etc. **2.** any continuous drumming, rapping, etc. —*vt., vi.* **-tooed', -too'ing** to beat or tap on (a drum, table, etc.)

tat·ty (tat/ē) *adj.* **-ti·er, -ti·est** [prob. akin to OE. *taetteca,* a ray] [Chiefly Brit.] shabby, decrepit, worn out, tawdry, etc. —**tat'ti·ly** *adv.* —**tat'ti·ness** *n.*

tau (tô, tou) *n.* [ME. *taw, tau* (esp. with ref. to the tau cross) < L. *tau* < Gr. *tau* < Sem., as in Heb. *tāw*] the nineteenth letter of the Greek alphabet (T, τ)

tau cross a cross shaped like a capital tau

taught (tôt) *pt. & pp.* of TEACH

taunt¹ (tônt, tänt) *adj.* [< ?] very tall: said of a ship's mast

taunt² (tônt, tänt) *vt.* [< Fr. *tant pour tant,* tit for tat] **1.** to reproach in scornful or sarcastic language; jeer at; mock **2.** to drive or provoke (a person) by taunting —*n.* **1.** a scornful or jeering remark; gibe **2.** [Obs.] an object of taunts, reproaches, etc. —*SYN.* see RIDICULE — **taunt'er** *n.* —**taunt'ing·ly** *adv.*

Taun·ton (tôn/t'n, tän/-) **1.** [after ff.] city in SE Mass.: pop. 44,000 **2.** county seat of Somersetshire, SW England: pop. 36,000

taupe (tōp) *n.* [Fr. < L. *talpa,* a mole] a dark, brownish gray, the color of moleskin —*adj.* of such a color

tau·rine¹ (tôr/īn, -in) *adj.* [L. *taurinus* < *taurus,* a bull: see TAURUS] **1.** of or like a bull **2.** of Taurus (sense 2)

tau·rine² (tôr/ēn, -in) *n.* [< L. *taurus,* bull, ox + -INE⁴: because first obtained (1826) from ox bile] a colorless, crystalline compound, NC₂H₇SO₃, which is found in the free form in invertebrates and as a constituent of taurocholic acid in the bile of mammals

tau·ro·cho·lic acid (tôr/ə kō/lik) [< TAUR(INE)² + CHOL- + -IC] a colorless, crystalline acid, NC₂₆H₄₅O₇S, that occurs in the bile of mammals as the sodium salt and promotes the intestinal absorption of lipids, as cholesterol

tau·rom·a·chy (tô räm/ə kē) *n.* [Gr. *tauromachia,* bull-fight < *tauros,* a bull (for IE. base see ff.) + *machē,* a battle] *literary term for* BULLFIGHTING

Tau·rus (tôr/əs) [ME. < L., a bull, prob. < IE. **tauros* < base **tēu-,* to swell, whence THUMB, L. *tumere,* to swell] **1.** a N constellation between Aries and Orion containing the Hyades and the Pleiades **2.** the second sign of the zodiac (♉), entered by the sun on or about April 20: see ZODIAC, illus.

Taurus Mountains mountain range along the S coast of Asia Minor, Turkey: highest peak, c.12,250 ft.

Taus·sig (tou/sig), **Frank William** 1859-1940; U.S. political economist

taut (tôt) *adj.* [ME. *toght,* tight, firm, prob. < pp. of *togen* (< OE. *togian*), to pull: cf. TOW¹] **1.** tightly stretched, as a rope **2.** showing strain; tense [*a* taut *smile*] **3.** trim, tidy, well-disciplined, efficient, etc. [*a* taut *ship*] —*SYN.* see TIGHT —**taut'ly** *adv.* —**taut'ness** *n.*

taut·en (tôt/'n) *vt., vi.* to make or become taut

tau·to- (tôt/ō, -ə) [Gr. *tauto-* < *tauto* < *to auto,* the same] *a combining form meaning* the same [*tautomerism*]

☆**tau·tog** (tô täg/) *n.* [AmInd. (Narragansett) *tautauog,* pl. of *tautau,* kind of blackfish] a black or greenish food

fish (*Tautoga onitis*) related to the wrasses and found off the Atlantic coast of the U.S.

tau·to·log·i·cal (tôt'ə lăj'i k'l) *adj.* of, involving, or using tautology —**tau'to·log'i·cal·ly** *adv.*

tau·tol·o·gize (tô täl'ə jīz') *vi.* **-gized'**, **-giz'ing** to use tautology; be repetitious —**tau·tol'o·gism** (-jiz'm) *n.* —**tau·tol'o·gist** (-jist) *n.*

tau·tol·o·gous (-gəs) *adj.* same as: **1.** TAUTOLOGICAL **2.** ANALYTIC (sense 3) —**tau·tol'o·gous·ly** *adv.*

tau·tol·o·gy (tô täl'ə jē) *n.*, *pl.* **-gies** [LL. *tautologia* < Gr. *tautologia:* see TAUTO- & -LOGY] **1.** needless repetition of an idea in a different word, phrase, or sentence; redundancy; pleonasm (Ex.: "necessary essentials") **2.** an instance of such repetition

tau·to·mer (tôt'ə mər) *n.* [back-formation < ff.] a substance exhibiting tautomerism

tau·tom·er·ism (tô täm'ər iz'm) *n.* [< TAUTO- + Gr. *meros*, a part + -ISM] *Chem.* the property of some substances of being in a condition of equilibrium between two isomeric forms and of reacting readily to form either —**tau·to·mer·ic** (tô'tə mer'ik) *adj.*

tau·to·nym (tôt'ə nim') *n.* [< TAUT(O)- + Gr. *onyma*, a NAME] *Biol.* **1.** a scientific name consisting of two terms, in which the generic name and specific name or epithet are the same (Ex.: *Rattus rattus*, the black rat): this kind of name is no longer permitted by the International Code of Botanical Nomenclature but is frequent in zoological nomenclature **2.** a scientific name consisting of three terms, in which the name of the typical subdivision of the species repeats the specific name or epithet: now required by the Botanical Code —**tau'to·nym'ic** *adj.* —**tau·ton·y·my** (tô tän'ə mē) *n.*

tav (tăf, täv) *n.* [Heb. *tāw*] the twenty-third letter of the Hebrew alphabet (ת): also sp. **taw**

tav·ern (tav'ərn) *n.* [ME. *taverne* < OFr. < L. *taberna*, a tavern, booth, stall made of boards, altered by dissimilation < *traberna* < *trabs*, a beam, roof < IE. *treb-*, a beamed structure, building, whence THORP] **1.** a place where liquors, beer, etc. are sold to be drunk on the premises; saloon; bar **2.** an inn

tav·ern·er (-ər nər) *n.* [ME. *tauerner* < OFr. *tavernier* < LL. *tabernarius*] [Archaic] the proprietor of a tavern

taw¹ (tô) *n.* [< ?] **1.** a relatively large and fancy marble used to shoot with in playing marbles **2.** *a)* the game of marbles *b)* the line from which the players shoot

taw² (tô) *vt.* [ME. *tawen* < OE. *tawian*, to prepare, akin to Goth. *taujan*, to do, make, prob. < IE. base *deu-*, to venerate, whence L. *bonus*, good] **1.** formerly, to prepare (a natural product) for further treatment or use **2.** to make (skins) into leather by treating with alum, salt, etc. **3.** [Obs. exc. Dial.] to whip; flog

taw·dry (tô'drē) *adj.* **-dri·er**, **-dri·est** [by syllabic merging of *St. Audrey*, esp. in *St. Audrey laces*, women's neckpieces sold at St. Audrey's fair in Norwich, England] cheap and showy; gaudy; sleazy —*SYN.* see GAUDY¹ —**taw'dri·ly** *adv.* —**taw'dri·ness** *n.*

Taw·ney (tô'nē) **R**(ichard) **H**(enry) 1880–1962; Brit. economic historian

taw·ny (tô'nē) *adj.* **-ni·er**, **-ni·est** [ME. *tauny* < OFr. *tanné*, pp. of *tanner*, to TAN] brownish-yellow; tan —*n.* tawny color —*SYN.* see DUSKY —**taw'ni·ness** *n.*

taws (tôz) *n.*, *pl.* **taws** [orig. pl. of obs. *taw*, a thong, tawed leather < TAW²] [Brit.] a leather thong split into strips at the end, used as a whip: also sp. **tawse**

tax (taks) *vt.* [ME. *taxen* < MFr. *taxer*, to tax < L. *taxare*, to appraise, tax, censure < base of *tangere*, to touch (see TACT): used interchangeably with *tasken* (cf. TASK) in ME.] **1.** orig., to determine the value of; assess **2.** *a)* to require to pay a percentage of income, property value, etc. for the support of a government *b)* to require to pay a special assessment, as in a society, labor union, etc. **3.** to assess a tax on (income, property, purchases, etc.) **4.** to impose a burden on; put a strain on [*to tax* one's strength] **5.** to accuse; charge [to be *taxed* with negligence] —*n.* [ME.] **1.** *a)* a compulsory payment, usually a percentage, levied on income, property value, sales price, etc. for the support of a government *b)* a special assessment, as in a society, labor union, etc. **2.** a heavy demand; burden; strain ☆**3.** [Old Colloq.] a charge, cost, bill, etc. —**tax'a·bil'i·ty** *n.* —**tax'a·ble** *adj.* —**tax'er** *n.*

tax·a (tak'sə) *n.* *pl. of* TAXON

tax·a·tion (tak sā'shən) *n.* [ME. *taxacion* < MFr. *taxation* < L. *taxatio* < pp. of *taxare:* see TAX] **1.** a taxing or being taxed **2.** the principle of levying taxes **3.** a tax or tax levy **4.** revenue from taxes

tax-de·duct·i·ble (taks'di dukt'ə b'l) *adj.* that is allowed as a deduction in computing income tax

☆**tax duplicate 1.** the certification of real-estate assessments to the taxing authorities **2.** the basis upon which the tax collector prepares tax bills and for which he is held accountable to the auditor

tax·eme (tak'sēm) *n.* [< Gr. *taxis*, arrangement (see TAXIS) + (PHON)EME] any of the minimal features in grammatical construction, such as selection of words, order of words or morphemes, modulation in stress and pitch, etc. —**tax·e·mic** (tak sē'mik) *adj.*

tax-ex·empt (taks'ig zempt') *adj.* **1.** exempt from taxation; that may not be taxed **2.** producing income that is exempt from taxation [*tax-exempt* bonds]

☆**tax·i** (tak'sē) *n.*, *pl.* **tax'is** clipped form of TAXICAB —*vi.* **tax'ied**, **tax'i·ing** or **tax'y·ing 1.** to go in a taxi **2.** to move slowly along the ground or on the water under its own power as before taking off or after landing: said of an airplane —*vt.* **1.** to carry in a taxi **2.** to cause (an airplane) to taxi

☆**tax·i·cab** (-kab') *n.* [< *taxi(meter) cab*] an automobile in which passengers are carried for a fare at a rate usually recorded by a taximeter

☆**taxi dancer** [so called (after prec.) because hired to dance] a girl employed at a dance hall to dance with patrons, who pay a fee

tax·i·der·my (tak'si dur'mē) *n.* [< Gr. *taxis* (see TAXIS) + *derma*, a skin] the art of preparing, stuffing, and mounting the skins of animals, esp. so as to make them appear lifelike —**tax'i·der'mal**, **tax'i·der'mic** *adj.* —**tax'i·der'mist** *n.*

tax·i·me·ter (tak'sē mēt'ər) *n.* [Fr. *taximètre*, altered (after Gr. *taxis:* see ff.) < *taxamètre* < G. *taxameter* < ML. *taxa*, TAX + -*meter*, -METER] an automatic device installed in taxicabs, that computes and registers the fare due

tax·is (tak'sis) *n.* [Gr. *taxis*, arrangement, division: see TACTICS] **1.** in ancient Greece, a unit of troops, of varying size **2.** [ModL. < Gr.] *Biol.* the movement of a whole and free-moving cell or organism toward or away from some external stimulus: applied to microscopic plants, animals, germ cells, etc. **3.** *Surgery* the replacement by hand of some displaced part, as a hernial protrusion, without cutting any tissue

-tax·is (tak'sis) [ModL. < Gr. < *taxis:* see prec.] a combining form meaning arrangement, order, taxis [*parataxis*]

☆**taxi stand** a place where taxicabs are stationed for hire

tax·ite (tak'sīt) *n.* [G. *taxit* < Gr. *taxis* (see TAXIS) + -*it*, -ITE¹] volcanic rock having a clastic appearance —**tax·it'ic** (-sit'ik) *adj.*

tax·i·way (tak'sē wā') *n.* any of the paved strips at an airport for use by airplanes in taxiing between the terminals or hangars and the runways

tax·on (tak'sän) *n.*, *pl.* **tax'a** (-sə) [back-formation < TAXONOMY] a taxonomic category or unit, as a species, genus, etc.

tax·on·o·my (tak sän'ə mē) *n.* [Fr. *taxonomie* < Gr. *taxis* (see TAXIS) + *nomos*, a law (see -NOMY)] **1.** the science of classification; laws and principles covering the classifying of objects **2.** *Biol.* a system of arranging animals and plants into natural, related groups based on some factor common to each, as structure, embryology, biochemistry, etc.: the basic taxa now in use are, in descending order from most inclusive, *phylum* (in botany, *division*), *class*, *order*, *family*, *genus*, and *species* —**tax'o·nom'ic** (-sə näm'ik), **tax'o·nom'i·cal** *adj.* —**tax'o·nom'i·cal·ly** *adv.* —**tax·on'o·mist** *n.*

tax·pay·er (taks'pā'ər) *n.* any person who pays a tax or is subject to taxation

tax rate the percentage of income, property value, etc. assessed as tax

tax stamp a stamp that shows that a tax has been paid

☆**tax title** the title conveyed to the purchaser of property sold for nonpayment of taxes

tax·us (tak'səs) *n.*, *pl.* **tax'us** [ModL. < L., akin ? to Gr. *toxon*, a bow < Scythian **tachša*] *same as* YEW (*n.* 1)

-tax·y (tak'sē) *same as* -TAXIS

Tay (tā) **1.** river in Perth, C Scotland, flowing east into the North Sea: c.120 mi. **2.** Firth of, estuary of this river: 25 mi.

Tay·lor (tā'lər) [after Zachary TAYLOR] city in SE Mich.: suburb of Detroit: pop. 70,000

Tay·lor (tā'lər) **1.** (James) **Bay·ard** (bī'ərd, bā'ärd), 1825–78; U.S. poet, journalist, & translator **2.** **Brook** (brook), 1685–1731; Eng. mathematician **3.** (Joseph) **Deems** (dēmz), 1885–1966; U.S. composer & music critic **4.** **Jeremy**, 1613–67; Eng. bishop & theological writer **5.** **Zachary**, 1784–1850; U.S. general; 12th president of the U.S. (1849–50)

taz·za (tät'sə) *n.* [It. < Ar. *tassa:* see TASS] a shallow, ornamental cup or vase, usually with a pedestal

Tb *Chem.* terbium

TB, T.B., tb, t.b. 1. tubercle bacillus **2.** tuberculosis

t.b. trial balance

T-bar (tē'bär') *n.* ☆a T-shaped bar suspended from a power-driven endless cable, used to pull two skiers at a time uphill as they stand on their skis

Tbi·li·si (t'bi li sē') capital of the Georgian S.S.R., on the Kura River: pop. 823,000

☆**T-bone steak** (tē'bōn') a steak from the short loin, with a T-shaped bone, containing some tenderloin

tbs., tbsp. tablespoon; tablespoons

Tc *Chem.* technetium

tc. tierce; tierces

Tchad (chäd) *Fr. spelling of* CHAD

Tchai·kov·sky (chī kôf'skē), **Peter Il·ich** (il'yich) 1840–93; Russ. composer: also **Pëtr Il·yich Tschai·kow·sky** (pyô'tr' il yēch' chī kôf'skē)

Tchekov *var. sp. of* CHEKHOV: also **Tchekhov**

TD 1. tank destroyer **2.** touchdown: also **td**

T.D. Treasury Department

Te *Chem.* tellurium

tea (tē) *n.* see PLURAL, II, D, 3 [Chin. dial. *t'e*, for Mandarin

ch'a, tea] **1.** a white-flowered, evergreen plant (*Thea sinensis*) of the tea family, grown in China, India, Japan, etc. **2.** its dried and prepared leaves, used to make a beverage **3.** the beverage made by soaking such leaves in boiling water **4.** any of several plants resembling or used as tea **5.** a tealike beverage made from such a plant or from a meat extract [camomile tea, beef tea] **6.** [Chiefly Brit.] a light meal in the late afternoon or the evening at which tea is the usual beverage **7.** a reception or other social gathering in the afternoon, at which tea, coffee, etc. are served ☆**8.** [Slang] marijuana —*adj.* designating a family (Theaceae) of evergreen trees, shrubs, or vines, often with showy flowers, found in warm regions and including the camellias, loblolly bay, and the tea plant

☆**tea bag** a small, porous bag, as of paper, containing tea leaves and used in making an individual cup of tea

☆**tea ball** a hollow, perforated metal ball used to hold tea leaves in making tea

tea·ber·ry (tē′ber′ē) *n., pl.* **-ries 1.** *same as* WINTERGREEN (sense 1) **2.** the berrylike fruit of the wintergreen

tea biscuit any of a variety of crackers or cookies often served with tea

☆**tea cart** a small table on wheels for holding a tea service, extra dishes at a dinner, etc.; serving cart

teach (tēch) *vt.* **taught, teach′ing** [ME. *techen* < OE. *tæcan* < base of *tacn*, a sign, symbol (see TOKEN); basic sense "to show, demonstrate," as in cognate G. *zeigen*] **1.** to show or help to learn how to do something; give instructions to [to *teach* a child how to swim] **2.** to give lessons to (a student, pupil, or class); guide the study of; instruct **3.** to give lessons in (a subject) **4.** to provide with knowledge, insight, etc.; cause to know, understand, etc. [the accident that *taught* her to be careful] —*vi.* to be a teacher, esp. in a school or college —**teach′a·bil′i·ty, teach′a·ble·ness** *n.* —**teach′a·ble** *adj.*

SYN.—**teach** is the basic, inclusive word for the imparting of knowledge or skills and usually connotes some individual attention to the learner [he *taught* her how to skate]; **instruct** implies systematized teaching, usually in some particular subject [she *instructs* in chemistry]; **educate** stresses the development of latent faculties and powers by formal, systematic teaching, esp. in institutions of higher learning [he was *educated* in European universities]; **train** implies the development of a particular faculty or skill, or instruction toward a particular occupation, as by methodical discipline, exercise, etc. [he was *trained* as a mechanic]; **school**, often equivalent to any of the preceding, sometimes specifically connotes a disciplining to endure something difficult [he had to *school* himself to obedience]

Teach (tēch), **Edward** *see* BLACKBEARD

teach·er (tē′chər) *n.* a person who teaches, esp. as a profession; instructor —**teach′er·ship′** *n.*

☆**teach-in** (tēch′in′) *n.* [see TEACH & -IN²] a special, extended meeting, as at a college or university, with lectures, discussion, and debate on a controversial issue, esp. one held to protest against some policy

teach·ing (tē′chiŋ) *n.* **1.** the action of a person who teaches; profession of a teacher **2.** something taught; precept, doctrine, or instruction: *usually in pl.*

☆**teaching fellow** a student in a graduate school under a grant that requires him to perform some teaching duties

☆**teaching machine** a mechanical or computerized device for presenting programmed educational material to a student, to be learned at his own rate of speed by means of a corrective feedback

tea·cup (tē′kup′) *n.* **1.** a cup for drinking tea, etc. **2.** *same as* TEACUPFUL

tea·cup·ful (-fool′) *n., pl.* **-fuls′** as much as a teacup will hold, about four fluid ounces

☆**tea dance** a dance held in the late afternoon, at teatime

tea·house (tē′hous′) *n.* in the Orient, a place where tea and other refreshments are served

teak (tēk) *n.* [Port. *teca* < Malayalam *tēkka*] **1.** a large East Indian tree (*Tectona grandis*) of the verbena family, with white flowers and hard, yellowish-brown wood used for shipbuilding, furniture, etc. **2.** its wood: also **teak′wood′**

tea·ket·tle (tē′ket′'l) *n.* a covered kettle with a spout and handle, for boiling water to make tea, etc.

teal (tēl) *n.* [ME. *tele*, akin to Du. *taling*, MLowG. *telink*, teal] **1.** *pl.* **teals, teal:** see PLURAL, II, D, 1 any of several small, short-necked, freshwater wild ducks (genus *Anas*) of the Old World and N. America **2.** a dark grayish or greenish blue: also **teal blue**

Teale (tēl), **Edwin Way** (wā) 1899– ; U.S. naturalist

team (tēm) *n.* [ME. < OE., offspring, brood, team of draft animals, akin to G. *zaum*, a bridle, rein < base of *tēon*, to draw: for IE. base see TUG] **1.** *a)* [Obs.] progeny, race, or lineage *b)* [Dial.] a brood of young animals, esp. of ducks or pigs **2.** two or more horses, oxen, etc. harnessed to the same vehicle or plow **3.** *a)* two or more draft animals and their vehicle *b)* one draft animal and its vehicle **4.** *a)* a group of people constituting one side in a contest or competition *b)* a group of people working together in a coordinated effort —*vt.* **1.** to harness or yoke together in a team **2.** to haul with a team —*vi.* **1.** to drive a team ☆**2.** to join in cooperative activity (often with *up*) [to

team up on a research project] —*adj.* of or done by a team

team·mate (tēm′māt′) *n.* a fellow member on a team

☆**team·ster** (-stər) *n.* a person whose occupation is driving teams or trucks for hauling loads

☆**team teaching** teaching by several teachers working cooperatively to integrate studies in various subjects for a single group of students

team·work (-wurk′) *n.* ☆**1.** joint action by a group of people, in which individual interests are subordinated to group unity and efficiency; coordinated effort, as of an athletic team **2.** work done by or with a team

tea party a social gathering at which tea is served

tea·pot (tē′pät′) *n.* a pot with a spout, handle, and lid, for brewing and pouring tea

tea·poy (tē′poi) *n.* [Hindi *tipāi* < *tir*, three + Per. *pāi*, foot: sp. infl. by association with *tea*] **1.** a small, three-legged stand **2.** a small table for holding a tea service

tear¹ (ter) *vt.* **tore, torn, tear′ing** [ME. *teren* < OE. *teran*, to rend, akin to G. *zehren*, to destroy, consume < IE. base *der-*, to flay, split, whence Sans. *dar-*, to make burst] **1.** to pull apart or separate into pieces by force; rip or rend (cloth, paper, etc.) **2.** to make or cause by tearing or puncturing [to *tear* a hole in a dress] **3.** to wound by tearing; lacerate [skin *torn* and bruised] **4.** to force apart or divide into factions; disrupt; split [ranks *torn* by dissension] **5.** to divide with doubt, uncertainty, etc.; agitate; torment [a mind *torn* between duty and desire] **6.** to remove by or as by tearing, pulling, etc. (with *up, out, away, off*, etc.) [to *tear* a plant up by its roots, to *tear* oneself away] —*vi.* **1.** to be torn **2.** to move violently or with speed; dash —*n.* **1.** the act of tearing **2.** the result of a tearing; torn place; rent **3.** a violent outburst; rage ☆**4.** [Slang] a carousal; spree —**tear at** to make violent, pulling motions at in an attempt to tear or remove —**tear down 1.** to wreck or demolish (a building, etc.) **2.** to dismantle or take apart [to *tear down* an engine] **3.** to cause to disintegrate **4.** to controvert or disprove (an argument, etc.) point by point —**tear into** [Colloq.] to attack impetuously and, often, devastatingly —**tear′er** *n.*

SYN.—**tear** implies a pulling apart by force, so as to lacerate or leave ragged edges [to *tear* paper wrapping]; **rip** suggests a forcible tearing, especially along a seam or in a straight line [to *rip* a hem]; **rend**, a somewhat literary term, implies a tearing with violence [the tree was *rent* by a bolt of lightning]

tear² (tir) *n.* [ME. *tere* < OE. *tear, teagor*, akin to G. *zähre* < IE. **dakru*, tear, whence L. *lacrima*, tear (cf. LACHRYMAL) < OL. *dacruma*] **1.** a drop of the salty fluid secreted by the lacrimal gland, which serves normally to lubricate the eyeball and in weeping flows from the eye **2.** anything resembling this, as a drop of transparent gum; tearlike mass **3.** [*pl.*] sorrow; grief —*vi.* to shed, or fill with, tears —**in tears** crying; weeping

tear·drop (tir′dräp′) *n.* a tear —*adj.* shaped like a tear

tear·ful (-fəl) *adj.* **1.** in tears; weeping **2.** causing tears; sad —**tear′ful·ly** *adv.* —**tear′ful·ness** *n.*

tear gas (tir) a volatile liquid or gas that causes irritation of the eyes, a heavy flow of tears, and temporary blindness: used as in warfare or by the police —**tear′-gas′** *vt.* **-gassed′, -gas′sing**

tear·ing (ter′iŋ) *adj.* violent; impetuous; rushing

☆**tear-jerk·er** (tir′jur′kər) *n.* [Slang] a play, motion picture, etc. that is sad or sentimental in a very maudlin way —**tear′-jerk′ing** *adj.*

tear·less (tir′lis) *adj.* **1.** without tears; not weeping **2.** unable to weep —**tear′less·ly** *adv.* —**tear′less·ness** *n.*

tea·room (tē′rōōm′) *n.* a restaurant that serves tea, coffee, light lunches, etc. and caters chiefly to women

tea rose 1. a species of rose (*Rosa odorata*) having a sweet scent: it is native to China but is the parent of a class known as hybrid tea roses **2.** a yellowish-pink color

☆**tear sheet** (ter) a sheet torn, or taken in unbound form, from a publication for special distribution

tear·y (tir′ē) *adj.* **tear′i·er, tear′i·est 1.** tearful; crying **2.** of or like tears —**tear′i·ly** *adv.* —**tear′i·ness** *n.*

Teas·dale (tēz′dāl), **Sara** 1884–1933; U.S. poet

tease (tēz) *vt.* **teased, teas′ing** [ME. *tesen* < OE. *tæsan*, to pull about, pluck, tease, akin to Du. *teezen* < IE. **di-s* < base **dā(i)-*, to part, cut apart, tear out] **1.** *a)* to separate the fibers of; card or comb (flax, wool, etc.) *b)* to fluff (the hair) by brushing or combing in strokes from the hair ends toward the scalp *c)* to shred or pull apart (tissues, etc.) for microscopic examination **2.** to raise a nap on (cloth) by brushing with teasels; teasel **3.** to annoy or harass by persistent mocking or poking fun, playful fooling, etc. **4.** to urge persistently; beg; importune **5.** *a)* to tantalize *b)* to excite sexually in a coquettish, unfulfilling way —*vi.* to indulge in teasing —*n.* **1.** a teasing or being teased **2.** a person who teases —**SYN.** see ANNOY —**teas′ing·ly** *adv.*

tea·sel (tē′z'l) *n.* [ME. *tasel* < OE. *tæsel* < base of *tæsan*, to TEASE] **1.** any of a genus (*Dipsacus*) of bristly plants of the teasel family, with prickly, cylindrical heads of yellowish or purplish flowers; esp., the **fuller's teasel** (*Dipsacus fullonum*) with flower heads having sharp, spinelike bracts **2.** a flower head of the fuller's teasel,

used when dried for raising a nap on cloth 3. any device for raising a nap on cloth —*adj.* designating a family (Dipsaceae) of plants bearing dense flower heads covered with stiff bracts, including scabiosa and teasel —*vt.* -seled or -selled, -sel·ing or -sel·ling to raise a nap on (cloth) by means of teasels —**tea′sel·er, tea′sel·ler** *n.*

teas·er (tē′zər) *n.* 1. a person or thing that teases 2. an annoying or puzzling problem

tea service a set, as of china or silver, for serving tea, including a teapot, creamer, sugar bowl, etc.

tea·spoon (tē′spoon′) *n.* 1. a spoon for stirring tea, coffee, etc. and eating some soft foods 2. *same as* TEASPOONFUL

tea·spoon·ful (-fool′) *n., pl.* -fuls′ as much as a teaspoon will hold; 1/3 tablespoonful (1 1/3 fluid drams)

teat (tēt, tit) *n.* [ME. *tete* < OFr. < Gmc. base akin to OE. *tit:* see TIT²] 1. the small protuberance on a breast or udder, through which the milk passes in suckling the young; nipple 2. any small projection like a teat

tea·ta·ble (tē′tā′b'l) *adj.* like that of people at a tea [*tea-table* talk]

tea table a small table at which tea, etc. is taken

tea·tast·er (-tās′tər) *n.* a person whose work is tasting tea for grading

tea·time (-tīm′) *n.* the time of day, esp. late afternoon, when some people customarily have tea, etc.

tea tray a tray for carrying cups, plates, spoons, etc. in serving tea or other light refreshment

tea wagon *same as* TEA CART

tea·zel, tea·zle (tē′z'l) *n., vt. same as* TEASEL

Te·bet, Te·beth (tā vāt′, tā′vəs) *n.* [Heb.] the fourth month of the Jewish year: see JEWISH CALENDAR

tech. 1. technical 2. technically 3. technology

tech·ne·ti·um (tek nē′shē əm) *n.* [ModL. < Gr. < *technasthai,* contrive by art < *technē* (see TECHNIC) + -IUM] a silver-gray, metallic chemical element obtained by the irradiation of molybdenum with deuterons and in the fission of uranium: technetium does not exist in nature and all its isotopes are radioactive: it is a superconductor and inhibitor of metal corrosion: symbol, Tc; at. wt., 97(?); at. no., 43; sp. gr., 11.5; melt. pt., 2200°C

☆**tech·ne·tron·ic** (tek′nə trän′ik) *adj.* [TECHN(OLOGY) + E(LEC)TRONIC] characterized by the application of technology and electronics to the solution of social, political, and economic problems [a *technetronic* society]

tech·nic (tek′nik; *for n.* 1, *also* tek nēk′) *adj.* [Gr. *technikos* < *technē,* an art, artifice < IE. base *tekth-,* to weave, build, join, whence Gr. *tektōn,* a carpenter, L. *texere,* to weave, build] *same as* TECHNICAL —*n.* 1. *same as* TECHNIQUE 2. [*pl.,* with *sing.* or *pl. v.*] the study or principles of an art or of the arts, esp. the practical arts

tech·ni·cal (tek′ni k'l) *adj.* [prec. + -AL] 1. having to do with the practical, industrial, or mechanical arts or the applied sciences [a *technical* school] 2. of, used or skilled in, or peculiar to a specific science, art, profession, craft, etc.; specialized [*technical* vocabulary] 3. of, in, or showing technique [*technical* skill] 4. in terms of some science, art, etc.; according to principles or rules [a *technical* difference] 5. concerned with or making use of technicalities or minute, formal points 6. *Finance* designating or of a market in which stock prices are sharply affected by short-run, speculative considerations [*technical* rally] —**tech′ni·cal·ly** *adv.*

tech·ni·cal·i·ty (tek′nə kal′ə tē) *n., pl.* -ties 1. the state or quality of being technical 2. the use of technical terms, methods, etc. 3. a point, detail, term, method, etc. of or peculiar to an art, science, code, or skill, esp. one that only a technical expert would likely be aware of 4. a minute formal point, detail, etc. brought to bear upon a main issue [convicted on a *technicality*]

technical knockout *Boxing* a victory won when the opponent, though not knocked out, is so badly hurt that the referee stops the match

☆**technical sergeant** 1. *U.S. Army* formerly, the second grade of enlisted man (now *sergeant first class*) 2. *U.S. Air Force* the second grade of enlisted man, ranking just below master sergeant 3. *U.S. Marine Corps* formerly, the second grade of enlisted man (now *staff sergeant*)

tech·ni·cian (tek nish′ən) *n.* 1. a person skilled in the technicalities of some subject; technical expert 2. an artist, writer, musician, etc. who has great technical skill or knowledge ☆3. *U.S. Army* formerly, any of several ranks of enlisted man

☆**Tech·ni·col·or** (tek′ni kul′ər) *a trademark for* a process of making color motion pictures by combining several separate, synchronized films each of which is sensitive to a single color —*n.* [t-] 1. this process 2. bright, intense colors —**tech′ni·col′ored** *adj.*

tech·nique (tek nēk′) *n.* [Fr. < Gr. *technikos:* see TECHNIC] 1. the method of procedure (with reference to practical or formal details), or way of using basic skills, in rendering an artistic work or carrying out a scientific or mechanical operation 2. the degree of expertness in following this [a pianist with good *technique* but poor expression] 3. any method or manner of accomplishing something

tech·no- (tek′nō, -nə) [< Gr. *technē:* see TECHNIC] *a combining form meaning:* 1. art, science, skill [*technography*] 2. technical, technological [*technocracy*]

☆**tech·noc·ra·cy** (tek näk′rə sē) *n.* [TECHNO- + -CRACY] government by technicians; specif., the theory or doctrine

of a proposed system of government in which all economic resources, and hence the entire social system, would be controlled by scientists and engineers —**tech′no·crat′** (-nə krat′) *n.* —**tech′no·crat′ic** *adj.*

tech·nog·ra·phy (tek näg′rə fē) *n.* [TECHNO- + -GRAPHY] the description or study of arts and applied sciences as they developed historically

tech·no·log·i·cal (tek′nə läj′i k'l) *adj.* 1. of or having to do with technology 2. due to developments in technology; resulting from technical progress in the use of machinery and automation in industry, agriculture, etc. [*technological* productivity, *technological* unemployment] Also **tech′no·log′ic** —**tech′no·log′i·cal·ly** *adv.*

tech·nol·o·gy (tek näl′ə jē) *n.* [Gr. *technologia,* systematic treatment: see TECHNIC & -LOGY] 1. the science or study of the practical or industrial arts, applied sciences, etc. 2. the terms used in a science, art, etc.; technical terminology 3. applied science 4. a method, process, etc. for handling a specific technical problem 5. the system by which a society provides its members with those things needed or desired

tech·y (tech′ē) *adj.* **tech′i·er, tech′i·est** [LME. *teche,* a quality, mark < ?] *var. of* TETCHY

tec·ton·ic (tek tän′ik) *adj.* [LL. *tectonicus* < Gr. *tektonikos* < *tektōn,* a carpenter, builder: see TECHNIC] 1. of or having to do with building; constructional 2. architectural 3. designating, of, or pertaining to changes in the structure of the earth's crust, the forces responsible for such deformation, or the external forms produced

tec·ton·ics (-iks) *n.pl.* [*with sing. v.*] [see prec.] 1. the constructive arts in general; esp., the art of making things that have both beauty and usefulness 2. *Geol.* the study of the earth's crustal structure and the forces that produce changes in it

tec·ton·ism (tek′tən iz'm) *n. same as* DIASTROPHISM

tec·trix (tek′triks) *n., pl.* **-tri·ces** (-tri sēz′) [ModL., fem. of L. *tector,* one who covers < *tectus,* pp. of *tegere,* to cover] a wing covert of a bird

tec·tum (tek′təm) *n., pl.* **tec′ta** (-tə) [ModL. < L., a roof < *tectus,* pp. of *tegere,* to cover] *Anat., Zool.* a rooflike structure or covering —**tec′tal** *adj.*

Te·cum·seh (ti kum′sə) 1768?–1813; chief of the Shawnee Indians: attempted to unite the W Indian tribes

ted (ted) *vt.* **ted′ded, ted′ding** [ME. *tedden,* prob. < ON. *tethja,* to spread manure: for IE. base see TEASE] to spread or scatter (newly cut grass) for drying as hay —**ted′der** *n.*

☆**ted·dy** (ted′ē) *n., pl.* **-dies** [prob. < the nickname *Teddy*] [*usually pl.*] a woman's one-piece undergarment, worn esp. in the 1920's, consisting of a chemise top combined with loose-fitting panties

☆**teddy bear** [after *Teddy,* nickname for Theodore ROOSEVELT: first used (1902) after a cartoon by C. K. Berryman, containing a small cub in jocular allusion to his fondness for big-game hunting] a child's stuffed toy made to look like a bear cub

Teddy boy [< *Teddy,* nickname for *Edward*] a British delinquent youth of the 1960's, esp. one wearing clothes of a dandified Edwardian style

Te De·um (tē dē′əm, tā dā′oom) [ME. < LL.(Ec.)] 1. an old Christian hymn beginning *Te Deum laudamus* (We praise thee, O God) 2. music for this hymn 3. a service of thanksgiving at which this hymn is featured

te·di·ous (tē′dē əs, tē′jəs) *adj.* [ME. < LL. *taediosus*] full of tedium; long or verbose and wearisome; tiresome; boring —**te′di·ous·ly** *adv.* —**te′di·ous·ness** *n.*

te·di·um (-dē əm) *n.* [L. *taedium* < *taedet,* it disgusts, offends] the condition or quality of being tiresome, wearisome, boring, or monotonous; tediousness

tee¹ (tē) *n., pl.* **tees** 1. the letter T, t 2. anything shaped like a T —*adj.* shaped like a T —**to a tee** exactly; precisely

tee² (tē) *n.* [< prec.: the mark was orig. T-shaped] a mark aimed at in quoits, curling, etc.

tee³ (tē) *n.* [prob. contr. < Scot. dial. *teaz* (< ?), but now associated with prec. in form and sense] 1. *a)* a small, cone-shaped mound as of sand, on which a golf ball was formerly placed to be driven *b)* a small, pointed holder of wood, plastic, etc. now used to hold the ball *c)* the place at each hole from which a player makes his first stroke ☆2. a device on which a football is positioned for a kickoff —*vt., vi.* **teed, tee′ing** to place (a ball) on a tee —**tee off** 1. to play a golf ball from a tee 2. to begin; start ☆3. [Slang] to make angry or disgusted

tee-hee (tē′hē′) *interj., n.* [ME.: echoic] the sound of a titter or snicker —*vi.* **-heed′, -hee′ing** to titter or snicker

teel (tēl) *n.* [< Hindi *til* < Sans. *tila*] 1. *same as* SESAME 2. the oil of sesame seed

teem¹ (tēm) *vi.* [ME. *temen* < OE. *tieman,* to produce, bear < base of *team,* progeny: see TEAM] 1. orig., to produce offspring; bear 2. to be full, as though ready to bring forth young; abound; swarm [a river *teeming* with fish]

teem² (tēm) *vt.* [ME. *temen* < ON. *tœma,* to empty] to empty; pour out —*vi.* to pour [a *teeming* rain]

teen¹ (tēn) *n.* [see -TEEN] 1. [*pl.*] the years from thirteen through nineteen (of a century or a person's age) 2. *same as* TEEN-AGER —*adj. same as* TEEN-AGE

teen² (tēn) *n.* [ME. *tene* < OE. *teona,* akin to OFris. *tiona,* ON. *tjōn,* injury < IE. base *du-,* to injure, destroy, whence Sans. *dū,* pain] [Archaic or Dial.] 1. injury or harm 2. anger; wrath 3. grief or suffering

-teen (tēn) [ME. -tene < OE. -tene, -tyne, inflected form of tien, TEN] a suffix meaning ten and: used to form the cardinal numbers from thirteen to nineteen

teen-age (tēn'āj') adj. 1. in one's teens 2. of, characteristic of, or for persons in their teens Also **teen'age'**

☆**teen-ag-er** (-āj'ər) n. a person in his teens

tee-ny (tē'nē) adj. -ni-er, -ni-est colloq. var. of TINY: also **teen'sy**

☆**teen-y-bop-per** (-bäp'ər) n. [TEEN¹ + -Y¹ + BOP² + -ER] [Slang] a young teen-ager, esp. a girl, of the 1960's, following the latest fads, esp. in imitation of hippies

tee-ny-wee-ny (-wē'nē) adj. [Colloq.] very small; tiny: a facetious imitation of child's talk: also **teen·sy·ween·sy** (tēn'sē wēn'sē)

☆**tee-pee** (tē'pē) n. alt. sp. of TEPEE

Tees (tēz) river in N England, flowing into the North Sea: 70 mi.

☆**tee shirt** same as T-SHIRT

tee-ter (tēt'ər) vi. [dial. titter < ME. titeren < ON. titra, to tremble, akin to G. zittern < redupl. of IE. base *drā-, to step: cf. TRAP¹, TRIP] to totter, wobble, waver, etc. —vt. to cause to teeter —n. clipped form of TEETER-TOTTER

☆**tee-ter-board** (-bôrd') n. same as SEESAW

tee-ter-tot-ter (-tät'ər, -tôt'-) n., vi. same as SEESAW

teeth (tēth) n. pl. of TOOTH: for phrases, see TOOTH

teethe (tēth) vi. teethed, teeth'ing [ME. tethen < tethe, teeth] to grow teeth; cut one's teeth

☆**teeth·ing ring** (tē'thiŋ) a ring of ivory, plastic, rubber, etc. for teething babies to bite on

teeth·ridge (tēth'rij') n. the ridge of gum along the inside of the upper front teeth

tee-to-tal (tē tōt''l, tē'tōt''l) adj. [formed by redupl., for emphasis, of initial letter of TOTAL] 1. [Colloq.] entire; complete 2. of or advocating teetotalism —**tee·to'tal·er, tee·to'tal·ler** n. —**tee·to'tal·ly** adv.

tee-to-tal-ism (-iz'm) n. [see prec.] the principle or practice of never drinking any alcoholic liquor —**tee·to'tal·ist** n.

tee-to-tum (tē tōt'əm) n. [earlier T totum < the T (for totum) marked on one side + totum, the name of the toy < L. totum, neut. of totus (see TOTAL): the four sides were orig. marked T (totum, all), A (au/er, take), D (depone, put), N (nihil, nothing)] a kind of top spun with the fingers, esp. one with four, lettered sides used in a game of chance

☆**Tef·lon** (tef'län) [< (poly)te(tra)fl(uoroethylene) + -on, arbitrary suffix for synthetic products] a trademark for an inert, tough, insoluble polymer, used in making non-sticking coatings, as for cookware, and in gaskets, bearings, electrical insulators, etc.

teg·men (teg'mən) n., pl. teg'mi·na (-mi nə) [L. < tegere, to cover: see THATCH] 1. a covering; integument 2. Bot. the inner coat of a seed 3. Zool. a) a beetle elytron b) a hardened forewing in some insects —**teg'mi·nal** adj.

Te·gu·ci·gal·pa (te gōō'sē gäl'pä) capital of Honduras, in the SC part: pop. 191,000

teg·u·lar (teg'yoo lər) adj. [< L. tegula, a tile < tegere, to cover (see THATCH)] 1. of or like a tile or tiles 2. arranged like tiles —**teg'u·lar·ly** adv.

teg·u·ment (teg'yoo mənt) n. [L. tegumentum < tegere, to cover: see THATCH] same as INTEGUMENT —**teg'u·men'tal** (-men't'l), **teg'u·men'ta·ry** (-tə rē) adj.

tc-hee (tē'hē') inter., n., vi. -heed', -hee'ing var. of TEE-HEE

Teh·ran, Te·he·ran (te hrän'; E. te ə rän', -ran') capital of Iran, in the NC part: pop. 2,803,000

Te·huan·te·pec (te wän'tə pek', -wän'tə pek') 1. Gulf of, arm of the Pacific, off the S coast of Mexico: c.300 mi. wide 2. Isthmus of, narrowest part of Mexico, between this gulf & the Gulf of Campeche: c.125 mi. wide

Te·huel·che (te wel'che) n., pl. -ches, -che [native word, lit., southeast, but said of northern Patagonian natives] any member of the dominant aboriginal people of Patagonia, known for their tallness

Tei·de (tā'the), **Pi·co de** (pē'kō the) volcanic mountain on Tenerife, Canary Islands: c.12,200 ft.

te ig·i·tur (tā ij'ə toor') [LL.(Ec.), thee therefore] R.C.Ch. the opening words of the Canon of the Mass

Teil·hard de Char·din (te yàr' də shàr dan'), **Pierre** 1881-1955; Fr. paleontologist, geologist, & philosopher

Te·jo (te'zhoo) Port. name of TAGUS River

☆**tek·tite** (tek'tīt) n. [< Gr. tēktos, molten (< lēkein, to melt < IE. base *tā-, whence THAW) + -ITE¹] any of certain small, dark green to black glassy bodies of various shapes, found esp. in areas of the East Indies, Australia, N. America, C Europe, and E Africa, and assumed to have originated in outer space

tel (tel) n. var. of TELL²

tel- (tel) same as: 1. TELE-. 2. TELO-²

tel. 1. telegram 2. telegraph 3. telephone

tel·a·mon (tel'ə män') n., pl. tel'a·mo'nes (-mō'nēz) [L. < Gr. telamōn, bearer < telassai, to bear: for IE. base see TOLERATE] Archit. a supporting column in the form of a man's figure: see also ATLANTES, CARYATID

tel·an·gi·ec·ta·sis (tel an'jē ek'tə sis) n., pl. -ses (-sēz) [ModL. < Gr. telos, an end (see TELO-²) + angeion, receptacle (see ANGIO-) + ektasis, extension, dilatation] Med.

chronic dilatation of capillaries and small arterial branches, producing small, reddish tumors in the skin, as of the face, thighs, etc.: also **tel·an'gi·ec·ta'sia** (-ek tā'zhə, -zhē ə) —**tel·an'gi·ec·tat'ic** (-tat'ik) adj.

☆**Tel·Au·to·graph** (tel ôt'ə graf', -gräf') [< TEL(E)- + AUTOGRAPH] a trademark for an apparatus for transmitting writing, pictures, etc.: it produces facsimiles at the receiving end by means of an electrically controlled pen that makes the same motions as the transmitting pen —n. (written **telautograph**) this apparatus

Tel A·viv-Jaf·fa (tel' ä vēv'yäf'ə, tel' ə vēv'jaf'ə) seaport in W Israel, incorporating the former cities of Tel Aviv & Jaffa: pop. 394,000: usually called **Tel Aviv**

tel·e- (tel'ə, -i) a combining form meaning: 1. [Gr. tēle- < tēle, far off < IE. base *kwel-, distant, remote, whence W. pell, distant] at, over, from, or to a distance [telegraph] 2. [< TELE(VISION)] of, in, or by television [telecast]

tel·e·cast (tel'ə kast', -käst') vt., vi. -cast' or -cast'ed, -cast'ing [TELE- + (BROAD)CAST] to broadcast by television —n. a television broadcast —**tel'e·cast'er** n.

tel·e·com·mu·ni·ca·tion (tel'ə kə myōō'nə kā'shən) n. [also pl., with sing. or pl. v.] communication by radio, telephone, telegraph, television, etc.

☆**tel·e·course** (tel'ə kôrs') n. a course of televised lectures offered for credit by a college or other school

tel·e·du (tel'ə dōō') n. [Malay teledu] a small, flesh-eating, badger-like, burrowing mammal (Mydaus javanensis), that ejects a vile-smelling fluid when molested: native to Java, Borneo, and Sumatra

teleg. 1. telegram 2. telegraph 3. telegraphy

tel·e·gen·ic (tel'ə jen'ik) adj. [TELE- + -GENIC] that looks or is likely to look attractive on television: said esp. of persons

tel·eg·o·ny (tə leg'ə nē) n. [G. telegonie: see TELE- & -GONY] the supposed transmission of characters of one sire to offspring subsequently born to other sires by the same female —**tel·e·gon·ic** (tel'ə gän'ik) adj.

☆**tel·e·gram** (tel'ə gram') n. [TELE- + -GRAM] a message transmitted by telegraph

tel·e·graph (tel'ə graf', -gräf') n. [Fr. télégraphe: see TELE- & -GRAPH: orig. used of a semaphore] 1. orig., any signaling apparatus 2. an apparatus or system for transmitting messages by electric impulses sent through a wire or converted into radio waves: orig., Morse code signals were produced by the closing and opening of an electric circuit by a key, but are now sent chiefly by high-frequency radio or teletypewriter —vt. 1. to send (a message) by telegraph 2. to send a telegram to 3. [Colloq.] to signal (an intended action, decision, etc.) unintentionally to another, as by a gesture or look —vi. to send a telegram —**te·leg·ra·pher** (tə leg'rə fər), **te·leg·ra·phist** n.

tel·e·graph·ic (tel'ə graf'ik) adj. 1. of or transmitted by telegraph 2. in the concise style of a telegram —**tel'e·graph'i·cal·ly** adv.

telegraph plant a tick trefoil (Desmodium gyrans) of tropical Asia: so called because the two lateral leaflets of each leaf move like a railroad semaphore signal

te·leg·ra·phy (tə leg'rə fē) n. 1. the operation of telegraph apparatus or the study of this 2. the transmission of messages by telegraph

tel·e·ki·ne·sis (tel'ə ki nē'sis) n. [ModL. < tele-, TELE- + Gr. kinēsis, motion < kinein, to move] Parapsychology the apparent initiation of movement in an object, as by a medium in spiritualism, without perceptible mechanical or other means —**tel'e·ki·net'ic** (-net'ik) adj.

Te·lem·a·chus (tə lem'ə kəs) [L. < Gr. Tēlemachos] Gr. Legend the son of Odysseus and Penelope, who helped his father slay his mother's suitors

Te·le·mann (tā'lə män'), **Ge·org Phi·lipp** (gā ôrk' fē'lip) 1681-1767; Ger. composer

tel·e·mark (tel'ə märk') n. [after Telemark, region in S Norway] Skiing a slow turning movement in which the outer ski is advanced and turned in at a widening angle until the turn is accomplished

tel·e·me·ter (tel'ə mēt'ər, te lem'ə tər) n. [TELE- + -METER] 1. an instrument for determining the distance of an object remote from the observer; range finder 2. any device for measuring physical phenomena, as temperature, radiation, etc., at some remote point and transmitting, esp. by radio, the values obtained to a distant indicator, recorder, or observer: used in rockets, space studies, etc. —vt., vi. to transmit by telemeter —**tel'e·met'ric** (-met'rik) adj. —**tel'e·met'ri·cal·ly** adv. —**te·lem·e·try** (tə lem'ə trē) n.

tel·en·ceph·a·lon (tel'en sef'ə län') n., pl. -la (-lə) [ModL.: see TELE- & ENCEPHALON] the most anterior part of the forebrain, including the cerebral hemispheres and olfactory lobes —**tel'en·ce·phal'ic** (-sə fal'ik) adj.

te·le·ol·o·gy (tē'lē äl'ə jē, tel'ē-) n. [ModL. teleologia < Gr. telos, teleos, an end (see TELO-) + -logia (see -LOGY)] 1. the study of final causes 2. the fact or quality of being directed toward a definite end or of having an ultimate purpose, esp. as attributed to natural processes 3. a) a belief, as that of vitalism, that natural phenomena are determined not only by mechanical causes but by an

overall design or purpose in nature b) the study of evidence for this belief 4. *Ethics* the evaluation of conduct, as in utilitarianism, in relation to the end or ends it serves — **te′le·o·log′i·cal** (-ə läj′i k'l) *adj.* —**te′le·ol′o·gist** n.

tel·e·ost (tel′ē äst′, tē′lē-). n. [< Gr. *teleos*, complete < *telos* (see TELO-¹) + *osteon*, bone] any of a large subclass of bony fishes (Neopterygii or Teleostei) including most fishes extant, usually with a symmetrical tail fin and an air bladder —*adj.* of or belonging to the teleosts Also **tel′e·os′te·an** (-äs′tē ən)

te·lep·a·thy (tə lep′ə thē) n. [TELE- + -PATHY: coined (1882) by F. W. Myers (1843–1901), Eng. writer] supposed communication between minds by some means other than the normal sensory channels; transference of thought —**tel·e·path·ic** (tel′ə path′ik) *adj.* —**tel′e·path′i·cal·ly** *adv.* —**te·lep′a·thist** n.

tel·e·phone (tel′ə fōn′) n. [TELE- + -PHONE: term adopted by Bell (1876) after use for other sound instruments] ☆an instrument or system for conveying speech over distances by converting sound into electric impulses sent through a wire wholly or in part: it consists of a transmitter and receiver, often with a dialing mechanism for connecting lines —☆*vi.* -**phoned′**, -**phon′ing** to talk over a telephone; convey a message by telephone —*vt.* **1.** to convey (a message) by telephone **2.** to speak to or reach (a person) by telephone; call —**tel′e·phon′er** n. —**tel′e·phon′ic** (-fän′ik) *adj.* —**tel′e·phon′i·cal·ly** *adv.*

☆**telephone book** a book in which are listed alphabetically the names of persons, businesses, etc. having telephones in a specified area, along with their addresses and telephone numbers: also **telephone directory**

☆**telephone booth** a booth in a public place containing a telephone, usually operated by inserting coins

☆**telephone receiver** *see* RECEIVER (sense 2 b)

tel·e·phon·ist (tel′ə fōn′ist, tə lef′ə nist) n. [Chiefly Brit.] a telephone switchboard operator

te·leph·o·ny (tə lef′ə nē) n. **1.** the science of telephonic transmission **2.** the making or operation of telephones

tel·e·pho·to (tel′ə fōt′ō) *adj.* **1.** *same as* TELEPHOTOGRAPHIC **2.** designating or of a compound lens that produces a large image of a distant object in a camera of ordinary focal length —[T-] *a trademark for* a telephotograph (sense 2) or a system of telephotography

tel·e·pho·to·graph (tel′ə fōt′ə graf′, -gräf′) n. **1.** a photograph taken with a telephoto lens **2.** a photograph transmitted by telephotography —*vt.*, *vi.* **1.** to take (photographs) with a telephoto lens **2.** to transmit (photographs) by telephotography

tel·e·pho·tog·ra·phy (tel′ə fə täg′rə fē) n. **1.** the art or process of photographing distant objects by using a telephoto lens **2.** the science or process of transmitting photographs over distances by converting light rays into electric signals which are sent over wire or radio channels: the receiver converts the electric signals back into light rays to which a photographic film is exposed —**tel′e·pho′to·graph′ic** (-fōt′ə graf′ik) *adj.*

☆**tel·e·play** (tel′ə plā′) n. a play written for, or produced on, television

tel·e·por·ta·tion (tel′ə pôr tā′shən) n. [TELE- + (TRANS)PORTATION] the theoretical transportation of matter through space by converting it into energy and then reconverting it at the terminal point —**tel′e·port′** *vt.*

tel·e·print·er (tel′ə prin′tər) n. *chiefly Brit.* term for TELETYPEWRITER

☆**Tel·e·Promp·Ter** (-prämp′tər) *a trademark for* an electronic device that, unseen by the audience, unrolls a prepared speech, script, etc. line by line, as a prompting aid to a speaker or actor on television —n. (written **teleprompter**) this device

☆**tel·e·ran** (-ran′) n. [*tele*(vision) *r*(adar) *a*(ir) *n*(avigation)] an electronic aid to aerial navigation by which data received by radar, maps of the terrain, etc. are transmitted to aircraft by television

tel·e·scope (-skōp′) n. [It. *telescopio* (Galileo, 1611) < ModL. *telescopium* < Gr. *tēleskopos*, seeing from a distance: see TELE- & -SCOPE] an instrument for making distant objects, as the stars, appear nearer and consequently larger: it consists of a tube or series of tubes containing combinations of lenses and is of two types, *refracting*, in which the image is focused on a lens, and *reflecting*, in which the image is focused on a concave mirror —*adj.* having parts that slide one inside another —*vi.* -**scoped′**, -**scop′ing** to slide or be forced one into another like the concentric tubes of a small, collapsible telescope —*vt.* **1.** to cause to telescope **2.** to condense; shorten

DIAGRAM OF REFRACTING TELESCOPE
(A, image; B, final image; C, objective; D, eyepiece; E, light from bottom of object; F, light from top of object)

tel·e·scop·ic (tel′ə skäp′ik) *adj.* **1.** of a telescope or telescopes **2.** seen or obtained by a telescope **3.** visible only with the aid of a telescope **4.** having distant vision; farseeing **5.** having sections that slide one inside another

[a *telescopic* drinking tumbler] Also **tel′e·scop′i·cal** —**tel′e·scop′i·cal·ly** *adv.*

te·les·co·py (tə les′kə pē) n. the art or practice of using a telescope —**te·les′co·pist** n.

☆**tel·e·sis** (tel′ə sis) n. [ModL. < Gr. *telein*, to fulfill, complete < *telos*, an end: see TELO-²] the purposeful use of natural and social forces; planned progress

tel·e·spec·tro·scope (tel′ə spek′trə skōp′) n. an instrument combining a telescope and a spectroscope, for producing the spectra of stars, etc.

tel·es·the·si·a (tel′əs thē′zhə, -zē ə) n. [ModL.: see TELE- & ESTHESIA] extrasensory perception of distant objects, events, etc. —**tel′es·thet′ic** (-thet′ik) *adj.*

te·les·tich, te·les·tic (tə les′tik, tel′ə stik′) n. [< Gr. *telos*, an end (see TELO-²) + *stichos*, a line, after ACROSTIC] a short poem, etc. in which the last letters of the lines spell a word or words when taken in order: cf. ACROSTIC

☆**tel·e·thon** (tel′ə thän′) n. [TELE(VISION) + (MARA)THON] a lengthy telecast, as to raise funds for charity, promote a politician, etc.

☆**Tel·e·type** (tel′ə tīp′) *a trademark for* a form of teletypewriter —n. [*often* t-] communication by means of Teletype —*vt.*, *vi.* -**typed′**, -**typ′ing** [*often* t-] to send (messages) by Teletype —**tel′e·typ′er, tel′e·typ′ist** n.

☆**Tel·e·type·set·ter** (tel′ə tīp′set′ər) *a trademark for* a telegraphic apparatus that activates a typesetting machine with a keyboard by means of perforated tape —n. [t-] such an apparatus

☆**tel·e·type·writ·er** (tel′ə tīp′rīt′ər) n. a form of telegraph in which the receiver prints messages typed on the keyboard (like that of a typewriter) of the transmitter: the striking of the keys produces electrical impulses that cause the corresponding keys on the receiver to register

te·leu·to·spore (tə lōōt′ə spôr′) n. [< Gr. *teleutē*, completion, end < *telos*, end (see TELEOLOGY) + SPORE] *same as* TELIOSPORE —**te·leu′to·spor′ic** *adj.*

tel·e·view (tel′ə vyōō′) *vt.*, *vi.* to view or watch (a performance, event, etc.) by television —**tel′e·view′er** n.

tel·e·vise (-vīz′) *vt.*, *vi.* -**vised′**, -**vis′ing** to transmit by television —**tel′e·vis′or** n.

tel·e·vi·sion (-vizh′ən) n. [TELE- + VISION] **1.** the practice or science of transmitting scenes or views by radio or, sometimes, by wire: the television transmitter, by means of a camera tube, such as an image orthicon or vidicon, converts light rays into electric signals for modulation upon a radio carrier wave or for transmission over wires; the television receiver reconverts the signals into electron beams that are projected against the fluorescent screen of the kinescope, or picture tube, reproducing the original image **2.** a) broadcasting by television as an industry, entertainment, art, etc. b) all the facilities and related activities of such broadcasting **3.** a television receiving set —*adj.* of, using, used in, or sent by television —**tel′e·vi′sion·al, tel′e·vi′sion·al·ly** *adv.*

tel·ex (tel′eks) n. [TEL(ETYPEWRITER) + EX(CHANGE)] **1.** a teletypewriter using a telephone dial to establish connections **2.** a message sent in this way —*vt.* to send (a message) by telex

tel·fer (tel′fər) n., *vt. same as* TELPHER

te·li·al (tē′lē əl, tel′ē-) *adj.* **1.** of a telium **2.** designating or of the final stage in the life cycle of the rust fungi

te·lic (tē′lik, tel′ik) *adj.* [Gr. *telikos* < *telos*, an end: see TELO-²] directed toward an end; purposeful

te·li·o·spore (tē′lē ə spôr′, tel′ē ə-) n. [< TELIUM + SPORE] a thick-walled resting spore that develops in the late summer during the telial stage of the rust fungi and germinates the following spring —**te′li·o·spor′ic** *adj.*

te·li·um (tē′lē əm, tel′ē-) n., *pl.* -**li·a** (-ə) [ModL. < Gr. *teleios*, complete < Gr. *telos*, an end: see TELO-²] the teliospore-bearing sorus of the rust fungi

tell¹ (tel) *vt.* **told, tell′ing** [ME. *tellen* < OE. *tellan*, lit., to calculate, reckon < Gmc. **taljan*, whence G. *zählen*, to reckon, count: for IE. base see TALE] **1.** orig., to enumerate; count; reckon **2.** to relate in order; narrate; recount [to *tell* a story] **3.** to express in spoken or written words; utter; say [tell the facts, *tell* the truth] **4.** to report; announce; publish **5.** to reveal; disclose; make known [a smile that *told* her joy] **6.** to recognize; distinguish; discriminate [unable to *tell* one from the other] **7.** to decide; know [one can't *tell* what will happen] **8.** to let know; inform; acquaint [tell me about the game] **9.** to request; direct; order; command [tell him to leave] **10.** to state emphatically; assure [it's there, I *tell* you] —*vi.* **1.** to give an account or description (of something) **2.** to give evidence or be an indication (of something) **3.** to carry tales; reveal secrets [to kiss and *tell*] **4.** to produce a result; be effective; have a marked effect [efforts that are beginning to *tell*] —**tell off 1.** to count (persons, etc.) and separate from the total number **2.** [Colloq.] to rebuke severely —**tell on 1.** to tire; wear out **2.** [Colloq.] to inform against or gossip about

SYN.—**tell**, in this connection, is the simple, general word meaning to convey the facts or details of some circumstance or occurrence [tell me what happened]; **relate** suggests the orderly telling of something that one has personally experienced or witnessed [relate your dream to us]; **recount** implies the telling of events in consecutive order and in elaborate detail and, hence, often takes a plural object [to *recount* one's adventures]; **narrate** suggests the use of the techniques of fiction, such as plot development,

building up to a climax, etc. *[to narrate the story of one's life]*; **report** suggests the recounting for others' information of something that one has investigated or witnessed *[he will report the convention proceedings]* See also REVEAL[1]

tell[2] (tel) *n.* *[Ar. tall, a mound]* *Archaeol.* an artificial mound or hill covering the successive remains of ancient communities

Tell (tel), **William** in Swiss legend, a hero in the fight for independence from Austria, forced, on pain of death, to shoot an apple off his son's head with bow and arrow

tell·a·ble (tel′ə b'l) *adj.* 1. that can be told 2. worth being told

tell·er (tel′ər) *n.* 1. a person who tells (a story, etc.); narrator; recounter 2. a person who counts; specif., *a)* one who counts votes, as in a legislative body *b)* a bank clerk who pays out or receives money

Tel·ler (tel′ər), **Edward** 1908– ; U.S. nuclear physicist, born in Hungary

tell·ing (tel′iŋ) *adj.* 1. having an effect; forceful; striking *[a telling retort]* 2. that tells or reveals much —*SYN.* see VALID —**tell′ing·ly** *adv.*

tell·tale (-tāl′) *n.* 1. a person who tells secrets or informs; talebearer; tattler 2. an outward indication of something secret 3. any of various devices for indicating or recording information; indicator; specif., ☆*a)* a row of strips hung over a railroad track to warn of an approaching low bridge, tunnel, etc. *b)* a device indicating the position of a ship's rudder *c)* a time clock *d)* a gauge on a pipe organ showing the air pressure —*adj.* revealing what is meant to be kept secret *[the telltale mud on his shoes]*

tel·lu·ri·an (te loor′ē ən) *adj.* *[< L. tellus, gen. telluris, the earth (< IE. base *tel(o)-, flat, level ground, whence THILL, DEAL[3]) + -AN]* of the earth; terrestrial —*n.* 1. an inhabitant of the earth 2. an apparatus for demonstrating how the earth's position and movement (diurnal rotation, annual revolution, etc.) causes day and night and the cycle of the seasons: also **tel·lu′ri·on** (-ən)

tel·lu·ric[1] (te loor′ik) *adj.* of, derived from, or containing tellurium, esp. in a higher valence than in the corresponding tellurious compounds

tel·lu·ric[2] (te loor′ik) *adj.* 1. terrestrial; tellurian 2. of or arising from the earth, or soil

telluric acid a heavy, white, crystalline acid, H_2TeO_4

tel·lu·ride (tel′yə rīd′) *n.* a compound of tellurium combined with an electropositive element or with a radical

tel·lu·rite (-rīt′) *n.* 1. a salt of tellurous acid 2. native tellurium dioxide, TeO_2

tel·lu·ri·um (te loor′ē əm) *n.* *[ModL. < L. tellus, the earth (see TELLURIAN): so named (1798) in contrast to URANIUM]* a rare, tin-white, brittle, nonmetallic chemical element, belonging to the same family of elements as sulfur and selenium and occurring naturally in mineral tellurite and tellurides: it is used as a glass tint, as an alloying material, and in thermoelectric converters: symbol, Te; at. wt., 127.60; at. no., 52; sp. gr., 6.24; melt. pt., 449.5°C; boil. pt., 989.8°C

tel·lu·rize (tel′yoo rīz′) *vt.* **-rized′, -riz′ing** to combine or treat with tellurium

tel·lu·rous (tel′yə rəs, te loor′əs) *adj.* of, derived from, or containing tellurium, esp. in a lower valence than in the corresponding tellurous compounds

tellurous acid a white, crystalline powder, H_2TeO_3

Tel·lus (tel′əs) *[L.: see TELLURIAN]* *Rom. Myth.* the goddess of the earth: identified with the Greek Gaea

tel·ly (tel′ē) *n.* *[altered < TELE(VISION)]* *Brit. colloq.* term for TELEVISION

tel·o-[1] (tel′ə, -ō) same as TELE-

tel·o-[2] (tel′ə, -ō) *[< Gr. telos, an end, completion, orig. prob. "turning point" < IE. base *kwel-, to turn, whence WHEEL, L. colere, to till]* a combining form meaning end *[telophase]*

tel·o·dy·nam·ic (tel′ō dī nam′ik) *adj.* *[TELO-[1] + DYNAMIC]* of or for the transmission of mechanical power to a distance by cables and pulleys

te·lome (tē′lōm) *n.* *[G. telom < tel- (< Gr. telos: see TELO-[2]) + -om < ModL. -oma, a stem, mass < L. -oma: see -OMA]* *Bot.* the terminal branchlet of a primitive vascular plant

tel·o·phase (tel′ə fāz′) *n.* *[TELO-[2] + PHASE]* *Biol.* the final stage of mitosis, in which the parent cell becomes completely divided into two cells, each having a re-organized nucleus

tel·pher (tel′fər) *n.* *[< TEL(E)- + Gr. pherein, to BEAR[1]]* an electrically driven car suspended from and run on overhead cables —*vt.* to transport by telpher

tel·pher·age (-ij) *n.* a transportation system using telphers

tel·son (tel′sən) *n.* *[ModL. < Gr. telson, a limit, boundary: for IE. base see TELO-[2]]* the last, stinging segment of the body of a scorpion, or a projection of the last body segment, as in many decapod crustaceans

☆**Tel·star** (tel′stär′) *[TEL(E)- + STAR]* a communications satellite for relaying microwave transmissions, first placed in earth orbit on July 10, 1962

Tel·u·gu (tel′ə gōō′) *n.* *[< the Telugu name]* 1. a Dravidian language spoken in E India 2. *pl.* **-gus′, -gu′** a

member of a Dravidian people living in Andhra Pradesh, India, who speak this language —*adj.* of Telugu or the Telugus Also sp. **Tel′e·gu′**

☆**tem·blor** (tem′blôr, -blər; *Sp.* tem blôr′) *n., pl.* **-blors**; *Sp.* **-blo′res** (-blô′res) *[< Sp. temblor (de tierra), lit., trembling (of the earth) < temblar, to tremble < VL. tremulare: see TREMBLE]* same as EARTHQUAKE

tem·er·ar·i·ous (tem′ə rer′ē əs, -rar′-) *adj.* *[L. temerarius < temere: see ff.]* reckless; rash —**tem′er·ar′i·ous·ly** *adv.*

te·mer·i·ty (tə mer′ə tē) *n.* *[ME. temeryte < L. temeritas < temere, rashly, blindly < IE. base *tem-, dark, whence OS. thimm, dark, L. tenebrae, darkness]* foolish or rash boldness; foolhardiness; recklessness

SYN.—**temerity** refers to a rashness or foolish boldness that results from underrating the dangers or failing to evaluate the consequences *[he had the temerity to criticize his employer]*; **audacity** suggests either great presumption or defiance of social conventions, morals, etc. *[shocked at the audacity of his proposal]*; **effrontery,** always derogatory in usage, connotes shamelessness or insolence in defying the rules of propriety, courtesy, etc. *[his effrontery in addressing the teacher by her first name]*; **nerve, cheek,** and **gall** are colloquial equivalents of **effrontery,** but **nerve** and **cheek** usually suggest mere impudence or sauciness and **gall,** unmitigated insolence

Tem·es·vár (tem′esh vär′) *Hung. name of* TIMIŞOARA

temp. 1. *[L. tempore]* in the time of 2. temperature 3. temporary

Tem·pe (tem′pē) 1. *[after ff.]* city in SC Ariz., on the Salt River: suburb of Phoenix: pop. 63,000 2. **Vale of,** valley of the Piniós River in NE Thessaly, Greece, between Mounts Olympus & Ossa: anciently regarded as sacred to Apollo

tem·per (tem′pər) *vt.* *[ME. tempren < OE. temprian & OFr. temprer, both < L. temperare, to observe proper measure, mix, regulate, forbear < tempus (gen. temporis), time, period, orig., a span < IE. *tempos, a span < base *temp-, to pull, stretch < base *ten-: see TENSE[1]]* 1. to make suitable, desirable, or free from excess by mingling with something else; reduce in intensity, esp. by the admixture of some other quality; moderate; assuage; mollify *[to temper criticism with reason]* 2. *a)* to bring to the proper texture, consistency, hardness, etc. by mixing with something or treating in some way *[to temper paints with oil, to temper steel by heating and sudden cooling, to temper clay by moistening and kneading]* *b)* to toughen, as by rigors or trying experiences 3. *[Rare]* to fit; adapt 4. *[Archaic]* to mix in proper proportions 5. *Music* to adjust the pitch of (a note) or tune (an instrument) according to some temperament —*vi.* to be or become tempered —*n.* 1. the state of being tempered; specif., *a)* formerly, a properly proportioned mixture *b)* the state of a metal with regard to the degree of hardness and resiliency 2. frame of mind; disposition; mood *[in a bad temper]* 3. calmness of mind; composure: now only in the phrases **lose one's temper, keep one's temper** 4. a tendency to become angry readily *[to have a temper]* 5. anger; rage *[to go into a temper]* 6. something used to temper a mixture, etc. 7. *[Archaic]* a middle course; mean 8. *[Obs.]* *a)* character; quality *b)* bodily constitution —*SYN.* see DISPOSITION, MOOD[1] —**tem′per·a·bil′i·ty** *n.* —**tem′per·a·ble** *adj.* —**tem′per·er** *n.*

tem·per·a (tem′pər ə) *n.* *[It. < temperare < L.: see prec.]* 1. *a)* a process of painting in which pigments are mixed with size, casein, or egg, esp. egg yolk, to produce a dull finish *b)* the paint used in this process 2. an opaque, water-base paint used as for posters

tem·per·a·ment (tem′prə mənt, -pər ə mənt, -pər mənt) *n.* *[ME. < L. temperamentum, proper mixing < temperare: see TEMPER]* 1. orig., the act or an instance of tempering; proportionate mixture or balance of ingredients 2. in medieval physiology, any of the four conditions of body and mind, the *sanguine, phlegmatic, choleric* (or *bilious*), and *melancholic temperaments,* attributed to an excess of one of the four corresponding humors: see HUMOR 3. one's customary frame of mind or natural disposition; nature *[a man of even temperament]* 4. a nature that is excitable, moody, capricious, volatile, etc. *[the temperament of a prima donna]* 5. *[Obs.]* *a)* climate *b)* temperature 6. *Music* a system of adjustment of the intervals between the tones of an instrument of fixed intonation: it may be **pure temperament,** in which the intervals are set exactly according to theory, or **equal temperament,** as in a piano, in which the pitch of the tones is slightly adjusted to make them suitable for all keys —*SYN.* see DISPOSITION

tem·per·a·men·tal (tem′prə men′t'l, -pər ə men′t'l, -pər men′t'l) *adj.* 1. of or caused by temperament 2. having an excitable temperament; easily upset 3. erratic in behavior; unpredictable —**tem′per·a·men′tal·ly** *adv.*

tem·per·ance (tem′pər əns, -prəns) *n.* *[ME. < MFr. < L. temperantia, moderation, sobriety < prp. of temperare: see TEMPER]* 1. the state or quality of being temperate; self-restraint in conduct, expression, indulgence of the appetites, etc.; moderation 2. moderation in drinking alcoholic liquors or total abstinence from alcoholic liquors

tem·per·ate (tem′pər it, -prit) *adj.* [ME. *temperat* < L. *temperatus*, pp. of *temperare*, to TEMPER] **1.** moderate in indulging the appetites; not self-indulgent; abstemious, esp. in the use of alcoholic liquors **2.** moderate in one's actions, speech, etc.; self-restrained **3.** characterized by moderation or restraint [a *temperate* reply] **4.** *a)* neither very hot nor very cold: said of climate, etc. *b)* having a temperate climate —*SYN.* see MODERATE —**tem′per·ate·ly** *adv.* —**tem′per·ate·ness** *n.*

Temperate Zone either of two zones of the earth (**North Temperate Zone** and **South Temperate Zone**) between the tropics and the polar circles: see ZONE, illus.

tem·per·a·ture (tem′prə chər, tem′pər ə-) *n.* [L. *temperatura* < *temperatus*, TEMPERATE] **1.** the degree of hotness or coldness of anything, usually as measured on a thermometer; specif., *a)* the degree of heat of a living body; also, an excess of this over the normal (about 98.6°F or 37°C in man); fever *b)* the degree of heat of the atmosphere **2.** [Obs.] *a)* temperateness, as of climate *b)* temperament

temperature gradient the rate of temperature change, esp. with increase in altitude

tem·pered (tem′pərd) *adj.* **1.** having been given the desired temper, consistency, hardness, etc. [*tempered* steel] **2.** modified by addition of or mixture with other qualities, ingredients, etc. [justice *tempered* with mercy] **3.** having a (specified kind of) temper [bad-*tempered*] **4.** *Music* adjusted to a temperament, esp. equal temperament

tem·pest (tem′pist) *n.* [ME. < OFr. *tempeste* < VL. *tempesta*, for L. *tempestas*, portion of time, weather, a calamity, storm, tempest < *tempus*, time: see TEMPER] **1.** a violent storm with high winds, esp. one accompanied by rain, hail, or snow **2.** a violent outburst; tumult —*vt.* [Poet.] to agitate violently —☆**tempest in a teapot** a great commotion over a small problem

tem·pes·tu·ous (tem pes′choo wəs) *adj.* [MFr. *tempestueus* < LL. *tempestuosus* < L. *tempestas*] **1.** of, involving, or like a tempest **2.** violent; turbulent —**tem·pes′tu·ous·ly** *adv.* —**tem·pes′tu·ous·ness** *n.*

tem·pi (tem′pē) *n. alt. pl.* of TEMPO

Tem·plar (tem′plər) *n.* [ME. *templer* < OFr. *templier* < ML. *templarius* < L. *templum* (see TEMPLE[1])] **1.** [from occupying quarters near the site of Solomon's Temple in Jerusalem] *same as* KNIGHT TEMPLAR **2.** [t-] a barrister or law student of the Temple in London

tem·plate (tem′plit) *n.* [altered (after PLATE) < *templet* < Fr., dim. of *temple* < L. *templum*, small timber, purlin, akin to TEMPLE[1]] **1.** a pattern, usually in the form of a thin metal, wooden, or paper plate, for forming an accurate copy of an object or shape **2.** *Archit. a)* a short stone or timber placed under a beam to help distribute the pressure *b)* a beam for supporting joists over an open space, as a doorway

tem·ple[1] (tem′p'l) *n.* [ME. < OE. *tempel* & OFr. *temple*, both < L. *templum*, a temple, sanctuary, orig., space marked out: for IE. base see TEMPER] **1.** a building for the worship of a god or gods **2.** [T-] any of three buildings for worshiping Jehovah, successively built by the Jews in ancient Jerusalem **3.** the synagogue of a Reform, or sometimes Conservative, congregation **4.** a Christian church **5.** [T-] either of two (**Inner** and **Middle Temple**) of four sets of London buildings housing England's principal law societies: their site was formerly occupied by the London branch of Knights Templars **6.** a building, usually of imposing size, etc., serving the public or an organization in some special way [a *temple* of art, a Masonic *temple*] —**tem′pled** *adj.*

tem·ple[2] (tem′p'l) *n.* [ME. < OFr. < VL. *tempula*, altered < L. *tempora*, the temples, pl. of *tempus*, prob. akin to *tempus*, time: see TEMPER] **1.** either of the flat surfaces alongside the forehead, in front of each ear ☆**2.** either of the sidepieces of a pair of glasses that fit against the temples and over the ears

tem·ple[3] (tem′p'l) *n.* [LME. < MFr.: see TEMPLATE] a device for keeping the cloth in a loom stretched to its correct width during weaving

Tem·ple (tem′p'l), Sir **William** 1628–99; Eng. diplomat & writer

Temple Bar a former London gateway before the Temple buildings: the heads of traitors and criminals were exhibited on it

tem·plet (tem′plit) *n. same as* TEMPLATE

tem·po (tem′pō) *n., pl.* **-pos, -pi** (-pē) [It. < L. *tempus*, time: see TEMPER] **1.** the rate of speed at which a musical composition is, or is supposed to be, played: it is indicated by such notations as *allegro, andante,* etc. or by reference to metronome timing **2.** rate of activity; pace [the *tempo* of modern living]

tem·po·ral[1] (tem′pər əl, -prəl) *adj.* [ME. < L. *temporalis* < *tempus*, time: see TEMPER] **1.** lasting only for a time; transitory; temporary, not eternal **2.** of this world; worldly, not spiritual **3.** civil or secular rather than ecclesiastical **4.** of or limited by time **5.** *Gram.* that expresses time —*n.* a temporal thing, power, etc. —**tem′po·ral·ly** *adv.*

tem·po·ral[2] (tem′pər əl, -prəl) *adj.* [LL. *temporalis* < L. *tempora:* see TEMPLE[2]] of or near the temple or temples (of the head)

temporal bone either of a pair of compound bones forming the sides of the skull: see SKULL, illus.

tem·po·ral·i·ty (tem′pə ral′ə tē) *n., pl.* **-ties** [ME. *temporalite* < LL.(Ec.) *temporalitas*] **1.** the quality or state of being temporal **2.** [usually *pl.*] secular properties of a church, esp. church revenues

tem·po·rar·y (tem′pə rer′ē) *adj.* [L. *temporarius* < *tempus*, time: see TEMPER] lasting, enjoyed, used, etc. for a time only; not permanent —**tem·po·rar·i·ly** (tem′pə rer′ə lē, tem′pə rer′ə lē) *adv.* —**tem′po·rar′i·ness** *n.*

SYN.—**temporary** applies to a post held (or to the person holding such a post) for a limited time, subject to dismissal by those having the power of appointment [a *temporary* mail carrier]; **provisional** is specifically applied to a government established for the time being in a new state until a permanent government can be formed; **ad interim** refers to an appointment for an intervening period, as between the death of an official and the election of his successor; **acting** is applied to one who temporarily takes over the powers of a regular official during the latter's absence [a vice-president often serves as *acting* president] —*ANT.* **permanent**

tem·po·rize (tem′pə rīz′) *vi.* **-rized′, -riz′ing** [MFr. *temporiser* < ML. *temporizare* < L. *tempus*, time: see TEMPER] **1.** to suit one's actions to the time, occasion, or circumstances, without reference to principle **2.** *a)* to give temporary compliance or agreement, evade immediate decision, etc., so as to gain time or avoid argument *b)* to parley or deal (*with* a person, etc.) so as to gain time **3.** to effect a compromise (*with* a person, etc., or *between* persons or parties); negotiate —**tem′po·ri·za′tion** *n.* —**tem′po·riz′er** *n.*

tempt (tempt) *vt.* [ME. *tempten* < OFr. *tempter* < LL.(Ec.) *temptare* < L., to try the strength of, urge < IE. base *temp-*, to stretch: cf. TEMPER] **1.** orig., to test; try **2.** to try to persuade; induce or entice, esp. to something immoral or sensually pleasurable **3.** to rouse desire in; be inviting to; attract **4.** to provoke or run the risk of provoking (fate, etc.) **5.** to incline strongly [to be *tempted* to accept] —*SYN.* see LURE —**tempt′a·ble** *adj.*

temp·ta·tion (temp tā′shən) *n.* [ME. < OFr. < LL.(Ec.) *temptatio*] **1.** a tempting or being tempted **2.** something that tempts; enticement

tempt·er (temp′tər) *n.* [ME. *temptour* < MFr. *tempteur* < L. *temptator*, a tempter, in LL.(Ec.), Satan] a person who tempts —**the Tempter** the Devil; Satan

tempt·ing (-tiŋ) *adj.* that tempts; alluring; attractive; seductive —**tempt′ing·ly** *adv.*

tempt·ress (-tris) *n.* a woman who tempts, esp. sexually

tem·pu·ra (tem′poo rä′, tem poor′ə) *n.* [Jap., lit., fried food] a Japanese dish consisting of shrimp, fish, vegetables, etc. dipped in an egg batter and deep-fried

‡**tem·pus fu·git** (tem′pəs fyoo′jit) [L.] time flies

Te·mu·co (te moo′kō) city in SC Chile: pop. 117,000

ten (ten) *adj.* [ME. < OE. *ten, tyn, tene,* akin to G. *zehn* < IE. **dékm,* ten, whence Sans. *dáça,* Gr. *dēka,* L. *decem*] totaling one more than nine —*n.* **1.** the cardinal number between nine and eleven; 10; X **2.** any group of ten people or things **3.** something numbered ten or having ten units, as *a)* a playing card, throw of dice, etc. ☆*b)* [Colloq.] a ten-dollar bill

ten- (ten) *same as* TENO-: used before a vowel

ten. **1.** tenor **2.** *Music* tenuto

ten·a·ble (ten′ə b'l) *adj.* [Fr. < OFr. < *tenir,* to hold < L.: see TENANT] that can be held, defended, or maintained —**ten′a·bil′i·ty, ten′a·ble·ness** *n.* —**ten′a·bly** *adv.*

ten·ace (ten′ās) *n.* [< Sp. *tenaza,* lit., tongs, pincers < L. *tenaces,* things that hold fast < *tenax:* see ff.] *Bridge* an imperfect sequence of high cards in the same suit, as the ace and queen without the king

te·na·cious (tə nā′shəs) *adj.* [L. *tenax* (gen. *tenacis*) < *tenere,* to hold: see TENANT] **1.** holding firmly [a *tenacious* grip] **2.** that retains well; retentive [a *tenacious* memory] **3.** that holds together strongly; cohesive; tough [a *tenacious* wood] **4.** that clings; adhesive; sticky **5.** persistent; stubborn [*tenacious* courage] —**te·na′cious·ly** *adv.* —**te·na′cious·ness** *n.*

te·nac·i·ty (tə nas′ə tē) *n.* [L. *tenacitas*] the quality or state of being tenacious —*SYN.* see PERSEVERANCE

te·nac·u·lum (tə nak′yoo ləm) *n., pl.* **-la** (-lə) [LL., instrument for holding < L. *tenere,* to hold: see TENANT] *Surgery* a pointed, hooked instrument for lifting and holding parts, as blood vessels

te·naille, te·nail (tə näl′) *n.* [Fr. *tenaille,* lit., pincers, tongs < VL. **tenacula,* for LL. *tenaculum:* see prec.] in old fortifications, an outwork before the curtain between two bastions

ten·an·cy (ten′ən sē) *n., pl.* **-cies** **1.** *a)* the condition of being a tenant; occupation of land, a building, etc. by rental or lease *b)* [Obs.] property occupied by a tenant *c)* the duration of such an occupancy **2.** possession or occupation of property, an office, etc. by any kind of title or right

ten·ant (ten′ənt) *n.* [ME. *tenaunt* < OFr. *tenant,* orig. prp. of *tenir,* to hold < L. *tenere,* to hold < IE. base **ten-,* to pull, stretch, hold taut, whence THIN] **1.** a person who pays rent to occupy or use land, a building, etc. **2.** an occupant of or dweller in a specified place **3.** a person who possesses lands, etc. by any kind of title or right —*vt.* to hold as a tenant; occupy —**ten′ant·a·ble** *adj.* —**ten′ant·less** *adj.*

tenant farmer a person who farms land owned by another and pays rent in cash or in a share of the crops

ten·ant·ry (ten'ən trē) *n., pl.* **-ries** [ME.: see TENANT & -RY] **1.** the tenants collectively, as of an estate **2.** the condition of being a tenant

☆**ten-cent store** (ten'sent') *shortened form of* FIVE-AND-TEN-CENT STORE

tench (tench) *n., pl.* **tench'es, tench:** see PLURAL, II, D, 1 [ME. & OFr. *tenche* < LL. *tinca*] a common European freshwater fish (*Tinca tinca*) of the carp family

Ten Commandments *Bible* the ten laws constituting the fundamental moral code of Israel, given to Moses by God on Mount Sinai; Decalogue: Ex. 20:2–17; Deut. 5:6–22

tend¹ (tend) *vt.* [ME. *tenden*, aphetic < *attenden:* see ATTEND] **1.** to take care of; minister to; watch over; look after; attend to [to *tend* plants or animals, to *tend* the sick] **2.** to be in charge of or at work at; manage or operate [to *tend* a store] **3.** *Naut.* to be on the alert to keep (a rope, diver's air line, etc.) from fouling —*vi.* to pay attention; attend —**tend on** to wait upon; serve

tend² (tend) *vi.* [ME. *tenden* < OFr. *tendre* < L. *tendere*, to stretch, extend, tend < IE. base *ten(d)-*, to stretch, pull, whence Sans. *tanōti*, (he) stretches, Gr. *teinein*, to extend: cf. THIN] **1.** to be directed; proceed or extend [the road *tends* south] **2.** to have an inclination, tendency, bias, etc. to do something; incline [*tending* to overeat] **3.** to lead or be directed (*to* or *toward* a specified result)

tend·ance (ten'dəns) *n.* **1.** a tending, attention, or care **2.** [Obs.] attendants collectively

tend·en·cy (ten'dən sē) *n., pl.* **-cies** [ML. *tendentia* < L. *tendens*, prp. of *tendere:* see TEND²] **1.** an inclination to move or act in a particular direction or way; constant disposition to some action or state; leaning; bias; propensity; bent **2.** a course or apparent course toward some purpose, object, or result; drift **3.** a definite purpose or point of view in something said or written
SYN.—**tendency** refers to an inclination or disposition to move in a particular direction or act in a certain way, esp. as a result of some inherent quality or habit [he has a *tendency* toward exaggeration]; **trend** suggests a general direction, with neither a definite course nor goal, subject to change or fluctuation by some external force [a recent *trend* in literature]; **current** differs from **trend** in connoting a clearly defined course, but one also subject to change [the *current* of one's life]; **drift** refers either to the course along which something is being carried or driven [the *drift* toward absolute conformity] or to a course taken by something that has unstated implications [what is the *drift* of this argument?]; **tenor**, equivalent in this connection to **drift**, connotes more strongly the clarity or purport of the unstated purpose or objective [the general *tenor* of the Bill of Rights]

ten·den·tious (ten den'shəs) *adj.* [G. *tendenziös* < *tendenz* (< ML. *tendentia*), TENDENCY] characterized by a deliberate tendency or aim; esp., advancing a definite point of view [*tendentious* writings]: also sp. **ten·den'cious** —**ten·den'tious·ly** *adv.* —**ten·den'tious·ness** *n.*

ten·der¹ (ten'dər) *adj.* [ME. *tendre* < OFr. < L. *tener*, soft, delicate, tender] **1.** soft or delicate and easily chewed, broken, cut, etc.; fragile, succulent, etc. **2.** weak of constitution or physique; unable to endure pain, hardship, etc.; feeble; frail **3.** having weakness due to youth; immature; young [the *tender* years] **4.** of soft quality or delicate tone; subdued [*tender* colors] **5.** that requires careful handling; ticklish; delicate [a *tender* question] **6.** gentle, mild, or light; not rough or heavy [a *tender* touch] **7.** *a)* that has or expresses affection, love, consideration, etc. [a *tender* smile] *b)* careful; considerate [*tender* of another's feelings] **8.** sparing; chary [*tender* of one's praise] **9.** *a)* acutely sensitive, as to pain, insult, etc. *b)* sensitive to impressions, emotions, moral influences, etc.; impressionable [a *tender* conscience] *c)* sensitive to others' feelings; sympathetic; compassionate [a *tender* heart] **10.** *Naut.* tending to lean over under sail; crank —*vt.* **1.** to make tender **2.** [Archaic] to treat with tenderness —**ten'der·ly** *adv.* —**ten'der·ness** *n.*
SYN.—**tender**, in this connection, implies a softness or gentleness in one's relations with others that is expressive of warm affection, concern, etc. [a *tender* caress]; **compassionate** is applied to one who is easily affected by another's troubles or pains and is quick to show pity or mercy [a *compassionate* judge]; **sympathetic** implies the ability or disposition to enter into another's mental state or emotions and thus to share his sorrows, joys, desires, etc. [a *sympathetic* interest in a colleague's career]; **warm** and **warmhearted** suggest a sympathetic interest or affection characterized by cordiality, generosity, etc. [*warm*, or *warmhearted*, hospitality]

ten·der² (ten'dər) *vt.* [Fr. *tendre* < L. *tendere*, to stretch, extend: see TEND²] **1.** to offer in payment of an obligation **2.** to present for acceptance; offer [to *tender* an invitation, apology, etc.] —*n.* **1.** an offer of money, services, etc. made to satisfy an obligation, avoid legal action, etc. **2.** a formal offer, as of marriage, contractual terms, etc. ☆**3.** something offered in payment, esp. money: cf. LEGAL TENDER —*SYN.* see OFFER —**ten'der·er** *n.*

ten·der³ (ten'dər) *n.* **1.** a person who tends, or has charge of, something **2.** *a)* an auxiliary ship for supplying or servicing another ship or a submarine, seaplane, buoys, etc. *b)* a boat for carrying passengers, etc. to or from a ship close to shore **3.** a railroad car carrying coal and water for a steam locomotive, to the rear of which it is attached

☆**ten·der·foot** (-foot') *n., pl.* **-foots', -feet'** **1.** a newcomer to the ranching and mining country of the West, unused to the hardships of the life **2.** any newcomer, novice, or beginner **3.** a beginner in the Boy Scouts

ten·der·heart·ed (-härt'id) *adj.* having a tender heart; quick to feel pity; sympathetic —**ten'der·heart'ed·ly** *adv.* —**ten'der·heart'ed·ness** *n.*

ten·der·ize (ten'də rīz') *vt.* **-ized', -iz'ing** to make (meat) tender by using a process or adding a substance that softens tissues —**ten'der·i·za'tion** *n.* —**ten'der·iz'er** *n.*

☆**ten·der·loin** (ten'dər loin') *n.* the tenderest part of a loin of beef, pork, etc., located under the short ribs and consisting of the psoas muscle —[*usually* T-] **1.** formerly, a district in New York City, below 42d Street west of Broadway, in which there was much vice and corruption: so called because regarded as a choice assignment for police seeking graft **2.** a similar district in any city

tender offer a public offer to purchase a block of stock in a corporation, often the controlling interest, within a specified period and at a stipulated price, usually well above the existing market price

ten·di·ni·tis (ten'də nīt'əs) *n.* [< ModL. *tendo* (gen. *tendinis*), TENDON + -*itis*, ITIS] inflammation of a tendon

ten·di·nous (ten'də nəs) *adj.* [Fr. *tendineux* < ML. *tendinosus*] **1.** of or like a tendon **2.** consisting of tendons

ten·don (ten'dən) *n.* [ML. *tendo*, altered (after L. *tendere*, to stretch: see TEND²) < Gr. *tenōn*, a sinew < *teinein*, to stretch] any of the inelastic cords of tough, fibrous connective tissue in which muscle fibers end and by which muscles are attached to bones or other parts; sinew

ten·dril (ten'drəl) *n.* [earlier *tendrell*, prob. altered < ME. *tendron*, a young tender shoot < OFr. *tendrum*, ult. < L. *tener*, TENDER¹] a threadlike part of a climbing plant, often in a spiral form, serving to support it by clinging to or coiling around an object

Ten·e·brae (ten'ə brā', -brē') *n.pl.* [L., pl., shadows, darkness: see TEMERITY] *R.C.Ch.* the matins and lauds sung for the following day in the afternoon or evening of Wednesday, Thursday, and Friday of Holy Week, at which the Crucifixion is commemorated by the extinguishing of candles

TENDRILS
(A, stem; B, leaflet; C, stem with adhesive disks)

ten·e·brif·ic (ten'ə brif'ik) *adj.* [< L. *tenebrae* (see prec.) + -FIC] making dark; obscuring

ten·e·brous (ten'ə brəs) *adj.* [ME. *tenebrus* < OFr. < L. *tenebrosus* < *tenebrae:* see TENEBRAE] dark; gloomy: also **te·neb·ri·ous** (tə neb'rē əs)

Ten·e·dos (ten'ə däs) Turk. island in the Aegean, near the Dardanelles: 15 sq. mi.: Turk. name, BOZCAADA

1080 (ten'āt'ē) *n.* [the manufacturer's laboratory serial number] *same as* SODIUM FLUOROACETATE

ten·e·ment (ten'ə mənt) *n.* [ME. < OFr., a holding < ML. *tenementum* < L. *tenere*, to hold: see TENANT] **1.** *Law* land, buildings, offices, franchises, etc. held of another by tenure **2.** a dwelling house **3.** a room or set of rooms tenanted as a separate dwelling; apartment; flat **4.** *same as* TENEMENT HOUSE **5.** [Poet.] a dwelling place; abode —**ten·e·men'tal, ten'e·men'ta·ry** *adj.*

☆**tenement house** a building divided into tenements, or apartments, now specif. one in the slums that is run-down, overcrowded, etc.

Ten·er·ife (ten'ə rēf'; *Sp.* te ne rē'fe) largest island of the Canary Islands: 795 sq. mi.

te·nes·mus (ti nez'məs, -nes'-) *n.* [ML. < L. *tenesmos* < Gr. *teinesmos* < *teinein*, to stretch: see TEND²] *Med.* a feeling of urgent need to defecate or urinate, with a straining but unsuccessful effort to do so

ten·et (ten'it) *n.* [L., he holds < *tenere:* see TENANT] a principle, doctrine, or belief held as a truth, as by some group —*SYN.* see DOCTRINE

ten·fold (ten'fōld') *adj.* [see -FOLD] **1.** having ten parts **2.** having ten times as much or as many —*adv.* ten times as much or as many

☆**ten-gal·lon hat** (ten'gal'ən) a wide-brimmed felt hat with a high, round crown, orig. worn by American cowboys

Ten·gri Nor (teŋ'grē nôr') *same as* NAM TSO

tenia, teniacide, etc. *alt. sp.* of TAENIA, TAENIACIDE, etc.

Ten·iers (ten'yərz; *Fl.* tə nirs') **David 1.** 1582–1649; Fl. painter: called *the Elder* **2.** 1610–90; Fl. painter: son of *prec.:* called *the Younger*

Ten·nes·see (ten'ə sē') [< *Tanasi*, Cherokee village name < ?] **1.** EC State of the U.S.: admitted, 1796; 42,244 sq. mi.; pop. 3,924,000; cap. Nashville: abbrev. **Tenn., TN** **2.** river flowing from NE Tenn. through N Ala. & W Tenn. into the Ohio River: 652 mi. —**Ten'nes·se'an** *adj., n.*

☆**Tennessee Valley Authority** a Federal corporation organized in 1933 to provide cheap electric power, flood control, irrigation, etc. by developing the entire basin of the Tennessee River, esp. by building dams and reservoirs

☆**Tennessee walking horse** any of a breed of saddle or light utility horse with an easy, ambling gait

Ten·niel (ten′yəl), Sir **John** 1820–1914; Eng. illustrator & caricaturist

ten·nis (ten′is) *n.* [ME. *tenetz*, prob. < Anglo-Fr. *tenetz*, receive, hold (imperative for OFr. *tenez*) < OFr. *tenir*, to hold (see TENANT): a cry by the server before play] **1.** a game (officially called **lawn tennis**), usually played outdoors, in which two players or two pairs of players using rackets hit a fabric-covered, hollow rubber ball back and forth over a net stretched across a marked, level, rectangular area (**tennis court**) **2.** a similar but more complex old indoor game (**court tennis**) in which the ball is bounced against the walls of a specially constructed court as well as hit over a net

tennis shoe *same as* SNEAKER (sense 2)

Ten·ny·son (ten′ə s'n), **Alfred,** 1st Baron Tennyson, 1809–92; Eng. poet: poet laureate (1850–92): called *Alfred, Lord Tennyson* —**Ten′ny·so′ni·an** (-sō′nē ən) *adj.*

ten·o- (ten′ō, -ə) [< Gr. *tenōn*, TENDON] *a combining form meaning* tendon [*tenotomy*]

ten·on (ten′ən) *n.* [ME. < MFr. < *tenir*, to hold (see TENANT)] a projecting part cut on the end of a piece of wood for insertion into a corresponding hole (*mortise*) in another piece to make a joint: see MORTISE, illus. —*vt., vi.* **1.** to make a tenon (on) **2.** to joint by mortise and tenon

ten·or (ten′ər) *n.* [ME. < OFr. < L. < *tenere*, to hold: see TENANT] **1.** general course or tendency [the even *tenor* of his life] **2.** general meaning; drift; purport **3.** general character or nature **4.** the exact wording or an exact copy of a legal document **5.** *a)* [ME. < MFr. *tenour* < It. *tenore* < L. *tenor*, a holding: the tenor voice "held" the melody (*canto fermo*)] the adult male voice between baritone and countertenor, or the range of this voice, usually from about an octave below middle C to an octave above *b)* a part for such a voice *c)* a singer with such a voice, or an instrument having this range **6.** in a set of bells for ringing changes, the bell with the lowest tone —*adj.* of, in, for, or having the range of a tenor [a tenor saxophone] —SYN. see TENDENCY

tenor clef the C clef on the fourth line, used in notation for the tenor trombone, the upper range of the cello and bassoon, etc.

ten·o·rite (ten′ə rīt′) *n.* [It., after M. *Tenore* (1780–1861), It. botanist + *-ite,* -ITE¹] an oxide of copper occurring in tiny black scales in volcanic regions or copper veins

te·nor·rha·phy (tə nôr′ə fē, -när′-) *n., pl.* -**phies** [TENO- + *-rrhaphy* < Gr. *rhaphē*, suture] *Surgery* the joining of a divided tendon by sutures

te·not·o·my (tə nät′ə mē) *n., pl.* -**mies** [TENO- + -TOMY] *Surgery* the cutting or dividing of a tendon

ten·pen·ny (ten′pen′ē, -pə nē) *adj.* **1.** worth ten (esp. Brit.) pennies **2.** designating a nail of large size (three inches in length)

ten·pins (-pinz′) *n.pl.* **1.** [*with sing. v.*] the game of bowling in which ten pins are used **2.** the pins

ten·pound·er (-poun′dər) *n. same as:* **1.** LADYFISH **2.** MACHETE (sense 2)

ten·rec (ten′rek) *n.* [Fr. *tanrec, tenrec* < Malagasy *tàn-draka*] any of various small, burrowing, hedgehoglike mammals (family Tenrecidae) of Madagascar and the Comoro Islands, that feed chiefly on insects

tense¹ (tens) *adj.* **tens′er, tens′est** [L. *tensus,* pp. of *tendere,* to stretch < IE. base *ten(d)-*, to pull, stretch, whence THIN: cf. TEND²] **1.** stretched tight; strained; taut **2.** undergoing or showing mental or nervous strain; anxious; apprehensive; jittery **3.** *Phonet.* pronounced with the jaw and tongue relatively rigid: said of certain vowels, as *e* in *he*: opposed to LAX —*vt., vi.* **tensed, tens′ing** to make or become tense —SYN. see TIGHT —**tense′ly** *adv.* — **tense′ness** *n.*

tense² (tens) *n.* [ME. < OFr. *tens* < L. *tempus,* time: see TEMPER] **1.** any of the forms of a verb that show the time of its action or state of being: English tenses are usually listed as *present, past, future, perfect, past perfect* (*pluperfect*), and *future perfect,* in accordance with Latin models; English tenses other than the simple present and simple past are formed by using an auxiliary verb with a participle or infinitive form of a verb **2.** a set of such forms for any given time [the present *tense* of *be*]

ten·si·ble (ten′sə b'l) *adj.* [ML. *tensibilis* < L. *tensus:* see TENSE¹] *same as* TENSILE (sense 2) —**ten′si·bil′i·ty** *n.*

ten·sile (ten′s'l; *chiefly Brit.,* -sīl) *adj.* [ModL. *tensilis* < L. *tensus:* see TENSE¹] **1.** of, undergoing, or exerting tension **2.** capable of being stretched —**ten·sil′i·ty** (-sil′ə tē) *n.*

tensile strength resistance to lengthwise stress, measured (in weight per unit area) by the greatest load pulling in the direction of length that a given substance can bear without tearing apart

ten·sim·e·ter (ten sim′ə tər) *n.* [TENSI(ON) + -METER] an instrument that measures small changes in gas or vapor pressure and is used to obtain the temperature point at which one phase of a substance, esp. a crystal, is changed into another

ten·si·om·e·ter (ten′sē äm′ə tər) *n.* [TENSIO(N) + -METER] any instrument for measuring tautness or tension, as of a stretched wire, fabric, etc., or of the eyeball

ten·sion (ten′shən) *n.* [< MFr. or L.: MFr. *tension* < L. *tensio* < *tensus:* see TENSE¹] **1.** a tensing or being tensed **2.** mental or nervous strain, often accompanied by muscular tautness **3.** a state of strained relations; uneasiness due to mutual hostility **4.** a device for regulating tension or tautness, as of thread in a sewing machine **5.** *same as* VOLTAGE **6.** loosely, the expansive force, or pressure, of a gas or vapor **7.** *a)* stress on a material produced by the pull of forces tending to cause extension *b)* a force or combination of forces exerting such a pull against the resistance of the material **8.** a balancing of forces or elements in opposition —*vt.* to subject to tension —**ten′sion·al** *adj.*

ten·si·ty (ten′sə tē) *n.* a tense state or quality

ten·sive (-siv) *adj.* [Fr. *tensif*] relating to or causing tension

ten·sor (ten′sər, -sôr) *n.* [ModL. < L. *tensus:* see TENSE¹] **1.** any muscle that stretches, or tenses, some part of the body **2.** *Math.* an abstract object representing a generalization of the vector concept and having a specified system of components that undergo certain types of transformation under changes of the coordinate system

☆**ten-strike** (ten′strīk′) *n.* **1.** *Bowling same as* STRIKE **2.** [Colloq.] any entirely successful action

tent¹ (tent) *n.* [ME. < OFr. *tente* < L. *tenta,* fem. pp. of *tentus,* alternative pp. of *tendere,* to stretch: see TENSE¹] **1.** a portable shelter consisting of canvas, skins, etc. stretched over poles and attached to stakes **2.** anything suggestive of a tent, as an airtight shelter placed over the bed of a patient receiving inhalation therapy; specif., *short for* OXYGEN TENT —*adj.* of or like a tent —*vi.* to live in a tent; encamp —*vt.* **1.** to lodge in tents **2.** to cover with or as if with a tent

tent² (tent) *n.* [ME. *tente* < OFr., a probe < *tenter,* to try, test < L. *tentare,* var. of *temptare:* see TEMPT] *Med.* a plug of gauze, lint, etc. placed into an opening or wound to dilate it or keep it open —*vt.* to insert such a plug in

ten·ta·cle (ten′tə k'l) *n.* [ModL. *tentaculum* < L. *tentare,* to touch: see prec.] **1.** any of a variety of long, slender, flexible growths, as about the head or mouth of some invertebrate animals, used variously for grasping, feeling, moving, etc. **2.** *Bot.* any of various sensitive hairs on the leaves of some plants, as those used in capturing insects —**ten′ta·cled** *adj.* —**ten·tac·u·lar** (ten tak′yə lər) *adj.*

ten·ta·tive (ten′tə tiv) *adj.* [LL. *tentativus* < pp. of L. *tentare,* to touch, try: see TENT²] **1.** made, done, proposed, etc. experimentally or provisionally; not definite or final [*tentative* plans, a *tentative* explanation] **2.** indicating timidity, hesitancy, or uncertainty [a *tentative* caress] —**ten′ta·tive·ly** *adv.* —**ten′ta·tive·ness** *n.*

☆**tent caterpillar** one of several kinds of caterpillar (genus *Malacosoma*) that live in colonies in large, tentlike webs spun among the branches of trees, which they defoliate

tent·ed (ten′tid) *adj.* **1.** covered by or sheltered in a tent or tents **2.** shaped like a tent

ten·ter (ten′tər) *n.* [ME. *tentoure* < L. *tentus:* see TENT¹] **1.** a frame on which cloth is stretched after having been milled, so as to dry evenly without shrinking: in full **tenter frame 2.** [Obs.] a tenterhook —*vt.* [ME. *tenteren*] to stretch (cloth) on a tenter or tenters

ten·ter·hook (-hook′) *n.* any of the hooked nails that hold cloth stretched on a tenter —**on tenterhooks** in suspense; filled with anxiety

tenth (tenth) *adj.* [Early ME. *tenthe,* replacing OE. *teogotha, teotha:* see TEN & -TH²] **1.** preceded by nine others in a series; 10th **2.** designating any of the ten equal parts of something —*n.* **1.** the one following the ninth **2.** any of the ten equal parts of something; 1/10 **3.** a tenth of a gallon —**tenth′ly** *adv.*

tent show a show, as a circus, given in a tent

tent stitch [< ? TENT¹] an embroidery stitch that forms a series of parallel slanting lines

ten·u·is (ten′yoo wis) *n., pl.* -**u·es′** (-yoo wēz′) [ML. < L. (see TENUOUS): used as transl. of Gr. *psilos,* bare, unaspirated (so applied by Aristotle)] in Greek, a voiceless stop (p, t, or k)

te·nu·i·ty (tə noo′ə tē, -nyoo′-) *n., pl.* -**ties** [MFr. *tenuité* < L. *tenuitas*] the quality or state of being tenuous; specif., *a)* thinness; slenderness; fineness *b)* lack of substance; rarity, as of air *c)* faintness, as of light or voice *d)* meagerness; slightness

ten·u·ous (ten′yoo wəs) *adj.* [< L. *tenuis,* thin (for IE. base see THIN) + -OUS] **1.** slender or fine, as a fiber **2.** rare, as air at high altitudes; not dense **3.** not substantial; slight; flimsy [*tenuous* evidence] —SYN. see THIN —**ten′u·ous·ly** *adv.* —**ten′u·ous·ness** *n.*

ten·ure (ten′yər, -yoor) *n.* [ME. < MFr. < *tenir,* to hold: see TENANT] **1.** the act or right of holding property, an office, a position, etc. **2.** the length of time, or the conditions under which, something is held **3.** the status of holding one's position on a permanent basis, granted to teachers, civil service personnel, etc. on the fulfillment of specified requirements —**ten′ured** *adj.* —**ten·u·ri·al** (ten yoor′ē əl) *adj.*

te·nu·to (tə noot′ō) *adj.* [It., pp. of *tenere* (< L. *tenere,* to hold] *Music* held for the full value; sustained: usually indicated by a short line over the note or chord —*adv.* so as to be tenuto —*n., pl.* -**tos** a tenuto note or chord

te·o·cal·li (tē′ə kal′ē; *Sp.* te′ō kä′yē) *n., pl.* -**cal′lis** (-ēz; *Sp.* -yēs) [Nahuatl < *teotl,* god + *calli,* house] an ancient Mexican or Central American temple of the Aztecs, usually a building on a truncated pyramid

te·o·sin·te (tē/ə sin/tē) *n.* [AmSp. < Nahuatl *teocentli*, lit., divine maize < *teotl*, god + *centli*, maize] a tall, cornlike, fodder grass (*Euchlaena mexicana*) native to Mexico and Central America, having a tassel resembling that of maize but with small, bony ears

☆**te·pee** (tē/pē) *n.* [AmInd. (Siouan) *tĭpi* < *ti*, to dwell + *pi*, used for] a cone-shaped tent of animal skins, used by the Plains Indians

tep·e·fy (tep/ə fī/) *vt., vi.* **-fied', -fy'ing** [L. *tepefacere* < *tepere* (see TEPID) + *facere*, to make: see DO[1]] to make or become tepid —**tep'e·fac'tion** (-fak/shən) *n.*

teph·ra (tef/rə) *n.pl.* [with *sing.* or *pl. v.*] [< Gr. *tephra*: see ff.] clastic volcanic materials, as dust, ashes, pumice, etc., ejected during an eruption and carried through the air before deposition

TEPEE

teph·rite (tef/rīt) *n.* [< Gr. *tephra*, ashes < IE. base *dhegwh-*, to burn (cf. FEVER) + -ITE[1]] a volcanic rock resembling basalt and consisting essentially of plagioclase, nepheline, etc. —**teph·rit'ic** (-rit/ik) *adj.*

tep·id (tep/id) *adj.* [ME. *leped* < L. *tepidus* < *tepere*, to be slightly warm < IE. base *tep-*, to be warm, whence Sans. *tapati*, (it) burns] **1.** barely or moderately warm; lukewarm: said of liquids **2.** lacking warmth of feeling or enthusiasm —**te·pid·i·ty** (tə pid/ə tē), **tep/id·ness** *n.* —**tep'id·ly** *adv.*

tep·i·dar·i·um (tep/ə der/ē əm) *n., pl.* **-i·a** (-ə) [L., orig. neut. of *tepidarius*, of a tepid bath < *tepidus*: see prec.] in an ancient Roman bath, the warm room, intermediate between the hot and the cold rooms

te·poy (tē/poi) *n. same as* TEAPOY

☆**te·qui·la** (tə kē/lə) *n.* [AmSp. < Nahuatl *Tequila*, district in Mexico, where orig. produced] **1.** a strong alcoholic liquor of Mexico, distilled from pulque or mescal **2.** a Mexican agave (*Agave tequilana*) that is a source of tequila and mescal

ter. 1. terrace **2.** territory

ter·a- (ter/ə) [< Gr. *teras*, monster] a combining form meaning one trillion; the factor 10[12] [*teraherts*]

te·rai (tə rī/) *n.* [< *Terai*, region in NW India, where first worn by travelers] a soft, broad-brimmed, double-crowned hat of felt, worn for protection against the sun

ter·a·phim (ter/ə fim) *n.pl., sing.* **ter'aph** (-əf) [ME. *theraphym* < LL.(Ec.) *theraphim* < Gr.(Ec.) *theraphin* < Heb. *tĕrāfim*] small idols representing household gods, used among ancient Semitic peoples

ter·a·tism (ter/ə tiz'm) *n.* [< ff. + -ISM] a malformed fetus; monstrosity

ter·a·to- (ter/ə tō, -tə) [< Gr. *teras* (gen. *teratos*), a wonder, monster < IE. base *kwer-*, to cast a spell upon, orig. prob. to form, make, whence Sans. *karōti*, (he) makes] a combining form meaning monster, monstrosity [*teratology*]: also, before a vowel, **terat-**

ter·a·to·gen (ter/ə tə jən) *n.* [prec. + -GEN] an agent, as a chemical, disease, etc., that causes malformation of a fetus —**ter'a·to·gen'ic** (-jen'ik) *adj.*

ter·a·toid (ter/ə toid') *adj.* [TERAT(O)- + -OID] *Biol.* resembling a monster; malformed or abnormal

ter·a·tol·o·gy (ter/ə täl/ə jē) *n.* [TERATO- + -LOGY] the scientific study of biological monstrosities and malformations —**ter'a·to·log'i·cal** (-tə läj'ik'l) *adj.*

ter·bi·a (tur/bē ə) *n.* [ModL. < ff.] terbium oxide, Tb₂O₃, a white powder soluble in dilute acids

ter·bi·um (-əm) *n.* [ModL. < *Ytterby*, town in Sweden] a metallic chemical element of the rare-earth group, found in gadolinite and other minerals: symbol, Tb; at. wt., 158.924; at. no., 65; sp. gr., 8.27; melt. pt., 1356°C; boil. pt., 2800°C

terbium metals a series of closely related metals belonging to the rare-earth group, including terbium, gadolinium, europium, and, sometimes, dysprosium

Ter Borch (tur bôrkh/), **Ge·rard** (gā/rärt) 1617–81; Du. painter: also written **Ter·borch'**

terce (turs) *n.* [often T-] *Eccles. same as* TIERCE

Ter·cei·ra (tər sā/rə) island of the C Azores: 153 sq. mi.

ter·cel (tur/s'l) *n. var. of* TIERCEL

ter·cen·te·nar·y (tur/sen ten/ər ē, tər sen/tə ner/ē) *adj., n., pl.* **-nar'ies** [L. *ter*, three times (akin to *tres*, THREE) + CENTENARY] *same as* TRICENTENNIAL: also **ter'cen·ten'ni·al** (-ten/ē əl) *adj., n.*

ter·cet (tur/sit, tər set/) *n.* [Fr. < It. *terzetto*, dim. of *terzo* < L. *tertius*, THIRD] a group of three lines that rhyme with one another or are connected by rhyme with an adjacent triplet or triplets

ter·e·bene (ter/ə bēn/) *n.* [Fr. *térébène* < *térébinthe*, TEREBINTH + -*ène*, -ENE] a mixture of terpenes obtained by the action of sulfuric acid on spirits of turpentine, used as an expectorant, deodorant, and inhalant

te·reb·ic acid (tə reb/ik, -rē/bik) [TEREB(INTH) + -IC] a white, crystalline acid, C₇H₁₀O₄, a product of the oxidation of spirits of turpentine

ter·e·binth (ter/ə binth/) *n.* [ME. *terebint* < MFr. *therebint(he)* < L. *terebinthus* < Gr. *terebinthos*, earlier *terminthos*, prob. of Aegean orig.] a small European tree (*Pistacia terebinthus*) of the cashew family, whose cut bark yields a turpentine

ter·e·bin·thine (ter/ə binth/thin) *adj.* **1.** of the terebinth tree **2.** of or like turpentine

te·re·do (tə rē/dō) *n., pl.* **-dos, -di·nes'** (-də nēz/) [ME. < L. < Gr. *terēdōn*, borer, akin to *teirein*, to rub: for IE. base see THROW] any of a genus (*Teredo*) of long, wormlike, bivalve, marine mollusks that bore into and destroy submerged wood, as of ships, pilings, etc.; shipworm

Ter·ence (ter/əns) [L. *Terentius*, name of a Roman gens] **1.** a masculine name: dim. **Terry 2.** (L. name *Publius Terentius Afer*) 190?–159? B.C.; Rom. writer of comedies

Te·re·sa (tə rē/sə; *Sp.* te re/sä) **1.** a feminine name: see THERESA **2.** Saint, 1515–82; Sp. Carmelite nun: called **Teresa of Ávila**: her day is Oct. 12

te·rete (tə rēt/, ter/ēt) *adj.* [L. *teres* (gen. *teretis*), round, smooth, orig., rubbed < *terere*, to rub: for IE. base see THROW] *Biol.* cylindrical and tapered

Te·reus (tir/ē əs, tir/yōōs) [L. < Gr. *Tēreus*] *Gr. Myth.* a king of Thrace: see PHILOMELA

Ter·e·zi·na (ter/e zē/nä) city in NE Brazil, on the Parnaíba River; capital of Piauí state: pop. 145,000

ter·gal (tur/g'l) *adj.* [< L. *tergum*, the back + -AL] *Zool.* of the tergum, or back; dorsal

ter·gi·ver·sate (tur/ji ver sāt/) *vi.* **-sat'ed, -sat'ing** [< L. *tergiversatus*, pp. of *tergiversari*, to turn one's back, decline, shift < *tergum*, the back + *versari*, to turn: see VERSE] **1.** to desert a cause, party, etc.; become a renegade; apostatize **2.** to use evasions or subterfuge; equivocate —**ter'gi·ver·sa'tion** *n.* —**ter'gi·ver·sa'tor** *n.*

ter·gum (tur/gəm) *n., pl.* **-ga** (-gə) [L.] *Zool.* the longitudinal, upper or dorsal surface of a body segment of most arthropods

ter·i·ya·ki (ter/ē yä/kē) *n.* [Jap.] a Japanese dish consisting of meat or fish marinated or dipped in soy sauce and broiled, grilled, or barbecued

term (turm) *n.* [ME. *terme* < OFr. < L. *terminus*, a limit, boundary, end < IE. *termŋ*, a boundary stake < base *ter-*, to cross over, go beyond, whence Gr. *terma*, goal, Sans. *tarati*, (he) crosses over] **1.** orig., a point of time designating the beginning or end of a period **2.** a set date, as for payment, termination of tenancy, etc. **3.** a set period of time; duration; specif., *a)* a division of a school year, as a semester or quarter, during which a course of studies is given ☆*b)* a stipulated length of time that a person may hold office *c)* the normal elapsed period for birth after conception; also, delivery at the end of this period; parturition **4.** [*pl.*] conditions of a contract, agreement, sale, etc. that limit or define its scope or the action involved **5.** [*pl.*] mutual relationship between or among persons; footing [on speaking *terms*] **6.** a word or phrase having a limiting and definite meaning in some science, art, etc. [*tergum* is a zoological *term*] **7.** any word or phrase used in a definite or precise sense; expression [a colloquial *term*] **8.** [*pl.*] words that express ideas in a specified form [to speak in derogatory *terms*] **9.** *a)* [Archaic or Rare] a limit; boundary; extremity *b)* [*pl.*] [Obs.] conditions; circumstances **10.** *Archit.* a boundary post, esp. one consisting of a pedestal topped by a bust, as of the god Terminus **11.** *Law a)* the time a court is in session *b)* the length of time for which an estate is granted *c)* the estate itself *d)* time allowed a debtor to pay **12.** *Logic a)* either of two concepts that have a stated relation, as the subject and predicate of a proposition *b)* any one of the three parts of a syllogism **13.** *Math. a)* either of the two quantities of a fraction or a ratio *b)* each of the quantities in a series *c)* each of the quantities connected by plus or minus signs in an algebraic expression —*vt.* to call by a term; name —**bring to terms** to reduce to submission; force to agree —**come to terms** to arrive at an agreement or accommodation —**in terms of** regarding; concerning

term. 1. terminal **2.** termination

Ter·ma·gant (tur/mə gənt) *n.* [ME. *Tervagant* < OFr., name of an imaginary Moslem deity prob. introduced by the Crusaders] an imaginary Moslem deity supposed by medieval Christians to be worshiped by Moslems and represented in morality plays as a boisterous, overbearing figure —*n.* [t-] a boisterous, quarrelsome, scolding woman; shrew —*adj.* [t-] of the nature of a termagant; quarrelsome; scolding —**ter'ma·gan·cy** *n.* —**ter'ma·gant·ly** *adv.*

Ter·man (tur/mən), **L(ewis) M(adison)** 1877–1956; U.S. psychologist

term·er (tur/mər) *n.* a person serving a specified term, esp. in prison: usually in hyphenated compounds [third-*termer*]

ter·mi·na·ble (tur/mi nə b'l) *adj.* **1.** that can be terminated **2.** that terminates after a specified time, as a contract —**ter'mi·na·bil'i·ty, ter'mi·na·ble·ness** *n.* —**ter'mi·na·bly** *adv.*

ter·mi·nal (tur/mə n'l) *adj.* [L. *terminalis*] **1.** of, at, or forming the end, extremity, or terminus of something [*terminal* feathers] **2.** occurring at the end of a series; concluding; closing; final [a *terminal* payment] **3.** of or in

the final stages of a fatal disease *[terminal* cancer*]* **4.** having to do with a term or established period of time; occurring regularly in each term **5.** of, at, or forming the end of a transportation line **6.** *Bot.* growing at the end of a stem or branch *[a* terminal *leaflet] —n.* **1.** a terminating part; end; extremity; limit **2.** a connective device or point on an electric circuit or conductor ☆**3.** *a)* either end of a transportation line, esp. a railroad, including yards, servicing facilities, etc. *b)* a station or city located there *c)* a station at any important point or junction of a transportation line **4.** *Archit. a) same as* TERM (sense 10) *b)* an ornamental carving at the end of a structural element —*SYN.* see LAST[1] —**ter′mi·nal·ly** *adv.*

terminal juncture *Linguis.* any of several kinds of pause differing in duration and sometimes very brief, following various well-defined methods of breaking off speech

☆**terminal leave** the final leave granted to a member of the armed forces immediately before his discharge, equal in duration to his accumulated unused leave

terminal velocity *Physics* the unchanging velocity reached by a falling body when the frictional resistance of the enveloping medium is equal to the force of gravity

ter·mi·nate (tur′mə nāt′) *vt.* **-nat′ed, -nat′ing** *[< L. terminatus,* pp. of *terminare,* to end, limit *< terminus:* see TERM] **1.** to bring to an end in space or time; form the end or conclusion of; limit, bound, finish, or conclude **2.** to put an end to; stop; cease —*vi.* **1.** to come to an end in space or time; stop; end **2.** to have its end *(in* something) *[a* road *terminating* in woods*] —SYN.* see CLOSE[2] —**ter′mi·na′tive** *adj.*

ter·mi·na·tion (tur′mə nā′shən) *n.* [L. *terminatio*] **1.** a terminating or being terminated **2.** the end of something in space or time; limit, bound, conclusion, or finish **3.** *Linguis.* the end of a word; final sound, morpheme, or syllable; specif., an inflectional ending **4.** a thing's outcome or result *[friendly* termination *of a dispute]* —**ter′mi·na′tion·al** *adj.*

ter·mi·na·tor (-nāt′ər) *n.* [LL.] **1.** a person or thing that terminates **2.** the line dividing the illuminated and dark parts of the disk of the moon or a planet

ter·mi·nol·o·gy (tur′mə näl′ə jē) *n., pl.* **-gies** [G. *terminologie < ML. terminus,* a term *< L.* (see TERM) + G. *-logie,* -LOGY] **1.** the terms or system of terms used in a specific science, art, etc.; nomenclature *[legal* terminology*]* **2.** the systematic study of terms —**ter′mi·no·log′i·cal** (-nə läj′i k'l) *adj.* —**ter′mi·no·log′i·cal·ly** *adv.* —**ter′mi·nol′o·gist** *n.*

term insurance life insurance which expires at the end of a specified period of time

ter·mi·nus (tur′mə nəs) *n., pl.* **-ni′** (-nī′), **-nus·es** [L.: see TERM] **1.** a boundary or limit **2.** a boundary stone or marker **3.** an end; final point; extremity or goal **4.** *a)* either end of a transportation line *b)* a station or town at the end of such a line **5.** [T-] the ancient Roman deity presiding over boundaries and landmarks

‡**ter·mi·nus ad quem** (tur′mi nəs äd kwem′) [L., lit., end toward which] a destination; conclusion; end

‡**ter·mi·nus a quo** (ä kwō′) [L., lit., end from which] a starting point; point of origin; beginning

ter·mite (tur′mīt) *n.* [L. *termes* (gen. *termitis*), wood-boring worm *<* base of *terere,* to rub, bore: see THROW] any of an order (Isoptera) of pale-colored social insects having a soft body and living in colonies composed of winged forms that mate and wingless workers and soldiers that are sterile: they are very destructive to wooden structures and are found in the temperate zones and esp. in the tropics

term·less (turm′lis) *adj.* **1.** limitless **2.** unconditional

term·or (tur′mər) *n.* [ME. *<* Anglo-Fr. *termer < terme:* see TERM & -ER] *Law* a person holding an estate for a certain period of years or for life

☆**term paper** a long paper or report assigned to be written by a student in a course during a school term

tern (turn) *n.* [*< ON. therna,* via East Anglian dial.] any of several sea birds (esp. genus *Sterna*), related to the gulls, but smaller, with a more slender body and beak, and a deeply forked tail; sea swallow

ter·na·ry (tur′nər ē) *adj.* [ME. *< L. ternarius < terni,* three each *< tres,* THREE] **1.** made up of three parts; threefold; triple **2.** third in order or rank **3.** *Chem.* of or containing three different atoms, elements, radicals, etc. **4.** *Math. a)* having three as a base *b)* involving three variables **5.** *Metallurgy* of an alloy of three elements —*n., pl.* **-ries** [Rare] a group or set of three

ter·nate (tur′nāt) *adj.* [ModL. *ternatus < ML.,* pp. of *ternare < L. terni:* see prec.] **1.** consisting of three **2.** arranged in threes **3.** *Bot. a)* having three leaflets *b)* growing in groups or whorls of three, as some leaves —**ter′nate·ly** *adv.*

terne·plate (turn′plāt′) *n.* [Fr. *terne,* dull (cf. TARNISH) + PLATE] steel plate coated with an alloy of lead and a small amount of tin

ter·ni·on (tur′nē ən) *n.* [L. *ternio,* a triad *< terni:* see TERNARY] [Now Rare] a set of three; triad

ter·pene (tur′pēn) *n.* [G. *terpen < terp(entin),* turpentine + *-en,* -ENE] **1.** any of a series of isomeric, unsaturated hydrocarbons of the general formula $C_{10}H_{16}$, found in resins, essential oils, etc.: they are used in perfumes, medicines, etc. **2.** any of various derivatives of the terpene hydrocarbons

ter·pin·e·ol (tər pin′ē ōl′, -ôl′) *n.* [*terpine,* $C_{10}H_{18}(OH)_2$, (*<* prec. + -INE[2]) + -OL[1]] any of three isomeric alcohols, $C_{10}H_{17}OH$, with a lilac odor, found in certain volatile oils and used in perfumes

ter·pin hydrate (tur′pin) [*< terpine:* see prec.] a colorless crystalline powder, $C_{10}H_{20}O_2 \cdot H_2O$, used chiefly, in the form of an elixir, as an expectorant or cough syrup

Terp·sich·o·re (tərp sik′ə rē′) [Gr. *Terpsichorē < terpsichoros,* delighting in the dance *< terpein,* to delight in + *choros,* a dance] *Gr. Myth.* the Muse of dancing

terp·si·cho·re·an (turp′si kə rē′ən) *adj.* **1.** [T-] of Terpsichore **2.** having to do with dancing —*n.* a dancer: now only in facetious use

terr. **1.** terrace **2.** territory

‡**ter·ra** (ter′ə) *n.* [L.] (the) earth

terra al·ba (al′bə) [L., lit., white earth] any of several white mineral substances, as *a)* finely ground gypsum, used in making paints, paper, etc. *b)* pulverized kaolin, used in ceramics, etc. *c) same as* MAGNESIA (sense 1)

ter·race (ter′əs) *n.* [OFr., walled platform, orig., mound of earth *< It. terrazzo < terra,* earth *< L. < IE. *tersa <* base *tters,* dry, whence THIRST] **1.** *a)* a raised, flat mound of earth with sloping sides *b)* any of a series of flat platforms of earth with sloping sides, rising one above the other, as on a hillside *c)* a geological formation of this nature **2.** an unroofed, paved area, immediately adjacent to a house, etc. and usually overlooking a lawn or garden **3.** *a)* a gallery, portico, or colonnade *b)* a usually spacious veranda; piazza **4.** a small, usually roofed balcony, as outside an apartment **5.** a flat roof, esp. of a house of Spanish or Oriental architecture **6.** *a)* a line of houses, esp. of row houses, on ground raised from the street *b)* a street in front of such houses: often used in street names ☆**7.** a parklike strip in the middle of a boulevard, etc. —*vt.* **-raced, -rac·ing** to form into, lay out in, or surround with a terrace or terraces

ter·ra cot·ta (ter′ə kät′ə) [It., lit., baked earth *< L.:* cf. TERRACE & COOK] **1.** a hard, brown-red, usually unglazed earthenware used for pottery, sculpture, etc. **2.** its brown-red color —**ter′ra-cot′ta** *adj.*

terra fir·ma (fur′mə) [L.] firm earth; solid ground

ter·rain (tə rān′, ter′ān) *n.* [Fr. *< L. terrenum < terrenus,* of earth, earthen *< terra,* earth: see TERRACE] **1.** ground or a tract of ground, esp. with regard to its natural or topographical features or fitness for some use **2.** *Geol. same as* TERRANE (sense 1)

ter·ra in·cog·ni·ta (ter′ə in käg′ni tə) *pl.* **ter·rae in·cog·ni·tae** (ter′ē in käg′ni tē′) [L.] **1.** an unknown land; unexplored territory **2.** an unknown or unexplored field of knowledge

☆**Ter·ra·my·cin** (ter′ə mī′s'n) [*< L. terra,* earth (see TERRACE) + MYC- + -IN[1]] a trademark for OXYTETRACYCLINE

ter·rane (tə rān′, ter′ān) *n.* [Fr. *terrain:* see TERRAIN] *Geol.* **1.** *a)* a geological formation or series of related formations *b)* a region where a specific rock or group of rocks predominates **2.** *same as* TERRAIN (sense 1)

☆**ter·ra·pin** (ter′ə pin) *n.* [of AmInd. (Algonquian) origin, prob. dim. of *torope,* tortoise] **1.** any of several N. American, freshwater or tidewater turtles (esp. genus *Malaclemys*); specif., *same as* DIAMONDBACK **2.** its edible flesh

ter·ra·que·ous (ter ā′kwē əs) *adj.* [*< L. terra,* earth (see TERRACE) + AQUEOUS] consisting of land and water

ter·rar·i·um (tə rer′ē əm) *n., pl.* **-i·ums, -i·a** (-ə) [ModL. *< L. terra,* earth (see TERRACE) + *-arium,* as in *aquarium*] **1.** an enclosure in which to keep small land animals **2.** a glass container enclosing a garden of small plants

ter·raz·zo (tə raz′ō, tə rät′sō, te-) *n.* [It., lit., TERRACE] flooring of small chips of marble set in cement and polished

Ter·re Haute (ter′ə hōt′, hut′) [Fr., lit., high land] city in W Ind., on the Wabash: pop. 70,000

ter·rene (te rēn′, ter′ēn) *adj.* [ME. *< L. terrenus:* see TERRAIN] **1.** of earth; earthy **2.** worldly; mundane —*n.* **1.** the earth **2.** a land or territory

terre·plein (ter′plān′) *n.* [Fr. *< It. terrepieno < terrapienare,* to fill with earth, terrace *< terra* (see TERRACE) + *pienare,* to fill *< L. plenus,* full: see PLENTY] a level platform behind a parapet, rampart, etc., where guns are mounted

ter·res·tri·al (tə res′trē əl) *adj.* [ME. *terrestrialle < L. terrestris < terra,* earth (see TERRACE)] **1.** of this world; worldly; earthly; mundane **2.** of, constituting, or representing the earth *[a* terrestrial *globe]* **3.** consisting of land as distinguished from water **4.** living on land rather than in water, in the air, in trees, etc. **5.** growing on or in the soil —*n.* an inhabitant of the earth —*SYN.* see EARTHLY —**ter·res′tri·al·ly** *adv.*

ter·ret (ter′it) *n.* [ME. *teret < OFr. toret,* dim. of *tour,* a TURN] **1.** a ring for attaching a chain or leash, as on a dog collar **2.** any of the rings on a harness, through which the reins pass

terre-verte (ter′vert′) *n.* [Fr. *< terre,* earth (*< L. terra:* see TERRACE) + *verte,* green (see VERT)] any of several greenish earths used as a green pigment by artists

ter·ri·ble (ter′ə b'l) *adj.* [ME. *< OFr. < L. terribilis < terrere,* to frighten: see TERROR] **1.** causing terror; fearful; frightful; dreadful **2.** extreme; intense; severe **3.** [Colloq.] very bad, unpleasant, disagreeable, etc. —**ter′ri·ble·ness** *n.*

ter·ri·bly (-blē) *adv.* **1.** in a terrible manner **2.** extremely; very *[a* terribly *funny man]*

ter·ric·o·lous (te rik′ə ləs) *adj.* [< L. *terricola*, earth dweller < *terra*, earth + *colere*, to dwell, till (see CULT) + -OUS] *Biol.* living in or on the ground

ter·ri·er¹ (ter′ē ər) *n.* [ME. *terrere* < MFr. (*chien*) *terrier*, hunting (dog) < *terrier*, hillock, burrow < ML. *terrarius*, of earth < L. *terra* (see TERRACE)] any of various breeds of active, typically small dog, orig. bred to burrow after small game

ter·ri·er² (ter′ē ər) *n.* [ME. *terrar* < MFr. *terrier* < ML. *terrarius* (*liber*), (book) concerning the land (or landed estates): see prec.] in England, a detailed inventory of the landholdings of persons or corporations

ter·rif·ic (tə rif′ik) *adj.* [L. *terrificus* < base of *terrere*, to frighten: see TERROR & -FIC] 1. causing great fear or dismay; terrifying; dreadful; appalling 2. [Colloq.] *a*) unusually great, intense, severe, etc. *b*) unusually fine, admirable, enjoyable, etc. —**ter·rif′i·cal·ly** *adv.*

ter·ri·fy (ter′ə fi′) *vt.* -fied′, -fy′ing [L. *terrificare* < *terrificus*, TERRIFIC] to fill with terror; frighten greatly; alarm —SYN. see FRIGHTEN —**ter′ri·fy′ing·ly** *adv.*

ter·rig·e·nous (te rij′ə nəs) *adj.* [L. *terrigenus* < *terra*, earth + *gignere*, to be born: see TERRACE & GENUS] 1. earthborn 2. designating or of sea-bottom sediment derived from the erosion of land

ter·rine (te rēn′) *n.* [Fr.: see TUREEN] a small earthenware dish or jar in which table delicacies are prepared or packed

ter·ri·to·ri·al (ter′ə tôr′ē əl) *adj.* [LL. *territorialis*] 1. of territory or land 2. of, belonging to, or limited to a specific territory, district, or jurisdictional area [*territorial waters*] ☆3. [T-] of a Territory or Territories 4. [often T-] organized in regional groups for home defense [the *Territorial* Army of Great Britain] 5. *Ethology* characterized by or displaying territoriality —*n.* a member of a territorial force; specif., [T-] a member of the British Territorial Army —**ter′ri·to′ri·al·ly** *adv.*

ter·ri·to·ri·al·ism (-iz′m) *n.* any territorial system —**ter′ri·to′ri·al·ist** *n.*

ter·ri·to·ri·al·i·ty (ter′ə tôr′ē al′ə tē) *n.* 1. the state or quality of being territorial 2. *Ethology* the behavior pattern exhibited by an animal in defending its territory

ter·ri·to·ri·al·ize (ter′ə tôr′ē ə līz′) *vt.* -ized′, -iz′ing 1. to add territory to 2. *a*) to establish as a territory *b*) to reduce to the status of a territory 3. to distribute among territories —**ter′ri·to′ri·al·i·za′tion** *n.*

ter·ri·to·ry (ter′ə tôr′ē) *n., pl.* -ries [ME. < L. *territorium* < *terra*, earth] 1. the land and waters under the jurisdiction of a nation, state, ruler, etc. 2. a part of a country or empire that does not have the full status of a principal division; specif., ☆*a*) [T-] formerly, a part of the United States having its own legislature but without the status of a State and under the administration of an appointed governor *b*) [T-] a similar region, as in Canada or Australia, without the status of a Province or State See also TRUST TERRITORY 3. any large tract of land; region; district ☆4. an assigned area, as of a traveling salesman or franchised dealer 5. a sphere or province of action, existence, thought, etc. 6. *Ethology* the particular area occupied by an animal or group of animals; esp., the specific area appropriated by an animal or pair of animals, usually for breeding, nesting, and foraging purposes, and forcibly defended against any intruders 7. *Football, Hockey*, etc. that half of the playing area defended by a specified team

ter·ror (ter′ər) *n.* [ME. *terrour* < MFr. *terreur* < L. *terror* < *terrere*, to frighten < IE. *ters-*, to tremble (whence Gr. *trein*, to tremble, flee) < base *ter-*, to wriggle] 1. intense fear 2. *a*) a person or thing causing intense fear *b*) the quality of causing such fear; terribleness 3. a program of terrorism or a party, group, etc. resorting to terrorism 4. [Colloq.] a very annoying or unmanageable person, esp. a child; nuisance; pest —SYN. see FEAR

ter·ror·ism (-iz′m) *n.* [Fr. *terrorisme*] 1. the act of terrorizing; use of force or threats to demoralize, intimidate, and subjugate, esp. such use as a political weapon or policy 2. the demoralization and intimidation produced in this way —**ter′ror·ist** *n., adj.* —**ter′ror·is′tic** *adj.*

ter·ror·ize (-īz′) *vt.* -ized′, -iz′ing 1. to fill with terror; terrify 2. to coerce, make submit, etc. by filling with terror, as by the use or threat of violence —SYN. see FRIGHTEN —**ter′ror·i·za′tion** *n.*

ter·ry (ter′ē) *n., pl.* -ries [prob. < Fr. *tiré*, pp. of *tirer*, to draw] 1. uncut loops forming the pile of some fabrics 2. cloth having a pile of such loops; esp., cotton cloth used for toweling: also **terry cloth**

Ter·ry (ter′ē), Dame **Ellen** (**Alice** or **Alicia**) 1848–1928; Eng. actress

terse (turs) *adj.* **ters′er, ters′est** [L. *tersus*, wiped off, clean, pp. of *tergere*, to wipe < IE. *terg-* < base *ter-*, to rub, turn: cf. THROW] free of superfluous words; concise in a polished, smooth way; succinct —SYN. see CONCISE —**terse′ly** *adv.* —**terse′ness** *n.*

ter·tial (tur′shəl) *adj.* [< L. *tertius*, THIRD + -AL] designating or of the flight feathers, forming the third row, on the basal part of a bird's wing —*n.* a tertial feather

ter·tian (tur′shən) *adj.* [ME. *tercian* < L. (*febris*) *tertiana*, tertian (fever) < *tertius*, THIRD] occurring every other day

(i.e., every third day, counting both days of occurrence): usually applied to fever or a disease causing it, esp. any of certain forms of malaria —*n.* a tertian fever or disease

ter·ti·ar·y (tur′shē er′ē, -shə rē) *adj.* [L. *tertiarius* < *tertius*, THIRD] 1. of the third rank, order, formation, stage, etc.; third 2. *Chem.* *a*) third in order or type; involving the substitution of three atoms or radicals *b*) characterized by or designating a carbon atom or group attached to three other carbon atoms or groups in a chain or ring 3. [T-] *Geol.* designating or of the first period preceding the Quaternary in the Cenozoic Era, comprising the Paleocene, Eocene, Oligocene, Miocene, and Pliocene Epochs 4. *Linguis.* designating, of, or being an accent, or stress, that is weaker than a secondary accent 5. *R.C.Ch.* of the Third Order: see THIRD ORDER 6. *Zool.* same as TERTIAL —*n., pl.* -ar′ies 1. *R.C.Ch.* a member of the Third Order 2. *Zool.* same as TERTIAL —**the Tertiary** the Tertiary Period or its rocks: see GEOLOGY, chart

ter·ti·um quid (tur′shē əm kwid) [L., lit., third something] something of uncertain or unclassifiable nature, related to, but distinct from, two, usually opposite, things

Ter·tul·li·an (tər tul′ē ən, -tul′yən) (L. name *Quintus Septimius Florens Tertullianus*) 160?–230? A.D.; Latin church father, born in Carthage

ter·va·lent (tər vā′lənt) *adj.* [L. *ter*, thrice (akin to *tres*, THREE) + -VALENT] 1. having three valences 2. same as TRIVALENT (sense 1)

Ter·y·lene (ter′ə lēn′) [arbitrary blend of *ter*(*ephthalate*) + (*polyeth*)*ylene*, components in its production] *a trademark for* a synthetic, polyester, textile fiber, used in making suits, shirts, rainwear, etc.

ter·za ri·ma (tert′sə rē′mə) [It., lit., third rhyme < L. *tertia*, THIRD + Fr. *rime*: see RHYME] a verse form of Italian origin, made up of tercets, the second line of each tercet rhyming with the first and third lines of the next one (*aba, bcb, cdc*, etc.)

tes·la (tes′lə) *n.* [after ff.] the international unit of magnetic flux density, equal to one weber per square meter

Tes·la (tes′lə), **Ni·ko·la** (nik′ə lə) 1856–1943; U.S. inventor, born in Croatia

tes·sel·late (tes′ə lāt′; *for adj.* -lit) *vt.* -lat′ed, -lat′ing [< L. *tessellatus* < *tessella*, little square stone, dim. of *tessera*, a square: see ff.] to lay out, inlay, or pave in a mosaic pattern of small, square blocks —*adj.* arranged in a mosaic pattern; tessellated —**tes′sel·la′tion** (-lā′shən) *n.*

tes·ser·a (tes′ər ə) *n., pl.* -ser·ae (-ē) [L., square piece, cube < Gr. (Ionic) *tesseres* (for *tessares*), four: see TETRA-] 1. in ancient Rome, a small tablet of wood, ivory, etc. used as a token, ticket, label, etc. 2. any of the small pieces used in mosaic work

Tes·sin (Fr. te san′; G. te sēn′) Fr. & Ger. name of TICINO

tes·si·tu·ra (tes′i toor′ə; It. tes′sē tōō′rä) *n., pl.* -ras; It. -re (-re) [It., lit., texture < L. *textura*, TEXTURE] the average level of pitch of a specific vocal composition, operatic role, etc.

test¹ (test) *n.* [ME., a cupel < OFr., a pot, cupel < L. *testum*, earthen vessel < *testa*, piece of burned clay, shell < IE. base *tekth-*, to weave, join, whence Sans. *tašta*, cup, Gr. *tektōn*, a carpenter: mod. meaning from use of the cupel in examining metals] 1. *former var.* of CUPEL (sense 1) 2. an examination, experiment, or trial, as to prove the value or ascertain the nature of something 3. *a*) a method, process, or means used in making such an examination or trial *b*) a standard or criterion by which the qualities of a thing are tried *c*) an oath or declaration required as proof of one's orthodoxy, loyalty, etc. 4. an event, set of circumstances, etc. that proves or tries a person's qualities [the delay was a *test* of his patience] 5. a set of questions, problems, or exercises for determining a person's knowledge, abilities, aptitude, or qualifications; examination 6. *Chem.* *a*) a trial or reaction for identifying a substance or ingredient *b*) the reagent used in the procedure *c*) a positive indication obtained by it —*vt.* 1. to refine (metal), as in a cupel 2. to subject to a test; try 3. *Chem.* to examine by means of a reagent or reagents —*vi.* 1. to give or undergo a diagnostic test or a test of quality, function, etc.: usually with *for* [to *test* for blood sugar] 2. to be rated as the result of a test [to *test* high in comprehension] —SYN. see TRIAL —**test′a·ble** *adj.*

test² (test) *n.* [L. *testa*: see prec.] the hard outer covering of certain invertebrate animals, as the shell of clams

Test. Testament

tes·ta (tes′tə) *n., pl.* -tae (-tē) [ModL. < L.: see TEST¹] *Bot.* the hard outer covering or integument of a seed

tes·ta·cean (tes tā′shən) *n.* [< ModL. *Testacea*, name of the order < L. *testaceum*, shellfish < *testaceus*: see ff.] any of an order (Testacea) of shell-covered rhizopods

tes·ta·ceous (-shəs) *adj.* [L. *testaceus*, consisting of brick, tile, or shell < *testa*: see TEST¹] 1. of, like, or from shells 2. having a hard shell 3. *Biol.* of the color of unglazed earthenware; light reddish-brown

tes·ta·cy (tes′tə sē) *n. Law* the state of being testate

tes·ta·ment (tes′tə mənt) *n.* [ME. < OFr. < LL.(Ec.) *testamentum*, Testament (in NT., transl. of Gr. *diathēkē*,

covenant) < L., a will < *testari*, to testify, make a will < *testis*, a witness: see TESTIFY] **1.** orig., a covenant, esp. one between God and man **2.** [T-] *a*) either of the two parts of the Christian Bible, the *Old Testament* and the *New Testament b*) [Colloq.] a copy of the New Testament **3.** *a*) a statement, act, etc. testifying to the fact, validity, or worth of something; testimonial [*a testament* to liberty] *b*) an affirmation of beliefs or convictions; profession [a freethinker's *testament*] **4.** *Law* a will: now rare except in the phrase **last will and testament** —**tes′ta·men′ta·ry** (-men′tə rē), **tes′ta·men′tal** *adj.*

tes·tate (tes′tāt) *adj.* [LME. < L. *testatus*, pp. of *testari*: see prec.] having made and left a legally valid will —*n.* a person who has died testate

tes·ta·tor (tes′tāt ər, tes tāt′-) *n.* [ME. *testatour* < L. *testator* < pp. of *testari*: see TESTAMENT] a person who has made a will, esp. one who has died leaving a valid will —**tes·ta′trix** (-tā′triks) *n.fem.*, *pl.* **-tri·ces′** (-tri sēz′)

test ban an agreement between or among nuclear powers to forgo tests of nuclear weapons, esp. in the atmosphere

test case *Law* **1.** a case that, after its determination, is likely to be used as a precedent ☆**2.** a case entered into with the intention of testing the constitutionality of a particular law

test·ee (tes tē′) *n.* [TEST¹ + -EE¹] a person who has been or is being tested

test·er¹ (tes′tər) *n.* a person or thing that tests

tes·ter² (tes′tər) *n.* [ME. *testere* < OFr. *testiere*, headpiece, crown of a hat < *teste*, the head < L. *testa*: see TEST¹] a canopy, as over a bed

tes·ter³ (tes′tər) *n.* [altered < MFr. *testart* < *teston*, TESTON + -*art*, -ARD] *same as* TESTON (sense *b*)

tes·tes (tes′tēz) *n. pl.* of TESTIS

tes·ti·cle (tes′ti k'l) *n.* [L. *testiculus*, dim. of *testis*, testicle, lit., witness: see TESTIFY] either of two oval sex glands in the male that are suspended in the scrotum and secrete spermatozoa; testis —**tes·tic′u·lar** (-tik′yoo lər) *adj.*

tes·tic·u·late (tes tik′yoo lit) *adj.* [< L. *testiculus* (see prec.) + -ATE¹] *Bot.* **1.** shaped like a testicle **2.** having two testicle-shaped tubers, as certain orchids

tes·ti·fy (tes′tə fī′) *vi.* **-fied′, -fy′ing** [ME. *testifien* < L. *testificari* < *testis*, a witness (prob. < **tri-sto-*, standing as a third: see TRI- & STAND) + *facere*, to make, DO] **1.** to make a serious declaration to substantiate a fact; bear witness or give evidence, esp. under oath in court **2.** to be evidence or an indication [a look *testifying* to his impatience] —*vt.* **1.** to bear witness to; affirm; declare, esp. under oath in court **2.** to be evidence of; indicate **3.** [Archaic] to profess or proclaim publicly —**tes′ti·fi·ca′tion** *n.* —**tes′ti·fi′er** *n.*

tes·ti·mo·ni·al (tes′tə mō′nē əl) *n.* [ME. < OFr. < LL. *testimonialis* < *testimonium*: see ff.] **1.** a statement testifying to a person's qualifications, character, etc. or to the merits of some product, service, etc.; letter or statement of recommendation **2.** something given or done as an expression of gratitude or appreciation

tes·ti·mo·ny (tes′tə mō′nē) *n., pl.* **-nies** [ME. < L. *testimonium* < *testis*, a witness: see TESTIFY] **1.** a declaration or statement made under oath or affirmation by a witness in a court, often in response to questioning, to establish a fact **2.** any affirmation or declaration **3.** any form of evidence, indication, etc.; proof [the smile that was *testimony* of his disbelief] **4.** public avowal, as of faith or of a religious experience **5.** *Bible a*) the tablet bearing the Mosaic law; Decalogue: Ex. 25:16 *b*) [*pl.*] the precepts of God —SYN. see PROOF

tes·tis (tes′tis) *n., pl.* **-tes** (-tēz) [L.] *same as* TESTICLE

tes·ton (tes′tən) *n.* [Fr. < It. *testone* < *testa*, the head < L. *testa*: see TEST¹] any of several old European coins with the image of a head on one side; specif., *a*) a silver French coin of the 16th century *b*) an English coin with the head of Henry VIII Also **tes·toon′** (-tōon′)

tes·tos·ter·one (tes täs′tə rōn′) *n.* [TEST(IS) + -o- + STER(OL) + -ONE] a male, steroid, sex hormone, $C_{19}H_{28}O_2$, produced as a white, crystalline substance by isolation from animal testes, or synthesized: used in medicine

test paper 1. a paper on which a test has been written **2.** paper, as litmus paper, prepared with a reagent for making chemical tests

test pilot a pilot who tests new or newly designed airplanes in flight, to determine their fitness for use

test-tube (tes′tōob′, -tyōob′) *adj.* **1.** made in or as in a test tube; experimental **2.** produced by artificial insemination [a *test-tube* baby]

test tube a tube of thin, transparent glass closed at one end, used in chemical experiments, etc.

tes·tu·di·nal (tes tōod′'n əl, -tyōod′-) *adj.* [< L. *testudineus* < *testudo* (see TESTUDO) + -AL] of or like a tortoise or its shell; testudinate: also **tes·tu′di·nar′i·ous** (-er′ē əs)

tes·tu·di·nate (-it) *adj.* [LL. *testudinatus* (see ff.)] **1.** arched or vaulted like a tortoise shell **2.** having a protective bony shell, as the turtle —*n.* a turtle

tes·tu·do (tes tōo′dō, -tyōo′-) *n., pl.* **-di·nes′** (-də nēz′) [L., tortoise, tortoise shell, hence protective covering, shed < *testa*, shell: see TEST²] **1.** a movable shelter or screen with a strong arched roof, used as a protection by ancient Roman soldiers **2.** a protective covering over a group of ancient Roman soldiers, formed by overlapping their shields above their heads

tes·ty (tes′tē) *adj.* **-ti·er, -ti·est** [ME. *testif* < Anglo-Fr. < OFr. *teste*, the head < L. *testa*: see TEST¹] irritable; touchy; peevish —**tes′ti·ly** *adv.* —**tes′ti·ness** *n.*

Tet (tet) *n.* [Vietnamese] a three-day Asian festival in winter, celebrating the arrival of the new year in accordance with the lunar calendar

te·tan·ic (ti tan′ik) *adj.* [L. *tetanicus* < Gr. *tetanikos* < *tetanos*, a spasm] of, like, characterized by, or producing tetanus —*n.* any drug, as strychnine, capable of producing tetanic spasms of the muscles

tet·a·nize (tet′'n īz′) *vt.* **-nized′, -niz′ing** to produce tetanic spasms in (a muscle)

tet·a·nus (tet′'n əs) *n.* [L. < Gr. *tetanos*, spasm (of muscles), lit., stretched: for IE. base see TEND²] **1.** an acute infectious disease, often fatal, caused by the specific toxin of a bacillus (*Clostridium tetani*) which usually enters the body through wounds: it is characterized by spasmodic contractions and rigidity of some or all of the voluntary muscles, esp. of the jaw, face, and neck; lockjaw **2.** *Physiol.* the state of continuous contraction of a muscle, esp. when caused experimentally by a series of rapidly repeated stimuli

tet·a·ny (-ē) *n.* [ModL. *tetania*: see prec.] an abnormal condition characterized by tetanic spasms of voluntary muscles, esp. in the extremities

te·tar·to- (ti tär′tō, -tə) [< Gr. *tetartos*, fourth, akin to *tetra*: see TETRA-] *a combining form meaning* (a) fourth [*tetartohedral*]

te·tar·to·he·dral (ti tär′tə hē′drəl) *adj.* [prec. + -HEDRAL] having one fourth of the planes needed for crystallographic symmetry of the system

tetched (techt) *adj.* [LME. *techyd*, prob. altered (after *teche*, a quality, mark: see ff.) < *touchede*, pp. of *touchen*, TOUCH] [Dial. or Humorous] touched; slightly demented

tetch·y (tech′ē) *adj.* **tetch′i·er, tetch′i·est** [< LME. *teche*, a mark (prob. < OFr., a spot: see TACHISME) + -Y²] touchy; irritable; peevish —**tetch′i·ly** *adv.* —**tetch′i·ness** *n.*

tête-à-tête (tāt′ə tāt′; Fr. te tá tet′) *n.* [Fr., lit., head-to-head] **1.** a private or intimate conversation between two people ☆**2.** a usually S-shaped seat on which two people can sit so as to face each other —*adj.* for or of two people in private —*adv.* together privately [to speak *tête-à-tête*]

tête-bêche (tet′besh′) *adj.* [Fr. < *tête*, head + *bêche*, contr. < *béchevet*, the head of one at the feet of the other (in bed)] designating a pair of postage stamps printed, as in error, so that one is inverted in relation to the other

teth, tet (tet) *n.* [Heb. *tēth*] the ninth letter of the Hebrew alphabet (ט)

teth·er (teth′ər) *n.* [ME., prob. < ON. *tjothr*, akin to OHG. *zeotar*, wagon shaft] **1.** a rope or chain fastened to an animal so as to keep it within certain bounds **2.** the limit of one's abilities, resources, etc. —*vt.* to fasten or confine with a tether —**at the end of one's tether** at the end of one's endurance, resources, etc.

☆**teth·er·ball** (-bôl′) *n.* **1.** a game played by two people who, using the hand or a paddle, hit from opposite directions at a ball hanging by a length of cord from a pole: the object of the game is to make the cord coil completely around the pole **2.** the ball so used

Te·thys (tē′this) [L. < Gr. *Tēthys*] *Gr. Myth.* a Titaness, daughter of Uranus and wife of Oceanus

Te·ton (tē′tän) *n.* **1.** *pl.* **-tons, -ton** any member of a Dakota tribe of W N. America **2.** their Dakota dialect

tet·ra (tet′rə) *n.* [contr. < ModL. *Tetragonopterus*, old genus designation < *tetragonum*, TETRAGON + *-pterus*, -PTEROUS] any of a number of brightly colored, tropical American, characin fishes, often kept in aquariums

tet·ra- (tet′rə) [Gr. *tetra-* < base of *tettares, tessares*, four < IE. base **kwetwer-*, whence FOUR] *a combining form meaning* four [*tetrachord*]: also, before a vowel, **tetr-**

tet·ra·bas·ic (tet′rə bā′sik) *adj.* [prec. + BASIC] designating or of an acid having four replaceable hydrogen atoms per molecule

tet·ra·brach (tet′rə brak′) *n.* [Gr. *tetrabrachys*, consisting of four short syllables: see TETRA- & BRACHY-] *Gr. & L. Prosody* a word or foot containing four short syllables

tet·ra·bran·chi·ate (tet′rə braŋ′kē āt′, -it) *adj.* [ModL. *tetrabranchiatus*: see TETRA-, BRANCHIAE, & -ATE¹] of or belonging to an order (Tetrabranchia) of cephalopods with two pairs of gills, including the nautilus

tet·ra·chlo·ride (-klôr′īd) *n.* any chemical compound with four chlorine atoms to the molecule

tet·ra·chord (tet′rə kôrd′) *n.* [Gr. *tetrachordon*, musical instrument < *tetrachordos*, four-stringed: see TETRA- & CHORD²] *Music* a series of four tones comprising a total interval of a perfect fourth; half an octave —**tet′ra·chor′dal** *adj.*

te·trac·id (te tras′id) *n.* [TETR(A)- + ACID] **1.** a base that can react with four molecules of a monobasic acid to form a salt **2.** an alcohol having four OH groups per molecule

tet·ra·cy·cline (tet′rə sī′klin, -klin) *n.* [< TETRA- + CYCL(IC) + -INE⁴] a yellow, odorless, crystalline powder, $C_{22}H_{24}N_2O_8$, prepared synthetically or obtained from certain streptomyces: it is a broad-spectrum antibiotic

tet·rad (tet′rad) *n.* [Gr. *tetras* (gen. *tetrados*), four: see TETRA-] **1.** a group or set of four **2.** *Bot.* a group of four cells formed by division within a spore mother cell during meiosis **3.** *Chem.* an atom, radical, or element having a valence of four **4.** *Genetics* a group of four similar chro-

matids formed by the longitudinal division of a pair of homologous chromosomes during meiotic prophase

te·trad·y·mite (te trad′ə mīt′) *n.* [G. *tetradymit* < Gr. *tetradymos*, fourfold: because it occurs in compound twin crystals] a pale, steel-gray mineral, Bi_2Te_2S, consisting chiefly of tellurium and bismuth

☆**tet·ra·eth·yl lead** (tet′rə eth′′l) a heavy, colorless, poisonous compound of lead, $Pb(C_2H_5)_4$, added to gasoline to increase power and prevent engine knock

tet·ra·gon (tet′rə gän′) *n.* [LL. *tetragonum* < Gr. *tetragōnon*: see TETRA- & -GON] a plane figure with four angles and four sides; quadrangle

te·trag·o·nal (te trag′ə n′l) *adj.* **1.** of, or having the form of, a tetragon; quadrangular **2.** designating or of a system of crystallization in which the three axes intersect at right angles and the two horizontal axes are equal

tet·ra·gram (tet′rə gram′) *n.* [Gr. *tetragrammon*: see TETRA- & -GRAM] a word of four letters; specif., [T-] same as TETRAGRAMMATON

Tet·ra·gram·ma·ton (tet′rə gram′ə tän′) *n.* [ME. < Gr. *tetragrammaton* < *tetra-*, four + *gramma*, a letter (see GRAM¹] the four consonants of the ancient Hebrew name for God (variously transliterated JHVH, IHVH, JHWH, YHVH, YHWH), considered too sacred to be spoken aloud: the word *Adonai* (Lord) is substituted for this name in utterance, and the vowels of *Adonai* or *Elohim* (God) are inserted in Hebrew texts, so that the modern reconstructions are *Yahweh, Jehovah,* etc.

tet·ra·he·dral (tet′rə hē′drəl) *adj.* of, or having the form of, a tetrahedron —**tet′ra·he′dral·ly** *adv.*

tet·ra·he·drite (-hē′drīt) *n.* [G. *tetraëdrit* < LGr. *tetraedros* (see ff.) + G. *-it*, -ITE¹] a gray to blackish mineral occurring in tetrahedral crystals, essentially a sulfide of copper and antimony, $Cu_3(Sb,As)S_3$: in many forms the copper is partly replaced by iron, lead, silver, etc. and the antimony by arsenic: it is an important ore of copper and, sometimes, silver

tet·ra·he·dron (-hē′drən) *n., pl.* **-drons, -dra** (-drə) [ModL. < neut. of LGr. *tetraedros*, four-sided: see TETRA- & -HEDRON] a solid figure with four triangular faces

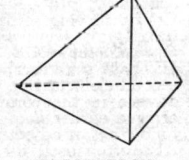

TETRAHEDRON

tet·ra·hy·dro·can·na·bi·nol (-hī′drō kan′ə bi nôl′) *n.* [TETRA- + HYDRO- + CANNABIN + -OL¹] a mind-affecting chemical, the principal and most active ingredient in marijuana

te·tral·o·gy (te tral′ə jē) *n., pl.* **-gies** [Gr. *tetralogia*: see TETRA- & -LOGY] **1.** a series of four dramas, three tragic and one satiric, performed together at the ancient Athenian festival of Dionysus **2.** any series of four related plays, novels, etc.

te·tram·er·ous (te tram′ər əs) *adj.* [TETRA- + -MEROUS] *Biol.* made up of four parts or divisions; in multiples of four: also written **4-merous**

te·tram·e·ter (te tram′ə tər) *n.* [LL. *tetrametrus* < Gr. *tetrametros*: see TETRA- & METER] **1.** a line of verse containing four metrical feet or measures **2.** verse consisting of tetrameters —*adj.* having four metrical feet or measures

tet·ra·pet·al·ous (tet′rə pet′′l əs) *adj.* four-petaled

tet·ra·ploid (tet′rə ploid′) *adj.* [TETRA- + -PLOID] *Biol.* having four times the haploid number of chromosomes —*n.* a tetraploid cell or organism —**tet′ra·ploi′dy** *n.*

tet·ra·pod (-päd′) *n.* [TETRA- + -POD] any object, as a caltrop, having four feet or projections coming from a central part so that it can rest on any three of the four feet

te·trap·ter·ous (te trap′tər əs) *adj.* [Gr. *tetrapteros*: see TETRA- & -PTEROUS] *Zool.* having four wings

te·trarch (te′trärk, tē′-) *n.* [ME. *tetrarche* < LL.(Ec.) *tetrarcha* < L. *tetrarches* < Gr. *tetrarchēs*: see TETRA- & -ARCH] **1.** in the ancient Roman Empire, the ruler of part (orig. a fourth part) of a province **2.** a subordinate prince, governor, etc. —**te·trarch′ic** *adj.*

te·trarch·y (-trär kē) *n., pl.* **-trarch·ies** [L. *tetrarchia* < Gr. *tetrarchia*] **1.** the rule or territory of a tetrarch **2.** government by four persons **3.** a group of four rulers **4.** a country divided into four subordinate governments Also **te′trarch·ate′** (-kāt′, -kit)

tet·ra·spo·ran·gi·um (tet′rə spô ran′jē əm) *n., pl.* **-gi·a** (-ə) *Bot.* a sporangium containing four asexual spores

tet·ra·spore (tet′rə spôr′) *n. Bot.* any of the asexual algal spores produced in groups of four in a tetrasporangium

tet·ra·stich (tet′rə stik′) *n.* [L. *tetrastichon* < Gr. *tetrastichon*: see TETRA- & STICH] a poem or stanza of four lines —**tet′ra·stich′ic** *adj.*

te·tras·ti·chous (te tras′ti kəs) *adj.* [Gr. *tetrastichos*, in four rows: see TETRA- & STICH] *Bot.* in four vertical rows, as the flowers on some spikes

tet·ra·syl·la·ble (tet′rə sil′ə b′l) *n.* a word of four syllables —**tet′ra·syl·lab′ic** (-si lab′ik) *adj.*

tet·ra·tom·ic (tet′rə täm′ik) *adj.* **1.** designating or of a molecule consisting of four atoms **2.** having four replaceable atoms or groups

tet·ra·va·lent (tet′rə vā′lənt) *adj.* **1.** having a valence of four **2.** *same as* QUADRIVALENT (sense 1)

Te·traz·zi·ni (te′trä tsē′nē; *E.* tet′rə zē′nē), **Lu·i·sa** (loo ē′zä) 1871–1940; It. operatic soprano

tet·rode (tet′rōd) *n.* [TETR(A)- + -ODE¹] an electron tube having four electrodes (a cathode, control grid, anode, and, usually, a screen grid): used to generate, amplify, modulate, or demodulate electrical signals

tet·ro·do·tox·in (tet′rə dō täk′sin) *n.* [< ModL. *Tetrodon*, a genus of fishes (short for *tetraodon* < *tetra-*, TETRA- + Gr. *odōn*, a TOOTH) + TOXIN] an extremely poisonous substance, found in the puffer fishes and a genus of newts, that blocks the conduction of nerve signals by stopping completely the movement of sodium ions into cells

te·trox·ide (te träk′sīd) *n.* any oxide with four atoms of oxygen in each molecule

tet·ryl (tet′ril) *n.* [*tetr(anitromethyl(aniline)*] a yellow powder, $C_7H_5N_5O_8$, used as a primer and as an explosive, esp. in detonators

tet·ter (tet′ər) *n.* [ME. *tetere* < OE. *teter*, akin to Sans. *dadru*, skin disease] any of various skin diseases, as eczema, characterized by itching

Te·tuán (te twän′) seaport in NE Morocco, on the Mediterranean: former cap. of Spanish Morocco: pop. 120,000

Tet·zel (tet′səl), **Jo·hann** (yō′hän) 1465?–1519; Ger. Dominican monk & inquisitor: opposed by Luther

Teu·cri·an (too′krē ən, tyoo′-) *adj., n.* [< *Teucer* (Gr. *Teukros*), first king of Troy] *same as* TROJAN

Teut. 1. Teuton **2.** Teutonic

Teu·to·burg Forest (too′tə burg′, tyoo′-) region of low, forested mountains, mostly in North Rhine-Westphalia, West Germany: highest point, c.1,500 ft.: Ger. name **Teu·to·bur·ger Wald** (toi′tô boor′gər vält′)

Teu·ton (toot′n, tyoot′-) *n.* **1.** a member of the Teutones **2.** a member of any Teutonic people; esp., a German

Teu·to·nes (-ēz′) *n.pl.* [L. < IE. *teutonos*, ruler < base *teutā*, people, country: cf. DEUTSCHLAND] an ancient tribe, variously considered as Teutonic or Celtic, that lived north of the Elbe in Jutland

Teu·ton·ic (too tän′ik, tyoo-) *adj.* **1.** of the ancient Teutons **2.** of the Germans; German **3.** designating or of a group of north European peoples including the German, Scandinavian, Dutch, English, etc. **4.** *Linguis.* earlier *var.* of GERMANIC —**Teu·ton′i·cal·ly** *adv.*

Teutonic Order a military and religious order of German knights (**Teutonic Knights**) organized in 1191 for service in the Crusades and later active in the military conquests by Germany of Baltic and Slavic lands

Teu·ton·ism (toot′n iz′m, tyoot′-) *n.* **1.** belief in the supposed racial superiority of the Teutons, esp. of the Germans **2.** Teutonic life, customs, etc. **3.** a Germanism Also **Teu·ton·i·cism** (too tän′ə siz′m, tyoo-) —**Teu′ton·ist** *n.*

Teu·ton·ize (-īz′) *vt., vi.* **-ized′, -iz′ing** to make or become Teutonic or German —**Teu′ton·i·za′tion** *n.*

Te·ve·re (te′ve re) *It. name of the* TIBER

Te·wa (tā′wə) *n.* **1.** *pl.* **-was, -wa** a member of any of six Indian tribes living in pueblo villages in New Mexico **2.** their Tanoan language

Tewkes·bur·y (tooks′ber′ē, tyooks′-; -bə rē) town in N Gloucestershire, England, on the Severn: site of a battle (1471) in the Wars of the Roses, reestablishing Edward IV on the English throne: pop. 6,000

Tex·ar·kan·a (tek′sär kan′ə) city on the Tex.-Ark. border, having a separate municipal government in each State: pop. (Tex.) 30,000, (Ark.) 22,000

Tex·as (tek′səs) [Sp. < AmInd. (Caddo) *techas*, allies (against the Apaches)] SW State of the U.S., on the Gulf of Mexico & the Mexican border: admitted, 1845; 267,339 sq. mi.; pop. 11,197,000; cap. Austin: abbrev.**Tex., TX** —*n.* [t-] [name given to officers' quarters on Mississippi steamboats because they were the largest cabins] a structure on the hurricane deck of a steamboat, containing the officers' quarters, etc. and having the pilothouse on top or in front —**Tex′an** *adj., n.*

Texas City seaport in SE Texas, on Galveston Bay: pop. 39,000

☆**Texas fever** an infectious disease of cattle caused by a sporozoan (*Babesia bigemina*) that invades the red blood cells and is carried by a cattle tick (*Boophilus annulatus*)

☆**Texas leaguer** [< the *Texas* (baseball) *League*] *Baseball* a fly ball that falls between the infield and outfield and is a safe hit

☆**Texas Ranger** a member of the mounted State police of Texas

☆**Texas tower** [so named after such structures, orig. for oil drilling, off the coast of *Texas*] an offshore platform erected on firm foundations or steel legs planted deeply in the sea bottom: used for supporting radar installations, navigation beacons, etc.

text (tekst) *n.* [ME. < OFr. *texte* < L. *textus*, fabric, structure, text < pp. of *texere*, to weave: see TECHNIC] **1.** the actual structure of words in a piece of writing; wording **2.** *a)* the actual or original words used by an author, as distinguished from notes, commentary, paraphrase, translation, etc. *b)* the exact or original words of a speaker **3.** any of the forms, versions, or editions in

which a written work exists **4.** the principal matter on a printed or written page, as distinguished from notes, headings, illustrations, etc. **5.** the main body of a book, excluding front and back matter **6.** the words of a song, oratorio, etc. **7.** *a)* a Biblical passage quoted as authority for a belief or as the topic of a sermon *b)* any passage, book, etc. used to support one's stand or as thematic material, etc. *c)* any topic or subject dealt with in **8.** *same as* TEXT HAND **9.** any of several black-letter styles of type: also **text letter 10.** *clipped form of* TEXTBOOK **11.** any of various versions or recensions of all or part of the Scriptures, taken to represent the authentic reading —*SYN.* see SUBJECT

text·book (tekst′book′) *n.* a book giving instructions in the principles of a subject of study, specif. one used as the basis or partial basis of a course of study

text hand large handwriting: so called from its former use to distinguish the text of manuscripts from notes

tex·tile (teks′tīl, -t'l, -til) *adj.* [L. *textilis* < *textus:* see TEXT] **1.** having to do with weaving or with woven fabrics **2.** that has been or can be woven [*textile* material] —*n.* **1.** a fabric made by weaving, knitting, etc.; cloth **2.** raw material suitable for this, as cotton, wool, nylon, etc.

tex·tu·al (teks′choo wəl) *adj.* [ME. *textuel* < L. *textus:* see TEXT] **1.** of, in, based on, or conforming to a text **2.** literal; word-for-word —**tex′tu·al·ly** *adv.*

textual criticism *see* CRITICISM (sense 5)

tex·tu·al·ism (-iz′m) *n.* **1.** strict adherence to the text, esp. of the Scriptures **2.** the art of textual criticism —**tex′tu·al·ist** *n.*

tex·tu·ar·y (teks′choo wer′ē) *adj. same as* TEXTUAL —*n., pl.* **-ar′ies** *same as* TEXTUALIST

tex·ture (teks′chər) *n.* [ME. < L. *textura* < *texere*, to weave: see TECHNIC] **1.** orig., a woven fabric **2.** the character of a woven fabric as determined by the arrangement, size, quality, etc. of the fabric's threads [*coarse texture*, twilled *texture*] **3.** the arrangement of the particles or constituent parts of any material, as wood, metal, etc., as it affects the appearance or feel of the surface; structure, composition, grain, etc. **4.** *a)* the structural quality of a work of art, resulting from the artist's method of using his medium *b)* the melodic and harmonic relationships of musical materials **5.** basic structure [the *texture* of society] —*vt.* **-tured, -tur·ing** to cause to have a particular texture —**tex′tur·al** *adj.* —**tex′tur·al·ly** *adv.*

Tey·de (tā′ǐħe), **Pico de** *same as* Pico de TEIDE

☆**T formation** *Football* an offensive formation with the quarterback behind the center, the fullback behind the quarterback, and a halfback at each side of the fullback

t.g. type genus

-th¹ [ME. *-th, -the* < OE. *-thu, -tho, -th,* akin to Goth. *-itha* (< IE. **-ita,* whence L. *-ta,* Sans. *-tā*): in words such as *height, sleight,* the *-th* has become *-t*] *a n.-forming suffix meaning:* **1.** the act of [*stealth*] **2.** the state or quality of being or having [*wealth*]

-th² [ME. *-the* < OE. *-tha, -the, -otha, -othe* < IE. **-tos,* whence Gr. *-tos,* L. *-tus;* in *fifth, sixth, eleventh, twelfth,* it replaced the orig. OE. *-ta, -te*] a suffix used in forming ordinal numerals [*fourth, ninth*]: also, after a vowel, **-eth**

-th³ [ME. < OE.: see -ETH²] *contracted form of* -ETH² [*hath, doth*]

Th *Chem.* thorium

Th. Thursday

Thack·er·ay (thak′ər ē), **William Make·peace** (māk′pēs′) 1811–63; Eng. novelist

Thad·de·us, Thad·e·us (thad′ē əs) [ME. < LL.(Ec.) *Thaddeus* < Gr.(Ec.) *Thaddaios*] a masculine name: dim. *Tad*

Thai (tī) *n.* **1.** a group of Asian languages considered to be a subbranch of the Sino-Tibetan language family **2.** the official language of Thailand **3.** *pl.* **Thais, Thai** *a)* any member of a group of Thai-speaking peoples of SE Asia *b)* a native or inhabitant of Thailand —*adj.* of Thailand, its people, culture, etc.

Thai·land (tī′land, -lənd) country in SE Asia, on the Indochinese & Malay peninsulas: 198,456 sq. mi.; pop. 33,693,000; cap. Bangkok See INDOCHINA, map

Tha·is (thā′is) 4th cent. B.C.; semihistorical Athenian courtesan, said to have accompanied Alexander the Great on his Asiatic campaign

thal·a·men·ceph·a·lon (thal′ə men sef′ə län′) *n., pl.* **-la** (-lə) [ModL.: see THALAMUS & ENCEPHALON] *same as* DIENCEPHALON —**thal′a·men′ce·phal′ic** (-sə fal′ik) *adj.*

thal·a·mus (thal′ə məs) *n., pl.* **-mi′** (-mī′) [ModL. < L., an inner chamber < Gr. *thalamos*] **1.** *Anat.* a mass of gray matter forming the lateral walls of the diencephalon and involved in the transmission and integration of certain sensations **2.** *Bot. same as* RECEPTACLE (sense 3a) —**tha·lam·ic** (thə lam′ik) *adj.*

thal·as·se·mi·a (thal′ə sē′mē ə) *n.* [ModL. < Gr. *thalassa,* sea + -EMIA] an inherited chronic anemia found chiefly among Mediterranean peoples, resulting from faulty hemoglobin production

tha·las·sic (thə las′ik) *adj.* [Fr. *thalassique* < Gr. *thalassa,* sea] **1.** of the sea or ocean; marine **2.** of bays, gulfs, etc. and inland seas, as distinguished from the ocean

tha·ler (tä′lər) *n., pl.* **-ler** *same as* TALER

Tha·les (thā′lēz) 636?–546? B.C.; Gr. philosopher, born in Miletus

Tha·li·a (thā′lē ə, thál′yə; *for 2, usually* thə lī′ə) [L. < Gr. *Thaleia* < *thallein,* to flourish, bloom < IE. base **dhal-,* to blossom, whence Alb. *dal,* (I) sprout] **1.** a feminine name **2.** *Gr. Myth. a)* the Muse of comedy and pastoral poetry *b)* one of the three Graces

tha·lid·o·mide (thə lid′ə mīd′) *n.* [THAL(LIC) + (IM)IDO- + (glutari)mide < GLUT(EN) + (TART)AR(IC) + IMIDE] a crystalline solid, $C_{13}H_{10}N_2O_4$, formerly used as a sedative and hypnotic: found to be responsible for severe birth deformities when taken during pregnancy

thal·lic (thal′ik) *adj.* designating or of a chemical compound containing thallium with a valence of three

thal·li·um (thal′ē əm) *n.* [ModL. < Gr. *thallos,* young, green shoot (see THALIA): from the green line that it gives in the spectrum] a rare, poisonous, bluish-white, soft, metallic chemical element, used in making antiknock compound, photoelectric cells, rat poisons, etc.: symbol, Tl; at. wt., 204.37; at. no., 81; sp. gr., 11.85; melt. pt., 303.5°C; boil. pt., 1457°C

thal·loid (thal′oid) *adj.* of or like a thallus

thal·lo·phyte (-ə fīt′) *n.* [< Gr. *thallos,* a young shoot < *thallein* (see THALIA) + -PHYTE] any of a subkingdom (Thallophyta) of nonvascular plants showing no clear distinction of roots, stem, or leaves and not producing flowers or seeds: it includes the bacteria, algae, fungi, and lichens —**thal′lo·phyt′ic** (-fit′ik) *adj.*

thal·lous (thal′əs) *adj.* designating or of a chemical compound containing thallium with a valence of one

thal·lus (-əs) *n., pl.* **thal′li** (-ī), **thal′lus·es** (-iz) [ModL. < Gr. *thallos,* young shoot, sprout, frond: see THALIA] the nonvascular plant body of a thallophyte, showing no clear distinction of roots, stem, or leaves

thal·weg (täl′veg) *n.* [G., obs. sp. of *talweg,* lit., valley way < *tal,* valley (for IE. base see DALE) + *weg,* WAY] *Geog., Geol.* the longitudinal profile of a river valley or a submarine canyon

Thames (temz; *for 3,* thāmz, tāmz) **1.** river in S England, flowing from Gloucestershire east through London into the North Sea: 210 mi. **2.** river in SE Ontario, Canada, flowing southwest into Lake St. Clair: 163 mi. **3.** estuary in SE Conn., flowing south into Long Island Sound: 15 mi.

than (ħan, *then; unstressed* ħən, th'n) *conj.* [ME. *than, thene, thonne* < OE. *thenne, thanne, thonne,* orig., then: for IE. base see THAT] a particle used *a)* to introduce the second element in a comparison, following an adjective or adverb in the comparative degree [A is taller *than* B; arrived earlier *than* the others] *b)* to express exception, following an adjective or adverb [none other *than* Sam] Also often used for "when" after usually inverted constructions introduced typically by *scarcely, hardly, barely* [*scarcely* had I seen her *than* she spoke to me] —*prep.* compared to: in *than whom, than which* [a writer *than whom* there is none finer]

than·age (thān′ij), *n.* [ME. < Anglo-Fr.: see THANE & -AGE] **1.** the land held by a thane **2.** the tenure of such holding **3.** the rank, jurisdiction, or allegiance of a thane

than·a·to- (than′ə tō, -tə) [< Gr. *thanatos,* death < IE. **dhwen-,* dark, clouded < base **dheu-,* to be smoky, stormy, whence L. *fumus,* smoke] *a combining form meaning* death [*thanatophobia*]: also, before a vowel, **thanat-**

than·a·to·pho·bi·a (than′ə tō fō′bē ə) *n.* [prec. + -PHOBIA] an abnormally great fear of death

☆**than·a·top·sis** (than′ə täp′sis) *n.* [coined by William Cullen BRYANT < Gr. *thanatos,* death + *opsis,* view] a view of or musing upon death

Than·a·tos (than′ə täs) [Gr.: see THANATO-] *Gr. Myth.* death personified

thane (thān) *n.* [ME. *thayne* < OE. *thegen,* akin to ON. *thegn* < IE. base **tek-,* to engender, beget, whence Sans. *takman-,* child; basic sense "freeborn man"] **1.** in early England, a member of a class of freemen who held land of the king or a lord in return for military services **2.** in early Scotland, a person of rank, often a clan chief, who held land of the king

thank (thaŋk) *vt.* [ME. *thankien* < OE. *thancian,* akin to G. *danken* < IE. base **tong-,* to think, whence THINK¹, L. *tongere,* to know] **1.** to show or express appreciation or gratitude to, as by saying "thank you" **2.** to hold responsible; blame: an ironic use [we have him to *thank* for our failure] —**thank you** *shortened form of* I thank you: the usual expression of appreciation today

thank·ful (-fəl) *adj.* feeling or expressing thanks; grateful —**thank′ful·ly** *adv.* —**thank′ful·ness** *n.*

thank·less (-lis) *adj.* **1.** not feeling or expressing thanks; ungrateful **2.** not receiving nor likely to receive thanks; unappreciated —**thank′less·ly** *adv.* —**thank′less·ness** *n.*

thanks (thaŋks) *n.pl.* [pl. of ME. *thank* < OE. *thanc,* thanks: for IE. base see THANK] an expression of gratitude; grateful acknowledgment of something received by or done for one —*interj.* I thank you —**thanks to 1.** thanks be given to **2.** on account of; because of

thanks·giv·ing (thaŋks′giv′iŋ) *n.* **1.** *a)* the act of giving thanks *b)* an expression of this; esp., a formal, often public, expression of thanks to God in the form of a prayer, etc. ☆**2.** [T-] *a)* an annual U.S. holiday observed on the fourth Thursday of November as a day of giving thanks and feasting: it commemorates the Pilgrims' celebration of the good harvest of 1621 *b)* a similar Canadian holiday on the second Monday of October In full **Thanksgiving Day**

thank·wor·thy (thaŋk′wur′thē) *adj.* worthy of thanks
Thant (thänt, thônt), U (o͞o) 1909– ; Burmese diplomat; secretary-general of the United Nations (1962–)
Thap·sus (thap′səs) ancient town in N Africa, in what is now NE Tunisia
Thar Desert (tur, tär) desert in NW India & E West Pakistan, chiefly in Rajasthan, India
Tha·sos (thā′sŏs) island of Greece in the N Aegean, a part of Macedonia: c.170 sq. mi.
that (that; *unstressed* thət) *pron., pl.* **those** [ME. < OE. that, nom. & acc. neut. of the def. article (nom. masc. *se,* nom. fem. *seo:* cf. THE), akin to G. neut. nom. *das* < IE. demonstrative base *-to-, *-tā-, whence THERE, THITHER, L. *istud,* that, *talis,* such] **I.** *as a demonstrative pronoun:* **1.** the person or thing mentioned or understood [*that* is John, *that* tastes good] **2.** the thing farther away than another referred to as "this" [this is larger than *that*] **3.** the more remote in thought of two contrasted things [of the two possibilities, this is more likely than *that*] **4.** [*pl.*] certain people [*those* who know] **II.** *as a relative pronoun:* **1.** who, whom, or which: used generally in restrictive clauses and often omitted [the road (*that*) we took] **2.** where; at which; on which [the place *that* I saw him] **3.** when; in which; on which [the year *that* he was born] —*adj., pl.* **those 1.** designating the person or thing mentioned or understood [*that* man is John, *that* pie tastes good] **2.** designating the thing farther away than the one referred to as "this" [this house is larger than *that* one] **3.** designating the more remote in thought of two contrasted things [of the two, this possibility is more likely than *that* one] **4.** designating something or someone not described but well known or easily recognizable: sometimes with implications of disparagement [*that* certain feeling, there comes *that* smile!, *that* George!] —*conj. used:* **1.** to introduce a noun clause expressing a supposed or actual fact [that he's gone is obvious, the truth was *that* we never saw him] **2.** to introduce an adverbial clause expressing purpose [they died *that* we might live] **3.** to introduce an adverbial clause expressing result [he ran so fast *that* I couldn't catch up] **4.** to introduce an adverbial clause expressing cause [I'm sorry *that* I caused you such annoyance] **5.** to introduce an elliptical sentence expressing surprise, indignation, or desire [*that* he should say such a thing!, oh, *that* this day were over!] —*adv.* to that extent; so [I can't see *that* far ahead]: also used colloquially before an adjective modified by a clause of result [I'm *that* tired I could drop] —**all that** [Colloq.] **1.** so very: used in negative constructions [he isn't *all that* rich] **2.** everything of the same or related sort [sex and *all that*] —**☆at that** [Colloq.] **1.** at that point; with no further discussion, etc.: also **with that 2.** all things considered; even so —**that is 1.** to be specific. **2.** in other words —**that's that!** that is done (or settled or decided, etc.)!
thatch (thach) *n.* [altered (after the *v.*) < older *thack* < ME. *thac* < OE. *thæc,* a thatch, roof: for base see the *v.*] **1.** *a)* a roof or roofing of straw, rushes, palm leaves, etc. *b)* material for such a roof **2.** any of a number of palms whose leaves are used for thatch: also **thatch palm 3.** anything suggestive of thatch on a roof as *a)* the hair growing on the head *b)* a matted layer of partly decayed leaves, stems, etc. between growing vegetation and the soil —*vt.* [ME. *thecchen* < OE. *thecc(e)an,* akin to G. *decken,* to cover < IE. base *(s)teg-, to cover, whence Gr. *stegos,* roof, L. *tegere,* to cover] to cover with or as with thatch —**thatch′y** *adj.* **thatch′i·er, thatch′i·est**
thatch·ing (-iŋ) *n.* **1.** the act of a person who thatches **2.** material for a thatch roof, etc.
thau·ma·tol·o·gy (thô′mə täl′ə jē) *n.* [< Gr. *thauma* (gen. *thaumatos*), a miracle (see THEATER) + -LOGY] the study or lore of miracles
thau·ma·trope (thô′mə trōp′) *n.* [Gr. *thauma* (see prec.) + -TROPE] a device consisting of a card or disk with different designs on either side, which, when the card or disk is twirled, appear to blend into one: it demonstrates the persistence of vision
thau·ma·turge (-turj′) *n.* [Fr. < ML. *thaumaturgus* < Gr. *thaumaturgos,* working wonders < *thauma,* a wonder (see THEATER) + -*ergos,* working < *ergon,* WORK] a person who supposedly works miracles: also **thau′ma·turg′ist**
thau·ma·tur·gy (-tur′jē) *n.* [Gr. *thaumatourgia:* see prec.] the supposed working of miracles; magic —**thau′ma·tur′gic, thau′ma·tur′gi·cal** *adj.*
thaw (thô) *vi.* [ME. *thawen* < OE. *thawian,* akin to Du. *dooien,* G. (*ver)dauen,* to digest < IE. base *tā-, to melt, dissolve, vanish, whence L. *tabere,* to melt, vanish] **1.** *a)* to become liquid or semiliquid; melt: said of ice, snow, etc. *b)* to pass to an unfrozen state: said of frozen foods **2.** to rise in temperature above the freezing point, so that snow, etc. melts: said of weather conditions, with impersonal *it* [it will *thaw* tomorrow] **3.** *a)* to get rid of the chill, stiffness, etc. resulting from extreme cold (often with *out) b)* to lose coldness or reserve of manner —*vt.* to cause to thaw —*n.* **1.** the act of thawing **2.** a spell of weather warm enough to allow thawing **3.** a becoming less reserved in manner —*SYN.* see MELT

Th.B. [L. *Theologiae Baccalaureus*] Bachelor of Theology
THC tetrahydrocannabinol
Th.D. [L. *Theologiae Doctor*] Doctor of Theology
the (thə; *before vowels* thi, thē) *adj., definite article* [ME., indeclinable article < OE. *se* (nom. masc. article) with *th-* < other case & gender forms (thone, thæs, thære, thæm, thy): for base see THAT; the meaning is controlled by the basic notion "a previously recognized, noticed, or encountered" in distinction to A[1], AN[1]] **I.** *the* (as opposed to *a, an*) is used to refer to a particular person, thing, or group, as: **1.** that (one) being spoken of or already mentioned [the story ended] **2.** that (one) which is present, close, nearby, etc., as distinguished from all others viewed as remote [the day just started, the heat is oppressive] **3.** that (one) designated or identified, as by a title [the President (of the U.S.), the Mississippi (River)] **4.** that (one) considered outstanding, most fashionable, etc. [that's the restaurant in town]: usually italicized in print **5.** that (one) belonging to a person previously mentioned or understood [take me by the hand, rub into the face] **6.** that (one) considered as a unit of purchase, etc. [at five dollars the half ton] **7.** one specified period of time, esp. a decade [the Dark Ages, the seventies] **8.** [Colloq.] that (one) who has a specific family relationship to one [the wife, the kid sister] **II.** *the* is used to refer to that one of a number of persons or things which is identified by a modifier, as by: **1.** an attributive adjective [the front door] **2.** a relative clause [the man who answered] **3.** a prepositional phrase [the hit of the week] **4.** an infinitive phrase [the right to strike] **5.** a participle [follow the directions given] **III.** *the* is used to refer to a person or thing considered generically or universally, as: **1.** one taken as the representative of the entire genus or type [learn to use *the* typewriter, *the* cow is a domestic animal] **2.** an adjective used as a noun [the good, the beautiful, the true] —*adv.* **1.** that much; to that extent [the better to see you with] **2.** by how much . . . by that much; to what extent . . . to that extent: used in a correlative construction expressing comparison [the sooner the better]
the- *same as* THEO-: used before a vowel
the·an·thro·pism (thē an′thrə piz′m) *n.* [< Gr. (Ec.) *theanthrōpos,* god-man < Gr. *theos,* god + *anthrōpos,* man (see THEO- & ANTHROPO-) + -ISM] **1.** the attributing of human characteristics to God or a god **2.** the theological doctrine of the union of divine and human natures in Jesus Christ —**the·an′thro·pic** (-thräp′ik) *adj.* —**the·an′thro·pist** *n.*
the·ar·chy (thē′är kē) *n., pl.* -**chies** [Gr.(Ec.) *thearchia* < Gr. *theos,* god + -*archia,* -ARCHY] **1.** government by God or gods; theocracy **2.** a system or order of ruling deities
the·a·ter, the·a·tre (thē′ə tər) *n.* [ME. *theatre* < OFr. < L. *theatrum* < Gr. *theatron* < base of *theasthai,* to see, view < IE. base *dhāu-, to see, whence Gr. *thauma,* a wonder] **1.** a place where plays, operas, motion pictures, etc. are presented; esp., a building or outdoor structure expressly designed for such presentations **2.** any place resembling a theater, esp. a lecture hall, surgical clinic, etc., having the floor of the seating space raked **3.** any place where events take place; scene of operations [journalists in the SE Asian *theater*] **4.** *a)* the dramatic art or dramatic works; drama *b)* the theatrical world; people engaged in theatrical activity *c)* the legitimate theater, as distinguished from motion pictures, television, etc. **5.** theatrical technique, production, etc. with reference to its effectiveness [a play that is good *theater*]
the·a·ter·go·er, the·a·tre·go·er (-gō′ər) *n.* a person who attends the theater, esp. one who goes often
☆the·a·ter-in-the-round (thē′ə tər in thə round′) *n. same as* ARENA THEATER
the·at·ri·cal (thē at′ri k'l) *adj.* [< LL. *theatricus* (< Gr. *theatrikos*) + -AL] **1.** having to do with the theater, the drama, a play, actors, etc. **2.** characteristic of the theater; dramatic; esp. (in disparagement), melodramatic, histrionic, or affected Also **the·at′ric** —**the·at′ri·cal·ism, the·at′ri·cal′i·ty** (-kal′ə tē) *n.* —**the·at′ri·cal·ly** *adv.*
the·at·ri·cals (-k'lz) *n.pl.* performances of stage plays, esp. by amateurs
the·at·rics (thē at′riks) *n.pl.* **1.** [*with sing. v.*] the art of the theater **2.** something done or said for theatrical effect; histrionic actions, manners, devices, etc.
theater of the absurd avant-garde, mid-20th-cent. drama made up of apparently absurd, incongruous, or pointless situations and dialogue, typically expressing the existential nature of man's self-isolation, anxiety, frustration, etc.
The·ba·id (thē′bā id) [L. *Thebais* (gen. *Thebaidis*) < *Thebae,* Thebes] district under the control of Egyptian Thebes or of Boeotian Thebes
the·ba·ine (thē′bə ēn′, thi bā′in) *n.* [< L. *Thebae* (Gr. *Thēbai*), Thebes + -INE[4]: after an Egyptian opium produced at Thebes] a colorless, crystalline, poisonous alkaloid, $C_{19}H_{21}NO_3$, obtained from opium and used in medicine
Thebes (thēbz) **1.** ancient city in S Egypt, on the Nile, on the site of modern Luxor and Karnak **2.** chief city of ancient Boeotia, EC Greece —**The·ban** (thē′bən) *adj., n.*

fat, āpe, cär; ten, ēven; is, bīte; gō, hôrn, to͞ol, look; oil, out; up, fur; get; joy; yet; chin; she; thin, then; zh, leisure; ŋ, ring; ə for *a* in *ago, e* in *agent, i* in *sanity, o* in *comply, u* in *focus;* ' as in *able* (ā′b'l); Fr. bâl; ë, Fr. coeur; ö, Fr. feu; ô, Fr. mon; ɔ̄, Fr. coq; ü, Fr. duc; r, Fr. cri; H, G. ich; kh, G. doch. See inside front cover. ☆ Americanism; ‡foreign; *hypothetical; < derived from

the·ca (thē′kə) *n.*, *pl.* **-cae** (-sē) [ModL. < L. < Gr. *thēkē*, a case < IE. *dhēkā* < base *dhē-*, to place, put, whence DO[1], L. *facere*] **1.** *Bot.* a spore case, sac, or capsule **2.** *Zool. & Anat.* any sac enclosing an organ or a whole organism, as the covering of an insect pupa —**the′cal** *adj.*

the·cate (-kit) *adj.* having a theca; sheathed

‡**thé dan·sant** (tā dän sän′) *pl.* **thés dan·sants′** (tā dän sän′) [Fr.] *same as* TEA DANCE

thee (thē) *pron.* [ME. *the* < OE., dat. & acc. of *thu*, THOU[1]] the objective case of THOU[1]: also used in place of *thou* by the Friends (Quakers) with the verb in the third person singular [*thee* speaks harshly]

thee·lin (thē′lin) *n.* [< Gr. *thēlys*, female (for IE. base see FEMALE) + -IN[1]] *earlier name for* ESTRONE

thee·lol (-lôl, -lōl) *n.* [< Gr. *thēlys* (see prec.) + -OL[1]] *earlier name for* ESTRIOL

theft (theft) *n.* [ME. *thefte* < OE. *thiefth*: see THIEF & -TH[1]] **1.** the act or an instance of stealing; larceny **2.** [Obs.] something stolen

SYN.—**theft** is the general term and **larceny** the legal term for the unlawful or felonious taking away of another's property without his consent and with the intention of depriving him of it; **robbery** in its strict legal sense implies the felonious taking of another's property from his person or in his immediate presence by the use of violence or intimidation; **burglary** in legal use implies a breaking into a house with intent to commit theft or other felony and is often restricted to such an act accomplished at night

thegn (thān) *n.* [OE.] *var. of* THANE

the·ine (thē′in, -ēn) *n.* [ModL. *theina* < *thea* (see THEOPHYLLINE)] *same as* CAFFEINE

their (*ther*; *unstressed ther*) *possessive pronominal adj.* [ME. *theyr* < ON. *theirra*, gen. pl. of the demonstrative pron. replacing ME. *here*, OE. *hira*: see THEY] of, belonging to, made, or done by them: often used colloquially with a singular antecedent (as *everybody*, *somebody*, *everyone*) [did everybody finish *their* lunch?]

theirs (*therz*) *pron.* [ME. *theires* < *theyr* (see prec.) + -es by analogy with *his*, HIS] that or those belonging to them: the absolute form of THEIR, used without a following noun, often after *of* [a friend of *theirs*, that book is *theirs*, *theirs* are better]: often used colloquially with a singular antecedent (as *everybody*, *somebody*, *everyone*) [he'll bring his wife if everyone else will bring *theirs*]

the·ism (thē′iz'm) *n.* [THE(O)- + -ISM] **1.** belief in a god or gods **2.** belief in one God; monotheism: opposed to PANTHEISM, POLYTHEISM **3.** belief in one God who is creator and ruler of the universe and known by revelation: distinguished from DEISM —**the′ist** *n.*, *adj.* —**the·is′tic**, **the·is′ti·cal** *adj.* —**the·is′ti·cal·ly** *adv.*

Thel·ma (thel′mə) [< ?, but often a var. of SELMA] a feminine name

them (*them*; *unstressed them*, *th'm*, *əm*) *pron.* [ME. *theim* < ON. *theim*, dat. of the demonstrative pron.: see THEY] *objective case of* THEY: also used colloquially as a predicate complement with a linking verb (Ex.: that's *them*)

the·mat·ic (thē mat′ik) *adj.* **1.** of or constituting a theme or themes **2.** *Linguis.* of or relating to the stem or a vowel ending a stem that precedes an inflectional ending —**the·mat′i·cal·ly** *adv.*

☆**Thematic Apperception Test** *Psychol.* a test for the analysis of personality, in which stories made up by the person being tested about a series of standard pictures of ambiguous situations are assumed to reveal elements of his psychological makeup

theme (thēm) *n.* [ME. < OFr. & L.: OFr. *teme* < L. *thema* < Gr. *thema*, what is laid down < base of *tithenai*, to put, place: see DO[1]] **1.** *a)* a topic or subject, as of a lecture, sermon, essay, etc. *b)* a recurring, unifying subject or idea; motif, often one used decoratively **2.** a short essay, esp. one written as an assignment in a school course **3.** *a)* a short melody used as the subject of a musical composition *b)* a musical phrase upon which variations are developed **4.** *same as* STEM[1] (*n.* 6) ☆**5.** *clipped form of* THEME SONG —*SYN.* see SUBJECT

☆**theme song** **1.** a recurring song or melody in a film, musical, etc., often one intended to set the mood, that becomes popularly identified with the work **2.** an identifying song or melody used by a dance band, singer, etc. or for a radio or television series; signature

The·mis (thē′mis) *Gr. Myth.* a goddess of law and justice, daughter of Uranus and Gaea: represented as holding aloft a scale for weighing opposing claims

The·mis·to·cles (thə mis′tə klēz′) 525?-460? B.C.; Athenian statesman & naval commander

them·selves (*them* selvz′, *them*-) *pron.* [Late (Northern) ME. *thaim selfe* for ME. *hemselve(n)* (cf. THEY) + -s, pl. suffix] a form of the 3d pers. pl. pronoun, used: *a)* as an intensive [they went *themselves*] *b)* as a reflexive [they hurt *themselves*] *c)* as a quasi-noun meaning "their real, true, or actual selves" [they are not *themselves* today]

then (*then*) *adv.* [ME.: see THAN] **1.** at that time [he was young *then*] **2.** soon afterward; next in time [he took his hat and *then* left] **3.** next in order [first comes alpha and *then* beta] **4.** in that case; therefore; accordingly: used with conjunctive force [if it rains, *then* there will be no picnic] **5.** besides; moreover [he likes to walk, and *then* it's good exercise] **6.** at another time or at other times: used as a correlative with *now*, *sometimes*, etc. [now it's

warm, *then* freezing] —*adj.* of that time; being such at that time [the *then* director] —*n.* that time [by *then*, they were gone] —**but then** but on the other hand; but at the same time —**then and there** at that time and in that place; at once —**what then?** what would happen in that case?

the·nar (thē′när) *n.* [ModL. < Gr. *thenar* < IE. base *dhen-*, palm of the hand, flat surface, whence DEN] **1.** the palm of the hand or, sometimes, the sole of the foot **2.** the bulge at the base of the thumb —*adj.* of a thenar

thence (*thens*, thens) *adv.* [ME. *thens*, *thannes* (with adv. gen. suffix -es) < OE. *thanan*, thence: for base see THAT] **1.** from that place; therefrom **2.** from that time; thenceforth **3.** on that account; therefore

thence·forth (-fôrth′) *adv.* from that time onward; after that; thereafter: also **thence′for′ward** (-fôr′wərd), **thence′for′wards** (-wərdz)

the·o- (thē′ō, -ə) [< Gr. *theos*, god < ? IE. *dhewes-*, to storm, breathe, whence L. *furere*, to rage] *a combining form meaning* a god or God [*theocentric*]

The·o·bald (thē′ə bôld′) [prob. via L. *Theobaldus*, altered after names beginning with *Theo-* (< Gr. *theos*, God, a god) < OG. *Theudobald*, *Theodbald* < *theuda*, folk, people + *bald*, brave, bold] a masculine name

the·o·bro·mine (thē′ə brō′mēn, -min) *n.* [< ModL. *Theobroma*, name of a genus of trees of the sterculia family (< Gr. *theos*, god + *brōma*, food) + -INE[4]] a bitter, crystalline alkaloid, $C_7H_8O_2N_4$, extracted from the leaves and seeds of the cacao plant, used in medicine as a diuretic and nerve stimulant: it is related to caffeine

the·o·cen·tric (thē′ə sen′trik) *adj.* [THEO- + CENTRIC] centering on or directed toward God —**the′o·cen′tri·cal·ly** *adv.* —**the′o·cen·tric′i·ty** (-tris′ə tē) *n.* —**the′o·cen′trism** (-triz′m) *n.*

the·oc·ra·cy (thē äk′rə sē) *n.*, *pl.* **-cies** [Gr. *theokratia*: see THEO- & -CRACY] **1.** lit., the rule of a state by God or a god **2.** government by priests claiming to rule with divine authority **3.** a country governed in this way —**the·o·crat** (thē′ə krat′) *n.* —**the′o·crat′ic**, **the′o·crat′i·cal** *adj.* —**the′o·crat′i·cal·ly** *adv.*

the·oc·ra·sy (-sē) *n.* [Gr. *theocrasia* < *theos* (see THEO-) + *krasis*, mixture] the process whereby two or more originally distinct deities are thought of or worshiped as a single deity

The·oc·ri·tus (thē äk′ri təs) 3d cent. B.C.; Gr. poet

the·od·i·cy (thē äd′ə sē) *n.*, *pl.* **-cies** [Fr. *théodicée*: coined by LEIBNITZ (1710) < Gr. *theos*, god + *dikē*, justice] a system of natural theology aimed at seeking to vindicate divine justice in allowing evil to exist

the·od·o·lite (thē äd′ 'l it′) *n.* [ModL. *theodelitus*: prob. invented (c.1571) by Eng. mathematician Leonard Digges] a surveying instrument used to measure vertical and horizontal angles —**the·od′o·lit′ic** (-ə lit′ik) *adj.*

The·o·do·ra (thē′ə dôr′ə) [Gr. *Theodōra*: see ff.] a feminine name: dim. *Dora*

The·o·dore (thē′ə dôr′) [L. *Theodorus* < Gr. *Theodōros* < *theos*, god + *dōron*, gift] a masculine name: dim. *Ted*, *Teddy*; fem. *Theodora*: also sp. **Theodor**

DIAGRAM OF THEODOLITE (A, vertical angles; B, horizontal angles)

The·od·o·ric (thē äd′ər ik) [LL. *Theodoricus*, altered (after *Theodorus*, Theodore) < Goth. *Thiudoreiks* < *thiuda*, folk, people (see DEUTSCHLAND) + *reiks*, ruler, leader: for IE. base see REGAL] **1.** a masculine name **2.** 454?-526 A.D.; king of the Ostrogoths (474-526)

The·o·do·si·a (thē′ə dō′shē ə, -shə) [Gr. *Theodosia*: see ff.] a feminine name

The·o·do·si·us (-shē əs, -shəs) [LL. < Gr. *Theodosios* < *theos*, god + *dosis*, a giving, gift] **1.** a masculine name: fem. *Theodosia* **2. Theodosius I** (*Flavius Theodosius*) 346?-395 A.D.; Rom. general: emperor of Rome (379-395): called the Great —**The′o·do′si·an** *adj.*

the·og·o·ny (thē äg′ə nē) *n.*, *pl.* **-nies** [Gr. *theogonia*: see THEO- & -GONY] the origin or genealogy of the gods, as told in myths —**the′o·gon′ic** (-ə gän′ik) *adj.*

theol. **1.** theologian **2.** theological **3.** theology

the·o·lo·gi·an (thē′ə lō′jən, -jē ən) *n.* [MFr. *théologien*] a student of or a specialist in theology or a theology

the·o·log·i·cal (-läj′i k'l) *adj.* of, having to do with, based on, or offering instruction in, theology or a theology: also **the′o·log′ic** —**the′o·log′i·cal·ly** *adv.*

theological virtues *Theol.* the three virtues (faith, hope, and charity) that have God as their immediate object

the·ol·o·gize (thē äl′ə jīz′) *vt.* **-gized′**, **-giz′ing** to put into theological terms; fit into a theology —*vi.* to speculate theologically —**the·ol′o·giz′er** *n.*

the·ol·o·gy (thē äl′ə jē) *n.*, *pl.* **-gies** [ME. *theologie* < LL.(Ec.) *theologia* < Gr. *theologia*: see THEO- & -LOGY] **1.** the study of God and the relations between God and the universe; study of religious doctrines and matters of divinity **2.** a specific form or system of this study, as expounded by a particular religion or denomination

the·om·a·chy (thē äm′ə kē) *n.*, *pl.* **-chies** [Gr. *theomachia*: see THEO- & -MACHY] **1.** a battle against the gods **2.** strife among the gods

the·o·mor·phic (thē′ə môr′fik) *adj.* [< Gr. *theomorphos* (see THEO- & -MORPH) + -IC] having the form, likeness, or aspect of God or a god —**the′o·mor′phism** *n.*

the·on·o·mous (thē än′ə məs) *adj.* [< THEO- + (AUTO)NO-

MOUS] ruled or controlled by God —**the·on'o·mous·ly** *adv.* —**the·on'o·my** (-mē) *n.*

the·op·a·thy (-äp'ə thē) *n., pl.* **-thies** [THEO- + -PATHY] openness to or absorption in religious rapture

the·oph·a·ny (-äf'ə nē) *n., pl.* **-nies** [LL.(Ec.) *theophania* < Gr. *theophaneia:* see THEO- & -PHANE] *Theol., Myth.* a visible appearance of God or a god to man —**the'o·phan'ic** (-ə fan'ik) *adj.*

The·o·phras·tus (thē'ə fras'təs) 372?–287? B.C.; Gr. philosopher & natural scientist

the·o·phyl·line (thē'ə fil'ēn, -in) *n.* [< ModL. *thea*, tea (after Gr. *thea*, goddess, as being a divine herb, but < source of TEA) + -PHYLL + -INE⁴] a colorless, crystalline alkaloid, $C_7H_8O_2N_4 \cdot H_2O$, extracted from tea leaves or prepared synthetically: an isomer of theobromine

theor. theorem

the·or·bo (thē ôr'bō) *n., pl.* **-bos** [Fr. *théorbe* < It. *tiorba* < ?] an obsolete type of lute with a double neck and two sets of strings

the·o·rem (thē'ə rəm, thir'əm) *n.* [< Fr. or L.: Fr. *théorème* < L. *theorema* < Gr. *theōrēma*, to look at, view < *theoros*, a spectator: for IE. base see THEATER] **1.** a proposition that is not self-evident but that can be proved from accepted premises and so is established as a law or principle **2.** an expression of relations in an equation or formula **3.** *Math., Physics* a proposition embodying something to be proved —**the'o·re·mat'ic** (-rə mat'ik) *adj.*

the·o·ret·i·cal (thē'ə ret'i k'l) *adj.* [< LL. *theoreticus* < Gr. *theōrētikos* + -AL] **1.** of or constituting theory **2.** limited to or based on theory; not practical or applied; hypothetical **3.** tending to theorize; speculative Also **the'o·ret'ic** —**the'o·ret'i·cal·ly** *adv.*

the·o·re·ti·cian (thē'ə rə tish'ən) *n.* a person who theorizes, esp. one who specializes in the theory of some art, science, etc.: also **the'o·rist** (-rist)

the·o·ret·ics (thē'ə ret'iks) *n.pl.* [*with sing. v.*] the theoretical part of a field of knowledge

the·o·rize (thē'ə rīz') *vi.* **-rized'**, **-riz'ing** to form a theory or theories; speculate —**the'o·riz'er** *n.* —**the'o·ri·za'tion** *n.*

the·o·ry (thē'ə rē, thir'ē) *n., pl.* **-ries** [< Fr. or LL.: Fr. *théorie* < LL. *theoria* < Gr. *theōria*, a looking at, contemplation, speculation, theory < *theōrein:* see THEOREM] **1.** orig., a mental viewing; contemplation **2.** a speculative idea or plan as to how something might be done **3.** a systematic statement of principles involved [the *theory* of equations in mathematics] **4.** a formulation of apparent relationships or underlying principles of certain observed phenomena which has been verified to some degree **5.** that branch of an art or science consisting in a knowledge of its principles and methods rather than in its practice; pure, as opposed to applied, science, etc. **6.** popularly, a mere conjecture, or guess

SYN.—**theory**, as compared here, implies considerable evidence in support of a formulated general principle explaining the operation of certain phenomena [the *theory* of evolution]; **hypothesis** implies an inadequacy of evidence in support of an explanation that is tentatively inferred, often as a basis for further experimentation [the nebular *hypothesis*]; **law** implies an exact formulation of the principle operating in a sequence of events in nature, observed to occur with unvarying uniformity under the same conditions [the *law* of the conservation of energy]

theory of games *same as* GAME THEORY

theos. **1.** theosophical **2.** theosophist **3.** theosophy

the·os·o·phy (thē äs'ə fē) *n., pl.* **-phies** [ML. *theosophia* < LGr. *theosophia*, knowledge of divine things < *theosophos*, wise in divine matters < Gr. *theos*, god + *sophos*, wise (see THEO- & -SOPHY)] **1.** any of various philosophies or religious systems that propose to establish direct, mystical contact with divine principle through contemplation, revelation, etc. **2.** [*often* T-] the doctrines and beliefs of a modern sect (**Theosophical Society**) of this nature that incorporates elements of Buddhism and Brahmanism —**the'o·soph'ic** (-ə säf'ik), **the'o·soph'i·cal** *adj.* —**the'o·soph'i·cal·ly** *adv.* —**the·os'o·phist** *n.*

ther·a·peu·tic (ther'ə pyōōt'ik) *adj.* [ModL. *therapeuticus* < Gr. *therapeutikos* < *therapeutēs*, attendant, servant, one who treats medically < *therapeuein*, to nurse, treat medically] **1.** *a)* serving to cure or heal; curative *b)* serving to preserve health [therapeutic abortion] **2.** of therapeutics Also **ther'a·peu'ti·cal** —**ther'a·peu'ti·cal·ly** *adv.*

ther·a·peu·tics (-iks) *n.pl.* [*with sing. v.*] the branch of medicine that deals with the treatment and cure of diseases; therapy

☆**ther·a·pist** (ther'ə pist) *n.* a specialist in a certain form of therapy: also **ther'a·peu'tist** (-pyōōt'ist)

ther·a·py (-pē) *n., pl.* **-pies** [ModL. *therapia* < Gr. *therapeia* < *therapeuein*, to nurse, cure] the treatment of disease or of any physical or mental disorder by medical or physical means, usually excluding surgery: sometimes used in compounds [hydrotherapy]

Ther·a·va·da (ther'ə vä'də) *n. same as* HINAYANA

there (ther) *adv.* [ME. *ther*, there, where < OE. *ther*, *thær*, there, where < IE. **tor-*, **ter-*, there < **to-*, **ta-*, demonstrative base, whence THAT, THEN] **1.** at or in that place: often used as an intensive [John *there* is a good

player]: in dialectal or nonstandard use, often placed between a demonstrative pronoun and the noun it modifies [that *there* man] **2.** toward, to, or into that place; thither [go *there*] **3.** at that point in action, speech, discussion, etc.; then [*there* he paused] **4.** in that matter, respect, etc.; as to that [*there* you are wrong] **5.** at the moment; right now [*there* goes the whistle] *There* is also used *a)* in interjectional phrases of approval, encouragement, etc. [*there's* a fine fellow!] *b)* with pronominal force in impersonal constructions in which the real subject follows the verb [*there* is very little time, there are three men here] —*n.* that place or point [we left *there* at six] —*interj.* an exclamation expressing: **1.** defiance, dismay, satisfaction, etc. [*there*, that's done!] **2.** sympathy, concern, etc. [*there*, *there!* don't worry] —(not) **all there** [Colloq.] (not) in full possession of one's wits; (not) mentally sound

there·a·bouts (ther'ə bouts') *adv.* **1.** near that place **2.** near that time or point in action, speech, etc. **3.** near that number, amount, degree, etc. Also **there'a·bout'**

there·aft·er (ther af'tər, -äf'-) *adv.* **1.** after that; from then on; subsequently **2.** [Archaic] accordingly

there·a·gainst (ther'ə genst') *adv.* against or contrary to that; in opposition

there·at (ther at') *adv.* **1.** at that place; there **2.** at that time; when that occurred **3.** for that reason

there·by (-bī') *adv.* **1.** by or through that; by that means **2.** connected with that [thereby hangs a tale] **3.** [Archaic] thereabouts

there·for (-fôr') *adv.* for this; for that; for it

there·fore (ther'fôr') *adv.* [ME. *ther fore:* see THERE & FORE] as a result of this or that; for this or that reason; consequently; hence: often used with conjunctive force

there·from (ther frum', -främ') *adv.* from this; from that; from it; from there

there·in (-in') *adv.* **1.** in there; in or into that place or thing **2.** in that matter, detail, etc.

there·in·aft·er (ther'in af'tər, -äf'-) *adv.* in the following part of that document, speech, etc.

there·in·to (ther in'tōō) *adv.* **1.** into that place or thing **2.** into that matter, condition, etc.

ther·e·min (ther'ə min) *n.* [after Leo *Theremin*, its Russ. inventor (c.1920)] an early electronic musical instrument whose tone and pitch are controlled by moving the hands through the air varying distances from two antennas

there·of (ther uv') *adv.* **1.** of that **2.** concerning that **3.** from that as a cause, reason, etc.; therefrom

there·on (-än') *adv.* **1.** on that or it **2.** *same as* THEREUPON

there's (therz) **1.** there is **2.** there has

The·re·sa (tə rē'sə) [< Fr. *Thérèse* or Port. *Theresa* < L. *Therasia* < ? Gr. *therizein*, to reap] **1.** a feminine name: dim. *Terry*, *Tess*; var. *Teresa* **2.** *same as:* *a)* Saint TERESA (OF ÁVILA) *b)* Saint THÉRÈSE (OF LISIEUX)

Thé·rèse (tā rez'; E. tə rēs'), Saint 1873–97; Fr. Carmelite nun: called **Thérèse of Lisieux:** her day is Oct. 31

there·to (ther tōō') *adv.* **1.** to that place, thing, etc.: also **there·un'to** (-un'tōō, ther'ən tōō') **2.** [Archaic] besides

there·to·fore (ther'tə fôr', ther'tə fôr') *adv.* up to then; until that time; before that

there·un·der (ther un'dər) *adv.* **1.** under that; under it **2.** under the terms stated there

there·up·on (ther'ə pän', ther'ə pän') *adv.* **1.** immediately following that; at once **2.** as a consequence of that **3.** upon that; concerning that subject, etc.

there·with (ther with', -with') *adv.* **1.** along with that **2.** in addition to that **3.** by that method or means **4.** immediately thereafter; thereupon

there·with·al (ther'with ôl') *adv.* **1.** with all that; in addition; besides **2.** [Obs.] along with that; therewith

the·ri·an·throp·ic (thir'ē an thräp'ik) *adj.* [< Gr. *thērion*, beast (< *thēr*, beast: see FIERCE) + *anthrōpos*, man] **1.** conceived of as being partly human and partly animal in form **2.** designating or of deities of this kind

the·ri·o·mor·phic (-ə môr'fik) *adj.* [< Gr. *thēriomorphos* (see prec. & -MORPH) + -IC] conceived of as having the form of an animal: said of certain gods

therm (thurm) *n.* [< Gr. *thermē*, heat: for IE. base see WARM] **1.** formerly, *a)* a great calorie *b)* a small calorie *c)* a unit of heat equal to 1,000 great calories **2.** a unit of heat equal to 100,000 British thermal units

Ther·ma (thur'mə) ancient name of SALONIKA

ther·mae (thur'mē) *n.pl.* [L. < Gr. *thermai*, pl. of *thermē*, heat: see WARM] hot or warm springs or baths; specif., the public baths or bathhouses of ancient Rome

ther·mal (thur'm'l) *adj.* [Fr. < Gr. *thermē*, heat: see WARM] **1.** having to do with heat, hot springs, etc. **2.** warm or hot ☆**3.** designating or of a loosely knitted material honeycombed with air spaces for insulation to help retain body heat [thermal underwear] —*n.* a rising column of warm air, caused by the uneven heating of the earth or sea by the sun —**ther'mal·ly** *adv.*

thermal barrier a limit to the speed of flight of vehicles in the atmosphere set by the effects of aerodynamic heating

thermal spring a spring whose water has a temperature greater than the mean annual temperature of the locality where it occurs

therm·an·es·the·si·a, therm·an·aes·the·si·a (thurm'-an əs thē'zhə, -zhē ə, -zē ə) *n.* [ModL.: see THERMO- & ANESTHESIA] insensibility to heat and cold

ther·mel (thur'mel) *n.* [< THERM(O)EL(ECTRIC)] a thermo-electric thermometer consisting of a single thermocouple or a series of thermocouples

therm·es·the·si·a, therm·aes·the·si·a (thurm'es thē'-zhə, -zhē ə, -zē ə) *n.* [ModL.: see THERMO- & ESTHESIA] sensibility to heat and cold

ther·mic (thur'mik) *adj.* [< Gr. *thermē*, heat (see WARM) + -IC] of or caused by heat

‡**Ther·mi·dor** (tər mē dôr'; *E.* thur'mə dôr') *n.* [Fr. < Gr. *thermē*, heat + *dōron*, gift] the eleventh month (July 19–Aug. 17) of the FRENCH REVOLUTIONARY CALENDAR

therm·i·on (thurm'ī'ən, thur'mē-) *n.* [THERM(O)- + ION] *Physics* a negative or positive ion emitted by an incandescent material —**therm'i·on'ic** (-än'ik) *adj.*

thermionic current a current resulting from directed thermionic emission, as the flow of emitted electrons from a heated cathode to the plate

thermionic emission the phenomenon of electron or ion emission from the heated surface of a conductor

therm·i·on·ics (thurm'ī än'iks, thur'mē-) *n.pl.* [with sing. v.] the study and science of thermionic activity

thermionic tube an electron tube having a cathode electrically heated in order to cause electron or ion emission: also [Brit.] **thermionic valve**

☆**therm·is·tor** (thər mis'tər, thur'mis'-) *n.* [THERM(O)- + (RES)ISTOR] a device constructed of solid semiconductor material, whose electrical resistance decreases with an increase in temperature: used to measure temperature differences in body cells, microwave or infrared power, etc.

Ther·mit (thur'mit) [G. < Gr. *thermē*, heat (see WARM) + G. *-it*, -ITE¹] *a trademark for* a mixture of finely granulated aluminum with an oxide of iron or other metal, which produces great heat and is used in welding and in incendiary bombs —*n.* [t-] such a mixture

ther·mo- (thur'mō, -mə) [< Gr. *thermē*, heat (see WARM)] *a combining form meaning:* **1.** heat [thermodynamics] **2.** thermoelectric [thermocouple]: also, before a vowel, **therm-**

ther·mo·ba·rom·e·ter (-bə räm'ə tər) *n. same as* HYPSOMETER (sense 1)

ther·mo·chem·is·try (-kem'is trē) *n.* the branch of chemistry that deals with the relationship of heat to chemical change —**ther'mo·chem'i·cal** *adj.*

ther·mo·cline (thur'mə klīn') *n.* [THERMO- + -cline, as in ANTICLINE] a layer of water between the warmer, surface zone and the colder, deep-water zone in a thermally stratified body of water, in which the temperature decreases rapidly with depth, usually at least 1°C with each meter of increased depth

ther·mo·cou·ple (-kup''l) *n.* a pair of dissimilar conductors joined in series to form a closed circuit so as to produce a thermoelectric current when heated: used in temperature measurements: also called **thermoelectric couple**

ther·mo·dy·nam·ic (thur'mō dī nam'ik) *adj.* **1.** of or having to do with thermodynamics **2.** caused or operated by heat converted into motive power —**ther'mo·dy·nam'i·cal·ly** *adv.*

ther·mo·dy·nam·ics (-dī nam'iks) *n.pl.* [with sing. v.] [THERMO- + DYNAMICS] the branch of physics dealing with the reversible transformation of heat into other forms of energy, esp. mechanical energy, and with the laws governing such conversions of energy

ther·mo·e·lec·tric (-i lek'trik) *adj.* of or having to do with the direct relations between heat and electricity: also **ther'mo·e·lec'tri·cal** —**ther'mo·e·lec'tri·cal·ly** *adv.*

ther·mo·e·lec·tric·i·ty (-i lek'tris'ə tē) *n.* electricity produced by heating the junction between two dissimilar conductors so as to produce an elecromotive force

ther·mo·e·lec·tro·mo·tive (-trə mōt'iv) *adj.* designating or of the electromotive force produced by a thermocouple

ther·mo·e·lec·tron (-i lek'trän) *n.* a negative ion, or electron, emitted from a body at high temperature

ther·mo·el·e·ment (-el'ə mənt) *n.* a device consisting of a thermocouple and a heating element arranged for measuring small currents, esp. at high frequencies

ther·mo·gen·e·sis (-jen'ə sis) *n.* [ModL.: see THERMO- & -GENESIS] the production of heat, esp. by physiological action in an animal —**ther'mo·ge·net'ic** (-jə net'ik) *adj.*

ther·mo·gram (thur'mə gram') *n.* [THERMO- + -GRAM] a record made by a thermograph

ther·mo·graph (-graf', -gräf') *n.* [THERMO- + -GRAPH] a thermometer for recording variations in temperature automatically; specif., an infrared camera for recording on film or on the face of an oscilloscope differences in temperature, as between normal and abnormal body tissues

ther·mog·ra·phy (thər mäg'rə fē) *n.* [THERMO- + -GRAPHY] **1.** the recording of temperature variations by means of a thermograph **2.** a process for imitating copperplate engraving, as on calling cards, by dusting the freshly printed surface with a resinous powder which, when heated, fuses with the ink to form a raised surface —**ther'mog'ra·pher** *n.* —**ther'mo·graph'ic** (thur'mə graf'ik) *adj.*

ther·mo·junc·tion (thur'mō junk'shən) *n.* the point of contact between the two conductors forming a thermocouple

ther·mo·la·bile (-lā'b'l, -lā'bil) *adj.* [THERMO- + LABILE] designating or of substances, as some toxins, enzymes, etc.,

that are destroyed or lose their characteristic properties when subjected to heat, esp. to a temperature of 55°C or above —**ther'mo·la·bil'i·ty** (-lā bil'ə tē) *n.*

ther·mo·lu·mi·nes·cence (-lōō'mə nes''ns) *n.* [THERMO- + LUMINESCENCE] the release in the form of light of stored energy from a substance when it is heated —**ther'mo·lu'mi·nes'cent** *adj.*

ther·mol·y·sis (thər mäl'ə sis) *n.* [ModL.: see THERMO- & -LYSIS] **1.** *Chem.* dissociation of a compound by heat **2.** *Physiol.* dispersion of heat from the body —**ther'mo·lyt'ic** (-mə lit'ik) *adj.*

ther·mo·mag·net·ic (thur'mō mag net'ik) *adj.* of or pertaining to the interrelations between heat and magnetism

ther·mom·e·ter (thər mäm'ə tər) *n.* [Fr. *thermomètre*: see THERMO- & -METER] **1.** an instrument for measuring temperatures, consisting of a graduated glass tube with a sealed, capillary bore in which mercury, colored alcohol, etc. rises or falls as it expands or contracts from changes in temperature: see FAHRENHEIT, CELSIUS, KELVIN, REAUMUR **2.** any similar instrument, as one operating by means of a thermocouple —**ther'mo·met'ric** (-mə met'rik) *adj.* —**ther'mo·met'ri·cal·ly** *adv.*

ther·mom·e·try (-trē) *n.* **1.** measurement of temperature **2.** the science of making or using thermometers

ther·mo·mo·tor (thur'mə mōt'ər) *n.* an engine operated by heat, esp. by the expansion of heated air

ther·mo·nu·cle·ar (thur'mō nōō'klē ər, -nyōō'-) *adj.* [THERMO- + NUCLEAR] *Physics* **1.** designating or of a reaction in which isotopes of a light element, esp. hydrogen, fuse at temperatures of millions of degrees into heavier nuclei **2.** designating, of, or employing the heat energy released in nuclear fusion [thermonuclear reactor]

ther·mo·phile (thur'mə fīl') *n.* [THERMO- + -PHILE] an organism adapted to living at high temperatures, as some bacteria and algae —**ther'mo·phil'ic** (-fil'ik) *adj.*

ther·mo·pile (-pīl') *n.* [THERMO- + PILE¹] a device consisting of a series of thermocouples, used for measuring minute changes in temperature or for generating thermo-electric current

ther·mo·plas·tic (thur'mə plas'tik) *adj.* becoming or remaining soft and moldable when subjected to heat: said of certain plastics —*n.* a thermoplastic substance

Ther·mop·y·lae (thər mäp'ə lē) in ancient Greece, a mountain pass in Locris, on an inlet of the Aegean Sea: scene of a battle (480 B.C.) in which the Persians under Xerxes destroyed a Spartan army under Leonidas

ther·mo·reg·u·la·tion (thur'mō reg'yə lā'shən) *n.* **1.** the regulation of temperature **2.** *Physiol.* the keeping of the temperature of a living body at a constant level by processes of heat production, heat transport, etc. —**ther'mo·reg'u·la'tor** *n.*

ther·mos (thur'məs) *n.* [orig. a trademark < Gr. *thermos*, hot: see WARM] a bottle, flask, or jug for keeping liquids at almost their original temperature for several hours: it has two walls enclosing a vacuum and is fitted in a metal outer case: in full **thermos bottle** (or **flask** or **jug**)

ther·mo·scope (thur'mə skōp') *n.* [THERMO- + -SCOPE] an instrument for indicating changes in temperature of a substance, without accurately measuring them, by observing the accompanying changes in volume —**ther'mo·scop'ic** (-skäp'ik) *adj.*

ther·mo·set·ting (thur'mō set'iŋ) *adj.* becoming permanently hard and unmoldable when once subjected to heat: said of certain plastics

ther·mo·si·phon (thur'mə sī'fən) *n.* an apparatus consisting of an arrangement of siphon tubes for inducing the circulation of a liquid, as in the water-cooling system of an internal-combustion engine

ther·mo·sta·ble (-stā'b'l) *adj.* [THERMO- + STABLE¹] designating or of substances, as some toxins, enzymes, etc., that can be heated to moderate temperatures above 55°C without losing their characteristic properties —**ther'mo·sta·bil'i·ty** (-stə bil'ə tē) *n.*

ther·mo·stat (thur'mə stat') *n.* [THERMO- + -STAT] **1.** an apparatus for regulating temperature, esp. one that automatically controls a heating unit **2.** a device that sets off a sprinkler, etc. at a certain heat —**ther'mo·stat'ic** *adj.* —**ther'mo·stat'i·cal·ly** *adv.*

ther·mo·stat·ics (thur'mə stat'iks) *n.pl.* [with sing. v.] [THERMO- + STATICS] the science that deals with the equilibrium of heat

ther·mo·tax·is (-tak'sis) *n.* [ModL.: see THERMO- & -TAXIS] **1.** *Biol.* movement of an organism toward or from a source of heat **2.** *Physiol.* the normal regulation of body temperature —**ther'mo·tax'ic, ther'mo·tac'tic** (-tik) *adj.*

ther·mo·ten·sile (-ten's'l) *adj.* of or having a tensile strength that varies with changes in temperature

ther·mot·ro·pism (thər mät'rə piz'm) *n.* [THERMO- + -TROPISM] *Biol.* growth or movement toward or away from a source of heat —**ther·mo·trop·ic** (thur'mə träp'ik) *adj.*

the·roid (thir'oid) *adj.* [Gr. *thēr*, a wild beast (see FIERCE) + -OID] suggestive of an animal; beastlike

the·ro·pod (thir'ə päd') *n.* [< ModL. *Theropoda* < Gr. *thēr*, a wild beast (see FIERCE) + ModL. *-poda*: see -PODA] any of a suborder (Theropoda) of flesh-eating dinosaurs that walked mainly on the hind legs

Ther·si·tes (thər sīt'ēz) [L. < Gr. *Thersitēs*] in the *Iliad*, an ugly, loud, abusive Greek soldier in the Trojan War

ther·sit·i·cal (thər sit′i k'l) *adj.* [after prec.] loud and abusive; scurrilous

the·sau·rus (thi sôr′əs) *n., pl.* **-sau′ri** (-ī), **-sau′rus·es** [L. < Gr. *thēsauros*, a treasure] **1.** a treasury or storehouse **2.** a book containing a store of words; specif., a book of synonyms and antonyms **3.** a categorized index of terms for use in information retrieval, as from a computer

these (thēz) *pron., adj. pl. of* THIS

The·seus (thē′sōōs, -syōōs, -sē əs) [L. < Gr. *Thēseus*] *Gr. Legend* the principal hero of Attica, son of Aegeus and king of Athens, famed esp. for his killing of the Minotaur —**The·se·an** (thi sē′ən) *adj.*

the·sis (thē′sis) *n., pl.* **the′ses** (-sēz) [L. < Gr. *thesis*, a placing, position, proposition < the base of *tithenai*, to put, place: see DO¹] **1.** *a)* in classical poetry, the accented syllable of a foot *b)* in later poetry, the unaccented syllable of a foot: usage due to a misunderstanding of the original Greek word *c)* in music, an accented note; downbeat **2.** a proposition maintained or defended in argument, formerly one publicly disputed by a candidate for a degree in a medieval university **3.** a formal and lengthy research paper, esp. one written in partial fulfillment of the requirements for a master's degree **4.** *Logic a)* an unproved statement assumed as a premise; postulate: distinguished from HYPOTHESIS *b)* a consequence of a hypothetical proposition *c)* with Kant, the affirmative member of one of the antinomies of pure reason *d)* with Hegel, the initial, least adequate phase of development in dialectic: see DIALECTIC (*n.* 3)

Thes·pi·an (thes′pē ən) *adj.* **1.** of Thespis **2.** [*often* t-] having to do with the drama; dramatic —*n.* [*often* t-] an actor or actress: a somewhat humorous or pretentious term

Thes·pis (thes′pis) 6th cent. B.C.; Gr. poet: traditionally the originator of Gr. tragedy

Thess. Thessalonians

Thes·sa·li·a (the sā′lē ə) *Gr. name of* THESSALY

Thes·sa·lo·ni·an (thes′ə lō′nē ən) *adj.* of Thessalonica or its people —*n.* a native or inhabitant of Thessalonica

Thes·sa·lo·ni·ans (-ənz) [*with sing. v.*] either of two books of the New Testament which were epistles from the Apostle Paul to the Christians of Thessalonica

Thes·sa·lon·i·ca (thes′ə län′i kə, -ə lə nī′kə) *ancient name of* SALONIKA

Thes·sa·lo·ni·ki, Thes·sa·lo·ni·ke (thes′ä lô nē′kē) *Gr. name of* SALONIKA

Thes·sa·ly (thes′ə lē) division of E Greece, between the Pindus Mountains & the Aegean Sea: an ancient region: 5,392 sq. mi.; pop. 695,000 See GREECE, map —**Thes·sa·li·an** (the sā′lē ən) *adj., n.*

the·ta (thāt′ə, thēt′-) *n.* [Gr. *thēta:* of Sem. origin, akin to Heb. *ṭēth*] the eighth letter of the Greek alphabet (Θ, θ, ϑ)

thet·ic (thet′ik) *adj.* [Gr. *thetikos*, fit for placing < *thetos*, placed < base of *tithenai:* see DO¹] **1.** set forth dogmatically; prescribed **2.** *Gr. & L. Poetry* beginning with, or constituting, the thesis Also **thet′i·cal** —**thet′i·cal·ly** *adv.*

The·tis (thēt′is) [L. < Gr. *Thetis*] *Gr. Myth.* Achilles' mother, one of the Nereids

the·ur·gy (thē′ər jē) *n., pl.* **-gies** [LL.(Ec.) *theurgia*, a summoning of spirits < LGr.(Ec.) *theourgia* < *theourgos*, divine worker < Gr. *theos*, god + *ergon*, WORK] **1.** supposed divine or supernatural intervention in human affairs **2.** magic; sorcery, esp. that practiced by certain Neoplatonists who professed to work miracles by the intervention of beneficent, divine spirits —**the·ur·gic** (thē ur′jik), **the·ur′gi·cal** *adj.* —**the·ur′gi·cal·ly** *adv.* —**the′ur·gist** *n.*

thew·less (thyōō′lis) *adj.* [Chiefly Scot.] without vigor or spirit

thews (thyōōz) *n.pl., sing.* **thew** [ME. *theawes*, good qualities, hence, later, good physical qualities, strength < OE. *theaw*, custom, habit, hence characteristic quality, akin to OS. *thau*, custom < IE. base *teu-*, to pay attention to, notice, whence L. *tueri*, to keep in sight, observe] **1.** muscular power; bodily strength **2.** muscles or sinews —**thew′y** *adj.* **thew′i·er, thew′i·est**

they (thā) *pron.* [for sing. see HE¹, SHE, IT] [ME. *thei* < ON. *their*, nom. masc. pl. of the demonstrative pron.; like THEIR & THEM (ME. *theim*), also < the ON. demonstrative forms, *thei* replaced earlier ME. *he* (hi) because the native pronouns were phonetically confused with the forms of the pers. pron. (ME. *he, hire, hem, him*, etc.): cf. THEIR, THEM, SHE] **1.** the persons, animals, or things previously mentioned: also used with a singular antecedent (as *everybody, somebody, everyone*) [everyone helped and it was good that *they* did] **2.** people (or a person) generally or indefinitely [*they* say it's so] *They* is the nominative case form, *them* the objective, *their* and *theirs* the possessive, and *themselves* the intensive and reflexive, of the third personal plural pronoun

they'd (thād) **1.** they had **2.** they would

they'll (thāl, thel) **1.** they will **2.** they shall

they're (ther, thā′ər) they are

they've (thāv) they have

thi- (thī) *same as* THIO-

thi·a·mine (thī′ə mēn′, -min) *n.* [altered < THI- + (VIT)AMIN] a factor of the vitamin B complex, a white,

crystalline compound, C₁₂H₁₇ON₄SCl, found in the outer coating of cereal grains, green peas, beans, egg yolk, liver, etc., and also prepared synthetically; vitamin B₁: a deficiency of this vitamin results in beriberi and certain nervous disorders: also **thi′a·min** (-min)

thi·a·zine (-zēn′, -zin) *n.* [THI- + AZINE] any of a group of heterocyclic compounds whose molecules contain one atom of nitrogen, one atom of sulfur, and four atoms of carbon, arranged in a ring

thi·a·zole (-zōl′) *n.* [THI- + AZOLE] **1.** a colorless liquid, C₃H₃NS, with a five-membered ring **2.** any of its various derivatives, used in dyes and drugs

Thi·bet (ti bet′) *var. of* TIBET —**Thi·bet′an** *adj., n.*

thick (thik) *adj.* [ME. *thikke* < OE. *thicce*, thick, dense, akin to G. *dick* < IE. base *tegu-*, thick, fat, whence OIr. *tiug*] **1.** having relatively great depth; of considerable extent from one surface or side to the opposite; not thin [a *thick* board] **2.** having relatively large diameter in relation to length [a *thick* pipe] **3.** as measured in the third dimension or between opposite surfaces [a wall six inches *thick*] **4.** having the constituent elements abundant and close together; specif., *a)* marked by profuse, close growth; luxuriant [*thick* hair, *thick* woods] *b)* great in number and packed closely together [a *thick* crowd] *c)* having much body; not thin in consistency; viscous [*thick* soup] *d)* dense and heavy [*thick* smoke, a *thick* snowfall] *e)* filled with smoke, fog, or other vapors *f)* covered to a considerable depth [roads *thick* with mud] *g)* sprinkled or studded profusely [a sky *thick* with stars] **5.** impenetrably dark, dismal, or obscure [the *thick* shadows of night] **6.** *a)* sounding blurred, slurred, muffled, fuzzy, etc., or husky, hoarse, etc. [a *thick* voice, *thick* speech] *b)* strongly marked; pronounced [speaking with a *thick* brogue] **7.** [Colloq.] slow to understand; stupid **8.** [Colloq.] close in friendly association; intimate **9.** [Chiefly Brit. Colloq.] too much to be tolerated; excessive —*adv.* in a thick way —*n.* the thickest part or the period of greatest activity [in the *thick* of the fight] —SYN. see CLOSE¹ —**through thick and thin** in good times and bad times; in every eventuality —**thick′ish** *adj.* —**thick′ly** *adv.*

thick·en (thik′ən) *vt., vi.* **1.** to make or become thick or thicker, as in dimension, density, consistency, articulation, etc. **2.** to make or become more complex or involved [the plot *thickened*] —**thick′en·er** *n.*

thick·en·ing (-iŋ) *n.* **1.** the action of a person or thing that thickens **2.** a substance or material used to thicken **3.** the thickened part of something

thick·et (thik′it) *n.* [ME. < OE. *thiccet* < *thicce* (see THICK)] a thick growth of shrubs, underbrush, or small trees —**thick′et·ed** *adj.*

thick·head (thik′hed′) *n.* a stupid person; blockhead —**thick′head′ed** *adj.* —**thick′head′ed·ness** *n.*

thick·ness (-nis) *n.* **1.** the quality or condition of being thick **2.** the measure of how thick a thing is, as distinguished from the length or width of any of its surfaces **3.** a layer, stratum, etc. [three *thicknesses* of cloth] **4.** the thickest place or part

thick·set (-set′) *adj.* **1.** planted thickly or closely **2.** thick in body; stocky —*n.* [Archaic] a thicket

thick-skinned (-skind′) *adj.* **1.** having a thick skin **2.** not easily hurt by criticism, insult, etc.; callous

thick-skulled (-skuld′) *adj.* stupid or obtuse

thick-wit·ted (-wit′id) *adj.* slow-witted; stupid

thief (thēf) *n., pl.* **thieves** (thēvz) [ME. < OE. *theof, thiof*, akin to G. *dieb* < IE. base *teup-*, to cower, lurk] a person who steals, esp. secretly; one guilty of theft, or larceny **thief knot** a kind of knot: see KNOT, illus.

Thiers (tyer) **Louis A·dolphe** (lwē à dôlf′) 1797–1877; Fr. statesman & historian

thieve (thēv) *vt., vi.* **thieved, thiev′ing** [via ME. dial. < OE. *theofian* < *theof*, THIEF] to commit, or get by, theft

thiev·er·y (thēv′ər ē) *n., pl.* **-er·ies** the act or practice of stealing or an instance of this; theft

thiev·ish (-ish) *adj.* **1.** addicted to thieving, or stealing **2.** of, like, or characteristic of a thief; stealthy; furtive —**thiev′ish·ly** *adv.* —**thiev′ish·ness** *n.*

thigh (thī) *n.* [ME. < OE. *theoh*, akin to MHG. *diech* < IE. *teuk-* < base *teu-*, to swell, whence L. *tumor*] **1.** that part of the leg in man and other vertebrates between the knee and the hip; region of the thighbone, or femur **2.** the region of the tibia, as in poultry

thigh·bone (-bōn′) *n.* the largest, longest, and heaviest bone in the body, extending from the hip to the knee; femur: also **thigh bone**

thig·mo·tax·is (thig′mə tak′sis) *n.* [ModL. < Gr. *thigma*, touch < *thinganein*, to touch with the hand + *-taxis*, -TAXIS] *same as* STEREOTAXIS —**thig′mo·tac′tic** (-tik) *adj.*

thig·mot·ro·pism (thig mät′rə piz′m) *n.* [ModL.: see prec. & -TROPISM] *same as* STEREOTROPISM —**thig′mo·trop′ic** (-mə träp′ik) *adj.*

thill (thil) *n.* [ME. *thille*, a stake, pole, plank < OE., akin to ON. *thil*, OHG. *dil*, board wall, plank floor < IE. base *tel-*, flat, flat surface, board, whence L. *tellus*, earth] either of the two shafts between which a horse is hitched to a wagon

thim·ble (thim′b'l) *n.* [ME. *thimbel* (with unhistoric -*b*-) < OE. *thymel*, thumbstall < *thuma*, THUMB + -*el*, dim. suffix] 1. a small cap of metal, plastic, etc. worn as a protection for the finger that pushes the needle in sewing 2. anything like this; esp., a grooved, metal ring inserted in a loop of rope or in a sail's rope hole to prevent wear

☆**thim·ble·ber·ry** (-ber′ē) *n.*, *pl.* -**ries** *same as* BLACK RASPBERRY

thim·ble·ful (-fool′) *n.*, *pl.* -**fuls′** 1. as much as a thimble will hold 2. a very small quantity

thim·ble·rig (-rig′) *n.* [cf. RIG] *same as* SHELL GAME —*vt.*, *vi.* -**rigged′**, -**rig′ging** to cheat or swindle, as in this game —**thim′ble·rig′ger** *n.*

☆**thim·ble·weed** (-wēd′) *n.* any of various plants with thimble-shaped receptacles; esp., *a*) any of several anemones with elongated cylindrical heads of woolly achenes *b*) any of several rudbeckias

thi·mer·o·sal (thī mer′ə sal′, -mur′-) *n.* [by contraction and transposition of (*sodium*) *mercurithiosalicylate*] a cream-colored, crystalline compound, $C_9H_9HgNaO_2S$: used chiefly in solutions as an antiseptic for surface wounds

thin (thin) *adj.* **thin′ner**, **thin′nest** [ME. *thinne* < OE. *thynne*, akin to G. *dünn* < IE. **tenu-*, thin (< base **ten-*, to stretch), whence L. *tenuis*, thin] 1. having relatively little depth; of little extent from one surface or side to the opposite [thin paper] 2. having relatively small diameter in relation to length [thin thread] 3. having little fat or flesh; lean; gaunt; slender 4. having the constituent elements small in number and not close together; specif., *a*) scanty in growth; sparsely distributed [thin hair] *b*) small in size or number [thin receipts] *c*) lacking body; not thick in consistency; watery [thin soup] *d*) not dense or heavy [thin smoke, a thin snowfall] *e*) rarefied, as air at high altitudes 5. of little intensity; dim; faint; pale [thin colors] 6. of little volume or resonance; high-pitched and weak [a thin voice] 7. light or sheer, as fabric 8. easily seen through; flimsy or unconvincing [a thin excuse] 9. lacking solidity, substance, or vigor; slight, weak, vapid, etc. [a thin plot, thin argument] 10. *Photog.* lacking contrast of light and shade: said of a negative or print —*adv.* in a thin way —*vt.*, *vi.* **thinned**, **thin′ning** [ME. *thinnen* < OE. (*ge*)*thynnian* < the *adj.*] to make or become thin or thinner, as in dimension, density, etc.: often with *out*, *down*, etc. —**thin′ly** *adv.* —**thin′ness** *n.*

SYN.—**thin** implies relatively little extent from one surface or side of a thing to the opposite and connotes lack of fleshiness, fullness, substance, etc.; **slender** and **slim** suggest a physical spareness that is more or less pleasing in proportion, but in extended senses, the words carry connotations of meagerness, scantiness, etc. [a slender income, a slim possibility]; **lean**, implying an absence of fat, figuratively connotes a lack of richness, productiveness, etc. [lean years]; **slight** implies smallness and lightness or fragility in form or build and, in extended senses, suggests inconsiderableness in amount, extent, significance, etc. [a slight figure, difference, etc.]; **tenuous** implies extreme physical thinness or fineness and, in extended senses, suggests insubstantiality, flimsiness, extreme subtlety, etc. [a tenuous film, plot, etc.] —**ANT. thick, substantial**

thine (thīn) *pron.* [ME. *thin* < OE., gen. of *thu*, THOU¹ (ME. loss of -*n* before a consonant gives THY)] [Archaic or Poet.] that or those belonging to thee (you): absolute form of THY [a friend of thine, this is thine] —*possessive pronominal adj.* [Archaic or Poet.] thy: used esp. before a word beginning with a vowel or unaspirated *h*

thing¹ (thin) *n.* [ME. < OE., a council, court, controversy, akin to G. *ding*, ON. *thing* (orig. sense, "public assembly," hence, "subject of discussion, matter, thing") < IE. **tenk-*, to stretch, period of time < base **ten-*, to stretch: cf. THIN, TEND²] 1. any matter, circumstance, affair, or concern: *often used in pl.* [how are things?] 2. that which is done, has been done, or is to be done; happening, act, deed, incident, event, etc. [to accomplish great things] 3. that which constitutes an end to be achieved, a step in a process, etc. [the next thing is to mix thoroughly] 4. anything conceived of or referred to as existing as an individual, distinguishable entity; specif., *a*) any single entity distinguished from all others [each thing in the universe] *b*) a tangible object, as distinguished from a concept, quality, etc. [paintings and other beautiful things] *c*) an inanimate object *d*) an item, detail, etc. [go over each thing in the list] *e*) the object or concept referred to or represented by a word, symbol, or sign; referent *f*) an object of thought; idea [think the right things] 5. *a*) [pl.] personal belongings; also, clothes or clothing *b*) a dress, garment, etc. [not a thing to wear] 6. [pl.] articles, devices, etc. used for some purpose 7. a person: used in expressions of affection, pity, contempt, etc. [poor thing!] 8. a being, object, or concept the exact term for which is not known or recalled or is avoided, as from disdain [where did you buy that thing?] 9. [Colloq.] a point of contention; issue [don't make a thing of it] ☆10. [Colloq.] a complex, often neurotic liking, fear, aversion, etc. with regard to some person, thing, or activity [to have a thing about flying] 11. *Law* that which may be owned; a property: distinguished from PERSON —☆**do one's (own) thing** [Colloq.] to express one's unique personality in one's own style or by doing what one feels motivated to do or is most adept at —**see things** [Colloq.] to have hallucinations —**the thing** 1. that which is wise, essen-

tial, etc. 2. that which is the height of fashion or style

‡**thing²** (tin; *E.* thin) *n.* [ON., assembly: see prec.] a Scandinavian legislative body

thing·a·ma·bob, thing·um·a·bob (thin′ə mə bäb′) *n.* [see ff.] [Colloq.] *same as* THINGAMAJIG: also **thing′um·bob′** (-əm bäb′), **thing′um·my** (-ə mē)

thing·a·ma·jig, thing·um·a·jig (-jig′) *n.* [extension of older *thingum*, THING¹] [Colloq.] any device, contrivance, gadget, etc.: jocular substitute for a name not known or temporarily forgotten

thing-in-it·self (thin′in it self′) *n.* [transl. of G. *ding an sich*] in Kantian philosophy, that aspect of a thing which has reality beyond perceptual knowledge and can never be known

think¹ (thin) *vt.* **thought**, **think′ing** [< ME. *thenchen*, to think, confused with *thinchen*, to seem < OE. *thencan*, to think, caus. of *thyncan*, to seem: for IE. base see THANK] 1. to form or have in the mind; conceive [thinking good thoughts] 2. to hold in one's opinion; judge; consider [many think her charming] 3. to believe; surmise; expect [they think they can come] 4. to determine, resolve, work out, etc. by reasoning [think what your next move should be] 5. [Now Rare] to purpose; intend [thinking to do right] 6. *a*) to bring to mind; form an idea of [think what the future holds] *b*) to recall; recollect [think what joy was ours] 7. to have the mind turned steadily toward; have constantly in mind [think success] —*vi.* 1. to use the mind for arriving at conclusions, making decisions, drawing inferences, etc.; reflect; reason [learn to think] 2. to have an opinion, belief, expectation, etc. [I just think so] 3. to weigh something mentally; reflect [think before you act] 4. to call to mind; recall; remember (with *of* or *about*) 5. to have an opinion, judgment, etc. (with *of* or *about*) 6. to allow oneself to consider (with *of* or *about*) 7. to have regard for; consider the welfare of (with *of* or *about*) 8. to discover or invent; conceive (*of*) —*n.* [Colloq.] the act of thinking [give it a good think] —*adj.* [Slang] having to do with thinking —**think (all) the world of** to admire or love greatly —**think better of** 1. to form a more favorable opinion of 2. to make a more sensible or practical decision about, after reconsidering —**think fit** to regard as proper or appropriate —**think little** (or **nothing) of** 1. to attach little (or no) importance, value, etc. to 2. to have little (or no) hesitancy about —**think on** (or **upon**) [Archaic] to give thought or consideration to —**think out** 1. to think about completely or to the end 2. to work out, solve, discover, or plan by thinking —**think out loud** to speak one's thoughts as they occur: also **think aloud** —**think over** to give thought to; ponder well, as for reconsideration —**think through** to think about until one reaches a conclusion or resolution —**think twice** to reconsider; pause to think about again —**think up** to invent, contrive, plan, etc. by thinking —**think′er** *n.*

SYN.—**think** is the general word meaning to exercise the mental faculties so as to form ideas, arrive at conclusions, etc. [learn to think clearly]; **reason** implies a logical sequence of thought, starting with what is known or assumed and advancing to a definite conclusion through the inferences drawn [he reasoned that she would accept]; **cogitate** is used, sometimes humorously, of a person who is, or appears to be, thinking hard [I was cogitating, not daydreaming]; **reflect** implies a turning of one's thoughts on or back on a subject and connotes deep or quiet continued thought [he reflected on the day's events]; **speculate** implies a reasoning on the basis of incomplete or uncertain evidence and therefore stresses the conjectural character of the opinions formed [to speculate on the possibility of life on Mars]; **deliberate** implies careful and thorough consideration of a matter in order to arrive at a conclusion [the jury deliberated on the case]

think² (thin) *v. impersonal* **thought** [< ME. *thinchen*, to seem, confused with *thenchen*, to think: see prec.] to seem: obs., except in archaic METHINKS, METHOUGHT

think·a·ble (-ə b'l) *adj.* 1. that can be thought; conceivable 2. that can be considered as a possibility

think·ing (-in) *adj.* 1. that thinks or can think; rational 2. given to thought; reflective —*n.* the action of one who thinks or the result of such action; thought —**put on one's thinking cap** to begin careful thinking about a problem

☆**think piece** [Slang] an article, column, etc., as in a newspaper or magazine, presenting news analysis, background material, personal opinion, etc., as distinguished from a straight news account

☆**think tank** (or **factory**) [Slang] a group or center organized, as by a government or business, to do intensive research and problem-solving, esp. with the aid of computers and other sophisticated equipment

thin·ner (thin′ər) *n.* a person or thing that thins; esp., a substance added, as turpentine to paint, for thinning

thin·nish (-ish) *adj.* somewhat thin

thin-skinned (-skind′) *adj.* 1. having a thin skin 2. easily hurt by criticism, insult, etc.; sensitive

thi·o- (thī′ō, -ə) [< Gr. *theion*, brimstone] *a combining form meaning* sulfur, used in many chemical terms to indicate the replacement of oxygen in an acid radical by negatively bivalent sulfur

thi·o·a·ce·tic acid (thī′ō ə sēt′ik, -set′-) [prec. + ACETIC] a yellow liquid, CH_3COSH, with a very pungent odor: used as a chemical reagent and tear gas

thi·o acid (thī′ō) [cf. THIO-] an acid in which part or all of the oxygen atoms in the molecule have been replaced by sulfur atoms

thi·o·al·de·hyde (thī′ō al′də hīd′) *n.* [THIO- + ALDEHYDE] any of a group of organic chemical compounds containing the monovalent radical –CHS; an aldehyde in which sulfur has replaced the oxygen

thi·o·an·ti·mo·nate (-an′tə mə nāt′) *n.* any of a group of chemical compounds considered salts of thioantimonic acid: also **thi·o·an′ti·mo′ni·ate′** (-mō′nē āt′)

thi·o·an·ti·mon·ic acid (-an′tə män′ik, -mō′nik) [THIO- + ANTIMONIC] a hypothetical acid, H_3SbS_4, known only in the form of its salts

thi·o·an·ti·mo·ni·ous acid (-an′tə mō′nē əs) [THIO- + ANTIMONIOUS] any of a group of hypothetical acids, H_3SbS_3, $HSbS_2$, and $H_4Sb_2S_5$, known only in the forms of their salts in solution

thi·o·an·ti·mo·nite (-an′tə mə nīt′) *n.* any of a group of chemical compounds considered salts of the thioantimonious acids

thi·o·ar·se·nate (-är′sə nāt′, -s′n it) *n.* any of a group of chemical compounds considered salts of the thioarsenic acids

thi·o·ar·sen·ic acid (-är sen′ik) [THIO- + ARSENIC] any of three hypothetical acids, H_3AsS_4, $HAsS_3$, and H_4AsS_7, known only in the forms of their salts

thi·o·ar·se·ni·ous acid (-är sē′nē əs) [THIO- + ARSENIOUS] any of a group of hypothetical acids, H_3AsS_3, $HAsS_2$, and $H_4As_2S_5$, known only in the forms of their salts

thi·o·ar·se·nite (-är′sə nīt′) *n.* any of a group of chemical compounds considered salts of the thioarsenious acids

thi·o·bac·te·ri·a (-bak tir′ē ə) *n.pl., sing.* **-ri·um** (-əm) [THIO- + BACTERIA] bacteria found esp. in stagnant water and at the bottom of the sea, that oxidize or reduce sulfur compounds, as hydrogen sulfide

thi·o·car·ba·mide (-kär′bə mīd′) *n. same as* THIOUREA

thi·o·cy·a·nate (-sī′ə nāt′) *n.* a salt or ester of thiocyanic acid, containing the monovalent radical –SCN

thi·o·cy·an·ic acid (-sī ən′ik) [THIO- + CYANIC] a colorless, unstable liquid, HSCN, with a penetrating odor, known chiefly in the form of its salts

☆**Thi·o·kol** (thī′ə kôl′, -kōl′) [arbitrary coinage] *a trademark for* any of various synthetic rubbery materials prepared by reacting aliphatic compounds containing two halogen atoms with an alkali polysulfide: they are resistant to oil, grease, and water and are used as sealants, for hosing and tank linings, etc.

thi·ol (thī′ōl, -ôl) *n.* [THI(O)- + -OL¹] *same as* MERCAPTAN

thi·o·nate (thī′ə nāt′) *n.* a salt or ester of a thionic acid

thi·on·ic (thī än′ik) *adj.* [< Gr. *theion*, brimstone, sulfur + -IC] of, containing, or derived from sulfur

thionic acid 1. any organic chemical compound containing the monovalent –CS·OH radical **2.** any of a group of acids with the general formula $H_2S_nO_6$, in which *n* varies from 2 to 6

thi·o·nine (thī′ə nēn′, -nin) *n.* [< Gr. *theion*, brimstone, sulfur + -INE⁴] a dark-green crystalline thiazine base, $C_{12}H_9N_3S$, producing a violet dye in solution, used esp. as a stain in microscopy

thi·o·nyl (-ə nil) *n.* [< Gr. *theion*, brimstone, sulfur + -YL] the bivalent radical –SO

thi·o·pen·tal (sodium) (thī′ə pen′tal, -tôl, -t′l) [THIO- + PENT(A)- + -AL] a yellowish-white, hygroscopic powder, $C_{11}H_{17}N_2O_2SNa$, injected intravenously in solution as a general anesthetic and hypnotic

thi·o·phene (thī′ə fēn′) *n.* [THIO- + obs. *phene*, benzene < Fr. *phène:* see PHEN-] a heterocyclic, colorless liquid, C_4H_4S, resembling benzene and found in coal tar

thi·o·phos·phate (thī′ō fäs′fāt) *n.* a salt or ester of a thiophosphoric acid

thi·o·phos·phor·ic acid (-fäs fôr′ik, -fär′-) **1.** a phosphoric acid in which one or more oxygen atoms have been replaced by a sulfur atom **2.** the unstable acid, H_3PO_3S, produced only in solution or as a salt

thi·o·sin·am·ine (-sin am′ēn, -sin′ə mēn′) *n.* [THIO- + *sinamine* (< L. *sinapis*, mustard + AMINE)] a colorless, crystalline chemical compound, $C_4H_8N_2S$, produced by the reaction of ammonia on mustard oil, used in medicine for resolving scar tissue and in industry as a reagent

thi·o·sul·fate (-sul′fāt) *n.* a salt or ester of thiosulfuric acid; esp., sodium thiosulfate

thi·o·sul·fu·ric acid (-sul fyoor′ik) [THIO- + SULFURIC] an unstable acid, $H_2S_2O_3$, whose salts are used in photography, as an antichlor in bleaching, etc.

thi·o·u·ra·cil (-yoor′ə sil) *n.* [THIO- + URACIL] a white, crystalline, bitter-tasting powder, $C_4H_4N_2OS$, used to reduce thyroid activity, and in treating angina pectoris

thi·o·u·re·a (-yoo rē′ə, -yoor′ē ə) *n.* [ModL.: see THIO- & UREA] a colorless, crystalline chemical compound, $CS(NH_2)_2$, used in organic synthesis, in photography, etc.

☆**thi·ram** (thī′ram) *n.* [< ? *thiuram* < THIOUR(EA) + AM(YL)] a yellow or white powder, $C_6H_{12}N_2S_4$, used as a fungicide, seed disinfectant, etc.

third (thurd) *adj.* [ME. *thirde*, altered by metathesis < *thridde* < OE. *thridda* < IE. **tr̥tiyo-* (< base **trei-*, THREE), whence L. *tertius*, Gr. *tritos*] **1.** preceded by two others in a series; 3d or 3rd **2.** next below the second in rank, power, value, merit, excellence, etc. **3.** designating any of the three equal parts of something —*adv.* in the third place, rank, group, etc. —*n.* **1.** the one following the second **2.** any person, thing, class, place, etc. that is third **3.** any of the three equal parts of something; 1/3 **4.** the third forward gear ratio of a motor vehicle: in most automobiles it is the highest **5.** [*usually pl.*] *Law* [Rare] *a)* the third part of a deceased man's estate, which, under certain conditions, goes unrestrictedly to his widow *b)* loosely, a widow's dower **6.** *Music a)* the third tone of an ascending diatonic scale, or a tone two degrees above or below any given tone in such a scale; mediant *b)* the interval between two such tones, or a combination of them

☆**third base** *Baseball* the base between second base and home plate, located on the pitcher's right

third-class (thurd′klas′, -kläs′) *adj.* **1.** of the class, rank, excellence, etc. next below the second **2.** designating or of accommodations next below the second ☆**3.** designating or of a lower-cost class of mail limited to merchandise weighing less than 16 oz. or bulk mailing of identical circulars, bulletins, advertisements, etc. —*adv.* **1.** with accommodations next below the second [to travel *third-class*] ☆**2.** as or by third-class mail

third degree 1. in Freemasonry, the degree of master mason ☆**2.** [orig. ? fig. use of ritual by Freemasons] [Colloq.] harsh, grueling treatment and questioning of a prisoner in order to force a confession or information —**third′-de·gree′** *adj.*

third-degree burn *see* BURN¹ (*n.* 1)

third dimension 1. *a)* the dimension of depth in something as distinguished from the two dimensions of any of its flat surfaces *b)* the quality of having, or of seeming to have, such depth, or solidity **2.** the quality of being true to life or seeming real —**third′-di·men′sion·al** *adj.*

third estate *see* ESTATE (sense 2)

third eyelid *same as* NICTITATING MEMBRANE

third force [occas. **T- F-**] a third element, group, bloc, etc. functioning as a counterbalancing, neutralizing, or moderating force or influence in a struggle between two established powers; specif., a coalition of nations for this purpose internationally

Third International *same as* COMINTERN

third·ly (thurd′lē) *adv.* in the third place; third: used chiefly in enumerating topics

☆**third market** large-scale, over-the-counter trading in listed stocks by dealers outside a stock exchange

Third Order [occas. **t- o-**] an association of persons (*tertiaries*) affiliated with a religious order

third party ☆**1.** a political party organized to compete against the two major parties in a two-party system **2.** a person in a case or matter other than the principals

third person 1. that form of a pronoun (as *he*) or verb (as *is*) which refers to the person or thing spoken of **2.** narration characterized by the general use of such forms

☆**third rail** an extra rail used in some electric railroads, instead of an overhead wire, for supplying power

third-rate (-rāt′) *adj.* **1.** third in quality or other rating; third-class **2.** inferior; very poor —**third′-rat′er** *n.*

Third Reich *see* REICH

Third Republic the republic established in France in 1870, after the fall of Napoleon III, lasting until the German occupation of France in World War II

☆**third stream** a kind of music that combines techniques of jazz improvisation with classical, esp. twelve-tone, composition —**third′-stream′** *adj.*

third ventricle one of the four cavities of the brain, lying on the midline between the cerebral hemispheres

third world [*often* **T- W-**] the underdeveloped or emergent countries of the world, esp. of Africa and Asia

thirl (thurl) *vt., vi.* [ME. *thirlen* < OE. *thyrlian*, to bore < *thyrel*, a hole < *thurh*, THROUGH] [Brit. Dial.] **1.** to pierce; perforate **2.** *var.* of THRILL

thirst (thurst) *n.* [ME. < OE. *thurst*, akin to G. *durst* < IE. base **ters-*, to dry, whence L. *torridus*, torrid, *terra*, earth] **1.** the uncomfortable or distressful feeling caused by a desire or need for water and characterized generally by a sensation of dryness in the mouth and throat **2.** [Colloq.] a craving for a specific liquid, esp. for alcoholic liquor **3.** any strong desire; craving [a *thirst* for fame] —*vi.* **1.** to be thirsty **2.** to have a strong desire or craving

thirst·y (thur′stē) *adj.* **thirst′i·er, thirst′i·est** [ME. *thyrsti* < OE. *thurstig*] **1.** feeling thirst; wanting to drink **2.** *a)* lacking water or moisture; dry; parched [*thirsty* fields] *b)* very absorbent **3.** [Colloq.] causing thirst [*thirsty* work] **4.** having a strong desire; craving —**thirst′i·ly** *adv.* —**thirst′i·ness** *n.*

thir·teen (thur′tēn′) *adj.* [ME. *thritteene* < OE. *threotyne:* see THREE & -TEEN] three more than ten —*n.* the cardinal number between twelve and fourteen; 13; XIII

thir·teenth (-tēnth′) *adj.* [ME. *thirtenth:* see THIRTEEN & -TH²] **1.** preceded by twelve others in a series; 13th **2.** designating any of the thirteen equal parts of something —*n.* **1.** the one following the twelfth **2.** any of the thirteen equal parts of something; 1/13

thir·ti·eth (thur′tē ith) *adj.* [< ME. *thrittythe* < OE. *thritigotha:* see ff. & -TH²] **1.** preceded by twenty-nine others

in a series; 30th **2.** designating any of the thirty equal parts of something —*n.* **1.** the one following the twenty-ninth **2.** any of the thirty equal parts of something; 1/30

thir·ty (thur'tē) *adj.* [LME. *thirti*, metathetic for *thritti* < OE. *thritig* < *thri*, THREE + *-tig*, -TY²] three times ten —*n., pl.* **-ties 1.** the cardinal number between twenty-nine and thirty-one; 30; XXX ✩2. [prob. orig. telegraphers' code for a concluding sentence] this number used to signify the end of a dispatch, story, etc., as for a newspaper —**the thirties** the numbers or years, as of a century, from thirty through thirty-nine

thir·ty-sec·ond note (thurt'ē sek'ənd) *Music* a note having 1/32 the duration of a whole note: see NOTE, illus.

thir·ty-two·mo (-tōō'mō') *n., pl.* **-mos** [see -MO] **1.** the page size of a book made up of printer's sheets folded into 32 leaves, each leaf being approximately 3 1/2 by 5 1/2 in. **2.** a book consisting of pages of this size Usually written 32*mo* or 32° —*adj.* consisting of pages of this size

Thirty Years' War a series of European wars (1618–48) on political and religious issues, fought originally between German Catholics and German Protestants, but later involving the Swedish, French, and Spanish

this (*this*) *pron., pl.* **these** [ME. *this, thes* < OE. *thes, theos, this*, neut. < base of the demonstrative pron.: see THAT] **1.** the person or thing mentioned or understood [*this* is John, *this* tastes good] **2.** the thing that is nearer than another referred to as "that" [*this* is larger than that] **3.** the less remote in thought of two contrasted things [of the two possibilities, *this* is more likely than that] **4.** the fact, idea, etc. that is being, or is about to be, mentioned, presented, etc. [*this* convinces us, now hear *this*] —*adj., pl.* **these 1.** designating the person or thing mentioned or understood [*this* man was John, *this* pie tastes good] **2.** designating the thing that is nearer than the one referred to as "that" [*this* desk is smaller than that one] **3.** designating the less remote in thought of two contrasted things [of the two, *this* possibility is more likely than that] **4.** designating something that is being, or is about to be, mentioned, presented, etc. [hear *this* song, *this* fact will convince you] **5.** [Colloq.] designating a particular but unspecified person or thing [there's *this* lady in Iowa] —*adv.* to this extent; so [it was *this* big]

Thisbe *see* PYRAMUS AND THISBE

this·tle (this'l) *n.* [ME. *thistel* < OE., akin to G. *distel* < IE. base *(s)teig-*, a point, whence Sans. *tiktá*, sharp, L. (*in*)*stigare*, to spur] any of various plants (as genera *Onopordum, Cirsium*, and *Cnicus*) of the composite family, with prickly leaves and heads of white, purple, pink, or yellow flowers; esp., the **Scotch thistle** (*Onopordum acanthium*) with white down and lavender flowers **this·tle·down** (-doun') *n.* the down attached to the flower head of a thistle

THISTLE

this·tly (this'lē, -'l ē) *adj.* **-tli·er, -tli·est 1.** like a thistle or thistles; prickly **2.** full of thistles

thith·er (thith'ər, thith'-) *adv.* [ME. *thider* < OE. < demonstrative base: see THAT] to or toward that place; there —*adj.* on or toward that side; farther

thith·er·to (-tōō'; thith'ər tōō', thith'-) *adv.* [ME. *thidir to*] until that time; till then

thith·er·ward (-wərd) *adv.* [ME. < OE. *thiderweard*] [Rare] toward that place; thither: also **thith'er·wards**

thix·ot·ro·py (thik sät'rə pē) *n.* [< Gr. *thixis*, touching (< *thinganein*, to touch < IE. base *dheigh-*, to knead, whence DOUGH) + Eng. *-o-* + *-TROPY*] the property of certain gels and emulsions of becoming fluid when agitated and then setting again when left at rest —**thix'o·trop'ic** (-sə träp'ik) *adj.*

tho, tho' (thō) *conj., adv. clipped form of* THOUGH

thole¹ (thōl) *n.* [ME. *tholle* < OE. *thol*, akin to ON. *thollr*, Du. *dol* < IE. *tuel-* < base *teu-*, to swell, rise, increase, whence Gr. *tylē*, a swelling, L. *tuber*] a pin or either of a pair of pins, made of metal or wood and set vertically in the gunwale of a boat to serve as a fulcrum for an oar: also **thole'pin'** (-pin')

thole² (thōl) *vt.* **tholed, thol'ing** [ME. *tholen* < OE. *tholian* < IE. base *tel-*, to bear: cf. TOLERATE] [Archaic or Brit. Dial.] to suffer; endure; undergo

Thom·as (täm'əs) [ME. < LL.(Ec.) < Gr.(Ec.) *Thōmas* < Ar. *tĕ'ōma*, lit., a twin] **1.** a masculine name: dim. *Tom, Tommy*; fem. *Thomasina* **2.** *Bible* one of the twelve apostles, who doubted at first the resurrection of Jesus: John 20:24–29: also called *Saint Thomas*: his day is Dec. 21 **3.** **Dyl·an** (Marlais) (dil'ən), 1914–53; Welsh poet **4.** **George Henry**, 1816–70; Union general in the Civil War **5.** **John Charles**, 1891–1960; U.S. operatic baritone **6.** **Norman** (Mattoon), 1884–1968; U.S. Socialist leader **7.** **Seth**, 1785–1859; U.S. clock manufacturer

Thomas à Becket *see* BECKET

Thomas à Kempis *see* KEMPIS

Thomas Aquinas *see* AQUINAS

Tho·mism (tō'miz'm) *n.* the theological and philosophical doctrines of Thomas Aquinas and his followers: it formed the basis of 13th-cent. scholasticism —**Tho'mist** *adj., n.* —**Tho·mis'tic** *adj.*

Thomp·son (tämp's'n, täm'-) **1. Benjamin**, Count Rumford, 1753–1814; Brit. scientist & statesman, born in America **2. David**, 1770–1857; Canad. explorer, born in England **3. Francis**, 1859–1907; Eng. poet

☆**Thompson submachine gun** [< the co-inventor, J. T. *Thompson* (1860–1940), U.S. army officer] *a trademark for* a type of submachine gun: see SUBMACHINE GUN

Thom·son (täm's'n) **1.** Sir **George Pag·et** (paj'ət), 1892– ; Eng. physicist **2. James**, *a*) 1700–48; Scot. poet *b*) (pseud. *B. V.*; i.e., *Bysshe Vanolis*) 1834–82; Scot. poet **3.** (Sir) **J(ohn) Arthur**, 1861–1933; Scot. naturalist & writer **4.** Sir **Joseph John**, 1856–1940; Eng. physicist: father of *George Paget* **5. Virgil**, 1896– ; U.S. composer **6. William**, *see* Baron KELVIN

Thon·bu·ri (tän'boo rē') city in Thailand, on the Chao Phraya River, opposite Bangkok: pop. 490,000

thong (thôŋ) *n.* [ME. < OE. *thwang*, a twisted string, thong: for IE. base see TWINGE] **1.** a narrow strip of leather, etc. used as a lace, strap, etc. **2.** a whiplash, as of plaited strips of hide

Thon·ga (thäŋ'gə) *n.* **1.** *pl.* **-gas, -ga** any member of a farming people of Mozambique **2.** their Bantu language

Thor (thôr) [ON. *Thorr*: for IE. base see THUNDER] *Norse Myth.* the god of thunder, war, and strength, and the son of Odin, armed with a magic hammer

tho·rac·ic (thô ras'ik, thə-) *adj.* [ModL. *thoracicus* < Gr. *thōrakikos*] of, in, or near the thorax

thoracic duct the main canal of the lymphatic system, passing along the front of the spinal column, collecting lymph and conveying it into the left subclavian vein

tho·ra·co- (thôr'ə kō) [Gr. *thōrako-*] *a combining form meaning:* **1.** the thorax [*thoracoplasty*] **2.** the thorax and [*thoracolumbar*] Also, before a vowel, **thorac-**

tho·ra·co·lum·bar (thôr'ə kō lum'bər) *adj.* **1.** of the thoracic and lumbar regions **2.** *same as* SYMPATHETIC (sense 4)

tho·ra·co·plas·ty (thôr'ə kō plas'tē) *n., pl.* **-ties** [THORA-CO- + -PLASTY] surgery of the thorax in which part of the rib cage is collapsed to diminish the thoracic cavity

tho·ra·cot·o·my (thôr'ə kät'ə mē) *n., pl.* **-mies** [THORACO- + -TOMY] surgical incision into the thorax

tho·rax (thôr'aks) *n., pl.* **-rax·es, -ra·ces'** (-ə sēz') [ME. < L. < Gr. *thōrax*, the chest, breastplate] **1.** in man and other higher vertebrates, the part of the body between the neck and the abdomen; specif., the cavity containing the heart, lungs, etc.; chest **2.** the middle one of the three main segments of an insect's body

☆**Tho·ra·zine** (thôr'ə zēn') [*thor-* (< ?) + (CHLORPROM)-AZINE] *a trademark for* CHLORPROMAZINE

Thor·eau (thôr'ō, thə rō'), **Henry David** (born *David Henry Thoreau*) 1817–62; U.S. naturalist & writer

tho·ri·a (thôr'ē ə) *n.* [ModL. < Sw. *Thorjord*, lit., Thor-earth (so named by BERZELIUS): see THORIUM] thorium oxide, ThO₂, a white, earthy powder: used esp. in gas mantles and in making refractory crucibles

tho·ri·a·nite (-nīt') *n.* [< prec. + -ITE¹] a black, crystal-line, radioactive mineral, consisting usually of 70% thori-um oxide, 12% uranium oxide, and various other rare earths

tho·rite (thôr'īt) *n.* [Sw. *thorit*: see ff. & -ITE¹] a dark-brown or black mineral, ThSiO₄, a native silicate of thorium

tho·ri·um (-ē əm) *n.* [ModL. < ON. *Thorr* (see THOR) + ModL. *-ium*: so named by BERZELIUS, who dis-covered it] a rare, grayish, radioactive chemical element occurring in monazite and thorite: it is used in making gas mantles, electronic equipment, etc. and as a nuclear fuel: symbol, Th; at. wt., 232.038; at. no., 90; sp. gr., 11.7; melt. pt., 1845°C; boil. pt., 4230°C —**tho'ric** *adj.*

thorn (thôrn) *n.* [ME. < OE., akin to G. *dorn* < IE. *(s)ter-*, prickly plant (< base *ster-*, to be stiff), whence Gr. *ternax*, cactus stem] **1.** *a*) a very short, hard, leafless branch or stem with a sharp point *b*) any small tree or shrub bearing thorns; esp., *same as* HAWTHORN *c*) the wood of any of these trees **2.** a sharp, pointed protuber-ance on an animal; spine **3.** anything that keeps troubling, vexing, or irritating one, like a constantly pricking thorn: usually in the phrase **thorn in one's side** (or **flesh**) **4.** in Old English and Old Norse, the runic character (þ), corresponding to either the voiced or unvoiced sound of English *th*: so called because it was the first letter of the word *thorn*: see YE¹

thorn apple ☆**1.** *a*) *same as* HAWTHORN *b*) its applelike fruit ✩**2.** a jimson weed or similar plant

thorn·back (thôrn'bak') *n.* **1.** any of several European rays with many tubercles on the back and a double row of spines on the tail **2.** a large European spider crab (*Maja squinado*) with a spiny back **3.** a California skate (*Platy-rhinoidis triseriata*) with spines on the back

Thorn·dike (thôrn'dīk'), **Edward Lee** 1874–1949; U.S. psychologist, educator, & lexicographer

thorn·y (thôr'nē) *adj.* **thorn'i·er, thorn'i·est 1.** full of thorns; brambly; prickly **2.** having thorns or spines: said of some animals **3.** like a thorn; sharp **4.** full of obstacles, vexations, pain, etc. [the *thorny* road to peace] **5.** full of controversial points; difficult; contentious [a *thorny* problem] —**thorn'i·ness** *n.*

thor·o (thûr'ō, -ə) *adj. clipped form of* THOROUGH

tho·ron (thôr'än) *n.* [ModL. < THORIUM + -*on* as in ARGON] a radioactive isotope of radon, resulting from the disintegration of thorium

thor·ough (thur'ō, -ə) *prep., adv.* [ME. *thoruh, thuruh,* an emphatic var. of *through,* THROUGH] *obs. var. of* THROUGH —*adj.* **1.** orig., passing through: now chiefly in combination, as in *thoroughfare* **2.** done or proceeding through to the end; omitting nothing; complete [a *thorough* checkup] **3.** that is completely (the thing specified); out-and-out; absolute [a *thorough* rascal] **4.** very exact, accurate, or painstaking, esp. with regard to details [a *thorough* researcher] —*n.* [T-] *Eng. History* the ruthlessly thoroughgoing administrative policies carried out by William Laud and the Earl of Strafford during the reign of Charles I —**thor'ough·ly** *adv.* —**thor'ough·ness** *n.*

thorough bass *Music* **1.** *a)* an old system for indicating accompanying chords by putting figures under the bass notes *b)* the figures used **2.** loosely, the theory of harmony

☆**thorough brace** either of a pair of leather straps supporting the body of a coach or other horse-drawn vehicle and often serving as springs

thor·ough·bred (thur'ə bred') *adj.* **1.** purebred, as a horse or dog; pedigreed **2.** thoroughly trained, educated, cultured, etc.; well-bred **3.** excellent; first-rate —*n.* **1.** a thoroughbred animal; specif., [T-] any of a breed of racehorses developed originally by crossing English mares with Arabian stallions **2.** a cultured, well-bred person

thor·ough·fare (-fer') *n.* [ME. *thurghfare:* see THROUGH & FARE] **1.** a way or passage through **2.** a public street open at both ends, esp. one through which there is much traffic; highway; main road

thor·ough·go·ing (-gō'iŋ) *adj.* very thorough; specif., *a)* precise and painstaking *b)* being wholly such; absolute; unmitigated [a *thoroughgoing* scoundrel]

thor·ough·paced (-pāst') *adj.* **1.** thoroughly trained in all paces or gaits: said of horses **2.** same as THOROUGHGOING

thor·ough·pin (-pin') *n.* a swelling in the sheath of a tendon in a horse's hock that shows on both sides of the leg like a pin going through

☆**thor·ough·wort** (-wurt') *n. same as* BONESET

thorp, thorpe (thôrp) *n.* [ME. < OE., akin to G. *dorf,* village < IE. base **treb-,* beamed structure, dwelling: cf. TAVERN] a village; hamlet: now mainly in place names

Thorpe (thôrp), **Jim** (*James Francis Thorpe*) 1888–1953; U.S. athlete

Thos. Thomas

those (thōz) *adj., pron.* [ME. *thas, thos* < OE. *thas, thæs,* pl. of *thes,* THIS] *pl. of* THAT

Thoth (thōth, tōt) [L. < Gr. *Thōth* < Egypt. *Ṭeḥuti*] the ancient Egyptian god of wisdom, learning, and magic, the scribe of the gods: represented as having a human body and the head of either a dog or an ibis

thou[1] (thou) *pron., pl. nom. & obj.* **you,** ye; *pl. poss.* **your, yours** [ME. < OE. *thu,* akin to G. *du* < IE. **tu,* whence L. *tu,* Sans. *tu*] the nominative second person singular of the personal pronoun: formerly used in familiar address but now replaced by *you* except in poetic or religious use and in some British dialects: *thee* is the objective case form, *thy* or *thine* the possessive, and *thyself* the intensive and reflexive

thou[2] (thou) *n., pl.* **thou, thous** *slang clipped form of* THOUSAND

though (thō) *conj.* [ME. *thah, thogh* < OE. *theah* & cognate ON. *tho,* akin to G. *doch,* yet, however, Goth. *thauh*] **1.** in spite of the fact that; notwithstanding that; although [*though* the car is new, it rattles] **2.** and yet; nevertheless; however [they will probably win, *though* no one thinks so] **3.** even if; supposing that [*though* he may fail, he will have tried] —*adv.* however; nevertheless [she sings well, *though*]

thought[1] (thôt) *n.* [ME. *thouht* < OE. *thoht* < PGmc. **thanht,* pret. of **thankjan* (whence OE. *thencan:* see THINK[1])] **1.** the act or process of thinking; reflection; meditation; cogitation **2.** the power of reasoning, or of conceiving ideas; capacity for thinking; intellect; imagination **3.** a result of thinking; idea, concept, opinion, etc. **4.** the ideas, principles, opinions, etc. prevalent at a given time or place or among a given people [modern *thought* in education] **5.** attention; consideration; heed [give it a moment's *thought*] **6.** mental engrossment; preoccupation; concentration [deep in *thought*] **7.** intention or expectation [no *thought* of leaving] **8.** a small amount, degree, etc.; a little; trifle [be a *thought* more careful] —*SYN.* see IDEA

thought[2] (thôt) *pt. & pp. of* THINK

thought·ful (-fəl) *adj.* **1.** full of thought; meditative; thinking **2.** showing or characterized by thought; serious [a *thoughtful* essay] **3.** heedful, careful, attentive, etc.; esp., considerate of others; kind —**thought'ful·ly** *adv.* —**thought'ful·ness** *n.*

SYN.—**thoughtful,** as compared here, implies the showing of thought for the comfort or well-being of others, as by anticipating their needs or wishes [it was *thoughtful* of you to call]; **considerate** implies a thoughtful or sympathetic regard for the feelings or circumstances of others, as in sparing them pain, distress, or discomfort [*considerate* enough to extend the time for payment]; **attentive** implies a constant thoughtfulness as shown by repeated acts of consideration, courtesy, or devotion [an *attentive* suitor] —*ANT.* **thoughtless**

thought·less (-lis) *adj.* **1.** not stopping to think; careless **2.** not given thought; ill-considered; rash **3.** not considerate of others; inconsiderate **4.** [Rare] stupid; senseless —**thought'less·ly** *adv.* —**thought'less·ness** *n.*

thou·sand (thou'z'nd) *n.* [ME. *thusend* < OE., akin to G. *tausend* < **thus-hundi,* "many hundred" < IE. base **teu-,* to swell, increase + PGmc. **hundi,* HUNDRED] **1.** ten hundred; 1,000; M **2.** an indefinite but very large number: a hyperbolic use —*adj.* amounting to one thousand in number

thou·sand·fold (-fōld') *adj.* having a thousand times as much or as many —*adv.* a thousand times as much or as many: with *a* —*n.* a number or an amount a thousand times as great

☆**Thousand Island dressing** a salad dressing made of mayonnaise with ketchup and minced pickles, capers, etc.

Thousand Islands group of c.1,000 islands in the St. Lawrence River at the outlet of Lake Ontario, some part of N.Y. State & some of Ontario, Canada

Thousand Oaks [after the many *oak* trees there] city in SW Calif., northwest of Los Angeles: pop. 36,000

thou·sandth (thou'z'ndth) *adj.* [THOUSAND + -TH[2]] **1.** coming last in a series of a thousand **2.** designating any of the thousand equal parts of something —*n.* **1.** the thousandth one of a series **2.** any of the thousand equal parts of something; 1/1000

Thrace (thrās) **1.** ancient region in the E Balkan Peninsula **2.** modern region in the SE Balkan Peninsula divided between Greece & Turkey

Thra·cian (thrā'shən) *adj.* of Thrace, its people, etc. —*n.* **1.** a native or inhabitant of Thrace **2.** the extinct language of ancient Thrace, usually assumed to belong to the Indo-European language family

thrall (thrôl) *n.* [ME. *thral* < OE. *thræl* < ON. *thræll* < Gmc. **thranhilaz,* lit., the constrained one < IE. base **trenk-,* to shove, press hard, whence THRONG] **1.** orig., a slave or bondman **2.** a person under the moral or psychological domination of someone or something **3.** slavery —*vt.* [Archaic] to enslave —*adj.* [Archaic] enslaved

thrall·dom, thral·dom (-dəm) *n.* the condition of being a thrall; servitude; slavery

thrash (thrash) *vt.* [ME. *threschen* < OE. *therscan,* akin to G. *dreschen,* to thresh < IE. base **ter-,* to rub, rub away, whence L. *terere,* to rub] **1.** same as THRESH **2.** to make move violently or wildly; beat [a bird *thrashing* its wings] **3.** to give a severe beating to; flog **4.** to defeat overwhelmingly —*vi.* **1.** same as THRESH **2.** to move or toss about violently, flinging the arms, legs, etc. about wildly or vigorously [*thrashing* in agony] **3.** to make one's way by thrashing —*n.* the act of thrashing —*SYN.* see BEAT —**thrash out** to settle by detailed discussion —**thrash over** to go over (a problem, etc.) in great detail

thrash·er[1] (-ər) *n.* a person or thing that thrashes

thrash·er[2] *n.* [E. dial. *thresher,* prob. akin to THRUSH[1]] ☆any of a group of gray to brownish American songbirds (genus *Toxostoma*) resembling the thrush by having a long, stiff tail and a long bill; esp., the **brown thrasher** (*Toxostoma rufum*) of the E U.S.

thrash·ing (thrash'iŋ) *n.* a beating; flogging

thra·son·i·cal (thrə sän'i k'l) *adj.* [< L. *Thraso* (< Gr. *Thrasōn* < *thrasos,* too bold), braggart in Terence's *Eunuch* + -ICAL] boastful; bragging —**thra·son'i·cal·ly** *adv.*

thrawn (thrôn) *adj.* [< *thraw,* dial. form of THROW] [Scot.] **1.** crooked; twisted **2.** perverse

thread (thred) *n.* [ME. *threde* < OE. *thræd* (akin to G. *draht*), akin to *thrawan,* to twist: see THROW] **1.** *a)* a light, fine, stringlike length of material made up of two or more fibers or strands of spun cotton, flax, silk, etc. twisted together and used in sewing *b)* a similar fine length of synthetic material, as nylon or plastic, or of glass or metal *c)* the fine, stringy filament extruded by a spider, silkworm, etc. *d)* any of the yarns of which a fabric is woven *e)* a fine, stringy length of syrup or other viscous material **2.** any thin line, stratum, vein, stream, ray, etc. **3.** an element suggestive of a thread in its continuousness, length, sequence, etc. [the *thread* of a story] **4.** the spiral or helical ridge of a screw, bolt, nut, etc. ☆**5.** [*pl.*] [Slang] a suit, or clothes generally —*vt.* **1.** *a)* to put a thread through the eye of (a needle, etc.) *b)* to arrange thread for use on (a sewing machine) **2.** to string (beads, etc.) on or as if on a thread **3.** to fashion a thread (sense 4) on or in (a screw, pipe, etc.) **4.** to interweave with or as if with threads [a red tapestry *threaded* with gold] **5.** *a)* to pass through by twisting, turning, or weaving in and out [to *thread* the streets] *b)* to make (one's way) in this fashion —*vi.* **1.** to go along or proceed in a winding way ☆**2.** to form a thread when dropped from a spoon: said of boiling syrup that has reached a certain consistency —**thread'er** *n.* —**thread'like'** *adj.*

thread·bare (-ber') *adj.* **1.** worn down so that the threads show; having the nap or surface fibers worn off [*threadbare* rugs] **2.** wearing old, worn clothes; shabby **3.** that has lost freshness or novelty; stale [a *threadbare* argument]

thread·fin (-fin') *n.* any of a family (Polynemidae) of saltwater fishes related to the mullets and having a divided pectoral fin that ends in threadlike rays

thread·worm (-wurm′) *n.* a nematode or gordian worm

thread·y (-ē) *adj.* **thread′i·er, thread′i·est** **1.** of or like a thread; stringy; fibrous; filamentous **2.** forming threads; viscid: said of liquids **3.** of or covered with threads or threadlike parts; fibrous **4.** thin, weak, feeble, etc. [a *thready* voice, a *thready* pulse] —**thread′i·ness** *n.*

threap (thrēp) *vt.* [ME. *threpen* < OE. *threapian*, to rebuke] [Scot. or Brit. Dial.] **1.** to scold; chide **2.** to maintain or assert obstinately

threat (thret) *n.* [ME. *threte* < OE. *threat*, a throng, painful pressure, akin to G. *(ver)driessen*, to grieve, annoy < IE. **treud-*, to push, press, whence L. *trudere*, to THRUST] **1.** an expression of intention to hurt, destroy, punish, etc., as in retaliation or intimidation **2.** *a)* an indication of imminent danger, harm, evil, etc. [the *threat* of war] *b)* a potential source of this —*vt., vi. obs. var. of* THREATEN

threat·en (thret′'n) *vt.* [ME. *thretnen* < OE. *threatnian*] **1.** *a)* to make threats against; express one's intention of hurting, punishing, etc. *b)* to express intention to inflict (punishment, reprisal, etc.) **2.** *a)* to be a menacing indication of (danger, harm, distress, etc.) [clouds *threatening* snow] *b)* to be a source of such danger, harm, etc. to [an epidemic that *threatens* the city] —*vi.* **1.** to make threats **2.** to be an indication or source of potential danger, harm, etc. —**threat′en·er** *n.* —**threat′en·ing·ly** *adv.*
SYN.—**threaten** implies a warning of impending punishment, danger, evil, etc. by words, actions, events, conditions, signs, etc. [he *threatened* to retaliate, the clouds *threaten* rain]; **menace** stresses the frightening or hostile character of that which threatens [he *menaced* me with a revolver]

three (thrē) *adj.* [ME. < OE. *threo, thrie*, akin to G. *drei* < IE. base **trei-*, whence L. *tres*, Gr. *treis*, Sans. *tri*] totaling one more than two —*n.* **1.** the cardinal number between two and four; 3; III **2.** any group of three people or things **3.** something numbered three or having three units, as a playing card, face of a die, etc.
☆**three-base hit** (thrē′bās′) *Baseball* a hit by which the batter can reach third base without benefit of an error: also [Slang] **three′-bag′ger** (-bag′ər) *n.*
☆**three-card mon·te** (thrē′kärd′ män′tē) a gambling game in which a person bets on the location of one of three cards shown and then, face down, shifted about
three-col·or (thrē′kul′ər) *adj.* designating or of a full-color printing process using three separate plates, each reproducing one primary color
three-cor·nered (-kôr′nərd) *adj.* having three corners or angles
☆**3-D** (thrē′dē′) *adj.* producing or designed to produce an effect of three dimensions; three-dimensional [a 3-D movie] —*n.* a system or effect that adds a three-dimensional appearance to visual images, as in films, slides, or drawings
three-deck·er (-dek′ər) *n.* **1.** *a)* formerly, a warship with three decks of cannon *b)* a ship with three decks **2.** any structure with three levels **3.** [Colloq.] a sandwich made with three slices of bread
three-di·men·sion·al (-də men′shən 'l) *adj.* **1.** *a)* of or having three dimensions *b)* appearing to have depth or thickness in addition to height and width **2.** having a convincing or lifelike quality
three·fold (-fōld′) *adj.* [see -FOLD] **1.** having three parts **2.** having three times as much or as many —*adv.* three times as much or as many
three-mile limit (-mīl′) the outer limit of a zone of water extending three miles offshore, sometimes regarded as the extent of the territorial jurisdiction of the coastal country
three·pence (thrip′'ns, thrup′-, threp′-) *n.* **1.** the sum of three British pennies **2.** a British coin of this value
three·pen·ny (thrē′pen′ē, thrip′ə nē) *adj.* **1.** worth or costing threepence **2.** of small worth; cheap **3.** designating a size of nail: see -PENNY
three-phase (thrē′fāz′) *adj. Elec.* designating or of a combination of three circuits energized by three alternating electromotive forces differing in phase by one third of a cycle, or 120 electrical degrees
three-piece (-pēs′) *adj.* composed of three separate pieces, as an outfit of skirt, sweater, and jacket
three-ply (-plī′) *adj.* having three thicknesses, interwoven layers, strands, etc.
three-point landing (-point′) a perfect airplane landing in which the main wheels and the tail wheel or nose wheel touch the ground at the same time
three-quar·ter (-kwôr′tər) *adj.* **1.** of or involving three fourths **2.** showing the face intermediate between profile and full face [a *three-quarter* portrait]
three-quarter binding a type of bookbinding in which the material of the back, usually leather, is extended onto the covers for one third of their width
☆**three-ring circus** (thrē′riŋ′) **1.** a circus having three rings for simultaneous performances **2.** any situation, performance, etc. hilariously or confusingly packed with action
Three Rivers *Eng. name of* TROIS RIVIÈRES
three R's, the *see* R (*n.*)
three·score (thrē′skôr′) *adj.* [see SCORE] three times twenty; sixty
three·some (-səm) *adj.* [ME. *thresum:* see -SOME²] of or engaged in by three —*n.* **1.** a group of three persons **2.** *Golf* a match in which one participant plays against two others, who alternate strokes on a single ball

three-square (-skwer′) *adj.* forming an equilateral triangle in cross section, as a three-cornered file
three-way (-wā′) *adj.* operating in three ways; specif., designating or for a light bulb with two filaments that can be switched on singly or together for three different wattages
three-wheel·er (-hwēl′ər, -wēl′-) *n.* a three-wheeled vehicle, as a tricycle or a three-wheeled motorcycle
threm·ma·tol·o·gy (threm′ə täl′ə jē) *n.* [< Gr. *thremma* (gen. *thremmatos*), a nursling (< IE. base **dherebh-*, to coagulate, whence Gr. *trephein*, to nourish, *thrombos*, a-clot) + -LOGY] [Rare] the branch of biology dealing with the breeding of domestic animals and plants
thren·o·dy (thren′ə dē) *n., pl.* **-dies** [Gr. *thrēnōidia* < *thrēnos*, lamentation (< IE. echoic base **dhren-*, to murmur, whence DRONE¹) + *ōidē*, song] a song of lamentation; funeral song; dirge: also **thre·node** (thrē′nōd, thren′ōd) —**thre·nod·ic** (thri näd′ik) *adj.* —**thren′o·dist** *n.*
thre·o·nine (thrē′ə nēn′, -nin) *n.* [prob. < *threon(ic acid)* + -INE⁴] an amino acid, C₄H₉NO₃, essential in nutrition, obtained from the hydrolysis of many proteins
thresh (thresh) *vt.* [ME. *threschen:* earlier form of THRASH] **1.** to beat out (grain) from its husk, as with a flail **2.** to beat grain out of (husks) **3.** to beat or strike as with a flail —*vi.* **1.** to thresh grain **2.** to toss about; thrash —**thresh out** *same as* THRASH OUT (see under THRASH)
thresh·er (-ər) *n.* **1.** a person who threshes **2.** *same as* THRESHING MACHINE **3.** a large shark (*Alopias vulpinus*) of temperate and tropical seas, having a very long upper tail lobe with which it is said to thresh the water and drive its prey together
threshing machine a machine for threshing grain
thresh·old (thresh′ōld, -hōld) *n.* [ME. *threschwold* < OE. *therscwold* (akin to ON. *threskǫlder*) < base of *therscan* (see THRASH)] **1.** *same as* DOORSILL **2.** the entrance or beginning point of something [at the *threshold* of a new career] **3.** *Physiol., Psychol.* the point at which a stimulus is just strong enough to be perceived or produce a response [the *threshold* of pain]
threw (throo) *pt. of* THROW
thrice (thrīs) *adv.* [ME. *thries < thrie* (< OE. *thriwa*, thrice, akin to *threo*, THREE) + -(*e*)*s*, adv. gen. suffix, after *ones* (see ONCE)] **1.** three times **2.** three times as much or as many; threefold **3.** greatly; highly
thrift (thrift) *n.* [ME. < ON. < *thrifast*, to prosper: see THRIVE] **1.** orig., *a)* the condition of thriving; prosperity *b)* physical thriving; vigorous growth **2.** careful management of one's money or resources; economy; frugality **3.** any of a genus (*Armeria*) of dwarf, evergreen perennials, with narrow leaves and small white, pink, red, or purplish flowers **4.** [Scot.] a means of thriving; work; labor
thrift·less (-lis) *adj.* without thrift; wasteful —**thrift′less·ly** *adv.* —**thrift′less·ness** *n.*
☆**thrift shop** a store where castoff clothes and rummage are sold, specif. to raise money for charity
thrift·y (-ē) *adj.* **thrift′i·er, thrift′i·est** **1.** practicing or showing thrift; economical; provident **2.** thriving; flourishing; prospering **3.** growing vigorously, as a plant —**thrift′i·ly** *adv.* —**thrift′i·ness** *n.*
SYN.—**thrifty** implies industry and clever management of one's money or resources, usually so as to result in some savings [the *thrifty* housewife watched for sales]; **frugal** stresses the idea of saving and suggests spending which excludes any luxury or lavishness and provides only the simplest fare, dress, etc. [the Amish are a *frugal* people]; **sparing** implies such restraint in spending as restricts itself to the bare minimum or involves deprivation [*sparing* to the point of niggardliness]; **economical** implies prudent management of one's money or resources so as to avoid any waste in expenditure or use [it is often *economical* to buy in large quantities]; **provident** implies management with the foresight to provide for future needs [never *provident*, he quickly spent his inheritance] —**ANT.** lavish, prodigal, wasteful
thrill (thril) *vt.* [ME. *thrillen*, by metathesis < *thyrlen* < OE. *thyr(e)lian*, to pierce < *thyrel*, perforation, hole < base of *thurh*, THROUGH] **1.** to cause sharply exhilarating excitement in; make shiver or tingle with excitement **2.** to produce vibrations or quivering in; cause to tremble —*vi.* **1.** to feel emotional excitement; shiver or tingle with excitement **2.** to tremble; vibrate; quiver —*n.* [new formation < the *v.*] **1.** a thrilling or being thrilled; tremor of excitement **2.** the quality of thrilling, or the ability to thrill [the *thrill* of the chase] **3.** something that causes emotional excitement **4.** a vibration; tremor; quiver; specif., *Med.* an abnormal tremor, as of the circulatory system, that can be felt by the hand on palpation
thrill·er (-ər) *n.* a person or thing that thrills; specif., a suspenseful novel, play, motion picture, etc., esp. [Chiefly Brit.] one dealing with crime and detection
thrips (thrips) *n., pl.* **thrips** [L. < Gr. *thrips*, woodworm] any of an order (Thysanoptera) of very small, destructive, usually winged insects, that suck the juices of plants
thrive (thrīv) *vi.* **thrived** or **throve, thrived** or **thriv·en** (thriv′'n), **thriv′ing** [ME. *thrifen* < ON. *thrifast*, to prosper, reflex. of *thrifa*, to grasp] **1.** to prosper or flourish; be successful, esp. as the result of economical management **2.** to grow vigorously or luxuriantly; improve physically —*SYN.* see SUCCEED
thro', thro (throo) *prep., adv., adj. archaic clipped form of* THROUGH

throat (thrōt) *n.* [ME. *throte* < OE., akin to G. *dross(el)*, *throat* < IE. **(s)treu-*, swollen, stretched < base **(s)ter-*, stiff: cf. STARE, STRETCH] 1. the front part of the neck 2. the upper part of the passage leading from the mouth and nose to the stomach and lungs, including the pharynx and the upper larynx, trachea, and esophagus 3. any narrow, throatlike passage or part, esp. one serving as an entrance [the *throat* of a chimney] —*vt.* [Archaic] to pronounce or sing in the throat, i.e., with a harsh, guttural quality —**cut each other's throats** [Colloq.] to ruin each other, as by underselling in business —**cut one's own throat** [Colloq.] to be the means of one's own ruin —**jump down someone's throat** [Colloq.] to attack or criticize someone suddenly and violently —**ram (something) down someone's throat** to force someone to accept, hear, etc. something —**stick in one's throat** to be hard for one to say, as from reluctance

-throat·ed (thrōt'id) *a combining form meaning* having a (specified kind of) throat [ruby-throated]

throat·latch (-lach') *n.* a strap that passes under a horse's throat, for holding a bridle or halter in place

throat·y (-ē) *adj.* **throat'i·er, throat'i·est** 1. produced in the throat, as some sounds or tones 2. characterized by such sounds; husky, hoarse, etc. [a *throaty* voice] — **throat'i·ly** *adv.* —**throat'i·ness** *n.*

throb (thräb) *vi.* **throbbed, throb'bing** [ME. *throbben,* prob. of echoic orig.] 1. to beat, pulsate, vibrate, etc. 2. to beat strongly or fast; palpitate, as the heart under exertion 3. to tingle or quiver with excitement —*n.* 1. the act of throbbing 2. a beat or pulsation, esp. a strong one of the heart —**throb'ber** *n.* —**throb'bing·ly** *adv.*

throe (thrō) *n.* [ME. *throwe,* prob. < OE. *thrawu,* pain, affliction, akin to ON. *thrā,* strong yearning < IE. **treu-* (whence Gr. *trauma,* a wound) < base **ter-,* to rub, grind: cf. THROW] a spasm or pang of pain: *usually used in pl.* [the *throes* of childbirth, death *throes*] —**in the throes of** in the act of struggling with (a problem, decision, task, etc.)

throm·bin (thräm'bin) *n.* [THROMB(US) + -IN[1]] the enzyme of the blood, formed from prothrombin, that causes clotting by converting fibrinogen to fibrin

thrombo- (thräm'bō) [< Gr. *thrombos,* a clot: see THROMBUS] *a combining form meaning* thrombus, blood clot

throm·bo·cyte (-bə sīt') *n.* [prec. + -CYTE] 1. a small nucleated blood cell in most nonmammalian vertebrates that initiates the process of blood clotting 2. *same as* PLATELET (sense 1) —**throm'bo·cyt'ic** (-sit'ik) *adj.*

throm·bo·em·bo·lism (thräm'bō em'bə liz'm) *n.* [THROMBO- + EMBOLISM] the obstruction of a blood vessel by an embolus that has broken away from a thrombus and moved into the vessel

throm·bo·gen (thräm'bə jən, -jen') *n.* [THROMBO- + -GEN] *same as* PROTHROMBIN

throm·bo·ki·nase (thräm'bō kī'nās, -kin'ās) *n.* [THROMBO- + KINASE] *same as* THROMBOPLASTIN

throm·bo·phle·bi·tis (-fli bīt'əs) *n.* [THROMBO- + PHLEBITIS] the formation of a clot in a vein, resulting from irritation of the vein's inner lining

throm·bo·plas·tic (-plas'tik) *adj.* 1. of or having the properties of a thromboplastin 2. initiating or hastening the clotting of blood —**throm'bo·plas'ti·cal·ly** *adv.*

throm·bo·plas·tin (-plas'tin) *n.* [THROMBO- + -PLAST + -IN[1]] a substance released from blood platelets and injured body tissues that assists in the clotting of the blood by initiating the conversion of prothrombin to thrombin

throm·bo·sis (thräm bō'sis) *n.* [ModL. < Gr. *thrombōsis,* coagulation < *thrombos,* a clot (see THROMBUS)] coagulation of the blood in the heart or a blood vessel, forming a clot —**throm·bot'ic** (-bät'ik) *adj.*

throm·bus (thräm'bəs) *n.,* pl. **throm'bi** (-bī) [ModL. < Gr. *thrombos,* a clot < IE. base **dherebh-,* to coagulate] the fibrinous clot attached at the site of thrombosis

throne (thrōn) *n.* [ME. *trone* < OFr. or L.: OFr. *trone* < L. *thronus* < Gr. *thronos,* a seat < IE. base **dher-,* to hold, support: cf. FIRM[1]] 1. the chair on which a king, cardinal, etc. sits on formal or ceremonial occasions: it usually is on a dais, covered with a canopy, and highly decorated 2. the power or rank of a king, etc.; sovereignty 3. a sovereign, ruler, etc. [orders from the *throne*] 4. [pl.] *Christian Theol.* the third order in the hierarchy of angels —*vt., vi.* **throned, thron'ing** to enthrone or be enthroned

throng (thrôŋ) *n.* [ME. < OE. *(ge)thrang* (akin to G. *drang*) < the base of *thringan,* to press, crowd: for IE. base cf. THRALL] 1. a great number of people gathered together; crowd 2. a crowding together of people; crowded condition 3. any great number of things massed or considered together; multitude —*vi.* to gather together, move, or press in a throng; crowd —*vt.* 1. to crowd or press upon in large numbers 2. to crowd into; fill with a multitude —*SYN.* see CROWD[1]

thros·tle (thräs'l) *n.* [ME. < OE., akin to G. *drossel* < IE. base **trozdos-,* whence THRUSH[1]] 1. [Now Chiefly Dial.] *same as* SONG THRUSH 2. [from the humming sound it makes] any of various machines for spinning wool, etc.

throt·tle (thrät'l) *n.* [prob. dim. of THROAT: see -LE] 1. [Rare] the throat or windpipe 2. the valve that regulates

the amount of fuel vapor entering an internal-combustion engine or controls the flow of steam in a steam line: also **throttle valve** 3. the hand lever or foot pedal that controls this valve —*vt.* **-tled, -tling** [ME. *throtlen* < *throte,* throat] 1. to choke; strangle 2. to stop the utterance or action of; censor or suppress 3. *a)* to reduce the flow of (fuel vapor, etc.) by means of a throttle *b)* to lessen the speed of (an engine, vehicle, etc.) by this or similar means; slow (down) —*vi.* to choke or suffocate —**throt'tler** *n.*

throt·tle·hold (-hōld') *n.* power to restrict or prevent freedom of development, movement, etc.; stranglehold

through (thrōō) *prep.* [ME. *thurgh, thrugh* < OE. *thurh,* akin to G. *durch* < IE. base **ter-,* through, beyond, whence L. *trans,* across, Sans. *tiráh,* through] 1. in one side and out the other side of; from end to end of 2. in the midst of; among 3. by way of 4. over the entire extent or surface of 5. to various places in; around [touring *through* France] 6. *a)* from the beginning to the end or conclusion of [to go *through* an experience, *through* the summer] **b)* up to and including [*through* Friday] 7. without making a stop [to go *through* a red light] 8. past the limitations or difficulties of [to fight one's way *through* red tape] 9. by means of [done *through* her help] 10. as a result of; because of [done *through* error] —*adv.* 1. in one side and out the other; from end to end 2. from the beginning to the end 3. completely to the end; to a conclusion [to see something *through*] 4. in every part or way; thoroughly; completely: also **through and through** [soaked *through*] —*adj.* 1. extending from one place to another; allowing free passage [a *through* street] *2. traveling to the destination without stops [a *through* train] *3. not necessitating changes; good for traveling without intermediate transfer [a *through* ticket] 4. arrived at the end; finished [*through* with an assignment] 5. at the end of one's usefulness, resources, etc. [*through* in politics] 6. having no further dealings, connections, etc. (*with* someone or something) *Through* is also used in various idiomatic expressions (e.g., *get through, see through*), many of which are entered in this dictionary under the key words

through·ly (thrōō'lē) *adv. archaic var. of* THOROUGHLY

through·out (thrōō out') *prep.* all the way through; in or during every part of —*adv.* 1. in or during every part; everywhere; from start to finish 2. in every respect

through·put (thrōō'poot') *n.* the amount of material put through a process in a given period, as by a computer

***through·way** (-wā') *n. same as* EXPRESSWAY

throve (thrōv) *alt. pt. of* THRIVE

throw (thrō) *vt.* **threw, thrown, throw'ing** [ME. *thrown,* to twist, wring, hurl < OE. *thrawan,* to throw, twist, akin to G. *drehen,* to twist, turn < IE. base **ter-,* to rub, rub with turning motion, bore, whence L. *terere,* to rub: cf. THREAD] 1. to twist strands of (silk, etc.) into thread or yarn 2. to cause to fly through the air by releasing from the hand while the arm is in rapid motion; cast; hurl 3. to discharge through the air from a catapult, pump, gun, etc. 4. to hurl violently, as in anger, etc.; dash 5. to cause to fall; upset; overthrow; dislodge [*thrown* by a horse] 6. to move or send rapidly; advance [to *throw* reinforcements into a battle] 7. to put suddenly and forcibly into or onto [she *threw* the clothes into the suitcase] 8. to put suddenly and forcibly into a specified condition or situation [*thrown* into prison, into confusion, etc.] 9. *a)* to cast or roll (dice) *b)* to make (a specified cast) at dice [to *throw* a five] 10. to cast off; shed [snakes *throw* their skins, the horse *threw* its shoe] 11. to bring forth (young): said of domesticated animals 12. to move (the lever of a switch, clutch, etc.) or connect, disconnect, engage, etc. by so doing 13. *a)* to direct, cast, turn, project, etc. (variously with *at, on, upon, over, toward,* etc.) [to *throw* a glance, a light, a shadow, etc.] *b)* to deliver (a punch) 14. to cause (one's voice) to seem to come from some other source, as in ventriloquism 15. to put (blame on, influence *into,* obstacles *before,* etc.) *16. [Colloq.] to lose (a game, race, etc.) deliberately, as by prearrangement *17. [Colloq.] to give (a party, dance, etc.) *18. [Colloq.] to have (a fit, tantrum, etc.) 19. [Colloq.] to confuse or disconcert [the question completely *threw* him] 20. *Card Games* to play or discard (a card) 21. *Ceramics* to shape on a potter's wheel —*vi.* to cast or hurl something —*n.* 1. the action of a person who throws; a cast 2. a cast of dice, or the numbers cast 3. the distance something is or can be thrown [a stone's *throw*] *4. *a)* a spread or coverlet for draping over a bed, sofa, etc. *b)* a woman's light scarf or wrap 5. *a)* the motion of a moving part, as a cam, eccentric, etc. *b)* the extent of such a motion, equal to the distance between the center of the crankshaft and the center of the cam, etc. 6. *Geol.* the amount of displacement at a fault 7. *Wrestling* a particular way or an instance of throwing an opponent —***throw a monkey wrench into** to stop or obstruct by direct interference; sabotage —**throw away** 1. to rid oneself of; discard 2. to be wasteful of; waste; squander 3. to fail to make use of 4. *Theater* to deliver (a line, speech, etc.) in a deliberately offhand manner —**throw back** 1. to check or stop from advancing 2. to revert to the type of an ancestor —**throw cold water**

on to discourage by indifference or disparagement —**throw in** 1. to engage (a clutch) or cause (gears) to mesh 2. to add extra or free 3. to add to others 4. [Colloq.] to join (*with*) in cooperative action —**throw off** 1. *a*) to rid oneself of; cast off   *b*) to recover from   *c*) *Card Games* to discard 2. *a*) to evade (a pursuer)   *b*) to mislead   *c*) to disconcert or confuse 3. to expel, emit, etc. 4. [Colloq.] to write or utter quickly, in an offhand manner —**throw on** to put on (a garment) carelessly or hastily —**throw oneself at** to try very hard to win the affection or love of —**throw oneself into** to engage in with great vigor —**throw oneself on** (or **upon**) rely on for support or aid —**throw open** 1. to open completely and suddenly 2. to remove all restrictions from —**throw out** 1. to get rid of; discard 2. to reject or remove, often with force 3. to emit 4. to put forth or utter (a hint or suggestion) 5. to disengage (a clutch)   ☆6. *Baseball* to throw the ball to a teammate who in turn retires (a runner) —**throw over** 1. to give up; abandon 2. to jilt —**throw together** 1. to make or assemble hurriedly and carelessly 2. to cause to become acquainted —**throw up** 1. to give up or abandon 2. to raise suddenly or rapidly 3. to vomit 4. to construct rapidly   ☆5. to mention repeatedly (*to* someone), as in reproach or criticism —**throw′er** *n.*

SYN.—**throw** is the general word meaning to cause to move through the air by a rapid propulsive motion of the arm, etc.; **cast**, the preferred word in certain connections [to *cast* a fishing line], generally has a more archaic or lofty quality [they *cast* stones at him]; to **toss** is to throw lightly or carelessly and, usually, with an upward or sidewise motion [to *toss* a coin]; **hurl** and **fling** both imply a throwing with force or violence, but **hurl** suggests that the object thrown moves swiftly for some distance [to *hurl* a javelin] and **fling**, that it is thrust sharply or vehemently so that it strikes a surface with considerable impact [she *flung* the plate to the floor]; **pitch** implies a throwing with a definite aim or in a definite direction [to *pitch* a baseball]

throw·a·way (thrō′ə wā′) *n.* a leaflet, handbill, etc. distributed as in the streets or from house to house —*adj.* ☆1. designed to be discarded after use [a *throwaway* bottle] 2. delivered in a deliberately offhand manner, as a line of dialogue in a play

throw·back (-bak′) *n.* 1. the act of throwing back; check or stop 2. reversion to an ancestral type or characteristic 3. an instance or example of this

☆**throw rug** *same as* SCATTER RUG

throw·ster (thrō′stər) *n.* [see THROW (*vt.* 1)] a person whose work is making threads of silk

thru (thrōō) *prep., adv., adj.* shortened *sp.* of THROUGH

thrum[1] (thrum) *n.* [ME. < OE. (in comp.), ligament, akin to G. *trumm* < IE. base *ter-*, to pass over, cross, whence Gr. *termōn*, border: cf. TERM] 1. *a*) the row of warp thread ends left on a loom when the web is cut off   *b*) any of these ends 2. any short end thread or fringe 3. [*pl.*] *Naut.* short pieces of woolen or hempen yarn for thrumming canvas —*vt.* thrummed, thrum′ming 1. to provide with or make of thrums; fringe 2. *Naut.* to insert thrums in (canvas) to make a rough surface for preventing chafing, stopping leaks, etc.

thrum[2] (thrum) *vt.* thrummed, thrum′ming [echoic] 1. to strum (a guitar, banjo, etc.) 2. to tell in a monotonous, tiresome way 3. to drum on with the fingers —*vi.* 1. *a*) to thrum a guitar, etc. *b*) to sound when so played 2. to drum with the fingers —*n.* a thrumming or the sound of this

thrush[1] (thrush) *n.* [ME. *thrusch* < OE. *thrysce* < IE. *trozdos-*, thrush: cf. THROSTLE] 1. any of a large family (Turdidae) of songbirds, most of which have plain plumage, including the robin, wood thrush, hermit thrush, etc. of N. America and the song thrush, blackbird, etc. of Europe   ☆2. [Slang] a woman singer of popular songs

thrush[2] (thrush) *n.* [prob. akin to Dan. *trøske*, Sw. *torsk*] 1. a disease, esp. of infants, caused by a fungus and characterized by the formation of milky-white lesions on the mouth, lips, and throat 2. a disease of the frog of a horse's foot, characterized by the formation of pus

thrust (thrust) *vt.* thrust, thrust′ing [ME. *thrusten, thristen* < ON. *thrysta*, prob. < IE. *treud-*, to squeeze, push, whence THREAT] 1. to push with sudden force; shove; drive 2. to pierce; stab 3. to force or impose (oneself or another) upon someone else or into some position or situation 4. to interject or interpose (a remark, question, etc.) 5. to extend, as in growth [the tree *thrusts* its branches high] —*vi.* 1. to push or shove against something 2. to make a thrust, stab, or lunge, as with a sword 3. to force one's way (*into, through,* etc.) 4. to extend, as in growth —*n.* 1. the act of thrusting; specif., *a*) a sudden, forceful push or shove   *b*) a lunge or stab, as with a sword   *c*) any sudden attack 2. continuous pressure of one part against another, as of a rafter against a wall 3. *a*) the driving force of a propeller in the line of its shaft   *b*) the forward force produced in reaction by the gases escaping rearward from a jet or rocket engine 4. *a*) forward movement; impetus [the *thrust* of machine technology]   *b*) energy; drive   ☆5. the basic meaning or purpose; point; force [the *thrust* of a speech] 6. *Geol.* an almost horizontal fault in which the hanging wall seems to have been pushed upward in relation to the footwall: in full **thrust fault** —*SYN.* see PUSH

thrust·er (thrus′tər) *n.* 1. a person or thing that thrusts

☆2. a rocket used to maneuver a spacecraft or to control its attitude

☆**thru·way** (thrōō′wā′) *n. same as* EXPRESSWAY

Thu·cyd·i·des (thōō sid′ə dēz′) 460?–400? B.C.; Athenian historian

thud (thud) *vi.* thud′ded, thud′ding [prob. < ME. *thudden*, to strike, thrust < OE. *thyddan*] to hit or fall with a dull sound —*n.* [prob. < the *v.*] 1. a heavy blow 2. a dull sound, as that of a heavy, solid object dropping on a soft but solid surface

thug (thug) *n.* [Hindi *thag*, swindler < Sans. *sthaga*, a cheat, rogue, akin to *sthagayati*, (he) hides < IE. base *(s)teg-*, to cover, whence THATCH] 1. [*also* T-] a member of a former religious organization of India that murdered and robbed in the service of Kali, a goddess of destruction 2. a rough, brutal hoodlum, gangster, robber, etc. —**thug′ger·y** *n.* —**thug′gish** *adj.*

thug·gee (thug′ē) *n.* [Hindi *thagī*: see prec.] murder and robbery as formerly practiced by the thugs of India

thu·ja (thōō′jə) *n.* [ModL., name of the genus < Gr. *thyia*, African tree with aromatic wood] *same as* ARBORVITAE (sense 1)

Thu·le (thōō′lē; *for 2* tōō′lē) [L. < Gr. *Thoulē, Thylē*] 1. among the ancients, the northernmost region of the world, possibly Norway, Iceland, Jutland, etc.: also **ultima Thule** 2. Eskimo settlement on the NW coast of Greenland: pop. c.100: site of U.S. air base

thu·li·a (thōō′lē ə) *n.* thulium oxide, Tm_2O_3

thu·li·um (thōō′lē əm) *n.* [ModL. < L. *Thule*, THULE: discovered in N Scandinavia] a metallic chemical element of the rare-earth group: symbol, Tm; at. wt., 168.934; at. no., 69; sp. gr., 9.33; melt. pt., 1545°C; boil. pt., 1727°C

thumb (thum) *n.* [ME. (with unhistoric *-b*) < OE. *thuma*, akin to G. *daume(n)* < IE. base *tēu-*, to swell, increase, whence L. *tumor*: basic sense, "enlarged finger"] 1. the short, thick digit of the human hand that is nearest the wrist and is apposable to the other fingers 2. a corresponding part in some other animals 3. that part of a glove or mitten which covers the thumb 4. *Archit. same as* OVOLO —*vt.* 1. to handle, turn, soil, or wear with or as with the thumb 2. [Colloq.] to solicit or get (a ride) or make (one's way) in hitchhiking by gesturing with the thumb extended in the direction one is traveling —**all thumbs** clumsy; fumbling —☆**thumb one's nose** to raise one's thumb to the nose with the fingers extended, as a coarse gesture of defiance or contempt —**thumbs down** a signal of rejection or disapproval —**thumbs up** a signal of acceptance or approval —**thumb through** to glance rapidly through (a book), as by releasing or turning pages along their edge with the thumb —**under one's thumb** under one's influence or sway

thumb index an index to the sections or divisions of a reference book, consisting of a series of rounded notches cut in the fore edge of a book with a labeled tab at the base of each notch —**thumb′-in′dex** *vt.*

thumb·nail (-nāl′) *n.* 1. the nail of the thumb 2. something as small as a thumbnail —*adj.* very small, brief, or concise [a *thumbnail* sketch]

thumb·screw (-skrōō′) *n.* 1. a screw with a head shaped in such a way that it can be turned with the thumb and forefinger 2. a former instrument of torture for squeezing the thumbs

thumb·stall (-stôl′) *n.* a kind of thimble or protective sheath of leather for the thumb

☆**thumb·tack** (-tak′) *n.* a tack with a wide, flat head, that can be pressed into a board, etc. with the thumb

THUMBSCREW

Thum·mim (tōō mēm′, tōōm′im; *E.* thum′im) [Heb. *tummīm*, pl. of *tōm*, perfection] *see* URIM AND THUMMIM

thump (thump) *n.* [echoic] 1. a blow with something heavy and blunt, as with a cudgel 2. the dull sound made by such a blow —*vt.* 1. to strike with a thump or thumps 2. *a*) to thrash; beat severely   *b*) to defeat decisively —*vi.* 1. to hit or fall with a thump 2. to make a dull, heavy sound; pound; throb —**thump′er** *n.*

thump·ing (thum′piŋ) *adj.* 1. that thumps 2. [Colloq.] very large; whopping —**thump′ing·ly** *adv.*

Thun (tōōn) 1. city in C Switzerland, on the Aar River where it leaves the Lake of Thun: pop. 32,000 2. **Lake of**, lake in Bern canton, C Switzerland: c.18 sq. mi.

thun·der (thun′dər) *n.* [ME. *thuner, thunder* (with unhistoric *-d-*) < OE. *thunor*, akin to G. *donner* < IE. base *(s)ten-*, loud rustling, deep noise, whence Gr. *stenein*, to moan, L. *tonare*, to thunder] 1. the sound that follows a flash of lightning, caused by the sudden heating and expansion of air by electrical discharge 2. any sound resembling this 3. a threatening, menacing, or extremely vehement utterance 4. [Archaic] a thunderbolt Also used in mild oaths and imprecations [yes, by *thunder!*, where in *thunder* is he]: also **thun′der·a′tion** —*vi.* 1. to produce thunder: usually in the impersonal construction [it is *thundering*] 2. to make, or move with, a sound like thunder 3. to make vehement speeches, denunciations, etc. —*vt.* 1. to say in a thundering voice 2. to strike, drive, attack, etc. with the sound or violence of thunder —**steal someone's thunder** to use someone's ideas or methods without

permission and without giving credit; esp., to lessen the effectiveness of someone's statement or action by anticipating him in its use —**thun′der·er** n.

thun·der·bird (-bʉrd′) n. ☆in the mythology of certain N. American Indians, an enormous bird that produces thunder, lightning, and rain

thun·der·bolt (-bōlt′) n. **1.** a flash of lightning and the accompanying thunder **2.** a bolt or missile imagined as hurled to earth by a stroke of lightning **3.** something that stuns with the speed and force of a thunderbolt, as bad news **4.** a person acting with sudden violence or force

thun·der·clap (-klap′) n. **1.** a clap, or loud crash, of thunder **2.** anything like this in being sudden, startling, violent, etc.

thun·der·cloud (-kloud′) n. a storm cloud charged with electricity and producing lightning and thunder

thun·der·head (-hed′) n. a round mass of cumulus clouds appearing before a thunderstorm

thun·der·ing (-iŋ) adj. **1.** that thunders **2.** [Colloq.] very large; thumping; whopping —**thun′der·ing·ly** adv.

thun·der·ous (-əs) adj. **1.** full of or making thunder **2.** making a noise like thunder —**thun′der·ous·ly** adv.

thun·der·peal (-pēl′) n. same as THUNDERCLAP

thun·der·show·er (-shou′ər) n. a shower accompanied by thunder and lightning

thun·der·squall (-skwôl′) n. a squall accompanied by thunder and lightning

thun·der·stone (-stōn′) n. any of various stones, fossils, prehistoric implements, etc. formerly thought to have been hurled to earth by lightning and thunder

thun·der·storm (-stôrm′) n. a storm accompanied by thunder and lightning

thun·der·struck (-struk′) adj. struck with amazement, terror, etc., as if by a thunderbolt: also **thun′der·strick′en** (-strik′'n)

thun·der·y (-ē) adj. **1.** that sounds like thunder **2.** accompanied with or betokening thunder

Thur·ber (thʉr′bər), **James** (**Grover**) 1894-1961; U.S. writer, humorist, & cartoonist

Thur·gau (toor′gou) canton of NE Switzerland, on Lake Constance: 388 sq. mi.; pop. 176,000: Fr. name **Thur·go·vie** (tür gō vē′)

thu·ri·ble (thoor′ə b'l, thyoor′-) n. [ME. thoryble < L. thuribulum < thus (gen. thuris), frankincense < Gr. thyos, incense: for ult. IE. base see FUME] same as CENSER

thu·ri·fer (-ə fər) n. [ModL. < L. thus (see prec.) + ferre, to BEAR¹] an acolyte or altar boy who carries a thurible

Thu·rin·gi·a (thoo rin′jē ə) region of SW East Germany, a former state: chief city, Erfurt: Ger. name **Thü·ring·en** (tü′riŋ ən)

Thu·rin·gi·an (-ən) adj. of Thuringia, its people, or culture —n. **1.** a member of an ancient Germanic tribe of C Germany **2.** a native or inhabitant of Thuringia

Thuringian Forest forested mountain range in Thuringia, East Germany: highest peak, 3,222 ft.: Ger. name **Thü·ring·er Wald** (tü′riŋ ər vält′)

THURINGIA

Thurs., Thur. Thursday

Thurs·day (thʉrz′dē, -dā) n. [ME. Thoresdai, Thunres dai < OE. Thunres dæg, ON. Thorsdagr, Thor's day, rendering LL. Jovis dies] the fifth day of the week

Thursday Island Australian island in Torres Strait: 1 1/4 sq. mi.; pop. 2,200

Thurs·days (-dēz, -dāz) adv. on or during every Thursday

thus (thus) adv. [ME. < OE.: for IE. base see THAT] **1.** in this or that manner; in the way just stated or in the following manner **2.** to this or that degree or extent; so **3.** according to this or that; consequently; therefore; hence: often used with conjunctive force **4.** for example

thwack (thwak) vt. [prob. echoic] to strike with something flat; whack —n. a blow with something flat

thwart (thwôrt) adj. [ME. thwert < ON. thvert, neut. of thverr, transverse < IE. *terk-, to turn (prob. < *ter-, to rub with rotary motion), whence L. torquere, to twist, turn] **1.** lying or extending across something else; transverse; oblique **2.** [Obs.] perverse —adv., prep. archaic var. of ATHWART —n. **1.** a rower's seat extending across a boat **2.** a brace extending across a canoe —vt. **1.** orig., to extend or place over or across **2.** to hinder, obstruct, frustrate, or defeat (a person, plans, wishes, etc.) —SYN. see FRUSTRATE —**thwart′er** n.

thy (thī) possessive pronominal adj. [ME. thi, contr. < thīn, thy: see THINE] of, belonging to, or done by thee: archaic or poetic var. of your: see also THINE, THOU¹

Thy·es·te·an banquet (or feast) (thī es′tē ən) [see ff.] a banquet at which human flesh is served

Thy·es·tes (thī es′tēz) [L. < Gr. Thyestēs] Gr. Myth. a brother of Atreus and son of Pelops: see ATREUS

thy·la·cine (thī′lə sin′, -sin) n. [Fr. < Gr. thylax, a pouch] same as TASMANIAN WOLF

thyme (tīm) n. [ME. < MFr. thym < L. thymum < Gr. thymon < thyein, to offer sacrifice: for IE. base see FUME] any of a genus (Thymus) of shrubby plants or aromatic herbs of the mint family, with white, pink, or red flowers and fragrant leaves used for seasoning

thy·mic¹ (thī′mik) adj. of the thymus

thym·ic² (tī′mik) adj. of or derived from thyme

thy·mi·dine (thī′mə dēn′, -din) n. [< THYM(INE) + -ID(E) + -INE⁴] a crystalline nucleoside, $C_{10}H_{14}N_2O_5$, one of the basic components of deoxyribonucleic acid: used chiefly in biochemical research

thy·mine (thī′mēn, -min) n. [G. thymin < Gr. thymos, spirit (< IE. *dhūmo < base *dheu-, to blow, whence L. fumus, smoke) + G. -in, -INE⁴] a white, crystalline, pyrimidine base, $C_5H_6N_2O_2$, one of the substances constituting the genetic code in DNA molecules: used chiefly in biochemical research

thy·mol (thī′môl, -mōl) n. [THYM(E) + -OL¹] an aromatic, colorless, crystalline compound, $C_{10}H_{14}O$, extracted from the volatile oil of thyme or made synthetically: used as an antiseptic, esp. in mouthwashes and nose and throat sprays and in perfumery, embalming, microscopy, etc.

thy·mo·nu·cle·ic acid (thī′mō noo klē′ik, -nyoo-) same as DEOXYRIBONUCLEIC ACID

thy·mus (thī′məs) n. [ModL. < Gr. thymos] a ductless, glandlike body, of undetermined function, situated in the upper thorax near the throat: it is most prominent at puberty, after which it disappears or becomes vestigial: the thymus of an animal, when used as food, is called sweetbread: also **thymus gland**

thy·my (tī′mē) adj. **1.** overgrown with thyme **2.** having the scent of thyme

☆**thy·ra·tron** (thī′rə trän′) n. [< Gr. thyris, a window, cell + Eng. -a- + -TRON] a hot-cathode, triode or tetrode, electronic tube containing low-pressure gas or metal vapor in which one or more electrodes start the current flow to the anode but exercise no further control over its flow

☆**thy·ris·tor** (thī ris′tər) n. [Gr. thyris, a window, cell + -tor, as in RESISTOR] any of various solid-state, semiconductor devices that convert alternating current to a unidirectional current; specif., a silicon-controlled rectifier

thy·ro- (thī′rō, -rə) a combining form meaning thyroid [thyrotoxicosis]: also, before a vowel, **thyr-**

thy·roid (thī′roid) adj. [ModL. thyroides < Gr. thyreoeidēs, shield-shaped < thyreos, large shield, door-shaped shield < thyra, DOOR + -eidēs, -OID] **1.** designating or of a large ductless gland lying in front and on either side of the trachea and secreting the hormone thyroxine, which regulates body growth and metabolism: the malfunctioning or congenital absence of this gland can cause goiter, cretinism, etc. **2.** designating or of the principal cartilage of the larynx, forming the Adam's apple —n. **1.** the thyroid gland **2.** the thyroid cartilage **3.** an artery, nerve, etc. in the region of the thyroid **4.** a preparation of the thyroid gland of certain animals, used in treating goiter, myxedema, etc.: also **thyroid extract**

thy·roid·ec·to·my (thī′roi dek′tə mē) n., pl. -mies [see -ECTOMY] the surgical removal of all or part of the thyroid gland

thy·roid·i·tis (-dīt′əs) n. [ModL.: see -ITIS] inflammation of the thyroid gland

thy·ro·tox·i·co·sis (thī′rō täk′sə kō′sis) n. [THYRO- + TOXICOSIS] same as HYPERTHYROIDISM

thy·rot·ro·phin (thī rät′rə fin) n. [THYRO- + TROPH(IC) + -IN¹] a hormone isolated from the anterior pituitary and responsible for the elaboration of thyroxine: also **thy·rot′ro·pin** (-pin)

thy·rox·ine (thī räk′sēn, -sin) n. [THYR(O)- + OX(Y)- + -INE⁴] a colorless, crystalline compound, $C_{15}H_{11}I_4NO_4$, the active hormone of the thyroid gland, often prepared synthetically and used in treating goiter, cretinism, and myxedema: also **thy·rox′in** (-sin)

thyr·soid (thʉr′soid) adj. [Gr. thyrsoeidēs < thyrsos, thyrsus + eidos, form] Bot. resembling a thyrsus: also **thyr·soi·dal** (thər soid′'l)

thyr·sus (thʉr′sas) n., pl. -si (-sī) [L. < Gr. thyrsos] **1.** a staff tipped with a pine cone and sometimes entwined with ivy or vine leaves, which Dionysus, the satyrs, etc. were represented as carrying **2.** Bot. a flower cluster in which the main stem is racemose and the secondary stems are cymose, as in the lilac: also **thyrse** (thʉrs)

thy·sa·nu·ran (thī′sə nyoor′ən, this′ə-; -noor′-) n. [< ModL. thysanura < Gr. thysanos, a tassel + oura, a tail) + -AN] any of an order (Thysanura) of very primitive wingless insects that have bristlelike appendages at the rear end and comprising the bristletails, including the silverfish —**thy′sa·nu′rous** adj.

thy·self (thī self′) pron. [ME. thi self, superseding earlier the self, lit., thee self < OE. the self; in ME., self, orig. adj., was regarded as n.] reflexive or intensive form of THOU¹: an archaic or poet. var. of yourself

ti¹ (tē) *n.* [altered < *si:* see GAMUT] *Music* a syllable representing the seventh tone of the diatonic scale: see SOLFEGGIO

ti² (tē) *n.* [Maori & Samoan] a Polynesian and Australian woody plant (*Cordyline terminalis*) of the agave family: the leaves are used for thatch, garments, fodder, etc. and the root for food and for making liquor

Ti *Chem.* titanium

Ti·a Jua·na (tē′ə hwän′ə, wän′ə) *former name of* TIJUANA

ti·ar·a (tē er′ə, -ar′-, -är′-; tī-) *n.* [L. < Gr. *tiara:* prob. of Oriental origin] **1.** an ancient Persian headdress **2.** the Pope's triple crown **3.** a woman's crownlike headdress of jewels or flowers; coronet

Ti·ber (tī′bər) river in C Italy, flowing from the Apennines south through Rome into the Tyrrhenian Sea: c.250 mi.: It. name, TEVERE

Ti·ber·i·as (tī bir′ē əs), **Sea of** *same as* the Sea of GALILEE

Ti·ber·i·us (tī bir′ē əs) (*Tiberius Claudius Nero Caesar*) 42 B.C.–37 A.D.; Rom. emperor (14 A.D.–37 A.D.)

Ti·bes·ti (tə bes′tē) mountain group of the Sahara, mostly in NW Chad: highest peak, 11,204 ft.

Ti·bet (ti bet′) autonomous region of SW China, occupying a high plateau area north of the Himalayas: 471,660 sq. mi.; pop. 1,321,000; cap. Lhasa

Ti·bet·an (ti bet′'n) *adj.* of Tibet, its people, their language, etc. —*n.* **1.** a member of the Mongolic people of Tibet **2.** the Tibeto-Burman language of Tibet

Ti·bet·o-Bur·man (ti bet′ō bur′mən) *n.* a branch of the Sino-Tibetan family of languages, including Tibetan and Burmese —*adj.* designating or of this branch

tib·i·a (tib′ē ə) *n., pl.* **-i·ae** (-i ē′), **-i·as** [L. < IE. **twibh-*, tubelike, hollow, whence Gr. *siphōn*, SIPHON] **1.** the inner and thicker of the two bones of the human leg between the knee and the ankle; shinbone **2.** a corresponding bone in the leg of other vertebrates **3.** the fourth segment (from the base) of an insect's leg **4.** an ancient flute, orig. made from an animal's tibia —**tib′i·al** *adj.*

Ti·bur (tī′bər) *ancient name of* TIVOLI (sense 1)

tic (tik) *n.* [Fr. < ?] any involuntary, regularly repeated, spasmodic contraction of a muscle, generally of neurotic origin; esp., *same as* TIC DOULOUREUX

ti·cal (ti käl′, -kôl′) *n.* [Malay *tikal*] the former monetary unit of Thailand, replaced by the baht

tic dou·lou·reux (tik′ dōō′loo rōō′; *Fr.* tēk dōō lōō rö′) [Fr., lit., painful tic] *same as* TRIGEMINAL NEURALGIA

Ti·ci·no (tē chē′nō) **1.** canton of S Switzerland, on the It. border: 1,085 sq. mi.; pop. 206,000 **2.** river flowing from this canton south into the Po River: c.160 mi.

tick¹ (tik) *n.* [ME. *tek*, prob. < Gmc. echoic base whence Du. *tikk*, MHG. *zicken*, to tick] **1.** orig., a light touch; pat **2.** a light clicking or tapping sound, as that made by the escapement of a watch or clock **3.** a mark made to check off items; check mark (√, /, etc.) **4.** [Brit. Colloq.] the time between two ticks of a clock; moment; instant —*vi.* **1.** to make a tick or series of ticks **2.** [Colloq.] to function characteristically or well; operate; work *[what makes him tick?]* —*vt.* **1.** to indicate, record, or count by a tick or ticks **2.** [Chiefly Brit.] to mark or check off (an item in a list, etc.) with a tick (usually with *off*) —**tick off 1.** [Slang] to make angry or irritable **2.** [Brit. Slang] to reprimand

tick² (tik) *n.* [ME. *teke* < OE. *ticia* (? for *tiica*, or *ticca*), akin to MDu. *teke*, G. *zecke* < IE. base **deiĝh-*, to prickle, itch, whence Arm. *tiz*, tick, MIr. *dega*, stag beetle] **1.** any of a superfamily (Ixodoidea) of wingless, blood-sucking arachnids, including many species that transmit diseases, that are larger than the related mites and are usually parasitic on man, cattle, sheep, etc. **2.** any of various degenerate, two-winged, parasitic insects

TICK
(1/4 in. long)

tick³ (tik) *n.* [LME. *tykke*, akin to MDu. *tyke*, both prob. < early WGmc. borrowing < L. *theca*, a cover, sheath: see THECA] **1.** the cloth case or covering that is filled with cotton, feathers, hair, etc. to form a mattress or pillow **2.** [Colloq.] *same as* TICKING

tick⁴ (tik) *n.* [contr. < TICKET] [Chiefly Brit. Colloq.] credit; trust *[to buy something on tick]*

tick·er (tik′ər) *n.* a person or thing that ticks; specif., ☆a) a telegraphic device that records stock market quotations, etc. on a paper tape   b) [Old Slang] a watch   c) [Slang] the heart

☆**ticker tape** paper tape used in a ticker for recording telegraphed stock market quotations, etc.

tick·et (tik′it) *n.* [apheltic < obs. Fr. *etiquet* (now *étiquette*): see ETIQUETTE] **1.** orig., any note, memorandum, voucher, etc. **2.** a printed card or piece of paper that gives a person a specified right, as to attend a theater, ride on a train, claim a purchase, etc. **3.** a license or certificate, as of a ship's captain or an airplane pilot **4.** a label or tag, as on a piece of merchandise, giving the size, color, price, quantity, etc. ☆**5.** the list of candidates nominated by a political party in an election; slate ☆**6.** [Colloq.] a summons to court for a traffic violation —*vt.* **1.** to label or tag with a ticket **2.** to provide a ticket or tickets for ☆**3.** [Colloq.] to issue or attach a ticket (*n.* 6) to —**that's the ticket!** [Slang] that's the correct or proper thing! that's right!

tick·et-of-leave man (-əv lēv′) [Brit.] formerly, a convicted person set at liberty, under certain restrictions, on

a permit (**ticket of leave**) granted before his sentence had expired

tick·et·y-boo (tik′ə tē bōō′) *adj.* [TICKET (as in THAT'S THE TICKET: see under TICKET) + -Y¹ + -boo] [Brit. Slang] fine, excellent, in working order, etc.

tick fever any infectious disease transmitted by the bite of a tick, as Rocky Mountain spotted fever

tick·ing (tik′iŋ) *n.* [see TICK³] strong, heavy cloth, often striped, used for casings of mattresses, pillows, etc.

tick·le (tik′'l) *vt.* **-led**, **-ling** [ME. *tikelen*, akin to G. dial. *zickeln*, OE. *tinclian*, to tickle: for IE. base see TICK²] **1.** to please, gratify, delight, etc.: often used in the passive voice with slang intensives, as tickled pink (or silly, to death, etc.) **2.** to stir to amusement or laughter; amuse **3.** to excite the surface nerves of, as by touching or stroking lightly with the finger, a feather, etc., so as to cause involuntary twitching, a pleasant tingling, laughter, etc. —*vi.* **1.** to have an itching, scratching, or tingling sensation *[a throat that tickles]* **2.** to be readily affected by excitation of the surface nerves; be ticklish —*n.* **1.** a tickling or being tickled **2.** a tickling sensation

tick·ler (tik′lər) *n.* **1.** a person or thing that tickles ☆**2.** a special memorandum pad, file, etc. for reminding one of matters requiring attention at certain dates in the future

tickler coil a small coil connected in series with the plate circuit of a vacuum tube and coupled inductively to the grid circuit to furnish feedback

tick·lish (-lish) *adj.* **1.** sensitive to tickling **2.** very sensitive or easily upset; touchy **3.** needing careful handling; precarious; delicate —**tick′lish·ly** *adv.* —**tick′lish·ness** *n.*

tick·seed (tik′sēd′) *n.* [TICK² + SEED: from the appearance] *popular name for:* **1.** COREOPSIS **2.** BUR MARIGOLD

tick-tack, tic·tac (tik′tak′) *n.* [echoic redupl. of TICK¹] **1.** a recurring sound like the ticking of a clock **2.** a device for making a tapping sound on a windowpane or door as a prank: it consists typically of a weight hung next to the window, etc. and manipulated from a distance by a string

tick-tack-toe, tic-tac-toe (tik′tak tō′) *n.* a game in which two players take turns marking either X's or O's in an open block of nine squares, the object being to complete a straight or diagonal row of three of one's mark before the other player can

tick-tock (tik′täk′) *n.* the sound made by a clock —*vi.* to make this sound

☆**tick trefoil** any of a genus (*Desmodium*) of plants of the legume family, with clusters of small purple flowers, leaves in groups of three, and jointed prickly pods

☆**tick·y tack·y** (tik′ē tak′ē) [redupl. of TACKY] dull, unimaginative, often shoddy uniformity, like that of houses in a real-estate development —**tick′y-tack′y** *adj.*

Ti·con·der·o·ga (tī′kän də rō′gə), **Fort** [< Iroquoian, lit., between two lakes] former fort in NE N.Y., taken from the British by the Green Mountain Boys in 1775

tid·al (tīd′'l) *adj.* of, having, caused by, determined by, or dependent on a tide or tides —**tid′al·ly** *adv.*

tidal wave 1. in popular usage, an unusually great, destructive wave sent inshore by an earthquake or a very strong wind ☆**2.** any great or widespread movement, expression of prevalent feeling, etc.

tid·bit (tid′bit′) *n.* [dial. *tid*, small object + BIT²] a pleasing or choice bit of food, news, gossip, etc.

tid·dly, tid·dley (tid′lē) *adj.* [prob. < *tiddly-wink*, illicit grogshop, rhyming slang for DRINK] [Chiefly Brit. Slang] drunk; tipsy

tid·dly·winks (tid′lē wiŋks′, tid′'l ē-) *n.* [prob. < *tiddly*, child's form of LITTLE: cf. prec.] a game in which the players try to snap little colored disks from a surface into a cup by pressing their edges with a larger disk: also **tid′dle·dy·winks′** (-'l dē wiŋks′)

tide¹ (tīd) *n.* [ME., tide, time, season < OE. *tid*, time, akin to G. *zeit* < IE. base **dā(i)-*, to part, divide up, whence TIME, Sans. *dāti*, (he) cuts off, Gr. *dēmos*, a district, people] **1.** orig., a period of time: now only in combination *[Eastertide, eventide]* **2.** [prob. influenced by MLowG. or MDu.] a) the alternate rise and fall of the surface of oceans, seas, and the bays, rivers, etc. connected with them, caused by the attraction of the moon and sun: it occurs twice in each period of 24 hours and 50 minutes (*lunar day*): see also FLOOD TIDE, EBB TIDE, SPRING TIDE, NEAP] b) *same as* FLOOD TIDE **3.** something that rises and falls like the tide **4.** a stream, current, etc. or trend, tendency, etc. *[the tide of public opinion]* **5.** the period during which something is at its highest or fullest point **6.** [Archaic] an opportune time or occasion —*adj. same as* TIDAL —*vi.* **tid′ed, tid′ing 1.** to flow or surge like a tide **2.** *Naut.* to drift with the tide, esp. in moving into or out of a harbor, river, etc. —*vt.* to carry with or as with the tide —**tide over** to help along temporarily, as through a period of difficulty —**turn the tide** to reverse a condition

tide² (tīd) *vi.* **tid′ed, tid′ing** [ME. *tiden* < OE. *tidan* < *tid:* see prec.] [Archaic] to betide; happen

☆**tide·land** (-land′, -lənd) *n.* **1.** land covered by water at high tide and uncovered at low tide **2.** [*pl.*] loosely, land under water just beyond this and within territorial limits

tide·mark (-märk′) *n.* a mark indicating the highest point of flood tide or, sometimes, the lowest point of ebb tide

tide·rip (-rip′) *n. same as* RIP²

tide·wait·er (-wāt′ər) *n.* formerly, a customs official who boarded incoming ships to prevent customs evasion

tide·wa·ter (-wôt'ər, -wät'-) *n.* **1.** water brought into an area by the action of the rising tide ☆**2.** water, as of a certain area or in certain streams, that is affected by the tide ☆**3.** an area in which water is affected by the tide; specif., [T-] the eastern part of Virginia ☆**4.** [T-] the English dialect of E Virginia —*adj.* **1.** of or along a tidewater ☆**2.** [T-] of (the) Tidewater

tide·way (-wā') *n.* **1.** a channel through which a tide runs **2.** the tidal part of a river **3.** a tidal current

ti·dings (tī'dinz) *n.pl.* [*sometimes with sing. v.*] [ME., pl. of *tidinge* < OE. *tidung* (< *tidan:* see TIDE²), akin to G. *zeitung,* newspaper] news; information

ti·dy (tī'dē) *adj.* **-di·er, -di·est** [ME. *tidi,* seasonable, honest, hence in good condition < *tide:* see TIDE¹] **1.** neat in personal appearance, ways, etc.; orderly **2.** neat in arrangement; in order; trim **3.** [Colloq.] *a*) fairly good; satisfactory *b*) rather large; considerable [a tidy sum of money] —*vt., vi.* **-died, -dy·ing** to make (things) tidy (often with *up*) —*n., pl.* **-dies 1.** *same as* ANTIMACASSAR **2.** a small container for odds and ends —SYN. see NEAT¹ —**ti'di·ly** *adv.* —**ti'di·ness** *n.*

☆**ti·dy·tips** (tī'dē tips') *n., pl.* **-tips'** a California wildflower (*Layia platyglossa*) of the composite family, with yellow, daisylike flowers, often tipped with white

tie (tī) *vt.* **tied, ty'ing** [ME. *tien* < OE. *tigan, tegan* < base of *teag,* a rope: for IE. base see TOW¹] **1.** to fasten, attach, or bind together or to something else, as with string, cord, or rope made secure by knotting, etc. [to tie someone's hands, to *tie* a boat to a pier] **2.** *a*) to draw together or join the parts, ends, or sides of by tightening and knotting laces, strings, etc. [to *tie* one's shoes] *b*) to make by fastening together parts [to *tie* fishing flies] **3.** *a*) to make (a knot or bow) *b*) to make a knot or bow in [to tie one's necktie] **4.** to fasten, connect, join, or bind in any way [tied by common interests] **5.** to confine; restrain; restrict **6.** *a*) to equal the score or achievement of, as in a contest *b*) to equal (a score, record, etc.) **7.** [Colloq.] to join in marriage **8.** *Music* to connect with a tie —*vi.* **1.** to be capable of being tied; make a tie **2.** to make an equal score or achievement, as in a contest —*n.* [ME. *tege, teige* < OE. *teag, teah,* a rope] **1.** a string, lace, cord, etc. used to tie things **2.** something that connects, binds, or joins; bond; link [a business *tie, ties* of affection] **3.** something that confines, limits, or restricts [legal *ties*] **4.** *short for* NECKTIE **5.** a beam, rod, etc. that holds together parts of a building and strengthens against stress ☆**6.** any of the parallel crossbeams to which the rails of a railroad are fastened; sleeper **7.** *a*) an equality of scores, votes, achievement, etc. in a contest *b*) a contest or match in which there is such an equality; draw; stalemate **8.** [*pl.*] low shoes fastened with laces, as oxfords **9.** *Music* a curved line above or below two notes of the same pitch, indicating that the tone is to be held unbroken for the duration of their combined values —*adj.* that has been tied, or made equal [a *tie* score] —**tie down** to confine; restrain; restrict —☆**tie in 1.** to bring into or have a connection **2.** to make or be consistent, harmonious, etc. —☆**tie in** [Colloq.] to attack vigorously —**tie off** to close off passage through by tying with something —☆**tie one on** [Slang] to get drunk —**tie up 1.** to tie firmly or securely **2.** to wrap up and tie with string, cord, etc. **3.** to moor (a ship or boat) to a dock ☆**4.** to obstruct; hinder; stop **5.** to cause to be already in use, retained, committed, etc.

SYN.—**tie** and **bind** are often interchangeable, but in discriminative use, **tie** specif. implies the connection of one thing with another by means of a rope, string, etc. which can be knotted [to *tie* a horse to a hitching post], and **bind** suggests the use of an encircling band which holds two or more things firmly together [to *bind* someone's legs]; **fasten,** a somewhat more general word, implies a joining of one thing to another, as by tying, binding, gluing, nailing, pinning, etc.; **attach** emphasizes the joining of two or more things in order to keep them together as a unit [to *attach* one's references to an application] —*ANT.* separate, part

tie·back (tī'bak') *n.* ☆**1.** a sash, ribbon, tape, etc. used to tie curtains or draperies to one side ☆**2.** a curtain with a tieback: *usually used in pl.*

tie beam a horizontal beam serving as a tie (*n.* 5)

tie clasp a decorative clasp for fastening a necktie to the shirt front: also **tie clip, tie bar**

tie-dye (tī'dī') *n.* **1.** a method of dyeing designs on cloth by tightly tying bunches of it with waxed thread so that the dye affects only exposed parts **2.** cloth so decorated or a design so made —*vt.* **-dyed', -dye'ing** to dye in this way

☆**tie-in** (-in') *adj.* designating or of a sale in which two or more articles, one of which is usually scarce or in demand, are offered in combination, often at a reduced price, and cannot be bought separately —*n.* **1.** a tie-in sale or advertisement **2.** an article sold in this way **3.** a connection or relationship

tie line ☆**1.** a direct telephone line between extensions in one or more PBX systems ☆**2.** a line used to connect one electric power or transportation system with another

tie·mann·ite (tē'mə nīt') *n.* [G. *tiemannit,* after its discoverer, W. *Tiemann,* 19th-c. G. mineralogist] a grayish mineral, HgSe, a compound of mercury and selenium

Tien Shan (tyen shän) mountain system in C Asia, extending across the Kirghiz S.S.R. & Sinkiang, China, to the Altai Mountains: highest peak, 24,406 ft.

Tien·tsin (tin'tsin'; *Chin.* tyen'jin') seaport in NE China: capital of Hopei province: pop. 3,278,000

tie·pin (tī'pin') *n.* same as STICKPIN

Tie·po·lo (tye'pô lō), **Gio·van·ni Bat·tis·ta** (jō vän'nē bät tēs'tä) 1696–1770; Venetian painter

tier¹ (tir) *n.* [< MFr. *tire,* order, rank, row: see ATTIRE] **1.** a row, or rank, of seats **2.** any of a series of rows, layers, ranks, etc. arranged one above or behind another —*vt., vi.* to arrange or be arranged in tiers

ti·er² (tī'ər) *n.* **1.** a person or thing that ties ☆**2.** a type of pinafore formerly worn by children

tierce (tirs) *n.* [ME. *terce* < OFr. < L. *tertia,* fem. of *tertius,* (a) third < base of *tres,* THREE] **1.** orig., a third **2.** [*often* T-] *same as* TERCE **3.** an old liquid measure, equal to 1/3 pipe (42 gallons) **4.** a cask of this capacity, between a barrel and a hogshead in size **5.** *Card Games* a sequence of three cards in the same suit **6.** *Fencing* the third defensive position, from which a lunge or parry can be made

tier·cel (tir'səl) *n.* [ME. *tercel* < OFr. < VL. **tertiolus* < L. *tertius,* third: reason for name uncertain] *Falconry* a male hawk, esp. the male peregrine

tie rod 1. a horizontal rod serving as a tie (*n.* 5) **2.** a rod connecting a front wheel of an automotive vehicle to the steering mechanism

Tier·ra del Fue·go (tyer'rä del fwe'gō; *E.* tē er'ə del' fōō ā'gō) **1.** group of islands at the tip of S. America, separated from the mainland by the Strait of Magellan: they are divided between Argentina & Chile: c.27,500 sq. mi. **2.** chief island of this group, divided between Argentina & Chile: c.18,500 sq. mi.

☆**tie tack** an ornamental pin with a short point that fits into a snap, used to fasten a necktie to the shirt front

tie-up (tī'up') *n.* ☆**1.** a temporary stoppage or interruption of work, production, traffic, service, etc. **2.** ☆*a*) a place for mooring a boat ☆*b*) [Dial.] a place for tying up cattle at night **3.** connection, relation, or involvement

tiff¹ (tif) *n.* [< ?] **1.** a slight fit of anger or bad humor; huff; pet **2.** a slight quarrel; spat —*vi.* to be in or have a tiff

tiff² (tif) *n.* [< ?] **1.** [Rare or Obs.] **1.** liquor; esp., weak liquor **2.** a little drink of weak liquor or punch

tif·fa·ny (tif'ə nē) *n., pl.* **-nies** [OFr. *tiphanie,* Epiphany < LL.(Ec.) *theophunia* < Gr. *theophania,* lit., manifestation of God: ? so called because worn on Epiphany] a thin gauze of silk or muslin

☆**Tiffany setting** (or **mounting**) [after Charles L. *Tiffany* (1812–1902), U.S. jeweler] a raised setting in a ring with a gem held in place by prongs

tif·fin (tif'in) *n., vi.* [Anglo-Ind. for *tiffing,* drinking, hence, by extension, eating < TIFF²] *Brit. term for* LUNCH

Ti·flis (tī'flis; *Russ.* tif lēs') *former name of* TBILISI

ti·ger (tī'gər) *n., pl.* **-gers, -ger:** see PLURAL, II, D, 1 [ME. *tygre* < OE. *tiger* & OFr. *tigre,* both < L. *tigris* < Gr. *tigris* < Iranian *tigra-,* sharp < IE. base **(s)teig-,* whence THISTLE, STICK] **1.** a large, fierce, flesh-eating animal (*Panthera tigris*) of the cat family, about the size of a lion, having a tawny coat striped with black: it is native to most of Asia **2.** any of several similar animals; esp., *a*) the S. American jaguar *b*) the African leopard *c*) *same as* TASMANIAN WOLF **3.** *a*) a very energetic or persevering person *b*) a fierce, belligerent person ☆**4.** a loud yell (often the word "tiger") at the end of a round of cheers —☆**have a tiger by the tail** to find oneself in a situation more difficult to handle than one expected —**ti'ger·ish** *adj.*

tiger beetle any of a family (Cicindelidae) of active, long-legged, brightly colored, often striped beetles with larvae that burrow in soil and feed on other insects

tiger cat 1. any of various wildcats smaller than, but somewhat resembling, the tiger, as the serval, ocelot, margay, etc. **2.** a domestic cat with tigerlike markings

tiger lily 1. a lily (*Lilium tigrinum*) having orange flowers with purplish-black spots **2.** any of several kinds of lilies resembling this flower

tiger moth any of a family (Arctiidae) of stout-bodied moths with brightly striped or spotted wings: the caterpillars (*woolly bears*) have a dense coat of fine hairs

☆**tiger salamander** a widely distributed N. American salamander (*Ambystoma tigrinum*) with a blackish body spotted with irregular yellow or white markings

tiger's eye a semiprecious, yellow-brown stone, silicified crocidolite, used for ornament: also **ti'ger·eye'** *n.*

tight (tīt) *adj.* [ME., altered (prob. after *tough:* see TAUT) < *thight* < OE. *-thight,* strong, akin to ON. *thēttr,* tight, thick < IE. base **tenk-,* to thicken, congeal, whence MIr. *tēcht,* coagulated] **1.** orig., dense **2.** so close or compact in structure that water, air, etc. cannot pass through [a *tight* boat] **3.** drawn, packed, spaced, etc. closely together [a *tight* weave, a *tight* schedule of events] **4.** [Dial.] snug; trim; neat **5.** fixed securely; held firmly; firm [a *tight* joint] **6.** fully stretched; taut, not slack or loose **7.** fitting closely, esp. too closely, so as to be uncomfortable **8.** strict; restraining; severe [*tight* control] **9.** difficult to manage; esp. in the phrase **a tight corner** (or **squeeze,** etc.), a

difficult situation **10.** showing tension or strain [a *tight* smile] **11.** almost even or tied; close [a *tight* race] **12.** of a short radius; sharp: said of a spiral, curve, turn, etc. **13.** *a)* difficult to get; scarce in relation to demand: said of commodities on a market, or of money available for loans *b)* characterized by such scarcity [a *tight* market] **14.** concise; condensed: said of language, style, etc. **15.** [Archaic or Dial.] well-proportioned; shapely **16.** [Dial.] competent; capable **17.** [Colloq.] stingy; parsimonious **18.** [Slang] drunk —*adv.* in a tight manner; esp., *a)* securely or firmly [hold *tight*, sit *tight*] *b)* [Colloq.] soundly [sleep *tight*] —**sit tight 1.** to maintain one's opinion; remain firm **2.** to maintain one's position; refrain from action —**tight′ly** *adv.* —**tight′ness** *n.*
SYN.—**tight**, in this connection, implies a constricting or binding encirclement [a *tight* collar] or such closeness or compactness of parts as to be impenetrable [*airtight*]; **taut** (and, loosely, also **tight**) is applied to a rope, cord, cloth, etc. that is pulled or stretched to the point where there is no slackness [*taut* sails]; **tense** suggests a tightness or tautness that results in great strain [*tense* muscles] —*ANT.* loose, slack, lax

-tight (tīt) [< prec.] *a combining form meaning* impervious to [*watertight, airtight*]
tight·en (tīt′'n) *vt., vi.* to make or become tight or tighter —**tight′en·er** *n.*
tight·fist·ed (tīt′fis′tid) *adj.* stingy; closefisted
tight·fit·ting (tīt′fit′iŋ) *adj.* fitting very tight
tight·knit (-nit′) *adj.* **1.** tightly knit **2.** well organized or put together in a concise or very orderly way
tight-lipped (-lipt′) *adj.* **1.** having the lips closed tightly **2.** not saying much; taciturn or secretive
tight·rope (-rōp′) *n.* a tightly stretched rope or cable on which aerialists walk or do balancing acts
tights (tīts) *n.pl.* a tightly fitting garment, with separate legs, for the lower half of the body, worn by acrobats, dancers, etc.
☆**tight·wad** (tīt′wäd′, -wôd′) *n.* [TIGHT + WAD¹] [Slang] a stingy person; miser
Tig·lath-pi·le·ser III (tig′lath pī lē′zər, -pi-) ?-727? B.C.; king of Assyria (745?-727?)
tig·lic acid (tig′lik) [< ModL. *tiglium*, croton-oil plant < Gr. *tilos*, thin feces: the seeds have a cathartic effect] a poisonous, monobasic acid, C₅H₈O₂, occurring in croton oil and camomile oil and used in perfumes, flavors, etc.
ti·glon (tī′glän′, -glon) *n.* [TIG(ER) + L(I)ON] the offspring of a male tiger and a female lion: also **ti′gon′** (-gän′, -gən)
Ti·gré (tē grā′) province of N Ethiopia, on the Eritrea border, a former kingdom —*n.* a modern Ethiopic language spoken in Eritrea
ti·gress (tī′gris) *n.* **1.** a female tiger **2.** a woman thought of as like a tiger in sensuous sleekness, ferocity, etc.
Ti·gri·nya (ti grēn′yə) *n.* a modern Ethiopic language developed from ancient Ethiopic
Ti·gris (tī′gris) river flowing from EC Turkey through Iraq, joining the Euphrates to form the Shatt al Arab: 1,150 mi.
Ti·jua·na (tē wä′nə, tē′ə wä′-; *Sp.* tē hwä′nä) city in Baja California, NW Mexico, on the U.S. border: pop. 203,000
tike (tīk) *n. same as* TYKE
Ti·ki (tē′kē) [Maori & Marquesan] *Polynesian Myth.* the first man, or the god who created him —*n.* [t-] a representation of an ancestor, god, etc., often a small, sculptured figure worn as an amulet
til (til, tēl) *n. var. of* TEEL
til·ak (til′ək) *n.* [Sans. *tilaka*] a small dot of a red cosmetic worn on the forehead variously by Hindu women and men
Til·burg (til′bərg; *Du.* til′bürkh) city in the S Netherlands, in North Brabant province: pop. 147,000
til·bu·ry (til′bər ē) *n., pl.* **-ries** [after the inventor, *Tilbury*, 19th-c. London coach builder] a light, two-wheeled carriage for two persons
til·de (til′də) *n.* [Sp. < L. *titulus*, TITLE] a diacritical mark (~) used: *a)* in Spanish, over an *n* to indicate a palatal nasal sound (ny), as in *señor b)* in Portuguese, over a vowel or the first vowel of a diphthong to indicate nasalization, as in *lã, pão*: the same mark is variously used, as in some phonetic systems, or in mathematics, logic, etc., with other significance
Til·den (til′d'n), **Samuel Jones** 1814-86; U.S. politician
tile (tīl) *n.* [ME. < OE. *tigele*, akin to G. *ziegel*, both < WGmc. *tegala* < L. *tegula*, a tile < *tegere*, to cover: for IE. base see THATCH] **1.** *a)* a thin, usually rectangular piece of unglazed, fired clay, stone, or concrete, used for roofing, flooring, etc. *b)* a thin, usually rectangular piece of glazed, fired clay, often decorated, used for fireplace borders, bathroom walls, etc. *c)* a similar piece of other material, as of metal, plastic, asphalt, rubber, etc., used to cover floors, walls, etc. **2.** tiles collectively; tiling **3.** a drain of semicircular tiles or earthenware pipe **4.** burnt-clay, hollow blocks, used variously in construction **5.** any of the pieces, or counters, in mah-jongg or other games **6.** [Colloq.] a high, stiff hat —*vt.* tiled, **til′ing** to cover with tiles —**on the tiles** [Brit. Colloq.] out carousing —**til′er** *n.*
☆**tile·fish** (-fish′) *n., pl.* **-fish′, -fish′es:** see FISH² [< ModL. (*Lophola*)*til*(*us*), name of the genus + FISH²] any of several large, deep-sea food fishes (family Branchiostegidae) with a golden-spotted blue or purple body,

yellow-spotted fins, and a fleshy crest on its head, esp. a species (*Lopholatilus chamaeleonticeps*) of the W Atlantic
til·ing (tīl′iŋ) *n.* **1.** the action of a person who tiles **2.** tiles collectively **3.** a covering or structure of tiles
till¹ (til) *prep.* [ME. < OE. *til*, akin to ON. *til*, to, till, OE. *til*, fitness: for IE. base see ff.] **1.** *same as* UNTIL **2.** [Obs. exc. Scot.] up to the point of; as far as **3.** [Scot.] to, concerning, for, by, etc. —*conj. same as* UNTIL
till² (til) *vt., vi.* [ME. < OE. *tilian*, lit., to strive for, work for, akin to G. *zielen*, to aim, strive, *ziel*, point aimed at < ? IE. base **ad-*, to order, establish] to work (land) in raising crops, as by plowing, fertilizing, etc.; cultivate —**till′a·ble** *adj.*
till³ (til) *n.* [earlier *tille* < ? ME. *tillen*, to draw < ?] **1.** a drawer or tray, as in a store or bank counter, for keeping money **2.** ready cash
till⁴ (til) *n.* [? var. of ME. *thill*, substratum of clay < ? *thille*, a board, flooring] unstratified, unsorted, glacial drift of clay, sand, boulders, and gravel
till·age (til′ij) *n.* [TILL² + -AGE] **1.** the tilling of land **2.** land that is tilled
til·land·si·a (ti land′zē ə) *n.* [ModL., after Elias *Tillands*, 17th-c. Swed. botanist] any of a genus (*Tillandsia*) of epiphytic plants of the pineapple family; esp., *same as* SPANISH MOSS
till·er¹ (til′ər) *n.* [ME. *tiler*, stock of a crossbow < OFr. *telier*, weaver's beam < ML. *telarium* < L. *tela*, a web (see TOIL²): nautical sense prob. infl. by ME. *tillen*, to pull, draw: cf. TILL²] a bar or handle for turning a boat's rudder
till·er² (til′ər) *n.* **1.** a person who tills the soil **2.** a machine for tilling; cultivator
till·er³ (til′ər) *n.* [< OE. *telgor* (extension of *telga*, a branch, bough, shoot)] a shoot growing from the base of the stem of a plant —*vi.* to send forth tillers
Til·lich (til′ik), **Paul (Johannes)** 1886-1965; U.S. theologian, born in Germany
☆**till·ite** (til′īt) *n.* [TILL⁴ + -ITE¹] rock made up of consolidated till
Til·ly (til′ē), **Count of,** (*Johann Tserklaes*) 1559-1632; Fl. general in the Thirty Years' War
tilt¹ (tilt) *vt.* [ME. *tilten*, to be overthrown, totter, prob. < OE. **tieltan* < *tealt*, shaky, unstable, akin to Sw. *tulta*, to totter < ? IE. base **del-*, to waddle, totter, whence Sans. *dulā*, she who totters] **1.** to cause to slope or slant; tip **2.** *a)* to poise or thrust (a lance) in or as in a tilt *b)* to charge at (one's opponent) in a tilt **3.** to forge or hammer with a tilt hammer —*vi.* **1.** to slope; incline; slant; tip **2.** to poise or thrust one's lance, or to charge (*at* one's opponent) in a tilt **3.** to take part in a tilt or joust **4.** to dispute, argue, contend, attack, etc. —*n.* **1.** a medieval contest in which two armed horsemen thrust with lances in an attempt to unseat each other; joust **2.** any spirited contest, contention, dispute, etc. between persons **3.** a thrust or parry, as with a lance **4.** *a)* the act of tilting, or sloping *b)* the condition or angle of being tilted; slope or slant —(**at**) **full tilt** at full speed; with the greatest force —**tilt′er** *n.*
tilt² (tilt) *n.* [ME. *telte* < OE. *teld*, a tent, akin to G. *zelt*] a cloth covering or canopy of a boat, stall, cart, etc. —*vt.* to furnish or cover with a tilt
tilth (tilth) *n.* [ME. *tilthe* < OE. < *tilian* (see TILL²), akin to OFris. *tilath*, cultivation] **1.** a tilling or being tilled; cultivation of land **2.** tilled land
tilt hammer a heavy drop hammer used in drop-forging
tilt·me·ter (tilt′mēt′ər) *n. same as* CLINOMETER
tilt-top (-täp′) *adj.* designating a table, stand, etc. designed so that the top, hinged to a pedestal, can be tipped to a vertical position
tilt·yard (-yärd′) *n.* a place where tilts were held
Tim. Timothy
tim·bal (tim′b'l) *n.* [Fr. *timbale*, altered (after *cymbale*, cymbal) < earlier *attabale* < Sp. *atabal: see* ATABAL] *same as* KETTLEDRUM
tim·bale (tim′b'l; *Fr.* taɴ bál′) *n.* [Fr., lit., kettledrum: see prec.] **1.** a custardlike, highly flavored dish made with chicken, lobster, fish, etc. and baked in a small drum-shaped mold **2.** a type of fried or baked pastry shell, filled with a cooked food: also **timbale case**
tim·ber (tim′bər) *n.* [ME. < OE., akin to G. *zimmer*, room (< OHG. *zimbar*, wooden structure) < IE. base **dem-*, **demā-*, to join together, build, whence L. *domus*, house] **1.** orig., *a)* a building *b)* building material **2.** wood suitable for building houses, ships, etc., whether cut or still in the form of trees **3.** a large, heavy, dressed piece of wood used in building; beam **4.** [Brit.] *same as* LUMBER¹ (*n.* 2) **5.** trees or forests collectively **6.** personal quality or character [a man of his *timber*] **7.** *Shipbuilding* a wooden rib —*vt.* to provide, build, or prop up with timbers —*adj.* of or for timber —*interj.* a warning shout by a lumberman that a cut tree is about to fall
tim·bered (-bərd) *adj.* **1.** made of or with timbers **2.** covered with trees; wooded **3.** having exposed timbers, as a wall
timber hitch *Naut.* a knot used for tying a rope to a spar: see KNOT, illus.
tim·ber·ing (tim′bər iŋ) *n.* **1.** timbers collectively **2.** work made of timber
☆**tim·ber·land** (-land′) *n.* land with trees suitable for timber; wooded land

☆**tim·ber·line** (-līn′) *n.* the line above or beyond which trees do not grow, as on mountains or in polar regions

☆**timber rattlesnake** a yellowish-brown to black rattlesnake (*Crotalus horridus*) with V-shaped bands on the back

timber wolf *same as* GRAY WOLF

tim·ber·work (-wurk′) *n.* work made of timber; timbering

tim·bre (tam′bər, tim′-; *Fr.* tan′br′) *n.* [Fr., timbre, earlier, sound of a bell < MFr., ball struck by a hammer < OFr., a kind of drum < LGr. *tymbanon* < Gr. *tympanon*: see TYMPAN] the characteristic quality of sound that distinguishes one voice or musical instrument from another or one vowel sound from another: it is determined by the harmonics of the sound and is distinguished from the *intensity* and *pitch*

tim·brel (tim′brəl) *n.* [dim. of ME. *timbre* < OFr.: see prec.] an ancient type of tambourine

Tim·buk·tu (tim′buk tōō′, tim buk′tōō) town in C Mali, near the Niger River: pop. 7,000

time (tim) *n.* [ME. < OE. *tima*, prob. < IE. *dī-men* < base *dā(i)-*, to part, divide up, whence TIDE] I. *duration; continuance* 1. indefinite, unlimited duration in which things are considered as happening in the past, present, or future; every moment there has ever been or ever will be 2. *a)* the entire period of existence of the known universe; finite duration, as distinguished from infinity *b)* the entire period of existence of

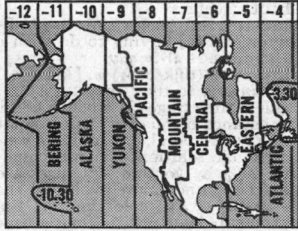

TIME ZONES

the world or of humanity; earthly duration, as distinguished from eternity 3. a system of measuring duration [solar *time*, standard *time*] 4. [T-] *same as* FATHER TIME II. *a period or interval* 1. the period between two events or during which something exists, happens, or acts; measured or measurable interval 2. [*usually pl.*] any period in the history of man or of the universe, often specif. with reference to a characteristic social structure, set of customs, famous person living then, etc. [prehistoric *times*, medieval *times*, geologic *time*, Lincoln's *time*] 3. *a)* a period characterized by a prevailing condition or specific experience [a *time* of peace, have a good *time*] *b)* [*usually pl.*] the prevailing conditions of a particular period [how were *times*?] 4. a period of duration set or thought of as set; specif., *a)* a period of existence; lifetime [his *time* is almost over] *b)* a term of apprenticeship *c)* a term of imprisonment *d)* a term of military service *e)* formerly, a period of indenture 5. a period or periods necessary, sufficient, or available for something [no *time* for play] 6. the specific, usual, or allotted period during which something is done [the runner's *time* was 1.47 minutes; baking *time*, 20 minutes] 7. *a)* the period regularly worked or to be worked by an employee *b)* the hourly rate of pay for the regular working hours 8. rate of speed in marching, driving, working, etc. [quick *time*, double *time*] 9. *Drama* one of the three unities: see UNITY 10. *Music a)* the grouping of rhythmic beats into measures of equal length *b)* the characteristic rhythm of a piece of music in terms of this grouping, indicated by the time signature *c)* the rate of speed at which a composition or passage is played; tempo *d)* loosely, the rhythm and tempo characteristic of a kind of composition [waltz *time*, march *time*] *e)* the duration of a note or rest 11. *Prosody* a unit of quantitative meter; esp., a mora, or short syllable ☆12. *Sports same as* TIMEOUT III. *a point in duration; moment; instant; occasion* 1. a precise instant, second, minute, hour, day, week, month, or year, determined by clock or calendar 2. the point at which something has happened, is happening, or will happen; occasion [game *time* is 2:00 o'clock] 3. the usual, natural, traditional, or appointed moment for something to happen, begin, or end [*time* to get up]; specif., *a)* the moment of death [his *time* is close at hand] *b)* the end of a period of pregnancy; moment of giving birth [her *time* had come] ☆*c)* one's turn at something [a *time* at bat] 4. the suitable, proper, favorable, or convenient moment [now is the *time* to act] 5. any one of a series of moments at which the same or nearly the same thing recurs; repeated occasion [told for the fifth *time*, *time* and *time* again] —*interj. Sports* an exclamation signaling that a period of play or activity is ended or that play is temporarily suspended —*vt.* **timed**, **tim′ing** 1. to arrange or set the time of so as to be acceptable, suitable, opportune, etc. [*time* an invasion] 2. to adjust, set, play, etc. so as to coincide in time with something else [to *time* one's watch with another's] 3. to regulate (a mechanism) for a given speed or length of operation 4. to set the duration of (a syllable or musical note) as a unit of rhythm 5. to calculate or record the pace, speed, finishing time, etc. of; clock [to *time* a runner] —*vi.* [Rare] to move

in time; keep time —*adj.* 1. having to do with time 2. set or regulated so as to explode, open, etc. at a given time [a *time* bomb] 3. payable later or on a specified future date [a *time* loan] ☆4. having to do with purchases in which payment is made over a period of time [a time payment] —**abreast of the times** 1. up-to-date, as in ideas, fashions, etc.; modern 2. informed about current matters —**against time** in an effort to finish in a given time —☆**ahead of time** sooner than due; early —**at one time** 1. simultaneously 2. formerly —**at the same time** 1. simultaneously; in the same period 2. nonetheless; however —**at times** occasionally; sometimes —**behind the times** out-of-date; old-fashioned —**behind time** late —**between times** now and then; occasionally —**do time** [Colloq.] to serve a prison term —**for the time being** for the present; temporarily —**from time to time** at intervals; now and then —**gain time** 1. to go too fast: said of a timepiece 2. to prolong a situation until a desired occurrence can take place —**in good time** 1. at the proper time 2. in a creditably short time; quickly —**in no time** almost instantly; very quickly —**in time** 1. in the course of time; eventually 2. before it is too late 3. keeping the set rhythm, tempo, pace, etc. —**kill time** to fill time, as between engagements, chores, etc., in some makeshift way —**lose time** 1. to go too slow: said of a timepiece 2. to let time go by without advancing one's objective —**make time** 1. to compensate for lost time by going faster, as a train ☆2. to travel, work, etc. at a specified, especially fast, rate of speed [we *made* (good) *time* between Boston and Albany] —☆**make time with** [Slang] to succeed in attracting or having an affair with (a person of the opposite sex) —**many a time** often; frequently —☆**on one's own time** during time for which one is not paid; during other than working hours —**on time** ☆1. at the appointed time; punctual or punctually ☆2. to be paid for in installments over a period of time —**out of time** 1. not at the usual time; unseasonable 2. not keeping the set rhythm, tempo, pace, etc. —**pass the time of day** to exchange a few words of greeting, etc. —**time after time** again and again; continually: also **time and again** —**time of life** age (of a person) —☆**time of one's life** [Colloq.] an experience of great pleasure for one —**time on one's hands** an interval with nothing to do —**time out of mind** *same as* TIME IMMEMORIAL (sense 1) —**time was** there was a time

time and a half a rate of payment one and a half times the usual rate, as for working overtime

☆**time capsule** a container holding articles, documents, etc. of current civilization, buried or otherwise preserved for a future age

☆**time clock** a clock with a mechanism for recording on a card (**timecard**) the time an employee begins and ends a work period

time-con·sum·ing (-kən sōōm′iŋ, -syōōm′-) *adj.* using up much or too much time [a *time-consuming* task]

☆**time deposit** a bank deposit payable at a specified future date or upon advance notice

time discount *Commerce* a discount in price for payment made before the bill is due

☆**time draft** a draft payable at a future specified date

time exposure 1. an exposure of photographic film for a relatively long period, generally longer than half a second 2. a photograph taken in this way

time-hon·ored (tīm′än′ərd) *adj.* honored or observed because in existence or usage for a long time

time immemorial 1. time so long past as to be vague 2. *Eng. Law* time beyond legal memory, fixed by statute as prior to 1189, the beginning of the reign of Richard I

time·keep·er (tīm′kē′pər) *n.* 1. *same as* TIMEPIECE 2. a person who keeps time; specif., *a)* a person employed to keep account of the hours worked by employees *b)* a person who keeps account of the elapsed time in the periods of play in certain sports

time-lapse (-laps′) *adj.* designating or of a technique of photographing a slow process, as the growth of a plant, on motion-picture film by exposing single frames at widely spaced intervals: the developed film is projected at regular speed to show the entire process greatly speeded up

time·less (-lis) *adj.* 1. that cannot be measured by time; unending 2. transcending time; eternal 3. restricted to no specific time; always valid, true, or applicable 4. [Obs.] untimely —**time′less·ly** *adv.* —**time′less·ness** *n.*

time limit a fixed period of time during which something is valid, or must be done, completed, or ended

time loan a loan to be repaid at a specified time

☆**time lock** a lock with a mechanism that prevents opening before the time set

time·ly (-lē) *adj.* **-li·er, -li·est** [ME. *tymeli* < OE. *timlice*: see TIME & -LY¹] 1. happening, done, said, etc. at a suitable time; well-timed; opportune 2. [Obs. or Rare] appearing in good time; early —*adv.* [Archaic or Poet.] early; soon —**time′li·ness** *n.*

SYN.—**timely** applies to that which happens or is done at an appropriate time, esp. at such a time as to be of help or service [a *timely* interruption]; **opportune** refers to that which is so timed, often as if by accident, as to meet exactly the needs of the

occasion *[the opportune* arrival of a supply train*]*; **seasonable** applies literally to that which is suited to the season of the year or, figuratively, to the moment or occasion *[seasonable* weather*]*

time·ous (tī′məs) *adj.* [Scot.] *same as* TIMELY

time-out (-out′) *n.* **1.** any time taken for rest or not counted toward a work record, score, etc. ☆**2.** *Football, Basketball,* etc. any suspension of play, with the time-keeper's clock stopped, to allow a team to make substitutions, discuss strategy, etc.

time·piece (-pēs′) *n.* any apparatus for measuring and recording time; esp., a clock or watch

tim·er (tī′mər) *n.* **1.** *same as:* a) TIMEKEEPER b) STOPWATCH ☆**2.** in internal-combustion engines, a mechanism for causing the spark to be produced in the cylinder at the required instant **3.** any of various devices for timing, or automatically starting and stopping at predetermined times, the operation of a machine

times (tīmz) *prep.* multiplied by: symbol, x *[two times* three is six*]*

time·sav·ing (-sā′viŋ) *adj.* that saves time because of greater efficiency, etc. —**time′sav′er** *n.*

time·serv·er (-sur′vər) *n.* a person who for his own advantage deliberately surrenders his principles and acts in conformity with the patterns of behavior prevailing at the time or sanctioned by those in authority; toady —**time′serv′ing** *n., adj.*

☆**time sharing** a system permitting the simultaneous employment of a computer or computer complex by many users at remote locations for solving their individual problems in real time —**time′-shared′** *adj.*

time sheet a sheet on which are recorded the hours worked by an employee or employees

time signature *Music* a sign like a numerical fraction, esp. after the key signature, showing how many beats occur in the following measure or measures (e.g., 3/4 means three quarter-note beats); also, a nonnumerical sign used in this way (e.g., C is often used instead of 4/4)

time study study of operational or production procedures and the time consumed by them, for the purpose of devising methods of increasing efficiency or productivity of workers: in full **time and motion study**

time·ta·ble (-tā′b'l) *n.* a schedule of the times certain things are to happen, esp. of the times of arrival and departure of airplanes, trains, buses, etc.

time-test·ed (-tes′tid) *adj.* having value proved by long use or experience

time·work (-wurk′) *n.* work paid for by the hour or day: cf. PIECEWORK —**time′work′er** *n.*

time·worn (-wôrn′) *adj.* **1.** worn or deteriorated by long use or existence **2.** hackneyed; trite

☆**time zone** *see* STANDARD TIME and chart at TIME

tim·id (tim′id) *adj.* [L. *timidus < timere,* to fear] **1.** easily frightened; lacking self-confidence; shy; timorous **2.** showing fear or lack of self-confidence; hesitant *[a timid* reply*]* —*SYN.* see AFRAID —**ti·mid·i·ty** (tə mid′ə tē), **tim′id·ness** *n.* —**tim′id·ly** *adv.*

tim·ing (tī′miŋ) *n.* **1.** a) the regulation of the speed, or of the moment of occurrence, of something so as to produce the most effective results *[the timing* of an engine, of a golfer's swing, of an announcement, etc.*]* b) the pacing of various scenes, as of a play, for total effect **2.** measurement of time, as with a stopwatch

Ti·miş·oa·ra (tē′mē shwä′rä) city in the Banat region of W Romania: pop. 170,000

ti·moc·ra·cy (tī mäk′rə sē) *n.* [MFr. *tymocracie < ML. timocratia < Gr. timokratia < timē,* honor, worth (< IE. base **kwei-,* to heed, value, whence Lith. *káina,* worth, price) + *-kratia* (see -CRACY)] **1.** in Plato's politics, a state in which love of wealth, property, and power is the guiding principle of the rulers **2.** in Aristotle's politics, a state in which political power is in direct proportion to property ownership —**ti·mo·crat·ic** (tī′mə krat′ik) *adj.*

Ti·mor (tē′môr, ti môr′) **1.** island in the SE Malay Archipelago, divided between Portugal (see PORTUGUESE TIMOR) & Indonesia: c.13,000 sq. mi. **2.** W portion of this island: c.5,800 sq. mi.

tim·or·ous (tim′ər əs) *adj.* [ME. *tymerouse < MFr. timoreus < ML. timorosus < L. timor,* fear] **1.** full of or subject to fear; timid **2.** showing or caused by timidity —**tim′or·ous·ly** *adv.* —**tim′or·ous·ness** *n.* —*SYN.* see AFRAID

Timor Sea arm of the Indian Ocean, between Timor & the NW coast of Australia: c.300 mi. wide

Tim·o·thy (tim′ə thē) [Fr. *Timothée < L. Timotheus < Gr. Timotheos < timē,* honor + *theos,* god] **1.** a masculine name: dim. *Tim* **2.** *Bible* a) a disciple of the Apostle Paul b) either of the Epistles to Timothy, books of the New Testament attributed to the Apostle Paul

tim·o·thy (tim′ə thē) *n.* [after *Timothy* Hanson, who took the seed from New York to the Carolinas, c.1720] ☆a perennial European grass (*Phleum pratense*) with dense, cylindrical spikes of bristly spikelets, widely grown for hay

tim·pa·ni (tim′pə nē) *n.pl., sing.* -**pa·no′** (-nō′) [It., pl. of *timpano < L. tympanum:* see TYMPAN] *[often with sing. v.]* kettledrums; esp., a set of kettledrums of different pitches played by one performer in an orchestra —**tim′pa·nist** *n.*

Ti·mur (tē mōōr′) *see* TAMERLANE

tin (tin) *n.* [ME. < OE., akin to G. *zinn;* only in Gmc. languages] **1.** a soft, silver-white, crystalline, metallic chemical element, malleable at ordinary temperatures, capable of a high polish, and used as an alloy in tinfoils, solders, utensils, type metals, etc. and in making tin plate: symbol, Sn; at. wt., 118.69; at. no., 50; sp. gr., 7.28; melt. pt., 231.9°C; boil. pt., 2260°C **2.** *same as* TIN PLATE **3.** *a)* a pan, box, etc. made of tin plate *b)* [Chiefly Brit.] *same as* CAN² (*n.* 2, 3) **4.** [Old Slang] money Variously used to connote cheapness, baseness, spuriousness, etc. of a material or thing —*vt.* **tinned, tin′ning 1.** to cover or plate with tin **2.** [Chiefly Brit.] *same as* CAN² (*vt.* 1)

tin·a·mou (tin′ə mōō′) *n.* [Fr. < the native (Carib) name] any of a family (Tinamidae) of South and Central American birds resembling the partridge and quail, but belonging to the ostrich group: they are strong runners

tin·cal (tiŋ′kəl, -kôl) *n.* [Malay *tiṅkal < Per. tiṅkāl, tiṅkar < Sans. ṭaṅkaṇa]* crude borax

☆**tin can** *same as:* **1.** CAN² (*n.* 2) **2.** [Slang] DESTROYER (*n.* 2)

tinct (tiŋkt) *adj.* [L. *tinctus,* pp. of *tingere:* see TINGE] [Archaic] tinged; tinted —*n.* [Now Rare] a color; tint —*vt.* [Obs.] to tincture

tinct. tincture

tinc·to·ri·al (tiŋk tôr′ē əl) *adj.* [< L. *tinctorius < tinctor,* dyer: see ff.] having to do with color, dyeing, or staining —**tinc·to′ri·al·ly** *adv.*

tinc·ture (tiŋk′chər) *n.* [ME. < L. *tinctura < tinctus,* pp. of *tingere,* to dye: see TINGE] **1.** orig., a dye **2.** a light color; tint; tinge **3.** a slight admixture or infusion of some substance or quality; trace, smattering, etc. **4.** *Heraldry* any color, metal, or fur **5.** *Pharmacy* an alcoholic or water-alcoholic solution of a medicinal substance, usually 10% to 20% by volume: tinctures are more dilute than fluidextracts and more volatile than spirits —*vt.* **-tured, -tur·ing 1.** to color lightly; tint; tinge **2.** to imbue or permeate lightly with some substance or quality *[a message inctured* with hope*]*

Tin·dale (or **Tin·dal**) (tin′d'l), **William** *same as* TYNDALE

tin·der (tin′dər) *n.* [ME. < OE. *tynder* (akin to G. *zunder*) < base of OE. *tendan,* to kindle] any dry, easily flammable material, esp. as formerly used for starting a fire from a spark made by flint and steel struck together

tin·der·box (-bäks′) *n.* **1.** formerly, a metal box for holding tinder, flint, and steel for starting a fire **2.** any highly flammable object, structure, etc. **3.** a place or situation likely to be the source of a flare-up of trouble, war, etc.

tine (tīn) *n.* [ME. *tind* < OE., akin to OHG. *zint,* a jag, prong] a slender, projecting part pointed at the end; prong *[the tines* of a fork*]* —**tined** *adj.*

tin·e·a (tin′ē ə) *n.* [ME. < L., a gnawing worm, moth] any of various skin diseases caused by a fungus; esp., ringworm

tin ear [Colloq.] ☆a lack of discriminating sensitivity to music, speech, etc.

tin·e·id (tin′ē id) *n.* [< L. *tinea,* gnawing worm, moth + -ID] any of a family (Tineidae) of small moths, including the common clothes moth (*Tinea pellionella*) that feeds on dry organic matter, as wool, hair, etc. —*adj.* of this family

tine test a tuberculin test in which the skin is punctured by small tines, or prongs, coated with a small amount of protein from dead tubercle bacilli

tin·foil (tin′foil′) *n.* a very thin sheet or sheets of tin or an alloy of tin and lead, etc., used as a wrapping for food products, in insulation, etc.

ting¹ (tin) *n.* [echoic] a single, light, ringing sound, as of a small bell being struck —*vt., vi.* to make or cause to make a ting

‡**ting²** (tiŋ) *n. same as* THING²

ting-a-ling (tiŋ′ə liŋ′) *n.* the sound of a small bell ringing repeatedly

tinge (tinj) *vt.* **tinged, tinge′ing** or **ting′ing** [L. *tingere,* to dye, stain < IE. base **teng-,* to moisten, whence Gr. *tengein,* to moisten, OHG. *dunkon,* to dip: cf. DUNK] **1.** to color slightly; give a tint to **2.** to give a trace, slight flavor or odor, shade, etc. to *[joy tinged* with sorrow*]* —*n.* **1.** a slight coloring; tint **2.** a slight trace, flavor, odor, etc.; smack; touch —*SYN.* see COLOR

tin·gle (tiŋ′g'l) *vi.* **-gled, -gling** [ME. *tynglen,* var. of *tinklen,* to TINKLE] **1.** to have a prickling or stinging feeling, as from cold, a sharp slap, excitement, etc. **2.** to cause this feeling —*vt.* to cause to have this feeling —*n.* this feeling —**tin′gler** *n.* —**tin′gling·ly** *adv.* —**tin′gly** *adj.* **-gli·er, -gli·est**

☆**tin god** a person unworthy of the veneration or respect he demands or receives

☆**tin·horn** (tin′hôrn′) *adj.* [< phr. *tin horn gambler,* so named from use of metal dice-shaker in chuck-a-luck games, scorned as petty by faro dealers] [Slang] pretending to have money, influence, ability, etc., though actually lacking in these; cheap and showy *[a tinhorn* sport*]* —*n.* [Slang] a tinhorn person, esp. a gambler

ti·ni·ly (tī′n'l ē) *adv.* to a tiny degree; minutely

ti·ni·ness (tī′nē nis) *n.* a tiny quality or condition

tin·ker (tiŋ′kər) *n.* [ME. *tinkere < ?* or akin to *tinken,* to make a tinkling sound] **1.** a person who mends pots, pans, etc., usually traveling at his trade **2.** a person who can make all kinds of minor repairs; jack-of-all-trades **3.** a clumsy or unskillful worker; bungler ☆**4.** a young mackerel —*vi.* **1.** to work as a tinker **2.** to make clumsy, futile attempts to mend or repair something **3.** to fuss or putter aimlessly or uselessly —*vt.* to mend as a tinker; patch up —**tink′er·er** *n.*

tinker's damn (or **dam**) [< prec. + DAMN: with reference to the lowly status and profane speech of tinkers] something of no value: esp. in **not worth a tinker's damn**

☆**Tin·ker·toy** (tiŋ′kər toi′) *a trademark for* a toy set of wooden dowels, joints, wheels, etc., used by children to assemble structures —*n.* [t-] anything resembling or suggesting such a structure

tin·kle (tiŋ′k'l) *vi.* **-kled, -kling** [ME. *tynclen*, freq. of *tinken*, to make a tingling sound, of echoic orig.] 1. to make a series of small, short, light, clinking sounds like those of a very small bell ☆2. [Colloq.] to urinate: child's term —*vt.* 1. to cause to tinkle 2. to indicate, signal, etc. by tinkling —*n.* the act or sound of tinkling —**give some-one a tinkle** [Brit.] to call someone on the telephone —**tin′kler** *n.* —**tin′kly** *adj.* **-kli·er, -kli·est**

☆**tin liz·zie** (liz′ē) [orig. nickname of an early model of Ford automobile] any cheap or old automobile

tin·man (tin′mən) *n., pl.* **-men** same as TINSMITH

tinned (tind) *adj.* 1. plated with tin 2. [Brit.] preserved in tins; canned

tin·ner (tin′ər) *n.* 1. a tin miner 2. same as TINSMITH

tin·ni·tus (ti nit′əs) *n.* [L. < pp. of *tinnire*, to tinkle, of echoic orig.] any ringing or buzzing in the ear not resulting from an external stimulus

tin·ny (tin′ē) *adj.* **-ni·er, -ni·est** 1. of, containing, or yielding tin 2. like tin, as in appearance, sound, value, etc. [*tinny* jewelry, *tinny* music] 3. tasting of tin —**tin′ni·ly** *adv.* —**tin′ni·ness** *n.*

☆**Tin Pan Alley** 1. the area of a city, esp. New York, where there are many songwriters, publishers of popular music, etc. 2. the publishers, writers, and promoters of popular music

tin·plate (tin′plāt′) *vt.* **-plat′ed, -plat′ing** to plate with tin

tin plate thin sheets of iron or steel plated with tin

tin·sel (tin′s'l, -z'l) *n.* [aphetic < MFr. *estincelle*, a spark, spangle: see STENCIL] 1. formerly, a cloth of wool, etc. interwoven with glittering threads of gold, silver, or other metal 2. thin sheets, strips, or threads of tin, metal foil, etc., used for inexpensive decoration 3. something that glitters like precious metal but has little worth; empty show; sham splendor —*adj.* 1. made of or decorated with tinsel 2. having sham splendor; showy; gaudy —*vt.* **-seled** or **-selled, -sel·ing** or **-sel·ling** 1. to make glitter with or as with tinsel 2. to give a false appearance of splendor to —**tin′sel·ly** *adj.*

tin·smith (tin′smith′) *n.* a person who works in tin or tin plate; maker of tinware

tin·stone (-stōn′) *n.* same as CASSITERITE

tint (tint) *n.* [earlier *tinct* < L. *tinctus*, a dyeing, dipping < pp. of *tingere*, to dye, TINGE] 1. a delicate or pale color or hue; tinge 2. a color or a shading of a color; esp., a gradation of a color with reference to its mixture with white 3. a dye for the hair 4. *Engraving* an even shading produced by fine parallel lines 5. *Printing* a light-colored background, as for an illustration —*vt.* to give a tint to —*SYN.* see COLOR —**tint′er** *n.*

Tin·tag·el Head (tin taj′əl) cape of NW Cornwall, England: legendary birthplace of King Arthur

tin·tin·nab·u·lar·y (tin′ti nab′yoo ler′ē) *adj.* [< L. *tintinnabulum*, little bell, dim. < *lintinnare*, to jingle, ring < *tinnire*, to jingle + -ARY] of bells or the ringing of bells: also **tin′tin·nab′u·lar** (-lər), **tin′tin·nab′u·lous** (-ləs)

☆**tin·tin·nab·u·la·tion** (tin′ti nab′yoo lā′shən) *n.* [see prec. & -TION] the ringing sound of bells

Tin·to·ret·to (tēn′tō ret′tō; *E.* tin′tə ret′ō), **Il** (ēl) (born *Jacopo Robusti*) 1518-94; Venetian painter

☆**tin·type** (tin′tip′) *n.* an old kind of photograph taken directly as a positive print on a sensitized plate of enameled tin or iron; ferrotype

tin·ware (-wer′) *n.* pots, pans, etc. made of tin plate

tin·work (-wurk′) *n.* 1. work done in tin 2. [*pl.*, *with sing. v.*] a place where tin is smelted, rolled, etc.

ti·ny (ti′nē) *adj.* **-ni·er, -ni·est** [< ME. *tine*, *n.*, a little (something)] very small; diminutive —*SYN.* see SMALL

-tion (shən) [< Fr., OFr., or L.: Fr. *-tion* < OFr. *-cion* < L. *-tio* (gen. *-tionis*) < *-t-* of pp. stem + *-io* (gen. *-ionis*), suffix] *n.-forming suffix meaning:* 1. the act of [*correction*] 2. the state of being [*elation*] 3. the thing that is [*creation*]

-tious (shəs) [< Fr. or L.: Fr. *-tieux* < L. *-tiosus* < *-t-* of pp. stem + *-iosus*, -OUS] *adj.-forming suffix corresponding to* -TION [*cautious*]

tip¹ (tip) *n.* [ME. *tippe*, akin to MLowG. *tip*, point, top, G. *zipf-* in *zipfel*, an end, tip, prob. < IE. base *dumb-*, tail, whence Avestan *duma-*, tail] 1. the pointed, tapering, or rounded end or top of something long and slim 2. something attached to the end, as a cap, ferrule, etc. 3. a top or apex, as of a mountain —*vt.* **tipped, tip′ping** 1. to make a tip on 2. to cover the tip or tips of (*with* something) 3. to serve as the tip of ☆4. to remove the stems from (berries, etc.) —**tip in** to insert (a map, picture, etc.) by pasting along the inner edge in bookbinding

tip² (tip) *vt.* **tipped, tip′ping** [akin ? to prec.] 1. to strike lightly and sharply; tap 2. to give a small present of money to (a waiter, porter, etc.) for some service 3. [Colloq.] *a)* to give secret information to in an attempt to be helpful (often with *off*) *b)* to reveal or divulge (a secret, plot, etc.) ☆4. *Baseball*, etc. *a)* to hit (the ball) a glancing blow *b)* to glance off (the bat, glove, etc.): said of the ball —*vi.* to give a tip or tips —*n.* 1. a light, sharp blow; tap: cf. FOUL TIP 2. a piece of secret information given confidentially in an attempt to be helpful [a *tip* on the race] 3. a suggestion, hint, warning, etc. 4. a small present of money given to a waiter, porter, etc. for services; gratuity —☆**tip one's hand** (or **mitt**) [Slang] to reveal a secret, one's plans, etc., often inadvertently

tip³ (tip) *vt.* **tipped, tip′ping** [ME. *tipen* < ?] 1. to overturn or upset (often with *over*) 2. to cause to tilt or slant 3. to raise slightly or touch the brim of (one's hat) in salutation —*vi.* 1. to tilt or slant 2. to overturn or topple (often with *over*) —*n.* 1. a tipping or being tipped; tilt; slant 2. [Brit.] a place for dumping rubbish, etc.; dump —**tip the scales at** to weigh (a specified amount)

tip cart a cart with a body that can be tipped for dumping its contents

tip·cat (tip′kat′) *n.* [TIP² + CAT] 1. a game in which a small piece of wood, usually tapered at both ends, is struck on one end with a bat or stick so that it is flipped into the air where it can be batted for distance 2. the small piece of wood used in this game

☆**ti·pi** (tē′pē′) *n., pl.* **-pis** alt. sp. of TEPEE

☆**tip-off** (tip′ôf′) *n.* 1. the act of tipping off 2. a tip; confidential disclosure, hint, or warning

Tip·pe·ca·noe (tip′ē kə noo′) [< Algonquian (Miami), lit., place of buffalo fish] 1. river in N Ind. flowing southwest into the Wabash: c.180 mi.: scene of a battle (1811) in which U.S. forces under William Henry Harrison defeated a band of Tecumseh's Indians 2. *nickname of* William Henry HARRISON

tip·per (tip′ər) *n.* a person who gives tips, or gratuities

Tip·per·ar·y (tip′ə rer′ē) county of S Ireland, in Munster province: 1,643 sq. mi.; pop. 123,000

tip·pet (tip′it) *n.* [ME. *tipet*, prob. dim. of *tip*, TIP¹] 1. formerly, a long, hanging part of a hood, cape, or sleeve 2. a scarflike garment of fur, wool, etc. for the neck and shoulders, hanging down in front 3. a long, black scarf worn by Anglican clergymen, etc.

tip·ple¹ (tip′'l) *vi., vt.* **-pled, -pling** [prob. back-formation < ME. *tipelar*, a tavern-keeper < ?] to drink (alcoholic liquor) habitually —*n.* alcoholic liquor —**tip′pler** *n.*

☆**tip·ple²** (tip′'l) *n.* [< obs. *lipple*, freq. of TIP³] 1. an apparatus for emptying coal, etc. from a mine car by tipping 2. the place where this is done

tip·py (tip′ē) *adj.* **-pi·er, -pi·est** [Colloq.] that tips easily; not steady; shaky

tip·py-toe, tip·py·toe (-tō′) *n., vi., adj., adv.* colloq. var. of TIPTOE

tip·staff (tip′staf′, -stäf′) *n., pl.* **-staffs′, -staves′** (-stāvz′) 1. a staff with a metal tip, formerly carried as an emblem by certain officials 2. an official who carried such a staff, esp., in England, a bailiff or constable

tip·ster (tip′stər) *n.* [Colloq.] a person who sells tips, as on horse races, for stock speculation, etc.

tip·sy (tip′sē) *adj.* **-si·er, -si·est** 1. that tips easily; not steady; shaky 2. crooked; awry 3. somewhat drunk; intoxicated enough to be somewhat unsteady, fuddled, etc. —**tip′si·ly** *adv.* —**tip′si·ness** *n.*

tip·toe (tip′tō′) *n.* the tip of a toe or the tips of the toes —*vi.* **-toed′, -toe′ing** to walk stealthily or cautiously on one's tiptoes —*adj.* 1. standing on one's tiptoes 2. *a)* lifted up; exalted *b)* eager; excited; alert *c)* stealthy; cautious —*adv.* on tiptoe —**on tiptoe** 1. on one's tiptoes 2. eager or eagerly 3. silently; stealthily

tip·top (-täp′) *n.* [TIP¹ + TOP¹] 1. the highest point; very top 2. [Colloq.] the highest in quality or excellence; best —*adj., adv.* 1. at the highest point, or top 2. [Colloq.] at the highest point of excellence, health, etc.

ti·rade (ti′rād, ti rād′) *n.* [Fr. < It. *tirata*, a volley < pp. of *tirare*, to draw, fire] a long, vehement speech, esp. one of denunciation; harangue

‡**ti·rail·leur** (tē rä yër′) *n.* [Fr. < *tirailler*, to tease, skirmish < *tirer*, to draw, fire] a sharpshooter

Ti·ra·na (ti rä′nə) capital of Albania, in the C part: pop. 153,000: also, Albanian **Ti·ra·në** (tē rä′nə)

tire¹ (tir) *vi.* **tired, tir′ing** [ME. *tiren* < OE. *tiorian*, to fail, be tired, prob. < Gmc. *tiuzōn*, to stay behind < IE. *deus-*, to cease] 1. to become in need of rest; become weary or fatigued through exertion 2. to lose interest or patience; become bored or impatient (usually with *of*) —*vt.* 1. to diminish the strength of by exertion, etc.; fatigue; weary 2. to diminish the patience or interest of, as by dull talk, etc.; make weary; bore

tire² (tir) *n.* [ME. *tyre*, prob. var. (in sense "equipment") of ff.] 1. a hoop of iron or rubber around the wheel of a vehicle, forming the tread 2. *a)* a rubber tube filled with air, fixed about the wheel of a vehicle to reduce shock: one type of automobile tire consists of a rubber inner tube filled with air at a specified pressure and enclosed in a heavy, treaded casing of rubber and fabric, etc.: see also TUBELESS TIRE *b)* the casing alone, as distinguished from the inner tube —*vt.* **tired, tir′ing** to furnish with tires

---

fat, āpe, cär; ten, ēven; is, bīte; gō, hôrn, tool, look; oil, out; up, fur; get; joy; yet; chin; she; thin, then; zh, leisure; ŋ, ring; ə for *a* in *ago*, *e* in *agent*, *i* in *sanity*, *o* in *comply*, *u* in *focus*; ' as in *able* (ā′b'l); Fr. bâl; ë, Fr. coeur; ö, Fr. feu; Fr. mon; δ, Fr. coq; ü, Fr. duc; r, Fr. cri; H, G. ich; kh, G. doch. See inside front cover. ☆ Americanism; ‡foreign; *hypothetical; < derived from

tire[3] (tīr) *vt.* **tired, tir′ing** [ME. *tiren,* aphetic for *atiren,* ATTIRE] [Archaic] to attire or dress —*n.* [ME. < *atir:* see *v.*] [Archaic] 1. attire 2. a woman's headdress

☆**tire chain** a device made of chains, attached to a tire of a motor vehicle to increase traction as on snow

tired (tīrd) *adj.* [ME. (Northern) *tyrit* < *tiren:* see TIRE[1]] 1. fatigued, worn-out, or weary 2. stale; hackneyed —**tired′ly** *adv.* —**tired′ness** *n.*
SYN.—**tired** is applied to one who has been drained of much of his strength and energy through exertion, boredom, impatience, etc. *[tired* by years of hard toil*]*; **weary** (or **wearied**) suggests such depletion of energy or interest as to make one unable or unwilling to continue *[weary* of study*]*; **exhausted** implies a total draining of strength and energy, as after a long, hard climb; **fatigued** refers to one who has lost so much energy through prolonged exertion that rest and sleep are essential *[fatigued* at the end of the day*]*; **fagged,** an informal word, suggests great exhaustion or fatigue from hard, unremitting work or exertion *[completely fagged* after a set of tennis*]*

tire·less (tīr′lis) *adj.* that does not become tired; untiring —**tire′less·ly** *adv.* —**tire′less·ness** *n.*

Ti·re·si·as (tī rē′sē əs) [L. < Gr. *Teiresias*] Gr. *Myth.* a blind soothsayer of Thebes

tire·some (tīr′səm) *adj.* [see -SOME] 1. tiring; boring; tedious 2. annoying; irksome —**tire′some·ly** *adv.* —**tire′some·ness** *n.*

tire·wom·an (tīr′woom′ən) *n., pl.* **-wom′en** [see TIRE[3]] [Archaic] a lady's maid

Ti·rich Mir (tē′rich mir′) mountain in N West Pakistan: highest peak of the Hindu Kush: 25,230 ft.

tir·ing room (tīr′iŋ) [see TIRE[3]] [Archaic] a dressing room, esp. in a theater

ti·ro (tī′rō) *n., pl.* **-ros** *var.* of TYRO

Tir·ol (tir′äl, ti′rōl, ti rōl′) 1. E Alpine region in W Austria & N Italy 2. province of W Austria in this region: 4,883 sq. mi.; pop. 463,000; cap. Innsbruck —**Ti·ro·le·an** (ti rō′lē ən) *adj., n.* —**Tir·o·lese** (tir′ə lēz′) *adj., n., pl.* **-lese′**

☆**Ti·ros** (tī′rōs) *n.* [*T*(elevision *and*) *I*(n-*fra-*)*R*(ed) *O*(bservation) *S*(atellite)] any of a series of satellites for televising and transmitting pictures of the earth's cloud cover

Tir·so de Mo·li·na (tir′sō *the* mō lē′nä) (pseud. of *Gabriel Téllez*) 1584?–1648; Sp. dramatist

Tir·u·chi·ra·pol·li (tir′ə chə rə pul′ē, -räp′ə lē) city in Madras state, S India: pop. 250,000

'tis (tiz) it is

ti·sane (ti zan′; *Fr.* tē zàn′) *n.* [ME. < MFr.: see PTISAN] *same as* PTISAN

Tish·ah b'Ab (tē shä′ bə äv′, tish′ə bôv′) [Heb. *tish'āh b'ābh,* ninth (day) of Ab] a Jewish fast day commemorating the destruction of the Temple, observed on the 9th day of Ab

Tish·ri (tish rē′, tish′rē) *n.* [Heb.] the first month of the Jewish year: see JEWISH CALENDAR

Ti·siph·o·ne (ti sif′ə nē′) Gr. & *Rom. Myth.* one of the three Furies

tis·sue (tish′oo; *chiefly Brit.,* tis′yoo) *n.* [ME. *tissu,* a rich cloth < OFr. < pp. of *tistre,* to weave < L. *texere,* to weave: see TEXT] 1. cloth; esp., light, thin cloth, as gauze 2. an interwoven or intricate mass or series; mesh; network; web *[a tissue* of lies*]* 3. a piece of soft, absorbent paper, used as a disposable handkerchief, as toilet paper, etc. 4. *a) same as* TISSUE PAPER *b)* a sheet of tissue paper 5. *Biol. a)* the substance of an organic body or organ, consisting of cells and intercellular material *b)* any of the distinct structural materials of an organism, having a particular function *[epithelial tissue]* —*vt.* **-sued, -su·ing** 1. to cover with tissue 2. [Archaic] to weave into tissue

tissue culture 1. the process or technique of growing tissue artificially in a special, sterile culture medium 2. the tissue thus grown

tissue paper very thin, unsized, nearly transparent paper, as for wrapping things, making tracings, etc.

Ti·sza (tē′sɔ) river in E Europe, flowing from the W Ukraine southwest through Hungary & Yugoslavia into the Danube: c.800 mi.: Romanian name **Ti·sa** (tē′sȯ)

tit[1] (tit) *n.* [TIT(MOUSE)] a titmouse or other small bird

tit[2] (tit) *n.* [ME. *titte* < OE. *tit,* TEAT] 1. *same as* TEAT 2. a breast: in this sense now vulgar

tit[3] (tit) *n.* [ME. *tit-* in *titmose* (cf. TITMOUSE), *titling:* prob. children's term for "little," seen also in ON. *tūllingr,* little bird, Norw. *titta,* little girl] [Now Rare] a small, worn-out, or inferior horse

Tit. Titus

tit. title

Ti·tan (tīt′'n) [ME. < L. < Gr. *Titan*] *poetic epithet for* HELIOS —*n.* 1. Gr. *Myth.* any of a race of giant deities who were overthrown by the Olympian gods 2. [t-] any person or thing of great size or power —*adj.* [also t-] same as TITANIC —**Ti′tan·ess** *n.fem.*

ti·tan·ate (tīt′'n āt′) *n.* a salt or ester of titanic acid

Ti·ta·ni·a (ti tā′nē ə, tī-) in early folklore, the queen of fairyland and wife of Oberon

Ti·tan·ic (tī tan′ik) *adj.* [Gr. *Titanikos*] 1. of or like the Titans 2. [t-] of great size, strength, or power —**ti·tan′i·cal·ly** *adv.*

ti·tan·ic (tī tan′ik, ti-) *adj.* designating or of a chemical compound containing titanium with a valence of four

titanic acid either of two weak acids, H_2TiO_3 or H_4TiO_4, derived from titanium dioxide

ti·tan·if·er·ous (tīt′'n if′ər əs) *adj.* [TITANI(UM) + -FEROUS] containing titanium

Ti·tan·ism (tīt′'n iz'm) *n.* [also t-] a spirit of revolt or defiance, like that of the Titans, against the established order, social conventions, etc.

ti·tan·ite (tīt′'n īt′) *n.* [G. *titanit:* see TITANIUM & -ITE[1]] *same as* SPHENE

ti·ta·ni·um (tī tā′nē əm, ti-) *n.* [ModL. < Gr. *Titanes,* pl. of *Titan,* a Titan] a silvery or dark-gray, lustrous, metallic chemical element found in rutile and other minerals and used as a cleaning and deoxidizing agent in molten steel, and in the manufacture of aircraft, satellites, chemical equipment, etc.: symbol, Ti; at. wt., 47.90; at. no., 22; sp. gr., 4.5; melt. pt., 1675°C; boil. pt., 3260°C

titanium dioxide a colorless to black crystalline compound, TiO_2, used as a paint pigment and ceramic glaze, and in making white rubber, plastics, etc.: also **titanium white, titanic oxide**

Ti·tan·om·a·chy (tīt′'n äm′ə kē) [Gr. *Titanomachia:* see TITAN & -MACHY] Gr. *Myth.* the war between the Titans and the Olympian gods

ti·tan·o·saur (tī tan′ə sôr′) *n.* [< ModL. *Titanosaurus:* see TITAN & -SAURUS] any of a genus (*Titanosaurus*) of large, plant-eating, amphibious dinosaurs of the Cretaceous

ti·tan·ous (tī tan′əs, ti-; tī′t'n əs) *adj.* designating or of a chemical compound containing titanium with a valence of three

tit·bit (tit′bit′) *n. chiefly Brit. var.* of TIDBIT

ti·ter (tīt′ər, tēt′-) *n.* [Fr. *titre,* standard, title < OFr. *title:* see TITLE] *Chem., Physiol.* 1. a standard strength or degree of concentration of a solution as established through titration 2. the minimum weight or volume of a substance necessary to cause a given result in titration 3. the point at which a fatty acid solidifies after being liberated by hydrolysis, separated, and washed free of other products

tit for tat [var. of earlier *tip for tap* (Fr. *tant pour tant*): see TIP[2]] retaliation in kind, as blow for blow

tithe (tīth) *n.* [ME. < OE. *teothe, teogotha,* a TENTH] 1. one tenth of the annual produce of one's land or of one's annual income, paid as a tax or contribution to support a church or its clergy 2. *a)* a tenth part *b)* any small part 3. any tax or levy —*vt.* **tithed, tith′ing** [ME. *iithen* < OE. *teothian* < the *n.*] 1. to pay a tithe of (one's produce, income, etc.) 2. to levy a tithe on or collect a tithe from —*vi.* to pay a tithe —**tith′a·ble** *adj.* —**tith′er** *n.*

tith·ing (tī′thiŋ) *n.* [ME. < OE. *teothung*] 1. a levying or paying of tithes 2. *same as* TITHE 3. formerly, in England, a unit of civil administration originally consisting of ten families

Ti·tho·nus (ti thō′nəs) [L. < Gr. *Tithōnos*] Gr. *Myth.* the son of Laomedon, loved by Eos, who got for him immortality but not eternal youth, so that he shriveled up and was turned into a grasshopper

☆**ti·ti**[1] (tēt′ē) *n.* [< ? AmInd. name] 1. a small evergreen tree (*Cliftonia monophylla*) with white or pinkish flowers, found in the S U.S. 2. *same as* LEATHERWOOD (sense 2)

ti·ti[2] (ti tē′) *n.* [Sp. *titi* < Aymara *titi*] 1. any of several marmosets (genus *Callithrix*) of Brazil and Bolivia, with short canine teeth 2. any of several small S. American monkeys (genus *Callicebus*) with a round head

Ti·tian (tish′ən) (It. name *Tiziano Vecellio*) 1490?–1576; Venetian painter

ti·tian (tish′ən) *n.* [from the color of the hair in many of *Titian's* portraits] reddish yellow; auburn

Ti·ti·ca·ca (tit′ē kä′kə; *Sp.* tē′tē kä′kä) Lake largest lake of S. America, on the border of SE Peru & W Bolivia: c.3,500 sq. mi.; altitude, 12,500 ft.

tit·il·late (tit′'l āt′) *vt.* **-lat′ed, -lat′ing** [< L. *titillatus,* pp. of *titillare,* to tickle] 1. *same as* TICKLE 2. to excite or stimulate pleasurably —**tit′il·lat′er** *n.* —**tit′il·la′tion** *n.* —**tit′il·la′tive** *adj.*

tit·i·vate (tit′ə vāt′) *vt., vi.* **-vat′ed, -vat′ing** [earlier *tidivate, tiddivate,* prob. < TIDY, with quasi-Latin suffix] to dress up; spruce up —**tit′i·va′tion** *n.*

tit·lark (tit′lärk′) *n.* [TIT[1] + LARK[1]] *same as* PIPIT

ti·tle (tīt′'l) *n.* [ME. < OFr. < L. *titulus,* inscription, label, title, sign] 1. the name of a book, chapter, poem, essay, picture, statue, piece of music, play, movie, etc. 2. *a) clipped form of* TITLE PAGE *b)* a literary work of a particular title *[150* new *titles* in the publisher's fall catalog*]* 3. a descriptive name or appellation; epithet 4. an appellation given to a person or family as a sign of privilege, distinction, rank, or profession 5. a claim or right 6. *a) Ch. of England,* etc. presentment to a benefice, specif. as a prerequisite to ordination *b) R.C.Ch.* a parish church in Rome having a cardinal for its head 7. *Law a)* the name of a statute or act; also, the heading designating a proceeding

b) a division of a law book, statute, etc., usually larger than a section or article *c)* a right to ownership, esp. of real estate *d)* evidence of such right of ownership *e)* a document stating such a right; deed **8.** in sports and other competition, a championship **9.** *Motion Pictures, TV* words shown on the screen that give credit to someone for work done, translate a segment of foreign dialogue, etc.; subtitle, credit, etc. —*vt.* **-tled, -tling** to give a title to; designate by a specified name, or title; entitle

ti·tled (-'ld) *adj.* having a title, esp. of nobility

title deed a document that establishes title to property

ti·tle·hold·er (tīt''l hōl'dər) *n.* the holder of a title; specif., the winner of a championship, as in some sport

title page the page in the front of a book that gives the title, author, publisher, etc.

title role (or **part** or **character**) the character in a play, movie, etc. whose name is used as or in its title

☆**ti·tlist** (tīt'list) *n.* a titleholder in some sport

tit·mouse (tit'mous') *n., pl.* **-mice'** (-mīs') [altered, after MOUSE < ME. *titemose,* prob. < *tit-,* little + OE. *mase,* titmouse, akin to G. *meise*] any of a family (Paridae) of small passerine birds found throughout the world except in S. America and Australia; ☆esp., the **tufted titmouse** (*Baeolophus bicolor*), with ashy-gray feathers and a prominent crest on the head, common in the E U.S.

Ti·to (tē'tō), Marshal (born *Josip Broz*) 1892– ; Yugoslav Communist party leader; prime minister (1945–53) & president (1953–) of Yugoslavia

Ti·to·grad (tē'tō grad', -gräd') city in S Yugoslavia; capital of Montenegro: pop. 31,000

Ti·to·ism (-iz'm) *n.* **1.** the policies and practices of Yugoslavia under Marshal Tito **2.** the practice of nationalistic socialism, as by Yugoslavia, independently of other socialist states and specif. of the U.S.S.R. —**Ti'to·ist** *adj., n.*

ti·trate (tī'trāt) *vt., vi.* **-trat·ed, -trat·ing** [< Fr. *titrer* < *titre* (see TITER) + -ATE[1]] to test by or be subjected to titration

ti·tra·tion (tī trā'shən) *n.* [< prec. + -ION] *Chem., Physiol.* the process of finding out how much of a certain substance is contained in a known volume of a solution by measuring volumetrically how much of a standard solution is required to produce a given reaction

ti·tre (tīt'ər, tēt'-) *n. Brit. sp. of* TITER

tit-tat-toe (tit'tat tō') *n. same as* TICK-TACK-TOE

tit·ter (tit'ər) *vi.* [of Gmc. echoic origin] to laugh in a half-suppressed way, suggestive of silliness, nervousness, etc.; giggle —*n.* the act or an instance of tittering —*SYN.* see LAUGH —**tit'ter·er** *n.*

tit·tie (tit'ē) *n.* [Scot.] a sister: also sp. **tit'ty**

tit·ti·vate (tit'ə vāt') *vt., vi.* **-vat·ed, -vat·ing** *var. of* TITIVATE

tit·tle (tit''l) *n.* [ME. *title,* orig. same word as TITLE] **1.** formerly, a dot or other small mark used as a diacritic **2.** a very small particle; iota; jot

tit·tle-tat·tle (tit''l tat''l) *n., vi.* **-tled, -tling** [redupl. of TATTLE] gossip; chatter

tit·tup (tit'əp) *n.* [prob. echoic of hoofbeats] a lively movement; frolicsome behavior; frisk; caper —*vi.* **-tuped** or **-tupped, -tup·ing** or **-tup·ping** to move in a frolicsome or prancing way; caper

tit·ty (tit'ē) *n., pl.* **-ties** a teat or breast: now vulgar

tit·u·ba·tion (tich'oo bā'shən) *n.* [L. *titubatio,* a staggering < *titubare,* to totter] a stumbling or staggering gait characteristic of certain nervous disorders

tit·u·lar (tich'ə lər; *chiefly Brit.,* tit'yə-) *adj.* [L. *titulus* (see TITLE) + -AR] **1.** of, or having the nature of, a title **2.** having a title **3.** existing only in title; in name only; nominal [a *titular* sovereign] **4.** from whom or which the title or name is taken **5.** designating a bishop holding the title of a defunct see —*n.* a person who holds a title, esp. without any obligations of office —**tit'u·lar·ly** *adv.*

Ti·tus (tīt'əs) [L. < Gr. *Titos*] **1.** a masculine name **2.** (L. name *Titus Flavius Sabinus Vespasianus*) 39?–81 A.D.; Rom. general & emperor (79–81): son of VESPASIAN **3.** *Bible* a book of the New Testament, which was an Epistle of the Apostle Paul to his disciple Titus

Ti·u (tē'ōō) [OE. *Tiw,* akin to OHG. *Ziu* < IE. **deiwos,* god (< base **dei-,* to shine, gleam): cf. JOVE, ZEUS, DEITY] *Ger. Myth.* a god of war and of the sky

Tiv·o·li (tiv'ə lē) **1.** (*It.* tē'vō lē') city in C Italy, near Rome: pop. 33,000 **2.** famous recreational & cultural garden center in Copenhagen, Denmark

tiz·zy (tiz'ē) *n., pl.* **-zies** [< ?] [Colloq.] a state of frenzied excitement, esp. over some trivial matter

tk. truck

TKO, T.K.O. *Boxing abbrev. of* TECHNICAL KNOCKOUT

tkt. ticket

Tl *Chem.* thallium

T.L. 1. total loss **2.** trade-last **3.** trade list **4.** truck load

Tlax·ca·la (tläs kä'lä) state of C Mexico: 1,555 sq. mi.; pop. 431,000

TLC, T.L.C., t.l.c. tender, loving care

Tlem·cen (tlem sen') city in NW Algeria: pop. 83,000

Tlin·git (tlin'git) *n.* [< AmInd. (Tlingit) name, lit. people] **1.** *pl.* **Tlin'gits, Tlin'git** a member of a tribe of seafaring American Indians of the coastal areas of S Alaska and N British Columbia **2.** their isolated language, the unique member of a family

Tm *Chem.* thulium

☆**T-man** (tē'man') *n., pl.* **T'-men'** (-men') [< T(*reasury*)-*man*] [Colloq.] a law-enforcement agent of the U.S. Department of the Treasury

tme·sis (tə mē'sis, mē'sis) *n.* [LL. < Gr. *tmēsis,* a cutting < *temnein,* to cut: see -TOMY] *Rhetoric, Prosody* separation of the parts of a compound word by an intervening word or words (Ex.: *what person soever* for *whatsoever person*)

tn. 1. ton(s) **2.** train

tng. training

TNT, T.N.T. trinitrotoluene

T number *Photog.* a measure of the relative aperture of a lens set to take correct account of the lens transmittance

to (tōō; *unstressed* too, tə) *prep.* [ME. < OE., akin to G. *zu* < IE. **-dō-,* up towards, whence L. (*quan*)*do,* when, then, *do*(*nec*), until] **1.** *a)* in the direction of; toward [turn to the left, traveling to Pittsburgh] *b)* in the direction of and reaching; as far as [he went to Boston, it dropped to the ground] **2.** as far as [wet to the skin, a fight to the death] **3.** *a)* toward or into a condition of [to grow to manhood, a rise to fame] *b)* so as to result in [sentenced to ten years in prison] **4.** on, onto, against, at, next, etc.: used to indicate nearness or contact [to apply lotion to the skin, a house to the right] **5.** *a)* until [no parking from four to six] *b)* before [the time is ten to six] **6.** for the purpose of; for [come to dinner] **7.** *a)* as concerns; in respect of; involving [that's all there is to it, open to attack] *b)* in the opinion of [it seems good to me] **8.** producing, causing, or resulting in [to his amazement, torn to pieces] **9.** with; along with; accompanied by; as an accompaniment for [add this to the others, dance to the music] **10.** being the proper appurtenance, possession, or attribute of; of [the key to the house] **11.** as compared with; as against [a score of 7 to 0, superior to the others] **12.** *a)* in agreement, correspondence, or conformity with [not to one's taste] *b)* as a reaction or in response to [the dog came to his whistle] **13.** comprising; constituting; in or for each [four quarts to a gallon] **14.** to the limit of [moderate to high in price] **15.** with (a specified person or thing) as the recipient, or indirect object, of the action [listen to him, give the book to her] **16.** in honor of [a toast to your success] **17.** [Colloq.] with [a field planted to corn] **18.** [Dial.] at or in (a specified place) [he's to home] *To* is also used before a verb as a sign of the infinitive (Ex.: it was easy to read, to live is sweet) or, elliptically, to denote the infinitive (Ex.: tell him if you want to) —*adv.* **1.** forward [his hat is on wrong side to] **2.** in the normal or desired direction, position, or condition; esp., shut or closed [the door was blown to] **3.** to the matter at hand [they took off their coats and fell to] **4.** at hand [we were close to when it happened] **5.** *Naut.* close to the wind: said of a sailing vessel *To* is used in many idiomatic phrases entered in this dictionary under their key words (e.g., *bring to, come to, go to*) —**to and fro** first in one direction and then in the opposite; back and forth

to- (tə, tōō) [ME. < OE., akin to G. *zer-,* L. *dis-:* see DIS-] *an obsolete prefix, formerly used as an intensive with verbs, meaning* to pieces, asunder, as in **to-broken,** broken to pieces

t.o. turn over

toad (tōd) *n.* [ME. *tode* < OE. *tade,* earlier *tadige* (cf. TADPOLE); there are no known cognates in other languages] **1.** any of a group of tailless, leaping amphibians (esp. family Bufonidae), with a rough, warty skin, that eat insects and live on moist land rather than in water, except during the breeding season **2.** a person regarded as loathsome, contemptible, etc.

TOAD (1/2 to 9 in. long)

toad·eat·er (-ēt'ər) *n. same as* TOADY

toad·fish (fish') *n., pl.* **-fish'**, **-fish'es:** see FISH[2] any of a family (Batrachoididae) of scaleless fishes with a broad, froglike head, found in shallows off the Atlantic coast of N. America

toad·flax (-flaks') *n.* [from the spotted and flaxlike appearance of the plant] *same as* BUTTER-AND-EGGS

toad spit (or **spittle**) *same as* CUCKOO SPIT (sense 1)

toad·stone (-stōn') *n.* [TOAD + STONE, after L. or Gr. *batrachitēs* or MFr. *crapaudine*] any stone or similar object formerly thought to have been formed inside a toad's head or body and often worn as a charm

toad·stool (-stōōl') *n.* [ME. *todestole:* see TOAD & STOOL] any of a number of fleshy, umbrella-shaped, basidiomycetous fungi; mushroom; esp., in popular usage, any poisonous mushroom

toad·y (tōd'ē) *n., pl.* **toad'ies** [short for TOADEATER, quack doctor's assistant who pretended to eat toads (thought to be poisonous) to show the efficacy of quack medicines] a servile flatterer; sycophant, esp. one who does distasteful or unprincipled things in order to gain favor —*vt., vi.* **toad'ied, toad'y·ing** to be a toady (to); flatter —*SYN.* see PARASITE —**toad'y·ism** *n.*

to-and-fro (tōō′ən frō′) *adj.* [ME.] moving forward and backward; back-and-forth

toast[1] (tōst) *vt.* [ME. *tosten* < OFr. *toster* < VL. *tostare* < L. *tostus*, pp. of *torrere*, to parch, roast: see THIRST] 1. to brown the surface of (bread, cheese, etc.) by heating in a toaster, over or near a fire, or in an oven 2. to warm thoroughly [*toasting* themselves by the campfire] —*vi.* to become toasted —*n.* sliced bread made brown and crisp by heat

toast[2] (tōst) *n.* [from the use of toasted spiced bread to flavor the wine, and the notion that the person honored also added flavor] 1. a person, thing, idea, etc. in honor of which a person or persons raise their glasses and drink 2. *a*) a proposal to drink to such a person, etc., or a sentiment expressed just before so drinking *b*) such a drink 3. any person greatly admired or acclaimed —*vt., vi.* to propose or drink a toast (to)

toast·er[1] (tōs′tər) *n.* any of various utensils or appliances for toasting bread

toast·er[2] (tōs′tər) *n.* a person who proposes or drinks a toast

toast·mas·ter (tōst′mas′tər, -mäs′-) *n.* the person at a banquet who proposes toasts, introduces after-dinner speakers, etc. —**toast′mis′tress** (-mis′trəs) *n.fem.*

toast·y (tōs′tē) *adj.* **toast′i·er, toast′i·est** 1. of or characteristic of toast 2. warm and comfortable or cozy

Tob. Tobit

to·bac·co (tə bak′ō) *n., pl.* **-cos** [Sp. *tobaco* < WInd. (Taino), pipe or tube in which the Indians smoked the plant: name transferred by the Spaniards to the plant itself] 1. any of a genus (*Nicotiana*) of chiefly tropical American plants of the nightshade family, with hairy, sticky foliage and long-tubed, white, yellow, greenish, or purple flowers; esp., the species (*Nicotiana tabacum*) now widely cultivated for its leaves 2. the leaves of certain of these plants, prepared for smoking, chewing, or snuffing 3. products prepared from these leaves; cigars, cigarettes, snuff, etc. 4. the use of tobacco for smoking, etc.

to·bac·co·nist (tə bak′ə nist) *n.* [TOBACCO + -*n*- + -IST: orig. applied to a user of tobacco] [Chiefly Brit.] a dealer in tobacco and other smoking supplies

☆**tobacco worm moth** a hawkmoth (*Protoparce sexta*) whose large, green caterpillar (**tobacco hornworm**) feeds on the leaves of tobacco plants

TOBACCO PLANT (3–6 ft. high)

To·ba·go (tō bā′gō, tə-) island in the West Indies, northeast of Trinidad: 116 sq. mi.; pop. 33,000: see TRINIDAD

To·bey (tō′bē), **Mark** 1890– ; U.S. painter

To·bi·ah (tō bī′ə, tə-) [Heb. *tōbhīyāh*, lit., the lord is good] a masculine name: dim. *Toby*

To·bi·as (-əs) [LL.(Ec.) *Tobias* < Gr.(Ec.) *Tobias* < Heb. *tōbhīyāh*: see prec.] 1. a masculine name: dim. *Toby* 2. *Douay Bible* name for TOBIT

To·bit (tō′bit) a book of the Apocrypha

to·bog·gan (tə bäg′ən) *n.* [CanadFr. *tabagan* < AmInd. (Algonquian) name] a long, narrow, flat sled without runners, made of thin boards curved back at the front end and often having side rails: now used for the sport of coasting down a prepared slope or chute —*vi.* 1. to coast, travel, etc. on a toboggan 2. to decline rapidly [*prices tobogganed*] —**to·bog′gan·er, to·bog′gan·ist** *n.*

To·bol (tō bōl′y′) river in W Siberia, flowing from the S Urals into the Irtysh: 1,042 mi.

To·by (tō′bē) *n., pl.* **-bies** [< *Toby*, dim. of TOBIAS] a jug or mug for ale or beer shaped like a stout man with a three-cornered hat: also **Toby jug**

TOBOGGAN

To·can·tins (tō′kän tēns′) river flowing from C Brazil north into the Pará River: c.1,700 mi.

toc·ca·ta (tə kät′ə) *n.* [It., orig. fem. of pp. of *toccare* < VL., to TOUCH] a composition in free style for the organ, piano, etc., generally characterized by the use of full chords and running passages and often used as the prelude of a fugue: it was originally designed to display the technique of the performer

To·char·i·an (tō ker′ē ən, -kar′-, -kär′-) *n.* [< *Tochri*, word used to designate the language in certain accompanying (Uigur) writings; identified with Gr. *Tocharoi*, Oriental people mentioned by STRABO] 1. any member of a people living in C Asia until about 1000 A.D. 2. their extinct Indo-European language, comprising two major dialects: the earliest record known is from the 7th cent. A.D. —*adj.* of the Tocharians or their language

to·col·o·gy (tō käl′ə jē) *n.* [< Gr. *tokos*, childbirth < *tiktein*, to bear (for IE. base see THANE) + -LOGY] same as OBSTETRICS —**to·col′o·gist** *n.*

to·coph·er·ol (tō käf′ə rōl′, -rōl′) *n.* [< Gr. *tokos* (see prec.) + *pherein*, to BEAR + -OL[1]] any of a group of four closely related viscous oils that constitute vitamin E and occur chiefly in wheat-germ oil, cottonseed oil, lettuce, etc.

Tocque·ville (tōk vēl′; E. tōk′vil), **A·lex·is** (**Charles Henri**

Maurice Clérel) **de** (à lek sē′ də) 1805–59; Fr. author & statesman

toc·sin (täk′sin) *n.* [Fr. < MFr. *touquesain* < Pr. *tocasenh* < *toc*, a stroke < *tocar* (< VL. *toccare*, to TOUCH) + *senh*, a bell < LL. *signum*, a signal, bell < L., a SIGN] 1. *a*) an alarm bell *b*) its sound 2. any alarm, or sound of warning

tod[1] (täd) *n.* [ME. *todde*, prob. < LowG. source, as in EFris. *todde*, *tod*, a bundle, pack, load, akin to G. *zotte*, tuft of hair < IE. **det-* < base **dā(i)-*, to divide, whence TEASE] 1. a former English weight for wool, about 28 pounds 2. a bushy clump of ivy, etc.

tod[2] (täd) *n.* [ME. < ?] [Scot.] a fox

to·day (tə dā′) *adv.* [ME. *to dai* < OE. *to dæg*: see TO & DAY] 1. on or during the present day 2. in the present time or age; nowadays —*n.* 1. the present day 2. the present time or period Also, esp. formerly, **to-day**

tod·dle (täd′l) *vi.* **-dled, -dling** [? freq. of TOTTER, via N dial. *doddle* (cf. DODDER[1])] to walk with short, uncertain steps, as in very early childhood —*n.* the act of toddling or a toddling movement —**tod′dler** *n.*

tod·dy (täd′ē) *n., pl.* **-dies** [Anglo-Ind. < Hindi *tārī*, fermented sap of palmyra tree < *tār*, palm tree < Sans. *tāla*, palmyra] 1. *a*) the sweet sap of various East Indian palms, used as a beverage *b*) an intoxicating liquor made by fermenting this sap 2. a drink of brandy, whiskey, etc. mixed with hot water, sugar, and, usually, spices: also **hot toddy**

toddy palm any of several palms (esp. genera *Arenga*, *Borassus*, *Phoenix*, and *Cocos*) yielding toddy

to-do (tə dōō′) *n.* [Colloq.] a commotion; stir; fuss

to·dy (tō′dē) *n., pl.* **-dies** [Fr. *todier* < L. *todus*, small bird] any of several small, insect-eating birds (genus *Todus*) of the West Indies, related to the kingfisher; esp., the **green tody** (*Todus viridis*) of Jamaica, with green upper parts, a red throat, and a yellow belly

toe (tō) *n.* [ME. < OE. *ta*, earlier *tahe*, akin to G. *zehe* < IE. base **deik-*, to show, whence L. *dicere*, to say; *digitus* (cf. DIGIT), TEACH, TOKEN] 1. *a*) any of the five digits of the human foot *b*) the forepart of the human foot *c*) that part of a shoe, sock, etc. which covers the toes 2. any of the digits of an animal's foot, or the forepart of a hoof, etc. 3. anything suggesting a toe in location, shape, or function; specif., *a*) a pivot or journal extending vertically in a bearing *b*) a projecting arm raised or moved by a cam —*vt.* **toed, toe′ing** 1. to provide with a toe or toes 2. to touch, follow, or kick with the toes [to *toe* a starting line] 3. *a*) to drive (a nail) slantingly *b*) to clinch or fasten with nails driven slantingly; toenail —*vi.* ☆to stand, walk, or be formed so that the toes are in a specified position [to *toe* in or *toe* out] —**on one's toes** [Colloq.] mentally or physically alert —**step** (or **tread**) **on someone's toes** to offend someone, esp. by trespassing or intruding on his prerogative or rights —**toe the line** (or **mark**) 1. to stand or crouch with the toes touching the starting line of a race, etc. 2. to follow orders, rules, doctrines, etc. strictly

toe·cap (tō′kap′) *n.* that part of a shoe or boot which covers the toes

toe crack a lesion (*quarter*, or *sand*, *crack*) in the front part of a horse's hoof

toed (tōd) *adj.* 1. having (a specified kind or number of) toes: usually in hyphenated compounds [*three-toed*] 2. *a*) driven slantingly: said of a nail *b*) fastened by nails driven slantingly

toe dance a dance performed on the tips of the toes, as in ballet —**toe′-dance′** *vi.* **-danced′, -danc′ing** —**toe′-danc′er** *n.*

toe·hold (-hōld′) *n.* 1. a small space or ledge for supporting the toe of the foot in climbing, etc. 2. any means of surmounting obstacles, gaining entry, etc. 3. a slight footing or advantage 4. *Wrestling* a hold in which one wrestler twists the other's foot

toe-in (tō′in′) *n.* an adjustment of the front wheels of an automobile or other motor vehicle so that they are not perfectly parallel but tend to converge slightly toward the front

toe·less (-lis) *adj.* 1. having no toe or toes 2. having the toe open or uncovered [a *toeless* shoe]

toe·nail (-nāl′) *n.* 1. the nail of a toe 2. *Carpentry* a nail driven slantingly, as through the side of a vertical plank to fasten it to the horizontal plank on which it is based —*vt. Carpentry* to fasten with a toenail

toff (täf, tôf) *n.* [< *toft*, var. of TUFT, slang term for "titled undergraduate," in reference to gold tassel on the caps of aristocratic students] [Brit. Slang] a fashionable, upper-class person; esp., a dandy

tof·fee, tof·fy (tôf′ē, täf′-) *n.* [later Brit. form of TAFFY] a hard, chewy candy made with brown sugar or molasses, often coated with nuts; kind of taffy

toft (tôft, täft) *n.* [ME. < Late OE. < ON. *topt*, a homestead, ground marked out for building, knoll: for IE. base see TIMBER] 1. [Brit.] *a*) orig., a house site or homestead *b*) a homestead with its arable land 2. [Brit. Dial.] a knoll; hillock

tog (täg, tôg) *n.* [prob. < cant *togeman*(s), *togman*, a cloak, coat, ult. < L. *toga*, toga] 1. [Old Slang] a coat 2. [*pl.*] [Colloq.] clothes; outfit [tennis *togs*] —*vt., vi.* **togged, tog′ging** [Colloq.] to put clothes on; dress (usually with *up* or *out*)

to·ga (tō′gə) *n., pl.* **-gas, -gae** (-jē) [L. < *tegere*, to cover: see THATCH] **1.** in ancient Rome, a loose, one-piece outer garment worn in public by citizens **2.** a robe of office; characteristic gown of a profession

to·gaed (tō′gəd) *adj.* wearing a toga

‡**to·ga vi·ri·lis** (vī rī′lis) [L., lit., toga of a man] the toga of manhood, put on by boys of ancient Rome in their fourteenth year

ROMAN TOGA

to·geth·er (tə geth′ər) *adv.* [ME. *togeder* < OE. *togædre, togadere < to* (see TO) + *gædre*, together < base of *gaderian* (see GATHER)] **1.** in or into one gathering, group, mass, or place [a reunion to bring the family *together*] **2.** in or into contact, collision, union, etc. with each other [the cars skidded *together*] **3.** considered collectively; added up [winning more than all the others *together*] **4.** *a*) with one another; in association or companionship [to spend a week *together*] *b*) by joint effort [*together* they were able to lift the sofa] **5.** at the same time; simultaneously [shots fired *together*] **6.** in succession; continuously [sulking for three whole days *together*] **7.** in or into agreement, cooperation, etc. [to get *together* on a deal] **8.** in or into a unified whole *Together* is also used colloquially as an intensive, as after *add, join,* etc. —☆*adj.* [Slang] having fully developed one's abilities, ambitions, etc.; having an integrated personality

to·geth·er·ness (-nis) *n.* the spending of much time together, as in social and leisure-time activities by the members of a family, esp. when regarded as resulting in a more unified, stable relationship

tog·ger·y (täg′ər ē, tôg′-) *n.* [< TOG + -ERY] [Colloq.] clothes; togs

tog·gle (täg′'l) *n.* [prob. naut. var. of dial. *tuggle*, freq. of TUG] **1.** a rod, pin, or bolt for insertion between the strands or through a loop of a rope, through a link of a chain, etc. to make an attachment, prevent slipping, or tighten by twisting **2.** a toggle joint or a device having one —*vt.* **-gled, -gling** to provide or fasten with a toggle or toggles

toggle joint a knee-shaped joint consisting of two bars pivoted together at one end: when pressure is put on the joint to straighten it, opposite, outward pressures are transmitted to the open ends

toggle switch a switch consisting of a projecting lever moved back or forth through a small arc to open or close an electric circuit

To·go (tō′gō) country in W Africa, on the Gulf of Guinea, east of Ghana: 21,853 sq. mi.; pop. 1,857,000; cap. Lomé —**To′go·lese′** (-lēz′) *adj., n. sing. & pl.*

TOGGLE JOINT (arrows indicate direction of pressure)

To·go·land (tō′gō land′) a former German territory in W Africa, now partly Togo and partly in Ghana

toil[1] (toil) *vi.* [ME. *toilen* < Anglo-Fr. *toiler*, to strive, dispute < OFr. *toeillier*, to pull about, begrime < L. *tudiculare*, to stir about < *tudicula*, small machine for bruising olives < *tudes*, mallet < base of *tundere*, to beat < IE. base *(s)teu-*, whence STOCK, STUB] **1.** to work hard and continuously; labor untiringly **2.** to proceed laboriously; advance or move with painful effort or difficulty [to *toil* up a mountain] —*vt.* [Now Rare] to make or accomplish with great effort —*n.* [ME. *toile* < Anglo-Fr. *toil* < OFr. *toeil*, turmoil, struggle < the *v.*] **1.** orig., contention; struggle; strife **2.** hard, exhausting work or effort; tiring labor **3.** a task performed by such effort —SYN. see WORK —**toil′er** *n.*

toil[2] (toil) *n.* [OFr. *toile*, a net, web, cloth < L. *tela*, a web, woven material < base of *texere*: see TEXT] **1.** [Archaic] a net for trapping **2.** [*pl.*] any snare suggestive of a net

toile (twäl) *n.* [Fr.: see prec.] any of various linen or sheer cotton fabrics

toi·let (toi′lit) *n.* [MFr. *toilette*, orig., cloth covering used in shaving or hairdressing < *toile*, cloth: see TOIL[2]] **1.** formerly, a dressing table **2.** the process of dressing or grooming oneself, esp., formerly, of dressing one's hair **3.** toilette; dress; attire; costume ☆**4.** *a*) a room, shelter, etc. for defecation or urination; specif., a small room with a bowl-shaped fixture for this purpose, fitted with a device for flushing with water *b*) such a fixture **5.** the cleaning and dressing of a wound, esp. in surgery —*adj.* **1.** of or for dressing or grooming oneself [*toilet* articles] ☆**2.** for a toilet (*n.* 4 *b*) [a *toilet* brush] —**make one's toilet** [Now Rare] to bathe and dress, arrange one's hair, etc.

toilet paper (or **tissue**) soft, absorbent paper, usually in a roll, for use in cleaning oneself after evacuation

toi·let·ry (toi′lə trē) *n., pl.* **-ries** soap, lotion, cologne, etc. used in cleaning and grooming oneself

toi·lette (twä let′, toi-) *n.* [Fr.: see TOILET] **1.** the process, esp. by a woman, of grooming and dressing oneself **2.** dress or manner of dress; attire; costume

toilet training the training of a young child to control defecation and urination

toilet water a perfumed, slightly alcoholic liquid applied to the skin after bathing, etc. or added to bath water

toil·ful (toil′fəl) *adj.* full of toil; laborious

toil·some (-səm) *adj.* [see -SOME[1]] requiring or involving toil; laborious —**toil′some·ly** *adv.* —**toil′some·ness** *n.*

toil·worn (-wôrn′) *adj.* worn by or showing the effects of toil

To·kay (tō kā′) *n.* **1.** a sweet, rich wine made in the vicinity of Tokay, a town in NE Hungary **2.** any wine like this **3.** a large, sweet grape used for the wine

toke (tōk) *n.* [? < ff.] ☆[Slang] a puff on a cigarette, esp. one of marijuana or hashish —☆*vt.* **toked, tok′ing** [Slang] to take a puff on (such a cigarette)

to·ken (tō′k'n) *n.* [ME. < OE. *tacn*, akin to G. *zeichen* < IE. base *deik-*, to point, show: cf. TOE, DIGIT, DICTION] **1.** a sign, indication, or symbol [a *token* of one's affection] **2.** something serving as a sign of authority, identity, genuineness, etc. **3.** a distinguishing mark or feature **4.** a keepsake **5.** a piece of stamped metal, etc. with a face value higher than its real value, issued for use as fare on a transportation line, etc. —*vt.* **1.** to be a token of; betoken or symbolize —*adj.* **1.** by way of a token, symbol, indication, etc. [a *token* gesture] **2.** merely simulated; slight or of no real account [*token* resistance] —SYN. see PLEDGE, SIGN —**by the same** (or **this**) **token** following from this —**in token of** as evidence of

to·ken·ism (-iz'm) *n.* a show of accommodation to a demand, principle, etc. by small, often merely formal concessions to it; specif., ☆token integration of Negroes, as in schools, jobs, etc.

token payment a partial payment made as a token of intention to pay the remainder of the debt later

To·khar·i·an (tō ker′ē ən, -kar′-, -kär′-) *n., adj. var. of* TOCHARIAN: also **To·khar′ic** (-ik)

To·ku·shi·ma (tō′koo shē′mä) seaport in E Shikoku, Japan, on the Inland Sea: pop. 183,000

To·kyo (tō′kē ō′; *Jap.* tō′kyō′) capital of Japan; seaport on an inlet (**Tokyo Bay**) of the Pacific, on S Honshu: pop. 8,991,000 (met. area 11,027,000) —**To′kyo·ite′** (-īt′) *n.*

to·la (tō′lä) *n.* [Hindi < Sans. *tulā*, a balance] in India, a unit of weight equal to 180 grains (the weight of one silver rupee)

to·lan (tō′lan) *n.* [TOL(UENE) + -AN(E)] a colorless, crystalline hydrocarbon, C₁₄H₁₀, used chiefly in organic synthesis

tol·booth (tōl′booth′) *n.* [ME. *tolbothe*, booth where toll is collected: see TOLL[1] & BOOTH] [Scot.] a jail or prison

☆**tol·bu·ta·mide** (täl byoot′ə mīd′) *n.* [TOL(U) + BUT(YRIC) + AMIDE] an oral antidiabetic drug, C₁₂H₁₈N₂O₃S, that releases insulin from the pancreas

told (tōld) *pt. & pp. of* TELL[1] —**all told** all (being) counted; in all [there were forty *all told*]

tole[1] (tōl) *vt.* **toled, tol′ing** [var. of TOLL[2]] [Archaic or Dial.] to allure; entice

tole[2] (tōl) *n.* [Fr. *tôle*, sheet iron, plate: dial. var. of *table*: see TABLE] a type of lacquered or enameled metalware popular in the 18th cent. and reproduced today for trays, lamps, etc.: it is commonly dark-green, ivory, or black

To·le·do (tə lē′dō; *also, for 2, Sp.* tō lā′thō) **1.** [after ff.] city & port in NW Ohio, on Lake Erie: pop. 384,000 (met. area 693,000) **2.** city in C Spain, on the Tagus River: pop. 38,000 —*n., pl.* **-dos** a fine-tempered sword or sword blade made in Toledo, Spain

tol·er·a·ble (täl′ər ə b'l) *adj.* [ME. *tollerabill* < MFr. *tolérable* < L. *tolerabilis*] **1.** that can be tolerated; endurable; bearable **2.** fairly good; passable **3.** [Colloq.] in reasonably good health —**tol′er·a·bil′i·ty, tol′er·a·ble·ness** *n.* —**tol′er·a·bly** *adv.*

tol·er·ance (-əns) *n.* [ME. *tolleraunce* < MFr. *tolerance* < L. *tolerantia*] **1.** *a*) a tolerating or being tolerant, esp. of views, beliefs, practices, etc. of others that differ from one's own *b*) freedom from bigotry or prejudice **2.** the amount of variation allowed from a standard, accuracy, etc.; specif., *a*) the amount that coins are legally allowed to vary from a standard of weight, fineness, etc. *b*) the difference between the allowable maximum and minimum sizes of some mechanical part, as a basis for determining the accuracy of a fitting **3.** [Rare] an enduring or the ability to endure **4.** *Med.* the natural or developed ability to endure, or resist the harmful effects of, the continued or increasing use of a drug, etc.

tol·er·ant (-ənt) *adj.* [L. *tolerans*, prp.] **1.** having or showing tolerance of others' beliefs, practices, etc. **2.** *Med.* of or having tolerance —**tol′er·ant·ly** *adv.*

tol·er·ate (täl′ə rāt′) *vt.* **-at′ed, -at′ing** [< L. *toleratus*, pp. of *tolerare*, to bear, sustain, tolerate < IE. base *tel-*, to lift up, bear, whence L. *tollere*, to lift up & THOLE[2]] **1.** to not interfere with; allow; permit [to *tolerate* heresy] **2.** to recognize and respect (others' beliefs, practices, etc.) without sharing them **3.** to bear, or put up with (someone or something not especially liked) **4.** *Med.* to have tolerance for (a specific drug, etc.) —SYN. see BEAR[1] —**tol′er·a′tive** *adj.* —**tol′er·a′tor** *n.*

tol·er·a·tion (täl'ə rā'shən) *n.* [Fr. *tolération* < L. *toleratio*] **1.** the act or an instance of tolerating **2.** tolerance; esp., freedom to hold religious views that differ from the established ones

tol·i·dine (täl'ə dēn', -din) *n.* [TOL(UOL) + (BENZ)IDINE] any of a group of isomeric dimethyl derivatives of benzidine, $C_{14}H_{16}N_2$, used in the manufacture of dyes and in the detection of gold and chlorine

To·li·ma (tō lē'mä) volcanic mountain of the Andes, in WC Colombia: 16,207 ft.

Tol·ki·en (tōl'kē ən), **J(ohn) R(onald) R(euel)** 1892– ; Eng. novelist, scholar, & linguist

toll[1] (tōl) *n.* [ME. < OE., akin to G. *zoll*, ON. *tollr* < early borrowing < VL. **toloneum*, toll(house), for L. *teloneum* < Gr. *telōnion* < *telōnēs*, tax collector < *telos*, tax, akin to *tlēnai*, to support, bear: for IE. base see TOLERATE] **1.** a tax or charge for a privilege, esp. for permission to pass over a bridge, along a highway, etc. **2.** the right to demand toll **3.** a charge for service or extra service, as for transportation, for a long-distance telephone call, or, formerly, for milling one's grain **4.** the number lost, taken, exacted, etc.; exaction [the tornado took a heavy *toll* of lives] —*vi.* [Now Rare] to collect toll —*vt.* [Now Rare] **1.** to take a part of as toll **2.** to impose a toll on **3.** to gather (something) as toll

toll[2] (tōl) *vt.* [ME. *tollen*, to pull, altered < ? OE. *-tillan*, to touch] **1.** [Dial. or Rare] to allure or entice; esp., to decoy (game, etc.) **2.** *a*) to ring (a church bell, etc.) slowly with regularly repeated strokes, esp. for announcing a death *b*) to sound (the hour, a knell, etc.) by this *c*) to announce, summon, or dismiss by this *d*) to announce the death of (someone) in this way —*vi.* to sound or ring slowly in regularly repeated strokes: said of a bell —*n.* **1.** the act or sound of tolling a bell **2.** a single stroke of the bell —**toll'er** *n.*

toll·age (tōl'ij) *n.* [see -AGE] **1.** toll, or tax **2.** payment or demand of toll

toll bar a bar, gate, etc. for stopping travel at a point where toll is taken

toll·booth (-bōōth') *n.* **1.** [Scot.] *var. of* TOLBOOTH ☆**2.** a booth at which toll is collected, as before entering a toll road

toll bridge a bridge at which toll is paid for passage

toll call a long-distance telephone call, for which there is a charge beyond the local rate

Tol·ler (tō'lər), **Ernst** (ernst) 1893–1939; Ger. playwright

toll·gate (tōl'gāt') *n.* a gate for stopping travel at a point where toll is taken

toll·house (-hous') *n.* **1.** a house at a tollgate, in which the tollkeeper lives **2.** a booth, etc. where toll is taken

☆**tollhouse cookie** [made according to a recipe used at the *Toll House* in Whitman, Mass., suburb of Brockton] a kind of cookie containing bits of solid chocolate and, often, nuts

toll·keep·er (-kēp'ər) *n.* a person who collects tolls at a tollgate

toll road a road for travel on which toll must be paid

Tol·stoy (tōl stoi'; E. täl'stoi, tōl'-), Count **Lev** (E. **Leo**) **Ni·ko·la·ye·vich** (lyev nē'kô lä'ye vich) 1828–1910; Russ. novelist & social theorist: also sp. **Tolstoi**

Tol·tec (täl'tek, tōl'-) *n.* [Nahuatl *Tolteca*] any member of an ancient group of Nahuatl Indians who lived in Mexico before the Aztecs: their culture shows Mayan influence —*adj.* of the Toltecs or their culture: also **Tol'tec·an**

tol·u·ate (täl'yoo wāt') *n.* a salt or ester of toluic acid

to·lu (balsam) (tō lōō') [Sp. *tolú* < *Tolú*, Caribbean seaport in Colombia] *same as* BALSAM OF TOLU

To·lu·ca (tō lōō'kä; E. tä lōō'kə) **1.** city in S Mexico; capital of Mexico state (see MEXICO, sense 2): pop. 77,000 **2.** volcanic mountain near this city: 15,020 ft.

tol·u·ene (täl'yoo wēn') *n.* [TOLU + (BENZ)ENE] a colorless, liquid, flammable, poisonous hydrocarbon, C_7H_8, obtained originally from balsam of Tolu but now generally from coal tar or petroleum, and used in making dyes, explosives, etc. and as a solvent

to·lu·ic acid (täl'yoo wik, täl'yoo wik) any of four isomeric acids, $C_8H_8O_2$, carboxyl derivatives of toluene, used in the manufacture of various resins, in organic synthesis, etc.

tol·u·ide (täl'yoo wid') *n.* any of a class of chemical compounds having the general formula $RCONHC_6H_4CH_3$, derived from the toluidines by the substitution of an acid radical for one of the amino H atoms: also **to·lu·i·dide** (tə lōō'i did')

to·lu·i·dine (tə lōō'ə dēn', -din) *n.* any of three isomeric amino derivatives, C_7H_9N, of toluene, used in organic synthesis, in dyes, as a test reagent, etc.

toluidine blue a dark green powder, $C_{15}H_{16}N_3SCl \cdot ZnCl_2$, used in dyeing textiles, as a biological stain, as a coagulant in medicine, etc.

tol·u·ol (täl'yoo wôl', -wōl') *n.* [TOLU + -OL[1]] *same as* TOLUENE; esp., crude commercial toluene

tolu tree the tree that yields tolu: see BALSAM OF TOLU

tol·u·yl (täl'yoo wil) *n.* [TOLU(IC ACID) + -YL] the univalent acid radical C_7H_7CO-

tol·yl (täl'il) *n.* [TOL(UIC ACID) + -YL] the univalent radical $CH_3C_6H_4-$, derived from toluene

Tom (täm) *n.* ☆[Colloq.] *same as* UNCLE TOM —☆*vi.* **Tommed**, **Tom'ming** [*also* t-] [Colloq.] to behave like an Uncle Tom

tom (täm) *n.* [< *Tom*, dim. of THOMAS, esp. after TOMCAT, earlier *Tom the Cat* (c.1760): cf. similar use of JACK[1]] the male of some animals, esp. of the cat —*adj.* male [a *tom* turkey] Sometimes used in compounds, occasionally with derived senses, as *tomcod*

☆**tom·a·hawk** (täm'ə hôk') *n.* [of AmInd. (Algonquian) origin] a light ax, typically having a stone or bone head, used by North American Indians as a tool and a weapon —*vt.* to hit, cut, or kill with a tomahawk —**bury the tomahawk** to stop fighting; make peace

tom·al·ley (täm'al'ē) *n.* [< Carib name] the liver of the lobster, which turns green when boiled and is considered a delicacy

Tom and Jerry [from names of two characters in Egan's *Life in London* (1821)] ☆a hot drink made of alcoholic liquor, beaten eggs, sugar, water or milk, and nutmeg

to·ma·to (tə māt'ō, -mät'ō) *n.*, *pl.* -**toes** [Sp. *tomate* < Nahuatl *tomatl*] **1.** a red or yellowish fruit with a juicy pulp, used as a vegetable: botanically it is a berry **2.** the annual plant (*Lycopersicon esculentum*) of the nightshade family, on which this berry grows ☆**3.** [Old Slang] an attractive young woman

☆**tomato worm moth** a hawkmoth (*Protoparce quinquemaculata*) whose large, green caterpillar (**tomato hornworm**) has a series of white stripes along the side of the body and feeds on tomato plants

tomb (tōōm) *n.* [ME. *toumbe* < Anglo-Fr. *tumbe* (OFr. *tombe*) < LL.(Ec.) *tumba* < Gr. *tymbos*, a tomb, funeral mound < IE. base **tu-*, var. of *tēu-*, to swell: cf. THUMB, TUMOR] **1.** a vault, chamber, or grave for the dead **2.** a burial monument or cenotaph —*vt.* [Rare] to entomb —**the tomb** death —**tomb'less** *adj.* —**tomb'like'** *adj.*

tom·bac, tom·bak (täm'bak) *n.* [Fr. *tombac* < Port. *tambaca* < Malay *tĕmbaga*, copper < Sans. *tamṛka*, lit., dark metal] an alloy of copper and zinc, used in making cheap jewelry

Tom·big·bee (täm big'bē) [< Choctaw, coffin maker < *itombi*, box, coffin + *ikbi*, maker: referring to burial boxes used by Choctaws] river flowing from NE Miss. through Ala., joining the Alabama River to form the Mobile River: 409 mi.

tom·bo·la (täm'bə lə) *n.* [It., prob. < *tombolare*, to tumble: akin to Fr. *tomber*, to fall] a British gambling game somewhat like bingo

tom·bo·lo (täm'bə lō') *n.*, *pl.* -**los'** [It. < L. *tumulus*, a mound: cf. TUMULUS] a bar of sand or other sediment tying an island to the mainland or another island

Tom·bouc·tou (tōn bōōk tōō') *Fr. name of* TIMBUKTU

tom·boy (täm'boi') *n.* [see TOM] a girl who behaves like a boisterous boy; hoyden —**tom'boy'ish** *adj.* —**tom'boy'ish·ly** *adv.* —**tom'boy'ish·ness** *n.*

tomb·stone (tōōm'stōn') *n.* a stone or monument, usually with an engraved inscription, marking a tomb or grave

tom·cat (täm'kat') *n.* [see TOM] a male cat —*vi.* -**cat'ted**, -**cat'ting** [Slang] to be sexually promiscuous: said of a man

☆**tom·cod** (-käd') *n.* [see TOM] **1.** a small, codlike saltwater food fish (*Microgadus tomcod*) of the N Atlantic coast **2.** a similar fish (*Microgadus proximus*) of the Pacific coast

Tom Collins *see* COLLINS

Tom, Dick, and Harry everyone; anyone; people taken at random: usually preceded by *every* and used disparagingly

tome (tōm) *n.* [Fr. < L. *tomus* < Gr. *tomos*, piece cut off, hence part of a book, volume < *temnein*, to cut: see -TOMY] **1.** orig., any volume of a work of several volumes **2.** a book, esp. a large, scholarly or ponderous one

-tome (tōm) [Gr. < *tomon* < *tomos*: see prec.] a combining form meaning: **1.** cutting instrument [*microtome*, *osteotome*] **2.** section, division [*dermatome*]

to·men·tose (tō men'tōs, tō'mən tōs') *adj.* [ModL. *tomentosus* < L. *tomentum*: see ff.] *Biol.* covered with a dense layer of short, matted, woolly hairs

to·men·tum (tō men'təm) *n.*, *pl.* -**ta** (-tə) [ModL. < L., a stuffing (of hair, wool, etc.): for IE. base see TUMOR] **1.** a growth of short, matted, woolly hairs, as on the stems or leaves of some plants **2.** a network of very small blood vessels in the pia mater and the cortex of the cerebrum

tom·fool (täm'fōōl') *n.* [earlier *Tom Fool*, as in *Tom o'Bedlam*, *poor Tom*, names formerly applied to the demented and retarded] a foolish, stupid, or silly person —*adj.* foolish, stupid, or silly

tom·fool·er·y (-ər ē) *n.*, *pl.* -**er·ies** [see prec.] foolish behavior; silliness; nonsense

-tom·ic (täm'ik) a combining form used to form adjectives *corresponding* to nouns ending in -TOME

Tom·my (täm'ē) *n.*, *pl.* -**mies** [clipped from *Tommy Atkins* (for *Thomas Atkins*, fictitious name used in Brit. army sample forms)] [*also* t-] *epithet for* a private in the British army

☆**Tommy gun** *alternate trademark for* THOMPSON SUB-MACHINE GUN —*n.* a submachine gun

tom·my·rot (täm'ē rät') *n.* [< the nickname *Tommy*, in dial. sense of "fool" (cf. TOMFOOL) + ROT] [Slang] nonsense; foolishness; rubbish

to·mog·ra·phy (tə mäg'rə fē) *n.* [< Gr. *tomos*, a piece cut off (see -TOMY) + -GRAPHY] a technique of X-ray photography by which a single plane is photographed, with the outline of structures in other planes eliminated

to·mor·row (tə mär'ō, -môr'ō) *adv.* [ME. *to morwe* < *to morwen* < OE. *to morgen*: see TO & MORNING] **1.** on or for the day after today **2.** at some time in the indefinite

future —n. 1. the day after today 2. some time in the indefinite future Also, esp. formerly, **to-morrow**

tom·pi·on (täm'pē ən) n. var. of TAMPION

Tomsk (tômsk) city in SC R.S.F.S.R., near Novosibirsk: pop. 311,000

Tom Thumb 1. a tiny hero of many English folk tales 2. any dwarf, midget, or small person

tom·tit (täm'tit') n. [see TOM] [Chiefly Brit.] a titmouse or any of various other small birds

tom-tom (täm'täm') n. [Hindi tam-tam, of echoic origin] 1. any of various drums, as of Indian or African tribes, usually beaten with the hands 2. same as TAM-TAM

-to·my (tə mē) [ModL. -tomia < Gr. -tomia < tomē, a cutting < temnein, to cut < IE. base *tem-, to cut, whence L. tondere, to shear] a combining form meaning: 1. a dividing [dichotomy] 2. a surgical operation [ovariotomy; lobotomy]

ton¹ (tun) n. [var. (differentiated in 17th c. for senses "weight, measure") of TUN] 1. a unit of weight equal to 2,000 pounds avoirdupois (or 907.20 kilograms), commonly used in the U.S., Canada, South Africa, etc.: in full **short ton** 2. a unit of weight equal to 2,240 pounds avoirdupois (or 1,016.06 kilograms), commonly used in Great Britain: in full **long ton, shipping ton** 3. same as METRIC TON 4. a unit of internal capacity of ships, equal to 100 cubic feet (or 2.8317 cubic meters): in full **register ton** 5. a unit of carrying capacity of ships, usually equal to 40 cubic feet: in full **measurement ton, freight ton** 6. a unit for measuring displacement of ships, equal to 35 cubic feet: it is approximately equal to the volume of a long ton of sea water: in full **displacement ton** ☆7. a unit of cooling capacity of an air conditioner, equal to 12,000 B.t.u. per hour 8. [often pl.] [Colloq.] a very large amount or number Abbrev. **T., t., tn.** (sing. & pl.)

‡ton² (tôn) n. [Fr.: see TONE] style; vogue

ton·al (tō'n'l) adj. [ML. tonalis] of a tone or tonality —**ton'al·ly** (-ē) adv.

to·nal·i·ty (tō nal'ə tē) n., pl. **-ties** 1. quality of tone 2. Art the arrangement of tones, or color scheme, in a painting 3. Music a) same as KEY¹ b) tonal character, as determined by the relationship of the tones to the keynote

ton·do (tän'dō) n., pl. **-di** (-dē), **-dos** [It., a plate, orig. round, aphetic for rotondo < L. rotundus: see ROTUND] a round painting

tone (tōn) n. [ME. < OFr. & L.: OFr. ton < L. tonus, a sound < Gr. tonos, a stretching, tone < teinein, to stretch: see TENANT] 1. a) a vocal or musical sound b) its quality 2. an intonation, pitch, modulation, etc. of the voice that expresses a particular meaning or feeling of the speaker [a tone of contempt] 3. a manner of speaking or writing that shows a certain attitude on the part of the speaker or writer, consisting in choice of words, phrasing, etc. [the friendly tone of her letter] 4. normal resiliency or elasticity [rubber that has lost its tone] 5. a) the prevailing or predominant style, character, spirit, trend, morale, or state of morals of a place or period [the cultured tone of their house] b) distinctive style; elegance [paintings that lent the room tone] 6. a) a quality or value of color; tint; shade b) any of the slight modifications of a particular color; hue [three tones of green] 7. Linguis. a) the relative height of pitch with which a syllable, word, etc. is pronounced b) the relative height of pitch that is a phoneme of a language and distinguishes meaning, as in the tone languages 8. Music a) a sound that is distinct and identifiable by its regularity of vibration, or constant pitch (as distinguished from a noise), and that may be put into harmonic relation with other such sounds b) the simple or fundamental tone of a musical sound as distinguished from its overtones c) any one of the full intervals of a diatonic scale; whole step d) any of several recitation melodies used in singing the psalms in plainsong 9. Painting the effect produced by the combination of light, shade, and color 10. Physiol. a) the condition of an organism, organ, or part with reference to its normal, healthy functioning b) the normal tension, or resistance to stretch, of a healthy muscle, independent of that caused by voluntary innervation; tonus —vt. **toned, ton'ing** 1. [Rare] same as INTONE 2. to give a tone to; specif., to give the proper or desired tone to (a musical instrument, a painting, etc.) 3. to change the tone of 4. Photog. to change or alter the color of (a print) by chemical means —vi. to assume a tone —SYN. see SOUND¹ —**tone down** 1. to give a lower or less intense tone to 2. to become softened 3. to make (something written or said) less harsh or more moderate —**tone in with** to harmonize with —**tone up** 1. to give a higher or more intense tone to 2. to become strengthened or heightened —**tone'less** adj. —**tone'less·ly** adv. —**tone'less·ness** n. —**ton'er** n.

tone arm the pivoted arm containing the pickup on a phonograph

tone cluster a number of close musical tones (not a chord) sounded together, as on a piano

tone color same as TIMBRE

tone control a device, as in a phonograph, by which the intensity of tones of varying frequencies is regulated

tone-deaf (-def') adj. not able to distinguish accurately differences in musical pitch —**tone'-deaf'ness** n.

tone language a language, as Mandarin or some Bantu languages, in which pitch variation is used to distinguish words that would otherwise sound alike

tone poem same as SYMPHONIC POEM

tone row (or **series**) see TWELVE-TONE

to·net·ic (tō net'ik) adj. [TON(E) + (PHON)ETIC] of or having to do with a tone language —**to·net'i·cal·ly** adv.

☆tong¹ (tôn, tän) vt. to seize, collect, handle, or hold with tongs —vi. to use tongs —**tong'er** n.

☆tong² (tôn, tän) n. [Chin. t'ang, a hall, meeting place, society] 1. a Chinese association or political party 2. in the U.S., a secret, fraternal society of Chinese

Ton·ga (täŋ'gə) 1. group of islands in the South Pacific, east of the Fiji Islands: also **Tonga Islands:** see FIJI ISLANDS, map 2. independent kingdom occupying these islands: a member of the Brit. Commonwealth: 270 sq. mi.; pop. 79,000

ton·ga (täŋ'gə) n. [Hindi tāṅgā] a light, two-wheeled carriage used in India

Ton·gan (-gən) n. 1. a native of Tonga 2. the Polynesian language of the Tongans

tongs (tôŋz, täŋz) n.pl. [sometimes with sing. v.] [ME. tongys, pl. of tonge < OE. tange, akin to G. zange < IE. base *denk-, to bite: basic sense "those that bite together"] a device for seizing or lifting objects, generally having two long arms pivoted or hinged together: also called **pair of tongs**

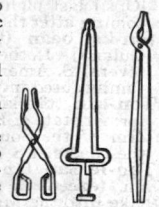

TONGS

tongue (tun) n. [ME. tunge < OE., akin to G. zunge < IE. base *dṅghū-, tongue, whence L. lingua (OL. dingua) 1. the movable muscular structure attached to the floor of the mouth in most vertebrates: it is an important organ in the ingestion of food, the perception of taste, and, in man, the articulation of speech sounds 2. an analogous part in invertebrate animals; specif., a) same as RADULA b) the proboscis in certain insects, as bees 3. an animal's tongue used as food 4. a) the human tongue as the organ of speech b) ideas expressed by speaking; talk; speech c) the act or power of speaking d) a manner or style of speaking, with reference to tone, diction, etc. [a glib tongue] 5. a) a language or dialect b) in the Bible, a nation or people speaking a distinct language 6. [pl.] see GLOSSOLALIA 7. the cry of a hunting dog, etc. in sight of game: chiefly in **give tongue**, to start barking 8. something resembling a tongue in shape, position, movement, or use; specif., a) the flap under the laces or strap of a shoe b) the clapper of a bell c) the pin of a buckle, etc. d) the pole of a wagon, etc. e) the projecting tenon of a tongue-and-groove joint f) in machines, a projecting flange, rib, etc. g) the vibrating end of the reed in a wind instrument h) a narrow strip of land extending into a sea, river, etc. i) a narrow inlet of water j) the movable rail in a railroad switch k) a long, narrow flame l) the pointer of a scale, etc. —vt. **tongued, tongu'ing** a) [Archaic] to reproach or scold b) to speak or say 2. to touch, lick, etc. with the tongue 3. a) to cut a tongue (sense 8 e) on or in b) to join by means of a tongue-and-groove joint 4. Music to play by tonguing: see TONGUING —vi. 1. [Rare] to talk or talk much 2. to project like a tongue 3. Music to use tonguing: see TONGUING —**find one's tongue** to recover the ability to talk, as after shock or embarrassment —**hold one's tongue** to refrain from speaking —**on everyone's tongue** prevailing as common gossip —**on the tip of one's** (or **the**) **tongue** 1. almost said by one 2. about to be said, esp. because almost but not quite recalled —**speak in tongues** to be subject to glossolalia

tongue-and-groove joint (tuŋ'n grōōv') a kind of joint in which a tongue or tenon on one board fits exactly into a groove in another

tongued (tuŋd) adj. having a (specified kind of) tongue: usually in hyphenated compounds [loose-tongued]

tongue-lash (tuŋ'lash') vt. [Colloq.] to scold or reprove harshly; reprimand —**tongue'-lash'ing** n.

tongue·less (-lis) adj. 1. having no tongue 2. speechless; mute; dumb

tongue-tie (-tī') n. limited motion of the tongue, usually caused by a short frenum and resulting in indistinct articulation —vt. **-tied', -ty'ing** to make tongue-tied

tongue-tied (-tīd') adj. 1. having a condition of tongue-tie 2. speechless from amazement, embarrassment, etc.

tongue twister a phrase or sentence hard to speak fast, usually because of alliteration or a sequence of nearly similar sounds (Ex.: six sick sheiks)

tongu·ing (tuŋ'iŋ) n. the use of the tongue in playing a musical wind instrument, esp. for more accurate intonation of rapid notes

ton·ic (tän'ik) adj. [Gr. tonikos < tonos: see TONE] 1. of, producing, or tending to produce good muscular tone, or tension 2. mentally or morally invigorating; stimulating 3. having to do with tones; specif., a) Music designating

or based on the first tone (*keynote*) of a diatonic scale [a *tonic* chord] *b*) *Painting* having to do with the tone or tones of a picture *c*) *Phonet.* [Now Rare] designating or of sounds characterized by resonance in the head cavities; also, accented **4.** *Med., Physiol. a*) of or characterized by tone, or tonus *b*) of or characterized by continuous muscular contraction [a *tonic* spasm] —*n.* **1.** anything that invigorates or stimulates; specif., *a*) a drug, medicine, or other agent for restoring or increasing body tone *b*) a hair or scalp dressing **2.** a carbonated beverage flavored with a little quinine and served in a mixed drink with gin, vodka, etc.; quinine water **3.** *Music* the first, or basic, tone of a diatonic scale; keynote **4.** *Phonet.* [Now Rare] a tonic sound or syllable —**ton′i·cal·ly** *adv.*

tonic accent *Phonet.* emphasis given to a syllable by changing, esp. by raising, the pitch rather than by stress

to·nic·i·ty (tō nis′ə tē) *n.* the quality or condition of being tonic; esp., *same as* TONUS

tonic sol-fa a system of musical notation based on the relationship between the tones of a key, using the syllables of solmization (*do, re, mi,* etc.) instead of the usual staff symbols: used in teaching singing

to·night (tə nīt′) *adv.* [ME. *to niht* < OE.: see TO & NIGHT] **1.** on or during the present or coming night **2.** [Obs.] last night —*n.* **1.** the present night **2.** the night coming after the present day Also, esp. formerly, **to-night**

ton·ka bean (tän′kə) [< the native (Tupi) name in Guiana] **1.** the fragrant, almond-shaped seed of any of several S. American trees (genus *Dipteryx*) of the legume family, used in perfumes and flavoring **2.** the tree

Ton·kin (tän′kin, tän′-) **1.** region of North Vietnam, a former state of Fr. Indochina: chief city, Hanoi **2. Gulf of,** arm of the South China Sea between Hainan Island & the coasts of S China & North Vietnam

Ton·le Sap (tän′lā säp′) **1.** lake in C Cambodia: 1,000 sq. mi. (except in flood season) **2.** river flowing from this lake into the Mekong River: c.70 mi.

ton·nage (tun′ij) *n.* [ME. < MFr.: see TUN & -AGE] **1.** a duty or tax on ships, based on tons carried **2.** a charge per ton on cargo or freight on a canal, at a port, etc. **3.** the total amount of shipping of a country or port, calculated in tons **4.** the carrying capacity of a ship, calculated in tons **5.** weight in tons

ton·neau (tu nō′) *n., pl.* **-neaus′, -neaux′** (-nōz′) [Fr., lit., a cask < *tonne:* see TUN] **1.** an enclosed rear compartment for passengers in an early type of automobile **2.** the whole body of such an automobile ☆**3.** a protective cover for the passenger compartment of a small, open sports car

to·nom·e·ter (tō näm′ə tər) *n.* [< Gr. *tonos,* TONE + -METER] **1.** an instrument for determining the pitch of a tone; specif., a tuning fork or, esp., a set of tuning forks **2.** an instrument for measuring vapor pressure **3.** *Med., Physiol.* any of various instruments for measuring tension, as of the eyeball, or pressure, as of the blood —**ton·o·met·ric** (tän′ə met′rik, tō′nə-) *adj.* —**to·nom′e·try** *n.*

ton·sil (tän′s'l) *n.* [L. *tonsillae, pl.*] either of a pair of oval masses of lymphoid tissue, one on each side of the throat at the back of the mouth —**ton′sil·lar** *adj.*

ton·sil·lec·to·my (-lə lek′tə mē) *n., pl.* **-mies** [prec. + -ECTOMY] the surgical removal of the tonsils

ton·sil·li·tis (-lī′təs) *n.* [ModL. < L. *tonsillae,* tonsils + -*itis,* -ITIS] inflammation of the tonsils —**ton′sil·lit′ic** (-lit′ik) *adj.*

ton·sil·lot·o·my (-lät′ə mē) *n., pl.* **-mies** [< L. *tonsillae,* tonsils + -TOMY] the surgical incision of a tonsil; esp., a tonsillectomy

ton·so·ri·al (tän sôr′ē əl) *adj.* [L. *tonsorius,* of clipping < *tonsor,* clipper < *tonsus,* pp. of *tondere,* to shear] of a barber or barbering: often used humorously [a *tonsorial* artist]

ton·sure (tän′shər) *n.* [ME. < MFr. < L. *tonsura* < *tonsus:* see prec.] **1.** the act or rite of clipping the hair or shaving the head, esp. the crown, of a person becoming a cleric or entering a monastic order, as in the Roman Catholic Church **2.** the state of being so shaven **3.** the part of the head left bare by so shaving —*vt.* **-sured, -sur·ing** to cause to undergo tonsure

TONSURE

ton·tine (tän′tēn, tän tēn′) *n.* [Fr. < It. *tontina* < Lorenzo *Tonti,* Neapolitan banker who introduced the system into France in the 17th c.] **1.** *a*) a fund to which a group of persons contribute, the benefits ultimately accruing to the last survivor or to those surviving after a specified time *b*) the subscribers to such a fund, collectively *c*) the total fund or the share of each subscriber **2.** any annuity or insurance system of this kind

to·nus (tō′nəs) *n.* [ModL. < L.: see TONE] the slight continuous contraction characteristic of a normal muscle in a state of rest

To·ny (tō′nē) a masculine name: see ANTHONY —*n., pl.* **-nies** [nickname of *Antoinette* Perry (1888–1946), U.S. theatrical figure] ☆[Slang] any of the awards made annually in the U.S. for special achievement in the theater in acting, directing, etc.

☆**ton·y** (tō′nē) *adj.* **ton′i·er, ton′i·est** [Slang] high-toned; luxurious; stylish: often ironic

too (tōō) *adv.* [stressed form of TO, with differentiated sp.] **1.** in addition; as well; besides; also **2.** more than enough;

superfluously; overly [the hat is *too* big] **3.** to a regrettable extent [that's *too* bad!] **4.** extremely; very [it was just *too* delicious!] *Too* is often used as a mere emphatic [I will *too* go!] and is sometimes construed as an adjective in modifying *much* or *many* [there was not *too* much to see]

took (took) *pt. of* TAKE

tool (tōōl) *n.* [ME. *toole* < OE. *tol,* akin to ON. *tol:* for IE. base see TAW[2]] **1.** any implement, instrument, or utensil held in the hand and used for cutting, hitting, digging, rubbing, etc.: knives, saws, hammers, shovels, rakes, etc. are tools **2.** *a*) any similar instrument that is the working part of a power-driven machine, as a drill, band-saw blade, etc. *b*) the whole machine; machine tool **3.** anything that serves in the manner of a tool; a means [books are a scholar's *tools*] **4.** a person used by another to accomplish his purposes, esp. when these are illegal or unethical; dupe; stooge **5.** *Law* any instrument or device necessary to one's profession or occupation: in full **tools of one's trade** —*vt.* **1.** to form, shape, or work with a tool **2.** to provide tools or machinery for (a factory, industry, etc.): often with *up* **3.** to drive (a vehicle) or convey (a person in a vehicle) **4.** to impress letters or designs on (leather, a book cover, etc.) with special tools —*vi.* **1.** to use a tool or tools **2.** to get or install the tools, equipment, etc. needed (often with *up*) **3.** to ride or drive in a vehicle —*SYN.* see IMPLEMENT —**tool′er** *n.*

tool·box (-bäks′) *n.* a box or chest, usually compartmented, in which tools are kept: also **tool chest**

tool·ing (-in) *n.* **1.** work or decoration done with tools **2.** the process of fitting out a factory with machine tools in readiness for going into production

tool·mak·er (-mā′kər) *n.* a machinist who makes, maintains, and repairs machine tools —**tool′mak′ing** *n.*

tool·room (-rōōm′) *n.* a room, as in a machine shop, where tools are stored, kept in repair, issued to workmen, etc.

tool·shed (-shed′) *n.* a small structure, as at the back of a house, where tools are kept: also **tool′house′**

toon (tōōn) *n.* [Hindi *tūn* < Sans. *tunna*] **1.** a large Australian and East Indian tree (*Cedrela toona*) of the mahogany family, with soft, closegrained, reddish wood used in furniture: its flowers yield a dye **2.** its wood

toot (tōōt) *vi.* [prob. via LowG. *tuten* < echoic base] **1.** to blow a horn, whistle, etc. in short blasts **2.** to sound in short blasts: said of a horn, whistle, etc. **3.** to make a sound like a horn or whistle —*vt.* **1.** to cause to sound in short blasts **2.** to sound (tones, blasts, etc.) as on a horn —*n.* **1.** a short blast of a horn, whistle, etc. ☆**2.** [prob. a play on (WET ONE'S) WHISTLE] [Slang] a drinking spree

tooth (tōōth; *for v., also* tōōth) *n., pl.* **teeth** (tēth) [ME. < OE. *toth* (< **tanth*), akin to G. *zahn* < IE. **edont-* (< base **ed-,* to eat) whence L. *dens,* Gr. *odous* (gen. *odontos*)] **1.** *a*) any of a set of hard, bonelike structures (normally 32 in the human adult) set in the jaws of most vertebrates and used for biting, tearing, and chewing: a tooth consists typically of a sensitive, vascular pulp surrounded by dentine and coated on the crown with enamel and on the root with cement *b*) any of various analogous processes in invertebrates *c*) [*pl.*] *same as* DENTURE (sense 2) **2.** something resembling a tooth; toothlike part, as on a saw, fork, rake, gearwheel, etc.; tine, prong, cog, etc. **3.** appetite or taste for something specified [a sweet *tooth*] **4.** something that bites, pierces, or gnaws like a tooth [the *teeth* of the storm] **5.** a rough surface, as on 'paper, metal, etc. **6.** [*pl.*] a sound or effective means of enforcing something [to put *teeth* into a law] **7.** *Bot.* any small, pointed lobe, as of a leaf or of the fringe surrounding the opening of a capsule in mosses —*vt.* **1.** to provide with teeth **2.** to make jagged; indent —*vi.* to mesh, or become interlocked, as gears —**armed (or dressed) to the teeth** as armed (or dressed up) as one can be —**get (or sink) one's teeth into** to become fully occupied or absorbed with —**in the teeth of 1.** directly against; in the face of **2.** in opposition to; defying —**long in the tooth** elderly; old —**set one's teeth** to prepare to meet firmly something difficult or unpleasant —**show one's teeth** to show hostility; threaten angrily —**throw (something) in someone's teeth 1.** to reproach someone for (something) **2.** to hurl (a challenge, taunt, etc.) at someone —**tooth and nail** with all one's strength or resources —**tooth′less** *adj.*

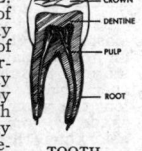

CROWN
DENTINE
PULP
ROOT

TOOTH

SYN.—**tooth** is the general, inclusive word (see the definition above); **tusk** refers to a long, pointed, enlarged tooth projecting outside the mouth in certain animals, as the elephant, wild boar, and walrus, and used for digging or as a weapon; **fang** refers either to one of the long, sharp teeth with which meat-eating animals tear their prey or to the long, hollow tooth through which poisonous snakes inject their venom

tooth·ache (tōōth′āk′) *n.* pain in or near a tooth

tooth·brush (-brush′) *n.* a brush for cleaning the teeth

toothed (tōōtht, tōōthd) *adj.* **1.** having (a specified kind or number of) teeth: often used in hyphenated compounds [big-*toothed*] **2.** notched; indented

toothed whale any of a suborder (Odontoceti) of whales, as the sperm whale, with conical teeth and a telescoped, nonsymmetrical skull: cf. WHALEBONE WHALE

tooth·paste (tōōth′pāst′) *n.* a paste used in cleaning the teeth with a toothbrush

tooth·pick (-pik′) *n.* a slender, pointed instrument, esp. a shaped sliver of wood, for dislodging food particles from between the teeth

tooth powder a powder used like toothpaste

tooth shell *same as* SCAPHOPOD

tooth·some (tōōth′səm) *adj.* [TOOTH + -SOME¹] pleasing to the taste; palatable —**tooth′some·ly** *adv.* —**tooth′some·ness** *n.*

tooth·wort (-wurt′) *n.* **1.** any of a genus (*Dentaria*) of small woodland plants of the mustard family, having scaly or toothed, pungent rhizomes and clusters of white or pinkish flowers in spring **2.** any of a genus (*Lathraea*) of European parasitic plants of the broomrape family, having a rhizome covered with tooth-shaped scales

tooth·y (tōō′thē) *adj.* **tooth′i·er, tooth′i·est** having or exposing teeth that show prominently [a *toothy* smile] —**tooth′i·ly** *adv.* —**tooth′i·ness** *n.*

too·tle (tōōt′'l) *vi.* **-tled, -tling** [freq. of TOOT] to toot softly and more or less continuously on a horn, flute, etc. —*n.* the act or sound of tootling —**toot′ler** *n.*

toots (tōōts) *n.* [< ff.] [Old Slang] darling; dear: affectionate or playful term of address, esp. for a girl or woman

toot·sy, toot·sie (tōōt′sē) *n., pl.* **-sies** [child's term] [Old Slang] **1.** a foot, esp. of a child or woman **2.** *same as* TOOTS **3.** a girl or woman

Too·woom·ba (tə wōōm′bə) city in SW Queensland, Australia, east of Brisbane: pop. 56,000

top¹ (täp) *n.* [ME. < OE., akin to ON. *toppr*, tuft, top, G. *zopf*, tuft of hair, summit] **1.** orig., *a*) a tuft of hair *b*) the hair of the head **2.** the head, or crown of the head: now chiefly in **top to toe 3.** the upper or highest part, section, point, or surface of anything [the *top* of a hill] **4.** the part of a plant that grows above ground [beet *tops*] **5.** something that constitutes the uppermost part or covering of something else; specif., *a*) a lid, cover, cap, etc. [a box *top*, bottle *top*] *b*) the upper part of an automobile body, esp. a folding roof or cover *c*) a platform around the head of each lower mast or a sailing ship, to which the rigging of the topmast is attached **6.** [*sometimes pl.*] the upper unit of a two-piece garment, as a pajama blouse **7.** a person or thing first in order, excellence, importance, etc.; specif., *a*) the highest degree or pitch; zenith; acme [at the *top* of one's voice, the *top* of one's career] *b*) the highest rank, position, etc. [at the *top* in one's profession] *c*) a person in this rank, etc. *d*) the choicest part; pick; cream [the *top* of the crop, *top* of the morning] *e*) the beginning, as of a piece of music [take it from the *top*] ☆*f*) *Baseball* the first half (of an inning) **8.** *Card Games* the card or [*pl.*] cards that will win the first or second round of a suit **9.** *Chem.* the most volatile part of a mixture **10.** *Sports a*) a stroke that hits the ball above center or near its top *b*) the forward spin given the ball by such a stroke —*adj.* of, situated at, or being the top; uppermost, highest, greatest, or foremost [the *top* drawer, *top* honors] —*vt.* **topped, top′ping 1.** to take off the top of (a plant, etc.) **2.** *a*) to provide or cover with a top *b*) to put or place on the top of **3.** to be a top for **4.** to reach the top of; be on a level with **5.** to exceed in amount, height, degree, etc. [a fish *topping* 75 pounds] **6.** to be better, more effective, funnier, etc. than; surpass; outdo **7.** to go over the top of (a rise of ground, etc.) **8.** to be at the top of; head; lead **9.** *Chem.* to remove the volatile parts from by distillation **10.** *Dyeing* to finish with a certain dye **11.** *Sports a*) to hit or stroke (a ball) at a point above its center, giving it a forward spin *b*) to make (a stroke) by hitting the ball in this way —*vi.* to top someone or something (in any sense) —☆**blow one's top** [Slang] **1.** to lose one's temper **2.** to become insane —**off the top** [Slang] from gross income —☆**off the top of one's head** speaking offhand, without careful thought —**on top** at the top; successful —**on top of 1.** on or at the top of **2.** resting upon **3.** in addition to; besides **4.** following immediately after **5.** controlling successfully —**over the top 1.** over the front of a trench, as in attacking **2.** exceeding the assigned quota or goal —(**the**) **tops** [Slang] preeminent in quality, ability, popularity, etc.; the very best: used predicatively —**top off** to complete by adding a finishing touch —☆**top out 1.** to complete the skeleton or framework of a building, esp. a skyscraper **2.** to level off

top² (täp) *n.* [ME. < OE. < ?] a child's toy shaped somewhat like an inverted cone, with a point at its apex upon which it is spun, as by quickly unwinding a string —**sleep like a top** to sleep soundly

to·paz (tō′paz) *n.* [ME. *topace* < OFr. *topase* < L. *topazus* < Gr. *topazos*] **1.** a native silicate of aluminum and fluorine, Al₂SiO₄(F, OH)₂, usually containing hydroxyl and occurring in white, yellow, pale-blue, or pale-green, orthorhombic crystals; esp., a yellow variety of this, used as a gem **2.** *a*) a yellow variety of sapphire *b*) a yellow variety of quartz **3.** either of two brightly colored hummingbirds (*Topaza pyra* or *Topaza pella*) of S. America

to·paz·o·lite (tō paz′ə lit′) *n.* [< Gr. *topazos*, topaz + -LITE] a yellow to greenish variety of andradite garnet

☆**top banana** [prob. so named in reference to the banana-shaped soft club carried by comedians] [Slang] **1.** a top performer in show business; specif., the star comedian in a burlesque show: cf. SECOND BANANA **2.** the most important person in any group

top boot any of several high boots reaching to just below the knee: its upper part is usually of a different material

☆**top brass** important officials: see BRASS (sense 7)

☆**top·coat** (täp′kōt′) *n.* a lightweight overcoat

top dog [Slang] the person, company, etc. in a dominant or leading position, esp. in a competitive situation

top-drawer (-drôr′) *adj.* of first importance, privilege, etc.

top-dress·ing (-dres′in) *n.* **1.** material applied to a surface, as fertilizer on land or crops, or stones on a road **2.** the applying of such material —**top′-dress** *vt.*

tope¹ (tōp) *vt., vi.* **toped, top′ing** [Fr. *toper*, to accept the stakes in gambling (prob. < ODu. *topp*, touch): present E. meaning prob. from the custom of drinking to the conclusion of the wager] [Archaic] to drink (alcoholic liquor) in large amounts and often

tope² (tōp) *n.* [Hindi *top*, ult. < Sans. *stūpa*, a mound, tope] a Buddhist shrine in the form of a dome with a cupola

tope³ (tōp) *n.* [< ? Cornish] a small, gray European shark (*Galeorhinus galeus*) about five feet long

to·pee (tō pē′, tō′pē) *n.* [Hindi *topī*] in India, a hat or cap, esp. a pith helmet worn as a sunshade

To·pe·ka (tə pē′kə) [< ? Siouan (Omaha), lit., good place to dig potatoes] capital of Kans., in the NE part, on the Kansas River: pop. 125,000

top·er (tō′pər) *n.* a person who topes; drunkard

top-flight (täp′flit′) *adj.* [Colloq.] best; first-rate

top-full (täp′fool′) *adj.* [Now Rare] filled to the top

top·gal·lant (täp′gal′ənt, tə gal′ənt) *adj.* **1.** designating or of a mast, sail, spar, etc. situated above the topmast and below the royal mast on a sailing ship **2.** higher than the adjoining parts of the ship: said of a rail, deck, etc. —*n.* a topgallant mast, sail, etc.

top-ham·per (täp′ham′pər) *n.* **1.** the upper masts, spars, and rigging of a sailing ship, usually kept aloft **2.** rigging, spars, etc. not needed immediately and an encumbrance aloft or on deck Also **top hamper**

top hat a tall, black, cylindrical hat, usually of silk, worn by men in formal dress

top-heav·y (täp′hev′ē) *adj.* too heavy at the top for the base below, so as to be likely to fall over or collapse: also used figuratively, as of an organization with too many executives —**top′-heav′i·ly** *adv.* —**top′-heav′i·ness** *n.*

To·phet, To·pheth (tō′fit) *n.* [ME. < Heb. *tōpheth*] **1.** *Bible* a place near Jerusalem where human sacrifices were made to Moloch **2.** hell

top-hole (täp′hōl′) *adj.* [Brit. Slang] first-rate

to·phus (tō′fəs) *n., pl.* **-phi** (-fi) [L., tufa] *Med.*, an abnormal mineral deposit, as of calcium carbonate, about the joints, on the roots of the teeth, etc., in a person who has the gout; chalkstone

to·pi (tō pē′, tō′pē) *n. same as* TOPEE

to·pi·ar·y (tō′pē er′ē) *adj.* [L. *topiarius*, concerning an ornamental garden < *topia* (opera), ornamental gardening < Gr. *topos*, place: see ff.] designating or of the art of trimming and training shrubs or trees into unnatural, ornamental shapes —*n., pl.* **-ar′ies 1.** topiary art or work **2.** a topiary garden

top·ic (täp′ik) *n.* [L. *topica* < Gr. *ta topika*, title of a work by Aristotle < *topikos*, local, concerning < *topoi*, commonplaces < *topos*, a place < IE. base *top-, to arrive, goal, whence OE. *thafian*, to endure] **1.** formerly, *a*) a class or category of considerations or arguments on which a rhetorician may draw *b*) one such consideration or argument **2.** the subject of a paragraph, essay, speech, etc. **3.** a subject for discussion or conversation **4.** a heading or item in an outline —*SYN.* see SUBJECT

top·i·cal (-i k'l) *adj.* **1.** of a particular place; local **2.** of, using, or arranged under topics, subjects, or headings **3.** having to do with topics of the day; of current or local interest [*topical* allusions in literature] **4.** *Med.* of or for a particular part of the body; esp., designating or by local application [a *topical* remedy] —**top′i·cal′i·ty** (-kal′ə tē) *n.* —**top′i·cal·ly** *adv.*

topic sentence the principal sentence, setting forth the main idea and coming usually at the beginning, in a paragraph or section of a discourse, esp. of an expository nature

top kick [Mil. Slang] *same as* FIRST SERGEANT

top·knot (täp′nät′) *n.* **1.** a knot of feathers, ribbons, etc. worn as a headdress **2.** *a*) a tuft of hair on the crown of the head *b*) a tuft of feathers on a bird's head

top·less (-lis) *adj.* **1.** without a top; specif., ☆designating or wearing a costume that exposes the breasts **2.** seeming to have no top; very high [a *topless* tower]

top-lev·el (-lev′'l) *adj.* **1.** of or by persons of the highest office or rank **2.** in the highest office or rank

top·loft·y (-lôf′tē) *adj.* [Colloq.] lofty in manner; haughty; pompous —**top′loft′i·ly** *adv.* —**top′loft′i·ness** *n.*

top·mast (täp′məst, -mast′, -mäst′) *n.* the second mast above the deck of a sailing ship, supported by the lower mast and often supporting a topgallant mast in turn

☆**top·min·now** (-min′ō) *n.* **1.** any of a family (Poeciliidae) of small, surface-feeding fishes, as the mosquitofish, that

produce their young fully formed **2.** any of several related egg-laying fishes (family Cyprinodontidae)

top·most (täp′mōst′) *adj.* at the very top; uppermost

☆**top-notch** (-näch′) *adj.* [Colloq.] first-rate; excellent

topog. 1. topographic **2.** topography

to·pog·ra·pher (tə päg′rə fər) *n.* **1.** an expert or specialist in topography **2.** a person who describes or maps the topography of a place or region

to·pog·ra·phy (-fē) *n., pl.* **-phies** [ME. *topographye* < LL. *topographia* < Gr. *topographia:* see TOPIC & -GRAPHY] **1.** orig., the accurate and detailed description of a place **2.** *a)* the science of drawing on maps and charts or otherwise representing the surface features of a region, including its relief and rivers, lakes, etc., and such manmade features as canals, bridges, roads, etc. *b)* these surface features **3.** topographic surveying **4.** a study or description of a region, system, or part of the body showing specific relations of component parts as to shape, size, position, etc. [cerebral *topography*] **5.** any similar study of an entity, as the mind, the atom, a particular discipline, etc. —**top·o·graph·ic** (täp′ə graf′ik), **top′o·graph′i·cal** *adj.* —**top′o·graph′i·cal·ly** *adv.*

to·pol·o·gy (tə päl′ə jē) *n., pl.* **-gies** [< Gr. *topos*, a place (see TOPIC) + -LOGY] **1.** a topographical study of a specific object, entity, place, etc. [the *topology* of the mind] **2.** *Math.* the study of those properties of geometric figures that remain unchanged even when under distortion, so long as no surfaces are torn: see MÖBIUS STRIP **3.** *Med.* the topographic anatomy of a body region —**top·o·log·i·cal** (täp′ə läj′i k′l) *adj.* —**to·pol′o·gist** *n.*

top·o·nym (täp′ə nim′) *n.* [back-formation < TOPONYMY] **1.** a name of a place **2.** a name that indicates origin, natural locale, etc., as in zoological nomenclature

top·o·nym·ic (täp′ə nim′ik) *adj.* **1.** toponyms **2.** having to do with toponymy Also **top′o·nym′i·cal**

to·pon·y·my (tə pän′ə mē) *n.* [< Gr. *topos*, a place (see TOPIC) + -onymia, a naming < *onyma*, NAME] **1.** the place names of a country, district, etc., or the study of these **2.** [Rare] *Anat.* the nomenclature of the regions of the body

top·per (täp′ər) *n.* **1.** a person or thing that tops **2.** [Colloq.] *a) same as* TOP HAT *b)* a woman's short, loose-fitting topcoat ☆**3.** [Slang] a remark, joke, etc. that tops, or surpasses, all preceding ones

top·ping (-iŋ) *n.* **1.** the action of a person or thing that tops **2.** something that forms the top of, or is put on top of, something else, as a sauce on food —*adj.* **1.** *a)* that excels in degree, rank, etc. *b)* that rises higher than another thing **2.** [Brit. Colloq.] superior; excellent; first-rate

top·ple (täp′'l) *vi.* **-pled, -pling** [< TOP[1], *v.* + -LE] **1.** to fall top forward; fall (*over*) from top-heaviness, etc. **2.** to lean forward as if on the point of falling; overbalance; totter —*vt.* **1.** to cause to topple; overturn **2.** to overthrow [to *topple* a monarch]

top·sail (täp′s'l, -sāl′) *n.* **1.** in a square-rigged vessel, the square sail, or either of a pair of square sails, next above the lowest sail on a mast: see SAIL, illus. **2.** in a fore-and-aft-rigged vessel, the small sail set above the gaff of a fore-and-aft sail

top-se·cret (-sē′krit) *adj.* designating or of the most highly restricted military or government information

☆**top sergeant** *colloq. var. of* FIRST SERGEANT

top·side (-sīd′) *n.* [*usually pl.*] the part of a ship's side above the waterline —*adv.* on or to an upper deck or the main deck of a ship

☆**top·soil** (-soil′) *n.* the upper layer of soil, usually darker and richer than the subsoil; surface soil

top·sy·tur·vy (täp′sē tur′vē) *adv., adj.* [earlier *topsy-tervy*, prob. < *top*, highest part + ME. *terven*, to roll] **1.** upside down; in a reversed condition **2.** in confusion or disorder —*n.* **1.** a topsy-turvy condition; inverted state **2.** a state of confusion —**top′sy-tur′vi·ly** *adv.* —**top′sy-tur′vi·ness** *n.*

toque (tōk) *n.* [Fr., a cap < Sp. *toca* < Basque *tauka*, kind of cap] a woman's small, round, closefitting hat, with or without a brim: a modification of a 16th-cent. small, plumed hat, worn by men and women

tor (tôr) *n.* [ME. < OE. *torr*, a tower, crag < L. *turris*, a tower] a high, rocky hill; crag

to·rah, to·ra (tō′rə, tō rä′) *n.* [Heb. *tōrāh*, law] *Judaism* **1.** *a)* learning, law, instruction, etc. *b)* [also T-] the whole body of Jewish religious literature, including the Scripture, the Talmud, etc. **2.** [usually T-] *a)* the Pentateuch *b) pl.* **-roth, -rot** (-rəs, -rōt′) a parchment scroll containing the Pentateuch

torch (tôrch) *n.* [ME. < OFr. *torche* < VL. **torca*, a twisted object, for L. *torqua* < *torquere*, to twist: see TORSION] **1.** a portable light consisting of a long piece of resinous wood, or twisted tow dipped in tallow, etc., flaming at one end; link; flambeau **2.** anything considered as a source of enlightenment, illumination, inspiration, etc. [the *torch* of science] **3.** any of various portable devices for producing a very hot flame, used in welding, burning off paint, etc. **4.** [Brit.] a flashlight —**carry a** (or **the**) **torch for** [Slang] to be in love with (someone), esp. without having one's love returned

torch·bear·er (-ber′ər) *n.* **1.** a person who carries a torch **2.** *a)* a person who brings enlightenment, truth, etc. *b)* an inspirational leader, as in some movement

torch·ier, torch·iere (tôr chir′) *n.* [< Fr. *torchère*, small, high candlestand < OFr. *torche:* see TORCH] a floor lamp

with a reflector bowl and no shade, for casting light upward so as to give indirect illumination

torch·light (tôrch′līt′) *n.* the light of a torch or torches —☆*adj.* done or carried on by torchlight

tor·chon lace (tôr′shän; *Fr.* tôr shôn′) [Fr. *torchon*, dishcloth, duster < *torche:* see TORCH] **1.** a strong, bobbin lace made of coarse linen or cotton thread in simple, open, geometric patterns **2.** an imitation of this made by machine

☆**torch song** [< phrase *carry a torch for:* see TORCH] a sentimental popular song, esp. of unrequited or unhappy love —**torch singer**

☆**torch·wood** (tôrch′wood′) *n.* **1.** any of a number of trees with resinous wood from which torches can be made **2.** any of a genus (*Amyris*) of tropical American trees and shrubs of the rue family, having hard, resinous wood **3.** the wood of any of these trees

tore[1] (tôr) *alt. pt. of* TEAR[1]

tore[2] (tôr) *n. Archit., Geom. same as* TORUS

tor·e·a·dor (tôr′ē ə dôr′) *n.* [Sp. < *torear*, to fight bulls < *toro*, a bull < L. *taurus*, a bull: see TAURUS] a bullfighter, esp. one on horseback: term no longer used in bullfighting

to·re·ro (tə rer′ō; *Sp.* tō re′rō) *n., pl.* **-ros** (-rōz; *Sp.* -rōs) [Sp. < LL. *taurarius* < L. *taurus* (see prec.)] a bullfighter, esp. a matador

to·reu·tic (tə rōōt′ik) *adj.* [Gr. *toreutikos* < *toreuein*, to work in relief, bore < IE. base **ter-:* cf. THROW] designating or of embossed or chased work, esp. in metal

to·reu·tics (-iks) *n.pl.* [with sing. *v.*] the art of making toreutic work

to·ri (tôr′ī) *n. pl. of* TORUS

tor·ic (tôr′ik) *adj.* of or shaped like a torus

toric lens a lens of which one surface is a segment of the surface of a torus: used esp. in eyeglasses

to·ri·i (tôr′i ē′) *n., pl.* **-ri·i** [Jap.] a gateway at the entrance to a Japanese Shinto temple, consisting of two uprights supporting a curved lintel, with a straight crosspiece below

To·ri·no (tō rē′nō) *It. name of* TURIN

TORII

tor·ment (tôr′ment; *for v., usually* tôr ment′) *n.* [ME. < OFr. < L. *tormentum*, a rack, instrument of torture, torture, pain, orig., machine for hurling missiles < *torquere*, to twist: see TORT] **1.** orig., an instrument of torture or the torture inflicted **2.** great pain or anguish, physical or mental; suffering; agony **3.** a source of pain, anxiety, or annoyance —*vt.* [ME. *tormenten* < OFr. *tourmenter* < the *n.*] **1.** [Rare] to torture **2.** to cause great physical or mental anguish in **3.** to annoy, harass, or tease **4.** [Obs.] to stir up; agitate —**tor·ment′ing·ly** *adv.*

SYN.—**torment** implies harassment or persecution by the continued or repeated infliction of suffering or annoyance [*tormented* by the mosquitoes]; **torture** implies the infliction of acute physical or mental pain, such as to cause agony [*tortured* by his memories]; **rack** suggests the excruciating pain suffered on the rack, an ancient instrument of torture on which the limbs were pulled out of place [*racked* by the pain of arthritis] See also BAIT —ANT. **comfort**

tor·men·til (tôr′men til′) *n.* [ME. < ML. *tormentilla* < L. *tormentum* (see prec.): from belief in the pain-killing power of the plant] a European cinquefoil (*Potentilla tormentilla*) with yellow flowers and rhizomes used in tanning and dyeing

tor·men·tor (tôr men′tər) *n.* [ME. < OFr. *tormenteor*] **1.** a person or thing that torments **2.** [because it can obstruct the view of those sitting at the sides] *Theater* a flat or curtain projecting out onto either side of a proscenium stage, for concealing the wings and backstage from the audience **3.** *Motion Pictures* a covered screen for absorbing echoes on a set Also sp. **tor·ment′er**

torn (tôrn) *alt. pp. of* TEAR[1]

tor·na·do (tôr nā′dō) *n., pl.* **-does, -dos** [altered (prob. after Sp. *tornar*, to turn) < Sp. *tronada*, thunder, thunderstorm < *tronar*, to thunder < L. *tonare*, to THUNDER] ☆**1.** a violently whirling column of air extending downward from a cumulonimbus cloud, esp. in Australia and the C U.S., almost always seen as a rapidly rotating, slender, funnel-shaped cloud that usually destroys everything along its narrow path **2.** in West Africa and the adjacent Atlantic, a severe thundersquall **3.** any whirlwind or hurricane —☆**tor·nad′ic** (-nad′ik) *adj.*

☆**tor·nil·lo** (tôr nē′yō, -nil′ō) *n., pl.* **-los** [Sp., lit., screw, dim. of *torno*, a winch, spindle, wheel < L. *tornus*, a turner's wheel, lathe: see TURN] *same as* SCREW BEAN

to·roid (tôr′oid) *n* [TOR(E)[2] + -OID] **1.** *Elec.* a doughnut-shaped coil **2.** *Geom.* a surface, or its enclosed solid, generated by any closed plane curve rotating about a straight line in its own plane —**to·roid′al** *adj.*

To·ron·to (tə rän′tō) [< Iroquoian < ?] capital of Ontario, Canada; port on Lake Ontario: pop. 665,000 (met. area 2,158,000)

to·rose (tôr′ōs, tô rōs′) *adj.* [L. *torosus*, full of muscle, brawny < *torus*, muscle] **1.** bulging, knobbed, etc. **2.** *Bot.* cylindrical, with swellings at intervals Also **to′rous** (-əs)

tor·pe·do (tôr pē′dō) *n., pl.* **-does** [L., numbness, crampfish < *torpere*, to be stiff: see TORPID] **1.** *same as* ELECTRIC RAY

☆**2.** a large, cigar-shaped, self-propelled, underwater projectile for launching against enemy ships from a submarine, airplane, etc.: it explodes on contact by means of a timing mechanism or by radio control **3.** a metal case containing explosives, esp. one used as an underwater mine **4.** a small firework consisting of a percussion cap and gravel wrapped in tissue paper, which explodes with a loud noise when thrown against a hard surface ☆**5.** an explosive cartridge placed on a railroad track and detonated by a train wheel as a signal to the crew ☆**6.** an explosive cartridge lowered into oil wells, where it is detonated to clear the bore or break through into the oil pocket ☆**7.** [Slang] a gangster or gunman hired as a bodyguard, assassin, etc. —*vt.* to attack, destroy, damage, or ruin with or as with a torpedo

☆**torpedo boat** a small, fast, maneuverable warship for attacking with torpedoes

tor·pe·do-boat destroyer (-bōt) *n.* a former warship like a torpedo boat but larger and more heavily armed, orig. designed to destroy torpedo boats

torpedo tube a tube for launching torpedoes, located in surface vessels below or close to the waterline

tor·pid (tôr′pid) *adj.* [L. *torpidus* < *torpere*, to be numb or torpid < IE. *(s)terp-* < base *(s)ter-*, to be stiff, whence STARE, STARVE] **1.** *a)* having lost temporarily all or part of the power of sensation or motion, as a hibernating animal; dormant *b)* sluggish in functioning **2.** slow and dull; apathetic —**tor·pid′i·ty**, **tor′pid·ness** *n.* —**tor′pid·ly** *adv.*

tor·por (tôr′pər) *n.* [L. < *torpere*: see prec.] **1.** a state of being dormant or inactive; temporary loss of all or part of the power of sensation or motion; sluggishness; stupor **2.** dullness; apathy —SYN. see LETHARGY

tor·por·if·ic (tôr′pə rif′ik) *adj.* inducing torpor

tor·quate (tôr′kwāt) *adj.* [L. *torquatus*] having a torques; collared

Tor·quay (tôr kē′) city in Devonshire, SW England, on the English Channel: pop. 52,000

torque (tôrk) *n.* [< L. *torques* (infl. in senses 2 & 3 by *torquere*): see TORQUES] **1.** a twisted metal collar or necklace worn by ancient Teutons, Gauls, Britons, etc. **2.** *Physics* a twisting or wrenching effect or moment exerted by a force acting at a distance on a body, equal to the force multiplied by the perpendicular distance between the line of action of the force and the center of rotation at which it is exerted **3.** popularly, the force that acts to produce rotation, as in an automotive vehicle

torque converter a hydraulic device for transferring and increasing torque

Tor·que·ma·da (tôr′ke mä′thä; *E.* tôr′ki mä′də), **To·más de** (tō mäs′ *the*) 1420–98; Sp. Dominican monk; first Grand Inquisitor of the Spanish Inquisition

tor·ques (tôr′kwēz) *n.* [L. *torques*, a twisted necklace < *torquere*, to twist: see TORT] a ring of hair, feathers, or modified skin around the neck of an animal or bird, of a distinctive color or form

torque wrench a wrench that indicates, as on a dial, the amount of torque exerted in tightening a bolt, nut, etc.

torr (tôr) *n.* [< TORRICELLI] a unit of pressure equal to 1,333.2 microbars, the pressure needed to support a column of mercury one millimeter high under standard conditions

Tor·rance (tôr′əns) [after Jared S. *Torrance*, local landowner] city in SW Calif.: suburb of Los Angeles: pop. 135,000

tor·re·fy (tôr′ə fī′, tär′-) *vt.* **-fied′, -fy′ing** [Fr. *torréfier* < L. *torrefacere* < *torrere*, to dry by heat (see THIRST) + *facere*, to make, DO] to dry or parch (certain drugs or ores) with heat —**tor′re·fac′tion** (-fak′shən) *n.*

Tor·ren·ize (tôr′ə niz′, tär′-) *vt.* **-ized′, -iz′ing** to register (property) under a Torrens law

Tor·rens (tôr′ənz, tär′-), **Lake** shallow salt lake in SE South Australia: c.2,230 sq. mi.

Tor·rens law (tôr′ənz, tär′-) [after Sir Robert *Torrens* (1814–84), Austral. statesman] any of various statutes that provide for the registration of the title to land with the government, which issues a warranted title deed (**Torrens certificate**) to said land

tor·rent (tôr′ənt, tär′-) *n.* [Fr. < L. *torrens*, burning, roaring, rushing, impetuous, prp. of *torrere*, to parch, dry, roast, consume: see THIRST] **1.** a swift, violent stream, esp. of water **2.** a rapid, profuse, or violent flow of words, mail, etc.; flood; rush **3.** a very heavy fall of rain —*adj.* [Rare] of or like a torrent

tor·ren·tial (tô ren′shəl, tə-) *adj.* **1.** of, having the nature of, or produced by, a torrent **2.** like a torrent, as in violence, swiftness, copiousness, etc.; overwhelming —**tor·ren′tial·ly** *adv.*

Tor·re·ón (tô′rā ōn′) city in NC Mexico, in Coahuila state: pop. 228,000

Tor·res Strait (tôr′iz, tär′-) strait between New Guinea & NE Australia: c.95 mi. wide

Tor·ri·cel·li (tôr′rē chel′lē; *E.* tôr′i chel′ē), **E·van·ge·lis·ta** (e′vän je lēs′tä) 1608–47; It. physicist & mathematician: discovered principle of the barometer

tor·rid (tôr′id, tär′-) *adj.* [L. *torridus* < *torrere*, to dry: see THIRST] **1.** dried by or subjected to intense heat, esp. of the sun; scorched; parched; arid **2.** so hot as to be parching

or oppressive; scorching **3.** highly passionate, ardent, zealous, etc. —**tor·rid·i·ty** (tô rid′ə tē), **tor′rid·ness** *n.* —**tor′rid·ly** *adv.*

Torrid Zone the area of the earth's surface between the Tropic of Cancer & the Tropic of Capricorn and divided by the equator: see ZONE, illus.

tor·sade (tôr säd′) *n.* [Fr. < ML. *torsus*, twisted, for L. *tortus*: see TORT] **1.** a twisted cord used in drapery, etc. **2.** a molded or worked ornament resembling this

tor·si (tôr′sē) *n. alt. pl. of* TORSO

tor·si·bil·i·ty (tôr′sə bil′ə tē) *n.* ability to undergo, or resistance to, torsion

tor·sion (tôr′shən) *n.* [ME. *torcion* < MFr. *torsion* < LL.(Ec.) *torsio* < pp. of L. *torquere*, to twist: see TORT] **1.** the process or condition of twisting or being twisted **2.** *Mech. a)* the stress or strain produced in a body, as a rod, wire, or thread, by turning one end along a longitudinal axis while the other end is held firm or twisted in the opposite direction *b)* the torque exerted by a body in reaction to being placed under torsion —**tor′sion·al** *adj.* —**tor′sion·al·ly** *adv.*

torsion balance an instrument for measuring small forces, such as those caused by gravitation, electric charges, or magnetism, by recording the amount of torsion they produce in a fine wire

torsion bar a metal bar exhibiting resilience under torsion, part of the wheel suspension on some automotive vehicles

torsk (tôrsk) *n., pl.* **torsk, torsks**: see PLURAL, II, D, 2 [< Norw. *torsk* < ON. *thorskr*: for IE. base see THIRST] a fish of the cod family

tor·so (tôr′sō) *n., pl.* **-sos, -si** (-sē) [It., a stump, trunk of a statue < L. *thyrsus*, a stalk, stem < Gr. *thyrsos*, a stem, wand] **1.** the trunk of a statue of the nude human figure, esp. of such a statue lacking the head and full limbs **2.** the trunk of the human body **3.** any unfinished or fragmentary piece of work

tort (tôrt) *n.* [ME. < OFr. < ML. *tortum* < neut. of L. *tortus*, pp. of *torquere*, to twist < IE. *terk-*, to turn < base *ter-*, to rub: cf. THROW] *Law* a wrongful act, injury, or damage (not involving a breach of contract), for which a civil action can be brought

torte (tôrt; *G.* tôr′tə) *n., pl.* **tortes**, *G.* **tor·ten** (tôr′tən) [G. < It. *torta* < LL., a twisted bread] a rich cake, variously made, as of eggs, finely chopped nuts, and crumbs or a little flour

tort-fea·sor (tôrt′fē′zər) *n.* [Fr. *tortfaiseur* < MFr. < *tort*, TORT + *faiseur*, one who does < *fais-*, stem of *faire*, to do < L. *facere*: see FACT] *Law* a person who commits or is guilty of a tort

tor·ti·col·lis (tôr′ti käl′is) *n.* [ModL. < L. *tortus*, twisted + *collum*, the neck: see TORT & COLLAR] *Med.* a condition of persistent involuntary contraction of the neck muscles, causing the head to be twisted to an abnormal position

tor·tile (tôr′t'l, -tīl) *adj.* [L. *tortilis* < *tortus*: see TORT] twisted or coiled

☆**tor·til·la** (tôr tē′ə) *n.* [Sp., dim. of *torta*, a cake < LL. *torta*, twisted loaf] a thin, flat, round cake of unleavened cornmeal, now sometimes of flour, baked on a griddle or, orig., a flat stone: a staple food throughout Mexico

tor·tious (tôr′shəs) *adj.* [ME. *torcious* < Anglo-Fr.] *Law* of or involving a tort —**tor′tious·ly** *adv.*

tor·toise (tôr′təs) *n., pl.* **-tois·es, -toise**: see PLURAL, II, D, 1 [ME. *tortuce* < ML. *tortuca*, altered (prob. by association with L. *tortus*, twisted) < VL. *tartaruca* < ? LGr. *tartarouchos*, evil demon, orig., controlling Tartarus] a turtle, esp. one that lives on land: see TURTLE

tortoise beetle any of various small, often brightly colored or iridescent, turtle-shaped beetles (family Chrysomelidae) that feed chiefly on plant leaves

tortoise shell 1. the hard, mottled, yellow-and-brown shell of some turtles and tortoises, used in inlaying and, esp. formerly, in making combs, frames for eyeglasses, etc. **2.** a synthetic substance made in imitation of this **3.** any of several common, black and yellow-brown butterflies (genus *Nymphalis*) with markings resembling those of tortoise shell —**tor′toise-shell′** *adj.*

Tor·to·la (tôr tō′lə) chief island of the Brit. Virgin Islands: 21 sq. mi.; pop. 6,000

tor·to·ni (tôr tō′nē) *n.* [prob. altered < It. *tortone*, lit., big tart < *torta*, tart < L., orig. fem. of *tortus*: see TART] an ice cream made with heavy cream, maraschino cherries, almonds, etc.

tor·tri·cid (tôr′trə sid) *n.* [< ModL. *Tortricidae*, name of the family < *Tortrix*, type genus < L. *tortus*, pp. of *torquere*: see TORT] any of a family (Tortricidae) of small, broad-bodied moths whose larvae feed on the leaves of shrubs and trees: the larvae of some species roll and fasten leaves together to form nests

Tor·tu·ga (tôr tōō′gə) island of Haiti, off the NW coast: c.70 sq. mi. Fr. name **La Tor·tue** (lä tôr tü′)

tor·tu·os·i·ty (tôr′chōō wäs′ə tē) *n.* [L. *tortuositas*] **1.** the quality or condition of being tortuous **2.** *pl.* **-ties** a twist, turn, winding, etc.

tor·tu·ous (tôr′chōō wəs) *adj.* [ME. < Anglo-Fr. < L. *tortuosus* < *tortus*, pp. of *torquere*: see TORT] **1.** full of

fat, āpe, cär; ten, ēven; is, bīte; gō, hôrn, tōōl, look; oil, out; up, fʉr; get; joy; yet; chin; she; thin, *then*; zh, leisure; ŋ, ring; ə for *a* in *ago*, *e* in *agent*, *i* in *sanity*, *o* in *comply*, *u* in *focus*; ' as in *able* (ā′b'l); Fr. bal; ë, Fr. coeur; ö, Fr. feu; ô, Fr. mon; б, Fr. coq; ü, Fr. duc; ɼ, Fr. cri; H, G. ich; kh, G. doch. See inside front cover. ☆ Americanism; ‡foreign; *hypothetical; < derived from

twists, turns, curves, or windings; winding; crooked **2.** not straightforward; devious; specif., deceitful or tricky — **tor′tu·ous·ly** *adv.* —**tor′tu·ous·ness** *n.*

tor·ture (tôr′chər) *n.* [Fr. < LL. *tortura,* a twisting, torture < pp. of L. *torquere,* to twist: see TORT] **1.** the inflicting of severe pain to force information or confession, get revenge, etc. **2.** any method by which such pain is inflicted **3.** any severe physical or mental pain; agony; anguish **4.** a cause of such pain or agony **5.** [Rare] a violent twisting, distortion, perversion, etc. —*vt.* **-tured, -tur·ing 1.** to subject to torture **2.** to cause extreme physical or mental pain to; agonize **3.** to twist or distort (meaning, language, etc.) —*SYN.* see TORMENT —**tor′tur·er** *n.* —**tor′tur·ous** *adj.* —**tor′tur·ous·ly** *adv.*

tor·u·la (tôr′oo lə) *n., pl.* **-lae′** (-lē′), **-las** [ModL. < L. *torus,* a swelling, protuberance + *-ula,* -ULE] any of a group of yeastlike fungi that reproduce by budding: some cause animal disease, others ferment food

To·ruń (tô′roon y′) city in NC Poland, on the Vistula: pop. 114,000

to·rus (tôr′əs) *n., pl.* **-ri** (-ī) [L., a bulge, protuberance] **1.** *Anat.* any rounded projection or swelling **2.** *Archit.* a large, convex molding used at the base of columns, etc., just above the plinth **3.** *Bot. a*) same as RECEPTACLE (sense 3 *a*) *b*) a thick spot at the center of the pit membrane in bordered pits of xylem cells **4.** *Geom.* a surface, or its enclosed solid, generated by the revolution of a conic, esp. a circle, about any line in its plane and external to it

To·ry (tôr′ē) *n., pl.* **-ries** [Ir. *tōruidhe,* robber, pursuer < *tōir,* to pursue, akin to Gael. *tōir,* pursuit] **1.** [*sometimes* t-] *a*) in the 17th cent. any of the dispossessed Irish who became outlaws, killed English settlers and soldiers, and lived by plundering *b*) later, an armed Irish Catholic or Royalist **2.** in 1679–1680, a person who opposed the exclusion of James, Duke of York, from succession to the English throne **3.** after 1689, a member of one of the two major political parties of England: opposed to *Whig,* and later, to *Liberal, Radical, Laborite;* changed officially c.1830 to *Conservative* **4.** in the American Revolution, a person who advocated or actively supported continued allegiance to Great Britain **5.** [*often* t-] any extreme conservative; reactionary —*adj.* [*also* t-] of, being, or having the conservative principles of a Tory —**To′ry·ism** *n.*

Tos·ca·na (tôs kä′nä) *It.* name of TUSCANY

Tos·ca·ni·ni (täs′kə nē′nē; *It.* tôs′kä nē′nē), **Ar·tu·ro** (är toor′ō; *It.* är too′rō) 1867–1957; It. orchestral conductor, esp. in the U.S.

tosh (täsh) *n., interj.* [< ?] [Chiefly Brit. Colloq.] nonsense

toss (tôs, täs) *vt.* [prob. < Scand., as in Norw. dial. *tossa,* to spread, strew, akin to MLowG. *tōsen,* to tear, ME. (*to*)*tusen,* to pull to pieces < IE. base **dā*(*i*), to part, tear, whence TEASE] **1.** to throw or pitch about; fling here and there; buffet [*a* boat *tossed* by a storm] ☆**2.** to mix lightly the parts or ingredients of (esp. a salad) **3.** to disturb; agitate; disquiet **4.** to throw (in various senses); specif., to throw upward, lightly and easily, from the hand **5.** to throw in or bandy (ideas, remarks, etc.) **6.** to lift quickly; jerk upward [*tossing* her head in disdain] **7.** to toss up with (someone *for* something): see phrase below —*vi.* **1.** to be flung to and fro; be thrown about or pitched about **2.** to fling oneself about in sleep, etc.; be restless in bed **3.** to move or go impatiently, angrily, or disdainfully, as with a toss of the head **4.** to toss up: see phrase below —*n.* **1.** a tossing or being tossed; a throw, fling, pitch, etc. **2.** *clipped form of* TOSSUP (sense 1) **3.** the distance that something is or can be tossed —*SYN.* see THROW —**toss off 1.** to make, do, write, etc. quickly, casually, and without effort **2.** to drink up in one draft —**toss up** to toss a coin for deciding something according to which side lands uppermost —**toss′er** *n.*

toss·pot (tôs′pät′, täs′-) *n.* [prec. + POT] a drunkard

toss·up (-up′) *n.* **1.** the act of tossing or flipping a coin to decide something according to which side lands uppermost **2.** an even chance

tost (tôst, täst) *archaic pt. & pp. of* TOSS

tos·ta·da (tôs tä′də) *n.* [AmSp., orig. fem. of *tostado,* fried < Sp., toasted, pp. of *tostar,* to toast, roast < VL. **tostare,* to TOAST[1]] ☆a tortilla fried until crisp: also **tos·ta′do** (-dō), *pl.* **-dos**

tot[1] (tät) *n.* [prob. < Scand., as in ON. *tuttr,* small chap, *tutta,* little girl] **1.** a young child **2.** [Chiefly Brit.] a small drink of alcoholic liquor

tot[2] (tät) *vt., vi.* **tot′ted, tot′ting** [contr. < TOTAL] [Chiefly Brit. Colloq.] to add; total (usually with *up*)

tot. total

to·tal (tōt′'l) *adj.* [ME. < MFr. < ML. *totalis* < L. *totus,* all, whole < IE. base **tēu-,* to swell, whence THUMB] **1.** constituting the (or a) whole; entire; whole **2.** complete; utter [*a* total *loss*] —*n.* the whole amount or number; sum; aggregate —*vt.* **-taled** or **-talled, -tal·ing** or **-tal·ling 1.** to find the total of; add **2.** to equal a total of; add up to ☆**3.** [Slang] to wreck completely; demolish —*vi.* to amount (*to*) as a whole —*SYN.* see COMPLETE, SUM

total depravity the utter depravity of man which Calvinists regard as due to original sin and as persisting until regeneration through the Spirit of God

to·tal·i·sa·tor (tōt′'l ī zāt′ər) *n. var. sp. of* TOTALIZATOR

to·tal·is·tic (tōt′'l is′tik) *adj. same as* TOTALITARIAN: also **to′tal·ist** —**to′tal·ism** *n.*

to·tal·i·tar·i·an (tō tal′ə ter′ē ən, tō′tal ə-) *adj.* [TOTAL + (AUTHOR)ITARIAN] **1.** designating, of, or characteristic of a government or state in which one political party or group maintains complete control under a dictatorship and bans all others **2.** completely authoritarian, autocratic, dictatorial, etc. —*n.* a person who favors such a government or state —**to·tal′i·tar′i·an·ism** *n.*

to·tal·i·ty (tō tal′ə tē) *n., pl.* **-ties 1.** the fact or condition of being total; entirety **2.** the total amount or sum —**in totality** as a whole; altogether

to·tal·i·za·tor (tōt′'l ī zāt′ər) *n.* [Fr. *totalisateur*] any machine for computing and showing totals of measurements, etc.; esp., a machine used in parimutuel betting for registering bets and, usually, computing the odds and payoffs while the bets are being placed

to·tal·ize (tōt′'l īz′) *vt.* **-ized′, -iz′ing** to make a total of; combine into a total —**to′tal·i·za′tion** *n.*

to·tal·iz·er (-ī′zər) *n.* a person or thing that totals; specif., *same as* TOTALIZATOR

to·tal·ly (-ē) *adv.* wholly; completely; altogether

☆**total recall** the ability of a person to recall the past accurately in seemingly complete detail

to·ta·quine (tō′tə kwēn′, -kwin) *n.* [< ModL. *totaquina* < LL. *totalis,* TOTAL + Sp. *quina,* cinchona bark (see QUININE): because it contains all the alkaloids of cinchona bark] a yellowish-white to gray powder containing a mixture of quinine and other alkaloids, obtained from cinchona bark and used as an antimalarial

☆**tote[1]** (tōt) *vt.* **tot′ed, tot′ing** [prob. < Afr. orig., as in Kongo *tota,* to pick up] [Colloq.] **1.** to carry or haul, esp. in the arms or on the back **2.** to be armed with (a gun, etc.) —*n.* **1.** [Colloq.] *a*) the act of toting *b*) something toted; load; haul **2.** *clipped form of* TOTE BAG —**tot′er** *n.*

tote[2] (tōt) *vt.* **tot′ed, tot′ing** *clipped form of* TOTAL (usually with *up*)

tote[3] (tōt) *n. clipped form of* TOTALIZATOR

tote bag ☆a large, open handbag of cloth, straw, etc., in which women can carry shoes, small packages, etc.

tote board [Colloq.] a large board facing the grandstand at a race track, on which the bets, odds, and payoffs recorded by a totalizator are flashed

to·tem (tōt′əm) *n.* [of AmInd. (Algonquian) origin, as in Ojibway *ototeman,* Cree *ototema,* his relations] **1.** among primitive peoples, an animal or natural object considered as being related by blood to a given family or clan and taken as its symbol **2.** an image of this —**to·tem′ic** (tō tem′ik) *adj.*

to·tem·ism (tōt′əm iz′m) *n.* **1.** belief in totems and totemic relationships **2.** the use of totems to distinguish families **3.** social customs based on this —**to′tem·ist** *n.*

totem pole **1.** a pole or post carved and painted with totems, often erected in front of their dwellings by Indian tribes of the NW coast of N. America **2.** a hierarchical system [at the top of the educational *totem pole*]

toth·er, t'oth·er, 'toth·er (tu th′ər) *adj., pron.* [ME. *the tother,* by faulty division of *thet other, that other*] [Chiefly Dial.] that (or the) other

to·ti- (tōt′ə) [< L. *totus,* whole: see TOTAL] a combining form meaning whole or wholly; entire or entirely [*totipalmate*]

to·ti·pal·mate (tōt′ə pal′māt) *adj.* [TOTI- + PALMATE] having all four toes completely united by a web, as ducks, geese, pelicans, etc. —**to′ti·pal·ma′tion** *n.*

to·tip·o·tent (tō tip′ə tənt) *adj.* [TOTI- + POTENT] *Zool.* capable of developing into a complete embryo or organ: said of a cleavage cell —**to·tip′o·ten·cy** (-tən sē) *n.*

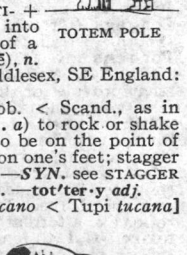

TOTEM POLE

Tot·ten·ham (tät′'n əm) city in Middlesex, SE England: suburb of London: pop. 113,000

tot·ter (tät′ər) *vi.* [ME. *toteren,* prob. < Scand., as in Norw. dial. *totra,* to quiver, shake] **1.** *a*) to rock or shake as if about to fall; be unsteady *b*) to be on the point of failure or collapse **2.** to be unsteady on one's feet; stagger —*n.* an unsteady walk or movement —*SYN.* see STAGGER —**tot′ter·ing** *adj.* —**tot′ter·ing·ly** *adv.* —**tot′ter·y** *adj.*

tou·can (tōō′kan) *n.* [Fr. < Port. *tucano* < Tupi *tucana*] any of a family (Ramphastidae) of brightly colored, fruit-eating birds of tropical America, distinguished by a very large beak

touch (tuch) *vt.* [ME. *touchen* < OFr. *tochier* (Fr. *toucher*) < VL. **toccare* < **tok,* light blow, of echoic origin] **1.** to put the hand, finger, or some other part of the body on, so as to feel; perceive by the sense of feeling **2.** to bring into contact with something else [*to touch* a match to kindling, to *touch* the ceiling with a stick] **3.** formerly, to lay the hand on (a person with scrofula), as some kings once did, supposedly to effect a cure **4.** to be or come into contact with **5.** to border on; adjoin **6.** to strike lightly **7.** to be effective on contact; have a

TOUCAN
(1 1/2–2 ft. long, including beak)

physical effect on: usually used in the negative [water won't *touch* these grease spots] **8.** to injure slightly [frost *touched* the plants] **9.** to give a light tint, aspect, etc. to: used chiefly in the past participle [clouds *touched* with pink] **10.** to stop at (a port, etc.) in passing: said of a ship **11.** to lay hands on; handle; use **12.** to manhandle or molest **13.** to taste or partake of: usually used in the negative [didn't *touch* his supper] **14.** to come up to; reach; attain **15.** to compare with; equal; rival: usually used in the negative [cooking that can't *touch* hers] **16.** to take or make use of without permission or wrongly; misappropriate **17.** to deal with or refer to, esp. in a light or passing way; mention **18.** to have to do with; affect; concern [a subject that *touches* our welfare] **19.** to arouse an emotion in, esp. one of sympathy, gratitude, etc. **20.** to hurt the feelings of; pain [*touched* him to the quick] **21.** [Slang] to ask for, or get by asking, a loan or gift of money from **22.** [Archaic] *a*) to strike the keys of, pluck the strings of, etc. (a musical instrument) *b*) to play (a few notes, an air, etc.) **23.** *Geom.* to be tangent to —*vi.* **1.** to touch a person or thing **2.** to be or come in contact **3.** to come near to something; verge (*on* or *upon*) **4.** to pertain; bear (*on* or *upon*) **5.** to treat a topic slightly or in passing (with *on* or *upon*) **6.** to stop briefly or land (*at* a port, etc.) during a voyage **7.** *Geom.* to be tangent —*n.* **1.** a touching or being touched; specif., *a*) a light tap, stroke, etc. *b*) a delicate stroke made with a brush in painting, etc. **2.** the sense by which physical objects are felt; tactile sense **3.** a sensation caused by touching, esp. one characteristic of a particular substance or texture; tactile quality; feel **4.** a mental capacity analogous to the sense of touch; mental or moral sensitivity **5.** a special or characteristic quality, skill, or manner [he lost his *touch*] **6.** an effect of being touched; specif., *a*) a mark, impression, etc. left by touching *b*) a subtle change or addition in a painting, story, or other work **7.** a very small amount, degree, etc.; specif., *a*) a trace, tinge, etc. [a *touch* of humor] *b*) a slight attack [a *touch* of the flu] **8.** *a*) formerly, a touchstone or the testing of the quality of gold, silver, etc. by use of a touchstone *b*) an official stamp attesting to the standard fineness of gold, silver, etc. **9.** any test or criterion **10.** contact or communication [to lose *touch* with reality, to keep in *touch* with friends] **11.** [Slang] *a*) the act of asking for, or getting in this way, a gift or loan of money [to make a *touch*] *b*) money so gotten *c*) a person with reference to the ease with which money can be so gotten from him **12.** *Music a*) the manner in which a performer strikes the keys of a keyboard instrument [a delicate *touch*] *b*) the manner in which the action of a piano, etc. responds to the fingers [a piano with a heavy *touch*] *c*) in bell ringing, a set of changes less than a peal **13.** *Rugby, Soccer* the part of the field outside the sidelines —*SYN.* see AFFECT¹ —**touch down** to land: said of an aircraft or spacecraft —**touch off 1.** to represent accurately or aptly **2.** to make explode or detonate; fire **3.** to motivate or initiate (esp. a violent action or reaction) —**touch up 1.** to stimulate or rouse, as by a tap or light blow **2.** to improve or finish (a painting, literary work, etc.) by minor changes or additions —**touch′a·bil′i·ty** *n.* —**touch′a·ble** *adj.* —**touch′er** *n.*

touch and go an uncertain, risky, or precarious situation —**touch-and-go** (tuch′ən gō′) *adj.*

☆**touch·back** (-bak′) *n. Football* a play in which a player grounds the ball behind his own goal line when the ball was caused to pass the goal line by an opponent: distinguished from SAFETY

☆**touch·down** (-doun′) *n.* **1.** *a*) the act of touching down, or landing *b*) the moment at which a landing aircraft or spacecraft touches the landing surface **2.** *Football a*) a scoring play in which a player grounds the ball on or past the opponent's goal line *b*) a score of six points so made

tou·ché (tōō shā′) *interj.* [Fr., pp.: see TOUCH] *Fencing* touched: said when one's opponent scores a point by a touch: also used to acknowledge a successful point in debate or a witty retort

touched (tucht) *adj.* **1.** emotionally affected; moved **2.** slightly demented or unbalanced: also **touched in the head**

☆**touch football** an informal variety of football in which a defensive player stops a play by touching the ball carrier (usually with both hands) rather than tackling him

touch·hole (tuch′hōl′) *n.* in early firearms, the hole in the breech through which the charge was touched off

touch·ing (-iŋ) *adj.* that touches the feelings; arousing tender emotion; affecting —*prep.* concerning; with regard to —*SYN.* see MOVING —**touch′ing·ly** *adv.*

touch·line (-līn′) *n. Rugby, Soccer* either of the sidelines bounding the field

touch-me-not (-mē nät′) *n. same as* JEWELWEED

touch·stone (-stōn′) *n.* **1.** a type of black stone formerly used to test the purity of gold or silver by the streak left on it when it was rubbed with the metal **2.** any test or criterion for determining genuineness or value

☆**touch system** a method of typing without looking at the keyboard, by regularly touching a given key with a specific finger

☆**Touch-Tone** (-tōn′) *a trademark for* a telephone that instead of a dial has push buttons, each of which activates an electronic sound having a fixed tone

☆**touch-type** (-tīp′) *vi.* **-typed′, -typ′ing** to type by means of the touch system —**touch′-typ′ist** *n.*

touch·wood (-wood′) *n.* [? altered (after TOUCH) < ME. *tache*, touchwood] dried, decayed wood or dried fungus used as tinder; punk

touch·y (tuch′ē) *adj.* **touch′i·er, touch′i·est** [TOUCH + -Y²: also (sense 1) altered < TECHY] **1.** easily offended; oversensitive; irritable **2.** sensitive to touch; easily irritated, as a part of the body **3.** very risky [a *touchy* situation] **4.** highly flammable or readily ignited —*SYN.* see IRRITABLE —**touch′i·ly** *adv.* —**touch′i·ness** *n.*

tough (tuf) *adj.* [ME. < OE. *toh*, akin to G. *zäh*, tough, viscous, prob. < IE. base **denk-*, to bite, whence TONGS] **1.** strong but pliant; that will bend, twist, etc. without tearing or breaking **2.** that will not cut or chew easily [*tough* steak] **3.** strongly cohesive; glutinous; viscous; sticky [*tough* putty] **4.** *a*) strong of physique; robust; hardy *b*) displaying mental or moral firmness **5.** hard to convince or influence; stubborn **6.** practical and realistic rather than emotional or sentimental ☆**7.** overly aggressive; brutal or rough **8.** *a*) very difficult; toilsome *b*) vigorous or violent [a *tough* fight] **9.** [Colloq.] unfavorable; bad [a *tough* break] ☆**10.** [Slang] fine; excellent: a generalized term of approval —*n.* a tough person; thug —*SYN.* see STRONG —**tough′ly** *adv.* —**tough′ness** *n.*

tough·en (-'n) *vt., vi.* to make or become tough or tougher —**tough′en·er** *n.*

tough·ie, tough·y (-ē) *n., pl.* **-ies** [Colloq.] **1.** a tough person; ruffian **2.** a difficult problem or situation

tough-mind·ed (-mīn′did) *adj.* shrewd and unsentimental; practical; realistic —**tough′mind′ed·ness** *n.*

Tou·lon (tōō län′; *Fr.* tōō lōn′) seaport in SE France, on the Mediterranean: pop. 162,000

Tou·louse (tōō lōōz′) city in S France, on the Garonne River: pop. 324,000

Tou·louse-Lau·trec (tōō lōōz′lō trek′), **Hen·ri (Marie Raymond) de** (än rē′ də) 1864-1901; Fr. painter & lithographer

tou·pee (tōō pā′) *n.* [Fr. *toupet*, dim. of OFr. *toup, top*, tuft of hair < Frank. **top*, akin to G. *zopf*: cf. TOP¹] **1.** formerly, a curl or lock of hair worn on top of the head, sometimes as part of a wig **2.** a man's wig, esp. a small one for covering a bald spot

tour (toor) *n.* [ME. < MFr. < OFr. *torn* < *torner*, to TURN] **1.** a turn or shift of work; esp., a period of duty or military service at a single place: in full **tour of duty 2.** a long trip, as for sightseeing **3.** any trip, as for inspection; round; circuit; specif., a trip, as by a theatrical company or speaker, to give performances, lectures, etc. at a number of cities —*vi.* to go on a tour —*vt.* **1.** to take a tour through **2.** to take (a play, theatrical company, etc.) on a tour —**on tour** touring, as to give performances, lectures, etc.

tou·ra·co (toor′ə kō′, toor′ə kō′) *n., pl.* **-cos′** [prob. via Fr. < WAfr. native name] any of several brightly colored, tropical forest birds (family Musophagidae) of Africa, with a short, stout bill, long tail, and erectile crest

Tou·raine (tōō rān′; *Fr.* tōō ren′) region & former province of WC France: chief city, Tours

tour·bil·lion (toor bil′yən) *n.* [LME. *turbilloun* < MFr. *tourbillon*, whirlwind, altered < VL. **turbinio* < L. *turbo*: see TURBINE] **1.** orig., a whirlwind **2.** a firework that rises with a spiral motion

Tour·coing (toor kwan′) city in N France, near the Belgian border: pop. 89,000

tour de force (toor′ də fôrs′) *pl.* **tours′ de force′** (toor′) [Fr., feat of strength] an unusually skillful or ingenious creation, production, or performance, sometimes one that is merely clever or spectacular

Tou·ré (tōō rā′), **Sé·kou** (sä′kōō), 1922– ; president of Guinea (1958–)

☆**touring car** an early type of open automobile, often with a folding top, seating five or more passengers

tour·ism (toor′iz'm) *n.* tourist travel, esp. when regarded as a source of income for a country, business, etc. —**tour·is′tic** *adj.*

tour·ist (-ist) *n.* **1.** a person who makes a tour, esp. for pleasure **2.** tourist class —*adj.* **1.** of or for tourists **2.** designating or of the lowest-priced accommodations, as on a ship —*adv.* in or by means of tourist class

☆**tourist court** *same as* MOTEL

☆**tourist home** a private home in which bedrooms are rented to tourists or travelers

tour·ma·line (toor′mə lin, -lēn′) *n.* [Fr., ult. < Singhalese *tōramalli*, a carnelian] a crystalline mineral that is a complex silicate of boron and aluminum, with some magnesium, iron, etc.: it occurs in a common black variety and in colored and transparent varieties used as gemstones and in optical equipment

Tour·nai (tōōr nā′) city in W Belgium, on the Scheldt River: pop. 33,000

tour·na·ment (toor′nə mənt, tur′-) *n.* [ME. *tournement* < OFr. *torneiement < torneier:* see TOURNEY] **1.** in the

Middle Ages, *a*) a sport consisting of an encounter between knights on horseback, in which the opponents tried to unseat one another with lances, the winner receiving a prize; jousting contest *b*) a series of such encounters presented as an entertainment 2. a series of contests in some sport, chess, or bridge, usually a competition for championship

‡**tour·ne·dos** (tŏōr nə dō′) *n., pl.* **-dos′** (-dō′) [Fr. < *tourner*, to TURN + *dos* (see DOSS)] a small, round beefsteak cut from the tenderloin and prepared with a sauce

tour·ney (tŏōr′nē, tur′-) *n., pl.* **-neys** [ME. *turnai* < OFr. *tornei* < *torneier* < base of *tourner*: see TURN] *same as* TOURNAMENT —*vi.* [ME. *tourneien* < OFr. *torneier*] to take part in a tournament; joust

tour·ni·quet (tŏōr′na kit, tur′-; -kā′) *n.* [Fr., altered in sense and form (after *tourner*, to TURN) < MFr. *turniquet*, earlier *turniquel*, coat of mail, upper garment < OFr. *tunicle* < L. *tunicula*, dim. of *tunica*, tunic] any device for compressing a blood vessel to stop bleeding or control the circulation of blood to some part, as a bandage twisted about a limb and released at intervals or a pad pressed down by a screw

TOURNI-QUET

Tours (toor; *Fr.* tŏōr) city in WC France, on the Loire: site of a battle (732 A.D.) in which the Franks under Charles Martel defeated the Saracens: pop. 93,000

tou·sle (tou′z'l) *vt.* **-sled, -sling** [freq. of ME. *tusen* (in comp.), to pull, tear, akin to TEASE, TOSS] to disorder, dishevel, muss, rumple, etc. —*n.* a tousled condition, mass of hair, etc.

Tous·saint L'Ou·ver·ture (tŏō san′ lŏō ver tür′) (born *Pierre François Dominique Toussaint*) 1743?-1803; Haitian Negro liberator & general

tout (tout) *vi.* [ME. *toten* < OE. *totian*, to peep, look out after] [Colloq.] 1. to solicit customers, patrons, votes, etc. 2. *a*) esp. in England, to spy on racehorses in training, etc. in order to secure tips for betting *b*) to provide betting tips on horse races —*vt.* [Colloq.] 1. to praise or recommend highly; puff 3. *a*) to solicit or importune, as for business 3. *a*) to spy out or otherwise get information on (racehorses) ☆*b*) to give a tip on (a racehorse) for a price —*n.* [Colloq.] a person who touts; esp., a person who makes a business of selling tips on racehorses —**tout′er** *n.*

‡**tout à fait** (tŏō tá fe′) [Fr., lit., all done] entirely; quite

‡**tout de suite** (tŏōt swēt′) [Fr., lit., all in succession] immediately; right away

‡**tout en·sem·ble** (tŏō tän sän′bl′) [Fr., lit., all (taken) together] 1. everything being considered; all in all 2. the general effect; total impression, as of a work of art

‡**tout le monde** (tŏō le mŏnd′) [Fr., lit., all the world] everyone

tou·zle (tou′z'l) *n., vt.* **-zled, -zling** *var. of* TOUSLE

to·va·rish, to·va·rich (tō vär′ish; *Russ.* tô vär′ishch) *n.* [Russ. *tovarishch*] *same as* COMRADE

To·vey (tō′vē), Sir **Donald Francis** 1875-1940; Eng. musicologist & music critic

tow¹ (tō) *vt.* [ME. *towen* < OE. *togian*, akin to OHG. *zogōn*, to draw, tug: for IE. base see TUG] 1. to pull by a rope or chain 2. to pull or drag behind —*n.* 1. a towing or being towed 2. something towed 3. *same as* TOWLINE —*SYN.* see PULL —**in tow** 1. being towed 2. in one's company or retinue [with several admirers in *tow*] 3. under one's control or charge

tow² (tō) *n.* [ME. < OE. *tow-*, for spinning, akin to *tawian*: see TAW²] the coarse and broken fibers of hemp, flax, etc. before spinning —*adj.* of or resembling tow

tow·age (tō′ij) *n.* [ME.] 1. a towing or being towed 2. the charge for this

to·ward (tôrd; *also for prep.,* tə wôrd′; *also, and for adj. usually,* tō′ərd) *prep.* [ME. < OE. *toweard*: see TO & -WARD] 1. in the direction of 2. so as to face; facing 3. in a manner designed to achieve or along a course likely to result in [steps *toward* peace] 4. concerning; regarding; about [a negative attitude *toward* abstract art] 5. close to or just before (in time) [*toward* daybreak] 6. in anticipation of; in order to get; for [saving *toward* a new car] 7. so as to help pay for [to contribute *toward* a new library] —*adj.* [Archaic or Rare] 1. favorable; propitious 2. ready to learn; promising 3. docile; compliant 4. at hand; imminent 5. being done; in progress: used predicatively

to·ward·ly (tō′ərd lē, tôrd′lē) *adj.* [prec. + -LY¹] [Archaic or Rare] 1. favorable, propitious, or promising 2. tractable; docile 3. friendly; affable

to·wards (tôrdz, tə wôrdz′) *prep.* [ME. *towardes* < OE. *toweardes* < *toweard* + *adv. gen.* (-*e*)*s*] *same as* TOWARD

tow·boat (tō′bōt′) *n.* 1. *same as* TUGBOAT ☆2. a boat used for pushing a barge or group of barges in inland waters

tow·el (tou′'l, toul) *n.* [ME. *towaille* < OFr. *toaille* (Fr. *touaille*) < Frank. **thwahlja*, akin to OHG. *dwahila*, towel < *dwahan*, to wash < IE. base **twak-*, to bathe, whence OPr. *twaxtan*, bath towel] a piece of absorbent cloth or paper for wiping or drying things or for drying oneself after washing or bathing [a dish *towel*, a bath *towel*] —*vt.* **-eled** or **-elled, -el·ing** or **-el·ling** to wipe or dry with a towel —**throw** (or **toss**, etc.) **in the towel** [Colloq.] to admit defeat —**towel off** to dry oneself, as after bathing

tow·el·ing, tow·el·ling (tou′'l iŋ, toul′iŋ) *n.* material for making towels

tow·er¹ (tou′ər) *n.* [ME. *tour, tur* < OE. *torr* & OFr. *tur*, both < L. *turris*, a tower, akin to Gr. *tyrsis*, fortified city] 1. a building or structure that is relatively high for its length and width, either standing alone or forming part of another building 2. such a structure used as a fortress or prison 3. a person or thing that resembles a tower in height, strength, dominance, etc. —*vi.* to rise high or stand high like a tower

tow·er² (tō′ər) *n.* a person or thing that tows

tow·ered (tou′ərd) *adj.* having a tower or towers

tow·er·ing (tou′ər iŋ) *adj.* 1. that towers; very high or tall 2. very great, intense, violent, etc. [a *towering* rage] —*SYN.* see HIGH

Tower of London a fortress on the Thames in London, serving in historic times as a palace, prison, etc.

tow·er·y (tou′ər ē) *adj.* 1. having towers; towered 2. towering; high; lofty

☆**tow·head** (tō′hed′) *n.* [see TOW²] 1. a head of pale-yellow hair 2. a person having such hair —**tow′head′ed** *adj.*

☆**tow·hee** (tou′hē, tō′-) *n.* [echoic of the note] any of various small, N. American, ground-feeding sparrows (family Fringillidae), esp. the chewink

tow·line (tō′lin′) *n.* a rope, chain, etc. used for towing

town (toun) *n.* [ME. < OE. *tun*, enclosed space, group of houses, village, town, akin to G. *zaun*, fence, hedge, OIr. *dūn*, fortified camp] 1. [Brit. Dial.] a group of houses; hamlet 2. a more or less concentrated group of houses and private and public buildings, larger than a village but smaller than a city 3. a city or other thickly populated urban place ☆4. *a*) in parts of the U.S., *same as* TOWNSHIP *b*) in New England and some other States, a unit of local government having its sovereignty vested in a town meeting 5. in England, a village that holds a market periodically 6. the business center of a city [to go into *town*] 7. the inhabitants, voters, etc. of a town 8. the local residents of a town as distinct from the members of a college within the town: cf. GOWN —*adj.* of, for, or characteristic of a town —**go to town** [Slang] 1. to go on a spree; indulge in something without restraint 2. to work or act fast and efficiently ☆3. to be eminently successful —☆**on the town** [Colloq.] out for a good time at the theater, nightclubs, bars, etc.

town clerk an official in charge of the records, legal business, etc. of a town

town crier a person who formerly cried public announcements through the streets of a village or town

town hall a building in a town, containing the offices of public officials, the council chamber, etc.

town house 1. a city residence, esp. as distinguished from a country residence of the same owner ☆2. a two-story dwelling that is one of a planned complex of such, often contiguous, dwellings

town·ie (tou′nē) *n.* [Colloq.] a resident of a town, ☆esp. one of college age, who is not a student at the local college

☆**town meeting** 1. a meeting of the people of a town 2. esp. in New England, a meeting of the qualified voters of a town to act upon town business

towns·folk (tounz′fōk′) *n.pl. same as* TOWNSPEOPLE

town·ship (toun′ship) *n.* [ME. *tunscipe* < OE. *tunscipe*, people living in a *tun*: see TOWN & -SHIP] 1. orig., in England, a parish or division of a parish, as a unit of territory and administration 2. in parts of the U.S., a division of a county, constituting a unit of local government with administrative control of local schools, roads, etc. 3. in New England, *same as* TOWN (sense 4 *b*) 4. a unit of territory in the U.S. land survey, generally six miles square, containing 36 mile-square sections, and sometimes, but not necessarily, coextensive with a governmental township 5. in Canada, a subdivision of a province

towns·man (tounz′mən) *n., pl.* **-men** [ME. *tunesman* < OE. < *gen.* of *tun*, TOWN + *man*, MAN] 1. a person who lives in, or has been reared in, a town 2. a fellow resident of the town in which one lives

towns·peo·ple (-pē′p'l) *n.pl.* 1. the people of a town 2. people brought up in a town or city, as distinguished from those brought up in the country

Towns·ville (tounz′vil) seaport on the E coast of Queensland, Australia: pop. 59,000

☆**tow·path** (tō′path′, -päth′) *n.* a path alongside a canal, used by men or animals towing canalboats

tow·rope (-rōp′) *n.* a rope used in towing

Tow·son (tou′sən) [after the *Towson* family, early settlers] suburb of Baltimore, in N Md.: pop. 78,000

☆**tow truck** a truck equipped for towing away vehicles that are disabled, illegally parked, etc.

tox·al·bu·min (täk′sal byōō′mən) *n.* [TOX(IC) + ALBUMIN] a poisonous protein found in certain plants and cultures of bacteria, and in snake venoms

☆**tox·a·phene** (täk′sa fēn′) *n.* [arbitrary blend < TOXIC + (CAM)PHENE] a commercial insecticide, $C_{10}H_{10}Cl_8$, made by chlorinating camphene

tox·e·mi·a (täk sē′mē ə) *n.* [ModL.: see TOXIC & -EMIA] a condition resulting from distribution throughout the body by the bloodstream of poisonous substances, esp. toxins produced by pathogenic bacteria or by cells of the body: also sp. **tox·ae′mi·a** (-mik) —**tox·e′mic** (-mik) *adj.*

tox·ic (täk′sik) *adj.* [ML. *toxicus* < L. *toxicum*, a poison < Gr. *toxikon*, a poison, orig., poison in which arrows were dipped < *toxikos*, of or for a bow < *toxon*, a bow]

1. of, affected by, or caused by a toxin, or poison 2. acting as a poison; poisonous —**tox·ic′i·ty** (-sis′ə tē) n.

tox·i·cant (-si kənt) adj. [LL. toxicans, prp. of toxicare, to smear with poison < L. toxicum: see prec.] poisonous; toxic —n. a poison; toxic agent

tox·i·co- (täk′si kō′, -kə) [ModL. < Gr. toxikon: see TOXIC] a combining form meaning poison [toxicogenic]: also, before a vowel, **tox′ic-**

tox·i·co·gen·ic (täk′si kō jen′ik) adj. [prec. + -GENIC] producing toxic substances

tox·i·col·o·gy (täk′si käl′ə jē) n. [Fr. toxicologie: see TOXIC & -LOGY] the science of poisons, their effects, antidotes, etc. —**tox′i·co·log′ic** (-kə läj′ik), **tox′i·co·log′i·cal** adj. —**tox′i·co·log′i·cal·ly** adv. —**tox′i·col′o·gist** n.

tox·i·co·sis (-kō′sis) n. [ModL.: see TOXIC & -OSIS] any diseased condition caused by poisoning

tox·in (täk′sin) n. [TOX(IC) + -IN[1]] 1. any of various unstable poisonous compounds produced by some microorganisms and causing certain diseases 2. any of various similar poisons, related to proteins, formed in certain plants, as ricin, or secreted by certain animals, as snake venom Toxins, when injected into animals or man, typically initiate the formation of antitoxins

tox·in-an·ti·tox·in (-an′ti täk′sin) n. a mixture of toxin and antitoxin formerly used for producing active immunity against a specific disease, esp. diphtheria: now superseded by toxoids

tox·oid (täk′soid) n. [TOX(IN) + -OID] a toxin that has been treated, as with chemicals or heat, so as to eliminate the toxic qualities while retaining the antigenic properties

tox·oph·i·lite (täk säf′ə lit′) n. [< Toxophilus, title of a book (1545) by R. ASCHAM < Gr. toxon, a bow + philos, lover + -ITE[1]] a person who is especially fond of archery —**tox·oph′i·lit′ic** (-lit′ik) adj. —**tox·oph′i·ly** (-lē) n.

tox·o·plas·mo·sis (täk′sō plaz mō′sis) n. [ModL.: see TOXIC, -PLASM, & -OSIS] a disease caused by a protozoan (Toxoplasma gondii), affecting man and animals, esp. in the tropics: in its congenital form it damages the central nervous system, eyes, and viscera

toy (toi) n. [ME. toye in sense 1 (< ?); other senses < ? MDu. toi, finery, ornament, akin to G. zeug, ON. tygi, stuff, gear: for IE. base see TUG] 1. orig., a) amorous behavior; flirtation b) pastime; sport 2. a thing of little value or importance; trifle 3. a little ornament; bauble; trinket 4. any article to play with, esp. a plaything for children 5. any small thing, person, or animal; specif., a dog of a small breed 6. [Scot.] formerly, a woman's headdress of linen or wool, with flaps that hang over the shoulders —adj. 1. like a toy, or plaything, in size, use, etc.; specif., designating a breed of dog of a small kind [a toy terrier] 2. made as a toy; esp., being a miniature imitation [a toy stove] —vi. 1. to play or trifle (with a thing, an idea, etc.) 2. to engage in flirtation; dally —SYN. see TRIFLE —**toy′er** n. —**toy′like′** adj.

To·ya·ma (tō′yä mä′) seaport on the N coast of C Honshu, Japan: pop. 240,000

Toyn·bee (toin′bē) **Arnold J(oseph)** 1889– ; Eng. historian

To·yo·ha·shi (tō′yō hä′shē) seaport on the S coast of Honshu, Japan: pop. 239,000

☆**to·yon** (tō′yən) n. [AmSp., also tollon, prob. < Nahuatl name] a large evergreen shrub or tree (Heteromeles arbutifolia) of the rose family, with clusters of white flowers and bright-red berries: it is native to California

To·yo·na·ka (tō′yō nä′kä) city in S Honshu, Japan, near Osaka: pop. 292,000

toy·shop (toi′shäp′) n. a shop where toys are sold

tp. township

t.p. title page

tpk. turnpike

T-R transmit-receive

tr. 1. trace 2. transitive 3. translated 4. translation 5. translator 6. transpose 7. treasurer 8. trustee

tra·be·at·ed (trā′bē āt′id) adj. [< L. trabem, acc. of trabs, a beam: see TAVERN] 1. built with horizontal beams or lintels, instead of arches 2. of such construction —**tra′be·a′tion** (-ā′shən) n.

tra·bec·u·la (trə bek′yoo lə) n., pl. **-lae** (-lē′), **-las** [ModL. < L., dim. of trabs, a beam: see TAVERN] 1. Anat., Zool. a) a small rod, bar, or bundle of fibers b) a small septum of fibers forming, with others of its kind, an essential part of the framework of an organ or part 2. Bot. a rodlike structure, plate, or bar of tissue, as any of the crossbars in the peristome teeth of mosses —**tra·bec′u·lar** (-lər), **tra·bec′u·late** (-lit) adj.

Trab·zon (träb zōn′) Turk. name of TREBIZOND

trace[1] (trās) n. [ME. < OFr. < tracier < VL. *tractiare < L. tractus, a drawing along, track < pp. of trahere, to DRAW] 1. orig., a way followed or path taken 2. a mark, footprint, etc. left by the passage of a person, animal, or thing ☆3. a beaten path or trail left by the repeated passage of persons, vehicles, etc. 4. any perceptible mark left by a past person, thing, or event; sign; evidence; vestige [the traces of war] 5. a barely perceptible amount; very small quantity [a trace of anger] 6. something drawn or traced, as a mark, sketch, etc. 7. the traced record of a recording instrument 8. a) the visible line or spot that moves across the face of a cathode-ray tube b) the path followed by this line or spot 9. Chem. a very small amount, usually one quantitatively immeasurable 10. Math. the intersection of a line or of a projecting plane of the line with the coordinate plane 11. Meteorol. precipitation amounting to less than 0.005 of an inch 12. Psychol. same as ENGRAM —vt. **traced**, **trac′ing** [ME. tracen < OFr. tracier: see the n.] 1. [Now Rare] to move along, follow, or traverse (a path, route, etc.) 2. to follow the trail or footprints of; track 3. a) to follow the development, process, or history of, esp. by proceeding from the latest to the earliest evidence, etc. b) to determine (a source, date, etc.) by this procedure 4. to discover or ascertain by investigating traces or vestiges of (something prehistoric, etc.) 5. to draw, sketch, outline, etc. 6. to ornament with tracery: used chiefly in the past participle 7. to copy (a drawing, etc.) by following its lines on a superimposed, transparent sheet 8. to form (letters, etc.) carefully or laboriously 9. to make or copy with a tracer 10. to record by means of a curved, broken, or wavy line, as in a seismograph —vi. 1. to follow a path, route, development, etc.; make one's way 2. to go back or date back (to something past) —**trace′a·bil′i·ty**, **trace′a·ble·ness** n. —**trace′a·ble** adj. —**trace′a·bly** adv.

SYN.—**trace**, literally applying to a mark, footprint, etc. left by the passage of an animal or vehicle, commonly refers to any mark showing that something has existed or occurred [a faint trace of egg on his vest]; **vestige** applies to some slight remains of something that is no longer in actual existence [the vestiges of an ancient civilization]; **track**, equivalent to trace in its literal sense, suggests a continuous mark or series of marks that can be followed for some distance [automobile tracks in the snow]

trace[2] (trās) n. [ME. traice < OFr. trais, pl. of trait: see TRAIT] 1. either of two straps, chains, etc. connecting a draft animal's harness to the vehicle drawn 2. a rod, pivoted at each end, that transmits motion from one moving part of a machine to another —**kick over the traces** to shake off control; show insubordination or independence

trace element 1. a chemical element, as iron, copper, zinc, etc., essential in plant and animal nutrition, but only in minute quantities 2. any element present in minute quantities in an organism, soil, water, etc.

trac·er (trā′sər) n. 1. a person or thing that traces; specif., a) a person whose work is tracing drawings, designs, etc. on transparent paper b) a person whose work is tracing lost or missing articles, persons, etc. c) an instrument for tracing designs on cloth, etc. ☆2. an inquiry sent out for a letter, package, etc. that is missing in transport 3. same as TRACER BULLET (or SHELL) 4. a substance, usually a labeled element, used to follow a complex sequence of biochemical reactions, as in an animal body, to locate diseased cells and tissues, to determine physical properties, etc. 5. a contrasting color woven into or stamped on wire insulation for identification and for aid in tracing a circuit

tracer bullet (or **shell**) a bullet or shell that traces its own course in the air with a trail of smoke or fire, so as to facilitate adjustment of the aim

trac·er·y (-ē) n., pl. **-er·ies** [< TRACE[1] + -ERY] ornamental work of interlacing or branching lines, as in a Gothic window, some kinds of embroidery, etc.

tra·che- (trā′kē) same as TRACHEO-: used before a vowel

tra·che·a (trā′kē ə; chiefly Brit., trə kē′ə) n., pl. **-che·ae′** (-ē′), **-che·as** [ME. trache < ML. trachea < LL. trachia, windpipe < Gr. tracheia (arteria), rough (windpipe) < trachys, rough, akin to thrassein, to confuse < IE. base *dher-, dark residue, dirt, whence DREGS] 1. in the respiratory tract of most land vertebrates, the tube extending from the larynx to its division into the two bronchi; windpipe 2. in the respiratory system of insects and certain other invertebrates, any of the small tubules branching throughout the body and conducting air from the exterior 3. Bot. same as VESSEL (sense 4b)

TRACERY

tra·che·al (-əl) adj. 1. of, like, or having a trachea or tracheae 2. of or composed of woody tissue having tracheae (vessels) or tracheids, or both

tra·che·ate (-āt′, -it) adj. breathing through tracheae, as insects

tra·che·id (-id) n. [TRACHE- + -ID] Bot. any of the long, nonliving, thick-walled, water-conducting, tubelike cells found in xylem, esp. of the conifers, communicating only by pits in their walls with adjacent tracheids —**tra·che·i·dal** (trā kē′i dəl) adj.

tra·che·i·tis (trā′kē īt′əs) n. [ModL.: see TRACHEA & -ITIS] inflammation of the trachea

tra·che·o- (trā′kē ō′) [< TRACHEA] a combining form meaning: 1. of the trachea [tracheotomy] 2. the trachea and [tracheobronchial]

tra·che·o·bron·chi·al (trā′kē ō brän′kē əl) adj. relating to the trachea and bronchi

tra·che·ole (trā′kē ōl′) n. [< TRACHE- + -ole, dim. suffix

< Fr. < L. *-olus, -olum, -ola*] any of the extremely small, thin-walled, respiratory tubules originating from the ends of the smallest insect tracheae

tra·che·o·phyte (-ə fīt′) *n.* [TRACHEO- + -PHYTE] any of a proposed division (Tracheophyta) of plants having specialized tissues (xylem and phloem) that conduct water and synthesized foods, comprising the pteridophytes and the spermatophytes; vascular plant

tra·che·ot·o·my (trā′kē ät′ə mē) *n., pl.* **-mies** [TRACHEO- + -TOMY] surgical incision of the trachea, as for making an artificial breathing hole

tra·cho·ma (trə kō′mə) *n.* [ModL. < Gr. *trachōma*, roughness < *trachys*, rough: see TRACHEA] a contagious infection of the conjunctiva and cornea, caused by a virus and characterized by scar formation and granulation — **tra·cho′ma·tous** (-käm′ə təs, -kō′mə-) *adj.*

tra·chyte (trā′kīt, trak′īt) *n.* [Fr. < Gr. *trachys*, rough: see TRACHEA] a fine-grained, light-colored, extrusive, igneous rock, consisting largely of alkalic feldspars and equivalent to syenite in composition

tra·chyt·ic (trə kit′ik) *adj.* of or pertaining to the internal structure of some igneous rocks, as trachyte, in which hairlike, feldspar crystals are in nearly parallel rows

trac·ing (trā′siŋ) *n.* 1. the action of one that traces 2. something made by tracing; specif., *a*) a copy of a drawing, etc. made by tracing the lines on a superimposed, transparent sheet *b*) the record of a recording instrument, in the form of a traced line

track (trak) *n.* [LME. *trak* < MFr. *trac*, a track, tract, trace < ?] 1. a mark or series of marks or other discoverable evidence left by a person, animal, or thing that has passed, as a footprint, wheel rut, wake of a boat, etc. 2. a trace or vestige 3. a beaten path or trail left by the repeated passage of persons, animals, or vehicles 4. *a*) a course or line of motion or action; route; way *b*) the projection of the flight path of an airplane, rocket, etc. on the surface of the earth 5. a sequence of ideas, events, etc.; succession 6. a path or circuit laid out for running, horse racing, etc. ☆7. any of the groups in a track system of education 8. a pair of parallel metal rails, with their crossties, etc., on which trains, streetcars, etc. run ☆9. the distance in inches between the centers of the tread of parallel wheels, as of an automobile 10. either of the two continuous roller belts with which tanks, some tractors, etc. are equipped for moving over rough ground 11. the tread of an automobile tire ☆12. *a*) athletic sports performed on a track, as running, hurdling, etc. *b*) track and field sports together 13. *a*) same as SOUND TRACK *b*) any of the bands on a phonograph record *c*) any of the separate, parallel recording surfaces extending along the length of a magnetic tape *d*) in a computer, that part of a magnetic drum, tape, or disc that passes under a given reading head position —*vt.* 1. *a*) to follow the track or footprints of [to *track* game] *b*) to follow (a path, etc.) 2. to trace by means of vestiges, evidence, etc. 3. to observe or plot the path or trajectory of, and record data from (an aircraft, spacecraft, etc.) using a telescope, radar, etc. 4. to tread or travel 5. *a*) to leave tracks or footprints on (often with *up*) ☆*b*) to leave in the form of tracks [to *track* dirt over a floor] ☆6. to provide with tracks or rails —*vi.* 1. to run in the same (width) track 2. to be in alignment, as wheels or gears, or the pickup of a phonograph with a groove on a record 3. to have a (specified) width between the wheels [a narrow-gauge car *tracks* less than 56 inches] —SYN. see TRACE¹ —**in one's tracks** where one is at the moment —**keep track of** to keep an account of; stay informed about —**lose track of** to fail to keep informed about; lose sight or knowledge of —☆**make tracks** [Colloq.] to proceed or depart hurriedly —**on** (or **off**) **the track** keeping to (or straying from) the subject, objective, or goal —☆**the wrong side of the tracks** that part of a community where those considered socially and culturally inferior live —**track down** 1. to pursue until caught, as by following tracks 2. to investigate or search for until found, by examining evidence, etc. —**track′er** *n.*

☆**track·age** (-ij) *n.* [see -AGE] 1. all the tracks of a railroad 2. *a*) permission for a railroad to use the tracks of another *b*) a charge for this

☆**tracking station** a station equipped to track the path of, and record data from, a spacecraft, satellite, etc.

track·less (-lis) *adj.* 1. *a*) without a track, trail, or path [a *trackless* wilderness] *b*) leaving no track, or trail 2. not running on tracks [a *trackless* trolley]: cf. TROLLEY BUS

☆**track·man** (-mən) *n., pl.* **-men** a person whose work is laying and repairing railroad tracks: also **track′lay′er**

☆**track man** an athlete who competes in track or field events, as a runner, hurdler, discus thrower, etc.

☆**track system** a system of education in which students are put in different groups according to test performance and are kept in them through the grades

☆**track·walk·er** (-wô′kər) *n.* a person whose work is walking along, and inspecting, sections of railroad track so as to report on parts in need of repair

tract¹ (trakt) *n.* [L. *tractus*, a drawing out, extent < pp. of *trahere*, to DRAW] 1. formerly, *a*) duration or lapse of time *b*) a period of time 2. a continuous expanse of land or of water, mineral deposit, etc.; stretch; extent; area ☆3. [Chiefly Western] a housing development: see DEVELOPMENT (sense 4) 4. *Anat., Zool. a*) a system of parts or

organs having some special function [the genitourinary *tract*] *b*) a bundle of nerve fibers having the same origin, termination, and function 5. [ML.(Ec.) *tractus*] R.C.Ch. a penitential chant of Lent, etc., preceding the Gospel and consisting either of a complete psalm or of a few verses of Scripture, often from the Psalms

tract² (trakt) *n.* [ME. *tracte* < LL. *tractatus*: see TRACTATE] 1. formerly, a treatise 2. a propagandizing pamphlet, esp. one on a religious or political subject

trac·ta·ble (trak′tə b'l) *adj.* [L. *tractabilis* < *tractare*, to drag, haul, freq. of *trahere*, to DRAW] 1. easily managed, taught, or controlled; docile; compliant 2. easily worked; malleable —SYN. see OBEDIENT —**trac′ta·bil′i·ty, trac′ta·ble·ness** *n.* —**trac′ta·bly** *adv.*

Trac·tar·i·an·ism (trak ter′ē ən iz′m) *n.* the principles of the Oxford movement, favoring a return to early Catholic doctrines and practices in the Church of England: from the ninety "Tracts for the Times," pamphlets issued at Oxford from 1833 to 1841 —**Trac·tar′i·an** *n., adj.*

trac·tate (trak′tāt) *n.* [LL. *tractatus*, a discussion, treatise < pp. of *tractare*: see TRACTABLE] a treatise or dissertation

trac·tile (trak′t'l; *chiefly Brit.,* -tīl) *adj.* [< L. *tractus* (see ff.) + -ILE] that can be drawn out in length; ductile; tensile —**trac·til′i·ty** (-til′ə tē) *n.*

trac·tion (trak′shən) *n.* [ML. *tractio* < L. *tractus*, pp. of *trahere*, to DRAW] 1. *a*) a pulling or drawing, esp. of a load, vehicle, etc. over a road, track, or other surface *b*) the state of being pulled or drawn 2. *a*) a pulling, as of the muscles of the leg, arm, etc., in order to bring a fractured or dislocated bone into place *b*) a constant pull of this kind maintained by means of some apparatus, as for relieving pressure 3. the kind of power used by a locomotive, street railway, etc. [steam *traction*, electric *traction*] 4. adhesive friction, as of tires on pavement —**trac′tion·al** *adj.*

traction engine a steam locomotive for pulling heavy wagons, farm equipment, etc. on roads or in fields

trac·tive (trak′tiv) *adj.* [ML. *tractivus*: see TRACTION & -IVE] used for pulling or drawing

☆**trac·tor** (trak′tər) *n.* [ModL. < L. *tractus*: see TRACTION] 1. a powerful vehicle with a gasoline or Diesel engine and huge rear wheels or a continuous tread rolling over cogged wheels, used for pulling farm machinery, hauling loads, etc. 2. a truck with a driver's cab and no body, designed for hauling one or more large trailers 3. an airplane with its propeller or propellers mounted in front of the engine

☆**trac·tor-trail·er** (-trā′lər) *n.* a combination of a tractor and a trailer or semitrailer, used in trucking

trade (trād) *n.* [ME., a track, course of action < MLowG., a track < OS. *trada*, a trace, trail, akin to ME. *trede*, TREAD] 1. orig., *a*) a track; path *b*) a course; regular procedure 2. *a*) a means of earning one's living; occupation, work, or line of business *b*) skilled work, as distinguished from unskilled work or from a profession or business; craft *c*) all the persons or companies in a particular line of business or work 3. the buying and selling of commodities or the bartering of goods; commerce 4. dealings or the market involving specified commodities, customers, seasons, etc. [the tourist *trade*, the Easter *trade*] 5. customers; clientele 6. a purchase or sale; deal; bargain 7. an exchange; swap 8. [*pl.*] the trade winds: see TRADE WIND —*adj.* 1. of or relating to trade or commerce 2. of, by, or for those in a particular business or industry [*trade* papers or journals] 3. [*also pl.*] of the members in the trades, or crafts, etc. [*trade* unions] —*vi.* **trad′ed, trad′ing** 1. to carry on a trade or business 2. to have business dealings (*with* someone) 3. to make an exchange (*with* someone) 4. [Colloq.] to be a customer (*at* a specified store or shop) —*vt.* 1. to exchange; barter; swap 2. to buy and sell (stocks, etc.) —SYN. see BUSINESS, SELL —**trade in** to give (one's used automobile, etc.) as part of the purchase price of a new one —**trade on** (or **upon**) to take advantage of; exploit —**trad′a·ble, trade′a·ble** *adj.*

trade acceptance a bill of exchange or draft drawn upon the purchaser by the seller and accepted by the purchaser for payment at a specified time

trade association an association of merchants or business firms for the unified promotion of their common interests

trade book a book intended for sale through regular trade outlets, as distinguished from a textbook, subscription book, etc.

trade discount a deduction from the list price allowed a retailer by a manufacturer, wholesaler, or distributor, or allowed one firm by another in the same trade

trade edition that edition of a book sold through regular trade outlets to the general public, as distinguished from a school edition, etc. of the same book

☆**trade-in** (trād′in′) *n.* 1. a used car, appliance, etc. given or taken as part payment in the purchase of a new one 2. a transaction involving a trade-in 3. the valuation allowed by the seller on a trade-in

trade journal a magazine devoted to the interests of a specific trade, business, or industry

☆**trade-last** (-last′, -läst′) *n.* [Colloq.] a compliment heard about another that one offers to tell him in exchange for one that he can similarly report about oneself

trade·mark (-märk′) *n.* a symbol, design, word, letter, etc. used by a manufacturer or dealer to distinguish a product or products from those of competitors, and usually registered and protected by law: cf. SERVICE MARK —*vt.* 1. to

put a trademark on (a product) **2.** to register (a symbol, word, etc.) as a trademark

trade name 1. the name by which a commodity is commonly known in trade **2.** a name used by a company to describe a product, service, etc., often specif., a name that is a trademark or service mark **3.** the name under which a company carries on business

trad·er (trā′dər) *n.* **1.** a person who trades; merchant **2.** a ship used in trade ☆**3.** a member of a stock exchange who trades esp. for his own account rather than customers' accounts

trade route any route customarily taken by trading ships, caravans, etc.

trad·es·can·ti·a (trad′is kan′shē ə) *n.* [ModL., name of the genus, after John *Tradescant* (1608–62), Eng. naturalist & traveler] *same as* SPIDERWORT

trade school a school where a trade or trades are taught

trade secret any device, method, formula, etc. known to the manufacturer who uses it but not to his competitors

trades·man (-mən) *n., pl.* **-men 1.** [Dial.] a craftsman or artisan **2.** [Chiefly Brit.] a person engaged in trade; esp., a storekeeper —**trades′wom′an** *n.fem., pl.* **-wom′en**

trades·peo·ple (-pē′p'l) *n.pl.* people engaged in trade; esp., storekeepers: also **trades′folk′**

trade union *same as* LABOR UNION: also [Chiefly Brit.] **trades union** —**trade′-un′ion** *adj.* —**trade unionism** —**trade unionist**

trade wind [earlier *trade*, adv., steadily, in phr. *to blow trade*] a wind that blows steadily toward the equator from the northeast in the tropics north of the equator and from the southeast in the tropics south of the equator

☆**trading post** a store or station in an outpost, settlement, etc., where trading is done, as with natives

☆**trading stamp** a stamp given by some merchants as a premium to customers, redeemable in specified quantities for various kinds of merchandise

tra·di·tion (trə dish′ən) *n.* [ME. *tradycion* < MFr. *tradicion* < L. *traditio*, a surrender, delivery, tradition < *traditus*, pp. of *tradere*, to deliver: see TREASON] **1.** orig., a surrender or betrayal **2.** *a)* the handing down orally of stories, beliefs, customs, etc. from generation to generation *b)* a story, belief, custom, proverb, etc. handed down this way **3.** a long-established custom or practice that has the effect of an unwritten law; specif., any of the usages of a school of art or literature handed down through the generations, and generally observed **4.** *Law same as* DELIVERY **5.** *Theol. a)* among Jews, the unwritten religious code and doctrine regarded as handed down from Moses *b)* among Christians, the unwritten teachings regarded as handed down from Jesus and the Apostles *c)* among Moslems, the sayings and acts attributed to Mohammed, not in the Koran, but orally transmitted —**tra·di′tion·less** *adj.*

tra·di·tion·al (-'l) *adj.* of, handed down by, or conforming to tradition; conventional: also **tra·di′tion·ar′y** (-er′ē), [Rare] **trad·i·tive** (trad′ə tiv) —**tra·di′tion·al·ly** *adv.*

tra·di·tion·al·ism (-'l iz'm) *n.* **1.** adherence to tradition; sometimes, specif., excessive respect for tradition **2.** the doctrine that the only valid religious belief is that handed down by tradition from an original divine revelation —**tra·di′tion·al·ist** *n.* —**tra·di′tion·al·is′tic** *adj.*

tra·di·tion·ist (-ist) *n.* **1.** an upholder of traditions **2.** a student, recorder, or transmitter of traditions

trad·i·tor (trad′ə tər) *n., pl.* **trad′i·to′res** (-tôr′ēz) [L., TRAITOR] among the early Christians, a traitor during the Roman persecutions

tra·duce (trə dōōs′, -dyōōs′) *vt.* **-duced′, -duc′ing** [L. *traducere*, to lead along, exhibit as a spectacle, disgrace < *tra(ns)*, across, over + *ducere*, to lead: see TRANS- & DUCT] **1.** to say untrue or malicious things about; defame; slander; vilify **2.** to make a mockery of; betray —**tra·duce′ment** *n.* —**tra·duc′er** *n.*

tra·du·cian·ism (trə dōō′shən iz'm, -dyōō′-) *n.* [< LL. *traducianus*, believer in this doctrine < *tradux*, a shoot, vine branch, lit., that which is brought over < *traducere*: see prec.] the theological doctrine that the soul is inherited, along with the body, from the parents: opposed to CREATIONISM —**tra·du′cian·ist** *n.*

Tra·fal·gar (trə fal′gər; *Sp.* trä′fäl gär′), **Cape** cape on the SW coast of Spain, between Cádiz & the Strait of Gibraltar: site of a naval battle (1805) in which Nelson's Brit. fleet defeated Napoleon's fleet

traf·fic (traf′ik) *n.* [Fr. *trafic* < It. *traffico* < *trafficare*, to trade < L. *trans*, across + It. *ficcare*, to thrust in, bring < VL. *figicare*, intens. for L. *figere*: see FIX] **1.** orig., *a)* transportation of goods for trading *b)* trading over great distances; commerce **2.** buying and selling; barter; trade, sometimes, specif., of a wrong or illegal kind [*traffic* in drugs] **3.** dealings, business, or intercourse (*with* someone) **4.** *a)* the movement or number of automobiles along a street, pedestrians along a sidewalk, ships up a port, etc. *b)* the automobiles, pedestrians, ships, etc. so moving **5.** the number of passengers, quantity of freight, etc. carried by a transportation company during a given period **6.** the volume of telegrams, calls, etc. transmitted by a communications company during a given

period **7.** the number of potential customers entering a retail store during a given period —*adj.* of or having to do with the regulation of traffic or with laws enforcing such regulation [a *traffic* policeman, *traffic* violation] —*vi.* **-ficked, -fick·ing 1.** to carry on traffic, esp. illegal trade (*in* a commodity) **2.** to have traffic, trade, or dealings (*with* someone) —**traf′fick·er** *n.*

☆**traffic circle** a circular street at the intersection of several streets with vehicles traveling in one direction only, designed to facilitate the flow of traffic

traffic island an area or platform marked in a roadway, from which vehicular traffic is diverted so as to separate such traffic, or to protect pedestrians (cf. SAFETY ZONE)

☆**traffic light** (or **signal**) a set of signal lights, usually changing from red to yellow to green and back, placed at intersections of streets to regulate traffic

☆**traffic pattern** a pattern of flight in the air above or around an airport normally followed by aircraft before landing or after taking off

trag·a·canth (trag′ə kanth′) *n.* [Fr. *tragacanthe* < L. *tragacantha* < Gr. *tragakantha* < *tragos*, goat (see TRAGEDY) + *akantha*, thorn (see ACANTHO-)] **1.** a white or reddish, tasteless and odorless gum, used in pharmacy, calico printing, etc. **2.** any of various, esp. Asiatic, plants (genus *Astragalus*) of the legume family, yielding this gum

tra·ge·di·an (trə jē′dē ən) *n.* [ME. *tragedien* < MFr.] **1.** a writer of tragedies **2.** an actor of tragedy

tra·ge·di·enne (trə jē′dē en′) *n.* [Fr. *tragédienne*] an actress of tragedy

trag·e·dy (traj′ə dē) *n., pl.* **-dies** [ME. *tragedie* < MFr. < L. *tragoedia* < Gr. *tragōidia*, tragedy, lit., the song of the goat < *tragos*, goat (< IE. *treg-*, to gnaw < base *ter-*, to rub, grind, whence THROW) + *ōidē*, song (see ODE): so named prob. because of the goatskin dress of the performers, representing satyrs] **1.** a serious play typically dealing with the problems of a central character, leading to an unhappy or disastrous ending brought on, as in ancient drama, by fate and a tragic flaw in this character, or, in modern drama, usually by moral weakness, psychological maladjustment, or social pressures: see CATHARSIS (sense 2), TRAGIC FLAW **2.** the branch of drama consisting of plays of this type **3.** the writing, acting, or theoretical principles of this kind of drama **4.** a novel or other literary work with similar characteristics **5.** the tragic element of such a literary work, or of a real event **6.** a very sad or tragic event or events; disaster

trag·ic (traj′ik) *adj.* [L. *tragicus* < Gr. *tragikos*] **1.** of, or having the nature of, tragedy **2.** like or characteristic of tragedy; bringing great harm, suffering, etc.; calamitous, disastrous, fatal, etc. **3.** appropriate to the acting of tragedy [in a *tragic* voice] **4.** writing or acting in tragedy Also **trag′i·cal** —*n.* the tragic element in art or life —**trag′i·cal·ly** *adv.* —**trag′i·cal·ness** *n.*

tragic flaw a flaw, as pride, in the character of the protagonist of a tragedy, that leads him to his downfall

trag·i·com·e·dy (traj′ə käm′ə dē) *n., pl.* **-dies** [Fr. *tragi-comédie* < LL. *tragicomedia* < L. *tragicocomoedia*: see TRAGIC & COMEDY] **1.** a play or other literary work combining tragic and comic elements **2.** a situation or incident in life like this —**trag′i·com′ic** (-käm′ik), **trag′i·com′i·cal** *adj.* —**trag′i·com′i·cal·ly** *adv.*

trag·o·pan (trag′ə pan′) *n.* [ModL., name of the genus < L., a fabulous bird < Gr. *tragopan*, lit., goat-Pan < *tragos*, goat (see TRAGEDY) + *Pan*, Pan] any of several brightly colored Asiatic pheasants (genus *Tragopan*) with two erectile, fleshy, hornlike protuberances on the head

tra·gus (trā′gəs) *n., pl.* **-gi** (-jī) [LL. < Gr. *tragos*, hairy part of the ear, lit., goat] the fleshy, cartilaginous protrusion at the front of the external ear, partly extending over the opening of the ear

trail (trāl) *vt.* [ME. *trailen* < MFr. *trailler* < VL. *tragulare* < L. *tragula*, small drag, sledge < *trahere*, to DRAW] **1.** *a)* to drag or let drag behind one, esp. on the ground, etc. *b)* to bring along behind [*trailing* exhaust fumes] *c)* to pull or tow **2.** *a)* to make or mark (a path, track, etc.), as by treading down *b)* to make a path in (grass, etc.) **3.** to follow the tracks of; track **4.** to hunt by tracking **5.** *a)* to follow behind, esp. in a lagging manner *b)* to be or lag behind, as in a contest **6.** *Mil.* to carry (a rifle, etc.) in the right hand with the arm extended downward so that the muzzle is tilted forward and the butt is near the ground —*vi.* **1.** to hang down, esp. behind, so as to drag on the ground, etc. **2.** to grow so long as to extend along the ground, over rocks, etc.: said of some plants **3.** to extend in an irregular line; straggle **4.** to flow behind in a long, thin stream, wisp, etc. [smoke *trailed* from the chimney] **5.** to move, walk, go along, etc. wearily, heavily, or slowly; crawl; drag **6.** *a)* to follow or lag behind *b)* to be losing, as in a sports contest [to *trail* by 13 points] **7.** to track game: said of hounds **8.** to grow gradually weaker, dimmer, less direct, etc. (with *off* or *away*) —*n.* [ME. *traille* < MFr. < the *v.*] **1.** something that trails or is trailed behind **2.** a mark, footprint, scent, etc. left by a person, animal, or thing that has passed ☆**3.** a path or track made by repeated passage or deliberately blazed

4. a series of events or conditions following something; train [an illness bringing debts in its *trail*] **5.** *Mil. a*) the position of trailing a rifle *b*) a beamlike part of a gun carriage, which may be lowered to the ground to form a rear brace —**trail′ing·ly** *adv.*

☆**trail·blaz·er** (-blā′zər) *n.* **1.** a person who blazes a trail **2.** a pioneer in any field —**trail′blaz′ing** *n.*

trail·er (trā′lər) *n.* **1.** a person, animal, or thing that trails another ☆**2.** a cart, wagon, or large van, designed to be pulled by an automobile, truck, or tractor, for hauling freight, animals, a boat, etc. ☆**3.** a closed vehicle designed to be pulled by an automobile or truck and equipped as a place to live or work in, as one with beds, cooking facilities, etc.: see also MOBILE HOME ☆**4.** *Motion Pictures a*) a short film made up of scenes from, and advertising, a coming movie: because originally attached to the end of a reel of film *b*) a blank piece of film at the end of a reel

☆**trailer park** an area, usually with piped water, electricity, etc., designed to accommodate trailers, esp. mobile homes: also **trailer camp, trailer court**

☆**trail·ing arbutus** (trā′liŋ) *same as* ARBUTUS (sense 2)

trailing edge *Aeron.* the rear edge of an airfoil, propeller blade, etc.

train (trān) *n.* [ME. *traine* < OFr. *trahin* < *trahiner*, to draw on < VL. **traginare* < L. *trahere*, to pull, DRAW] **1.** something that hangs down and drags behind; specif., *a*) a part of a dress, skirt, etc. that trails behind *b*) the tail feathers of a bird [the *train* of a peacock] *c*) a stream of something trailing behind **2.** a group of persons following as attendants in a procession; retinue; suite **3.** a group of persons, animals, vehicles, etc. that follow one another in a line; procession; caravan; cortege **4.** the persons, vehicles, etc. carrying supplies, ammunition, food, etc. for combat troops **5.** a series of events or conditions that follow some happening; aftermath [a war bringing famine and disease in its *train*] **6.** any connected order or arrangement; series; sequence [a *train* of thought] **7.** a line of gunpowder that serves as a fuse for an explosive charge **8.** a series of connected mechanical parts for transmitting motion [a *train* of gears] **9.** a line of connected railroad cars pulled or pushed by a locomotive or locomotives —*vt.* [ME. *trainen* < OFr. *trahiner*] **1.** [Rare] to trail or drag **2.** to guide the growth of (a plant), as by tying, pruning, etc. **3.** to subject to certain action, exercises, etc. in order to bring to a desired condition [a surgeon's hand *trained* to be steady] **4.** to guide or control the mental, moral, etc. development of; bring up; rear **5.** to instruct so as to make proficient or qualified [to *train* nurses at a hospital] **6.** to discipline or condition (animals) to perform tricks or obey commands **7.** to prepare or make fit for an athletic contest, etc. as by exercise, diet, etc. **8.** to aim (a gun, binoculars, etc.) at something; bring to bear (usually with *on*) **9.** [Colloq.] to condition (a child, puppy, etc.) to defecate and urinate in the required place —*vi.* to administer or undergo training —*SYN.* see TEACH —**train′a·ble** *adj.*

train·band (-band′) *n.* [contr. of *trained band*] formerly, a band of citizens trained locally as a militia

train·ee (trā nē′) *n.* a person undergoing vocational training, military training, etc. —**train·ee′ship′** *n.*

train·er (trān′ər) *n.* **1.** a person who trains; specif., *a*) a person who trains animals, as racehorses, show dogs, circus beasts, etc. *b*) a person who trains athletes for sports contests **2.** an apparatus used in training, as, in aeronautics, a flight simulator

train·ing (-iŋ) *n.* **1.** the action or method of one that trains **2.** the process or experience of being trained

training school a school that gives training in some vocation or profession, as nursing, acting, etc.

training ship a ship used for training persons in seamanship, esp. in a navy

☆**training table** a table or dining room where athletes in training eat supervised meals

☆**train·man** (trān′mən) *n.*, *pl.* -men (-mən) a person who works on a railroad train or in a railroad yard, usually as a conductor's assistant; esp., a brakeman

train·mas·ter (-mas′tər, -mäs′-) *n.* **1.** formerly, the man in charge of a wagon train **2.** a railroad official in charge of some division of a line

train oil [earlier *trane* < MDu. *traen*, akin to G. *träne*, a tear: basic sense "exuded oil"] whale oil, or, formerly, oil from seals, codfish, etc.

traipse (trāps) *vi.*, *vt.* **traipsed**, **traips′ing** [< ?] [Dial. or Colloq.] to walk, wander, tramp, or gad —*n.* [Dial. or Colloq.] the act of traipsing

trait (trāt) *n.* [Fr., a draft, line, stroke < L. *tractus*, pp. of *trahere*, to DRAW] **1.** a distinguishing quality or characteristic, as of personality **2.** [Rare] a stroke, trace, or touch —*SYN.* see QUALITY

trai·tor (trāt′ər) *n.* [ME. *traitour* < OFr. *traitor* < L. *traditor*, one who betrays < *traditus*, pp. of *tradere*, to hand over, betray: see TREASON] a person who betrays his country, cause, friends, etc.; one guilty of treason or treachery —**trai·tress** (-tris) *n.fem.*

trai·tor·ous (-əs) *adj.* **1.** of, or having the nature of, a traitor; treacherous; faithless **2.** of or involving treason; treasonable —*SYN.* see FAITHLESS —**trai′tor·ous·ly** *adv.* —**trai′tor·ous·ness** *n.*

Tra·jan (trā′jən) (L. name *Marcus Ulpius Trajanus*) 53?–117 A.D.; Rom. general & statesman, born in Spain; Rom. emperor (98–117)

tra·ject (trə jekt′) *vt.* [< L. *trajectus*, pp. of *trajicere*, to throw or fling over or across < *tra-* (see TRANS-) + *jacere*, to throw: see JET[1]] [Now Rare] to transmit or transport —**tra·jec′tion** *n.*

tra·jec·to·ry (trə jek′tə rē) *n.*, *pl.* -ries [ML. *trajectorius* < L. *trajectus*: see prec.] **1.** the curved path of something hurtling through space, esp. that of a projectile from the time it leaves the muzzle of the gun **2.** *Math. a*) a curve or surface that passes through all the curves of a given family at the same angle *b*) a curve or surface that fits a particular law such as passing through a given set of points

tra·la (trä lä′) *interj.* syllables conventionally used in singing, esp. as a short refrain, to express gaiety, carefreeness, etc.: often **tra′-la-la′**

Tra·lee (trə lē′) county seat of Kerry, SW Ireland: pop. 11,000

tram[1] (tram) *n.* [Fr. *trame* < L. *trama*, the woof] a double, twisted silk thread used as the weft in fine silks and velvets

tram[2] (tram) *n.* [E. dial., shaft, wooden frame for carrying, rail, coal wagon, prob. < LowG. *traam*, a beam] **1.** an open railway car for carrying loads in mines: also **tram′car′** (-kär′) **2.** the basket or car of an overhead conveyor **3.** *clipped form of* TRAMROAD **4.** [Brit.] *a*) a streetcar; trolley car: in full **tram′car′** (-kär′) *b*) a streetcar line: in full **tram′line′** (-līn′) —*vt.*, *vi.* **trammed**, **tram′ming** to convey or be conveyed by tram

tram[3] (tram) *n. clipped form of* TRAMMEL (sense 6) —*vt.*, *vi.* **trammed**, **tram′ming** to adjust, align, or measure with a trammel (sense 6)

tram·mel (tram′'l) *n.* [ME. *tramaile* < MFr. *tramail*, a net < ML. *tremaculum*, kind of fishing net < L. *tres*, THREE + *macula*, a mesh] **1.** *a*) a fishing net consisting of two outer layers of coarse mesh and a loosely hung middle layer of fine mesh *b*) a fowling net Also **trammel net 2.** a kind of shackle for a horse, esp. one to teach ambling **3.** [*usually pl.*] something that confines, restrains, or shackles **4.** a device with links or openings at different heights for hanging a pothook in a fireplace **5.** *a*) an instrument for drawing ellipses *b*) *same as* BEAM COMPASS **6.** any of several devices for adjusting or aligning parts of a machine —*vt.* -meled or -melled, -mel·ing or -mel·ling **1.** to entangle in or as in a trammel **2.** to confine, restrain, or shackle —**tram′mel·er, tram′mel·ler** *n.*

tra·mon·tane (trə män′tān) *adj.* [It. *tramontano* < L. *transmontanus*, beyond the mountains < *tra-* (see TRANS-) < *mons* (gen. *montis*), MOUNT[1]] located beyond or coming from beyond the mountains, specif. the Alps (from an Italian viewpoint) —*n.* **1.** orig., a tramontane person **2.** a foreigner; stranger

tramp (tramp) *vi.* [ME. *trampen* < or akin to LowG. *trampen*, to trample < nasalized form of the base in TRAP[1]] **1.** *a*) to walk with heavy steps *b*) to step heavily; stamp [to *tramp* on someone's foot] **2.** *a*) to travel about on foot; trudge; hike *b*) to travel as or like a vagabond, hobo, etc. —*vt.* **1.** to step on firmly and heavily; trample **2.** to walk or ramble through —*n.* **1.** a person who travels about on foot, esp. one doing odd jobs or begging for a living; hobo; vagrant **2.** the sound of heavy steps, as of people marching **3.** the act of tramping; esp., a journey on foot; hike **4.** a freight ship that has no regular schedule, arranging for cargo, passengers, and ports of call as it goes along **5.** an iron plate on the sole of a shoe to protect it, to prevent slipping, etc. **6.** [Slang] a woman who is sexually promiscuous —*SYN.* see VAGRANT —**tramp′er** *n.*

tram·ple (tram′p'l) *vt.* -pled, -pling [ME. *trampelen*, freq. of *trampen*: see prec.] to tread heavily; tramp —*vt.* to crush, destroy, hurt, violate, etc. by or as by treading heavily on —*n.* the sound of trampling —**trample under foot 1.** to crush or hurt by trampling **2.** to treat harshly or ruthlessly; domineer over Also **trample on, trample upon** —**tram′pler** *n.*

tram·po·line (tram′pə lēn′, -lin; tram′pə lēn′) *n.* [It. *trampolino*, a springboard, akin to *trampoli*, stilts < G. *trampeln*, to trample, freq. of *trampen*: cf. TRAMP] ☆a sheet of strong canvas stretched tightly on a frame, used for performing various feats of acrobatic tumbling —**tram′po·lin′er, tram′po·lin′ist** *n.*

tram·road (tram′rōd′) *n.* [TRAM[2] + ROAD] *Mining* a road for trams, having tracks of wood, stone, or metal

tram·way (-wā′) *n.* **1.** *same as* TRAMROAD **2.** [Brit.] a streetcar line; tramline ☆**3.** a system in which carriers or cars are supported by overhead cables

TRAMPOLINE

trance (trans, träns) *n.* [ME. < OFr. *transe*, great anxiety, fear < *transir*, to perish < L. *transire*, to die, lit., go across: see TRANSIT] **1.** a state of altered consciousness, somewhat resembling sleep, during which voluntary movement is lost, as in hypnosis **2.** a stunned condition; daze; stupor **3.** a condition of great mental concentration or abstraction, esp. one induced by religious fervor or mysticism **4.** a

condition in which a spiritualist medium allegedly loses consciousness and passes under the control of some external force, as for the supposed transmission of communications from the dead —*vt.* **tranced, tranc'ing** *chiefly poet. var. of* ENTRANCE²

tran·quil (traŋ′kwəl, tran′-) *adj.* **-quil·er** or **-quil·ler, -quil·est** or **-quil·lest** [L. *tranquillus,* calm, quiet, still < *trans-,* beyond (see TRANS-) + base akin to *quies,* rest, calm, QUIET] **1.** free from disturbance or agitation; calm, serene, peaceful, placid, etc. **2.** quiet or motionless; even, steady [*tranquil* waters] —*SYN.* see CALM —**tran'quil·ly** *adv.* —**tran'quil·ness** *n.*

tran·quil·ize, tran·quil·lize (traŋ′kwə līz′, tran′-) *vt., vi.* **-ized'** or **-lized', -iz'ing** or **-liz'ing** to make or become tranquil; specif., to calm by the use of a tranquilizer —**tran'quil·i·za'tion, tran'quil·li·za'tion** *n.*

tran·quil·iz·er, tran·quil·liz·er (-lī′zər) *n.* a person or thing that tranquilizes; specif., any of certain drugs, as chlorpromazine, meprobamate, etc., used as a calming agent in relieving and controlling various emotional disturbances, anxiety neuroses, certain psychoses, etc.

tran·quil·li·ty, tran·quil·i·ty (traŋ kwil′ə tē, tran-) *n.* the quality or state of being tranquil; calmness; serenity

trans- (trans, tranz) [L. *trans-* (contr. to *tra-* before *d-, m-, n-, l-, v-, j-*) < *trans,* across, over, orig., prob. prp. of **trare,* to pass, seen in *intrare, extrare* < IE. base **ter-,* over, beyond, whence Sans. *tiras,* over, THROUGH] *a prefix meaning:* **1.** on the other side of, to the other side of, over, across, through [*transatlantic*] **2.** so as to change thoroughly [*transliterate*] **3.** above and beyond; transcending [*trans-*sonic] **4.** *Chem.* designating an isomer having certain atoms or groups on opposite sides of a given plane in the molecule

trans. **1.** transaction(s) **2.** transferred **3.** transitive **4.** translated **5.** translation **6.** translator **7.** transportation **8.** transpose **9.** transverse

trans·act (tran sakt′, -zakt′) *vt.* [< L. *transactus,* pp. of *transigere,* to drive through, settle < *trans-* + *agere,* to drive: see TRANS- & ACT] to carry on, perform, conduct, or complete (business, etc.) —*vi.* [Rare] to do business; negotiate —**trans·ac'tor** *n.*

trans·ac·tion (-sak′shən, -zak′-) *n.* [L. *transactio*] **1.** a transacting or being transacted **2.** something transacted; specif., *a)* a business deal or agreement *b)* [*pl.*] a record of the proceedings of a society, convention, etc., esp. a published one —**trans·ac'tion·al** *adj.*

trans·al·pine (trans al′pin, tranz-; -pin) *adj.* [L. *transalpinus:* see TRANS- & ALPINE] on the other (the northern) side of the Alps: from the viewpoint of Rome

trans·am·i·nase (-am′ə nās′, -nāz′) *n.* [< ff. + -ASE] an enzyme that causes transamination

trans·am·i·na·tion (-am′ə nā′shən) *n.* [TRANS- + AMIN(E) + -ATION] the transfer of an amino group from one molecule to another usually by the action of a transaminase

trans·at·lan·tic (trans′ət lan′tik, tranz′-) *adj.* **1.** crossing or spanning the Atlantic **2.** on the other side of the Atlantic

trans·ca·lent (trans kā′lənt) *adj.* [< TRANS- + L. *calens,* prp. of *calere,* to be hot: for IE. base see CALDARIUM] conducting heat readily; pervious to heat

Trans·cau·ca·sia (trans′kô kā′zhə, -shə) that part of the Caucasus south of the Caucasus Mountains, containing the republics of Armenia, Azerbaijan, & Georgia — **Trans'cau·ca'sian** *adj., n.*

☆**trans·ceiv·er** (tran sē′vər) *n.* [TRANS(MITTER) + (RE)CEIVER] an apparatus contained in a single housing, functioning alternately as a radio transmitter and receiver

tran·scend (tran send′) *vt.* [ME. *transcenden* < L. *transcendere,* to climb over < *trans-,* over + *scandere,* to climb: see SCAN] **1.** to go beyond the limits of; overstep; exceed [*a story that transcends* belief] **2.** to be superior to; surpass; excel **3.** *Philos., Theol.* to be separate from or beyond (experience, the material universe, etc.) —*vi.* to be transcendent; excel —*SYN.* see EXCEL

tran·scend·ent (-sen′dənt) *adj.* [L. *transcendens,* prp. of *transcendere*] **1.** transcending; surpassing; excelling; extraordinary **2.** *Philos. a)* beyond the limits of possible experience *b)* in Kantianism, beyond human knowledge **3.** *Theol.* existing apart from the material universe: said of God —**tran·scend'ence, tran·scend'en·cy** *n.* —**tran·scend'ent·ly** *adv.*

tran·scen·den·tal (tran′sen den′t'l) *adj.* [ML. *transcendentalis*] **1.** *same as:* *a)* TRANSCENDENT (sense 1) *b)* SUPERNATURAL **2.** abstract; metaphysical **3.** of or having to do with transcendentalism **4.** in Kantian philosophy, not derived from experience but based on the a priori elements of experience, which are the necessary conditions of human knowledge; transcending sense experience but not knowledge **5.** *Math. a)* not capable of being a root of any algebraic equation with rational coefficients *b)* of, pertaining to, or being a function, as a logarithm, trigonometric function, exponential, etc., that is not expressible algebraically in terms of the variables and constants —**tran'scen·den'tal·ly** *adv.*

tran·scen·den·tal·ism (-iz'm) *n.* [< 18th-c. G. *transcen-*

dentalismus: see prec. & -ISM] **1.** any of various philosophies that propose to discover the nature of reality by investigating the process of thought rather than the objects of sense experience: the philosophies of Kant, Hegel, and Fichte are types of transcendentalism ☆**2.** by extension, the philosophical ideas of Ralph Waldo Emerson and some other 19th-cent. New Englanders, based on a search for reality through spiritual intuition **3.** popularly, any obscure, visionary, or idealistic thought —**tran'scen·den'·tal·ist** *n., adj.*

trans·con·duct·ance (trans′kən duk′təns) *n. Electronics* the ratio of the small change in anode current of an electron tube to a small change in grid voltage which produced the change in anode current, usually expressed in mhos

☆**trans·con·ti·nen·tal** (trans′kän tə nen′t'l) *adj.* **1.** that crosses a (or the) continent **2.** on the other side of a (or the) continent —**trans'con·ti·nen'tal·ly** *adv.*

tran·scribe (tran skrīb′) *vt.* **-scribed', -scrib'ing** [L. *transcribere:* see TRANS- & SCRIBE] **1.** to write out or type out in full (shorthand notes, a speech, etc.) **2.** to represent (something spoken or written) in phonetic or phonemic symbols **3.** to translate or transliterate **4.** to arrange or adapt (a piece of music) for an instrument, voice, or ensemble other than that for which it was originally written **5.** to make a recording of; specif., *Radio & TV* to record (a program, commercial, etc.) for broadcast at some later time —**tran·scrib'er** *n.*

tran·script (tran′skript′) *n.* [ME. *transcripte* < ML. *transcriptum* < L. *transcriptus,* pp. of *transcribere*] **1.** something made by or based on transcribing; written, typewritten, or printed copy **2.** any copy or reproduction, ☆esp. one that is official, as a copy of a student's record in school or college, listing courses, credits, grades, etc.

tran·scrip·tion (tran skrip′shən) *n.* [L. *transcriptio* < *transcriptus:* see prec.] **1.** the act or process of transcribing **2.** something transcribed; specif., *a)* a transcript; copy *b)* an arrangement of a piece of music for an instrument, voice, or ensemble other than that for which it was originally written *c)* a recording made for radio or television broadcasting; also, the act or practice of using such recordings —**tran·scrip'tion·al** *adj.*

trans·duc·er (trans dōōs′ər, tranz-; -dyōōs′-) *n.* [< L. *transducere,* to lead across < *trans-,* over + *ducere,* to lead (see DUCT) + -ER] any of various devices that transmit energy from one system to another, sometimes one that converts the energy in form

trans·duc·tion (trans duk′shən) *n.* [< L. *transductus,* pp. of *transducere:* see prec.] **1.** the transfer of energy from one system to another **2.** *Biol.* the transfer of genetic material from one bacterium to another by a bacteriophage

tran·sect (tran sekt′) *vt.* [< TRANS- + L. *sectus,* pp. of *secare,* to cut: see SAW¹] to cut across or divide by cutting —**tran·sec'tion** *n.*

tran·sept (tran′sept) *n.* [ModL. *transeptum* < L. *trans-,* across + *septum,* enclosure: see SEPTUM] **1.** the part of a cross-shaped church at right angles to the long, main section, or nave **2.** either arm of this part, outside the nave —**tran·sep'tal** (-sep′t'l) *adj.*

transf. transferred

trans·fer (trans fur′; *also, and for n. always,* trans′fər) *vt.* **-ferred', -fer'ring** [ME. *transferren* < L. *transferre* < *trans-,* across + *ferre,* to BEAR¹] **1.** to convey, carry, remove, or send from one person, place, or position to another **2.** to make over or convey (property, title to property, etc.) to another **3.** to convey (a picture, design, etc.) from one surface to another by any of several processes —*vi.* **1.** to transfer oneself or be transferred; move ☆**2.** to withdraw from one school, college, course of study, etc. and be admitted to another ☆**3.** to change from one bus, streetcar, etc. to another, usually by presenting a transfer —*n.* **1.** *a)* a transferring or being transferred *b)* a means of transferring **2.** a thing or person that is transferred; specif., a picture or design transferred or to be transferred from one surface to another ☆**3.** a ticket, provided free or at a small extra charge, entitling the bearer to change from one bus, streetcar, etc. to another as specified ☆**4.** a place for transferring ☆**5.** a form or document effecting a transfer, as of a student ☆**6.** a person who transfers or is transferred from one school, post, position, etc. to another **7.** *Law a)* the transferring of a title, right, etc. from one person to another *b)* the document effecting this —*SYN.* see MOVE —**trans·fer'a·ble, trans·fer'ra·ble** *adj.* —**trans·fer'al, trans·fer'ral** *n.,* **trans·fer'rer,** *Law* **trans·fer'or** *n.*

trans·fer·ase (trans′fər ās′, -āz′) *n.* [TRANSFER + -ASE] any of a class of enzymes whose actions cause the transfer of radicals from one molecule to another

trans·fer·ee (trans′fər ē′) *n.* **1.** a person to whom something is transferred, esp. in law **2.** a person who is transferred; transfer

trans·fer·ence (trans fur′əns, trans′fər-) *n.* **1.** a transferring or being transferred **2.** *Psychoanalysis* a reproduction of emotions relating to repressed experiences, esp. of childhood, and the substitution of another person, esp. the psychoanalyst, for the original object of the repressed impulses

trans·fer·en·tial (trans'fə ren'shəl) *adj.* of or involving a transfer or transference

trans·fer·rin (trans fer'in) *n.* [< TRANS- + L. *ferrum*, iron + -IN[1]] an iron-binding, crystalline globulin, a plasma protein important as an iron carrier

trans·fig·u·ra·tion (trans fig'yoo rā'shən, trans'fig-) *n.* a transfiguring or being transfigured —[T-] 1. *Bible* the change in the appearance of Jesus on the mountain: Matt. 17 2. a church festival (Aug. 6) commemorating this

trans·fig·ure (trans fig'yər) *vt.* -ured, -ur·ing [ME. *transfiguren* < L. *transfigurare*: see TRANS- & FIGURE] 1. to change the figure, form, or outward appearance of; transform 2. to transform so as to exalt or glorify —*SYN.* see TRANSFORM

trans·fi·nite (-fī'nīt) *adj.* 1. extending beyond or surpassing the finite 2. *Math.* designating or of a cardinal or ordinal number that is larger than any positive integer

trans·fix (trans fiks') *vt.* [< L. *transfixus*, pp. of *transfigere*, to transfix < *trans-*, through + *figere*, to FIX] 1. to pierce through with or as with something pointed 2. to fasten in this manner; impale 3. to make motionless, as if impaled [*transfixed* with horror] —**trans·fix'ion** (-fik'shən) *n.*

trans·form (trans fôrm'; *for n.*, trans'fôrm) *vt.* [ME. *transformen* < L. *transformare* < *trans-*, over + *formare*, to form < *forma*, FORM] 1. to change the form or outward appearance of 2. to change the condition, nature, or function of; convert 3. to change the personality or character of 4. *Elec.* to change (a voltage or current value) by use of a transformer 5. *Math.* to change (an algebraic expression or equation) to a different form having the same value 6. *Physics* to change (one form of energy) into another —*vi.* [Rare] to be or become transformed —*n.* ☆1. *Linguis.* a) any of a set of rules for producing grammatical transformations of a kernel sentence b) a sentence produced by using such a rule 2. *Math.* the process or result of a mathematical transformation —**trans·form'a·ble** *adj.* —**trans·form'a·tive** *adj.*

SYN.—**transform**, the broadest in scope of these terms, implies a change either in external form or in inner nature, in function, etc. [she was *transformed* into a happy girl]; **transmute**, from its earlier use in alchemy, suggests a change in basic nature that seems almost miraculous [*transmuted* from a shy youth into a gay man about town]; **convert** implies a change in details so as to be suitable for a new use [to *convert* an attic into an apartment]; **metamorphose** suggests a startling change produced as if by magic [a tadpole is *metamorphosed* into a frog]; **transfigure** implies a change in outward appearance which seems to exalt or glorify [his whole being *transfigured* by love] See also CHANGE

trans·for·ma·tion (trans'fər mā'shən) *n.* [LL.(Ec.) *transformatio*] 1. a transforming or being transformed 2. [Now Rare] a woman's wig ☆3. *Linguis.* a) the process of obtaining, by the application of certain rules, all the sentences of a given language from a basic group of kernel sentences b) the result obtained by applying any of these rules 4. *Math.* the process of setting up correspondences between the elements of two sets or spaces so that every element of the first set corresponds to a unique element of the second set —**trans'for·ma'tion·al** *adj.*

☆**transformational (generative) grammar** a grammatical system characterized by the view that all sentences in a given language are either kernel sentences or transformations of kernel sentences resulting from the application of transformational rules: cf. GENERATIVE GRAMMAR

trans·form·er (trans fôr'mər) *n.* 1. a person or thing that transforms 2. *Elec.* a device containing no moving parts and consisting essentially of two or more coils of insulated wire that transfers alternating-current energy by electromagnetic induction from one winding to another at the same frequency but usually with changed voltage and current values

trans·fuse (-fyooz') *vt.* -fused', -fus'ing [ME. *transfusen* < L. *transfusus*, pp. of *transfundere*, to pour from one container into another < *trans-*, across + *fundere*, to pour: see FOUND[3]] 1. a) to transfer or transmit by or as by causing to flow or be diffused b) to permeate, instill, imbue, infuse, etc. 2. *Med.* a) to transfer or introduce (blood, blood plasma, saline solution, etc.) into a blood vessel, usually a vein b) to give a transfusion to — **trans·fus'i·ble** *adj.* —**trans·fu'sive** (-fyoo'siv) *adj.*

trans·fu·sion (-fyoo'zhən) *n.* the act or an instance of transfusing, esp. blood, blood plasma, etc.

trans·gress (trans gres', tranz-) *vt.* [Fr. *transgresser* < L. *transgressus*, pp. of *transgredi*, to step over, pass over < *trans-*, over, across + *gradi*, to step, walk: see GRADE] 1. to overstep or break (a law, commandment, etc.) 2. to go beyond (a limit, boundary, etc.) —*vi.* to break a law, commandment, etc.; sin —**trans·gres'sive** *adj.* —**trans·gres'sor** *n.*

trans·gres·sion (-gresh'ən) *n.* the act or an instance of transgressing; breach of a law, duty, etc.; sin

tran·ship (tran ship') *vt. var. sp.* of TRANSSHIP

trans·hu·mance (trans hyōō'məns, tranz-) *n.* [Fr. *transhumer*, to practice transhumance < Sp. *trashumar* < *tras-*, trans- (< L., TRANS-) + L. *humus*, earth: see HUMUS] seasonal and alternating movement of livestock, together with the persons who tend the herds, between two regions, as lowlands and highlands —**trans·hu'mant** *adj.*

tran·sient (tran'shənt) *adj.* [L. *transiens*, prp. of *transire*: see TRANSIT] 1. *a)* passing away with time; not permanent;

temporary; transitory *b)* passing quickly or soon; fleeting; ephemeral ☆2. staying only for a short time [the *transient* population at resorts] —*n.* ☆1. a transient person or thing [*transients* at a hotel] 2. *Elec.* a temporary component of a current, resulting from a voltage surge, a change from one steady-state condition to another, etc. —**tran'sience**, **tran'sien·cy** *n.* —**tran'sient·ly** *adv.*

SYN.—**transient** applies to that which lasts or stays but a short time [a *transient* guest, feeling, etc.]; **transitory** refers to that which by its very nature must sooner or later pass or end [life is *transitory*]; **ephemeral** literally means existing only one day and, by extension, applies to that which is markedly short-lived [*ephemeral* glory]; **momentary** implies duration for a moment or an extremely short time [a *momentary* lull in the conversation]; **evanescent** applies to that which appears momentarily and fades quickly away [*evanescent* mental images]; **fleeting** implies of a thing that it passes swiftly and cannot be held [a *fleeting* thought] —*ANT.* lasting, permanent

tran·sil·i·ent (tran sil'ē ənt, -sil'yənt) *adj.* [L. *transiliens*, prp. of *transilire*, to leap across < *trans-*, over, across + *salire*: see SALIENT] passing abruptly or leaping from one thing, condition, etc. to another —**tran·sil'i·ence** *n.*

trans·il·lu·mi·nate (trans'i lōō'mə nāt', tranz'-) *vt.* -nat'ed, -nat'ing [TRANS- + ILLUMINATE] *Med.* to pass a light through the walls of (a body cavity) in examination —**trans'il·lu'mi·na'tion** *n.*

☆**tran·sis·tor** (tran zis'tər, -sis'-) *n.* [TRAN(SFER) + (RE)SISTOR: it transfers a current across a resistor] 1. a solid-state, electronic device, composed of semiconductor material, as germanium, silicon, etc., that controls current flow without use of a vacuum: transistors are similar in function to electron tubes, but have the advantages of being compact, long-lived, and low in power requirements 2. popularly, a transistorized radio

☆**tran·sis·tor·ize** (-tə rīz') *vt.* -ized', -iz'ing to equip (a device) with transistors

trans·it (tran'sit, -zit) *n.* [ME. *transite* < L. *transitus*, pp. of *transire* < *trans-*, over, across + *ire*, to go: see YEAR] 1. *a)* passage through or across *b)* a transition; change 2. *a)* a carrying or being carried through or across; conveyance [goods in *transit*] *b)* a system of urban public transportation: cf. RAPID TRANSIT 3. a surveying instrument for measuring horizontal angles, a kind of theodolite: in full **transit theodolite** 4. *Astron. a)* the apparent passage of a heavenly body across a given meridian or through the field of a telescope *b)* the apparent passage of a smaller heavenly body across the disk of a larger one, as of Mercury across the sun —*vt.* 1. to make a transit through or across 2. to revolve (the telescope of a transit) so as to reverse its direction —*vi.* to make a transit, or passage

TRANSIT THEODOLITE

transit instrument 1. a telescope mounted at right angles to a horizontal east-west axis so that it can be rotated only in the vertical plane of the meridian at its site, for observing and timing the transit of heavenly bodies across the meridian 2. *same as* TRANSIT (sense 3)

tran·si·tion (tran zish'ən, -sish'-; *Brit.* -sizh'-) *n.* [L. *transitio* < *transitus*: see TRANSIT] 1. *a)* a passing from one condition, form, stage, activity, place, etc. to another *b)* the period of such passing 2. a word, phrase, sentence, or group of sentences that relates a preceding topic to a succeeding one or that smoothly connects parts of a speech or piece of writing 3. *Music a)* a shifting from one key to another; modulation; esp., a brief or passing modulation *b)* an abrupt change into a remote key *c)* a passage connecting two sections of a composition —**tran·si'tion·al**, **tran·si'tion·ar'y** *adj.* —**tran·si'tion·al·ly** *adv.*

transition element any element of several groups of elements formed by adding electrons to an inner shell as the atomic number increases

tran·si·tive (tran'sə tiv, -zə-) *adj.* [LL. *transitivus* < L. *transitus*: see TRANSIT] 1. [Rare] of, showing, or characterized by transition; transitional 2. *Gram.* expressing an action that is thought of as passing over to and taking effect on some person or thing; taking a direct object to complete the meaning: said of certain verbs 3. *Math.* designating a relation having the property that, whenever a first element bears a particular relation to a second that in turn bears this same relation to a third, then the third element bears this relation to the first [identity and equality are *transitive* relations] —*n. Gram.* a transitive verb —**tran'si·tive·ly** *adv.* —**tran'si·tive·ness**, **tran'si·tiv'i·ty** *n.*

tran·si·to·ry (tran'sə tôr'ē, -zə-) *adj.* [ME. *transitorie* < MFr. *transitoire* < LL.(Ec.) *transitorius* < L., adapted for passing through < *transitus*: see TRANSIT] of a passing nature; not enduring or permanent; temporary, fleeting, or ephemeral; transient —*SYN.* see TRANSIENT —**tran'si·to'ri·ly** *adv.* —**tran'si·to'ri·ness** *n.*

Trans·jor·dan (trans jôr'd'n, tranz-) *earlier name for* JORDAN: also **Trans'jor·da'ni·a** (-dā'nē ə)

Trans·kei (trans kā', -kī') self-governing region in E Cape Province, South Africa, set aside as a reserve for the

native Bantu peoples: 16,500 sq. mi.; pop. c.1,300,000 —**Trans·kei′an** *adj.*

transl. 1. translated 2. translation

trans·late (trans lāt′, tranz-; trans′lāt, tranz′-) *vt.* **-lat′ed, -lat′ing** [ME. *translaten* < ML. & L.: ML. *translatare* < L. *translatus*, transferred, used as pp. of *transferre:* see TRANSFER] 1. to change from one place, position, or condition to another; transfer; specif., *a) Theol.* to convey to heaven, orig. without death *b) Eccles.* to transfer (a bishop) from one see to another; also, to move (a saint's body, relics, etc.) from one place of interment to another 2. to put into the words of a different language 3. to change into another medium or form [to *translate* ideas into action] 4. to put into different words; rephrase or paraphrase in explanation 5. to retransmit (a telegraphic message) by means of an automatic relay 6. [Archaic] to enrapture; entrance 7. *Mech.* to impart translation to —*vi.* 1. to make a translation into another language 2. to be capable of being translated —**trans·lat′a·ble** *adj.*

trans·la·tion (-lā′shən) *n.* [ME. *translacioun* < MFr. *translation* < L. *translatio*] 1. a translating or being translated 2. the result of a translating; esp., writing or speech translated into another language 3. *Mech.* motion in which every point of the moving object has simultaneously the same velocity and direction of motion —**trans·la′tion·al** *adj.*

SYN.—**translation** implies the rendering from one language into another of something written or spoken [a German *translation* of Shakespeare]; **version** is applied to a particular translation of a given work, specif. of the Bible [the King James *Version*]; **paraphrase**, in this connection, is applied to a free translation of a passage or work from another language; **transliteration** implies the writing of words with characters of another alphabet that represent the same sound or sounds [in this dictionary Greek words are *transliterated* with letters of the English alphabet.]

trans·la·tor (-lāt′ər) *n.* [ME. *translatour* < LL.(Ec.) *translator* < L., one who transfers] a person who translates; specif., *a)* a person who translates books, articles, etc. from one language into another *b)* a person who translates speech; interpreter

trans·lit·er·ate (trans lit′ə rāt′, tranz-) *vt.* **-at′ed, -at′ing** [< TRANS- + L. *litera, littera*, LETTER[1] + -ATE[1]] to write or spell (words, etc.) in corresponding characters of another alphabet —**trans·lit·er·a′tion** *n.*

trans·lo·cate (-lō′kāt) *vt.* **-cat′ed, -cat′ing** to cause to change location or position; dislocate; displace

trans·lo·ca·tion (trans′lō kā′shən, tranz′-) *n.* 1. a translocating; dislocation 2. *Bot.* the transport of organic food materials in solution through tissues from one part of a plant to another 3. *Genetics* the transfer of a broken portion of a chromosome to a different part of a homologous chromosome or into a nonhomologous chromosome

trans·lu·cent (trans lōō′s'nt, tranz-) *adj.* [L. *translucens*, prp. of *translucere*, to shine through: see TRANS- & LIGHT[1]] 1. orig., shining through 2. [Rare] transparent 3. letting light pass but diffusing it so that objects on the other side cannot be clearly distinguished; partially transparent, as frosted glass: also **trans·lu′cid** (-lōō′sid) 4. easily perceived; lucid; clear —*SYN.* see CLEAR —**trans·lu′cence, trans·lu′cen·cy** *n.* —**trans·lu′cent·ly** *adv.*

trans·ma·rine (trans′mə rēn′, tranz′-) *adj.* [L. *transmurinus:* see TRANS- & MARINE] 1. crossing the sea 2. coming from or being on the other side of the sea

trans·mi·grant (trans mī′grənt, tranz-) *adj.* [L. *transmigrans*, prp. of *transmigrare*] that transmigrates —*n.* a person or thing that transmigrates; specif., an emigrant passing through a country or place on his way to the country in which he will be an immigrant

trans·mi·grate (-mī′grāt) *vi.* **-grat′ed, -grat′ing** [ME. *transmigraten, vt.* < L. *transmigratus*, pp. of *transmigrare:* see TRANS- & MIGRATE] 1. to move from one habitation, country, etc. to another 2. in some religions, to pass into some other body at death: said of the soul —**trans·mi′gra·tor** *n.* —**trans·mi′gra·to·ry** (-grə tôr′ē) *adj.*

trans·mi·gra·tion (trans′mi grā′shən, tranz′-) *n.* [LL. (Ec.) *transmigratio*] the act or process of transmigrating; specif., the supposed passing of the soul at death into some other body

trans·mis·si·ble (trans mis′ə b'l, tranz-) *adj.* [LL. *transmissibilis* < L. *transmissus* (see ff. & -IBLE)] capable of being transmitted —**trans·mis′si·bil′i·ty** *n.*

trans·mis·sion (-mish′ən) *n.* [L. *transmissio* < *transmissus*, pp. of *transmittere*] 1. *a)* a transmitting or being transmitted *b)* something transmitted 2. the part of an automobile, truck, etc. that transmits motive force from the engine to the wheels, usually by means of gears or hydraulic cylinders 3. the passage of radio waves through space between the transmitting station and the receiving station —**trans·mis′sive** *adj.*

trans·mit (-mit′) *vt.* **-mit′ted, -mit′ting** [ME. *transmitten* < L. *transmittere* < *trans-*, over, across + *mittere*, to send: see MISSION] 1. to send or cause to go from one person or place to another, esp. across intervening space or distance; transfer; dispatch; convey 2. to pass along;

impart (a disease, etc.) 3. to hand down to others by heredity, inheritance, etc. 4. to communicate (news, etc.) 5. *a)* to cause (light, heat, sound, etc.) to pass through air or some other medium [the sun *transmits* heat and light] *b)* to allow the passage of; conduct [water *transmits* sound] 6. to convey (force, movement, etc.) from one mechanical part to another 7. to send out (radio or television broadcasts, etc.) by electromagnetic waves —*vi.* to send out radio or television signals —*SYN.* see CARRY —**trans·mit′tal** *n.* —**trans·mit′ti·ble, trans·mit′ta·ble** *adj.*

trans·mit·tance (-mit′'ns) *n.* 1. the act or process of transmitting 2. the ratio of the radiant energy transmitted by a body to the total radiant energy received by the body

trans·mit·tan·cy (-mit′'n sē) *n.* 1. the ratio of the transmittance of a solution to that of an equivalent thickness of the pure solvent 2. same as TRANSMITTANCE (sense 2)

trans·mit·ter (-mit′ər; *for* 2, *often* trans′mit ər, tranz′-) *n.* 1. a person who transmits 2. a thing that transmits; specif., *a)* the part of a telegraphic instrument by which messages are sent *b)* the part of a telephone, behind or including the mouthpiece, that converts speech sound into electric impulses for transmission *c)* the apparatus that generates radio waves, modulates their amplitude or frequency, and transmits them by means of an antenna

trans·mog·ri·fy (trans mäg′rə fī′, tranz-) *vt.* **-fied′, -fy′ing** [humorous pseudo-L. formation] to change completely; transform, esp. in a grotesque or strange manner —**transmog′ri·fi·ca′tion** *n.*

trans·mon·tane (trans män′tān, tranz-, ⸬rans′män tān′, tranz′-) *adj.* [L. *transmontanus*] same as TRAMONTANE

trans·mun·dane (-mun′dān) *adj.* [TRANS- + MUNDANE] beyond the world or worldly matters

trans·mu·ta·tion (trans′myōō tā′shən, tranz′-) *n.* [ME. *transmutacioun* < LL. *transmutatio* < pp. of L. *transmutare*] 1. a transmuting or being transmuted; change of one thing into another 2. [Rare] a fluctuation 3. in the Middle Ages, the supposedly possible conversion of base metals into gold and silver by alchemy 4. *Chem.* the conversion of atoms of a given element into atoms of a different isotope or of a different element, as in radioactive disintegration or by nuclear bombardment —**trans′mu·ta′tion·al** *adj.* —**trans·mut′a·tive** (-myōōt′ə tiv) *adj.*

trans·mute (trans myōōt′, tranz-) *vt., vi.* **-mut′ed, -mut′ing** [ME. *transmuten* < L. *transmutare* < *trans-*, over, across + *mutare*, to change: see MUTATE] to change from one form, species, condition, nature, or substance into another; transform; convert —*SYN.* see TRANSFORM —**trans·mut′a·ble** *adj.* —**trans·mut′a·bly** *adv.*

trans·na·tion·al (-nash′ə n'l) *adj.* transcending the limits, interests, etc. of a single nation

trans·o·ce·an·ic (trans′ō shē an′ik, tranz′-) *adj.* 1. crossing or spanning the ocean 2. coming from or being on the other side of the ocean

tran·som (tran′səm) *n.* [LME. *traunsom*, prob. altered < L. *tarnstrum*, crossbeam, lit., that which is across < *trans:* see TRANS-] 1. a crosspiece in a structure; specif., *a)* a lintel *b)* a horizontal crossbar across the top or middle of a window or the top of a door ☆2. a small window or shutterlike panel directly over a door or window, usually hinged to the transom (sense 1 *b*) 3. any crosspiece; specif., *a)* the horizontal beam of a gallows *b)* any of the transverse beams attached to the sternpost of a wooden ship

tran·son·ic (tran sän′ik) *adj.* [TRAN(S)- + SONIC] designating, of, or moving at a speed within the range of change from subsonic to supersonic speed

transp. transportation

trans·pa·cif·ic (trans′pə sif′ik) *adj.* 1. crossing or spanning the Pacific 2. on the other side of the Pacific

trans·pa·dane (trans′pə dān′, trans pā′dān) *adj.* [L. *transpadanus* < *trans-*, over, across + *Padus*, the Po] on the other (the northern) side of the river Po: from the viewpoint of Rome

trans·par·en·cy (trans per′ən sē, -par′) *n.* 1. the quality or state of being transparent: also **trans·par′ence** 2. *pl.* **-cies** something transparent; specif., a piece of transparent or translucent material, esp. a positive film or slide, having a picture or design that is visible when light shines through it or that can be projected on a screen

trans·par·ent (-ənt) *adj.* [ME. *transparaunt* < ML. *transparens*, prp. of *transparere*, to be transparent < L. *trans-*, over, across, through + *parens*, prp. of *parere*, to appear] 1. transmitting light rays so that objects on the other side may be distinctly seen; capable of being seen through; neither opaque nor translucent 2. so fine in texture or open in mesh that objects on the other side may be seen relatively clearly; sheer; gauzy; diaphanous 3. easily understood; very clear 4. easily recognized or detected; obvious 5. without guile or concealment; open; frank; candid —*SYN.* see CLEAR —**trans·par′ent·ly** *adv.* —**trans·par′ent·ness** *n.*

tran·spic·u·ous (tran spik′yoo wəs) *adj.* [ModL. *transpicuus* < L. *transpicere*, to see through < *trans-*, TRANS- + *specere*, to look at: see SPY] transparent; esp., easily understood —**tran·spic′u·ous·ly** *adv.*

trans·pierce (trans pirs′) *vt.* **-pierced′, -pierc′ing** [Fr.

transpercer: see TRANS- & PIERCE] **1.** to pierce through completely **2.** to pierce; penetrate

tran·spi·ra·tion (tran'spə rā'shən) *n.* [ML. *transpiratio*] the act or process of transpiring; specif., the giving off of moisture, etc. through the pores of the skin or through the surface of leaves and other parts of plants

tran·spire (tran spīr') *vt.* -spired', -spir'ing [Fr. *transpirer* < ML. *transpirare* < L. *trans*-, over, across, through + *spirare*, to breathe: see SPIRIT] to cause (vapor, moisture, etc.) to pass through tissue or other permeable substances, esp. through the pores of the skin or the surface of leaves, etc. —*vi.* **1.** to give off vapor, moisture, etc., as through the pores of the skin **2.** to be given off, passed through pores, exhaled, etc. **3.** to leak out; become known ☆**4.** to come to pass; happen: in this sense, still regarded by some as a loose usage —SYN. see HAPPEN

trans·plant (trans plant', -plänt'; *for n.* trans'plant', -plänt') *vt.* [ME. *transplaunten* < LL. *transplantare*: see TRANS- & PLANT] **1.** to dig up (a growing plant) from one place and plant in another **2.** to remove (people) from one place and resettle in another **3.** *Surgery* to transfer (tissue or an organ) from one individual or part of the body to another; graft —*vi.* **1.** to do transplanting **2.** to be capable of enduring transplantation —*n.* **1.** the act or an instance of transplanting **2.** something transplanted, as a body organ or seedling —**trans·plant'a·ble** *adj.* —**trans'plan·ta'tion** (-plan tā'shən) *n.* —**trans·plant'er** *n.*

tran·spon·der (tran spän'dər) *n.* [TRAN(SMITTER) + (RE)SPONDER] a radio or radar transceiver that automatically transmits electrical signals when actuated by a specific signal from an interrogator

trans·pon·tine (trans pän'tin, -tīn) *adj.* [< TRANS- + L. *pons* (gen. *pontis*), a bridge: see PONS] **1.** on the other side of a bridge **2.** south of the Thames in London

trans·port (trans pôrt'; *for n.* trans'pôrt') *vt.* [ME. *transporten* < MFr. *transporter* < L. *transportare*, to carry across < *trans*-, over, across + *portare*, to carry: see PORT[3]] **1.** to carry from one place to another, esp. over long distances **2.** to carry away with emotion; enrapture; entrance **3.** to carry off to a penal colony, etc.; banish; deport —*n.* **1.** the act, process, or means of transporting; transportation; conveyance **2.** strong emotion, esp. of delight or joy; rapture **3.** a ship, airplane, train, etc. used for transporting soldiers, freight, etc. **4.** a convict sentenced to transportation —SYN. see BANISH, CARRY, ECSTASY —**trans·port'a·bil'i·ty** *n.* —**trans·port'a·ble** *adj.* —**trans·port'er** *n.*

trans·por·ta·tion (trans'pər tā'shən) *n.* [Fr. < L. *transportatio*] **1.** a transporting or being transported ☆**2.** *a)* a means or system of conveyance *b)* the work or business of conveying passengers or goods ☆**3.** fare or a ticket for being transported **4.** banishment for crime, as to a penal colony; deportation —**trans'por·ta'tion·al** *adj.*

trans·pose (trans pōz') *vt.* -posed', -pos'ing [ME. *transposen* < MFr. *transposer* (for L. *transponere*): see TRANS- & POSE[1]] **1.** to transfer or shift; now, specif., to change the usual, normal, relative, or respective order or position of; interchange [inadvertently *transposed* the *e* and the *i* in "weird"] **2.** to transfer (an algebraic term) from one side of an equation to the other, reversing the plus or minus value **3.** to rewrite or play (a musical composition) in a different key **4.** [Obs.] to transform; convert —*vi.* to play music in a key different from the one in which it is written —*n.* *Math.* a matrix obtained by interchanging the rows and columns of a given matrix —SYN. see REVERSE —**trans·pos'a·ble** *adj.* —**trans·pos'er** *n.*

trans·po·si·tion (trans'pə zish'ən) *n.* [ML. *transpositio* < L. *transpositus*, pp. of *transponere*: see TRANS- & POSE[1]] **1.** a transposing or being transposed **2.** the result of this; something transposed —**trans'po·si'tion·al** *adj.*

☆**trans·sex·u·al** (tran sek'shoo wəl, trans-) *n.* a person who is predisposed to identify with the opposite sex, or one who has undergone surgery and hormone injections to effect a change of sex —**trans·sex'u·al·ism** *n.*

trans·ship (tran ship', trans-) *vt.* -shipped', -ship'ping to transfer from one ship, train, truck, etc. to another for reshipment —**trans·ship'ment** *n.*

trans·son·ic (-sän'ik) *adj.* same as TRANSONIC

☆**tran·stage** (tran'stāj') *n.* [TRAN(S)- + STAGE] an unmanned, third-stage rocket that can be re-started in space and that can change orbit, perform maneuvers, etc.

tran·sub·stan·ti·ate (tran'səb stan'shē āt') *vt.* -at'ed, -at'ing [< ML.(Ec.) *transsubstantiatus*, pp. of *transsubstantiare* < L. *trans*-, over, across + *substantia*, SUBSTANCE] **1.** to change one substance into another; transmute; transform **2.** *R.C. & Orthodox Eastern Ch.* to bring about transubstantiation in (bread and wine)

tran·sub·stan·ti·a·tion (-stan'shē ā'shən) *n.* [ML.(Ec.) *transsubstantiatio*] **1.** the act of transubstantiating; change of one substance into another **2.** *R.C. & Orthodox Eastern Ch.* the doctrine that, in the Eucharist, the whole substances of the bread and of the wine are changed into the body and blood of Christ, only the accidents of bread and wine remaining

tran·su·date (tran'soo dāt', ɛyoo-) *n.* [ModL. *transudatus*, pp. of *transudare*] something transuded

tran·su·da·tion (tran'soo dā'shən, -syoo-) *n.* [Fr. *transsudation*] **1.** an act or instance of transuding **2.** same as TRANSUDATE

tran·sude (tran sōōd', -syōōd') *vi.* -sud'ed, -sud'ing [ModL. *transudare* < L. *trans*-, over, across, through + *sudare*, to SWEAT] to ooze or exude through pores or interstices, as, esp., blood serum through the vessel walls

trans·u·ran·ic (trans'yoo ran'ik, tranz'-) *adj.* designating or of the elements having atomic numbers higher than that of uranium, as plutonium, prepared by nuclear bombardment: also **trans'u·ra'ni·um** (-rā'nē əm)

Trans·vaal (trans väl', tranz-) province of South Africa, in the NE part: 109,621 sq. mi.; pop. 6,273,000; cap. Pretoria See SOUTH AFRICAN REPUBLIC

trans·val·ue (trans val'yōō, tranz-) *vt.* -val'ued, -val'u·ing to evaluate by a new principle, esp. one rejecting conventional or accepted standards —**trans'val·u·a'tion** *n.*

trans·ver·sal (-vur'səl) *adj.* [ME. < ML. *transversalis*] same as TRANSVERSE —*n.* a line that intersects two or more other lines —**trans·ver'sal·ly** *adv.*

trans·verse (trans vurs', tranz-; *also, and for n. usually,* trans'vurs, tranz'-) *adj.* [L. *transversus*, pp. of *transvertere*: see TRAVERSE] **1.** lying, situated, placed, etc. across; crossing from side to side; crosswise **2.** *Geom.* designating the axis that passes through the foci of a hyperbola, or the part of that axis between the vertices —*n.* **1.** a transverse part, beam, etc. **2.** *Geom.* a transverse axis —**trans·verse'ly** *adv.*

transverse colon the central portion of the large intestine, crossing the abdominal cavity from right to left and lying between the ascending and descending colons

transverse process a process projecting laterally from a vertebra

trans·ves·tite (trans ves'tīt, tranz-) *n.* [< TRANS- + L. *vestire*, to clothe (see VEST) + -ITE[1]] a person who derives sexual pleasure from dressing in the clothes of the opposite sex —**trans·ves'tism, trans·ves'ti·tism** *n.*

Tran·syl·va·ni·a (tran'sil vā'nē ə, -vän'yə) plateau region in C Romania, north of the Transylvanian Alps: c.24,000 sq. mi.; chief city, Cluj —**Tran'syl·va'ni·an** *adj., n.*

Transylvanian Alps range of the Carpathian Mountains, in C & SW Romania, between Transylvania & Walachia: highest peak, 8,361 ft.

trap[1] (trap) *n.* [ME. *trappe* < OE. *træppe*, akin to *treppan*, to step, G. *treppe*, stairway < IE. **dreb*-, to run, step, trip (var. of **drā*-) whence Pol. *drabina*, a ladder] **1.** any device for catching animals, as one that snaps shut tightly when stepped on, or a pitfall; gin, snare, etc. **2.** any stratagem or ambush designed to catch or trick unsuspecting persons **3.** any of various devices for preventing the escape of gas, offensive odors, etc.; specif., a U-shaped or S-shaped part of a drainpipe, in which standing water seals off sewer gas **4.** an apparatus for throwing disks into the air to be shot at in trapshooting **5.** a light, two-wheeled carriage with springs **6.** same as TRAPDOOR ☆**7.** [*pl.*] the percussion devices, as cymbals, blocks, bells, etc., attached to the set of drums, as in a jazz band **8.** [Slang] the mouth, specif. as the organ of speech **9.** *Golf* same as SAND TRAP —*vt.* **trapped, trap'ping 1.** to catch in or as in a trap; entrap **2.** to hold back or seal off by a trap **3.** to furnish with a trap or traps ☆**4.** *Sports* to seize (a batted or thrown ball) just off the ground as it rebounds from it —*vi.* **1.** to set traps for game ☆**2.** to trap animals, esp. for their furs

TRAP

SYN.—**trap**, as applied to a device for capturing animals, specif. suggests a snapping device worked by a spring, **pitfall**, a concealed pit with a collapsible cover, and **snare**, a noose which jerks tight upon the release of a trigger; in extended senses, these words apply to any danger into which unsuspecting or unwary persons may fall; **trap** specifically suggesting a deliberate stratagem or ambush [a speed *trap*], **pitfall**, a concealed danger, source of error, etc. [the *pitfalls* of the law], and **snare**, enticement and entanglement [the *snares* of love] See also CATCH

trap[2] (trap) *n.* [Sw. *trapp* < *trappa*, stair, akin to prec.] **1.** any of several dark-colored, usually fine-grained, extrusive, igneous rocks; esp., such a rock, as basalt, used in road making **2.** a geologic structure forming a reservoir enclosing an accumulation of oil or gas

trap[3] (trap) *vt.* **trapped, trap'ping** [ME. *trappen* < *trappe*, trappings < OFr. *drap*, cloth: see DRAPE] to cover, equip, or adorn with trappings; caparison —*n.* **1.** [Obs.] an ornamental covering for a horse **2.** [*pl.*] [Colloq.] a person's clothes, personal belongings, etc.

tra·pan (trə pan') *n., vt.* **-panned', -pan'ning** *archaic var. of* TREPAN[2]

Tra·pa·ni (trä'pä nē') seaport on the NW coast of Sicily: pop. 76,000

trap·door (trap'dôr') *n.* a hinged or sliding door in a roof, ceiling, or floor

trapdoor spider any of various, often large spiders (esp. family Ctenizidae), that dig a burrow and cover the entrance with a hinged lid like a trapdoor

trapes (trāps) *vi., vt., n. var. sp.* of TRAIPSE

tra·peze (tra pēz', trə-) *n.* [Fr. *trapèze* < ModL. *trapezium*: see TRAPEZIUM] a short horizontal bar, hung at a height by two ropes, on or from which gymnasts, circus aerialists, etc. swing, performing various stunts

tra·pe·zi·form (trə pē'zə fôrm') *adj.* shaped like a trapezium

tra·pe·zi·um (trə pē′zē əm) *n., pl.* **-zi·ums, -zi·a** (-ə) [ModL. < Gr. *trapezion,* trapezium, lit., small table, dim. of *trapeza,* table, lit., four-footed bench < *tra-,* for *tetra,* FOUR + *peza,* a foot, akin to *pous,* FOOT] **1.** a plane figure with four sides no two of which are parallel **2.** [Brit.] *same as* TRAPEZOID (sense 1) **3.** *Anat.* a small bone of the wrist near the base of the thumb

TRAPEZIUM

trap·e·zo·he·dron (trap′i zō hē′drən, trə pē′zō-) *n.* [ModL.: see prec. & -HEDRON] a solid figure, esp. a crystal, all of whose faces are trapeziums

trap·e·zoid (trap′ə zoid′) *n.* [ModL. *trapezoides* < Gr. *trapezoeides,* shaped like a trapezoid: see TRAPEZIUM & -OID] **1.** a plane figure with four sides only two of which are parallel **2.** [Brit.] *same as* TRAPEZIUM (sense 1) **3.** *Anat.* a small bone of the wrist near the base of the index finger —*adj.* shaped like a trapezoid: also **trap′e·zoi′dal**

TRAPEZOID

trap·per (trap′ər) *n.* a person who traps; esp., one who traps fur-bearing animals for their skins

trap·pings (trap′iŋz) *n.pl.* [< ME. *trappe:* see TRAP³] **1.** an ornamental covering for a horse; caparison **2.** articles of dress, esp. of an ornamental kind; adornments **3.** the accouterments usually associated with something [an expense account and the other *trappings* of success]

Trap·pist (trap′ist) *n.* [Fr. *trappiste* < (La) *Trappe,* abbey near the village of Soligny-la-*Trappe,* in Normandy, where the rule was established in 1664] a monk of a branch of the Cistercian order, known for austerity and perpetual silence —*adj.* of or having to do with the Trappists

trap·rock (trap′räk′) *n. same as* TRAP²

trapse (traps) *vi., vt., n.* **trapsed, traps′ing** *var. sp.* of TRAIPSE

trap·shoot·ing (trap′shoot′iŋ) *n.* the sport of shooting at clay pigeons, or disks, sprung into the air from traps —**trap′shoot′er** *n.*

trapt (trapt) *archaic pt. & pp. of* TRAP¹

tra·pun·to (trə poon′tō) *n., pl.* **-tos** [It. < pp. of *trapungere,* to embroider < *tra-,* through (< L. *trans-,* TRANS-) + *pungere,* to prick (< L.: see POINT] a kind of padded quilting with the design, in high relief, outlined with single stitches: used for upholstery, robes, etc.

trash¹ (trash) *n.* [prob. < Scand., as in Norw. dial. *trask,* lumber, trash, akin to ON. *tros,* broken twigs < IE. base *der-,* to tear, split off, whence TEAR] **1.** parts that have been broken off, stripped off, etc., esp. leaves, twigs, husks, and other plant trimmings **2.** broken, discarded, or worthless things; rubbish; refuse **3.** *a)* any worthless, unnecessary, or offensive matter [literary *trash*] *b)* foolish talk; nonsense **4.** a person or people regarded as disreputable, insignificant, etc. **5.** the refuse of sugar cane after the juice has been pressed out —*vt.* to trim (trees or plants) of trash

trash² (trash) *vt.* [prob. ≤ OFr. *trachier,* var. of *tracier,* see TRACE¹] [Archaic] to restrain, as by a leash —*n.* [Archaic] a leash for restraining an animal

trash·y (-ē) *adj.* **trash′i·er, trash′i·est** containing, consisting of, or like trash; worthless —**trash′i·ness** *n.*

Tra·si·me·no (trä′sē me′nō) lake in C Italy: scene of a victory by Hannibal over the Romans (217 B.C.): L. name **Tras·i·me·nus** (tras′ə mē′nəs)

trass (tras) *n.* [G. < Du. *tras* < earlier *terras* < MFr. *terrace:* see TERRACE] a volcanic rock, powdered and used in making a hydraulic cement

‡**trat·tor·i·a** (trät′tō rē′ä) *n., pl.* **-i·e** (-e) [It. < *trattore,* innkeeper < *trattare,* to manage, handle < L. *tractare:* see TREAT] a small, inexpensive restaurant in Italy

trau·ma (trou′mə, trô′-) *n., pl.* **-mas, -ma·ta** (-mə tə) [ModL. < Gr. *trauma* (gen. *traumatos*): for IE. base see THROE] **1.** *Med.* a bodily injury, wound, or shock **2.** *Psychiatry* a painful emotional experience, or shock, often producing a lasting psychic effect and, sometimes, a neurosis —**trau·mat′ic** (-mat′ik) *adj.* —**trau·mat′i·cal·ly** *adv.*

trau·ma·tism (-tiz′m) *n.* [< Gr. *trauma* (see prec.) + -ISM] **1.** the abnormal condition caused by a trauma **2.** *same as* TRAUMA

trau·ma·tize (-tīz′) *vt.* **-tized′, -tiz′ing 1.** *Med.* to injure or wound (tissues) **2.** *Psychiatry* to subject to a trauma

trav. 1. traveler **2.** travels

trav·ail (trav′āl, trə väl′) *n.* [ME. < OFr. < VL. *tripalium,* instrument of torture composed of three stakes < *tri-,* three + *palus,* a stake: see PALE²] **1.** very hard work; toil **2.** labor pains; pains of childbirth **3.** intense pain; agony —*vi.* [ME. *travaillen* < OFr. *travaillier,* to labor, toil < VL. *tripaliare,* to torment < *tripalium*] **1.** to work very hard; toil **2.** to have labor pains; suffer the pains of childbirth —*SYN.* see WORK

Trav·an·core (trav′ən kôr′) former native state of SW India: merged with Cochin (1949) to form a state (**Travancore-Cochin**), incorporated into Kerala (1956)

trave (trāv) *n.* [ME. < MFr. < L. *trabs* (gen. *trabis*), a beam: see TAVERN] [Now Rare] **1.** *a)* a crossbeam *b)* a

section between crossbeams, as in a ceiling **2.** a wooden frame for enclosing a restive horse while it is being shod

trav·el (trav′'l) *vi.* **-eled** or **-elled, -el·ing** or **-el·ling** [var. of TRAVAIL] **1.** to go from one place to another; make a journey or journeys **2.** to go from place to place as a traveling salesman **3.** to walk or run **4.** to move, pass, or be transmitted from one point or place to another **5.** to move or be capable of moving in a given path or for a given distance: said of mechanical parts, etc. **6.** to advance or progress ☆**7.** *Basketball* to move more than the prescribed distance (generally two steps) while holding the ball **8.** [Colloq.] to associate or spend time (*with*) **9.** [Colloq.] to move with speed —*vt.* **1.** to make a journey over or through; traverse **2.** [Colloq.] to cause to move or pass along —*n.* **1.** the act or process of traveling **2.** [*pl.*] *a)* the trips, journeys, tours, etc. taken by a person or persons *b)* an account of these **3.** passage or movement of any kind **4.** traffic on a route, through a place, etc. **5.** *a)* mechanical motion, esp. reciprocating motion *b)* the distance of a mechanical stroke, etc.

travel agency an agency that makes travel arrangements for tourists or other travelers, as for transportation, hotels, itineraries, etc. —**travel agent**

trav·eled, trav·elled (-'ld) *adj.* **1.** that has traveled much **2.** much used by travelers [a *traveled* road]

trav·el·er, trav·el·ler (-lər, -lər) *n.* **1.** a person who travels **2.** a traveling salesman; commercial traveler **3.** a thing that travels; specif., *a)* any mechanical device, as a traveling crane, that moves or slides along a support *b)* *Naut.* a metal ring that slides on a rope, rod, or spar; also, the rope, rod, or spar it slides on

☆**traveler's check** a check or draft, usually one of a set, issued by a bank, etc. in any of several denominations and sold to a traveler who signs it at issuance and again in the presence of the person cashing it

☆**traveling salesman** a salesman who travels from place to place soliciting orders for the business firm he represents

☆**trav·e·logue, trav·e·log** (trav′ə lôg′, -läg′) *n.* [< TRAVEL + -LOGUE] **1.** a lecture on travels, usually accompanied by the showing of pictures **2.** a motion picture of travels

trav·erse (tra vʉrs′, trə-; *also, & for n., adj., & adv., always,* trav′ərs) *vt.* **-ersed′, -ers′ing** [ME. *traversen* < OFr. *traverser* < VL. *transversare,* pp. of *transvertere,* to turn across < *trans-,* over, across + *vertere,* to turn: see VERSE] **1.** *a)* to pass, move, or extend over, across, or through; cross *b)* to go back and forth over or along; cross and recross **2.** to go counter to; oppose; thwart **3.** to survey, inspect, or examine carefully **4.** to turn (a gun, lathe, etc.) laterally; swivel **5.** to make a traverse of in surveying **6.** *Law a)* to deny or contradict formally (something alleged by the opposing party in a lawsuit) *b)* to join issue upon (an indictment) or upon the validity of (an inquest of office) **7.** *Naut.* to brace (a yard) fore and aft —*vi.* **1.** to move across; cross over **2.** to move back and forth over a place, etc.; cross and recross **3.** to swivel or pivot **4.** to move across a mountain slope, as in skiing, in an oblique direction **5.** to make a traverse in surveying **6.** *Fencing* to move one's blade toward the opponent's hilt while pressing one's foil hard against his —*n.* **1.** something that traverses or crosses; specif., *a)* a line that intersects others *b)* a crossbar, crosspiece, crossbeam, transom, etc. *c)* a parapet or wall of earth, etc. across a rampart or trench *d)* a gallery, loft, etc. crossing a building *e)* a single line of survey across a plot, region, etc. *f)* [Obs.] a screen, curtain, etc. placed crosswise **2.** [Now Rare] something that opposes or thwarts; obstacle **3.** the act or an instance of traversing; specif., *a)* a passing across or through; crossing *b)* a lateral, pivoting, oblique, or zigzagging movement **4.** a part, device, etc. that causes a traversing movement **5.** a passage by which one may cross; way across **6.** *a)* a zigzagging course or route taken by a vessel, as in sailing against the wind *b)* a single leg of such a course **7.** a formal denial in a lawsuit —*adj.* [ME. *travers* < OFr. < L. *transversus:* see the *v.*] **1.** passing or extending across; transverse **2.** designating or of drapes (and the rods and hooks for them) usually hung in pairs that can be drawn together or apart by pulling a cord at the side —*adv.* [Obs.] across; crosswise —**trav·ers′a·ble** *adj.* —**trav·ers′al** *n.* —**trav·ers′er** *n.*

traverse jury *same as* PETIT JURY

trav·er·tine (trav′ər tēn′, -tin) *n.* [It. *travertino,* altered < *tiburtino* < L. (*lapis*) *Tiburtinus,* (stone) of Tibur (now Tivoli)] a light-colored, usually concretionary limestone deposited around limy springs, lakes, or streams

trav·es·ty (trav′is tē) *n., pl.* **-ties** [orig. an adj. < Fr. *travesti,* pp. of *travestir,* to disguise, travesty < It. *travestire* < L. *trans-,* over, across + *vestire,* to dress, attire: see VEST] **1.** a grotesque or farcical imitation for purposes of ridicule; burlesque **2.** a crude, distorted, or ridiculous representation (*of* something) [a trial that was a *travesty* of justice] —*vt.* **-tied, -ty·ing** to make a travesty of; burlesque —*SYN.* see CARICATURE

tra·vois (trə voi′) *n., pl.* **-vois′** (-voiz′), **-vois′es** (-voi′zəz) [CanadFr. < *travail,* a brake, load < Fr.: see TRAVAIL] a crude sledge of the N. American Plains Indians, consist-

ing of a net or platform dragged along the ground on the two poles that support it and serve as shafts for the frame or, orig., dog pulling it: also **tra·voise′** (-voiz′)

trawl (trôl) n. [< ? MDu. *traghel*, a dragnet] 1. a large, baglike net dragged by a boat along the bottom of a fishing bank: also **trawl′net′** ☆2. a long line supported by buoys, from which many short fishing lines are hung: also **trawl line** —vt., vi. to fish or catch with a trawl

trawl·er (trô′lər) n. a boat used in trawling

tray (trā) n. [ME. *treie* < OE. *treg, trig*, wooden board, akin to *treow*, TREE] 1. a flat receptacle made of wood, metal, glass, plastic, etc., often with slightly raised edges, used for holding or carrying articles 2. a tray with its contents [a tray of food] 3. a shallow, boxlike, removable compartment of a trunk, cabinet, etc.

treach·er·ous (trech′ər əs) adj. [ME. *trecherous* < OFr. *trecheros*] 1. characterized by treachery; traitorous; disloyal; perfidious 2. giving a false appearance of safety or reliability; untrustworthy or insecure [treacherous rocks] —SYN. see FAITHLESS —**treach′er·ous·ly** adv. —**treach′er·ous·ness** n.

treach·er·y (-ē) n., pl. **-er·ies** [ME. *trecherie* < OFr. *tricherie*, trickery < *trichier*, to cheat: cf. TRICK] 1. betrayal of trust, faith, or allegiance; perfidy, disloyalty, or treason 2. an act of perfidy or treason

trea·cle (trē′k'l) n. [ME. *triacle* < OFr. < L. *theriaca*, antidote for poison < Gr. *thēriakē*, remedy for bites of venomous beasts < *thērion*, wild beast, dim. of *thēr*: see FIERCE] 1. orig., a) a remedy for poison b) any effective remedy 2. [Brit.] molasses —**trea′cly** (-klē) adj.

tread (tred) vt. **trod**, **trod′den** or **trod**, **tread′ing** [ME. *treden* < OE. *tredan*, akin to G. *treten* < IE. *dreu-* < base *drā-*, to run, step: see TRAP¹] 1. to walk on, in, along, across, over, etc. 2. to do or follow by walking, dancing, etc. [treading the measures gaily] 3. to press or beat with the feet so as to crush or injure; trample 4. to oppress or subdue, as if by stepping on 5. to copulate with (the female): said of a bird —vi. 1. to move on foot; step; walk 2. to set one's foot (on, across, etc.); make a step; step 3. to trample (on or upon) 4. to copulate: said of birds —n. 1. the act, manner, or sound of treading 2. something on which a person or thing treads or moves, as the part of a shoe sole, wheel, etc. that touches the ground, the endless roller belt over cogged wheels of a tractor, tank, etc., the part of a rail on which a car wheel runs, the horizontal surface of a step in a stairway, etc. 3. a) the thick outer layer of an automotive tire, containing grooves for added traction b) the thickness of this layer, as measured by the depth of the grooves c) the pattern of the grooves 4. same as TRACK (n. 9) 5. [Rare] a footprint —**tread the boards** to act in plays on the stage —**tread water** pt. now usually **tread′ed** Swimming to keep the body upright and the head above water as by moving the legs in a treading motion without moving forward

trea·dle (tred′'l) n. [ME. *tredel* < OE. < *tredan*: see prec.] a lever or pedal moved by the foot so as to turn a wheel —vi. **-dled**, **-dling** to work a treadle

tread·mill (tred′mil′) n. 1. a kind of mill wheel turned by the weight of persons treading steps arranged around its circumference: formerly used as an instrument of prison discipline 2. a mill driven by an animal treading a sloping, endless belt 3. any monotonous round of duties, work, etc. in which one seems to get nowhere

treas. 1. treasurer 2. treasury

trea·son (trē′z'n) n. [ME. *treison* < OFr. *traïson* < L. *traditio* < pp. of *tradere*, to give or deliver over or up < *trans-*, over + *dare*, to give] 1. [Now Rare] betrayal of trust or faith; treachery 2. violation of the allegiance owed to one's sovereign or state; betrayal of one's country, specif., in the U.S. (as declared in the Constitution), consisting only in levying war against the U.S. or in giving aid and comfort to its enemies —SYN. see SEDITION

trea·son·a·ble (-ə b'l) adj. of, having the nature of, or involving treason; traitorous —**trea′son·a·bly** adv.

trea·son·ous (-əs) adj. treasonable; traitorous

treas·ure (trezh′ər, trā′zhər) n. [ME. *tresoure* < OFr. *tresor* < L. *thesaurus* < Gr. *thēsauros*, a store, treasure: see THESAURUS] 1. accumulated or stored wealth, esp. in the form of money, precious metals, jewels, etc. 2. any person or thing considered very valuable —vt. **-ured**, **-ur·ing** 1. to store away or save up (money, valuables, etc.) as for future use; hoard 2. to value greatly; cherish —SYN. see APPRECIATE

treasure house any place where treasure is kept or where things of great value are to be found

treasure hunt a game in which players, with the aid of clues, compete in trying to find hidden articles

treas·ur·er (-ər) n. [ME. *tresorer* < Anglo-Fr. *tresorer*, for OFr. *tresorier* < *tresor*: see TREASURE] a person in charge of a treasure or treasury; specif., an officer in charge of the funds or finances of a government, corporation, society, etc. —**treas′ur·er·ship′** n.

treas·ure-trove (-trōv′) n. [Anglo-Fr. *tresor trové* < OFr. *tresor* (see TREASURE) + *trové*, pp. of *trover*, to find: see TROVER] 1. treasure, as gold, bullion, etc., found hidden, the original owner being unknown 2. any valuable discovery

treas·ur·y (-ē) n., pl. **-ur·ies** [ME. *tresorie* < OFr.] 1. a place where treasure is preserved; room or building where valuable objects are preserved 2. a place where public

or private funds are kept, received, disbursed, and recorded 3. the funds or revenues of a state, corporation, society, etc. 4. [T-] the department of a state or nation that is in charge of revenue, taxation, and public finances 5. a collection of treasures in art, literature, etc. [a treasury of verse]

treasury bill ☆a short-term obligation of the U.S. Treasury, usually maturing in 91 days, bearing no interest and sold periodically on the open market on a discount basis

treasury bond ☆any of various series of bonds issued by the U.S. Treasury, usually maturing over long periods

☆**treasury certificate** an intermediate-term obligation of the U.S. Treasury, usually maturing in one year, paying interest periodically on a coupon basis

treasury note ☆any of the interest-bearing obligations of the U.S. Treasury with maturities between one and five years

☆**treasury stock** shares of issued stock reacquired by the issuing corporation and held by it

treat (trēt) vi. [ME. *treten* < OFr. *traitier*, to handle, meddle, treat < L. *tractare*, freq. of *trahere*, to DRAW] 1. to discuss terms (with a person or for a settlement); negotiate 2. to deal with a subject in writing or speech; speak or write (of) 3. to stand the cost of another's or others' entertainment —vt. 1. to deal with (a subject) in writing, speech, music, painting, etc., esp. in a specified manner or style 2. to act or behave toward (a person, animal, etc.) in a specified manner 3. to have a specified attitude toward and deal with accordingly [to treat a mistake as a joke] 4. a) to pay for the food, drink, entertainment, etc. of (another or others) b) to provide with something that pleases 5. to subject to some process or to some substance in processing, as in a chemical procedure 6. to give medical or surgical care to (someone) or for (some disorder) —n. 1. a meal, drink, entertainment, etc. given or paid for by someone else 2. anything that gives great or unusual pleasure; a delight 3. a) the act of treating or entertaining b) one's turn to treat —**treat′a·bil′i·ty** n. —**treat′a·ble** adj. —**treat′er** n.

trea·tise (trēt′is) n. [ME. *tretis* < Anglo-Fr. *tretiz* < OFr. *treiteiz* < *traitier*: see prec.] 1. a formal, systematic article or book on some subject, esp. a discussion of facts, evidence, or principles and the conclusions based on these 2. [Obs.] a narrative; tale

treat·ment (-mənt) n. 1. act, manner, method, etc. of treating, or dealing with, a person, thing, subject in art or literature, etc. 2. medical or surgical care, esp. a systematic course of this

trea·ty (trēt′ē) n., pl. **-ties** [ME. *trete* < ML. *traité* < LL. *tractatus*: see TRACTATE] 1. formerly, a) negotiation b) entreaty c) any agreement or contract 2. a) a formal agreement between two or more nations, relating to peace, alliance, trade, etc. b) the document embodying such an agreement

treaty port a port that must be kept open for foreign trade according to the terms of a treaty, as, formerly, any of certain ports in China or Japan

Treb·bia (treb′byä) river in NW Italy, flowing north into the Po: scene of a victory by Hannibal over the Romans (218 B.C.): ancient name **Tre·bia** (trē′byə)

Treb·i·zond (treb′ə zänd′) 1. empire (1204–1461) on the SE coast of the Black Sea 2. seaport in NE Turkey; former capital of the empire of Trebizond: pop. 53,000: Turk. name, TRABZON

tre·ble (treb′'l) adj. [ME. < OFr. < L. *triplus*, TRIPLE] 1. threefold; triple 2. a) of or for the highest part in musical harmony b) playing or singing this part 3. high-pitched or shrill —n. 1. the highest part in musical harmony; soprano 2. a singer or instrument that takes this part 3. a high-pitched voice or sound —vt., vi. **-bled**, **-bling** to make or become threefold —**tre′bly** adv.

TREBIZOND (c. 1450)

treble clef Music 1. a sign on a staff, indicating the position of G above middle C on the second line: see CLEF, illus. 2. the range of notes on a staff so marked

Treb·link·a (tre bleŋ′kä) Nazi concentration camp & extermination center in C Poland, northeast of Warsaw

treb·u·chet (treb′yoo shet′) n. [ME. < OFr. < *trebucher*, to stumble < *tre-* (< L. *trans-*, over) + *buc*, trunk, body < Frank. *buk*, trunk] a medieval engine of war for hurling large stones: also **tre·buck·et** (trē′buk it)

tre·cen·to (tre chen′tō) n. [It., lit., three hundred, short for *mil trecento*, one thousand three hundred] the 14th cent. as a period in Italian art and literature

tree (trē) n. [ME. < OE. *treow*, akin to Goth. *triu*, ON. *trē* < IE. base *derw-*, tree, prob. orig. oak tree, whence Gr. *drys*, oak, (den)*dreon*, tree] 1. a woody perennial plant

with one main stem or trunk which develops many branches, usually at some height above the ground: most trees are over ten feet tall and over six inches in diameter at a height of about five feet **2.** a treelike bush or shrub [a rose *tree*] **3.** a wooden beam, bar, pole, post, stake, etc. **4.** anything resembling a tree in form, as in having a stem and branches; specif., *a)* short for FAMILY TREE *b)* *Chem.* a treelike formation of crystals **5.** [Archaic] *a)* the cross on which Jesus was crucified *b)* a gallows **6.** [Obs.] wood —*vt.* **treed, tree′ing** ☆**1.** to chase up a tree **2.** to place or stretch on a boot or shoe tree ☆**3.** [Colloq.] to corner, as if chased up a tree; place in a difficult position —☆**up a tree** [Colloq.] in a situation without escape; cornered

Tree (trē), **Sir Herbert Beerbohm** (born *Herbert Beerbohm*) 1853–1917; Eng. actor & theatrical manager: half brother of Max BEERBOHM

treed (trēd) *adj.* provided or planted with trees

tree fern any of various, tropical treelike ferns (esp. genera *Cyathea, Alsophila,* and *Hemitelia*) with an elongated, woody trunk bearing fronds at the top

tree frog any of various frogs (family Hylidae) that live in trees, which they climb with the aid of adhesive discs on the toes: many are called *tree toads*

tree heath same as BRIER² (sense 1)

tree·hop·per (-häp′ər) *n.* any of a family (Membracidae) of homopterous hopping insects that feed on plant sap and are characterized by the backward prolongation over the abdomen of the prothorax, which is often extended

tree house a houselike structure built in the branches of a tree, ☆as for children to play in

☆**tree lawn** in some cities, the strip of ground between a street and its parallel sidewalk, often planted with lawns and trees: also **tree′lawn′** *n.*

☆**tree line** same as TIMBERLINE

tree·nail (trē′nāl′; tren′′l, trun′-) *n.* [ME. *trenayle* < *tre,* TREE (in early sense "wood") + *nayle,* NAIL] a very dry wooden peg used to join timbers, esp. in shipbuilding: it swells from moisture and assures a tight joint

tree of heaven a fast-growing ailanthus (*Ailanthus altissima*), native to China but widely cultivated in the U.S. as a shade tree

tree of knowledge *Bible* the tree whose fruit Adam and Eve tasted in disobedience of God: in full **tree of knowledge of good and evil:** Gen. 2, 3

tree of life *Bible* **1.** a tree in the Garden of Eden bearing fruit which, if eaten, gave everlasting life: Gen. 2:9; 3:22 **2.** a tree in the heavenly Jerusalem whose leaves are for healing the nations: Rev. 22:2

tree ring same as ANNUAL RING

tree shrew any of a number of small, squirrellike, insect-eating primates (suborder Tupaioidea) of SE Asia

tree squirrel any of various squirrels that live in trees; esp., any squirrel of the genus (*Sciurus*) that includes the gray squirrel, red squirrel, etc.

☆**tree surgery** treatment of damaged or diseased trees as by filling cavities, removing parts, treating fresh wounds, etc. —**tree surgeon**

☆**tree toad** see TREE FROG

tree·top (trē′täp′) *n.* the topmost part of a tree

tref (trāf) *adj.* [Yid. *treif* < Heb. *ṭerēfāh,* animal torn by predatory beast] *Judaism* not clean or fit to eat according to the dietary laws; not kosher

tre·foil (trē′foil) *n.* [ME. *treyfoyle* < Anglo-Fr. *trifoil* < L. *trifolium,* three-leaved plant < *tri-,* three + *folium,* a leaf (see FOIL²)] **1.** *a)* any of a number of plants with leaves divided into three leaflets, as the clover, tick trefoil, and certain species of lotus *b)* a flower or leaf with three lobes **2.** any ornamental figure resembling a threefold leaf

TREFOILS

trefoil knot a kind of knot: see KNOT, illus.

tre·ha·lose (trē′hə lōs′, tri häl′ōs) *n.* [< ModL. *trehala,* material composing the cocoons of a certain beetle and the orig. source of the sugar (< Turk. *tīghāleh* < Per. *tīghāl*) + -OSE¹] a crystalline sugar, $C_{12}H_{22}O_{11}$, extracted from yeast, mushrooms, and other fungi

treil·lage (trāl′ij, tre yäzh′) *n.* [Fr. < *treille,* a bower, trellis < L. *trichila,* a bower] a lattice for vines; trellis

Treitsch·ke (trīch′kə), **Hein·rich von** (hīn′riH fōn) 1834–96; Ger. historian

trek (trek) *vi.* **trekked, trek′king** [Afrik. < Du. *trekken,* to draw, akin to MHG. *trecken*] **1.** in South Africa, to travel by ox wagon **2.** to travel slowly or laboriously **3.** [Colloq.] to go, esp. on foot —*vt.* in South Africa, to draw (a wagon): said of an ox —*n.* **1.** in South Africa, a journey made by ox wagon, or one leg of such a journey **2.** any journey or leg of a journey **3.** a migration **4.** [Colloq.] a short trip, esp. on foot —**trek′ker** *n.*

trel·lis (trel′is) *n.* [ME. *trelis* < OFr. *treliz* < VL. *trilicius,* a coarse cloth < L. *trilix,* triple-twilled (see DRILL³)] infl. by OFr. *treille,* arbor < L. *trichila,* bower, arbor] **1.** a structure of thin strips, esp. of wood, crossing each other

in an open pattern of squares, diamonds, etc., on which vines or other creeping plants are trained; lattice **2.** a bower, archway, etc. of this —*vt.* **1.** to furnish with, or train on, a trellis **2.** to cross or interweave like a trellis

trel·lis·work (-wurk′) *n.* open network of strips, usually of wood; latticework

trem·a·tode (trem′ə tōd′, trē′mə-) *n.* [ModL. *Trematoda,* name of the class < Gr. *trēmatōdēs,* perforated < *trēma* (gen. *trēmatos*), a hole (< IE. base *ter-,* to rub, bore: see THROW) + *eidos,* form] any of a large class (Trematoda) of parasitic flatworms with one or more external, muscular suckers; fluke —*adj.* of a trematode

trem·ble (trem′b′l) *vi.* **-bled, -bling** [ME. *tremblen* < OFr. *trembler* < VL. *tremulare* < L. *tremulus,* trembling < *tremere,* to tremble < IE. *trem-,* whence Gr. *tremein,* to tremble] **1.** to shake involuntarily from cold, fear, excitement, fatigue, etc.; shiver **2.** to feel great fear or anxiety **3.** to quiver, quake, totter, vibrate, etc. **4.** to quaver [a *trembling* voice] —*n.* **1.** *a)* the act or condition of trembling *b)* [sometimes *pl.*] a fit or state of trembling ☆**2.** [*pl.*] a disease of cattle and sheep caused by a poisonous, oily alcohol contained in certain plants, as white snakeroot, and characterized by muscular tremors and a stumbling gait: communicated to man as milk sickness: cf. MILK SICKNESS —*SYN.* see SHAKE —**trem′bler** *n.* —**trem′bling·ly** *adv.* —**trem′bly** *adj.*

tre·men·dous (tri men′dəs) *adj.* [L. *tremendus* < *tremere,* to TREMBLE] **1.** such as to make one tremble; terrifying; dreadful **2.** *a)* very large; great; enormous *b)* [Colloq.] wonderful, amazing, extraordinary, etc. —*SYN.* see ENORMOUS —**tre·men′dous·ly** *adv.* —**tre·men′dous·ness** *n.*

trem·o·lite (trem′ə līt′) *n.* [after the *Tremola* valley, in Switzerland, where it was found] a white or gray variety of amphibole, a hydrated silicate of calcium and magnesium, occurring as distinct crystals or fibrous aggregates

trem·o·lo (trem′ə lō′) *n., pl.* **-los′** [It. < L. *tremulus:* see TREMULOUS] *Music* **1.** a tremulous effect produced by the rapid reiteration of the same tone, as by the rapid up-and-down movement of the bow or plectrum: in singing, sometimes, same as VIBRATO **2.** a device, as in an organ, for producing such a tone

trem·or (trem′ər; *occas.* trē′mər) *n.* [ME. < OFr. *tremour* < L. *tremor* < *tremere,* to TREMBLE] **1.** a trembling, shaking, or shivering **2.** a vibratory or quivering motion **3.** a nervous thrill; trembling sensation **4.** a trembling sound **5.** a state of tremulous excitement [in a *tremor* of delight] —**trem′or·ous** *adj.*

trem·u·lant (trem′yoo lant) *adj.* [VL. *tremulans,* prp. of *tremulare:* see TREMBLE] same as TREMULOUS

trem·u·lous (-las) *adj.* [L. *tremulus* < *tremere,* to TREMBLE] **1.** trembling; quivering; palpitating **2.** fearful; timid; timorous **3.** marked by or showing trembling or quivering [*tremulous* excitement, *tremulous* handwriting] —**trem′u·lous·ly** *adv.* —**trem′u·lous·ness** *n.*

tre·nail (trē′nāl′; tren′′l, trun′-) *n.* same as TREENAIL

trench (trench) *vt.* [LME. *trenchen* < OFr. *trenchier* (Fr. *trancher*), to cut, hack < ? L. *truncare,* to cut off] **1.** to cut, cut into, cut off, etc.; slice, gash, etc. **2.** *a)* to cut a deep furrow or furrows in *b)* to dig a ditch or ditches in **3.** to surround or fortify with trenches —*vi.* **1.** to dig a ditch or ditches, as for fortification **2.** to infringe (*on* or *upon* another's land, rights, time, etc.) **3.** to verge or border (*on*); come close —*n.* [ME. < OFr. *trenche* (Fr. *tranche,* a slice) < *trencher*] **1.** a deep furrow in the ground, ocean floor, etc. **2.** a long, narrow ditch from which the earth is thrown up in front as a parapet, used in battle for cover and concealment

trench·ant (tren′chənt) *adj.* [ME. < OFr., prp. of *trenchier:* see TRENCH] **1.** orig., cutting; sharp **2.** keen; penetrating; incisive [*trenchant* words] **3.** forceful; vigorous; effective [a *trenchant* argument] **4.** clear-cut; distinct [a *trenchant* pattern] —*SYN.* see INCISIVE —**trench′an·cy** *n.* —**trench′ant·ly** *adv.*

trench coat a belted raincoat in a military style, usually with shoulder straps

trench·er¹ (tren′chər) *n.* [ME. < OFr. *trencheor* < *trenchier:* see TRENCH] [Archaic] **1.** a wooden board or platter on which to carve or serve meat **2.** *a)* food served on a trencher *b)* a supply of food

trench·er² (tren′chər) *n.* a person who digs trenches

trench·er·man (-mən) *n., pl.* **-men 1.** an eater; esp., a person who eats much and heartily **2.** [Archaic] a person who frequents a patron's table; parasite; hanger-on

trench fever [from its prevalence among soldiers in the trenches in World War I] an infectious disease caused by a rickettsia (*Rickettsia quintana*) transmitted by body lice, characterized by a remittent fever, muscular pains, etc.

trench foot a diseased condition of the feet resulting from prolonged exposure to wet and cold and the circulatory disorders caused by inaction, as of soldiers in trenches

trench knife a double-edged military knife or dagger, for hand-to-hand combat

trench mortar (or **gun**) any of various portable mortars for shooting projectiles at a high trajectory and short range

trench mouth [from its prevalence among soldiers in

trenches] an infectious disease characterized by ulceration of the mucous membranes of the mouth and throat and caused by a bacterium (*Fusobacterium fusiforme*) often in conjunction with a spirochete (*Borrelia vincentii*)

trend (trend) *vi.* [ME. *trenden*, to roll < OE. *trendan*, to turn, roll, akin to *trinde*, round lump < IE. base *der-*, to split off (cf. TEAR¹); prob. basic sense "split-off piece of a tree trunk, as a disk or wheel"] 1. to extend, turn, incline, bend, etc. in a specific direction; tend; run [the river *trends* northward] 2. to have a general tendency: said of events, conditions, opinions, etc. —*n.* 1. the general direction of a coast, river, road, etc. 2. the general or prevailing tendency or course, as of events, a discussion, etc.; drift 3. a vogue, or current style, as in fashions —*SYN.* see TENDENCY

trend·y (-ē) *adj.* **trend′i·er, trend′i·est** [Colloq.] of or in the latest style, or trend; ultra-fashionable; faddish —**trend′i·ly** *adv.* —**trend′i·ness** *n.*

Treng·ga·nu (treŋ gä′nōō) state of the Federation of Malaya, on the E coast: 5,027 sq. mi.; pop. 357,000

Trent (trent) 1. commune in N Italy, on the Adige River: pop. 75,000 2. river in C England, flowing from Staffordshire northeast to the Humber: 170 mi. 3. **Council of,** the council of the Roman Catholic Church held intermittently at Trent, Italy, 1545–63: it condemned the Reformation, undertook Catholic reform, and defined Catholic doctrines

‡trente et qua·rante (trän tā kå ränt′) [Fr., lit., thirty and forty] *same as* ROUGE ET NOIR

Tren·ti·no-Al·to A·di·ge (tren tē′nō äl′tō ä′dē je) autonomous region of N Italy: the N part (*Alto Adige*) is in the S Tirol: 5,256 sq. mi.; pop. 785,000; cap. Trent

Tren·to (tren′tō) *It. name of* TRENT

Tren·ton (tren′tən) [after Wm. Trent (1655–1724), colonist] capital of N.J., on the Delaware River: pop. 105,000

tre·pan¹ (tri pan′) *n.* [ME. *trepane* < ML. *trepanum* < Gr. *trypanon*, carpenters' tool, auger, trepan < *trypan*, to bore < IE. *treup-* < base *ter-*, to bore, rub: cf. THROW] 1. an early form of the trephine 2. a heavy boring tool for sinking shafts, quarrying, etc. —*vt.* **-panned′, -pan′ning** 1. *same as* TREPHINE 2. to cut a disk out of (a metal plate, ingot, etc.) —**trep·a·na·tion** (trep′ə nā′shən) *n.*

tre·pan² (tri pan′) *n.* [older *trapan*, prob. < TRAP¹, but infl. by fig. use of prec.] [Archaic] 1. a person or thing that tricks, traps, or ensnares 2. a trick; stratagem; trap —*vt.* **-panned′, -pan′ning** [Archaic] to trick, trap, or lure —**tres′pass·er** *n.*

tre·pang (tri paŋ′) *n.* [Malay *tĕripang*] the eviscerated, boiled, smoked, and dried body of any of several species of sea cucumbers, used, esp. in the Orient, for making soup

tre·phine (tri fīn′, -fēn′) *n.* [earlier *trafine*, formed after TREPAN¹ < L. *tres*, THREE + *fines*, ends] a type of small crown saw used in surgery to remove a circular section of tissue, esp. of bone from the skull —*vt.* **-phined′, -phin′ing** to operate on with a trephine —**treph·i·na·tion** (tref′ə nā′shən) *n.*

trep·i·da·tion (trep′ə dā′shən) *n.* [L. *trepidatio* < *trepidatus*, pp. of *trepidare*, to tremble < *trepidus*, disturbed, alarmed < IE. *trep-*, to trip, tramp (< base *ter-*, to tremble), whence OE. *thrafian*, to press] 1. tremulous or trembling movement; quaking; tremor 2. fearful uncertainty, anxiety, etc.; apprehension

trep·o·ne·ma (trep′ə nē′mə) *n., pl.* **-mas, -ma·ta** (-mə tə) [ModL., name of the genus < Gr. *trepein*, to turn (see TROPE) + *nēma*, a thread < IE. base *(s)nē-*, whence NEEDLE] any of a genus (*Treponema*) of slender spirochetes parasitic in mammals and birds, including some that are pathogenic to man, as the organisms causing syphilis and yaws —**trep′o·ne′mal, trep′o·ne′ma·tous** (-mə təs) *adj.*

tres·pass (tres′pəs; *also, esp. for v.,* -pas′) *vi.* [ME. *trespassen* < OFr. *trespasser* < VL. *transpassare*, to pass across < L. *trans-*, over, across + VL. *passare*, to pass: see PACE¹] 1. to go beyond the limits of what is considered right or moral; do wrong; transgress 2. to go on another's land or property without permission or right 3. to intrude or encroach [to *trespass* on one's time] 4. *Law* to commit a trespass —*n.* [ME. *trespas* < OFr. < the *v.*] the act or an instance of trespassing; specif., *a)* a moral offense; transgression *b)* an encroachment or intrusion *c)* *Law* an illegal act done forcefully against another's person, rights, or property; also, legal action for damages resulting from this *SYN.*—**trespass** implies an unlawful or unwarranted entrance upon the property, rights, etc. of another [to *trespass* on a private beach]; to **encroach** is to make such inroads by stealth or gradual advances [squatters *encroaching* on his lands]; **infringe** implies an encroachment that breaks a law or agreement or violates the rights of others [to *infringe* on a patent]; **intrude** implies a thrusting oneself into company, situations, etc. without being asked or wanted [to *intrude* on one's privacy]; **invade** implies a forcible or hostile entrance into the territory or rights of others [to *invade* a neighboring state]

tress (tres) *n.* [ME. *tresse* < OFr. *tresce* (Fr. *tresse*) < ? Frank. *thrēhja*, twisted object] 1. orig., a braid or plait of hair 2. a lock of human hair 3. [pl.] a woman's or girl's hair, esp. when long and falling loosely

-tress (tris) *see* -ESS

tressed (trest) *adj.* 1. having tresses of a specified kind [black-*tressed*] 2. arranged in tresses; braided

tres·sure (tresh′ər) *n.* [ME. *tressour* < MFr. *tresseour* < OFr. *tresce*: see TRESS] *Heraldry* a narrow band following

the contour, and somewhat inside the edge, of a coat of arms, often ornamented with fleurs-de-lis

tres·tle (tres′'l) *n.* [ME. *trestel* < OFr. < VL. **transtellum*, dim. of L. *transtrum*, a beam: see TRANSOM] 1. a frame consisting of a horizontal beam fastened to two pairs of spreading legs, used to support planks to form a table, platform, etc. 2. *a)* a framework of vertical or slanting uprights and crosspieces, supporting a bridge, etc. *b)* a bridge with such a framework

TRESTLE

tres·tle·tree (-trē′) *n.* either of two horizontal fore-and-aft beams, one on each side of a mast, that support the crosstrees, top, and fid of the mast above

☆**tres·tle·work** (-wurk′) *n.* 1. a system of trestles for supporting a bridge, etc. 2. a structure made of trestles

tret (tret) *n.* [Anglo-Fr. (Fr. *trait*), a pull < OFr. *traire* (< L. *trahere*, to DRAW)] a fixed allowance on weight, after the deduction of tare, formerly made to buyers of certain commodities for waste and deterioration

Tre·vel·yan (tri vil′yən, -vel′-) 1. **George Macaulay,** 1876–1962; Eng. historian 2. **Sir George Otto,** 1838–1928; Eng. historian & politician: father of *prec.*

Treves (trēvz) *Eng. name of* TRIER: Fr. name **Trèves** (trev)

trews (trōōz) *n.pl.* [ScotGael. *triubhas*] [Scot.] closefitting tartan trousers

trey (trā) *n.* [ME. < OFr. *trei, treis* < L. *tres*, THREE] 1. a playing card with three spots 2. the side of a die bearing three spots, or a throw of the dice totaling three

t.r.f., trf tuned radio frequency

tri- (trī, tri) [< Fr., L., or Gr.: Fr. *tri-* < L. *tri-* (< *tres*, THREE) or Gr. *tri-* (< *treis*, THREE, *tris*, THRICE)] *a combining form meaning:* 1. having, combining, or involving three [*triangular*] 2. triply, in three ways or directions [*trilingual*] 3. three times, into three [*trisect*] 4. every three, every third [*triannual*] 5. *Chem.* having three atoms, groups, or equivalents of (the thing specified) [*tribasic*]

tri·a·ble (trī′ə b'l) *adj.* 1. that can be tried or tested 2. subject to trial in a law court —**tri′a·ble·ness** *n.*

☆**tri·ac** (trī′ak) *n.* [*tri*(*ode*) *a*(*lternating*) *c*(*urrent switch*)] *Electronics* a device used to control power

tri·ac·e·tate (trī as′ə tāt′) *n.* a compound containing three acetate radicals in the molecule

tri·ac·id (trī as′id) *adj.* 1. capable of reacting with three molecules of a monobasic acid: said of a base 2. containing three replaceable hydrogen atoms: said esp. of an acid

tri·ad (trī′ad) *n.* [< LL. *trias* (gen. *triadis*) < Gr. *trias* (gen. *triados*) < *treis*, THREE] 1. a group of three persons, things, ideas, etc.; trinity 2. a musical chord of three tones, esp. one consisting of a root tone and its third and fifth: a triad with a major third and perfect fifth is called a *major triad;* a triad with a minor third and perfect fifth is called a *minor triad* —**tri·ad′ic** *adj.*

tri·age (trē äzh′) *n.* [Fr., a sifting < *trier*, to sift: see TRY & -AGE] a system of assigning priorities of medical treatment to battlefield casualties on the basis of urgency, chance for survival, etc.

tri·al (trī′əl, trīl) *n.* [Anglo-Fr. < *trier*: see TRY] 1. *a)* the act or process of trying, testing, or putting to the proof; test *b)* a testing of qualifications, attainments, or progress; probation *c)* experimental treatment or operation; experiment 2. *a)* the fact or state of being tried by suffering, temptation, etc. *b)* a hardship, suffering, etc. that tries one's endurance *c)* a person or thing that is a source of annoyance or irritation 3. a formal examination of the facts of a case by a court of law to decide the validity of a charge or claim 4. an attempt; endeavor; effort —*adj.* 1. of a trial or trials 2. made, done, or used for the purpose of trying, testing, etc. —**on trial** in the process of being tried *SYN.*—**trial** implies the trying of a person or thing in order to establish his or its worth in actual performance [hired on *trial*]; **experiment** implies a showing by trial whether a thing will be effective [the honor system was instituted as an *experiment*] and, in addition, is used of any action or process undertaken to discover something not yet known or to demonstrate something known [*experiments* in nuclear physics]; **test** implies a putting of a thing to decisive proof by thorough examination or trial under controlled conditions and with fixed standards in mind [a *test* of a new jet plane] See also AFFLICTION

trial and error the process of making repeated trials, tests, etc. and eliminating faulty or unproductive methods to find a desired result or solution —**tri′al-and-er′ror** *adj.*

trial balance a statement of the debit and credit balances of all open accounts in a double-entry bookkeeping ledger to test their equality

☆**trial balloon** 1. *same as* PILOT BALLOON 2. any action, statement, etc. intended to test public opinion on an issue

trial jury *same as* PETIT JURY

trial of the pyx the annual examination of a random sample of silver coins made in the preceding year at a U.S. mint

tri·an·gle (trī′aŋ′g'l) *n.* [ME. < MFr. < L. *triangulum:* see TRI- & ANGLE¹] 1. a geometrical figure having three angles and three sides 2. any three-sided or three-cornered figure, area, object, part, etc. 3. a right-angled, flat, triangular instrument used as in mechanical drawing

4. a situation involving three persons, as when one person is having love affairs with two others **5.** a musical percussion instrument consisting of a steel rod bent in a triangle with one angle open; it produces a high-pitched, tinkling sound

tri·an·gu·lar (trī aŋ′gyə lər) *adj.* [LL. *triangularis*] **1.** of or shaped like a triangle; three-cornered **2.** of or involving three persons, factions, units, or parts **3.** having bases that are triangles, as a prism —**tri·an′gu·lar′i·ty** (-ler′ə tē) *n.* —**tri·an′gu·lar·ly** *adv.*

tri·an·gu·late (-lāt′; *for adj., usually* -lit) *vt.* **-lat′ed**, **-lat′ing** [< ML. *triangulatus*, pp. of *triangulare < L. *triangulum* (see TRIANGLE)] **1.** to divide into triangles **2.** to survey or map (a region) by triangulation **3.** to make triangular —*adj.* **1.** of triangles; triangular **2.** marked with triangles

tri·an·gu·la·tion (trī aŋ′gyə lā′shən) *n.* [LL. *triangulatio*] **1.** *Surveying, Navigation* the process of determining the distance between points on the earth's surface, or the relative positions of points, by dividing up a large area into a series of connected triangles, measuring a base line between two points, and then locating a third point by computing both the size of the angles made by lines from this point to each end of the base line and the lengths of these lines **2.** the triangles thus marked out

tri·arch·y (trī′är kē) *n., pl.* **-arch·ies** [Gr. *triarchia*: see TRI- & -ARCHY] **1.** *a)* government by three rulers; triumvirate *b)* a country governed by three rulers **2.** a country with three districts, each governed by its own ruler

Tri·as·sic (trī as′ik) *adj.* [ModL. < LL. *Trias* (see TRIAD: because divisible into three groups) + -IC] designating or of the first period of the Mesozoic Era, following the Permian Period of the Paleozoic Era and characterized by the appearance of many reptiles, including the dinosaurs, and the dominance of cycads and ferns —the **Triassic** the Triassic Period or its rocks: also the **Tri′as** (-əs): see GEOLOGY, chart

tri·at·ic stay (trī at′ik) [< ?] *Naut.* **1.** a rope or stay secured to the heads of the foremast and mainmast, to which hoisting tackles can be attached **2.** a wire running from the foremast to the after stack or mast

tri·a·tom·ic (trī′ə täm′ik) *adj.* designating or of: *a)* a molecule consisting of three atoms *b)* a molecule containing three replaceable atoms or groups

tri·ax·i·al (trī ak′sē əl) *adj.* having three axes

tri·a·zine (trī′ə zēn′, -zin; trī az′ēn, -in) *n.* [TRI- + AZINE] **1.** any of three isomeric heterocyclic compounds having the formula $C_3H_3N_3$ **2.** any derivative of these

tri·a·zole (trī′ə zōl′, trī az′ōl) *n.* [TRI- + AZOLE] **1.** any of four isomeric heterocyclic compounds having the formula $C_2H_3N_3$ **2.** any derivative of these

trib·ad·ism (trib′əd iz′m) *n.* [< Fr. *tribade*, lesbian + -ISM] homosexuality between women; lesbianism

trib·al (trī′b'l) *adj.* of, relating to, or characteristic of a tribe or tribes —**trib′al·ly** *adv.*

trib·al·ism (-iz′m) *n.* **1.** tribal organization, culture, loyalty, etc. **2.** a strong sense of identifying with and being loyal to one's tribe, group, etc. —**trib′al·ist** *adj., n.* —**trib′al·is′tic** *adj.*

tri·bas·ic (trī bā′sik) *adj.* [TRI- + BASIC] **1.** containing in its molecule three atoms of hydrogen that are replaceable by basic atoms or radicals: said of an acid **2.** producing three hydrogen ions per molecule in solution **3.** containing three univalent basic atoms or groups

tribe (trīb) *n.* [ME. *trybe* < L. *tribus*, one of the three groups into which Romans were orig. divided, tribe < *tri-* (see TRI-) + IE. base **bhū-*, to grow, flourish, whence BE] **1.** esp. among preliterate peoples, a group of persons, families, or clans believed to be descended from a common ancestor and forming a close community under a leader, or chief **2.** a group of this kind having recognized ancestry; specif., *a)* any of the three divisions of the ancient Romans, traditionally of Latin, Sabine, and Etruscan origin *b)* any of the later political and territorial divisions of the ancient Romans, orig. thirty and subsequently thirty-five in number *c)* any of the phylae of ancient Greece *d)* any of the twelve divisions of the ancient Israelites **3.** any group of people having the same occupation, habits, ideas, etc.: often in a somewhat derogatory sense [the *tribe* of drama critics] **4.** a taxonomic category that is a subdivision of a subfamily of plants or animals and consists of several closely related genera **5.** a natural group of plants or animals classified together without regard for their taxonomic relations **6.** in stock breeding, the animals descended from the same female through the female line **7.** [Colloq.] a family, esp. a large one

tribes·man (trībz′mən) *n., pl.* **-men** a member of a tribe

tri·bo- (trī′bō) [< Gr. *tribein*, to rub: for IE. base see THROW] a combining form meaning friction [*triboelectricity*]

tri·bo·e·lec·tric·i·ty (trī′bō i lek′tris′ə tē) *n.* [prec. + ELECTRICITY] electric charge developed upon the surface of a material by friction, as by rubbing silk upon glass —**tri′bo·e·lec′tric** (-trik) *adj.*

tri·bo·lu·mi·nes·cence (-lōō′mə nes′'ns) *n.* [TRIBO- + LUMINESCENCE] luminescence resulting from friction, observed at the surface of certain crystalline materials —**tri′bo·lu′mi·nes′cent** *adj.*

tri·brach (trī′brak, trib′rak) *n.* [L. *tribrachys* < Gr. *tribrachys*: see TRI- & BRACHY-] a metrical foot consisting of three short syllables, two belonging to the thesis and one to the arsis —**tri·brach′ic** *adj.*

tri·bro·mide (trī brō′mid) *n.* [TRI- + BROMIDE] a compound containing three bromine atoms in the molecule

tri·bro·mo·eth·a·nol (trī brō′mō eth′ə nōl′, -nôl′) *n.* [< TRI- + BROM(INE) + ETHANOL] a colorless, crystalline bromine derivative of ethyl alcohol, CBr_3CH_2OH, used as a basal anesthetic

trib·u·la·tion (trib′yə lā′shən) *n.* [ME. *tribulacion* < OFr. < LL.(Ec.) *tribulatio* < *tribulare*, to afflict, oppress < L., to press < *tribulum*, threshing sledge, akin to *terere*, to rub: for IE. base see THROW] **1.** great misery or distress, as from oppression; deep sorrow **2.** something that causes suffering or distress; affliction; trial —*SYN.* see AFFLICTION

tri·bu·nal (trī byōō′n'l, tri-) *n.* [L. < *tribunus*: see TRIBUNE¹] **1.** a seat or bench upon which a judge or judges sit in a court **2.** a court of justice **3.** any seat of judgment [the *tribunal* of popular sentiment]

trib·u·nate (trib′yoo nit, -nāt′) *n.* [Fr. *tribunat* < L. *tribunatus*] **1.** the rank, office, or authority of a tribune **2.** a group of tribunes

trib·une¹ (trib′yōōn; *in names of newspapers, often* tri byōōn′) *n.* [L. *tribunus*, a tribune, magistrate, lit., chief of a tribe < *tribus*, Roman tribal division: see TRIBE] **1.** in ancient Rome *a)* any of several magistrates, esp. one appointed to protect the interests and rights of plebeians against violation by patricians *b)* any of the six officers who rotated command over a legion for a period of a year **2.** a champion of the people: often used in newspaper names —**trib′une·ship′** (-ship′) *n.*

trib·une² (trib′yōōn) *n.* [Fr. < It. *tribuna* < L. *tribunal*: see TRIBUNAL] a raised platform or dais for speakers

trib·u·tar·y (trib′yoo ter′ē) *adj.* [ME. *tributarie* < L. *tributarius*] **1.** paying tribute **2.** under another's control; subject [a *tributary* nation] **3.** in the nature of tribute; owed or paid as tribute **4.** *a)* making additions or furnishing supplies; contributory *b)* flowing into a larger one [a *tributary* stream] —*n., pl.* **-tar′ies** **1.** a tributary nation or ruler **2.** a tributary stream or river —**trib′u·tar′i·ly** *adv.*

trib·ute (trib′yōōt) *n.* [ME. *tribut* < MFr. < L. *tributum*, neut. of *tributus*, pp. of *tribuere*, to assign, allot, pay < *tribus*, Roman tribal division: see TRIBE] **1.** *a)* money paid regularly by one ruler or nation to another as acknowledgment of subjugation, for protection from invasion, etc. *b)* a tax levied for this **2.** *a)* under feudalism, a tax paid by a vassal to his overlord *b)* the obligation to make such a payment **3.** any forced payment or contribution, as through bribery, or the need to make this **4.** something given, done, or said, as a gift, testimonial, etc., to show gratitude, respect, honor, or praise

SYN.—**tribute**, the broadest in scope of these words, is used of praise manifested by any act, situation, etc. as well as that expressed in speech or writing [their success was a *tribute* to his leadership]; **encomium** suggests an enthusiastic, sometimes high-flown expression of praise [*encomiums* lavished on party leaders at a convention]; **eulogy** generally applies to a formal speech or writing in exalting praise, especially of a person who has just died; **panegyric** suggests superlative or elaborate praise expressed in poetic or lofty language [Cicero's *panegyric* upon Cato]

tri·car·box·yl·ic (trī kär′bäk sil′ik) *adj.* containing three carboxyl groups in the molecule

tri·car·pel·lar·y (trī kär′pə ler′ē) *adj. Bot.* having a compound ovary consisting of three united carpels

trice (trīs) *vt.* **triced**, **tric′ing** [ME. *trisen* < MDu. *trisen*, to pull, hoist < *trise*, windlass, roller] to haul up (a sail, etc.) and secure with a small line (usually with *up*) —*n.* [< the *v.*, orig. meaning "one pull or effort"] a very short time; instant; moment: now only in **in a trice**

tri·cen·ten·ni·al (trī′sen ten′ē əl) *adj.* **1.** happening once in a period of 300 years **2.** lasting for 300 years —*n.* a 300th anniversary or its celebration

tri·ceps (trī′seps) *n., pl.* **-cep·ses**, **-ceps** [ModL. < L., triple-headed < *tri-*, TRI- + *caput*, a HEAD] a muscle having three heads, or points of origin; esp., the large muscle at the back of the upper arm that extends the forearm when contracted

tri·cer·a·tops (trī ser′ə täps′) *n.* [ModL. < *tri-* (see TRI-) + *cerat-* (see CERATO-) + Gr. *ōps*, EYE] any of a genus (*Triceratops*) of massive, four-legged, plant-eating dinosaurs having a large, bony crest over the neck, a long horn above each eye, and a short horn on the nose

TRICERATOPS (to 30 ft. long, including tail)

tri·chi·a·sis (tri kī′ə sis) *n.* [LL. < Gr. *trichiasis*: see ff. & -IASIS] an abnormal condition in which hairs, esp. the eyelashes, grow inward

tri·chi·na (tri kī′na) *n., pl.* **-nae** (-nē) [ModL. < Gr. *trichinos*, hairy < *thrix* (gen. *trichos*), hair] a very small

nematode worm (*Trichinella spiralis*), whose larvae infest the intestines and voluntary muscles of man, pigs, etc., causing trichinosis —**tri·chi′nal** *adj.*

trich·i·nize (trik′ə nīz′) *vt.* **-nized′, -niz′ing** to infest with trichinae

trich·i·no·sis (trik′ə nō′sis) *n.* [ModL.: see TRICHINA & -OSIS] a disease caused by the presence of trichinae in the intestines and muscle tissues and usually acquired by eating insufficiently cooked pork from an infested hog: it is characterized by fever, nausea, diarrhea, and muscular pains

trich·i·nous (trik′ə nəs, tri kī′nəs) *adj.* 1. infested with trichinae 2. of or having trichinosis

trich·ite (trik′īt) *n.* [< Gr. *thrix* (gen. *trichos*), hair + -ITE[1]] a hairlike crystallite occurring in volcanic rocks in irregular or radiating groups

tri·chlo·ride (trī klôr′īd) *n.* a chloride having three chlorine atoms to the molecule

tri·chlo·ro·a·ce·tic acid (trī klôr′ō ə sēt′ik) [TRI- + CHLORO- + ACETIC] a colorless, corrosive, deliquescent, crystalline substance, CCl₃COOH, with a sharp, pungent odor: it is used as an antiseptic and astringent

tri·chlo·ro·eth·yl·ene (-eth′ə lēn′) *n.* [TRI- + CHLORO- + ETHYLENE] a toxic, colorless liquid, CHCl:CCl₂, with an odor resembling chloroform: it is used as a solvent for fats, oils, and waxes, and in dry cleaning, etc.

tri·chlo·ro·phe·nox·y·a·ce·tic acid (-fi näk′sē ə sēt′ik) [TRI- + CHLORO- + PHENOXY + ACETIC] a trichloride derivative of phenoxy acetic acid, Cl₃C₆H₂OCH₂·COOH, used as a weed killer

trich·o- (trik′ō, -ə) [Gr. *tricho-* < *thrix* (gen. *trichos*), hair] a combining form meaning hair [*trichosis*]

trich·o·cyst (trik′ə sist′) *n.* [prec. + -CYST] any of the many tiny, rodlike, stinging and attachment organelles embedded in the ectoplasm of many ciliate protozoans —**trich′o·cys′tic** (-sis′tik) *adj.*

trich·o·gyne (trik′ə jin′, -jin) *n.* [TRICHO- + Gr. *gynē*, woman, female] the long, hairlike part of a procarp in red algae, certain fungi, and lichens, acting as a receptor for the male fertilizing bodies —**trich′o·gyn′i·al** (-jin′ē əl), **trich′o·gyn′ic** *adj.*

tri·choid (trik′oid) *adj.* resembling a hair; hairlike

tri·chol·o·gy (tri käl′ə jē) *n.* [TRICHO- + -LOGY] the science dealing with the hair and its diseases —**tri·chol′o·gist** *n.*

tri·chome (trī′kōm, trik′ōm) *n.* [G. *trichom* < Gr. *trichōma*, growth of hair < *trichoun*, to cover with hair < *thrix* (gen. *trichos*), hair] 1. any hairlike outgrowth from an epidermal cell of a plant, as a bristle, prickle, root hair, etc. 2. any of the threadlike structures, or filaments, of certain algae —**tri·chom′ic** (-käm′ik, -kō′mik) *adj.*

trich·o·mon·ad (trik′ə män′ad, -mō′nad) *n.* [ModL. *trichomonas* (gen. *trichomonadis*), name of the genus: see TRICHO- & MONAD] any of a genus (*Trichomonas*) of flagellated protozoans, parasitic or commensal in man and other animals

trich·o·mo·ni·a·sis (-mə nī′ə sis) *n.* [ModL. < *Trichomonas*, name of the genus (< *tricho-*, TRICHO- + *-monas*, simple organism < LL. *monas*: see MONAD) + -IASIS] infestation with trichomonads; esp., *a*) a vaginitis in women caused by a trichomonad (*Trichomonas vaginalis*) and characterized by a heavy discharge *b*) a disease of cows caused by a trichomonad (*Trichomonas foetus*) and producing temporary infertility and sometimes abortion

tri·chop·ter·an (tri käp′tər ən) *n.* [ModL. *Trichoptera*, name of the order (see TRICHO- & PTERO-) + -AN] *same as* CADDIS FLY —**tri·chop′ter·ous** *adj.*

tri·cho·sis (tri kō′sis) *n.* [ModL.: see TRICHO- & -OSIS] any disease of the hair

tri·chot·o·my (tri kät′ə mē) *n.* [Gr. *tricha*, threefold (< *treis*, THREE) + -TOMY] division into three parts, elements, groups, etc. —**tri·chot′o·mize** (-mīz′) *vt.* **-mized′, -miz′ing** —**tri·chot′o·mous** (-məs) *adj.* —**tri·chot′o·mous·ly** *adv.*

tri·chro·ism (trī′krō iz′m) *n.* [< Gr. *trichroos*, of three colors < *tri-*, TRI- + *chroia*, color: for base see CHROMA] the property that some crystals have of transmitting light of three different colors when looked at from three different directions —**tri·chro′ic** *adj.*

tri·chro·mat (trī′krō mat′) *n.* [back-formation < ff.] a person having trichromatic vision

tri·chro·mat·ic (trī′krō mat′ik) *adj.* [TRI- + CHROMATIC] 1. of, having, or using three colors, as in the three-color process in printing and photography 2. of, pertaining to, or having normal vision, in which the three primary colors are fully distinguished Also **tri·chro′mic** —**tri·chro′ma·tism** (-krō′mə tiz′m) *n.*

trick (trik) *n.* [ME. *trik* < ONormFr. *trique* < *trikier* < OFr. *trichier*, to trick, cheat, prob. < VL. *triccare*, altered < ? LL. *tricare*, to delay, for L. *tricari*, to make trouble, trifle, play tricks] 1. an action or device designed to deceive, cheat, outwit, etc.; artifice; dodge; ruse; stratagem 2. *a*) a practical joke; mischievous or playful act; prank *b*) a deception or illusion [the light played a *trick* on his eyes] 3. a freakish, foolish, mean, or stupid act 4. a clever or difficult act intended to amuse; specif., *a*) an act of jugglery or sleight of hand; also, an illusion of the kind created by legerdemain *b*) an action, feat, or routine performed by an animal as a result of training 5. any feat requiring skill 6. the art or knack of doing

something easily, skillfully, quickly, etc. [the *trick* of making good pastry] 7. an expedient or convention of an art, craft, or trade [to learn the *tricks* of the trade] 8. a personal habit or mannerism [a *trick* of tugging at his ear] 9. *a*) a turn or round of duty or work; shift *b*) [Slang] the time spent by a prostitute with a customer; also, the customer ☆10. [Colloq.] a child or girl, esp. one viewed as attractive 11. *Card Games* the cards played and won in a single round —*vt.* to deceive, swindle, cheat, fool, etc. —*adj.* 1. having to do with or used for a trick or tricks 2. that tricks 3. apt to malfunction or become stiff; of uncertain reliability [a *trick* knee] —**do** (or **turn**) **the trick** to bring about the desired result —**trick out** (or **up**) to dress up; deck; adorn; array —**trick′er** *n.*

SYN.—**trick** is the common word for an action or device in which ingenuity and cunning are used to outwit others and implies deception either for fraudulent purposes or as a prank, etc.; **ruse** applies to that which is contrived as a blind for one's real intentions or for the truth [her apparent illness was merely a *ruse*]; a **stratagem** is a more or less complicated ruse, by means of which one attempts to outwit or entrap an enemy or antagonist [military *stratagems*]; **maneuver**, specifically applicable to military tactics, in general use suggests the shrewd manipulation of persons or situations to suit one's purposes [a political *maneuver*]; **artifice** stresses inventiveness or ingenuity in the contrivance of an expedient, trick, etc. [*artifices* employed to circumvent the tax laws]; **wile** implies the use of allurements or beguilement to ensnare [womanly *wiles*] See also CHEAT

trick·er·y (-ər ē) *n., pl.* **-er·ies** the act or practice of tricking; use of tricks; deception; fraud —*SYN.* see DECEPTION

trick·ish (-ish) *adj.* 1. given to trickery; deceitful 2. characterized by or full of tricks —**trick′ish·ness** *n.*

trick·le (trik′'l) *vi.* **-led, -ling** [ME. *triklen*, prob. < *striklen*, freq. of *striken*, to STRIKE] 1. to flow slowly in a thin stream or fall in drops 2. to move, come, go, etc. little by little [the crowd *trickled* away] —*vt.* to cause to trickle —*n.* 1. the act of trickling 2. a slow, small flow —**trick′ly** *adj.*

☆**trick or treat!** give me a treat or I will play a trick on you!: traditional greeting used by children going from door to door in costume on Halloween asking for treats

trick·ster (trik′stər) *n.* a person who tricks; cheat

trick·sy (trik′sē) *adj.* **-si·er, -si·est** 1. [Archaic] tricked out; spruce; smart 2. full of tricks; playful; mischievous 3. *same as* TRICKY —**trick′si·ness** *n.*

trick·y (trik′ē) *adj.* **trick′i·er, trick′i·est** 1. given to or characterized by trickery; deceitful 2. like a trick in deceptiveness; intricate; difficult 3. requiring special skill or care —*SYN.* see SLY —**trick′i·ly** *adv.* —**trick′i·ness** *n.*

tri·clin·ic (trī klin′ik) *adj.* [< TRI- + Gr. *klinein*, to incline (see LEAN[1]) + -IC] designating of or a system of crystallization having three unequal axes intersecting at oblique angles

tri·clin·i·um (-ē əm) *n., pl.* **-i·a** (-ə) [L. < Gr. *triklinion*, dim. of *triklinos* < *tri-*, TRI- + *klinē*, a couch < *klinein* (cf. prec.)] 1. a couch extending around three sides of an ancient Roman dining table, for reclining at meals 2. an ancient Roman dining room, esp. one with such a couch

tri·col·or (trī′kul′ər) *n.* [Fr. *tricolore*, orig., three-colored < LL. *tricolor*: see TRI- & COLOR] a flag having three colors in large areas; esp., the flag of France, with three broad, vertical stripes of blue, white, and red —*adj.* having three colors

tri·corn (trī′kôrn) *adj.* [Fr. *tricorne* < L. *tricornis* < *tri-*, TRI- + *cornu*, HORN] having three horns or corners, as a hat with the brim folded up against the crown to form three sides —*n.* a tricorn hat; cocked hat: also sp. **tri′corne**

tri·cos·tate (trī käs′tāt) *adj.* [TRI- + COSTATE] *Bot., Zool.* having three ribs or riblike parts

tri·cot (trē′kō) *n.* [Fr. < *tricoter*, to knit < MFr., to move, dance < *tricot*, dim. of *trique*, a stick, cane < *estriquer*, to strike < MDu. *striken*, akin to STRIKE] 1. a fabric of thin texture that is knitted, or woven to resemble knitting 2. a type of ribbed cloth for dresses

tric·o·tine (trik′ə tēn′) *n.* [Fr.: see TRICOT & -INE[4]] a twilled woolen cloth resembling gabardine

tri·crot·ic (trī krät′ik) *adj.* [< Gr. *trikrotos*, (rowed) with triple stroke < *tri-*, TRI- + *krotein*, to beat (< IE. *kret-*, to strike, whence OE. *hrindan*, to push) + -IC] *Physiol.* designating or of a pulse having three separate rhythmic waves to each beat —**tri·cro·tism** (trī′krə tiz′m) *n.*

tric·trac (trik′trak′) *n.* [Fr., echoic of the sound made by the pegs] backgammon, esp. a variety using both pegs and pieces

tri·cus·pid (trī kus′pid) *adj.* [L. *tricuspis* (gen. *tricuspidis*): see TRI- & CUSP] 1. having three cusps, or points [a *tricuspid* tooth]: also **tri·cus′pi·date′** (-pə dāt′) 2. designating or of a valve with three flaps, between the right auricle and right ventricle of the heart —*n.* 1. a tricuspid tooth 2. the tricuspid valve

tri·cy·cle (trī′si k'l) *n.* [Fr.: see TRI- & CYCLE] a light, three-wheeled vehicle, esp. one for children, with one wheel in front and two in back, operated by pedals

tri·cy·clic (trī sī′klik, -sik′lik) *adj.* containing three fused rings of atoms in the molecule

tri·dac·tyl (trī dak′t'l) *adj.* [< Gr. *tridaktylos*: see TRI- & DACTYL] *Zool.* having three digits, or fingers

tri·dent (trīd′'nt) *n.* [L. *tridens* (gen. *tridentis*) < *tri-*, TRI- + *dens*, TOOTH] 1. a three-pronged spear used by the retiarius in ancient Roman gladiatorial combats 2. a three-

pronged fish spear **3.** *Gr. & Rom. Myth.* a three-pronged spear borne as a scepter by the sea god Poseidon, or Neptune —*adj.* three-pronged

tri·den·tate (trī den′tāt) *adj.* [ModL. *tridentatus:* see TRI- & DENTATE] having three teeth, prongs, or points

Tri·den·tine (trī den′tin, -tīn, -tēn) *adj.* [ML. *Tridentinus* < *Tridentum,* Trent] **1.** of Trent, Italy **2.** of the Council of Trent, or in accord with its decrees

Tri·den·tum (trī den′təm) *ancient name of* TRENT, Italy

tri·di·men·sion·al (trī′də men′shən 'l) *adj.* of or having three dimensions; having depth as well as length and width

tried (trīd) *pt. & pp. of* TRY —*adj.* **1.** tested; proved **2.** trustworthy; faithful **3.** having endured trials and troubles

tri·en·ni·al (trī en′ē əl) *adj.* [< L. *triennium,* three years < *tri-,* TRI- + *annus,* a year: see ANNUAL] **1.** happening every three years **2.** lasting three years —*n.* a triennial event or occurrence —**tri·en′ni·al·ly** *adv.*

tri·en·ni·um (-əm) *n., pl.* **-ni·ums, -ni·a** (-ə) [L., see prec.] a period of three years

Trier (trir) city in W West Germany, in Rhineland-Palatinate, on the Moselle River: pop. 85,000

tri·er (trī′ər) *n.* a person or thing that tries

tri·er·arch (trī′ə rärk′) *n.* [L. *trierarchus* < Gr. *triērarchos* < *triērēs,* a trireme (< *tri-,* TRI- + *-ērēs* < IE. base **erē-,* to row, oar: cf. ROW², RUDDER) + *archos,* leader, chief: see -ARCH] in ancient Greece, **1.** the commander of a trireme **2.** at Athens, a person who built, outfitted, and maintained a trireme for the service of the state

tri·er·arch·y (-rär′kē) *n., pl.* **-arch′ies** [Gr. *triērarchia*] **1.** the rank, authority, or duties of a trierarch **2.** trierarchs collectively **3.** the system by which trierarchs built, outfitted, and maintained triremes for the state

Tri·este (trē est′; *It.* trē es′te) **1.** seaport in NE Italy, on an inlet (Gulf of Trieste) of the Adriatic: pop. 281,000 **2. Free Territory of,** former region surrounding this city, administered by the United Nations and divided between Italy & Yugoslavia in 1954: 285 sq. mi.

tri·eth·yl (trī eth′'l) *adj.* [TRI- + ETHYL] containing three ethyl groups in the molecule

tri·fa·cial (trī fā′shəl) *adj., n. same as* TRIGEMINAL

tri·fid (trī′fid) *adj.* [L. *trifidus* < *tri-,* three + the base of *findere,* to divide: see FISSION] divided into three lobes or parts by deep clefts, as some leaves

tri·fle (trī′f'l) *n.* [ME. < OFr. *trufle,* mockery, dim. of *truffe,* deception] **1.** something of little value or importance; trivial thing, idea, etc.; paltry matter **2.** a small amount of money **3.** a small amount; bit **4.** esp. in England, a dessert consisting of spongecake soaked in wine, spread with jam, and covered with custard, whipped cream, etc. **5.** *a)* a kind of pewter of medium hardness *b)* [*pl.*] utensils made of this —*vi.* **-fled, -fling 1.** to talk or act jokingly, mockingly, etc.; deal lightly [not a person to *trifle* with] **2.** to play or toy (*with* something) **3.** to play fast and loose (*with* a person's affections, etc.); dally —*vt.* to spend idly; waste [to *trifle* the hours away] —**tri′fler** *n.* **SYN.—trifle** is the general term meaning to treat without earnestness, full attention, definite purpose, etc. [to *trifle* with a person, an idea, etc.]; **flirt** implies a light, transient interest or attention that quickly moves on to another person or thing [she's always *flirting* with men]; **dally** implies a playing with a subject or thing that one has little or no intention of taking seriously [to *dally* with painting]; **coquet** suggests the behavior of a flirtatious woman who promiscuously seeks attention or admiration without serious intent; **toy** implies a trifling or dallying with no purpose beyond that of amusement or idling away time [to *toy* with an idea]

tri·fling (trī′fliŋ) *adj.* **1.** that trifles; frivolous; shallow; fickle **2.** having little value or importance; trivial —*SYN.* see PETTY —**tri′fling·ly** *adv.*

☆**tri·fo·cal** (trī fō′k'l; *also, esp. for the n.,* trī′fō′k'l) *adj.* adjusted to three different focal lengths —*n.* **1.** a lens like a bifocal but with an additional narrow area ground to adjust the eye for intermediate focus (about 30 inches) **2.** [*pl.*] a pair of glasses with trifocal lenses

tri·fo·li·ate (trī fō′lē it, -āt′) *adj.* [TRI- + FOLIATE] **1.** having three leaves **2.** *loose var. of* TRIFOLIOLATE Also **tri·fo′li·at′ed** (-āt′id)

tri·fo·li·o·late (trī fō′lē ə lāt′) *adj.* [< TRI- + ModL. *foliolum,* dim. of L. *folium,* a leaf (see FOIL²) + -ATE¹] divided into three leaflets, as the leaf of a clover

tri·fo·li·um (-fō′lē əm) *n.* [L., TREFOIL] *same as* CLOVER (sense 1)

tri·fo·ri·um (-fôr′ē əm) *n., pl.* **-ri·a** (-ə) [ML. < L. *tri-,* TRI- + *foris,* DOOR] a gallery or arcade in the wall above the arches of the nave, choir, or transept of a church

tri·form (trī′fôrm) *adj.* [L. *triformis* < *tri-,* TRI- + *forma,* FORM] having three parts, forms, etc.: also **tri′formed**

tri·fur·cate (trī fur′kit, -kāt) *adj.* [< L. *trifurcus* < *tri-,* TRI- + *furca,* a fork + -ATE¹] having three forks or branches: also **tri·fur′cat·ed** —**tri′fur·ca′tion** *n.*

trig¹ (trig) *adj.* [ME. *trigg* < ON. *tryggr,* trusty, firm: for IE. base see TRUE] [Chiefly Brit.] **1.** trim; neat; spruce **2.** in good condition; strong; sound **3.** prim; precise —*vt.* **trigged, trig′ging** [Chiefly Brit. Dial.] to make trig (often with *out* or *up*)

trig² (trig) *vt.* **trigged, trig′ging** [< ? Scand., as in Dan. *trykke,* to press] [Chiefly Dial.] **1.** to prevent (a wheel, cask, etc.) from rolling by placing a wedge, stone, etc. under it **2.** to prop or support —*n.* [Dial.] a stone, wedge, etc. used in trigging

trig³ (trig) *n. clipped form of* TRIGONOMETRY

trig. 1. trigonometric(al) **2.** trigonometry Also **trigon.**

tri·gem·i·nal (trī jem′ə n'l) *adj.* [< ModL. *trigeminus* < L., born three together (< *tri-,* TRI- + *geminus,* twin) + -AL] designating or of either of the fifth pair of cranial nerves, each of which divides into three branches supplying the head and face —*n.* a trigeminal nerve

trigeminal neuralgia a disorder of unknown cause, characterized by severely painful paroxysms along one or more branches of a trigeminal nerve

trig·ger (trig′ər) *n.* [earlier *tricker* < Du. *trekker* < *trekken,* to draw, pull: see TREK] **1.** a small lever or part which when pulled or pressed releases a catch, spring, etc. **2.** in firearms, a small lever pressed back by the finger to activate the firing mechanism **3.** an act, impulse, etc. that initiates an action, series of events, etc. —*vt.* **1.** to fire or activate by pulling a trigger **2.** to initiate (an action); set off [the fight that *triggered* the riot] —☆**quick on the trigger** [Colloq.] **1.** quick to fire a gun **2.** quick to act, understand, retort, etc.; alert

trigger finger the finger used to press the trigger of a firearm; specif., the forefinger

trig·ger·fish (-fish′) *n., pl.* **-fish′, -fish′es:** see FISH² [because depression of the second spine of the fin causes the first to snap down] any of a group of brightly colored tropical fishes (family Balistidae) having a prominent first dorsal fin with two or three spines

☆**trig·ger-hap·py** (-hap′ē) *adj.* [see HAPPY, *adj.* 4] [Colloq.] **1.** inclined to resort to force rashly or irresponsibly **2.** ready to start a war at the slightest provocation; bellicose

tri·glyc·er·ide (trī glis′ər id′) *n.* [TRI- + GLYCERIDE] any of a group of esters derived from glycerol and containing one, two, or three fatty acid radicals

tri·glyph (trī′glif) *n.* [L. *triglyphus* < Gr. *triglyphos:* see TRI- & GLYPH] in a Doric frieze, a slightly projecting, rectangular block occurring at regular intervals and having two vertical grooves (*glyphs*) and two chamfers or half grooves at the sides —**tri·glyph′ic** *adj.*

tri·gon (trī′gän) *n.* [L. *trigonum* < Gr. *trigōnon,* triangle, lyre < *trigōnos,* triangular: see TRI- & -GON] **1.** [Archaic] a triangle **2.** an ancient, triangular lyre or harp **3.** *Astrol. a)* any of the four sets of three signs, each 120 degrees distant from the other two, into which the zodiac is divided *b) same as* TRINE (*n.* 2)

trig·o·nal (trig′ə n'l) *adj.* [L. *trigonalis*] **1.** of a triangle; triangular **2.** of a trigon **3.** designating or of a system of crystallization having three unequal axes, equally inclined

trigonometric function any of the basic functions (as sine, cosine, tangent, etc.) of an angle or arc usually expressed as the ratio of pairs of sides of a right triangle

trig·o·nom·e·try (trig′ə näm′ə trē) *n., pl.* **-tries** [ModL. *trigonometria* < Gr. *trigōnon,* triangle (see TRIGON) + *-metria,* measurement (see -METRY)] the branch of mathematics that deals with the ratios between the sides of a right triangle with reference to either acute angle (*trigonometric functions*), the relations between these ratios, and the application of these facts in finding the unknown sides or angles of any triangle, as in surveying, navigation, engineering, etc. —**trig′o·no·met′ric** (-nə met′rik), **trig′o·no·met′ri·cal** *adj.* —**trig′o·no·met′ri·cal·ly** *adv.*

trig·o·nous (trig′ə nəs) *adj.* [L. *trigonus* < Gr. *trigōnos:* see TRIGON] having three angles or corners

tri·graph (trī′graf′, -gräf′) *n.* [TRI- + -GRAPH] three letters representing one sound (Ex.: *eau* in *bureau*)

tri·he·dral (trī hē′drəl) *adj.* [TRI- + HEDRAL] having three sides or faces [a *trihedral* angle] —*n.* a figure formed by three lines, each in a different plane, that intersect at a point

tri·hy·drate (-hī′drāt) *n.* [TRI- + HYDRATE] a chemical compound containing three molecules of water —**tri·hy′drat·ed** *adj.*

tri·hy·drox·y (trī′hī dräk′sē) *adj.* containing three hydroxyl groups

tri·i·o·do·thy·ro·nine (trī ī′ə dō thī′rə nēn′) *n.* [< TRI- + IODO- + THYR(O)- + -INE⁴] a crystalline material, $C_{15}H_{12}I_3NO_4$, found in the thyroid gland and in the blood: used medically esp. to treat hypothyroidism

tri·ju·gate (trī′joo gāt′; trī joo′git, -gāt) *adj.* [< L. *trijugus,* threefold < *tri-,* TRI- + *jugum,* a YOKE + -ATE¹] *Bot.* having three pairs of leaflets: also **tri′ju·gous** (-gəs)

trike (trīk) *n.* [Colloq.] *same as* TRICYCLE

tri·lat·er·al (trī lat′ər əl) *adj.* [< L. *trilaterus,* three-sided: see TRI- & LATERAL] three-sided —**tri·lat′er·al·ly** *adv.*

tril·by (tril′bē) *n., pl.* **-bies** [orig. worn in a stage version (1895) of the novel *Trilby,* by George DU MAURIER] a type of soft felt hat popular in England

tri·lin·e·ar (trī lin′ē ər) *adj.* [TRI- + LINEAR] of, enclosed by, or involving three lines

tri·lin·gual (trī liŋ′gwəl) *adj.* [< L. *trilinguis* (< *tri-,* TRI- + *lingua,* tongue) + -AL] **1.** of or in three languages

2. using or capable of using three languages, esp. with equal or nearly equal facility —**tri·lin'gual·ly** adv.

tri·lit·er·al (-lit'ər əl) adj. [< TRI- + L. litera, a letter + -AL] consisting of three letters, esp. three consonants [most roots of Semitic languages are triliteral] —**tri·lit'er·al·ism** n.

trill (tril) n. [It. trillo < trillare, to trill, of echoic orig.] 1. a) a rapid alternation of a given musical tone with the tone immediately above it b) same as VIBRATO 2. the warbling sound made by some birds 3. a) a rapid vibration of the tongue or uvula, as in pronouncing r in some languages b) a consonant so pronounced —vt., vi. [It. trillare] to sound, speak, sing, or play with a trill —**trill'er** n.

tril·lion (tril'yən) n. [Fr. < tri-, TRI- + (mi)llion] 1. in the U.S. and France, the number represented by 1 followed by 12 zeros 2. in Great Britain and Germany, the number represented by 1 followed by 18 zeros —adj. amounting to one trillion in number

tril·lionth (-yənth) adj. 1. coming last in a series of a trillion 2. designating any of the trillion equal parts of something —n. 1. the last in a series of a trillion 2. any of the trillion equal parts of something

tril·li·um (tril'ē əm) n. [ModL., name of the genus < L. tri-, three] any of a genus (Trillium) of perennial plants of the lily family, having a short rootstock and an erect stem that bears a whorl of three leaves and a single flower with three green sepals and three petals of various colors

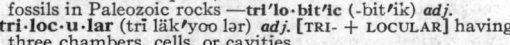

TRILLIUM

tri·lo·bate (tri lō'bāt) adj. having three lobes, as some leaves: also **tri·lo'bat·ed, tri'lobed'** (-lōbd')

tri·lo·bite (tri'lə bit') n. [ModL. Trilobites, Trilobita: see TRI-, LOBE, -ITE¹] any of a large class (Trilobita) of extinct, marine arthropods having the body divided by two furrows into three parts, found as fossils in Paleozoic rocks —**tri'lo·bit'ic** (-bit'ik) adj.

tri·loc·u·lar (tri läk'yoo lər) adj. [TRI- + LOCULAR] having three chambers, cells, or cavities

tril·o·gy (tril'ə jē) n., pl. -gies [Gr. trilogia: see TRI- & -LOGY] a set of three related plays, novels, etc. which together form an extended, unified work, though each has its own unity

trim (trim) vt. trimmed, trim'ming [via ME. dial. < OE. trymman, to make firm, set in order, array < trum, strong, firm: for IE. base see TREE] 1. orig., to prepare; fit out; dress 2. to put in proper order; make neat or tidy, esp. by clipping, lopping, etc. [to trim one's mustache] 3. to clip, lop, cut, etc. (often with off) [to trim dead branches off a tree] 4. to cut (something) down to the required size or shape 5. ☆a) to decorate or embellish as by adding ornaments, contrasting materials, etc. [to trim a Christmas tree] ☆b) to arrange an attractive display of merchandise in or on [to trim a store window] 6. a) to balance (a ship) by ballasting, shifting cargo, etc. b) to put (sails or yards) in order for sailing 7. to balance (an aircraft) in flight by adjusting stabilizers, tabs, etc. 8. to modify according to expediency; adjust; adapt 9. [Colloq.] a) to scold; chide; rebuke b) to beat, punish, thrash, etc. c) to defeat decisively d) to cheat —vi. 1. a) to change one's opinions or viewpoint so as to satisfy opposing factions, etc.; keep a middle-of-the-road policy; compromise b) to change one's opinions or viewpoint opportunistically 2. a) to keep in balance: said of a ship b) to keep a ship in balance, as by adjusting the sails or yards —n. 1. order; arrangement; condition [in proper trim] 2. good condition or order [to keep in trim for sports] 3. equipment; gear; dress 4. a trimming by clipping, cutting, etc. 5. ☆a) same as WINDOW DRESSING ☆b) decorative molding or borders, esp. around windows and doors ☆c) the interior furnishings of an automobile body; also, external ornamental metalwork on an automobile d) any ornamental trimming [a dress with lace trim] 6. a) the condition of being ready to sail: said of a vessel b) the position of a vessel in the water in relation to the horizontal, esp. a fore-and-aft horizontal axis c) correct position in the water: a ship is in trim if stable and floating on an even keel, out of trim if not d) the difference between the draft of a ship forward and the draft aft e) the adjustment of the sails or yards in managing a vessel f) the degree of buoyancy of a submarine 7. the position of an airplane in relation to a fore-and-aft horizontal axis 8. something that is trimmed, as sections of motion-picture film cut out in editing 9. [Obs.] character (of a person) —adj. trim'mer, trim'mest 1. orderly; neat; tidy 2. well-proportioned; smartly designed 3. in good condition 4. [Obs.] fine; nice —adv. in a trim manner —SYN. see NEAT¹ —trim one's sails to adjust one's opinions, actions, expenditures, etc. to meet changing conditions —**trim'ly** adv. —**trim'ness** n.

tri·ma·ran (tri'mə ran') n. [TRI- + (CATA)MARAN] a boat similar to a catamaran, but with three parallel hulls

tri·mer (tri'mər) n. [TRI- + Gr. meros, a part] Chem. 1. a molecule composed of three identical, simpler molecules 2. a substance composed of such molecules [C₆H₆ is a trimer of C₂H₂] —**tri·mer'ic** (-mer'ik) adj.

trim·er·ous (trim'ər əs) adj. [TRI- + -MEROUS] 1. having the parts in sets of three: said of a flower: also written 3-merous 2. having two-jointed tarsi: said of insects

tri·mes·ter (tri mes'tər, tri'mes-) n. [Fr. trimestre < L. trimestris, of three months < tri-, three + mensis, month: see MOON] 1. a period or term of three months 2. in some colleges and universities, any of the three periods into which the academic year is divided

trim·e·ter (trim'ə tər) n. [L. trimetrus < Gr. trimetros: see TRI- & METER¹] 1. a line of verse containing three metrical feet or measures 2. verse consisting of trimeters —adj. having three metrical feet

tri·meth·a·di·one (tri meth'ə di'ōn) n. [trimeth(yl) < TRI- + METHYL + -a- + DI-¹ + -ONE] a white, crystalline material, C₆H₉NO₃, used in treating epilepsy

tri·met·ric (tri met'rik) adj. 1. having three metrical feet 2. same as ORTHORHOMBIC Also **tri·met'ri·cal**

trimetric projection in mechanical drawing, a type of display by projection in which the three axes are inclined at arbitrary angles and are often scaled differently as well

tri·met·ro·gon (tri met'rə gän') n. [< TRI- + Gr. metron, a measure + -GON] a system of aerial photography in which three wide-angle cameras are used side by side to take photographs of the earth from horizon to horizon

trim·mer (trim'ər) n. 1. a person, thing, machine, etc. that trims 2. a beam in a floor frame that receives the ends of headers, as around a stair well

trim·ming (-iŋ) n. 1. the action of a person who trims; specif., [Colloq.] a) a beating; thrashing b) a decisive defeat c) a cheating or fleecing 2. something used to trim; specif., a) decoration; ornament b) [pl.] the side dishes or garnishings of a meal [steak with all the trimmings] 3. [pl.] parts trimmed off

tri·mo·lec·u·lar (tri'mə lek'yoo lər) adj. of or formed from three molecules

tri·month·ly (tri munth'lē) adj. happening or appearing every three months

tri·morph (tri'môrf) n. [TRI- + -MORPH: cf. ff.] 1. a substance that crystallizes in three distinct forms 2. any of these forms

tri·mor·phism (tri môr'fiz'm) n. [< Gr. trimorphos, of three forms < tri-, three + morphē, form + -ISM] 1. Crystallography the property of crystallizing in three distinct forms 2. Bot. the existence of three distinct forms of flowers, leaves, or other organs on the same plant or on different plants of the same species 3. Zool. the existence of three distinct forms in the same species —**tri·mor'phic,** tri·mor'phous adj.

Tri·mur·ti (tri moor'tē) [Sans. trimūrti, lit., of three forms < tri, THREE + mūrti, body, shape] the trinity of Hindu gods (Brahma, Vishnu, and Siva)

Tri·na·cri·a (tri nā'krē ə, tri-) ancient Latin name for SICILY —**Tri·na'cri·an** adj.

tri·nal (tri'n'l) adj. [LL. trinalis < L. trinus: see TRINE] having three parts; threefold; triple

tri·na·ry (tri'nər ē) adj. [LL.(Ec.) trinarius, of three kinds: see ff. & -ARY] threefold; ternary

trine (trin) adj. [ME. < MFr. < L. trinus, triple < tres, THREE] 1. threefold; triple 2. Astrol. in trine, i.e., favorable —n. 1. a group of three; triad 2. Astrol. the aspect of two planets 120 degrees apart, considered favorable —[T-] the Trinity

Trin·i·dad (trin'ə dad'; Sp. trē nē thäth') island in the West Indies, off the NE coast of Venezuela: see ff.: 1,864 sq. mi. —**Trin'i·dad'i·an** adj., n.

Trinidad and Tobago country in the West Indies, comprising the islands of Trinidad & Tobago: a member of the Brit. Commonwealth: 1,980 sq. mi.; pop. 1,010,000; cap. Port-of-Spain

Trin·i·tar·i·an (trin'ə ter'ē ən) adj. [ModL. trinitarius < LL.(Ec.) trinitas] 1. a) having to do with the Trinity or the doctrine of the Trinity b) believing in this doctrine 2. [t-] forming a trinity; threefold —n. one who believes in the doctrine of the Trinity —**Trin'i·tar'i·an·ism** n.

tri·ni·tro·cre·sol (tri ni'tro krē'sôl, -sōl) n. [TRI- + NITRO- + CRESOL] a yellow, crystalline chemical compound, C₇H₅N₃O₇, used as an antiseptic and in explosives

tri·ni·tro·glyc·er·in (-glis'ər in) n. same as NITROGLYCERIN

tri·ni·tro·tol·u·ene (-täl'yoo wēn') n. [TRI- + NITRO- + TOLUENE] a high explosive, one of several isomeric derivatives, CH₃C₆H₂(NO₂)₃, of toluene, used for blasting, in artillery shells, etc.: also **tri·ni'tro·tol'u·ol** (-ôl', -ōl'): abbrev. TNT

trin·i·ty (trin'ə tē) n., pl. -ties [ME. trinite < OFr. trinité < L. trinitas, triad, in LL.(Ec.), the Trinity (after Gr. trias) < trinus: see TRINE & -ITY] 1. the condition of being three or threefold 2. a set of three persons or things that form a unit 3. [T-] Christian Theol. a) the union of the three divine persons (Father, Son, and Holy Spirit, or Holy Ghost) in one Godhead b) same as TRINITY SUNDAY

Trinity Sunday the Sunday next after Whitsunday or Pentecost, dedicated to the Trinity

trin·ket (triŋ'kit) n. [ME. trenket, shoemakers' knife, ladies' toy knife, ornament < ONormFr. trenquet < OFr. trenchet < trenchier, to cut: cf. TRENCH] 1. a small ornament, piece of jewelry, etc. 2. a trifle or toy

tri·no·mi·al (tri nō'mē əl) adj. [TRI- + (BI)NOMIAL] consisting of three terms —n. 1. a mathematical expression consisting of three terms connected by plus or minus signs

2. the scientific name of a plant or animal taxon, consisting of three words designating in order the genus, species, and subspecies or variety

tri·o (trē′ō) *n., pl.* **tri′os** [Fr. < It. < *tri-*, TRI- (after *duo*, DUO)] **1.** any group of three persons or things **2.** *Music* **a)** a composition for three voices or three instruments **b)** the three performers of such a composition **c)** the middle section of a minuet, scherzo, etc., orig. written in three voices, or parts

tri·ode (trī′ōd) *n.* [TRI- + (ELECTR)ODE] a vacuum tube containing three electrodes (an anode, cathode, and control grid)

tri·oe·cious (trī ē′shəs) *adj.* [< TRI- + LL. *oecus*, a room (< Gr. *oikos*, a house) + -OUS] having male, female, and bisexual flowers on separate plants

tri·ol (trī′ôl, -ōl) *n.* [TRI- + -OL¹] a compound with three hydroxyl groups in the molecule

tri·o·let (trī′ə lit, trē′ə let′) *n.* [Fr., ? fig. use of *triolet*, clover, ult. < Gr. *triphyllon*, trefoil] a poem or stanza having eight lines and two rhymes, the first line being repeated as the fourth and seventh, and the second as the eighth: the rhyme scheme is *abaaabab*

tri·ose (trī′ōs) *n.* [TRI- + -OSE¹] a carbohydrate, $C_3H_6O_3$, with three carbon atoms

tri·ox·ide (trī äk′sīd) *n.* an oxide having three oxygen atoms to the molecule

trip (trip) *vi.* **tripped, trip′ping** [ME. *trippen* < OFr. *treper* < Gmc. *trippon (whence OE. *treppan*, to step): for the IE. base see TRAP¹] **1.** to walk, run, or dance with light, rapid steps; skip; caper **2.** to stumble, esp. by catching the foot **3.** to make a false step, inaccuracy, or mistake; err **4.** to falter in speaking **5.** to run past the pallet of the escapement: said of a tooth of the escapement wheel of a watch, etc. **6.** [Rare] to take a trip; journey ☆**7.** [Slang] to experience a trip (*n.* sense 6) —*vt.* **1.** to make stumble, esp. by catching the foot (sometimes with *up*) **2.** *a)* to cause to make a false step or mistake *b)* to cause to fail or stop; obstruct **3.** to catch (a person) in a lie, error, etc. (often with *up*) **4.** *a)* to release (a spring, wheel, or other mechanical part), as by the action of a detent *b)* to start or operate by this **5.** [Now Rare] to perform (a dance) lightly and nimbly **6.** *Naut. a)* to raise (an anchor) clear of the bottom *b)* to tilt (a yard) into position for lowering *c)* to raise (an upper mast) so that the fid may be removed before lowering —*n.* **1.** a light, quick tread **2.** *a)* a traveling from one place to another and returning; journey, esp. a short one, excursion, voyage, jaunt, etc. *b)* a going to a place and returning [made three *trips* to the kitchen] **3.** *a)* a stumble *b)* a maneuver for causing someone to stumble or fall, as by catching his foot **4.** a mistake; blunder **5.** *a)* any mechanical contrivance for tripping a part, as a pawl *b)* its action ☆**6.** [Slang] *a)* the hallucinations, sensations, etc. experienced under the influence of a psychedelic drug, esp. LSD *b)* the period or experience of being under such an influence —**trip the light fantastic** to dance

SYN.—**trip** strictly implies a relatively short course of travel, although it is also commonly used as an equivalent for **journey** [a vacation *trip*]; **journey**, a more formal word, generally implies travel of some length, usually over land, and does not necessarily suggest the idea of return [the *journey* was filled with hardships]; **voyage**, in current use, implies a relatively long journey by water [a *voyage* across the Atlantic]; **jaunt** is applied to a short, casual trip taken for pleasure or recreation [a *jaunt* to the city]; **expedition** is applied to a journey, march, etc. taken by an organized group for some definite purpose [a military *expedition*, a zoological *expedition* to Africa]

☆**TRIP** (trip) *adj.* [*tr*(*ansformation-*)*i*(*nduced*) *p*(*lasticity*)] designating or of any of several high-strength, highly ductile steel alloys containing chromium, molybdenum, nickel, and carbon

tri·par·tite (trī pär′tīt) *adj.* [ME. < L. *tripartitus* < *tri-*, three + *partitus*, PARTITE] **1.** divided into three parts; threefold **2.** having three corresponding parts or copies **3.** made or existing between three parties, as an agreement —**tri·par′tite·ly** *adv.*

tri·par·ti·tion (trī′pär tish′ən) *n.* [LL.(Ec.) *tripartitio*] division into three parts or among three parties

tripe (trīp) *n.* [ME. < MFr., prob. ult. < Ar. *tharb*, entrails, a net, lit., fold of fat] **1.** part of the stomach of an ox or similar animal, used as food **2.** [Slang] anything worthless, offensive, etc.; nonsense

tri·per·son·al (trī pur′s'n əl) *adj. Theol.* consisting of or existing in three persons: said of the Godhead

tri·pet·al·ous (-pet′'l əs) *adj.* having three petals

☆**trip·ham·mer** (trip′ham′ər) *n.* a heavy, power-driven hammer, alternately raised and allowed to fall by a tripping device: also **trip hammer**

tri·phen·yl·meth·ane (trī fen′'l meth′ān, -fē′n'l-) *n.* [TRI- + PHENYL + METHANE] a colorless, crystalline hydrocarbon, $CH(C_6H_5)_3$, used in organic synthesis and in making dyes

tri·phib·i·an (trī fib′ē ən) *adj.* [TRI- + (AM)PHIBIAN] **1.** that can function, operate, or carry on

TRIPHAMMER

warfare on land, at sea, or in the air ☆**2.** designating an aircraft that can take off from, or land on, water, land, or snow and ice

triph·thong (trif′thôŋ, trip′-) *n.* [TRI- + (DI)PHTHONG] **1.** a complex vowel sound involving three continuous vowel sounds in one syllable Ex.: *fire* (in the British pronunciation, IPA [faɪə]) **2.** *loose term for* TRIGRAPH —**triph·thon′gal** (-thôŋ′gəl) *adj.*

triph·y·lite (trif′ə līt′) *n.* [altered < earlier *triphyline* < G. *triphylin* < Gr. *tri-*, TRI- + *phylē*, a class, family + G. -*in*, -INE⁴: it contains three bases] a greenish-blue, orthorhombic mineral, Li(Fe,Mn)PO₄, a native phosphate of lithium and iron or manganese

tri·pin·nate (trī pin′āt) *adj. Bot.* bipinnate with each division pinnate, as some fern leaves —**tri·pin′nate·ly** *adv.*

tri·plane (trī′plān′) *n.* an early type of airplane with three sets of wings arranged one above another

tri·ple (trip′'l) *adj.* [Fr. < L. *triplus*: see the v.] **1.** consisting of or including three; threefold **2.** done, used, said, etc. three times; repeated twice **3.** three times as much, as many, as large, etc. **4.** *Music* containing three (or a multiple of three) beats to the measure [*triple* time] —*n.* [ME. < L. *triplus*] **1.** an amount three times as much or as many **2.** a group of three; triad ☆**3.** *Baseball* a hit on which the batter reaches third base —*vt.* **trip′led, trip′ling** [ME. *tryplen* < ML. *triplare* < L. *triplus*, threefold < *tri-*, TRI- + *-plus*, as in *duplus*, DOUBLE] **1.** to make three times as much or as many ☆**2.** *Baseball* to advance (a runner) by hitting a triple —*vi.* **1.** to become three times as much or as many ☆**2.** *Baseball* to hit a triple

Triple Alliance 1. an alliance of England, Sweden, and the Netherlands against France in 1668 **2.** an alliance of Great Britain, France, and the Netherlands against Spain in 1717 **3.** an alliance of Great Britain, Austria, and Russia against France in 1795 **4.** an alliance of Germany, Austria-Hungary, and Italy from 1882 to 1915, chiefly against Russia and France

triple bond *Chem.* the sharing of three pairs of electrons between two atoms in a molecule, usually represented in structural formulas by —C⋮C—

Triple Entente 1. the military understanding reached by Great Britain, France, and Russia before World War I as a counterbalance to the Triple Alliance **2.** these three countries as parties to the understanding

tri·ple-nerved (-nurvd′) *adj. Bot.* having three nerves arising from or near the base, as some leaves

☆**triple play** *Baseball* a single play in which three players are put out

triple point a pressure and temperature combination at which the solid, liquid, and vapor phases of a substance exist in contact and in equilibrium with one another: the triple point of water is 273.16°K

tri·ple-space (-spās′) *vt., vi.* **-spaced′, -spac′ing** to type (copy) so as to leave two full spaces between lines

tri·plet (trip′lit) *n.* [TRIPL(E) + -ET] **1.** a collection or group of three, usually of one kind; specif., *a)* a group of three successive lines of poetry, usually rhyming *b)* a group of three musical notes to be played in the time of two of the same value **2.** *a)* one of three offspring born at a single birth *b)* [*pl.*] three offspring born at a single birth

tri·ple·tail (trip′'l tāl′) *n.* a large food fish (*Lobotes surinamensis*) of warm W Atlantic waters, characterized by long dorsal and anal fins that extend back along the caudal fin giving the effect of a three-lobed tail

☆**triple threat 1.** a football player who is a skillful runner, passer, and kicker **2.** a person who is expert or adept in three fields, skills, etc.

tri·plex (trip′leks, trī′pleks) *adj.* [L. < *tri-*, TRI- + *-plex*: see DUPLEX] triple; threefold —*n.* a thing that is triplex

trip·li·cate (trip′lə kit; *for v.* -kāt′) *adj.* [ME. < L. *triplicatus*, pp. of *triplicare*, to treble < *triplex*: see prec.] **1.** threefold **2.** designating the third of identical copies —*n.* any of three identical copies or things —*vt.* **-cat′ed, -cat′ing** to make three identical copies of —**in triplicate** in three identical copies —**trip′li·ca′tion** *n.*

tri·plic·i·ty (tri plis′ə tē) *n., pl.* **-ties** [ME. *triplicite* < ML. *triplicitas* < L. *triplex*: see TRIPLEX] **1.** the quality or condition of being triple **2.** a group of three **3.** same as TRIGON (sense 3)

trip·lite (trip′līt) *n.* [G. *triplit* < Gr. *triplous*, threefold + G. -*it*, -ITE¹: because of its triple cleavage] a dark-brown, monoclinic mineral, a phosphate of iron and manganese, commonly containing some calcium and magnesium

trip·lo·blas·tic (trip′lō blas′tik) *adj.* [< Gr. *triploos*, triple < *tri-*, TRI- + *-ploos* (see DOUBLE) + BLAST- + -IC] *Zool.* of or pertaining to the metazoan body structure, except that of coelenterates, with three basic cellular layers, the ectoderm, the endoderm, and the mesoderm

trip·loid (trip′loid) *adj.* [< L. *triplus*, TRIPLE + -OID] *Biol.* having three times the haploid number of chromosomes —*n.* a triploid cell or organism —**trip′loi′dy** (-loi′dē) *n.*

tri·ply (trip′lē) *adv.* in a triple amount or degree

tri·pod (trī′päd) *n.* [L. *tripus* (gen. *tripodis*) < Gr. *tripous* < *tri-*, TRI- + *pous*, FOOT] **1.** a three-legged caldron, stool, table, etc. **2.** a three-legged support for a camera,

etc., usually adjustable for height —**trip·o·dal** (trip′ə d'l),
tri·pod·ic (trī päd′ik) *adj.*
trip·o·dy (trip′ə dē) *n.*, *pl.* **-dies** [TRI- + (DI)PODY] a verse
or phrase of three metrical feet
Trip·o·li (trip′ə lē) **1.** former Barbary State on the N
coast of Africa **2.** seaport on the NW coast of Libya &
one of its two capitals: pop. c.170,000 **3.** seaport on the
NW coast of Lebanon: pop. c.100,000 —**Tri·pol·i·tan**
(tri päl′ə t'n) *adj.*, *n.*
trip·o·li (trip′ə lē) *n.* [Fr. < *Tripoli*, town in Syria, from
which it was imported] a usually light-colored, very finely
divided, essentially siliceous material consisting either of
weathered chert or siliceous limestone: used as a polishing
powder: also called **trip′o·lite** (-līt′)
Trip·ol·i·ta·ni·a (trip′äl i tā′nē ə) region of NW Libya,
on the Mediterranean: 110,000 sq. mi.; chief city, Tripoli
tri·pos (trī′päs) *n.* [altered < L. *tripus*, TRIPOD] **1.** orig.,
a tripod **2.** at Cambridge University, *a)* formerly, a
scholar who sat on a three-legged stool at commencement
and disputed humorously with candidates for a degree
b) any examination for the B.A. degree with honors,
orig. in mathematics
trip·per (trip′ər) *n.* a person or thing that trips; specif.,
a) a mechanical part for tripping a cam, pawl, etc.; also,
a tripping device that operates a signal on a railroad
b) [Brit. Colloq.] a person who takes a trip; tourist
trip·pet (-it) *n.* [< TRIP + -ET] a cam or other mechanical
part designed to strike another part at regular intervals
trip·ping (-iŋ) *adj.* moving lightly and quickly; nimble
—**trip′ping·ly** *adv.*
trip·tane (trip′tān) *n.* [contr. < *tripentane*: see TRI- &
PENTANE] a liquid hydrocarbon, C_7H_{16}, a high antiknock
fuel for use in internal-combustion engines, esp. in airplanes
trip·ter·ous (trip′tər əs) *adj.* [TRI- + -PTEROUS] having
three winglike parts, as some fruits or seeds
trip·tych (trip′tik) *n.* [< Gr. *triptychos*, threefold < *tri-*,
TRI- + *ptychē* (gen. *ptychos*), a fold] **1.** an ancient writing
tablet of three leaves hinged together **2.** a set of three
panels with pictures, designs, or carvings, often hinged so
that the two side panels may be folded over the central
one, commonly used as an altarpiece
Tri·pu·ra (trī′poo rä′) territory of NE India: 4,036 sq.
mi.; pop. 1,143,000
☆**trip·wire** (trip′wīr′) *n.* a wire that will set off a trap,
snare, etc. when tripped on unsuspectingly
tri·que·trous (trī kwē′trəs, -kwet′rəs) *adj.* [L. *triquetrus*
< *tri-*, TRI- + **qued-* < IE. base **kwēd-*, to spur, bore,
sharpen, whence OE. *hwæt*, sharp (cf. WHET): hence orig.,
three-pointed] **1.** three-sided; triangular **2.** having a
triangular cross section
tri·ra·di·ate (trī rā′dē it, -āt′) *adj.* having three rays or
raylike projections —**tri·ra′di·ate·ly** *adv.*
tri·reme (trī′rēm) *n.* [L. *triremis*, trireme (orig., having
three banks of oars) < *tri-*, TRI- + *remus*, oar: for IE.
base see ROW²] an ancient Greek or Roman galley, usually
a warship, with three banks of oars on each side
tri·sac·cha·ride (trī sak′ə rīd′) *n.* a carbohydrate yielding
three monosaccharides upon hydrolysis
tri·sect (trī sekt′, trī′sekt) *vt.* [< TRI- + L. *sectus*, pp. of
secare, to cut (see SAW¹)] **1.** to cut into three parts **2.** *Geom.*
to divide into three equal parts —**tri·sec′tion** *n.* —**tri·sec′tor** *n.*
tri·sep·tate (trī sep′tāt) *adj.* [TRI- + SEPTATE] *Biol.* having
three septa, or dividing walls
tri·shaw (trī′shô′) *n.* [< TRI- + (JINRIKI)SHA] same as
PEDICAB
tris·kai·dek·a·pho·bi·a (tris′kī dek′ə fō′bē ə) *n.* [ModL.
< Gr. *triskaideka*, thirteen (< *treis*, THREE + *kai*, and +
deka, TEN) + -*phobia*, -PHOBIA] fear of the number 13
tris·kel·i·on (tris kel′ē än, tris kel′-) *n.*, *pl.* **-i·a** (-ə) [<
Gr. *triskelēs*, three-legged < *tri-*, TRI-
+ *skelos*, a leg < IE. base **(s)kel-*, to
bend, a joint of the body, whence L.
calx, heel, Gr. *kylindros*, a cylinder] a
design, usually symbolic, consisting of
three curved branches or three bent
legs or arms radiating from a center:
also **tris·kele** (tris′kēl, trī′skēl)
Trismegistus *see* HERMES TRISMEGISTUS
tris·mus (triz′məs, tris′-) *n.* [ModL.
< Gr. *trismos*, gnashing of the teeth, a
grinding, akin to *trizein*, to chirp, gnash
< IE. echoic base **(s)trei-*: cf. STRIDENT]
continuous contraction of the muscles
of the jaw, specif. as a symptom of
tetanus, or lockjaw —**tris′mic** *adj.*
tris·oc·ta·he·dron (tris äk′tə hē′drən)
n. [Gr. *tris*, thrice + OCTAHEDRON] an
isometric solid figure or crystal with
twenty-four plane surfaces, every three of which correspond to a single surface of an octahedron imagined as
underlying them: trisoctahedrons are of two kinds, the
trigonal trisoctahedron, having triangular surfaces, and
the **tetragonal trisoctahedron**, or **trapezohedron**, having
quadrilateral surfaces —**tris·oc′ta·he′dral** *adj.*
tri·so·di·um (trī sō′dē əm) *adj.* containing three sodium
atoms in the molecule
tri·so·mic (trī sō′mik) *adj.* [TRI- + -SOM(E)³ + -IC] having
a single extra chromosome in the cell in addition to the

BRONZE FROM IRELAND

SHELL DISK FROM TENNESSEE

GREEK SHIELD

TRISKELIONS

normal diploid number —*n.* a trisomic cell or organism
—**tri·so′my** (-mē) *n.*
Tris·tam (tris′təm) a masculine name: see TRISTRAM
Tris·tan (-tən) a masculine name: see TRISTRAM
Tris·tan da Cun·ha (tris′tən də kōon′yə) group of four
Brit. islands in the South Atlantic, administered as a
dependency of St. Helena: 38 sq. mi.; pop. c.250
‡**triste** (trēst) *adj.* [Fr.] sad; sorrowful
‡**tris·tesse** (trēs tes′) *n.* [Fr.] sadness; melancholy
trist·ful (trist′fool) *adj.* [LME. *trystefull* < *trist*, sad (<
OFr. *triste* < L. *tristis*) + *-ful*, -FUL] [Archaic] sad; sorrowful; melancholy
tris·tich (tris′tik) *n.* [TRI- + (DI)STICH] a group or stanza
of three lines of verse; triplet
tris·tich·ous (tris′ti kəs) *adj.* [Gr. *tristichos*, in three rows
< *tri-*, TRI- + *stichos*, a row (see STICH)] arranged in three
rows, specif. *Bot.* three vertical rows
Tris·tram (tris′trəm) [OFr. *Tristran*, *Tristan*, altered
(after L. *tristis*, sad) < Celt. *Drystan* < *drest*, tumult,
din] **1.** a masculine name: dim. *Tris*; var. *Tristam*,
Tristan **2.** *Medieval Legend* a knight sent to Ireland by
King Mark of Cornwall to bring back the princess Isolde
to be the king's bride: Isolde and Tristram fall in love
and tragically die together; in some versions, Tristram
marries another Isolde, a princess of Brittany
tri·sub·sti·tut·ed (trī sub′stə tōōt′id, -tyōōt′-) *adj.* containing three groups or atoms introduced into the molecule
in place of three original groups or atoms
tri·sul·fide (trī sul′fīd) *n.* a sulfide having three sulfur
atoms to the molecule
tri·syl·la·ble (trī sil′ə b'l, trī′sil′-) *n.* a word of three
syllables —**tri·syl·lab·ic** (trī′si lab′ik) *adj.*
trit. triturate
trite (trīt) *adj.* **trit′er, trit′est** [L. *tritus*, pp. of *terere*, to
rub, wear out < IE. base **ter-*, to rub, bore, whence
THROW, Gr. *tryein*, to wear away] worn out by constant
use; no longer having freshness, originality, or novelty;
stale *[a trite idea, remark, etc.]* —**trite′ly** *adv.* —**trite′ness** *n.*
SYN.—**trite** is applied to something, especially an expression or
idea, which through repeated use or application has lost its original
freshness and impressive force (e.g., "like a bolt from the blue");
hackneyed refers to such expressions which through constant use
have become virtually meaningless (e.g., "last but not least");
stereotyped applies to those fixed expressions which seem invariably to be called up in certain situations (e.g., "I point with pride"
in a political oration); **commonplace** is used of any obvious or
conventional remark or idea (e.g., "it isn't the heat, it's the
humidity") —*ANT.* original, fresh
tri·the·ism (trī′thē iz'm) *n.* [TRI- + THEISM] belief in three
gods; specif., the doctrine that the Christian Father, Son,
and Holy Spirit are three distinct Gods —**tri′the·ist** *n.*
tri·ti·at·ed (trit′ē āt′id, trish′-) *adj.* containing tritium
trit·i·um (trit′ē əm, trish′-) *n.* [ModL. < Gr. *tritos*,
THIRD + L. *-ium*, *n.* suffix] a radioactive isotope of hydrogen having an atomic weight of 3 and a half-life of about
12.5 years: it decays by beta-particle emission and is
used in thermonuclear bombs, as a radioactive tracer, etc.
trit·o·ma (trit′ə ma) *n.* [ModL. < Gr. *tritomos*, cut three
times < *tri-*, THREE + *-tomos*, cut off: see TOME] any of a
genus (*Kniphofia*) of African plants of the lily family, with
dense spikes of red to yellow tubular flowers in the autumn
Tri·ton (trīt′n) [L. < Gr. *Tritōn*] **1.** *Gr. Myth.* *a)* a sea
god, son of Poseidon and Amphitrite, pictured as having
the head and upper body of a man and the tail of a fish
and as carrying a conch-shell trumpet *b)* later, one of
many attendants of the sea gods **2.** the larger of Neptune's
two moons —*n.* [t-] **1.** *a)* any of several large sea snails
(esp. family Cymatiidae) with a long, spiral shell, often
brightly colored *b)* the shell **2.** any of a genus (*Triton*)
of old-world salamanders
tri·ton (trī′tän) *n.* [Gr., neut. of *tritos*, third: for base, see
THREE, THIRD] the nucleus of the tritium atom containing
one proton and two neutrons, used as a projectile in
nuclear reactions
tri·tone (trī′tōn′) *n.* [ML. *tritonum* < Gr. *tritonon*: see
TRI- & TONE] *Music* an interval of three whole tones
trit·u·rate (trich′ə rāt′) *vt.* **-rat′ed, -rat′ing** [< LL.
trituratus, pp. of *triturare*, to grind < L. *triura*, a rubbing
< *tritus*: see TRITE] to rub, crush, or grind into very fine
particles or powder; pulverize —*n.* something triturated;
specif., same as TRITURATION (sense 2) —**trit′u·ra·ble**
(-ər ə b'l) *adj.* —**trit′u·ra′tor** *n.*
trit·u·ra·tion (trich′ə rā′shən) *n.* **1.** a triturating or
being triturated **2.** *Pharmacy* a triturated preparation,
esp. one containing a pulverized mixture of a medicinal
substance with lactose
tri·umph (trī′əmf) *n.* [ME. *triumphe* < OFr. < L. *tri-
′umphus* < OL. *triumpus*, akin to Gr. *thriambos*, hymn to
Bacchus sung in festal processions] **1.** in ancient Rome, a
procession celebrating the return of a victorious general
and his army **2.** the act or fact of being victorious; victory;
success; achievement **3.** exultation or joy over a victory,
achievement, etc. **4.** [Obs.] any public spectacle or celebration —*vi.* [MFr. *triumpher* < L. *triumphare* < the *n.*]
1. to gain victory or success; win mastery **2.** to rejoice
or exult over victory, achievement, etc. **3.** to celebrate a
Roman triumph —*vt.* [Obs.] to conquer —*SYN.* see
VICTORY
tri·um·phal (trī um′f'l) *adj.* **1.** of, or having the nature

of, a triumph **2.** celebrating or commemorating a triumph [a *triumphal* procession]

tri·um·phant (-fənt) *adj.* [L. *triumphans*, prp. of *triumphare*: see TRIUMPH] **1.** successful; victorious **2.** rejoicing for victory; exulting in success; elated **3.** *rare* var. of TRIUMPHAL **4.** [Obs.] magnificent —**tri·um'phant·ly** *adv.*

tri·um·vir (trī um'vər) *n., pl.* **-virs, -vir·i'** (-vi rī') [L., back-formation < *trium virum*, gen. pl. of *tres viri*, three men < *tres*, THREE + *vir*, a man (for IE. base see WERE-WOLF)] **1.** in ancient Rome, any of a group of three administrators sharing authority equally **2.** any of three persons associated in office or authority

tri·um·vi·ral (-əl) *adj.* of a triumvir or triumvirate

tri·um·vi·rate (-it) *n.* [L. *triumviratus*] **1.** the office, functions, or term of a triumvir **2.** government by three men or by a coalition of three parties **3.** any association of three in authority **4.** any group or set of three

tri·une (trī'yōōn) *adj.* [< TRI- + L. *unus*, ONE] being three in one [a *triune* God] —*n.* **1.** same as TRIAD **2.** [T-] same as TRINITY —**tri·u'ni·ty** *n.*

tri·va·lent (trī vā'lənt, triv'ə-) *adj.* [TRI- + -VALENT] **1.** *Biol.* triple: said of a chromosome formed by three homologous chromosomes that lie close together or appear to join completely during meiosis **2.** *Chem. a)* having a valence of three *b)* same as TERVALENT (sense 1) —**tri·va'lence, tri·va'len·cy** *n.*

tri·valve (trī'valv) *adj.* having three valves, as a shell

Tri·van·drum (tri van'drəm) seaport on the Malabar Coast of S India, in Kerala state: pop. 240,000

triv·et (triv'it) *n.* [ME. *trevet* < OE. *trefet* < L. *tripes*, tripod, three-footed < *tri-*, three + *pes*, FOOT] **1.** a three-legged stand for holding pots, kettles, etc. over or near a fire **2.** a short-legged metal or ceramic plate for holding hot dishes on a table

triv·i·a (triv'ē ə) *n.pl.* [*often with sing. v.*] [ModL., back-formation < ff.] unimportant matters; trivialities

triv·i·al (triv'ē əl, triv'yəl) *adj.* [L. *trivialis*, of the cross-roads, hence commonplace < *trivium*, place where three roads meet < *tri-*, three + *via*, a road: see VIA] **1.** unimportant; insignificant; trifling **2.** [Rare] commonplace —*SYN.* see PETTY —**triv'i·al·ism** *n.* —**triv'i·al·ly** *adv.*

triv·i·al·i·ty (triv'ē al'ə tē) *n.* [TRIVIAL + -ITY] **1.** the quality or state of being trivial **2.** *pl.* **-ties** a trivial thing, matter, idea, etc.; trifle

triv·i·al·ize (triv'ē ə līz') *vt., vi.* **-ized', -iz'ing** to regard or treat as trivial; make seem unimportant —**triv'i·al·i·za'tion** *n.*

trivial name 1. a common or vernacular name, as of a plant or animal **2.** formerly, the specific name of an animal or epithet of a plant as distinct from the generic name in binomial nomenclature

triv·i·um (triv'ē əm) *n., pl.* **-i·a** (-ə) [ML. < L.: see TRIVIAL] in the Middle Ages, the lower division of the seven liberal arts; specif., the three arts of grammar, logic, and rhetoric: cf. QUADRIVIUM

tri·week·ly (trī wēk'lē) *adj., adv.* **1.** once every three weeks ☆**2.** three times a week —☆*n., pl.* **-lies** a publication that appears triweekly

-trix (triks) *pl.* **-trix'es, -tri·ces'** (tri sēz', trī'sēz) [L.] *an ending of some feminine nouns of agent, corresponding to* -OR

TRM trademark

Tro·as (trō'as) region surrounding ancient Troy, in NW Asia Minor: also called **the Tro'ad** (-ad)

Tro·bri·and Islands (trō'brē and') group of small islands off SE New Guinea: part of Papua: c.170 sq. mi.

tro·car (trō'kär) *n.* [Fr. *trocart* < *trois* (< L. *tres*, THREE) + *carre*, a side, face < *carrer*, to make square < L. *quadrare* (see QUADRATE): from the shape of the point] a surgical instrument consisting of a sharp stylet enclosed in a tube (*cannula*) and inserted through the wall of a body cavity: the stylet is withdrawn permitting fluid to drain off through the tube: also sp. **tro'char**

tro·cha·ic (trō kā'ik) *adj.* [MFr. *trochaïque* < L. *trochaïcus* < Gr. *trochaïkos*] of or made up of trochees —*n.* **1.** a trochaic verse **2.** same as TROCHEE

tro·chal (trō'k'l) *adj.* [< Gr. *trochos* (see TROCHE) + -AL] *Zool.* resembling a wheel

tro·chan·ter (trō kan'tər) *n.* [Gr. *trochantēr* < *trechein*, to run: see ff.] **1.** any of several jutting processes (in man, two) at the upper end of the femur of many vertebrates **2.** the second segment from the base of an insect leg —**tro·chan'ter·ic** *adj.*

tro·che (trō'kē) *n.* [altered < *trochisk* < Fr. *trochisque* < LL. *trochiscus*, a pill, small ball < Gr. *trochiskos*, a small wheel, lozenge < *trochos*, a wheel < *trechein*, to run < IE. base *dhregh-*, to run, whence OIr. *droch*, a wheel] a small, usually round, medicinal lozenge

tro·chee (trō'kē) *n.* [L. *trochaeus* < Gr. *trochaios*, running < *trechein*, to run: see prec.] a metrical foot of two syllables, the first accented and the other unaccented, as in English verse, or the first long and the other short, as in Latin verse (Ex.: "Pé·tĕr, | pén·cil | púmp·kin | éat·ĕr")

troch·el·minth (träk'l minth') *n.* [< ModL. *Trochelminthes* < Gr. *trochos*, a wheel (see TROCHE) + ModL. *helminthes*, parasitic worms: see HELMINTH] any member

of a former phylum (Trochelminthes) of very small invertebrates, including the rotifers and gastrotrichs

troch·i·lus (träk'i ləs) *n., pl.* **-li'** (-lī') [L. < Gr. *trochilos*, lit., a runner < *trechein*, to run: see TROCHE] **1.** any of various old-world birds, esp. warblers **2.** any of certain hummingbirds

troch·le·a (träk'lē ə) *n., pl.* **-le·ae'** (-lē ē') [ModL. < L., a pulley block < Gr. *trochilia* < *trochos*, a wheel: see TROCHE] *Anat.* a pulley-shaped part or structure, as the lower part of the humerus, which articulates with a corresponding part of the ulna

troch·le·ar (-ər) *adj.* **1.** *Anat.* of, having the nature of, or forming a trochlea **2.** *Bot.* shaped like a pulley; round and contracted in the middle

tro·choid (trō'koid) *n.* [< Gr. *trochoeides*, round like a wheel < *trochos* (see TROCHE) + *eidos*, form (cf. -OID)] a curve produced by any point on the radius, or the radius extended, of a circle rolling along a straight line —*adj.* having a wheellike rotary motion on an axis, as a joint: also **tro·choi'dal**

troch·o·phore (träk'ə fôr') *n.* [Gr. *trochos*, a wheel (see TROCHE) + -PHORE] a free-swimming ciliated larva of several invertebrate groups, including many marine annelid worms, mollusks, brachiopods, nemerteans, etc.

trod (träd) *pt. & alt. pp.* of TREAD

trod·den (-'n) *alt. pp.* of TREAD

trode (trōd) *archaic pt.* of TREAD

☆**trof·fer** (träf'ər) *n.* [altered < TROUGH + -ER] a trough-shaped ceiling recess having the lower surface flush with the ceiling: used esp. to enclose fluorescent lamps

trog·lo·dyte (träg'lə dīt') *n.* [L. *troglodyta* < Gr. *trōglodytēs*, one who creeps into holes, cave dweller < *trōglē*, a hole, cave (< *trōgein*, to gnaw < IE. *trōg-* < base *ter-*, to rub, grind, whence THROW) + *dyein*, to creep in, enter] **1.** any of the prehistoric people who lived in caves; cave man **2.** *a)* a person who chooses to live alone in seclusion; recluse *b)* anyone who lives in a primitive, low, or degenerate fashion **3.** an anthropoid ape —**trog'lo·dyt'ic** (-dit'ik), **trog'lo·dyt'i·cal** *adj.*

tro·gon (trō'gän) *n.* [ModL. < Gr. *trogōn*, gnawing, prp. of *trogein*, to gnaw: see prec.] any of a family (Trogonidae) of bright-colored, fruit-eating tropical birds

troi·ka (troi'kə) *n.* [Russ. < *troe*, three < IE. *troio-* < base *trei-*, THREE] **1.** *a)* a Russian vehicle drawn by a specially trained team of three horses abreast *b)* the team of horses **2.** any group of three; esp., an association of three in authority; triumvirate

Troi·lus (troi'ləs, trō'i ləs) [ME. < L. < Gr. *Trōilos*] *Gr. Legend* a son of King Priam, killed by Achilles: in medieval romance and in works by Boccaccio, Chaucer, and Shakespeare, Troilus was the lover of Cressida

☆**troilus butterfly** [after prec.] a large, black, American swallowtail butterfly (*Papilio troilus*) with yellow spots on the edge of the front wings and blue on the rear

Trois-Ri·vières (trwä rē vyer') city in S Quebec, Canada, on the St. Lawrence: pop. 58,000: Eng. name *Three Rivers*

Tro·jan (trō'jən) *adj.* [ME. *Troyan* < L. *Trojanus* < *Troja*, TROY] of ancient Troy, its people, or culture —*n.* **1.** a native or inhabitant of ancient Troy **2.** a strong, hard-working, determined person **3.** [Obs.] a merry, dissolute companion

Trojan horse 1. *Gr. Legend* a huge, hollow wooden horse filled with Greek soldiers and left at the gates of Troy: when it was brought into the city, the soldiers came out at night and opened the gates to the Greek army, which destroyed the city **2.** any person, group, or thing that seeks to subvert a nation, organization, etc. from within

Trojan War *Gr. Legend* the ten-year war waged against Troy by the Greeks in order to get back King Menelaus' wife, Helen, who had been abducted by Paris

troll[1] (trōl) *vt.* [ME. *trollen*, to roll, troll, wander, prob. < MFr. *troller* < ? MHG. *trollen*, to walk or run with short steps: cf. ff.] **1.** to roll; revolve **2.** [Now Rare] to pass (a vessel) around in drinking **3.** *a)* to sing the parts of (a round, catch, etc.) in succession *b)* to sing lustily or in a full, rolling voice; chant merrily **4.** *a)* to fish for with a moving line, esp. one with a revolving lure trailed behind a moving boat *b)* to move (a lure, bait, etc.) through water in fishing *c)* to fish in (a lake, etc.) by this method —*vi.* **1.** [Now Rare] *a)* to speak fast *b)* to wag: said of the tongue **2.** to sing in a round, catch, etc. **3.** *a)* to sing lustily or in a full, rolling voice *b)* to be uttered in such a voice **4.** to fish with a moving line, esp. one with a revolving lure trailed behind a moving boat **5.** to roll, spin, or whirl —*n.* **1.** a trolling, or moving round **2.** a song having parts sung in succession; round **3.** *a)* the method of trolling in fishing *b)* a lure, or a lure and line, used in trolling —**troll'er** *n.*

troll[2] (trōl) *n.* [ON., prob. < *truzla* < IE. *dreu-*, var. of base *dra-*, to run, whence TRAP[1], MHG. *trollen*, to run with short steps, G. *trolle*, wench: readopted < Norw. by 19th-c. antiquaries] in Scandinavian folklore, any of a race of supernatural beings, variously conceived of as giants or dwarfs, living underground or in caves

trol·ley (träl'ē) *n., pl.* **-leys** [< East Anglian dial. <

TROLL[1] **1.** a wheeled carriage, basket, etc. that runs suspended from an overhead track ☆**2.** an apparatus, as a grooved wheel at the end of a pole, for collecting electric current from an overhead wire and transmitting it to a motor of a streetcar, etc. ☆**3.** a trolley car; streetcar **4.** [Brit.] any of various low carts or trucks —*vt., vi.* **-leyed, -ley·ing** ☆to carry or ride on a trolley car —☆**off one's trolley** [Slang] crazy; insane

☆**trolley bus** an electric bus that gets its motive power from overhead wires by means of trolleys, but does not run on tracks; trackless trolley

☆**trolley car** an electric streetcar that gets its motive power from an overhead wire by means of a trolley

☆**trolley line** an electric streetcar system or route

trol·lop (träl′əp) *n.* [prob. < G. *trolle,* wench: see TROLL²] **1.** [Now Rare] a slovenly, dirty woman; slattern **2.** a sexually promiscuous woman; specif., a prostitute

Trol·lope (träl′əp) **1. Anthony,** 1815–82; Eng. novelist **2. Frances Milton,** 1780–1863; Eng. writer: mother of *prec.*

trol·ly (träl′ē) *n., pl.* **-lies,** *vt., vi.* **-lied, -ly·ing** *var. of* TROLLEY

trom·bi·di·a·sis (träm′bə dī′ə sis) *n.* [ModL. < *Trombidium,* a genus of mites + *-iasis:* see -IASIS] the state of being infested with chiggers: also **trom′bi·di·o′sis** (-dī ō′sis)

trom·bone (träm bōn′, träm′bōn) *n.* [It. < *tromba,* a trumpet < OHG. *trumba:* cf. TRUMP²] a large, brass-wind instrument consisting of a long tube bent parallel to itself twice and ending in a bell mouth: it is of two types, the **slide trombone,** in which different tones are produced by moving the slide, or movable section of the tube, in or out, and the **valve trombone,** played, like the trumpet, with valves —**trom·bon′ist** *n.*

trom·mel (träm′'l) *n.* [G., a drum < MHG. *trumel* < *trume,* of echoic orig.] a sieve, usually a revolving cylindrical one, used in screening ore, coal, etc.

tromp (trämp) *vt., vi. var. of* TRAMP

trompe (trämp) *n.* [Fr., lit., TRUMPET] an apparatus formerly used for producing a blast, as in a blast furnace, by means of water falling through a tube and sucking in air which is diverted to the furnace

TROMBONE

‡**trompe l'oeil** (trōnp lö′y′) [Fr., lit., trick of the eye] **1.** a painting, etc. that creates such a strong illusion of reality that the viewer on first sight is in doubt as to whether the thing depicted is real or a representation **2.** an illusion or effect of this kind

-tron (trän) [Gr. *-tron,* suffix of instrument, akin to L. *-trum*] *a combining form meaning* instrument: used esp. in forming names of devices in electronics and nuclear physics [*calutron*]

tro·na (trō′nə) *n.* [Sw. < Ar. *tron,* contr. < *natrūn:* see NATRON] an impure type of hydrous sodium carbonate, $Na_2CO_3 \cdot NaHCO_3 \cdot 2H_2O$, gray or yellowish-white

Trond·heim (trōn′hām) seaport in C Norway, on an inlet (**Trondheim Fjord**) of the Norwegian Sea: pop. 114,000

troop (trōōp) *n.* [Fr. *troupe* < OFr., back-formation < *troupeau* < ML. *troppus,* a flock < Frank. ***throp,* crowd, akin to OE. *thorp,* village: see THORP] **1.** a group of persons, animals, or, formerly, things; herd, flock, band, etc. **2.** loosely, a great number; lot **3.** [*pl.*] *a*) a body of soldiers *b*) soldiers [45 *troops* were killed] **4.** a subdivision of a cavalry regiment that corresponds to a company of infantry **5.** a unit of Boy Scouts or Girl Scouts under an adult leader **6.** [Archaic] a group of actors; troupe —*vi.* **1.** to gather or go in or as in troops [the crowd *trooping* out of the stadium] **2.** to walk, go, etc. [children *trooping* along the sidewalk] **3.** [Archaic] to associate or consort —*vt.* to form into a troop or troops

SYN.—**troop** is applied to a group of people organized as a unit [a cavalry *troop*], or working or acting together in close cooperation [*troops* of sightseers]; **troupe** is the preferred form with reference to a group of performers, as in the theater, a circus, etc.; **company** is the general word for any group of people associated in any of various ways; **band** suggests a relatively small group of people closely united for some common purpose [a *band* of thieves, a brass *band*]

troop·er (trōō′pər) *n.* [TROOP + -ER] **1.** an enlisted soldier in the cavalry **2.** a cavalry horse **3.** a mounted policeman ☆**4.** [Colloq.] a State policeman **5.** [Chiefly Brit.] a troopship

troop·ship (-ship′) *n.* a ship for carrying troops; transport

☆**troost·ite** (trōōs′tīt) *n.* [after G. *Troost* (1776–1850), U.S. mineralogist] a kind of willemite, occurring in large crystals, in which zinc is partially replaced by manganese

‡**trop** (trō) *adv.* [Fr. < ML. *troppus:* see TROOP] too; too much; too many

trop. 1. tropic **2.** tropical

tro·pae·o·lin (trō pē′ə lin) *n.* [< ff. + -IN(E)⁴: from resembling the hues of the flowers] any of a group of orange or orange-yellow azo dyes: also sp. **tro·pe′o·lin, tro·pe′o·line**

tro·pae·o·lum (-ləm) *n., pl.* **-lums, -la** (-lə) [ModL., name of the genus, dim. < Gr. *tropaion* (see TROPHY): from the shieldlike leaves] *same as* NASTURTIUM

-tro·pal (trə pəl) [< -TROP(E) + -AL] *same as* -TROPIC

trope (trōp) *n.* [L. *tropus* < Gr. *tropos,* a turning, turn, figure of speech (akin to *trope,* a turn) < *trepein,* to turn < IE. base **trep-,* to turn] **1.** *a)* the use of a word in a figurative sense *b)* a figure of speech *c)* figurative language in general **2.** in the medieval church, *a)* the interpolation of a phrase or passage into the authorized service: such passages were later developed into semidramatic dialogues *b)* any such passage

-trope (trōp) [Gr. *-tropos:* see prec.] *a combining form meaning* turning: see -TROPIC

troph·al·lax·is (träf′ə lak′sis) *n., pl.* **-lax′es** (-sēz) [ModL. < Gr. *trophē,* nourishment (see TROPHIC) + *allaxis,* barter < *allassein,* to exchange < *allos,* other: see ELSE] the exchange of regurgitated food, glandular secretions, etc. among members of a colony of social insects: such exchange is thought to also involve message communication —**troph′al·lac′tic** (-lak′tik) *adj.*

troph·ic (träf′ik) *adj.* [Gr. *trophikos* < *trophē,* food < *trephein,* to feed < IE. base **dherebh-,* to coagulate, whence Gr. *thrombos,* a clot] of nutrition; having to do with the processes of nutrition

-troph·ic (träf′ik) *var. of* -TROPIC

tro·phied (trō′fēd) *adj.* decorated with trophies

troph·o- (träf′ō, -ə) [< Gr. *trophē,* nourishment: see TROPHIC] *a combining form meaning* of nutrition [*trophoplasm*]: also, before a vowel, **troph-**

troph·o·blast (träf′ə blast′) *n.* [prec. + -BLAST] a layer of nutritive ectoderm outside the blastoderm, by which the fertilized ovum is attached to the uterine wall and the developing embryo receives its nourishment —**troph′o·blas′tic** *adj.*

troph·o·plasm (-plaz′m) *n.* [TROPHO- + -PLASM] the nutritive or vegetative substance of an organic cell, as fat or yolk granules: cf. IDIOPLASM

troph·o·zo·ite (träf′ə zō′it) *n.* [TROPHO- + ZO- + -ITE¹] a protozoan, esp. of certain parasitic species, during the active feeding and growing stage in contrast with reproductive and infective stages

tro·phy (trō′fē) *n., pl.* **-phies** [MFr. *trophée* < L. *trophaeum,* altered < *tropaeum,* sign of victory < Gr. *tropaion,* a token of an enemy's defeat < *tropaios,* of a rout, turning < *trope,* a turning, defeat < *trepein:* see TROPE] **1.** *a)* in ancient Greece and Rome, a memorial of victory erected on the battlefield or in some public place, orig. a display of captured arms or other spoils *b)* a representation of this on a medal **2.** an architectural ornament representing a group of weapons **3.** something taken from the enemy and kept as a memorial of victory, as captured arms **4.** a lion's skin, deer's head, etc. displayed as evidence of hunting prowess **5.** a prize, usually a silver cup, awarded in a sports contest or other competition **6.** any memento

-tro·phy (trə fē) [Gr. *-trophia* < *trephein,* to nourish: see TROPHIC] *a combining form meaning* nutrition, nourishment, growth [*hypertrophy*]

trop·ic (träp′ik) *n.* [ME. *tropik* < LL. *tropicus* < Gr. *tropikos,* belonging to a turn (of the sun at the solstices) < *trope:* see TROPE] **1.** *Astron.* either of two circles of the celestial sphere parallel to the celestial equator, one, the **Tropic of Cancer,** c. 23 1/2° north, and the other, the **Tropic of Capricorn,** c. 23 1/2° south: they are the limits of the apparent north - and - south journey of the sun **2.** *Geog.* either of two parallels of latitude (**Tropic of Cancer** and **Tropic of Capricorn**) situated on either side of the earth's equator that correspond to the astronomical tropics **3.** [*also* T-] [*pl.*] the region of the earth lying between these latitudes; Torrid Zone —*adj.* of the tropics; tropical

THE TROPICS

-trop·ic (träp′ik, trō′pik) [< Gr. *-tropos,* turning (< *trepein:* see TROPE) + -IC] *a combining form meaning* turning, changing, or otherwise responding to (a specified kind of) stimulus [*phototropic*]

trop·i·cal (träp′i k'l) *adj.* **1.** of, in, characteristic of, or suitable for the tropics **2.** very hot; sultry; torrid **3.** [L. *tropicus* < Gr. *tropikos*] of, or having the nature of, a trope; figurative —**trop′i·cal·ly** *adv.*

tropical cyclone *Meteorol.* a cyclone, originating over tropical seas, ranging in diameter from 60 to 1,000 miles and developing winds up to 200 miles per hour

tropical fish any of various usually brightly colored fish, orig. from the tropics, kept in an aquarium (**tropical aquarium**) maintained at a constant, warm temperature

tropical year *see* YEAR (sense 2)

Tropical Zone *same as* TORRID ZONE

tropic bird any of a genus (*Phaëthon*) of tropical sea birds, related to the pelicans and characterized by white plumage with black markings and a pair of long tail feathers

Tropic of Cancer (or **Capricorn**) *see* TROPIC (*n.* 1 & 2)

tro·pine (trō′pēn) *n.* [< (A)TROPINE] a poisonous, colorless heterocyclic alkaloid, C₈H₁₅ON, produced by the hydrolysis of atropine or hyoscyamine

tro·pism (trō′piz'm) *n.* [< ff.] 1. the tendency of a plant, animal, or part to grow or turn in response to an external stimulus, either by attraction or repulsion, as a sunflower turns toward light 2. any movement, action, etc. in response to stimuli —**tro·pis′tic** *adj.*

-tro·pism (trə piz'm) [< -TROP(E) + -ISM] *a combining form meaning* tropism, tendency to turn or grow toward or away from (something specified) [*heliotropism*]

tro·pol·o·gy (trō päl′ə jē) *n.* [LL. *tropologia* < LGr. *tropologia*: see TROPE & -LOGY] 1. the use of tropes or figurative language 2. a method of considering or interpreting Scripture in a figurative, moralistic way rather than in a literal sense 3. *pl.* -gies a treatise on figurative language —**trop·o·log·i·cal** (träp′ə läj′i k'l) *adj.* —**trop′o·log′i·cal·ly** *adv.*

trop·o·pause (träp′ə pôz′, trō′pə-) *n.* [TROPO(SPHERE) + PAUSE] a transition zone between the troposphere and the stratosphere, at which the drop in temperature with increasing height ceases

tro·poph·i·lous (trō päf′ə ləs) *adj.* [< Gr. *tropos*, a turning (see TROPE) + -PHILOUS] *Bot.* able to adjust to conditions of heat or cold, dryness or moisture, etc., as in seasonal changes: said of plants

trop·o·phyte (träp′ə fīt′, trō′pə-) *n.* [< Gr. *tropos*, a turning (see TROPE) + -PHYTE] any tropophilous plant, as a deciduous tree —**trop′o·phyt′ic** (-fit′ik) *adj.*

☆**trop·o·scat·ter** (-skat′ər) *n. same as* TROPOSPHERIC SCATTER

trop·o·sphere (-sfir′) *n.* [Fr. *troposphère* < Gr. *tropos*, a turning (see TROPE) + Fr. *sphère* (see SPHERE)] the atmosphere from the earth's surface to the tropopause, about 12 miles in extent at the equator and 6 miles at the poles: in this stratum clouds form, convective disturbances occur, and the temperature usually decreases with the altitude —**trop′o·spher′ic** (-sfer′ik, -sfir′-) *adj.*

☆**tropospheric scatter** scattering in the earth's troposphere, used in scatter communication at VHF and UHF for ranges beyond line of sight

-tro·pous (trə pəs) [< Gr. *tropos*, a turning (see TROPE) + -OUS] *a combining form meaning* turning or turned (in a specified way or in response to a specified stimulus): used in forming botanical terms [*phototropous*]

‡**trop·po** (trôp′pō) *adv.* [It. < Fr. *trop*: see TROP] too; too much so: used in musical directions (Ex.: *adagio ma non troppo*, slowly but not too much so)

-tro·py (trə pē) [< Gr. *tropē*: see TROPE] *same as* -TROPISM

Tros·sachs (träs′əks) valley in SW Perth, Scotland

trot (trät) *vi.* **trot′ted, trot′ting** [ME. *trotten* < OFr. *troter* < OHG. *trottōn*, to tread: for base see TREAD] 1. to move, ride, drive, run, or go at a trot 2. to move quickly; hurry; run —*vt.* to cause to go at a trot —*n.* 1. a gait of a horse, etc. in which the legs are lifted in alternating diagonal pairs 2. a jogging gait of a person, between a walk and a run 3. the sound of a trotting horse 4. *same as* TROTLINE 5. a horse race for trotters 6. [Rare] a small child; tot ☆7. [Slang] *same as* PONY (*n.* 3) 8. [Archaic] an old woman: a contemptuous term —**the trots** [Slang] a case of diarrhea —**trot out** [Colloq.] 1. to bring out for others to see or admire 2. to submit for approval

troth (trôth, trōth, träth) *n.* [ME. *trouthe* (see TRUTH) with specialized form & meaning] [Archaic] 1. faithfulness; loyalty 2. truth: chiefly in phrase **in troth**, truly; indeed 3. one's pledged word; promise: see also PLIGHT ONE'S TROTH at entry PLIGHT —*vt.* [Archaic] to pledge to marry

troth·plight (-plīt′) *n.* [Archaic] betrothal —*adj.* [Archaic] betrothed —*vt.* [Archaic] to betroth

trot·line (trät′līn′) *n.* [TROT + LINE¹] a strong fishing line suspended over the water, with short, baited lines hung from it at intervals

Trot·sky (trät′skē; *Russ.* trôt′skē), **Leon** (born *Lev Davidovich Bronstein*) 1879-1940; *Russ.* revolutionist; commissar of war (1918-24) under Lenin: exiled (1929) —**Trot′sky·ism** *n.* —**Trot′sky·ist, Trot′sky·ite′** *adj.*

trot·ter (trät′ər) *n.* 1. an animal that trots; esp., a horse bred and trained for trotting races 2. a person who moves about energetically and constantly 3. the foot of a sheep or pig used as food

tro·tyl (trō′til) *n.* [(TRINI)TROT(OLUENE) + -YL] *same as* TRINITROTOLUENE

trou·ba·dour (trōo′bə dôr′) *n.* [Fr. < Pr. *trobador* < trobar, to find, compose in verse < VL. *tropare* < ? L. *tropus*, TROPE] 1. any of a class of lyric poets and poet-musicians who lived in Provence, Catalonia, southern France, and northern Italy in the 11th, 12th, and 13th cent. and wrote poems of love and chivalry, usually with intricate stanza form and rhyme scheme 2. loosely, any minstrel

trou·ble (trub′'l) *vt.* **-bled, -bling** [ME. *trublen* < OFr. *trubler* < VL. *turbulare*, altered (after L. *turbula*, disorderly group, dim. of *turba*, crowd) < LL. *turbidare*, to trouble, make turbid < L. *turbidus*, TURBID] 1. to disturb or agitate [*troubled* waters] 2. to cause mental agitation to; worry; harass; perturb; vex 3. to cause pain or discomfort to; afflict [*troubled* by her back] 4. to cause difficulty or inconvenience to; incommode [don't *trouble* yourself to rise] 5. to pester, annoy, tease, bother, etc. —*vi.* 1. to make an effort; take pains; bother [don't *trouble* to return it] 2. to be distressed; worry —*n.* 1. a state of mental distress; worry 2. *a)* a misfortune; calamity; mishap *b)* a distressing or difficult happening or situation *c)* a condition of being out of order, needing repair, etc. [tire *trouble*] 3. a person, circumstance, or event that causes annoyance, distress, difficulty, etc. 4. public disturbance; civil disorder 5. effort; bother; pains [to take the *trouble* to look it up] 6. an illness; ailment; disease —**in trouble** [Colloq.] pregnant when unmarried —**trouble** (someone) **for** to ask (someone) to pass (something) —**trou′bler** *n.*

trou·ble·mak·er (-mā′kər) *n.* a person who habitually makes trouble for others; esp., one who incites others to quarrel, rebel, etc. —**trou′ble·mak′ing** *n.*

☆**trou·ble·shoot·er** (-shōōt′ər) *n.* 1. a person who locates and repairs mechanical breakdowns 2. a person charged with locating and eliminating the source of trouble in any flow of work —**trou′ble·shoot′ing** *n.*

trou·ble·some (-səm) *adj.* characterized by or causing trouble, irritation, inconvenience, etc. —**trou′ble·some·ly** *adv.* —**trou′ble·some·ness** *n.*

trou·blous (trub′ləs) *adj.* [ME. *troubelous* < OFr. *troubleus*] [Chiefly Literary] 1. troubled; agitated; disturbed; unsettled 2. *same as* TROUBLESOME

trou-de-loup (trōo′də lōo′) *n., pl.* **trous′-de-loup′** (trōo′-) [Fr., wolf hole] *Mil.* any of the conical pits with a vertical pointed stake in the center of each, formerly built in rows as an obstacle to the enemy, esp. to enemy cavalry

trough (trôf; *occas.* trôth, trō) *n.* [ME. < OE. *trog*, akin to G. *trog* < IE. *druk-* < base *deru-*, TREE: basic sense, "hollowed wooden object"] 1. a long, narrow, open container of wood, stone, etc. for holding water or food for animals 2. any similarly shaped vessel, as one for kneading or washing something 3. a channel or gutter, esp. one under the eaves of a building, for carrying off rain water 4. a long, narrow hollow or depression, as between waves 5. a low in an economic cycle 6. a long, narrow area of low barometric pressure

trounce (trouns) *vt.* **trounced, trounc′ing** [< ?] 1. to beat; thrash; flog 2. [Colloq.] to defeat —**trounc′er** *n.*

☆**troupe** (trōop) *n.* [Fr., a troop] a troop, esp. of actors, singers, etc.; company —*vi.* **trouped, troup′ing** to travel as a member of such a company —*SYN.* see TROOP

☆**troup·er** (trōo′pər) *n.* 1. a member of a troupe 2. an experienced, dependable actor

troup·i·al (trōo′pē əl) *n.* [Fr. *troupiale* < *troupe* (see TROOP): from their gregarious habit] any of a new-world family (Icteridae) of gregarious birds including the bobolinks, blackbirds, and orioles; specif., a large, orange and black oriole (*Icterus icterus*) of Central and South America

trou·sers (trou′zərz) *n.pl.* [lengthened (prob. after DRAWERS) < obs. *trouse* < ScotGael. *triubhas*: cf. TREWS] an outer garment, esp. for men and boys, extending from the waist generally to the ankles, and divided into separate coverings for the legs; pants —**trou′ser** *adj.*

trous·seau (trōo′sō, trōo sō′) *n., pl.* **-seaux** (-sōz), **-seaus** [Fr. < OFr., dim. of *trousse*, a bundle (see TRUSS)] a bride's outfit of clothes, linen, etc.

trout (trout) *n., pl.* **trout, trouts**: see PLURAL, II, D, 2 [ME. *troute* < OE. *truht* < LL. *tructus*, *tructa* < Gr. *trōktēs*, kind of fish < *trōgein*, to gnaw: see TROGLODYTE] 1. any of various food and game fishes (genera *Salmo, Salvelinus*, and *Cristivomer*) of the salmon family, usually spotted, smaller than the related salmons, and found chiefly in fresh water: the most common types in N. America are the brown trout, rainbow trout, brook trout, and lake trout 2. any of several unrelated troutlike fishes

☆**trout lily** *same as* DOGTOOTH VIOLET (sense 1)

☆**trout-perch** (-purch′) *n., pl.* **-perch′, -perch′es**: see PLURAL, II, D, 2 [TROUT + PERCH¹] either of two small freshwater fishes having both spiny and fleshy fins, specif. a species (*Percopsis omiscomaycus*) of Canada and the E U.S. and a species (*Percopsis transmontana*) of the Columbia River basin

trou·vère (trōo ver′) *n.* [Fr. < OFr. *trovere* < *trover*, to find, compose (akin to Pr. *trobar*: see TROUBADOUR)] any of a class of narrative poets in N France from the 11th to the 14th cent.: also **trou·veur′** (-vur′)

Trou·ville (trōo vēl′) resort town in NW France, on the English Channel: pop. 7,000: also **Trou·ville′-sur′-Mer′** (-sür′mer′)

trove (trōv) *n.* short for TREASURE-TROVE

tro·ver (trō′vər) *n.* [substantive use of OFr. *trover*, to find: see TROUVÈRE] *Law* 1. orig., an action against a person who found another's goods and refused to return them 2. an action to recover damages for goods withheld or used by another illegally

trow (trō, trou) *vi., vt.* [ME. *trowen* < OE. *treowian*, to have trust in (akin to G. *trauen*) < *treow*, faith, belief: see TRUE] [Archaic] to believe, think, suppose, etc.

trow·el (trou′əl) *n.* [ME. *truel* < MFr. *truelle* < LL. *truella* for L. *trulla,* small ladle, scoop, trowel < *trua,* stirring spoon, ladle, prob. < IE. base **twer-,* to stir, whence TURBID] any of several small hand tools for spreading, smoothing, scooping, etc.; specif., *a)* a tool with a thin, flat, rectangular blade, used for smoothing plaster *b)* a tool with a thin, flat, pointed blade for applying and shaping mortar, as in bricklaying *c)* a tool with a pointed scoop for loosening soil, digging holes, etc. in a garden —*vt.* **-eled** or **-elled, -el·ing** or **-el·ling** to spread, smooth, shape, dig, etc. with a trowel

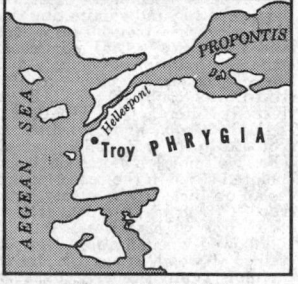

TROWELS
(A, brick; B, garden)

Troy (troi) [L. *Troja* < Gr. *Trōia,* after *Trōs,* father of *Ilos:* see ILIAD] **1.** ancient Phrygian city in Troas, NW Asia Minor: scene of the Trojan War **2.** [after prec.] *a)* city in E N.Y., on the Hudson: pop. 63,000: see SCHENECTADY *b)* city in SE Mich.: suburb of Detroit: pop. 39,000

troy (troi) *adj.* by or in troy weight

Troyes (trwä) city in NE France, on the Seine: pop. 67,000

Troyes, Chrétien de see CHRÉTIEN DE TROYES

troy weight [ME., after TROYES, where first used at medieval fairs] a system of weights for gold, silver, precious stones, etc.: see TABLES OF WEIGHTS AND MEASURES in Supplements

tru·an·cy (trōō′ən sē) *n.* **1.** *pl.* **-cies** the act or an instance of playing truant **2.** the state of being truant; truant behavior Also **tru′ant·ry,** *pl.* **-ries**

tru·ant (-ənt) *n.* [ME. < OFr., a beggar, vagabond < Celt., as in Ir. *trōgán,* dim. of *truag,* wretched] **1.** formerly, a lazy, idle person **2.** a pupil who stays away from school without permission **3.** a person who shirks or neglects his work or duties —*adj.* **1.** that is a truant; that plays truant **2.** idle; shiftless **3.** characteristic of a truant; errant; straying —*vi.* to be or play truant

☆**truant officer** a school official who deals with cases of truancy: term now generally replaced by *attendance officer*

truce (trōōs) *n.* [ME. *trewes,* pl. of *trewe,* a pledge < OE. *treow,* compact, faith; akin to *treowe,* TRUE] **1.** a temporary cessation of warfare by agreement between the belligerents; armistice; cease-fire **2.** any pause in or respite from quarreling, conflict, trouble, etc.

Tru·cial O·man (trōō′shəl ō′ män′) region in E Arabia, on the coast (**Trucial Coast**) of the Persian Gulf

Trucial States seven semi-independent Arab sheikdoms in Trucial Oman, under Brit. protection: 32,300 sq. mi.; pop. 130,000

truck[1] (truk) *n.* [prob. < L. *trochus,* a hoop < Gr. *trochos,* a wheel, disk: see TROCHE] **1.** a small, solid wheel or roller, esp. one for a gun carriage **2.** a small wooden block or disk with holes for halyards, esp. one at the top of a flagpole or mast **3.** a kind of barrow, consisting of an open frame with a pair of wheels at one end and handles at the other, used to carry trunks, crates, etc.: also called **hand truck 4.** any of various low frames or platforms on wheels, sometimes motor-driven, for carrying heavy articles, as in a warehouse ☆**5.** an automotive vehicle for hauling loads along highways, streets, etc.; motor truck **6.** a swiveling frame with two or more pairs of wheels, usually provided with brakes and springs, forming the wheel unit under each end of a railroad car, streetcar, etc. **7.** [Brit.] an open railroad freight car —*vt.* to carry or transport on a truck or trucks —*vi.* **1.** to do trucking **2.** to drive a truck as one's work

truck[2] (truk) *vt., vi.* [ME. *trukken* < MFr. *troquer,* to exchange, barter < ?] **1.** to exchange; barter **2.** [Rare] to peddle —*n.* [Anglo-Fr. *truke* < MFr. *troque* < the *v.*] **1.** *same as* BARTER **2.** payment of wages in goods produced instead of money **3.** small commercial articles **4.** small articles of little value ☆**5.** vegetables raised for sale in markets **6.** [Colloq.] dealings [have no further *truck* with them] **7.** [Colloq.] trash; rubbish

truck·age (truk′ij) *n.* **1.** transportation of goods by truck **2.** the charge for this

truck·er[1] (-ər) *n.* **1.** a person who drives a truck; truck driver **2.** a person or company engaged in trucking

truck·er[2] (-ər) *n.* ☆**1.** a truck farmer **2.** a person who sells commodities or engages in barter

☆**truck farm** a farm where vegetables are grown to be marketed —**truck farmer** —**truck farming**

truck·ing (-iŋ) *n.* the business or process of carrying goods by truck

truck·le (truk′'l) *n.* [ME. *trocle* < L. *trochlea,* a pulley, roller: see TROCHLEA] **1.** orig., a small wheel or caster **2.** *clipped form of* TRUCKLE BED —*vi.* **-led, -ling** [< TRUCKLE (BED): with reference to its low position] to be servile; cringe, submit, toady, etc. (usually with *to*) —*vt.* [Archaic] to move on small wheels or casters

truckle bed *same as* TRUNDLE BED

truck·man (truk′mən) *n., pl.* **-men** *same as* TRUCKER[1]

truck system the system of payment by truck (see TRUCK[2], *n.* 2)

truc·u·lent (truk′yoo lənt) *adj.* [< L. *truculentus* < *trux* (gen. *trucis*), fierce, savage] **1.** fierce; cruel; savage; ferocious **2.** rude, harsh, mean, scathing, etc.: said esp. of speech or writing **3.** pugnacious or bellicose —**truc′u·lence, truc′u·len·cy** *n.* —**truc′u·lent·ly** *adv.*

Tru·deau (trōō dō′; *Fr.* trü dō′) **Pierre Elliott** 1921–   ; prime minister of Canada (1968–   )

trudge (truj) *vi.* **trudged, trudg′ing** [< ?] to walk, esp. wearily or laboriously —*n.* a walk or tramp, esp. a wearying, tedious one —**trudg′er** *n.*

trudg·en stroke (truj′ən) [after John *Trudgen,* Eng. amateur who introduced it (1868) from Argentina] a swimming stroke in which a double overarm motion and a scissors kick are used: also **trudg′en** *n.*

true (trōō) *adj.* **tru′er, tru′est** [ME. *treue* < OE. *treowe,* akin to G. *treu* < IE. **drew-,* TREE: basic sense "firm (as a tree)"] **1.** faithful; loyal; constant **2.** reliable; certain [a *true* indication] **3.** in accordance with fact; that agrees with reality; not false **4.** *a)* conforming to an original, pattern, rule, standard, etc. *b)* exact; accurate; right; correct **5.** rightful; lawful; legitimate [the *true* heirs] **6.** accurately fitted, placed, or shaped [a door that is not *true* to the frame] **7.** *a)* real; genuine; authentic [a *true* diamond] *b)* conforming to the ideal character or having all the basic characteristics of such; rightly so called [a *true* scholar] **8.** determined by the poles of the earth's axis, not by the earth's magnetic poles [*true* north] **9.** [Archaic] honest, virtuous, or truthful —*adv.* **1.** in a true manner; truly, truthfully, accurately, etc. **2.** *Biol.* in accordance with the parental type; without variation [a plant that breeds *true*] —*vt.* **trued, tru′ing** or **true′ing** to make true; esp., to fit, place, or shape accurately —*n.* that which is true; truth or reality (with *the*) —**come true** to happen according to prediction or expectation; become a realized fact—**in true** properly set, adjusted, etc.; exact —**out of true** not properly set, adjusted, etc.; inexact —**true to form** behaving as might be expected —**true up** to fit, place, or shape accurately —**true′ness** *n.*

SYN.—**true, actual,** and **real** are often used interchangeably to imply correspondence with fact, but in discriminating use, **true** implies conformity with a standard or model [a *true* democrat] or with what actually exists [a *true* story], **actual** stresses existence or occurrence and is, hence, strictly applied to concrete things [*actual* and hypothetical examples], and **real** implies conformity between what something is and what it seems or pretends to be [*real* rubber, *real* courage]

true bill a bill of indictment endorsed by a grand jury as supported by evidence sufficient to warrant a trial

true-blue (trōō′blōō′) *adj.* very loyal; staunch

true-born (-bôrn′) *adj.* being genuinely such, specif. by birth [a *trueborn* New Yorker]

true-bred (-bred′) *adj.* same as: **1.** WELL-BRED **2.** PURE-BRED

true fruit *Bot.* a fruit derived from a single carpel or from the united carpels of a single flower

true-heart·ed (-härt′id) *adj.* **1.** loyal; faithful **2.** honest or sincere —**true′heart′ed·ness** *n.*

true level an imaginary surface that is perpendicular at every point to the plumb line, or line of gravity; specif., the mean sea level, or the geoid of the earth

true-life (-līf′) *adj.* corresponding to what happens in real life; true to reality [a *true-life* story]

true·love (-luv′) *n.* **1.** a person who loves or is loved truly; (one's) sweetheart **2.** *same as* HERB PARIS

truelove knot a kind of bowknot that is hard to untie, a symbol of lasting love: also **true′-lov′er's knot**

true·pen·ny (-pen′ē) *n., pl.* **-nies** [Archaic] an honest or trusty person

true ribs ribs that are attached by cartilage directly to the sternum; in man, the upper seven pairs of ribs

truf·fle (truf′'l, trōō′f'l) *n.* [< Fr. *truffe* < OIt. *truffa* < VL. **trufera* < Oscan-Umbrian **tufer,* for L. *tuber,* a knob, mushroom, truffle: see TUBER] any of a number of related fleshy, edible, potato-shaped, ascomycetous fungi that grow underground; esp., any of a European genus (*Tuber*) regarded as a delicacy

trug (trug) *n.* [prob. via Scand. < base akin to TRAY, TROUGH] [Brit.] a shallow, broad, gardener's basket made of strips of wood, for carrying flowers, vegetables, etc.

tru·ism (trōō′iz'm) *n.* a statement the truth of which is obvious and needs no proof; commonplace —**SYN.** see PLATITUDE —**tru·is′tic** *adj.*

Tru·jil·lo (trōō hē′yō) city in NW Peru: pop. 115,000

Truk Islands (truk, trook) island group in the E Caroline Islands, W Pacific: c.40 sq. mi.; pop. 27,000

trull (trul) *n.* [< G. *trulle* (via thieves' slang) < earlier *trolle:* see TROLL[2]] a prostitute or trollop

tru·ly (trōō′lē) *adv.* **1.** in a true manner; accurately, genuinely, faithfully, factually, etc. **2.** really; indeed:

often used as an interjection of surprise, confirmation, etc.
3. sincerely: used in the formal complimentary close of a letter [*yours truly*, very *truly yours*] **4.** rightfully; legally

Tru·man (trōō′mən), **Harry S** 1884– ; 33d president of the U.S. (1944–53)

Trum·bull (trum′b'l) **1. John**, 1756–1843; U.S. painter **2. Jonathan**, 1710–85; Am. Revolutionary patriot: father of *prec.*

trump[1] (trump) *n.* [altered < TRIUMPH (cf. Fr. *triomphe*, It. *trionfo*, a trump)] **1.** *a)* any playing card of a suit that ranks higher than any other suit during the playing of a hand: a trump can take any card of any other suit **2.** [*occas. pl.*, *with sing. v.*] a suit of trumps **3.** any advantage held in reserve until needed **4.** [Colloq.] a fine person, good fellow, etc. —*vt.* **1.** to take (a trick, another card, etc.) by playing a trump **2.** to surpass; outdo —*vi.* to play a trump —**trump up** to devise or make up (a charge against a person, etc.) fraudulently

trump[2] (trump) *n.*, *vt.*, *vi.* [ME. *trumpe* < OFr. *trompe*, prob. < OHG. *trumba*, of echoic orig.] *archaic or poet.* *var. of* TRUMPET

trumped-up (trumpt′up′) *adj.* fraudulently devised or concocted; false

trump·er·y (trum′pər ē) *n.*, *pl.* **-er·ies** [ME. *trompery* < MFr. *tromperie* < *tromper*, to deceive, cheat < ? *tromper*, to play the trumpet: cf. TRUMP[2]] **1.** something showy but worthless **2.** nonsense; rubbish —*adj.* showy but worthless; trashy; paltry

trum·pet (trum′pit) *n.* [ME. *trompette* < MFr., dim. of *trompe*: see TRUMP[2]] **1.** a brass-wind instrument with a blaring tone, consisting of a tube in an oblong loop or loops, with a flared bell at one end, a cupped mouthpiece at the other, and three valves for producing changes in tone **2.** a person who plays the trumpet **3.** something shaped like a trumpet; esp., *same as* EAR TRUMPET ☆**4.** [*pl.*] a pitcher plant (*Sarracenia flava*) of the SE U.S., with slender, erect, hollow leaves **5.** a sound like that of a trumpet, esp. one made by an elephant **6.** a trumpet-toned organ stop —*vi.* **1.** to blow a trumpet **2.** to make a sound like a trumpet —*vt.* **1.** to sound on a trumpet **2.** to sound or utter with a trumpetlike tone **3.** to proclaim loudly

TRUMPET

☆**trumpet creeper 1.** a high-climbing vine (*Campsis radicans*) of the S U.S., with red, trumpet-shaped flowers **2.** a related vine (*Campsis chinensis*) of China

trum·pet·er (-ər) *n.* **1.** *a)* orig., a soldier, herald, etc. who signals on a trumpet *b)* any person who plays the trumpet, as in a band or orchestra **2.** a person who proclaims or heralds something **3.** any of several long-legged, long-necked, cranelike, S. American birds (family Psophiidae) having a loud cry ☆**4.** *same as* TRUMPETER SWAN **5.** any of a breed of domestic pigeons with feathered feet and a rounded crest **6.** any of numerous ocean fishes (order Gasterosteiformes) with a tubular snout

☆**trumpeter swan** a N. American wild swan (*Cygnus buccinator*) with a loud, resonant cry

trumpet flower 1. any of a number of plants with trumpet-shaped flowers, as the trumpet creeper and the trumpet honeysuckle **2.** the flower of any of these

☆**trumpet honeysuckle** an American honeysuckle (*Lonicera sempervirens*) with trumpet-shaped flowers

☆**trumpet vine** any of various plants having trumpet-shaped flowers, as the trumpet creeper

trum·pet·weed (-wēd′) *n.* any of several eupatoriums, as joe-pye weed or boneset

trun·cate (truŋ′kāt) *vt.* **-cat·ed, -cat·ing** [< L. *truncatus*, pp. of *truncare*, to cut off < *truncus*, a stem, TRUNK] to cut off a part of; shorten by cutting; lop —*adj.* **1.** *same as* TRUNCATED **2.** *Biol.* having a square, flattened, or broad end: see LEAF, illus. **3.** *Zool.* lacking a normal apex, as some snail shells —**trun·ca′tion** *n.*

trun·cat·ed (-id) *adj.* **1.** cut short or appearing as if cut short **2.** *a)* cut off or replaced by a plane face: said of the angles or edges of a crystal or solid figure *b)* having its angles or edges cut off or replaced in this way: said of the crystal or solid figure **3.** having the vertex cut off by a plane: said of a cone or pyramid **4.** *same as* TRUNCATE (*adj.* 2 & 3)

trun·cheon (trun′chən) *n.* [ME. *tronchoun* < OFr. *tronchon* < VL. **truncio* < L. *truncus*, a stem, TRUNK] **1.** a short, thick cudgel; club **2.** any staff or baton of authority **3.** [Chiefly Brit.] a policeman's stick or billy **4.** [Archaic] the shaft of a spear **5.** [Obs.] a trunk or stem, esp. one with the branches lopped off —*vt.* to beat with a truncheon

trun·dle (trun′d'l) *n.* [altered < earlier *trendle* < OE. *trendel*, a ring, circle < *trendan*, to roll: see TREND] **1.** a small wheel or caster **2.** *clipped form of* TRUNDLE BED **3.** *a)* *same as* LANTERN PINION *b)* any of its bars **4.** [Obs.] a small cart or truck with low wheels —*vt.*, *vi.* **-dled, -dling 1.** to roll along **2.** to move along in a wheeled vehicle **3.** to rotate —**trun′dler** *n.*

trundle bed a low bed on small wheels or casters, that can be rolled under another bed when not in use

trunk (truŋk) *n.* [ME. *tronke* < OFr. *tronc* < L. *truncus*, a stem, trunk < *truncus*, maimed, mutilated < IE. **tronkus* < base **trenk-*, to press together, crowd, whence THRONG] **1.** the main stem of a tree **2.** the body of a human being or animal, not including the head and limbs **3.** the thorax of an insect **4.** the main body or stem of a nerve, blood vessel, etc., as distinguished from its branches **5.** a long, flexible snout or proboscis, as of an elephant **6.** a large, reinforced box or chest for carrying a traveler's clothing, etc., a salesman's samples, or the like **7.** a large, long, boxlike pipe, shaft, etc. for conveying air, water, etc. **8.** [*pl.*] *same as* TRUNK HOSE ☆**9.** [*pl.*] shorts worn by men for athletics, esp. for boxing or swimming ☆**10.** *clipped form of* TRUNK LINE ☆**11.** a compartment in an automobile, usually in the rear, for holding a spare tire, luggage, etc. **12.** *Archit.* the shaft of a column **13.** *Naut. a)* the part of a cabin above the upper deck *b)* a boxlike or funnellike casing, as for a centerboard, for connecting upper and lower hatches, etc.

trunk·fish (-fish′) *n.*, *pl.* **-fish**, **-fish′es:** see FISH[2] any of a family (Ostraciidae) of tropical fishes whose bodies are encased in fused, bony plates, with only the mouth, eyes, fins, and tail projecting through

trunk hose full, baggy breeches reaching about halfway down the thigh, worn in the 16th and 17th cent.

☆**trunk line** a main line of a railroad, canal, telephone system, etc.

trun·nel (trun′'l) *n.* *same as* TREENAIL

trun·nion (trun′yən) *n.* [Fr. *trognon*, a stump, trunk] **1.** either of two projecting journals or gudgeons on each side of a cannon, on which it pivots **2.** either of any similar pair of pins or pivots

truss (trus) *vt.* [ME. *trussen* < OFr. *trousser*, to bundle together, pack < ? VL. **torsare* < **torsus*, for L. *tortus*, pp. of *torquere*, to twist: cf. TORT] **1.** orig., to tie into a bundle **2.** to tie or bind (often with *up*) **3.** to skewer or bind the wings, etc. of (a fowl) before cooking **4.** to support or strengthen with a truss —*n.* [ME. *trusse* < OFr. *trousse* < *trousser*] **1.** a bundle or pack; specif., in England, a bundle of hay in any of various unit weights **2.** an iron band around a mast, having a gooseneck for securing a yard **3.** an architectural bracket or modillion **4.** a flower cluster growing at the tip of a stem **5.** a rigid framework of beams, girders, struts, bars, etc. for supporting a roof, bridge, etc. **6.** an appliance for giving support in cases of rupture or hernia, usually consisting of a pad on a special belt —**truss′er** *n.*

☆**truss bridge** a bridge supported chiefly by trusses

truss·ing (-iŋ) *n.* **1.** the act of a person who trusses **2.** the beams, rods, etc. forming a truss **3.** constructional trusses collectively **4.** bracing by or as by trusses

trust (trust) *n.* [ME. < ON. *traust*, trust, lit., firmness: for IE. base see TRUE] **1.** *a)* firm belief or confidence in the honesty, integrity, reliability, justice, etc. of another person or thing; faith; reliance *b)* the person or thing trusted **2.** confident expectation, anticipation, or hope [to have *trust* in the future] **3.** *a)* the fact of having confidence placed in one *b)* responsibility or obligation resulting from this **4.** keeping; care; custody **5.** something entrusted to one; charge, duty, etc. **6.** confidence in a purchaser's intention or future ability to pay for goods, etc. delivered; credit [to sell on *trust*] **7.** *a)* an industrial or business combination, now illegal in the U.S., in which management and control of the member corporations are vested in a single board of trustees, who are thus able to control a market, absorb or eliminate competition, fix prices, etc. *b)* *same as* CARTEL (sense 3): see also MONOPOLY **8.** *Law a)* the confidence reposed in a person by giving him nominal ownership of property, which he is to keep, use, or administer for another's benefit *b)* property under the charge of a trustee or trustees *c)* a trustee or group of trustees *d)* a person's right to property held in trust for him. **9.** [Archaic] trustworthiness; loyalty —*vi.* [ME. *trusten*, altered (after the *n.*) < ON. *treysta*, to trust, confide < base of *traust*] **1.** to have trust or faith; place reliance; be confident **2.** to hope (*for*) **3.** to give business credit —*vt.* **1.** *a)* to believe in the honesty, integrity, justice, etc. of; have confidence in *b)* to rely or depend on [*trust* him to be on time] **2.** to commit (*to* a person's care); entrust (*to* a person) **3.** to put something confidently in the charge of [to *trust* a lawyer with one's case] **4.** to allow to do something without fear of the outcome [to *trust* a child to go to the store] **5.** to believe or suppose **6.** to expect confidently; hope **7.** to grant business credit to —*adj.* **1.** relating to a trust or trusts **2.** held in trust **3.** managing for an owner; acting as trustee —*SYN.* see BELIEF, MONOPOLY, RELY —**in trust** in the condition of being entrusted to another's care —**trust to** to rely on —**trust′a·ble** *adj.* —**trust′er** *n.*

trust account 1. *same as* TRUST (*n.* 8 *b*) **2.** a savings account in a bank, the balance of which, at the death of the depositor, goes to a predesignated beneficiary

☆**trust·bust·er** (-bus′tər) *n.* a person, esp. a federal official,

who seeks to dissolve corporate trusts through the vigorous enforcement of antitrust laws —**trust′bust′ing** *n.*

☆**trust company** 1. a company formed to act as trustee 2. a bank organized to handle trusts and carry on all banking operations except the issuance of bank notes

trus·tee (trus tē′) *n.* 1. a person to whom another's property or the management of another's property is entrusted 2. a nation under whose authority a trust territory is placed 3. any of a group or board of persons appointed to manage the affairs of an institution or organization ☆4. in some States, a person in whose hands the property of a debtor is attached by means of garnishment; garnishee —*vt.* -teed′, -tee′ing 1. to commit (property or management) to a trustee or trustees ☆2. to attach by means of garnishment

trus·tee·ship (-ship′) *n.* 1. the position or function of a trustee 2. *a)* a commission from the United Nations to a country to administer a trust territory *b)* the condition or fact of being a trust territory

trust·ful (trust′fəl) *adj.* full of trust; ready to confide or believe; trusting —**trust′ful·ly** *adv.* —**trust′ful·ness** *n.*

trust fund money, stock, etc. held in trust

trust·ing (trus′tin) *adj.* that trusts; trustful —**trust′ing·ly** *adv.* —**trust′ing·ness** *n.*

trust·less (trust′lis) *adj.* [Now Rare] 1. not to be trusted; untrustworthy 2. not trusting; distrustful

trust territory a territory placed under the administrative authority of a country by the United Nations

trust·wor·thy (-wur′thē) *adj.* -thi·er, -thi·est worthy of trust; dependable; reliable —*SYN.* see RELIABLE —**trust′wor′thi·ly** *adv.* —**trust′wor′thi·ness** *n.*

trust·y (trus′tē) *adj.* trust′i·er, trust′i·est 1. that can be relied upon; dependable; trustworthy 2. *obs. var.* of TRUSTFUL —*n.*, *pl.* trust′ies a trusted person; ☆specif., a convict granted special privileges as a trustworthy person —*SYN.* see RELIABLE —**trust′i·ly** *adv.* —**trust′i·ness** *n.*

truth (trōōth) *n.*, *pl.* truths (trōōthz, trōōths) [ME. *treuthe* < OE. *treowth*: see TRUE & -TH¹] 1. the quality or state of being true; specif., *a)* orig., loyalty; trustworthiness *b)* sincerity; genuineness; honesty *c)* the quality of being in accordance with experience, facts, or reality; conformity with fact *d)* reality; actual existence *e)* agreement with a standard, rule, etc.; correctness; accuracy 2. that which is true; statement, etc. that accords with fact or reality 3. an established or verified fact, principle, etc. 4. a particular belief or teaching regarded by the speaker as the true one (often with *the*) —**in truth** truly; in fact —**of a truth** certainly

SYN.—**truth** suggests conformity with the facts or with reality, either as an idealized abstraction ["What is *truth?*" said jesting Pilate] or in actual application to statements, ideas, acts, etc. [there is no *truth* in that rumor]; **veracity**, as applied to persons or to their utterances, connotes habitual adherence to the truth [I cannot doubt his *veracity*]; **verity**, as applied to things, connotes correspondence with fact or with reality [the *verity* of his thesis]; **verisimilitude**, as applied to literary or artistic representations, connotes correspondence with actual, especially universal, truths [the *verisimilitude* of the characterizations in a novel] —*ANT.* falseness, falsity

Truth (trōōth), **So·journ·er** (sō′jurn ər) (orig. a slave called *Isabella*) 1797?-1883; U.S. abolitionist

truth drug an anesthetic or hypnotic, as thiopental sodium, regarded as tending to make a subject responsive while being questioned: also ☆**truth serum**

truth·ful (-fəl) *adj.* 1. telling the truth; presenting the facts; veracious; honest 2. corresponding with fact or reality, as an artistic representation —**truth′ful·ly** *adv.* —**truth′ful·ness** *n.*

try (trī) *vt.* tried, try′ing [ME. *trien* < OFr. *trier* < ? VL. *tritare*, to cull out, grind < L. *tritus*, pp. of *terere*, to rub, thresh grain: see TRITE] 1. orig., to separate; set apart 2. *a)* to melt or render (fat, etc.) to get (the oil) *b)* to extract or refine (metal, etc.) by heating Usually with *out* 3. [Now Rare] to settle (a matter, quarrel, etc.) by a test or contest; fight out 4. *a)* to examine and decide (a case) in a law court *b)* to determine legally the guilt or innocence of (a person) *c)* to preside as judge at the trial of (a case or person) 5. to put to the proof; test 6. to subject to trials, annoyance, etc.; afflict [Job was sorely *tried*] 7. to subject to a severe test or strain [rigors that *try* one's stamina] 8. to test the operation or effect of; experiment with; make a trial of [to *try* a new recipe] 9. to attempt to find out or determine by experiment or effort [to *try* one's fortune in another city] 10. to make an effort at; attempt; endeavor: followed by an infinitive [*try* to remember] 11. to attempt to open (a door or window) in testing to see whether it is locked 12. [Obs.] to find to be so by test or experience; prove —*vi.* 1. to make an effort, attempt, or endeavor: colloquially, *try* in this sense is often followed by *and* and a coordinate verb [please *try* and behave] 2. to make an experiment —*n.*, *pl.* tries 1. the act or an instance of trying; attempt; effort; trial 2. Rugby a scoring play in which the ball is grounded on or behind the opponent's goal line —**try on** to test the fit or appearance of (a garment) by putting it on —**try one's hand at** to attempt (to do something), esp. for the first time —**try out** ☆1. to test the quality, result, value, etc. of, as by putting to use; experiment with ☆2. to test one's fitness, as for a job, a place on an athletic team, a role in a play, etc.

SYN.—**try** is commonly the simple direct word for putting forth effort to do something [*try* to come], but specifically it connotes experimentation in testing or proving something [I'll *try* your recipe]; **attempt**, somewhat more formal, suggests a setting out to accomplish something but often connotes failure [he had *attempted* to take his life]; **endeavor** suggests exertion and determined effort in the face of difficulties [we shall *endeavor* to recover your loss]; **essay** connotes a tentative experimenting to test the feasibility of something difficult [he will not *essay* the high jump]; **strive** suggests great, earnest exertion to accomplish something [*strive* to win]; **struggle** suggests a violent striving to overcome obstacles or to free oneself from an impediment [he *struggled* to reach the top]

try·ing (-in) *adj.* that tries one's patience; annoying; exasperating; irksome —**try′ing·ly** *adv.*

☆**try·out** (trī′out′) *n.* [Colloq.] 1. an opportunity to prove, or a test to determine, fitness for a place on an athletic team, a role in a play, etc. 2. a performance of a play before its official opening, as to test audience reaction

tryp·a·no·some (trip′ə nə sōm′) *n.* [ModL. *Trypanosoma*, name of the genus < Gr. *trypanon*, borer (see TREPAN) + ModL. *-soma*, -SOME³] any of a genus (*Trypanosoma*) of flagellate protozoans that live as parasites in the blood of man and other vertebrates, are usually transmitted by an insect bite, and often cause serious diseases, as sleeping sickness, Chagas' disease, etc.

tryp·a·no·so·mi·a·sis (trip′ə nō′sō mī′ə sis) *n.* [ModL.: see prec. & -IASIS] any disease caused by a trypanosome

tryp·ars·a·mide (trip är′sə mid′) *n.* [TRYP(ANOSOMIASIS) + ARS(ENIC) + AMIDE] a drug containing arsenic, used in the treatment of trypanosomiasis

tryp·sin (trip′sin) *n.* [G., prob. < Gr. *tryein*, to wear away (see TRITE) + G. *(pe)psin*: see PEPSIN] 1. a proteolytic enzyme in the pancreatic juice that hydrolyzes proteins to smaller polypeptides 2. any of several similar enzymes —**tryp′tic** (-tik) *adj.*

tryp·sin·o·gen (trip sin′ə jən) *n.* [prec. + -o- + -GEN] the inactive precursor of trypsin, secreted by the pancreas

tryp·to·phan (trip′tə fan′) *n.* [< TRYPTIC + -PHANE] an aromatic, crystalline, essential amino acid, $C_{11}H_{12}O_2N_2$, produced synthetically and in digestion by the action of trypsin on proteins: also **tryp′to·phane** (-fān′)

try·sail (trī′s'l, -sāl′) *n.* [< naut. phr. *a try*, the position of lying to in a storm] a small, stout, fore-and-aft sail hoisted when other canvas has been lowered, to keep a vessel's head to the wind in a storm

try square an instrument consisting of two pieces set at right angles, used for testing the accuracy of square work and for marking off right angles

tryst (trist, trīst) *n.* [ME. *triste* < OFr., hunting station, hence hunting rendezvous, prob. < ON. *treysta*: see TRUST, *v.*] 1. an appointment to meet at a specified time and place, esp. one made secretly by lovers 2. *a)* a meeting held by appointment *b)* the place of such a meeting: also **trysting place** 3. [Scot.] a market; fair —*vi.*, *vt.* [Scot.] to agree to meet —**tryst′er** *n.*

TRY SQUARE

tsa·di (tsä′dē) *n.* [Heb. *şādhē*] the 18th letter of the Hebrew alphabet (צ, ץ)

Tsang·po (tsän′pō′) the upper course of the Brahmaputra, in Tibet: c.900 mi.

tsar (tsär, zär) *n. var. sp.* of CZAR —**tsar′dom** *n.* —**tsar′ism** *n.* —**tsar′ist** *n.*

Tsa·ri·tsyn (tsä rit′sin) *a former name of* VOLGOGRAD

Tschaikowsky *see* TCHAIKOVSKY

tset·se fly (tset′sē, tsēt′-, set′-, sēt′-) [Afrik. < native (Bantu) name] any of several small, two-winged flies (genus *Glossina*) of C and S Africa, including species that carry the trypanosomes that cause nagana and sleeping sickness

TSgt, T/Sgt Technical Sergeant

Tshi (chwē) *n. var.* of TWI

Tshi·lu·ba (chē lōō′bə) *n.* a Bantu language used as a lingua franca over a wide area of Congo (sense 2)

☆**T-shirt** (tē′shurt′) *n.* [so named because T-shaped] 1. a collarless, cotton undershirt with short sleeves 2. a similar pullover knit sport shirt

tsim·mes (tsim′əs) *n.* [Yid., lit., a kind of carrot stew] a commotion; fuss; to-do

Tsi·nan (jē′nän′) city in NE China; capital of Shantung province: pop. 882,000

Tsing·hai (chin′hī′) 1. province of NW China, northeast of Tibet: 278,378 sq. mi.; pop. 2,050,000; cap. Sining 2. salt lake in the NE part of this province: c.2,200 sq. mi.

Tsing·tao (chin′dou′) seaport in Shantung province, NE China, on the Yellow Sea: pop. 1,144,000

Tsin·ling Mountains (chin′lin′) mountain range in C China, in Kansu, Shensi, & Honan provinces: highest peak, over 12,000 ft.

Tsi·tsi·har (chē′chē′här′) *former name of* CHICHIHAERH

tsk (tisk: *conventionalized pronun.*) *interj.*, *n.* a clicking or sucking sound made with the tongue, usually repeated one or more times, to express disapproval, genuine or mock sympathy, etc. —*vi.* to utter "tsks"

tsor·is (tsôr′is, tsoor′-) *n.* [Yid., *pl.* of *tsore*, calamity < Heb. *tsarāh*] trouble, distress, woe, misery, etc.: also written **tsor′es, tsor′riss, tsoor′is,** etc.

tsp. 1. teaspoon(s) 2. teaspoonful(s)

T square a T-shaped ruler for drawing parallel lines by fitting the short, thick crosspiece over the edge of a drawing board

☆**T-strap** (tē′strap′) *n.* **1.** a T-shaped strap over the instep of a shoe **2.** a woman's or girl's shoe with such a strap

tsu·na·mi (tsōō nä′mē) *n.* [Jap. < *tsu,* a harbor + *nami,* wave] a huge sea wave caused by a submarine disturbance, as an earthquake or volcanic eruption: also popularly, but inaccurately, called *tidal wave* —**tsu·na′mic** (-mik) *adj.*

Tsun·i (dzoon′yē′) city in Kweichow province, S China: pop. 200,000

Tsu·shi·ma (tsōō′shē mä′) island of Japan in the Korea Strait, between Kyushu & Korea: 271 sq. mi.

tsu·tsu·ga·mu·shi disease (tsōō′tsōō gə mōō′shē) [Jap. *tsutsugamushi,* lit., dangerous insect] a disease of the Asiatic-Pacific area, transmitted to man by the bite of the larva of a mite (esp. *Trombicula akamushi*) and caused by a rickettsia (*Rickettsia tsutsugamushi*): it is characterized by fever and a rash

Tu. Tuesday

T.U. Trade Union

Tu·a·mo·tu Archipelago (tōō′ä mō′tōō) group of islands of French Polynesia: 330 sq. mi.; pop. 7,000

‡**tu·an** (tōō wän′) *n.* [Malay] sir; mister: a title of respect in SE Asia

Tua·reg (twä′reg) *n.* **1.** *pl.* **-regs, -reg** any member of a group of Berber tribes of the W and C Sahara **2.** their Berber dialect

tu·a·ta·ra (tōō′ə tä′rə) *n.* [Maori *tuatàra* < *tua,* back + *tara,* spine] a primitive, amphibious, lizardlike reptile (*Sphenodon punctatum*) of islands near New Zealand, with a row of spines in the middle of the back and a well-developed third eye: it is the only extant rhynchocephalian

tub (tub) *n.* [ME. *tubbe* < MDu., akin to MLowG. *tobbe,* EFris. *tubbe*] **1.** *a)* a round, broad, open, wooden container, usually formed of staves and hoops fastened around a flat bottom *b)* any similarly large, open container of metal, stone, etc., as for washing *c)* as much as a tub will hold **2.** a bucket or tram for carrying coal, ore, etc. in a mine **3.** *a) short for* BATHTUB *b)* [Brit. Colloq.] a bath in a tub **4.** [Colloq.] a slow-moving, clumsy ship or boat —*vt., vi.* **tubbed, tub′bing 1.** [Colloq.] to wash in a tub **2.** [Brit. Colloq.] to bathe (oneself) —**tub′ba·ble** *adj.* —**tub′ber** *n.*

tu·ba (tōō′bə, tyōō′-) *n., pl.* **tu′bas, tu′bae** (-bē) [L., a trumpet] **1.** in ancient Rome, a straight war trumpet **2.** any of a family of brass instruments of semi-conical bore, having a cup mouthpiece and three to five valves, esp. the large contrabass member **3.** a powerful, organ reed stop of 8-foot pitch

tub·al (tōō′b'l, tyōō′-) *adj.* of or in a tube, esp. a Fallopian tube *[a tubal pregnancy]*

Tu·bal-cain (tōō′bal kān′, tyōō′-) *Bible* a worker in brass and iron: Gen. 4:22

tu·bate (tōō′bāt, tyōō′-) *adj.* having or forming a tube or tubes; tubular

tub·by (tub′ē) *adj.* **-bi·er, -bi·est 1.** shaped like a tub **2.** fat and short —**tub′bi·ness** *n.*

TUBA

tube (tōōb, tyōōb) *n.* [Fr. < L. *tubus,* a pipe] **1.** *a)* a hollow cylinder or pipe of metal, glass, rubber, etc., usually long in proportion to its diameter, used for conveying fluids, etc. *b)* an instrument, part, organ, etc. resembling a tube *[bronchial tubes]* **2.** a rubber casing inflated with air and used, esp. formerly, with an outer casing to form an automotive tire **3.** an enclosed, hollow cylinder of thin, pliable metal, plastic, etc., fitted at one end with a screw cap and used for holding pastes or semiliquids, which can be squeezed out ☆**4.** *short for: a)* ELECTRON TUBE *b)* VACUUM TUBE **5.** *a)* a tunnel through rock, under water, etc., for a railroad, subway, etc. *b)* [Brit. Colloq.] an underground electric railway; subway **6.** *Bot.* the lower, united part of a gamopetalous corolla or a gamosepalous calyx **7.** *Elec.* in a vector field, the tubular space bounded by the lines of electric or magnetic force passing through every point on a closed curve on the outside of a charged body: in full **field tube** —*vt.* **tubed, tub′ing 1.** to provide with, place in, or pass through a tube or tubes **2.** to make tubular —☆**the tube** [Colloq.] television —**tube′like′** *adj.*

tube foot any of numerous small, water-filled, fleshy tubes in most echinoderms, projecting outside the body, ending in a suction disc, and used in locomotion, food handling, etc.

☆**tube·less tire** (-lis) a tire for an automotive vehicle, consisting of a single air-filled unit without an inner tube

tu·ber (tōō′bər, tyōō′-) *n.* [L., lit., a swelling, knob, truffle < IE. **teubh-* < base **teu-,* to swell, whence THIGH, L. *tumere,* to swell] **1.** a short, thickened, fleshy part of an underground stem, as a potato: new plants develop

from the buds, or eyes, that grow in the axils of the minute scale leaves of a tuber **2.** *Anat.* a tubercle or swelling

tu·ber·cle (-k'l) *n.* [L. *tuberculum,* dim. of *tuber:* see prec.] any small, rounded projection or process; specif., *a) Bot.* any of the wartlike growths on the roots of some plants *b) Anat.* a knoblike elevation, as on a bone *c) Med.* any abnormal hard nodule or swelling; specif., the typical nodular lesion of tuberculosis

tubercle bacillus the bacterium (*Mycobacterium tuberculosis*) causing tuberculosis

tu·ber·cu·lar (tōō bur′kyə lər, tyōō-) *adj.* [< L. *tuberculum* (see TUBERCLE) + -AR] **1.** of, like, or having a tubercle or tubercles **2.** of, relating to, or having tuberculosis **3.** caused by the tubercle bacillus —*n.* a person having tuberculosis

tu·ber·cu·late (-lit, -lāt′) *adj.* [ModL. *tuberculatus:* see TUBERCLE & -ATE[1]] **1.** having or characterized by a tubercle or tubercles: also **tu·ber′cu·lat′ed 2.** *same as* TUBERCULAR —**tu·ber′cu·la′tion** *n.*

tu·ber·cu·lin (-lin) *n.* [< L. *tuberculum* (see TUBERCLE) + -IN[1]] a sterile liquid preparation made from the growth products or extracts of a tubercle bacillus culture and injected into the skin as a test for tuberculosis

tu·ber·cu·lo- (-lō) [< L. *tuberculum:* see TUBERCLE] *a combining form meaning:* **1.** tuberculous **2.** tubercle bacillus **3.** tuberculosis

tu·ber·cu·loid (-loid′) *adj.* resembling a tubercle or tuberculosis

tu·ber·cu·lo·sis (tōō bur′kyə lō′sis, tyōō-) *n.* [ModL.: see TUBERCLE & -OSIS] an infectious disease caused by the tubercle bacillus and characterized by the formation of tubercles in various tissues of the body; specif., tuberculosis of the lungs; pulmonary phthisis; consumption

tu·ber·cu·lous (-bur′kyə ləs) *adj. same as* TUBERCULAR

tube·rose[1] (tōōb′rōz′, tyōōb′-) *n.* [ModL. *tuberosa* < L. *tuberosus,* TUBEROUS] a perennial Mexican plant (*Polianthes tuberosa*) of the agave family, with a tuberous rootstock and white, sweet-scented flowers borne in racemes

tu·ber·ose[2] (tōō′bər ōs′, tyōō′-) *adj. same as* TUBEROUS

tu·ber·os·i·ty (tōō′bə räs′ə tē, tyōō′-) *n., pl.* **-ties** [Fr. *tuberosité* < VL. *tuberositas*] **1.** the quality or condition of being tuberous **2.** a rounded swelling or projection, as on a bone for the attachment of a muscle or tendon

tu·ber·ous (tōō′bər əs, tyōō′-) *adj.* [Fr. *tubéreux* < L. *tuberosus:* see TUBER & -OUS] **1.** covered with rounded, wartlike swellings; knobby **2.** *Bot.* of, like, or having a tuber or tubers

tuberous root a tuberlike root without buds or scale leaves, as of the dahlia —**tu′ber·ous-root′ed** *adj.*

tu·bi·fex (tōō′bə feks′, tyōō′-) *n., pl.* **-fex′es, -fex′** [ModL. < L. *tubus* (see TUBE) + -fex < facere, to make, DO[1]] any of a genus (*Tubifex*) of small, freshwater, oligochaete worms, often living in chimneylike tubes: found esp. in polluted waters and often used as food for aquarium fish

tub·ing (tōōb′iŋ, tyōōb′-) *n.* **1.** a series or system of tubes **2.** material in the form of a tube **3.** a piece or length of tube

Tub·man (tub′mən) **1. Harriet,** 1820?–1913; U.S. abolitionist **2. William V(acanarat) S(hadrach),** 1895–1971; president of Liberia (1943–71)

tu·bu·lar (tōō′byə lər, tyōō′-) *adj.* [< L. *tubulus,* dim. of *tubus,* a tube, pipe] **1.** of or shaped like a tube **2.** made or furnished with a tube or tubes **3.** sounding as if produced by blowing through a tube —**tu′bu·lar′i·ty** (-lar′ə tē) *n.* —**tu′bu·lar·ly** *adv.*

tu·bu·late (-lāt′; *for adj., usually* -lit) *adj.* [L. *tubulatus*] *same as* TUBULAR (senses 1 & 2) —*vt.* **-lat′ed, -lat′ing** to shape into or provide with a tube —**tu′bu·la′tion** *n.*

tu·bule (tōōb′yool, tyōōb′-) *n.* [< L. *tubulus,* dim. of *tubus,* a tube] a small tube; minute tubular structure in an animal or plant

tu·bu·li- (-tōō′byə lə, tyōō′-) [< L. *tubulus:* see prec.] *a combining form meaning* tubule or tubular

tu·bu·li·flo·rous (tōō′byə lə flō′rəs, tyōō′-) *adj.* [prec. + -FLOROUS] having flowers all or some of whose corollas are tubular: said of certain plants of the composite family

tu·bu·lous (tōō′byə ləs, tyōō′-) *adj.* [TUBUL(E) + -OUS] **1.** *same as* TUBULAR (senses 1 & 2) **2.** having small, tubelike flowers —**tu′bu·lous·ly** *adv.*

tu·bu·lure (-loor′) *n.* [Fr. < L. *tubulus:* see TUBULE & -URE] a short tubular opening as at the top of a retort

tuck[1] (tuk) *vt.* [ME. *tuken* < MDu. *tucken,* to tuck & cognate OE. *tucian,* to ill-treat, lit., to tug, akin to G. *zucken,* to jerk: for IE. base see TUG] **1.** to pull up or gather up in a fold or folds; draw together so as to make shorter *[to tuck up one's skirt for wading]* **2.** to sew a fold or folds in (a garment) **3.** *a)* to thrust the edges of (a sheet, napkin, shirt, etc.) under or in, in order to make secure (usually with *up, in,* etc.) *b)* to cover or wrap snugly in or as in this way *[to tuck a baby in bed]* **4.** to put or press snugly into a small space; cram; fit *[to tuck shoes in a suitcase]* **5.** *a)* to put into an empty or convenient place *b)* to put into a secluded or isolated spot *[a cabin tucked in the hills]* **6.** to put (one's legs) in the position of a tuck (sense 3) —*vi.* **1.** to draw together; pucker **2.** to make tucks —*n.* **1.** a sewed fold in a garment, for shortening or decoration **2.** the part of a ship under the stern

where the ends of the bottom planks meet **3.** a position of the body, esp. in diving, in which the knees are drawn up tightly to the chest **4.** [Brit. Slang] food —**tuck away 1.** to eat or drink heartily **2.** to put aside or apart, as for future use —**tuck in 1.** to pull in or contract (one's chin, stomach, etc.) **2.** to eat or drink heartily

tuck² (tuk) *n.* [Fr. *estoc* < OFr. *estoquier* < MDu. *stocken,* to stick, pierce, poke (see STOKE)] [Archaic] a thin sword

tuck³ (tuk, tŏŏk) *vt.* [ME. *tukken* < ONormFr. *toker, toquer,* var. of OFr. *toucher,* to TOUCH] [Scot.] to beat or tap (a drum) —*n.* a beat or tap, as on a drum

☆**tuck⁴** (tuk) *n.* *clipped form of* TUXEDO

☆**tuck·a·hoe** (tuk′ə hō′) *n.* [< AmInd., as in Virginian *tockawhoughe*] **1.** a brown, massive, underground, basidiomycetous fungus (*Poria cocos*) producing an edible, carbohydrate substance **2.** any of various roots and tubers eaten by certain Indians of E. N. America

tuck·er¹ (tuk′ər) *n.* [ME. *toukere,* person who dresses cloth stretched on tenterhooks < *touken:* see TUCK¹] **1.** a person or device that makes tucks **2.** *a)* a neck and shoulder covering worn with a low-cut bodice by women in the 17th and 18th centuries *b)* later, a detachable collar or chemisette of thin muslin, etc. **3.** [Austral. Slang] food

☆**tuck·er²** (tuk′ər) *vt.* [prob. < TUCK¹, in obs. sense′ "to punish, rebuke"] [Colloq.] to tire (*out*); weary

tuck·et (tuk′it) *n.* [< TUCK³] [Archaic] a flourish on a trumpet

tuck-shop (tuk′shäp′) *n.* [TUCK¹ (*n.* 4) + SHOP] [Brit. Slang] a bakery or confectionery, esp. one near a school

Tuc·son (tōō′sän, tōō sän′) [Sp. < Piman *tu-uk-so-on,* black base, referring to a dark stratum, in a nearby mountain] city in S Ariz.: pop. 263,000

Tu·cu·mán (tōō kōō män′) city in N Argentina: pop. 287,000

-tude (tōōd, tyōōd) [Fr. < L. *-tudo* (gen. *-tudinis*)] a *n.*-forming suffix corresponding to -NESS [*certitude*]

Tu·dor (tōō′dər, tyōō′-) ruling family of England (1485–1603), descended from Owen Tudor (?–1461), a Welsh nobleman who married the widow of Henry V —*adj.* designating or of a style of architecture popular under the Tudors: it is characterized by slightly rounded arches, shallow moldings, extensive paneling, etc.

Tues·day (tōōz′dē, tyōōz′-; -dā) *n.* [ME. *Twisdai* < OE. *Tiwes dæg,* Tiu's day, rendering L. *Martis dies:* see TIU & DAY] the third day of the week

Tues·days (-dēz, -dāz) *adv.* on or during every Tuesday

tu·fa (tōō′fə, tyōō′-) *n.* [It. *tufo, tufa,* kind of porous stone < L. *tofus,* tuff, tufa] *Geol.* **1.** same as SINTER (*n.* 1) **2.** an obsolete name for TUFF —**tu·fa′ceous** (-fā′shəs) *adj.*

tuff (tuf) *n.* [Fr. *tuf,* earlier *tufe, tuffe* < It. *tufo,* TUFA] a porous rock, usually stratified, formed by consolidation of volcanic ash, dust, etc. —**tuff·a′ceous** (-ā′shəs) *adj.*

tuf·fet (tuf′ət) *n.* [altered < TUFT] **1.** a tuft of grass **2.** [by misunderstanding of a nursery rhyme] a low stool

tuft (tuft) *n.* [ME. (with unhistoric -*t*) < OFr. *tufe,* prob. < L. *tufa,* a kind of helmet crest] **1.** a bunch of hairs, feathers, grass, etc. growing closely together or attached at the base **2.** any similar cluster; specif., *a)* a clump of plants or trees *b)* the fluffy ball forming the end of any of the clusters of threads drawn tightly through a mattress, quilt, etc. to hold the padding in place *c)* a decorative button to which such a tuft is fastened —*vt.* **1.** to provide or decorate with a tuft or tufts **2.** to secure the padding of (a quilt, mattress, etc.) by regularly spaced tufts —*vi.* to grow in or form into tufts —**tuft′er** *n.* —**tuft′y** *adj.*

tuft·ed (tuf′tid) *adj.* **1.** provided or decorated with tufts **2.** formed into or growing in a tuft or tufts

tug (tug) *vi.* **tugged, tug′ging** [ME. *tuggen,* prob. < ON. *toga,* to draw, pull, akin to OE. *togian* (see TOW¹), *teon,* to pull < IE. base *deuk-,* to draw, pull, whence L. *ducere,* to lead, draw] **1.** to exert great effort in pulling; pull hard; drag; haul (often with *at*) **2.** to labor; toil; struggle —*vt.* **1.** to pull at with great force; strain at **2.** to drag; haul **3.** to tow with a tugboat —*n.* **1.** an act or instance of tugging; hard pull **2.** a great effort or strenuous contest **3.** a rope, chain, etc. used for tugging or pulling; esp., a trace of a harness **4.** *clipped form of* TUGBOAT —*SYN.* see PULL —**tug′ger** *n.*

tug·boat (-bōt′) *n.* a sturdily built, powerful boat designed for towing or pushing ships, barges, etc.

tug of war 1. a contest in which two teams pull at opposite ends of a rope, each trying to drag the other across a central line **2.** any power struggle between two parties

tu·grik (tōō′grik) *n.* [Mongol. *dughurik,* lit., wheel, circular object] the monetary unit of the Mongolian People's Republic: see MONETARY UNITS, table

tu·i (tōō′ē) *n.* [Maori] a greenish-blue, New Zealand honey eater (*Prosthemadera novaeseelandiae*), with white feathers under the throat: it can mimic human speech

Tui·ler·ies (twē′lər ēz; Fr. twēl rē′) former royal palace in Paris, burned in 1871: site now a public garden

tuille (twēl) *n.* [ME. *toile* < MFr. *tuile* < OFr. *tiule* < L. *tegula:* see TILE] in medieval plate armor, any of the lower plates of the tasse, protecting the thigh

☆**Tu·i·nal** (tōō′ə nôl′) *a trademark for* a combination of equal parts of Seconal sodium and amobarbital, used as a quick and relatively long-acting sedative or hypnotic

tu·i·tion (tōō wish′ən, tyōō-) *n.* [ME. *tuicion* < OFr. < L. *tuitio,* protection < *tuitus,* pp. of *tueri,* to watch,

protect] **1.** orig., guardianship **2.** the charge for instruction, esp. at a college or private school **3.** [Now Rare] teaching; instruction —**tu·i′tion·al** *adj.*

Tu·la (tōō′lä) city in C European R.S.F.S.R.: pop. 371,000

☆**tu·la·re·mi·a** (tōō′lə rē′mē ə) *n.* [ModL. < *Tulare* County, California (< Sp. *tulares,* pl., regions overgrown with tules: see ff.) + -EMIA] an infectious disease of rodents, esp. rabbits, caused by a bacterium (*Pasturella tularensis*) and transmitted to man in handling the flesh of infected animals or by the bite of certain insects: it is characterized by an irregular fever, aching, inflammation of the lymph glands, etc.: also sp. **tu′la·rae′mi·a** —**tu′la·re′mic** *adj.*

☆**tu·le** (tōō′lē) *n.* [Sp. < Nahuatl *tullin,* bulrush] either of two large bulrushes (*Scirpus acutus* or *Scirpus validus*) found in lakes and marshes of the SW U.S.

tu·lip (tōō′lip, tyōō′-) *n.* [Fr. *tulipe* (obs. *tulipan*) < Turk. *tülbend,* TURBAN: the flower somewhat resembles a turban] **1.** any of a number of related bulb plants (genus *Tulipa*) of the lily family, mostly spring-blooming, with long, broad, pointed leaves and, usually, a single large, cup-shaped, variously colored flower **2.** the flower or bulb

☆**tulip tree** a N. American forest tree (*Liriodendron tulipifera*) of the magnolia family, with tulip-shaped, greenish-yellow flowers, and conelike fruit: also called **tulip poplar**

☆**tu·lip·wood** (-wood′) *n.* **1.** the light, soft wood of the tulip tree **2.** *a)* any of several woods with stripes or streaks of color *b)* any tree having such wood

tulle (tōōl; Fr. tül) *n.* [after *Tulle,* city in France, where first made] a thin, fine netting of silk, rayon, nylon, etc., used for veils, scarfs, etc.

tul·li·bee (tul′ə bē′) *n.* [CanadFr. *toulibi* < Cree *otonabi,* mouth water] either of two kinds of chub (*Leucichthys nipigon* or *Leucichthys artedi*) of the upper Great Lakes

Tul·ly (tul′ē) *Englished name of* (Marcus) Tullius (CICERO)

Tul·sa (tul′sə) [< Muskogean (Creek) town name, akin to TALLAHASSEE] city in NE Okla., on the Arkansas River: pop. 332,000 —**Tul′san** *n., adj.*

tum·ble (tum′b'l) *vi.* **-bled, -bling** [ME. *tumblen,* freq. of *tumben* < OE. *tumbian,* to fall, jump, dance, akin to G. *tummeln* < Gmc. base borrowed in Fr. *tomber,* to fall] **1.** to do somersaults, handsprings, or similar acrobatic feats **2.** *a)* to fall suddenly, clumsily, or helplessly *b)* to experience a sudden fall or decline, as from power, high value, etc. *c)* to come down in ruins; collapse **3.** to stumble or trip **4.** to toss about or roll around **5.** to move, go, issue, etc. in a hasty, awkward, or disorderly manner **6.** [Colloq.] to have sudden awareness or understanding of some situation (with *to*) —*vt.* **1.** to cause to tumble; make fall, overthrow, topple, roll over, etc. **2.** to put into disorder by or as by tossing here and there; disarrange **3.** to whirl in a tumbler (sense 10) —*n.* **1.** the act or an instance of tumbling; specif., *a)* a somersault, handspring, etc. *b)* a fall *c)* a stumble **2.** disorder; confusion **3.** a confused heap —**give** (or **get**) **a tumble** [Colloq.] to give (or get) some favorable or affectionate notice, attention, etc.

☆**tum·ble·bug** (-bug′) *n.* any of several dung beetles that roll and bury in soil balls of dung, upon which the females deposit their eggs and in which the larvae develop

tum·ble·down (-doun′) *adj.* ready to tumble down; dilapidated

tum·bler (tum′blər) *n.* **1.** an acrobat or gymnast who does somersaults, handsprings, etc. **2.** a type of small greyhound formerly used to hunt rabbits **3.** a kind of pigeon that does somersaults in flight **4.** *a)* an ordinary drinking glass without foot or stem: orig., such a glass with a rounded or pointed bottom, that would tumble over when set down *b)* its contents **5.** the part of a gunlock through which the mainspring acts upon the hammer **6.** a part of a lock whose position must be changed by a key in order to release the bolt **7.** a projecting piece, as on a revolving or rocking part, that strikes and moves another part **8.** a part moving a gear into place in an automobile transmission **9.** an easily tipped toy that rights itself because of the way it is weighted **10.** *a)* a device for tumbling laundered clothes about in hot air until they are dry *b)* same as TUMBLING BOX

☆**tum·ble·weed** (tum′b'l wēd′) *n.* any of a number of plants, as the pigweed, Russian thistle, etc., that break off near the ground in autumn and are blown about by the wind

tumbling box (or **barrel**) a revolving box or drum into which loose materials are loaded and tumbled about, as for mixing, polishing, etc.

tum·brel, tum·bril (tum′brəl) *n.* [ME. *tomberel* < MFr. tip cart < *tomber,* to fall, tumble, leap: see TUMBLE] **1.** formerly, an instrument of punishment, as the cucking stool **2.** a farmer's cart or wagon that can be tilted for emptying **3.** any of the carts used to carry the condemned to the guillotine during the French Revolution **4.** an old two-wheeled military cart for carrying ammunition, etc.

tu·me·fa·cient (tōō′mə fā′shənt, tyōō′-) *adj.* [L. *tumefaciens,* prp. of *tumefacere:* see TUMEFY] causing or tending to cause swelling

tu·me·fac·tion (-fak′shən) *n.* [MFr.] **1.** a swelling up or becoming swollen **2.** a swollen part

tu·me·fy (tōō′mə fi′, tyōō′-) *vt., vi.* **-fied′, -fy′ing** [Fr. *tuméfier,* as if < L. *tumeficere,* for *tumefacere,* to cause to swell < *tumere,* to swell (see TUMOR) + *facere,* to make (see DO¹)] to make or become swollen; swell

tu·mes·cence (tōō mes′'ns, tyōō-) *n.* [< L. *tumescens*, prp. of *tumescere*, to swell up, inceptive of *tumere*, to swell (see TUMOR)] **1.** a swelling; distention **2.** a swollen or distended part —**tu·mes′cent** *adj.*

tu·mid (tōō′mid, tyōō′-) *adj.* [L. *tumidus* < *tumere*, to swell (see TUMOR)] **1.** swollen or as if swollen; bulging; distended **2.** inflated or pompous; bombastic —**tu·mid′i·ty, tu′mid·ness** *n.* —**tu′mid·ly** *adv.*

tum·my (tum′ē) *n., pl.* -**mies** stomach: a child's word

tu·mor (tōō′mər, tyōō′-) *n.* [L., a swelling < *tumere*, to swell < IE. base **teu-*, to swell, whence THUMB] **1.** a swelling on some part of the body; esp., a mass of new tissue growth independent of its surrounding structures, having no physiological function; neoplasm: tumors are classified as benign or malignant **2.** [Obs.] high-flown language; bombast Brit. sp. **tu′mour** —**tu′mor·ous** *adj.*

tump (tump) *n.* [< ?] [Brit. Dial.] **1.** a little mound; hillock **2.** a clump, as of grass

☆**tump·line** (tump′lin) *n.* [*tump*, a tumpline < AmInd. (Algonquian) word (as in Massachusett *tâmpân*) + LINE[1]] a broad band passed across the forehead and behind across the shoulders to support a pack on the back

tu·mu·lar (tōō′myə lər, tyōō′-) *adj.* of or like a tumulus

tu·mu·lose (-lōs′) *adj.* [L. *tumulosus*] full of tumuli, or mounds: also **tu′mu·lous** (-ləs)

tu·mult (tōō′mult, tyōō′-) *n.* [ME. *tumulte* < MFr. < L. *tumultus*, a swelling or surging up, tumult < *tumere*, to swell (see TUMOR)] **1.** noisy commotion, as of a crowd; uproar **2.** confusion; agitation; disturbance **3.** great emotional disturbance; agitation of mind or feeling

tu·mul·tu·ar·y (too mul′choo wer′ē, tyoo-) *adj.* **1.** irregular; disorderly **2.** *same as* TUMULTUOUS

tu·mul·tu·ous (-choo wəs) *adj.* [MFr. < L. *tumultuosus*] **1.** full of or characterized by tumult; wild and noisy; uproarious; riotous **2.** making a tumult; turbulent **3.** greatly disturbed or agitated —**tu·mul′tu·ous·ly** *adv.* —**tu·mul′tu·ous·ness** *n.*

tu·mu·lus (tōō′myə ləs, tyōō′-) *n., pl.* -**li′** (-lī′), -**lus·es** [L., a mound, hillock, akin to *tumere*: see TUMOR] an artificial mound; esp., an ancient burial mound

tun (tun) *n.* [ME. *tonne* < OE. *tunne*, a large cask & OFr. *tonne*, both < ML. *tunna* < Celt. base] **1.** a large cask, esp. for wine, beer, or ale **2.** a measure of capacity for liquids, usually 252 wine gallons —*vt.* **tunned, tun′ning** to put into or store in a tun or tuns

☆**tu·na[1]** (tōō′nə, tyōō′-) *n., pl.* **tu′nas** or **tu′na:** see PLURAL, II, D, 2 [AmSp. < Sp. *atún* < Ar. *tūn* < L. *tunnus:* see TUNNY] **1.** a large, ocean, food and game fish (*Thunnus thynnus*) of the mackerel group, with coarse, somewhat oily flesh, weighing up to 1,000 pounds, and found in Atlantic and Pacific waters: also called **bluefin tuna 2.** any of various related fishes, as the albacore **3.** the flesh of the tuna, often canned for food: also called **tuna fish**

tu·na[2] (tōō′nə, tyōō′-) *n.* [Sp., of WInd. (Taino) orig.] **1.** any of various prickly pears (esp. *Opuntia tuna*), cultivated for their edible fruits **2.** the fruit

tun·a·ble (tōōn′ə b'l, tyōōn′-) *adj.* **1.** capable of being tuned **2.** [Archaic] tuneful; melodious Also sp. **tune′a·ble** —**tun′a·ble·ness** *n.* —**tun′a·bly** *adv.*

Tun·bridge Wells (tun′brij welz′) city & spa in Kent, SE England: pop. 40,000

tun·dra (tun′drə, toon′-) *n.* [Russ., of Lapp orig.] any of the vast, nearly level, treeless plains of the arctic regions

tune (tōōn, tyōōn) *n.* [ME., var. of *tone*, TONE] **1.** orig., a tone **2.** *a)* a succession of musical tones forming a rhythmic, catchy whole; melody; air *b)* a musical setting of a hymn, psalm, poem, etc. **3.** the condition of having correct musical pitch, or of being in key; also, harmony; agreement; concord: now used chiefly in the phrases **in tune, out of tune** [a violin that is *in tune*, a person *out of tune* with the times] —*vt.* **tuned, tun′ing 1.** to adjust (a musical instrument) to some standard of pitch; put in tune **2.** to adapt (music, the voice, etc.) to some pitch, tone, or mood **3.** to adapt to some condition, mood, etc.; bring into harmony or agreement **4.** [Now Rare] to utter or express musically **5.** to adjust (an electronics circuit or system, a motor, etc.) to the proper or desired performance —*vi.* to be in tune; harmonize —SYN. see MELODY —**call the tune** to direct proceedings; be in control —**change one's tune** to change one's attitude or manner, as from scorn to respect —**sing a different tune** to talk or act differently because of a change of attitude —**to the tune of** [Colloq.] to the sum, price, or extent of —**tune in 1.** to adjust a radio or television receiver to a given frequency or channel so as to receive (a specified station, program, etc.) ☆**2.** [Slang] to become or make aware, knowing, hip, etc. —**tune out 1.** to adjust a radio or television receiver so as to eliminate (interference, etc.) **2.** [Slang] to turn one's attention, sympathies, etc. away from —**tune up 1.** to adjust (musical instruments) to the same pitch, as in an orchestra **2.** to bring (an engine) to the proper condition, as by replacing parts, making adjustments, etc.

tune·ful (-fəl) *adj.* **1.** full of music or melody; melodious; harmonious **2.** producing musical sounds —**tune′ful·ly** *adv.* —**tune′ful·ness** *n.*

tune·less (-lis) *adj.* **1.** not musical or melodious **2.** not producing music; silent —**tune′less·ly** *adv.* —**tune′less·ness** *n.*

tun·er (tōō′nər, tyōō′-) *n.* a person or thing that tunes; specif., *a)* a person who tunes musical instruments [a piano *tuner*] *b)* the part of a radio receiver that detects signals; esp., a separate unit of a high-fidelity system

☆**tune·smith** (tōōn′smith′, tyōōn′-) *n.* [Colloq.] a composer of popular songs

tune·up, tune-up (-up′) *n.* an adjusting, as of an engine, to the proper or required condition

tung oil (tuŋ) [< Chin. *yu-t'ung* < *yu*, oil + *t'ung*, name of the tree] a fast-drying oil derived from the seeds of the tung tree, used in place of linseed oil in paints, varnishes, etc. for a more water-resistant finish

tung·state (tuŋ′stāt) *n.* a salt or ester of tungstic acid

tung·sten (tuŋ′stən) *n.* [Sw., lit., heavy stone < *tung*, heavy + *sten*, STONE] a hard, heavy, gray-white, metallic chemical element, found in wolframite, scheelite, tungstite, etc., and used in steel for high-speed tools, in electric contact points and lamp filaments, etc.: symbol, W; at. wt., 183.85; at. no., 74; sp. gr., 19.35; melt. pt., 3410°C; boil. pt., 5927°C —**tung·sten′ic** (-sten′ik) *adj.*

tungsten lamp an electric lamp having filaments of tungsten and a very low wattage

tungsten steel a very hard steel made with tungsten

tung·stic (tuŋ′stik) *adj.* designating or of a chemical compound containing tungsten, esp. with a valence of five or six

tungstic acid any of a group of acids produced by the combination of tungstic trioxide, WO_3, with water; specif., the monohydrate acid, H_2WO_4

tung·stite (-stīt) *n.* a yellow or yellow-green mineral, WO_3, native tungstic trioxide: also called **tungstic ocher**

Tung·ting (dooŋ′tiŋ′) lake in Hunan province, SE China: c.1,450 sq. mi.: during floods, over 4,000 sq. mi.

tung tree (tuŋ) a subtropical tree (*Aleurites fordii*) of the spurge family, whose seeds yield tung oil

Tun·gus (toon gooz′) *n. 1. pl.* -**gus′es**, -**gus′** any member of a group of Tungusic-speaking peoples of Mongolian descent, including the Manchu, living in Siberia east of the Yenisei in the Amur basin, and, formerly, in Manchuria **2.** their Tungusic language —*adj.* of the Tunguses, their language, or culture Also sp. **Tun·guz′**

Tun·gus·ic (-goo′zik) *n.* a subfamily of the Altaic language family, spoken in C and NE Asia and including Tungus and Manchu —*adj.* **1.** of the Tunguses **2.** of Tungusic

Tun·gus·ka Basin (toon goos′kə) large coal basin in E R.S.F.S.R., between the Yenisei & Lena rivers: it is drained by three rivers, the **Lower Tunguska, Stony Tunguska,** & **Upper Tunguska,** which flow west into the Yenisei

tu·nic (tōō′nik, tyōō′-) *n.* [L. *tunica*, ult. of Sem. orig. (whence Gr. *chitōn*), as in Aram. *kithuna*, garment worn next to the skin] **1.** a loose, gownlike garment worn by men and women in ancient Greece and Rome **2.** a blouselike garment extending to the hips or lower, usually gathered at the waist, often with a belt **3.** [Chiefly Brit.] a short coat forming part of the uniform of soldiers, policemen, etc. **4.** a vestment worn by a subdeacon over the alb or by a bishop under the dalmatic **5.** a natural covering of a plant, animal, etc.

tu·ni·ca (tōō′ni kə, tyōō′-) *n., pl.* -**cae** (-sē′) [ModL.: see prec.] *Anat., Zool.* an enclosing or covering layer of tissue or membrane, as of the ovaries

tu·ni·cate (-kit, -kāt′) *adj.* [L. *tunicatus*, pp. of *tunicare*, to put on a tunic < *tunica*, a TUNIC] **1.** *Bot.* of or covered with concentric layers or tunics, as an onion **2.** *Zool.* having a tunic or mantle Also **tu′ni·cat′ed** (-kāt′id) —*n.* any of a subphylum (Tunicata) of solitary or colonial sea chordates, having a saclike body enclosed by a thick cellulose tunic, and including the salpas and ascidians

tu·ni·cle (-k'l) *n.* [ME. < L. *tunicula*, dim. of *tunica*, a tunic] *same as* TUNIC (sense 4)

tuning fork a small steel instrument with two prongs, which when struck sounds a certain fixed tone in perfect pitch: it is used as a guide in tuning instruments, in testing hearing, etc.

Tu·nis (tōō′nis, tyōō′-) **1.** capital of Tunisia, a seaport near the site of ancient Carthage: pop. 662,000 **2.** a former Barbary State, which became Tunisia

Tu·ni·sia (tōō nē′zhə, tyōō′-; -nish′ə, -nish′ē ə) country in N Africa, on the Mediterranean: 48,332 sq. mi.; pop. 4,533,000; cap. Tunis —**Tu·ni′sian** *adj., n.*

tun·nage (tun′ij) *n. same as* TONNAGE

tun·nel (tun′'l) *n.* [ME. *tonel*, a net with wide opening and narrow end < MFr. *tonnelle*, arbor, semicircular vault < OFr. *tonnel*, dim. of *tonne*, a TUN] **1.** orig., *a)* a flue *b)* a funnel **2.** an underground or underwater passageway, as for automotive traffic, a railroad, etc. **3.** an animal's burrow **4.** any tunnellike passage, as one in a mine —*vt.* **-neled** or **-nelled, -nel·ing** or **-nel·ling 1.** to dig (a passage) in the form of a tunnel **2.** to make a tunnel through or under **3.** to make (one's way) by digging a tunnel —*vi.* to make a tunnel —**tun′nel·er, tun′nel·ler** *n.*

TUNING FORK

☆**tunnel diode** a semiconductor diode, containing many impurities, in which an increase in voltage across the diode first produces an increase in current, then a decrease, and finally another increase: used as an amplifier, oscillator, or computer switching element

tunnel disease *same as* DECOMPRESSION SICKNESS

tun·ny (tun′ē) *n.*, *pl.* **-nies, -ny:** see PLURAL, II, D, 1 [MFr. *thon* < L. *thunnos* < Gr. *thynnos*] *same as* TUNA¹ (senses 1 & 2)

tup (tup) *n.* [ME. *tupe*] **1.** a male sheep; ram **2.** the striking part of a pile driver or power hammer —*vt.* **tupped,** **tup′ping** to copulate with (a ewe): said of a ram

☆**tu·pe·lo** (tōō′pə lō′) *n.*, *pl.* **-los′** [< Creek Indian *ito,* tree + *opilwa,* swamp] **1.** *same as* BLACK GUM **2.** its fine-textured wood used for mallets, furniture, etc.

Tu·pi (tōō pē′, tōō′pē) *n.* [Tupi, comrade] **1.** *pl.* **Tu·pis′, Tu·pi′** any member of a group of S. American Indian peoples living in parts of Brazil, chiefly along the coast and along the lower Amazon, and in part of Paraguay **2.** their dialect of the Tupi-Guaraní language, which in an earlier form was used as a lingua franca in the Amazon region **3.** a S. American Indian language family including Tupi-Guaraní and over three dozen other languages spoken over a wide area in S. America —**Tu·pi′an** *adj.*

Tu·pi-Gua·ra·ní (-gwä′rä nē′) *n.* **1.** a Tupi language spoken in some seven major dialects, including Guaraní and Tupi, esp. in Paraguay, Brazil, Argentina, and Bolivia **2.** *same as* TUPI (sense 3)

tup·pence (tup′ns) *n. same as* TWOPENCE

Tu·pun·ga·to (tōō′poon gä′tō) mountain of the Andes on the Argentina-Chile border: 22,310 ft.

tuque (tōōk, tyōōk) *n.* [CanadFr. < Fr. *toque:* see TOQUE] a winter cap consisting of a knitted bag tapered and closed at both ends, worn with one end tucked into the other

‡**tu quo·que** (tōō kwō′kwē) [L.] thou ·also; you too: a retort accusing an accuser of the same charge

Tu·ra·ni·an (too rā′nē ən, tyoo-) *n.* [< Per. *Tūrān,* area in S Turkestan + -IAN] *earlier term for* URAL-ALTAIC

tur·ban (tur′bən) *n.* [earlier *turbant* < MFr. < It. or Port. *turbante* < Turk. *tülbend,* dial. form of *dülbend* < Per. *dulbänd,* turban, sash] **1.** a headdress of Moslem origin, consisting of a length of cloth wound in folds about the head, often over a cap **2.** any similar headdress; esp., *a)* a scarf or bandana wound around the head, worn by women *b)* a woman's hat with no brim or a very short brim turned up closely —**tur′baned** (-bənd) *adj.*

TURBAN

tur·ba·ry (tur′bər ē) *n.*, *pl.* **-ries** [ME. *turbarye* < OFr. *turberie* < *tourbe,* turf < Frank. *turba:* for IE. base see TURF] **1.** land where turf or peat is dug **2.** *Eng. Law* the right to dig turf or peat on another's land

tur·bel·lar·i·an (tur′bə ler′ē ən) *n.* [< ModL. *Turbellaria,* name of the class < L. *turbellae,* a bustle, stir, dim. of *turba,* a crowd (see ff.), disturbance (from water currents caused by the cilia) + -AN] any of a class (Turbellaria) of flatworms, mostly aquatic and nonparasitic, characterized by a leaf-shaped body covered with many cilia —*adj.* of or pertaining to flatworms of this class

tur·bid (tur′bid) *adj.* [L. *turbidus* < *turba,* a crowd < IE. *turb-* < base *twer-,* to stir up, whence OE. *thwirel,* stirring rod, churn handle] **1.** muddy or cloudy from having the sediment stirred up **2.** thick, dense, or dark, as clouds or smoke **3.** confused; perplexed; muddled —**tur·bid′i·ty,** **tur′bid·ness** *n.* —**tur′bid·ly** *adv.*

tur·bi·dim·e·ter (tur′bə dim′ə tər) *n.* [TURBID(ITY) + -METER] a device for measuring the turbidity of a liquid, as in a water-purification plant —**tur·bi·di·met·ric** (tur′bə di met′rik) *adj.* —**tur′bi·dim′e·try** (-trē) *n.*

tur·bi·dite (tur′bə dīt′) *n.* [TURBID + -ITE¹] *Geol.* rock consisting of sediment deposited from a turbidity current

turbidity current *Geol.* a current of highly turbid water carrying large amounts of suspended sediment that increase its density and cause it to flow downward through less dense water along the bottom slope of a sea or lake

tur·bi·nate (tur′bə nit, -nāt′) *adj.* [L. *turbinatus* < *turbo* (gen. *turbinis*), a whirl, rotation (for base see TURBID)] **1.** shaped like a cone resting on its apex; top-shaped, as a molluskan shell **2.** shaped like a scroll or spiral; specif., *Anat., Zool.* designating or of any of certain spiral, spongy bones in the nasal passages Also **tur′bi·nat′ed** (-nāt′id), **tur′bi·nal** (-n'l) —*n.* **1.** a turbinate shell **2.** a turbinate bone —**tur′bi·na′tion** *n.*

tur·bine (tur′bin, -bīn) *n.* [Fr. < L. *turbo,* whirl: see TURBINATE] an engine or motor driven by the pressure of steam, water, air, etc. against the curved vanes of a wheel or set of wheels fastened to a driving shaft

tur·bit (tur′bət) *n.* [< ? L. *turbo,* a top: from the shape] any of a variety of domestic pigeons distinguished by a short head and beak and a ruffled breast

tur·bo (tur′bō) *n. clipped form of* TURBOSUPERCHARGER

tur·bo- (tur′bō) [< TURBINE] *a combining form meaning* consisting of or driven by a turbine

tur·bo·fan (tur′bō fan′) *n.* **1.** a turbojet engine in which additional thrust is obtained from the part of the air that bypasses the engine and is accelerated by a fan in an enclosed duct: in full **turbofan engine 2.** a fan driven by a turbine

tur·bo·gen·er·a·tor (-jen′ə rāt′ər) *n.* a generator driven by and directly coupled to a turbine

tur·bo·jet (-jet′) *n.* **1.** a jet engine using a turbine to drive an air compressor that takes in and compresses air for fuel combustion and employing the resulting hot gases to rotate the turbine before forming the propulsive stream: in full **turbojet engine 2.** an aircraft propelled by such an engine

tur·bo·prop (-präp′) *n.* [TURBO- + PROP(ELLER)] **1.** a turbojet engine whose turbine shaft, through reduction gears, drives a propeller that develops most of the thrust, with some thrust usually being added by a jet of the turbine exhaust gases: in full **turboprop engine 2.** an aircraft propelled by such an engine

tur·bo·su·per·charg·er (-sōō′pər chär′jər) *n.* a device using a turbine driven by exhaust gases to compress air before delivering it to the intake of a reciprocating engine: used to maintain air-intake pressure at high altitudes

tur·bot (tur′bət) *n.*, *pl.* **-bot, -bots:** see PLURAL, II, D, 2 [ME. *turbut* < OFr. *tourbout,* prob. < OSw. *törnbut* < *törn,* a thorn (akin to THORN) + *but,* BUTT¹ (so named from the spines)] **1.** any of several large European flatfishes highly regarded as food **2.** any of several American flounders and halibuts

tur·bu·lence (tur′byə ləns) *n.* [LL. *turbulentia*] the condition or quality of being turbulent; specif., *a)* commotion or wild disorder *b)* violent, irregular motion or swirling agitation of water, air, gas, etc. Also **tur′bu·len·cy**

tur·bu·lent (-lənt) *adj.* [Fr. < L. *turbulentus* < *turba,* a crowd: see TURBID] full of commotion or wild disorder; specif., *a)* marked by or causing turmoil; unruly or boisterous *[a turbulent mob] b)* violently agitated; tumultuous *[turbulent grief] c)* marked by wildly irregular motion *[turbulent air currents]* —**tur′bu·lent·ly** *adv.*

turbulent flow the random motion of layers of a fluid, causing high resistance to movement through this fluid

Tur·co- (tur′kō, -kə) *var. of* TURKO-

turd (turd) *n.* [ME. < OE. *tord,* akin to MHG. *zurch,* dung, Lett. *dirsa,* anus < IE. base *der-,* to split, whence TEAR¹] a piece of excrement: now a vulgar term

tu·reen (too rēn′) *n.* [earlier *terreen* < MFr. *terrine,* earthen vessel < VL. *terrinus* < L. *terra,* earth] a large, deep dish with a lid, for serving soup, stew, etc.

Tu·renne (tü ren′), vicomte de (də), (Henri de la Tour d'Auvergne) 1611–75; Fr. marshal

turf (turf) *n.*, *pl.* **turfs,** rarely **turves** (turvz) [ME. < OE. akin to ON. *torf* < IE. *dorbhos,* sod, lit., twisted together < base *derbh-,* to twist together] **1.** *a)* a surface layer of earth containing grass plants with their matted roots; sod; sward *b)* a piece of this layer **2.** peat, or a piece of it for use as fuel **3.** a track for horse racing; also, the sport of horse racing: usually with *the* ☆**4.** [Slang] a neighborhood area regarded by a street gang as its own territory to be defended against other gangs —*vt.* **1.** to cover with turf **2.** [Brit. Colloq.] to shove, push, or dismiss

turf·man (-mən) *n.*, *pl.* **-men** a person interested in horse racing, esp. an owner, trainer, etc. of racehorses

turf·y (tur′fē) *adj.* **turf′i·er, turf′i·est 1.** of, like, or covered with turf **2.** having to do with horse racing

Tur·ge·nev (toor gā′nyif), **I·van Ser·ge·e·vich** (ē vän′ syer gā′yə vich) 1818–83; Russ. novelist: also sp. **Turge-nieff, Turgeniev**

tur·gent (tur′jənt) *adj.* [L. *turgens,* prp. of *turgere,* to swell] [Now Rare] swelling or swollen

tur·ges·cent (tur jes′'nt) *adj.* [L. *turgescens,* prp. of *turgescere,* to swell up (see ff. & -ESCENT)] becoming turgid or swollen; swelling —**tur·ges′cence, tur·ges′cen·cy** *n.*

tur·gid (tur′jid) *adj.* [L. *turgidus* < *turgere,* to swell] **1.** swollen; distended **2.** bombastic; pompous; grandiloquent —SYN. see BOMBASTIC —**tur·gid′i·ty, tur′gid·ness** *n.* —**tur′gid·ly** *adv.*

tur·gite (tur′jīt′) *n.* [< *Turginsk,* copper mine in the Ural Mountains + -ITE¹] a crimson iron ore, probably intermediate in composition between limonite and hematite

tur·gor (tur′gər) *n.* [LL. < L. *turgere,* to swell] **1.** turgescence; turgidity **2.** the normal distention or rigidity of living animal and plant cells due to pressure against the cell membrane from within by the cell contents

Tur·got (tür gō′), **Anne Ro·bert Jacques** (än′ rō ber zhåk′), baron de l'Aulne, 1727–81; Fr. economist & statesman

Tu·rin (toor′in, tyoor′-; too rin′, tyoo-) commune in the Piedmont, NW Italy, on the Po River: pop. 1,107,000: It. name, TORINO

Turk (turk) *n.* [ME. *Turke* < MFr. *Turc* < ML. *Turcus* < Turk. *Türk*] **1.** a native or inhabitant of Turkey; esp., a member of the Moslem people of Turkey or, formerly, of the Ottoman Empire **2.** a member of any of the peoples speaking Turkic languages and living in a region extending from the Balkans to E Siberia **3.** a horse of a breed developed in Turkey See also YOUNG TURK

Turk. 1. Turkey **2.** Turkish

Tur·ke·stan (tur′ki stan′, -stän′) region in C Asia, extending from the Caspian Sea to the Gobi Desert, inhabited by Turkic-speaking peoples: generally divided by the Tien Shan into two divisions, **Western** (or **Russian**) **Turkestan & Eastern** (or **Chinese**) **Turkestan**

Tur·key (tur′kē) country occupying Asia Minor & a SE part of the Balkan Peninsula: 301,381 sq. mi.; pop. 33,823,000; cap. Ankara

tur·key (tur′kē) n., pl. **-keys, -key:** see PLURAL, II, D, 1 [earlier *Turkey-cock,* term orig. applied to the guinea fowl, sometimes imported through Turkey and for a time identified with the Am. fowl] ☆1. *a)* any of several sub-species of large, wild or domesticated, N. American birds (*Meleagris gallopavo*), with a small, naked head and spreading tail, bred as poultry in many parts of the world *b)* a related wild bird (*Agriocharis ocellata*) of Central America, with eyespots on the tail *c)* the flesh of a turkey ☆2. [Slang] a failure or flop: said esp. of a theatrical production ☆3. *Bowling* three strikes in a row —☆**talk turkey** [Colloq.] to talk bluntly and directly, without subterfuge or circumlocution

☆**turkey buzzard** a dark-colored vulture (*Cathartes aura*) of temperate and tropical America, resembling a turkey in having a naked, reddish head: also called **turkey vulture**

turkey cock 1. a male turkey **2.** a strutting or pompous person

Turkey red 1. a bright red produced on cotton cloth by alizarin **2.** cotton cloth of this color

☆**turkey trot** [cf. FOXTROT] a ballroom dance to ragtime music, popular in the early 20th cent.

Tur·ki (toor′kē, tur′-) n. [Per. < *Turk* < Turk. *Türk*] **1.** the Turkic languages collectively or any individual Turkic language; esp., *same as* UIGHUR (sense 2) **2.** a member of any Turkic people —*adj.* designating or of the Turkic languages or the peoples who speak them

Tur·kic (tur′kik) *adj.* **1.** designating or of a subfamily of the Altaic languages divided into several branches, including Turkish, Azerbaijani, Tatar, Uighur, Uzbek, and Turkoman **2.** designating or of the peoples who speak any of these —*n.* the Turkic subfamily of languages

Turk·ish (tur′kish) *adj.* of Turkey, the Turks, their language, etc. —*n.* **1.** the Turkic language of Turkey: in full **Ottoman-Turkish 2.** loosely, *same as* TURKIC

Turkish bath 1. a kind of bath in which the bather, after a period of heavy perspiration in a room of hot air or steam, is washed, massaged, and cooled **2.** a place where such a bath is given

Turkish delight (or **paste**) a kind of candy consisting of cubes of a sweetened and flavored jellylike substance covered with powdered sugar

Turkish Empire *same as* OTTOMAN EMPIRE

Turkish tobacco a dark, highly aromatic tobacco, grown in Turkey, Greece, etc. and used chiefly in cigarettes

Turkish towel [*also* t-] a thick cotton towel of terry cloth

Turk·ism (tur′kiz'm) n. Turkish culture, beliefs, etc.

Tur·ki·stan (tur′ki stan′, -stän′) *same as* TURKESTAN

Turk·man (turk′mən) n., pl. **-men** (-mən) a native or inhabitant of the Turkmen S.S.R.

Turk·men (-men) n. *same as* TURKOMAN (sense 2)

Turkmen Soviet Socialist Republic republic of the U.S.S.R., in C Asia, on the Caspian Sea, north of Iran: 188,400 sq. mi.; pop. 1,900,000; cap. Ashkhabad: also **Turk′men·i·stan′** (-i stan′, -i stän′). **Turk·me·ni·a** (turk mē′nē ə) —**Turk·me′ni·an** *adj.*

Tur·ko- (tur′kō, -ka) *a combining form meaning:* **1.** of Turkey or the Turks **2.** Turkey and, or the Turks and

Tur·ko·man (tur′kə mən) n. [Per. *Turkumān,* one like a Turk] **1.** pl. **-mans** any member of a group of seminomadic tribes living in the Turkmen, Uzbek, and Kazakh Soviet Socialist Republics and in parts of Iran and Afghanistan **2.** the Turkic language of the Turkomans

Turks and Caicos Islands (turks) Brit. crown colony in the West Indies, consisting of two groups of small islands southeast of the Bahamas: 166 sq. mi.; pop. 6,000

Turk's-cap lily (turks′kap′) any of various lilies having flowers whose petals and sepals are strongly recurved, resembling a rolled turban

Turk's-head (-hed′) n. *Naut.* a turbanlike knot made on a rope by means of a small line

Tur·ku (toor′koo) seaport in SW Finland: pop. 146,000

tur·mer·ic (tur′mər ik) n. [earlier also *tormerik* < MFr. *terre-mérite* < ML. *terra merita,* lit., deserved (or deserving) earth < ?] **1.** *a)* an East Indian plant (*Curcuma longa*) of the ginger family, whose rhizome in powdered form is used as a yellow dye or a seasoning, and in medicine *b)* its aromatic rhizome or the powder made from it **2.** any of several other plants having tuberous rhizomes

turmeric paper paper impregnated with turmeric, used as a test for alkali, which turns it brown, or for boric acid, which turns it reddish-brown

tur·moil (tur′moil) n. [*tur-* (< ? TURBULENT) + *moil*] tumult; commotion; uproar; confusion

turn (turn) vt. [ME. *turnen* < OE. *turnian* & OFr. *turner, tourner,* both < L. *tornare,* to turn in a lathe, turn < *tornus,* a lathe < Gr. *tornos,* a lathe, carpenter's compasses, akin to *terein,* to bore through: for IE. base see TRITE] **I.** *to cause to revolve or rotate* **1.** to make (a wheel, etc.) move about a central point or axis; revolve or rotate **2.** to give circular motion to; move around or partly around [to *turn* a somer-

sault] **II.** *to form by revolving, etc.* **1.** to give circular shape to by rotating against a tool, as in a lathe **2.** to give rounded shape or form to in any way **3.** to give a well-rounded or graceful form to [to *turn* a pretty phrase] **III.** *to change in position* **1.** to change the position of, as by a rotating motion [to *turn* a chair around] **2.** to revolve in the mind; ponder (often with *over*) **3.** *a)* to bend, fold, twist, etc. [*turn* the sheet back] *b)* to twist or wrench (one's ankle) **4.** to bend back (a cutting edge); blunt **5.** to reverse the position or sides of; invert; specif., *a)* to move so that the undersurface is on top and vice versa [to *turn* a phonograph record] *b)* to spade, plow, etc. so that the undersoil comes to the surface *c)* to reverse (a collar, coat, etc.) so that the inner surface becomes the outer **6.** to cause to become upside down, topsy-turvy, etc. **7.** to upset or unsettle (the stomach) **IV.** *to change the movement or course of* **1.** to bend the course of; deflect; divert [to *turn* a blow] **2.** to cause to change intentions, actions, etc. [to *turn* someone from his purpose]; specif., *a)* to convert or persuade *b)* to change in feelings, attitudes, etc. [to *turn* people against someone] **3.** to go around (a corner, an army's flank, etc.) **4.** to reach or pass (a certain age, amount, etc.) **5.** to reverse the course of; specif., *a)* to stop or repel [to *turn* an attack] *b)* to cause to recoil, rebound, etc. [criticism *turned* against the critic] **6.** to drive, set, let go, etc. in some way [to *turn* someone adrift] **7.** to keep (money, goods, etc.) circulating or moving **V.** *to change the direction, trend, etc. of* **1.** to change the direction of (one's eyes, face, etc.) **2.** to direct, point, aim, etc. [to *turn* a gun on someone] **3.** to change the trend, focus, etc. of [to *turn* one's thoughts to practical matters] **4.** to put to (a specified) use or result; employ; apply [to *turn* knowledge to good account, to *turn* one's hand to writing] **VI.** *to change the nature or condition of* **1.** to change; convert; transmute [to *turn* cream into butter, a writer *turned* actor] **2.** to exchange for [to *turn* produce into hard cash] **3.** to subject [to *turn* another's remarks to ridicule] **4.** to translate or paraphrase **5.** to derange, dement, distract, or infatuate **6.** to make sour **7.** to affect in some way [*turned* sick by the sight] **8.** to change the color of —vi. **I.** *to revolve, rotate, etc.* **1.** to move in a circle or around an axis; rotate or revolve; pivot **2.** to move in a circular manner; move around or partly around [they won't *turn*] **3.** *a)* to seem to be whirling or moving, as to one who is dizzy *b)* to reel or be giddy: said of the head **II.** *to form something by revolving* **1.** to run a lathe **2.** to be shaped on a lathe **III.** *to change position* **1.** *a)* to move in a rotary manner so as to change position *b)* to shift or twist the body as if on an axis **2.** to become curved or bent **3.** to reverse position so that bottom becomes top; become reversed or inverted **4.** to become upset or unsettled: said of the stomach **IV.** *to change course or movement* **1.** to change one's or its course so as to be moving, going, etc. in a different direction; deviate **2.** to reverse one's or its course; start to move, go, etc. in the opposite direction [the tide has *turned*] **3.** to consult; refer (*to*) **4.** to go or apply (*to*) for help **V.** *to change in direction, trend, etc.* **1.** to change one's or its direction; face about; shift **2.** to direct or shift one's attention, abilities, thoughts, etc. [to *turn* from one's work to a hobby] **3.** to make a sudden attack (*on* or *upon*) [the dog *turned* on him] **4.** to reverse one's feelings, attitude, allegiance, etc. [to *turn* against former friends] **5.** to be contingent or depend (*on* or *upon*) **6.** [Obs.] to vacillate **VI.** *to become changed in nature or condition* **1.** to enter into a specified condition; become [to *turn* bitter with age] **2.** to change into another form, type, or sort [the rain *turned* to sleet] **3.** to become rancid, putrid, sour, etc. **4.** to change color [leaves *turning* in the fall] —n. **I.** *rotation, circular motion, etc.* **1.** the act of turning around; complete or partial rotation, as of a wheel, handle, etc.; revolution **2.** *a)* a winding of one thing around another *b)* a single twist, coil, winding, etc.; convolution **3.** *a)* the condition of being twisted, bent, etc. in a circular form *b)* the direction of this **4.** a musical ornament consisting usually of four tones, the second and fourth of which are the same, or principal, tone, the first, normally, being a degree above, and the third a degree below **II.** *change of movement, direction, etc.* **1.** a change of position or posture, as by rotating motion **2.** a change or reversal of course or direction [the *turn* of the tide] **3.** *a)* a walk taken about a building, area, etc., as for inspection; tour *b)* a short walk or ride, returning to the starting place, as for exercise **4.** the place where a change in direction occurs; bend; curve **III.** *change of nature, condition, etc.* **1.** *a)* a change in trend, circumstances, events, policy, health, etc. [a *turn* for the better] *b)* same as TURNING POINT **2.** the time of a chronological change [at the *turn* of the century] **3.** a sudden, brief shock or fright; start **IV.** *an occasional or repeated action, performance, etc.* **1.** an action that harms or, more usually, benefits another [to do someone a good *turn*] **2.** a bout; spell; try [a *turn* at gardening] **3.** an attack of illness, dizziness, rage, etc.; fit **4.** the right, duty, or opportunity to do something, esp. as coming to each of a number of people in regular order [one's *turn* at bat]

5. [Brit.] a shift of work **6.** *a)* a short performance given as part of a variety show; act *b)* its performer or performers ☆**7.** *Finance* a transaction on the stock exchange involving both purchase and sale of particular securities **V.** *trend, form, style, character, etc.* **1.** a distinctive form, manner, cast, detail, etc. /a quaint *turn* to her speech/ **2.** natural inclination or aptitude; flair /an inquisitive *turn* of mind/ **3.** a tendency; drift; trend /the discussion took a new *turn*/ **4.** a variation or interpretation of the original /to give an old story a new *turn*/ —**at every turn** in every instance; constantly —**by turns** one after another; alternately; in succession —☆**call the turn** to predict successfully —**in turn** in proper sequence or succession —**out of turn 1.** not in proper sequence or order **2.** at the wrong time; esp., unwisely or imprudently /to talk *out of turn*/ —**take turns** to speak, do, etc. one after another in regular order —**to a turn** to just the right degree; perfectly —**turn and turn about** one after another in regular order; by turns: also **turn about** —**turn down** ☆**1.** *a)* to reject (a request, advice, etc.) *b)* to reject the request, advice, etc. of (someone) **2.** to lessen the intensity or volume of (light or sound) by manipulating controls —**turn in 1.** to make a turn into; enter **2.** to point (the toes) inward ☆**3.** to deliver; hand in ☆**4.** to inform on or hand over, as to the police **5.** to give back; return **6.** to fold over; double **7.** [Colloq.] to go to bed —**turn off 1.** to leave (a road, path, etc.) and enter another branching off **2.** to branch off: said of a road, path, etc. **3.** *a)* to stop a flow of (water, gas, electricity, etc.) *b)* to close (a faucet, etc.) so as to stop a flow *c)* to make (an electrical device) stop functioning by operating the controls **4.** to stop displaying or showing, suddenly or automatically /to *turn off* a smile/ **5.** to deflect; divert ☆**6.** [Slang] to cause (someone) to become bored, depressed, uninterested, etc. **7.** [Brit.] to discharge (an employee) —**turn on 1.** *a)* to start a flow of (water, gas, electricity, etc.) *b)* to open (a faucet, etc.) so as to start a flow *c)* to make (an electrical device) start functioning by operating the controls **2.** to show or display suddenly or automatically /to *turn on* the charm/ ☆**3.** [Slang] *a)* to initiate in the use of a psychedelic drug *b)* to stimulate or be stimulated with or as with a psychedelic drug; make or become elated, euphoric, etc. —**turn out 1.** to put out (a light, etc.) **2.** to put outside **3.** to drive out; dismiss or discharge **4.** to turn inside out **5.** to come or go out, as to assemble somewhere **6.** to produce as the result of work **7.** to result; eventuate **8.** to prove to be; be discovered to be **9.** to come to be; become **10.** to equip, dress, etc. **11.** [Colloq.] to get out of bed —**turn over 1.** to change the position of, as by rolling **2.** to reverse the position of; turn upside down; invert **3.** to shift one's position, as from one side to the other; roll over **4.** to begin, or make begin, to operate, as an engine or motor **5.** to think about carefully; ponder **6.** to hand over; transfer **7.** to relinquish; delegate **8.** to put to a different use; convert **9.** to sell and replenish (a stock of goods) **10.** to buy and sell, or do business, to the amount of —**turn to** to get to work; get busy —**turn up 1.** to fold or bend back or over upon itself **2.** to shorten (a dress, etc.) by folding back the bottom edge and making a new hem **3.** to lift up or turn face upward, as to see the other side **4.** to bring to light, as by digging **5.** to increase the flow, speed, intensity, loudness, etc. of, as by turning a control **6.** *a)* to make a turn onto and ascend (a street on a hill, etc.) *b)* to make a turn into any street or road **7.** to have an upward direction **8.** to come about; happen **9.** to make an appearance; arrive **10.** to be found

SYN.—**turn,** the general word in this connection, implies motion around, or partly around, a center or axis /a wheel *turns*, he *turned* on his heel/; **rotate** implies movement of a body around its own center or axis /the earth *rotates* on its axis/; **revolve** is sometimes interchangeable with **rotate,** but in strict discrimination, it suggests movement in an orbit around a center /the earth *revolves* around the sun/; **gyrate** implies movement in a circular or spiral course, as by a tornado; **spin** and **whirl** suggest very fast and continuous rotation or revolution /a top *spins,* the leaves *whirled* about the yard/ See also CURVE

turn·a·bout (turn′ə bout′) *n.* **1.** the act of turning about, as to face the other way **2.** a shift or reversal of allegiance, opinion, tendency, etc.; about-face: also **turn′-a-bout′-face′** ☆**3.** a merry-go-round

turn-and-bank indicator (-ən baŋk′) an airplane instrument that indicates the rate of turn and degree of bank at the same time, to help the pilot judge whether the airplane is properly banked for a turn

☆**turn·a·round** (-ə round′) *n.* **1.** *same as* TURNABOUT (senses 1 & 2) **2.** a wide area, as in a driveway, to allow for turning a vehicle around **3.** the time needed to unload, refuel, service, and reload an aircraft

turn·buck·le (-buk′'l) *n.* **1.** orig., a catch for shutters or casement windows **2.** a metal sleeve with opposite internal threads at each end for the threaded ends of two rods or for ringbolts, forming a coupling that can be turned to tighten or loosen the united rod or wire attached to the ringbolts

TURNBUCKLE

turn·coat (-kōt′) *n.* [from the notion of a coat worn right side out or inside out, according to circumstances] a person who goes over to the opposite side or party; renegade; traitor

turn·down (-doun′) *adj.* **1.** that can be turned down **2.** having the upper part folded down /a *turndown* collar/ —*n.* **1.** a rejection; rebuff **2.** a decline; downturn

turn·er[1] (tur′nər) *n.* **1.** a thing that turns or is used for turning /a pancake *turner*/ **2.** a person who turns, specif. one who operates a lathe

☆**turn·er**[2] (tur′nər) *n.* [G. < *turnen,* to engage in gymnastics < OHG., to turn < L. *tornare:* see TURN] a gymnast or tumbler; esp., a member of a Turnverein

Tur·ner (tur′nər) **1.** Frederick Jackson, 1861-1932: U.S. historian **2.** J(oseph) M(allord) W(illiams), 1775-1851: Eng. painter **3.** Nat, 1800-31; U.S. Negro slave, who led an abortive revolt (1831)

turn·er·y (tur′nər ē) *n., pl.* -**er·ies** [TURNER[1] + -Y[4]] the work or shop of a lathe operator

turn·ing (tur′niŋ) *n.* **1.** the action of a person or thing that turns **2.** a place where a road, etc. turns or turns off **3.** the art or process of shaping things on or as on a lathe

turning point 1. a point at which something turns or changes direction **2.** a point in time at which a decisive change occurs; crisis

tur·nip (tur′nip) *n.* [earlier *turnep,* prob. < TURN or Fr. *tour,* in the sense of "turned, round" + ME. *nepe* < OE. *næp,* a turnip < L. *napus*] **1.** *a)* a biennial plant (*Brassica rapa*) of the mustard family, with edible, hairy leaves and a roundish, light-colored, fleshy root used as a vegetable *b)* *same as* RUTABAGA **2.** the root of either of these plants **3.** [Old Slang] a pocket watch

turn·key (turn′kē′) *n., pl.* -**keys′** a person in charge of the keys of a prison; warder; jailer

turn·off (-ôf′) *n.* **1.** the act of turning off ☆**2.** a place where one turns off; esp., a road or ramp leading off a highway

turn·out (-out′) *n.* **1.** the act of turning out **2.** *a)* a gathering of people, as for a meeting *b)* the number of people assembled **3.** an amount produced; output **4.** *a)* a wider part of a narrow road, enabling vehicles to pass one another *b)* an exit road or side road *c)* a railroad siding **5.** a carriage with its horse or horses; equipage **6.** *a)* equipment; furnishings *b)* a particular set of clothes; costume **7.** [Chiefly Brit.] a labor strike or striker

turn·o·ver (-ō′vər) *n.* **1.** the act or an instance of turning over; specif., *a)* an upset *b)* a change from one use, side, opinion, management, etc. to another **2.** a small pie made by folding one half of the crust back over the other half, with a filling in between **3.** *a)* the number of times a stock of goods is sold and replenished in a given period of time *b)* the amount of business done during a given period of time in terms of the money used in buying and selling *c)* the number of shares sold in a stock market during a given period of time **4.** *a)* the number of workers hired to replace those who have left during a given period of time *b)* the ratio of this to the average number of workers employed —*adj.* that turns over or is turned over /a *turnover* collar/

turn·pike (-pīk′) *n.* [ME. *turnpyke,* a spiked barrier across a road: see TURN & PIKE[4]] **1.** formerly, a turnstile **2.** *same as* TOLLGATE **3.** a toll road, esp. one that is an expressway

turn·sole (-sōl′) *n.* [ME. *turnesole* < MFr. *tournesol* < It. *tornasole* or Sp. *tornasol* < *tornar*(*e*), to TURN + *sol*(*e*), sun (see SOL)] **1.** any of a number of plants whose flowers supposedly turn with the sun, as the sunflower and heliotrope **2.** *a)* a Mediterranean plant (*Croton tinctoria*) of the spurge family, yielding a purple dye *b)* this dye

turn·spit (-spit′) *n.* **1.** a person who turns a spit **2.** formerly, a breed of small dog trained to turn a spit by means of a treadmill **3.** a spit that can be turned

turn·stile (-stīl′) *n.* **1.** a post with revolving horizontal bars, placed in an entrance to allow the passage of persons but not of horses, cattle, etc. **2.** a similar apparatus, often coin-operated, used at entrances to admit persons one at a time and to count those passing through

turn·stone (-stōn′) *n.* any of several small, ploverlike, migratory shore birds (genus *Arenaria*) related to the sandpipers; esp., the ruddy turnstone (*Arenaria interpres*) of nearly worldwide distribution: so called because they turn over shells, stones, etc. in search of food

turn·ta·ble (-tā′b'l) *n.* a circular rotating platform; specif., *a)* a platform of this kind for supporting a phonograph record being played *b)* a platform carrying track to turn a locomotive around

turn·up (turn′up′) *n.* something turned up; a turned-up part —*adj.* that turns up or is turned up

‡**Turn·ver·ein** (toorn′fer in′; *E.* turn′fə rin′) *n.* [G. < *turnen,* to exercise (see TURNER[2]) + *verein,* a union, association] a club of turners, or gymnasts

tur·pen·tine (tur′pən tīn′) *n.* [ME. *turpentyne* < OFr. *terbentine* < L. *terebinthinus,* of the turpentine tree < *terebinthus:* see TEREBINTH] **1.** the brownish-yellow, sticky, semifluid oleoresin exuding from the terebinth **2.** any of the various sticky, viscid oleoresins obtained from pines and other coniferous trees: in full **gum turpentine 3.** a colorless, volatile essential oil, $C_{10}H_{16}$, distilled from such oleoresins and used in paints, varnishes, etc., and in medicine: in full **spirits** (or **oil**) **of turpentine** —*vt.* -**tined′,** -**tin′ing 1.** to apply turpentine to ☆**2.** to extract turpentine

from (trees) —**tur·pen·tin·ic** (-tin'ik), **tur'pen·tin'ous** (-tī'nəs) *adj.*

Tur·pin (tur'pin), **Dick** 1706–39; Eng. highwayman: hanged

tur·pi·tude (tur'pə tōōd', -tyōōd') *n.* [MFr. < L. *turpitudo* < *turpis*, base, vile] 1. baseness; vileness; depravity 2. an instance of this

turps (turps) *n.pl.* [*with sing. v.*] same as TURPENTINE (*n.* 3)

tur·quoise (tur'koiz, -kwoiz) *n.* [ME. *turkeis* < MFr. *turqueise*, fem. of OFr. *turqueis*, Turkish (see TURK): orig. brought to western Europe through Turkey] 1. a semiprecious stone, typically greenish-blue, a hydrous phosphate of aluminum containing a small amount of copper 2. the color of turquoise; greenish-blue —*adj.* greenish-blue Also sp. **tur'quois**

tur·ret (tur'it) *n.* [ME. *turet* < OFr. *tourete*, dim. of *tour*: see TOWER¹] 1. a small tower projecting from a building, usually at a corner and often merely ornamental 2. a wooden, usually square tower on wheels, carrying soldiers, battering-rams, catapults, etc., used in ancient warfare for attacking fortresses and walled cities 3. *a*) a low, armored, usually revolving, towerlike structure for a gun or guns, as on a warship, tank, or fortress *b*) a transparent dome for a gun and gunner, as on a bomber 4. an attachment for a lathe, drill, etc., consisting of a block holding several cutting tools, which may be rotated to present any of the tools to the work: also **tur'ret·head'** (-hed') 5. an adjustable device on a camera for holding various lenses

tur·ret·ed (-id) *adj.* 1. having a turret or turrets 2. shaped like a turret 3. having whorls forming a high, conical spiral, as some shells

tur·ric·u·late (tə rik'yōo lit, -lāt') *adj.* [< L. *turricula*, dim. of *turris*, a tower + -ATE¹] having or resembling a small turret or turrets: also **tur·ric'u·lat'ed**

tur·tle (tur't'l) *n.*, *pl.* **-tles, -tle:** see PLURAL, II, D, 1 [altered (after TURTLEDOVE) < Fr. *tortue*, tortoise < VL. *tartaruca:* see TORTOISE] 1. any of a large and widely distributed order (Chelonia) of land, freshwater, and saltwater reptiles having a toothless beak and a soft body encased in a hard shell into which, in most species, the head, tail, and four legs may be withdrawn: although water, esp. sea, species are usually called *turtle* and land species are usually called *tortoise*, the terms are properly interchangeable for all species 2. the flesh of some turtles, used as food 3. *archaic var. of* TURTLEDOVE —*vi.* **-tled, -tling** to hunt for turtles —**turn turtle** to turn upside down; capsize

tur·tle·back (-bak') *n.* an arched structure built over the deck of a ship as a protection against heavy seas

tur·tle·dove (-duv') *n.* [ME. < OE. *turtle, turtla* < L. *turtur*, of echoic origin] 1. any of several old-world wild doves noted for their plaintive cooing and the affection that the mates are traditionally thought of as showing toward each other 2. same as MOURNING DOVE

tur·tle·head (-hed') *n.* ☆any of a genus (*Chelone*) of perennial N. American plants of the figwort family, with showy, tubular, white or pink flowers

tur·tle·neck (-nek') *n.* ☆1. a high, snugly fitting, turndown collar on a pullover sweater, shirt, etc. ☆2. a sweater, shirt, etc. with such a neck

turves (turvz) *n. archaic pl. of* TURF

Tus·ca·loo·sa (tus'kə lōō'sə) [after a Choctaw chief, lit., Black Warrior < *taska*, warrior + *lusa*, black] city in WC Ala., near Birmingham: pop. 66,000

Tus·can (tus'kən) *adj.* [ME. < L. *Tuscanus* < *Tuscus*, an Etruscan] 1. of Tuscany, its people, etc. 2. designating or of a classical (Roman) order of architecture characterized by unfluted columns with a ringlike capital and no decoration —*n.* 1. a native or inhabitant of Tuscany 2. any of the Italian dialects of Tuscany, esp. that one accepted as standard literary Italian

TUSCAN CAPITAL

Tus·ca·ny (tus'kə nē) region of C Italy, formerly a grand duchy: 8,876 sq. mi.; pop. 3,267,000; chief city, Florence: It. name, TOSCANA

Tus·ca·ro·ra (tus'kə rôr'ə) *n.* [< the native name, lit., hemp gatherers] 1. *pl.* **-ras, -ra** any member of a tribe of Indians at one time living in Virginia and North Carolina but later, after joining the Iroquois Confederacy in 1722, living in New York and Ontario 2. their Iroquoian language

tush¹ (tush) *interj., n.* [ME. *tussch*] an exclamation expressing impatience, reproof, contempt, etc.

tush² (tush) *n.* [ME. *tusch* < OE. *tucs:* see ff.] 1. same as TUSK 2. any of the canine teeth of a horse

tusk (tusk) *n.* [ME. *tusk*, by metathesis < OE. *tucs*, akin to OFris. *tusk* < Gmc. *tunth-ska* < *tunth-:* for IE. base see TOOTH] 1. in elephants, wild boars, walruses, etc., a very long, large, pointed tooth, usually one of a pair, projecting outside the mouth and used for defense, digging up food, etc. 2. any tooth or projection suggestive of a tusk —*vt.* to dig, gore, etc. with a tusk or tusks —SYN. see TOOTH —**tusked** (tuskt) *adj.* —**tusk'like'** (-līk') *adj.*

Tus·ke·gee (tus kē'gē) [< Muskogean town name; ? akin to Creek *taskáya*, warrior] city in E Ala.: pop. 11,000

tusk·er (tus'kər) *n.* an animal with tusks

tus·sah (tus'ə) *n.* [Hindi *tasar* < Sans. *tasara*, lit., a shuttle, kind of silkworm] 1. a semidomesticated Asiatic silkworm (*Antheraea paphia*), that produces a coarse, tough silk 2. *a*) this silk: in full **tussah silk** *b*) a fabric made from this

Tus·saud (tus sō'), **Madame** (born *Marie Gresholtz*) 1760–1850; Swiss waxworks exhibitor in London

tus·sis (tus'is) *n.* [L.] *Med.* a cough —**tus'sive** (-iv) *adj.*

tus·sle (tus''l) *vi.* **-sled, -sling** [LME. *tussillen*, freq. of *tusen* (in comp.), to pull: cf. TOUSLE] to fight, struggle, contend, etc. vigorously or vehemently; wrestle; scuffle —*n.* a vigorous or vehement struggle or contest; scuffle

tus·sock (tus'ək) *n.* [prob. < ME. (*to*)*tusen*, to rumple + -OCK] a thick tuft or clump of grass, sedge, twigs, etc. —**tus'sock·y** (-ē) *adj.*

tussock moth any of a large group of moths (family Lymantriidae) whose caterpillars are covered with long tufts of hair: many are destructive pests of certain trees

tus·sore, tus·sor (tus'ôr) *n. var. of* TUSSAH

tut (tut: *conventionalized pronun.*) *interj., n.* a clicking or sucking sound made with the tongue, usually repeated one or more times, to express impatience, annoyance, mild rebuke, etc. —*vi.* **tut'ted, tut'ting** to utter "tuts"

Tut·ankh·a·men (tōōt'äŋk ä'mən) fl. c.1355 B.C.; Egyptian king of the 18th dynasty: tomb discovered in 1922: also sp. **Tut'ankh·a'mon**

☆**tu·tee** (tōō tē', tyōō-) *n.* [TUT(OR) + -EE¹] a person who is being tutored

tu·te·lage (tōōt'l ij, tyōōt'-) *n.* [< L. *tutela*, protection < *tutus* (see TUTOR) + -AGE] 1. the function of a guardian; guardianship; care, protection, etc. 2. teaching; instruction 3. the condition of being under a guardian or tutor

tu·te·lar·y (-er'ē) *adj.* [L. *tutelarius* < *tutela:* see prec.] 1. that watches over or protects 2. of or serving as a guardian Also **tu'te·lar** (-ər) —*n.*, *pl.* **-lar'ies** a tutelary god, spirit, etc.

tu·tor (tōōt'ər, tyōōt'-) *n.* [ME. < MFr. *tuteur* < L. *tutor* < *tutus* for *tuitus*, pp. of *tueri*, to look after, guard] 1. a teacher who gives individual instruction to a student; private teacher 2. a legal guardian of a minor and his property 3. in English universities, a college official in charge of the studies of an undergraduate ☆4. in some American universities and colleges, a teacher ranking below an instructor; teaching assistant —*vt.* 1. to act as a tutor to; teach; esp., to give individual instruction to 2. to train under discipline; discipline; admonish —*vi.* 1. to act as a tutor, or instructor 2. [Colloq.] to be instructed, esp. by a tutor —**tu'tor·age, tu'tor·ship'** *n.*

tu·to·ri·al (tōō tôr'ē əl, tyōō-) *adj.* [< L. *tutorius* + -AL] of a tutor or tutors —*n.* a class in a tutorial system

tutorial system a system of instruction, as in some universities, in which a tutor directs the studies of and has general supervision over each of the small group of students assigned to him

tu·toy·er (tōō'twä yā', Fr. tü twä yā') *vt.* [Fr. < MFr. < *tu*, (familiar form for you, thou < L.: see THOU¹) + *toi* (acc. of *tu*) + *-er*, inf. ending] to speak to familiarly, as, in French, by using the singular forms (*tu* and *toi*) of "you" rather than the more formal plural form (*vous*)

tut·ti (tōōt'ē; It. tōōt'tē) *adj.* [It. (pl. of *tutto*), lit., all < VL. *tottus* for L. *totus*, all, whole: see TOTAL] for all instruments or voices: a musical direction to the performers —*n., pl.* **-tis** 1. a passage played or sung by all performers 2. the tonal effect produced by playing such a passage

☆**tut·ti-frut·ti** (tōōt'ē frōōt'ē) *n.* [It., lit., all fruits: cf. prec.] 1. ice cream or other sweet food containing bits of candied fruits 2. a flavoring combining the flavors of a number of fruits

tut-tut (tut'tut') *interj., n.* see TUT

tut·ty (tut'ē) *n.* [ME. *tutie* < MFr. < Ar. *tūtiyā*, zinc oxide, prob. via Per. < Sans. *tuttha*, blue vitriol] crude zinc oxide obtained from the flues of smelting furnaces

tu·tu (tōō'tōō; Fr. tü tü') *n.* [Fr., orig. baby talk alteration < *cul*, bottom, backside (see BASCULE)] a very short, full, projecting skirt worn by ballerinas

Tu·tu·i·la (tōō'tōō ē'lä) chief island of American Samoa, in the South Pacific: with nearby islets, 53 sq. mi.; pop. 25,000; chief town, Pago Pago

tu-whit tu-whoo (tōō hwit' tōō hwōō'; -wit', -wōō') the characteristic vocal sound made by an owl

☆**tux** (tuks) *n. clipped form of* TUXEDO

☆**tux·e·do** (tək sē'dō) *n., pl.* **-dos** [< the name of a country club at *Tuxedo* Park, near *Tuxedo* Lake, N.Y.] 1. a man's tailless, semiformal jacket for evening wear, orig. black and with satin lapels; dinner jacket 2. a suit of such a jacket and dark trousers, worn with a dark bow tie

tu·yère (twē yer', tōō-; twir) *n.* [Fr. *tuyère*, nozzle < *tuyau*, a pipe < Frank. *thuta*, akin to EFris. *tute*, a pipe, tube] the pipe or nozzle through which air is forced into a blast furnace, forge, etc.

TV (tē'vē') *n., pl.* **TVs, TV's** television or a television receiving set

TVA, T.V.A. Tennessee Valley Authority

☆**TV dinner** [because it can conveniently be eaten while viewing television] a frozen, precooked dinner packaged in a compartmented tray for heating and serving

twa (twä) *adj., n.* [ME. (Northern & Scot.) < OE., TWO] *Scot. var.* of TWO

twad·dle (twäd′'l) *n.* [earlier *twattle*, prob. collateral form of *tattle*, in *twittle-twattle* for TITTLE-TATTLE] foolish, empty talk or writing; nonsense —*vt., vi.* **-dled, -dling** to talk or write in a foolish or senseless manner; prattle —**twad′dler** *n.*

twain (twān) *n., adj.* [ME. *twene* < OE. *twegen*, nom. & acc. masc. form of *twa*, TWO] *archaic var.* of TWO

Twain (twān), **Mark** *see* Samuel Langhorne CLEMENS

twang (twaŋ) *n.* [echoic] **1.** *a*) a quick, sharp, vibrating sound, as of a taut string suddenly plucked or released *b*) an act of plucking that makes this sound **2.** *a*) a sharply nasal way of speaking; ringing nasal quality *b*) a dialect characterized by this **3.** [Dial.] a twinge —*vi.* **1.** to make a twang, as a bowstring, banjo, etc. **2.** to speak with a twang **3.** to be released with a twang: said of an arrow —*vt.* **1.** to cause to twang **2.** to say with a twang **3.** to shoot (an arrow), release (a bowstring), etc. with a twang Also [Rare] **twan′gle** (-g'l) **-gled, -gling** —**twang′y** *adj.*

'twas (twuz, twäz; *unstressed* twəz) it was

twat·tle (twät′'l) *n., vi., vt.* **-tled, -tling** *var.* of TWADDLE

tway·blade (twā′blād′) *n.* [archaic *tway*, two (ME. *twei*, var. of *twene*: see TWAIN) + BLADE] any of various native, soil-inhabiting orchids (esp. genera *Listera* and *Liparis*) having opposite, paired leaves

tweak (twēk) *vt.* [var. of dial. *twick* < ME. *twikken* < OE. *twiccan*, to TWITCH] to give a sudden, twisting pinch to (someone's nose, ear, cheek, etc.) —*n.* such a pinch

twee (twē) *adj.* [back-formation < *tweet*, in same sense < child's pronun. of SWEET] [Brit. Colloq.] affectedly clever, dainty, elegant, etc.; mincingly cute or sweet

Tweed (twēd) river in SE Scotland flowing east through NE England into the North Sea: 97 mi.

tweed (twēd) *n.* [< misreading of *tweel*, Scot. form of TWILL: later associated with prec.] **1.** a wool fabric with a rough surface, in any of various twill weaves of two or more colors or shades **2.** a suit, etc. of this **3.** [*pl.*] clothes of tweed

Tweed (twēd), **William Mar·cy** (mär′sē) 1823–78; U.S. politician & corrupt Tammany leader: called *Boss Tweed*

Tweed·dale (twēd′dāl) *same as* PEEBLES

twee·dle (twēd′'l) *vi., vt.* **-dled, -dling** [echoic of a reed pipe] **1.** to pipe, whistle, sing, etc. shrilly **2.** [infl. by WHEEDLE] to cajole or wheedle —*n.* a shrill, piping sound

twee·dle·dum and twee·dle·dee (twēd′'l dum′ 'n twēd′'l dē′) [< prec. + *dum & dee*, echoic of musical notes: first used of two 18th-c. rival composers] **1.** two persons or things so much alike as to be almost indistinguishable **2.** [T- T-] two almost identical brothers in *Through the Looking Glass*, by Lewis Carroll

Tweeds·muir (twēdz′myoor), 1st Baron, *see* BUCHAN

tweed·y (twēd′ē) *adj.* **tweed′i·er, tweed′i·est 1.** of or like tweed **2.** *a*) habitually wearing tweeds *b*) characterized by the casually tailored look, fondness for the outdoors, etc. of a person given to wearing tweeds —**tweed′i·ness** *n.*

'tween (twēn) *prep.* [ME. *twene*, aphetic for *atwene*, *betwene*, BETWEEN] [Poet.] between

'tween deck *Naut.* any deck on a ship below the main deck

tween·y (twēn′ē) *n., pl.* **-ies** [< *tween*, aphetic for *between-maid* + -Y¹] [Brit. Colloq.] a housemaid, esp. a scullery maid

tweet (twēt) *n., interj.* [echoic] the thin, chirping sound of a small bird —*vi.* to make this sound

tweet·er (-ər) *n.* a small, high-fidelity loudspeaker for reproducing high-frequency sounds: cf. WOOFER

tweeze (twēz) *vt.* **tweezed, tweez′ing** [back-formation < TWEEZERS] [Colloq.] to pluck with or as with tweezers

tweez·er (twē′zər) *n.* [back-formation < ff.] *same as* TWEEZERS

tweez·ers (-zərz) *n.pl.* [*with sing. or pl. v.*] [extended < obs. *tweeze*, surgical set < Fr. *étuis*, pl. of *étui*: see ETUI] small pincers for plucking out hairs, handling little objects, etc.: often **pair of tweezers**

twelfth (twelfth) *adj.* [ME. *twelfthe* < OE. *twelfta*: see TWELVE & -TH²] **1.** preceded by eleven others in a series; 12th **2.** designating any of the twelve equal parts of something —*n.* **1.** the one following the eleventh **2.** any of the twelve equal parts of something; 1/12

Twelfth Day the twelfth day (Jan. 6) after Christmas; Epiphany: the evening before, or sometimes the evening of, this day is called **Twelfth Night**

TWEEZERS

twelve (twelv) *adj.* [ME. *twelfe* < OE. *twelf*, akin to G. *zwölf*, Goth. *twalif* < Gmc. compound < IE. bases whence TWO & LEAVE¹: basic sense, "two left" (i.e., after ten): cf. ELEVEN] two more than ten —*n.* **1.** the cardinal number between eleven and thirteen; 12; XII **2.** any group of twelve persons or things; dozen **3.** something numbered twelve or having twelve units, as a throw of dice, etc. —**the Twelve** the Twelve Apostles

Twelve Apostles the twelve disciples chosen by Jesus to go forth to teach the gospel: see APOSTLE (sense 1)

twelve·fold (twelv′fōld′) *adj.* **1.** having twelve parts **2.** having twelve times as much or as many —*adv.* twelve times as much or as many

twelve·mo (-mō) *adj., n., pl.* **-mos** *same as* DUODECIMO

twelve·month (-munth′) *n.* a year

twelve-tone (-tōn′) *adj. Music* designating or of a system or technique of composition, developed by Arnold SCHÖNBERG, in which the twelve tones of the chromatic scale are arranged into some arbitrary, fixed succession (*tone row*) which then forms a basis for further thematic development

twen·ti·eth (twen′tē ith, twun′-) *adj.* [ME. *twentithe*, new formation for OE. *twentigotha*: see ff. & -TH²] **1.** preceded by nineteen others in a series; 20th **2.** designating any of the twenty equal parts of something —*n.* **1.** the one following the nineteenth **2.** any of the twenty equal parts of something; 1/20

twen·ty (twen′tē, twun′-) *adj.* [ME. *twenti* < OE. *twegentig*, lit., two tens (akin to G. *zwanzig*, Goth. *twai tigjus*) < *twegen*, TWAIN & -*tig*, -TY²] two times ten —*n., pl.* **-ties 1.** the cardinal number between nineteen and twenty-one; 20; XX ☆**2.** [Colloq.] a twenty-dollar bill —**the twenties** the numbers or years, as of a century, from twenty through twenty-nine

twen·ty·fold (-fōld′) *adj.* **1.** having twenty parts **2.** having twenty times as much or as many —*adv.* twenty times as much or as many

twen·ty-one (-wun′) *n.* ☆a gambling game at cards, in which each player's aim is to obtain from the dealer cards totaling twenty-one points or as near as possible to that total without exceeding it; blackjack

twen·ty-twen·ty (or 20/20) **vision** (twen′tē twen′tē) normal acuity of vision, which is the ability to see clearly at twenty feet what the normal eye sees at that distance

'twere (twur) [Poet.] it were [*if 'twere time*]

twerp (twurp) *n.* [ult. < ? or akin to Dan. *tver*, perverse: for base see THWART] [Slang] a person regarded as insignificant, contemptible, presumptuous, ridiculous, etc.

Twi (chwē) *n.* **1.** a language belonging to the Kwa branch of languages and spoken principally in Ghana **2.** *pl.* **Twis, Twi** any member of a Twi-speaking people

twi- (twī) [ME. < OE.: for IE. base see TWO] *a prefix meaning* two, double, twice

twi·bil, twi·bill (twī′bil′) *n.* [ME. *twibil* < OE.: see TWI- & BILL³] **1.** a double-bladed battle-ax **2.** [Brit. Dial.] a mattock or reaping hook

twice (twīs) *adv.* [ME. *twies* < OE. *twiges* < *twiga*, twice, akin to *twa*, TWO + -*es*, gen. sing. ending] **1.** on two occasions or in two instances **2.** two times **3.** two times as much or as many; twofold; doubly

twice-laid (-lād′) *adj.* **1.** made from strands of old rope **2.** made from remnants or used material

twice-told (-tōld′) *adj.* **1.** told twice **2.** told so often as to be hackneyed or trite

Twick·en·ham (twik′ən əm, twik′nəm) city in Middlesex, England, on the Thames, near London: pop. 102,000

twid·dle (twid′'l) *vt.* **-dled, -dling** [prob. < TW(IST) + (D)IDDLE¹] to twirl or play with lightly or idly —*vi.* **1.** to toy or trifle with some object **2.** to be busy about trifles **3.** to move in a twirling manner —*n.* a light, twirling motion, as with the thumbs —**twiddle one's thumbs 1.** to twirl one's thumbs idly around one another **2.** to do nothing; be idle —**twid′dler** *n.* —**twid′dly** *adj.*

twig¹ (twig) *n.* [ME. *twigge* < OE., akin to G. *zweig* < IE. *dwigho- < base *dwōu-*, two (cf. TWO): prob. with reference to the forking of the twig] a small, slender branch or shoot of a tree or shrub

twig² (twig) *vt., vi.* **twigged, twig′ging** [via thieves' slang < Ir. *tuigim*, I understand] [Brit. Colloq.] **1.** to observe; notice **2.** to understand

twig·gy (-ē) *adj.* **-gi·er, -gi·est 1.** slender, delicate, etc. like a twig **2.** full of or covered with twigs

twi·light (twī′līt′) *n.* [ME. (see TWI- & LIGHT¹), akin to G. *zwielicht*: basic sense prob. "the light between"] **1.** *a*) the subdued light just after sunset or, in less common usage, just before sunrise *b*) the period from sunset to dark **2.** any growing darkness **3.** a condition or period of gradual decline following full development, achievement, glory, etc. —*adj.* of or like twilight; dim, obscure, etc.

Twilight of the Gods *see* RAGNAROK

twilight sleep [transl. of G. *dämmerschlaf*] a state of partial anesthesia induced by the injection of morphine and scopolamine, formerly used to lessen the pains of childbirth

twi·lit (twī′lit) *adj.* full of or bathed in the softly diffused light of twilight

twill (twil) *n.* [ME. *twyll* < OE. *twilic*, woven of double thread (akin to OHG. *zwilih*) < WGmc. partial transl. (with *twi-*, TWI-) of L. *bilix*, with a double thread < *bi-*, BI-¹ + *licium*, a thread] **1.** a cloth woven so as to have parallel diagonal lines or ribs **2.** the pattern of this weave or its appearance —*vt.* to weave so as to produce a twill

'twill (twil) [Poet.] it will

twin (twin) *adj.* [ME. < OE. *twinn* & ON. *tvinnr*, double, both < base of TWO] **1.** *a*) consisting of or being two separate but similar or closely related things; forming a pair; double; paired [*twin* beds] *b*) being one of a pair of such things; being a counterpart **2.** *a*) being two that have been born at the same birth [*twin* girls] *b*) being either one of two born at the same birth [a *twin* sister] —*n.* **1.** either one of two born at the same birth: twins are either *identical* (produced from the same ovum) or *fraternal* (produced from separate ova) **2.** either one of two persons or things very much alike in appearance, shape, structure, etc. **3.** a compound crystal of two crystals or parts having a common face but in reversed positions with respect to each

other —*vi.* **twinned, twin′ning 1.** to give birth to twins **2.** to be paired or coupled (with another) **3.** [Archaic] to be born at the same birth —*vt.* **1.** to give birth to as twins **2.** to be or provide a counterpart to **3.** to pair or couple

☆**twin·ber·ry** (-ber′ē) *n., pl.* **-ries 1.** a N. American variety of honeysuckle (*Lonicera involucrata*) with purple flowers **2.** *same as* PARTRIDGEBERRY

☆**twin bill** [Colloq.] *same as:* **1.** DOUBLE FEATURE **2.** DOUBLE-HEADER (sense 2)

twin·born *adj.* born as a twin or twins

Twin Cities Minneapolis & St. Paul, Minn.

twine (twin) *n.* [ME. *twin* < OE., double thread, akin to *twegen*, TWAIN] **1.** strong thread, string, or cord of two or more strands twisted together **2.** a twining or being twined **3.** a twining thing or part; twist; convolution **4.** a tangle; snarl **5.** a twining branch or spray of a plant —*vt.* **twined, twin′ing** [ME. *twinen* < the *n.*] **1.** *a)* to twist together; intertwine; interlace *b)* to form by twisting, intertwining, or interlacing **2.** to encircle or wreathe (one thing) with another **3.** to wind (something) around something else **4.** to enfold, embrace, etc. [a wreath *twining* his brow] —*vi.* **1.** to twist, interlace, etc. **2.** to twist and turn

twin-en·gined (twin′en′jand) *adj.* powered by two engines: said of an airplane: also **twin′-en′gine**

☆**twin·flow·er** (-flou′ər) *n.* a trailing plant (*Linnaea borealis*) of the honeysuckle family, with glossy leaves and small, fragrant, pink, bell-shaped flowers growing in pairs

twinge (twinj) *vt.* **twinged, twing′ing** [ME. *twengen* < OE. *twengan*, to squeeze, press, pinch, akin to MHG. *twengen*, to pinch, squeeze (< OHG. *dwengan*, caus. of *dwingan*, to constrain) & OE. *thwang*, a thong, prob. < IE. base *tuengh-*, to constrain] to cause to have a sudden, brief, darting pain or pang —*vi.* to feel a sudden, brief, darting pain or pang —*n.* **1.** a sudden, brief, darting pain or pang **2.** a sudden, brief feeling of remorse, shame, etc.; qualm

☆**twi-night, twi·night** (twi′nit′) *adj.* [TWI(LIGHT) + NIGHT] *Baseball* designating a double-header that starts in the late afternoon and continues into the evening

twin·kle (twin′k'l) *vi.* **-kled, -kling** [ME. *twinklen* < OE. *twinclian*, freq. of base seen in G. *zwinken*, to wink] **1.** to shine with quick, intermittent flashes of light, as some stars; sparkle **2.** to light up, as with amusement: said of the eyes **3.** to move about or back and forth quickly and lightly, as a dancer's feet; flicker **4.** [Archaic] to wink or blink —*vt.* **1.** to make twinkle **2.** to emit (light) in quick, intermittent flashes —*n.* **1.** a flicker or wink of the eye **2.** a quick flash of amusement, etc. in the eye **3.** a quick, intermittent flash of light; sparkle **4.** the very brief time it takes to wink; twinkling —**twin′kler** *n.*

twin·kling (-klin) *n.* **1.** the action of a thing that twinkles **2.** *a)* the winking of an eye *b)* the very brief time it takes to wink; instant

twinned (twind) *adj.* **1.** born as a twin or twins **2.** paired or coupled **3.** consisting of two crystals forming a twin

twin·ning (twin′in) *n.* **1.** the bearing of twins **2.** a pairing or coupling **3.** the formation of a twin crystal or crystals

twin-screw (-skrōō′) *adj.* having two screw propellers, usually rotating in opposite directions, as some ships

twirl (twurl) *vt., vi.* [prob. < Scand., as in Norw. dial. *tvirla*, to twirl, akin to OE. *thwirel*, a stirring rod: cf. TURBID] **1.** to rotate rapidly; spin **2.** to turn rapidly in a circle; whirl around **3.** to twist or coil [to *twirl* one's mustache] ☆**4.** *Baseball* to pitch —*n.* **1.** a twirling or being twirled **2.** something twirled; specif., *a)* a twist, coil, etc. *b)* a twisting line; flourish —**twirl′er** *n.*

twirp (twurp) *n.* [Slang] *var. of* TWERP

twist (twist) *vt.* [ME. *twisten* < OE. *-twist*, a rope (in *mæst-twist*, rope to stay a mast), akin to TWAIN, TWINE, ON. *tvistra*, to separate, G. *zwist*, a quarrel (for IE. base see TWO)] **1.** *a)* to wind (two or more threads or strands) around one another, as by spinning *b)* to wind two or more threads or strands of (cotton, silk, etc.) around one another so as to produce thread or cord *c)* to produce (thread, cord, etc.) in this way **2.** to wreathe; twine **3.** to wind or coil (thread, rope, etc.) around something **4.** to encircle with a coil of **5.** to entwine or interweave in something else **6.** to make (one's or its way) by turning one way and then another **7.** to give spiral shape to by turning the ends in opposite directions **8.** *a)* to subject to torsion *b)* to put out of shape in this manner; wrench; sprain [to *twist* one's ankle] **9.** *a)* to contort or distort (the face, etc.) *b)* to cause to be malformed [fingers *twisted* with arthritis] **10.** to cause to become confused or mentally or emotionally disturbed **11.** to distort or pervert the meaning of **12.** to cause to turn around or rotate **13.** to break off by turning the end (often with *off*) **14.** to make (a ball) go in a curve by throwing or striking it so as to give it a spinning motion —*vi.* **1.** to undergo twisting and thus take on a spiral or coiled form [the wire *twists* easily] **2.** to spiral, coil, twine, etc. (*around* or *about* something) **3.** to revolve or rotate **4.** to turn to one side; change direction **5.** to turn one way and then another, as a path; wind; meander **6.** to squirm; writhe **7.** to move in a curved path, as a ball given a spinning motion ☆**8.** to dance the twist —*n.* **1.** the number of turns given to a specified

length of fiber, thread, cord, etc. along its axis **2.** a strong, closely twisted silk thread used for making buttonholes, etc. ☆**3.** tobacco leaves twisted into the shape of a roll **4.** a loaf of bread or roll made of one or more twisted pieces of dough **5.** a knot, etc. made by twisting **6.** a sliver of peel from a lemon, lime, etc. twisted and added to a drink for flavor **7.** rotation; spin, turn, twirl, etc. **8.** a spin given to a ball in throwing or striking it **9.** spiral movement along and around an axis **10.** *a)* the condition of being twisted in a spiral; torsional stress *b)* the degree of this; angle of torsion **11.** a contortion, as of the face **12.** a wrench or sprain **13.** a turning aside; turn; bend **14.** a place at which something twists or turns [a *twist* in the road] **15.** a personal tendency, esp. an eccentric one; quirk **16.** distortion or perversion, as of meaning **17.** an unexpected direction given to or taken by a situation **18.** a special or different meaning, method, or slant [a new *twist* to an old story] ☆**19.** a rock-and-roll dance characterized by movement of the arms and hips while standing in one place **20.** [Slang] a girl or woman —*SYN.* see CURVE

twist drill a kind of drill with deep helical grooves for carrying out chips

twist·er (twis′tər) *n.* **1.** a person who twists **2.** a thing that twists; specif., *a)* a machine for twisting threads, etc. *b)* a thrown or batted ball that has been given a twist ☆**3.** a tornado or cyclone

twit¹ (twit) *vt.* **twit′ted, twit′ting** [aphetic < ME. *atwiten*, to twit < OE. *ætwitan* < *æt*, at + *witan*, to accuse, akin to *witan*, to know: see WISE¹] to reproach, tease, taunt, etc., esp. by reminding of a fault or mistake —*n.* **1.** the act of twitting **2.** a reproach or taunt

twit² (twit) *n.* [prob. < TWI(RP) + (twa)t, slang for "fool"] [Brit. Slang] a foolish, contemptible, little person

twit³ (twit) *n.* [< TWITTER] ☆a state of nervous excitement

twitch (twich) *vt., vi* [ME. *twicchen* < OE. **twiccan*, var. of *twiccian*, to pluck, catch hold of: akin to G. *zwicken*, prob. < base of TWIG¹] **1.** to pull (at) with a quick, slight jerk; pluck **2.** to move with a quick, slight jerk or jerks or spasmodically **3.** to ache with a sudden, sharp pain —*n.* **1.** a quick, slight jerk **2.** a sudden, quick motion, esp. a spasmodic one; tic [a facial *twitch*] **3.** a sudden, sharp pain; twinge

twit·ter¹ (twit′ər) *vi.* [ME. *twiteren*, akin to G. *zwitschern*: orig. echoic] **1.** to make a series of light, sharp, intermittent vocal sounds; chirp continuously or tremulously, as birds do **2.** *a)* to talk in a rapid, tremulous manner expressive of agitation, timidity, etc.; chatter *b)* to giggle or titter **3.** to tremble with excitement, eagerness, etc. —*vt.* to express or say in a twittering manner —*n.* **1.** a light, sharp, intermittent vocal sound of a bird; chirping **2.** any similar sound **3.** a condition of trembling excitement; flutter —**twit′ter·er** *n.* —**twit′ter·y** *adj.*

twit·ter² (twit′ər) *n.* a person who twits

'twixt (twikst) *prep.* [Poet.] betwixt

two (tōō) *adj.* [ME. *two, tu* < OE. *twa*, fem. & neut., *tu*, neut. (cf. TWAIN), akin to G. *zwei* < IE. base **dwou-*, two, whence L. *duo*, two, Gr. *duo*, Sans. *dvau*] totaling one more than one —*n.* **1.** the cardinal number between one and three; 2; II **2.** any two people or things; pair; couple **3.** something numbered two or having two units, as a playing card, domino, face of a die, etc. —**in two** in two parts; asunder —**put two and two together** to reach an obvious conclusion by considering several facts together

☆**two-base hit** (tōō′bās′) *Baseball* a hit by which the batter can reach second base without benefit of an error: also [Slang] **two′-bag′ger** (-bag′ər) *n.*

☆**two-bit** (bit′) *adj.* [acc BIT⁹, sense 2] **1.** [Colloq.] worth or costing twenty-five cents **2.** [Slang] *a)* cheap; tawdry *b)* mediocre, inferior, or insignificant

☆**two bits** [see prec.] [Colloq.] twenty-five cents

☆**two-by-four** (tōō′bə fôr′, -bī-) *adj.* **1.** that measures two inches by four inches, two feet by four feet, etc. **2.** [Colloq.] small, narrow, cramped, etc. —*n.* any length of lumber two inches thick and four inches wide when untrimmed: in the building trades, applied to a trimmed piece 1 5/8 by 3 5/8 inches

two-cy·cle (-si′k'l) *adj.* having a cycle of two strokes of the piston, as some internal-combustion engines

two-edged (-ejd′) *adj.* **1.** that has two cutting edges **2.** that can be used or taken two ways, as a remark

two-faced (-fāst′) *adj.* **1.** having two faces, surfaces, etc. **2.** deceitful; hypocritical —**two′-fac′ed·ly** (-fās′id lē) *adv.*

☆**two-fer** (tōō′fər) *n.* [altered < *two for*] [*usually pl.*] [Colloq.] two (esp. theater tickets) for the price of one

two-fist·ed (-fis′tid) *adj.* [Colloq.] **1.** having, and able to use, both fists ☆**2.** vigorous; virile

two-fold (-fōld′) *adj.* [see -FOLD] **1.** having two parts; double; dual **2.** having twice as much or as many —*adv.* twice as much or as many

two-four (tōō′fôr′) *adj.* designating or of a musical rhythm with two quarter notes to a measure

☆**2,4-D** (tōō′fôr dē′) *n.* a white, crystalline plant hormone, $C_8H_6Cl_2O_3$, used as a weed killer

☆**2,4,5-T** (-fiv′tē′) *n.* trichlorophenoxyacetic acid

two-hand·ed (-han′did) *adj.* **1.** that needs to be used or

wielded with both hands **2.** needing two people to operate [a *two-handed* saw] **3.** for two people [a *two-handed* card game] **4.** having two hands **5.** able to use both hands equally well; ambidextrous

two·leg·ged (-leg'id, -legd') *adj.* having two legs

two-name (-nām') *adj.* designating or of commercial paper bearing the names of two parties, the maker and the endorser, as liable

two·pence (tup'ns) *n.* **1.** the sum of two pence, or two British pennies **2.** a former British coin of this value

two·pen·ny (tup'ə nē; *also, esp. of nails,* tōō'pen'ē) *adj.* **1.** worth or costing twopence **2.** cheap; worthless **3.** designating a size of nails one inch long

two-phase (tōō'fāz') *adj. Elec. same as* QUARTER-PHASE

two-piece (tōō'pēs') *adj.* consisting of two separate parts [a *two-piece* bathing suit]

two-ply (-plī') *adj.* **1.** having two thicknesses, layers, strands, etc. **2.** woven double

Two Sic·i·lies (sis'l ēz) a former kingdom including Naples (with lower Italy) and Sicily: united with the Kingdom of Italy in 1861

two-sid·ed (tōō'sīd'id) *adj.* **1.** having two sides **2.** having two aspects [a *two-sided* question]

two·some (-səm) *n.* **1.** two people together; a couple **2.** *a)* a golf match between two people *b)* the players —*adj.* consisting of or engaged in by two

two-step (-step') *n.* **1.** a ballroom dance in 2/4 time **2.** a piece of music for this dance

☆**two-time** (tōō'tīm') *vt.* **-timed'**, **-tim'ing** [Slang] to deceive or double-cross; esp., to be unfaithful to (one's wife or husband, or one's lover) —**two'-tim'er** *n.*

'twould (twood) [Poet.] it would

two-way (-wā') *adj.* **1.** having two lanes for vehicles going in opposite directions [a *two-way* street] **2.** involving reciprocity, mutual obligation, etc. [a *two-way* cultural exchange, contract, etc.] **3.** involving two persons, groups, etc. [a *two-way* political race] **4.** *a)* used for both transmission and reception [a *two-way* radio] *b)* moving, operating, or allowing movement in either of two directions [a *two-way* faucet, stretch, etc.] **5.** adapted for use in either of two ways; esp., reversible [a *two-way* raincoat]

twp. township

-ty¹ (tē, ti) [ME. *-tee, -tie, -te* < OFr. *-té* < L. *-tas* (gen. *-tatis*)] a *n.-forming suffix meaning* quality of, condition of [*novelty*]

-ty² (tē, ti) [ME. *-ti, -tie* < OE. *-tig*, akin to G. *-zig*, Goth. *tigus*, ten < IE. ***dekṃ-mi(s)*, dat. pl. < ***dekṃ*, TEN] a *suffix meaning* tens, times ten [*sixty*]

Ty. Territory

Ty·burn (tī'bərn) former place of public execution in London, England, in what is now Hyde Park

Ty·che (tī'kē) [Gr. *Tychē*, akin to *teuchein*, to prepare: for IE. base see DOUGHTY] *Gr. Myth.* the goddess of chance, identified with the Roman Fortuna

☆**ty·coon** (tī kōōn') [Jap. *taikun*, mighty lord < Chin. *ta*, great + *kiun*, prince] **1.** a title applied by foreigners to the former shogun of Japan **2.** a wealthy and powerful industrialist, financier, etc.

Ty·deus (tī'dyōōs, -dē əs; tid'ē əs) [L. < Gr. *Tydeus*] *Gr. Legend* the father of Diomedes, and one of the Seven against Thebes: see SEVEN AGAINST THEBES

ty·ing (tī'in) *prp. of* TIE

tyke (tīk) *n.* [ME. *tike* < ON. *tik*, a bitch < IE. base ***digh-*, goat, whence OE. *ticcen*, a kid] **1.** [Colloq.] a small child **2.** [Chiefly Brit. Dial.] *a)* a dog, esp. a mongrel or cur *b)* a boor

Ty·ler (tī'lər) city in E Tex.: pop. 58,000

Ty·ler (tī'lər) **1.** John, 1790–1862; 10th president of the U.S. (1841–45) **2.** Wat (wät) (or **Walter**), ?–1381; Eng. rebel; leader of the Peasants' Revolt

tym·bal (tim'b'l) *n. var. of* TIMBAL

tym·pan (tim'pən) *n.* [ME. < OE. *timpana* & OFr. *tympan* < L. *tympanum* < Gr. *tympanon*, a drum, area of a pediment, panel of a door < *typtein*, to strike, beat < IE. ***(s)teup-*, to strike (see STEEP¹)] **1.** orig., a drum **2.** the paper, cardboard, etc. stretched over the platen or impression cylinder of a printing press to cushion the paper being printed and equalize type pressure **3.** the membranelike part **4.** [L. *tympanum*] *Archit. same as* TYMPANUM

tym·pa·ni (tim'pə nē) *n.pl., sing.* **-no'** (-nō') *var. of* TIMPANI —**tym'pa·nist** *n.*

tym·pan·ic (tim pan'ik) *adj.* **1.** of or like a drum or drumhead **2.** *Anat., Zool.* of the tympanum or eardrum

tympanic bone a bone in the skull of mammals, supporting the eardrum and partly enclosing the tympanum

tympanic membrane a thin membrane that separates the middle ear from the external ear and vibrates when struck by sound waves; eardrum

tym·pa·ni·tes (tim'pə nīt'ēz) *n.* [ME. < LL. < Gr. *tympaniētēs* < *tympanon:* see TYMPAN] a distention of the abdomen by the accumulation of gas or air in the intestines or peritoneal cavity —**tym'pa·nit'ic** (-nit'ik) *adj.*

tym·pa·ni·tis (-nīt'əs) *n. same as* OTITIS MEDIA

tym·pa·num (tim'pə nəm) *n., pl.* **-nums, -na** (-nə) [L.: see TYMPAN] **1.** *Anat. same as:* a) MIDDLE EAR b) TYMPANIC MEMBRANE **2.** *Zool. a)* a drumlike structure serving as a vibratory membrane for the hearing organs of certain insects *b)* the resonating chamber of the syrinx in birds

3. a drum or drumhead **4.** *Archit. a)* the recessed space, usually triangular, enclosed by the slanting cornices of a pediment, often ornamented with sculpture *b)* a corresponding semicircular space enclosed by an arch and the top of the door or window below it **5.** *Elec.* the diaphragm of a telephone

tym·pa·ny (-nē) *n., pl.* **-nies** [ML. *tympanias* < Gr. *tympanias* < *tympanon*, drum: see TYMPAN] **1.** inflated or distended condition **2.** bombast; pomposity

Tyn·dale (tin'd'l), **William** 1494?–1536; Eng. religious reformer & translator of the Bible: executed for heresy

Tyn·dall effect (tin'd'l) [after John *Tyndall* (1820–93), Brit. physicist] *Physics* the scattering and polarization of a light beam by colloidal particles in a dispersed system

Tyn·da·re·us (tin der'ē əs) [L. < Gr. *Tyndareos*] a legendary Spartan king: see LEDA

Tyne (tīn) river in Northumberland, N England, flowing east into the North Sea: c.30 mi.

Tyne·mouth (tīn'məth, tīn'-) seaport in Northumberland, N England, at the mouth of the Tyne: pop. 72,000

typ. **1.** typographer **2.** typographical **3.** typography

typ·al (tīp'l) *adj.* **1.** of or pertaining to a type **2.** serving as a type; typical

type (tīp) *n.* [LL.(Ec.) *typus*, a model, symbol < L. & Gr.: L., a figure < Gr. *typos*, a figure, archetype, model, orig., a blow, mark made by a blow < *typtein* (see TYMPAN)] 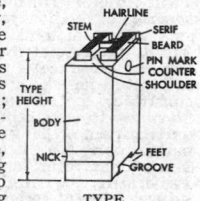 **1.** a person, thing, or event that represents or symbolizes another, esp. another that it is thought will appear later; symbol; token; sign **2.** [Rare] a distinguishing mark, sign, or impress **3.** the general form, structure, plan, style, etc. characterizing or distinguishing the members of a class or group **4.** a kind, class, or group having distinguishing characteristics in common [a new *type* of airplane, an animal of the dog *type*]: in colloquial usage, often used elliptically immediately preceding the noun [a new *type* airplane] **5.** a person, animal, or thing that is representative of, or has the distinctive characteristics of, a class or group; typical individual or instance **6.** a perfect example; model; pattern; archetype **7.** [Colloq.] an odd or eccentric person; character **8.** *Agric.* the combination of characters of an animal or breed that make it most suitable for a particular use [beef *type*, dairy *type*] **9.** *Biol. a)* the single specimen designated as the one on which the original description and name of a taxon has been based *b) same as* TYPE GENUS or TYPE SPECIES **10.** *Math.* the simplest of a set of equivalent forms **11.** *Printing a)* a rectangular piece of metal or, sometimes, wood, with a raised letter, figure, etc. in reverse on its upper end, which when inked and pressed against a piece of paper or other material, as in a printing press, leaves an ink impression of its face *b)* such pieces collectively, or the photographic reproductions used in photocomposition; also, a particular face of type *c)* a printed or photographically reproduced character or characters [small *type* is hard to read] —*vt.* **typed, typ'ing** **1.** [Now Rare] *a)* to prefigure *b)* to typify; represent **2.** to classify according to type [to be *typed* as a villain in the theater] **3.** to write with a typewriter; typewrite **4.** *Med.* to determine the type of (a blood sample) —*vi.* to use a typewriter —**typ'a·ble, type'a·ble** *adj.*

SYN.—type is used of a group or category of persons or things whose distinguishing characteristics held in common clearly set it apart from related groups or categories [a new *type* of shock absorber]; **kind** basically refers to a natural group or division [the rodent *kind*], but it is sometimes interchangeable with **sort** when used in vague reference to a less explicit group [all *sorts*, or *kinds*, of games]; **nature**, in precise use, implies that the distinguishing characteristics are inherent or innate [earthquakes and other phenomena of that *nature*]

-type (tīp) [Gr. *-typon* < *typos:* see TYPE] a *combining form meaning:* **1.** type, representative form, example [*prototype*] **2.** stamp, print, printing type [*daguerreotype, monotype*]

☆**type·bar** (tīp'bär') *n.* any of the slender bars to which are fastened the raised letters, figures, etc. in a typewriter

type·cast (-kast', -käst') *vt.* **-cast', -cast'ing** to cast (an actor) repeatedly in the same type of part, or in the part of a character whose traits are very much like his own

type-cast (-kast', -käst') *vt., vi.* **-cast', -cast'ing** to cast (type) —**type'-cast'er** *n.*

type·face (tīp'fās') *n. same as* FACE (*n.* 12)

type founder a person who casts metal type —**type founding**

type foundry a place where metal type is cast

type genus *Biol.* the particular genus that is theoretically most typical of a family and whose name serves as the base for the family name

type-high (tīp'hī') *adj.* exactly as high as type of standard height (.9186 inch)

type metal an alloy of tin, lead, and antimony, and sometimes copper, used for making type, etc.

☆**type·script** (-skript') *n.* typewritten matter or copy

type·set (-set') *vt.* **-set', -set'ting** [back-formation < ff.] to set in type; compose

type·set·ter (-set′ər) *n.* **1.** a person who sets type; compositor **2.** a machine for setting type —**type′set′ting** *n., adj.*

type species *Biol.* the particular species that is theoretically most typical of a genus and from which the genus is named

type specimen *same as* TYPE (*n.* 9 *a*)

☆**type·write** (tīp′rīt′) *vt., vi.* **-wrote′, -writ′ten, -writ′ing** [back-formation < ff.] to write with a typewriter: now usually clipped to *type*

☆**type·writ·er** (-rīt′ər) *n.* [TYPE + WRITER: so named (1867), prob. by C. L. Sholes (1819–1890), U.S. journalist, who patented the first practical machine in 1868] **1.** a writing machine with a keyboard for reproducing letters, figures, etc. that resemble printed ones: when the keys are struck, raised letters, figures, etc. are pressed as against an inked ribbon, making an impression on an inserted piece of paper, or cutting a perforation as for a stencil **2.** a style of printer's type that looks like typewriter print **3.** *earlier term for* TYPIST

type·writ·ing (-rīt′iŋ) *n.* **1.** the art, act, or process of using a typewriter **2.** writing done on a typewriter

typh·li·tis (tif līt′əs) *n.* [ModL. < Gr. *typhlon*, cecum < *typhlos*, blind, closed + ModL. *-itis*, -ITIS] [Obs.] inflammation of the cecum —**typh·lit′ic** (-lit′ik) *adj.*

ty·pho- (tī′fō, -fə) [< Gr. *typhos*: see TYPHUS] *a combining form meaning* typhus, typhoid *[typhogenic]*: also, before a vowel, **typh-**

Ty·pho·eus (tī fō′yoōs, -fē′əs) [L. < Gr. *Typhōeus*] *Gr. Myth.* a monster with a hundred heads, killed by Zeus —**Ty·phoe′an** (-fē′ən) *adj.*

ty·pho·gen·ic (tī′fə jen′ik) *adj.* [TYPHO- + -GENIC] causing typhus or typhoid fever

ty·phoid (tī′foid) *n.* [TYPH(US) + -OID] **1.** orig., any typhuslike disorder **2.** an acute infectious disease caused by a bacillus (*Salmonella typhosa*) and acquired by ingesting food or water contaminated by excreta: it was formerly considered a form of typhus and is characterized by fever, intestinal disorders, etc.: in full **typhoid fever** —**ty·phoi′dal** *adj.*

☆**Typhoid Mary** [orig. nickname for *Mary Mallon* (d. 1938), typhoid-carrying cook in New York] **1.** a person who is a carrier of typhoid **2.** a person who spreads any kind of disease, infection, or corruption

Ty·phon (tī′fän) [L. < Gr. *Typhōn*: see ff.] *Gr. Myth.* a monster, variously regarded as a son of Typhoeus or as Typhoeus himself

ty·phoon (tī fōōn′) *n.* [< Chin. dial. *tai-fung*, lit., great wind (or < ? *Tai*, Formosa: hence, Formosa wind); merged with earlier *tuphan, tufan* < Port. *tufāo* < Ar. *ṭūfān* < Gr. *typhōn*, hurricane, akin to *typhos*: see ff.] any violent tropical cyclone originating in the W Pacific, esp. in the South China Sea —**ty·phon′ic** (-fän′ik) *adj.*

ty·phus (tī′fas) *n.* [ModL. < Gr. *typhos*, a vapor, fever, stupor, akin to *typhein*, to smoke < IE. base **dheu-*, see FUME] an acute infectious disease caused by a rickettsia (*Rickettsia prowazekii*) transmitted to man by the bite of fleas, lice, etc., and characterized by fever, headache, and an eruption of red spots on the skin: in full **typhus fever** —**ty′phous** (-fas) *adj.*

typ·i·cal (tip′i k'l) *adj.* [ML. *typicalis* < L. *typicus* < Gr. *typikos*] **1.** serving as a type; symbolic **2.** having or showing the characteristics, qualities, etc. of a kind, class, or group so fully as to be a representative example **3.** of or belonging to a type or representative example; characteristic Also **typ′ic** —SYN. see NORMAL —**typ′i·cal·ly** *adv.* —**typ′i·cal·ness, typ′i·cal′i·ty** (-kal′ə tē) *n.*

typ·i·fy (tip′ə fī′) *vt.* **-fied′, -fy′ing** [see TYPE & -FY] **1.** to be a type or emblem of; symbolize; prefigure **2.** to have or show the distinctive characteristics of; be typical of; exemplify —**typ′i·fi·ca′tion** *n.* —**typ′i·fi′er** *n.*

typ·ist (tīp′ist) *n.* a person who operates a typewriter, esp. one whose work is typing

☆**ty·po** (tī′pō) *n.* [Colloq.] a typographical error; mechanical mistake made in setting type or in typing

ty·po- (tī′pō, tī′pə) [< Gr. *typos*: see TYPE] *a combining form meaning* type *[typography]*

typo., typog. **1.** typographer **2.** typographic **3.** typographical **4.** typography

ty·pog·ra·pher (tī pāg′rə fər) *n.* a person skilled in typography; printer, compositor, etc.

ty·po·graph·i·cal (tī′pə graf′i k'l) *adj.* of typography; having to do with the setting of type, printing, etc.: also **ty′po·graph′ic** —**ty′po·graph′i·cal·ly** *adv.*

ty·pog·ra·phy (tī pāg′rə fē) *n.* [Fr. *typographie* < ML. *typographia*: see TYPO- & -GRAPHY] **1.** the art or process of printing from type **2.** the art or process of setting and arranging type for printing **3.** the arrangement, style, or general appearance of matter printed from type

ty·pol·o·gy (tī pāl′ə jē) *n.* [TYPO- + -LOGY] **1.** the study of types, symbols, or symbolism **2.** symbolic meaning or representation; symbolism —**ty′po·log′i·cal** *adj.*

ty·poth·e·tae (tī päth′ə tē′, tī′pə thet′ē) *n.pl.* [ModL. < Gr. *typos* (see TYPE) + *tithenai*, to place, DO¹] **1.** [*with sing.* v.] an association of master printers **2.** printers: used in the names of organizations of printers

Tyr (tir) [ON.: for base see TIU] *Norse Myth.* the god of war and son of Odin

ty·ra·mine (tī′rə mēn′, -min) *n.* [TYR(OSINE) + AMINE] a crystalline amine, C₈H₁₁NO, found in ergot, cheeses, mistletoe, etc., and used in the treatment of hypotension

ty·ran·ni·cal (ti ran′i k'l, tī-) *adj.* [L. *tyrannicus* < Gr. *tyrannikos*] **1.** of or suited to a tyrant; arbitrary; despotic **2.** harsh, cruel, unjust, oppressive, etc. Also **ty·ran′nic** —**ty·ran′ni·cal·ly** *adv.*

ty·ran·ni·cide (-ə sīd′) *n.* [in sense 1 < L. *tyrannicidium*; in sense 2 < L. *tyrannicida*: see TYRANT & -CIDE] **1.** the act of killing a tyrant **2.** a person who kills a tyrant —**ty·ran′ni·ci′dal** *adj.*

tyr·an·nize (tir′ə nīz′) *vi.* **-nized′, -niz′ing** [MFr. *tyranniser* < ML. *tyrannizare*] **1.** to govern as a tyrant; rule with absolute power **2.** to govern or use authority harshly or cruelly; be oppressive —*vt.* to treat tyrannically; oppress —**tyr′an·niz′er** *n.*

☆**ty·ran·no·saur** (ti ran′ə sôr′, tī-) *n.* [< ModL. *tyrannosaurus* < Gr. *tyrannos*, tyrant + ModL. *-saurus*, -SAURUS] any of a genus (*Tyrannosaurus*) of huge, two-footed, flesh-eating dinosaurs of the Upper Cretaceous Period in N. America: also **ty·ran′no·saur′us** (-əs)

tyr·an·nous (tir′ə nəs) *adj.* tyrannical; despotic, oppressive, unjust, etc. —**tyr′an·nous·ly** *adv.*

tyr·an·ny (tir′ə nē) *n., pl.* **-nies** [ME. *tirannie* < OFr. < ML. *tyrannia* < Gr. *tyrannia*] **1.** the office, authority, government, or jurisdiction of a tyrant, or absolute ruler **2.** oppressive and unjust government; despotism **3.** very cruel and unjust use of power or authority **4.** harshness; rigor; severity **5.** a tyrannical act

tyr·ant (tī′rant) *n.* [ME. *tirant* < OFr. *tiran, tirant* (with *-t* after ending *-ant* of prp.) < L. *tyrannus* < Gr. *tyrannos*] **1.** an absolute ruler; specif., in ancient Greece, etc., one who seized sovereignty illegally; usurper **2.** a cruel, oppressive ruler; despot **3.** any person who exercises authority in an oppressive manner; cruel master **4.** a tyrannical influence

tyrant flycatcher any of a family (Tyrannidae) of American flycatchers

Tyre (tīr) [ME. < L. *Tyrus* < Gr. *Tyros*] seaport in SW Lebanon, on the Mediterranean: center of ancient Phoenician culture: pop. 12,000

tyre (tīr) *n. Brit. sp. of* TIRE²

Tyr·i·an (tir′ē ən) *adj.* [L. *Tyrius*] **1.** of ancient Tyre, its people, culture, etc. **2.** of Tyrian purple —*n.* a native of Tyre

Tyrian purple (or **dye**) **1.** a purple or crimson dye used by the ancient Romans and Greeks: it was made from certain mollusks, orig. at Tyre **2.** bluish red

ty·ro (tī′rō) *n., pl.* **-ros** [ML. < L. *tiro*, young soldier, beginner] a beginner in learning something; novice —SYN. see AMATEUR

ty·ro·ci·dine (tī′rə sīd′n, -sī′dēn) *n.* [TYRO(SINE) + -CID(E) + -INE⁴] an antibiotic drug obtained from a soil bacillus (*Bacillus brevis*) that is one of the two components of tyrothricin

Tyr·ol (tir′äl, tī′rōl, ti rōl′) *same as* TIROL —**Ty·ro·le·an** (ti rō′lē ən) *adj., n.* —**Tyr·o·lese** (tir′ə lēz′) *adj., n., pl.* **-lese′**

‡**Ty·ro·lienne** (tē rō lyen′) *n.* [Fr., fem. of *Tyrolien*, Tyrolese] **1.** a Tyrolese folk dance **2.** music for this

Ty·rone (ti rōn′) county of W Northern Ireland: 1,261 sq. mi.; pop. 137,000

ty·ro·si·nase (tī′rə si nās, tī räs′ə nās′) *n.* [< ff. + -ASE] an enzyme, found in plants and animals, that catalyzes the oxidation of the amino acid tyrosine and is involved in the formation of the dark pigment melanin

ty·ro·sine (tī′rə sēn′, -sin) *n.* [Gr. *tyros*, cheese + -INE⁴] a white, crystalline, nonessential amino acid, C₉H₁₁NO₃, formed by the decomposition of proteins, as in the putrefaction of cheese

ty·ro·thri·cin (tī′rə thrī′sin, -thris′in) *n.* [< prec. + Gr. *thrix*, a hair + -IN¹] an antibiotic drug obtained from a soil bacillus (*Bacillus brevis*) and used in treating infections of the body surface

Tyr·rhe·ni·an Sea (ti rē′nē ən) part of the Mediterranean, between the W coast of Italy & the islands of Corsica, Sardinia, & Sicily

Tyu·men (tyoō men′y′) city in W Asiatic R.S.F.S.R., near the Urals: pop. 218,000

tzar (tzär, zär) *n. var. of* CZAR —**tzar′dom** *n.* —**tzar′ism** *n.* —**tzar′ist** *adj., n.*

Tza·ra (tsä′rä), **Tristan** 1896– ; Romanian poet & editor in France

tzar·e·vitch (tsär′ə vich, zär′-) *n. var. of* CZAREVITCH

tza·ri·na (-rē′nə) *n. var. of* CZARINA

tza·rit·za (-rēt′sə) *n. var. of* CZARITZA

tzet·ze fly (tset′sē, tsē′tsē) *var. of* TSETSE FLY

‡**tzi·gane** (tsē gän′) *n.* [Fr. < Hung. *czigány*] a gypsy; esp., a Hungarian gypsy

Tzu·kung (dzoō′goon′) city in Szechwan province, SC China: pop. 280,000

Tzu·po (dzoō′pō′) city in Shantung province, NE China: pop. 875,000

U

U, u (yōō) *n., pl.* **U's, u's** **1.** the twenty-first letter of the English alphabet: formerly a variant of *V, v*; not until the 18th cent. was it established as a vowel symbol only **2.** a sound of *U* or *u:* in English, esp. the mid-back, unrounded vowel (u) of *cut*, the high-back, rounded vowel (ōō) of *crude*, or the lower high-back, rounded vowel (ōō) of *bush:* it is also often silent after *g*, as in *guide, guilt* **3.** a type or impression for *U* or *u* **4.** *a symbol for* the twenty-first (or the twentieth if J is omitted) in a sequence or group —*adj.* **1.** of *U* or *u* **2.** twenty-first (or twentieth if J is omitted) in a sequence or group

U (yōō) *n.* **1.** an object shaped like *U* **2.** *Chem.* uranium —*adj.* **1.** shaped like *U* **2.** [Colloq.] of the upper or wealthy class, esp. British upper class, as characterized by supposedly definitive usages, accent, behavior, tastes, etc.

U., U **1.** Uncle **2.** Union **3.** United **4.** University

U., U, u, u unit; units

U.A.R. United Arab Republic

U.A.W., UAW United Automobile, Aerospace, and Agricultural Implement Workers of America

U·ban·gi (ōō bäŋ′gē, yōō baŋ′-) river in C Africa, formed on the N Congo border by the juncture of the Uele & Bomu rivers & flowing west & south into the Congo River: c.700 mi. —*n. a nickname for* any of the women among the Sara, a people living near the Ubangi in the Central African Republic, with pierced lips enlarged by saucerlike disks

‡**Ü·ber·mensch** (ü′bər mensh′) *n., pl.* **-mensch'en** (-ən) [G.] *same as* SUPERMAN

u·bi·e·ty (yōō bī′ə tē) *n.* [ModL. *ubietas* < L. *ubi*, where] [Now Rare] the condition of being in a particular place

u·biq·ui·tous (yōō bik′wə təs) *adj.* [see ff. & -OUS] present, or seeming to be present, everywhere at the same time; omnipresent —*SYN.* see OMNIPRESENT —**u·biq′ui·tous·ly** *adv.* —**u·biq′ui·tous·ness** *n.*

u·biq·ui·ty (-tē) *n.* [Fr. *ubiquité* < L. *ubique*, everywhere < *ubi*, where + *-que*, any, akin to *qui:* see WHO] the state, fact, or capacity of being, or seeming to be, everywhere at the same time; omnipresence

‡**u·bi su·pra** (ōō′bē sōō′prə, yōō′bī) [L.] where (mentioned) above

U-boat (ōō′bōt′) *n.* [< G. *U-boot*, abbrev. of *Unterseeboot*, undersea boat] a German submarine

U bolt a U-shaped bolt with threads and a nut at each end

u.c. *Printing* upper case

U·ca·ya·li (ōō′kä yä′lē) river in E Peru, flowing north to join the Marañón & form the Amazon: c.1,200 mi.

U·dall (yōō′d'l), **Nicholas** 1505-56; Eng. schoolmaster, translator, & playwright

ud·der (ud′ər) *n.* [ME. *uddre* < OE. (rare) *udr*, akin to G. *euter* < IE. base **ūdh-*, udder, whence Sans. *ūdhar*, L. *uber*, udder] a mammary gland, esp. one that is relatively large and pendulous, with two or more teats, as in cows

U·di·ne (ōō′dē ne) commune in NE Italy: pop. 85,000

u·do (ōō′dō) *n., pl.* **u′dos** [Jap.] a Japanese plant (*Aralia cordata*) of the ginseng family, whose blanched shoots are used like asparagus and in salads

Ue·le (wā′lə) river flowing from the NE Congo (sense 2) west to join the Bomu & form the Ubangi: c.700 mi.

U·fa (ōō fä′) city in E European R.S.F.S.R., in the W foothills of the Urals: pop. 683,000

☆**UFO** (yōō′fō′, yōō′ef ō′) *n., pl.* **UFOs, UFO's** [*u(nidentified) f(lying) o(bject)*] any of a number of unidentified objects frequently reported, esp. since 1947, to have been seen flying at varying heights and speeds and variously regarded as light phenomena, hallucinations, secret military missiles, spacecraft from another planet, etc.

u·fol·o·gist (yōō fäl′ə jist) *n.* [< prec. + -LOGY + -IST] a person interested in the study of UFOs, esp. one who believes them to be craft from outer space —**u·fol′o·gy** *n.*

U·gan·da (yōō gan′də, ōō gän′dä) country in EC Africa: a member of the Brit. Commonwealth: 93,981 sq. mi.; pop. 7,934,000; cap. Kampala —**U·gan′dan** (-dən) *adj., n.*

U·ga·rit·ic (ōō′gə rit′ik, yōō′-) *n.* [< *Ugarit*, ancient city in W Syria + -IC] an extinct Semitic language closely related to classical Hebrew and known from cuneiform inscriptions from the middle of the 2d millenium B.C., found in Syria —*adj.* of this language or its speakers

ugh (ookh, uH, oo, *etc.*; ug *is a conventionalized pronun.*) *interj.* [echoic] an exclamation of disgust, horror, etc.

ug·li (ug′lē) *n.* [altered < UGLY; from its misshapen appearance] a Jamaican citrus fruit that is a three-way cross between a grapefruit, orange, and tangerine: also called **ugli fruit**

ug·li·fy (ug′lə fī′) *vt.* **-fied′, -fy′ing** to make ugly; disfigure

ug·ly (ug′lē) *adj.* **-li·er, -li·est** [ME. *uglike* < ON. *uggligr*, fearful, dreadful < *uggr*, fear, prob. < IE. base **ak-*, sharp, whence Gr. *akē*, a point: cf. ACID] **1.** unpleasing to look at; aesthetically offensive or unattractive; unsightly **2.** bad, vile, disagreeable, repulsive, offensive, objectionable, etc. [an *ugly* lie, habit, etc.] **3.** threatening; ominous; dangerous [*ugly* storm clouds] **4.** [Colloq.] ill-tempered; cross [an *ugly* disposition] —**ug′li·ly** *adv.* —**ug′li·ness** *n.*

ugly duckling [from a story by H. C. ANDERSEN about a supposed ugly duckling that turns out to be a swan] a very plain child or unpromising thing that in time becomes or could become beautiful, admirable, important, etc.

U·gri·an (ōō′grē ən, yōō′-) *adj.* [< Russ. *Ugri*, an Asiatic people living east of the Urals + -AN] **1.** designating or of a group of Finno-Ugric peoples of W Siberia and Hungary, including the Magyars **2.** *same as* UGRIC (*adj.* 1) —*n.* **1.** a member of any of the Ugrian peoples **2.** *same as* UGRIC

U·gric (-grik) *adj.* **1.** designating or of a branch of the Finno-Ugric subfamily of languages comprising Hungarian (Magyar), Vogul, and Ostyak **2.** *same as* UGRIAN (*adj.* 1) —*n.* the Ugric languages

uh (u, un) *interj.* **1.** *same as* HUH **2.** a prolonged sound made in speaking, as while searching for a word or collecting one's thoughts

UHF, U.H.F., uhf, u.h.f. ultrahigh frequency

uh-huh (ə hu′; *for 2* un′un′) *interj.* **1.** an exclamation indicating: *a*) an affirmative response *b*) that one is listening attentively **2.** *var. of* UH-UH

uh·lan (ōō′län, yōō′-; -lən; ōō län′) *n.* [obs. G. (now *ulan*) < Pol. *ulan*, a lancer < Turk. *oghlān*, a youth] formerly, a mounted lancer or a cavalryman in Poland, Prussia, etc.

Uh·land (ōō′länt), **Jo·hann Lud·wig** (yō′hän lōot′viH) 1787-1862; Ger. poet & literary historian

uh-uh (un′un′, -un′) *interj.* an exclamation indicating a negative response

‡**u·hu·ru** (ōō hoo′rōō) *n., interj.* [Swahili] freedom: a slogan of African Nationalists

Ui·ghur, Ui·gur (wē′goor) *n.* [Uighur *uighur* < *ui*, to follow + *-gur*, adj. suffix] **1.** a member of a Turkic people ruling in Mongolia and Turkestan from the 8th to the 12th cent. A.D. **2.** their Turkic language, the chief language of Sinkiang: also called New Uighur

☆**u·in·ta·ite, u·in·tah·ite** (yōō win′tə īt′) *n.* [after ff.] a black, brilliantly lustrous, natural variety of asphalt, found in parts of Utah and W Colorado

U·in·ta Mountains (yoo win′tə) [after the *Uinta* Indians, a division of the Utes = ?] range of the Rockies, in NE Utah: highest peak, 13,498 ft.

‡**uit·land·er** (ūt′län′dər; E. īt′lan/dər, āt′-) *n.* [Afrik. < Du. *uit*, out + *land*, land] [*sometimes* U-] in South Africa, a foreigner; specif., one not a Boer in the Transvaal

U.K. United Kingdom

u·kase (yōō′kās, -kāz; yōō kās′, -kāz′) *n.* [Russ. *ukaz*, edict < *ukasati*, to order] **1.** in Czarist Russia, an imperial order or decree, having the force of law **2.** any official, esp. arbitrary, decree or proclamation

U·krain·i·an (yōō krā′nē ən, -krī′-) *adj.* of the Ukraine, its people, their language, etc. —*n.* **1.** a native or inhabitant of the Ukraine **2.** the East Slavic language of the Ukrainians, very closely related to Russian

Ukrainian Soviet Socialist Republic republic of the U.S.S.R., in the SW European part: 231,990 sq. mi.; pop. 46,400,000; cap. Kiev: also called **the U·kraine** (yōō krān′, -krīn′; yōō′krān) or Russ. **U·kra·i·na** (ōō krä ē′nä)

☆**u·ku·le·le** (yōō′kə lā′lē; *Haw.* ōō′koo lā′lā) *n.* [Haw., lit., flea < *uku*, insect + *lele*, to jump: a nickname first applied to a nimble player, later to the instrument itself] a small, four-stringed guitarlike musical instrument introduced from Portugal into the Hawaiian Islands about 1879: colloquially shortened to **uke** (yōōk)

UL, U.L. Underwriters' Laboratories

u·la·ma (ōō′lə mä′, ōō′lə mä′) *n.pl. var. of* ULEMA

u·lan (ōō′län, yōō′lən) *n. same as* UHLAN

U·lan Ba·tor (ōō′län bä′tôr) capital of the Mongolian People's Republic, in the NC part: pop. 250,000

UKULELE

U·la·no·va (o͞o lä′nô vä), **Ga·li·na** (Sergeyevna) (gä lē′nä) 1910– ; Soviet ballerina

U·lan-U·de (o͞o′län o͞o′də) city in SE R.S.F.S.R., near Lake Baikal: pop. 220,000

Ul·bricht (o͞ol′briHt), **Wal·ter** (väl′tər) 1893– ; chief of state of East Germany (1960–)

ul·cer (ul′sər) n. [L. ulcus (gen. ulceris) < IE. *elkos-, abscess, whence Sans. ársas-, hemorrhoids, Gr. helkos, abscess, wound] 1. an open sore (other than a wound) on the skin or some mucous membrane, as the lining of the stomach (peptic ulcer), characterized by the disintegration of the tissue and, often, the discharge of pus 2. any corrupting or festering condition or influence

ul·cer·ate (ul′sə rāt′) vt., vi. -at′ed, -at′ing [< L. ulceratus, pp. of ulcerare] to make or become ulcerous —**ul′cer·a′tion** n. —**ul′cer·a′tive** adj.

ul·cer·ous (-sər əs) adj. [L. ulcerosus] 1. having an ulcer or ulcers 2. of, being, or characterized by an ulcer or ulcers 3. causing an ulcer or ulcers —**ul′cer·ous·ly** adv.

-ule (yo͞ol, yool) [Fr. or L.: Fr. -ule < L. -ulus, -ula, -ulum] a n.-forming suffix meaning little [sporule, umbellule]

u·le·ma (o͞o′lə mä′, o͞o′lə mä′) n.pl. [Turk. 'ulema < Ar. 'ulamā, pl. of 'alim, wise < 'alama, to know] 1. Moslem scholars or men of authority in religion and law, esp. in Turkey 2. [with sing. v.] a) a council or college of such men b) a member of such a council

-u·lent (yoo lənt) [< Fr. or L.: Fr. -ulent < L. -ulentus] a suffix meaning full of, abounding in [fraudulent]

Ul·fi·las (ul′fi ləs) 311?–383? A.D.; bishop of the Goths: translated the Bible into Gothic: also **Ul′fi·la** (-lə)

ull·age (ul′ij) n. [ME. ulage < Anglo-Fr. ulliage < OFr. ouillage, a filling up to the brim or the bunghole < ouiller, to fill (a cask) to the bunghole < ueil, an eye, fig. bunghole < L. oculus, an EYE] the amount by which a container, esp. of liquid, falls short of being full

Ulm (o͞olm) city in Baden-Württemberg, S West Germany, on the Danube: pop. 90,000

ul·na (ul′nə) n., pl. -nae (-nē), -nas [ModL. < L., the elbow: for base see ELBOW] 1. the larger of the two bones of the forearm of man, on the side opposite the thumb 2. a homologous bone in the forelimb of other land vertebrates —**ul′nad** (-nad) adv. —**ul′nar** (-nər) adj.

ul·no (ul′nō, ul′nə) a combining form meaning the ulna and

-u·lose (yoo lōs′) [L. -ulosus: see -ULE & -OSE²] a suffix meaning characterized by, marked by [granulose]

u·lot·ri·chous (yoo lät′ri kəs) adj. [< Gr. oulothrix, woolly-haired < oulos, crisp, woolly + thrix, hair + -OUS] having wool or tightly twisted hair

-u·lous (yoo ləs) [< L. -ulosus: see -ULOSE] a suffix meaning tending to, full of, or characterized by [tremulous, populous]

Ul·pi·an (ul′pē ən) (L. name Domitius Ulpianus) 170?–228 A.D.; Roman jurist

Ul·ster (ul′stər) n. 1. former province of Ireland, divided in 1920 to form Northern Ireland & a province of Ireland 2. a province of Ireland, in the N part; 3,094 sq. mi.; pop. 208,000 —**Ul′ster·man** (-mən), pl. -men, **Ul′ster·ite′** (-īt′) n.

ul·ster (ul′stər) n. [< prec.: the fabric was orig. made in Ulster] a long, loose, heavy overcoat, esp. one with a belt, orig. made of Irish frieze

ult. 1. ultimate 2. ultimately 3. ultimo

ul·te·ri·or (ul tir′ē ər) adj. [L., compar. of *ulter, beyond, farther (see ULTRA-)] 1. lying beyond or on the farther side 2. later, subsequent, or future 3. further; more remote; esp., beyond what is expressed, implied, or evident; undisclosed [an ulterior motive] —**ul·te′ri·or·ly** adv.

ul·ti·ma (ul′ti mə) n. [L., fem. of ultimus, last, superl. of *ulter, farther (see ULTRA)] the last syllable of a word

ul·ti·mate (ul′tə mit) adj. [LL. ultimatus, pp. of ultimare, to come to an end < L. ultimus: see prec.] 1. beyond which it is impossible to go; farthest; most remote or distant 2. by which a process or series comes to an end; final; conclusive 3. beyond which further analysis, division, etc. cannot be made; elemental; fundamental; primary 4. greatest or highest possible; maximum; utmost —n. something ultimate; final point or result, fundamental principle, etc. —SYN. see LAST¹ —**ul′ti·ma·cy** (-mə sē), **ul′ti·mate·ness** n.

ultimate constituent Linguis. see CONSTITUENT (n. 4)

ul·ti·mate·ly (-lē) adv. finally; at last; in the end

ul·ti·ma Thu·le (ul′ti mə tho͞o′lē) [L., farthest Thule] 1. same as THULE (sense 1) 2. any far-off, unknown region 3. a) the farthest possible point or limit b) the uttermost degree or goal attainable

ul·ti·ma·tum (ul′tə māt′əm) n., pl. -tums, -ta (-ə) [ModL. < LL., neut. of ultimatus: see ULTIMATE] a final offer or demand, esp. by one of the parties engaged in negotiations, the rejection of which usually leads to a break in relations and unilateral action, the use of force, etc. by the party issuing the ultimatum

ul·ti·mo (ul′tə mō′) adv. [L. ultimo (mense), (in the) last (month), abl. sing. of ultimus: see ULTIMA] in the preceding month: an old-fashioned usage [yours of the 13th (day) ultimo received]: cf. PROXIMO

ul·ti·mo·gen·i·ture (ul′tə mō jen′ə chər) n. [< L. ultimus, last + -geniture as in PRIMOGENITURE] inheritance or succession by the youngest son of the family

ul·tra (ul′trə) adj. [< ff.] going beyond the usual limit; excessive; extreme, esp. in opinions —n. an extremist, as in opinions held or policies favored

ultra- (ul′trə) [L. < ultra, fem. of *ulter, beyond, on the other side of < IE. *ol-, var. of base *al-, beyond, whence ALL, L. alius, other] a prefix meaning: 1. beyond, on the farther side of [ultraviolet] 2. (something) excessive, to an extreme degree [ultramodern, ultraism] 3. beyond the range of [ultramicroscopic]

ul·tra·cen·tri·fuge (ul′trə sen′trə fyo͞oj′) n. a high-speed centrifuge for segregating microscopic and submicroscopic materials to determine the sizes and molecular weights of colloidal and other small particles —vt. -fuged′, -fug′ing to subject to the action of an ultracentrifuge —**ul′tra·cen·trif′u·gal** (-trif′yə gəl) adj.

ul·tra·con·serv·a·tive (-kən sur′və tiv) adj. conservative to an extreme degree —n. an ultraconservative person

ul·tra·high frequency (ul′trə hī′) any radio frequency between 300 and 3,000 megahertz

ul·tra·ism (ul′trə iz′m) n. [ULTRA- + -ISM] 1. the opinions, principles, etc. of those who are extreme; extremism 2. an instance of this —**ul′tra·ist** n., adj. —**ul′tra·is′tic** adj.

ul·tra·ma·rine (ul′trə mə rēn′) adj. [ML. ultramarinus (see ULTRA- & MARINE)] 1. beyond the sea 2. deep-blue —n. 1. a blue pigment orig. made by grinding lapis lazuli to a powder 2. a blue pigment of similar chemical composition prepared from other substances 3. any of certain other pigments [yellow ultramarine] 4. deep blue

ul·tra·mi·crom·e·ter (-mī kräm′ə tər) n. a micrometer for making very small measurements

ul·tra·mi·cro·scope (-mī′krə skōp′) n. an instrument equipped to pick up the reflections of light rays dispersed by ultramicroscopic objects lighted from the side and against a dark background, thus making them visible: used esp. in the study of colloidal particles —**ul′tra·mi·cros′co·py** (-mī kräs′kə pē) n.

ul·tra·mi·cro·scop·ic (-mī′krə skäp′ik) adj. 1. too small to be seen with an ordinary microscope 2. of an ultramicroscope

ul·tra·mod·ern (-mäd′ərn) adj. modern to an extreme degree —**ul′tra·mod′ern·ism** n. —**ul′tra·mod′ern·ist** n.

ul·tra·mon·tane (-män′tān, -mən tān′) adj. [ML. ultramontanus < L. ultra, beyond + mons (gen. montis), MOUNT¹] 1. beyond the mountains, specif. the Alps: applied to the Italians by peoples to the north 2. a) historically, of the party in the Roman Catholic Church advocating the doctrine of papal supremacy b) of or favoring this doctrine —n. 1. a person living beyond the mountains, esp. south of the Alps 2. an adherent of the ultramontane party —**ul′tra·mon′ta·nism** (-tə niz′m) n.

ul·tra·mun·dane (-mun′dān, -mən dān′) adj. [L. ultramundanus: see ULTRA- & MUNDANE] 1. being beyond the world or the limits of our solar system 2. beyond life

ul·tra·na·tion·al·ism (-nash′ən ′l iz′m) n. nationalism that is excessive or extreme —**ul′tra·na′tion·al·ist** adj., n. —**ul′tra·na′tion·al·is′tic** adj.

ul·tra·red (-red′) adj. nontechnical var. of INFRARED

ul·tra·short (-shôrt′) adj. very short; specif., designating or of radio waves shorter than 10 meters in wavelength and above 30 megahertz in frequency

ul·tra·son·ic (-sän′ik) adj. [ULTRA- + SONIC] designating or of a frequency of mechanical vibrations above the range audible to the human ear, i.e., above 20,000 vibrations per second —**ul′tra·son′i·cal·ly** adv.

ul·tra·son·ics (-sän′iks) n.pl. [with sing. v.] the science dealing with ultrasonic phenomena

ul·tra·sound (ul′trə sound′) n. ultrasonic waves, used in medical diagnosis and therapy, in surgery, etc.

ul·tra·struc·ture (-struk′chər) n. the minute, invisible, elemental structure of protoplasm —**ul′tra·struc′tur·al** adj.

ul·tra·vi·o·let (ul′trə vī′ə lit) adj. 1. lying just beyond the violet end of the visible spectrum and having wavelengths shorter than approximately 4,000 angstroms 2. of, pertaining to, or producing light rays of such wavelengths —n. ultraviolet radiation

‡ul·tra vi·res (ul′trə vī′rēz) [L.] beyond the legal power or authority of a person, corporation, etc.

ul·tra·vi·rus (ul′trə vī′rəs) n. [ModL.: see ULTRA- & VIRUS] an ultramicroscopic virus, so small as to pass through the pores of the finest filter

u·lu (o͞o′lo͞o) n. [Esk.] a knife with a rounded blade, used by Eskimo women

u·lu·late (yo͞ol′yoo lāt′, ul′-) vi. -lat′ed, -lat′ing [< L. ululatus, pp. of ululare, to howl: echoic] 1. to howl or hoot 2. to wail or lament loudly —**ul′u·lant** (-lət) adj. —**ul′u·la′tion** n.

Ul·ya·novsk (o͞ol yä′nôfsk) river port in SW R.S.F.S.R., on the Volga: pop. 275,000

U·lys·ses (yoo lis′ēz) [ML., for L. *Ulixes* < ?] **1.** a mascu-line name **2.** *same as* ODYSSEUS

U·may·yad (⊙⊙ mī′ad) *n., pl.* **-yads, -ya·des′** (-ə dēz′) *var. of* OMAYYAD

um·bel (um′b'l) *n.* [L. *umbella*, a parasol: see UMBRELLA] a cluster of flowers with stalks of nearly equal length which spring from about the same point, like the ribs of an umbrella

um·bel·late (-it, -āt′) *adj.* [ModL. *umbellatus*] having, consisting of, resembling, or forming an umbel or umbels: also **um′bel·lat′ed** **—um′bel·late′ly** *adv.*

um·bel·lif·er·ous (um′bə lif′ər əs) *adj.* [ModL. *umbellifer* (see UMBEL & -FER) + -OUS] having an umbel or umbels, as plants of the parsley family

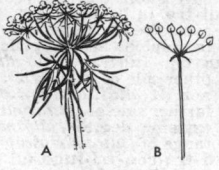

UMBEL
(A, compound;
B, simple)

um·bel·lule (um′b'l y⊙⊙l′, əm bel′y⊙⊙l) *n.* [ModL. *umbellula*, dim.] a small or simple umbel, esp. any of the secondary umbels of a compound umbel **—um·bel′lu·late** (-yoo lit) *adj.*

um·ber¹ (um′bər) *n.* [Fr. (*terre d′*)*ombre* < It. (*terra d′*)*ombra*, lit., (earth of) shade, prob. < L. *umbra*, a shade, shadow (but < ? UMBRIA)] **1.** a kind of earth containing oxides of manganese and iron, used as a pigment: raw umber is yellowish-brown; burnt, or calcined, umber is reddish-brown **2.** a yellowish-brown or reddish-brown color **—*adj.*** of the color of raw umber or burnt umber **—*vt.*** to color with or as with umber

um·ber² (um′bər) *n.* [ME. < OFr. *umbre* (Fr. *ombre*) < L. *umbra*: see prec.] **1.** [Now Dial.] shade; shadow **2.** a common European grayling (*Thymallus thymallus*)

um·bil·i·cal (um bil′i k'l) *adj.* [ML. *umbilicalis*] **1.** of or like an umbilicus, or navel, or an umbilical cord **2.** situated at or near the navel; central to the abdomen **3.** linked together by or as if by an umbilical cord **—*n.*** **1.** a flexible, detachable cable serving as a tether or supplying oxygen, electric power, etc. as to an astronaut or aquanaut when he goes outside his craft **2.** a similar cable for testing the components of a spacecraft, detached just before liftoff

umbilical cord **1.** a tough, cordlike structure projecting from the navel, that connects a fetus with the placenta and serves to convey food to, and remove waste from, the fetus: it is severed at birth ☆**2.** *same as* UMBILICAL (*n.*)

um·bil·i·cate (-kit, -kāt′) *adj.* [L. *umbilicatus*] **1.** having an umbilicus, or navel **2.** shaped or depressed like an umbilicus, or navel Also **um·bil′i·cat′ed**

um·bil·i·ca·tion (um bil′ə kā′shən) *n.* **1.** the condition of being umbilicate **2.** a navellike pit, as in a pustule

um·bil·i·cus (um bil′i kəs, um′bi li′kəs) *n., pl.* **-ci′** (-sī′, -sī) [L., NAVEL] **1.** *same as* NAVEL **2.** a navellike depression, as the hilum of a seed

um·bil·i·form (um bil′ə fôrm′) *adj.* [< prec. + -FORM] shaped like an umbilicus, or navel

um·ble pie (um′b'l) *var. of* HUMBLE PIE

um·bles (um′b'lz) *n.pl. var. of* NUMBLES

um·bo (um′bō) *n., pl.* **um·bo·nes** (um bō′nēz), **um′bos** [L., akin to *umbilicus*, NAVEL] **1.** the boss, or knob, at the center of a shield **2.** something resembling this; specif., *a*) the elevation beside the hinge on each half of a bivalve shell *b*) the prominence on the eardrum at the point of attachment of the malleus **—um′bo·nal** (-bə n'l), **um′bo·nate** (-nit, -nāt′), **um·bon·ic** (um bän′ik) *adj.*

um·bra (um′brə) *n., pl.* **-brae** (-brē), **-bras** [L., a shade, shadow] **1.** shade or a shadow **2.** the dark cone of shadow projecting from a planet or satellite on the side opposite the sun: see ECLIPSE, illus. **3.** the dark central part of a sunspot **4.** [Rare] a phantom, or ghost **5.** *Physics* a perfect or complete shadow, in which no direct light is received from the source of illumination **—um′bral** *adj.*

um·brage (um′brij) *n.* [ME. < OFr. < L. *umbraticus*, of shade < *umbra*, a shade, shadow] **1.** [Obs. or Poet.] shade; shadow **2.** foliage, considered as shade-giving **3.** offense or resentment [to take *umbrage* at a remark] **4.** [Archaic] a semblance or shadowy appearance **—*SYN.*** see OFFENSE

um·bra·geous (um brā′jəs) *adj.* [Fr. *ombrageux*, shy, suspicious, orig., shady < *ombrage* < OFr. *umbrage*: see prec.] **1.** giving shade; shady **2.** easily offended; taking, or inclined to take, umbrage **—um·bra′geous·ly** *adv.*

um·brel·la (um brel′ə) *n.* [It. *ombrella* < L. *umbrella* (altered after *umbra*, shade) < *umbella*, parasol, dim. of *umbra*, shade] **1.** a screen or shade, usually of cloth stretched over a folding radial frame, carried for protection against the rain or sun **2.** something suggestive of this; specif., *a*) the disk or body of a jellyfish *b*) any comprehensive, protective organization, alliance, strategy, or device [the *umbrella* of insurance] *c*) a force of military aircraft sent up to screen ground or naval forces [air *umbrella*]

umbrella bird any of several large, black South and Central American birds (genus *Cephalopterus*) with a large, umbrellalike, erectile crest and a long, feathered wattle

☆**umbrella leaf** a perennial plant (*Diphylleia cymosa*) of the

barberry family, native to the S Appalachians and having one or two lobed, peltate leaves and a cyme of white flowers

umbrella plant a common, cultivated, aquatic sedge (*Cyperus alternifolius*), having naked triangular stems surmounted by an umbrellalike whorl of grasslike leaves and greenish spikelets: also called **umbrella palm**

umbrella tree ☆**1.** an American magnolia (*Magnolia tripetala*) with clusters of long leaves at the ends of the branches, foul-smelling white flowers, and reddish fruit **2.** any of a number of other trees or shrubs whose leaves are umbrella-shaped or grow with an umbrellalike effect, including the CHINABERRY (sense 1)

um·brette (um bret′) *n.* [< Fr. or ModL.: Fr. *ombrette*, dim. of *ombre*, shade, or ModL. *umbretta*, dim., both < L. *umbra*, shade] *same as* HAMMERHEAD (sense 5)

Um·bri·a (um′brē ə; *It.* ⊙⊙m′brē ä′) [L. < *Umbri*, the Umbrians] region in C Italy: in ancient times a district extending from the Tiber to the Adriatic: 3,270 sq. mi.; pop. 789,000; chief city, Perugia

Um·bri·an (-ən) *adj.* of Umbria, its people, etc. **—*n.*** **1.** a native or inhabitant of Umbria **2.** the extinct Osco-Umbrian language of ancient Umbria

u·mi·ak, u·mi·ack (⊙⊙′mē ak′) *n.* [Esk. (Eastern dial.)] a large, open boat made of skins stretched on a wooden frame, used by Eskimos for transporting goods and traditionally rowed by women

UMIAK

um·laut (⊙⊙m′lout) *n.* [G., change of sound < *um*, about + *laut*, a sound (see LOUD): first use in these senses by Jakob GRIMM] *Linguis.* **1.** *a*) a historical change in the sound of a vowel, caused by its assimilation to another vowel or semivowel originally occurring in the next syllable but later generally lost; mutation: in English, the differences of vowel in certain singulars and plurals (Ex.: *foot—feet, mouse—mice*) or causative verbs and the words from which they are derived (Ex.: *gold—gild*) are due to the effects of umlaut on the second word of each pair *b*) a vowel resulting from such assimilation **2.** the diacritical mark (¨) placed over a vowel, esp. in German, to indicate umlaut: cf. DIERESIS **—*vt.*** to modify, sound, or write with an umlaut

ump (ump) *n., vt., vi. clipped form of* UMPIRE

um·pir·age (um′pīr ij) *n.* **1.** the position or authority of an umpire **2.** an action or ruling of an umpire

um·pire (um′pīr) *n.* [ME. *oumpere*, altered by faulty separation of *a noumpire* < *noumpere* (cf. ADDER², APRON) < MFr. *nomper*, uneven, hence an uneven number, third person < *non*, not + *per*, even < L. *par*, PAR] **1.** a person chosen to render a decision in a dispute; judge; arbiter **2.** an official who administers the rules in certain team sports, as baseball or cricket **—*vt.* -pired, -pir·ing** to act as umpire in or of **—*vi.*** to act as umpire **—*SYN.*** see JUDGE

ump·teen (ump′tēn′) *adj.* [*ump*-, indefinite sound for an uncertain number + -TEEN] [Slang] a great number of; very many **—ump′teenth′** *adj.*

UMW, U.M.W. United Mine Workers of America

un- (un; *unstressed, also* ən) *either of two prefixes, meaning:* **1.** [ME. < OE., akin to Gr. *an-, a-* (cf. A-², AN-¹), L. *in-* (cf. IN-²), and to the negative elements in *not, nor*] not, lack of, the opposite of [*untruth, unable, unhappily, unceasing*]: see NON- **2.** [ME., *un-, on-* < OE. *un-, on-,* and-, back, akin to G. *ent-,* Du. *ont-*: cf. ANSWER] back; the reverse or removal of: it is added to verbs to indicate a reversal of the action of the verb [*unfasten, unchain*] and to nouns to indicate a removal or release of the thing mentioned or from the condition, place, etc. indicated by the noun [*unbonnet, unbosom*]; sometimes it has a mere intensive force [*unloosen*] The list at the bottom of the following pages includes many of the more common compounds formed with un- (either prefix) that do not have special meanings

UN, U.N. United Nations

U·na (⊙⊙′nə, yoo′-) [Ir. *Una, Oonagh;* also < L. *una,* one] a feminine name

un·a·ble (un ā′b'l) *adj.* **1.** not able; incompetent **2.** help-less; feeble; ineffectual

un·a·bridged (un′ə brijd′) *adj.* **1.** not abridged; complete **2.** designating or of a dictionary that is not abridged from a larger work: an arbitrary designation for any of various large, extensive dictionaries **—**☆*n.* an unabridged dictionary

un·ac·com·mo·dat·ed (un′ə käm′ə dāt′id) *adj.* **1.** not accommodated or adapted **2.** having no accommodations

un·ac·com·pa·nied (-kum′pə nēd) *adj.* **1.** not accompanied **2.** *Music* without an accompaniment

un·ac·com·plished (-käm′plisht) *adj.* **1.** not accomplished or completed **2.** having no accomplishments or skills

un·ac·count·a·ble (-koun′tə b'l) *adj.* **1.** that cannot be explained or accounted for; strange; mysterious **2.** not accountable; not responsible **—un′ac·count′a·bil′i·ty, un′ac·count′a·ble·ness** *n.* **—un′ac·count′a·bly** *adv.*

un·ac·count·ed-for (-koun′tid fôr′) *adj.* **1.** not explained or accounted for

un·ac·cus·tomed (-kus′təmd) *adj.* **1.** not accustomed or

---

unabashed	unabetted	unacademic	unacclimated
unabated	unabsolved	unaccented	unaccommodating
unabbreviated	unabsorbed	unacceptable	unaccredited

habituated; not used (to) [*unaccustomed* to such kindness]
2. not usual; strange [an *unaccustomed* action]

u·na cor·da (ōō′nə kôr′də) [It., lit., one string: the pedal
allows the hammers to strike only one of the strings
provided for each key] with the soft pedal depressed:
musical direction to a pianist

un·ad·vised (-əd vīzd′) *adj.* 1. without counsel or advice
2. thoughtlessly hasty; indiscreet; rash —**un′ad·vis′ed·ly**
(-vīz′id lē) *adv.* —**un′ad·vis′ed·ness** *n.*

un·af·fect·ed (-ə fek′tid) *adj.* 1. not changed, affected,
or influenced 2. without affectation; simple; sincere;
natural —*SYN.* see SINCERE —**un′af·fect′ed·ly** *adv.*
—**un′af·fect′ed·ness** *n.*

U·na·las·ka (ōō′nə las′kə, un′ə-) [Russ. < Aleut *a′u-an
alakska*, lit., this Alaska] island of Alas., in the E Aleutians:
c.75 mi. long

un·A·mer·i·can (un′ə mer′ə kən) *adj.* not American; regarded as not characteristically or properly American;
esp., regarded as opposed or dangerous to the U.S., its
institutions, etc. —**un′·A·mer′i·can·ism** *n.*

U·na·mu·no (ōō′nä mōō′nō), **Mi·guel de** (mē gel′ *the*)
1864–1936; Sp. philosopher & writer

un·a·neled (un′ə nēld′) *adj.* [Archaic] not aneled; not
having received extreme unction

u·nan·i·mous (yoo nan′ə məs) *adj.* [L. *unanimus, unani-
mis < unus,* ONE + *animus,* the mind (see ANIMAL)]
1. agreeing completely; united in opinion 2. showing, or
based on, complete agreement —**u·na·nim·i·ty** (yōō′nə
nim′ə tē) *n.* —**u·nan′i·mous·ly** *adv.*

un·ap·proach·a·ble (un′ə prōch′ə b′l) *adj.* 1. not to be
approached; inaccessible; aloof 2. having no rival or equal;
unmatched —**un′ap·proach′a·bil′i·ty, un′ap·proach′a·
ble·ness** *n.* —**un′ap·proach′a·bly** *adv.*

un·ap·pro·pri·at·ed (-prō′prē āt′id) *adj.* not appropriated; specif., *a)* not owned by or assigned to any particular
person or agent *b)* not granted or set aside for any particular use or purpose: said of sums of money, etc.

un·apt (un apt′) *adj.* 1. not fitting or suitable 2. not likely
or inclined 3. not quick or skillful, as in learning; dull
—**un·apt′ly** *adv.* —**un·apt′ness** *n.*

un·arm (-ärm′) *vt.* 1. [Archaic] to strip of armor 2. *same
as* DISARM

un·armed (-ärmd′) *adj.* 1. having no weapons, esp. firearms, or armor; defenseless 2. lacking scales, claws, or
the like: said of plants or animals

un·asked (-askt′) *adj.* 1. *a)* not asked or requested *b)* not
asked for 2. not invited

un·as·sail·a·ble (un′ə sāl′ə b′l) *adj.* not assailable; specif.,
a) that cannot be successfully attacked or assaulted
b) that cannot be successfully denied or contested —
un′as·sail′a·ble·ness, un′as·sail′a·bil′i·ty *n.* —**un′as·sail′
a·bly** *adv.*

un·as·sum·ing (-ə sōō′miŋ, -syōō′-) *adj.* not assuming,
pretentious, or forward; modest; retiring —**un′as·sum′-
ing·ly** *adv.* —**un′as·sum′ing·ness** *n.*

un·at·tached (-ə tacht′) *adj.* 1. not attached or fastened
2. not connected with any particular group, institution,
etc.; independent 3. not engaged or married 4. *Law* not
taken or held as security for a judgment

un·at·tend·ed (-ə ten′did) *adj.* 1. not attended or waited
on 2. unaccompanied (*by* or *with*) 3. neglected or ignored

u·nau (yoo nô′, ōō nou′) *n.* [Fr. < Tupi name] the two-toed
sloth (*Choloepus hoffmanni*) of S. America

un·a·vail·ing (un′ə vā′liŋ) *adj.* not availing; futile; ineffectual —**un′a·vail′ing·ly** *adv.*

un·a·void·a·ble (-ə voi′də b′l) *adj.* 1. that cannot be
avoided; inevitable 2. that cannot be voided or nullified
—**un′a·void′a·ble·ness** *n.* —**un′a·void′a·bly** *adv.*

un·a·ware (-ə wer′) *adj.* 1. not aware or conscious [*unaware*
of danger] 2. [Rare] unwary; heedless —*adv. same as*
UNAWARES —**un′a·ware′ness** *n.*

un·a·wares (-ə werz′) *adv.* 1. without knowing or being
aware; unintentionally 2. unexpectedly; suddenly; by
surprise [to sneak up on someone *unawares*]

un·backed (un bakt′) *adj.* 1. not broken to the saddle:
said of a horse 2. not backed, supported, etc. 3. without
a back or backing 4. having no backers in betting

un·bal·ance (-bal′əns) *vt.* **-anced, -anc·ing** 1. to disturb
the balance or equilibrium of 2. to disturb the functioning
of; derange (the mind) —*n.* the condition of being unbalanced; lack of balance; imbalance

un·bal·anced (-bal′ənst) *adj.* 1. not in balance or equilibrium 2. not equal as to debit and credit 3. *a)* mentally
deranged *b)* erratic or unstable

un·bal·last·ed (-bal′ə stid) *adj.* not steadied by ballast;
wavering; unsteady

un·bar (-bär′) *vt.* **-barred′, -bar′ring** to remove the bar or
bars from; unbolt; unlock; open

un·bat·ed (-bāt′id) *adj.* 1. [Poet.] not abated or diminished
2. [Archaic] not blunted [*unbated* lance]

un·bear·a·ble (-ber′ə b′l) *adj.* that cannot be endured or
tolerated —**un·bear′a·ble·ness** *n.* —**un·bear′a·bly** *adv.*

un·beat·a·ble (-bēt′ə b′l) *adj.* that cannot be defeated

un·beat·en (-bēt′n) *adj.* 1. not struck, pounded, etc. 2.
untrodden or untraveled 3. undefeated or unsurpassed

un·be·com·ing (un′bi kum′iŋ) *adj.* not appropriate or
suited to one's appearance, status, character, etc.; unattractive, indecorous, etc. —**un′be·com′ing·ly** *adv.* —
un′be·com′ing·ness *n.*

un·be·known (-bi nōn′) *adj.* unknown or unperceived;
without one's knowledge (usually with *to*): also **un′be·
knownst′** (-nōnst′)

un·be·lief (-bə lēf′) *n.* [ME. *unbeleve*] a withholding or lack
of belief; esp. in religion or certain religious doctrines
SYN.—**unbelief** implies merely a lack of belief, as because of
insufficient evidence, esp. in matters of religion or faith; **disbelief**
suggests a positive refusal to believe an assertion, theory, etc.
because one is convinced of its falseness or unreliability; **incredulity** implies a general skepticism or disinclination to believe—**ANT.**
belief, credulity

un·be·liev·a·ble (-bə lēv′ə b′l) *adj.* beyond belief; astounding; incredible —**un′be·liev′a·bly** *adv.*

un·be·liev·er (-bə lē′vər) *n.* 1. a person who does not
believe; doubter 2. a person who does not accept any, or
any particular, religious belief —*SYN.* see ATHEIST

un·be·liev·ing (-bə lē′viŋ) *adj.* not believing, doubting;
skeptical; incredulous —**un′be·liev′ing·ly** *adv.*

un·bend (-bend′) *vt.* **-bent′** or **-bend′ed, -bend′ing** [ME.
unbenden: see UN- (not) & BEND[1]] 1. to release (a bow,
etc.) from strain or tension 2. to relax (the mind) from
strain or effort 3. to straighten (something bent or crooked)
4. *Naut. a)* to loosen or unfasten (a rope, sail, etc.) *b)* to
untie (a rope) —*vi.* 1. to become straight or less bent
2. to become free from constraint, stiffness, or severity;
relax and be less formal, more natural, etc.

un·bend·ing (-ben′diŋ) *adj.* not bending; specif., *a)* rigid;
stiff *b)* firm; resolute *c)* aloof; austere —*n.* [< prec.] a
relaxation of restraint, severity, etc. —**un·bend′ing·ly** *adv.*
—**un·bend′ing·ness** *n.*

un·bi·ased, un·bi·assed (-bī′əst) *adj.* without bias or
prejudice; objective; impartial

un·bid·den (-bid′n) *adj.* [ME. *unbiden*: see UN- (not) &
BID[1]] 1. not commanded 2. not invited; unasked, undesired, etc. Also **un·bid′**

un·bind (-bīnd′) *vt.* **-bound′, -bind′ing** [ME. *unbinden <*
OE. *unbindan*: see UN- (back) & BIND] 1. to untie; unfasten
2. to free from bonds or restraints; release

un·bit·ted (-bit′id) *adj.* 1. having no bit or bridle on
2. unrestrained; uncontrolled; ungoverned

un·blessed, un·blest (-blest′) *adj.* 1. not hallowed or
consecrated 2. not given a blessing 3. accursed; wicked
4. wretched; unhappy

un·blood·ed (-blud′id) *adj.* 1. not thoroughbred 2. uninitiated: see BLOOD (*vt.* 2, 3)

un·blush·ing (-blush′iŋ) *adj.* 1. not blushing 2. shameless
—**un·blush′ing·ly** *adv.*

un·bod·ied (-bäd′ēd) *adj.* having no body or form; incorporeal, disembodied, formless, etc.

unacknowledged	unalterable	unapproached	unattired
unacquainted	unambiguous	unarguable	unattractive
unadaptable	unambitious	unarmored	unauspicious
unadjustable	unamplified	unartistic	unauthentic
unadorned	unamusing	unascertained	unauthenticated
unadulterated	unanalyzable	unashamed	unauthorized
unadventurous	unannealed	unaspirated	unavailable
unadvertised	unannounced	unaspiring	unavenged
unadvisable	unanswerable	unassignable	unavowed
unaffiliated	unanticipated	unassigned	unawakened
unafraid	unapologetic	unassimilable	unawed
unaggressive	unappalled	unassimilated	unbaked
unaided	unapparent	unassisted	unbaptized
unaimed	unappealable	unassociated	unbathed
unalienable	unappealing	unassorted	unbefitting
unalike	unappeasable	unassured	unbelt
unalleviated	unappetizing	unatoned	unblamable
unallied	unappreciated	unattainable	unbleached
unallowable	unappreciative	unattempted	unblemished
unalloyed	unapprehensive	unattested	unblinking

un·bolt (-bōlt′) *vt.*, *vi.* to withdraw the bolt or bolts of (a door, etc.); unbar; open

un·bolt·ed[1] (-id) *adj.* not fastened with a bolt

un·bolt·ed[2] (-id) *adj.* not bolted or sifted, as flour

un·bon·net (-bän′it) *vt.*, *vi.* to take the bonnet or head covering off; uncover —**un·bon′net·ed** *adj.*

un·born (-bôrn′) *adj.* **1.** not born or brought into being **2.** still within the mother's womb; not yet delivered **3.** yet to come or be; future

un·bos·om (-booz′əm, -boo′zəm) *vt.* [UN- (back) + BOSOM] to give vent to (feelings, secrets, etc.); tell; reveal —*vi.* to reveal what one feels, knows, etc. —**unbosom oneself** to tell or reveal one's feelings, secrets, etc.

un·bound (-bound′) *pt. & pp. of* UNBIND —*adj.* **1.** released from bonds, ties, or shackles **2.** without a binding, as a book **3.** not held in physical or chemical union with another element, substance, etc. free [*unbound* electrons]

un·bound·ed (-boun′did) *adj.* **1.** without bounds or limits; boundless **2.** not restrained; uncontrolled

un·bowed (-boud′) *adj.* **1.** not bowed or bent **2.** not yielding or giving in; unsubdued

un·brace (-brās′) *vt.* **-braced′, -brac′ing 1.** to free from braces or bands **2.** to loosen; relax **3.** to make feeble

un·bred (-bred′) *adj.* **1.** formerly, ill-bred **2.** untrained or uninstructed **3.** not (yet) bred, as a filly

un·bri·dled (-brī′d'ld) *adj.* **1.** having no bridle on: said of a horse, etc. **2.** unrestrained; uncontrolled

un·bro·ken (-brō′k'n) *adj.* not broken; specif., *a)* whole, intact *b)* not tamed or subdued *c)* continuous; uninterrupted *d)* not disordered or disorganized *e)* not plowed or spaded *f)* not surpassed [an *unbroken* record]

un·buck·le (-buk′'l) *vt.* **-led, -ling** to unfasten the buckle or buckles of

un·build (-bild′) *vt.* **-built′, -build′ing** to tear down (something built); demolish; raze

un·built (-bilt′) *adj.* not yet built (on)

un·bur·den (-burd′'n) *vt.* **1.** to free from a burden **2.** to relieve (oneself or one's soul, mind, etc.) by revealing or disclosing (something hard to bear, as guilt)

un·but·ton (-but′'n) *vt.* **1.** to free (a button) from the buttonhole **2.** to unfasten the button or buttons of (a garment, etc.) —*vi.* to unfasten buttons, as in disrobing

un·but·toned (-but′'nd) *adj.* **1.** with buttons unfastened **2.** free and easy; casual; informal

un·called-for (un kôld′fôr′) *adj.* **1.** not called for or required **2.** unnecessary and out of place; impertinent

un·can·ny (-kan′ē) *adj.* [see UN- (not) & CANNY] **1.** mysterious or unfamiliar, esp. in such a way as to frighten or make uneasy; preternaturally strange; eerie; weird **2.** so remarkable, acute, etc. as to seem preternatural [uncanny shrewdness] **3.** [Scot. & North Eng. Dial.] *a)* dangerous *b)* severe —*SYN.* see WEIRD —**un·can′ni·ly** *adv.* —**un·can′ni·ness** *n.*

un·cap (-kap′) *vt.* **-capped′, -cap′ping 1.** to remove the cap from the head of (a person) **2.** to remove the cap, or cover, from (a bottle, etc.)

un·cared-for (-kerd′fôr′) *adj.* not cared for or looked after; neglected

un·caused (-kôzd′) *adj.* not caused or created; self-existent

un·cer·e·mo·ni·ous (un′ser ə mō′nē əs) *adj.* **1.** less formal and ceremonious than is usual or expected; informal; familiar **2.** so curt or abrupt as to be discourteous —**un′cer·e·mo′ni·ous·ly** *adv.* —**un′cer·e·mo′ni·ous·ness** *n.*

un·cer·tain (un surt′'n) *adj.* [ME. *uncertayn*] **1.** *a)* not surely or certainly known; questionable; problematical *b)* not sure or certain in knowledge; doubtful **2.** not definite or determined; vague **3.** liable to vary or change; not dependable or reliable **4.** not steady or constant; varying —**un·cer′tain·ly** *adv.* —**un·cer′tain·ness** *n.*

un·cer·tain·ty (-tē) *n.* [ME. *uncerteynte*] **1.** lack of certainty; doubt **2.** *pl.* **-ties** something uncertain

SYN.—**uncertainty** ranges in implication from a mere lack of absolute sureness [uncertainty about a date of birth] to such vagueness as to preclude anything more than guesswork [the uncertainty of the future]; **doubt** implies such a lack of conviction, as through absence of sufficient evidence, that there can be no certain opinion or decision [there is doubt about his guilt]; **dubiety** suggests uncertainty characterized by wavering between conclusions; **dubiosity** connotes uncertainty characterized by vagueness or confusion; **skepticism** implies an unwillingness to believe, often a habitual disposition to doubt, in the absence of absolute certainty or proof —*ANT.* conviction, assurance, certitude

uncertainty principle in quantum mechanics, the axiom that it is impossible to measure simultaneously and

exactly two related quantities, as both the position and momentum of an electron

un·chanc·y (un chan′sē, -chän′-) *adj.* [UN- (not) + CHANCY] [Scot.] **1.** unlucky; ill-fated **2.** dangerous

un·charged (-chärjd′) *adj.* not charged; specif., *a)* not formally accused *b)* without an electrical charge

un·char·i·ta·ble (-char′i tə b'l) *adj.* harsh or severe, as in opinion; unforgiving, ungenerous, or censorious —**un·char′i·ta·ble·ness** *n.* —**un·char′i·ta·bly** *adv.*

un·chart·ed (-chär′tid) *adj.* not marked on a chart or map; unexplored or unknown

un·chris·tian (-kris′chən) *adj.* **1.** not having or practicing a Christian religion **2.** not in accord with the principles of Christianity **3.** [Colloq.] outrageous; dreadful

un·church (-church′) *vt.* **1.** to deprive (a person) of membership in a given church **2.** to deprive (an entire congregation or sect) of its rights as a church

un·churched (-churcht′) *adj.* **1.** not belonging to or attending any church **2.** not having a church

un·ci·al (un′shē əl, -shəl) *adj.* [L. *uncialis*, of an inch, inch-high < *uncia*, a twelfth part, INCH[1]] designating or of a form of large, rounded letter used in the script of Greek and Latin manuscripts between 300 and 900 A.D. —*n.* **1.** an uncial letter **2.** an uncial manuscript **3.** uncial script

un·ci·form (un′si fôrm′) *adj.* [ModL. *unciformis* < L. *uncus*, a hook (< IE. *onko-* < base *ank-*, to bend, whence ANGLE[1]) + *-formis*, -FORM] **1.** hook-shaped **2.** *Anat. a)* designating or of a hook-shaped bone in the distal row of the wrist, on the same side as the ulna *b)* designating a hooked process on the uniform bone, or a similar process on the ethmoid bone —*n.* an unciform bone

Bellum   caveat   emplor   caesar   LATIN UNCIALS

un·ci·na·ri·a·sis (un′si nə rī′ə sis) *n.* [ModL. < *Uncinaria*, name of a genus including the hookworm (< L. *uncinus*, a hook): see -IASIS] *same as* HOOKWORM DISEASE

un·ci·nate (un′si nit, -nāt′) *adj.* [L. *uncinatus* < *uncinus*, a hook < *uncus*: see UNCIFORM] bent like a hook; hooked

un·cir·cum·cised (un sur′kəm sīzd′) *adj.* **1.** not circumcised; specif., not Jewish; gentile **2.** [Archaic] heathen

un·cir·cum·ci·sion (un′sur kəm sizh′ən) *n.* the condition of being uncircumcised —**the uncircumcision** *Bible* the gentiles

un·civ·il (un siv′'l) *adj.* **1.** not civilized; barbarous **2.** not civil or courteous; ill-mannered —*SYN.* see RUDE —**un·civ′il·ly** *adv.* —**un·civ′il·ness** *n.*

un·civ·i·lized (-siv′ə līzd′) *adj.* **1.** not civilized; barbarous; unenlightened **2.** far from civilization

un·clad (-klad′) *alt. pt. & pp. of* UNCLOTHE —*adj.* not clad; wearing no clothes; naked

un·clasp (-klasp′, -kläsp′) *vt.* **1.** to unfasten the clasp of **2.** to release from a clasp or grasp —*vi.* **1.** to become unfastened **2.** to relax the clasp or grasp

un·clas·si·fied (-klas′i fīd) *adj.* **1.** not classified; not put in a category **2.** not under security classification; not secret or restricted

un·cle (uŋ′k'l) *n.* [ME. < OFr. < L. *avunculus*, one's mother's brother, dim. of *avo* < IE. *awos*, maternal grandfather, whence OE. *eam*, OHG. *oheim*, uncle, L. *avus*, grandfather] **1.** the brother of one's father or mother **2.** the husband of one's aunt **3.** [Colloq.] any elderly man: a term of address **4.** [Old Slang] a pawnbroker —☆say (or cry) uncle to surrender or admit defeat

un·clean (un klēn′) *adj.* [ME. *unclene* < OE. *unclæne*: see UN- (not) + CLEAN] **1.** dirty; filthy; foul **2.** ceremonially impure **3.** morally impure; unchaste, obscene, or vile —**un·clean′ness** *n.*

un·clean·ly[1] (-klen′lē) *adj.* [see UN- & CLEANLY[1]] not cleanly; unclean; dirty —**un·clean′li·ness** *n.*

un·clean·ly[2] (-klēn′lē) *adv.* in an unclean manner

un·clench (-klench′) *vt.*, *vi.* to open: said of something clenched, or clinched: also **un·clinch′** (-klinch′)

☆**Uncle Sam** [extended < abbrev. *U.S.*] [Colloq.] the U.S. (government or people), personified as a tall, spare man with chin whiskers, dressed in a red, white, and blue costume of swallow-tailed coat, striped trousers, and tall hat with a band of stars

☆**Uncle Tom** [after the main character, an elderly Negro slave, in H. B. STOWE's antislavery novel, *Uncle Tom's Cabin* (1852)] [Colloq.] a Negro whose behavior toward whites is regarded as fawning or servile: a term of contempt —**Uncle Tom′ism**

unboned	unburned	unceasing	unchecked
unbought	unburnt	uncelebrated	uncherished
unbraid	unbusinesslike	uncensored	unchewed
unbranched	unbuttered	uncensured	unchilled
unbranded	uncaged	uncertified	unchivalrous
unbreakable	uncalculating	unchain	unchosen
unbreathable	uncanceled	unchallenged	unchristened
unbribable	uncancelled	unchangeable	unclaimed
unbridgeable	uncanonical	unchanged	unclarified
unbrotherly	uncaring	unchaperoned	unclassifiable
unbruised	uncarpeted	uncharacteristic	uncleaned
unbrushed	uncasked	unchartered	unclear
unbudgeted	uncataloged	unchaste	uncleared
unburied	uncaught	unchastened	unclipped

un·cloak (un klōk′) *vt., vi.* **1.** to remove a cloak or other covering (from) **2.** to reveal; expose

un·close (-klōz′) *vt., vi.* **-closed′, -clos′ing** [ME. *unclosen:* see UN- (back) + CLOSE²] **1.** to make or become no longer closed; open **2.** to disclose or reveal

un·clothe (-klōth′) *vt.* **-clothed′** or **-clad′, -cloth′ing** [ME. *unclothen*] to strip of or as of clothes; uncover; divest

un·co (uŋ′kō) *adj.* [ME. *unkow*, contr. < *uncouth*, UNCOUTH] [Scot.] **1.** unknown; strange **2.** weird; uncanny **3.** notable; remarkable —*adv.* [Scot.] remarkably; extremely; very — *n., pl.* **-cos** [Scot.] **1.** a strange person or thing **2.** [*pl.*] news

un·coil (un koil′) *vt., vi.* [UN- (back) + COIL¹] to unwind or release from being coiled

un·com·fort·a·ble (-kumf′tər b'l, -kum′fər tə b'l) *adj.* **1.** not comfortable; feeling discomfort **2.** not pleasant or agreeable; causing discomfort **3.** ill at ease —**un·com′fort·a·ble·ness** *n.* —**un·com′fort·a·bly** *adv.*

un·com·mer·cial (un′kə mur′shəl) *adj.* **1.** of or concerned with things other than trade or commerce **2.** not in accordance with the principles or methods of commerce **3.** not commercially profitable

un·com·mit·ted (-kə mit′id) *adj.* **1.** not committed or carried out, as a crime **2.** *a)* not bound or pledged, as to certain principles *b)* not having taken a position; neutral **3.** not imprisoned **4.** not committed to a mental hospital

un·com·mon (un käm′ən) *adj.* **1.** rare; not common or usual **2.** strange; remarkable; extraordinary —*SYN.* see RARE¹ —**un·com′mon·ly** *adv.* —**un·com′mon·ness** *n.*

un·com·mu·ni·ca·tive (un′kə myōō′nə kāt′iv, -ni kə tiv) *adj.* not communicative; tending to withhold information, opinions, feelings, etc.; reserved; taciturn —**un′com·mu′ni·ca′tive·ly** *adv.* —**un′com·mu′ni·ca′tive·ness** *n.*

un·com·pro·mis·ing (un käm′prə mī′ziŋ) *adj.* not compromising or yielding; firm; inflexible; determined

un·con·cern (un′kən surn′) *n.* **1.** lack of interest; apathy; indifference **2.** lack of concern, or worry

un·con·cerned (-kən surnd′) *adj.* not concerned; specif., *a)* not interested; indifferent *b)* not solicitous or anxious —*SYN.* see INDIFFERENT —**un′con·cern′ed·ly** (-sur′nid lē) *adv.* —**un′con·cern′ed·ness** *n.*

un·con·di·tion·al (-kən dish′ən 'l) *adj.* without conditions or reservations; absolute —**un′con·di′tion·al·ly** *adv.*

un·con·di·tioned (-kən dish′ənd) *adj.* **1.** *same as* UNCONDITIONAL **2.** *Philos.* infinite; absolute **3.** *Psychol.* not acquired by conditioning; natural; inborn [an *unconditioned* reflex]

un·con·form·a·ble (-kən fôr′mə b'l) *adj.* **1.** not conformable or conforming **2.** *Geol.* showing unconformity —**un′con·form′a·bly** *adv.*

un·con·form·i·ty (-kən fôr′mə tē) *n., pl.* **-ties 1.** a lack of conformity; inconsistency; incongruity **2.** *Geol. a)* a break in the continuity of rock strata in contact, separating younger from older rocks and usually resulting from erosion of the surface of the older bed before the younger bed was laid down *b)* the surface of contact between such strata

un·con·nect·ed (-kə nek′tid) *adj.* **1.** not connected; separate **2.** disconnected; incoherent

un·con·scion·a·ble (un kän′shən ə b'l) *adj.* **1.** not guided or restrained by conscience; unscrupulous **2.** unreasonable, excessive, or immoderate —**un·con′scion·a·bly** *adv.*

un·con·scious (-kän′shəs) *adj.* **1.** *a)* not endowed with consciousness; mindless *b)* temporarily deprived of consciousness [*unconscious* from a blow on the head] **2.** not aware (of) [*unconscious* of his mistake] **3.** not known, realized, or intended; not done, said, etc. on purpose [an *unconscious* habit, *unconscious* humor] **4.** not aware of one's own existence; not conscious of self **5.** having to do with those of one's mental processes that one is unable to bring into one's consciousness —**the unconscious** *Psychoanalysis* the sum of all thoughts, memories, impulses, desires, feelings, etc. of which the individual is not con-

scious but which influence his emotions and behavior; that part of one's psyche which comprises repressed material of this nature —**un·con′scious·ly** *adv.* —**un·con′scious·ness** *n.*

un·con·sid·ered (un′kən sid′ərd) *adj.* **1.** not considered; not taken into account **2.** done without consideration; not based upon careful reflection [a hasty, *unconsidered* remark]

un·con·sti·tu·tion·al (-kän stə tōō′shən 'l, -tyōō′-) *adj.* not in accordance with or permitted by a constitution, specif. the U.S. Constitution; not constitutional —☆**un′-con·sti·tu′tion·al′i·ty** (-shə nal′ə tē) *n.* —**un′con·sti·tu′tion·al·ly** *adv.*

un·con·ven·tion·al (un′kən ven′shən 'l) *adj.* not conventional; not conforming to customary, formal, or accepted practices, standards, rules, etc. —**un′con·ven′tion·al′i·ty** (-shə nal′ə tē) *n.* —**un′con·ven′tion·al·ly** *adv.*

un·cork (un kôrk′) *vt.* **1.** to pull the cork out of **2.** [Colloq.] to let out, let loose, release, etc.

un·count·ed (-koun′tid) *adj.* **1.** not counted **2.** inconceivably numerous; innumerable

un·cou·ple (-kup′'l) *vt.* **-pled, -pling 1.** to release (dogs) from being leashed together in couples **2.** to unfasten (things coupled); disconnect —*vi.* to become unfastened

un·couth (-kōōth′) *adj.* [ME. < OE. *uncuth*, unknown < *un-*, not + *cuth*, pp. of *cunnan*, to know: see CAN¹] **1.** formerly, not known or familiar; strange **2.** awkward; clumsy; ungainly **3.** uncultured; crude; boorish —**un·couth′ly** *adv.* —**un·couth′ness** *n.*

un·cov·e·nant·ed (-kuv′ə nən tid) *adj.* **1.** not promised, secured, or sanctioned by a covenant **2.** not bound by or committed to the terms of a covenant

un·cov·er (-kuv′ər) *vt.* **1.** to make known; disclose; reveal **2.** to lay bare or open by removing a covering **3.** to remove the cover or protection from **4.** to remove the hat, cap, etc. from (the head), as a conventional gesture of respect —*vi.* **1.** to bare the head, as in respect **2.** to remove a cover or coverings

un·cov·ered (-kuv′ərd) *adj.* **1.** having no covering; exposed **2.** not covered or protected by insurance, collateral, etc. **3.** wearing no hat, cap, etc.

un·cre·at·ed (un′krē āt′id) *adj.* **1.** not yet created; not existing **2.** *Theol.* existing eternally

un·cross (un krôs′) *vt.* to change back from a crossed position [to *uncross* one's legs]

un·crowned (-kround′) *adj.* **1.** not crowned; not officially installed as ruler by a coronation ceremony **2.** ruling without the title of king, queen, etc.

unc·tion (uŋk′shən) *n.* [ME. *unccioun* < L. *unctio* < *ungere*, to anoint: see UNGUENT] **1.** *a)* the act of anointing, as in medical treatment or a religious ceremony *b)* the oil, ointment, etc. used for this **2.** anything that soothes or comforts **3.** *a)* a fervent or earnest quality or manner of speaking or behaving, esp. in dealing with religious matters *b)* pretended or affected fervor or earnestness in speech or manner; unctuous quality

unc·tu·ous (uŋk′chōō wəs) *adj.* [ME. < ML. *unctuosus*, greasy < L. *unctum*, ointment < *ungere*, to anoint: see UNGUENT] **1.** *a)* of, like, or characteristic of an ointment or unguent; oily or greasy *b)* made up of or containing fat or oil **2.** like oil, soap, or grease to the touch: said of certain minerals **3.** soft and rich: said of soil **4.** plastic; moldable **5.** characterized by a smug, smooth pretense of spiritual feeling, fervor, or earnestness, as in seeking to persuade; too suave or oily in speech or manner —**unc′tu·os′i·ty** (-wäs′ə tē), **unc′tu·ous·ness** *n.* —**unc′tu·ous·ly** *adv.*

un·curl (un kurl′) *vt.* to straighten (something curled)

un·cus (uŋ′kəs) *n., pl.* **un·ci** (-sī) [ModL. < L., a hook < IE. base *ank-*: see ANGLE¹] *Anat.* a hooked process

un·cut (un kut′) *adj.* not cut; specif., *a)* not trimmed *b)* having untrimmed margins: said of the pages of a book *c)* not ground to shape: said of a gem *d)* not abridged

unclog	uncomplimentary	unconsecrated	uncorrected
unclouded	uncomplying	unconsoled	uncorroborated
uncluttered	uncompounded	unconsolidated	uncorrupted
uncoagulated	uncomprehending	unconstituted	uncountable
uncoated	uncomprehensible	unconstrained	uncrate
uncocked	uncompressed	unconstricted	uncredited
uncoined	unconcealed	unconsumed	uncrippled
uncollectable	unconciliated	uncontaminated	uncritical
uncollected	unconcluded	uncontemplated	uncropped
uncolonized	uncondemned	uncontested	uncrowded
uncolored	uncondensed	uncontradictable	uncrushable
uncombed	unconducive	uncontrived	uncrystallized
uncombinable	unconfessed	uncontrollable	uncultivable
uncombined	unconfined	uncontrolled	uncultivated
uncomely	unconfirmed	uncontrovertible	uncultured
uncomforted	unconfused	unconverted	uncurable
uncommissioned	uncongealed	unconvinced	uncurbed
uncompanionable	uncongenial	unconvincing	uncurtailed
uncompensated	uncongeniality	uncooked	uncurtained
uncomplaining	unconquerable	uncooled	uncushioned
uncompleted	unconquered	uncooperative	uncustomary
uncomplicated	unconscientious	uncoordinated	undamaged

un·damped (-dampt′) *adj.* not damped; specif., *a*) not disheartened or discouraged *b*) *Elec.* not decreasing in amplitude

un·daunt·ed (-dôn′tid, -dän′-) *adj.* not daunted; not faltering or hesitating because of fear or discouragement; undismayed; intrepid —**un·daunt′ed·ly** *adv.*

un·dé, un·dée (un′dā) *adj.* [OFr. *unde* (Fr. *ondé*) < L. *unda*, a wave: see WATER] *Heraldry* wavy

un·dec·a·gon (un dek′ə gän′) *n.* [< L. *undecim*, eleven (see UNDECYLENIC ACID) + Gr. *gōnia*, a corner, angle: see -GON] a plane figure with eleven angles and eleven sides

un·de·ceive (un′di sēv′) *vt.* -ceived′, -ceiv′ing to cause to be no longer deceived, mistaken, or misled

un·de·cid·ed (-di sīd′id) *adj.* 1. that is not decided or settled 2. not having come to a decision; irresolute —**un′de·cid′ed·ly** *adv.* —**un′de·cid′ed·ness** *n.*

un·dec·y·le·nic acid (un′des ə lē′nik, -len′ik) [< *undecylene*, C₁₁H₂₂ (< L. *undecim*, eleven < base of *unus*, ONE + *decem*, TEN + -YL + -ENE) + -IC] a light-colored liquid or crystalline mass, C₁₁H₂₀O₂, used in treating fungus infections of the skin, in making perfumes, etc.

un·de·mon·stra·tive (-di män′strə tiv) *adj.* not demonstrative; giving little outward expression of feeling; restrained; reserved —**un′de·mon′stra·tive·ly** *adv.* —**un′de·mon′stra·tive·ness** *n.*

un·de·ni·a·ble (-di nī′ə b′l) *adj.* 1. that cannot be denied; indisputable; incontestable 2. unquestionably good or excellent —**un′de·ni′a·bly** *adv.*

un·der (un′dər) *prep.* [ME. < OE., akin to G. *unter* < IE. *ṇdhos*, *ṇdheri*, under, whence L. *infra*, below: cf. INFRA-] 1. in, at, or to a position down from; lower than; below [shoes *under* the bed] 2. beneath the surface of [*under* water] 3. below and to the other side of [to drive *under* a bridge] 4. covered, surmounted, enveloped, or concealed by [to wear a vest *under* a coat] 5. *a*) lower in authority, position, power, etc. than *b*) lower in value, amount, etc. than; less than *c*) lower than the required or standard degree of [*under* age] 6. in a position or condition regarded as lower or inferior or implying subordination; specif., *a*) subject to the control, limitations, government, direction, instruction, or influence of [*under* orders from the President, *under* oath] *b*) burdened, oppressed, or distressed by [*under* a strain] *c*) subjected to; undergoing [*under* an anesthetic, *under* repair] 7. with the character, pretext, disguise, or cover of [*under* an alias] 8. in or included in (the designated category, division, class, etc.) [spiders are classified *under* arachnids] 9. in the time of [literature flourished *under* Elizabeth I] 10. being the subject of [the question *under* discussion] 11. having regard for; because of [*under* the circumstances] 12. authorized or attested by [*under* one's signature] 13. planted with; sowed with [an acre *under* corn] —*adv.* 1. in or to a position below something; beneath 2. beneath the surface, as of water 3. in or to a condition that is subordinate 4. so as to be covered or concealed 5. less in amount, value, etc.; not so much [costs two dollars or *under*] —*adj.* 1. located or moving below something else or on the lower surface 2. lower in authority or position; subordinate 3. held in control: used predicatively 4. lower in amount, degree, etc.: used predicatively

un·der- (un′dər) [ME. < OE. *under-*: see prec.] *a prefix meaning:* 1. in, on, to, or from a lower place or side; beneath or below [*undershirt*] 2. in an inferior or subordinate position or rank [*undergraduate*] 3. too little, not enough, below normal or standard [*underdeveloped*]: the list below includes some common compounds formed with *under-* that can be understood if *too little* or *insufficiently* is added to the meaning of the base word

underactive	underorganized
underbake	underpopulated
undercolored	underpowered
underconsumption	underpraise
undercook	underprice
underdose	underripe
undereducated	underspend
underemphasize	undersubscribe
underexercise	undersupply
undermanned	undertrained

☆**un·der·a·chieve** (un′dər ə chēv′) *vi.* -chieved′, -chiev′ing to fail to do as well in school studies as might be expected from scores made on intelligence tests —**un′der·a·chieve′ment** *n.* —**un′der·a·chiev′er** *n.*

un·der·act (-akt′) *vt., vi.* to act (a theatrical role) with insufficient emphasis or too great restraint

un·der·age¹ (-āj′) *adj.* 1. not of full or mature age 2. below the age required by law

un·der·age² (un′dər ij) *n.* [UNDER- + -AGE] a shortage; insufficiency

un·der·arm (un′dər ärm′) *adj.* 1. of, for, in, or used on the area under the arm, or the armpit 2. *same as* UNDERHAND —*adv. same as* UNDERHAND

un·der·armed (un′dər ärmd′) *adj.* not sufficiently armed; not provided with enough weapons

un·der·bel·ly (un′dər bel′ē) *n.* 1. the lower, posterior part of an animal's belly 2. any vulnerable or unprotected area, region, point, etc.

un·der·bid (un′dər bid′; *for n.* un′dər bid′) *vt., vi.* -bid′, -bid′ding 1. to bid lower than (another person) 2. to bid less than the worth of (a thing, as one's hand in bridge) —*n.* a lower or inadequate bid

un·der·bod·y (un′dər bäd′ē) *n.* 1. the underpart of an animal's body 2. the undersurface of a vehicle

un·der·bred (un′dər bred′) *adj.* 1. lacking good manners; ill-bred 2. not of pure breed

☆**un·der·brush** (un′dər brush′) *n.* small trees, shrubs, etc. that grow beneath large trees in woods or forests

un·der·buy (un′dər bī′) *vt., vi.* -bought′, -buy′ing 1. to buy at less than the real value or asking price 2. to buy more cheaply than (another or others) 3. to buy less of (something) than is needed

un·der·cap·i·tal·ize (-kap′ə tə liz′) *vt., vi.* -ized′, -iz′ing to provide (a business) with too little capital for efficient operation —**un′der·cap′i·tal·i·za′tion** *n.*

un·der·car·riage (un′dər kar′ij) *n.* 1. a supporting frame or structure, as of an automobile 2. [Chiefly Brit.] the landing gear of an aircraft

un·der·charge (un′dər chärj′; & *for n.* un′dər chärj′) *vt., vi.* -charged′, -charg′ing 1. to charge too low a price (to) 2. to load (a gun) with an insufficient charge —*n.* an insufficient charge

☆**un·der·class·man** (un′dər klas′mən, -kläs′-) *n., pl.* -men a freshman or sophomore

un·der·clay (un′dər klā′) *n.* a bed of clay lying immediately beneath a coal seam, often used as a fireclay

un·der·clothes (-klōz′, -klōthz′) *n.pl. same as* UNDERWEAR: also **un′der·cloth′ing** (-klōth′iŋ)

un·der·coat (-kōt′) *n.* 1. orig., a coat worn under another 2. an under layer of short hair in an animal's coat 3. a coating as of tarlike material applied to the exposed undersurface of an automobile to retard rust, etc. 4. a coat of paint, varnish, etc. applied as a first coat or before the final coat Also (for 3 & 4) **un′der·coat′ing** —*vt.* to apply an undercoat to

un·der·cool (un′dər kōōl′) *vt., vi. same as* SUPERCOOL

☆**un·der·cov·er** (-kuv′ər) *adj.* acting or carried out in secret [*undercover* work as a spy]

un·der·croft (un′dər krôft′, -kräft′) *n.* [ME. < *under* + *croft*, a vault (ult. < L. *crypta*: see CRYPT)] an underground room or vault, esp. beneath a church

un·der·cur·rent (-kur′ənt) *n.* 1. a current, as of water or air, flowing below another or beneath the surface 2. a hidden or underlying tendency, opinion, etc., usually one at variance with another that is obvious or out in the open

un·der·cut (un′dər kut′; *for v.* un′dər kut′) *n.* 1. *a*) a cut made below another so as to leave an overhang or concave profile *b*) the part cut out in this way ☆2. a notch cut in a tree below the level of the major cut and on the side to which the tree is to fall 3. [Chiefly Brit.] a tenderloin or fillet of beef 4. *Sports* the act or an instance of undercutting —*adj.* that is undercut —*vt.* -cut′, -cut′ting 1. to make an undercut (senses 1 & 2) in 2. to cut out the underpart of 3. to undersell or work for lower wages than 4. to weaken the position of; lessen the force or impact of; undermine 5. *Sports* to strike (a ball) with an oblique downward motion, as in golf, or to chop with an underhand stroke, as in tennis, esp. so as to impart backspin —*vi.* to undercut something or someone

un·der·de·vel·op (un′dər di vel′əp) *vt.* 1. to develop to a point below what is needed 2. *Photog.* to develop (a film, plate, etc.) too short a time or with too weak a developer

un·der·de·vel·oped (-əpt) *adj.* not developed to the proper or desirable degree; specif., inadequately developed economically and industrially so as to have a relatively low standard of living [*underdeveloped* nations]

un·der·do (-dōō′) *vt.* -did′, -done′, -do′ing to do less than is usual, needed, or desired

☆**un·der·dog** (un′dər dôg′) *n.* 1. orig., the dog that is losing in a dogfight 2. a person or group that is losing, or is expected to lose, in a contest or struggle 3. a person who is handicapped or at a disadvantage because of injustice, discrimination, etc.

un·der·done (un′dər dun′) *adj.* not cooked enough or thoroughly: said esp. of meat

un·der·drain·age (un′dər drān′ij) *n.* drainage by an underground system of drains, as in agriculture

un·der·draw·ers (-drôrz′) *n. same as* DRAWERS

un·der·dress (un′dər dres′) *vi.* to dress more plainly or informally than is indicated by the occasion

un·der·em·ployed (-im ploid′) *adj.* 1. inadequately employed; esp., employed at less than full time so that, usually, one has a low standard of living 2. working at low-skilled, poorly paid jobs when one is trained for, or

undated	undecomposable	undefiled	undemocratically
undaughterly	undecorated	undefinable	undemonstrable
undebatable	undefaced	undefined	undemonstrably
undecayed	undefeatable	undelegated	undenied
undecipherable	undefeated	undeliverable	undenominational
undeclared	undefended	undemanding	undependable
undeclinable	undefensible	undemocratic	undepreciated

could be trained for, more skilled work —**the underemployed** underemployed people —**un′der·em·ploy′ment** *n.*

un·der·es·ti·mate (-es′tə māt′; *for n.* -mit) *vt., vi.* **-mat′ed, -mat′ing** to set too low an estimate on or for —*n.* an estimate that is too low —**un′der·es′ti·ma′tion** *n.*

un·der·ex·pose (-ik spōz′) *vt.* **-posed′, -pos′ing** to expose (a photographic film, etc.) to inadequate light or for too short a time —**un′der·ex·po′sure** (-spō′zhər) *n.*

un·der·feed (-fēd′) *vt.* **-fed′, -feed′ing** 1. to feed less than is needed 2. to stoke (a fire) from below

un·der·fired (un′dər fird′) *adj.* fired, or heated, from beneath, as a hot water tank

un·der·foot (un′dər foot′) *adv., adj.* 1. under the foot or feet [to trample flowers *underfoot*] ☆2. in the way, as of one walking

un·der·fur (un′dər fur′) *n.* the softer, finer fur under the outer coat of some animals, as beavers and seals

un·der·gar·ment (-gär′mənt) *n.* a piece of underwear

un·der·gird (un′dər gurd′) *vt.* **-gird′ed** or **-girt′, -gird′ing** 1. to gird, strengthen, or brace from the bottom side 2. to supply support or a strong basis for

un·der·glaze (un′dər glāz′) *adj. Ceramics* designating colors, designs, etc. applied before the glaze is put on, as in painting porcelain —*n.* such colors, designs, etc.

un·der·go (un′dər gō′) *vt.* **-went′, -gone′, -go′ing** 1. to experience; endure; go through 2. [Obs.] to undertake

un·der·grad·u·ate (-graj′oo wit) *n.* a student at a university or college who has not yet received the first, or bachelor's, degree —*adj.* 1. of, for, consisting of, or characteristic of undergraduates 2. having the status of an undergraduate

un·der·ground (un′dər ground′; *for n.* -ground′) *adj.* 1. occurring, working, placed, used, etc. beneath the surface of the earth 2. secret; hidden; undercover 3. designating or of noncommercial newspapers, movies, etc. that are unconventional, experimental, radical, etc. —*adv.* 1. beneath the surface of the earth 2. in or into secrecy or hiding; so as to be undercover; surreptitiously —*n.* 1. the entire region beneath the surface of the earth 2. an underground space or passage 3. a secret movement organized in a country to oppose or overthrow the government in power or enemy forces of occupation 4. [Brit.] a subway

underground railroad 1. a subway: also **underground railway** ☆2. [*often* U- R-] in the U.S. before the Civil War, a system set up by certain opponents of slavery to help fugitive slaves escape to free States and Canada

un·der·grown (un′dər grōn′) *adj.* 1. not grown to full or normal size or development 2. having undergrowth

un·der·growth (un′dər grōth′) *n.* 1. small trees, shrubs, etc. that grow beneath large trees in woods or forests; underbrush 2. an undercoat (sense 2) 3. the state of being undergrown

un·der·hand (un′dər hand′) *adj.* 1. performed with the hand below the level of the elbow or the arm below the level of the shoulder [an *underhand* throw] 2. *same as* UNDERHANDED (sense 1) —*adv.* 1. with an underhand motion 2. underhandedly

un·der·hand·ed (un′dər han′did) *adj.* 1. not open or straightforward; secret, sly, deceitful, etc. 2. lacking workers, players, etc.; shorthanded —*SYN.* see SECRET —**un′der·hand′ed·ly** *adv.* —**un′der·hand′ed·ness** *n.*

un·der·hung (un′dər hun′) *adj.* 1. *a)* projecting beyond the upper jaw: said of the lower jaw *b)* having such a lower jaw 2. *same as* UNDERSLUNG 3. resting or moving on a track or rail beneath, as some sliding doors

un·der·laid (-lād′) *adj.* 1. laid or placed underneath 2. having an underlay or underlying layer, support, etc.

un·der·lap (-lap′) *vt.* **-lapped′, -lap′ping** to lie or extend partly under (something)

un·der·lay¹ (un′dər lā′; *for n.* un′dər lā′) *vt.* **-laid′, -lay′ing** [ME. *underlein* < OE. *underlecgan*] 1. to cover, line, or extend over the bottom of 2. to lay (something) under something else, esp. as a support, wedge, etc. 3. to raise or support with something laid underneath; specif., *Printing* to provide with an underlay —*n.* something laid underneath; specif., *Printing* a patch or patches of paper laid under type, cuts, etc. to raise the level of the face

un·der·lay² (un′dər lā′) *pt. of* UNDERLIE

un·der·let (-let′) *vt.* **-let′, -let′ting** 1. to let at a price below the real value 2. *same as* SUBLET

un·der·lie (-lī′) *vt.* **-lay′, -lain′, -ly′ing** [ME. *underlien* < OE. *underlicgan*] 1. to lie under or beneath 2. to be the basis for; form the foundation of 3. *Finance* to have priority over (another) in order of claim, as a bond

un·der·line (un′dər līn′; *also, for v.*, un′dər līn′) *vt.* **-lined′, -lin′ing** 1. to draw a line beneath; underscore 2. to stress or emphasize —*n.* a line underneath, as an underscore

un·der·ling (-liŋ) *n.* [ME. < OE.: see UNDER- & -LING¹] a person in a subordinate position; inferior: usually contemptuous or disparaging

un·der·lin·ing (-līn′iŋ) *n.* a garment lining formed of pieces cut to the shape of and attached to the separate sections of a garment which are then sewed together

un·der·lip (-lip′) *n.* the lower lip

un·der·ly·ing (-lī′iŋ) *adj.* 1. lying under; placed

beneath 2. fundamental; basic 3. not clearly evident, but implicit 4. *Finance* having priority, as a claim

un·der·mine (un′dər mīn′) *vt.* **-mined′, -min′ing** 1. to dig beneath; excavate ground from under, so as to form a tunnel or mine 2. to wear away at the base or foundation 3. to injure, weaken, or impair, esp. by subtle, stealthy, or insidious means —*SYN.* see WEAKEN

un·der·most (un′dər mōst′) *adj., adv.* lowest in place, position, rank, etc.

un·der·neath (un′dər nēth′) *adv.* [ME. *undernethe* < OE. *underneothan* < *under*, UNDER + *neothan*, below: see NETHER] 1. under; below; beneath 2. on the underside; at a lower level —*prep.* 1. under; below; beneath 2. under the form, guise, or authority of —*adj.* under or lower —*n.* the underpart; bottom side

un·der·nour·ish (-nur′ish) *vt.* to give insufficient nourishment to; provide with less food than is needed for health and growth —**un′der·nour′ish·ment** *n.*

☆**un·der·pants** (un′dər pants′) *n.pl.* an undergarment, long or short, for the lower part of the body, with a separate opening for each leg

un·der·part (un′dər pärt′) *n.* 1. the lower part or side, as of an animal's body or an airplane's fuselage 2. a secondary or subsidiary position or part

☆**un·der·pass** (-pas′, -päs′) *n.* a passage, road, etc. running under something; esp., a passageway for vehicles or pedestrians that runs under a railway or highway

un·der·pay (un′dər pā′) *vt.* **-paid′, -pay′ing** 1. to pay too little, or less than (the due amount) 2. to pay too little to (someone) —**un′der·pay′ment** *n.*

un·der·pin (-pin′) *vt.* **-pinned′, -pin′ning** 1. to support or strengthen from beneath, as with props 2. to support or strengthen in any way; corroborate, substantiate, etc.

un·der·pin·ning (un′dər pin′iŋ) *n.* 1. a supporting structure or foundation, esp. one placed beneath a wall 2. a support or prop ☆3. [*pl.*] [Colloq.] the legs

un·der·play (un′dər plā′) *vt., vi.* 1. to play, or act (a role or scene) with less than the usual emphasis, in an intentionally restrained manner 2. *same as* UNDERACT

un·der·plot (un′dər plät′) *n.* a secondary or subordinate plot in a story, play, etc.

un·der·priv·i·leged (un′dər priv′'l ijd, -priv′lijd) *adj.* deprived of fundamental social rights and security through poverty, discrimination, etc. —**the underprivileged** those who are underprivileged

un·der·pro·duce (-prə doos′, -dyoos′) *vt., vi.* **-duced′, -duc′ing** to produce in a quantity insufficient to meet the need or demand —**un′der·pro·duc′tion** *n.*

un·der·proof (-proof′) *adj.* containing less alcohol than proof spirit does

un·der·prop (-präp′) *vt.* **-propped′, -prop′ping** to prop underneath; support

un·der·quote (-kwōt′) *vt.* **-quot′ed, -quot′ing** 1. to quote (goods) at a price lower than another price or than the market price 2. to quote a lower price than (other sellers)

un·der·rate (-rāt′) *vt.* **-rat′ed, -rat′ing** to rate, assess, or estimate too low

un·der·run (-run′) *vt.* **-ran′, -run′, -run′ning** to run, go, or pass under —*n.* something running or passing underneath, as an undercurrent

un·der·score (un′dər skôr′; *for n.* un′dər skôr′) *vt.* **-scored′, -scor′ing** *same as* UNDERLINE —*n.* a line drawn under a word, passage, etc., as for emphasis

un·der·sea (-sē′) *adj., adv.* beneath the surface of the sea: also **un′der·seas′** (-sēz′) *adv.*

un·der·sec·re·tar·y (-sek′rə ter′ē) *n., pl.* **-tar′ies** an assistant secretary: in U.S. government, **under secretary**

un·der·sell (un′dər sel′) *vt.* **-sold′, -sell′ing** 1. to sell at a lower price than (another seller) ☆2. to promote, try to persuade, etc. in a restrained or inadequate manner

un·der·set (un′dər set′) *n.* an ocean undercurrent

☆**un·der·sexed** (un′dər sekst′) *adj.* characterized by a weaker than normal sexual drive or interest

un·der·sher·iff (un′dər sher′if) *n.* a deputy sheriff

☆**un·der·shirt** (-shurt′) *n.* a collarless, usually sleeveless undergarment worn under an outer shirt, esp. by men

un·der·shoot (un′dər shoot′) *vt.* **-shot′, -shoot′ing** 1. to shoot or fall short of (a target, mark, etc.) 2. to bring an aircraft down short of (the runway, landing field, etc.) while trying to land —*vi.* to shoot or go short of the mark

☆**un·der·shorts** (un′dər shôrts′) *n.pl.* short underpants worn by men and boys

un·der·shot (-shät′) *adj.* 1. with the lower part or half extending past the upper [an *undershot* jaw] 2. driven by water flowing along the lower part [an *undershot* water wheel]

un·der·shrub (-shrub′) *n.* any low-growing, woody, bushy plant; specif., *same as* SUBSHRUB

un·der·side (-sīd′) *n.* the side or surface that is underneath

un·der·sign (un′dər sīn′) *vt.* to sign one's name at the end of (a letter, document, etc.)

UNDERSHOT WHEEL

un·der·signed (un′dər sīnd′) *adj.* **1.** signed at the end **2.** whose name is signed at the end —**the undersigned** the person or persons having signed at the end

un·der·sized (-sīzd′) *adj.* smaller in size than is usual, average, or proper: also **un′der·size′** (-sīz′)

un·der·skirt (un′dər skurt′) *n.* a skirt worn under another; petticoat

un·der·slung (-slun′) *adj.* **1.** attached to the underside of the axles: said of an automobile frame **2.** having an underslung frame **3.** projecting: said of the lower jaw

un·der·soil (-soil′) *n.* same as SUBSOIL

un·der·song (-sôn′) *n.* a song or refrain sung as accompaniment to another song

un·der·staffed (un′dər staft′, -stäft′) *adj.* having too small a staff; having insufficient personnel

un·der·stand (un′dər stand′) *vt.* **-stood′, -stand′ing** [ME. *understanden* < OE. *understandan,* lit., to stand under or among] **1.** to get or perceive the meaning of; know or grasp what is meant by; comprehend [to *understand* a question] **2.** to gather or assume from what is heard, known, etc.; infer [are we to *understand* that you want to go?] **3.** to take as meant or meaning; interpret [to *understand* his silence as refusal] **4.** to take for granted or as a fact [it is *understood* that no one is to leave] **5.** to supply mentally (an idea, word, etc.), as for grammatical completeness **6.** to get as information; learn **7.** to know thoroughly; grasp or perceive clearly and fully the nature, character, functioning, etc. of **8.** to have a sympathetic rapport with [no one *understands* me] —*vi.* **1.** to have understanding, comprehension, sympathetic awareness, etc., either in general or with reference to some specific statement, situation, etc. **2.** to be informed; believe; assume [he is, I *understand,* no longer here] —**un′der·stand′a·ble** *adj.* —**un′der·stand′a·bly** *adv.*

SYN.—**understand** and **comprehend** are used interchangeably to imply clear perception of the meaning of something, but, more precisely, **understand** stresses the full awareness or knowledge arrived at, and **comprehend**, the process of grasping something mentally [a foreigner may *comprehend* the words in an American idiom without *understanding* at all what is meant]; **appreciate** implies sensitive, discriminating perception of the exact worth or value of something [to *appreciate* the difficulties of a situation]

un·der·stand·ing (-in) *n.* **1.** the mental quality, act, or state of a person who understands; comprehension, knowledge, discernment, sympathetic awareness, etc. **2.** the power or ability to think, learn, judge, etc.; intelligence; sense **3.** a specific interpretation or inference [one's *understanding* of a matter] **4.** *a)* mutual comprehension, as of ideas, intentions, etc. *b)* mutual agreement, esp. one that settles differences or is informal and not made public —*adj.* that understands; having or characterized by comprehension, sympathy, etc. —**un′der·stand′ing·ly** *adv.*

un·der·state (un′dər stāt′) *vt.* **-stat′ed, -stat′ing 1.** to make a weaker statement of than is warranted by truth, accuracy, or importance; state too weakly **2.** to state, express, etc. in a style that is restrained and often makes use of irony or litotes —**un′der·state′ment** *n.*

un·der·stock (-stäk′) *vt.* to stock less of than is needed or desired

un·der·stood (-stood′) *pt. & pp.* of UNDERSTAND —*adj.* **1.** known; comprehended **2.** agreed upon **3.** implied but not expressed; assumed

un·der·strap·per (un′dər strap′ər) *n.* [UNDER- + STRAPPER] a subordinate or underling

un·der·stud·y (-stud′ē) *n., pl.* **-stud′ies 1.** an actor who learns the part of another actor so that he can serve as a substitute when necessary **2.** any person who learns the duties of another so that he can serve as a substitute —*vt., vi.* **-stud′ied, -stud′y·ing 1.** to act as an understudy (to) **2.** to learn (a part) as an understudy (sense 2)

un·der·sur·face (-sur′fis) *n.* same as UNDERSIDE

un·der·take (un′dər tāk′) *vt.* **-took′, -tak′en, -tak′ing** [ME. *undertaken:* see UNDER- & TAKE] **1.** to take upon oneself; agree to do; enter into or upon (a task, journey, etc.) **2.** to give a promise or pledge that; contract [he *undertook* to be their guide] **3.** to promise; guarantee **4.** to make oneself responsible for; take over as a charge —*vi.* **1.** [Archaic] to take on responsibility, pledge oneself, guarantee, or be surety (for) ☆**2.** [Old Colloq.] to work as an undertaker (sense 2)

un·der·tak·er (un′dər tā′kər; *for 2* un′dər tā′kər) *n.* **1.** a person who undertakes something **2.** earlier term for FUNERAL DIRECTOR

un·der·tak·ing (un′dər tā′kin; *also, & for 3 always,* un′dər tā′kin) *n.* **1.** something undertaken; task; charge; enterprise **2.** a promise; guarantee **3.** the business of an

undertaker (sense 2) **4.** the act of one who undertakes some task, responsibility, etc.

un·der-the-count·er (un′dər *tha* koun′tər) *adj.* [Colloq.] done, sold, given, etc. secretly in an unlawful or unethical way: also **under-the-ta′ble**

un·der·things (-thinz′) *n.pl.* women's or girls' underwear

un·der·tint (-tint′) *n.* a faint or subdued tint

un·der·tone (-tōn′) *n.* **1.** a low tone of sound or voice **2.** a faint or subdued color, esp. one seen through other colors, as in some glazes **3.** *a)* any underlying quality, factor, element, etc. [an *undertone* of horror] *b) Finance* the underlying tendency of a market

un·der·took (un′dər took′) *pt.* of UNDERTAKE

un·der·tow (un′dər tō′) *n.* [UNDER- + TOW¹] a current of water moving beneath and in a different direction from that of the surface water: said esp. of a seaward current beneath breaking surf

un·der·trick (-trik′) *n. Bridge* any of the tricks by which one falls short of making one's contract

un·der·val·ue (un′dər val′yōō) *vt.* **-ued, -u·ing 1.** to value too low, or below the real worth **2.** to regard or esteem too lightly —**un′der·val′u·a′tion** *n.*

un·der·vest (un′dər vest′) *n.* [Brit.] *same as* UNDERSHIRT

☆**un·der·waist** (-wāst′) *n.* an undergarment worn under a waist

un·der·wa·ter (un′dər wôt′ər, -wät′ər) *adj.* **1.** being, placed, done, etc. beneath the surface of the water **2.** used or for use under water **3.** below the waterline of a ship —*adv.* beneath the surface of the water

un·der·way (un′dər wā′) *adj. Naut.* not at anchor or moored or aground

un·der·wear (un′dər wer′) *n.* clothing worn under one's outer clothes, usually next to the skin, as undershirts, undershorts, slips, brassieres, etc.

un·der·weight (un′dər wāt′; *also, for adj.,* un′dər wāt′) *adj.* below the normal, desirable, or allowed weight —*n.* less weight than is needed, desired, or allowed

un·der·went (un′dər went′) *pt.* of UNDERGO

un·der·wing (un′dər win′) *n.* **1.** either of the pair of hind wings of an insect **2.** any of a genus (*Catocala*) of noctuid moths, having brightly colored hind wings that are hidden under drab forewings except during flight

un·der·wood (un′dər wood′) *n. same as* UNDERBRUSH

un·der·world (-wurld′) *n.* **1.** formerly, the earth **2.** the mythical world of the dead; Hades **3.** the opposite side of the earth; antipodes **4.** the criminal members of society, or people living by vice or crime, regarded as an organized social group

un·der·write (un′dər rīt′) *vt.* **-wrote′, -writ′ten, -writ′ing** [ME. *underwriten,* orig. used as transl. of L. *subscribere* (see SUBSCRIBE)] **1.** to write under something, esp. under something written; subscribe **2.** to agree to buy (an issue of stocks, bonds, etc.) on a given date and at a fixed price, or to guarantee the purchase of (stocks or bonds to be made available to the public for subscription) **3.** to subscribe or agree to, as by signature **4.** to agree to pay for or finance (an undertaking, etc.) **5.** *Insurance a)* to write one's signature at the end of (an insurance policy), thus assuming liability in the event of specified loss or damage *b)* to insure *c)* to assume liability to the amount of (a specified sum) —*vi.* **1.** to underwrite something **2.** to be in business as an underwriter

un·der·writ·er (-ər) *n.* **1.** a person who underwrites, or finances something **2.** a person who underwrites issues of stocks, bonds, etc. **3.** *a)* an employee of an insurance company who determines the acceptability of risks, the premiums that should be charged, etc. *b)* an agent who underwrites insurance

un·de·sign·ing (un′di zī′nin) *adj.* not designing; straightforward; honest; not crafty or underhanded

un·de·sir·a·ble (-di zīr′ə b'l) *adj.* not desirable or pleasing; objectionable —*n.* an undesirable person —**un′de·sir′a·bil′i·ty** *n.* —**un′de·sir′a·bly** *adv.*

un·did (-did′) *pt.* of UNDO

un·dies (un′dēz) *n.pl.* [dim. euphemistic abbrev.] [Colloq.] women's or girls' underwear

un·dine (un dēn′; un′dēn, -din) *n.* [G. < ModL. *Undina* < L. *unda,* a wave: see WATER] *Folklore* a female water spirit who could acquire a soul by marrying, and having a child by, a mortal: orig. a spirit in Paracelsus' system

un·di·rect·ed (un′di rek′tid, -dī-) *adj.* **1.** not directed; not guided **2.** not addressed, as a letter

un·dis·posed (-dis pōzd′) *adj.* **1.** not disposed (of) **2.** indisposed; unwilling

un·dis·so·ci·at·ed (-di sō′shē āt′id, -sē-) *adj. Chem.* not separated into ions, radicals, or simpler atoms or molecules

undescribable	undeviating	undiplomatic	undisguised
undescried	undevoured	undiscernible	undisheartened
undeserving	undevout	undiscernibly	undishonored
undesignated	undifferentiated	undiscerning	undismantled
undesired	undiffused	undischarged	undismayed
undesirous	undigested	undisciplined	undismembered
undestroyed	undigestible	undisclosed	undispelled
undetachable	undignified	undiscouraged	undisputable
undetected	undiluted	undiscoverable	undisputed
undeterminable	undiminishable	undiscovered	undissected
undeterred	undiminished	undiscriminating	undissolved
undeveloped	undimmed	undiscussed	undissolving

un·do (un dōō′) *vt.* -did′, -done′, -do′ing [ME. *undon* < OE. *undon* < *un-*, UN- + *don*, to DO[1]] 1. *a*) to release or untie (a fastening) *b*) to open (a parcel, door, etc.) by this means 2. to reverse the doing of (something accomplished); do away with; cancel; annul 3. to put an end to; bring to ruin, disgrace, or downfall 4. to upset emotionally; perturb 5. [Obs.] to interpret; explain —**un·do′er** *n.*

un·do·ing (-in) *n.* 1. the act of opening, untying, etc. 2. a reversal of the doing of something done or accomplished; canceling or annulling 3. the act of bringing to ruin, disgrace, or destruction 4. the cause or source of ruin, disgrace, or destruction

un·done[1] (-dun′) *pp.* of UNDO —*adj.* 1. ruined, disgraced, etc. 2. emotionally upset; greatly perturbed

un·done[2] (-dun′) *adj.* not done; not performed, accomplished, completed, etc.

un·dou·ble (-dub′'l) *vt.* -bled, -bling to cause to be no longer doubled or double; unfold

un·doubt·ed (-dout′id) *adj.* not doubted, called in question, or disputed; certain —**un·doubt′ed·ly** *adv.*

un·draw (-drô′) *vt., vi.* -drew′, -drawn′, -draw′ing to draw (a curtain, drapes, etc.) open, back, or aside

un·dreamed (-drēmd′) *adj.* not even dreamed (*of*) or imagined; inconceivable: also **un·dreamt′** (-dremt′)

un·dress (un dres′; *for n., usually* un′dres′) *vt.* 1. to take off the clothing of; strip 2. to divest of ornament 3. to remove the dressing from (a wound) —*vi.* to take off one's clothes; strip —*n.* 1. the state of being naked, only partially dressed, or in night clothes, a robe, etc. 2. ordinary or informal dress, as opposed to uniform, full dress, etc.

Und·set (ōōn′set), **Si·grid** (si′gri; *E.* si′grid) 1882-1949; Norw. novelist

un·due (un dōō′, -dyōō′) *adj.* 1. not yet due or payable, as a debt 2. not appropriate or suitable; improper 3. excessive; unreasonable; immoderate

un·du·lant (un′joo lənt, -dyoo-; -doo-) *adj.* moving in or as in waves; undulating

undulant fever a persistent form of brucellosis, transmitted to man from lower, esp. domestic, animals, or their products, and characterized by an undulating, or recurrent, fever, sweating, and pains in the joints

un·du·late (-lāt′; *for adj., usually* -lit) *vt.* -lat′ed, -lat′ing [< L. *undulatus*, undulated < *undula*, dim. of *unda*, a wave: see WATER] 1. to cause to move in waves 2. to give a wavy form, margin, or surface to —*vi.* 1. to move in or as in waves; move sinuously 2. to have a wavy form, margin, or surface —*adj.* having a wavy form, margin, or surface; undulating: also **un′du·lat′ed** —SYN. see SWING

un·du·la·tion (un′joo lā′shən, -dyoo-, -doo-) *n.* 1. *a*) the act of undulating *b*) an undulating motion, as of a wave 2. a wavy, curving form or outline, esp. one of a series 3. *Physics* wave motion, as of light or sound, or a wave or vibration

un·du·la·to·ry (un′joo lə tôr′ē, -dyoo-, -doo-) *adj.* 1. of, caused by, or characterized by undulations 2. having a wavelike form or motion; undulating

un·du·ly (un dōō′lē, -dyōō′-) *adv.* 1. improperly; unjustly 2. to an undue degree; excessively

un·dy·ing (-dī′in) *adj.* not dying; immortal or eternal

un·earned (-urnd′) *adj.* 1. not earned by work or service; specif., obtained as a return on an investment [*unearned* income] 2. not deserved; unmerited

unearned increment an increase in the value of land or other property through no work or expenditure by the owner, as through an increase in area population

un·earth (-urth′) *vt.* 1. to dig up from out of the earth 2. to bring to light as by searching; discover; disclose —SYN. see LEARN

un·earth·ly (-urth′lē) *adj.* 1. not, or as if not, of this earth 2. supernatural; ghostly 3. weird; mysterious 4. [Colloq.] fantastic, outlandish, absurd, etc. —SYN. see WEIRD —**un·earth′li·ness** *n.*

un·eas·y (-ē′zē) *adj.* -eas′i·er, -eas′i·est 1. having, showing, or allowing no ease of body or mind; uncomfortable 2. awkward; constrained 3. disturbed by anxiety or apprehension; restless; unsettled; perturbed —**un·ease′**, **un·eas′i·ness** *n.* —**un·eas′i·ly** *adv.*

un·ed·it·ed (-ed′it id) *adj.* 1. not edited for publication 2. not assembled for presentation [an *unedited* film]

un·em·ploy·a·ble (un′im ploi′ə b'l) *adj.* not employable; specif., that cannot be employed because of age, physical or mental deficiency, etc. —*n.* an unemployable person

un·em·ployed (-im ploid′) *adj.* 1. not employed; without work 2. not being used; idle —**the unemployed** people who are out of work

un·em·ploy·ment (-im ploi′mənt) *n.* 1. the state of being unemployed; lack of employment 2. the number or percentage of persons in the normal labor force out of work

unemployment compensation payment, as by a State government, of a certain amount of money to an unemployed person, usually at regular intervals and over a fixed period of time

un·e·qual (un ē′kwəl) *adj.* 1. not equal, as in size, strength, ability, value, rank, number, amount, etc. 2. *a*) not balanced or symmetrical [an *unequal* pattern] *b*) that matches unequal contestants [an *unequal* battle] 3. not even, regular, or uniform; variable; fluctuating 4. not equal or adequate (with *to*) [*unequal* to the task] 5. [Now Rare] not equitable; unjust; unfair —*n.* a person or thing not equal to another —**un·e′qual·ly** *adv.*

un·e·qualed, un·e·qualled (-ē′kwəld) *adj.* not equaled; unmatched; unrivaled; supreme

un·e·quiv·o·cal (un′i kwiv′ə k'l) *adj.* not equivocal; not ambiguous; plain; clear —**un·e·quiv′o·cal·ly** *adv.*

un·err·ing (un ur′in, -er′-) *adj.* 1. free from error 2. not missing or failing; certain; sure; exact —**un·err′ing·ly** *adv.*

UNESCO (yoo nes′kō) United Nations Educational, Scientific, and Cultural Organization

un·es·sen·tial (un′i sen′shəl) *adj.* not essential; that can be dispensed with —*n.* an unessential thing

un·e·ven (un ē′vən) *adj.* [ME. < OE. *unefen*] not even; specif., *a*) not level, smooth, or flat; rough; irregular *b*) not straight or parallel *c*) unequal, as in length, thickness, etc. *d*) not uniform; varying; fluctuating *e*) not equally balanced or matched *f*) not equitable; unfair *g*) *Math.* odd; not evenly divisible by two —SYN. see ROUGH —**un·e′ven·ly** *adv.* —**un·e′ven·ness** *n.*

un·e·vent·ful (un′i vent′fəl) *adj.* with no outstanding or unusual event; peaceful, routine, etc. [an *uneventful* day] —**un·e·vent′ful·ly** *adv.*

un·ex·am·pled (-ig zam′p'ld, -zäm′-) *adj.* having no precedent, parallel, or similar case; unprecedented

un·ex·cep·tion·a·ble (-ik sep′shə nə b'l) *adj.* not exceptionable; without flaw or fault; not warranting even the slightest criticism —**un′ex·cep′tion·a·bly** *adv.*

un·ex·cep·tion·al (-ik sep′shən 'l) *adj.* 1. not exceptional; not uncommon or unusual; ordinary 2. not admitting of any exception 3. *var. of* UNEXCEPTIONABLE: regarded by some as a loose usage —**un′ex·cep′tion·al·ly** *adv.*

un·ex·pect·ed (-ik spek′tid) *adj.* not expected; unforeseen —**un′ex·pect′ed·ly** *adv.* —**un′ex·pect′ed·ness** *n.*

un·ex·press·ive (-ik spres′iv) *adj.* 1. *same as* INEXPRESSIVE 2. [Obs.] that cannot be expressed; inexpressible

un·fail·ing (un fāl′in) *adj.* 1. not failing 2. never ceasing or falling short; inexhaustible 3. always reliable; certain; sure —**un·fail′ing·ly** *adv.*

---

undistilled	uneatable	unenriched	unexcitable
undistinguishable	uneaten	unenrolled	unexcited
undistinguished	uneconomical	unenslaved	unexciting
undistorted	unedible	unentangled	unexcused
undistracted	unedifying	unentered	unexecuted
undistressed	uneducable	unenterprising	unexercised
undistributed	uneducated	unentertaining	unexpanded
undisturbed	uneffaced	unenthralled	unexpendable
undiversified	unemancipated	unenthusiastic	unexperienced
undiverted	unembarrassed	unentitled	unexpert
undivested	unembellished	unenviable	unexpiated
undivided	unemotional	unenvious	unexpired
undivulged	unemphatic	unequipped	unexplainable
undocumented	unenclosed	unerased	unexplained
undogmatic	unencumbered	unescapable	unexplicit
undomestic	unendearing	unescorted	unexploded
undomesticated	unending	unestablished	unexploited
undrained	unendorsed	unesthetic	unexplored
undramatic	unendowed	unethical	unexported
undramatically	unendurable	unexacting	unexposed
undramatized	unenforceable	unexaggerated	unexpunged
undraped	unengaged	unexalted	unexpurgated
undried	unengaging	unexamined	unextended
undrinkable	un-English	unexcavated	unextinguished
undutiful	unenjoyable	unexcelled	unfaded
undyed	unenlightened	unexchangeable	unfading

---

fat, āpe, cär; ten, ēven; is, bīte; gō, hôrn, tōōl, look; oil, out; up, fur; get; joy; yet; chin; she; thin, *th*en; zh, leisure; ŋ, ring; ə for *a* in ago, *e* in agent, *i* in sanity, *o* in comply, *u* in focus; ′ as in able (ā′b'l); Fr. bâl; ë, Fr. coeur; ö, Fr. feu; Fr. mon; ô, Fr. coq; ü, Fr. duc; r, Fr. cri; H, G. ich; kh, G. doch. See inside front cover. ✩ Americanism; ‡foreign; *hypothetical; < derived from

un·fair (-fer′) *adj.* [ME. < OE. *unfæger*, unfair, frightful < *un-*, not + *fæger*, FAIR] **1.** not just or impartial; biased; inequitable **2.** dishonest, dishonorable, or unethical in business dealings —**un·fair′ly** *adv.* —**un·fair′ness** *n.*

un·faith·ful (-fāth′fəl) *adj.* **1.** failing to observe the terms of a vow, promise, understanding, etc., or false to allegiance or duty; faithless; disloyal **2.** not true, accurate, or reliable; untrustworthy **3.** guilty of adultery; adulterous **4.** [Archaic] lacking good faith; dishonest **5.** [Obs.] infidel —**un·faith′ful·ly** *adv.* —**un·faith′ful·ness** *n.*

un·fa·mil·iar (un′fə mil′yər) *adj.* **1.** not familiar or well-known; strange **2.** having no acquaintance (*with*); not conversant [*unfamiliar* with the novels of Kafka] —**un′·fa·mil′i·ar′i·ty** (-yer′ə tē, -ē er′-) *n.* —**un′fa·mil′iar·ly** *adv.*

un·fas·ten (un fas′'n) *vt.* to open or make loose; untie, unlock, undo, etc. —*vi.* to become unfastened

un·fa·thered (-fā′thərd) *adj.* **1.** having no father; fatherless **2.** of unknown paternity; bastard **3.** of unknown authorship or unestablished authenticity

un·fa·vor·a·ble (-fā′vər ə b'l, -fāv′rə b'l) *adj.* not favorable; specif., *a*) not propitious *b*) adverse, contrary, or disadvantageous —**un·fa′vor·a·bly** *adv.*

un·feel·ing (-fēl′in) *adj.* **1.** incapable of feeling or sensation; insensate or insensible **2.** incapable of sympathy or mercy; hardhearted; callous; cruel —**un·feel′ing·ly** *adv.*

un·feigned (-fānd′) *adj.* not feigned; genuine; real; sincere —*SYN.* see SINCERE —**un·feign′ed·ly** (-fān′id lē) *adv.*

un·fet·ter (-fet′ər) *vt.* to free from fetters; free from restraint of any kind; liberate

un·fil·i·al (-fil′ē əl) *adj.* unlike, or unsuitable to, a loving, respectful son or daughter —**un·fil′i·al·ly** *adv.*

un·fin·ished (-fin′isht) *adj.* **1.** not finished; not completed or perfected; incomplete **2.** having no finish, or final coat, as of paint **3.** not processed after looming, as woolen cloth

un·fit (-fit′) *adj.* **1.** incapable of meeting requirements or qualifications; not suitable or qualified **2.** not physically or mentally fit or sound **3.** not adapted or fitted for a given purpose —*vt.* **-fit′ted, -fit′ting** to make unfit; disqualify or incapacitate —**un·fit′ly** *adv.* —**un·fit′ness** *n.*

un·fix (-fiks′) *vt.* [UN- (back) + FIX] **1.** to unfasten; loosen; detach **2.** to unsettle

un·flap·pa·ble (-flap′ə b'l) *adj.* [< UN- + FLAP (*n.* 4) + -ABLE] [Colloq.] not easily excited or disconcerted; imperturbable; calm —**un·flap′pa·bil′i·ty** *n.*

un·fledged (-flejd′) *adj.* **1.** not fully fledged; unfeathered, as a young bird **2.** immature; undeveloped

un·flinch·ing (-flin′chin) *adj.* not flinching, yielding, or shrinking; steadfast; resolute —**un·flinch′ing·ly** *adv.*

un·fold (-fōld′) *vt.* [ME. *unfolden* < OE. *unfealdan* < *un-*, back + *fealdan*, to FOLD¹] **1.** to open and spread out (something folded) **2.** to make known or lay open to view, esp. in stages or little by little; reveal, disclose, display, or explain **3.** to open up; unwrap —*vi.* **1.** to become unfolded; open out or open up **2.** to develop fully

un·for·get·ta·ble (un′fər get′ə b'l) *adj.* so important, beautiful, forceful, shocking, etc. as never to be forgotten —**un′for·get′ta·bly** *adv.*

un·formed (un fôrmd′) *adj.* **1.** having no regular form or shape; shapeless **2.** not organized or developed **3.** not made; uncreated

un·for·tu·nate (-fôr′chə nit) *adj.* **1.** *a*) having bad luck; unlucky *b*) bringing, or coming by, bad luck; inauspicious; unfavorable **2.** not suitable or successful —*n.* an unfortunate person —**un·for′tu·nate·ly** *adv.*

un·found·ed (-foun′did) *adj.* **1.** not founded on fact or truth; baseless **2.** not established

un·freeze (-frēz′) *vt.* **-froze′, -froz′en, -freez′ing** [UN- (back) + FREEZE] **1.** to cause to thaw ☆**2.** to remove financial controls from (prices, a raw material, etc.)

un·friend·ed (-fren′did) *adj.* having no friends; friendless

un·friend·ly (-frend′lē) *adj.* **1.** not friendly or kind; hostile **2.** not favorable or propitious —*adv.* in an unfriendly manner —**un·friend′li·ness** *n.*

un·frock (-fräk′) *vt.* **1.** to remove a frock from **2.** to deprive of the rank or function of priest or minister

un·fruit·ful (-frōōt′fəl) *adj.* **1.** not reproducing; barren; unproductive **2.** yielding no worthwhile result; fruitless;

unprofitable —*SYN.* see STERILE —**un·fruit′ful·ly** *adv.*

un·furl (-furl′) *vt., vi.* to open or spread out from a furled state; unfold

un·gain·ly (-gān′lē) *adj.* [ME. *ungeinliche* < *ungein*, perilous (< *un-*, not + ON. *gegn*, ready, serviceable, akin to OE. *gegn:* see AGAIN) + *-liche*, -LY¹] **1.** awkward; clumsy **2.** coarse and unattractive —*adv.* [Archaic] in an ungainly manner —**un·gain′li·ness** *n.*

Un·ga·va (uŋ gā′və, -gä′-) region in N Quebec, Canada, between Labrador & Hudson Bay: 351,780 sq. mi.

un·gen·er·ous (un jen′ər əs) *adj.* **1.** not generous; stingy; mean **2.** not liberal or charitable; harsh [an ungenerous remark] —**un·gen′er·ous·ly** *adv.*

un·gird (-gurd′) *vt.* [ME. *ungirden* < OE. *ongyrdan* < *un-*, back + *gyrdan*, to GIRD¹] **1.** to remove the belt or girdle of **2.** to remove by unfastening a belt

un·girt (-gurt′) *adj.* [ME. *ungyrt* < *ungirden:* see prec.] **1.** having the belt or girdle off or slackened; not girded **2.** loose; not braced or drawn tight; slack

un·glued (-glōōd′) *adj.* broken open; separated: said of things glued together —☆**come unglued** [Slang] to become emotionally upset and lose one's composure

un·god·ly (-gäd′lē) *adj.* **1.** not godly or religious; impious **2.** sinful; wicked **3.** [Colloq.] outrageous; dreadful —*adv.* **1.** [Archaic] in an impious, sinful, or wicked manner **2.** [Colloq.] outrageously; dreadfully [*ungodly* noisy] —**un·god′li·ness** *n.*

un·gov·ern·a·ble (-guv′ər nə b'l) *adj.* that cannot be governed or controlled; unruly, wild, etc. —*SYN.* see UNRULY —**un·gov′ern·a·bly** *adv.*

un·gra·cious (-grā′shəs) *adj.* **1.** not gracious or affable; rude; discourteous; impolite **2.** unpleasant; unattractive —**un·gra′cious·ly** *adv.* —**un·gra′cious·ness** *n.*

un·gram·mat·i·cal (un′grə mat′i k'l) *adj.* **1.** not in accordance with the rules of a grammar **2.** using ungrammatical language —**un′gram·mat′i·cal·ly** *adv.*

un·gual (uŋ′gwəl) *adj.* [< L. *unguis*, a claw, NAIL + -AL] of, like, or having a nail, claw, or hoof

un·guard·ed (un gärd′id) *adj.* **1.** having no guard; unprotected **2.** without guile or cunning; open **3.** careless; thoughtless; imprudent —**un·guard′ed·ly** *adv.*

un·guent (uŋ′gwənt) *n.* [L. *unguentum* < *unguere*, to anoint < IE. base *ongw-*, whence Sans. *anákti*, (he) anoints, MHG. *anke*, butter] a salve or ointment —**un′·guen·tar′y** (-gwən ter′ē) *adj.*

un·guic·u·late (uŋ gwik′yoo lit, -lāt′) *adj.* [< L. *unguiculus*, fingernail, dim. of *unguis*, claw, talon, NAIL + -ATE¹] **1.** having nails, claws, or talons instead of hoofs **2.** *Bot.* having an unguis —*n.* a mammal having claws or nails

un·guis (uŋ′gwis) *n., pl.* **-gues** (-gwēz) [L., a NAIL] **1.** *Bot.* the narrow, stalklike, claw-shaped base of certain petals **2.** *Zool.* a nail, claw, or hoof

un·gu·la (uŋ′gyoo lə) *n., pl.* **-lae′** (-lē′) [L., a hoof < *unguis*, a hoof, NAIL] same as UNGUIS (sense 2) —**un′gu·lar** *adj.*

un·gu·late (-lit, -lāt′) *adj.* [LL. *ungulatus* < L. *ungula*, a hoof < *unguis*, a NAIL] **1.** having hoofs; of or belonging to a former group of all mammals having hoofs **2.** shaped like a hoof —*n.* a mammal having hoofs

un·hair (un her′) *vt., vi.* to make or become free from hair, as hides before tanning

un·hal·low (-hal′ō) *vt.* to desecrate; profane

un·hal·lowed (-hal′ōd) *adj.* **1.** not hallowed or consecrated; unholy **2.** wicked; profane; impious

un·hand (-hand′) *vt.* to loose or release from the hand or hands or one's grasp; let go of

un·hand·some (-han′səm) *adj.* **1.** not handsome or attractive; plain; homely **2.** not gracious or courteous; rude; unbecoming **3.** stingy; mean —**un·hand′some·ly** *adv.*

un·hand·y (-han′dē) *adj.* **-hand′i·er, -hand′i·est** **1.** not handy; inconvenient or inaccessible **2.** not clever with the hands; awkward —**un·hand′i·ly** *adv.* —**un·hand′i·ness** *n.*

un·hap·py (-hap′ē) *adj.* **-pi·er, -pi·est** **1.** unlucky; unfortunate **2.** sad; wretched; sorrowful **3.** not suitable or apt; ill-chosen **4.** [Obs.] evil; reprehensible —**un·hap′pi·ly** *adv.* —**un·hap′pi·ness** *n.*

un·har·ness (-här′nis) *vt.* **1.** to remove the harness or gear from **2.** to remove the armor from (a knight, etc.)

unfaltering	unflattering	unfrequented	ungrateful
unfashionable	unflavored	unfulfilled	ungratified
unfatherly	unforbidden	unfunded	ungreased
unfathomable	unforced	unfunny	ungrounded
unfathomed	unfordable	unfurnished	ungrudging
unfeared	unforeknown	ungarnished	unguessable
unfearful	unforeseeable	ungathered	unguided
unfeasible	unforeseen	ungentlemanly	unhackneyed
unfeathered	unforested	ungenuine	unhammered
unfed	unforfeited	ungifted	unhampered
unfederated	unforged	unglazed	unhandled
unfelt	unforgivable	unglorified	unhanged
unfeminine	unforgivably	unglossed	unhardened
unfenced	unforgiven	ungloved	unharmed
unfermented	unforgotten	ungot	unharmful
unfertile	unformulated	ungotten	unharmonious
unfertilized	unforsaken	ungowned	unharnessed
unfilled	unfortified	ungraced	unharrowed
unfiltered	unfought	ungraceful	unharvested
unfired	unframed	ungraded	unhasty
unflagging	unfree	ungraduated	unhatched

un·health·y (-hel'thē) *adj.* **-health'i·er, -health'i·est** **1.** having or showing poor health; sickly; not well **2.** harmful to health; unwholesome **3.** harmful to morals or character **4.** dangerous or risky *[an unhealthy situation]* —**un·health'i·ly** *adv.* —**un·health'i·ness** *n.*

un·heard (-hurd') *adj.* **1.** not heard; not perceived by the ear **2.** not given a hearing **3.** *earlier var. of* UNHEARD-OF

un·heard-of (-hurd'uv') *adj.* **1.** not heard of before; unprecedented or unknown **2.** unacceptable or outrageous *[unheard-of effrontery]*

un·helm (-helm') *vt., vi.* [Archaic] to remove the helm or helmet (of)

un·hinge (-hinj') *vt.* **-hinged', -hing'ing** **1.** *a)* to remove from the hinges *b)* to remove the hinges from **2.** to dislodge or detach **3.** to throw (the mind, etc.) into confusion; unbalance or upset

un·his·tor·ic (un'his tôr'ik, -tär'-) *adj.* not historic or historical; specif., *Linguis.* not having a historical basis; accidental, as the *b* in *thumb:* also **un'his·tor'i·cal**

un·hitch (un hich') *vt.* **1.** to free from a hitch **2.** to unfasten; release; detach

un·ho·ly (-hō'lē) *adj.* **-li·er, -li·est** [ME. < OE. *unhalig* < *un-*, not + *halig,* HOLY] **1.** not sacred, hallowed, or consecrated **2.** wicked; profane; impious **3.** [Colloq.] outrageous; dreadful —**un·ho'li·ness** *n.*

un·hook (-hook') *vt.* **1.** to remove or loosen from a hook **2.** to undo or unfasten the hook or hooks of —*vi.* to become unhooked

un·hoped-for (-hōpt'fôr') *adj.* not hoped for; unexpected *[an unhoped-for advantage]:* also [Now Rare] **un·hoped'**

un·horse (-hôrs') *vt.* **-horsed', -hors'ing** **1.** to throw (a rider) from a horse **2.** to overthrow; upset

un·hu·man (-hyōō'mən, -yōō'-) *adj.* **1.** *rare var. of: a)* INHUMAN *b)* SUPERHUMAN **2.** not human in kind, quality, etc. —**un·hu'man·ly** *adv.*

un·hur·ried (-hur'ēd) *adj.* not hurried; leisurely; deliberate —**un·hur'ried·ly** *adv.*

u·ni- (yōō'nə, -ni; before a vowel, often -nē) [L. < *unus,* ONE] *a combining form meaning* having or consisting of one only *[unicellular]*

U·ni·ate, U·ni·at (yōō'nē ət, -at') *n.* [Russ. *uniyat* < *uniya,* a union < L. *unus,* ONE: so named from union with the Roman Church] a member of any Eastern Christian Church in union with the Roman Catholic Church but with its own rite, custom, etc. —*adj.* of such a church Often regarded as an offensive term

u·ni·ax·i·al (yōō'ni ak'sē əl) *adj.* having a single axis

u·ni·cam·er·al (yōō'nə kam'ər əl) *adj.* [UNI- + CAMERAL] of or having a single legislative chamber

UNICEF (yōō'nə sef') United Nations International Children's Emergency Fund

u·ni·cel·lu·lar (yōō'nə sel'yoo lər) *adj.* [UNI- + CELLULAR] having or consisting of a single cell

u·ni·corn (yōō'nə kôrn') *n.* [ME. *unicorne* < OFr. < L.: *unicornis,* one-horned < *unus,* ONE + *cornu,* a HORN] **1.** a mythical horselike animal with a single horn growing from the center of its forehead **2.** [< a mistranslation of Heb. *re'ēm,* wild ox] *Bible* a two-horned, oxlike animal: Deut. 33:17

u·ni·cos·tate (yōō'nə käs'tāt) *adj.* *Bot.* having only one main rib: said of a leaf

☆**u·ni·cy·cle** (yōō'nə sī'k'l) *n.* [UNI- + (BI)CYCLE] a trick riding device with only one wheel, which is straddled by the rider, who pushes its pedals

UNICORN

u·ni·di·men·sion·al (yōō'nə də men'shən 'l) *adj.* having only a single dimension

u·ni·di·rec·tion·al (-də rek'shən 'l, -dī-) *adj.* having, or moving in, only one direction

unidirectional current *same as* DIRECT CURRENT

u·ni·fi·a·ble (yōō'nə fī'ə b'l) *adj.* that can be unified

u·ni·fi·ca·tion (yōō'nə fi kā'shən) *n.* the act of unifying or the state of being unified

u·ni·fi·er (yōō'nə fī'ər) *n.* a person or thing that unifies

u·ni·fi·lar (yōō'nə fī'lər) *adj.* [UNI- + FILAR] of or having only one thread, wire, etc.

u·ni·fo·li·ate (-fō'lē it, -āt') *adj.* [UNI- + FOLIATE] **1.** bearing only one leaf **2.** *var. of* UNIFOLIOLATE

u·ni·fo·li·o·late (-fō'lē ə lāt', -lit) *adj.* [UNI- + FOLIOLATE] **1.** bearing only one leaflet although compound in structure, as a leaf of the orange **2.** having leaves of this sort

u·ni·form (yōō'nə fôrm') *adj.* [MFr. *uniforme* < L. *uniformis* < *unus,* ONE + *-formis,* -FORM] **1.** *a)* always the same; not varying or changing in form, rate, degree, manner, etc.; constant *[a uniform speed]* *b)* identical throughout a state, country, etc. *[a uniform minimum wage]* **2.** *a)* having the same form, appearance, manner, etc. as others of the same class; conforming to a given standard *[a row of uniform houses]* *b)* being or looking the same in all parts; undiversified *[a uniform surface]* **3.** consistent in action, intention, effect, etc. *[a uniform policy]* —*n.* the official or distinctive clothes or outfit worn by the members of a particular group, as policemen or soldiers, esp. when on duty —*vt.* ☆**1.** to clothe or supply with a uniform **2.** to make uniform —*SYN.* see STEADY —**uniform with** having the same form, appearance, etc. as —**u'ni·form'ly** *adv.*

☆**Uniform Code of Military Justice** the body of laws governing members of the U.S. armed forces: superseded the Articles of War in 1951

u·ni·formed (-fôrmd') *adj.* wearing a uniform

u·ni·form·i·tar·i·an (yōō'nə fôr'mə ter'ē ən) *adj.* **1.** of or holding the doctrine of uniformitarianism **2.** of or adhering to uniformity in something —*n.* a person who adheres to some doctrine of uniformity

u·ni·form·i·tar·i·an·ism (-iz'm) *n.* the doctrine that all geologic changes may be explained by existing physical and chemical processes, as erosion, deposition, volcanic action, etc., that have operated in essentially the same way throughout geologic time

u·ni·form·i·ty (yōō'nə fôr'mə tē) *n., pl.* **-ties** [ME. *uniformite* < MFr. < L. *uniformitas*] state, quality, or instance of being uniform

u·ni·fy (yōō'nə fī') *vt., vi.* **-fied', -fy'ing** [MFr. *unifier* < LL. *unificare:* see UNI- & -FY] to combine into one; become or make united; consolidate

u·nij·u·gate (yoo nij'ə gāt'; yōō'nə jōō'gāt, -git) *adj.* [UNI- + JUGATE] *Bot.* having only one pair of leaflets: said of a pinnate leaf

u·ni·lat·er·al (yōō'nə lat'ər əl) *adj.* [ModL. *unilateralis:* see UNI- & LATERAL] **1.** of, occurring on, or affecting one side only **2.** involving or obligating one only of several persons or parties; done or undertaken by one only; not reciprocal *[a unilateral contract]* **3.** taking into account one side only of an issue, matter, etc.; one-sided **4.** showing descent through only one line of the family **5.** turned to one side **6.** *Biol.* arranged or produced on one side of an axis —**u'ni·lat'er·al·ism** *n.* —**u'ni·lat'er·al·ly** *adv.*

u·ni·lin·e·ar (-lin'ē ər) *adj.* of or following a single, consistent path of development or progression

u·ni·loc·u·lar (-läk'yə lər) *adj.* having, or made up of, only one loculus, compartment, cell, or chamber

un·im·peach·a·ble (un'im pēch'ə b'l) *adj.* not impeachable; that cannot be doubted, questioned, or discredited; irreproachable —**un'im·peach'a·bly** *adv.*

un·im·proved (un'im prōōvd') *adj.* **1.** not bettered, improved, or developed, as land by planting, building, etc. **2.** not used to good advantage **3.** not improved in health

un·in·cor·po·rat·ed (-in kôr'pə rāt'id) *adj.* not organized as a legal corporation *[an unincorporated village]*

un·in·hib·it·ed (-in hib'it id) *adj.* without inhibition; esp., free from the usual social or psychological restraints, as in behavior, expression, etc.

un·in·tel·li·gent (-in tel'ə jənt) *adj.* having or showing a lack or deficiency of intelligence —**un'in·tel'li·gence** *n.* —**un'in·tel'li·gent·ly** *adv.*

un·in·tel·li·gi·ble (-tel'i jə b'l) *adj.* not intelligible; that cannot be understood; incomprehensible —**un'in·tel'li·gi·bil'i·ty** *n.* —**un'in·tel'li·gi·bly** *adv.*

un·in·ten·tion·al (-in ten'shən 'l) *adj.* not done on purpose —**un'in·ten'tion·al·ly** *adv.*

un·in·ter·est·ed (un in'trist id, -in'tər ist-) *adj.* not interested; indifferent —**un·in'ter·est·ed·ly** *adv.*

un·in·ter·est·ing (-in) *adj.* lacking interest; dull; tedious —**un·in'ter·est·ing·ly** *adv.*

unhealed	unhoused	unimpassioned	uninflected
unhealthful	unhung	unimpeded	uninfluential
unheated	unhurt	unimplemented	uninformed
unheeded	unhusk	unimportance	uninhabitable
unheeding	unhygienic	unimportant	uninitiated
unhelpful	unhyphenated	unimposing	uninjured
unheralded	unidentified	unimpregnated	uninspiring
unheroic	unidiomatic	unimpressionable	unstructed
unhesitating	unilluminated	unimpressive	uninsurable
unhewn	unillustrated	unindemnified	uninsured
unhindered	unimaginable	unindulged	unintegrated
unhired	unimaginably	unindustrialized	unintended
unhomogeneous	unimaginative	unindustrious	unintermittent
unhonored	unimitated	uninfected	uninterpolated
unhostile	unimpaired	uninfested	uninterpreted

un·ion (yōōn'yən) n. [ME. < MFr. < LL.(Ec.) unio < L., oneness, unity < unus, ONE] **1.** a uniting or being united; combination; junction; fusion; specif., a) a combining, joining, or grouping together of nations, states, political groups, etc. for some specific purpose b) a marrying or being married; marriage **2.** something united or unified; a whole made up of united parts; specif., a) an organization or confederation uniting various individuals, groups, political units, etc. b) short for LABOR UNION c) in England, formerly, a combination of parishes for the joint administration of relief for the poor; also, a workhouse kept up by such a union **3.** a device symbolizing political union, used in a flag or ensign, as the white stars on a blue field in the flag of the U.S. **4.** a facility for social recreation on a college or university campus: in full **student union 5.** a device for joining together parts, as of a machine; esp., a coupling for linking the ends of pipes **6.** a fabric made of two or more different kinds of material, as cotton and linen **7.** Math. the set containing all the elements of two or more given sets, and no other elements —SYN. see ALLIANCE, UNITY —☆the Union the United States of America
☆**union card** a card serving to identify one as a member in good standing of a specified labor union
☆**union catalog** a library catalog combining the catalogs of different libraries or different divisions
Union City [formed by the union of two older towns] city in NE N.J.: suburb of Jersey City: pop. 59,000
un·ion·ism (-iz'm) n. **1.** a) the principle of union b) support of this principle or of a specified union **2.** the system or principles of labor unions ☆**3.** [U-] loyalty to the Federal union of the U.S., esp. during the Civil War
un·ion·ist (-ist) n. **1.** a person who believes in unionism **2.** a member of a labor union ☆**3.** [U-] a supporter of the Federal union of the U.S., esp. during the Civil War —**un'ion·is'tic** adj.
un·ion·ize (-īz') vt. -ized', -iz'ing **1.** to form into a union; esp., to organize (a group of workers in a shop, industry, etc.) into a labor union **2.** to bring into conformity with the rules, standards, etc. of a labor union —vi. to join or organize a union, esp. a labor union —**un'ion·i·za'tion** n.
un·i·on·ized (un ī'ə nīzd') adj. not ionized
union jack 1. a jack or flag consisting only of a union, esp. of the union of a national flag **2.** [U- J-] the national flag of the United Kingdom
Union of South Africa see SOUTH AFRICA
Union of Soviet Socialist Republics country in E Europe & N Asia, extending from the Arctic Ocean to the Black Sea & from the Baltic Sea to the Pacific: it is a union of fifteen constituent republics: 8,603,000 sq. mi.; pop. 240,000,000; cap. Moscow See also RUSSIA
☆**union shop** a factory, business, etc. operating under a contract between the employer and a labor union, which permits the hiring of nonunion workers but requires that all new employees join the union within a specified period
☆**union suit** a suit of men's or boys' underwear uniting shirt and drawers in a single garment
u·nip·a·rous (yoo nip'ə rəs) adj. [UNI- + -PAROUS] **1.** Bot. producing only one axis at each branching, as a cyme **2.** Zool. producing only one egg or offspring at a time
u·ni·per·son·al (yōō'nə pur's'n əl) adj. **1.** existing as or in, consisting of, or manifested in the form of, only one person **2.** Gram. used in only one person (specif., the third person singular): said of certain verbs, as methinks
u·ni·pet·al·ous (-pet'l əs) adj. having a corolla of only one petal, the others being undeveloped
u·ni·pla·nar (-plā'nər) adj. extending or occurring in one plane
u·ni·pod (yōō'nə päd') n. [UNI- + (TRI)POD] a one-legged prop or support
un·i·po·lar (yōō'nə pō'lər) adj. **1.** Elec. of or having only one magnetic or electric pole **2.** Zool. designating a nerve cell, as in spinal ganglia, having only one process —**u'ni·po·lar'i·ty** (-ler'ə tē) n.
u·nip·o·tent (yoo nip'ə tənt) adj. [UNI- + POTENT] Zool. capable of developing into only a single type of cell or tissue: said of certain, esp. embryonic, cells
u·nique (yōō nēk') adj. [Fr. < L. unicus, single < unus, ONE] **1.** one and only; single; sole [a unique specimen] **2.** having no like or equal; unparalleled [a unique achievement] **3.** highly unusual, extraordinary, rare, etc.: a common usage still objected to by some —SYN. see SINGLE —**u·nique'ly** adv. —**u·nique'ness** n.
u·ni·ra·mous (yōō'nə rā'məs) adj. [UNI- + RAMOUS] having a single branch
☆**u·ni·sex** (yōō'nə seks') adj. [Colloq.] designating, of, or involving a fashion, as in garments, hair styles, etc., that is undifferentiated for the sexes
u·ni·sex·u·al (yōō'nə sek'shoo wəl) adj. [ModL. unisexualis: see UNI- & SEXUAL] of only one sex; specif., a) Bot. same as DICLINOUS b) Zool. producing either eggs or sperm, not both; not hermaphroditic; dioecious —**u'ni·sex'u·al'i·ty** (-shoo wal'ə tē) n. —**u'ni·sex'u·al·ly** adv.
u·ni·son (yōō'nə sən, -zən) n. [MFr. < ML. unisonus, having the same sound < L. unus, ONE + sonus, a SOUND¹] **1.** identity of musical pitch, as of two or more voices or tones, or the interval of a perfect prime **2.** complete agree-

ment; concord; harmony —**in unison 1.** sounding the same note at the same time **2.** sounding together in octaves **3.** with all the voices or instruments performing the same part: said of a musical composition or passage **4.** uttering the same words, or producing the same sound, at the same time
u·nis·o·nous (yoo nis'ə nəs) adj. produced or sounding in unison: also **u·nis'o·nal, u·nis'o·nant**
u·nit (yōō'nit) n. [back-formation (prob. after DIGIT) < UNITY] **1.** a) the smallest whole number; one b) a magnitude or number regarded as an undivided whole c) the number in the position just to the left of the decimal point **2.** any fixed quantity, amount, distance, measure, etc. used as a standard; specif., ☆a) a fixed amount of work used as a basis in awarding scholastic credits, usually determined by the number of hours spent in class b) the amount of a drug, vaccine, serum, or antigen needed to produce a given result, as on a certain animal or on animal tissues **3.** a) a single person or group, esp. as distinguished from others or as part of a whole b) a single, distinct part or object, esp. one used for a specific purpose [the lens unit of a camera] **4.** Mil. an organized body of troops, airplanes, etc. forming a subdivision of a larger body
u·nit·age (-ij) n. a designation of the amount or quantity of a unit of measure
U·ni·tar·i·an (yōō'nə ter'ē ən) n. [< ModL. unitarius, unitary + -AN: also in part < UNIT(Y) + -ARIAN] **1.** a person who denies the doctrine of the Trinity, accepting the moral teachings, but rejecting the divinity, of Jesus, and holding that God exists in only one person **2.** a member of a Christian denomination based on these beliefs and characterized by congregational autonomy, tolerance of differing religious views, absence of creed, etc. —adj. **1.** of Unitarians or their doctrines, or adhering to Unitarianism **2.** [u-] same as UNITARY —**U'ni·tar'i·an·ism** n.
u·ni·tar·y (yōō'nə ter'ē) adj. **1.** of a unit or units **2.** of, based on, or characterized by unity **3.** having the nature of or used as a unit
unit cell the smallest unit of structure of a crystal, having sides parallel to the crystal axes and whose exact repetition in three dimensions along these axes generates the space lattice of a given crystal
unit character Genetics a character or trait determined by a single gene or gene pair: see MENDEL'S LAWS
u·nite¹ (yoo nīt') vt. -nit'ed, -nit'ing [ME. unyten < L. unitus, pp. of unire, to unite < unus, ONE] **1.** to put or bring together so as to make one; combine or join into a whole **2.** a) to bring together in common cause, interest, opinion, etc.; join, as in action, through fellowship, agreement, legal bonds, etc. b) to join in marriage **3.** to have or show (qualities, characteristics, etc.) in combination **4.** to cause to adhere —vi. **1.** to become combined or joined together; become one or as one, by adhering, associating, etc. **2.** to act together —SYN. see JOIN
u·nite² (yōō'nīt, yoo nīt') n. [< ME., united < L. unitus (see prec.): with reference to the union of England and Scotland] a former English gold coin of James I, equal to 20 shillings
u·nit·ed (yoo nīt'id) adj. **1.** combined; joined; made one **2.** of or resulting from joint action or association **3.** in agreement or harmony —**u·nit'ed·ly** adv.
United Arab Republic 1. former name of Egypt and Syria, united as a single nation (1958–61) **2.** former name of Egypt (1971–71)
United Church of Christ a Protestant denomination formed by the merger in 1957 of the Congregational Christian Church with the Evangelical and Reformed Church
United Kingdom 1. country in W Europe, consisting of Great Britain & Northern Ireland: 94,217 sq. mi.; pop. 55,229,000; cap. London: in full **United Kingdom of Great Britain and Northern Ireland 2.** formerly (1801–1922), country consisting of Great Britain & Ireland: in full **United Kingdom of Great Britain and Ireland**
☆**United Nations** an international organization of nations pledged to promote world peace and security, maintain treaty obligations & the observance of international law, & cooperate in furthering social progress: the organization was formed at San Francisco in 1945 under a permanent charter (ratified by 50 countries) that had its inception in conferences (1941–45) held by nations opposed to the fascist coalition of Germany, Japan, Italy, & their satellites: the headquarters has been in New York City since 1946 and the membership (1971) consists of 127 nations
United Press International a large, privately owned news agency, formed (1958) by the merger of **United Press** and **International News Service**
United Provinces former name of UTTAR PRADESH
United States Air Force the aviation branch of the United States military force
United States Army the Regular Army, or permanent military land force, of the United States: cf. ARMY OF THE UNITED STATES
United States Marine Corps a branch of the United States Navy responsible especially for amphibious operations
United States Navy the naval branch of the United States military force

---

uninterrupted	uninventive	uninvited	uninvoked
unintimidated	uninvested	uninviting	uninvolved

United States of America country made up of the N. American area extending from the Atlantic Ocean to the Pacific Ocean between Canada and Mexico, together with Alaska & Hawaii: 3,615,211 sq. mi.; pop. 203,185,000; cap. Washington, D.C.: also called **United States**

unit factor a gene involved in the inheritance of a given unit character

u·ni·tive (yōō′nə tiv) adj. [ML. unitivus] **1.** having or characterized by unity **2.** tending to unite

u·nit·ize (yōō′nə tiz′) vt. **-ized′, -iz′ing** [UNIT + -IZE] to make into a single unit —**u′nit·i·za′tion** n.

unit (magnetic) pole a magnetic pole that, when placed in a vacuum at a distance of one centimeter from an equal and like pole, will repel it with a force of one dyne

☆**unit rule** a rule, as in national conventions of the Democratic Party, that the entire vote of a delegation, if the State's party apparatus so chooses, shall be cast as a unit, disregarding minority votes in the delegation

u·ni·ty (yōō′nə tē) n., pl. **-ties** [ME. unite < OFr. unité < L. unitas, oneness < unus, ONE] **1.** the state of being one, or united; oneness; singleness **2.** something complete in itself; single, separate thing **3.** the quality of being one in spirit, sentiment, purpose, etc.; harmony; agreement; concord; uniformity **4.** a) unification b) a unified group or body **5.** the quality or fact of being a totality or whole, esp. a complex that is a union of related parts **6.** a) an arrangement of parts or material that will produce a single, harmonious design or effect in an artistic or literary production b) a design or effect so produced **7.** constancy, continuity, or fixity of purpose, action, etc. **8.** Math. a) any quantity, magnitude, etc. considered or identified as a unit, or 1 b) the numeral or unit 1 —**the (three) unities** the three principles of dramatic construction derived by French neoclassicists from Aristotle's Poetics, holding that a play should have one unified plot (**unity of action**), that all the action should occur within one day (**unity of time**), and that there should be one locale (**unity of place**)
SYN.—**unity** implies the oneness, as in spirit, aims, interests, feelings, etc., of that which is made up of diverse elements or individuals [national unity]; **union** implies the state of being united into a single organization for a common purpose [a labor union]; **solidarity** implies such firm and complete unity in an organization, group, class, etc. as to make for the greatest possible strength in influence, action, etc.

Univ. 1. Universalist **2.** University

univ. 1. universal **2.** universally **3.** university

u·ni·va·lent (yōō′nə vā′lənt, yōō niv′ə lənt) adj. [UNI- + -VALENT] **1.** Biol. single; unpaired: said of a chromosome **2.** Chem. a) having one valence b) having a valence of one —**u′ni·va′lence, u′ni·va′len·cy** n.

u·ni·valve (yōō′nə valv′) n. [UNI- + VALVE] **1.** a mollusk having a one-piece shell, as a snail **2.** such a one-piece shell —adj. **1.** designating or having a one-piece shell **2.** having one valve only: also **u′ni·valved′** adj.

u·ni·ver·sal (yōō′nə vur′s'l) adj. [ME. universel < OFr. < L. universalis < universus: see UNIVERSE] **1.** of the universe; present or occurring everywhere or in all things **2.** of, for, affecting, or including all or the whole of something specified; not limited or restricted **3.** being, or regarded as, a complete whole; entire; whole **4.** broad in knowledge, interests, ability, etc. **5.** that can be used for a great many or all kinds, forms, sizes, etc.; highly adaptable [a universal voltage regulator] **6.** used, intended to be used, or understood by all **7.** Logic not restricted or particular in application; predicating something of every member of a specified class —n. **1.** clipped form of UNIVERSAL JOINT **2.** Logic a) a universal proposition b) same as PREDICABLE (n. 2) c) a general term or concept, or that which such a term or concept covers **3.** Philos. a metaphysical entity characterized by repeatability and unchanging nature through a series of changing relations, as substance —**u′ni·ver′sal·ness** n.
SYN.—**universal** implies applicability to every case or individual, without exception, in the class, category, etc. concerned [a universal practice among primitive peoples]; **general** implies applicability to all, nearly all, or most of a group or class [a general election]; **generic** implies applicability to every member of a class or, specif. in biology, of a genus [a generic name]

u·ni·ver·sal·ism (-iz'm) n. **1.** same as UNIVERSALITY **2.** [U-] the theological doctrine that all souls will eventually find salvation in the grace of God

u·ni·ver·sal·ist (-ist) n. **1.** a person characterized by universality, as of interests or activities **2.** [U-] a believer in Universalism, ☆specif. a member of a Protestant denomination founded in the U.S. (c.1780) and now merged with the Unitarians —adj. **1.** marked by universality; comprehensive ☆**2.** [U-] of Universalism or Universalists —**u′ni·ver′sal·is′tic** adj.

u·ni·ver·sal·i·ty (yōō′nə vər sal′ə tē) n., pl. **-ties 1.** quality, state, or instance of being universal **2.** unlimited range, application, occurrence, etc.; comprehensiveness

u·ni·ver·sal·ize (yōō′nə vur′sə liz′) vt. **-ized′, -iz′ing** to make universal —**u′ni·ver′sal·i·za′tion** n.

universal joint (or **coupling**) a joint or coupling that permits a swing of limited angle in any direction, esp. one used to transmit rotary motion from one shaft to another not in line with it, as in the drive shaft of an automobile

u·ni·ver·sal·ly (yōō′nə vur′s'l ē) adv. in a universal manner; specif., a) in every instance b) in every part or place

universal suffrage suffrage for all adult citizens

UNIVERSAL JOINT

u·ni·verse (yōō′nə vurs′) n. [L. universum, the universe < neut. of universus, all together < unus, ONE + versus, pp. of vertere, to turn: see VERSE] **1.** the totality of all the things that exist; creation; the cosmos **2.** the world, or earth, as the scene of human activity **3.** an area, province, or sphere, as of thought or activity, regarded as a distinct, comprehensive system —SYN. see EARTH

universe of discourse Logic the totality of facts, things, or ideas implied or assumed in a given discussion, argument, or discourse

u·ni·ver·si·ty (yōō′nə vur′sə tē) n., pl. **-ties** [ME. university < MFr. université < ML. universitas < L., the whole, universe, society, guild < universus: see UNIVERSE] **1.** an educational institution of the highest level, typically, in the U.S., with one or more undergraduate colleges, together with a program of graduate studies and a number of professional schools, and authorized to confer various degrees, as the bachelor's, master's, and doctor's **2.** the grounds, buildings, etc. of a university **3.** the students, faculty, or administrators of a university

University City [from its being adjacent to Washington University] city in E Mo.: suburb of St. Louis: pop. 46,000

u·niv·o·cal (yoo niv′ə k'l, yōō′nə vō′k'l) adj. having a single, sharply defined sense or nature; unambiguous

un·joint (un joint′) vt. **1.** to separate (a joint) **2.** to separate the joints of

un·just (-just′) adj. **1.** not just or right; unfair; contrary to justice **2.** [Obs.] dishonest or unfaithful

un·kempt (-kempt′) adj. [UN- + kempt, pp. of dial. kemben, to comb < ME. kemben < OE. cemban < camb, a COMB¹] **1.** not combed **2.** not tidy, neat, or groomed; slovenly **3.** not polished or refined; crude; rough —SYN. see SLOVENLY —**un·kempt′ness** n.

un·kenned (-kend′) adj. [Scot.] unknown; strange

un·ken·nel (-ken′l) vt. **-neled** or **-nelled, -nel·ing** or **-nel·ling 1.** to drive or release from a kennel or hole **2.** to bring to light; uncover; disclose

un·kind (-kind′) adj. not kind; specif., a) not sympathetic to or considerate of others b) harsh, severe, cruel, rigorous, etc. —**un·kind′ness** n.

un·kind·ly (-kind′lē) adj. same as UNKIND —adv. in an unkind manner —**un·kind′li·ness** n.

un·knit (-nit′) vt., vi. **-knit′ted** or **-knit′, -knit′ting** [ME. unknytten < OE. uncnyttan] to untie, undo, or unravel (something knitted or knotted)

un·knot (-nät′) vt. **-knot′ted, -knot′ting 1.** to untie (a knot) **2.** to undo or untangle a knot or knots in

un·know·a·ble (-nō′ə b'l) adj. not knowable; that cannot be known; specif., beyond the range of human comprehension or experience —n. anything unknowable

un·known (-nōn′) adj. not known; specif., a) not in the knowledge, understanding, or acquaintance of someone; unfamiliar (to) b) not discovered, identified, determined, explored, etc. —n. an unknown person or thing; specif., Math. an unknown quantity; also, a symbol for this

Unknown Soldier [also u- s-] an unidentified soldier, killed in a war, who has been chosen and enshrined as representative of a nation's war dead

un·lace (-lās′) vt. **-laced′, -lac′ing 1.** to undo or unfasten the laces of **2.** to loosen or remove the clothing of by or as by unfastening laces

un·lade (-lād′) vt., vi. **-lad′ed, -lad′ed** or **-lad′en, -lad′ing 1.** to unload (a ship, etc.) **2.** to discharge (a cargo, etc.)

un·lash (-lash′) vt. to untie or loosen (something lashed, or tied with a rope, etc.)

un·latch (-lach′) vt., vi. to open by release of a latch

un·law·ful (-lô′fəl) adj. **1.** against the law; illegal **2.** against moral or ethical standards; immoral —**un·law′ful·ly** adv. —**un·law′ful·ness** n.

un·lay (-lā′) vt., vi. **-laid′, -lay′ing** [UN- (back) + LAY¹, 14] Naut. to untwist: said of a rope

un·lead·ed (-led′id) adj. **1.** not covered or weighted with lead **2.** Printing not spaced with leads

un·learn (-lurn′) vt., vi. [ME. unlernen: see UN- & LEARN] to seek to forget (something learned), as in reeducation

un·learn·ed (-lur′nid; for 2 -lurnd′) adj. **1.** a) not learned or educated; ignorant b) showing a lack of learning or

unjaded	unjustifiable	unknowing	unladylike
unjoined	unkept	unlabeled	unlamented
unjudicial	unkissed	unlabored	unlaundered

education 2. *a*) not learned or mastered [*unlearned* lessons] *b*) known or acquired without conscious study [an *unlearned* sense of tact] —*SYN.* see IGNORANT

un·leash (-lēsh′) *vt.* to release from or as from a leash

un·less (ən les′) *conj.* [ME. *onlesse*, earlier *on lesse that*, *in lesse that*, in less that, at less than, for less] in any case other than that; except that; except if [*unless* it rains, the game will be played] —*prep.* except; save [nothing, *unless* a miracle, can save him]

un·let·tered (un let′ərd) *adj.* 1. *a*) not lettered; ignorant; uneducated *b*) illiterate 2. not marked with letters —*SYN.* see IGNORANT

un·like (-līk′) *adj.* [ME. *unliche*: see UN- (not) & LIKE¹] 1. having little or no resemblance; not alike; different; dissimilar 2. [Archaic or Dial.] unlikely —*prep.* 1. not like; different from [a case *unlike* any previous one] 2. not characteristic of [it's *unlike* her to cry] —**un·like′ness** *n.*

un·like·ly (-līk′lē) *adj.* [ME. *unlikly*, prob. after ON. *ūlīklīgr*] 1. not likely to happen or be true; improbable 2. not likely to succeed; not promising —*adv.* improbably [he may, not *unlikely*, join us] —**un·like′li·hood, un·like′li·ness** *n.*

un·lim·ber¹ (-lim′bər) *adj.* not limber, or supple; stiff [*unlimber* fingers] —*vt., vi.* to make or become supple

un·lim·ber² (-lim′bər) *vt., vi.* [UN- (back) + LIMBER²] 1. to prepare (a field gun) for use by detaching the limber (of the gun carriage) 2. to get ready for use or action

un·lim·it·ed (-lim′it id) *adj.* 1. without limits or restrictions [*unlimited* power] 2. lacking or seeming to lack boundaries; vast; illimitable [*unlimited* space]

un·link (-liŋk′) *vt.* 1. to unfasten the links of (a chain, etc.) 2. to separate (things linked together)

un·list·ed (-lis′tid) *adj.* not listed; specif., *a*) not constituting an entry in a list *b*) not publicly listed; privately assigned [an *unlisted* telephone number] *c*) not listed among those admitted for the purpose of trading on the stock exchange: said of securities

un·live (-liv′) *vt.* **-lived′, -liv′ing** 1. to live so as to wipe out the consequences or results of; live down 2. to annul or wipe out (past experience, etc.)

un·load (-lōd′) *vt.* 1. *a*) to remove or take off (a load, cargo, etc.) *b*) to take a load or cargo from 2. *a*) to give vent to (one's grief, troubles, etc.); express or tell without restraint *b*) to relieve of something that troubles, burdens, etc. 3. to remove the charge from (a gun) 4. to get rid of [*unloading* surplus goods] —*vi.* to unload something

un·lock (-läk′) *vt.* 1. *a*) to open (a lock) *b*) to open the lock of (a door, chest, etc.) 2. to let loose as if by opening a lock; release [*unlocked* a torrent of grief] 3. to cause to separate; part [to *unlock* clenched jaws] 4. to lay open; reveal [to *unlock* a secret] —*vi.* to become unlocked

un·looked-for (-lookt′fôr′) *adj.* not looked for; not expected or foreseen

un·loose (-lōōs′) *vt.* **-loosed′, -loos′ing** to make or set loose; loosen, release, undo, etc.: also **un·loos′en**

un·love·ly (-luv′lē) *adj.* not lovely, pleasing, or attractive; disagreeable —**un·love′li·ness** *n.*

un·luck·y (-luk′ē) *adj.* **-luck′i·er, -luck′i·est** not lucky; having, attended with, bringing, or involving bad luck; unfortunate, ill-fated, or ill-omened —**un·luck′i·ly** *adv.*

un·make (-māk′) *vt.* **-made′, -mak′ing** 1. to cause to be as before being made; cause to revert to the original form, elements, or condition 2. to ruin; destroy 3. to depose from a position, rank, or authority

un·man (-man′) *vt.* **-manned′, -man′ning** 1. to deprive of manly courage, nerve, self-confidence, etc. 2. to emasculate; castrate 3. to deprive of men or personnel: now usually in the pp.: cf. UNMANNED —*SYN.* see UNNERVE

un·man·ly (-man′lē) *adj.* not manly; specif., *a*) lacking courage, resoluteness, etc.; cowardly, weak, etc. *b*) not befitting a man; effeminate; womanish —**un·man′li·ness** *n.*

un·manned (-mand′) *adj.* not manned; ☆specif., without men aboard and operating by automatic or remote control, as a pilotless aircraft or spacecraft

un·man·ner·ly (-man′ər lē) *adj.* [ME. *unmannerli*] having or showing poor manners; rude; discourteous —*adv.* in an unmannerly way; rudely —**un·man′ner·li·ness** *n.*

un·mask (-mask′, -mäsk′) *vt.* 1. to remove a mask or disguise from 2. to disclose the true nature of; expose; reveal —*vi.* 1. to take off a mask or disguise 2. to appear in true character

un·mean·ing (-mēn′iŋ) *adj.* 1. lacking in meaning, sense, or significance 2. showing no sense or intelligence; empty; expressionless

un·meet (-mēt′) *adj.* [ME. *unmete* < OE. *unmæte*] not meet, fit, or proper; unsuitable; unseemly

un·men·tion·a·ble (un men′shən ə b'l) *adj.* not fit to be mentioned, esp. in polite conversation

un·men·tion·a·bles (-b'lz) *n.pl.* things regarded as improper to be mentioned or talked about; specif., undergarments or (formerly) trousers: a jocular usage

un·mer·ci·ful (un mur′si fəl) *adj.* 1. having or showing no mercy; cruel; relentless; pitiless 2. beyond what is proper or usual; excessive —**un·mer′ci·ful·ly** *adv.*

un·mind·ful (-mīnd′fəl) *adj.* not mindful or attentive; forgetful; heedless; careless —**un·mind′ful·ly** *adv.*

un·mis·tak·a·ble (un′mis tāk′ə b'l) *adj.* that cannot be mistaken or misinterpreted; leaving room for no misunderstanding; clear; plain —**un′mis·tak′a·bly** *adv.*

un·mit·i·gat·ed (un mit′ə gāt′id) *adj.* 1. not lessened or eased [*unmitigated* suffering] 2. unqualified; out-and-out; absolute [an *unmitigated* fool] —**un·mit′i·gat′ed·ly** *adv.*

un·moor (-moor′) *vt.* 1. to free (a ship, etc.) from moorings 2. to heave up all anchors of (a ship) but one —*vi.* to become unmoored

un·mor·al (-môr′əl) *adj. var.* of AMORAL —**un·mo·ral·i·ty** (un′mə ral′ə tē, -mô-) *n.*

un·muf·fle (-muf′'l) *vt.* **-fled, -fling** 1. to remove a covering from (the face, head, etc.) 2. to remove the muffling from (oars, a drum, etc.) —*vi.* to take off something that muffles

un·muz·zle (-muz′'l) *vt.* **-zled, -zling** 1. to free (a dog, etc.) from a muzzle 2. to free from restraint or censorship of what is written or spoken

un·nat·u·ral (-nach′ər əl) *adj.* not natural or normal; specif., *a*) contrary to, or at variance with, nature; abnormal; strange *b*) artificial, affected, or strained [an *unnatural* smile] *c*) characterized by a lack of the emotions, attitudes, or behavior regarded as natural, normal, or right *d*) abnormally evil or cruel —*SYN.* see IRREGULAR —**un·nat′u·ral·ly** *adv.* —**un·nat′u·ral·ness** *n.*

un·nec·es·sar·y (-nes′ə ser′ē) *adj.* not necessary or required; needless —**un·nec′es·sar′i·ly** *adv.*

un·nerve (-nurv′) *vt.* **-nerved′, -nerv′ing** 1. to cause to lose one's nerve, courage, self-confidence, etc. 2. to make feel weak, nervous, etc.

SYN.—**unnerve** implies a causing to lose courage or self-control as by shocking, dismaying, etc. [the screams *unnerved* her]; **enervate** implies a gradual loss of strength or vitality, as because of climate, indolence, etc. [*enervating* heat]; **unman** implies a loss of manly courage, fortitude, or spirit [he was so *unmanned* by the news that he broke into tears]

un·num·bered (-num′bərd) *adj.* 1. not counted 2. same as INNUMERABLE 3. having no identifying number

un·oc·cu·pied (-äk′yə pīd′) *adj.* 1. having no occupant; vacant; empty 2. at leisure; idle

unleased	unmanufacturable	unmilled	unnavigated
unleavened	unmanufactured	unmingled	unneeded
unlessened	unmarked	unmirthful	unneedful
unlessoned	unmarketable	unmistaken	unneighborly
unlevel	unmarred	unmitigable	unnoted
unlevied	unmarriageable	unmixed	unnoticeable
unlibidinous	unmarried	unmodified	unnoticed
unlicensed	unmastered	unmodish	unnurtured
unlifelike	unmatchable	unmodulated	unobjectionable
unlighted	unmatched	unmoistened	unobliged
unlikable	unmated	unmold	unobliging
unlikeable	unmatted	unmolested	unobscured
unlined	unmatured	unmolten	unobservant
unliquefiable	unmeant	unmortgaged	unobserved
unlit	unmeasurable	unmotherly	unobserving
unlived	unmechanical	unmotivated	unobstructed
unlively	unmedicated	unmounted	unobtainable
unlocated	unmeditated	unmourned	unobtrusive
unlovable	unmelodious	unmovable	unoffending
unloved	unmelted	unmoved	unoffensive
unloving	unmenacing	unmoving	unoffered
unlubricated	unmendable	unmown	unofficial
unmagnified	unmended	unmusical	unofficious
unmaidenly	unmentioned	unmystified	unoiled
unmalleable	unmercenary	unnail	unopen
unmanageable	unmerchantable	unnamable	unopened
unmanful	unmerited	unnameable	unopposed
unmanifested	unmesh	unnamed	unoppressed
unmannered	unmethodical	unnaturalized	unordained
unmannish	unmilitary	unnavigable	

un·or·gan·ized (-ôr′gə nīzd′) *adj.* 1. having no organic structure 2. having no regular order, system, or organization 3. not behaving, thinking, etc. in an orderly way 4. not having or belonging to a labor union

un·pack (-pak′) *vt.* 1. to open and remove the packed contents of 2. to take from a crate, trunk, etc. 3. to remove a pack or load from —*vi.* 1. to remove the contents of a packed trunk, suitcase, etc. 2. to admit of being unpacked

un·paged (-pājd′) *adj.* having the pages unnumbered: said of a book, etc.

un·par·al·leled (-par′ə leld′) *adj.* that has no parallel, equal, or counterpart; unmatched

un·par·lia·men·ta·ry (-pär′lə men′tər ē, -trē) *adj.* contrary to parliamentary law or usage

un·peg (-peg′) *vt.* **-pegged′, -peg′ging** 1. to remove a peg or pegs from 2. to unfasten or detach in this way

un·peo·ple (-pē′p'l) *vt.* **-pled, -pling** to depopulate

un·per·son (un′pur′s'n) *n.* a person completely ignored, as if he did not exist

un·pin (un pin′) *vt.* **-pinned′, -pin′ning** 1. to remove a pin or pins from 2. to unfasten or detach in this way

un·pleas·ant (un plez′'nt) *adj.* not pleasant; offensive; disagreeable —**un·pleas′ant·ly** *adv.*

un·pleas·ant·ness (-nis) *n.* 1. an unpleasant quality or condition 2. an unpleasant situation, relationship, etc. 3. a quarrel or disagreement

un·plumbed (-plumd′) *adj.* 1. not sounded, measured, or explored with or as with a plumb 2. not fully plumbed or understood

un·polled (-pōld′) *adj.* [UN- + pp. of POLL, *v.*] 1. a) not canvassed in a poll b) not cast or registered: said of votes 2. unshorn

un·pop·u·lar (-päp′yə lər) *adj.* not popular; not liked or approved of by the public or by the majority —**un′pop·u·lar′i·ty** (-yə lar′ə tē) *n.*

un·prac·ticed (-prak′tist) *adj.* 1. not practiced; not habitually or repeatedly done, performed, etc. 2. not skilled or experienced; inexpert

un·prec·e·dent·ed (-pres′ə den′tid) *adj.* having no precedent or parallel; unheard-of; novel

un·prej·u·diced (-prej′ə dist) *adj.* 1. without prejudice or bias; impartial 2. not affected detrimentally; unimpaired

un·pre·med·i·tat·ed (un′pri med′ə tāt′id) *adj.* not premeditated; done without plan or forethought

un·prin·ci·pled (un prin′sə p'ld) *adj.* characterized by lack of moral principles; unscrupulous

un·print·a·ble (-print′ə b'l) *adj.* not printable; not fit to be printed, as because of obscenity

un·pro·fes·sion·al (un′prə fesh′ən 'l) *adj.* 1. violating the rules or ethical code of a given profession 2. not of, characteristic of, belonging to, or connected with a profession; nonprofessional —**un′pro·fes′sion·al·ly** *adv.*

un·pub·lished (un pub′lisht) *adj.* not published; specif., in copyright law, designating a literary work that has neither been given public distribution nor been reproduced for sale, as of the time of registration

un·qual·i·fied (-kwäl′ə fīd′) *adj.* 1. lacking the necessary or desirable qualifications; not fit 2. not limited or modified; absolute [an *unqualified* endorsement, an *unqualified* success] —**un·qual′i·fied′ly** *adv.*

un·ques·tion·a·ble (-kwes′chən ə b'l) *adj.* 1. not to be questioned, doubted, or disputed; certain 2. with no exception or qualification; unexceptionable —**un·ques′tion·a·bly** *adv.*

un·ques·tioned (-kwes′chənd) *adj.* not questioned; specif., a) not interrogated b) not disputed; accepted c) not subjected to inquiry

un·qui·et (-kwī′ət) *adj.* not quiet; specif., a) full of turmoil; restless, disturbed, agitated, etc. b) anxious; uneasy —*n.* a lack of quiet or rest; disturbance, agitation, etc. —**un·qui′et·ly** *adv.* —**un·qui′et·ness** *n.*

un·quote (un′kwōt′) *interj.* ☆ end the quotation: used in speech to signal the conclusion of a quotation

un·rav·el (un rav′'l) *vt.* **-eled** or **-elled, -el·ing** or **-el·ling** 1. to undo (something woven, tangled, or raveled up); untangle or separate the threads of 2. to make clear of confusion or involvement; solve —*vi.* to become unraveled —**un·rav′el·ment** *n.*

un·read (-red′) *adj.* 1. not read, as a book 2. having read little or nothing 3. unlearned (*in* a subject)

un·read·a·ble (-rēd′ə b'l) *adj.* not readable; specif., a) not legible or decipherable b) too dull, difficult, etc. to read

un·read·y (-red′ē) *adj.* not ready; specif., a) not prepared, as for action or use b) not prompt or alert; slow; hesitant —**un·read′i·ly** *adv.* —**un·read′i·ness** *n.*

un·re·al (-rē′əl, -rēl′) *adj.* not real, actual, or genuine; imaginary, fanciful, insubstantial, false, etc.

un·re·al·is·tic (un′rē ə lis′tik) *adj.* dealing with ideas or matters in a way that is not realistic; impractical or visionary —**un′re·al·is′ti·cal·ly** *adv.*

un·re·al·i·ty (-rē al′ə tē) *n., pl.* **-ties** 1. the state or quality of being unreal 2. something unreal or imaginary 3. inability to deal with reality; impracticality

un·rea·son (un rē′z'n) *n.* lack of reason; irrationality

un·rea·son·a·ble (-ə b'l) *adj.* not reasonable; specif., a) having or showing little sense or judgment; not rational b) excessive; immoderate; exorbitant *SYN.* see IRRATIONAL —**un·rea′son·a·ble·ness** *n.* —**un·rea′son·a·bly** *adv.*

un·rea·son·ing (-iŋ) *adj.* not reasoning or reasoned; marked by a lack of reason or judgment; irrational —**un·rea′son·ing·ly** *adv.*

☆**un·re·con·struct·ed** (un′rē kən struk′tid) *adj.* 1. not reconstructed 2. holding to an earlier, outmoded practice or point of view; specif., not reconciled to the Reconstruction

un·reel (un′rēl′) *vt., vi.* to unwind as from a reel

unoriginal	unperturbable	unprescribed	unpunishable
unornamental	unperturbed	unpresentable	unpunished
unornamented	unphilosophic	unpreserved	unpure
unorthodox	unphilosophical	unpressed	unpurged
unorthodoxy	unpicked	unpresumptuous	unpurified
unostentatious	unpierced	unpretending	unpurposed
unowned	unpile	unpretentious	unquaking
unoxidized	unpitied	unprevailing	unqualifying
unpacified	unpitying	unpreventable	unquelled
unpaid	unplaced	unpriced	unquenchable
unpaid-for	unplanned	unprimed	unquenched
unpainful	unplanted	unprincely	unquestioning
unpainted	unplayable	unprinted	unquotable
unpaired	unplayed	unprivileged	unquoted
unpalatable	unpleased	unprizable	unransomed
unpardonable	unpleasing	unprized	unrated
unpardoned	unpledged	unprobed	unratified
unparted	unpliable	unprocessed	unravaged
unpasteurized	unploughed	unprocurable	unreachable
unpatched	unplowed	unproductive	unrealizable
unpatented	unplucked	unprofaned	unrealized
unpatriotic	unplug	unprofessed	unreasoned
unpatriotically	unpoetic	unprofitable	unrebuked
unpaved	unpoetical	unprogressive	unreceivable
unpeaceable	unpointed	unprohibited	unreceived
unpeaceful	unpoised	unpromising	unreceptive
unpedigreed	unpolarized	unprompted	unreciprocated
unpen	unpolished	unpronounceable	unreclaimable
unpenetrated	unpolite	unpronounced	unreclaimed
unpensioned	unpolitic	unpropitiable	unrecognizable
unperceivable	unpolitical	unpropitious	unrecognized
unperceived	unpolluted	unproportionate	unrecommended
unperceiving	unpopulated	unproposed	unrecompensed
unperceptive	unposed	unprosperous	unreconcilable
unperfect	unposted	unprotected	unreconciled
unperfected	unpotted	unproved	unrecorded
unperformed	unpractical	unproven	unrecoverable
unperplexed	unpredictable	unprovided	unrecruited
unpersuadable	unpreoccupied	unprovoked	unrectified
unpersuaded	unprepared	unpruned	unredeemed
unpersuasive	unprepossessing	unpunctual	unredressed

un·reeve (un′rēv′) *vt.* **-rove′** or **-reeved′**, **-reev′ing** to withdraw (a rope, etc.) from a block, deadeye, or the like —*vi.* **1.** to become unreeved **2.** to unreeve a rope, etc.

un·re·gen·er·ate (un′ri jen′ər it) *adj.* **1.** not regenerate; not spiritually reborn or converted **2.** not converted to a particular belief, viewpoint, etc. **3.** recalcitrant or obstinate Also **un′re·gen′er·at′ed** —**un′re·gen′er·ate·ly** *adv.*

un·re·lent·ing (-ri len′tiŋ) *adj.* **1.** refusing to yield or relent; inflexible; relentless **2.** without mercy or compassion **3.** not relaxing or slackening, as in effort, speed, etc.

un·re·li·gious (-ri lij′əs) *adj.* **1.** *same as* IRRELIGIOUS **2.** not connected with or involving religion; nonreligious

un·re·mit·ting (-ri mit′iŋ) *adj.* not stopping, relaxing, or slackening; incessant; persistent

un·re·serve (-ri zurv′) *n.* lack of reserve; frankness

un·re·served (-ri zurvd′) *adj.* not reserved; specif., *a)* frank or open in speech *b)* not restricted or qualified; unlimited *c)* not set aside for advance sale [*unreserved* seats] —**un′re·serv′ed·ly** (-zur′vid lē) *adv.*

un·rest (un rest′) *n.* a troubled or disturbed state; restlessness; disquiet; uneasiness; specif., a condition of angry discontent and protest verging on revolt

un·rid·dle (-rid′'l) *vt.* **-dled, -dling** to solve or explain (a riddle, mystery, etc.)

un·rig (-rig′) *vt.* **-rigged′, -rig′ging** to strip of rigging, or of equipment, clothes, etc.

un·right·eous (-rī′chəs) *adj.* **1.** not righteous; wicked; sinful **2.** not right; unjust; unfair —**un·right′eous·ly** *adv.* —**un·right′eous·ness** *n.*

un·rip (-rip′) *vt.* **-ripped′, -rip′ping** **1.** to rip open; take apart or detach by ripping **2.** [Now Rare] to make known

un·ripe (-rip′) *adj.* **1.** not ripe or mature; green **2.** not yet fully developed [*unripe* plans] **3.** [Obs.] premature: said esp. of death —**un·ripe′ness** *n.*

un·ri·valed, un·ri·valled (-rī′v'ld) *adj.* having no rival, equal, or competitor; matchless; peerless

un·roll (-rōl′) *vt.* **1.** to open or extend (something rolled up) **2.** to present to view; display **3.** [Obs.] to remove from a roll or list —*vi.* to become unrolled

un·roof (-rōōf′, -roof′) *vt.* to take off the roof or covering of

un·root (-rōōt′, -root′) *vt. same as* UPROOT

un·round (-round′) *vt. Phonet.* **1.** to pronounce (a vowel usually rounded) without rounding of the lips **2.** to keep (the lips) from being rounded, as in pronouncing the vowel in *she* —**un·round′ed** *adj.*

un·rove (-rōv′) *alt. pt. & pp. of* UNREEVE

UNRRA (un′rə, -rä) United Nations Relief and Rehabilitation Administration: also **U.N.R.R.A.**

un·ruf·fled (un ruf′'ld) *adj.* not ruffled, disturbed, or agitated; calm; smooth; serene —*SYN.* see COOL

un·rul·y (-rōō′lē) *adj.* **-rul′i·er, -rul′i·est** [ME. *unruely* < *un-,* not + *reuly,* orderly < *reule,* RULE] hard to control, restrain, or keep in order; disobedient, unmanageable, disorderly, etc. —**un·rul′i·ness** *n.*

SYN.—**unruly** implies a lack of submissiveness or obedience to rule or restraint [an *unruly* child]; **unmanageable** and **ungovernable** both imply incapability of being controlled or directed [a delirious, *unmanageable* patient, an *ungovernable* temper]; **intractable** and **refractory** both imply stubborn resistance to or a balking at direction, control, manipulation, etc. [an *intractable,* or *refractory,* will]; **recalcitrant** implies defiant resistance to authority or control [a *recalcitrant* prisoner] —*ANT.* tractable, manageable, docile

un·sad·dle (-sad′'l) *vt.* **-dled, -dling** **1.** to take the saddle off (a horse, etc.) **2.** to throw from the saddle; unhorse —*vi.* to take the saddle off a horse, etc.

un·said (-sed′) *pt. & pp. of* UNSAY —*adj.* not expressed

un·sat·u·rat·ed (-sach′ə rāt′id) *adj.* **1.** not saturated **2.** *Chem. a)* designating of a compound in which some element possesses the capacity of combining further with other elements *b)* designating or of a solution that is not in equilibrium with the undissolved solute *c)* designating an organic compound with a double or triple bond that links two atoms, usually of carbon —**un′sat·u·ra′tion** *n.*

un·sa·vor·y (-sā′vər ē) *adj.* **1.** orig., without flavor; tasteless **2.** unpleasant to taste or smell **3.** offensive, disagreeable, or unpleasant, esp. so as to be or seem immoral —**un·sa′vor·i·ly** *adv.* —**un·sa′vor·i·ness** *n.*

un·say (-sā′) *vt.* **-said′, -say′ing** to take back or retract (what has been said)

un·scathed (-skā*th*d′) *adj.* [see SCATHED] not hurt; uninjured; unharmed

un·schooled (-skōōld′) *adj.* **1.** not educated or trained, esp. by formal schooling **2.** not acquired or altered by schooling; natural

☆**un·scram·ble** (-skram′b'l) *vt.* **-bled, -bling** to cause to be no longer scrambled, disordered, or mixed up; specif., *Electronics* to make (incoming scrambled signals) intelligible at the receiver —**un·scram′bler** *n.*

un·screw (-skrōō′) *vt.* **1.** to remove a screw or screws from **2.** *a)* to remove, detach, or loosen by removing a screw or screws, or by turning *b)* to remove a threaded top, cover, etc. from (a jar, etc.) —*vi.* to become unscrewed or admit of being unscrewed

un·scru·pu·lous (-skrōōp′yə ləs) *adj.* not scrupulous; not restrained by ideas of right and wrong; unprincipled —**un·scru′pu·lous·ly** *adv.* —**un·scru′pu·lous·ness** *n.*

un·seal (-sēl′) *vt.* **1.** to break or remove the seal of **2.** to open (something sealed or closed as if sealed)

un·seam (-sēm′) *vt.* to open the seam or seams of; rip

un·search·a·ble (-surch′ə b'l) *adj.* that cannot be searched into; mysterious; inscrutable —**un·search′a·bly** *adv.*

un·sea·son·a·ble (-sē′z'n ə b'l) *adj.* **1.** not usual for or appropriate to the season [*unseasonable* heat] **2.** not in season [*unseasonable* seafood] **3.** coming, said, etc. at the wrong time; untimely; inopportune —**un·sea′son·a·ble·ness** *n.* —**un·sea′son·a·bly** *adv.*

un·sea·soned (-sē′z'nd) *adj.* not seasoned; specif., *a)* not ripened, dried, etc. by enough seasoning [*unseasoned* wood] *b)* not matured by experience; inexperienced *c)* not flavored with seasoning: said of food

un·seat (-sēt′) *vt.* **1.** to throw or dislodge from a seat; specif., *same as* UNHORSE **2.** to remove from office, deprive of rank, etc.

un·se·cured (un′si kyoord′) *adj.* **1.** not made secure or firm; not kept firmly in place **2.** not secured or guaranteed, as by collateral [an *unsecured* loan]

un·seem·ly (un sēm′lē) *adj.* not seemly; not decent or proper; unbecoming; indecorous —*adv.* in an unseemly manner —*SYN.* see IMPROPER —**un·seem′li·ness** *n.*

un·seen (-sēn′) *adj.* **1.** not seen, perceived, or observed; invisible **2.** not noticed or discovered **3.** not studied previously, as a translation

un·self·ish (-sel′fish) *adj.* not selfish; putting the good of others above one's own interests; altruistic; generous —**un·self′ish·ly** *adv.* —**un·self′ish·ness** *n.*

---

unrefined	unrepentant	unrevised	unsatisfied
unreflecting	unrepented	unrevoked	unsatisfying
unreformable	unrepenting	unrewarded	unsaved
unreformed	unreplaceable	unrewarding	unsayable
unrefreshed	unreplaced	unrhymed	unscalable
unregarded	unreplenished	unrhythmic	unscaled
unregistered	unreported	unrhythmical	unscanned
unregretted	unrepresentative	unrightful	unscarred
unregulated	unrepresented	unripened	unscented
unrehearsed	unrepressed	unroasted	unsceptical
unrelated	unreprieved	unrobe	unscheduled
unrelaxed	unreprimanded	unromantic	unscholarly
unreliability	unreprovable	unromantically	unscientific
unreliable	unrequested	unroped	unscientifically
unreliably	unrequited	unruled	unscorched
unrelievable	unresentful	unrumpled	unscourged
unrelieved	unresigned	unrusted	unscratched
unremarked	unresistant	unsafe	unscreened
unremedied	unresisting	unsaintly	unscriptural
unremembered	unresolved	unsalability	unsculptured
unremittable	unrespectful	unsalable	unsealed
unremitted	unresponsive	unsalaried	unseasonal
unremorseful	unrested	unsaleability	unseaworthy
unremovable	unrestful	unsaleable	unseconded
unremunerated	unrestrained	unsalted	unseeded
unremunerative	unrestraint	unsampled	unseeing
unrendered	unrestricted	unsanctified	unsegmented
unrenewed	unretentive	unsanctioned	unsegregated
unrenowned	unretracted	unsanitary	unselected
unrentable	unretrieved	unsated	unselective
unrented	unreturned	unsatiable	unsensational
unrepaid	unrevealed	unsatiated	unsent
unrepairable	unrevenged	unsatiating	unsentimental
unrepaired	unreversed	unsatisfactorily	unseparated
unrepealed	unreviewed	unsatisfactory	unserved

un·set (-set′) *adj.* **1.** not mounted in a setting [an *unset* gem] **2.** not yet hardened [*unset* cement]

un·set·tle (-set′'l) *vt.* **-tled, -tling** to make unsettled, insecure, or unstable; disturb, displace, disarrange, or disorder —*vi.* to become unsettled —**un·set′tle·ment** *n.*

un·set·tled (-set′'ld) *adj.* **1.** not settled or orderly; disordered **2.** not stable or fixed; changeable; uncertain **3.** not decided or determined **4.** not paid, allotted, or otherwise disposed of [an *unsettled* debt or estate] ☆**5.** having no settlers; unpopulated **6.** not established in a place or abode —**un·set′tled·ness** *n.*

un·sex (-seks′) *vt.* **1.** to deprive of sexual potency **2.** to deprive of the qualities considered characteristic of one's sex; esp., to make unwomanly

un·shack·le (-shak′'l) *vt.* **-led, -ling 1.** to loosen or remove the shackles from **2.** to free

un·shap·en (-shā′pən) *adj.* [ME.] **1.** without shape; shapeless **2.** badly shaped; misshapen; malformed

un·sheathe (-shēth′) *vt.* **-sheathed′, -sheath′ing** to draw or remove (a sword, knife, etc.) from or as if from a sheath

un·ship (-ship′) *vt.* **-shipped′, -ship′ping** [ME. *unshippen:* see UN- & SHIP] **1.** to take (cargo, etc.) out of or off from a ship **2.** to remove (an oar, mast, etc.) from the proper position for use **3.** to disembark (passengers) —*vi.* to become detached

un·sight·ly (-sīt′lē) *adj.* not sightly; not pleasant to look at; ugly —**un·sight′li·ness** *n.*

un·skilled (-skild′) *adj.* not skilled; specif., *a)* having no special skill or training *b)* requiring or using no special skill or training [*unskilled* labor] *c)* showing a lack of skill

un·skill·ful (-skil′fəl) *adj.* not skillful; having little or no skill or dexterity; awkward; clumsy —**un·skill′ful·ly** *adv.* —**un·skill′ful·ness** *n.*

un·sling (-sliŋ′) *vt.* **-slung′, -sling′ing 1.** to take (a rifle, etc.) from a slung position **2.** *Naut.* to release from slings

un·snap (-snap′) *vt.* **-snapped′, -snap′ping** to undo the snap or snaps of, so as to loosen or detach

un·snarl (-snärl′) *vt.* to free of snarls; untangle

un·so·cia·ble (-sō′shə b'l) *adj.* **1.** avoiding association with others; not sociable or friendly **2.** not conducive to sociability —**un·so′cia·bil′i·ty, un·so′cia·ble·ness** *n.* —**un·so′cia·bly** *adv.*

un·so·cial (-sō′shəl) *adj.* having or showing a dislike for the society of others —**un·so′cial·ly** *adv.*

SYN.—**unsocial** implies an aversion for the society or company of others [an *unsocial* neighbor]; **asocial** implies complete indifference to the interests, welfare, etc. of society and connotes abnormal or irresponsible self-centeredness [the *asocial* behavior of a sociopath]; **antisocial** applies to that which is believed to be detrimental or destructive of the social order, social institutions, etc. [*antisocial* racism]; **nonsocial** expresses simple absence of social relationship [*nonsocial* fields of interest] —**ANT. social**

un·sol·der (-säd′ər) *vt.* **1.** to take apart (things soldered together) **2.** to disunite; separate; sunder

un·son·sy (-sän′sē) *adj.* [UN- + SONSY] [Scot.] bringing or indicating bad luck; ominous

un·so·phis·ti·cat·ed (-un′sə fis′tə kāt′id) *adj.* not sophisticated; specif., *a)* artless, simple, ingenuous, etc. *b)* not complex, refined, developed, etc. *c)* not adulterated; genuine or pure —**SYN.** see NAIVE —**un′so·phis′ti·cat′ed·ly** *adv.* —**un′so·phis′ti·ca′tion** *n.*

un·sound (un sound′) *adj.* not sound or free from defect; specif., *a)* not normal or healthy physically or mentally *b)* not safe, firm, or solid; insecure *c)* not safe and secure financially *d)* not based on truth or valid reasoning; not accurate, reliable, judicious, sensible, etc. *e)* not deep; light: said of sleep —**un·sound′ly** *adv.* —**un·sound′ness** *n.*

un·spar·ing (-sper′iŋ) *adj.* **1.** not sparing or stinting; lavish; liberal; profuse **2.** not merciful or forgiving; severe —**un·spar′ing·ly** *adv.*

un·speak (-spēk′) *vt.* **-spoke′, -spok′en, -speak′ing** [Obs.] to unsay, or retract

un·speak·a·ble (-spēk′ə b'l) *adj.* **1.** that cannot be spoken **2.** marvelous, awesome, etc.; beyond human expression; ineffable **3.** so bad, evil, etc. as to defy description —**un·speak′a·bly** *adv.*

un·sphere (-sfir′) *vt.* **-sphered′, -spher′ing** to remove from its sphere or from one's sphere

un·sta·ble (-stā′b'l) *adj.* [ME.] not stable; specif., *a)* not fixed, firm, or steady; easily upset or unbalanced *b)* changeable; variable; fluctuating *c)* unreliable; fickle *d)* emotionally unsettled *e) Chem.* tending to decompose or change into other compounds —**SYN.** see INCONSTANT —**un·sta′ble·ness** *n.* —**un·sta′bly** *adv.*

un·stead·y (-sted′ē) *adj.* not steady; specif., *a)* not firm or stable; shaky *b)* changeable; inconstant; wavering *c)* erratic in habits, purpose, or behavior —*vt.* **-stead′ied, -stead′y·ing** to make unsteady —**un·stead′i·ly** *adv.*

un·steel (-stēl′) *vt.* to deprive of strength, resoluteness, etc.

un·step (-step′) *vt.* **-stepped′, -step′ping** *Naut.* to remove (a mast) from its step or socket

un·stick (-stik′) *vt.* **-stuck′, -stick′ing** to loosen or free (something stuck)

un·stop (-stäp′) *vt.* **-stopped′, -stop′ping** [ME. *unstoppen:* see UN- & STOP] **1.** to remove the stopper from **2.** to clear (a pipe, etc.) of a stoppage or obstruction; open **3.** to pull out (an organ stop)

un·strap (-strap′) *vt.* **-strapped′, -strap′ping** to loosen or remove the strap or straps of

un·string (-striŋ′) *vt.* **-strung′, -string′ing 1.** to loosen or remove the string or strings of **2.** to remove from a string **3.** to loosen; relax **4.** to cause to be unstrung; make nervous, weak, upset, etc.

un·struc·tured (-struk′chərd) *adj.* not formally or systematically organized; loose, free, open, etc.

un·strung (-struŋ′) *pt. & pp. of* UNSTRING —*adj.* **1.** nervous or upset; unnerved **2.** having the string or strings loosened or detached, as a bow, racket, etc.

un·stuck (-stuk′) *pt. & pp. of* UNSTICK —*adj.* loosened or freed from being stuck

un·stud·ied (-stud′ēd) *adj.* **1.** not got by study or conscious effort **2.** spontaneous; natural; unaffected **3.** not having studied; unlearned or unversed (*in*)

un·sub·stan·tial (un′səb stan′shəl) *adj.* not substantial; specif., *a)* having no material substance *b)* not solid or heavy; flimsy; light *c)* unreal; visionary —**un′sub·stan′ti·al′i·ty** (-stan′shē al′ə tē) *n.* —**un′sub·stan′tial·ly** *adv.*

un·suit·a·ble (un sōōt′ə b'l, -syōōt′-) *adj.* not suitable; unbecoming; inappropriate —**un·suit′a·bly** *adv.*

un·sung (un suŋ′) *adj.* [LME. *unsonge*] **1.** not sung **2.** not honored or celebrated, as in song or poetry

un·sus·pect·ed (un′sə spek′tid) *adj.* not suspected; specif., *a)* not under suspicion *b)* not imagined to be existent, probable, etc. —**un′sus·pect′ed·ly** *adv.*

---

unserviceable	unsingable	unspecified	unstocked
unsewn	unsinkable	unspectacular	unstoppable
unsexual	unsisterly	unspeculative	unstrained
unshaded	unsized	unspent	unstrategic
unshadowed	unskeptical	unspilled	unstratified
unshakable	unslackened	unspiritual	unstressed
unshakeable	unslaked	unspirituality	unstriated
unshaken	unsleeping	unsplit	unstriped
unshaped	unsliced	unspoiled	unstripped
unshapely	unsmiling	unspoken	unstuffed
unshared	unsmoked	unsporting	unstylish
unsharpened	unsnagged	unsportsmanlike	unsubdued
unshaved	unsober	unspotted	unsubmissive
unshaven	unsoftened	unsprung	unsubscribed
unshelled	unsoiled	unsquandered	unsubsidized
unsheltered	unsold	unsquared	unsubstantiated
unshielded	unsoldierly	unstack	unsuccessful
unshod	unsolicited	unstained	unsufferable
unshorn	unsolicitous	unstalked	unsuggestive
unshortened	unsolid	unstamped	unsuited
unshrinkable	unsolidified	unstandardized	unsullied
unshrinking	unsolvable	unstarched	unsunk
unshrunk	unsolved	unstarred	unsupervised
unshuffled	unsoothed	unstated	unsupportable
unshut	unsorted	unstatesmanlike	unsupported
unshuttered	unsought	unsteadfast	unsuppressed
unsifted	unsounded	unstemmed	unsure
unsighted	unsoured	unsterilized	unsurmountable
unsigned	unsowed	unstigmatized	unsurpassable
unsilenced	unsown	unstinted	unsurpassed
unsimilar	unspecialized	unstinting	unsurprised
unsimplified	unspecific	unstitched	unsusceptible

un·swathe (un swā*th*′) *vt.* -**swathed**′, -**swath**′**ing** to remove a swathe or wrappings from

un·swear (-swer′) *vt.*, *vi.* -**swore**′, -**sworn**′, -**swear**′**ing** to recant or take back (something sworn to), as by another oath; abjure

un·tan·gle (-taŋ′g'l) *vt.* -**gled**, -**gling** 1. to free from a snarl or tangle; disentangle 2. to free from confusion; clear up; put in order

un·taught (-tôt′) *pt. & pp.* of UNTEACH —*adj.* [ME. *untaght*] 1. not taught or instructed; uneducated; ignorant 2. got without being taught; natural

un·teach (-tēch′) *vt.* -**taught**′, -**teach**′**ing** 1. to try to make forget something learned, as in the process of re-education 2. to teach the opposite of

un·ten·a·ble (-ten′ə b'l) *adj.* 1. that cannot be held, defended, or maintained 2. incapable of being tenanted or occupied —**un′ten·a·bil′i·ty**, **un·ten′a·ble·ness** *n.*

Un·ter·mey·er (un′tər mī′ər), **Louis** 1885– ; U.S. poet, anthologist, & critic

Un·ter·wal·den (ō͞on′tər väl′dən) canton of C Switzerland: 296 sq. mi.; pop. 48,000

un·thank·ful (un thaŋk′fəl) *adj.* 1. not thankful; ungrateful 2. thankless; unappreciated —**un·thank′ful·ly** *adv.* —**un·thank′ful·ness** *n.*

un·think (-thiŋk′) *vt.* -**thought**′ (-thôt′), -**think**′**ing** to rid one's mind of, or change one's mind about

un·think·a·ble (-thiŋk′ə b'l) *adj.* [ME. *unthenkable*] 1. not thinkable; too great, too many, etc. to be imagined; inconceivable 2. not to be considered; impossible —**un·think′a·bly** *adv.*

un·think·ing (-thiŋk′iŋ) *adj.* 1. *a*) not stopping to think; thoughtless; heedless *b*) showing lack of thought, attention, or consideration 2. lacking the ability to think; nonrational —**un·think′ing·ly** *adv.*

un·thread (-thred′) *vt.* 1. to remove the thread or threads from 2. to disentangle; unravel 3. to find one's way through (a labyrinth, etc.)

un·throne (-thrōn′) *vt.* -**throned**′, -**thron**′**ing** *same as* DETHRONE —**un·throne′ment** *n.*

un·ti·dy (-tī′dē) *adj.* -**di·er**, -**di·est** [ME. *untydi*] not tidy; not neat or in good order; slovenly; messy —*SYN.* see SLOVENLY —**un·ti′di·ly** *adv.* —**un·ti′di·ness** *n.*

un·tie (-tī′) *vt.* -**tied**′, -**ty**′**ing** or -**tie**′**ing** [ME. *unteien* < OE. *untigan*: see UN- & TIE] 1. to loosen, undo, or unfasten (something tied or knotted) 2. to free, as from difficulty, restraint, etc. 3. to resolve (perplexities, etc.) —*vi.* to become untied

un·til (un til′, ən-) *prep.* [ME. *untill* < *un-* (see UNTO) + *till*, to, TILL[1]] 1. up to the time of; till (a specified time or occurrence) [*until* payday] 2. before (a specified time): used with a negative [not *until* tomorrow] 3. [Chiefly Scot.] to or toward —*conj.* 1. up to the time when or that [*until* you leave] 2. to the point, degree, or place that [cook *until* done] 3. before: used with a negative [not *until* he tells you]

un·time·ly (un tīm′lē) *adj.* 1. coming, said, done, etc. before the usual or expected time; premature [to come to an *untimely* end] 2. coming, said, done, etc. at the wrong time; poorly timed; inopportune —*adv.* 1. prematurely 2. inopportunely —**un·time′li·ness** *n.*

un·time·ous (-tīm′əs) *adj.* [Scot.] *same as* UNTIMELY

un·ti·tled (-tīt′'ld) *adj.* 1. not having a title [an *untitled* book, *untitled* nobility] 2. having no right or claim

un·to (un′tō͞o, -too) *prep.* [ME. < *un-*, until, akin to ON. *unz* (< *und es*), Goth. *und* < IE. **ṇti* < base **ant-*, front, fore (whence Gr. *anti*, L. *ante*, before) + ME. *to*, TO] *archaic or poet. var. of:* 1. TO 2. UNTIL

un·told (un tōld′) *adj.* [ME. *untald* < OE. *unteald*] 1. not told, related, or revealed 2. too great or too numerous to be counted or measured; incalculable [*untold* wealth] 3. indescribably great or intense [*untold* misery]

un·touch·a·ble (un tuch′ə b'l) *adj.* that cannot or should not be touched —*n.* 1. an untouchable person or thing 2. in India, formerly, any member of the lowest class of people, whose touch was regarded as defiling to higher caste Hindus: discrimination against these people (now called *Scheduled Castes*) was abolished in 1955 —**un′touch·a·bil′i·ty** *n.*

un·to·ward (un tō′ərd, -tôrd′) *adj.* [UN- + TOWARD] 1. inappropriate, improper, unseemly, etc. [an *untoward* remark] 2. not favorable or fortunate; adverse, inauspicious, etc. [*untoward* circumstances] 3. [Archaic] stubborn or unruly 4. [Obs.] awkward; clumsy

un·trav·eled, un·trav·elled (un trav′'ld) *adj.* 1. not used or frequented by travelers: said of a road, etc. 2. not having done much traveling, esp. to far places

un·tread (-tred′) *vt.* -**trod**′, -**trod**′**den** or -**trod**′, -**tread**′**ing** to retrace (a path, one's steps, etc.)

un·tried (-trīd′) *adj.* 1. not tried; not attempted, tested, or proved 2. not tried in court

un·true (-trō͞o′) *adj.* [ME. *untrewe* < OE. *untreowe; un-*, not + *treowe*, TRUE] 1. contrary to fact or truth; false or incorrect 2. not agreeing with a standard, rule, or measure 3. not faithful or loyal —**un·tru′ly** *adv.*

un·truss (-trus′) *vt.* 1. to release as from being trussed up 2. [Obs.] to undress

un·truth (-trō͞oth′) *n.* [ME. *untrouthe* < OE. *untreowth* < *un-*, not + *treowth*, TRUTH] 1. the quality or state of being untrue; falsity 2. an untrue statement; falsehood; lie 3. [Obs.] unfaithfulness or disloyalty

un·truth·ful (-trō͞oth′fəl) *adj.* 1. not in accordance with the truth; untrue 2. given to telling untruths; likely to tell lies —*SYN.* see DISHONEST —**un·truth′ful·ly** *adv.* —**un·truth′ful·ness** *n.*

un·tuck (-tuk′) *vt.* to undo a tuck or tucks in; free from a tuck or fold

un·tu·tored (-tō͞ot′ərd, -tyō͞ot′-) *adj.* 1. not tutored or taught; uneducated 2. simple; naive; unsophisticated —*SYN.* see IGNORANT

un·twine (-twīn′) *vt.* -**twined**′, -**twin**′**ing** [ME. *untwynen*] to undo (something twined or twisted); disentangle or unwind —*vi.* to become untwined

un·twist (-twist′) *vt.*, *vi.* to turn in the opposite direction so as to loosen or separate; untwine

un·used (-yō͞ozd′) *adj.* 1. not used; not in use 2. that has never been used 3. unaccustomed (*to*)

un·u·su·al (-yō͞o′zhoo wəl) *adj.* not usual or common; strange; rare; exceptional —*SYN.* see RARE[1] —**un·u′su·al·ly** *adv.* —**un·u′su·al·ness** *n.*

un·ut·ter·a·ble (-ut′ər ə b'l) *adj.* 1. [Rare] that cannot easily be pronounced 2. that cannot be expressed or described; inexpressible —**un·ut′ter·a·bly** *adv.*

un·var·nished (-vär′nisht) *adj.* 1. not varnished 2. plain; simple; unadorned [the *unvarnished* truth]

un·veil (un vāl′) *vt.* to reveal or make visible by or as by removing a veil or covering from; disclose —*vi.* to take off a veil or covering; reveal oneself

un·veil·ing (-iŋ) *n.* a formal or ceremonial removal of a covering from a new statue, tombstone, etc.

un·voice (un vois′) *vt.* -**voiced**′, -**voic**′**ing** *Phonet.* to make (a normally voiced sound) voiceless by uttering the corresponding voiceless sound; make surd [to *unvoice* the *s* in *has* when saying "has to"]

un·voiced (-voist′) *adj.* 1. not expressed; not spoken or uttered 2. *Phonet.* made voiceless; surd

un·war·y (-wer′ē) *adj.* not wary; not watchful or cautious; not alert to possible danger, trickery, etc.; unguarded —**un·war′i·ly** *adv.* —**un·war′i·ness** *n.*

---

unsuspecting	untarnished	untracked	unuttered
unsuspicious	untasted	untrained	unvaccinated
unsustainable	untaxed	untrammeled	unvacillating
unsustained	unteachable	untransferable	unvalued
unswayed	untechnical	untransferred	unvanquished
unsweetened	untempered	untranslatable	unvaried
unswept	untenanted	untranslated	unvarying
unswerving	untended	untransmitted	unveiled
unswollen	unterrified	untransported	unventilated
unsworn	untested	untransposed	unverifiable
unsymmetrical	unthanked	untrapped	unverified
unsymmetry	unthankful	untraversed	unversed
unsympathetic	unthatched	untreated	unvexed
unsympathetically	unthawed	untrimmed	unvindicated
unsympathizing	untheatrical	untrod	unviolated
unsystematic	unthoughtful	untroubled	unvisited
unsystematically	unthought-of	untrustful	unvocal
unsystematized	unthrifty	untrustworthy	unvocalized
untabulated	unticketed	untufted	unvulcanized
untack	untillable	untunable	unwakened
untactful	untilled	untuned	unwalled
untagged	untinged	untuneful	unwaning
untainted	untipped	unturned	unwanted
untalented	untired	untwilled	unwarlike
untalked-of	untiring	untwisted	unwarmed
untamable	untorn	untypical	unwarned
untamed	untouched	unusable	unwarped
untanned	untraceable	unutilizable	unwarrantable
untapped	untraced	unutilized	unwarranted

un·wea·ried (-wir′ēd) *adj.* [ME. *unweried* (see UN- & WEARY), for OE. *ungewerged*] **1.** not weary or tired **2.** never wearying; tireless; indefatigable

un·well (-wel′) *adj.* not well; ailing; ill; sick

un·wept (-wept′) *adj.* **1.** not shed [*unwept* tears] **2.** not wept for; unmourned

un·whole·some (-hōl′səm) *adj.* [ME. *unholsom*] not wholesome; specif., *a)* harmful to body or mind; unhealthful *b)* having unsound health or an unhealthy appearance *c)* morally harmful or corrupt —**un·whole′some·ly** *adv.*

un·wield·y (-wēl′dē) *adj.* **1.** hard to wield, manage, handle, or deal with, as because of large size or weight, or awkward form **2.** [Now Rare] awkward; clumsy —**un·wield′i·ness** *n.*

un·will·ing (-wil′iŋ) *adj.* [altered (in 16th c.) < ME. *unwilland* < OE. *unwillende* < *un-*, not + prp. of *willan*: see WILL²] **1.** not willing or inclined; reluctant; loath; averse **2.** done, said, given, etc. reluctantly —**un·will′ing·ly** *adv.* —**un·will′ing·ness** *n.*

un·wind (-wind′) *vt.* **-wound′, -wind′ing** [ME. *unwinden* < OE. *unwindan*] **1.** to wind off or undo (something wound) **2.** same as UNCOIL **3.** to straighten out or untangle (something confused or involved) **4.** to make relaxed, less tense, etc. —*vi.* **1.** to become unwound **2.** to become relaxed, less tense, etc.

un·wise (-wīz′) *adj.* [ME. < OE. *unwis*: see UN- & WISE¹] having or showing a lack of wisdom or sound judgment; foolish; imprudent —**un·wise′ly** *adv.*

un·wish (-wish′) *vt.* **1.** *a)* to retract (a wish) *b)* to stop wishing for **2.** [Obs.] to do away with by wishing

un·wit·ting (-wit′iŋ) *adj.* [ME. *unwiting*, altered < OE. *unwitende* < *un-*, not + prp. of *witan*, to know: see WIT²] **1.** not knowing or aware; unconscious **2.** not intended; unintentional —**un·wit′ting·ly** *adv.*

un·wont·ed (-wun′tid, -wôn′-) *adj.* [UN- + WONTED] **1.** not common, usual, or habitual; infrequent; rare [to speak with *unwonted* severity] **2.** [Archaic] not accustomed, familiar, or used (usually with *to*) —**un·wont′ed·ly** *adv.*

un·world·ly (-wurld′lē) *adj.* **1.** not of or limited to this world; unearthly **2.** not concerned with the affairs, pleasures, etc. of this world; otherworldly **3.** not worldly wise; unsophisticated —**un·world′li·ness** *n.*

un·wor·thy (-wur′thē) *adj.* **-thi·er, -thi·est** [ME.] **1.** lacking merit or value; worthless **2.** not deserving (often with *of*) **3.** not fit or becoming (usually with *of*) [a remark *unworthy* of a gentleman] **4.** not deserved or warranted —**un·wor′thi·ly** *adv.* —**un·wor′thi·ness** *n.*

un·wound (-wound′) *pt.* & *pp.* of UNWIND

un·wrap (-rap′) *vt.* **-wrapped′, -wrap′ping** to take off the wrapping of; open or undo (something wrapped) —*vi.* to become unwrapped

un·writ·ten (-rit′'n) *adj.* **1.** not in writing; not written or printed **2.** operating only through custom or tradition [an *unwritten* rule] **3.** not written on; blank

unwritten law 1. law originating in custom, usage, court decisions, etc., rather than in the action of any lawmaking body **2.** the traditionally assumed rule that a man may, with impunity, criminally assault the seducer or raper of his wife or daughter

un·yoke (-yōk′) *vt.* **-yoked′, -yok′ing** [ME. *unyoken* < OE. *ungeocian*] **1.** to release from a yoke **2.** to separate or disconnect —*vi.* **1.** to become unyoked **2.** to remove a yoke **3.** [Obs.] to stop working

☆**un·zip** (-zip′) *vt., vi.* **-zipped′, -zip′ping 1.** to open (a zipper) **2.** to separate the edges of (a garment, etc.) by opening a zipper

up¹ (up) *adv.* [ME. < OE. *up, uppe,* akin to G. *auf,* ON. *upp* < IE. **upo,* up from below, whence also SUB-, HYPO-, OVER] **1.** from a lower to a higher place; away from or out of the ground **2.** in or on a higher position or level; off the ground, or from a position below to one at the surface of the earth or water **3.** in a direction or place thought of as higher or above **4.** above the horizon **5.** to a later period [from childhood *up*] **6.** to a higher or better condition or station **7.** to a higher amount, greater degree, etc. [with prices going *up*] **8.** *a)* in or into a standing or upright position *b)* out of bed **9.** in or into existence, action, view, evidence, consideration, etc. [to bring a matter *up*] **10.** into an excited or troubled state [to get worked *up*] **11.** aside; away; by [lay *up* grain for the winter] **12.** so as to be even with in space, time, degree, etc. [keep *up* with the times] **13.** so as to be tightly closed, bound, packed, etc. [tie *up* the package] **14.** to the point of completeness; entirely;

thoroughly [eat *up* the pie] **15.** so as to stop [to rein *up* a horse] ☆**16.** *Baseball* to one's turn at batting; at bat **17.** *Naut.* to the windward point [put *up* the helm] **18.** *Sports & Games* ahead of an opponent with reference to the number of points, goals, strokes, etc. ☆**19.** [Colloq.] served without ice cubes; not on the rocks: said of a cocktail The adverb *up* is used idiomatically *a)* to form a verb-adverb combination with a meaning different from the meaning of the simple verb (Ex.: look *up* this word, he didn't turn *up*) *b)* as an intensive with verbs (Ex.: dress *up*, eat *up*, clean *up*) *c)* as a virtually meaningless element added, esp. colloquially, to almost any verb (Ex.: light *up* a cigarette, write *up* a story) —*prep.* **1.** to, toward, or at a higher place on or in **2.** to, toward, or at a higher condition or station on or in [*up* the social ladder] **3.** at, along, or toward the higher or more distant part of [*up* the road] **4.** toward the source of, or against the current, flow, or movement of (a river, the wind, etc.) **5.** in or toward the interior or more northerly part of (a country, territory, etc.) —*adj.* **1.** tending or directed toward a position that is higher or is regarded as being higher **2.** *a)* in a higher position, condition, or station *b)* mounted on a horse or horses **3.** *a)* above the ground *b)* above the horizon **4.** advanced in amount, degree, etc. [rents are *up*] **5.** *a)* in a standing position *b)* out of bed **6.** in an active, excited, or agitated state [her anger was *up*] **7.** even with in space, time, degree, etc. **8.** living or located in the inner or elevated part of a country, territory, etc. **9.** at an end; over [time is *up*] ☆**10.** at stake in gambling [to have two dollars *up* on a horse] **11.** [Colloq.] going on; happening [what's *up*?] ☆**12.** *Baseball* having one's turn at batting; at bat **13.** *Golf* on the green: said of the ball **14.** *Sports & Games a)* ahead of an opponent with reference to the number of points, goals, strokes, etc. *b)* needed for winning or ending the game: said of the specified number of points, etc. As an adjective, *up* is usually predicative —*n.* a person or thing that is up, moves upward, etc.; specif., *a)* an upward slope *b)* an upward movement or course *c)* an upbound train, bus, elevator, etc. *d)* a period or state of prosperity, good luck, etc. —*vt.* **upped, up′ping** [Colloq.] to get up; rise: sometimes used colloquially in the uninflected form to emphasize another, following verb [he *up* and left] —*vt.* [Colloq.] **1.** to put up, lift up, or take up **2.** to bring to a higher level or cause to rise [to *up* prices] **3.** to raise, or bet more than (a preceding bet or bettor) —**it's all up with** there is no further hope for; the end is near for —☆**on the up and up** [Slang] open and aboveboard; honest —☆**up against** [Colloq.] face to face with; confronted with —☆**up against it** [Colloq.] in difficulty; esp., in financial difficulty —**up and around** (or *about*) out of bed and resuming one's normal activities, as after an illness —**up and doing** busy; active —**up for 1.** presented or considered for (an elective office, an election, sale, auction, etc.) **2.** before a court for (trial) or for (some criminal charge) —**up on** (or **in**) [Colloq.] well-informed concerning —**ups and downs** good periods and bad periods —**up to** [Colloq.] **1.** occupied with; doing; scheming; devising [*up* to no good?] **2.** equal to (a task, challenge, etc.); capable of (doing, undertaking, etc.) **3.** as many as [*up* to four may play] **4.** as far as [*up* to now, *up* to his hips] ☆**5.** dependent upon; incumbent upon [entirely *up* to her] —**up to the ears** (or **eyes, neck,** etc.) very deeply: said of involvement in work, debt, trouble, etc. —**up with** put in or restore (a specified person or thing) to power, authority, favor, etc.

up² (up) *adv.* [phonetic respelling of AP(IECE), infl. by prec.] apiece; each [the score is seven *up*]

up- (up) [ME. < OE., identical with *up,* UP¹] *a combining form meaning* up [*up*grade, *up*hill]

☆**up-and-com·ing** (up′n kum′iŋ) *adj.* **1.** enterprising, alert, and promising **2.** gaining in importance or status

up-and-down (-doun′) *adj.* **1.** going alternately up and down, to and fro, etc. **2.** variable; fluctuating

U·pan·i·shad (oo pan′i shad′, oo pän′ē shäd′) *n.* [Sans. *upaniṣad*] any of a group of late Vedic metaphysical treatises dealing with man in relation to the universe

u·pas (yoo′pəs) *n.* [short for Malay *pohon upas,* tree of poison] **1.** a tall Javanese tree (*Antiaris toxicaria*) of the mulberry family, whose whitish bark yields a poisonous milky juice used as an arrow poison **2.** the juice of this tree **3.** something harmful or deadly in its influence

up·beat (up′bēt′) *n.* **1.** an upward trend; upswing **2.** *Music a)* an unaccented beat, esp. when on the last note

unwashed	unweathered	unwinking	unworkmanlike
unwasted	unweave	unwished	unworn
unwatched	unwed	unwished-for	unworried
unwatchful	unwedded	unwithered	unworshiped
unwatered	unweeded	unwithering	unwounded
unwavering	unweighed	unwitnessed	unwoven
unwaxed	unwelcome	unwomanly	unwrinkle
unweakened	unwelded	unwon	unwrought
unweaned	unwetted	unwooded	unyielding
unwearable	unwhipped	unwooed	unyouthful
unweary	unwifely	unworkable	unzealous
unwearying	unwilled	unworked	unzoned

of a bar *b*) the upward stroke of a conductor's baton marking such a beat —*adj.* lively; cheerful; optimistic

up·bow (up′bō′) *n.* a stroke on a violin, cello, etc. in which the bow is drawn across the strings from the tip to the heel of the bow: symbol (∨)

up·braid (up brād′) *vt.* [ME. *upbreiden* < OE. *upbregdan* < *up-*, UP- + *bregdan*, to pull: see BRAID] to rebuke severely or bitterly; censure sharply —*SYN.* see SCOLD

up·bring·ing (up′briŋ′iŋ) *n.* [obs. *upbring*, to rear, train (< ME. *upbryngen:* see UP- & BRING) + -ING] the training and education received while growing up; rearing; nurture

up·build (up bild′) *vt.* -**built′**, -**build′ing** to build up

up·cast (up′kast′, -käst′) *n.* 1. something cast or thrown up 2. *Geol.* same as UPTHROW (sense 2) 3. *Mining* a ventilating shaft through which air is returned to the surface —*adj.* 1. thrown upward 2. directed upward

☆**up·chuck** (up′chuk′) *vi.*, *vt.*, *n.* [Slang] same as VOMIT

up·com·ing (-kum′iŋ) *adj.* coming soon; forthcoming

up·coun·try (up′kun′trē) *adj.* of or located in the interior of a country; inland —*n.* the interior of a country —*adv.* ☆in or toward the interior of a country

up·date (up dāt′) *vt.* -**dat′ed**, -**dat′ing** to bring up to date; make conform to the most recent facts, methods, ideas, etc.

up·draft (up′draft′, -dräft′) *n.* an upward air current

up·end (up end′) *vt.*, *vi.* 1. to set, turn, or stand on end 2. to upset or topple

☆**up·grade** (up′grād′; *for v., usually* up grād′) *n.* an upward slope, esp. in a road —*adj.*, *adv.* uphill; upward —*vt.* -**grad′ed**, -**grad′ing** 1. to promote to a more skilled job at higher pay 2. to raise in importance, value, esteem, etc. —**on the upgrade** gaining in status, influence, health, etc.

up·growth (up′grōth′) *n.* 1. upward growth; rise or development 2. anything produced by this

up·heav·al (up hē′v′l) *n.* 1. a heaving up or violent uplifting, as of part of the earth's crust, by volcanic or earthquake activity 2. a sudden, violent change or disturbance in affairs

up·heave (up hēv′) *vt.* -**heaved′** or -**hove′**, -**heav′ing** to heave or lift up; raise from beneath —*vi.* to rise as if forced up; be raised from beneath —**up·heav′er** *n.*

up·hill (up′hil′) *adj.* 1. going or sloping up; rising 2. calling for prolonged effort; laborious 3. located on high ground —*n.* a sloping rise or ascent —*adv.* 1. toward the top of a hill or incline; upward 2. with difficulty; laboriously

up·hold (up hōld′) *vt.* -**held′**, -**hold′ing** 1. to hold up; raise 2. to keep from falling; support 3. to give moral or spiritual support or encouragement to 4. to decide in favor of; agree with and support against opposition; sustain —*SYN.* see SUPPORT —**up·hold′er** *n.*

☆**up·hol·ster** (up hōl′stər, ə pōl′-) *vt.* [back-formation < ff.] to fit out (furniture, etc.) with covering material, padding, springs, etc.

up·hol·ster·er (-stər ər) *n.* [altered < ME. *upholdster*, altered < *upholder*, dealer in small or secondhand wares < *upholden*, to repair (< *up-*, UP- + *holden*, to keep, HOLD¹): cf. -STER] a person whose business is upholstering furniture

up·hol·ster·y (-stər ē, -strē) *n.*, *pl.* -**ster·ies** [see prec. & -ERY] 1. the fittings and material used in upholstering 2. the business or work of an upholsterer

UPI United Press International

up·keep (up′kēp′) *n.* 1. the act of keeping up buildings, equipment, etc.; maintenance 2. the condition of being kept up; repair 3. the cost of maintenance

up·land (-lənd, -land′) *n.* land elevated above other land, as above land along a river —*adj.* of or situated in upland

☆**upland cotton** any of various, mostly short-staple, cottons (*Gossypium hirsutum*) of the U.S., China, etc.

☆**upland plover** a large, short-billed sandpiper (*Bartramia longicauda*) with streaked brownish plumage, found in the fields and uplands of the interior of N. and S. America

up·lift (up lift′; *for n.* up′lift′) *vt.* 1. to lift up, or elevate 2. to raise to a higher moral, social, or cultural level or condition —☆*n.* 1. the act or process of lifting up; elevation 2. *a)* the act or process of raising to a higher moral, social, or cultural level *b)* any influence, movement, etc. intended to improve society morally, culturally, etc. 3. a brassiere designed to lift and support the breasts: in full **uplift brassiere** 4. *Geol.* *a)* a raising of land above the surrounding area *b)* land so raised —**up·lift′er** *n.* —**up·lift′ment** *n.*

up·man·ship (up′mən ship′) *n.* short for ONE-UPMANSHIP

up·most (up′mōst′) *adj.* same as UPPERMOST

U·po·lu (ōō pō′lōō) smaller of the two main islands of Western Samoa: 435 sq. mi.; pop. 93,000: cf. SAVAII

up·on (ə pän′) *prep.* [ME. < *up*, UP¹ + *on*, ON, prob. infl. by ON. *upp á* (< *upp*, upward + *á*, on)] on (in various senses), or up and on: *on* and *upon* are generally interchangeable, the choice being governed by idiom, sentence rhythm, etc. —*adv.* 1. on: used only for completing a verb [a canvas not painted *upon*] 2. [Obs.] on it; on one's person 3. [Obs.] thereupon; thereafter

up·per (up′ər) *adj.* [ME., compar. of *up*, UP¹] 1. higher in place or physical position 2. farther north or farther inland 3. higher in rank, authority, dignity, etc.; superior 4. [U-] *Geol.* more recent; later: used of a division of a period [*Upper* Cambrian] —*n.* 1. something above another similar thing, related part, etc.; specif., *a)* the part of a shoe or boot above the sole ☆*b)* [*pl.*] cloth gaiters ☆*c)* [Colloq.] an upper berth, as in a Pullman car 2. [Slang] any drug containing a stimulant; esp., an amphetamine —☆**on one's**

uppers [Colloq.] 1. wearing shoes with soles worn through 2. in need or want; poor; shabby

Upper Arlington [so called to distinguish it from the nearby village of *Arlington*, now called Marble Cliff] city in C Ohio: suburb of Columbus: pop. 39,000

upper bound *Math.* a number that is greater than or equal to any number in a set

Upper Canada *former name of* ONTARIO, Canada

up·per-case (up′ər kās′) *adj. Printing* designating, of, or in upper case —*vt.* -**cased′**, -**cas′ing** to set up in, or to change to, upper case

upper case [from their being kept in the upper of two cases of type] capital-letter type used in printing, as distinguished from small letters (*lower case*)

upper class the social class above the middle class; rich, socially prominent, or aristocratic class

☆**up·per-class·man** (up′ər klas′mən) *n.*, *pl.* -**men** a student in the junior or senior class of a high school or college

upper crust 1. the top crust, as of a loaf of bread ☆2. [Colloq.] same as UPPER CLASS

up·per·cut (up′ər kut′) *n. Boxing* a short, swinging blow directed upward, as to the chin —*vt.*, *vi.* -**cut′**, -**cut′ting** to hit with an uppercut

upper hand the position of advantage or control

Upper House [*often* **u- h-**] in a legislature having two branches, that branch which is usually smaller and less representative, as the Senate of the U.S. Congress

up·per·most (up′ər mōst′) *adj.* highest in place, position, power, authority, influence, etc.; topmost; predominant; foremost —*adv.* in the highest place, position, rank, etc.

Upper Peninsula NW section of Mich., a peninsula separated from the rest of the State by the Straits of Mackinac: 16,538 sq. mi.

Upper Volta country in W Africa, north of Ghana: 108,880 sq. mi.; pop. 5,330,000; cap. Ouagadougou

upper works *Naut.* those parts of a loaded ship that project above the surface of the water

up·pish (up′ish) *adj.* [< UP¹ + -ISH] [Colloq.] inclined to be haughty, arrogant, snobbish, etc.: also ☆**up′pi·ty** (-ə tē) —**up′pish·ly** *adv.* —**up′pish·ness** *n.*

Upp·sa·la (ōōp′sä′lä; *E.* up′sə lə) city in EC Sweden: pop. 87,000: also sp. **Up′sa·la**

up·raise (up rāz′) *vt.* -**raised′**, -**rais′ing** to raise up; lift

up·rear (-rir′) *vt.* 1. to lift up 2. to erect; build 3. to elevate in dignity; exalt 4. to bring up; rear —*vi.* to rise up

up·right (up′rit′; *also, for adv.*, up rit′) *adj.* [ME. < OE. *upriht:* see UP¹ & RIGHT] 1. standing, pointing, or directed straight up; in a vertical or perpendicular position; erect 2. honest and just; honorable —*adv.* in an upright position or direction —*n.* 1. the state of being upright or vertical 2. something having an upright position; vertical part or member 3. *clipped form of* UPRIGHT PIANO 4. [*pl.*] *a)* goal posts, as in football ☆*b)* the standards supporting the crossbar in the high jump or pole vault —**up′right′ly** *adv.* —**up′right′ness** *n.*

SYN.—**upright** implies an unbending moral straightness and integrity; **honest** implies complete fairness and openness in one's dealings with others and stresses freedom from deceit or fraud; **just**, of things, stresses fairness or equitableness and, of persons, high moral rectitude; **honorable** implies a keen sense of, and strict adherence to, what is considered morally or ethically right, esp. in one's social class, profession, position, etc.; **scrupulous** implies meticulous conscientiousness with regard to the morality of one's actions, aims, etc. —*ANT.* dishonest, unjust

upright piano a piano with a vertical, rectangular body

up·rise (up rīz′; *for n.* up′rīz′) *vi.* -**rose′**, -**ris′en**, -**ris′ing** 1. to get up; rise 2. to move or slope upward; ascend 3. to rise into view, being, or activity 4. to be or become erect or upright 5. to increase in size, volume, etc.; swell, as sound 6. to rise in revolt —*n.* 1. the act or process of rising up 2. an upward slope or ascent

up·ris·ing (up′rīz′iŋ) *n.* 1. the action of rising up; specif., an outbreak against a government; revolt 2. an upward slope or ascent —*SYN.* see REBELLION

up·roar (-rôr′) *n.* [Du. *oproer*, a stirring up (akin to G. *aufruhr*) < *op*, up + *roeren*, to stir (akin to OE. *hreran* < IE. base **kere-*, to mix, stir up): form and sense infl. by ROAR] 1. violent disturbance or commotion, esp. one accompanied by loud, confused noise, as of shouting; tumult 2. loud, confused noise; din —*SYN.* see NOISE

up·roar·i·ous (up rôr′ē əs) *adj.* 1. making, or characterized by, an uproar; tumultuous 2. *a)* loud and boisterous, as laughter *b)* causing such laughter [an *uproarious* joke] —**up·roar′i·ous·ly** *adv.* —**up·roar′i·ous·ness** *n.*

up·root (up rōōt′, -root′) *vt.* 1. to tear up by the roots 2. to destroy or remove utterly; eradicate

up·rouse (-rouz′) *vt.* -**roused′**, -**rous′ing** to rouse; stir up

up·sa·dai·sy (up′sə dā′zē) *interj. var. of* UPSY-DAISY

up·set (up set′; *for n., and occas. adj.*, up′set′) *vt.* -**set′**, -**set′ting** [ME. *upsetten:* see UP¹ & SET] 1. orig., to set up; erect 2. *a)* to tip over; overturn [to *upset* a vase] *b)* to overthrow or defeat, esp. unexpectedly 3. *a)* to disturb the functioning, fulfillment, or completion of [to *upset* a busy schedule] *b)* to disturb mentally or emotionally [*upset* by bad news] *c)* to disturb physically; make sick [to *upset* the stomach] 4. *Mech.* *a)* to shorten and thicken (a red-hot iron) by beating on the end; swage *b)* to shorten (a metal tire) in the process of resetting it —*vi.* to become overturned or upset —*n.* 1. an upsetting or being upset; specif.,

a) a tipping over, knocking over, etc. *b)* an overthrow or defeat, esp. when unexpected *c)* a disturbance or disorder, specif. of an emotional or physical nature **2.** *Mech.* *a)* a swage used for upsetting *b)* an upset piece or part —*adj.* **1.** [Rare] set up; erected **2.** *a)* tipped over; overturned *b)* overthrown or defeated *c)* disturbed or disordered —**up·set′ter** *n.*

SYN.—upset is the ordinary word implying a toppling, disorganization, etc. as a result of a loss of balance or stability [*to upset* a glass, one's plans, etc., emotionally *upset*]; **overturn** implies a turning of a thing upside down or flat on its side and, in extended use, connotes the destruction of something established [*to overturn* a chair, a government, etc.]; **capsize** specifically implies the overturning or upsetting of a boat

upset price the price fixed as the minimum at which something will be sold at an auction

up·shot (up′shät′) *n.* [orig., the final shot in an archery match] the conclusion; result; outcome

up·side (-sīd′) *n.* the upper side or part

upside down [ME. *up so doun,* lit., up as if down: altered by folk etym.] **1.** with the top side or part underneath or turned over; inverted **2.** in disorder or confusion; topsy-turvy —**up′side′-down′** *adj.*

☆**upside-down cake** a cake baked with a bottom layer of fruit and turned upside-down before serving

up·si·lon (yo͞op′sə län′, up′-; -lən; *Brit.* yo͞op sī′lən) *n.* [LGr. *y psilon,* lit., simple *u* (to distinguish from *oi,* of the same sound in LGr.)] the twentieth letter of the Greek alphabet (Υ, υ)

up·spring (up spriŋ′; *for n.* up′spriŋ′) *vi.* **-sprang′** or **-sprung′, -sprung′, -spring′ing** to spring up (in various senses) —*n.* a spring upward

up·stage (up′stāj′; *for v.* up stāj′) *adv.* toward or at the rear of a stage —*adj.* **1.** of or having to do with the rear of a stage **2.** haughtily or disdainfully aloof —*vt.* **-staged′, -stag′ing 1.** to draw the attention of the audience away from (a fellow actor) and to oneself by moving upstage so that the other actor must face away from the audience **2.** to draw attention to oneself at the expense of (another) as by treating disdainfully

up·stairs (up′sterz′) *adv.* **1.** up the stairs or to an upper floor or higher level —*adj.* situated on an upper floor —*n.* an upper floor or floors —**kick upstairs** [Colloq.] to promote to a higher level so as to be rid of on a lower, but more effective, level

up·stand·ing (up stan′diŋ) *adj.* **1.** standing straight; erect **2.** upright in character and behavior; honorable

up·start[1] (up′stärt′) *n.* a person who has recently come into wealth, power, etc., esp. one who behaves in a presumptuous, aggressive manner; parvenu —*adj.* **1.** newly rich, powerful, etc. **2.** of or characteristic of an upstart

up·start[2] (up stärt′) *vi., vt.* to start, or spring, up or cause to spring up

☆**up·state** (up′stāt′) *n.* that part of a State farther to the north or away from a large city; esp., the northern part of New York —*adj., adv.* in, to, or from upstate —**up′stat′er** *n.*

up·stream (-strēm′) *adv., adj.* in the direction against the current of a stream

up·stretched (up strecht′) *adj.* stretched upward

up·stroke (up′strōk′) *n.* **1.** an upward stroke or movement **2.** a line, brush mark, etc. made with an upward stroke

up·surge (up surj′; *for n.* up′surj′) *vi.* **-surged′, -surg′ing** to surge up —*n.* a surge upward

up·sweep (up′swēp′; *for v.* up swēp′) *n.* **1.** a sweep or curve upward **2.** an upswept hairdo —*vt., vi.* **-swept′, -sweep′ing** to sweep or curve upward

up·swell (up swel′) *vi.* **-swelled′, -swelled′** or **-swol′len, swell′ing** to swell up

up·swept (up′swept′) *pt. & pp. of* UPSWEEP —*adj.* **1.** curved or sloped upward **2.** designating or of a style of hairdo in which the hair is combed up smoothly in the back and piled on the top of the head

up·swing (up′swiŋ′; *for v.* up swiŋ′) *n.* a swing, trend, or movement upward; specif., an upward trend in business —*vi.* **-swung′, -swing′ing 1.** to swing or move upward **2.** to advance or improve

up·sy-dai·sy (up′sə dā′zē) *interj.* baby-talk extension of UP[1] up you go: used playfully as when lifting a small child

up·take (up′tāk′) *n.* **1.** the act of taking up; a drawing up, absorbing, etc. **2.** *a)* a pipe carrying smoke and gases from a furnace to its chimney *b)* a ventilating shaft or pipe —☆**quick (or slow) on the uptake** [Colloq.] quick (or slow) to understand or comprehend

up·throw (-thrō′) *n.* **1.** a throwing up; upheaval **2.** *Geol.* that side of a fault which has moved upward relative to the other side

up·thrust (-thrust′) *n.* **1.** an upward push or thrust **2.** *Geol.* an upheaval of a part of the earth's crust

☆**up·tight, up·tight** (up′tīt′) *adj.* [Slang] **1.** very tense, nervous, anxious, etc. **2.** overly conventional or strict in attitudes **3.** in a bad way or state Also **up tight**

up·tilt (up tilt′) *vt.* to tilt up

up-to-date (up′tə dāt′) *adj.* **1.** extending to the present time; using or including the latest facts, methods, ideas,

data, etc. **2.** keeping up with what is most recent in style, taste, information, etc. —**up′-to-date′ness** *n.*

up·town (up′toun′) *adj., adv.* of, in, like, to, or toward the upper part of a city or town, usually the part away from the main business district —☆*n.* the uptown, usually residential, section of a city or town

up·turn (up turn′; *for n.* up′turn′) *vt., vi.* to turn up, upward, or over —*n.* an upward turn, curve, or trend —**up′turned′** *adj.*

up·ward (up′wərd) *adv., adj.* [ME. < OE. *upweard:* see UP[1] & -WARD] **1.** toward a higher place, position, degree, amount, etc. **2.** from an earlier to a later time **3.** beyond (an indicated price, amount, etc.) [tickets cost two dollars and *upward*] Also **up′wards** *adv.* —**upwards (or upward) of** more than —**up′ward·ly** *adv.*

☆**upward mobility** movement from a lower to a higher social and economic status

up·wind (up′wind′) *adv., adj.* in the direction from which the wind is blowing or usually blows

Ur (ur) ancient Sumerian city on the Euphrates River, in what is now S Iraq

ur- (oor) [G.] *a prefix meaning* original, primitive

u·ra·cil (yoor′ə sil) *n.* [UR(O)-[1] + AC(ETIC) + -IL] a colorless, crystalline, pyrimidine base, $C_4H_4O_2N_2$, that occurs as a constituent of ribonucleic acid

u·rae·us (yoo rē′əs) *n., pl.* **-rae′i** (-ī) [ModL. < LGr. *ouraios,* cobra: form prob. infl. by Gr. *oura,* a tail] the figure of the sacred asp or cobra on the headdress of ancient Egyptian rulers

URAEUS

U·ral (yoor′əl) **1.** [*pl.*] mountain system in the W R.S.F.S.R., extending from the Arctic Ocean south to the N border of the Kazakh S.S.R.: traditionally regarded as the boundary between Europe & Asia: highest peak, c.6,180 ft.: also **Ural Mountains 2.** river flowing from the S section of these mountains into the N end of the Caspian Sea: 1,575 mi.

U·ral-Al·ta·ic (-al tā′ik) *n.* the postulated group of languages which includes, among others, the Uralic and Altaic families —*adj.* **1.** designating or of this group of languages **2.** of the peoples speaking these languages

U·ral·ic (yoo ral′ik, -rā′lik) *adj.* designating or of the family of languages including the Finno-Ugric and Samoyed subfamilies —*n.* this family of languages Also **U·ra′li·an** (-ē ən)

u·ral·ite (yoor′ə līt′) *n.* [G. *uralit* < Ural, URAL + -*it,* -ITE[1]] a fibrous, monoclinic amphibole, a variety of hornblende altered from pyroxene —**u′ral·it′ic** (-ə lit′ik) *adj.*

U·ra·ni·a (yoo rā′nē ə) *n.* [L. < Gr. *Ourania,* lit., the heavenly one] *Gr. Myth.* the Muse of astronomy

U·ra·ni·an[1] (-ən) *adj.* **1.** of Urania **2.** heavenly; celestial

U·ra·ni·an[2] (-ən) *adj.* of Uranus

u·ran·ic[1] (yoo ran′ik) *adj.* [< Gr. *ouranos,* heaven, sky + -IC] of the heavens; celestial; astronomical

u·ran·ic[2] (yoo ran′ik) *adj.* [URAN(IUM) + -IC] of or containing uranium, esp. in its higher valence

u·ra·nide (yoor′ə nīd′) *n.* any of the transuranic elements

u·ran·i·nite (yoo ran′ə nīt′) *n.* [< URAN(IUM) + -IN[1] + -ITE[1]] a black, opaque mineral, essentially uranium oxide, but often containing radium, thorium, or lead, and, sometimes, the gases helium and argon: the chief ore of uranium

u·ra·ni·um (yoo rā′nē əm) *n.* [ModL. < earlier G. *uranit,* after URANUS, then (1781) the most recently discovered planet] a very hard, heavy, silvery, moderately malleable, radioactive metallic chemical element: it is found only in combination, chiefly in pitchblende, and is important in work on atomic energy, esp. in the isotope (**uranium 235**), which can undergo continuous fission, and in the more plentiful isotope (**uranium 238**) from which plutonium is produced: symbol, U; at. wt., 238.03; at. no., 92; sp. gr., 19.05; melt. pt., 1132.3°C; boil. pt., 3818°C

u·ra·nog·ra·phy (yoor′ə näg′rə fē) *n.* [Gr. *ouranographia* < *ouranos,* heaven + *graphein,* to write: see GRAPHIC] the branch of astronomy dealing with the description of the heavens and the mapping of the stars —**u′ra·nog′ra-**

URALS

pher *n.* —**u·ra·no·graph·ic** (yoor′ə nō graf′ik), **u′ra·no·graph′i·cal** *adj.*

u·ra·nol·o·gy (-näl′ə jē) *n.* [< Gr. *ouranos*, heaven + -LOGY] *an old term for* ASTRONOMY

u·ra·nom·e·try (-näm′ə trē) *n.* [ModL. *uranometria* < Gr. *ouranos*, heaven + ModL. *-metria*, -METRY] 1. the measurement of the positions, magnitudes, distances, etc. of the stars 2. a map or chart prepared from the stars

u·ra·nous (yoor′ə nəs, yoo rā′-) *adj.* [URAN(IUM) + -OUS] of or containing uranium, esp. in its lower valence

U·ra·nus (yoor′ə nəs, yoo rā′nəs) [LL. < Gr. *Ouranos*, lit., heaven] 1. *Gr. Myth.* a god who was the personification of the heavens, the husband or son of Gaea (Earth) and father of the Titans, Furies, and Cyclopes: he was overthrown by his son Cronus (Saturn) 2. a planet of the solar system, seventh in distance from the sun, having five satellites: mean diameter, c.29,500 mi.; period of revolution, c.84 tropical years; period of rotation, c.10 hrs., 45 min.; symbol, ♅

u·ra·nyl (yoor′ə nil) *n.* [URAN(IUM) + -YL] the bivalent radical UO₂, present in many compounds of uranium

u·rate (yoor′āt) *n.* a salt of uric acid

ur·ban (ur′bən) *adj.* [L. *urbanus* < *urbs*, a city] 1. of, in, constituting, or comprising a city or town 2. characteristic of the city as distinguished from the country; citified ☆3. in U.S. census use, designating or of an incorporated or unincorporated place with at least 2,500 inhabitants

Ur·ban II (ur′bən) 1042?-99; Pope (1088-99)

urban district in the British Isles, a densely populated community, like a borough but lacking a borough charter

ur·bane (ur bān′) *adj.* [L. *urbanus*: see URBAN] polite and courteous in a smooth, polished way; refined —*SYN.* see SUAVE —**ur·bane′ly** *adv.* —**ur·bane′ness** *n.*

ur·ban·ism (ur′bən iz′m) *n.* 1. *a)* the character of life in the cities; urban life, organization, problems, etc. *b)* the study of this 2. movement of the population to, or concentration of the population in, the cities —**ur′ban·ist** *n., adj.* —**ur′ban·is′tic** *adj.*

ur·ban·ite (-īt′) *n.* a person living in a city

ur·ban·i·ty (ur ban′ə tē) *n., pl.* -**ties** 1. the quality of being urbane 2. [*pl.*] civilities, courtesies, or amenities

ur·ban·ize (ur′bə nīz′) *vt.* -**ized′**, -**iz′ing** 1. to change from rural to urban in character; make like or characteristic of a city 2. [Rare] to make urbane —**ur′ban·i·za′tion** *n.*

ur·ban·ized (-nīzd′) *adj.* 1. made urban in character ☆2. in U.S. census use, designating or of a population area that includes one or more cities and adjoining densely settled urban places, whether incorporated or unincorporated, at least one of the cities having a population of 50,000 or more

ur·ban·ol·o·gist (ur′bə näl′ə jist) *n.* [URBAN + -O- + -LOG(Y) + -IST] a student of, or specialist in, urban problems

☆**urban renewal** rehabilitation of deteriorated or distressed urban areas, as by slum clearance and redevelopment construction in housing and public facilities

☆**urban town** (or **township**) in U.S. census use, a New England town or a New Jersey or Pennsylvania township with no incorporated municipalities as subdivisions and with a population of at least 25,000 or, if less, a density of at least 1,500 persons per square mile

ur·bi·a (ur′bē ə) *n.* cities collectively, as distinguished from suburbs (*suburbia*) and exurbs (*exurbia*)

‡**ur·bi et or·bi** (oor′bē et ôr′bē) [L.] to the city (Rome) and to the world: said of certain special papal blessings

ur·ce·o·late (ur′sē ə lit, -lāt′) *adj.* [ModL. *urceolatus* < L. *urceolus*, dim. of *urceus*, vase] shaped like a vase or urn

ur·chin (ur′chin) *n.* [ME. *irchoun* < OFr. *heriçun* < L. *ericius*, a hedgehog < *er*, hedgehog, for earlier **her* < IE. base **ĝher-*, to bristle, be stiff, whence L. *horrere*, to bristle, Gr. *chēr*, porcupine] 1. orig., a hedgehog 2. *same as* SEA URCHIN 3. a small boy, or any youngster, esp. one who is roguish or mischievous 4. [Obs.] an elf

urd (urd) *n.* [Hindi] a hairy annual bean (*Phaseolus mungo*) of the legume family, with small, black, edible seeds

Ur·du (oor′doo) *n.* [Hindi *urdū*, short for *zabān-i-urdū*, language of the camp < Per. *urdu*, camp < Turk. *ordū*: cf. HORDE] an Indic language, a variant of Hindi written with Arabic characters: an official language of Pakistan

-ure (ər) [Fr. < L. *-ura*] *a suffix meaning:* 1. act or result of being [*exposure*] 2. agent, instrument, or scope of [*legislature*] 3. state of being [*composure*]

u·re·a (yoo rē′ə, yoor′ē ə) *n.* [ModL. < Fr. *urée* < Gr. *ouron*, URINE] a highly soluble, crystalline solid, CO(NH₂)₂, found in the urine and other body fluids of mammals or produced synthetically: used in making plastics, fertilizer, adhesives, etc. —**u·re′al, u·re′ic** *adj.*

u·re·a-form·al·de·hyde resins (-fôr mal′də hīd′) strong, odorless, thermosetting resins formed by condensing urea and formaldehyde in the presence of a catalyst: used in making buttons, tableware, etc.

u·re·ase (yoor′ē ās′, -āz′) *n.* [URE(A) + -ASE] an enzyme that catalyzes the hydrolysis of urea into ammonia and carbon dioxide or ammonium carbonate

u·re·din·i·um (yoor′ə din′ē əm) *n., pl.* -**i·a** (-ə) [ModL. < L. *uredo* (gen. *uredinis*), a blight: see UREDO & -IUM] *Bot.* a pustule, often found on the epidermis of grasses, formed by a rust fungus and consisting of uredospores: also **u·re·di·um** (yoo rē′dē əm) —**u·re·din′i·al** *adj.*

u·re·do (yoo rē′dō) *n.* [ModL. < L., a blight, blast, burning itch < *urere*, to burn < IE. base **eus-*, to burn: cf. EMBER] *same as* URTICARIA

u·re·do·spore (yoo rē′də spôr′) *n.* [L. *uredo* (see prec.) + SPORE] *Bot.* a thin-walled, red, summer spore of a rust fungus, produced usually on the leaves or stems of grasses and capable of reinfecting other grasses of the same species: also **u·re′di·o·spore′** (-dē ə spôr′)

u·re·do·stage (-stāj′) *n.* [L. *uredo* (see UREDO) + STAGE] *Bot.* the stage in which rust fungi develop uredospores

u·re·ide (yoor′ē id′, -id) *n.* [URE(A) + -IDE] any of several compounds derived from urea by the replacement of one or more hydrogen atoms by an acid radical

u·re·mi·a (yoo rē′mē ə, -rēm′yə) *n.* [ModL. < Gr. *ouron*, URINE + *haima*, blood] a toxic condition caused by the presence in the blood of waste products normally eliminated in the urine and resulting from a failure of the kidneys to secrete urine —**u·re′mic** *adj.*

-u·ret [< ModL. *-uretum* (replacing earlier -URE)] *an obsolete suffix meaning* -IDE

u·re·ter (yoo rēt′ər) *n.* [ModL. < Gr. *ourētēr* < *ourein*, to urinate] a duct or tube that carries urine from a kidney to the bladder or cloaca —**u·re·ter′al, u·re·ter′ic** (yoor′ə ter′ik) *adj.*

u·re·ter·o- (yoo rēt′ər ō′, -ə) [< URETER] *a combining form meaning* the ureter [*ureterostomy*]

u·re·ter·os·to·my (yoo rēt′ə räs′tə mē) *n., pl.* -**mies** [prec. + -STOMY] the surgical creation of an artificial opening for the direct discharge of urine from the ureter

u·re·thane (yoor′ə thān′, yoo reth′ān) *n.* [Fr. *uréthane*: see UREA, ETHER, -ANE] 1. a white, crystalline compound, C₂H₇NO₂, produced by the action of ammonia on ethyl carbonate or by heating urea nitrate and ethyl alcohol: it is used as a hypnotic and sedative, a solvent, etc. 2. any ester of carbamic acid Also **u′re·than′** (-than′)

u·re·thra (yoo rē′thrə) *n., pl.* -**thrae** (-thrē), -**thras** [LL. < Gr. *ourēthra* < *ouron*, URINE] the membranous canal through which urine is discharged from the bladder in most mammals: in the male, semen is also discharged through the urethra —**u·re′thral** *adj.*

u·re·thri·tis (yoor′i thrīt′əs) *n.* [ModL.: see URETHRA & -ITIS] inflammation of the urethra

u·re·thro- (yoo rē′thrō, -thrə) [< URETHRA] *a combining form meaning* the urethra [*urethroscope*]: also, before a vowel, **urethr-**

u·re·thro·scope (yoo rē′thrə skōp′) *n.* [prec. + -SCOPE] an instrument for examining the interior of the urethra —**u·re′thro·scop′ic** (-skäp′ik) *adj.*

u·ret·ic (yoo ret′ik) *adj.* [LL. *ureticus* < Gr. *ourētikos*] 1. of the urine; urinary 2. *same as* DIURETIC

U·rey (yoor′ē), **Harold Clay·ton** (klā′t'n) 1893- ; U.S. chemist

Ur·fa (oor fä′) city in SE Turkey, near the Syrian border: pop. 60,000: cf. EDESSA

urge (urj) *vt.* **urged**, **urg′ing** [L. *urgere*, to press hard] 1. *a)* to press upon the attention; present or speak of earnestly and repeatedly; plead, allege, or advocate strongly [to *urge* caution] *b)* to entreat or plead with; ask, persuade, or solicit earnestly; press; exhort 2. to stimulate or incite; provoke 3. to drive or force onward; press forward; impel 4. to ply (oars, etc.) vigorously —*vi.* 1. to make an earnest presentation of arguments, claims, charges, entreaties, etc. 2. to exert a force that drives or impels, as to action —*n.* 1. the act of urging 2. an impulse to do a certain thing; impelling influence or force, esp. an inner drive —**urg′er** *n.*

SYN.—**urge** implies a strong effort to persuade one to do something, as by entreaty, argument, or forceful recommendation [he *urged* us to accept the offer]; **exhort** implies an earnest urging or admonishing to action or conduct considered proper or right [the minister *exhorted* his flock to work for peace]; **press** suggests a continuous, insistent urging that is difficult to resist [we *pressed* him to stay]; **importune** implies persistent efforts to break down resistance against a demand or request, often to the point of being annoying or wearisome [not too proud to *importune* for help]

ur·gen·cy (ur′jən sē) *n., pl.* -**cies** 1. the quality or state of being urgent; need for action, haste, etc.; stress or pressure, as of necessity 2. insistence; importunity 3. something urgent

ur·gent (-jənt) *adj.* [LME. < MFr. < L. *urgens*, prp. of *urgere*, to press hard, urge] 1. calling for haste, immediate action, etc.; grave; pressing 2. insistent; importunate —**ur′gent·ly** *adv.*

-ur·gy (ur′jē) [Gr. *-ourgia* < *-ourgos*, worker < *ergon*, WORK] *a combining form meaning* the science, technique, or process of working with or by means of (something specified) [*crystallurgy, zymurgy*]

U·ri (oo′rē) canton of EC Switzerland: 415 sq. mi.; pop. 33,000

-u·ri·a (yoor′ē ə) [ModL. < Gr. *-ouria* < *ouron*, urine] *a combining form meaning* a (diseased) condition of the urine [*glycosuria, albuminuria*]

U·ri·ah (yoo rī′ə) [Heb. *ūriyāh*, lit., God is light] 1. a masculine name 2. *Bible* a Hittite captain whose beautiful wife, Bathsheba, aroused David's lust: David arranged for Uriah to die in battle and then married Bathsheba: II Sam. 11: in the Douay Bible, **U·ri′as** (-əs)

u·ric (yoor′ik) *adj.* [Fr. *urique* < *urine* + -*ique*, -IC] of, contained in, or derived from urine

uric acid a white, odorless, crystalline substance, $C_5H_4N_4O_3$, found in urine, the excreta of birds and reptiles, etc.: it is slightly soluble in water

u·ri·co- (yoor'i kō, -kə) [< URIC] *a combining form meaning* uric acid [*uricotelic*]: also, before a vowel, **uric-**

u·ri·cos·u·ric (yoor'i kō syoor'ik) *adj.* [URICO- + -s- + URIC] increasing or promoting the urinary excretion of uric acid

u·ri·dine (yoor'ə dēn') *n.* [UR(O)-¹ + -ID(E) + -INE²] a nucleoside, $C_9H_{12}N_2O_6$, formed from uracil and ribose and found in ribonucleic acid

U·ri·el (yoor'ē əl) [Heb. *ūrī'ēl*, lit., light of God] *Bible* one of the archangels

U·rim and Thum·mim (yoor'im 'n thum'im) [Heb. *ūrīm b'tummīm*] certain unidentified objects mentioned in the Bible (cf. Ex. 28:30) as being worn in the breastplate of the high priest

u·ri·nal (yoor'ə n'l) *n.* [ME. < OFr. < LL. < *urinalis*, of urine < *urina*, urine] **1.** a portable receptacle used for urinating, esp. by the bedridden **2.** a place for urinating; specif., a fixture for use by men in urinating, esp. one installed in a men's restroom

☆**u·ri·nal·y·sis** (yoor'ə nal'ə sis) *n.*, *pl.* **-ses** (-sēz') [ModL.] chemical or microscopic analysis of the urine

u·ri·nar·y (yoor'ə ner'ē) *adj.* [< L. *urina*, urine | -ARY] **1.** of or relating to urine **2.** of the organs involved in the secretion and discharge of urine

urinary bladder a saclike structure in many animals, serving for temporary storage of fluid or semifluid excretions, as urine

urinary calculus a calculus in the urinary tract

urinary tubule any of the long, winding tubules of the vertebrate kidney in which urine is formed: also called **uriniferous tubule**

u·ri·nate (yoor'ə nāt') *vi.* **-nat·ed, -nat·ing** [< ML. *urinatus*, pp. of *urinare*] to discharge urine from the body; micturate —*vt.* to discharge as or with the urine —**u'ri·na'tion** *n.* —**u'ri·na'tive** *adj.*

u·rine (yoor'in) *n.* [ME. < OFr. < L. *urina*, urine < IE. **ŭr-*, var. of base **awer-*, to moisten, flow, whence WATER, Gr. *ouron*, urine] a waste product of vertebrates and many invertebrates, secreted by the kidneys or other excretory structures: in mammals, it is a yellowish liquid containing urea, certain salts, etc., which is stored in the bladder and discharged periodically from the body through the urethra; in birds, reptiles, etc., it is a solid or almost solid substance formed chiefly of uric acid

u·ri·nif·er·ous (yoor'ə nif'ər əs) *adj.* conveying urine

u·ri·no- (yoor'ə nō) [< L. *urina*, urine] *a combining form meaning* urine, urinary tract [*urinogenital*]: also, before a vowel, **urin-**

u·ri·no·gen·i·tal (yoor'ə nō jen'ə t'l) *adj.* same as URO-GENITAL

u·ri·nous (yoor'ə nəs) *adj.* [ModL. *urinosus*] of, like, or containing urine: also **u'ri·nose'** (-nōs')

Ur·mi·a (oor'mē ə), **Lake** large saltwater lake in NW Iran: 1,500 to 2,300 sq. mi.

urn (urn) *n.* [ME. < L. *urna*, urn, akin to *urceus*, a jug] **1.** a) a vase, esp. one with a foot or pedestal b) such a vase used to hold the ashes of a cremated body **2.** a large metal container with a faucet, used for making or serving hot coffee, tea, etc. **3.** *Bot.* the part of a moss capsule that bears the spores

u·ro-¹ (yoor'ō, -ə) [< Gr. *ouron*, URINE] *a combining form meaning* urine, urination, urinary tract [*urolith*]: also, before a vowel, **ur-**

u·ro-² (yoor'ō, -ə) [< Gr. *oura*, tail < IE. *orsos, var. of base **ers-*, the buttocks, tail, whence ARSE] *a combining form meaning* tail [*uropod*]: also, before a vowel, **ur-**

u·ro·chord (yoor'ə kôrd') *n.* [prec. + CHORD¹] **1.** same as TUNICATE **2.** *Zool.* the notochord when confined to the tail region in larval, and sometimes adult, tunicates —**u'ro·chor'dal** *adj.*

u·ro·chrome (-krōm') *n.* [URO-¹ + CHROME] the pigment that gives urine its characteristic yellow color

u·ro·dele (-dēl') *n.* [Fr. *urodèle* < ModL. *Urodela* < *uro-* (see URO-²) + Gr. *-dēlos*, visible < IE. base **dei-*, to shine, whence L. *dies*, day, OE. *tætan*, to cheer] any of a subclass (Caudata) of amphibians, including salamanders, newts, etc., that retain the tail throughout life

u·ro·gen·i·tal (yoor'ō jen'ə t'l) *adj.* designating or of the urinary and genital organs; genitourinary

u·rog·e·nous (yoo rāj'ə nəs) *adj.* [URO-¹ + -GENOUS] **1.** producing urine **2.** contained in or obtained from urine

☆**u·ro·ki·nase** (yoor'ō ki nās, -kin'ās) *n.* [URO-¹ + KINASE] an enzyme found as a trace in human urine, used for dissolving blood clots

u·ro·lith (yoor'ō lith) *n.* [URO-¹ + -LITH] same as URINARY CALCULUS —**u'ro·lith'ic** *adj.*

u·rol·o·gy (yoo räl'ə jē) *n.* [URO-¹ + -LOGY] the branch of medicine dealing with the urogenital or urinary system and its diseases —**u·ro·log·ic** (yoor'ə läj'ik), **u'ro·log'i·cal** *adj.* —**u·rol'o·gist** *n.*

u·ro·pod (yoor'ə päd') *n.* [URO-² + -POD] an appendage of the last abdominal segment in certain crustaceans, as

either of the pair in the tailfan of the lobster, shrimp, etc.

uropygial gland a large gland located at the base of the tail in most birds, that secretes an oil used in preening

u·ro·pyg·i·um (yoor'ə pij'ē əm) *n.*, *pl.* **-i·a** (-ə), **-i·ums** [ModL. < Gr. *ouropygion*, altered (after *oura*, tail: see URO-²) < *orrhopygion* < *orrhos*, end of the os sacrum + *pygē*, rump] the hump at the rear extremity of a bird's body, from which the tail feathers grow —**u'ro·pyg'i·al** *adj.*

u·ros·co·py (yoo räs'kə pē) *n.*, *pl.* **-pies** [URO-¹ + -SCOPY] examination of the urine, as for the diagnosis of disease —**u·ro·scop·ic** (yoor'ə skäp'ik) *adj.*

Ur·quhart (ur'kart, -kärt), **Sir Thomas** 1611?-60?; Scot. writer & translator

Ursa Major [L., lit., Great Bear] the most conspicuous constellation in the northern sky: it contains fifty-three visible stars, seven of which form the Big Dipper

Ursa Minor [L., lit., Little Bear] the northernmost constellation: it contains twenty-three visible stars, including those forming the Little Dipper: the most important of these is the North Star at the end of the handle

ur·si·form (ur'sə fôrm') *adj.* [< L. *ursus*, a bear + -FORM] having the form or appearance of a bear

ur·sine (ur'sīn, -sin) *adj.* [L. *ursinus* < *ursus*, a bear, akin to Gr. *arktos*, a bear] of, like, or characteristic of a bear or the bear family; bearlike

‡**Ur·spra·che** (oor'shprä'khə) *n.* [G. < *ur-*, original + *sprache*, language] a reconstructed, hypothetical parent language, as proto-Germanic

Ur·su·la (ur'sə lə) [ModL., dim. of L. *ursa*, she-bear] **1.** a feminine name **2.** Saint, a legendary Christian Brit. princess said to have been killed in the 4th cent. along with 11,000 virgins, by the Huns at Cologne

Ur·su·line (-lin, -līn') *n.* [ModL. *Ursulina*: after Saint URSULA] *R.C.Ch.* any member of a teaching order of nuns founded c.1537 —*adj.* of this order

ur·ti·car·i·a (ur'tə ker'ē ə) *n.* [ModL. < L. *urtica*, a nettle] a skin condition characterized by itching, burning, stinging, and the formation of smooth patches, or wheals, usually red —**ur'ti·car'i·al** *adj.*

ur·ti·cate (ur'tə kāt') *vt.*, *vi.* **-cat·ed, -cat·ing** [< ML. *urticatus*, pp. of *urticare*, to sting < L. *urtica*, a nettle] to sting with or as with nettles

ur·ti·ca·tion (ur'tə kā'shən) *n.* [ML. *urticatio*] *Med.* **1.** formerly, the flogging of a paralyzed limb, etc. with nettles for the stimulating effect produced **2.** any sensation of stinging or itching **3.** the formation of urticarial wheals

U·ru·guay (yoor'ə gwā', -gwī'; *Sp.* ōō'rōō gwī') **1.** country in SE S. America, on the Atlantic: 72,171 sq. mi.; pop. 2,818,000; cap. Montevideo **2.** river in SE S. America flowing from S Brazil into the Río de la Plata: c.1,000 mi. —**U'ru·guay'an** *adj.*, *n.*

U·rum·chi (ōō rōōm'chē) city in NW China; capital of Sinkiang region: pop. c.400,000

U·run·di (oo roon'dē) the S portion of the former Ruanda-Urundi that is now Burundi

u·rus (yoor'əs) *n.* [L. < Gmc. name, as in OE. & OHG. *ur*: see AUROCHS] an extinct, shaggy, long-horned wild ox (*Bos primigenius*), formerly common in Europe and thought to be an ancestor of modern domestic cattle

u·ru·shi·ol (ōō'rōō shē ôl', oo rōō'-; -ōl') *n.* [Jap. *urushi*, lacquer + -OL¹] a poisonous, irritant liquid, $C_{21}H_{32}O_2$, present in poison ivy and the Japanese lac tree

us (us) *pron.* [ME. *us*, *ous* (acc. & dat. of *we*: see WE) < OE. *us*, dat., but also used, beside *usic*, as acc., akin to G. *uns* < IE. base **ns-* < **nes-*, **nos-*, pl. of **ne-*, **no-*, we, whence L. *nos*, we] *objective case of* WE: also used colloquially as a predicate complement with a linking verb (Ex.: that's *us*)

U.S. 1. United Service **2.** United States: also **US**

u.s. 1. [L. *ut supra*] as above **2.** [L. *ubi supra*] where (mentioned) above

USA, U.S.A. 1. United States of America **2.** United States Army

us·a·ble (yōō'zə b'l) *adj.* that can be used; fit, convenient, or available for use —**us'a·bil'i·ty** (-bil'ə tē), **us'a·ble·ness** *n.* —**us'a·bly** *adv.*

USAF, U.S.A.F. United States Air Force

USAFI United States Armed Forces Institute

us·age (yōō'sij, -zij) *n.* [ME. < OFr. < ML. *usagium* < L. *usus*: see USE] **1.** the act, way, or extent of using or treating; treatment; use **2.** long-continued or established practice; habitual or customary use or way of acting; custom; habit **3.** the way in which a word, phrase, etc. is used to express a particular idea; customary manner of using the words of a given language in speaking or writing, or an instance of this —*SYN.* see HABIT

us·ance (yōō'z'ns) *n.* [ME. < MFr. < *usant*, prp. of *user*: see USE] **1.** income or other benefits derived from wealth or the use of wealth **2.** the time allowed for the payment of a foreign bill of exchange, as established by custom **3.** [Obs.] same as: a) USE b) USAGE c) USURY

USCG, U.S.C.G. United States Coast Guard

USDA United States Department of Agriculture

use (yōōz; *for n.* yōōs) *vt.* **used** (yōōzd; *for vt.* 6 & *vi.* 1, *with the following "to,"* yōōs'tə or yōōs'too), **us'ing** [ME.

usen < OFr. *user* < VL. **usare* < L. *usus*, pp. of *uti*, to use] **1.** to put or bring into action or service; employ for or apply to a given purpose **2.** to practice; exercise [to *use* one's judgment] **3.** to act or behave toward; treat [to *use* a friend badly] **4.** to consume, expend, or exhaust by use (often with *up*) [to *use* up one's energy] **5.** *a)* to smoke or chew (tobacco) *b)* to take or consume habitually [to *use* drugs] **6.** to make familiar; accustom (used in the passive with *to*) [to become *used* to certain ways] **7.** to exploit or treat (a person) as a means to some selfish end —*vi.* **1.** to be accustomed; be wont (now only in the past tense, with an infinitive, meaning "did at one time") [he *used* to live in Iowa] **2.** [Archaic or Dial.] to frequent; resort —*n.* [ME. & OFr. *us* < L. *usus*] **1.** the act of using or the state of being used **2.** the power or ability to use [to regain the *use* of an injured hand] **3.** the right or permission to use [to grant a neighbor the *use* of one's car] **4.** the need, opportunity, or occasion to use [no further *use* for his services] **5.** an instance or way of using **6.** the quality that makes a thing useful or suitable for a given purpose; advantage; usefulness; worth; utility **7.** the object, end, or purpose for which something is used **8.** function, service, or benefit **9.** constant, continued, customary, or habitual employment, practice, or exercise, or an instance of this; custom; habit; practice; wont **10.** the particular form of ritual or liturgy practiced in a given church, diocese, etc. [the Lutheran *use*] **11.** *Law a)* the enjoyment of property, as from occupying, employing, or exercising it *b)* [influenced by OFr. *ues*, gain < L. *opus*, a work] profit, benefit, or advantage, esp. that of lands and tenements held in trust by another —**have no use for 1.** to have no need of **2.** to have no wish to deal with; be impatient with ☆**3.** to have no affection or respect for; dislike strongly —**in use** in the process of being used —**make use of** to use; have occasion to use —**put to use** to use; find a use for —*SYN.*—**use** implies the putting of a thing (or, usually in an opprobrious sense, a person regarded as a passive thing) to a given purpose so as to accomplish an end [to *use* a pencil, a suggestion, etc., he *used* his brother to advance himself]; **employ**, a somewhat more elevated term, implies the putting to useful work of something not in use at that moment [to *employ* a vacant lot as a playground] and, with reference to persons, suggests a providing of work and pay [he *employs* five mechanics]; **utilize** implies the putting of something to a practical or profitable use [to *utilize* byproducts].

use·a·ble (yōō′zə b'l) *adj. same as* USABLE —**use′a·bil′i·ty** (-bil′ə tē), **use′a·ble·ness** *n.* —**use′a·bly** *adv.*

used (yōōzd: *see note at* USE) *pt. & pp. of* USE —*adj.* **1.** that has been used **2.** *same as* SECOND-HAND

use·ful (yōōs′fəl) *adj.* that can be used to advantage; serviceable; helpful; beneficial; often, having practical utility —**use′ful·ly** *adv.* —**use′ful·ness** *n.*

use·less (-lis) *adj.* **1.** having no use; unserviceable; worthless **2.** to no purpose; ineffectual; of no avail —*SYN.* see FUTILE —**use′less·ly** *adv.* —**use′less·ness** *n.*

us·er (yōō′zər) *n.* [sense 1 < US(E) + -ER; in sense 2 a substantive use of OFr. *user*, to use] **1.** a person or thing that uses; specif., ☆a person who uses drugs; addict **2.** *Law a)* the exercise of a right of use (see USE, *n.* 11 *a*) *b)* a right of use, based on long use

USES United States Employment Service

USGS, U.S.G.S. United States Geological Survey

U-shaped (yōō′shāpt′) *adj.* having the shape of a U

U·shas (ōō′shäs) [Sans. *Uṣas*, dawn] the Hindu, or Vedic, goddess of the dawn

ush·er (ush′ər) *n.* [ME. *ussher* < OFr. *uissier* < L. *ostiarius*, doorkeeper: see OSTIARY] **1.** an official doorkeeper **2.** a person whose duty it is to show people to their seats in a theater, church, etc. **3.** a person whose official duty is to precede someone of rank, as in a procession **4.** any of the groom's attendants at a wedding, accompanying the bridesmaids **5.** [Obs.] in Great Britain, an assistant teacher in a boys' school —*vt.* **1.** to act as an usher to; escort or conduct (others) to seats, etc. **2.** to precede, or be a forerunner of (often with *in*)

☆**ush·er·ette** (ush′ə ret′) *n.* a woman or girl usher, as in a theater

USIA, U.S.I.A. United States Information Agency

USIS, U.S.I.S. United States Information Service

Usk (usk) river flowing from S Wales through Monmouth-shire into the Severn estuary: 60 mi.

Üs·kü·dar (üs′kü där′) section of Istanbul, Turkey, on the Asian side of the Bosporus

U.S.M., USM **1.** United States Mail **2.** United States Mint

USMC, U.S.M.C. **1.** United States Marine Corps **2.** United States Maritime Commission

USN, U.S.N. United States Navy

USNG, U.S.N.G. United States National Guard

USO, U.S.O. United Service Organizations

U.S.P., U.S. Pharm. United States Pharmacopoeia

Us·pal·la·ta Pass (ōōs′pä yä′tä) mountain pass in the Andes, on the Chile-Argentina border: c.12,650 ft. high

U.S.P.H.S., USPHS United States Public Health Service

U.S.P.O., USPO United States Post Office

us·que·baugh (us′kwi bô′, -bä′) *n.* [IrGael. *uisce beathadh*: see WHISKEY] [Ir. & Scot.] *same as* WHISKEY

U.S.S. **1.** United States Senate **2.** United States Service **3.** United States Ship, Steamer, or Steamship

Ussh·er (ush′ər), **James** 1581–1656; Ir. archbishop & theologian

U.S.S.R., USSR Union of Soviet Socialist Republics

Us·su·ri (ōō sōō′rē) river in SE R.S.F.S.R., flowing north along the Manchurian border into the Amur River: 365 mi. (incl. principal headstream, 540 mi.)

us·tu·late (us′choo lit, -lāt′) *adj.* [L. *ustulatus*, pp. of *ustulare*: see ff.] discolored or blackened, as if scorched

us·tu·la·tion (us′choo lā′shən) *n.* [ML. *ustulatio* < L. *ustulare*, to scorch < base of *urere*, to burn < IE. base **eus-*, to burn: cf. EMBER¹] the act of burning, scorching, or searing

u·su·al (yōō′zhoo wəl, -zhwəl, -zhəl) *adj.* [ME. < MFr. < LL. *usualis* < L. *usus*: see USE] such as is in common or ordinary use; such as is most often seen, heard, used, etc.; common; ordinary; customary —**as usual** as is or was customary; in the usual way —**u′su·al·ly** *adv.* —**u′su·al·ness** *n.*

SYN.—**usual** applies to that which past experience has shown to be the normal, common, hence expected thing [the *usual* results, price, answer, etc.]; **customary** refers to that which accords with the usual practices of some individual or with the prevailing customs of some group [his *customary* mid-morning coffee, it was *customary* to dress for dinner]; **habitual** implies a fixed practice as the result of habit [her *habitual* tardiness]; **wonted** is a somewhat literary equivalent for **customary** or **habitual** [according to their *wonted* manner]; **accustomed** is equivalent to **customary** but suggests less strongly a settled custom [he sat in his *accustomed* place]. See also NORMAL. —*ANT.* extraordinary, unusual

u·su·fruct (yōō′zyoo frukt′, -zoo-, -syoo-, -soo-) *n.* [LL. *usufructus* < L. *usus*, a USE + *fructus*, enjoyment, FRUIT] *Roman & Civil Law* the right of using and enjoying all the advantages and profits of the property of another without altering or damaging the substance

u·su·fruc·tu·ar·y (yōō′zyoo fruk′choo wer′ē, -zoo-, -syoo-, -soo-) *n.*, *pl.* **-ar′ies** [LL. *usufructuarius*] a person or agent having the usufruct of property —*adj.* of, or having the nature of, a usufruct

u·su·rer (yōō′zhoo rər) *n.* [ME. < MFr. *usurier* < ML. *usurarius*, usurer < L. *usura*: see USURY] a person who lends money at interest, now specif., at a rate of interest that is excessive or unlawfully high

u·su·ri·ous (yōō zhoor′ē əs) *adj.* **1.** practicing usury **2.** of or constituting usury —**u·su′ri·ous·ly** *adv.* —**u·su′ri·ous·ness** *n.*

u·surp (yōō surp′, -zurp′) *vt.* [ME. *usurpen* < MFr. *usurper* < L. *usurpare* < *usus*, a USE + *rapere*, to seize: see RAPE¹] to take or assume (power, a position, property, rights, etc.) and hold in possession by force or without right —*vi.* to practice or commit usurpation (*on* or *upon*) —**u·surp′er** *n.* —**u·surp′ing·ly** *adv.*

u·sur·pa·tion (yōō′sər pā′shən, -zər-) *n.* [ME. *usurpacion* < L. *usurpatio*] the act of usurping; esp., the unlawful or violent seizure of a throne, power, etc.

u·su·ry (yōō′zhoo rē) *n.*, *pl.* **-ries** [ME. *usurie* < ML. *usuria* < L. *usura* < *usus*: see USE] **1.** the act or practice of lending money at interest, now specif., at a rate of interest that is excessive or unlawfully high **2.** interest at such a high rate

usw, u.s.w. [G. *und so weiter*] and so forth

ut (ut, ōōt) *n.* [ME. < ML.: see GAMUT] *Music* a syllable formerly used in solmization: now replaced by *do*

U·tah (yōō′tô, -tä) [< Sp. *Yutta* < tribal name, lit. ? hill dwellers] Mountain State of the W U.S.: admitted, 1896; 84,916 sq. mi.; pop. 1,059,000; cap. Salt Lake City: abbrev. Ut., UT —**U′tah·an** *adj.*, *n.*

ut dict. [L. *ut dictum*] as directed

Ute (yōōt, yōōt′ē) *n.* [akin to UTAH] **1.** *pl.* Utes, Ute any member of a tribe of nomadic Shoshonean Indians that lived in Colorado and Utah, ranging down into New Mexico and Arizona **2.** their Shoshonean language

u·ten·sil (yōō ten′s'l) *n.* [ME. *utensele* < MFr. *utensile* < L. *utensilia*, materials, utensils < neut. pl. of *utensilis*, fit for use < *uti*, to use] **1.** any implement or container ordinarily used as in a kitchen [cooking *utensils*] **2.** an implement or tool, as for use in farming, etc. —*SYN.* see IMPLEMENT

u·ter·ine (yōō′tər in, -tə rīn′) *adj.* [ME. < LL. *uterinus*] **1.** of the uterus **2.** having the same mother but a different father [uterine sisters]

u·ter·o- (yōōt′ə rō′) [< ff.] *a combining form meaning:* **1.** the uterus **2.** the uterus and

u·ter·us (yōōt′ər əs) *n.*, *pl.* **u′ter·i′** (-ī′) [L.] **1.** a hollow, muscular organ of female mammals in which the ovum is deposited and the embryo and fetus are developed; womb: it is usually paired, but is single in man and other primates **2.** a similar structure in many invertebrates

U Thant *see* THANT

U·ther (yōō′thər) a legendary king of Britain, father of King Arthur

U·ti·ca (yōō′ti kə) **1.** [after ff.] city in C N.Y., on the Mohawk River: pop. 92,000 **2.** city of ancient times in N Africa, just north of modern Tunis

u·tile (yōōt′'l) *adj.* [LME. < MFr. < L. *utilis* < *uti*, to use] [Obs.] *same as* USEFUL

u·ti·lise (yōōt′'l īz′) *vt.* -ised′, -is′ing *Brit. sp.* of UTILIZE

u·til·i·tar·i·an (yoo til′ə ter′ē ən) *adj.* [UTILIT(Y) + -ARIAN: coined by J. Bentham] **1.** of or having to do with utility **2.** stressing usefulness over beauty or other considerations **3.** made for or aiming at utility **4.** of, or having belief in, utilitarianism —*n.* a person who believes in utilitarianism

also, and for adj. & v. usually,
-u·a (-yoo wə) [L., with nothing at all in it;
space with an enclosed space, as that
2. a) an enclosed space of the air or gas
of which most of the degree to which
pumping b) the degree to which
ght below atmospheric pressure
the removal or absence of some-
it; void: often used figuratively
M CLEANER —adj. 1. of a vacuum
m 3. having a vacuum; partially
d of air or gas 4. working by
of a partial vacuum —vt., vi. to
aner: in full vac'u·um-clean'
or jug] same as THERMOS
chine for cleaning carpets, floors,
ion: also vacuum sweeper
ument for measuring the pressure
artial vacuum
kt') adj. packed in an airtight const of the air was exhausted before
ain freshness
ump used to draw air or gas out of
as PULSOMETER (sense 1)
tron tube from which the air has
highest possible degree, containing
ed as an amplifier, rectifier, etc.
same as VACUUM TUBE
mē'kam, vä'-) [L., lit., go with me]
out by a person for constant use,
andbook or manual

[< L. vadosus, shallow < vadum, a
akin to vadere, to go: for IE. base see
of water lying in the zone of aeration
surface and the water table
capital of Liechtenstein: pop. 3,900
häud') adj. [ME. < MFr. < L. vaga-
ng about < vagari, to wander < vagus:
ing from place to place, with no fixed
2. living an unsettled, drifting, or
agrant 3. shiftless; worthless; good-for-
haracteristic of a wandering, shiftless,
ay of life 5. aimlessly following an
path; drifting —n. 1. a person who
ce to place, having no fixed abode
le, disreputable, or shiftless person —vi.
see VAGRANT —vag'a·bond'ish adj.
-ij) n. [Fr.: see prec. & -AGE] 1. the
of being a vagabond; vagrant way of
2. vagabonds collectively
[VAG(US) + -AL] of or having to do with

ger'ē əs, -gar'-) adj. 1. full of or charac-
ries; capricious 2. wandering; roaming
, -gar'-; və'gər ē) n., pl. -gar'ies [earlier
wander < L. vagari, to wander < vagus:
n odd, eccentric, or unexpected action or
2. an odd, whimsical, or freakish idea or
caprice —SYN. see CAPRICE
ə) n., pl. -nas, -nae (-nē) [L., a sheath]
a sheath or sheathlike structure; specif.,
mals, the canal leading from the vulva to
ot, the sheath formed by the base of certain
envelops a stem
n'l, və ji'n'l) adj. Anat. Zool. 1. of or like
or for the vagina of a female mammal
'o nit·'nat') adj. [ModL. vaginatus] 1. hav-
sheath; sheathed 2. like a sheath
aj'ə nit'əs) n. [ModL.: see VAGINA & -ITIS]
of the vagina; colpitis
ə nō', -nə) [< L. vagina] 2. vagina and Also,
vagina [vaginitis]
, vagin- [< VAGUS] a combining form meaning vagus

.or (vā'gō di pres'ər) adj. depressing the
ctivity —n. a vagodepressor drug
(vā gät'ə mē) n., pl. -mies [VAGO- + -TOMY]
cutting of the vagus nerve, as to relieve
by reducing the flow of gastric juice
(vā'gə tō'nē ə) n. [ModL.: see VAGO-, TONE,
order: resulting from overstimulation of the
causing a slowing of the heart rate, fainting,
ton'ic (-tän'ik) adj.
on, the vagus nerve [VAGO- + -TROPIC] affecting,
(və'grən sē) n., pl. -cies [< ff.] 1. a wandering
or talk; digression 2. a wandering from place
vagabondage 3. shiftless or idle wandering
oney or work, as of tramps, beggars, etc.: often
offense chargeable as a misdemeanor
vä'grənt) n. [ME. vagraunt, prob. < Anglo-Fr.
alcrant < OFr. walcrer, to wander < Frank.
WALK'] < infl. prob. by L. vagari, to wander]
n who wanders from place to place or lives a
life; rover 2. a person who wanders from place
without a regular job, supporting himself by
etc.; idle wanderer; vagabond 3. Law a tramp,
prostitute, or similar idle or disorderly person

t'ər) vt. [ME. uttren < utter, outward (see prec.)]
o give out; put forth: now used only of the passing
erfeit money or forged checks 2. to pronounce,
express audibly (words, thoughts, vocal sounds,
to express in any way 4. to emit (nonvocal
s if speaking 5. to make known; divulge; reveal
o publish (a book, etc.) 7. [Obs.] to sell (goods,
ter·a·ble adj. —ut'ter·er n.
r implies the communication of an idea or feeling by
cal sounds, such as words, exclamations, etc. [he
n of relief]; express, the broadest of these terms,
vealing of ideas, feelings, one's personality, etc. by
ch, action, or creative work [to express oneself in
suggests expression through words, either spoken or
g one's opinions in letters to the editor]; broach
tterance or mention of an idea to someone for the
broach the subject to him at dinner]; enunciate
nouncement or open attestation of some idea [to
ry, doctrine, etc.]
ut'ər əns, ut'rəns) n. [ME.: see prec. &
ct of uttering, or expressing by voice 2. the
of speaking 3. that which is uttered; esp., a
ttered, whether written or spoken
t'ər əns, ut'rəns) n. [ME., altered (after
. outrance: see OUTRANCE] [Obs.] the ut-
tremity; i.e., death
ər mōst') adj., n. same as UTMOST
') n. a turning completely around, esp.
n the width of a street or road, so as to
ite direction

ä'rôf it') n. [G. uwarowit, after S. S.
5), Russ. statesman and author] an
et, Ca₃Cr₂(SiO₄)₃, containing chromium
[ML. < L. uva, a grape (see UVULA)]
y, and choroid, together forming the
ascular layer of the eye —u've·al adj.
Nicholas same as Nicholas UDALL
əs) n. [ModL.: see UVEA & -ITIS]
uvea —u've·it'ic (it'ik) adj.
., pl. -las, -lae (-lē') [ML., dim. of
E. base *el-, reddish,
iw, YEW] the small,
down from the middle
he back of the tongue
L. uvularis] 1. of or
e uvula 2. Phonet.
ration of the uvula,
tongue near or in
—n. Phonet. a uvular

UVULA

y in Middlesex, SE England:
5,000
Mayan city in the N Yucatán

zôr'-) adj. [< L. uxorius (see
fitting, or characteristic of a

L. uxor, wife (see ff.) + -CIDE]
her husband 2. a man who

uxorius < uxor, wife < ? IE.
ox] dotingly or irrationally
s wife —ux·o'ri·ous·ly adv.
member of a Turkic people
zbek S.S.R. 2. the Turkic
Uz'beg (-beg)
lic republic of the U.S.S.R.,
hen S.S.R. & the Tadzhik
0,600,000; cap. Tashkent:
än')

tted) —adj. 1. of V
st if J is omitted) in

a Roman numeral
. Chem. vanadium

tory 4. volt(s)

h, leisure; ŋ, ring;
, Fr. mon; ö, Fr. coq;
gn; *hypothetical; <derived from

V. 1. Venerable 2. Vicar 3. Vice 4. Viscount
v. 1. [L. *vice*] in the place of 2. [G. *von*] of 3. [L. *vide*] see
4. valve 5. ventral 6. verb 7. *pl.* **vv.** verse 8. version
9. verso 10. versus 11. village ☆12. *pl.* **vv.** violin ☆13. vise
14. vocative 15. voice 16. volt 17. voltage 18. volume
VA, V.A. Veterans' Administration
Va. Virginia
V.A. 1. Vicar Apostolic 2. Vice Admiral
Vaal (väl) river in South Africa, flowing from SE Transvaal
into the Orange River in N Cape Province: c.700 mi.
va·can·cy (vā′kən sē) *n.*, *pl.* **-cies** [L. *vacantia* < *vacans*]
1. the state of being vacant, or empty; emptiness 2. *a)*
empty space *b)* a vacant space; gap, blank, opening, etc.
3. the state of being empty in mind; lack of intelligence,
interest, or thought; vacuity 4. [Now Rare] the state of
being free from work, activity, etc.; idleness 5. an unoccupied position or office; unfilled post, situation, or job
6. untenanted quarters, as in a hotel 7. *Physics* a lattice
defect in a crystal due to a displaced or missing ion or atom
va·cant (vā′kənt) *adj.* [ME. < OFr. < L. *vacans*, prp. of
vacare, to be empty] 1. having nothing in it, as a space;
devoid of contents; empty; void 2. not held, filled, or
occupied, as a position or office 3. having no occupant [a
vacant seat] 4. untenanted, as a room or house 5. not filled
with activity or work; free; leisure [*vacant* time] 6. *a)* having or showing emptiness of mind or lack of intelligence,
interest, thought, etc. *b)* empty of thought: said of the
mind 7. *Law a)* unoccupied or unused, as land *b)* having
no claimant, as an estate or succession *c)* not yet granted,
as public lands —*SYN.* see EMPTY —**va′cant·ly** *adv.*
—**va′cant·ness** *n.*
va·cate (-kāt) *vt.* **-cat·ed, -cat·ing** [< L. *vacatus*, pp. of
vacare, to be empty] 1. to make vacant; specif., *a)* to
cause (an office, position, etc.) to be unfilled or unoccupied,
as by resignation *b)* to leave (a house, room, etc.) uninhabited or untenanted; give up the occupancy of 2. *Law*
to make void; annul —*vi.* 1. to make an office, position,
place, etc. vacant ☆2. [back-formation < ff.] [Colloq.] to
spend a vacation
va·ca·tion (və kā′shən, vā-) *n.* [ME. *vacacion* < MFr. <
L. *vacatio*] 1. freedom from any activity; rest; respite;
intermission ☆2. a period of rest and freedom from work,
study, etc.; time of recreation, usually a specific interval
in a year 3. [Rare] the act of making vacant 4. *Law* a
formal recess between terms of a court —*vi.* 1. to take a
vacation 2. to spend one's vacation [to *vacation* in Maine]
☆**va·ca·tion·er** (-ər) *n.* a person taking a vacation, esp.
one who is traveling or at a resort: also **va·ca′tion·ist**
va·ca·tion·land (-land′) *n.* an area attractive to vacationers because of recreational facilities, historic sights, etc.
vac·ci·nal (vak′sə n'l) *adj.* of vaccine or vaccination
vac·ci·nate (vak′sə nāt′) *vt.* **-nat′ed, -nat′ing** [VACCIN(E)
+ -ATE¹] to inoculate with a specific vaccine in order to
prevent disease; specif., to inoculate with cowpox vaccine
in order to immunize against smallpox —*vi.* to practice
vaccination —**vac′ci·na′tor** *n.*
vac·ci·na·tion (vak′sə nā′shən) *n.* 1. the act or practice
of vaccinating 2. the scar on the skin where the vaccine
has been applied
vac·cine (vak sēn′; vak′sēn, -sin) *n.* [L. *vaccinus* < *vacca*,
a cow] 1. orig., lymph, or a preparation of this, from a
cowpox vesicle, containing the causative virus and used
in vaccination against cowpox or smallpox 2. any preparation of killed microorganisms, living weakened organisms,
etc. introduced into the body to produce immunity to a
specific disease by causing the formation of antibodies
—*adj.* [Rare] of cowpox or vaccination
vac·cin·i·a (vak sin′ē ə) *n.* [ModL. < *vaccinus*: see prec.]
same as COWPOX —**vac·cin′i·al** *adj.*
vac·il·lant (vas′ə lənt) *adj.* vacillating; wavering
vac·il·late (-lāt′) *vi.* **-lat′ed, -lat′ing** [< L. *vacillatus*, pp.
of *vacillare*, to sway to and fro, waver < IE. *wek-*, to be
bent, prob. < base *wā-*, to bend apart, turn, whence L.
varus, bent, diverse] 1. to sway to and fro; waver; totter;
stagger 2. to fluctuate or oscillate 3. to waver in mind;
show indecision —*SYN.* see HESITATE —**vac′il·la′tion** *n.*
—**vac′il·la′tor** *n.* —**vac′il·la·to′ry** (-lə tôr′ē) *adj.*
vac·il·lat·ing (-lāt′iŋ) *adj.* wavering or tending to waver
in motion, opinion, etc. —**vac′il·lat′ing·ly** *adv.*
vac·u·a (vak′yoo wə) *n. alt. pl.* of VACUUM
vac·u·i·ty (va kyōō′ə tē) *n.*, *pl.* **-ties** [L. *vacuitas* < *vacuus*,
empty] 1. the quality or state of being empty; emptiness
2. an empty space; void or vacuum 3. emptiness of mind;
lack of intelligence, interest, or thought 4. an inane or
senseless thing, remark, or quality; inanity
vac·u·o·late (vak′yoo wə lāt′, -lit) *adj.* having a vacuole
or vacuoles: also **vac′u·o·lat′ed**
vac·u·o·la·tion (vak′yoo wə lā′shən) *n.* the formation or
arrangement of vacuoles
vac·u·ole (vak′yoo wōl′) *n.* [Fr. < L. *vacuus*, empty]
Biol. a relatively clear, fluid-filled cavity within the plasma
membrane of a cell, believed to have the function of
discharging excess water or wastes —**vac′u·o·lar** (-wə lər,
vak′yoo wō′lər) *adj.*
vac·u·ous (-wəs) *adj.* [L. *vacuus*] 1. empty of matter
2. having or showing lack of intelligence, interest, or
thought; stupid; senseless; inane 3. characterized by lack
of purpose, of profitable employment, etc.; idle —*SYN.*
see EMPTY —**vac′u·ous·ly** *adv.* —**vac′u·ous·ness** *n.*

vac·u·um (vak′yoo wəm;
vak′yoom) *n.*, *pl.* **-u·ums**
of *vacuus*, empty] 1. a
completely empty space
inside a vacuum tube, ou
has been taken, as by p
pressure has been brou
3. a space left empty by
thing usually found in
☆4. *clipped form of* VACUU
2. used to make a vacuu
or completely exhauste
suction or the creation
clean with a vacuum cle
vacuum bottle (or **flas**
vacuum cleaner a ma
upholstery, etc. by suc
vacuum gauge an inst
of the air or gas in a p
☆**vacuum-packed** (-pa
tainer from which mo
sealing, so as to maint
vacuum pump 1. a p
sealed space 2. *same*
vacuum tube an ele
been evacuated to the
one or more grids, us
vacuum valve [Brit.]
va·de me·cum (vā′d
something carried a
reference, etc., as a h
va·dose (vā′dōs) *adj.*
shallow place, ford,
WADE] designating
between the earth's
Va·duz (vä′doots)
vag·a·bond (vag′ə
bundus, *adj.*, strolli
see VAGUE] 1. mov
abode; wandering
irresponsible life; v
nothing 4. of or c
or irresponsible w
irregular course o
wanders from pla
2. a tramp 3. an i
to wander —*SYN*
vag·a·bond·age (
state or condition
life: also **vag′a·b**
va·gal (vā′g′l) *adj*
the vagus nerve
va·gar·i·ous (və
terized by vaga
va·gar·y (və ger′
used as a *v.*, to
see VAGUE] 1. a
bit of conduct
notion; oddity;
va·gi·na (və jī′n
1. *Anat.*, *Zool.*
in female mam
the uterus 2. *B*
leaves where it
vag·i·nal (vaj′ə
a sheath 2. of
vag·i·nate (vaj
ing a vagina o
vag·i·ni·tis (v
inflammation
vag·i·no- (vaj
meaning: 1.
before a vowe
va·go- (vā′gō
(nerve) [*vago*
va·go·de·pres
vagus nerve
va·got·o·my
the surgical
peptic ulcer
va·go·to·ni
& -IA] a dis
vagus nerve
etc. —**va′go**
va·go·trop
or acting u
va·gran·cy
in thought
to place;
without m
a statutory
va·grant (
wacrant, *w*
walken (
1. a pers
wandering
to place;
begging,
beggar,

whose way of living makes him liable to be arrested and jailed —*adj.* **1.** wandering from place to place or living a wandering life; roaming; nomadic **2.** living the life of a vagabond or tramp **3.** of or characteristic of a vagrant **4.** characterized by straggling growth: said of plants **5.** following no fixed direction, course, or pattern; random, wayward, fleeting, erratic, etc. **—va′grant·ly** *adv.*
SYN.—vagrant refers to a person without a fixed home who wanders about from place to place, supporting himself by begging, etc., and in legal usage, implies such a person regarded as a public nuisance, subject to arrest; **vagabond** orig. implying shiftlessness, rascality, etc., now often connotes no more than a carefree, roaming existence; **bum, tramp,** and **hobo** are informal equivalents for the preceding, variously discriminated, but **bum** always connotes an idle, dissolute, often alcoholic person who never works, **tramp** connotes a vagrant, whether he lives by begging or by doing odd jobs, and **hobo** is now most commonly restricted to a migratory laborer who follows seasonal work, etc. See also ITINERANT
va·grom (vā′grəm) *adj.* archaic var. of VAGRANT
vague (vāg) *adj.* [Fr. < L. *vagus,* wandering < IE. *wag-,* to be bent, prob. < base *wā-:* cf. VACILLATE] **1.** not clearly, precisely, or definitely expressed or stated **2.** indefinite in shape, form, or character; hazily, obscurely, or indistinctly seen or sensed **3.** not sharp, certain, or precise in thought, feeling, or expression [*vague* in his answers, a *vague* hope] **4.** not precisely determined or known; uncertain **—SYN.** see OBSCURE **— vague′ly** *adv.* **—vague′ness** *n.*
va·gus (vā′gəs) *n.,* pl. **va′gi** (-jī) [ModL. < L., wandering: see prec.] either of the tenth pair of cranial nerves, arising in the medulla oblongata and providing parasympathetic innervation to the larynx, lungs, heart, esophagus, and most of the abdominal organs: also **vagus nerve**
va·hi·ne (vä hē′nä) *n.* [Tahitian, akin to Haw. *wahine,* WAHINE] a Polynesian woman, esp. of Tahiti
vail¹ (vāl) *vi.* [ME. *vailen* < pres. indic. stem of OFr. *valoir,* to be of worth: see AVAIL] [Archaic] to be of use, service, or profit; avail **—n.** [Archaic] a tip; gratuity
vail² (vāl) *vt.* [ME. *valen* < OFr. *valer* or aphetic < *avaler,* to descend < *à val,* down < L. *ad vallum,* lit., to the valley] [Archaic] **1.** to lower; let sink or fall down **2.** to take off or tip (one's hat, etc.) as a sign of respect or submission
vail³ (vāl) *n., vt. obs. sp.* of VEIL
vain (vān) *adj.* [ME. < OFr. < L. *vanus,* empty, vain: for IE. base see WANT] **1.** having no real value or significance; worthless, empty, idle, hollow, etc. [*vain* pomp] **2.** without force or effect; futile, fruitless, unprofitable, unavailing, etc. [a *vain* endeavor] **3.** having or showing an excessively high regard for one's self, looks, possessions, ability, etc.; indulging in or resulting from personal vanity; conceited **4.** [Archaic] lacking in sense; foolish **—in vain 1.** fruitlessly; vainly **2.** lightly; profanely **—vain′ness** *n.*
SYN.—vain, in this connection, applies to that which has little or no real value, worth, or meaning [*vain* studies]; **idle** refers to that which is baseless or worthless because it can never be realized or have a real effect [*idle* hopes, *idle* talk]; **empty** and **hollow** are used of that which lacks real substance and only appears to be genuine, sincere, worthwhile, etc. [*empty* threats, *hollow* pleasures]; **otiose** applies to that which has no real purpose or function and is therefore useless or superfluous [*otiose* remarks] See also FUTILE
vain·glo·ri·ous (vān′glôr′ē əs) *adj.* [LME. *vanegloreous* < ML. *vaniglorius:* see ff.] **1.** boastfully vain and proud of oneself **2.** showing or characterized by boastful vanity **—vain′glo′ri·ous·ly** *adv.* **—vain′glo′ri·ous·ness** *n.*
vain·glo·ry (vān′glôr′ē, vān glôr′ē) *n.* [ME. *vainglorie* < OFr. *vaine gloire* < L. *vana gloria,* empty boasting: see VAIN & GLORY] **1.** extreme self-pride and boastfulness; excessive and ostentatious vanity **2.** vain show or empty pomp **—SYN.** see PRIDE
vain·ly (vān′lē) *adv.* **1.** in vain; uselessly; fruitlessly; without success **2.** with vanity; conceitedly
vair (ver) *n.* [ME. < OFr., *vair,* orig., variegated < L. *varius:* see VARIOUS] **1.** [Archaic] a fur, usually from a gray and white squirrel, used for trimming and lining clothes in the Middle Ages **2.** *Heraldry* a fur, represented by rows of small bells, alternately upright and turned down
Vaish·na·va (vish′nə və) *n.* [Sans. *vaiṣṇava,* of Vishnu < *Viṣṇu,* VISHNU] in Hinduism, a devotee of Vishnu
Vais·ya (vīs′yə) *n.* a member of the Hindu business and agricultural caste, next below the Kshatriya
val. 1. valuation **2.** value
Va·lais (vå le′) canton of SW Switzerland: 2,020 sq. mi.; pop. 180,000
val·ance (val′əns, vāl′-) *n.* [ME. < ? VALENCE, center for textile manufacturing] **1.** a short drapery or curtain hanging from the edge of a bed, shelf, table, etc., often to the floor **2.** a short drapery or facing of wood or metal across the top of a window, concealing curtain rods, etc. **—val′anced** *adj.*
Val·dai Hills (väl dī′) range of hills in W R.S.F.S.R., between Leningrad & Moscow, forming a watershed for rivers flowing to the Baltic & those flowing south & southeast, esp. the Volga

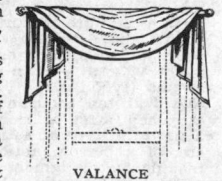
VALANCE

Val d'A·os·ta (väl′dä ôs′tä) same as VALLE D'AOSTA
Val·de·mar I (väl′də mär′) same as WALDEMAR I
vale¹ (vāl) *n.* [ME. < OFr. *val* < L. *vallis,* VALLEY] [Chiefly Poet.] same as VALLEY
‡va·le² (vā′lē, wä′lā) *interj., n.* [L.] farewell
val·e·dic·tion (val′ə dik′shən) *n.* [< L. *valedictus,* pp. of *valedicere,* to say farewell < *vale,* farewell (imperative of *valere,* to be well: see VALUE) + *dicere,* to say: see DICTION] **1.** the act of bidding or saying farewell **2.** something said in parting; farewell utterance
☆**val·e·dic·to·ri·an** (val′ə dik tôr′ē ən) *n.* in schools and colleges, the, student, usually the one ranking highest in the class in scholarship, who delivers the valedictory
val·e·dic·to·ry (val′ə dik′tər ē) *adj.* [< L. *valedictus* (see VALEDICTION) + -ORY] said or done at parting, by way of farewell; uttered as a valediction **—**☆*n., pl.* **-ries** a farewell speech, esp. one delivered at graduation from a school or college
Va·lence (vá läns′) city in SE France, on the Rhone: pop. 53,000
va·lence (vā′ləns) *n.* [ML. *valentia,* worth, value < LL., capacity < L., vigor < *valens,* prp. of *valere,* to be strong: see VALUE] *Chem.* **1.** the capacity of an element or radical to combine with another to form molecules, as measured by the number of hydrogen or chlorine atoms which one radical or one atom of the element will combine with or replace (e.g.: oxygen has a *valence* of two, i.e., one atom of oxygen combines with two hydrogen atoms to form the water molecule, H_2O) **2.** any of the units of valence which a particular element may have Also **va′len·cy,** *pl.* **-cies**
valence electrons the orbital electrons in the outermost shell of an atom which largely determine its properties
Va·len·ci·a (və len′shē ə, -shə, -sē ə; *Sp.* vä len′thyä) **1.** region & former kingdom in E Spain, on the Mediterranean **2.** seaport in this region: pop. 583,000 **3.** city in N Venezuela: pop. 164,000
Va·len·ci·ennes (vo len′sē enz′; *Fr.* vå län syen′) city in N France, near the Belg. border: pop. 45,000 **—n.** a flat bobbin lace having a simple floral pattern on a background of fine, diamond-shaped mesh: also **Va·lenciennes lace, Val lace**
Va·lens (vā′lanz), (**Fla·vius**) 328?–378 A.D.; emperor of the Eastern Roman Empire (364–378): brother of VALENTINIAN I

VALENCIA

-va·lent (vā′lənt) [< L. *valens:* see VALENCE] *Chem. a suffix meaning:* **1.** having a specified valence **2.** having a specified number of valences Although both the Greek set of prefixes (*mono-, di-, tri-, tetra-,* etc.) and the Latin (*uni-, bi-, ter-, quadri-,* etc.) are used with *-valent,* the latter set is preferred when designating the number of valences an element exhibits and the former when designating the specific valence of some atom or radical
Val·en·tine (val′ən tīn′) [ME. < L. *Valentinus* < *Valens,* a masculine name < *valens,* prp.: see VALENCE] **1.** a masculine name **2.** Saint, 3d cent. A.D.; Christian martyr of Rome: his day is Feb. 14
val·en·tine (val′ən tīn′) *n.* [ME. < OFr.] **1.** *a)* a sweetheart chosen or complimented on Saint Valentine's Day *b)* one's sweetheart **2.** *a)* a greeting card or note sent to a real or pretended sweetheart on this day, and containing lines of sentimental love *b)* a burlesque of this, often sent anonymously **3.** a gift presented on Saint Valentine's Day
Val·en·tin·i·an (val′ən tin′ē ən) [ME. name *Valentinianus*) name of three Roman emperors **1. Valentinian I** 321?–375 A.D.; ruled, 364–375: brother of VALENS **2. Valentinian II** 371?–392 A.D.; ruled, 375–392: son of *prec.* **3. Valentinian III** 419?–455 A.D.; ruled, 425–455
Valera, Eamon De see DE VALERA
val·er·ate (val′ə rāt′) *n.* a salt or ester of valeric acid
Va·ler·i·a (və lir′ē ə) [L., fem. of *Valerius,* name of a Roman gens, prob. < *valere,* to be strong (see VALUE)] a feminine name: equiv. Fr. *Valérie:* also **Valerie**
Va·ler·i·an (və lir′ē ən) (L. name *Publius Licinius Valerianus*) 190?–after 260 A.D.; Roman emperor (253–260)
va·le·ri·an (və lir′ē ən) *n.* [ME. < MFr. *valériane* < ML. *valeriana,* valerian, prob. < *Valeria,* province in Pannonia, where the plants were grown] **1.** any of a genus (*Valeriana*) of plants of the valerian family, with clusters or spikes of white, pink, red, or purplish flowers **2.** a drug made from the dried rhizomes and roots of the garden heliotrope (*Valeriana officinalis*), formerly used as a sedative and antispasmodic **—adj.** designating a family (Valerianaceae) of plants, chiefly of the Northern Hemisphere, including corn salad, spikenard, and valerian

va·ler·ic acid (və ler′ik, -lir′-) any of four isomeric fatty acids, C₄H₉COOH, some originally found in valerian root, but all now made synthetically: used in the manufacture of pharmaceuticals, flavors, perfumes, etc.: also called **va·le′ri·an′ic acid** (-lir′ē ən′ik)

Val·er·ie (val′ər ē) a feminine name: see VALERIA

Va·lé·ry (vȧ lā rē′), **Paul (Ambroise)** (pôl) 1871–1945; Fr. poet & essayist

val·et (val′it, val′ā; *Fr.* vȧ lā′) *n.* [Fr., a groom, yeoman < OFr. *vaslet*, young man, page < VL. *vassellittus*, double dim. < Gaul. *vasso-*, servant (akin to MIr. *foss*, W. *gwas*) < IE. *uposto-*, one who stands by < *upo-* (cf. UP¹) + base *stā-*, to STAND] **1.** a man's personal manservant who takes care of the man's clothes, helps him in dressing, etc. **2.** an employee, as of a hotel, who cleans or presses clothes, or performs other personal services ☆**3.** a rack for coats, pants, etc. —*vt.*, *vi.* to serve (a person) as a valet

‡**va·let de cham·bre** (vȧ lā′ də shän′br′) *pl.* **va·lets de cham′bre** (vȧ lā) [Fr., chamber servant] *same as* VALET (sense 1)

val·e·tu·di·nar·i·an (val′ə tōō′də ner′ē ən) *n.* [< L. *valetudinarius*, sickly, infirm, an invalid < *valetudo* (gen. *valetudinis*), state of health, sickness < *valere*, to be strong: see VALUE] **1.** a person in poor health; invalid **2.** a person who thinks constantly and anxiously about his health —*adj.* **1.** in poor health; sickly; invalid **2.** anxiously concerned about one's health **3.** characterized by poor health Also **val′e·tu′di·nar′y**, *pl.* **-nar′ies** —**val′e·tu′di·nar′i·an·ism** *n.*

val·gus (val′gəs) *n.* [ModL. < L., bowlegged: for IE. base see WALK] **1.** clubfoot in which the foot is turned outward **2.** any similar bent or twisted position, as of the knee, hip, or great toe —*adj.* **1.** bent or twisted outward **2.** loosely, knock-kneed

Val·hal·la (val hal′ə) [ModL. < ON. *valhöll*, gen. *valhallar*, hall of the slain < *valr*, slaughter, the slain (< IE. base *wel-*, to tear, wound, corpse, whence L. *volnus*, Gr. *oulē*, a wound) + *höll*, hall: for IE. base see HALL] *Norse Myth.* the great hall where Odin receives and feasts the souls of heroes fallen bravely in battle: also **Val·hall′** (-hal′)

val·iant (val′yənt) *adj.* [ME. < OFr. *vaillant*, prp. of *valoir* < L. *valere*, to be strong: see VALUE] full of or characterized by valor or courage; brave —*SYN.* see BRAVE —**val′iance, val′ian·cy** *n.* —**val′iant·ly** *adv.*

val·id (val′id) *adj.* [Fr. *valide* < L. *validus*, strong, powerful (in ML., valid) < *valere*, to be strong: see VALUE] **1.** having legal force; properly executed and binding under the law **2.** well-grounded on principles or evidence; able to withstand criticism or objection, as an argument; sound **3.** effective, effectual, cogent, etc. **4.** [Rare] robust; strong; healthy **5.** *Logic* correctly derived or inferred according to the rules of logic —**val′id·ly** *adv.* —**val′id·ness** *n.*
SYN.—**valid** applies to that which cannot be objected to because it conforms to law, logic, the facts, etc. [a *valid* criticism]; **sound** refers to that which is firmly grounded on facts, evidence, logic, etc. and is therefore free from error or superficiality [a *sound* method]; **cogent** implies such a powerful appeal to the mind, as because of validity, as to appear conclusive [*cogent* reasoning]; **convincing** implies such validity as to persuade or overcome doubts, opposition, etc. [a *convincing* argument]; **telling** suggests the power to have the required effect by being forcible, striking, relevant, etc. [a *telling* rejoinder] —*ANT.* fallacious

val·i·date (val′ə dāt) *vt.* **-dat′ed, -dat′ing** [< ML. *validatus*, pp. of *validare*, to validate: see prec.] **1.** to make binding under the law; give legal force to; declare legally valid **2.** to prove to be valid; confirm the validity of —*SYN.* see CONFIRM —**val′i·da′tion** *n.*

va·lid·i·ty (və lid′ə tē) *n.*, *pl.* **-ties** [Fr. *validité* < LL. *validitas*] the state, quality, or fact of being valid in law or in argument, proof, authority, etc.

val·ine (val′ēn, vāl′-) *n.* [< *(iso)val(eric acid)* + -INE⁴] a white, crystalline, essential amino acid, C₅H₁₁NO₂, found in small quantities in many proteins

va·lise (və lēs′) *n.* [Fr. < It. *valigia* < ?] a piece of hand luggage: an old-fashioned term

Val·kyr·ie (val kir′ē, val′ki rē) *n.* [ON. *valkyrja*, lit., chooser of the slain < *valr*, those slain (see VALHALLA) + *kjōsa*, to CHOOSE] *Norse Myth.* any of the maidens of Odin who conduct the souls of heroes slain in battle to Valhalla and wait on them there —**Val·kyr′i·an** *adj.*

Val·la·do·lid (val′ə dō′lid; *Sp.* vä′lyä thō lēth′) city in NC Spain: pop. 172,000

val·la·tion (va lā′shən) *n.* [LL. *vallatio* < L. *vallatus*, pp. of *vallare*, to protect with a rampart < *vallum*, a rampart, WALL] **1.** a wall or earthwork formerly used for military defense; rampart **2.** the art or process of building such a military defense

val·lec·u·la (va lek′yoo lə) *n.*, *pl.* **-lae′** (-lē′) [ModL. < LL., dim. < L. *vallis*, VALLEY] a groove or furrow in a plant or animal structure, as the depression between the epiglottis and the base of the tongue, or any of the grooves on celery —**val·lec′u·lar, val·lec′u·late** (-lit, -lāt′) *adj.*

Val·le d'A·os·ta (väl′ā dä ōs′tä) autonomous region of NW Italy: 1,260 sq. mi.; pop. 100,000

Val·le·jo (və lā′hō, -ō) [after Mariano G. *Vallejo* (1807–90), owner of the site] seaport in W Calif., just north of Oakland: pop. 67,000

Val·let·ta (vä let′ä) seaport & capital of Malta, on the island of Malta: pop. 18,000

val·ley (val′ē) *n.*, *pl.* **-leys** [ME. *valey* < OFr. *valee* < *val* < L. *vallis*, a vale < IE. base *wel-*, to turn, roll, whence WALK, WELL¹] **1.** a stretch of low land lying between hills or mountains and usually having a river or stream flowing through it **2.** the land drained or watered by a great river system [the Mississippi *valley*] **3.** any long dip or hollow, as the trough of a wave **4.** *Archit.* the trough formed where two slopes of a roof meet, or where the roof meets a wall

Valley Forge [after an iron *forge* located on *Valley* Creek] village in SE Pa., on the Schuylkill River: scene of Washington's winter encampment (1777–78)

Valley of Ten Thousand Smokes region in Katmai National Monument, SW Alas., in which steam and gases are emitted from thousands of earth vents

Valley Stream village on SW Long Island, N.Y., adjacent to the borough of Queens: pop. 40,000

Val·lom·bro·sa (väl′lōm brō′sä; *E.* val′əm brō′sə) village in Tuscany, Italy, near Florence

Val·ois (vál wä′) **1.** former duchy in NC France **2.** ruling family of France (1328–1589)

Va·lo·na (vä lō′nä) *same as* VLONË

va·lo·ni·a (və lō′nē ə) *n.* [It. *vallonia* < ModGr. *balania*, evergreen oak < Gr. *balanos*, acorn (see GLAND¹)] the acorn cups of an oak (*Quercus aegilops*) of Europe and Asia, used in dyeing, tanning, etc.

val·or (val′ər) *n.* [ME., monetary worth < OFr. *valour* < LL. *valor*, worth < L. *valere*, to be strong: see VALUE] marked courage or bravery: also, Brit. sp., **val′our**

☆**val·or·i·za·tion** (val′ər i zā′shən) *n.* [Port. *valorização* < *valorizar*, to valorize < *valor*, a price, worth < LL. *valor*: see prec.] a maintenance or fixing of prices, usually by government action, as by buying up a commodity at the fixed price or lending money to producers so that they can keep their goods off the market

val·or·ize (val′ə rīz′) *vt.*, *vi.* **-ized′, -iz′ing** [Port. *valorizar*: see prec.] to fix or control the price of (a commodity) by valorization

val·or·ous (-ər əs) *adj.* [ME. < OFr. *valeureux* < ML. *valorosus*] having or showing valor; courageous; brave —**val′or·ous·ly** *adv.* —**val′or·ous·ness** *n.*

Val·pa·rai·so (val′pə rā′zō, -rī′sō) seaport in C Chile: pop. 262,000: also **Val·pa·ra·í·so** (*Sp.* väl′pä rä ē′sō)

Val·sal·va maneuver (val sal′və) [after Antonio *Valsalva* (1666–1723), It. anatomist] the act of equalizing pressure in the ears, as during ascents or descents in aircraft, by holding the nose and mouth firmly shut and blowing hard

‡**valse** (vȧls) *n.* [Fr. < G. *walzer*: see WALTZ] a waltz

val·u·a·ble (val′yoo b'l, -yoo wə b'l) *adj.* **1.** *a*) having material value; being worth money *b*) having great value in terms of money [a *valuable* diamond] **2.** of great merit, use, or service; highly important, esteemed, etc. —*n.* an article of value, esp. one of small size, as a piece of jewelry: *usually used in pl.* —*SYN.* see COSTLY —**val′u·a·bly** *adv.*

val·u·ate (val′yoo wāt′) *vt.* **-at′ed, -at′ing** [back-formation < ff.] to set a value on; appraise —**val′u·a′tor** *n.*

val·u·a·tion (val′yoo wā′shən) *n.* [OFr. *valuacion*] **1.** the act of determining the value or price of anything; evaluation; appraisal **2.** determined or estimated value or price on the market **3.** estimation of the worth, merit, etc. of anything —**val′u·a′tion·al** *adj.* —**val′u·a′tion·al·ly** *adv.*

val·ue (val′yōō) *n.* [ME. < OFr., fem. of *valu*, pp. of *valoir*, to be strong, be worth < L. *valere* < IE. base *wal-*, to be strong, whence WIELD] **1.** a fair or proper equivalent in money, commodities, etc., esp. for something sold or exchanged; fair price or return **2.** the worth of a thing in money or goods at a certain time; market price **3.** estimated or appraised worth or price; valuation **4.** purchasing power [the fluctuating *value* of the dollar] **5.** that quality of a thing according to which it is thought of as being more or less desirable, useful, estimable, important, etc.; worth or the degree of worth **6.** that which is desirable or worthy of esteem for its own sake; thing or quality having intrinsic worth **7.** [pl.] the social principles, goals, or standards held or accepted by an individual, class, society, etc. **8.** precise meaning, as of a word **9.** denomination, as of a postage stamp, playing card, etc. **10.** *Art a*) relative lightness or darkness of a color *b*) proportioned effect, as of light and shade, in an artistic work **11.** *Math.* the quantity or amount for which a symbol stands [to determine the *value* of x] **12.** *Music* the relative duration of a note, tone, or rest **13.** *Phonet.* the quality of a speech sound [the several *values* of a vowel in English] —*vt.* **val′ued, val′u·ing 1.** to estimate the value of; set a price for or determine the worth of; appraise **2.** to place a certain estimate of worth on in a scale of values [to *value* health above wealth] **3.** to think highly of; esteem; prize [to *value* someone's friendship] —*SYN.* see APPRECIATE, WORTH¹ —**val′u·er** *n.*

val·ued (-yōōd) *adj.* **1.** estimated; appraised [a painting *valued* at ten thousand dollars] **2.** highly thought of; esteemed [a *valued* friend]

value judgment an estimate made of the worth, goodness, etc. of a person, action, event, or the like, esp. when making such judgment is improper or undesirable

val·ue·less (-yoo lis) *adj.* of no value or use; worthless

va·lu·ta (və lōōt′ə) *n.* [It., value] the value of a currency; specif., the exchange value of the currency of any of certain European countries with reference to the currency of a specified country

val·vate (val′vāt) *adj.* [L. *valvatus*, having folding doors < *valva*: see ff.] 1. having a valve or valves 2. *Bot.* meeting without overlapping, as the petals of some flower buds *b)* opening by valves, as a pea pod

valve (valv) *n.* [ME., a door leaf < L. *valva*, leaf of a folding door, akin to *volvere*, to roll: see WALK; senses 3, 4, 8 < ModL. *valva* < L.] 1. orig., either of the halves of a double door or any of the leaves of a folding door 2. a gate regulating the flow of water in a sluice, channel, etc. 3. *Anat.* a membranous fold or structure which permits body fluids to flow in one direction only, or opens and closes a tube or opening 4. *Bot. a)* one of the segments into which a pod or capsule separates when it bursts open *b)* a lidlike part in some anthers, through which pollen is discharged *c)* either of the boxlike halves forming the cell walls of a diatom 5. *Elec., Radio a)* a device consisting of a metal in contact with a solution or compound across the boundary of which current flows in one direction only *b) Brit.* term for ELECTRON TUBE 6. *Mech. a)* any device in a pipe or tube that permits a flow in one direction only, or regulates the flow of whatever is in the pipe, by means of a flap, lid, plug, etc. acting to open or block passage *b)* the flap, lid, plug, etc. 7. *Music* a device in certain brass-wind instruments, as the trumpet, that opens an auxiliary to the main tube, lengthening the air column and lowering the pitch 8. *Zool. a)* one of the two or more parts making up the shell of a mollusk, barnacle, clam, etc. *b)* any of the parts forming the sheath of an ovipositor in certain insects —*vt., vi.* **valved**, **valv′ing** 1. to fit with or make use of a valve or valves 2. to regulate the flow of (a fluid) by means of a valve or valves —**valve′less** *adj.*

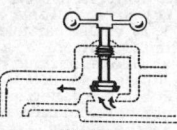
VALVE
(in a faucet)

valve-in-head engine (-in hed′) an internal-combustion engine, as in some automobiles, having the intake and exhaust valves in the cylinder head instead of the block

val·vu·lar (val′vyə lər) *adj.* 1. having the form or function of a valve 2. having a valve or valves 3. of a valve or valves; esp., of the valves of the heart Also **val′var** (-vər)

val·vule (-vyōōl) *n.* [Fr. < ModL. *valvula*, dim. < L. *valva*] a small valve: also **valve′let**

val·vu·li·tis (valv′yə līt′əs) *n.* [ModL. < *valvula* (see prec.) + -ITIS] inflammation of a valve, esp. of the heart

☆**va·moose** (va mōōs′) *vi., vt.* -**moosed′**, -**moos′ing** [Sp. *vamos*, let us go] [Old Slang] to leave quickly; go away (from) hurriedly: also **va·mose′** (-mōs′) -**mosed′**, -**mos′ing**

vamp¹ (vamp) *n.* [ME. *vampe* < OFr. *avampié* < *avant*, before + *pié, pied*, a foot < L. *pes* (gen. *pedis*), FOOT] 1. the part of a boot or shoe covering the instep and, in some styles, the toes 2. [< the *v.*] *a)* something patched up or fixed up to seem new; patchwork *b)* something patched on *c) Music* a simple, improvised introduction or interlude, esp. a series of chords, as between popular numbers by a dance band —*vt.* 1. to put a vamp on; provide or mend with a new vamp 2. to patch (*up*); repair 3. to invent; fabricate 4. *Music* to improvise —*vi. Music* to play a vamp

 VAMP

vamp² (vamp) *n. clipped form of* VAMPIRE (sense 3) —*vt.* to seduce or beguile (a man) by the use of feminine charms —*vi.* to act the part of a vamp

vam·pire (vam′pīr) *n.* [Fr. < G. *vampir*, of Slav. orig., as in Serb. *vâmpir*] 1. in folklore and popular superstition, a corpse that becomes reanimated and leaves its grave at night to suck the blood of sleeping persons 2. an unscrupulous person who preys ruthlessly on others, as a blackmailer or usurer 3. a beautiful but unscrupulous woman who seduces men and leads them to their ruin 4. *clipped form of* VAMPIRE BAT

vampire bat 1. any of several species of tropical American bats (family Desmodontidae) that live on vertebrate blood, esp. of stock animals, and sometimes transmit rabies and a trypanosome disease of horses 2. any of various other bats mistakenly believed to feed on blood

vam·pir·ism (vam′pīr iz′m, -pi riz′m) *n.* 1. superstitious belief in vampires 2. the habits or practices of vampires in folklore; specif., bloodsucking 3. the act or practice of preying ruthlessly on other people

Van (vän) salt lake in E Turkey: c.1,450 sq. mi.

van¹ (van) *n.* [abbrev. < VANGUARD] 1. the front of an army or fleet when advancing or in battle array 2. the foremost position in a line, movement, field of endeavor, etc., or those in the foremost position

van² (van) *n.* [ME. *vanne* < MFr. *van* < L. *vannus*, a van, FAN¹] 1. [Archaic] a winnowing machine 2. [Poet.] a wing

van³ (van) *n.* [contr. < CARAVAN] 1. a large, closed truck or wagon for moving furniture, carrying freight, etc. 2. [Brit.] *a)* a closed railway car for baggage, etc. *b)* a delivery wagon or truck

van⁴ (van; *Du.* vän) *prep.* [Du., akin to G. *von*] of; from: in Dutch family names it originally indicated place of origin

van·a·date (van′ə dāt′) *n.* a salt or ester of vanadic acid

va·nad·ic (və nad′ik, -nā′dik) *adj.* designating or of compounds containing trivalent or pentavalent vanadium

vanadic acid any of a series of acids containing vanadium that apparently do not exist in the free state but are represented in various vanadates

va·nad·i·nite (və nad′ n īt′) *n.* [VANAD(IUM) + -IN¹ + -ITE¹] a hexagonal mineral, $Pb_3(VO_4)_3Cl$, an ore of vanadium consisting of lead vanadate and lead chloride, occurring in bright, usually red, yellow, or brown, crystals

va·na·di·um (və nā′dē əm) *n.* [ModL. < ON. *Vanadis*, a name of the goddess Freya] a rare, malleable, ductile, silver-white metallic chemical element: it is alloyed with steel, to which it adds tensile strength, and is used in nuclear applications, etc.: symbol, V; at. wt., 50.42; at. no., 23; sp. gr., 5.96; melt. pt., 1890°C; boil. pt., c.3000°C

vanadium steel a steel alloy containing 0.15 to 0.25 percent vanadium to harden and toughen it

van·a·dous (van′ə dəs, və nā′dəs) *adj.* designating or of compounds containing divalent or trivalent vanadium

☆**Van Al·len (radiation) belt** (van al′ən) [after James A. Van Allen (1914–), U.S. physicist] a broad, doughnut-shaped belt of radiation, composed of high-intensity protons and electrons temporarily trapped by the earth's magnetic field and encircling the earth at varying levels, starting at c.600 mi. and extending to 40,000 mi. or more

Van·brugh (van brōō′; *Brit. usually* van′brə), Sir John 1664–1726; Eng. dramatist & architect

Van Bu·ren (van byoor′ən), **Martin** 1782–1862; 8th president of the U.S. (1837–41)

Van·cou·ver (van kōō′vər) [after Capt. George *Vancouver* (1758–98), Brit. explorer] 1. island of British Columbia, Canada, off the SW coast: 12,408 sq. mi. 2. seaport in SW British Columbia, opposite this island, on the Strait of Georgia: pop. 410,000 (met. area 892,000) 3. city in SW Wash., on the Columbia River, opposite Portland, Oreg.: pop. 42,000 4. **Mount**, mountain of the St. Elias Range, on the Alas.-Yukon border: 15,700 ft.

van·da (van′də) *n.* [ModL. < Hindi *vandā*, mistletoe < Sans., a parasitic plant] any of a genus (*Vanda*) of small-flowered tropical orchids of the E Hemisphere, having racemes of fragrant white, lilac, blue, or greenish flowers

Van·dal (van′d'l) *n.* [L. *Vandalus* < Gmc. base seen also in OE. *Wendil*, ON. *Vendill*] 1. a member of an East Germanic tribe that ravaged Gaul, Spain, and N Africa and sacked Rome (455 A.D.) 2. [v-] a person who, out of malice or ignorance, destroys or spoils any public or private property, esp. that which is beautiful or artistic —*adj.* 1. of the Vandals: also **Van·dal·ic** (van dal′ik) 2. [v-] like or characteristic of a vandal; ruthlessly destructive

van·dal·ism (van′d'l iz'm) *n.* the actions or attitudes of the Vandals or of a vandal; malicious or ignorant destruction of public or private property, esp. of that which is beautiful or artistic —**van′dal·is′tic** *adj.*

van·dal·ize (-īz′) *vt.* -**ized′**, -**iz′ing** to destroy or damage (public or private property) maliciously

☆**Van de Graaff generator** (van′ di gräf′) [after R. J. *Van de Graaff* (1901–), U.S. physicist] an electrostatic generator using a movable insulating belt to produce potentials of millions of volts

Van·der·bilt (van′dər bilt), **Cornelius** 1794–1877; U.S. capitalist & railroad & steamship industrialist

van der Waals (vän dər välz′), **Jo·han·nes Di·de·rik** (yō hä′nəs dē′də rik) 1837–1923; Du. physicist

van der Waals' forces [after prec.] weak attractive forces between electrically neutral atoms and molecules

Van Die·man's Land (van dē′mənz) *former name of* TASMANIA

Van Do·ren (van dôr′ən) 1. **Carl (Clinton)**, 1885–1950; U.S. editor & writer 2. **Mark (Albert)**, 1894– ; U.S. poet & literary critic: brother of *prec.*

Van Dyck (van dīk′), Sir Anthony 1599–1641; Fl. painter, in England after 1632: also sp. **Van·dyke′**

Van·dyke (van dīk′) *n. clipped form of:* 1. VANDYKE BEARD 2. VANDYKE COLLAR —*adj.* of, or in the style of, Van Dyck or in the fashion of the subjects of his portraits

Vandyke beard a closely trimmed, pointed beard

Vandyke brown 1. a deep-brown pigment used by Van Dyck 2. any of several other brown pigments or colors

Vandyke collar a broad linen or lace collar with a deeply indented edge

vane (vān) *n.* [South Brit. var. of *fane*, small flag or pennon < OE. *fana*, a flag: for IE. base see PANE] 1. a flat piece of metal, strip of cloth, etc. set up high to swing with the wind and show which way it is blowing; weather vane 2. any of several flat or curved pieces set around an axle and rotated about it by moving air, water, etc. [the *vanes* of a windmill], or mechanically rotated to move the air or water [the *vanes* of a turbine], or to compress the air [the

VANDYKE BEARD

vanes of a supercharger*]* **3.** a projecting fixed plate or strip of metal attached to a rocket, missile, etc. to provide stability or guidance **4.** a target set to slide on a leveling rod, for use in surveying **5.** any of the sights on a compass, quadrant, etc. **6.** *a)* the web or flat part of a feather, containing the barbs: see FEATHER, illus. *b)* a feather on an arrow —**vaned** *adj.*

Vane (vān), **Sir Henry** (or **Harry**) 1613–62; Eng. Puritan statesman; colonial governor of Mass. (1636–37)

Vä·nern (ve'nərn), **Lake** largest lake in Sweden, in the SW part: c.2,150 sq. mi.: also **Vä'ner** (-nər)

vang (vaŋ) *n.* [Du. *vang*, a catch < *vangen*, to catch: for base see FANG] *Naut.* either of two ropes running from the end of a gaff to the deck, used to steady the gaff

van Gogh (van gō', gôkh; *Du.* vän khôkh'), **Vincent** 1853–90; *Du.* painter

van·guard (van'gärd') *n.* [ME. *vaunt garde* < OFr. *avant-garde* < *avant*, before (see AVAUNT) + *garde* (see GUARD)] **1.** the part of an army which goes ahead of the main body in an advance; the van **2.** the leading position or persons in a movement

va·nil·la (və nil'ə) *n.* [ModL., name of the genus < Sp. *vainilla*, small pod, husk, dim. of *vaina*, a pod < L. *vagina*, a case, pod, sheath] **1.** any of a genus (*Vanilla*) of climbing tropical American orchids with fragrant, greenish-yellow flowers **2.** the podlike, immature capsule (**vanilla bean**) of some of these plants **3.** an extract of these capsules, used as a flavoring in cooking, confections, etc.

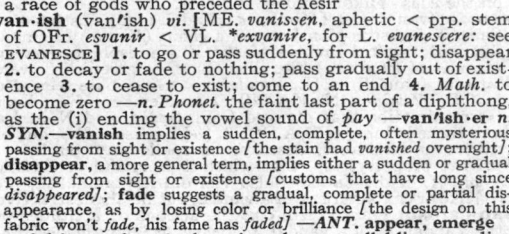

VANILLA

va·nil·lic (-ik) *adj.* of or derived from vanilla or vanillin

va·nil·lin (və nil'in, van'ə lin) *n.* a fragrant, white, crystalline substance, $C_8H_8O_3$, produced from the vanilla bean or made synthetically: used for flavoring, in the manufacture of perfumes, etc.

Va·nir (vä'nir) *n.pl.* [ON.] *Norse Myth.* a race of gods who preceded the Aesir

van·ish (van'ish) *vi.* [ME. *vanissen*, aphetic < prp. stem of OFr. *esvanir* < VL. **exvanire*, for L. *evanescere*: see EVANESCE] **1.** to go or pass suddenly from sight; disappear **2.** to decay or fade to nothing; pass gradually out of existence **3.** to cease to exist; come to an end **4.** *Math.* to become zero —*n. Phonet.* the faint last part of a diphthong, as the (i) ending the vowel sound of *pay* —**van'ish·er** *n.* *SYN.*—**vanish** implies a sudden, complete, often mysterious passing from sight or existence *[the stain had vanished overnight]*; **disappear**, a more general term, implies either a sudden or gradual passing from sight or existence *[customs that have long since disappeared]*; **fade** suggests a gradual, complete or partial disappearance, as by losing color or brilliance *[the design on this fabric won't fade, his fame has faded]* —*ANT.* appear, emerge

vanishing point 1. the point where parallel lines receding from the observer seem to come together **2.** a time, place, or stage at which something disappears or ceases to exist

van·i·ty (van'ə tē) *n., pl.* **-ties** [ME. *vanite* < OFr. *vanité* < L. *vanitas*, emptiness, worthlessness < *vanus*, vain: see WANT] **1.** any thing or act that is vain, futile, idle, or worthless **2.** the quality or fact of being vain, or worthless; futility **3.** the quality or fact of being vain, or excessively proud of oneself or one's qualities or possessions; self-conceit **4.** a thing about which one is vain or conceited ☆**5.** *clipped form of* VANITY CASE ☆**6.** a small table or ledge with a mirror for use while putting on cosmetics, combing one's hair, etc.; dressing table —*SYN.* see PRIDE

vanity case a woman's small traveling case fitted for carrying cosmetics, toilet articles, etc.

Vanity Fair 1. in Bunyan's *Pilgrim's Progress*, a fair always going on in the town of Vanity, symbolic of worldly folly, frivolity, and show **2.** the world, esp. the social world, or a city, society, etc., regarded as dominated by folly, frivolity, and show

☆**vanity press** (or **publisher**) a press or publishing house that publishes books only at the author's own expense

van·quish (vaŋ'kwish, van'-) *vt.* [ME. *venquissen* < OFr. *veinquis-*, inflectional stem of *veinquir* < L. *vincere*, to conquer: see VICTOR] **1.** to conquer or defeat in battle; force into submission **2.** *a)* to defeat in any conflict, as in argument *b)* to overcome (a feeling, condition, etc.); suppress —*SYN.* see CONQUER —**van'quish·er** *n.*

Van Rens·se·laer (van ren'sə lər, -lir'), **Stephen** 1764–1839; U.S. politician & general

van·tage (van'tij) *n.* [ME. < Anglo-Fr., aphetic for OFr. *avantage*: see ADVANTAGE] **1.** *a)* a position, situation, etc. more advantageous than that of an opponent *b)* a position that allows a clear and broad view, understanding, etc.: also **vantage point 2.** [Chiefly Brit.] *Tennis* same as AD²

van't Hoff (vänt hôf'), **Ja·co·bus Hen·ri·cus** (yä kō'bəs hen rē'kəs) 1852–1911; Du. physical chemist

Va·nu·a Le·vu (vä noo'ä le'voo) second largest of the Fiji Islands, northeast of Viti Levu: 2,137 sq. mi.

van·ward (van'wərd) *adj.* in the van, or front, as of an army —*adv.* toward the van

Van·zet·ti (van zet'ē), **Bar·to·lo·me·o** (bär'tō lō mā'ō) 1888–1927; It. anarchist in the U.S.: see SACCO

vap·id (vap'id) *adj.* [L. *vapidus*, stale, insipid, akin to *vappa*, stale wine: for base see VAPOR] **1.** tasteless; flavor-

less; flat **2.** uninteresting; lifeless; dull; boring *[vapid talk]* —*SYN.* see INSIPID —**vap'id·ly** *adv.* —**vap'id·ness** *n.*

va·pid·i·ty (va pid'ə tē) *n.* **1.** the state or quality of being vapid; flatness; dullness; insipidity **2.** *pl.* **-ties** a dull or uninteresting remark, idea, etc.

va·por (vā'pər) *n.* [ME. *vapour* < Anglo-Fr. < MFr. *vapeur* < L. *vapor* < IE. base **wep-*, to give off vapors] **1.** *a)* visible particles of moisture floating in the air, as fog, mist, or steam *b)* any cloudy or imperceptible exhalation, as smoke, noxious fumes, etc. **2.** the gaseous form of any substance which is usually a liquid or a solid **3.** *a)* any substance vaporized for use in machinery, medical therapy, etc. *b)* a mixture of such a vaporized substance with air, as the explosive mixture in an automotive cylinder **4.** [Now Rare] anything insubstantial or worthless **5.** [*pl.*] [Archaic] *a)* exhalations from the stomach believed to be harmful to one's health *b)* hypochondria or depressed spirits (often with *the*) —*vi.* **1.** to rise or pass off in the form of vapor; evaporate **2.** to give off vapor **3.** to indulge in idle talk or boasting; brag or bluster —*vt.* same as VAPORIZE —**va'por·er** *n.* —**va'por·like'** *adj.*

‡**va·po·ret·to** (vä'pô ret'tō; *E.* vap'ə ret'ō) *n., pl.* **-ret'ti** (-tē), *E.* **-tos** [It., dim. of *vapore*, steamboat < Fr. *vapeur*, short for *bateau à vapeur*, calque of Eng. STEAMBOAT] a large motorboat used for public transportation on the canals of Venice

va·por·if·ic (vā'pə rif'ik) *adj.* same as VAPOROUS

va·por·im·e·ter (vā'pə rim'ə tər) *n.* an instrument for measuring vapor pressure or volume

va·por·ing (vā'pər iŋ) *adj.* boastful, bombastic, etc. —*n.* boastful or extravagant talk or behavior

va·por·ish (-ish) *adj.* **1.** like or full of vapor **2.** [Archaic] having, or inclined to have, the vapors; in low spirits

va·por·ize (vā'pə rīz') *vt., vi.* **-ized', -iz'ing** to change into vapor, as by heating or spraying —**va'por·iz'a·ble** *adj.* —**va'por·i·za'tion** *n.*

va·por·iz·er (-rī'zər) *n.* a device for vaporizing liquids; specif., *a)* an atomizer, esp. one for creating steam or vaporizing medicated liquid for medicinal purposes *b)* a jet in a carburetor

☆**vapor lock** a blocking of the flow of fuel in an internal-combustion engine as the result of vaporized fuel in the fuel line, caused by excessive heat

va·por·ous (vā'pər əs) *adj.* [LL. *vaporosus*] **1.** giving off or forming vapor **2.** full of vapor; foggy; misty **3.** like, having the nature of, or characteristic of vapor **4.** *a)* fleeting, unsubstantial, fanciful, etc.: said of things, ideas, etc. *b)* given to such ideas or talk —**va'por·ous·ly** *adv.* —**va'por·ous·ness, va'por·os'i·ty** (-pə räs'ə tē) *n.*

vapor pressure the pressure at any given temperature of a vapor in equilibrium with its liquid or solid form: also called **vapor tension**

vapor trail same as CONTRAIL

va·por·y (vā'pə rē) *adj.* same as VAPOROUS

va·pour (-pər) *n., vi., vt.* Brit. sp. of VAPOR

☆**va·que·ro** (vä ker'ō) *n., pl.* **-ros** [Sp. < *vaca*, a cow < L. *vacca*] in the Southwest, a man who herds cattle; cowboy

var (vär) *n.* [< *v(olt) a(mpere) r(eactive)*] *Elec.* the unit of reactive power, equal to one reactive volt-ampere

VAR visual-aural (radio) range

var. 1. variant(s) **2.** variation **3.** variety **4.** various

☆**va·ra** (vä'rä) *n.* [Sp. & Port., lit., a rod, stick < L., a forked pole < *varus*, bent: for base see VARY] in Spain and Spanish America, *a)* a unit of linear measure, varying from about 31 to 33 inches *b)* a unit of area, the square vara

☆**va·rac·tor** (və rak'tər) *n.* [VAR(IABLE) + (RE)ACT(ANCE) + -OR] *Electronics* a semiconductor diode capacitor whose capacitance varies with the voltage applied

Va·ra·na·si (və rän'ə sē') city in Uttar Pradesh, NE India, on the Ganges: pop. 490,000

Va·ran·gi·an (və ran'jē ən) *n.* any of a Scandinavian people who settled in Russia in the 9th cent. and, under Rurik, founded the first Russian dynasty

Var·dar (vär'där) river in SE Yugoslavia & N Greece, flowing into the Gulf of Salonika: c.230 mi.

var·i·a·ble (ver'ē ə b'l, var'-) *adj.* [ME. < MFr. < LL. *variabilis*] **1.** apt or likely to change or vary; changeable, inconstant, fickle, fluctuating, etc. **2.** that can be changed or varied **3.** *Biol.* tending to deviate in some way from the type; aberrant **4.** *Math.* having no fixed value —*n.* **1.** anything changeable; thing that varies or may vary **2.** *Astron. clipped form of* VARIABLE STAR **3.** *Math. a)* a quantity that may have a number of different values *b)* a symbol for such a quantity **4.** *Naut.* a shifting wind —**var'i·a·bil'i·ty, var'i·a·ble·ness** *n.* —**var'i·a·bly** *adv.*

variable star a star whose brightness varies from time to time as the result of causes operating outside the earth's atmosphere: see CEPHEID (VARIABLE), RR Lyrae VARIABLES

var·i·ance (ver'ē əns, var'-) *n.* [ME. < OFr. < L. *variantia* < L. *varians*, prp. of *variare*, to vary] **1.** the quality, state, or fact of varying or being variant; a changing or tendency to change **2.** degree of change or difference; divergence; discrepancy **3.** official permission to bypass regulations; specif., permission to make nonconforming use of zoned property **4.** an active disagreement; quarrel; dispute **5.** *Accounting* the difference between the actual costs of production and the standard or expected costs **6.** *Law* a lack of agreement between two parts of a legal proceeding which should agree, as between a statement

and the evidence offered in support of it **7.** *Physical Chem.* the number of degrees of freedom of a system: see PHASE RULE **8.** *Statistics* the square of the standard deviation —**at variance** not in agreement or accord; conflicting

var·i·ant (-ənt) *adj.* [ME. < OFr. < L. *varians:* see prec.] **1.** varying; different; esp., different in some way from others of the same kind or class, or from some standard or type **2.** [Archaic] variable; changeable —*n.* anything that is variant, as a different spelling of the same word, a different version of a tale, myth, or literary passage, etc.

var·i·ate (-it) *n. same as:* **1.** VARIANT **2.** RANDOM VARIABLE

var·i·a·tion (ver′ē ā′shən, var′-) *n.* [ME. *variacion* < OFr. < L. *variatio*] **1.** *a)* the act, fact, or process of varying; change or deviation in form, condition, appearance, extent, etc. from a former or usual state, or from an assumed standard *b)* the degree or extent of such change **2.** the angular difference between magnetic north, as indicated on a magnetic compass, and true north; declination **3.** a thing that is somewhat different from another of the same kind **4.** *Astron.* a change in or deviation from the mean motion or orbit of a planet, satellite, etc. **5.** *Ballet* a solo dance **6.** *Biol. a)* a deviation from the usual or parental type in structure or form *b)* an organism showing such deviation **7.** *Math.* a relation between two quantities so that one changes with the other in the same ratio **8.** *Music* the repetition of a theme or musical idea with changes or embellishments in harmony, rhythm, key, etc., esp. any of a series of such repetitions developing a single theme —**var′i·a′tion·al** *adj.*

var·i·cel·la (var′ə sel′ə) *n.* [ModL., dim. of *variola:* see VARIOLA] *same as* CHICKEN POX —**var′i·cel′loid** (-oid) *adj.*

var·i·cel·late (var′ə sel′it, -āt) *adj.* [< *varicella* (dim. of VARIX) + -ATE¹] *Zool.* marked with small or indistinct ridges: said of certain shells

var·i·ces (var′ə sēz′) *n. pl.* of VARIX

var·i·co- (var′ə kō) [< L. *varix:* see VARIX] *a combining form meaning* an enlarged vein *[varicocele]:* also, before a vowel, **var′ic-**

var·i·co·cele (var′ə kō sēl′) *n.* [prec. + -CELE] *a varicose condition of the veins of the spermatic cord in the scrotum*

var·i·col·ored (ver′i kul′ərd, var′-) *adj.* [< L. *varius,* varied + COLORED] of several or many colors

var·i·cose (var′ə kōs′) *adj.* [L. *varicosus* < *varix* (gen. *varicis*), enlarged vein] **1.** abnormally and irregularly swollen or dilated *[varicose veins]* **2.** resulting from varicose veins *[varicose ulcer]*

var·i·co·sis (var′ə kō′sis) *n.* [ModL.: see VARICO- & -OSIS] a varicose condition of the veins

var·i·cos·i·ty (-käs′ə tē) *n.* **1.** the condition of being varicose **2.** *pl.* **-ties** *same as* VARIX

var·i·cot·o·my (-kät′ə mē) *n., pl.* **-mies** [VARICO- + -TOMY] the surgical excision of a varix, esp. of a varicose vein

var·ied (ver′ēd, var′-) *adj.* **1.** of different kinds; various **2.** showing different colors; variegated **3.** changed; altered —**var′ied·ly** *adv.*

var·i·e·gate (ver′ē ə gāt′, ver′ə gāt′; var′-) *vt.* **-gat′ed,** **-gat′ing** [< L. *variegatus,* pp. of *variegare* < *varius:* see VARY] **1.** to make varied in appearance by differences, as in colors **2.** to give variety to; diversify

var·i·e·gat·ed (-id) *adj.* **1.** marked with different colors in spots, streaks, etc.; parti-colored **2.** having variety in character, form, etc.; varied; diversified

var·i·e·ga·tion (ver′ē ə gā′shən, ver′ə gā′; var′-) *n.* **1.** a variegating or being variegated **2.** diversity or variety in character or appearance; specif., varied coloration

var·i·er (ver′ē ər, var′-) *n.* a person who varies

va·ri·e·tal (və rī′ə t′l) *adj.* **1.** of, connected with, or characterizing a variety **2.** constituting a distinct variety; specif., designating a wine that bears the name of the variety of grape from which it is made —**va·ri′e·tal·ly** *adv.*

va·ri·e·ty (və rī′ə tē) *n., pl.* **-ties** [Fr. *variété* < L. *varietas*] **1.** the state or quality of being various or varied; absence of monotony or sameness **2.** a different form of something, condition, or quality; sort; kind *[varieties of cloth]* **3.** a number of different things thought of together; collection of varied things *[a variety of items in the attic]* **4.** [Chiefly Brit.] *clipped form of* VARIETY SHOW **5.** *a) Bacteriology same as* SUBSPECIES *b) Biol.* loosely, a group having characteristics of its own within a species or subspecies; subdivision of a species *c) Bot.* a variant form of wild plants that has been recognized as a true taxon ranking below subspecies, even though it may have been brought under cultivation: e.g., cabbage (*Brassica oleracea* var. *capitata*) *d) Zool.* any of a group of widely separated variants within a single interbreeding population —*adj.* of or in a variety show

variety meat meat other than flesh; specif., any of the edible organs, as the liver, kidneys, heart, etc.

variety show a show, as on television or in a nightclub, made up of different kinds of acts, as comic skits, songs, dances, etc.: see also VAUDEVILLE

☆**variety store** a retail store that sells a wide variety of relatively small and inexpensive items

var·i·form (ver′ə fôrm′, var′-) *adj.* varied in form; having various forms

var·i·o·coup·ler (ver′ē ō kup′lər, var′-) *n.* [VARIO(US) + COUPLER] a radio-frequency transformer consisting of a movable coil within a fixed coil

va·ri·o·la (və rī′ə lə) *n.* [ModL. < ML., a pustule < L. *varius,* various, mottled: see VARY] any of a group of virus diseases characterized by pustular eruptions and including smallpox, cowpox, horsepox, etc.

va·ri·o·lar (-lər) *adj. same as* VARIOLOUS

var·i·ole (ver′ē ōl′) *n.* [Fr. < ML. *variola:* see VARIOLA] **1.** a tiny pit or depression, as on some parts of an insect **2.** any of the whitish spherules in variolite

var·i·o·lite (ver′ē ə līt′) *n.* [G. *variolit* < ML. *variola* (see VARIOLA): from its pitted surface] a basaltic or andesite rock in which whitish spherules of feldspar are embedded

var·i·o·loid (ver′ē ə loid′, var′-) *n.* [ModL. *varioloides:* see VARIOLA & -OID] a mild form of variola occurring in a person who has had a previous attack or who has been vaccinated

va·ri·o·lous (və rī′ə ləs) *adj.* [ModL. *variolosus*] of or relating to variola, or smallpox

var·i·om·e·ter (ver′ē äm′ə tər, var′-) *n.* [VARIO(US) + -METER] **1.** any of various devices designed to measure or record small variations in some quantity, as air pressure **2.** a geophysical instrument for measuring magnetic forces or determining variations of magnetic force, esp. at different places on the earth **3.** *Radio* an instrument consisting of a movable coil mounted within and in series with a fixed coil, with the inner coil capable of rotation so as to vary the mutual inductance of the unit

var·i·o·rum (ver′ē ôr′əm, var′-) *n.* [L., of various (scholars), gen. pl. of *varius:* see ff.] **1.** an edition or text, as of a literary work, containing notes by various editors, scholars, etc. **2.** an edition of a work containing variant versions of the text —*adj.* of such an edition or text

var·i·ous (ver′ē əs, var′-) *adj.* [L. *varius,* diverse, parti-colored: see VARY] **1.** differing one from another; of several kinds **2.** *a)* several or many *[found in various sections of the country]* *b)* individual; distinct *[bequests to the various heirs]* **3.** many-sided; versatile **4.** characterized by variety; varied in nature or appearance **5.** [Obs.] changeable —SYN. see DIFFERENT —**var′i·ous·ly** *adv.*

va·ris·tor (və ris′tər) *n.* [VAR(IOUS) + (RES)ISTOR] *Electronics* a semiconductor resistor whose resistance varies with the voltage applied

var·ix (var′iks) *n., pl.* **var′i·ces′** (-ə sēz′) [L.] **1.** *Med.* a permanently and irregularly swollen or dilated blood or lymph vessel, esp. a vein; varicose vein **2.** *Zool.* a prominent ridge across the whorls of various spiral shells, showing an earlier position of the outer lip

var·let (vär′lit) *n.* [ME. < OFr., a servant, page, var. of *vaslet* (see VALET): for sense development cf. KNAVE] [Archaic] **1.** an attendant **2.** a youth serving as a knight's page **3.** a scoundrel; knave

var·let·ry (-li trē) *n.* [Archaic] **1.** varlets collectively **2.** the rabble; mob

var·mint, var·ment (vär′mənt) *n.* [dial. var. of VERMIN, with unhistoric -*t*] [Dial. or Colloq.] a person or animal regarded as troublesome or objectionable: also used as a generalized epithet of disparagement

Var·na (vär′nä) seaport in NE Bulgaria, on the Black Sea: pop. 180,000

var·na (vur′nə) *n.* [Hindi *varṇa,* color < Sans., orig. prob. covering < IE. base *wer-,* to close, cover, whence WEIR] *same as* CASTE (sense 1)

var·nish (vär′nish) *n.* [ME. *vernisch* < OFr. *verniz* < ML. *veronix, veronice,* a resin < Gr. *Berenikē* (now Benghazi), ancient city in Cyrenaica] **1.** *a)* a preparation made of resinous substances dissolved in oil (*oil varnish*) or in a liquid such as alcohol which evaporates quickly (*spirit varnish*), used to give a glossy surface to wood, metal, etc. *b)* any of various natural or prepared products used for the same purpose **2.** the smooth, hard, glossy surface of this after it has dried **3.** a surface gloss or smoothness, as of manner —*vt.* **1.** to cover with varnish; brush varnish on **2.** to impart a smooth surface or appearance to, as with varnish **3.** to make superficially attractive or acceptable, as by embellishing **4.** to polish up; brighten —**var′nish·er** *n.*

varnish tree any of a number of trees whose sap or juice can be made into a varnish or lacquer (*n.* 2)

va·room (və rōōm′) *n., vi. var. of* VROOM

Var·ro (var′ō), (**Marcus Terentius**) 116–27? B.C.; Roman scholar & writer

var·si·ty (vär′sə tē) *n., pl.* **-ties** [contr. & altered < UNIVERSITY] **1.** the main team that represents a university, college, or school in some competition, esp. an athletic one **2.** [Brit. Colloq.] a university —*adj.* designating or of a university, college, or school team or competition

Var·u·na (vur′ōō nə, var′-, vär′-) [Sans.] the Hindu god of the cosmos

var·us (ver′əs, var′-) *n.* [ModL. < L., bent, knock-kneed: see VACILLATE] an abnormal bent or turned condition, esp. of the foot —*adj.* abnormally bent or turned: said of the hip, knee, or foot

varve (värv) *n.* [Sw. *varv,* a layer < *varva,* to turn, change < ON. *hverfa* < IE. base *kwerp-,* to turn, whence CARPUS]

---

an annual layer of sedimentary material deposited in lakes and fiords by glacial meltwaters, consisting of two distinct bands of sediment deposited in summer and winter

var·y (ver′ē, var′-) *vt.* **var′ied, var′y·ing** [ME. *varien* < OFr. *varier* < L. *variare,* to vary, change < *varius,* various, prob. < IE. base **wa-,* to bend, turn (cf. VACILLATE)] **1.** to change in form, appearance, nature, substance, etc.; alter; modify **2.** to make different from one another **3.** to give variety to; diversify [to *vary* one's reading] **4.** *Music* to repeat (a theme or idea) with changes in harmony, rhythm, key, etc. —*vi.* **1.** to undergo change in any way; become different **2.** to be different or diverse; differ [*varying* opinions] **3.** to deviate, diverge, or depart (*from*) **4.** *Biol.* to show variation **5.** *Math.* to change (directly or inversely) in the same ratio —*SYN.* see CHANGE

vas (vas) *n., pl.* **va·sa** (vā′sə) [L., a vessel, dish] *Anat., Biol.* a vessel or duct —**va·sal** (vā′s'l) *adj.*

Va·sa·ri (vä zä′rē), **Gior·gio** (jôr′jō) 1511–74; It. architect, painter, & biographer of artists

Vas·con·ga·das (väs′kôn gä′t̶h̶äs) *Sp. name of the* BASQUE PROVINCES

vas·cu·lar (vas′kyə lər) *adj.* [ModL. *vascularis* < L. *vasculum,* small vessel, dim. of *vas,* a vessel, dish] of or having vessels or ducts; specif., *a) Anat., Zool.* designating or of the vessels, or system of vessels, for conveying blood or lymph *b) Bot.* of or pertaining to the specialized conducting cells, xylem and phloem, that convey water and foods in plants; also, of or pertaining to plants that have xylem and phloem —**vas′cu·lar′i·ty** (-lar′ə tē) *n.*

vascular bundle *Bot.* an isolated unit of the conducting system of higher plants, consisting of xylem and phloem, frequently with other interspersed cells or a sheath of thick-walled cells

vascular cylinder *same as* STELE (sense 3)
vascular plant *same as* TRACHEOPHYTE
vascular ray *same as* MEDULLARY RAY (sense 2)
vascular tissue *Bot.* tissue composed of the xylem and phloem ducts that carry sap and food through any of the higher plants

vas·cu·lum (vas′kyə ləm) *n., pl.* **-la** (-lə) **-lums** [ModL. < L.: see VASCULAR] a covered metal case, often cylindrical, used by botanists to carry specimen plants

vas de·fe·rens (vas def′ə renz′) *pl.* **va·sa de·fe·ren·ti·a** (vā′sə def′ə ren′shē ə) [ModL. < L. *vas,* a vessel + *deferens,* carrying down (see DEFERENCE)] the highly convoluted duct that conveys sperm from the testicle to the ejaculatory duct of the penis

vase (vās, vāz; *chiefly Brit.,* väz) *n.* [Fr. < L. *vas,* a vessel, dish] an open container of metal, glass, pottery, etc., usually rounded and of greater height than width, used for decoration, for holding flowers, etc.

vas·ec·to·my (vas ek′tə mē) *n., pl.* **-mies** [VAS(O)- + -ECTOMY] the surgical removal of all or part of the vas deferens: cf. VASOTOMY

☆**Vas·e·line** (vas′ə lēn′) [arbitrary coinage < G. *was(ser),* WATER + Gr. *el(aion),* OIL + -INE⁴] *a trademark for* petrolatum —*n.* [v-] petrolatum, or petroleum jelly

Vash·ti (vash′tī, väsh′tē) [Heb. *washtī*] *Bible* the queen of Ahasuerus of Persia, disowned by him when she slighted his command for her presence at a feast: Esth. 1

vas·o- (vas′ō, -ə) [< L. *vas,* a vessel] *a combining form meaning:* **1.** the blood vessels [*vasomotor*] **2.** the vas deferens [*vasectomy*] **3.** vasomotor [*vasoinhibitor*] Also, before a vowel, **vas-**

vas·o·con·stric·tor (vas′ō kən strik′tər) *adj.* [prec. + CONSTRICTOR] *Physiol.* causing constriction of the blood vessels —*n.* a nerve or drug causing such constriction —**vas′o·con·stric′tion** *n.*

vas·o·di·la·tor (-dī′lāt′ər) *adj.* [VASO- + DILATOR] *Physiol.* causing dilatation of the blood vessels —*n.* a nerve or drug causing such dilatation —**vas′o·dil′a·ta′tion** (-dil′ə tā′shən), **vas′o·di·la′tion** (-dī lā′shən) *n.*

vas·o·in·hib·i·tor (-in hib′ə tər) *n.* [VASO- + INHIBITOR] a drug or agent inhibiting the action of the vasomotor nerves —**vas′o·in·hib′i·to·ry** (-tôr′ē) *adj.*

vas·o·mo·tor (-mōt′ər) *adj.* [VASO- + MOTOR] *Physiol.* regulating the caliber, or size in diameter, of blood vessels by causing contraction or dilatation: said of a nerve, nerve center, or drug

vas·o·pres·sin (-pres′'n) *n.* [< VASO- + PRESS(URE) + -IN¹] a hormone secreted by the posterior pituitary gland that increases blood pressure by constricting the arterioles

vas·o·pres·sor (-pres′ər) *adj.* [VASO- + PRESS(URE) + -OR] causing a rise in blood pressure by constricting blood vessels —*n.* a substance causing such rise

vas·o·spasm (vas′ə spaz′m) *n.* [VASO- + SPASM] a spastic constriction of a blood vessel

vas·ot·o·my (vas ät′ə mē) *n., pl.* **-mies** [VASO- + -TOMY] a surgical cutting of the vas deferens, as for the purpose of sterilizing sexually

vas·o·va·gal (vas′ō vā′g'l) *adj.* [VASO- + VAGAL] pertaining to the action of the vagus nerve upon the circulatory system, as in causing a fainting spell

vas·sal (vas′'l) *n.* [ME. < OFr. < ML. *vassalus,* man-servant, extension of *vassus,* servant < Celt.: for base see VALET] **1.** in the Middle Ages, a person who held land under the feudal system, doing homage and pledging fealty to an overlord, and performing military or other duties in return for his protection; feudal tenant **2.** a subordinate, subject, servant, slave, etc. —*adj.* **1.** of or like a vassal; dependent, servile, etc. **2.** being a vassal

vas·sal·age (-ij) *n.* [ME. < OFr. < ML. *vassallagium*] **1.** the state of being a vassal **2.** the homage, loyalty, and service required of a vassal **3.** dependence, subservience, or subjection **4.** lands held by a vassal; fief **5.** a body of vassals

vast (vast, väst) *adj.* [L. *vastus:* see WASTE] very great in size, extent, amount, number, degree, etc. —*n.* [Archaic] a vast space —**vast′ly** *adv.* —**vast′ness** *n.*

Väs·te·rås (ves′tə rôs′) city in SC Sweden, on Lake Malar: pop. 85,000

vas·ti·tude (vas′tə tood′, väs′-; -tyood′) *n.* **1.** the quality or condition of being vast **2.** a vast extent or space

vast·y (vas′tē, väs′-) *adj.* **vast′i·er, vast′i·est** [Archaic] vast; immense; huge

vat (vat) *n.* [ME., Southern dial. var. of *fat* < OE. *fæt,* a cask, vessel, akin to G. *fass,* container < IE. base **pēd-,* **pōd-,* to seize, hold, whence Lett. *pußds,* a pot] **1.** a large tank, tub, or cask for holding liquids to be used in a manufacturing process or to be stored for fermenting or ripening **2.** a liquid containing a vat dye: see VAT DYE —*vt.* **vat′ted, vat′ting 1.** to place or store in a vat **2.** to dip into a vat (*n.* 2)

vat dye a colorfast dye made soluble for application to cloth, then oxidized and thus rendered insoluble in the cloth —**vat′-dyed′** *adj.*

vat·ic (vat′ik) *adj.* [< L. *vates,* a prophet < IE. base **wāt-,* to be mentally excited, whence OE. *wōd,* mad, MIr. *fāth,* prophecy] of or characteristic of a prophet; prophetic

Vat·i·can (vat′i k'n) [L. *Vaticanus* (*mons*), Vatican (hill)] **1.** the papal palace, consisting of a group of buildings in Vatican City **2.** the papal government or authority —*adj.* **1.** of this palace or government **2.** designating either of the Roman Catholic Ecumenical Councils held in St. Peter's Basilica in 1869–1870 (**Vatican I**) or 1962–1965 (**Vatican II**)

Vatican City independent papal state constituted in 1929 as an enclave in Rome: it includes the Vatican & St. Peter's Basilica: 108 acres; pop. c.1,000

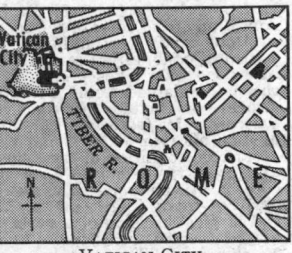

VATICAN CITY

va·tic·i·nal (və tis′ə n'l) *adj.* [< L. *vaticinus* (see VATICINATE) + -AL] having the nature of or characterized by prophecy; prophetic

va·tic·i·nate (-nāt′) *vt.,* *vi.* **-nat′ed, -nat′ing** [< L. *vaticinatus,* pp. of *vaticinari,* to foretell, prophesy < *vaticinus,* prophetic < *vates,* a seer, prophet: see VATIC] to prophesy; foretell —**vat·i·ci·na·tion** (vat′ə si nā′shən) *n.* —**va·tic′i·na′tor** *n.*

Vat·ter (vet′ər), **Lake** lake in SC Sweden: 733 sq. mi.: Swed. name **Vät·tern** (vet′tərn)

Vau·ban (vō bän′), **marquis de** (də) (*Sébastien le Prestre*) 1633–1707; Fr. military engineer

Vaud (vō) canton of W Switzerland: 1,240 sq. mi.; pop. 473,000; cap. Lausanne

vaude·ville (vôd′vil, vôd′-; vō′də-, vô′də-) *n.* [Fr., earlier *vau-de-vire* < *Vau-de-Vire,* the valley of the Vire (in Normandy), famous for light, convivial songs] ☆**1.** *a)* a stage show consisting of mixed specialty acts, including songs, dances, comic skits, acrobatic performances, etc. *b)* this branch of entertainment generally **2.** [Now Rare] a comic theatrical piece interspersed with songs and dances **3.** [Obs.] a satirical or topical song, often with pantomime

☆**vaude·vil·lian** (vôd vil′yən, vôd-; vō′də-, vô′də-) *n.* one who performs in vaudeville —*adj.* of or like vaudeville

Vau·dois (vō dwä′) *n.pl.* [Fr. < ML. *Valdenses:* see WALDENSES] *same as* WALDENSES

Vaughan (vôn) **1.** [< a family name] a masculine name: also sp. **Vaughn 2.** Henry, 1622–95; Eng. poet & metaphysician: called *the* Silurist

Vaughan Williams, Ralph 1872–1958; Eng. composer

vault¹ (vôlt) *n.* [ME. *voute* < OFr. < VL. **volvita,* an arch, vault < **volvitus,* pp. of **volvitare,* intens. of L. *volvere,* to turn around, roll (see WALK)] **1.** an arched roof, ceiling, or covering of masonry **2.** an arched chamber or space, esp. when underground **3.** a cellar room used for storage, as of wine **4.** *a)* a burial chamber *b)* a concrete or metal enclosure in the ground, into which the casket is lowered at burial ☆**5.** a secure room, often with individual safe-deposit boxes, for the safekeeping of valuables or money, as in a bank **6.** an underground cave with a naturally arched roof **7.** the sky as a vaultlike canopy **8.** *Anat.* any arched cavity or structure [the cranial *vault*] —*vt.* **1.** to make a vault over; cover with a vault **2.** to build in the form of a vault —*vi.* to curve like a vault

GROINED VAULT

vault² (vôlt) *vi.* [MFr. *volter* < OIt. *voltare* < VL. **volvitare:* see prec.] to jump, leap, or spring, as over a barrier or

from one position to another, esp. with the help of the hands supported on the barrier, etc., or holding a long pole —*vt.* to vault over *[to vault a fence]* —*n.* [sense 1 the *v.*; sense 2 < Fr. *volte,* a turn, bound, leap < It. *volta* < LL. **volta:* see prec.] **1.** an act of vaulting **2.** a leap or bound made by a horse; curvet —**vault′er** *n.*

vault·ed (vôl′tid) *adj.* **1.** having the form of a vault; arched **2.** built with an arched roof; having a vault

vault·ing¹ (-tin) *n.* **1.** the building of a vault or vaults **2.** the arched work forming a vault **3.** a vault or vaults

vault·ing² (-tin) *adj.* **1.** leaping or leaping over **2.** over-reaching; unduly confident *[vaulting* ambition*]* **3.** used in vaulting

vaunt (vônt, vänt) *vi.* [ME. *vaunten* < OFr. *vanter* < LL.(Ec.) *vanitare* < L. *vanus,* VAIN] to boast; brag —*vt.* to boast about (something); brag of —*n.* a boast; brag —SYN. see BOAST¹ —**vaunt′ed** *adj.* —**vaunt′er** *n.*

vaunt-cour·i·er (vônt′koor′ē ər, vänt′-) *n.* [Fr. *avant-courrier*] **1.** [Obs.] a soldier sent out in advance of an army **2.** a forerunner; precursor

vaunt·y (vôn′tē) *adj.* [Scot.] boastful; vain

v.aux. auxiliary verb

vav (väv, vôv) *n.* [Heb. *vāv,* lit., a hook] the sixth letter of the Hebrew alphabet (ٵ)

vav·a·sor (vav′ə sôr′) *n.* [ME. *vavasour* < OFr. < ML. *vavassor,* prob. < *vassus vassorum,* vassal of vassals: cf. VASSAL, VALET] in the Middle Ages, a feudal vassal next in rank below a baron, holding lands from a superior lord and having vassals under himself: also **vav′a·sour′** (-soor′)

va·ward (vä′wôrd) *n.* [LME., contr. < *vaumwarde,* for ONormFr. *avantwarde* < OFr. *avant-garde:* see VANGUARD] *archaic var. of* VANGUARD

vb. 1. verb **2.** verbal

VC, V.C. Viet Cong

V.C. 1. Veterinary Corps **2.** Vice-Chairman **3.** Vice-Chancellor **4.** Vice-Consul **5.** Victoria Cross

VD, V.D. venereal disease

☆**V-Day** (vē′dā′) *n.* Victory Day

've contraction of HAVE *[we've* seen it*]*

Ve·a·dar (vā′ä där′, vē′ä där′) *n.* [Heb. *wĕ-adhār,* lit., and Adar, hence second Adar] an extra month of the Jewish year, occurring about once every three years between Adar and Nisan: see JEWISH CALENDAR

veal (vēl) *n.* [ME. *vel* < OFr. *veel* < L. *vitellus,* little calf, dim. of *vitulus,* a calf, orig. prob. yearling, akin to *vetus,* old; see VETERAN, WETHER] **1.** the flesh of a young calf used as food **2.** *same as* VEALER

☆**veal·er** (-ər) *n.* a calf, esp. as intended for food

Veb·len (veb′lən), **Thor·stein (Bunde)** (thôr′stin) 1857–1929; U.S. political economist & social scientist

vec·tor (vek′tər) *n.* [ModL. < L., a bearer, carrier < *vectus,* pp. of *vehere,* to carry: see WAY] **1.** *Biol.* an animal, as an insect, that transmits a disease-producing organism from one host to another **2.** *Math.* *a)* a physical quantity with both magnitude and direction, such as a force or velocity: distinguished from SCALAR *b)* a directed line segment representing such a physical quantity *c)* a directed line segment without physical interpretation *d)* a set of *n* real numbers arranged either horizontally in a row or vertically in a column **3.** the particular course followed or to be followed, as by an aircraft; compass heading —*vt.* to guide (a pilot, aircraft, missile, etc.) by means of a vector sent by radio —**vec·to′ri·al** (-tôr′ē əl) *adj.* —**vec·to′ri·al·ly** *adv.*

VECTOR
(AB, x-component of vector V; CD, y-component of vector V; O, origin; T, terminus)

vector analysis the branch of mathematics dealing with the geometry of vectors and with mathematical operations performed on vectors

vector product a vector perpendicular to two given vectors whose magnitude is equal to the product of their lengths and the sine of the angle between their positive directions

Ve·da (vā′də, vē′-) *n.* [Sans. *veda,* knowledge < IE. base **weid-,* to see, know, whence WISE¹, L. *videre,* to see] **1.** any of four ancient sacred books of Hinduism, consisting of psalms, chants, sacred formulas, etc.: see RIG-VEDA **2.** these books collectively —**Ve·da·ic** (vi dā′ik) *adj.* —**Ve′da·ism** *n.*

ve·da·li·a (və dā′lē ə, -dāl′yə) *n.* [ModL. < ?] an Australian ladybug (*Rodolia cardinalis*), now widely introduced all over the world to combat certain scale insects

Ve·dan·ta (vi dän′tə, -dan′-) *n.* [Sans. *Vedānta* < *Veda* (see VEDA) + *anta,* an END] a system of Hindu monistic or pantheistic philosophy based on the Vedas —**Ve·dan′tic** *adj.* —**Ve·dan′tism** *n.*

☆**V-E Day** (vē′ē′) May 8, 1945, the day on which the surrender of Germany was announced, officially ending the European phase of World War II

Ved·da (ved′ə) *n., pl.* **-das, -da** [Singh., a hunter] any member of the aboriginal people of Ceylon: also sp. **Ved′dah** —**Ved′doid** (-oid) *adj.*

ve·dette (vi det′) *n.* [Fr. < It. *vedetta,* altered (after *vedere,* to see) < *veletta,* sentry box < Sp. *vela,* a vigil < *velar,* to watch < L. *vigilare:* see VIGIL] **1.** formerly, a mounted sentinel posted in advance of the outposts of an army **2.** a well-known personality, esp. of the entertainment world

Ve·dic (vā′dik, vē′-) *adj.* of the Vedas —*n.* the Old Indic language of the Vedas, an early form of Sanskrit

vee (vē) *n.* the letter V, v, or anything shaped like it —*adj.* shaped like V

☆**Veep** (vēp) *n.* [altered from *veepee* (for *V. P.*)] [*sometimes* v-] [Colloq.] a vice-president; specif., the Vice President of the U.S.

veer¹ (vir) *vi.* [altered (after ff.) < Fr. *virer,* to turn around, prob. < VL. **virare,* contr. < L. *vibrare:* see VIBRATE] **1.** to change direction; shift; turn or swing around **2.** to change sides; shift, as from one opinion or attitude to another **3.** *Meteorol.* to shift clockwise (in the Northern Hemisphere): said of the wind: opposed to BACK¹ (*vi.* 2) **4.** *Naut. a)* to change the direction of a ship by swinging its stern to the wind; wear ship *b)* to be so turned: said of a ship —*vt.* **1.** to turn or swing; change the course of **2.** *Naut.* to change the direction or course of (a ship) by swinging its stern to the wind; wear —*n.* a change of direction —SYN. see DEVIATE —**veer′ing·ly** *adv.*

veer² (vir) *vt., vi.* [ME. *veren* < MDu. *vieren,* to let out] *Naut.* to let out (a line, chain, anchor, etc.): often with *out*

☆**veer·y** (vir′ē) *n., pl.* **veer′ies** [prob. echoic] a brown and cream-colored thrush (*Hylocichla fuscescens*) of the E U.S.

Ve·ga (vē′gə, vā′-) *n.* [ML. < Ar. (*ar nasr*) *al waqi',* the falling (vulture)] a very bright star in the constellation Lyra

Ve·ga (ve′gä), **Lo·pe de** (lō′pe *the*) (born *Lope Félix de Vega Carpio*) 1562–1635; Sp. dramatist & poet

veg·e·ta·ble (vej′tə b'l, vej′ə tə-) *adj.* [ME. < ML. *vegetabilis,* vegetative, capable of growth < LL., animating, enlivening < L. *vegetare:* see VEGETATE] **1.** of, or having the nature of, plants in general *[the vegetable* kingdom*]* **2.** of, having the nature of, made from, consisting of, or produced by, edible vegetables —*n.* [< ML. *vegetabilia* (pl.), growing things, vegetables] **1.** broadly, any plant, as distinguished from animal or inorganic matter **2.** *a)* specif., any herbaceous plant that is eaten whole or in part, raw or cooked, generally with an entree or in a salad but not as a dessert *b)* the edible part of such a plant, as the root (e.g., a carrot), tuber (a potato), seed (a pea), fruit (a tomato), stem (celery), leaf (lettuce), etc. **3.** a person thought of as like a vegetable, as because of leading a dull, unthinking existence or because of having lost consciousness, the use of the mind, etc.

vegetable butter any of various vegetable fats that are solid at ordinary temperatures

vegetable ivory 1. the fully ripe, ivorylike seed of a S. American palm (*Phytelephas macrocarpa*) used to make buttons, ornaments, etc. **2.** the shell of the coquilla nut

vegetable marrow [Chiefly Brit.] **1.** any of various large, elongated, smooth-skinned, meaty varieties of summer squash **2.** the flesh of any of these

vegetable oil any of various liquid fats derived from the fruits or seeds of plants, used in food products

vegetable oyster ☆*same as* SALSIFY

vegetable silk *same as* KAPOK

☆**vegetable sponge** *same as* LUFFA (sense 2)

vegetable tallow any of various fatty, tallowlike substances got from the fruits or seeds of plants

vegetable wax any of various waxes found on the leaves or fruits of some plants and the stems of others

veg·e·tal (vej′ə t'l) *adj.* [ME. *vegytalle* < ML. **vegetalis* < *vegetare,* to grow < L.: see VEGETATE] *same as:* **1.** VEGETABLE **2.** VEGETATIVE (sense 3)

veg·e·tar·i·an (vej′ə ter′ē ən) *n.* [VEGET(ABLE) + -ARIAN] a person who eats no meat, and sometimes no animal products (as milk, eggs, etc.); esp., one who advocates a diet of only vegetables, fruits, grains, and nuts as the proper one for all people for reasons of health or because of principles opposing the killing of animals —*adj.* **1.** of vegetarians or vegetarianism **2.** consisting only of vegetables, fruits, etc.

veg·e·tar·i·an·ism (-iz'm) *n.* the principles or practices of vegetarians

veg·e·tate (vej′ə tāt′) *vi.* **-tat′ed, -tat′ing** [< L. *vegetatus,* pp. of *vegetare,* to enliven < *vegetus,* lively < *vegere,* to quicken, WAKE¹; senses 1 & 2 infl. by VEGETABLE] **1.** to grow as plants **2.** to exist with little mental and physical activity; lead a dull, inactive life **3.** *Med.* to grow or increase in size, as a wart or other abnormal outgrowth

veg·e·ta·tion (vej′ə tā′shən) *n.* [ML. *vegetatio,* growth < LL., an enlivening: see prec.] **1.** the act or process of vegetating **2.** plant life in general **3.** a dull, passive, unthinking existence **4.** *Med.* any abnormal outgrowth on a part of the body —**veg′e·ta′tion·al** *adj.*

veg·e·ta·tive (vej′ə tāt′iv) *adj.* [ME. < ML. *vegetativus* < L. *vegetatus:* see VEGETATE] **1.** *a)* of vegetation, or plants *b)* of or concerned with vegetation, or plant growth **2.** growing, or capable of growing, as plants **3.** designating or of those functions or parts of plants concerned with

growth and nutrition as distinguished from reproduction **4.** capable of causing growth in plants; fertile *[vegetative material]* **5.** *same as* VEGETATIONAL **6.** involuntary or passive like the growth of plants; showing little mental activity *[a vegetative existence]* **7.** *Zool.* of or pertaining to reproduction by budding or other asexual method Also **veg′e·tive** (-tiv) **—veg′e·ta′tive·ly** *adv.* **—veg′e·ta′tive-ness** *n.*

ve·he·ment (vē′ə mənt; *occas.* vē′hi-) *adj.* [LME. < MFr. *véhément* < L. *vehemens*, eager, vehement < base of *vehere*, to carry: see WAY] **1.** acting or moving with great force; violent; impetuous **2.** having or characterized by intense feeling or strong passion; fervent, impassioned, etc. **—ve′he·mence, ve′he·men·cy** *n.* **—ve′he·ment·ly** *adv.*

ve·hi·cle (vē′ə k'l; *occas.* vē′hi-) *n.* [Fr. *véhicule* < L. *vehiculum*, carriage < *vehere*, to carry: see WAY] **1.** any device or contrivance for carrying or conveying persons or objects, including land conveyances, vessels, aircraft, and spacecraft: sometimes specif. restricted to land conveyances on wheels, runners, treads, etc. **2.** a means by which thoughts are expressed or made known *[music as the vehicle for one's ideas]* **3.** a play thought of as a means of communication or as a means of presenting a specified actor or company **4.** *Painting* a liquid, as water or oil, with which pigments are mixed for use **5.** *Pharmacy* a substance, as sweet syrup, in which medicines are given

ve·hic·u·lar (vē hik′yoo lər) *adj.* [LL. *vehicularis*] **1.** of or for vehicles *[a vehicular tunnel]* **2.** serving as a vehicle **3.** resulting from collisions, etc. of vehicles, as accidents

☆**V-8** (vē′āt′) *adj.* designating or of an internal-combustion engine with two opposing rows of cylinders, four to a row, and with each pair of cylinders opposed at a V-shaped angle **—n. 1.** a V-8 engine **2.** an automotive vehicle with a V-8 engine

Ve·ii (vē′yī) ancient Etruscan city just northwest of Rome: destroyed by the Romans in 396 B.C.

veil (vāl) *n.* [ME. *veile*, veil, sail, curtain < ONormFr. < L. *vela*, neut. pl., taken as fem. of *velum*, a sail, cloth, curtain < IE. base *weg-*, to weave, attach, a textile, whence OIr. *figim*, I weave, OE. *wecca*, wick] **1.** a piece of light fabric, as of net or gauze, worn, esp. by women, over the face or head or draped from a hat to conceal, protect, or enhance the face **2.** any piece of cloth used as a concealing or separating screen or curtain **3.** anything like a veil in that it covers or conceals *[a veil of mist, a veil of silence]* **4.** *a)* a part of a nun's headdress, draped along the sides of the face and over the shoulders *b)* the state or life of a nun or novice: chiefly in **take the veil,** to become a nun **5.** *short for* HUMERAL VEIL **6.** [Dial.] *same as* CAUL **7.** *Bot., Zool. same as* VELUM **—vt. 1.** to cover with or as with a veil **2.** to conceal, hide, disguise, screen, obscure, etc.

veiled (vāld) *adj.* **1.** wearing a veil **2.** covered with or as with a veil **3.** concealed, hidden, disguised, obscured, etc. **4.** not openly expressed *[a veiled threat]*

veil·ing (vā′liŋ) *n.* **1.** the act of covering with or as with a veil **2.** a veil; curtain **3.** thin, transparent fabric used for veils

vein (vān) *n.* [ME. *veine* < OFr. < L. *vena*] **1.** *a)* any blood vessel that carries blood from some part of the body back toward the heart *b)* loosely, any blood vessel **2.** any of the riblike supports strengthening the membranous wings of an insect **3.** any of the bundles of vascular tissue forming the framework of a leaf blade **4.** a more or less continuous body of minerals, igneous or sedimentary rock, etc., occupying a fissure or zone, differing in nature, and abruptly separated, from the enclosing rock and usually deposited from solution by circulating water **5.** *same as* LODE (senses 1 & 2) **6.** a streak or marking of a different color or substance from the surrounding material, as in marble or wood **7.** *a)* any distinctive quality or strain regarded as running through one's character, or a speech, writing, etc. *[a vein of humor in the essay]* *b)* course or tenor of thought, feeling, action, etc. **8.** a temporary state of mind; mood *[speaking in a serious vein]* **—vt. 1.** to streak or mark with or as with veins **2.** to branch out through in the manner of veins **—SYN.** see MOOD¹

veined (vānd) *adj.* having veins or veinlike markings

vein·ing (vā′niŋ) *n.* the formation or arrangement of veins or veinlike markings

vein·let (vān′lit) *n. same as* VENULE

vein·stone (-stōn′) *n. same as* GANGUE

vein·ule (-yōōl) *n.* [VEIN + -ULE] *same as* VENULE

vein·y (vā′nē) *adj.* **vein′i·er, vein′i·est 1.** having or showing veins **2.** full of veins, as flesh, leaves, marble, etc.

vel. vellum

Ve·la (vē′lə) [ModL. < L.: see VEIL] a constellation in the S Milky Way directly north of Carina

ve·la (vē′lə) *n. pl. of* VELUM

ve·la·men (vē lā′mən) *n., pl.* **-lam′i·na** (-lam′i nə) [L., a covering < *velare*, to cover: for base see VEIL] **1.** *Anat.* a membrane or velum **2.** *Bot.* the corky outer layer of the aerial roots of certain orchids **—vel·a·men·tous** (vel′ə men′təs) *adj.*

ve·lar (vē′lər) *adj.* [L. *velaris*, belonging to a veil or curtain < *velum*, a VEIL] **1.** of a velum; esp., of the soft palate in the mouth **2.** *Phonet.* pronounced with the back of the tongue touching or near the soft palate, as the sound of *k* when followed by a back vowel such as (ōō) or (ô) **—n.** a velar sound

ve·lar·i·um (və ler′ē əm, -lar′-) *n., pl.* **-i·a** (-ə) [L. < *velum*, a covering, VEIL] in ancient Rome, a large awning over an amphitheater or theater

ve·lar·ize (vē′lə rīz′) *vt.* **-ized′, -iz′ing** *Phonet.* to modify the pronunciation of (a sound) by an adjacent velar sound **—ve′lar·i·za′tion** *n.*

ve·late (vē′lāt, -lit) *adj.* [L. *velatus*, pp. of *velare*, to cover: for base see VEIL] having a velum

Ve·láz·quez (və läth′keth; *E.* və las′kes, -kwez), **Die·go Ro·drí·guez de Sil·va y** (dye′gō rō thrē′geth *the* sēl′vä ē) 1599-1660; Sp. painter: also **Ve·lás·quez** (ve läs′keth)

☆**Vel·cro** (vel′krō) [arbitrary formation based on VEL(VET)] *a trademark for* a nylon material made with both a surface of tiny hooks and a complementary surface of an adhesive pile, used, as in garments, in matching strips that can be pressed together or pulled apart for easy fastening and unfastening **—n.** this material

veld, veldt (velt) *n.* [Afrik. < MDu. *veld*, a FIELD] in South Africa, open grassy country, with few bushes and almost no trees; grassland

vel·i·ta·tion (vel′ə tā′shən) *n.* [L. *velitatio* < *velitatus*, pp. of *velitari*, to skirmish < *velites*, VELITES] a hostile encounter; skirmish or dispute

vel·i·tes (vē′lə tēz′) *n.pl.* [L., pl. of *veles* (gen. *velitis*), akin to *velox*, swift & *vehere*, to carry: see WAY] in ancient Rome, lightly armed foot soldiers

vel·le·i·ty (və lē′ə tē) *n., pl.* **-ties** [ML. *velleitas* < L. *velle*, to wish: see WILL²] **1.** the weakest kind of desire or volition **2.** a mere wish that does not lead to the slightest action

vel·li·cate (vel′ə kāt′) *vt., vi.* **-cat′ed, -cat′ing** [L. *vellicatus*, pp. of *vellicare*, to twitch, pinch < *vellere*, to pluck < IE. base *wel-*, to tear, pluck out, whence OE. *wæl*, battlefield] [Now Rare] to twitch, pluck, etc. **—vel′li·ca′tion** *n.*

vel·lum (vel′əm) *n.* [ME. *velim* < MFr. *velin*, vellum, prepared calfskin < *veel*: see VEAL] **1.** a fine kind of parchment prepared from calfskin, lambskin, or kidskin, used as writing parchment or for binding books **2.** a manuscript written on vellum **3.** a strong paper made to resemble vellum **—adj.** of or like vellum

ve·loc·i·pede (və läs′ə pēd′) *n.* [Fr. *vélocipède* < L. *velox* (gen. *velocis*), swift, speedy (for base see WAY) + *pes* (gen. *pedis*), a FOOT] **1.** any of various early bicycles or tricycles **2.** [Now Rare] a child's tricycle **3.** an old type of handcar for use on railroad tracks

ve·loc·i·ty (-tē) *n., pl.* **-ties** [Fr. *vélocité* < L. *velocitas* < *velox*: see prec.] **1.** quickness or rapidity of motion or action; swiftness; speed **2.** *a)* rate of change of position, in relation to time *b)* rate of motion in a particular direction, as of the rotation of a sphere, in relation to time

ve·lo·drome (vē′lə drōm′, vel′ə-) *n.* [Fr. *vélodrome* < *vélo* (contr. < *vélocipède*, VELOCIPEDE) + *-drome*, -DROME] an indoor arena with a track banked for bicycle races

ve·lour, ve·lours (və loor′) *n., pl.* **ve·lours′** [Fr.: see VELURE] a fabric with a soft nap like velvet, used for upholstery, draperies, hats, clothing, etc.

ve·lou·té (və lōō tā′) *n.* [Fr., velvety] a rich white sauce made from meat or fish stock thickened with flour and butter: also **velouté sauce**

Vel·sen (vel′sən) city in W Netherlands: pop. 68,000

†**vel·skoen** (vel′skün′, fel′-) *n.pl.* [Afrik. < *vel*, skin (< MDu., akin to FELL⁴) + *skoen*, shoe (akin to OE. *scoh*, SHOE)] sturdy shoes of untanned hide, worn in South Africa: also **veld′skoen** (velt′-, felt′-)

ve·lum (vē′ləm) *n., pl.* **-la** (-lə) [L., a VEIL] *Biol.* any of various veillike membranous partitions or coverings; specif., *a) same as* SOFT PALATE *b)* a lobed, ciliated swimming organ in front of the mouth of some mollusk larvae

ve·lure (və loor′) *n.* [Fr. *velours*, altered < OFr. *velous* < LL. *villosus*, shaggy < *villus*, shaggy hair: for IE. base see WOOL] velvet or a fabric like velvet

ve·lu·ti·nous (və lōōt′'n əs) *adj.* [< It. *velluto*, velvet (ult. < L. *villus*: see prec.) + -OUS] *Bot., Zool.* covered with short, dense, silky, upright hairs; soft and velvety

vel·vet (vel′vit) *n.* [ME. < OFr. *veluotte* < VL. *villutus* < L. *villus*, shaggy hair: see WOOL] **1.** a rich fabric of silk, rayon, nylon, etc. with a soft, thick pile: **pile velvet** has the pile uncut, standing in loops; **cut velvet** has the loops cut apart **2.** anything with a surface like that of velvet **3.** a soft, furry skin on a deer's growing antlers ☆**4.** [Old Slang] extra or clear profit or winnings; gain **—adj. 1.** made of or covered with velvet **2.** smooth or soft like velvet

☆**velvet ant** any of a family (Mutillidae) of wasps, often with brightly colored hairs: the females are wingless

☆**velvet bean** a coarse, twining, annual vine (*Stizolobium deeringianum*) of the legume family, grown for forage

vel·vet·een (vel′və tēn′) *n.* [< VELVET] **1.** a cotton cloth with a short, thick pile, resembling velvet **2.** [*pl.*] clothes, esp. trousers, made of velveteen

vel·vet·y (vel′vi tē) *adj.* **1.** smooth or soft like velvet **2.** smooth-tasting; mellow; not harsh: said of liquors

Ven. 1. Venerable **2.** Venice

†**ve·na** (vē′nə) *n., pl.* **ve′nae** (-nē) [L.] a vein

vena ca·va (kā′və) *pl.* **venae ca′vae** (-vē) [ModL. < L. *vena*, vein + *cava*, fem. of *cavus*, hollow] *Anat.* either of two large veins conveying blood to the right atrium of the heart

ve·nal (vē′n'l) *adj.* [L. *venalis*, salable, for sale < *venus*, sale < IE. *wesno-*, price, whence Sans. *vasná-*, price, payment, Gr. *ônos*, price] **1.** [Now Rare] capable of being obtained for a price *[venal services]* **2.** that can readily be

bribed or corrupted [a venal judge] 3. characterized by corruption or bribery [a venal bargain] —**ve′nal·ly** adv.

ve·nal·i·ty (vē nal′ə tē) n., pl. **-ties** [< Fr. or LL.: Fr. venalité < LL. venalitas] state, quality, or instance of being venal; willingness to be bribed or bought off, or to prostitute one's talents for mercenary considerations

ve·nat·ic (vē nat′ik) adj. [L. venaticus, of hunting < venatus, hunting < venari, to hunt: see VENISON] [Now Rare] of or engaging in hunting: also **ve·nat′i·cal**

ve·na·tion (vē nā′shən) n. [< L. vena, a vein] 1. an arrangement or system of veins, as in an animal part, an insect's wing, or a leaf 2. such veins collectively

vend (vend) vt. [Fr. vendre < L. vendere, contr. < venum dare, to offer for sale < venus, sale (see VENAL) + dare, to give] 1. to sell, esp. by peddling 2. to give public expression to (opinions); publish —vi. 1. to sell goods 2. to be disposed of by sale —SYN. see SELL

ven·dace (ven′dās) n., pl. **-dace, -dac·es:** see PLURAL, II, D, 2 [OFr. vandoise, dace] a freshwater whitefish (Coregonus vandesius) native to a few lakes of England and Scotland

Ven·dée (vän dā′) department of W France: scene of a royalist revolt (1793–96) —**Ven·de·an** (-dē′ən) adj., n.

vend·ee (ven′dē′) n. [VEND + -EE¹] the person to whom a thing is sold; buyer

vend·er (ven′dər) n. var. of VENDOR

ven·det·ta (ven det′ə) n. [It. < L. vindicta, vengeance: see VINDICTIVE] 1. a feud in which the relatives of a murdered or wronged person seek vengeance on the wrongdoer or members of his family 2. any bitter quarrel or feud —**ven·det′tist** n.

vend·i·ble (ven′də b'l) adj. [ME. < L. vendibilis < vendere: see VEND] 1. capable of being sold: also sp. **vend′a·ble** 2. [Obs.] same as VENAL —n. something vendible —**vend′i·bil′i·ty** n. —**vend′i·bly** adv.

vending machine a coin-operated machine for selling certain kinds of articles, refreshments, etc.

ven·di·tion (ven dish′ən) n. [L. venditio < venditus, pp. of vendere: see VEND] the act of vending; sale

Ven·dôme (vän dōm′), duc (**Louis Joseph**) **de** (də) 1654–1712; Fr. general; marshal of France

ven·dor (ven′dər) n. [Anglo-Fr. < Fr. vendre] 1. one who vends, or sells; seller 2. same as VENDING MACHINE

☆**ven·due** (ven dōō′, -dyōō′) n. [obs. Fr. vendue, sale < vendu, pp. of vendre: see VEND] a public auction

ve·neer (və nir′) vt. [G. furnieren, to veneer < Fr. fournir, to FURNISH] 1. to cover with a thin layer of more costly material; esp., to cover (wood) with wood of finer quality 2. to give a superficially attractive appearance to 3. to cement (thin layers of wood) to form plywood —n. 1. a thin surface layer of fine wood or costly material laid over a base of common material 2. any of the thin layers glued together in plywood 3. any attractive but superficial appearance or display [a veneer of culture]

ve·neer·ing (-iŋ) n. 1. the act of one who veneers 2. material used for veneer

ven·e·punc·ture (ven′ə puŋk′chər, vē′nə-) n. [< L. vena, vein + PUNCTURE] var. of VENIPUNCTURE

ven·er·a·ble (ven′ər ə b'l, ven′rə b'l) adj. [ME. < MFr. vénérable < L. venerabilis, to be reverenced < venerari: see VENERATE] 1. worthy of respect or reverence by reason of age and dignity, character, position, etc. 2. impressive on account of age or historic or religious associations [a venerable monument] In the Anglican Church, it is a title given to an archdeacon; in the Roman Catholic Church, it is a title given to persons who have attained the lowest of the three degrees of sanctity, the others being beatification and canonization —**ven′er·a·bil′i·ty, ven′er·a·ble·ness** n. —**ven′er·a·bly** adv.

Venerable Bede, the see BEDE

ven·er·ate (ven′ə rāt′) vt. **-at′ed, -at′ing** [< L. veneratus, pp. of venerari, to worship, reverence < venus (gen. veneris), love: see VENUS] to look upon with feelings of deep respect; regard as venerable; revere —SYN. see REVERE —**ven′er·a′tor** n.

ven·er·a·tion (ven′ə rā′shən) n. [ME. veneracion < OFr. < L. veneratio] 1. a venerating or being venerated 2. a feeling of deep respect and reverence 3. an act of showing this —SYN. see AWE

ve·ne·re·al (və nir′ē əl) adj. [ME. venerealle < L. venereus < venus, love (see VENUS)] 1. a) having to do with sexual love or intercourse b) serving to arouse sexual desire; aphrodisiac 2. a) transmitted only or chiefly by sexual intercourse with an infected individual [syphilis and gonorrhea, the venereal diseases] b) infected with a venereal disease c) of or dealing with venereal disease

ve·ne·re·ol·o·gy (və nir′ē äl′ə jē) n. [< VENERE(AL) + -o- + -LOGY] the branch of medicine dealing with venereal disease —**ve·ne′re·ol′o·gist** n.

ven·er·y¹ (ven′ər ē) n. [LME. venerie < L. Venus (gen. Veneris): see VENUS] [Archaic] the indulgence of sexual desire; specif., sexual intercourse

ven·er·y² (ven′ər ē) n. [ME. venerie < MFr. < vener, to hunt < L. venari: see VENISON] [Archaic] the act or practice of hunting game; the chase

ven·e·sec·tion (ven′ə sek′shən, vē′nə-) n. [< ModL. venae

sectio, cutting of a vein: see VEIN & SECTION] Med. same as PHLEBOTOMY

Ve·ne·ti·a (və nē′shē ə, -shə) [L.] 1. ancient district at the head of the Adriatic, north of the Po River: with Istria it formed a Roman province 2. former region of NE Italy, the E portion of which was ceded to Yugoslavia in 1947 3. same as VENETO

Ve·ne·tian (və nē′shən) adj. of Venice, its people, culture, etc. —n. a native or inhabitant of Venice

Venetian blind [also v- b-] a window blind made of a number of thin, horizontal wooden, metal, or plastic slats that can be set together at any angle to regulate the light and air passing through or drawn up together to the top of the window by means of cords

Venetian glass a fine glassware made in or near Venice, esp. on a nearby island (Muranó)

Venetian red 1. a red pigment formerly made from ferric oxides, now prepared synthetically 2. a brownish-red color

Ve·net·ic (və net′ik) n. [< L. Veneticus, of the Veneti < Veneti, a people living in VENETIA] an extinct Italic language known through about 200 short inscriptions

Ve·ne·to (ve′ne tō′) region of N Italy, on the Adriatic: 7,095 sq. mi.; pop. 3,834,000; chief city, Venice

Ve·ne·zi·a (ve ne′tsyä) 1. It. name of VENICE 2. former region of N Italy, generally corresponding to ancient Venetia: it now forms most of Veneto

Ven·e·zue·la (ven′i zwā′lə, -zwē′-; Sp. ve′ne swe′lä) 1. country in N S. America: 352,143 sq. mi.; pop. 9,686,000; cap. Caracas 2. Gulf of, inlet of the Caribbean, on the NW coast of Venezuela: c.150 mi. wide —**Ven′e·zue′lan** adj., n.

venge·ance (ven′jəns) n. [ME. < OFr. < venger, to avenge < L. vindicare: see VINDICATE] 1. the return of an injury for an injury, in punishment or retribution; avenging of an injury or offense; revenge 2. the desire to make such a return —**with a vengeance** 1. with great force or fury 2. excessively; to an unusual extent

venge·ful (venj′fəl) adj. [obs. venge, vengeance < venge, to avenge < ME. vengen < OFr. venger (see prec.) + -FUL] 1. desiring or seeking vengeance; vindictive 2. arising from or showing a desire for vengeance: said of actions or feelings 3. inflicting or serving to inflict vengeance —SYN. see VINDICTIVE —**venge′ful·ly** adv. —**venge′ful·ness** n.

ve·ni·al (vē′nē al, vēn′yəl) adj. [ME. < OFr. < LL.(Ec.) venialis, pardonable, orig., gracious < L. venia, a grace, favor, akin to venus, love: see VENUS] 1. that may be forgiven; pardonable 2. that may be excused or overlooked, as an error or fault; excusable 3. Theol. not causing death of the soul; committed without awareness of its seriousness or without full consent and hence not totally depriving the soul of sanctifying grace: said of sin: distinguished from MORTAL —**ve′ni·al′i·ty** (-al′ə tē), n. —**ve′ni·al·ly** adv.

Ven·ice (ven′is) 1. seaport in N Italy built on more than 100 small islands in the Lagoon of Venice: formerly a maritime city-state extending over most of Venetia & Dalmatia: pop. 364,000: It. name, VENEZIA 2. Gulf of, N end of the Adriatic: c.60 mi. wide 3. Lagoon of, arm of this gulf, on the coast of Veneto: c.180 sq. mi.

ven·in (ven′in) n. [< VEN(OM) + -IN¹] any of the specific toxic constituents of animal venoms

ven·i·punc·ture (ven′i puŋk′chər, vē′ni-) n. [< L. vena, vein + PUNCTURE] the puncture of a vein, as with a hypodermic needle

ve·ni·re (və nī′rē) n. [L., to come: see ff.] 1. clipped form of VENIRE FACIAS 2. a list or group of people from among whom a jury or juries will be selected

venire fa·ci·as (fā′shē as′) [ME. < ML., cause to come] Law a writ issued by a judge to a sheriff or coroner, instructing him to summon persons to serve as jurors

☆**ve·ni·re·man** (və nī′rē mən) n., pl. **-men** a member of a venire (sense 2)

ven·i·son (ven′i s'n, -z'n; Brit. ven′zən) n. [ME. veneison < OFr., hunting < L. venatio, the chase < venatus, pp. of venari, to hunt < IE. base *wen-, to strive for, desire, whence WIN, L. venus, love] the flesh of a game animal, now esp. the deer, used as food

Ve·ni·te (ve nē′te) n. [L., come, 2d pers. pl., imper., of venire, to COME: from the opening word of the 94th Psalm in the Vulgate (95th in the KJV)] 1. a canticle sung at matins or morning prayer, consisting of parts of Psalms 95 and 96 in the King James Version 2. music for this

‡**ve·ni, vi·di, vi·ci** (vā′nē vē′dē vē′chē, wā′nē wē′dē wē′kē, vē′nī vī′dī vī′sī) [L.] I came, I saw, I conquered: Julius Caesar's report to the Roman Senate of a victory

Venn diagrams (ven) [after John Venn (1834–1923), Eng. logician] Math. diagrams, esp. in symbolic logic, using overlapping circles, often shaded or crosshatched, to show relationships between sets

ven·om (ven′əm) n. [ME. < OFr. venim, var. of venin < L. venenum, a poison, orig., a juice, potion, prob. akin to venus, love: see VENUS] 1. the poison secreted by some snakes, spiders, insects, etc., introduced into the body of the victim by bite or sting 2. [Rare] poison of any kind 3. malignancy; spite; malice

ven·om·ous (-əs) adj. [ME. venimous < OFr. venimeux] 1. containing or full of venom; poisonous 2. malignant;

spiteful; malicious **3.** *Zool.* having a poison gland or glands and able to inflict a poisonous wound by biting or stinging —**ven'om·ous·ly** *adv.* —**ven'om·ous·ness** *n.*

ve·nose (vē'nōs) *adj.* veined or veiny, as an insect's wing

ve·nos·i·ty (vē nä/s/ə tē) *n.* the state or quality of being venose or venous

ve·nous (vē'nəs) *adj.* [L. *venosus*] **1.** *Biol.* a) of a vein or veins b) having veins or full of veins; veiny **2.** *Physiol.* designating blood being carried in the veins back to the heart and lungs: venous blood has given up oxygen and taken up carbon dioxide, and in vertebrates is characterized by a dark-red color —**ve'nous·ly** *adv.*

vent[1] (vent) *n.* [ME. *venten* < OFr. *venter*, to blow (or aphetic < OFr. *esventer*, to expose to the air, let out < *es-*, out + *venter*) < VL. *ventare* < L. *ventus*, WIND[2]] **1.** the action of escaping or passing out, or the means or opportunity to do this; issue; outlet; passage; escape **2.** expression; release [giving *vent* to emotion] **3.** a) a small hole or opening to permit passage or escape, as of a gas ☆b) a small triangular window, as in an automobile door, for ventilation without a direct draft **4.** in old guns, the small hole at the breech through which a spark passes to set off the charge **5.** the crusted opening in a volcano from which gas and molten rock erupt **6.** *Zool.* the excretory opening in animals; esp., the external opening of the cloaca in birds, reptiles, amphibians, and fishes —*vt.* **1.** to make a vent in or provide a vent for **2.** to allow (steam, gas, etc.) to escape through an opening **3.** to give release or expression to **4.** to relieve or unburden by giving vent to feelings [to *vent* oneself in curses]

vent[2] (vent) *n.* [ME. *vent*, altered (after prec.) < *fente* < OFr. < VL. *findita*, fem. pp., for L. *fissus*, pp. of *findere*, to split: see FISSION] a vertical slit in a garment, esp. at the back or sides of a coat —*vt.* to make a vent or vents in

vent·age (-ij) *n.* [see -AGE] a small hole or opening; vent

ven·tail (ven'tāl) *n.* [ME. *ventaylle* < OFr. *ventaille* < *vent* (L. *ventus*), a WIND[2]] the movable piece of armor forming the lower front part of a metal helmet

ven·ter (ven'tər) *n.* [Anglo-Fr. < L. *venter*: see VENTRAL] **1.** *Anat., Zool.* a) the belly, or abdomen b) a protuberance like a belly, as on a muscle c) a cavity or hollowed surface **2.** *Law* the womb: used in designating maternal parentage, as in *children of the first venter*, meaning "children of the first wife"

ven·ti·duct (ven'ti dukt') *n.* [< L. *ventus*, a WIND[2] + DUCT] an air ventilating duct or passage

ven·ti·fact (-fakt') *n.* [< L. *ventus*, a WIND[2] + (ART)IFACT] any stone shaped by the abrasion of windblown sand

ven·ti·late (ven't'l āt') *vt.* **-lat'ed, -lat'ing** [< L. *ventilatus*, pp. of *ventilare*, to fan, ventilate < *ventus*, a WIND[2]] **1.** a) to circulate fresh air in (a room, etc.), driving out foul air b) to circulate in (a room, etc.) so as to freshen: said of air **2.** to provide with an opening for the escape of air, gas, etc.; furnish a means for airing **3.** to expose (a substance) to fresh air so as to keep in good condition **4.** to examine and discuss in public; bring (a grievance, problem, etc.) out into the open **5.** to aerate (blood); oxygenate **6.** [Obs.] to winnow (grain) —**ven'ti·la'tive** *adj.*

ven·ti·la·tion (ven't'l ā/shən) *n.* [L. *ventilatio*] **1.** a ventilating or being ventilated **2.** a system or equipment for ventilating

ven·ti·la·tor (ven't'l āt'ər) *n.* a thing that ventilates; esp., any device used to bring in fresh air and drive out foul air

ven·ti·la·to·ry (-ə tôr'ē) *adj.* **1.** of, having, or pertaining to ventilation **2.** *Med.* of, pertaining to, or involved in breathing and the oxygenation of the blood

ven·tral (ven'trəl) *adj.* [Fr. < L. *ventralis* < *venter*, belly < IE. base *udero-*, belly, whence L. *uterus*, womb, G. *wanst*, paunch] **1.** *Anat., Zool.* of, near, on, or toward the belly or the side of the body where the belly is located; in man, anterior (or front), in most other animals, inferior (or lower) **2.** *Bot.* of or belonging to the inner or lower surface —**ven'tral·ly** *adv.*

ven·tri·cle (ven'tri k'l) *n.* [ME. < L. *ventriculus*, a stomach, ventricle, dim. of *venter*: see prec.] *Anat., Zool.* any of various cavities or hollow organs; specif., a) either of the two lower chambers of the heart which receive blood from the atria and pump it into the arteries: see HEART, illus. b) any of the four small continuous cavities within the brain

ven·tri·cose (-kōs') *adj.* [ModL. *ventricosus* < L. *venter*, belly: see VENTRAL] **1.** large-bellied **2.** *Biol.* swelling out on one side —**ven'tri·cos'i·ty** (-käs'ə tē) *n.*

ven·tric·u·lar (ven trik'yə lər) *adj.* [< L. *ventriculus* (see VENTRICLE) + -AR] **1.** of, involving, or being a ventricle **2.** having a bulge or belly

ven·tric·u·lus (-ləs) *n., pl.* **-u·li'** (-lī') [ModL. < L.: see VENTRICLE] *Zool.* **1.** that part of the alimentary tract of an insect, analogous to the stomach, where digestion takes place **2.** the gizzard of a bird

ven·tri·lo·qui·al (ven'tri lō'kwē əl) *adj.* of, having to do with, or using ventriloquism —**ven'tri·lo'qui·al·ly** *adv.*

ven·tril·o·quism (ven tril'ə kwiz'm) *n.* [< L. *ventriloquus*, lit., one who speaks from the belly < *venter*, belly (see VENTRAL) + *loqui*, to speak + -ISM] the art or practice of speaking so that the voice seems to come from some source other than the speaker: also **ven·tril'o·quy** (-kwē)

ven·tril·o·quist (-kwist) *n.* a person who practices ventriloquism; specif., an entertainer who uses ventriloquism

to carry on a pretended conversation as with a large puppet, or dummy —**ven·tril'o·quis'tic** *adj.*

ven·tril·o·quize (-kwīz') *vi., vt.* **-quized', -quiz'ing** to utter (words or sounds) as a ventriloquist

ven·tro- (ven'trō, -trə) [< L. *venter*, belly: see VENTRAL] a combining form meaning: **1.** abdomen, belly **2.** ventral and *[ventrodorsal]*

ven·tro·dor·sal (ven'trə dôr's'l) *adj.* [prec. + DORSAL[1]] of or involving both the ventral and dorsal surfaces

ven·tro·lat·er·al (-lat'ər əl) *adj.* [VENTRO- + LATERAL] of or involving both the ventral and lateral surfaces

Ven·tur·a (ven toor'ə) [< (San Buena)ventura (the official name) < Sp., lit., saint of good fortune] city in SW Calif., northwest of Los Angeles: pop. 56,000

ven·ture (ven'chər) *n.* [ME., aphetic for *aventure*: see ADVENTURE] **1.** a risky or dangerous undertaking; esp., a business enterprise in which there is danger of loss as well as chance for profit **2.** something on which a risk is taken, as the merchandise in a commercial enterprise or a stake in gambling **3.** chance; fortune: now only in **at a venture**, by mere chance, at random —*vt.* **-tured, -tur·ing 1.** to expose to danger or risk [to *venture* one's life] **2.** to expose (money, merchandise, etc.) to chance of loss **3.** to undertake the risk of; brave [to *venture* a storm] **4.** to express at the risk of criticism, objection, denial, etc. [to *venture* an opinion] —*vi.* to do or go at some risk —**ven'tur·er** *n.*

☆**venture capital** funds invested or available for investment at considerable risk of loss in potentially highly profitable enterprises

ven·ture·some (-səm) *adj.* **1.** inclined to venture; daring **2.** venturous; risky; hazardous —**ven'ture·some·ly** *adv.* —**ven'ture·some·ness** *n.*

ven·tu·ri (**tube**) (ven toor'ē) [after G. B. *Venturi* (1746–1822), It. physicist] a short tube with a constricted, throatlike passage that increases the velocity and lowers the pressure of a fluid conveyed through it: used to measure the flow of a fluid or operate certain instruments, as in aircraft, to regulate the mixture in a carburetor, etc.

ven·tur·ous (ven'chər əs) *adj.* **1.** inclined to venture, or take chances; bold **2.** involving danger or risk; risky; hazardous —**ven'tur·ous·ly** *adv.* —**ven'tur·ous·ness** *n.*

☆**vent window** same as VENT[1] (n. 3 b)

ven·ue (ven'yōo, -ōo) *n.* [ME. < OFr., a coming, arrival, approach < *venir*, to come < L. *venire*: see COME] *Law* **1.** the county or locality in which a cause of action occurs or a crime is committed **2.** the county or locality in which a jury is drawn and a case tried **3.** that part of a declaration in an action that designates the county in which the trial is to occur **4.** [Rare] the clause in an affidavit designating the place where it was sworn to —**change of venue** *Law* the substitution of another place of trial, as when the jury or court is likely to be prejudiced

ven·ule (ven'yōol) *n.* [L. *venula*, dim. of *vena*, vein] **1.** *Anat.* a small vein; veinlet **2.** *Biol.* any of the small branches of a vein in a leaf or in the wing of an insect —**ven'u·lar** (-yōo lər) *adj.* —**ven'u·lose'** (-yōo lōs') *adj.*

Ve·nus (vē'nəs) [ME. < L., lit., love < IE. *wenos*, desire < base *wen-*, to strive for, attain, whence OE. *wine*, friend, *winnan*, to WIN] **1.** *Rom. Myth.* the goddess of love and beauty: identified with the Greek Aphrodite **2.** the most brilliant planet in the solar system, second in distance from the sun, anciently or poetically called Lucifer as the morning star and Hesperus as the evening star: diameter, c.7,600 mi.; period of revolution, 243 days; period of rotation, unknown; symbol, ♀ —*n.* **1.** a statue or image of Venus **2.** a very beautiful woman **3.** *alchemists' term for* COPPER[1]

Ve·nus·berg (vē'nəs burg'; *G.* vā'noos berkh') [G., Venus mountain] *Medieval Legend* a mountain somewhere in Germany where Venus held court in a cavern, enticing travelers who became loath to leave

☆**Ve·nus' fly·trap** (flī'trap') a white-flowered swamp plant (*Dionaea muscipula*) of the sundew family, native to the Carolinas, having leaves with two hinged blades that snap shut to trap insects

Ve·nus'-hair (vē'nəs her') *n.* a maidenhair fern (*Adiantum capillus-veneris*) of tropical America and the S U.S.

Ve·nu·sian (vi nōo'shən) *adj.* of the planet Venus —*n.* an imagined inhabitant of Venus, as in science fiction

Ver. Version

ver. verse; verses

Ver·a (vir'ə) [Russ. *Vjera*, faith; also < L. *vera*, fem. of *verus*, true: see VERY] a feminine name

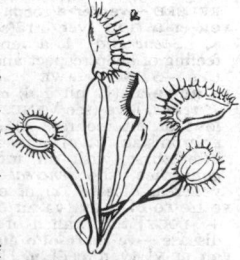
VENUS' FLYTRAP

ve·ra·cious (və rā'shəs) *adj.* [< L. *verax*, speaking truly < *verus*, true: see VERY] **1.** habitually truthful; honest **2.** true; accurate —**ve·ra'cious·ly** *adv.* —**ve·ra'cious·ness** *n.*

ve·rac·i·ty (və ras'ə tē) *n., pl.* **-ties** [ML. *veracitas*, truthfulness < L. *verus*, true: see VERY] **1.** habitual truthfulness; honesty **2.** accuracy of statement; accordance with truth **3.** accuracy or precision, as of perception **4.** that which is true; truth —*SYN.* see HONESTY, TRUTH

Ver·a·cruz (ver′ə krōōz′; *Sp.* ve′rä krōōs′) **1.** state of Mexico, on the E coast: 27,759 sq. mi.; pop. 3,409,000; cap. Jalapa **2.** seaport in this state: pop. 186,000

ve·ran·da, ve·ran·dah (və ran′də) *n.* [Anglo-Ind. < Port. *varanda*, a balcony < *vara*, a pole, staff < L., a wooden trestle, forked stick (for spreading out nets) < IE. base *wa-, to bend apart: cf. VACILLATE, VARY] an open porch or portico, usually roofed, along the outside of a building

ve·rat·ri·dine (və rat′rə dēn′, -din) *n.* [< L. *veratrum*, hellebore (see ff.) + -IDE + -INE⁴] an amorphous alkaloid, C₃₆H₅₁O₁₁N, found in sabadilla seeds

ver·a·trine (ver′ə trēn′, -trin) *n.* [ModL. *veratrina* < L. *veratrum*, hellebore, prob. orig. "plant which reveals truth" < *verus*, true (see VERY): the pulverized root causes sneezing, regarded in primitive belief as confirmation of truth] **1.** a poisonous mixture of colorless, crystalline alkaloids obtained from sabadilla seeds **2.** *same as* VERATRIDINE Also **ve·ra·tri·a** (və rā′trē ə)

ve·ra·trum (və rā′trəm) *n.* [L.: see prec.] **1.** *same as* HELLEBORE (sense 2) **2.** the dried rhizomes of a hellebore (*Veratrum viride*), once used in medicine

verb (vurb) *n.* [ME. *verbe* < OFr. < L. *verbum*, a WORD (used as transl. of Gr. *rhēma*, verb, orig., word)] **1.** any of a class of words expressing action, existence, or occurrence, or used as an auxiliary or copula, and constituting usually the main element of a predicate **2.** any phrase or construction used as a verb —*adj.* of, or having the nature or function of, a verb

ver·bal (vur′b'l) *adj.* [LME. < MFr. < LL. *verbalis*, of a word < *verbum*: see prec.] **1.** of, in, or by means of words [*a verbal image*] **2.** concerned merely with words, as distinguished from facts, ideas, or actions **3.** in speech; oral rather than written [*a verbal contract*] **4.** [Now Rare] word for word; verbatim [*a verbal translation*] **5.** *a*) of, or made up of, verbs [*a verbal auxiliary*] *b*) of, having the nature of, or derived from a verb [*a verbal noun*] *c*) used to form verbs [*-ate* is a *verbal* suffix] —*n.* a verbal noun or some other word, as an adjective, derived from a verb: in English, gerunds, infinitives, and participles are verbals —SYN. see ORAL —**ver′bal·ly** *adv.*

ver·bal·ism (-iz'm) *n.* **1.** a verbal expression; expression in words; a word or phrase **2.** words only, without any real meaning; mere verbiage **3.** any virtually meaningless phrase or form of words

ver·bal·ist (-ist) *n.* **1.** a person skilled in verbal expression; one who uses words well **2.** a person who fixes his attention or emphasis on mere words, rather than on facts or ideas —**ver′bal·is′tic** *adj.*

ver·bal·ize (vur′bə līz′) *vi.* **-ized′, -iz′ing** [< Fr. *verbaliser* (see VERBAL & -IZE)] **1.** to be wordy, or verbose **2.** to use words to express or communicate meaning —*vt.* **1.** to express in words **2.** to change (a noun, etc.) into a verb —**ver′bal·i·za′tion** *n.* —**ver′bal·iz′er** *n.*

verbal noun *Gram.* a noun derived from a verb and acting in some respects like a verb: in English, it is either a noun ending in -*ing* (a gerund) or an infinitive (Ex.: *walking* is healthful, *to err* is human)

ver·ba·tim (vər bāt′əm) *adv.* [LME. < ML. < L. *verbum*, a WORD] word for word; in exactly the same words —*adj.* following the original word for word [*a verbatim account*]

ver·be·na (vər bē′nə) *n.* [ModL., name of the genus < L., foliage, branches, vervain < IE. *werb-, to turn, bend < base *wer-, whence WORM] any of a genus (*Verbena*) of plants of the verbena family, with spikes or clusters of showy red, white, or purplish flowers, widely grown for ornament —*adj.* designating a family (Verbenaceae) of mostly tropical American plants including verbena, vervain, and lantana, and some trees, as teak

ver·bi·age (vur′bē ij) *n.* [Fr. < OFr. *verbier*, to speak, chatter < *verbe*: see VERB] **1.** an excess of words beyond those needed to express concisely what is meant; wordiness **2.** style of expression; diction

ver·bid (vur′bid) *n. Gram.* a gerund, infinitive, or participle that functions in part as a verb, as in taking an object (Ex.: *watching* television can be tiring)

verb·i·fy (-bə fī′) *vt.* **-fied′, -fy′ing** *same as* VERBALIZE (*vt.* 2)

ver·bose (vər bōs′) *adj.* [L. *verbosus*, full of words < *verbum*, a WORD] using or containing too many words; wordy; long-winded; prolix —SYN. see WORDY —**ver·bose′ly** *adv.* —**ver·bos′i·ty** (-bäs′ə tē), **ver·bose′ness** *n.*

‡ver·bo·ten (fer bō′tən) *adj.* [G.] forbidden; prohibited

‡ver·bum sat sa·pi·en·ti (est) (vur′bəm sat sap′ē en′tī est) [L.] a word to the wise (is) enough: often clipped to **ver·bum sap** (vur′bəm sap)

Ver·cin·get·o·rix (vur′sin jet′ə riks, -get′-) 72?–46? B.C.; Gallic chieftain defeated by Julius Caesar

ver·dant (vur′d'nt) *adj.* [prob. < VERD(URE) + -ANT, after MFr. *verdoyant* < OFr. *verdoiant*, prp. of *verdoier*, to be green < *verd*, green: see VERDURE] **1.** green **2.** covered with green vegetation **3.** inexperienced; immature [*verdant* youth] —**ver′dan·cy** (-d'n sē) *n.* —**ver′dant·ly** *adv.*

verd antique (vurd) [older form of Fr. *vert antique* < OFr. *verd*, green + *antique*, ancient] **1.** a green mottled or veined marble, used for interior decoration **2.** any of various green porphyritic rocks **3.** *same as* VERDIGRIS (sense 2)

Verde (vurd), **Cape** peninsula on the Atlantic coast of Senegal: westernmost point of Africa

ver·der·er, ver·der·or (vur′dər ər) *n.* [Anglo-Fr. *verderer*, extended < *verder* < OFr. *verdier* < *verd*, green: see VERDURE] in medieval England, a judicial officer appointed to handle all matters of trespass, etc. on the king's forests

Ver·di (ver′dē), **Giu·sep·pe** (**Fortunino Francisco**) (jōō zep′pe) 1813–1901; It. operatic composer

ver·dict (vur′dikt) *n.* [ME. *verdit* < Anglo-Fr. < ML. *veredictum*, true saying, verdict < L. *vere*, truly + *dictum*, a thing said: see VERY & DICTUM] **1.** *Law* the formal and unanimous finding of a jury on the matter submitted to them in a trial **2.** any decision or judgment

ver·di·gris (vur′di grēs′, -gris) *n.* [ME. *vertegrez* < MFr. *verdegris* < OFr. *vert de Grece*, lit., green of Greece < *verd*, green + *de*, of + *Grece*, Greece] **1.** a green or greenish-blue poisonous compound, a basic acetate of copper, prepared by treating copper with acetic acid and used as a pigment, dye, etc. **2.** a green or greenish-blue coating (**false verdigris**) that forms like rust on brass, bronze, or copper

☆**ver·din** (vur′din) *n.* [Fr., yellowhammer] a small gray titmouse (*Auriparus flaviceps*) with a bright-yellow head, found in the SW U.S. and N Mexico

ver·di·ter (vur′di tər) *n.* [MFr. *verd de terre*, lit., green of the earth, earth green] either of two basic copper carbonate pigments, the one (**blue verditer**) usually consisting of ground azurite, the other (**green verditer**) ground malachite

Ver·dun (ver dun′, vur-; *Fr.* ver dön′) **1.** city in NE France, on the Meuse River: scene of much battle in World War I: pop. 22,000 **2.** city on Montreal Island, SW Quebec, Canada: suburb of Montreal: pop. 77,000

ver·dure (vur′jər) *n.* [ME. < OFr. < *verd*, green < VL. *virdis*, for L. *viridis*, akin to *virere*, to be green] **1.** the fresh green color of growing things; greenness **2.** green growing plants and trees; green vegetation **3.** vigorous or flourishing condition —**ver′dured** *adj.*

ver·dur·ous (vur′jər əs) *adj.* **1.** covered with or consisting of verdure **2.** of or characteristic of verdure

verge¹ (vurj) *n.* [ME. < OFr., a rod, wand, stick, yard, hoop < L. *virga*, a twig, rod, wand < IE. *wizga- < base *wei-, to bend, twist, whence WIRE, WHISK] **1.** *a*) the edge, brink, or margin (*of* something) [the *verge* of the forest]: also used figuratively [on the *verge* of hysteria] *b*) [Brit.] a grassy border, as along a road **2.** *a*) an enclosing line or border; boundary, esp. of something more or less circular *b*) the area so enclosed **3.** the edge of the tiling that projects over a gable **4.** the spindle of a balance wheel in a clock with an old vertical escapement **5.** a rod or staff symbolic of an office, as that carried before a church official in processions **6.** *English Feudal Law a*) a rod held in the hand by a feudal tenant as he swore fealty to his lord *b*) the area over which an official had special jurisdiction, as the land surrounding the royal palace, under the jurisdiction of the king's marshal —*vi.* **verged, verg′ing** to be on the verge, edge, brink, or border (usually with *on* or *upon*) [streets *verging* on the slum area]: also used figuratively [talk that *verges* on the ridiculous]

verge² (vurj) *vi.* **verged, verg′ing** [L. *vergere*, to bend, turn < IE. *werg- < base *wer-, to turn, bend, whence WARP, WORM] **1.** to tend or incline (*to* or *toward*) **2.** to be in the process of change or transition into something else; pass gradually (*into*) [dawn *verging* into daylight]

verg·er (vur′jər) *n.* [ME. < base VERGE¹ & -ER] [Chiefly Brit.] **1.** a person who carries a verge before a bishop, dean, etc. in a procession **2.** a church caretaker or usher

Ver·gil (vur′jəl) *var.* of VIRGIL —**Ver·gil′i·an** (-jil′ē ən) *adj.*

ver·glas (ver glä′) *n.* [Fr. < MFr. *verreglaz* < *verre*, glass + *glaz*, *glace*, ice: see GLACIER] *same as* GLAZE (n. 5)

ve·rid·i·cal (və rid′i k'l) *adj.* [< L. *veridicus*, speaking the truth < *verus*, truth + *dicere*, to speak (see VERY & DICTION)] **1.** truthful; veracious **2.** corresponding with reality or facts —**ve·rid′i·cal′i·ty** (-kal′ə tē) *n.*

ver·i·est (ver′ē ist) *adj.* [superl. of VERY, *adj.*] being such to the highest degree; utter [the *veriest* nonsense]

ver·i·fi·a·ble (ver′ə fī′ə b'l) *adj.* capable of verification; that can be proved to be true or accurate

ver·i·fi·ca·tion (ver′ə fi kā′shən) *n.* [MFr. *verificacion* < ML. *verificatio*] **1.** a verifying or being verified; establishment or confirmation of the truth or accuracy of a fact, theory, etc. **2.** *Law* a statement at the end of a pleading to the effect that the pleader is ready to prove his allegations —**ver′i·fi·ca′tion·al** *adj.*

ver·i·fy (ver′ə fī′) *vt.* **-fied′, -fy′ing** [ME. *verifien* < MFr. *verifier* < ML. *verificare*, to make true < L. *verus*, true (see VERY) + -*ficare*, -FY] **1.** to prove to be true by demonstration, evidence, or testimony; confirm or substantiate **2.** to test or check the accuracy or correctness of, as by investigation, comparison with a standard, or reference to the facts **3.** *Law a*) to add a verification to (a pleading) *b*) to affirm on oath —SYN. see CONFIRM —**ver′i·fi′er** *n.*

ver·i·ly (ver′ə lē) *adv.* [ME. *verrayly*: see VERY & -LY²] [Archaic] in very truth; truly

ver·i·sim·i·lar (ver′ə sim′ə lər) *adj.* [< L. *verisimilis* < *verus*, true (see VERY) + *similis*, SIMILAR] seeming to be true or real; plausible; likely

ver·i·si·mil·i·tude (ver'ə si mil'ə tōōd', -tyōōd') *n.* [L. *verisimilitudo* < *verisimilis*: see prec.] 1. the appearance of being true or real 2. something having the mere appearance of being true or real —*SYN.* see TRUTH

ver·ism (vir'iz'm, ver'-) *n.* [It. *verismo* < *vero*, true < L. *verus* (see VERY) + -ISM] realism in the arts, esp. as applied in opera —**ver'ist** *adj.*, *n.* —**ve·ris·tic** (vi ris'tik) *adj.*

ver·i·ta·ble (ver'i tə b'l) *adj.* [LME. < OFr. < *verite*, VERITY] being such truly or in fact; actual *[a veritable* feast*]* —**ver'i·ta·bly** *adv.*

ver·i·ty (ver'ə tē) *n., pl.* -ties [ME. *verite* < OFr. *verite*(*t*) < L. *veritas*, truth < *verus*, true: see VERY] 1. conformity to truth or fact; truth; reality 2. a principle, belief, etc. taken to be fundamentally and permanently true; a truth; a reality —*SYN.* see TRUTH

ver·juice (vur'jōōs') *n.* [ME. *vergeous* < MFr. *verjus* < *vert*, green (see VERDURE) + *jus*, JUICE] 1. the sour, acid juice of green, or unripe, fruit, as of crab apples, grapes, etc. 2. sourness of temper, looks, etc.

Ver·laine (ver len'), **Paul** (pôl) 1844-96; Fr. poet

Ver·meer (vər mer'; E. var yän'), **Jan** (yän) 1632-75; Du. painter: also called *Jan van der Meer van Delft*

ver·meil (vur'mil) *n.* [ME. *vermayle* < OFr. *vermeil* < LL.(Ec.) *vermiculus*, kermes < L., dim. of *vermis*, a WORM] 1. [Obs. or Poet.] the color vermilion 2. gilded copper, bronze, or silver —*adj.* vermilion

ver·mi- (vur'mə) [< L. *vermis*, a WORM] *a combining form meaning* worm *[vermicide]*

ver·mi·cel·li (vur'mə sel'ē, -chel'ē) *n.* [It., pl. of *vermicello*, lit., little worm < L. *vermiculus*, dim. of *vermis*, a WORM] pasta like spaghetti, but in thinner strings

ver·mi·cide (vur'mə sid') *n.* [VERMI- + -CIDE] an agent used to kill worms, esp. intestinal worms

ver·mic·u·lar (vər mik'yə lər) *adj.* [ModL. *vermicularis*: see ff. & -AR] 1. *a)* suggestive of a worm or worms in shape or movement *b)* covered with irregularly twisting lines, ridges, or indentations suggestive of worm tracks 2. *a)* of or having to do with worms *b)* formed or caused by worms

ver·mic·u·late (vər mik'yə lāt'; *for adj., usually* -lit) *vt.* -**lat'ed**, -**lat'ing** [< L. *vermiculatus*, pp. of *vermiculari*, to be full of worms < *vermiculus*, dim. of *vermis*, a WORM] to make vermicular; esp., to cover, as by inlaying, with vermicular markings or traceries —*adj. same as* VERMICULAR: also **ver·mic'u·lat·ed** (-lāt'id)

ver·mic·u·la·tion (vər mik'yə lā'shən) *n.* [L. *vermiculatio*: see prec.] 1. a vermiculating or being vermiculated 2. vermicular markings 3. movement marked by alternate contraction and dilation, as in peristalsis

☆**ver·mic·u·lite** (vər mik'yə līt') *n.* [< L. *vermiculus*, dim. of *vermis*, WORM + -ITE[1]] any of a number of hydrous silicate minerals resulting usually from alterations of mica and occurring in tiny, leafy scales that expand greatly when heated: used for insulation, water adsorption, etc.

ver·mi·form (vur'mə fôrm') *adj.* [VERMI- + -FORM] shaped like a worm

vermiform appendix *same as* APPENDIX (sense 2)

vermiform process *Anat.* 1. the median lobe of the cerebellum 2. *same as* APPENDIX (sense 2)

ver·mi·fuge (vur'mə fyōōj') *adj.* [VERMI- + -FUGE] serving to expel worms and other parasites from the intestinal tract —*n.* a vermifuge drug

ver·mil·ion (vər mil'yən) *n.* [ME. < OFr. *vermillon* < *vermeil*, bright-red: see VERMEIL] 1. *a)* bright-red mercuric sulfide, used as a pigment *b)* any of several other red pigments resembling this 2. a bright red or scarlet —*adj.* of the color vermilion

ver·min (vur'min) *n., pl.* -**min** [ME. < OFr. *vermine* < L. *vermis*, a WORM] 1. *a)* any of various insects, bugs, or small animals regarded as objectional because destructive, disease-carrying, etc., as flies, lice, rats, or weasels *b)* such pests collectively 2. [Chiefly Brit.] collectively, birds or animals that kill game on preserves 3. *a)* a vile, loathsome person *b)* such persons collectively

ver·mi·na·tion (vur'mi nā'shən) *n.* [L. *verminatio*] [Archaic] infestation with, or the spreading of, vermin

ver·min·ous (vur'mi nəs) *adj.* [L. *verminosus*] 1. of, having the nature of, or resembling vermin 2. infested with vermin 3. caused or produced by vermin

Ver·mont (vər mänt') *n.* [< Fr. *Verd Mont* (1647), green mountain] New England State of the U.S.: admitted, 1791; 9,609 sq. mi.; pop. 444,000; cap. Montpelier: abbrev. Vt., VT —**Ver·mont'er** *n.*

ver·mouth (vər mōōth') *n.* [Fr. *vermout* < G. *wermut*, WORMWOOD] a fortified, sweet or dry white wine flavored with aromatic herbs, used in cocktails and as an aperitif

ver·nac·u·lar (vər nak'yə lər) *adj.* [< L. *vernaculus*, belonging to homeborn slaves, indigenous < *verna*, a homeborn slave] 1. using the native language of a country or place *[a vernacular* writer*]* 2. commonly spoken by the people of a particular country or place *[a vernacular*, as distinguished from the literary, dialect*]* 3. of or in the native language 4. native to a country *[the vernacular* arts of Brittany*]* 5. designating or of the common name of an animal or plant, as distinguished from the scientific name in Modern Latin taxonomic classification —*n.* 1. the native speech, language, or dialect of a country or place 2. the common, everyday language of ordinary people in a particular locality 3. the shoptalk or idiom of a profession or trade 4. *a)* a vernacular word or term *b)* the vernacular name of an animal or plant —*SYN.* see DIALECT —**ver·nac'u·lar·ly** *adv.*

ver·nac·u·lar·ism (-iz'm) *n.* 1. a vernacular word, phrase, or usage 2. the use of vernacular language

ver·nal (vur'n'l) *adj.* [L. *vernalis* < *vernus*, belonging to spring < *ver*, spring < IE. base *wesr*, spring, whence Sans. *vasanta*, OBulg. *vesna*, spring] 1. of, relating to, or appearing or occurring in, the spring 2. springlike; fresh, warm, and mild 3. fresh and young; youthful —**ver'nal·ly** *adv.*

ver·nal·ize (-īz') *vt.* -**ized'**, -**iz'ing** [prec. + -IZE] to stimulate the growth and flowering of (a plant) by artificially shortening the dormant period —**ver'nal·i·za'tion** *n.*

ver·na·tion (vər nā'shən) *n.* [ModL. *vernatio* < pp. of L. *vernare*, to be verdant < *ver*, spring: see VERNAL] *Bot.* the arrangement of leaves in a leaf bud

Verne (vurn; *Fr.* vern), **Jules** (jōōlz; *Fr.* zhül) 1828-1905; Fr. novelist

Ver·ner's law (vur'nərz, ver'-) [formulated (1875) by Karl *Verner* (1846-96), Dan. philologist] an explanation for a series of apparent exceptions to Grimm's law stating that the proto-Germanic medial voiceless spirants (f, **th**, h, s), derived from the proto-Indo-European voiceless stops (p, t, k, s), regularly became the voiced spirants (v, *th*, g, z), respectively, and final (s) became (z), when the vowel immediately preceding these did not in proto-Indo-European bear the principal accent of the word

ver·ni·er (vur'nē ər, -nir) *n.* [after Pierre *Vernier* (1580-1637), Fr. mathematician who invented it] 1. a short graduated scale that slides along a longer graduated instrument and is used to indicate fractional parts of divisions, as in a micrometer: also **vernier scale** 2. any device that makes possible a finer setting of a tool or measuring instrument —*adj.* of or fitted with a vernier

†**ver·nis·sage** (ver nē säzh') *n., pl.* -**sages'** (-säzh') [Fr., lit., varnishing (see VARNISH & -AGE): in allusion to the former practice of varnishing paintings before exhibiting] the opening, or first showing, of an art exhibit

Ver·non (vur'nən) [< the surname *Vernon*, prob. < *Vernon*, a town in France] 1. a masculine name 2. **Edward**, 1684-1757; Eng. admiral

Ve·ro·na (və rō'nə; *It.* ve rō'nä) commune in Veneto, N Italy: pop. 245,000 —**Ver·o·nese** (ver'ə nēz') *adj., n.*

Ver·o·nal (ver'ə n'l) [G.: so named by the inventor, about to leave on a trip to VERONA] *a trademark for* BARBITAL

Ve·ro·ne·se (ve'rō ne'se; *E.* ver'ə nēz'), **Pa·o·lo** (pä'ô lô') (born *Paolo Cagliari*) 1528-88; Venetian painter, born in Verona

Ve·ron·i·ca (və rän'i kə) [ML.] 1. a feminine name 2. **Saint**, woman of Jerusalem who, according to legend, wiped the bleeding face of Jesus on the way to Calvary: her day is July 12 —*n.* 1. [*often* v-] *a)* the image of Jesus' face supposed to have appeared on the veil or handkerchief used by Saint Veronica to wipe the bleeding face of Jesus *b)* any cloth or garment with a representation of the face of Jesus 2. [v-] [ModL.] *same as* SPEEDWELL 3. [v-] *Bullfighting* a move in which the matador holds his cape out and pivots slowly as the bull charges past him

Ver·ra·za·no (ver'rä tsä'nô), **Gio·van·ni da** (jō vän'nē dä) 1480?-1527?; It. explorer in the service of France: also sp. **Verrazzano**

Ver·roc·chio (ver rôk'kyô), **An·dre·a del** (än dre'ä del) (born *Andrea di Michele di Francesco di Cioni*) 1435-88; Florentine sculptor and painter

ver·ru·ca (və rōō'kə) *n., pl.* -**cae** (-sē) [L., WART] 1. *same as* WART 2. a wartlike elevation, as on a toad's back —**ver·ru·cose** (ver'oo kōs'), **ver'ru·cous** (-kəs) *adj.*

Ver·sailles (vər sī', -sālz'; *Fr.* ver sä'y') city in NC France, near Paris: site of a palace built by Louis XIV: the Allies & German signed a peace treaty here (1919) ending World War I: pop. 95,000

ver·sant (vur'sənt) *n.* [Fr. < L. *versans*, prp. of *versare*: see ff.] 1. the slope of a mountain or mountain chain 2. the general slope, or declination, of a region

ver·sa·tile (vur'sə t'l; *chiefly Brit.*, -tīl') *adj.* [Fr. < L. *versatilis*, that turns around, movable, versatile < *versatus*, pp. of *versare*, to turn often, freq. of *vertere*, to turn: see VERSE] 1. *a)* competent in many things; able to turn easily from one subject or occupation to another; many-sided *b)* adaptable to many uses or functions 2. [Rare] *a)* that can be turned or moved around, as on a hinge or pivot *b)* fickle; inconstant 3. *Bot.* turning about freely on the filament to which it is attached, as an anther 4. *Zool.* *a)* moving forward or backward, as the toes of a bird *b)* movable in any direction, as the antenna of an insect —**ver'sa·tile·ly** *adv.* —**ver'sa·til'i·ty** (-til'ə tē) *n.*

†**vers de so·ci·é·té** (ver' də sô sya tā') [Fr., verse of society] witty, polished, light verse

verse (vurs) *n.* [ME. *vers* < OE. *fers* & OFr. *vers*, both < L. *versus*, a turning, verse, line, row, pp. of *vertere*, to turn < IE. *wert-*, to turn < base *wer-*, whence WARP, WORM, -WARDS] 1. a sequence of words arranged metrically in accordance with some rule or design; single line of poetry 2. *a)* metrical writing or speaking; poetry in general; sometimes, specif., *short for* LIGHT VERSE *b)* a particular form of metrical composition *[blank verse*, trochaic *verse]* 3. *a)* a single metrical composition; poem *b)* a body of poetry, as of a specific writer or period 4. a stanza or similar short subdivision of a metrical composition, sometimes specif. as distinguished from the chorus, or

refrain **5.** *Bible* any of the single, usually numbered, short divisions of a chapter, generally a sentence —*vt.*, *vi.* **versed, vers′ing** [Now Rare] *same as* VERSIFY

versed (vurst) *adj.* [< L. *versatus*, pp. of *versari*, to occupy oneself: form as if pp. of prec., *v.*] acquainted by experience and study; skilled or learned (*in* a specified subject)

versed sine (vurst) [< ModL. *versus* < L., pp. of *vertere*, to turn (see VERSE) + -ED] *Trigonometry* 1 minus the cosine of a given angle

ver·si·cle (vur′si k'l) *n.* [ME. < L. *versiculus*, dim. of *versus*] a short or little verse; esp., one of the short sentences said or sung in a church service by a minister and followed by the response of the congregation

ver·si·col·or (vur′si kul′ər) *adj.* [L. < *versare*, to change (see VERSATILE) + *color*, COLOR] **1.** having many colors; variegated **2.** changing in color; iridescent

ver·si·fi·ca·tion (vur′sə fi kā′shən) *n.* [L. *versificatio*] **1.** the act of versifying **2.** the art, practice, or theory of poetic composition **3.** the form or style of a poem; metrical structure **4.** a metrical version (*of* something)

ver·si·fi·er (vur′sə fī′ər) *n.* **1.** a person who versifies; poet **2.** a writer of mediocre verse; poetaster —*SYN.* see POET

ver·si·fy (-fī′) *vi.* **-fied′**, **-fy′ing** [ME. *versifien* < MFr. *versifier* < L. *versificare* < *versus*: see VERSE & -FY] to compose verses —*vt.* **1.** to tell about, treat of, or describe in verse **2.** to put into verse form

ver·sion (vur′zhən, -shən) *n.* [Fr. < ML. *versio*, a turning < L. *versus*: see VERSE] **1.** *a)* a translation *b)* [*often* V-] a translation of the Bible, in whole or part [the Douay and King James *versions*] **2.** an account showing one point of view; particular description or report given by one person or group [the two *versions* of the accident] **3.** a particular form or variation of something, esp. as modified in a different art form [the movie *version* of the novel] **4.** *Med. a)* displacement of the uterus in which it is deflected but not bent upon itself *b)* the operation of turning the fetus during childbirth to make delivery easier —*SYN.* see TRANSLATION —**ver′sion·al** *adj.*

‡vers li·bre (ver lē′br′) *French term for* FREE VERSE

ver·so (vur′sō) *n.*, *pl.* **-sos** [ModL. (*folio*) *verso* < L., abl. of *versus*: see VERSE] *Printing* any left-hand page of a book; back of a leaf: opposed to RECTO

verst (vurst, verst; *Russ.* vyôrst) *n.* [Russ. *versta* < OSlav. *vrista*, a turning < IE. *wert-*: see VERSE] a former Russian unit of linear measure, equal to c.3,500 feet

ver·sus (vur′səs) *prep.* [ML. < L., toward, turned in the direction of < *vertere*, to turn: see VERSE] **1.** in contest against [plaintiff *versus* defendant] **2.** in contrast with; by way of alternative to [peace *versus* war]

vert (vurt) *n.* [ME. *verte* < OFr. < L. *viridis*, green] **1.** [Brit.] *a)* the green growth of a forest, as cover for deer *b)* [Archaic] the right to cut green wood in a forest **2.** *Heraldry* the color green

vert. vertical

ver·te·bra (vur′tə brə) *n.*, *pl.* **-brae′** (-brē′), **-bras** [L., a joint, vertebra < *vertere*, to turn: see VERSE] any of the single bones or segments of the spinal column, articulating in the higher vertebrates with those adjacent to it by means of elastic fibrous disks

ver·te·bral (-brəl) *adj.* [ModL. *vertebralis*] **1.** of, or having the nature of, a vertebra or vertebrae **2.** having or composed of vertebrae [*vertebral* column]

ver·te·brate (-brit, -brāt′) *adj.* [L. *vertebratus* < *vertebra*: see VERTEBRA] **1.** having a backbone, or spinal column **2.** of or belonging to the vertebrates —*n.* any of a large subphylum (Vertebrata) of chordate animals, including all mammals, fishes, birds, reptiles, and amphibians, characterized by a segmented spinal column and a brain enclosed in a brainpan or cranium

VERTEBRAE (A, section of spinal column; B, single vertebra)

ver·te·bra·tion (vur′tə brā′shən) *n.* vertebral formation; segmentation into vertebrae

ver·tex (vur′teks) *n.*, *pl.* **-tex·es**, **-ti·ces′** (-tə sēz′) [L., the top, properly the turning point < *vertere*, to turn: see VERSE] **1.** *a)* the highest or topmost point; top; summit; apex *b)* *same as* ZENITH **2.** *Anat.*, *Zool.* the top or crown of the head **3.** *Geom. a)* the point of intersection of the two sides of an angle *b)* a corner point of a triangle, square, cube, parallelepiped, or other geometric figure bounded by lines, planes, or lines and planes **4.** *Optics* the point at the center of a lens at which the axis of symmetry intersects the curve of the lens

ver·ti·cal (vur′ti k'l) *adj.* [Fr. < LL. *verticalis* < L. *vertex* (gen. *verticis*): see prec.] **1.** of, at, or in the vertex, or zenith; directly overhead **2.** *a)* perpendicular, or at a right angle, to the plane of the horizon; upright; straight up and down *b)* at a right angle to the plane of the supporting surface **3.** at, or made up of elements at, different levels, as of industrial production and distribution or of social status **4.** *Anat.*, *Zool.* of the vertex of the head **5.** *Biol.* in the direction in which the axis lies; lengthwise —*n.* **1.** a vertical line, plane, circle, etc. **2.** upright position —**ver′ti·cal′i·ty** (-kal′ə tē) *n.* —**ver′ti·cal·ly** *adv.* *SYN.*—**vertical** is specifically applied to that which rises in a straight line so as to form a right angle with the plane of the horizon [the *vertical* studs in a wall]; **perpendicular**, the preferred term in geometry, refers to a straight line forming a right angle with any other line or plane [a line *perpendicular* to the hypotenuse of a triangle]; **plumb** is a term used by carpenters, masons, etc. with reference to the perpendicularity or, esp., verticality of something, as determined by dropping a weight at the end of a line [this door is now *plumb*]—*ANT.* **horizontal**

vertical circle *Astron.* any great circle in the celestial sphere passing through the zenith and the nadir, its plane cutting the plane of the horizon at a right angle

vertical union *same as* INDUSTRIAL UNION

ver·ti·ces (vur′tə sēz′) *n.* *alt. pl.* of VERTEX

ver·ti·cil (vur′tə sil) *n.* [ModL. *verticillus* < L., a whirl, dim. of *vertex*: see VERTEX] *Bot.* a circular arrangement of leaves or flowers around a stem; whorl

ver·ti·cil·las·ter (vur′tə sil las′tər) *n.* [ModL.: see prec. & -ASTER¹] *Bot.* an almost circular flower arrangement formed by a pair of dichasia facing each other on the stem, as in some mints

ver·tic·il·late (vər tis′'l it, -āt′; vur′tə sil′āt) *adj.* [ModL. *verticillatus* < *verticillus*] *Bot.* arranged in or having verticils: also **ver·tic′il·lat′ed** —**ver·tic′il·la′tion** *n.*

ver·tig·i·nous (vər tij′ə nəs) *adj.* [L. *vertiginosus*] **1.** of, affected by, or causing vertigo; dizzy or dizzying **2.** whirling about; spinning **3.** marked by quick or frequent change; unstable —**ver·tig′i·nous·ly** *adv.*

ver·ti·go (vur′ti gō′) *n.*, *pl.* **-goes′**, **ver·tig·i·nes** (vər tij′ə nēz′) [L., dizziness < *vertere*: see VERSE] *Med.* a subjective sensation of dizziness in which an individual feels that he, or his surrounding, is whirling about sickeningly

ver·tu (vər tōō′, vur′tōō) *n.* *same as* VIRTU

Ver·tum·nus (vər tum′nəs) [L., of Etruscan orig.] *Rom. Myth.* the god of the changing seasons and of growing flowers and fruits, husband of Pomona

Ver·u·lam (ver′yoo ləm), Baron *see* Francis BACON

ver·vain (vur′vān) *n.* [ME. *verveine* < OFr₁. < L. *verbena*: see VERBENA] any of a number of verbenas; esp., *a)* the European vervain (*Verbena officinalis*), formerly used in folk medicine *b)* any of several species of N. American verbena, not generally cultivated —*adj. same as* VERBENA

verve (vurv) *n.* [Fr. < OFr., caprice, fantasy, manner of speech < L. *verba*, pl. of *verbum*, a WORD] **1.** vigor and energy, as in movement, portrayal, etc. **2.** exuberant enthusiasm; spirit, dash, etc. **3.** [Archaic] aptitude

ver·vet (vur′vit) *n.* [Fr. < ? *vert*, green + *grivet*, GRIVET] a small guenon monkey (*Cercopithecus pygerythrus*) found in E and S Africa, related to the grivet and green monkey

ver·y (ver′ē) *adj.* **ver′i·er**, **ver′i·est** [ME. *verai*, true < OFr. < VL. *veraius* < L. *verus*, true < IE. *weros*, true < base *wer-*, to be friendly, true, whence G. *wahr*, true, OE. *wær*, a compact] **1.** in the fullest sense; complete; absolute [the *very* opposite of the truth] **2.** same; identical [the *very* hat he lost] **3.** being just what is needed or suitable [the *very* sofa to fit into the space] **4.** even; even the: used as an intensive [the *very* rafters shook] **5.** actual [caught in the *very* act] **6.** [Archaic] *a)* real; true; genuine *b)* legitimate; lawful; rightful —*adv.* **1.** in a high degree; to a great extent; extremely; exceedingly **2.** truly; really: used as an intensive [the *very* same man] —*SYN.* see SAME

very high frequency any radio frequency between 30 and 300 megahertz

very low frequency any radio frequency between 10 and 30 kilohertz

Ver·y signal (or **light**) (ver′ē, vir′ē) [after E. W. *Very* (1847–1910), U.S. ordnance expert, who invented it] a colored flare fired from a special pistol (**Very pistol**) for signaling at night

Ve·sa·li·us (vi sā′lē əs), **An·dre·as** (an′drē əs) 1514–64; Fl. anatomist in Italy, Spain, etc.

ve·si·ca (vi sī′kə) *n.*, *pl.* **-cae** (-sē) [L.] *same as* BLADDER

ves·i·cal (ves′i k'l) *adj.* [ModL. *vesicalis* < L. *vesica*, bladder] of a bladder, esp. the urinary bladder

ves·i·cant (ves′i kənt) *adj.* [< L. *vesica*, a blister] causing blisters —*n.* a vesicant agent; specif., in chemical warfare, any agent, as mustard gas, used to blister and burn body tissues by contact with the skin or inhalation Also **ves′i·ca·to′ry** (-kə tôr′ē) *adj.*, *n.*, *pl.* **-to′ries**

ves·i·cate (-kāt′) *vt.*, *vi.* **-cat′ed**, **-cat′ing** [< L. *vesica*, a bladder, blister] to blister —**ves′i·ca′tion** *n.*

ves·i·cle (ves′i k'l) *n.* [< Fr. or L.: Fr. *vésicule* < L. *vesicula*, dim. of *vesica*, bladder] a small membranous cavity, sac, or cyst; specif., *a)* *Anat.*, *Zool.*, *Med.* a small cavity or sac filled with fluid; esp., a small, round elevation of the skin containing a serous fluid; blister *b)* *Bot.* a small, bladderlike sac filled with air *c)* *Geol.* a small, spherical cavity in volcanic rock, produced by bubbles of air or gas in the molten rock

ves·i·co- (ves′i kō, -kə) [< L. *vesica*, the bladder] a combining form meaning: **1.** bladder **2.** bladder and

ve·sic·u·lar (və sik′yə lər) *adj.* [ModL. *vesicularis*] **1.** of, composed of, or having vesicles **2.** having the form or structure of a vesicle

---

ve·sic·u·late (-lit; *for v.* -lāt′) *adj.* same as VESICULAR —*vt.,* *vi.* -**lat′ed,** -**lat′ing** to make or become vesicular — **ve·sic′u·la′tion** *n.*

Ves·pa·si·an (ves pā′zhē ən, -zhən) (L. name *Titus Flavius Sabinus Vespasianus*) 9–79 A.D.; Rom. emperor (69–79): father of DOMITIAN & TITUS

ves·per (ves′pər) *n.* [ME., evening star < L. *vesper,* masc., *vespera,* fem., evening < IE. **wesperos* (prob. < base **we-:* cf. WEST), whence Gr. *hesperos*] 1. *a)* orig., evening or eventide *b)* [Poet.] [V-] *same as* EVENING STAR 2. an evening prayer or service; specif., [*pl.*] [*often* V-] *a)* R.C.Ch. the sixth of the seven canonical hours, recited or sung in the late afternoon *b)* *Anglican Ch.* same as EVEN-SONG —*adj.* 1. of evening 2. of vespers

ves·per·al (-əl) *adj.* [LL. *vesperalis* < L. *vespera*] [Rare] of evening or vespers —*n.* *Eccles.* 1. a book containing the chants, psalms, etc. used at vespers 2. a cloth cover for protecting the altar cloth between services

☆**vesper sparrow** a gray N. American sparrow (*Pooecetes gramineus*) with white markings on its outer tail feathers: so called from its practice of singing in the evening

ves·per·til·i·o·nid (ves′pər til′ē ə nid) *n.* [< L. *vespertilio* (gen. *vespertilionis*), a bat (< *vesper,* evening: see VESPER) + -ID] any of a large family (Vespertilionidae) of long-tailed bats that are widely distributed, esp. in temperate regions, including most of the small, insect-eating species

ves·per·tine (ves′pər t′n, -tin′) *adj.* [L. *vespertinus* < *vesper:* see VESPER] 1. of or occurring in the evening 2. *Bot.* opening or blossoming in the evening 3. *Zool.* becoming active or flying in the early evening Also **ves·per·ti·nal** (ves′pər ti′n′l)

ves·pi·ar·y (ves′pē er′ē) *n.,* *pl.* -**ar′ies** [< L. *vespa,* a WASP + (AP)IARY] a nest or colony of social wasps

ves·pid (ves′pid) *n.* [< ModL. *Vespidae,* name of the family < L. *vespa,* a WASP] any of a worldwide family (Vespidae) of social wasps, as the hornet and yellow jacket, that live in colonies consisting of a queen, males, and workers —*adj.* of these wasps

ves·pine (ves′pin, -pin) *adj.* [< L. *vespa,* a WASP + -INE¹] of, pertaining to, or like wasps

Ves·puc·ci (ves pōōt′chē), **A·me·ri·go** (ä′me rē′gô) (L. name *Americus Vespucius*) 1451?–1512; It. navigator & explorer: see AMERICA (etym.)

ves·sel (ves′'l) *n.* [ME. < OFr. *vaissel* < LL. *vascellum,* dim. of L. *vas,* a vessel] 1. a utensil for holding something, as a vase, bowl, pot, kettle, etc. 2. [Chiefly Biblical] a person thought of as being the receiver or repository of some spirit, influence, etc. [*a vessel* of wrath] 3. a boat or ship, esp. a relatively large one 4. *a)* *Anat., Zool.* a tube or duct containing or circulating a body fluid [*a blood vessel*] *b)* *Bot.* a continuous, water-conducting tube in the xylem, composed of a vertical row of single-cell segments whose end walls have disappeared

vest (vest) *n.* [Fr. *veste* < It. < L. *vestis,* a garment < IE. base **wes-,* to clothe, whence OE. *werian,* to WEAR¹] 1. *a)* a short, tight-fitting, sleeveless garment worn, esp. under a suit coat, by men; waistcoat *b)* a similar, jacketlike garment worn by women *c)* an insert or trimming worn under the bodice by women, simulating the front of a man's vest 2. *a)* a long, cassocklike garment worn by men in the time of Charles II *b)* [Rare] any long robe 3. [Brit.] *same as* UNDERSHIRT 4. [Obs.] vesture; clothing —*vt.* [ME. *vesten* < OFr. *vestir* < L. *vestire* < the *n.*] 1. to dress, as in church vestments; clothe 2. to place (authority, power, property rights, etc.) in the control of a person or group (with *in*) 3. to put (a person) in possession or control of, as power or authority; invest (*with* something) —*vi.* 1. to put on garments or vestments; clothe oneself 2. to pass to a person; become vested (*in* a person), as property

Ves·ta (ves′tə) [L.] *Rom. Myth.* the goddess of the hearth, identified with the Greek Hestia —*n.* [v-] 1. orig., a short, wax friction match 2. later, a short wooden match

ves·tal (ves′t′l) *adj.* 1. of or sacred to Vesta 2. of the vestal virgins 3. chaste; pure —*n.* 1. *clipped form of* VESTAL VIRGIN 2. a chaste woman; specif., a virgin

vestal virgin in ancient Rome, any of a small group of virgin priestesses of Vesta, who, sworn to remain chaste, tended the sacred fire in her temple

vest·ed (ves′tid) *adj.* [pp. of VEST] 1. clothed; robed, esp. in church vestments 2. *Law* not contingent upon anything; fixed; settled; absolute [*a vested right*]

vested interest 1. the close involvement of a person or group of people in promoting personal advancement or advantage, usually at the expense of others 2. [*pl.*] a number of such groups cooperating or competing in pursuing selfish goals and exerting powerful controlling influence

☆**vest·ee** (ves tē′) *n. dim. of* VEST (*n.* 1 *c*)

ves·ti·ar·y (ves′tē er′ē) *adj.* [ME. < OFr. *vestiairie:* see VESTRY] [Rare] of clothes or vestments —*n.,* *pl.* -**ar·ies** a supply room for clothing, as in a monastery

ves·ti·bule (ves′tə byōōl′) *n.* [L. *vestibulum,* entrance hall] 1. a small entrance hall or room, either to a building or to a room within a building ☆2. the enclosed passage between passenger cars of a train, having doors for entrance or exit 3. *Anat., Zool.* any cavity or space serving as an entrance to another cavity or space [the *vestibule* of the inner ear leading into the cochlea] —☆*vt.* -**buled′,** -**bul′ing** to furnish (railroad cars) with vestibules —**ves·tib·u·lar** (ves tib′-yə lər) *adj.*

ves·tige (ves′tij) *n.* [Fr. < L. *vestigium,* a footprint] 1. a trace, mark, or sign of something that once existed but has passed away or disappeared [*vestiges* of the ancient wall] 2. a trace; bit [*not a vestige* of hope left] 3. *Biol.* a degenerate, atrophied, or rudimentary organ or part, more fully developed or functional in an earlier stage of development of the individual or species: also **ves·tig·i·um** (ves tij′ē əm), *pl.* -**i·a** (-ə) —*SYN.* see TRACE¹ —**ves·tig′i·al** (-tij′ē əl, -tij′əl) *adj.* —**ves·tig′i·al·ly** *adv.*

vest·ing (ves′tin) *n.* 1. cloth for vests 2. the retention by an employee of all or part of his pension rights regardless of whether or not he changes employers, retires early, etc.

vest·ment (vest′mənt) *n.* [ME. *vestement* < OFr. < L. *vestimentum* < *vestire,* to clothe: see VEST] 1. a garment; robe; gown; esp., an official robe or gown 2. *Eccles.* any of the garments worn by officiants and their assistants, choir members, etc. during certain services and rites

vest-pocket (vest′päk′it) *adj.* 1. small enough to fit into a vest pocket [*a vest-pocket* dictionary] 2. quite small or compact [*a vest-pocket* park]

ves·try (ves′trē) *n.,* *pl.* -**tries** [ME. *vestrie* < OFr. *vestiarie* < L. *vestiarium,* a wardrobe < *vestis,* a garment: see VEST] 1. a room in a church, where the clergy put on their vestments and the sacred vessels are kept; sacristy 2. a room in a church or church building, where prayer meetings, Sunday school, etc. are held 3. *Anglican & Episcopal Ch.* a group of church members who manage the temporal affairs of the church 4. *Anglican Ch. a)* a meeting of such a group or of the parishioners in general *b)* the place for this

ves·try·man (-mən) *n.,* *pl.* -**men** a member of a vestry

ves·ture (ves′chər) *n.* [ME. < OFr. < VL. *vestitura* < L. *vestire,* to clothe: see VEST] 1. [Now Rare] *a)* clothing; garments; apparel *b)* a covering; wrapper 2. *Law* everything growing on land except trees, as grass or grain —*vt.* -**tured, -tur·ing** [Rare or Archaic] to cover; clothe

Ve·su·vi·an (və sōō′vē ən) *adj.* of or like Mount Vesuvius; volcanic —*n.* [v-] an early type of match; fusee

ve·su·vi·an·ite (-ə nit′) *n.* [< prec. + -ITE¹] a glassy mineral, brown to green in color, a complex hydrated silicate of calcium and aluminum; idocrase

Ve·su·vi·us (və sōō′vē əs) active volcano in S Italy, on the Bay of Naples: eruption of 79 A.D. destroyed Pompeii & Herculaneum: 4,000 ft.: It. name **Ve·su·vio** (ve zōō′vyô)

vet¹ (vet) *n. clipped form of* VETERINARIAN —*vt.* **vet′ted, vet′ting** [Colloq.] 1. to examine or treat as a veterinarian does 2. to examine, investigate, or evaluate in a thorough or expert way —*vi.* [Colloq.] to work as a veterinarian

☆**vet²** (vet) *n. clipped form of* VETERAN

vet. 1. veteran 2. veterinarian 3. veterinary

vetch (vech) *n.* [ME. *feche, veche* < ONormFr. *veche* < L. *vicia,* vetch < IE. **weik-* (< base **wei-,* to bend), whence OE. *wagian,* to shake, totter] any of a number of leafy, climbing or trailing plants (esp. genus *Vicia*) of the legume family, grown chiefly for fodder and as a green manure

vetch·ling (-lin) *n.* [prec. + -LING¹] any of a genus (*Lathyrus*) of tendril-climbing plants of the legume family

vet·er·an (vet′ər ən, vet′rən) *adj.* [L. *veteranus* < *vetus* (gen. *veteris*), old < IE. base **wet-,* year, whence WETHER, Gr. *etos,* year] 1. old and experienced; long-practiced, esp. in war or military service 2. of a veteran or veterans —*n.* 1. a person of long experience in some service or position, esp. in military service 2. any person who has served in the armed forces of a country, esp. in time of war

☆**Veterans Administration** a consolidated Federal agency that administers all laws governing benefits for veterans of the armed forces

☆**Veterans Day** the fourth Monday in October, a legal holiday in the U.S. honoring all veterans of the armed forces: celebrated (1954–70) on ARMISTICE DAY

☆**Veterans of Foreign Wars** an organization of U.S. veterans who have served in foreign wars: founded in 1899

vet·er·i·nar·i·an (vet′ər ə ner′ē ən, vet′rə ner′-) *n.* [< L. *veterinarius* (see ff.) + -AN] a person licensed to practice veterinary medicine or surgery

vet·er·i·nar·y (vet′ər ə ner′ē, vet′rə-) *adj.* [L. *veterinarius,* of beasts of burden < *veterina,* beasts of burden < *veterinus,* pertaining to beasts of burden < *vetus* (gen. *veteris*), old, in the sense "beasts of a certain age"] designating or of the branch of medicine dealing with the prevention and treatment of diseases and injuries in animals, esp. domestic animals —*n.,* *pl.* -**nar′ies** same as VETERINARIAN

vet·i·ver (vet′ə vər) *n.* [Fr. *vétiver* < Tamil *veṭṭivēru,* lit., root that is dug up < *vēr,* root] 1. an East Indian grass (*Vetiveria zizanioides*) whose roots yield a fragrant oil used in perfumes, cosmetics, etc. 2. its fibrous roots, also used for making screens, mats, etc.

ve·to (vē′tō) *n.,* *pl.* -**toes** [L., I forbid < *vetare,* to forbid] 1. *a)* an order prohibiting some proposed or intended act; prohibition, esp. by a person in authority *b)* the power to prevent action by such prohibition 2. the constitutional right or power of a ruler or legislature to reject bills passed by another branch of the government; specif., ☆in the U.S., *a)* the power of the President to refuse to sign a bill passed by Congress, preventing it from becoming law unless it is passed again (with a two-thirds majority) by both houses *b)* a similar power held by the governors of States *c)* the exercise of this power ☆3. a document or message giving the reasons of the executive for rejecting a bill: also **veto message** 4. the power of any of the five

permanent members of the Security Council of the United Nations to cast a negative vote, affirmative votes of all five being required to take action on other than procedural matters —*vt.* **-toed, -to·ing** 1. to prevent (a bill) from becoming law by a veto 2. to forbid; prohibit; refuse consent to —**ve′to·er** *n.*

vex (veks) *vt.* [ME. *vexen* < MFr. *vexer*, to vex, torment < L. *vexare*, to shake, agitate] 1. to give trouble to, esp. in a petty or nagging way; disturb, annoy, irritate, etc. 2. to distress, afflict, or plague *[vexed* with rheumatism] 3. to keep bringing up, going over, or returning to (a matter difficult to solve) 4. [Obs.] to shake or toss about —*SYN.* see ANNOY —**vex′er** *n.*

vex·a·tion (vek sā′shən) *n.* [ME. *vexacion* < MFr. < L. *vexatio*] 1. a vexing or being vexed 2. something that vexes; cause of annoyance or distress

vex·a·tious (-shəs) *adj.* 1. characterized by or causing vexation; annoying, troublesome, etc. 2. *Law* instituted without real grounds, chiefly to cause annoyance to the defendant: said of legal actions —**vex·a′tious·ly** *adv.*

vex·il·lar·y (vek′sə ler′ē) *adj.* [L. *vexillarius* < *vexillum*: see VEXILLUM] 1. of an ensign or standard 2. *Bot., Zool.* of a vexillum —*n., pl.* **-lar′ies** in ancient Rome, a veteran soldier serving under a special standard

vex·il·late (vek′sə lit, -lāt′) *adj.* having a vexillum or vexilla

vex·il·lum (vek sil′əm) *n., pl.* **-il′la** (-ə) [L., a standard, flag, dim. < base of *velum*: see VEIL] 1. in ancient Rome, *a)* a square flag, or standard, carried by troops *b)* a company of soldiers serving under one standard 2. *same as: a) Bot.* STANDARD (n. 9 a) *b) Zool.* VANE (sense 6)

vex·ing (vek′sin) *adj.* that vexes —**vex′ing·ly** *adv.*

VFR Visual Flight Rules

V.F.W., VFW Veterans of Foreign Wars

V.G. Vicar-General

VHF, V.H.F., vhf, v.h.f. very high frequency

vi., v.i. intransitive verb

V.I. Virgin Islands

v.i. [L. *vide infra*] see below

vi·a (vī′ə, vē′ə) *prep.* [L., abl. sing. of *via*, a way < IE. base *"wei-*, to go, strive toward, whence OE. *wathan*, to hunt] 1. by a route passing through, along, or over; by way of *[from* Rome to London *via* Paris] 2. by means of; by the medium of *[via* airmail]

vi·a·ble (vī′ə b'l) *adj.* [Fr., likely to live < *vie*, life < L. *vita*: see VITAL] 1. able to live; specif., *a)* having developed sufficiently within the uterus to be able to live and continue normal development outside the uterus *[a premature but viable* infant] *b)* able to take root and grow *[viable* seeds] 2. workable and likely to survive or to have real meaning, pertinence, etc. *[a viable* economy, *viable* ideas] —**vi′a·bil′i·ty** *n.* —**vi′a·bly** *adv.*

vi·a·duct (vī′ə dukt′) *n.* [L. *via* (see VIA) + (AQUE)DUCT] 1. a long bridge consisting of a series of short concrete or masonry spans supported on piers or towers, usually to carry a road or railroad over a valley, gorge, etc. 2. a similar structure of steel girders and towers

vi·al (vī′əl) *n.* [ME. *viole*, var. of *fiole* < OFr. < OPr. *fiola*: see PHIAL] a small vessel or bottle, usually of glass, for containing medicines or other liquids; phial —*vt.* **-aled** or **-alled, -al·ing** or **-al·ling** to put or keep in or as in a vial

‡**vi·a me·di·a** (vī′ə mē′dē ə, vē′ə mä′-) [L.] a middle way; course between two extremes

vi·and (vī′ənd) *n.* [ME. *vyaunde* < OFr. *viande* < VL. *"vivanda*, for L. *vivenda*, neut. pl. gerundive of *vivere*, to live] 1. an article of food 2. *[pl.]* food of various kinds; esp., choice dishes

vi·at·i·cum (vī at′i kəm) *n., pl.* **-ca** (-kə), **-cums** [L., provision for a journey < *viaticus*, of a way or road < *via*, a way: see VIA] 1. *a)* in ancient Rome, money or supplies provided as traveling expenses to an officer on an official mission *b)* money or supplies for any journey 2. *[often* V-] the Eucharist as given to a dying person or to one in danger of death

vi·a·tor (vī āt′ər) *n., pl.* **-tor′es** (vī′ə tôr′ēz) [L. < *viare*, to travel < *via*: see VIA] a traveler; wayfarer

☆**vibes** (vībz) *n.pl.* 1. [Colloq.] *same as* VIBRAPHONE 2. [Slang] *same as* VIBRATION (sense 3)

Vi·borg (vē′bôr y′) Swed. name of VYBORG

vi·brac·u·lum (vī brak′yoo ləm) *n., pl.* **-u·la** (-lə) [ModL., dim. < L. *vibrare*, to shake, VIBRATE] *Zool.* any of the specially modified zooids in a colony of bryozoans, with a whiplike, movable form —**vi·brac′u·lar** *adj.*

☆**vi·bra·harp** (vī′brə härp′) *n. same as* VIBRAPHONE

vi·bran·cy (vī′brən sē) *n.* a vibrant state or quality

vi·brant (vī′brənt) *adj.* [L. *vibrans*, prp. of *vibrare*, to VIBRATE] 1. quivering or vibrating, esp. in such a way as to produce sound 2. produced by vibration; resonant: said of sound 3. throbbing with life and activity; lively *[vibrant* streets] 4. vigorous, energetic, radiant, sparkling, vivacious, etc. *[a vibrant* woman] —**vi′brant·ly** *adv.*

vi·bra·phone (vī′brə fōn′) *n.* [VIBRA(TE) + -PHONE] a musical instrument resembling the marimba, but with electrically operated valves in the resonators, that produce a gentle vibrato —**vi′bra·phon′ist** *n.*

vi·brate (vī′brāt) *vt.* **-brat·ed, -brat·ing** [< L. *vibratus*, pp. of *vibrare*, to vibrate, shake < IE. *"weib-* (> WIPE) 1. to give off (light or sound) by vibration 2. to set in to-and-fro motion; oscillate 3. to cause to quiver —*vi.* 1. to swing back and forth; oscillate, as a pendulum 2. to move rapidly back and forth; quiver, as a plucked string 3. to resound: said of sounds 4. to be emotionally stirred; thrill 5. to waver or vacillate, as between two choices —*SYN.* see SWING

vi·bra·tile (vī′brə til, -tīl) *adj.* [Fr. < L. *vibratus* (see VIBRATE) + -ile, -ILE] 1. of or characterized by vibration 2. capable of vibrating or of being vibrated 3. having a vibratory motion —**vi′bra·til′i·ty** (-til′ə tē) *n.*

vi·bra·tion (vī brā′shən) *n.* [L. *vibratio*] 1. the action of vibrating; specif., *a)* movement back and forth, as of a pendulum; oscillation *b)* rapid rhythmic movement back and forth; quiver 2. vacillation or wavering, as between two choices or opinions ☆3. *[pl.]* one's emotional reaction to a person or thing as being in or out of harmony with one 4. *Physics a)* rapid, periodic, to-and-fro motion or oscillation of an elastic body or the particles of a fluid when displaced from the rest position or position of equilibrium, as in transmitting sound *b)* a single, complete oscillation —**vi·bra′tion·al** *adj.*

vi·bra·tive (vī′brə tiv) *adj. same as* VIBRATORY

vi·bra·to (vi brät′ō, vē-) *n., pl.* **-tos** [It., pp. of *vibrare*: see VIBRATE] *Music* a pulsating effect, less extreme than a tremolo, produced by rapid alternation of a given tone with a barely perceptible variation in pitch, as by the slight oscillation of the finger on a violin string or by a slight wavering of the tone in singing

vi·bra·tor (vī′brāt′ər) *n.* something that vibrates or causes vibration; specif., *a)* the hammer of an electric bell *b)* a vibrating electrical device used in massage *c)* Electronics an electromagnetic device with contacts on a tuned, vibrating steel reed that periodically interrupt a steady direct current to generate a pulsating current

vi·bra·to·ry (vī′brə tôr′ē) *adj.* 1. of, like, or causing vibration 2. vibrating or capable of vibration

vib·ri·o (vib′rē ō′) *n., pl.* **-ri·os′** [ModL. < L. *vibrare*, to shake: *sec* VIBRATE] any of a genus (*Vibrio*) of short, flagellate, Gram-negative bacteria shaped like a comma or the letter S: one species (*Vibrio comma*) causes cholera

vi·bris·sa (vī bris′ə) *n., pl.* **-sae** (-ē) [ModL. < L. *vibrissae*, pl., akin to *vibrare*, to VIBRATE] *Anat., Zool.* 1. any of the stiff hairs growing in or near the nostrils of certain animals and often serving as organs of touch, as a cat's whiskers 2. any of the bristlelike feathers growing near the mouth of certain insect-eating birds, as the whippoorwill

vi·bur·num (vī bur′nəm) *n.* [ModL., name of the genus < L., the wayfaring tree] 1. any of a large genus (*Viburnum*) of shrubs or small trees of the honeysuckle family, with white flowers 2. the bark of several species of this plant, sometimes used in medicine

vic. 1. vicar 2. vicarage 3. vicinity

vic·ar (vik′ər) *n.* [ME. < OFr. *vicaire* < L. *vicarius*, orig., vicarious < *vicis*, a change, alteration < IE. *"weik-* < base *"wei-*, to bend, whence WEEK] 1. a person who acts in place of another; deputy 2. *Anglican Ch.* a parish priest who is not a rector and receives a stipend instead of the tithes 3. *Protestant Episcopal Ch.* a minister in charge of one chapel in a parish, as deputy of another minister 4. *R.C.Ch. a)* a church officer acting as deputy of a bishop *b)* [V-] the Pope, regarded as earthly representative of Christ: in full **Vicar of (Jesus) Christ** —**vic′ar·ship′** *n.*

vic·ar·age (-ij) *n.* [ME. *vicerege*: see prec. & -AGE] 1. the residence of a vicar 2. the benefice or salary of a vicar 3. the position or duties of a vicar

vicar apostolic *pl.* **vicars apostolic** *R.C.Ch.* 1. formerly, a bishop or archbishop to whom the Pope delegated part of his jurisdiction 2. a titular bishop administering a vacant diocese, etc., or a missionary bishop acting as a delegate of the Holy See in a region where no regular see has yet been organized

vicar fo·rane (fô rān′) [VICAR + ML. *foraneus*, outside the episcopal city, rural, for LL. *foranus*: see FOREIGN] *R.C.Ch. same as* DEAN (sense 1 b)

vic·ar-gen·er·al (vik′ər jen′ər əl) *n., pl.* **vic′ars-gen′er·al** [ME. *vicare generale* < ML. *vicarius generalis*: see VICAR & GENERAL] 1. *Anglican Ch.* a layman serving as administrative deputy to an archbishop or bishop 2. *R.C.Ch.* a priest, etc. acting as administrative deputy to a bishop or to the general superior of a religious order, society, etc. 3. in English history, the title given to Thomas Cromwell as vicegerent of Henry VIII

vi·car·i·al (vī ker′ē əl, vi-) *adj.* [Fr.] 1. of a vicar 2. acting as a vicar 3. vicarious, or delegated *[vicarial* powers]

vi·car·i·ate (-it, -āt′) *n.* [ML. *vicariatus* < L. *vicarius*] 1. the office or authority of a vicar 2. the district administered by a vicar Also **vi·car′ate** (-ər it, -ə rāt′)

vi·car·i·ous (-ē əs) *adj.* [L. *vicarius*, substituted: see VICAR] 1. *a)* taking the place of another thing or person; substitute; deputy *b)* held or handled by one person as the deputy of another; delegated *[vicarious* powers] 2. *a)* endured, suffered, or performed by one person in place of

another [*vicarious* punishment] b) shared in or experienced by imagined participation in another's experience [a *vicarious* thrill] **3.** *Physiol.* designating or of a function abnormally performed by other than the usual organ or part [*vicarious* menstruation] —**vi·car'i·ous·ly** adv. —**vi·car'i·ous·ness** n.

vice[1] (vīs) n. [ME. < OFr. < L. *vitium*, vice, fault < IE. base *wi-*, apart, in two, whence Sans. *viṣu-*, in opposite directions: cf. WITH] **1.** a) an evil or wicked action, habit, or characteristic b) evil or wicked conduct or behavior; depravity or corruption c) prostitution d) [V-] in old English morality plays, a character, often a buffoon, representing a vice or vice in general **2.** any trivial fault or failing, act of self-indulgence, etc. **3.** a defect or flaw, as in a work of art **4.** any physical or functional defect or imperfection of the body **5.** a bad or harmful trick or habit, as of a horse or dog —*SYN.* see FAULT

vi·ce[2] (vī'sē, -sə) prep. [L.: see VICE-] in the place of; as the deputy or successor of

vice[3] (vīs) n., vt. chiefly Brit. sp. of VISE

vice- (vīs) [< L. *vice*, in the place of another, abl. of *vicis*: see VICAR] a *prefix meaning* one who acts in the place of; subordinate; deputy [*vice-president*]

vice admiral a naval officer next in rank above a rear admiral and below an admiral —**vice admiralty**

vice-chair·man (vīs'cher'mən) n., pl. **-men** an assistant or deputy chairman

vice-chan·cel·lor (-chan'sə lər, -chän'-) n. **1.** an official next in rank below a chancellor, as of a university, and authorized to act as his deputy **2.** *Law* a judge serving as assistant to a chancellor

vice-con·sul (-kän's'l) n. an officer who is subordinate to or a substitute for a consul —**vice'-con'su·lar** adj. —**vice'-con'su·late** (-it) n. —**vice'-con'sul·ship'** n.

vice·ge·ren·cy (vīs'jir'ən sē) n., pl. **-cies** the office of, or district ruled by, a vicegerent

vice·ge·rent (-jir'ənt) n. [ML. *vicegerens:* see VICE- & GERENT] a person appointed by another, esp. by a ruler, to exercise the latter's power and authority; deputy; vicar —adj. of a vicegerent: also **vice'ge'ral**

vic·e·nar·y (vis'ə ner'ē) adj. [L. *vicenarius* < *viceni*, twenty each] **1.** of or consisting of twenty **2.** using twenty as the basic unit of notation

vi·cen·ni·al (vī sen'ē əl) adj. [< L. *vicennium*, period of twenty years < *vicies*, twenty times + *annus*, year (see ANNUAL)] **1.** happening every twenty years **2.** lasting or existing for twenty years

Vi·cen·za (vē chen'tsä) commune in N Italy: pop. 106,000

vice-pres·i·dent (vīs'prez'i dənt) n. **1.** a) an officer next in rank below a president, acting in his place during his absence or incapacity b) [V- P-] the elected officer of this rank in the U.S. government, acting as president of the Senate but not as executive assistant to the President: he succeeds to the Presidency in the event of the President's death, incapacity, or removal: in this sense, usually **Vice President 2.** any of several officers of a company, institution, etc., each in charge of a separate department —☆**vice'-pres'i·den·cy** n. —☆**vice'-pres'i·den'tial** adj.

vice·re·gal (vīs'rē'g'l) adj. [VICE- + REGAL] of a viceroy —**vice're'gal·ly** adv.

vice·re·gent (-rē'jənt) n. a deputy of a regent

vice·reine (vīs'rān) n. [Fr. < *vice-* (see VICE-) + *reine*, queen < L. *regina* (see REGINA)] the wife of a viceroy

vice·roy (-roi) n. [MFr. < *vice-* (see VICE-) + *roy*, king < L. *rex:* see REGAL] **1.** a person ruling a country, province, or colony as the deputy of a sovereign ☆**2.** an American butterfly (*Limenitis archippus*) of striking red and black coloring, much like the monarch butterfly, but smaller

vice·roy·al·ty (vīs'roi'əl tē) n., pl. **-ties** [< Fr. *vice-royauté:* see VICE- & ROYALTY] the office or tenure of, or the area ruled by, a viceroy: also **vice'roy·ship'**

vice squad a police squad assigned to the suppression or control of prostitution, gambling, etc.

vi·ce ver·sa (vī'sē vur'sə, vī'sə; vis') [L.] the order or relation being reversed; conversely

Vi·chy (vish'ē, vē'shē') city in C France: capital of unoccupied France (1940–44): pop. 31,000

vi·chy·ssoise (vē'shē swäz', vish'ē-) n. [Fr., orig. fem. of *Vichyssois*, of VICHY] a thick cream soup of potatoes, onions, etc., usually served cold

Vichy (water) 1. a sparkling mineral water from springs at Vichy **2.** a natural or processed water like this

vic·i·nage (vis'ə nij) n. [ME. *vesinage* < MFr. *visenage* < *veisin*, near < VL. *vecinus*, for L. *vicinus*: see VICINITY] **1.** same as VICINITY **2.** the people living in a particular neighborhood

vic·i·nal (-n'l) adj. [L. *vicinalis* < *vicinus*: see ff.] **1.** neighboring; nearby **2.** designating a road that is local and not a highway **3.** *Mineralogy* designating faces on a crystal that approximate or take the place of fundamental planes

vi·cin·i·ty (və sin'ə tē) n., pl. **-ties** [L. *vicinitas* < *vicinus*, near < *vicus*, group of houses, village < IE. base *weik-*, house, settlement, whence Gr. *oikos*, house, Goth. *weihs*, village] **1.** the state of being near or close by; nearness; proximity [two theaters in close *vicinity*] **2.** the region or area surrounding a particular place; neighborhood

vi·cious (vish'əs) adj. [ME. < OFr. *vicieus* < L. *vitiosus*, full of faults, corrupt, vicious < *vitium*, VICE[1]] **1.** a) given to or characterized by vice; evil, corrupt, or depraved

b) tending to deprave or corrupt; pernicious [*vicious* interests] c) harmful, unwholesome, or noxious [a *vicious* concoction] **2.** ruined by defects, flaws, or errors; full of faults [a *vicious* argument] **3.** having bad or harmful habits; unruly [a *vicious* horse] **4.** malicious; spiteful; mean [a *vicious* rumor] **5.** very intense, forceful, sharp, etc. [a *vicious* blow] —**vi'cious·ly** adv. —**vi'cious·ness** n.

SYN. **vicious** suggests such reprehensible qualities as wickedness, depravity, cruelty, etc. [a *vicious* bigot, remark, etc.]; **villainous**, more or less synonymous with **vicious**, suggests the evil or criminality of a villain [a *villainous* attack]; **iniquitous** implies the absence of all righteousness or justice and indifference to moral principles [the *iniquitous* practices of colonialism]; **nefarious** implies unspeakable wickedness and total disregard of morality and ethics [a *nefarious* scheme for robbing the poor]; **infamous** suggests scandalous or notorious wickedness [an *infamous* crime] —*ANT.* virtuous, righteous

vicious circle 1. a situation in which the solution of one problem gives rise to another, but the solution of this, or of other problems rising out of it, brings back the first, often with greater involvement **2.** a situation in which one disease or disorder results in another which in turn aggravates the first **3.** *Logic* a) an argument which is invalid because its conclusion rests on a premise which itself depends on the conclusion b) the definition of a word by another which is in turn defined by the first

vi·cis·si·tude (vi sis'ə tōōd', -tyōōd') n. [Fr. < L. *vicissitudo* < *vicis*, a turn, change: see VICAR] **1.** a) a condition of constant change or alternation, as a natural process; mutability [the *vicissitude* of the sea] b) regular succession or alternation, as of night and day **2.** [pl.] unpredictable changes or variations that keep occurring in life, fortune, etc.; shifting circumstances; ups and downs —*SYN.* see DIFFICULTY —**vi·cis'si·tu'di·nar'y, vi·cis'si·tu'di·nous** adj.

Vicks·burg (viks'burg) [after Rev. Newitt *Vick* (?–1819), early settler] city in W Miss., on the Mississippi River: besieged by Grant in the Civil War (1863): pop. 25,000

vi·comte (vē kônt') n., pl. **-comtes** (-kônt') Fr. equivalent of VISCOUNT (sense 2)

vic·tim (vik'təm) n. [L. *victima*, victim, beast for sacrifice < IE. base *weik-*, to separate, whence OE. *wig*, idol, *wicce*, WITCH] **1.** a person or animal killed as a sacrifice to a god in a religious rite **2.** someone or something killed, destroyed, injured, or otherwise harmed by, or suffering from, some act, condition, agency, or circumstance [victims of war] **3.** a person who suffers some loss, esp. by being swindled; dupe

vic·tim·ize (vik'tə mīz') vt. **-ized', -iz'ing** to make a victim of; specif., a) to kill, destroy, etc. as or like a sacrificial victim b) to dupe or cheat —**vic'tim·i·za'tion** n. —**vic'tim·iz'er** n.

Vic·tor (vik'tər) [L.: see ff.] a masculine name: dim. *Vic;* fem. *Victoria*

vic·tor (vik'tər) n. [ME. < L. < pp. of *vincere*, to conquer < IE. base *weik-*, vigorous or hostile display of force, whence OHG. *wic*, battle, OE. *wigan*, to fight] the winner in a battle, struggle, etc. —adj. same as VICTORIOUS

Victor Emmanuel I 1759–1824; king of Sardinia (1802–21): abdicated

Victor Emmanuel II 1820–78; king of Sardinia (1849–61) & 1st king of Italy (1861–78)

Victor Emmanuel III 1869–1947; king of Italy (1900–46): abdicated & the monarchy dissolved (1946)

Vic·to·ri·a[1] (vik tôr'ē ə, -tôr'yə) [L., VICTORY] **1.** a feminine name; dim. *Vicky;* equiv. Fr. *Victoire,* It. *Vittoria,* Sp. *Vitoria* **2. (Alexandrina)**, 1819–1901; queen of Great Britain & Ireland (1837–1901); empress of India (1876–1901): granddaughter of GEORGE III —n. [v-] **1.** a four-wheeled carriage for two passengers, with a folding top and high seat in front for the coachman **2.** an early touring automobile with a folding top over the rear seat **3.** any of a genus (*Victoria*) of S. American waterlilies with platterlike leaves up to seven feet wide and large, night-blooming flowers

VICTORIA

Vic·to·ri·a[2] (vik tôr'ē ə, -tôr'yə) **1.** state of Australia, in the SE part: 87,884 sq. mi.; pop. 3,218,000; cap. Melbourne **2.** capital of Hong Kong; seaport on Hong Kong Island: pop. c.1,000,000 **3.** capital of British Columbia, Canada; seaport on SE Vancouver Island: pop. 57,000 **4.** [orig. name Sp. *Guadalupe Victoria*, lit., our Lady of Guadalupe triumphant] city in SE Tex.: pop. 41,000 **5. Lake**, lake in E Africa, bounded by Kenya, Uganda, & Tanzania: 26,828 sq. mi.

Victoria Cross the highest British military decoration, given for deeds of exceptional valor

Victoria Day a legal holiday in Canada, celebrated on the Monday immediately preceding May 25

Victoria Falls waterfall of the Zambezi River, between Rhodesia & Zambia: c.350 ft. high; c.1 mi. wide

Victoria Island island of the Northwest Territories, Canada, east of Banks Island: 81,930 sq. mi.

Victoria Land mainland region of Antarctica, along the Ross Sea: part of the Ross Dependency

Vic·to·ri·an (-ən) *adj.* **1.** of or characteristic of the time when Victoria was queen of England (1837–1901) **2.** showing the middle-class respectability, prudery, bigotry, etc. generally attributed to Victorian England **3.** designating or of a style of furniture of the 19th cent., characterized by ornate, flowery carving and patterned upholstery —*n.* a person, esp. a British writer, of the time of Queen Victoria —**Vic·to'ri·an·ism** *n.*

Victoria Nile upper course of the Nile, flowing from Lake Victoria into Lake Albert: c.250 mi.

vic·to·ri·ous (vik tôr'ē əs, -tôr'yəs) *adj.* [ME. < L. *victoriosus*] **1.** having won a victory; winning; triumphant **2.** of, typical of, or bringing about victory —**vic·to'ri·ous·ly** *adv.*

vic·to·ry (vik'tər ē, -trē) *n., pl.* **-ries** [ME. < OFr. *victorie* < L. *victoria* < *victor*, a VICTOR] **1.** final and complete supremacy or superiority in battle or war **2.** a specific military engagement ending in triumph **3.** success in any contest or struggle involving the defeat of an opponent or the overcoming of obstacles
SYN.—**victory** implies the winning of a contest or struggle of any kind [a *victory* in battle, in sports, etc.]; **conquest** implies a victory in which one subjugates others and brings them under complete control [the *conquests* of Napoleon]; **triumph** implies a victory in which one exults because of its outstanding and decisive character [the *triumphs* of modern medicine] —*ANT.* **defeat**

vic·tress (vik'tris) *n.* [Now Rare] a female victor

☆**Vic·tro·la** (vik trō'lə) *a trademark for* a phonograph —*n.* [v-] *old-fashioned term for* PHONOGRAPH

vict·ual (vit'') *n.* [ME. *vitaille*, provisions < MFr. < LL. *victualia*, provisions < L. *victualis*, of food < *victus*, food < pp. of *vivere*, to live: see QUICK] **1.** [Archaic or Dial.] food or other provisions **2.** [pl.] [Dial. or Colloq.] articles of food, esp. when prepared for use —*vt.* **-ualed** or **-ualled**, **-ual·ing** or **-ual·ling** to supply with victuals —*vi.* **1.** [Archaic] to eat or feed **2.** to lay in a supply of food

vict·ual·er, vict·ual·ler (-ər) *n.* [ME. *vittailler* < MFr. *vitailleur*] **1.** formerly, *a*) a person who supplied victuals, as to an army or a ship; sutler *b*) a supply ship **2.** [Brit.] an innkeeper

vi·cu·ña (vī kōōn'yə, vi-; -kōōn'ə, -kyōōn'ə) *n., pl.* **-ñas**, **-ña**: see PLURAL, II, D, 1 [Sp., of Quechuan orig.] **1.** a cud-chewing animal (*Vicugna vicugna*) of the camel family, found wild in the S. American Andes, related to the guanaco, llama, and alpaca, with soft, shaggy wool **2.** this wool **3.** a fabric made from it or in imitation of it

Vi·da (vē'də, vī'-) [W., dim. of *Davida*, fem. of *David*] a feminine name

‡**vi·de** (vī'dē, vē'dā) [L., imperative sing. of *videre*, to see] see; refer to: used to direct attention to a particular page, book, etc.

VICUÑA
(to 40 in. high
at shoulder)

‡**vide an·te** (an'tē) [L.] see before (in the book, etc.)

‡**vide in·fra** (in'frə) [L.] see below; see further on (in the book, etc.)

‡**vi·de·li·cet** (vi del'ə sit) *adv.* [L. < *videre licet*, it is permitted to see] that is; namely

vid·e·o (vid'ē ō') *adj.* [L., I see < *videre*: see VISION: used by analogy with AUDIO] **1.** of or used in television **2.** designating or of the picture portion of a telecast, as distinguished from the *audio* (or sound) portion —*n. same as* TELEVISION

video tape a magnetic tape on which the electronic impulses of the video and audio portions of a television program can be recorded as for later broadcasting

‡**vide post** (pōst) [L.] see after; see further on (in the book, etc.)

‡**vide su·pra** (sōō'prə) [L.] see above; see earlier (in the book, etc.)

vi·dette (vi det') *n. alt. sp. of* VEDETTE

‡**vide ut su·pra** (ut sōō'prə, oot) [L.] see what is stated above

☆**vid·i·con** (vid'ə kän) *n.* [VID(EO) + ICON(OSCOPE)] a television camera pickup tube of high sensitivity in which the image is focused on a transparent, thin, metal film backed with a layer of photoconductive material that is scanned with a low-velocity electron beam for transmission as signals

vie (vī) *vi.* **vied**, **vy'ing** [ME. *vien*, aphetic for *envien* < OFr. *envier*, to invite, vie in games < L. *invitare*, to INVITE] to struggle for superiority (*with* someone) or enter into competition (*for* something); compete —*vt.* **1.** [Obs.] to bet; wager; hazard **2.** [Archaic] to do, offer, display, or match in rivalry —**vi'er** *n.*

Vi·en·na (vē en'ə) capital of Austria, in the NE part, on the Danube: pop. 1,628,000: Ger. name, WIEN —**Vi·en·nese** (vē'ə nēz') *adj., n., pl.* **-nese'**

Vienna, Congress of a conference of the major European powers held at Vienna (1814–15) at the end of the Napoleonic wars: its purpose was to restore monarchies and readjust territories throughout Europe

Vienne (vyen) **1.** city in SE France: pop. 27,000 **2.** river in WC France, flowing into the Loire: 230 mi.

Vien·tiane (vyen tyän') administrative capital of Laos, on the Mekong River: pop. c.125,000

Vi·et (vē'ət, -et; vyet) *n., adj. colloq. clipped form of* VIETNAM, VIETNAMESE

‡**vi et ar·mis** (vī' et är'mis) [L., with force and arms] with actual violence: used in law to refer to a trespass that is the direct cause of damage

Viet Cong (kän) [< Vietnamese *Viet Nam Cong San*, Vietnamese Communist] **1.** collectively, native guerrilla and combat groups that compose the military force of the National Liberation Front of Vietnam **2.** any member of such a group **3.** of or having to do with these groups A loose, orig. derogatory, term Also **Vi'et·cong'** *n.*

Vi·et·minh (vē'ət min', vyet'-) *n.* [Vietnamese, contr. < *Viet Nam Doc-Lap Dong Minh*, the Revolutionary League for the Independence of Vietnam] **1.** an organization formed of nationalist and communist parties in 1941 to resist the Japanese and later the French, and to win independence for Vietnam **2.** [*with pl. verb*] the members of this organization —*adj.* of this organization

Vi·et·nam (vē'ət näm', vyet'-; -nam') country on the E coast of the Indochinese Peninsula: formed (1945) by the union of the Fr. territories of Annam, Cochin-China, & Tonkin: since 1954, divided into two zones: *a*) **North Vietnam** 63,344 sq. mi.; pop. 16,400,000; cap. Hanoi *b*) **South Vietnam** 66,263 sq. mi.; pop. 17,414,000; cap. Saigon See INDOCHINA, map Also sp. **Viet-Nam, Viet Nam**

Vi·et·nam·ese (vē'ət nə mēz', vē et'-, vyet'-; -mēs') *adj.* of Vietnam, its people, etc. —*n.* **1.** *pl.* **-ese'** a native or inhabitant of Vietnam **2.** the Austro-Asiatic language of Vietnam, written in the Latin alphabet Also **Vi'et·Nam·ese'**

view (vyōō) *n.* [ME. *vewe* < OFr. *veue* < *veoir*, to see < L. *videre*: see VISION] **1.** a seeing or looking, as in inspection or examination **2.** sight or vision; esp., range of vision [not a person in *view*] **3.** mental examination or survey; critical contemplation [to take a correct *view* of a situation] **4.** that which is seen; esp., a scene or prospect, as of a landscape [a room with a *view*] **5.** a picture, sketch, or photograph of a scene, esp. of a landscape **6.** visual appearance or aspect of something **7.** manner of regarding or considering something; judgment; opinion [one's *views* on a matter] **8.** that which is worked toward or sought; object; aim; goal [to have a *view* to bettering one's condition] **9.** a general survey or summary **10.** *Law* a formal inspection by the jury of the scene of an alleged crime —*vt.* **1.** to inspect; scrutinize **2.** to look at or see; behold **3.** to survey mentally; consider **4.** to regard in a particular way [to *view* a situation with fear] —**in view 1.** in sight **2.** under consideration **3.** in mind or memory **4.** as an end or object aimed at **5.** in expectation, as a hope or wish —**in view of** in consideration of; because of —**on view** displayed or exhibited publicly —**with a view to 1.** with the purpose of **2.** with a hope of; looking forward to
SYN.—**view** is the general word for that which is exposed to the sight or lies within the range of vision [the *view* is cut off by the next building]; **prospect** suggests an extensive view as afforded by a position from which one can look out to a distance [a commanding *prospect* of the countryside]; **scene** has aesthetic or dramatic connotations with reference to a view or a representation of a view [a rustic *scene*]; **vista** suggests a view seen through a long narrow passage, as between rows of trees See also OPINION, SEE[1]

view·er (-ər) *n.* **1.** a person who views a scene, exhibit, movie, television show, etc.; spectator **2.** an optical device for individual viewing of slides, filmstrips, etc.

view·find·er (-fīn'dər) *n. same as* FINDER (sense 2)

view halloo a shout by a huntsman when he sees the fox break into the open: also **view hallo, view halloa**

view·less (-lis) *adj.* **1.** affording no view, or prospect **2.** [Rare] that cannot be seen; invisible **3.** having or expressing no views, or opinions —**view'less·ly** *adv.*

view·point (-point') *n.* the mental position from which things are viewed and judged; point of view

view·y (-ē) *adj.* **view'i·er, view'i·est** [Old Colloq.] **1.** fanciful or visionary **2.** showy; ostentatious

☆**vi·ga** (vē'gə) *n.* [Sp., beam] any of the heavy beams or rafters across the ceiling in a house of the old Spanish type in the Southwest

vi·ges·i·mal (vī jes'ə m'l) *adj.* [< L. *vigesimus*, var. of *vicesimus* < *viceni*, twenty each < *viginti*, twenty < IE. *wikmti*, two decades < *wi-*, apart, two (cf. WITH) + *dkmt-*, TEN] **1.** of or based on the number twenty **2.** twentieth

vig·il (vij'əl) *n.* [ME. *vigile* < OFr. < L. *vigilia*, a watch < *vigil*, awake: see WAKE[1]] **1.** *a*) a purposeful or watchful staying awake during the usual hours of sleep *b*) a watch kept, or the period of this **2.** *Eccles.* the evening or day before a festival, or the church service or devotional watch held then

vig·i·lance (vij'ə ləns) *n.* [Fr. < L. *vigilantia*] the quality or state of being vigilant; watchfulness

☆**vigilance committee** a group extralegally assuming authority for summary action professedly to keep order and punish crime because of the alleged lack or failure of the usual law-enforcement agencies

vig·i·lant (vij'ə lənt) *adj.* [Fr. < L. *vigilans*, prp. of *vigilare*, to watch < *vigil*, awake: see WAKE[1]] staying watchful and alert to danger or trouble —*SYN.* see WATCHFUL —**vig'i·lant·ly** *adv.*

☆**vig·i·lan·te** (vij'ə lan'tē) *n.* [Sp., watchman, orig., vigilant] a member of a vigilance committee

☆**vig·i·lan·tism** (vij'ə lan tiz'm) *n.* the lawless, violent methods, spirit, etc. of vigilantes —**vig'i·lan'tist** *adj.*

vigil light a candle burned before a shrine or icon, as in a church, as an act of devotion or petition

vi·gnette (vin yet') *n.* [Fr., dim. < *vigne*, a VINE] **1.** an ornamental design (orig. one of vine leaves, tendrils, and grapes) or illustration used on a page of a book, magazine, etc., as at the beginning or end of a chapter or section **2.** a picture or photograph with no definite border, shading off gradually at the edges into the background **3.** a short, delicate literary sketch —*vt.* **-gnet'ted, -gnet'ting** to make a vignette of —**vi·gnet'tist** (-nyet'ist) *n.*

Vi·gny (vē nyē'), **Al·fred Vic·tor** (ȧl fred' vēk tôr'), comte **de** (də), 1797–1863; Fr. poet & man of letters

Vi·go (vē'gō) seaport in NW Spain: pop. 166,000

vig·or (vig'ər) *n.* [ME. *vigour* < OFr. < L. *vigor* < *vigere*, to be strong: see WAKE[1]] **1.** active physical or mental force or strength; vitality **2.** active or healthy growth [the *vigor* of a plant] **3.** intensity, force, or energy [the *vigor* of her denial] **4.** effective legal or binding force; validity [a law that is still in *vigor*] Also, Brit. sp., **vig'our**

☆**vig·or·ish** (vig'ər ish) *n.* [altered (as if < VIGOR + -ISH), prob. < Russ. *vyigrysh*, winnings, profit] [Slang] **1.** the advantage in betting odds that a bookmaker or gambler creates to produce his profit **2.** excessive interest as charged by a loan shark

vi·go·ro·so (vig'ə rō'sō; *It.* vē'gō rō'sō) *adj.* [It.] *Music* vigorous; energetic: a direction to the performer

vig·or·ous (vig'ər əs) *adj.* [ME. *vigerous* < OFr. *viguereus*: see VIGOR & -OUS] **1.** living or growing with full vital strength; strong; robust **2.** of, characterized by, or requiring vigor or strength **3.** forceful or powerful; strong; energetic **4.** acting, or ready to act, with energy and force —*SYN.* see ACTIVE —**vig'or·ous·ly** *adv.* —**vig'or·ous·ness** *n.*

Vii·pu·ri (vē'poo rē') *Finn. name of* VYBORG

Vi·ja·ya·wa·da (vē'jə yə wä'də) city in Andhra Pradesh, SE India, on the Kistna River: pop. 230,000

vik·ing (vī'kiŋ) *n.* [ON. *vikingr*] [*also* V-] any of the Scandinavian sea rovers and pirates who ravaged the coasts of Europe from the 8th to the 10th centuries

vil. village

vile (vīl) *adj.* [ME. *vil* < OFr. < L. *vilis*, cheap, base] **1.** morally base or evil; wicked; depraved; sinful **2.** offensive to the senses or sensibilities; repulsive; disgusting **3.** cheap; worthless **4.** degrading; low; mean **5.** highly disagreeable or most inferior; very bad: a generalized term of disapproval [*vile* weather] —*SYN.* see BASE[2] —**vile'ly** *adv.* —**vile'ness** *n.*

vil·i·fy (vil'ə fī') *vt.* **-fied', -fy'ing** [LL.(Ec.) *vilificare*: see VILE & -FY] **1.** to use abusive or slanderous language about or of; calumniate; revile; defame **2.** [Rare] to degrade —**vil'i·fi·ca'tion** *n.*

vil·i·pend (vil'ə pend') *vt.* [ME. *vilipenden* < MFr. *vilipender* < L. *vilipendere* < *vilis*, VILE + *pendere*, to weigh (see PEND)] **1.** to treat or regard contemptuously or slightingly; disparage; belittle **2.** to vilify; revile

vil·la (vil'ə) *n.* [It. < L., a country seat, farm, akin to *vicus*, village: see VICINITY] **1.** a country house or estate, esp. when large or luxurious and used as a retreat or summer house **2.** [Brit.] a small suburban house

Vi·lla (vē'yä), **Fran·cis·co** (frän sēs'kō) (born *Doroteo Arango*) 1877?–1923; Mex. revolutionary leader: called *Pancho Villa*

vil·la·dom (vil'ə dəm) *n.* [VILLA + -DOM] [Chiefly Brit.] villas and their occupants, collectively; suburban society, regarded as smug, dull, etc.; suburbia

Vil·la·fran·chi·an (vil'ə franʹkē ən) *adj.* [after *Villafranca*, town in NW Italy] designating or of the Lower Pleistocene before the first glaciation

vil·lage (vil'ij) *n.* [ME. < OFr. < L. *villaticus*, belonging to a country house < *villa*, a country house, farm (see VILLA)] **1.** *a)* a group of houses in the country, larger than a hamlet and smaller than a city or town *b)* such a community incorporated as a municipality *c)* the people of a village, collectively; villagers **2.** a group or cluster of the habitations of animals or birds —*adj.* of a village

village community a primitive type of organized farming community, regarded as the basic self-governing political unit from which the modern state developed, and characterized by communal ownership of land

vil·lag·er (-ər) *n.* a person who lives in a village

Vi·lla·her·mo·sa (vē'yä er mō'sä) city in SE Mexico; capital of Tabasco state: pop. 52,000

vil·lain (vil'ən) *n.* [ME. *vilein* < OFr. *vilain* < VL. *villanus*, a farm servant < L. *villa*, a farm (see VILLA)] **1.** a person guilty of committing or likely to commit great crimes; evil or wicked person; scoundrel **2.** a wicked or unprincipled character in a novel, play, etc. who opposes the protagonist or hero **3.** *same as* VILLEIN **4.** [Obs.] a boor; lout —**vil'lain·ess** *n.fem.*

vil·lain·ous (-əs) *adj.* **1.** of, like, or characteristic of a villain; evil; wicked **2.** very bad, disagreeable, or objectionable —*SYN.* see VICIOUS —**vil'lain·ous·ly** *adv.*

vil·lain·y (-ē) *n., pl.* **-lain·ies** [ME. *vileinie* < Anglo-Fr. & OFr. *vilainie* < *vilain*] **1.** the fact or state of being villainous **2.** villainous conduct **3.** a villainous act; wicked, detestable, or criminal deed

Vil·la-Lo·bos (vēʹlä lōʹboos; *E.* vēʹlə lōʹbəs), **Hei·tor** (ā tôrʹ) 1887?–1959; Brazilian composer

vil·la·nel·la (vil'ə nelʹə; *It.* vēlʹlä nelʹlä) *n., pl.* **-le** (-ē; *It.* -lē) [It., fem. dim. of *villano* < VL. *villanus:* see VILLAIN] **1.** an old rustic Italian song and accompanying dance **2.** a Neapolitan 16th-cent. part song for unaccompanied voices, like the madrigal

vil·la·nelle (vil'ə nel') *n.* [Fr. < It. *villanella:* see prec.] a short poem of fixed form, French in origin, consisting usually of five three-line stanzas and a final four-line stanza and having only two rhymes throughout

Vil·lard (vi lärd'), **Oswald Garrison** 1872–1949; U.S. journalist, editor, & writer, born in Germany

vil·lat·ic (vi lat'ik) *adj.* [L. *villaticus*] of a villa, country house, or farm; rustic; rural

-ville (vil) [< Fr. *ville*, town, city < L. *villa:* see VILLA] *a combining form meaning:* **1.** town, city: used in many place names [*Evansville*] ☆**2.** place or condition characterized by, fit for, or filled with: freely used in coining slang terms, typically derogatory [*"squaresville," "dullsville"*]

vil·lein (vil'ən) *n.* [ME.: see VILLAIN] in feudal England, any of a class of serfs who by the 13th cent. had become freemen in their legal relations to all except their lord, to whom they remained subject as slaves

vil·lein·age, vil·len·age (-ij) *n.* [ME. *villenage* < OFr.: see VILLAIN] **1.** the status of a villein **2.** the conditions of tenure by which a villein held his land

Ville·ur·banne (vēl ür bȧn') city in EC France; suburb of Lyon: pop. 105,000

vil·li (vil'ī) *n. pl. of* VILLUS

Vil·liers (vil'ərz, -yərz), **George** *see* BUCKINGHAM

vil·li·form (vil'ə fôrm') *adj.* [< VILLUS + -FORM] **1.** like villi in form **2.** designating the small teeth of some fishes, so closely set as to resemble the pile of velvet

Vil·lon (vē yōn'), **Fran·çois** (frän swä') (born *François de Montcorbier* or *des Loges*) 1431–?; Fr. poet

vil·los·i·ty (vi läs'ə tē) *n., pl.* **-ties 1.** the condition of being villous **2.** a villus **3.** a coating or surface of villi

vil·lous (vil'əs) *adj.* [ME. < L. *villosus*] of, having the nature of, or covered with villi: also **vil'lose** (-ōs)

vil·lus (vil'əs) *n., pl.* **vil'li** (-ī) [L., shaggy hair, tuft of hair, var. of *vellus*, a fleece, WOOL] **1.** *Anat.* any of numerous hairlike or fingerlike vascular processes on certain mucous membranes of the body, as of the small intestine, serving to secrete mucus, absorb fats, etc., or of the chorion in the mammalian placenta, serving in the exchange of food materials, etc. between the mother and the fetus **2.** *Bot.* any of the long, soft, fine hairs on certain plants, as mosses

Vil·ni·us (vil'nē oos') capital of the Lithuanian S.S.R.: pop. 305,000; Russ. name **Vil·na** (vēlʹnä; *E.* vilʹnə)

☆**vim** (vim) *n.* [prob. echoic, associated with L. *vim*, acc. of *vis*, strength (for IE. base see VIA)] energy; vigor

vi·men (vī'men) *n., pl.* **vim·i·na** (vim'ə nə) [L., an osier, twig, akin to *viere*, to bend, twist < IE. base *wei-*, whence WITHE, WIRE] *Bot.* a long, flexible shoot or branch —**vi·min·e·ous** (vi min'ē əs), **vim·i·nal** (vim'ə nəl) *adj.*

Vim·i·nal (vim'ə n'l) *see* SEVEN HILLS OF ROME

v.imp. verb impersonal

Vi·my (vē mē') town in N France, near the site of a fierce battle (1917) of World War I: pop. 2,700

‡**vin** (van; *Anglicized* vin) *n.* [Fr.] wine

vi·na (vē'nä) *n.* [Sans. *viṇā*] an ancient musical instrument of India: four strings on a long, fretted fingerboard are plucked for melody, three others along one side are plucked in accompaniment, and one to three attached gourds serve as resonators

vi·na·ceous (vī nā'shəs) *adj.* [L. *vinaceus* < *vinum:* see VINE] **1.** of or like wine or grapes **2.** wine-colored; red

Vi·ña del Mar (vēʹnyä del mär') seaport in C Chile, near Valparaiso: pop. 108,000

vin·ai·grette (vin'i gret') *n.* [Fr. < *vinaigre*, VINEGAR] a small ornamental box or bottle with a perforated lid, used for holding aromatic vinegar, smelling salts, etc.

vinaigrette sauce a savory sauce made of vinegar, oil, herbs, etc., and used esp. on cold meats

Vin·cent (vin's'nt) [LL. *Vincentius* < *vincens*, prp. of *vincere*, to conquer: see VICTOR] a masculine name: equiv. Ger. *Vincens*, It. *Vincenzo*, Sp. *Vicente*

Vincent de Paul (də pôl'), **Saint** 1580?–1660; Fr. priest who founded charitable orders: his day is July 19

Vin·cent's angina (vin's'nts) [after J. H. *Vincent* (1862–1950), Fr. physician] *same as* TRENCH MOUTH: also called **Vincent's infection**

Vinci, Leonardo da *see* DA VINCI

vin·ci·ble (vin'sə b'l) *adj.* [L. *vincibilis*, easily overcome < *vincere*, to overcome: see VICTOR] that can be overcome or defeated; conquerable —**vin'ci·bil'i·ty** *n.*

☆**vin·cris·tine** (vin kris'tēn, -tin) *n.* [< L. *vinca*, periwinkle + *crista*, crest < -INE[4]] an alkaloid obtained from the periwinkle (*Vinca rosea*): used esp. in treating leukemia

vin·cu·lum (viŋ'kyoo ləm) *n., pl.* **-la** (-lə) [L. < *vincere*, to bind: for IE. base see VIMEN] **1.** that which binds; bond; tie **2.** *Anat.* a band or connecting fold **3.** *Math.* a line drawn over two or more terms of a compound quantity to show that they are to be treated together (Ex.: a − $\overline{x + y}$)

Vind·hya Pra·desh (vind′yä prä′desh) former state of C India: since 1956, part of Madhya Pradesh

Vindhya Range chain of hills across C India, north of the Narbada River, marking the N edge of the Deccan Plateau: also called **Vindhya Mountains** (or **Hills**)

vin·di·ca·ble (vin′di kə b'l) *adj.* [ME. *vindicabilis*] that can be vindicated; justifiable

vin·di·cate (vin′də kāt′) *vt.* -cat′ed, -cat′ing [< L. *vindicatus*, pp. of *vindicare*, to claim, avenge < *vim*, force (see VIM) + *dicere*, to say: see DICTION] **1.** to clear from criticism, blame, guilt, suspicion, etc.; uphold by evidence or argument **2.** to defend or maintain (a cause, claim, etc.) against opposition **3.** to serve as justification for; justify [a success which *vindicated* their belief in him] **4.** to lay claim to or establish possession of (something *for* oneself or another) **5.** [Obs.] *a)* to avenge *b)* to punish —*SYN.* see ABSOLVE —**vin′di·ca′tor** *n.*

vin·di·ca·tion (vin′də kā′shən) *n.* [LME. *vyndycacion* < L. *vindicatio*, a claiming < *vindicare*: see prec.] **1.** a vindicating or being vindicated **2.** a fact or circumstance that vindicates, or justifies

vin·dic·a·tive (vin′də kāt′iv, vin dik′ə tiv) *adj.* [ML. *vindicativus*] serving to vindicate; justifying

vin·di·ca·to·ry (vin′di kə tôr′ē) *adj.* **1.** serving to vindicate; vindicative **2.** bringing retribution; punitive

vin·dic·tive (vin dik′tiv) *adj.* [< L. *vindicta*, revenge, vindication < *vindicatus* (see VINDICATE) + -IVE] **1.** revengeful in spirit; inclined to seek vengeance **2.** said or done in revenge; characterized by vengeance [*vindictive* punishment] —**vin·dic′tive·ly** *adv.* —**vin·dic′tive·ness** *n.* *SYN.* —**vindictive** stresses the unforgiving nature of one who is animated by a desire to get even with another for a wrong, injury, etc. [*vindictive* feelings]; **vengeful and revengeful** more directly stress the strong impulsion to action and the actual seeking of vengeance [a *vengeful*, or *revengeful*, foe]; **spiteful** implies a mean or malicious vindictiveness [*spiteful* gossip]

vine (vīn) *n.* [ME. < OFr. *vine* < L. *vinea*, a vine < *vineus*, pertaining to wine < *vinum*, wine, akin to Gr. *oinē*, vine, prob. a loanword from a pre-IE. language of the Pontus region (whence Heb. *yayin*)] **1.** *a)* any plant with a long, thin stem that grows along the ground or climbs a wall or other support by means of tendrils, etc. *b)* the stem of such a plant **2.** *same as* GRAPEVINE (sense 1)

vine·dress·er (-dres′ər) *n.* a person who cultivates or prunes grapevines

vin·e·gar (vin′i gər) *n.* [ME. *vinegre* < MFr. *vinaigre* < *vin*, wine + *aigre*, sour < L. *acris* (see ACRID] **1.** a sour liquid with a pungent odor, containing acetic acid, made by fermenting dilute alcoholic liquids, as cider, wine, malt, etc.: it is used as a condiment and preservative **2.** sour or ill-tempered speech, character, etc. ☆**3.** forceful vigor

vinegar eel (or **worm**) a small nematode worm (*Anguillula aceti*) often found in unsterilized vinegar

☆**vin·e·gar·roon** (vin′i gə rōōn′) *n.* [AmSp. *vinagrón* < Sp. *vinagre*, vinegar + -*ón*, augmentative suffix] a large whip scorpion (*Mastigoproctus giganteus*) found in the S U.S. and in Mexico that, when disturbed, excretes a substance having a vinegary odor

vin·e·gar·y (vin′i gər ē) *adj.* **1.** of, or having the nature of, vinegar **2.** sour in speech or disposition; ill-tempered Also **vin′e·gar·ish**

Vine·land (vīn′lənd) [after the vineyards there] city in S N.J.: pop. 47,000

vin·er·y (vīn′ər ē) *n.*, *pl.* -er·ies [ME. *vinary* < ML. *vinarium* < L. *vinea*, VINE] **1.** an enclosed area or building in which vines, esp. grapevines, are grown ☆**2.** vines collectively

vine·yard (vin′yərd) *n.* [VINE + YARD², after OE. *wingeard*] **1.** land devoted to cultivating grapevines **2.** a field of activity, esp. of spiritual labor

†**vingt-et-un** (van tā ën′) *n.* [Fr., lit., twenty and one, twenty-one] *same as* TWENTY-ONE

vin·i- (vin′i) [< L. *vinum*, wine (see VINE)] *a combining form meaning* wine grapes or wine [*viniculture*]

vi·nic (vī′nik, vin′ik) *adj.* [< L. *vinum*, wine (see VINE) + -IC] of, found in, or derived from wine

vin·i·cul·ture (vin′i kul′chər) *n.* [VINI- + CULTURE] the cultivation of wine grapes —**vin′i·cul′tur·al** *adj.* —**vin′i·cul′tur·ist** *n.*

vi·nif·er·ous (vī nif′ər əs) *adj.* [VINI- + -FEROUS] that produces or yields wine

Vin·land (vin′lənd) region, now believed to be part of N. America, discovered by Norsemen led by Leif Ericsson in c.1000 A.D.

†**vi·no** (vē′nō) *n.* [It. & Sp.] wine

†**vin or·di·naire** (van ôr dē ner′) [Fr., lit., ordinary wine] any inexpensive wine routinely served with meals

vi·nos·i·ty (vī näs′ə tē) *n.* [LL. *vinositas*] **1.** the state or quality of being vinous **2.** addiction to wine

vi·nous (vī′nəs) *adj.* [L. *vinosus*, full of wine < L. *vinum*: see VINE] **1.** *a)* of, having the nature of, or characteristic of wine *b)* wine-colored; specif., red like wine **2.** *a)* addicted to drinking wine *b)* resulting from drinking wine

†**vin ro·sé** (van rō zā′; *often Anglicized* vin′ rō zā′) [Fr., pink wine] *same as* ROSÉ

Vin·son (vin′sən), **Fred(erick) M(oore)** 1890–1953; U.S. jurist; chief justice of the U.S. (1946–53)

vin·tage (vin′tij) *n.* [ME., earlier *vendage* < OFr. *vendange* < L. *vindemia*, vintage < *vinum*, wine (see VINE) + *demere*, to remove < *de-*, off + *emere*, to take: see REDEEM] **1.** *a)* the crop or yield of a particular vineyard or grape-growing region in a single season, with reference either to the grapes or to the wine made from them *b)* wine; specif., the wine, esp. a prized wine, of a particular region in a specified year *c)* the region or year of a particular wine **2.** the act or season of gathering grapes or of making wine **3.** the type or model of a particular year or period [a car of prewar *vintage*] —*adj.* **1.** *a)* of a good vintage or period; choice [*vintage* wine] *b)* representative of the best **2.** representative of or dating from a period long past [*vintage* clothes]

vin·tag·er (-ər) *n.* [< prec. + -ER] a person who harvests grapes for making wine

vint·ner (vint′nər) *n.* [altered < ME. *viniter*, a vintner < OFr. *vinetier* < ML. *vinetarius* < L. *vinetum*, a vineyard < *vinum*: see VINE] a person who sells wine; wine merchant

vin·y (vī′nē) *adj.* **vin′i·er**, **vin′i·est** **1.** of or like vines **2.** filled or covered with vines

vi·nyl (vī′n'l) *n.* [< L. *vinum*, wine (see VINE) + -YL] the univalent radical, CH_2:CH-, characteristic of many derivatives of ethylene, its hydride: various vinyl compounds are polymerized to form resins and plastics for a wide variety of industrial products

vinyl alcohol an alcohol, CH_2:CHOH, known only in the form of its esters or ethers, or its polymer, polyvinyl alcohol

vinyl chloride a colorless gas, CH_2:CHCl, made by reacting acetylene with hydrogen chloride or by cracking ethylene dichloride: it is used to make polyvinyl chloride, etc.

vi·nyl·i·dene (vī nil′ə dēn′) *n.* [VINYL + -ID(E) + -INE⁴] the bivalent radical CH_2:C=, derived from ethylene

vinylidene resin any synthetic resin in which the basic structure consists of the (-H_2CCR_2-) group, where R usually is a halogen

☆**vinyl plastic** any of various plastics made from polymerized vinyl compounds or copolymers of vinyl and other resins, used in various molded or extruded products, coatings, adhesives, sizes, etc.

☆**vinyl resin** a polymer formed from vinyl compounds, used with other resins, plasticizers, etc. to produce various solid vinyl plastics

vi·ol (vī′əl) *n.* [MFr. *viole* < OPr. *viula* < ?] any of an early family of stringed instruments played with a curved bow, characterized generally by six strings, frets, a flat back, and C-shaped sound holes: used chiefly in the 16th and 17th cent. in sizes from the treble viol to the bass viol

Vi·o·la (vī ō′lə, vē-; vī′ə lə) [< L. *viola*, a violet] a feminine name: dim. *Vi*

vi·o·la¹ (vē ō′lə, vī-) *n.* [It. < OPr. *viula*, viol] a stringed instrument of the violin family, slightly larger than a violin and tuned a fifth lower

vi·o·la² (vī′ə lə, vī ō′lə) *n.* [ME. < L., a violet] *same as* VIOLET (sense 1); esp., any of various violets developed from a pansy (*Viola cornuta*), grown as garden plants

vi·o·la·ble (vī′ə lə b'l) *adj.* [L. *violabilis* < *violare*: see VIOLATE] that can be, or is likely to be, violated —**vi′o·la·bil′i·ty**, **vi′o·la·ble·ness** *n.* —**vi′o·la·bly** *adv.*

vi·o·la·ceous (vī′ə lā′shəs) *adj.* [L. *violaceus*, violet-colored < *viola*, violet] violet in color

viola clef *same as* ALTO CLEF

vi·o·la da brac·cio (vē ō′lə də brä′chō) [It., lit., viol for the arm] an early stringed instrument of the viol family, comparable in range to the viola

viola da gam·ba (gam′bə, gäm′-) [It., lit., viol for the leg] an early stringed instrument of the viol family, held between the knees and comparable in range to the cello

viola d'a·mo·re (dä mō′rā) [It., lit., viol of love] an early stringed instrument of the viol family having a set of wire strings that are stretched behind the bowed gut strings, and whose sympathetic vibrations produce soft, clear, ringing tones

vi·o·late (vī′ə lāt′) *vt.* -lat′ed, -lat′ing [ME. *violaten* < L. *violatus*, pp. of *violare*, to use force or violence, akin to *vis*, force: for IE. base see VIA] **1.** to break (a law, rule, promise, etc.); fail to keep or observe; infringe on **2.** to commit a sexual assault on; esp., to rape (a woman) **3.** to desecrate or profane (something sacred) **4.** to break in upon; interrupt; disturb [to *violate* someone's privacy] **5.** to offend, insult, or outrage [to *violate* one's sense of decency] **6.** [Obs.] to treat (someone) roughly or abusively; mistreat —**vi′o·la′tive** *adj.* —**vi′o·la′tor** *n.*

vi·o·la·tion (vī′ə lā′shən) *n.* [ME. *violacion* < L. *violatio*] a violating or being violated; specif., *a)* infringement or breach, as of a law, rule, right, etc. *b)* sexual assault; rape *c)* desecration of something sacred, as a church *d)* interruption; disturbance

vi·o·lence (vī′ə ləns) *n.* [ME. < MFr. < L. *violentia* < *violentus*: see ff.] **1.** physical force used so as to injure, damage, or destroy; extreme roughness of action **2.** intense, often devastatingly or explosively powerful force or energy, as of a hurricane or volcano **3.** *a)* unjust or callous use of force or power, as in violating another's rights, sensibilities,

etc. b) the harm done by this 4. great force or strength of feeling, conduct, or expression; vehemence; fury 5. a twisting or wrenching of a sense, phrase, etc., so as to distort the original or true sense or form [to do *violence* to a text/ 6. an instance of violence; violent act or deed

vi·o·lent (-lənt) *adj.* [ME. < L. *violentus*, violent, akin to *violare*, to VIOLATE] 1. a) acting with or characterized by great physical force, so as to injure, damage, or destroy b) acting or characterized by force unlawfully or callously used 2. caused by violence [a *violent* death/ 3. a) showing, or resulting from, strong feeling or emotion; vehement; furious [*violent* language/ b) emotionally disturbed to an uncontrollable degree 4. extreme; intense; very strong [a *violent* storm/ 5. tending to distort the meaning [to put a *violent* construction on a text/ —**vi'o·lent·ly** *adv.*

vi·o·les·cent (vī'ə les''nt) *adj.* [< L. *viola*, a violet + -ESCENT] shading off toward a violet color

Vi·o·let (vī'ə lit) [< ff.] a feminine name: dim. *Vi*

vi·o·let (vī'ə lit) *n.* [ME. < OFr. *violette*, dim. of *viole* < L. *viola*, a violet] 1. a) any of a genus (*Viola*) of plants of the violet family, having white, blue, purple, or yellow irregular flowers with short spurs b) the flower of any of these plants 2. any of various similar but unrelated plants, as the African violet, or their flowers 3. a bluish-purple color —*adj.* 1. designating a family (Violaceae) of temperate and tropical plants having five-parted flowers, a one-celled ovary, and a three-valved fruit capsule, including the violets, pansies, heartsease, etc. 2. of a violet color

violet ray 1. the shortest ray of the visible spectrum 2. loosely, an ultraviolet ray

vi·o·lin (vī'ə lin') *n.* [It. *violino*, dim. of *viola*, VIOLA¹] any instrument of the modern family of stringed instruments played with a bow, characterized by four strings tuned in fifths, a lack of frets, a somewhat rounded back, and *f*-shaped sound holes; specif., the smallest and highest-pitched instrument of this family, held horizontally under the chin, held against the collarbone; fiddle

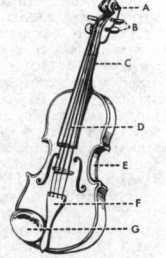

VIOLIN
(A, scroll; B, pegs; C, neck; D, fingerboard; E, waist; F, tailpiece; G, chinboard)

vi·o·lin·ist (-ist) *n.* [It. *violinista*] a violin player

vi·ol·ist (vī'ə list; *for 2* vē ō'list) *n.* 1. a viol player 2. a viola player

vi·o·lon·cel·list (vē'ə län chel'ist, vī'ə lən-) *n.* a cello player; cellist

vi·o·lon·cel·lo (-chel'ō) *n., pl.* -los [It., dim. of *violone*, bass viol < *viola*, viol] *same as* CELLO

vio·lo·ne (vyō lō'nā) *n.* [It., augmentative of *viola*, a viol, VIOLA¹] *same as* DOUBLE BASS

vi·os·ter·ol (vī äs'tə rôl', -rōl') *n.* [(UL-TRA)VIO(LET) + (ERGO)STEROL] *same as* CALCIFEROL

VIP, V.I.P. [Colloq.] very important person

vi·per (vī'pər) *n.* [OFr. < L. *vipera*, contr. < ? *vivipara*, producing live young < *vivus*, living + *parere*, to bear (from the notion that the viper does not lay eggs)] 1. a) any of a family (Viperidae) of venomous snakes found in Europe, Africa, and Asia, including the puff adder (sense 1), the horned adder, etc. b) *same as* PIT VIPER c) *same as* ADDER² (sense 1) 2. any of various other poisonous or supposedly poisonous snakes 3. a) a malicious or spiteful person b) a treacherous person

vi·per·ine (-in, -īn') *adj.* [L. *viperinus*] of, having the nature of, or like that of a viper; venomous

vi·per·ous (-əs) *adj.* of, having the nature of, or like a viper; esp., spiteful or malicious: also **vi'per·ish** —**vi'per·ous·ly** *adv.*

viper's bugloss *same as* BLUEWEED

vi·ra·go (vi rā'gō, vī-; -rä'-) *n., pl.* -goes, -gos [ME. < OE. < L., a manlike maiden < *vir*, a man: see WEREWOLF] 1. a quarrelsome, shrewish woman; scold 2. [Archaic] a strong, manlike woman; amazon

vi·ral (vī'rəl) *adj.* of, involving, or caused by a virus

vi·re·lay (vir'ə lā') *n.* [ME. *vyrelaye* < MFr. *virelai*, prob. altered after *lai* (cf. LAY⁴, kind of poem) < OFr. *virli*, *vireli*, jingle used as the refrain of a song] 1. an old French form of short poem, consisting of short lines with two rhymes and having two opening lines repeated at intervals 2. any similar verse form, esp. one with stanzas made up of alternating long lines and short lines, the rhyme of the short lines of one stanza being echoed by the rhyme of the long lines of the next stanza Also **vir'e·lai'** (-lā' ; Fr. vir lā')

☆**vir·e·o** (vir'ē ō') *n., pl.* -os' [L., greenfinch, akin to *virere*, to be green] any of a family (Vireonidae) of small, insect-eating, American songbirds, with olive-green or gray plumage —**vir'e·o·nine'** (-ə nīn', -nin) *adj., n.*

†**vi·res** (vī'rēz) *n.* [L.] *pl.* of VIS

vi·res·cence (vi res''ns, vī-) *n.* [< ff.] the condition of becoming green; specif., *Bot.* the turning green of petals or other parts that are not normally so, due to the abnormal presence of chlorophyll

vi·res·cent (-'nt) *adj.* [L. *virescens*, prp. of *virescere*, to grow green < *virere*, to be green] 1. turning or becoming green 2. greenish

vir·ga (vur'gə) *n.* [ModL. < L., a twig, streak in the heavens: see ff.] *Meteorol.* long streamers or wispy streaks of water or ice particles falling from the base of a cloud but evaporating completely before reaching the ground

vir·gate¹ (vur'git, -gāt) *n.* [ML. *virgata* (*terrae*) < L. *virga*, a rod (see VERGE¹): used as transl. of OE. *gierdland*, *yardland*] an old English measure of land varying greatly in size, but most commonly equal to about thirty acres

vir·gate² (-git, -gāt) *adj.* [ModL. *virgatus* < L., made of twigs < *virga*, a twig: see VERGE¹] 1. rod-shaped 2. *Bot.* long, thin, and stiff, with few branches

Vir·gil (vur'jəl) [< L. *Vergilius*, name of the Roman gens to which the poet belonged] 1. a masculine name 2. (L. name *Publius Vergilius Maro*) 70–19 B.C.; Rom. poet: author of the *Aeneid* —**Vir·gil'i·an** (-jil'ē ən) *adj.*

vir·gin (vur'jin) *n.* [ME. < OFr. *virgine* < L. *virgo* (gen. *virginis*), a maiden: ? akin to *virga*, slender branch, twig, shoot] 1. a) a woman, esp. a young woman, who has never had sexual intercourse b) an unmarried girl or woman 2. less commonly, a man, esp. a youth, who has never had sexual intercourse 3. *Zool.* a) a female animal that has not copulated b) a female insect that lays eggs without impregnation by the male —[V-] *Astron. same as* VIRGO —*adj.* 1. being a virgin 2. composed of virgins 3. characteristic of or proper to a virgin; chaste; modest 4. like or suggesting a virgin because untouched, unmarked, pure, clean, etc. [*virgin* snow/ 5. up to this time unused, untrod, unworked, undiscovered, etc. by man [a *virgin* forest/ 6. occurring uncombined in its native form [*virgin* silver/ 7. being the first; initial [a *virgin* effort/ 8. a) obtained from the first pressing, without the use of heat: said of an oil, as of olives b) obtained directly from an ore: said of a metal —**the Virgin** Mary, the mother of Jesus

vir·gin·al¹ (-ji n l) *adj.* [ME. < OFr. < L. *virginalis*] 1. of, characteristic of, or proper to a virgin; maidenly 2. remaining in a state of virginity 3. pure; fresh; untouched; unsullied 4. *Zool.* not fertilized

vir·gin·al² (-ji n'l) *n.* [prob. akin to prec.: reason for name obscure] [*sometimes pl.*] a harpsichord; esp., a small, rectangular harpsichord of the 16th cent., placed on a table or held in the lap to be played: also called **pair of virginals**

virgin birth 1. [*usually* V- B-] *Christian Theol.* the doctrine that Jesus was born to Mary without violating her virginity and that she was his only human parent: cf. IMMACULATE CONCEPTION 2. *Zool.* parthenogenesis

Vir·gin·ia (vur jin'yə, -ē ə) [L., fem. of *Virginius*, *Verginius*, name of a Roman gens] 1. a feminine name: dim. *Ginny*; equiv. Fr. *Virginie* 2. [after ELIZABETH I, the *Virgin* Queen] Southern State of the U.S., on the Atlantic: one of the 13 original States; 40,815 sq. mi.; pop. 4,648,000; cap. Richmond: abbrev. **Va., VA** —**Vir·gin'ian** *adj., n.*

Virginia Beach city in SE Va., on the Atlantic, near Norfolk: pop. 172,000

Virginia City [after a miner nicknamed "*Virginia*"] township in W Nev., near Reno: formerly a center of gold & silver mining (site of the Comstock Lode): pop. 700

☆**Virginia cowslip** (or **bluebell**) a perennial woodland plant (*Mertensia virginica*) of the borage family, native to E N. America and having clusters of blue or purple, bell-shaped flowers that develop from pink buds

☆**Virginia creeper** *same as* WOODBINE (sense 2)

☆**Virginia deer** *same as* WHITE-TAILED DEER

☆**Virginia fence** a zigzag fence made of rails laid across each other at the ends: also **Virginia rail fence**

☆**Virginia reel** 1. a country dance, the American variety of the reel, performed by a number of couples facing each other in two parallel lines 2. music for this dance

Virgin Islands [< Sp. *Las Virgenes*, the virgins, in honor of St. Ursula and her maids] group of islands of the Leeward group in the West Indies, east of Puerto Rico: a) **British Virgin Islands** easternmost islands of this group, constituting a Brit. colony: 59 sq. mi.; pop. 9,000 b) **Virgin Islands of the United States** the islands of this group closest to Puerto Rico, constituting a territory of the U.S.: 132 sq. mi.; pop. 63,000; cap. Charlotte Amalie: abbrev. **VI**

Virgin Islands National Park national park on the island of St. John in the Virgin Islands: 8 sq. mi.

vir·gin·i·ty (vər jin'ə tē) *n.* [ME. *virginite* < OFr. *virginité* < L., *virginitas*] 1. the state or fact of being a virgin; maidenhood, chastity, spinsterhood, etc. 2. the state of being virgin, pure, clean, untouched, etc.

Virgin Mary Mary, the mother of Jesus

Virgin Queen epithet of ELIZABETH I

vir·gin's-bow·er (vur'jinz bou'ər) *n.* any of several small-flowered forms of clematis; esp., a climbing vine (*Clematis virginiana*) with white flowers, native to E N. America

virgin wool wool that has never before been processed

Vir·go (vur'gō) [ME. < L., lit., virgin] 1. a large equatorial constellation between Leo and Libra, in which the brightest member is the first-magnitude star Spica 2. the sixth sign of the zodiac (♍), which the sun enters about August 22: see ZODIAC, illus.

†**vir·go in·tac·ta** (vur'gō in tak'tə) [L., lit., untouched virgin] a virgin; esp., a woman or girl whose hymen is intact

vir·gu·late (vur'gyoo lit, -lāt') *adj.* [< L. *virgula* (see ff.) + -ATE¹] rod-shaped

vir·gule (-gyool) *n.* [Fr. < L. *virgula*, a small rod, twig, dim. of *virga*, a slender branch, twig: see VERGE¹] a short

diagonal line (/) used between two words to show either is applicable (and/or), in dates or fractions (3/8), to express "per" (feet/second), etc.

vi·ri·cide (vī'rə sīd') *n.* [< VIR(US) + -*i*- + -CIDE] an agent capable of destroying or inhibiting viruses —**vi'ri·ci'dal** *adj.*

vir·i·des·cent (vir'ə des''nt) *adj.* [LL. *viridescens,* prp. of *viridescere,* to become green < *viridis,* green] turning or having turned green; greenish —**vir'i·des'cence** *n.*

vi·rid·i·an (və rid'ē ən) *n.* [< L. *viridis,* green] a bluish-green pigment, hydrated chromic oxide, Cr₂O₃

vi·rid·i·ty (-ə tē) *n.* [ME. *viridite* < MFr. *viridité* < L. *viriditas* < *viridis,* green] 1. greenness, as of young leaves or grass; verdancy 2. freshness; liveliness

vir·ile (vir'əl; *chiefly Brit.,* -īl) *adj.* [L. *virilis* < *vir,* man: for IE. base see WEREWOLF] 1. of, belonging to, or characteristic of an adult man; manly; masculine; male 2. having manly strength or vigor; forceful 3. of or capable of copulation; sexually potent —*SYN.* see MALE —**vi·ril·i·ty** (vi ril'ə tē) *n.*

vir·i·lism (-iz'm) *n.* [< prec. + -ISM] *Med.* the development of secondary male sex characteristics in a woman

vi·ri·on (vī'rē än') *n.* [< VIRUS + -ON (sense 2)] the smallest unit of a mature virus, made up of a molecule of nucleic acid enveloped by a specific number of protein molecules in a definite arrangement

vi·rol·o·gy (vī räl'ə jē) *n.* [< VIR(US) + -*o*- + -LOGY] the study of viruses and virus diseases —**vi·ro·log·ic** (vī'rə läj'ik), **vi'ro·log'i·cal** *adj.* —**vi·rol'o·gist** *n.*

vi·ro·sis (vī rō'sis) *n., pl.* -**ses** (-sēz) [VIR(US) + -OSIS] any disease caused by a virus

vir·tu (vər tōō', vur'tōō) *n.* [It. *virtù,* excellence, virtue < L. *virtus,* strength, VIRTUE] 1. a love of, or taste for, artistic objects, esp. curios, antiques, etc. 2. such objects, collectively 3. the quality of being artistic, beautiful, rare, or otherwise such as to interest a collector of such objects

vir·tu·al (vur'chōō wəl) *adj.* [ME. *vertual* < ML. *virtualis* < L. *virtus,* strength, VIRTUE] 1. being such practically or in effect, although not in actual fact or name [a *virtual* impossibility] 2. [Now Rare] effective because of certain inherent powers —**vir'tu·al'i·ty** (-wal'ə tē) *n.*

virtual image an image, as produced by a convex mirror, having virtual foci and appearing to be formed by divergent rays

vir·tu·al·ly (-chōō wəl ē, -chōō lē) *adv.* in effect although not in fact; for all practical purposes [*virtually* identical]

vir·tue (vur'chōō) *n.* [ME. *vertue* < OFr. *vertu,* virtue, goodness, power < L. *virtus,* manliness, worth < *vir,* man: see WEREWOLF] 1. general moral excellence; right action and thinking; goodness or morality 2. a specific moral quality regarded as good or meritorious: see also CARDINAL VIRTUES, THEOLOGICAL VIRTUES 3. chastity, esp. in a woman 4. *a)* excellence in general; merit; value [the *virtue* in planning ahead] *b)* a specific excellence; good quality or feature [the *virtues* of teaching as a profession] 5. effective power or force; efficacy; potency; esp., the ability to heal or strengthen [the *virtue* of a medicine] 6. [Now Rare] manly quality; strength, courage, etc. —**by** (or **in**) **virtue of** because of; on the grounds of —**make a virtue of necessity** to do or accept with an agreeable or positive attitude that which must be done anyway

vir·tu·os·i·ty (vur'chōō wäs'ə tē) *n., pl.* -**ties** [< ff. + -ITY] 1. [Now Rare] interest in or taste for the fine arts; esp., a sensitive but amateur or trifling interest; dilettantism 2. great technical skill in some fine art, esp. in the performance of music

vir·tu·o·so (vur'chōō wō'sō) *n., pl.* -**sos,** -**si** (-sē) [It., skilled, learned < LL. *virtuosus:* see ff.] 1. orig., *a)* a person who has a general or broad interest in the arts and sciences; savant or dilettante *b)* a collector or connoisseur of art objects or curios 2. a person displaying great technical skill in some fine art, esp. in the performance of music 3. [Obs.] a person learned in the arts or sciences; scholar; savant —*adj.* of or like that of a virtuoso: also **vir'tu·os'ic** (-wäs'ik, -wō'sik) —*SYN.* see AESTHETE —**vir'tu·o'sa** (-sə) *n.fem., pl.* -**se** (-sā)

vir·tu·ous (vur'chōō wəs) *adj.* [ME. *vertuous* < OFr. *vertuos* < LL. *virtuosus* < L. *virtus,* worth, VIRTUE] 1. having, or characterized by, moral virtue; righteous 2. chaste: said of a woman 3. [Archaic] having effective virtue, or potency; efficacious —*SYN.* see CHASTE, MORAL —**vir'tu·ous·ly** *adv.* —**vir'tu·ous·ness** *n.*

vi·ru·cide (vī'rə sīd') *n. var. of* VIRICIDE —**vi'ru·ci'dal** *adj.*

vir·u·lence (vir'yoo ləns, -ə-) *n.* [LL. *virulentia*] 1. the quality of being virulent, or very poisonous, noxious, malignant, etc. 2. bitter animosity; venom; rancor 3. the relative infectiousness of a microorganism causing disease Also **vir'u·len·cy** (-lən sē)

vir·u·lent (-lənt) *adj.* [ME. < L. *virulentus,* full of poison < *virus:* see ff.] 1. *a)* extremely poisonous or injurious; deadly *b)* bitterly antagonistic or spiteful; full of hate and enmity; venomous; rancorous 2. *Med. a)* violent and rapid in its course; highly malignant: said of a disease *b)* able to overcome the natural defenses of the host; highly infectious: said of a microorganism —**vir'u·lent·ly** *adv.*

vi·rus (vī'rəs) *n.* [L., a slimy liquid, poison < IE. base **weis-,* to flow (used of foul or malodorous fluids), whence OOZE², WEASEL, Gr. *ios,* poison] 1. orig., venom, as of a snake 2. *a) same as* FILTERABLE VIRUS; specif., any of a group of ultramicroscopic or submicroscopic infective agents that cause various diseases in animals, as measles, mumps, etc., or in plants, as mosaic diseases: viruses are capable of multiplying only in connection with living cells and are regarded both as living organisms and as complex proteins sometimes involving nucleic acid, enzymes, etc. *b)* a disease caused by a virus 3. anything that corrupts or poisons the mind or character; evil or harmful influence

†vis (vis) *n., pl.* **vi·res** (vī'rēz) [L.: see VIM] force; strength

vi·sa (vē'zə) *n.* [Fr. < L. fem. of *visus,* pp. of *videre,* to see: see VISION] an endorsement on a passport, showing that it has been examined by the proper officials of a country and granting entry into or passage through that country —*vt.* -**saed,** -**sa·ing** 1. to put a visa on (a passport) 2. to give a visa to (someone)

vis·age (viz'ij) *n.* [ME. < OFr. < *vis,* a face < L. *visus,* a look, a seeing < pp. of *videre:* see VISION] 1. the face, with reference to the form and proportions of the features or to the expression; countenance 2. appearance; aspect —*SYN.* see FACE

-vis·aged (viz'ijd) *a combining form meaning* having a (specified) kind of visage [stern-*visaged*]

Vi·sa·kha·pat·nam (vi sä'kə put'nəm) seaport in Andhra Pradesh, E India, on the Bay of Bengal: pop. 182,000

vis-à-vis (vē'zə vē'; *Fr.* vē zà vē') *adj., adv.* [Fr.] face to face; opposite —*prep.* 1. face to face with; opposite to 2. in comparison with or in relation to —*n., pl.* **vis-à-vis** (-vēz', -vē'; *Fr.* -vē') 1. *a)* a person who is face to face with another *b)* one's opposite number or counterpart 2. *a)* a carriage with facing seats *b)* an S-shaped seat or sofa on which two people can sit facing each other

Vi·sa·yan (vi sä'yən) *n.* 1. a member of a large ethnic group of the Visayas and N Mindanao 2. their Indonesian language —*adj.* of the Visayans or their language

Vi·sa·yas (vi sä'yəs) group of islands in the C Philippines, including Cebu, Leyte, Negros, Panay, Samar, & many smaller islands: also called **Visayan Islands**

Vis·by (vis'bē, *Swed.* vēs'bü) seaport on the W coast of the Swed. island of Gotland: pop. 15,000

Visc. 1. Viscount 2. Viscountess Also **Vis.,** **Visct.**

vis·ca·cha (vis kä'chə) *n.* [Sp. *vizcacha* < Quechua *uiscacha*] any of a genus (*Lagostomus*) of large, burrowing rodents of the S. American pampas, related to the chinchilla

vis·cer·a (vis'ər ə) *n.pl., sing.* **vis'cus** (-kəs) [L., pl. of *viscus,* an inner part of the body] the internal organs of the body, esp. of the thorax and abdomen, as the heart, lungs, liver, kidneys, intestines, etc.; specif., in popular usage, the intestines

vis·cer·al (-əl) *adj.* [ML. *visceralis*] 1. of, having the nature of, situated in, or affecting the viscera 2. intuitive, instinctive, emotional, etc. rather than intellectual [a *visceral* reaction] —**vis'cer·al·ly** *adv.*

visceral cleft any of a series of paired openings leading from the pharynx to the ectoderm on each side of the neck area in a chordate embryo: in fish and some amphibians the clefts develop into gills, but in land animals they are either lost or transformed into other structures

vis·cid (vis'id) *adj.* [LL. *viscidus,* sticky < L. *viscum,* birdlime: see VISCOUS] 1. having a cohesive and sticky fluid consistency; viscous 2. covered with a viscid substance —**vis·cid·i·ty** (vi sid'ə tē) *n.* —**vis'cid·ly** *adv.*

vis·co·e·las·tic (vis'kō i las'tik) *adj.* [< VISCO(US) + ELASTIC] having or exhibiting viscous and elastic properties

vis·coid (vis'koid) *adj.* somewhat viscous: also **vis'coi'dal**

vis·com·e·ter (vis käm'ə tər) *n.* a device for measuring viscosity, as by metering the rate of flow through a small opening: also **vis·co·sim·e·ter** (vis'kə sim'ə tər)

vis·cose (vis'kōs) *adj.* [LL. *viscosus:* see VISCOUS] 1. *same as* VISCOUS 2. of, containing, or made of viscose —*n.* 1. an amber-colored, syruplike solution made by treating cellulose with sodium hydroxide and carbon disulfide: used in making rayon thread and fabrics, and cellophane 2. thread or fabric made from viscose: in full **viscose rayon**

vis·cos·i·ty (vis käs'ə tē) *n., pl.* -**ties** [ME. *viscosite* < ML. *viscositas*] 1. the state or quality of being viscous 2. *Physics* the internal friction of a fluid, caused by molecular attraction, which makes it resist a tendency to flow

vis·count (vī'kount) *n.* [ME. < OFr. *viscomte* < ML. *vice comes:* see VICE- & COUNT²] 1. formerly, *a)* a deputy of a count or earl *b)* a sheriff 2. a nobleman next below an earl or count and above a baron

vis·count·cy (-sē) *n., pl.* -**cies** the title, rank, or station of a viscount: also **vis'count·ship'** (-ship')

vis·count·ess (vī'koun tis) *n.* 1. the wife of a viscount 2. a peeress with a rank equivalent to that of a viscount

vis·count·y (-tē) *n., pl.* -**count·ies** *same as* VISCOUNTCY

vis·cous (vis'kəs) *adj.* [ME. *viscouse* < LL. *viscosus* < L. *viscum,* birdlime made from mistletoe berries, mistletoe, prob. < IE. base **weis-:* see VIRUS] 1. having a cohesive and sticky fluid consistency; viscid 2. *Physics* having viscosity —**vis'cous·ly** *adv.* —**vis'cous·ness** *n.*

vis·cus (vis′kəs) *n.* [L.] [Rare] a visceral organ

vise (vīs) *n.* [ME. *vis*, a screw < OFr., a winding object, spiral staircase < L. *vitis*, a vine, lit., that which winds < IE. base *wei-*, to twist, whence WIRE] a device, usually fastened to a workbench, consisting of two jaws opened and closed by a screw, lever, etc. and used for holding firmly an object being worked on —*vt.* **vised**, **vis′ing** to hold or squeeze with or as with a vise

vi·sé (vē′zā, vē zā′) *n.*, *vt.* **-séed**, **-sé·ing** [Fr., pp. of *viser*, to view, inspect < L. *visus:* see VISION] *same as* VISA

Vish·nu (vish′nōō) [Sans. *Viṣṇu*, lit., prob. all-pervader] *Hindu Theol.* the second member of the trinity (Brahma, Vishnu, and Siva), called "the Preserver" and popularly held to have had several human incarnations, most important of which is Krishna —**Vish′nu·ism** *n.*

vis·i·bil·i·ty (viz′ə bil′ə tē) *n.*, *pl.* **-ties** [LL. *visibilitas*] 1. the fact or condition of being visible 2. *a)* the relative possibility of being seen under the conditions of distance, light, and atmosphere prevailing at a particular time *b)* the maximum distance at which an object can be seen under the prevailing conditions; range of vision

vis·i·ble (viz′ə b'l) *adj.* [ME. < OFr. < L. *visibilis* < *visus*, pp. of *videre*, to see: see VISION] 1. that can be seen; perceptible by the eye 2. that can be perceived or observed; apparent; evident; manifest [no *visible* improvement] 3. on hand or available [*visible* supply] 4. so constructed as to bring to view parts or elements that are normally not perceptible —**vis′i·bly** *adv.*

Vis·i·goth (viz′ə gäth′, -gôth′) *n.* [LL. *Visigothi*, pl. < *visi-* (< Gmc. base prob. meaning "west") + *Gothi*, Goths] any of the West Goths, a Teutonic people who invaded the Roman Empire late in the 4th cent. A.D. and set up a kingdom in France and in Spain —**Vis′i·goth′ic** *adj.*

vi·sion (vizh′ən) *n.* [ME. < OFr. < L. *visio* < *visus*, pp. of *videre*, to see < IE. *w(e)idē*, var. of *w(e)di-*, to view, see, whence WISE[1]] 1. the act or power of seeing with the eye; sense of sight 2. *a)* something supposedly seen by other than normal sight; something perceived in a dream, trance, etc. or supernaturally revealed, as to a prophet *b)* the experience of having such a perception or revelation 3. a mental image; esp., an imaginative contemplation [to have *visions* of power] 4. *a)* the ability to perceive something not actually visible, as through mental acuteness or keen foresight [a project made possible by one man's *vision*] *b)* force or power of imagination [a statesman of great *vision*] 5. something or someone, esp. a woman, of extraordinary beauty 6. [Rare] something actually seen —*vt.* to see in or as in a vision; imagine

vi·sion·al (-əl) *adj.* 1. of, or having the nature of, a vision or visions 2. seen, or as if seen, in a vision; unreal

vi·sion·ar·y (-er′ē) *adj.* 1. of, having the nature of, or seen in a vision 2. *a)* existing only in the mind; not real; imaginary [*visionary* achievements] *b)* not capable of being put into effect; not realistic; impractical [a *visionary* scheme] 3. seeing or disposed to see visions 4. characterized by impractical ideas or schemes —*n.*, *pl.* **-ar′ies** 1. a person who sees visions; prophet or seer 2. a person whose ideas, plans, etc. are impractical, too idealistic, or fantastic; dreamer —*SYN.* see IMAGINARY

vis·it (viz′it) *vt.* [ME. *visiten* < OFr. *visiter* < L. *visitare*, freq. < *visere*, to go to see < *visus*, pp. of *videre:* see VISION] 1. to go or come to see (someone) out of friendship or for social reasons 2. to stay with as a guest for a time 3. to go or come to see in a professional or business capacity [to *visit* a doctor (or a patient)] 4. to go or come to (a place) in order to inspect or investigate 5. to go or come to for a time so as to make use of, look at, etc. [to *visit* an art gallery] 6. to occur or come to [*visited* by an odd idea] 7. to bring suffering, trouble, etc. to; assail [a drought *visited* the land] 8. *a)* to inflict (punishment, suffering, etc.) upon someone *b)* to afflict (*with* punishment, suffering, etc.) *c)* to inflict punishment for (wrongdoing); avenge [*visiting* the sins of the fathers upon the children] —*vi.* to visit someone or something; specif., *a)* to inflict punishment or revenge ☆*b)* to make a social call or calls (often followed by *with*) *c)* to stay with someone as a guest ☆*d)* [Colloq.] to converse or chat, as during a visit —*n.* the act or an instance of visiting; specif., *a)* a social call *b)* a stay as a guest; sojourn *c)* an official or professional call, as of a doctor *d)* an official call as for inspection or investigation; esp., *Marine Law* the boarding of a ship of a neutral nation by an officer of a nation at war to search it for contraband, etc. ☆*e)* [Colloq.] a friendly conversation or chat

vis·it·a·ble (-ə b'l) *adj.* 1. that can be visited 2. suitable for or worth visiting 3. subject to visitation, or inspection

vis·it·ant (-ənt) *n.* [< Fr. or L.: Fr. *visitant* < L. *visitans*, prp. of *visitare:* see VISIT] 1. a visitor, esp. one from a strange or foreign place 2. a supernatural being, as supposedly perceived by a person; ghost, phantom, etc. 3. *Zool.* a migratory bird in any of its temporary resting places —*adj.* [Archaic] paying a visit —*SYN.* see VISITOR

vis·it·a·tion (viz′ə tā′shən) *n.* [ME. < OFr. < L. *visitatio*] 1. the act or an instance of visiting; esp., an official visit to inspect or examine, as that made by a bishop to a church in his diocese 2. a visiting of reward or, esp., punishment, as by God 3. any affliction or disaster thought of as an act of God 4. *Zool.* migration of animals or birds to a particular place at an unusual time or in unusual numbers —**the Visitation** *R.C.Ch.* 1. the visit of the Virgin Mary to Elizabeth: Luke 1:39–56 2. a church feast (July 2) commemorating this —**vis′it·a′tion·al** *adj.*

vis·it·a·to·ri·al (viz′i tə tôr′ē əl) *adj.* of or for visitation or inspection: also **vis′i·to′ri·al**

vis·it·ing card (viz′it iŋ) *same as* CALLING CARD

☆**visiting fireman** [Colloq.] 1. an important person, esp. any of a group, visiting a city, organization, etc. and given an official welcome, special entertainment, etc. 2. a free-spending tourist, conventioneer, etc.

☆**visiting nurse** a registered nurse employed by a community to promote public health, esp. by giving nursing care to the sick in their homes

☆**visiting professor** a professor at a college or university invited to teach at another for a specified period

☆**visiting teacher** a teacher who visits pupils' homes, as for giving instruction to those too ill or disabled to attend regular classes

vis·i·tor (viz′it ər) *n.* [ME. *visitour* < Anglo-Fr. < MFr. *visiteur*] a person making a visit *SYN.—***visitor** is the general term for one who comes to see a person or spend some time in a place, whether for social, business, or professional reasons, or for sightseeing, etc.; **visitant** now generally suggests a supernatural rather than a human visitor and, in biology, is applied to a migratory bird in any of its temporary resting places; **guest** applies to one who is hospitably entertained at the home of another, as at dinner, or, by extension, to one who pays for his lodgings, meals, etc. at a hotel; **caller** applies to one who makes a brief, often formal visit, as for business or social reasons

‡**vis ma·jor** (vis mā′jər) [L., greater force] *same as* ACT OF GOD

vis·or (vī′zər) *n.* [ME. *visere* < Anglo-Fr. *viser* < OFr. *visiere* < *vis*, a face: see VISAGE] 1. *a)* in ancient armor, a movable part of a helmet that could be lowered to cover the upper part of the face, with slits for seeing *b)* a movable section, made usually of safety glass, that is part of a protective head covering, as for welders 2. a mask, as for disguise ☆3. the projecting front brim of a cap, for shading the eyes 4. a fixed or movable shade fastened to the windshield of a car, for shading the eyes —*vt.* to cover or provide with a visor —**vis′ored** *adj.*

VISORS

☆**VIS·TA** (vis′tə) [*V*(*olunteers*) *i*(*n*) *S*(*ervice*) *t*(*o*) *A*(*merica*)] a U.S. government program established in 1964 to provide volunteers to work at improving the living conditions of persons in impoverished areas of the U.S., its possessions, and Puerto Rico

vis·ta (vis′tə) *n.* [It., sight < pp. of *vedere*, to see < L. *videre:* see VISION] 1. a view or outlook, esp. one seen through a long passage, as between rows of houses or trees 2. a comprehensive mental view of a series of remembered or anticipated events —*SYN.* see VIEW

Vis·tu·la (vis′choo lə) river in Poland, flowing from the Carpathians into the Baltic: 677 mi.: Pol. name, WISŁA

vis·u·al (vizh′oo wəl) *adj.* [ME. < LL. *visualis* < L. *visus*, a sight < pp. of *videre:* see VISION] 1. *a)* of, connected with, or used in seeing *b)* based on, designed for, or controlled by the use of sight [*visual* flight rules] 2. that is or can be seen; visible 3. of, having the nature of, or occurring as a mental image, or vision 4. *Optics same as* OPTICAL —**vis′u·al·ly** *adv.*

visual acuity the ability of the eye to discriminate detail, usually tested by comparison with the power of the normal eye to distinguish certain letters on a standard chart at a given distance, generally 20 feet

visual aids motion pictures, slides, charts, and other devices involving the sense of sight (other than books), used in teaching, illustrating lectures, etc.

☆**vis·u·al-au·ral (radio) range** (-ôr′əl) a radio range that sends out signals as an aid to air navigation; esp., a very-high-frequency range that beams four signals, two for reception by the ear and two for viewing on an indicator

visual binary a binary star appearing to the naked eye as a single star, but separable into its two components by the telescope: also called **visual double**

vis·u·al·ize (vizh′oo wə līz′, -oo līz′) *vt.* **-ized′**, **-iz′ing** [VISUAL + -IZE] to form a mental image of (something not present to the sight, an abstraction, etc.); envision —*vi.* to form a mental image —**vis′u·al·i·za′tion** *n.*

visual purple *same as* RHODOPSIN

vis·u·o·mo·tor (vizh′oo wō mōt′ər) *adj.* [VISU(AL) + -o- + MOTOR] of or involving the use of both vision and muscular movement [*visuomotor* reflexes]

‡**vi·ta** (vīt′ə; vē′tə, wē′-) *n.*, *pl.* **-tae** (vīt′ē; vē′tī, wē′-) *n.* [L., life] 1. a biography or autobiography, often a brief one 2. *same as* CURRICULUM VITAE

vi·tal (vīt′'l) *adj.* [ME. < MFr. < L. *vitalis*, vital < *vita*, life, akin to *vivere*, to live: see QUICK] 1. of, concerned

with, or manifesting life *[vital energy]* **2.** *a)* necessary or essential to life; being a source or support of life *[vital organs]* *b)* affecting, esp. destroying, life; critical, esp. fatal *[a vital wound]* **3.** *a)* essential to the existence or continuance of something; indispensable *[a vital function]* *b)* of crucial importance *[a vital matter]* **4.** affecting the validity, truth, etc. of something *[a vital error]* **5.** full of life and vigor; energetic *[a vital personality]* —*n.* *[pl.]* **1.** the vital organs, as the heart, brain, lungs, etc. **2.** the essential parts of anything, indispensable for its existence, continuance, etc. —*SYN.* see LIVING —**vi′tal·ly** *adv.*

vital force 1. a basic force or principle regarded as the source and cause of life in living organisms: see VITALISM **2.** *same as* ÉLAN VITAL Also called **vital principle**

vi·tal·ism (-iz′m) *n.* [Fr. *vitalisme*] the doctrine that the life in living organisms is caused and sustained by a vital force that is distinct from all physical and chemical forces and that life is, in part, self-determining and self-evolving —**vi′tal·ist** *n., adj.* —**vi′tal·is′tic** *adj.*

vi·tal·i·ty (vī tal′ə tē) *n., pl.* **-ties** [L. *vitalitas*] **1.** *same as* VITAL FORCE **2.** power to live or go on living **3.** power, as of an institution, to endure or survive **4.** mental or physical vigor; energy

vi·tal·ize (vīt′'l īz′) *vt.* **-ized′**, **-iz′ing 1.** to make vital; give life to **2.** to give vigor or animation to; make lively —*SYN.* see ANIMATE —**vi′tal·i·za′tion** *n.*

Vi·tal·li·um (vī tal′ē əm) *a trademark for* a noncorrosive alloy of cobalt, chromium, and molybdenum, used for dentures, in bone surgery and prosthetics, in castings, etc.

vital staining the staining of living cells with dyes that are not poisonous

vital statistics data on births, deaths, marriages, etc.

vi·ta·min (vīt′ə min; *Brit. & sometimes Canad.* vit′-) *n.* [earlier *vitamine* < L. *vita*, life (see VITAL) + AMINE: from the orig. mistaken idea that these substances all contain amino acids] any of a number of unrelated, complex organic substances found variously in most foods, or sometimes synthesized in the body, and essential, in small amounts, for the regulation of the metabolism and normal growth and functioning of the body —**vi′ta·min′ic** *adj.*

vitamin A a fat-soluble aliphatic alcohol, $C_{20}H_{30}OH$, found in fish-liver oil, egg yolk, butter, etc. or derived from carotene in carrots and other vegetables: a deficiency of this vitamin results in night blindness, a general susceptibility to infections, and degeneration of epithelial tissue: it occurs in two forms, **vitamin A₁**, having the formula above, and **vitamin A₂**, $C_{20}H_{27}OH$

vitamin B (complex) a group of unrelated water-soluble substances found in liver, yeast, etc., including: *a)* **vitamin B₁** (*see* THIAMINE) *b)* **vitamin B₂** (*see* RIBOFLAVIN) *c)* **vitamin B₆** (*see* PYRIDOXINE) *d)* NICOTINIC ACID *e)* PANTOTHENIC ACID *f)* BIOTIN: also called **vitamin H** *g)* INOSITOL *h)* PARA-AMINOBENZOIC ACID *i)* CHOLINE *j)* FOLIC ACID *k)* **vitamin B₁₂** a complex vitamin, $C_{63}H_{90}N_{14}O_{14}PCo$, containing trivalent cobalt, essential for the normal maturation of erythrocytes, and for normal growth and neurological function, and used esp. in treating pernicious anemia and as an animal feed supplement

vitamin C a water-soluble, acid hexose sugar, $C_6H_8O_6$, occurring in citrus fruits, tomatoes, rose hips, and leafy vegetables and produced synthetically: it is essential for the building of intercellular material, and a deficiency produces scurvy

vitamin D any of several fat-soluble vitamins essential for deposition of calcium and phosphorus in teeth and bones and occurring in fish-liver oils, milk, egg yolk, etc. or produced by irradiation of provitamins; specif., *a)* **vitamin D₂** (*see* CALCIFEROL) *b)* **vitamin D₃** the most abundant natural vitamin D, $C_{27}H_{44}OH$, found esp. in fish-liver oils and produced by irradiation of the skin by sunlight *c)* **vitamin D₄**, $C_{28}H_{46}OH$, produced by irradiation of a derivative of ergosterol *d)* **vitamin D₅**, $C_{29}H_{47}OH$, produced by irradiation of a derivative of sitosterol A deficiency of vitamin D tends to produce rickets

vitamin E the tocopherols collectively, necessary for fertility in the rat and certain other animals: a deficiency of vitamin E in the diet of various animals, as the rabbit, sheep, etc., results in muscular dystrophy, sterility, etc.

vitamin H *same as* BIOTIN

vitamin K a fat-soluble vitamin, synthesized constantly by intestinal bacteria in mammals and occurring in certain green vegetables, fish meal, etc., that promotes blood clotting and is required for the synthesis of prothrombin by the liver: the two naturally occurring varieties are **vitamin K₁**, $C_{31}H_{46}O_2$, found chiefly in alfalfa leaves, and **vitamin K₂**, $C_{41}H_{56}O_2$, found chiefly in fish meal: **vitamin K₃** (MENADIONE) and **vitamin K₄** are prepared synthetically

vitamin P the bioflavonoids, occurring esp. in citrus fruits and paprika and acting to decrease the permeability of capillary walls and the susceptibility to hemorrhaging

Vi·tebsk (vē′tepsk′) city in NE Byelorussian S.S.R., on Western Dvina River; pop. 194,000

vi·tel·lin (vi tel′in, vī-) *n.* [< L. *vitellus*, the yolk of an egg, orig., a calf (see VEAL) + -IN¹] a phosphoprotein occurring in the yolk of eggs

vi·tel·line (-in, -ēn) *adj.* [ME. *vitellyn* < L. *vitellus* (see prec.)] **1.** of or having to do with the egg yolk **2.** yellow like an egg yolk

vi·tel·lus (-əs) *n.* [L., orig., calf: see VEAL] the yolk of an egg

vi·ti·a·ble (vish′ē ə b'l) *adj.* that can be vitiated

vi·ti·ate (vish′ē āt′) *vt.* **-at′ed**, **-at′ing** [< L. *vitiatus*, pp. of *vitiare*, to vitiate < *vitium*, a VICE¹] **1.** to make imperfect, faulty, or impure; spoil; corrupt **2.** to weaken morally; debase; pervert **3.** to make (a contract, etc.) legally ineffective; invalidate —**vi′ti·a′tion** *n.* —**vi′ti·a′tor** *n.*

vit·i·cul·ture (vit′ə kul′chər, vīt′-) *n.* [< L. *vitis*, a vine (see WITHE) + CULTURE] the cultivation of grapes; science or art of grape-growing —**vit′i·cul′tur·al** *adj.* —**vit′i·cul′tur·ist** *n.*

Vi·ti Le·vu (vē′tē lē′vōō) largest island of the Fiji Islands: 4,010 sq. mi.; chief city, Suva

vit·i·li·go (vit′ə li′gō) *n.* [L., a kind of cutaneous eruption, tetter < *vitium*, a blemish, VICE¹] *Med.* a disorder in which there is a loss of pigment resulting in white patches of skin

Vi·to·ria (vē tô′ryä) city in the Basque Provinces, N Spain: pop. 93,000

Vi·tó·ria (vē tô′ryə) seaport in E Brazil, on the Atlantic; capital of Espírito Santo state: pop. 85,000

vit·rain (vit′rān) *n.* [< L. *vitrum*, glass + *-ain*, as in FUSAIN] thin, bright, horizontal bands in bituminous coal that usually break with a conchoidal fracture

vit·re·ous (vit′rē əs) *adj.* [L. *vitreus*, glassy < *vitrum*, glass] **1.** *a)* of, having the nature of, or like glass; glassy *b)* derived from or made of glass **2.** of the vitreous humor —**vit′re·ous·ness** *n.*

vitreous body (or **humor**) the transparent, colorless, jellylike substance that fills the eyeball between the retina and lens: see EYE, illus.

vitreous silica *same as* FUSED QUARTZ

vi·tres·cent (vi tres′'nt) *adj.* [< L. *vitrum*, glass + -ESCENT] **1.** that can be formed into glass **2.** becoming, or tending to become, glass —**vi·tres′cence** (-'ns) *n.*

vit·ric (vit′rik) *adj.* [< L. *vitrum*, glass + -IC] of, having the nature of, or like glass

vit·rics (-riks) *n.pl.* [see prec. & -ICS] **1.** [*with sing. v.*] the art or study of making and decorating articles of glass **2.** articles of glass; glassware

vit·ri·form (vit′rə fôrm′) *adj.* [< L. *vitrum*, glass + -FORM] having the form or appearance of glass

vit·ri·fy (vit′rə fī′) *vt., vi.* **-fied′**, **-fy′ing** [Fr. *vitrifier* < L. *vitrum*, glass + Fr. *-fier*, -FY] to change into glass or a glasslike substance by fusion due to heat; make or become vitreous —**vit′ri·fi′a·ble** *adj.* —**vit′ri·fi·ca′tion** (-fi kā′shən), **vit′ri·fac′tion** (-fak′shən) *n.*

vit·rine (vi trēn′) *n.* [Fr. < *vitre*, pane of glass < L. *vitrum*, glass] a glass-paneled cabinet or glass display case for art objects, curios, etc.

vit·ri·ol (vit′rē əl, -ōl′) *n.* [ME. < MFr. < ML. *vitriolum*, vitriol < LL. *vitreolus*, glassy < L. *vitreus*, glassy: from the glassy appearance] **1.** *a)* any of several sulfates of metals, as copper sulfate (*blue vitriol*), iron sulfate (*green vitriol*), zinc sulfate (*white vitriol*), etc. *b)* *same as* SULFURIC ACID: in full **oil of vitriol 2.** sharpness or bitterness of feeling, as in speech or writing; venom —*vt.* **-oled** or **-olled**, **-ol·ing** or **-ol·ling** to treat with or as with vitriol

vit·ri·ol·ic (vit′rē äl′ik) *adj.* [Fr. *vitriolique*] **1.** of, like, or derived from a vitriol **2.** extremely biting or caustic; sharp and bitter *[vitriolic talk]*

vit·ri·ol·ize (vit′rē ə līz′) *vt.* **-ized′**, **-iz′ing 1.** to convert into vitriol **2.** to subject to the action of vitriol

Vi·tru·vi·us (vi trōō′vē əs) (full name *Marcus Vitruvius Pollio*) born 1st cent. B.C.; Rom. architect & engineer —**Vi·tru′vi·an** *adj.*

Vi·try-sur-Seine (vē trē sür sen′) city in NC France; suburb of Paris: pop. 66,000

vit·ta (vit′ə) *n., pl.* **-tae** (-ē) [ModL. < L., headband, fillet, akin to *viere*, to tie, *vitis*, vine: see WITHE] **1.** *Biol.* a band or streak of color **2.** *Bot.* an oil tube in the fruit of most plants of the parsley family

vit·tate (-āt) *adj.* [ModL. *vittatus:* see prec.] **1.** *Biol.* striped lengthwise **2.** *Bot.* having a vitta or vittae

vit·tle (vit′'l) *n., v. obs. or dial. var. of* VICTUAL

vit·u·line (vich′ōo lin′, -lin) *adj.* [L. *vitulinus* < *vitulus*, a calf: see VEAL] of or like a calf or veal

vi·tu·per·ate (vī tōō′pər āt′, vi-; -tyōō′-) *vt.* **-at′ed**, **-at′ing** [< L. *vituperatus*, pp. of *vituperare*, to blame < *vitium*, a fault, VICE¹ + *parare*, to PREPARE] to speak abusively to or about; berate; revile —*SYN.* see SCOLD —**vi·tu′per·a·tive** *adj.* —**vi·tu′per·a·tive·ly** *adv.* —**vi·tu′per·a·tive·ness** *n.* —**vi·tu′per·a′tor** *n.*

vi·tu·per·a·tion (vī tōō′pə rā′shən, vi-; -tyōō′-) *n.* [L. *vituperatio*] **1.** the act of vituperating **2.** abusive language

‡vi·va (vē′vä) *interj.* [It., Sp.] (long) live (someone or something specified)!: an exclamation of acclaim

vi·va·ce (vi vä′chā) *adj., adv.* [It. < L. *vivax:* see ff.] *Music* in a lively, spirited manner: a direction to the performer

vi·va·cious (vi vā′shəs, vī-) *adj.* [L. *vivax* (gen. *vivacis*), vigorous < *vivere*, to live (see QUICK) + -OUS] **1.** full of life and animation; spirited; lively **2.** [Obs.] long-lived, or

---

hard to kill or destroy —*SYN.* see LIVELY —**vi·va′cious·ly** *adv.* —**vi·va′cious·ness** *n.*

vi·vac·i·ty (vi vas′ə tē, vī-) *n.* [ME. *vivacite* < L. *vivacitas*] 1. the quality or state of being vivacious 2. liveliness of spirit; animation 3. *pl.* **-ties** [Now Rare] a vivacious act

Vi·val·di (vē väl′dē; *E.* vi-), **An·to·nio** (än tô′nyô) 1675?–1741; It. composer

vi·var·i·um (vī ver′ē əm) *n., pl.* **-i·ums, -i·a** (-ə) [L. < *vivarius*, concerning living creatures < *vivere*, to live: see QUICK] an enclosed place for keeping and studying animals in an environment corresponding as closely as possible in soil, vegetation, etc. to the animals' natural environment

vi·va vo·ce (vī′və vō′sē) [ML., with living voice, abl. fem. of L. *vivus*, living + abl. of *vox*, VOICE] by word of mouth; orally —**vi′va-vo′ce** *adj.*

‡**vive** (vēv) *interj.* [Fr.] (long) live (someone or something specified)!: an exclamation of acclaim

vi·ver·rine (vī ver′in, vi-; -īn) *adj.* [< L. *viverra*, a ferret < redupl. of IE. base *wer-*, whence Per. *vavrarah*, OPrus. *weware*, OE. (*ac*)*weorna*, squirrel + -INE¹] of or belonging to a family (Viverridae) of small, slender, flesh-eating mammals, including the civets and mongooses —*n.* an animal of this family

Viv·i·an (viv′ē ən, viv′yən) [L. *Vivianus* < *vivus*, alive] 1. a masculine name: equiv. Fr. *Vivien* 2. a feminine name: equiv. Fr. *Vivienne* 3. *Arthurian Legend* an enchantress, mistress of Merlin

viv·id (viv′id) *adj.* [L. *vividus*, lively < *vivere*, to live: see QUICK] 1. full of life; vigorous; lively; striking *[a vivid personality]* 2. *a)* bright; intense; brilliant: said of colors, light, etc. *b)* brightly colored *[a vivid tapestry]* 3. forming clear or striking mental images; strong; active; daring *[a vivid imagination]* 4. clearly perceived by the mind, as a recollection 5. bringing strikingly realistic or lifelike images to the mind *[a vivid description]* —*SYN.* see GRAPHIC —**viv′id·ly** *adv.* —**viv′id·ness** *n.*

viv·i·fy (viv′ə fī′) *vt.* **-fied′, -fy′ing** [Fr. *vivifier* < LL.(Ec.) *vivificare* (as opposed to *mortificare*: see MORTIFY) < L. *vivus*, alive (see QUICK) + *facere*, to make, DO¹] 1. to give life to; make come to life; animate 2. to make more lively, active, striking, etc. —**viv′i·fi·ca′tion** *n.* —**viv′i·fi′er** *n.*

vi·vip·a·rous (vī vip′ər əs) *adj.* [L. *viviparus* < *vivus*, alive (see QUICK) + *parere*, to produce (see -PAROUS)] 1. bearing or bringing forth living young (as most mammals and some other animals do) instead of laying eggs; also, designating or of this type of reproduction: opposed to OVIPAROUS 2. *Bot. a)* germinating while still on the parent plant, as certain seeds or bulbs *b)* producing such seeds or bulbs; proliferous —**vi·vip′a·rar′i·ty** (viv′ə pa′rə tē), **vi·vip′a·rous·ness** *n.* —**vi·vip′a·rous·ly** *adv.*

viv·i·sect (viv′ə sekt′) *vt.* [back-formation < ff., after DISSECT] to perform vivisection on —*vi.* to practice vivisection —**viv′i·sec′tor** *n.*

viv·i·sec·tion (viv′ə sek′shən) *n.* [< L. *vivus*, alive (see QUICK) + SECTION] medical research consisting of surgical operations or other experiments performed on living animals to study the structure and function of living organs and parts, and to investigate the effects of diseases and therapy —**viv′i·sec′tion·al** *adj.*

viv·i·sec·tion·ist (-ist) *n.* 1. a person who practices vivisection 2. a person who advocates or defends vivisection as essential to scientific progress

vix·en (vik′s′n) *n.* [ME. (southern dial.) *fixen* < OE. *fyxe*, she-fox (or *fyxen*, adj., of a fox) < *fox*, FOX] 1. a female fox 2. an ill-tempered, shrewish, or malicious woman —**vix′en·ish** *adj.* —**vix′en·ish·ly** *adv.*

Vi·yel·la (vī yel′ə, vi-) [arbitrary coinage] *a trademark for* a soft, light, flannellike fabric made of a blend of lamb's wool and fine cotton —*n.* this fabric

viz., viz (viz; *often read* "namely") [ML., altered (because abbrev. for L. *et* resembled a *z*) < earlier *viet.*, contr. for L. *videlicet*] videlicet; that is; namely

viz·ard (viz′ərd) *n.* [altered < earlier *visar*, var. of VISOR] *same as* VISOR (esp. sense 2)

vi·zier (vi zir′, viz′yər) *n.* [Turk. *vezir* < Ar. *wazīr*, a vizier, lit., bearer of burdens, porter < *wazara*, to bear a burden: the vizier bears the duties actually incumbent upon the ruler] in Moslem countries, a high officer in the government; esp., a minister of state: also sp. **vi·zir′** —**vi·zier′ate** (-it, -āt), **vi·zier′ship** *n.* —**vi·zier′i·al** *adj.*

viz·or (vī′zər) *n. alt. sp. of* VISOR

vizs·la (vēz′lə; *Hung.* vēzh′lä) *n.* [Hung. < *vizslatni*, to track (game)] any of a breed of medium-sized Hungarian hunting dog with a smooth, short, rusty-gold coat

V-J Day (vē′jā′) the day on which the fighting with Japan officially ended in World War II (Aug. 15, 1945) or the day the surrender was formally signed (Sept. 2, 1945)

VL. Vulgar Latin

Vlaar·ding·en (vlär′diŋ ən) seaport in SW Netherlands, just west of Rotterdam: pop. 74,000

Vlad·i·mir (vlä dē′mir) city in W R.S.F.S.R., east of Moscow: pop. 203,000

Vlad·i·mir I (vlad′ə mir; *Russ.* vlä dē′mür) 956?–1015; Russ. ruler & prince of Kiev (980–1015): converted to Christianity (989), which he introduced into Russia: called *the Great & Saint Vladimir* (his day is July 15)

Vla·di·vos·tok (vlä′di väs′täk; *Russ.* vlä′di vôs tôk′) seaport in SE R.S.F.S.R., on the Sea of Japan: the E terminus of the Trans-Siberian Railroad: pop. 379,000

Vla·minck (vlȧ maNk′), **Mau·rice de** (mô rēs′ də) 1876–1958; Fr. painter

VLF, V.L.F., vlf, v.l.f. very low frequency

Vlo·në, Vlo·na (vlô′nə) seaport in SW Albania, on the Strait of Otranto: pop. 45,000: also **Vlo′rë, Vlo′ra** (-rə)

Vl·ta·va (v′l′tä vä) river in W Czechoslovakia, flowing from the Bohemian Forest into the Elbe: c.265 mi.

☆**V-mail** (vē′māl′) *n.* mail to or from the armed forces in World War II, reduced to microfilm to conserve shipping space, and enlarged and printed for delivery

V.M.D. [L. *Veterinariae Medicinae Doctor*] Doctor of Veterinary Medicine

v.n. neuter verb

V-neck (vē′nek′) *n.* a neckline V-shaped in front

voc. vocative

vocab. vocabulary

vo·ca·ble (vō′kə b′l) *n.* [Fr. < L. *vocabulum*, a name, title, word < *vocare*, to call < *vox*, VOICE] a word or term; esp., a word regarded as a unit of sounds or letters rather than as a unit of meaning

vo·cab·u·lar·y (vō kab′yə ler′e, və-) *n., pl.* **-lar′ies** [ML. *vocabularium* < L. *vocabulum*, a word: see prec.] 1. a list of words and, often, phrases, abbreviations, inflectional forms, etc., usually arranged in alphabetical order and defined or otherwise identified, as in a dictionary or glossary 2. all the words of a language 3. *a)* all the words used by a particular person, class, profession, etc.: in full **active vocabulary** *b)* all the words recognized and understood by a particular person, although not necessarily used by him: in full **passive vocabulary** 4. an interrelated group of nonverbal symbols, signs, gestures, etc. used for communication or expression in a particular art, skill, etc.

vo·cal (vō′k′l) *adj.* [ME. < L. *vocalis* < *vox* (gen. *vocis*), a VOICE] 1. *a)* uttered or produced by the voice; esp., spoken; oral *[vocal sounds]* *b)* sung or to be sung *[vocal music]* 2. having a voice; capable of speaking or making oral sounds 3. of, used in, connected with, or belonging to the voice *[vocal organs]* 4. full of voice or voices; sounding 5. expressing or inclined to express oneself in speech; speaking freely or vociferously 6. *Phonet. same as: a)* VOCALIC *b)* VOICED —*n.* 1. a vocal sound 2. the part of a popular song that is, or is to be, sung, rather than played by the instruments —**vo′cal·ly** *adv.*

vocal cords either of two pairs of membranous cords or folds in the larynx, consisting of a thicker upper pair **(false vocal cords)** and a lower pair **(true vocal cords)**: voice is produced when air from the lungs causes the lower (true) cords to vibrate: pitch is controlled by varying the tension on the cords, and volume, by regulating the air passing through the larynx

vo·cal·ic (vō kal′ik) *adj.* 1. *a)* of, having the nature of, or consisting of a vowel or vowels *b)* composed mainly or entirely of vowels 2. producing or involving vowel change or vowel modification —**vo·cal′i·cal·ly** *adv.*

vo·cal·ise (vō′k′l ēz′) *n.* [Fr. < *vocaliser*, to vocalize] 1. a singing exercise using sol-fa syllables or other vowel sounds 2. a vocal composition or passage using vowel sounds instead of words

vo·cal·ism (vō′k′l iz′m) *n.* 1. the use of the voice, as in speaking or singing; vocalization 2. the act or art of singing 3. *a)* the system of vowels peculiar to a given language, dialect, etc. *b)* a vocalic sound; vowel

vo·cal·ist (-ist) *n.* [VOCAL + -IST] one who sings; singer

vo·cal·ize (vō′k′l iz′) *vt.* **-ized′, -iz′ing** 1. *a)* to give utterance to; express with the voice; speak or sing *b)* to make capable of vocal expression; make vocal, or articulate 2. to add diacritical vowel marks to (the exclusively consonantal characters of certain languages such as Hebrew) 3. *Phonet. a)* to change into or use as a vowel *b)* to voice —*vi.* 1. to make vocal sounds; speak or sing; specif., to do a singing exercise, using various vowel sounds 2. to be changed into a vowel; become vocalic —**vo′cal·i·za′tion** *n.* —**vo′cal·iz′er** *n.*

vo·ca·tion (vō kā′shən) *n.* [ME. *vocacion* < LL.(Ec.) *vocatio*, a calling < L., an invitation, court summons < *vocare*, to call < *vox*, VOICE] 1. *a)* a call, summons, or impulsion to perform a certain function or enter a certain career, esp. a religious one *b)* the function or career toward which one believes himself to be called 2. any trade, profession, or occupation

vo·ca·tion·al (-′l) *adj.* 1. of a vocation, trade, occupation, etc. 2. designating or of education, training, etc. intended to prepare one for an occupation, sometimes specif. in a trade —**vo·ca′tion·al·ism** *n.* —**vo·ca′tion·al·ly** *adv.*

☆**vocational guidance** the work of testing and interviewing persons in order to guide them toward the choice of a suitable vocation or toward training for such vocation

voc·a·tive (väk′ə tiv) *adj.* [ME. *vocatif* < OFr. or L.: OFr. *vocatif* < L. *vocativus* < pp. of *vocare*, to call < *vox*, VOICE] *Gram.* in certain inflected languages, designating or of the case of nouns, pronouns, or adjectives used in direct address to indicate the person or thing addressed —*n.* 1. the vocative case 2. a word in this case —**voc′a·tive·ly** *adv.*

vo·cif·er·ant (vō sif′ər ənt) *adj.* [L. *vociferans*, prp. of *vociferari*: see ff.] vociferating; shouting; clamorous

vo·cif·er·ate (vō sif′ə rāt′) *vt., vi.* **-at′ed, -at′ing** [< L. *vociferatus*, pp. of *vociferari*, to cry out < *vox*, VOICE + *ferre*, to BEAR¹] to utter or shout loudly or vehemently; bawl; clamor —**vo·cif′er·a′tion** *n.* —**vo·cif′er·a′tor** *n.*

vo·cif·er·ous (vō sif′ər əs) *adj.* [L. *vociferari* (see prec.) + -OUS] **1.** loud, noisy, or vehement in making one's feelings known; clamorous **2.** characterized by clamor or vehement outcry —**vo·cif′er·ous·ly** *adv.* —**vo·cif′er·ous·ness** *n.*
SYN.—**vociferous** suggests loud and unrestrained shouting or crying out [a *vociferous* crowd, *vociferous* cheers]; **clamorous** suggests an urgent or insistent vociferousness, as in demand or complaint [*clamorous* protests]; **blatant** implies a bellowing loudness and, hence, suggests vulgar or offensive noisiness, clamor, etc. [*blatant* heckling]; **strident** suggests a harsh, grating loudness [a *strident* voice]; **boisterous** implies roughness or turbulence and, hence, suggests unrestrained exuberance in noisemaking [*boisterous* revels]; **obstreperous** implies an unruliness that is noisy or boisterous in resisting control [an *obstreperous* child]
☆**vo·cod·er** (vō′kō′dər) *n.* [VO(ICE) + CODER] an electronic system for analyzing the frequency spectrum of speech and constructing a code that can be transmitted and reconstructed into a replica of the original speech
vod·ka (väd′kə; *Russ.* vôd′kä) *n.* [Russ., brandy, dim. of *voda*, WATER] a colorless alcoholic liquor distilled from wheat, rye, etc.
vogue (vōg) *n.* [Fr., a fashion, reputation, lit., rowing of a ship < *voguer*, to row, sail < MLowG. *wagon*, to sail, float, akin to OE. *wæg*, a wave, billow: for IE. base see WEIGH¹] **1.** the accepted fashion or style at any particular time; mode: often with *the* **2.** general favor or acceptance; popularity [coming into *vogue*] —*adj.* in vogue: also **vogu·ish** (vō′gish) —**SYN.** see FASHION
Vo·gul (vō′gool) *n.* **1.** any member of a Finno-Ugric people living in W Siberia **2.** their Ugric language
voice (vois) *n.* [ME. < OFr. *vois* < L. *vox* (gen. *vocis*), a voice < IE. base *wekw-*, to speak, whence Sans. *vákti*, (he) speaks, Gr. *ossa*, voice, OE. *woma*, noise] **1.** sound made through the mouth, esp. by human beings in talking, singing, etc. **2.** the ability to make sounds orally or to speak, sing, etc. [to lose one's *voice*] **3.** *a)* any sound regarded as like vocal utterance [the *voice* of the sea] *b)* anything regarded as like vocal utterance in communicating to the mind [the *voice* of one's conscience] **4.** a specified condition, quality, or tone of vocal sound [an angry *voice*] **5.** the characteristic speech sounds normally made by a particular person [to recognize someone's *voice* over the phone] **6.** *a)* an expressed wish, choice, opinion, etc. [the *voice* of the people] *b)* the right to express one's wish, choice, opinion, etc., or to make it prevail; vote [to have a *voice* in one's government] **7.** utterance or expression [giving *voice* to his joy] **8.** the person or other agency by which something is expressed or made known [a newspaper known to be the *voice* of the administration] **9.** [Obs.] *a)* rumor; report *b)* fame; reputation **10.** *Gram.* *a)* any of the forms of a verb showing the connection between the subject and the verb, either as performing (*active voice*) or receiving (*passive voice*) the action *b)* such forms or categories, collectively **11.** *Music a)* musical sound made with the mouth; singing *b)* the quality of a particular person's singing [a good *voice*] *c)* a singer *d)* any of the individual parts sung or played together in a musical composition **12.** *Phonet.* sound made by vibrating the vocal cords with air forced from the lungs, as in pronouncing all vowels and such consonants as (b), (d), (g), (m), etc. —*vt.* **voiced, voic′ing 1.** to give utterance or expression to; utter or express in words **2.** *Music* to regulate the tone of (organ pipes, etc.) **3.** *Phonet.* to utter with voice —**SYN.** see UTTER² —**in voice** with the voice in good condition, as for singing —**with one voice** unanimously —**voic′er** *n.*
voiced (voist) *adj.* **1.** having a voice **2.** having or using (a specified kind or tone of) voice: often in hyphenated compounds [deep-*voiced*] **3.** expressed by the voice **4.** *Phonet.* made by vibrating the vocal cords with air forced from the lungs; sonant: said of certain consonants
voice·ful (vois′fəl) *adj.* [Poet.] vocal; esp., full of voice or voices; sounding —**voice′ful·ness** *n.*
voice·less (vois′lis) *adj.* **1.** having no voice; dumb; mute **2.** not speaking; silent **3.** not spoken; not uttered [a *voiceless* wish] **4.** lacking a musical voice or the ability to sing **5.** having no vote; lacking suffrage **6.** *Phonet.* uttered without voice; surd [p, t, k, etc. are *voiceless* consonants] —**voice′less·ly** *adv.* —**voice′less·ness** *n.*
SYN.—**voiceless** is applied to one who has no voice, either from birth or through deprivation [the throat operation left him *voiceless*]; **speechless** usually implies temporary or momentary deprivation of the ability to speak [*speechless* with horror]; **dumb** implies a lack of the power of speech and is now more often applied to brute animals and inanimate objects than to persons with impaired speech organs [a *dumb* beast]; **mute** is applied to persons incapable of speech, specif. as because of congenital deafness and not through absence or impairment of the speech organs —**ANT.** articulate
voice-o·ver (-ō′vər) *n.* the voice commenting or narrating off camera, as for a television commercial
☆**voice·print** (-print′) *n.* a pattern of wavy lines and whorls recorded by a device actuated by the sound of a person's voice: the pattern is supposed to be distinctive for each individual, like a fingerprint —**voice′print′ing** *n.*
void (void) *adj.* [ME. *voide* < OFr. < VL. **vocitus*, for L.

vocivus, var. of *vacivus* < *vacare*, to be empty: cf. VACANT] **1.** not occupied; vacant: said of benefices, offices, etc. **2.** *a)* holding or containing nothing *b)* devoid or destitute (of) [*void* of sense] **3.** having no effect or result; ineffective; useless **4.** *Law a)* of no legal force; not binding; invalid; null *b)* loosely, capable of being nullified **5.** *Bridge* holding no cards in a suit as dealt to the hand [*void* in clubs] —*n.* **1.** total emptiness; an empty space or vacuum **2.** *a)* total absence of something normally present *b)* a feeling of emptiness or deprivation [the *void* left by his death] **3.** a break or open space, as in a surface; gap —*vt.* [ME. *voiden* < MFr. *voidier* < *voide*, adj.] **1.** [Now Rare] *a)* to make empty or vacant; clear *b)* to vacate **2.** *a)* to empty (the contents of something) *b)* to evacuate, or discharge (urine or feces) **3.** to make void, or of no effect; nullify; annul —*vi.* to defecate or, esp., to urinate —**SYN.** see EMPTY, NULLIFY —**void′a·ble** *adj.* —**void′er** *n.*
void·ance (-'ns) *n.* [ME. *voydaunce* < Anglo-Fr. *voidaunce* < OFr. *vuidance*] the act of voiding; specif., *a)* annulment, as of a contract *b)* vacancy, as of a benefice
void·ed (-id) *adj.* **1.** made void **2.** *Heraldry* with the field showing through the space outlined by a bearing
†**voi·là** (vwä lä′) [Fr., see there] behold; there it is: often used as an interjection
voile (voil; *Fr.* vwál) *n.* [Fr., a veil: see VEIL] a thin, sheer fabric, as of cotton, used for garments, curtains, etc.
voir dire (vwär′ dir′) [Fr. < *voir(e)*, truly + *dire*, to say] *Law* **1.** an oath taken by a person to speak the truth in an examination testing his competence as a witness or juror **2.** the examination itself
voix cé·leste (vwä sä lest′) [Fr., lit., heavenly voice] an organ stop producing a soft, tremulous effect
vol. 1. volcano **2.** *pl.* **vols.** volume **3.** volunteer
vo·lant (vō′lənt) *adj.* [< Fr. or L.; Fr. *volant* < L. *volans*, prp. of *volare*, to fly] **1.** flying or capable of flying **2.** nimble; agile; quick **3.** *Heraldry* represented as flying
Vo·la·pük (vō′lä pük′) *n.* [< Volapük *vol*, world (altered < WORLD) + *pük*, language (altered < SPEAK)] an artificial language invented about 1879 by J. M. Schleyer of Baden, Germany, for proposed international use as an auxiliary language: also **Vol·a·puk** (väl′ə pook′)
vo·lar (vō′lər) *adj.* [< L. *vola*, palm of the hand, sole of the foot (for IE. base see WALE¹) + -AR] *Anat.* of the palm of the hand or sole of the foot
vol·a·tile (väl′ə t'l; *chiefly Brit.*, -til′) *adj.* [MFr. < L. *volatilis* < *volare*, to fly] **1.** orig., flying or able to fly; volitant **2.** vaporizing or evaporating quickly, as alcohol **3.** *a)* likely to shift quickly and unpredictably; unstable; explosive [a *volatile* social condition] *b)* moving capriciously from one idea, interest, etc. to another; fickle *c)* not lasting long; fleeting —*n.* [Now Rare] **1.** any flying creature **2.** a volatile substance —**vol·a·til′i·ty** (-til′ə tē) *n.*, **vol′a·tile·ness** *n.*
volatile oil same as ESSENTIAL OIL
vol·a·til·ize (väl′ə t'l iz′) *vt.* **-ized′, -iz′ing** to make volatile; cause to pass off as vapor —*vi.* to become volatile —**vol′a·til·iz′a·ble** *adj.* —**vol·a·til·i·za′tion** *n.*
‡**vol-au-vent** (vô lō vän′) *n.* [Fr., lit., flight in the wind] a baked pastry shell of puff paste, filled with a stew of chicken, game, fish, etc.
vol·can·ic (väl kan′ik) *adj.* [Fr. *volcanique* < It. *volcanico*] **1.** of, thrown from, caused by, or characteristic of a volcano **2.** having, or composed of, volcanoes **3.** bursting forth or threatening to burst forth like a volcanic eruption; violently explosive —**vol·can′i·cal·ly** *adv.*
volcanic glass natural glass, as obsidian, formed by the very rapid cooling of molten lava
vol·can·ic·i·ty (väl′kə nis′ə tē) *n.* [Fr. *volcanicité*] the quality or state of being volcanic; volcanic activity
volcanic rock igneous rock, fine-textured and sometimes glassy, that solidified rapidly from molten lava at or very near the surface of the earth
vol·can·ism (väl′kə niz′m) *n.* [Fr. *volcanisme*] volcanic activity or phenomena
vol·can·ist (-nist) *n.* same as VOLCANOLOGIST
vol·can·ize (-niz′) *vt.* **-ized′, -iz′ing** to subject to, or change by, volcanic heat —**vol′can·i·za′tion** *n.*
vol·ca·no (väl kā′nō) *n.*, *pl.* **-noes, -nos** [It. < L. *Volcanus*, VULCAN] **1.** a vent in the earth's crust through which molten rock (lava), rock fragments, gases, ashes, etc. are ejected from the earth's interior: a volcano is *active* while erupting, *dormant* during a long period of inactivity, or *extinct* when all

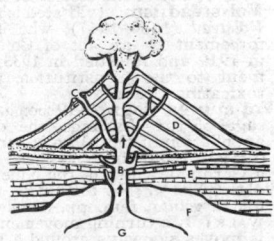

VOLCANO
(A, crater; B, conduit through which molten rock & gases rise to surface; C, parasitic cone; D, ashes & lava; E, sedimentary & metamorphic rock; F, igneous rock; G, reservoir of hot magma)

activity has finally ceased 2. a cone-shaped hill or mountain, wholly or chiefly of volcanic materials, built up around the vent, usually so as to form a crater

Volcano Islands group of small Japanese islands, including Iwo Jima, in the W Pacific: 11 sq. mi.

vol·can·ol·o·gist (väl′kə näl′ə jist) *n.* a student of or specialist in volcanology

vol·can·ol·o·gy (-jē) *n.* [VOLCANO + -LOGY] the science dealing with volcanoes and volcanic activity —**vol′can·o·log′i·cal** *adj.*

vole[1] (vōl) *n.* [earlier *vole mouse* < Scand., as in Norw. *voll*, meadow, field (akin to WEALD, WOLD[1]) + MOUSE] any of a number of small rodents (subfamily Microtinae), with a stout body and short tail; esp., *same as* FIELD MOUSE

vole[2] (vōl) *n.* [Fr., prob. < *voler*, to fly < L. *volare*] in old card games, the winning of all the tricks in a deal

Vol·ga (väl′gə, vōl′-; *Russ.* vôl′gä) river in W R.S.F.S.R., flowing from the Valdai Hills into the Caspian Sea: 2,290 mi.

Vol·go·grad (väl′gə grad′; *Russ.* vôl′gô grät′) city in SC European R.S.F.S.R., on the Volga: scene of a decisive Soviet victory (1943) over German troops in World War II: pop. 720,000: formerly called *Stalingrad, Tsaritsyn*

vol·i·tant (väl′ə tənt) *adj.* [L. *volitans*, prp. of *volitare*, to fly to and fro, freq. of *volare*, to fly] 1. flying, flitting, or constantly in motion 2. capable of flight

vol·i·ta·tion (väl′ə tā′shən) *n.* [ML. *volitatio* < L. *volitare*: see prec.] 1. the act of flying; flight 2. the ability to fly

vo·li·tion (vō lish′ən, və-) *n.* [Fr. < ML. *volitio* < L. *volo*, pres. indic., of *velle*, to be willing, to will[2]] 1. the act of using the will; exercise of the will as in deciding what to do 2. a conscious or deliberate decision or choice thus made 3. the power or faculty of using the will —*SYN.* see WILL[1] —**vo·li′tion·al** *adj.* —**vo·li′tion·al·ly** *adv.*

vol·i·tive (väl′ə tiv) *adj.* [ML. *volitivus* < L. *volo:* see prec.] 1. of or arising from the will 2. *Gram.* expressing a wish, as a verb, mood, etc.

‡Volks·lied (fôlks′lēt′) *n., pl.* **Volks′lied′er** (-lē′dər) [G.] a folk song

vol·ley (väl′ē) *n., pl.* **-leys** [MFr. *volee* < VL. *volata* < fem. of L. *volatus*, pp. of *volare*, to fly] 1. *a)* the simultaneous discharge of a number of firearms or other weapons *b)* the bullets, arrows, etc. discharged in this way 2. a burst of words or acts suggestive of this *[a volley of curses, questions, etc.]* 3. *Sports a)* the act of returning the ball, shuttlecock, etc. in certain games before it touches the ground *b)* the flight of the ball, etc. before it touches the ground *c)* loosely, any extended exchange of shots, as in tennis or volleyball, esp. such an exchange in warming up for a game —*vt.* **-leyed, -ley·ing** 1. to discharge in or as in a volley 2. *Sports* to return (the ball, etc.) as a volley —*vi.* 1. to be discharged in or as in a volley 2. *Sports* loosely, to engage in a volley —**vol′ley·er** *n.*

☆**vol·ley·ball** (-bôl′) *n.* 1. a game played on a court by two teams who hit a large, light, inflated ball back and forth over a high net with the hands, each team trying to return the ball before it touches the ground 2. this ball

Vo·log·da (vô′lôg dä) city in NC European R.S.F.S.R.: pop. 166,000

vo·lost (vō′läst) *n.* [Russ. *volost′*] 1. formerly, a small administrative district of peasants in czarist Russia 2. a rural soviet in the Soviet Union

vol·plane (väl′plān′) *vi.* **-planed′, -plan′ing** [Fr. *vol plané* < *vol*, flight < *voler*, to fly (< L. *volare*) + *plané*, pp. of *planer*, to glide: see PLANE[4]] to glide down as or in an airplane with the engine cut off —*n.* such a glide

vols. volumes

Vol·sci (väl′sī) *n.pl.* [L.] an ancient people of Latium, conquered by the Romans in the 4th cent. B.C.

Vol·scian (väl′shən) *adj.* of the Volsci, their language, etc. —*n.* 1. any of the Volsci 2. the Italic dialect of the Volsci

☆**Vol·stead·ism** (väl′sted iz′m) *n.* [after Rep. A. J. *Volstead* (1860–1947), who introduced the act] the enforcement by an act of Congress (**Volstead Act,** passed in 1919 and repealed in 1933) of the Eighteenth Amendment to the Constitution, prohibiting the sale of intoxicating liquor

Vol·sun·ga Saga (väl′soon gə) [ON. *Völsunga saga*, lit., saga of the Volsungs, the descendants of *Volsi*, prob. appellation of Odin] an Icelandic saga relating the legend of Sigurd and the Nibelungs: also told, with variations, in a Germanic version, the Nibelungenlied

volt[1] (vōlt) *n.* [Fr. *volte* < It. *volta*, a turn < VL. *volvita*, for L. *voluta*, fem. pp. of *volvere*, to roll, turn about: see WALK] 1. a turning movement or gait of a horse, in which it moves sideways around a center 2. *Fencing* a leap to avoid a thrust

volt[2] (vōlt) *n.* [after A. VOLTA] the practical mks unit of electromotive force or difference in potential between two points in an electric field that requires one joule of work to move a positive charge of one coulomb from the point of lower potential to the point of higher potential

Vol·ta (väl′tə) river in Ghana, flowing south into the Bight of Benin: c.300 mi.: formed by the confluence of the **Black Volta** (c.550 mi.) & the **White Volta** (c.550 mi.)

Vol·ta (vôl′tä), Conte A·les·san·dro (ä′les sän′drô) 1745–1827; It. physicist

volt·age (vōl′tij) *n.* electromotive force, or difference in electrical potential, expressed in volts

voltage divider a device consisting of a resistor or series of resistors connected across a voltage and having one or more fixed or adjustable intermediate contacts: from any two terminals a desired reduced voltage may be obtained

Vol·ta·ic (väl tā′ik) *adj.* 1. of or pertaining to Upper Volta or the peoples of Upper Volta 2. of or pertaining to the Voltaic branch of languages —*n.* a branch of the Niger-Congo subfamily of languages, centered in the valley of the Volta River in Upper Volta and Ghana

vol·ta·ic (väl tā′ik, vōl-) *adj.* [< A. VOLTA + -IC] 1. designating or of electricity produced by chemical action; galvanic 2. used in so producing electricity

voltaic battery *Elec.* 1. a battery composed of voltaic cells 2. *same as* VOLTAIC CELL

voltaic cell *Elec.* a device for producing an electric current by the action of two plates of different metals in an electrolyte

voltaic pile *same as* PILE[1] (*n.* 5)

Vol·taire (vōl ter′, väl-; *Fr.* vôl ter′), (**François Marie Arouet de**) (born *François Marie Arouet*) 1694–1778; Fr. writer and philosopher

vol·ta·ism (väl′tə iz′m, vōl′-) *n.* [< VOLTA (cf. VOLTAIC) + -ISM] *same as* GALVANISM

vol·tam·e·ter (väl tam′ə tər, vōl-) *n.* [VOLTA(IC) + -METER] *Physics* an electrolytic cell for measuring a current by the amount of gas liberated or metal deposited from an electrolyte —**vol′ta·met′ric** (-tə met′rik) *adj.*

volt·am·me·ter (vōlt′am′mēt′ər) *n.* a dual-purpose instrument for measuring either voltage or amperage

volt-am·pere (-am′pir) *n. Elec.* the unit of apparent power in an alternating-current circuit or device containing reactance, equal to the product of the voltage in volts and the current in amperes without regard to phase

volte-face (vält′fäs′; *Fr.* vôlt fås′) *n.* [Fr. < It. *volta faccia* < *volta*, a turn (see VOLT[1]) + *faccia* < VL. *facia*, FACE] 1. a turn so as to face the opposite way; about-face 2. a complete reversal of opinion, attitude, etc.

volt·me·ter (vōlt′mēt′ər) *n.* [VOLT[2] + -METER] *Elec.* an instrument for measuring voltage

Vol·tur·no (vôl toor′nô) river in SC Italy, flowing from the Apennines into the Tyrrhenian Sea: c.110 mi.

vol·u·ble (väl′yoo b'l) *adj.* [Fr. < L. *volubilis*, easily turned about < *volutus*, pp. of *volvere*, to roll, turn about: see WALK] 1. characterized by a great flow of words; talking much and easily; talkative, glib, etc. 2. [Rare] rolling easily on an axis; rotating 3. *Bot.* twining or twisting, as a vine —*SYN.* see TALKATIVE —**vol′u·bil′i·ty, vol′u·ble·ness** *n.* —**vol′u·bly** *adv.*

vol·ume (väl′yoom, -yəm) *n.* [ME. < MFr. < L. *volumen*, a roll, scroll, hence a book written on a parchment < *volutus*, pp. of *volvere*, to roll: see WALK] 1. orig., a roll of parchment, a scroll, etc. 2. *a)* a collection of written, typewritten, or printed sheets bound together; book *b)* any of the separate books making up a matched set or a complete work 3. a set of the issues of a periodical over a fixed period of time, usually a year 4. any of the individual phonograph records of a multirecord album, esp. of literary readings 5. the amount of space occupied in three dimensions; cubic contents or cubic magnitude 6. *a)* a quantity, bulk, mass, or amount *b)* a large quantity; bulk, amount, etc. 7. the quantity, strength, or loudness of sound 8. *Music* fullness of tone —*SYN.* see BULK[1] —**speak volumes** to be very expressive or meaningful

vol·umed (-yoomd, -yəmd) *adj.* 1. [Now Rare] consisting of (a specified number or kind of) volumes: used in hyphenated compounds *[a ten-volumed encyclopedia]* 2. [Poet.] forming a bulky mass

vo·lu·me·ter (və loo′mə tər) *n.* [VOLU(ME) + -METER] *Physics* an instrument used to measure the volume of liquids and gases directly, and of solids by the amount of liquid they displace

vol·u·met·ric (väl′yoo met′rik) *adj.* [VOLU(ME) + -METRIC] of or based on the measurement of volume: also **vol′u·met′ri·cal** —**vol′u·met′ri·cal·ly** *adv.*

volumetric analysis the quantitative analysis of an unknown chemical solution by determining the amount of reagent of known concentration necessary to effect a reaction in a known volume of the solution

volume unit a unit equal to a decibel for expressing the magnitude of a complex audio signal, as that of speech or music, above a reference level of one milliwatt

vo·lu·mi·nous (və loo′mə nəs) *adj.* [LL. *voluminosus*, full of rolls or folds < *volumen*: see VOLUME] 1. writing, producing, consisting of, or forming enough material to fill volumes 2. of great volume; large; bulky; full 3. [Archaic] characterized by many coils or windings —**vo·lu′mi·nos′i·ty** (-näs′ə tē) *n.* —**vo·lu′mi·nous·ly** *adv.*

vol·un·ta·rism (väl′ən tər iz′m) *n.* 1. *a)* voluntary or willing participation in a course of action *b)* a doctrine or system based on such participation 2. *Philos.* any theory which holds that reality is ultimately of the nature of will or that the will is the primary factor in experience —**vol′un·ta·rist** *n., adj.* —**vol′un·ta·ris′tic** *adj.*

vol·un·tar·y (väl′ən ter′ē) *adj.* [ME. *voluntarie* < L. *voluntarius*, voluntary < *voluntas*, free will < *volo*, I will, pres. indic. of *velle*, to WILL[1]] 1. brought about by one's own free choice; given or done of one's own free will; freely chosen or undertaken 2. acting in a specified capacity willingly or of one's own accord 3. intentional; not

accidental [*voluntary* manslaughter] **4.** controlled by one's mind or will [*voluntary* muscles] **5.** having free will or the power of free choice [man is a *voluntary* agent] **6.** *a)* supported by contributions or freewill offerings; not supported or maintained by the state [*voluntary* churches] *b)* done or carried on by or made up of volunteers rather than by people paid or conscripted **7.** arising in the mind without external constraint; spontaneous **8.** *Law a)* acting or done without compulsion or persuasion *b)* done without profit, payment, or any valuable consideration —n., *pl.* -tar'ies *Music* a piece or solo, often an improvisation, played on the organ before, during, or after a church service —vol·un·tar·i·ly (väl'ən ter'ə lē, väl'ən ter'-) *adv.* **SYN.** voluntary implies the exercise of one's own free choice or will in an action, whether or not external influences are at work [*voluntary* services]; **intentional** applies to that which is done on purpose for a definite reason and is in no way accidental [an *intentional* slight]; **deliberate** implies full realization of the significance of what one intends to do and of its effects [a *deliberate* lie]; **willful** implies obstinate and perverse determination to follow one's own will despite influences, arguments, advice, etc. in opposition [a *willful* refusal]

vol·un·tar·y·ism (-iz'm) *n.* **1.** the doctrine that churches, schools, etc. should be supported by voluntary contributions and not by the state **2.** a system based on this principle

vol·un·teer (väl'ən tir') *n.* [earlier *voluntier* < obs. Fr. *voluntaire* < L. *voluntarius*, VOLUNTARY] **1.** a person who enters or offers to enter into any service of his own free will **2.** a person who enters naval or military service of his own free will, without being compelled to do so by law: opposed to CONSCRIPT, DRAFTEE **3.** *Law a)* a person who enters into any transaction of his own free will with no promise of compensation *b)* a person to whom property is transferred without valuable consideration —*adj.* **1.** composed of volunteers, as an army **2.** serving as a volunteer, usually without compensation **3.** of a volunteer or volunteers **4.** *same as* VOLUNTARY **5.** *Bot.* growing from seed that has fallen naturally to the ground, not planted by man —*vt.* to offer or give of one's own free will without being asked or obliged —*vi.* to enter or offer to enter into any service of one's own free will; enlist

☆**Volunteers of America** a private welfare organization, somewhat like the Salvation Army, established in 1896 to provide help for the handicapped, needy, etc.

vo·lup·tu·ar·y (və lup'choo wer'ē) *n.*, *pl.* -ar'ies [L. *voluptuarius* < *voluptas*, pleasure: see ff.] a person devoted to luxurious living and sensual pleasures; sensualist; sybarite —*adj.* of or characterized by luxury and sensual pleasures

vo·lup·tu·ous (-choo wəs) *adj.* [ME. < L. *voluptuosus*, full of pleasure < *voluptas*, pleasure < IE. base *wel-*, to wish, choose, whence WILL²] **1.** full of, producing, or characterized by sensual delights and pleasures; sensual **2.** fond of or directed toward luxury, elegance, and the pleasures of the senses **3.** *a)* suggesting or expressing sensual pleasure or gratification *b)* sexually attractive because of a full, shapely figure **4.** arising from sensual gratification —*SYN.* see SENSUOUS —**vo·lup'tu·ous·ly** *adv.* —**vo·lup'tu·ous·ness** *n.*

vo·lute (və lōōt') *n.* [L. *voluta*, orig., fem. of *volutus*, pp. of *volvere*, to roll: see WALK] **1.** a spiral or twisting form; turn; whorl **2.** *Archit.* a spiral scroll forming one of the chief features of Ionic and Corinthian capitals **3.** *Zool. a)* any of the turns or whorls of a spiral shell *b)* any of various saltwater gastropods (family Volutidae) having a shell with a tapering spire and often brightly colored —*adj.* **1.** rolled up; spiraled **2.** having a spirally shaped part —**vo·lut'ed** *adj.*

vo·lu·tion (və lōō'shən) *n.* [< L. *volutus:* see VOLUTE] **1.** a revolving or rolling **2.** a spiral turn or twist; coil; convolution **3.** a whorl of a spiral shell or structure

vol·va (väl'və) *n.* [ModL. < L., var. of *vulva:* see VULVA] the membranous covering enclosing certain mushrooms in the early stage of growth, becoming a cup at the base of the stalk at maturity —**vol'vate'** (-vāt') *adj.*

vol·vox (väl'väks) *n.* [ModL. < L. *volvere*, to roll (see WALK) + -*ox* (as in *atrox*, fierce)] any of a genus (*Volvox*) of multicellular, free-swimming, flagellated algae whose cells form a pale green globular colony that rolls about in the water

vol·vu·lus (väl'vyoo ləs) *n.* [ModL. < L. *volvere*, to roll: see WALK] a twisting or displacement of the intestines resulting in intestinal obstruction

vo·mer (vō'mər) *n.* [ModL. < L., plowshare] *Anat.* a thin, flat bone forming part of the nasal septum separating the nasal passages —**vo·mer·ine** (vō'mə rin', -rin; väm'ə-) *adj.*

vom·it (väm'it) *n.* [ME. < L. *vomitus*, a discharging, vomiting < *vomere*, to discharge, vomit < IE. base *wemē-*, whence Gr. *emein*, to vomit, OE. *wamm*, stain, disgrace] **1.** the act or process of ejecting the contents of the stomach through the mouth **2.** matter ejected in this way **3.** [Archaic] a drug that causes vomiting; emetic —*vi.* **1.** to eject the contents of the stomach through the mouth; throw up **2.** to be thrown up or out with force or violence; rush out —*vt.* **1.** to throw up (food) **2.** to discharge or throw out with force or in copious quantities; belch forth —**vom'it·er** *n.*

vom·i·tive (-ə tiv) *adj.* of or causing vomiting; emetic

vom·i·to·ry (väm'ə tôr'ē) *adj.* [L. *vomitorius*] [Archaic] vomitive; emetic —*n.*, *pl.* -ries **1.** *obs. var.* of EMETIC **2.** any opening, funnel, etc. through which matter is to be discharged **3.** [LL. *vomitorium:* the spectators were discharged through these] in Roman amphitheaters, etc., any of the entrances leading to the tiers of seats

vom·i·tu·ri·tion (väm'i choo rish'ən) *n.* **1.** repeated but unsuccessful attempts to vomit; retching **2.** vomiting that brings up but little matter

vom·i·tus (väm'it əs) *n.* [L., a vomiting: see VOMIT] matter that has been vomited

†**von** (fôn; *E.* vän) *prep.* [G.] of; from: a prefix occurring in many names of German and Austrian families, esp. of the nobility

von Braun (fôn broun'; *E.* vän broun'), **Wern·her** (ver'nər; *E.* wur'nər) 1912— ; U.S. rocket engineer, born in Germany

☆**voo·doo** (vōō'dōō) *n.*, *pl.* -doos [Creole Fr., of WAfr. orig., as in Ewe (Dahomey and Togo) *vodu*, a fetish, demon] **1.** a primitive religion based on a belief in sorcery and in the power of charms, fetishes, etc.: it originated in Africa and is still practiced, chiefly by natives of the West Indies **2.** a person who practices voodoo **3.** a voodoo charm, fetish, etc. —*adj.* of voodoos or voodooism —*vt.* to affect by voodoo magic

☆**voo·doo·ism** (-iz'm) *n.* the system of voodoo beliefs and practices —**voo'doo·ist** *n.* —**voo'doo·is'tic** *adj.*

vo·ra·cious (vô rā'shəs, və-) *adj.* [L. *vorax* (gen. *voracis*), greedy to devour < *vorare*, to devour < IE. base **gwer-*, to devour, gorge, whence Gr. *bora*, food (of carnivorous beasts), L. *gurges*, gorge] **1.** greedy in eating; devouring or eager to devour large quantities of food; ravenous; gluttonous **2.** very greedy or eager in some desire or pursuit; insatiable [a *voracious* reader] —**vo·ra'cious·ly** *adv.* —**vo·rac'i·ty** (-ras'ə tē), **vo·ra'cious·ness** *n.*

Vo·ro·nezh (vô rô'nesh) city in SC European R.S.F.S.R., near the Don: pop. 592,000

Vo·ro·shi·lov·grad (vô'rô shē'lôf grät') *former name of* LUGANSK

-**vo·rous** (və rəs) [L. -*vorus* < *vorare:* see VORACIOUS] a combining form meaning feeding on, eating [*omnivorous*]

vor·tex (vôr'teks) *n.*, *pl.* vor'tex·es, vor'ti·ces' (-tə sēz') [L. *vortex*, var. of *vertex:* see VERTEX] **1.** a whirling mass of water forming a vacuum at its center, into which anything caught in the motion is drawn; whirlpool **2.** a whirl or powerful eddy of air; whirlwind **3.** any activity, situation, or state of affairs that resembles a whirl or eddy in its rush, absorbing effect, catastrophic power, etc.

vor·ti·cal (vôr'ti k'l) *adj.* **1.** of, characteristic of, or like a vortex **2.** moving in a vortex; whirling —**vor'ti·cal·ly** *adv.*

vor·ti·cel·la (vôr'tə sel'ə) *n.*, *pl.* -cel'lae (-ē) [ModL., dim. < L. *vortex:* see VORTEX] any of a genus (*Vorticella*) of one-celled animals living in water, with a bell-shaped body on a thin, contractile stem serving as a holdfast

vor·ti·cose (vôr'tə kōs') *adj.* [L. *vorticosus* < *vortex:* see VORTEX] whirling; vortical

vor·tig·i·nous (vôr tij'ə nəs) *adj.* [L. *vertiginosus* < *vertigo:* see VERTIGO] [Archaic] **1.** whirling: said of motion **2.** moving in or like a vortex

Vor·tum·nus (vôr tum'nəs) *same as* VERTUMNUS

Vosges (Mountains) (vōzh) mountain range in NE France, west of the Rhine: highest peak, c.4,700 ft.

vot·a·ble (vōt'ə b'l) *adj.* that can be submitted to a vote; subject to a vote: also sp. **vote'a·ble**

vo·ta·ry (vōt'ə rē) *n.*, *pl.* -ries [< L. *votus*, pp. of *vovere*, to vow (see ff.) + -ARY] **1.** a person bound by a vow or promise, esp. one bound to religious vows, as a monk or nun **2.** a person devoted to a particular religion or object of worship; devout worshiper **3.** a devoted or ardent supporter, as of a cause, ideal, etc. **4.** a person who is devoted to any game, study, pursuit, etc. Also **vo'ta·rist** —*adj.* **1.** consecrated by a vow **2.** of, or having the nature of, a vow —**vo'ta·ress** (-ris) *n.fem.*

vote (vōt) *n.* [LME. (Scot.) < L. *votum*, a wish, vow < neut. of *votus*, pp. of *vovere*, to vow < IE. base *ewegwh-*, to speak solemnly, vow, whence Sans. *vāghát*, one who vows, Gr. *euche*, a vow, prayer] **1.** *a)* a decision by a group on a proposal, resolution, bill, etc., or a choice between candidates for office, expressed by written ballot, voice, show of hands, etc. *b)* the decision of any individual in the group **2.** *a)* the expression or indication of such a decision or choice *b)* the ticket, ballot, voice, or other means by which it is expressed **3.** the right to exercise such a decision or choice, as in a meeting, election, etc.; suffrage **4.** *a)* the total number of ballots cast [a light *vote*] *b)* votes collectively [to get out the *vote*] *c)* a specified group of voters, or their votes, collectively [the farm *vote*] **5.** [Archaic] a voter **6.** [Obs.] *a)* a vow *b)* a prayer —*vi.* **vot'ed, vot'ing** to express the will or a preference in a matter by ballot, voice, etc.; give or cast a vote —*vt.* **1.** *a)* to decide, choose, enact, or authorize by vote *b)* to grant or confer by vote *c)* to support (a specified party ticket) in voting **2.** to declare by general opinion [*voted* the picnic a success] **3.** [Colloq.] to suggest —**vote down** to defeat by

voting; decide against —**vote in** to elect —**vote out** to defeat (an incumbent) in an election —**vote′less** *adj.*

vot·er (vōt′ər) *n.* a person who has a right to vote; elector, esp. one who actually votes

☆**voting machine** a machine on which votes in an election are cast, registered, and counted

vo·tive (vōt′iv) *adj.* [L. *votivus* < *votum:* see VOTE] 1. given, dedicated, consecrated, done, etc. in fulfillment of a vow or pledge [*votive* offerings] 2. R.C.Ch. designating or of a special or extraordinary Mass said at the priest's option

vouch (vouch) *vt.* [ME. *vouchen* < OFr. *vocher* < L. *vocare,* to call < *vox,* VOICE] 1. to uphold by demonstration or evidence 2. [Archaic] *a)* to attest, affirm, or guarantee *b)* to call as witness *c)* to cite (authority, books, etc.) in support of one's views or actions 3. in old English law, to call (a person) into court to give warranty of title —*vi.* 1. to give assurance, affirmation, or a guarantee (with *for)* [to *vouch* for someone's honesty] 2. to serve as evidence or assurance (*for)* [references *vouching* for his ability] —*n.* [Obs.] the act of vouching; assertion or attestation

vouch·er (vou′chər) *n.* [substantive use of Anglo-Fr. *voucher,* to VOUCH] 1. a person who vouches, as for the truth of a statement 2. a paper serving as evidence or proof; specif., a receipt or statement attesting to the expenditure or receipt of money, the accuracy of an account, etc. 3. in old English law, the summoning of a person into court to warrant another's title to a property: in full **voucher of warranty**

vouch·safe (vouch sāf′) *vt.* -**safed′**, -**saf′ing** [contr. of ME. *vouchen safe,* to vouch as safe] to be gracious enough or condescend to give or grant [to *vouchsafe* a reply] — **vouch·safe′ment** *n.*

vous·soir (vōō swär′) *n.* [Fr. < OFr. *volsoir,* curvature of a vault < VL. *volsorium* < *volsus,* for L. *volutus,* pp. of *volvere,* to roll: see WALK] *Archit.* any of the wedge-shaped stones of which an arch or vault is built

vow (vou) *n.* [ME. *vou* < OFr. < L. *votum:* see VOTE] 1. a solemn promise or pledge, esp. one made to God or a god, dedicating oneself to an act, service, or way of life 2. a solemn promise of love and fidelity [marriage *vows*] 3. a solemn affirmation or assertion —*vt.* 1. to promise solemnly 2. to make a solemn resolution to do, get, etc. 3. to declare emphatically, earnestly, or solemnly —*vi.* to make a vow —**take vows** to enter a religious order —**vow′er** *n.*

vow·el (vou′əl, voul) *n.* [ME. *vowelle* < MFr. *vouel* < L. *vocalis* (*littera*), vocal (letter), vowel < *vox,* VOICE] 1. a voiced speech sound characterized by generalized friction of the air passing in a continuous stream through the pharynx and opened mouth but with no constriction narrow enough to produce local friction; the sound of the greatest prominence in most syllables 2. a letter, as *a, e, i, o, u,* and sometimes *y,* representing such a sound Cf. CONSONANT —*adj.* of a vowel or vowels

vow·el·ize (vou′ə līz′) *vt.* -**ized′**, -**iz′ing** to add vowel points or signs to [to *vowelize* a Hebrew text] —**vow′el·i·za′tion** *n.*

vowel point in certain languages whose written form normally consists only of consonants, as Hebrew, a diacritical mark accompanying a consonant (to indicate the following vowel sound) or a neutral letter (to indicate an initial vowel sound)

†**vox** (väks) *n., pl.* **vo·ces** (vō′sēz) [L.] voice

vox an·ge·li·ca (an jel′i kə) [L., lit., angelic voice] *same as* VOIX CÉLESTE

vox hu·ma·na (hyōō mā′nə, -män′ə) [L., human voice] a reed organ stop with very short pipes in which only the higher harmonics are reinforced

†**vox po·pu·li** (päp′yoo li′) [L.] the voice of the people; public opinion or sentiment: abbrev. **vox pop.**

voy·age (voi′ij) *n.* [ME. *viage* < OFr. *veiage,* a voyage < L. *viaticum,* provision for a journey < *viaticus,* of a journey < *via,* way, journey: see VIA] 1. a relatively long journey or passage by water or, formerly, by land 2. a journey by aircraft or spacecraft 3. a written account of a voyage 4. [Obs.] a project; enterprise —*vi.* -**aged**, -**ag·ing** to make a voyage; travel —*vt.* to sail or travel over or on —*SYN.* see TRIP —**voy′ag·er** *n.*

†**vo·ya·geur** (vwä yá zhër′) *n., pl.* -**geurs′** (-zhër′) [Fr., a traveler] in Canada, 1. formerly, a person who transported goods and men by rivers and lakes to trading posts for the fur companies 2. any woodsman or boatman of the Canadian wilds

vo·yeur (vwä yur′, voi ur′) *n.* [Fr. < *voir,* to see < L. *videre:* see VISION] a person who has an exaggerated interest in viewing sexual objects or activities to obtain sexual gratification; peeping Tom —**vo·yeur′ism** *n.* —**vo′yeur·is′tic** *adj.*

V.P., VP Vice-President

V.R. [L. *Victoria Regina*] Queen Victoria

V.Rev. Very Reverend

Vries, Hugo De *see* DE VRIES

vroom (vrōōm) *n.* [echoic] any of the sounds made by a motor vehicle in accelerating —*vi.* [Colloq.] to make, or move off with, such sounds

vs. versus

V.S. Veterinary Surgeon

v.s. [L. *vide supra*] see above

V-shaped (vē′shāpt′) *adj.* shaped like the letter V

V.S.O. very superior (or special) old: of brandy

V.S.O.P. very superior (or special) old pale: of brandy

vss. versions

VT variable time

Vt. Vermont

vt., v.t. transitive verb

☆**VTOL** [*v(ertical) t(ake)o(ff* and) *l(anding)*] an aircraft, usually other than a helicopter, that can take off and land vertically

V-type engine (vē′tīp′) a gasoline engine in which the cylinders are set at an angle, or in two banks forming a V

VU volume unit

vug, vugg, vugh (vug, voog) *n.* [Corn. *vooga,* a cave] *Mining* a cavity or hollow in a rock or lode, often lined with crystals —**vug′gy** *adj.* -**gi·er,** -**gi·est**

Vuil·lard (vwē yàr′), **Jean É·douard** (zhän ā dwär′) 1868–1940; Fr. painter

Vul·can (vul′kən) [L. *Vulcanus, Volcanus*] *Rom. Myth.* the god of fire and of metalworking: later identified with the Greek god Hephaestus

Vul·ca·ni·an (vul kā′nē ən) *adj.* [L. *Vulcanius,* of Vulcan] 1. of, characteristic of, associated with, or made by, Vulcan 2. [v-] having to do with metalworking 3. [v-] *Geol.* *a) same as* VOLCANIC *b)* of or pertaining to a volcanic explosion emitting a large cloud of gases bearing fine ash and a mass of viscous lava that hardens in the air

vul·can·ism (vul′kə niz'm) *n. same as* VOLCANISM

vul·can·ite (-nīt′) *n.* [VULCAN + -ITE[1]] a hard rubber made by treating crude rubber with a large amount of sulfur and subjecting it to intense heat; ebonite: used in combs, electrical insulation, etc.

vul·can·i·za·tion (vul′kən i zā′shən) *n.* [< ff. + -ATION] 1. the process of treating crude rubber with sulfur or its compounds and subjecting it to heat in order to make it nonplastic and increase its strength and elasticity 2. a process somewhat like this, for hardening some substance

vul·can·ize (vul′kə nīz′) *vt.* -**ized′**, -**iz′ing** [VULCAN + -IZE] to subject to vulcanization —*vi.* to undergo vulcanization —**vul′can·iz′er** *n.*

vul·can·ol·o·gy (vul′kə näl′ə jē) *n. same as* VOLCANOLOGY —**vul′can·ol′o·gist** *n.*

Vulg. Vulgate

vulg. 1. vulgar 2. vulgarly

vul·gar (vul′gər) *adj.* [ME. < L. *vulgaris* < *vulgus, volgus,* the common people < IE. base *wel-,* to crowd, throng, whence Gr. *eilein,* to press, swarm] 1. of, characteristic of, belonging to, or common to the great mass of people in general; common; popular [a *vulgar* superstition] 2. designating, of, or in the popular, or vernacular, speech 3. *a)* characterized by a lack of culture, refinement, taste, restraint, sensitivity, etc.; coarse; crude; boorish *b)* indecent or obscene —*n.* 1. [Archaic] the common people (with *the*) 2. [Obs.] the vernacular —*SYN.* see COARSE, COMMON —**vul′gar·ly** *adv.*

vulgar fraction *same as* COMMON FRACTION

vul·gar·i·an (vul ger′ē ən, -gar′-) *n.* a vulgar person; esp., a rich person with coarse, ostentatious manners or tastes

vul·gar·ism (vul′gər iz'm) *n.* 1. a word, phrase, or expression that is used widely but is regarded as nonstandard, unrefined, coarse, or obscene 2. vulgar behavior, quality, etc.; vulgarity

vul·gar·i·ty (vul gar′ə tē) *n.* [LL. *vulgaritas*] 1. the state or quality of being vulgar, crude, coarse, unrefined, etc. 2. *pl.* -**ties** a vulgar act, habit, usage in speech, etc.

vul·gar·i·za·tion (vul′gə ri zā′shən) *n.* 1. the act or an instance of making something, as abstruse or highly technical information, more readily intelligible or widely known 2. the act or an instance of making vulgar, coarse, unrefined, obscene, etc.

vul·gar·ize (vul′gə rīz′) *vt.* -**ized′**, -**iz′ing** 1. to cause to be more widely known, more easily understood, etc.; popularize 2. to make vulgar, coarse, unrefined, obscene, etc. —**vul′gar·iz′er** *n.*

Vulgar Latin the everyday speech of the Roman people, from which the Romance languages developed; popular Latin as distinguished from standard or literary Latin

Vul·gate (vul′gāt, -git) *n.* [ML. *vulgata (editio)*, popular (edition) < L. *vulgatus,* common, usual, orig. pp. of *vulgare,* to make common < *vulgus:* see VULGAR] 1. a Latin version of the Bible prepared by St. Jerome in the 4th cent., serving as an authorized version of the Roman Catholic Church 2. [v-] *a)* any text or version in common acceptance *b)* the vernacular, or common speech —*adj.* 1. of or in the Vulgate 2. [v-] commonly accepted; popular; specif., of or in the vernacular, or common speech

vul·ner·a·ble (vul′nər ə b'l) *adj.* [LL. *vulnerabilis,* wounding, likely to injure (also, in pass. sense, vulnerable) < L. *vulnerare,* to wound < *vulnus* (gen. *vulneris*), a wound < IE. base *wel-,* to tear, wound, whence OE. *wæl,* carnage: cf. VALKYRIE] 1. that can be wounded or physically injured 2. *a)* open to criticism or attack [a *vulnerable* reputation] *b)* easily hurt, as by adverse criticism; sensitive *c)* affected by a specified influence, temptation, etc. [*vulnerable* to political pressure] 3. open to attack by armed forces 4. *Bridge* liable to increased penalties and entitled to increased bonuses: said of a team which has won one game —**vul′ner·a·bil′i·ty** *n.* —**vul′ner·a·bly** *adv.*

vul·ner·ar·y (vul′nə rer′ē) *adj.* [L. *vulnerarius* < *vulnus,* a wound: see prec.] used for healing wounds —*n., pl.* -**ar′ies** any vulnerary drug, plant, etc.

vul·pine (vul′pīn, -pin) *adj.* [L. *vulpinus*, foxlike < *vulpes*, a fox] 1. of or like a fox or foxes 2. clever, cunning, etc.

vul·ture (vul′chər) *n.* [ME. *vultur* < L., akin to *vellere*, to tear: for IE. base see VULNERABLE] 1. any of a number of large birds (family Accipitridae) related to the eagles and hawks, with a naked, usually brightly colored head and dark plumage: vultures feed chiefly or entirely on carrion and are found in tropical and temperate regions ☆2. same as TURKEY BUZZARD 3. any greedy and ruthless person who preys on others

vul·tur·ine (-chər īn′, -in) *adj.* [L. *vulturinus* < *vultur*: see prec.] 1. of the vulture family 2. of, characteristic of, or like a vulture or vultures; voracious

VULTURE
(to 32 in. long;
wingspread to 6 ft.)

vul·tur·ous (-əs) *adj.* like a vulture; voracious; greedy

vul·va (vul′və) *n., pl.* **-vae** (-vē), **-vas** [ModL. < L. *vulva*, *volva*, wrapper, covering, womb < *volvere*, to roll or turn about: see WALK] the external genital organs of the female, including the labia majora, labia minora, clitoris, and the entrance to the vagina —**vul′val, vul′var** *adj.*, —**vul′vate** (-vāt, -vit) *adj.*

vul·vi·form (-və fôrm′) *adj.* like a vulva in form or appearance

vul·vi·tis (vul vīt′əs) *n.* inflammation of the vulva

vul·vo- (vul′vō, -və) [< L. *vulva*] *a combining form meaning:* 1. vulva 2. vulva and Also, before a vowel, **vulv-**

vul·vo·vag·i·ni·tis (vul′vō vaj′ə nīt′əs) *n.* [< prec. + VAGINITIS] inflammation of the vulva and the vagina

vv. 1. verses 2. violins

v.v. vice versa

V.W. Very Worshipful

Vy·borg (vē′bôrg) seaport in NW R.S.F.S.R., on the Gulf of Finland: pop. 51,000

vy·ing (vī′iŋ) *adj.* [prp. of VIE] that vies; that competes

W

W, w (dub′l yōō, -yə) *n., pl.* **W's, w's** 1. the twenty-third letter of the English alphabet: its sound was represented in Anglo-Saxon manuscripts by *uu* or *u* until about 900 A.D., then by þ (*wen*) borrowed from the runic alphabet; in the 11th cent. a ligatured *VV* or *vv* was introduced by Norman scribes to replace the *wen* 2. the sound of *W* or *w*: in English, it is a lip-rounded tongue-back semivowel or continuant before a vowel or a *u* glide concluding a diphthong; before *r*, as in *wrist*, and in some words, as *answer*, *sword*, *two*, it is silent 3. a type or impression for *W* or *w* 4. a symbol for the twenty-third in a sequence or group (or the twenty-second if J is omitted) —*adj.* 1. of *W* or *w* 2. twenty-third (or twenty-second if J is omitted) in a sequence or group

W *Chem.* tungsten

W, w watt, watts

W', W., -, w, w. 1. west 2. western

W. 1. Wales 2. Washington 3. Wednesday 4. Welsh

W., w. 1. warden 2. warehouse 3. watt(s) 4. weight 5. width 6. won 7. *Physics* work

w. 1. week(s) 2. wide 3. wife 4. with

wa' (wô, wä) *n. Scot. clipped form of* WALL

W.A. Western Australia

WAAC 1. Women's Auxiliary Army Corps 2. (British) Women's Army Auxiliary Corps

Waadt (vät) *Ger. name of* VAUD

WAAF (British) Women's Auxiliary Air Force

Waal (wäl) southernmost of two arms of the Rhine, flowing west through the Netherlands & joining the Meuse in the Rhine delta on the North Sea: c.50 mi.

Waals, Johannes Diderik van der *see* VAN DER WAALS

Wa·bash (wô′bash) [< Algonquian (cf. Fr. *Ouabachi, Ouabash*), stream and tribal name < ?] river flowing from W Ohio across Ind. into the Ohio River: 475 mi.

wab·ble (wäb′'l) *n., vt., vi.* **-bled, -bling** *var. of* WOBBLE

☆**Wac** (wak) *n.* a member of the Women's Army Corps

WAC Women's Army Corps

Wace (wās, wäs) 12th cent.; Anglo-Norman poet & chronicler: also, prob. erroneously, called **Robert Wace**

wack·e (wak′ə) *n.* [G. < OHG. *wacko*, earlier *waggo*, gravel, stone] old name for any of several rocks

wack·y (wak′ē) *adj.* **wack′i·er, wack′i·est** [< ? WHACK + -Y²: cf. SLAP-HAPPY] [Slang] ☆erratic, eccentric, or irrational —**wack′i·ly** *adv.* —**wack′i·ness** *n.*

Wa·co (wā′kō) [< AmInd. tribal name < ?] city in EC Tex., on the Brazos River: pop. 95,000

wad[1] (wäd, wôd) *n.* [ML. *wadda*, wadding < ?] 1. a small, soft mass or ball, as a handful of cotton, crumpled paper, etc. 2. a lump or small, compact mass (*of something*) [a *wad* of chewing tobacco] 3. a mass of soft or fibrous material used for padding, packing, stuffing, etc. 4. a plug of hemp, tow, paper, etc. stuffed against a charge to keep it firmly in the breech of a muzzleloading gun or in a cartridge ☆5. [Colloq.] a roll of paper money ☆6. [Slang] a large amount, esp. of money —*vt.* **wad′ded, wad′ding** 1. to compress into a wad ☆2. to roll up (paper, etc.) into a wad 3. *a)* to plug with a wad *b)* to force or stuff [to *wad* oakum into a crack] 4. to line or pad with or as with wadding 5. to hold (a charge) in place by a wad —**wad′der** *n.*

wad[2] (wäd; *unstressed* wəd) *v. Scot. var. of* WOULD

Wad·den·zee, Wad·den Zee (väd′ən zā′) shallow section of the North Sea, between the North Frisian Islands & the Netherlands mainland

wad·ding (wäd′iŋ, wôd′-) *n.* 1. any soft or fibrous material for use in padding, packing, stuffing, etc.; esp., cotton made up into loose, fluffy sheets, or batting 2. any soft material for making wads, as for guns or cartridges 3. a wad, or wads collectively

wad·dle (wäd′'l, wôd′-) *vi.* **-dled, -dling** [freq. of WADE] 1. to walk with short steps, swaying from side to side, as a duck 2. to move clumsily with a motion like this; toddle, as a baby —*n.* 1. the act of waddling 2. a waddling gait —**wad′dler** *n.*

wad·dy[1] (wäd′ē) *n., pl.* **-dies** [< the native name] in Australia, a short, thick club used by aborigines as a weapon —*vt.* **-died, -dy·ing** to strike or beat with a waddy

☆**wad·dy**[2] (wäd′ē) *n., pl.* **-dies** [< ?] [Western] a cowboy

wade (wād) *vi.* **wad′ed, wad′ing** [ME. *waden* < OE. *waden*, to go, akin to G. *waten*, to wade < IE. base *wādh-*, to go, stride forward, whence L. *vadere*, to go, *vadare*, to wade] 1. to walk through any substance, as water, mud, snow, sand, tall grass, etc., that offers resistance 2. to walk about in shallow water, as for amusement 3. to go forward with effort or difficulty [to *wade* through a long report] ☆4. [Colloq.] to move energetically into action; attack with vigor (*with in* or *into*) 5. [Obs.] to go; proceed; pass —*vt.* to go across or through by wading [to *wade* a brook] —*n.* an act of wading

wad·er (wād′ər) *n.* 1. a person or thing that wades 2. *same as* WADING BIRD 3. *a)* [*pl.*] high waterproof boots ☆*b)* [*usually pl.*] waterproof trousers with bootlike parts for the feet, worn by fishermen, etc. for wading in deep water

wa·di (wä′dē) *n., pl.* **-dis, -dies** [Ar. *wādī*, channel of a river, a river, ravine, valley] in Arabia, N Africa, etc., 1. a valley, ravine, or watercourse that is dry except during the rainy season 2. the stream or rush of water that flows through it Also sp. **wa′dy** *pl.* **-dies**

wading bird any of various unrelated long-legged shore birds that wade the shallows and marshes for food, as the crane, heron, rail, coot, sandpiper, and snipe

wad·na (wäd′nə) [Scot.] would not

wae (wā) *n.* [Scot.] woe or sorrow

wae·sucks (wā′suks′) *interj.* [Scot. *wae*, woe + *sucks*, sakes: see SAKE¹] [Scot.] alas!

☆**Waf** (waf) *n.* a member of the WAF

WAF Women in the Air Force

wa·fer (wā′fər) *n.* [ME. *wafre* < ONormFr. *waufre* < MDu. *wafel*, a wafer, WAFFLE¹] 1. *a)* a thin, flat, crisp cracker or cookie *b)* anything resembling this, as a thin, flat disk of candy 2. a thin cake of unleavened bread used in the Eucharist 3. a small adhesive disk, as of paper, dried paste, gelatin, etc., used as a seal on letters, documents, etc. —*vt.* [Archaic] to seal, close, or attach, or fasten with a wafer or wafers

waff[1] (waf, wäf) *n.* [var. of WAVE] [Scot. & N. Eng. Dial.] 1. a wave, or waving motion, as in signaling 2. a puff or gust, as of air 3. a glimpse 4. a ghost

waff[2] (waf, wäf) *adj.* [var. of WAIF] [Scot.] worthless

☆**waf·fle**[1] (wäf′'l, wôf′-) *n.* [Du. *wafel*, akin to OHG. *waba*, honeycomb, OE. *wefan*, to WEAVE] a batter cake like a pancake but crisper, baked in a waffle iron —*adj.* having a gridlike surface resembling a waffle: also **waf′fled**

waf·fle[2] (wäf′'l, wôf′-) *vi.* -**fled**, -**fling** [orig., to yelp < echoic *waff*, to yelp] [Chiefly Brit. Colloq.] to speak or write in a wordy, vague, or indecisive manner —*n.* [Chiefly Brit. Colloq.] wordy, vague, or indecisive talk or writing

☆**waffle iron** [transl. of Du. *wafelijzer*] a utensil for cooking waffles, having two flat, studded plates, now usually of aluminum and heated electrically, pressed together so that the waffle bakes between them

waft (waft, wäft) *vt.* [back-formation < obs. *wafter*, a convoy < LME. *waughter* < Du. *wachter*, lit., a watcher < *wachten*, to watch: for IE. base see WAKE[1]] **1.** *a)* to carry or propel (objects, sounds, odors, etc.) lightly through the air or over water *b)* to transport as if in this manner **2.** [altered < WAFF[1]] [Obs.] to beckon or signal to, as by a wave of the hand —*vi.* **1.** to float, as on the wind **2.** to blow gently: said of breezes —*n.* **1.** the act or fact of floating or being carried lightly along **2.** an odor, sound, etc. carried through the air **3.** a breath or gust of wind **4.** a wave, waving, or wafting movement **5.** *Naut.* [Now Rare] a signal flag or pennant, or a signal made by a flag or pennant, usually rolled or furled

waft·age (waf′tij, wäf′-) *n.* [Archaic] a wafting or being wafted; conveyance by wafting

waft·er (-tər) *n.* a person or thing that wafts; esp., a revolving fan in a blower

waf·ture (waf′chər, wäf′-) *n.* **1.** the act of waving or wafting **2.** something wafted, as by a breeze

wag[1] (wag) *vt.* **wagged**, **wag′ging** [ME. *waggen*, prob. < ON. *vaga*, to move back and forth, rock, akin to OE. *wagian*, to shake, totter < IE. base *weĝh-*, to move, whence L. *vehere*, to carry] **1.** *a)* to cause (something fastened or held at one end) to move rapidly and repeatedly back and forth, from side to side, or up and down [the dog *wagged* his tail] *b)* to shake (a finger) or nod (the head), as in summoning, reproving, etc. **2.** to move (the tongue) in talking, esp. in idle or malicious gossip —*vi.* **1.** to move rapidly and repeatedly back and forth, from side to side, or up and down, as a part of the body **2.** to keep moving in talk, esp. in idle or malicious gossip: said of the tongue **3.** to walk or move with a swaying motion; waddle —*n.* the act or an instance of wagging —**wag′ger** *n.*

wag[2] (wag) *n.* [prob. a shortening of obs. *waghalter*, a gallows bird, applied to a joker, rogue] a comical or humorous person; joker; wit

wage (wāj) *vt.* **waged**, **wag′ing** [ME. *wagen* < ONormFr. *wagier* (OFr. *gagier*) < *wage* (OFr. *gage*), a stake, pledge < Frank. *wadi*, akin to Goth. *wadi*, a pledge: for IE. base see WED] **1.** to engage in or carry on (a war, struggle, campaign, etc.) **2.** [Chiefly Brit. Dial.] to hire **3.** [Obs.] *a)* to pledge *b)* to wager; bet *c)* to pay —*vi.* [Obs.] to struggle or contend —*n.* **1.** [often *pl.*] money paid to an employee for work done, and usually figured on an hourly, daily, or piecework basis **2.** [usually *pl.*] what is given in return; recompense; requital: formerly the plural form was often construed as singular ["The *wages* of sin is death"] **3.** [pl.] *Econ.* the share of the total product of industry that goes to labor, as distinguished from the share taken by capital

SYN.—**wage** (also often **wages**) applies to money paid an employee at relatively short intervals, often daily, or weekly, esp. for manual or physical labor; **salary** applies to fixed compensation usually paid at longer intervals, often monthly or semimonthly, esp. to clerical or professional workers; **stipend** is a somewhat lofty substitute for **salary**, or it is applied to a pension or similar fixed payment; **fee** applies to the payment requested or given for professional services, as of a doctor, lawyer, artist, etc.; **pay** is a general term equivalent to any of the preceding, but it is specifically used of compensation to members of the armed forces; **emolument** is an elevated, now somewhat jocular, substitute for **salary** or **wages**

wage earner a person who works for wages

wa·ger (wā′jər) *n.* [ME. < ONormFr. *wageure* < *wagier*: see WAGE] **1.** same as BET[1] (*n.* 1, 2) **2.** formerly, a pledge to do something or abide by an outcome: esp. in **wager of battle**, a challenge by a defendant to prove his innocence by personal combat —*vt.*, *vi.* same as BET[1] —**wag′er·er** *n.*

wage scale 1. a schedule of wages paid for the performance of related jobs or tasks in a given industry, plant, locality, etc. **2.** the schedule of wages paid by a given employer

☆**wage·work·er** (wāj′wur′kər) *n.* one who works for wages

wag·ger·y (wag′ər ē) *n.*, *pl.* -**ger·ies** [< WAG[2] + -ERY] **1.** the action, spirit, or manner of a wag; roguish jocularity or merriment **2.** a joke or jest; esp., a practical joke

wag·gish (-ish) *adj.* [< WAG[2] + -ISH] **1.** like, characteristic of, or befitting a wag; roguishly merry **2.** done, said, or made in jest; playful [a *waggish* remark] —**wag′gish·ly** *adv.*

wag·gle (wag′'l) *vt.* -**gled**, -**gling** [freq. of WAG[1]] to wag, esp. with short, quick movements —*vi.* to move in a shaky or wobbly manner; totter —*n.* the act or an instance of waggling —**wag′gly** *adj.*

wag·gon (wag′ən) *n.*, *vt.* Brit. var. of WAGON

Wag·ner (väg′nər), (Wilhelm) **Rich·ard** (riH′ärt) 1813–83; Ger. composer

Wag·ne·ri·an (väg nir′ē ən) *adj.* **1.** of or like Richard Wagner or his music, theories, methods, etc.: cf. MUSIC DRAMA **2.** designating or of an operatic singer specializing in Wagner's operas [a *Wagnerian* soprano] —*n.* an admirer or follower of Wagner's music, theories, etc.

wag·on (wag′ən) *n.* [Du. *wagen*, akin to WAIN] **1.** any of various types of four-wheeled vehicles; specif., *a)* a horse-drawn vehicle for hauling heavy loads *b)* a small cart pulled or steered by means of a pole handle and used by children in play ☆**2.** *short for:* *a)* PATROL WAGON *b)* STATION WAGON **3.** [Brit.] a railroad freight car **4.** [Obs.] a chariot —[**W**-] same as CHARLES'S WAIN —*vt.*, *vi.* to carry or transport (goods) by wagon; move or go in a wagon —☆**fix someone's wagon** [Slang] to hurt someone in some way so as to get even with him —**hitch one's wagon to a star** to set oneself an ambitious goal —☆**on** (or **off**) **the wagon** [Slang] no longer (or once again) drinking alcoholic liquors: also **on** (or **off**) **the water wagon**

wag·on·age (-ij) *n.* **1.** *a)* transport by wagon ☆*b)* money paid for this **2.** a collection of wagons

wag·on·er (-ər) *n.* **1.** a person who drives a wagon **2.** [Obs.] a charioteer —[**W**-] same as AURIGA

wag·on·ette (wag′ə net′) *n.* [dim. of WAGON] a light, open, four-wheeled carriage with two seats set lengthwise facing each other behind the driver's seat

‡**wag·on-lit** (vȧ gōn lē′) *n.*, *pl.* **wag·ons-lits′** (-gōn lē′) [Fr.: *wagon*, a car, railway coach (< E. WAGON) + *lit*, a bed] in Europe, a railroad sleeping car

wag·on·load (wag′ən lōd′) *n.* the load that a wagon carries or will carry

wagon train a line or convoy of wagons traveling together, as one carrying military supplies, or one in which pioneers crossed the Western plains

Wa·gram (vä′gräm) town in NE Austria, near Vienna: site (1809) of a Napoleonic victory over the Austrians

wag·tail (wag′tāl′) *n.* **1.** any of numerous small birds (family Motacillidae) related to the pipits, mostly native to Europe, characterized by long wing feathers and a very long tail that wags up and down ☆**2.** any of various similar birds, as an American water thrush

Wah·ha·bi, Wa·ha·bi (wä hä′bē) *n.* [Ar. *wahhābī*] any member of a strict Moslem sect which adheres closely to the Koran: it was founded by Abdul-Wahhab (1703?–92?) and flourishes in Saudi Arabia —**Wah·ha′bism, Wa·ha′bism** (-biz′m) *n.* —**Wah·ha′bite** (-bīt) *n.*, *adj.*

☆**wa·hi·ne** (wä hē′nä) *n.* [Maori & Haw.] a Polynesian woman, esp. of Hawaii

☆**wa·hoo**[1] (wä′hōō, wä hōō′) *n.* [< AmInd. (Dakota) *wanhu*, lit., arrowwood] same as: **1.** BURNING BUSH (sense 1) **2.** STRAWBERRY BUSH

☆**wa·hoo**[2] (wä′hōō, wä hōō′) *n.* [< AmInd. (Creek) *úhawhu*, cork elm] **1.** a small elm (*Ulmus alata*) of the S U.S., with spreading branches having winglike, corky ridges **2.** any of various other N. American trees or shrubs, as the cascara

☆**wa·hoo**[3] (wä′hōō, wä hōō′) *n.*, *pl.* -**hoo**, -**hoos**: see PLURAL, II, D, 2 [< ?] a large game and food fish (*Acanthocybium solanderi*), related to the mackerels and found in warm seas

☆**wa·hoo**[4] (wä hōō′, wä′hōō) *interj.* [Western] a shout expressing unrestrained enthusiasm, exhilaration, etc.

waif (wāf) *n.* [ME. < ONormFr., prob. < ON. *veif*, anything flapping about < *veifa*, to wave, swing < IE. base *weip-*, to turn, var. of *weib-*, whence L. *vibrare*, to VIBRATE] **1.** anything found by chance that is without an owner **2.** a person without home or friends; esp., a homeless child **3.** a stray animal **4.** same as WAFT (*n.* 5) **5.** *Law* *a)* a piece of property found but claimed by nobody *b)* [pl.] [Obs.] goods stolen and discarded by the thief in his flight

Wai·ki·ki (wī′kē kē′, wī′kē kē′) [Haw., lit., spurting water] famous bathing beach in Honolulu, Hawaii

wail (wāl) *vi.* [ME. *wailen* < ON. *væla*, to lament < *væ*, WOE] **1.** to express grief or pain by long, loud cries **2.** to make a plaintive, sad, crying sound [the wind *wailing* in the trees] **3.** *Jazz* [Slang] to play in an intense or inspired manner —*vt.* [Archaic] **1.** to lament; mourn [to *wail* someone's death] **2.** to cry out in mourning or lamentation —*n.* **1.** a long, pitiful cry of grief and pain **2.** a sound like this **3.** the act of wailing —**SYN.** see CRY —**wail′er** *n.*

wail·ful (-fəl) *adj.* **1.** wailing; sorrowful **2.** like, or giving forth, a wail or cry of sorrow —**wail′ful·ly** *adv.*

Wailing Wall same as WESTERN WALL

wain (wān) *n.* [ME. < OE. *wægn*, wheeled vehicle, akin to Du. & G. *wagen* (cf. WAGON) < IE. *woĝhno-* < base *weĝh-*, to move, whence L. *vehere*, to carry: cf. WEIGH[1]] [Archaic exc. Dial.] a wagon or cart —**the Wain** same as CHARLES'S WAIN

wain·scot (wān′skət, -skät′) *n.* [ME. *waynescote* < MDu. *wagenschot*, wainscot, prob. < *wagen*, a carriage (see WAIN) + *schot*, an enclosure or partition of boards < ?] **1.** a wood lining or paneling on the walls of a room; sometimes, specif., such a paneling on the lower part of the walls only **2.** *a)* the lower part of the walls of a room when having a finish different from the upper *b)* any applied finish, as tile, linoleum, etc., on a wall **3.** [Brit.] a fine imported oak used for interior paneling —*vt.* -**scot·ed** or -**scot·ted**, -**scot·ing** or -**scot·ting** to line (a wall, etc.) with wainscoting

wain·scot·ing, wain·scot·ting (-in) *n.* **1.** same as WAINSCOT (*n.* 1, 2) **2.** material used to wainscot

wain·wright (wān′rīt′) *n.* [WAIN + WRIGHT] a person who builds or repairs wagons

waist (wāst) *n.* [ME. *wast* < base of OE. *weaxan*, to grow, WAX[2]: sense development: growth (of body), hence size,

thickness] **1.** the part of the body between the ribs and the hips **2.** *a)* the part of a garment that covers the waist *b)* same as WAISTLINE (sense 2 *a)* *c)* the part of a garment covering the body from the shoulders to a line above the hips *d)* the upper part of a woman's dress; bodice *e)* same as BLOUSE ☆*f)* a child's undershirt to which other undergarments may be fastened **3.** the narrow part of any object that is wider at the ends [the *waist* of a violin] ☆**4.** *Aeron.* the middle section of the fuselage of an airplane, esp. a bomber **5.** *Naut.* the central section of a ship; specif., the part of the deck between the forecastle and the quarterdeck **6.** *Zool.* the narrow part of the front of the abdomen of certain insects, as ants, wasps, etc.

waist·band (wāst′band′) *n.* a band encircling the waist, esp. one at the top of a skirt, trousers, etc.

waist·cloth (-klôth′) *n.* same as LOINCLOTH

waist·coat (wes′kət, wāst′kōt′) *n.* **1.** [Brit.] same as VEST (*n.* 1) *b)* a similar garment worn by women **2.** a somewhat longer, heavily ornamented sleeveless jacket formerly worn under a doublet —**waist′coat·ed** *adj.*

waist-high (wāst′hī′) *adj.* reaching up to the waist

waist·line (-līn′) *n.* **1.** the line of the waist, between the ribs and the hips **2.** *a)* the narrow part of a woman's dress, etc., worn at the waist or above or below it as styles change *b)* the line where the waist and skirt of a dress join **3.** the distance around the waist

wait (wāt) *vi.* [ME. *waiten* < ONormFr. *waitier* < Frank. *wahten*, to guard, akin to OHG. *wahta*, a guard, watch: for IE. base see WAKE¹] **1.** to stay in a place or remain in readiness or in anticipation (*until* something expected happens or *for* someone to arrive or catch up) **2.** to be ready or at hand [dinner was *waiting* for them] **3.** to remain temporarily undone or neglected [let that job *wait*] **4.** to serve food at a meal (with *at* or *on*) [to *wait* at table, to *wait* on a person] —*vt.* **1.** to be, remain, or delay in expectation or anticipation of; await [to *wait* orders, to *wait* one's turn] **2.** [Colloq.] to delay serving (a meal) as in waiting for someone [to *wait* dinner] **3.** [Obs.] to attend upon or escort, esp. as a token of respect or honor **4.** [Obs.] to attend as a consequence —*n.* **1.** the act or fact of waiting **2.** a period of waiting [a four-hour *wait*] **3.** in England, any of a group of singers and musicians who go through the streets at Christmas time performing carols for small gifts of money **4.** [Obs.] a member of a band of musicians formerly employed by a city or town in England to play at entertainments **5.** [Obs.] a watchman —*SYN.* see STAY³ —**lie in wait** (**for**) to wait so as to catch after planning an ambush or trap (*for*) —**wait on** (or **upon**) **1.** to act as a servant to **2.** to call on or visit (esp. a superior) in order to pay one's respects, ask a favor, etc. **3.** to result from; be a consequence of **4.** to supply the needs or requirements of (a person at table, a customer in a store, etc.), as a waiter, clerk, etc. **5.** [Dial. or Colloq.] to wait for; await —**wait out** to remain inactive during the course of —**wait table** to serve food as a waiter or servant to people at a table —**wait up 1.** to put off going to bed until someone expected arrives or something expected happens **2.** [Colloq.] to stop and wait for someone to catch up

wait-a-bit (wāt′ə bit′) *n.* [transl. of Afrik. *wacht-en-beetje:* so named for their clinging thorns] any of a number of plants having sharp or hooked thorns

Waite (wāt), **Mor·ri·son Rem·ick** (môr′i s'n rem′ik) 1816-88; U.S. jurist; chief justice (1874-88)

wait·er (wāt′ər) *n.* [ME. *waitere*, watchman] **1.** a person who waits or awaits **2.** a man who waits on table, as in a restaurant **3.** a tray for carrying dishes; salver

wait·ing (-iṅ) *adj.* **1.** that waits **2.** of or for a wait **3.** that serves or is in attendance —*n.* **1.** the act of one that waits **2.** a period of waiting —**in waiting** in attendance, as on a king or other person of royalty

waiting game a scheme by means of which one outwits or wins out over another by delaying or postponing action until one has an advantage

waiting list a list of applicants, as for a vacancy or an item in short supply, in the order of their application

waiting room a room in which people wait, as in a railroad station, a dentist's office, etc.

wait·ress (wā′tris) *n.* a woman or girl who waits on table, as in a restaurant

waive (wāv) *vt.* **waived, waiv′ing** [ME. *weiven* < Anglo-Fr. *waiver*, to renounce, abandon < ON. *veifa*, to fluctuate: see WAIF] **1.** to give up or forgo (a right, claim, privilege, etc.) **2.** to refrain from insisting on or taking advantage of **3.** to put off until later; postpone; defer **4.** *Law* to forgo or relinquish voluntarily (a right, privilege, claim, etc. which one is legally entitled to enforce) **5.** [Obs.] to leave, reject, or abandon —*SYN.* see RELINQUISH

waiv·er (wā′vər) *n.* [substantive use of Anglo-Fr. *weyver*, to waive: see prec.] *Law* **1.** the act or an instance of waiv-

ing, or relinquishing voluntarily, a right, claim, privilege, etc. **2.** a formal written statement of such relinquishment

Wa·ka·ya·ma (wä′kä yä′mä) seaport on the S coast of Honshu, Japan: pop. 329,000

wake¹ (wāk) *vi.* **woke** or **waked, waked** or **wok′en** or, occas. Brit., **woke, wak′ing** [ME. *wakien* < OE. *wacian*, to be awake & *wacan*, to arise, akin to G. *wachen* < IE. base *weĝ-*, to be active, whence L. *vegere*, to arouse, be active, Sans. *vāja-*, strength, speed] **1.** to come out of sleep or a state like or suggestive of sleep, as a stupor, trance, etc.; awake (often with *up*) **2.** to be or stay awake **3.** to become active or animated after inactivity or dormancy (often with *up*) **4.** to become alert (*to* a realization, possibility, etc.) **5.** [Chiefly Dial.] *pt.* & *pp.* **waked** to keep watch or vigil; esp., to hold a wake over a corpse —*vt.* **1.** to cause to wake from or as from sleep: often with *up* **2.** to arouse, excite, or stir up (passions, etc.) or evoke (a sound, echo, etc.) **3.** [Chiefly Dial.] *pt.* & *pp.* **waked** to keep watch or vigil over; esp., to hold a wake over (a corpse) —*n.* **1.** [Now Rare] the state of being awake **2.** an all-night vigil over a corpse before burial, formerly often with festivities **3.** *Anglican Ch.* an annual parish festival, orig. held in honor of the dedication of a parish church

wake² (wāk) *n.* [< ON. *vök*, a hole, opening in the ice: for IE. base see HUMOR] **1.** the track or trail left in the water by a moving ship or boat **2.** the track or course of anything that has gone before or passed by —**in the wake of 1.** following directly or close behind **2.** following as a consequence

Wake·field (wāk′fēld′) city in NC England, in West Riding, Yorkshire: pop. 60,000

wake·ful (wāk′fəl) *adj.* **1.** keeping awake; not sleeping **2.** alert; watchful; vigilant **3.** *a)* unable to sleep *b)* sleepless [a *wakeful* night] —**wake′ful·ly** *adv.* —**wake′ful·ness** *n.*

Wake Island (wāk) coral atoll in the N Pacific between Midway & Guam: a U.S. possession: 3 sq. mi.; pop. 1,000

wake·less (-lis) *adj.* unbroken; deep: said of sleep

wak·en (wāk′'n) *vi.* [ME. *waknen* < OE. *wacnian, wæcnan*, to become awake, akin to ON. *vakna*, to waken: for IE. base see WAKE¹] **1.** to become awake; come to one's senses after sleep or a state like sleep **2.** to become active, animated, or alive after inactivity or dormancy —*vt.* **1.** to cause to wake; awake **2.** to urge or stir into action or activity; arouse; excite —*SYN.* see STIR¹ —**wak′en·er** *n.*

wake·rife (wāk′rīf′) *adj.* [LME. (Scot.) *walkryfe* < ME. *waken*, to WAKE¹ + *ryfe*, RIFE] [Scot. & N. Eng. Dial.] same as WAKEFUL

wake-rob·in (wāk′räb′in) *n.* ☆**1.** same as TRILLIUM **2.** [Brit.] any of several arums; esp., same as CUCKOOPINT

☆**wake-up** (-up′) *n.* [echoic] *colloq.* name for FLICKER²

Waks·man (waks′mən), **Sel·man** A(braham) (sel′mən) 1888- ; U.S. microbiologist, born in Russia

Wal. 1. Walachian: also **Walach. 2.** Walloon

Wa·la·chi·a (wä lā′kē ə) region in E Europe, south of the Transylvanian Alps: merged with Moldavia (1861) to form Romania

Wa·la·chi·an (-ən) *adj.* of Walachia, its people, or their language —*n.* **1.** a native or inhabitant of Walachia **2.** the Romanian dialect of the Walachians

Wał·brzych (väl′bzhikh) city in SW Poland, near Wrocław: pop. 125,000

Wal·de·mar (väl′də mär′) 1131-82; king of Denmark (1157-82): called *the Great*

Wal·den Pond (wôl′dən) [prob. after Saffron *Walden*, town in Essex, England + POND] pond in E Mass.: site of Thoreau's cabin (1845-47)

WALACHIA

Wal·den·ses (wäl den′sēz) *n.pl.* [ME. *waldensis* < ML. *waldenses*, after Peter *Waldo*, 12th-c. Fr. merchant and founder of the sect] a sect of dissenters from the Roman Catholic Church which arose about 1170 in S France: excommunicated in 1184, they survive in the Alps of France and Italy —**Wal·den′si·an** *adj., n.*

Wal·do (wôl′dō, wäl′-) [Frank. or OHG. < *waldan*, to rule; also G., contr. for names beginning with *Walde-* (e.g., *Waldemar*), of same origin] a masculine name

☆**Wal·dorf salad** (wôl′dôrf) [after the old *Waldorf*-Astoria Hotel in New York City] a salad made of diced raw apples, celery, and walnuts, with mayonnaise

wale¹ (wāl) *n.* [ME. < OE. *walu*, a weal < IE. *wolos*, round < base *wel-*, to turn, roll, whence WALK] **1.** a raised line or streak made on the skin by the slash of a stick or whip; welt; weal **2.** *a)* a ridge on the surface of cloth, as corduroy *b)* texture of cloth **3.** a band or ridge woven around the body of a basket to brace it **4.** *Naut.* any of several strakes or heavy planks fastened to the outside of the hull of a wooden ship: *usually used in pl.*

—vt. waled, wal′ing 1. to mark (the skin) with wales **2.** to make (cloth) or weave (wickerwork) with wales
wale² (wāl) *n.* [ME. *wal* < ON. *val*, akin to G. *wahl*, choice, a choosing: for IE. base see WILL²] [Scot. & N. Eng. Dial.] **1.** choice; selection **2.** that chosen as best **—vt. waled, wal′ing** [Scot. & N. Eng. Dial.] to choose; pick out; select
Wal·er (wā′lər) *n.* [Anglo-Ind.: < (NEW SOUTH WALES) [Colloq.] an Australian range horse, bred chiefly in New South Wales, of a kind formerly exported to India for use as cavalry horses or polo ponies
Wales (wālz) division of the United Kingdom, occupying a peninsula of WC Great Britain: incl. Monmouthshire, 8,016 sq. mi.; pop. 2,662,000; chief city, Cardiff
Wa·ley (wā′lē), **Arthur** (born *Arthur David Schloss*) 1889–1966; Eng. translator of Chin. & Jap. literature
Wal·hal·la (väl häl′ə, wal hal′ə) *n. var. of* VALHALLA
walk (wôk) *vi.* [ME. *walken* < OE. *wealcan*, to roll, journey, akin to G. *walken*, to full (cloth), cudgel < IE. **wolg-* < base **wel-*, to turn, roll, whence L. *volvere*, to roll, Gr. *eilyein*, to roll up, wrap] **1.** to go along or move about on foot at a moderate pace; specif., *a)* to move by placing one foot firmly on the ground before lifting the other, as two-legged creatures do, or by placing two feet firmly on the ground before lifting either of the others, as four-legged creatures do *b)* to go about on foot for exercise or pleasure; hike **2.** to return after death and appear on earth as a ghost **3.** to advance or move in a manner suggestive of walking: said of inanimate objects **4.** *a)* to follow a certain course of life; conduct oneself in a certain way *[let us walk in peace]* *b)* to join with others in a cooperative action, a cause, etc. **5.** [Obs.] to be active or in motion, or to keep moving ☆**6.** *Baseball* to be advanced to first base as a result of being pitched four balls ☆**7.** *Basketball same as* TRAVEL **—vt. 1.** to go through, over, or along at a moderate pace on foot *[to walk the deck, the streets, etc.]* **2.** to traverse (a boundary, fence, etc.) on foot in order to survey, inspect, or repair **3.** *a)* to cause (a horse, dog, etc.) to move at a walk; lead, ride, or drive at a walk *b)* to train and exercise (a horse, dog, etc.) in this way **4.** to push (a bicycle, motorcycle, etc.) while walking alongside **5.** to accompany (a person) on a walk or stroll *[to walk a friend home]* **6.** *a)* to force (a person) to move at a walk, as by grasping the shoulders and pushing *b)* to help (a disabled person) to walk **7.** to bring (a person or animal) to a specified state by walking *[to walk someone to exhaustion]* **8.** to move (a bulky or heavy object) by rocking along from one side or corner to another in a manner suggestive of walking ☆**9.** *Baseball a)* to advance (a batter) to first base by pitching four balls *b)* to force (a run) *in* by doing this when the bases are loaded **—n. 1.** the act of walking **2.** a period or course of walking for pleasure or exercise; stroll or hike **3.** a route traversed by walking **4.** a distance walked, often in terms of the time required *[an hour's walk from home]* **5.** the relatively slow pace of a person or animal that walks **6.** a manner of walking *[to know someone by his walk]* **7.** a particular station in life, sphere of activity, occupation, etc. *[people from all walks of life]* **8.** [Now Rare] mode of living; general conduct or behavior **9.** a path, avenue, etc. specially prepared or set apart for walking; specif., *same as* SIDEWALK **10.** *same as* ROPEWALK **11.** *a)* a plantation of trees in rows with a space between *b)* the space between any two such rows **12.** a place or enclosure for grazing or exercising animals; specif., *same as* SHEEPWALK **13.** [Brit.] the route covered in one's round of duty or work, as in patrolling, street selling, etc. **14.** [Obs.] a resort or haunt **15.** a race between walking contestants: in this sport, the heel of each foot must touch the ground before the toe ☆**16.** *Baseball* the act of walking a batter or of being walked **—walk (all) over** [Colloq.] **1.** to defeat overwhelmingly **2.** to treat in a domineering, unfeeling way **—walk away from** outdistance easily; defeat handily **—walk away with 1.** to steal **2.** to win easily **—walk off 1.** to go away, esp. without warning **2.** to get rid of by walking *[to walk off pounds]* **—walk off with 1.** to steal **2.** to win (a contest) or gain (a prize), esp. easily **—walk out 1.** to leave abruptly or angrily ☆**2.** to go on strike **—**☆**walk out on** [Colloq.] to leave; desert; abandon **—walk through** *Theater* to carry out a walk-through of **—walk with God** to lead a godly, morally upright life
walk·a·way (wôk′ə wā′) *n.* an easily won victory
walk·er (wôk′ər) *n.* **1.** a person or animal that walks; specif., a contestant in a walking race ☆**2.** a tubular frame on wheels for use by babies who are learning to walk ☆**3.** a somewhat similar frame used as a support in walking by the lame, convalescents, etc.
☆**walk·ie-talk·ie** (wôk′ē tôk′ē) *n.* a compact radio transmitter and receiver that can be carried by one person
☆**walk-in** (-in′) *adj.* **1.** large enough for one to walk inside *[a walk-in closet]* **2.** that can be entered directly from the street rather than through a lobby **—n. 1.** a walk-in closet, apartment, etc. **2.** an easily won victory
walk·ing (wôk′iŋ) *adj.* **1.** that walks or is able to walk **2.** for use by a walker, hiker, etc. **3.** characterized by walking, hiking, etc. *[a walking trip through Wales]* **4.** in human form *[a walking encyclopedia]* ☆**5.** that is drawn by an animal and guided by a person walking *[a walking plow]* **6.** that moves back and forth or up and down *[a walking beam]* **7.** that moves in a manner suggestive of walking *[a walking crane]* **8.** permitting the patient to be ambulatory *[walking pneumonia]* **—n. 1.** the act of a

person or thing that walks **2.** manner of walking; gait **3.** the condition of the ground, a path, etc. with reference to its suitability for walking on
☆**walking delegate** formerly, a labor-union official who investigated working conditions, represented the union to its locals, etc.
walking fern ☆a native American fern (*Camptosorus rhizophyllus*) having simple lanceolate leaves with a protracted tip that roots when it touches the ground
walking leaf *same as:* **1.** LEAF INSECT **2.** WALKING FERN
☆**walking papers** [Colloq.] dismissal from a job
☆**walking shorts** *same as* BERMUDA SHORTS
walking stick 1. a stick carried when walking; cane **2.** any of various elongated, wingless, phasmid insects resembling a twig, esp. a N. American species (*Diapheromera femorata*) feeding on plants: also **walk′ing·stick′** *n.*
walk-on (wôk′än′) *n.* a minor role in which the actor has no speaking lines or just a very few
☆**walk-out** (-out′) *n.* **1.** a strike of workers **2.** the abrupt departure of a group of people from a meeting, etc. in a show of protest
walk·o·ver (-ō′vər) *n.* **1.** a race in which the one horse entered has merely to walk over the course to win **2.** an easily won victory
walk-through (-thrōō′) *n.* an early rehearsal of a play in which the actors begin to carry out actions on stage
☆**walk-up** (-up′) *n.* **1.** an apartment house of two or more stories without an elevator **2.** an apartment above the ground floor in such a building
‡**Wal·kü·re, Die** (dē väl kü′rə) [G.: cf. VALKYRIE] the second in a tetralogy of music dramas by Richard Wagner: see RING OF THE NIBELUNG
☆**walk·way** (wôk′wā′) *n.* a path, passage, etc. for pedestrians, esp. one that is sheltered
Wal·kyr·ie (väl kir′ē, wal-) *n. same as* VALKYRIE
☆**walk·y-talk·y** (wôk′ē tôk′ē) *n., pl.* **-talk′ies** *var. of* WALKIE-TALKIE
wall (wôl) *n.* [ME. *wal* < OE. *weall* (akin to G. *wall*) < L. *vallum*, a rampart < *vallus*, a stake, palisade: for IE. base see WALK] **1.** an upright structure of wood, stone, brick, etc., serving to enclose, divide, support, or protect; specif., *a)* such a structure forming a side or inner partition of a building *b)* such a continuous structure serving to enclose an area, to separate fields, etc. *c)* [*usually pl.*] such a structure used as a military defense; fortification *d)* such a structure used to hold back water; levee; dike **2.** something resembling a wall in appearance or function, as the side or inside surface of a container, body cavity, etc. **3.** something suggestive of a wall in that it holds back, divides, hides, etc. *[a wall of secrecy]* **—adj. 1.** of or along a wall **2.** placed or growing on, in, or against a wall **—vt. 1.** to furnish, line, enclose, divide, protect, etc. with or as with a wall or walls *[to wall a room with books, to wall off the old wing, a mind walled in by fears]* **2.** to close up (an opening) with a wall (usually with *up*) **—drive (or push) to the wall** to place in a desperate or extreme position **—drive (or send, etc.) up the wall** [Colloq.] to make frantic, emotionally tense, crazy, etc. **—go to the wall 1.** to be forced to retreat or yield in a conflict; suffer defeat **2.** to fail in business; become bankrupt **—wall′-like′** *adj.*
wal·la·by (wäl′ə bē) *n., pl.* **-bies, -by:** see PLURAL, II, D, 1 [< Australian native name *wolabā*] any of various small and medium-sized marsupials (esp. genera *Lagorchestes* and *Petrogale*), related to the kangaroos and including some about the size of a rabbit
Wal·lace (wôl′is, wäl′-) [< the surname *Wallace* < Anglo-Fr. *Waleis* or ME. *Walisc*, foreign, WELSH] **1.** a masculine name: dim. *Wally* **2. Alfred Russel**, 1823–1913; Eng. naturalist **3. Henry A**(gard), 1888–1965; U.S. agriculturist & politician; vice president of the U.S. (1941–45) **4. Lew**(is), 1827–1905; U.S. general & novelist **5. Sir William**, 1272?–1305?; Scot. patriot & leader in struggle against Edward I of England
Wal·la·chi·a (wä lā′kē ə) *same as* WALACHIA
wal·lah (wäl′ə) *n.* [Anglo-Ind. < Hindi *-wālā*, a suffix of agency] [Anglo-Indian] a person connected with a particular thing or function Also sp. **wal′la**
wal·la·roo (wäl′ə rōō′, wäl′ə rōō′) *n.* [< Australian native name *wolarū*] any of a number of kangaroos characterized by a stocky body and broad, thickly padded feet; esp., any of a genus (*Osphranter*) living in rocky areas
Wal·la·sey (wäl′ə sē) seaport in Cheshire, NW England, on the Mersey River opposite Liverpool: pop. 103,000
wall·board (wôl′bôrd′) *n.* fibrous material, commonly prepared with gypsum, made up into thin slabs for use in making or covering walls, partitions, and ceilings, in place of plaster, paneling, etc.
wall creeper a small bird (*Tichodroma muraria*) related to the brown creepers and living in cliffs and town walls, mainly in Europe, Asia, and N Africa
walled (wôld) *adj.* **1.** having, or enclosed by, a wall or walls **2.** fortified *[a walled town]* **3.** enclosed or hedged in as if by a wall
Wal·len·stein (väl′ən shtīn′; *E.* wôl′ən stīn′), **Al·brecht Eu·se·bi·us Wen·zel von** (äl′breHt oi zā′bē ōōs ven′tsəl fôn) 1583–1634; Austrian general in the Thirty Years' War
Wal·ler (wôl′ər, wäl′-), **Edmund** 1606–87; Eng. poet
wal·let (wôl′it, wäl′-) *n.* [ME. *walet* < ?] **1.** [Now Rare] a bag for carrying provisions, clothing, etc. on a journey

on foot; knapsack ☆**2.** a pocketbook, as of leather, with compartments for paper money, cards, etc.; billfold

wall·eye (wôl′ī′) *n.* [back-formation < ff.] **1.** an eye, as of a horse, with a whitish iris or white, opaque cornea **2.** *a)* an eye that turns outward, showing more white than is normal *b)* divergent strabismus **3.** leucoma of the cornea **4.** a large, staring eye, as of some fishes **5.** any of several fishes with large, staring eyes; esp., ☆*same as* WALLEYED PIKE

wall·eyed (-īd′) *adj.* [altered by folk etym. < ME. *wawil-eyed* < ON. *valdeygthr*, altered < *vagl eygr* < *vagl*, a beam (whence Sw. *vagel*, sty) + *eygr*, having eyes, akin to EYE] **1.** having one or both eyes with a whitish iris or white, opaque cornea **2.** having eyes that turn outward, showing more white than is normal, because of divergent strabismus **3.** having leucoma of the cornea **4.** having large, staring eyes, as some fishes **5.** having or characterized by crazed, glaring eyes

☆**walleyed pike** a N. American freshwater food and game fish (*Stizostedion vitreum*) of the perch family

☆**walleye pollack** a black ocean food fish (*Theragra chalcogrammus*), common off the W coast of N. America

☆**walleye surfperch** a common black and silvery surfperch (*Hyperprosopon argenteum*) found off the coast of California

wall fern a small, hardy fern (*Polypodium virginianum*), with densely matted, creeping stems, found on cliffs and walls in E N. America and often grown in gardens

wall·flow·er (-flou′ər) *n.* **1.** a common garden perennial (*Cheiranthus cheiri*), having racemes of fragrant yellow, orange, brown, red, or purple flowers, native to S Europe **2.** any of a number of perennial or annual garden plants (genera *Cheiranthus* and *Erysimum*) of the mustard family, having racemes of cross-shaped flowers, usually yellow or orange **3.** [Colloq.] a person, esp. a girl, who merely looks on at a dance, etc. as from shyness or from lack of a partner

Wal·ling·ford (wäl′iŋ fard) [for *Wallingford*, England] town in SC Conn.: pop. 36,000

Wal·lis (väl′is) *Ger. name of* VALAIS

Wal·lis and Futuna (wôl′is) Fr. overseas territory in the South Pacific, northeast of the Fiji Islands: it consists of two groups of islands (**Wallis Islands & Futuna Islands**): c.100 sq. mi.; pop. 9,000

Wal·loon (wä loōn′) *n.* [Fr. *Wallon* < ML. *Wallo*, of Gmc. orig., as in OHG. *walh*, foreigner, OE. *Wealh*, Briton, foreigner: cf. WELSH] **1.** any member of a chiefly Celtic people living mostly in S and SE Belgium and nearby parts of France **2.** the French dialect of the Walloons

wal·lop (wäl′əp, wôl′-) *vi.* [ME. *walopen*, to gallop < ONormFr. *waloper* (OFr. *galoper*): see GALLOP] [Dial. or Colloq.] **1.** *a)* to move along in a rapid, reckless, awkward way *b)* to move heavily and clumsily; flounder **2.** to boil vigorously, with noisy bubbling —*vt.* [Colloq.] **1.** to beat soundly; thrash **2.** to strike with a very hard blow **3.** to defeat convincingly or crushingly —*n.* **1.** [Dial. or Colloq.] a heavy, clumsy movement of the body **2.** [Colloq.] *a)* a hard blow *b)* the power to strike a hard blow *c)* effective force; vigor ☆**3.** [Colloq.] a feeling of pleasurable excitement; thrill **4.** [Brit. Slang] beer —**wal′lop·er** *n.*

wal·lop·ing (-in) *adj.* [prp. of WALLOP] [Colloq.] impressively large; enormous —*n.* [Colloq.] **1.** a thrashing or beating **2.** a crushing defeat

wal·low (wäl′ō, wôl′-) *vi.* [ME. *walwen* < OE. *wealwian*, to roll around; for IE. base see WALK] **1.** to roll about or flounder, as in mud, dust, water, slime, etc. **2.** to move heavily and clumsily; roll and pitch, as a ship **3.** to live or indulge oneself fully with immoderate enjoyment (*in* a specified thing, condition, etc.) [to *wallow* in self-pity] **4.** to surge up or billow forth, as smoke, flame, etc. —*n.* **1.** the act or an instance of wallowing ☆**2.** a muddy or dusty place in which animals wallow ☆**3.** a pit or depression produced by animals' wallowing —**wal′low·er** *n.*

wall·pa·per (wôl′pā′pər) *n.* paper, usually with colored patterns printed on it, for covering the walls or ceiling of a room —*vt.* to hang or apply wallpaper on or in

wall pellitory *same as* PELLITORY (sense 1)

wall plate a timber laid horizontally along a wall to support the ends of joists, girders, etc. and distribute their weight

☆**wall rock** *Geol., Mining* the rock mass on either side of a fault or vein

wall rocket a yellow-flowered European plant (*Diplotaxis tenuifolia*) of the mustard family, found on rocky walls

wall rue either of two small, delicate, light-green ferns (*Asplenium cryptolepis* or *Asplenium rutamuraria*) usually growing on cliffs or walls in N. America and Europe

Walls·end (wôlz′end′) city in Northumberland, N England, on the Tyne: pop. 50,000

Wall Street [from a defensive wall built there by the Dutch in 1653] **1.** a street in lower Manhattan, New York City: the main financial center of the U.S. **2.** U.S. financiers and their power, influence, policies, etc., or the U.S. money market

wall-to-wall (wôl′tə wôl′) *adj.* that completely covers a floor [wall-to-wall carpeting]

wal·ly (wā′lē) *adj.* [cf. WALE²] [Scot.] **1.** fine; first-rate **2.** large, strong, or robust **3.** pleasing; agreeable

wal·ly·drag (wä′lē drag′) *n.* [Scot.] **1.** a weak, underdeveloped creature **2.** a slovenly person; esp., a slovenly woman Also **wal′ly·drai′gle** (-drā′g'l)

wal·nut (wôl′nut′, -nət) *n.* [ME. *walnot* < OE. *walhhnutu* < *wealh*, foreign (cf. WELSH) + *hnutu*, a NUT] **1.** any of a genus (*Juglans*) of trees of the walnut family, valued as shade trees, for their nuts, and for their wood, used in making furniture, paneling, etc. **2.** the edible nut of any of these trees, having a two-lobed seed **3.** their wood **4.** a shade of brown characteristic of the heartwood of the black walnut ☆**5.** *local name for* SHAGBARK —*adj.* designating a family (Juglandaceae) of trees native to the temperate parts of the Northern Hemisphere, including the black walnut, English walnut, pecan, hickory, etc.

Walnut Creek [transl. of Sp. *Arroyo de los Nogales*, Creek of the Walnuts, after the native black walnuts] city in W Calif., near Oakland: pop. 40,000

Wal·pole (wôl′pōl, wäl′-) **1.** *Horace*, 4th Earl of Orford, (born *Horatio Walpole*) 1717–97; Eng. writer **2.** Sir *Hugh* (*Seymour*), 1884–1941; Eng. novelist, born in New Zealand **3.** Sir *Robert*, 1st Earl of Orford, 1676–1745; Eng. statesman; prime minister (1721–42): father of *Horace*

Wal·pur·gis Night (väl poor′gis) [after St. *Walpurgis*, Eng. missionary in Germany in the 8th cent.: her day is April 30] the eve of May Day (April 30), when witches supposedly gathered on Brocken mountain for a demonic orgy: also [G.] **Wal·pur·gis·nacht** (väl poor′gis näkht′)

wal·rus (wôl′rəs, wäl′-) *n., pl.* **-rus·es -rus:** see PLURAL, II, D, 1 [Du. < Dan. *hvalros*, prob. by metathesis < ON. *hrosshvalr*, lit., horse whale < *hross*, HORSE + *hvalr*, a WHALE¹] either of two massive sea mammals (*Obodenus divergens*) native to the N Pacific and (*Obodenus rosmarus*) native to the N Atlantic, related to the seals and having two tusks projecting from the upper jaw, a thick mustache, a very thick hide, and a heavy layer of blubber —*adj.* of, characteristic of, or suggestive of a walrus; specif., designating a mustache with long, drooping ends

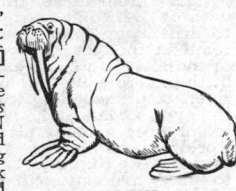

WALRUS
(to 12 ft. long
& 5 ft. high)

Wal·sall (wôl′sôl) city in Staffordshire, WC England, near Birmingham: pop. 183,000

Wal·sing·ham (wôl′sin əm), Sir *Francis* 1530?–90; Eng. statesman; secretary of state to Elizabeth I (1573–90)

Wal·ter (wôl′tər; *for 2*, väl′tər) [ONormFr. *Waltier* < Frank. *Waldheri* < *waldan*, to rule (akin to WIELD) + *heri, hari*, army, host; also < G. *Walter, Walther* < OHG. form of same name] **1.** a masculine name: dim. *Walt, Wat* **2.** *Bruno*, (born *Bruno Walter Schlesinger*) 1876–1962; Ger. orchestra conductor in the U.S.

Wal·tham (wôl′tham, -thəm) [? after *Waltham* Abbey in England, home of some of the first settlers] city in E Mass., on the Charles River: pop. 62,000

Wal·tham·stow (wôl′thəm stō′, -təm-) city in Essex, SE England, near London: pop. 107,000

Wal·ther von der Vo·gel·wei·de (väl′tər fôn dər fō′gəl vī′də) 1170?–1230?; Ger. minnesinger

Wal·ton (wôl′t'n) **1.** *I·zaak* (ī′zək), 1593–1683; Eng. writer **2.** Sir *William* (*Turner*), 1902– ; Eng. composer

waltz (wôlts, wôls) *n.* [abbrev. < G. *walzer* < *walzen*, to roll, dance about, waltz: for IE. base see WALK] **1.** a ballroom dance for couples, in moderate 3/4 time with marked accent on the first beat of the measure **2.** music for this dance or in its characteristic rhythm —*adj.* of, for, or characteristic of a waltz —*vi.* **1.** to dance a waltz **2.** to move lightly and nimbly; whirl **3.** [Colloq.] to move effortlessly and with apparent success (usually with *through*) —*vt.* **1.** to dance with in a waltz **2.** to take and lead peremptorily —**waltz′er** *n.*

Wal·vis Bay (wôl′vis) [< Du. *walvis*, a whale < MDu. *walvisc*: cf. WHALE¹ & FISH²] **1.** *a)* a seaport on an inlet of the Atlantic, on the coast of South West Africa *b)* this inlet **2.** small exclave of Cape Province, South Africa, surrounding this seaport: administered by South West Africa: 434 sq. mi.; pop. 13,000

wam·ble (wäm′'l, wam′-; -b'l) *vi.* **-bled, -bling** [ME. *wamlen*, akin to Norw. *vamla*, to stagger, Dan. *vamle*, to feel nausea: for IE. base see VOMIT] [Chiefly Dial.] **1.** to turn, twist, or roll about **2.** to move unsteadily; stagger or reel **3.** *a)* [Obs.] to be nauseated *b)* to give the sensation of nausea: said of the stomach —*n.* [Chiefly Dial.] **1.** *a)* a wambling, twisting, etc. *b)* an unsteady movement **2.** a sensation of nausea —**wam′bly** *adj.* **-bli·er, -bli·est**

wame (wām) *n.* [var. of WOMB] [Scot. & N. Eng. Dial.] the belly; abdomen

Wam·pa·no·ag (wäm′pə nō′ag) *n., pl.* **-no′ag, -no′ags** any member of a tribe of Algonquian Indians that lived in SE Mass. at the time of the Pilgrims

☆**wam·pum** (wäm′pəm) *n.* [< AmInd. (Algonquian) *wampumpeage*, lit., white string of beads < *wap*, white + *umpe*, string + *-ag*, pl. suffix] **1.** small beads made of shells

and used by N. American Indians as money, for ornament, etc.: they were of two varieties, white and the more valuable black (or dark purple) **2.** [Slang] money

wan[1] (wän, wôn) *adj.* **wan′ner, wan′nest** [ME. < OE. *wann,* dark] **1.** sickly pale; pallid; colorless *[a wan complexion]* **2.** faint, feeble, or weak in a way suggestive of a sickly condition or great weariness, sadness, etc. *[a wan smile]* **3.** [Obs.] dark; gloomy —*vt., vi.* **wanned, wan′ning** [Now Rare] to make or become sickly pale —*SYN.* see PALE[1] —**wan′ly** *adv.* —**wan′ness** *n.*

wan[2] (wan) *obs. pt. of* WIN

Wan·a·ma·ker (wän′ə mā′kər), **John** 1838–1922; U.S. merchant

wand (wänd, wônd) *n.* [ME. < ON. *vǫndr,* akin to Goth. *wandus:* for IE. base see WIND[1]] **1.** a slender, supple switch or shoot, as of a young tree, esp. a willow **2.** a rod or staff carried as a symbol of authority; scepter **3.** a rod with supposed or pretended magical powers, as one used by a magician, conjurer, or fairy ☆**4.** *Archery* a slat 6 feet high and 2 inches wide, used as a target at a distance of 100 yards for men and 60 yards for women

wan·der (wän′dər, wôn′-) *vi.* [ME. *wandren* < OE. *wandrian,* akin to G. *wandern:* for IE. base see WIND[1]] **1.** to move or go about aimlessly, without plan or fixed destination; ramble; roam **2.** to go to a destination in a casual way or by an indirect route; idle; stroll **3.** *a)* to turn aside or astray *(from* a path, course, etc.); lose one's way *b)* to stray from home, friends, familiar places, etc. (often with *off)* **4.** to go astray in mind or purpose; specif., *a)* to drift away from a subject, as in discussion; stray or roam in thought *b)* to turn away from accepted belief or morals *c)* to be disjointed, disordered, incoherent, etc. **5.** to pass or extend in an irregular course; meander, as a river **6.** to move idly from one object to another: said of the eyes, a glance, the hands, etc. —*vt.* to roam through, in, or over without plan or destination *[to wander the world]* —**wan′der·er** *n.*

wan·der·ing (-iŋ) *adj.* **1.** that wanders; moving from place to place; roaming, roving, straying, etc. **2.** nomadic: said of tribes **3.** winding: said of rivers and roads —*n.* **1.** an aimless going about **2.** [*pl.*] travels, esp. when extended and apparently purposeless **3.** [*pl.*] incoherent or disordered thoughts or utterances, as in delirium —**wan′der·ing·ly** *adv.*

wandering albatross a large white sea bird (*Diomedea exulans*) with black wings, native to southern seas

Wandering Jew 1. in medieval folklore, a Jew condemned to wander the earth restlessly until the second coming of Christ because of his scornful attitude just before the Crucifixion **2.** [w- J-] any of several trailing plants (esp. genera *Tradescantia* and *Zebrina*) of the spiderwort family, having smooth stems and leaves, and white, red, or blue flowers; esp., a purplish plant (*Zebrina pendula*)

‡**Wan·der·jahr** (vän′dər yär′) *n.* [G., lit., wander-year] **1.** a year of travel before settling down to one's vocation: orig. a custom of European journeymen **2.** any lengthy period of travel

wan·der·lust (wän′dər lust′, wôn′-) *n.* [G. < *wandern,* to travel, WANDER + *lust,* joy (see LUST)] an impulse, longing, or urge to wander or travel

Wands·worth (wändz′wurth′) metropolitan borough of London, on the south bank of the Thames: pop. 331,000

wane (wän) *vi.* **waned, wan′ing** [ME. *wanien* < OE. *wanian,* to decrease, grow less, akin to *wan,* lacking: for IE. base see WANT] **1.** to grow gradually less in extent: said of the visible face of the moon during the period after it has become full: opposed to WAX[2] (sense 2) **2.** to become less intense, bright, strong, etc.; grow dim or faint, as a light **3.** to decline in power, importance, prosperity, influence, etc. **4.** to approach the end: said of a period of time *[the day wanes]* —*n.* **1.** *a)* the gradual decrease in the visible face of the moon after it has become full *b)* the time when this takes place **2.** a gradual decrease in power, importance, prosperity, intensity, etc., esp. after a gradual climb to a peak **3.** a period of decline **4.** the beveled, defective, bark-covered edge or corner of a board or plank cut from an unsquared log or block of wood —**on the wane** waning, declining, decreasing, etc.

SYN.—**wane** implies a fading or weakening of that which has reached a peak of force, excellence, etc. *[his fame waned rapidly];* **abate** suggests a progressive lessening in degree, intensity, etc. *[the fever is abating];* **ebb,** applied specifically to a fluctuating force, refers to one of the periods of recession or decline *[their ebbing fortunes];* **subside** suggests a quieting or slackening of violent activity or turbulence *[her temper had subsided]* —*ANT.* wax, increase, revive

wan·ey (wā′nē) *adj.* **wan′i·er, wan′i·est 1.** waning; decreasing, declining, etc. **2.** having a wane (*n.* 4)

wan·gle (waŋ′g'l) *vt.* **wan′gled, wan′gling** [altered < ? WAGGLE] [Colloq.] **1.** to get, make, or bring about by persuasion, influence, adroit manipulation, contrivance, etc. **2.** to manipulate or change (statistics, accounts, etc.) for a selfish or dishonest purpose; falsify; juggle **3.** to wiggle or wriggle —*vi.* [Colloq.] **1.** to make use of contrivance, adroit manipulation, or tricky and indirect methods in order to achieve one's aims **2.** to wriggle, as out of a difficult situation —**wan′gler** *n.*

Wan·hsien (wän′shyen′) city in Szechwan province, C China, on the Yangtze River: pop. c.300,000

☆**wan·i·gan** (wän′i gən) *n.* [< AmInd. (Abnaki) *wanīgan,* a trap, container for stray objects] **1.** a trunk, chest, etc. for storing supplies, as in a lumbering camp **2.** a small, rough shelter for sleeping, cooking, etc., now often one mounted on runners or wheels Also sp. **wan′ni·gan**

wan·ion (wän′yən, wôn′-) *n.* [altered < ME. *waneand,* Northern dial. prp. of *wanien,* to WANE: sense < notion of the waning of the moon as unlucky time] [Archaic] bad luck; curse; plague: used in **with** (or **in**) **a wanion**

Wan·kel engine (väŋ′k'l, waŋ′-) [after Felix *Wankel* (1902–), G. engineer and inventor] a rotary combustion engine having a spinning piston and requiring fewer parts and much less fuel than that used in a comparable turbine engine: used in automobiles, air compressors, etc.

Wan·ne-Ei·ckel (vän′ə ī′kəl) city in the Ruhr Basin of North Rhine-Westphalia, West Germany: pop. 108,000

want (wänt, wônt) *vt.* [ME. *wanten* < ON. *vanta,* to be lacking, want: see the *n.*] **1.** to have too little of; be deficient in; lack **2.** to be short by (a specified amount) *[it wants twelve minutes of midnight]* **3.** to feel the need of; long for; crave *[to want adventure]* **4.** to desire; wish or long (followed by the infinitive) *[to want to travel]* **5.** *a)* to wish to see or speak with (someone) *[wanted on the phone]* *b)* to wish to apprehend, as for questioning or arrest *[wanted by the police]* **6.** [Chiefly Brit.] to require; need *[this wants attending to]* *Want* is also used colloquially as an auxiliary meaning *ought* or *should [you want to be careful crossing streets]* —*vi.* **1.** to have a need or lack (usually with *for) [to want for money]* **2.** to lack the necessities of life; be destitute or impoverished *["Waste not, want not"]* **3.** [Rare] to be lacking or missing for completeness or a certain result *[there wants but his approval]* —*n.* [ME. < ON. *vant,* neut. of *vanr,* deficient < IE. base *(e)wā-,* to lack, whence L. *vanus,* empty] **1.** the state or fact of lacking, or having too little of, something needed or desired; scarcity; shortage; lack *[to suffer from want of adequate care]* **2.** a lack of the necessities of life; poverty; destitution *[to live in want]* **3.** a wish or desire for something; craving **4.** something needed or desired but lacking; need —*SYN.* see DESIRE, LACK, POVERTY —**want in** (or **out, off,** etc.) [Colloq.] to want to get, go, or come in (or out, off, etc.) —**want′er** *n.*

☆**want ad** [Colloq.] a classified advertisement in a newspaper or magazine stating that one wants a job, an apartment to rent, a specified type of employee, etc., or that one wishes to sell, buy, or trade something

want·ing (wän′tiŋ, wôn′-) *adj.* **1.** absent; lacking; missing *[a coat with some buttons wanting]* **2.** not up to some standard; inadequate in some essential *[weighed and found wanting]* —*prep.* **1.** lacking (something); without *[a watch wanting a minute hand]* **2.** minus *[a year, wanting one week]* —**wanting in** deficient in (some quality, etc.)

wan·ton (wän′t'n, wôn′-) *adj.* [ME. *wantowen,* var. of *wantogen,* wanton, irregular < OE. *wan-,* used as negative prefix < *wan,* lacking, deficient + *togen,* pp. of *teon,* to draw, educate, bring up (see TOW[1])] **1.** orig., undisciplined; unmanageable *[a wanton child]* **2.** *a)* sexually loose or unrestrained *[a wanton woman]* *b)* [Poet.] frisky; playful; frolicsome *c)* [Poet.] capricious; unrestrained *[wanton winds]* **3.** senseless, unprovoked, unjustifiable, or deliberately malicious *[wanton cruelty, a wanton insult]* **4.** recklessly or arrogantly ignoring justice, decency, morality, etc. *[wanton disregard of human rights]* **5.** *a)* [Now Rare] luxuriant: said of vegetation, etc. *b)* lavish, luxurious, or extravagant: said of speech, dress, etc. —*n.* a wanton person or thing; esp., a sexually loose or unrestrained woman —*vi.* to be wanton in behavior, action, manner, etc. —*vt.* to waste carelessly or in luxurious pleasures —**wan′ton·ly** *adv.* —**wan′ton·ness** *n.*

wan·y (wā′nē) *adj.* **wan′i·er, wan′i·est** *var. of* WANEY

wap (wäp, wap) *n., vt., vi.* **wapped, wap′ping** [Dial. or Archaic] *same as* WHOP

wap·en·take (wäp′ən tāk′, wap′-) *n.* [ME. < OE. *wapentac* < ON. *vapnatak,* lit., a weapon-taking (< *vapn,* WEAPON + *tak,* a taking < *taka,* to TAKE): prob. used territorially from brandishing of weapons as symbol of an assent vote: cf. WAPPENSCHAWING] in England, formerly, **1.** a subdivision of certain northern counties originally under Norse domination, corresponding to the hundred in other counties **2.** a law court in such a subdivision

☆**wap·i·ti** (wäp′ə tē) *n., pl. -ti, -tis:* see PLURAL, II, D, 1 [< AmInd. (Algonquian) name, as in Shawnee *wapiti,* pale, white] the American elk (*Cervus canadensis*), the largest N. American deer, with widely branching antlers and a short tail, related to the European red deer

wap·pen·schaw·ing (wäp′ən shô′iŋ, wap′-) *n.* [ME. *wapynschawing* < *wapen,* WEAPON + *schawing,* a showing (see SHOW)] *Scot. History* a review or mustering of men under arms, held at periodic intervals in each district: also **wap′pen·schaw**

wap·per·jaw (wäp′ər jô′) *n.* [< ?] [Colloq.] an underjaw that projects or is crooked —**wap′per·jawed′** *adj.*

war[1] (wôr) *n.* [ME. *werre* < ONormFr. < Frank. *werra,* confusion, strife] **1.** open armed conflict between countries or between factions within the same country **2.** any active hostility, contention, or struggle; conflict *[the war against disease]* **3.** military operations as a profession or science **4.** [Obs.] a battle —*adj.* of, used in, or resulting from war —*vi.* **warred, war′ring 1.** to carry on war;

engage in military conflict **2.** to be in a state of hostility or contention; contend; strive —**at war** in a state of active armed conflict —**declare war (on) 1.** to make a formal declaration of being at war (with) **2.** to announce one's hostility (to) —**go to war 1.** to enter into a war **2.** to become a member of the armed forces during a war

war² (wär) *adj., adv.* [ME. < ON. *verre,* adj., *verr,* adv.: see WORSE] [Scot. & N. Eng. Dial.] *same as* WORSE

War between the States the U.S. Civil War (1861–65): term used by those sympathetic to the Confederacy

war·ble¹ (wôr′b'l) *vt.* **-bled, -bling** [ME. *werblen* < ONormFr. *werbler* < Frank. *wirbilon,* akin to G. *wirbeln,* to whirl, warble: cf. WHIRL] **1.** to sing (a song, notes, etc.) melodiously, with trills, quavers, runs, etc., as a bird **2.** to express in song —*vi.* **1.** to sing melodiously, with trills, etc. **2.** to make a musical sound; babble, as a stream ☆**3.** *same as* YODEL —*n.* **1.** the act of warbling **2.** a warbling sound; trill

war·ble² (wôr′b'l) *n.* [prob. < Scand., as in obs. Sw. *varbulde,* a boil < *var,* pus + *bulde,* tumor] **1.** a small, hard tumor on the back of a horse, caused by the rubbing and pressing of a saddle **2.** a lump or swelling under the hide of an animal, esp. on the back, caused by the presence of a larva of the warble fly or botfly —**war′bled** *adj.*

warble fly any of a family (Hypodermatidae) of two-winged flies whose larvae burrow beneath the hide of cattle, horses, and other animals, producing warbles

war·bler (wôr′blər) *n.* **1.** a bird or person that warbles; singer; songster ☆**2.** any of a large family (Mniotiltidae) of small, insect-eating birds of the New World, many of which are brightly colored, as the yellow warbler, the prothonotary warbler, the American redstart, etc. **3.** any of a family (Sylviidae) of small songbirds, as the whitethroats, related to the thrushes

☆**war bonnet** a ceremonial headdress worn by some N. American Indian warriors, consisting of a headband and trailing part studded with feathers

☆**war chest** a fund, as of contributions from individuals, created for a particular purpose, as a political campaign

war crime any crime in violation of international law or accepted laws of war or of assumed norms of humane behavior, committed in connection with a war as by a member of a belligerent nation's military forces or government —**war criminal**

war cry 1. a name, phrase, slogan, etc. shouted in a charge or battle **2.** a phrase or slogan adopted by a party in any conflict, contest, election, etc.

ward (wôrd) *vt.* [ME. *warden* < OE. *weardian,* to protect, guard, akin to OHG. *warten,* to wait < IE. base **wer-,* to heed, whence L. *vereri,* to respect, fear; E. form and sense infl. by ONormFr. *warder* (for OFr. *guarder,* to GUARD)] **1.** to turn aside; fend off; parry (usually with *off*) **2.** [Now Rare] to keep watch over; guard; protect —*n.* [ME. < OE. *weard,* akin to OHG. *warta,* a watching] **1.** the act of guarding: see WATCH AND WARD **2.** the state of being under guard **3.** *a)* [Now Rare] guardianship, as of a child or person not capable of handling his own affairs *b)* [Now Rare] the condition of being under the control of a guardian; wardship *c)* a child or legally incompetent person placed under the care of a guardian or court *d)* any person under another's protection or care **4.** each of the parts or divisions of a jail or prison **5.** a room or division of a hospital set apart for a specific class or group of patients [a maternity *ward*] **6.** a district or division of a city or town, for purposes of administration, representation, voting, etc. **7.** any of the administrative districts into which some counties in N England and Scotland are divided, corresponding to the hundred and wapentake ☆**8.** in the Mormon Church, a local unit presided over by a bishop and two counselors **9.** a means of defense or protection **10.** a defensive posture, position, or motion, as in fencing **11.** an open space enclosed by the walls of a castle or fortification **12.** [Archaic] a garrison; the guard or watch **13.** *Lockmaking a)* a projecting ridge in a keyhole or lock face that allows only the right key to enter *b)* the notch in a key that matches this ridge

-ward (wərd) [ME. *-werd* < OE. *-weard* < base of *weorthan,* to become (see WORTH¹)] *a suffix meaning* in a (specified) direction or course [*backward, eastward*]

Ward (wôrd) **1. Ar·te·mus** (är′ti məs), (pseud. of *Charles Farrar Browne*) 1834–67; U.S. humorist **2. Barbara,** 1914– ; Eng. writer **3.** Mrs. **Humphry,** (born *Mary Augusta Arnold*) 1851–1920; Brit. novelist, born in Tasmania

☆**war dance** a ceremonial dance performed as by some American Indian tribes before battle or after victory

ward·ed (wôr′did) *adj.* having wards, as a lock or key

Ward·en (wôr′d'n) *n.* [ME. *wardon,* prob. < ONormFr. *warder,* to keep: see WARD, *v.*] [*sometimes* w-] an old variety of winter pear used chiefly for cooking

war·den (wôr′d'n) *n.* [ME. *wardein* < ONormFr., warden (for OFr. *gardein,* warden): see GUARDIAN, WARD] **1.** a person who guards, or has charge of, something; keeper, custodian, or special supervisory official [fire *warden,* game *warden*] **2.** the chief administrative official of a prison **3.** in England, a high government official: now

obsolete except in titles; specif., *a)* a governor *b)* an officer in charge of a certain department of government *c)* the superintendent of a port or market **4.** in England, *a)* a governing officer in certain guilds, hospitals, etc.; trustee *b)* the head of certain Oxford colleges and of some schools **5.** in Connecticut, the chief executive of a borough **6.** *same as* CHURCHWARDEN (sense 1) **7.** [Archaic] a gatekeeper or watchman —**war′den·ship′** *n.*

ward·er¹ (wôr′dər) *n.* [ME. *wardere* < Anglo-Fr. *wardour,* for OFr. *guarder:* see GUARD, WARD] **1.** a person who guards; watchman **2.** a person who guards an entrance **3.** [Chiefly Brit.] a warden in a jail —**war′der·ship′** *n.*

ward·er² (wôr′dər) *n.* [LME. < ? *warden,* WARD] formerly, a staff or rod carried by a king, commander, etc. as a mark of authority, and used to signal his wishes

☆**ward heeler** a hanger-on of a ward committee or politician, who solicits votes for his party and performs minor tasks for his political bosses: a contemptuous term

ward·ress (wôr′dris) *n.* [Chiefly Brit.] a prison matron

ward·robe (wôrd′rōb′) *n.* [ME. *warderobe* < ONormFr.: see WARD & ROBE] **1.** a closet or movable cabinet, usually relatively tall and provided with hangers, etc., for holding clothes **2.** a room where clothes are kept; esp., a room in a theater where costumes are kept **3.** a collection of clothes; esp., *a)* the complete supply of clothes of a person *b)* a supply of clothes for a particular season or purpose [a spring *wardrobe*] *c)* the collection of costumes of a theater or theatrical company **4.** in a royal or noble household, the department in charge of clothes

wardrobe mistress the woman in charge of the wardrobe of a theater or theatrical company

☆**wardrobe trunk** a large trunk for carrying clothing, etc. and, when standing upright, for hanging suits, dresses, etc.

ward·room (wôrd′rōōm′) *n.* [WARD, *n.* + ROOM] **1.** in a warship, a compartment used for eating and lounging by commissioned officers, except, usually, the captain **2.** these officers collectively

-wards (wərdz) *same as* -WARD

ward·ship (wôrd′ship′) *n.* **1.** the office of a guardian; guardianship; custody, as of a minor **2.** the condition of being a ward, or in the care of a guardian

ware¹ (wer) *n.* [ME. < OE. *waru,* merchandise, specialized use of *waru,* watchful care, in the sense "what is kept safe": for IE. base see WARD] **1.** any piece or kind of goods that a store, merchant, peddler, etc. has to sell; also, any skill or service that one seeks to sell: *usually used in pl.* **2.** things, usually of the same general kind, that are for sale; a (specified) kind of merchandise, collectively: generally in compounds [*hardware, earthenware, glassware*] **3.** dishes made of baked and glazed clay; pottery, or a specified kind or make of pottery

ware² (wer) *adj.* [ME. *war* < OE. *wær* < base of *waru:* see prec.] [Archaic] **1.** aware; conscious (*of*) **2.** on one's guard; ready; wary **3.** prudent; cautious; wise —*vt.* **wared, war′ing** [ME. *waren* < OE. *warian*] to beware of: usually in the imperative, esp. in hunting [*ware* hounds!]

ware³ (wer) *vt.* **wared, war′ing** [ME. *waren* < ON. *verja,* akin to OE. *werian* (see WEAR¹)] [Scot.] to spend or squander (money, time, etc.)

ware·house (wer′hous′; *for v., usually* -houz′) *n.* [ME.: see WARE¹ & HOUSE] **1.** a building where wares, or goods, are stored, as before distribution to retailers, or are kept in reserve, in bond, etc. **2.** [Chiefly Brit.] a wholesale store or, sometimes, a large retail store —*vt.* **-housed′, -hous′ing** to place or store in a warehouse —**ware′house′man** (-mən) *n., pl.* **-men**

ware·room (-rōōm′) *n.* a room used for storing or displaying things for sale

war·fare (wôr′fer′) *n.* **1.** the action of waging war; armed conflict **2.** conflict or struggle of any kind

☆**war·fa·rin** (wôr′fə rin) *n.* [W(isconsin) A(lumni) R(esearch) F(oundation) + (COUM)ARIN] **1.** a colorless, odorless, tasteless rat poison, $C_{19}H_{16}O_4$, a crystalline powder that causes fatal internal bleeding in rodents **2.** this drug neutralized with sodium hydroxide, used in medicine as an anticoagulant

war game 1. *same as* KRIEGSPIEL **2.** [*pl.*] practice maneuvers involving actual troops and military equipment

☆**war hawk** *same as* HAWK¹ (*n.* 2)

war·head (-hed′) *n.* the head, or forward section, as of a self-propelled torpedo or projectile, containing the charge of explosive, chemical, etc.

war horse 1. a horse used in battle; charger **2.** [Colloq.] a person who has been through many battles or struggles; veteran **3.** [Colloq.] a symphony, play, opera, etc. that has been performed so often as to seem trite and stale For **2** & **3,** now usually **war′horse′** *n.*

war·i·ly (wer′ə lē) *adv.* in a wary manner; cautiously

war·i·ness (-ē nis) *n.* the quality or state of being wary

war·i·son (wer′ə s'n) *n.* [ME. < ONormFr., for OFr. *garison:* see GARRISON] **1.** [Obs.] a reward or gift given by a superior **2.** [from such an erroneous use by Sir Walter SCOTT] a note sounded to signal an attack

war·like (wôr′līk) *adj.* **1.** fit for, fond of, or ready for war; bellicose; martial **2.** of or appropriate to war **3.** threaten-

ing, or suggesting the likelihood of, war —*SYN*. see MARTIAL

war·lock (wôr′läk′) *n*. [ME. *warloghe* < OE. *wærloga*, a traitor, liar < *wær*, faith + *leogan*, to LIE²] 1. a person who practices black magic; sorcerer or wizard: the male equivalent of a *witch* 2. a conjurer or magician

war·lord (wôr′lôrd′) *n*. 1. a high military officer in a warlike nation 2. an aggressive tyrant 3. a local ruler or bandit leader, as formerly in China, with some sort of military following in a district where the established government is weak —**war′lord′ism** *n*.

warm (wôrm) *adj*. [ME. < OE. *wearm*, akin to G. *warm* < IE. base *gwher-*, hot, whence Gr. *thermos*, warm, *theros*, summer, L. *formus*, warm, *fornax*, furnace] 1. *a*) having or giving off a moderate degree of heat [*a warm* iron, *warm* coffee] *b*) giving off pleasurable heat [*a warm* fire] *c*) uncomfortably warm; hot [*a warm* night] 2. having the natural heat of living beings: said of the body, blood, etc. 3. *a*) heated or overheated, as with exercise or hard work *b*) such as to make one heated or overheated [*warm* exercise, work, etc.] 4. effective in keeping body heat in [*warm* clothing] 5. characterized by lively disagreement: said of argument or controversy 6. fervent; ardent; enthusiastic [*warm* encouragement] 7. lively, vigorous, brisk, or animated 8. quick to anger; irascible; heated 9. *a*) genial; cordial [*a warm* welcome] *b*) sincere; grateful [*warm* thanks] *c*) sympathetic, affectionate, or loving *d*) passionate; amorous 10. suggesting warmth; having yellow, orange, or red hue: said of colors 11. newly made; fresh; strong: said of a scent or trail 12. [Colloq.] close to discovering something; on the verge of guessing or finding, as in games 13. [Colloq.] disagreeable; uncomfortable [to make things *warm* for someone] 14. [Brit. Colloq.] well-to-do; well-off —*adv*. so as to be warm; warmly —*vt*. [ME. *warmen* < OE. *wearmian*] 1. to make warm; raise the temperature of to a moderate extent 2. to make excited, animated, ardent, enthusiastic, lively, etc. 3. to fill with pleasant or kindly emotions [a sight to *warm* the heart] —*vi*. 1. to become warm 2. to become friendly, kindly, affectionate, or sympathetic (*to* or *toward*) 3. to become excited, ardent, enthusiastic, lively, etc. (often with *to*) 4. to feel a glow of pleasure; bask —*n*. [Colloq.] a warming or being warmed —*SYN*. see TENDER¹ —**warm up** 1. *a*) to heat or be heated; make or become warm *b*) to make or become sufficiently warm to operate effectively or efficiently [to *warm up* an engine] 2. to reheat (cooked food, etc.): also **warm over** 3. to make or become more animated, excited, ardent, lively, etc. 4. *Sports* to practice or exercise a while before going into a game, race, etc. —**warm′er** *n*. —**warm′ly** *adv*. —**warm′ness** *n*.

warm·blood·ed (-blud′id) *adj*. 1. having a body temperature that remains relatively constant, independent of and usually higher than that of the surroundings [mammals and birds are *warmblooded* animals] 2. having or characterized by an eager, lively, or passionate temperament; ardent; fervent; impetuous —**warm′blood′ed·ness** *n*.

☆**warmed-o·ver** (wôrmd′ō′vər) *adj*. 1. reheated [*warmed-over* hash] 2. presented again, without freshness or significant change [*warmed-over* ideas]

warm front *Meteorol*. the forward edge of an advancing mass of warm air replacing colder air

warm·heart·ed (wôrm′härt′id) *adj*. kind, sympathetic, friendly, loving, etc. —*SYN*. see TENDER¹ —**warm′heart′-ed·ly** *adv*. —**warm′heart′ed·ness** *n*.

warming pan a long-handled, covered pan for holding live coals: formerly used to warm beds

warm·ish (wôr′mish) *adj*. somewhat warm

war·mon·ger (wôr′muŋ′gər, -män′-) *n*. a person or agency that advocates war or tries to bring about a war —**war′mon′ger·ing** *adj*., *n*.

☆**war·mouth** (wôr′mouth′) *n*., *pl*. **-mouth′**, **-mouths′**: see PLURAL, II, D, 2 [< ?] a freshwater sunfish (*Chaenobryttus gulosus*) of the E U.S. and the Mississippi basin, usually olive-green or bronze mottled with darker colorings

warmth (wôrmth) *n*. [ME. *wermthe*: see WARM & -TH¹] 1. *a*) the state or quality of having or giving off a moderate degree of heat *b*) the degree of heat in a substance, esp. when it is moderate; mild heat 2. *a*) excitement or vigor of feeling; enthusiasm, ardor, zeal, etc. *b*) sympathetic, cordial, or affectionate feelings or nature *c*) slight anger 3. a glowing effect obtained by using red, yellow, etc.

☆**warm-up** (wôrm′up′) *n*. the act or an instance of warming up

warn (wôrn) *vt*. [ME. *warnien* < OE. *wearnian*, akin to G. *warnen*: for IE. base see WARD] 1. to tell (a person) of a danger, coming evil, misfortune, etc.; put on guard; caution 2. to caution about certain acts; admonish [*warned* against smoking in the building] 3. to notify in advance; inform 4. to give notice to (a person) to stay or keep (*off*, *away*, etc.) —*vi*. to give warning —*SYN*. see ADVISE —**warn′er** *n*.

warn·ing (wôr′niŋ) *n*. 1. the act of one that warns, or the state of being warned 2. something that serves to warn —*adj*. that warns; serving to warn —**warn′ing·ly** *adv*.

warning coloration bright and striking coloration, as the conspicuous stripes of the skunk, occurring in many distasteful or poisonous animals, thought to warn attackers

War of American Independence *Brit. name for* AMERICAN REVOLUTION

War of 1812 a war (1812–15) between the U.S. and Great Britain

War of Independence *same as* AMERICAN REVOLUTION

war of nerves a conflict or campaign utilizing psychological means to unsettle an opponent or to destroy his morale

War of Secession the U.S. Civil War: also called **War between the States**, **War of the Rebellion**

warp (wôrp) *n*. [ME. *wearp* < the base of *weorpan*, to throw, akin to G. *werfen* < IE. *werb-* < base *wer-*, to turn, bend, whence WORM] 1. *a*) a distortion, as a twist or bend, in wood or in an object made of wood, caused by contraction in drying *b*) any similar distortion, as in metal *c*) the state or fact of being so distorted 2. a mental twist, quirk, aberration, or bias 3. *a*) silt, sediment, or mud deposited as by a stream *b*) a deposit of this 4. *Naut*. a rope or line run from a boat, etc. to a dock, buoy, anchor, etc., and used to warp the vessel into position 5. *a*) *Weaving* the threads running lengthwise in the loom and crossed by the weft or woof *b*) the very fiber or essential part of something; foundation; base —*vt*. [ME. *warpen*, to throw, bend < OE. *weorpan*, to throw] 1. to bend, curve, or twist out of shape; distort 2. *a*) to turn from the true, natural, or right course *b*) to turn from a healthy, sane, or normal condition; pervert; bias: said of the mind, character, judgment, etc. *c*) to twist or distort in telling; misinterpret [a *warped* account] 3. *Naut*. to move (a boat, etc.) by hauling on a line fastened to a pile, dock, anchor, etc. 4. *Weaving* to arrange (threads or yarns) so as to form a warp —*vi*. 1. to become bent or twisted out of shape, as wood in drying 2. to turn aside from the true, natural, or right course 3. *Naut*. to move into position by warping or being warped, as a boat —*SYN*. see DEFORM —**warp′er** *n*.

☆**war paint** 1. a pigment applied to the face and body, as by some American Indian tribes, in preparation for war 2. [Slang] ceremonial dress; regalia 3. [Slang] cosmetics, as used by women; makeup

☆**war·path** (wôr′path′, -päth′) *n*. the path or course taken by American Indians on a warlike expedition —**on the warpath** 1. at war, ready for war, or looking for war 2. actively angry; ready to fight

warp beam the roller on which the warp is wound in a loom

war·plane (wôr′plān′) *n*. any airplane for use in war

war·rant (wôr′ənt, wär′-) *n*. [ME. *warant* < ONormFr. (OFr. *garant*), a warrant < Frank. *warand* < prp. of *warjan*, akin to OE. *werian*, to guard, defend: see WEIR] 1. *a*) authorization or sanction, as by a superior or the law *b*) justification or reasonable grounds for some act, course, statement, or belief 2. something that serves as an assurance, or guarantee, of some event or result 3. a writing serving as authorization or certification for something; specif., *a*) authorization in writing for the payment or receipt of money *b*) a short-term note issued by a municipality or other governmental agency, usually in anticipation of tax revenues *c*) an option issued by a company granting the holder the right to buy certain securities, generally common stock, at a specified price and usually for a limited time *d*) [Brit.] a receipt for goods stored in a warehouse *e*) *Law* a writ or order authorizing an officer to make an arrest, seizure, or search, or perform some other designated act *f*) *Mil*. the certificate of appointment to the grade of warrant officer: cf. WARRANT OFFICER —*vt*. 1. *a*) to give (someone) authorization or sanction to do something *b*) to authorize (the doing of something) 2. to serve as justification or reasonable grounds for (an act, belief, etc.) [a remark that did not *warrant* such anger] 3. to give formal assurance, or guarantee, to (someone) or for (something); specif., *a*) to guarantee the quality, quantity, condition, etc. of (goods) to the purchaser *b*) to guarantee to (the purchaser) that goods sold are as represented *c*) to guarantee to (the purchaser) the title of goods purchased; assure of indemnification against loss *d*) *Law* to guarantee the title of granted property to (the grantee) 4. [Colloq.] to state with confidence; affirm emphatically [I *warrant* he'll be late] —*SYN*. see ASSERT —**war′rant·a·ble** *adj*.

war·ran·tee (wôr′ən tē′, wär′-) *n*. *Law* a person to whom a warranty is given

warrant officer an officer of the U.S. armed forces ranking above an enlisted man but below a commissioned officer and holding his office on a warrant instead of a commission

war·ran·tor (wôr′ən tôr′, wär′-; -tər) *n*. *Law* a person who warrants, or gives warranty: also **war′rant·er** (-tər)

war·ran·ty (-tē) *n*., *pl*. **-ties** [ME. *warantie* < ONormFr. (OFr. *garantie*): see WARRANT] 1. official authorization or sanction 2. justification; reasonable grounds, as for an opinion or action 3. *Law* a guarantee; specif., *a*) a guarantee or an assurance, explicit or implied, of something having to do with a contract, as of sale; esp., the seller's assurance to the purchaser that the goods or property is or shall be as represented *b*) a guarantee by the insured that the facts are as stated in regard to an insurance risk, or that specified conditions shall be fulfilled: it constitutes a part of the contract and must be fulfilled to keep the contract in force *c*) a covenant by which the seller of real estate assures, and binds himself to defend, the security of the title: in full **covenant of warranty**

warranty deed *Law* a deed to real estate containing a covenant of warranty: see WARRANTY (sense 3 *c*)

War·ren[1] (wôr′ən, wär′-) [ONormFr. *warin* < ? OHG. *Warin*, the Varini, a people mentioned by Tacitus] **1.** a masculine name **2. Earl**, 1891– ; U.S. jurist; chief justice (1953–69) **3. Robert Penn**, 1905– ; U.S. writer & poet

War·ren[2] (wôr′ən, wär′-) **1.** [after Dr. Joseph *Warren* (1741–75), killed at Bunker Hill] city in SE Mich.: suburb of Detroit: pop. 179,000 **2.** [after Moses *Warren*, 19th cent. U.S. surveyor] city in NE Ohio: pop. 63,000: see YOUNGSTOWN

war·ren (wôr′ən, wär′-) *n.* [ME. *wareine* < ONormFr. *warenne* < *warir*, to preserve < Frank. *warjan: see WARRANT] **1.** orig., a piece of land enclosed for the breeding of game **2.** a space or limited area in which rabbits breed or are numerous **3.** any building or group of buildings crowded like a rabbit warren

war·ren·er (-ər) *n.* the owner or keeper of a warren

War·ring·ton (wôr′iŋ t′n, wär′-) city in Lancashire, NW England, on the Mersey River: pop. 74,000

war·ri·or (wôr′ē ər, wär′-; -yər) *n.* [ME. *werreour* < ONormFr. *werreiur* < *werrier*, to make war < *werre*, WAR[1]] a man taking part or experienced in conflict, esp. war; fighting man; soldier

War·saw (wôr′sô) capital of Poland, on the Vistula River: pop. 1,249,000 Pol. name, **War·sza·wa** (vär shä′vä)

☆**war·saw** (wôr′sô) *n.* [altered < AmSp. *guasa*] a very large, black grouper (*Epinephelus nigritus*) found in the warm waters about the West Indies and Florida

war·ship (wôr′ship′) *n.* any ship constructed or armed for combat use, as a battleship, destroyer, etc.

war·sle (wôr′s'l) *n., vi., vt.* **-sled, -sling** [Scot. & N. Eng. Dial.] same as WRESTLE —**war′sler** *n.*

Wars of the Roses the English civil war (1455–85) fought between the house of York, whose emblem was a white rose, and the house of Lancaster, whose emblem was a red rose: the war ended with the establishment of the house of Tudor on the English throne

wart (wôrt) *n.* [ME. *warte* < OE. *wearte*, akin to G. *warze* < IE. base **wer-*, a raised place, whence L. *verruca*, wart (cf. VERRUCA)] **1.** a small, usually hard, tumorous growth on the skin, caused by a virus **2.** any small protuberance, as a glandular protuberance on a plant —**wart′y** *adj.*

War·ta (vär′tä) river in Poland, flowing from the S part northwest into the Oder: 502 mi.

Wart·burg (värt′boork) medieval castle in Thuringia, Germany, where Martin Luther completed his translation of the New Testament (1521–22)

wart hog a wild African hog (*Phacochoerus aethiopicus*) having a broad, flat face, very large, incurved tusks, and a number of conical warts on the cheeks between the eyes and tusks

war·time (wôr′tim′) *n.* a time of war —*adj.* of or characteristic of such a time

☆**war whoop** a loud shout or yell uttered, as by N. American Indians, on going into battle, etc.

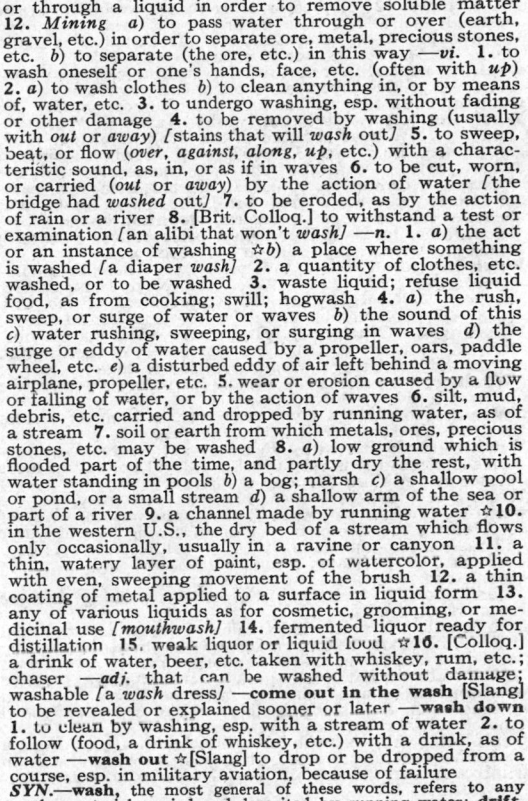

WART HOG
(2–2-1/2 ft. high at shoulder)

War·wick (wôr′ik, wär′-; *for 2, usually* wôr′wik) **1.** same as WARWICKSHIRE **2.** [after the Earl of *Warwick*, friend of the founder] city in SE R.I., on Narragansett Bay: pop. 84,000: see PROVIDENCE

War·wick (wôr′ik, wär′-), Earl of, (*Richard Neville*) 1428–71; Eng. statesman & military leader

War·wick·shire (wôr′ik shir′, wär′-) county of C England: 983 sq. mi.; pop. 2,077,000

war·y (wer′ē) *adj.* **war′i·er, war′i·est** [< WARE[2] + -Y[2]] **1.** cautious; on one's guard **2.** characterized by caution [a *wary* look] —*SYN.* see CAREFUL —**wary of** careful of

was (wuz, wäz; *unstressed* wəz) [ME. < OE. *wæs*, 1st & 3d pers. sing. of *wesan*, to be < IE. base **wes-*, to dwell, stay, whence Sans. *vastū*, house: not orig. connected with BE: cf. WERE] *1st & 3d pers. sing., pt., of* BE

Wa·satch Range (wô′sach) [< AmInd. (Ute), lit., mountain pass] range of the Rockies, extending from C Utah to SE Ida.: highest peak, 12,008 ft.

wash (wôsh, wäsh) *vt.* [ME. *wasshen* < OE. *wæscan*, akin to G. *waschen*: for prob. IE. base see WATER] **1.** to clean by means of water or other liquid, as by dipping, tumbling, or scrubbing, often with soap, a detergent, etc. **2.** to make clean in a religious or moral sense; purify **3.** to make wet, or moisten; drench or flush with water or other liquid **4.** to cleanse (itself or another) by licking, as a cat does **5.** to flow over, past, or against: said of a sea, river, lake, waves, etc. **6.** to soak (*out*), flush (*off*), or carry (*away*) by or as by the use or action of water [to *wash* out dirt, a bridge *washed* away by the flood] **7.** *a*) to make by flowing over and wearing away substance [a heavy rain that *washed* gullies in the bank] *b*) to cut into or erode; wear (*out* or *away*) by flowing over [the flood *washed* out the road] **8.** to act as a suitable cleaning agent for [soap that will *wash* silks] **9.** to cover with a thin or watery coating of paint, esp. of water color **10.** to cover with a thin layer of metal **11.** *Chem.* *a*) to pass distilled water through (a precipitate in a filter) *b*) to pass (a gas) over

or through a liquid in order to remove soluble matter **12.** *Mining* *a*) to pass water through or over (earth, gravel, etc.) in order to separate ore, metal, precious stones, etc. *b*) to separate (the ore, etc.) in this way —*vi.* **1.** to wash oneself or one's hands, face, etc. (often with *up*) **2.** *a*) to wash clothes *b*) to clean anything in, or by means of, water, etc. **3.** to undergo washing, esp. without fading or other damage **4.** to be removed by washing (usually with *out* or *away*) [stains that will *wash* out] **5.** to sweep, beat, or flow (*over, against, along, up*, etc.) with a characteristic sound, as, in, or as if in waves **6.** to be cut, worn, or carried (*out* or *away*) by the action of water [the bridge had *washed* out] **7.** to be eroded, as by the action of rain or a river **8.** [Brit. Colloq.] to withstand a test or examination [an alibi that won't *wash*] —*n.* **1.** *a*) the act or an instance of washing ☆*b*) a place where something is washed [a diaper *wash*] **2.** a quantity of clothes, etc. washed, or to be washed **3.** waste liquid; refuse liquid food, as from cooking; swill; hogwash **4.** *a*) the rush, sweep, or surge of water or waves *b*) the sound of this *c*) water rushing, sweeping, or surging in waves *d*) the surge or eddy of water caused by a propeller, oars, paddle wheel, etc. *e*) a disturbed eddy of air left behind a moving airplane, propeller, etc. **5.** wear or erosion caused by a flow or falling of water, or by the action of waves **6.** silt, mud, debris, etc. carried and dropped by running water, as of a stream **7.** soil or earth from which metals, ores, precious stones, etc. may be washed **8.** *a*) low ground which is flooded part of the time, and partly dry the rest, with water standing in pools *b*) a bog; marsh *c*) a shallow pool or pond, or a small stream *d*) a shallow arm of the sea or part of a river **9.** a channel made by running water ☆**10.** in the western U.S., the dry bed of a stream which flows only occasionally, usually in a ravine or canyon **11.** a thin, watery layer of paint, esp. of watercolor, applied with even, sweeping movement of the brush **12.** a thin coating of metal applied to a surface in liquid form **13.** any of various liquids as for cosmetic, grooming, or medicinal use [*mouthwash*] **14.** fermented liquor ready for distillation **15.** weak liquor or liquid food ☆**16.** [Colloq.] a drink of water, beer, etc. taken with whiskey, rum, etc.; chaser —*adj.* that can be washed without damage; washable [a *wash* dress] —**come out in the wash** [Slang] to be revealed or explained sooner or later —**wash down 1.** to clean by washing, esp. with a stream of water **2.** to follow (food, a drink of whiskey, etc.) with a drink, as of water —**wash out** ☆[Slang] to drop or be dropped from a course, esp. in military aviation, because of failure

SYN.—**wash**, the most general of these words, refers to any earthy material carried and deposited by running water; **drift**, the more precise term as used in geology, is usually qualified by a word descriptive of the manner in which the material is transported [glacial or fluvial *drift*]; **alluvium** usually refers to a deposit of relatively fine particles, such as soil, left by a flood, etc.; **silt** applies to material composed of very fine particles, such as that deposited on river beds or suspended in standing water

Wash (wôsh, wäsh), **The** shallow inlet of the North Sea, on the E coast of England: c.20 mi. long

Wash. Washington (State)

wash·a·ble (wôsh′ə b'l, wäsh′-) *adj.* that can be washed without damage —☆*n.* a washable fabric or garment

☆**wash-and-wear** (-'n wer′) *adj.* designating or of fabrics or garments that need little or no ironing after washing

wash·board (-bôrd′) *n.* ☆**1.** *a*) a board or frame with a ridged surface of metal, glass, etc., used for scrubbing dirt out of clothes *b*) the worn surface of a paved road resembling this **2.** same as BASEBOARD **3.** *Naut.* a thin, broad plank fastened along the gunwale of a boat or on the sill of a lower deck port to keep out the sea and spray

wash·bowl (-bōl′) *n.* ☆a bowl or basin for use in washing one's hands and face, etc., esp. a bathroom fixture fitted with water faucets and a drain: also **wash′ba·sin** (-bā′s'n)

☆**wash·cloth** (-klôth′) *n.* a small cloth, usually of terry, used in washing the face or body

wash·day (-dā′) *n.* a day, often the same day every week, when the clothes of a household are washed

wash drawing a painting done in transparent watercolors, usually in shades of black and gray

washed-out (wôsht′out′, wäsht′-) *adj.* **1.** faded in color, specif. from washing **2.** [Colloq.] tired; spiritless **3.** [Colloq.] tired-looking; pale and wan

washed-up (-up′) *adj.* **1.** cleaned up **2.** [Colloq.] tired; exhausted ☆**3.** [Slang] finished; done for; having failed

wash·er (wôsh′ər, wäsh′-) *n.* **1.** a person who washes **2.** a flat disk or ring of metal, leather, rubber, etc., used to make a seat for the head of a bolt or for a nut or faucet valve, to lock a nut in place, to provide a bearing surface, to serve as a sealer, etc. **3.** a machine for washing something, as clothes, dishes, etc. **4.** a device for washing gases

wash·er·wom·an (-woom′ən) *n., pl.* **-wom′en** a woman whose work is washing clothes; laundress —**wash′er·man** (-mən) *n.masc., pl.* **-men**

wash goods washable fabrics or garments

wash·ing (wôsh′iŋ, wäsh′-) *n.* **1.** the act of a person or thing that washes; a cleaning, flushing, etc. in water or

other liquid **2.** clothes or other things washed or to be washed, esp. at one time **3.** matter obtained or removed by washing **4.** a thin coating, as of metal, put on in liquid form **5.** *Finance* the act of making a wash sale

washing machine a machine for washing clothes, linens, etc., now usually operated automatically; washer

washing soda a crystalline form of sodium carbonate

Wash·ing·ton (wôsh′iŋ tən, wäsh′-) [after G. WASHINGTON] **1.** NW coastal State of the U.S.: admitted, 1889; 68,192 sq. mi.; pop. 3,409,000; cap. Olympia: abbrev. **Wash., WA 2.** capital of the U.S., coextensive with the District of Columbia: pop. 757,000 (met. area, incl. parts of Md. & Va., 2,861,000) **3. Lake,** lake in WC Wash., near Seattle: c.20 mi. long **4. Mount,** mountain of the White Mountains, in N H.: highest peak in New England: 6,288 ft. —**Wash′ing·to′ni·an** (-tō′nē ən) *adj., n.*

Wash·ing·ton (wôsh′iŋ tən, wäsh′-) **1. Book·er T(alia-ferro)** (book′ər), 1856–1915; U.S. Negro educator & author **2. George,** 1732–99; 1st president of the U.S. (1789–97); commander in chief of the Continental army

Washington (National) Monument white marble obelisk in Washington, D.C., on a mall west of the Capitol, in memory of George Washington: 555 ft. high

☆**Washington palm** a tall, slender fan palm (*Washingtonia filifera*) native to S California

☆**Washington pie** a layer cake with a filling of cream, custard, chocolate, fruit jelly, or the like

Washington's Birthday February 22, George Washington's birthday: it is celebrated as a legal holiday in most States on the third Monday in February

Wash·i·ta (wäsh′i tô, wôsh′-) *same as* OUACHITA

wash·out (wôsh′out′, wäsh′-) *n.* ☆**1.** the washing away of soil, earth, rocks, etc. by a sudden, strong flow of water ☆**2.** a hole or gap made by such washing away, as in a railroad bed **3.** [Slang] a complete failure

☆**wash·rag** (-rag′) *n. same as* WASHCLOTH

☆**wash·room** (-rōōm′) *n.* **1.** a room for washing **2.** *same as* RESTROOM

☆**wash sale** the pretended trading of stock, accomplished by buying shares at one broker and simultaneously selling an equal number of shares at another broker, in order to make trade in that stock appear active: an illegal practice

wash·stand (-stand′) *n.* **1.** a table holding a bowl and pitcher, etc. for washing the face and hands **2.** a washbowl that is a bathroom fixture

wash·tub (-tub′) *n.* a tub for washing clothes, etc.; often, a stationary metal tub fitted with water faucets and a drain

wash·wom·an (-woom′ən) *n., pl.* **-wom′en** *same as* WASHERWOMAN

wash·y (-ē) *adj.* **wash′i·er, wash′i·est 1.** watery; weak **2.** weak in color; pale **3.** without force or substance; insipid

☆**was·n't** (wuz′'nt, wäz′-) was not

☆**WASP, Wasp** (wäsp, wôsp) *n.* a white Anglo-Saxon Protestant

wasp (wäsp, wôsp) *n.* [ME. *waspe* < OE. *wæsp,* akin to G. *wespe* < Gmc. base *waps-* < IE. *wobhsā* < base *webh-,* to WEAVE (in reference to the cocoonlike nest)] any of a large, worldwide group of winged hymenopterous insects, characterized by a slender body with the abdomen attached by a narrow stalk, biting mouthparts, and, in the females and workers, a vicious sting that can be used repeatedly: some wasps, as the hornet, are characterized by a colonial or social organization

WASP
(1/2–3 in. long)

wasp·ish (wäs′pish, wôs′-) *adj.* **1.** of or like a wasp **2.** having a slender waist, like a wasp **3.** bad-tempered; snappish —**wasp′ish·ly** *adv.* —**wasp′ish·ness** *n.*

wasp waist a very slender or tightly corseted waist

wasp·y (wäs′pē, wôs′-) *adj.* **wasp′i·er, wasp′i·est** of, like, or characteristic of a wasp —**wasp′i·ness** *n.*

was·sail (wäs′'l, was′-; -āl) *n.* [ME., earlier *wæs hæil* < ON. *ves heill,* lit., be hale, be hearty (replacing cognate OE. *wes hal,* lit., be whole)] **1.** a salutation formerly given in drinking the health of a person, as at a festivity **2.** the spiced ale or other liquor with which such healths were drunk **3.** a celebration with much drinking, esp. at Christmas time; carousal —*vi.* to drink wassails —*vt.* to drink to the health or prosperity of —**was′sail·er** *n.*

Was·ser·mann (väs′ər män′; *E.* wäs′ər mən) **1. Au·gust von** (ou′goost fôn), 1866–1925; Ger. bacteriologist **2. Ja·kob** (yä′kōp), 1873–1934; Ger. novelist

Wassermann test (or **reaction**) [after A. von WASSERMANN, who devised it] a complement-fixation test for the diagnosis of syphilis by determining the presence of syphilitic antibodies in the blood serum

wast (wäst; *unstressed* wəst) *archaic 2d pers. sing., past indic., of* BE: *used with* thou

wast·age (wās′tij) *n.* **1.** loss by use, decay, deterioration, etc. **2.** anything wasted, or the amount of this; waste **3.** *Geol.* **a)** the processes by which snow and ice masses are reduced by melting, evaporation, etc. **b)** the amount of material lost through these processes

waste (wāst) *vt.* **wast′ed, wast′ing** [ME. *wasten* < ONormFr. *waster* < L. *vastare,* to lay waste, devastate (< *vastus:*

see VAST): infl. by cognate Gmc. *wostjan,* whence OHG. *wuosten*] **1.** to destroy; devastate; ruin **2.** to wear away; consume gradually; use up **3.** to make weak, feeble, or emaciated; wear away the strength, vigor, or life of [a man *wasted* by age and disease] **4.** to use up or spend without real need, gain, or purpose; squander **5.** to fail to take proper advantage of [to *waste* an opportunity] —*vi.* **1.** to lose strength, health, vigor, flesh, etc., as by disease; become weak or enfeebled (often with *away*) **2.** to be used up or worn down gradually; become smaller or fewer by gradual loss **3.** [Now Rare] to pass or be spent: said of time **4.** to be wasted, or not put to full or proper use —*adj.* [ME. *wast* < ONormFr. < L. *vastus:* see VAST] **1.** uncultivated or uninhabited, as a desert; wild; barren; desolate **2.** left over, superfluous, refuse, or no longer of use [a *waste* product] **3.** produced in excess of what is or can be used [*waste* energy] **4.** excreted from the body as useless or superfluous material, as feces or urine **5.** used to carry off or hold waste or refuse [a *waste* pipe, *wastebasket*] —*n.* [ME. < ONormFr. < the *adj.;* also in part < L. *vastum,* neut. of *vastus*] **1.** uncultivated or uninhabited land, as a desert or wilderness **2. a)** a desolate, uncultivated, or devastated stretch, tract, or area **b)** a vast expanse, as of the sea **3.** a wasting or being wasted; specif., **a)** a useless or profitless spending or consuming; squandering, as of money, time, etc. **b)** a failure to take advantage (of something) **c)** a gradual loss, decrease, or destruction by use, wear, decay, deterioration, etc. **4.** useless, superfluous, or discarded material, as ashes, garbage, sewage, etc. **5.** superfluous matter excreted from the body, as feces or urine **6.** cotton fiber or yarn left over from the process of milling, used for wiping machinery, packing bearings, etc. **7.** [Rare or Obs.] ruin or devastation, as by war, fire, etc. **8.** *Physical Geography* material derived by land erosion or disintegration of rock, and carried to the sea by rivers and streams —**go to waste** to be or become wasted —**lay waste (to)** to destroy; devastate; make desolate

SYN.—**waste,** in this connection, is the general word for any stretch of uncultivable, hence uninhabitable, land; a **desert** is a barren, arid, usually sandy tract of land; **badlands** is applied to a barren, hilly waste where rapid erosion has cut the soft rocks into fantastic shapes; **wilderness** refers to an uninhabited waste where a lack of paths or trails makes it difficult to find one's way, specif. to such a region thickly covered with trees and underbrush

waste·bas·ket (wāst′bas′kit, -bäs′-) *n.* a basket or other open container for wastepaper, bits of trash, etc.: also **wastepaper basket**

waste·ful (-fəl) *adj.* in the habit of wasting or characterized by waste; squandering; extravagant —**waste′ful·ly** *adv.* —**waste′ful·ness** *n.*

waste·land (-land′) *n.* **1.** land that is uncultivated, barren, or without vegetation **2.** a neglected, improperly managed, or intellectually unproductive activity, endeavor, etc.

waste·pa·per (-pā′pər) *n.* paper thrown away after use or as useless: also **waste paper**

waste pipe a pipe for carrying off waste water, sink drainage, excess steam, etc.

wast·er (wās′tər) *n.* a person or thing that wastes; esp., a spendthrift or prodigal; wastrel

wast·ing (-tiŋ) *adj.* **1.** desolating; destructive [a *wasting* war] **2.** destructive to health, as a disease —**wast′ing·ly** *adv.*

wast·rel (wās′trəl) *n.* [dim. of WASTER] **1.** a person who wastes; esp., a spendthrift **2.** *same as* GOOD-FOR-NOTHING

‡**wat** (wät) *n.* [Thai < Sans. *vāṭa,* enclosed area] a Buddhist temple in Thailand

watch (wäch, wôch) *n.* [ME. *wacche* < OE. *wæcce* < the base of *wacian:* see WAKE¹] **1.** the act or fact of keeping awake, esp. of keeping awake and alert, in order to look after, protect, or guard **2. a)** any of the several periods into which the night was divided in ancient times **b)** a part of the night [the still *watches* of the night] **3. a)** close observation for a time, in order to see or find out something **b)** the act or process of vigilant, careful guarding [to keep *watch* over a house] **4.** a person or group on duty, esp. at night, to protect or guard; lookout or guard **5. a)** the period of duty of a guard **b)** the post of a guard **6.** a small timepiece designed to be carried in the pocket or worn on the wrist, a pendant, etc. **7.** [Obs.] **a)** a vigil; wake **b)** vigilance **8.** [Obs.] a candle marked off into sections, used for keeping time **9.** [Obs.] a watchman's cry **10.** *Naut.* **a)** any of the periods of duty (five of four hours, and two of two hours), into which the day is divided on shipboard, so that the work is shared among alternating shifts of the crew **b)** the part of the crew on duty during any such period **c)** a ship's chronometer —*vi.* **1.** to stay awake at night in devotion; keep religious vigil **2.** to stay awake and alert at night; care for or guard something at night **3.** to be on the alert; be on the lookout **4.** to look or observe, esp. attentively **5.** to be looking or waiting attentively (with *for*) [to *watch* for one's chance] —*vt.* **1.** to guard **2.** to keep looking at; observe carefully and constantly **3.** to view mentally; keep informed about **4.** to be on the alert for; wait for and look for [to *watch* one's chance] **5.** to keep watch over or tend (a flock, a baby, etc.) —**on the watch** watching; on the lookout, as for something or person expected —☆**watch oneself** to be careful, cautious, or discreet —☆**watch out** to be alert and on one's guard; be careful —**watch over** protect from harm or danger

watch and ward the act of watching as a sentinel: now

chiefly in the titles of societies self-appointed as guardians of a community's morals

☆**watch·band** (-band′) *n.* a band of leather, metal, cloth, etc. for holding a watch on the wrist

☆**watch cap** a closefitting, knitted wool cap of a kind worn by sailors during cold weather

watch·case (-kās′) *n.* the metal case, or outer covering, of a watch

watch chain a chain attached at one end to a pocket watch, with an ornament (or fob) or fastener at the other end

watch·dog (-dôg′, -däg′) *n.* 1. a dog kept to guard property, as by barking 2. a person or group that keeps watch in order to prevent waste, unethical practices, etc.

watch·er (-ər) *n.* 1. a person who watches, esp. one who keeps watch beside a sick or dead person 2. an observer; esp., ☆a person authorized to keep watch at a polling place to detect irregularities

watch fire a fire kept burning at night as a signal or for the use of those staying awake to watch, or guard

watch·ful (-fəl) *adj.* 1. watching closely; vigilant; alert 2. characterized by vigilance 3. [Archaic] wakeful; unsleeping —**watch′ful·ly** *adv.* —**watch′ful·ness** *n.*
SYN.—**watchful** is the general word implying a being observant and prepared, as to ward off danger or seize an opportunity [under the *watchful* eye of her guardian]; **vigilant** implies an active, keen watchfulness and connotes the immediate necessity for this [a *vigilant* sentry]; **alert** implies a quick intelligence and a readiness to take prompt action [alert to the danger that confronted them]; **wide-awake** more often implies an alertness to opportunities than to dangers and connotes an awareness of all the surrounding circumstances [a *wide-awake* young salesman]

watch guard a chain, cord, or strap used to fasten a watch to clothing

watch·mak·er (-mā′kər) *n.* a person who makes or repairs watches —**watch′mak′ing** *n.*

watch·man (-mən) *n., pl.* -**men** 1. formerly, a person whose duty was to guard or police the streets at night 2. a person hired to guard a building or other property against thieves, vandals, or trespassers, esp. at night

watch night a religious service held on New Year's Eve: also **watch meeting** or **watch-night service**

watch pocket a small pocket, usually in a vest or trousers, for carrying a watch

watch·tow·er (-tou′ər) *n.* a high tower from which a sentinel watches for enemies, forest fires, etc.; lookout

watch·word (-wurd′) *n.* 1. a password, or countersign 2. a word or phrase embodying a principle or precept, esp. as the slogan or cry of a group or party

wa·ter (wôt′ər, wät′-) *n.* [ME. < OE. *wæter*, akin to G. *wasser* < IE. **wodōr* < base **wed-*, to wet, whence Gr. *hydōr*, water, L. *unda*, a wave, Russ. *voda*, water, IrGael. *uisce*, water] 1. the colorless, transparent liquid occurring on earth as rivers, lakes, oceans, etc., and falling from the clouds as rain: chemically a compound of hydrogen and oxygen, H_2O, it freezes, forming ice, at 32° F (0° C) and boils, forming steam, at 212° F (100° C) 2. water in a specified form or amount, or occurring or distributed in a specified way, or for a specified use, as drinking, washing, etc. 3. [*often pl.*] *a*) a large body of water, as a river, lake, sea, etc. *b*) the part of the sea contiguous with a specified country, land mass, etc. or the parts away from this [international *waters*] 4. water with reference to its depth [ten feet of *water* at the dam], its displacement [a boat that draws six feet of *water*], its surface [above *water*, under *water*], or its level in a sea, river, etc. [high *water*, low *water*] 5. [*pl.*] the water of mineral springs [to take the *waters* at Saratoga] 6. any body fluid or secretion, as urine, saliva, tears, gastric and pancreatic juices, etc.; specif., *a*) the fluid surrounding the fetus in pregnancy; amniotic fluid *b*) a watery fluid retained abnormally [*water* on the knee] 7. a solution of any substance in water [mineral *water*, ammonia *water*] 8. *a*) the degree of transparency and luster of a precious stone as a measure of its quality [a diamond of the first *water*] *b*) degree of quality or conformity to type [an artist of the first or purest *water*] 9. a wavy, lustrous finish given to linen, silk, rayon, etc., or to a metal surface 10. a watercolor painting 11. *Finance a*) a valuation wrongfully given to the assets of a business in excess of their real value *b*) an issue of capital stock which brings the face value of all the stock issued by a business to a figure higher than the actual value of its assets: now prohibited by SEC regulations —*vt.* [ME. *wateren* < OE. *wæterian* < the n.] 1. to supply with water; specif., *a*) to give (animals) water to drink *b*) to give water to (soil, crops, etc.) by sprinkling, pouring, or irrigating *c*) to bring water to (land): said of a river, canal, etc. *d*) to put water on by sprinkling, hosing, etc.; soak or moisten with water (often with *down*) *e*) to add water to so as to weaken; dilute [to *water* the milk] 2. to give a wavy luster to the surface of (silk, etc.) 3. *Finance* to issue (stock) so as to add illegally to the total face value without increasing assets to justify this valuation —*vi.* 1. to fill with tears: said of the eyes 2. to secrete or fill with saliva [his mouth *watered* at the sight of the roast] 3. to take on a supply of water 4. to drink water: said of animals

—*adj.* 1. of or having to do with water 2. in or on water [*water* sports] 3. growing in or living on or near water [*water* plants, *water* birds] 4. *a*) operated by water [a *water* wheel] *b*) derived from running water [*water* power] 5. containing water or fluid [a *water* blister] 6. prepared with water, as for thinning or hardening —**by water** by ship or boat —**hold water** 1. to contain water without leaking 2. to remain sound, consistent, or logical, with no breaks or weaknesses [an argument that *holds* no *water*] 3. to keep a boat at a standstill by holding the oars steady in the water —**like water** lavishly; freely: said of money spent, etc. —**make one's mouth water** to create a desire or appetite in one; be or seem tasty —**make water** 1. to urinate: also **pass water** 2. to take in water, as through a leak: said of a boat, etc. —**water down** to weaken the potency or effectiveness of

wa·ter·age (-ij) *n.* [Brit.] 1. the movement of goods by water 2. the fee for this

☆**water back** a tank or coil behind the firebox of a stove, for heating water

water bag 1. a bag designed to hold water, esp. one with tiny surface pores that allow evaporation, keeping the water cool 2. the fluid-filled amnion surrounding the fetus in human beings and other placental mammals

Water Bearer same as AQUARIUS

water beetle any of numerous unrelated beetles that live in freshwater ponds and streams, sometimes having one or two pairs of swimming legs fringed and functioning as oars

water bird any bird that lives on or near water; swimming or wading bird

water biscuit a cracker made of water, flour, and often some shortening

water blister a blister containing a clear, watery fluid without pus or blood

water boatman any of various hemipterous water bugs (family Corixidae) that swim about in ponds and streams by vigorous movement of the fringed, oarlike hind legs

wa·ter·borne (-bôrn′) *adj.* floating on or carried by water

wa·ter·brain (-brān′) *n.* same as GID

water brash same as PYROSIS

wa·ter·buck (-buk′) *n., pl.* -**buck′**, -**bucks′**: see PLURAL, II. D, 2 any of a number of African antelopes (genus Kobus) that frequent streams or rivers; esp., either of two species (*Kobus ellipsiprymnus* and *Kobus defassa*) of large, reddish or grayish antelopes of E and S Africa, having lyre shaped horns

water buffalo a slow, powerful, oxlike animal (*Bubalus bubalis*) native to S Asia, Malaya, and the Philippine Islands, having a pair of large, strong horns growing from the sides of the head: it likes to wallow in mud and is used as a draft animal

water bug 1. any of a large group of hemipterous insects that live in fresh waters, including the backswimmers and the water boatmen ☆2. loosely, same as CROTON BUG

WATERBUCK
(2-1/2—4 ft. high at shoulder)

Wa·ter·bur·y (wôt′ər bār′ē, wät′-) [from the many streams there] city in WC Conn.: pop. 108,000

water chestnut ☆1. *a*) a Chinese sedge (*Eleocharis dulcis*) with erect cylindrical leaves, growing in dense clumps in water *b*) the large, button-shaped, submerged tubers of this plant, used in Chinese cooking 2. a floating aquatic weed (*Trapa natans*) native to the Old World, with black, hard, horned fruit, the seed of which is sometimes eaten

☆**water chinquapin** 1. a perennial American waterlily (*Nelumbo lutea*) with large, emersed, umbrella-shaped leaves and yellow flowers 2. its edible fruit

water clock a mechanism for measuring time by the fall or flow of water; clepsydra

water closet same as TOILET (*n.* 4)

wa·ter·col·or (-kul′ər) *n.* 1. a pigment or coloring matter that is mixed with water for use as a paint 2. a painting done with such paints 3. the art of painting with watercolors —*adj.* painted with watercolors —**wa′ter·col′or·ist** *n.*

wa·ter·cooled (-kōōld′) *adj.* kept from overheating by having water circulated around or through it, as in pipes or a water jacket [a *water-cooled* engine] —**wa′ter·cool′** *vt.*

☆**water cooler** a device for cooling water, esp. by refrigeration, for drinking, as from a bubbler

wa·ter·course (-kôrs′) *n.* 1. a stream of water; river, brook, etc. 2. a channel for water, as a canal or stream bed

wa·ter·craft (-kraft′, -kräft′) *n.* 1. skill in handling boats or ships 2. skill in water sports, as swimming 3. *pl.* -**craft′** a boat, ship, or other water vehicle

wa·ter·cress (-kres′) *n.* [ME. *watercresse*; see WATER & CRESS] a white-flowered plant (*Nasturtium officinale*) of the mustard family, growing generally in running water, as from springs: its leaves are used in salads, soups, etc.

water cure same as: 1. HYDROPATHY 2. HYDROTHERAPY

wa·ter·cy·cle (-sī′k'l) *n.* any of various small watercraft that are moved by working pedals or treadles

water dog 1. any of various dogs especially fond of the water, as the water spaniel 2. any of several hunting dogs trained to retrieve waterfowl ☆3. *same as* MUD PUPPY 4. [Colloq.] a person who is at home in or on the water; esp., an old, experienced sailor

wa·tered (wôt′ərd, wät′-) *adj.* 1. sprinkled with water 2. supplied with water; having streams: said of land 3. having a wavy, lustrous pattern: said of cloth, metal surfaces, etc. 4. treated, prepared, or diluted with water ☆5. *Finance* issued in amounts producing a total face value beyond its true worth: said of stock, etc.

Wa·ter·ee (wôt′ə rē′) [< ? Siouan (Catawba) *wateran*, to float] river in N.C. & S.C., flowing from the Blue Ridge Mountains south to join the Congaree & form the Santee: c.300 mi. (in its upper course, c.225 mi., called *Catawba*)

wa·ter·fall (wôt′ər fôl′, wät′-) *n.* a steep fall of water, as of a stream, from a height; cascade

☆**wa·ter·find·er** (-fin′dər) *n.* a person who seeks out underground water by means of a divining rod

water flea any of many minute crustaceans which swim with spasmodic leaps; esp., any of various cladocerans

Wa·ter·ford (wôt′ər fərd) 1. county of Munster province, S Ireland, on the Atlantic: 709 sq. mi.; pop. 73,000 2. its county seat; a seaport: pop. 30,000

wa·ter·fowl (-foul′) *n., pl.* **-fowls′, -fowl′:** see PLURAL, II, D, 1 a water bird, esp. one that swims: the collective plural is used esp. of swimming game birds

☆**wa·ter·front** (-frunt′) *n.* 1. land at the edge of a stream, harbor, etc. 2. the part of a city or town on such land; wharf or dock area

☆**water gap** a break in a mountain ridge, with a stream flowing through it

water gas a fuel gas that is a poisonous mixture of hydrogen, carbon dioxide, carbon monoxide, and nitrogen, made by forcing steam over incandescent coke or coal

water gate a gate controlling the flow of water; floodgate

water gauge 1. a gauge for measuring the level or flow of water in a stream or channel 2. a device, as a glass tube, that shows the water level in a tank, boiler, etc.

water glass 1. *a)* a drinking glass or goblet *b)* a glass container for water, etc. 2. *same as* WATER GAUGE (sense 2) 3. a glass-bottomed tube or box for looking at things under water 4. sodium silicate or, sometimes, potassium silicate, occurring as a stony powder, usually dissolved in water to form a colorless, syrupy liquid used as an adhesive, as a protective or waterproofing coat, as a preservative for eggs, etc. 5. *same as* WATER CLOCK Also **wa′ter·glass′** *n.*

water gum ☆a black gum tree (*Nyssa biflora*) with greenish-white flowers, purplish fruit, and a swollen, submerged trunk base, growing in swampy ground

water hammer 1. a sealed glass tube partially filled with water but containing no air: when it is shaken, the water strikes against the ends with a hammerlike sound, demonstrating that solids and liquids fall at the same rate in a vacuum 2. *a)* the hammering sound caused in a pipe containing water when live steam is passed through it *b)* the thump of water in a pipe, caused by an air lock, when a faucet is suddenly closed

water hemlock any of a genus (*Cicuta*) of perennial plants of the parsley family, with compound umbels of small white flowers and intensely poisonous, tuberous roots, found in the Northern Hemisphere in moist places

water hen 1. any of various birds of the rail family, as the gallinule, moorhen, etc. ☆2. the American coot (*Fulica americana*)

water hole 1. a dip or hole in the surface of the ground, in which water collects; pond or pool, esp. one left in the dry bed of a stream and used as a drinking place by animals 2. a hole in the ice on a body of water

☆**water hyacinth** a S. American aquatic plant (*Eichhornia crassipes*) related to the pickerelweed, with swollen petioles that float on water and spikes of showy lavender flowers: a pest that blocks water traffic in the S U.S., esp. Florida

water ice 1. ice formed directly by the freezing of fresh water or salt water, as in a lake, bay, etc., rather than by the packing down of snow 2. [Brit.] water and sugar flavored and frozen as a confection

wa·ter·inch (-inch′) *n.* a former unit of hydraulic measure, calculated as the discharge of water through a circular opening one inch in diameter and equal to about fourteen pints per minute

wa·ter·i·ness (-ē nis) *n.* the state or quality of being watery

watering place 1. a place at a stream, lake, etc. where animals go to drink 2. a place where water, esp. fresh water, can be obtained 3. [Chiefly Brit.] a resort or spa with mineral springs for drinking or bathing or with a beach suitable for swimming, water sports, etc.

watering pot (or **can**) a container, esp. a can with a spout having a perforated nozzle, for watering plants, etc.; sprinkling can

wa·ter·ish (-ish) *adj. same as* WATERY

water jacket a casing holding water, placed around something to be cooled or kept at a constant temperature, as by the circulation of the water; esp., such a casing around the cylinder or cylinders of an internal-combustion engine

water jump a strip, ditch, or channel of water that a horse must jump, as in a steeplechase

wa·ter·leaf (-lēf′) *n., pl.* **-leafs′** any of a genus (*Hydrophyllum*) of perennial plants of the waterleaf family, with white or bluish, bell-shaped flowers —*adj.* designating a family (Hydrophyllaceae) of chiefly N. American plants, with a cymose inflorescence and capsular fruit, including baby blue-eyes, the nemophilas, the waterleafs, etc.

wa·ter·less (-lis) *adj.* 1. without water; dry 2. not needing water, as for cooking —**wa′ter·less·ness** *n.*

water lettuce a floating aquatic plant (*Pistia stratiotes*) of the arum family, with rosettes of thick, blunt, velvety, ribbed leaves and a hanging mass of feathery roots

water level 1. *a)* the surface of still water *b)* the height of this 2. *same as* WATER TABLE 3. a leveling instrument containing water in a glass tube 4. *same as* WATERLINE

wa·ter·lil·y (-lil′ē) *n., pl.* **-lil′ies** 1. any of various related water plants (esp. genera *Nymphaea*, *Nuphar*, and *Nelumbo*) of the water-lily family, having large, flat, floating leaves and showy flowers in a wide range of color 2. the flower of such a plant —*adj.* designating a family (Nymphaeaceae) of aquatic plants found worldwide in warm and temperate regions, including various African and Asiatic lotuses, the water chinquapin, the spatterdocks, etc.

WATERLILY

wa·ter·line (-lin′) *n.* 1. the line to which the surface of the water comes on the side of a ship or boat 2. any of several lines parallel to this, marked at various heights on the hull of a ship, indicating the various degrees of submergence when the ship is fully or partly loaded, or unloaded, and on an even keel ☆3. a pipe, tube, or other line connected to a source of water 4. *same as* WATERMARK (sense 1)

☆**water locust** a thorny tree (*Gleditsia aquatica*) of the legume family, native to the SE U.S., with a dark, heavy wood that takes a high polish

wa·ter·logged (-lôgd′, -lägd′) *adj.* 1. soaked or filled with water so as to be almost awash, and heavy and sluggish in movement: said of boats or floating objects 2. soaked with water; swampy

Wa·ter·loo (wôt′ər loō′, wät′-; wôt′ər loō′, wät′-) 1. [after ff.] city in NE Iowa: pop. 76,000 2. town in C Belgium, south of Brussels: scene of Napoleon's final defeat (June 18, 1815) by the Allies under Wellington & Blücher: pop. 10,000 —*n.* any disastrous or decisive defeat

water main a main pipe in a system of water pipes

wa·ter·man (wôt′ər mən, wät′-) *n., pl.* **-men** a person who works on or with boats; esp., an oarsman

wa·ter·man·ship (-ship′) *n.* the work, business, or skill of a waterman; esp., oarsmanship

wa·ter·mark (wôt′ər märk′, wät′-) *n.* 1. a mark showing the limit to which water has risen 2. *Papermaking a)* a translucent mark in paper, produced by pressure of a projecting design, as in the mold, during manufacture *b)* the design —*vt.* 1. to mark (paper) with a watermark 2. to impress (a design) as a watermark

water mass *Oceanography* a large body of oceanic water of nearly uniform temperature and chemical content, often a mixture of two or more such bodies, each having a specified temperature and salinity

wa·ter·mel·on (-mel′ən) *n.* [WATER + MELON: from its abundant watery juice] 1. a large, round or oblong, edible fruit with a hard, green rind and juicy, pink or red pulp containing many seeds 2. the widely cultivated African, tropical, trailing vine (*Citrullus vulgaris*) of the gourd family, on which it grows

water meter an instrument that measures and records the amount of water flowing through a pipe, etc.

water milfoil any of a genus (*Myriophyllum*) of graceful, feathery plants of a family (Haloragidaceae) related to the myrtle family, growing under water: used in aquariums

water mill a mill whose machinery is driven by water

☆**water moccasin** a large, poisonous, olive-brown pit viper (*Agkistrodon piscivorus*) with dark crossbars, related to the copperhead and found along or in rivers and swamps in the SE U.S.: often confused with various harmless snakes, esp. several water snakes (genus *Natrix*)

water nymph *Gr. & Rom. Myth.* a goddess having the form of a lovely young girl, supposed to dwell in a stream, pool, lake, etc.; naiad, Nereid, Oceanid, etc.

☆**water oak** an oak (*Quercus nigra*) of the SE U.S., found mainly along rivers, streams, etc.

water of crystallization water that occurs as a constituent of crystalline substances and can be removed from them by the application of heat at 100° C: the loss of water usually results in the loss of crystalline structure

water of hydration water which is chemically combined with a substance to form a hydrate and which can be removed, as by heating

water ouzel any of several birds of Europe, Asia, and America; esp., the American dipper (*Cinclus mexicanus*) of W N. America that dives and swims in mountain streams

water parting *same as* WATERSHED (sense 1)

water pepper any of several polygonums growing in wet places and having an acrid juice, as smartweed

water pimpernel 1. either of two small, white-flowered plants (*Samolus floribundus* or *Samolus valerandi*) of the primrose family, usually found along the edges of brooks 2. *same as* SCARLET PIMPERNEL: see PIMPERNEL

water pipe 1. a pipe for carrying water 2. a kind of

smoking pipe in which the smoke is drawn through water; narghile; hookah

water pistol a toy gun that shoots water in a stream

water plant any plant living submerged in water or with only the roots in or under water

water plantain any of a genus (*Alisma*) of hardy aquatic perennials of a family (Alismaceae) of water plants with large, heart-shaped leaves and small, usually white, flowers

water polo a water game played with a round, partly inflated ball by two teams of seven swimmers, the object of the game being to pass or take the ball over the opponent's goal line

water power 1. the power of running or falling water, used to drive machinery, etc., or capable of being so used **2.** a fall of water that can be so used **3.** a water right or privilege owned by a mill Also **wa′ter·pow′er** *n.*

wa·ter·proof (-prōōf′) *adj.* that keeps out water completely; esp., treated with rubber, plastic, etc., so that water will not penetrate —*n.* **1.** waterproof cloth or other material **2.** [Chiefly Brit.] a raincoat or other outer garment of waterproof material —*vt.* to make waterproof —**wa′ter·proof′er** *n.*

wa·ter·proof·ing (-iŋ) *n.* **1.** the act or process of making something waterproof **2.** any substance used for this

☆**water purslane 1.** a red-stemmed trailing plant (*Ludwigia palustris*) of the evening-primrose family, found in watery or muddy places **2.** a small aquatic plant (*Peplis diandra*) of the loosestrife family, with linear leaves

water rat 1. any of various rodents that live on the banks of streams and ponds ☆**2.** same as MUSKRAT

wa·ter·re·pel·lent (-ri pel′ənt) *adj.* that repels water but is not thoroughly waterproof

wa·ter·re·sist·ant (-ri zis′tənt) *adj.* that repels water for a short time but is not thoroughly waterproof

☆**water right** the right, sometimes limited, to use water from a stream, canal, etc. for general or specific purposes, as irrigation

water sapphire [transl. of Fr. *saphir d'eau*] a deep-blue, transparent variety of cordierite, sometimes used as a gem

wa·ter·scape (-skāp′) *n.* [WATER + (LAND)SCAPE] **1.** a view of a body of water; esp., a picture containing such a view **2.** same as SEASCAPE

water scorpion any of a family (Nepidae) of elongated, sticklike, four-winged insects, characterized by a long breathing tube at the anal end of the abdomen

wa·ter·shed (-shed′) *n.* **1.** a ridge or stretch of high land dividing the areas drained by different rivers or river systems ☆**2.** the area drained by a river or river system **3.** a crucial turning point affecting action, opinion, etc.

water shield ☆**1.** a purple-flowered water plant (*Brasenia schreberi*) of the waterlily family, having floating leaves coated underneath with a jellylike substance **2.** same as CABOMBA

wa·ter·side (-sīd′) *n.* land at the edge of a body of water; shore —*adj.* of, at, or on the waterside

☆**wa·ter·ski** (-skē′) *vi.* **-skied′, -ski′ing** to be towed, as a sport, on skilike boards (**water skis**) by a line attached to a speedboat —**wa′ter·ski′er** *n.*

water snake any of numerous saltwater or freshwater snakes; esp., any of a widely distributed genus (*Natrix*) of thick-bodied, nonpoisonous, freshwater snakes that feed chiefly on fish and amphibians

wa·ter·soak (-sōk′) *vt.* to soak with or in water

water softener 1. a chemical compound added to hard water to soften it, as by precipitating out the minerals **2.** a tank or other container in which water is filtered through any of various chemicals for softening

wa·ter·sol·u·ble (-säl′yoo b'l) *adj.* that can be dissolved in water

water spaniel either of two breeds of spaniel used in hunting to retrieve waterfowl and having a curly coat

wa·ter·spout (-spout′) *n.* **1.** a hole, pipe, or spout from which water runs **2.** *a)* a tornado occurring over water, close to or touching the surface, and appearing as a rapidly rotating, funnel-shaped or tubelike column of air full of spray *b)* [Rare] a similar whirlwind of lesser intensity

water sprite in folklore, a spirit, nymph, etc. dwelling in or haunting the water

water sprout a fast-growing sprout arising from the base, the trunk, or a main limb, of a tree or shrub, often with leaves different from those of adult parts of the same plant

water strider any of an insect-eating family (Gerridae) of usually slender-bodied, hemipterous insects, having long legs with which they glide swiftly on the surface film of calm waters, esp. of ponds and streams

water supply 1. the water available for use of a community or in an area **2.** the system for storing and supplying such water, as the reservoirs, mains, etc.

water system 1. a river with all its tributaries **2.** same as WATER SUPPLY

water table 1. the level below which the ground is saturated with water **2.** *Archit.* a projecting ledge or molding which throws off rainwater

water thrush ☆any of several N. American warblers (genus *Seiurus*), usually found near streams

wa·ter·tight (-tīt′) *adj.* **1.** so snugly put together that no water can get in or through **2.** that cannot be misconstrued, refuted, defeated, nullified, etc.; flawless [a *watertight* excuse, plan, etc.] —**wa′ter·tight′ness** *n.*

Wa·ter·ton Lakes National Park (wôt′ər tən, wät′-) national park in S Alberta, Canada: 203 sq. mi.: with Glacier National Park of Montana, it forms **Waterton-Glacier International Peace Park**

water tower 1. an elevated tank used for water storage and for maintaining equalized pressure on a water system ☆**2.** a firefighting apparatus that can be used to lift high-pressure hose and nozzles to great heights

Wa·ter·town (wôt′ər toun′) [orig., *Waterton*, after a place or family in Yorkshire, England, later understood as *Watertown*, the place being well watered] town in E Mass., on the Charles River: suburb of Boston: pop. 39,000

☆**water turkey** same as DARTER (sense 2)

water vapor water in the form of mist or tiny diffused particles, esp. when below the boiling point, as in the air: distinguished from STEAM

wa·ter·vas·cu·lar system (-vas′kyə lər) in echinoderms, a system of closed tubes and ducts filled with sea water containing some protein, and functioning variously, as in locomotion, food gathering, clinging, and respiration

wa·ter·way (-wā′) *n.* **1.** a channel or runnel through or along which water runs **2.** any body of water wide enough and deep enough for boats, ships, etc., as a stream, canal, or channel; water route

wa·ter·weed (-wēd′) *n.* **1.** any of various water plants having inconspicuous flowers, as pondweed **2.** a N. American aquatic plant (*Anacharis canadensis*) with white flowers: used in aquariums

water wheel a wheel turned by water running against or falling on paddles, used as a source of power **2.** a wheel with buckets on its rim, used for lifting water

water wings a device, inflated with air, used to keep one afloat as while learning to swim: it is shaped somewhat like a pair of wings and is worn under the arms

water witch ☆**1.** a person who professes to have the power to find underground water with a divining rod; dowser ☆**2.** any of various diving birds, as certain grebes —**water witching**

wa·ter·works (-wurks′) *n.pl.* [often with sing. v. for 1] **1.** *a)* a system of reservoirs, pumps, pipes, etc., used to bring a water supply to a town or city *b)* a pumping station in such a system, with its machinery, filters, etc. **2.** [Slang] tears: usually in **turn on the waterworks**, to shed tears; weep

wa·ter·worn (-wôrn′) *adj.* worn, smoothed, or polished by the action of running water

wa·ter·y (-ē) *adj.* **1.** of or like water **2.** containing or full of water; moist **3.** bringing rain, as clouds **4.** thin; diluted [*watery* tea] **5.** tearful; weeping **6.** in or consisting of water [a *watery* grave] **7.** weak; insipid; without force **8.** soft, soggy, or flabby **9.** full of, secreting, or giving off a morbid discharge resembling water —**wa′ter·i·ness** *n.*

Wat·ling Island (wät′liŋ) same as SAN SALVADOR (island): also **Wat′lings Island**

Wat·son (wät′s'n, wôt′-) **1. James Dewey,** 1928– ; U.S. biochemist: helped determine the structure of DNA **2. John B**(roadus), 1878–1958; U.S. psychologist

watt (wät, wôt) *n.* [after ff.: name proposed (1882) by Sir W. SIEMENS] the practical mks unit of electrical power, equal to one joule per second or to the power developed in a circuit by a current of one ampere flowing through a potential difference of one volt; 1/746 of a horsepower

Watt (wät, wôt), **James** 1736–1819; Scot. engineer & inventor: pioneer in the development of the steam engine

watt·age (wät′ij, wôt′-) *n.* **1.** amount of electrical power, expressed in watts **2.** the amount of watts required to operate a given appliance or device

Wat·teau (vá tō′; *E.* wä tō′), **Jean An·toine** (zhän′ än twän′) 1684–1721; Fr. genre painter —*adj.* designating any of certain styles of dress found in Watteau paintings; esp., a back panel or train for a dress, that hangs straight from the shoulders

watt-hour (wät′our′, wôt′-) *n.* a unit of electrical energy or work, equal to one watt acting for one hour, or 3,600 joules

wat·tle (wät′'l, wôt′-) *n.* [ME. *wattel* < OE. *watul*, a hurdle, woven twigs, prob. < IE. base *wedh-*, to knit, bind] **1.** a sort of woven work made of sticks intertwined with twigs or branches, used for walls, fences, and roofs **2.** [Brit. Dial.] *a)* a stick, rod, twig, or wand *b)* a hurdle or framework made of sticks, rods, etc. **3.** [pl.] rods or poles used as the support of a thatched roof **4.** in Australia, any of various acacias: the flexible branches were much used by early settlers for making wattles **5.** a fleshy, wrinkled, often brightly colored piece of skin which hangs from the chin or throat of certain birds, as the turkey, or of some lizards **6.** a barbel of a fish —*adj.* made of or roofed with wattle or wattles —*vt.* **-tled, -tling** **1.** to twist or intertwine (sticks,

WATTLES

twigs, branches, etc.) so as to form an interwoven structure or fabric 2. to construct (a fence) by intertwining sticks, twigs, etc. 3. to build of, or roof, fence, etc. with, wattle **wat·tle·bird** (-bʉrd′) *n.* any of a number of honey eaters (genus *Anthochaera*) of Australia and Tasmania, with wattles hanging from the corners of the jaws
wat·tled (wät′'ld, wôt′-) *adj.* 1. built with wattles 2. having wattles, as a bird
watt·me·ter (wät′mēt′ər, wôt′-) *n.* an instrument for measuring in watts the power in an electric circuit
Watts (wäts, wôts), Isaac 1674–1748; Eng. clergyman & writer of hymns
Wa·tu·si (wä tōō′sē) *n., pl.* -sis, -si any member of a tall, slender, cattle-owning class of the Rundi of Burundi and Rwanda: also **Wa·tut′si** (-tōōt′sē)
Waugh (wô), **Evelyn (Arthur St. John)** 1903–66; Eng. novelist
Wau·ke·gan (wô kē′gən) [< Algonquian, lit., trading place] city in NE Ill., on Lake Michigan: pop. 65,000
Wau·ke·sha (wô′ki shô′) [< Algonquian dial., ? lit., fox] city in SE Wis.: suburb of Milwaukee: pop. 40,000
waul (wôl) *vi., n.* [cf. CATERWAUL] wail, squall, or howl
Wau·wa·to·sa (wô′wə tō′sa) [< AmInd. *wawatosi,* ? firefly] city in SE Wis.: suburb of Milwaukee: pop. 59,000
Wave (wāv) *n.* a member of the WAVES
wave (wāv) *vi.* **waved, wav′ing** [ME. *waven* < OE. *wafian,* akin to G. *waben,* to fluctuate < IE. base *webh-,* to move to and fro, prob. identical with *webh-,* to WEAVE] 1. to move up and down or back and forth in a curving or undulating motion; swing, sway, or flutter to and fro: said of flexible things free at one end [flags *waving* in the breeze] 2. to signal by moving a hand, arm, light, etc. to and fro 3. to have the form of a series of curves or undulations [hair that *waves* naturally] —*vt.* 1. to cause to wave, undulate, or sway to and fro 2. to swing or brandish (a weapon) 3. *a)* to move or swing (something) as a signal; motion with (the hand, arms, etc.) *b)* to signal (something) by doing this [to *wave* farewell] *c)* to signal or signify something to (someone) by doing this [he *waved* us on] 4. to give an undulating form to; make sinuous [to *wave* one's hair] 5. to give a wavy, or watered, appearance to (silk, etc.) —*n.* [altered (after the *v.*) < ME. *wawe,* a wave] 1. a ridge or swell moving along the surface of a liquid or body of water as a result of disturbance, as by wind 2. *a)* an undulation or series of undulations in or on a surface, such as that caused by wind over a field of grain *b)* a curve or series of curves or curls, as in the hair *c)* a wavy or undulating line on a watered fabric 3. a motion to and fro or up and down, such as that made by the hand in signaling 4. something like a wave in action or effect; specif., *a)* an upsurge or rise, as to a crest, or a progressively swelling manifestation [a crime *wave,* heat *wave, wave* of emotion, etc.] *b)* a movement of people, etc., in groups or masses, which recedes or grows smaller before subsiding or being followed by another [a *wave* of immigrants] 5. [Poet.] water; esp., the sea or other body of water 6. *Physics* a disturbance or state of motion that periodically rises and falls, or advances and retreats, as it is transmitted progressively from one particle or region in a medium to the next in a given direction or directions with no actual transport of matter, as in the propagation of light, sound, etc. —**make waves** to disturb the prevailing calm, complacency, etc. —**wave′less** *adj.* —**wave′like′** *adj.* —**wav′er** *n.*
SYN.—**wave** is the general word for a curving ridge or swell in the surface of the ocean or other body of water; **ripple** is used of the smallest kind of wave, such as that caused by a breeze ruffling the surface of water; **roller** is applied to any of the large, heavy, swelling waves that roll in to the shore, as during a storm; **breaker** is applied to such a wave when it breaks, or is about to break, into foam upon the shore or upon rocks; **billow** is a somewhat poetic or rhetorical term for a great, heaving ocean wave
wave band *Radio, TV* a specific range of wave frequencies
wave base the depth in a body of standing water at which the action of surface waves stops stirring the sediments
wave front *Physics* a surface, at right angles to a propagated disturbance, that passes at any given moment through those parts of the wave motion that are in the same phase and are moving in the same direction
wave·guide (wāv′gīd′) *n.* an electric conductor consisting of a metal tubing, usually circular or rectangular in cross section, used for the conduction or directional transmission of microwaves: also **wave guide**
wave·length (-leŋkth′, -leŋth′) *n. Physics* the distance, measured in the direction of progression of a wave, from any given point to the next point characterized by the same phase: also **wave length**
wave·let (wāv′lit) *n.* a little wave; ripple
Wa·vell (wā′v'l), **Archibald (Percival),** 1st Earl Wavell, 1883–1950; Brit. field marshal
wa·vell·ite (wā′və līt′) *n.* [after W. *Wavell* (?–1829), Eng. physician who discovered it] an orthorhombic hydrous phosphate of aluminum, vitreous and translucent
wave mechanics the branch of physics that deals with the dual nature of matter, i.e., matter exhibiting both particle and wave phenomena, and with the representation, in mathematical terms, of this behavior
wa·ver (wā′vər) *vi.* [ME. *waveren,* freq. of *waven,* to WAVE] 1. to swing or sway to and fro; flutter 2. to show doubt

or indecision; find it hard, or be unable, to decide; vacillate 3. to become unsteady; begin to give way; falter 4. to tremble; quaver: said of the voice, etc. 5. to vary in brightness; flicker: said of light 6. to fluctuate 7. to totter —*n.* the act of wavering, trembling, vacillating, etc. —**SYN.** see HESITATE —**wa′ver·er** *n.* —**wa′ver·ing·ly** *adv.*
WAVES (wāvz) [orig., *W(omen) A(ppointed for) V(oluntary) E(mergency) S(ervice)*] the women's branch of the U.S. Navy
wave train *Physics* a series of waves passing along the same course at regular intervals
wav·y (wā′vē) *adj.* **wav′i·er, wav′i·est** 1. having waves 2. moving in a wavelike motion 3. having undulating curves; forming waves and hollows; sinuous 4. like, characteristic of, or suggestive of waves 5. wavering; fluctuating; unsteady —**wav′i·ly** *adv.* —**wav′i·ness** *n.*
wawl (wôl) *vt., v.* [Chiefly Scot.] *same as* WAUL
wax¹ (waks) *n.* [ME. < OE. *weax,* akin to G. *wachs* < IE. *wokso-* < base *weg-,* to weave, whence WICK¹: from the appearance, etc.] 1. a plastic, dull-yellow substance secreted by bees for building cells; beeswax: it is hard when cold, easily molded when warm, melts at about 148°F, cannot be dissolved in water, and is used for candles, modeling, etc. 2. any plastic substance like this; specif., *a)* paraffin *b)* a waxlike substance exuded by the ears; earwax; cerumen *c)* a waxy substance produced by scale insects *d)* any waxlike substance yielded by plants or animals *e)* a resinous substance used by shoemakers to rub on thread *f) same as* SEALING WAX 3. any of a group of substances with a waxy appearance made up variously of esters, fatty acids, free alcohols, and solid hydrocarbons 4. [Colloq.] a phonograph record: orig. made with wax —*vt.* 1. to rub, polish, cover, smear, or treat with wax 2. [Colloq.] to make a phonograph record of —*adj.* made of wax —**wax′er** *n.* —**wax′like′** *adj.*
wax² (waks) *vi.* **waxed, waxed** or archaic **wax′en, wax′ing** [ME. *waxen* < OE. *weaxan,* to grow, akin to G. *wachsen* < IE. base *aweg-, *aug-,* whence EKE¹, L. *augere,* to increase] 1. to grow gradually larger, more numerous, etc.; increase in strength, intensity, volume, etc. 2. to increase in the size of its lighted portion; become gradually full: said of the moon: opposed to WANE (*vi.* 1) 3. to become; grow [to *wax* angry]
wax³ (waks) *n.* [< ? prec., as in phr. *wax angry* [Chiefly Brit. Colloq.] a fit of anger or temper; a rage
☆**wax bean** 1. a variety of kidney bean with long, narrow, yellow pods 2. the edible immature seed pod of this
wax·ber·ry (waks′ber′ē) *n., pl.* -ries *same as:* 1. SNOWBERRY (senses 1 & 3) ☆2. BAYBERRY (sense 1)
wax·bill (waks′bil′) *n.* any of a group of finchlike, old-world birds of the weaverbird family, with waxy pink, scarlet, or white bills: some species are kept as cage birds
wax·en¹ (wak′s'n) *adj.* 1. made of wax 2. like wax, as in being white, soft, smooth, lustrous, pale, plastic, pliable, impressionable, etc. 3. covered with wax
wax·en² (wak′s'n) *archaic pp. of* WAX²
wax·i·ness (wak′sē nis) *n.* a waxy state or quality
wax insect any of various homopterous insects, esp. scale insects, that secrete a waxy substance sometimes used commercially; specif., a Chinese scale insect (*Ericerus pela*)
☆**wax-myr·tle** (-mʉr′t'l) *adj.* designating a family (Myricaceae) of trees and shrubs with aromatic foliage and decorative fruits that in some species are covered with a wax, including bayberry, sweet fern, sweet gale, etc.
☆**wax myrtle** *same as* BAYBERRY; esp., an evergreen shrub (*Myrica cerifera*) native to E N. America and having grayish-white berries coated with a wax used for candles
wax palm 1. *same as* CARNAUBA 2. a palm (*Ceroxylon andicola*) of the Andes, whose trunk yields a wax used in making candles, polishes, etc.
wax paper a kind of paper made moistureproof by a wax, or paraffin, coating: also **waxed paper**
☆**wax·weed** (-wēd′) *n.* a plant (*Cuphea petiolata*) of the loosestrife family, with sticky stems and purple flowers
wax·wing (-wiŋ′) *n.* any of several fruit-eating birds (family Bombycillidae) found in many parts of the Northern Hemisphere, with silky-brown plumage, a showy crest, and scarlet spines, suggesting sealing wax, at the ends of the secondary quill feathers, as the CEDAR WAXWING
wax·work (-wʉrk′) *n.* 1. work, as objects, figures, etc., made of wax 2. a human figure made of wax
wax·works (-wʉrks′) *n.pl.* [*with sing. v.*] an exhibition of wax figures, usually representations of famous and notorious persons: also **wax museum**
wax·y (wak′sē) *adj.* **wax′i·er, wax′i·est** 1. full of, covered with, or made of wax 2. like wax in nature or appearance 3. *Med.* designating, of, or characterized by degeneration resulting from the deposit of an insoluble, waxlike substance in an organ
way (wā) *n.* [ME. < OE. *weg,* akin to G. *weg* < IE. base *weĝh-,* to go, whence L. *vehere,* to carry, ride, Gr. *ochos,* wagon] 1. a means of passing from one place to another, as a road, highway, street, path, etc. [the Appian *Way*] 2. room or space for passing; free area; an opening, as in a crowd or traffic [clear a *way* for the ambulance] 3. a route or course that is or may be used to go from one place to another: often used in combination [highway, railway, one-*way* street, etc.] 4. a specified route or direction [on the *way* to town] 5. a path in life; course or habits of life or conduct [to fall into evil *ways*] 6. *a)* a course of action;

method or manner of doing something [do it this *way*] *b)* a means to an end; method [a *way* to cut costs] **7.** a usual or customary manner of living, acting, or being [the *way* of the world] **8.** a characteristic manner of acting or doing [to learn the *ways* of other people] **9.** manner or style [to have a pleasant *way*] **10.** distance [a long *way* off] **11.** direction of movement or action [go this *way*, look this *way*] **12.** respect; point; particular; feature [to be right in some *ways*] **13.** what one desires; wish; will [to have or get one's own *way*] **14.** range or scope, as of experience [a method that never came in his *way*] **15.** relationship as to those taking part: used in hyphenated compounds [a four-*way* conversation] **16.** [Colloq.] a (specified) state or condition [to be in a bad *way*] **17.** [Colloq.] a district; locality; area [out our *way*] **18.** *Law* the privilege that a person or group of persons, as residents in a village, have to go over certain ground; right of way **19.** *Mech.* a surface or slide on which the carriage of a lathe, etc. moves along its bed **20.** *Naut.* a ship's movement or momentum through water **21.** [*pl.*] *Shipbuilding* a timber framework on which a ship is built and along which it slides in launching —*adv.* [Colloq.] away; far; to a considerable extent or at some distance [*way* behind] —*SYN.* see METHOD —**by the way 1.** incidentally **2.** on or beside the way —**by way of 1.** passing through; through; via **2.** as a way, method, mode, or means of **3.** [Chiefly Brit.] in the condition or position of [by *way of* being a fine pianist] —**come one's way 1.** to come within one's scope or range; come to one **2.** [Colloq.] to turn out successfully for one: also **go one's way** —**give way 1.** to withdraw; yield **2.** to break down; collapse —**give way to 1.** to step aside for; yield **2.** to give free expression to [to *give way to* tears] —**go out of the** (or **one's**) **way** to inconvenience oneself; do something that one would not ordinarily do, or that requires extra or deliberate effort or trouble —**in the way** in such a position or of such a nature as to obstruct, hinder, impede, or prevent —**lead the way** to be a guide or example —**make one's way 1.** to advance or proceed **2.** to advance in life or succeed, as by one's own efforts —**make way 1.** to make room; clear a passage **2.** to make progress —**on the way out 1.** becoming unfashionable, obsolescent, etc. **2.** dying —**out of the way 1.** in a position so as not to hinder or interfere **2.** disposed of **3.** out of existence; (put) to death **4.** not on the right or usual route or course **5.** *a)* improper; wrong; amiss *b)* unusual; uncommon *c)* [Obs.] lost —**parting of the ways** an ending of a relationship as because of a disagreement —**see one's way** (**clear**) **1.** to be willing (to do something) **2.** to find it convenient or possible —**take one's way** [Poet.] to go on a journey; travel —**the way** according to the way that; as [with things *the way* they are] —**under way 1.** moving; advancing; making progress **2.** *Naut. see* UNDERWAY

way·bill (wā′bil′) *n.* ☆a paper giving a list of goods and shipping instructions, sent with goods in transit

way·far·er (-fer′ər) *n.* a person who travels, esp. from place to place on foot —**way′far′ing** *adj., n.*

way·go·ing (wā′gō′iŋ) *adj.* **1.** [Chiefly Scot.] going away; departing **2.** *Law* designating a crop that will not ripen until after a tenant's term of occupancy has expired, and in which he has an interest —*n.* [Chiefly Scot.] the act of leaving or departing

Way·land (wā′lənd) in Germanic & English folklore, an invisible smith: also **Wayland** (**the**) **Smith**

way·lay (wā′lā′, wā′lā′) *vt.* **-laid′**, **-lay′ing** [WAY + LAY[1], after MLowG. *wegelagen*, to waylay < *wegelage*, an ambush] **1.** to lie in wait for and attack; ambush **2.** to wait for and accost (a person) on the way —**way′lay′er** *n.*

Wayne (wān) [< surname *Wayne*] **1.** a masculine name **2. Anthony**, 1745–96; Am. general in the Revolutionary War: called **Mad Anthony Wayne**

Way of the Cross *same as* STATIONS OF THE CROSS

☆**way-out** (wā′out′) *adj.* [Colloq.] very unusual, unconventional, experimental, nonconformist, esoteric, etc.

ways (wāz) *n.pl.* [with *sing. v.*] [Colloq.] *same as* WAY (*n.* 10)

-ways (wāz) [ME. < *way* (see WAY) + *adv. gen.* -*s*] *an adv.-forming suffix meaning* in a (specified) direction, position, or manner [endways]: equivalent to *-wise* (sense 1)

ways and means 1. methods and resources at the disposal of a person, company, etc. **2.** methods of raising money, specif. such methods, including legislation, in government

way·side (wā′sīd′) *n.* the edge of a road; area close to the side of a road —*adj.* on, near, or along the side of a road —**go by the wayside** to be put aside, shelved, or discarded

☆**way station** a small railroad station between more important ones, where through trains stop only on signal

☆**way train** a train stopping at way stations; local

way·ward (-wərd) *adj.* [ME. *weiward*, aphetic for *aweiward*: see AWAY & -WARD] **1.** insistent upon having one's own way contrary to others' advice, wishes, or orders; headstrong, willful, disobedient, delinquent, etc. **2.** conforming to no fixed rule or pattern; unpredictable; irregular; capricious; erratic **3.** [Archaic] not expected or wanted [his *wayward* fate] —**way′ward·ly** *adv.* —**way′ward·ness** *n.*

way·worn (-wôrn′) *adj.* tired from traveling

Wa·zir·i·stan (wä zir′i stän′) mountainous region in West Pakistan, on the Afghanistan border: c.5,000 sq. mi.

W.B., W/B waybill

w.b. 1. *Naut.* water ballast **2.** westbound

WbN west by north

WbS west by south

W.C. West Central (postal district in London)

w.c. 1. water closet **2.** without charge

W.C.T.U. Woman's Christian Temperance Union

wd. 1. ward **2.** word

we (wē) *pron.* [for sing. see I] [ME. < OE., akin to G. *wir*, Goth. *weis* < IE. base **we-*, we, whence Sans. *vayám*] **1.** the persons speaking or writing: sometimes used by a person in referring to two or more persons including himself and often the person or persons addressed, or by a monarch, author, editor, judge, etc. in referring to himself **2.** you: used in direct address as in encouraging or admonishing a child, invalid, etc. [shall we take the medicine now?] *We* is the nominative case form, *us* the objective, *our* and *ours* the possessive, and *ourselves* (or, by a king, etc., *ourself*) the intensive and reflexive, of the first personal plural pronoun

weak (wēk) *adj.* [ME. *waik* < ON. *veikr*, akin to OE. *wac*, feeble (which the ON. word replaced) < IE. base **weig-*, to bend, yield, whence WICKER, L. *vicis*, change] **1.** *a)* lacking in strength of body or muscle; not physically strong *b)* lacking vitality; feeble; infirm **2.** lacking in skill or strength in combat or competition [a *weak* team] **3.** lacking in moral strength or will power; yielding easily to temptation, the influence of others, etc. **4.** lacking in mental power, or in the ability to think, judge, decide, etc. **5.** *a)* lacking ruling power, or authority [a *weak* government] *b)* having few resources; relatively low in wealth, numbers, supplies, etc. [the *weaker* nations] **6.** lacking in force or effectiveness [*weak* discipline] **7.** *a)* lacking in strength of material or construction; unable to resist strain, pressure, etc.; easily torn, broken, bent, etc. [a *weak* railing] *b)* not sound or secure; unable to stand up to an attack, etc. [a *weak* fortification] **8.** *a)* not functioning normally or well: said of a body organ or part [*weak* eyes] *b)* easily upset; queasy [a *weak* stomach] **9.** indicating or suggesting moral or physical weakness [*weak* features] **10.** lacking in volume, intensity, etc.; faint [a *weak* voice, a *weak* current] **11.** lacking the usual or proper strength; specif., *a)* having only a small amount of its essential ingredient; diluted [*weak* tea] *b)* not as potent as usual or as others of the kind [a *weak* drug] *c)* lacking, poor, or deficient in something specified [*weak* in grammar, a baseball team *weak* in pitchers] **12.** *a)* ineffective; unconvincing [a *weak* argument] *b)* faulty [*weak* logic] **13.** tending toward lower prices: said of a stock or stock market **14.** *Chem.* having a low ion concentration, as certain acids and bases **15.** *Gram. a)* inflected by the addition of a suffix such as *-ed* or *-d* rather than by an internal vowel change: said of verbs popularly called *regular b)* inflected by the addition of a suffix originally belonging to a stem ending in *-n:* said of Germanic adjectives and nouns **16.** *Phonet.* unstressed or lightly stressed **17.** *Photog.* lacking contrast; thin: said of a negative **18.** *Prosody* designating or of a verse ending in which the stress falls on a word or syllable that is normally unstressed, often a preposition whose object occurs in the following line —**weak′ish** *adj.*

SYN.—**weak**, the broadest in application of these words, basically implies a lack or inferiority of physical, mental, or moral strength [a *weak* muscle, mind, character, foundation, excuse, etc.]; **feeble** suggests a pitiable weakness or ineffectiveness [a *feeble* old man, a *feeble* joke]; **frail** suggests an inherent or constitutional delicacy or weakness, so as to be easily broken or shattered [her *frail* body, conscience, etc.]; **infirm** suggests a loss of strength or soundness, as through illness or age [his *infirm* old grandfather]; **decrepit** implies a being broken down, worn out, or decayed, as by old age or long use [a *decrepit* old pensioner, a *decrepit* sofa] —*ANT.* strong, sturdy, robust

weak·en (-'n) *vt., vi.* to make or become weak or weaker —**weak′en·er** *n.*

SYN.—**weaken**, the most general of these words, implies a lessening of strength, power, soundness, etc. [weakened by disease, to *weaken* an argument]; **debilitate** suggests a partial or temporary weakening, as by disease or dissipation [debilitated by alcoholic excesses]; **enervate** implies a lessening of force, vigor, energy, etc., as through indulgence in luxury [enervated by idleness]; **undermine** and **sap** both suggest a weakening or impairing by subtle or stealthy means [his authority had been *undermined* by rumors, her strength was *sapped* by disease] —*ANT.* strengthen, energize

☆**weak·fish** (-fish′) *n., pl.* -**fish′**, -**fish′es**: see FISH[2] [< obs. Du. *weekvisch* < *week*, soft (akin to WEAK) + *visch*, FISH[2]] any of several ocean food fishes (genus *Cynoscion*), esp. a species (*Cynoscion regalis*), off the E coast of the U.S.

weak-kneed (-nēd′) *adj.* **1.** having weak knees **2.** lacking in courage, determination, resistance, etc.

weak·ling (-liŋ) *n.* **1.** a person or animal low in physical strength or vitality **2.** a person of weak character or intellect —*adj.* weak; feeble

weak·ly (-lē) *adj.* -**li·er**, -**li·est** sickly; feeble; weak —*adv.* in a weak manner —**weak′li·ness** *n.*

weak·mind·ed (-mīn′did) *adj.* 1. not firm of mind; indecisive; unable to refuse or deny 2. mentally deficient; feebleminded 3. showing weakness of resolve or thought [a *weak-minded* decision] —**weak′-mind′ed·ness** *n.*

weak·ness (-nis) *n.* 1. the state or quality of being weak 2. a weak point; fault or defect, as in one's character 3. *a)* a liking; esp., an unreasonable fondness (*for* something) *b)* something of which one is unreasonably fond [candy is his one *weakness*] —*SYN.* see FAULT

weak sister ☆[Slang] one who is cowardly, unreliable, etc.

weal¹ (wēl) *n.* [var. of WALE¹] a mark, line, or ridge raised on the skin, as by a blow; welt; wale

weal² (wēl) *n.* [ME. *wele* < OE. *wela*, wealth, well-being, akin to OS. *wela*: for IE. base see WILL¹] 1. a sound or prosperous state; well-being; welfare [the public *weal*] 2. [Obs.] *a)* wealth *b)* the body politic

weald (wēld) *n.* [readoption of OE. (WS.) *weald* (ME. *weeld*), forest, wold, wilderness, akin to WOLD¹, G. *wald*, forest] [Poet.] 1. a wooded area; forest 2. wild open country —**The Weald** region in SE England, in Surrey, Kent, & Sussex: formerly heavily forested

wealth (welth) *n.* [ME. *welthe*, wealth, happiness: see WEAL² & -TH¹] 1. *a)* much money or property; great amount of worldly possessions; riches *b)* the state of having much money or property; affluence [a man of *wealth*] 2. a large amount (*of* something); abundance [a *wealth* of ideas] 3. valuable products, contents, or derivatives [the *wealth* of the oceans] 4. [Obs.] weal; well-being 5. *Econ. a)* everything having economic value measurable in price *b)* any useful material thing capable of being bought, sold, or stocked for future disposition

Wealth·y (wel′thē) *n.* ☆a red, medium-sized fall apple

wealth·y (wel′thē) *adj.* **wealth′i·er**, **wealth′i·est** 1. having wealth; rich; prosperous; affluent 2. of, characterized by, or suggestive of wealth 3. rich or abundant (*in* something specified) [talk *wealthy* in nuances] —*SYN.* see RICH —**wealth′i·ly** *adv.* —**wealth′i·ness** *n.*

wean¹ (wēn) *vt.* [ME. *wenen* < OE. *wenian*, to accustom, wean, with sense affected by *awenian*, to wean (akin to G. *entwöhnen*, to wean) < IE. base *wen-*, to desire, attain, be satisfied, whence WONT, L. *venus*, love] 1. to cause (a child or young animal) to become accustomed gradually to food other than its mother's milk; cause to give up suckling; now, often, to cause to give up drinking milk from a bottle with a nipple 2. to withdraw (a person) by degrees (*from* a habit, object of affection, occupation, etc.), as by substituting some other interest —**wean′er** *n.*

wean² (wēn) *n.* [contr. of Scot. *wee ane*, little one] [Scot.] a child or baby

wean·ling (-liŋ) *n.* a child or young animal that has just been weaned —*adj.* recently weaned

weap·on (wep′ən) *n.* [ME. *wepen* < OE. *wæpen*, akin to G. *waffe*, ON. *vāpn*: base found only in Gmc.] 1. an instrument or device of any kind used for fighting, as specif. in warfare 2. any organ or part (of an animal or plant) so used 3. any means of attack or defense [the *weapon* of the law] —**weap′oned** *adj.* —**weap′on·less** *adj.*

☆**weap·on·eer** (wep′ə nir′) *n.* an expert in the design and production of weapons, esp. nuclear weapons

weap·on·ry (wep′ən rē) *n.* [WEAPON + -RY] 1. the design and production of weapons 2. weapons collectively; esp., a nation's stockpile of weapons of war

wear¹ (wer) *vt.* **wore**, **worn**, **wear′ing** [ME. *werian*, akin to ON. *verja*, Goth. *wasjan*, to clothe < IE. base *wes-*, to clothe, whence Sans. *vastra-*, L. *vestis*, clothing, *vestire*, to clothe] 1. *a)* to have on the body or carry on the person (clothing, jewelry, a weapon, etc.) *b)* to hold the position or rank symbolized by [to *wear* the heavyweight crown] *c)* to dress in (a specified kind of attire) so as to be in style [what the college girl is *wearing* this spring] 2. to have or show in one's expression or appearance [to *wear* a smile, *wearing* an air of expectancy] 3. to be fitted with or have on the person habitually [to *wear* dentures] 4. to have or bear as a characteristic or attribute [to *wear* a beard, to *wear* one's hair long] 5. to fly or show (its flag): said of a ship 6. to impair, consume, or diminish by constant use, handling, friction, etc. (often with *away*) 7. to bring by use to a specified state [to *wear* a coat to rags] 8. to make, cause, or produce by the friction of rubbing, scraping, flowing, etc. [to *wear* a hole in the sole of one's shoe] 9. to tire or exhaust (a person) 10. to pass (time) slowly or tediously (often with *away* or *out*) —*vi.* 1. to become impaired, consumed, or diminished by constant use, friction, etc. [shoes that have begun to *wear*] 2. to hold up in use as specified; bear continued use or handling; last [a suit that *wears* well] 3. to become in time; grow gradually [courage that is *wearing* thin] 4. to pass away gradually (often with *away* or *on*): said of time [the year *wore* on] 5. to have an irritating or exhausting effect (*on*) [noise *wearing* on his nerves] —*n.* 1. the act of wearing or the state of being worn 2. things, esp. clothes, worn, or for wearing, on the body [men's *wear*]: often in combination [sportswear, footwear] 3. the fashion or proper style of dress or the like 4. *a)* the gradual impairment, loss, or diminution from use, friction, etc. *b)* the amount of such loss 5. the ability to resist impairment or loss from use, friction, etc. [a lot of *wear* left in the tire] —**wear down** 1. to make or become worn; lose or cause to lose thickness or height by use, friction, etc. 2. to tire out, or exhaust (a person); weary 3. to overcome the resistance of by persistence —**wear off** to pass away or diminish by degrees —**wear out** 1. to make or become useless from continued wear or use 2. to waste or consume by degrees 3. to tire out; exhaust —**wear the pants** (or **trousers**) [Colloq.] to be master of the house —**wear′er** *n.*

wear² (wer) *vt.* **wore**, **worn**, **wear′ing** [altered (after prec.) < VEER²] to turn or bring (a ship) about by swinging its bow away from the wind; veer: opposed to TACK —*vi.* to turn or come about by having the bow swung away from the wind —*n.* the act of wearing a ship

wear·a·ble (wer′ə b'l) *adj.* that can be worn; suitable for wear —*n.* [*pl.*] wearable things; garments; clothing —**wear′a·bil′i·ty** *n.*

wear and tear loss and damage resulting from use

wea·ri·ful (wir′ē fəl) *adj.* that makes weary; tiresome —**wea′ri·ful·ly** *adv.* —**wea′ri·ful·ness** *n.*

wea·ri·less (-lis) *adj.* unwearying; tireless —**wea′ri·less·ly** *adv.* —**wea′ri·less·ness** *n.*

wea·ri·ness (-nis) *n.* 1. the condition or quality of being weary; fatigue or tedium 2. something that wearies

wear·ing (wer′iŋ) *adj.* 1. of or intended for wear [*wearing* apparel] 2. causing wear, or gradual impairment or diminution 3. wearying; tiring —**wear′ing·ly** *adv.*

wea·ri·some (wir′ē səm) *adj.* causing weariness; tiring, tiresome, or tedious —**wea′ri·some·ly** *adv.*

wear·proof (wer′prōōf′) *adj.* resistant to normal wear or continued use

wea·ry (wir′ē) *adj.* **-ri·er**, **-ri·est** [ME. *weri* < OE. *werig*, akin to OHG. *wuorag*, drunk < IE. base *wōr-*, giddiness, faintness, whence Gr. *hōrakian*, to be giddy] 1. tired; worn out 2. without further liking, patience, tolerance, zeal, etc.; bored (with *of*) [*weary* of jokes] 3. tiring [*weary* work] 4. irksome; tedious; tiresome [his *weary* explanation] —*vt.*, *vi.* **-ried**, **-ry·ing** to make or become weary —*SYN.* see TIRED —**wea′ri·ly** *adv.* —**wea′ri·ness** *n.*

wea·sand (wē′z'nd) *n.* [ME. *wesand* < OE. *wæsend*, the windpipe, akin to OHG. *weisant*, prp. form prob. < IE. base *weis-*, to flow out, with basic sense "the flowing": cf. ff.] 1. the esophagus; gullet 2. [Archaic] the trachea

wea·sel (wē′z'l) *n.*, *pl.* **-sels**, **-sel**: see PLURAL, II, D, 1 [ME. *wesel* < OE. *wesle*, akin to G. *wiesel*, prob. < IE. base *weis-*, to flow out (with reference to the rank odor emitted by the animal): cf. VIRUS, BISON]

WEASEL (6–14 in. long, including tail)

1. any of a worldwide group of agile, flesh-eating mammals (genus *Mustela*) related to the martens, with a long, slender body, short legs, and a long, bushy tail: they feed on rats, mice, birds, eggs, etc. 2. a sly, cunning, or sneaky person —*vi.* 1. to use weasel words 2. [Colloq.] to avoid or evade a commitment or responsibility (with *out*) —**wea′sel·ly** *adj.*

☆**weasel words** [prob. in allusion to the weasel's habit of sucking out the contents of an egg without destroying the shell] words or remarks that are equivocal or deliberately ambiguous or misleading

weath·er (weth′ər) *n.* [ME. *weder* < OE., akin to ON. *vethr*, G. *wetter* < IE. base *we-*, *awe-*, to blow, whence OSlav. *vedro*, fair weather] 1. the general condition of the atmosphere at a particular time and place, with regard to the temperature, moisture, cloudiness, etc. 2. disagreeable or harmful atmospheric conditions; storm, rain, etc. [protected against the *weather*] —*vt.* 1. to expose to the action of weather or atmosphere, as for airing, drying, seasoning, etc. 2. to wear away, discolor, disintegrate, or otherwise change for the worse by exposure to the atmosphere 3. to pass through safely or survive [to *weather* a storm] 4. to slope (masonry, cornices, etc.) so as to throw off rain, etc. 5. *Naut.* to pass to the windward of (a cape, reef, etc.) —*vi.* 1. to become discolored, disintegrated, etc. by exposure to the weather or atmosphere 2. to endure such exposure in a specified manner [canvas that *weathers* well] —*adj.* 1. designating or of the side of a ship, etc. toward the wind; windward 2. exposed to the elements [*weather* deck] —☆**under the weather** [Colloq.] 1. not feeling well; somewhat sick; ailing 2. somewhat drunk —**weather through** to pass or go safely through a storm, peril, difficulty, etc.

weath·er·beat·en (-bēt′'n) *adj.* showing the effect of weather, as, *a)* stained, damaged, or worn down *b)* sun-burned, roughened, etc.: said of a person, his face, etc.

weath·er·board (-bôrd′) *n.* 1. a board so shaped that its thin upper edge is overlapped by the board above, and its thick lower edge covers the top edge of the one below, in order to shed water; siding 2. *Naut.* the windward side of a ship —*vt.* to nail weatherboards on (a roof or wall)

weath·er·board·ing (-bôr′diŋ) *n.* weatherboards collectively

weath·er·bound (-bound′) *adj.* delayed or halted by bad weather, as a ship, airplane, etc.

☆**Weather Bureau** *former name of the* NATIONAL WEATHER SERVICE

weath·er·cock (-käk′) *n.* 1. a weather vane in the form of a cock 2. a fickle or changeable person or thing

weath·ered (we*th*′ərd) *adj.* **1.** seasoned by the weather; stained, worn, or beaten by the weather **2.** given a stained or discolored finish intended to resemble that produced by exposure to the weather **3.** *Archit.* made sloping, as sills, so as to shed water

weather eye 1. an eye alert to signs of changing weather **2.** a close watch for change of any kind /to keep a *weather eye* on a touchy situation/ —**keep one's weather eye open** to be on the alert; stay on guard

weath·er·glass (we*th*′ər glas′, -gläs′) *n.* same as BAROMETER (sense 1)

weath·er·ing (-iŋ) *n.* **1.** *Archit.* a slope built to shed water **2.** *Geol.* the physical and chemical effects of the forces of weather on rock surfaces, as in forming soil, sand, etc.

weath·er·ly (-lē) *adj. Naut.* that can sail close to the wind with very little drift to leeward —**weath′er·li·ness** *n.*

weath·er·man (-man′) *n., pl.* -**men′** (-men′) ☆a person who forecasts the weather, or, esp., one who reports weather conditions and forecasts, as on television

☆**weather map** a map or chart showing the condition of the weather in a certain area at a given time by indicating barometric pressures, temperatures, wind direction, etc.

weath·er·proof (-prōōf′) *adj.* that can withstand exposure to wind, rain, snow, etc. without being damaged —*vt.* to make weatherproof

weather station a post or office where weather conditions are recorded and studied and forecasts are made

☆**weath·er·strip** (-strip′) *n.* a thin strip of metal, felt, wood, etc., used to cover the joint between a door or window sash and the jamb, casing, or sill, so as to keep out drafts, rain, etc.: also **weather strip** —*vt.* -**stripped′**, -**strip′ping** to fit or provide with weatherstrips: also **weath′er·strip′**

☆**weath·er·strip·ping** (-strip′iŋ) *n.* **1.** same as WEATHERSTRIP **2.** weatherstrips collectively

weather vane a vane that swings in the wind to show the direction from which the wind is blowing

weath·er·wise (-wīz′) *adj.* **1.** skilled in predicting weather **2.** skilled in predicting shifts of opinion, feeling, etc.

weath·er·worn (-wôrn′) *adj. same as* WEATHER-BEATEN

weave (wēv) *vt.* **wove** or, chiefly for *vt.* 6 & *vi.* 3, **weaved**, **wov′en** or **wove** or, chiefly for *vt.* 6 & *vi.* 3, **weaved**, **weav′ing** [ME. *weven* < OE. *wefan*, akin to ON. *vefa*, G. *weben* < IE. base *webh-*, to weave, plait, whence Gr. *hyphē*, weaving: cf. WAVE, WEFT¹] **1.** *a)* to make (a fabric), esp. on a loom, by interlacing threads or yarns *b)* to form (threads) into a fabric **2.** *a)* to construct in the mind or imagination *b)* to work (details, incidents, etc.) into a story, poem, etc. **3.** *a)* to make by interlacing twigs, straw, rush, wicker, etc. /to *weave* baskets/ *b)* to twist or interlace (straw, wicker, etc.) so as to form something **4.** to twist or interlace (something) into, through, or among /to *weave* flowers into one's hair/ **5.** to make or spin (a web): said of spiders, etc. **6.** *a)* to cause (a vehicle, etc.) to move from side to side or in and out *b)* to make (one's way) by moving in this fashion —*vi.* **1.** to do weaving; make cloth **2.** to become interlaced or intertwined **3.** to move from side to side or in and out /*weaving* through traffic/ —*n.* a method, manner, or pattern of weaving /a cloth of English *weave*/

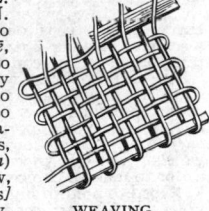

WEAVING

weav·er (wē′vər) *n.* **1.** a person who weaves; esp., one whose work is weaving **2.** same as WEAVERBIRD

weav·er·bird (-bʉrd′) *n.* any of a number of old-world, finchlike birds (family Ploceidae) that weave elaborate domed nests of sticks, grass, and other vegetation

weaver's hitch (or **knot**) *same as* SHEET BEND

web (web) *n.* [ME. < OE. *webb*, akin to ON. *vefr*, OHG. *weppi* < IE. base *webh-*, to WEAVE] **1.** any woven fabric; esp., a length of cloth being woven on a loom or just taken off **2.** *a)* the woven or spun network of a spider; cobweb *b)* a similar network spun by the larvae of certain insects **3.** a carefully woven trap or snare **4.** a complicated work of the mind, imagination, etc. /a *web* of lies/ **5.** anything like a web, as in intricacy of pattern, interconnection of elements, etc.; network **6.** *Anat. a)* a tissue or membrane *b)* an abnormal membrane joining fingers or toes at the base **7.** *Archit.* the portion of a ribbed vault between the ribs **8.** *Mech. a)* the plate joining the flanges of a joist, girder, rail, etc. *b)* the blade of a saw, key, etc. **9.** *Printing* a large roll of paper for continuously feeding a type of rotary press (**web press**) **10.** *Zool. a)* the vane of a feather *b)* a membrane partly or completely joining the digits of various water birds, water animals, etc. —*vt.* **webbed**, **web′bing** **1.** to join by a web **2.** to cover with or as with a web **3.** to catch or snare in or as in a web —**web′like′** *adj.*

Webb (web), **Beatrice** (**Potter**) 1858–1943 & her husband **Sidney** (**James**), 1st Baron Passfield, 1859–1947; Eng. economists & socialist reformers

webbed (webd) *adj.* **1.** formed like a web or made of web-

bing **2.** joined by a web /*webbed* toes/ **3.** having the digits joined by a web /a *webbed* foot/

web·bing (web′iŋ) *n.* **1.** a strong, tough fabric, as of jute or cotton, woven in strips and used for belts, in upholstery, etc. **2.** a membrane uniting the digits, as of a duck, goose, frog, etc. **3.** a part like this, as between the thumb and forefinger of a baseball glove **4.** a netlike structure of interwoven cord, etc., as the strung part of rackets

web·by (-ē) *adj.* **web′bi·er**, **web′bi·est** **1.** of, having the nature of, or like a web **2.** webbed or palmated

we·ber (web′ər; vä′bər, wē′-) *n.* [after W. E. WEBER] the practical mks unit of magnetic flux, equal to 10⁸ maxwells

We·ber (vā′bər) **1. Carl Ma·ri·a** (**Friedrich Ernst**) **von** (mä rē′ä fôn), 1786–1826; Ger. composer **2. Ernst Hein·rich** (ernst hīn′riH), 1795–1878; Ger. physiologist & anatomist **3. Max**, *a)* 1864–1920; Ger. sociologist & political economist *b)* 1881–1961; U.S. painter, born in Russia **4. Wil·helm E·du·ard** (vil′helm ā′dōō ärt), 1804–91; Ger. physicist: brother of *Ernst*

We·bern (vā′bərn), **An·ton** (**von**) (än′tôn) 1883–1945; Austrian composer

web·foot (web′foot′) *n., pl.* -**feet′** **1.** a foot with the toes webbed **2.** an animal with webbed feet —**web′-foot′ed** *adj.*

web spinner any of an order (Embioptera) of small, secretive, tropical and subtropical insects that live in silk-lined tunnels underground

web·ster (web′stər) *n.* [ME. < *webbestre*, fem. of *webba*, weaver: see WEB & -STER] [Obs.] a weaver

Web·ster (web′stər) **1. Daniel**, 1782–1852; U.S. statesman & orator **2. John**, 1580?–1625?; Eng. dramatist **3. Noah**, 1758–1843; U.S. lexicographer —**Web·ster′i·an** (-stir′ē ən) *adj.*

web-toed (web′tōd′) *adj.* having webfeet

☆**web·worm** (-wʉrm′) *n.* any of various caterpillars that spin large, irregular webs, as the **fall webworm** (*Hyphantria cunea*), whose webs envelop whole branches of trees

wed (wed) *vt.* **wed′ded**, **wed′ded** or **wed**, **wed′ding** [ME. *wedden* < OE. *weddian*, lit., to pledge, engage < *wed*, a pledge, akin to G. *wetten*, to pledge, wager < IE. base *wadh-*, a pledge, to redeem a pledge, whence L. *vas* (gen. *vadis*), a pledge: cf. WAGE] **1.** to marry; specif., *a)* to take for one's husband or wife *b)* to conduct the marriage ceremony for; join in wedlock **2.** to unite or join closely /a project that *weds* science and art/ —*vi.* to become married; take a husband or wife

we'd (wēd) **1.** we had **2.** we should **3.** we would

Wed. Wednesday

wed·ded (wed′id) *adj.* **1.** married /the *wedded* pair/ **2.** of or arising from marriage /*wedded* bliss/ **3.** devoted /*wedded* to one's work/ **4.** joined /*wedded* by common interests/

Wed·dell Sea (wed′əl, wə del′) section of the Atlantic east of Antarctic Peninsula: see ANTARCTICA, map

wed·ding (-iŋ) *n.* [ME. < OE. *weddung* < *weddian*: see WED] **1.** *a)* the act or ceremony of becoming married; marriage *b)* the marriage ceremony with its attendant festivities **2.** an anniversary of a marriage, or the celebration of this /a golden *wedding*/ **3.** a joining or blending together —*SYN.* see MARRIAGE

wedding ring a ring, typically a band of gold, platinum, etc., placed on the bride's finger by the groom during the marriage ceremony; also, a similar ring sometimes given to the groom by the bride

wed·eln (vād′′ln) *n.* [G. < *wedeln*, to wag < MHG. *wedelen* < *wedel*, a tail < OHG. *wadil* (akin to ON. *vēli*, bird's tail), orig., something that moves about < IE. *wēt-* < base *we-*, to hover, blow, whence WIND²] *Skiing* a series of short parallel turns executed in rapid succession at a constant speed —*vi.* to execute a wedeln

wedge (wej) *n.* [ME. *wegge* < OE. *wecg*, akin to G. dial. *weck* < IE. *wogwhyo-*, wedge, akin to *wogwhni-s*, ploughshare, whence L. *vomis*, OHG. *waganso*] **1.** a piece of hard material, as wood or metal, tapering from a thick back to a thin edge that can be driven or forced into a narrow opening, as to split wood, lift a weight, reinforce a structure, etc. **2.** anything shaped like a wedge or having a wedge-shaped part /a *wedge* of pie/; specif., *a)* a wedge-shaped stroke in cuneiform writing *b)* a wedge-shaped tactical formation, as of troops, used to penetrate a narrow front to a great depth *c)* *Golf* an iron with the face angled to give the most loft, as for shots out of bunkers ☆*d)* same as WEDGIE **3.** any action or procedure that serves to open the way for a gradual change, disruption, intrusion, etc. —*vt.* **wedged**, **wedg′ing** **1.** to split or force apart with or as with a wedge **2.** to fix solidly in place by driving a wedge or wedges under, beside, etc. **3.** to force or pack (in) **4.** to force or crowd together in a narrow space —*vi.* to push or be forced as or like a wedge —**wedge′like′** *adj.*

☆**wedg·ie** (wej′ē) *n.* a style of women's shoe having a wedge-shaped piece under the heel, which forms a solid sole, flat from heel to toe: *usually used in pl.*

Wedg·wood (wej′wood′) *n.* [after J. *Wedgwood* (1730–95),

WEDGE

Eng. potter] *a trademark for* a fine English pottery, typically with delicate neoclassical figures applied in a white, cameolike relief on a tinted background: also **Wedgwood ware**

wedg·y (wej′ē) *adj.* **wedg′i·er, wedg′i·est** shaped or used like a wedge

wed·lock (wed′läk′) *n.* [ME. *wedlok* < OE. *wedlac* < *wed*, a compact, pledge + *-lac*, an offering, gift, akin to ON. *leikr*, play, Goth. *laiks*, a dance] the state of being married; matrimony —*SYN.* see MARRIAGE

Wednes·day (wenz′dē, -dā) *n.* [ME. *Wednes dei* < OE. *Wodnes dæg*, Woden's day (see WODEN & DAY), like ON. *Othinsdagr* (lit., Odin's day), early transl. of L. *dies Mercurii*, Mercury's day] the fourth day of the week

Wednes·days (-dēz, -dāz) *adv.* on or during every Wednesday

wee (wē) *adj.* **we′er, we′est** [ME. *we, wei*, small quantity (only in north Eng. & Scot. dial.) < OE. (Anglian) *wege, weg* < base of *wegan*, to bear: see WEIGH¹] **1.** very small; tiny **2.** very early [*wee* hours of the morning] —*n.* [Scot. & Eng. Dial.] a little bit; esp., a short time [*bide a wee*]

weed¹ (wēd) *n.* [ME. *weede* < OE. *weod*, akin to LowG. *wēd*: base only in WGmc.] **1.** any undesired, uncultivated plant, esp. one growing in profusion so as to crowd out a desired crop, disfigure a lawn, etc. **2.** [Colloq.] *a)* tobacco: with *the b)* a cigar or cigarette *c)* a marijuana cigarette **3.** something useless; specif., a horse that is unfit for racing or breeding **4.** [Archaic] wild, luxuriant growth, as of underbrush —*vt.* **1.** to remove the weeds from (a garden, lawn, etc.) **2.** to remove (a weed): often with *out* **3.** to remove as useless, harmful, etc.: often with *out* **4.** to rid of elements regarded as useless, harmful, etc. —*vi.* to remove weeds, etc. —**weed′er** *n.* —**weed′less** *adj.*

weed² (wēd) *n.* [ME. *wede* < OE. *wæde*, a garment, akin to OHG. *wāt* (G. *-wand*, in *leinwand*, linen) < IE. base *(a)wē-*, to weave, whence (in reference to the spinning by the fate goddesses) < ON. *authna*, fate] **1.** [Archaic] a garment or clothing **2.** [*pl.*] black mourning clothes, esp. those worn by a widow **3.** a black mourning band, as of crepe, worn on a man's hat or sleeve

weed·kill·er (-kil′ər) *n. same as* HERBICIDE

weed·y (-ē) *adj.* **weed′i·er, weed′i·est 1.** having weeds; full of weeds **2.** of or like a weed or weeds, as in rapid, rank growth **3.** lean, lanky, ungainly, etc. —**weed′i·ness** *n.*

week (wēk) *n.* [ME. *weke* < OE. *wicu* with lengthened & lowered vowel, akin to G. *woche* (OHG. *wohha*) < IE. *weig-*, to bend, yield (cf. WEAK), seen also in L. *vicis*, change, G. *wechsel*, exchange: basic sense "period of change, or which changes"] **1.** a period of seven days, esp. one beginning with Sunday and ending with Saturday **2.** a particular or specified week [Easter *week*, freshman *week*] **3.** the hours or days of work in a seven-day period [to work a 40-hour *week*] —**Sunday** (or **Monday, Tuesday,** etc.) **week** [Chiefly Brit.] a week (counting backward or forward) from Sunday (or Monday, Tuesday, etc.) —**this day** (or **yesterday,** etc.) **week** [Chiefly Brit.] a week (counting backward or forward) from today (or yesterday, etc.) —**week after week** every week —**week by week** each week —**week in, week out** every week

week·day (-dā′) *n.* **1.** any day of the week except Sunday (or, as in Judaism, Saturday) **2.** any day not in the weekend —*adj.* of, for, or on a weekday

week·days (-dāz′) *adv.* on or during every weekday or most weekdays

week·end, week-end (-end′) *n.* the period from Friday night or Saturday to Monday morning; end of the week: also **week end** —*adj.* of, for, or on a weekend —*vi.* to spend the weekend (*at* or *in* a specified place) —**long weekend** a weekend plus one or two days before or after

week·end·er (-en′dər) *n.* **1.** a person who takes a vacation or goes for a visit on a weekend **2.** a small piece of luggage for use on a weekend trip: also **weekend case** (or **bag**)

week·ends (-endz′) *adv.* on or during every weekend or most weekends

Week·ley (wēk′lē), **Ernest** 1865-1954; Eng. etymologist & lexicographer

week·ly (wēk′lē) *adj.* **1.** continuing or lasting for a week **2.** done, happening, appearing, payable, etc. once a week, or every week [a *weekly* visit] **3.** of a week, or of each week [a *weekly* wage] —*adv.* once a week; every week —*n., pl.* **-lies** a periodical published once a week

Weems (wēmz), **Mason Locke** 1759-1825; U.S. clergyman & writer: called *Parson Weems*

ween (wēn) *vi., vt.* [ME. *wenen* < OE. *wenan*, akin to G. *wähnen* < IE. base *wen-*, to desire, attain, whence WIN, WEAN¹, L. *venus*, love] [Archaic] to think; suppose; imagine

☆**wee·nie, wee·ny¹** (wē′nē) *n., pl.* **-nies** [Colloq.] *same as* WIENER

wee·ny² (wē′nē) *adj.* [WEE + (TI)NY] small; tiny

weep (wēp) *vi.* **wept, weep′ing** [ME. *wepen* < OE. *wepan*, akin to *woþ*, outcry, Goth. *wōpjan*, OS. *wōpian* < IE. base *wab-*, to cry, complain, whence OSlav. *vabiti*, to call to] **1.** to manifest or give expression to a strong emotion, usually grief or sorrow, by crying, wailing, or, esp., shedding tears **2.** to lament or mourn (with *for*) **3.** to let fall drops of water or other liquid; esp., to drop moisture condensed from the air [cold pipes *weep* in hot weather] **4.** to exude water or other liquid, as a wound, the stem of a plant, etc. —*vt.* **1.** to weep for; lament; bewail; mourn [to *weep* one's misfortune] **2.** to shed (tears or other drops

of liquid) **3.** to bring to a specified condition by weeping [to *weep* oneself to sleep] —*n.* **1.** [*often pl.*] a fit of weeping **2.** an exudation or dripping of moisture —*SYN.* see CRY

weep·er (wē′pər) *n.* **1.** a person who weeps, esp. habitually **2.** a hired mourner, as, formerly, at a funeral **3.** a conventional badge of mourning, as the long, black band of crepe formerly worn **4.** *same as* CAPUCHIN (sense 3)

weep·ing (-piŋ) *n.* the act of one who or that which weeps —*adj.* **1.** that weeps tears or other liquid **2.** having graceful, drooping branches —**weep′ing·ly** *adv.*

weeping willow a Chinese willow (*Salix babylonica*), grown as an ornamental for its delicate, drooping branches

weep·y (wē′pē) *adj.* **weep′i·er, weep′i·est 1.** *a)* inclined to weep; tearful *b)* exuding liquid **2.** characterized by or apt to cause weeping —**weep′i·ness** *n.*

wee·ver (wē′vər) *n.* [ONormFr. *wivre* (OFr. *guivre*), orig., serpent, dragon < L. *vipera*, VIPER] any of a number of edible ocean fishes (family Trachinidae) with sharp, very poisonous spines on the gill cover and the first dorsal fin

wee·vil (wē′v′l) *n.* [ME. < OE. *wifel*, akin to MLowG. *wevel* < IE. base *webh-*, to move to and fro, whence WAVE] any of numerous beetles; esp., any beetle (family Curculionidae) having the head prolonged into a projecting beak that usually curves downward, and including many pest species that feed, esp. as larvae, on cotton, fruits, grain, etc. —**wee·vil·y, wee·vil·ly** (-ē) *adj.* infested with weevils

wee-wee (wē′wē′) *vi.* **-weed′, -wee′ing** [baby talk] to urinate —*n.* urine Child's term

weft¹ (weft) *n.* [ME. < OE. < base of *wefan*, to WEAVE] **1.** the yarns carried by the shuttle back and forth across the warp in weaving; woof; filling **2.** something woven

weft² (weft) *n. same as* WAFT (n. 5)

‡**Wehr·macht** (vār′mäkht′) *n.* [G., lit., defense force] the armed forces of Germany, esp. of Nazi Germany

Wei (wā) river in NC China, flowing from Kansu province east into the Yellow River: c.500 mi.

wei·ge·la (wī jē′lə, -gē′-) *n.* [ModL., after C. E. *Weigel* (1748-1831), G. physician] any of a genus (*Weigela*) of shrubs of the honeysuckle family, with clusters of bell-shaped flowers; esp., a widely cultivated species (*Weigela florida*) with dark red flowers: also called **wei·ge·lia** (-jēl′yə)

weigh¹ (wā) *vt.* [ME. *weien*, to weigh, bear < OE. *wegan*, to carry, bear, akin to G. *weigen, wägen* < IE. base *wegh-*, to move, draw, whence OE. *wæg*, a wave, L. *vehere*, to carry, bring] **1.** to determine the weight of by means of a scale or balance **2.** to have (a specified) weight [it *weighs* ten pounds]: orig. construed as a *vi.* and still so construed when used with an adverb **3.** *same as* WEIGHT (*vt.* 1) **4.** to lift or balance (an object) in the hand or hands, in order to estimate its heaviness or weight **5.** to measure out, dole out, or apportion, by or as by weight (often with *out*) **6.** *a)* to consider and choose carefully [to *weigh* one's words] *b)* to balance or ponder in the mind; consider in order to make a choice [to *weigh* one plan against another] **7.** [Obs.] to hold in high regard; esteem; value **8.** *Naut.* to hoist, or lift (an anchor) —*vi.* **1.** to have significance, importance, or influence [his word *weighed* heavily with the jury] **2.** to be a burden; press or bear down (with *on* or *upon*) [the theft *weighed* on his mind] **3.** *Naut.* *a)* to hoist anchor *b)* to start to sail —*SYN.* see CONSIDER —**weigh down 1.** to make bend toward the earth as with added weight **2.** to burden or bear down on so as to oppress or depress —**weigh in 1.** to weigh (a boxer, jockey, etc.) before or after a contest in order to verify his declared weight **2.** to be so weighed —**weigh′a·ble** *adj.*

weigh² (wā) *n.* [modified by the notion of "weighing anchor"] *var. of* WAY, in **under weigh,** progressing, advancing: cf. UNDERWAY

weight (wāt) *n.* [ME. *weiht*, altered (after *weien*, WEIGH¹) < OE. *wiht* < *wegan*: see WEIGH¹] **1.** a portion or quantity weighing a definite or specified amount [ten pounds *weight* of lead] **2.** heaviness as a quality of things; specif., *Physics* the force of gravity acting on a body, equal to the mass of the body multiplied by the acceleration of gravity **3.** *a)* quantity or amount of heaviness; how much a thing weighs *b)* the amount a specified thing should weigh **4.** *a)* any unit of heaviness or mass *b)* any system of such units [troy *weight*, avoirdupois *weight*]: see TABLES OF WEIGHTS AND MEASURES in Supplements *c)* a piece of metal, etc. of a specific standard heaviness, used on a balance or scale in weighing **5.** any block or mass of material used for its heaviness; specif., *a)* one used to hold light things down or in position [a *paperweight*] *b)* one used to drive a mechanism [the *weights* in a clock] *c)* one used to maintain balance [*weights* placed on an automobile wheel] *d)* one of a particular heaviness, lifted as an athletic exercise **6.** *a)* any heavy thing or load *b)* a burden or oppressiveness, as of responsibility or sorrow **7.** importance or consequence [a matter of great *weight*] **8.** influence, power, or authority [to throw one's *weight* to the losing side] **9.** the relative thickness or heaviness of a fabric or an article of clothing as proper to a particular season, use, etc. [a suit of summer *weight*] **10.** *Printing* the relative thickness of the lines in type fonts **11.** *Sports a)* any of the several classifications into which boxers and wrestlers are placed according to how much they weigh *b)* the number of pounds a horse is required to carry for a particular race, including the weight of the jockey, the saddle, and, often, added lead weights **12.** *Statistics* a constant assigned to a

single item in a frequency distribution, indicative of the item's relative importance —*vt.* **1.** to add weight to; make heavy or heavier **2.** to burden; load down; oppress **3.** to treat (thread or fabric) with a solution of metallic salts, in order to increase its weight **4.** to manage, control, or influence in a particular direction or so as to favor a particular side; slant [*evidence weighted* against the defendant] **5.** *Statistics* to assign a weight to in a frequency distribution —*SYN.* see IMPORTANT, INFLUENCE —**by weight** as determined by weighing —**carry weight** to be important, influential, etc. —**pull one's weight** to do one's share —**throw one's weight around** to take undue advantage of one's authority or rank; be overbearing

weight·less (-lis) *adj.* having little or no apparent weight; specif., lacking acceleration of gravity or other external force, as a satellite in earth orbit when the gravitational pull of the earth is counterbalanced by the centrifugal force imparted to the satellite by its initial rocket blast —**weight'less·ly** *adv.* —**weight'less·ness** *n.*

weight lifting the athletic exercise or competitive sport of lifting barbells —**weight lifter**

weight·y (-ē) *adj.* **weight'i·er, weight'i·est 1.** having much weight; very heavy; ponderous **2.** burdensome; oppressive [*weighty* responsibilities] **3.** of great significance or moment; serious [*weighty* matters of state] **4.** of great influence or importance —*SYN.* see HEAVY —**weight'i·ness** *n.*

Weill (wīl; *G.* vīl), **Kurt** (kurt) 1900–50; U.S. composer, born in Germany

Wei·mar (vī'mär; *E.* wī'mär) city in SW East Germany, near Erfurt: pop. 64,000

Wei·ma·ra·ner (vī'mə rän'ər, wī'-) *n.* [< prec., where the breed was developed] any of a breed of lean, medium-sized hunting dog with a smooth, gray coat

Weimar Republic German Republic (1919–33): created by a constitutional assembly at Weimar (1919) & dissolved after Hitler became chancellor

weir (wir) *n.* [ME. *were* < OE. *wer*, a weir, dam (akin to G. *wehr*) < base of *werian*, to defend, dam up < IE. base *wer-*, to shut up, cover, whence WARN] **1.** a low dam built in a river to back up or divert water, as for a mill; milldam **2.** a fence, as of brushwood or stakes, built in a stream, channel, etc., for catching fish **3.** an obstruction placed in a stream, diverting the water through a prepared aperture for measuring the rate of flow

weird (wird) *adj.* [ME. *werde*, orig. *n.*, fate < OE. *wyrd*, fate < the base of *weorthan*, to become (basic sense "what is to come") < IE. *wert-*, to turn, whence -WARD, L. *vertere*, to turn] **1.** orig., of fate or destiny **2.** suggestive of ghosts, evil spirits, or other supernatural things; unearthly, mysterious, eerie, etc. **3.** strikingly odd, strange, queer, etc.; fantastic; bizarre [a *weird* costume] —*n.* [Scot. or Archaic] **1.** fate or destiny **2.** *a)* any of the Fates *b)* a soothsayer **3.** a prophecy **4.** a spell or supernatural event —**weird'ly** *adv.* —**weird'ness** *n.*

SYN. —**weird** applies to that which is supernaturally mysterious or fantastically strange [a *weird* experience]; **eerie** applies to that which inspires a vague, superstitious uneasiness or dread [the *eerie* howling of a dog]; **uncanny** applies to that which is unnaturally strange or remarkable [*uncanny* insight]; **unearthly** applies to that which is so strange or extraordinary as to seem to belong to another world [an *unearthly* light]

weird·o (wir'dō) *n., pl.* **-os** [Slang] a person or thing that is weird, queer, bizarre, etc.: also **weird'ie** (-dē)

Weird Sisters the three Fates

Weis·mann (vīs'män), **Au·gust** (ou'goost) 1834–1914; Ger. biologist

Weis·mann·ism (vīs'män iz'm) *n.* [after prec.] a theory of heredity that emphasizes the continuity of the germ plasm from generation to generation and the rigid separation of the somatoplasm which dies in every generation, thus prohibiting the transmission of acquired characters

Weiss·horn (vīs'hôrn') mountain of the Pennine Alps, S Switzerland: c.14,800 ft.

Weiz·mann (vīts'män; *E.* wīts'mən), **Cha·im** (khī'im) 1874–1952; Israeli chemist & Zionist leader, born in Russia; first president of Israel (1948–52)

we·ka (wā'kä, wē'kə) *n.* [Maori: from its cry] any of a genus (*Gallirallus*) of large flightless rails of New Zealand

Welch (welch, welsh) *adj., n. var. of* WELSH —**Welch'man** *n., pl.* **-men**

welch (welch, welsh) *vt., vi.* [Slang] *var. of* WELSH

wel·come (wel'kəm) *adj.* [ME. *welcume*, altered after *wel*, WELL² (as if transl. of OFr. *bien venu*) < *wilcume* < OE. *wilcuma*, orig. *n.*, a welcome guest < *willa*, pleasure, WILL¹ + *cuma*, a guest < *cuman*, to COME] **1.** gladly and cordially received [a *welcome* guest] **2.** agreeable or gratifying [*welcome* news] **3.** freely and willingly permitted or invited [*welcome* to use the library]: also used in a conventional response to thanks ("you're welcome," meaning "you're under no obligation for the favor given") —*n.* an act or expression of welcoming [a hearty (or cold) *welcome*] —*interj.* you are welcome: an expression of cordial greeting —*vt.* **-comed, -com·ing 1.** to greet with pleasure and hospitality **2.** to receive or accept with pleasure or satisfaction [to *welcome* criticism] **3.** to meet, receive, or

acknowledge in a specified way; greet —**bid welcome** to receive with cordial greetings —☆**wear out one's welcome** to come so often or stay so long that one is no longer welcome —**wel'com·er** *n.*

☆**welcome mat** a doormat: chiefly in the phrase **put out the welcome mat,** to give an enthusiastic or sincere welcome, reception, or acceptance

weld¹ (weld) *vt.* [altered (with unhistoric -d) < obs. *well*, to weld < ME. *wellen*, to weld, WELL¹, *v.*] **1.** to unite (pieces of metal, etc.) by heating until molten and fused or until soft enough to hammer or press together **2.** to bring into close or intimate union; unite in a single, compact whole —*vi.* to be welded or capable of being welded [alloys that *weld* at different heats] —*n.* **1.** a welding or being welded **2.** the joint formed by welding —**weld'-a·bil'i·ty** *n.* —**weld'a·ble** *adj.* —**weld'er** *n.*

weld² (weld) *n.* [ME. *welde*, akin to MLowG. *wolde*, MDu. *wouw*] **1.** a European mignonette (*Reseda luteola*) that yields a yellow dye **2.** the dye

wel·fare (wel'fer') *n.* [ME. < *wel faren*, to fare well: see WELL² & FARE] **1.** the state of being or doing well; condition of health, happiness, and comfort; well-being; prosperity **2.** those government agencies concerned with granting aid to those suffering from poverty, unemployment, etc. **3.** *same as* WELFARE WORK —**on welfare** receiving government aid because of poverty, unemployment, etc.

Welfare Island island in the East River, between the boroughs of Manhattan & Queens, in New York City

welfare state a state in which the welfare of its citizens, with regard to employment, medical care, social security, etc. is considered to be the responsibility of the government

welfare work the organized effort of a community or organization to improve the living conditions and standards of its needy members —**welfare worker**

☆**wel·far·ism** (wel'fer'iz'm) *n.* **1.** the policies and practices of a welfare state or of public welfare agencies **2.** aid given or benefits made available by a welfare state or by public welfare agencies —**wel'far'ist** *n., adj.*

wel·kin (wel'kin) *n.* [ME. *welkne* < OE. *wolcen*, cloud, akin to G. *wolke* < IE. base *welg-*, wet, whence Russ. *vológa*, a fluid & *Wolga*, VOLGA] [Archaic or Poet.] the vault of heaven, the sky, or the upper air: now chiefly in **make the welkin ring,** to make a very loud sound

well¹ (wel) *n.* [ME. *welle* < OE. *wella*, akin to *weallan*, to boil up, akin to G. *welle*, wave, *wallen*, to boil < IE. base *wel-*, to turn, roll, whence L. *volvere*, to roll: see WALK] **1.** a flow of water from the earth; natural spring and pool **2.** a hole or shaft sunk into the earth to tap an underground supply of water, gas, oil, etc. **3.** a source of abundant supply; fount [a book that is a *well* of information] **4.** any of various shafts or deep enclosed spaces resembling a well; esp., *a)* an open shaft in a building for a staircase; stairwell *b)* a shaft in a building or between buildings, open to the sky for light and air; airshaft *c)* an elevator shaft *d)* in English law courts, an open space before the bench, for solicitors *e) Naut.* an enclosure in the hold of a ship for containing the pumps and protecting them from damage *f)* a compartment in a fishing boat where freshly caught fish are kept **5.** any of various vessels, containers, etc. for holding liquid, as an inkwell **6.** a depression, as on a platter, broiler, etc. for catching meat juices —*vi.* [ME. *wellen*, to well up, bubble, boil, weld < OE. *wiellan, wyllan,* to bubble, caus. of *weallan:* see the *n.*] to flow or spring from or as from a well; gush (*up, forth, down, out,* etc.) —*vt.* to pour forth; gush [eyes that *welled* tears]

well² (wel) *adv.* **bet'ter, best** [ME. *wel* < OE., akin to G. *wohl:* for IE. base see WILL¹: basic sense "according to desire"] **1.** in a pleasing or desirable manner; satisfactorily [work that is going *well*] **2.** in a proper, friendly, or attentive manner [to treat a person *well*] **3.** skillfully; expertly [to sing *well*] **4.** in an appropriate manner; fittingly [spoken *well*] **5.** *a)* prosperously; in comfort and plenty [to live *well*] *b)* to one's advantage or well-being [to marry *well*] **6.** with good reason; in justice; properly [one may *well* ask] **7.** satisfactorily in regard to health or physical condition [the patient is doing *well*] **8.** to a considerable extent, degree, or distance [*well* advanced] **9.** thoroughly; fully [stir *well* before cooking] **10.** with certainty; definitely [to know perfectly *well* what one must do] **11.** intimately; familiarly; closely [to know a person *well*] **12.** in good spirit; with good grace [he took the news *well*] *Well* is sometimes used in hyphenated compounds meaning *properly, satisfactorily, thoroughly,* etc. [*well-defined, well-able, well-worn*] —*adj.* **1.** suitable, proper, fit, right, etc. [it is *well* that he came] **2.** in good health [she is quite *well*] **3.** in a good or satisfactory condition; favorable; comfortable [things are *well* with us] —*interj.* an exclamation used to express surprise, acquiescence, agreement, resignation, expostulation, etc., or merely to preface or resume one's remarks —*SYN.* see HEALTHY —**as well 1.** besides; in addition **2.** with equal justification, propriety, or effect; equally —**as well as 1.** equally with; just as much or as good as **2.** in addition to —**wish someone well** to wish success or good fortune for someone

we'll (wēl, wil) **1.** we shall **2.** we will

well-ad·vised (-əd vīzd′) *adj.* showing or resulting from careful consideration or sound advice; wise; prudent

Wel·land (wel′ənd) port in SE Ontario, Canada, on the Welland Canal: pop. 40,000

Welland (Ship) Canal [ult. after *Welland* River, in England] canal of the St. Lawrence Seaway, in Ontario, Canada, between Lake Ontario & Lake Erie: 27 1/2 mi. long: see ST. LAWRENCE SEAWAY, map

well-ap·point·ed (wel′ə poin′tid) *adj.* excellently furnished or equipped [a *well-appointed* office]

well-a·way (-ə wā′) *interj.* [ME. *wei la wei*, lit., woe! lo! woe!: *wei* < ON. *vei*, WOE + OE. *la*, LO] [Archaic] alas!: an exclamation of sorrow, regret, etc.: also **well′a·day′** (-dā′)

well-bal·anced (-bal′ənst) *adj.* 1. nicely or exactly balanced, adjusted, or regulated [a *well-balanced* meal] 2. sane, sensible, and reliable

well-be·haved (-bi hāvd′) *adj.* behaving well; conducting oneself properly; displaying good manners

well-be·ing (-bē′iŋ) *n.* the state of being well, happy, or prosperous; welfare

well-be·loved (-bi luvd′, -luv′id) *adj.* 1. deeply or greatly loved 2. highly respected: used in formal ceremonies or correspondence —*n.* a well-beloved person

well-born (-bôrn′) *adj.* born into a family of high social position

well-bred (-bred′) *adj.* 1. showing good breeding; courteous and considerate 2. of good stock: said of animals

well-chos·en (-chō′z′n) *adj.* chosen with care and judgment; proper; appropriate [*well-chosen* words]

well-con·tent (-kən tent′) *adj.* thoroughly pleased or satisfied: also **well′-con·tent′ed**

well-dis·posed (-dis pōzd′) *adj.* 1. suitably or properly placed or arranged 2. inclined to be friendly, kindly, or favorable (*toward* a person) or receptive (*to* an idea, etc.)

well-do·ing (-dōō′iŋ) *n.* 1. good or benevolent action or conduct 2. prosperity or success

well-done (-dun′) *adj.* 1. performed with skill and efficiency 2. thoroughly cooked: said esp. of meat —*interj.* an exclamation of approval of another's action

Welles (welz) 1. **(George) Orson**, 1915– ; U.S. motion-picture actor & producer 2. **Sumner**, 1892–1961; U.S. diplomat

well-fa·vored (wel′fā′vərd) *adj.* handsome; pretty

well-fed (-fed′) *adj.* showing the effect of eating much good food; specif., plump, or fat

well-fixed (-fikst′) *adj.* [Colloq.] ☆wealthy; well-to-do

well-found (-found′) *adj.* properly and adequately equipped [a *well-found* ship]

well-found·ed (-foun′did) *adj.* based on facts, good evidence, or sound judgment [a *well-founded* suspicion]

well-groomed (-grōōmd′) *adj.* 1. carefully cared for [a *well-groomed* horse, a *well-groomed* lawn] 2. clean and neat; carefully washed, combed, dressed, etc.

well-ground·ed (-groun′did) *adj.* 1. having a thorough basic knowledge of a subject 2. based on good reasons

well-han·dled (-han′d'ld) *adj.* efficiently managed

well-head (wel′hed′) *n.* 1. the source of a spring of water; spring 2. a source; fountainhead

☆**well-heeled** (wel′hēld′) *adj.* [Slang] rich; prosperous

well-in·formed (-in fôrmd′) *adj.* 1. having thorough knowledge of a subject 2. having considerable knowledge of many subjects, esp. those of current interest

Wel·ling·ton (wel′iŋ tən) capital of New Zealand; seaport on Cook Strait, S North Island: pop. 132,000

Wel·ling·ton (wel′iŋ tən), 1st Duke of, (*Arthur Wellesley*) 1769–1852; Brit. general & statesman, born in Ireland: prime minister (1828–30): called *the Iron Duke*

Wellington (boot) [after prec.] [*also* w- b-] a high boot, traditionally extending just above the knee in front, and just below in back, now usually just below the knee

well-in·ten·tioned (-in ten′shənd) *adj.* having or showing good, kindly, or benevolent intentions: usually connoting failure or miscarriage of intention

well-knit (-nit′) *adj.* 1. well constructed; firm and strong 2. having a sturdy body build; not lanky

well-known (-nōn′) *adj.* 1. widely or generally known; famous or notorious 2. thoroughly known

well-made (-mād′) *adj.* 1. well-proportioned; strongly built; skillfully and soundly put together 2. *Literature & Drama a)* skillfully constructed or contrived [a *well-made* plot] *b)* having a skillfully contrived plot [a *well-made* play]

well-man·nered (-man′ərd) *adj.* having or showing good manners; polite; courteous

well-mean·ing (-mē′niŋ) *adj.* 1. having good or kindly intentions 2. said or done with good intentions, but often unwisely or ineffectually: also **well′-meant′** (-ment′)

well-nigh (-nī′) *adv.* very nearly; almost

well-off (-ôf′) *adj.* 1. in a favorable or fortunate condition or circumstance 2. prosperous; well-to-do

well-or·dered (-ôr′dərd) *adj.* properly or carefully organized

well-pre·served (-pri zurvd′) *adj.* in good condition or of good appearance, in spite of age

well-read (-red′) *adj.* 1. having read much (*in* a particular subject) 2. having a wide knowledge of books through having read much

well-round·ed (-roun′did) *adj.* 1. well planned for proper balance [a *well-rounded* education, a *well-rounded* program] 2. *a)* showing interest or ability in many fields *b)* showing many facets of personality [a *well-rounded* character] 3.

fully developed; shapely [a *well-rounded* figure]: also [Slang] ☆**well′-stacked′**

Wells (welz), **H(erbert) G(eorge)** 1866–1946; Eng. novelist & historian

well-spo·ken (wel′spō′k'n) *adj.* 1. speaking easily or fluently 2. speaking in a courteous or gracious manner 3. properly or aptly spoken

well-spring (wel′spriŋ) *n.* 1. the source of a stream, spring, etc.; fountainhead 2. a source of abundant and continual supply [a *wellspring* of knowledge]

well-thought-of (wel′thôt′uv′) *adj.* having a good reputation; of good repute

well-timed (-tīmd′) *adj.* timely; opportune

well-to-do (-tə dōō′) *adj.* prosperous; well-off; wealthy —*SYN.* see RICH

well-turned (-turnd′) *adj.* 1. gracefully formed or shaped [a *well-turned* ankle] 2. expressed or worded well; felicitous [a *well-turned* phrase]

well-wish·er (-wish′ər) *n.* a person who wishes well to another, or to a cause, etc. —**well′-wish′ing** *adj., n.*

well-worn (-wôrn′) *adj.* 1. much worn; much used 2. overused, trite [a *well-worn* joke] 3. worn becomingly

Wels·bach burner (welz′bak; *G.* vels′bäkh) [after C. A. von *Welsbach* (1858–1929), Austrian chemist, its inventor] *a trademark for* a gas burner with a gauze mantle impregnated with thorium oxide and cerium oxide: when lighted, the gauze gives off an incandescent, greenish light

Welsh (welsh, welch) *adj.* [ME. *Wel(i)sch* < OE. *Welisc* < *Wealh*, Briton, foreigner < Celt. name whence L. *Volcae*, name of a Celtic people of S France] of Wales, its people, their language, etc. —*n.* the Brythonic language spoken in Wales —**the Welsh** the people of Wales

welsh (welsh, welch) *vt., vi.* [19th-c. slang, prob. < prec., with opprobrious reference to alleged propensities] [Slang] 1. to cheat or swindle by failing to pay a bet or other debt 2. to evade (an obligation) Often with *on* —**welsh′er** *n.*

Welsh cor·gi (kôr′gē) [WELSH + W. *corgi* < *corr*, dwarf + *ci*, dog] either of two breeds of short-legged dog with a foxlike head, orig. from Wales: the **Cardigan Welsh corgi** has a long tail and rounded ears; the **Pembroke Welsh corgi**, a short tail and pointed, erect ears

Welsh·man (welsh′mən, welch′-) *n., pl.* -men a native or inhabitant of Wales

Welsh rabbit [orig. a humorous usage] a dish of melted cheese, often mixed with ale or beer, served on crackers or toast: also, through faulty etymologizing, **Welsh rarebit**

Welsh terrier any of a breed of lean wire-haired terrier closely resembling the Airedale, but smaller: believed to have originated in Wales

welt (welt) *n.* [ME. *welte*, prob. akin to OE. *wealtan*, to roll (for IE. base see WALK)] 1. a strip of leather stitched into the seam between the sole and upper of a shoe to strengthen the joining 2. a strip of material, often folded over a cord, placed at the edge or seam of a garment, cushion, etc. to reinforce or trim it 3. *a)* a raised ridge left on the skin by a slash or blow, as of a whip; wale; weal *b)* such a slash or blow —*vt.* 1. to furnish with a welt 2. [Colloq.] to beat severely; thrash so as to raise welts

‡**Welt·an·schau·ung** (velt′än′shou′ŏŏŋ) *n.* [G., lit., world view] a comprehensive, esp. personal, philosophy or conception of the universe and of human life

welt·er (wel′tər) *vi.* [ME. *weltren* < MDu. *welteren*, freq. formation akin to OE. *wealtan*, to roll: for IE. base see WELL¹] 1. *a)* to roll about or wallow, as a pig in mud *b)* to be deeply or completely involved [to *welter* in sin] 2. to be soaked, stained, or bathed [to *welter* in blood] 3. to tumble and toss about, as the sea —*n.* 1. a tossing and tumbling, as of waves 2. a confusion; turmoil

welt·er·weight (wel′tər wāt′) *n.* [prob. < WELT (*vt.* 2) + -ER + WEIGHT] a boxer or wrestler between a lightweight and a middleweight (in boxing, 136–147 pounds)

‡**Welt·schmerz** (velt′shmerts′) *n.* [G., world pain] sentimental pessimism or melancholy over the state of the world

Wel·ty (wel′tē), **Eu·do·ra** (yŏŏ dôr′ə) 1909– ; U.S. short-story writer & novelist

Wem·bley (wem′blē) city in Middlesex, SE England: suburb of London: pop. 125,000

wen¹ (wen) *n.* [ME. *wenne* < OE. *wenn*, akin to *wund*, a WOUND¹] a benign skin tumor, esp. of the scalp, consisting of a cyst in which sebaceous matter has been retained

wen² (wen) *n.* [ME. < OE., var. of *winn*, joy, bliss] an Old English rune (þ), replaced in the 11th cent. by the letter *w*

Wen·ces·laus (wen′səs lôs′) 1361–1419; Holy Roman emperor (1378–1400); as **Wenceslaus IV**, king of Bohemia (1378–1419): Ger. name **Wen·zel** (ven′tsəl)

wench (wench) *n.* [ME. *wenche*, contr. < *wenchel*, child, boy, girl, young woman < OE. *wencel*, a child, akin to *wancol*, unsteady (? in reference to an infant's gait): for IE. base see WINCH¹] 1. a girl or young woman: now a somewhat derogatory or jocular term 2. [Archaic] *a)* a country girl *b)* a female servant *c)* a prostitute or loose woman —*vi.* to be sexually promiscuous with prostitutes or loose women —**wench′er** *n.*

Wen·chou, Wen·chow (wen′chou′; *Chin.* wun′jō′) seaport in Chekiang province, SE China: pop. 250,000

Wend (wend) *n.* [G. *wende*, akin to OE. *Winedas*, the Wends] *same as* SORB —**Wend′ish** *adj., n.*

wend (wend) *vt.* **wend′ed** or archaic **went**, **wend′ing** [ME. *wenden* < OE. *wendan*, to turn, akin to Du. & G. *wenden*,

caus. formation < base of WIND¹] to proceed or go on (one's way) —*vi.* [Archaic] to go; journey; travel

went (went) [old *pt.* of WEND, used to replace missing form of GO¹] *pt. of* GO¹

wen·tle·trap (wen′t'l trap′) *n.* [Du. *wenteltrap*, lit., a winding staircase < *wentel*, a winding, akin to *wenden* (cf. WEND) + *trap*, stair: see TRAP¹] any of a number of deep-sea gastropod mollusks (esp. genus *Epitonium*) enclosed in a single, usually white, spiral shell

wept (wept) *pt. & pp. of* WEEP

were (wur; *unstressed* wər) [ME. *weren* < OE. *wæron*, akin to G. *waren* < Gmc. base *wæz-* < IE. base *wes-* (cf. WAS)] *pl. & 2d pers. sing., past indic., and the past subj., of* BE

we're (wir) we are

weren't (wurnt) were not

were·wolf (wir′woolf′, wur′-, wer′-) *n., pl.* **-wolves′** (-woolvz′) [ME. *werwolf* < OE. *werwulf* < *wer*, a man < IE. *wiros*, man (prob. orig., "the strong one") < base *wei-*, to be strong, whence L. *vis*, power (cf. VIM) + OE. *wulf*, WOLF] *Folklore* a person changed into a wolf, or one capable of assuming the form of a wolf at will; lycanthrope: also sp. **werwolf**

Wer·fel (ver′fəl), **Franz** (fränts) 1890–1945; Austrian novelist, playwright, & poet, born in Prague

wer·geld (wur′geld′, wer′-) *n.* [ME. *weregylt* < OE. *wergild* < *wer*, a man (see WEREWOLF) + *geld*, payment: see GELD²] in early Germanic and Anglo-Saxon law, a price paid by the family of a manslayer to the family of the person killed, to atone for the killing and avoid reprisals: also **were′gild′, wer′gild′** (-gild′)

wer·ner·ite (wur′nə rīt′) *n.* [< A. G. *Werner* (1750–1817), G. geologist + -ITE¹] *same as* SCAPOLITE

wert (wurt; *unstressed* wərt) *archaic 2d pers. sing., past indic. & subj., of* BE: *used with* thou

We·ser (vā′zər) river in West Germany, flowing from S Lower Saxony north into the North Sea: c.300 mi.

wes·kit (wes′kit) *n.* [altered < WAISTCOAT] a vest or waistcoat

Wes·ley (wes′lē, wez′-) [< the surname *Wesley*] **1.** a masculine name **2. Charles,** 1707–88; Eng. clergyman & hymn writer: brother of *ff.* **3. John,** 1703–91; Eng. clergyman & evangelist: founder of Methodism

Wes·ley·an (wes′lē ən, wez′-) *adj.* of John Wesley or the Methodist Church —*n.* a follower of John Wesley; Methodist —**Wes′ley·an·ism** *n.*

Wes·sex (wes′iks) **1.** former Anglo-Saxon kingdom in S England **2.** corresponding section in modern England, chiefly in Dorsetshire, as the locale of Hardy's novels

west (west) *n.* [ME. < OE., akin to G. *west* < IE. base *we-*, down from, away from, whence Gr. *hesperos*, L. *vesper*, evening] **1.** the direction to the left of a person facing north; direction in which sunset occurs: it is properly the point on the horizon at which the center of the sun sets at the equinox **2.** the point on a compass at 270°, directly opposite east **3.** a region or district in or toward this direction **4.** [W-] the western part of the earth, esp. the Western Hemisphere or the Western Hemisphere and Europe; Occident **5.** [W-] the Western Roman Empire —*adj.* **1.** in, of, to, toward, or facing the west **2.** from the west [a *west* wind] **3.** [W-] designating the western part of a continent, country, etc. [*West* Pakistan] **4.** in, of, or toward that part of a church directly opposite the altar —*adv.* in or toward the west; in a westerly direction —**the West 1.** the western part of the U.S.; specif., *a)* formerly, the region west of the Allegheny Mountains *b)* the region west of the Mississippi, esp. the northwestern part of this region **2.** the U.S. and its non-Communist allies in Europe and the Western Hemisphere

West (west) **1. Benjamin,** 1738–1820; Am. painter, in England after 1763 **2. Dame Rebecca,** (pseud. of *Cicily Isabel Fairfield*; Mrs. *H. M. Andrews*) 1892– ; Brit. novelist & critic, born in Ireland

West Al·lis (al′is) [after the *Allis*-Chalmers Co. there] city in SE Wis.: suburb of Milwaukee: pop. 72,000

West Bengal state of NE India, created (1947) by the division of Bengal: 33,829 sq. mi.; pop. 34,926,000; cap. Calcutta

☆**west·bound** (-bound′) *adj.* bound west; going westward

West Brom·wich (brum′ich, -ij; bräm′ich) city in Staffordshire, England, near Birmingham: pop. 172,000

west by north the direction, or the point on a mariner's compass, halfway between due west and west-northwest; 11°15′ north of due west

west by south the direction, or the point on a mariner's compass, halfway between due west and west-southwest; 11°15′ south of due west

West Co·vi·na (kō vē′nə) [*Covina* said locally to mean "place of vines"] city in SW Calif.: suburb of Los Angeles: pop. 68,000

West End W section of London, England, essentially a fashionable residential section

west·er (wes′tər) *vi.* to move, turn, or shift to the west —*n.* a wind from the west, esp. one bringing a storm with it —**west′er·ing** *adj.*

west·er·ly (-lē) *adj.* **1.** in, of, or toward the west **2.** from

the west [a *westerly* wind] —*n., pl.* **-lies** a wind blowing from the west —*adv.* **1.** toward the west **2.** from the west

Wes·ter·marck (wes′tər märk′; *Finn.* ves′tər márk′), **Edward Alexander** 1862–1939; Finn. anthropologist

west·ern (wes′tərn) *adj.* [ME. < OE. *westerne*] **1.** in, of, toward, or facing the west **2.** from the west **3.** [W-] of or characteristic of the West **4.** [W-] of the Western Church —*n.* **1.** *same as* WESTERNER ☆**2.** a story, motion picture, etc. about cowboys or frontiersmen in the western U.S.

Western Australia state of Australia, in the W third of the continent: 975,920 sq. mi.; pop. 836,000; cap. Perth

Western Church 1. that part of the Catholic Church which recognizes the Pope and follows the Latin Rite; the Roman Catholic Church **2.** broadly, all the Christian churches of Western Europe and America

west·ern·er (wes′tər nər) *n.* **1.** a native or inhabitant of the west ☆**2.** [W-] a native or inhabitant of the western part of the U.S.

Western Hemisphere that half of the earth which includes North & South America

west·ern·ism (wes′tərn iz'm) *n.* a word, expression, or practice peculiar to the west; ☆specif., a term or idiom peculiar to the western U.S.

west·ern·ize (-īz′) *vt.* **-ized′, -iz′ing** to make western in character, habits, ideas, etc. —**west′ern·i·za′tion** *n.*

west·ern·most (-mōst′) *adj.* farthest west

Western Ocean *ancient name of the* ATLANTIC OCEAN

☆**Western (omelet)** an omelet prepared with diced green pepper, onion, and ham

Western Reserve section of the Northwest Territory, on Lake Erie: reserved by Conn. for settlers when its other W lands were ceded to the Federal government in 1786: incorporated into the Ohio territory in 1800

Western Roman Empire the W part of the Roman Empire, after it was divided in 395 A.D. by Theodosius until it was overthrown by Odoacer in 476

Western Samoa country in the South Pacific, consisting of two large islands & several small ones: a member of the Brit. Commonwealth: 1,130 sq. mi.; pop. 141,000

Western Wall a high wall in Jerusalem believed to be part of the western wall of Herod's Temple: Jews have traditionally gathered at this site for prayer

West·fa·len (vest fä′lən) *Ger. name of* WESTPHALIA

West Flanders province of NW Belgium, on the North Sea: 1,249 sq. mi.; pop. 1,029,000

West Germany Federal Republic of Germany: see GERMANY

West Ham (ham) city in Essex, SE England, on the Thames: suburb of London: pop. 157,000

West Hartford suburb of Hartford, in C Conn.: pop. 68,000

West Haven city in SW Conn., on Long Island Sound: suburb of New Haven: pop. 53,000

West Indies large group of islands between N. America & S. America: it includes the Greater Antilles, Lesser Antilles, & Bahamas —**West Indian**

west·ing (wes′tin) *n.* **1.** *Naut.* the distance covered sailing in a westerly direction **2.** a westerly direction

West·ing·house (wes′tin hous′), **George** 1846–1914; U.S. inventor & manufacturer

West Ir·i·an (ir′ē ən) province of Indonesia, occupying the W half of the island of New Guinea: c.160,000 sq. mi.; pop. 896,000; cap. Kotabaru

West·land (west′lənd, -land′) [from its location in the western part of the county] city in SE Mich.: suburb of Detroit: pop. 87,000

West Lo·thi·an (lō′*th*ē ən) county of SC Scotland, on the Firth of Forth: 120 sq. mi.; pop. 103,000

West·min·ster (west′min′stər) **1.** metropolitan borough (officially a city) of London: site of the Houses of Parliament: pop. 87,000 **2.** [from the sympathy of its settlers with the Presbyterian principles of the Westminster Assembly (1643–49)] city in SW Calif.: suburb of Los Angeles: pop. 60,000

Westminster Abbey Gothic church (orig. a Benedictine abbey) in Westminster where English monarchs are crowned: it is also a burial place for English monarchs, outstanding statesmen, famous writers, etc.

West·mor·land (west′mər land) county of NW England: 789 sq. mi.; pop. 67,000

West New York town in NE N.J., across the Hudson from New York City: pop. 41,000

west-north·west (west′nôrth′west′; *in naut. usage,* -nôr′-) *n.* the direction, or the point on a mariner's compass, halfway between due west and northwest; 22°30′ north of due west —*adj., adv.* **1.** in or toward this direction **2.** from this direction [a *west-northwest* wind]

West Orange [see ORANGE] town in NE N.J.: suburb of Newark: pop. 44,000

West Pakistan one of the two provinces of Pakistan, on the Arabian Sea: formed from the Sind, Baluchistan, part of Punjab, & other sections of Brit. India: 310,403 sq. mi.; pop. 42,900,000; cap. Lahore

West Palm Beach city in SE Fla., on a lagoon opposite Palm Beach: winter resort: pop. 57,000

West·pha·li·a (west fā'lē ə, -fāl'yə) **1.** region in West Germany, a part of the state of North Rhine-Westphalia: formerly a duchy, a kingdom, & a province of Prussia **2.** **Peace of,** treaties signed (1648) at Osnabrück & Münster ending the Thirty Years' War — **West·pha·li·an** *adj.*, *n.*

West Point military reservation in SE N.Y., on the west bank of the Hudson River: site of the U.S. Military Academy

West Prussia former province of Prussia, since 1945 part of Poland: chief city, Gdansk

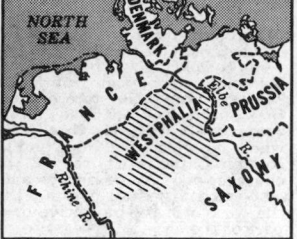

WESTPHALIA (1812)

West Riding administrative division of Yorkshire county, NE England: 2,790 sq. mi.; pop. 3,697,000

West Saxon 1. the old English dialect of the West Saxons, the major literary dialect of the Anglo-Saxons before the Conquest **2.** a native or inhabitant of Wessex (sense 1)

west-south·west (west'south'west'; *in naut. usage,* -sou'-) *n.* the direction, or the point on a mariner's compass, halfway between due west and southwest; 22°30' south of due west —*adj., adv.* **1.** in or toward this direction **2.** from this direction [a *west-southwest* wind]

West Suffolk *see* SUFFOLK

West Sussex *see* SUSSEX

West Virginia [see VIRGINIA] E state of the U.S., northwest of Va.: admitted, 1863; 24,181 sq. mi.; pop. 1,744,000; cap. Charleston: abbrev. **W.Va., WV** —**West Virginian**

west·ward (west'wərd) *adv., adj.* toward the west —*n.* a westward direction, point, or region

west·ward·ly (-lē) *adv., adj.* **1.** toward the west **2.** from the west [a *westwardly* wind]

west·wards (west'wərdz) *adv.* same as WESTWARD

wet (wet) *adj.* **wet'ter, wet'test** [ME. < OE. *wæt,* akin to ON. *vatr:* for IE. base see WATER] **1.** moistened, covered, or saturated with water or other liquid **2.** rainy; foggy; misty [a *wet* day] **3.** not yet dry [*wet* paint] **4.** preserved or bottled in a liquid **5.** using water; done with or in water or other liquid [*wet* sanding] ☆**6.** permitting or favoring the manufacture or sale of alcoholic liquor; opposing, or not enforcing, prohibition [a *wet* candidate, *wet* town] —*n.* **1.** that which moistens or makes wet; water or other liquid; moisture **2.** rain or rainy weather [come in out of the *wet*] ☆**3.** a person who favors the manufacture or sale of alcoholic liquor; one opposed to prohibition —*vt., vi.* **wet** or **wet'ted, wet'ting 1.** to make or become wet (often with *through* or *down*) **2.** to make (a bed, oneself, etc.) wet by urination —☆**all wet** [Slang] wrong; mistaken; in error —**wet behind the ears** young and inexperienced; immature —**wet'ly** *adv.* —**wet'ness** *n.*

SYN.—**wet** is applied to something covered or soaked with water or other liquid [*wet* streets, clothes, etc.] or to something not yet dry [*wet* paint]; **damp** implies slight, usually undesirable or unpleasant wetness [a *damp* room]; **dank** suggests a disagreeable, chilling, unwholesome dampness [a *dank* fog]; **moist** implies slight wetness but, unlike **damp,** often suggests that the absence of dryness is desirable [*moist* air]; **humid** implies such permeation of the air with moisture as to make for discomfort [a hot, *humid* day] —ANT. **dry**

☆**wet·back** (wet'bak') *n.* [from the fact that many cross the border by swimming or wading the Rio Grande] [Colloq.] a Mexican agricultural laborer who illegally enters or is brought into the U.S. to work

☆**wet bar** a bar or serving counter, as in a recreation room, equipped with running water

wet blanket a person or thing whose presence or influence lessens the enthusiasm or gaiety of others

wet-bulb thermometer (wet'bulb') *Meteorol.* that one of a pair of thermometers in a psychrometer having its bulb covered with a wet cloth, while the other (**dry-bulb thermometer**) is left uncovered: the rate of water evaporation from the wet bulb and its resultant cooling depend on the water vapor content in the air, which can be determined by comparison of readings on the two thermometers

wet cell a voltaic cell in which the electrolyte is a liquid

wet dream an involuntary emission of semen during sleep, usually accompanying a sexual dream

wet fly *see* FLY² (sense 2)

weth·er (weth'ər) *n.* [ME. < OE., akin to G. *widder* < IE. base *wet-,* a year, whence Gr. *etēsios,* annual, L. *vetus,* old, *vitulus,* calf] a castrated male sheep

wet·land (wet'land') *n.* [usually pl.] swamps or marshes, ☆esp. as an area preserved for wildlife

wet-nurse (-nurs') *vt.* -nursed', -nurs'ing **1.** to act as wet nurse to **2.** to give overly careful attention to

wet nurse a woman hired to suckle another's child

wet pack *Med.* a type of bath, as for therapy, in which the patient is wrapped in wet sheets or blankets

wet suit a closefitting, usually one-piece suit of rubber, esp. of foam neoprene, worn by skin divers for warmth

wet·ta·bil·i·ty (wet'ə bil'ə tē) *n.* **1.** the condition or state of being wettable **2.** *Chem., Physics* the degree to which a solid is wetted by a liquid, measured by the force of adhesion between the solid and liquid phases

wet·ta·ble (wet'ə b'l) *adj.* **1.** capable of being wetted **2.** *Chem., Physics* able to be made adhesive or absorptive, as by the addition of a liquid, hydrocarbon, etc.

wet·ter (wet'ər) *n.* a person or thing that wets

Wet·ter·horn (vet'ər hôrn') mountain of the Bernese Alps, SC Switzerland: c.12,150 ft.

wetting agent any of a group of surface-active agents which, when added to a liquid, cause the liquid to spread more easily over, or penetrate into, a solid surface

wet·tish (wet'ish) *adj.* somewhat wet

☆**wet wash 1.** laundry washed and left damp without ironing **2.** a washing at a carwash in which the car is not wiped dry

we've (wēv) we have

Wex·ford (weks'fərd) county of Leinster province, SE Ireland: 908 sq. mi.; pop. 83,000

Wey·mouth (wā'məth) [prob. after *Weymouth,* town in England] suburb of Boston, in E Mass., on an inlet of Boston Bay: pop. 55,000

wf, w.f. *Printing* wrong font

WFTU, W.F.T.U. World Federation of Trade Unions

W.G., w.g. wire gauge

WGmc. West Germanic

whack (hwak, wak) *vt., vi.* [echoic] [Colloq.] **1.** to strike or slap with a sharp, resounding blow **2.** to cut (*up*) or divide, as into shares —*n.* [Colloq.] **1.** *a)* a sharp, resounding blow *b)* the sound of this **2.** a share; portion —**at a** (or **one**) **whack** [Colloq.] at one time and quickly or without pausing —☆**have** (or **take**) **a whack at** [Colloq.] **1.** to aim a blow at **2.** to make an attempt at —☆**out of whack** [Colloq.] not in proper condition —**whack off** [Colloq.] to separate or remove by or as by a blow —**whack'er** *n.*

whack·ing (-iŋ) *adj.* [prp. of prec.] [Chiefly Brit. Colloq.] very large; tremendous

whack·y (-ē) *adj.* **whack'i·er, whack'i·est** same as WACKY

whale¹ (hwāl, wāl) *n., pl.* **whales, whale:** see PLURAL, II, D, 1 [ME. < OE. *hwæl,* akin to OHG. *hwal* < IE. *(s)kwalos,* a large fish, whence prob. L. *squalus,* big sea fish] any of various large, warmblooded, fishlike mammals (order Cetacea), esp. as distinguished from the smaller dolphins and porpoises, that breathe air, bear live young, and have front limbs that have been modified into flippers, and a flat, horizontal tail: see TOOTHED WHALE, WHALEBONE WHALE —*vi.* **whaled, whal'ing** to engage in the work of hunting whales —☆**a whale of a** [Colloq.] an exceptionally large, fine, etc. example of a (class of persons or things)

whale² (hwāl, wāl) *vt.* **whaled, whal'ing** [prob. var. of WALE¹] [Colloq.] to beat; whip; thrash

whale·back (hwāl'bak', wāl'-) *n.* **1.** something rounded on top like the back of a whale ☆**2.** a freight steamer with the bow and upper deck rounded so that heavy seas will wash right over: formerly used on the Great Lakes

☆**whale·boat** (-bōt') *n.* **1.** a large, long rowboat, pointed at both ends to increase maneuverability: used formerly by whalers **2.** a similar boat, now often one with a motor (**motor whaleboat**), used as a ship's lifeboat

whale·bone (-bōn') *n.* **1.** the horny, elastic material that hangs in fringed, parallel, platelike sheets from the upper jaw or palate of whalebone whales and serves to strain the minute sea animals on which they feed; baleen **2.** something made of whalebone; esp., a strip of this used, esp. formerly, for corset stays, whips, etc.

whalebone whale any of a suborder (Mysticeti) of whales, as the blue whale, with toothless jaws, whalebone in the mouth, and a symmetrical skull: cf. TOOTHED WHALE

whal·er (hwā'lər, wā'-) *n.* **1.** a ship used in whaling **2.** a man whose work is whaling: also ☆**whale'man** *n., pl.* -men

Whales, Bay of inlet of the Ross Sea, in the Ross Ice Shelf, Antarctica, near Little America

whale shark a large, spotted, egg-laying shark (*Rhincodon typus*) that lives in warm seas, has many small teeth, and feeds on plankton and small fishes by means of gill strainers: the largest of fishes, reaching 50 ft. in length

whal·ing¹ (hwā'liŋ, wā'-) *n.* the work or trade of hunting and killing whales for their blubber, whalebone, etc.

whal·ing² (hwā'liŋ, wā'-) *n.* [< WHALE² + -ING] [Colloq.] a sound thrashing; whipping

wham (hwam, wam) *interj.* a sound in imitation of a heavy blow or explosion —*n.* a heavy blow or impact —*vt., vi.* **whammed, wham'ming** to strike, explode, etc. with a loud, sharp sound

☆**wham·my** (-ē) *n., pl.* -mies [Slang] a jinx or the evil eye: usually in **put a** (or **the**) **whammy on**

whang¹ (hwaŋ, waŋ) *vt.* [of echoic origin] **1.** to strike with a resounding blow **2.** [Dial.] to beat or thrash —*vi.* to make a whanging noise —*n.* **1.** a whanging noise **2.** a whack or blow

whang² (hwaŋ, waŋ) *n.* [altered < ME. *thwang,* THONG] [Dial.] **1.** a thong of leather **2.** leather for thongs, etc.

whang·ee (hwaŋ'ē, waŋ'-) *n.* [prob. < Chin. *huang-li* < *huang,* yellow + *li,* bamboo cane] **1.** any of a number of related Chinese and Japanese bamboos (genus *Phyllostachys*); esp., **blackjoint bamboo** (*Phyllostachys nigra*), growing to 25 ft. in height **2.** a walking stick of whangee

whap (hwap, wap) *vi.* **whapped, whap'ping** *var. of* WHOP

whap·per (-ər) *n. colloq. var. of* WHOPPER

wharf (hwôrf, wôrf) *n.*, *pl.* **wharves, wharfs** [ME. < OE. *hwerf*, a dam or bank to keep out water, lit., a turning < base of *hweorfan*, to turn < IE. **kwerp-*, to turn, whence Gr. *karpos*, wrist] **1.** a structure of wood or stone, sometimes roofed over, built at the shore of a harbor, river, etc. for ships to lie alongside, as during loading or unloading; pier; dock **2.** [Obs.] a band at the water's edge; shore —*vt.* **1.** to bring to a wharf; moor at a wharf **2.** to unload or store on a wharf **3.** to furnish with a wharf or wharves

wharf·age (hwôr′fij, wôr′-) *n.* **1.** the use of a wharf for mooring, loading, or unloading a ship, or for storing goods **2.** a fee charged for this **3.** wharves collectively

wharf·in·ger (-fin jər) *n.* [altered < earlier *wharfager* < prec.] a person who owns or manages a wharf

☆**wharf rat 1.** any of various rats found around wharves; esp., same as BROWN RAT: see RAT (*n.* 1 *a*) **2.** a vagrant or petty criminal who haunts wharves

Whar·ton (hwôr′t'n, wôr′-), **Edith** (born *Edith Newbold Jones*) 1862–1937; U.S. novelist

wharve (hwôrv, wôrv) *n.* [ME. *wherve* < OE. *hweorfa* < base of *hweorfan*, to turn: see WHARF] **1.** orig., a small flywheel on the spindle of a spinning wheel **2.** a small drive pulley on a spindle of a modern spinning machine

wharves (hwôrvz, wôrvz) *n. alt. pl.* of WHARF

what (hwut, hwät, wut, wät; *unstressed* hwət, wət) *pron.* [ME. < OE. *hwæt*, neut. of *hwa*, who < IE. interrogative base **kwo-*, **kwe-*, whence L. *qui*, who, what, Lith. *kàs*, what, who: cf. WHERE, WHO] **1.** which thing, event, circumstance, etc.: used interrogatively in asking for the specification of an identity, quantity, quality, etc.; specif., *a)* in asking about the nature, class, name, purpose, etc. of a thing [*what* is that object? *what* is his address?] *b)* in asking for an explanation or repetition of something previously said [you told him *what?*] *c)* in asking for a quantity, sum, etc. [*what* will it cost?] *d)* in asking about the value, importance, or effect of something [*what* is home without a wife?] *What* is often used elliptically with the sense of 1 *b*, or, esp., as a Brit. colloquialism, to end a sentence with a general or rhetorical interrogative force [it's rather late, *what?*] **2.** that which or those which [to know *what* one wants]: used to introduce a parenthetical element in a sentence [he has, *what* is rare, true tolerance] and also used as a compound relative pronoun with the specific senses of *a)* anything that [do *what* you will] *b)* the exact person or thing that [not *what* he was five years ago] *c)* that or who: now regarded as substandard [the man *what* gave it to me] except in **but what**, but that or but who [there is no one *but what* would approve]: also used elliptically for "what it is," "what to do," etc. [I'll tell you *what*] and with an intensive force in exclamations [*what* he said about her!] —*n.* the true or basic quality of something [to uncover the *what* and why of their relationship] —*adj.* **1.** which or which kind of: used interrogatively or relatively in asking for or specifying the nature, identity, etc. of a person or thing [*what* man told you that? he knows *what* role she played] **2.** as much, or as many, as [take *what* time (or men) you need] **3.** how great, surprising, magnificent, disappointing, etc.: in exclamations [*what* a man! *what* nonsense!] —*adv.* **1.** in what respect? to what degree? how? [*what* does it matter?] **2.** in some manner or degree; in part; partly (usually followed by *with*) [*what* with singing and joking, the time passed quickly] **3.** how greatly, surprisingly, etc.: in exclamations [*what* tragic news!] **4.** [Obs.] why? —*conj.* **1.** that: in **but what**, but that [never doubt *but what* he loves you] **2.** [Dial.] so far as; as much as [we warned them *what* we could] —*interj.* an exclamation of surprise, anger, confusion, etc. [*what!* no dinner?] —**and what not** and other things of all sorts —**what about** what do you think, know, feel, etc. concerning? —**what for 1.** for what purpose? why? **2.** [Slang] punishment; esp., a whipping [he gave his son *what for!*] —☆**what have you** [Colloq.] anything else of a similar sort [selling games, toys, or *what have you*] —**what if 1.** what would happen if **2.** what difference would it make if —☆**what it takes** [Colloq.] whatever is necessary for success or popularity, as wealth, beauty, or intelligence —**what's what** [Colloq.] the true state of affairs —**what the (heck, deuce,** etc.) **1.** an exclamatory remark of surprise **2.** what: used emphatically —**what though** what difference does it make that

what·ev·er (hwət ev′ər, wət-) *pron.* what: an emphatic variant; specif., *a)* which thing, event, circumstance, etc.: used as an interrogative expressing perplexity or wonder [*whatever* can he mean by that?] *b)* anything that [tell her *whatever* you like] *c)* no matter what [*whatever* you may think, he's innocent] —*adj.* **1.** of no matter what type, degree, quality, etc. [to make *whatever* repairs are needed] **2.** being who it may be [*whatever* man told you that, it is not true] **3.** of any kind: used following the word that it modifies [I have no plans *whatever*] Also [Poet.] **what·e′er** (-er′)

what·not (hwut′nät′, hwät′-, wut′-, wät′-) *n.* **1.** a nondescript or indescribable thing or, sometimes, person **2.** a set of open shelves, as for bric-a-brac

what's (hwuts, hwäts, wuts, wäts) what is

what·so·ev·er (hwut′sō ev′ər, hwät′-, wut′-, wät′-) *pron.*, *adj.* whatever: an emphatic form: also [Poet.] **what′so·e′er** (-er′)

whaup (hwôp, wôp) *n.* [prob. < or akin to OE. *whilpe*, curlew, akin to *hwelp:* see WHELP] [Scot. or Eng. Dial.] same as CURLEW

wheal[1] (hwēl, wēl) *n.* [ME. *whele*, akin to OE. *hwelian*, to suppurate] **1.** formerly, a pustule; pimple **2.** a small, itching elevation of the skin, as from the bite of an insect

wheal[2] (hwēl, wēl) *n.* [altered (after prec.) < WEAL[1]] a raised stripe or ridge on the skin, as from a lash of a whip

wheat (hwēt, wēt) *n.* see PLURAL, II, D, 3 [ME. *whete* < OE. *hwæte*, akin to G. *weizen* < IE. base **kweit-*, to gleam, bright, white, whence WHITE: from the white seed] **1.** any of several cereal grasses (genus *Triticum*) having dense, erect spikes containing grains which thresh free of the chaff; esp., **bread wheat** (*Triticum aestivum*), a cultigen with large, nutritious grains **2.** the grain of any of these grasses; esp., bread wheat, used in making flour, cereals, pastries, cakes, etc., and durum, used in making macaroni, noodles, etc.: next to rice, the most widely used grain

☆**wheat cake** a pancake made with whole-wheat flour

wheat·ear (-ir′) *n.* [earlier *white ears* < WHITE + *eeres*, *ers*, var. of ARSE: in reference to its white rump] a small, long-legged, migrating bird (*Oenanthe oenanthe*) of the chat family, native to N Europe, Asia, and N. America

wheat·en (hwēt′'n, wēt′-) *adj.* **1.** made of wheat or wheat flour **2.** of the pale-yellow color of wheat

☆**wheat germ** the fat-rich embryo of the wheat kernel, milled out as an oily flake and used to enrich breads, cereals, etc. with vitamins

Wheat·ley (hwēt′lē, wēt′-), **Phillis** 1753?–84; Am. poet, born in Africa & brought to America as a slave

Wheat·on (hwēt′'n, wēt′-) [after U.S. Army Maj. Gen. Frank *Wheaton* (1833–1903)] suburb of Washington, D.C., in C Md.: pop. 66,000

wheat rust a disease of wheat, caused by various rust fungi; esp., any of numerous stem rusts caused by a fungus (*Puccinia graminis*) harbored by certain barberries

Wheat·stone bridge (hwēt′stōn′, wēt′-; *chiefly Brit.*, -stən) [after Sir Charles *Wheatstone* (1802–75), Eng. physicist] **1.** a divided bridge circuit (see BRIDGE[1], *n.* 10) used for the measurement of electrical resistance **2.** a device containing such a circuit

wheat·worm (hwēt′wurm′, wēt′-) *n.* a small roundworm (*Anguina tritici*) that feeds on wheat, oats, etc.

whee (hwē, wē: *with prolonged vowel*) *interj.* an exclamation expressing joy, thrill, exultation, etc.

whee·dle (hwē′d'l, wē′-) *vt.*, *vi.* **-dled, -dling** [17th-c. cant < ? G. *wedeln*, to wag the tail, fan, hence to flatter < *wedel*, a fan, tail] **1.** to influence or persuade (a person) by flattery, soothing words, coaxing, etc. **2.** to get (something) by coaxing or flattery —*SYN.* see COAX —**whee′dler** *n.* —**whee′dling·ly** *adv.*

wheel (hwēl, wēl) *n.* [ME. *whele* < OE. *hweol*, earlier *hweogol* < IE. **kwekwlo-*, wheel (whence Gr. *kyklos*, a circle) < base **kwel-*, to turn, be around, dwell, whence Gr. *telos*, turning point, end, *polos*, axis, L. *colere*, to till, dwell, G. *hals*, neck] **1.** a solid disk, or a circular frame connected by spokes to a central hub, capable of turning on a central axis and used as to move vehicles or transmit power in machinery **2.** anything like a wheel in shape, movement, action, etc., as a firework (**Catherine wheel**) that revolves in a circular orbit while burning **3.** a device or apparatus of which the principal element is a wheel or wheels; specif., *a)* in the Middle Ages, an instrument of torture consisting of a circular frame on which the victim's limbs were painfully stretched *b)* a wheel with projecting handles for controlling the rudder of a ship *c)* short for PADDLE WHEEL, POTTER'S WHEEL, SPINNING WHEEL, STEERING WHEEL, etc. *d)* any of various rotating disks used for gambling [a roulette *wheel*] ☆*e)* [Colloq.] a bicycle ☆*f)* [*pl.*] [Slang] an automobile **4.** [*usually pl.*] the moving, propelling, or controlling forces or agencies [the *wheels* of progress] **5.** a turning about; circular, rotating, or revolving movement; specif., a turning movement as of troops or ships in line, with one end of the line as the pivot; also, any pivoting movement like this, as of dancers ☆**6.** [Slang] an important, influential, or authoritative person: also **big wheel 7.** [Archaic] the refrain of a song —*vt.* **1.** *a)* to move or roll on wheels [to *wheel* a baby buggy] *b)* to transport in a wheeled vehicle **2.** to cause to turn, revolve, or rotate **3.** to perform in a circular movement **4.** to furnish with a wheel or wheels —*vi.* **1.** to turn on or as on an axis; pivot, rotate, revolve, etc. **2.** to reverse one's course of action, movement, opinion, attitude, etc. (often with *about*) **3.** to turn in a swooping, circular motion: said of birds **4.** to move or roll along on or as on wheels —**at the wheel 1.** steering a ship, motor vehicle, etc. **2.** in charge; directing activities —☆**wheel and deal** [Slang] to behave in an aggressive, flamboyant way, as in

R1 R2
R3 R4

WHEATSTONE
BRIDGE

arranging business or political deals —**wheel of fortune 1.** the wheel which the goddess of fortune was believed to rotate to bring about the alternations or reverses in human affairs **2.** the changes or vicissitudes of life —**wheels within wheels** a series of involved circumstances, motives, etc. reacting upon one another

wheel and axle a grooved wheel fixed to a shaft or drum, used for lifting weights: the turning of the wheel, as by a rope in the groove, winds a rope on the shaft or drum

wheel animalcule *same as* ROTIFER

wheel·bar·row (-bar′ō, -ber′ō) *n.* [ME. *wilberwe:* see WHEEL & BARROW¹] a shallow, open box for moving small loads, having a single wheel in front forming a tripod with two legs in back, and two shafts with handles for raising the vehicle off its legs and pushing or pulling it —*vt.* to move or transport in a wheelbarrow

wheel·base (-bās′) *n.* in a motor vehicle, the distance in inches from the center of the hub of a front wheel to the center of the hub of the corresponding back wheel

☆**wheel bug** a large N. American hemipterous insect (*Arilus cristatus*) distinguished by a high, saw-toothed crest on the prothorax: it sucks the blood of other insects

wheel·chair (-cher′) *n.* ☆a mobile chair mounted on large wheels, for persons unable to walk

wheeled (hwēld, wēld) *adj.* **1.** having a wheel or wheels **2.** having wheels of a specified number or kind: used in hyphenated compounds [four-*wheeled*]

wheel·er (hwēl′ər, wēl′-) *n.* **1.** a person or thing that wheels **2.** *same as* WHEEL HORSE (sense 1) **3.** something having a specified kind or number of wheels: used in hyphenated compounds [side-*wheeler*, two-*wheeler*]

Wheel·er (hwēl′ər), **Joseph** 1836–1906; Confederate general in the Civil War & U.S. general in the Spanish-American War

☆**wheel·er-deal·er** (hwēl′ər dēl′ər, wēl′-) *n.* [Slang] a person who wheels and deals: see phrase at entry WHEEL

wheel horse 1. the horse, or one of the horses, harnessed nearest the front wheels of a vehicle ☆**2.** a person who works especially hard and steadily in any enterprise

☆**wheel·house** (-hous′) *n. same as* PILOTHOUSE

Wheel·ing (hwēl′in) [< AmInd. (Lenape), lit., place of the head (of a slain enemy exhibited there)] city in N W.Va., on the Ohio River: pop. 48,000

wheel lock 1. an early type of gunlock in which a rough wheel is spun on a flint to throw sparks into the pan and set off the charge **2.** a gun with such a lock

wheel·man (-mən) *n., pl.* **-men 1.** [Rare] a cyclist ☆**2.** *same as* HELMSMAN: also **wheels′man 3.** [Slang] the driver of an automobile; esp., the driver of a getaway car

wheel·work (-wurk′) *n.* an arrangement of wheels or gears in a machine or mechanical contrivance

wheel·wright (-rīt′) *n.* [see WHEEL & WRIGHT] a person who makes and repairs wheels and wheeled vehicles

wheen (hwēn, wēn) *n.* [ME. *qwheyn(e)* < OE. *whēne*, *whæne*, instrumental case of *whōn*, (a) few] [Scot. & Eng. Dial.] a few or, sometimes, a considerable number

wheeze (hwēz, wēz) *vi.* **wheezed**, **wheez′ing** [ME. *whesen* < ON. *hvaesa*, to hiss < IE. *kwes-*, to wheeze, snort, whence L. *queri*, to lament] **1.** to breathe hard with a whistling, breathy sound, as in asthma **2.** to make a sound like this [the old organ *wheezed*] —*vt.* to utter with a sound of wheezing —*n.* **1.** an act or sound of wheezing **2.** [Slang] an overworked or trite remark, joke, or gag —**wheez′er** *n.* —**wheez′ing·ly** *adv.*

wheez·y (hwē′zē, wē′-) *adj.* **wheez′i·er, wheez′i·est** wheezing or characterized by wheezing —**wheez′i·ly** *adv.*

whelk¹ (hwelk, welk) *n.* [ME. *welke* < OE. *wioluc* < IE. base *wel-*, to turn (with reference to the spiral shell): cf. WALK] any of various large marine snails (esp. genera *Buccinum* and *Busycon*) with spiral shells, esp. those species used in Europe for food

whelk² (hwelk, welk) *n.* [ME. *whelke* < OE. *hwylca*, a pustule < base of *hwelian*, to exude pus] **1.** a pimple or pustule **2.** *same as* WHEAL¹

WHELK

whelm (hwelm, welm) *vt.* [ME. *welmen, whelmen:* ? merging of OE. *-hwelfan*, to overwhelm, with *helmian*, to cover (cf. HELM¹)] **1.** to submerge, cover, or engulf **2.** to overpower or crush; overwhelm

whelp (hwelp, welp) *n.* [ME. < OE. *hwelp*, akin to G. *welf*, ON. *hvelpr*, puppy, prob. < IE. *kwel-*, to yelp, cry out, whence W. *colwyn*, puppy] **1.** a young dog; puppy **2.** the young of any of various flesh-eating animals, as of a lion, tiger, leopard, bear, wolf, etc. **3.** a youth or child: a contemptuous usage **4.** any of the teeth on a sprocket wheel **5.** *Naut.* any of the ribs or ridges along the barrel of a capstan or the drum of a windlass: *usually used in pl.* —*vt., vi.* to bring forth (young); give birth to: said of animals, and contemptuously of a woman

when (hwen, wen; *unstressed* hwən, wən) *adv.* [ME. *whenne* < OE. *hwænne*, akin to G. *wann*, when, *wenn*, if, akin to *hwa*, who: for IE. base see WHAT] **1.** *a)* at what time? [*when* did they leave? he asked *when* he should go] *b)* on what occasion or under what circumstances? [*when* do you double the final consonant?] *c)* at what point? [*when* shall I stop pouring?] **2.** at an earlier time and

under different circumstances [I knew him *when*] Used interrogatively and in indirect questions —*conj.* **1.** at what time or point [he told us *when* to eat] **2.** at which time [he came at six, *when* the sun was setting] **3.** at which [a time *when* men must speak out] **4.** at the time that [*when* we were at college] **5.** as soon as [the runners started *when* the gun went off] **6.** at whatever time; whenever [she smiles *when* you praise her] **7.** although; whereas; while on the contrary [to complain of one's lot *when* one might change it] **8.** if; considering the fact that [how can he help *when* they won't let him?] —*pron.* what or which time [until *when* will you remain? we came a week ago, since *when* we've had no rest] —*n.* the time or moment (*of* an event) [the *when* and where of his arrest]

when·as (hwen az′, wen-) *conj.* [WHEN + AS¹] [Archaic] **1.** when **2.** inasmuch as **3.** whereas

whence (hwens, wens) *adv.* [ME. *whennes* (< *whenne*, WHEN + adv. gen. *-s*), replacing OE. *hwanan*] **1.** from what place; from where [*whence* do you come? I know *whence* he comes] **2.** from what source or cause [*whence* does he get his strength?] —*conj.* **1.** to the place from which [return *whence* you came] **2.** from which fact [there was no reply, *whence* he inferred that all had gone]

whence·so·ev·er (hwens′sō ev′ər, wens′-) *adv., conj.* from whatever place, source, or cause

when·ev·er (hwen ev′ər, wen-, hwən-, wən-) *adv.* [Colloq.] when: an emphatic form expressing surprise or bewilderment [*whenever* will he learn?] —*conj.* **1.** at whatever time [leave *whenever* you're ready] **2.** on whatever occasion [visit us *whenever* you can] Also [Poet.] **when′e′er′** (-er′)

when·so·ev·er (hwen′sō ev′ər, wen′-) *adv., conj.* whenever: an emphatic form: also [Poet.] **when′so·e′er′** (-er′)

where (hwer, wer; *unstressed* hwər, wər) *adv.* [ME. *wher* < OE. *hwær*, akin to G. *wo* & to *war-* in *warum*: for IE. base see WHAT] **1.** in or at what place? [*where* is the car?] **2.** to or toward what place or point? [*where* did he go?] **3.** in what situation or position [*where* will we be if we lose?] **4.** in what respect? [*where* is she to blame?] **5.** from what place or source? [*where* did you get your information?] —*conj.* **1.** in or at what place [he knows *where* they are] **2.** in or at which place [we came home, *where* we had dinner] **3.** in or at the place or situation in which [he is *where* he should be] **4.** in whatever place, situation, or respect in which [there is never peace *where* men are greedy] **5.** *a)* to or toward the place to which [the bus will take you *where* you're going] *b)* to a place in which [she never goes *where* she's not wanted] **6.** to or toward whatever place [go *where* you please] **7.** [Colloq.] *same as* WHEREAS The use of *where* in place of *that* to introduce a noun clause, though widespread in informal usage, is objected to by some [I see *where* the tax rates are going up] —*pron.* **1.** the place or situation in, at, or to which [he lives two miles from *where* he works] **2.** what or which place [*where* do you come from?] —*n.* the place (*of* an event) [to announce the when and *where* of the marriage]

where·a·bouts (hwer′ə bouts′, wer′-) *adv.* **1.** near or at what place? where? **2.** [Obs.] about or concerning which —*n.* the place where a person or thing is [to know the *whereabouts* of a person] Also [Rare] **where′a·bout′** (-bout′)

where·as (hwer az′, wer-, hwər-, wər-) *conj.* **1.** it being the case that; in view of the fact that: used in the preamble to a formal document [*whereas* the following incidents have occurred] **2.** while on the contrary; but on the other hand [she is slender, *whereas* he is stout] —*n., pl.* **-as·es** a statement beginning with "whereas"

where·at (-at′) *adv.* [Archaic] at what? [*whereat* was he offended?] —*conj.* [Archaic] at which point [he turned to leave, *whereat* she began to weep]

where·by (-bī′) *adv.* [Archaic] by what? how? [*whereby* did you expect to profit?] —*conj.* by which; by means of which [a device *whereby* to make money]

where·fore (hwer′fôr′, wer′-) *adv.* [ME. *hwarfore:* see WHERE & FOR] [Archaic] for what reason or purpose? why? [*wherefore* are you angry?] —*conj.* **1.** for which [the reason *wherefore* we have met] **2.** on account of which; because of which; therefore [we are victorious, *wherefore* let us rejoice] —*n.* the reason; cause [never mind the why and *wherefore*]

where·from (hwer frum′, wer′-) *adv., conj.* from which

where·in (-in′) *adv.* [ME. *hwerin:* see WHERE & IN] [Archaic] in what way? how? [*wherein* is it wrong?] —*conj.* in which [the room *wherein* he lay]

where·in·to (-in′tōō, -in tōō′) *conj.* into which

where·of (-uv′) *adv., conj.* [ME.: see WHERE & OF] of what, which, or whom [the things *whereof* he spoke]

where·on (-än′) *adv.* [Archaic] on what? [*whereon* do you rely?] —*conj.* on which [the hill *whereon* we stand]

where·so·ev·er (hwer′sō ev′ər, wer′-) *adv., conj.* [ME. *wher so ever*] at, in, or to whatever place; wherever: an emphatic form: also [Poet.] **where′so·e′er′** (-er′)

where·through (hwer thrōō′, wer-) *conj.* [Archaic] through which

where·to (-tōō′) *adv.* [ME. *hwerto*] to what? toward what place, direction, or end? —*conj.* to which [the place *whereto* they hurry]

where·un·to (-un′tōō, -ən tōō′) *adv., conj.* archaic var. of WHERETO

where·up·on (hwer′ə pän′, wer′-; hwer′ə pän, wer′-) *adv.* [Archaic] upon what? whereon? —*conj.* **1.** upon which [the ground *whereupon* he had fallen] **2.** at which; upon

which; as a consequence of which [she told a tale, *whereupon* he laughed heartily]

wher·ev·er (hwer ev′ər, wer-, hwər-, wər-) *adv.* [ME.] [Colloq.] where: an emphatic form expressing surprise or bewilderment [*wherever* did you hear that?] —*conj.* in, at, or to whatever place or situation [he thinks of us, *wherever* he is] Also [Poet.] **wher·e'er′** (-er′)

where·with (hwer with′, wer-; -with′) *adv.* [ME. *wher with*] [Archaic] with what? [*wherewith* shall he be saved?] —*conj.* with which [lacking the money *wherewith* to pay his debts] —*pron.* that with which [to have *wherewith* to stock one's larder] —*n.* [Rare] *same as* WHEREWITHAL

where·with·al (hwer′with ôl′, wer′-; -with-) *n.* that with which something can be done; necessary means, esp. money (usually with *the*) [the *wherewithal* to continue one's education] —*adv., conj. archaic var. of* WHEREWITH

wher·ry (hwer′ē, wer′-) *n., pl.* **-ries** [ME. *whery* < ? *whirren*, WHIR, with suggestion of fast movement] **1.** a light rowboat used on rivers **2.** a racing scull for one person **3.** [Brit.] a large, broad, but light barge, used for moving freight —*vt.* **-ried, -ry·ing** to transport in a wherry

whet (hwet, wet) *vt.* **whet′ted, whet′ting** [ME. *whetten* < OE. *hwettan*, to make keen < *hwæt*, sharp, keen, bold < IE. base *kwed-*, to pierce, sharpen, whet, whence prob. L. (*tri*)*quetrus*, (three-)cornered] **1.** to sharpen by rubbing or grinding (the edge of a knife or tool); hone **2.** to make keen; stimulate [to *whet* the appetite] —*n.* **1.** an act of whetting **2.** something that whets (the appetite, etc.) —**whet′ter** *n.*

wheth·er (hweth′ər, weth′-) *conj.* [ME. < OE. *hwæther* (akin to G. *weder*, neither) < IE. *kwotero-*, which (of two) < base *kwo-*, who (cf. WHAT) + compar. suffix] **1.** if it be the case or fact that: used to introduce an indirect question [ask *whether* she will help] **2.** in case; in either case that: used to introduce alternatives, the second of which is introduced by *or* or by *or whether* [*whether* he drives or (*whether* he) flies, he'll be on time]: the second alternative is sometimes merely implied or understood [we don't know *whether* he'll improve (or not)] **3.** either [taxation to support the war, *whether* just or unjust] —*pron.* [Archaic] which (esp. of two): used interrogatively and relatively —**whether or no** in any case

whet·stone (hwet′stōn′, wet′-) *n.* [ME. *whetston* < OE. *hwetstan* < *hwettan* (see WHET) + *stan*, STONE] an abrasive stone for sharpening knives or other edged tools

whew (hyoo, hwyoo; *often unvoiced*) *interj.* [echoic] an exclamation or sharp, breathing sound of relief, surprise, disgust, dismay, etc.

whey (hwā, wā) *n.* [ME. *whei* < OE. *hwæg*, akin to Du. *wei* < ? IE. base *kwei-*, slime, mud, whence L. *caenum*, mire (cf. OBSCENE)] the thin, watery part of milk, that separates from the thicker part (curds) after coagulation, as in cheesemaking —**whey′ey** (-ē) *adj.*

whey·face (-fās′) *n.* [WHEY + FACE] **1.** a pale or pallid face **2.** a person having such a face —**whey′faced′** *adj.*

which (hwich, wich) *pron.* [ME. *whiche* < OE. *hwylc, hwelc*, for *hwa-lic*, lit., who like (Goth. *hwileiks*, OHG. *hwelih*, G. *welch*): see WHO & -LY¹] **1.** what one (or ones) of the number of persons, things, or events mentioned or implied? [*which* of the men answered? *which* do you want?] **2.** the one (or ones) that [he knows *which* he wants] **3.** who, whom, or that: used as a relative in a restrictive or nonrestrictive clause referring to the thing or event (or, archaically, person) specified in the antecedent word, phrase, or clause [the black hat, *which* is on the table; the war *which* had just ended]: also used with a preposition and referring to a specified antecedent [the town in *which* he was born] **4.** either, or any, of the persons, things, or events previously mentioned or implied; whichever [take *which* you prefer] **5.** a thing or fact that [you are late—*which* reminds me, where were you yesterday?] —*adj.* **1.** what one or ones (of the number mentioned or implied) [*which* man (or men) answered? *which* books did he choose?] **2.** whatever; no matter what [try *which* method he pleased, he could not succeed] **3.** being the one just mentioned [he is very old, *which* fact is important]

which·ev·er (hwich ev′ər, wich-) *pron., adj.* **1.** any one (of two or more) [he may choose *whichever* (he wishes] **2.** no matter which [*whichever* (desk) he chooses, they won't be pleased]

which·so·ev·er (hwich′sō ev′ər, wich′-) *pron., adj.* whichever: an emphatic form

whick·er (hwik′ər, wik′-) *vi.* [echoic] **1.** to utter a partly stifled laugh; snicker; titter **2.** to neigh or whinny

whid (hwid, wud) *vi.* **whid′ded, whid′ding** [< ? ON. *hvitha*, a squall] [Scot.] to move nimbly

whid·ah bird (hwid′ə, wud′ə) *same as* WHYDAH BIRD

whiff (hwif, wif) *n.* [echoic] **1.** a light puff or gust of air or wind; breath **2.** a slight wave of odor; faint momentary smell [a *whiff* of garlic] **3.** a puff of smoke or vapor; esp., an exhaling of tobacco smoke **4.** an inhaling of tobacco smoke ☆**5.** [Colloq.] an unsuccessful attempt at hitting the ball in golf or baseball —*vt.* **1.** to blow or propel with a puff or gust; waft **2.** to blow out (tobacco smoke) in puffs **3.** to smoke (a pipe, etc.) ☆**4.** [Colloq.] to cause (a batter) to strike out in baseball —*vi.* **1.** to blow

or move in puffs **2.** to inhale or exhale whiffs, as in smoking ☆**3.** [Colloq.] to miss the ball, as in golf, or strike out, as in baseball —**whiff′er** *n.*

☆**whif·fet** (-it) *n.* [dim. of prec.] **1.** a little whiff, or puff **2.** [var. of WHIPPET] a small dog **3.** [Colloq.] an insignificant, esp. young, person

whif·fle (-'l) *vi.* **-fled, -fling** [freq. of WHIFF] **1.** to blow fitfully; blow in puffs or gusts: said of the wind **2.** to shift or veer about; vacillate —*vt.* **1.** to blow or scatter with or as with a puff of wind

whif·fler (-lər) *n.* [< prec. + -ER] a person who vacillates or shifts position frequently in argument

☆**whif·fle·tree** (-'l trē′) *n. var. of* WHIPPLETREE

Whig (hwig, wig) *n.* [shortened form of *whiggamore* (applied to Scot. Covenanters who marched on Edinburgh in 1648), an erratic form of WScot. *whiggamaire* < *whig*, a cry to urge on horses + *mare*, a horse] **1.** a member of a political party in England (fl. 18th to mid-19th cent.) which championed reform and parliamentary rights: it later became the Liberal Party ☆**2.** in the American Revolution, a person who opposed continued allegiance to Great Britain and supported the Revolution ☆**3.** a member of an American political party (c.1836–1856) opposing the Democratic Party and advocating protection of industry and limitation of the power of the executive branch of government —*adj.* **1.** that is a Whig **2.** composed of Whigs **3.** adhering to, or characteristic of, Whiggism —**Whig′gish** *adj.*

Whig·gism (-iz'm) *n.* the doctrines and principles of Whigs, esp. of English Whigs: also **Whig′ger·y**

whig·ma·lee·rie, whig·ma·lee·ry (hwig′mə lir′ē, wig′-) *n., pl.* **-ries** [fanciful coinage] [Chiefly Scot.] **1.** a fanciful notion, whim, etc. **2.** a fanciful contrivance; gewgaw

while (hwīl, wīl) *n.* [ME. < OE. *hwil*, akin to G. *weile* < IE. base *kwoyo-*, to rest, whence L. *quies*, quiet] a period or space of time [a short *while*] —*conj.* **1.** during or throughout the time that [we waited *while* he dined] **2.** at the same time that [*while* you're up, close the door] **3.** *a)* although on the one hand [*while* he was not poor, he had no ready cash] *b)* whereas; and on the other hand [the walls are green, *while* the ceiling is white] **4.** [Dial.] until —*prep.* [Archaic] until —*vt.* **whiled, whil′ing** [< the *n.*, but prob. influenced in meaning by *wile*] to spend (time) in a pleasant way; cause to pass idly (often with *away*) [to *while* away the afternoon] —**between whiles** now and then; at intervals —**the while** at the same time; during this very time —**worth (one's) while** worth one's time, consideration, etc.; profitable to one in some way

whiles (hwīlz, wīlz) *adv.* [ME. < *while* (see prec.) + adv. gen. -s] [Chiefly Scot.] *same as* SOMETIMES —*conj.* [Archaic or Dial.] *same as* WHILE

whi·lom (hwī′ləm, wī′-) *adv.* [ME. *whilum* < OE. *hwilum*, dat. pl. of *hwil*, WHILE] [Archaic] at one time; formerly —*adj.* formerly such; former [their *whilom* friends]

whilst (hwīlst, wīlst) *conj.* [ME. *whilest*, extended < *whiles*, WHILES] [Now Chiefly Brit. or U.S. Dial.] *same as* WHILE

whim (hwim, wim) *n.* [short for WHIM-WHAM] **1.** a sudden fancy; idle and passing notion; capricious idea or desire **2.** a kind of winch or capstan, consisting of a vertical drum with extended arms to which one or more horses may be hitched: formerly used in mines to raise ore or water —*SYN.* see CAPRICE

whim·brel (hwim′brəl, wim′-) *n.* [earlier *whimrel*, prob. echoic of its cry] a small European curlew (*Numenius phaeopus*), with a pale stripe along the dark-brown crown

whim·per (hwim′pər, wim′-) *vi.* [? akin to WHINE] to make low, whining, broken sounds, as in crying or in fear —*vt.* to utter or say with a whimper —*n.* a whimpering sound or cry —*SYN.* see CRY —**whim′per·ing·ly** *adv.*

whim·si·cal (hwim′zi k'l, wim′-) *adj.* **1.** full of or characterized by whims or whimsy **2.** oddly out of the ordinary; fanciful; freakish **3.** subject to sudden change; unpredictable —**whim′si·cal·ly** *adv.*

whim·si·cal·i·ty (hwim′zi kal′ə tē, wim′-) *n.* **1.** the quality of being whimsical: also **whim′si·cal·ness** **2.** *pl.* **-ties** a whimsical speech, notion, or action; caprice

whim·sy (hwim′zē, wim′-) *n., pl.* **-sies** [prob. < ff.] **1.** an odd fancy; idle notion; whim **2.** curious, quaint, or fanciful humor [poems full of *whimsy*] ☆**3.** a small piece of shaped veiling worn as a hat, usually decorated with bows, etc. Also sp. **whim′sey,** *pl.* **-seys** —*SYN.* see CAPRICE

whim-wham (hwim′hwam′, wim′wam′) *n.* [< ?] **1.** a fanciful ornament; bauble; trinket **2.** an odd notion; fancy; whim —☆**the whim-whams** [Colloq.] an uneasy, nervous feeling; the jitters

whin¹ (hwin, win) *n.* [ME., prob. < Scand., as in obs. Dan. *hvine,* Sw. *hven,* applied to coarse grasses; the IE. base is *kwei-*, slime, dirt: cf. WHEY] *same as* FURZE

whin² (hwin, win) *n.* [ME. (Northern) *quin* < ?] [Brit. Dial.] any of several hard, igneous or basaltic rocks, occurring as dikes or flows: also **whin′stone**

whin·chat (hwin′chat′, win′-) *n.* [WHIN¹ + CHAT¹, *n.*] a brown and buff migrating European songbird (*Saxicola rubetra*) that frequents heaths and meadows

whine (hwīn, wīn) *vi.* **whined, whin′ing** [ME. *whinen* < OE. *hwinan*, akin to ON. *hvina* < IE. echoic base *kwei-*,

to whiz, hiss, whence WHISTLE, WHISPER] **1.** *a)* to utter a peevish, high-pitched, somewhat nasal sound, as in complaint, distress, fear, etc. *b)* to make a prolonged, high-pitched sound like this **2.** to complain or beg in a childishly undignified way, as with a whine —*vt.* to utter with or as with a whine —*n.* **1.** the act or sound of whining **2.** a complaint uttered in a whining tone —**whin′er** *n.* —**whin′ing·ly** *adv.*

☆**whing·ding** (hwiŋ′diŋ′, wiŋ′-) *n. var. of* WINGDING

whin·ny[1] (hwin′ē, win′-) *adj.* **-ni·er, -ni·est** [WHIN[1] + -Y[2]] covered with whin, or furze

whin·ny[2] (hwin′ē, win′-) *vi.* **whin′nied, whin′ny·ing** [prob. < or akin to WHINE] to neigh in a low, gentle, contented way: said of a horse —*vt.* to express with a whinny —*n., pl.* **-nies** the whinnying of a horse, or a similar sound

whin·y (hwī′nē, wī′-) *adj.* **whin′i·er, whin′i·est** of, given to, or characterized by whining [a *whiny* child]: also say. **whin′ey** —**whin′i·ness** *n.*

whip (hwip, wip) *vt.* **whipped, whip′ping** [ME. *whippen* < MDu. *wippen*, to swing, move up and down < IE. base *weib-*, to turn, swing, whence WIPE, L. *vibrare*, to set in rapid motion] **1.** to move, pull, jerk, snatch, throw, etc. suddenly (usually with *out*, *off*, *up*, etc.) [to *whip* out a knife] **2.** *a)* to strike, as with a strap, rod, etc.; lash; beat *b)* to punish in this manner **3.** to force, drive, compel, urge, etc. by or as by whipping **4.** to strike as a whip does [the rain *whipped* her face] **5.** to attack with stinging words; flay **6.** *a)* to cover (a cord, rope, etc.) with cord or thread wound round and round, so as to prevent fraying *b)* to wind or bind (cord, etc.) around something **7.** to fish (a stream, etc.) by making repeated casts with a rod and line **8.** to beat (egg whites, cream, etc.) with a fork, whisk, mixer, etc. so as to incorporate air and make frothy **9.** to sew (a seam, etc.) with a loose, overcasting or overhand stitch **10.** [Colloq.] to defeat or outdo, as in a contest **11.** *Naut.* to hoist by means of a rope passing through an overhead pulley —*vi.* **1.** to move, go, pass, etc. quickly and suddenly [he *whipped* down the stairs] **2.** to flap or thrash about in a whiplike manner [flags *whipping* in high wind] **3.** to cast with a fishing rod, using a quick, whiplike motion —*n.* [ME. *whippe* < MDu. *wippe*] **1.** an instrument for striking or flogging, consisting generally of a stiff or flexible rod with a lash attached to one end **2.** a blow, cut, etc. made with or as with a whip **3.** a person who uses a whip, as a coachman, a huntsman who whips on the hounds, etc. **4.** *a)* an officer of a political party in Congress, Parliament, etc. who maintains discipline, enforces attendance, etc.: also **party whip** *b)* [Brit.] a call issued to party members in a lawmaking body to be in attendance at a certain time **5.** a whipping motion **6.** a dessert made of sugar and whipped cream, stiffly beaten egg whites, or gelatin, and often fruit **7.** something resembling a whip in its action, as a windmill vane, kind of egg beater, etc. **8.** a hoisting apparatus consisting of a single rope passing through an overhead pulley —*SYN.* see BEAT —**whip in** to bring together or assemble, as a party whip does —**whip into shape** [Colloq.] to bring by vigorous action into the proper or desired condition —**whip up 1.** to rouse; excite [to *whip up* enthusiasm] **2.** [Colloq.] to prepare quickly and efficiently

whip·cord (-kôrd′) *n.* **1.** a hard, twisted or braided cord used for whiplashes, etc. **2.** a strong worsted cloth with a hard, diagonally ribbed surface

whip hand 1. the hand in which a driver holds his whip **2.** the position of advantage or control

whip·lash (-lash′) *n.* **1.** the lash of a whip ☆**2.** a sudden, severe bending and jolting of the neck backward and then forward, as caused by the impact of a rear-end automobile collision, sometimes resulting in injury to the soft tissues and to the vertebrae of the neck

whipped cream rich sweet cream stiffened as by whipping and used as a topping on desserts, etc.: also **whip cream**

whip·per (-ər) *n.* a person or thing that whips

whip·per·in (-ər in′) *n., pl.* **-pers-in′ 1.** [Chiefly Brit.] a huntsman's assistant who keeps the hounds together in the pack **2.** *same as* WHIP (*n.* 4 *a*)

whip·per·snap·per (hwip′ər snap′ər, wip′-) *n.* [extended < *whip-snapper*, one who snaps whips] an insignificant, esp. young, person who appears impertinent or presumptuous

whip·pet (hwip′it, wip′-) *n.* [dim. < WHIP] a swift dog resembling a small greyhound, used in coursing and racing

whip·ping (-iŋ) *n.* **1.** the action of a person or thing that whips; esp., a flogging or beating, as in punishment **2.** cord, twine, etc. used to whip, or bind

whipping boy 1. orig., a boy brought up together with a young prince and required to take the punishment for the latter's misdeeds **2.** *same as* SCAPEGOAT (sense 2)

whipping cream sweet cream with a high percentage of butterfat, that can be whipped until stiff

whipping post a post to which offenders are tied to be whipped as a legal punishment

whip·ple·tree (hwip′l trē′, wip′-) *n.* [< WHIP + TREE] *same as* SINGLETREE

WHIPPET
(18–22 in. high
at shoulder)

☆**whip·poor·will** (hwip′ər wil′, wip′-) *n., pl.* **-wills′, -will′:** see PLURAL, II, D, 1 [echoic of its cry] a grayish, insect-eating goatsucker (*Caprimulgus vociferus*) of E N. America, related to the nightjar and active at night

whip·saw (hwip′sô′, wip′-) *n.* any of several long-bladed saws; esp., a crosscut saw with a tapering blade, from 5 to 7 1/2 feet long and with a handle at each end, used usually by two persons —☆*vt.* **1.** to cut with a whipsaw **2.** to defeat or get the best of (a person) two ways at once, as, in faro, by winning two different bets in a single play

whip scorpion any of an order (Pedipalpi) of tropical or subtropical arachnids resembling the scorpion but having a long, whiplike tail at the end of the abdomen and no sting

whip snake 1. any of a genus (*Masticophis*) of long, slender, nonpoisonous snakes of N. and S. America that often live in trees **2.** any of several similar, but poisonous, snakes (genera *Demansia* and *Denisonia*) of Australia

☆**whip·stall** (-stôl′) *n.* a stunt in flying in which the airplane first goes into a stall during a steep climb, then drops or whips suddenly nose downward

whip·stitch (-stich′) *vt., vi.* Sewing to overcast or whip —*n.* **1.** a stitch made in this way **2.** [Old Colloq.] a short period of time

whip·stock (-stäk′) *n.* the handle of a whip

whip·worm (-wurm′) *n.* any of a genus (*Trichuris*) of roundworms, about two inches in length with a whiplike front portion, parasitic in the intestines of mammals

whir, whirr (hwur, wur) *vi., vt.* **whirred, whir′ring** [ME. (Northern) *quirren*, prob. < Scand., as in Dan. *hvirre*, Norw. *kvirra*, akin to ON. *hverfa*, to turn: for IE. base see WHARF] to fly, revolve, vibrate, or otherwise move quickly with a whizzing or buzzing sound —*n.* a sound like this, as that made by a bird's wings, a propeller, etc.

whirl (hwurl, wurl) *vi.* [ME. *whirlen* < ON. *hvirfla*, akin to *hverfa*: see prec.] **1.** to move rapidly in a circular manner or as in an orbit; circle swiftly [couples *whirling* round the dance floor] **2.** to rotate or spin fast; gyrate **3.** to move, go, drive, etc. swiftly **4.** to seem to spin; reel [her head beginning to *whirl*] —*vt.* **1.** to cause to rotate, revolve, or spin rapidly **2.** to move, carry, drive, etc. with a rotating motion [the wind *whirled* the leaves] **3.** [Obs.] to hurl or throw —*n.* [ME. *wherwille* < ON. *hverfill*, akin to G. *wirbel*] **1.** the act of whirling **2.** a whirling motion **3.** something whirling or being whirled [a *whirl* of dust] **4.** a round of parties, etc., one after another **5.** a tumult; uproar; stir **6.** a confused or giddy condition [his head in a *whirl*] —*SYN.* see TURN —☆**give it a whirl** [Colloq.] to try something; make an attempt —**whirl′er** *n.*

whirl·i·gig (hwur′li gig′, wur′-) *n.* [ME. *whirlgigge:* see WHIRL & GIG[1]] **1.** a child's toy that whirls or spins, as a pinwheel **2.** a merry-go-round **3.** something that seems to whirl, or revolve in a cycle **4.** a whirling motion or course

whirligig beetle any of a small family (Gyrinidae) of bluish-black gregarious beetles found darting about in circles on the surface of ponds, streams, etc.

whirl·pool (hwurl′pool′, wurl′-) *n.* **1.** water in rapid, violent, whirling motion caused by two meeting currents, by winds meeting tides, etc. and tending to form a circle into which floating objects are drawn; vortex or eddy of water **2.** anything like a whirlpool, as in violent motion

☆**whirlpool bath** a bath, as used in hydrotherapy, in which an agitating device propels a current of warm water with a swirling motion

whirl·wind (-wind′) *n.* [ME. *whirlwynd;* prob. after ON. *hvirfilvindr*] **1.** a current of air whirling violently upward in a spiral motion around a more or less vertical axis that has a forward motion **2.** anything resembling a whirlwind, as in violent or destructive force, etc. —*adj.* impetuous and speedy [a *whirlwind* courtship] —**sow the wind and reap the whirlwind** to engage in, and suffer the consequences of, evil or folly: Hos. 8:7

whirl·y·bird (hwur′lē burd′, wur′-) *n. colloq. term for* HELICOPTER

whir·ry (hwur′ē, wur′-) *vt., vi.* **-ried, -ry·ing** [Scot.] to whirl; hurry

whish (hwish, wish) *vi.* [echoic] to move with a soft, rushing sound; whiz; swish —*n.* a sound so made

whisht (hwisht, wisht) *interj., n., vt.* [Chiefly Scot. & Ir.] hush; silence

whisk (hwisk, wisk) *n.* [ME. *wysk* < ON. *visk*, a wisp, brush < IE. *weisk-* (< *weis-*, supple twig, broom) whence G. *wischen*, to wipe] **1.** *a)* the act of brushing with a quick, light, sweeping motion *b)* such a motion **2.** a small bunch of straw, twigs, hair, etc. used for brushing **3.** a kitchen utensil consisting of wire loops fixed in a handle, for whipping egg whites, cream, etc. —*vt.* **1.** to move, remove, carry, brush (*away*, *off*, *out*, etc.) with a quick, sweeping motion [to *whisk* out a handkerchief, to *whisk* off crumbs] **2.** [Chiefly Brit.] to whip (egg whites, cream, etc.) —*vi.* to move quickly, nimbly, or briskly

whisk broom a small, short-handled broom for brushing clothes, etc.

whisk·er (hwis′kər, wis′-) *n.* [ME. *wisker*, something used for whisking: see WHISK & -ER] **1.** [pl.] *a)* formerly, a mustache *b)* the hair growing on a man's face; esp., the beard on the cheeks **2.** *a)* a hair of a man's beard *b)* any of the long bristly hairs growing on the upper lip of a cat, rat, etc. at each side; vibrissa **3.** a very small, hairlike, single-crystal filament of high tensile strength, grown on

certain metals, alloys, crystals, etc. and serving to reinforce the material 4. *Naut.* either of two spars extending laterally one on each side of the bowsprit, for spreading the jib and flying jib guys: also **whisker boom** —**whisk′-ered, whisk′er·y** *adj.*

whis·key (hwis′kē, wis′kē) *n., pl.* -**keys**, -**kies** [short for USQUEBAUGH < IrGael. *uisce beathadh* (or cognate Scot-Gael. *uisge beatha*) < *uisce*, WATER + *beathadh*, life < IE. base **gwi-*, **gwei-*, to live, whence QUICK, Gr. *bios*, L. *vita*, life] **1.** a strong alcoholic liquor distilled from the fermented mash of grain, esp. of rye, wheat, corn, or barley **2.** a drink of whiskey —*adj.* of, for, or made with whiskey Also sp. **whis′ky,** *pl.* -**kies** *Note:* In general, U.S. and Irish usage favors **whiskey,** and Brit. and Canad. usage favors **whisky**

☆**whiskey sour** a cocktail of lemon juice, sugar, and whiskey, shaken with cracked ice

whis·ky-jack (-jak′) *n.* [altered < *whisky john,* itself altered (after WHISKY + JOHN) < AmInd. (Algonquian) name, as in Cree *wiskatjân*] *same as* CANADA JAY

whis·per (hwis′pər, wis′-) *vi.* [ME. *whisperen* < OE. *hwisprian,* akin to G. *wispern* < IE. base **kwei-,* to whiz, hiss, whence WHINE, WHISTLE] **1.** to speak very softly, esp. without the resonance produced by the vibration of the vocal cords **2.** to talk quietly or furtively, as in gossiping, maligning, or plotting **3.** to make a soft, rustling sound like a whisper, as the leaves of a tree —*vt.* **1.** to say very softly, esp. by whispering **2.** to tell (something) to (someone) privately or as a secret —*n.* **1.** the act or an instance of whispering; specif., soft, low speech produced with breath but, usually, without voice **2.** *a)* something whispered *b)* a secret, hint, rumor, etc. **3.** a soft rustling sound like a whisper —**whis′per·er** *n.*

whis·per·ing (-iŋ) *adj.* that whispers or is like a whisper: also **whis′per·y** —*n.* **1.** the act of one who whispers **2.** something whispered; whispered sound, speech, etc. —**whis′per·ing·ly** *adv.*

☆**whispering campaign** the organized dissemination of defamatory rumors by word of mouth, intended to discredit a political candidate, group, cause, etc.

whist[1] (hwist, wist) *interj.* [ME.; echoic] [Archaic or Dial.] hush! silence! —*vt., vi.* to be or become quiet

whist[2] (hwist, wist) *n.* [altered < earlier *whisk:* prob. from the habit of whisking the tricks from the table as soon as played] a card game played with a full pack of 52 cards, usually by two pairs of players, and similar to bridge, of which it is the forerunner

whis·tle (hwis′'l, wis′-) *vi.* -**tled, -tling** [ME. *whistlen* < *hwistlian;* for IE. base see WHINE, WHISPER] **1.** *a)* to make a clear, shrill sound or note, or a series of these, by forcing breath between the teeth or through a narrow opening made by puckering the lips *b)* to make a similar sound by sending steam through a small opening **2.** to make a clear, shrill cry: said of some birds and animals **3.** to move, pass, go, etc. with a high, shrill sound, as the wind **4.** *a)* to blow a whistle *b)* to have its whistle blown [the train *whistled*] —*vt.* **1.** to produce (a tune, etc.) by whistling **2.** to summon, signal, direct, etc. by whistling —*n.* **1.** an instrument for making whistling sounds, as by forcing the breath or steam through a slit into a cavity or against a thin edge **2.** a clear, shrill sound made by whistling or blowing a whistle **3.** the act of whistling **4.** a signal, summons, etc. made by whistling **5.** a whistling sound, as of the wind —☆**blow the whistle (on)** [Slang] **1.** to report or inform (on) **2.** to cause to stop; call a halt (to) —**wet one's whistle** to take a drink —**whistle for** to seek, expect, or demand but fail to get —☆**whistle in the dark** to pretend to be confident when faced with danger or defeat —**whis′tle·a·ble** *adj.*

whis·tler (-lər) *n.* **1.** a person, animal, or thing that whistles **2.** *a)* any of various birds having a whistling call or making a whistling sound in flight, as the goldeneye ☆*b)* *same as* HOARY MARMOT *c)* a horse affected with whistling (sense 2) *d)* a radio wave, generated by lightning, high-energy electrons, etc. that travels along the earth's magnetic field lines and is heard as a whistling sound on radio receivers

Whis·tler (hwis′lər, wis′-), **James Abbott Mc·Neill** (mək nēl′) 1834–1903; U.S. painter & etcher in England — **Whis·tle′ri·an** (-lir′ē ən) *adj.*

☆**whistle stop** **1.** a small town, orig. one at which a train stopped only upon signal **2.** a brief stop in a small town as part of a tour, esp. in a political campaign; orig., such a stop in which the candidate spoke from the rear platform of his train —**whis′tle-stop′** *vi.* -**stopped′, -stop′ping**

whis·tling (hwis′liŋ, wis′-) *n.* [ME. *whistlinge* < OE. *hwistlung*] **1.** the act or sound of a person, animal, or thing that whistles **2.** shrill, noisy breathing by a horse, caused by a disorder of the air passages

whit (hwit, wit) *n.* [Early ModE. respelling of *wiht,* a WIGHT[1]] the least bit; jot; iota: chiefly in negative constructions [not a *whit* the wiser]

white (hwit, wit) *adj.* **whit′er, whit′est** [ME. *whit* < OE. *hwit,* akin to G. *weiss* < IE. **kweid-,* to gleam, bright, white, whence WHEAT, OSlav. *svěšta,* a light, candle] **1.** having the color of pure snow or milk; of the color of radiated, transmitted, or reflected light containing all of the visible rays of the spectrum; opposite to black: see COLOR **2.** of a light or pale color; specif., *a)* gray; silvery; hoary *b)* very blond *c)* pale; wan; pallid; ashen [a face *white* with terror] *d)* light-yellow or amber [*white* wines] *e)* blank: said of a space unmarked by printing, writing, etc. *f)* of a light-gray color and lustrous appearance: said of silver and other metals *g)* made of silver *h)* snowy [a *white* Christmas] **3.** lacking color; colorless [*white* creme de menthe] **4.** clothed in white; wearing a white habit [the *White* Friars] **5.** morally or spiritually pure; spotless; innocent **6.** free from evil intent; harmless [*white* magic] **7.** *a)* having a light-colored skin; Caucasoid *b)* of, controlled by, or restricted to Caucasoids ☆*c)* [< notions of racial superiority] [Slang] honest; honorable; fair; decent **8.** being at white heat **9.** reactionary, counterrevolutionary, or royalist, as opposed to *red* (radical or revolutionary) **10.** [Rare] happy; fortunate; auspicious: said of times and seasons —*n.* **1.** *a)* white color *b)* a white pigment or paint **2.** whiteness; specif., *a)* fairness of complexion *b)* purity; innocence **3.** a white or light-colored part; specif., *a)* the albumen of an egg *b)* the white part of the eyeball *c)* a blank space in printing, writing, etc. *d)* the white or light-colored part of meat, wood, etc. **4.** something white or nearly white in color; specif., *a)* white cloth *b)* [*pl.*] white garments or vestments; white uniform *c)* white wine *d)* white pigment *e)* a white breed, esp. of pig *f)* [*pl.*] a highly refined, usually bleached flour *g)* clipped form of WHITE BREAD **5.** a person with a light-colored skin; member of the Caucasoid division of mankind **6.** a member of a reactionary or counterrevolutionary faction, party, etc. in certain European countries **7.** [*pl.*] *same as* LEUKORRHEA **8.** *Archery a)* [Archaic] a white target *b)* the outermost ring of a target *c)* a hit on this ring —*vt.* **whit′ed, whit′ing** [ME. *whiten* < OE. *hwitian* < the *adj.*] **1.** to make white; whiten **2.** to leave blank spaces in or around (printed or written matter, illustrations, etc.): often with *out* —**bleed white** to drain (a person) completely of money, resources, etc.

White (hwit, wit) **1. Byron R(aymond),** 1917– ; U.S. jurist; associate justice, U.S. Supreme Court (1962–) **2. Edward Douglass,** 1845–1921; U.S. jurist; chief justice of the U.S. (1910–21) **3. E(lwyn) B(rooks),** 1899– ; U.S. humorist **4. Gilbert,** 1720–93; Eng. naturalist **5. Stan·ford** (stan′fərd), 1853–1906; U.S. architect **6. Walter (Francis),** 1893–1955; U.S. Negro leader **7. William Allen,** 1868–1944; U.S. newspaper editor

white admiral a butterfly (*Limenitis arthemis*) of Canada and the NE U.S., with showy, white bands on its wings

white alkali **1.** refined soda ash **2.** the white crust formed on some alkali soils, consisting of a mixture of sodium and magnesium sulfates and sodium chloride

white ant *popular name for* TERMITE

white·bait (-bāt′) *n., pl.* -**bait** **1.** any of various small, silvery, European fishes, as the fry of the herring or of similar fish, used as food ☆**2.** a smelt (*Allosmerus elongatus*) of inshore Pacific waters of N. America

☆**white bass** (bas) a bluish and silver food and game fish (*Roccus chrysops*) with blackish stripes on the sides

white·beard (-bird′) *n.* a white-bearded old man

white birch ☆**1.** *same as* PAPER BIRCH **2.** a European birch (*Betula pendula*) with silvery-white bark, widely grown in the U.S.

white blood cell *same as* LEUKOCYTE: also called **white blood corpuscle**

white book an official government report bound in white, fuller in detail, or viewed as more important, than a white paper

white bread bread of a light color, made from finely sifted wheat flour

☆**white bush (scallop)** a variety of summer squash having a saucer-shaped, white fruit, scalloped around the edges

white·cap (-kap′) *n.* a wave with its crest broken into white foam

☆**white cedar** **1.** *a)* an evergreen tree (*Chamaecyparis thyoides*) of the cypress family, growing in swampy land in the E U.S. *b)* its soft, light-colored wood, used for shingles, woodenware, etc. **2.** *a)* the American arborvitae (*Thuja occidentalis*), growing in cool areas of the NE U.S. *b)* its soft, brittle, durable wood

White·chap·el (hwit′chap′'l) district in the borough of Stepney, E London

white clover a creeping species of clover (*Trifolium repens*) with white flower clusters, grown as a forage plant

white coal water as a source of power

white-col·lar (-käl′ər) *adj.* [from the white shirt typically worn] ☆designating or of clerical or professional workers or others, usually salaried, employed in work not essentially manual

☆**white crappie** *see* CRAPPIE

white damp carbon monoxide, occurring in coal mines

whited sepulcher a hypocrite: Matt. 23:27

white dwarf any of a class of small, extremely dense stars of low luminosity, often no larger than the earth but weighing as much as the sun

white elephant 1. an albino elephant, regarded as sacred by the Siamese, Burmese, etc. **2.** something from which little profit or use is derived; esp., such a possession maintained at much expense ☆**3.** any object no longer desired by its owner, but of possible value to others

white-eye (hwīt′ī′, wīt′-) *n.* any of various small songbirds (family Zosteropidae) of E Asia, S Africa, Australia, etc., usually having rings of white feathers around the eyes

white-faced (-fāst′) *adj.* **1.** having a pale face; pallid **2.** having a white mark on the front of the head, as a horse

white feather [from the notion that a white feather in the tail of a gamecock indicates bad breeding, hence cowardice] an indication of cowardice: chiefly in the phrase **show the white feather**

White·field (hwīt′fēld′, wīt′-), George 1714–70; Eng. Methodist evangelist

white·fish (hwīt′fish′, wīt′-) *n., pl.* **-fish′, -fish′es:** see FISH² **1.** any of various white or silvery freshwater food fishes (esp. genera *Prosopium* and *Coregonus*) of the salmon family, found in the lakes of the N U.S. and Canada **2.** any of various other similarly colored fishes, as the ocean whitefish (*Caulolatilus princeps*) of S California waters **3.** same as BELUGA (sense 2)

white flag a white banner or cloth hoisted as a signal of truce or surrender

☆**white·fly** (-flī′) *n., pl.* **-flies′** any of a family (Aleyrodidae) of tiny homopterous insects having scalelike larvae and winged adults covered with a white powdery wax

white fox the arctic fox in winter, when its fur is white

White Friar a Carmelite friar: so called from the white mantle of the habit

White·fri·ars (hwīt′frī′ərz, wīt′-) district in London, near Fleet Street: formerly the site of a Carmelite monastery

☆**white gasoline** (or **gas**) gasoline without any tetraethyl lead additive

white gold gold alloyed variously with nickel, zinc, or rarely platinum, to give it a white, platinumlike appearance for use in jewelry

☆**white goods** [from their typical color] **1.** household linens, as sheets, pillowcases, towels, etc. **2.** large household appliances, as refrigerators, stoves, etc.

white-haired (-herd′) *adj.* **1.** having white or very light hair **2.** [Colloq.] same as FAIR-HAIRED (sense 2)

White·hall (hwīt′hôl′, wīt′-) **1.** former royal palace in Westminster, London: also **Whitehall Palace 2.** street in Westminster, east of Trafalgar Square, site of several government offices —*n.* the British government

white·head (hwīt′hed′, wīt′-) *n.* **1.** any of a number of unrelated birds that are white about the head and neck **2.** *popular name for* MILIUM

White·head (-hed′), Alfred North 1861–1947; Eng. mathematician & philosopher, in the U.S. after 1924

white·head·ed (-hed′id) *adj.* **1.** having a white head; specif., having white or very light hair, feathers, etc. on the head **2.** [Colloq.] same as FAIR-HAIRED (sense 2)

white heat 1. the degree of intense heat (beyond red heat) at which metal, etc. glows white **2.** a state of intense emotion, excitement, etc.

☆**white hope** [term orig. applied to Caucasoid boxers who it was thought might defeat Negro heavyweight champion Jack Johnson (c.1910)] [Colloq.] any person who is expected to bring honor, glory, etc. to some group, place, etc.

White·horse (hwīt′hôrs′, wīt′-) capital of the Yukon Territory, Canada, in the S part: pop. 5,000

white-hot (hwīt′hät′, wīt′-) *adj.* **1.** glowing white with heat **2.** extremely angry, excited, enthusiastic, etc.

White House, the ☆**1.** official residence of the President of the U.S.: a white mansion in Washington, D.C. ☆**2.** the executive branch of the U.S. government

white lead 1. a poisonous, heavy, white powder, basic lead carbonate, 2PbCO₃·Pb(OH)₂, used as an exterior paint pigment, for pottery glazes, etc. **2.** any of several white pigments containing lead, as lead sulfate

white leather soft leather suitable for babies' shoes, etc., made by tanning hides with alum and salt

white lie a lie concerning a trivial matter, often one told to spare someone's feelings

white light *Physics* light, as sunlight, composed of rays of all the wavelengths ranging from red to violet

☆**white lightning** [Slang] homemade whiskey, esp. corn whiskey, usually unaged and strong and typically colorless

white-liv·ered (hwīt′liv′ərd, wīt′-) *adj.* cowardly; craven

white lupine an annual Mediterranean lupine (*Lupinus albus*) having large, white seeds often eaten after processing to remove a poison

white·ly (-lē) *adv.* so as to be white; with a white or pale appearance

white man's burden the alleged duty of the white, or Caucasoid, peoples to bring their civilization to other peoples regarded as backward: phrase popularized by Kipling and other apologists for imperialism

white matter whitish nerve tissue of the brain and spinal cord, consisting chiefly of medullated nerve fibers: distinguished from GRAY MATTER (sense 1)

white meat 1. any light-colored meat, as veal, pork, the breast of poultry, etc. **2.** [ME. *wyttemel:* see WHITE & MEAT] [Obs. or Dial.] cheese, butter, or some other dairy product

white metal any of various light-colored alloys, esp. any of those, as pewter, containing much lead or tin

White Mountains [from the appearance of the higher peaks] range of the Appalachian system, in N N.H.: highest peak, Mt. WASHINGTON

white mustard an annual mustard (*Brassica hirta*), often cultivated for its seeds, which are ground and made into a paste used as a condiment

whit·en (hwīt′'n, wīt′-) *vt., vi.* [ME. *whitnen:* see WHITE & -EN] to make or become white or whiter

whit·en·er (-ər) *n.* a person or thing that whitens; specif., a bleach or other substance used for whitening

white·ness (hwīt′nis, wīt′-) *n.* **1.** the quality or condition of being white; specif., *a)* white color or appearance *b)* pallor *c)* freedom from stain **2.** a white substance or part

White Nile *see* NILE

whit·en·ing (hwīt′'n iŋ, wīt′-) *n.* **1.** the act or process of making or becoming white **2.** a preparation used for making something white, as whiting

white noise [by analogy with WHITE LIGHT] a sound containing a blend of all the audible frequencies distributed equally over the range of the frequency band

white oak 1. any of a number of oaks having leaves with rounded lobes, acorns that mature in one season, whitish or grayish bark, and hard, impervious wood; esp., the **American white oak** (*Quercus alba*) of E N. America **2.** the wood of any such tree, used in barrels, furniture, etc.

white·out (-out′) *n. Meteorol.* an optical phenomenon occurring in polar regions in which the snow-covered ground blends into a uniformly white sky blotting out shadows, clouds, horizon, etc. and destroying all sense of depth, direction, or distance

white paper 1. an official government report bound in white, less detailed or viewed as of less importance than a white book or blue book **2.** any lengthy, pretentiously authoritative report or piece of political propaganda

white pepper pepper ground from the husked, dried seeds of the nearly ripe pepper berry

☆**white perch 1.** a small, silvery food fish (*Roccus americanus*) found in coastal waters and streams of the U.S. **2.** a freshwater drum (*Aplodinotus grunniens*) of the C U.S. **3.** *same as: a)* SILVER PERCH *b)* [South] WHITE CRAPPIE

☆**white pine 1.** *a)* a pine (*Pinus strobus*) of E N. America, with bluish-green or grayish-green needles in bundles of five, hanging brown cones, and soft, light wood *b)* the wood of this tree **2.** any of various closely related pines having needles in groups of five

☆**white plague** tuberculosis, esp. of the lungs

White Plains [? after the AmInd. *quaropas,* white marshes] city in SE N.Y., near New York City: scene of a battle (1776) of the Revolutionary War: pop. 50,000

white poplar 1. a large old-world poplar (*Populus alba*), having lobed leaves with white or gray down on the undersides, now widespread in the U.S. ☆**2.** *same as: a)* TULIP TREE *b)* TULIPWOOD (sense 1)

☆**white potato** *same as* POTATO (sense 2 *a*)

☆**white primary** in some Southern States of the U.S., a direct primary election with Negroes barred from voting: declared unconstitutional by U.S. Supreme Court in 1944

white race loosely, the Caucasoid group of mankind: see CAUCASOID

white rat an albino rat; esp., any of a breed of albino Norway rats used in biological experiments

White River river flowing from NW Ark. through S Mo. into the Mississippi: 690 mi.

☆**white room** a room from which all contaminants have been eliminated and in which temperature, humidity, and pressure are controlled: used for assembly and repair of precision mechanisms, in preventing infection, etc.

White Russia *same as* BYELORUSSIAN SOVIET SOCIALIST REPUBLIC

White Russian 1. *same as* BYELORUSSIAN **2.** a Russian member of, or sympathizer with, a faction which fought the Bolsheviks (Reds) in the Russian civil war

white sale a sale of household linens

white sapphire a colorless variety of corundum

white sauce a sauce for vegetables, meat, fish, etc., made of fat or butter, flour, milk or stock, and seasoning

White Sea arm of the Barents Sea, extending into NW U.S.S.R.: c.36,000 sq. mi.

white slave a woman enticed or forced into or held in prostitution for the profit of others —**white′-slave′** *adj.*

☆**White-Slave Act** [Colloq.] *same as* MANN ACT

white slaver a person who entices or forces women to become white slaves —**white slavery**

white·smith (-smith′) *n.* **1.** a worker in white metals; esp., a tinsmith **2.** a worker in iron who does finishing, polishing, or galvanizing

white squall a sudden squall supposed to arise at sea in the tropics with no accompanying cloud formation

☆**white supremacy** the social, economic, and political repression and exploitation of colored peoples, esp. Negroes, by white people, based on notions of racial superiority —**white supremacist**

white·tail (-tāl′) *n.* any of various animals with white about the tail, esp. the deer

☆**white-tailed deer** (-tāld′) a common American deer (*Odocoileus virginianus*) having a tail that is white on the undersurface, a white-spotted red coat in summer, and a diffuse brownish-gray coat in winter

white·throat (-thrōt′) *n.* **1.** any of several birds having white around the throat; esp., any of several old-world warblers (genus *Sylvia*) with a whitish throat and belly ☆**2.** *same as* WHITE-THROATED SPARROW

☆**white-throat·ed sparrow** (-thrōt′id) a common N. American sparrow (*Zonotrichia albicollis*) having a square white patch on the throat

white tie 1. a white bow tie, properly worn with a swallow-tailed coat **2.** a swallow-tailed coat and its accessories

white vitriol *same as* ZINC SULFATE

White Volta *see* VOLTA

☆**white·wall** (-wôl′) *adj.* designating or of a pneumatic tire with a circular white band on the outer sidewall: also **white′-wall′** —*n.* a whitewall tire

☆**white walnut** *same as* BUTTERNUT (senses 1 & 2)

white·wash (-wôsh′, -wäsh′) *n.* **1.** a mixture of lime, whiting, size, water, etc., for whitening walls, etc. **2.** a cosmetic formerly used for making the skin fair **3.** *a)* a glossing over or concealing of faults or defects in an effort to exonerate or give the appearance of soundness *b)* something said or done for this purpose ☆**4.** [Colloq.] *Sports* a defeat in which the loser scores no points at all —*vt.* **1.** to cover with whitewash **2.** to gloss over or conceal the faults or defects of; give a favorable interpretation of or a falsely virtuous appearance to ☆**3.** [Colloq.] *Sports* to defeat (an opponent) without permitting him to score —**white′wash′er** *n.*

white water 1. foaming, whitish water, as in whitecaps, rapids, etc. **2.** a light-colored water over a shallow area

white whale *same as* BELUGA (sense 2)

white·wing (-wiŋ′) *n.* ☆[Old Colloq.] a street cleaner wearing a white uniform

white·wood (-wood′) *n.* **1.** any of a number of trees with white or light-colored wood, as the tulip tree, linden, cottonwood, etc. **2.** the wood of any of these trees

whith·er (hwith′ər, with′-) *adv.* [ME. *whider* < OE. *hwider*: for bases see WHAT & HITHER] to what place, point, condition, result, etc.? where?: used to introduce questions [*whither* are we drifting?] —*conj.* **1.** to which place, point, condition, result, etc.: used relatively [the island *whither* we drifted] **2.** to whatever place, point, condition, result, etc.; wherever [let them go *whither* they will] *Whither* is now largely replaced by *where* except in poetical or rhetorical usage

whith·er·so·ev·er (hwith′ər sō ev′ər, with′-) *adv., conj.* [Archaic or Poet.] to whatever place; wheresoever

whith·er·ward (hwith′ər wərd, with′-) *adv., conj.* [Archaic or Poet.] in what or which direction; where: used relatively or interrogatively

whit·ing (hwīt′iŋ, wīt′-) *n., pl.* **-ings, -ing**: see PLURAL, II, D, 1 [ME. < MDu. *wijting* < *wit*, WHITE] any of numerous unrelated ocean food fishes of N. America, Europe, and Australia, including several hakes and king-fishes; specif. *a)* the European whiting (*Merlangus merlangus*) of the cod family ☆*b)* *same as* SILVER HAKE, WALLEYE POLLACK, CORVINA (sense 1)

whit·ing (hwīt′iŋ, wīt′-) *n.* [ME. *whytyng*: see WHITE, *v.* + -ING] powdered chalk used in making paints, inks, etc.

whit·ish (-ish) *adj.* somewhat white —**whit′ish·ness** *n.*

whit·leath·er (hwit′leth′ər, wit′-) *n. same as* WHITE LEATHER

whit·low (hwit′lō, wit′-) *n.* [ME. *whitflowe, whitflawe*: of disputed origin; cf. WHITE & FLAW] *same as* FELON[2]

Whit·man (hwit′s n, wit′-) **1. Marcus**, 1802–47; U.S. pioneer & missionary in the Northwest **2. Walt(er)**, 1819–92; U.S. poet

Whit·mon·day (hwit′mun′dē, wit′-; -dā) *n.* [after *Whitsunday*] the Monday immediately following Whitsunday: in England, a bank holiday

Whit·ney (hwit′nē, wit′-), **Eli** 1765–1825; U.S. inventor, esp. of the cotton gin

Whit·ney (hwit′nē), **Mount** [after J. D. *Whitney* (1819–96), U.S. geologist] mountain of the Sierra Nevada Range, EC Calif., in Sequoia National Park: highest peak in the U.S. outside of Alas., 14,495 ft.

Whit·sun (hwit′s n, wit′-) *adj.* [ME. *whitsone* < *whitsondei* analyzed as *Whitsun Day*: see ff.] of or observed on Whit-sunday or at Whitsuntide

Whit·sun·day (hwit′sun′dē, wit′-; -dā; -s′n dā′) *n.* [ME. *whitsondei* < OE. *Hwita Sunnandæg*, lit., white Sunday: from the white garments of candidates for baptism] *same as* PENTECOST (sense 2)

Whit·sun·tide (-s′n tīd′) *n.* [ME. *whitsunetide*: see WHITSUN & TIDE[1]] the week beginning with Whitsunday, esp. the first three days of that week

Whit·ti·er (hwit′ē ər, wit′-) [after ff.] city in SW Calif.: suburb of Los Angeles: pop. 73,000

Whit·ti·er (hwit′ē ər, wit′-), **John Green·leaf** (grēn′lēf′) 1807–92; U.S. poet

Whit·ting·ton (hwit′iŋ tən, wit′-), **Richard** 1358?–1423; Eng. merchant; lord mayor of London: associated with various Eng. legends of a Dick Whittington

whit·tle (hwit′l, wit′-) *vt.* **-tled, -tling** [< obs. *whittle*, a knife < ME. *whyttel*, var. of *thwitel*, dim. < OE. *thwitan*, to cut < IE. *twei-*, to strike, cut] **1.** *a)* to cut or pare thin

shavings from (wood) with a knife *b)* to make or fashion (an object) in this manner **2.** to reduce, destroy, or get rid of gradually, as if by whittling away with a knife: usually with *down, away*, etc. [to whittle down the cost of a project] —*vi.* to whittle wood; esp., to cut away aimlessly at a stick, etc. —*n.* [Obs.] a large knife —**whit′tler** *n.*

Whit·tle (hwit′l), **Sir Frank** 1907– ; Eng. engineer & pioneer developer of jet propulsion engines

whit·y (hwīt′ē, wīt′-) *adj.* **-i·er, -i·est** *same as* WHITISH

whiz, whizz (hwiz, wiz) *vi.* **whizzed, whiz′zing** [echoic] **1.** to make the buzzing or hissing sound of something moving swiftly through the air **2.** to move swiftly by with or as with this sound [the bus *whizzed* by him] —*vt.* to cause to whiz, esp. by rotating rapidly —*n.* **1.** a whizzing sound or movement ☆**2.** [cf. WIZ] *a)* [Slang] a person who is very quick, adroit, or skilled at something; expert [a *whiz* at football] *b)* [Old Slang] something strikingly excellent, attractive, etc. [a *whiz* of a car]

whiz-bang, whizz-bang (-baŋ′) *n.* **1.** [Old Slang] a high explosive shell of great speed whose sound of explosion occurs immediately after its sound of flight; also, a fire-work suggestive of this ☆**2.** [Slang] *same as* WHIZ (sense 2) —☆*adj.* [Slang] extremely clever, useful, impressive, etc.

who (hōō) *pron.*, obj. **whom**, poss. **whose** [ME. *who, ho, hwo* < OE. *hwa*, masc. & fem., *hwæt*, neut., who? what? (akin to L. *qui*): for IE. base see WHAT] **1.** what or which person or persons: used to introduce a direct, indirect, or implied question [*who* is he? I asked *who* he was, I don't know *who* he is] **2.** *a)* (the, or a, person or persons) that: used to introduce a relative clause [the man *who* came to dinner] *b)* any person or persons that; whoever: used as an indefinite relative with an implied antecedent ["*who* steals my purse steals trash"] The use of *who* rather than *whom* as the object of a verb or preposition [*who* did you see there? *who* was it written by?], although widespread at all levels of speech, is still objected to by some —as **who should say** as if one should say —**who's who 1.** who the important people are **2.** [often W- W-] a book or list containing the names and short biographies of prominent persons of a certain place, group, profession, etc.

WHO World Health Organization

whoa (hwō, wō, hō) *interj.* [for HO] stop!: used esp. in directing a horse to stand still

☆**who·dun·it** (hōō dun′it) *n.* [< WHO + DONE + IT: coined in 1930 by D. Gordon in *American News of Books*] [Colloq.] a mystery novel, play, etc.: cf. MYSTERY[1] (sense 2 b)

who·ev·er (-ev′ər) *pron.* **1.** any person that; whatever person [*whoever* wins gets a prize] **2.** no matter what person [*whoever* said it, it's not so] **3.** what person? who?: an emphatic usage [*whoever* told you that?]

whole (hōl) *adj.* [ME. *hol* < OE. *hal*, healthy, whole, hale: akin to G. *heil*, ON. *heill* (cf. HALE[1]) < IE. base *kailo-*, sound, uninjured, auspicious, whence W. *coel*, omen] **1.** *a)* in sound health; not diseased or injured *b)* [Archaic] healed: said of a wound **2.** not broken, damaged, defective, etc.; intact [a *whole* yolk] **3.** containing all the elements or parts; entire; complete [a *whole* set, *whole* blood] **4.** not divided up; in a single unit [a *whole* cheese] **5.** constituting the entire amount, extent, number, etc. [the *whole* night] **6.** having both parents in common [a *whole* brother] **7.** in all aspects of one's being including the physical, mental, social, etc. [the *whole* man] **8.** *Arith.* integral and not mixed or fractional [28 is a *whole* number] —*n.* **1.** the entire amount, quantity, extent, or sum; totality [the *whole* of the estate] **2.** a thing complete in itself, or a complete organization of integrated parts; a unity, entirety, or system —*SYN.* see COMPLETE —**as a whole** as a complete unit; altogether —☆**made out of whole cloth** completely fictitious or false; made up —**on the whole** all things considered; in general —**whole′ness** *n.*

whole blood 1. blood for transfusion from which none of the elements has been removed **2.** *same as* FULL BLOOD (sense 1)

☆**whole gale** a wind whose speed is 55 to 63 miles per hour: see BEAUFORT SCALE

☆**whole·heart·ed** (-här′tid) *adj.* doing or done with all one's energy, enthusiasm, etc.; hearty; sincere; earnest —**whole′heart′ed·ly** *adv.* —**whole′heart′ed·ness** *n.*

whole-hog (hōl′hôg′, -häg′) *adj., adv.* [Slang] ☆without reservation; complete(ly)

whole milk milk from which none of the butterfat or other elements have been removed

whole note *Music* a note having four times the duration of a quarter note: see NOTE, illus.

whole number zero or any positive or negative multiple of 1; integer [28 is a *whole number*]

whole·sale (-sāl′) *n.* [ME. *holesale* (< phr. *by hole sale*, by wholesale): see WHOLE & SALE] the selling of goods in relatively large quantities and usually at lower prices than at retail; esp., such selling to retailers for resale to consumers —*adj.* **1.** of, connected with, or engaged in such selling [*wholesale* prices] **2.** extensive, sweeping, or indiscriminate [*wholesale* criticism] —*adv.* **1.** in wholesale amounts or at wholesale prices **2.** extensively, sweepingly, or indiscriminately [to reject proposals *wholesale*] —*vt.,*

vi. **-saled′, -sal′ing** to sell wholesale —**at wholesale** in wholesale quantities or at wholesale prices —**by wholesale** 1. at wholesale 2. extensively, sweepingly, or indiscriminately —**whole′sal′er** *n.*

whole·some (-səm) *adj.* [ME. *holsom*, akin to ON. *heilsamr*, G. *heilsam*: see WHOLE & -SOME¹] 1. promoting or conducive to good health or well-being; healthful [a *wholesome* climate] 2. tending to improve the mind or character [a *wholesome* movie for children] 3. characterized by health and vigor of mind and body; sound [a *wholesome* girl] 4. tending to suggest health, or soundness [a *wholesome* look about the boys] —**whole′some·ly** *adv.*—**whole′some·ness** *n.*

☆**whole-souled** (-sōld′) *adj. same as* WHOLEHEARTED

whole step *Music* an interval consisting of two adjacent half steps; a major second: also **whole tone**

☆**whole-wheat** (-hwēt′) *adj.* 1. made of the entire cleaned kernels of wheat [*whole-wheat* flour] 2. made of whole-wheat flour [*whole-wheat* bread]

who·lism (hō′liz'm) *n. var. of* HOLISM —**who·lis′tic** *adj.*

who′ll (hōōl) 1. who shall 2. who will

whol·ly (hō′lē, hōl′lē) *adv.* [ME. *holi*: see WHOLE & -Y²] to the whole amount or extent; totally; entirely

whom (hōōm) *pron.* [ME. < OE. *hwam*, dat. of *hwa*, WHO] *objective case of* WHO: *who* is often used colloquially instead of *whom*

whom·ev·er (hōōm ev′ər) *pron. objective case of* WHOEVER

whomp (hwämp) *vt.* [echoic] 1. to beat, strike, hit, thump, etc. 2. to defeat decisively —*n.* the act or sound of whomping —**whomp up** to prepare quickly; whip up; concoct

whom·so·ev·er (hōōm′sō ev′ər) *pron. objective case of* WHOSOEVER

whoop (hōōp, hwōōp, wōōp, woop) *n.* [ME. *houpen*, to call, shout < OFr. *houper*, to call afar off, cry out] a loud shout, cry, or noise; specif., *a*) a shrill and prolonged cry, as of excitement, exultation, ferocity, etc. *b*) a hoot, as of an owl *c*) the gasping sound marking the convulsive intake of air that immediately follows a fit of coughing in whooping cough —*vi.* to utter, or move along with, a whoop or whoops —*vt.* 1. to utter with a whoop or whoops 2. to drive, urge on, chase, bring about, etc. with whoops —*interj.* an exclamation of excitement, joy, exultation, etc. —**not worth a whoop** [Colloq.] worth nothing at all —☆**whoop it** (or **things**) **up** [Slang] 1. to create a noisy disturbance, as in celebrating 2. to create enthusiasm (*for*) —**whoop′er** *n.*

☆**whoop-de-do, whoop-de-doo** (hōōp′dē dōō′, hwōōp′-) *n.* [extended < WHOOP] [Colloq.] noisy or excited activity, commotion, or fuss; hoopla, ballyhoo, to-do, etc.

whoop·ee (wōō′pē, hwōō′-, woo′-, hwoo′-) *interj.* [< prec.] an exclamation of great joy, exultation, gay abandonment, etc. —☆*n.* 1. a shout of "whoopee!" 2. hilarious revelry; noisy fun —**make whoopee** [Slang] to revel boisterously

whoop·ing cough (hōō′piŋ, hoo′-) an acute infectious disease, usually affecting children, caused by a bacillus (*Bordetella pertussis*) and characterized by a mucous discharge from the nose and later by repeated attacks of coughing that end in a forced intake of breath, or whoop

☆**whooping crane** a large, white, N. American crane (*Grus americana*), noted for its whooping call: now nearly extinct

☆**whoop·la** (hōōp′lä′, hwōōp′-, hoop′-) *n. var. of* HOOPLA

whoops (hwoops, woops, hwōōps, wōōps) *interj.* an exclamation uttered as in regaining one's balance after stumbling or one's composure after a slip of the tongue

whoosh (hwoosh, woosh) *vi.* [echoic] 1. to make the quick, hissing or rushing sound of something moving swiftly through the air 2. to move swiftly with or as with this sound [rockets *whooshed* by] —*vt.* to cause to whoosh —*n.* a whooshing sound or movement —*interj.* an exclamation imitating this or expressing surprise, fatigue, etc.

☆**whoo·sis** (hōō′zis) *n. var. of* WHOSIS

whop (hwäp, wäp) *vt., vi.* **whopped, whop′ping** [< ME. *whappen*, prob. echoic] [Colloq.] 1. to hit, strike, beat, etc. 2. to defeat decisively —*n.* [Colloq.] a sharp, resounding blow, stroke, thump, etc.

whop·per (-ər) *n.* [< prec.] [Colloq.] 1. anything extraordinarily large 2. a great lie

whop·ping (-iŋ) *adj.* [< WHOP + -ING] [Colloq.] extraordinarily large or great; colossal

whore (hôr) *n.* [ME. < OE. < or akin to ON. *hora* < IE. base *kā-*, to like, be fond of, desire, whence L. *carus*, dear, precious, Lett. *kārs*, lecherous: cf. CHARITY] 1. *same as* PROSTITUTE 2. any woman who engages in promiscuous sexual intercourse —*vi.* **whored, whor′ing** 1. to be a whore 2. to fornicate with whores —*vt.* [Obs.] to make a whore of —**whore after** to seek or pursue ardently that which is immoral, idolatrous, etc.

who′re (hōō′ər, hoor) who are

whore·dom (hôr′dəm) *n.* [ME. *hordom* < ON. *hordomr*] 1. prostitution or fornication 2. the fact of being false to God; idolatry: so used in the Bible

whore·house (-hous′) *n.* [ME. *horehowse*] a place where prostitutes are for hire; brothel

whore·mon·ger (-muŋ′gər, -mäŋ′gər) *n.* a man who fornicates or associates with whores; specif., a pimp, or pander: also **whore′mas′ter**

whore·son (-s'n) *n.* [ME. *hores son*, lit., son of a whore, bastard, after OFr. *fiz a putain*] [Archaic] 1. a bastard 2. a scoundrel; knave: a general epithet of abuse —*adj.* [Archaic] vile, knavish, etc.

whor·ish (-ish) *adj.* of or typical of a whore; lewd

whorl (hwôrl, wôrl, hwurl, wurl) *n.* [ME. *whorwyl*, dial. var. of *wherwille*, WHIRL] 1. a small flywheel on a spindle, as for regulating the speed of a spinning wheel 2. anything with a coiled or spiral appearance; specif., *a*) any of the circular ridges that form the design of a fingerprint *b*) *Bot.* a circular growth of leaves, petals, etc. about the same point on a stem *c*) *Zool.* any of the turns in a spiral shell —**whorled** *adj.*

whor·tle·ber·ry (hwur′t'l ber′ē, wur′-) *n., pl.* **-ries** [< SW Brit. dial. form of earlier HURTLEBERRY] 1. *a*) either of two European blueberries (*Vaccinium myrtillus* or *Vaccinium uliginosum*) having pink flowers and blue or blackish edible berries with a mealy bloom *b*) any of these berries ☆2. any of various American plants, as the huckleberry

who's (hōōz) 1. who is 2. who has

whose (hōōz) *pron.* [ME. *whos, hwas* < OE. *hwæs*, gen. of *hwa*, WHO] that or those belonging to whom: used without a following noun [*whose* is this? *whose* will last longer?] —*possessive pronominal adj.* of, belonging to, made, or done by whom or which [*whose* book is lost? a play *whose* popularity endures]

whose·so·ev·er (hōōz′sō ev′ər) *pron.* of whomsoever

whos·ev·er (hōōz ev′ər) *pron.* of whomever

☆**who·sis** (hōō′zis) *n.* [contr. < *who is this*] [Slang] a person or thing whose name is not known or is forgotten

who·so (hōō′sō) *pron.* [ME. *wha swa* < OE.: see WHO & SO¹] [Archaic] whoever; whosoever

who·so·ev·er (hōō′sō ev′ər) *pron.* whoever: an emphatic form

whr. watt-hour

whump (hwump) *n., vt., vi.* [Colloq.] *same as* THUMP

why (hwī, wī) *adv.* [ME. *hwi* < OE., instrumental case of *hwæt*, WHAT] for what reason, cause, or purpose? with what motive?: used in direct, indirect, and implied questions [*why* did he go? he told her *why* he went] —*conj.* 1. because of which; on account of which [he knows of no reason *why* you shouldn't go] 2. the reason for which [that is *why* he went] —*n., pl.* **whys** the reason, cause, motive, purpose, etc. [never mind the *why* and wherefore] —*interj.* an exclamation used to express surprise, impatience, indignation, etc., or merely as an expletive, as to preface a remark

whyd·ah (**bird**) (hwid′ə, wid′-) [altered < *widow bird*, by association with *Ouidah* (sometimes sp. *Whidah*), seaport in Dahomey] any of several chiefly brown and black West African weaverbirds (subfamily Viduinae): the male has long drooping tail feathers during the breeding season

W.I. 1. West Indian 2. West Indies

Wich·i·ta (wich′ə tô′) [< AmInd. < ?] city in S Kans., on the Arkansas River: pop. 255,000

Wichita Falls [see prec.] city in NC Tex.: pop. 102,000

wick¹ (wik) *n.* [ME. *wicke* < OE. *weoca*, akin to G. *wieche*, wick yarn < IE. base **weg-*, to weave, knit together, fabric, whence L. *velum*, sail, cloth] a piece of cord or tape, or a thin bundle of threads, in a candle, oil lamp, cigarette lighter, etc., designed to absorb fuel by capillary attraction and, when lighted, to burn with a small, steady flame

wick² (wik) *n.* [ME. *wik* < OE. *wic*, akin to MHG. *wich*, a village < early WGmc. borrowing < L. *vicus*, group of houses: see VICINITY] a village, town, or hamlet: now archaic except as compounded in *bailiwick* and (often in the form **-wich**) in place names, as in *Warwick, Greenwich*

wick·ed (wik′id) *adj.* [ME. < *wikke*, evil, akin to OE. *wicce*, WITCH] 1. morally bad or wrong; acting or done with evil intent; depraved; iniquitous 2. generally bad, painful, unpleasant, etc., but without any moral considerations involved [a *wicked* blow on the head] 3. naughty in a playful way; mischievous ☆4. [Slang] showing great skill [he plays a *wicked* game of golf] —*SYN.* see BAD¹ —**wick′ed·ly** *adv.* —**wick′ed·ness** *n.*

wick·er (wik′ər) *n.* [ME. *wiker* < Scand., as in Sw. dial. *viker*, Dan. dial. *vigger*, willow, Sw. *vika*, to bend: for IE. base see WEAK] 1. a thin, flexible twig; withe 2. *a*) such twigs or long, woody strips woven together, as in making baskets or furniture *b*) *same as* WICKERWORK (sense 1) —*adj.* made of or covered with wicker

wick·er·work (-wurk′) *n.* 1. things made of wicker 2. *same as* WICKER (sense 2 *a*)

wick·et (wik′it) *n.* [ME. *wiket* < ONormFr. (for OFr. *guichet*), dim. < Gmc. base appearing in ON. *vīk*, a bay, MDu. *wijk*, a curve < IE. **weig-* < base **wei-*, to bend, turn: cf. WEEK] 1. a small door or gate, esp. one set in or near a larger door or gate 2. a small window or opening, as for a bank teller or in a box office 3. a small gate for regulating the flow of water to a water wheel or for emptying a canal lock 4. [from orig. resemblance to a gate] *Cricket a*) either of two sets of three vertical sticks (*stumps*) each, with two small pieces (*bails*) resting on top of them *b*) the playing space between the two wickets *c*) an unplayed or unfinished inning *d*) a player's turn at bat ☆5. *Croquet* any of the small wire arches through which the balls must be hit; hoop

wick·et·keep·er (-kē′pər) *n. Cricket* the fielder stationed immediately behind the wicket

wick·ing (wik′iŋ) *n.* cord, yarn, etc. for wicks

☆**wick·i·up** (wik′ē up′) *n.* [< AmInd. (Algonquian) name (as in Sauk & Fox *wikiyap*): akin to WIGWAM] a kind of hut built by the nomadic Indians of the SW U.S., consisting of an oval-shaped frame covered with grass, brush, etc.

Wick·liffe, Wic·lif (wik′lif) *vars. of* WYCLIFFE

Wick·low (wik′lō) county of Leinster province, SE Ireland, on the Irish Sea: 782 sq. mi.; pop. 60,000

☆**wic·o·py** (wik′ə pē) n. [< AmInd. (Algonquian) name (as in Massachusett *wik′pi*, inner bark)] **1.** *same as: a)* LEATHERWOOD (sense 1) *b)* BASSWOOD (sense 1) **2.** any of several species of willow herb, as fireweed

wid·der·shins (wid′ər shinz′) adv. var. of WITHERSHINS

wide (wīd) adj. [ME. < OE. *wid*, akin to G. *weit* < IE. **wi-itos*, lit., gone apart (< **wi-*, apart + base *ei-*, to go), whence L. *vitare*, lit., to go away from, avoid] **1.** extending over a large area; esp., extending over a larger area from side to side than is usual or normal [a *wide* bed] **2.** of a specified extent from side to side [three miles *wide*] **3.** of great extent, range, or inclusiveness [a *wide* variety, *wide* reading] **4.** roomy; ample; loose; full [*wide* pants] **5.** open or extended to full width [eyes *wide* with fear] **6.** landing, striking, or ending far from the point, issue, etc. aimed at: usually with of [*wide* of the target] ☆**7.** having a relatively low proportion of protein: said of livestock feed **8.** [Brit. Slang] shrewd and unscrupulous [a *wide* boy] **9.** *Phonet. same as* LAX (sense 5) —adv. **1.** over a relatively large area; widely [to travel far and *wide*] **2.** to a large or full extent; fully [with the door *wide* open] **3.** so as to miss the point, issue, etc. aimed at; astray [shots that went *wide*] —n. **1.** [Rare or Poet.] a wide area or extent **2.** *Cricket* a ball that is bowled out of the batsman's reach, counted as a run for the team at bat —SYN. see BROAD —**wide′ly** adv. —**wide′ness** n.

-wide (wīd) *a combining form meaning* existing or extending throughout [nationwide]

wide-an·gle (wīd′aŋ′g'l) adj. **1.** designating or of a kind of camera lens that covers a wider angle of view than the ordinary lens **2.** designating or of any of several motion-picture systems employing one or more cameras (and projectors) and an especially wide, curved screen to simulate normal panoramic vision

wide-a·wake (-ə wāk′) adj. **1.** completely awake **2.** alert —SYN. see WATCHFUL —**wide′-a·wake′ness** n.

wide-eyed (-īd′) adj. with the eyes opened widely, as because of surprise, fear, lack of sophistication, etc.

wid·en (wīd′'n) vt., vi. to make or become wide or wider —**wid′en·er** n.

wide-o·pen (wīd′ō′p'n) adj. **1.** opened wide ☆**2.** having no laws, or lax in enforcing laws, prohibiting or regulating prostitution, gambling, liquor sales, etc. [a *wide-open* city]

wide·spread (-spred′) adj. spread widely; esp., *a)* widely extended [with *widespread* arms] *b)* distributed, circulated, or occurring over a wide area or extent [*widespread* benefits, *widespread* rumors]

wide·spread·ing (-iŋ) adj. spreading out widely

widg·eon (wij′ən) n., pl. -eons, -eon [prob. < MFr. *vigeon* < ? L. *vipio*, small crane] any of a genus (*Mareca*) of wild, freshwater ducks found in various parts of the world; esp., *a)* the **European widgeon** (*Mareca penelope*), the male of which has a cream-colored crown and reddish-brown head and neck *b)* *same as* BALDPATE

☆**wid·get** (wij′it) n. [altered < GADGET] any small, unspecified gadget or device, esp. one that is hypothetical

wid·ow (wid′ō) n. [ME. *widwe* < OE. *widewe*, akin to G. *witwe* < IE. **widhewo-*, separated < **weidh-*, to separate, whence G. *waise*, orphan, L. *vidua*, a widow, (*di*)*videre*, to DIVIDE] **1.** a woman who has outlived the man to whom she was married at the time of his death; esp., such a woman who has not remarried ☆**2.** *Cards* a number of cards dealt into a separate pile, typically for the use of the highest bidder **3.** *Printing* an incomplete line, as that ending a paragraph, carried over to the top of a new page or column: generally avoided by rewriting copy to eliminate the line or fill it out **4.** [Colloq.] *a)* short for GRASS WIDOW ☆*b)* a woman whose husband is often away indulging a specified hobby, sport, etc. [a golf *widow*] —vt. **1.** to cause to become a widow: usually in the past participle [*widowed* by the war] **2.** [Rare] to deprive of something important **3.** [Obs.] *a)* to survive as the widow of *b)* to endow with the rights of a widow —**wid′ow·hood′** n.

widow bird [after Port. *viuva*, widow bird, lit., widow (< L. *vidua*: see prec.): from the resemblance of its dark plumage to a widow's clothing] *same as* WHYDAH BIRD

wid·ow·er (wid′ə wər) n. [ME. *widewer*, extended < *wedow*, a widower < OE. *widewa*, masc. of *widewe*, widow] a man who has outlived the woman to whom he was married at the time of her death; esp., such a man not remarried

widow's cruse a supply that is apparently inexhaustible: I Kings 17:10–17; II Kings 4:1–7

widow's mite a small gift or contribution freely given by one who can scarcely afford it: Mark 12:41–44

widow's peak a point formed by hair growing down in the middle of a forehead: formerly supposed to foretell early widowhood

☆**widow's walk** a platform with a rail around it, built onto the roof of some early New England coastal homes, usually for observing ships at sea

width (width, witth) n. [< WIDE, by analogy with LENGTH, BREADTH] **1.** the fact, quality, or condition of being wide; wideness **2.** the size of something in terms of how wide it is; distance from side to side **3.** a piece of something of a certain width [two *widths* of cloth]

width·wise (-wīz′) adv., adj. in the direction of the width: also **width′ways′** (-wāz′)

Wi·du·kind (vē′dŏŏ kint) 8th cent. A.D.; Saxon warrior; leader of the Saxons against Charlemagne

Wie·land (vē′länt), **Chris·toph Mar·tin** (kris′tôf mär′tēn) 1733–1813; Ger. novelist, poet, & translator

wield (wēld) vt. [ME. *welden*, a blend of OE. *wealdan* & *wieldan*, with form < the latter: akin to G. *walten* < IE. base **wal-*, to be strong, whence L. *valere*, to be strong] **1.** to handle and use (a tool or weapon), esp. with skill and control **2.** to exercise (power, influence, etc.) **3.** [Obs.] to govern or rule —SYN. see HANDLE —**wield′er** n.

wield·y (wēl′dē) adj. **wield′i·er**, **wield′i·est** that can be wielded easily; manageable

Wien (vēn) Ger. name of VIENNA

☆**wie·ner** (wē′nər) n. [short for *wienerwurst* < G. *Wiener wurst*, Vienna sausage] a smoked sausage of beef or beef and pork, usually enclosed in a membranous casing and made in cylindrical links a few inches long; frankfurter: also **wie′ner·wurst′** (-wurst′)

Wie·ner (wē′nər), **Norbert** 1894–1964; U.S. mathematician & pioneer in cybernetics

Wie·ner schnit·zel (vē′nər shnit′s'l) [G. < *Wiener*, of Vienna + *schnitzel*, cutlet, dim. of *schnitz*, a cut, piece < *schneiden*, to cut] a breaded veal cutlet with a garnish on it, esp. a lemon slice and rolled anchovy

☆**wie·nie** (wē′nē) n. [Colloq.] *same as* WIENER

Wies·ba·den (vēs′bäd′'n) resort city in W West Germany, on the Rhine; capital of Hesse: pop. 260,000

wife (wīf) n., pl. **wives** (wīvz) [ME. < OE. *wif*, a woman, akin to Sw. *viv*, G. *weib* < ? IE. **weip-*, to twist, turn, wrap, in sense "the hidden or veiled person"] **1.** orig., a woman: still so used in *midwife*, *housewife*, etc. **2.** a married woman; specif., a woman in her relationship to her husband —**take to wife** to marry (a specified woman) —**wife′hood** n. —**wife′less** adj. —**wife′ly** adj. **-li·er**, **-li·est**

wig (wig) n. [shortened < PERIWIG] **1.** *a)* a false covering of real or synthetic hair for the head, worn as part of a costume, to conceal baldness, etc. *b)* *same as* TOUPEE ☆**2.** [Slang] variously, the hair, head, or mind —vt. **wigged**, **wig′ging 1.** to furnish with a wig or wigs ☆**2.** [Slang] *a)* to annoy, upset, anger, etc. *b)* to make excited, ecstatic, frenzied, crazy, etc. (often with *out*) **3.** [Brit. Colloq.] to scold, censure, rebuke, etc. —☆vi. [Slang] to be or become wigged, or upset, excited, crazy, etc. (often with *out*)

Wig·an (wig′ən) city in Lancashire, NW England: pop. 79,000

wig·an (wig′ən) n. [after prec., where first made] a canvas-like cotton cloth used to stiffen hems, lapels, etc.

wi·geon (wij′ən) n. var. of WIDGEON

wig·ger·y (wig′ər ē) n. [Rare] **1.** wigs collectively **2.** the practice of wearing a wig

Wig·gin (wig′in), **Kate Douglas** (born *Kate Smith*) 1856–1923; U.S. educator & writer of children's novels

wig·gle (wig′'l) vt., vi. **-gled**, **-gling** [ME. *wigelen*, prob. < MDu. & MLowG. *wiggelen*, freq. of *wiggen*, to move from side to side, akin to OE. *wegan*, to move: for IE. base see WAG[1]] to move or cause to move with short, jerky or twisting motions from side to side; wriggle shakily or sinuously —n. the act or an instance of wiggling

wig·gler (wig′lər) n. **1.** a person or thing that wiggles **2.** the larva of a mosquito; wriggler

wig·gly (-lē) adj. **-gli·er**, **-gli·est 1.** that wiggles; wiggling **2.** having a form that suggests wiggling; wavy [a *wiggly* line]

wig·gy (wig′ē) adj. **-gi·er**, **-gi·est 1.** [Now Rare] *a)* wearing a wig *b)* pompously formal or elegant ☆**2.** [Slang] wild, exciting, crazy, etc.

wight[1] (wīt) n. [ME. *wiht* < OE., akin to G. *wicht*, creature < IE. base **wekti-*, thing, whence Russ. *rech′*, speech] **1.** [Obs.] a living being; creature **2.** [Archaic] a human being; person: now sometimes used in a patronizing or commiserating sense

wight[2] (wīt) adj. [ME. *wihte* < ON. *vigt*, neut. of *vigr*, skilled in arms, akin to OE. *wigan*, to fight: for IE. base see VICTOR] [Archaic exc. Dial.] strong, brisk, active, brave, etc.

Wight (wīt), **Isle of** island in the English Channel, off the S coast of Hampshire, constituting a county of England: 147 sq. mi.; pop. 75,000: cf. HAMPSHIRE (sense 2)

☆**wig·let** (wig′lit) n. a small wig; specif., a woman's hair-piece designed to supplement her own hair

Wig·town (wig′tən) county of SW Scotland: 487 sq. mi.; pop. 29,000: also **Wig′town·shire′** (-shir′)

wig·wag (wig′wag′) vt., vi. **-wagged′**, **-wag′ging** [< obs. *wig*, to move + WAG[1]] **1.** to move back and forth; wag **2.** to send (a message) by waving flags, lights, etc. back and forth in accordance with a code —n. **1.** the act or practice of sending messages in this way **2.** a message so sent —**wig′wag′ger** n.

WIGGLER
(of mosquito)

☆**wig·wam** (wig′wäm, -wôm) *n.* [< AmInd. (Algonquian) name, as in Ojibwa *wigiwam*, lodge, lit., their dwelling, akin to *wigiw*, he dwells] **1.** a domed shelter made by the Indians of E and C N. America, consisting of a framework of arched poles covered with rushes, bark, leaves, branches, etc. **2.** a readily movable, conical shelter of these Indians, resembling a tepee but made of bark and having a second, outer set of poles lashed together

WIGWAM

☆**wik·i·up** (wik′ē up′) *n.* same as WICKIUP

Wil·ber·force (wil′bər fôrs′), **William** 1759–1833; Eng. statesman & vigorous opponent of slavery

Wil·bert (wil′bərt) [G. *Willebert* < OHG. *willeo*, a WILL¹ + *beraht, berht*, BRIGHT] a masculine name

Wil·bur (wil′bər) [OE. *Wilburh:* prob. a place name < *Wiligburh*, lit., willow town] a masculine name

☆**wil·co** (wil′kō) *interj.* [*wil*(l) *co*(*m*ply] I will comply with your request: used in radiotelephony

wild (wīld) *adj.* [ME. *wilde* < OE., akin to G. *wild*, prob. < IE. base *wel-*, shaggy hair, unkempt, whence WOOL; cf. WOLD¹] **1.** living or growing in its original, natural state and not normally domesticated or cultivated [*wild* flowers, *wild* animals] **2.** not lived in or cultivated; overgrown, waste, etc. [*wild* land] **3.** not civilized; savage [a *wild* tribe] **4.** not easily restrained or regulated; not controlled or controllable; unruly, rough, lawless, etc. [*wild* children] **5.** characterized by a lack of social or moral restraint; unbridled in pursuing pleasure; dissolute, orgiastic, etc. [a *wild* rake, a *wild* party] **6.** violently disturbed; turbulent; stormy [a *wild* seacoast] **7.** in a state of intense excitement; specif., *a)* eager or enthusiastic, as with desire or anticipation [*wild* with delight] *b)* angered, frenzied, frantic, crazed, etc. [*wild* with desperation] **8.** in a state of disorder, disarrangement, confusion, etc. [*wild* hair] **9.** fantastically impractical; visionary [a *wild* scheme] **10.** showing a lack of sound judgment; reckless; imprudent [a *wild* wager] **11.** going wide of the mark aimed at; missing the target [a *wild* swing in boxing] **12.** *Card Games* having any value specified by the holder: said of a card [deuces, when *wild* in poker, may be counted as aces, kings, etc.] —*adv.* in a wild manner; wildly; without aim or control [to shoot *wild*] —*n.* [*usually pl.*] a wilderness or wasteland —**run wild** to grow, exist, or behave without control or regulation —**the wild** the wilderness, nature, the out-of-doors, etc. [the call of *the wild*] —**wild′ly** *adv.* —**wild′ness** *n.*

☆**wild allspice** same as SPICEBUSH (sense 1)

wild boar a variety of hog (*Sus scrofa*) living wild in Europe and Asia, from which most domestic hogs are believed to be derived: recently introduced into the U.S.

wild brier any kind of wild rose; esp., *same as* EGLANTINE or DOG ROSE

wild carrot a common biennial weed (*Daucus carota*) of the parsley family, with finely divided foliage and umbels of white flowers: the cultivated carrot is derived from it

wild·cat (wīld′kat′) *n., pl.* **-cats′, -cat′:** see PLURAL, II, D, 1 **1.** *a)* any of a large group of fierce, medium-sized, undomesticated animals of the cat family, found throughout N. America, including the Canada lynx and the bay lynx *b)* any of several similar cats, as the ocelot, serval, caracal, margay, etc. *c)* an undomesticated cat (*Felis sylvestris*) of Europe, similar to but slightly larger than the domestic cat *d)* a house cat that has escaped from domestication: in this sense, usually **wild cat 2.** any person regarded as like a wildcat in fierceness, aggressiveness, etc. ☆**3.** an unsound or risky business scheme ☆**4.** an oil well drilled in an area not previously known to have oil **5.** *Naut.* a drum on a windlass, constructed to engage the links of a chain cable ☆**6.** *Railroading* a locomotive without cars sent out on special tasks, as to help haul a train —*adj.* ☆**1.** unsound or financially risky [a *wildcat* venture] ☆**2.** designating or of an enterprise or undertaking that is illegal, unethical, irregular, unauthorized, etc.; specif., designating a labor strike not officially authorized by the union representing the strikers ☆**3.** *Railroading* running without authorization or on an irregular schedule —*vi.* **-cat′ted, -cat′ting 1.** to drill for oil in an area previously considered unproductive **2.** to engage in wildcat enterprises, etc. —**wild′cat′ter** *n.*

Wilde (wīld), **Oscar (Fingal O'Flahertie Wills)** 1854–1900; Brit. playwright, poet, & novelist, born in Ireland

wil·de·beest (wil′də bēst′, vil′-) *n., pl.* **-beests′, -beest′:** see PLURAL, II, D, 1 [Afrik. < Du. *wild*, wild + *beeste*, beast] *same as* GNU

wil·der (wil′dər) *vt., vi.* [prob. < WILDERNESS] [Archaic or Poet.] **1.** to lose or cause to lose one's way **2.** to bewilder or become bewildered

Wil·der (wil′dər), **Thorn·ton (Niven)** (thôrn′t'n) 1897– ; U.S. novelist & playwright

Wil·der·ness (wil′dər nis) woodland region in NE Va., south of the Rapidan River: scene of a Civil War battle (May, 1864) between the armies of Grant and Lee

wil·der·ness (wil′dər nis) *n.* [ME. *wildernesse* < *wilderne*, wild place (< OE. *wilddeor*, wild animal < *wilde*, WILD + *deor*, animal, DEER) + *-nesse, -NESS*] **1.** an uncultivated,

uninhabited region; waste; wild **2.** any barren, empty, or open area, as of ocean **3.** a large, confused mass or tangle of persons or things **4.** [Obs.] a wild condition or quality —*SYN.* see WASTE

wild-eyed (wīld′īd′) *adj.* **1.** staring in a wild, distracted, or demented way **2.** fantastically foolish, impractical, or extreme [wild-eyed ideas]

wild fig same as CAPRIFIG

wild·fire (-fīr′) *n.* **1.** orig., *a)* a highly destructive fire *b)* a highly flammable substance; specif., *same as* GREEK FIRE: now mainly in **spread like wildfire**, to be disseminated widely and rapidly, as a rumor **2.** [Now Rare] *same as: a)* HEAT LIGHTNING *b)* WILL-O′-THE-WISP

wild·flow·er (-flou′ər) *n.* **1.** any plant growing without cultivation in fields, woods, etc. **2.** its flower Also **wild flower**

wild·fowl (-foul′) *n., pl.* **-fowls′, -fowl′:** see FOWL a wild bird, esp. a game bird, as a wild duck, pheasant, quail, etc.: also **wild fowl**

wild goose any undomesticated goose, as the graylag or the Canada goose

wild-goose chase (-gōos′) any search, pursuit, or endeavor as futile as trying to catch a wild goose by chasing it

wild hog same as: **1.** WILD BOAR **2.** PECCARY

Wild Hunt *European Folklore* a nighttime ride of spectral huntsmen across the countryside or the sky —**Wild Huntsman**

wild hyacinth ☆**1.** a camass (*Camassia scilloides*) of the E U.S., with bluish flowers **2.** same as WOOD HYACINTH

☆**wild indigo** same as BAPTISIA

wild·ing (wīl′diŋ) *n.* **1.** *a)* a wild plant; esp., a wild apple tree *b)* its fruit **2.** a plant originally cultivated, but growing wild **3.** [Rare] a wild animal —*adj.* [Poet.] not cultivated or domesticated; wild

wild lettuce any of various wild, weedy species of lettuce, having small, dandelionlike flower heads with yellow or blue flowers, milky juice, and often prickly foliage; esp., a horseweed (*Lactuca canadensis*) of E N. America

wild·life (wīld′līf′) *n.* wild animals and birds, collectively

wild·ling (wīld′liŋ) *n.* [WILD + -LING¹] an uncultivated plant or undomesticated animal

wild mustard any of several weedy mustards; esp., *same as* CHARLOCK

wild oats ☆**1.** a woodland plant (*Uvularia sessilifolia*) of the lily family, with small, drooping, yellowish flowers, native to E N. America **2.** any of several wild grasses (genus *Avena*); esp., the wild progenitor (*Avena fatua*) of the cultivated oat, having strong, twisted awns and commonly occurring as a weed, esp. in the W U.S.: also **wild oat** —**sow one's wild oats** to be promiscuous or dissolute in youth before settling down: usually said of a man

wild olive any of various trees resembling the olive or bearing olivelike fruits, as the Russian olive

wild pansy an uncultivated pansy, esp. a European species (*Viola tricolor*) with petals in combinations of white, yellow, and purple, that is the ancestor of the garden pansy

wild parsnip a tall, stout biennial weed (*Pastinaca sativa*) of the parsley family, with pinnately compound leaves: regarded as the ancestor of the cultivated parsnip

wild pink 1. any of several catchflies; esp., ☆an early flowering species (*Silene caroliniana*) of the E U.S., having lance-shaped leaves and bright pink flowers in clusters ☆**2.** same as ARETHUSA (*n.*)

☆**wild pitch** *Baseball* a pitch so erratic that the catcher cannot reasonably control it and a runner advances to another base

wild rice 1. a tall, annual, aquatic grass (*Zizania aquatica*) of the U.S. and Canada, found along the swampy borders of lakes and streams **2.** its edible grain

wild rose any of various roses growing wild, as eglantine

wild rubber rubber obtained from uncultivated trees

wild rye any of a genus (*Elymus*) of perennial grasses having erect or drooping, usually bristly, spikes: native to most parts of N. America

☆**wild turkey** the wild, original form, now rare, of the N. American domesticated turkey, which was derived from a Mexican variety: see TURKEY (sense 1 *a*)

wild type the ordinary phenotype that is characteristic of most members of a species under natural conditions

☆**wild vanilla** a perennial plant (*Trilisa odoratissima*) of the composite family, with vanilla-scented foliage: found in the SE U.S.

☆**Wild West** [also w- W-] the western U.S. in its early frontier period of lawlessness

☆**Wild West show** a circuslike spectacle featuring horsemanship and other feats by cowboys, Indians, etc.

wild·wood (wīld′wood′) *n.* a natural woodland or forest, esp. when unfrequented by man

wile (wīl) *n.* [ME. < Late OE. *wil* < OE. *wigle*, magic, divination, akin to *wiglian*, to take auspices, *wicce*, WITCH] **1.** a sly trick; deceitful artifice; stratagem **2.** a beguiling or coquettish trick: *usually used in pl.* **3.** [Now Rare] craftiness; guile —*vt.* **wiled, wil′ing** to beguile; lure —*SYN.* see TRICK —**wile away** to while away (time, etc.): by confusion with WHILE

Wil·fred, Wil·frid (wil′frid) [OE. *Wilfrith* < *willa*, a wish, WILL¹ + *frith*, peace] a masculine name

wil·ful (wil′fəl) *adj. var. of* WILLFUL

Wil·helm (vil′helm) *Ger. form of* WILLIAM

esidence of English sovereigns since the ne Conqueror, located in Windsor
a style of wooden pular in 18th-cent. merica, with spreading f spindles, and usually

WINDSOR CHAIR

ot a form of double slip- a four-in-hand necktie, n a wider, bulkier knot
e a wide necktie of silk cut s, tied in a loose double bow
rm (wind′stôrm′) *n.* a storm strong wind but little or no il, etc.
uck·ing (-suk′iŋ) *n.* the habit ome horses have of swallowing s in crib biting —**wind′-suck′er** *n.*
-swept (-swept′) *adj.* swept by or exposed to winds
nd tee a large T-shaped weather vane placed on a nding field to show wind direction to aircraft
wind tunnel a tunnellike chamber through which air is forced and in which scale models of airplanes, etc. are tested to determine the effects of wind pressure
wind·up (wind′up′) *n.* **1.** a winding up, or conclusion; close; end ☆**2.** *Baseball* the swinging of the arm preparatory to pitching the ball
wind·ward (wind′wərd; *in nautical usage,* win′dərd) *n.* the direction or side from which the wind blows —*adv.* in the direction from which the wind blows; toward the wind —*adj.* **1.** moving windward **2.** on the side from which the wind blows Opposed to LEEWARD —**to windward of** advantageously situated in respect to
Windward Islands **1.** S group of islands in the Lesser Antilles of the West Indies, extending from the Leeward Islands south to Trinidad, but usually excluding Barbados **2.** former Brit. colony in this group, constituted in 1960 as four separate colonies
Windward Passage strait between Cuba & Hispaniola, in the West Indies: 50 mi. wide
wind·y (win′dē) *adj.* **wind′i·er, wind′i·est** **1.** characterized by or accompanied by wind [*a windy day*] **2.** exposed to wind; swept by strong or frequent winds [*a windy city*] **3.** like wind; stormy, blustery, violent, etc. [*windy anger*] **4.** *a*) without substance; empty, flimsy, etc. *b*) long-winded, pompous, boastful, etc. **5.** *same as* FLATULENT
wine (win) *n.* [ME. < OE. *win,* akin to ON. *vin,* G. & Goth. *wein* < early Gmc. borrowing < L. *vinum,* wine: see VINE] **1.** the fermented juice of grapes, used as an alcoholic beverage and in cooking, religious ceremonies, etc.: wines vary in color (*red, white, rosé,* etc.) and sugar content (*sweet, dry, sec,* etc.), may be effervescent (*sparkling*) or noneffervescent (*still*), and are sometimes strengthened with additional alcohol (*fortified*) **2.** the fermented juice of other fruits or plants, used as a beverage [*dandelion wine*] **3.** anything having an intoxicating or exhilarating effect **4.** a dark, purplish red resembling the color of red wines —*vt., vi.* **wined, win′ing** to provide with or drink wine: usually in the phrase **wine and dine,** to entertain lavishly with food, drink, etc.
wine·bib·ber (-bib′ər) *n.* [coined by Coverdale to transl. G. *weinsäufer,* Luther's transl. of Gr. *oinopotēs,* wine drinker: cf. Matt. 11:19] a person given to drinking much or too much wine —**wine′bib′bing** *adj., n.*
wine cellar **1.** a cellar where wine is stored **2.** a stock of wine
wine-col·ored (-kul′ərd) *adj.* having the color of red wine; dark purplish-red
wine gallon the old English gallon of 231 cu. in., now the standard gallon in the U.S.
wine·glass (-glas′, -gläs′) *n.* a small glass, usually stemmed, for serving wine —**wine′glass·ful′** *n., pl.* **-fuls′**
wine·grow·ing (-grō′iŋ) *n.* the art or process of cultivating grapes and making wine from them —**wine′grow′er** *n.*
wine palm any of certain palms yielding a sap drunk as a beverage, often in fermented form: cf. TODDY (sense 1)
wine press a vat in which grapes are trodden, or a machine for pressing them, to extract the juice for making wine
☆**win·er·y** (win′ər ē) *n., pl.* **-er·ies** an establishment where wine is made
☆**Wine·sap** (win′sap′) *n.* a dark-red winter apple
wine·skin (win′skin′) *n.* in Eastern countries, a large bag for holding wine, made of the skin of an animal
Win·fred (win′frid) [OE. *Winfrith* < *wine,* friend + *frithu,* peace] a masculine name
wing (wiŋ) *n.* [ME. *winge, weng* < ON. *vaengir,* pl. of *vaengr* (for IE. base see WIND[2]): the word replaced OE. *fethra,* wings, pl. of *fether,* FEATHER] **1.** *a*) either of the two feathered forelimbs of a bird, fully developed for flying, as in eagles, gulls, swallows, etc., or insufficiently developed for flight and used for balance in running, etc., as in chickens, ostriches, etc., or for swimming, as in penguins *b*) either of the paired organs of flight of a bat, the lifting surface of which is formed by the membranous skin connecting the long, modified digits *c*) either of the paired organs of flight of insects, light membranous structures that are lateral outgrowths of the thorax supported by a network of veins *d*) any of various winglike structures used by certain animals for gliding movements, as the patagium of flying squirrels or the enlarged pectoral fins of flying fish **2.** in art, mythology, etc., either of a pair of winglike structures associated with or attributed to gods, angels, demons, dragons, etc., or used as a symbol of speed or the like **3.** something used as or like a wing; esp., *a*) an (or the) main lateral supporting surface of an airplane *b*) either of the inflatable pouches of a pair of water wings **4.** something resembling a wing in position or in relation to the main part; esp., *a*) a part, extension, or annex of a building, with reference to its location at a side of the main part or its specialized use [*the east wing, the surgical wing of a hospital*] *b*) either of the longer sides of an outwork that connect it with the main fortification *c*) an outlying area, as of an estate *d*) either of the two side extensions of the back of a wing chair *e*) either part of a double door, screen, etc. *f*) any of the sidepieces used in stage scenery; also, either side of the stage out of sight of the audience *g*) any winglike anatomical or botanical part, as on some leafstalks or seeds; ala *h*) a vane, as of a windmill *i*) [Brit.] a fender or mudguard **5.** a group of persons having a winglike relation to another group or to the entire body; specif., *a*) the section of an army, fleet, etc. to the right (or left) of the center *b*) a section or faction, as of a political party, with reference to its radicalism or conservatism *c*) an organization affiliated with or subsidiary to a parent organization **6.** *a*) in hockey and certain other goal games, a position played forward and right (or left) of center *b*) the player at such a position **7.** *a*) any of various units in an air force; specif., in the U.S. Air Force, a unit below the division level and above the group level *b*) [*pl.*] the insignia worn by pilots and crew of military aircraft **8.** the act of flying, or a means or manner of flying: now chiefly in **give wing to, take wing** (see phrases below) **9.** anything represented as flying or soaring, or as carrying one to soaring heights of rapture, joy, etc. [*on wings of song*] **10.** [Slang] a person's arm; specif., ☆*Baseball* a pitcher's throwing arm —*vt.* **1.** to provide with wings **2.** to feather (an arrow) **3.** *a*) to cause to fly or speed as on wings [*to wing an arrow at a target*] *b*) to make (one's way) by flying *c*) to pass through or over by or as if by flying **4.** to transport by or as by flight **5.** to wound, as with a bullet, in the wing, arm, etc. —*vi.* to go swiftly on or as on wings; fly —**give wing** (or **wings**) **to** to enable to fly or soar on or as if on wings —**on the wing** **1.** flying, or while in flight **2.** in motion or while moving or traveling —**take wing** **1.** to take flight; fly away **2.** to become joyous, jubilant, or enraptured —**under one's wing** under one's protection, patronage, etc. —**wing′less** *adj.*
wing and wing *Naut.* with sails extended on either side by booms
☆**wing·back** (-bak′) *n.* *Football* **1.** an offensive back, flanking the end of the line **2.** the position this back plays
wing bow (bō) the color at the bend of a bird's wing formed by distinctive coloration of the lesser coverts
wing chair an upholstered armchair with a high back from each side of which extend high sides, or wings, orig. to give protection from drafts
wing collar a stiff, stand-up collar having the top corners in front turned down: worn by men in formal dress, as with a swallow-tailed or cutaway coat
wing covert any of the coverts of the wing quills
☆**wing·ding** (wiŋ′diŋ′) *n.* [< earlier *whing-ding* < ?] [Slang] **1.** an event, action, party, celebration, etc. that is very festive, lively, unrestrained, etc. **2.** something very striking, exciting, etc. of its kind
winged (wiŋd; *often poet.* wiŋ′id) *adj.* **1.** having wings or winglike parts **2.** moving, esp. swiftly, on or as if on wings **3.** lofty; sublime [*winged words*]
wing-foot·ed (wiŋ′foot′id) *adj.* having or as if having winged feet; swift
wing·let (-lit) *n.* **1.** a small wing **2.** *same as* ALULA
wing loading the total weight of a loaded airplane, divided by the area of the wings: also **wing load**
wing·man (-mən) *n., pl.* **-men** ☆**1.** in a formation of aircraft, the pilot who flies behind and to the side of the leader ☆**2.** the aircraft flown in this position
☆**wing nut** a nut with flared sides for turning with the thumb and forefinger
wing·o·ver (wiŋ′ō′vər) *n.* an aerial maneuver in which an airplane enters a steep climbing turn until almost stalled, rolls beyond a vertical bank, then noses down and dives until normal flight is resumed in a direction approximately opposite to the original direction of flight
wing shot **1.** a shot made at a flying bird, clay pigeon, etc. **2.** a person skilled in making these —**wing shooting**
wing·span (-span′) *n.* the distance between the tips of an airplane's wings
wing·spread (-spred′) *n.* **1.** the distance between the tips of a pair of fully spread wings **2.** *same as* WINGSPAN
wing tip **1.** the outermost end of a wing ☆**2.** *a*) a man's shoe, esp. a brogue, of a style characterized by a decorative piece of leather over the vamp, peaked toward the tongue, with perforations on it and along the sides extending back from it *b*) this piece of leather Also **wing′-tip′, wing′tip′**
Win·i·fred (win′ə frid) [earlier *Winefred, Wynifreed,* altered (after WINFRED) < W. *Gwenfrewi,* lit., white wave] a feminine name: dim. *Winnie*
wink (wiŋk) *vi.* [ME. *winken* < OE. *wincian,* akin to G. *winken:* for IE. base see WINCH[1]] **1.** to close the eyel

Wil·hel·mi·na (wil′hel mē′nə; *Du.* vil′hel mē′nä) [G. *Wilhelmine,* fem. of *Wilhelm:* see WILLIAM] **1.** a feminine name **2.** (*Wilhelmina Helena Pauline Maria*) 1880–1962; queen of the Netherlands (1890–1948)
Wilhelmina, Mount mountain in West Irian, C New Guinea: 15,585 ft.
Wil·helms·ha·ven (vil′helms hä′fən) seaport in Lower Saxony, N West Germany, on the North Sea: pop. 101,000
wil·i·ly (wī′lə lē) *adv.* in a wily manner
wil·i·ness (-lē nis) *n.* a wily quality or condition
Wilkes (wilks) **1. Charles,** 1798–1877; U.S. naval officer & explorer **2. John,** 1727–97; Eng. political reformer
Wilkes-Bar·re (wilks′bar′ē, -ber′-; -ə) [after J. WILKES & Col. Isaac *Barré,* Brit. officer] city in NE Pa., on the Susquehanna River: pop. 64,000
Wilkes Land (wilks) region of Antarctica, on the Indian Ocean south of Australia
Wil·kins (wil′kinz) **1.** Sir **(George) Hubert,** 1888–1958; Australian polar explorer **2. Maurice H(ugh) F(rederick),** 1916– ; Eng. biophysicist, born in New Zealand: helped determine the structure of DNA
Wil·kins·burg (wil′kinz burg′) [after Wm. *Wilkins,* local citizen] borough in SW Pa.: suburb of Pittsburgh: pop. 30,000
will[1] (wil) *n.* [ME. *wille* < OE. *willa,* akin to G. *wille,* *willen* < IE. base **wel-,* to wish, choose, whence L. *velle,* to wish, *voluptas,* pleasure] **1.** the power of making a reasoned choice or of controlling one's own actions [*a man of weak will*] **2.** *a*) strong and fixed purpose; determination [*where there's a will there's a way*] *b*) energy and enthusiasm [*to work with a will*] **3.** disposition or attitude toward others [*a man of good will*] **4.** *a*) the particular desire, purpose, pleasure, choice, etc. of a certain person or group [*what is your will?*] *b*) a compelling command or decree [*the will of the people*] **5.** *Law* *a*) the legal statement of a person's wishes concerning the disposal of his property after death *b*) the document containing this —*vt.* [ME. *willien* < OE. *willian* < *willan,* to desire: cf. ff.] **1.** to have as the object of one's will; desire; want [*to will another's happiness, to will to survive*] **2.** to control or influence by the power of the will [*to will oneself into an action, to will others into submission*] **3.** *Law* to bequeath by a will —*vi.* **1.** to exert one's will [*to succeed by willing*] **2.** to wish, desire, prefer, or choose [*to do as one wills*] —**at will** when one wishes; at one's discretion
SYN.—**will,** the more inclusive term here, basically denotes the power of choice and deliberate action or the intention resulting from the exercise of this power [*freedom of the will, the will to succeed*]; **volition** stresses the exercise of the will in making a choice or decision [*he came of his own volition*]
will[2] (wil; *unstressed* wəl) *v.,* pt. **would;** archaic 2d pers. sing., pres. indic., **wilt;** archaic 2d pers. sing., pt., **wouldest, wouldst;** obs. pp. **wold, would** [ME. *willen* < OE. *willan,* to be willing, desire, akin to G. *wollen,* will: for IE. base see prec.] an auxiliary used: **1.** to express simple futurity, usually with implications of intention, determination, compulsion, obligation, or necessity: in this sense *will* is formally used instead of *shall* except in questions in the first person, singular or plural [*shall we go tomorrow?*]; *shall* and *will* are used interchangeably to express determination, compulsion, obligation, and necessity **2.** in formal speech, *a*) to express determination, compulsion, obligation, or necessity in the first person [*I will finish on time*] and futurity in the second and third persons [*they will all die*] *b*) in a question expecting *will* in the answer [*will you have some wine?*] *c*) in an indirect quotation, if *would* would be used in the direct form of the quotation These formal conventions, however, do not reflect and have not reflected prevailing usage See also SHALL, SHOULD, WOULD **3.** to express: *a*) willingness [*will you go?*] *b*) ability, capability, or capacity [*it will hold another quart*] *c*) habit or customary practice [*she will talk for hours on end*] *d*) inclination or inevitability [*boys will be boys*] *e*) expectation, surmise, etc. [*that will be his wife with him, I suppose*] —*vt., vi.* to wish; desire [*what will you, master?*]
will·a·ble (wil′ə b′l) *adj.* that can be willed, wished, determined, etc.
Wil·lam·ette (wi lam′it) [< AmInd. place name < ?] river in W Oreg., flowing north into the Columbia River near Portland: c.190 mi.
Wil·lard (wil′ərd) [< the surname *Willard*] **1.** a masculine name **2. Frances (Elizabeth Caroline),** 1839–98; U.S. temperance leader
will call the department, as of a large store, at which articles are held to be picked up, as when paid for
willed (wild) *adj.* having a will, esp. a specified kind of will: used in hyphenated compounds [*strong-willed*]
wil·lem·ite (wil′ə mīt′) *n.* [Du. *willemit,* after *Willem* I (1772–1843), king of the Netherlands] native silicate of zinc, Zn_2SiO_4, found in massive, granular, or crystalline form in various colors from pale yellow-green to red
Wil·lem·stad (wil′əm stät′, vil′-) capital of the Netherlands Antilles, on the island of Curaçao: pop. 44,000
Willes·den (wilz′dən) city in Middlesex, SE England: suburb of London: pop. 172,000
☆**wil·let** (wil′it) *n., pl.* **-lets, -let:** see PLURAL, II, D, 1 [echoic of its cry] a large, gray and white, long-legged, snipelike wading bird (*Catoptrophorus semipalmatus*) of N. and S. America, living along shallow shores
will·ful (wil′fəl) *adj.* **1.** said or done deliberately or intentionally **2.** following one's own will unreasonably; obstinate; stubborn —*SYN.* see VOLUNTARY —**will′ful·ly** *adv.* —**will′ful·ness** *n.*
Wil·liam (wil′yəm) [ONormFr. *Willaume* < OHG. *Willehelm* < *willeo,* WILL[1] + *helm,* protection (see HELM[1])] **1.** a masculine name: dim. *Bill, Billy, Will, Willy;* equiv. It. *Guglielmo,* Du. *Willem,* Fr. *Guillaume,* G. *Wilhelm,* Sp. *Guillermo* **2. William I** *a*) 1027?–87; duke of Normandy who invaded England & defeated Harold at Battle of Hastings; king of England (1066–87): called *William the Conqueror* *b*) 1533–84; prince of Orange (1544–84) & count of Nassau (1559–84); founder and 1st stadholder (1579–84) of the Netherlands republic: called *William the Silent* *c*) 1797–1888; king of Prussia (1861–88) & emperor of Germany (1871–88): son of FREDERICK WILLIAM III **3. William II** *a*) 1056?–1100; king of England (1087–1100): son of WILLIAM THE CONQUEROR: called *William Rufus* *b*) 1859–1941; emperor of Germany & king of Prussia (1888–1918): called *Kaiser Wilhelm* **4. William III** 1650–1702; king of England, Scotland, & Ireland (1689–1702); stadholder of the Netherlands (1672–1702): see MARY II
William of Malmesbury 1095?–1143?; Eng. historian
Wil·liams (wil′yəmz) **1. Ralph Vaughan,** *see* VAUGHAN WILLIAMS **2. Roger,** 1603?–83; Eng. clergyman & colonist in America: founder of Rhode Island **3. Tennessee,** (born *Thomas Lanier Williams*) 1914– ; U.S. playwright **4. William Car·los** (kär′lōs), 1883–1963; U.S. poet, writer, & physician
Wil·liams·burg (wil′yəmz burg′) [after King WILLIAM III] city in SE Va.: colonial capital of Va., now restored to its 18th-cent. appearance: pop. 7,000
Wil·liams·port (-pôrt′) [prob. after *William* Russell, early settler] city in NC Pa., on the Susquehanna River: pop. 42,000
William Tell *see* William TELL
William the Conqueror *see* WILLIAM (2 *a*)
☆**wil·lies** (wil′ēz) *n.pl.* [< ?] [Slang] a state of nervousness; jitters: with *the*
will·ing (wil′iŋ) *adj.* [ME. < OE. *willung* < *willian,* to WILL[1], *v.*] **1.** favorably disposed or consenting (*to* do something specified or implied) **2.** acting, giving, etc. readily and cheerfully [*a willing assistant*] **3.** done, given, offered, etc. readily or gladly; voluntary —**will′ing·ly** *adv.* —**will′ing·ness** *n.*
Wil·lis (wil′is) [< the surname *Willis,* prob. < *Willson, Wilson* (< *Will's son*)] a masculine name
wil·li·waw, wil·ly·waw (wil′i wô′) *n.* [prob. altered < WILLY-WILLY] **1.** a sudden, violent cold wind blowing down from mountain passes toward the coast in far northern or southern latitudes, as on the Alaskan coast and Aleutians, and in the Strait of Magellan **2.** a state of extreme confusion, turmoil, or agitation
Will·kie (wil′kē), **Wendell L(ewis)** 1892–1944; U.S. lawyer & political leader
will-o'-the-wisp (wil′ə *th*ə wisp′) *n.* [earlier *Will with the wisp* < *Will* (nickname for WILLIAM) + WISP] **1.** a shifting, elusive light seen over marshes at night; ignis fatuus **2.** a delusive hope, goal, or influence
wil·low (wil′ō) *n.* [ME. *wilwe* < OE. *welig,* akin to Du. *wilg* < IE. base **wel-,* to turn, twist, bend, whence Gr. *helikē,* willow] **1.** *a*) any of a genus (*Salix*) of trees and shrubs of the willow family, having usually narrow leaves, single, slipper-shaped bud scales, and staminate and pistillate catkins borne on separate plants: the flexible twigs of certain species are used in weaving baskets, chair seats, etc. *b*) the wood of any of these trees **2.** a machine with revolving spikes for cleaning raw wool, cotton, etc. **3.** [orig. made of willow] [Colloq.] a baseball or cricket bat —*adj.* designating a family (Salicaceae) of trees and shrubs consisting of the willows and poplars —*vt.* to clean (wool, cotton, etc.) with a willow —**wil′low·er** *n.*
willow herb **1.** any of a genus (*Epilobium*) of perennial plants of the evening-primrose family, with narrow leaves, whitish or purple flowers, and slender pods filled with plumed seeds, as the fireweed **2.** *same as* PURPLE LOOSESTRIFE: see LOOSESTRIFE (*n.* 2)
☆**willow oak** a N. American oak (*Quercus phellos*) with oblong, unlobed leaves, found near swamps and streams
willow pattern a design for china, originated in England (1780) and picturing a river, pagodas, willow trees, etc., usually in blue on a white background
☆**wil·low·ware** (wil′ō wer′) *n.* articles of china decorated with the willow pattern
wil·low·y (wil′ə wē) *adj.* **1.** covered or shaded with willows **2.** like a willow; specif., *a*) gracefully slender *b*) pliant, supple, lithe, etc.
will·pow·er (wil′pou′ər) *n.* strength of will, mind, or determination; self-control

fat, āpe, cär; ten, ēven; is, bīte; gō, hôrn, tōōl, look; oil, out; up, fur; get; joy; yet; chin; she; thin, *then;* zh, leisure; ŋ, ring; ə *for* a *in* ago, e *in* agent, i *in* sanity, o *in* comply, u *in* focus; ′ as in able (ā′b′l); Fr. bál; ë, Fr. coeur; ö, Fr. feu; Fr. mon; ô, Fr. coq; ü, Fr. duc; r, Fr. cri; H, G. ich; kh, G. doch. See inside front cover. ☆ Americanism; ‡foreign; *hypothetical; <derived from

wil·ly (wil′ē) *n., vt.* **-lied, -ly·ing** *var. of* WILLOW (*n.* 2, *vt.*)
wil·ly-nil·ly (wil′ē nil′ē) *adv.* [contr. < *will I, nill I:* see WILL¹ & NILL] whether one wishes it or not; willingly or unwillingly —*adj.* that is or happens whether one wishes it or not
wil·ly-wil·ly (-wil′ē) *n., pl.* **-lies** [prob. reduplication of *willy,* altered < *whirly,* short for WHIRLWIND] [Austral.] **1.** a severe tropical cyclone **2.** a whirlwind over a desert
Wil·ma (wil′mə) [G., contr. < *Wilhelmina:* see WILLIAM] a feminine name
Wil·ming·ton (wil′miŋ tən) [after Spencer Compton (1673?–1743), Earl of *Wilmington*] **1.** a seaport in N Del., on the Delaware River: pop. 96,000 **2.** a seaport in SE N.C.: pop. 44,000
Wil·no (vil′nô; *Pol.* vēl′nô) *Pol. name of* VILNIUS
Wil·son (wil′s'n) **1. Alexander,** 1766–1813; Am. ornithologist, born in Scotland **2. Edmund,** 1895– ; U.S. writer & critic **3. (James) Harold,** 1916– ; Eng. politician; prime minister (1964–) **4. (Thomas) Woodrow,** 1856–1924; 28th president of the U.S. (1913–21)
Wil·son (wil′s'n), **Mount** [after Ben D. *Wilson,* early settler] mountain of the Coast Ranges, SW Calif., near Pasadena: site of an astronomical observatory: 5,710 ft.
Wilson (cloud) chamber [after C. T. R. *Wilson* (1869–1959), Scot. physicist] *same as* CLOUD CHAMBER
Wilson Dam [after President WILSON] dam on the Tennessee River, in NW Ala.: 137 ft. high
☆**Wil·son·i·an** (wil sō′nē ən) *adj.* of Woodrow Wilson or his political ideas, policies, etc.
☆**Wilson's thrush** [see ff.] *same as* VEERY
☆**Wilson's warbler** [after Alexander WILSON] a small, green and yellow N. American warbler (*Wilsonia pusilla*)
wilt¹ (wilt) *vi.* [var. of obs. *welk,* to wither < ME. *welken,* to fade, wither, dry up, akin to OHG. *welc,* damp, wilted < IE. **welg-,* var. of *welk-,* moist, damp, whence OE. *wealg,* nauseous] **1.** to become limp, as from heat or lack of water; wither; droop: said of plants **2.** to become weak or faint; lose strength; languish **3.** to lose courage; quail —*vt.* to cause to wilt —*n.* **1.** a wilting or being wilted **2.** *a)* a highly infectious disease of some caterpillars, in which the carcasses liquefy *b)* any of several plant diseases caused by certain bacteria or fungi and characterized by wilting of the leaves: also, esp. for 2 *a,* **wilt disease**
wilt² (wilt) *archaic 2d pers. sing., pres. indic., of* WILL²
Wil·ton (wilt′'n) *n.* [after *Wilton,* city in S England, where it was first made] a kind of carpet with a velvety pile of cut loops: also **Wilton carpet, Wilton rug**
Wilt·shire (wilt′shir; *for n., also* -shər) county of S England: 1,345 sq. mi.; pop. 447,000 —*n.* any of an old breed of pure-white sheep originating in England and characterized by a long head and long curved horns
wi·ly (wī′lē) *adj.* **-li·er, -li·est** full of wiles; crafty; sly —*SYN.* see SLY
wim·ble (wim′b'l) *n.* [ME. < Anglo-Fr. < MDu. *wimmel* (or Fl. *wemel*), an auger: cf. GIMLET] any of various tools for boring, as a gimlet, auger, etc. —*vt.* **-bled, -bling** to bore with a wimble
Wim·ble·don (wim′b'l dən) city in Surrey, SE England: suburb of London: scene of international lawn tennis matches: pop. 57,000
wim·ple (wim′p'l) *n.* [ME. *wimpel* < OE., akin to G. *wimpel,* wimple, pennon < IE. base **weib-,* to turn, swing, whence WIPE] **1.** a woman's head covering of medieval times, consisting of a cloth arranged about the head, cheeks, chin, and neck, leaving only the face exposed: now worn only by certain orders of nuns **2.** [Scot.] *a)* a fold or plait *b)* a winding; turn; curve *c)* a ripple —*vt.* **-pled, -pling 1.** to cover or clothe with or as with a wimple **2.** to lay in folds **3.** to cause to ripple or undulate, as the surface of a lake —*vi.* **1.** to lie in folds **2.** to ripple **3.** [Scot.] to meander, as a brook

WIMPLE

win (win) *vi.* **won, win′ning** [ME. *winnen* < OE. *winnan,* to fight, endure, struggle, akin to G. *winnen,* to struggle, contend < IE. base **wen-,* to desire, strive for, whence WISH, L. *venus,* love] **1.** *a)* to gain a victory; be victorious; triumph (sometimes with *out*) *b)* to finish in first place in a race, contest, etc. **2.** to succeed in reaching or achieving a specified condition or place; get (with various prepositions, adverbs, or complementary adjectives) *[to win loose from a pressing crowd, to win free from bias and prejudice]* —*vt.* **1.** to get by effort, labor, struggle, etc.; specif., *a)* to gain or acquire through accomplishment *[to win distinctions]* *b)* to achieve or attain (one's point, demands, etc.) *c)* to gain (a prize or award) in competition *d)* to obtain or earn (a livelihood, security, etc.) **2.** to be successful or victorious in (a contest, game, dispute, etc.) **3.** to get to, usually with effort; reach *[they won the top of the hill by noon]* **4.** to prevail upon; influence; persuade: often with *over [to win someone over to one's side]* **5.** *a)* to gain the sympathy, favor, affection, or love of *[to win a supporter, friend, etc.]* *b)* to gain (someone's sympathy, affection, love, etc.) **6.** to persuade to marry one **7.** *a)* to extract (metal, minerals, etc.) from ore *b)* to obtain (coal, ore, etc.) by mining *c)* to prepare (a vein, shaft, etc.) for mining —*n.* **1.** [Colloq.] an act of winning; victory, as in a contest **2.** *Racing* first position at the finish
wince¹ (wins) *vi.* **winced, winc′ing** [ME. *wynsen* < Anglo-Fr. var. of OFr. *guenchir* < Frank. **wenkjan,* akin to OHG. *wankon,* to totter, turn: for IE. base see WENCH] to shrink or draw back slightly, usually with a grimace, as in pain, embarrassment, alarm, etc. —*n.* the act or an instance of wincing —*SYN.* see RECOIL —**winc′er** *n.*
wince² (wins) *n.* [var. of WINCH¹] a roller used between dyeing vats to facilitate the transfer of pieces of cloth
win·cey·ette (win′sē et′) *n.* [*wincey,* a kind of fabric, altered < LINSEY(-WOOLSEY) + -ETTE] [Brit.] a kind of flannelette or cotton flannel
winch¹ (winch) *n.* [ME. *winche* < OE. *wince* < IE. **weng-,* to be curved, bowed, whence WINK] **1.** a crank with a handle for transmitting motion, as to a grindstone **2.** an apparatus operated by hand or machine, for hoisting or hauling, consisting of a drum or cylinder upon which is wound the rope or cable which is attached to the object to be lifted or moved —*vt.* to hoist or haul with a winch
winch² (winch) *vi., n.* [Obs. or Dial.] *var. of* WINCE¹
Win·ches·ter (win′ches′tər, -chis-) county seat of Hampshire, S England: capital of the Anglo-Saxon kingdom of Wessex: pop. 30,000
☆**Win·ches·ter (rifle)** (win′ches′tər, -chis-) [after Oliver F. *Winchester* (1810–80), the manufacturer] *a trademark for* a type of repeating rifle with a tubular magazine set horizontally under the barrel
Winck·el·mann (viŋ′kəl män′), **Jo·hann Jo·a·chim** (yō′hän yō′ä khim) 1717–68; Ger. archaeologist & art historian
wind¹ (wīnd) *vt.* **wound** or rarely **wind′ed, wind′ing** [ME. *winden* < OE. *windan,* akin to ON. *vinda,* G. *winden* < IE. base **wendh-,* to turn, wind, twist, whence Arm. *gind,* a ring] **1.** *a)* to turn, or make revolve *[to wind a crank]* *b)* to move by or as if by cranking **2.** *a)* to turn or coil (string, ribbon, etc.) around itself to form a ball or around something else so as to encircle it closely; twine; wreathe *[winding the bandage on his finger]* *b)* to wrap or cover by encircling with something turned in the manner of a coil; entwine *[to wind a spool with thread]* **3.** *a)* to make (one's way) in a winding or twisting course *b)* to cause to move in a winding or twisting course **4.** to introduce deviously; insinuate *[winding his prejudices through all his writings]* **5.** to hoist or haul by or as by winding rope on a winch (often with *up*) **6.** to tighten the operating spring of (a clock, mechanical toy, etc.) by turning a stem or the like (often with *up*) —*vi.* **1.** to move, go, or extend in a curving, zigzagging, or sinuous manner; meander **2.** to double on one's track, so as to throw off pursuers **3.** to take a circuitous, devious, or subtle course in behavior, argument, etc. **4.** to insinuate oneself **5.** to coil, twine, or spiral (*about* or *around* something) **6.** to warp or twist: said of wood **7.** to undergo winding *[a watch that winds easily]* —*n.* **1.** the act of winding **2.** a single turn of something wound **3.** a turn; twist; bend; curve —**wind off** to unwind or remove by unwinding —**wind up 1.** to wind or roll into a ball, etc. **2.** to entangle or involve **3.** to bring or come to an end or final settlement; conclude; finish **4.** to make very tense, nervous, excited, etc. ☆**5.** *Baseball* to swing the arm preparatory to pitching the ball
wind² (wind; *for n., also poet.* wīnd) *n.* [ME. < OE., akin to ON. *vindr,* G. *wind* < IE. **wentos* (whence L. *ventus*) < base **we-,* to blow, whence Sans. *vāti,* (it) blows] **1.** air in motion; specif., *a)* any noticeable natural movement of air parallel to the earth's surface: see BEAUFORT SCALE *b)* air artificially put in motion, as by an air pump or fan **2.** a strong, fast-moving, or destructive natural current of air; gale or storm **3.** the direction from which a wind blows: now chiefly in *the four winds,* with reference to the cardinal points of the compass **4.** a natural current of air regarded as a bearer of odors or scents, as in hunting *[to lose (the) wind of the fox]* **5.** figuratively, air regarded as bearing information, indicating trends, etc. *[a rumor that's in the wind]* **6.** breath or the power of breathing *[to get the wind knocked out of one]* **7.** *a)* idle or empty talk; nonsense *b)* bragging; pomposity; conceit **8.** gas in the stomach or intestines; flatulence **9.** [*pl.*] the wind instruments of an orchestra, or the players of these —*vt.* **1.** to expose to the wind or air, as for drying; air **2.** to get or follow the scent of; scent **3.** to cause to be out of breath *[to be winded by a long run]* **4.** to rest (a horse, etc.) so as to allow recovery of breath —**between wind and water 1.** close to the waterline of a ship **2.** in a dangerous spot —**break wind** to expel gas from the bowels —**get** (or **have**) **the wind up** to become nervous or alarmed —**get** (or **have**) **wind of** to get (or have) information or a hint concerning; hear (or know) of —**how the wind blows** (or **lies**) what the trend of affairs, public opinion, etc. is —**in the teeth of the wind** straight against the wind: also **in the wind's eye** —**in the wind** happening or about to happen —**into the wind** in the direction from which the wind is blowing —**off the wind** with the wind coming from behind —**on the wind** approximately in the direction from which the wind is blowing —**sail close to the wind 1.** to sail as nearly as possible straight against the wind **2.** to be economical in one's affairs **3.** to border on indecency, foolhardiness, etc. —**take the wind out of one's sails** to remove one's advantage, nullify one's argument, etc. suddenly
SYN.—**wind** is the general term for any natural movement of

air, whether of high or low velocity or great or little force; **breeze** is popularly applied to a light, fresh wind and meteorologically, to a wind having a velocity of from 4 to 31 miles an hour; **gale** is popularly applied to strong, somewhat violent wind and, meteorologically, to a wind having a velocity of from 32 to 63 miles an hour; **gust** and **blast** apply to sudden, brief winds, **gust** suggesting a light puff, and **blast** a driving rush, of air; **zephyr** is a poetic term for a soft, gentle breeze
wind³ (wīnd, wind) *vt., vi.* **wound** or rarely **wind′ed, wind′ing** [Early ModE. < prec.] [Poet.] **1.** to blow (a horn, etc.) **2.** to sound (a signal, etc.), as on a horn
wind·age (win′dij) *n.* **1.** the disturbance of air around a moving projectile **2.** *a)* the deflection of a projectile by the effects of the wind *b)* the degree of this *c)* in aiming a gun, the degree of adjustment of the wind gauge to compensate for such deflection **3.** the space between the inside wall of the barrel of a firearm and its projectile, to allow for the expansion of gas in firing, as measured by the difference in diameters of the bore and projectile **4.** the part of a ship's surface exposed to the wind
wind·bag (wind′bag′) *n.* [Colloq.] a person who talks much and pretentiously but says little of importance
wind·blown (-blōn′) *adj.* **1.** blown by the wind **2.** twisted in growth by the prevailing wind: said of a tree
wind-borne (-bôrn′) *adj.* carried by the wind, as pollen
☆**wind·break** (-brāk′) *n.* a hedge, fence, or row of trees that serves as a protection from wind
☆**Wind·break·er** (-brā′kər) *a trademark for* a warm sports jacket of leather, wool, etc., having a closefitting elastic waistband and cuffs —*n.* [**w-**] such a jacket
wind-bro·ken (-brō′k'n) *adj.* having the heaves: *see* HEAVES
wind·burn (-burn′) *n.* a roughened, reddened, sore condition of the skin, caused by overexposure to the wind
Wind Cave National Park national park in SW S.Dak.: it contains a limestone cavern (**Wind Cave**): 43 1/2 sq. mi.
wind cone *same as* WINDSOCK
wind·ed (win′did) *adj.* out of breath
wind·er (wīn′dər) *n.* **1.** a person who winds material or operates a winding machine in textile and other industries **2.** an apparatus for winding or on which winding is done **3.** a key, knob, etc. for winding a spring-operated mechanism **4.** any of the steps in a winding staircase
Win·der·mere (win′dər mir′) lake in NW England, between Westmorland & Lancashire: largest lake in England: 10 1/2 mi. long
wind·fall (wind′fôl′) *n.* **1.** something blown down by the wind, as fruit from a tree **2.** any unexpected acquisition, gain, or stroke of good luck
wind·flaw (-flô′) *n.* a gust of wind: see FLAW²
wind·flow·er (-flou′ər) *n. same as* ANEMONE (sense 1)
wind·gall (-gôl′) *n.* [WIND² + GALL²] a soft swelling on the fetlock joint of a horse —**wind′galled′** *adj.*
☆**wind gap** a notch in a mountain ridge, formerly serving as the bed of a small stream
wind gauge 1. *same as* ANEMOMETER **2.** a graduated attachment on a gun sight for indicating the degree of deflection necessary to counteract windage
Wind·hoek (vint′hook) capital of South West Africa, in the C part: pop. c.48,000
wind·hov·er (wind′huv′ər, -häv′-) *n.* [Brit.] *same as* KESTREL
wind·i·ly (win′də lē) *adv.* in a windy manner
wind·i·ness (-dē nis) *n.* a windy quality or condition
wind·ing (wīn′diŋ) *n.* **1.** the action or effect of a person or thing that winds; specif., *a)* a sinuous path or course *b)* [*usually pl.*] devious methods, actions, etc. *c)* a coiling, spiraling, or twining *d)* a single turn **2.** something that winds; specif., *a)* wire, thread, etc. wound around something *[the winding on an electric coil]* *b)* a single turn of this *c)* the manner in which this is wound *[a shunt winding]* **3.** the condition or fact of being warped or twisted *[a board in winding]* **4.** a defective gait of horses in which one leg tends to twist around the other —*adj.* that winds, turns, coils, spirals, etc.
winding sheet a cloth in which the body of a dead person is wrapped for burial; shroud
wind instrument (wind) a musical instrument played by blowing air through it, esp. a portable one played with the breath, as a flute, oboe, tuba, trumpet, etc.
☆**wind·jam·mer** (wind′jam′ər) *n. Naut.* **1.** a sailing ship, esp. a large one: so called orig. in contempt by seamen on early steamships **2.** a crew member of such a ship
wind·lass (wind′ləs) *n.* [ME. *wyndlas,* altered (after *-wyndel,* a winding device < *winden,* WIND¹) < *windas,* windlass < ON. *vindass* < *vinda,* to WIND¹ + *ass,* a beam] *same as* WINCH¹; esp., a simple kind of winch worked by a crank, as for lifting a bucket in a well, an anchor, etc. —*vt., vi.* to hoist or haul with a windlass
wind·less (wind′lis) *adj.* **1.** devoid of any wind or breeze **2.** out of breath —**wind′less·ly** *adv.* —**wind′-less·ness** *n.*

WINDLASS

win·dle·straw (win′d'l ... Scot. dial.) < *windel ... straw,* STRAW] [Scot ... or weak person o...
wind·mill (wind... rotation of la... vanes radiat... as a sourc... grain, pu... thing li... lerlike to... wind —**figh**... to fight imag... nents: from Do... ing at windmills ... that they were gia... rotate like a windmi...
win·dow (win′dō) *n.* [M... < ON. *vindauga,* a windo... + *auga,* an eye: for IE. ba... in a building, vehicle, or con... air or for looking through, usua... of glass, etc. set in a frame or sa... able so that it can be opened an... panes, or the sash or sashes in the... similar opening, as that before a bank... parent panel of a window envelope **4.** ... into the atmosphere to yield a perceptib... usually used for tracking an airborne object ... of wind *b)* *same as* CHAFF (*n.* 4) **5.** *same* ... WINDOW **6.** any portion of the frequency spectr... earth's atmosphere through which light, heat, o... waves can penetrate to the earth's surface due to th... absorption or dissipation of electromagnetic energy in ... particular portion —*vt.* to provide with a window ... windows —**win′dow·less** *adj.*
window box 1. a long, narrow box on or outside a window ledge, for growing plants **2.** any of the grooves along the sides of a window frame for containing the weights that counterbalance the sash
window dressing 1. the arrangement or display of goods and trimmings in a store window to attract customers **2.** statements, actions, or display designed to make something seem better than it really is —**win′dow-dress′** *vt.* —**window dresser**
window envelope an envelope with a transparent panel, through which the address on the enclosure can be seen
win·dow·pane (-pān′) *n.* a pane of glass in a window
window seat 1. a seat built in beneath a window or windows and usually containing storage space **2.** a seat near a window, as in an airplane
☆**window shade** a shade for a window, esp. one consisting of a piece of stiffened cloth or heavy paper on a spring roller, with a pull to lower and raise it
win·dow-shop (-shäp′) *vi.* **-shopped′, -shop′ping** to look at displays of goods in store windows without entering the stores to buy —**win′dow-shop′per** *n.*
win·dow·sill (-sil′) *n.* the sill of a window
wind·pipe (wind′pīp′) *n. same as* TRACHEA (sense 1)
wind-pol·li·nat·ed (-päl′ə nāt′id) *adj. Bot.* fertilized by pollen carried by the wind
wind·proof (-proof′) *adj.* impervious to or unaffected by the wind *[a windproof coat, a windproof lighter]*
Wind River 1. [from the severe winds near its head] river in WC Wyo., flowing southeast into the Bighorn: c.110 mi. **2.** range of the Rocky Mountains, in WC Wyo.: highest peak, 13,787 ft.: in full **Wind River Range**
wind rose a diagram that shows for a particular place the frequency and intensity of wind from different directions
wind·row (wind′rō′) *n.* **1.** a row of hay raked together to dry before being made into heaps or cocks **2.** any similar row, as of grain **3.** a row of dry leaves, dust, etc. that has been swept together by the wind —*vt.* to rake, sweep, etc. into a windrow or windrows
wind scale a scale used in meteorology to designate relative wind intensities, as the Beaufort scale
wind shake a condition of timber in which there is separation of the concentric rings, supposedly due to strain from strong winds during growth —**wind′-shak′en** *adj.*
☆**wind·shield** (-shēld′) *n.* in automobiles, trucks, speedboats, motorcycles, etc., a transparent screen, as of glass, in front, that protects the riders from wind, etc.: also, chiefly Brit., **wind′screen′**
wind·sock (-säk′) *n.* a long, cone-shaped cloth bag, open at both ends and attached to the top of a mast, as at an airfield to show wind direction: also called **wind sleeve**
Wind·sor¹ (win′zər) **1.** ruling family of Great Britain since 1917, when the name was officially changed from *Saxe-Coburg Gotha* **2.** Duke of, (*Edward Albert Christian George Andrew Patrick David*) 1894– ; king of England, as Edward VIII (1936): abdicated: son of GEORGE V
Wind·sor² (win′zər) **1.** city in Berkshire, SE England, on the Thames, just west of London: site of Windsor Castle: pop. 28,000: official name **New Windsor 2.** port in SE Ontario, Canada, opposite Detroit: pop. 193,000

Windsor C... **Windsor Castle** ... time of William ... **Windsor chair** ... chair, esp. ... England and ... legs, a back ... a saddle seat ... **Windsor kn...** knot in ... resulting ... **Windsor** ... on the bl... **wind·sto...** with a ... rain, ... **wind-...** air, ... **win...** la...

and open them again quickly 2. *a)* to close one eyelid and open it again quickly, as a signal, etc. *b)* to be closed and opened in this way: said of the eye 3. to shine intermittently; twinkle —*vt.* 1. to make (the eyes or an eye) wink 2. to move, remove, etc. by winking (usually with *back* or *away)* [*to* wink *back tears]* 3. to signal or express by winking —*n.* 1. the act of winking 2. *a)* the time occupied by this; an instant *b)* a tiny interval (*of* sleep) [*not get a* wink *of sleep]:* cf. FORTY WINKS 3. a signal, hint, etc. given by winking 4. a twinkle or twinkling —**wink at** to pretend not to see, as in connivance

SYN.—**wink** usually implies a deliberate movement in the quick closing and opening of one or both eyelids one or more times [*he* winked *at her knowingly];* **blink** implies a rapid series of such movements, usually performed involuntarily and with the eyes half-shut [*to* blink *in the harsh sunlight]*

wink·er (wiŋ'kər) *n.* 1. a person or thing that winks 2. a blinder for a horse 3. [Colloq.] an eyelash or eye

win·kle[1] (wiŋ'k'l) *n.* 1. *short for* PERIWINKLE[2] 2. any of numerous large whelks (as genus *Busycon*) that are very destructive to oysters and clams

win·kle[2] (wiŋ'k'l) *vt.* -**kled**, -**kling** [< ?] [Colloq.] to pry or rout from cover, secrecy, etc. (with *out, out of,* etc.)

win·kle-pick·er (-pik'ər) *n.* [reason for name unc.] [Slang] a shoe or boot with a narrow, sharply pointed toe

Win·ne·ba·go (win'ə bā'gō) *n.* [< Fr. < Algonquian, lit., muddy water people: cf. WINNIPEG] 1. *pl.* -**gos,** -**goes,** -**go** any member of a tribe of N. American Indians living in E Wisconsin and now also in Nebraska 2. their Siouan language

Winnebago, Lake lake in E Wis.: 215 sq. mi.

win·ner (win'ər) *n.* one that wins; esp., [Colloq.] one that seems destined to win or be successful

☆**win·ner's circle** (win'ərz) an area, usually circular, at a race track where the winning horse and its jockey, owner, etc. are brought for recognition

win·ning (-iŋ) *adj.* 1. that wins; victorious 2. attractive; charming —*n.* 1. the action of a person that wins; victory 2. [*pl.*] something won, esp. money 3. a shaft, bed, etc. in a coal mine, opened for mining —**win'ning·ly** *adv.*

winning gallery *Court Tennis* an opening in the side wall of the court to the left of the server and on the hazard side of the net: a ball played into it wins a point

winning opening *Court Tennis* any of three openings, the dedans, grille, or winning gallery: a ball played into any of these wins a point

winning post a post marking the end of a racecourse

Win·ni·peg (win'ə peg') [< Fr. < Algonquian *winipig,* filthy water] 1. capital of Manitoba, Canada, on the Red River: pop. 257,000 (met. area 509,000) 2. river in S Canada, flowing from the Lake of the Woods into Lake Winnipeg: (with its principal headstream) 475 mi. 3. **Lake,** large lake in SC Manitoba: 9,465 sq. mi.

Win·ni·pe·go·sis (win'i pə gō'sis), **Lake** [< Algonquian, lit., little Winnipeg] lake in SW Manitoba, Canada, west of Lake Winnipeg: 2,103 sq. mi.

Win·ni·pe·sau·kee (win'ə pə sô'kē) [< Algonquian tribal name < ?] lake in EC N.H.: 25 mi. long, 12 mi. wide: former sp. **Win'ne·pe·sau'kee**

win·now (win'ō) *vt.* [ME. *winewen* < OE. *windwian,* to winnow < *wind,* WIND[2]] 1. *a)* to blow the chaff from (grain) by wind or a forced current of air *b)* to blow off (chaff) in this manner 2. to blow away; scatter 3. to analyze or examine carefully in order to separate the various elements; sift 4. *a)* to separate out or eliminate (the poor or useless parts) *b)* to sort out or extract (the good or useful parts) 5. [Now Rare] to fan with or as with the wings —*vi.* to winnow grain —*n.* 1. the act of winnowing 2. an apparatus for winnowing —**win'now·er** *n.*

☆**win·o** (wī'nō) *n., pl.* -**os** [WIN(E) + -o] [Slang] a person who habitually becomes drunk on wine; esp., an alcoholic derelict who drinks only cheap wine

Wins·low (winz'lō), **Edward** 1595-1655; Eng. colonist in America; a founder & governor of Plymouth Colony

win·some (win'səm) *adj.* [ME. *winsum* < OE. *wynsum,* pleasant, delightful < *wynn,* delight, joy (for base see WIN) + -*sum,* -SOME[1]] attractive in a sweet, engaging way; charming —**win'some·ly** *adv.* —**win'some·ness** *n.*

Win·ston-Sa·lem (win'stən sā'ləm) [a merging of two towns, after Major Joseph *Winston* (1746-1815) & SALEM] city in NC N.C.: pop. 133,000: see GREENSBORO

win·ter (win'tər) *n.* [ME. < OE., akin to ON. *vetr,* Goth. *wintrus,* prob. < IE. base *wed-,* to make wet, whence WATER, WET] 1. *a)* the coldest season of the year, regarded in the North Temperate Zone as including the months of December, January, and February: in the astronomical year, that period between the winter solstice and the vernal equinox *b)* the typically cold weather of this season 2. a year as reckoned by this season [*a man of eighty* winters] 3. any period or condition regarded, like winter, as a time of decline, dreariness, adversity, etc. —*adj.* 1. of or characteristic of the winter 2. done, used, played, etc. during the winter [winter *sports]* 3. that will keep during the winter [winter *apples]* 4. planted in the fall to be harvested in the spring [winter *wheat]* —*vi.* 1. to

pass the winter 2. to be supplied with food and shelter in the winter —*vt.* to keep or maintain during the winter —**win'ter·er** *n.*

winter aconite a small plant (*Eranthis hyemalis*) of the buttercup family, bearing yellow flowers early in spring

win·ter·ber·ry (-ber'ē) *n., pl.* -**ries** ☆any of several tall hollies of E N. America, as the inkberry and the black alder, with thin, evergreen or deciduous leaves and brilliant red, black, purple, or yellow berries that persist over winter

win·ter·bourne (-bôrn', -boorn') *n.* [OE. *winter burna:* see WINTER & BURN[2]] a stream that flows only or principally in winter

win·ter·feed (-fēd') *vt.* -**fed'**, -**feed'ing** to feed (animals, esp. livestock) during the winter

☆**winter flounder** a common, brownish-gray flatfish (*Pseudopleuronectes americanus*) of the Atlantic coast of N. America, valued as a food fish, esp. in winter

win·ter·green (-grēn') *n.* [after G. *wintergrün,* Du. *wintergroen:* so named because evergreen] ☆1. *a)* any of several gaultherias; esp., a creeping subshrub (*Gaultheria procumbens*) having small, rounded evergreen leaves, bell-shaped white flowers, and red, edible berries *b)* an aromatic compound (**oil of wintergreen**), made from the leaves of this plant or the bark of the sweet birch (*Betula lenta*), or synthetically from salicylic acid: sometimes used in medicine or as a flavoring *c)* the flavor or anything flavored with it 2. any of a number of similar plants; esp., *same as:* *a)* SHINLEAF *b)* PIPSISSEWA 3. fringed polygala (*Polygala paucifolia*), with large rose-lavender flowers

☆**win·ter·ize** (-īz') *vt.* -**ized'**, -**iz'ing** to put into condition for or equip for winter [*to* winterize *an automobile with antifreeze]* —**win'ter·i·za'tion** *n.*

☆**win·ter·kill** (-kil') *vt., vi.* to kill or die by exposure to winter cold or excessive snow or ice —*n.* the process or an instance of winterkilling

win·ter·ly (-lē) *adj. same as* WINTRY

winter melon *same as* CASABA

winter solstice the time in the Northern Hemisphere when the sun is farthest south of the equator; December 21 or 22

☆**winter squash** any of several squashes (*Cucurbita moschata* and *Cucurbita maxima*), as the acorn, butternut, Hubbard, etc., with a thick, hard rind and good keeping qualities

Win·ter·thur (vin'tər toor) city in N Switzerland, near Zürich: pop. 88,000

win·ter·time (win'tər tīm') *n.* the season of winter: also [Archaic or Poet.] **win'ter·tide'**

Win·throp (win'thrəp), **John** 1. 1588-1649; Eng. colonist in America; 1st governor of Massachusetts Bay colony 2. 1606-76; governor of Connecticut colony (1657, 1659-76): son of *prec.*

win·try (win'trē) *adj.* -**tri·er,** -**tri·est** of or like winter; cold, bleak, etc. [*a* wintry *day, a* wintry *stare]:* also **win'ter·y** (-tər ē, -trē) —**win'tri·ly** (-trə lē) *adv.* —**win'tri·ness** (-trē nis) *n.*

win·y (wī'nē) *adj.* **win'i·er, win'i·est** like wine in taste, smell, color, etc.

winze (winz) *n.* [prob. < *winds,* pl. of *wind,* winder, windlass] an inclined shaft from one level to another in a mine

wipe (wīp) *vt.* **wiped, wip'ing** [ME. *wipen* < OE. *wīpian,* akin to OHG. *wīfan,* to wind around < IE. base *weip-,* *weib-,* to turn, twist, turning motion, whence L. *vibrare,* to vibrate] 1. *a)* to rub or pass over with a cloth, mop, etc., as for cleaning or drying *b)* to clean or dry in this manner [wipe *the dishes]* 2. to rub or pass (a cloth, the hand, etc.) over something 3. to apply by wiping [wipe *oil over the surface]* 4. to remove by or as by wiping (with *away, off, up, out)* 5. to form (a joint in lead pipe) by applying liquid solder and rubbing with a leather pad, greased cloth, etc. —*n.* 1. an act or instance of wiping 2. [Old Slang] *a)* a blow; swipe *b)* a gibe; jeer —**wipe out** 1. to remove; erase 2. to kill off 3. to destroy or demolish ☆4. [Slang] to be capsized by a wave in surfing

wipe·out (-out') *n.* [Slang] ☆1. the act of being capsized by a wave in surfing 2. any fall, failure, debacle, etc.

wip·er (wī'pər) *n.* 1. a person or thing that wipes 2. something used for wiping, as a towel or rag 3. a moving electrical contact, as in a rheostat 4. a projecting piece on a rotating or rocking part, which raises and lowers or trips another, usually reciprocating, part; cam; eccentric

wire (wīr) *n.* [ME. < OE. *wir,* akin to LowG. *wir* < IE. *weir-* base *wei-,* to bend, turn, whence Gr. *iris,* rainbow, L. *vitis,* a vine: cf. WITHE] 1. metal that has been drawn into a very long, thin thread or rod, usually circular in cross section 2. a length of this, used for various purposes, such as conducting electric current, stringing musical instruments, etc. 3. wire netting or other wirework 4. anything made of wire or wirework, as a telephone cable, barbed wire fence, a snare, etc. 5. *a)* telegraph [*reply by* wire] *b)* a telegram ☆6. *Horse Racing* a wire above the finish line of a race —*adj.* made of wire or wirework —*vt.* **wired, wir'ing** 1. to furnish, connect, bind, attach, string, etc. with a wire or wires 2. to supply with a system of wires for electric current 3. to telegraph 4. [Archaic] to snare with a wire or wires —*vi.* to telegraph —**down to the wire** to the very end or the very last

moments —☆**get (in) under the wire** to manage to enter or achieve barely on time —☆**pull wires** [from the wires used to operate puppets] to use private influence to achieve a purpose —**wire′like′** *adj.*

wire cloth a type of fine wire netting for strainers, etc.

wired radio a system for transmitting modulated electromagnetic waves of radio frequency over wires or cables: also [Brit.] **wired wireless**

wire·draw (-drô′) *vt.* **-drew′, -drawn′, -draw′ing** [back-formation < *wire-drawer* < WIRE + DRAWER] **1.** to draw (metal) into wire **2.** to draw out; spin out; protract; prolong **3.** to reduce to the finest subtleties; overrefine or strain (a point in argument)

wire gauge an instrument for measuring the diameter of wire, thickness of sheet metal, etc.: it usually consists of a disk with notches of graduated sizes along its edge

wire gauze very fine, gauzelike wire netting

☆**wire glass** sheet glass containing wire netting

☆**wire grass** any of several grasses with wiry stems; esp. *a)* a European meadow grass (*Poa compressa*), naturalized in Canada and the U.S. *b)* any of several coarse grasses (genus *Aristida*) *c)* a cultivated grass (*Eleusine indica*)

wire·hair (-her′) *n.* a fox terrier with a wiry coat: also **wire-haired terrier**

wire-haired (-herd′) *adj.* having coarse, or wiry, hair

wire·less (-lis) *adj.* **1.** without wire or wires; specif., operating with electromagnetic waves and not with conducting wire **2.** [Chiefly Brit.] *same as* RADIO —*n.* **1.** *same as: a)* WIRELESS TELEGRAPHY *b)* WIRELESS TELEPHONY *c)* [Chiefly Brit.] RADIO **2.** a message sent by wireless —*vt., vi.* to communicate (with) by wireless

wireless telegraphy (or **telegraph**) telegraphy by radio-transmitted signals

wireless telephone a telephone operating by radio-transmitted signals —**wireless telephony**

wire·man (-mən) *n., pl.* **-men** (-mən) a person who installs and repairs electrical wiring, cables, etc.

wire netting netting of woven wire, used in various sizes for fences, guards, etc.

Wire·pho·to (-fōt′ō) *a trademark for:* **1.** a system of reproducing photographs at a distance by means of electric impulses transmitted by wire **2.** a photograph so produced

☆**wire·pull·er** (-pool′ər) *n.* a person who uses private or secret influence to gain his ends —**wire′pull′ing** *n.*

wir·er (wīr′ər) *n.* a person who wires

wire recorder a machine for recording sound electromagnetically on a thin wire on a spool: replaced by the tape recorder

wire rope rope made of twisted wires

wire service a business organization that sends news stories, features, etc. by direct telegraph to subscribing or member newspapers and radio and television stations

wire-stitched (-sticht′) *adj.* stitched with wire, as some book bindings

☆**wire·tap** (-tap′) *vi., vt.* **-tapped′, -tap′ping** to tap (a telephone wire, etc.) to get information secretly or underhandedly —*n.* **1.** the act or an instance of wiretapping **2.** a device used in wiretapping —*adj.* of or relating to wiretapping —**wire′tap′per** *n.*

wire·work (-wurk′) *n.* netting, mesh, etc. made of wire

wire·works (-wurks′) *n.pl.* [*often with sing. v.*] a factory where wire or wire articles are made

wire·worm (-wurm′) *n.* **1.** any of the slender, hard-bodied, wormlike larvae of click beetles that often live underground and attack the roots of crops **2.** a millepede (genus *Julus*) **3.** a roundworm (*Haemonchus contortus*) parasitic in the stomach and small intestine of cattle and sheep

wire-wove (-wōv′) *adj.* **1.** designating or of a very fine grade of paper with a smooth surface, made in a frame of wire gauze **2.** made of woven wire

wir·ing (wīr′iŋ) *n.* **1.** the action of a person or thing that wires **2.** a system of wires, as to provide a house with electricity —*adj.* **1.** that wires **2.** used in wiring

wir·ra (wir′ə) *interj.* [short for *o wirra*, altered < IrGael. *a Muire*, O Mary, a cry to the Virgin] [Irish] an exclamation of sorrow, lament, etc.

wir·y (wir′ē) *adj.* **wir′i·er, wir′i·est 1.** of wire **2.** like wire in shape and substance; stiff [*wiry hair*] **3.** lean, sinewy, and strong: said of persons and animals **4.** produced by or as if by a vibrating wire [*a wiry sound*] —**wir′i·ness** *n.*

wis (wis) *vt.* [< IWIS, erroneously understood as "I know"] [Archaic] to suppose; imagine; deem

Wis·con·sin (wis kän′s'n) [< Fr. *Ouisconsin*, name of the river < Algonquian < ?] **1.** Middle Western State of the NC U.S.: admitted, 1848; 56,154 sq. mi.; pop. 4,418,000; cap. Madison: abbrev. **Wis., Wisc., WI 2.** river in Wis., flowing into the Mississippi: 430 mi. —**Wis·con′sin·ite′** (-īt′) *n.*

wis·dom (wiz′dəm) *n.* [ME. < OE. < *wis*, WISE[1] + *-dom*, -DOM] **1.** the quality of being wise; power of judging rightly and following the soundest course of action, based on knowledge, experience, understanding, etc.; good judgment; sagacity **2.** learning; knowledge; erudition [*the wisdom of the ages*] **3.** wise discourse or teaching **4.** a wise plan or course of action —*SYN.* see INFORMATION

Wisdom of Jesus, Son of Si·rach (sī′rak) *same as* ECCLESIASTICUS

Wisdom of Solomon one of the books of the Apocrypha, included as canonical (and called **Wisdom**) in the Douay Bible: abbrev. **Wisd.**

wisdom tooth [so called (after Gr. *sōphronistēres*) from their late appearance] the back tooth on each side of each jaw in human beings, the third molar, appearing usually between the ages of 17 and 25 —**cut one's wisdom teeth** to arrive at the age of discretion

wise[1] (wīz) *adj.* **wis′er, wis′est** [ME. *wis* < OE., akin to *witan*, to know < PGmc. **wisa-*, wise < IE. base **weid-*, to see, know, whence Sans. *vēdas*, knowledge, Gr. *idris*, knowing, L. *videre*, to see] **1.** having or showing good judgment; sagacious; prudent; discreet **2.** prompted by wisdom; judicious; sound [*a wise* saying, *wise* action] **3.** having information; informed [*none the wiser*] **4.** learned; erudite **5.** shrewd; crafty; cunning **6.** [Obs. or Dial.] having knowledge of black magic, etc. ☆**7.** [Slang] *a)* annoyingly self-assured, knowing, conceited, etc. *b)* impudent; fresh —☆**be (or get) wise to** [Slang] to be (or become) aware of; have (or attain) a proper understanding of —☆**get wise** [Slang] **1.** to become aware of the true facts or circumstances **2.** to become impudent —☆**put wise (to)** [Slang] to give (someone) information, an explanation, etc. (about); enlighten (concerning) —☆**wise up** [Slang] to make or become informed —**wise′ly** *adv.*

SYN.—**wise** implies the ability to judge and deal with persons, situations, etc. rightly, based on a broad range of knowledge, experience, and understanding [*a wise* parent]; **sage** suggests the venerable wisdom of age, experience, and philosophical reflection [*sage* counsel]; **sapient**, a literary term now sometimes used ironically, implies sageness or learnedness [*a sapient* assembly]; **judicious** implies the ability to make wise decisions, based on the possession and use of sound judgment [*a judicious* approach to a problem]; **prudent**, as compared here, suggests the wisdom of one who is able to discern the most suitable or politic course of action in practical matters [*a prudent* policy] —*ANT.* foolish, stupid

wise[2] (wīz) *n.* [ME. < OE., akin to G. *weise* (orig. sense prob. "appearance"): for IE. base see prec.] way; manner: used chiefly in such phrases as **in no wise, in this wise,** etc.

wise[3] (wīz) *vt.* **wised, wis′ing** [ME. *wisen* < OE. *wisian*, akin to ON. *visa*, Goth (*fulla-*)*weisjan*, OHG. *wisen* < base of WISE[1]] [Scot.] **1.** to direct or guide **2.** to convey or conduct

-wise (wīz) [< WISE[2]] *an adv.-forming suffix meaning:* **1.** in a (specified) direction, position, or manner [*sidewise, anywise*]: in this sense, equivalent to *-ways* **2.** in a manner characteristic of [*clockwise*] **3.** with regard to; in connection with: in this sense a revival of an earlier usage [*weatherwise, budgetwise*]

Wise (wīz), **Stephen Samuel** 1874–1949; U.S. rabbi & Jewish leader, born in Hungary

wise·a·cre (wīz′ā′kər) *n.* [altered by folk etymology < MDu. *wijssegger*, altered (after *wijs,* WISE[1] + *zeggen,* to say) < OHG. *wizzago*, a prophet < Gmc. **witag-,* knowing: for IE. base see WISE[1]] a person who acts as though he were much wiser than he really is

☆**wise·crack** (-krak′) *n.* [Slang] a flippant or facetious remark, often a gibe or retort —*vi.* [Slang] to make a wisecrack or wisecracks —*vt.* [Slang] to say as a wisecrack —*SYN.* see JOKE —**wise′crack′er** *n.*

☆**wise guy** [Slang] a person who is brashly and annoyingly conceited, knowing, etc.; smart aleck

☆**wis·en·heim·er** (wī′z'n hīm′ər) *n.* [WIS(E)[1] + *-enheimer*, as in G. family names, e.g., *Oppenheimer, Altenheimer*] [Slang] a wiseacre or wise guy

wi·sent (vē′zənt) *n.* [G. < OHG. *wisunt,* BISON] the European bison (*Bison bonasus*), now nearly extinct

wish (wish) *vt.* [ME. *wisshen* < OE. *wyscan,* akin to G. *wüschen* < IE. base **wen-,* to strive (for), desire, whence WIN, L. *Venus*] **1.** to have a longing for; want; desire; crave **2.** to have or express a desire concerning [*to wish* the day were over] **3.** to have or express a desire concerning the fortune, circumstances, etc. of [*to wish* someone good luck] **4.** to give a (specified) greeting to; bid [*to wish* a person good morning] **5.** to request or order [*to wish* a person to come] **6.** to impose (something burdensome or unpleasant) *on* someone —*vi.* **1.** to have a desire; long; yearn **2.** to make a wish —*n.* **1.** the act of wishing; felt or expressed desire for something **2.** something wished for [*to get one's wish*] **3.** a polite request with some of the force of an order **4.** [*pl.*] expressed desire for a person's health, good fortune, etc. [*to offer one's best wishes*] —*SYN.* see DESIRE —**wish′er** *n.*

wish·bone (-bōn′) *n.* the forked bone in front of the breastbone of most birds; furcula: so called from the custom whereby two persons make wishes and snap a dried wishbone in two, the longer fragment being a token of fulfillment of the holder's wish

wish·ful (-fəl) *adj.* having or showing a wish; desirous; longing —**wish′ful·ly** *adv.* —**wish′ful·ness** *n.*

wish fulfillment 1. the realization of a desire or wish **2.** *Psychoanalysis* the symbolic attainment, in the form of dreams, fantasies, etc., of an often unconscious wish or impulse, even if opposed by the conscious personality

wishful thinking thinking in which one consciously or unconsciously interprets facts in terms of what he would like to believe —**wishful thinker**

wish·y-wash·y (wish′ē wôsh′ē, -wäsh′ē) *adj.* [redupl. of WASHY] [Colloq.] **1.** watery; insipid; thin **2.** *a)* weak; feeble *b)* vacillating; indecisive —**wish′y-wash′i·ly** *adv.*

Wis·la (vē′slä) *Pol. name of the* VISTULA

wisp (wisp) *n.* [ME., prob. < Scand., as in Sw. *visp,* a

bundle of rushes or twigs, akin to ON. *visk:* see WHISK]
1. a small bundle or bunch, as of straw **2.** a thin, slight, or filmy piece, strand, etc. *[a wisp of smoke]* **3.** something delicate, frail, etc. *[a wisp of a girl]* **4.** same as WILL-O'-THE-WISP —*vt.* to roll into a wisp —**wisp′y, wisp′l·er, wisp′l·est** *adj.*

wist (wist) *pt. & pp.* of WIT²

Wis·ter (wis′tər), **Owen** 1860–1938; U.S. novelist

☆**wis·te·ri·a** (wis tir′ē ə) *n.* [ModL., after Casper *Wistar* (1761–1818), U.S. anatomist] any of a genus (*Wisteria*) of twining woody vines or shrubs of the legume family, with fruits that are pods and showy clusters of bluish, white, pink, or purplish flowers: native to the E U.S. and E Asia: also **wis·tar′i·a** (-ter′-)

wist·ful (wist′fəl) *adj.* [altered (after WISHFUL) < earlier *wistly,* attentive] showing or expressing vague yearnings; longing pensively —**wist′ful·ly** *adv.* —**wist′ful·ness** *n.*

wit¹ (wit) *n.* [ME. < OE., akin to G. *witz:* for IE. base see WISE¹] **1.** orig., the mind **2.** [*pl.*] *a)* powers of thinking and reasoning; intellectual and perceptive powers *b)* mental faculties with respect to their state of balance, esp. in their normal condition of sanity **3.** alert, practical intelligence; good sense **4.** *a)* the ability to make lively, clever remarks in a sharp, amusing way *b)* the ability to perceive incongruous relationships and express them in a surprising or epigrammatic manner *c)* a person characterized by wit *d)* writing or speech expressing wit; esp., any clever disparagement or raillery **5.** [Archaic] intellect; reason —**at one's wits' end** at a point where one's mental resources are exhausted; at a loss as to what to do —**keep (or have) one's wits about one** to remain mentally alert; function with undiminished acumen, as in an emergency —**live by one's wits** to live by trickery or craftiness

SYN.—**wit** refers to the ability to perceive the incongruous and to express it in quick, sharp, spontaneous, often sarcastic remarks that delight or entertain; **humor** is applied to the ability to perceive and express that which is comical, ludicrous, or ridiculous, but connotes kindliness, geniality, sometimes even pathos, in the expression and a reaction of sympathetic amusement from the audience; **irony** refers to the humor implicit in the contradiction between literal expression and intended meaning or in the discrepancy between appearance and reality in life; **satire** applies to the use, especially in literature, of ridicule, sarcasm, irony, etc. in exposing and attacking vices or follies; **repartee** refers to the ability to reply or retort with quick, skillful wit or humor

wit² (wit) *vt., vi.* **wist, wit′ting** [ME. *witen* < OE. *witan,* to know: see WISE¹] [Archaic] to know or learn *Wit* is conjugated in the present indicative: (I) *wot,* (thou) *wost* or *wot(t)est,* (he, she, it) *wot* or *wot(t)eth,* (we, ye, they) *wite* or *witen* —**to wit** that is to say; namely

wit·an (wit′n) *n.pl.* [OE., pl. of *wita,* one who knows, wise man, councilor < *witan,* to know: see WISE¹] the members of the witenagemot

witch (wich) *n.* [ME. *wicche* < OE. *wicce,* fem. of *wicca,* sorcerer, akin to MDu. *wicken,* to use magic < IE. base *weik-,* to separate (hence set aside for religious worship), whence Goth. *weihs,* holy, OE. *wig,* idol] **1.** *a)* a woman supposedly having supernatural power by a compact with the devil or evil spirits; sorceress *b)* [Obs.] a man with such power: cf. WARLOCK **2.** an ugly and ill-tempered old woman; hag; crone ☆**3.** *short for* WATER WITCH (sense 1) **4.** [Colloq.] a bewitching or fascinating woman or girl —*vt.* **1.** to put a magic spell on; bewitch **2.** to charm; fascinate —*vi.* ☆*same as* DOWSE² —**witch′like′** *adj.*

witch·craft (-kraft′, -kräft′) *n.* [ME. *wicchecrafte* < OE. *wiccecræft*] **1.** *a)* the power or practices of witches; black magic; sorcery *b)* an instance of this **2.** bewitching attraction or charm —*SYN.* see MAGIC

witch doctor among certain tribes, esp. in Africa, a person who practices a type of primitive medicine involving the use of magic, witchcraft, etc.

witch elm (wich′ elm′) *var.* of WYCH-ELM

witch·er·y (wich′ər ē) *n., pl.* **-er·ies 1.** witchcraft; sorcery **2.** bewitching charm; fascination

witch·es'-broom (wich′iz brōōm′) *n.* an abnormal growth of closely bunched, slender twigs at the ends of branches of various woody plants, caused by fungi, viruses, etc.

witches' Sabbath a midnight meeting of witches, sorcerers, and demons, supposed in medieval times to have been held annually as a demonic orgy

☆**witch grass** [altered < QUITCH (GRASS)] a common, weedy N. American grass (*Panicum capillare*) having hairy foliage and a large, dome-shaped panicle of small spikelets

witch hazel [altered (after WITCH) < *wyche hazel* < ME. *wyche* < OE. *wice,* applied to trees with pliant branches, akin to ON. *veikr,* WEAK] **1.** any of a genus (*Hamamelis*) of small, N. American and Asiatic trees and shrubs of the witch hazel family; esp., a tall shrub (*Hamamelis virginiana*) of E N. America, having yellow, wavy-petaled flowers in late autumn and woody fruit **2.** a lotion consisting of an alcoholic solution of an extract from the leaves and bark of this shrub, used on bruises, inflammations, etc. **3.** designating a family (Hamamelidaceae) of trees and shrubs of temperate regions, having flowers in heads or spikes, including the witch hazels, the liquidambars, etc.

witch hunt [so named in allusion to persecutions of persons alleged to be witches] an investigation usually conducted with much publicity, supposedly to uncover subversive political activity, disloyalty, etc., but really to harass and weaken political opposition —**witch hunter**

witch·ing (wich′in) *n.* the action or practice of a person who witches; witchcraft —*adj.* that witches; bewitching

witch moth any of several noctuid moths (genus *Erebus*) of the S U.S., S. America, and the West Indies

wite (wit) *n., vt.* **wit′ed, wit′ing** [ME. *witen* < OE. *witan,* akin to *witan,* to know: see WISE¹] [Scot.] blame; censure

wit·e·na·ge·mot, wit·e·na·ge·mote (wit′'n ə gə mōt′) *n.* [OE. *witena-gemot* < *witena,* gen. pl. of *wita* (see WITAN) + (*ge*)*mot,* a meeting: lit., assembly of the wise men] the king's council of the Anglo-Saxons

with (with, with) *prep.* [ME. < OE., orig., against, in opposition to, contr. < or akin to *wither,* against < IE. *witero-* (< base *wi-,* asunder, separate + compar. suffix), whence G. *wider,* against] **1.** in opposition to; against *[to argue with* a friend] **2.** *a)* alongside of; near to *b)* in the company of *c)* into; among *[mix blue with yellow]* **3.** as an associate, or companion, of *[to play golf with* one's son] **4.** *a)* as a member of *[to play with* a string quartet] *b)* working for, serving under, etc. *[having been with* the firm for 20 years] **5.** in regard or relation to; concerning *[pleased with* her gift] **6.** in the same terms as; compared to; contrasted to *[having equal standing with* the others] **7.** as well, completely, etc. as *[able to run with* the best] **8.** of the same opinions, belief, etc. as *[I'm with* you there] **9.** in support of; on the side of *[voting with* the Tories] **10.** in the opinion or estimation of *[her decision is all right with* him] **11.** as the result of; because of *[faint with* hunger] **12.** *a)* by means of; using *[to stir with* a spoon, to play *with* a toy] *b)* by the use, presence, etc. of; by *[filled with* air] **13.** *a)* accompanied by, attended by, circumstanced by, etc. *[enter with* confidence] *b)* having received *[with* your permission, he'll go] **14.** having as a possession, attribute, accouterment, etc.; bearing, wearing, or owning *[the man with* brown hair] **15.** showing or exhibiting *[to play with* skill] **16.** in the keeping, care, etc. of *[children were left with* the baby sitter] **17.** *a)* added to; and *[those, with* the ones we have, will be enough] *b)* including *[with* the stepchildren, the family numbers ten] **18.** in spite of; notwithstanding *[with* all his boasting, he is a coward] **19.** *a)* at the same time as *[to rise with* the chickens] *b)* in the same direction as *[to travel with* the sun] *c)* in the same degree as; in proportion to *[wages that vary with* skill] *d)* in the course of *[grief that lessened with* time] **20.** to; onto *[to join one end with* the other] **21.** from *[to part with* one's gains] **22.** following upon; after *[with* that remark, he left] —**with that** after, or as a consequence of, that

with- (with, with) [ME. < OE. < *with:* see prec.] *a combining form meaning:* **1.** away, back *[withdraw]* **2.** against, from *[withhold]*

with·al (with ôl′, with-) *adv.* [ME. *with alle:* see WITH & ALL] **1.** in addition; besides **2.** despite that; notwithstanding **3.** [Archaic] with that; therewith —*prep.* [Archaic] with: used at the end of a clause or sentence

with·draw (-drô′) *vt.* **-drew′, -drawn′, -draw′ing** [ME. *withdrawen:* see WITH- & DRAW] **1.** *a)* to take back or draw back; remove *b)* to remove from use, consideration, etc. **2.** to retract or recall (a statement, etc.) —*vi.* **1.** to move back; go away; retire; retreat **2.** to remove oneself (*from* an organization, activity, society, etc.) **3.** *Psychiatry* to retreat from reality, as in schizophrenia **4.** in parliamentary procedure, to retract a motion, statement, etc. —*SYN.* see GO¹ —**with·draw′er** *n.*

with·draw·al (-drô′əl) *n.* **1.** a withdrawing, as of money from the bank, a person or thing from its place or position, etc.: also [Rare] **with·draw′ment** (-mənt) **2.** the act or process of giving up the use of a narcotic drug to which one has become addicted, typically accompanied by distressing physiological and mental effects (**withdrawal symptoms**)

withdrawing room *archaic var.* of DRAWING ROOM

with·drawn (-drôn′) *pp.* of WITHDRAW —*adj.* withdrawing within oneself; shy, reserved, introverted, etc.

withe (with, with, with) *n.* [ME. *wythe* < OE. *withthe,* willow, twig of willow < IE. base *wei-,* to bend, twist, whence WIRE, L. *vitis,* a vine] a tough, flexible twig of willow, osier, etc., used for binding things; withy —*vt.* **withed, with′ing** to bind with withes

with·er (with′ər) *vi.* [ME. *widren,* var. of *wederen,* lit., to weather, expose to the weather < *weder,* WEATHER, *v.*] **1.** to dry up, as from great heat; shrivel; wilt: said esp. of plants **2.** to lose vigor or freshness; become wasted or decayed **3.** to weaken; languish *[affection that soon withered]* —*vt.* **1.** to cause to wither **2.** to cause to quail or feel abashed, as by a scornful glance —**with′er·ing·ly** *adv.*

SYN.—**wither** implies a drying up, decaying, wilting, fading, etc., as from a loss of natural juices *[apples withering on the bough]*; **shrivel** implies a shrinking, wrinkling, or curling, as from exposure to intense heat *[blossoms shriveling in the hot sun]*; **wizen,** now usually in the past participle, implies a shrinking and wrinkling,

as from advanced age, malnourishment, etc. *[the wizened face of the old beggar]*

with·er·ite (wi*th*'ə rīt') *n.* [G. *witherit*, after its discoverer, W. *Withering* (1741–99), Eng. scientist] native barium carbonate, BaCO₃, occurring in white, yellowish, or grayish orthorhombic crystals, and often in masses

☆**withe rod** either of two N. American viburnums (*Viburnum cassinoides* or *Viburnum nudum*) with osierlike shoots and clusters of white flowers in June

with·ers (wi*th*'ərz) *n.pl.* [< ME. *wither*, resistance (prob. in sense "that which the horse opposes to his load") < OE. *withre*, resistance < *wither*, against: see WITH] the highest part of the back of a horse or similar animal, located between the shoulder blades

with·er·shins (wi*th*'ər shinz') *adv.* [< MLowG. *weddersinnes* < MHG. *widdersinnes* < *wider*, against (akin to WITH) + *sinnes*, gen. of *sin*, way, direction] in a direction contrary to the apparent course of the sun

With·er·spoon (wi*th*'ər spo͞on'), **John** 1723–94; Am. clergyman & educator, born in Scotland; signer of the Declaration of Independence

with·hold (with hōld', with-) *vt.* **-held', -hold'ing** [ME. *withholden:* see WITH- & HOLD¹, *v.*] **1.** *a)* to hold back; keep back; restrain ☆*b)* to take out or deduct (taxes, etc.) from wages or salary **2.** to refrain from granting, permitting, etc.; refuse —*vi.* to refrain; forbear —*SYN.* see KEEP —**with·hold'er** *n.*

☆**withholding tax** the amount of income tax paid by employees through the employer's withholding of part of their wages or salaries

with·in (with in', with-) *adv.* [ME. *withinne* < OE. *withinnan* < 'with, WITH + *innan*, within, into < *in*, IN] **1.** in or into the interior; on the inside; internally **2.** indoors **3.** inside the body, mind, heart, etc.; inwardly —*prep.* **1.** in the inner part of; inside **2.** not beyond in distance, time, degree, range, scope, etc. *[within a mile, within one's experience]* **3.** inside the limits of *[within the law]* —*n.* the inside or the interior

with·in·doors (-dôrz') *adv.* same as INDOORS

with·out (with out', with-) *adv.* [ME. *withuten* < OE. *withutan* < *with*, WITH + *utan*, from outside, without < *ut*, OUT] **1.** on the outside; externally **2.** outside a building or place; out of doors —*prep.* **1.** at, on, to, or toward the outside of **2.** beyond *[without his reach]* **3.** not with; lacking *[a shirt without buttons]* **4.** free from *[without fear]* **5.** with avoidance of *[to pass by without speaking]* **6.** [Obs.] besides —*n.* the outside or the exterior —*conj.* [Dial.] unless: often followed by *that [they can't go, without (that) they get permission]* —**go** (or **do**) **without** to manage although lacking something implied or previously mentioned

with·out·doors (-dôrz') *adv.* archaic var. of OUTDOORS

with·stand (with stand', with-) *vt., vi.* **-stood', -stand'ing** [ME. *withstanden* < OE. *withstandan:* see WITH & STAND] to oppose, resist, or endure, esp. in a successful way —*SYN.* see OPPOSE

with·y (with'ē, with'ē) *n., pl.* **with'ies** [ME. < OE. *withig*, a willow, twig of willow: for base see WITHE] a tough, flexible twig of willow, osier, etc., used for binding things; withe —*adj.* tough and flexible; wiry

wit·less (wit'lis) *adj.* lacking wit or intelligence; foolish —**wit'less·ly** *adv.* —**wit'less·ness** *n.*

wit·ling (wit'liŋ) *n.* one who fancies himself a wit

wit·ness (wit'nis) *n.* [ME. *witnesse* < OE. *gewitnes*, witness, knowledge, testimony < *witan*, to know: for IE. base see WISE¹] **1.** an attesting of a fact, statement, etc.; evidence; testimony **2.** a person who saw, or can give a firsthand account of, something **3.** a person who testifies in court **4.** a person called upon to observe a transaction, signing, etc. in order to testify concerning it if it is later held in question **5.** something providing or serving as evidence —*vt.* **1.** to testify to **2.** to serve as evidence of **3.** to act as witness of, often by signing a statement to that effect **4.** to be present at; see personally **5.** to be the scene or setting of *[a hall that has witnessed many conventions]* —*vi.* **1.** to give, or serve as, evidence; testify **2.** to testify to religious beliefs or faith —**bear witness** to be or give evidence; testify

☆**witness stand** the place from which a witness gives his testimony in a law court: also, Brit., **wit'ness-box'** *n.*

wit·ted (wit'id) *adj.* having (a specified kind of) wit: used in hyphenated compounds *[slow-witted]*

Wit·te·kind (vit'ə kint) same as WIDUKIND

Wit·ten·berg (wit''n bûrg'; *G.* vit'ən berk') city in C East Germany, on the Elbe: the Reformation originated here in 1517: pop. 48,000

Witt·gen·stein (vit'gən shtīn', -stīn'), **Lud·wig (Josef Johann)** (lo͞od'vig) 1889–1951; Brit. philosopher, born in Austria

wit·ti·cism (wit'ə siz'm) *n.* [< WITTY + -CISM, as in ANGLICISM, CRITICISM] a witty remark —*SYN.* see JOKE

wit·ting (wit'iŋ) *adj.* [ME. *wytting* < *witen:* see WIT²] done knowingly; deliberate; intentional —**wit'ting·ly** *adv.*

wit·tol (wit''l) *n.* [LME. *wetewold*, formed, after *cokewold* (cf. CUCKOLD) < *weten*, to know: see WIT²] [Archaic] a man who knows of his wife's adultery and tolerates it

wit·ty (wit'ē) *adj.* **-ti·er, -ti·est** [ME. *witti* < OE. *wittig* < *wit*, knowledge: see WIT¹] **1.** having, showing, or characterized by wit; cleverly amusing **2.** [Obs. or Dial.] intelligent; clever —**wit'ti·ly** *adv.* —**wit'ti·ness** *n.*

SYN.—**witty** implies sharp cleverness and spontaneity in perceiving and expressing, sometimes sarcastically, the incongruous, esp. as evidenced in quick repartee; **humorous** connotes more geniality, gentleness, or whimsicality in saying or doing something that is deliberately comical or amusing; **facetious** is now usually derogatory in suggesting an attempt to be witty or humorous that is unsuccessful because it is inappropriate or in bad taste; **jocular** implies a happy or playful disposition characterized by the desire to amuse others; **jocose** suggests a mildly mischievous quality in joking or jesting, sometimes to the point of facetiousness —*ANT.* serious, solemn, sober

Wit·wa·ters·rand (wit wôt'ərz rand', -wät'-; -ränt') region in SW Transvaal, South Africa, near Johannesburg, consisting of ranges of hills which contain rich gold fields

wive (wīv) *vi.* **wived, wiv'ing** [ME. *wiven* < OE. *wifian*, to take a wife < *wif*, a woman, WIFE] [Archaic] to marry a woman; take a wife —*vt.* [Archaic] **1.** to marry (a woman); take for a wife **2.** to provide with a wife

wi·vern (wī'vərn) *n.* same as WYVERN

wives (wīvz) *n., pl. of* WIFE

☆**wiz** (wiz) *n. clipped form of* WIZARD (*n.* 3)

wiz·ard (wiz'ərd) *n.* [ME. *wisard*, prob. < *wis*, WISE¹ + -*ard*, -ARD] **1.** orig., a sage **2.** a magician; conjurer; sorcerer **3.** [Colloq.] a person exceptionally gifted or clever at a specified activity —*adj.* **1.** of wizards or wizardry **2.** magic **3.** [Chiefly Brit.] excellent —**wiz'ard·ly** *adj.*

wiz·ard·ry (-rē) *n.* the art or practice of a wizard; witchcraft; magic; sorcery —*SYN.* see MAGIC

wiz·en (wiz'n, wēz'-) *vt., vi.* [ME. *wisenen* < OE. *wisnian*, to become dry < IE. base *wei-*, to wither, whence L. *viescere*, Lith. *výsti*, to wither] to dry up; wither; shrivel —*adj.* same as WIZENED —*SYN.* see WITHER

wiz·ened (-'nd) *adj.* dried up; shriveled; withered

wk. *pl.* **wks. 1.** week **2.** work

wkly. weekly

WL, w.l. 1. waterline **2.** wavelength

Wm. William

wmk. watermark

WNW, W.N.W., w.n.w. west-northwest

wo (wō) *n., interj. archaic var. of* WOE

WO, W.O. 1. wait order **2.** War Office **3.** Warrant Officer

woad (wōd) *n.* [ME. *wod* < OE. *wad*, akin to G. *waid*, L. *vitrum*, woad] any of a genus (*Isatis*) of plants of the mustard family; esp., same as DYER'S WOAD

woad·wax·en (-wak's'n) *n.* [ME. *wodewexen* < OE. *wuduweaxe* < *wudu*, WOOD¹ + *weaxe* < base of *weaxan*, to grow, WAX²] an ornamental plant (*Genista tinctoria*) of the legume family, with simple leaves and flowers that yield a yellow dye used by the ancient Britons

wob·ble (wäb'l) *vi.* **-bled, -bling** [prob. < LowG. *wabbeln*, to wobble: for IE. base see WAVE] **1.** to move unsteadily from side to side, as in walking **2.** to rotate unevenly so as to move from side to side **3.** to shake or tremble, as jelly does **4.** to waver in one's opinions, etc.; vacillate —*vt.* to cause to wobble —*n.* wobbling motion —*SYN.* see SHAKE —**wob'bler** *n.* —**wob'bling** *adj.* —**wob'bling·ly** *adv.*

☆**wobble pump** *Aeron.* an emergency hand pump for supplying fuel to the carburetor of an airplane engine

wob·bly¹ (wäb'lē) *adj.* **-bli·er, -bli·est** inclined to wobble; shaky —**wob'bli·ness** *n.*

☆**wob·bly²** (wäb'lē) *n., pl.* **-blies** [said to be < Chin. mispronunciation of *I.W.W.* as I *wobbly wobbly*] [also **W-**] [Slang] a member of the Industrial Workers of the World

Wo·burn (wō'bərn, wo͞o'-) [after *Woburn*, town in S England] city in E Mass.: suburb of Boston: pop. 37,000

W.O.C. without compensation

Wo·den, Wo·dan (wōd'n) [OE. *Woden*, akin to G. *Wotan* & ON. *Odinn:* see EDDA, cf. WEDNESDAY] the chief Germanic god, identified with the Norse Odin

woe (wō) *n.* [ME. *wo* < OE. *wa*, woe < an IE. interj. *wai-*, whence ON. *væ*, Goth. *wai*, W. *gwae*, L. *vae*] **1.** great sorrow; grief; misery **2.** a cause of sorrow; affliction; trouble —*interj.* alas! —*SYN.* see SORROW

woe·be·gone (wō'bi gôn', -gän') *adj.* [ME. *wo begon* < *wo*, WOE + *begon*, pp. of *begon*, to go around < OE. *began* < *be-*, BE + *gan*, to GO¹] **1.** [Archaic] woeful **2.** of woeful appearance; looking sorrowful, mournful, or wretched

woe·ful (-fəl) *adj.* **1.** full of woe; sad; mournful **2.** of, causing, or involving woe **3.** pitiful; wretched; miserable Also [Archaic] **wo'ful** —**woe'ful·ly** *adv.* —**woe'ful·ness** *n.*

Wof·fing·ton (wäf'iŋ tən), **Peg** (peg) (born *Margaret Woffington*) 1714?–60; Irish actress in England

wok (wäk) *n.* [Chin.] a metal cooking pan with a convex bottom, for frying, braising, steaming, etc.: often used with a ringlike stand for holding it steady

woke (wōk) *alt. pt. and occas. Brit. pp. of* WAKE¹

wok·en (wō'k'n) *occas. Brit. pp. of* WAKE¹

wold¹ (wōld) *n.* [ME. *wold* < OE. (Anglian) *wald*, corresponding to WS. *weald*, akin to OHG. *wald*, forest, ON. *vollr*, meadow, prob. < IE. base *wel-*, shaggy hair, grass] a treeless, rolling plain, esp. a high one

wold² (wōld) *n. same as* WELD²

wold³ (wōld) *alt. obs. pp. of* WILL²

wolf (woolf) *n., pl.* **wolves** [ME. < OE. *wulf*, akin to G. *wolf*, ON. *ulfr* < IE. base *wlp-*, *lup-*, name of animals of prey, whence L. *lupus* (cf. LUPINE), Gr. *lykos* (cf. LYCANTHROPY)] **1.** *a)* any of a large group of wild, flesheating, doglike mammals (genus *Canis*), esp. the gray wolf, widely distributed throughout the Northern Hemi-

sphere: domestic dogs are thought to be descended from wolves *b*) the fur of a wolf **2.** *a*) a fierce, cruel, or greedy person ☆*b*) [Slang] a man who flirts aggressively with many women; philanderer **3.** *a*) the dissonance of some chords on an organ, piano, etc. that has been tuned in a system of unequal temperament; also, a chord in which such dissonance is heard *b*) an unsteadiness or breaking of certain tones in instruments of the violin group, due to faulty vibration —*vt.* to eat ravenously, as a wolf does (often with *down*) —**cry wolf** to give a false alarm —**keep the wolf from the door** to provide the necessities of life in sufficient quantity to prevent privation —**wolf in sheep's clothing** a person who hides malicious intent under a benign manner: see Matt. 7:15

Wolf (vôlf) **1. Frie·drich Au·gust** (frē′driH ou gσ̄σst′), 1759–1824; Ger. classical scholar **2. Hu·go** (hōō′gō), 1860–1903; Austrian composer

☆**wolf·ber·ry** (woolf′ber′ē) *n.*, *pl.* **-ries** a hardy plant (*Symphoricarpos occidentalis*) of the honeysuckle family, with pink, globular flowers and white, spongy berries

wolf call ☆a characteristic whistle of two notes, the second sliding from a high to a low note, or a wolflike howl, etc., made by a man to express his admiration of a sexually attractive woman

Wolf Cub *Brit. & Canad. term for* Cub Scout

wolf dog 1. *same as* WOLFHOUND **2.** a hybrid of a wolf and a dog

Wolfe (woolf) **1. James,** 1727–59; Eng. general: defeated the Fr. forces under Montcalm at Quebec (1759) **2. Thomas (Clayton),** 1900–38; U.S. novelist

☆**wolf·er** (wool′fər) *n.* a person who hunts wolves

Wolf-Fer·ra·ri (vôlf′fer rä′rē), **Er·man·no** (er mä′nō) 1876–1948; It. composer

Wolff·i·an body (wool′fē ən, vôl′-) [after K. F. *Wolff* (1733–94), G. embryologist who described it] the transitory mesonephros of higher vertebrates that functions as a kidney in the embryo and is replaced by the adult kidney

wolf·fish (woolf′fish′) *n.*, *pl.* **-fish′**, **-fish′es:** see FISH² any of a family (Anarhichadidae) of large, savage sea fishes related to the blennies, with a long, tapered body

wolf·hound (-hound′) *n.* a large dog of any of several breeds formerly used for hunting wolves: see IRISH WOLFHOUND, BORZOI (*Russian wolfhound*)

wolf·ish (wool′fish) *adj.* of or like a wolf; rapacious —**wolf′ish·ly** *adv.* —**wolf′ish·ness** *n.*

wolf·ram (-frəm) *n.* [G. < *wolf*, WOLF + MHG. *ram*, dirt, soot (akin to OE. *romig*, dirty < IE. base *rēmo-*, dark, whence Sans. *rāmá-*, black): prob. because considered of little value in comparison to tin] *same as* TUNGSTEN

wolf·ram·ite (-frə mīt′) *n.* [G. *wolframit:* see prec.] a brownish or blackish monoclinic mineral, (Fe,Mn)WO₄, a tungstate of iron and manganese occurring in columnar or granular masses: the principal ore of tungsten

Wol·fram von Esch·en·bach (vôl′främ fôn esh′ən bäkh′) 1170?–1220?; Ger. epic poet

wolfs·bane (woolfs′bān′) *n.* [transl. of L. *lycoctonum* < Gr. *lykoktonon* < *lykos*, a WOLF + base of *kteinein*, to kill] *same as* ACONITE; esp., a tall, Eurasian plant (*Aconitum lycoctonum*) with showy, hooded, yellow flowers

wolf spider any of a family (Lycosidae) of active hunting spiders that are wanderers, living in ground tunnels or natural crevices and not building webs

wol·las·ton·ite (wool′əs tə nīt′) *n.* [after William H. *Wollaston* (1766–1828), Eng. physicist] a white, monoclinic mineral, CaSiO₃, a native calcium silicate

Wo·lof (wō′lôf) *n.* **1.** *pl.* **-lofs, -lof** any member of a people of Senegal and Gambia **2.** their Niger-Congo language

Wol·sey (wool′zē), **Thomas** 1475?–1530; Eng. statesman & cardinal; lord chancellor (1515–29) under Henry VIII

wol·ver (wool′vər) *n.* ☆*same as* WOLFER

Wol·ver·hamp·ton (wool′vər hamp′tən) city in Staffordshire, WC England, near Birmingham: pop. 266,000

wol·ver·ine (wool′və rēn′, wool′və rēn′) *n.*, *pl.* **-ines′**, **-ine′:** see PLURAL, II, D, 1 [irreg. dim. < WOLF, prob. because of its ferocity] **1.** *a*) a stocky, ferocious, flesh-eating mammal (*Gulo gulo*) with thick fur, found in the N U.S., N Eurasia, and Canada: the European variety is the GLUTTON (sense 3) *b*) its fur Also, Brit. sp., **wol′ver·ene′** ☆**2.** [W-] [Colloq.] a native or inhabitant of Michigan, called **the Wolverine State**

wolves (woolvz) *n. pl. of* WOLF

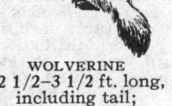

WOLVERINE
(2 1/2–3 1/2 ft. long, including tail; 12–16 in. high at shoulder)

wom·an (woom′ən) *n.*, *pl.* **wom′en** (wim′in) [ME. *wumman* < OE. *wifmann*, later *wimmann* < *wif*, a female, WIFE + *mann*, a human being, MAN: change of vowel due to influence of the initial *w*-] **1.** the female human being, or women collectively, as distinguished from *man* **2.** an adult female human being **3.** a female servant **4.** *a*) [Dial.] a wife *b*) a sweetheart or a mistress **5.** a man with qualities conventionally regarded as feminine, such as

weakness, timidity, inclination to gossip, etc. **6.** womanly qualities or characteristics; femininity [the *woman* in her] —*adj.* **1.** of or characteristic of a woman or women; feminine **2.** female [a *woman* scientist] —**the little woman** ☆[Slang] one's wife

SYN.—**woman** is the standard general term for the adult human being of the sex distinguished from *man;* **female,** referring specif. to sex, is applied to plants and animals, but is now regarded as a contemptuous equivalent for **woman** [that strong-minded *female* is here again], except in scientific, technical, or statistical use, as in population tables; **lady,** once restricted to a woman of the upper classes or high social position, is now used in polite or genteel reference to any woman [there's a *lady* to see you, the *ladies'* room] or, in the plural, in addressing a group of women [*ladies* and gentlemen]

wom·an·hood (-hood′) *n.* **1.** the condition of being a woman **2.** womanly qualities; womanliness **3.** women; womankind

wom·an·ish (-ish) *adj.* like, characteristic of, or suitable to a woman; feminine or effeminate —*SYN.* see FEMALE —**wom′an·ish·ly** *adv.* —**wom′an·ish·ness** *n.*

wom·an·ize (-īz′) *vt.* -ized′, -iz′ing to make effeminate —*vi.* [Colloq.] to be sexually promiscuous with women —**wom′an·iz′er** *n.*

wom·an·kind (-kīnd′) *n.* women in general

wom·an·like (-līk′) *adj.* like or fit for a woman; womanly

wom·an·ly (-lē) *adj.* **1.** like a woman; womanish **2.** characteristic of or fit for a woman; womanlike —*adv.* [Archaic] in a womanly manner —*SYN.* see FEMALE —**wom′an·li·ness** *n.*

woman suffrage the right of women to vote in governmental elections —**wom′an-suf′fra·gist** *n.*

womb (woom) *n.* [ME. < OE. *wamb*, akin to G. *wamme*] **1.** orig., the belly **2.** *same as* UTERUS (sense 1) **3.** any place or part that holds, envelops, generates, etc. [the *womb* of time]

wom·bat (wäm′bat) *n.* [altered < Australian native name] any of a family (Phascolomidae) of burrowing marsupials resembling small bears, found in Australia, Tasmania, and several Pacific islands

wom·en (wim′in) *n. pl. of* WOMAN

wom·en·folk (-fōk′) *n.pl.* [Dial. or Colloq.] women; womankind: also **wom′en·folks′**

women's rights the rights claimed by and for women of equal privileges and opportunities with men: cf. FEMINISM: also **woman's rights**

wom·er·a (wäm′ər ə) *n.* [Australian native name] a spear-throwing device used by Australian aborigines

WOMBAT
(2–4 ft. long)

won¹ (wun) *pt. & pp. of* WIN

won² (wun, wŏn) *vi.* **wonned, won′ning** [ME. *wonen* < OE. *wunian:* see WONT] [Archaic or Brit. Dial.] to dwell; abide

won³ (wän) *n.*, *pl.* **won** [Kor.] the basic monetary unit of North Korea and South Korea: see MONETARY UNITS, table

won·der (wun′dər) *n.* [ME. < OE. *wundor*, akin to G. *wunder:* only in Gmc.] **1.** a person, thing, or event that causes astonishment and admiration; prodigy; marvel **2.** the feeling of surprise, admiration, and awe aroused by something strange, unexpected, incredible, etc. [gazing in *wonder* at the comet] **3.** a miraculous or apparently miraculous thing or act; miracle —*vi.* [OE. *wundrian*, to wonder] **1.** to be seized or filled with wonder; feel amazement; marvel **2.** to have curiosity, sometimes mingled with doubt —*vt.* to have curiosity or doubt about; want to know [he *wondered* what happened] —**for a wonder** surprisingly —**no wonder!** now I know why! —**won′der·er** *n.*

won·der·ful (-fəl) *adj.* [ME. < OE. *wundorfull*] **1.** that causes wonder; marvelous; amazing **2.** [Colloq.] very good, excellent, fine, etc.: generalized term of approval —**won′der·ful·ly** *adv.* —**won′der·ful·ness** *n.*

won·der·ing (-iŋ) *adj.* feeling or showing wonder

won·der·land (-land′) *n.* **1.** an imaginary land full of wonders **2.** any place of great beauty, strangeness, etc.

won·der·ment (-mənt) *n.* **1.** a state or expression of wonder; amazement; astonishment **2.** something causing wonder; a marvel

won·der·struck (-struk′) *adj.* struck with wonder, surprise, admiration, etc.: also **won′der·strick′en** (-strik′'n)

won·der·work (-wurk′) *n.* [ME. *wonder werk* < OE. *wundorweorc*] **1.** a wonderful work; wonder **2.** a miraculous act; miracle —**won′der-work′er** *n.* —**won′der·work′ing** *adj.*

won·drous (wun′drəs) *adj.* [altered (as if < WONDER + -OUS) < ME. *wundres*, adv. gen. of *wunder*, WONDER] wonderful —*adv.* extraordinarily; surprisingly Now only literary or rhetorical —**won′drous·ly** *adv.* —**won′drous·ness** *n.*

wonk (wäŋk) *n.* [back-formation < ff.] [Slang] a student who studies very hard; grind —*vi.* [Slang] to cram or grind, as some students

won·ky (wäŋ′kē) *adj.* -ki·er, -ki·est [prob. < or suggested by dial. words based on OE. *wancol*, shaky, tottering] [Brit. Slang] shaky, tottery, feeble, etc.

Won·san (wän′sän′) seaport in North Korea, on the E coast: pop. 113,000

wont (wônt, wŏnt, wunt, wänt) *adj.* [ME. *wunt*, *woned*, pp.

of *wunien*, to be accustomed, dwell < OE. *wunian*, to dwell: for IE. base see WIN] accustomed: used predicatively [he was *wont* to rise early] —*n.* [prob. altered (after the adj.) < ME. *wune*, custom, habit < OE. (*ge*)*wuna*] usual practice; habit —*vt.* **wont**, **wont** or **wont'ed**, **wont'ing** to accustom: usually in the passive —*vi.* to be accustomed —*SYN.* see HABIT

won't [contr. < ME. *wol not*, will not] will not

wont·ed (wôn'tid, wōn'-, wun'-, wän'-) *adj.* [ME.: see WONT, *n.* & -ED] **1.** customary; habitual **2.** accustomed; habituated —*SYN.* see USUAL —**wont'ed·ness** *n.*

won ton (wän' tän') a Chinese dish consisting of casings of noodle dough filled with ground meat and boiled: served in a broth (**won-ton soup**) or fried and served as a side dish

woo (wōō) *vt.* [ME. *wowen* < OE. *wogian*] **1.** to make love to, usually with the intention of proposing marriage; court **2.** to try to get; seek [to *woo* fame] **3.** to entreat solicitously; coax; urge —*vi.* **1.** to make love; court **2.** to make entreaty

wood[1] (wood) *n.* [ME. *wode* < OE. *wudu*, earlier *widu*, akin to OHG. *wito* < IE. base *widhu-*, tree, whence OIr. *fid*, W. *gwŷdd*, tree, forest] **1.** [*usually pl.*] a thick growth of trees; forest or grove **2.** the hard, fibrous substance beneath the bark in the stems and branches of trees and shrubs; xylem **3.** trees cut and prepared for use in making things; lumber or timber **4.** *short for* FIREWOOD **5.** something made of wood; specif., *a*) a cask or other wooden container for alcoholic liquor [whiskey aged in *wood*] *b*) [*pl.*] woodwind instruments, collectively **6.** *Golf* any of a set of numbered clubs with wooden heads having various lofts —*adj.* **1.** made of wood; wooden **2.** for cutting, shaping, or holding wood **3.** growing or living in woods —*vt.* **1.** to plant or cover thickly with trees **2.** to furnish with wood, esp. firewood —*vi.* to get or take on a supply of wood —☆**out of the woods** [Colloq.] out of difficulty, danger, etc.

wood[2] (wood) *adj.* [ME. < OE. *wod*, akin to G. *wut*, madness] [Archaic] **1.** out of one's mind; insane **2.** violently angry; enraged

Wood (wood) **1. Grant**, 1892–1942; U.S. painter **2. Leonard**, 1860–1927; U.S. general & political administrator

wood alcohol *same as* METHANOL

wood anemone any of several anemones; esp., *a*) a forest species (*Anemone quinquefolia*) of the E U.S. with starlike flowers *b*) a similar species (*Anemone nemorosa*) of Europe

wood betony ☆*same as* LOUSEWORT

wood·bin (wood'bin') *n.* a bin for firewood

wood·bine (-bīn') *n.* [ME. *wodebinde* < OE. *wudubinde* < *wudu*, WOOD[1] + *binde* < *bindan*, to BIND] **1.** *a*) a European climbing honeysuckle (*Lonicera periclymenum*), with fragrant, yellowish-white flowers *b*) any of various other honeysuckles ☆**2.** a tendril-climbing vine (*Parthenocissus quinquefolia*) of the grape family, growing in E N. America and having palmately compound leaves with five leaflets and green flower clusters that produce dark blue inedible berries

wood block a block of wood, esp. one used in making a woodcut —**wood'block'** *adj.*

wood·carv·ing (-kär'vin) *n.* **1.** the art or craft of carving wood by hand to make art objects or decorative features **2.** an object so made —**wood'carv'er** *n.*

wood·chat (-chat') *n.* [WOOD[1] + CHAT[1], *n.*] **1.** any of several small Asiatic birds of the thrush group **2.** a European shrike (*Lanius senator*)

☆**wood·chuck** (wood'chuk') *n.* [altered by folk etym. < AmInd. (Algonquian) name, as in Cree *otchek*, Chippewa *otchig*] **1.** a common N. American burrowing and hibernating marmot (*Marmota monax*) with coarse, redbrown fur **2.** any of several marmots of W N. America, as the hoary marmot

wood coal *same as:* **1.** CHARCOAL **2.** LIGNITE

wood·cock (-käk') *n., pl.* **-cocks'**, **-cock'**: see PLURAL, II, D, 1 [ME. *wodekoc* < OE. *wuducoc* < *wudu*, WOOD[1] + *coc*, a COCK[1]] **1.** a widespread, European, migratory game bird (*Scolopax rusticola*), with short legs and a long bill, related to the snipe and sandpiper ☆**2.** a smaller, related game bird (*Philohela minor*) of E N. America, that frequents bogs and swampy places **3.** [Obs.] a fool; dupe

wood·craft (-kraft', -kräft') *n.* **1.** matters relating to the woods, as camping, hunting, etc. **2.** *same as:* *a*) WOODWORKING *b*) WOODCARVING **3.** skill in any of these

wood·crafts·man (-krafts'mən, -kräfts'-) *n., pl.* **-men** a person who practices, or has skill in, woodcraft

wood·cut (-kut') *n.* **1.** a wooden block engraved with a design, etc. **2.** a print made from this See also WOOD ENGRAVING

☆**wood·cut·ter** (-kut'ər) *n.* a person who fells trees, cuts wood, etc. —**wood'cut'ting** *n.*

☆**wood duck** a brilliantly colored N. American duck (*Aix sponsa*) that nests in hollow trees near woodland lakes

wood·ed (-id) *adj.* covered with trees or woods

wood·en (wood'n) *adj.* **1.** made of or consisting of wood **2.** stiff, lifeless, expressionless, etc., as if made of wood **3.** dull; insensitive —**wood'en·ly** *adv.* —**wood'en·ness** *n.*

wood engraving 1. the art or process of engraving on wood **2.** *same as* WOODCUT: a wood engraving is often distinguished from a woodcut in that the former uses a block of

wood cut *across* the grain and the latter a block of wood cut *along* the grain —**wood engraver**

wood·en·head (wood'n hed') *n.* [Colloq.] a stupid person; blockhead —**wood'en·head'ed** *adj.*

wooden horse *same as* TROJAN HORSE (sense 1)

☆**wooden Indian 1.** a wooden image of an American Indian in a standing position, formerly placed in front of cigar stores as an advertisement **2.** [Colloq.] a person who is dull, spiritless, or inarticulate

wood·en·ware (-wer') *n.* bowls, dishes, etc. made of wood

wood hen *same as:* **1.** WOODCOCK **2.** WEKA

wood hyacinth a European scilla (*Scilla nonscripta*) with racemes of drooping, blue, white, or rose, bell-shaped flowers

☆**wood ibis** a large, white, heronlike stork (*Mycteria americana*) with a slender, downward curving bill and naked head, found in the wooded swamps of the S U.S. and southward into S. America

wood·i·ness (wood'ē nis) *n.* the condition or quality of being woody

wood·land (wood'land'; *also, and for adj. always,* -lənd) *n.* land covered with woods or trees; forest —*adj.* of, living in, or relating to the woods —**wood'land·er** *n.*

wood lark a European lark (*Lullula arborea*) similar to but smaller than a skylark

☆**wood lot** a piece of land on which trees are cultivated

wood louse *same as* SOW BUG

wood·man (-mən) *n., pl.* **-men** *same as* WOODSMAN

wood·note (-nōt') *n.* a sound of a forest bird or animal

wood nymph 1. a nymph that lives in the woods; dryad **2.** any of several S. American hummingbirds (genus *Thalurania*) **3.** any of several moths (genus *Euthisanotia*) with brightly colored larvae **4.** any of a family (Satyridae) of brown and gray butterflies with eyespots on the wings

wood·peck·er (-pek'ər) *n.* any of various tree-climbing birds (family Picidae), distinguished by stiff, sharp tail feathers used for support, a strong, pointed, chisel-shaped bill used for drilling holes in bark to get insects, and a long, protrusile tongue with a spearlike tip

☆**wood pewee** *see* PEWEE

wood pigeon any of several pigeons; esp., *same as:* *a*) RINGDOVE (sense 1) *b*) PASSENGER PIGEON

wood·pile (-pīl') *n.* a pile of wood, esp. of firewood

wood pulp pulp made from wood fiber, used as in paper manufacture

☆**wood pussy** [Dial.] *same as* SKUNK

☆**wood rat** *same as* PACK RAT

wood ray *same as* XYLEM RAY

Wood·row (wood'rō) [< the surname *Woodrow*] a masculine name: dim. *Woody*

wood·ruff (-ruf') *n.* [ME. *woderove* < OE. *wudurofe* < *wudu*, WOOD[1] + *-rofe*, prob. akin to (*a*)*rafian*, to unravel: prob. because of its creeping rootstock] any of a genus (*Asperula*) of plants of the coffee family, with small white, pink, or blue, lily-shaped flowers, and whorled leaves, esp. a European species (*Asperula odorata*) used to flavor wine and in perfumery

Woods, Lake of the *see* LAKE OF THE WOODS

wood screw a metal screw with a sharp point and a thread of coarse pitch, for use in wood: see SCREW, illus.

wood·shed (-shed') *n.* a shed for storing firewood

wood·si·a (wood'zē ə) *n.* [ModL., after Joseph *Woods* (1776–1864), Eng. botanist] any of a genus (*Woodsia*) of ferns with wiry leafstalks, found chiefly on rock ledges

☆**Wood's light** (woodz) [after R. W. *Wood* (1868–1955), U.S. physicist] ultraviolet light filtered through glass containing nickel oxide, used as in detecting forgeries

woods·man (woodz'mən) *n., pl.* **-men 1.** a person who lives or works in the woods, as a hunter, woodcutter, etc. **2.** a person at home in the woods or skilled in woodcraft

wood sorrel [transl. of MFr. *sorrel de boys*] any of a genus (*Oxalis*) of creeping plants with white, pink, red, or yellow, five-parted flowers and cloverlike compound leaves that contain oxalic acid: found in cool, shaded, damp woods

wood spirit *same as* METHANOL

wood sugar *same as* XYLOSE

☆**wood·sy** (wood'zē) *adj.* **-si·er**, **-si·est** of, characteristic of, or like the woods —**wood'si·ness** *n.*

wood tar a dark, sticky, syruplike substance obtained by the dry distillation of wood and used in the preservation of timber, rope, etc.

wood thrush ☆ a large thrush (*Hylocichla mustelina*) of E N. America, having a brown mantle, a white breast, and a sweet, clear song: also called ☆**wood robin**

wood turning the art or process of turning, or shaping, wood on a lathe —**wood'-turn'er** *n.* —**wood'-turn'ing** *adj.*

wood vinegar *same as* PYROLIGNEOUS ACID

☆**wood warbler** *same as* WARBLER (sense 2)

wood·wax·en (-wak's'n) *n. var. of* WOADWAXEN

wood·wind (-wind') *n.* **1.** [*pl.*] the wind instruments of an orchestra made, esp. originally, of wood: the principal modern woodwinds are the clarinet, oboe, bassoon, flute, and English horn **2.** any of these instruments —*adj.* of or for such instruments

wood·work (-wurk') *n.* **1.** work done in wood **2.** things

WOODPECKER (10–20 in. long)

WOODCHUCK (head & body to 15 in. long; tail to 6 in. long)

made of wood, esp. the interior moldings, doors, stairs, etc. of a house

wood·work·ing (-wur'kiŋ) *n.* the art or work of making things of wood —*adj.* of woodworking —**wood'work'er** *n.*

wood·worm (-wurm') *n.* any of a number of insect larvae that live on and burrow in wood

wood·y (wood'ē) *adj.* **wood'i·er, wood'i·est** **1.** covered with trees; wooded **2.** consisting of or forming wood; ligneous *[a woody plant]* **3.** like or characteristic of wood *[a woody texture, odor, etc.]*

woo·er (wōō'ər) *n.* a person who woos; suitor

woof¹ (woof, wōōf) *n.* [altered (prob. after WARP, WEFT¹) < ME. *oof* < OE. *owef* < o- (< *on*) + *-wef* < base of *wefan*, to WEAVE] **1.** the horizontal threads crossing the warp in a woven fabric; weft **2.** a woven fabric or its texture

woof² (woof) *n.* a gruff barking sound of or like that of a dog —*vi.* to make such a sound

woof·er (woof'ər) *n.* [prec. + -ER] in an assembly of two or more loudspeakers, a large speaker for reproducing low-frequency sounds: cf. TWEETER

wool (wool) *n.* see PLURAL, II, D, 3 [ME. *wolle* < OE. *wull,* akin to G. *wolle* < IE. base *wel*-, hair, wool, grass, whence L. *vellus,* fleece, *lana,* wool, Gr. *lēnos,* wool] **1.** *a)* the soft, curly or crisped hair of sheep *b)* the hair of some other animals, as the goat, llama, or alpaca, having a similar texture **2.** *a)* yarn spun from the fibers of such fleece, esp. the fleece of sheep *b)* cloth, clothing, etc. made of this yarn **3.** short, thick, curly or crispy human hair **4.** anything that looks or feels like wool, as a fibrous mass of inorganic material *[rock wool]* or the hairy or furry coating on some insects, insect larvae, and plants —*adj.* of wool or woolen goods —☆**all wool and a yard wide** genuine or admirable; truly and thoroughly as described —☆**pull the wool over someone's eyes** to deceive or trick someone

wool clip annual production of wool

wool·en (-ən) *adj.* [ME. *wullen* < OE.] **1.** made of wool **2.** of or relating to wool or woolen cloth —*n.* *[pl.]* woolen goods or clothing Also, chiefly Brit. sp., **wool'len**

Woolf (woolf) **1. Leonard (Sidney),** 1880– ; Eng. publisher & writer **2. Virginia,** (born *Adeline Virginia Stephen*) 1882–1941; Eng. novelist & critic: wife of *prec.*

wool fat 1. the natural grease found in sheep's wool, yielding lanolin: also **wool grease 2.** *same as* LANOLIN

wool·fell (wool'fel') *n.* [WOOL + FELL⁴] the pelt of a wool-bearing animal with the wool still on it

wool·gath·er·ing (-gath'ər iŋ) *n.* [from random wandering to gather tufts of wool caught on thorns and hedges] absent-mindedness or daydreaming —**wool'gath'er·er** *n.*

wool·grow·er (-grō'ər) *n.* a person who raises sheep for wool —**wool'grow'ing** *n.*

Wooll·cott (wool'kət), **Alexander (Humphreys)** 1887–1943; U.S. writer & critic

wool·ly (wool'ē) *adj.* **-li·er, -li·est** **1.** of or like wool **2.** bearing wool **3.** covered with wool or something resembling wool in texture ☆**4.** having characteristics of the early frontier life of the western U.S.; rough and uncivilized: used chiefly in **wild and woolly 5.** tangled and confused; fuzzy *[woolly ideas]* —*n.*, *pl.* **-lies 1.** [Western] a sheep **2.** a woolen garment, esp. one with a fleecelike surface; specif., *[pl.]* long underwear —**wool'li·ness** *n.*

woolly aphid any of a number of homopterous, aphidlike insects (family Eriosomatidae) that secrete a hairlike covering of wax

woolly bear *see* TIGER MOTH

wool·ly-head·ed (-hed'id) *adj.* confused, unclear, impractical, etc. in thought: also **wool'ly-mind'ed** (-mīn'did)

wool·pack (-pak') *n.* **1.** a large bag of canvas, cotton, etc. in which to pack wool or fleece for sale **2.** a bale of wool so packed, esp., formerly, one weighing 240 pounds **3.** a fleecy cumulus cloud

wool·sack (-sak') *n.* **1.** a sack of wool **2.** *a)* a cushion stuffed with wool, on which the British Lord Chancellor sits in the House of Lords *b)* the office of Lord Chancellor

wool·shed (-shed') *n.* a building in which sheep are sheared and the wool is packed for market

wool·sort·ers' disease (-sôr'tərz) pulmonary anthrax, an occupational disease of workers in unprocessed wool, contracted by inhaling the spores of the anthrax bacillus

☆**wool sponge** any of several commercial sponges with durable, soft, fibrous skeletons; esp., the **sheepswool sponge** (*Hippospongia glossypina*) of the Caribbean area

wool stapler 1. a person who sells wool **2.** a person who sorts wool according to its staple, or fiber

Wool·wich (wool'ij, -ich) metropolitan borough of London, on the S bank of the Thames: pop. 149,000

Wool·worth (wool'wərth), **Frank Win·field** (win'fēld) 1852–1919; U.S. merchant

wool·y (wool'ē) *adj.* **wool'i·er, wool'i·est, n.,** *pl.* **wool'ies** *same as* WOOLLY —**wool'i·ness** *n.*

woo·mer·a (wōō'mər ə) *n. same as* WOMERA

Woon·sock·et (wōōn säk'it) [< AmInd. (*mis*)*wosakit* < ?] city in N R.I.: pop. 47,000

woops (woops, wōōps) *vi., vt.* [altered < OOPS] [Colloq.] *same as* VOMIT

woo·ra·li (wōō rä'lē) *n.* [var. of CURARE] *same as* CURARE

woosh (woosh) *vi., vt., n., interj. var. of* WHOOSH

☆**wooz·y** (wōō'zē, wooz'ē) *adj.* **wooz'i·er, wooz'i·est** [prob. < *wooze,* var. of OOZE¹] [Colloq.] **1.** dizzy, faint, and sickish **2.** befuddled, muddled, or dazed, as from drink, drugs, a blow, etc. —**wooz'i·ly** *adv.* —**wooz'i·ness** *n.*

Worces·ter (woos'tər) **1.** *a)* city in E England; county seat of Worcestershire: pop. 69,000 *b) same as* WORCESTERSHIRE **2.** [after prec.] city in C Mass.: pop. 177,000

Worces·ter (woos'tər), **Joseph Emerson** 1784–1865; U.S. lexicographer

Worcester china (or **porcelain**) a fine china (or porcelain) made at Worcester, England, from 1751

Worces·ter·shire (woos'tər shir') county of W England: 700 sq. mi.; pop. 588,000; county seat, Worcester

Worcestershire sauce a spicy sauce for meats, poultry, etc., containing soy, vinegar, and other ingredients: orig. made in Worcester, England

word (wurd) *n.* [ME. < OE., akin to G. *wort* < IE. *werdh*- (extension of base *wer*-, to speak, say), whence L. *verbum,* a word] **1.** *a)* a speech sound, or series of them, serving to communicate meaning and consisting of at least one base morpheme with or without prefixes or suffixes but with a superfix; unit of language between the morpheme and the complete utterance *b)* a letter or group of letters representing such a unit of language, written or printed usually in solid or hyphenated form **2.** a brief expression, statement, remark, etc. *[a word of advice]* **3.** a promise, affirmation, or assurance *[to give a person one's word]* **4.** news; information; tidings *[no word from home, what's the good word?]* **5.** *a)* a password or signal *b)* a command, order, or authorization *[waiting for the word to go ahead]* **6.** *[usually pl.]* *a)* talk; speech *b)* the lyrics, text, libretto, etc. of a musical composition that is sung **7.** *[pl.]* a quarrel; dispute; argument **8.** an ordered combination of characters carrying at least one meaning that is stored in one location in a computer and that is regarded as a unit when stored or transferred by the computer circuits **9.** [Archaic] a saying; proverb —*vt.* to express in words; phrase —**a good word** a favorable comment, or commendation —**at a word** in quick response to a request or command; immediately —**be as good as one's word** to live up to one's promises —**break one's word** to fail to keep one's promise —**by word of mouth** by speech, not by writing; orally —**hang on someone's words** to listen to someone eagerly —**have a word with** to have a brief conversation with —**have no words for** to be incapable of describing —**have words with** to argue angrily with —**in a word** in short; briefly —**in so many words** precisely; succinctly —**man** (or **woman**) **of his** (or **her**) **word** a person who keeps his promises —**of few words** not talkative; laconic —**of many words** wordy; talkative; garrulous —**take one at one's word** to take one's words literally or seriously and, often, act accordingly —**take the words out of one's mouth** to say what one was about to say oneself —**the Word 1.** *same as* LOGOS **2.** the Bible; Scriptures **3.** *same as* GOSPEL (sense 1) —**(upon) my word!** indeed! really!: an exclamation of surprise, irritation, etc. —**word for word** in precisely the same words; exactly; verbatim

word·age (-ij) *n.* **1.** words collectively, or the number of words (*of a story, novel, etc.*) **2.** verbiage; wordiness **3.** wording; diction

word blindness *same as* ALEXIA —**word'-blind'** *adj.*

word·book (-book') *n.* a dictionary, lexicon, or vocabulary

word deafness a cerebral disorder characterized by loss of ability to understand spoken words; auditory aphasia —**word'-deaf'** *adj.*

word-for-word (-fər wurd') *adj.* in exactly the same words

word·ing (-iŋ) *n.* choice and arrangement of words; diction

word·less (-lis) *adj.* **1.** without words; speechless **2.** not expressed or not capable of being expressed in words —**word'less·ly** *adv.* —**word'less·ness** *n.*

Word of God the Bible

word of honor pledged word; solemn promise; oath

word-of-mouth (-əv mouth') *adj.* transmitted orally

word order the arrangement of words in a phrase, clause, or sentence

word·play (-plā') *n.* **1.** subtle or clever exchange of words; repartee **2.** punning or a pun

word square a square made of letters so arranged that they spell the same words in the same order horizontally and vertically

Words·worth (wurdz'wərth), **William** 1770–1850; Eng. poet; poet laureate (1843–50)

word·y (wur'dē) *adj.* **word'i·er, word'i·est 1.** of words; verbal **2.** containing or using many or too many words; verbose —**word'i·ly** *adv.* —**word'i·ness** *n.*

SYN.—**wordy** is the general word implying the use of more words in speaking or writing than are necessary for communication *[a wordy document]*; **verbose** suggests a wordiness that results in obscurity, tediousness, bombast, etc. *[a verbose acceptance speech]*; **prolix** implies such a tiresome elaboration of trivial details as to be boring or dull *[his prolix sermons]*; **diffuse** suggests such verbosity and loose construction as to lose all force and sharpness *[a*

D A T E
A C I D
T I N G
E D G E

rambling, *diffuse* harangue*]*; **redundant,** in this connection, implies the use of unnecessary or repetitious words or phrases *[a redundant literary style]* —ANT. **concise, terse, pithy**

wore (wôr) *pt. of* WEAR

work (wurk) *n.* [ME. *werk* < OE. *weorc,* akin to G. *werk* < IE. base *werǧ-,* to do, act, whence Gr. *ergon* (for *wergon*), action, work, *organon,* tool, instrument] **1.** physical or mental effort exerted to do or make something; purposeful activity; labor; toil **2.** employment at a job or in a position **3.** occupation, profession, business, trade, craft, etc. **4.** *a)* something one is making, doing, or acting upon, esp. as part of one's occupation or duty; task; undertaking *[to bring work home from the office]* *b)* the amount of this *[a day's work]* **5.** something that has been made or done; result of a specific kind of activity or way of working *[to have dental work done, skillful brushwork]*; specif., *a)* an act; deed: *usually used in pl. [a person of good works]* *b)* *[pl.]* collected writings *[the works of Poe]* *c)* *[pl.]* engineering structures, as bridges, dams, docks, etc. *d)* a fortification *e)* needlework; embroidery *f)* same *as* WORK OF ART **6.** material that is being or is to be processed, as in a machine tool, in some stage of manufacture **7.** *[pl.]* a place where work is done, as a factory, public utility plant, etc.: often in combination *[steelworks, gasworks]* **8.** manner, style, quality, rate, etc. of working; workmanship **9.** foam due to fermentation, as in cider **10.** the action of, or effect produced by, natural forces **11.** *Mech.* transference of force from one body or system to another, measured by the product of the force and the amount of displacement in the line of force **12.** *[pl.]* *Theol.* moral actions, esp. those regarded as just, merciful, etc. —*adj.* of, for, or used in work —*vi.* **worked** or **wrought, work'ing** [OE. *wyrcan, wercan*] **1.** to exert oneself in order to do or make something; do work; labor; toil **2.** to be employed **3.** *a)* to perform its required or expected function; operate or act as specified *b)* to operate effectively; be effectual *[a makeshift arrangement that works]* **4.** to undergo fermentation **5.** to produce results or exert an influence *[let it work in their minds]* **6.** to be manipulated, kneaded, etc. *[putty that works easily]* **7.** to move, proceed, etc. slowly and with or as with difficulty **8.** to move, twitch, etc. as from agitation *[his face worked with emotion]* **9.** to change into a specified condition, as by repeated movement *[the door worked loose]* **10.** *Naut.* to strain, as in a storm, so that the fastenings become slack: said of a ship —*vt.* **1.** to cause; bring about; effect *[an idea that worked harm]* **2.** to mold; shape; form *[to work silver]* **3.** to sew, embroider, etc. *[to work a sampler]* **4.** to solve (a mathematical problem, puzzle, etc.) **5.** to draw, paint, carve, etc. (a portrait or likeness) **6.** to manipulate; knead *[to work dough]* **7.** to bring into a specified condition, as by movement back and forth *[to work a nail loose]* **8.** to cultivate (soil) **9.** to cause to function; operate; manage; use *[to work a pump]* **10.** to cause fermentation in **11.** to cause to work *[to work a crew hard]* **12.** to influence; persuade; induce *[to work someone to one's way of thinking]* **13.** to make (one's way, passage, etc.) by work or effort **14.** to provoke; rouse; excite *[to work oneself into a rage]* **15.** to carry on activity in, along, etc.; cover *[a salesman working his territory]* **16.** [Colloq.] to make use of, esp. by artful contriving *[to work one's connections]* ☆**17.** [Colloq.] to use one's influence, charm, etc. on (a person) to gain some profits or advantage —**at work 1.** working or engaged in work **2.** in operation —☆**get the works** [Slang] to be the victim of extreme measures —☆**give (someone) the works** [Slang] **1.** to murder (someone) **2.** to subject (someone) to an ordeal, either maliciously or jokingly —**in the works** [Colloq.] in the process of being planned or done —**make short** (or **quick**) **work of** to deal with or dispose of quickly —**out of work** without a job; unemployed —☆**shoot the works** [Slang] **1.** to risk everything on one chance or play **2.** to make a supreme effort or attempt —**the works 1.** the working parts or mechanism (*of* a watch, clock, etc.) ☆**2.** [Colloq.] all possible accessories, extras, etc.; also (usually *the whole works*), everything that can be included —**work in 1.** to introduce or insert **2.** to be introduced or inserted —**work off 1.** to get rid of or dissipate, as by exertion ☆**2.** to pay (a debt or obligation) by work rather than with money —**work on** (or **upon**) **1.** to influence **2.** to try to persuade —**work out 1.** to make its way out, as from being embedded **2.** to exhaust (a mine, etc.) **3.** *same as* WORK OFF (sense 2) **4.** to bring about by work; accomplish **5.** to solve **6.** to calculate **7.** to result in some way **8.** to add up to a total (*at* a specified amount) **9.** to develop; elaborate **10.** to put into practice **11.** to engage in a training session or program for physical fitness or athletic skill —**work over 1.** to work or do again ☆**2.** [Colloq.] to subject to harsh or cruel treatment, as by beating, torture, etc. —**work up** ☆**1.** to make one's (or its) way up; advance; rise **2.** to manipulate, mix, etc. into a specified object or shape **3.** to develop; elaborate **4.** to acquire knowledge of or skill at **5.** to arouse; excite **6.** [Slang] to bring about or cause (a sweat) by vigorous activity

SYN.—**work,** in this connection, is the general word for effort put forth in doing or making something, whether physical or mental, easy or difficult, pleasant or unpleasant, etc.; **labor** more often implies strenuous physical work *[sentenced to three years*

at hard *labor]*; **travail,** now a somewhat literary word, suggests painful exertion or oppressive labor *[wearied by long travail]*; **toil** implies long, exhausting work, whether physical or mental *[the irksome toil of cataloging]*; **grind** suggests prolonged, tedious, uninspiring work *[the grind of routine tasks]* —ANT. **rest, play**

work·a·ble (wur'kə b'l) *adj.* **1.** that can be worked **2.** practicable or feasible *[a workable plan]* —**work'a·bil'i·ty, work'a·ble·ness** *n.*

work·a·day (wur'kə dā') *adj.* [ME. *werkedai* < *werk,* WORK + *-e-* (prob. as in *sunnedai,* SUNDAY, *messeday,* "mass day") + *dai,* DAY] **1.** of or suitable for working days; everyday **2.** commonplace; ordinary

work·bag (wurk'bag') *n.* a bag for holding implements and materials for work, as for knitting, crocheting, etc.

work basket a basket for holding sewing equipment

work·bench (-bench') *n.* a table at which work is done, as by a mechanic, carpenter, repairman, etc.

work·book (-book') *n.* ☆**1.** a book for the use of students, containing questions and exercises based on a textbook or course of study **2.** a book containing instructions on the method of operation **3.** a book in which one keeps a record of work planned or done

work·box (-bäks') *n.* a box for work tools and materials

☆**work camp 1.** a prison camp for people sentenced to hard labor **2.** a camp where work is done by volunteer workers, as for a religious organization

work·day (-dā') *n.* [LME. *werkdai,* prob. < *werk* + *dai* (OE. had *weorcdæg*)] **1.** a day on which work is done; working day ☆**2.** the part of a day during which work is done *[a 7-hour workday]* —*adj. same as* WORKADAY

work·er (wur'kər) *n.* **1.** a person, animal, or thing that works; specif., a person who is employed to do physical or mental work for wages, esp. in order to earn a living, as in a trade, industry, business, office, etc. or on a farm, ranch, etc. **2.** a person who works for a cause, organization, etc. *[volunteer workers,* a party *worker]* **3.** any of a class of sterile or sexually imperfect female ants, bees, wasps, etc. that do work for the colony **4.** *Printing* an electrotype used to print from, as distinguished from one used as a mold for making duplicate electrotypes

work farm a farm on which the workers are short-term prisoners convicted of less serious crimes

work·folk (wurk'fōk') *n.pl.* [Now Rare] working people, esp. farm workers: also **work'folks'** (-fōks')

work force the total number of workers actively employed in, or available for work in, a nation, region, plant, etc.

work function *Physics* the energy needed for a free electron to escape through the surface of a metal

work·horse (-hôrs') *n.* **1.** a horse used for working, as for pulling a plow **2.** a steady, responsible worker who assumes a heavy workload **3.** a machine, vehicle, etc. that proves to be durable and dependable

work·house (-hous') *n.* **1.** orig., a workshop **2.** in England, formerly, a poorhouse ☆**3.** a kind of prison, where petty offenders are confined and made to work

work·ing (wur'kin) *adj.* **1.** that works **2.** of, for, used in, or taken up by work *[a working day, working clothes]* **3.** sufficient to get work done *[a working majority]* **4.** on which further work is or may be based *[a working hypothesis]* **5.** moving or jerking convulsively, as from emotion: said of the face, features, etc. —*n.* **1.** the act or process of a person or thing that works **2.** the process of forming or shaping something **3.** convulsive movement or jerking, as of the face **4.** slow or gradual progress involving great effort or exertion **5.** [usually *pl.*] a part of a mine, quarry, etc. where work is or has been done

working capital 1. *Accounting* excess of readily convertible assets over current liabilities **2.** *Finance* the part of a company's capital readily convertible into cash

working class workers as a class; esp., industrial or manual workers as a class; proletariat —**work'ing-class'** *adj.*

working day 1. a day on which work is done, esp. as distinguished from a Sunday, holiday, etc.; workday **2.** the part of a day during which work is done; specif., the number of hours constituting the required day's work for the regular wage or salary

working drawing a drawing made to scale, for the guidance of those doing the work illustrated by it

work·ing·man (-man') *n., pl.* **-men'** a worker; esp., an industrial or manual worker; wage earner; laborer

working papers any official papers that legalize the employment of a minor or of an alien

working substance the air, gas, or liquid that works the pistons, vanes, etc. of an engine

work·ing·wom·an (-woom'ən) *n., pl.* **-wom'en** a woman worker; esp., a woman industrial or manual worker

work·load (wurk'lōd') *n.* the amount of work assigned for completion within a given period of time

work·man (wurk'mən) *n., pl.* **-men 1.** *same as* WORKINGMAN **2.** a craftsman

work·man·like (-līk') *adj.* characteristic of a good workman; skillful: also **work'man·ly**

work·man·ship (-ship') *n.* **1.** skill of a workman, or the quality of his work; craftsmanship *[furniture of fine workmanship]* **2.** something produced by this skill

workmen's compensation the compensation to an employee for injury or occupational disease suffered in connection with his employment, paid under a government-supervised insurance system contributed to by employers

work of art 1. something produced in one of the fine arts, esp. in one of the graphic or plastic arts, as a painting, sculpture, carving, etc. 2. anything made, done, performed, etc. with great skill and beauty

☆**work·out** (wurk′out′) n. 1. a training session of exercises to maintain or improve one's physical fitness or athletic skill 2. any strenuous exercise, work, etc.

work·peo·ple (-pē′p'l) n.pl. [Chiefly Brit.] workers; esp., industrial or manual workers

work·room (-rōōm′) n. a room in which work is done

works council [Brit.] a committee of workers in a factory, business, etc. organized by an employer to discuss industrial relations

work sheet 1. a sheet of paper on which a record of work, working time, etc. is kept 2. a sheet of paper printed with practice exercises, problems, etc., to be worked on directly by students 3. a sheet of paper containing working notes, preliminary formulations, etc.

work·shop (-shäp′) n. 1. a room or building where work, as home repairs or light manufacturing, is done 2. a seminar or series of meetings for intensive study, work, discussion, etc. in some field [a writers' workshop]

work song a folk song sung by laborers, as in the fields, with a marked rhythm matching the rhythm of their work

work·ta·ble (-tā′b'l) n. a table at which work is done, esp. one with drawers for tools, materials, etc.

work-up (-up′) n. Printing an unwanted mark on a printed page caused by the rising of spacing material

☆**work·week** (-wēk′) n. the total number of hours or days worked in a week for the regular wage or salary

work·wom·an (-woom′ən) n., pl. -wom′en var. of WORK-INGWOMAN

world (wurld) n. [ME. < OE. werold, world, humanity, long time, akin to OHG. weralt < early WGmc. compound < *wera-, man (see WEREWOLF) + *alth-, an age, mankind (for IE. base see OLD): basic sense "the age of man"] 1. a) the planet earth b) the whole universe c) any heavenly body thought of hypothetically as inhabited [worlds in space] 2. the earth and its inhabitants 3. a) the human race; mankind b) people generally; the public [a discovery that startled the world] 4. a) [also W-] some part of the earth [the Old World] b) some period of history, its society, etc. [the ancient world] c) any sphere or domain [the animal world] d) any sphere of human activity [the world of music] e) any sphere or state of existence [the world of tomorrow] 5. individual experience, outlook, etc. [a man whose world is narrow] 6. a) secular or social life and interests, as distinguished from the religious or spiritual b) people primarily concerned with secular affairs and pursuits 7. [often pl.] a large amount; great deal [the rest did him a world (or worlds) of good] 8. a star or planet —SYN. see EARTH —**bring into the world** to give birth to —**come into the world** to be born —**for all the world** 1. for any reason or consideration at all 2. in every respect; exactly —**in the world** 1. on earth or in the universe; anywhere 2. at all; ever —☆**on top of the world** [Colloq.] elated with joy, pride, success, etc.; exultant —☆**out of this world** [Slang] exceptionally fine; extraordinary; remarkable —**world without end** forever

World Bank an agency (officially **International Bank for Reconstruction and Development**) of the UN, established in 1945 to make loans to member nations so as to encourage foreign trade, industrial development, etc.

☆**world·beat·er** (-bēt′ər) n. [Colloq.] one that is, or that has the qualities needed to become, a great success

World Council of Churches an international organization of over 200 Protestant, Anglican, and Orthodox churches, founded in 1948 to foster ecumenism and cooperation

World Court a court (**Permanent Court of International Justice**) set up by the League of Nations to settle disputes between nations: cf. INTERNATIONAL COURT OF JUSTICE

world·ling (-lin) n. a worldly person

world·ly (wurld′lē) adj. -li·er, -li·est 1. of or limited to this world; temporal or secular 2. devoted to or concerned with the affairs, pleasures, etc. of this world: also **world′ly-mind′ed** 3. worldly-wise; sophisticated —SYN. see EARTHLY —**world′li·ness** n.

world·ly-wise (-wīz′) adj. wise in the ways or affairs of the world; sophisticated

world power [transl. of G. weltmacht] a nation or organization large or powerful enough to have a worldwide influence

☆**World Series** [also w- s-] an annual series of games between the winning teams of the two major U.S. baseball leagues to decide the championship

☆**world's fair** any of various expositions of the arts, crafts, industrial and agricultural products, scientific advances, etc. of various countries of the world

world-shak·ing (wurld′shā′kin) adj. of great significance, effect, or influence; momentous

world soul a universal animating principle conceived of as analogous to the soul of a person

☆**World War I** the war (1914–18) between the Allies (Great Britain, France, Russia, the U.S., Italy, Japan, etc.) and the Central Powers (Germany, Austria-Hungary, etc.)

☆**World War II** the war (1939–45) between the United Na-
tions (Great Britain, France, the Soviet Union, the U.S., etc.) and the Axis (Germany, Italy, Japan, etc.)

world-wea·ry (wurld′wir′ē) adj. weary of the world; bored with living

world·wide (-wīd′) adj. extending throughout the world

worm (wurm) n. [ME. < OE. wyrm, serpent, dragon, akin to G. wurm < IE. base *wer-, to twist, curve, whence L. vermis, worm: cf. WARP, WRINKLE[1]] 1. any of many long, slender, soft-bodied, creeping animals, some segmented, that live by burrowing underground or as parasites, including the annelids, flatworms, roundworms, ribbon worms, gordian worms, and spiny-headed worms 2. popularly, a) an insect larva, as a caterpillar, grub, or maggot b) any of several mollusks, as the shipworms c) any of various wormlike animals, as a rotifer, a blindworm, etc. d) [Obs.] a snake; serpent 3. an abject, wretched, or contemptible person 4. something that gnaws or distresses one inwardly, suggesting a parasitic worm [the worm of conscience] 5. something thought of as being wormlike because of its spiral shape, etc.; specif., a) the thread of a screw b) the coil of a still c) an Archimedean screw or similar apparatus d) a short, rotating screw that meshes with the teeth of a worm wheel or a rack 6. Anat. any organ or part resembling a worm, as the vermiform process 7. [pl.] Med. any disease or disorder caused by the presence of parasitic worms in the intestines, etc. 8. Zool. same as LYTTA —vi. to move, proceed, etc. like a worm, in a winding, creeping, or devious manner —vt. 1. to bring about, make, etc. in a winding, creeping, or devious manner [to worm one's way through a tunnel] 2. to insinuate (oneself) into a situation, conversation, etc. 3. to extract (information, secrets, etc.) by insinuation, cajolery, or subtle questioning 4. to purge of intestinal worms 5. Naut. to wind yarn or small rope around (a rope or cable), filling the spaces between the strands ☆6. to rid (tobacco plants) of worms or grubs —**worm′er** n. —**worm′like**′ adj.

worm-eat·en (-ēt′'n) adj. 1. eaten into by worms, termites, etc. 2. worn-out, out-of-date, etc.

☆**worm fence** a zigzag fence of rails; snake fence

worm gear 1. same as WORM WHEEL 2. a gear consisting of a worm and worm wheel

worm·hole (-hōl′) n. a hole made, as in wood, by a worm, termite, etc.

worm lizard any of a family (Amphisbaenidae) of legless, cylindrical, burrowing lizards, resembling the earthworm and found chiefly in tropical America and Africa

WORM GEAR

worm·root (-rōōt′) n. same as PINKROOT

Worms (vôrmz; E. wurmz) city in Hesse, West Germany, on the Rhine: scene of an assembly (Diet of Worms), 1521, at which Martin Luther was condemned for heresy: pop. 60,000

worm·seed (wurm′sēd′) n. 1. any of a number of plants, as santonica, whose seeds are used in medicine as a remedy for worms, including the **American wormseed** (Chenopodium ambrosoides) of the goosefoot family 2. the seed of any of these plants 3. same as SANTONICA (sense 2)

worm snake any of a number of wormlike, nonpoisonous snakes (families Typhlopidae and Leptotyphlopidae)

worm wheel a toothed wheel designed to gear with the thread of a worm

worm·wood (-wood′) n. [ME. wormwode, altered by folk etym. (after worm, WORM + wode, WOOD[1]: from use as a vermifuge) < wermode < OE. wermod, akin to G. wermut (whence Fr. vermout: cf. VERMOUTH)] 1. any of a genus (Artemisia) of strong-smelling plants of the composite family, with white or yellow flowers; esp., a Eurasian perennial (Artemisia absinthium) that yields a bitter-tasting, dark-green oil (wormwood oil) used in making absinthe 2. a bitter, unpleasant, or mortifying experience

worm·y (wur′mē) adj. worm′i·er, worm′i·est 1. containing a worm or worms; worm-infested 2. same as WORM-EATEN 3. like a worm 4. debased; groveling —worm′i·ness n.

worn (wôrn) pp. of WEAR[1] —adj. 1. showing the effects of use, wear, etc. 2. damaged by use or wear 3. showing the effects of worry or anxiety 4. exhausted; spent

worn-out (-out′) adj. 1. used or worn until no longer effective, usable, or serviceable 2. exhausted; tired out

wor·ri·ment (wur′ē mənt) n. 1. a worrying or being worried; mental disturbance; anxiety 2. a cause of worry

wor·ri·some (-səm) adj. 1. causing worry or anxiety 2. having a tendency to worry —wor′ri·some·ly adv.

wor·ry (wur′ē) vt. -ried, -ry·ing [ME. wirwen < OE. wyrgan, to strangle, injure, akin to G. würgen, to strangle < IE. *wergh-, to twist, choke < base *wer-, to twist, whence WORM] 1. a) to harass or treat roughly with or as with continual biting or tearing with the teeth [a dog worrying a bone] b) to pluck at, push on, touch, etc. repeatedly in a nervous or determined way [worrying the loose tooth with his tongue] 2. to annoy, bother, harass, vex, etc. 3. to cause to feel troubled or uneasy; make anxious; distress —vi. 1. to bite, pull, or tear (at an object) with or as with the teeth 2. to feel distressed in the mind; be anxious, troubled, or uneasy 3. to manage to get

fat, āpe, cär; ten, ēven; is, bīte; gō, hôrn, tōōl, look; oil, out; up, fur; get; joy; yet; chin, she; thin, then; zh, leisure; ŋ, ring; ə for a in ago, e in agent, i in sanity, o in comply, u in focus; ' as in able (ā′b'l); Fr. bāl; ë, Fr. coeur; ö, Fr. feu; ô, Fr. mon; ô, Fr. coq; ü, Fr. duc; r, Fr. cri; H, G. ich; kh, G. doch. See inside front cover. ☆ Americanism; ‡foreign; *hypothetical; <derived from

(*along* or *through*) in the face of trials and difficulties —*n.*, *pl.* -ries 1. the act of worrying 2. a troubled state of mind; anxiety; distress; care; uneasiness 3. something that causes anxiety —*SYN.* see CARE —wor'ri·er *n.*

☆wor·ry·wart (-wôrt') *n.* [WORRY + WART] [Colloq.] a person who tends to worry, esp. over insignificant details

worse (wurs) *adj. compar. of* BAD¹ & ILL [ME. < OE. *wiersa* (used as compar. of *yfel*, bad, EVIL), akin to OHG. *wirsiro*, prob. < base of OHG. & OS. *werran*, to confuse] 1. *a)* bad, evil, harmful, unpleasant, etc. in a greater degree; less good *b)* of inferior quality or condition 2. in poorer health or physical condition; more ill; less well 3. in a less favorable condition; in a less satisfactory situation —*adv. compar. of* BADLY & ILL in a worse manner or way; to a worse extent or degree —*n.* that which is worse —for the worse to a worse condition —worse off in a worse condition

wors·en (wur's'n) *vt., vi.* [orig., a dial. word < prec. + -EN] to make or become worse

wors·er (-sər) *adj., adv.* worse: a redundant form now considered dial. or substandard

wor·ship (wur'ship) *n.* [ME. *worschip* < OE. *weorthscipe*, honor, dignity, worship: see WORTH¹ & -SHIP] 1. *a)* reverence or devotion for a deity; religious homage or veneration *b)* a church service or other rite showing this 2. extreme devotion or intense love or admiration of any kind 3. something worshiped 4. [Chiefly Brit.] a title of honor (preceded by *your* or *his*) used in addressing magistrates and certain others holding high rank 5. [Rare] a distinct type of religious group, as a sect 6. [Archaic] greatness of character; honor; dignity; worthiness —*vt.* -shiped or -shipped, -ship·ing or -ship·ping 1. to show religious devotion or reverence for; adore or venerate as a deity 2. to have intense love or admiration for; adore or idolize —*vi.* to engage in worship, or perform an act of religious devotion; specif., to offer prayers, attend church services, etc. —*SYN.* see REVERE¹ —wor'ship·er, wor'ship·per, *n.*

wor·ship·ful (-fəl) *adj.* 1. [Chiefly Brit.] worthy of being worshiped; honorable; respected: used as a title of respect for magistrates, certain lodge officials, etc. 2. feeling or offering great devotion or respect; worshiping —wor'ship·ful·ly *adv.* —wor'ship·ful·ness *n.*

worst (wurst) *adj. superl. of* BAD¹ & ILL [ME. *worste* < OE. *wyrsta* < the base of *wiersa*, WORSE + -*st*, superl. suffix] 1. *a)* bad, evil, harmful, unpleasant, etc. in the highest degree; least good *b)* of the lowest quality or condition 2. in the least favorable condition or least satisfactory situation —*adv. superl. of* BADLY & ILL in the worst manner; to a degree that is most bad, evil, unpleasant, etc. —*n.* that which is worst —*vt.* to get the better of; defeat —at worst under the worst circumstances; at the greatest disadvantage —give one the worst of it to defeat or get the better of one —if (the) worst comes to (the) worst if the worst possible thing happens —☆(in) the worst way [Slang] very much; greatly —make the worst of to be pessimistic about

wor·sted (woos'tid, wur'stid) *n.* [ME. *wurstede*, after *Worsted*, now *Worstead*, England, where first made] 1. a smooth, hard-twisted thread or yarn made from long-staple wool 2. fabric made from this, with a smooth, hard surface —*adj.* made of worsted

wort¹ (wurt) *n.* [ME. < OE. *wyrt-* (in compounds), akin to G. *würze*, a spice < IE. base **wrād-*, twig, root, whence L. *radix*, ROOT¹] a liquid prepared with malt which, after fermenting, becomes beer, ale, etc.

wort² (wurt) *n.* [ME. < OE. *wyrt*, a root, herb, plant < same base as prec.] a plant, vegetable, or herb: now usually in compounds [*spleenwort, liverwort*]

worth¹ (wurth) *n.* [ME. < OE. *weorth*, akin to *weorthian*, to honor, G. *wert*, worth, *werden*, to become < IE. base **wer-* < **wer-*, to turn] 1. material value, esp. as expressed in terms of money or some other medium of exchange 2. that quality of a person or thing that lends importance, value, merit, etc. and that is measurable by the esteem in which the person or thing is held 3. the amount or quantity of something that may be had for a given sum [a dime's *worth* of nuts] 4. wealth; possessions; riches —*adj.* [*with prepositional force*] 1. deserving or worthy of; meriting [not *worth* the effort] 2. equal in worth or value to [a book that is *worth* $50] 3. having wealth or possessions amounting to [a man *worth* half a million] —☆for all one is worth to the extent of one's powers or ability; to the utmost —☆put in one's two cents worth to give one's own opinion; speak up

SYN.—worth and value are used interchangeably when applied to the desirability of something material as measured by its equivalence in money, goods, etc. [the *worth* or *value* of a used car], but, in discrimination, worth implies an intrinsic excellence resulting as from superior moral, cultural, or spiritual qualities, and value suggests the excellence attributed to something with reference to its usability, importance, etc. [the true *worth* of Shakespeare's plays cannot be measured by their *value* to the commercial theater]

worth² (wurth) *vi.* [ME. *worthen* < OE. *weorthan*, to become, used as auxiliary of the passive voice, akin to G. *werden:* for IE. base see prec.] [Archaic] to betide; befall; become [woe *worth* the day]

worth·less (wurth'lis) *adj.* without worth or merit; useless, valueless, etc. —worth'less·ly *adv.* —worth'less·ness *n.*

worth·while (-hwil', -wil') *adj.* important or valuable enough to repay time or effort spent; of true value

wor·thy (wur'thē) *adj.* -thi·er, -thi·est [ME. *worthi*] 1. having worth, value, or merit 2. having enough worth or merit (for someone or something specified); meriting (often with *of* or an infinitive) [a man *worthy* of her, a candidate *worthy* to be supported] —*n., pl.* -thies a person of outstanding worth or importance: often used humorously —wor'thi·ly *adv.* —wor'thi·ness *n.*

wot (wät) *1st & 3d pers. sing., pres. indic.,* of WIT²

would (wood; *unstressed* wad) *v.* [ME. *wolde* < OE., pt. of *willan*, to wish, WILL¹] 1. *pt. & alt. obs. pp.* of WILL² 2. an auxiliary used: *a)* to express condition [he *would* write if you *would* answer] *b)* in indirect discourse to express futurity [he said he *would* bring it] *c)* to express habitual action [Sundays he *would* sleep late] *d)* to soften the force of a statement or request [*would* you please leave?] 3. I wish [*would* that she were here] Cf. SHOULD

would-be (wood'bē') *adj.* [ME. (northern) *walde be*] 1. wishing or pretending to be [a *would-be* expert] 2. intended to be [a *would-be* help]

would·n't (wood''nt) would not

wouldst (woodst) *archaic 2d pers. sing. pt.* of WILL²: used with *thou:* also would·est (wood'ist)

wound¹ (woond) *n.* [ME. *wunde* < OE. *wund*, akin to G. *wunde* < IE. base **wen-*, to hit, wound, whence WEN¹] 1. an injury to the body in which the skin or other tissue is broken, cut, pierced, torn, etc. 2. an injury to a plant caused by cutting, scraping, or other external force 3. any hurt or injury to the feelings, honor, etc. —*vt., vi.* [ME. *wundien* < OE. *wundian* < the *n.*] to inflict a wound or wounds (on or upon); hurt; injure —the wounded persons wounded, esp. in warfare

wound² (wound) 1. *pt. & pp.* of WIND¹ 2. *pt. & pp.* of WIND³

wound·wort (woond'wurt') *n.* [WOUND¹ + WORT²] any of various plants formerly used in dressing wounds; esp., *same as* BETONY

wove (wōv) *pt. & alt. pp.* of WEAVE

wo·ven (-'n) *alt. pp.* of WEAVE

wove paper paper made on a mold in which the wires are so closely woven together that the finished sheets do not readily show wire marks as on laid paper

wow¹ (wou) *interj.* an exclamation of surprise, wonder, pleasure, pain, etc. —*n.* ☆[Slang] a remarkable, successful, exciting, etc. person or thing —☆*vt.* [Slang] to be a great success with; arouse enthusiasm in

☆wow² (wou) *n.* [echoic] a distortion in reproduced sound resulting from variations in the speed of the turntable, tape, etc. either in recording or playing

wow·ser (wou'zər) *n.* [Chiefly Austral. Slang] a person who is rigorously puritanical, strait-laced, etc.

WPA, W.P.A. Works Progress (later, Work Projects) Administration

wpm words per minute

WRAC, W.R.A.C. Women's Royal Army Corps

wrack¹ (rak) *n.* [ME. *wrak*, damage, wrecked ship < OE. *wræc*, misery, something driven (< *wrecan*, to WREAK) & < cognate MDu. *wrak*, a wreck, wrecked ship] 1. ruin; destruction: now chiefly in the phrase wrack and ruin 2. a wrecked ship 3. *a)* wreckage *b)* a fragment of something that has been destroyed 4. seaweed or other marine plant life cast up on shore 5. [Scot. & Dial.] weeds —*vt., vi.* [Archaic] to wreck or be wrecked

wrack² (rak) *vt.* [altered (after prec.) < RACK¹] *same as* RACK¹; esp., *a)* to subject to extreme mental or physical suffering; torture *b)* to disturb violently; convulse

wrack³ (rak) *n.* a rack of clouds or other vapor

WRAF, W.R.A.F. Women's Royal Air Force

wraith (rāth) *n.* [Scot., earlier *warth*, guardian angel < ON. *vorthr*, guardian < *vartha*, to ward, guard: for IE. base see WARD] 1. a ghost 2. the spectral figure of a person supposedly seen as a premonition just before his death

Wran·gel Island (raŋ'g'l; *Russ.* vrän'gel/y') island of the U.S.S.R. in the Chukchi Sea: c.2,000 sq. mi.

Wran·gell (raŋ'g'l) [after Baron F. von *Wrangel(l)*, 1796–1870, Russ. explorer] 1. mountain range in SE Alas.: highest peak, Mount BLACKBURN 2. Mount, active volcano in these mountains: 14,006 ft.

wran·gle¹ (raŋ'g'l) *vi.* -gled, -gling [ME. *wranglen*, freq. of *wringen:* see WRING] 1. to quarrel angrily and noisily 2. to argue; dispute —*vt.* to argue (a person) *into* or *out of* something —*n.* an angry, noisy dispute or quarrel —*SYN.* see QUARREL

wran·gle² (raŋ'g'l) *vt.* -gled, -gling [back-formation < WRANGLER²] ☆to herd (livestock, esp. saddle horses)

wran·gler¹ (-glər) *n.* [WRANGLE¹ + -ER] a person who wrangles, or argues, esp. in a contentious way

wran·gler² (-glər) *n.* [< (*horse*) *wrangler*, partial transl. of AmSp. *caballerango*, a groom, footman] ☆a cowboy who herds livestock, esp. saddle horses

wrap (rap) *vt.* wrapped or wrapt, wrap'ping [ME. *wrappen*] 1. *a)* to wind or fold (a covering) around something *b)* to cover by this means 2. to envelop, surround, overspread, etc. or hide, conceal, veil, etc. as by enveloping [a town *wrapped* in fog] 3. to enclose and fasten as a package in a wrapper of paper, etc. 4. to wind or fold [to *wrap* one's arms around someone] —*vi.* to twine, extend, coil, etc. (usually with *over, around,* etc.) —*n.* 1. an outer covering; esp., *a)* something worn by being wrapped around the body, as a shawl *b)* [*usually pl.*] an outer garment, as an overcoat *c)* a blanket 2. [*pl.*] secrecy; censorship; conceal-

ment [plans kept under *wraps*] **3.** same as WRAPAROUND (*n.* 2) —**wrapped up in 1.** devoted to; absorbed or engrossed in (work, etc.) **2.** involved or implicated in —**wrap up 1.** to enfold in a covering **2.** to put on warm clothing ☆**3.** [Colloq.] *a*) to bring to an end; make final; conclude; settle *b*) to give a concluding, summarizing statement, report, etc.

wrap·a·round (rap′ə round′) *adj.* **1.** that has a full-length opening and is wrapped around the body [a *wraparound* skirt] **2.** molded, constructed, etc. so as to curve [a *wraparound* windshield] —*n.* **1.** a wraparound garment, esp. a skirt **2.** in bookbinding, a folded section of four pages or of multiples of four pages placed on the outside of a folded signature and sewed together with it

wrap·per (-ər) *n.* **1.** a person or thing that wraps **2.** that in which something is wrapped; covering; cover; specif., *a*) the leaf of tobacco forming the covering of a cigar *b*) the dust jacket of a book *c*) the paper wrapping in which a newspaper, magazine, etc. is enclosed for mailing **3.** a loose garment that is wrapped around the body; esp., a woman's dressing gown or baby's robe

wrap·ping (-iŋ) *n.* [often *pl.*] the material, as paper, in which something is wrapped

wrapt (rapt) *alt. pt. & pp.* of WRAP

wrap-up (rap′up′) *adj.* [Colloq.] **1.** that wraps something up; concluding ☆**2.** that comes at the end and summarizes —*n.* **1.** [Colloq.] *a*) the concluding event, action, etc. in a sequence *b*) a concluding, summarizing statement, report, etc. ☆**2.** [Slang] a quick, easy sale or the customer to whom such a sale is made

wrasse (ras) *n., pl.* **wrass′es, wrasse:** see PLURAL, II, D, 1 [Corn. *wrach*] any of a number of fishes (family Labridae), as the tautog, cunner, and hogfish (sense 2), having thick lips, spiny fins, strong teeth, and bright coloring, found esp. in tropical seas: some species are valued as food fishes

wras·tle (ras′'l) *n., vi., vt.* -**tled,** -**tling** *dial. or colloq. var.* of WRESTLE: also **wras′sle** -**sled,** -**sling**

wrath (rath, räth; *chiefly Brit.,* rôth) *n.* [ME. *wraththe* < OE. *wræththo* < *wrath,* WROTH] **1.** intense anger; rage; fury **2.** any action carried out in great anger, esp. for punishment or vengeance —*adj.* [Archaic] wrathful —SYN. see ANGER

wrath·ful (-fəl) *adj.* **1.** full of wrath; intensely angry **2.** resulting from, characterized by, or expressing wrath —**wrath′ful·ly** *adv.* —**wrath′ful·ness** *n.*

wrath·y (-ē) *adj.* **wrath′i·er, wrath′i·est** [Old Colloq.] wrathful; angry

wreak (rēk) *vt.* [ME. *wreken* < OE. *wrecan,* to revenge, punish, akin to G. *rächen,* Goth. *wrikan* < IE. base **wreg-,* to shove, oppress, hunt down, whence L. *urgere,* to press, URGE] **1.** to give vent or free play to (one's anger, malice, rage, etc.) **2.** to inflict (vengeance), cause (harm or havoc), etc. **3.** [Archaic] to avenge —**wreak′er** *n.*

wreath (rēth) *n., pl.* **wreaths** (rēthz) [ME. *wrethe* < OE. *writha,* a ring, a twisted band < *writhan,* to twist: see WRITHE] **1.** a twisted band or ring of leaves, flowers, etc.; esp., *a*) a chaplet worn as a mark of honor or victory *b*) a garland laid upon a grave or hung on a door, window, etc. **2.** something suggesting this in shape; twisted or circular band [*wreaths* of smoke] —**wreath′like′** *adj.*

wreathe (rēth) *vt.* **wreathed, wreath′ed** or *archaic* **wreath′-en, wreath′ing** [in Early ModE., back-formation < ME. *wrethen,* pp. of *writhen,* WRITHE; in later use < WREATH] **1.** to coil, twist, or entwine, esp. so as to form into a wreath **2.** to coil, twist, or entwine around; encircle [clouds *wreathed* the mountains] **3.** to decorate with wreaths **4.** to cover or envelop [a face *wreathed* in smiles] —*vi.* **1.** to have a twisting or coiling movement **2.** to move or take the form of a wreath

wreck (rek) *n.* [ME. *wrek* < Anglo-Fr. *wrec* < ON. *vrek,* driftwood, wreckage, akin to MDu. *wrak,* wrack: for IE. base see WREAK] **1.** goods or wreckage cast ashore after a shipwreck **2.** *a*) the disabling or destruction of a ship by any disaster of navigation; shipwreck *b*) a ship that has been disabled or destroyed by any disaster of navigation **3.** the remains of anything that has been destroyed or badly damaged **4.** a person in very poor health physically or mentally **5.** a wrecking or being wrecked; destruction; ruin —*vt.* **1.** to cause the wreck of; destroy or damage badly **2.** to tear down or dismantle (a building, etc.) **3.** to bring to ruin or disaster; overthrow; thwart; defeat **4.** to destroy the health, or physical or mental soundness, of —*vi.* **1.** to be wrecked **2.** to work as a wrecker

wreck·age (-ij) *n.* **1.** a wrecking or being wrecked **2.** the remains of something that has been wrecked

wreck·er (-ər) *n.* **1.** a person or thing that wrecks **2.** a person who causes ruin, obstruction, or disruption of any kind; specif., a person using false lights, etc. to lead ships to destruction in order to plunder the wreckage **3.** a person, car, train, boat, etc. that salvages or clears away wrecks; specif., a truck equipped to tow away wrecked or disabled automobiles **4.** a person who demolishes or dismantles old buildings, motor vehicles, etc., salvaging usable materials and parts [house *wrecker,* auto *wrecker*]

wreck·ing (-iŋ) *n.* the act or work of a wrecker —*adj.* engaged or used in dismantling or salvaging wrecks

☆**wrecking bar** a crowbar with a chisellike point at one end and a curved claw at the other

Wren (ren) *n.* [Colloq.] a member of the (British) Women's Royal Naval Service

wren (ren) *n.* [ME. *wrenne* < OE. *wrenna,* akin to OHG. *rentilo,* ON. *rindill*] **1.** any of a large family (Troglodytidae) of small, insect-eating songbirds having a long bill, rounded wings, and a stubby, erect tail; ☆esp., the **house wren** (*Troglodytes aëdon*) that often nests in birdhouses in N. America **2.** any of various similar, unrelated birds

Wren (ren), Sir **Christopher** 1632–1723; Eng. architect

wrench (rench) *n.* [ME. < OE. *wrenc,* a trick, deceit; akin to G. *ränke,* a bend, twist < IE. **wreng-* < base **wer-,* to twist, turn, whence WORM] **1.** a sudden, sharp twist or pull **2.** an injury caused by a twist or jerk, as to the back, a joint, etc. **3.** a sudden feeling of anguish, grief, etc., as at parting with someone [☆esp., the machine] **4.** any of a number of tools used for holding and turning nuts, bolts, pipes, etc. **5.** a false or strained interpretation of an original meaning —*vt.* **1.** to twist, pull, or jerk suddenly and violently **2.** to injure (a part of the body) with a twist or wrench **3.** to distort, strain, or give a false interpretation of (a meaning, statement, etc.) —*vi.* to pull or tug (at something) with a wrenching movement

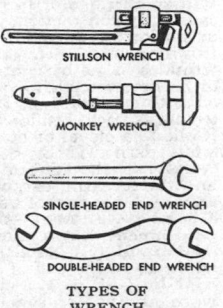

STILLSON WRENCH

MONKEY WRENCH

SINGLE-HEADED END WRENCH

DOUBLE-HEADED END WRENCH

TYPES OF WRENCH

wrest (rest) *vt.* [ME. *wresten* < OE. *wræstan,* to twist violently, akin to ON. *reista* < IE. base **wer-,* to turn, bend, twist, whence WRITHE] **1.** to turn or twist; esp., to pull or force away violently with a twisting motion **2.** to take or extract by force; usurp; extort; wring **3.** to distort or change the true meaning, purpose, use, etc. of; pervert; twist —*n.* **1.** the act of wresting; a twist; wrench **2.** [Now Rare] a wrenchlike key used in tuning pianos, harps, etc., for turning the pins (**wrest pins**) around which the strings are coiled —**wrest′er** *n.*

wres·tle (res′'l) *vi.* -**tled,** -**tling** [ME. *wrestlen, wrastlen* < OE. *wræstlian,* freq. of *wræstan,* to twist: see prec.] **1.** to struggle hand to hand with an opponent in an attempt to throw or force him to the ground without striking blows **2.** to struggle in opposition; strive; contend —*vt.* **1.** to struggle or fight with by wrestling; wrestle with **2.** to move, lift, etc. with great effort, using wrestling or grappling movements [to *wrestle* a boulder into place] ☆**3.** in the W U.S., to throw (a calf, etc.) for branding —*n.* **1.** the action of wrestling; wrestling bout **2.** a struggle or contest —**wres′tler** *n.*

wres·tling (-liŋ) *n.* a form of sport in which the opponents struggle hand to hand attempting to throw or force each other to the ground without striking blows

wretch (rech) *n.* [ME. *wrecche* < OE. *wrecca,* an outcast, lit., one driven out < *wrecan,* to drive out: see WREAK] **1.** a miserable or unhappy person; person in deep distress or misfortune **2.** a person who is despised or scorned

wretch·ed (-id) *adj.* [ME. *wrecched < wrecche* < OE. *wræcc,* wretched < *wrecan:* see prec.] **1.** deeply distressed or unhappy; miserable; unfortunate **2.** characterized by or causing distress or misery; dismal [*wretched* slums] **3.** poor in quality; very inferior [a *wretched* meal] **4.** contemptible; despicable —**wretch′ed·ly** *adv.* —**wretch′ed·ness** *n.*

wrick (rik) *vt., n.* [via dial. < ME. *wrikken,* to move jerkily: for base see WRY] [Brit.] sprain or wrench

wrig·gle (rig′'l) *vi.* -**gled,** -**gling** [MLowG. *wriggeln,* akin to WRY] **1.** to move to and fro with a twisting, writhing motion; twist and turn; squirm **2.** to move along with a wriggling motion **3.** to make one's way, or manage to get (out of a difficulty, etc.) by subtle or shifty means; dodge; equivocate —*vt.* **1.** to cause to wriggle **2.** to bring into a specified condition, form, etc. by wriggling —*n.* a wriggling movement or action —**wrig′gly** *adj.* -**gli·er,** -**gli·est**

wrig·gler (-lər) *n.* **1.** a person or thing that wriggles **2.** the larva of a mosquito

wright (rīt) *n.* [ME. < OE. *wyrhta,* a worker, maker < *wyrcan,* to WORK] a person who makes, constructs, or repairs: used chiefly in compounds [*wheelwright, shipwright*]

Wright (rīt) **1. Frank Lloyd,** 1869–1959; U.S. architect **2. Joseph,** 1855–1930; Eng. linguist & lexicographer **3. Orville,** 1871–1948 & his brother **Wilbur,** 1867–1912; U.S. airplane inventors **4. Richard,** 1908–60; U.S. novelist

wring (riŋ) *vt.* **wrung** or *rare* **wringed, wring′ing** [ME. *wringen* < OE. *wringan,* to press, compress, strain, akin to G. *ringen,* to struggle, wrestle < IE. **wreng-* < base **wer-,* to turn, bend (cf. WARP)] **1.** *a*) to squeeze, press, twist, or compress, esp. so as to force out water or other liquid *b*) to force out (water or other liquid) by this means, as from wet clothes (usually with *out*) **2.** to clasp and twist (the hands) together as an expression of distress

3. to clasp (another's hand) forcefully in greeting **4.** to wrench or twist forcibly **5.** to get or extract by force, threats, persistence, etc.; extort **6.** to afflict with anguish, distress, pity, etc. [a story to *wring* one's heart] —*vi.* to writhe, squirm, or twist with force or great effort —*n.* the action of wringing or twisting

wring·er (-ər) *n.* [ME., an oppressor] **1.** a person or thing that wrings **2.** a machine or device for squeezing out water or other liquid, esp. one fitted with opposed rollers to squeeze water from wet clothes

wrin·kle¹ (riŋ'k'l) *n.* [ME. *wrinkel*, a wrinkle, prob. back-formation < *wrinkled* < OE. (*ge*)*wrinclod*, pp. of (*ge*)*wrin-clian*, to wind about, akin to *wringan*, to press, WRING] **1.** a small ridge or furrow in a normally smooth surface, caused by contraction, crumpling, folding, etc. **2.** a crease or pucker in the skin, as any of those caused by aging, frowning, etc. —*vt.* **-kled, -kling** to form a wrinkle or wrinkles in, as by contracting; pucker; crease —*vi.* to be or become wrinkled —**wrin'kly** *adj.* **-kli·er, -kli·est**

wrin·kle² (riŋ'k'l) *n.* [prob. altered after prec. < obs. *wrench*, a trick, artifice, ult. < OE. *wrenc*, akin to WRENCH] [Colloq.] a clever or novel trick, idea, or device

wrist (rist) *n.* [ME. < OE. < base of *wræstan*, to twist, WREST] **1.** the joint or part of the arm between the hand and the forearm; carpus **2.** the corresponding part in an animal **3.** the part of a sleeve, glove, etc. covering the wrist **4.** *same as* WRIST PIN —☆**a slap** (or **tap**) **on the wrist** a token punishment that is much less severe than seems called for

wrist·band (rist'band') *n.* a band that goes around the wrist, as on the cuff of a sleeve

wrist·let (-lit) *n.* **1.** a closefitting band or strip of material worn around, or sometimes sewed on a sleeve at, the wrist, as for warmth **2.** a bracelet

wrist·lock (-läk') *n.* a wrestling hold in which one wrestler secures a lock on his opponent's wrist and twists his arm

wrist pin the stud or pin by which a connecting rod is attached to a wheel, crank, etc.

wrist·watch (-wäch', -wôch') *n.* a watch worn on a strap or band that fits around the wrist

writ (rit) *n.* [ME. < OE. < *writan:* see ff.] **1.** [Rare or Archaic] something written; writing; document **2.** a formal legal document ordering or prohibiting some action

write (rīt) *vt.* **wrote, writ'ten, writ'ing;** archaic pt. & pp. **writ** [ME. *writen* < OE. *writan,* to scratch, engrave, write, akin to G. *reissen,* to tear < IE. base *wer-,* to tear off, scratch, whence Russ. *véred,* a wound, Gr. *rhīnē,* a rasp] **1.** *a)* to form or inscribe (words, letters, symbols, etc.) on a surface, as by cutting, carving, embossing, or, esp., marking with a pen or pencil *b)* to form the words, letters, or symbols of with pencil, chalk, typewriter, etc.; put down in a form to be read [to *write* a paragraph, a formula, etc.] **2.** to form or inscribe (words) in cursive style: opposed to PRINT (*vt.* 7) **3.** to spell (a name, word, etc.) [words *written* alike are often pronounced differently] **4.** to know (a specific alphabet, language, etc.) well enough to communicate in writing **5.** to be the author or composer of (literary or musical material) **6.** to draw up or compose in legal form **7.** to fill in (a check, printed form, etc.) with necessary writing **8.** to cover with writing [to *write* three pages] **9.** to communicate in writing [he *wrote* that he would be late] **10.** to communicate with in writing; write a letter or note to [*write* her before you go] **11.** to entitle or designate in writing [he *writes* himself "Judge"] **12.** to underwrite **13.** to record (information) in a computer's memory or on a tape, etc. for use by a computer **14.** to leave marks, signs, or evidence of; show clearly [greed was *written* on his face] —*vi.* **1.** to form or inscribe words, letters, symbols, etc. on a surface, esp. by making marks with a pen or pencil **2.** to form words in cursive style: opposed to PRINT (*vi.* 3) **3.** to write books or other literary matter; be an author or writer **4.** to write a letter or letters **5.** to be employed at written work, as a clerk, copyist, etc. **6.** to produce writing of a specified kind [to *write* legibly, a pen that *writes* scratchily] —**write down 1.** to put into written form; write a record of **2.** to disparage or depreciate in writing **3.** to write in a pointedly simple style, as for readers considered to be less cultivated than the writer —**write in** ☆to vote for (someone not officially on a ballot) by inserting his name on the ballot —**write off 1.** to cancel or remove from accounts (bad debts, claims, etc.) **2.** to drop from consideration **3.** *same as* AMORTIZE (sense 2) —**write out 1.** to put into writing **2.** to write in full **3.** to exhaust (oneself) of ideas by writing prolifically —**write up 1.** to write a record or account of **2.** to complete in writing **3.** to praise or make much of in writing **4.** *Accounting* to set down an excessive value for (an asset)

☆**write-in** (-in') *n.* **1.** the act of voting for some person whose name is not on the ballot by inserting his name **2.** a person whose name is so inserted —*adj.* of or relating to a write-in [*write-in* campaign]

write-off (-ôf') *n.* something written off, amortized, etc.

writ·er (rīt'ər) *n.* **1.** a person who writes **2.** a person whose work or occupation is writing; now, specif., an author, journalist, or the like **3.** [Scot.] a solicitor or lawyer

writ·er's cramp (rīt'ərz) painful, spasmodic contraction of the muscles of the hand and fingers, resulting from excessive use in writing

☆**write-up** (rīt'up') *n.* **1.** [Colloq.] a written report or description, as in a newspaper, magazine, etc.; sometimes,

specif., a favorable account, as for a publicity release **2.** *Finance* a statement of the alleged assets of a corporation in excess of the true value

writhe (rīth) *vt.* **writhed, writhed** or archaic or poet. **with·en** (rith'n), **writh'ing** [ME. *writhen* < OE. *writhan,* to twist, wind about, akin to ON. *rītha* < IE. base *wer-,* to bend, twist: cf. WREATH, WRY] to cause to twist or turn; contort —*vi.* **1.** to make twisting or turning movements; contort the body, as in agony; squirm **2.** to suffer great emotional distress, as from embarrassment, revulsion, etc. —*n.* a writhing movement; contortion —**writh'er** *n.*

writh·en (rith'n) *adj.* [ME. *wrythen,* pp. of *writhen,* to WRITHE] [Archaic or Poet.] writhed; twisted; contorted

writ·ing (rīt'iŋ) *n.* **1.** the act of a person who writes **2.** something written, as a letter, document, inscription, etc. **3.** written form **4.** *short for* HANDWRITING **5.** a book, poem, article, or other literary work **6.** the profession or occupation of a writer **7.** the art, style, etc. of literary composition —*adj.* **1.** that writes **2.** used in writing

writing paper paper for writing on, esp. stationery

writ of assistance a writ issued by a court of equity, as an aid to the enforcement of its decree, for the transfer of real property to the rightful owner

writ of certiorari *same as* CERTIORARI

writ of error a writ directed to a lower court by an appellate court requiring the submission of the record of a legal action for review, in order to ascertain whether or not errors have been committed and so that the judgment may be upheld, reversed, or corrected

writ of prohibition an order from a higher court to a lower one directing it to cease hearing or prosecuting some matter outside its jurisdiction

writ of right *Eng. Law* formerly, a legal writ protecting or restoring title rights in freehold real estate

writ·ten (rit'n) *pp. of* WRITE —*adj.* put down in a form to be read; not spoken or oral

wrnt. warrant

Wroc·ław (vrôts'läf) city in Silesia, SW Poland, on the Oder River: pop. 471,000

wrong (rôŋ) *adj.* [ME., crooked, twisted, wrong < OE. *wrang* < ON. *rangr, wrangr,* wrong, twisted: for IE. base see WRING] **1.** not in accordance with justice, law, morality, etc.; unlawful, immoral, or improper **2.** not in accordance with an established standard, previous arrangement, given intention, etc. [the *wrong* method, came on the *wrong* day] **3.** not suitable or appropriate [the *wrong* thing to say] **4.** *a)* contrary to fact, reason, some set standard, etc.; incorrect; inaccurate; false *b)* acting, judging, believing, etc. incorrectly; mistaken **5.** unsatisfactory; in a bad state or condition **6.** not functioning properly; out of order [something *wrong* with her eyes] **7.** designating the side, surface, etc. that is not meant to be seen; designating the unfinished, inner, or under side [the *wrong* side of a fabric] —*adv.* in a wrong manner, direction, etc.; so as to be wrong; incorrectly; amiss —*n.* **1.** that which is not right, or not just, proper, correct, etc.; esp., an unjust or immoral act **2.** *Law* a violation or invasion of a legal right; injurious act, as a tort —*vt.* **1.** to treat badly or unjustly; do wrong to; injure **2.** to think badly of without real justification **3.** to malign; dishonor **4.** to seduce (a woman) —☆**get (someone) in wrong** [Colloq.] to bring (someone) into disfavor —**get (someone or something) wrong** [Colloq.] to fail to understand (someone or something) properly —**go wrong 1.** to turn out badly **2.** to change from good behavior to bad; go astray —**in the wrong** not on the side supported by truth, justice, etc. —**wrong'er** *n.* —**wrong'ly** *adv.* —**wrong'ness** *n.*

SYN.—**wrong** implies the inflicting of unmerited injury or harm upon another [he was *wronged* by false charges]; **oppress** implies a burdening with harsh, rigorous impositions or the cruel or unjust use of power [*oppressed* by heavy taxation]; **persecute** suggests constant harassment or the relentless infliction of cruelty and suffering [the *persecuted* minorities of Nazi Germany]; **aggrieve** suggests the inflicting of such wrongs or injuries as seem a just cause for complaint or resentment [*aggrieved* by her ill-treatment of him]; **abuse** suggests improper or hurtful treatment, as by the use of insulting or coarse language [her much *abused* husband] See also INJUSTICE

wrong·do·ing (-dōo'iŋ) *n.* any act or behavior that is wrong; the doing of wrong; transgression —**wrong'do'er** *n.*

wrong font the incorrect font: used in proofreading to designate a type face of the wrong size or style

wrong·ful (-fəl) *adj.* **1.** full of wrong; unjust, unfair, or injurious **2.** without legal right; unlawful —**wrong'ful·ly** *adv.* —**wrong'ful·ness** *n.*

wrong·head·ed (-hed'id) *adj.* stubborn in adhering to wrong opinions, ideas, etc.; perverse —**wrong'head'ed·ly** *adv.* —**wrong'head'ed·ness** *n.*

wrong number 1. *a)* a telephone number reached through error, as by dialing incorrectly *b)* the person reached by so dialing **2.** [Slang] someone or something considered to be unsuitable, undesirable, untrustworthy, etc.

wrote (rōt) *pt. of* WRITE

wroth (rôth; *chiefly Brit.,* rōth) *adj.* [ME. < OE. *wrath,* bad, wroth < the pt. stem of *writhan,* to twist, WRITHE] angry; wrathful; incensed

wrought (rôt) *alt. pt. & pp. of* WORK —*adj.* **1.** formed; fashioned **2.** shaped by hammering or beating: said of metals **3.** elaborated with care **4.** decorated; ornamented

wrought iron a kind of iron that contains some slag and very little carbon: it is resistant to corrosion, tough, and ductile, and is used in fences, grating, rivets, etc. —**wrought′-i′ron** *adj.*

wrought-up (rôt′up′) *adj.* very disturbed or excited

wrung (ruŋ) *pt. & pp. of* WRING

wry (rī) *vt., vi.* **wried, wry′ing** [ME. *wrien*, to twist, bend < OE. *wrigian*, to turn, twist, akin to OFris. *wrigia*, to bend, stoop < IE. base **wreik-* (whence L. *rica*, head veil) < **wer-*, to turn, bend] to writhe or twist —*adj.* **wri′er, wri′est 1.** turned or bent to one side; twisted; distorted **2.** made by twisting or distorting the features [a *wry* face expressing distaste] **3.** stubbornly contrary **4.** distorted in meaning, interpretation, etc. **5.** perverse, ironic, etc. [*wry* humor] —**wry′ly** *adv.* —**wry′ness** *n.*

wry·neck (-nek′) *n.* **1.** *a) same as* TORTICOLLIS *b)* a person afflicted with this **2.** any of several old-world birds (genus *Jynx*), related to the woodpecker but with soft tail feathers, noted for its habit of twisting its neck

WS. West Saxon

WSW, W.S.W., w.s.w. west-southwest

wt. weight

Wu·chang (wōō′chäŋ′) former city in EC China: see WUHAN

Wu·han (wōō′hän′) city in EC China, formed by the merger of the cities of Hankow, Hanyang, & Wuchang; capital of Hupeh province: pop. 2,500,000

Wu·hsi (wōō′shē′) city in Kiangsu province, E China, on the Grand Canal: pop. 616,000

Wu·hu (wōō′hōō′) city in Anhwei province, E China, on the Yangtze River: pop. 380,000

wul·fen·ite (wool′fə nīt′) *n.* [G. *wulfenit*, after F. X. von *Wulfen* (1728–1805), Austrian mineralogist] a mineral, lead molybdate, PbMoO₄, having a high luster and occurring usually as yellow tetragonal crystals

‡**wun·der·bar** (voon′dər bär′) *adj., interj.* [G.] wonderful

‡**Wun·der·kind** (-kint′) *n., pl.* **-kin′der** (-kin′dər) [G. < *wunder*, WONDER + *kind*, child < OHG.: for IE. base see KIND] a child prodigy

Wundt (voont), **Wil·helm (Max)** (vil′helm) 1832–1920; Ger. physiologist & psychologist

Wup·per·tal (vōōp′ər täl′) city in the Ruhr Basin of North Rhine-Westphalia, West Germany: pop. 422,000

wurst (wurst, woorst; *G.* voorsht) *n.* [G. < OHG.] sausage: often used in combination [*bratwurst, knackwurst*]

Würt·tem·berg (wurt′əm burg′; *G.* vür′təm berk′) former state in SW West Germany: see BADEN-WÜRTTEMBERG

Würz·burg (wurts′bərg; *G.* vürts′boork) city in NW Bavaria, West Germany, on the Main River: pop. 122,000

Wu·sih (wōō′shē′) *var. of* WUHSI

W.Va. West Virginia

WWI World War I

WWII World War II

WWW World Weather Watch

Wy·an·dot (wī′ən dät′) *adj., n., pl.* **-dots′, -dot′** [< Iroquoian < ?] *same as* HURON

Wy·an·dotte (wī′ən dät′) [after prec.] city in SE Mich., on the Detroit River: suburb of Detroit: pop. 41,000 —*n.* **1.** *var. of* WYANDOT **2.** any of a breed of American chickens, a cross between the Brahma and the Hamburg

Wy·att (wī′ət), **Sir Thomas** 1503?–42; Eng. poet & diplomat

wych-elm (wich′elm′) *n.* [< ME. *wyche* (see WITCH HAZEL) + ELM: from the pliant branches] **1.** a small variety of elm (*Ulmus glabra*), native to Europe and N Asia **2.** its wood

Wych·er·ley (wich′ər lē), **William** 1640?–1716; Eng. dramatist

Wyc·liffe (or **Wyc·lif**) (wik′lif), **John** 1324?–84; Eng. religious reformer: made the first complete translation of the Bible into English (from the Vulgate) —**Wyc′lif·fite′** (-li fīt′) *adj., n.*

Wye (wī) river in SE Wales & W England, flowing southeast into the Severn estuary: c.130 mi.

wye (wī) *n., pl.* **wyes 1.** the letter Y **2.** something shaped like Y

Wy·eth (wī′əth) **1. Andrew (Newell)**, 1917– ; U.S. painter: son of *ff.* **2. N(ewell) C(onvers)**, 1882–1945; U.S. painter & illustrator

Wyld (wīld), **Henry Cecil (Kennedy)** 1870–1945; Eng. linguist & lexicographer

wynd (wind) *n.* [MScot. *wynde* < ME. *winden*, to WIND¹] [Scot.] a narrow lane or alley

Wy·o·ming (wī ō′miŋ) [after *ff.*] **1.** Mountain State of the W U.S.: admitted, 1890; 97,914 sq. mi.; pop. 332,000; cap. Cheyenne: abbrev. **Wyo., WY 2.** city in SW Mich.: suburb of Grand Rapids: pop. 57,000 —**Wy·o′ming·ite′** (-īt′) *n.*

Wyoming Valley [< Algonquian (Delaware), lit., large plains] valley of the Susquehanna River, NE Pa., near Wilkes-Barre: site of a massacre (1778)

Wythe (with), **George** 1726–1806; Am. jurist & patriot

wy·vern (wī′vərn) *n.* [ME. *wivere* < ONormFr. *wivre* (OFr. *guivre*), dragon, serpent < L. *vipera:* see VIPER] *Heraldry* a two-legged dragon with wings and a barbed tail

X

X, x (eks) *n., pl.* **X's, x's 1.** the twenty-fourth letter of the English alphabet: from a western Greek alphabet **2.** a sound of X or x: in English, (ks), as in *lax;* (gz), as in *exact;* (ksh), as in *anxious;* (gzh), as in *luxurious;* and (z), as in *xylophone* **3.** a type or impression for X or x **4.** *a symbol for* the twenty-fourth in a sequence or group (or the twenty-third if J is omitted) —*adj.* **1.** of X or x **2.** twenty-fourth (or twenty-third if J is omitted) in a sequence or group

X (eks) *n.* **1.** an object shaped like X **2.** a mark shaped like an X used: *a)* to represent the signature of a person who cannot write *b)* to indicate a particular point on a map, diagram, etc. *c)* as a symbol for a kiss in letters, etc. *d)* to indicate the degree of fineness of flour, sugar, etc. **3.** the Roman numeral 10: with a superior bar (X̄), 10,000: XX = 20, XXX = 30, and X before another Roman numeral expresses a number 10 less than that numeral (XC = 90) **4.** a person or thing unknown or unrevealed **5.** Christ: used also in combination, as in *Xmas* —*adj.* shaped like X

x (eks) *vt.* **x-ed** or **x'd, x-ing** or **x'ing 1.** to indicate (one's choice or answer) by or as by marking with an X **2.** to delete or cross (*out*) written or printed matter with or as with an X or a series of X's

x 1. *Math. a symbol for: a)* an unknown quantity or a variable *b)* times (in multiplication) [3 x 3 = 9] *c)* an abscissa **2.** *a symbol for: a)* by (in indicating dimensions) [3 ft. x 4 ft.] *b)* power of magnification (in optical instruments) *c)* one's choice or answer (on a ballot, test, etc.)

xan·thate (zan′thāt) *n.* a salt or ester of xanthic acid

xan·the·in (-thē in) *n.* [Fr. *xanthéine*, arbitrarily differentiated from *xanthine*, XANTHINE] the water-soluble part of the yellow pigment present in the cell sap of some plants

xan·thene (zan′thēn) *n.* [XANTH(O)- + -ENE] a ring system, C₆H₄CH₂OC₆H₄, occurring as yellowish, crystalline leaflets in the molecules of many dyes

xanthene dye any of various dyes that contain the xanthene ring structure in their molecules

xan·thic (zan′thik) *adj.* [Fr. *xanthique:* cf. XANTHO- & -IC] **1.** yellow or yellowish in color **2.** of or having to do with xanthine

xanthic acid 1. an unstable, oily, colorless liquid, C₃H₆OS₂, that decomposes into ethyl alcohol and carbon disulfide at 24°C **2.** any of a series of acids having the general formula ROC(S)SH, in which R is any hydrocarbon radical

xan·thine (-thēn, -thin) *n.* [Fr.: cf. XANTHO- & -IN¹] **1.** a white, crystalline nitrogenous compound, C₅H₄N₄O₂, resembling uric acid: it is present in blood, urine, and certain plants **2.** any of various derivatives of this compound

Xan·thip·pe (zan tip′ē) 5th cent. B.C.; wife of Socrates: the prototype of the quarrelsome, nagging wife

xan·tho- (zan′thō, -thə) [< Gr. *xanthos*, yellow < ? IE. **ḱasno-* < base **ḱas*, gray, whence OE. *hasu*, ashen] a combining form meaning yellow [*xanthochroid*]: also, before a vowel, **xanth-**

xan·tho·chroid (zan′thə kroid′) *adj.* [Gr. *xanthochroos* (see XANTHO- & -CHROOUS), taken as if < *xanthos*, yellow + *ōchros*, pale] [Rare] having light-colored hair and complexion —*n.* [Rare] a xanthochroid person

xan·tho·ma (zan thō′mə) *n., pl.* **-mas, -ma·ta** (-mə tə) [XANTH(O)- + -OMA] a small tumor, esp. of the skin, formed by a deposit of lipids, often in a soft, rounded, yellowish mass —**xan·tho′ma·tous** (-thäm′ə təs, -thō′mə-) *adj.*

xan·thone (zan′thōn) *n.* [XANTH(O)- + -ONE] a ring ketone, C₆H₄(CO)OC₆H₄, occurring in some plant pigments and dyes

xan·tho·phyll (-thə fil) *n.* [XANTHO- + -PHYLL] a yellow crystalline pigment, C₄₀H₅₆O₂, found in plants; lutein: it is

related to carotene and is the basis of the yellow seen in autumn leaves —**xan'tho·phyl'lous** (-fil'əs) *adj.*

xan·thous (zan'thəs) *adj.* [Gr. *xanthos*, yellow (cf. XAN-THO-)] yellow or yellowish

Xan·thus (zan'thəs) ancient city in Lycia, SW Asia Minor

Xa·vi·er (zā'vē ər, zav'ē-; zāv'yər), Saint **Francis** 1506-52; Sp. Jesuit missionary: his day is Dec. 3: called the *Apostle of the Indies*

x-ax·is (eks'ak'sis) *n.*, *pl.* **x'-ax'es** (-sēz) *Geom.* **1.** the horizontal, or more nearly horizontal, axis in a plane Cartesian coordinate system along which the abscissa is measured **2.** one of the three axes in a three-dimensional Cartesian coordinate system

X chromosome *Genetics* one of the sex chromosomes: see SEX CHROMOSOME

X.D., x.d., x-div. ex (without) dividend

Xe *Chem.* xenon

xe·bec (zē'bek) *n.* [altered (after Sp. form) < earlier *chebec* < Fr. *chébec* < It. *sciabecco*, prob. via Sp. *xabeque* (now *jabeque*) < Ar. *shabbāk*] a small, three-masted ship having an overhanging bow and stern and both square and lateen sails: once common in the Mediterranean, esp. as used by corsairs

xe·ni·a (zē'nē ə, zēn'yə) *n.* [ModL. < Gr. *xenia*, hospitality < *xenos*, a guest, stranger] *Bot.* the immediate influence of pollen from one strain of a plant upon the endosperm of another strain, resulting in hybrid characters in the form, color, etc. of the resulting growth, as in the colors of corn grains

xen·o- (zen'ō, -ə) [< Gr. *xenos*, strange, foreign, a stranger] *a combining form meaning:* **1.** stranger, foreigner [*xenophobia*] **2.** strange, foreign, extraneous [*xenolith*] Also, before a vowel, **xen-**

Xe·noc·ra·tes (zi näk'rə tēz') 396-314 B.C.; Gr. philosopher, born at Chalcedon

xe·nog·a·my (zi näg'ə mē) *n.* [XENO- + -GAMY] *Bot.* cross-fertilization between different plants of the same species —**xe·nog'a·mous** *adj.*

xen·o·gen·e·sis (zen'ə jen'ə sis) *n.* [ModL.: see XENO- & -GENESIS] *Biol.* **1.** *same as:* a) SPONTANEOUS GENERATION b) ALTERNATION OF GENERATIONS **2.** the supposed production of an individual completely different from either of its parents —**xen'o·ge·net'ic** (-jə net'ik), **xen'o·gen'ic** (-jen'ik) *adj.*

xen·o·lith (zen'ə lith) *n.* [XENO- + -LITH] *Geol.* a rock fragment different in kind from the igneous rock in which it is embedded —**xen'o·lith'ic** *adj.*

xen·o·mor·phic (zen'ə môr'fik) *adj.* [XENO- + -MORPHIC] *Mineralogy* not showing their characteristic crystal faces, but distorted by the pressure of adjacent minerals: said of the granular constituents of igneous rocks

xe·non (zē'nän, zen'än) *n.* [Gr., neut. of *xenos*, strange] a heavy, colorless, noble, gaseous chemical element present in the air in minute quantities, found to react with fluorine and other reactive compounds and to form salts and acids in solution: used in bubble chambers, electric luminescent tubes, lasers, vacuum tubes, etc.: symbol, Xe; at. wt. 131.30; at. no., 54; density, 5.887 g/l (0°C); melt. pt., −111.9°C; boil. pt., −107.1°C

xenon hex·a·flu·o·ride (hek'sə floor'id, -flôr'-; -floo'ə rid') large, colorless crystals, XeF₆, prepared from gaseous xenon and fluorine

xenon tet·ra·flu·o·ride (tet'rə floor'id, -flôr'-; -floo'ə rid') a stable compound, XeF₄, prepared by mixing gaseous xenon and fluorine, heating to 400°C in a nickel container, and then cooling to form large, colorless crystals

Xe·noph·a·nes (zi näf'ə nēz') 570?-475? B.C.; Gr. Eleatic philosopher

xen·o·pho·bi·a (zen'ə fō'bē ə) *n.* [ModL.: see XENO- & -PHOBIA] fear or hatred of strangers or foreigners or of anything foreign or strange —**xen'o·phobe'** (-fōb') *n.* —**xen'o·pho'bic** (-fō'bik, -fäb'ik) *adj.*

Xen·o·phon (zen'ə fən) 430?-355? B.C.; Gr. historian, essayist, & military leader

xe·rarch (zir'ärk) *adj.* [XER(O)- + -ARCH] *Ecol.* developing in dry or desert sites: said of a sere

xe·ric (-ik) *adj.* [XER(O)- + -IC] **1.** of, pertaining to, or having dry or desertlike conditions **2.** *same as* XEROPHYTIC

xe·ro- (zir'ō, -ə) [< Gr. *xēros*, dry < IE. *ksero-*, dry (< base *ksā-*, to burn): cf. SERENE] *a combining form meaning* dry [*xerophyte*]: also, before a vowel, **xer-**

xe·ro·der·ma (zir'ə dur'mə) *n.* [prec. + DERMA¹] *same as* ICHTHYOSIS

☆**xe·rog·ra·phy** (zi räg'rə fē) *n.* [XERO- + -GRAPHY] a process for copying printed material, pictures, etc., in which the latent image of the original material is transferred by the action of light to an electrically charged surface to which the image attracts oppositely charged dry ink particles, which are then fused in place on the copy paper, reproducing the original image —**xe·ro·graph·ic** (zir'ə graf'ik) *adj.*

xe·roph·i·lous (zi räf'ə ləs) *adj.* [XERO- + -PHILOUS] capable of thriving in a hot, dry climate, as certain plants and animals —**xe·roph'i·ly** *n.*

xe·roph·thal·mi·a (zir'äf thal'mē ə) *n.* [LL. < Gr. *xēroph-thalmia*: see XERO- & OPHTHALMIA] a form of conjunctivitis characterized by a dry and lusterless condition of the eyeball and caused by a deficiency of vitamin A —**xe'roph·thal'mic** *adj.*

xe·ro·phyte (zir'ə fit') *n.* [XERO- + -PHYTE] a plant structurally adapted to growing under very dry or desert conditions, often having greatly reduced leaf surfaces for avoiding water loss, thick, fleshy parts for water storage, and hairs, spines, or thorns —**xe'ro·phyt'ic** (-fit'ik) *adj.*

xe·ro·sere (zir'ō sir') *n.* [XERO- + SERE¹] *Ecol.* a sere beginning in a dry area

xe·ro·sis (zi rō'sis) *n.* [Gr. *xērosis*: see XERO- & -OSIS] *Med.* abnormal dryness, as of the skin or eyeball

xe·ro·ther·mic (zir'ə thur'mik) *adj.* [XERO- + THERMIC] of or pertaining to a hot and dry climatic period, as one of the postglacial periods

☆**Xe·rox** (zir'äks) *a trademark for* a process for copying graphic or printed material by xerography —*vt.*, *vi.* to reproduce by xerography

Xer·xes I (zurk'sēz) 519?-465? B.C.; king of Persia (486?-465?): son of DARIUS I: called *the Great*

Xho·sa (kō'sä, -zä; *the* k *is actually a click*) *n.* **1.** *pl.* **Xho'sas, Xho'sa** any member of a pastoral people living in Cape Province, South Africa **2.** their Bantu language, characterized by the use of clicks Also sp. **Xo'sa**

xi (zī, sī; *Gr.* ksē) *n.* [Gr. *xi*, earlier *xei*] the fourteenth letter of the Greek alphabet (Ξ, ξ)

X.i., x-i., x-int. ex (without) interest

Xin·gu (shin goo') river in NC Brazil, flowing north into the Amazon: c.1,200 mi.

-xion *Brit. sp. of* -(c)tion [*connexion* (connection)]

xiph·i·ster·num (zif'ə stur'nəm) *n.*, *pl.* **-na** (-nə) [ModL. < Gr. *xiphos*, sword + ModL. *sternum*, STERNUM] *Anat.*, *Zool.* the cartilaginous process at the lowermost end of the sternum —**xiph'i·ster'nal** *adj.*

xiph·oid (zif'oid) *adj.* [Gr. *xiphoeides*, sword-shaped < *xiphos*, a sword + *eidēs*, a form] *Anat.*, *Zool.* shaped like a sword; ensiform —*n. same as* XIPHISTERNUM: in full **xiphoid process**

xiph·o·su·ran (zif'ə soor'ən, -syoor'-) *n.* [< Gr. *xiphos*, a sword + *oura*, a tail: see URO-²] any of an order (Xiphosura) of arthropods made up of the horseshoe crabs and related extinct forms —*adj.* of or pertaining to this order

XL extra large

Xmas (kris'məs; *popularly* eks'məs) *n.* [see XP] *same as* CHRISTMAS

Xn. Christian

Xnty. Christianity

XP [first two letters (chi & rho) of Gr. ΧΡΙΣΤΟΣ, *Khristos*] a symbol or emblem for Christ

X-ray (eks'rā') *n.* [transl. of G. *x-strahl* (< *x*, algebraic symbol for an unknown quantity + *strahl*, ray): so named by W. ROENTGEN, in 1895, because of its unknown character] **1.** a nonluminous electromagnetic ray or radiation of extremely short wavelength, generally less than 2 angstroms, produced by the bombardment of a substance (usually one of the heavy metals) by a stream of electrons moving at great velocity, as in a vacuum tube: X-rays are capable of penetrating opaque or solid substances, ionizing gases and body tissues through which they pass or, by extended exposure, destroying tissue, and affecting photographic plates and fluorescent screens: they are widely used in medicine for study, diagnosis, and treatment of certain organic disorders, esp. of internal structures of the body **2.** a photograph made by means of X-rays —*adj.* of, by, or having to do with X-rays —*vt.* to examine, treat, or photograph with X-rays Also **X ray**, **x-ray, x ray**

X-ray therapy medical treatment by controlled use of X-rays

X-ray tube an evacuated tube containing a metal target that is bombarded by electrons from a cathode and that subsequently emits X-rays

xy·lan (zī'lan) *n.* [XYL(O)- + -AN] a yellow, gummy pentosan that is found in woody tissues and yields xylose upon hydrolysis

xy·lem (zī'ləm, -lem) *n.* [G. < Gr. *xylon*, wood] the woody vascular tissue of a plant, characterized by the presence of vessels or tracheids or both, fibers, and parenchyma, that conducts water and mineral salts in the stems, roots, and leaves and gives support to the softer tissues

xylem ray a transverse sheet of soft, living cells wholly within the wood or xylem and extending from the pith of a stem to the phloem

xy·lene (zī'lēn) *n.* [XYL(O)- + -ENE] any of three isomeric, colorless hydrocarbons, C₈H₁₀, having the characteristics of benzene and derived from coal tar, wood tar, and petroleum: used as solvents, antiseptics, etc.

xy·lic acid (zī'lik, zil'ik) any of six isomeric crystalline acids, C₉H₁₀O₂, carboxyl derivatives of xylene

xy·li·dine (zī'lə dēn, zil'ə-) *n.* [XYL(ENE) + -ID(E) + -INE⁴] **1.** any of the six poisonous, liquid, isomeric compounds having the formula C₈H₁₁N, resembling aniline and derived from xylene **2.** a mixture of these isomeric compounds, used in making certain dyes and in organic synthesis

xy·lo- (zī'lō, -lə) [< Gr. *xylon*, wood] *a combining form meaning* wood [*xylograph*]: also, before a vowel, **xyl-**

xy·lo·graph (zī'lə graf', -gräf') *n.* [prec. + -GRAPH] [Rare] a woodcut or a wood engraving

xy·log·ra·phy (zī läg'rə fē) *n.* [Fr. *xylographie*: see XYLO- & -GRAPHY] [Rare] the art of making woodcuts or wood engravings —**xy·log'ra·pher** *n.* —**xy'lo·graph'ic** (-lə graf'ik), **xy'lo·graph'i·cal** *adj.*

xy·loid (zī′loid) *adj.* [XYL(O)- + -OID] of or like wood; woody
xy·lol (-lôl, -lōl) *n.* [XYL(O)- + -OL²] *a commercial name for* XYLENE
xy·loph·a·gous (zī läf′ə gəs) *adj.* [Gr. *xylophagos:* see XYLO- & -PHAGOUS] eating, boring into, or destroying wood, as certain mollusks or the larvae of certain insects
xy·lo·phone (zī′lə fōn′) *n.* [XYLO- + -PHONE] a musical percussion instrument consisting of a series of wooden

XYLOPHONE

bars graduated in length so as to sound the notes of the scale when struck with small, wooden hammers —**xy′lo·phon′ist** (-fō′nist, zī läf′ə nist) *n.*
xy·lose (zī′lōs) *n.* [XYL(AN) + -OSE¹] a colorless, crystalline pentose, C₅H₁₀O₅, formed by the hydrolysis of xylan, straw, corncobs, etc.
xy·lot·o·mous (zī lät′ə məs) *adj.* [< XYLO- + Gr. *tomos,* cutting (see -TOMY)] that can bore into or cut wood: said of certain insects
xy·lot·o·my (-mē) *n.* [XYLO- + -TOMY] the preparation of sections of wood for microscopic inspection —**xy·lot′o·mist** *n.*
xys·ter (zis′tər) *n.* [ModL. < Gr. *xystēr* < *xyein,* to scrape] [Obs.] a surgical instrument for scraping bones

Y

Y, y (wī) *n.,* *pl.* **Y's, y's** 1. the twenty-fifth letter of the English alphabet: from the Greek *upsilon* 2. the sound of *Y* or *y*: in English, a tongue-front semivowel glide when it begins a syllable, as in *yes* or *beyond,* or a high, front, lax vowel (i), as in *myth,* or the diphthong (ī), as in *my* 3. a type or impression for *Y* or *y* 4. *a symbol for* the twenty-fifth in a sequence or group (or the twenty-fourth if *J* is omitted) —*adj.* 1. of *Y* or *y* 2. twenty-fifth (or twenty-fourth if *J* is omitted) in a sequence or group
Y (wī) *n.* 1. an object shaped like Y, as a branched piece of piping, a forked support for a telescope, etc. 2. *Chem.* yttrium —*adj.* shaped like Y
y *Math.* a symbol for: 1. the second of a set of unknown quantities, *x* usually being the first 2. a variable 3. an ordinate
y- (i) [ME. *y-, i-* < OE. *ge-,* perfective prefix (basic sense "together"): for IE. base see COM-] an obsolete or archaic prefix formerly used regularly with the past participles of verbs: its use, as a poetic archaism, survived until the end of the 16th cent., as in *yclept*
-y¹ (ē, i) [ME. *-y, -i, -ie,* prob. after OFr. *-i, -e,* in such familiar names as *Davi* (for *David*), *Mathe* (for *Matheu*), etc.] a suffix meaning little, dear: used in forming diminutives, nicknames, and terms of endearment or familiarity [*kitty, Billy, daddy*]
-y² (ē, i) [ME. *-y, -ie* < OE. *-ig,* akin to L. *-ic(us)*, Gr. *-ik(os)*] an adj.-forming suffix meaning: 1. having, full of, or characterized by [*dirty, healthy*] 2. rather, somewhat [*yellowy, chilly, dusky*] 3. inclined or tending to [*drowsy, sticky*] 4. suggestive of, somewhat like [*wavy, horsy*] Sometimes used with a slight intensive force that does not change the meaning of the root adjective [*stilly*]
-y³ (ē, i) [ME. *-ie* < OFr. < L. *-ia* < or akin to Gr. *-ia, -eia*] a n.-forming suffix meaning: 1. quality or condition [*jealousy*] 2. a shop or goods of a specified kind [*bakery*] 3. a collective body of a specified kind [*soldiery*]
-y⁴ (ē, i) [ME. *-ie* < Anglo-Fr. < L. *-ium*] a n.-forming suffix meaning action of [*inquiry, entreaty*]
Y., Y *clipped form of:* 1. Y.M.C.A. or Y.W.C.A. 2. Y.M.H.A. or Y.W.H.A.
y. 1. yard(s) 2. year(s)
yab·ber (yab′ər) *vi., n.* [< native Australian *yabba*] [Australian Colloq.] talk; jabber
Ya·blo·no·vyy Range (yä′blō nô vī) range of mountains in SE R.S.F.S.R., a watershed between areas of Pacific & Arctic drainage: highest peak, c.9,000 ft.: also **Ya′blo·noi′** (-noi′)
yacht (yät) *n.* [Du. *jacht,* earlier *jaghte,* short for *jaghtschip,* pursuit ship (i.e., against pirates) < *jaght,* a hunt < *jagen,* to chase + *schip,* a SHIP] any of various relatively small ships for pleasure cruises, racing, etc. —*vi.* to sail or cruise in a yacht
yacht·ing (-in) *n.* the action, sport, or recreation of sailing or cruising in a yacht
yachts·man (yäts′mən) *n., pl.* **-men** a person who owns or sails a yacht —**yachts′man·ship′** *n.* —**yachts′wom′an** (-woom′ən) *n.fem., pl.* **-wom′en**
yack, yack-yack, yackety-yak *var. of* YAK², YAK-YAK, etc.
Yad·kin (yad′kin) [< AmInd. < ?] upper course of the Pee Dee River, in N.C.
ya·gi (antenna) (yä′gē, yag′ē) [after H. *Yagi,* 20th-cent. Jap. engineer] a VHF or UHF directional antenna array in which a basic dipole antenna is supplemented by several parallel reflector and director elements: widely used for television reception in weak-signal areas

yah (yä, ya) *interj.* a shout of derision, defiance, etc.
Ya·ha·ta (yä′hä tä′) *same as* YAWATA
Ya·hoo (yä′hōō) *n.* 1. in Swift's *Gulliver's Travels,* any of a race of brutish, degraded creatures subject to the Houyhnhnms and having the form and all the vices of man: see also HOUYHNHNM 2. [y-] a vicious, coarse person
yahr·zeit (yär′tsīt, yôr′-) *n.* [< Yid. *yartsayt* < MHG. *jarzit,* anniversary < *jar* (G. *jahr*), YEAR + *zit* (G. *zeit*), time: see TIDE¹] *Judaism* the anniversary according to the Jewish calendar of the death of a parent or other member of the immediate family, commemorated by the lighting of a 24-hour candle (**yahrzeit candle**), the saying of kaddish, etc.
Yah·weh, Yah·we (yä′we) [Heb.: see JEHOVAH] God: a form of the Hebrew name in the Old Testament: see TETRAGRAMMATON: also **Yah·ve, Yah·veh** (yä′ve)
Yah·wism (-wiz′m) *n.* 1. the worship of Yahweh (Jehovah) 2. the use of *Yahweh* as a name for God
Yah·wist (-wist) *n.* the unidentified writer or writers of certain Old Testament passages in which *Yahweh* (Jehovah) instead of *Elohim* is used as the name for God: cf. ELOHIST —**Yah·wis′tic** *adj.*
yak¹ (yak) *n., pl.* **yaks, yak:** see PLURAL, II, D, 1 [Tibet. *gyak*] a stocky, long-haired wild ox (*Bos grunniens*) of Tibet and C Asia, often domesticated as a beast of burden
☆**yak²** (yak; *also, for n.* 2, yäk) *vi.* **yakked, yak′king** [echoic] [Slang] to talk much or idly; chatter —*n.* [Slang] 1. idle or voluble talk 2. *a*) a loud laugh, esp. as audience response to comedy *b*) a joke or comic bit that evokes such a laugh Also, for *vi.* & *n.* (sense 1), **yak′-yak′, yak·e·ty-yak** (yak′ə tē yak′) —**yak′ker** *n.*

YAK
(to 5 ft. high at shoulder)

Yak·i·ma¹ (yak′ə mə) *n.* [< Sahaptin, ? lit., runaway] 1. *pl.* **-mas, -ma** any member of a Sahaptin Indian tribe living in the State of Washington 2. their Sahaptin language
Yak·i·ma² (yak′ə mô′, -ə mə) [after prec.] city in SC Wash.: pop. 46,000
Ya·kut (yä kōōt′) *n.* 1. *pl.* **Ya·kuts′, Ya·kut′** any of a people living in NE Siberia 2. their Turkic language
Ya·kutsk (yä kōōtsk′) city in EC R.S.F.S.R., on the Lena River: pop. 82,000
☆**Yale (lock)** [< its U.S. inventor, Linus *Yale,* 1821–68] *a trademark for* a key-operated, pin-tumbler cylinder lock
Yal·ta (yäl′tə) seaport in the S Crimea, R.S.F.S.R., on the Black Sea: site of a conference (Feb., 1945) of Roosevelt, Churchill, and Stalin: pop. 47,000
Ya·lu (yä′lōō′; *Chin.* yä′lü′) river flowing from Kirin province, China, along the Manchuria–North Korea border into the Yellow Sea: c.500 mi.
yam (yam) *n.* [Port. *inhame,* prob. < WAfr. native name] 1. *a*) the edible, starchy, tuberous root of any of several tropical climbing plants (genus *Dioscorea*) of the yam family, widely grown in the tropics for food *b*) any of these plants 2. any of various other plants of this same genus, as barbasco ☆3. [South] any of certain large varieties of sweet potato 4. [Scot.] *same as* POTATO (sense 2) —*adj.* designating a family (Dioscoreaceae) of climbing, chiefly tropical plants including the yams, barbasco, etc.
ya·mal·ka, ya·mul·ka (yäm′əl kə) *n. var. of* YARMULKE

---

ya·men (yä′mən) *n.* [Chin.] formerly in China, the office or residence of a mandarin or public official

yam·mer (yam′ər) *vi.* [ME. *yameren* < OE. *geomerian*, to lament, groan < *geomor*, sad, mournful, wretched: infl. by cognate MDu. & MLowG. *jammeren*] [Colloq. or Dial.] 1. to whine, whimper, or complain 2. to shout, yell, clamor, etc. —*vt.* to say in a complaining tone —*n.* the act of yammering —**yam′mer·er** *n.*

yang (yäŋ, yan) *n.* [< Chin. dial.] in Chinese philosophy, the active, positive, masculine force or principle in the universe, source of light and heat: it is always both contrasted with and complementary to the *yin*: cf. YIN²

Yang·chu·an (yäŋ′chōō än′) city in Shansi province, NE China: pop. c.200,000

Yang·tze (yaŋ′sē; *Chin.* yäŋ′tse′) river in C China, flowing from the Tibetan highlands into the East China Sea near Shanghai: c.3,400 mi.

Ya·ni·na (yä′nē nä′) *a former name of* IOANNINA

☆**Yank** (yaŋk) *n.* [Slang] a Yankee; esp., a U.S. soldier in World Wars I and II —*adj.* of or like a Yank or Yanks

yank (yaŋk) *n.* [< ?] ☆[Colloq.] a sudden, strong pull; jerk —*vt., vi.* [Colloq.] to jerk

Yan·kee (yaŋ′kē) *n.* [< ? Du. *Jan Kees* (taken as pl.) < *Jan*, John & *Kees*, dial. form of *kaas*, cheese; orig. (*Jan Kaas*) used as disparaging nickname for a Hollander, later for Dutch freebooter; applied by colonial Dutch in New York to English settlers in Connecticut: cf. H. L. Mencken, *Am. Lang. Suppl. I*, pp. 192–197] ☆1. a native or inhabitant of New England ☆2. *a)* a native or inhabitant of a Northern State; Northerner *b)* a Union soldier in the Civil War ☆3. a native or inhabitant of the U.S. —*adj.* of, like, or characteristic of the Yankees

☆**Yan·kee·dom** (-dəm) *n.* 1. Yankees collectively 2. the United States; esp., the northern States or New England

☆**Yankee Doo·dle** (dōō′d'l) [< YANKEE + (?) TOOTLE, in reference to sound made in tonguing a flute or fife, for which the tune was apparently first written] an early American song with several versions of humorous verses, popular during the Revolutionary War

☆**Yan·kee·ism** (-iz'm) *n.* 1. Yankee character or characteristics 2. a particular Yankee mannerism, idiom, etc.

‡**Yan·qui** (yän′kē) *n., pl.* **-quis** (-kēs) *Sp.* American respelling of YANKEE (sense 3)

Ya·oun·dé (yá ōōn dā′) capital of Cameroun, in the SW part: pop. 90,000

Yap (yäp, yap) group of islands in the W Carolines, W Pacific: c.80 sq. mi.; pop. 7,000

yap (yap) *vi.* **yapped, yap′ping** [echoic] 1. to make a sharp, shrill bark or yelp 2. [Slang] to talk noisily and stupidly; jabber —*n.* 1. a sharp, shrill bark or yelp 2. [Slang] noisy, stupid talk; jabber 3. [Slang] a crude, noisy, or contemptible person 4. [Slang] the mouth —**yap′per** *n.* —**yap′ping·ly** *adv.*

ya·pok, ya·pock (yə päk′) *n.* [< *Oyapok*, river in Guiana] a small, water-dwelling marsupial (*Chironectes minimus*) of Central and South America, with webbed hind feet

Ya·qui (yä′kē) *n.* [Sp. < Nahuatl (Piman), ? lit., chief river] 1. *pl.* **-quis, -qui** any member of a tribe of N. American Indians living in S Arizona and Sonora, Mexico 2. their Uto-Aztecan language

Yar·bor·ough (yär′bur′ō, -bər ə) *n.* [said to be so named after an Earl of *Yarborough*, who would bet 1,000 to 1 against its occurring] a bridge or whist hand containing no card higher than a nine

yard¹ (yärd) *n.* [ME. *yerde* < OE. *gierd*, a rod, staff, yard measure, akin to obs. G. *gerte*, a rod < IE. base *ghasto-*, a rod, pole, whence L. *hasta*, a pole, spear] 1. *a)* a measure of length, equal to 3 feet, or 36 inches: one yard is equivalent to .9144 meter: abbrev. **yd., y.** (sing. & pl.) *b)* a cubic yard [*a yard* of topsoil] 2. *Naut. a)* a slender rod or spar, tapering toward the ends, fastened at right angles across a mast to support a sail *b)* the transverse member of a mast on non-sailing ships: used to hold signal flags, lights, etc. 3. [Slang] one hundred dollars or, sometimes, one thousand dollars

yard² (yärd) *n.* [ME. *yerd* < OE. *geard*, enclosure, akin to ON. *garthr*, OHG. *gart*, GARDEN < IE. base *gherdh-*, to enclose, surround, whence GIRDLE, Russ. *górod*, town] 1. *a)* the space or grounds surrounding or surrounded by a building or group of buildings: often in combination [*churchyard*, *farmyard*, etc.] *b)* a plot of grass adjacent to a building, house, etc. 2. a pen or other enclosure for livestock or poultry 3. an enclosed place used for a particular purpose or business [a lumber *yard*, shipyard] 4. a place where wild deer, moose, etc. herd together for feeding during the winter 5. a railroad center where trains are made up, serviced, switched from track to track, etc. —*vt.* to put, keep, or enclose in a yard (often with *up*) —**the Yard** clipped form of SCOTLAND YARD

yard·age¹ (yär′dij) *n.* 1. measurement in yards 2. the extent or amount of something so measured ☆3. distance covered in advancing a football

yard·age² (yär′dij) *n.* 1. the use of a yard for storage, as for cattle at a railroad station 2. the charge for this

yard·arm (yärd′ärm′) *n. Naut.* either end of a yard supporting a square sail, signal lights, etc.

☆**yard·bird** (-burd′) *n.* [Slang] 1. a military recruit; rookie, esp. one frequently assigned to cleanup or other menial duties 2. a prisoner; convict

yard goods textiles made in standard width, usually sold by the yard

yard·land (-land′) *n.* same as VIRGATE¹

yard·man (yärd′mən) *n., pl.* **-men** a man who works in a yard, esp. a railroad yard

☆**yard·mas·ter** (-mas′tər, -mäs′-) *n.* a man in charge of a railroad yard

☆**yard·stick** (-stik′) *n.* 1. a graduated stick or rod one yard in length, used in measuring 2. any test or standard used in measuring, judging, etc. —*SYN.* see STANDARD

yare (yer) *adj.* [ME. < OE. *gearo* (akin to G. *gar*, OS. *garu*): prob. < *ge-* (cf. Y-) + *earu*, ready (for IE. base see RISE)] [Archaic or Dial.] 1. ready; prepared 2. brisk; active; quick 3. responding quickly and truly to the helm: said of a ship —*adv.* [Obs.] quickly; promptly Also for *adj.* 1 & 2, **yar** (yär)

Yar·kand (yär′känd′) same as SOCHE

Yar·mouth (yär′məth) same as GREAT YARMOUTH

yar·mul·ke (yär′məl kə) *n.* [Yid. < Pol. *yarmułka*] a skullcap often worn by Jewish men and boys when at prayer or study, at meals, etc.: also **yar′mal·ke, yar′mel·ke**

yarn (yärn) *n.* [ME. < OE. *gearn*, yarn, akin to G. *garn* < IE. base *gher-*, intestine, whence L. *haru-spex*, soothsayer, lit., intestine-seer, Gr. *chordē* (cf. CORD)] 1. any fiber, as wool, silk, flax, cotton, nylon, glass, etc., spun into strands for weaving, knitting, or making thread 2. coarse fibers woven into strands for rope-making 3. [Colloq.] a tale or story, esp. one that seems exaggerated or hard to believe —*vi.* [Old Colloq.] to tell yarns —**spin a yarn** [Colloq.] to tell a yarn

yarn-dyed (-dīd′) *adj.* woven of yarn dyed before weaving

Ya·ro·slavl, Ya·ro·slavl′ (yä′rō släv′l′) city in W European R.S.F.S.R., on the Volga: pop. 486,000

yar·o·vize (yär′ə vīz′) *vt.* **-vized′, -viz′ing** same as VERNALIZE

yar·row (yar′ō) *n.* [ME. *yarowe* < OE. *gæruwe*, akin to G. *garbe*] any of a genus (*Achillea*) of perennial plants of the composite family; esp., the **common yarrow** (*Achillea millefolium*), having a strong smell and taste, finely divided leaves, and clusters of small, pink or white flower heads

yash·mak, yash·mac (yäsh mäk′, yash′mak) *n.* [Ar. *yashmaq*] the double veil worn by Moslem women in public

yat·a·ghan, yat·a·gan (yat′ə gan′, -gən) *n.* [Turk. *yātāghan*] a type of Turkish short saber with a double-curved blade and a handle without a guard; ataghan

yat·ter (yat′ər) *vi.* [prob. < YA(K)² + (CHA)TTER] [Slang] to talk idly and foolishly about trivial things; chatter continuously —*n.* the act of yattering

yaud (yôd, yäd) *n.* [Scot.] an old, worn-out mare; jade

yauld (yôld, yäld) *adj.* [Scot.] active, nimble, etc.

yaup (yôp, yäp) *vi., n. var.* of YAWP

☆**yau·pon** (yô′pən) *n.* [AmInd. (Catawba) *yopún*, dim. of *yop*, a shrub] an evergreen holly (*Ilex vomitoria*) of the SE U.S.: its leaves are sometimes used as a substitute for tea

yaw (yô) *vi.* [ON. *jaga*, to sway (like a door on its hinges) < or akin to MHG. *jagen*, to hunt: cf. YACHT] 1. to turn or deviate unintentionally from the planned course or heading: said of a ship or boat 2. to swing on the vertical axis so that the longitudinal axis forms an angle with the line of flight; esp., to rotate or oscillate about the vertical axis: said of a projectile, aircraft, spacecraft, etc. —*vt.* to cause to yaw —*n.* 1. an act of yawing 2. the angle formed by a yawing craft

Ya·wa·ta (yä′wä tä′) city in N Kyushu, Japan, on an inlet of the Sea of Japan: pop. 332,000

yawl¹ (yôl) *n.* [< MLowG. *jolle* or Du. *jol*] 1. a ship's boat; jolly boat 2. a small sailboat rigged fore-and-aft, with a short mizzenmast astern of the rudder post: distinguished from KETCH

yawl² (yôl) *vi., n. Brit. dial. var. of* YOWL

yawn (yôn) *vi.* [ME. *yanen*, prob. merging OE. *ginian* & the synonymous *ganian*, to gape, akin to G. *gähnen* < IE. base *ghei-*, to gape, prob. echoic of the yawning sound, whence L. *hiare* (cf. HIATUS)] 1. to open the mouth wide, esp. involuntarily, and with a deep inhalation, as a result of fatigue, drowsiness, or boredom 2. to be or become wide open; gape [a *yawning* chasm] —*vt.* to express or utter with a yawn —*n.* 1. an act of yawning or opening wide 2. a wide opening; chasm —**yawn′er** *n.*

YAWL

yawp (yôp) *vi.* [ME. *yolpen*, prob. echoic var. of *yelpen*, YELP] 1. *a)* to utter a loud, harsh call or cry *b)* [Slang] to talk noisily and stupidly 2. [Colloq.] to yawn aloud; gape —*n.* the act or sound of yawping

yaws (yôz) *n.pl.* [*with sing. v.*] [of WInd. (Cariban) origin] a tropical infectious disease caused by a spirochete (*Treponema pertenue*) and characterized by raspberrylike skin eruptions followed sometimes by destructive lesions of the skin and bones; frambesia

y-ax·is (wī′ak′sis) *n., pl.* **y′-ax′es** (-sēz) *Geom.* 1. the vertical, or more nearly vertical, axis in a plane Cartesian coordinate system along which the ordinate is measured

2. one of the three axes in a three-dimensional Cartesian coordinate system

Yaz·oo (yaz′ōō) [< Fr. < AmInd. < ?] river flowing from NW Miss. southwest into the Mississippi River near Vicksburg: 188 mi.

Yb *Chem.* ytterbium

Y.B., YB Yearbook

Y chromosome *Genetics* one of the sex chromosomes: see SEX CHROMOSOME

y·clept, y-clept (i klept′) *pp.* [ME. *ycleped* < OE. *geclypod;* Y- + pp. of *clipian,* to call, CLEPE (popularized by Spenser & Milton) [Archaic] called; named; known as [*a* giant *yclept* Barbarossa]: also sp. **ycleped, y-cleped**

yd. *pl.* **yd., yds.** yard

ye¹ (*th*ə, *th*i, *th*ē; *now often erroneously or facetiously* yē) *adj. archaic form of* THE: *y* was substituted by early printers for the thorn (þ), the Old and Middle English character representing the sound (*th*): sometimes written yᵉ, as though a contraction

ye² (yē; *unstressed* yi) *pron.* [ME. < OE. *ge,* ye, nom. pl. corresponding to *thu,* thou, akin to Goth. *jus,* but with vowel modified after *we* (cf. WE): for IE. base see YOU] *archaic form of* YOU: orig. used only as nominative plural, later as nominative singular, and still later, esp. in dialectal speech, as accusative singular and plural

yea (yā) *adv.* [ME. *ye* < OE. *gea,* akin to G. *ja*] **1.** yes: used to express affirmation **2.** indeed; truly; verily: used to introduce a question or statement **3.** [Archaic] not only that, but more; moreover [*a* thousand, *yea,* ten thousand] —*n.* **1.** an affirmative statement or vote **2.** a person voting in the affirmative —*interj.* ☆an exclamation used in cheering on an athletic team, etc.

☆**yeah** (ya, ye, ye′ə, *etc.*) *adv.* [prob. < Du. & G. *ja,* merged with cognate YEA] [Colloq.] yes

yean (yēn) *vt., vi.* [ME. *genen* < OE. **ge-eanian* (cf. *geean,* pregnant) < *ge* (cf. Y-) + *eanian,* to bring forth lambs, akin to Du. *oonen* < IE. base **agwhnos,* lamb, whence Gr. *amnos,* L. *agnus,* lamb) to bring forth (young): said of a sheep or goat

yean·ling (-lin) *n.* [prec. + -LING¹] a lamb or kid —*adj.* newborn; infant

year (yir) *n.* [ME. *yere* < OE. *gear,* akin to G. *jahr* < IE. **yēro-,* year, summer (whence Gr. *hōros,* time, year, OBulg. *jara,* spring) < base **ei-,* to go (whence L. *ire,* to go): basic sense "that which passes"] **1.** *a)* a period of 365 days (in leap year, 366 days) divided into 12 months and regarded in the Gregorian calendar as beginning January 1 and ending the following December 31 *b)* a period of more or less the same length in other calendars **2.** the period (365 days, 5 hours, 48 minutes, and 46 seconds of mean solar time) spent by the sun in making its apparent passage from vernal equinox to vernal equinox: the year of the seasons: also **tropical, equinoctial,** or **solar year 3.** the period (365 days, 6 hours, 9 minutes, and 9.54 seconds of mean solar time) spent by the sun in its apparent passage from a fixed star and back to the same position again: it is the true period of the earth's revolution, and the difference in time between this and the tropical year is due to the precession of the equinoxes: also **sidereal year 4.** a period of 12 lunar months, as in the Jewish calendar: also **lunar year 5.** the period of time occupied by any planet in making one complete revolution from perihelion to perihelion: for the earth this period is 365 days, 6 hours, 13 minutes, and 53 seconds: also **anomalistic year 6.** a period of 12 calendar months reckoned from any date [six *years* old in July, a *year* from today] **7.** a calendar year of a specified number in a particular era [the *year* 500 B.C.] **8.** a particular annual period of less than 365 days [a school *year*] **9.** [*pl.*] *a)* age [old for his *years*] *b)* time; esp., a long time [he died *years* ago] —**year after year** every year —**year by year** each year —**year in, year out** every year

year·book (-book′) *n.* a book published yearly; specif., *a)* a book giving statistics and data of the preceding year *b)* same as ANNUAL (sense 1)

year·ling (yir′lin, yur′-) *n.* **1.** an animal one year old or in its second year **2.** *Horse Racing* a horse one year old: all thoroughbreds' birthdays are arbitrarily set at January 1, at which time a foal born on any date of the preceding year is reckoned one year old —*adj.* being a year old

year·long (yir′lôn′) *adj.* continuing for a full year

year·ly (-lē) *adj.* **1.** continuing or lasting for a year **2.** done, happening, appearing, payable, etc. once a year, or every year [a *yearly* event] **3.** of a year, or each year —*adv.* annually; every year

yearn (yurn) *vi.* [ME. *yernen* < OE. *gyrnan* < *georn,* eager, akin to G. *gern,* gladly: see HORTATORY] **1.** to be filled with longing or desire **2.** to be deeply moved, esp. with tenderness or sympathy —**yearn′er** *n.*

yearn·ing (yur′nin) *n.* [ME. *yerning* < OE. *girninge:* see prec. + -ING] deep or anxious longing, desire, etc.

year-round (yir′round′) *adj.* open, in use, operating, etc. throughout the year

yea·say·er (yā′sā′ər) *n.* [YEA + SAY + -ER] a person who is affirmative, positive, etc. in his attitude toward life

yeast (yēst) *n.* [ME. *yest* < OE. *gist,* akin to G. *gischt,* spray, froth & OHG. *jesan,* to ferment < IE. base **yes-,* to foam, boil up, whence Gr. *zein,* to boil, seethe: cf. ENZYME] **1.** *a)* any of various single-celled ascomycetous fungi (esp. genus *Saccharomyces*) in which little or no mycelium develops and that ordinarily reproduce by budding: they live on sugary solutions, ferment sugars to form alcohol and carbon dioxide, and are used in making beer, whiskey, etc. and as a leavening in baking *b)* same as BREWER'S YEAST Also **yeast plant 2.** *a)* the yellowish, moist mass of yeast plants occurring as a froth on fermenting solutions *b)* this substance dried in flakes or granules or compressed into cakes for preservation **3.** foam; froth **4.** *a)* something that agitates or causes ferment; leaven *b)* ferment; agitation —*vi.* [Rare] to froth or ferment

yeast·y (yēs′tē) *adj.* **yeast′i·er, yeast′i·est 1.** of, like, or containing yeast **2.** frothy; foamy **3.** light; superficial; frivolous **4.** in a ferment; restless —**yeast′i·ness** *n.*

Yeats (yāts), **William Butler** 1865–1939; Ir. poet, playwright, & essayist

Yed·o, Yed·do (ye′dō) former name of TOKYO

☆**yegg** (yeg) *n.* [< ?] [Slang] a criminal; esp., a safecracker or burglar: also **yegg′man** (-mən), *pl.* **-men**

yeld (yeld) *adj.* [ME. < OE. *gelde,* akin to ON. *geldr:* see GELD¹] [Scot.] **1.** barren **2.** not giving milk

yelk (yelk) *n.* [Archaic or Dial.] *var. of* YOLK

yell (yel) *vi.* [ME. *yellen* < OE. *giellan,* akin to ON. *gjalla,* OHG. *gellan* < IE. base **ghel-,* to cry out, whence Gr. *chelidōn,* a swallow] to cry out loudly; shriek; scream —*vt.* to utter by yelling —*n.* **1.** a loud outcry or shout; shriek; scream ☆**2.** a rhythmic cheer given in unison, as by students at a school or college football game —**yell′er** *n.*

yel·low (yel′ō) *adj.* [ME. *yelwe* < OE. *geolu,* akin to G. *gelb* < IE. base **ĝhel-,* to gleam, whence Gr. *cholos,* gall, L. *helvus,* tawny] **1.** of the color of gold, butter, or ripe lemons **2.** changed to a yellowish color as by age, as old paper **3.** having a yellowish pigmentation of the skin ☆**4.** [Colloq.] cowardly; craven ☆**5.** [see YELLOW JOURNALISM] cheaply sensational: said of certain newspapers —*n.* **1.** a yellow color; color lying between orange and green in the color spectrum **2.** a pigment or dye that is yellow or capable of producing yellow **3.** the yolk of an egg **4.** [*pl.*] any of several fungus or virus diseases of plants, causing yellowing of the leaves, stunting of growth, etc. **5.** [*pl.*] jaundice, esp. in farm animals —*vt., vi.* to make or become yellow —**yel′low·ness** *n.*

☆**yellow-bellied sapsucker** a sapsucker (*Sphyrapicus varius*) with a red head and yellowish underparts

☆**yel·low-bel·ly** (-bel′ē) *n., pl.* **-lies** [Slang] a contemptible coward —**yel′low-bel′lied** *adj.*

yel·low·bird (-burd′) *n.* any of various birds that are mostly yellow in color, as the yellow warbler, any of several American goldfinches, etc.

yel·low·cake (-kāk′) *n.* a uranium oxide, U₃O₈, that is processed into fuel for nuclear reactors: also **yellow cake**

yellow daisy ☆*popular name for* BLACK-EYED SUSAN

☆**yel·low-dog contract** (-dôg′) an employer-employee contract, now illegal, by which an applicant for a job must agree not to be a member of a labor union while employed

yellow enzyme any of several yellow respiratory enzymes that are members of the flavoprotein group, found in yeast and other natural sources

☆**yellow fever** an acute, infectious tropical disease caused by a virus transmitted by the bite of the **yellow-fever mosquito** (*Aëdes aegypti*) and characterized by fever, jaundice, vomiting, etc.

yel·low-green algae (-grēn′) a group (Xanthophyceae) of algae that contain a yellowish or brownish pigment that obscures the chlorophyll and whose motile cells have two unequal flagella: the cell walls are made of silica

yel·low·ham·mer (-ham′ər) *n.* [altered by folk etym. < earlier *yelambre* < OE. *geolu,* YELLOW + *amore,* akin to OHG. *amaro,* a kind of finch that fed on emmer: cf. EMMER] **1.** a small European finch (*Emberiza citrinella*), having a yellow head, neck, and breast: also called **yellow bunting** ☆**2.** the golden-winged flicker (*Colaptes auratus*)

yel·low·ish (yel′ə wish) *adj.* somewhat yellow

☆**yellow jack 1.** *same as* YELLOW FEVER **2.** a yellow flag used as a signal of quarantine **3.** a carangoid food fish (*Caranx bartholomaei*) of Florida and the West Indies, having a gold and silver coloring

☆**yellow jacket** any of several small social wasps or hornets (family Vespidae), having bright-yellow markings

yellow jasmine ☆a slender gelsemium (*Gelsemium semper-virens*) with funnel-shaped, yellow flowers, native to the SE U.S.: also **yellow jessamine**

☆**yellow journalism** [< the use of yellow ink, to attract readers, in printing the "Yellow Kid," a comic strip, in the *New York World* (1895)] the use of cheaply sensational or unscrupulous methods in newspapers, etc. to attract or influence the readers

Yel·low·knife (yel′ō nīf′) town in Mackenzie District, Canada, on Great Slave Lake: capital of Northwest Territories: pop. 4,000

yel·low·legs (-legz′) *n.*, *pl.* **-legs′** ☆either of two black and white sandpipers, the **greater yellowlegs** (*Totanus melanoleucus*) or the **lesser yellowlegs** (*Totanus flavipes*), having long, yellow legs, found in N. and S. America

yellow metal 1. gold **2.** brass that is approximately 60 parts copper and 40 parts zinc with a small admixture (c.1%) of lead

yellow ocher a paint pigment, a variety of limonite, consisting of iron oxide and clay

☆**Yellow Pages** [*also* y- p-] the section or volume of a telephone directory, usually printed on yellow paper, containing classified listings of subscribers according to business, profession, etc.

yellow peril the alleged danger to the world supremacy of the white, or Caucasoid, peoples created by the vast numbers and potential political power of the yellow, or Mongoloid, peoples

☆**yellow pine 1.** any of several N. American pines, as the longleaf pine, having yellowish wood **2.** this wood

☆**yellow poplar** *same as:* **1.** TULIP TREE **2.** TULIPWOOD (sense 1)

yellow race loosely, the Mongoloid group of mankind: see MONGOLOID

Yellow River *same as* HWANG HO

Yellow Sea arm of the East China Sea, between China & Korea: c.400 mi. wide

☆**yel·low-shaft·ed flicker** (or **woodpecker**) (-shaf′tid) *same as* YELLOWHAMMER (sense 2)

yellow spot *same as* MACULA LUTEA

Yel·low·stone (yel′ō stōn′) [transl. of Fr. *Roche Jaune*, ? transl. of native name] river flowing from NW Wyo. through Mont. into the Missouri River: 671 mi.

Yellowstone Falls two waterfalls on the Yellowstone River in Yellowstone National Park: upper falls, 109 ft.; lower falls (or **Grand Falls**), 308 ft.

Yellowstone Lake lake in Yellowstone National Park, fed by the Yellowstone River: 137 sq. mi.

Yellowstone National Park national park mostly in NW Wyo., but including narrow strips of S Mont. & E Ida.: it contains geysers, boiling springs, etc.: 3,458 sq. mi.

☆**yellow streak** a tendency to be cowardly, craven, etc.

yel·low·tail (-tāl′) *n.*, *pl.* **-tails′**, **-tail′**: see PLURAL, II, D, 1 ☆any of several fishes having a yellowish tail; specif., *a*) a rockfish (*Sebastodes flavidus*) of the Pacific coast of the U.S. *b*) a carangoid fish (*Seriola dorsalis*) found along the California coast *c*) a croaker (*Umbrina roncador*) found in warm waters along the coasts of N. America *d*) a flounder (*Limanda ferruginea*) of the Atlantic coast of N. America *e*) a snapper (*Ocyurus chrysurus*) of the western Atlantic *f*) *same as* SILVER PERCH (sense 1)

yel·low·throat (-thrōt′) *n.* ☆any of various American warblers (genus *Geothlypis*) with a yellow breast and throat, living in dense underbrush

yel·low-throat·ed warbler (-thrōt′id) a wood warbler (*Dendroica dominica*) of the SE U.S., with a yellow throat

☆**yellow warbler** a small, bright-yellow N. American warbler (*Dendroica petechia*)

yel·low·weed (-wēd′) *n.* any of various weedy, yellow-flowered plants; specif., *a*) any of several goldenrods *b*) the European ragwort (*Senecio jacobaea*)

yel·low·wood (-wood′) *n.* **1.** any of several trees yielding yellow wood; esp., ☆*a*) a white-flowered tree (*Cladrastis lutea*) of the legume family, native to the SE U.S. *b*) *same as* SATINWOOD (sense 2 *b*) **2.** the wood of any of these

yel·low·y (yel′ə wē) *adj.* somewhat yellow

yelp (yelp) *vi.* [ME. *yelpen*, to boast < OE. *gielpan*, to boast noisily, akin to MHG. *gelfen*: for IE. base see YELL] **1.** to utter a short, sharp cry or bark, as a dog **2.** to cry out sharply, as in pain —*vt.* to utter or express by yelping —*n.* a short, sharp cry or bark —**yelp′er** *n.*

Yem·en (yem′ən) country in the S Arabian Peninsula, on the Red Sea: c.75,000 sq. mi.; pop. 5,000,000; cap. Sanʻa —**Yem′en·ite′** (-ə nīt′), **Yem′e·ni** (-ə nē) *adj.*, *n.*

yen[1] (yen) *n.*, *pl.* **yen** [Jap. < Chin. *yüan*, round, yuan] the monetary unit of Japan: see MONETARY UNITS, table

yen[2] (yen) *n.* [Chin. (Cantonese) *yăn*, opium, craving for opium] ☆[Colloq.] a strong longing or desire —*vi.* **yenned**, **yen′ning** [Colloq.] to have a yen (*for*); long; yearn

Ye·ni·sei, Ye·ni·sey (ye′ni sā′) river in C Siberian R.S.F.S.R., flowing from the Sayan Mountains north into the Kara Sea: c.2,600 mi.

yen·ta, yen·te (yen′tə) *n.* [Yid.] a woman gossip or busybody

Yen·tai (yen′tī′) seaport on the Shantung Peninsula, NE China, on the Po Hai: pop. 116,000

yeo·man (yō′mən) *n.*, *pl.* **-men** [ME. *yeman*, prob. contr. < *yengman*, *yung man*, lit., young man] **1.** orig., *a*) an attendant or manservant in a royal or noble household *b*) an assistant or subordinate, as to a sheriff *c*) a freeholder of a class below the gentry, who worked his own land **2.** [Brit.] *a*) a small landowner *b*) *same as* YEOMAN OF THE GUARD *c*) a member of the yeomanry (sense 2) **3.** *U.S. Navy* a petty officer assigned to clerical duty —*adj.* of or characteristic of yeomen: see also YEOMAN'S SERVICE

yeo·man·ly (-lē) *adj.* **1.** of, characteristic of, or befitting a yeoman **2.** brave; sturdy —*adv.* in a yeomanly manner

yeoman of the (royal) guard any of the 100 men forming a ceremonial guard for the English royal family: instituted in 1485 by Henry VII

yeo·man·ry (-rē) *n.* **1.** yeomen collectively **2.** a British volunteer cavalry force organized in 1761 as a home guard, but since 1907, a part of the Territorial Army

yeoman's service exceptionally good, useful, or loyal service or assistance: also **yeoman service**

☆**yep** (yep) *adv.* [Slang] yes: an affirmative reply

-yer (yər) *same as* -IER: usually after *w*, as in *lawyer*

☆**yer·ba bue·na** (yer′bə bwā′nə, yur′-) [Sp., lit., good herb] a trailing evergreen plant (*Micromeria chamissonis*) of the mint family, native to the Pacific coast of N. America and formerly used in medicine

Ye·re·van (ye re vän′) capital of the Armenian S.S.R., at the foot of Mt. Ararat: pop. 643,000

yerk (yurk) *vt.*, *n.* *dial. var. of* JERK[1] (sense 1)

yes (yes) *adv.* [ME. < OE. *gese*, yes, prob. < *gea*, yea + *si*, be it so, 3d pers. sing., pres. subj., of *beon*, to be (cf. BE)] **1.** aye; yea; it is so: the opposite of *no*, and used to express agreement, consent, affirmation, or confirmation **2.** not only that, but more; moreover [ready, *yes*, eager to help] *Yes* is sometimes used alone in inquiry to signify "What is it?", "Do you wish to say (or add) something?" or as a mere expression of interest equivalent to "Is it so?" —*n.*, *pl.* **yes′es 1.** the act of saying *yes*; affirmative reply; agreement **2.** an affirmative vote or a person voting this way: usually *aye* —*vt.*, *vi.* **yessed**, **yes′sing** to say *yes* (to)

ye·shi·va (yə she′və; *Heb.* ye she vä′) *n.*, *pl.* **-vas**; *Heb.* **-vot′** (-vōt′) [< Heb. *yeshīvāh*, lit., a sitting] **1.** a school or college for Talmudic studies; esp., a seminary for the training of orthodox rabbis **2.** a Jewish school combining religious and secular studies

☆**yes man** [Slang] a person who indicates indiscriminating approval of every suggestion or opinion offered by his superior; servile sycophant

yes·ter (yes′tər) *adj.* [< ff.] **1.** of yesterday **2.** previous to this Usually in combination [*yestereve*, *yesteryear*]

yes·ter·day (yes′tər dē, -dā′) *n.* [ME. *yistredai* < OE. *geostrandæg* < *geostran*, yesterday (akin to G. *gestern* < IE. **ĝhyes*, whence Sans. *hyáḥ*, L. *heri*, yesterday) + *dæg*, DAY] **1.** the day before today; day just past **2.** a recent day or time **3.** [*usually pl.*] time gone by —*adv.* **1.** on the day before today **2.** recently —*adj.* of yesterday [*yesterday* morning]

yes·ter·eve·ning (-ēv′niŋ) *n.*, *adv.* [Archaic or Poet.] (on) the evening of yesterday: also **yes′ter·eve′**

yes·ter·morn·ing (-môr′niŋ) *n.*, *adv.* [Archaic or Poet.] (on) the morning of yesterday: also **yes′ter·morn′**

yes·tern (yes′tərn) *adj.* *archaic var. of* YESTER

yes·ter·night (yes′tər nīt′) *n.*, *adv.* [Archaic or Poet.] (on) the night before today; last night

yes·ter·year (-yir′) *n.*, *adv.* [used by D. G. ROSSETTI to translate Fr. *antan*] [Poet.] **1.** last year **2.** (in) recent years

yes·treen (yes trēn′) *n.*, *adv.* [contr. < MScot. *yystrewin*: cf. YESTER & E'EN] [Scot. or Poet.] *same as* YESTEREVENING

yet (yet) *adv.* [ME. *yit* < OE. *giet*, *gieta*, akin to OFris. *ieta*] **1.** up to now or to the time specified; thus far [he hasn't gone *yet*] **2.** at the present time; now [we can't leave just *yet*] **3.** still; even now; in the time still remaining [there is *yet* a chance for peace] **4.** at some future time; sooner or later [she will thank you *yet*] **5.** now or at a particular time, implying continuance from a preceding time [we could hear him *yet*] **6.** in addition; further; still; even (usually with a comparative) [he was *yet* more kind] **7.** as much as; even [he did not come, nor *yet* write] **8.** now, after all the time that has elapsed [hasn't he finished *yet*?] **9.** nevertheless [she is comfortable, *yet* lonely] —*conj.* nevertheless; however [she seems happy, *yet* she is troubled] —**as yet** up to now

ye·ti (yet′ē) *n.* [Tibet.] [*often* Y-] *same as* ABOMINABLE SNOWMAN

yew (yōō) *n.* [ME. *ew* < OE. *iw*, *eow*, akin to G. *eibe* (OHG. *iwa*) < IE. **(e)iwā* < base **ei-*, reddish, whence L. *uva*, grape: orig. name because of color of the wood] **1.** *a*) any of a genus (*Taxus*) of evergreen shrubs and trees of the yew family, having red, cuplike, waxy cones containing a single seed, broad, flattened leaves that are needles, and fine-grained, elastic wood *b*) the wood, used esp. for making archers' bows **2.** [Archaic] an archer's bow of yew —*adj.* designating a family (Taxaceae) of resinous evergreen trees and shrubs with needlelike leaves, including the yews, ground hemlock, etc.

Ye·zo (ye′zō) former name of HOKKAIDO

Yg·dra·sil, Ygg·dra·sill (ig′drə sil′) [ON.] *Norse Myth.* the great ash tree whose roots and branches hold together the universe

YHVH, YHWH Yahweh: see JEHOVAH, TETRAGRAMMATON

Yid·dish (yid′ish) *n.* [Yid. *yidish*, for G. *jüdisch-(deutsch)*, Jewish-(German) < *jüdisch*, Jewish < *Jude*, a Jew < L. *Judaeus*: see JEW] a language derived from medieval High German, spoken by East European Jews and their descendants in other countries: it is written in the Hebrew alphabet and contains vocabulary borrowings from Hebrew, Russian, Polish, English, etc.: abbrev. **Yid.** —*adj.* of or in this language

yield (yēld) *vt.* [ME. *yelden* < OE. *gieldan*, to pay, give, akin to G. *gelten*, to be worth < IE. **ghel-tō*, (I) give, pay: cf. GUILD] **1.** to produce; specif., *a*) to give or furnish as a natural process or as the result of cultivation [an orchard that *yielded* a good crop] *b*) to give in return; produce as a result, profit, etc. [an investment that

yielded high profits*]* **2.** to give up under pressure; surrender: sometimes used reflexively with *up [*to *yield* oneself up to pleasure*]* **3.** to give; concede; grant *[*to *yield* the right of way, to *yield* a point*]* **4.** [Archaic] to pay; recompense —*vi.* **1.** to produce or bear *[*a mine that has *yielded* poorly*]* **2.** to give up; surrender; submit **3.** to give way to physical force *[*the gate would not *yield* to their blows*]* **4.** to give place; lose precedence, leadership, etc. (often with *to*); specif., *a)* to let another, esp. a motorist, have the right of way *b)* to give up willingly a right, position, privilege, etc. —*n.* **1.** the act of yielding, or producing **2.** the amount yielded or produced; return on labor, investment, taxes, etc.; product **3.** *Finance* the ratio of the annual cash dividends or of the earnings per share of a stock to the market price **4.** *Physics, Chem. a)* the total products actually obtained from given raw materials, usually expressed as a percentage of the amount theoretically obtainable *b)* the force in kilotons or megatons of a nuclear or thermonuclear explosion —**yield′er** *n.*
SYN.—**yield** implies a giving way under the pressure or compulsion of force, entreaty, persuasion, etc. *[*to *yield* to demands*]*; **capitulate** implies surrender to a force that one has neither the strength nor will to resist further *[*to *capitulate* to the will of the majority*]*; **succumb** stresses the weakness of the one who gives way or the power and irresistibility of that which makes one yield *[*she *succumbed* to his charms*]*; **relent** suggests the yielding or softening of one in a dominant position who has been harsh, stern, or stubborn *[*he *relented* at the sight of her grief*]*; **defer** implies a yielding to another because of respect for his dignity, authority, knowledge, etc. *[*to *defer* to another's judgment*]* See also SURRENDER —*ANT.* resist

yield·ing (yēl′diŋ) *adj.* **1.** producing a good yield; productive **2.** bending easily; flexible **3.** submissive; obedient
yill (yil) *n.* [Scot.] *same as* ALE
yin[1] (yin) *adj., pron., n.* [Scot.] *same as* ONE
yin[2] (yin) *n.* [< Chin. dial.] in Chinese philosophy, the passive, negative, feminine force or principle in the universe: it is always both contrasted with and complementary to the *yang:* cf. YANG
Yin·chuan (yin′chwän′) city in N China; capital of the Ningsia-Hui autonomous region: pop. 84,000
Ying·kou, Ying·kow (yiŋ′kou′) seaport in Liaoning province, NE China, on an arm of the Po Hai: pop. 131,000
☆**yip** (yip) *n.* [echoic] [Colloq.] a yelp, or bark —*vi.* **yipped, yip′ping** [Colloq.] to yelp, or bark
yipe (yīp) *interj.* an exclamation of pain, dismay, alarm, etc.
yip·pee (yip′ē) *interj.* an exclamation of joy, delight, etc.
☆**yip·pie** (yip′ē) *n.* [< Y(outh) I(nternational) P(arty), a supposed, but nonexistent group + (HIP)PIE] [Slang] any of a group of young people in the U.S. loosely organized in 1968 as self-styled radical activists
yird (yurd) *n.* [Scot.] *same as* EARTH
-yl (il; *now rarely* ēl) [< Gr. *hylē,* wood, substance] *Chem. a combining form meaning:* **1.** a monovalent hydrocarbon radical *[*ethyl*]* **2.** a radical containing oxygen *[*hydroxyl*]*
y·lang-y·lang (ē′läŋ ē′läŋ) *n.* [Tagalog] **1.** an East Indian tree (*Cananga odorata*) of the custard-apple family, with fragrant, greenish-yellow flowers **2.** the oil obtained from these flowers, used in perfumes
y·lem (ī′ləm) *n.* [ME. < MFr. *ilem* < ? ML. *hylem,* acc. of *hyle,* matter, orig., wood < Gr. *hylē*] in some theories of cosmogony, the primordial material substance from which all the elements are supposed to have been derived
Y.M.C.A., YMCA Young Men's Christian Association
Y.M.H.A., YMHA Young Men's Hebrew Association
Y·mir (ē′mir) [ON.] *Norse Myth.* the giant from whose body the gods created the world
yob (yäb) *n.* [inversion of BOY] [Brit. Slang] a hoodlum or lout: also **yob·bo** (yä′bō)
☆**yock** (yäk) *n.* [var. of YAK[2]] [Slang] a loud laugh or something evoking loud laughter; yak
yod, yodh (yōd, yood) *n.* [Heb. *yōdh,* lit., hand] the tenth letter of the Hebrew alphabet (ʼ)
yo·del (yō′d'l) *vt., vi.* **-deled** or **-delled, -del·ing** or **-del·ling** [G. *jodeln*] to sing with abrupt alternating changes between the normal chest voice and the falsetto —*n.* **1.** the act or sound of yodeling **2.** a song or refrain sung in this way to meaningless syllables: popular among the mountain people of Switzerland and Austria —**yo′del·er, yo′del·ler** *n.*
yo·ga (yō′gə) *n.* [Sans., union, lit., a yoking: for base see YOKE] **1.** *Hinduism* a mystic and ascetic discipline by which one seeks to achieve liberation of the self and union with the supreme spirit or universal soul through intense concentration, deep meditation, and practices involving prescribed postures, controlled breathing, etc. **2.** a system of exercising involving the postures, breathing, etc. practiced in yoga —**yo′gic** (-gik) *adj.*
yogh (yōkh) *n.* [ME.] the name of the Middle English character 3, representing: *a)* a voiceless velar fricative, or guttural, similar to Modern German *ch,* as in *doch:* it is now written *gh* and is usually silent, as in *though,* or pronounced (f), as in *cough b)* a voiced palatal fricative, now represented by the *y* of *yes*
yo·gi (yō′gē) *n., pl.* **-gis** [Hindi *yogī* < Sans. *yogin*] a person who practices yoga: also **yo′gin** (-gin)

yo·gurt (yō′gərt) *n.* [Turk. *yōghurt*] a thick, semisolid food made from milk fermented by a bacterium (*Lactobacillus bulgaricus*) believed to have a beneficial effect on the intestines: it is now often prepared with various flavors: also sp. **yo′ghurt, yo′ghourt**
yo-heave-ho (yō′hēv′hō′) *interj.* a chant formerly used by sailors while pulling or lifting together in rhythm
yo·him·bine (yō him′bēn) *n.* [< *yohimbé,* a tropical African tree (of Bantu origin) + -INE[4]] a poisonous alkaloid, $C_{21}H_{26}O_3N_2$, obtained from quebracho bark and the bark of a West African tree (*Corynanthe yohimbé*): formerly used as an aphrodisiac
yoicks (yoiks) *interj.* [earlier *hoik, hike,* also *yoaks*] [Brit.] a cry used for urging on the hounds in fox hunting
☆**yok** (yäk) *n.* [Slang] *var. of* YAK[2] (sense 2)
yoke (yōk) *n., pl.* **yokes;** for 2, usually **yoke** [ME. *yok* < OE. *geoc,* akin to G. *joch* < IE.

YOKE
(on pair of oxen)

*yugo- (whence L. *jugum,* Gr. *zeugma,* W. *iau,* OSlav. *igo*) < base **yeu-,* to join] **1.** a wooden frame or bar with loops or bows at either end, fitted around the necks of a pair of oxen, etc. for harnessing them together **2.** a pair of animals harnessed together *[*a *yoke* of oxen*]* **3.** *a)* a device symbolizing a yoke, as an arch of spears, under which the conquered were forced to pass in ancient times *b)* any mark or symbol of bondage or servitude *c)* subjection; bondage; servitude **4.** something that binds, unites, or connects *[*the *yoke* of matrimony*]* **5.** something like a yoke in shape or function; specif., *a)* a frame fitting over the shoulders for carrying pails, etc., one on either end *b)* a clamp, coupling, slotted piece, etc. used to hold two parts together *c)* the crosspiece to which the steering cables are attached on a ship's rudder *d)* the bar used in double harnessing to connect the horse's collar to the tongue of the wagon or carriage **6.** a part of a garment fitted closely to the shoulders, as of a dress, or to the hips, as of a skirt, as a support for gathered parts **7.** *Elec.* a piece of magnetic material, without windings, that permanently connects two or more magnet cores **8.** *Electronics* an assembly of coils and magnetic material placed about the neck of a cathode-ray tube to provide electromagnetic deflection fields for the electron beam —*vt.* **yoked, yok′ing 1.** to put a yoke on **2.** to harness (an animal) to (a plow, etc.) **3.** *a)* to join together; link *b)* to join in marriage **4.** [Rare] to associate —*vi.* to be joined together or closely united —*SYN.* see PAIR
yoke·fel·low (-fel′ō) *n.* **1.** a companion, partner, or associate **2.** a husband or wife; mate
yo·kel (yō′k'l) *n.* [prob. < dial. *yokel,* green woodpecker] a person living in a rural area; rustic; country bumpkin: a contemptuous term
Yo·ko·ha·ma (yō′kə hä′mə; *Jap.* yō kō hä′mä) seaport on Tokyo Bay, Japan, south of Tokyo: pop. 1,789,000
Yo·ko·su·ka (yō′kə soō′kä; *Jap.* yō kōs′kä, yō kō′soo kä) seaport on Tokyo Bay, Japan: pop. 317,000
yolk (yōk) *n.* [ME. *yolke* < OE. *geolca,* yolk, lit., yellow part, akin to *geolu,* YELLOW] **1.** the yellow, principal substance of an egg, as distinguished from the albumen, or white **2.** *Biol.* the protein and fat contents of the ovum, serving as nourishment for the growing embryo **3.** *same as* SUINT —**yolked, yolk′y** *adj.*
yolk sac *Zool. a)* a saclike membrane containing yolk, an outgrowth from the ventral surface of very yolky vertebrate embryos, as those of fishes, birds, reptiles, etc., that contains many blood vessels, and supplies nourishment to the embryo *b)* a homologous organ in most mammalian embryos that contains no yolk and that becomes a vestige at an early embryonic stage
yolk stalk a short, thick, tubular stalk between the embryo and the yolk sac
Yom Kip·pur (yäm kip′ər, yôm-; *Heb.* yōm′ kē pōōr′) [Heb. *yōm kipūr,* day of atonement] one of the Jewish High Holidays, the Day of Atonement, a fast day observed on the 10th day of Tishri: Lev. 16:29–34
yon (yän) *adj., adv.* [ME. *yone* < OE. *geon,* akin to G. *jener,* Goth. *jains,* that] [Archaic or Dial.] yonder —*pron.* [Archaic or Dial.] that or those at a distance
yond (yänd) *adv., adj.* [ME. *yond* < OE. *geond,* akin to prec.] [Archaic or Dial.] *same as* YONDER
yon·der (yän′dər) *adj.* [ME., extension of *yond:* see prec.] **1.** farther; more distant (with *the*) **2.** being at a distance, but within, or as within, sight; that or those over there —*adv.* at or in that place; over there
yo·ni (yō′nē) *n.* [Sans., vulva, womb] *Hinduism* a representation of the vulva, a symbol used in the worship of Shakti: cf. LINGAM
Yon·kers (yäŋ′kərz) [< Du. *De Jonkers* (*Land*), the young nobleman's (land)] city in SE N.Y., on the Hudson: suburb of New York City: pop. 204,000
☆**yoo-hoo** (yoō′hoō′) *interj., n.* a shout or call used to attract someone's attention

yore (yôr) *adv.* [ME. < OE. *geara,* adv. formation < *gear,* YEAR] [Obs.] long ago; in times long past —*n.* time long past: now only in **of yore,** formerly

York (yôrk) ruling family of England (1461–85): founded by Edward III, who created his son (later Edward IV) the first Duke of York in 1385

York (yôrk) 1. city in West Riding, Yorkshire, on the Ouse River: county seat of Yorkshire, administratively separate from any of the three ridings: pop. 104,000 2. same as YORKSHIRE 3. city in SE Pa.: pop. 50,000 4. **Cape,** see CAPE YORK PENINSULA

York·ist (yôr′kist) *n.* a member or supporter of the English royal house of York —*adj.* of or supporting the house of York, esp. in the Wars of the Roses

York rite a system of ceremonial procedure in Freemasonry

York·shire (yôrk′shir) largest county of England, in the N part, on the North Sea: it is divided into East Riding, North Riding, & West Riding: 6,090 sq. mi.; pop. 4,801,000; county seat, York —*n.* any of several breeds of pure white hogs orig. developed in Yorkshire, with pink skin and erect ears

Yorkshire pudding [after prec.] a batter of flour, eggs, and milk baked in the drippings of roasting meat

Yorkshire terrier a breed of toy terrier, originating in Yorkshire, England, with long, silky, grayish-blue hair on the back and tan hair on the head and chest

York·town (yôrk′toun′) [after the Duke of *York,* later CHARLES I] town in SE Va.: scene of the surrender of Cornwallis to Washington: pop. 300

Yo·ru·ba (yō′roo bə, yō′roo bä′) *n.* 1. *pl.* **-bas, -ba** any member of a large ethnic group of SW Nigeria and SE Dahomey 2. their Kwa language —**Yo′ru·ban** *adj.*

Yo·sem·i·te Falls (yō sem′ə tē) [< AmInd. name of the Valley Indians, lit., grizzly bears, killers] series of waterfalls in Yosemite National Park, falling into Yosemite Valley: upper falls, 1,430 ft.; lower falls, 320 ft.; total drop, with intermediate cascades, 2,565 ft.

Yosemite National Park national park in EC Calif., in the Sierra Nevadas, notable for its steep-walled valley **(Yosemite Valley),** high waterfalls, etc.: 1,189 sq. mi.

you (yoo; *unstressed* yoo, yə) *pron.* [ME. *you, ou, eow* < OE. *eow,* dat. & acc. pl. of *ge,* YE², akin to Du. *u* < IE. base *iw-,* you, whence Sans. *yuvám,* you] 1. the person or persons to whom one is speaking or writing: *you* is the nominative and objective form (sing. & pl.), *your* and *yours* the possessive (sing. & pl.), and *yourself* (sing.) and *yourselves* (pl.) the intensive and reflexive, of the second personal pronoun 2. a person or people generally: equivalent in sense to indefinite *one* [*you* can never tell!]

you-all (yoo ôl′, yôl) *pron.* ☆*Southern colloq. for* YOU: chiefly used as a plural form

you'd (yood; *unstressed* yood, yəd) 1. you had 2. you would

you'll (yool; *unstressed* yool, yəl) 1. you will 2. you shall

young (yuŋ) *adj.* [ME. *yonge* < OE. *geong,* akin to G. & Du. *jung* < IE. **yuwen-,* whence L. *juvenis,* Sans. *yuvan-,* young] 1. being in an early period of life or growth; not old 2. characteristic of youth in quality, appearance, or behavior; fresh; vigorous; strong; lively; active 3. representing or embodying a new tendency, social movement, progressivism, etc. [the *Young* Turks] 4. of or having to do with youth or early life 5. lately begun; not advanced or developed; in an early stage 6. lacking experience or practice; immature; raw; ignorant; green 7. younger than another of the same name or family; junior [*young* Jones or his father] 8. *Geol.* a) in a stage of increasing and more effective activity, as a stream cutting deep valleys or gorges b) having undergone little erosion, as a mountain range showing rugged topography —*n.* 1. young people 2. offspring, esp. young offspring, collectively [a bear and her *young*] —**with young** pregnant **SYN.**—**young** is the general word for one in an early period of life and variously connotes the vigor, strength, immaturity, etc. of this period [a *young* child, man, etc., *young* blood]; **youthful** applies to one who is, or appears to be, in the period between childhood and maturity or to that which is appropriate to such a person [a *youthful* executive, *youthful* hopes]; **juvenile** applies to that which relates to, is suited to, or is intended for young persons [*juvenile* delinquency, behavior, books, etc.]; **puerile** implies reference to adults who unbecomingly display the immature qualities of a child [*puerile* petulance]; **adolescent** applies to one in the period between puberty and maturity and especially suggests the awkwardness, emotional instability, etc. of this period [*adolescent* yearnings] —ANT. old, mature

Young (yuŋ) 1. **Art(hur Henry),** 1866–1943; U.S. satiric cartoonist 2. **Brig·ham** (brig′əm), 1801–77; U.S. Mormon leader 3. **Edward,** 1683–1765; Eng. poet 4. **Thomas,** 1773–1829; Eng. physician, physicist, & linguist

☆**young·ber·ry** (yuŋ′ber′ē) *n., pl.* **-ries** [after B. M. *Young,* 19th-cent. U.S. horticulturist] 1. a large, sweet, dark-purple berry, a cross between a blackberry and a dewberry 2. the trailing bramble bearing this fruit

young blood 1. young people; youth 2. youthful strength, vigor, ideas, etc.

young-eyed (yuŋ′īd′) *adj.* 1. having the bright, clear, keen eyes associated with youth 2. having a youthful or fresh outlook; enthusiastic, optimistic, etc.

young·ish (-ish) *adj.* rather young

young·ling (-liŋ) *n.* [ME. *yongling* < OE. *geongling,* dim. of *geong,* YOUNG] 1. a young person; youth 2. a young animal or plant 3. [Now Rare] a novice —*adj.* young

Young Pretender *epithet* of Charles Edward STUART

young·ster (yuŋ′stər) *n.* 1. a child 2. a youth 3. a young animal ☆4. in the U.S. Naval Academy, a member of the second-year, or sophomore, class

Youngs·town (yuŋz′toun′) [after John *Young,* an early (c. 1800) settler] city in NE Ohio: pop. 140,000 (met. area, with Warren, 536,000)

Young Turk [orig., member of early 20th-c. revolutionary party in Turkey] [*also* **y- T-**] any of a group of younger people seeking to take control of an organization, party, country, etc. from an entrenched, usually conservative, group of older people

☆**youn·ker** (yuŋ′kər) *n.* [Du. *jonker* < *jong,* YOUNG + *heer,* lord, gentleman: cf. JUNKER] 1. orig., a young nobleman or gentleman 2. [Now Rare] a youngster

your (yoor, yôr; *unstressed* yər) *possessive pronominal adj.* [ME. *your, eower* < OE. *eower,* gen. of *ge,* ye: see YOU] of, belonging to, or done by you: also used before some formal titles [*your* Honor, *your* Majesty]

you're (yoor, yoor; *unstressed* yər) you are

yours (yoorz, yôrz) *pron.* [ME. *youres* < *your* + gen. *-es:* hence, in form, a double possessive] that or those belonging to you: the absolute form of *your,* used without a following noun, often after *of* [a friend of *yours,* that book is *yours, yours* are better]

your·self (yər self′, yoor-) *pron., pl.* **-selves** (-selvz′) 1. a form of the second person singular pronoun, used: *a)* as an intensive [you *yourself* said so] *b)* as a reflexive [you hurt *yourself*] *c)* as a quasi-noun meaning "your real, true, or actual self" (Ex.: you are not *yourself* when you rage like that): in this construction *your* may be considered a possessive pronominal adjective and *self* a noun, and they may be separated [*your* own sweet *self*] 2. same as ONESELF [it is best to do it *yourself*]

yours truly 1. a phrase or formula used before the signature in ending a letter 2. [Colloq.] I or me

youth (yooth) *n., pl.* **youths** (yooths, yoothz) [ME. *youthe* < OE. *geoguthe* < **jugunthi* < **juwunthi* with g for w after **dugunthi-* (*dugoth,* the doughty ones, veterans): akin to Du. *jeugd*: for IE. base see YOUNG; formation parallel to cognate L. *juvencus,* youth] 1. the state or quality of being young, esp. of being vigorous and lively, or immature, impetuous, etc. 2. the period of life coming between childhood and maturity; adolescence 3. an early stage of growth or existence 4. young people collectively 5. a young person; esp., a young man

youth·ful (-fəl) *adj.* 1. young; possessing youth; not yet old or mature 2. of, characteristic of, or suitable for youth 3. fresh; vigorous; active 4. new; early; in an early stage 5. *Geol.* same as YOUNG (sense 8) —SYN. see YOUNG —**youth′ful·ly** *adv.* —**youth′ful·ness** *n.*

youth hostel any of a system of supervised shelters providing cheap lodging on a cooperative basis for young people on bicycle tours, hikes, etc.

you've (yoov; *unstressed* yoov, yəv) you have

yow (you) *interj.* an exclamation of pain, surprise, etc.

yowl (youl) *vi.* [ME. *goulen, youlen* < ON. *gaula,* to howl] to utter a long, mournful cry; howl —*n.* such a cry

☆**yo-yo** (yō′yō′) *n.* [< Tagalog name: the toy came to the U.S. from the Philippines] 1. a spoollike toy with a string attached to the pin holding its two halves together: it may be reeled up and then let down by manipulating the string 2. [Slang] a dull, stupid, or gullible person

Y·pres (ē′pr′) town in NW Belgium, near the Fr. border: center of heavy fighting in World War I: pop. 18,000

Yp·si·lan·ti (ip′sə lan′tē; *Gr.* ēp′sē län′tē) 1. **Alexander** 1792–1828 and his brother **De·me·tri·os** (də mē′trē əs) 1793–1832; Gr. revolutionary leaders against the Turks

Y·quem (ē kem′) *n.* [< the Château *Yquem,* an estate in SW France] a fine variety of sauterne wine

yr. 1. year(s) 2. younger 3. your

yrs. 1. years 2. yours

Y·sä·ye (ē zá ē′), **Eu·gène** (ö zhen′) 1858–1931; Belg. violinist, composer, & conductor

Y·seult (ē soolt, -zoolt) *var.* of ISEULT (Isolde)

Y.T. Yukon Territory

yt·ter·bi·a (i tur′bē ə) *n.* [ModL. < YTTERBIUM] colorless ytterbium oxide, Yb_2O_3

yt·ter·bic (-bik) *adj.* of or containing ytterbium, esp. with a valence of three

yt·ter·bi·um (i tur′bē əm) *n.* [ModL. < *Ytterby,* village in Sweden] a scarce, divalent or trivalent, silvery, malleable, metallic chemical element of the rare-earth group, resembling and found with yttrium in gadolinite and certain other minerals: symbol, Yb; at. wt., 173.04; at. no., 70; sp. gr. 6.98; melt. pt., 824°C; boil. pt., 1427°C

yt·ter·bous (-bəs) *adj.* of or containing ytterbium, esp. with a valence of two

yt·tri·a (it′rē ə) *n.* [ModL. < *Ytterby,* village in Sweden] yttrium oxide, Y_2O_3, a heavy, white powder, insoluble in water: used in electronics, color television tubes, etc.

yt·tric (-rik) *adj.* of or containing yttrium

yt·tri·um (it′rē əm) *n.* [ModL. < YTTRIA] a rare, trivalent, silvery, metallic chemical element found in combination in gadolinite, samarskite, etc.: symbol, Y; at. wt., 88.905; at. no., 39; sp. gr., 4.34; melt. pt., 1495°C; boil. pt., 2927°C

yttrium garnet any of various single crystals of synthetic garnets containing iron, aluminum, etc. and having special magnetic properties: used in lasers and in microwave and other electronic devices

yttrium metals a series of closely related metals belonging, with the exception of yttrium, to the rare-earth group, including yttrium, dysprosium, holmium, erbium, thulium, ytterbium, lutetium, and, sometimes, terbium and gadolinium

Yü·an (yōō än′) river in SE China flowing from Kweichow province through Hunan into Tungting Lake: c.550 mi.

yu·an (yōō än′) *n.* [Chin. *yüan*, round, yuan] the basic monetary unit of China: see MONETARY UNITS, table

Yu·ca·tán, Yu·ca·tan (yōō′kä tän′; *E.* yōō′kə tan′) **1.** peninsula comprising SE Mexico, Brit. Honduras, & part of W Guatemala: it extends north separating the Gulf of Mexico from the Caribbean: c.70,000 sq. mi. **2.** state of Mexico, at the N end of this peninsula: 14,868 sq. mi.; pop. 775,000; cap. Mérida

Yucatán Channel strait between the Yucatán Peninsula & Cuba, joining the Gulf of Mexico & the Caribbean: 135 mi. wide

Yu·ca·tec (yōō′kə tek′) *n.* **1.** *pl.* **-tecs′, -tec′** any member of a tribe of American Indians living on the Yucatán Peninsula **2.** their Maya language —**Yu′ca·tec′an** *adj.*

yuc·ca (yuk′ə) *n.* [ModL., name of the genus < Sp. *yuca*, of WInd. (prob. Taino) orig.] **1.** any of a genus (*Yucca*) of plants of the agave family, having stiff, sword-shaped leaves and white flowers in an erect raceme, found in the U.S. and Latin America **2.** the flower of any of these plants

☆**yuck** (yuk) *n., vi. var. of* YUK

Yu·ga (yoog′ə) *n.* [Sans. *yuga*, an age, YOKE] any of the four ages or eras of the world according to Hindu religious writings, each period being shorter, darker, and less righteous than the preceding

Yugo. Yugoslavia

Yu·go·slav (yōō′gō släv′, -gə-) *adj.* of Yugoslavia or its people: also **Yu′go·slav′ic** —*n.* a member of a Slavic people, including Serbs, Croats, and Slovenes, who live in Yugoslavia Also **Yu′go·sla′vi·an** (-slä′vē ən, -släv′yən)

Yu·go·sla·vi·a (yōō′gō slä′vē ə, -gə släv′yə) country in the NW Balkan Peninsula, bordering the Adriatic: established as a nation in 1918 (called **Kingdom of the Serbs, Croats, and Slovenes,** 1918–29): 98,766 sq. mi.; pop. 20,538,000; cap. Belgrade

☆**yuk** (yuk) *n.* [echoic] [Slang] a loud laugh of amusement, or something evoking such a laugh —*vi.* **yukked, yuk′king** to laugh loudly

yu·ka·ta (yōō kä′tä) *n.* [Jap.] a lightweight kimono for informal wear, as at home, esp. by Japanese men

Yu·kon (yōō′kän) [< Athapascan stream name < ?] **1.** territory of NW Canada, east of Alas.: 207,076 sq. mi.; pop. 14,000; cap. Whitehorse: in full **Yukon Territory 2.** river flowing through this territory & Alas. into the Bering Sea: 1,979 mi.

Yukon Standard Time a standard time used in a zone which includes Yukon, Canada, corresponding to the mean local time of the 135th meridian west of Greenwich, England: it is nine hours behind Greenwich time: see TIME, chart

yule (yōōl) *n.* [ME. < OE. *geol, iul,* Christmas, the feast of the nativity, orig., name of a heathen festival at the winter solstice, akin to ON. *jol:* cf. JOLLY] Christmas or the Christmas season

yule log a large log formerly used as the foundation for the ceremonial Christmas Eve fire

yule·tide (-tīd′) *n.* Christmas time

Yu·ma (yōō′mə) *n.* **1.** *pl.* **-mas, -ma** any member of a tribe of N. American Indians living along the lower Colorado River in Ariz. and Calif. **2.** their dialect of a Yuman language

Yu·man (-mən) *adj.* **1.** of the Yumas or their language **2.** designating or of a N. American Indian language family of the SW U.S. and NW Mexico, including Yuma and Mohave, dialects of one of the languages of this family —*n.* this language family

Yü·men (yōō′men′) city in Kansu province, NW China: pop. c.200,000

yum·my (yum′ē) *adj.* **-mi·er, -mi·est** [echoic of a sound made in expressing pleasure at a taste] [Colloq.] very tasty; delectable; delicious: also used, chiefly by women, as a generalized term of approval

Yun·nan (yoo′nän′; *Chin.* yün′nän′) province of S China: 168,417 sq. mi.; pop. 19,100,000; cap. Kunming

☆**yup** (yup) *adv.* [Slang] yes: an affirmative reply

yurt (yoort) *n.* [< Russ. *yurta*, of Turkic orig., lit., dwelling, home] a circular tent of felt or skins on a framework of poles, used by the nomads of Mongolia

Y.W.C.A., YWCA Young Women's Christian Association

Y.W.H.A., YWHA Young Women's Hebrew Association

y·wis (i wis′) *adv. var. of* IWIS

Z

Z, z (zē; *Brit. & usually Canad.*, zed) *n., pl.* **Z's, z's 1.** the twenty-sixth and last letter of the English alphabet: via Latin from the Greek *zeta* **2.** the sound of Z or z, normally a voiced palatal fricative formed by the apex of the tongue: the letter Z is sometimes repeated in a series, often hyphenated, to represent a buzzing sound, as of a person snoring, a bee in flight, a power saw, etc. **3.** a type or impression for Z or z **4.** *a symbol for* the twenty-sixth in a sequence or group (or the twenty-fifth if J is omitted) —*adj.* **1.** of Z or z **2.** twenty-sixth (or twenty-fifth if J is omitted) in a sequence or group

Z 1. *Chem., Physics* atomic number **2.** *Elec.* impedance **3.** *Astron.* zenith distance

Z (zē; *Brit. & usually Canad.*, zed) *n.* an object shaped like Z —*adj.* shaped like Z

z *Math. a symbol for:* **1.** the third of a set of unknown quantities, *x* and *y* usually being the first two **2.** a variable

Z., z. 1. zero **2.** zone

za·ba·glio·ne (zab′əl yō′nē; *It.* dzä′bä lyô′ne) *n.* [It., augmentative of *zabaione*, ult. < LL. *sabaia*, an Illyrian barley drink, beer, ult. < IE. base **sab-*, to taste, whence SAP¹] a frothy dessert made of eggs, sugar, and wine, typically Marsala, beaten together over boiling water

Zab·rze (zäb′zhe) city in Silesia, S Poland, near Katowice: pop. 200,000

Za·ca·te·cas (sä′kä te′käs) **1.** state of NC Mexico: 28,360 sq. mi.; pop. 1,031,000 **2.** its capital: pop. 32,000

☆**za·ca·tón** (sä′kä tōn′) *n.* [Sp.: see SACATON] **1.** any of various tough, wiry grasses found or cultivated in the SW U.S. and Mexico: used in making brushes, brooms, paper, etc. **2.** *same as* SACATON

Zach·a·ri·ah (zak′ə rī′ə) [LL.(Ec.) *Zacharias* < Gr.(Ec.) *Zacharias* < Heb. *zĕharyah*, lit., God remembers] a masculine name: dim. **Zach;** var. **Zacharias, Zachary, Zechariah**

Zach·a·ri·as (-əs) **1.** a masculine name: see ZACHARIAH **2.** *Bible a)* the father of John the Baptist: Luke 1:5 *b)* a man named as a martyr by Jesus: Matt. 23:35 *c) Douay Bible name of* ZECHARIAH

Zach·a·ry (zak′ər ē) a masculine name: see ZACHARIAH

zaf·fer, zaf·fre (zaf′ər) *n.* [< Fr. *zafre* or It. *zaffera*, prob. < Ar. *ṣufr*, yellow copper, brass] a mixture of impure oxides and arsenates of cobalt, used in making smalt and as a blue pigment in ceramic glazes, glassmaking, etc.

zaf·tig (zäf′tig) *adj.* [< Yid., lit., juicy, succulent < MHG. *saft*, earlier *saf*, juice, SAP¹ + *-ig*, -Y²] [Slang] having a full, shapely figure: said of a woman

Za·greb (zä′greb) city in NW Yugoslavia, on the Sava River; capital of Croatia: pop. 457,000

Zag·ros Mountains (zag′rəs) mountain system in W & S Iran, extending along the borders of Turkey & Iraq & along the Persian Gulf: highest peaks, over 14,000 ft.

zai·ba·tsu (zī′bät sōō′) *n.pl., sing.* **-tsu′** [Jap. *zai*, property + *batsu*, family] the few families that dominate Japanese finance, commerce, and industry

za·ire (zä ir′) *n., pl.* **za·ire′** the monetary unit of the Congo (Kinshasa): see MONETARY UNITS, table

Zá·kin·thos, Zá·kyn·thos (zä′kēn thôs′) one of the southernmost islands of the Ionian group, Greece: 155 sq. mi.; pop. 36,000

Za·ma (zä′mə, zä′mä) ancient town in N Africa, southwest of Carthage: scene of a battle (202 B.C.) in which Scipio defeated Hannibal, ending the 2d Punic War

Zam·be·zi (zam bē′zē) river in S Africa, flowing from NW Zambia into the Mozambique Channel: c.1,600 mi.

Zam·bi·a (zam′bē ə) country in S Africa, formerly the Brit. protectorate of Northern Rhodesia: a member of the Brit. Commonwealth: 290,323 sq. mi.; pop. 4,144,000; cap. Lusaka —**Zam′bi·an** adj.

Zam·bo·an·ga (zäm′bō än′gä) seaport in the Philippines, on the SW coast of Mindanao: pop. 153,000

za·mi·a (zā′mē ə) n. [ModL., name of the genus < L. zamiae (pl.), false reading in Pliny for (nuces) azaniae, pine (nuts)] any of a genus (Zamia) of cycads growing in Florida and tropical regions, having a short, thick trunk, pinnately compound, palmlike leaves, and short, thick cones

za·min·dar (zə mēn′där′) n. [Hindi zamīndār, an occupant of land, landholder < Per. < zamīn, land, earth + -dār, holding] in India, formerly, **1.** a collector of the revenue for land **2.** a landowner, esp. one paying revenue

Zan·gwill (zaŋ′gwil), **Israel** 1864–1926; Eng. novelist & playwright

Zan·te (zän′te) same as ZÁKINTHOS

za·ny (zā′nē) n., pl. **-nies** [Fr. zani < It. zanni, a zany, clown, orig. a familiar abbrev. pronun. of Giovanni, JOHN] **1.** a clown or buffoon; specif., a former stock character in comedies who clownishly aped the principal actors **2.** a silly or foolish person; simpleton —adj. **-ni·er, -ni·est** or characteristic of a zany; specif., a) comical in an extravagantly ludicrous or slapstick manner b) foolish or crazy —**za′ni·ly** adv. —**za′ni·ness** n.

Zan·zi·bar (zan′zə bär′) **1.** island off the E coast of Africa: 640 sq. mi. **2.** former Brit. protectorate including this island, Pemba, & small nearby islands, now part of Tanzania **3.** seaport on the island of Zanzibar: pop. 58,000

☆**zap** (zap) vt., vi. **zapped, zap′ping** [echoic blend < ? z(IP) and (SL)AP, popularized in comic strip use] [Slang] to move, strike, stun, smash, kill, defeat, etc. with sudden speed and force —n. [Slang] energy, verve, pep, zip, etc. —interj. an exclamation used to express sudden, swift action or change

Za·po·rozh·e, Za·po·rozh·ye (zä′pô rôzh′ye) city in the SE Ukrainian S.S.R., on the Dnepr: pop. 571,000

Za·po·tec (zä′pə tek′) n. **1.** pl. **-tecs′, -tec′** any member of a large tribe of American Indians who live in the Mexican state of Oaxaca **2.** their Zapotecan language

Za·po·tec·an (zä′pə tek′ən) n. any of a family of American Indian languages spoken in Mexico

Za·ra·go·za (thä′rä gô′thä) city in NE Spain, on the Ebro River: pop. 377,000: Eng. name, SARAGOSSA

Zar·a·thus·tra (zar′ə thōōs′trə) Persian, or Avestan, name of ZOROASTER

za·ra·tite (zä′rə tīt′) n. [Sp. zaratita, after a Señor Zarate] a hydrated, basic carbonate of nickel, found in emerald-green incrustations on chromite and magnetite

za·re·ba, za·ree·ba (zə rē′bə) n. [Ar. zarība, a pen] in the Sudan and surrounding territory, a camping place or enclosure formed by a palisade or thorn hedge

zarf (zärf) n. [Ar. ẓarf, a saucer] a small, metal, cuplike holder, usually ornamented, used in the Levant for a hot coffee cup

zar·zue·la (zär zwä′lə) n. [Sp.: after La Zarzuela, royal palace near Madrid, where first performed in 1629] in Spain, **1.** an operetta of a traditional type, with spoken dialogue, lyrical music, etc. **2.** a seafood stew

zax (zaks) n. [var. of sax < ME., a knife, dagger < OE. seax] a tool used for trimming roofing slates

z-ax·is (zē′ak′sis) n., pl. **z-ax′es** (-sēz) Geom. one of the three axes in a three-dimensional Cartesian coordinate system along which values of z are measured

za·yin (zä′yin) n. [Heb. zāyin] the seventh letter of the Hebrew alphabet (ז)

zeal (zēl) n. [ME. zele < LL.(Ec.) zelus, zeal, emulation < Gr. zēlos, zeal, ardor < IE. base *yā-, to be excited, praise, whence OSlav. jaru, furious] intense enthusiasm, as in working for a cause; ardent endeavor or devotion; ardor; fervor —SYN. see PASSION

Zea·land (zē′lənd) largest island of Denmark, between Jutland & Sweden: 2,912 sq. mi.; chief city, Copenhagen: Dan. name, SJÆLLAND

zeal·ot (zel′ət) n. [LL.(Ec.) zelotes, one who is jealous < Gr. zēlōtēs, a zealous follower < zēloun, to be zealous < zēlos, ZEAL] **1.** a person who is zealous, esp. to an extreme or excessive degree; fanatic **2.** [Z-], among the ancient Jews, a member of a radical political and religious sect who openly resisted Roman rule in Palestine —**zeal′ot·ry** n.

SYN.—**zealot** implies extreme or excessive devotion to a cause and vehement activity in its support [zealots of reform]; **fanatic** suggests the unreasonable overzealousness of one who goes to any length to maintain or carry out his beliefs [a temperance fanatic]; an **enthusiast** is one who is animated by an intense and eager interest in an activity, cause, etc. [a sports enthusiast]; **bigot** implies blind and intolerant devotion to a creed, opinion, etc. [a religious bigot]

zeal·ous (zel′əs) adj. [ML. zelosus < LL.(Ec.) zelus: see ZEAL] full of, characterized by, or showing zeal; ardently devoted to a purpose; fervent; enthusiastic —**zeal′ous·ly** adv. —**zeal′ous·ness** n.

ze·bec, ze·beck (zē′bek) n. same as XEBEC

Zeb·e·dee (zeb′ə dē′) [LL.(Ec.) Zebedaeus < Gr.(Ec.) Zebedaios, prob. < Heb. zĕbhadyāh, lit., God has bestowed] Bible father of the disciples James and John

ze·bra (zē′brə; Brit. & Canad., also zeb′rə) n., pl. **-bras, -bra:** see PLURAL, II, D, 1 [Port., zebra, earlier used of a wild ass (now extinct), prob. ult. < L. equiferus, a wild horse (see EQUINE & FIERCE)] **1.** any of several swift African mammals (genus Equus) related to and resembling the horse and ass but having dark stripes on a white or tawny body; esp., the **mountain zebra** (Equus zebra) of South Africa **2.** a butterfly (Heliconius charitonius) with black wings crossed by several yellowish bands: in full **zebra butterfly** —**ze′brine** (-brīn, -brin) adj.

ZEBRA
(4–4 1/2 ft. high at shoulder)

zebra finch a small Australian finch (Poephila castanotis), with a grayish back and head, a whitish belly, and a brown patch on each cheek: often kept as a cage bird

zebra fish any of a number of unrelated fishes with barred, zebralike markings, as the **zebra danio** (Brachydanio rerio), often kept in aquariums

ze·brass (zē′bras′) n. [ZEBR(A) + ASS¹] the offspring of a male zebra and a female ass

ze·bra·wood (zē′brə wood′) n. **1.** the hard, striped wood of a tree (Connarus guianensis) native to Guiana, used in cabinetmaking **2.** the striped wood of various other trees or shrubs **3.** any of these trees or shrubs

ze·bu (zē′byōō) n., pl. **-bus, -bu:** see PLURAL, II, D, 1 [Fr. zébu < ?] an oxlike domestic animal (Bos indicus) native to Asia and parts of Africa: it has a large hump over the shoulders, short, curving horns, pendulous ears, and a large dewlap and is resistant to heat and insect-borne diseases: see BRAHMAN (sense 2)

ZEBU
(5–5 1/2 ft. high at shoulder)

Zeb·u·lun (zeb′yə lən) [Heb., prob. orig. akin to Assyr. zabālu, to carry, exalt (hence, lit. ? prince)] **1.** a masculine name [Bible a) the tenth son of Jacob b) the tribe of Israel descended from him

Zech. Zechariah

Zech·a·ri·ah (zek′ə rī′ə) **1.** a masculine name: see ZACHARIAH **2.** Bible a) a Hebrew prophet of the 6th cent. B.C. who urged the rebuilding of the Temple b) the book containing his prophecies

zech·in (zek′in) n. [It. zecchino: see SEQUIN] same as SEQUIN (sense 1)

zed (zed) n. [ME. < MFr. zede < LL. zeta < Gr. zēta] Brit. and usual Canad. name for the letter Z, z

zed·o·ar·y (zed′ō er′ē) n. [ME. zeduarye < ML. zedoaria < Ar. jadwār < Per. zadwār] **1.** an aromatic substance obtained from the dried, pulverized rhizome of an East Indian turmeric (Curcuma zedoaria) and used as a condiment, in flavoring, in perfumery, and, in India, as a stimulant and carminative **2.** this plant

zee (zē) n., pl. **zees** the letter Z, z

Zee·land (zē′lənd; Du. zā′länt) province of the SW Netherlands, on the North Sea: 660 sq. mi.; pop. 292,000

Zee·man effect (zā′män) [after Pieter Zeeman (1865–1943), Du. physicist] Physics the effect produced upon the structure of the spectrum lines of light emitted or absorbed by atoms subjected to a moderately strong magnetic field, resulting in the splitting of each spectrum line into two or three lines (**normal Zeeman effect**) or into many lines (**anomalous Zeeman effect**)

☆**ze·in** (zē′in) n. [ModL. Zea, a genus of grasses (< Gr. zea, one-seeded wheat < IE. base *yewo-, grain, barley, whence Sans. yava-, Lith. jāvas, a kind of grain) + -IN¹] a white, tasteless, odorless protein extracted from corn, used in plastics, coatings, paints, inks, etc.

Zeist (zīst) city in the C Netherlands, near Utrecht: pop. 55,000

‡**Zeit·geist** (tsīt′gīst′) n. [G., time spirit] the spirit of the age; trend of thought and feeling in a period

ze·min·dar (zi mēn′där′) n. var. of ZAMINDAR

zem·stvo (zemst′vô) n., pl. **-stvos** [Russ. < zemlya, earth, land] a local administrative body in Czarist Russia

Zen (zen) n. [Jap. < Chin. ch'an, ult. < Sans. dhyāna, thinking, meditation < IE. base *dhya-, to see, contemplate, whence Gr. sēma, a sign, symbol] **1.** an anti-rational Buddhist sect developed in India and now widespread in Japan: it differs from other Buddhist sects in seeking enlightenment through introspection and intuition rather than in Pali scripture **2.** the beliefs and practices of this sect

☆**ze·nai·da** (dove) (zə nā′də, -nī′-) [ModL.: after Zénaïde, wife of C. L. Bonaparte (1803–57), Fr. ornithologist] either of two wild doves (Zenaida aurita) of Florida and the Caribbean or (Zenaida asiatica) of the SW U.S. to Chile

ze·na·na (zə nä′nə) n. [Hindi zanāna < Per. zanāna < zan, woman, akin to Gr. gynē, woman: for IE. base see QUEEN] in India and Persia, the part of the house reserved for women

Zend (zend) n. [Per., interpretation] **1.** the Middle Persian translation of and commentary on the Zoroastrian Avesta **2.** formerly, same as AVESTAN —**Zend′ic** adj.

Zend-A·ves·ta (-ə ves′tə) n. [Fr., altered < Avestā-va-Zend < MPer. avastāk va zand, lit., (sacred) text and interpretation) the sacred writings of the Zoroastrians

☆**ze·ner diode** (zē′nər) [after Clarence Zener (1905–), U.S. physicist] a semiconductor rectifier diode in which there is a sharp transition from a very low current below a predetermined voltage (**zener voltage**) to a large current above this voltage

Zeng·er (zeŋ′ər, -gər), **John Peter** 1697–1746; Am. journalist & publisher, born in Germany

ze·nith (zē′nith; Brit., zen′ith) n. [ME. senyth < MFr. cenith < ML. cenit < senit, scribal error for Ar. semt, road, path (as in semt-ar-ras, zenith, lit., way of the head) < L. semita, path, way] 1. the point in the sky directly overhead; that point of the celestial sphere directly opposite to the nadir 2. the highest point; culmination; peak; summit —SYN. see SUMMIT —**ze′nith·al** adj.

zenith distance the angular distance of a heavenly body from the zenith

Ze·no (zē′nō) 1. 5th cent. B.C.; Gr. Eleatic philosopher: also **Zeno of E·le·a** (ē′lē·ə), (town in Italy: fl. 334?–261? B.C.; Gr. philosopher: founder of Stoicism: also **Zeno of Ci·ti·um** (si′shē əm), city in Cyprus

Ze·no·bi·a (zə nō′bē ə) [L. < Gr. Zēnobia] 1. a feminine name 2. 3d cent. A.D.; queen of Palmyra

ze·o·lite (zē′ə līt′) n. [Sw. zeolit < Gr. zein, to boil (see YEAST): from its swelling up when heated] 1. any of a large group of natural hydrous aluminum silicates of sodium, calcium, potassium, or barium, chiefly found in cavities in igneous rocks and characterized by a ready loss or gain of water of hydration: many are capable of ion exchange with solutions 2. a similar natural or synthetic silicate, used for softening water —**ze′o·lit′ic** (-lit′ik) adj.

Zeph. Zephaniah

Zeph·a·ni·ah (zef′ə nī′ə) [Heb. tsĕphanyāh, lit., the Lord has hidden] Bible 1. a Hebrew prophet of the 7th cent. B.C. 2. the book containing his prophecies

zeph·yr (zef′ər) n. [ME. zeferus < L. zephyrus < Gr. zephyros, the west wind] 1. the west wind; specif., [Z-] same as ZEPHYRUS 2. a soft, gentle breeze 3. a fine, soft, lightweight yarn, cloth, or garment —SYN. see WIND²

Zeph·y·rus (zef′ər əs) [L.: see prec.] Gr. Myth. the god of the west wind

zep·pe·lin (zep′ə lin, zep′lin) n. [after Count Ferdinand von Zeppelin (1838–1917), G. general who designed it] [often Z-] a type of dirigible airship designed around 1900

ze·ro (zir′ō, zē′rō) n., pl. **-ros, -roes** [Fr. zéro < It. zero < Ar. ṣifr, CIPHER] 1. the symbol or numeral 0; cipher; naught 2. the point, marked 0, from which positive or negative quantities are reckoned on a graduated scale, as on a thermometer; specif., a) on a centigrade thermometer, the freezing point of water b) on a Fahrenheit thermometer, a point 32° below the freezing point of water 3. a temperature that causes a thermometer to register zero 4. the point intermediate between positive and negative quantities 5. nothing 6. the lowest point /his chances of success sank to zero/ 7. Gunnery a sight setting for a range, allowing for both elevation and windage —adj. 1. of or at zero 2. without measurable value 3. Aeron. a) designating or of a ceiling that is at or near the ground, specif. one at a height of fifty feet or lower b) designating or of visibility along the ground regarded as within the limit of a few feet 4. Linguis. designating a hypothetical inflectional form /the plural of deer is said to be formed by the addition of a zero allomorph of the plural morpheme/ —vt. **-roed, -ro·ing** to adjust (an instrument, etc.) to a zero point or to an arbitrary point from which all positive and negative readings are to be measured —**zero in** 1. to adjust the sight settings of (a rifle) by calibrated firing on a standard range when there is no deflection due to wind 2. to aim (a gun) or concentrate (firepower) directly at or on (a target) —**zero in on** 1. to adjust gunfire so as to be aiming directly at (a target) 2. to concentrate attention on; focus on

zero gravity Physics a condition in which gravitational attraction is zero; weightlessness

zero hour 1. the time set for the beginning of an attack or other military operation 2. any crucial or decisive moment; critical point

ze·ro-ze·ro (-zir′ō, -zē′rō) adj. having or characterized by weather conditions in which both ceiling and visibility are zero

zest (zest) n. [Fr. zeste, partition membrane in a nut, hence piece of orange or orange peel used to give piquancy] 1. something that gives flavor, relish, or piquancy 2. stimulating or exciting quality; flavor; relish; piquancy 3. keen enjoyment or inclination; gusto (often with for) /a zest for life/ —**zest′ful** adj. —**zest′ful·ly** adv. —**zest′ful·ness** n. —**zest′y** adj.

ze·ta (zāt′ə, zēt′ə) n. [Gr. zēta] the sixth letter (Z, ζ) of the Greek alphabet

Zet·land (zet′lənd) same as SHETLAND

zeug·ma (zōōg′mə) n. [L. < Gr. zeugma, lit., YOKE] a figure of speech in which a single word, usually a verb or adjective, is syntactically related to two or more words, with only one of which it seems logically connected (Ex.:

The room was not light, but his fingers were) —**zeug·mat′ic** (-mat′ik) adj.

Zeus (zōōs) [Gr. Zeus: for IE. base see DEITY] the supreme deity of the ancient Greeks, son of Cronus and Rhea and husband of Hera: identified with the Roman god Jupiter

Zeux·is (zōōk′sis) 5th cent. B.C.; Gr. painter: known only through ancient writers

Zhda·nov (zhdän′ôf) city in the SE Ukrainian S.S.R., on the Sea of Asov: pop. 373,000

Zhu·kov (zhōō′kôf), **Ge·or·gi K(onstantinovich)** (gye ôr′gē) 1895?– ; Soviet marshal

zib·el·ine, zib·el·line (zib′ə lin′, -lēn′, -lin) adj. [Fr. zibeline < It. zibellino < Slav. base: see SABLE] of or having to do with sables —n. 1. the fur of the sable 2. a soft woolen dress material with a furlike nap

zib·et, zib·eth (zib′it) n. [< ML. zibethum or It. zibetto, CIVET] a civet (Viverra zibetha) of S Asia

Zieg·feld (zig′feld), **Flor·enz** (flôr′ənz) 1869–1932; U.S. theatrical producer

zig·gu·rat (zig′oo rat) n. [Assyr. ziqquratu, height, pinnacle] a temple tower of the ancient Assyrians and Babylonians, in the form of a terraced pyramid with each story smaller than the one below it

zig·zag (zig′zag′) n. [Fr., prob. < G. zickzack, redupl. < zacke, a tooth, sharp prong or point] 1. a series of short, sharp angles or turns in alternate directions, as in a line or course 2. something characterized by such a series, as a design, path, etc. —adj. having the form of or characterized by a zigzag [zigzag stitching] —adv. so as to form a zigzag; in a zigzag course —vt., vi. **-zagged′, -zag′ging** to move or form in a zigzag

zik·ku·rat, zik·u·rat (zik′oo rat) n. same as ZIGGURAT

☆**zilch** (zilch) n. [nonsense syllable, orig. used in the 1930's as name of a character in the magazine Ballyhoo] [Slang] 1. nothing; zero 2. [Z-] a name used to refer to anyone whose name is unknown or to the average person, an insignificant person, etc.

zil·lah (zil′ə) n. [Hindi ḍil′ < Ar. ḍil′, a part] in India under British rule, an administrative district

☆**zil·lion** (zil′yən) n. [arbitrary coinage, after MILLION] [Colloq.] a very large, indefinite number

Zil·pah (zil′pə) [Heb. zilpāh] Bible the mother of Gad and Asher: Gen. 30:10-13

Zim·ba·bwe (zim bä′bwe) n. 1. Bantu name of RHODESIA 2. ruined city in SE Rhodesia, probably dating from the 15th cent.: thought to have been built by a Bantu people

Zim·bal·ist (zim′bə list), **Ef·rem** (ef′rəm) 1889– ; U.S. violinist, born in Russia

zinc (ziŋk) n. [G. zink, Dan. orig., prong, point: from the form of the crystals on smelting] a bluish-white, metallic chemical element, usually found in combination, used as a protective coating for iron, as a constituent in various alloys, as an electrode in electric batteries, and, in the form of salts, in medicines: symbol, Zn; at. wt. 65.37; at. no., 30; sp. gr., 7.14; melt. pt., 419.4°C; boil. pt., 907°C —vt. **zincked** or **zinced, zinck′ing** or **zinc′ing** to coat or treat with zinc; galvanize —**zinc′ic** (-ik), **zinc′ous** (-əs), **zinck′y** (-ē), **zink′y, zinc′y** adj.

zinc·ate (-āt) n. a salt produced by the reaction of amphoteric zinc hydroxide as an acid

zinc blende same as SPHALERITE

zinc·if·er·ous (ziŋ kif′ər əs, zin sif′-) adj. [ZINC + -i- + -FEROUS] yielding or containing zinc

zinc·i·fy (ziŋ′kə fī′) vt. **-fied′, -fy′ing** [ZINC + -i- + -FY] to coat or impregnate with zinc —**zinc′i·fi·ca′tion** n.

zinc·ite (-kīt) n. a native oxide of zinc, ZnO, a deep-red to yellowish hexagonal mineral, usually containing some manganese: a minor ore of zinc

zin·cog·ra·phy (ziŋ käg′rə fē) n. [ZINC + -o- + -GRAPHY] the art or process of engraving or etching on zinc plates for printing —**zin·cog′ra·pher** n. —**zin′co·graph′ic** (-kə graf′ik), **zin′co·graph′i·cal** adj.

zinc·oid (ziŋ′koid) adj., of, pertaining to, or resembling zinc

zinc ointment an ointment containing zinc oxide

zinc oxide a white powder, ZnO, used as a pigment and in the manufacture of rubber articles, glass, cosmetics, ointments, etc.

zinc sulfate a colorless, crystalline powder, $ZnSO_4 \cdot 7H_2O$, used as an antiseptic and emetic in medicine, as a mordant in dyeing, etc.

zinc white zinc oxide used as a white pigment

☆**zin·eb** (zin′eb) n. [zin(c) e(thylene) b(is-dithiocarbamate)] an insecticide and fungicide, $Zn(CS_2NHCH_2)_2$, obtained as a light tan dust or wettable powder, used on plants and fruit

☆**zin·fan·del** (zin′fən del′) n. [< ?] 1. a dry, red wine like claret, made in California 2. the dark grape from which it is made, orig. imported from Hungary

zing (ziŋ) n. [echoic] [Slang] 1. a shrill, high-pitched sound, as of something moving at high speed 2. a lively, zestful quality; zest, vigor, animation, force, vitality, etc. —vi. [Slang] to make a shrill, high-pitched sound —**zing′y** adj. **zing′i·er, zing′i·est**

zing·er (ziŋ′ər) n. [Slang] something said or done that has zing, as a retort, punch line, etc.

Zin·jan·thro·pus (zin jan'thrə pəs) *n.* [ModL. < Ar. *Zinj*, East Africa + Gr. *anthrōpos*, man] a type of primitive man (*Australopithecus boisei*) who lived about 1,500,000 years ago, known from fossil remains found in Tanganyika in 1959

zin·ken·ite (ziŋ'kə nīt') *n.* [G. *zinkenit*, after J. K. *Zincken*, 19th-c. G. geologist] a steel-gray metallic mineral, PbSb₂S₄, a sulfide of lead and antimony

zin·ni·a (zin'ē ə, zin'yə) *n.* [ModL., after J. G. *Zinn* (d. 1759), G. botanist] any of a genus (*Zinnia*) of plants of the composite family, having colorful flower heads, native to N. and S. America

Zins·ser (zin'sər), **Hans** 1878–1940; U.S. bacteriologist

Zi·on (zī'ən) [ME. *Syon* < OE. *Sion* < LL.(Ec.) *Sion* < Heb. *tsiyōn*, a hill] **1.** *a)* orig., a Canaanite fortress in Jerusalem captured by David and called in the Bible "City of David" *b)* later, the hill in Jerusalem on which the Temple was built: Zion has historically been regarded by Jews as a symbol of the center of Jewish national life **2.** *a)* Jerusalem *b)* the land of Israel **3.** the Jewish people **4.** heaven; the heavenly city **5.** the theocracy of God

Zi·on·ism (-iz'm) *n.* a movement formerly for reestablishing, now for supporting, the Jewish national state of Israel —**Zi'on·ist** *n., adj.* —**Zi'on·is'tic** *adj.*

Zion National Park national park in SW Utah, noted for its spectacular rock formations: 206 sq. mi.

zip (zip) *n.* [echoic] **1.** a short, sharp hissing or whizzing sound, as of a passing bullet **2.** [Colloq.] energy; vigor; vim **3.** [Brit.] *same as* ZIPPER: also **zip'-fas'ten·er 4.** [Slang] a score of zero —☆*vi.* **zipped, zip'ping 1.** to make, or move with, a zip **2.** [Colloq.] to act or move with speed or energy **3.** to become fastened or unfastened by means of a zipper —☆*vt.* to fasten or unfasten with a zipper

☆**ZIP code** (zip) [z(*oning*) i(*mprovement*) p(*lan*)] a system devised to speed mail deliveries, under which the post office assigns a code number to individual areas and places

☆**zip gun** a crude, improvised pistol, usually consisting of a piece of pipe attached to a wooden stock with a firing pin actuated by a rubber band or a spring

☆**zip·per** (zip'ər) *n.* **1.** a person or thing that zips **2.** a device used to fasten and unfasten two adjoining edges of material, as on the placket of a dress, the fly of a pair of trousers, etc.: it consists of two rows of interlocking tabs which are joined or separated by sliding a part up or down —*vt., vi.* to fasten or become fastened by means of a zipper

zip·py (-ē) *adj.* **-pi·er, -pi·est** [< ZIP + -Y²] [Colloq.] full of vim and energy; brisk

☆**zi·ram** (zī'ram) *n.* [ZI(NC) + (THI)RAM] a white powder, Zn(SCSN(CH₃)₂), used as a vegetable fungicide and as a rubber accelerator

zir·con (zur'kän) *n.* [G. *zirkon*, altered < Fr. *jargon* < It. *giargone* < Ar. *zarqūn*, cinnabar < Per. *zargūn*, gold-colored < *zar*, gold] a silicate of zirconium, ZrSiO₄, a mineral found in igneous and sedimentary rocks and occurring in tetragonal crystals colored yellow, brown, red, etc.: transparent varieties are used as gems

zir·con·ate (zur'kə nāt') *n.* a salt produced by the high-temperature fusion of zirconium oxide with other metal oxides

zir·co·ni·a (zər kō'nē ə) *n.* [ModL.: see ZIRCON] *same as* ZIRCONIUM OXIDE

zir·co·ni·um (zər kō'nē əm) *n.* [ModL.: see ZIRCON] a fairly soft, ductile, gray or black metallic chemical element found combined in zircon, etc., and used in alloys, ceramics, and cladding for nuclear fuel in reactors, as a deoxidizer, etc.: symbol, Zr; at. wt., 91.22; at. no., 40; sp. gr., 6.49; melt. pt., 1852°C; boil. pt., 3578°C —**zir·con'ic** (-kän'ik) *adj.*

zirconium oxide zirconium dioxide, ZrO₂, a white, infusible powder used in making crucibles, furnace linings, pigments, etc. and, because of its luminosity, in incandescent burners

Zis·ka (tsis'kä), **Jo·hann** (yō'hän) *Ger. name of* Jan ŽIŽKA

zith·er (zith'ər, zith'-) *n.* [G. < L. *cithara* < Gr. *kithara*, a lute (cf. GUITAR)] a musical instrument having from thirty to forty strings stretched across a flat soundboard and played with a plectrum and the fingers

zi·zit, zi·zith (tsē tsēt', tsi'tsis) *n.pl.* [Heb. *tsītsīth*] the fringes or tassels worn by orthodox Jewish men, formerly on the corners of the outer garment, now on the four corners of the tallit: Deut. 22:12

Žiž·ka (zhish'kä), **Jan** (yän) 1360?–1424; Bohemian general & leader of the Hussites

Zla·to·ust (zlä'tə ōōst') city in SW R.S.F.S.R., in the Ural Mountains, near Chelyabinsk: pop. 176,000

zło·ty (zlô'tē) *n., pl.* **-tys** [Pol., lit., golden] **1.** the monetary unit of Poland: see MONETARY UNITS, table **2.** a coin of this value Abbrev. **zl.**

Zn *Chem.* zinc

zo- (zō) *same as* ZOO-: used before a vowel

zo·a (zō'ə) *n., pl. of* ZOÖN

-zo·a (zō'ə) [ModL. < Gr. *zōia*, pl. of *zōion*, an animal:

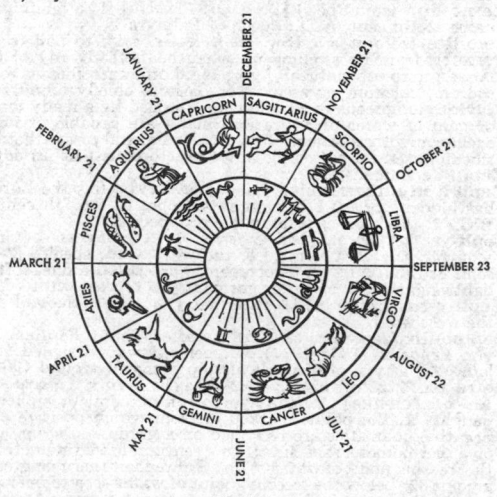

ZODIAC

see QUICK] *a combining form used in zoology to form names of groups* [*Hydrozoa, Protozoa*]

Zo·an (zō'an) *Biblical name of* TANIS

zo·an·thar·i·an (zō'an ther'ē ən) *n.* [< ModL. *Zoantharia* (< *Zoanthis*, a genus of polyps < ZO- + Gr. *anthos*, flower: see ANTHO-) + -AN] any of a subclass (Zoantharia) of anthozoan coelenterates having few or many tentacles and a solid exoskeleton or no skeleton: it includes the true corals and the sea anemones —*adj.* of the zoantharians

zo·an·thro·py (zō an'thrə pē) *n.* [ModL. *zoanthropia:* see -ZOA & ANTHROPO- & -Y³] a form of mental disorder in which the patient imagines himself to be a beast

zo·di·ac (zō'dē ak') *n.* [ME. *zodiak* < MFr. *zodiaque* < L. *zodiacus*, zodiac < Gr. *zōdiakos* (*kyklos*), zodiac (circle), lit., circle of animals < *zōidion*, dim. of *zōion*, animal: see QUICK] **1.** an imaginary belt in the heavens extending for about eight degrees on either side of the apparent path of the sun and including the paths of the moon and the principal planets: it is divided into twelve equal parts, or signs, each named for a different constellation **2.** a figure or diagram representing the zodiac and its signs: used in astrology **3.** [Rare] a circle or circuit —**zo·di'a·cal** (-dī'ə k'l) *adj.*

zodiacal light a faint, elliptical disk of light around the sun, sometimes visible in the west during or after twilight and in the east before daybreak

Zo·e (zō'ē) [Gr. *Zoe*, lit., life] a feminine name

zo·e·a (zō ē'ə) *n., pl.* **zo·e'ae'** (-ē'), **zo·e'as** [ModL. < Gr. *zōē*, life (cf. ZOO-) + -ea < L., fem. of -*eus*, -EOUS] an early, free-swimming larval stage of various saltwater crabs, characterized by long curved anterior and dorsal spines on the carapace —**zo·e'al** *adj.*

zof·tig (zäf'tig) *adj. var. of* ZAFTIG

Zo·har (zō'här) *n.* [< Heb. *zōhar*, lit., brightness] a mystical commentary on the Pentateuch, written from the 2d to the 13th cent.: a principal source of the cabala

-zo·ic (zō'ik) *an adj.-forming suffix meaning:* **1.** [< Gr. *zōikos*, pertaining to animals < *zōon*, animal (see QUICK) + -*ikos*, -IC] having a (specified) animal way of life [*saprozoic*] **2.** [< Gr. *zōē*, life + -IC] of, pertaining to, or being a geologic era having a (specified) type of life [*Cenozoic*]

zois·ite (zoi'sīt) *n.* [G. *zoisit*, after Baron *Zois* von Edelstein (1747–1819), its discoverer] a vitreous ortho-rhombic mineral, a silicate of calcium and aluminum, Ca₂Al₃(SiO₄)₃(OH), in which the aluminum may be replaced by iron

Zo·la (zō lä'; *E.* zō'lə), **É·mile** (**Édouard Charles Antoine**) (ā mēl') 1840–1902; Fr. novelist

‡**Zoll·ver·ein** (tsôl'fer in') *n.* [G. < *zoll*, custom, duty, TOLL¹ + *verein*, union, association] a customs union formed by the German states during the 19th cent.

Zom·ba (zäm'bə) capital of Malawi, in the S part: pop. 20,000

☆**zom·bie** (zäm'bē) *n.* [of Afr. orig., as in Congo *zumbi*, fetish] **1.** in West African voodoo cults, the python deity **2.** any voodoo snake deity, as in Haiti and parts of the S U.S. **3.** *a)* in West Indian superstition, a supernatural power through which a corpse supposedly is brought to a state of trancelike animation and made to obey the commands of the person exercising the power *b)* a corpse so animated **4.** [Slang] *a)* a person considered to be like a zombie in listlessness, mechanical behavior, etc. *b)* a weird, eccentric, or unattractive person **5.** an iced drink made with fruit juices, various kinds of rum, and apricot brandy For 1, 2, & 3 *a* usually, and for 3 *b* sometimes, sp. **zom'bi**

zon·al (zōn'l) *adj.* **1.** of or having to do with a zone or zones **2.** formed or divided in zones; zoned **3.** designating a kind of soil having a permanent type of profile, determined largely by the influence of the prevailing climate and vegetation —**zon'al·ly** *adv.*

zon·a·ry (-ər ē) *adj.* [L. *zonarius*] *same as* ZONAL (senses 1 & 2)

zon·ate (-āt, -it) *adj.* marked with zones or bands; belted: also **zon'at·ed**

zo·na·tion (zō nā'shən) *n.* **1.** the state of being zonal or arranged in zones **2.** arrangement in zones, or bands, as of color **3.** the distribution of plants or animals in biogeographic zones

zone (zōn) *n.* [Fr. < L. *zona* < Gr. *zōnē*, a belt < *zōnnynai*, to gird < IE. *yosmen- < base *yos-, to gird, whence OSlav. *pojašĕ*, to gird] **1.** an encircling band, stripe, course, etc. distinct in color, texture, structure, etc. from the surrounding medium **2.** any of the five great latitudinal divisions of the earth's surface, named according to the prevailing climate; specif., the **torrid zone,** bounded by the Tropic of Cancer and the Tropic of Capricorn, two **temperate** (or **variable**) **zones,** bounded by the Tropics and the polar circles, and two **frigid zones,** lying between the polar circles and the poles **3.**

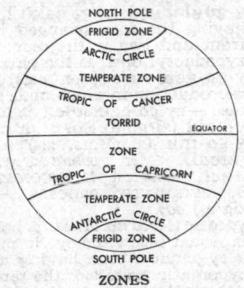

ZONES

any area or region considered as separate or distinct from others because of its particular use, crops, plant or animal life, status in time of war, geological features, etc. [a canal *zone,* cotton *zone,* demilitarized *zone*] ✰**4.** *a)* any section or district in a city restricted by law for a particular use, as for homes, parks, businesses, etc. *b)* any space along a street or road restricted in a specified way, esp. by traffic regulations [no parking *zone*] ✰**5.** *a)* any of the numbered sections into which a large metropolitan area is divided, as in ZIP code, to facilitate mail delivery *b)* any of a series of ring-shaped areas concentric upon a given point, each having a different postage rate for materials shipped from that point ✰**6.** any similar area used by railroads, telephone companies, etc. in determining the fare or tariff charged from one point to another **7.** *short for* TIME ZONE **8.** [Archaic] a belt or girdle **9.** *Math.* a part of the surface of a sphere lying between two parallel planes that intersect the figure **10.** *Sports* any of the areas into which a football field, basketball court, etc. is divided, as for defense —*vt.* **zoned, zon'ing 1.** to mark off or divide into zones; ✰specif., *a)* to divide (a city, etc.) into areas determined by specific restrictions on types of construction, as into residential and business areas *b)* to limit to a certain use by designating as or placing in a zone (sense 4 *a)* **2.** to surround with or as with a belt or zone; encircle **3.** to mark with bands or stripes

✰**zonked** (zäŋkt) *adj.* [pp. of *zonk,* to strike, beat; echoic term, intens. of CONK¹] [Slang] highly intoxicated or under the influence of a drug

zon·ule (zōn'yōol) *n.* [L. *zonula,* dim. of *zona,* a ZONE] a small zone, belt, band, girdle, etc. —**zon'u·lar** (-yə lər) *adj.*

zoo (zōō) *n.* [< ZOO(LOGICAL GARDEN)] **1.** a place where wild animals are kept for public showing **2.** a collection of wild animals

zo·o- (zō'ə) [< Gr. *zōion,* an animal: see QUICK] *a combining form meaning:* **1.** animal, animals [zoology] **2.** zoology and [zoogeography] Words beginning with zoo- are sometimes also written **zoö-**

zo·o·chem·is·try (zō'ə kem'is trē) *n.* [prec. + CHEMISTRY] the chemistry of the solids and fluids in the animal body —**zo'o·chem'i·cal** (-i k'l) *adj.*

zo·o·flag·el·late (-flaj'ə lit, -lāt') *n.* [ZOO- + FLAGELLATE] any flagellated protist cell that does not contain chlorophyll, ingests food, and has the same general type of nutrition as animals

zo·o·gam·ete (-gam'ēt, -gə mēt') *n. Biol.* a motile gamete

zo·o·gen·ic (-jen'ik) *adj.* [ZOO- + -GENIC] caused by or starting in animals, as a disease: also **zo·og·e·nous** (zō äj'ə nəs)

zo·o·ge·og·ra·phy (zō'ə jē äg'rə fē) *n.* [ZOO- + GEOGRA- PHY] the science dealing with the geographical distribution of animals; specif., the study of the relationship between specific animal forms and species and the regions in which they live —**zo'o·ge·og'ra·pher** (-jē'ə graf'ik), **zo'o·ge'o·graph'i·cal** *adj.* —**zo'o·ge'o·graph'i·cal·ly** *adv.*

zo·o·gloe·a (-glē'ə) *n.* [ModL. < ZOO- + Gr. *gloios,* glutinous substance, gum: for IE. base see CLAY] a colony of bacteria forming a jellylike mass as the result of the swelling of the cell walls through the absorption of water —**zo'o·gloe'al, zo'o·gloe'ic** *adj.*

zo·og·ra·phy (zō äg'rə fē) *n.* [ZOO- + -GRAPHY] the branch of zoology concerned with the description of animals, their habits, etc. —**zo·o·graph·ic** (zō'ə graf'ik), **zo'o·graph'i·cal** *adj.*

zo·oid (zō'oid) *n.* [ZO- + -OID] **1.** a comparatively independent animal organism produced by other than sexual methods, as by fission, gemmation, etc. **2.** any of the individual members of a colonial or compound animal: used esp. of hydroids, corals, or ectoprocts —*adj.* of, or having the nature of, an animal: also **zo·oi'dal**

zool. 1. zoological **2.** zoology

zo·ol·a·try (zō äl'ə trē) *n.* [ZOO- + -LATRY] worship of animals

zo·o·log·i·cal (zō'ə läj'i k'l) *adj.* **1.** of or having to do with zoology **2.** of, pertaining to, or concerned with animals Also **zo'o·log'ic** —**zo'o·log'i·cal·ly** *adv.*

zoological garden a place where a collection of wild animals is kept for public showing; zoo

zo·ol·o·gist (zō äl'ə jist) *n.* a student of or specialist in zoology

zo·ol·o·gy (-jē) *n.* [ModL. *zoologia:* see ZOO- & -LOGY] **1.** the science, a branch of biology, that deals with animals, their life, structure, growth, classification, etc. **2.** the animal life of an area; fauna **3.** the characteristics or properties of an animal or animal group

zoom (zōōm) *vi.* [echoic] **1.** to make a loud, low-pitched, buzzing or humming sound **2.** to move with a zooming sound **3.** to climb in an airplane suddenly and sharply at an angle greater than normal, using the energy of momentum **4.** to rise rapidly [prices *zoomed*] **5.** to focus a camera by using a zoom lens —*vt.* to cause to zoom —*n.* **1.** the act of zooming **2.** a zooming sound **3.** *same as* ZOOM LENS —*adj.* equipped with or having to do with a zoom lens [a *zoom* telescope]

zo·om·e·try (zō äm'ə trē) *n.* [ZOO- + METRY] the measurement and comparison of the relative sizes of the different parts of animals —**zo'o·met'ric** (-ə met'rik) *adj.*

zoom lens a system of lenses, as in a motion-picture or television camera, that can be rapidly adjusted for close-up shots or distance views while keeping the image in focus

zo·o·mor·phic (zō'ə môr'fik) *adj.* [ZOO- + -MORPHIC] of or having animal form [a *zoomorphic* deity]

zo·o·mor·phism (-fiz'm) *n.* [ZOO- + -MORPH + -ISM] **1.** the attributing of animal form or characteristics to God or a god **2.** the representation of animal forms in decorative art or symbolism

zo·on (zō'än) *n., pl.* **zo·a** (-ə) [ModL. < Gr. *zōion,* an animal: see QUICK] *rare var.* of ZOOID (sense 2) —**zo·on'al** *adj.*

-zo·on (zō'än) [ModL.: see prec.] *a combining form meaning* animal or living being [*spermatozoon, protozoon*]

zo·o·no·sis (zō än'ə sis, zō'ə nō'sis) *n., pl.* **-no'ses** (-än'ə sēz', -ə nō'sēz) [ModL. < Gr. *zōion,* an animal + *nosos,* disease] a disease that can be transmitted to man by vertebrate animals —**zo'o·not'ic** (-nät'ik) *adj.*

zo·o·par·a·site (zō'ə par'ə sīt') *n.* a parasitic animal —**zo'o·par'a·sit'ic** (-sit'ik) *adj.*

zo·oph·a·gous (zō äf'ə gəs) *adj.* [ZOO- + -PHAGOUS] *same as* CARNIVOROUS

zo·oph·i·lism (zō äf'ə liz'm) *n.* [ZOO- + PHIL- + -ISM] extreme love for animals; specif., abnormal sexual attraction to animals: also **zo·oph'i·ly, zo·o·phil·i·a** (zō'ə fil'ē ə) —**zo'o·phil'ic** *adj.*

zo·oph·i·lous (-ləs) *adj.* [ZOO- + -PHILOUS] **1.** having zoophilism **2.** adapted to pollination by animals other than insects: said of plants

zo·o·pho·bi·a (zō'ə fō'bē ə) *n.* [ZOO- + -PHOBIA] an abnormal fear of animals

zo·o·phyte (zō'ə fīt') *n.* [ModL. *zoophyton* < Gr. *zōophy- ton:* see ZOO- & -PHYTE] any animal, as a coral, sponge, etc., having somewhat the appearance and character of a plant; esp., *same as* ECTOPROCT —**zo'o·phyt'ic** (-fit'ik), **zo'o·phyt'i·cal** *adj.*

zo·o·plank·ton (zō'ə plaŋk'tən) *n.* plankton consisting of animals, as protozoans —**zo'o·plank·ton'ic** (-tän'ik) *adj.*

zo·o·spo·ran·gi·um (-spə ran'jē əm) *n., pl.* **-gi·a** (-ə) [ModL.: see ZOO- & SPORANGIUM] *Bot.* a sporangium in certain fungi and algae, producing zoospores —**zo'o·spo·ran'gi·al** (-əl) *adj.*

zo·o·spore (zō'ə spôr') *n.* [ZOO- + SPORE] **1.** *Bot.* an asexual sporangial spore, esp. of certain fungi or algae, capable of independent motion usually by means of cilia or flagella **2.** *Zool.* a motile flagellate or amoeboid reproductive cell arising from a sporocyst in certain protozoans —**zo'o·spor'ic** (-spôr'ik), **zo·os'po·rous** (-äs'pə rəs) *adj.*

zo·os·ter·ol (zō äs'tə rôl', -rōl') *n.* [ZOO- + STEROL] any of several steroid alcohols, as cholesterol, found in animals

zo·ot·o·my (zō ät'ə mē) *n.* [ModL. *zootomia:* see ZOO- & -TOMY] the anatomy or dissection of animals other than man —**zo'o·tom'ic** (-ə täm'ik), **zo'o·tom'i·cal** *adj.* —**zo·ot'o·mist** *n.*

✰**zoot suit** (zōōt) [redupl.] a man's suit of a former, exaggerated style, with high-waisted, baggy trousers narrowing at the cuffs and a long, draped coat

Zor·ach (zôr'äk, -ak), **William** 1887-1966; U.S. sculptor & painter, born in Lithuania

---

zo·ri (zôr′ē) *n.*, *pl.* **zo′ris, zo′ri** [Jap.] a sandal of a Japanese style, consisting of a flat sole held on the foot by means of a thong slipped between the big toe and the toe next to it

zor·ille, zor·il (zôr′il, zär′-) *n.* [Fr. *zorille* < Sp. *zorilla*, *zorillo*, dim. of *zorra*, *zorro*, a fox] a small, striped, black and white, weasellike mammal (*Ictonyx striatus*) of the drier parts of Africa, closely resembling the skunk in its appearance and fetid odor

Zorn (sôrn), **An·ders Le·o·nhard** (än′dərs lā′ô nárd′) 1860–1920; Swed. painter, etcher, & sculptor

Zo·ro·as·ter (zō′rō as′tər, zôr′ō as′-) ? 6th or 7th cent. B.C.; Per. religious teacher; founder of Zoroastrianism

Zo·ro·as·tri·an (zō′rō as′trē ən, zôr′ō-) *adj.* of or having to do with Zoroaster or Zoroastrianism —*n.* an adherent of Zoroastrianism

Zo·ro·as·tri·an·ism (-iz′m) *n.* the religious system of the Persians before their conversion to Islam: it was founded by Zoroaster, and its principles, contained in the Zend-Avesta, include belief in an afterlife and in the continuous struggle of the universal spirit of good (*Ormazd*) with the spirit of evil (*Ahriman*), the good ultimately to prevail

Zor·ri·lla (y Moral) (thô rē′lyä), **Jo·sé** (hô se′) 1817–93; Sp. poet & playwright

zos·ter (zäs′tər) *n.* [L. < Gr. *zoster*, a belt, girdle, akin to zone: see ZONE] *short for* HERPES ZOSTER

Zou·ave (zoo äv′, zwäv) *n.* [Fr. < Ar. *Zwāwa*, a Kabyle tribe living in the Jurjura Mountains of Algeria, from whom the Zouaves were originally recruited] **1.** a member of a former infantry unit in the French army, noted for the precision of its close-order drill and characterized by a colorful Oriental uniform **2.** a member of any military group having a similar uniform; ☆specif., a member of any of various volunteer regiments in the American Civil War

Zoug (zoog) *Fr. name of* ZUG

zounds (zoundz) *interj.* [altered < the oath (*by*) *God's wounds*] [Archaic] a mild oath used as an exclamation of surprise or anger

☆**zow·ie** (zou′ē) *interj.* an exclamation expressing excitement, enthusiasm, admiration, etc.

zoy·si·a (zoi′sē ə) *n.* [ModL., altered < *Zoisia*, so named after Karl von *Zois*, 18th-c. G. botanist] ☆any of a genus (*Zoysia*) of creeping, wiry grasses, often used for lawns, esp. in warm, dry regions

Zr *Chem.* zirconium

zuc·chet·to (zoo ket′ō, -ə; *It.* tsoo ket′tô) *n.*, *pl.* **-tos**; *It.* **-ti** (-tē) [altered < It. *zucchetta*, a cap, orig., dim. of *zucca*, a gourd < LL. *cucutia*] a skullcap worn by Roman Catholic ecclesiastics: a priest's is black, a bishop's purple, a cardinal's red, and the Pope's white

☆**zuc·chi·ni** (zoo kē′nē) *n.*, *pl.* **-ni, -nis** [It., pl. of *zucchino*, dim. of *zucca*, a gourd: see prec.] a summer squash of a variety that is green-skinned and shaped somewhat like a cucumber

Zug (tsookh) **1.** canton of NC Switzerland, on the Lake of Zug: 92 sq. mi.; pop. 58,000 **2.** its capital, on the Lake of Zug: pop. 21,000 **3.** Lake of, lake in NC Switzerland, in the cantons of Zug & Schwyz: 15 sq. mi.

Zui·der Zee, Zuy·der Zee (zī′dər zē′; *Du.* zöi′dər zā′) former arm of the North Sea, which extended into the Netherlands: its S section was shut off from the North Sea by dikes: see IJSSELMEER & WADDENZEE

Zu·lo·a·ga (thoo′lô ä′gä), **Ig·na·cio** (ēg nä′thyô) 1870–1945; Sp. painter

Zu·lu (zoo′loo) *n.* **1.** *pl.* **-lus, -lu** any member of a pastoral people living in Natal, South Africa **2.** their Bantu language —*adj.* of the Zulus, their culture, or their language

Zu·lu·land (zoo′loo land′) region, formerly a Zulu kingdom, in NE Natal province, South Africa, on the Indian Ocean: 10,427 sq. mi.

Zu·ñi (zoon′yē) *n.* [AmSp. < AmInd.] **1.** *pl.* **-ñis, -ñi** any member of a tribe of N. American Indians living in a pueblo in W New Mexico **2.** their isolated language, the unique member of a family —**Zu′ñi·an** *adj.*,

Zur·ba·rán (thoor′bä rän′), **Fran·cis·co de** (frän thēs′kô *the*) 1598–1664; Sp. painter

Zur·ich (zoor′ik) **1.** canton of N Switzerland: 668 sq. mi.; pop. 1,019,000 **2.** its capital, on the Lake of Zurich: pop. 440,000: also written **Zür′ich** (G. tsü′riH) **3.** Lake of, lake in N Switzerland, mostly in Zurich canton: 34 sq. mi.

Zweig (tsviH; *E.* tswig, swig) **1. Ar·nold** (är′nôlt), 1887– ; Ger. novelist, playwright & essayist **2. Stef·an** (shte′fän), 1881–1942; Austrian biographer, novelist, & playwright

Zwick·au (tsvik′ou) city in Saxony, S East Germany: pop. 129,000

☆**zwie·back** (swē′bak, swī′-, tswē′-, zwī′-; -bäk; *G.* tsvē′bäk′) *n.* [G. < *zwie-*, two, twice, var. of *zwei*, TWO + *backen*, to BAKE] a kind of rusk or biscuit that is sliced and toasted after baking

Zwing·li (tsvin′lē; *E.* zwiŋ′glē, swiŋ′-), **Ul·rich** (ool′riH) or **Hul·dreich** (hool′driH) 1484–1531; Swiss Protestant reformer

Zwing·li·an (zwiŋ′glē ən, swiŋ′-, tsviŋ′-) *adj.* of Zwingli or his doctrines, esp. the doctrine that the body of Christ is not actually present in the Eucharist and that the ceremony is merely a commemorative one —*n.* a follower of Zwingli —**Zwing′li·an·ism** *n.*

zwit·ter·i·on (tsvit′ər i′ən) *n.* [G. < OHG. *zwitarn* < *zwi-*, double, akin to OE. *twi-*: for IE. base see TWO) + *ion*, ION] an ion carrying both a positive and a negative charge in different parts of the molecule, as in certain amino acids and protein molecules —**zwit′ter·i·on′ic** (-ī än′ik) *adj.*

Zwol·le (zvôl′ə) city in the NE Netherlands: pop. 59,000

zyg·a·poph·y·sis (zig′ə päf′ə sis, zī′gə-) *n.*, *pl.* **-ses′** (-sēz′) [ModL. < Gr. *zygon*, YOKE + APOPHYSIS] any of the processes of the neural arch of a vertebra by which it articulates with the adjoining vertebrae —**zyg′ap·o·phys′e·al** (-ap ə fiz′ē əl) *adj.*

zy·go- (zī′gə, zig′ə) [< Gr. *zygon*, a YOKE] a combining form meaning yoke or yoked, pair or paired [*zygodactyl*]: also, before a vowel, **zyg-**

zy·go·dac·tyl (zī′gə dak′t'l, zig′ə-) *adj.* [prec. + DACTYL] having the toes arranged in two opposed pairs, two in front and two in the rear: also **zy′go·dac′tyl·ous** —*n.* a zygodactyl bird, as the parrot —**zy′go·dac′tyl·ism** *n.*

zy·go·gen·e·sis (-jen′ə sis) *n.* [ZYGO- + GENESIS] *Biol.* reproduction in which male and female gametes and nuclei fuse —**zy′go·ge·net′ic** (-jə net′ik) *adj.*

zy·goid (zī′goid) *adj.* of or pertaining to a zygote; zygotic

zy·go·ma (zī gō′mə, zi-) *n.*, *pl.* **-ma·ta** (-mə tə), **-mas** [ModL. < Gr. *zygōma* < *zygoun*, to yoke < *zygon*, YOKE] *Anat. same as:* **1.** ZYGOMATIC ARCH **2.** ZYGOMATIC BONE **3.** ZYGOMATIC PROCESS —**zy·go·mat·ic** (zī′gə mat′ik, zig′ə-) *adj.*

zygomatic arch *Anat.* a bony arch on either side of the face just below the eye in many vertebrates, consisting of a zygomatic bone having a process that fuses with the zygomatic process of the temporal bone

zygomatic bone *Anat.* a bone of the zygomatic arch on either side of the face, forming the prominence of each cheek; cheekbone

zygomatic process *Anat.* any of several bony processes that form part of the zygomatic arch

zy·go·mor·phic (zī′gə môr′fik, zig′ə-) *adj.* [ZYGO- + -MORPHIC] *Biol.* bilaterally symmetrical; that can be divided in two identical halves by a single plane passing through the axis: said of organisms, organs, or parts: also **zy′go·mor′phous** —**zy′go·mor′phism**, **zy′go·mor′phy** *n.*

zy·go·spore (zī′gə spôr′, zig′ə-) *n.* [ZYGO- + SPORE] *Bot.* a thick-walled, resting spore formed by conjugation of two isogametes, as in certain phycomycetous fungi and certain green algae —**zy′go·spor′ic** (-spôr′ik) *adj.*

zy·gote (zī′gōt, zig′ōt) *n.* [< Gr. *zygōtos*, yoked < *zygon*, a YOKE] a cell formed by the union of male and female gametes; fertilized egg cell before cleavage —**zy·got′ic** (-gät′ik) *adj.* —**zy·got′i·cal·ly** *adv.*

zy·go·tene (zī′gə tēn′, zig′ə-) *n.* [Fr. *zygotène* < Gr. *zygon*, YOKE + *tainia*, ribbon, tape: see TAENIA] the synaptic stage of the first prophase in meiosis, during which longitudinal pairing of homologous chromosomes occurs

zy·mase (zī′mās) *n.* [Fr. *zymase*: see ff. & -ASE] an enzyme, present in yeast, that promotes fermentation by breaking down glucose and some other carbohydrates into alcohol and carbon dioxide

zyme (zīm) *n.* [Gr. *zymē*, a leaven < ? IE. base *yeu-*, to mix (foods), whence Sans. *yuṣ*, broth] [Obs.] **1.** a ferment or enzyme **2.** the principle regarded as the specific cause of a zymotic disease

zy·mo- (zī′mō, -mə) [< Gr. *zymē*: see prec.] *a combining form meaning* fermentation [*zymology*]: also, before a vowel, **zym-**

zy·mo·gen (zī′mə jən) *n.* [Fr. *zymogène*: see ZYMO- & -GEN] *Biochem.* an inactive antecedent form of an active enzyme that becomes functional by the action of an appropriate kinase or other activator

zy·mo·gen·e·sis (zī′mə jen′ə sis) *n.* [ModL.: see ZYMO- & -GENESIS] the process by which a zymogen becomes an enzyme

zy·mo·gen·ic (-jen′ik) *adj. Biochem.* **1.** of, having to do with, or producing a zymogen **2.** causing fermentation Also **zy′mog·e·nous** (zī mäj′ə nəs)

zy·mol·o·gy (zī mäl′ə jē) *n.* [ZYMO- + -LOGY] the science dealing with fermentation —**zy′mo·log′ic** (-mə läj′ik), **zy′mo·log′i·cal** *adj.* —**zy′mol·o·gist** *n.*

zy·mol·y·sis (zī mäl′ə sis) *n.* [ModL.: see ZYMO- & -LYSIS] *Biochem.* **1.** the fermentative action of enzymes **2.** fermentation or other changes resulting from this —**zy′mo·lyt′ic** (-mə lit′ik) *adj.*

zy·mom·e·ter (zī mäm′ə tər) *n.* [ZYMO- + -METER] an instrument used to measure the degree of fermentation

zy·mo·sis (zī mō′sis) *n.*, *pl.* **-ses** (-sēz) [ModL. < Gr. *zymōsis*, fermentation < *zymē*, a leaven, ferment: see ZYME] [Obs.] **1.** a process like fermentation by which infectious diseases were formerly believed to be developed **2.** a zymotic disease

zy·mot·ic (zī mät′ik) *adj.* [Gr. *zymōtikos*, causing to ferment < *zymoun*, to ferment < *zymē*, a ferment: see ZYME] **1.** of, causing, or caused by or as by, fermentation **2.** [Obs.] designating or of any infectious disease, as smallpox, formerly believed to be caused by a fermentative process

zy·mur·gy (zī′mər jē) *n.* [ZYM(O)- + -URGY] the branch of chemistry dealing with fermentation, as applied in wine making, brewing, etc.

COLLEGES AND UNIVERSITIES OF THE UNITED STATES

This list includes colleges and universities of the United States that offer a four-year program of college-level curriculum and generally offer a bachelor's degree or higher; it has been compiled according to the latest available information which has been supplied by the institutions themselves. After the name of the institution the following information is given: the general size of its enrollment; its location; its date of founding; the principal source of financial control (state, county, private, etc.); the nature of its enrollment (for men, for women, or coeducational); the type of degrees offered (Bachelor's, Master's, etc.).

Key: C., College; U., University; P., Private; S., State; Mun., Municipal; Fed., Federal; Dist., District; Co., County; Ter., Territory: degrees offered—I, Associate; II, Bachelor's; III, Bachelor's & Master's; IV, Master's; V, Professional; VI, Ph.D.; VII, Bachelor's, Master's, Professional, & Ph.D.; D, diploma offered: enrollment, *3,000 to 8,000;** over 8,000

Abilene Christian C. Abilene, Tex.; 1906; P.; coed.; III, V
Abraham Baldwin Agricultural C. Tifton, Ga.; 1908; S.; coed.; I
Adams State C. Alamosa, Colo.; 1921; S.; coed.; III
Adelphi U.* Garden City, N.Y.; 1896; P.; coed.; I, III, VI
Adrian C. Adrian, Mich.; 1859; P.; coed.; II
Aero-Space Institute Chicago, Ill.; 1959; coed.; I, II
Agnes Scott C. Decatur, Ga.; 1889; P.; women; II
Air Force Institute of Technology* Wright-Patterson AFB (Dayton), Ohio; 1919; Fed.; coed.; III, V
Akron, U. of* Akron, Ohio; 1870; S.; coed.; I, VII
Alabama, U. of* University (Tuscaloosa), Ala.; 1831; S.; coed.; VII: ext. centers—Birmingham, Gadsden, Huntsville, Montgomery
Alabama Agricultural & Mechanical C. Normal, Ala.; 1875; S.; coed.; III
Alabama C. Montevallo, Ala.; 1896; S.; coed.; III
Alabama State C. Montgomery, Ala.; 1874; S.; coed.; III
Alaska, U. of College (Fairbanks), Alas.; 1917; S.; coed.; I, III, VI
Alaska Bible C. Glennallen, Alas.; 1966; P.; coed.; II
Alaska Methodist U. Anchorage, Alas.; 1957; P.; coed.; III
Albany State C. Albany, Ga.; 1903; S. & Mun.; coed.; II
Albertus Magnus C. New Haven, Conn.; 1925; P.; women; II
Albion C. Albion, Mich.; 1835; P.; coed.; II
Albright, C. Reading, Pa.; 1856; P.; coed.; II
Albuquerque, The U. of Albuquerque, N.Mex.; 1940; P.; coed.; I, II
Alcorn Agricultural & Mechanical C. Lorman, Miss.; 1871; S.; coed.; II
Alderson-Broaddus C. Philippi, W.Va.; 1871; P.; coed.; II
Alfred U. Alfred, N.Y.; 1836; P.; coed.; III, VI
Allegheny C. Meadville, Pa.; 1815; P.; coed.; III
Allentown C. of St. Francis de Sales Center Valley, Pa.; 1964; P.; men; II
Allen U. Columbia, S.C.; 1870; P.; coed.; II
Alliance C. Cambridge Springs, Pa.; 1912; P.; coed.; II
Alma C. Los Gatos, Calif.; 1934; P.; men; IV, VI
Alma C. Alma, Mich.; 1886; P.; coed.; II
Alma White C. Zarephath, N.J.; 1921; P.; coed.; II
Alvernia C. Reading, Pa.; 1958; P.; women; II
Alverno C. Milwaukee, Wis.; 1936; P.; women; II
Ambassador C. Pasadena, Calif.; 1947; P.; coed.; III, VI
American Conservatory of Music Chicago, Ill.; 1886; P.; coed.; III, V
American Institute for Foreign Trade, The Phoenix, Ariz.; 1946; P.; coed.; IV, V
American International C. Springfield, Mass.; 1885; P.; coed.; I, III
American U., The* Washington, D.C.; 1893; P.; coed.; I, VII
Amherst C. Amherst, Mass.; 1821; P.; men; II
Anderson C. Anderson, Ind.; 1917; P.; coed.; II, V
Andover Newton Theological School Newton Centre, Mass.; 1807; P.; coed.; IV, V
Andrews U. Berrien Springs, Mich.; 1874; P.; coed.; I, III, V
Angelo State C. San Angelo, Tex.; 1928; S.; coed.; II
Anna Maria C. for Women Paxton, Mass.; 1946; P.; women; II
Annhurst C. South Woodstock, Conn.; 1941; P.; women; II
Antioch C. Yellow Springs, Ohio; 1852; P.; coed.; III
Appalachian State U.* Boone, N.C.; 1903; S.; coed.; III
Aquinas C. Grand Rapids, Mich.; 1886; P.; coed.; II
Aquinas Institute of Philosophy & Theology River Forest, Ill.; 1939; P.; coed.; III, V
Arizona, U. of* Tucson, Ariz.; 1885; S.; coed.; VII
Arizona Bible C. Phoenix, Ariz.; 1935; P.; coed.; II
Arizona State U.* Tempe, Ariz.; 1885; S.; coed.; VII
Arkansas, State C. of* Conway, Ark.; 1907; S.; coed.; III
Arkansas, U. of* Fayetteville, Ark.; 1871; S.; coed.; VII
Arkansas Agricultural & Mechanical C. College Heights (Monticello), Ark.; 1909; S.; coed.; II
Arkansas Agricultural, Mechanical, & Normal C.* Pine Bluff, Ark.; 1875; S.; coed.; II
Arkansas Baptist C. Little Rock, Ark.; 1884; P.; coed.; II
Arkansas C. Batesville, Ark.; 1872; P.; coed.; II
Arkansas Polytechnic C. Russellville, Ark.; 1909; S.; coed.; I, II

Arkansas State U.* State University (Jonesboro), Ark.; 1909; S.; coed.; III: J. C. branch—Beebe
Armstrong C. Berkeley, Calif.; 1918; P.; coed.; I, III
Armstrong State C. Savannah, Ga.; 1935; S.; coed.; I, II
Aroostook State C. Presque Isle, Me.; 1903; S.; coed.; II
Art Academy of Cincinnati Cincinnati, Ohio; 1887; P.; coed.; affiliated with U. of Cincinnati, II
Art Center C. of Design Los Angeles, Calif.; 1930; P.; coed.; III
Artesia, C. of Artesia, N.Mex.; 1965; P.; coed.; II
Art Institute of Chicago, The School of the Chicago, Ill.; 1866; P.; coed.; III
Art School of the Society of Arts & Crafts Detroit, Mich.; 1926; P.; coed.; II
Asbury C. Wilmore, Ky.; 1890; P.; coed.; II
Asbury Theological Seminary Wilmore, Ky.; 1923; P.; coed.; IV, V
Asheville-Biltmore C. Asheville, N.C.; 1927; S.; coed.; II
Ashland C. Ashland, Ohio; 1878; P.; coed.; I, II
Assumption C. Worcester, Mass.; 1904; P.; men (coed., eve. & grad. school); III
Athenaeum of Ohio, The Cincinnati, Ohio; 1829; P.; men; III
Athens C. Athens, Ala.; 1822; P.; coed.; I, III
Atlanta Christian C. East Point, Ga.; 1937; P.; coed.; II
Atlanta School of Art Atlanta, Ga.; 1927; P.; coed.; II
Atlanta U. Atlanta, Ga.; 1865; P.; coed.; IV, VI
Atlantic Christian C. Wilson, N.C.; 1902; P.; coed.; II
Atlantic Union C. South Lancaster, Mass.; 1882; P.; coed.; I, II
Auburn U.* Auburn, Ala.; 1856; S.; coed.; VII: branch—Montgomery
Augsburg C. Minneapolis, Minn.; 1869; P.; coed.; II
Augusta C. Augusta, Ga.; 1925; S.; coed.; II
Augustana C. Rock Island, Ill.; 1860; P.; coed.; II
Augustana C. Sioux Falls, S.Dak.; 1860; P.; coed.; III
Aurora C. Aurora, Ill.; 1893; P.; coed.; II
Austin C. Sherman, Tex.; 1849; P.; coed.; III
Austin Peay State U. Clarksville, Tenn.; 1929; S.; coed.; III
Austin Presbyterian Theological Seminary Austin, Tex.; 1902; P.; coed.; IV, V
Avila C. Kansas City, Mo.; 1916; P.; women (coed., part time); I
Azusa Pacific C. Azusa, Calif.; 1899; P.; coed.; III

Babson Institute of Business Administration Babson Park (Wellesley), Mass.; 1919; P.; men; III
Baker U. Baldwin City, Kans.; 1858; P.; coed.; II
Baldwin-Wallace C. Berea, Ohio; 1845; P.; coed.; II
Ball State U.* Muncie, Ind.; 1918; S.; coed.; VII
Baltimore, U. of* Baltimore, Md.; 1925; P.; coed.; II, V
Baltimore C. of Commerce Baltimore, Md.; 1909; P.; coed.; II
Baltimore Hebrew C. Baltimore, Md.; 1919; P.; coed.; II
Bangor Theological Seminary Bangor, Me.; 1814; P.; coed.; II, V
Bank Street C. of Education New York, N.Y.; 1917; P.; coed.; IV
Baptist Bible C. Denver, Colo.; 1952; P.; coed.; I, III
Baptist Bible C. Springfield, Mo.; 1950; P.; coed.; II
Baptist Bible Seminary Clarks Summit, Pa.; 1932; P.; coed.; I, II
Baptist Christian C. Shreveport, La.; 1961; P.; coed.; II, V
Baptist C. at Charleston Charleston, S.C.; 1960; P.; coed.; II
Barat C. Lake Forest, Ill.; 1919; P.; women; II
Barber-Scotia C. Concord, N.C.; 1867; P. & Co.; coed.; II
Bard C. Annandale-on-Hudson, N.Y.; 1860; P.; coed.; II
Barnard C. New York, N.Y.; 1889; women; II: affiliated with Columbia U.
Barrington C. Barrington, R.I.; 1900; P.; coed.; II
Barry C. Miami, Fla.; 1940; P.; women; III, V
Bartlesville Wesleyan C. Bartlesville, Okla.; 1959; P.; coed.; I, II
Bates C. Lewiston, Me.; 1864; P.; coed.; II
Baylor U.* Waco, Tex.; 1845; P.; coed.; VII: branches—Dallas, Houston, San Antonio
Beaver C. Glenside, Pa.; 1853; P.; women; II
Belhaven C. Jackson, Miss.; 1883; P.; coed.; II
Belknap C. Center Harbor, N.H.; 1963; P.; coed.; I, II

1657

Bellarmine-Ursuline C. Louisville, Ky.; 1950; P.; coed.; II
Bellevue C. Bellevue, Nebr.; 1966; P.; coed.; II
Belmont Abbey C. Belmont, N.C.; 1878; P.; coed. (women only in jr. & sr. yrs.); II
Belmont C. Nashville, Tenn.; 1951; P.; coed.; II
Beloit C. Beloit, Wis.; 1846; P.; coed.; II
Bemidji State C.* Bemidji, Minn.; 1918; S.; coed.; I, III
Benedict C. Columbia, S.C.; 1870; P.; coed.; II
Benjamin Franklin U. Washington, D.C.; 1925; P.; coed.; I, II
Bennet C. Greensboro, N.C.; 1873; P.; women; II
Bennington C. Bennington, Vt.; 1932; P.; women; II
Bentley C.* Waltham, Mass.; 1917; P.; coed.; I, II
Berea C. Berea, Ky.; 1855; P.; coed.; II
Berkeley Baptist Divinity School Berkeley, Calif.; 1871; P.; coed.; IV, V
Berkeley Divinity School New Haven, Conn.; 1854; P.; coed.; V
Berklee School of Music Boston, Mass.; 1945; P.; coed.; II
Berkshire Christian C. Lenox, Mass.; 1897; P.; coed.; II
Bernard M. Baruch C. *see* The City U. of NEW YORK
Berry C. Mount Berry, Ga.; 1902; P.; coed.; II
Bethany Bible C. Santa Cruz, Calif.; 1919; P.; coed.; II
Bethany C. Lindsborg, Kans.; 1881; P.; coed.; II
Bethany C. Bethany, W.Va.; 1840; P.; coed.; II
Bethany Nazarene C. Bethany, Okla.; 1899; P.; coed.; III
Bethany Theological Seminary Oak Brook, Ill.; 1905; P.; coed.; V
Bethel C. Mishawaka, Ind.; 1947; P.; coed.; II
Bethel C. North Newton, Kans.; 1887; P.; coed.; I, II
Bethel C. St. Paul, Minn.; 1871; P.; coed.; I, II
Bethel C. McKenzie, Tenn.; 1842; P.; coed.; II
Bethel Theological Seminary St. Paul, Minn.; 1871; P.; coed.; V
Bethune-Cookman C. Daytona Beach, Fla.; 1904; P.; coed.; II
Bible Baptist Seminary Arlington, Tex.; 1939; P.; coed.; II, V
Biola C. La Mirada, Calif.; 1907; P.; coed.; II
Birmingham-Southern C. Birmingham, Ala.; 1856; P.; coed.; III
Biscayne C. Miami, Fla.; 1961; P.; men; II
Bishop C. Dallas, Tex.; 1881; P.; coed.; II
Blackburn C. Carlinville, Ill.; 1837; P.; coed.; II
Black Hills State C. Spearfish, S.Dak.; 1883; S.; coed.; III: branch—Ellsworth AFB
Bliss C. Columbus, Ohio; 1899; P.; coed.; I, II
Bloomfield C. Bloomfield, N.J.; 1868; P.; coed.; II
Bloomsburg State C.* Bloomsburg, Pa.; 1839; S.; coed.; III
Bluefield State C. Bluefield, W.Va.; 1895; S.; coed.; I, II
Blue Mountain C. Blue Mountain, Miss.; 1873; P.; women; II
Bluffton C. Bluffton, Ohio; 1900; P.; coed.; II
Bob Jones U.* Greenville, S.C.; 1927; P.; coed.; VII
Boise State C.* Boise, Ida.; 1932; S.; coed.; I, II
Borromeo Seminary of Ohio Wickliffe, Ohio; 1954; P.; men; II
Boston C.* Chestnut Hill, Mass.; 1863; P.; coed.; VII
Boston Conservatory of Music Boston, Mass.; 1867; P.; coed.; III
Boston U.* Boston, Mass.; 1864; P.; coed.; I, VII
Bowdoin C. Brunswick, Me.; 1794; P.; men; III
Bowie State C. Bowie, Md.; 1867; S.; coed.; II
Bowling Green State U.* Bowling Green, Ohio; 1910; S.; coed.; III, VI: ext. centers—Bryan, Fostoria, Fremont, Sandusky
Bradley U.* Peoria, Ill.; 1897; P.; coed.; I, III
Brandeis U. Waltham, Mass.; 1948; P.; coed.; III, VI
Brenau C. Gainsville, Ga.; 1878; P.; women; II
Brentwood C. Brentwood, N.Y.; 1955; P.; women; II
Brescia C. Owensboro, Ky.; 1925; P.; coed.; II
Briarcliff C. Briarcliff Manor, N.Y.; 1903; P.; women; I, II
Briar Cliff C. Sioux City, Iowa; 1930; P.; coed.; II
Bridgeport, U. of* Bridgeport, Conn.; 1927; P.; coed.; I, III
Bridgeport Engineering Institute, The Bridgeport, Conn.; 1924; P.; coed.; I, II
Bridgewater C. Bridgewater, Va.; 1880; P.; coed.; II
Brigham Young U.* Provo, Utah; 1875; P.; coed.; VII: ext. centers—Ogden, Salt Lake City, & Idaho Falls, Ida., Inglewood, Calif.
Brooklyn, The Polytechnic Institute of* Brooklyn, N.Y.; 1854; P.; coed.; II
Brooklyn C. *see* The City U. of NEW YORK
Brooklyn C. of Pharmacy *see* LONG ISLAND U.
Brooklyn Law School Brooklyn, N.Y.; 1901; P.; coed.; V
Brooks Institute of Photography Santa Barbara, Calif.; 1946; P.; coed.; II
Brown U.* Providence, R.I.; 1764; P.; men (coed., grad. school); III, VI: see PEMBROKE C.
Bryant C. of Business Administration Providence, R.I.; 1863; P.; coed.; I, II
Bryn Mawr C. Bryn Mawr, Pa.; 1885; P.; women (coed., grad. school); III, VI
Bucknell U. Lewisburg, Pa.; 1846; P.; coed.; III
Buena Vista C. Storm Lake, Iowa; 1891; P.; coed.; II
Butler U.* Indianapolis, Ind.; 1855; P.; coed.; I, III

Cabrini C. Radnor, Pa.; 1957; P.; women; II
Caldwell C. for Women Caldwell, N.J.; 1939; P.; women; II
California, U. of* Berkeley, Calif.; 1868; S.; coed.; VII: other campuses at Davis** (1908), Irvine (1965), Los Angeles** (1919), Riverside* (1907), San Diego (1912), San Francisco* (1873), Santa Barbara** (1944), Santa Cruz (1965)
California Baptist C. Riverside, Calif.; 1950; P.; coed.; II
California Baptist Theological Seminary Covina, Calif.; 1944; P.; coed.; V
California C. of Arts and Crafts Oakland, Calif.; 1907; P.; coed.; III
California C. of Medicine Los Angeles, Calif.; 1914; coed.; V: part of the U. of California, Irvine
California C. of Podiatric Medicine San Francisco, Calif.; 1914; P.; coed.; II, V
California Institute of Technology Pasadena, Calif.; 1891; P.; men (coed., grad. school); III, VI
California Institute of the Arts Los Angeles, Calif.; 1921; P.; coed.; V
California Lutheran C. Thousand Oaks, Calif.; 1959; P.; coed.; II
California Maritime Academy Vallejo, Calif.; 1929; S. & Fed.; men; II
California State Colleges Los Angeles (hdqrs.); 1961: 19 campuses, all S., all coed.
  California State C., Bakersfield Bakersfield; 1967; II
  California State C., Dominguez Hills Dominguez Hills; 1960; III
  California State C. at Fullerton* Fullerton; 1957; III
  California State C. at Hayward* Hayward; 1957; III
  California State C. at Long Beach* Long Beach; 1949; III
  California State C. at Los Angeles* Los Angeles; 1947; III, VI
  California State C. at San Bernardino San Bernardino; 1960; III
  California State Polytechnic C., Kellogg-Voorhis* Pomona; 1938; III
  California State Polytechnic C., San Luis Obispo* San Luis Obispo; 1901; III
  Chico State C.* Chico; 1887; III
  Fresno State C.* Fresno; 1910; III
  Humboldt State C.* Arcata; 1913; III
  Sacramento State C.* Sacramento; 1947; III
  San Diego State C.* San Diego; 1897; III, VI
  San Fernando Valley State C.* Los Angeles; 1958; III
  San Francisco State C.* San Francisco; 1899; III, VI
  San Jose State C.* San Jose; 1857; III
  Sonoma State C. Rohnert Park (Cotati); 1960; III
  Stanislaus State C. Turlock; 1959; III
California State C.* California, Pa.; 1852; S.; coed.; III
California Western U. San Diego, Calif.; 1952; P.; coed.; III, VI
Calvary Bible C. Kansas City, Mo.; 1932; P.; coed.; III
Calvary C. Letcher, Ky.; 1966; P.; coed.; II
Calvin C.* Grand Rapids, Mich.; 1876; P.; coed.; II
Calvin Coolidge C. Boston, Mass.; 1936; P.; coed.; II
Calvin Theological Seminary Grand Rapids, Mich.; 1876; P.; coed.; V
Cameron State Agricultural C. Lawton, Okla.; 1909; S.; coed.; I, II
Campbell C. Buies Creek, N.C.; 1887; P.; coed.; I, II
Campbellsville C. Campbellsville, Ky.; 1906; P.; coed.; II
Canaan C. Canaan, N.H.; 1955; P.; coed.; II
Canisius C. Buffalo, N.Y.; 1870; P.; coed.; III
Capital U. Columbus, Ohio; 1850; P.; coed.; II, V
Capitol Institute of Technology Washington, D.C.; 1927; P.; coed.; I, II
Capuchin Seminary of St. Mary Crown Point, Ind.; 1959; P.; men; II
Capuchin Theological Seminary Garrison, N.Y.; 1952; P.; men; IV, V
Cardinal Cushing C. Brookline, Mass.; 1952; P.; women; I, II
Cardinal Glennon C. St. Louis, Mo.; 1900; P.; men; II
Cardinal Stritch C. Milwaukee, Wis.; 1937; P.; women (coed., grad. & summer schools); III
Carleton C. Northfield, Minn.; 1866; P.; coed.; II
Carnegie-Mellon U.* Pittsburgh, Pa.; 1900; P.; coed.; III, VI
Carroll C. Helena, Mont.; 1909; P.; coed.; II
Carroll C. Waukesha, Wis.; 1846; P.; coed.; II
Carson-Newman C. Jefferson City, Tenn.; 1851; P.; coed.; II
Carthage C. Kenosha, Wis.; 1847; P.; coed.; II
Cascade C. Portland, Oreg.; 1918; P.; coed.; I, II
Case Western Reserve U.* Cleveland, Ohio; 1826; P.; coed.; VII
Castleton State C. Castleton, Vt.; 1787; S.; coed.; I, II
Catawba C. Salisbury, N.C.; 1851; P.; coed.; II
Cathedral C. of the Immaculate Conception Douglaston, N.Y.; 1914; P.; men; II
Catherine Spalding C. Louisville, Ky.; 1920; P.; women; III
Catholic U. of America, The* Washington, D.C.; 1887; P.; coed.; VII

Cedar Crest C. Allentown, Pa.; 1867; P.; women; II
Cedarville C. Cedarville, Ohio; 1887; P.; coed.; II
Centenary C. of Louisiana Shreveport, La.; 1825; P.; coed.; II
Central Baptist Theological Seminary Kansas City, Kans.; 1901; P.; coed.; IV, V
Central Bible C. Springfield, Mo.; 1922; P.; coed.; II
Central Christian C. of the Bible Moberly, Mo.; 1957; coed.; V
Central C. Pella, Iowa; 1853; P.; coed.; II
Central Connecticut State C.* New Britain, Conn.; 1849; S.; coed.; I, III
Central Methodist C. Fayette, Mo.; 1854; P.; coed.; II
Central Michigan U.* Mt. Pleasant, Mich.; 1892; S.; coed.; III
Central Missouri State C.* Warrensburg, Mo.; 1870; S.; coed.; III
Central State C.* Edmond, Okla.; 1890; S.; coed.; III
Central State U. Wilberforce, Ohio; 1887; S.; coed.; III
Central Washington State C.* Ellensburg, Wash.; 1891; S.; coed.; III
Central Wesleyan C. Central, S.C.; 1906; P.; coed.; II
Centre C. of Kentucky Danville, Ky.; 1819; P.; coed.; II
Chadron State C.* Chadron, Nebr.; 1911; S.; coed.; III
Chaminade C. of Honolulu Honolulu, Hawaii; 1955; P.; coed.; I, II
Chapman C. Orange, Calif.; 1861; P.; coed.; III
Charleston, The C. of Charleston, S.C.; 1770; P.; coed.; II
Chatham C. Pittsburgh, Pa.; 1869; P.; women; II
Chattanooga, U. of Chattanooga, Tenn.; 1886; P.; coed.; III
Chestnut Hill C. Philadelphia, Pa.; 1871; P.; women; II
Cheyney State C. Cheyney, Pa.; 1837; S.; coed.; II
Chicago, The U. of Chicago, Ill.; 1892; P.; coed.; VII
Chicago Academy of Fine Arts Chicago, Ill.; 1902; P.; coed.; I, II
Chicago Baptist Institute Chicago, Ill.; 1935; P.; coed.; II
Chicago C. of Osteopathy Chicago, Ill.; 1913; P.; coed.; V
Chicago Conservatory C. Chicago, Ill.; 1857; P.; coed.; III
Chicago-Kent C. of Law Chicago, Ill.; 1887; P.; coed.; V
Chicago Medical School, The Chicago, Ill.; 1912; P.; coed.; V
Chicago State C.* Chicago, Ill.; 1869; S.; coed.; III
Chicago Technical C. Chicago, Ill.; 1904; P.; men; I, II
Chicago Theological Seminary, The Chicago, Ill.; 1855; P.; coed.; V
Chico State C. see CALIFORNIA STATE COLLEGES
Christian Brothers C. Memphis, Tenn.; 1871; P.; men; II
Christian Theological Seminary Indianapolis, Ind.; 1958; P.; coed.; V
Christ the Saviour Seminary Johnstown, Pa.; 1940; P.; men; II
Church Divinity School of the Pacific, The Berkeley, Calif.; 1893; P.; coed.; V
Cincinnati, U. of Cincinnati, Ohio; 1819; S. & Mun.; coed.; I, VII
Cincinnati Bible Seminary, The Cincinnati, Ohio; 1924; P.; coed.; I, III, V
Citadel, The — The Military C. of South Carolina Charleston, S.C.; 1842; S.; men; II
City C. of New York see The City U. of NEW YORK
Claflin U. Orangeburg, S.C.; 1869; P.; coed.; II
Claremont Colleges Claremont, Calif.; 1925; P.; six affiliated, but independent institutions—
  Claremont Graduate School 1925; coed.; IV, VI
  Claremont Men's C. 1946; men; II
  Harvey Mudd C. 1955; coed.; II
  Pitzer C. 1963; women; II
  Pomona C. 1887; coed.; II
  Scripps C. 1926; women; II
Clarion State C.* Clarion, Pa.; 1867; S.; coed.; III; branch—Oil City
Clark C. Atlanta, Ga.; 1869; P.; coed.; II
Clarke C. Dubuque, Iowa; 1843; P.; women; III
Clarkson C. of Technology Potsdam, N.Y.; 1896; P.; coed.; III, VI
Clark U. Worcester, Mass.; 1887; P.; coed.; III, V, VI
Cleary C. Ypsilanti, Mich.; 1883; P.; coed.; I, II: ext.— Tecumseh
Clemson U.* Clemson, S.C.; 1893; S.; coed.; I, III, VI: 2-yr. ext. centers—Greenville, Sumter
Cleveland Institute of Art, The Cleveland, Ohio; 1882; P.; coed.; II
Cleveland Institute of Music, The Cleveland, Ohio; 1920; P.; coed.; III, V
Cleveland State U., The* Cleveland, Ohio; 1965; S.; coed.; I, III
Clinch Valley C. see U. of VIRGINIA
Coe C. Cedar Rapids, Iowa; 1851; P.; coed.; II
Coker C. for Women Hartsville, S.C.; 1908; P.; women; II
Colby C. Waterville, Me.; 1813; P., coed.; II
Colgate U. Hamilton, N.Y.; 1819; P.; men (coed., grad. school); III
Colombiere C. Clarkston, Mich.; 1959; men; affiliated with U. of Detroit, III
Colorado, U. of Boulder, Colo.; 1876; S.; coed.; VII: ext. centers—Colorado Springs, Denver

Colorado Alpine C. Steamboat Springs, Colo.; 1962; P.; coed.; II
Colorado C., The Colorado Springs, Colo.; 1874; P.; coed.; III
Colorado School of Mines Golden, Colo.; 1874; S.; coed.; VII
Colorado State C.* Greeley, Colo.; 1890; S.; coed.; III, VI
Colorado State U.* Fort Collins, Colo.; 1870; S.; VII
Colorado Western C. Montrose, Colo.; 1967; P.; coed.; II
Columbia Bible C. Columbia, S.C.; 1923; P.; coed.; III, V
Columbia C. Chicago, Ill.; 1890; P.; coed.; II
Columbia C. Columbia, S.C.; 1854; P.; women; II
Columbia Theological Seminary Decatur, Ga.; 1828; P.; coed.; V
Columbia Union C. Takoma Park, Md.; 1904; P.; coed.; II
Columbia U. in the City of New York* New York, N.Y.; 1754; P.; coed.; VII
Columbus C. Columbus, Ga.; 1958; S.; coed.; I, II
Columbus C. of Art & Design, The Columbus, Ohio; 1879; P.; coed.; II
Combs C. of Music Philadelphia, Pa.; 1885; P.; coed.; III, VI
Concord C. Athens, W.Va.; 1872; S.; coed.; II
Concordia C. Moorhead, Minn.; 1891; P.; coed.; II
Concordia C. St. Paul, Minn.; 1893; P.; coed.; I, II
Concordia Seminary St. Louis, Mo.; 1839; P.; men (coed., grad. school); IV, V
Concordia Senior C. Fort Wayne, Ind.; 1957; P.; men; II
Concordia Teachers C. River Forest, Ill.; 1864; P.; coed.; III
Concordia Teachers C. Seward, Nebr.; 1894; P.; coed.; III
Concordia Theological Seminary Springfield, Ill.; 1846; P.; men; V
Connecticut, U. of Storrs, Conn.; 1881; S.; coed.; VII
Connecticut C. New London, Conn.; 1911; P.; women (coed., grad. school); III
Conservative Baptist Theological Seminary Denver, Colo.; 1950; P.; coed.; V
Converse C. Spartanburg, S.C.; 1889; P.; women (coed., music school); III
Cooper Union for the Advancement of Science & Art, The New York, N.Y.; 1859; P.; coed.; III, VI
Coppin State C. Baltimore, Md.; 1900; S.; coed.; II
Cornell C. Mount Vernon, Iowa; 1853; P.; coed.; II
Cornell U.* Ithaca, N.Y.; 1865; P. (operates 4 units of State U. of NEW YORK); coed.; VII
Corpus Christi, U. of Corpus Christi, Tex.; 1947; P.; coed.; II
Covenant C. Lookout Mountain, Tenn.; 1955; P.; coed.; II
Covenant Theological Seminary St. Louis, Mo.; 1956; men; V: grad. school of Covenant C., Tenn.
Cranbrook Academy of Art Bloomfield Hills, Mich.; 1927; P.; coed.; III
Creighton U., The* Omaha, Nebr.; 1878; P.; coed.; III, V
Crosier House of Studies Fort Wayne, Ind.; 1930; P.; men; affiliated with St. Francis C., Ind., & Catholic U. of America, III
Crozer Theological Seminary Chester, Pa.; 1867; P.; coed.; V
Culver-Stockton C. Canton, Mo.; 1853; P.; coed.; II
Cumberland C. Williamsburg, Ky.; 1889; P.; coed.; II
Curry C. Milton, Mass.; 1879; P.; coed.; II
Curtis Institute of Music, The Philadelphia, Pa.; 1924; P.; coed.; II

Dakota Wesleyan U. Mitchell, S.Dak.; 1885; P.; coed.; II
Dallas, U. of University of Dallas Station (Irving), Tex.; 1956; P.; coed.; III, VI
Dallas Baptist C. Dallas, Tex.; 1898; P.; coed.; II
Dallas Bible C. Dallas, Tex.; 1940; P.; coed.; II
Dallas Christian C. Dallas, Tex.; 1950; P.; coed.; V
Dallas Theological Seminary & Graduate School of Theology Dallas, Tex.; 1924; P.; men; V
Dana C. Blair, Nebr.; 1884; P.; coed.; II
Daniel Payne C. Birmingham, Ala.; 1889; P.; coed.; II
Dartmouth C.* Hanover, N.H.; 1769; P.; men; III, VI
David Lipscomb C. Nashville, Tenn.; 1891; P.; coed.; II
Davidson C. Davidson, N.C.; 1837; P.; men; II
Davis & Elkins C. Elkins, W.Va.; 1904; P.; coed.; II
Dayton, U. of Dayton, Ohio; 1850; P.; coed.; I, III
Defiance C., The Defiance, Ohio; 1850; P.; coed.; II
Delaware, U. of Newark, Del.; 1833; P. & S.; coed.; I, III, VI: ext. centers—Dover, Georgetown, Wilmington, & Aberdeen, Md.
Delaware State C. Dover, Del.; 1891; S.; coed.; II
Delaware Valley C. of Science & Agriculture Doylestown, Pa.; 1896; P.; men (coed., evening div.); II
De Lourdes C. Des Plaines, Ill.; 1927; P.; women; II
Delta State C. Cleveland, Miss.; 1924; S.; coed.; III
Denison U. Granville, Ohio; 1831; P.; coed.; II
Denver, U. of Denver, Colo.; 1864; P.; coed.; VII
De Paul U.* Chicago, Ill.; 1898; P.; coed.; VII
DePauw U. Greencastle, Ind.; 1837; P.; coed.; III
Detroit, U. of Detroit, Mich.; 1877; P.; coed.; VII
Detroit Bible C. Detroit, Mich.; 1945; P.; coed.; V
Detroit C. of Business Dearborn, Mich.; 1936; P.; coed.; I, II

Detroit C. of Law Detroit, Mich.; 1891; P.; coed.; V
Detroit Institute of Technology Detroit, Mich.; 1891; P.; coed.; II
Dickinson C. Carlisle, Pa.; 1773; P.; coed.; II
Dickinson School of Law, The Carlisle, Pa.; 1834; P.; coed.; V
Dickinson State C. Dickinson, N.Dak.; 1918; S.; coed.; I, II
Dillard U. New Orleans, La.; 1869; P.; coed.; II
Diocesan Sisters C. Bloomfield, Conn.; 1949; P.; women; II
District of Columbia Teachers C. Washington, D.C.; 1851; Mun.; coed.; II
Divine Word C. Epworth, Iowa; 1964; P.; men; II
Divine Word Seminary Techny, Ill.; 1909; P.; men; II
Divinity School of the Protestant Episcopal Church in Philadelphia, The Philadelphia, Pa.; 1857; P.; coed.; V
Doane C. Crete, Nebr.; 1872; P.; coed.; II
Dominican C. Houston, Tex.; 1945; P.; women; II
Dominican C. Racine, Wis.; 1946; P.; coed.; II
Dominican C. of Blauvelt Blauvelt, N.Y.; 1952; P.; coed.; I, II
Dominican C. of San Rafael San Rafael, Calif.; 1890; P.; women (coed., grad. school); III
Don Bosco C. Newton, N.J.; 1928; P.; men; II
Dordt C. Sioux Center, Iowa; 1955; P.; coed.; II
Dowling C. Oakdale, N.Y.; 1959; P.; coed.; II
Drake C. of Florida Fort Lauderdale, Fla.; 1940; P.; coed.; I, II
Drake U.* Des Moines, Iowa; 1881; P.; coed.; III, V
Drew U. Madison, N.J.; 1866; P.; coed.; V
Drexel Institute of Technology* Philadelphia, Pa.; 1891; P.; coed.; III, VI
Dr. Martin Luther C. New Ulm, Minn.; 1884; P.; coed.; II
Dropsie C. for Hebrew & Cognate Learning, The Philadelphia, Pa.; 1907; P.; coed.; IV, VI
Drury C. Springfield, Mo.; 1873; P.; coed.; III
D.T. Watson School of Physiatrics Leetsdale, Pa.; 1920; P.; coed.; affiliated with U. of Pittsburgh & Thiel C., II
Dubuque, U. of Dubuque, Iowa; 1852; P.; coed.; II
Duke U.* Durham, N.C.; 1838; P.; coed.; VII
Dunbarton C. of Holy Cross Washington, D.C.; 1935; P.; women; II
Duns Scotus C. Southfield, Mich.; 1930; P.; men; II
Duquesne U.* Pittsburgh, Pa.; 1878; P.; coed.; VII
Dyke C. Cleveland, Ohio; 1848; P.; coed.; I, II
D'Youville C. Buffalo, N.Y.; 1908; P.; women; II

Earlham C. Richmond, Ind.; 1847; P.; coed.; III
East Carolina U.** Greenville, N.C.; 1907; S.; coed.; I, III: branches—Camp Lejeune, Cherry Point, Seymour Johnson AFB
East Central State C. Ada, Okla.; 1909; S.; coed.; III
East Coast U. Brooksville, Fla.; 1947; P.; coed.; VII
Eastern Baptist C. St. Davids, Pa.; 1952; P.; coed.; II
Eastern Baptist Theological Seminary, The Philadelphia, Pa.; 1925; P.; coed.; IV, V
Eastern C. Baltimore, Md.; 1928; P.; coed.; I, II, V
Eastern Connecticut State C. Willimantic, Conn.; 1889; S.; coed.; I, III
Eastern Illinois U.* Charleston, Ill.; 1895; S.; coed.; II
Eastern Kentucky U.** Richmond, Ky.; 1906; S.; coed.; I, III
Eastern Mennonite C. Harrisonburg, Va.; 1917; P.; coed.; II, V
Eastern Michigan U.** Ypsilanti, Mich.; 1849; S.; coed.; III
Eastern Montana C.* Billings, Mont.; 1927; S.; coed.; III
Eastern Nazarene C. Wollaston Park (Quincy), Mass.; 1918; P.; coed.; I, III
Eastern New Mexico U.* Portales, N.Mex.; 1934; S.; coed.; I, III: ext. centers—Artesia, Hobbs, Clovis, Roswell, Tucumcari
Eastern Oregon C. La Grande, Oreg.; 1929; S.; coed.; I, III
Eastern Pilgrim C. Allentown, Pa.; 1921; P.; coed.; I, II
Eastern Washington State C.* Cheney, Wash.; 1890; S.; coed.; III
East Stroudsburg State C. East Stroudsburg, Pa.; 1893; S.; coed.; III
East Tennessee State U.* Johnson City, Tenn.; 1909; S.; coed.; I, III: ext. centers—Bristol, Greeneville, Kingsport
East Texas Baptist C. Marshall, Tex.; 1912; P.; coed.; II
East Texas State U.* Commerce, Tex.; 1889; S.; coed.; III, VI: ext. centers—15 throughout NE Texas
Eden Theological Seminary Webster Groves, Mo.; 1850; P.; coed.; IV, V
Edgewood C. Madison, Wis.; 1927; P.; women; II
Edinboro State C.* Edinboro, Pa.; 1857; S.; coed.; III: ext. centers—Sharon, Warren
Edward Waters C. Jacksonville, Fla.; 1866; P.; coed.; II
Eisenhower C. Seneca Falls, N.Y.; 1968; P.; coed.; II
Elizabeth City State C. Elizabeth City, N.C.; 1891; S.; coed.; II
Elizabethtown C. Elizabethtown, Pa.; 1899; P.; coed.; II
Elmhurst C. Elmhurst, Ill.; 1871; P.; coed.; II
Elmira C. Elmira, N.Y.; 1855; P.; women (coed., evening & summer sessions); I, III
Elon C. Elon College, N.C.; 1889; P.; coed.; II

Embry-Riddle Aeronautical Institute Daytona Beach, Fla.; 1926; P.; coed.; I, II
Emerson C. Boston, Mass.; 1880; P.; coed.; III
Emmanuel C. Boston, Mass.; 1919; P.; women (coed., evening & summer sessions); III
Emmanuel School of Religion Milligan College, Tenn.; 1961; P.; coed.; V: affiliated with Milligan College
Emory & Henry C. Emory, Va.; 1836; P.; coed.; II
Emory U.* Atlanta, Ga.; 1836; P.; coed.; VII
Emporia, The C. of Emporia, Kans.; 1882; P.; coed.; II
Episcopal Theological School, The Cambridge, Mass.; 1867; P.; coed.; V
Episcopal Theological Seminary of the Southwest, The Austin, Tex.; 1951; P.; coed.; V
Erskine C. Due West, S.C.; 1839; P.; coed.; II, V
Eureka C. Eureka, Ill.; 1855; P.; coed.; II
Evangel C. Springfield, Mo.; 1955; P.; coed.; II
Evangelical Congregational School of Theology, The Myerstown, Pa.; 1953; P.; men (& pastor's wives); V
Evangelical Lutheran Theological Seminary, The Columbus, Ohio; 1830; P.; coed.; V
Evangelical Theological Seminary, The Naperville, Ill.; 1873; P.; coed.; V
Evansville, U. of* Evansville, Ind.; 1854; P.; coed.; I, III

Fairfield U. Fairfield, Conn.; 1947; P.; men (coed., grad. school); III
Fairleigh Dickinson U.* Rutherford, N.J.; 1941; P.; coed.; I, III, V
Fairmont State C. Fairmont, W.Va.; 1867; S.; coed.; I, II
Faith Theological Seminary Elkins Park, Pa.; 1937; P.; coed.; IV, V
Farmington State C. Farmington, Me.; 1864; S.; coed.; II
Fayetteville State C. Fayetteville, N.C.; 1877; S.; coed.; II
Federal City C. Washington, D.C.; 1967; Mun.; coed.; I, III
Felician C. Lodi, N.J.; 1942; P.; women; I, II
Ferris State C.* Big Rapids, Mich.; 1884; S.; coed.; I, II
Finch C. New York, N.Y.; 1900; P.; women; I, II
Findlay C. Findlay, Ohio; 1882; P.; coed.; II
Fisk U. Nashville, Tenn.; 1866; P.; coed.; III
Flagler C. St. Augustine, Fla.; 1963; P.; women; II
Florence State C.* Florence, Ala.; 1872; S.; coed.; III
Florida, U. of** Gainesville, Fla.; 1853; S.; coed.; VII
Florida Agricultural & Mechanical U.* Tallahassee, Fla.; 1887; S.; coed.; III, V
Florida Atlantic U.* Boca Raton, Fla.; 1961; S.; coed.; III
Florida Beacon C. & Seminary Clearwater, Fla.; 1947; P.; coed.; II, V
Florida Institute of Technology Melbourne, Fla.; 1958; P.; coed.; II
Florida Memorial C. Miami, Fla.; 1892; P.; coed.; II
Florida Presbyterian C. St. Petersburg, Fla.; 1958; P.; coed.; II
Florida Southern C. Lakeland, Fla.; 1885; P.; coed.; II
Florida State U., The** Tallahassee, Fla.; 1857; S.; coed.; VII
Florida Technological U. Orlando, Fla.; 1968; S.; coed.; III
Fontbonne C. St. Louis, Mo.; 1917; P.; women; II
Fordham U.* New York, N.Y.; 1841; P.; coed.; VII
Fort Hays Kansas State C.* Hays, Kans.; 1902; S.; coed.; III
Fort Kent State C. Fort Kent, Me.; 1878; S.; coed.; II
Fort Lewis C. Durango, Colo.; 1911; S.; coed.; II
Fort Valley State C., The Fort Valley, Ga.; 1895; S.; coed.; III
Fort Wayne Art Institute Fort Wayne, Ind.; 1921; P.; coed.; II
Fort Wayne Bible C. Fort Wayne, Ind.; 1904; P.; coed.; II
Fort Wright C. of the Holy Names Spokane, Wash.; 1907; P.; women (coed., special programs); III
Francis T. Nicholls State C.* Thibodaux, La.; 1948; S.; coed.; III
Franconia C. Franconia, N.H.; 1961; P.; coed.; I, II
Frankfort Pilgrim C. Frankfort, Ind.; 1927; P.; coed.; II
Franklin & Marshall C. Lancaster, Pa.; 1787; P.; men; I, III
Franklin C. of Indiana Franklin, Ind.; 1834; P.; coed.; II
Franklin Pierce C. Rindge, N.H.; 1962; P.; coed.; II
Franklin U. Columbus, Ohio; 1902; P.; coed.; I, II
Free Will Baptist Bible C. Nashville, Tenn.; 1942; P.; coed.; II
Fresno State C. see CALIFORNIA STATE COLLEGES
Friends Bible C. Haviland, Kans.; 1917; P.; coed.; II
Friends U. Wichita, Kans.; 1898; P.; coed.; II
Friends World C. Westbury, N.Y.; 1965; P.; coed.; II
Frostburg State C. Frostburg, Md.; 1898; S.; coed.; II
Fuller Theological Seminary Pasadena, Calif.; 1947; P.; coed.; IV, V, VI
Furman U. Greenville, S.C.; 1826; P.; coed.; III

Gallaudet C. Washington, D.C.; 1864; P.; coed.; III
Gannon C. Erie, Pa.; 1944; P.; men (coed., aft. & evening div.); III
Garrett Theological Seminary Evanston, Ill.; 1853; P.; coed.; IV, V, VI

General Beadle State C. Madison, S.Dak.; 1881; S.; coed.; II

General Motors Institute Flint, Mich.; 1919; P.; coed.; II

General Theological Seminary, The New York, N.Y.; 1817; P.; men; V

Geneva C. Beaver Falls, Pa.; 1848; P.; coed.; II

George Fox C. Newberg, Oreg.; 1891; P.; coed.; II

George Mason C. see U. of VIRGINIA

George Peabody C. for Teachers Nashville, Tenn.; 1785; P.; coed.; III, VI

Georgetown C. Georgetown, Ky.; 1829; P.; coed.; III

Georgetown U.* Washington, D.C.; 1789; P.; coed.; VII

George Washington U., The* Washington, D.C.; 1821; P.; coed.; I, VII

George Williams C. Downers Grove, Ill.; 1890; P.; coed.; III, V

Georgia, Medical C. of Augusta, Ga.; 1828; S.; coed.; VII

Georgia, U. of* Athens, Ga.; 1785; S.; coed.; VII

Georgia C. at Milledgeville Milledgeville, Ga.; 1889; S.; coed.; III

Georgia Institute of Technology* Atlanta, Ga.; 1885; S.; coed.; III, VI

Georgian Court C. Lakewood, N.J.; 1908; P.; women; II

Georgia Southern C.* Statesboro, Ga.; 1908; S.; coed.; III

Georgia Southwestern C. Americus, Ga.; 1908; S.; coed.; I, II

Georgia State C.** Atlanta, Ga.; 1913; S.; coed.; I, III, VI

Gettysburg C. Gettysburg, Pa.; 1832; P.; coed.; II

Glassboro State C.* Glassboro, N.J.; 1923; S.; coed.; III

Glenville State C. Glenville, W.Va.; 1872; S.; coed.; II

Goddard C. Plainfield, Vt.; 1938; P.; coed.; II

Golden Gate Baptist Theological Seminary Mill Valley, Calif.; 1944; P.; coed.; III, V

Golden Gate C. San Francisco, Calif.; 1901; P.; coed.; I, III, V

Gonzaga U. Spokane, Wash.; 1887; P.; coed.; III, V

Good Counsel C. White Plains, N.Y.; 1923; P.; women; II

Gordon C. Wenham, Mass.; 1889; P.; coed.; III

Gorham State C. Gorham, Me.; 1878; S.; coed.; III

Goshen C. Goshen, Ind.; 1903; P.; coed.; II, V

Goucher C. Towson (Baltimore), Md.; 1885; P.; women (coed., grad. school); III

Grace Bible C. Grand Rapids, Mich.; 1939; P.; coed.; I, II, V

Grace Bible Institute Omaha, Nebr.; 1943; P.; coed.; II

Graceland C. Lamoni, Iowa; 1895; P.; coed.; I, II

Grace Theological Seminary & Grace C. Winona Lake, Ind.; 1937; P.; coed.; II, V

Graduate Theological Union Berkeley, Calif.; 1962; P.; coed.; V, VI

Grambling C.* Grambling, La.; 1901; S.; coed.; II

Grand Canyon C. Phoenix, Ariz.; 1949; P.; coed.; II

Grand Rapids Baptist Bible C. & Seminary Grand Rapids, Mich.; 1941; P.; coed.; II, V

Grand Valley State C. Allendale, Mich.; 1960; S.; coed.; II

Gratz C. Philadelphia, Pa.; 1895; P.; coed.; II

Great Falls, The C. of Great Falls, Mont.; 1932; P.; coed.; II

Great Lakes Bible C. Lansing, Mich.; 1949; P.; coed.; II

Greensboro C. Greensboro, N.C.; 1838; P.; coed.; II

Greenville C. Greenville, Ill.; 1892; P.; coed.; II

Grinnell C. Grinnell, Iowa; 1846; P.; coed.; II

Grove City C. Grove City, Pa.; 1876; P.; coed.; II

Guam, C. of Mangilao, Guam; 1952; Ter.; coed.; I, II

Guilford C. Greensboro, N.C.; 1837; P.; coed.; I, III

Gulf-Coast Bible C. Houston, Tex.; 1953; P.; coed.; I, II

Gustavus Adolphus C. St. Peter, Minn.; 1862; P.; coed.; II

Gwynedd-Mercy C. Gwynedd Valley, Pa.; 1948; P.; women; I, II

Hahneman Medical C. & Hospital Philadelphia, Pa.; 1848; P.; coed.; VII

Hamilton C. Clinton, N.Y.; 1812; P.; men; II

Hamline U. St. Paul, Minn.; 1854; P.; coed.; II

Hampden C. of Pharmacy Willimansett, Mass.; 1927; P.; coed.; V

Hampden-Sydney C. Hampden-Sydney, Va.; 1776; P.; men; II

Hampshire C. South Amherst, Mass.; 1965; P.; coed.; II

Hampton Institute* Hampton, Va.; 1868; P.; coed.; III

Hanover C. Hanover, Ind.; 1827; P.; coed.; II

Harding C. Searcy, Ark.; 1924; P.; coed.; II

Harding Graduate School of Religion Memphis, Tenn.; 1958; P.; coed.; IV, V

Hardin-Simmons U. Abilene, Tex.; 1891; P.; coed.; III

Harris Teachers C. St. Louis, Mo.; 1857; S. & Mun.; coed.; I

Hartford, U. of West Hartford, Conn.; 1957; P.; coed.; I, III

Hartford Seminary Foundation Hartford, Conn.; 1834; P.; coed.; IV, V, VI

Hartwick C. Oneonta, N.Y.; 1928; P.; coed.; II

Harvard U.** Cambridge, Mass.; 1636; P.; coed.; VII

Harvey Mudd C. see CLAREMONT COLLEGES

Hastings C. Hastings, Nebr.; 1882; P.; coed.; II

Hastings C. of Law San Francisco, Calif.; 1878; S.; coed.; V: affiliated with the U. of California

Haverford C. Haverford, Pa.; 1833; P.; men; II

Hawaii, The Church C. of Laie, Hawaii; 1955; P.; coed.;

Hawaii, U. of** Honolulu, Hawaii; 1907; S.; coed.; VII: branch—Hilo

Hawaii Loa C. Honolulu, Hawaii; 1963; P.; coed.; II

Hawaii Pacific C. Honolulu, Hawaii; 1965; P.; coed.; II

Heald Engineering C. San Francisco, Calif.; 1863; P.; coed.; II

Hebrew Teachers C. Brookline, Mass.; 1921; P.; coed.; III

Hebrew Theological C. Skokie, Ill.; 1922; P.; men; I, III, V

Hebrew Union C.-Jewish Institute of Religion Cincinnati, Ohio; 1875; P.; coed.; VII: branches—New York, N.Y., Los Angeles, Calif.

Heidelberg C. Tiffin, Ohio; 1850; P.; coed.; II

Hellenic C. Brookline, Mass.; 1937; P.; men; II, V

Henderson State C.* Arkadelphia, Ark.; 1890; S.; coed.; III

Hendrix C. Conway, Ark.; 1884; P.; coed.; II

Herbert H. Lehman C. see The City U. of NEW YORK

High Point C. High Point, N.C.; 1924; P.; coed.; II

Hillsdale C. Hillsdale, Mich.; 1844; P.; coed.; II

Hiram C. Hiram, Ohio; 1850; P.; coed.; II

Hiram Scott C. Scottsbluff, Nebr.; 1965; P.; coed.; II

Hobart & William Smith Colleges Geneva, N.Y.; 1822; P.; coed.; III

Hofstra U.** Hempstead, N.Y.; 1935; P.; coed.; III, VI

Hollins C. Hollins College, Va.; 1842; P.; women (coed., grad. school); III

Hollywood C. Hollywood, Fla.; 1965; P.; coed.; II

Holy Apostles Seminary Cromwell, Conn.; 1956; P.; men; II

Holy Cross, C. of the Worcester, Mass.; 1843; P.; men; III

Holy Family C. Philadelphia, Pa.; 1954; P.; women; II

Holy Family C. Manitowoc, Wis.; 1935; P.; women; II

Holy Family Seminary Overland, Mo.; 1944; P.; men; II

Holy Names, C. of the Oakland, Calif.; 1880; P.; women (coed., grad. school); III

Holy Redeemer C. Waterford, Wis.; 1968; P.; men; II

Holy Trinity Orthodox Seminary Jordanville, N.Y.; 1948; P.; men; II

Hood C. Frederick, Md.; 1893; P.; women; II

Hope C. Holland, Mich.; 1866; P.; coed.; II

Houghton C. Houghton, N.Y.; 1884; P.; coed.; I, II

Houston, U. of** Houston, Tex.; 1934; S.; coed.; I, VII

Houston Baptist C. Houston, Tex.; 1960; P.; coed.; II

Howard Payne C. Brownwood, Tex.; 1887; P.; coed.; III

Howard U.* Washington, D.C.; 1867; P.; coed.; VII

Humboldt State C. see CALIFORNIA STATE COLLEGES

Hunter C. see The City U. of NEW YORK

Huntingdon C. Montgomery, Ala.; 1854; P.; coed.; II

Huntington C. Huntington, Ind.; 1897; P.; coed.; II, V

Huron C. Huron, S.Dak.; 1883; P.; coed.; II

Husson C. Bangor, Me.; 1898; P.; coed.; I, II

Huston-Tillotson C. Austin, Tex.; 1876; P.; coed.; II

Idaho, The C. of Caldwell, Ida.; 1891; P.; coed.; III

Idaho, U. of* Moscow, Ida.; 1889; S.; coed.; VII

Idaho State U.* Pocatello, Ida.; 1901; S.; coed.; I, III

Iliff School of Theology, The Denver, Colo.; 1892; P.; coed.; V

Illinois, U. of** Urbana, Ill.; 1868; S.; coed.; VII: branch—Chicago

Illinois C. Jacksonville, Ill.; 1829; P.; coed.; II

Illinois C. of Optometry Chicago, Ill.; 1872; P.; coed.; V

Illinois C. of Podiatric Medicine Chicago, Ill.; 1912; P.; coed.; V

Illinois Institute of Technology* Chicago, Ill.; 1892; P.; coed.; III, VI

Illinois State U.** Normal, Ill.; 1857; S., coed.; III VI

Illinois Wesleyan U. Bloomington, Ill.; 1850; P.; cc ; II

Immaculata C. Immaculata, Pa.; 1920; P.; women II

Immaculate Conception, Cathedral C. of the Do .glaston, N.Y.; 1914; P.; men; II

Immaculate Conception Seminary Conception, Mo.; 1891; P.; men; II

Immaculate Conception Seminary Darlington (Ramsey), N.J.; 1860; P.; men; affiliated with Seton Hall U., II

Immaculate Heart C. Los Angeles, Calif.; 1916; P.; women (coed., grad. school); III

Incarnate Word C. San Antonio, Tex.; 1881; P.; w men (coed., grad. school); III

Indiana Central C. Indianapolis, Ind.; 1902; P.; coed.; I, III

Indiana Institute of Technology Fort Wayne, Ind.; 1930; P.; coed.; II

Indiana State U.** Terre Haute, Ind.; 1870; S.; coed.; III

Indiana U.** Bloomington, Ind.; 1820; S.; coed.; VII: branches—Fort Wayne, Gary, Indianapolis, Jeffersonville, Kokomo, & South Bend

Indiana U. of Pennsylvania** Indiana, Pa.; 1875; S.; coed.; III, IV; ext. centers—Kittanning, Punxsutawney

Institute for Advanced Study, The Princeton, N.J.; 1930; P.; coed.; post-doctoral research, no degrees awarded

Insurance, The C. of New York, N.Y.; 1962; P.; coed.; III

Inter American U. of Puerto Rico* San Germán, P.R.; 1912; P.; coed.; III

Interdenominational Theological Center Atlanta, Ga.; 1958; P.; coed.; V

Iona C. New Rochelle, N.Y.; 1940; P.; men (coed., grad., eve., & summer schools); III

Iowa, The U. of** Iowa City, Iowa; 1847; S.; coed.; VII

Iowa State U. of Science & Technology** Ames, Iowa; 1858; S.; coed.; III, VI

Iowa Wesleyan C. Mt. Pleasant, Iowa; 1842; P.; coed.; II

Ithaca C.* Ithaca, N.Y.; 1892; P.; coed.; III

Jackson State C.* Jackson, Miss.; 1877; S.; coed.; III

Jacksonville State U.* Jacksonville, Ala.; 1883; S.; coed.; III

Jacksonville U. Jacksonville, Fla.; 1934; P.; coed.; III

Jamestown C. Jamestown, N.Dak.; 1884; P.; coed.; II

Jarvis Christian C. Hawkins, Tex.; 1912; P.; coed.; II

Jefferson Medical C. Philadelphia, Pa.; 1824; P.; coed.; IV, V, VI

Jersey City State C. Jersey City, N.J.; 1927; S.; coed.; III

Jewish Religion, Academy for New York, N.Y.; 1956; P.; men; V

Jewish Studies, The C. of Chicago, Ill.; 1925; P.; coed.; VII

Jewish Theological Seminary of America New York, N.Y.; 1886; P.; men (coed., some divisions); VII

John Brown U. Siloam Springs, Ark.; 1919; P.; coed.; II

John Carroll U.* University Heights (Cleveland), Ohio; 1886; P.; coed.; III

John F. Kennedy C. Wahoo, Nebr.; 1965; P.; coed.; II

John F. Kennedy U. Martinez, Calif.; 1964; P.; coed.; III, V

John Jay C. of Criminal Justice *see* The City U. of NEW YORK

John J. Pershing C. Beatrice, Nebr.; 1966; P.; coed.; II

John Marshall Law School, The Chicago, Ill.; 1899; P.; coed.; V

John Marshall U. Atlanta, Ga.; 1933; P.; coed.; I, V

Johns Hopkins U., The Baltimore, Md.; 1876; P.; men (coed., grad. school); VII: branch—Washington, D.C.

Johnson Bible C. Kimberlin Heights, Tenn.; 1893; P.; coed.; II

Johnson C. Smith U. Charlotte, N.C.; 1867; P.; coed.; II, V

Johnson State C. Johnson, Vt.; 1867; S.; coed.; II

John Wesley C. Greensboro, N.C.; 1932; P.; coed.; II, V

Jones C. Jacksonville, Fla.; 1918; P.; coed.; I, II: branch —Orlando

Judge Advocate General's School, The Charlottesville, Va.; 1942; Fed.; coed.; grad. program, non-degree-granting

Judson C. Marion, Ala.; 1838; P.; women; II

Judson C. Elgin, Ill.; 1963; P.; coed.; II

Juilliard School of Music New York, N.Y.; 1906; P.; coed.; III, VI

Juniata C. Huntingdon, Pa.; 1876; P.; coed.; II

Kalamazoo C. Kalamazoo, Mich.; 1833; P.; coed.; III

Kansas, The U. of** Lawrence, Kans.; 1866; S.; coed.; VII

Kansas City Art Institute Kansas City, Mo.; 1885; P.; coed.; II

Kansas City C. of Osteopathy & Surgery Kansas City, Mo.; 1916; P.; coed.; V

Kansas State C. of Pittsburg* Pittsburg, Kans.; 1903; S.; coed.; III

Kansas State Teachers C.* Emporia, Kans.; 1863; S.; coed.; III

Kansas State U.** Manhattan, Kans.; 1863; S.; coed.; III, VI

Kansas Wesleyan U. Salina, Kans.; 1886; P.; coed.; II

Kearney State C.* Kearney, Nebr.; 1905; S.; coed.; III

Keene State C. Keene, N.H.; 1909; coed.; III: division of the U. of New Hampshire

Kenrick Seminary St. Louis, Mo.; 1869; P.; men; affiliated with St. Louis U., IV, V

Kent State U.** Kent, Ohio; 1910; S.; coed.; I, VII: 10 branches in NE Ohio

Kentucky, U. of** Lexington, Ky.; 1865; S.; coed.; VII: 13 affiliated community colleges throughout the State

Kentucky Christian C. Grayson, Ky.; 1919; P.; coed.; II

Kentucky Southern C. Louisville, Ky.; 1960; P.; coed.; III

Kentucky State C. Frankfort, Ky.; 1886; S.; coed.; I, II

Kentucky Wesleyan C. Owensboro, Ky.; 1866; P.; coed.; II

Kenyon C. Gambier, Ohio; 1824; P.; men; II

Keuka C. Keuka Park, N.Y.; 1890; P.; women; II

Kilroe Seminary of the Sacred Heart Honesdale, Pa.; 1955; P.; men; II

King C. Bristol, Tenn.; 1867; P.; coed.; II

King's C., The Briarcliff Manor, N.Y.; 1938; P.; coed.; I, II

King's C. Wilkes-Barre, Pa.; 1946; P.; men (coed., summer & eve. courses); II

Kirkland C. Clinton, N.Y.; 1965; P.; women; II

Kirksville C. of Osteopathy & Surgery Kirksville, Mo.; 1892; P.; coed.; V

Knox C. Galesburg, Ill.; 1837; P.; coed.; II

Knoxville C. Knoxville, Tenn.; 1875; P.; coed.; II

Kutztown State C.* Kutztown, Pa.; 1866; S.; coed.; III

Ladycliff C. Highland Falls, N.Y.; 1933; P.; women (coed., summer); II

Lafayette C. Easton, Pa.; 1826; P.; men; II

LaGrange C. LaGrange, Ga.; 1831; P.; coed.; II

Lake Erie C. Painsville, Ohio; 1856; P.; women; II

Lake Forest C. Lake Forest, Ill.; 1857; P.; coed.; II

Lakeland C. Sheboygan, Wis.; 1862; P.; coed.; II

Lake Superior State C. Sault Ste. Marie, Mich.; 1946; S.; coed.; I, II: branch of Michigan Technological U.

Lamar State C. of Technology** Beaumont, Tex.; 1923; S.; coed.; III

Lambuth C. Jackson, Tenn.; 1843; P.; coed.; II

Lancaster Theological Seminary of the United Church of Christ Lancaster, Pa.; 1825; P.; coed.; V

Lander C. Greenwood, S.C.; 1872; Co.; coed.; I, II

Lane C. Jackson, Tenn.; 1882; P.; coed.; II

Langston U. Langston, Okla.; 1897; S.; coed.; I, II

La Roche C. Allison Park, Pa.; 1963; P.; women; II

La Salle C.* Philadelphia, Pa.; 1863; P.; men (coed., eve. division); III

La Verne C. La Verne, Calif.; 1891; P.; coed.; III

Lawrence Institute of Technology* Southfield (Detroit), Mich.; 1932; P.; coed.; I, II

Lawrence U. Appleton, Wis.; 1847; P.; coed.; III, VI

Layton School of Art Milwaukee, Wis.; 1920; P.; coed.; II

Lea C. Albert Lea, Minn.; 1966; P.; coed.; II

Lebanon Valley C. Annville, Pa.; 1866; P.; coed.; II

Lee C. Cleveland, Tenn.; 1918; P.; coed.; I, II

Lehigh U.* Bethlehem, Pa.; 1865; P.; men (coed., grad. school); III, VI

Le Moyne C. Syracuse, N.Y.; 1946; P.; coed.; II

LeMoyne-Owen C. Memphis, Tenn.; 1870; P.; coed.; II

Lenoir Rhyne C. Hickory, N.C.; 1891; P.; coed.; II

Lesley C. Cambridge, Mass.; 1909; P.; women (coed., grad. school); III

LeTourneau C. Longview, Tex.; 1946; P.; coed.; II

Lewis & Clark C. Portland, Oreg.; 1867; P.; coed.; III, V

Lewis-Clark Normal School Lewiston, Ida.; 1893; S.; coed.; I, II

Lewis C. Lockport, Ill.; 1930; P.; men; II

Lexington Theological Seminary Lexington, Ky.; 1865; P.; coed.; V

L.I.F.E. Bible C. Los Angeles, Calif.; 1925; P.; coed.; II

Limestone C. Gaffney, S.C.; 1845; P.; women; II

Lincoln Christian C. Lincoln, Ill.; 1944; P.; coed.; III, V

Lincoln Memorial U. Harrogate, Tenn.; 1897; P.; coed.; II

Lincoln U. Jefferson City, Mo.; 1866; S.; coed.; III

Lincoln U. Lincoln University, Pa.; 1854; P. & S.; coed.; II

Linda Vista Baptist Bible C. & Seminary El Cajon, Calif.; 1946; P.; coed.; III, V

Lindenwood C. St. Charles, Mo.; 1827; P.; women; II

Linfield C. McMinnville, Oreg.; 1849; P.; coed.; III

Little Rock U. Little Rock, Ark.; 1927; P.; coed.; I, II

Livingstone C. Salisbury, N.C.; 1879; P.; coed.; II

Livingston U. Livingston, Ala.; 1840; S.; coed.; III

Lock Haven State C. Lock Haven, Pa.; 1870; S.; coed.; II

Loma Linda U. Loma Linda & Riverside, Calif.; 1905; P.; coed.; I, VII

Long Island U.* Brooklyn, N.Y.; 1926; P.; coed.; III, VI: includes 3 other units, all coed.—

    Brooklyn C. of Pharmacy Brooklyn; 1886; V

    C.W. Post C.* Brookville; 1954; III

    Southampton C. Southampton; 1963; II

Longwood C. Farmville, Va.; 1884; S.; women (coed., grad. school); III

Loras C. Dubuque, Iowa; 1839; P.; men; III

Loretto Heights C. Denver, Colo.; 1918; P.; women; II

Los Angeles Baptist C. & Theological Seminary Newhall, Calif.; 1927; P.; coed.; II, V

Los Angeles C. of Chiropractic Glendale, Calif.; 1911; P.; coed.; II, V

Los Angeles C. of Optometry Los Angeles, Calif.; 1904; P.; coed.; II, V

Louisiana C. Pineville, La.; 1906; P.; coed.; II

Louisiana Polytechnic Institute* Ruston, La.; 1894; S.; coed.; III, VI

Louisiana State U. & Agricultural & Mechanical C.** Baton Rouge, La.; 1860; S.; coed.; VII: branch (1958) & medical center (1931) in New Orleans; 2-year colleges at Alexandria (1960), Eunice (1967), & Shreveport (1967)

Louisville, U. of** Louisville, Ky.; 1798; Mun.; coed.; I, VII

Louisville Presbyterian Theological Seminary Louisville, Ky.; 1853; P.; coed.; V

Lowell Technological Institute* Lowell, Mass.; 1897; S.; coed.; III, V

Loyola C. Baltimore, Md.; 1852; P.; men (coed., eve. & grad. divisions); III

Loyola U. of Chicago** Chicago, Ill.; 1870; P.; coed.; VII

Loyola U. of Los Angeles Los Angeles, Calif.; 1911; P.; coed.; III, V

Loyola U.—New Orleans* New Orleans, La.; 1849; P.; coed.; VII

Lutheran School of Theology at Chicago Chicago, Ill.; 1860; P.; coed.; III, V

Lutheran Theological Seminary at Gettysburg Gettysburg, Pa.; 1826; P.; coed.; V

Lutheran Theological Seminary at Philadelphia, The Philadelphia, Pa.; 1864; P.; coed.; IV, V

Lutheran Theological Southern Seminary Columbia, S.C.; 1830; P.; coed.; V
Luther C. Decorah, Iowa; 1861; P.; coed.; II
Luther Rice Seminary Jacksonville, Fla.; 1962; P.; coed.; V
Luther Theological Seminary St. Paul, Minn.; 1869; P.; men; V
Lycoming C. Williamsport, Pa.; 1812; P.; coed.; II
Lynchburg C. Lynchburg, Va.; 1903; P.; coed.; III
Lyndon State C. Lyndonville, Vt.; 1911; S.; coed.; II

Macalester C. St. Paul, Minn.; 1874; P.; coed.; III
Mackinac C. Mackinac Island, Mich.; 1965; P.; coed.; II
MacMurray C. Jacksonville, Ill.; 1846; P.; coed.; II
Madison Business C. Madison, Wis.; 1856; P.; coed.; I, II
Madison C.* Harrisonburg, Va.; 1908; S.; coed.; III
Madonna C. Livonia, Mich.; 1937; P.; women; II
Maine, U. of* Orono, Me.; 1865; S.; coed.; I, VII; branches—Augusta, Portland
Maine Maritime Academy Castine, Me.; 1941; S.; men; II
Malone C. Canton, Ohio; 1892; P.; coed.; II
Manchester C. North Manchester, Ind.; 1895; P.; coed.; II
Manhattan Bible C. Manhattan, Kans.; 1927; P.; cocd.; II
Manhattan C.* Bronx, N.Y.; 1853; P.; coed.; III
Manhattan School of Music New York, N.Y.; 1917; P.; coed.; III
Manhattanville C. Purchase, N.Y.; 1841; P.; women; III
Mankato State C.* Mankato, Minn.; 1867; S.; coed.; III
Mannes C. of Music, The New York, N.Y.; 1916; P.; coed.; II
Mansfield State C. Mansfield, Pa.; 1857; S.; coed.; III
Marian C. Indianapolis, Ind.; 1851; P.; coed.; II
Marian C. of Fond du Lac Fond du Lac, Wis.; 1936; P.; women; II
Marietta C. Marietta, Ohio; 1835; P.; coed.; II
Marillac C. St. Louis, Mo.; 1955; P.; women; II
Marion C. Marion, Ind.; 1920; P.; coed.; II
Marist C. Poughkeepsie, N.Y.; 1929; P.; men; II
Mark Hopkins C. Brattleboro, Vt.; 1964; P.; coed.; II
Marlboro C. Marlboro, Vt.; 1946; P.; coed.; II
Marquette U.* Milwaukee, Wis.; 1864; P.; coed.; I, VII: branch—*Jesuit C.*, St. Bonifacius, Minn.
Marshall U.* Huntington, W.Va.; 1837; S.; coed.; I, III: branches—Logan, Williamson
Mars Hill C. Mars Hill, N.C.; 1856; P.; coed.; I, II
Mary Baldwin C. Staunton, Va.; 1842; P.; women; II
Mary C. Bismarck, N.Dak.; 1955; P.; coed.; II
Marycrest C. Davenport, Iowa; 1939; P.; women (coed., part time); II
Maryglade C. Memphis, Mich.; 1960; P.; men; II
Marygrove C. Detroit, Mich.; 1910; P.; women (coed., grad. school); III
Mary Hardin-Baylor C. Belton, Tex.; 1845; P.; women (& some men); II: ext. center—Ft. Hood
Mary Immaculate Seminary & C. Northampton, Pa.; 1939; P.; men; II
Maryknoll Seminary Glen Ellyn, Ill.; 1949; P.; men; II
Maryknoll Seminary Ossining, N.Y.; 1912; P.; men; IV, V
Maryland, U. of* College Park, Md.; 1856; S.; coed.; I, VII: divisions—Baltimore & Princess Anne
Maryland Institute C. of Art Baltimore, Md.; 1826; P.; coed.; III
Marylhurst C. Marylhurst (Portland), Oreg.; 1893; P.; women (coed., eve. & summer school); II
Mary Manse C. Toledo, Ohio; 1922; P.; women; II
Marymount C. Salina, Kans.; 1922; P.; coed.; II
Marymount C. Tarrytown, N.Y.; 1919; P.; women; II
Marymount Manhattan C. New York, N.Y.; 1936; P.; women; II
Mary Rogers C. Maryknoll, N.Y.; 1931; P.; women; I, II
Maryville C. Maryville, Tenn.; 1819; P.; coed.; II
Maryville C. of the Sacred Heart St. Louis, Mo.; 1872; P.; women; II
Marywood C. Scranton, Pa.; 1915; P.; women; III
Massachusetts, U. of* Amherst, Mass.; 1863; S.; coed.; I, III, VI: branch—Boston
Massachusetts C. of Art Boston, Mass.; 1873; S.; coed.; II
Massachusetts C. of Optometry, The Boston, Mass.; 1894; P.; coed.; V
Massachusetts C. of Pharmacy Boston, Mass.; 1823; P.; coed.; III, VI
Massachusetts Institute of Technology* Cambridge, Mass.; 1861; P.; coed.; VII
Massachusetts Maritime Academy Buzzards Bay, Mass.; 1891; S.; men; II
Massachusetts State Colleges all S., all coed.
  State C. at Boston* 1852; III
  State C. at Bridgewater 1840; III
  State C. at Fitchburg* 1894; III
  State C. at Framingham 1839; III
  State C. at Lowell 1897; III
  State C. at North Adams 1894; III
  State C. at Salem* 1854; III
  State C. at Westfield 1839; III
  State C. at Worcester 1874; III
Mayville State C. Mayville, N.Dak.; 1889; S.; coed.; I, II

McCormick Theological Seminary Chicago, Ill.; 1829; P.; coed.; IV, V
McKendree C. Lebanon, Ill.; 1828; P.; coed.; II
McMurry C. Abilene, Tex.; 1926; P.; coed.; II
McNeese State C.* Lake Charles, La.; 1939; S.; coed.; I, III, V
McPherson C. McPherson, Kans.; 1887; P.; coed.; II
Meadville Theological School of Lombard C. Chicago, Ill.; 1851; P.; coed.; IV, V
Medaille C. Buffalo, N.Y.; 1937; P.; coed.; III
Meharry Medical C. Nashville, Tenn.; 1876; P.; coed.; V
Memphis Academy of Arts, The Memphis, Tenn.; 1936; P.; coed.; II
Memphis State U.* Memphis, Tenn.; 1912; S.; coed.; I, VII
Memphis Theological Seminary Memphis, Tenn.; 1908; P.; coed.; V
Menlo C. Menlo Park, Calif.; 1915; P.; men; I, II
Mennonite Biblical Seminary Elkhart, Ind.; 1945; P.; coed.; IV, V
Mercer U. Macon, Ga.; 1833; P.; coed.; III, V
Mercy C. Dobbs Ferry, N.Y.; 1950; P.; women; II
Mercy C. of Detroit Detroit, Mich.; 1941; P.; coed.; II
Mercyhurst C. Erie, Pa.; 1926; P.; women; II
Meredith C. Raleigh, N.C.; 1891; P.; women; II
Merrill-Palmer Institute Detroit, Mich.; 1920; P.; coed.: non-degree-granting with undergrad. & grad. programs
Merrimack C. North Andover, Mass.; 1947; P.; coed.; I, II
Mesivta Talmudical Seminary Brooklyn, N.Y.; 1915; P.; men; III
Mesivtha Tifereth Jerusalem of America New York, N.Y.; 1907; P.; men; V
Messiah C. Grantham, Pa.; 1909; P.; coed.; II
Methodist C. Fayetteville, N.C.; 1956; P.; coed.; II
Methodist Theological School in Ohio Delaware, Ohio; 1958; P.; coed.; V
Metropolitan State C.* Denver, Colo.; 1963; S.; coed.; II
Miami, U. of* Coral Gables, Fla.; 1925; P.; coed.; VII
Miami U.* Oxford, Ohio; 1809; S.; coed.; I, III, VI; branches—Hamilton, Middletown
Michigan, The U. of* Ann Arbor, Mich.; 1817; S.; oocd.; VII: ext. centers—Dearborn, Detroit, Flint, Grand Rapids, Saginaw
Michigan Lutheran C. Detroit, Mich.; 1962; P.; oocd.; I, II
Michigan State U.* East Lansing, Mich.; 1855; S.; coed.; VII: ext. centers—Benton Harbor, Grand Rapids, Marquette, Pontiac, Saginaw, Traverse City
Michigan Technological U.* Houghton, Mich.; 1885; S.; coed.; I, III, VI
Mid-America Nazarene C. Olathe, Kans.; 1968; P.; coed.; II
Middlebury C. Middlebury, Vt.; 1800; P.; coed.; III, V
Middle Tennessee State U.* Murfreesboro, Tenn.; 1911; S.; coed.; I, III
Midland Lutheran C. Fremont, Nebr.; 1883; P.; coed.; II
Midwest Christian C. Oklahoma City, Okla.; 1946; P.; coed.; I, II
Midwestern Baptist C. Pontiac, Mich.; 1954; P.; coed.; II
Midwestern Baptist Theological Seminary Kansas City, Mo.; 1957; P.; coed.; V
Midwestern C. Denison, Iowa; 1965; P.; coed.; II
Midwestern U.* Wichita Falls, Tex.; 1922; S.; coed.; III
Midwest Institute Eureka, Kans.; 1946; P.; coed.; I, II
Miles C. Birmingham, Ala.; 1905; P.; coed.; II
Millersville State C.* Millersville, Pa.; 1855; S.; coed.; III
Milligan C. Milligan College, Tenn.; 1881; P.; coed.; II
Millikin U. Decatur, Ill.; 1901; P.; coed.; II
Millsaps C. Jackson, Miss.; 1890; P.; coed.; II
Mills C. Oakland, Calif.; 1852; P.; women; III
Mills C. of Education New York, N.Y.; 1909; P.; women; II
Milton C. Milton, Wis.; 1867; P.; cocd.; II
Miltonvale Wesleyan C. Miltonvale, Kans.; 1909; P.; coed.; I, II
Milwaukee School of Engineering Milwaukee, Wis.; 1903; P.; coed.; I, III
Minneapolis School of Art Minneapolis, Minn.; 1886; P.; coed.; II
Minnesota, The U. of* Minneapolis, Minn.; 1851; S.; coed.; I, VII: branches—Crookston, Duluth, Morris, Rochester
Minnesota Bible C. Minneapolis, Minn.; 1913; P.; coed.; II
Minot State C. Minot, N.Dak.; 1913; S.; coed.; III
Mirrer Yeshiva Central Institute Brooklyn, N.Y.; 1947; P.; men; V
Misericordia, C. Dallas, Pa.; 1924; P.; women; II
Mississippi, The U. of* University, Miss.; 1848; S.; coed.; VII
Mississippi C. Clinton, Miss.; 1826; P.; coed.; III
Mississippi Industrial C. Holly Springs, Miss.; 1905; P.; coed.; II
Mississippi State C. for Women* Columbus, Miss.; 1884; S.; women; III
Mississippi State U.* State College (Starkville), Miss.; 1878; S.; coed.; VII: ext. centers—Columbus, Gulfport, Jackson, Vicksburg

Mississippi Valley State C. Itta Bena, Miss.; 1950; S.; coed.; I, II

Missouri, U. of ** Columbia, Mo.; 1839; S.; coed.; VII: branches—Kansas City, Rolla, St. Louis

Missouri School of Religion, The Columbia, Mo.; 1895; P.; coed.; V

Missouri Southern C. Joplin, Mo.; 1937; S.; coed.; I, II

Missouri Valley C. Marshall, Mo.; 1889; P.; coed.; II

Missouri Western C. St. Joseph, Mo.; 1915; S. & Dist.; coed.; I, II

M. J. Lewi C. of Podiatry New York, N.Y.; 1912; P.; coed.; V

Mobile C. Mobile, Ala.; 1963; P.; coed.; II

Molloy Catholic C. for Women Rockville Centre, N.Y.; 1955; P.; women; II

Monmouth C., The Monmouth, Ill.; 1853; P.; coed.; II

Monmouth C. * West Long Branch, N.J.; 1933; P.; coed.; I, III

Montana, U. of * Missoula, Mont.; 1893; S.; coed.; VII

Montana C. of Mineral Science & Technology Butte, Mont.; 1893; S.; coed.; III

Montana State U. * Bozeman, Mont.; 1893; S.; coed.; III, VI

Montclair State C. * Upper Montclair, N.J.; 1908; S.; coed.; III

Monterey Institute of Foreign Studies Monterey, Calif.; 1955; P.; coed.; III

Moody Bible Institute Chicago, Ill.; 1886; P.; coed.; II

Moore C. of Art Philadelphia, Pa.; 1844; P.; women; III

Moorhead State C. * Moorhead, Minn.; 1885; S.; coed.; I, III

Moravian C. Bethlehem, Pa.; 1742; P.; coed.; II, V

Morehead State U. * Morehead, Ky.; 1922; S.; coed.; I, III

Morehouse C. Atlanta, Ga.; 1867; P.; men; II

Morgan State C. * Baltimore, Md.; 1867; S.; coed.; III

Morningside C. Sioux City, Iowa; 1894; P.; coed.; III

Morris Brown C. Atlanta, Ga.; 1881; P.; coed.; II

Morris C. Sumter, S.C.; 1908; P.; coed.; II

Morris Harvey C. Charleston, W.Va.; 1888; P.; coed.; I, II

Mt. Alvernia C. Newton, Mass.; 1959; P.; women; II

Mt. Angel C. Mt. Angel, Oreg.; 1887; P.; coed.; II

Mt. Angel Seminary Saint Benedict, Oreg.; 1887; P.; men; II

Mt. Holyoke C. South Hadley, Mass.; 1837; P.; women; III

Mt. Marty C. Yankton, S.Dak.; 1936; P.; women (coed., part time); II

Mt. Mary C. Milwaukee, Wis.; 1913; P.; women; II

Mt. Mercy C. Cedar Rapids, Iowa; 1928; P.; women; II

Mt. Mercy C. Pittsburgh, Pa.; 1929; P.; women; II

Mt. Senario C. Ladysmith, Wis.; 1962; P.; coed.; II

Mt. Sinai School of Medicine see City U. of NEW YORK

Mt. St. Agnes C. Baltimore, Md.; 1890; P.; women (coed., part time); II

Mt. St. Alphonsus Seminary Esopus, N.Y.; 1907; P.; men; IV, V

Mt. St. Joseph C. Wakefield, R.I.; 1953; P.; women; II

Mt. St. Joseph on the Ohio, C. of Mount St. Joseph, Ohio; 1854; P.; women (coed., eve. & summer school); II

Mt. St. Mary C. Hooksett, N.H.; 1934; P.; women; II

Mt. St. Mary C. Newburgh, N.Y.; 1959; P.; coed.; II

Mt. St. Mary's C. Los Angeles, Calif.; 1925; P.; women (coed., grad. school & selected depts.); I, III

Mt. St. Mary's C. Emmitsburg, Md.; 1808; P.; men; II

Mt. St. Paul C. Waukesha, Wis.; 1961; P.; coed.; II

Mt. St. Scholastica C. Atchison, Kans.; 1863; P.; women; II

Mt. St. Vincent, C. of Riverdale (Bronx), N.Y.; 1847; P.; women; II

Mt. Union C. Alliance, Ohio; 1846; P.; coed.; II

Muhlenberg C. Allentown, Pa.; 1848; P.; coed.; II

Multnomah School of the Bible Portland, Oreg.; 1936; P.; coed.; I, V

Mundelein C. Chicago, Ill.; 1929; P.; women; II

Murray State U. * Murray, Ky.; 1922; S.; coed.; I, III

Museum Art School Portland, Oreg.; 1908; P.; coed.; affiliated with Reed C.; II

Museum of Fine Arts, School of the Boston, Mass.; 1876; P.; coed.: affiliated with Tufts U.; II

Muskingum C. New Concord, Ohio; 1837; P.; coed.; II

Nashotah House Nashotah, Wis.; 1842; P.; men; V

Nasson C. Springvale, Me.; 1912; P.; coed.; I, II

Nathaniel Hawthorne C. Antrim, N.H.; 1962; P.; coed.; II

National C. of Business Rapid City, S.Dak.; 1935; P.; coed.; I, II

National C. of Chiropractic Lombard, Ill.; 1906; P.; coed.; II, V

National C. of Education Evanston, Ill.; 1886; P.; coed.; III

Nazarene Theological Seminary Kansas City, Mo.; 1945; P.; coed.; V

Nazareth C. Kalamazoo, Mich.; 1924; P.; women; II

Nazareth C. of Kentucky Nazareth, Ky.; 1814; P.; women; II

Nazareth C. of Rochester Rochester, N.Y.; 1924; P.; women; II

Nebraska, The U. of ** Lincoln, Nebr.; 1869; S.; coed.; VII: branch—Omaha

Nebraska at Omaha, The U. of * Omaha, Nebr.; 1908; S.; coed.; I, III

Nebraska Christian C. Norfolk, Nebr.; 1945; P.; coed.; II, V

Nebraska Wesleyan U. Lincoln, Nebr.; 1897; P.; coed.; II

Ner Israel Rabbinical C. Baltimore, Md.; 1933; P.; men; IV, V

Nevada, Reno, U. of * Reno, Nev.; 1864; S.; coed.; I, VII

Nevada, Las Vegas, U. of * Las Vegas, Nev.; 1955; S.; coed.; I, III

Newark C. of Engineering Newark, N.J.; 1881; S. & Mun.; coed.; III, V

Newark State C. * Union, N.J.; 1855; S.; coed.; III: ext. centers—Denville, Neptune

Newberry C. Newberry, S.C.; 1856; P.; coed.; II

New Brunswick Theological Seminary New Brunswick, N.J.; 1784; P.; men; V

New Church, The Academy of the Bryn Athyn, Pa.; 1877; P.; coed.; II, V

New C. Sarasota, Fla.; 1960; P.; coed.; II

Newcomb C. see TULANE U.

New England C. Henniker, N.H.; 1946; P.; coed.; II

New England Conservatory Boston, Mass.; 1867; P.; coed.; III

New England Institute Ridgefield, Conn.; 1966; P.; coed.; IV, V

New Hampshire, U. of * Durham, N.H.; 1866; S.; coed.; I, III, VI

New Hampshire C. of Accounting & Commerce Manchester, N.H.; 1932; P.; coed.; I, II

New Haven C. * West Haven, Conn.; 1926; P.; coed.; I, II

New Jersey C. of Medicine & Dentistry Jersey City, N.J.; 1954; S.; coed.; IV, V, VI

New Mexico, The U. of ** Albuquerque, N.Mex.; 1889; S.; coed.; VII: branches—Gallup, Holloman AFB, Los Alamos

New Mexico Highlands U. Las Vegas, N.Mex.; 1893; S.; coed.; I, III

New Mexico Institute of Mining & Technology Socorro, N.Mex.; 1889; S.; coed.; III, VI

New Mexico State U. * Las Cruces, N.Mex.; 1888; S.; coed.; I, III, VI: J.C. branches—Alamogordo, Carlsbad, Farmington

New Orleans Baptist Theological Seminary, The New Orleans, La.; 1917; P.; coed.; V

New Rochelle, The C. of New Rochelle, N.Y.; 1904; P.; women; II

New School for Social Research New York, N.Y.; 1919; P.; coed.; III, VI

Newton C. of the Sacred Heart Newton, Mass.; 1946; P.; women; II

New York, The City U. of New York, N.Y.; 1847; Mun.; coed.: it is comprised of six community colleges and
  Bernard M. Baruch C. ** New York; 1968; III, VI
  Brooklyn C. ** Brooklyn; 1930; I, III
  City C. ** New York; 1847; I, III, VI
  Herbert H. Lehman C. * Bronx; 1931; III, VI
  Hunter C. ** New York; 1870; III, VI
  John Jay C. of Criminal Justice New York; 1964; I, III
  Mt. Sinai School of Medicine New York; 1963; V
  Queens C. ** Flushing; 1937; I, III
  Richmond C. Staten Island; 1965; III
  York C. Flushing; 1966; II

New York, State U. of Albany, N.Y.; 1948; S.; coed.: comprised of 30 community colleges; six 2-yr. agricultural & technical colleges; university centers at **Albany** * (1844, III, VI), **Binghamton** * (1946, III, VI), **Buffalo** ** (1846, VII), **Stony Brook** * (1957, III, VI); colleges of arts & sciences at **Brockport** * (1867, III, VI), **Buffalo** * (1871, III), **Cortland** * (1868, III), **Fredonia** (1866, III), **Geneseo** (1871, III), **New Paltz** * (1886, III), **Oneonta** * (1889, III), **Oswego** * (1861, III), **Oyster Bay** (1967, II), **Plattsburgh** * (1889, III), **Potsdam** (1816, III); and several specialized colleges including—**C. of Agriculture at Cornell U.** * (1904, III, VI), **C. of Ceramics at Alfred U.** (1900, III, VI), **Downstate Medical Center** (Brooklyn, 1860, V, VI), **C. of Forestry at Syracuse U.** (1911, III, VI), **C. of Home Economics at Cornell U.** (1925, III), **School of Industrial & Labor Relations at Cornell U.** (1944, III), **Maritime C.** (Fort Schuyler, Bronx, 1874, men, II), **Upstate Medical Center** (Syracuse, 1950, I, VII), **Veterinary C. at Cornell U.** (1894, VII)

New York Institute of Technology * New York, N.Y.; 1957; P.; coed.; I, II: branch—Old Westbury

New York Law School New York, N.Y.; 1891; P.; coed.; V

New York Medical C. New York, N.Y.; 1860; P.; coed.; IV, V, VI

New York-Phoenix School of Design New York, N.Y.; 1892; P.; coed.; C

New York Theological Seminary New York, N.Y.; 1900; P.; coed.; V

New York U. ** New York, N.Y.; 1832; P.; coed.; I, VII

Niagara U. Niagara University, N.Y.; 1856; P.; coed.; III

Nichols C. of Business Administration Dudley, Mass.; 1815; P.; men; II

North American Baptist Seminary Sioux Falls, S.Dak.; 1850; P.; coed.; V

North Carolina Agricultural & Technical State U.* Greensboro, N.C.; 1891; S.; coed.; I, III

North Carolina at Chapel Hill, The U. of** Chapel Hill, N.C.; 1793; S.; coed.; VII: three other campuses of U. of North Carolina—

North Carolina at Charlotte, The U. of 1946; II

North Carolina at Greensboro, The U. of* 1891; III, VI

North Carolina State U. at Raleigh** 1887; I, III, VI

North Carolina C. at Durham* Durham, N.C.; 1910; S.; coed.; III, V

North Carolina School of the Arts Winston-Salem, N.C.; 1965; S.; coed.; II

North Carolina Wesleyan C. Rocky Mount, N.C.; 1956; P.; coed.; II

North Central Bible C. Minneapolis, Minn.; 1930; P.; coed.; II

North Central C. Naperville, Ill.; 1861; P.; coed.; II

North Dakota, U. of* Grand Forks, N.Dak.; 1883; S.; coed.; I, VII

North Dakota State U. of Agriculture & Applied Science* Fargo, N.Dak.; 1890; S.; coed.; I, III, VI

Northeast Bible Institute Green Lane, Pa.; 1938; P.; coed.; II

Northeastern Collegiate Bible Institute Essex Fells, N.J.; 1950; P.; coed.; II

Northeastern Illinois State C.* Chicago, Ill.; 1869; S.; coed.; III

Northeastern State C.* Tahlequah, Okla.; 1846; S.; coed.; III

Northeastern U.** Boston, Mass.; 1898; P.; coed.; I, VII

Northeast Louisiana State C.* Monroe, La.; 1931; S.; coed.; III, VI

Northeast Missouri State C.* Kirksville, Mo.; 1867; S.; coed.; III

Northern Arizona U.* Flagstaff, Ariz.; 1899; S.; coed.; I, III

Northern Baptist Theological Seminary Oak Brook, Ill.; 1913; P.; coed.; V

Northern Conservatory of Music Bangor, Me.; 1949; P.; coed.; II

Northern Illinois U.** De Kalb, Ill.; 1895; S.; coed.; III, VI

Northern Iowa, U. of** Cedar Falls, Iowa; 1876; S.; coed.; III

Northern Michigan U.* Marquette, Mich.; 1899; S.; coed.; I, III

Northern Montana C. Havre, Mont.; 1925; S.; coed.; I, II

Northern State C.* Aberdeen, S.Dak.; 1901; S.; coed.; III

North Georgia C. Dahlonega, Ga.; 1876; S.; coed.; II

Northland C. Ashland, Wis.; 1892; P.; coed.; II

North Park C. & Theological Seminary Chicago, Ill.; 1891; P.; coed.; II, V

Northrop Institute of Technology Inglewood, Calif.; 1942; P.; coed.; II

North Texas State U.** Denton, Tex.; 1890; S.; coed.; III, VI

Northwest Bible C. Minot, N.Dak.; 1934; P.; coed.; II

Northwest Christian C. Eugene, Oreg.; 1895; P.; coed.; II

Northwest C. Kirkland, Wash.; 1934; P.; coed.; I, II

Northwestern C. Orange City, Iowa; 1882; P.; coed.; I, II

Northwestern C. Watertown, Wis.; 1864; P.; men; II

Northwestern Lutheran Theological Seminary St. Paul, Minn.; 1920; P.; men; V

Northwestern State C. Alva, Okla.; 1897; S.; coed.; III

Northwestern State C. of Louisiana* Natchitoches, La.; 1884; S.; coed.; I, III, V

Northwestern U.** Evanston, Ill.; 1851; P.; coed.; VII: branch—Chicago

Northwest Missouri State C.* Maryville, Mo.; 1905; S.; coed.; III

Northwest Nazarene C. Nampa, Ida.; 1913; P.; coed.; II

Norwich U. Northfield, Vt.; 1819; P.; men; III

Notre Dame, C. of Belmont, Calif.; 1868; P.; women (coed., selected depts.); II

Notre Dame, U. of* Notre Dame, Ind.; 1842; P.; men (coed., grad. school); VII

Notre Dame C. St. Louis, Mo.; 1954; P.; women; II

Notre Dame C. Manchester, N.H.; 1950; P.; women (coed., part time); II

Notre Dame C. Cleveland, Ohio; 1922; P.; women; II

Notre Dame C. of Staten Island Staten Island, N.Y.; 1931; P.; women; II

Notre Dame of Maryland, C. of Baltimore, Md.; 1895; P.; women; II

Notre Dame of Wilton, C. of Wilton, Conn.; 1961; P.; women; II

Notre Dame Seminary New Orleans, La.; 1923; P.; men; III

Nova U. Fort Lauderdale, Fla.; 1964; P.; coed.; VI

Nyack Missionary C. Nyack, N.Y.; 1882; P.; coed.; II

Oakland City C. Oakland City, Ind.; 1885; P.; coed.; II

Oakland U.* Rochester, Mich.; 1957; S.; coed.; III

Oakwood C. Huntsville, Ala.; 1896; P.; coed.; II

Oberlin C. Oberlin, Ohio; 1833; P.; coed.; III

Oblate C. Washington, D.C.; 1917; P.; men; III

Oblate C. & Seminary Natick, Mass.; 1927; P.; men; II

Oblate C. of the Southwest San Antonio, Tex.; 1903; P.; men; V

Occidental C. Los Angeles, Calif.; 1887; P.; coed.; III

Oglethorpe C. Atlanta, Ga.; 1835; P.; coed.; II

Ohio C. of Podiatry Cleveland, Ohio; 1916; P.; coed.; V

Ohio Dominican C. Columbus, Ohio; 1911; P.; coed.; II

Ohio Northern U. Ada, Ohio; 1871; P.; coed.; II, V: branch—Celina

Ohio State U., The** Columbus, Ohio; 1870; S.; coed.; VII: branches—Lima, Mansfield, Marion, Newark

Ohio U.** Athens, Ohio; 1804; S.; coed.; I, III, VI

Ohio Wesleyan U. Delaware, Ohio; 1842; P.; coed.; II

Oklahoma, U. of** Norman, Okla.; 1890; S.; coed.; VII: military ext. centers—Altus, Lawton, Midwest City

Oklahoma Baptist U. Shawnee, Okla.; 1910; P.; coed.; II

Oklahoma Christian C. Oklahoma City, Okla.; 1950; P.; coed.; II

Oklahoma City U. Oklahoma City, Okla.; 1904; P.; coed.; I, III, V

Oklahoma C. of Liberal Arts Chickasha, Okla.; 1908; S.; coed.; II

Oklahoma Panhandle State C. of Agriculture & Applied Sciences Goodwell, Okla.; 1909; S.; coed.; II

Oklahoma State U.** Stillwater, Okla.; 1890; S.; coed.; I, VII: ext. centers—Enid, Oklahoma City, Tulsa

Old Dominion C.** Norfolk, Va.; 1930; S.; coed.; I, III

Olivet C. Olivet, Mich.; 1844; P.; coed.; II

Olivet Nazarene C. Kankakee, Ill.; 1907; P.; coed.; III

Oral Roberts U. Tulsa, Okla.; 1963; P.; coed.; II

Oregon, U. of** Eugene, Oreg.; 1872; S.; coed.; VII

Oregon C. of Education Monmouth, Oreg.; 1882; S.; coed.; I, III

Oregon State U.** Corvallis, Oreg.; 1868; S.; coed.; III, VI

Oregon Technical Institute Klamath Falls, Oreg.; 1947; S.; coed.; I, II

Osteopathic Medicine & Surgery, C. of Des Moines, Iowa; 1898; P.; coed.; V

Otis Art Institute of Los Angeles County Los Angeles, Calif.; 1918; Co.; coed.; IV

Ottawa U. Ottawa, Kans.; 1865; P.; coed.; II

Otterbein C. Westerville, Ohio; 1847; P.; coed.; II

Ouachita Baptist U. Arkadelphia, Ark.; 1883; P.; coed.; III

Our Lady of Angels C. Glen Riddle, Pa.; 1962; P.; women; II

Our Lady of Cincinnati C. Cincinnati, Ohio; 1935; P.; women; II

Our Lady of Holy Cross C. New Orleans, La.; 1916; P.; coed.; II

Our Lady of Providence Seminary Warwick, R.I.; 1939; P.; men; II

Our Lady of the Elms, C. of Chicopee, Mass.; 1928; P.; women; II

Our Lady of the Lake C. San Antonio, Tex.; 1911; P.; women (coed., grad. school); III

Owosso C. Owosso, Mich.; 1909; P.; coed.; II

Ozark Bible C. Joplin, Mo.; 1942; P.; coed.; II, V

Ozarks, C. of the Clarksville, Ark.; 1834; P.; coed.; II

Ozarks, The School of the Point Lookout, Mo.; 1906; P.; coed.; II

Pace C.* New York, N.Y.; 1906; P.; coed.; I, III, V: branch—Westchester

Pacific, U. of the* Stockton, Calif.; 1851; P.; coed.; VII

Pacific Christian C. Long Beach, Calif.; 1928; P.; coed.; II

Pacific C. Fresno, Calif.; 1944; P.; coed.; II

Pacific Lutheran Theological Seminary Berkeley, Calif.; 1950; P.; coed.; IV, V, VI

Pacific Lutheran U. Tacoma, Wash.; 1890; P.; coed.; III

Pacific Oaks C. Pasadena, Calif.; 1945; P.; coed.; II

Pacific School of Religion Berkeley, Calif.; 1866; P.; coed.; V

Pacific States U. Los Angeles, Calif.; 1928; P.; coed.; II

Pacific Union C. Angwin, Calif.; 1882; P.; coed.; I, III

Pacific U. Forest Grove, Oreg.; 1849; P.; coed.; III, V

Paine C. Augusta, Ga.; 1883; P.; coed.; II

Palm Beach Atlantic C. West Palm Beach, Fla.; 1968; P.; coed.; II

Palmer C. of Chiropractic Davenport, Iowa; 1895; P.; coed.; V

Pan American C.* Edinburg, Tex.; 1927; S.; coed.; I, II

Paper Chemistry, The Institute of Appleton, Wis.; 1929; P.; coed.; affiliated with Lawrence U., IV, VI

Park C. Parkville (Kansas City), Mo.; 1875; P.; coed.; II

Parsons C. Fairfield, Iowa; 1875; P.; coed.; II

Pasadena C. Pasadena, Calif.; 1902; P.; coed.; III

Pasadena Playhouse C. of Theatre Arts Pasadena, Calif.; 1928; P.; coed.; II

Passionist Monastic Seminary, The Jamaica (Queens), N.Y.; 1929; P.; men; II

Paterson State C.* Wayne, N.J.; 1855; S.; coed.; III

Paul Quinn C. of the African Methodist Episcopal Church Waco, Tex.; 1872; P.; coed.; II

Payne Theological Seminary Wilberforce, Ohio; 1844; P.; coed.; V

Peabody Institute of the City of Baltimore Baltimore, Md.; 1868; P.; coed.; III, V
Pembroke C. Providence; 1891; II: women's college in Brown U.
Pembroke State C. Pembroke, N.C.; 1887; S.; coed.; II
Pennsylvania, U. of** Philadelphia, Pa.; 1740; P.; coed.; I, VII
Pennsylvania C. of Optometry Philadelphia, Pa.; 1919; P.; coed.; II, V
Pennsylvania C. of Podiatric Medicine Philadelphia, Pa.; 1960; P.; coed.; V
Pennsylvania State U., The** University Park, Pa.; 1855; S.; coed.; I, VII: branches—Abington, Allentown, Altoona, Chester, DuBois, Erie, Hazleton, McKeesport, Middletown, Monaca, Mont Alto, New Kensington, Schuylkill Haven, Scranton, Sharon, Uniontown, Wilkes-Barre, Wyomissing, York
Pentecostal Bible Institute Tupelo, Miss.; 1945; P.; coed.; I, II
Pepperdine C. Los Angeles, Calif.; 1937; P.; coed.; III
Peru State C. Peru, Nebr.; 1867; S.; coed.; II
Pestalozzi Froebel Teachers C. Chicago, Ill.; 1896; P.; coed.; II
Pfeiffer C. Misenheimer, N.C.; 1885; P.; coed.; II
Philadelphia C. of Art Philadelphia, Pa.; 1876; P.; coed.; I, III
Philadelphia C. of Bible Philadelphia, Pa.; 1913; P.; coed.; II
Philadelphia C. of Osteopathic Medicine Philadelphia, Pa.; 1899; P.; coed.; V
Philadelphia C. of Pharmacy & Science Philadelphia, Pa.; 1821; P.; coed.; VII
Philadelphia C. of Textiles & Science Philadelphia, Pa.; 1884; P.; coed.; I, II
Philadelphia Musical Academy Philadelphia, Pa.; 1870; P.; coed.; II
Philander Smith C. Little Rock, Ark.; 1877; P.; coed.; II
Phillips U. Enid, Okla.; 1907; P.; coed.; III, V
Piedmont Bible C. Winston-Salem, N.C.; 1945; P.; coed.; II
Piedmont C. Demorest, Ga.; 1897; P.; coed.; II
Pikeville C. Pikeville, Ky.; 1889; P.; coed.; II
Pittsburgh, U. of** Pittsburgh, Pa.; 1787; P.; coed.; VII
Pittsburgh Theological Seminary Pittsburgh, Pa.; 1794; P.; coed.; IV, V, VI
Pitzer C. see CLAREMONT COLLEGES
Plano, U. of Plano, Tex.; 1964; P.; coed.; II
Platte Valley Bible C. Scottsbluff, Nebr.; 1951; P.; coed.; II
Plymouth State C. Plymouth, N.H.; 1871; coed.; III: division of the U. of New Hampshire
PMC Colleges Chester, Pa.; 1821; P.; coed.; I, III
Point Park C. Pittsburgh, Pa.; 1960; P.; coed.; I, II
Pomona C. see CLAREMONT COLLEGES
Pontifical C. Josephinum, The Worthington, Ohio; 1892; P.; men; IV
Portia Law School Boston, Mass.; 1908; P.; coed.; II, V
Portland, U. of Portland, Oreg.; 1901; P.; coed.; III, VI
Portland State C.** Portland, Oreg.; 1955; S.; coed.; III
Prairie View A & M C. see TEXAS A & M U.
Pratt Institute* Brooklyn, N.Y.; 1887; P.; coed.; I, III
Presbyterian C. Clinton, S.C.; 1880; P.; coed.; II
Presbyterian School of Christian Education Richmond, Va.; 1914; P.; coed.; III
Prescott C. Prescott, Ariz.; 1966; P.; coed.; II
Princeton Theological Seminary Princeton, N.J.; 1812; P.; coed.; V
Princeton U.* Princeton, N.J.; 1746; P.; men (coed., grad. school); III, VI
Principia C. Elsah, Ill.; 1910; P.; coed.; II
Protestant Episcopal Theological Seminary in Virginia, The Alexandria, Va.; 1823; P.; coed.; IV, V
Providence C. Providence, R.I.; 1917; P.; men; III, VI
Puerto Rico, Catholic U. of* Ponce, P.R.; 1948; P.; coed.; I, III, V
Puerto Rico, U. of* Río Piedras, P.R.; 1903; Ter.; coed.; I, VII: other campuses—Mayaguez, San Juan: branches—Arecibo, Cayey, Humacao
Puget Sound, U. of Tacoma, Wash.; 1888; P.; coed.; III
Puget Sound C. of the Bible Seattle, Wash.; 1950; P.; coed.; II: ext. centers—Caldwell, Ida., Ashland & Portland, Oreg.
Purdue U.** Lafayette, Ind.; 1869; S.; coed.; I, VII: branches—Fort Wayne, Hammond, Indianapolis, Westville

Queen of Apostles C. & Seminary Dedham, Mass.; 1946; P.; men; II
Queen of Peace Mission Seminary Jaffrey Center, N.H.; 1939; P.; men; V
Queens C. see The City U. of NEW YORK
Queens C. Charlotte, N.C.; 1857; P.; women; II
Quincy C. Quincy, Ill.; 1860; P.; coed.; II
Quinnipiac C. Hamden, Conn.; 1929; P.; coed.; I, II

Rabbinical C. Kamenitz Yeshiva of America Brooklyn, N.Y.; 1927; P.; men; IV, V

Rabbinical Seminary of America Forest Hills, N.Y.; 1934; P.; men; V
Radcliffe C. Cambridge; 1879; II: women's college in Harvard U.
Radford C.* Radford, Va.; 1910; S.; women (coed., grad. school); III
Randolph-Macon C. Ashland, Va.; 1830; P.; men; II
Randolph-Macon Woman's C. Lynchburg, Va.; 1891; P.; women; II
Redlands, U. of Redlands, Calif.; 1907; P.; coed.; III
Redwoods, C. of the* Eureka, Calif.; 1964; Dist.; coed.; II
Reed C. Portland, Oreg.; 1908; P.; coed.; III
Reformed Episcopal Church, Theological Seminary of the Philadelphia, Pa.; 1886; P.; coed.; II, V
Reformed Presbyterian Theological Seminary Pittsburgh, Pa.; 1810; P.; men; V
Regis C. Denver, Colo.; 1877; P.; coed.; II
Regis C. Weston, Mass.; 1927; P.; women; II: branch—Framingham
Rensselaer Polytechnic Institute* Troy, N.Y.; 1824; P.; coed.; III, VI: branch—(Hartford Graduate Center) East Windsor Hill, Conn., IV
Rhode Island, U. of* Kingston, R.I.; 1892; S.; coed.; I, VII
Rhode Island C.* Providence, R.I.; 1854; S.; coed.; III
Rhode Island School of Design Providence, R.I.; 1877; P.; coed.; III
Rice U. (officially, *William Marsh Rice U.*) Houston, Tex.; 1912; P.; coed.; III, VI
Richmond, U. of* Richmond, Va.; 1830; P.; coed.; I, III, V
Richmond C. see The City U. of NEW YORK
Richmond Professional Institute** Richmond, Va.; 1917; S.; coed.; I, III
Ricker C. Houlton, Me.; 1848; P.; coed.; II
Rider C.* Trenton, N.J.; 1865; P.; coed.; I, III: branches—Mt. Holly, Willingboro
Ringling School of Art Sarasota, Fla.; 1931; P.; coed.; II
Rio Grande C. Rio Grande, Ohio; 1876; P.; coed.; II
Ripon C. Ripon, Wis.; 1851; P.; coed.; II
Rivier C. Nashua, N.H.; 1933; P.; women (coed., grad. school); III
Roanoke C. Salem, Va.; 1842; P.; coed.; II
Roberts Wesleyan C. North Chili, N.Y.; 1866; P.; coed.; II
Rochester, U. of** Rochester, N.Y.; 1850; P.; coed.; VII
Rochester Institute of Technology* Rochester, N.Y.; 1829; P.; coed.; I, III
Rockefeller U., The New York, N.Y.; 1901; P.; coed.; VI
Rockford C. Rockford, Ill.; 1847; P.; coed.; I, III
Rockhurst C. Kansas City, Mo.; 1910; P.; men (coed., eve. & summer session); II
Rockmont C. Denver, Colo.; 1914; P.; coed.; II
Rocky Mountain C. Billings, Mont.; 1883; P.; coed.; II
Roger Williams C. Bristol, R.I.; 1948; P.; coed.; I, II
Rollins C. Winter Park, Fla.; 1885; P.; coed.; III
Roosevelt U.* Chicago, Ill.; 1945; P.; coed.; III: ext. centers—Fort Sheridan, Great Lakes Naval Station
Rosary C. River Forest, Ill.; 1848; P.; women (coed., grad. school); III
Rosary Hill C. Buffalo, N.Y.; 1947; P.; women (coed., selected programs); II: ext. center—Stella Niagara
Rosemont C. Rosemont, Pa.; 1921; P.; women; II
Rose Polytechnic Institute Terre Haute, Ind.; 1874; P.; men; III
Royalton C. South Royalton, Vt.; 1965; P.; coed.; II
Russell C. Burlingame, Calif.; 1928; P.; women; II
Russell Sage C.* Troy, N.Y.; 1916; P.; women (coed., eve. & J.C. divisions); I, III: branch—Albany
Rust C. Holly Springs, Miss.; 1866; P.; coed.; II
Rutgers—The State U.** New Brunswick, N.J.; 1766; S.; coed.; I, VII: branches—Camden, Newark, Paterson

Sacramento State C. see CALIFORNIA STATE COLLEGES
Sacred Heart, C. of the Santurce, P.R.; 1880; P.; women; I, II
Sacred Heart C. Wichita, Kans.; 1933; P.; coed.; II
Sacred Heart C. Belmont, N.C.; 1892; P.; women; I, II
Sacred Heart Novitiate Monroe, Mich.; 1962; P.; men; II
Sacred Hearts, C. of the Fall River, Mass.; 1934; P.; women; II
Sacred Heart Seminary Detroit, Mich.; 1919; P.; men; II
Sacred Heart U. Bridgeport, Conn.; 1963; P.; coed.; I, II
Saginaw Valley C. University Center, Mich.; 1963; S.; coed.; II
Salem C. Winston-Salem, N.C.; 1772; P.; women; II
Salem C. Salem, W.Va.; 1888; P.; coed.; I, II
Salisbury State C. Salisbury, Md.; 1925; S.; coed.; III
Salmon P. Chase C., School of Law Cincinnati, Ohio; 1893; P.; coed.; V
Salve Regina C. Newport, R.I.; 1947; P.; women; II
Samford U. Birmingham, Ala.; 1842; P.; coed.; III, V
Sam Houston State C.* Huntsville, Tex.; 1879; S.; coed.; III
San Diego, U. of San Diego, Calif.; 1949; P.; coed.; III
San Diego State C. see CALIFORNIA STATE COLLEGES
San Fernando Valley State C. see CALIFORNIA STATE COLLEGES

San Francisco, U. of* San Francisco, Calif.; 1855; P.; coed.; III, V

San Francisco Art Institute, C. of the San Francisco, Calif.; 1874; P.; coed.; III

San Francisco C. for Women, The San Francisco, Calif.; 1921; P.; women; III

San Francisco Conservatory of Music, The San Francisco, Calif.; 1917; P.; coed.; II

San Francisco State C. see CALIFORNIA STATE COLLEGES

San Francisco Theological Seminary San Anselmo, Calif.; 1871; P.; coed.; V

San Jose Bible C. San Jose, Calif.; 1939; P.; coed.; II

San Jose State C. see CALIFORNIA STATE COLLEGES

San Luis Rey C. San Luis Rey, Calif.; 1929; P.; men; II

Santa Clara, U. of* Santa Clara, Calif.; 1851; P.; coed.; VII

Santa Fe, C. of Santa Fe, N.Mex.; 1947; P.; coed.; II

Sarah Lawrence C. Bronxville, N.Y.; 1928; P.; women; III

Savannah State C. Savannah, Ga.; 1890; S.; coed.; III

Scarritt C. for Christian Workers Nashville, Tenn.; 1892; P.; coed.; III

Scranton, U. of Scranton, Pa.; 1888; P.; men (coed., eve. & grad. schools); I, III

Scripps C. see CLAREMONT COLLEGES

Seabury-Western Theological Seminary Evanston, Ill.; 1858; P.; coed.; IV, V

Seattle Pacific C. Seattle, Wash.; 1891; P.; coed.; III

Seattle U.* Seattle, Wash.; 1891; P.; coed.; III

Selma U. Selma, Ala.; 1878; P.; coed.; I, V

Seton Hall U.* South Orange, N.J.; 1856; P.; coed.; VII

Seton Hill C. Greensburg, Pa.; 1883; P.; women; II

Shaw U. Raleigh, N.C.; 1865; P.; coed.; II, V

Shelton C. Cape May, N.J.; 1941; P.; coed.; II

Shenandoah C. & Shenandoah Conservatory of Music Winchester, Va.; 1875; P.; coed.; I, II

Shepherd C. Shepherdstown, W.Va.; 1871; S.; coed.; I, II

Sherwood Music School Chicago, Ill.; 1895; P.; coed.; II

Shimer C. Mount Carroll, Ill.; 1853; P.; coed.; II

Shippensburg State C.* Shippensburg, Pa.; 1871; S.; coed.; III

Shorter C. Rome, Ga.; 1873; P.; coed.; II

Siena C. Loudonville, N.Y.; 1937; P.; men (coed., eve. & summer sessions); III

Siena C. Memphis, Tenn.; 1922; P.; coed.; II

Siena Heights C. Adrian, Mich.; 1919; P.; women (coed., grad. school); III

Simmons C. Boston, Mass.; 1899; P.; women (coed., grad. school); III

Simpson Bible C. San Francisco, Calif.; 1921; P.; coed.; II

Simpson C. Indianola, Iowa; 1860; P.; coed.; II

Sioux Falls C. Sioux Falls, S.Dak.; 1883; P.; coed.; II

Skidmore C. Saratoga Springs, N.Y.; 1911; P.; women; II

Slippery Rock State C.* Slippery Rock, Pa.; 1889; S.; coed.; III

Smith C. Northampton, Mass.; 1871; P.; women (coed., grad. school); III, VI

Sonoma State C. see CALIFORNIA STATE COLLEGES

South, U. of the Sewanee, Tenn.; 1858; P.; men; III, V

South Alabama, U. of Mobile, Ala.; 1963; S.; coed.; III

South Carolina, The Medical C. of Charleston, S.C.; 1823; S.; coed.; VII

South Carolina, U. of** Columbia, S.C.; 1801; S.; coed.; VII: 7 two-year branches throughout the State, I

South Carolina State C. Orangeburg, S.C.; 1896; S.; coed.; III

South Dakota, U. of* Vermillion, S.Dak.; 1882; S.; coed.; I, VII

South Dakota School of Mines & Technology Rapid City, S.Dak.; 1885; S.; coed.; III, VI

South Dakota State U.* Brookings, S.Dak.; 1881; S.; coed.; III, VI

Southeastern Baptist Theological Seminary Wake Forest, N.C.; 1951; P.; coed.; V

Southeastern Bible C. Birmingham, Ala.; 1935; P.; coed.; II, V

South-Eastern Bible C. Lakeland, Fla.; 1935; P.; coed.; II

Southeastern Louisiana C.* Hammond, La.; 1925; S.; coed.; III

Southeastern Massachusetts Technological Institute North Dartmouth, Mass.; 1895; S.; coed.; III

Southeastern State C. Durant, Okla.; 1909; S.; coed.; III

Southeastern U. Washington, D.C.; 1879; P.; coed.; I, II: branch—Alexandria, Va.

Southeast Missouri State C.* Cape Girardeau, Mo.; 1873; S.; coed.; I, III

Southern Baptist Theological Seminary, The Louisville, Ky.; 1859; P.; coed.; V

Southern Bible C. Houston, Tex.; 1958; P.; coed.; I, II, V

Southern California, U. of** Los Angeles, Calif.; 1880; P.; coed.; VII

Southern California C. Costa Mesa, Calif.; 1920; P.; coed.; II

Southern California School of Theology Claremont, Calif.; 1885; P.; coed.; V

Southern C. of Optometry Memphis, Tenn.; 1932; P.; coed.; II, V

Southern Colorado State C.* Pueblo, Colo.; 1933; S.; coed.; I, II: ext. centers—Canon City, Fort Carson

Southern Connecticut State C.* New Haven, Conn.; 1893; S.; coed.; I, III

Southern Illinois U.** Carbondale, Ill.; 1869; S.; coed.; I, III, VI: branch—Edwardsville; ext. centers—Alton, East St. Louis

Southern Methodist C. Orangeburg, S.C.; 1956; P.; coed.; I, II

Southern Methodist U.** Dallas, Tex.; 1911; P.; coed.; VII

Southern Missionary C. Collegedale, Tenn.; 1892; P.; coed.; I, II

Southern Mississippi, U. of** Hattiesburg, Miss.; 1910; S.; coed.; III, VI: ext. centers—Keesler AFB, Jackson, Natchez

Southern Oregon C.* Ashland, Oreg.; 1926; S.; coed.; III

Southern Pilgrim C. Kernersville, N.C.; 1946; P.; coed.; I, II

Southern State C. Magnolia, Ark.; 1909; S.; coed.; II

Southern State C. Springfield, S.Dak.; 1897; S.; coed.; I, II

Southern U. & Agricultural & Mechanical C.* Baton Rouge, La.; 1880; S.; coed.; III, V: branches—New Orleans, Shreveport

Southern Utah, C. of Cedar City, Utah; 1897; S.; coed.; II

South Florida, U. of** Tampa, Fla.; 1956; S.; coed.; III, V

South Texas C. Houston, Tex.; 1923; P.; coed.; consists of a J.C. & a C. of Law, I, V

Southwest, C. of the Hobbs, N.Mex.; 1956; P.; coed.; II

Southwest Baptist C. Bolivar, Mo.; 1878; P.; coed.; II

Southwestern Assemblies of God C. Waxahachie, Tex.; 1927; P.; coed.; I, II

Southwestern at Memphis Memphis, Tenn.; 1848; P.; coed.; II

Southwestern Baptist Theological Seminary Fort Worth, Tex.; 1908; P.; coed.; V

Southwestern C. Winfield, Kans.; 1885; P.; coed.; II

Southwestern Louisiana, The U. of** Lafayette, La.; 1901; S.; coed.; III, VI

Southwestern State C.* Weatherford, Okla.; 1901; S.; coed.; III

Southwestern Union C. Keene, Tex.; 1894; P.; coed.; II

Southwestern U. Georgetown, Tex.; 1840; P.; coed.; II

Southwest Minnesota State C. Marshall, Minn.; 1963; S.; coed.; I, II

Southwest Missouri State C.* Springfield, Mo.; 1906; S.; coed.; III: ext. center—West Plains

Southwest Texas State C.* San Marcos, Tex.; 1899; S.; coed.; III

Spelman C. Atlanta, Ga.; 1881; P.; women; II

Spring Arbor C. Spring Arbor, Mich.; 1873; P.; coed.; II

Springfield C. Springfield, Mass.; 1885; P.; coed.; III, V

Spring Hill C. Mobile, Ala.; 1830; P.; coed.; II

St. Alphonsus C. Suffield, Conn.; 1963; P.; men; II

St. Ambrose C. Davenport, Iowa; 1882; P.; coed.; II

St. Andrews Presbyterian C. Laurinburg, N.C.; 1858; P.; coed.; II

Stanford U. (officially, Leland Stanford Jr. U.)** Stanford, Calif.; 1885; P.; coed.; VII

Stanislaus State C. see CALIFORNIA STATE COLLEGES

St. Anselm's C. Manchester, N.H.; 1889; P.; men (women in nursing dept.); II

St. Anthony Seminary Hudson, N.H.; 1955; P.; men; II

Starr King School for the Ministry Berkeley, Calif.; 1904; P.; coed.; V

St. Augustine's C. Raleigh, N.C.; 1867; P.; coed.; II

St. Basil's C. Stamford, Conn.; 1939; P.; men; II

St. Benedict, C. of St. Joseph, Minn.; 1913; P.; women; II

St. Benedict C. Ferdinand, Ind.; 1914; P.; coed.; II

St. Benedict's C. Atchison, Kans.; 1858; P.; men; II

St. Bernard C. St. Bernard, Ala.; 1892; P.; men (coed., jr. & sr. classes); II

St. Bernard's Seminary Rochester, N.Y.; 1893; P.; men; II

St. Bonaventure U. St. Bonaventure, N.Y.; 1856; P.; coed.; III, VI

St. Catherine, The C. of St. Paul, Minn.; 1905; P.; women; II

St. Charles Borromeo Seminary Philadelphia, Pa.; 1832; P.; men; II

St. Cloud State C.* St. Cloud, Minn.; 1869; S.; coed.; I, III

St. Dominic C. St. Charles, Ill.; 1963; P.; coed.; II

St. Edward's U. Austin, Tex.; 1885; P.; coed.; II

Steed C. Johnson City, Tenn.; 1940; P.; coed.; I, II

St. Elizabeth, The C. of Convent Station, N.J.; 1899; P.; women; II

Stephen F. Austin State C.** Nacogdoches, Tex.; 1923; S.; coed.; III

Stephens C. Columbia, Mo.; 1833; P.; women; I, II

Sterling C. Sterling, Kans.; 1887; P.; coed.; II

Stetson U. DeLand, Fla.; 1883; P.; coed.; III, V

Steubenville, The C. of Steubenville, Ohio; 1946; P.; coed.; II

Stevens Institute of Technology Hoboken, N.J.; 1870; P.; men (coed., grad. school); III, VI

St. Fidelis C. Herman, Pa.; 1877; P.; men; II

St. Francis, C. of Joliet, Ill.; 1925; P.; women; II

St. Francis C. Fort Wayne, Ind.; 1890; P.; coed.; III

St. Francis C. Biddeford, Me.; 1953; P.; coed.; II
St. Francis C. Brooklyn, N.Y.; 1884; P.; men; II
St. Francis C. Loretto, Pa.; 1847; P.; coed.; III
St. Francis C. Burlington, Wis.; 1931; P.; men; II
St. Francis Seminary Milwaukee, Wis.; 1856; P.; men; III
St. Hyacinth C. & Seminary Granby, Mass.; 1957; P.; men; II
Stillman C. Tuscaloosa, Ala.; 1876; P.; coed.; II
St. John C. of Cleveland Cleveland, Ohio; 1928; P.; women; III
St. John Fisher C. Rochester, N.Y.; 1948; P.; men; II
St. John's C. Annapolis, Md.; 1696; P.; coed.; III: branch—Santa Fe, N.Mex.
St. John's C. Camarillo, Calif.; 1939; P.; men; III
St. John's Provincial Seminary Plymouth, Mich.; 1949; P.; men; V
St. John's Seminary Brighton, Mass.; 1884; P.; men; III
St. John's U. Collegeville, Minn.; 1857; P.; men (coed., grad. school); III
St. John's U.** Brooklyn & Jamaica, N.Y.; 1870; P.; coed.; I, VII
St. John Vianney Seminary East Aurora, N.Y.; 1961; P.; men; III
St. Joseph C. West Hartford, Conn.; 1932; P.; women (coed., grad. school); III
St. Joseph C. Emmitsburg, Md.; 1809; P.; women; II
St. Joseph C. of Orange Orange, Calif.; 1959; P.; women; II
St. Joseph's C. Rensselaer, Ind.; 1889; P.; coed.; II: branch—East Chicago
St. Joseph's C. North Windham, Me.; 1915; P.; women; II
St. Joseph's C. Philadelphia, Pa.; 1851; P.; men (coed., eve. classes); I, III
St. Joseph's C. for Women Brooklyn, N.Y.; 1916; P.; women; II
St. Joseph Seminary St. Benedict, La.; 1891; P.; coed.; II
St. Joseph's Seminary Washington, D.C.; 1888; P.; men; III
St. Joseph's Seminary & C. Yonkers, N.Y.; 1833; P.; men; III, V
St. Joseph the Provider, The C. of Rutland, Vt.; 1954; P.; women; II
St. Lawrence U. Canton, N.Y.; 1856; P.; coed.; III
St. Leo C. St. Leo, Fla.; 1889; P.; coed.; II
St. Louis Christian C. Florissant, Mo.; 1956; P.; coed.; II
St. Louis C. of Pharmacy St. Louis, Mo.; 1864; P.; coed.; II
St. Louis Institute of Music St. Louis, Mo.; 1924; P.; coed.; III
St. Louis U.** St. Louis, Mo.; 1818; P.; coed.; VII
St. Martin's C. Olympia, Wash.; 1895; P.; coed.; II
St. Mary, The C. of Omaha, Nebr.; 1923; P.; women (coed., summer & part-time programs); III
St. Mary C. Xavier (Leavenworth), Kans.; 1923; P.; women; III
St. Mary of the Lake Seminary, U. of Mundelein, Ill.; 1844; P.; men; V
St. Mary of the Plains C. Dodge City, Kans.; 1952; P.; coed.; II
St. Mary-of-the-Woods C. St. Mary-of-the-Woods, Ind.; 1840; P.; women; II
St. Mary's C. Notre Dame, Ind.; 1844; P.; women; III
St. Mary's C. St. Mary, Ky.; 1821; P.; men; II
St. Mary's C. Orchard Lake, Mich.; 1885; P.; men; II
St. Mary's C. Winona, Minn.; 1912; P.; men; III
St. Mary's C. of California St. Mary's College, Calif.; 1863; P.; men; I, III
St. Mary's C. of Maryland St. Mary's City, Md.; 1839; S.; coed.; II
St. Mary's Dominican C. New Orleans, La.; 1910; P.; women; II
St. Mary's Seminary Perryville, Mo.; 1818; P.; men; II
St. Mary's Seminary Cleveland, Ohio; 1848; P.; men; affiliated with Catholic U. of America, II
St. Mary's Seminary & U. Baltimore, Md.; 1791; P.; men; II, V
St. Mary's U.* San Antonio, Tex.; 1852; P.; coed.; III, V
St. Meinrad C. St. Meinrad, Ind.; 1861; P.; men; II
St. Michael's C. Winooski, Vt.; 1903; P.; men; III
St. Michael's Monastery Union City, N.J.; 1866; P.; men; III
St. Norbert C. West De Pere, Wis.; 1898; P.; coed.; II
St. Olaf C. Northfield, Minn.; 1874; P.; coed.; II
Stonehill C. North Easton, Mass.; 1948; P.; coed.; II
Stout State U.* Menomonie, Wis.; 1893; S.; coed.; III: J.C. branch—Rice Lake
St. Patrick's C. Menlo Park, Calif.; 1898; P.; men; II
St. Paul Bible C. St. Paul, Minn.; 1916; P.; coed.; II
St. Paul's C. Washington, D.C.; 1889; P.; men; III
St. Paul's C. Lawrenceville, Va.; 1888; P.; coed.; II
St. Paul School of Theology Methodist Kansas City, Mo.; 1958; P.; coed.; V
St. Paul Seminary St. Paul, Minn.; 1894; P.; men; II
St. Peter's C.* Jersey City, N.J.; 1872; P.; coed.; II
St. Procopius C. Lisle, Ill.; 1885; P.; coed.; II
Stratford C. Danville, Va.; 1852; P.; women; II
St. Rose, The C. of Albany, N.Y.; 1920; P.; women (coed., grad. school); III

St. Scholastica, C. of Duluth, Minn.; 1912; P.; coed.; II
St. Stephen's C. Dover, Mass.; 1955; P.; men; III, VI
St. Teresa, C. of Winona, Minn.; 1907; P.; women; II
St. Thomas, C. of St. Paul, Minn.; 1885; P.; men; III
St. Thomas, U. of Houston, Tex.; 1947; P.; coed.; III
St. Thomas Aquinas C. Sparkill, N.Y.; 1952; P.; women; II
St. Thomas Seminary Denver, Colo.; 1907; P.; men; III
St. Vincent C. Latrobe, Pa.; 1846; P.; men; II
St. Vincent de Paul, Seminary of Boynton Beach, Fla.; 1963; P.; men; II, V
St. Vladimir's Orthodox Theological Seminary Tuckahoe, N.Y.; 1938; P.; coed.; V
St. Xavier C. Chicago, Ill.; 1847; P.; women; III
Suffolk U. Boston, Mass.; 1906; P.; coed.; III, V
Sulpician Seminary of the Northwest Kenmore, Wash.; 1931; P.; men; II
Sul Ross State C. Alpine, Tex.; 1919; S.; coed.; III
Susquehanna U. Selinsgrove, Pa.; 1858; P.; coed.; II
Swarthmore C. Swarthmore, Pa.; 1864; P.; coed.; III
Sweet Briar C. Sweet Briar, Va.; 1901; P.; women; II
Syracuse U.** Syracuse, N.Y.; 1870; P.; coed.; I, VII: branch—Utica

Tabor C. Hillsboro, Kans.; 1908; P.; coed.; II
Talbot Theological Seminary La Mirada, Calif.; 1952; P.; coed.; IV, V; affiliated with Biola C.
Talladega C. Talladega, Ala.; 1867; P.; coed.; II
Tampa, U. of Tampa, Fla.; 1931; P.; coed.; II
Tarkio C. Tarkio, Mo.; 1883; P.; coed.; II
Tarleton State C. see Texas A & M U.
Taylor U. Upland, Ind.; 1846; P.; coed.; II
Telshe, Rabbinical C. of Wickliffe, Ohio; 1875; P.; men; V: branch—Chicago, Ill.
Temple Buell C. Denver, Colo.; 1888; P.; women; II
Temple U.** Philadelphia, Pa.; 1884; P. & S.; coed.; I, VII: 25-30 extension centers
Tennessee, U. of** Knoxville, Tenn.; 1794; S.; coed.; VII: branches—Chattanooga, Martin, Memphis, Nashville
Tennessee Agricultural & Industrial State U.* Nashville, Tenn.; 1912; S.; coed.; I, III
Tennessee Technological U.* Cookeville, Tenn.; 1915; S.; coed.; III: ext. centers—Crossville, McMinnville
Tennessee Temple C. Chattanooga, Tenn.; 1946; P.; coed.; II
Tennessee Wesleyan C. Athens, Tenn.; 1857; P.; coed.; II
Texas, The U. of** Austin, Tex.; 1883; S.; coed.; VII: the main university of a system that includes—
   The U. of Texas at Arlington** 1895; coed.; III
   The U. of Texas at El Paso** 1913; coed.; III
Texas A & I U.* Kingsville, Tex.; 1925; S.; coed.; III
Texas A & M U.** College Station, Tex.; 1876; S.; men (coed., limited basis); VII: the main university of a system that includes—
   Prairie View Agricultural & Mechanical C.* Prairie View; 1876; coed.; I, III
   Tarleton State C. Stephenville; 1899; coed.; II
Texas Christian U.* Fort Worth, Tex.; 1873; P.; coed.; VII
Texas C. Tyler, Tex.; 1894; P.; coed.; II
Texas Lutheran C. Seguin, Tex.; 1891; P.; coed.; I, II
Texas Southern U.* Houston, Tex.; 1947; S.; coed.; III, V
Texas Technological C.** Lubbock, Tex.; 1923; S.; coed.; III, VI
Texas Wesleyan C. Fort Worth, Tex.; 1891; P.; coed.; II
Texas Woman's U.* Denton, Tex.; 1902; S.; women; III, VI
Textile Technology, Institute of Charlottesville, Va.; 1944; P.; men; IV
Thiel C. Greenville, Pa.; 1866; P.; coed.; III
Thomas C. Waterville, Me.; 1894; P.; coed.; I, II
Thomas More C. Fort Mitchell, Ky.; 1921; P.; coed.; I, II
Tiffin U. Tiffin, Ohio; 1918; P.; coed.; I, II
Tift C. Forsyth, Ga.; 1847; P.; women; II
Toccoa Falls Institute Toccoa Falls, Ga.; 1911; P.; coed.; II
Toledo, The U. of** Toledo, Ohio; 1872; S.; coed.; I, VII
Tougaloo C. Tougaloo, Miss.; 1869; P.; coed.; II
Towson State C.* Baltimore, Md.; 1865; S.; coed.; III
Transylvania U. Lexington, Ky.; 1780; P.; coed.; II
Trenton State C.* Trenton, N.J.; 1855; S.; coed.; III
Trevecca Nazarene C. Nashville, Tenn.; 1901; P.; coed.; II
Trinity Christian C. Palos Heights, Ill.; 1959; P.; coed.; II
Trinity C. Hartford, Conn.; 1823; P.; men (coed., grad. & summer divisions); III
Trinity C. Deerfield, Ill.; 1897; P.; coed.; II
Trinity C. Burlington, Vt.; 1925; P.; women; II
Trinity C. Washington, D.C.; 1897; P.; women; III
Trinity U. San Antonio, Tex.; 1869; P.; coed.; III
Tri-State C. Angola, Ind.; 1894; P.; coed.; II
Troy State U. Troy, Ala.; 1887; S.; coed.; III: ext. centers—Fort Rucker, Maxwell AFB
Tufts U.* Medford, Mass.; 1852; P.; coed.; VII
Tulane U.* New Orleans, La.; 1834; P.; coed.; VII: women's div. (Newcomb C.)—1886; II
Tulsa, The U. of* Tulsa, Okla.; 1894; P.; coed.; VII
Tusculum C. Greeneville, Tenn.; 1794; P.; coed.; II
Tuskegee Institute* Tuskegee Institute, Ala.; 1881; P.; coed.; III, V

UCLA (U. of California, Los Angeles) *see* U. of CALIFORNIA

Union C. Barbourville, Ky.; 1879; P.; coed.; III

Union C. Lincoln, Nebr.; 1891; P.; coed.; I, II

Union Theological Seminary New York, N.Y.; 1836; P.; coed.; V

Union Theological Seminary Richmond, Va.; 1812; P.; coed.; V

Union U. Schenectady, N.Y.; 1795; P.; men (coed., eve. division); III: branch—Albany; 1839; coed.; IV, V, VI

Union U. Jackson, Tenn.; 1825; P.; coed.; I, II

United States Air Force Academy* USAFA (Colorado Springs), Colo.; 1955; Fed.; men; II

United States Army Command & General Staff C. Fort Leavenworth, Kans.; 1881; Fed.; coed.; IV equivalent program, no degree

United States Coast Guard Academy New London, Conn.; 1876; Fed.; men; II

United States Department of Agriculture, Graduate School* Washington, D.C.; 1921; Fed.; coed.; III programs, no degrees

United States International U. San Diego, Calif.; 1952; P.; coed.; III, VI

United States Merchant Marine Academy Kings Point, N.Y.; 1943; Fed.; men; II

United States Military Academy* West Point, N.Y.; 1802; Fed.; men; II

United States Naval Academy* Annapolis, Md.; 1845; Fed.; men; II

United States Naval Postgraduate School Monterey, Calif.; 1909; Fed.; coed.; VII, II

United States Naval War C. Newport, R.I.; 1884; Fed.; men: non-degree-granting postgraduate school

United Theological Seminary Dayton, Ohio; 1871; P.; coed.; V

United Theological Seminary of the Twin Cities New Brighton, Minn.; 1960; P.; coed.; V

Unity C. of Liberal Arts & Sciences Unity, Me.; 1966; P.; coed.; II

Upper Iowa C. Fayette, Iowa; 1857; P.; coed.; II

Upsala C. East Orange, N.J.; 1893; P.; coed.; II

Urbana C. Urbana, Ohio; 1850; P.; coed.; I, II

Ursinus C. Collegeville, Pa.; 1869; P.; coed.; I, II

Ursuline C. for Women Cleveland, Ohio; 1871; P.; women; II

Utah, U. of* Salt Lake City, Utah; 1850; S.; coed.; I, VII

Utah State U.* Logan, Utah; 1888; S.; coed.; VII: J.C. branch (*Snow C.*)—Ephraim

Valdosta State C. Valdosta, Ga.; 1906; S.; coed.; III

Valley City State C. Valley City, N.Dak.; 1889; S.; coed.; II

Valparaiso Technical Institute Valparaiso, Ind.; 1874; P.; coed.; I, II

Valparaiso U.* Valparaiso, Ind.; 1859; P.; coed.; III, V

Vanderbilt U.* Nashville, Tenn.; 1873; P.; coed.; VII

VanderCook C. of Music Chicago, Ill.; 1909; P.; coed.; III

Vassar C. Poughkeepsie, N.Y.; 1861; P.; women; III

Vennard C. University Park, Iowa; 1910; P.; coed.; I, II

Vermont, The U. of* Burlington, Vt.; 1791; S.; coed.; I, VII

Vermont C. Montpelier, Vt.; 1834; P.; women; I, II

Villa Maria C. Erie, Pa.; 1925; P.; women; III

Villanova U.* Villanova, Pa.; 1842; P.; coed.; III, V

Virginia, U. of* Charlottesville, Va.; 1819; S.; coed.; VII: main university of a system that includes branches at Martinsville (*Patrick Henry*) & Wallops Island (*Eastern Shore*), several extension centers, and
  Clinch Valley C. Wise; 1954; coed.; II
  George Mason C. Fairfax; 1956; coed.; II
  Mary Washington C. Fredericksburg; 1908; women; II

Virginia Commonwealth U.* Richmond, Va.; 1838; S.; coed.; I, VII

Virginia Military Institute Lexington, Va.; 1839; S.; men; II

Virginia Polytechnic Institute* Blacksburg, Va.; 1872; S.; coed.; III, VI

Virginia Seminary & C. Lynchburg, Va.; 1887; P.; coed.; I, II, V

Virginia State C. Petersburg, Va.; 1882; S.; coed.; III

Virginia Union U. Richmond, Va.; 1865; P.; coed.; II

Virginia Wesleyan C. Norfolk, Va.; 1961; P.; coed.; II

Virgin Islands, C. of the St. Thomas, V.I.; 1963; Ter.; coed.; I, II

Viterbo C. La Crosse, Wis.; 1931; P.; women; II

Voorhees C. Denmark, S.C.; 1897; P.; coed.; I, II

Wabash C. Crawfordsville, Ind.; 1832; P.; men; II

Wadhams Hall Ogdensburg, N.Y.; 1924; P.; men; II

Wagner C. Staten Island, N.Y.; 1883; P.; coed.; III

Wake Forest U.* Winston-Salem, N.C.; 1834; P.; coed.; VII

Walla Walla C. College Place, Wash.; 1892; P.; coed.; III

Walsh C. Canton, Ohio; 1960; P.; coed.; II

Warner Pacific C. Portland, Oreg.; 1937; P.; coed.; II

Warren Wilson C. Swannanoa, N.C.; 1894; P.; coed.; II

Wartburg C. Waverly, Iowa; 1852; P.; coed.; II

Wartburg Theological Seminary Dubuque, Iowa; 1854; P.; men; V

Washburn U. of Topeka* Topeka, Kans.; 1865; Mun.; coed.; III, V

Washington, U. of* Seattle, Wash.; 1861; S.; coed.; VII

Washington & Jefferson C. Washington, Pa.; 1787; P.; men; III

Washington & Lee U. Lexington, Va.; 1749; P.; men; II, V

Washington Bible C. Washington, D.C.; 1938; P.; coed.; II, V

Washington C. Chestertown, Md.; 1782; P.; coed.; II

Washington Musical Institute, Inc. Washington, D.C.; 1928; P.; coed.; II

Washington School of Psychiatry, The Washington, D.C.; 1936; P.; coed.; grad. program, no degrees awarded

Washington State C. Machias, Me.; 1909; S.; coed.; II

Washington State U.* Pullman, Wash.; 1890; S.; coed.; I, VII: ext. center—Spokane

Washington U.* St. Louis, Mo.; 1853; P.; coed.; VII

Wayland Baptist C. Plainview, Tex.; 1908; P.; coed.; II

Waynesburg C. Waynesburg, Pa.; 1850; P.; coed.; II

Wayne State C. Wayne, Nebr.; 1910; S.; coed.; III

Wayne State U.* Detroit, Mich.; 1868; S.; coed.; VII

Webber C. Babson Park, Fla.; 1927; P.; women; I, II

Webb Institute of Naval Architecture Glen Cove, N.Y.; 1889; P.; men; III

Weber State C.* Ogden, Utah; 1889; S.; coed.; I, II

Webster C. St. Louis, Mo.; 1915; P.; coed.; III

Wellesley C. Wellesley, Mass.; 1870; P.; women; III

Wells C. Aurora, N.Y.; 1868; P.; women; III

Wesleyan C. Macon, Ga.; 1836; P.; women; II

Wesleyan U. Middletown, Conn.; 1831; P.; men; III, VI

Wesley Theological Seminary of the United Methodist Church Washington, D.C.; 1882; P.; coed.; V

West Chester State C.* West Chester, Pa.; 1812; S.; coed.; III

West Coast U. Los Angeles, Calif.; 1909; P.; coed.; III

Western Baptist Bible C. & Theological Seminary El Cerrito, Calif.; 1935; P.; coed.; II

Western Carolina U.* Cullowhee, N.C.; 1889; S.; coed.; III

Western C. for Women Oxford, Ohio; 1853; P.; women; II

Western Connecticut State C. Danbury, Conn.; 1903; S.; coed.; I, III

Western Evangelical Seminary Portland, Oreg.; 1945; P.; coed.; V

Western Illinois U.* Macomb, Ill.; 1899; S.; coed.; III

Western Kentucky U.* Bowling Green, Ky.; 1906; S.; coed.; I, III, VI

Western Maryland C. Westminster, Md.; 1867; P.; coed.; III

Western Michigan U.* Kalamazoo, Mich.; 1903; S.; coed.; III, VI

Western Montana C. Dillon, Mont.; 1893; S.; coed.; III

Western New England C. Springfield, Mass.; 1919; P.; coed.; III, V

Western New Mexico U. Silver City, N.Mex.; 1893; S.; coed.; I, III

Western State C. of Colorado* Gunnison, Colo.; 1901; S.; coed.; III

Western States C. of Engineering Inglewood, Calif.; 1946; P.; coed.; I, II

Western Theological Seminary Holland, Mich.; 1866; P.; coed.; IV, V

Western Washington State C.* Bellingham, Wash.; 1893; S.; coed.; III

West Florida, The U. of Pensacola, Fla.; 1964; S.; coed.; II

West Georgia C.* Carrollton, Ga.; 1933; S.; coed.; III

West Liberty State C. West Liberty, W.Va.; 1837; S.; coed.; I, II: branches—Weirton, Wheeling

Westmar C. Le Mars, Iowa; 1890; P.; coed.; II

Westminster Choir C. Princeton, N.J.; 1926; P.; coed.; II

Westminster C. Fulton, Mo.; 1851; P.; men; II

Westminster C. New Wilmington, Pa.; 1852; P.; coed.; III

Westminster C. Salt Lake City, Utah; 1875; P.; coed.; II

Westminster Theological Seminary Chestnut Hill (Philadelphia), Pa.; 1929; P.; men; V

Westmont C. Santa Barbara, Calif.; 1940; P.; coed.; II

West Texas State U.* Canyon, Tex.; 1910; S.; coed.; III

West Virginia Institute of Technology Montgomery, W.Va.; 1895; S.; coed.; I, II

West Virginia State C.* Institute, W.Va.; 1891; S.; coed.; I, II

West Virginia U.* Morgantown, W.Va.; 1867; S.; coed.; VII: ext. centers—Charleston, Parkersburg

West Virginia Wesleyan C. Buckhannon, W.Va.; 1890; P.; coed.; II

Wheaton C. Wheaton, Ill.; 1860; P.; coed.; III, V

Wheaton C. Norton, Mass.; 1834; P.; women; II

Wheeling C. Wheeling, W.Va.; 1954; P.; coed.; II

Wheelock C. Boston, Mass.; 1888; P.; women (coed., grad. school); III

Whitman C. Walla Walla, Wash.; 1859; P.; coed.; II

Whittier C. Whittier, Calif.; 1901; P.; coed.; III

Whitworth C. Brookhaven, Miss.; 1858; P.; coed.; II

Whitworth C. Spokane, Wash.; 1890; P.; coed.; III

Wichita State U.* Wichita, Kans.; 1895; S.; coed.; III

Wilberforce U. Wilberforce, Ohio; 1856; P.; coed.; II, V

Wiley C. Marshall, Tex.; 1873; P.; coed.; II

Wilkes C. Wilkes-Barre, Pa.; 1933; P.; coed.; I, III
Willamette U. Salem, Oreg.; 1842; P.; coed.; III, V
William & Mary, C. of* Williamsburg, Va.; 1693; S.; coed.; VII: J.C. branches—Newport News, Petersburg; ext. centers—Hampton, Henrico, Hopewell, Portsmouth, Princess Anne
William Carey C. Hattiesburg, Miss.; 1911; P.; coed.; II
William Jennings Bryan C. Dayton, Tenn.; 1930; P.; coed.; II
William Jewell C. Liberty, Mo.; 1849; P.; coed.; II
William Mitchell C. of Law St. Paul, Minn.; 1900; P.; coed.; V
William Penn C. Oskaloosa, Iowa; 1873; P.; coed.; II
Williams C. Williamstown, Mass.; 1793; P.; men; III
William Smith C. 1908; women's div. of HOBART & WM. SMITH C.
William Woods C. Fulton, Mo.; 1870; P.; women; II
Wilmington C. New Castle, Del.; 1967; P.; coed.; II
Wilmington C. Wilmington, N.C.; 1947; S.; coed.; II
Wilmington C. Wilmington, Ohio; 1870; P.; coed.; III, VI
Wilson C. Chambersburg, Pa.; 1869; P.; women; II
Windham C. Putney, Vt.; 1951; P.; coed.; III
Winebrenner Theological Seminary Findlay, Ohio; 1942; P.; coed.; IV
Winona State C. Winona, Minn.; 1858; S.; coed.; I, III
Winston-Salem State C. Winston-Salem, N.C.; 1892; S.; coed.; I
Winthrop C.* Rock Hill, S.C.; 1886; S.; women; III
Wisconsin, The U. of** Madison, Wis.; 1848; S.; coed.; VII: major div.—Milwaukee; 11 2-yr. ext. centers
Wisconsin College-Conservatory Milwaukee, Wis.; 1898; P.; coed.; III
Wisconsin Lutheran Seminary Mequon, Wis.; 1863; P.; men; V
Wisconsin State U.* Eau Claire, Wis.; 1916; S.; coed.; III
Wisconsin State U.* La Crosse, Wis.; 1908; S.; coed.; III
Wisconsin State U.** Oshkosh, Wis.; 1871; S.; coed.; III: 2-yr. branch—Fond du Lac
Wisconsin State U.* Platteville, Wis.; 1866; S.; coed.; III: 2-yr. branch—Richland Center

Wisconsin State U.* River Falls, Wis.; 1874; S.; coed.; III
Wisconsin State U.* Stevens Point, Wis.; 1894; S.; coed.; III
Wisconsin State U.* Superior, Wis.; 1893; S.; coed.; III
Wisconsin State U.** Whitewater, Wis.; 1868; S.; coed.; III
Wittenberg U. Springfield, Ohio; 1845; P.; coed.; II, V
Wofford C. Spartanburg, S.C.; 1854; P.; men; II
Woman's Medical C. of Pennsylvania Philadelphia, Pa.; 1850; P.; women, M.D. program; coed., grad. program; IV, V, VI
Woodbury C. Los Angeles, Calif.; 1884; P.; coed.; II
Woods Hole Oceanographic Institution Woods Hole, Mass.; 1930; P.; coed.; VI
Woodstock C. Woodstock, Md.; 1869; P.; men; IV, V
Wooster, The C. of Wooster, Ohio; 1866; P.; coed.; III
Worcester Art Museum, School of the Worcester, Mass.; 1898; P.; coed.; affiliated with Clark U., II
Worcester Polytechnic Institute Worcester, Mass.; 1865; P.; coed.; III, VI
Wright State U.* Dayton, Ohio; 1964; S.; coed.; III, V: ext. centers—Celina, Piqua
Wyoming, The U. of* Laramie, Wyo.; 1886; S.; coed.; VII

Xavier U. Cincinnati, Ohio; 1831; P.; men (coed., grad., eve., & summer divisions); I, III
Xavier U. of Louisiana New Orleans, La.; 1917; P.; coed.; III

Yale U.** New Haven, Conn.; 1701; P.; men (coed., grad. & prof. schools); II, V, VI
Yankton C. Yankton, S.Dak.; 1881; P.; coed.; II
Yeshiva Beth Shearim Rabbinical Institute Brooklyn, N.Y.; 1860; P.; men; II, V
Yeshiva U.* New York, N.Y.; 1886; P.; coed.; I, VII
York C. of Pennsylvania York, Pa.; 1941; P.; coed.; I, II
Youngstown State U.** Youngstown, Ohio; 1908; S.; coed.; I, II

JUNIOR COLLEGES OF THE UNITED STATES

This list includes junior colleges, community colleges, and other colleges of the United States that are essentially two-year schools (i.e., colleges offering freshman and sophomore programs and, frequently, conferring associate degrees). **Key:** C., College; U., University; C.C., Community College; J.C., Junior College; P., Private; S., State; Mun., Municipal; Fed., Federal; Dist., District; Co., County; Ter., Territory: D, diploma offered; C, certificate offered; I, Associate degree offered: enrollment, *3,000 to 8,000; **over 8,000

Adirondack C.C. Glens Falls, N.Y.; 1961; S.& Co.; coed.; I
Aeronautics, Academy of Flushing, N.Y.; 1932; P.; men; I
Aims J.C. Greeley, Colo.; 1967; S.; coed.; I
Alabama Christian C. Montgomery, Ala.; 1942; P.; coed.; I
Alabama Lutheran C. Selma, Ala.; 1922; P.; coed.; I
Alamance, Technical Institute of Burlington, N.C.; 1958; S.; coed.; I
Alameda, C. of Alameda, Calif.; 1970; Dist.; coed.; I
Albany, J.C. of Albany, N.Y.; 1957; P.; coed.; I
Albany J.C. Albany, Ga.; 1966; S.; coed.; I
Albemarle, C. of The Elizabeth City, N.C.; 1961; Co.; coed.; I
Alexander City State J.C. Alexander City, Ala.; 1965; S.; coed.; I
Alice Lloyd C. Pippa Passes, Ky.; 1916; P.; coed.; I
Allan Hancock J.C. Santa Maria, Calif.; 1920; Dist.; coed.; I
Allegany C.C. Cumberland, Md.; 1961; Co.; coed.; I
Allegheny County, C.C. of Pittsburgh, Pa.; 1965; Co.; coed.; I: branches—Monroeville, West Mifflin
Allen Academy J.C. Bryan, Tex.; 1927; P.; coed.; I
Allen County Community J.C. Iola, Kans.; 1923; Co.; coed.; I
Alpena C.C. Alpena, Mich.; 1952; Dist.; coed.; I
Alphonsus C. Woodcliff Lake, N.J.; 1961; P.; women; I
Altus J.C. Altus, Okla.; 1926; Mun.; coed.; I
Alvin J.C. Alvin, Tex.; 1949; Dist.; coed.; I
Amarillo C.* Amarillo, Tex.; 1929; Dist.; coed.; I
American River C.* Sacramento, Calif.; 1955; Dist.; coed.; I
American Technical Institute Akron, Ohio; 1947; P.; men; I
Anchorage C.C. Anchorage, Alas.; 1954; S.; coed.; I
Ancilla Domini C. Donaldson, Ind.; 1937; P.; coed.; I
Anderson C. Anderson, S.C.; 1911; P.; coed.; I
Andrew C. Cuthbert, Ga.; 1854; P.; coed.; I
Angelina C. Lufkin, Tex.; 1966; Dist.; coed.; I
Anne Arundel C.C. Arnold, Md.; 1961; Co.; coed.; I
Annunciation C. Victoria, Tex.; 1959; P.; women; I
Anoka-Ramsey State J.C. Coon Rapids, Minn.; 1965; S.; coed.; I
Anson Technical Institute Ansonville, N.C.; 1967; S.; coed.; I

Antelope Valley C. Lancaster, Calif.; 1929; S.; coed.; I
Appalachian Bible Institute Bradley, W.Va.; 1950; P.; coed.; 3-yr. D
Aquinas C. Nashville, Tenn.; 1961; P.; coed.; I
Aquinas J.C. of Business Milton, Mass.; 1956; P.; women; I
Arapahoe J.C. Littleton, Colo.; 1965; Dist.; coed.; I
Area Ten C.C. Cedar Rapids, Iowa; 1966; S.; coed.; I
Arizona Western C. Yuma, Ariz.; 1963; Co.; coed.; I
Arlington Baptist J.C. Arlington, Tex.; 1939; P.; coed.; I
Asheville-Buncombe Technical Institute Asheville, N.C.; 1959; S.; coed.; I
Ashland C.C. Ashland; 1957; I: see U. of KENTUCKY
Ashland County Teachers C. Ashland, Wis.; 1914; S. & Co.; coed.; I
Assumption C. Richardton, N.Dak.; 1962; P.; coed.; I
Assumption C. for Sisters Mendham, N.J.; 1953; P.; women; I
Atlantic C.C. Mays Landing, N.J.; 1964; Co.; coed.; I
Auburn C.C. Auburn, N.Y.; 1953; Dist.; coed.; I
Austin State J.C. Austin, Minn.; 1940; S.; coed.; I
Averett C. Danville, Va.; 1859; P.; women; I

Bacone C. Bacone, Okla.; 1880; P.; coed.; I
Bakersfield C.* Bakersfield, Calif.; 1913; Dist.; coed.; I: ext. centers—Edwards AFB, Ridgecrest
Baltimore, C.C. of Baltimore, Md.; 1947; Mun.; coed.; I
Barstow C. Barstow, Calif.; 1960; Dist.; coed.; I
Barton County Community J.C. Great Bend, Kans.; 1965; Co.; coed.; I
Bay de Noc C.C. Escanaba, Mich.; 1962; Co.; coed.; I
Bay Path J.C. Longmeadow, Mass.; 1897; P.; women; I
Beal Business C. Bangor, Me.; 1891; P.; coed.; I
Beaver County, C.C. of Freedom, Pa.; 1966; S.; coed.; I
Becker J.C. Worcester, Mass.; 1887; P.; coed.; I
Beckley C. Beckley, W.Va.; 1933; P.; coed.; I
Bee County C. Beeville, Tex.; 1967; S.; coed.; I
Bellevue C.C. Bellevue, Wash.; 1965; S.; coed.; I
Bennett C. Millbrook, N.Y.; 1891; P.; women; I
Bergen C.C. Paramus, N.J.; 1965; Co.; coed.; I
Berkeley-Charleston-Dorchester Technical Education Center North Charleston, S.C.; 1964; S. & Co.; coed.; I
Berkshire C.C. Pittsfield, Mass.; 1960; S.; coed.; I
Bethany Lutheran C. Mankato, Minn.; 1911; P.; coed.; I

Big Bend C.C. Moses Lake, Wash.; 1962; S.; coed.; I
Birdwood J.C. Thomasville, Ga.; 1954; P.; coed.; I
Bismarck J.C. Bismarck, N.Dak.; 1939; Mun.; coed.; I
Black Hawk C.* Moline, Ill.; 1946; Dist.; coed.; I: branch
—Kewanee
Bladen Technical Institute Elizabethtown, N.C.; 1967;
S. & Co.; coed.; I
Blinn C. Brenham, Tex.; 1883; Co.; coed.; I
Bliss C. Lewiston, Me.; 1897; P.; coed.; I
Bluefield C. Bluefield, Va.; 1922; P.; coed.; I
Blue Mountain C.C. Pendleton, Oreg.; 1962; Dist.; coed.;
I
Blue Ridge C.C. Weyers Cave, Va.; 1967; S.; coed.; I
Boone J.C. Boone, Iowa; 1927; Dist.; coed.; I
Bradford J.C. Bradford, Mass.; 1803; P.; women; D, I
Brainerd State J.C. Brainerd, Minn.; 1938; S.; coed.; I
Brandywine J.C. Wilmington, Del.; 1965; P.; coed.; I
Brazosport J.C. Freeport, Tex.; 1968; Dist.; coed.; I
Brevard C. Brevard, N.C.; 1853; P.; coed.; I
Brevard J.C.* Cocoa, Fla.; 1960; S. & Co.; coed.; I:
branch—Eau Gallie
Brewton Parker C. Mt. Vernon, Ga.; 1904; P.; coed.; I
Bristol C.C. Fall River, Mass.; 1966; S.; coed.; I: ext.
center—Attleboro
Bronx C.C. 1957; coed.; I: part of City U. of NEW YORK
Broome Technical C.C. Binghamton, N.Y.; 1947; Co.;
coed.; I
Broward J.C.* Fort Lauderdale, Fla.; 1960; S.; coed.; I
Brunswick J.C. Brunswick, Ga.; 1961; S.; coed.; I
Bryant & Stratton C. of Commerce San Jose, Calif.;
1963; P.; coed.; I
Bucks County C.C. Newtown, Pa.; 1965; Co.; coed.; I
Buffalo Bible Institute Buffalo, N.Y.; 1940; P.; coed.; D
Buffalo County Teachers C. Alma, Wis.; 1902; S. & Co.;
coed.; D
Buffalo Diocesan Preparatory Seminary Buffalo, N.Y.;
1925; P.; men; I
Burdett C. Boston, Mass.; 1879; P.; coed.; D
Burlington C.C. Pemberton, N.J.; 1966; S. & Co.; coed.;. I
Butler C. Tyler, Tex.; 1905; P.; coed.; I
Butler County C.C. Butler, Pa.; 1965; Co.; coed.; I
Butler County Community J.C. El Dorado, Kans.; 1927;
Co.; coed.; I
Butte C. Durham, Calif.; 1967; Dist.; coed.; I

Cabrillo C. Aptos, Calif.; 1959; Dist.; coed.; I
Caldwell Technical Institute Lenoir, N.C.; 1964; S.;
coed.; I
California Concordia C. Oakland, Calif.; 1906; P.; coed.;
D
Camden County C. Blackwood, N.J.; 1966; Co.; coed.; I
Canada C. Redwood City, Calif.; 1968; Dist.; coed.; I
Canal Zone C. Balboa, C.Z.; 1933; Fed.; coed.; I
Cape Cod C.C. Hyannis, Mass.; 1961; S.; coed.; I
Cape Fear Technical Institute Wilmington, N.C.; 1958;
S.; coed.; I
Carl Sandburg C. Galesburg, Ill.; 1966; Dist.; coed.; I
Carteret Technical Institute Morehead City, N.C.;
1963; S.; coed.; I
Casa Loma C. Pacoima, Calif.; 1966; P.; coed.; I
Casper C. Casper, Wyo.; 1945; Co.; coed.; I
Catawba Valley Technical Institute Hickory, N.C.;
1958; S. & Co.; coed.; I
Catonsville C.C. Catonsville, Md.; 1957; Co.; coed.; I
Cazenovia C. Cazenovia, N.Y.; 1824; P.; women; I
Centenary C. for Women Hackettstown, N.J.; 1867;
P.; women; I, II
Centerville C.C. Centerville, Iowa; 1930; Dist.; coed.; I
Central Arizona C. Coolidge, Ariz.; 1962; Co.; coed.; I
Central Baptist C. Conway, Ark.; 1892; P.; coed.; I
Central Carolina Technical Institute Sanford, N.C.;
1961; S. & Co.; coed.; I
Central C. McPherson, Kans.; 1914; P.; coed.; I
Central Florida J.C. Ocala, Fla.; 1958; S. & Dist.; coed.; I
Centralia C. Centralia, Wash.; 1925; S.; coed.; I
Central Nebraska Tech Hastings, Nebr.; 1966; Dist.;
coed.; I
Central Oregon C.C. Bend, Oreg.; 1957; Dist.; coed.; I
Central Piedmont C.C.* Charlotte, N.C.; 1963; Co.;
coed.; I
Central Technical Institute Kansas City, Mo.; 1931; P.;
coed.; I
Central Texas C. Killeen, Tex.; 1965; Dist.; coed.; I
Central Virginia C.C. Lynchburg, Va.; 1966; S.; coed.; I
Central Wyoming C. Riverton, Wyo.; 1966; Dist.; coed.; I
Central YMCA C.C. Chicago, Ill.; 1961; P.; coed.; I
Cerritos C.* Norwalk, Calif.; 1955; S.; coed.; I
Chabot C.* Hayward, Calif.; 1961; Dist.; coed.; I
Chaffey C.* Alta Loma, Calif.; 1922; Dist.; coed.; I
Chamberlayne J.C. Boston, Mass.; 1892; P.; coed.; D
Champlain C. Burlington, Vt.; 1878; P.; coed.; I
Charles County C.C. La Plata, Md.; 1958; S. & Co.; coed.;
I
Chattanooga City C. Chattanooga, Tenn.; 1964; P.;
coed.; I
Chattanooga State Technical Institute Chattanooga,
Tenn.; 1965; S.; coed.; I
Chesapeake C. Wye Mills, Md.; 1965; Dist.; coed.; I

Chesterfield-Marlboro Technical Education Center
Cheraw, S.C.; 1968; S. & Co.; coed.; I
Chicago City C.** Chicago, Ill.; 1911; Co. & S.; coed.; I:
eight branch campuses in Chicago
Chipola J.C. Marianna, Fla.; 1947; S. & Co.; coed.; I
Chowan C. Murfreesboro, N.C.; 1848; P.; coed.; I
Christian C. Columbia, Mo.; 1851; P.; women; I
Christian C. of the Southwest Dallas, Tex.; 1962; P.;
coed.; I
Christopher Newport C. Newport News; 1961; I: J.C.
branch of C. of WILLIAM & MARY
Cisco J.C. Cisco, Tex.; 1941; S.; coed.; I
Citrus C. Azusa, Calif.; 1915; S.; coed.; I
Clackamas C.C. Oregon City, Oreg.; 1966; S. & Dist.;
coed.; I
Clarendon C. Clarendon, Tex.; 1898; S.; coed.; I
Clark C. Vancouver, Wash.; 1933; Dist.; coed.; I
Clarke Memorial C. Newton, Miss.; 1908; P.; coed.; I
Clatsop C.C. Astoria, Oreg.; 1958; S. & Dist.; coed.; I
Cleveland County Technical Institute Shelby, N.C.;
1965; S.; coed.; I
Cleveland State C.C. Cleveland, Tenn.; 1966; S.; coed.; I
Clinton J.C. Rock Hill, S.C.; 1894; P.; coed.; I
Cloud County Community J.C. Concordia, Kans.; 1965;
S.; coed.; I
Coahoma J.C. Clarksdale, Miss.; 1949; S.; coed.; I
Coalinga C. Coalinga, Calif.; 1941; Dist.; coed.; I
Cochise C. Douglas, Ariz.; 1961; Co.; coed.; I
Coffeyville Community J.C. Coffeyville, Kans.; 1923;
Dist.; coed.; I
Cogswell Polytechnical C. San Francisco, Calif.; 1887; P.;
coed.; I
Colby Community J.C. Colby, Kans.; 1964; Co.; coed.; I
Colby J.C. for Women New London, N.H.; 1838; P.;
women; I, II
Coleman Technical Institute La Crosse, Wis.; 1966;
S.; coed.; I
Colorado Mountain C. Leadville & Glenwood Springs,
Colo.; 1965; Dist.; coed.; I
Columbia Basin C. Pasco, Wash.; 1955; S.; coed.; I
Columbia Christian C. Portland, Oreg.; 1956; P.; coed.; I
Columbia County Teachers C. Columbus, Wis.; 1912;
S. & Co.; coed.; D
Columbia J.C. Columbia, Calif.; 1968; Dist.; coed.; I
Columbia State C.C. Columbia, Tenn.; 1966; S.; coed.; I
Columbus Technical Institute Columbus, Ohio; 1963;
S.; coed.; I
Commonwealth C. of Sciences Houston, Tex.; 1936; P.;
coed.; I
Compton District J.C. Compton, Calif.; 1927; Dist.;
coed.; I
Concordia C. Portland, Oreg.; 1950; P.; coed.; I
Concordia C. Milwaukee, Wis.; 1881; P.; coed.; I
Concordia J.C. Bronxville, N.Y.; 1881; P.; coed.; I
Concordia Lutheran C. Austin, Tex.; 1926; P.; coed.; D
Concordia Lutheran J.C. Ann Arbor, Mich.; 1962; P.;
coed.; I
Connecticut, The J.C. of Bridgeport, Conn.; 1927; P.;
coed.; I
Connors State C. Warner, Okla.; 1908; S.; coed.; I
Contra Costa C.* San Pablo, Calif.; 1948; Dist.; coed.; I
Cooke County J.C. Gainesville, Tex.; 1924; Co.; coed.; I
Copiah-Lincoln J.C. Wesson, Miss.; 1928; Co.; coed.; I
Corbett J.C. Crookston, Minn.; 1957; P.; women; I
Corning C.C. Corning, N.Y.; 1957; S.; coed.; I
Cottey J.C. Nevada, Mo.; 1884; P.; women; I
Cowley County Community J.C. Arkansas City, Kans.;
1922; Co.; coed.; I
Craven County Technical Institute New Bern, N.C.;
1965; S.; coed.; I
Crosier Seminary Onamia, Minn.; 1922; P.; men; C
Crowder C. Neosho, Mo.; 1963; Dist.; coed.; I
Crowley's Ridge C. Paragould, Ark.; 1964; P.; coed.; I
Cuesta C. San Luis Obispo, Calif.; 1964; Dist.; coed.; I
Cumberland C. of Tennessee Lebanon, Tenn.; 1842; P.;
coed.; I
Cumberland County C. Vineland, N.J.; 1964; Co.; coed.;
I
Cuyahoga C.C.* Cleveland, Ohio; 1963; S. & Co.; coed.; I
Cypress J.C. Cypress, Calif.; 1966; Dist.; coed.; I

Dabney S. Lancaster C.C. Clifton Forge, Va.; 1964; S.;
coed.; I
Dalton J.C. Dalton, Ga.; 1963; S.; coed.; I
Danville C.C. Danville, Va.; 1936; S.; coed.; I
Danville J.C.** Danville, Ill.; 1949; Dist.; coed.; I
Davenport C. of Business Grand Rapids, Mich.; 1866;
P.; coed.; I
Davidson County C.C. Lexington, N.C.; 1961; S. & Co.;
coed.; I
Davis J.C. of Business Toledo, Ohio; 1858; P.; coed.; I
Dawson C. Glendive, Mont.; 1940; Dist.; coed.; I
Daytona Beach J.C. Daytona Beach, Fla.; 1958; Dist.;
coed.; I
Dean Academy & J.C. Franklin, Mass.; 1865; P.; coed.; I
De Anza C. Cupertino, Calif.; 1967; Dist.; coed.; I
Deep Springs C. Deep Springs, Calif.; 1917; P.; men
DeKalb C.* Clarkston, Ga.; 1964; Co.; coed.; I

Delaware County, C.C. of Concordville, Pa.; 1967; Dist.; coed.; I
Delaware Technical & C.C. Georgetown, Del.; 1967; S.; coed.; I
Delgado J.C.* New Orleans, La.; 1921; S. & Mun.; coed.; I
DeLima J.C. Oxford, Mich.; 1959; P.; women; I
DeLisle J.C. New Orleans, La.; 1959; P.; women; I
Del Mar C.* Corpus Christi, Tex.; 1935; S.; coed.; I
Delta C.* University Center, Mich.; 1961; Dist.; coed.; I
Desert, C. of the Palm Desert, Calif.; 1959; Dist.; coed.; I
Des Moines Area C.C.* Ankeny, Iowa; 1966; Dist.; coed.; I
Detroit Engineering Institute Detroit, Mich.; 1910; P.; men; I
Detroit Institute of Musical Art Detroit, Mich.; 1914; P.; coed.; D & C
DeVry Institute of Technology Chicago, Ill.; 1931; P.; coed.; I
Diablo Valley C.* Pleasant Hill, Calif.; 1948; Dist.; coed.; I
Dixie J.C. St. George, Utah; 1913; S.; coed.; I
Dodge City Community J.C. Dodge City, Kans.; 1935; Co.; coed.; I
Dodge County Teachers C. Mayville, Wis.; 1925; S. & Co.; coed.; I
Donnelly C. Kansas City, Kans.; 1949; P.; coed.; I
Door-Kewaunee County Teachers C. Algoma, Wis.; 1905; S. & Co.; coed.; I
Du Page, C. of Naperville, Ill.; 1967; S. & Dist.; coed.; I
Durham Technical Institute Durham, N.C.; 1958; S.; coed.; I: ext. centers—Henderson, Hillsborough, Roxboro
Dutchess C.C. Poughkeepsie, N.Y.; 1958; Co.; coed.; I
Dyersburg State C.C. Dyersburg, Tenn.; 1969; S.; coed.; I

Early Education, Center for Los Angeles, Calif.; 1939; P.; coed.; I
East Central J.C. Decatur, Miss.; 1928; S.; coed.; I
Eastern Arizona C. Thatcher, Ariz.; 1888; S. & Co.; coed.; I
Eastern Iowa C.C. Bettendorf, Iowa; 1966; Dist.; coed.; I: branches—Clinton (1946), Muscatine (1929)
Eastern Oklahoma State C. Wilburton, Okla.; 1909; S.; coed.; I
Eastern Utah, C. of Price; 1938: J.C. branch of U. of Utah
Eastern Wyoming C. Torrington, Wyo.; 1948; Dist.; coed.; I
East Los Angeles C.* Los Angeles, Calif.; 1945; Dist.; coed.; I
East Mississippi J.C. Scooba, Miss.; 1927; S.; coed.; I
Edison J.C. Fort Myers, Fla.; 1962; S. & Co.; coed.; I
Edmonds C.C. Edmonds, Wash.; 1967; S.; coed.; I
Edward Williams C. Hackensack, N.J.; 1964; P.; coed.; I: J.C. division of Fairleigh Dickinson U.
El Camino C.* Torrance, Calif.; 1946; S. & Dist.; coed.; I
El Centro C.* Dallas, Tex.; 1966; Co.; coed.; I
Elgin C.C. Elgin, Ill.; 1949; Dist.; coed.; I
Elizabeth Seton C. Westchester, N.Y.; 1960; P.; women; I
Elizabethtown C.C. Elizabethtown; 1962; I: see U. of KENTUCKY
Elko C.C. Elko, Nev.; 1967; S.; coed.; I
Ellen Cushing J.C. Bryn Mawr, Pa.; 1892; P.; women; I
Ellsworth C. Iowa Falls, Iowa; 1890; S.; coed.; I
El Paso C.C. Colorado Springs, Colo.; 1968; S.; coed.; I
El Reno C., The El Reno, Okla.; 1938; Dist.; coed.; I
Emmanuel C. Franklin Springs, Ga.; 1919; P.; coed.; I
Emmetsburg C.C. Emmetsburg, Iowa; 1930; Dist.; coed.; I
Endicott J.C. Beverly, Mass.; 1939; P.; women; I
Englewood Cliffs C. Englewood Cliffs, N.J.; 1962; P.; women; I
Enterprise State J.C. Enterprise, Ala.; 1965; S.; coed.; I
Epiphany Apostolic C. Newburgh, N.Y.; 1925; P.; men
Erie County Technical Institute Williamsville, N.Y.; 1948; Co.; coed.; I
Essex C.C. Essex, Md.; 1957; Co.; coed.; I
Essex County C. Newark, N.J.; 1968; S. & Co.; coed.; I
Everett C.C.* Everett, Wash.; 1941; Dist.; coed.; I

Fairbury J.C. Fairbury, Nebr.; 1941; Dist.; coed.; I
Fashion Institute of Technology New York, N.Y.; 1944; S. & Mun.; coed.; I
Father Judge Mission Seminary Monroe, Va.; 1932; P.; men; I
Fayetteville Technical Institute Fayetteville, N.C.; 1961; S.; coed.; I
Felician C., The Chicago, Ill.; 1926; P.; women; I
Fergus Falls State J.C. Fergus Falls, Minn.; 1960; S.; coed.; I
Ferrum J.C. Ferrum, Va.; 1913; P.; coed.; I
Finger Lakes, C.C. of the Canandaigua, N.Y.; 1965; Co.; coed.; I
Fisher J.C. Boston, Mass.; 1903; P.; women; I
Flathead Valley C.C. Kalispell, Mont.; 1967; S.; coed.; I
Flint Community J.C.* Flint, Mich.; 1923; Dist.; coed.; I
Florence-Darlington Technical Education Center* Florence, S.C.; 1963; S. & Co.; coed.; I

Florida C. Temple Terrace, Fla.; 1944; P.; coed.; I
Florida J.C. at Jacksonville* Jacksonville, Fla.; 1965; S.; coed.; I
Florida Keys J.C. Key West, Fla.; 1965; Co.; coed.; I
Florissant Valley C.C.* Ferguson, Mo.; 1962; Mun.; coed.; I
Foothill C.* Los Altos Hills, Calif.; 1957; Dist.; coed.; I
Forest Park C.C.* St. Louis, Mo.; 1962; Dist.; coed.; I
Forsyth School for Dental Hygienists Boston, Mass.; 1910; P.; women; C: affiliated with Northeastern U., I
Forsyth Technical Institute Winston-Salem, N.C.; 1963; S. & Co.; coed.; I
Fort Knox C.C. Fort Knox; 1959; I: see U. of KENTUCKY
Fort Scott Community J.C. Fort Scott, Kans.; 1919; S.; coed.; I
Fort Steilacoom C.C. Tacoma, Wash.; 1965; S. & Dist.; coed.; I
Fort Worth Christian C. Fort Worth, Tex.; 1959; P.; coed.; I
Franklin Institute of Boston Boston, Mass.; 1908; P.; coed.; I
Frank Phillips C. Borger, Tex.; 1948; S.; coed.; I
Frederick C.C. Frederick, Md.; 1957; Co.; coed.; I
Frederick C.C. Portsmouth, Va.; 1958; S.; coed.; I
Freed-Hardeman C. Henderson, Tenn.; 1908; P.; coed.; I
Freeman J.C. Freeman, S.Dak.; 1900; P.; coed.; I
Fresno City C.** Fresno, Calif.; 1910; Dist.; coed.; I
Friendship J.C. Rock Hill, S.C.; 1891; P.; coed.; I
Fullerton J.C.** Fullerton, Calif.; 1913; Dist.; coed.; I
Fulton-Montgomery C.C. Johnstown, N.Y.; 1964; Co.; coed.; I

Gadsden State J.C. Gadsden, Ala.; 1965; S.; coed.; I
Gainesville J.C. Oakwood, Ga.; 1964; S.; coed.; I
Galveston C.C. Galveston, Tex.; 1966; S. & Dist.; coed.; I
Garden City Community J.C. Garden City, Kans.; 1919; Dist.; coed.; I
Gardner-Webb C. Boiling Springs, N.C.; 1905; P.; coed.; I
Garland J.C. Boston, Mass.; 1872; P.; women; I
Gaston C. Dallas, N.C.; 1964; S.; coed.; I
Gavilan C. Gilroy, Calif.; 1919; S. & Co.; coed.; I
Genesee C.C. Batavia, N.Y.; 1967; S. & Co.; coed.; I
George C. Wallace State Technical J.C. Dothan, Ala.; 1965; S.; coed.; I
Georgia Military C. Milledgeville, Ga.; 1879; Mun.; men; I
Glendale C.* Glendale, Calif.; 1927; Dist.; coed.; I
Glendale C.C.* Glendale, Ariz.; 1965; S.; coed.; I
Glen Oaks C.C. Centreville, Mich.; 1965; Co.; coed.; I
Gloucester County C. Sewell, N.J.; 1966; S. & Co.; coed.; I
Gogebic C.C. Ironwood, Mich.; 1932; Co.; coed.; I
Golden Valley Lutheran C. Minneapolis, Minn.; 1967; P.; coed.; I
Golden West C. Huntington Beach, Calif.; 1966; Dist.; coed.; I
Goldey Beacom J.C. Wilmington, Del.; 1886; P.; coed.; I
Gordon Military C. Barnesville, Ga.; 1852; P.; coed.; I
Grahm J.C. Boston, Mass.; 1950; P.; coed.; I
Grand Rapids J.C.* Grand Rapids, Mich.; 1914; Dist.; coed.; I
Grand View C. Des Moines, Iowa; 1896; P.; coed.; I
Grantham School of Electronics Hollywood, Calif.; 1951; P.; coed.; I
Grays Harbor C. Aberdeen, Wash.; 1930; S.; coed.; I
Grayson County C. Denison, Tex.; 1963; S.; coed.; I
Greater Hartford C.C. Hartford, Conn.; 1967; S.; coed.; I
Greenbrier C. Lewisburg, W.Va.; 1812; P.; women; I
Greenfield C.C. Greenfield, Mass.; 1962; S.; coed.; I
Green Mountain C. Poultney, Vt.; 1834; P.; women; I
Green River C.C. Auburn, Wash.; 1963; S.; coed.; I
Greenville Technical Education Center Greenville, S.C.; 1961; S.; coed.; I
Grossmont C.* El Cajon, Calif.; 1961; Dist.; coed.; I
Guilford Technical Institute Jamestown, N.C.; 1959; S.; coed.; I
Gulf Coast J.C. Panama City, Fla.; 1957; S.; coed.; I
Gulf Park C. Long Beach, Miss.; 1919; P.; women; I
Gunstock J.C. Laconia, N.H.; 1965; P.; coed.; I

Hagerstown J.C. Hagerstown, Md.; 1946; Co.; coed.; I
Halifax County Technical Institute Weldon, N.C.; 1967; S.; coed.; I
Harcum J.C. Bryn Mawr, Pa.; 1915; P.; women; I
Harford J.C. Bel Air, Md.; 1957; Co.; coed.; I
Harriman C. Harriman, N.Y.; 1956; P.; women; I
Harrisburg Area C.C. Harrisburg, Pa.; 1964; Dist.; coed.; I
Harris J.C. Meridian, Miss.; 1956; Mun.; coed.; I
Hartford C. for Women Hartford, Conn.; 1939; P.; women; I
Hartford State Technical C. Hartford, Conn.; 1946; S.; coed.; I
Hartnell C. Salinas, Calif.; 1920; Dist.; coed.; I
Haskell Institute Lawrence, Kans.; 1884; Fed.; coed.; D
Haywood Technical Institute Clyde, N.C.; 1965; S. & Co.; coed.; I

Henderson C.C. Henderson; 1960; I: see U. of KENTUCKY
Henderson County J.C. Athens, Tex.; 1946; S. & Dist.; coed.; I
Henry Ford C.C.* Dearborn, Mich.; 1938; Mun.; coed.; I
Herkimer County C.C. Ilion, N.Y.; 1966; Co.; coed.; I
Hesston C. Hesston, Kans.; 1909; P.; coed.; I
Hibbing State J.C. Hibbing, Minn.; 1916; S.; coed.; I
Highland C.C. Freeport, Ill.; 1962; Dist.; coed.; I
Highland Community J.C. Highland, Kans.; 1857; S.; coed.; I
Highland Park C.* Highland Park, Mich.; 1918; S. & Dist.; coed.; I
Highline C. Midway, Wash.; 1963; S.; coed.; I
Hill J.C. Hillsboro, Tex.; 1923; Dist.; coed.; I
Hillsborough J.C. Tampa, Fla.; 1967; S. & Dist.; coed.; I
Hinds J.C.* Raymond, Miss.; 1917; Dist.; coed.; I
Hiwassee C. Madisonville, Tenn.; 1849; P.; coed.; I
Holmes J.C. Goodman, Miss.; 1925; Dist.; coed.; I
Holy Cross J.C. Notre Dame, Ind.; 1966; P.; coed.; I
Holy Names, The C. of the Albany, N.Y.; 1961; P.; women; I
Holyoke C.C. Holyoke, Mass.; 1946; S.; coed.; I
Honolulu Business C. Honolulu, Hawaii; 1917; P.; coed.; I
Honolulu C.C. Honolulu, Hawaii; 1920; S.; coed.; I
Hopkinsville C.C. Hopkinsville; 1965; I: see U. of KENTUCKY
Horry-Marion-Georgetown Technical Education Center Conway, S.C.; 1966; S. & Co.; coed.; I
Housatonic C.C. Stratford, Conn.; 1967; S.; coed.; I
Howard County J.C. Big Spring, Tex.; 1946; Co.; coed.; I
Hudson Valley C.C.* Troy, N.Y.; 1953; S. & Co.; coed.; I
Humacao Regional C. Humacao, P.R.; 1962; S.; coed.; I
Humphreys C. Stockton, Calif.; 1896; P.; coed.; I
Hutchinson Community J.C. Hutchinson, Kans.; 1928; S. & Co.; coed.; I

Illinois Central C. East Peoria, Ill.; 1966; S., Co., & Dist.; coed.; I
Illinois J.C. District 522* Belleville, Ill.; 1946; Dist.; coed.; I
Illinois J.C. District 525 Joliet, Ill.; 1967; Dist.; coed.; I
Illinois Valley C.C. La Salle, Ill.; 1924; Dist.; coed.; I
Immaculata C. Bartlett, Ill.; 1955; P.; women; I
Immaculata C. Hamburg, N.Y.; 1957; P.; women; I
Immaculata C. of Washington Washington, D.C.; 1905; P.; women; I
Imperial Valley C. Imperial Valley, Calif.; 1922; Dist.; coed.; I
Independence Community J.C. Independence, Kans.; 1925; Dist.; coed.; I
Indian River J.C. Fort Pierce, Fla.; 1960; S.; coed.; I
Iowa Central C.C. Fort Dodge, Iowa; 1967; Dist.; coed.; I: branches—Eagle Grove, Webster City
Iowa Lakes C.C. Estherville, Iowa; 1924; Dist.; coed.; I
Iowa State Technical Institute Ames, Iowa; 1960; S.; coed.; I
Iowa Western C.C. Clarinda, Iowa; 1923; S. & Dist.; coed.; I: ext. centers—Atlantic, Council Bluffs, Harlan
Isothermal C.C. Spindale, N.C.; 1965; S.; coed.; I
Itasca State J.C. Grand Rapids, Minn.; 1922; S.; coed.; I
Itawamba J.C. Fulton, Miss.; 1948; S.; coed.; I

Jackson C.C. Jackson, Mich.; 1928; Co.; coed.; I
Jackson County J.C. Gautier, Miss.; 1964; S.; coed.; I
Jackson State C.C. Jackson, Tenn.; 1967; S.; coed.; I
Jacksonville C. Jacksonville, Tex.; 1899; P.; coed.; I
James Connally Technical Institute Waco, Tex.; 1965; S.; coed.; I
James Sprunt Institute Kenansville, N.C.; 1964; S. & Co.; coed.; I
Jamestown C.C. Jamestown, N.Y.; 1950; S. & Mun.; coed.; I
Jefferson C. Hillsboro, Mo.; 1963; Co.; coed.; I
Jefferson C.C. Watertown, N.Y.; 1961; S. & Co.; coed.; I
Jefferson Davis J.C. Handsboro, Miss.; 1965; S. & Co.; coed.; I: branch of Perkinston C.
Jefferson Davis State J.C. Brewton, Ala.; 1965; S.; coed.; I
Jefferson State J.C.* Birmingham, Ala.; 1963; S.; coed.; I
John A. Gupton C. Nashville, Tenn.; 1946; P.; coed.; I
John A. Logan C. Herrin, Ill.; 1967; Dist.; coed.; I
John C. Calhoun J.C. & Technical School Decatur, Ala.; 1965; S.; coed.; I
John Curtis J.C. New Orleans, La.; 1963; P.; coed.; I
Johnson & Wales J.C. of Business Providence, R.I.; 1914; P.; coed.; I
John Tyler C.C. Chester, Va.; 1966; Dist.; coed.; I
Jones County J.C. Ellisville, Miss.; 1927; Dist.; coed.; I
Juneau County Teachers C. New Lisbon, Wis.; 1916; S. & Co.; coed.; D
Juneau-Douglas C.C. Juneau, Alas.; 1956; S.; coed.; I

Kalamazoo Valley C.C. Kalamazoo, Mich.; 1966; Dist.; coed.; I

Kankakee C.C. Kankakee, Ill.; 1966; S. & Dist.; coed.; I
Kansas City Kansas Community J.C. Kansas City, Kans.; 1923; Dist.; coed.; I
Kansas Technical Institute Salina, Kans.; 1965; S.; coed.; I
Kapiolani C.C. Honolulu, Hawaii; 1957; S.; coed.; I
Kaskaskia C. Centralia, Ill.; 1966; Dist.; coed.; I
Kauai C.C. Lihue, Hawaii; 1965; S.; coed.; I
Kellogg C.C. Battle Creek, Mich.; 1956; Dist.; coed.; I
Kemper Military School & C. Boonville, Mo.; 1844; P.; men; I
Kenai Peninsula C.C. Kenai, Alas.; 1964; S.; coed.; I
Kendall C. Evanston, Ill.; 1934; P.; coed.; I
Kennesaw J.C. Marietta, Ga.; 1963; S.; coed.; I
Kenosha Technical Institute Kenosha, Wis.; 1912; Dist.; coed.; I
Ketchikan C.C. Ketchikan, Alas.; 1954; S.; coed.; I
Kettering C. of Medical Arts Kettering, Ohio; 1967; P.; coed.; I
Keystone J.C. La Plume, Pa.; 1868; P.; coed.; I
Kilgore C.* Kilgore, Tex.; 1935; Dist.; coed.; I
Kingsborough C.C. Brooklyn; 1964; coed.; I: part of The City U. of NEW YORK
King's C. Charlotte, N.C.; 1901; P.; coed.; I
Kirkland Hall C. Easton, Md.; 1967; P.; coed.; I
Kirtland C.C. Roscommon, Mich.; 1966; Dist.; coed.; I
Kishwaukee C. Malta, Ill.; 1967; Dist.; coed.; I
Kittrell C. Kittrell, N.C.; 1886; P.; coed.; I

Labette Community J.C. Parsons, Kans.; 1923; Co.; coed.; I
Lackawanna J.C. Scranton, Pa.; 1894; P.; coed.; I
Lain Technical Institute Indianapolis & Evansville, Ind.; 1903; P.; coed.; I
Lake City J.C. & Forest Ranger School Lake City, Fla.; 1962; S.; coed.; I
Lake County, C. of Waukegan, Ill.; 1967; Dist.; coed.; I
Lake Land C. Mattoon, Ill.; 1966; Dist.; coed.; I
Lakeland C.C. Mentor, Ohio; 1966; Co.; coed.; I
Lake Michigan C. Benton Harbor, Mich.; 1946; Co.; coed.; I
Lake Region J.C. Devils Lake, N.Dak.; 1941; Dist.; coed.; I
Lake-Sumter J.C. Leesburg, Fla.; 1962; S. & Co.; coed.; I
Lakewood State J.C. White Bear Lake, Minn.; 1967; S.; coed.; I
Lamar C. Lamar, Colo.; 1937; S.; coed.; I
Lane C.C.* Eugene, Oreg.; 1964; Dist.; coed.; I
Laney C. Oakland, Calif.; 1953; Dist.; coed.; I
Langlade County Teachers C. Antigo, Wis.; 1906; S. & Co.; coed.; D
Lansing C.C.* Lansing, Mich.; 1957; Dist.; coed.; I
Laredo J.C. Laredo, Tex.; 1947; S.; coed.; I
La Salette Seminary Altamont, N.Y.; 1952; P.; men; I
Lasell J.C. Auburndale, Mass.; 1851; P.; women; I
Lassen C. Susanville, Calif.; 1925; S.; coed.; I
L.D.S. Business C. Salt Lake City, Utah; 1886; P.; coed.; I
Lee C. Baytown, Tex.; 1934; Dist.; coed.; I
Lees J.C. Jackson, Ky.; 1883; P.; coed.; I
Lees-McRae C. Banner Elk, N.C.; 1900; P.; coed.; I
Lehigh County C.C. Allentown, Pa.; 1967; Dist.; coed.; I
Leicester C. Leicester, Mass.; 1784; P.; coed.; I
Lenoir County C.C. Kinston, N.C.; 1960; S.; coed.; I
Lincoln Land C.C. Springfield, Ill.; 1967; Dist.; coed.; I
Lincoln U. Lincoln, Ill.; 1865; P.; coed.; I
Lindsey Wilson C. Columbia, Ky.; 1903; P.; coed.; I
Linn Benton C.C. Albany, Oreg.; 1966; Dist.; coed.; I
Lomax-Hannon J.C. Greenville, Ala.; 1893; P.; coed.; I
Long Beach City C.** Long Beach, Calif.; 1927; Dist.; coed.; I
Lon Morris C. Jacksonville, Tex.; 1873; P.; coed.; I
Loop C., The* Chicago, Ill.; 1962; Mun.; coed.; I
Lorain County C.C. Elyria, Ohio; 1964; S.; coed.; I
Los Angeles City C.** Los Angeles, Calif.; 1929; Dist.; coed.; I
Los Angeles Harbor C.* Wilmington, Calif.; 1949; Dist.; coed.; I
Los Angeles Pierce C.** Woodland Hills, Calif.; 1947; Dist.; coed.; I
Los Angeles Southwest C. Los Angeles, Calif.; 1967; Dist.; coed.; I
Los Angeles Trade-Technical C.** Los Angeles, Calif.; 1949; Dist.; coed.; I
Los Angeles Valley C.** Van Nuys, Calif.; 1949; Dist.; coed.; I
Louisburg C. Louisburg, N.C.; 1787; P.; coed.; I
Lourdes J.C. Sylvania, Ohio; 1958; P.; women; I
Lower Columbia C. Longview, Wash.; 1934; S. & Dist.; coed.; I
Lubbock Christian C. Lubbock, Tex.; 1957; P.; coed.; I
Luther Rice C. Alexandria, Va.; 1966; P.; coed.; I
Luzerne County C.C. Wilkes-Barre, Pa.; 1966; Co.; coed.; I

MacCormac C. Chicago, Ill.; 1904; P.; coed.; I
Macomb County C.C.** Warren, Mich.; 1954; Dist. & Co.; coed.; I

Macon J.C. Macon, Ga.; 1965; S.; coed.; I
Madison Area Technical C. Madison, Wis.; 1912; Dist.; coed.; I
Magic Valley Christian C. Albion, Ida.; 1958; P.; coed.; I
Mainland C. of the Texas City, Tex.; 1966; Dist.; coed.; I
Mallinckrodt C. Wilmette, Ill.; 1918; P.; women; I
Manatee J.C. Bradenton, Fla.; 1957; S.; coed.; I
Manchester C.C. Manchester, Conn.; 1963; S.; coed.; I
Manhattan C.C., Borough of 1963; coed.; I: part of The City U. of NEW YORK
Manitowoc County Teachers C. Manitowoc, Wis.; 1902; S. & Co.; coed.; D
Manor J.C. Jenkintown, Pa.; 1959; P.; women; I
Maria C. Albany, N.Y.; 1958; P.; women; I
Maria J.C. Chicago, Ill.; 1948; P.; women; I
Maria Regina C. Syracuse, N.Y.; 1961; P.; women; I
Maricopa Technical C. Phoenix, Ariz.; 1963; S. & Dist.; coed.; I
Marin, C. of* Kentfield, Calif.; 1926; Dist.; coed.; I
Marion Institute, The Marion, Ala.; 1842; P.; men; I
Marjorie Webster J.C. Washington, D.C.; 1920; P.; women; I
Marshalltown C.C. Marshalltown, Iowa; 1927; Dist.; coed.; I
Martin C. Pulaski, Tenn.; 1870; P.; coed.; I
Martin Technical Institute Williamston, N.C.; 1968; S.; coed.; I
Mary Allen J.C. Crockett, Tex.; 1885; P.; coed.; I
Mary Holmes C. West Point, Miss.; 1892; P.; coed.; I
Marymount C. Boca Raton, Fla.; 1963; P.; coed.; I
Marymount C. of Virginia Arlington, Va.; 1950; P.; women; I
Massachusetts Bay C.C. Watertown, Mass.; 1961; S.; coed.; I
Massasoit C.C. North Abington, Mass.; 1966; S.; coed.; I
Massey J.C. Atlanta, Ga.; 1963; P.; coed.; I
Matanuska-Susitna C.C. Palmer, Alas.; 1958; S.; coed.; I
Mater Christi Seminary Albany, N.Y.; 1954; P.; men; I
Mater Dei C. Ogdensburg, N.Y.; 1960; P.; women; C
Mattatuck C.C. Waterbury, Conn.; 1967; S.; coed.; I
Maui C.C. Kahului, Hawaii; 1931; S.; coed.; I
Mauna Olu C. Paia, Hawaii; 1861; P.; coed.; I
McCook C. McCook, Nebr.; 1926; Dist.; coed.; I
McDowell Technical Institute Marion, N.C.; 1964; S. & Co.; coed.; I
McHenry County C. Crystal Lake, Ill.; 1967; Dist.; coed.; I
McIntosh C. Dover, N.H.; 1896; P.; coed.; I
McLennan C.C. Waco, Tex.; 1966; Co.; coed.; I
Memphis, State Technical Institute at Memphis, Tenn.; 1967; S.; coed.; I
Meramec C.C.* Kirkwood, Mo.; 1964; Dist.; coed.; I
Merced C. Merced, Calif.; 1962; Dist.; coed.; I
Mercer County C.C. Trenton, N.J.; 1966; Co.; coed.; I
Mercy J.C. St. Louis, Mo.; 1952; P.; women; I
Meridian J.C. Meridian, Miss.; 1937; S.; coed.; I
Merritt C.* Oakland, Calif.; 1953; Dist.; coed.; I
Mesabi State J.C. Virginia, Minn.; 1966; S.; coed.; I
Mesa C. Grand Junction, Colo.; 1925; Co.; coed.; I
Mesa C.C. Mesa, Ariz.; 1965; Co.; coed.; I
Metropolitan J.C.* Kansas City, Mo.; 1915; Dist.; coed.; I
Metropolitan State J.C. Minneapolis, Minn.; 1965; S.; coed.; I
Miami-Dade J.C.** Miami, Fla.; 1960; S. & Co.; coed.; I
Miami-Jacobs J.C. of Business Dayton, Ohio; 1860; P.; coed.; I
Michigan Christian J.C. Rochester, Mich.; 1959; P.; coed.; I
Middle Georgia C. Cochran, Ga.; 1887; S.; coed.; I
Middlesex C. Stowe, Vt.; 1964; P.; coed.; 3-yr. non-degree-granting program
Middlesex C.C. Center Middletown, Conn.; 1966; Dist.; coed.; I
Middlesex County C. Edison, N.J.; 1964; S. & Co.; coed.; I
Mid Michigan C.C. Harrison, Mich.; 1965; Dist.; coed.; I
Midway J.C. Midway, Ky.; 1849; P.; women; I
Midwestern C. Fort Wayne, Ind.; 1956; P.; men; I
Midwest Montessori Teacher Training Center Chicago, Ill.; 1963; P.; coed.; D
Miles C.C. Miles City, Mont.; 1939; Co.; coed.; I
Milwaukee Technical C.* Milwaukee, Wis.; 1934; Mun.; coed.; I
Mineral Area C. Flat River, Mo.; 1922; Dist.; coed.; I
Mira Costa C. Oceanside, Calif.; 1934; S.; coed.; I
Missionary Aviation Institute Glendale, Ariz.; 1965; P.; coed.; I
Mississippi Delta J.C. Moorhead, Miss.; 1926; S.; coed.; I
Missouri Baptist C. Hannibal, Mo.; 1858; P.; coed.; I
Mitchell C. New London, Conn.; 1938; P.; coed.; I
Mitchell C. Statesville, N.C.; 1853; P.; coed.; I
Moberly J.C. Moberly, Mo.; 1927; Mun.; coed.; I
Mobile State J.C. Mobile, Ala.; 1965; S.; coed.; I
Modesto J.C.* Modesto, Calif.; 1921; Dist.; coed.; I
Mohawk Valley C.C. Utica, N.Y.; 1946; S. & Co.; coed.; I
Monroe C.C.* Rochester, N.Y.; 1961; S. & Co.; coed.; I
Monroe County C.C. Monroe, Mich.; 1964; Co.; coed.; I
Montcalm C.C. Sidney, Mich.; 1965; Dist.; coed.; I

Monterey Peninsula C. Monterey, Calif.; 1947; Dist.; coed.; I
Montgomery County C.C. Conshohocken, Pa.; 1964; S. & Co.; coed.; I
Montgomery J.C. Takoma Park & Rockville, Md.; 1946; Co.; coed.; I
Montgomery Technical Institute Troy, N.C.; 1967; S.; coed.; I
Monticello C. Godfrey, Ill.; 1835; P.; women; I
Montreat-Anderson C. Montreat, N.C.; 1916; P.; coed.; I
Moorpark C. Moorpark, Calif.; 1967; Dist.; coed.; I
Moraine Valley C.C. Palos Hills, Ill.; 1967; S.; coed.; I
Morris, County C. of Dover, N.J.; 1965; Co.; coed.; I
Morristown C. Morristown, Tenn.; 1881; P.; coed.; I
Morse C. Hartford, Conn.; 1860; P.; coed.; D
Morton J.C. Cicero, Ill.; 1924; Dist.; coed.; I
Motlow State C.C. Tullahoma, Tenn.; 1969; S.; coed.; I
Mt. Aloysius J.C. Cresson, Pa.; 1939; P.; women; I
Mt. Hood C.C.* Gresham, Oreg.; 1964; S.; coed.; I
Mt. Ida J.C. Newton Centre, Mass.; 1899; P.; women; I
Mt. Olive J.C. Mount Olive, N.C.; 1951; P.; coed.; I
Mt. Providence J.C. Baltimore, Md.; 1963; P.; women; I
Mt. Sacred Heart C. Hamden, Conn.; 1954; P.; women; I
Mt. San Antonio C.* Walnut, Calif.; 1946; Dist.; coed.; I
Mt. San Jacinto J.C. Gilman Hot Springs, Calif.; 1961; S. & Dist.; coed.; I
Mt. St. Clare C. Clinton, Iowa; 1928; P.; coed.; I
Mt. St. Mary C. North Plainfield, N.J.; 1965; P.; women; I
Mt. Vernon J.C. Washington, D.C.; 1875; P.; women; I
Mt. Vernon Nazarene C. Mt. Vernon, Ohio; 1966; P.; coed.; I
Mt. Wachusett C.C. Gardner, Mass.; 1963; S.; coed.; I
Multnomah C. Portland, Oreg.; 1897; P.; coed.; I
Murray State C. Tishomingo, Okla.; 1908; S.; coed.; I
Muskegon Business C. Muskegon, Mich.; 1885; P.; coed.; I
Muskegon County C.C.* Muskegon, Mich.; 1926; Co.; coed.; I

Napa C. Napa, Calif.; 1942; Dist.; coed.; I
Nassau C.C.* Garden City, N.Y.; 1959; Co.; coed.; I
Natchez J.C. Natchez, Miss.; 1952; P.; coed.; I
National Business C. Roanoke, Va.; 1886; P.; coed.; I
National Technical Schools Los Angeles, Calif.; 1905; P.; men; I
Navarro J.C. Corsicana, Tex.; 1946; Co.; coed.; I
Neosho County Community J.C. Chanute, Kans.; 1936; Co.; coed.; I
Nevada C.C. Elko, Nev.; 1967; Dist.; coed.; I
New England Aeronautical Institute Nashua, N.H.; 1965; P.; coed.; I
New Hampshire Technical Institute Concord, N.H.; 1961; S.; coed.; I
New Hampshire Vocational Institute Berlin, N.H.; 1966; S.; coed.; I
New Hampshire Vocational Institute Claremont, N.H.; 1967; S.; coed.; I
New Hampshire Vocational Institute Laconia, N.H.; 1965; S.; coed.; I
New Hampshire Vocational Institute Manchester, N.H.; 1945; S.; coed.; I
New Hampshire Vocational Institute Portsmouth, N.H.; 1945; S.; coed.; I
New Mexico J.C. Hobbs, N.Mex.; 1965; Dist.; coed.; I
New Mexico Military Institute Roswell, N.Mex.; 1891; S.; men; I
New River Vocational Technical School Radford, Va.; 1967; S.; coed.; I
Newton J.C. Newtonville, Mass.; 1946; Mun.; coed.; I
New York Agricultural & Technical C., State U. of Alfred, 1908; Canton, 1907; Cobleskill, 1948; Delhi, 1915; Farmingdale, 1912; Morrisville, 1908; S.; coed.; I
New York City C.C.* Brooklyn; 1946; coed.; I: part of The City U. of NEW YORK
Niagara County C.C. Niagara Falls, N.Y.; 1962; S. & Co.; coed.; I: branches—Lockport, Tonawanda
Norfolk J.C. Norfolk, Nebr.; 1928; Dist.; coed.; I
Norman C. Norman Park, Ga.; 1900; P.; coed.; I
Normandale State J.C. Bloomington, Minn.; 1968; S.; coed.; I
North American Technical Institute Albuquerque, N.Mex.; 1958; P.; coed.; I
Northampton Commercial C. Northampton, Mass.; 1896; P.; coed.; I
Northampton County Area C.C. Bethlehem, Pa.; 1966; S. & Dist.; coed.; I
North Central Michigan C. Petoskey, Mich.; 1958; Co.; coed.; I
North Central Technical Institute Wausau, Wis.; 1911; Dist.; coed.; I
North Country C.C. Saranac Lake, N.Y.; 1967; Dist.; coed.; I
North Dakota School of Forestry Bottineau, N.Dak.; 1906; S.; coed.; I
North Dakota State School of Science Wahpeton, N.Dak.; 1903; S.; coed.; I
Northeast Alabama State J.C. Rainsville, Ala.; 1965; S.; coed.; I

Northeastern Christian J.C. Villanova, Pa.; 1959; P.; coed.; I
Northeastern J.C. Sterling, Colo.; 1941; Co.; coed.; I
Northeastern Oklahoma A & M C. Miami, Okla.; 1919; S.; coed.; I
Northeast Mississippi J.C., The Booneville, Miss.; 1948; Dist.; coed.; I
Northern C.C. Covington; 1948; I: *see* U. of KENTUCKY
Northern Essex C.C. Haverhill, Mass.; 1960; S.; coed.; I
Northern Oklahoma C. Tonkawa, Okla.; 1901; S.; coed.; I
Northern Virginia C.C.* Annandale, Va.; 1965; S.; coed.; I
Northern Wyoming C.C. Sheridan, Wyo.; 1948; Dist.; coed.; I
North Florida J. C. Madison, Fla.; 1958; S.; coed.; I
North Greenville J.C. Tigerville, S.C.; 1892; P.; coed.; I
North Hennepin State J.C. Osseo, Minn.; 1966; S.; coed.; I
North Idaho J.C. Coeur d'Alene, Ida.; 1939; Dist.; coed.; I
North Iowa Area C.C. Mason City, Iowa; 1918; Dist.; coed.; I
Northland State J.C. Thief River Falls, Minn.; 1965; S.; coed.; I
North Platte C. North Platte, Nebr.; 1965; Dist.; coed.; I
North Shore C.C. Beverly, Mass.; 1965; S.; coed.; I
Northwest Alabama State J.C. Phil Campbell, Ala.; 1961; S.; coed.; I
Northwest C.C. Powell, Wyo.; 1947; Dist.; coed.; I
Northwestern C. Minneapolis, Minn.; 1902; P.; coed.; I
Northwestern Connecticut C.C. Winsted, Conn.; 1965; S.; coed.; I
Northwestern Michigan C. Traverse City, Mich.; 1951; S.; coed.; I
Northwest Mississippi J.C. Senatobia, Miss.; 1927; S.; coed.; I
Northwood Institute of Michigan Midland, Mich.; 1959; P.; coed.; I: branches—Alma, Mich.; West Baden, Ind.; Cedar Hills, Tex.
Norwalk C.C. Norwalk, Conn.; 1961; S.; coed.; I
Norwalk State Technical C. Norwalk, Conn.; 1961; S.; coed.; I

Oakland C.C.* Bloomfield Hills, Mich.; 1964; Dist.; coed.; I
Ocean County C. Toms River, N.J.; 1964; Co.; coed.; I
Odessa C. Odessa, Tex.; 1946; Co.; coed.; I
Ohio C. of Applied Science Cincinnati, Ohio; 1828; P.; coed.; I
Ohio Technical C. Columbus, Ohio; 1952; P.; coed.; I
Ohio Valley C. Parkersburg, W.Va.; 1959; P.; coed.; I
Ohlone C. Fremont, Calif.; 1966; Dist.; coed.; I
Okaloosa-Walton J.C. Valparaiso, Fla.; 1963; Co.; coed.; I
Oklahoma Military Academy Claremore, Okla.; 1909; S.; men; I
Oklahoma School of Business, Accountancy, Law, & Finance Tulsa, Okla.; 1919; P.; coed.; I
Olney Central C. Olney, Ill.; 1963; Dist.; coed.; I
Olympic C. Bremerton, Wash.; 1946; S.; coed.; I
Onondaga C.C. Syracuse, N.Y.; 1962; Co.; coed.; I
Onslow Technical Institute Jacksonville, N.C.; 1963; Co., coed.; I
Orangeburg-Calhoun Technical Education Center Orangeburg, S.C.; 1968; S. & Co.; coed.; I
Orange Coast C.* Costa Mesa, Calif.; 1948; Dist.; coed.; I
Orange County C.C.* Middletown, N.Y.; 1950; S.; coed.; I
Orlando J.C. Orlando, Fla.; 1941; P.; coed.; I
Oshkosh Technical Institute Oshkosh, Wis.; 1957; S.; coed.; I
Otero J.C. La Junta, Colo.; 1941; S.; coed.; I
Ottumwa Heights C. Ottumwa, Iowa; 1925; P.; coed.; I
Our Lady of Hope Mission Seminary Newburgh, N.Y.; 1946; P.; men; I
Our Lady of the Angels J.C. Enfield, Conn.; 1945; P.; women; I
Outagamie County Teachers C. Kaukauna, Wis.; 1912; S. & Co.; coed.; I

Packer Collegiate Institute, J.C. of the Brooklyn, N.Y.; 1845; P.; women; I
Paducah J.C. Paducah, Ky.; 1932; S.; coed.; I
Palm Beach J.C.* Lake Worth, Fla.; 1933; Co.; coed.; I
Palmer C. Charleston, S.C.; 1954; P.; coed.; I
Palmer J.C. Davenport, Iowa; 1965; P.; coed.; I
Palomar C.* San Marcos, Calif.; 1946; Dist.; coed.; I
Palo Verde C. Blythe, Calif.; 1947; S.; coed.; I
Panola J.C. Carthage, Tex.; 1947; Co.; coed.; I
Paris J.C. Paris, Tex.; 1924; S.; coed.; I
Parkland C. Champaign, Ill.; 1966; Dist.; coed.; I
Pasadena City C.** Pasadena, Calif.; 1924; S.; coed.; I
Patrick Henry State J.C. Monroeville, Ala.; 1965; S.; coed.; I
Paul Smith's C. of Arts & Sciences Paul Smiths, N.Y.; 1937; P.; coed.; I
Peace C. Raleigh, N.C.; 1857; P.; women; I
Pearl River J.C. Poplarville, Miss.; 1922; Dist.; coed.; I

Peirce J.C. Philadelphia, Pa.; 1865; P.; coed.; I
Peninsula C. Port Angeles, Wash.; 1961; S.; coed.; I
Penn Hall J.C. Chambersburg, Pa.; 1906; P.; women; I
Pennsylvania Institute of Technology Upper Darby, Pa.; 1953; P.; coed.; I
Pensacola J.C.* Pensacola, Fla.; 1948; Dist.; coed.; I
Penta County Technical Institute Perrysburg, Ohio; 1965; S.; coed.; I: branch—Lima
Perkinston C. Perkinston, Miss.; 1914; Dist.; coed.; I
Perry Normal School, Inc. Boston, Mass.; 1898; P.; women; 3-yr. D
Philadelphia, C.C. of Philadelphia, Pa.; 1964; S. & Mun.; coed.; I
Phillips County C.C. Helena, Ark.; 1965; Dist.; coed.; I
Phoenix C.* Phoenix, Ariz.; 1920; Co.; coed.; I
Piedmont Technical Education Center Greenwood, S.C.; 1966; S. & Co.; coed.; I
Pine Manor J.C. Chestnut Hill, Mass.; 1911; P.; women; I
Piney Woods School Piney Woods, Miss.; 1915; P.; coed.; I
Pitt Technical Institute Greenville, N.C.; 1961; S. & Co.; coed.; I
Platte C. Columbus, Nebr.; 1967; Co.; coed.; I
Polk County Teachers C. Frederic, Wis.; 1905; S. & Co.; coed.; C
Polk J.C. Winter Haven, Fla.; 1964; S.; coed.; I
Porterville C. Porterville, Calif.; 1927; Dist.; coed.; I
Portland C.C.** Portland, Oreg.; 1961; Dist.; coed.; I
Post J.C. Waterbury, Conn.; 1890; P.; coed.; I
Poteau Community J.C. Poteau, Okla.; 1933; Mun. & Dist.; coed.; I
Potomac State C. of West Virginia U. Keyser, W.Va.; 1901; S.; coed.; I: under direction of West Virginia U.
Prairie State C. Chicago Heights, Ill.; 1958; Dist.; coed.; I
Pratt Community J.C. Pratt, Kans.; 1938; Dist.; coed.; I
Prentiss Institute Prentiss, Miss.; 1931; P.; coed.; C
Presentation C. Aberdeen, S.Dak.; 1951; P.; coed.; I
Presentation J.C. of the Sacred Heart Newburgh, N.Y.; 1953; P.; women; I
Prestonsburg C.C. Prestonsburg; 1964; I: *see* U. of KENTUCKY
Prince George's C.C.* Largo, Md.; 1958; Co.; coed.; I
Puerto Rico J.C. Rio Piedras, P.R.; 1949; P.; coed.; I

Queensborough C.C.* Bayside (Long Island); 1958; coed.; I: part of The City U. of NEW YORK
Quincy J.C. Quincy, Mass.; 1958; Mun.; coed.; I
Quinsigamond C.C. Worcester, Mass.; 1963; S.; coed.; I

Racine-Kenosha County Teachers C. Union Grove, Wis.; 1916; S. & Co.; coed.; D
Rainy River State J.C. International Falls, Minn.; 1967; S.; coed.; I
Randolph Technical Institute Asheboro, N.C.; 1962; S. & Co.; coed.; I
Rangely C. Rangely, Colo.; 1960; Dist.; coed.; I
Ranger J.C. Ranger, Tex.; 1926; S. & Mun.; 1926; coed.; I
Reedley C. Reedley, Calif.; 1926; Dist.; coed.; I
Reinhardt C. Waleska, Ga.; 1883; P.; coed.; I
Rend Lake C. Mt. Vernon, Ill.; 1956; S.; coed.; I
Rhode Island J.C. Providence, R.I.; 1964; S.; coed.; I
Richard Bland C. Petersburg; 1961; I: J.C. branch of C. of WILLIAM & MARY
Richland Technical Education Center Columbia, S.C.; 1962; S.; coed.; I
Richmond Technical Institute Hamlet, N.C.; 1964; S. & Co.; coed.; I
Ricks C.* Rexburg, Ida.; 1888; P.; coed.; I
Rio Hondo J.C.* Whittier, Calif.; 1960; S. & Dist.; coed.; I
Riverside City C. Riverside, Calif.; 1916; Dist.; coed.; I
Robert Morris C. Carthage, Ill.; 1965; P.; coed.; I
Robert Morris J.C. Coraopolis, Pa.; 1921; P.; coed.; I
Rochester State J.C. Rochester, Minn.; 1915; S.; coed.; I
Rockingham C.C. Wentworth, N.C.; 1966; Co.; coed.; I
Rockland C.C. Suffern, N.Y.; 1959; S. & Co.; coed.; I
Rock Valley C. Rockford, Ill.; 1964; Dist.; coed.; I
Rowan Technical Institute Salisbury, N.C.; 1962; S.; coed.; I

Sacramento City C.* Sacramento, Calif.; 1916; Dist.; coed.; I
Sacred Heart C. Cullman, Ala.; 1941; P.; women; I
Sacred Heart J.C. Fargo, N.Dak.; 1943; P.; women; I
Sacred Heart J.C. Yardley, Pa.; 1962; P.; women; I
Saddleback C. Mission Viejo, Calif.; 1967; Dist.; coed.; I
Saints J.C. Lexington, Miss.; 1918; P.; coed.; I
Salem Technical Vocational C.C. Salem, Oreg.; 1925; Dist.; coed.; I
Salesian C. Paterson, N.J.; 1948; P.; women; I
San Antonio C.** San Antonio, Tex.; 1925; S.; coed.; I
San Bernardino Valley C.** San Bernardino, Calif.; 1926; S.; coed.; I
Sandhills C.C. Southern Pines, N.C.; 1963; S.; coed.; I
San Diego Junior Colleges San Diego, Calif.; Dist.; coed.; I: administrative unit for—**San Diego City C.** 1914; **San Diego Evening C.** 1962; **San Diego Mesa C.*** 1963

San Francisco, City C. of* San Francisco, Calif.; 1935; Mun.; coed.; I
San Francisco C. of Mortuary Science San Francisco, Calif.; 1930; P.; coed.; I
San Jacinto C.* Pasadena, Tex.; 1960; S.; coed.; I
San Joaquin Delta C.* Stockton, Calif.; 1963; Dist.; coed.; I
San Jose City C.* San Jose, Calif.; 1921; S.; coed.; I
San Mateo, C. of** San Mateo, Calif.; 1924; Co.; coed.; I
Santa Ana C. Santa Ana, Calif.; 1915; S. & Mun.; coed.; I
Santa Barbara City C. Santa Barbara, Calif.; 1911; Dist.; coed.; I
Santa Fe J.C. Gainesville, Fla.; 1965; Dist.; coed.; I
Santa Monica City C.* Santa Monica, Calif.; 1929; Dist.; coed.; I
Santa Rosa J.C.* Santa Rosa, Calif.; 1918; Dist.; coed.; I
Sauk County Teachers C. Reedsburg, Wis.; 1906; S. & Co.; coed.; D
Sauk Valley C. Dixon, Ill.; 1965; S.; coed.; I
Sayre J.C. Sayre, Okla.; 1938; Mun.; coed.; I
Schoolcraft C.* Livonia, Mich.; 1961; Dist.; coed.; I
Schreiner Institute Kerrville, Tex.; 1923; P.; men; I
Scotts Bluff County C. Scottsbluff, Nebr.; 1932; Co.; coed.; I
Seattle C.C.** Seattle, Wash.; 1966; S.; coed.; I
Seminole J.C. Sanford, Fla.; 1966; S.; coed.; I
Seminole J.C. Seminole, Okla.; 1931; Dist.; coed.; I
Sequoias, C. of the Visalia, Calif.; 1925; Dist.; coed.; I
Shasta C. Redding, Calif.; 1950; Dist.; coed.; I
Shawnee C.C. Karnak, Ill.; 1967; Dist.; coed.; I
Sheboygan County Teachers C. Sheboygan Falls, Wis.; 1921; S. & Co.; coed.; D
Sheldon Jackson C. Sitka, Alas.; 1944; P.; coed.; I
Shoreline C.C. Seattle, Wash.; 1964; S.; coed.; I
Shorter C. North Little Rock, Ark.; 1885; P.; coed.; I
Sierra C. Rocklin, Calif.; 1935; Dist.; coed.; I
Silvermine C. of Art New Canaan, Conn.; 1960; P.; coed.; I
Sinclair C.C. Dayton, Ohio; 1966; S.; coed.; I
Sioux Empire C. Hawarden, Iowa; 1965; P.; coed.; I
Siskiyous, C. of the Weed, Calif.; 1957; Dist.; coed.; I
Sitka C.C. Sitka, Alas.; 1962; S.; coed.; I
Skagit Valley C. Mt. Vernon, Wash.; 1926; S.; coed.; I
Snead State J.C. Boaz, Ala.; 1935; S.; coed.; I
Snow C. Ephraim; 1888; coed.; I: branch of Utah State U.
Solano C.* Vallejo, Calif.; 1945; S.; coed.; I
Somerset C.C. Somerset; 1965; I: see U. of KENTUCKY
Somerset County C. Green Brook, N.J.; 1966; Co.; coed.; I
South Central C.C. New Haven, Conn.; 1967; S.; coed.; I
Southeast C.C. Cumberland; 1960; I: see U. of KENTUCKY
Southeastern Baptist C. Laurel, Miss.; 1947; P.; coed.; I
Southeastern Christian C. Winchester, Ky.; 1949; P.; coed.; I
Southeastern C.C. Whiteville, N.C.; 1964; S.; coed.; I
Southeastern Illinois C. Harrisburg, Ill.; 1960; Dist.; coed.; I
Southeastern Iowa Area C.C. Burlington, Iowa; 1967; Dist.; coed.; I: ext. centers—Keokuk, Mt. Pleasant
Southern Baptist C. Walnut Ridge, Ark.; 1941; P.; coed.; I
Southern Idaho, C. of Twin Falls, Ida.; 1965; Dist.; coed.; I
Southern Maine Vocational Technical Institute South Portland, Me.; 1946; S.; coed.; I
Southern Seminary J.C. Buena Vista, Va.; 1867; P.; women; I
Southern Technical Institute Marietta, Ga.; 1948; S.; coed.; I
Southern Union State J.C. Wadley, Ala.; 1922; S.; coed.; I
South Florida J.C. Avon Park, Fla.; 1965; S.; coed.; I
South Georgia C. Douglas, Ga.; 1908; S.; coed.; I
South Plains C. Levelland, Tex.; 1957; S.; coed.; I
South Texas J.C.* Houston, Tex.; 1948; P.; coed.; I
Southwestern Christian C. Terrell, Tex.; 1948; P.; coed.; I
Southwestern C.* Chula Vista, Calif.; 1961; S.; coed.; I
Southwestern C. Oklahoma City, Okla.; 1946; P.; coed.; I
Southwestern C.C. Creston, Iowa; 1966; S.; coed.; I
Southwestern Michigan C. Dowagiac, Mich.; 1964; Co.; coed.; I
Southwestern Oregon C.C.* Coos Bay, Oreg.; 1961; S.; coed.; I
Southwest Mississippi J.C. Summit, Miss.; 1918; Dist.; coed.; I
Southwest Texas J.C. Uvalde, Tex.; 1946; S.; coed.; I
Southwest Virginia C.C. Richlands, Va.; 1967; S.; coed.; I
Southwood C. Salemburg, N.C.; 1875; P.; coed.; I
Sowela Technical Institute Lake Charles, La.; 1938; S.; coed.; I
Spartanburg County Technical Education Center Spartanburg, S.C.; 1961; S. & Co.; coed.; I
Spartanburg J.C. Spartanburg, S.C.; 1911; P.; coed.; I
Spokane C.C.* Spokane, Wash.; 1963; S.; coed.; I
Spoon River J.C. Canton, Ill.; 1959; S.; coed.; I
Springfield J.C. Springfield, Ill.; 1929; P.; coed.; I
Springfield Technical C.C. Springfield, Mass.; 1964; S.; coed.; I

Spring Garden Institute Philadelphia, Pa.; 1850; P.; coed.; I
State Fair C.C. Sedalia, Mo.; 1966; Dist.; coed.; I
Staten Island C.C.* Staten Island; 1955; coed.; I: part of The City U. of NEW YORK
St. Catharine C. St. Catharine, Ky.; 1931; P.; coed.; I
St. Clair County C.C. Port Huron, Mich.; 1923; Co.; coed.; I
St. Clare C. Williamsville, N.Y.; 1957; P.; women; I
Stevens Henager C. Salt Lake City, Utah; 1907; P.; coed.; I
St. Gertrude, C. of Cottonwood, Ida.; 1956; P.; coed.; I
St. Gregory's C. Shawnee, Okla.; 1875; P.; coed.; I
St. John's C. Winfield, Kans.; 1893; P.; coed.; I
St. Johns River J.C. Palatka, Fla.; 1958; S. & Co.; coed.; I·
St. John Vianney Minor Seminary Miami, Fla.; 1961; P.; men; I
St. Joseph C. Old Bennington, Vt.; 1962; P.; coed.; I
St. Joseph C. of Florida Jensen Beach, Fla.; 1890; P.; coed.; I·
St. Joseph J.C. Tipton, Ind.; 1960; P.; women; I
St. Joseph's C. Princeton, N.J.; 1914; P.; men; I
St. Lawrence Seminary Mt. Calvary, Wis.; 1860; P.; men; I
St. Mary's C. of O'Fallon O'Fallon, Mo.; 1921; P.; coed.; I
St. Mary's J.C. Minneapolis, Minn.; 1964; P.; coed.; I
St. Mary's J.C. Raleigh, N.C.; 1842; P.; women; I
St. Paul's C. Concordia, Mo.; 1883; P.; coed.; I
St. Petersburg J.C.* St. Petersburg & Clearwater, Fla.; 1927; Co.; coed.; I
Strayer J.C. Washington, D.C.; 1904; P.; coed.; I
St. Thomas Seminary Bloomfield, Conn.; 1897; P.; men; I
Sue Bennett C. London, Ky.; 1896; P.; coed.; I
Suffolk County C.C.* Selden, N.Y.; 1959; Co.; coed.; I
Sullins C. Bristol, Va.; 1870; P.; women; I
Sullivan County C.C. South Fallsburg, N.Y.; 1963; S. & Co.; coed.; I
Sumter Area Technical Education Center Sumter, S.C.; 1963; S.; coed.; I
Suomi C. Hancock, Mich.; 1896; P.; coed.; I
Surry C.C. Dobson, N.C.; 1965; S.; coed.; I

Tacoma C.C. Tacoma, Wash.; 1963; S.; coed.; I
Taft C. Taft, Calif.; 1922; Dist.; coed.; I
Tallahassee J.C. Tallahassee, Fla.; 1965; Dist.; coed.; I
Tampa C. Tampa, Fla.; 1890; P.; coed.; I
Tarrant County J.C.* Fort Worth, Tex.; 1965; Dist.; coed.; I
Taylor County Teachers C. Medford, Wis.; 1911; S. & Co.; coed.; I
Temple J.C. Temple, Tex.; 1926; S.; coed.; I
Texarkana C. Texarkana, Tex.; 1927; S.; coed.; I
Texas Southmost C. Brownsville, Tex.; 1926; S. & Co.; coed.; I
Thames Valley State Technical C. Norwich, Conn.; 1963; S.; coed.; I
Thomas Nelson C.C. Hampton, Va.; 1967; S.; coed.; I
Thornton J.C. Harvey, Ill.; 1927; Dist.; coed.; I
Three Rivers J.C. Poplar Bluff, Mo.; 1967; Dist.; coed.; I
T. J. Harris J.C. Meridian, Miss.; 1956; Mun.; coed.; I
Tombrock C. West Paterson, N.J.; 1956; P.; women; I
Tomlinson C. Cleveland, Tenn.; 1966; P.; coed.; I
Tompkins-Cortland C.C. Groton, N.Y.; 1967; Co.; coed.; I
Treasure Valley C.C. Ontario, Oreg.; 1962; Dist.; coed.; I
Trenton J.C. Trenton, Mo.; 1925; Dist.; coed.; I
Tri-County Technical Education Center Pendleton, S.C.; 1968; S. & Co.; coed.; I
Trinidad State J.C. Trinidad, Colo.; 1925; S.; coed.; I
Trinitarian C. Baltimore, Md.; 1956; P.; men; I
Triton C. Northlake, Ill.; 1964; Dist.; coed.; I
Trocaire C. Buffalo, N.Y.; 1958; P.; women; I
Truett McConnell C. Cleveland, Ga.; 1946; P.; coed.; I
Tyler J.C.* Tyler, Tex.; 1926; Dist.; coed.; I

Ulster County C.C. Stone Ridge, N.Y.; 1961; Co.; coed.; I
Umpqua C.C. Roseburg, Oreg.; 1964; Co.; coed.; I
Union C. Cranford, N.J.; 1933; P.; coed.; I
Utah Technical C. at Provo* Provo, Utah; 1941; S.; coed.; I
Utah Technical C. at Salt Lake Salt Lake City, Utah; 1947; S.; coed.; I
Utica J.C. Utica, Miss.; 1954; Dist.; coed.; I

Valencia J.C. Orlando, Fla.; 1967; S. & Co.; coed.; I
Valley Forge Military C. Wayne, Pa.; 1934; P.; men; I
Vardell Hall J.C. Red Springs, N.C.; 1964; P.; women; I
Ventura C.* Ventura, Calif.; 1929; Dist.; coed.; I
Vermilion State J.C. Ely, Minn.; 1922; S.; coed.; I
Vermont Technical C. Randolph Center, Vt.; 1957; S.; coed.; I
Vernon County Teachers C. Viroqua, Wis.; 1907; S. & Co.; coed.; D
Victoria C., The Victoria, Tex.; 1926; Dist.; coed.; I

Victor Valley C. Victorville, Calif.; 1961; Dist.; coed.; I
Villa Julie C. Stevenson, Md.; 1952; P.; women; I
Villa Maria C. of Buffalo Buffalo, N.Y.; 1960; P.; women; I
Villa Walsh C. Morristown, N.J.; 1928; P.; women; I
Vincennes U. Vincennes, Ind.; 1801; Co.; coed.; I
Virginia Highlands C.C. Abingdon, Va.; 1968; S.; coed.; I
Virginia Intermont C. Bristol, Va.; 1884; P.; women; I
Virginia Southern C. Roanoke, Va.; 1933; P.; coed.; I
Virginia Western C.C. Roanoke, Va.; 1966; S.; coed.; I
Voorhees Technical Institute New York, N.Y.; 1881; P.; coed.; I

Wabash Valley C. Mt. Carmel, Ill.; 1960; Dist.; coed.; I
Waldorf C. Forest City, Iowa; 1903; P.; coed.; I
Walker C. Jasper, Ala.; 1938; P.; coed.; I
Walla Walla C.C. Walla Walla, Wash.; 1967; S.; coed.; I
Ward Technical Institute Hartford, Conn.; 1948; P.; men; I: division of U. of Hartford
Washington County Technical School Abingdon, Va.; 1938; Co.; coed.; C & D
Washington Technical Institute Washington, D.C.; 1966; Fed.; coed.; I
Washtenaw C.C. Ann Arbor, Mich.; 1965; Co.; coed.; I
Waterbury State Technical C. Waterbury, Conn.; 1964; S.; coed.; I
Waubonsee C.C. Aurora, Ill.; 1966; Dist.; coed.; I
Waukesha County Technical Institute Waukesha, Wis.; 1963; Co.; coed.; I
Waushara County Teachers C. Wautoma, Wis.; 1908; S. & Co.; coed.; C
Wayne C.C. Goldsboro, N.C.; 1957; S.; coed.; I
Weatherford C. Weatherford, Tex.; 1869; Co.; coed.; I
Wenatchee Valley C.C. Wenatchee, Wash.; 1939; S.; coed.; I
Wenonah State J.C. Birmingham, Ala.; 1963; S.; coed.; I
Wentworth Institute Boston, Mass.; 1904; P.; men; I
Wentworth Military Academy J.C. Lexington, Mo.; 1880; P.; men; I
Wesley C. Dover, Del.; 1873; P.; coed.; I
Westark J.C. Fort Smith, Ark.; 1928; Co.; coed.; I
Westbrook J.C. Portland, Me.; 1831; P.; women; I, II
Westchester C.C.* Valhalla, N.Y.; 1946; S. & Co.; coed.; I
Western Iowa Technical C. Sioux City, Iowa; 1966; Dist.; coed.; I

Western Piedmont C.C. Morganton, N.C.; 1964; S.; coed.; I
Western Wyoming C. Rock Springs, Wyo.; 1959; Dist.; coed.; I
West Los Angeles C. Culver City, Calif.; 1969; Dist.; coed.; I
West Shore C.C. Scottville, Mich.; 1967; Dist.; coed.; I
West Valley Joint J.C.* Campbell, Calif.; 1963; Dist.; coed.; I
Wharton County J.C. Wharton, Tex.; 1946; S.; coed.; I
White Pines C. Chester, N.H.; 1965; P.; coed.; I
Wilkes C.C. Wilkesboro, N.C.; 1964; S.; coed.; I
William Rainey Harper C.* Elk Grove, Ill.; 1965; S. & Dist.; coed.; I
Williamsport Area C.C., The Williamsport, Pa.; 1965; S.; coed.; I
Willmar State J.C. Willmar, Minn.; 1962; S.; coed.; I
Wilson County Technical Institute Wilson, N.C.; 1958; S.; coed.; I
Wingate C. Wingate, N.C.; 1896; P.; coed.; I
Winston Churchill C. Pontiac, Ill.; 1965; P.; coed.; I
Wisconsin, U. of 2-yr. extension centers at Green Bay, Janesville, Kenosha, Manitowoc, Marinette, Marshfield, Menasha, Milwaukee, Racine, Sheboygan, & Wausau
Wisconsin School of Electronics Madison, Wis.; 1948; P.; men; I
W.L. Yancey State J.C. Bay Minette, Ala.; 1965; S.; coed.; I
Wood J.C. Mathiston, Miss.; 1936; P.; coed.; I
Worcester J.C. Worcester, Mass.; 1938; P.; coed.; I
Worthington State J.C. Worthington, Minn.; 1936; S.; coed.; I
W.W. Holding Technical Institute Raleigh, N.C.; 1963; S.; coed.; I
Wytheville C.C. Wytheville, Va.; 1963; S.; coed.; I

Xaverian C. Silver Spring, Md.; 1931; P.; men; I

Yakima Valley C. Yakima, Wash.; 1928; S.; coed.; I
Yavapai C. Prescott, Ariz.; 1967; S.; coed.; I
York C. York, Nebr.; 1890; P.; coed.; I
York County Technical Education Center Rock Hill, S.C.; 1964; S. & Co.; coed.; I
Young Harris C. Young Harris, Ga.; 1886; P.; coed.; I
Yuba C. Marysville, Calif.; 1926; Dist.; coed.; I

CANADIAN COLLEGES AND UNIVERSITIES

Institutions conferring the bachelor's degree, an advanced degree, or a professional degree

Key: C., College; U., University; J.C., Junior College; P., Private; Prov., Provincial; Mun., Municipal; Fed., Federal: degrees offered—I, Associate; II, Bachelor's; III, Bachelor's & Master's; IV, Master's; V, Master's; V, Professional; VI, Ph.D.; VII, Bachelor's, Master's, Professional, & Ph.D.; D, diploma offered: enrollment, *3,000 to 8,000; **over 8,000

Acadia U. Wolfville, N.S.; 1839; P.; coed.; III, V
Alberta, The U. of** Edmonton, Alta.; 1906; Prov.; coed.; VII

Bishop's U. Lennoxville, Que.; 1843; P.; coed.; III, V
Brandon U. Brandon, Man.; 1899; Prov.; coed.; II
British Columbia, The U. of** Vancouver, B.C.; 1908; Prov.; coed.; VII
Brock U. St. Catharines, Ont.; 1963; Prov.; coed.; III

Calgary, The U. of* Calgary, Alta.; 1966; Prov.; coed.; VII
Canadian Union C. Lacombe, Alta.; 1907; P.; coed.; II
Carleton U.* Ottawa, Ont.; 1942; Prov.; coed.; VII, VI
Christ the King, Seminary of Mission City, B.C.; 1934; P.; men; II, V

Dalhousie U.* Halifax, N.S.; 1818; P.; coed.; VII

Guelph, U. of* Guelph, Ont.; 1964; P.; coed.; VII

Lakehead U. Port Arthur, Ont.; 1946; Prov.; coed.; III
Laurentian U. Sudbury, Ont.; 1960; Prov.; coed.; II
Laval, U.** Quebec, Que.; 1852; P.; coed.; VII
Lethbridge, U. of Lethbridge, Alta.; 1967; Prov.; coed.; II

Manitoba, The U. of** Winnipeg, Man.; 1877; Prov.; coed.; VII
McGill U.** Montreal, Que.; 1821; P.; coed.; VII
McMaster U.* Hamilton, Ont.; 1887; P.; coed.; VII
Moncton, U. de Moncton, N.B.; 1864; P.; coed.; III
Montréal, U. de** Montreal, Que.; 1919; P.; coed.; VII
Mt. Allison U. Sackville, N.B.; 1840; P.; coed.; III
Mt. Carmel C. Niagara Falls, Ont.; 1875; P.; men; II
Mt. St. Vincent U. Halifax, N.S.; 1925; P.; women; III

New Brunswick, The U. of* Fredericton, N.B.; 1785; Prov.; coed.; VII
Newfoundland, Memorial U. of* St. John's, Nfld.; 1949; Prov.; coed.; III, V

Notre Dame U. of Nelson Nelson, B.C.; 1950; P.; coed.; II

Ottawa, The U. of* Ottawa, Ont.; 1849; Prov.; coed.; VII

Philathea C. London, Ont.; 1935; P.; coed.; III, VI
Prince of Wales C. Charlottetown, P.E.I.; 1834; Prov.; coed.; II

Queen's U.* Kingston, Ont.; 1841; Prov.; coed.; VII

Royal Military C. of Canada Kingston, Ont.; 1876; Fed.; men; III, V

Saskatchewan, U. of** Saskatoon & Regina, Sask.; 1907; Prov.; coed.; VII
Sherbrooke, U. de* Sherbrooke, Que.; 1954; P.; coed.; VII
Simon Fraser U.* Burnaby, B.C.; 1963; Prov.; coed.; III, VI
Sir George Williams U.* Montreal, Que.; 1926; P.; coed.; III
St. Dunstan's U. Charlottetown, P.E.I.; 1855; P.; coed.; II
Ste-Anne, C. Church Point, N.S.; 1890; P.; coed.; II
St. Francis Xavier U. Antigonish, N.S.; 1853; P.; coed.;
St. Mary's U. Halifax, N.S.; 1841; P.; men; II

Toronto, U. of** Toronto, Ont.; 1827; Prov.; coed.; VII
Trent U. Peterborough, Ont.; 1963; P.; coed.; III, VI

Victoria, U. of* Victoria, B.C.; 1963; Prov.; coed.; III, VI

Waterloo, U. of* Waterloo, Ont.; 1957; P.; coed.; III, VI
Waterloo Lutheran U. Waterloo, Ont.; 1924; P.; coed.; III, V
Western Ontario, The U. of** London, Ont.; 1878; Prov.; coed.; VII
Windsor, U. of* Windsor, Ont.; 1857; Prov.; coed.; III, VI
Winnipeg, The U. of Winnipeg, Man.; 1871; Prov.; coed.; II

York U.* Toronto, Ont.; 1959; Prov.; coed.; VII

OTHER INSTITUTIONS OF HIGHER EDUCATION IN CANADA

This list includes technological institutes, junior colleges, and other schools offering pre-university level courses, as well as institutions federated or affiliated with a degree-granting university

Ahuntsic, C. d'* Montreal, Que.; 1967; Prov.; coed.: C.E.G.E.P.#
Algoma C. Sault Ste. Marie, Ont.; 1966; Prov.; coed.: affiliated with Laurentian U.
Algonquin C. of Applied Arts & Technology Ottawa, Ont.; 1967; Prov.; coed.; D
Anglican Theological C. of British Columbia Vancouver, B.C.; 1915; P.; coed.: affiliated with U. of British Columbia
Assomption, C. de l' L'Assomption, Que.; 1832; P.; coed.; II
Assumption U. Windsor, Ont.; 1857; P.; coed.: federated with U. of Windsor

Basile-Moreau, C. Montreal, Que.; 1955; P.; coed.; II
Bathurst, Le C. de Bathurst, N.B.; 1899; P.; coed.: affiliated with U. de Moncton
Bois-de-Boulogne, C. Montreal, Que.; 1968; Prov.; coed.: C.E.G.E.P.
Brescia C. London, Ont.; 1919; P.; women: affiliated with U. of Western Ontario
British Columbia Institute of Technology Burnaby, B.C.; 1964; Prov.; coed.; D

Cambrian C. of Applied Arts & Technology North Bay, Sault Ste. Marie, & Sudbury, Ont.; 1967; Prov.; coed.; D
Campion C. Regina, Sask.; 1924; Prov.; coed.: affiliated with U. of Saskatchewan
Camrose Lutheran C. Camrose, Alta.; 1959; P.; coed.: affiliated with U. of Alberta
Canadian Mennonite Bible C. Winnipeg, Man.; 1947; P.; coed.: affiliated with U. of Manitoba
Canterbury C. Windsor, Ont.; 1957; P.; coed.: affiliated with U. of Windsor
Centennial C. of Applied Arts & Technology Scarborough, Ont.; 1966; Prov.; coed.; D
Chicoutimi, C. de Chicoutimi, Que.; 1967; Prov.; coed.: C.E.G.E.P.
Concordia Lutheran C. Edmonton, Alta.; 1921; P.; coed.
Conestoga C. of Applied Arts & Technology Kitchener, Ont.; 1968; Prov.; coed.; D
Confederation C. of Applied Arts & Technology Fort William & Port Arthur, Ont.; 1967; Prov.; coed.; D

Durham C. of Applied Arts & Technology Oshawa, Ont.; 1966; Prov.; coed.; D

Edouard-Montpetit, C. d' Jacques-Cartier, Que.; 1968; Prov.; coed.: C.E.G.E.P.
Emmanuel C., U. of Saskatoon, Sask.; 1879; P.; coed.: affiliated with U. of Saskatchewan
Emmanuel C. of Victoria U. Toronto, Ont.; 1928; P.; coed.: part of Victoria U. & federated with U. of Toronto

Fanshawe C. of Applied Arts & Technology London, Ont.; 1967; Prov.; coed.; D
Fisheries, C. of St. John's, Nfld.; 1964; Prov.; coed.; D

Gaspé, Séminaire de Gaspé, Que.; 1926; P.; coed.: affiliated with U. Laval
Gaspésie, C. de la Gaspé, Que.; 1968; Prov.; coed.: C.E.G.E.P.
George Brown C. of Applied Arts & Technology* Toronto, Ont.; 1968; Prov.; coed.; D
Georgian C. of Applied Arts & Technology Barrie, Ont.; 1967; Prov.; coed.; D
Grande Prairie J.C. Grande Prairie, Alta.; 1965; Prov.; coed.: affiliated with U. of Alberta

Hauterive, C. de Hauterive, Que.; 1954; P.; coed.: affiliated with U. Laval
Hearst C. Hearst, Ont.; 1953; P.; coed.: affiliated with Laurentian U.
Holy Heart Seminary Halifax, N.S.; 1895; P.; coed.: affiliated with U. Laval
Hull, C. de Hull, Que.; 1967; Prov.; coed.: C.E.G.E.P.
Humber C. of Applied Arts & Technology Toronto, Ont.; 1967; Prov.; coed.; D
Huron C. London, Ont.; 1863; P.; coed.: affiliated with U. of Western Ontario

Jean-de-Brébeuf, C. Montreal, Que.; 1929; P.; coed.; II
Jésuites, Le C. de Quebec, Que.; 1930; P.; coed.: affiliated with U. Laval
Jésus-Marie, C. Shippagan, N.B.; 1960; P.; women: affiliated with U. de Moncton
Joliette, C. de Joliette, Que.; 1847; Prov.; coed.: C.E.G.E.P.
Jonquière, C. de Jonquière, Que.; 1967; Prov.; coed.: C.E.G.E.P.

Kemptville C. of Agricultural Technology Kemptville, Ont.; 1917; Prov.; coed.; D
King's C. London, Ont.; 1912; P.; men: affiliated with U. of Western Ontario
King's C., U. of Halifax, N.S.; 1789; P.; coed.: associated with Dalhousie U.
Kingsway C. Oshawa, Ont.; 1916; P.; coed.; D
Knox C. Toronto, Ont.; 1844; P.; coed.: federated with U. of Toronto

Lambton C. of Applied Arts & Technology Sarnia, Ont.; 1966; Prov.; coed.; D
Lethbridge J.C. Lethbridge, Alta.; 1962; Prov.; coed.: affiliated with U. of Calgary
Lévis, C. de Lévis, Que.; 1853; P.; coed.: affiliated with U. Laval
Lévis-Lauzon, C. de Lauzon, Que.; 1969; Prov.; coed.: C.E.G.E.P.
Limoilou, C. de Quebec, Que.; 1967; Prov.; coed.: C.E.G.E.P.
Lionel-Groulx, C. Ste-Thérèse-de-Blainville, Que.; 1825; Prov.; coed.: C.E.G.E.P.
Loyola C.* Montreal, Que.; 1899; P.; coed.; II
Luther C. of Regina Regina, Sask.; 1926; P.; coed.: federated with U. of Saskatchewan

Maillet, C. St-Basile, N.B.; 1947; P.; women: affiliated with C. St-Louis
Maisonneuve, C. de Montreal, Que.; 1967; Prov.; coed.: C.E.G.E.P.
Manitoba Institute of Technology Winnipeg, Man.; 1963; Prov.; coed.; D
Marguerite-Bourgeoys, C. Montreal, Que.; 1908; P.; women; II
Marianopolis C. Montreal, Que.; 1908; P.; women; II
Marie-Anne, C. Montreal, Que.; 1932; P.; women; I
Marie-Reine-du-Clérge, Séminaire Métabetchouan, Que.; 1956; P.; men; II
Maritime School of Social Work Halifax, N.S.; 1941; P.; coed.: professional school associated with Acadia U., King's C., Mt. Allison U., St. Francis Xavier U., & St. Mary's U.
McMaster Divinity C. Hamilton, Ont.; 1957; P.; coed.: affiliated with McMaster U.
Medicine Hat J.C. Medicine Hat, Alta.; 1965; Prov.; coed.: affiliated with U. of Calgary
Mohawk C. of Applied Arts & Technology Hamilton, Ont.; 1966; Prov.; coed.; D
Montreal Diocesan Theological C. Montreal, Que.; 1873; P.; men: affiliated with McGill U.
Mt. Royal J.C. Calgary, Alta.; 1910; Mun.; coed.: affiliated with U. of Calgary
Mt. St. Bernard C. Antigonish, N.S.; 1894; P.; women: affiliated with St. Francis Xavier U.

New Brunswick Institute of Technology Moncton, N.B.; 1947; Prov.; coed.; D
Newfoundland C. of Trades & Technology St. John's, Nfld.; 1963; Prov.; coed.; D
Niagara C. of Applied Arts & Technology Welland, Ont.; 1967; Prov.; coed.; D
Niagara Parks Commission School of Horticulture Niagara Falls, Ont.; 1936; Prov.; men; D
Nipissing C. North Bay, Ont.; 1967; Prov.; coed.: affiliated with Laurentian U.
Northern Alberta Institute of Technology Edmonton, Alta.; 1962; Prov.; coed.; D
Northern C. of Applied Arts & Technology Haileybury & Kirkland Lake, Ont.; 1945; Prov.; coed.; D
Northern Manitoba Vocational Centre The Pas, Man.; 1966; Fed. & Prov.; coed.; D
Notre-Dame de Bellevue, C. Quebec, Que.; 1864; P.; women; II

#C.E.G.E.P. College d'Enseignement Général et Professionnel (College of General and Professional Instruction), an institution in the province of Quebec offering programs in general studies and technological training designed to prepare the student for transfer to a university or for entrance into an occupation

Notre-Dame de Foy, École Normale Cap-Rouge, Que.; 1965; P.; coed.; III
Notre-Dame-du-Sacré-Coeur, C. Montreal, Que.; 1869; men; II
Nova Scotia Agricultural C. Truro, N.S.; 1905; Prov.; coed.; D
Nova Scotia C. of Art Halifax, N.S.; 1887; Prov.; coed.: affiliated with Dalhousie U.
Nova Scotia Eastern Institute of Technology Sydney, N.S.; 1968; Prov.; coed.; D
Nova Scotia Institute of Technology Halifax, N.S.; 1963; Prov.; coed.; D
Nova Scotia Land Survey Institute Lawrencetown, N.S.; 1947; Prov.; coed.; D
Nova Scotia Technical C. Halifax, N.S.; 1907; Prov.; coed.; V

Ontario C. of Art Toronto, Ont.; 1912; Prov.; coed.; D
Osgoode Hall Law School Toronto, Ont.; 1882; P.; coed.: affiliated with York U.

Presbyterian C. Montreal, Que.; 1865; P.; coed.: affiliated with McGill U.
Prince George C. Prince George, B.C.; 1962; P.; coed.: affiliated with U. of British Columbia

Québec, Académie de Quebec, Que.; 1862; Prov.; coed.: C.E.G.E.P.
Québec, Petit Séminaire de Quebec, Que.; 1668; P.; men: affiliated with U. Laval
Queen's C. St. John's, Nfld.; 1841; P.; coed.: affiliated with Memorial U. of Newfoundland & Bishop's U.
Queen's Theological C. Kingston, Ont.; 1841; P.; coed.: affiliated with Queen's U.

Red Deer J.C. Red Deer, Alta.; 1964; Prov.; coed.: affiliated with U. of Alberta
Regis C. Toronto, Ont.; 1930; P.; men: affiliated with St. Mary's U.
Ridgetown C. of Agricultural Technology Ridgetown, Ont.; 1951; Prov.; coed.; D
Rigaud-de-Vaudreuil, C. Vaudreuil, Que.; 1968; P.; coed.; D
Rimouski, C. de Rimouski, Que.; 1967; Prov.; coed.: C.E.G.E.P.
Rosemont, C. de Montreal, Que.; 1968; Prov.; coed.: C.E.G.E.P.
Rouyn-Noranda, C. de Rouyn, Que.; 1967; Prov.; coed.: C.E.G.E.P.
Royal Roads Military C. Victoria, B.C.; 1942; Fed.; men: affiliated with Royal Military C. of Canada
Ryerson Polytechnical Institute* Toronto, Ont.; 1948; Prov.; coed.; D

Sacred Heart, J.C. of the Halifax, N.S.; 1925; P.; women: affiliated with Dalhousie U.
Salaberry-de-Valleyfield, C. Salaberry-de-Valleyfield, Que.; 1967; Prov.; coed.: C.E.G.E.P.
Saskatchewan Institute of Applied Arts & Sciences Saskatoon, Sask.; 1963; Prov.; coed.; D
Saskatchewan Technical Institute Moose Jaw, Sask.; 1958; Prov.; coed.; D
Selkirk C. Castlegar, B.C.; 1965; Prov.; coed.; D
Seneca C. of Applied Arts & Technology Willowdale, Ont.; 1967; Prov.; coed.; D
Sherbrooke, C. de Sherbrooke, Que.; 1968; Prov.; coed.: C.E.G.E.P.
Sheridan C. of Applied Arts & Technology Brampton, Ont.; 1966; Prov.; coed.; D
Sir Sanford Fleming C. of Applied Arts & Technology Peterborough, Ont.; 1967; Prov.; coed.; D
Southern Alberta Institute of Technology Calgary, Alta.; 1917; Prov.; coed.; D
Stanislas, C. Montreal, Que.; 1938; Prov.; men; II
St-Augustin, Séminaire Cap-Rouge, Que.; 1965; P.; men: affiliated with U. Laval
St. Augustine's C. Scarborough, Ont.; 1910; P.; men: affiliated with U. of Ottawa
St-Boniface, C. de St. Boniface, Man.; 1871; P.; coed.: affiliated with U. of Manitoba
St. Bride's C. St. John's, Nfld.; 1884; P.; women: affiliated with Memorial U. of Newfoundland
St. Clair C. of Applied Arts & Technology Windsor, Ont.; 1967; Prov.; coed.; D
Ste-Anne-de-la-Pocatière, C. de La Pocatière, Que.; 1827; P.; coed.: affiliated with U. Laval
Ste-Foy, C. de Quebec, Que.; 1967; Prov.; coed.: C.E.G.E.P.
Ste-Marie, C. Montreal, Que.; 1848; P.; coed.; II
Ste-Marie de Shawinigan, Le Séminaire Shawinigan, Que.; 1947; P.; coed.: affiliated with U. Laval

St-Georges, Séminaire de St-Georges, Que.; 1946; P.; coed.: affiliated with U. Laval
St-Ignace, Le C. Montreal, Que.; 1927; Prov.; coed.; II
St-Jean, C. Edmonton, Alta.; 1911; P.; coed.: affiliated with U. of Alberta
St-Jean, C. Militaire Royal de St-Jean, Que.; 1952; Fed.; men: affiliated with Royal Military C. of Canada
St-Jean, Séminaire de St-Jean, Que.; 1911; P.; coed.; II
St-Jean-Vianney, C. Montreal, Que.; 1956; P.; men; II
St. Jerome's C., U. of Waterloo, Ont.; 1864; P.; coed.: federated with U. of Waterloo
St. John Institute of Technology St. John, N.B.; 1963; Prov.; coed.; D
St. John's C. Winnipeg, Man.; 1849; P.; coed.: affiliated with U. of Manitoba
St-Joseph, C. Moncton, N.B.; 1964; P.; coed.: affiliated with U. de Moncton
St. Joseph's C. Yorkton, Sask.; 1964; Prov.; coed.: affiliated with U. of Saskatchewan
St-Laurent, C. de Montreal, Que.; 1847; Prov.; coed.: C.E.G.E.P.
St. Lawrence C. Quebec, Que.; 1958; P.; coed.: affiliated with U. Laval
St. Lawrence C. of Applied Arts & Technology Cornwall & Kingston, Ont.; 1966; Prov.; coed.; D
St-Louis, C. Edmundston, N.B.; 1946; P.; coed.: affiliated with U. de Moncton
St. Mark's C. Vancouver, B.C.; 1956; P.; coed.: affiliated with U. of British Columbia
St-Maurice, C. St-Hyacinthe, Que.; 1935; P.; women; II
St. Michael's C., U. of Toronto, Ont.; 1852; P.; coed.: federated with U. of Toronto
St-Paul, C. Montreal, Que.; 1957; P.; coed.; II
St. Paul's C. Winnipeg, Man.; 1926; P.; coed.: affiliated with U. of Manitoba
St. Paul U. Ottawa, Ont.; 1848; P.; coed.: federated with U. of Ottawa
St. Peter's J.C. Muenster, Sask.; 1927; P.; coed.: affiliated with U. of Saskatchewan
St-Sacrement, Séminaire des Pères du Très Terrebonne, Que.; 1903; Prov.; men: affiliated with U. de Montréal
Sts-Apôtres, Séminaire des Ste-Catherine, Que.; 1952; P.; men; II
St. Stephen's C. Edmonton, Alta.; 1903; P.; coed.: affiliated with U. of Alberta
St. Thomas C. North Battleford, Sask.; 1932; P.; men: affiliated with U. of Ottawa
St-Thomas d'Aquin, Grand Séminaire Chicoutimi, Que.; 1950; P.; men: affiliated with U. Laval
St. Thomas More C. Saskatoon, Sask.; 1936; P.; coed.: federated with U. of Saskatchewan
St. Thomas U. Fredericton, N.B.; 1910; P.; coed.: federated with U. of New Brunswick
Sudbury, U. of Sudbury, Ont.; 1913; P.; coed.: federated with Laurentian U.

Technologie Agricole, Institut de La Pocatière, Que.; 1962; Prov.; coed.; D
Technologie Agricole, Institut de St-Hyacinthe, Que.; 1962; Prov.; coed.; D
Thetford, C. de Thetford Mines, Que.; 1956; Prov.; coed.: C.E.G.E.P.
Thorneloe U. Sudbury, Ont.; 1961; P.; coed.: federated with Laurentian U.
Trades & Technology, C. of St. John's, Nfld.; 1963; Prov.; coed.; D
Très-Ste-Trinité, Séminaire de St-Bruno, Que.; 1953; P.; men: affiliated with U. de Montréal
Trinity C., U. of Toronto, Ont.; 1852; P.; coed.: federated with U. of Toronto
Trinity J.C. Langley, B.C.; 1962; P.; coed.; D
Trois-Rivières, C. de Trois-Rivières, Que.; 1968; Prov.; coed.: C.E.G.E.P.
Trois-Rivières, Grand Séminaire de Trois-Rivières, Que.; 1874; P.; men: affiliated with U. Laval

Union C. of British Columbia Vancouver, B.C.; 1927; P.; coed.: affiliated with U. of British Columbia
United Theological C. Montreal, Que.; 1928; P.; coed.: affiliated with McGill U.

Vancouver City C. Vancouver, B.C.; 1965; Mun.; coed.; D
Victoria U. Toronto, Ont.; 1836; P.; coed.: affiliated with U. of Toronto
Victoriaville, C. de Victoriaville, Que.; 1872; P.; coed.: affiliated with U. Laval
Vieux-Montréal, C. de Montreal, Que.; 1968; Prov.; coed.: C.E.G.E.P.

Westbury C. Montreal, Que.; 1965; P.; coed.; I
Wycliffe C. Toronto, Ont.; 1877; P.; men: federated with U. of Toronto

MARKS OF PUNCTUATION

The Period [.]

1. Use a period at the end of declarative sentences, indirect questions, and most imperative sentences.

Tutors will be asked to assess the student's performance during the tutoring sessions. (*declarative sentence*)
He asked what the score was. (*indirect question*)
Write your name at the top of each sheet. (*imperative sentence*)

2. Use a period after most abbreviations. (See the section on abbreviations, p. 1684.)

3. Use three periods (called *suspension points* or *ellipsis marks*) to show that material has been omitted from a quotation. Use four periods when the omission comes at the end of a sentence.

"There are four ways . . . to remedy the situation."
Original: "There are four ways, none of which has been mentioned by my opponent, to remedy the situation."
"There is only one way to settle the matter. . . . We must sit at the conference table."
Original: "There is only one way to settle the matter, whatever my opponent may say. We must sit at the conference table."

4. A period may be used after a polite request phrased as a question.

Would you please send me a copy of your catalog.

5. Do *not* use a period at the end of the title of a book, magazine, article, poem, or the title of an essay or paper you yourself write.

6. In a typed manuscript there should be two spaces between a period and the beginning of the next sentence.

7. In a typed manuscript, abbreviations and the initials of names do not have any spacing between the periods.

U.S.A.
T. S. Eliot
e.g.
B.A.

The Question Mark [?]

1. Use a question mark at the end of a direct question.

Do you have the money?
"Do you have the money?" he asked. (Note that a comma is not used after the question mark.)
You do have the money?

2. Use a question mark after each query in a series if you wish to emphasize each element.

Have you heard the candidate give his views on civil rights? the war? urban problems? or the farm problem?

3. Use a question mark enclosed in parentheses to express doubt about a word, fact, or number.

He was born in 1572 (?) and died in 1622.

4. Do *not* use the question mark at the end of an indirect question.

He asked what we wanted.

5. Do *not* use a question mark in parentheses to indicate humor or irony.

6. In a typed manuscript there should be two spaces between a question mark and the beginning of the next sentence.

The Exclamation Mark [!]

1. Use the exclamation mark after a particularly forceful interjection or imperative sentence.

Help!
Oh! You hit me!

2. Do not overuse the exclamation mark. In expository writing the exclamation mark is seldom needed.

3. Do not use the exclamation mark after a word, phrase, or sentence to indicate irony or humor. Let the words speak for themselves.

4. In a typed manuscript there should be two spaces between an exclamation mark and the beginning of the next sentence.

The Comma [,]

1. Use a comma before the conjunctions *and, but, for, or, yet,* and *nor* when they join the clauses of a compound sentence.

We inquired for him at the address he gave us, but no one there had ever heard of a person by that name.
We had never before eaten such wonderful meals, and we were delighted with the service.
Note: Between most short clauses and between many long ones when the meaning is clear, the comma is omitted.
First he stopped at the bank and then he went to his office.

2. Use a comma to separate an introductory clause or phrase from a main clause.

When he had tired of the mad pace of New York, he moved to Dubuque.
In the beginning, he liked the work.
Note: If the introductory clause or phrase is short, as in the examples given, or if there is no danger of ambiguity, the comma may be omitted. The following examples require commas because their omission slows up comprehension.
In spite of all that, she got a passing grade.
If the police shoot, the woman may be wounded.
Note: Use a comma, however, after a phrase that begins a sentence, if you want to set the phrase off for rhetorical effect.
From this balcony, he spoke to the crowd.

3. Use a comma to set off introductory *yes* and *no*, mild exclamations, words of direct address, and transitional introductory words (*however, nevertheless, anyway,* etc.)

Yes, I am going too.
Oh, I didn't really much care one way or the other.
John, bring the book with you.
Nevertheless, he was there when the trouble started.

4. Use a comma to set off a question at the end of a statement.

You are coming too, aren't you?

5. Use a comma to set off dates, addresses, and titles.

The letter was dated June 20, 1968, and was mailed from Paris.
He lived at 21 Baker Street, Elyria, Ohio, for twenty years.
Dr. Peter Haws, Director of Admissions.

6. Use a comma to set off contrasted sentence elements.

Fred, not Jim, was first in his class.

7. Use a comma to indicate an omitted word or words in parallel constructions within a sentence.

Bert is studying hard; Susan, scarcely at all.

8. Use a comma to set off sentence elements out of natural order.

That he would accept the money, none of us seriously doubted.

9. Use a comma to separate words, phrases, and clauses in a series.

The menu offered the usual choice of steak, chops, or chicken.
If he studies hard, if he takes good notes, and if he participates in class discussion, he will probably pass.
Note: The comma is frequently omitted before the conjunction in a series of words.
On the counter were displayed needles, thread, pencils, nails and paper clips.
It is a good habit, however, to supply a comma in this position to prevent any ambiguity. Naturally, when the last two elements of a series are considered as a single unit, they are not broken by a comma.
I had orange juice, toast, and ham and eggs for breakfast.

10. Use a comma to set off absolute and parenthetical elements in the sentence.

This year having passed rapidly, we found ourselves at home again.
We finished within the allotted time, however.
He did not say that, as you will realize when we play the recording, but he did imply it.

11. Use a comma to separate coordinate adjectives modifying the same noun. (If you can substitute *and* for the comma, the adjectives are coordinate.)

It was a quaint, old-fashioned, vine-covered cottage.
She had bright, mischievous, laughing brown eyes.
But do not use a comma to separate noncoordinate adjectives modifying the same noun.
Professor Jones is a kind old gentleman.

12. Use a comma or commas to set off nonrestrictive phrases or clauses from the rest of the sentence. (A nonrestrictive phrase or clause is one not essential to the meaning of the sentence.)

My gun, which is now over the mantelpiece, hasn't been used for years.
He found the paper on the roof, where the newsboy had thrown it.

13. Use a comma to set off direct quotations from such expressions as *he said, she replied,* etc.

He said, "I'll never believe you again."
"I know you can pass this course," he said, "if you will only try."
But note that if the *he said* (or similar expression) comes between two independent clauses, then it must be followed by a period or semicolon, not by a comma.
"Try this book," he said; "I think you will like it."

14. Use a comma following the salutation of a personal letter and following the closing phrase of every letter.

Dear John,
Very truly yours,

15. Use a comma before and after a dependent clause that comes in the middle of a sentence.

> The apples, although they had been freshly picked, became spoiled in shipment.

16. Use a comma after terms (*e.g.*, *i.e.*, *namely*) that introduce a series or examples.

> Some of our presidents, e.g., Jefferson, J. Q. Adams, and Buchanan, had previously been secretaries of state.
> *But note:* "Such as" should not have a comma preceding or following it.
> I enjoy sports such as football, basketball, and track.

17. Use a comma to set off the one spoken to in direct address.

> "John, you're the troublemaker in this class."
> "Yes, sir, I guess I am."

18. Use a comma to separate thousands in numbers of one thousand or over.

> The area of the earth is approximately 196,950,000 sq. mi.

19. Use a comma to separate inverted names, phrases, etc., as in a bibliography, index, or catalog.

> Jones, Harold T.
> Persia, architecture of
> radios, portable

20. In a typed manuscript a comma is followed by one space.

Misused and Unnecessary Commas

1. Do not use a comma to separate independent clauses not joined by a conjunction. This error is called the *comma splice* or *comma fault*.

> Evanston is by no means a resort city; however, its recreation facilities are of the finest. (*not* . . . a resort city, however, . . .)
> John told me he was an officer in the army; that isn't what I heard from others, however. (*not* . . . in the army, that isn't what . . .)
> *Note:* Good writers sometimes separate independent clauses by a comma alone (rather than by a semicolon or conjunction and comma), so that they will be read more closely together. We always translate Caesar's famous sentences as "I came, I saw, I conquered."
> His body did not even jerk when the shots hit him, the tortured breathing continued without pause. (George Orwell)

2. Do not use a comma or commas to set off restrictive phrases or clauses—that is, phrases or clauses necessary to the proper identification of the words they modify.

> The book which I am reading is a history text.
> A student who is president of his fraternity has little time for study.

3. Do not use a comma to separate a verb from a noun clause used as its subject or as its object.

> That the professor enjoyed his subject was evident. (*not* That the professor enjoyed his subject, was evident.)
> I cannot imagine what made me do it. (*not* I cannot imagine, what made me do it.)

4. Do not use a comma between a noun and an immediately preceding adjective.

> It was a cold, wet, miserable day. (*not* . . . a cold, wet, miserable, day.)

5. Do not use a comma before *that* introducing an indirect statement.

> He said that he would go. (*not* He said, that he would go.)

The Semicolon [;]

1. Use a semicolon between two independent clauses when they are not joined by a coordinating conjunction.

> Since interest in the past is induced solely by books, the savage can take no interest in the past; the events of the past are, in fact, completely lost. (Lord Raglan)
> *Note:* A period could have been used in place of the semicolon in the sentence above. The writer used the semicolon because he wished to indicate a closer connection between the ideas than a period would suggest.

2. Use a semicolon to separate independent clauses joined only by conjunctive adverbs (*however*, *furthermore*, *nevertheless*, *consequently*, *also*, *besides*, *thus*, *otherwise*, *accordingly*, *hence*, *moreover*, *then*, etc.)

> He has passed all his examinations; consequently, we must award him a degree.
> The bill was sent to the Senate; however, it was buried there in committee.

3. Use a semicolon with a coordinating conjunction if the independent clauses themselves contain commas.

> During the years when English schools and colleges required the composition of Latin quatrains on the Gospel for the Day, innumerable youths must, with pious conscientiousness, have filled their manuscript books; but, of all this diligence, Crawshaw's epigrams alone possessed the brilliance and maturity to invite publication. (Austin Warren)

4. Use a semicolon to separate elements of a series when the elements themselves contain internal punctuation.

> A thorough examination of Johnson's criticism would require, first, a study of the eighteenth-century background; second, a study of Johnson himself, not as the subject of anecdote, but in his other works, and in his religious and political opinions; and finally, a much more detailed study of his criticism of the greater poets who come under his observation: Shakespeare, Milton, Dryden, Pope, Gray. (T. S. Eliot)

5. Do *not* use a semicolon as the equivalent of a colon. Although a semicolon is often interchangeable with a period, it is never interchangeable with a colon.

6. Do *not* use a semicolon as the equivalent of a comma. Except for the special uses described in *3* and *4* above, the semicolon should never be used as a substitute for the comma.

7. In a typed manuscript a semicolon is followed by one space.

The Colon [:]

1. Use a colon before a long, formal quotation, formal statement, or list of items.

> The Commencement speaker, Dr. Reginald Huntington Bysshe, spoke as follows: ". . . ."
> I still think that the rule which I formulated for my own guidance is more concise than any other, and so I give it here: A play should lead up to and away from a central crisis, and this crisis should consist in a discovery by the leading character which has an indelible effect on his thought and emotion and completely alters his course of action. (Maxwell Anderson)
> This is the somber reality behind the organized—and often ludicrous—courting of engineering students: the full-page ads in the college newspapers, expense-paid tours of the company plants during winter and spring vacations, and reams of propaganda done up in the glossiest Madison Avenue style. (George S. Odiorne)

2. Use a colon after a main clause when the succeeding clause or clauses explain the first clause.

> As a student of literature you must be sincere with yourself and your teacher: you must not say that you like certain works because you think you ought to, or because it has been suggested to you by a critic or a reviewer that it is the proper thing to do; and you must not, in general, read uncomprehendingly books which you think you ought to read, rather than simpler ones that you could read and understand. (E. G. Biaggini)
> English usage is like table etiquette: it is conventional and its sanction is a social one.

3. Use a colon following the salutation of a formal letter. In informal letters a comma may be used.

> Dear Mr. Brown:
> Dear Sir:
> Dear Bob,

4. Use a colon to separate parts of a Biblical citation.

> Exodus 4:6

5. In a typed manuscript a colon is followed by one space.

The Dash [—]

1. Use a dash to indicate an abrupt break in the structure of the sentence or an unfinished statement.

> He is—how shall I say it?—an ineffably officious oaf.
> He said, "I am at a loss to understand—"
> *Note:* When the dash comes at the end of the sentence, it is not followed by a period.

2. Use a dash to set off a summary or a long appositive.

> I shall, however, take this opportunity of giving a specimen from the writings of Robert Southey, whose style is a model of consistent "workmanlike" qualities—the style of a man who writes swiftly and voluminously, and who has discovered the true economy of a clear mind and a clean pen. (Herbert Read)
> Behind his apparent solicitude for her health, comfort, and happiness, one motive was evident to us—his avarice.
> Three campus leaders—Shirley Mann, president of the All Student Association; Bert Flynn, editor of the student paper; and Susan Sarachek, president of the Student Senate—came out strongly for the proposal.

3. Use a dash to set off strongly parenthetical expressions.

> I was offended—no, enraged would be more accurate—by his actions.
> We have never seen in our own generation—indeed, the world has not seen more than once or twice in all the course of history—a literature which has exercised such prodigious influence over the minds of men, over every cast and shade of intellect, as that which emanated from Rousseau between 1749 and 1762. (Sir Henry Maine)

4. Do not use dashes indiscriminately as a substitute for other marks of punctuation.

5. A dash is made in typing by using two hyphens with no space between them and the preceding and following words.

Parentheses [( )]

1. Use parentheses to enclose material that is explanatory, supplementary, or exemplifying.

> The passive voice is the natural voice of science. Not only officialdom but scientific objectivity tempts us to it. It sounds dispassionate and impersonal; it stops time and holds life still so we can catalogue it. (Flowers never grow in this dry land; they "are found.") (Sheridan Baker)

2. Use parentheses to enclose material that is strongly parenthetical.

> The world is worth nothing, after such a death, says Sannazaro (and God knows how many times the same thing had been said before!). (Mario Praz)

3. Use parentheses to enclose figures and letters in the text of a piece of writing to indicate order of enumeration.

> The subjects of the medieval quadrivium were (1) arithmetic, (2) geometry, (3) astronomy, and (4) music.

4. Use parentheses to enclose cross-references.

> The amount of this yearly increase is astonishing (see Appendix A).
> "Unexceptionable" is not to be confused with "unexceptional" (consult the dictionary).

5. Use parentheses in formal business transactions to confirm a sum previously given in words.

> I enclose my check for five hundred dollars ($500.00) to cover payment in full.

6. The conventions governing the use of parentheses with other marks of punctuation are as follows:

a. When a complete sentence within parentheses stands alone (that is, not as part of another sentence), the terminal punctuation is enclosed within parentheses.

> He said that knowledge is sometimes useful. (That must be the unexceptionable statement of the century.)

b. When a complete sentence within parentheses is part of another sentence:

- It does not begin with a capital letter unless the first word is a proper noun.
- No period is used within the parentheses.
- If it is a question, a question mark is used within the parentheses.

> Later in his Preface on Bosses in his volume of plays of 1936, he was back praising Mussolini again and even throwing a few kind words to Hitler, whom he described as "not a stupid German" (did Bernard Shaw prefer a crazy Austrian?) and whose persecution of the Jews he characterized considerately as "a craze, a complex, a bee in his bonnet, a hole in his armor, a hitch in his statesmanship, one of those lesions which sometimes prove fatal." (Edmund Wilson)

c. When a word, phrase, or clause within parentheses is part of a sentence:

- A comma, semicolon, or period is never used after the last word in the parentheses.
- A comma, semicolon, or period is used following the second parenthesis only if the sentence without the parenthetical material requires punctuation at that point.
- A question mark or exclamation mark is used within the parentheses if it applies to the material within the parentheses.

> But the man finds himself faced with the question he imagines the horse to be asking: what *is* there to stop for out there in the cold, away from bin and stall (house and village and mankind?) and all that any self-respecting beast could value on such a night? (John Ciardi)

7. In a typed manuscript a parenthesis within a sentence is separated from the words on either side of it by a single space. A sentence standing by itself within parentheses is separated from the preceding and following sentences by two spaces.

Quotation Marks [" "]

1. Use quotation marks to enclose all direct quotations.

> "Are you," she asked, "the man who helped my son?"
> "Yes," he said, "I helped him. I didn't do much, though."

2. Use single quotation marks to enclose a quotation within another quotation.

> In *Literary Symbolism*, Maurice Beebe says, "Mary McCarthy admits that a writer does not always know beforehand just what he intends to accomplish in a story, which is always for him, as well as for the reader, 'a little act of discovery.'"

3. Use quotation marks to enclose titles of articles, chapters of a book, essays, short stories, short poems, and musical compositions.

> The third chapter, "Some Solutions to the Problem," is perhaps the most valuable in the book.
> One of Emerson's characteristic essays is "Self Reliance."
> I enjoyed Steinbeck's short story "The Leader of the People."
> She made us memorize the poem "Dover Beach," which none of us liked.
> She sang "Over the Bounding Waves" loudly and with appropriate gestures.

4. Use quotation marks to enclose words spoken of as words, words used in special senses, or words emphasized. (Italics may also be used in such cases.)

> Some people consider that all such words as "good," "bad," "beautiful," "ugly" only indicate one's own emotional reactions towards actions or things and in no sense properties of the actions or things themselves. (Robert H. Thouless)
> Power is assumed to be always "brute" power, crude, ugly, and undiscriminating, the way an elephant appears to be. (Lionel Trilling)

5. Use indentation and single spacing with no quotation marks for a quotation of more than three or four lines.

6. Generally speaking, do not use quotation marks to redeem slang. If the slang expression is the best and most exact expression for the context, then use it without the apology of quotation marks; if it is not, putting it in quotation marks probably will not improve it or make it acceptable.

7. The conventions governing the use of quotation marks with other forms of punctuation are as follows:

a. The comma and the period are *always* enclosed within quotation marks.

> "I'm sorry," he said, "but I don't believe you."

b. The colon and semicolon are *never* enclosed within quotation marks.

> I had not read Francis Bacon's essay, "Of Truth"; in fact, I had never heard of it.

c. The dash, question mark, and exclamation mark are enclosed within quotation marks if they apply to the quoted material. They are placed after the quotation marks if they apply to the whole sentence.

> "Am I going too?" she asked.
> Did she say, "I am going too"?

Brackets [ ]

1. Use brackets to enclose matter which you insert in the text of a quoted passage to explain, comment, or correct.

> "He was born in 1805 [actually in 1802] in . . . ."
> According to *Time* magazine, "It [*Rabbit, Run*] was a flawlessly turned portrait of a social cripple who understood somehow that, running, he was more alive than he would be standing still."

2. Use brackets to enclose the Latin word *sic*, meaning "thus," when you insert it into a quotation following a mistake in fact, spelling, grammar, etc. to indicate to the reader that you are quoting verbatim from your source and that the mistake was in your source and was not yours.

> "Andrew Johnson never attended school and was scarcely able to read when he met Eliza McCardle, whom he married on May 5, 1927 [sic]."

3. In a typed manuscript insert brackets in ink if your typewriter lacks these characters.

Apostrophe [']

1. Use the apostrophe to indicate the possessive case of the noun or pronoun.

> the student's book
> John's golf clubs
> one's obligation

2. **a.** For nouns not ending in *s* add the apostrophe followed by *s*.

> children's shoes
> dog's collar
> men's suits

b. For singular nouns ending in an *s*, *sh*, or *z* sound, the possessive is formed either by adding the apostrophe to the final *s* or by adding the apostrophe and another *s*.

> James' book *or* James's book
> Mr. Jones' house *or* Mr. Jones's house
> conscience' sake *or* conscience's sake

c. For plural nouns ending in an *s*, *sh*, or *z* sound, use the apostrophe alone.

> the Joneses' house
> dogs' collars
> the ladies' purses

d. In compound constructions place the apostrophe and *s* on the word standing immediately before the word being modified.

> the King of England's daughter
> anyone else's opinion
> sister-in-law's cousin

e. Joint possession is denoted by adding the apostrophe and *s* to the last name only or to all the names.

> Wendy, Tony, and Christopher's home
> Wendy's, Tony's, and Christopher's home

f. Separate ownership is denoted by the apostrophe and *s* after each name and the plural form of the modified word.

> Wendy's, Tony's, and Christopher's homes
> Selma's and Debbie's typewriters

3. Use the apostrophe to indicate the omission of letters or figures.

> we've, won't, it's, can't, '69

4. Use an apostrophe to indicate the plurals of figures, letters, and words referred to as such.

> Watch your p's and q's.
> There are too many 5's in the number.
> There are too many "and's" in your sentence.
> It was a party of V.I.P.'s.

5. Do not use the apostrophe with the personal and relative pronouns to indicate possession.

> Is it yours? (*not* Is it your's?)
> Its color is faded. (*not* It's color is faded.)

6. The apostrophe is often omitted in the names of organizations.

> Teachers College
> Citizens Bank
> Ladies Aid Society

Italics

Italics (slanted type in printing) are indicated in a typed or handwritten manuscript by underlining.

1. Use italics for titles of books, magazines, plays, movies, long musical compositions, and names of trains, planes, and ships.

I read Austin Warren's *Rage for Order*.
Esquire is one of my favorite magazines.
We saw Alec Guinness in *The Horse's Mouth*
We sailed on the *Cristoforo Colombo*.
Jim Frantz gave us Menotti's *The Medium* for Christmas.
Mort Walker directed Garcia Lorca's *Blood Wedding*.

2. Use italics to emphasize a word or larger element in a sentence or to refer to a word as a word.

Moderation and *pragmatism* are the key terms to describe Lincoln's reconstruction policies.
The dictionary under the word *get* lists dozens of meanings.
I said stomach *ulcers*, not *ulsters*.

Note: Do not overuse italics for emphasis.

3. Use italics to indicate a foreign word or phrase which has not been Anglicized. Check the dictionary to see whether the foreign word or phrase you want to use has been Anglicized.

His motto was *ars gratia artis*, which means "art for art's sake."
I thought the bullfighter would never deliver the *coup de grâce*.
He received a per diem allowance while on the trip.

(Note that the phrase "per diem," a Latin phrase, is now considered English and, hence, is not italicized.)

The Hyphen [-]

1. Use a hyphen to divide a word at the end of a line.
But note:
 • Words of one syllable cannot be divided (this includes verbs such as "worked").
 • Words of more than one syllable can be divided only between syllables. (Consult the dictionary.)
 • Suffixes of fewer than three letters should not be separated from the rest of the word.
 • Never divide a word so that only one letter stands at the end of the line.
 • Hyphenated words should be divided only at the hyphen.

2. Use a hyphen between parts of a compound modifier preceding a noun except when the compound includes an adverb ending in *ly*. Compound modifiers following a noun are usually not hyphenated.

It was their twenty-fifth anniversary.
(All compound numerical modifiers between twenty-one and ninety-nine are hyphenated.)
She was a well-dressed woman.
The woman was well dressed.
(Here the compound follows the noun.)
She was a smartly dressed woman.
(Here the compound includes an adverb ending in *ly*.)

3. Use the dictionary to check on the hyphenation of other compound words. The practice of hyphenating words varies, and, moreover, dictionaries differ about which compounds should be hyphenated. Your only recourse is to consult the dictionary and to be consistent in your practice regarding any one word.

NUMBERS

1. Use figures to express dates, hours, street numbers, decimals, measures, percentages, and volume, chapter, and page numbers.

April 22, 1969	Vol. II
12:05 P.M. or p.m.	Chapter V
21 Baker Street	p. 83
.3715	73% or 73 percent
16 pounds	80° or 80 degrees

2. Use figures to record uneven sums of money, and numbers over one hundred except when the numbers can be written as two words.

$4.19
122 *but* five thousand

3. Be consistent in your use of numbers within any piece of writing; do not, for example, spell out a number which can be expressed in two words (fifteen thousand) and later use figures for the same kind of number (20,000).

4. Usually spell out ordinal numbers.

Third Reich	Tenth Street
eighteenth century	Twenty-third Psalm

5. Do not begin a sentence with a figure. If spelling out the number, however, would be awkward, recast the sentence so that it does not begin with a number.

Nine hundred and sixty students attended the rally.
He received 2,694,386 votes. (*not* Two million six hundred and ninety-four thousand three hundred and eighty-six votes were cast for him.)

CAPITALIZATION

1. Capitalize the first word of a sentence.
2. Capitalize the pronoun *I* and the interjection *O*.
3. Capitalize the first word in a quotation.

He asked, "Are you going too?"
But note: When a sentence is interrupted by such an expression as "he said," do not use a capital letter for the first word of what follows (unless, of course, it is a word which would normally be capitalized in the middle of a sentence, as *I*, *O*, a name, etc.).
"Is it," he asked, "because I am so ugly?"

4. Capitalize the first word of a direct question falling within a sentence.

This story answers the question, Where does true happiness really lie?

5. Capitalize all nouns referring to the deity and to the Bible and other sacred books.

God	The Ten Commandments	the Holy Bible
Christ	The Blessed Virgin	the Koran
The Holy Spirit	the Incarnate Word	

When Christ performed His first miracle, He was attending a wedding feast.
(Pronouns referring to the deity are capitalized by many, but not all, writers. It depends on the religious position of the individual writer.)

6. Capitalize the names of gods and goddesses of polytheistic religions.

Isis	Venus
Zeus	Thor

7. Use a capital letter for *President* and *Presidency* when these refer to the office of President of the United States.

The President will speak at 9:00 P.M.
But note: The president [of a company] will address the luncheon.

8. Use a capital letter for official titles before the names of officials.

Mayor Davis	Governor Blair
President Kennedy	Queen Elizabeth

But note: Mr. Williams was governor of Michigan.

9. Capitalize proper nouns, and adjectives formed from proper nouns. (Consult the dictionary when in doubt.)

Michael Mardikes	Germany	Catholicism	Fifth Avenue
London	Maine	Protestant	Shakespearean

10. Capitalize every word except conjunctions, articles, and short prepositions in the titles of works of literature, music, art, titles of books, magazines, etc. The first word of the title is always capitalized.

The Decline and Fall of the Roman Empire
The Taming of the Shrew
The Atlantic Monthly
The Magic Flute

11. Capitalize every word except conjunctions, articles, and short prepositions in the names (or derived adjectives, verbs, etc.) of organizations, institutions, businesses, agencies, movements, religions, holidays, holy days, etc. Sometimes the initial article is capitalized as part of the official name.

The World Publishing Company	Memorial Day
the Boy Scouts of America	Corpus Christi
Internal Revenue Service	Buddhism
Yom Kippur	Library of Congress

12. Capitalize the names of nationalities, languages, and the anthropological terms for races.

Italian	Mongolian
English	Negro
Latin	Caucasian

But note: Do not capitalize *white*, *black*, *yellow*, or *red* when referring to races.

13. Capitalize the names of all heavenly bodies.

Mars	Virgo
Sirius	Big Dipper

But note: Earth, sun, and moon are not capitalized except when cited along with other heavenly bodies.
The moon shines by means of light reflected from the sun. (*But:* Mercury is the planet closest to the Sun.)

14. Capitalize a title, rank, etc. followed by a proper name or of an epithet used with or in place of a proper name.

Dr. Culver	General MacArthur
Bishop Helmsing	the Senator from New York
Lord Byron	Richard the Lion-Hearted
The Great Emancipator	

15. Capitalize the names of trademarks.

Dacron
Vaseline

16. Capitalize compass directions and adjectives derived from them when they refer to a specific geographical area.

He lives in the East.
She lives in the Middle West.
He is a Southern congressman.
But note: Chicago is east of Kansas City.

17. Capitalize words denoting family relationships only

when they precede the name of a person or when they stand unmodified as a substitute for a person's name.

> I wrote to Grandfather Smith.
> I wrote Mother a letter.
> I wrote my mother a letter.

18. Capitalize the names of abstract or inanimate things that are personified.

> It has been said that Justice is lame as well as blind.
> It was the work of Fate.
> And now Spring came scattering her vexatious dandelions.

19. Capitalize geographical terms when they are part of a proper name.

Long Island Sound	the Gobi Desert
the Great Lakes	Mount Hood
the Dead Sea	the Straits of Mackinac

But note: Do not capitalize geographical terms when they are used with two or more proper names (e.g., the Missouri River, *but* the Missouri and Mississippi rivers).

20. Capitalize government departments and offices.

Senate	Supreme Court
House of Representatives	Court of Appeals

ABBREVIATIONS

In general, do not use abbreviations in formal or informal writing (including business letters), except for the universally recognized cases given below.

1. Use abbreviations for the titles *Mr., Mrs., Dr.* These are never spelled out.

2. You may use abbreviations for the titles of college faculty, clergy, government officials, military personnel, etc. if the title is followed by a full name (first name and surname); if only the surname is used, the title must be written out.

> Prof. Ralph King, Jr. *but* Professor King (*never* Professor King, Jr. Use *Jr.* and *Sr.* only with full names)
> Rev. William Clancy *but* The Reverend Dr. *or* Mr. *or* Father Clancy (*never* Reverend Clancy)
> Gov. Warren Hearnes *but* Governor Hearnes
> Hon. Warren Hearnes *but* The Honorable Warren Hearnes or The Honorable Mr. Hearnes
> Col. John Daniel   *but* Colonel Daniel

3. Use abbreviations for academic degrees following the full name and a comma and with no title preceding the name.

> Robert Smithey, Ph.D. *not* Dr. *or* Mr. Robert Smithey, Ph.D.

4. Use abbreviations for titles of religious orders, following the full name and a comma. Women's names are preceded by their title and followed by a surname if that is the custom of the order. Men's names may or may not be preceded by a title, according to one's choice.

> Sister Bede Sullivan, O.S.B.
> Mother Angela Therese, I.H.M.
> Father James Agattas, S.J. *or* Fr. James Agattas, S.J. *or* James Agattas, S.J. *or* Rev. James Agattas, S.J.
> (the last form is now the most usual)

5. Abbreviate the names of organizations when the full names the abbreviations stand for are universally known.

AFL–CIO	NAACP
DAR	SDS

6. Abbreviate the names of government agencies and military services and terms when the abbreviations are universally used. These abbreviations do not usually have periods (consult the dictionary entry for an abbreviation when in doubt about the use of periods with it).

CIA	USN
FBI	USAF
NATO	MP
HEW	PX
USA (United States Army, used following a military title and name)	

7. Abbreviate certain foreign terms in frequent use.

> etc.
> e.g.
> i.e.

8. Abbreviate terms used in footnotes and bibliographies. (See *Terms and Abbreviations Used in Scholarly Writing,* p. 1686.)

9. Do *not* abbreviate in formal writing, except in footnotes or bibliographies, the days of the week, months of the year, States, countries (except U.S.S.R.), weights and measures, or the words *street* and *avenue.*

MANUSCRIPT FORM

The following regulations concerning manuscript form apply specifically to college term papers and research papers in the humanities. Manuscripts in the sciences and business observe the regulations as to paper size, margins, spacing, and, generally, bibliographical form given here, but often do not use footnotes for reference to books and articles (using instead numbers in the text of the paper which refer to a numbered bibliography at the end). Most scholarly journals in the humanities and most university presses follow "The MLA [Modern Language Association] Style Sheet." The regulations which follow are in general accord with that publication, but differ in a few particulars because "The MLA Style Sheet" is concerned exclusively with preparation of a manuscript for publication in one of the scholarly journals or by one of the university presses (the spacing of quotations, for example, is different in such a manuscript). Other publishers use essentially the same form as given here, but may differ in a few respects; therefore, it would be wise for a writer intending to submit a manuscript to a publishing company to inquire of the company about the form it desires. Many publishing companies make available their own style guide.

1. Type your manuscript on 8 1/2″ x 11″ paper of good quality. Do not use highly glazed paper because your instructor will not be able to make comments on it in ink. It is a good practice to make a carbon copy for yourself.

2. Use a one-inch margin on all sides of the paper, a one and one-half inch margin on the left side if you use a binder, and observe these margins strictly.

3. Put page numbers, following the first page of the text (which is unnumbered), at the center top of each page or at the right-hand top margin.

4. Include a title page with the title of your paper centered between the margins, your name centered beneath the title, and down below at the right side of the page, the title of the course for which you are submitting it, with your instructor's name below that.

5. The first page of the text should have the title centered at the top margin (and, hence, no page number).

6. Double-space throughout the text of the paper except for quotations longer than three lines, which are single-spaced and indented five spaces from both the right and left margins *and have no quotation marks.*

FOOTNOTES

Purposes of Footnotes

1. To give the source of any direct or indirect quotations you use. (An example of an indirect quotation: In a lecture delivered on his American tour, Matthew Arnold said that by the term *literature* he meant a great deal more than what Thomas Huxley regarded as *belles lettres.*[1]) [Since Matthew Arnold is being quoted, though indirectly, this sentence must be footnoted.]

2. To give the source of facts which are not common knowledge. Obviously, if you mention in your paper the date of the Battle of Hastings, you need not document the date. Nor need you document any fact which may be new to you when you begin work on a subject but which, from your reading, you discover is known to everybody who has written on the subject.

3. To give the source of theories, ideas, and opinions which are original with one of the books or articles you read and should, therefore, not be used in your paper without giving credit to the source.

4. To give additional information about some point in the paper or to explain some point when you do not wish to interrupt the flow of the writing by inserting the information or explanation in the text proper.

> **a.** Example of a footnote giving additional information:
> [1]See Jesperson, pp. 37–41, for a detailed criticism.
> **b.** Example of an explanatory footnote:
> [1]That is, taking into account all the synonyms for the 60,000 entries.
> (This footnote explains a puzzling figure which appeared in the text of the paper from which the footnote was taken.)

Placement of Footnotes

1. Footnotes should be numbered consecutively throughout the paper, beginning with number 1. A paper which is not a research paper (an informal essay, for example) and which has only two or three footnotes may use asterisks to indicate the footnotes, but papers which have many footnotes should always make use of Arabic numerals.

2. The number in the text to which the footnote refers is always an Arabic superscript number (placed slightly above the line).

a. Numbers in the text referring to footnotes which identify sources of quotations are always placed *after the last word of the quotation.*

b. Numbers in the text referring to informational or explanatory footnotes come wherever in the text the information or explanation would logically be given if it were included in the text. (This might be following a word in the middle of a sentence.)

c. Numbers in the text referring to footnotes are always placed after a word, never in front of it, and they always come after any punctuation.

3. Unless your instructor gives you permission to put all the footnotes on a separate page or pages at the end of the paper, all footnotes will appear at the foot of the page to which they refer.

a. One space below the last line of text on any page make a straight line (using the underlining character on the typewriter) either all the way across the page or two or three inches in from the left margin.

b. Begin the footnote two spaces below this line and indented five spaces from the left margin.

c. Begin the footnote with a superscript number not followed by any punctuation.

d. Bring the second line of the footnote out to the left margin.

e. Single-space within footnotes, but double-space between them (for easier reading).

f. The last footnote on any page should end at the one-inch bottom margin or just above it.

g. Avoid, if at all possible, running a footnote onto the next page.

Form of Footnotes

1. When a bibliography is not included in a paper (and sometimes when it is, according to the preference of your instructor), the facts of publication for a book cited are given in a footnote the first time the source is cited. Following is an example in the proper form:

[1]Thomas Pyles, *The Origins and Development of the English Language* (New York: Harcourt, Brace and World, Inc., 1964), p. 23.

a. The author's name in normal order, followed by a comma.

b. Title of the book underlined. The author's name and the title of the book should be given as they appear on the title page of the book.

c. The last word of the title followed by a parenthesis with no intervening punctuation.

d. The place of publication followed by a colon.

e. The publishing company, as its name is given on the title page, followed by a comma, the date (the last copyright date as given on the back of the title page), parenthesis, and comma.

f. The page reference with the abbreviation for page followed by a period and with the footnote ended with a period.

2. When a bibliography is part of a paper, then the place of publication, the publisher, and the date of publication are omitted from all footnotes (unless your instructor insists on that information) because that information is given in the bibliography.

Examples of Initial Book and Periodical Footnotes

A book by one author:

[1]J. Middleton Murray, *The Problem of Style*, p. 57.

(1) The author's name in normal order, followed by a comma.

(2) Title of book underlined, followed by a comma.

(3) Page number, followed by a period.

A book by two authors:

[2]Roma A. King, Jr. and Frederick R. McLeod, *Modern American Writer*, p. 423.

A book by more than two authors:

[3]Donna Worrall Brown and others, *Form in Modern English*, p. 81.

Note: Instead of "and others" the Latin abbreviation *et al.* is sometimes used.

A book with both an author and editor:

[4]Mark Twain, *Adventures of Huckleberry Finn*, ed. Leo Marx, p. 21.

An edited collection:

[5]E. B. White and Katherine S. White, eds., *A Subtreasury of American Humor*, p. 97.

A translated work:

[6]Charles Baudelaire, *The Mirror of Art*, trans. and ed. Jonathan Mayne, pp. 33-44.

A work of more than one volume:

[7]Harley Granville-Barker, *Prefaces to Shakespeare*, II, 64.

A book with a "corporate author":

[8]National Council of Teachers of English, Commission on the English Curriculum, *Language Arts for Today's Children*, p. 108.

An edition other than the first:

[9]Louis E. Glorfeld, and others, *A Concise Guide for Writers*, 2nd ed., p. 63.

An article in a larger work:

[10]Erwin Panofsky, "Style and Medium in the Motion Picture," *Problems in Aesthetics*, ed. Morris Weitz, p. 527.

(1) The author's name in normal order, followed by a comma.

(2) Title of article in quotation marks, followed by a comma (within the second quotation marks).

(3) Name of book underlined, followed by a comma.

(4) The abbreviation for "editor" followed by the name of the editor and a comma.

(5) Page number, followed by a period.

An article in a magazine or scholarly journal:

[11]Constance M. Drake, "An Approach to Blake," *College English*, XXIX (April 1968), 541-547.

(1) The author's name in normal order, followed by a comma.

(2) Title of article in quotation marks and followed by a comma.

(3) Name of periodical underlined and followed by a comma.

(4) Volume number in Roman numerals (no comma following).

(5) Date within parentheses with comma following second parenthesis.

(6) Page in Arabic numerals and followed by a period. *Note:* No *vol.* precedes the volume number and no *p.* or *pp.* precedes the page number when both volume and page references are given.

A signed article in a newspaper:

[12]Warren French, "A Stable Force in a Crumbling World," *The Kansas City Star*, October 13, 1968, p. 8 F.

An unsigned newspaper article:

[13]"Reading Teachers Put on Spot," *The Kansas City Star*, May 1, 1969, p. 16 A.

A signed article in an encyclopedia:

[14]William Solzbacher, "Esperanto," *The Encyclopedia Americana*, X, 501-503.

An unsigned article in an encyclopedia:

[15]"Islam," *Hutchinson's New 20th Century Encyclopedia*, p. 580.

Note: The lack of volume number means this is a one-volume encyclopedia, and figures are used for *20th* because that is the way it appears on the title page.

These are the basic initial footnote forms. Cases not covered by these examples can easily be figured out by analogy with one or more of the examples given here. (For example, an unsigned article in a magazine would be treated like the example of an article in a magazine or scholarly journal above, except that the entry would begin with the title of the article.) And to repeat, the assumption of these sample footnotes is that there will be a bibliography at the end of the paper; hence, the place and year of publication are omitted. If your instructor wants that information given in the initial footnotes, too, then follow the form given in the first example under *Form of Footnotes*, above, putting the place and date of publication within parentheses, and spacing and punctuating as indicated in that example. (This applies only to books, since the information given for magazine and journal articles is the same in both the bibliography and initial footnotes.)

Subsequent Footnote Citations

Second and subsequent references to a work are not accompanied by a complete footnote.

1. If a footnote refers to the same work cited in the immediately preceding footnote, then the Latin abbreviation Ibid. (meaning "in the same place" or, in effect, "the same work I have just cited") may be used.

[4]Richard Poirier, "Learning from the Beatles," *Partisan Review*, XXXIV (Fall 1967), 529.

[5]Ibid., p. 531.

[6]Ibid.

a. Ibid. always refers to the *immediately preceding* footnote, so that footnote 5 in the examples above refers to the article by Poirier.

b. Ibid. always refers to as much of the preceding footnote as is the same in both; i.e., footnote 6 in the examples above has no page reference because the footnote refers to the same article and to the same page as given in footnote 5, i.e., to Poirier's article, p. 531.

c. Ibid. is a Latin abbreviation, but it is not usually underlined; this is an exception to the rule that foreign terms are underlined.

d. It is followed by a period.

e. It is always capitalized because it is always the first word in the footnote in which it is used.

f. Do not use Ibid. if the immediately preceding footnote to which it refers is two or three pages back, because the reader is forced to turn back the pages to find out to what it refers; in fact, it would be a favor to the reader not to use it as the first footnote on a page.

2. Instead of using Ibid., many writers prefer to use simply the author's last name and the page reference.

    ⁴Richard Poirier, "Learning from the Beatles," *Partisan Review*, XXXIV (Fall 1967), 529.
    ⁵Poirier, p. 531.
    ⁶Poirier, p. 531.

3. When two works by the same author are cited, the footnote includes the author's name and the title of the work referred to.

    ⁴Eliot, *Notes Towards the Definition of Culture*, p. 41.
    ⁵Eliot, *Poetry and Drama*, p. 31.

4. When citing two works by one author, if one or both works have a long, cumbersome title, the title may be shortened after the first citation if that fact is noted in the initial entry.

    ¹T. S. Eliot, *Notes Towards the Definition of Culture*, p. 41. Hereafter referred to as *Notes*.
    ⁶Eliot, *Notes*, p. 6.

5. The traditional way to cite works already noted earlier but separated from the present citation by intervening footnotes is to use the Latin abbreviation *op. cit.* (for *opere citato*, "in the work already cited").

    ³Leon Edel, "The Literary Convictions of Henry James," *Modern Fiction Studies*, III (Spring 1957), 5.
    ⁹Edel, *op. cit.*, p. 14.

6. Modern practice is to omit *op. cit.* and *loc. cit.* (which is explained under *Terms and Abbreviations Used in Scholarly Writing*, below) because they add no real information to the footnote and impress many readers as pedantic and superfluous.

7. Any information about the author, book, or article given in the text of the paper need not be repeated in the footnote. For example, if a writer were to say in the text of his paper: "As T. S. Eliot said in his book *Poetry and Drama*," and then were to go on to quote the passage, the footnote would only give the page number.

    ⁴P. 43.

8. If a book has an editor, his name is shown in the entry; a magazine or journal editor's name is never shown in the entry.

TERMS AND ABBREVIATIONS USED IN SCHOLARLY WRITING

Many of the following terms and abbreviations you will not have occasion to use in your own research papers, but since they occur frequently, particularly in articles in scholarly journals, they are listed here for reference. The use of Latin terms and abbreviations, once quite general in scholarly writing, is now considered either pedantic (*infra*, *supra*) because the English words are just as short, or else superfluous (*op. cit.*, *loc. cit.*) because they add no real information. Notice that the Latin terms in the following list are italicized (and hence would be underlined in a typewritten manuscript) because they are foreign terms, that all the abbreviations have a period following them, and that the term is capitalized whenever it begins a footnote—for example, Ibid.

ante	"before"
art(s).	article(s)
c. or *ca.*	*circa*—"about," used with a date to indicate that the exact date is unknown. Not always italicized.
cf.	*confer*—"compare," used to invite the reader to compare the passage which has been footnoted with the reference cited in the footnote. Not italicized.
ch(s).	chapter(s)
col(s).	column(s)
comp.	compiled by *or* compiler
diss.	dissertation
ed(s).	editor(s) *or* edition(s)
ed. cit.	*editio citato*—"in the edition cited"
et al.	*et alii*—"and others," used when citing a work by three or more authors to substitute for all the authors' names except the first. The English translation "and others" is now often used.
et seq.	*et sequens*—"and following." The English abbreviation f(f). is now often used—for example, pp. 9 ff. rather than pp. 9 et seq. (But why not give the exact page references—pp. 9–15?)
f(f).	and the following. See *et seq.*
fig(s).	figure(s)
fl.	*floruit*—"he (or she) flourished"
Ibid.	*Ibidem*—"in the same place"—see examples and comment under *Subsequent Footnote Citations*, above. This abbreviation is capitalized here because when used it is always the first word of the footnote. It is usually not underlined.

infra	"below," as in "See *infra*." Most writers now use the English word.
l(l).	line(s)
loc. cit.	*loco citato*—"in the place cited," used to refer to the same passage referred to in a recent footnote and also to refer to a magazine or encyclopedia article. It is not only useless but confusing.
MS(S). *or* ms(s).	manuscript(s)
n(n).	note(s). A reference to a footnote—p. 35n.
N.D. *or* n.d.	no date. Used to indicate that the book or article has no date of publication given.
op. cit.	See the examples and comment under *Subsequent Footnote Citations*, above.
passim	"throughout," used to indicate that whatever is spoken of in the footnote occurs here and there throughout the source cited—pp. 43–68 *passim*.
pl(s).	plural or plate(s), depending on context.
post	"after." The English word is now most often used.
pseud.	pseudonym
q.v.	*quod vide*—"which see," used to direct the reader to look up a reference mentioned in the footnote in which this abbreviation is used.
supra	"above," as in "See *supra*." Most writers now use the English word.

BIBLIOGRAPHY

1. The bibliography of the ordinary research or term paper usually includes only the books actually cited in the footnotes of the paper.

2. The bibliography is generally the last page(s) of the manuscript (never begin a bibliography on the last page of the text, even if that page has only one or two lines on it).

3. The title *Bibliography* is centered between the margins at the top of the page.

4. The entries begin at the left-hand margin, and second and succeeding lines of an entry are indented one or two spaces.

5. Single-space within entries and double-space between entries.

6. Unless the bibliography is unusually long, or unless your instructor requests otherwise, no division into books, magazines, journals, etc. is made; all items are simply listed together in alphabetical order.

7. Unsigned articles are listed by title.

8. If more than one work by an author is cited, the listing under the author is usually alphabetical by title; in the second and subsequent references, the author's name is replaced by five unspaced hyphens followed by a period.

9. All information about a book (author's name, title, place of publication, publishing company, date of publication) should be taken from the title page and the reverse of the title page (for the latest date of publication).

Following is a diverse list of books and articles put into proper form and alphabetical order, as though for a bibliography. Notice the differences between the forms in the bibliography and the forms in the footnotes.

(1) The author's name (only the first author in the case of works by more than one author) is in reverse order—last name first. This, of course, is for purposes of alphabetizing.

(2) The punctuation for book entries in the bibliography is quite different from that in the footnotes. Notice the use of periods and the colon in the bibliography entry.

(3) Journal entries are the same in both footnotes and bibliography, except that the author's name is reversed in the bibliography and is followed by a period, and the bibliography entry gives the inclusive paging of the article.

(4) Notice that encyclopedia entries are punctuated like journal entries.

Brown, Donna Worrall, and others. *Form in Modern English*. New York: Oxford University Press, 1958.

Burke, Kenneth. *A Grammar of Motives*. New York: Prentice-Hall, Inc., 1952.

------. *A Rhetoric of Motives*. New York: Prentice-Hall, Inc., 1952.

Croce, Benedetto. "Art as Intuition," *Problems in Aesthetics*. ed. Morris Weitz. New York: The Macmillan Company, 1959.

Granville-Barker, Harley. *Prefaces to Shakespeare*. 2 vols. [or vol. I or vol. II if only one or the other is used] Princeton: Princeton University Press, 1947.

Morrison, Samuel Eliot, and Henry Steele Commager. *The Growth of the American Republic*. 5th ed., rev. and enl. 2 vols. New York: Oxford University Press, 1962.

National Council of Teachers of English, Commission of the English Curriculum. *Language Arts for Today's Children*. New York: Appleton-Century-Crofts, 1954.

Poirier, Richard. "Learning from the Beatles," *Partisan Review*, XXXIV (Fall 1967), 526–546.

"Reading Teachers Put on Spot," *The Kansas City Star*, May 1, 1969, p. 16 A.

Solzbacher, William. "Esperanto," *The Encyclopedia Americana*, X (1960), 501–503.

⌐⌐ Delete	tr Transpose	⌐⌐ Superscript
⌒ Close up	eq. # or ∨∧ Equalize space	⌐⌐ Subscript
⌐⌐ Delete and close up	⊔ Indent 1 em	?/ Question mark
⌐⌐ Push down lead that prints	ld Insert lead between lines	!/ Exclamation point
⊗ Broken letter	⌐⌐ ld Take out lead	=/ Hyphen
# Space or more space	stet Let it stand	(/) Parentheses
⊅ Reverse; turn over	sp Spell out	[/] Brackets
¶ Begin a paragraph	⌐¦⌐ M Em dash	⌒ or lig Use ligature
⌐⌐ Center	⌐¦⌐ N En dash	wf Wrong font
⌐ Move to right	⊙ Period	lf Lightface type
⌐ Move to left	⌐ Comma	bf Boldface type
⌐⌐ Lower letters or words	;/ Semicolon	rom Roman type
⌐⌐ Raise letters or words	:/ Colon	ital Italic type
‖ Align type vertically	∨ Apostrophe or 'single quote'	caps CAPITALS
⎓ Straighten line	⌐/⌐ Quotation marks	sm. c. SMALL CAPITALS
∧ Insert from margin	run on No paragraph	lc Lower case

The following passage shows the use of proofreaders' marks. They are placed in the margins and corresponding marks are inserted within the copy to indicate where a change is to be made. If a line has more than one correction or change, the marginal proofreaders' marks are separated by diagonal lines.

For whatever reasons—and they are not entirely clear—dictionaries have become a sort of specialty of the English-speaking world. A possible explanation may be sought in the size of the vocabulary, since English seems to have more words and more uses for words—many more than 2 million named uses—than any other known language. Speakers of English have uncommon need for dictionaries, and Americans, who constitute the largest single body of English speakers and who been have uncommonly well provided with the means of buying reference works, have augmented this need with what would seem to be a mania for linguistic correctness, a zeal for rectitude which they have built into their elaborate school system.

This, for whatever reason, the speakers of no other known language have ever brought to fruition work as such a the *Oxford English Dictionary* (also called *A New English Dictionary on Historical Principles*) whose editors endeavored to trace every use of every word that has ever gained wide currency in the native tongue. The creation of the modern American desk dictionary is scarcely less remarkable. American lexicography has its own glories and its own character. The founder of the American school was Noah Webster, whose *An American Dictionary of the English Language* (1828 and frequently revised & enlarged was a truly remarkable work, especially for its day and place, a New world still very much a colony, socially and intellectually, of the old. Webster was an untiring and self assertive as Samuel Johnson himself, and if he was less well read and probably less intellectually endowed, he suffered from no false modesty and he possessed a genius for definition. His work was rivaled in many ways by that of his onetime employee, Joseph E. Worcester, and the "War of the Dictionaries waged between the successors to Websters volume and Worcester's *A Dictionary of the English Language* (1860), lent to lexicography the zest of a sporting event.

TABLES OF WEIGHTS AND MEASURES

Linear Measure

1 mil = 0.001 inch		=	0.0254 millimeter
1 inch = 1,000 mils		=	2.54 centimeters
12 inches = 1 foot		=	0.3048 meter
3 feet = 1 yard		=	0.9144 meter
5½ yards or 16½ feet = 1 rod (or pole or perch)		=	5.029 meters
40 rods = 1 furlong		=	201.168 meters
8 furlongs or 1,760 yards or 5,280 feet = 1 (statute) mile		=	1.6093 kilometers
3 miles = 1 (land) league		=	4.83 kilometers

Square Measure

1 square inch		=	6.452 square centimeters
144 square inches = 1 square foot		=	929.03 square centimeters
9 square feet = 1 square yard		=	0.8361 square meter
30¼ square yards = 1 square rod (or square pole or square perch)	=	25.292 square meters
160 square rods or 4,840 square yards or 43,560 square feet = 1 acre		=	0.4047 hectare
640 acres = 1 square mile		=	259.00 hectares or 2.590 square kilometers

Cubic Measure

1 cubic inch	=	16.387 cubic centimeters
1,728 cubic inches = 1 cubic foot	=	0.0283 cubic meter
27 cubic feet = 1 cubic yard	=	0.7646 cubic meter
(in units for cordwood, etc.)		
16 cubic feet = 1 cord foot	=	0.453 cubic meter
128 cubic feet or 8 cord feet = 1 cord	=	3.625 cubic meters

Chain Measure

(for Gunter's, or surveyor's, chain)

7.92 inches = 1 link	=	20.12	centimeters
100 links or 66 feet = 1 chain	=	20.12	meters
10 chains or 220 yards = 1 furlong	=	201.17	meters
80 chains = 1 mile	=	1.6093	kilometers

(for engineer's chain)

1 foot = 1 link	=	0.3048	meter
100 feet = 1 chain	=	30.48	meters
52.8 chains = 1 mile	=	1,609.3	meters

Surveyor's (Square) Measure

625 square links = 1 square pole	=	25.29	square meters
16 square poles = 1 square chain	=	404.7	square meters
10 square chains = 1 acre	=	0.4047	hectare
640 acres = 1 square mile or 1 section	=	259.00	hectares or 2.59 square kilometers
36 square miles = 1 township	=	9,324.0	hectares or 93.24 square kilometers

Nautical Measure

6 feet = 1 fathom	=	1.829 meters
100 fathoms = 1 cable's length (ordinary)		
(In the U.S. Navy 120 fathoms or 720 feet, or 219.456 meters, = 1 cable's length; in the British Navy, 608 feet, or 185.319 meters, = 1 cable's length.)		
10 cables' length = 1 international nautical mile (6,076.11549 feet, by international agreement)	=	1.852 kilometers (exactly)
1 international nautical mile = 1.150779 statute miles (the length of a minute of longitude at the equator)		
3 nautical miles = 1 marine league (3.45 statute miles)	=	5.56 kilometers
60 nautical miles = 1 degree of a great circle of the earth = 69.047 statute miles		

Dry Measure

1 pint =	33.60 cubic inches =	0.5506 liter
2 pints = 1 quart =	67.20 cubic inches =	1.1012 liters
8 quarts = 1 peck =	537.61 cubic inches =	8.8098 liters
4 pecks = 1 bushel =	2,150.42 cubic inches =	35.2390 liters

According to United States government standards, the following are the weights avoirdupois for single bushels of the specified grains: for wheat, 60 pounds; for barley, 48 pounds; for oats, 32 pounds; for rye, 56 pounds; for shelled corn, 56 pounds. Some States have specifications varying from these.

The British dry quart = 1.032 U.S. dry quarts

Liquid Measure

1 gill = 4 fluid ounces =	7.219 cubic inches =	0.1183 liter
(see next table)		
4 gills = 1 pint =	28.875 cubic inches =	0.4732 liter
2 pints = 1 quart =	57.75 cubic inches =	0.9464 liter
4 quarts = 1 gallon =	231 cubic inches =	3.7854 liters

The British imperial gallon (4 imperial quarts) = 277.42 cubic inches = 4.546 liters. The barrel in Great Britain equals 36 imperial gallons, in the United States, usually 31½ gallons.

Apothecaries' Fluid Measure

	1 minim	=	0.0038 cubic inch	=	0.0616 milliliter
60 minims	= 1 fluid dram	=	0.2256 cubic inch	=	3.6966 milliliters
8 fluid drams	= 1 fluid ounce	=	1.8047 cubic inches	=	0.0296 liter
16 fluid ounces	= 1 pint	=	28.875 cubic inches	=	0.4732 liter

See table immediately preceding for quart and gallon equivalents.
The British pint = 20 fluid ounces.

Circular (or Angular) Measure

60 seconds ('')	= 1 minute (')
60 minutes	= 1 degree (°)
90 degrees	= 1 quadrant or 1 right angle
180 degrees	= 2 quadrants or 1 straight angle
4 quadrants or 360 degrees	= 1 circle

Avoirdupois Weight

(The grain, equal to 0.0648 gram, is the same in all three tables of weight.)

1 dram or 27.34 grains		=	1.772 grams
16 drams or 437.5 grains	= 1 ounce	=	28.3495 grams
16 ounces or 7,000 grains	= 1 pound	=	453.59 grams
100 pounds	= 1 hundredweight	=	45.36 kilograms
2,000 pounds	= 1 ton	=	907.18 kilograms

In Great Britain, 14 pounds (6.35 kilograms) = 1 stone, 112 pounds (50.80 kilograms) = 1 hundredweight, and 2,240 pounds (1,016.05 kilograms) = 1 long ton.

Troy Weight

(The grain, equal to 0.0648 gram, is the same in all three tables of weight.)

3.086 grains	= 1 carat	=	200.00 milligrams
24 grains	= 1 pennyweight	=	1.5552 grams
20 pennyweights or 480 grains	= 1 ounce	=	31.1035 grams
12 ounces or 5,760 grains	= 1 pound	=	373.24 grams

Apothecaries' Weight

(The grain, equal to 0.0648 gram, is the same in all three tables of weight.)

20 grains	= 1 scruple	=	1.296 grams
3 scruples	= 1 dram	=	3.888 grams
8 drams or 480 grains	= 1 ounce	=	31.1035 grams
12 ounces or 5,760 grains	= 1 pound	=	373.24 grams

THE METRIC SYSTEM

Linear Measure

	1 millimeter	=	0.03937 inch
10 millimeters	= 1 centimeter	=	0.3937 inch
10 centimeters	= 1 decimeter	=	3.937 inches
10 decimeters	= 1 meter	=	39.37 inches or 3.2808 feet
10 meters	= 1 decameter	=	393.7 inches
10 decameters	= 1 hectometer	=	328.08 feet
10 hectometers	= 1 kilometer	=	0.621 mile or 3,280.8 feet
10 kilometers	= 1 myriameter	=	6.21 miles

Square Measure

	1 square millimeter	=	0.00155 square inch
100 square millimeters	= 1 square centimeter	=	0.15499 square inch
100 square centimeters	= 1 square decimeter	=	15.499 square inches
100 square decimeters	= 1 square meter	=	1,549.9 square inches or 1.196 square yards
100 square meters	= 1 square decameter	=	119.6 square yards
100 square decameters	= 1 square hectometer	=	2.471 acres
100 square hectometers	= 1 square kilometer	=	0.386 square mile or 247.1 acres

Land Measure

1 square meter	= 1 centiare	=	1,549.9 square inches
100 centiares	= 1 are	=	119.6 square yards
100 ares	= 1 hectare	=	2.471 acres
100 hectares	= 1 square kilometer	=	0.386 square mile or 247.1 acres

Volume Measure

1,000 cubic millimeters	= 1 cubic centimeter	=	0.06102 cubic inch
1,000 cubic centimeters	= 1 cubic decimeter	=	61.023 cubic inches or 0.0353 cubic foot
1,000 cubic decimeters	= 1 cubic meter	=	35.314 cubic feet or 1.308 cubic yards
	(the unit is called a *stere* in measuring firewood)		

Capacity Measure

10 milliliters	= 1 centiliter	=	0.338 fluid ounce
10 centiliters	= 1 deciliter	=	3.38 fluid ounces or 0.1057 liquid quart
10 deciliters	= 1 liter	=	1.0567 liquid quarts or 0.9081 dry quart
10 liters	= 1 decaliter	=	2.64 gallons or 0.284 bushel
10 decaliters	= 1 hectoliter	=	26.418 gallons or 2.838 bushels
10 hectoliters	= 1 kiloliter	=	264.18 gallons or 35.315 cubic feet

Weights

10 milligrams	= 1 centigram	=	0.1543 grain or 0.000353 ounce (avdp.)
10 centigrams	= 1 decigram	=	1.5432 grains
10 decigrams	= 1 gram	=	15.432 grains or 0.035274 ounce (avdp.)
10 grams	= 1 decagram	=	0.3527 ounce
10 decagrams	= 1 hectogram	=	3.5274 ounces
10 hectograms	= 1 kilogram	=	2.2046 pounds
10 kilograms	= 1 myriagram	=	22.046 pounds
10 myriagrams	= 1 quintal	=	220.46 pounds
10 quintals	= 1 metric ton	=	2,204.6 pounds

SPECIAL SIGNS AND SYMBOLS

ASTRONOMY

SUN, MOON, PLANETS, ETC.

☉ the sun
☾, ☽ the moon
● new moon
☽, ◐, ☽ first quarter
○ full moon
☾, ◑, ☾ last quarter
✱, ✳ fixed star
☿ Mercury
♀ Venus
⊕, ⊖, ♁ Earth
♂ Mars
♃ Jupiter
♄ Saturn
♅, ♅ Uranus
♆ Neptune
♇ Pluto
☄ comet
①, ②, ③, *etc.* asteroids in the order of their discovery
α, β, γ, *etc.* stars (of a constellation) in the order of their brightness: the Greek letter is followed by the Latin genitive of the name of the constellation

SIGNS OF THE ZODIAC

Spring Signs

1. ♈ Aries (the Ram)
2. ♉ Taurus (the Bull)
3. Ⅱ, □, ♊ Gemini (the Twins)

Summer Signs

4. ♋, ⊗ Cancer (the Crab)
5. ♌ Leo (the Lion)
6. ♍ Virgo (the Virgin)

Autumn Signs

7. ♎ Libra (the Balance)
8. ♏ Scorpio (the Scorpion)
9. ♐ Sagittarius (the Archer)

Winter Signs

10. ♑, ♑ Capricorn (the Goat)
11. ♒ Aquarius (the Water Bearer)
12. ♓ Pisces (the Fishes)

ASPECTS AND NODES

☌ conjunction: with reference to bodies having the same longitude, or right ascension
□ quadrature: being 90° apart in longitude, or right ascension
☍ opposition: being 180° apart in longitude, or right ascension
☊ ascending node
☋ descending node

SIGNS AND ABBREVIATIONS USED IN ASTRONOMICAL NOTATION

A albedo
a mean distance
α, R.A. right ascension
A.U. astronomical unit
β celestial latitude
γ vernal equinox of the earth
D diameter
δ declination
Δ distance
e eccentricity of orbit
G universal gravitational constant
h, ^{h} hours [5h *or* 5^h]
i inclination to the ecliptic
L mean longitude in orbit
λ longitude
l.y. light year
M mass
m, ^{m} minutes of time [5m *or* 5^m]
μ, η mean daily motion
\+ north
☊ longitude of ascending node
π, ω longitude of perihelion
P sidereal period of rotation
p parallax
ps parsec
q perihelion distance
R radius
− south
$\bar{S}$ mean position of satellite
s, ^{s} seconds of time [16s *or* 16^s]
ϕ geographical latitude
° degrees of arc
′ minutes of arc
″ seconds of arc

BIOLOGY

♃ perennial herb
♂, ♂ 1. male organism or cell 2. staminate plant or flower
♀ 1. female organism or cell 2. pistillate plant or flower
☿ perfect, or hermaphroditic, plant or flower
○ individual, especially female, organism
□ individual, especially male, organism
∞ indefinite number, as of stamens when there are more than twenty
× crossed with: used of a hybrid
P parental generation
F filial generation; offspring
F_1, F_2, F_3, *etc.* offspring of the first, second, third, etc. filial generation

CHEMISTRY

The symbol for each of the chemical elements is formed of the initial or an abbreviation of its English, Latin, or Modern Latin name, as C for carbon, K for potassium (ModL. ***kalium***), Mn for manganese, Au for gold (L. ***aurum***). A complete list of these symbols can be found on p. 452.

The formula for a chemical compound is expressed by combining the symbols of its constituent elements, with a small subscript at the right of each specifying the number of atoms of each element in a molecule of the compound. Where only one atom is involved, no subscript is used. Examples: MgO (magnesium oxide), a compound in which one atom of magnesium is combined with one atom of oxygen; H_2O (water), a compound in which two atoms of hydrogen are combined with one atom of oxygen; $NaHCO_3$ (sodium bicarbonate), a compound in which one atom each of sodium, hydrogen, and carbon, and three atoms of oxygen are combined.

In equations, the number of molecules of the element or compound entering into a reaction is indicated by a figure placed before the symbol or formula (unless there is only one molecule), as $3O_2$, three molecules of oxygen; 2NaCl, two molecules of sodium chloride.

· 1. separates the water of crystallization from a substance, as in $CaSO_4 \cdot 2H_2O$ (gypsum, or hydrated calcium sulfate) 2. designates free radicals, as ethyl $CH_3CH_2\cdot$ *or* phenyl $C_6H_5\cdot$
, indicates elements which are interchangeable, as (Er, Y) PO_4 means $ErPO_4$ and YPO_4 in proportions that vary
( ) indicates a radical within a compound, as in $(NH_4)_2S$, ammonium sulfide, or is used to set off elements that are interchangeable, as in (Er, Y)
[ ] is used together with parentheses to indicate certain radicals, as in $Fe_3[Fe(CN)_6]_2$, ferrous ferricyanide, or in coordination formulas to indicate relationship to the central atom

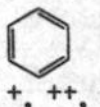
is used in structural formulas to indicate the benzene ring

$^+, ^{++}, ^{+++}$, *etc.* *or* $^{1+}, ^{2+}, ^{3+}$, *etc.* indicate the unit charges of positive electricity, as Al^{+++}, an aluminum ion with three positive charges
$^-, ^{--}, ^{---}$, *etc.* *or* $^{1-}, ^{2-}, ^{3-}$, *etc.* indicate the unit charges of negative electricity, as S^{--}, a sulfide ion with two negative charges
−, =, ≡, *etc.* indicate: 1. the same as the symbols immediately preceding, as S= 2. a single, double or triple bond, as in HC≡CH, acetylene
·, :, ⁝, *etc.* indicate a single, double, or triple bond, as in $C_6H_5C⁝CH$, phenylacetylene
′, ″, ‴, *etc.* indicate: 1. valence of one, two, three, etc. as Fe‴, trivalent iron 2. the unit charges of negative electricity, as SO_4'', a sulfate ion with two negative charges
1−, 2−, 3−, *etc.* *or* $\alpha-, \beta-, \gamma-$, *etc.* used in names of compounds to designate one of the several possible positions of substituting groups in a parent compound, as in 2-ethylnaphthalene, γ-resorcylic acid
− indicates levorotation, as −130°
\+ 1. means "with the addition of *or* together with," and is used in chemical equations between the formulas of the reacting substances 2. indicates dextrorotation, as +130°
= means "form *or* result in," and is used in chemical equations between the formulas of the reacting substances and those of the reaction products
→ indicates the direction of the reaction
⇄ indicates a reversible reaction; i.e., one that can proceed in either direction, or in both directions at the same time, in a state of equilibrium
↓ indicates that the specified reaction product (after which it is written) appears as a precipitate

↑   indicates that the specified reaction product (after which it is written) appears as a gas

≡, ⇌   means "is equivalent to" and is used in quantitative equations to indicate the quantities of specified substances that will react with each other completely, so as to leave no excess matter

<   indicates a bivalent element

>   indicates a bivalent radical

°/₀₀   salinity

R indicates a hydrogen atom *or* a saturated hydrocarbon radical

X indicates a halogen *or* acid radical

COMMERCE AND FINANCE

$ dollar *or* dollars [$100]

¢   cent *or* cents [13¢]

£   pound *or* pounds sterling [£100]

/   shilling *or* shillings [2/6, two shillings and sixpence]

℔   pound (in weight)

@   at [200 @ $1 each]

⅌   per

%   percent [5%]

1. number (before a figure) [#5 can]   2. pounds (after a figure) [25#]

A/C, a/c   1. account   2. account current

A/O, a/o   account of

B/D   bank draft

B/E   bill of exchange

B/L   bill of lading

B/P   bills payable

B/R   bills receivable

B/V   book value

C/D   1. *Bookkeeping* carried down   2. certificate of deposit

C/O   1. care of   2. *Bookkeeping* carried over   3. cash order

C/N   1. circular note   2. credit note

d/d   delivered

D/O   delivery order

G/A   general average

L/C, l/c   letter of credit

M/D, m/d   month's date (i.e., months after date)

N/S, n/s   *Banking* not sufficient funds

o/c   overcharge

O/S   out of stock

P/A   power of attorney

P/C, p/c   1. petty cash   2. prices current

P/N   promissory note

w/   with

W/B   waybill

w/o   without

MATHEMATICS
NUMERATION

Arabic	Greek	Roman
0	…	…
1	α	I
2	β	II
3	γ	III
4	δ	IV *or* IIII
5	ϵ	V
6	s	VI
7	ζ	VII
8	η	VIII *or* IIX
9	θ	IX *or* VIIII
10	ι	X
11	$\iota\alpha$	XI
12	$\iota\beta$	XII
13	$\iota\gamma$	XIII *or* XIIV
14	$\iota\delta$	XIV *or* XIIII
15	$\iota\epsilon$	XV
16	ιs	XVI
17	$\iota\zeta$	XVII
18	$\iota\eta$	XVIII *or* XIIX
19	$\iota\theta$	XIX *or* XVIIII
20	κ	XX
30	λ	XXX
40	μ	XL *or* XXXX
50	ν	L
60	ξ	LX
70	o	LXX
80	π	LXXX *or* XXC
90	φ	XC *or* LXXXX
100	ρ	C
200	σ	CC
300	τ	CCC
400	υ	CƆ *or* CCCC
500	ϕ	Ɔ *or* IƆ
600	χ	ƆC *or* IƆC
700	ψ	ƆCC *or* IƆCC
800	ω	ƆCCC *or* IƆCCC
900	$\mathcal{D}'$	CM, DCCCC, *or* IƆCCCC
1,000	…	M *or* CIƆ
2,000	…	MM *or* CIƆCIƆ

The alternative Roman numerals shown above are not commonly used today. Capital letters were sometimes used for the Greek numerals, and lower-case letters are often used for the Roman. In the Roman notation, the value of a character to the right of a larger numeral is added to that of the numeral (Ex.: VI = V + I = 6). I, X, and sometimes C, are also placed to the left of larger numerals and when so situated their value is subtracted from that of such numerals (Ex.: IV, that is, V − I = 4). After the sign IƆ for D, each time the character Ɔ was repeated it indicated the number of times ten was to be used as a factor (Ex.: IƆƆ, 5,000; IƆƆƆ, 50,000). In writing numbers twice as great as these, C was placed as many times before the stroke I as the Ɔ was written after it. Sometimes a line was drawn over a numeral to indicate thousands (Ex.: C̄ = 100,000).

CALCULATION

+   1. plus, the sign of addition: used also to indicate that figures are only approximately exact, some figures being omitted at the end [2.1557+]   2. positive

−   1. minus, the sign of subtraction: used also to indicate that figures have been left off from the end of a number, and that the last figure has been increased by one [2.9378 = 2.94−]   2. negative

±, ∓   plus or minus: indicating that either of the signs + or − may properly be used: also used to introduce the probable error after a figure obtained by experimentation, etc.

×   multiplied by (5 × 4 = 20): multiplication is also indicated by a centered dot (5 · 4 = 20) or by placing the factors in immediate juxtaposition ($2ab = 2 \times a \times b$)

÷   divided by: division is also indicated by the sign : ($x \div y = x : y$), by a straight line between the dividend and the divisor $\left(\dfrac{x}{y}\right)$, or by an oblique line (x/y)

=   equal to; equals

≠   not equal to

>   greater than, as $x > y$; that is, x is greater than y

<   less than, as $x < y$; that is, x is less than y

≮   not less than

≯   not greater than

≥   equal to or greater than

≤   equal to or less than

| | absolute value (Ex.: |3| is the absolute value for −3 and +3)

∪   logical sum; union (Ex.: the logical sum A ∪ B is the union of all points in A and B: if A = 1,2,3,4 and B = 3,4,5,6, then A ∪ B = 1,2,3,4,5,6)

∩   logical product; intersection (Ex.: the logical product A ∩ B is the intersection of all the points common to both A and B: when A and B have the same values as above, then A ∩ B = 3,4)

⊂   is contained in (Ex.: B = 1,2 and A = 0,1,2,3, then B ⊂ A *or* A contains B)

→   approaches the limit of

⇌   equivalent to: applied to magnitudes or quantities that are equal in area or volume, but are not of the same form

≡   identical with

≅   congruent to

∼   1. difference: used to designate the difference between two quantities without indicating which is the greater, as $x \sim z$ = the difference between x and z 2. equivalent, as ∠A ∼ ∠B

∝   varies as; is directly proportional to, as $x \propto y$; that is, x varies as y varies

⚏   geometric proportion, as ⚏ $x : y : : a : b$; that is, the geometric proportion, x is to y as a is to b

:   is to; the ratio of

: :   as; equals: used between ratios

∞   indefinitely great: the symbol for infinity

!   the factorial of *or* the continued product of numbers from one upward, as $5! = 5 \times 4 \times 3 \times 2 \times 1$

∴   therefore

∵   since; because

…   and so on

∠   angle, as ∠XYZ

∟   right angle

⊥   perpendicular; is perpendicular to, as EF ⊥ MN = EF is perpendicular to MN

∥   parallel; is parallel to, as EF ∥ DG

○   circle; circumference; 360°

⌒   arc of a circle

△   triangle

□   square

▭   rectangle

▱   parallelogram

⌀   diameter

◖   ellipse

⌔   sector

⌓   segment

𝒳   quantic

$\sqrt{\ }$, $\sqrt{\ }$　radical sign; root: indicating, when used without a figure placed above it, the square root, as $\sqrt{9} = 3$: when any other than the square root is meant, a figure (called the *index*) expressing the degree of the required root, is placed above the sign, as $\sqrt[3]{27} = 3$

$^1, ^2, ^3$, *etc.*　exponents, placed above and to the right of a quantity to indicate that it is raised to the first, second, third, etc. power, as a^2, $(a + b)^3$

$'$, $''$, $'''$, *etc.*　prime, double (or second) prime, triple (or third) prime, etc.: used to distinguish between different values of the same variable, as x', x'', x''', etc.

———　vinculum, as $\overline{x + y}$

( )　parentheses, as $2(x + y)$

[ ]　brackets, as $a[2(x + y)]$

{ }　braces, as $b + \{2 - a[2(x + y)]\}$

These signs indicate that the quantities connected or enclosed by them are to be taken together, as a single quantity.

f, F, ϕ　function; function of, as $f(a)$

d　differential of, as da

δ, ∂　variation of, as δa

$\triangle$　finite difference; increment

D　differential coefficient; derivative

$\int$　integral; integral of: indicating that the expression following it is to be integrated, as $\int f(x)\,dx$ indicates the indefinite integral of $f(x)$ with respect to x

$\int_a^b$　definite integral: indicating the limits of integration, as $\int_a^b f(x)\,dx$ indicates the integral of $f(x)$ with respect to x, between the limits a and b

Σ　sum; algebraic sum: when used to indicate the summation of finite differences, it has a sense similar to that of the symbol $\int$

Π　the continued product of all terms such as (those indicated)

π　pi, the number 3.14159265+: the ratio of the circumference of a circle to its diameter, of a semicircle to its radius, and of the area of a circle to the square of its radius

e, ϵ　1. 2.7182818+: the base of the natural system of logarithms　2. the eccentricity of a conic section

M　modulus of a system of logarithms, especially of the natural system of logarithms, where it is equal to 0.4342944819+

g　acceleration of gravity

$°$　degrees, as 90°

$'$　1. minutes of arc　2. feet

$''$　1. seconds of arc　2. inches

h　hours

m　minutes of time

s　seconds of time

MEDICINE AND PHARMACY

Å　angstrom unit

Ā, ĀĀ, āā, āa　[Gr. *ana*] of each

a.c.　[L. *ante cibum*] before meals

ad　[L.] up to; so as to make [*ad* ʒij, so as to make two drams]

add.　[L. *adde*] let there be added; add

ad lib.　[L. *ad libitum*] at pleasure; as needed or desired

agit.　[L. *agita*] shake

aq.　[L. *aqua*] water

b. (i.) d.　[L. *bis (in) die*] twice daily

c̄　[L. *cum*] with

cap.　1. [L. *capiat*] take　2. [L. *capsula*] capsule

coch.　[L. *cochleare*] a spoonful

d.　[L. *da*] give

dil.　[L. *dilue*] dilute *or* dissolve

fldxt.　[L. *fluid extractum*] fluid extract

ft.　[L. *fiat*] make

ft. mist.　[L. *fiat mistura*] let a mixture be made

ft. pulv.　[L. *fiat pulvis*] let a powder be made

gr.　[L. *granum*] a grain

gtt.　[L. *guttae*] drops

H.　[L. *hora*] hour

haust.　[L. *haustus*] a draft

in d.　[L. *in dies*] daily

lot.　[L. *lotio*] a lotion

m̄, M.　[L. *misce*] mix

℔, ℞　minim

μ　micron

$\mu\mu$　micromicron

mod. praesc.　[L. *modo praescripto*] in the manner prescribed

O., o.　[L. *octarius*] a pint

ol.　[L. *oleum*] oil

oz.　ounce (avoirdupois)

p.c.　[L. *post cibum*] after meals

pil.　[L. *pilula(e)*] pill(s)

p.r.n.　[L. *pro re nata*] as circumstances may require

pulv.　[L. *pulvis*] powder

q. (i.) d.　[L. *quater (in) die*] four times daily

q.l.　[L. *quantum libet*] as much as you please

q.s.　[L. *quantum sufficit*] as much as will suffice

q.v.　[L. *quantum vis*] as much as you like

℞　[L. *recipe*] take: used at the beginning of a prescription

rep.　[L. *repetatur*] let it be repeated

σ　1/1000 of a second

S, Sig.　[L. *signa*] write: used in prescriptions to indicate the directions to be placed on the label of the medicine

sol.　[L. *solutio*] solution

s.o.s.　[L. *si opus sit*] if necessary

s̄　[L. *sans*] without

s̄s̄　[L. *semis*] one half

tab.　[L. *tabella*] tablet

t. (i.) d.　[L. *ter (in) die*] three times daily

ut dict.　[L. *ut dictum*] as directed

w/v　weight in volume

℥　ounce: ℥i = one ounce; ℥ij = two ounces; ℥ss = half an ounce; ℥iss = one ounce and a half, etc.; f℥ = a fluid ounce

ʒ　dram: ʒi = one dram; ʒij = two drams; ʒss = half a dram; ʒiss = one dram and a half, etc.; fʒ = a fluid dram

℈　scruple: ℈i = one scruple; ℈ij = two scruples; ℈ss = half a scruple; ℈iss = one scruple and a half, etc.

$*$　birth

$\dagger$　death

○, ♀　female

□, ♂　male

PHYSICS, ELECTRICITY, ETC.

A/m　ampere per meter

β　specific heat constant

γ　1. electric conductivity　2. surface tension

cd/m²　candela per square meter

ϵ　dielectric constant

η　coefficient of viscosity

HP　horsepower

J　radiance

L　inductance

Λ　1. equivalent conductivity　2. permeance

λ　1. wavelength　2. decay constant　3. linear density

m/s²　meter per second squared

ν　1. frequency　2. reluctivity

ρ　1. specific resistance　2. density

Φ　magnetic flux

φ　fluidity

Ψ　1. dielectric flux　2. electrostatic flux　3. luminous flux

R　1. thermal resistance　2. gas constant

$\Re$　reluctance

rad/s　radian per second

rad/s²　radian per second squared

S　entropy

V/m　volt per meter

X　reactance

Z　impedance

Ω　ohm

ω　angular frequency

$+$　unit positive charge of electricity

$-$　unit negative charge of electricity

$\leftrightarrows$　electric current

$\rightarrow$　direction of flow

MISCELLANEOUS

&, &　(the ampersand) and: as A. B. Smith & Co.

&c.　[L. *et cetera*] and others; and so forth

©　copyright; copyrighted

®　registered; officially recorded: said of a trademark

℞, R　response: in certain religious services, used to mark the part to be uttered by the congregation in answer to the officiant

$*$　in Roman Catholic service books, a mark used to divide each verse of a psalm into two parts, indicating where the response begins

℣, V', V℟　versicle: in certain religious services, used to mark the part to be uttered by the officiant

✠　1. a sign of the cross used by the Pope, by archbishops, and by bishops, before their names　2. in certain religious services, used to mark the places where the sign of the cross is to be made

🕎　menorah, a candelabrum with seven branches: a traditional symbol of Judaism

✡　Star of David, a six-pointed star: a symbol of Judaism

$\dagger$　died: used in genealogies etc.

$\times$　1. by: used in dimensions, as paper 8 × 11 inches　2. a mark representing a signature, as on a legal document, made by someone unable to write; the name is added by someone else; e.g.

　　　　　　　　　　　his
　　　John　×　Doe
　　　　　　　　　　mark